PETERSON'S®
GRADUATE & PROFESSIONAL PROGRAMS

AN OVERVIEW

2018

About Peterson's®

Peterson's®, a Nelnet company, has been your trusted educational publisher for over 50 years. It's a milestone we're quite proud of, as we continue to offer the most accurate, dependable, high-quality educational content in the field, providing you with everything you need to succeed. No matter where you are on your academic or professional path, you can rely on Peterson's for its books, online information, expert test-prep tools, the most up-to-date education exploration data, and the highest quality career success resources—everything you need to achieve your education goals. For our complete line of products, visit **www.petersons.com**.

For more information, contact Peterson's Publishing, 3 Columbia Circle, Suite 205, Albany, NY 12203-5158; 800-338-3282 Ext. 54229; or find us on the World Wide Web at www.petersonsbooks.com.

ISSN 1093-8443
ISBN: 978-0-7689-4165-4

Printed in the United States of America

10 9 8 7 6 5 4 3 2 1   20 19 18

Fifty-second Edition

CONTENTS

A Note from the Peterson's Editors

The six volumes of Peterson's *Graduate and Professional Programs*, the only annually updated reference work of its kind, provide wideranging information on the graduate and professional programs offered by accredited colleges and universities in the United States, U.S. territories, and Canada and by those institutions outside the United States that are accredited by U.S. accrediting bodies. Nearly 36,000 individual academic and professional programs at more than 2,200 institutions are listed. Peterson's *Graduate and Professional Programs* have been used for more than forty years by prospective graduate and professional students, placement counselors, faculty advisers, and all others interested in postbaccalaureate education.

Graduate & Professional Programs: An Overview contains information on institutions as a whole, while the other books in the series are devoted to specific academic and professional fields:

Graduate Programs in the Humanities, Arts & Social Sciences
Graduate Programs in the Biological/Biomedical Sciences & Health-Related Medical Professions
Graduate Programs in the Physical Sciences, Mathematics, Agricultural Sciences, the Environment & Natural Resources
Graduate Programs in Engineering & Applied Sciences
Graduate Programs in Business, Education, Information Studies, Law & Social Work

The books may be used individually or as a set. For example, if you have chosen a field of study but do not know what institution you want to attend or if you have a college or university in mind but have not chosen an academic field of study, it is best to begin with the Overview guide.

Graduate & Professional Programs: An Overview presents several directories to help you identify programs of study that might interest you; you can then research those programs further in the other books in the series by using the Directory of Graduate and Professional Programs by Field, which lists 500 fields and gives the names of those institutions that offer graduate degree programs in each.

For geographical or financial reasons, you may be interested in attending a particular institution and will want to know what it has to offer. You should turn to the Directory of Institutions and Their Offerings, which lists the degree programs available at each institution. As in the Directory of Graduate and Professional Programs by Field, the level of degrees offered is also indicated.

All books in the series include advice on graduate education, including topics such as admissions tests, financial aid, and accreditation. **The Graduate Adviser** includes two essays and information about accreditation. The first essay, "The Admissions Process," discusses general admission requirements, admission tests, factors to consider when selecting a graduate school or program, when and how to apply, and how admission decisions are made. Special information for international students and tips for minority students are also included. The second essay, "Financial Support," is an overview of the broad range of support available at the graduate level. Fellowships, scholarships, and grants; assistantships and internships; federal and private loan programs, as well as Federal Work-Study; and the GI bill are detailed. This essay concludes with advice on applying for need-based financial aid. "Accreditation and Accrediting Agencies" gives information on accreditation and its purpose and lists institutional accrediting agencies first and then specialized accrediting agencies relevant to each volume's specific fields of study.

With information on more than 44,000 graduate programs in more than 500 disciplines, Peterson's *Graduate and Professional Programs* give you all the information you need about the programs that are of interest to you in three formats: **Profiles** (capsule summaries of basic information), **Displays** (information that an institution or program wants to emphasize), and **Close-Ups** (written by administrators, with more expansive information than the **Profiles**, emphasizing different aspects of the programs). By using these various formats of program information, coupled with **Appendixes** and **Indexes** covering directories and subject areas for all six books, you will find that these guides provide the most comprehensive, accurate, and up-to-date graduate study information available.

Peterson's publishes a full line of resources with information you need to guide you through the graduate admissions process. Peterson's publications can be found at college libraries and career centers and your local bookstore or library—or visit us on the Web at www.petersonsbooks.com. Peterson's books are now also available as ebooks.

Colleges and universities will be pleased to know that Peterson's helped you in your selection. Admissions staff members are more than happy to answer questions, address specific problems, and help in any way they can. The editors at Peterson's wish you great success in your graduate program search!

THE GRADUATE ADVISER

The Admissions Process

Generalizations about graduate admissions practices are not always helpful because each institution has its own set of guidelines and procedures. Nevertheless, some broad statements can be made about the admissions process that may help you plan your strategy.

Factors Involved in Selecting a Graduate School or Program

Selecting a graduate school and a specific program of study is a complex matter. Quality of the faculty; program and course offerings; the nature, size, and location of the institution; admission requirements; cost; and the availability of financial assistance are among the many factors that affect one's choice of institution. Other considerations are job placement and achievements of the program's graduates and the institution's resources, such as libraries, laboratories, and computer facilities. If you are to make the best possible choice, you need to learn as much as you can about the schools and programs you are considering before you apply.

The following steps may help you narrow your choices.

- Talk to alumni of the programs or institutions you are considering to get their impressions of how well they were prepared for work in their fields of study.
- Remember that graduate school requirements change, so be sure to get the most up-to-date information possible.
- Talk to department faculty members and the graduate adviser at your undergraduate institution. They often have information about programs of study at other institutions.
- Visit the websites of the graduate schools in which you are interested to request a graduate catalog. Contact the department chair in your chosen field of study for additional information about the department and the field.
- Visit as many campuses as possible. Call ahead for an appointment with the graduate adviser in your field of interest and be sure to check out the facilities and talk to students.

General Requirements

Graduate schools and departments have requirements that applicants for admission must meet. Typically, these requirements include undergraduate transcripts (which provide information about undergraduate grade point average and course work applied toward a major), admission test scores, and letters of recommendation. Most graduate programs also ask for an essay or personal statement that describes your personal reasons for seeking graduate study. In some fields, such as art and music, portfolios or auditions may be required in addition to other evidence of talent. Some institutions require that the applicant have an undergraduate degree in the same subject as the intended graduate major.

Most institutions evaluate each applicant on the basis of the applicant's total record, and the weight accorded any given factor varies widely from institution to institution and from program to program.

The Application Process

You should begin the application process at least one year before you expect to begin your graduate study. Find out the application deadline for each institution (many are provided in the **Profile** section of this guide). Go to the institution's website and find out if you can apply online. If not, request a paper application form. Fill out this form thoroughly and neatly. Assume that the school needs all the information it is requesting and that the admissions officer will be sensitive to the neatness and overall quality of what you submit. Do not supply more information than the school requires.

The institution may ask at least one question that will require a three- or four-paragraph answer. Compose your response on the assumption that the admissions officer is interested in both what you think and how you express yourself. Keep your statement brief and to the point, but, at the same time, include all pertinent information about your past experiences and your educational goals. Individual statements vary greatly in style and content, which helps admissions officers differentiate among applicants. Many graduate departments give considerable weight to the statement in making their admissions decisions, so be sure to take the time to prepare a thoughtful and concise statement.

If recommendations are a part of the admissions requirements, carefully choose the individuals you ask to write them. It is generally best to ask current or former professors to write the recommendations, provided they are able to attest to your intellectual ability and motivation for doing the work required of a graduate student. It is advisable to provide stamped, preaddressed envelopes to people being asked to submit recommendations on your behalf.

Completed applications, including references, transcripts, and admission test scores, should be received at the institution by the specified date.

Be advised that institutions do not usually make admissions decisions until all materials have been received. Enclose a self-addressed postcard with your application, requesting confirmation of receipt. Allow at least ten days for the return of the postcard before making further inquiries.

If you plan to apply for financial support, it is imperative that you file your application early.

ADMISSION TESTS

The major testing program used in graduate admissions is the Graduate Record Examinations (GRE®) testing program, sponsored by the GRE Board and administered by Educational Testing Service, Princeton, New Jersey.

The Graduate Record Examinations testing program consists of a General Test and eight Subject Tests. The General Test measures critical thinking, verbal reasoning, quantitative reasoning, and analytical writing skills. It is offered as an Internet-based test (iBT) in the United States, Canada, and many other countries.

The GRE® General Test's questions were designed to reflect the kind of thinking that students need to do in graduate or business school and demonstrate that students are indeed ready for graduate-level work.

- **Verbal Reasoning**—Measures ability to analyze and evaluate written material and synthesize information obtained from it, analyze relationships among component parts of sentences, and recognize relationships among words and concepts.
- **Quantitative Reasoning**—Measures problem-solving ability, focusing on basic concepts of arithmetic, algebra, geometry, and data analysis.
- **Analytical Writing**—Measures critical thinking and analytical writing skills, specifically the ability to articulate and support complex ideas clearly and effectively.

The computer-based GRE® General Test is offered year-round at Prometric™ test centers and on specific dates at testing locations outside of the Prometric test center network. Appointments are scheduled on a first-come, first-served basis. The GRE® General Test is also offered as a paper-based test three times a year in areas where computer-based testing is not available.

You can take the computer-based GRE® General Test once every twenty-one days, up to five times within any continuous rolling twelve-month period (365 days)—even if you canceled your scores on a previously taken test. You may take the paper-based GRE® General Test as often as it is offered.

Three scores are reported on the revised General Test:

1. A **Verbal Reasoning score** is reported on a 130–170 score scale, in 1-point increments.

2. A **Quantitative Reasoning score** is reported on a 130–170 score scale, in 1-point increments.

3. An **Analytical Writing score** is reported on a 0–6 score level, in half-point increments.

The GRE® Subject Tests measure achievement and assume undergraduate majors or extensive background in the following eight disciplines:

- Biochemistry, Cell and Molecular Biology
- Biology
- Chemistry
- Computer Science
- Literature in English
- Mathematics
- Physics
- Psychology

The Subject Tests are available three times per year as paper-based administrations around the world. Testing time is approximately 2 hours and 50 minutes. You can obtain more information about the GRE® by visiting the ETS website at www.ets.org or consulting the *GRE® Information and Registration Bulletin*. The *Bulletin* can be obtained at many undergraduate colleges. You can also download it from the ETS website or obtain it by contacting Graduate Record Examinations, Educational Testing Service, P.O. Box 6000, Princeton, NJ 08541-6000; phone: 609-771-7670.

If you expect to apply for admission to a program that requires any of the GRE® tests, you should select a test date well in advance of the application deadline. Scores on the computer-based General Test are reported within ten to fifteen days; scores on the paper-based Subject Tests are reported within six weeks.

Another testing program, the Miller Analogies Test® (MAT®), is administered at more than 500 Controlled Testing Centers, licensed by Harcourt Assessment, Inc., in the United States, Canada, and other countries. The MAT® computer-based test is now available. Testing time is 60 minutes. The test consists of 120 partial analogies. You can obtain the *Candidate Information Booklet,* which contains a list of test centers and instructions for taking the test, from http://www.milleranalogies.com or by calling 800-328-5999 (toll-free).

Check the specific requirements of the programs to which you are applying.

How Admission Decisions Are Made

The program you apply to is directly involved in the admissions process. Although the final decision is usually made by the graduate dean (or an associate) or the faculty admissions committee, recommendations from faculty members in your intended field are important. At some institutions, an interview is incorporated into the decision process.

A Special Note for International Students

In addition to the steps already described, there are some special considerations for international students who intend to apply for graduate study in the United States. All graduate schools require an indication of competence in English. The purpose of the Test of English as

a Foreign Language (TOEFL®) is to evaluate the English proficiency of people who are nonnative speakers of English and want to study at colleges and universities where English is the language of instruction. The TOEFL® is administered by Educational Testing Service (ETS) under the general direction of a policy board established by the College Board and the Graduate Record Examinations Board.

The TOEFL® iBT assesses the four basic language skills: listening, reading, writing, and speaking. It was administered for the first time in September 2005, and ETS continues to introduce the TOEFL® iBT in selected cities. The Internet-based test is administered at secure, official test centers. The testing time is approximately 4 hours. Because the TOEFL® iBT includes a speaking section, the Test of Spoken English (TSE) is no longer needed.

The TOEFL® is also offered in the paper-based format in areas of the world where Internet-based testing is not available. The paper-based TOEFL® consists of three sections—listening comprehension, structure and written expression, and reading comprehension. The testing time is approximately 3 hours.

The TOEFL® paper-based test (TOEFL® PBT) began being phased out in mid-2012. For those who may have taken the TOEFL® PBT, scores remain valid for two years after the test date. The Test of Written English (TWE®) is also given. The TWE® is a 30-minute essay that measures the examinee's ability to compose in English. Examinees receive a TWE® score separate from their TOEFL® score. The *Information Bulletin* contains information on local fees and registration procedures.

Additional information and registration materials are available from TOEFL® Services, Educational Testing Service, P.O. Box 6151, Princeton, New Jersey 08541-6151. Phone: 609-771-7100. Website: www.toefl.org.

International students should apply especially early because of the number of steps required to complete the admissions process. Furthermore, many United States graduate schools have a limited number of spaces for international students, and many more students apply than the schools can accommodate.

International students may find financial assistance from institutions very limited. The U.S. government requires international applicants to submit a certification of support, which is a statement attesting to the applicant's financial resources. In addition, international students *must* have health insurance coverage.

Tips for Minority Students

Indicators of a university's values in terms of diversity are found both in its recruitment programs and its resources directed to student success. Important questions: Does the institution vigorously recruit minorities for its graduate programs? Is there funding available to help with the costs associated with visiting the school? Are minorities represented in the institution's brochures or website or on their faculty rolls? What campus-based resources or services (including assistance in locating housing or career counseling and placement) are available? Is funding available to members of underrepresented groups?

At the program level, it is particularly important for minority students to investigate the "climate" of a program under consideration. How many minority students are enrolled and how many have graduated? What opportunities are there to work with diverse faculty and mentors whose research interests match yours? How are conflicts resolved or concerns addressed? How interested are faculty in building strong and supportive relations with students? "Climate" concerns should be addressed by posing questions to various individuals, including faculty members, current students, and alumni.

Information is also available through various organizations, such as the Hispanic Association of Colleges & Universities (HACU), and publications such as *Diverse Issues in Higher Education* and *Hispanic Outlook* magazine. There are also books devoted to this topic, such as *The Multicultural Student's Guide to Colleges* by Robert Mitchell.

Financial Support

The range of financial support at the graduate level is very broad. The following descriptions will give you a general idea of what you might expect and what will be expected of you as a financial support recipient.

Fellowships, Scholarships, and Grants

These are usually outright awards of a few hundred to many thousands of dollars with no service to the institution required in return. Fellowships and scholarships are usually awarded on the basis of merit and are highly competitive. Grants are made on the basis of financial need or special talent in a field of study. Many fellowships, scholarships, and grants not only cover tuition, fees, and supplies but also include stipends for living expenses with allowances for dependents. However, the terms of each should be examined because some do not permit recipients to supplement their income with outside work. Fellowships, scholarships, and grants may vary in the number of years for which they are awarded.

In addition to the availability of these funds at the university or program level, many excellent fellowship programs are available at the national level and may be applied for before and during enrollment in a graduate program. A listing of many of these programs can be found at the Council of Graduate Schools' website: http://www.cgsnet.org. There is a wealth of information in the "Programs" and "Awards" sections.

Assistantships and Internships

Many graduate students receive financial support through assistantships, particularly involving teaching or research duties. It is important to recognize that such appointments should not be viewed simply as employment relationships but rather should constitute an integral and important part of a student's graduate education. As such, the appointments should be accompanied by strong faculty mentoring and increasingly responsible apprenticeship experiences. The specific nature of these appointments in a given program should be considered in selecting that graduate program.

TEACHING ASSISTANTSHIPS

These usually provide a salary and full or partial tuition remission and may also provide health benefits. Unlike fellowships, scholarships, and grants, which require no service to the institution, teaching assistantships require recipients to provide the institution with a specific amount of undergraduate teaching, ideally related to the student's field of study. Some teaching assistants are limited to grading papers, compiling bibliographies, taking notes, or monitoring laboratories. At some graduate schools, teaching assistants must carry lighter course loads than regular full-time students.

RESEARCH ASSISTANTSHIPS

These are very similar to teaching assistantships in the manner in which financial assistance is provided. The difference is that recipients are given basic research assignments in their disciplines rather than teaching responsibilities. The work required is normally related to the student's field of study; in most instances, the assistantship supports the student's thesis or dissertation research.

ADMINISTRATIVE INTERNSHIPS

These are similar to assistantships in application of financial assistance funds, but the student is given an assignment on a part-time basis, usually as a special assistant with one of the university's administrative offices. The assignment may not necessarily be directly related to the recipient's discipline.

RESIDENCE HALL AND COUNSELING ASSISTANTSHIPS

These assistantships are frequently assigned to graduate students in psychology, counseling, and social work, but they may be offered to students in other disciplines, especially if the student has worked in this capacity during his or her undergraduate years. Duties can vary from being available in a dean's office for a specific number of hours for consultation with undergraduates to living in campus residences and being responsible for both counseling and administrative tasks or advising student activity groups. Residence hall assistantships often include a room and board allowance and, in some cases, tuition assistance and stipends. Contact the Housing and Student Life Office for more information.

Health Insurance

The availability and affordability of health insurance is an important issue and one that should be considered in an applicant's choice of institution and program. While often included with assistantships and fellowships, this is not always the case and, even if provided, the benefits may be limited. It is important to note that the U.S. government requires international students to have health insurance.

The GI Bill

This provides financial assistance for students who are veterans of the United States armed forces. If you are a veteran, contact your local Veterans Administration office to determine your eligibility and to get full details about benefits. There are a number of programs that offer educational benefits to current military enlistees. Some states have tuition assistance programs for members of the National Guard. Contact the VA office at the college for more information.

Federal Work-Study Program (FWS)

Employment is another way some students finance their graduate studies. The federally funded Federal Work-Study Program provides eligible students with employment opportunities, usually in public and private nonprofit organizations. Federal funds pay up to 75 percent of the wages, with the remainder paid by the employing agency. FWS is available to graduate students who demonstrate financial need. Not all schools have these funds, and some only award them to undergraduates. Each school sets its application deadline and workstudy earnings limits. Wages vary and are related to the type of work done. You must file the Free Application for Federal Student Aid (FAFSA) to be eligible for this program.

Loans

Many graduate students borrow to finance their graduate programs when other sources of assistance (which do not have to be repaid) prove insufficient. You should always read and understand the terms of any loan program before submitting your application.

FEDERAL DIRECT LOANS

Federal Direct Loans. The Federal Direct Loan Program offers a variable-fixed interest rate loan to graduate students with the Department of Education acting as the lender. Students receive a new rate with each new loan, but that rate is fixed for the life of the loan. Beginning with loans made on or after July 1, 2013, the interest rate for loans made each July 1st to June 30th period are determined based on the last 10-year Treasury note auction prior to June 1st of that year, plus an added percentage. The interest rate can be no higher than 9.5%.

Beginning July 1, 2012, the Federal Direct Loan for graduate students is an unsubsidized loan. Under the *unsubsidized* program, the grad borrower pays the interest on the loan from the day proceeds are issued and is responsible for paying interest during all periods. If the borrower chooses not to pay the interest while in school, or during the grace periods, deferment, or forbearance, the interest accrues and will be capitalized.

Graduate students may borrow up to $20,500 per year through the Direct Loan Program, up to a cumulative maximum of $138,500, including undergraduate borrowing. No more than $65,500 of the $138,500 can be from subsidized loans, including loans the grad borrower may have received for periods of enrollment that began before July 1, 2012, or for prior undergraduate borrowing. You may borrow up to the cost of attendance at the school in which you are enrolled or will attend, minus estimated financial assistance from other federal, state, and private sources, up to a maximum of $20,500. Grad borrowers who reach the aggregate loan limit over the course of their education cannot receive additional loans; however, if they repay some of their loans to bring the outstanding balance below the aggregate limit, they could be eligible to borrow again, up to that limit.

For Unsubsidized loans first disbursed on or after July 1, 2016, and before July 1, 2017, the interest rate was 5.31%. For those first disbursed on or after July 1, 2017, and before July 1, 2018, the interest rate is 6%.

A fee is deducted from the loan proceeds upon disbursement. Loans with a first disbursement on or after July 1, 2010 but before July 1, 2012, have a borrower origination fee of 1 percent. For loans disbursed after July 1, 2012, these fee deductions no longer apply. The Budget Control Act of 2011, signed into law on August 2, 2011, eliminated Direct Subsidized Loan eligibility for graduate and professional students for periods of enrollment beginning on or after July 1, 2012, and terminated the authority of the Department of Education to offer most repayment incentives to Direct Loan borrowers for loans disbursed on or after July 1, 2012.

Under the *subsidized* Federal Direct Loan Program, repayment begins six months after your last date of enrollment on at least a half-time basis. Under the *unsubsidized* program, repayment of interest begins within thirty days from disbursement of the loan proceeds, and repayment of the principal begins six months after your last enrollment on at least a half-time basis. Some borrowers may choose to defer interest payments while they are in school. The accrued interest is added to the loan balance when the borrower begins repayment. There are several repayment options.

Federal Perkins Loans. The Federal Perkins Loan is available to students demonstrating financial need and is administered directly by the school. Not all schools have these funds, and some may award them to undergraduates only. Eligibility is determined from the information you provide on the FAFSA. The school will notify you of your eligibility.

Eligible graduate students may borrow up to $8,000 per year, up to a maximum of $60,000, including undergraduate borrowing (even if your previous Perkins Loans have been repaid). The interest rate for Federal Perkins Loans is 5 percent, and no interest accrues while you remain in school at least half-time. Students who are attending less than half-time need to check with their school to determine the length of their grace period. There are no guarantee, loan, or disbursement fees. Repayment begins nine months after your last date of enrollment on at least a half-time basis and may extend over a maximum of ten years with no prepayment penalty.

Federal Direct Graduate PLUS Loans. Effective July 1, 2006, graduate and professional students are eligible for Graduate PLUS loans. This program allows students to borrow up to the cost of attendance, less any other aid received. These loans have a fixed interest rate (7.0% for the 2017–2018 academic year), and interest begins to accrue at the time of disbursement. Beginning with loans made on or after July 1, 2013, the interest rate for loans made each July 1st to June 30th period are determined based on the last 10-year Treasury note auction prior to June 1st of that year. The interest rate can be no higher than 10.5%. The PLUS loans do involve a credit check; a PLUS borrower may obtain a loan with a cosigner if his or her credit is not good enough. Grad PLUS loans may be deferred while a student is in school and for the six months following a drop below half-time enrollment. For more information, you should contact a representative in your college's financial aid office.

Deferring Your Federal Loan Repayments. If you borrowed under the Federal Direct Loan Program, Federal Direct PLUS Loan Program, or the Federal Perkins Loan Program for previous undergraduate or graduate study, your payments may be deferred when you return to graduate school, depending on when you borrowed and under which program.

There are other deferment options available if you are temporarily unable to repay your loan. Information about these deferments is provided at your entrance and exit interviews. If you believe you are eligible for a deferment of your loan payments, you must contact your lender or loan servicer to request a deferment. The deferment must be filed prior to the time your payment is due, and it must be re-filed when it expires if you remain eligible for deferment at that time.

SUPPLEMENTAL (PRIVATE) LOANS

Many lending institutions offer supplemental loan programs and other financing plans, such as the ones described here, to students seeking additional assistance in meeting their education expenses. Some loan programs target all types of graduate students; others are designed specifically for business, law, or medical students. In addition, you can use private loans not specifically designed for education to help finance your graduate degree.

If you are considering borrowing through a supplemental or private loan program, you should carefully consider the terms and be sure to read the fine print. Check with the program sponsor for the most current terms that will be applicable to the amounts you intend to borrow for graduate study. Most supplemental loan programs for graduate study offer unsubsidized, credit-based loans. In general, a credit-ready borrower is one who has a satisfactory credit history or no credit history at all. A creditworthy borrower generally must pass a credit test to be eligible to borrow or act as a cosigner for the loan funds.

Many supplemental loan programs have minimum and maximum annual loan limits. Some offer amounts equal to the cost of attendance minus any other aid you will receive for graduate study. If you are planning to borrow for several years of graduate study, consider whether there is a cumulative or aggregate limit on the amount you may borrow. Often this cumulative or aggregate limit will include any amounts you borrowed and have not repaid for undergraduate or previous graduate study.

The combination of the annual interest rate, loan fees, and the repayment terms you choose will determine how much you will repay over time. Compare these features in combination before you decide which loan program to use. Some loans offer interest rates that are adjusted monthly, quarterly, or annually. Some offer interest rates that are lower during the in-school, grace, and deferment periods and then increase when you begin repayment. Some programs include a loan origination fee, which is usually deducted from the principal amount you receive when the loan is disbursed and must be repaid along with the interest and other principal when you graduate, withdraw from school, or drop below half-time study. Sometimes the loan fees are reduced if you borrow with a qualified cosigner. Some programs allow you to defer interest and/or principal payments while you are enrolled in graduate school. Many programs allow you to capitalize your interest payments; the interest due on your loan is added to the outstanding balance of your loan, so you don't have to repay immediately, but this increases the amount you owe. Other programs allow you to pay the interest as you go, which reduces the amount you later have to repay. The private loan market is very competitive, and your financial aid office can help you evaluate these programs.

Applying for Need-Based Financial Aid

Schools that award federal and institutional financial assistance based on need will require you to complete the FAFSA and, in some cases, an institutional financial aid application.

If you are applying for federal student assistance, you **must** complete the FAFSA. A service of the U.S. Department of Education, the FAFSA is free to all applicants. Most applicants apply online at www.fafsa.ed.gov. Paper applications are available at the financial aid office of your local college.

After your FAFSA information has been processed, you will receive a Student Aid Report (SAR). If you provided an e-mail address on the FAFSA, this will be sent to you electronically; otherwise, it will be mailed to your home address.

Follow the instructions on the SAR if you need to correct information reported on your original application. If your situation changes after you file your FAFSA, contact your financial aid officer to discuss amending your information. You can also appeal your financial aid award if you have extenuating circumstances.

If you would like more information on federal student financial aid, visit the FAFSA website or download the most recent version of *Funding Education Beyond High School: The Guide to Federal Student Aid* at http://studentaid.ed.gov/students/publications/student_guide/index.html. This guide is also available in Spanish.

The U.S. Department of Education also has a toll-free number for questions concerning federal student aid programs. The number is 1-800-4-FED AID (1-800-433-3243). If you are hearing impaired, call toll-free, 1-800-730-8913.

Summary

Remember that these are generalized statements about financial assistance at the graduate level. Because each institution allots its aid differently, you should communicate directly with the school and the specific department of interest to you. It is not unusual, for example, to find that an endowment vested within a specific department supports one or more fellowships. You may fit its requirements and specifications precisely.

Accreditation and Accrediting Agencies

Colleges and universities in the United States, and their individual academic and professional programs, are accredited by nongovernmental agencies concerned with monitoring the quality of education in this country. Agencies with both regional and national jurisdictions grant accreditation to institutions as a whole, while specialized bodies acting on a nationwide basis—often national professional associations—grant accreditation to departments and programs in specific fields.

Institutional and specialized accrediting agencies share the same basic concerns: the purpose an academic unit—whether university or program—has set for itself and how well it fulfills that purpose, the adequacy of its financial and other resources, the quality of its academic offerings, and the level of services it provides. Agencies that grant institutional accreditation take a broader view, of course, and examine university-wide or college-wide services with which a specialized agency may not concern itself.

Both types of agencies follow the same general procedures when considering an application for accreditation. The academic unit prepares a self-evaluation, focusing on the concerns mentioned above and usually including an assessment of both its strengths and weaknesses; a team of representatives of the accrediting body reviews this evaluation, visits the campus, and makes its own report; and finally, the accrediting body makes a decision on the application. Often, even when accreditation is granted, the agency makes a recommendation regarding how the institution or program can improve. All institutions and programs are also reviewed every few years to determine whether they continue to meet established standards; if they do not, they may lose their accreditation.

Accrediting agencies themselves are reviewed and evaluated periodically by the U.S. Department of Education and the Council for Higher Education Accreditation (CHEA). Recognized agencies adhere to certain standards and practices, and their authority in matters of accreditation is widely accepted in the educational community.

This does not mean, however, that accreditation is a simple matter, either for schools wishing to become accredited or for students deciding where to apply. Indeed, in certain fields the very meaning and methods of accreditation are the subject of a good deal of debate. For their part, those applying to graduate school should be aware of the safeguards provided by regional accreditation, especially in terms of degree acceptance and institutional longevity. Beyond this, applicants should understand the role that specialized accreditation plays in their field, as this varies considerably from one discipline to another. In certain professional fields, it is necessary to have graduated from a program that is accredited in order to be eligible for a license to practice, and in some fields the federal government also makes this a hiring requirement. In other disciplines, however, accreditation is not as essential, and there can be excellent programs that are not accredited. In fact, some programs choose not to seek accreditation, although most do.

Institutions and programs that present themselves for accreditation are sometimes granted the status of candidate for accreditation, or what is known as "preaccreditation." This may happen, for example, when an academic unit is too new to have met all the requirements for accreditation. Such status signifies initial recognition and indicates that the school or program in question is working to fulfill all requirements; it does not, however, guarantee that accreditation will be granted.

Institutional Accrediting Agencies—Regional

MIDDLE STATES ASSOCIATION OF COLLEGES AND SCHOOLS

Accredits institutions in Delaware, District of Columbia, Maryland, New Jersey, New York, Pennsylvania, Puerto Rico, and the Virgin Islands.

Dr. Elizabeth Sibolski, President
Middle States Commission on Higher Education
3624 Market Street, Second Floor West
Philadelphia, Pennsylvania 19104
Phone: 267-284-5000
Fax: 215-662-5501
E-mail: info@msche.org
Website: www.msche.org

NEW ENGLAND ASSOCIATION OF SCHOOLS AND COLLEGES

Accredits institutions in Connecticut, Maine, Massachusetts, New Hampshire, Rhode Island, and Vermont.

Dr. Barbara E. Brittingham, President/Director
Commission on Institutions of Higher Education
3 Burlington Woods Drive, Suite 100
Burlington, Massachusetts 01803-4531
Phone: 855-886-3272 or 781-425-7714
Fax: 781-425-1001
E-mail: cihe@neasc.org
Website: http://cihe.neasc.org

THE HIGHER LEARNING COMMISSION

Accredits institutions in Arizona, Arkansas, Colorado, Illinois, Indiana, Iowa, Kansas, Michigan, Minnesota, Missouri, Nebraska, New Mexico, North Dakota, Ohio, Oklahoma, South Dakota, West Virginia, Wisconsin, and Wyoming.

Dr. Barbara Gellman-Danley, President
The Higher Learning Commission
230 South LaSalle Street, Suite 7-500
Chicago, Illinois 60604-1413
Phone: 800-621-7440 or 312-263-0456
Fax: 312-263-7462
E-mail: info@hlcommission.org
Website: www.hlcommission.org

NORTHWEST COMMISSION ON COLLEGES AND UNIVERSITIES

Accredits institutions in Alaska, Idaho, Montana, Nevada, Oregon, Utah, and Washington.

Dr. Sandra E. Elman, President
8060 165th Avenue, NE, Suite 100
Redmond, Washington 98052
Phone: 425-558-4224
Fax: 425-376-0596
E-mail: selman@nwccu.org
Website: www.nwccu.org

SOUTHERN ASSOCIATION OF COLLEGES AND SCHOOLS

Accredits institutions in Alabama, Florida, Georgia, Kentucky, Louisiana, Mississippi, North Carolina, South Carolina, Tennessee, Texas, and Virginia.

Dr. Belle S. Wheelan, President
Commission on Colleges
1866 Southern Lane
Decatur, Georgia 30033-4097
Phone: 404-679-4500 Ext. 4504
Fax: 404-679-4558
E-mail: questions@sacscoc.org
Website: www.sacscoc.org

WESTERN ASSOCIATION OF SCHOOLS AND COLLEGES

Accredits institutions in California, Guam, and Hawaii.

Dr. Mary Ellen Petrisko, President
Accrediting Commission for Senior Colleges and Universities
985 Atlantic Avenue, Suite 100
Alameda, California 94501
Phone: 510-748-9001
Fax: 510-748-9797
E-mail: wasc@wascsenior.org
Website: http://www.wascsenior.org/

Institutional Accrediting Agencies—Other

ACCREDITING COUNCIL FOR INDEPENDENT COLLEGES AND SCHOOLS
Anthony S. Bieda, Executive in Charge
750 First Street, NE, Suite 980
Washington, DC 20002-4241
Phone: 202-336-6780
Fax: 202-842-2593
E-mail: info@acics.org
Website: www.acics.org

DISTANCE EDUCATION AND ACCREDITING COMMISSION (DEAC)
Accrediting Commission
Leah Matthews, Executive Director
1101 17th Street, NW, Suite 808
Washington, DC 20036-4704
Phone: 202-234-5100
Fax: 202-332-1386
E-mail: info@deac.org
Website: www.deac.org

Specialized Accrediting Agencies

ACUPUNCTURE AND ORIENTAL MEDICINE
Mark S. McKenzie, LAc MsOM DiplOM, Executive Director
Accreditation Commission for Acupuncture and Oriental Medicine
8941 Aztec Drive
Eden Prairie, Minnesota 55347
Phone: 952-212-2434
Fax: 301-313-0912
E-mail: coordinator@acaom.org
Website: www.acaom.org

ALLIED HEALTH
Kathleen Megivern, Executive Director
Commission on Accreditation of Allied Health Education Programs (CAAHEP)
25400 US Hwy 19 North, Suite 158
Clearwater, Florida 33763
Phone: 727-210-2350
Fax: 727-210-2354
E-mail: mail@caahep.org
Website: www.caahep.org

ART AND DESIGN
Karen P. Moynahan, Executive Director
National Association of Schools of Art and Design (NASAD)
Commission on Accreditation
11250 Roger Bacon Drive, Suite 21
Reston, Virginia 20190-5248
Phone: 703-437-0700
Fax: 703-437-6312
E-mail: info@arts-accredit.org
Website: http://nasad.arts-accredit.org

ATHLETIC TRAINING EDUCATION
Micki Cuppett, Executive Director
Commission on Accreditation of Athletic Training Education (CAATE)
6850 Austin Center Blvd., Suite 100
Austin, Texas 78731-3184
Phone: 512-733-9700
E-mail: micki@caate.net
Website: www.caate.net

AUDIOLOGY EDUCATION
Doris Gordon, Executive Director
Accreditation Commission for Audiology Education (ACAE)
11480 Commerce Park Drive, Suite 220
Reston, Virginia 20191
Phone: 202-986-9550
Fax: 202-986-9500
E-mail: info@acaeaccred.org
Website: www.acaeaccred.org

AVIATION
Dr. Gary J. Northam, Executive Director
Aviation Accreditation Board International (AABI)
3410 Skyway Drive
Auburn, Alabama 36830
Phone: 334-844-2431
Fax: 334-844-2432
E-mail: bayenva@auburn.edu
Website: www.aabi.aero

BUSINESS
Robert D. Reid, Executive Vice President and Chief Accreditation Officer
AACSB International—The Association to Advance Collegiate Schools of Business
777 South Harbour Island Boulevard, Suite 750
Tampa, Florida 33602
Phone: 813-769-6500
Fax: 813-769-6559
E-mail: bob@aacsb.edu
Website: www.aacsb.edu

BUSINESS EDUCATION
Dennis N. Gash, President and Chief Executive Officer
International Assembly for Collegiate Business Education (IACBE)
11257 Strang Line Road
Lenexa, Kansas 66215
Phone: 913-631-3009
Fax: 913-631-9154
E-mail:iacbe@iacbe.org
Website: www.iacbe.org

CHIROPRACTIC
Craig S. Little, President
Council on Chiropractic Education (CCE)
Commission on Accreditation
8049 North 85th Way
Scottsdale, Arizona 85258-4321
Phone: 480-443-8877 or 888-443-3506
Fax: 480-483-7333
E-mail: cce@cce-usa.org
Website: www.cce-usa.org

CLINICAL LABORATORY SCIENCES
Dianne M. Cearlock, Ph.D., Chief Executive Officer
National Accrediting Agency for Clinical Laboratory Sciences
5600 North River Road, Suite 720
Rosemont, Illinois 60018-5119
Phone: 773-714-8880 or 847-939-3597
Fax: 773-714-8886
E-mail: info@naacls.org
Website: www.naacls.org

CLINICAL PASTORAL EDUCATION
Trace Haythorn, Executive Director
Association for Clinical Pastoral Education, Inc.
1549 Clairmont Road, Suite 103
Decatur, Georgia 30033-4611
Phone: 404-320-1472
Fax: 404-320-0849
E-mail: acpe@acpe.edu
Website: www.acpe.edu

DANCE
Karen P. Moynahan, Executive Director
National Association of Schools of Dance (NASD)
Commission on Accreditation
11250 Roger Bacon Drive, Suite 21
Reston, Virginia 20190-5248
Phone: 703-437-0700
Fax: 703-437-6312
E-mail: info@arts-accredit.org
Website: http://nasd.arts-accredit.org

DENTISTRY
Dr. Sherin Tooks, Director
Commission on Dental Accreditation
American Dental Association
211 East Chicago Avenue, Suite 1900
Chicago, Illinois 60611
Phone: 312-440-4643 or 800-621-8099
E-mail: accreditation@ada.org
Website: www.ada.org

DIETETICS AND NUTRITION
Mary B. Gregoire, Ph.D., Executive Director; RD, FADA, FAND
Academy of Nutrition and Dietetics
Accreditation Council for Education in Nutrition and Dietetics (ACEND)
120 South Riverside Plaza, Suite 2000
Chicago, Illinois 60606-6995
Phone: 800-877-1600 Ext. 5400 or 312-899-0040
Fax: 312-899-4817
E-mail: acend@eatright.org
Website: www.eatright.org/ACEND

EDUCATION PREPARATION
Christopher Koch, President
Council for the Accreditation of Education Preparation (CAEP)
1140 19th Street NW, Suite 400
Washington, DC 20036
Phone: 202-223-0077
Fax: 202-296-6620
E-mail: caep@caepnet.org
Website: www.caepnet.org

ENGINEERING
Michael Milligan, Ph.D., PE, Executive Director
Accreditation Board for Engineering and Technology, Inc. (ABET)
415 North Charles Street
Baltimore, Maryland 21201
Phone: 410-347-7700
E-mail: accreditation@abet.org
Website: www.abet.org

FORENSIC SCIENCES
Nancy J. Jackson, Director of Development and Accreditation
American Academy of Forensic Sciences (AAFS)
Forensic Science Education Program Accreditation Commission (FEPAC)
410 North 21st Street
Colorado Springs, Colorado 80904
Phone: 719-636-1100
Fax: 719-636-1993
E-mail: njackson@aafs.org
Website: www.fepac-edu.org

FORESTRY
Carol L. Redelsheimer
Director of Science and Education
Society of American Foresters
5400 Grosvenor Lane
Bethesda, Maryland 20814-2198
Phone: 301-897-8720 or 866-897-8720
Fax: 301-897-3690
E-mail: redelsheimerc@safnet.org
Website: www.safnet.org

HEALTHCARE MANAGEMENT
Commission on Accreditation of Healthcare Management Education (CAHME)
Anthony Stanowski, President and CEO
1700 Rockville Pike
Suite 400
Rockville, Maryland 20852
Phone: 301-998-6101
E-mail: info@cahme.org
Website: www.cahme.org

HEALTH INFORMATICS AND HEALTH MANAGEMENT
Claire Dixon-Lee, Executive Director
Commission on Accreditation for Health Informatics and Information Management Education (CAHIIM)
233 North Michigan Avenue, 21st Floor
Chicago, Illinois 60601-5800
Phone: 312-233-1100
Fax: 312-233-1948
E-mail:E-mail: claire.dixon-lee@cahiim.org
Website: www.cahiim.org

HUMAN SERVICE EDUCATION
Dr. Elaine Green, President
Council for Standards in Human Service Education (CSHSE)
3337 Duke Street
Alexandria, Virginia 22314
Phone: 571-257-3959
E-mail: info@cshse.org
Web: http://www.cshse.org

INTERIOR DESIGN
Holly Mattson, Executive Director
Council for Interior Design Accreditation
206 Grandview Avenue, Suite 350
Grand Rapids, Michigan 49503-4014
Phone: 616-458-0400
Fax: 616-458-0460
E-mail: info@accredit-id.org
Website: www.accredit-id.org

JOURNALISM AND MASS COMMUNICATIONS
Susanne Shaw, Executive Director
Accrediting Council on Education in Journalism and Mass Communications (ACEJMC)
School of Journalism
Stauffer-Flint Hall
University of Kansas
1435 Jayhawk Boulevard
Lawrence, Kansas 66045-7575
Phone: 785-864-3973
Fax: 785-864-5225
E-mail: sshaw@ku.edu
Website: http://www2.ku.edu/~acejmc/

LANDSCAPE ARCHITECTURE
Kristopher D. Pritchard, Executive Director
Landscape Architectural Accreditation Board (LAAB)
American Society of Landscape Architects (ASLA)
636 Eye Street, NW
Washington, DC 20001-3736
Phone: 202-216-2359
Fax: 202-898-1185
E-mail: info@asla.org
Website: www.asla.org

LAW
Barry Currier, Managing Director of Accreditation & Legal Education
American Bar Association
321 North Clark Street, 21st Floor
Chicago, Illinois 60654
Phone: 312-988-6738
Fax: 312-988-5681
E-mail: legaled@americanbar.org
Website: http://www.americanbar.org/groups/legal_education/
    resources/accreditation.html

LIBRARY
Karen O'Brien, Director
Office for Accreditation
American Library Association
50 East Huron Street
Chicago, Illinois 60611-2795
Phone: 312-280-2432
Fax: 312-280-2433
E-mail: accred@ala.org
Website: www.ala.org/accreditation/

MARRIAGE AND FAMILY THERAPY
Tanya A. Tamarkin, Director of Educational Affairs
Commission on Accreditation for Marriage and Family Therapy
    Education (COAMFTE)
American Association for Marriage and Family Therapy
112 South Alfred Street
Alexandria, Virginia 22314-3061
Phone: 703-838-9808
Fax: 703-838-9805
E-mail: coa@aamft.org
Website: www.aamft.org

MEDICAL ILLUSTRATION
Kathleen Megivern, Executive Director
Commission on Accreditation of Allied Health Education Programs
    (CAAHEP)
1361 Park Street
Clearwater, Florida 33756
Phone: 727-210-2350
Fax: 727-210-2354
E-mail: mail@caahep.org
Website: www.caahep.org

MEDICINE
Liaison Committee on Medical Education (LCME)
Robert B. Hash, M.D., LCME Secretary
American Medical Association
Council on Medical Education
330 North Wabash Avenue, Suite 39300
Chicago, Illinois 60611-5885
Phone: 312-464-4933
E-mail: lcme@aamc.org
Website: www.ama-assn.org

Liaison Committee on Medical Education (LCME)
Heather Lent, M.A., Director
Accreditation Services
Association of American Medical Colleges
655 K Street, NW
Washington, DC 20001-2399
Phone: 202-828-0596
E-mail: lcme@aamc.org
Website: www.lcme.org

MUSIC
Karen P. Moynahan, Executive Director
National Association of Schools of Music (NASM)
Commission on Accreditation
11250 Roger Bacon Drive, Suite 21
Reston, Virginia 20190-5248
Phone: 703-437-0700
Fax: 703-437-6312
E-mail: info@arts-accredit.org
Website: http://nasm.arts-accredit.org/

NATUROPATHIC MEDICINE
Daniel Seitz, J.D., Ed.D., Executive Director
Council on Naturopathic Medical Education
P.O. Box 178
Great Barrington, Massachusetts 01230
Phone: 413-528-8877
E-mail: www.cnme.org/contact.html
Website: www.cnme.org

NURSE ANESTHESIA
Francis R.Gerbasi, Ph.D., CRNA, COA Executive Director
Council on Accreditation of Nurse Anesthesia Educational Programs
    (CoA-NAEP)
American Association of Nurse Anesthetists
222 South Prospect Avenue, Suite 304
Park Ridge, Illinois 60068-4010
Phone: 847-655-1160
Fax: 847-692-7137
E-mail: accreditation@coa.us.com
Website: http://home.coa.us.com

NURSE EDUCATION
Jennifer L. Butlin, Executive Director
Commission on Collegiate Nursing Education (CCNE)
One Dupont Circle, NW, Suite 530
Washington, DC 20036-1120
Phone: 202-887-6791
Fax: 202-887-8476
E-mail: jbutlin@aacn.nche.edu
Website: www.aacn.nche.edu/accreditation

Marsal P. Stoll, Chief Executive Officer
Accreditation Commission for Education in Nursing (ACEN)
3343 Peachtree Road, NE, Suite 850
Atlanta, Georgia 30326
Phone: 404-975-5000
Fax: 404-975-5020
E-mail: mstoll@acenursing.org
Website: www.acenursing.org

NURSE MIDWIFERY
Heather L. Maurer, M.A., Executive Director
Accreditation Commission for Midwifery Education (ACME)
American College of Nurse-Midwives
8403 Colesville Road, Suite 1550
Silver Spring, Maryland 20910
Phone: 240-485-1800
Fax: 240-485-1818
E-mail: info@acnm.org
Website: www.midwife.org/Program-Accreditation

NURSE PRACTITIONER
Gay Johnson, CEO
National Association of Nurse Practitioners in Women's Health
Council on Accreditation
505 C Street, NE
Washington, DC 20002
Phone: 202-543-9693 Ext. 1
Fax: 202-543-9858
E-mail: info@npwh.org
Website: www.npwh.org

NURSING

Marsal P. Stoll, Chief Executive Director
Accreditation Commission for Education in Nursing (ACEN)
3343 Peachtree Road, NE, Suite 850
Atlanta, Georgia 30326
Phone: 404-975-5000
Fax: 404-975-5020
E-mail: info@acenursing.org
Website: www.acenursing.org

OCCUPATIONAL THERAPY

Heather Stagliano, DHSc, OTR/L, Executive Director
The American Occupational Therapy Association, Inc.
4720 Montgomery Lane, Suite 200
Bethesda, Maryland 20814-3449
Phone: 301-652-6611 Ext. 2682
TDD: 800-377-8555
Fax: 240-762-5150
E-mail: accred@aota.org
Website: www.aoteonline.org

OPTOMETRY

Joyce L. Urbeck, Administrative Director
Accreditation Council on Optometric Education (ACOE)
American Optometric Association
243 North Lindbergh Boulevard
St. Louis, Missouri 63141-7881
Phone: 314-991-4100, Ext. 4246
Fax: 314-991-4101
E-mail: accredit@aoa.org
Website: www.theacoe.org

OSTEOPATHIC MEDICINE

Director, Department of Accreditation
Commission on Osteopathic College Accreditation (COCA)
American Osteopathic Association
142 East Ontario Street
Chicago, Illinois 60611
Phone: 312-202-8048
Fax: 312-202-8202
E-mail: predoc@osteopathic.org
Website: www.aoacoca.org

PHARMACY

Peter H. Vlasses, PharmD, Executive Director
Accreditation Council for Pharmacy Education
135 South LaSalle Street, Suite 4100
Chicago, Illinois 60603-4810
Phone: 312-664-3575
Fax: 312-664-4652
E-mail: csinfo@acpe-accredit.org
Website: www.acpe-accredit.org

PHYSICAL THERAPY

Sandra Wise, Senior Director
Commission on Accreditation in Physical Therapy Education (CAPTE)
American Physical Therapy Association (APTA)
1111 North Fairfax Street
Alexandria, Virginia 22314-1488
Phone: 703-706-3245
Fax: 703-706-3387
E-mail: accreditation@apta.org
Website: www.capteonline.org

PHYSICIAN ASSISTANT STUDIES

Sharon L. Luke, Executive Director
Accredittion Review Commission on Education for the Physician
    Assistant, Inc. (ARC-PA)
12000 Findley Road, Suite 150
Johns Creek, Georgia 30097
Phone: 770-476-1224
Fax: 770-476-1738
E-mail: arc-pa@arc-pa.org
Website: www.arc-pa.org

PLANNING

Ms. Shonagh Merits, Executive Director
American Institute of Certified Planners/Association of Collegiate
    Schools of Planning/American Planning Association
Planning Accreditation Board (PAB)
2334 West Lawrence Avenue, Suite 209
Chicago, Illinois 60625
Phone: 773-334-7200
E-mail: smerits@planningaccreditationboard.org
Website: www.planningaccreditationboard.org

PODIATRIC MEDICINE

Alan R. Tinkleman, M.P.A., Executive Director
Council on Podiatric Medical Education (CPME)
American Podiatric Medical Association (APMA)
9312 Old Georgetown Road
Bethesda, Maryland 20814-1621
Phone: 301-581-9200
Fax: 301-571-4903
Website: www.cpme.org

PSYCHOLOGY AND COUNSELING

Jacqueline Remondet Wall, CEO of the Accrediting Unit,
Office of Program Consultation and Accreditation
American Psychological Association
750 First Street, NE
Washington, DC 20002-4202
Phone: 202-336-5979 or 800-374-2721
TDD/TTY: 202-336-6123
Fax: 202-336-5978
E-mail: apaaccred@apa.org
Website: www.apa.org/ed/accreditation

Carol L. Bobby, Ph.D., Executive Director
Council for Accreditation of Counseling and Related Educational
    Programs (CACREP)
1001 North Fairfax Street, Suite 510
Alexandria, Virginia 22314
Phone: 703-535-5990
Fax: 703-739-6209
E-mail: cacrep@cacrep.org
Website: www.cacrep.org

Richard M. McFall, Executive Director
Psychological Clinical Science Accreditation System (PCSAS)
1101 East Tenth Street
IU Psychology Building
Bloomington, Indiana 47405-7007
Phone: 812-856-2570
Fax: 812-322-5545
E-mail: rmmcfall@pcsas.org
Website: www.pcsas.org

PUBLIC HEALTH

Laura Rasar King, M.P.H., MCHES, Executive Director
Council on Education for Public Health
1010 Wayne Avenue, Suite 220
Silver Spring, Maryland 20910
Phone: 202-789-1050
Fax: 202-789-1895
E-mail: Lking@ceph.org
Website: www.ceph.org

PUBLIC POLICY, AFFAIRS AND ADMINISTRATION

Crystal Calarusse, Chief Accreditation Officer
Commission on Peer Review and Accreditation
Network of Schools of Public Policy, Affairs, and Administration
(NASPAA-COPRA)
1029 Vermont Avenue, NW, Suite 1100
Washington, DC 20005
Phone: 202-628-8965
Fax: 202-626-4978
E-mail: copra@naspaa.org
Website: www.naspaa.org

RADIOLOGIC TECHNOLOGY
Leslie Winter, Chief Executive Officer Joint Review Committee on Education in Radiologic Technology (JRCERT)
20 North Wacker Drive, Suite 2850
Chicago, Illinois 60606-3182
Phone: 312-704-5300
Fax: 312-704-5304
E-mail: mail@jrcert.org
Web: www.jrcert.org

REHABILITATION EDUCATION
Frank Lane, Ph.D., Executive Director
Council on Rehabilitation Education (CORE)
Commission on Standards and Accreditation
1699 Woodfield Road, Suite 300
Schaumburg, Illinois 60173
Phone: 847-944-1345
Fax: 847-944-1346
E-mail: flane@core-rehab.org
Website: www.core-rehab.org

RESPIRATORY CARE
Thomas Smalling, Executive Director
Commission on Accreditation for Respiratory Care (CoARC)
1248 Harwood Road
Bedford, Texas 76021-4244
Phone: 817-283-2835
Fax: 817-354-8519
E-mail: tom@coarc.com
Website: www.coarc.com

SOCIAL WORK
Dr. Stacey Borasky, Director of Accreditation
Office of Social Work Accreditation
Council on Social Work Education
1701 Duke Street, Suite 200
Alexandria, Virginia 22314
Phone: 703-683-8080
Fax: 703-519-2078
E-mail: info@cswe.org
Website: www.cswe.org

SPEECH-LANGUAGE PATHOLOGY AND AUDIOLOGY
Patrima L. Tice, Accreditation Executive Director
American Speech-Language-Hearing Association
Council on Academic Accreditation in Audiology and Speech-Language Pathology
2200 Research Boulevard #310
Rockville, Maryland 20850-3289
Phone: 301-296-5700
Fax: 301-296-8750
E-mail: accreditation@asha.org
Website: http://caa.asha.org

TEACHER EDUCATION
Christopher A. Koch, President
National Council for Accreditation of Teacher Education (NCATE)
Teacher Education Accreditation Council (TEAC)
1140 19th Street, Suite 400
Washington, DC 20036
Phone: 202-223-0077
Fax: 202-296-6620
E-mail: caep@caepnet.org
Website: www.ncate.org

TECHNOLOGY
Michale S. McComis, Ed.D., Executive Director
Accrediting Commission of Career Schools and Colleges
2101 Wilson Boulevard, Suite 302
Arlington, Virginia 22201
Phone: 703-247-4212
Fax: 703-247-4533
E-mail: mccomis@accsc.org
Website: www.accsc.org

TECHNOLOGY, MANAGEMENT, AND APPLIED ENGINEERING
Kelly Schild, Director of Accreditation
The Association of Technology, Management, and Applied Engineering (ATMAE)
275 N. York Street, Suite 401
Elmhurst, Illinois 60126
Phone: 630-433-4514
Fax: 630-563-9181
E-mail: Kelly@atmae.org
Website: www.atmae.org

THEATER
Karen P. Moynahan, Executive Director
National Association of Schools of Theatre Commission on Accreditation
11250 Roger Bacon Drive, Suite 21
Reston, Virginia 20190
Phone: 703-437-0700
Fax: 703-437-6312
E-mail: info@arts-accredit.org
Website: http://nast.arts-accredit.org/

THEOLOGY
Dr. Bernard Fryshman, Executive VP
Emeritus and Interim Executive Director
Association of Advanced Rabbinical and Talmudic Schools (AARTS)
Accreditation Commission
11 Broadway, Suite 405
New York, New York 10004
Phone: 212-363-1991
Fax: 212-533-5335
E-mail: k.sharfman.aarts@gmail.com

Daniel O. Aleshire, Executive Director
Association of Theological Schools in the United States and Canada (ATS)
Commission on Accrediting
10 Summit Park Drive
Pittsburgh, Pennsylvania 15275
Phone: 412-788-6505
Fax: 412-788-6510
E-mail: ats@ats.edu
Website: www.ats.edu

Dr. Timothy Eaton, Interim President
Transnational Association of Christian Colleges and Schools (TRACS)
Accreditation Commission
15935 Forest Road
Forest, Virginia 24551
Phone: 434-525-9539
Fax: 434-525-9538
E-mail: info@tracs.org
Website: www.tracs.org

VETERINARY MEDICINE
Dr. Karen Brandt, Director of Education and Research
American Veterinary Medical Association (AVMA)
Council on Education
1931 North Meacham Road, Suite 100
Schaumburg, Illinois 60173-4360
Phone: 847-925-8070 Ext. 6674
Fax: 847-285-5732
E-mail: info@avma.org
Website: www.avma.org

How to Use This Guide

As you identify the particular programs and institutions that interest you, you can use both the *Graduate & Professional Programs: An Overview* volume and the specialized volumes to obtain detailed information--*Graduate & Professional Programs: An Overview* for information on the institutions overall and the specialized volumes for details about the individual graduate units and their degree programs.

Directory of Graduate and Professional Programs by Field

This directory lists the more than 500 fields covered in *Peterson's Graduate and Professional Programs*, with an alphabetical listing of each of the institutions offering graduate or professional work in that field. Institutions in the United States and U.S. territories and those in Canada, Mexico, Europe, and Africa that are accredited by U.S. accrediting bodies are included. The directory enables readers who are interested in a particular academic area to quickly identify the colleges and universities that they might wish to attend. In each field, degree levels are given if an institution provided the information in response to *Peterson's Annual Survey of Graduate and Professional Institutions*. An *M* indicates that a master's degree program is offered; a *D* indicates that a doctoral program is offered; and an *O* signifies that other advanced degrees (e.g., certificates and specialist degrees) are offered. If no degree is listed, the school offers a degree in a subdiscipline of the field, not in the field itself.

All of the programs listed in this directory are profiled, and many are described in detail in **Close-Ups** or **Displays** in the specialized volumes. These **Displays** and **Close-Ups** are indicated in the directory listings by an asterisk, and their page numbers may be found by consulting the indexes of the specialized volumes. The **Profiles, Displays**, and **Close-Ups Index** at the back of this book indicate the institutions that chose to place a **Close-Up** or a **Display** in this volume.

Directory of Institutions and Their Offerings

This directory contains information identical to that in the **Directory of Graduate and Professional Programs by Field** but conversely presented. Accredited institutions in the United States and U.S. territories and those in Canada, Mexico, Europe, and Africa that are accredited by U.S. accrediting bodies are given here, with an alphabetical listing of which programs they offer out of the selected fields that are covered in the guides. The directory will be of value to readers who are interested in the range of programs at particular institutions, as well as those who wish to compare programs and degree levels. The degree levels are shown if the institution provided information in response to *Peterson's Annual Survey of Graduate and Professional Institutions*; the degree levels included are master's, doctorate, and other advanced degrees (e.g., certificates and specialist degrees), included as *M, D,* and *O*, respectively.

All of the programs listed in this directory are profiled, and many are described in detail in **Close-Ups** or outlined briefly in **Displays** in the specialized volumes. A note at the end of each institution's listing refers the reader to the specific page number if a **Display** or **Close-Up** appears in this book. If there is such information in the specialized volumes, an asterisk appears in the column that lists the degree level offered. The reader should then refer to the **Profiles, Displays, and Close-Ups Index** in the appropriate volume.

Profiles of Institutions Offering Graduate and Professional Work

This section presents profiles of accredited colleges and universities in the United States and U.S. territories and those in Canada, Mexico, Europe, and Africa that are accredited by U.S. accrediting bodies. Together with the other sections of this book, it is both a basic reference source and a foundation for the specialized volumes of *Peterson's Graduate and Professional Programs*. (The specialized volumes provide descriptions of graduate programs in the humanities, arts, and social sciences; the biological/biomedical sciences and health-related medical professions; the physical sciences, mathematics, agricultural sciences, the environment, and natural resources; engineering and applied sciences; and business, education, information studies, law, and social work, respectively.) The profiles in this section include the data on graduate and professional units that were submitted in 2016 by each institution in response to *Peterson's Annual Survey of Graduate and Professional Institutions*. If an institution provided all of the information requested, the profile includes all of the items listed below. A number of graduate school administrators have submitted and paid for **Displays**, which appear near their profiles. In these, readers will find information an institution wants to emphasize. In addition, bolded reference lines at the end of a profile indicate the page number on which the reader will find a **Display** and/or **Close-Up**, if the institution has chosen to submit one or both. The absence of a **Display** or **Close-Up** does not reflect any type of editorial judgment on the part of Peterson's.

A ★ graphic next to the school's name indicates the institution has additional detailed information in a "Premium Profile" on Petersons.com. After reading their information here, you can learn more about the school by visiting www.petersons.com and searching for that particular institution's graduate program.

General Information

Type. An institution's control is indicated as independent (private nonprofit), independent with religious affiliation, proprietary (private profit-making), or state-supported or state-related (public). Whether an institution is coeducational or primarily for men or women is indicated. A few schools are designated as undergraduate: women (or men) only; graduate: coed. Institutional type is given as university, comprehensive, graduate only, or upper level.

CGS Membership. Membership in the Council of Graduate Schools in the United States and in Canada is indicated here.

Enrollment. Enrollment figures include total matriculated students (graduate, professional, and undergraduate), total full- and part-time matriculated graduate and professional students, and the number of women in each category.

Enrollment by Degree Level. Figures include the total number of students enrolled at each degree level--master's, doctoral, and other advanced degrees.

Graduate Faculty. The numbers of full-time and part-time/adjunct faculty members actively involved with graduate students through teaching or research are given, followed by numbers of women.

Graduate Expenses. Tuition and fees for the overall institution for 2017–18 are indicated on a full-time (per academic year, semester, quarter, etc.) and/or a part-time (per credit, semester hour, quarter hour, course, etc.) basis. In-state and out-of-state figures are supplied where applicable. For exact costs at any given time, contact the schools and programs directly. Keep in mind that the tuition of Canadian institutions is usually given in Canadian dollars.

Graduate Housing. Institutions were asked to indicate whether housing for single and married students is guaranteed or available on a first-come, first-served basis and whether that includes board and to indicate the typical cost per year.

Student Services. Each institution was asked which of the following services are available to graduate and professional students: campus employment opportunities, campus safety program, career counseling, child day-care facilities, disabled student services, exercise/wellness program, free psychological counseling, grant writing training, international student services, low-cost health insurance, multicultural affairs office, teacher training, and writing training.

Library Facilities. The main library name and the number of additional on-campus libraries, if any, are provided. Also provided are online resources, such as library catalog, Web page, and other libraries' catalogs, and numbers of titles, current serial subscriptions, and audiovisual materials.

Research Affiliations. Institutions were asked to name up to six independent research centers, laboratories, or institutes with which they maintain formal arrangements providing extra research or study opportunities for graduate students.

Computer Facilities

Institutions were asked to provide the total number of PCs and/or terminals available for student use, whether a campuswide network is available, and whether Internet access and/or online class registration is available. The institution's website also appears here if that information was supplied.

General Application Contact

The name, title, phone number, fax number, and e-mail address of the person to contact for further information about applying to graduate and professional programs appear here.

Graduate Units

Each major graduate and professional unit within the institution (school, college, institute, center, etc.) is listed below the general information. These units are arranged to show the hierarchical structure of the institution. Those units offering advanced degree programs through the graduate school are listed immediately beneath it. Professional schools not connected with the graduate school are listed separately.

Enrollment. The number of full- and part-time matriculated students and the number of women, minority-group members, and international students are given. Average age is indicated, followed by the number of applicants, percentage accepted, and the number enrolled.

Faculty. Full-time and part-time/adjunct figures are given, and the number of women is indicated.

Expenses. For individual program expenses, readers are advised to contact the institution.

Financial Support. Information is given on the number of fellowships and assistantships awarded in 2016–17 and the availability of other types of aid. The financial aid application deadline is also indicated.

Degree Program Information. The number of degrees awarded in calendar year 2017 is given, broken down by degree level, followed by the availability of part-time and evening/weekend programs. Degree programs offered through the subunits and the specific degrees awarded are listed. Special degree information is also included, such as that a degree is offered jointly with another university.

Applying. The application deadline (for domestic and international students) and application fee are given, followed by a person to contact and a phone number, fax number, and e-mail address (if provided).

Head. The head of the unit and his or her title are indicated, along with a phone number, fax number, and e-mail address (if provided).

Close-Ups of Institutions Offering Graduate and Professional Work

The **Close-Ups** in this section present an overview of accredited graduate and professional schools in the United States and U.S. territories and institutions in Canada, Mexico, Europe, and Africa that are accredited by U.S. accrediting bodies. Critical information sought by all prospective graduate students—regardless of their intended field of study—has been supplied by the schools themselves.

In addition to listing the degree programs available, each entry gives valuable information on research facilities, financial aid opportunities, tuition rates, living and housing costs, students, the faculty, location, the university, and application criteria—in short, facts that all prospective graduate students need to know about an institution when selecting a graduate program.

After using the **Close-Ups** and the other sections of this volume to identify those universities that are appropriate to your needs, refer to the specialized volumes for specific program information. Graduate and professional schools and colleges within the institutions represented in this book are considered in detail in the specialized volumes, which cover the humanities, arts, and social sciences; the biological/biomedical sciences and health-related medical professions; the physical sciences, mathematics, agricultural sciences, the environment, and natural resources; engineering and applied sciences; and business, education, information studies, law, and social work, respectively.

Appendixes

This section contains two appendixes. The first, *Institutional Changes Since the 2017 Edition,* lists institutions that have closed, moved, merged, or changed their name or status since the last edition of the guides. The second, *Abbreviations Used in the Guides,* gives abbreviations of degree names, along with what those abbreviations stand for. These appendixes are identical in all six volumes of *Peterson's Graduate and Professional Programs.*

Indexes

There are two indexes in this section. The first, **Profiles, Displays, and Close-Ups,** gives page references for all information on all graduate and professional schools in this volume. Location of the institution's **Profile** is indicated in normal type. An *italic* page number indicates that a **Display** follows the institution's **Profile**. A **boldface** page number indicates the location of an institution's **Close-Up**. The second, **Directories and Subject Areas in the Specialized Volumes**, gives references to the directories in other volumes of this set and also includes cross-references for subject area names not used in the directory structure, for example, City and Regional Planning (see Urban and Regional Planning).

Data Collection Procedures

The information published in the directories and **Profiles** of all the books is collected through *Peterson's Annual Survey of Graduate and Professional Institutions.* The survey is sent each spring to more than 2,200 institutions offering postbaccalaureate degree programs, including accredited institutions in the United States, U.S. territories, and Canada and those institutions outside the United States that are accredited by U.S. accrediting bodies. Deans and other administrators complete these surveys, providing information on programs in over 500 academic and professional fields covered in the guides as well as overall institutional information. While every effort has been made to ensure the accuracy and completeness of the data, information is sometimes unavailable or changes occur after publication deadlines. All usable information received in time for publication has been included. The omission of any particular item from a directory or **Profile** signifies either that the item is not applicable to the institution or program or that information was not available. **Profiles** of programs scheduled to begin during the 2016–17 academic year cannot, obviously, include statistics on enrollment or, in many cases, the number of faculty members. If no usable data were submitted by an institution, its name, address, and program name appear in order to indicate the availability of graduate work.

Criteria for Inclusion in This Guide

To be included in this guide, an institution must have full accreditation or be a candidate for accreditation (preaccreditation) status by an institutional or specialized accrediting body recognized by the U.S. Department of Education or the Council for Higher Education Accreditation (CHEA). Institutional accrediting bodies, which review each institution as a whole, include the six regional associations of schools and colleges (Middle States, New England, North Central, Northwest, Southern, and Western), each of which is responsible for a specified portion of the United States and its territories. Other institutional accrediting bodies are national in scope and accredit specific kinds of institutions (e.g., Bible colleges, independent colleges, and rabbinical and Talmudic schools). Program registration by the New York State Board of Regents is considered to be the equivalent of institutional accreditation, since the board requires that all programs offered by an institution meet its standards before recognition is granted. A Canadian institution must be chartered and authorized to grant degrees by the provincial government, affiliated with a chartered institution, or accredited by a recognized U.S. accrediting body. This guide also includes institutions outside the United States that are accredited by these U.S. accrediting bodies. There are recognized specialized or professional accrediting bodies in more than fifty different fields, each of which is authorized to accredit institutions or specific programs in its particular field. For specialized institutions that offer programs in one field only, we designate this to be the equivalent of institutional accreditation. A full explanation of the accrediting process and complete information on recognized institutional (regional and national) and specialized accrediting bodies can be found online at www.chea.org or at www.ed.gov/admins/finaid/accred/index.html.

DIRECTORY OF GRADUATE AND PROFESSIONAL PROGRAMS BY FIELD

ACCOUNTING

Institution	Degree
Abilene Christian University	M
Adelphi University	M
Adrian College	M
Alabama State University	M
Albany State University	M
Albertus Magnus College	M
Alfred University	M
American Business & Technology University	M
American InterContinental University Online	M
American International College	M,D,O
American Public University System	M
American University	M,O
American University of Sharjah	M
Anderson University (IN)	M,D
Andrews University	M
Angelo State University	M
Appalachian State University	M
Argosy University, Atlanta	M,D
Argosy University, Chicago	M,D
Argosy University, Dallas	M,D,O
Argosy University, Denver	M,D
Argosy University, Hawai`i	M,D,O
Argosy University, Inland Empire	M,D
Argosy University, Los Angeles	M,D
Argosy University, Nashville	M,D
Argosy University, Northern Virginia	M,D,O
Argosy University, Orange County	M,D,O
Argosy University, Phoenix	M,D
Argosy University, Salt Lake City	M,D
Argosy University, San Diego	M,D
Argosy University, San Francisco Bay Area	M,D
Argosy University, Sarasota	M,D,O
Argosy University, Schaumburg	M,D,O
Argosy University, Seattle	M,D
Argosy University, Tampa	M,D
Argosy University, Twin Cities	M,D
Arizona State University at the Tempe campus	M,D
Arkansas State University	M
Assumption College	M,O
Auburn University	M
Auburn University at Montgomery	M
Aurora University	M
Averett University	M
Avila University	M
Babson College	M,O
Baker College Center for Graduate Studies–Online	M,D
Baldwin Wallace University	M
Ball State University	M
Barry University	M
Baruch College of the City University of New York	M,D
Bayamón Central University	M
Baylor University	M
Bay Path University	M
Belmont University	M
Benedictine University	M
Bentley University	M,D
Binghamton University, State University of New York	M
Bloomfield College	M
Bloomsburg University of Pennsylvania	M
Bluffton University	M
Bob Jones University	M,D,O
Boise State University	M
Boston College	M
Bowling Green State University	M
Bradley University	M
Brandman University	M
Brenau University	M
Bridgewater State University	M
Brock University	M
Brooklyn College of the City University of New York	M
Bryant University	M,O
Butler University	M
Cabrini University	M
Cairn University	M,O
Caldwell University	M
California Baptist University	M
California Polytechnic State University, San Luis Obispo	M
California State Polytechnic University, Pomona	M
California State University, East Bay	M
California State University, Fullerton	M
California State University, Los Angeles	M
California State University, Sacramento	M
California State University, San Bernardino	M
California Western School of Law	M,D
Canisius College	M
Capella University	M,D
Carnegie Mellon University	D
Case Western Reserve University	M,D
The Catholic University of America	M
Centenary University	M
Central Connecticut State University	M
Central Michigan University	M,O
Central Washington University	M
Chaminade University of Honolulu	M
Chapman University	M
Charleston Southern University	M
Chatham University	M
Christian Brothers University	M,O
City University of Seattle	M,O
Clarion University of Pennsylvania	M
Clark Atlanta University	M
Clark University	M
Clayton State University	M
Clemson University	M
Cleveland State University	M
Coastal Carolina University	M,O
The College at Brockport, State University of New York	M,O
College of Charleston	M
The College of Saint Rose	M
College of Staten Island of the City University of New York	M
The College of William and Mary	M
Colorado State University	M
Colorado State University–Global Campus	M
Colorado Technical University Aurora	M
Colorado Technical University Colorado Springs	M,D
Columbia College (MO)	M
Columbia University	M,D
Cornell University	M,D
Creighton University	M
Culver-Stockton College	M
Daemen College	M
Dallas Baptist University	M
Davenport University	M
Delaware Valley University	M
Delta State University	M
DePaul University	M
DeSales University	M
DeVry University–Folsom Campus	M
Dominican College	M
Dominican University	M
Drexel University	M,D,O
Duke University	D
Duquesne University	M
East Carolina University	M
Eastern Connecticut State University	M
Eastern Illinois University	M
Eastern Michigan University	M
East Tennessee State University	M
Edgewood College	M
Elms College	M
Emory University	M,D
Emporia State University	M
Everest University	M
Everglades University	M
Fairfield University	M,O
Fairleigh Dickinson University, College at Florham	M
Fairleigh Dickinson University, Metropolitan Campus	M,O
Fitchburg State University	M
Florida Agricultural and Mechanical University	M
Florida Atlantic University	M
Florida Gulf Coast University	M
Florida International University	M
Florida Southern College	M
Florida State University	M,D
Fontbonne University	M
Fordham University	M
Franklin University	M
Freed-Hardeman University	M
Friends University	M
George Fox University	M,D
George Mason University	M,O
The George Washington University	M
Georgia College & State University	M
Georgia Southern University	M
Georgia State University	M
Golden Gate University	M,D,O
Gonzaga University	M
Governors State University	M
The Graduate Center, City University of New York	D
Grand Canyon University	M
Grand Valley State University	M
Harvard University	D
Hawai`i Pacific University	M
HEC Montreal	M,O
Hendrix College	M
Herzing University Online	M
Hodges University	M
Hofstra University	M,O
Holy Family University	M,D
Hood College	M
Howard University	M
Hunter College of the City University of New York	M
IGlobal University	M
Illinois State University	M
Indiana Tech	M
Indiana University Kokomo	M,O
Indiana University Northwest	M,O
Indiana University–Purdue University Indianapolis	M
Indiana University South Bend	M,O
Indiana Wesleyan University	M,O
Instituto Tecnologico de Santo Domingo	M,O
Inter American University of Puerto Rico, Aguadilla Campus	M
Inter American University of Puerto Rico, Arecibo Campus	M
Inter American University of Puerto Rico, Barranquitas Campus	M
Inter American University of Puerto Rico, Metropolitan Campus	M
Inter American University of Puerto Rico, Ponce Campus	M
Inter American University of Puerto Rico, San Germán Campus	M,D
Iona College	M,O
Iowa State University of Science and Technology	M
Ithaca College	M
Jackson State University	M
Jacksonville University	M
James Madison University	M
John Carroll University	M
Johnson & Wales University	M
Juniata College	M
Kansas State University	M
Kean University	M
Keiser University	M
Kennesaw State University	M
Kent State University	M,D
Keystone College	M
King University	M
Lakeland University	M
Lamar University	M
La Roche College	M
La Salle University	M,O
La Sierra University	M,O
Lehigh University	M
Lehman College of the City University of New York	M
Lenoir-Rhyne University	M
Lewis University	M
Liberty University	M,D,O
Lincoln University (MO)	M
Lindenwood University	M
Lipscomb University	M,O
Long Island University–LIU Brooklyn	M,O
Long Island University–LIU Post	M
Louisiana State University and Agricultural & Mechanical College	M,D
Louisiana Tech University	M,D
Loyola Marymount University	M
Loyola University Chicago	M
Loyola University Maryland	M
Maharishi University of Management	M,D
Manhattanville College	M
Marquette University	M
Marshall University	M
Maryville University of Saint Louis	M,O
McGill University	M,D,O
Mercer University	M
Mercy College	M
Mercyhurst University	M,O
Merrimack College	M
Metropolitan State University of Denver	M
Miami University	M
Michigan State University	M,D
Michigan Technological University	M
Middle Tennessee State University	M
Millennia Atlantic University	M
Millsaps College	M
Minnesota State University Mankato	M
Minnesota State University Moorhead	M
Misericordia University	M
Mississippi College	M,O
Mississippi State University	M
Missouri State University	M
Missouri Western State University	M
Molloy College	M,O
Monmouth University	M,O
Monroe College	M
Montana State University	M
Montclair State University	M,O
Moravian College	M
Mount Aloysius College	M
Murray State University	M
Neumann University	M
New England College	M
New Jersey City University	M,O
New Mexico State University	M
New York Institute of Technology	M
New York University	M,D
Niagara University	M
North Carolina Agricultural and Technical State University	M
North Carolina State University	M
North Dakota State University	M
Northeastern Illinois University	M
Northeastern State University	M
Northeastern University	M
Northern Illinois University	M
Northern Kentucky University	M
Northwest Christian University	M
Northwestern University	M
Nova Southeastern University	M
Oakland University	M,O
Ohio Christian University	M
Ohio Dominican University	M
Ohio Northern University	M
The Ohio State University	M,D
Oklahoma Christian University	M
Oklahoma State University	M,D
Old Dominion University	M
Oral Roberts University	M
Oregon State University	M,D
Our Lady of the Lake University	M
Pace University	M,O
Pacific Lutheran University	M
Pacific States University	M,D
Penn State Erie, The Behrend College	M
Penn State Harrisburg	M,O
Penn State University Park	M,D
Pepperdine University	M
Pittsburg State University	M
Polytechnic University of Puerto Rico, Miami Campus	M
Polytechnic University of Puerto Rico, Orlando Campus	M
Pontifical Catholic University of Puerto Rico	M,O
Post University	M
Prairie View A&M University	M
Providence College	M
Purdue University Northwest	M
Queens College of the City University of New York	M
Regent University	M,D,O
Regis University	M,O
Rhode Island College	M
Rhodes College	M
Rider University	M
Robert Morris University Illinois	M
Rochester Institute of Technology	M
Rockhurst University	M,O
Rocky Mountain College	M
Roosevelt University	M
Rutgers University–Newark	M,D
Sacred Heart University	M
St. Ambrose University	M
St. Bonaventure University	M
St. Edward's University	M,O
St. Francis College	M
St. John's University (NY)	M
St. Joseph's College, Long Island Campus	M
St. Joseph's College, New York	M
Saint Joseph's College of Maine	M
Saint Joseph's University	M,O
Saint Leo University	M,D,O
Saint Louis University	M
Saint Mary's College of California	M
St. Mary's University (United States)	M
Saint Mary's University of Minnesota	M
Saint Peter's University	M
St. Thomas University	M,O
Samford University	M
Sam Houston State University	M
San Diego State University	M
San Francisco State University	M
San Jose State University	M
Seattle University	M
Seton Hall University	M,O
Seton Hill University	M
Shorter University	M
Siena College	M
Slippery Rock University of Pennsylvania	M
Southeast Missouri State University	M
Southern Adventist University	M
Southern Illinois University Carbondale	M,D
Southern Illinois University Edwardsville	M
Southern Methodist University	M
Southern New Hampshire University	M,O
Southern Oregon University	M,O
Southern Utah University	M
Southwestern Adventist University	M
State University of New York at New Paltz	M
State University of New York College at Geneseo	M
State University of New York College at Old Westbury	M
State University of New York Polytechnic Institute	M
Stephen F. Austin State University	M
Stetson University	M
Stony Brook University, State University of New York	M,O
Stratford University (VA)	M
Strayer University	M
Suffolk University	M,O
Syracuse University	M
Tabor College	M
Tarleton State University	M
Temple University	M,D
Tennessee Technological University	M
Tennessee Wesleyan University	M
Texas A&M International University	M
Texas A&M University	M
Texas A&M University–Central Texas	M,O
Texas A&M University–Commerce	M
Texas A&M University–Corpus Christi	M
Texas A&M University–San Antonio	M
Texas A&M University–Texarkana	M
Texas Christian University	M
Texas Lutheran University	M
Texas State University	M
Texas Tech University	M,D
Texas Woman's University	M
Thomas Edison State University	M
Towson University	M
Trinity University	M
Troy University	M
Truman State University	M
Tulane University	M,D
Union University	M
Universidad del Este	M
Universidad del Turabo	M
Universidad Metropolitana	M
Université de Sherbrooke	M
Université du Québec à Montréal	M,O
Université du Québec à Trois-Rivières	M
Université du Québec en Outaouais	M,O
Université Laval	M,O
University at Albany, State University of New York	M
University at Buffalo, the State University of New York	M,D
The University of Akron	M
The University of Alabama	M,D
The University of Alabama at Birmingham	M
The University of Alabama in Huntsville	M,O
University of Alberta	D
The University of Arizona	M
University of Arkansas	M
University of Baltimore	M,O
University of Bridgeport	M
The University of British Columbia	D
University of California, Berkeley	D,O
University of California, Davis	M
University of California, Irvine	M

University of California, Los Angeles	M,D
University of Central Arkansas	M
University of Central Florida	M
University of Central Missouri	M,D,O
University of Central Oklahoma	M
University of Charleston	M
University of Chicago	M,O
University of Cincinnati	M,D
University of Colorado Denver	M
University of Connecticut	M
University of Dallas	M,D
University of Dayton	M
University of Delaware	M
University of Denver	M
University of Detroit Mercy	M,O
The University of Findlay	M,D
University of Florida	M,D
University of Georgia	M
University of Hartford	M,O
University of Hawaii at Manoa	M,D
University of Houston	M,D
University of Houston–Clear Lake	M
University of Houston–Victoria	M
University of Idaho	M
University of Illinois at Chicago	M
University of Illinois at Springfield	M
University of Illinois at Urbana–Champaign	M,D
The University of Iowa	M,D
The University of Kansas	M,D
University of Kentucky	M
University of La Verne	M
University of Lethbridge	M,D
University of Louisville	M
The University of Manchester	M
University of Mary Hardin-Baylor	M
University of Maryland University College	M
University of Massachusetts Amherst	M,D
University of Massachusetts Boston	M
University of Massachusetts Dartmouth	M,O
University of Memphis	M,D
University of Michigan	M,D
University of Michigan–Dearborn	M
University of Michigan–Flint	M,O
University of Minnesota, Twin Cities Campus	M,D
University of Mississippi	M,D
University of Missouri	M,D,O
University of Missouri–Kansas City	M,D
University of Missouri–St. Louis	M,D,O
University of Montana	M
University of Nebraska at Kearney	M
University of Nebraska at Omaha	M
University of Nebraska–Lincoln	M,D
University of Nevada, Las Vegas	M,O
University of Nevada, Reno	M
University of New Hampshire	M
University of New Haven	M,O
University of New Mexico	M
University of New Orleans	M
University of North Alabama	M
The University of North Carolina at Chapel Hill	M,D
The University of North Carolina at Charlotte	M
The University of North Carolina at Greensboro	M,O
The University of North Carolina Wilmington	M
University of Northern Colorado	M
University of Northern Iowa	M
University of North Florida	M,D,O
University of North Texas	M,D,O
University of North Texas at Dallas	M
University of Notre Dame	M
University of Oklahoma	M,D
University of Oregon	M,D
University of Pennsylvania	M,D
University of Phoenix–Atlanta Campus	M
University of Phoenix–Augusta Campus	M
University of Phoenix–Bay Area Campus	M,D
University of Phoenix–Central Valley Campus	M
University of Phoenix–Charlotte Campus	M
University of Phoenix–Colorado Campus	M
University of Phoenix–Colorado Springs Downtown Campus	M
University of Phoenix–Columbus Georgia Campus	M
University of Phoenix–Dallas Campus	M
University of Phoenix–Hawaii Campus	M
University of Phoenix–Jersey City Campus	M
University of Phoenix–Las Vegas Campus	M
University of Phoenix–New Mexico Campus	M
University of Phoenix–North Florida Campus	M

University of Phoenix–Online Campus	M,O
University of Phoenix–Phoenix Campus	M,O
University of Phoenix–Sacramento Valley Campus	M
University of Phoenix–San Antonio Campus	M
University of Phoenix–San Diego Campus	M
University of Phoenix–Southern Arizona Campus	M
University of Phoenix–Southern California Campus	M
University of Phoenix–South Florida Campus	M
University of Phoenix–Utah Campus	M
University of Phoenix–Washington D.C. Campus	M,D
University of Pittsburgh	M,D
University of Puerto Rico, Río Piedras Campus	M,D
University of Rhode Island	M,D
University of Rochester	M,D
University of St. Francis (IL)	M,O
University of St. Thomas (TX)	M
University of St. Thomas (MN)	M
University of San Diego	M
University of Saskatchewan	M
The University of Scranton	M
University of South Africa	M,D
University of South Alabama	M
University of South Carolina	M
The University of South Dakota	M
The University of Iowa	M
University of Southern California	M
University of Southern Indiana	M
University of Southern Maine	M
University of Southern Mississippi	M
University of South Florida	M,D
The University of Tampa	M
The University of Tennessee	M
The University of Tennessee at Chattanooga	M
The University of Texas at Arlington	M,D
The University of Texas at Austin	M,D
The University of Texas at Dallas	M
The University of Texas at El Paso	M
The University of Texas at San Antonio	M,D
The University of Texas at Tyler	M
The University of Texas of the Permian Basin	M
The University of Texas Rio Grande Valley	M
University of the Cumberlands	M
University of the Sacred Heart	M,O
The University of Toledo	M
The University of Tulsa	M
University of Utah	M,D
University of Vermont	M
University of Virginia	M
University of Washington	M,D
University of Washington, Tacoma	M
University of Waterloo	M,D
University of West Florida	M
University of West Georgia	M
University of Wisconsin–Madison	M,D
University of Wisconsin–Whitewater	M
University of Wyoming	M
Upper Iowa University	M
Ursuline College	M
Utah State University	M
Utah Valley University	M
Utica College	M
Vanderbilt University	M
Villanova University	M
Virginia Commonwealth University	M
Virginia International University	M,O
Virginia Polytechnic Institute and State University	M,D
Wagner College	M
Wake Forest University	M
Walden University	M,D,O
Walsh College of Accountancy and Business Administration	M
Warner University	M
Washburn University	M
Washington & Jefferson College	M,O
Washington State University	M
Washington University in St. Louis	M,D
Wayland Baptist University	M,D,O
Wayne State University	M
Webber International University	M
Weber State University	M
Webster University	M
Western Carolina University	M
Western Connecticut State University	M
Western Illinois University	M
Western Michigan University	M
Western New England University	M
Westfield State University	M
Westminster College (UT)	M,O
West Virginia University	M,D
Wheeling Jesuit University	M
Wichita State University	M
Wilfrid Laurier University	M,D
Wilkes University	M
Wilmington University	M
Wilson College	M
Wingate University	M
Worcester State University	M
Wright State University	M
Xavier University	M
Yale University	D
Yeshiva University	M
York University	M,D

Youngstown State University	M

ACOUSTICS

Naval Postgraduate School	M,D
Penn State University Park	M,D
Rensselaer Polytechnic Institute	M,D
The University of Kansas	M,D,O
University of Massachusetts Dartmouth	M,D,O

ACTUARIAL SCIENCE

Ball State University	M
Boston University	M
California State University, East Bay	M
Central Connecticut State University	M,O
Columbia University	M
Florida State University	M,D
Georgia State University	M
Lock Haven University of Pennsylvania	M
Maryville University of Saint Louis	M
Middle Tennessee State University	M
The Ohio State University	M,D
Oregon State University	M,D
Roosevelt University	M
St. John's University (NY)	M
Simon Fraser University	M,D
Temple University	M
Université du Québec à Montréal	O
University of Illinois at Urbana–Champaign	M,D
The University of Iowa	M,D
The University of Manchester	M,D
University of Nebraska–Lincoln	M
The University of Texas at Austin	M,D
The University of Texas at Dallas	M,D
University of Waterloo	M,D
University of Wisconsin–Milwaukee	M,D

ACUPUNCTURE AND ORIENTAL MEDICINE

Academy for Five Element Acupuncture	M
Academy of Chinese Culture and Health Sciences	M
Acupuncture & Integrative Medicine College, Berkeley	M
Acupuncture and Massage College	M
American Academy of Acupuncture and Oriental Medicine	M,D
American College of Acupuncture and Oriental Medicine	M
AOMA Graduate School of Integrative Medicine	M,D
Arizona School of Acupuncture and Oriental Medicine	M
Atlantic Institute of Oriental Medicine	M,D
Bastyr University	M,D,O
California Institute of Integral Studies	M,D
Canadian Memorial Chiropractic College	O
Colorado School of Traditional Chinese Medicine	M
Dongguk University Los Angeles	M
Dragon Rises College of Oriental Medicine	M
East West College of Natural Medicine	M
Emperor's College of Traditional Oriental Medicine	M,D
Five Branches University	M,D
Florida College of Integrative Medicine	M
Institute of Clinical Acupuncture and Oriental Medicine	M
Institute of Taoist Education and Acupuncture	M
Maryland University of Integrative Health	M,D,O
MCPHS University	M
Midwest College of Oriental Medicine	M,O
National University of Health Sciences	M,D
National University of Natural Medicine	M
New York Chiropractic College	M
New York College of Health Professions	M
New York College of Traditional Chinese Medicine	M
Northwestern Health Sciences University	M
Oregon College of Oriental Medicine	M,D
Pacific College of Oriental Medicine	M,D
Pacific College of Oriental Medicine–Chicago	M
Pacific College of Oriental Medicine-New York	M
Phoenix Institute of Herbal Medicine & Acupuncture	M
Seattle Institute of Oriental Medicine	M
South Baylo University	M
Southern California University of Health Sciences	M,D
Southwest Acupuncture College	M
Swedish Institute, College of Health Sciences	M
Tri-State College of Acupuncture	M,O
University of Bridgeport	M
University of East-West Medicine	M,D

WON Institute of Graduate Studies	M,O
World Medicine Institute	M
Yo San University of Traditional Chinese Medicine	M

ACUTE CARE/CRITICAL CARE NURSING

Augusta University	D
Barry University	M,O
Case Western Reserve University	M
The College of New Rochelle	M,O
Columbia University	M
Drexel University	M
Duke University	M,D,O
Georgetown University	M,D
Goldfarb School of Nursing at Barnes-Jewish College	M
Grand Canyon University	M,D,O
Indiana University–Purdue University Indianapolis	M
Inter American University of Puerto Rico, Arecibo Campus	M
Marquette University	M,D,O
Maryville University of Saint Louis	M,D
Moravian College	M
Mount Carmel College of Nursing	M,D
New York University	M,D,O
Northeastern University	M,D,O
Purdue University Northwest	M
San Francisco State University	M,O
Southern Adventist University	M
Texas Tech University Health Sciences Center	M,D,O
Texas Woman's University	M,D
Universidad de Iberoamerica	M,D
The University of Alabama in Huntsville	M,D,O
University of Cincinnati	M,D
University of Guelph	M,D,O
University of Illinois at Chicago	M,O
University of Miami	M,D
The University of North Carolina at Charlotte	M,D,O
University of Northern Colorado	M,D
University of Pennsylvania	M
University of Pittsburgh	M,D
University of Puerto Rico, Medical Sciences Campus	M
University of Rhode Island	M,D
University of Rochester	M,D
University of South Africa	M,D
University of South Carolina	M,O
University of South Florida	M,D,O
The University of Texas Health Science Center at San Antonio	M,D,O
University of Virginia	M,D
Vanderbilt University	M,D,O
Winona State University	M,D,O
Wright State University	M

ADDICTIONS/SUBSTANCE ABUSE COUNSELING

Adler Graduate School	M
Adler University	M,D,O
Alliant International University–Los Angeles	M
Antioch University New England	M
Argosy University, Hawai'i	O
Arkansas State University	M,O
Assumption College	O
Bay Path University	M
Cambridge College	M,O
Capella University	M,D
Carlow University	M,O
The College of New Jersey	M,O
College of St. Joseph	M
The College of William and Mary	M,D
Coppin State University	M
East Carolina University	M,D,O
Fairfield University	M,O
The George Washington University	M
Governors State University	M
Hazelden Graduate School of Addiction Studies	M,O
Hofstra University	M,O
Indiana University Northwest	M,O
Indiana University–Purdue University Indianapolis	M,D
Indiana University South Bend	M,O
Indiana Wesleyan University	M
Johnson & Wales University	M
Johnson State College	M
Kean University	M
Lenoir-Rhyne University	M
Lewis & Clark College	M
Liberty University	M,D,O
Loma Linda University	M,D,O
Long Island University–Hudson	M,O
Maryville University of Saint Louis	M
McNeese State University	M
Monmouth University	M,O
Montclair State University	O
Northeastern State University	M
Northwest Nazarene University	M
Pace University	M,D
Palm Beach Atlantic University	M
Post University	M
Saint Mary's University of Minnesota	M,O
Salve Regina University	M,O
Springfield College	M
Stephens College	M,O
Stony Brook University, State University of New York	M,O
Syracuse University	M,O
United States International University–Africa	M
Universidad Central del Caribe	M
University of California, Berkeley	O

University	Program
University of Central Oklahoma	M
University of Cincinnati	M,D,O
University of Detroit Mercy	M,D,O
University of Illinois at Springfield	M,O
University of Lethbridge	M
University of Louisville	M,D,O
University of Nevada, Las Vegas	M,D,O
University of New Hampshire	M,O
The University of North Carolina at Charlotte	M,D,O
University of Oklahoma	M
The University of South Dakota	M
University of Southern Maine	M,O
University of South Florida	M,D
The University of Tennessee at Martin	M
Viterbo University	M
Walden University	M,D
Washburn University	M
Waynesburg University	M,D
Winona State University	M,O

ADULT EDUCATION

University	Program
Alverno College	M
Antioch University Seattle	M
Argosy University, Chicago	M,D,O
Argosy University, Hawai'i	M,D
Argosy University, Phoenix	M,D
Argosy University, Seattle	M,D
Armstrong State University	M,O
Athabasca University	M,O
Auburn University	M,D,O
Aurora University	M,D
Ball State University	M,D
Buffalo State College, State University of New York	M,O
California Baptist University	M
Capella University	M
Carroll University	M
Cleveland State University	M,D
Colorado State University	M,D
Concordia University (Canada)	M,O
Coppin State University	M
Cornell University	M,D
Dallas Theological Seminary	M
Delaware State University	M
DePaul University	M
East Carolina University	M
Eastern Washington University	M
Edgewood College	M,D,O
Florida Agricultural and Mechanical University	M,D
Florida Atlantic University	M,D,O
Florida International University	M,D
The George Washington University	O
Grand Valley State University	M
Indiana University of Pennsylvania	M
Instituto Tecnologico de Santo Domingo	M,O
Kansas State University	M,D,O
Lesley University	M,D,O
Marshall University	M
Memorial University of Newfoundland	M,O
Merrimack College	M,O
Michigan State University	M,D,O
Montana State University	M,D,O
Morehead State University	M,O
Mount Saint Vincent University	M
National Louis University	M,D,O
North Carolina Agricultural and Technical State University	M
North Carolina State University	M,D
North Dakota State University	M,D,O
Northern Illinois University	M,D
Northwestern Oklahoma State University	M
Northwestern State University of Louisiana	M
Oregon State University	M,D
Penn State Harrisburg	M,D,O
Penn State University Park	M,D,O
Plymouth State University	D
Point Park University	M,D
Regent University	M,D,O
St. Francis Xavier University	M
Saint Joseph's College of Maine	M
San Francisco State University	M
Seattle University	M,O
Southern Arkansas University–Magnolia	M
State University of New York Empire State College	M
Teachers College, Columbia University	M,D
Texas A&M University–Kingsville	M,D
Texas A&M University–Texarkana	M
Texas State University	M,D
Trident University International	M
Troy University	M
Universidad del Este	M
Universidad Metropolitana	M
University of Alberta	M,D,O
University of Arkansas	M,D
University of Arkansas at Little Rock	M
The University of British Columbia	M,D
University of Calgary	M,D
University of Central Arkansas	M,O
University of Central Oklahoma	M
University of Cincinnati	M,D,O
University of Colorado Denver	M
University of Connecticut	M,O
University of Georgia	D,O
University of Houston–Victoria	M
University of Manitoba	M
University of Memphis	M,D,O
University of Minnesota, Twin Cities Campus	M,O
University of Missouri	M
University of Missouri–St. Louis	M,D,O
University of Nebraska–Lincoln	M,D,O
The University of North Carolina at Greensboro	M,D,O
University of North Florida	M
University of Oklahoma	M
University of Phoenix–Bay Area Campus	M,D,O
University of Phoenix–Online Campus	M,O
University of Phoenix–Phoenix Campus	M
University of Phoenix–Sacramento Valley Campus	M,O
University of Phoenix–Southern Arizona Campus	M,O
University of Phoenix–Southern California Campus	M,O
University of Phoenix–Washington D.C. Campus	M
University of Regina	M
University of South Africa	M,D
The University of South Dakota	M,D,O
University of Southern Maine	M,O
University of South Florida	M,D,O
The University of Tennessee	M,D
University of the District of Columbia	O
The University of West Alabama	M
University of Wisconsin–Milwaukee	M,D,O
University of Wisconsin–Platteville	M
Virginia Commonwealth University	M
Walden University	M,D,O
Western Kentucky University	M,D,O
Western Washington University	M
Widener University	M,D

ADULT NURSING

University	Program
Adelphi University	M
Allen College	M,D
Armstrong State University	M,O
Bloomsburg University of Pennsylvania	M
Boston College	M,D
California Baptist University	M
Clarkson College	M,O
College of Staten Island of the City University of New York	M,O
Columbia University	M,O
Creighton University	M,D,O
Daemen College	M,D,O
Duke University	M,D,O
Eastern Michigan University	M,O
Emory University	M
Felician University	M,O
Florida International University	M,D
Florida Southern College	M
The George Washington University	M,D,O
Georgia State University	M,D,O
Gwynedd Mercy University	M,D
Hampton University	M,D
Hunter College of the City University of New York	M
Indiana University–Purdue University Fort Wayne	M,O
Kent State University	M,D
La Salle University	M,D,O
Lehman College of the City University of New York	M
Lewis University	M,O
Loma Linda University	M
Long Island University–LIU Brooklyn	M,O
Madonna University	M
Marian University (WI)	M
Marquette University	M,D,O
Maryville University of Saint Louis	M,D
Medical University of South Carolina	M,D
Monmouth University	M,D,O
Mount Carmel College of Nursing	M,D
Mount Saint Mary College	M,O
Neumann University	M,O
New York University	M,D,O
North Park University	M
Old Dominion University	M,D
Purdue University Northwest	M
Quinnipiac University	D
Research College of Nursing	M
Rush University	D
Rutgers University–Newark	M,D,O
St. Catherine University	M,D
Saint Peter's University	M,D,O
Seattle Pacific University	M,O
Seattle University	M
Seton Hall University	M,D
Shenandoah University	M,D,O
Southern Adventist University	M
South University	M
Spalding University	M,D,O
Stony Brook University, State University of New York	M,D,O
Temple University	D
Texas Christian University	M,O
Texas Woman's University	M,D
Troy University	M,D
Universidad del Turabo	M,O
University at Buffalo, the State University of New York	M,D
The University of Alabama at Birmingham	M,D
University of Central Arkansas	M,D
University of Cincinnati	M,D
University of Colorado Colorado Springs	M,D
University of Colorado Denver	M,D
University of Delaware	M,O
University of Hawaii at Manoa	M,D,O
University of Illinois at Chicago	M,O
The University of Kansas	M,D,O
University of Massachusetts Amherst	M,D
University of Massachusetts Dartmouth	M,D,O
University of Massachusetts Medical School	M,D,O
University of Miami	M,D
University of Missouri	M,D,O
University of Missouri–Kansas City	M,D
University of Missouri–St. Louis	D,O
The University of North Carolina at Chapel Hill	M,D,O
The University of North Carolina at Greensboro	M,D,O
University of Pennsylvania	M
University of Puerto Rico, Medical Sciences Campus	M
University of Rochester	M,D
University of San Diego	M,D
University of South Carolina	M
University of Southern Maine	M,D,O
University of South Florida	M,D,O
The University of Tampa	M
The University of Texas at Austin	M,D
The University of Texas Rio Grande Valley	M
University of Wisconsin–Eau Claire	M,D
University of Wisconsin–Madison	D
University of Wisconsin–Oshkosh	M
Ursuline College	M,D
Vanderbilt University	M,D,O
Villanova University	M,D
Virginia Commonwealth University	M,D,O
Walden University	M,D
Walsh University	M,D
Western Connecticut State University	M,D
Wilmington University	M,D
Winona State University	M,D,O
Wright State University	M
York College of Pennsylvania	M,D,O

ADVERTISING AND PUBLIC RELATIONS

University	Program
Academy of Art University	M
Arcadia University	M
Ball State University	M
Boston University	M
California Baptist University	M
Clarion University of Pennsylvania	O
Colorado State University	M,D
DePaul University	M
Emerson College	M
Georgetown University	M
Golden Gate University	M,D,O
Hofstra University	M
Iona College	M,O
Kansas State University	M
Kent State University	M
La Salle University	M,O
Lasell College	M,O
La Sierra University	M
Liberty University	M,D,O
Marquette University	M,O
Marshall University	M
Michigan State University	M,D
Mississippi College	M
Monmouth University	M,O
Montana State University Billings	M
Montclair State University	M
New York University	M
Northern Kentucky University	M,O
Quinnipiac University	M
Rowan University	M
Royal Roads University	O
San Diego State University	M
Savannah College of Art and Design	M
Seton Hall University	M
Southern Illinois University Edwardsville	M
Southern Methodist University	M
Suffolk University	M
Syracuse University	M
Universidad Autonoma de Guadalajara	M,D
Université Laval	O
The University of Alabama	M
University of Colorado Boulder	M,D
University of Florida	M,D
University of Houston	M
University of Illinois at Urbana–Champaign	M
University of Maryland, College Park	M,D
University of Miami	M,D
University of Nebraska–Lincoln	M,D
University of North Texas	M,D,O
University of Saint Mary	M
University of Southern California	M
University of Southern Mississippi	M,D
The University of Tennessee	M,D
The University of Texas at Austin	M,D
The University of Texas Rio Grande Valley	M,O
University of the Sacred Heart	M
University of Wisconsin–Stevens Point	M
Virginia Commonwealth University	M
Virginia International University	M,O
Wayne State University	M,D,O
Webster University	M
Western New England University	M
William Woods University	M,D,O

AEROSPACE/AERONAUTICAL ENGINEERING

University	Program
Air Force Institute of Technology	M,D
American Public University System	M
Arizona State University at the Tempe campus	M,D
Auburn University	M,D
California Institute of Technology	M,D,O
California Polytechnic State University, San Luis Obispo	M
California State Polytechnic University, Pomona	M
Carleton University	M,D
Case Western Reserve University	M,D
The Citadel, The Military College of South Carolina	M,O
Concordia University (Canada)	M
Cornell University	M,D
École Polytechnique de Montréal	M,D,O
Embry-Riddle Aeronautical University–Daytona	M,D
Embry-Riddle Aeronautical University–Worldwide	M
Florida Institute of Technology	M
The George Washington University	M,D,O
Georgia Institute of Technology	M,D
Illinois Institute of Technology	M,D
Inter American University of Puerto Rico, Bayamón Campus	M
Iowa State University of Science and Technology	M,D
Johns Hopkins University	M
Massachusetts Institute of Technology	M,D,O
McGill University	M,D
Middle Tennessee State University	M
Mississippi State University	M,D
Missouri University of Science and Technology	M,D
Naval Postgraduate School	M,D,O
New Mexico State University	M,D
North Carolina State University	M,D
The Ohio State University	M,D
Old Dominion University	M,D
Penn State University Park	M,D
Princeton University	M,D
Purdue University	D
Rensselaer Polytechnic Institute	M,D
Rutgers University–New Brunswick	M,D
San Diego State University	M,D
Stanford University	M,D,O
Stevens Institute of Technology	M,D
Syracuse University	M,D
Texas A&M University	M,D
Université Laval	M
University at Buffalo, the State University of New York	M,D
The University of Alabama	M,D
The University of Alabama in Huntsville	M,D
The University of Arizona	M,D
University of California, Davis	M,D,O
University of California, Irvine	M,D
University of California, Los Angeles	M,D
University of California, San Diego	M,D
University of Central Florida	M
University of Central Missouri	M,D,O
University of Cincinnati	M,D
University of Colorado Boulder	M,D
University of Colorado Colorado Springs	M,D
University of Dayton	M,D
University of Florida	M,D
University of Illinois at Urbana–Champaign	M,D
The University of Kansas	M,D
The University of Manchester	M,D
University of Maryland, College Park	M,D
University of Miami	M,D
University of Michigan	M,D
University of Minnesota, Twin Cities Campus	M,D
University of Missouri	M,D
University of Nevada, Las Vegas	M,D,O
University of Notre Dame	M,D
University of Oklahoma	M,D
University of Ottawa	M,D
University of Puerto Rico, Mayagüez Campus	M,D
University of Southern California	M,D,O
The University of Tennessee	M,D
The University of Texas at Arlington	M,D
The University of Texas at Austin	M,D
University of Toronto	M,D
University of Virginia	M,D
University of Washington	M,D
Utah State University	M,D
Virginia Polytechnic Institute and State University	M,D,O
Washington University in St. Louis	M,D
Webster University	M,D,O
Western Michigan University	M,D
West Virginia University	M,D
Wichita State University	M,D
Worcester Polytechnic Institute	M,D
Wright State University	M,D

AFRICAN-AMERICAN STUDIES

University	Program
Boston University	M
Carnegie Mellon University	D
Clark Atlanta University	M,D
Columbia University	M,D
Cornell University	M,D
Eastern Michigan University	O
Georgia State University	M
Harvard University	D
Indiana University Bloomington	M,D
Michigan State University	M,D
Morgan State University	M,D
North Carolina Agricultural and Technical State University	M
Northwestern University	D

Oblate School of Theology — M,D,O
The Ohio State University — M,D
Rutgers University–New
  Brunswick — D
Syracuse University — M
Temple University — M,D
Trinity Lutheran Seminary — M
University at Albany, State
  University of New York — M
University of California, Berkeley — D
University of California, Los
  Angeles — M
University of California, Santa
  Barbara — D
The University of Kansas — M,O
University of Louisville — M
University of Massachusetts
  Amherst — M,D
University of Memphis — M,D,O
University of Wisconsin–
  Madison — M
West Virginia University — M,D
Yale University — D

AFRICAN STUDIES
Arizona State University at the
  Tempe campus — M,D,O
California State University, Long
  Beach — M
Carnegie Mellon University — D
Claremont Graduate University — M,D,O
College of Staten Island of the
  City University of New York — M
Columbia University — M,D
Cornell University — M,D
Florida International University — M
Harvard University — D
Howard University — M
Indiana University Bloomington — M
Michigan State University — M
New York University — M,D,O
Northwestern University — O
The Ohio State University — M,D
Ohio University — M
Rice University — D
Rutgers University–New
  Brunswick — D
Stony Brook University, State
  University of New York — M,O
Syracuse University — M
University at Albany, State
  University of New York — M
The University of Arizona — M,D,O
University of California, Los
  Angeles — M
University of Illinois at
  Urbana–Champaign — M
The University of Kansas — M,O
University of Louisville — M
The University of North Carolina
  at Charlotte — O
University of Pennsylvania — M,D
University of Pittsburgh — O
University of South Florida — M,O
The University of Texas at Austin — M,D
University of Wisconsin–
  Madison — M,D
University of Wisconsin–
  Milwaukee — D
Wayne State University — M,D,O
West Virginia University — M,D
Yale University — M

AGRICULTURAL ECONOMICS AND AGRIBUSINESS
Alcorn State University — M
American University of Beirut — M
Arizona State University at the
  Tempe campus — D
Auburn University — M
California Polytechnic State
  University, San Luis Obispo — M
Colorado State University — M,D
Cornell University — M,D
Delaware Valley University — M
Illinois State University — M
Instituto Centroamericano de
  Administración de Empresas — M
Iowa State University of Science
  and Technology — M,D
Kansas State University — M,D
Louisiana State University and
  Agricultural & Mechanical College — M,D
McGill University — M
Michigan State University — M,D
Mississippi State University — M
New Mexico State University — M,D
North Carolina Agricultural and
  Technical State University — M
North Carolina State University — M
North Dakota State University — M
Northwest Missouri State
  University — M
The Ohio State University — M,D
Oklahoma State University — M,D
Penn State University Park — M,D,O
Presidio Graduate School (CA) — M,O
Purdue University — M,D
Rutgers University–New
  Brunswick — M
South Carolina State University — M
Southern Illinois University
  Carbondale — M
Texas A&M University — M,D
Texas A&M University–
  Kingsville — M,D
Texas Tech University — M,D
Tropical Agriculture Research and
  Higher Education Center — M,D
Tuskegee University — M
Universidad del Este — M

Université Laval — M
University of Alberta — M,D
The University of Arizona — M
University of Arkansas — M
University of California, Berkeley — D
University of California, Davis — M
University of California, Santa
  Barbara — M,D
University of Connecticut — M,D
University of Delaware — M
University of Florida — M,D
University of Georgia — M,D
University of Guelph — M,D
University of Idaho — M
University of Illinois at
  Urbana–Champaign — M,D
University of Kentucky — M,D
University of Maine — M
University of Manitoba — M,D
University of Maryland, College
  Park — M,D
University of Massachusetts
  Amherst — M,D
University of Missouri — M,D,O
University of Nebraska–
  Lincoln — M,D
University of Nevada, Reno — M,D
University of Puerto Rico,
  Mayagüez Campus — M
University of Saskatchewan — M,D,O
The University of Tennessee at
  Martin — M
University of Vermont — M
University of Wisconsin–Madison — M,D
University of Wyoming — M
Virginia Polytechnic Institute and
  State University — M,D
Washington State University — M,D,O
West Texas A&M University — M
West Virginia University — M

AGRICULTURAL EDUCATION
Alcorn State University — M,O
Arkansas State University — M,O
California Polytechnic State
  University, San Luis Obispo — M
California State University, Chico — M
Clemson University — M
Cornell University — M,D
Eastern Kentucky University — M
Iowa State University of Science
  and Technology — M,D
Ithaca College — M
Kansas State University — M
Louisiana State University and
  Agricultural & Mechanical College — M,D
Mississippi State University — M,D
Montana State University — M
Murray State University — M
New Mexico State University — M
North Carolina Agricultural and
  Technical State University — M
North Carolina State University — M,D
North Dakota State University — M
Northwest Missouri State
  University — M
The Ohio State University — M
Oklahoma State University — M,D
Oregon State University — M,D
Penn State University Park — M,D,O
Purdue University — M,D,O
Saint Leo University — M
South Dakota State University — M
State University of New York at
  Oswego — M
Stephen F. Austin State University — M
Tennessee State University — M,D
Texas A&M University — M,D
Texas State University — M
Texas Tech University — M,D
The University of Arizona — M,O
University of Arkansas — M
University of Connecticut — M,D
University of Delaware — M
University of Florida — M,D
University of Illinois at
  Urbana–Champaign — M
University of Missouri — M,D,O
University of Nebraska–
  Lincoln — M
University of Puerto Rico,
  Mayagüez Campus — M
The University of Tennessee — M
University of Wisconsin–
  River Falls — M
Utah State University — M
West Virginia University — M,D

AGRICULTURAL ENGINEERING
Cornell University — M,D
Dalhousie University — M,D
Illinois Institute of Technology — M
Instituto Tecnológico y de
  Estudios Superiores de Monterrey,
  Campus Monterrey — M,D
Iowa State University of Science
  and Technology — M,D
Kansas State University — M,D
Louisiana State University and
  Agricultural & Mechanical College — M,D
McGill University — M,D
New York University — M,D
North Carolina State University — M,D,O
The Ohio State University — M,D
Oklahoma State University — M,D
Oregon State University — M,D
Penn State University Park — M,D
Purdue University — M,D
South Dakota State University — M,D
Texas A&M University — M,D
Université Laval — M

The University of Arizona — M,D
University of Arkansas — M,D
University of Florida — M,D,O
University of Illinois at
  Urbana–Champaign — M,D
University of Kentucky — M,D
University of Missouri — M,D
University of Nebraska–
  Lincoln — M,D
The University of Tennessee — M
University of Wisconsin–
  Madison — M,D
Utah State University — M,D
Virginia Polytechnic Institute and
  State University — M,D
Washington State University — M,D

AGRICULTURAL SCIENCES—GENERAL
Alabama Agricultural and
  Mechanical University — M,D
Alcorn State University — M
Angelo State University — M
Arkansas State University — M,O
Auburn University — M
Brigham Young University — M,D
California Polytechnic State
  University, San Luis Obispo — M
California State Polytechnic
  University, Pomona — M
California State University, Chico — M
Clemson University — M,D
Colorado State University — M,D
Dalhousie University — M
Illinois State University — M
Instituto Tecnológico y de
  Estudios Superiores de Monterrey,
  Campus Monterrey — M,D
Iowa State University of Science
  and Technology — M,D
Kansas State University — M,D,O
Louisiana State University and
  Agricultural & Mechanical College — M,D
McGill University — M,D,O
McNeese State University — M
Michigan State University — M
Mississippi State University — M,D
Missouri State University — M
Montana State University — M
Morehead State University — M
Murray State University — M
New Mexico State University — M,D
North Carolina Agricultural and
  Technical State University — M
North Carolina State University — M,D,O
North Dakota State University — M,D
Northwest Missouri State
  University — M
The Ohio State University — M,D
Oklahoma State University — M,D
Penn State University Park — M,D,O
Prairie View A&M University — M
Purdue University — M,D
Sam Houston State University — M
South Dakota State University — M
Southern Arkansas University–
  Magnolia — M
Southern Illinois University
  Carbondale — M
Southern University and
  Agricultural and Mechanical College — M
Tarleton State University — M
Tennessee State University — M,D
Texas A&M University — M,D
Texas A&M University–
  Commerce — M
Texas A&M University–
  Kingsville — M,D
Texas Tech University — M,D
Tropical Agriculture Research and
  Higher Education Center — M,D
Universidad Nacional Pedro
  Henriquez Urena — M
Université Laval — M,D,O
University of Alberta — M,D
The University of Arizona — M,D,O
University of Arkansas — M,D
The University of British Columbia — M
University of California, Davis — M
University of Connecticut — M,D
University of Delaware — M,D,O
University of Florida — M,D,O
University of Georgia — M,D
University of Guelph — M,D,O
University of Hawaii at Manoa — M,D
University of Illinois at
  Urbana–Champaign — M
The University of Iowa — M,D,O
University of Kentucky — M,D
University of Lethbridge — M,D
University of Maine — M,D,O
University of Manitoba — M,D
University of Maryland, College
  Park — M,D
University of Maryland Eastern
  Shore — M,D
University of Minnesota, Twin
  Cities Campus — M,D
University of Missouri — M,D,O
University of Nebraska–
  Lincoln — M,D
University of Nevada, Reno — M,D
University of Puerto Rico,
  Mayagüez Campus — M
University of Saskatchewan — M,D,O
University of South Africa — M,D
The University of Tennessee — M,D
The University of Tennessee at
  Martin — M
University of Vermont — M,D
University of Wisconsin–Madison — M,D

University of Wisconsin–
  River Falls — M
University of Wyoming — M,D
Utah State University — M,D
Virginia Polytechnic Institute and
  State University — M,D,O
Western Kentucky University — M
West Texas A&M University — M,D
West Virginia University — M,D

AGRONOMY AND SOIL SCIENCES
Alabama Agricultural and
  Mechanical University — M,D
Alcorn State University — M
Auburn University — M,D
Colorado State University — M,D
Cornell University — M,D
Dalhousie University — M
Iowa State University of Science
  and Technology — M,D
Kansas State University — M,D,O
McGill University — M,D
Michigan State University — M,D
Mississippi State University — M,D
North Carolina Agricultural and
  Technical State University — M
North Carolina State University — M,D
North Dakota State University — M,D
The Ohio State University — M,D
Oklahoma State University — M,D
Oregon State University — M,D
Penn State University Park — M,D
Purdue University — M,D
South Dakota State University — M,D
Southern Illinois University
  Carbondale — M
Tennessee State University — M,D
Texas A&M University — M,D
Texas A&M University–
  Kingsville — M
Texas Tech University — M,D
Tuskegee University — M
Université Laval — M,D
University of Alberta — M,D
The University of Arizona — M,D,O
University of Arkansas — M,D
The University of British Columbia — M,D
University of California, Davis — M,D
University of California,
  Riverside — M,D
University of Connecticut — M,D
University of Delaware — M,D
University of Florida — M,D
University of Georgia — M,D
University of Guelph — M,D
University of Idaho — M,D
University of Illinois at
  Urbana–Champaign — M,D
University of Kentucky — M,D
University of Manitoba — M,D
University of Minnesota, Twin
  Cities Campus — M,D
University of Missouri — M,D,O
University of Nebraska–
  Lincoln — M,D
University of Puerto Rico,
  Mayagüez Campus — M
University of Saskatchewan — M,D,O
University of Vermont — M,D
University of Wisconsin–
  Madison — M,D
University of Wyoming — M,D
Utah State University — M,D
Virginia Polytechnic Institute and
  State University — M,D
Washington State University — M,D,O
West Virginia University — M

ALLIED HEALTH—GENERAL
Alabama State University — M,D
American College of Healthcare
  Sciences — M,O
Andrews University — M
Athabasca University — M,O
A.T. Still University — M,D,O
Augusta University — D
Baylor University — M,D
Belmont University — M,D
Bennington College — O
Boston University — M,D
Brock University — M,O
Canisius College — M
Cleveland State University — M
Concordia University, St. Paul — M,D
Creighton University — M,D
Dominican College — M,D
Drexel University — M,D,O
Duquesne University — M,D,O
East Carolina University — M,D,O
Eastern Kentucky University — M
East Tennessee State University — M,D,O
Emory University — M,D
Ferris State University — M
Florida Agricultural and
  Mechanical University — M,D
Florida Gulf Coast University — M,D
Geisinger Commonwealth School of
  Medicine — D
Georgia Southern University — M,D,O
Georgia State University — M,D
Grand Valley State University — M,D
Hampton University — M
Harding University — M,D
Idaho State University — M,D,O
Ithaca College — M
Jacksonville University — M
Loma Linda University — M,D
Long Island University–LIU
  Post — M,O
Marymount University — M,D,O

Maryville University of Saint Louis	M,D
Medical University of South Carolina	M,D
Mercy College	M,D
Midwestern University, Downers Grove Campus	D
Midwestern University, Glendale Campus	M,D
Minnesota State University Mankato	M,D,O
Misericordia University	M,D
Moravian College	M
New Jersey City University	M
Northeastern University	M,D,O
Northern Arizona University	M,D,O
Northern Kentucky University	M
Nova Southeastern University	M,D
Oakland University	M,D,O
The Ohio State University	M
Old Dominion University	M,D
Oregon State University	M,D
Purdue University	M,D
Quinnipiac University	M
Regis University	M,D,O
Rosalind Franklin University of Medicine and Science	M,D,O
Rutgers University–Newark	M,D,O
Saint Louis University	M,D,O
Sam Houston State University	M
Seton Hall University	D
Shenandoah University	M,D,O
South Carolina State University	M
Southwestern Oklahoma State University	M
Temple University	M,D
Tennessee State University	M,D,O
Texas A&M University	M,D
Texas Christian University	M,D,O
Texas State University	M,D
Texas Woman's University	M,D
Towson University	M
University at Buffalo, the State University of New York	M,D,O
The University of Alabama at Birmingham	M,D,O
University of Detroit Mercy	M,D,O
University of Florida	M,D,O
University of Illinois at Chicago	M,D,O
The University of Kansas	M,D,O
University of Kentucky	M,D
University of Massachusetts Lowell	M,D
University of Memphis	M,O
University of Mississippi Medical Center	M
University of Nebraska Medical Center	M,D,O
University of Nevada, Las Vegas	M,D,O
University of New Mexico	M,D,O
The University of North Carolina at Chapel Hill	M,D
University of Northern Iowa	M,D
University of North Florida	M,D,O
University of Oklahoma Health Sciences Center	M,D,O
University of Phoenix–Las Vegas Campus	M
University of Puerto Rico, Medical Sciences Campus	M,D,O
University of South Alabama	M,D
The University of South Dakota	M,D,O
The University of Tennessee Health Science Center	M,D
The University of Texas at El Paso	D
The University of Texas Medical Branch	M,D
University of Vermont	M,D
University of Wisconsin–Milwaukee	M,D,O
Virginia Commonwealth University	D
Western University of Health Sciences	M,D
Wichita State University	M,D

ALLOPATHIC MEDICINE

Albany Medical College	D
Albert Einstein College of Medicine	D
American University of Beirut	M,D
Augusta University	D
Baylor College of Medicine	D
Boston University	D
Brown University	D
Case Western Reserve University	D
Charles R. Drew University of Medicine and Science	D
Columbia University	M,D
Creighton University	D
Dalhousie University	M,D
Dartmouth College	D
Drexel University	D
Duke University	D
East Carolina University	D
Eastern Virginia Medical School	D
East Tennessee State University	D
Emory University	D
Florida International University	M,D
Georgetown University	D
The George Washington University	D
Harvard University	D
Hofstra University	D
Howard University	D
Icahn School of Medicine at Mount Sinai	D
Indiana University–Purdue University Indianapolis	M,D
Instituto Tecnológico de Santo Domingo	M,D
Johns Hopkins University	D
Loma Linda University	M,D
Louisiana State University Health Sciences Center	M,D
Louisiana State University Health Sciences Center at Shreveport	D
Marshall University	D

Mayo Clinic School of Medicine	D
McGill University	M,D
Medical College of Wisconsin	D
Medical University of South Carolina	D
Meharry Medical College	D
Mercer University	M,D
Michigan State University	D
Morehouse School of Medicine	D
New York Medical College	D
New York University	M,D
Northeast Ohio Medical University	D
Northwestern University	D
The Ohio State University	D
Oregon Health & Science University	D
Penn State Hershey Medical Center	M,D
Ponce Health Sciences University	D
Pontificia Universidad Católica Madre y Maestra	D
Queen's University at Kingston	D
Quinnipiac University	D
Rosalind Franklin University of Medicine and Science	D
Rush University	D
Rutgers University–Newark	D
Rutgers University–New Brunswick	D
Saint Louis University	D
Stanford University	D
State University of New York Downstate Medical Center	M,D
State University of New York Upstate Medical University	D
Stony Brook University, State University of New York	D
Temple University	D
Texas Tech University Health Sciences Center	D
Thomas Jefferson University	D
Tufts University	D
Tulane University	D
Universidad Autónoma de Guadalajara	D
Universidad Central del Caribe	M,D
Universidad Central del Este	D
Universidad de Ciencias Médicas	M,D,O
Universidad de Iberoamerica	M,D
Universidad Iberoamericana	D
Universidad Nacional Pedro Henriquez Ureña	D
Université de Montréal	D
Université de Sherbrooke	D
Université Laval	D,O
University at Buffalo, the State University of New York	D
The University of Alabama at Birmingham	D
The University of Arizona	M,D
University of Arkansas for Medical Sciences	D
The University of British Columbia	M,D
University of Calgary	D
University of California, Berkeley	D
University of California, Davis	D
University of California, Irvine	D
University of California, Los Angeles	D
University of California, San Diego	D
University of California, San Francisco	D
University of Central Florida	M,D
University of Chicago	D
University of Cincinnati	D
University of Colorado Denver	D
University of Connecticut Health Center	D
University of Florida	D
University of Hawaii at Manoa	D
University of Illinois at Chicago	D
University of Illinois at Urbana–Champaign	D
The University of Iowa	D
The University of Kansas	D
University of Kentucky	D
University of Louisville	D
University of Maryland, Baltimore	D
University of Massachusetts Medical School	D
University of Miami	D
University of Michigan	D
University of Minnesota, Duluth	D
University of Minnesota, Twin Cities Campus	M,D
University of Mississippi Medical Center	D
University of Missouri	D
University of Missouri–Kansas City	M,D
University of Nebraska Medical Center	D,O
University of New Mexico	D
The University of North Carolina at Chapel Hill	D
University of Oklahoma Health Sciences Center	D
University of Ottawa	M,D
University of Pennsylvania	D
University of Pittsburgh	D
University of Puerto Rico, Medical Sciences Campus	D
University of Rochester	D
University of Saskatchewan	D
University of South Alabama	D
University of South Carolina	D
The University of South Dakota	D
University of Southern California	D
University of South Florida	M,D
The University of Tennessee Health Science Center	D
The University of Texas Health Science Center at Houston	D

The University of Texas Health Science Center at San Antonio	M,D
The University of Texas Medical Branch	D
The University of Texas Rio Grande Valley	D
The University of Texas Southwestern Medical Center	D
University of Toronto	M,D
University of Utah	D
University of Virginia	M,D
University of Washington	D
The University of Western Ontario	M,D
University of Wisconsin–Madison	D
Vanderbilt University	M,D
Virginia Commonwealth University	D
Wake Forest University	D
Washington University in St. Louis	D
Wayne State University	D
West Virginia University	D
Wright State University	D
Yale University	D

AMERICAN INDIAN/NATIVE AMERICAN STUDIES

Central Michigan University	M
Montana State University	M
Navajo Technical University	M
Northeastern State University	M
Trent University	M
The University of Arizona	M,D
University of California, Davis	M,D
University of California, Los Angeles	M
University of Idaho	D
The University of Kansas	M,O
University of Lethbridge	M,D
University of Manitoba	M
University of New Mexico	M
University of Oklahoma	M
The University of Tulsa	M,D,O

AMERICAN STUDIES

American Public University System	M
American University	M,D,O
American University of Beirut	M,D
Appalachian State University	M
Armstrong State University	M
Baylor University	M
Boston University	D
Bowling Green State University	M,D
Brown University	M,D
California State University, Fullerton	M
The Catholic University of America	M
Central Michigan University	M,O
Claremont Graduate University	M,D,O
Clark University	D
The College at Brockport, State University of New York	M
College of Staten Island of the City University of New York	M
The College of William and Mary	M,D
The Colorado College	M
Columbia University	M,D
Cornell University	M,D
Drew University	M,D,O
East Carolina University	M
Emory & Henry College	M
Fairfield University	M
Florida State University	M,D
Georgetown University	M,D
The George Washington University	M,D
Harvard University	D
Inter American University of Puerto Rico, Metropolitan Campus	M,D
James Madison University	M
Kennesaw State University	M
Lake Forest College	M
La Salle University	M,O
Lehigh University	M,D,O
Michigan State University	M,D
Mississippi State University	M,D
Monmouth University	M
New Mexico Highlands University	M
New York University	M,D
Northwestern Oklahoma State University	M
Northwestern University	M
Penn State Harrisburg	M,D,O
Pepperdine University	M
Providence College	M
Purdue University	M
Regent University	M
Rice University	D
Rutgers University–Newark	M,D
Saint Louis University	M,D
Salisbury University	M,O
Stockton University	M,O
Texas Christian University	M,D
Trinity College (United States)	M
Universidad de las Américas Puebla	M
University at Buffalo, the State University of New York	M,D,O
The University of Alabama	M
University of Colorado Denver	M
University of Dallas	M
University of Delaware	M
University of Hawaii at Manoa	M,D,O
The University of Iowa	M,D
The University of Kansas	M,D
University of Louisiana at Lafayette	D
University of Maryland, College Park	M,D
University of Massachusetts Amherst	M,D
University of Massachusetts Boston	M
University of Michigan	D
University of Michigan–Flint	M
University of Minnesota, Twin Cities Campus	D

University of Missouri–St. Louis	M,D
University of New Mexico	M,D
University of Rochester	M,D
University of Southern California	D
University of Southern Maine	M,O
University of South Florida	M,D
The University of Texas at Austin	M,D
University of Utah	M,D
University of West Florida	M
University of Wisconsin–Madison	M,D
University of Wyoming	M
Utah State University	M
Washington State University	M,D
Wayne State University	M,D,O
West Virginia University	M,D
Wilfrid Laurier University	M,D
Yale University	D

ANALYTICAL CHEMISTRY

Auburn University	M,D
Binghamton University, State University of New York	M,D
Brigham Young University	M,D
California State University, Los Angeles	M
Cornell University	D
Eastern New Mexico University	M
Florida State University	M,D
Georgetown University	D
The George Washington University	M,D
Georgia State University	M,D
Governors State University	M
Howard University	M,D
Illinois Institute of Technology	M,D
Indiana University Bloomington	M,D
Iowa State University of Science and Technology	M,D
Laurentian University	M
Marquette University	M,D
McMaster University	M,D
Old Dominion University	M,D
Oregon State University	M,D
Purdue University	M,D
Rutgers University–Newark	M,D
Seton Hall University	M,D
Southern University and Agricultural and Mechanical College	M
Stevens Institute of Technology	M,D,O
University of Calgary	M,D
University of Cincinnati	M,D
University of Georgia	M,D
University of Louisville	M,D
The University of Manchester	M,D
University of Maryland, College Park	M,D
University of Massachusetts Lowell	M,D
University of Memphis	M,D
University of Michigan	D
University of Missouri	M,D
University of Missouri–Kansas City	M,D
University of Montana	M,D
University of Nebraska–Lincoln	M,D
University of Oklahoma	M,D
University of Regina	M,D
The University of Tennessee	M,D
The University of Texas at Austin	D
The University of Toledo	M,D
University of Wisconsin–Milwaukee	M,D
Vanderbilt University	M,D
Virginia Commonwealth University	M,D
Wake Forest University	M,D
Wayne State University	M,D
West Virginia University	M,D
Youngstown State University	M

ANATOMY

Albert Einstein College of Medicine	D
Augusta University	D
Barry University	M
Boston University	M,D
Case Western Reserve University	M
Columbia University	M,D
Cornell University	D
Creighton University	M
Dalhousie University	M,D
Des Moines University	M
Duke University	D
East Carolina University	D
East Tennessee State University	M
Howard University	M,D
Indiana University–Purdue University Indianapolis	M,D
Johns Hopkins University	D
Loma Linda University	D
Louisiana State University Health Sciences Center	D
Louisiana State University Health Sciences Center at Shreveport	M,D
McGill University	M,D
New York Academy of Art	M
New York Chiropractic College	M
The Ohio State University	M,D
Palmer College of Chiropractic	M
Penn State Hershey Medical Center	M,D
Purdue University	M,D
Queen's University at Kingston	M,D
Rosalind Franklin University of Medicine and Science	D
Rush University	M,D
Saint Louis University	M,D
State University of New York Upstate Medical University	M,D
Stony Brook University, State University of New York	D
Universidad Central del Caribe	M,D
Universidad de Ciencias Médicas	M,D,O
Université Laval	O
University at Buffalo, the State University of New York	M,D

University of California, Irvine M,D
University of California, Los Angeles M,D
University of Chicago D
University of Colorado Denver M,D
University of Connecticut Health Center D
University of Guelph M,D
University of Illinois at Chicago M
The University of Iowa D
The University of Kansas M,D
University of Kentucky D
University of Louisville M,D
University of Manitoba M,D
University of Mississippi Medical Center M,D
University of Missouri M
University of Nebraska Medical Center M,D
University of North Texas Health Science Center at Fort Worth M,D
University of Prince Edward Island M,D
University of Puerto Rico, Medical Sciences Campus M,D
University of Rochester D
University of Saskatchewan M,D
University of South Florida M,D
The University of Tennessee M,D
University of Utah D
The University of Western Ontario M,D
Virginia Commonwealth University M
Wake Forest University D
Wayne State University M,D,O
Wright State University M
Youngstown State University

ANESTHESIOLOGIST ASSISTANT STUDIES
Case Western Reserve University M
Emory University M
Nova Southeastern University M,D
Quinnipiac University M
South University (GA) M
Université Laval O
University of Colorado Denver M
University of Guelph M,D,O

ANIMAL BEHAVIOR
Arizona State University at the Tempe campus M,D
Bucknell University M
Cornell University D
Emory University D
Hunter College of the City University of New York M,O
Illinois State University M,D
Oregon State University M,D
University of California, Davis D
University of Colorado Denver M,D
University of Massachusetts Amherst M,D
University of Minnesota, Twin Cities Campus M,D
University of Montana M,D,O
The University of Tennessee M,D
The University of Texas at Austin D
University of Washington D

ANIMAL SCIENCES
Alcorn State University M
American University of Beirut M
Angelo State University M
Auburn University M,D
Bergin University of Canine Studies M
Boise State University M,D
Brigham Young University M,D
California State University, Fresno M
Colorado State University M,D
Cornell University M,D
Dalhousie University M
Fort Valley State University M
Iowa State University of Science and Technology M,D
Kansas State University M,D
Louisiana State University and Agricultural & Mechanical College M,D
McGill University M,D
Michigan State University M,D
Mississippi State University M,D
Missouri Western State University M
Montana State University M,D
New Mexico State University M,D
North Carolina Agricultural and Technical State University M
North Carolina State University M,D
North Dakota State University M,D
The Ohio State University M,D
Oklahoma State University M,D
Oregon State University M,D
Penn State University Park M,D
Purdue University M,D
Rutgers University–New Brunswick M,D
South Dakota State University M,D
Southern Illinois University Carbondale M
Sul Ross State University M
Texas A&M University M,D
Texas A&M University–Kingsville M
Texas Tech University M,D
Tufts University M
Tuskegee University M
Universidad Nacional Pedro Henriquez Urena M
Université Laval M,D
The University of Arizona M,D
University of Arkansas M,D
The University of British Columbia M,D
University of California, Davis M,D

University of Connecticut M,D
University of Delaware M,D
University of Florida M,D
University of Georgia M,D
University of Guelph M,D
University of Hawaii at Manoa M
University of Idaho M,D
University of Illinois at Urbana–Champaign M,D
University of Kentucky M,D
University of Manitoba M,D
University of Maryland, College Park M,D
University of Massachusetts Amherst M,D
University of Minnesota, Twin Cities Campus M,D
University of Missouri M,D
University of Nebraska–Lincoln M,D
University of Nevada, Reno M
University of New Hampshire D
University of Puerto Rico, Mayagüez Campus M
University of Rhode Island M,D
University of Saint Joseph M
University of Saskatchewan M,D
The University of Tennessee M,D
University of Vermont M,D
University of Wisconsin–Madison M,D
University of Wyoming M,D
Utah State University M,D
Virginia Polytechnic Institute and State University M,D
Washington State University M,D
West Texas A&M University M

ANTHROPOLOGY
American University M,D,O
American University of Beirut M,D
Arizona State University at the Tempe campus M,D,O
Ball State University M,O
Binghamton University, State University of New York M,D
Biola University M,D,O
Boise State University M,D
Boston University M,D
Brandeis University M
Brigham Young University M
Brown University M,D
California State University, Bakersfield M
California State University, Chico M
California State University, East Bay M
California State University, Fullerton M
California State University, Long Beach M
California State University, Los Angeles M
California State University, Northridge M
California State University, Sacramento M
Canisius College M
Carleton University M
Case Western Reserve University M,D
The Catholic University of America M
Central European University M,D
The College of William and Mary M,D
Colorado State University M
Columbia University M,D
Concordia University (Canada) M,D
Cornell University D
Creighton University M
Dalhousie University M,D
East Carolina University M
Eastern New Mexico University M
Edinboro University of Pennsylvania M
Emory University D
Florida Atlantic University M
George Mason University M,D
The George Washington University M,D
Georgia State University M
The Graduate Center, City University of New York D
Harvard University M,D
Humboldt State University M
Hunter College of the City University of New York M
Idaho State University M
Indiana University Bloomington M,D
Iowa State University of Science and Technology M
Johns Hopkins University D
Kent State University M
Louisiana State University and Agricultural & Mechanical College M,D
McGill University M,D
McMaster University M,D
Memorial University of Newfoundland M,D
Mercyhurst University M
Michigan State University M,D
Minnesota State University Mankato M
Mississippi State University M
Monmouth University M
New Mexico Highlands University M
New Mexico State University M,O
The New School M,D
New York University M,D
North Carolina State University M
North Dakota State University M
Northern Arizona University M
Northern Illinois University M
Northwestern University D
The Ohio State University M,D

Oregon State University M,D
Penn State University Park M,D
Portland State University M,D,O
Princeton University D
Purdue University M,D
Rice University M,D
Rutgers University–New Brunswick M,D
San Diego State University M
San Francisco State University M
San Jose State University M,O
Simon Fraser University M,D
Sonoma State University M
Southern Illinois University Carbondale M,D
Southern Methodist University M,D
Stanford University M,D
Stony Brook University, State University of New York M,D
Syracuse University M,D
Teachers College, Columbia University M,D
Temple University D
Texas A&M University M,D
Texas State University M
Texas Tech University M
Trent University M
Tulane University D
Universidad de las Américas Puebla M
Université de Montréal M
Université Laval M,D
University at Albany, State University of New York M,D
University at Buffalo, the State University of New York M,D
The University of Alabama M,D
The University of Alabama at Birmingham M,D
University of Alaska Anchorage M
University of Alaska Fairbanks M
University of Alberta M,D
The University of Arizona M,D,O
University of Arkansas M
The University of British Columbia M,D
University of Calgary M,D
University of California, Berkeley D
University of California, Davis M
University of California, Irvine M,D
University of California, Los Angeles M,D
University of California, Riverside M,D
University of California, San Diego D
University of California, San Francisco D
University of California, Santa Barbara M,D
University of California, Santa Cruz D
University of Central Florida M,O
University of Chicago D
University of Cincinnati M
University of Colorado Boulder M,D
University of Colorado Denver M
University of Connecticut M,D
University of Denver M
University of Florida M,D
University of Georgia M,D
University of Guelph M,D
University of Hawaii at Manoa M,D
University of Houston M
University of Idaho M
University of Illinois at Chicago M,D
University of Illinois at Urbana–Champaign M,D
University of Indianapolis M
The University of Iowa M,D
The University of Kansas M,D
University of Kentucky M,D
University of Lethbridge M,D
University of Louisville M
University of Maine D
The University of Manchester M,D
University of Manitoba M,D
University of Maryland, College Park M
University of Massachusetts Amherst M,D
University of Memphis M
University of Michigan D
University of Minnesota, Duluth M
University of Minnesota, Twin Cities Campus M,D
University of Mississippi M,D
University of Missouri M,D
University of Montana M,D
University of Nebraska–Lincoln M
University of Nevada, Las Vegas M,D
University of Nevada, Reno M,D
University of New Brunswick Fredericton M
University of New Mexico M,D
The University of North Carolina at Chapel Hill M,D
The University of North Carolina at Charlotte M
University of North Georgia M
University of North Texas M,D,O
University of Oklahoma M,D
University of Oregon M,D
University of Ottawa M,D
University of Pennsylvania M,D
University of Pittsburgh M,D
University of Regina M
University of Rhode Island M
University of Saskatchewan M,D
University of South Africa M,D
University of South Carolina M,D

University of Southern Mississippi M
University of South Florida M,D,O
The University of Tennessee M,D
The University of Texas at Arlington M
The University of Texas at Austin M,D
The University of Texas at El Paso M,O
The University of Texas at San Antonio M,D
The University of Texas Rio Grande Valley M
University of Toronto M,D
The University of Tulsa M,D
University of Utah M,D
University of Victoria M,D
University of Virginia M,D
University of Washington M,D
University of Waterloo M
The University of Western Ontario M,D
University of West Florida M
University of Wisconsin–Madison D
University of Wisconsin–Milwaukee M,D,O
University of Wyoming M,D
Vanderbilt University M,D
Washington State University M,D
Washington University in St. Louis D
Wayne State University M,D,O
Western Kentucky University M
Western Michigan University M
Western Washington University M
Wichita State University M
Yale University M,D
York University M,D

APPLIED ARTS AND DESIGN—GENERAL
Academy of Art University M
Alfred University M
Arizona State University at the Tempe campus M,D
The Art Institute of Dallas, a branch of Miami International University of Art & Design M
Bowling Green State University M
California College of the Arts M
California Institute of the Arts M,O
California State University, Fresno M
California State University, Los Angeles M
Carnegie Mellon University M,D
College for Creative Studies M
Concordia University (Canada) M,O
Drexel University M
Emily Carr University of Art + Design M
Fashion Institute of Technology M
Ferris State University M
Florida Atlantic University M
Howard University M
Illinois Institute of Technology M,D
Indiana University Bloomington M
Iowa State University of Science and Technology M,D
Louisiana State University and Agricultural & Mechanical College M
Louisiana Tech University M
Maryland Institute College of Art M
Massachusetts College of Art and Design M,O
Memphis College of Art M
Miami International University of Art & Design M
Millersville University of Pennsylvania M
Minneapolis College of Art and Design M
The New School M
New York Institute of Technology M
New York University M
North Carolina State University M,D
Northeastern University M
NSCAD University M
Oklahoma State University M,D
Pacific Northwest College of Art M
Pratt Institute M,O
Purdue University M
Rhode Island School of Design M
Rutgers University–New Brunswick M
Samford University M
San Diego State University M
San Francisco State University M
Savannah College of Art and Design M
School of the Art Institute of Chicago M
School of Visual Arts (NY) M
Southern Illinois University Carbondale M
Stanford University M,D,O
Stephen F. Austin State University M
Suffolk University M
Syracuse University M
Texas State University M
University of Alberta M
University of Baltimore M
University of Bridgeport M
University of California, Berkeley O
University of California, Los Angeles M
University of Central Oklahoma M
University of Cincinnati M
University of Connecticut M
University of Delaware M
University of Illinois at Chicago M
University of Illinois at Urbana–Champaign M,D
The University of Kansas M
University of Kentucky M
University of Louisville M,D

---

*M—masters degree; D—doctorate; O—other advanced degree; *—Close-Up and/or Display*

University of Massachusetts
Dartmouth — M
University of Michigan — M,D
University of Minnesota, Twin
Cities Campus — M,D,O
University of North Texas — M,D,O
University of Notre Dame — M
The University of Texas at Austin — M
University of Washington — M
University of Wisconsin–
Madison — M,D
University of Wisconsin–
Milwaukee — M
Western Carolina University — M
Western Michigan University — M
Yale University — M
York University — M

APPLIED BEHAVIOR ANALYSIS

Antioch University New England — M,O
Arcadia University — M
Arizona State University at the
Tempe campus — M,D
Assumption College — M,O
Aurora University — M
Ball State University — M
Baylor University — M,D,O
Bay Path University — M
Cairn University — M,O
Caldwell University — M,D,O
California State University,
Fresno — M,O
California State University,
Sacramento — M
California State University,
Stanislaus — M
Capella University — M
The Chicago School of Professional
Psychology — M,D
The Chicago School of Professional
Psychology at Downtown
Los Angeles — M,D
Drexel University — M,D
Eastern University — M,O
Endicott College — M,D
Fairfield University — M,O
Florida Institute of Technology — M,D
Florida International University — M,D
Florida State University — M
Georgian Court University — M,O
Hofstra University — M,D,O
James Madison University — M
Johns Hopkins University — O
Johnson State College — M
Lipscomb University — M,D,O
Long Island University–LIU
Brooklyn — M,O
Long Island University–LIU
Post — M,O
McNeese State University — M
Mercyhurst University — M
Missouri State University — M,O
Monmouth University — M,D,O
Montana State University Billings — M
Northeastern University — M,D,O
Northern Michigan University — M,O
Oakland University — M,O
Oklahoma City University — M
Oklahoma State University — M,D,O
Penn State Harrisburg — M,D,O
Philadelphia College of
Osteopathic Medicine — M,D,O
Queens College of the City
University of New York — M,O
Regis College (MA) — M,D,O
Rollins College — M
Rowan University — M,O
Sage Graduate School — M,O
St. Cloud State University — M
Saint Peter's University — M,D,O
Shenandoah University — M
Simmons College — M,D,O
Teachers College, Columbia
University — M,D,O
Temple University — M,D,O
Tennessee Technological University — D
The University of Kansas — M,D,O
University of Louisville — M,D,O
University of Massachusetts
Dartmouth — M,O
University of Memphis — M,D
University of Nebraska at Omaha — M,D,O
University of Nebraska Medical
Center — M,D
The University of North Carolina
Wilmington — M
University of North Florida — M
University of North Texas — M,D,O
University of Oklahoma — M,D
University of Pittsburgh — M,D
University of Saint Joseph — M,O
University of San Francisco — M
University of Southern Maine — M,O
University of Southern Mississippi — M,D
University of South Florida — M,D
The University of Texas at San
Antonio — M,O
University of West Florida — M
University of Wisconsin–
Milwaukee — M,D
Wayne State University — M,D,O
Western New England University — M,D
Westfield State University — M
Wright State University — M
Youngstown State University — M

APPLIED ECONOMICS

Auburn University — D
Buffalo State College, State
University of New York — M
Clemson University — M,D
Cornell University — M,D
DePaul University — M
East Carolina University — M
Florida State University — M,D

Georgia Southern University — M,O
HEC Montreal — M
Johns Hopkins University — M
Mills College — M
New York University — M,D,O
North Carolina Agricultural and
Technical State University — M
Ohio University — M
Portland State University — M,D
St. Cloud State University — M
Southern Methodist University — M,D
Texas Tech University — M,D
Thomas Jefferson University — M,D,O
University of California, Santa
Cruz — M
University of Cincinnati — M
University of Georgia — M,D
University of Houston — M,D
University of Idaho — M
University of Illinois at
Urbana–Champaign — M,D
University of Massachusetts Boston — M
University of Michigan — M
University of Minnesota, Twin
Cities Campus — M,D
University of Nevada, Las Vegas — M,O
University of Nevada, Reno — M,D
University of New Brunswick
Fredericton — M
The University of North Carolina
at Charlotte — M,O
The University of North Carolina
at Greensboro — M
University of North Dakota — M
University of Oklahoma — M,D
University of Pennsylvania — D
University of Regina — M
University of Vermont — M
University of Wisconsin–
Madison — M,D
University of Wyoming — M
Utah State University — M
Virginia Polytechnic Institute and
State University — M,D
Washington & Jefferson College — M,O
Western Kentucky University — M
Western Michigan University — M,D
Wright State University — M

APPLIED MATHEMATICS

Acadia University — M
Air Force Institute of Technology — M,D
Arizona State University at the
Tempe campus — M,D,O
Auburn University — M,D
Bowie State University — M
Brown University — M,D
California Baptist University — M
California Institute of Technology — M,D
California State Polytechnic
University, Pomona — M
California State University, East
Bay — M
California State University,
Fullerton — M
California State University, Long
Beach — M,D
California State University, Los
Angeles — M
California State University,
Northridge — M
Case Western Reserve University — M,D
Central European University — M,D
Claremont Graduate University — M,D
The College of William and Mary — M,D
Colorado School of Mines — M,D
Columbia University — M,D
Cornell University — M,D
Dalhousie University — M,D
Delaware State University — M,D
DePaul University — M,D
Ecole Polytechnique de
Montréal — M,D,O
Elizabeth City State University — M
Florida Atlantic University — M,D
Florida Institute of Technology — M,D
Florida State University — M,D
The George Washington University — M,D,O
Hampton University — M
Harvard University — M,D
Howard University — M,D
Hunter College of the City
University of New York — M
Illinois Institute of Technology — M,D
Indiana University Bloomington — M,D
Indiana University of Pennsylvania — M
Indiana University–Purdue
University Fort Wayne — M,O
Indiana University–Purdue
University Indianapolis — M,D
Indiana University South Bend — M
Inter American University of
Puerto Rico, San Germán Campus — M
Iowa State University of Science
and Technology — M,D
Jackson State University — M
Johns Hopkins University — M,D,O
Kent State University — M,D
Lehigh University — M,D
Long Island University–LIU
Post — M,O
Manhattan College — M
McGill University — M,D
Michigan State University — M,D
Michigan Technological University — M,D
Missouri University of Science and
Technology — M,D
Montclair State University — M
Naval Postgraduate School — M,D
New Jersey Institute of Technology — M,D,O
New Mexico Institute of Mining and
Technology — M,D
North Carolina Agricultural and
Technical State University — M

North Carolina Central University — M
North Carolina State University — M,D
North Dakota State University — M,D
Northeastern Illinois University — M
Northeastern University — M,D
Northwestern University — M,D
Oakland University — M,D
Oklahoma State University — M,D
Old Dominion University — M,D
Oregon State University — M
Princeton University — D
Rensselaer Polytechnic Institute — M
Rice University — M,D
Rochester Institute of Technology — M
Rutgers University–Camden — M
Rutgers University–New
Brunswick — M,D
St. John's University (NY) — M
San Diego State University — M
Santa Clara University — M,D,O
Simon Fraser University — M,D
Southern Illinois University
Edwardsville — M
Southern Methodist University — M,D
Stevens Institute of Technology — M
Stony Brook University, State
University of New York — M,D,O
Temple University — M,D
Texas Christian University — M,D
Texas State University — M
Towson University — M
The University of Akron — M
The University of Alabama — M,D
The University of Alabama at
Birmingham — D
The University of Alabama in
Huntsville — M,D
University of Alberta — M,D,O
The University of Arizona — M,D
University of Arkansas at Little
Rock — M,O
University of California, Berkeley — M,D
University of California, Davis — M,D
University of California, Irvine — M,D
University of California, Merced — M,D
University of California, San
Diego — M,D
University of California, Santa
Barbara — M,D
University of California, Santa
Cruz — M,D
University of Central Arkansas — M
University of Central Missouri — M,D,O
University of Central Oklahoma — M
University of Cincinnati — M,D
University of Colorado Boulder — M,D
University of Colorado Colorado
Springs — M
University of Colorado Denver — M,D
University of Connecticut — M
University of Dayton — M
University of Delaware — M,D
University of Georgia — M,D
University of Guelph — M,D
University of Houston — M,D
University of Illinois at
Urbana–Champaign — M,D
The University of Iowa — D
The University of Kansas — M,D,O
University of Kentucky — M,D
University of Louisville — M,D
The University of Manchester — M,D
University of Maryland, Baltimore
County — M,D
University of Maryland, College
Park — M,D
University of Massachusetts
Amherst — M,D
University of Memphis — M,D
University of Michigan–
Dearborn — M
University of Minnesota, Duluth — M
University of Missouri — M,D
University of New Hampshire — M,D,O
The University of North Carolina
at Charlotte — M,D
University of Northern Iowa — M
University of Notre Dame — M,D
University of Pennsylvania — D
University of Pittsburgh — M,D
University of Puerto Rico,
Mayagüez Campus — M
University of Rhode Island — M,D
University of Southern California — M,D
The University of Tennessee — M,D
The University of Tennessee at
Chattanooga — M
The University of Texas at
Arlington — M,D
The University of Texas at Austin — M,D
The University of Texas at Dallas — M,D
The University of Texas at San
Antonio — M
The University of Toledo — M,D
The University of Tulsa — M
University of Washington — M,D
University of Waterloo — M,D
The University of Western Ontario — M,D
University of Wisconsin–
Milwaukee — M,D
University of Wisconsin–
Stout — M
Utah State University — M,D
Virginia Commonwealth University — M
Washington State University — M,D
Wayne State University — M,D
West Chester University of
Pennsylvania — M,O
Western Michigan University — M,D
West Virginia University — M,D
Wichita State University — M,D
Worcester Polytechnic Institute — M,D,O
Wright State University — M
Yale University — M,D

York University — M,D
Youngstown State University — M

APPLIED PHYSICS

Air Force Institute of Technology — M,D
Binghamton University, State
University of New York — M,D
California Institute of Technology — M,D
Carnegie Mellon University — M,D
Christopher Newport University — M
The College of William and Mary — M,D
Colorado School of Mines — M,D
Columbia University — M,D
Cornell University — M,D
East Carolina University — M,D
George Mason University — M
Georgia Southern University — M
Harvard University — M,D
Idaho State University — M,D
Illinois Institute of Technology — M,D
Iowa State University of Science
and Technology — M,D
Johns Hopkins University — M,O
Laurentian University — M
Louisiana Tech University — M
Michigan Technological University — M,D
Naval Postgraduate School — M,D,O
New Jersey Institute of Technology — M,D,O
New York University — M,D
Northern Arizona University — M,D
Northwestern University — D
Rice University — M,D
Rutgers University–Newark — M,D
Southern Illinois University
Carbondale — M,D
Stanford University — M,D
Texas A&M University — M,D
Towson University — M
University of Arkansas — M,D
University of California, San
Diego — M,D
University of Massachusetts Boston — M
University of Michigan — D
University of Missouri–St.
Louis — M,D
The University of North Carolina
at Charlotte — M,D
University of South Florida — M,D
The University of Texas at Austin — M,D
University of Washington — M,D
Virginia Commonwealth University — M,D
West Virginia University — M,D
Yale University — M,D

APPLIED PSYCHOLOGY

Angelo State University — M
Antioch University Midwest — M
Antioch University New England — M,D,O
Arizona State University at the
Tempe campus — M
Athabasca University — M,O
Boston College — M,D
Brigham Young University — D
California State University, Chico — M
The Catholic University of America — M,D
Central Michigan University — M,D
The Chicago School of Professional
Psychology: Online — M,O
Clayton State University — M
Clemson University — M
DEREE - The American College of
Greece — M
Eastern Washington University — M
Fairfield University — M,O
Fordham University — M,D
Francis Marion University — M,O
George Mason University — M,D,O
The George Washington University — D
Laurentian University — M
London Metropolitan University — M,D
Loras College — M
Lynn University — M
New York University — M,D,O
Oklahoma State University — M,D,O
Old Dominion University — D
Penn State Harrisburg — M,D,O
Rider University — M
Rutgers University–New
Brunswick — M,D
Sacred Heart University — M
Saint Mary's University
(Canada) — M,D
Tarleton State University — M
Teachers College, Columbia
University — M,D
University of Arkansas at Little
Rock — M
University of Baltimore — M
University of Calgary — M,D
University of Central Florida — M,D
University of Guelph — M,D
University of Maryland, Baltimore
County — D
University of Pennsylvania — M
University of Pittsburgh — M,D
University of Regina — M,D
University of South Carolina Aiken — M
The University of Tennessee — M,D
The University of Texas at El Paso — M,O
The University of Texas of the
Permian Basin — M
University of West Florida — M
University of Windsor — M,D
University of Wisconsin–
Stout — M
Walden University — M,D,O
William James College — M,D,O

APPLIED SCIENCE AND TECHNOLOGY

The College of William and Mary — M,D
Colorado State University–
Pueblo — M
Harvard University — M,O
Kansas State University — M,O

Louisiana State University and Agricultural & Mechanical College M
Missouri State University M
Naval Postgraduate School M,D
Saint Mary's University (Canada) M
Southeastern Louisiana University M
Southern Methodist University M,D
Thomas Edison State University M,O
University of Arkansas at Little Rock M,D
University of California, Berkeley D
University of California, Davis M,D
University of Colorado Denver M,D
University of Mississippi M,D

APPLIED SOCIAL RESEARCH
American University M,O
California State University, Dominguez Hills M
Concordia University Irvine M
Florida State University M,D
Hunter College of the City University of New York M
Laurentian University M
Loma Linda University M,D
The New School M,D
New York University M
Portland State University M,D
Queens College of the City University of New York M
University of California, Los Angeles M,D

APPLIED STATISTICS
American University M,O
Bay Path University M
Binghamton University, State University of New York M,D
Bowling Green State University M
Brigham Young University M
California State University, East Bay M
California State University, Long Beach M
Cleveland State University M
Colorado School of Mines M,D
Cornell University M,D
DePaul University M,D
Florida State University M,D
Fordham University M
Indiana University Bloomington M,D
Indiana University–Purdue University Fort Wayne M,O
Indiana University–Purdue University Indianapolis M,D
Instituto Tecnológico y de Estudios Superiores de Monterrey, Campus Monterrey M,D
Kennesaw State University M
Louisiana State University and Agricultural & Mechanical College M
Loyola University Chicago M
McMaster University M
Michigan State University M,D
Minnesota State University Mankato M
New Jersey Institute of Technology M,D,O
New Mexico State University M,D,O
New York University M
Northern Arizona University M,O
Oakland University M
Oregon State University M
Penn State University Park M,D
Rochester Institute of Technology M,O
Rutgers University–New Brunswick M,D
St. Cloud State University M
Stevens Institute of Technology O
Syracuse University M
Teachers College, Columbia University M,D
The University of Alabama M,D
University of Arkansas at Little Rock M,O
University of California, Santa Barbara M,D
University of Chicago M
University of Colorado Denver M,D
University of Guelph M,D
University of Illinois at Urbana–Champaign M,D
The University of Kansas M,D,O
University of Memphis M,D
University of Michigan M,D
University of Northern Colorado M,D
University of Notre Dame M,D
University of Pittsburgh M,D
University of South Carolina M,D,O
The University of Tennessee at Chattanooga M
The University of Texas at San Antonio M,D
University of the Incarnate Word M
Villanova University M
Virginia Polytechnic Institute and State University M,D
West Chester University of Pennsylvania M,O
Western Illinois University M
Worcester Polytechnic Institute M,D,O
Wright State University M

AQUACULTURE
American University of Beirut M
Auburn University M,D
Dalhousie University M
Kentucky State University M
Memorial University of Newfoundland M
Oregon State University M,D
Purdue University M,D

Texas A&M University–Corpus Christi M
University of Arkansas at Pine Bluff M,D
University of Florida M,D
University of Guelph M,D
University of Rhode Island M,D

ARCHAEOLOGY
American University of Beirut M,D
Arizona State University at the Tempe campus M,D,O
Boston University M,D
Brown University D
Bryn Mawr College M,D
California State University, Northridge M
California State University, San Bernardino M
Columbia University M,D
Cornell University M,D
Florida State University M,D
Gordon-Conwell Theological Seminary M,D
The Graduate Center, City University of New York D
Harvard University M,D
Illinois State University M
Indiana University Bloomington M,D
Indiana University of Pennsylvania M
Johns Hopkins University D
Massachusetts Institute of Technology M,D,O
Memorial University of Newfoundland M,D
Mercyhurst University M
Michigan Technological University M,D
New York University M,D
Northern Arizona University M
Princeton University D
Rice University M,D
St. Cloud State University M
San Francisco State University M
Simon Fraser University M,D
Stanford University M,D
Trinity International University M,D,O
Tufts University M
Universidad de las Américas Puebla M
Université Laval M,D
University of Alberta M,D
The University of British Columbia M,D
University of Calgary M
University of California, Berkeley M,D
University of California, Los Angeles M,D
University of Chicago D
University of Colorado Denver M
University of Denver M
University of Lethbridge M,D
The University of Manchester M,D
University of Massachusetts Boston M
University of Memphis M,D,O
University of Michigan M,D
University of Minnesota, Twin Cities Campus M,D
University of Missouri M,D
University of Nebraska–Lincoln M,D
University of New Mexico M,D
The University of North Carolina at Chapel Hill M,D
University of Oklahoma M,D
University of Pennsylvania M,D
University of Rhode Island M
University of Saskatchewan M,D
University of South Africa M,D
University of South Florida M,D,O
The University of Tennessee M,D
The University of Texas at Austin M,D
University of West Florida M
University of Wisconsin–Madison D
University of Wisconsin–Milwaukee M,D,O
Washington State University M,D
Washington University in St. Louis M,D
Wheaton College M,D
Yale University M,D

ARCHITECTURAL ENGINEERING
California Polytechnic State University, San Luis Obispo M
California State University, Fullerton M
Carnegie Mellon University M,D
Drexel University M,D
Illinois Institute of Technology M,D
Kansas State University M
Lawrence Technological University M,D
Milwaukee School of Engineering M
Penn State University Park M,D
University of California, San Diego M
University of Colorado Boulder M,D
University of Detroit Mercy M
The University of Kansas M
University of Louisiana at Lafayette M
University of Massachusetts Amherst M,D
University of Miami M,D
University of Nebraska–Lincoln M,D
The University of Texas at Austin M

ARCHITECTURAL HISTORY
Arizona State University at the Tempe campus D
Cornell University M,D
The Graduate Center, City University of New York D

Harvard University D
Massachusetts Institute of Technology M,D
New York University M
Roger Williams University M
Savannah College of Art and Design M
University of California, Berkeley M
University of Colorado Denver D
University of Pittsburgh M,D
The University of Texas at Austin M,D
University of Virginia M,D

ARCHITECTURE
Academy of Art University M
Andrews University M
Arizona State University at the Tempe campus M,D
Athabasca University M,O
Auburn University M
Ball State University M
Boston Architectural College M
California Baptist University M
California College of the Arts M
California Polytechnic State University, San Luis Obispo M
California State Polytechnic University, Pomona M
Carleton University M
Carnegie Mellon University M,D
The Catholic University of America M,O
City College of the City University of New York M
Clemson University M,O
Columbia University M,D
Cooper Union for the Advancement of Science and Art M
Cornell University M,D
Cranbrook Academy of Art M
Dalhousie University M
Ferris State University M
Florida Agricultural and Mechanical University M
Florida International University M
Florida State University M
Georgia Institute of Technology M,D
Hampton University M
Harvard University M,D
Illinois Institute of Technology M,D
Instituto Tecnológico y de Estudios Superiores de Monterrey, Campus Estado de México M,D
Instituto Tecnológico y de Estudios Superiores de Monterrey, Campus Irapuato M,D
Iowa State University of Science and Technology M
Judson University M
Kansas State University M
Kennesaw State University M
Kent State University M
Lawrence Technological University M,O
London Metropolitan University M,D
Louisiana State University and Agricultural & Mechanical College M
Louisiana Tech University M
Marywood University M
Massachusetts College of Art and Design M
Massachusetts Institute of Technology M,D
McGill University M,D,O
Miami University M
Montana State University M
Morgan State University M
New Jersey Institute of Technology M,D
The New School M
NewSchool of Architecture and Design M
New York Institute of Technology M
North Carolina State University M
North Dakota State University M
Northeastern University M
The Ohio State University M,D
Penn State University Park M,D
Philadelphia University M
Pontificia Universidad Catolica Madre y Maestra M
Portland State University M
Prairie View A&M University M
Pratt Institute M
Princeton University M,D
Rensselaer Polytechnic Institute M,D
Rhode Island School of Design M
Rice University M,D
Rochester Institute of Technology M
Roger Williams University M
Savannah College of Art and Design M
School of Architecture at Taliesin M
School of the Art Institute of Chicago M
Southern California Institute of Architecture M
Southern Illinois University Carbondale M
Syracuse University M
Temple University M
Texas A&M University M,D
Texas Tech University M,D
Tulane University M
Universidad Autonoma de Guadalajara M,D
Universidad Nacional Pedro Henriquez Urena M
Université Laval M
University at Buffalo, the State University of New York M
The University of Arizona M
The University of British Columbia M
University of Calgary M,D
University of California, Berkeley M,D

University of California, Los Angeles M,D
University of Cincinnati M
University of Colorado Denver M
University of Florida M,D
University of Hartford M
University of Hawaii at Manoa D
University of Houston M
University of Idaho M
University of Illinois at Chicago M
University of Illinois at Urbana–Champaign M,D
The University of Kansas M,D,O
University of Kentucky M
The University of Manchester M,D
University of Manitoba M
University of Maryland, College Park M
University of Massachusetts Amherst M
University of Memphis M
University of Miami M
University of Michigan M
University of Minnesota, Twin Cities Campus M
University of Missouri M,D
University of Nebraska–Lincoln M,D
University of Nevada, Las Vegas M,O
University of New Mexico M,D
The University of North Carolina at Charlotte M
The University of North Carolina at Greensboro M,O
University of Notre Dame M
University of Oklahoma M,D
University of Oregon M
University of Pennsylvania M,D,O
University of Puerto Rico, Río Piedras Campus M
University of Southern California M,D
University of South Florida M
The University of Tennessee M
The University of Texas at Arlington M
The University of Texas at Austin M
The University of Texas at San Antonio M
University of the District of Columbia M
University of Toronto M
University of Utah M
University of Washington M,D,O
University of Waterloo M
University of Wisconsin–Milwaukee M,D,O
Virginia Polytechnic Institute and State University M,D,O
Washington State University M
Washington University in St. Louis M
Wentworth Institute of Technology M
Woodbury University M
Yale University M

ARCHIVES/ARCHIVAL ADMINISTRATION
Claremont Graduate University M,D,O
Clayton State University M
Columbia University M
Drexel University M
East Tennessee State University M,O
Middle Tennessee State University M,D,O
Montclair State University M
New York University M,D,O
The University of British Columbia M,D
University of California, Los Angeles M,D,O
University of California, Riverside M,D
University of Manitoba M,D
University of Massachusetts Boston M
University of Rochester M
University of South Carolina M,O
Wayne State University M,O

ART/FINE ARTS
Academy of Art University M
Adams State University M
Adelphi University M
Alfred University M,D
Anna Maria College M,O
Arizona State University at the Tempe campus M,D
ArtCenter College of Design M
Azusa Pacific University M
Ball State University M
Bard College M
Barry University M
Bob Jones University M,D,O
Boise State University M
Boston University M
Bowling Green State University M
Bradley University M
Brandeis University O
Brigham Young University M
Brooklyn College of the City University of New York M
Butler University M
California College of the Arts M
California Institute of the Arts M,O
California State University, Chico M
California State University, Fresno M
California State University, Long Beach M
California State University, Los Angeles M
California State University, Northridge M
California State University, Sacramento M

---

*M—masters degree; D—doctorate; O—other advanced degree; *—Close-Up and/or Display*

California State University, San Bernardino	M
Carnegie Mellon University	M
Central Washington University	M
Christie's Education	O
City College of the City University of New York	M
Claremont Graduate University	M
The College at Brockport, State University of New York	M
College for Creative Studies	M
Colorado State University	M
Columbia University	M,D
Concordia University (Canada)	M
Cornell University	M
Cranbrook Academy of Art	M
Drew University	M,D,O
Duke University	M,D
East Carolina University	M
Eastern Illinois University	M
Eastern Michigan University	M
East Tennessee State University	M
Edinboro University of Pennsylvania	M
Emily Carr University of Art + Design	M
Fairleigh Dickinson University, Metropolitan Campus	M
Ferris State University	M
Florida Atlantic University	M
Florida International University	M,O
Florida State University	M
Fontbonne University	M
Fort Hays State University	M
Framingham State University	M
Full Sail University	M
George Mason University	M
The George Washington University	M,O
Georgia Southern University	M
Georgia State University	M
Governors State University	M
Hollins University	M
Hood College	M,O
Houston Baptist University	M
Howard University	M
Hunter College of the City University of New York	M
Idaho State University	M
Illinois State University	M
Indiana State University	M
Indiana University Bloomington	M
Indiana University of Pennsylvania	M
Indiana University–Purdue University Indianapolis	M
Institute for Doctoral Studies in the Visual Arts	D
Inter American University of Puerto Rico, San Germán Campus	M
Iowa State University of Science and Technology	M
Ithaca College	M
Jacksonville University	M
James Madison University	M
John F. Kennedy University	M
Johnson State College	M
Kansas State University	M
Kent State University	M
Laguna College of Art & Design	M
Lake Forest College	M
Lee University	M,O
Lehman College of the City University of New York	M
Lesley University	M,D,O
Liberty University	M
Long Island University–LIU Post	M
Louisiana State University and Agricultural & Mechanical College	M
Louisiana Tech University	M
Maine College of Art	M
Maryland Institute College of Art	M,O
Marywood University	M
Massachusetts College of Art and Design	M,O
Memphis College of Art	M
Miami University	M
Michigan State University	M
Millersville University of Pennsylvania	M
Mills College	M
Minneapolis College of Art and Design	M,O
Minnesota State University Mankato	M
Mississippi College	M
Missouri State University	M
Montana State University	M
Montclair State University	M
Moore College of Art & Design	M
Morehead State University	M
New Hampshire Institute of Art	M
New Jersey City University	M
New Mexico State University	M
The New School	M
New York Academy of Art	M
New York Institute of Technology	M
New York Studio School of Drawing, Painting and Sculpture	M,O
New York University	M,D,O
Norfolk State University	M
Northeastern University	M
Northern Illinois University	M
Northwestern State University of Louisiana	M
Northwestern University	M
Nova Southeastern University	M,D,O
NSCAD University	M
The Ohio State University	M
Ohio University	M
Oregon College of Art and Craft	M
Otis College of Art and Design	M
Pace University	M,O
Pacific Northwest College of Art	M
Paris College of Art	M
Penn State University Park	M,D,O

Pennsylvania Academy of the Fine Arts	M,O
Pensacola Christian College	M,D,O
Philadelphia University	M
Pontifical Catholic University of Puerto Rico	M
Portland State University	M
Pratt Institute	M
Prescott College	M
Purchase College, State University of New York	M
Purdue University	M,D
Queens College of the City University of New York	M
Radford University	M
Rensselaer Polytechnic Institute	D
Rhode Island College	M
Rhode Island School of Design	M
Rochester Institute of Technology	M
Rutgers University–New Brunswick	M
San Diego State University	M
San Francisco Art Institute	M,O
San Francisco State University	M
Savannah College of Art and Design	M
School of the Art Institute of Chicago	M
School of Visual Arts (NY)	M
Sotheby's Institute of Art–London	M
Sotheby's Institute of Art–New York	M
Southern Illinois University Carbondale	M
Southern Illinois University Edwardsville	M
Southern Methodist University	M
Southwest University of Visual Arts	M
Spring Hill College	M,O
Stanford University	M,D
State University of New York at New Paltz	M
State University of New York at Oswego	M
Stephen F. Austin State University	M
Stony Brook University, State University of New York	M
Sul Ross State University	M
Syracuse University	M
Temple University	M
Texas A&M University	M
Texas A&M University–Commerce	M,D,O
Texas A&M University–Corpus Christi	M
Texas Christian University	M
Texas Southern University	M
Texas Tech University	M,D
Texas Woman's University	M
Tiffin University	M
Towson University	M
Tufts University	M,O
Tulane University	M
United Theological Seminary of the Twin Cities	M,D,O
Universidad del Turabo	M
Université du Québec à Chicoutimi	M
Université du Québec à Montréal	M
Université Laval	M
University at Albany, State University of New York	M
University at Buffalo, the State University of New York	M,D
The University of Alabama	M
University of Alaska Fairbanks	M
University of Alberta	M
The University of Arizona	M
University of Arkansas	M
University of Arkansas at Little Rock	M
The University of British Columbia	M,D
University of Calgary	M
University of California, Berkeley	M,O
University of California, Davis	M
University of California, Irvine	M,D
University of California, Los Angeles	M
University of California, Riverside	M
University of California, San Diego	M,D
University of California, Santa Barbara	M
University of California, Santa Cruz	M,D
University of Central Florida	M
University of Chicago	M
University of Cincinnati	M
University of Colorado Boulder	M
University of Colorado Denver	M
University of Dallas	M
University of Delaware	M
University of Denver	M
University of Florida	M,D
University of Georgia	M,D
University of Guam	M
University of Guelph	M
University of Hartford	M
University of Hawaii at Manoa	M
University of Houston	M
University of Idaho	M
University of Illinois at Chicago	M,D
University of Illinois at Urbana–Champaign	M
University of Indianapolis	M
The University of Iowa	M
The University of Kansas	M,D
University of Kentucky	M
University of Lethbridge	M,D
University of Maine	M
The University of Manchester	M,D

University of Maryland, College Park	M
University of Massachusetts Amherst	M
University of Massachusetts Dartmouth	M,O
University of Memphis	M,O
University of Miami	M
University of Michigan	M
University of Michigan–Flint	M
University of Minnesota, Duluth	M
University of Minnesota, Twin Cities Campus	M
University of Mississippi	M,D
University of Missouri	M
University of Missouri–Kansas City	M,D
University of Montana	M
University of Nebraska at Omaha	M
University of Nebraska–Lincoln	M
University of Nevada, Las Vegas	M
University of Nevada, Reno	M
University of New Mexico	M
University of New Orleans	M
The University of North Carolina at Chapel Hill	M
The University of North Carolina at Greensboro	M
University of North Dakota	M
University of Northern Colorado	M
University of Northern Iowa	M
University of North Texas	M,D,O
University of Notre Dame	M
University of Oklahoma	M
University of Oregon	M
University of Pennsylvania	M,O
University of Regina	M
University of Rochester	D
University of Saint Francis (IN)	M
University of Saskatchewan	M
The University of Scranton	M
University of South Alabama	M
University of South Carolina	M
The University of South Dakota	M
University of Southern California	M,D,O
University of South Florida	M
The University of Tennessee	M
The University of Texas at Arlington	M
The University of Texas at Austin	M
The University of Texas at El Paso	M
The University of Texas at San Antonio	M
The University of Texas at Tyler	M
The University of Texas Rio Grande Valley	M
The University of the Arts	M
The University of Tulsa	M
University of Utah	M
University of Victoria	M
University of Washington	M
University of Waterloo	M
University of Windsor	M
University of Wisconsin–Madison	M
University of Wisconsin–River Falls	M
University of Wisconsin–Stout	M
University of Wisconsin–Superior	M
Utah State University	M
Vermont College of Fine Arts	M
Virginia Commonwealth University	M,D
Washington State University	M
Washington University in St. Louis	M
Wayne State University	M
Webster University	M
Western Carolina University	M
Western Connecticut State University	M
West Texas A&M University	M
West Virginia University	M
Wichita State University	M
Wilson College	M
Winthrop University	M
Yale University	M
York University	M,D

ART EDUCATION

Academy of Art University	M
Adelphi University	M
Alabama Agricultural and Mechanical University	M
American University of Puerto Rico	M
Arcadia University	M,D,O
Arizona State University at the Tempe campus	M,D
Art Academy of Cincinnati	M
Boise State University	M
Boston University	M
Bowling Green State University	M
Bridgewater State University	M
Brigham Young University	M
Brooklyn College of the City University of New York	M
Buffalo State College, State University of New York	M
California State University, Long Beach	M
California State University, Los Angeles	M
California State University, Northridge	M
Carthage College	M,O
Case Western Reserve University	M
Central Connecticut State University	M,O
Chatham University	M
Cleveland State University	M
The College of New Rochelle	M
The Colorado College	M

Colorado State University–Pueblo	M
Columbus State University	M
Concordia University (Canada)	M,D
Concordia University Wisconsin	M
Converse College	M
Delaware State University	M
East Carolina University	M
Eastern Illinois University	M
Eastern Kentucky University	M
Eastern Michigan University	M
Edinboro University of Pennsylvania	M
Ferris State University	M
Fitchburg State University	M,O
Florida Atlantic University	M
Florida International University	M,D,O
Florida State University	M,D
Fontbonne University	M
George Mason University	M
The George Washington University	M
Georgia State University	M
Harding University	M,O
Harvard University	M
Hofstra University	M,D,O
Indiana University Bloomington	M,D,O
James Madison University	M
Kean University	M
Kennesaw State University	M
Kent State University	M
Kutztown University of Pennsylvania	M
Lake Forest College	M
Lesley University	M,D,O
Long Island University–LIU Post	M,D,O
Manhattanville College	M
Mansfield University of Pennsylvania	M
Maryland Institute College of Art	M
Marywood University	M
Massachusetts College of Art and Design	M,O
Memphis College of Art	M
Miami University	M
Millersville University of Pennsylvania	M
Minnesota State University Mankato	M
Mississippi College	M,D,O
Montclair State University	M
Moore College of Art & Design	M
Morehead State University	M
Nazareth College of Rochester	M
New Hampshire Institute of Art	M
New Jersey City University	M
New York University	M,O
The Ohio State University	M,D
Penn State University Park	M,D,O
Piedmont University	M,O
Plymouth State University	M
Pratt Institute	M,O
Purdue University	M,D,O
Queens College of the City University of New York	M,O
Rhode Island College	M
Rhode Island School of Design	M
Rochester Institute of Technology	M
Rocky Mountain College of Art + Design	M
Saint Michael's College	M,O
Salem College	M
Salem State University	M
School of the Art Institute of Chicago	M
School of Visual Arts (NY)	M
School of Visual Arts (NY)	M
Simon Fraser University	M,D
Southern Connecticut State University	M
Southwestern Oklahoma State University	M
Spalding University	M
State University of New York at New Paltz	M
State University of New York at Oswego	M
Sul Ross State University	M
Syracuse University	M
Teachers College, Columbia University	M,D,O
Temple University	M
Texas Tech University	M
Towson University	M,O
Tufts University	M,D,O
The University of Akron	M
The University of Alabama at Birmingham	M
The University of Arizona	M,D
University of Arkansas at Little Rock	M
The University of British Columbia	M,D
University of Central Florida	M
University of Cincinnati	M
University of Denver	M,O
University of Florida	M,D
University of Illinois at Urbana–Champaign	M,D
University of Indianapolis	M,D
The University of Iowa	M,D
University of Kansas	M
University of Kentucky	M
University of Louisiana at Monroe	M,D
University of Louisville	M,D,O
University of Maryland, Baltimore County	M
University of Massachusetts Amherst	M
University of Massachusetts Dartmouth	M
University of Minnesota, Twin Cities Campus	M
University of Missouri	M,D,O
University of Montana	M
University of Nebraska at Kearney	M

University of New Mexico	M
The University of North Carolina at Charlotte	M,D,O
The University of North Carolina at Pembroke	M
University of Northern Colorado	M
University of Northern Iowa	M
University of North Texas	M,D,O
University of Rio Grande	M
University of St. Francis (IL)	M,D,O
University of South Alabama	M,D
University of South Carolina	M,D
The University of South Dakota	M
The University of Tennessee	M,D,O
The University of Texas at Austin	M
The University of Texas at El Paso	M
The University of the Arts	M
The University of Toledo	M,D,O
University of Utah	M
University of Victoria	M,D
University of Wisconsin–Madison	M,D
University of Wisconsin–Milwaukee	M,D,O
University of Wisconsin–Superior	M
Vermont College of Fine Arts	M
Virginia Commonwealth University	M,D
Wayne State University	M,D,O
Western Kentucky University	M
Western Michigan University	M
West Virginia University	M
Wilkes University	M,D
William Carey University	M,O
Winthrop University	M

ART HISTORY

Academy of Art University	M
American University	M
American University of Beirut	M,D
Arizona State University at the Tempe campus	M,D
Bard Graduate Center	M,D
Binghamton University, State University of New York	M,D
Boston University	M,D,O
Bowling Green State University	M
Brooklyn College of the City University of New York	M
Brown University	D
Bryn Mawr College	M
California State University, Chico	M
California State University, Los Angeles	M
California State University, Northridge	M
Caribbean University	M,D
Carleton University	M
Case Western Reserve University	M,D
Christie's Education	M
City College of the City University of New York	M
Cleveland State University	M
Colorado State University	M
Columbia University	M,D
Concordia University (Canada)	D
Cornell University	D
Dominican University of California	M
Duke University	M,D
Emory University	D
Fashion Institute of Technology	M
Florida State University	M,D
George Mason University	M
The George Washington University	M
Georgia State University	M
The Graduate Center, City University of New York	D
Graduate Theological Union	M,D,O
Harvard University	D
Howard University	M
Hunter College of the City University of New York	M
Illinois State University	M
James Madison University	M
Johns Hopkins University	M,D
Kent State University	M
Lancaster Theological Seminary	M,D,O
Louisiana State University and Agricultural & Mechanical College	M
Massachusetts Institute of Technology	M,D
McGill University	M,D
Montana State University	M
New Mexico State University	M
New York University	M,D
Northwestern University	D
The Ohio State University	M,D
Ohio University	M
Oklahoma State University	M
Penn State University Park	M,D
Pratt Institute	M
Purchase College, State University of New York	M
Queens College of the City University of New York	M
Rice University	D
Richmond, The American International University in London	M
Roger Williams University	M
Rutgers University–New Brunswick	M,D,O
San Diego State University	M
San Francisco Art Institute	M
San Francisco State University	M
San Jose State University	M,O
Savannah College of Art and Design	M
School of the Art Institute of Chicago	M
School of Visual Arts (NY)	M
Southern Methodist University	M,D

Stony Brook University, State University of New York	M,D
Sul Ross State University	M
Syracuse University	M,D
Temple University	M,D
Texas Christian University	M
Texas Tech University	M
Towson University	M
Tufts University	M
Tulane University	M
Université de Montréal	M,D
Université du Québec à Montréal	M,D
Université Laval	M,D
University at Buffalo, the State University of New York	M
The University of Alabama	M
The University of Alabama at Birmingham	M
University of Alberta	M
The University of Arizona	M,D
University of Arkansas at Little Rock	M
The University of British Columbia	M,D
University of California, Berkeley	D
University of California, Davis	M
University of California, Los Angeles	M,D
University of California, Riverside	M,D
University of California, San Diego	M,D
University of California, Santa Barbara	D
University of Chicago	M,D
University of Cincinnati	M
University of Colorado Boulder	M
University of Delaware	M
University of Denver	M
University of Florida	M,D
University of Georgia	M,D
University of Hawaii at Manoa	M
University of Houston	M
University of Illinois at Chicago	M
University of Illinois at Urbana–Champaign	M,D
The University of Iowa	M,D
The University of Kansas	M,D
University of Kentucky	M
University of Louisville	M,D
The University of Manchester	D
University of Maryland, College Park	M,D
University of Massachusetts Amherst	M
University of Memphis	M,O
University of Miami	M
University of Michigan	M,D
University of Minnesota, Twin Cities Campus	M,D
University of Missouri	M,D
University of Montana	M
University of Nebraska–Lincoln	M
University of New Mexico	M,D
The University of North Carolina at Chapel Hill	M,D
University of Northern Colorado	M
University of North Texas	M,D,O
University of Notre Dame	M
University of Oklahoma	M,D
University of Oregon	M,D
University of Pennsylvania	M,D
University of Pittsburgh	M,D
University of Rochester	D
University of St. Thomas (MN)	M
University of South Africa	M,D
University of South Carolina	M
University of Southern California	M,D,O
University of South Florida	M,D
The University of Texas at Austin	M,D
The University of Texas at San Antonio	M
The University of Texas at Tyler	M
University of Toronto	M,D
University of Utah	M
University of Victoria	M,D
University of Virginia	M,D
University of Washington	M,D
University of Wisconsin–Madison	M,D
University of Wisconsin–Milwaukee	M
University of Wisconsin–Superior	M
Virginia Commonwealth University	M,D
Washington University in St. Louis	M
Wayne State University	M
Webster University	M
West Virginia University	M
Williams College	M
Yale University	D
York University	M,D

ARTIFICIAL INTELLIGENCE/ROBOTICS

The American University in Cairo	M,D,O
California State University, Northridge	M
Carnegie Mellon University	M,D
The College of William and Mary	M,D
Cornell University	M,D
Georgia Institute of Technology	D
Illinois Institute of Technology	M,D
Indiana University Bloomington	D
Instituto Tecnológico y de Estudios Superiores de Monterrey, Campus Monterrey	M,D
Johns Hopkins University	M,D
Northwestern University	M
Oregon State University	M,D
Portland State University	M,D,O

South Dakota School of Mines and Technology	M
Stevens Institute of Technology	M,D,O
Temple University	M,D
University of California, Riverside	M,D
University of California, San Diego	M,D
University of Georgia	M
University of Michigan	M,D
University of Nebraska at Omaha	M,O
University of Pennsylvania	M
University of Pittsburgh	M,D
University of Southern California	M,D
Villanova University	M,O
Worcester Polytechnic Institute	M,D

ARTS ADMINISTRATION

American University	M,O
Arizona State University at the Tempe campus	M,D
Baruch College of the City University of New York	M
Boston University	M,O
Brooklyn College of the City University of New York	M
Carnegie Mellon University	M
Christie's Education	M,O
Claremont Graduate University	M
The College at Brockport, State University of New York	M,O
College of Charleston	O
Colorado State University	M
Columbia College Chicago	M
Daemen College	M
Drexel University	M
Eastern Michigan University	M
Fashion Institute of Technology	M
Florida State University	M,D
George Mason University	M,O
Goucher College	M
HEC Montreal	O
Indiana University Bloomington	M
Le Moyne College	M
London Metropolitan University	M,D
Montclair State University	M
Moore College of Art & Design	M
New York Institute of Technology	M
New York University	M
Northwestern University	M
The Ohio State University	M
Pratt Institute	M
Rhode Island College	M
Robert Morris University Illinois	M
Rocky Mountain College of Art + Design	M
Roosevelt University	M,O
Rowan University	M
Ryerson University	M
Saint Mary's University of Minnesota	M
St. Thomas University	M
Savannah College of Art and Design	M
School of the Art Institute of Chicago	M
Seattle University	M
Sotheby's Institute of Art–London	M
Sotheby's Institute of Art–New York	M
Southern Methodist University	M
Southern Utah University	M
Teachers College, Columbia University	M,D
Temple University	M
Universidad del Turabo	M
University at Buffalo, the State University of New York	M
The University of Akron	M
University of Cincinnati	M,D
University of Kentucky	M
The University of Manchester	D
University of Michigan–Flint	M
University of New Orleans	M
The University of North Carolina at Charlotte	M,O
University of Oregon	M
University of Southern California	M
University of Wisconsin–Madison	M
Valparaiso University	M
Winthrop University	M

ARTS JOURNALISM

Academy of Art University	M
School of the Art Institute of Chicago	M
Syracuse University	M

ART THERAPY

Adler Graduate School	M
Adler University	M,D,O
Albertus Magnus College	M
Athabasca University	M,O
Caldwell University	M,O
California Institute of Integral Studies	M,D
California State University, Los Angeles	M
Cedar Crest College	M
The College of New Rochelle	M
Concordia University (Canada)	M
Drexel University	M,O
Eastern Virginia Medical School	M
Edinboro University of Pennsylvania	M,O
Emporia State University	M
The George Washington University	M
Georgia College & State University	M
Goddard College	M
Hofstra University	M,O

Indiana University–Purdue University Indianapolis	M
Lesley University	M,D,O
Long Island University–LIU Post	M
Marylhurst University	M,O
Marywood University	M,O
Mount Mary University	M,D
Naropa University	M
Nazareth College of Rochester	M
New York University	M
Notre Dame de Namur University	M
Ottawa University	M
Phillips Graduate University	M
Pratt Institute	M
Prescott College	M
Saint Mary-of-the-Woods College	M,O
School of the Art Institute of Chicago	M
School of Visual Arts (NY)	M
Seton Hill University	M
Southern Illinois University Edwardsville	M
Southwestern College (NM)	M
Springfield College	M,O
University of Louisville	M,D
University of Maryland, College Park	M,D,O
University of Wisconsin–Superior	M
Ursuline College	M

ASIAN-AMERICAN STUDIES

Binghamton University, State University of New York	M,O
California State University, Long Beach	M
San Francisco State University	M
Stony Brook University, State University of New York	M
University of California, Los Angeles	M

ASIAN LANGUAGES

Cornell University	M,D
Harvard University	M,D
Indiana University Bloomington	M,D
The Ohio State University	M,D
St. John's College (NM)	M
Stanford University	M
University of California, Berkeley	M,D
University of California, Irvine	M,D
University of California, Los Angeles	M,D
University of California, Santa Barbara	M,D
University of Chicago	D
University of Hawaii at Manoa	M,D
University of Illinois at Urbana–Champaign	M,D
The University of Iowa	M
The University of Kansas	M,O
University of Michigan	D
University of Minnesota, Twin Cities Campus	D
University of Oregon	M,D
University of Southern California	M,D
The University of Texas at Austin	M,D
University of Washington	M,D
University of Wisconsin–Madison	M,D
Washington University in St. Louis	M,D
Yale University	D

ASIAN STUDIES

American University	O
Binghamton University, State University of New York	M,O
Brown University	D
California Institute of Integral Studies	M,D
California State University, Long Beach	M
Columbia University	M,D,O
Cornell University	M,D
Creighton University	M
Dallas Baptist University	M
Duke University	M,O
Florida International University	M
Florida State University	M
Georgetown University	M
The George Washington University	M
Harvard University	M,D
Indiana University Bloomington	M,D
Johns Hopkins University	M,D,O
Maharishi University of Management	M,D
McGill University	M,D
New York University	M,D
The Ohio State University	M
Ohio University	M
Princeton University	D
Rutgers University–New Brunswick	M
St. John's College (NM)	M
St. John's College (NY)	M
San Diego State University	M
Seton Hill University	M
Stanford University	M
Stony Brook University, State University of New York	M
United Theological Seminary of the Twin Cities	M,D,O
University of Alberta	M
The University of Arizona	M,D
University of Bridgeport	M
The University of British Columbia	M,D
University of California, Berkeley	M,D
University of California, Los Angeles	M,D
University of California, Riverside	M

M—masters degree; D—doctorate; O—other advanced degree; *—Close-Up and/or Display

University of California, Santa Barbara	M,D
University of Chicago	M,D
University of Colorado Boulder	M,D
University of Hawaii at Manoa	O
University of Illinois at Urbana–Champaign	M,D
The University of Iowa	M
The University of Kansas	M,O
The University of Manchester	M,D
University of Michigan	M,D,O
University of Minnesota, Twin Cities Campus	D
University of Oregon	M
University of Pennsylvania	M,D
University of Pittsburgh	M,O
University of San Francisco	M
University of Southern California	M,D
The University of Texas at Austin	M,D
University of Toronto	M,D
University of Utah	M
University of Victoria	M
University of Virginia	M
University of Washington	M,D
University of Wisconsin–Madison	M,D
Washington University in St. Louis	M,D
Wayne State University	M,D,O
West Virginia University	M,D
Yale University	M

ASTRONOMY

Boston University	M,D
Brigham Young University	M,D
California Institute of Technology	D
Case Western Reserve University	M,D
Columbia University	M,D
Cornell University	D
Dartmouth College	D
George Mason University	M,D
Georgia State University	D
Harvard University	D
Hunter College of the City University of New York	M,D
Indiana University Bloomington	M,D
Johns Hopkins University	D
Louisiana State University and Agricultural & Mechanical College	M,D
Michigan State University	M,D
Minnesota State University Mankato	M
New Mexico State University	D
Northwestern University	D
The Ohio State University	M,D
Ohio University	M,D
Penn State University Park	M,D
Princeton University	D
Rice University	M,D
Rutgers University–New Brunswick	M,D
Saint Mary's University (Canada)	M,D
San Diego State University	M
San Francisco State University	M
Stony Brook University, State University of New York	D
Texas A&M University	M,D
Texas Tech University	M,D
Université de Moncton	M
The University of Alabama	M,D
The University of Alabama in Huntsville	M,D
The University of Arizona	D
The University of British Columbia	M,D
University of Calgary	M,D
University of California, Los Angeles	M,D
University of California, Santa Cruz	D
University of Chicago	D
University of Delaware	M,D
University of Florida	M,D
University of Hawaii at Manoa	M,D
University of Illinois at Urbana–Champaign	M,D
The University of Iowa	M
The University of Kansas	M,D
University of Kentucky	M,D
The University of Manchester	M,D
University of Maryland, College Park	M,D
University of Massachusetts Amherst	M,D
University of Michigan	D
University of Missouri	M,D
University of Nebraska–Lincoln	M,D
University of Nevada, Las Vegas	M,D
The University of North Carolina at Chapel Hill	M,D
University of Pittsburgh	D
University of Rochester	M,D
University of South Carolina	M,D
The University of Texas at Austin	M,D
University of Toronto	M,D
University of Victoria	M,D
University of Virginia	M,D
University of Washington	M,D
The University of Western Ontario	M,D
University of Wisconsin–Madison	D
Vanderbilt University	M,D
Wesleyan University	M
West Chester University of Pennsylvania	M,O
Yale University	M,D
York University	M,D

ASTROPHYSICS

Air Force Institute of Technology	M,D
Arizona State University at the Tempe campus	M,D
Cornell University	D
Harvard University	D
Indiana University Bloomington	M,D

Iowa State University of Science and Technology	M,D
Louisiana State University and Agricultural & Mechanical College	M,D
McMaster University	D
Michigan State University	M,D
New Mexico Institute of Mining and Technology	M,D
New Mexico State University	M,D
Penn State University Park	M,D
Princeton University	D
Rochester Institute of Technology	M,D
Texas Christian University	M,D
Tufts University	M,D
University of Alaska Fairbanks	M,D
University of Alberta	M,D
University of California, Berkeley	D
University of California, Los Angeles	M,D
University of California, Santa Cruz	D
University of Chicago	D
University of Colorado Boulder	M,D
The University of Manchester	M,D
University of Michigan	D
University of Minnesota, Twin Cities Campus	M,D
University of Missouri–St. Louis	M,D
The University of North Carolina at Chapel Hill	M,D
University of North Dakota	M,D
The University of Toledo	M,D
University of Toronto	M,D
University of Victoria	M,D
Yale University	M,D

ATHLETIC TRAINING AND SPORTS MEDICINE

Adrian College	M
Armstrong State University	M,O
A.T. Still University	M,D,O
Azusa Pacific University	M
Barry University	M
Bloomsburg University of Pennsylvania	M
Boston University	D
Bridgewater College	M
Brigham Young University	M,D
California Baptist University	M
California State University, Long Beach	M
California University of Pennsylvania	M
Chapman University	M
The College of St. Scholastica	M
Eastern Michigan University	M,O
East Stroudsburg University of Pennsylvania	M
Florida International University	M
Franklin College	M
Gannon University	M
Georgia State University	M
Grand View University	M,O
Indiana State University	M,D
Indiana University Bloomington	M,D
Inter American University of Puerto Rico, Metropolitan Campus	M
Kent State University	M,D
Lebanon Valley College	M
Lenoir-Rhyne University	M
Life University	M
Lock Haven University of Pennsylvania	M
London Metropolitan University	M,D
Long Island University–LIU Brooklyn	M,D,O
Manchester University	M
Marshall University	M
Merrimack College	M
Missouri State University	M
Montana State University Billings	M
Moravian College	M
North Dakota State University	M,D
Ohio University	M
Old Dominion University	M
Oregon State University	M
Pacific University	M,D
Philadelphia University	M
Plymouth State University	M
Saint Louis University	M,D
Salisbury University	M
Samford University	M,D
San Jose State University	M,O
Seton Hall University	M
Shenandoah University	M,D,O
South Dakota State University	M
Spalding University	M
Springfield College	M,D
Stephen F. Austin State University	M
Tarleton State University	M
Temple University	M,D
Texas A&M University	M,D
Texas State University	M
Texas Tech University Health Sciences Center	M
Trinity International University	M
United States Sports Academy	M
Universidad del Turabo	M
University of Arkansas	M
University of Central Oklahoma	M
University of Evansville	M
The University of Findlay	M,D
University of Florida	M,D
University of Idaho	M,D
The University of Iowa	M,D
University of Kentucky	M
University of Miami	M,D
University of Nebraska at Omaha	M,D
The University of North Carolina at Chapel Hill	M
The University of North Carolina at Greensboro	M,D
University of Northern Iowa	M

University of Pittsburgh	M
University of St. Augustine for Health Sciences	M
University of South Florida	M,D
The University of Tennessee	M,D
The University of Tennessee at Chattanooga	M
The University of Texas at Arlington	M,D
University of Utah	D
University of Wisconsin–La Crosse	M
University of Wisconsin–Milwaukee	M,D
Weber State University	M
West Chester University of Pennsylvania	M,O
Western Michigan University	M
West Virginia University	M,D
West Virginia Wesleyan College	M
Xavier University	M

ATMOSPHERIC SCIENCES

Bard College	M,O
Carnegie Mellon University	D
City College of the City University of New York	M
The College of William and Mary	M,D
Colorado State University	M,D
Columbia University	M,D
Cornell University	M,D
Florida State University	M,D
George Mason University	D
Georgia Institute of Technology	M,D
Hampton University	M,D
Howard University	M,D
Jackson State University	M,D
Massachusetts Institute of Technology	M,D
McGill University	M,D
Michigan Technological University	M,D,O
Millersville University of Pennsylvania	M
Mississippi State University	M,D
New Mexico Institute of Mining and Technology	M,D
North Carolina State University	M,D
Northern Arizona University	M,D
The Ohio State University	M,D
Oregon State University	M,D
Princeton University	D
Purdue University	M,D
Rutgers University–New Brunswick	M,D
South Dakota School of Mines and Technology	M,D
Southern Methodist University	M,D
Stevens Institute of Technology	M,D,O
Stony Brook University, State University of New York	M,D
Texas Tech University	M,D
Université du Québec à Montréal	M,D,O
University at Albany, State University of New York	M,D
The University of Alabama in Huntsville	M,D
University of Alaska Fairbanks	M,D
The University of Arizona	M,D
The University of British Columbia	M,D
University of California, Davis	M,D
University of California, Los Angeles	M,D
University of Chicago	D
University of Colorado Boulder	M,D
University of Guelph	M,D
University of Houston	M,D
University of Illinois at Urbana–Champaign	M,D
The University of Kansas	M,D,O
The University of Manchester	M,D
University of Maryland, Baltimore County	M,D
University of Michigan	M,D
University of Nevada, Reno	M,D
University of North Dakota	M,D
University of Utah	M,D
University of Washington	M,D
University of Wisconsin–Madison	M,D
University of Wisconsin–Milwaukee	M,D
University of Wyoming	M,D
Yale University	D

AUTOMOTIVE ENGINEERING

Clemson University	M,D
College for Creative Studies	M
Lawrence Technological University	M,D
Michigan Technological University	M,D,O
Minnesota State University Mankato	M
University of Michigan	M,D
University of Michigan–Dearborn	M,D
The University of Tennessee at Chattanooga	M
University of Wisconsin–Madison	M,D
Wayne State University	M,O

AVIATION

Embry-Riddle Aeronautical University–Prescott	M
Everglades University	M
Florida Institute of Technology	M,D
Lewis University	M
National Test Pilot School	M
Southeastern Oklahoma State University	M
University of North Dakota	M
The University of Tennessee	M

AVIATION MANAGEMENT

Arizona State University at the Tempe campus	M

Delta State University	M
Embry-Riddle Aeronautical University–Daytona	M
Embry-Riddle Aeronautical University–Worldwide	M
Florida Institute of Technology	M
Lewis University	M
Lynn University	M
Middle Tennessee State University	M
Purdue University	M
Southeastern Oklahoma State University	M
Vaughn College of Aeronautics and Technology	M

BACTERIOLOGY

Illinois State University	M,D
The University of Iowa	M,D
University of Prince Edward Island	M,D
University of Wisconsin–Madison	M

BIOCHEMICAL ENGINEERING

Brown University	M,D
Cornell University	M,D
Dartmouth College	M,D
Drexel University	M
Lehigh University	M,D
Rutgers University–New Brunswick	M,D
University of California, Irvine	M,D
University of Georgia	M
The University of Iowa	M,D
The University of Manchester	M,D
University of Maryland, Baltimore County	M,D,O
The University of Western Ontario	M,D
Villanova University	M,O

BIOCHEMISTRY

Albert Einstein College of Medicine	D
American University of Beirut	M,D
Arizona State University at the Tempe campus	M,D
Auburn University	M,D
Augusta University	D
Baylor College of Medicine	D
Baylor University	M,D
Boston College	M,D
Boston University	M,D
Bradley University	M
Brandeis University	M,D
Brigham Young University	M,D
Brown University	M,D
California Institute of Technology	M,D
California Polytechnic State University, San Luis Obispo	M
California State University, East Bay	M
California State University, Long Beach	M
California State University, Los Angeles	M
California State University, Northridge	M
California State University, Sacramento	M
Carnegie Mellon University	M,D
Case Western Reserve University	M,D
City College of the City University of New York	M,D
Clark University	D
Clemson University	D
Colorado State University	M,D
Colorado State University–Pueblo	M
Columbia University	M,D
Cornell University	M,D
Dalhousie University	M,D
Dartmouth College	M,D
Drexel University	M,D
Duke University	D
East Carolina University	M,D
Eastern New Mexico University	M
East Tennessee State University	D
Emory University	D
Florida Institute of Technology	M
Florida State University	M,D
George Mason University	M,D
Georgetown University	M,D
The George Washington University	D
Georgia State University	M,D
The Graduate Center, City University of New York	D
Harvard University	D
Howard University	M,D
Hunter College of the City University of New York	M,D
Illinois Institute of Technology	M,D
Illinois State University	M,D
Indiana University Bloomington	M,D
Indiana University–Purdue University Indianapolis	M,D
Irell & Manella Graduate School of Biological Sciences	D*
Johns Hopkins University	M,D
Kansas State University	M,D
Kennesaw State University	M
Laurentian University	M
Lehigh University	M,D
Loma Linda University	M,D
Louisiana State University and Agricultural & Mechanical College	M,D
Louisiana State University Health Sciences Center at Shreveport	M,D
Loyola University Chicago	M,D
Massachusetts Institute of Technology	D
Mayo Clinic Graduate School of Biomedical Sciences	D
McGill University	M,D
McMaster University	M,D
Medical College of Wisconsin	D

Medical University of South Carolina	M,D
Meharry Medical College	D
Memorial University of Newfoundland	M,D
Miami University	M,D
Michigan State University	M,D
Michigan Technological University	M,D,O
Mississippi College	M
Mississippi State University	M,D
Montana State University	M,D
Montclair State University	M
New York Medical College	M,D
North Carolina State University	D
North Dakota State University	M,D
Northern Michigan University	M
Northwestern University	D
The Ohio State University	M,D
Ohio University	M,D
Oklahoma State University	M,D
Old Dominion University	M,D
Oregon Health & Science University	M,D
Oregon State University	M,D
Pace University	M
Penn State Hershey Medical Center	M,D
Penn State University Park	M,D
Purdue University	M,D
Queen's University at Kingston	M,D
Rensselaer Polytechnic Institute	M,D
Rice University	M,D
Rosalind Franklin University of Medicine and Science	D
Rush University	M,D
Rutgers University–Newark	M,D
Rutgers University–New Brunswick	M,D
Saint Louis University	D
San Diego State University	M,D
San Francisco State University	M
Seton Hall University	M,D
Simon Fraser University	M,D,O
Sonoma State University	M
Southern Illinois University Carbondale	M,D
Southern University and Agricultural and Mechanical College	M
Stanford University	D
State University of New York College of Environmental Science and Forestry	M,D
State University of New York Upstate Medical University	M,D
Stevens Institute of Technology	M,D,O
Stony Brook University, State University of New York	M,D
Texas A&M University	M,D
Texas Christian University	M,D
Texas State University	M
Thomas Jefferson University	D
Tufts University	D
Tulane University	M
Universidad Central del Caribe	M,D
Université de Moncton	M
Université de Montréal	M,D,O
Université de Sherbrooke	M
Université Laval	M,D,O
University at Buffalo, the State University of New York	M,D
The University of Alabama at Birmingham	D
University of Alaska Fairbanks	M,D
University of Alberta	M,D
The University of Arizona	M,D
University of Arkansas for Medical Sciences	M,D,O
The University of British Columbia	M,D
University of Calgary	M,D
University of California, Berkeley	D
University of California, Davis	M,D
University of California, Irvine	M,D
University of California, Los Angeles	M,D
University of California, Merced	M,D
University of California, Riverside	M,D
University of California, San Diego	M,D
University of California, San Francisco	D
University of California, Santa Barbara	D
University of California, Santa Cruz	M,D
University of Cincinnati	M,D
University of Colorado Boulder	M,D
University of Colorado Denver	D
University of Connecticut Health Center	D
University of Delaware	M,D
University of Florida	D
University of Georgia	M,D
University of Guelph	M,D
University of Houston	M,D
University of Idaho	M,D
University of Illinois at Chicago	D
University of Illinois at Urbana–Champaign	M,D
The University of Iowa	M,D
The University of Kansas	D
University of Kentucky	D
University of Lethbridge	M,D
University of Louisville	M,D
The University of Manchester	M,D
University of Manitoba	M,D
University of Maryland, Baltimore	M,D
University of Maryland, Baltimore County	M,D,O
University of Maryland, College Park	M,D
University of Massachusetts Amherst	M,D
University of Massachusetts Dartmouth	M,D
University of Massachusetts Lowell	M,D
University of Massachusetts Medical School	M,D
University of Miami	D
University of Michigan	M,D
University of Minnesota, Duluth	M,D
University of Minnesota, Twin Cities Campus	D
University of Mississippi Medical Center	D
University of Missouri	M,D
University of Missouri–Kansas City	D
University of Missouri–St. Louis	M,D
University of Montana	D
University of Nebraska–Lincoln	M,D
University of Nebraska Medical Center	M,D
University of Nevada, Las Vegas	M,D
University of Nevada, Reno	M,D
University of New Hampshire	M,D
University of New Mexico	M,D
The University of North Carolina at Chapel Hill	M,D
The University of North Carolina at Greensboro	M
University of North Texas	M,D,O
University of North Texas Health Science Center at Fort Worth	M,D
University of Notre Dame	M,D
University of Oklahoma	M,D
University of Oklahoma Health Sciences Center	M,D
University of Oregon	M,D
University of Ottawa	M,D
University of Pennsylvania	D
University of Puerto Rico, Medical Sciences Campus	M,D
University of Regina	M,D
University of Rhode Island	M,D
University of Rochester	D
University of Saint Joseph	M
University of Saskatchewan	M,D
The University of Scranton	M
University of South Carolina	M,D
University of Southern California	M
University of Southern Mississippi	M,D
The University of Tennessee	M,D
The University of Texas at Austin	D
The University of Texas Health Science Center at Houston	M,D
The University of Texas Health Science Center at San Antonio	M,D
The University of Texas Medical Branch	D
The University of Texas Southwestern Medical Center	D
University of the Sciences	M,D
The University of Toledo	M,D
University of Toronto	M,D
The University of Tulsa	M,D
University of Utah	M,D
University of Victoria	M,D
University of Virginia	D
University of Washington	D
University of Waterloo	M,D
The University of Western Ontario	M,D
University of Windsor	M,D
University of Wisconsin–Madison	M,D
University of Wisconsin–Milwaukee	M,D
Utah State University	M,D
Vanderbilt University	M,D
Virginia Commonwealth University	M,D
Wake Forest University	D
Washington State University	M,D
Washington University in St. Louis	D
Wayne State University	M,D,O
Weill Cornell Medicine	M,D
Wesleyan University	D
West Virginia University	D
Worcester Polytechnic Institute	M,D
Wright State University	M
Yale University	D
Youngstown State University	M

BIOENGINEERING

Alfred University	M,D
Baylor College of Medicine	D
California Institute of Technology	M,D
Carnegie Mellon University	M,D
Clemson University	M,D,O
Colorado School of Mines	M,D
Colorado State University	M,D
Cornell University	M,D
Dalhousie University	M,D
Florida Atlantic University	M,D
George Mason University	D
Georgia Institute of Technology	M,D
Harvard University	M,D
Illinois Institute of Technology	M,D
Johns Hopkins University	M,D
Kansas State University	M,D
Lehigh University	M,D
Louisiana State University and Agricultural & Mechanical College	M,D
Massachusetts Institute of Technology	M,D
McGill University	M,D
Mississippi State University	M,D
North Carolina Agricultural and Technical State University	M,D
North Carolina State University	M,D,O
Northeastern University	M,D,O
Northwestern University	D
The Ohio State University	M,D
Oklahoma State University	M,D
Oregon State University	M,D
Penn State University Park	M,D
Rensselaer Polytechnic Institute	M,D
Rice University	M,D
Santa Clara University	M,D,O
South Dakota School of Mines and Technology	D
Stanford University	M,D
Syracuse University	M,D
Temple University	M,D
Texas A&M University	M,D
Texas Tech University	M
Tufts University	M,D,O
University at Buffalo, the State University of New York	M,D
University of Arkansas	M
The University of British Columbia	M,D
University of California, Berkeley	M,D
University of California, Davis	M,D
University of California, Los Angeles	M,D
University of California, Merced	M,D
University of California, Riverside	M,D
University of California, San Diego	M,D
University of California, San Francisco	D
University of California, Santa Barbara	M,D
University of Chicago	M,D
University of Colorado Denver	M,D
University of Dayton	M
University of Denver	M,D
University of Florida	M,D,O
University of Guelph	M,D
University of Hawaii at Manoa	M
University of Idaho	M
University of Illinois at Chicago	M,D
University of Illinois at Urbana–Champaign	M,D
The University of Kansas	M,D
University of Louisville	M
University of Maryland, College Park	M,D
University of Michigan–Dearborn	M
University of Missouri	M,D
University of Nebraska–Lincoln	M,D
University of Notre Dame	M,D
University of Ottawa	M,D
University of Pennsylvania	M,D
University of Pittsburgh	M,D
University of Puerto Rico, Mayagüez Campus	M,D
University of Saskatchewan	M,D
The University of Texas at Arlington	M,D
The University of Toledo	M,D
University of Utah	M,D
University of Washington	M,D
Virginia Polytechnic Institute and State University	M,D
Washington State University	M,D
Wilkes University	M

BIOETHICS

Albany Medical College	M,D,O
Case Western Reserve University	M
Clarkson University	M,O
Cleveland State University	M,O
Columbia University	M
Duke University	M
Duquesne University	M,D,O
Emory University	M
Icahn School of Medicine at Mount Sinai	M
Indiana University–Purdue University Indianapolis	M,D,O
Instituto Tecnologico de Santo Domingo	M,O
Johns Hopkins University	M,D
Kansas City University of Medicine and Biosciences	M
Loma Linda University	M,O
Loyola Marymount University	M
Loyola University Chicago	M,D,O
McGill University	M,D,O
Medical College of Wisconsin	M,O
New York University	M,D
Northeast Ohio Medical University	M,D,O
Saint Louis University	D,O
Stony Brook University, State University of New York	
Trinity International University	M,D
Université de Montréal	M,D,O
University of Louisville	M,D
University of Mary	M
University of Pennsylvania	M
University of Pittsburgh	M
University of South Florida	O
The University of Tennessee	M,D
University of Toronto	M,D
University of Washington	M
Washington State University	M,D,O
Washington University in St. Louis	M

BIOINFORMATICS

Arizona State University at the Tempe campus	M,D
Boston University	M,D
Brandeis University	M
California State University Channel Islands	M
California State University, Dominguez Hills	M
Dalhousie University	M,D
Duke University	D,O
Emory University	M,D
George Mason University	M,D,O
Georgetown University	M,O
Georgia Institute of Technology	M,D
Georgia State University	M,D
Grand Valley State University	M
Hood College	M,O
Hunter College of the City University of New York	M
Indiana University Bloomington	M,D,O
Indiana University–Purdue University Indianapolis	M,D
Iowa State University of Science and Technology	M,D
Johns Hopkins University	M,D
Lawrence Technological University	M,O
Marquette University	M,D
Massachusetts Institute of Technology	M,D
McGill University	M,D
Morgan State University	M
New Jersey Institute of Technology	M,D,O
New Mexico State University	M,D
New York University	M,D
North Carolina State University	M,D
North Dakota State University	M,D
Northeastern University	M,D
Nova Southeastern University	M,D,O
Oregon Health & Science University	M,D,O
Oregon State University	D
Rice University	M,D
Rochester Institute of Technology	M
Rowan University	M
Rutgers University–Newark	M,D
Simon Fraser University	M,D,O
Stevens Institute of Technology	M,D,O
Stony Brook University, State University of New York	M,D
Tufts University	M,D
Université de Montréal	M,D
University at Buffalo, the State University of New York	M,D
The University of Alabama at Birmingham	D
University of Arkansas at Little Rock	M,D
University of Arkansas for Medical Sciences	M,D,O
The University of British Columbia	M,D
University of California, Los Angeles	D
University of California, Riverside	D
University of California, San Diego	D
University of California, San Francisco	D
University of California, Santa Cruz	M,D
University of Cincinnati	D,O
University of Colorado Denver	D
University of Georgia	M,D
University of Idaho	M,D
University of Illinois at Chicago	M,D
University of Illinois at Urbana–Champaign	M,D,O
The University of Iowa	M,D,O
University of Louisville	M,D
University of Maine	M,D
The University of Manchester	M,D
University of Maryland, College Park	D
University of Massachusetts Medical School	M,D
University of Memphis	M,D
University of Michigan	D
University of Minnesota Rochester	M,D
University of Missouri	D
University of Missouri–Kansas City	M,D,O
University of Nebraska at Omaha	M,D
University of Nebraska–Lincoln	M,D
University of Nebraska Medical Center	M,D
The University of North Carolina at Chapel Hill	D
The University of North Carolina at Charlotte	M,D,O
University of Pittsburgh	M,D,O
University of Southern California	D
University of South Florida	M,D,O
The University of Texas at El Paso	M,D
The University of Texas Health Science Center at Houston	M,D,O
The University of Texas Medical Branch	D
University of the Sciences	M
The University of Toledo	M,O
University of Utah	M,D,O
University of Washington	M,D
University of Wisconsin–Madison	M
Vanderbilt University	M,D
Virginia Polytechnic Institute and State University	M,D
Wayne State University	M,D
Wesleyan University	M,D
Worcester Polytechnic Institute	M,D
Yale University	D

BIOLOGICAL AND BIOMEDICAL SCIENCES—GENERAL

Acadia University	M
Adelphi University	M
Alabama Agricultural and Mechanical University	M,D
Alabama State University	M,D
Albert Einstein College of Medicine	D

M—masters degree; D—doctorate; O—other advanced degree; *—Close-Up and/or Display

Institution	Degree
Alcorn State University	M
American Museum of Natural History–Richard Gilder Graduate School	D
American University of Beirut	M,D
Andrews University	M
Angelo State University	M
Appalachian State University	M
Arizona State University at the Tempe campus	M,D
Arkansas State University	M,O
A.T. Still University	M,D
Auburn University	M,D
Austin Peay State University	M
Ball State University	M,D
Barry University	M
Baylor College of Medicine	M,D
Baylor University	M,D
Bemidji State University	M
Binghamton University, State University of New York	M,D
Bloomsburg University of Pennsylvania	M
Boise State University	M,D
Boston College	D
Boston University	M,D
Bowling Green State University	M,D
Bradley University	M
Brandeis University	M,D,O
Brigham Young University	M,D
Brock University	M,D
Brooklyn College of the City University of New York	M
Brown University	M,D
Bucknell University	M
Buffalo State College, State University of New York	M
California Institute of Technology	D
California Polytechnic State University, San Luis Obispo	M
California State Polytechnic University, Pomona	M
California State University, Bakersfield	M
California State University, Chico	M
California State University, Dominguez Hills	M
California State University, East Bay	M
California State University, Fresno	M
California State University, Fullerton	M
California State University, Long Beach	M
California State University, Los Angeles	M
California State University, Northridge	M
California State University, Sacramento	M
California State University, San Bernardino	M
California State University, San Marcos	M
Carleton University	M,D
Carnegie Mellon University	M,D
Case Western Reserve University	M,D
The Catholic University of America	M,D
Cedars-Sinai Medical Center	D
Central Connecticut State University	M,O
Central Michigan University	M
Central Washington University	M
Chatham University	M
Chicago State University	M
The Citadel, The Military College of South Carolina	M,O
City College of the City University of New York	M,D
Clark Atlanta University	M,D
Clarkson University	M
Clark University	D
Clayton State University	M
Clemson University	M
Cleveland State University	M,D
Cold Spring Harbor Laboratory	D
The College at Brockport, State University of New York	M,O
College of Staten Island of the City University of New York	M
The College of William and Mary	M
Colorado State University	M,D
Colorado State University–Pueblo	M
Columbia University	M,D,O
Columbus State University	M
Concordia University (Canada)	M,D,O
Cornell University	M,D
Creighton University	M,D
Dalhousie University	M,D
Dartmouth College	D
Delaware State University	M
Delta State University	M
DePaul University	M,D
Des Moines University	M
Dominican University of California	M
Drew University	M,D,O
Drexel University	M,D,O
Duke University	M,D
Duquesne University	D
East Carolina University	M,D
Eastern Illinois University	M
Eastern Kentucky University	M
Eastern Mennonite University	M
Eastern Michigan University	M
Eastern New Mexico University	M
Eastern Virginia Medical School	M,D
Eastern Washington University	M
East Stroudsburg University of Pennsylvania	M
East Tennessee State University	M,D
Elizabeth City State University	M
Emory University	D
Emporia State University	M
Fairleigh Dickinson University, College at Florham	M
Fairleigh Dickinson University, Metropolitan Campus	M
Fayetteville State University	M
Fisk University	M
Fitchburg State University	M,O
Florida Atlantic University	M
Florida Institute of Technology	M,D
Florida International University	M,D
Florida State University	M,D
Fordham University	M,D,O
Fort Hays State University	M
Frostburg State University	M
Geisinger Commonwealth School of Medicine	M
George Mason University	M,D,O
Georgetown University	M,D
The George Washington University	M,D
Georgia College & State University	M
Georgia Institute of Technology	M,D
Georgia Southern University	M
Georgia State University	M,D
Gerstner Sloan Kettering Graduate School of Biomedical Sciences	D
Goucher College	O
The Graduate Center, City University of New York	D
Grand Valley State University	M
Hampton University	M
Harvard University	M,D,O
Hofstra University	M
Hood College	M
Howard University	M,D
Humboldt State University	M
Hunter College of the City University of New York	M,D
Icahn School of Medicine at Mount Sinai	M,D
Idaho State University	M,D
Illinois Institute of Technology	M,D
Illinois State University	M,D
Indiana State University	M,D
Indiana University Bloomington	M,D
Indiana University of Pennsylvania	M
Indiana University–Purdue University Fort Wayne	M
Indiana University–Purdue University Indianapolis	M,D
Iowa State University of Science and Technology	M,D
Irell & Manella Graduate School of Biological Sciences	D*
Ithaca College	M
Jackson State University	M
Jacksonville State University	M
James Madison University	M
John Carroll University	M
Johns Hopkins University	M,D
Kansas City University of Medicine and Biosciences	M
Kansas State University	M,D
Keck Graduate Institute	M,D,O
Kennesaw State University	M
Kent State University	M,D
Kutztown University of Pennsylvania	M
Lake Erie College of Osteopathic Medicine	M,D,O
Lakehead University	M
Lamar University	M
Laurentian University	M,D
Lee University	M,O
Lehigh University	M,D
Lehman College of the City University of New York	M
Liberty University	M
London Metropolitan University	M,D
Long Island University–LIU Brooklyn	M,D,O
Long Island University–LIU Post	M,O
Louisiana State University and Agricultural & Mechanical College	M,D
Louisiana State University Health Sciences Center	D
Louisiana State University Health Sciences Center at Shreveport	M
Louisiana State University in Shreveport	M
Louisiana Tech University	M
Loyola University Chicago	M,D
Marquette University	M,D
Marshall University	M,D
Massachusetts Institute of Technology	M,D
Mayo Clinic Graduate School of Biomedical Sciences	D
McGill University	M,D
McMaster University	M,D
Medical College of Wisconsin	M,D,O
Medical University of South Carolina	M,D
Meharry Medical College	D
Memorial University of Newfoundland	M,D,O
Miami University	M,D
Michigan State University	M,D
Michigan Technological University	M,D
Middle Tennessee State University	M
Midwestern State University	M
Midwestern University, Downers Grove Campus	M
Midwestern University, Glendale Campus	M
Mills College	O
Minnesota State University Mankato	M
Mississippi College	M
Mississippi State University	M,D
Missouri State University	M
Missouri University of Science and Technology	M
Missouri Western State University	M
Molloy College	M,O
Montana State University	M,D
Montclair State University	M
Morehead State University	M
Morehouse School of Medicine	M,D
Morgan State University	M,D
Mount Allison University	M
Murray State University	M
National University	M,O
New Jersey Institute of Technology	M,D,O
New Mexico Institute of Mining and Technology	M,D
New Mexico State University	M,D
New York Medical College	M
New York University	M,D,O
North Carolina Agricultural and Technical State University	M
North Carolina Central University	M
North Carolina State University	M,D,O
North Dakota State University	M,D
Northeastern Illinois University	M
Northeastern University	M,D
Northern Arizona University	M,D
Northern Illinois University	M,D
Northern Michigan University	M
Northwestern University	D
Northwest Missouri State University	M,O
Nova Southeastern University	M,D
Oakland University	M,D,O
Occidental College	M
The Ohio State University	M,D
Ohio University	M,D
Oklahoma State University	M,D
Oklahoma State University Center for Health Sciences	M,D
Old Dominion University	M,D
Oregon Health & Science University	M,D,O
Oregon State University	M,D
Pace University	M,O
Penn State Hershey Medical Center	M,D
Penn State University Park	M,D
Philadelphia College of Osteopathic Medicine	M
Pittsburg State University	M
Plymouth State University	M
Point Loma Nazarene University	M
Ponce Health Sciences University	D
Pontifical Catholic University of Puerto Rico	M
Portland State University	M,D
Purdue University	M,D
Purdue University Northwest	M
Queens College of the City University of New York	M,O
Queen's University at Kingston	M,D
Regis University	M
Rensselaer Polytechnic Institute	M,D
Rhode Island College	M,O
Rochester Institute of Technology	M,D
The Rockefeller University	M,D
Rocky Vista University	M
Rosalind Franklin University of Medicine and Science	M,D
Rowan University	M
Rutgers University–Camden	M
Rutgers University–Newark	M,D,O
Rutgers University–New Brunswick	M,D
Sacred Heart University	M
St. Cloud State University	M
Saint Francis University	M
St. Francis Xavier University	M
St. John Fisher College	M
St. John's University (NY)	M,D
Saint Joseph's University	M
Saint Louis University	M,D
Salisbury University	M
Sam Houston State University	M
San Diego State University	M,D
Sanford Burnham Prebys Medical Discovery Institute	D
San Francisco State University	M
San Jose State University	M,O
The Scripps Research Institute	D
Seton Hall University	M,D
Shippensburg University of Pennsylvania	M
Simon Fraser University	M,D,O
Smith College	M
Sonoma State University	M
South Carolina State University	M
South Dakota State University	M
Southeastern Louisiana University	M
Southeast Missouri State University	M
Southern Connecticut State University	M
Southern Illinois University Carbondale	M,D
Southern Illinois University Edwardsville	M
Southern Methodist University	M,D
Southern University and Agricultural and Mechanical College	M
Stanford University	M,D
State University of New York at Fredonia	M
State University of New York College at Oneonta	M
State University of New York Downstate Medical Center	M,D
State University of New York Upstate Medical University	M
Stephen F. Austin State University	M
Stevenson University	M
Stony Brook University, State University of New York	M,D,O
Sul Ross State University	M
Syracuse University	M,D
Tarleton State University	M
Teachers College, Columbia University	M
Temple University	M,D
Tennessee State University	D
Tennessee Technological University	M,D
Texas A&M International University	M
Texas A&M University	M,D,O
Texas A&M University–Commerce	M,O
Texas A&M University–Corpus Christi	M
Texas A&M University–Kingsville	M
Texas Christian University	M
Texas Southern University	M
Texas State University	M
Texas Tech University	M,D
Texas Tech University Health Sciences Center	M,D
Texas Woman's University	M,D
Thomas Jefferson University	M,D,O
Towson University	M
Trent University	M,O
Troy University	M
Truman State University	M
Tufts University	M,D,O
Tulane University	M,D
Tuskegee University	M,D
Uniformed Services University of the Health Sciences	M,D
Universidad Central del Caribe	M,D
Universidad de Ciencias Medicas	M,D,O
Université de Moncton	M
Université de Montréal	M,D
Université de Sherbrooke	M,D,O
Université du Québec à Montréal	M,D
Université du Québec en Abitibi-Témiscamingue	M,D
Université du Québec, Institut National de la Recherche Scientifique	M,D
Université Laval	M,D,O
University at Albany, State University of New York	M,D
University at Buffalo, the State University of New York	M,D
The University of Akron	M,D
The University of Alabama	M,D
The University of Alabama at Birmingham	M,D
The University of Alabama in Huntsville	M,D
University of Alaska Anchorage	M
University of Alberta	M,D
The University of Arizona	M,D
University of Arkansas	M,D
University of Arkansas at Little Rock	M
University of Arkansas for Medical Sciences	M,D,O
University of Calgary	M,D
University of California, Berkeley	D
University of California, Irvine	M,D
University of California, Los Angeles	M,D
University of California, Merced	M,D
University of California, Riverside	M,D
University of California, San Diego	M,D
University of California, San Francisco	D
University of Central Arkansas	M
University of Central Florida	M,D
University of Central Missouri	M,D,O
University of Central Oklahoma	M
University of Chicago	D
University of Cincinnati	M,D,O
University of Colorado Denver	M,D
University of Connecticut Health Center	D
University of Dayton	M,D
University of Delaware	M,D
University of Denver	M,D
University of Florida	M,D
University of Georgia	D
University of Guam	M
University of Guelph	M,D
University of Hartford	M
University of Hawaii at Manoa	M,D
University of Houston	M,D
University of Houston–Clear Lake	M
University of Houston–Victoria	M
University of Idaho	M,D
University of Illinois at Chicago	M,D
University of Illinois at Springfield	M
University of Illinois at Urbana–Champaign	M,D
University of Indianapolis	M
The University of Iowa	M,D
The University of Kansas	D
University of Kentucky	M,D
University of Lethbridge	M,D
University of Louisiana at Lafayette	M,D
University of Louisiana at Monroe	M,D
University of Louisville	M,D
University of Maine	M,D
The University of Manchester	M,D
University of Manitoba	M,D
University of Maryland, Baltimore	M,D,O
University of Maryland, Baltimore County	M,D,O
University of Maryland, College Park	M,D
University of Massachusetts Amherst	M,D
University of Massachusetts Boston	M,D
University of Massachusetts Dartmouth	M
University of Massachusetts Lowell	M

University of Massachusetts Medical School	M,D
University of Memphis	M,D
University of Miami	M,D
University of Michigan	M,D
University of Michigan–Flint	M
University of Minnesota, Duluth	M,D
University of Minnesota, Twin Cities Campus	M
University of Mississippi	M,D
University of Mississippi Medical Center	M,D
University of Missouri	M,D
University of Missouri–Kansas City	M,D
University of Missouri–St. Louis	M,D,O
University of Montana	M,D
University of Nebraska at Kearney	M
University of Nebraska at Omaha	M,O
University of Nebraska–Lincoln	M,D
University of Nebraska Medical Center	M,D
University of Nevada, Las Vegas	M,D
University of Nevada, Reno	M
University of New Brunswick Fredericton	M,D
University of New Brunswick Saint John	M,D
University of New England	M
University of New Hampshire	M,D
University of New Mexico	M,D
University of New Orleans	M,D
The University of North Carolina at Chapel Hill	M,D
The University of North Carolina at Charlotte	M,D
The University of North Carolina at Greensboro	M
The University of North Carolina Wilmington	M,D
University of North Dakota	M,D
University of Northern Colorado	M
University of Northern Iowa	M
University of North Florida	M
University of North Texas	M,D,O
University of North Texas Health Science Center at Fort Worth	M,D
University of Notre Dame	M,D
University of Oklahoma	D
University of Oklahoma Health Sciences Center	M,D
University of Oregon	M,D
University of Ottawa	M,D
University of Pennsylvania	M,D
University of Pittsburgh	D
University of Prince Edward Island	M,D
University of Puerto Rico, Mayagüez Campus	M
University of Puerto Rico, Medical Sciences Campus	M,D
University of Puerto Rico, Río Piedras Campus	M,D
University of Regina	M,D
University of Rhode Island	M,D
University of Rochester	M,D
University of Saint Joseph	M
University of San Francisco	M
University of Saskatchewan	M,D
University of South Alabama	M,D
University of South Carolina	M,D,O
The University of South Dakota	M,D
University of Southern California	M,D,O
University of Southern Maine	M
University of Southern Mississippi	M,D
University of South Florida	M,D
The University of Tennessee	M,D
The University of Tennessee Health Science Center	M,D
The University of Tennessee–Oak Ridge National Laboratory	M,D
The University of Texas at Arlington	M,D
The University of Texas at Austin	M,D
The University of Texas at Dallas	M,D
The University of Texas at El Paso	M,D
The University of Texas at San Antonio	M,D
The University of Texas at Tyler	M
The University of Texas Health Science Center at Houston	M,D
The University of Texas Health Science Center at San Antonio	D
The University of Texas Medical Branch	M,D
The University of Texas of the Permian Basin	M
The University of Texas Rio Grande Valley	M
The University of Texas Southwestern Medical Center	M,D
University of the Incarnate Word	M
University of the Pacific	M,D
The University of Toledo	M,D,O
The University of Tulsa	M,D
University of Utah	M,D,O
University of Vermont	M,D,O
University of Victoria	M,D
University of Virginia	M,D
University of Washington	M,D
University of Waterloo	M,D
The University of Western Ontario	M,D
University of West Florida	M
University of West Georgia	M,O
University of Windsor	M,D
University of Wisconsin–La Crosse	M
University of Wisconsin–Madison	

University of Wisconsin–Milwaukee	M,D
University of Wisconsin–Oshkosh	M
Utah State University	M,D
Vanderbilt University	M,D
Villanova University	M
Virginia Commonwealth University	M,D,O
Virginia Polytechnic Institute and State University	M,D
Virginia State University	M
Wake Forest University	M,D
Walla Walla University	M
Washington State University	M,D
Washington University in St. Louis	D
Wayne State University	M,D
Weill Cornell Medicine	M,D
Wesleyan University	D
West Chester University of Pennsylvania	M,O
Western Carolina University	M
Western Connecticut State University	M
Western Illinois University	M,O
Western Kentucky University	M
Western Michigan University	M,D,O
Western University of Health Sciences	M
Western Washington University	M
West Texas A&M University	M
West Virginia University	M,D
Wichita State University	M
Wilfrid Laurier University	M
William Paterson University of New Jersey	M,D
Winthrop University	M
Worcester Polytechnic Institute	M,D
Wright State University	M,D
Yale University	D
York University	M,D
Youngstown State University	M

BIOLOGICAL ANTHROPOLOGY

Duke University	D
Kent State University	M,D
Mercyhurst University	M
University of Wisconsin–Milwaukee	M,D,O

BIOMATHEMATICS

The College of William and Mary	M,D
North Carolina State University	M,D
University of California, Los Angeles	M,D

BIOMEDICAL ENGINEERING

American University of Beirut	M,D
American University of Sharjah	M
Arizona State University at the Tempe campus	M,D
Baylor College of Medicine	D
Baylor University	M,D
Binghamton University, State University of New York	M,D
Boston University	M,D
Brown University	M,D
Carleton University	M
Carnegie Mellon University	M,D
Case Western Reserve University	M,D
The Catholic University of America	M,D
City College of the City University of New York	M,D
Clemson University	M,D,O
Cleveland State University	D
Colorado State University	M,D
Columbia University	M,D
Cornell University	M,D
Dalhousie University	M,D
Dartmouth College	M,D
Drexel University	M,D
Duke University	M,D
East Carolina University	M
École Polytechnique de Montréal	M,D,O
Florida Agricultural and Mechanical University	M,D
Florida Institute of Technology	M,D
Florida International University	M,D
Florida State University	M,D
The George Washington University	M,D
Georgia Institute of Technology	D
The Graduate Center, City University of New York	D
Harvard University	D
Illinois Institute of Technology	M,D
Indiana University–Purdue University Indianapolis	M,D
Johns Hopkins University	M,D,O
Lawrence Technological University	M,D
Louisiana Tech University	D
Marquette University	M,D
Massachusetts Institute of Technology	M,D
Mayo Clinic Graduate School of Biomedical Sciences	D
McGill University	M,D
Mercer University	M
Michigan Technological University	M,D
Mississippi State University	M,D
New Jersey Institute of Technology	M,D
New York University	M,D
North Carolina State University	M,D
Northwestern University	M,D
The Ohio State University	M,D
Ohio University	M
Old Dominion University	M,D
Oregon Health & Science University	D
Purdue University	M,D
Rensselaer Polytechnic Institute	M,D
Rice University	M,D
Rose-Hulman Institute of Technology	M

Rutgers University–Newark	O
Rutgers University–New Brunswick	M,D
St. Cloud State University	M
Saint Louis University	M,D
South Dakota School of Mines and Technology	M
Southern Illinois University Carbondale	M
Stanford University	M,D,O
State University of New York Downstate Medical Center	M,D
Stevens Institute of Technology	M,D
Stony Brook University, State University of New York	M,D,O
Tennessee State University	M,D
Texas A&M University	M,D
Tufts University	M,D
Tulane University	M,D
Université de Montréal	M,D,O
University at Buffalo, the State University of New York	M,D
The University of Akron	M,D
The University of Alabama at Birmingham	M,D
University of Alberta	M,D
The University of Arizona	M,D
University of Arkansas	M
University of Bridgeport	M,D
University of Calgary	M,D
University of California, Davis	M,D
University of California, Irvine	M,D
University of California, Los Angeles	M,D
University of Central Oklahoma	M
University of Cincinnati	M,D
University of Connecticut	M,D
University of Florida	M,D,O
University of Houston	D
The University of Iowa	M,D
University of Kentucky	M,D
University of Maine	M,D
University of Massachusetts Boston	D
University of Massachusetts Dartmouth	M,D
University of Memphis	M,D
University of Miami	M,D
University of Michigan	M,D
University of Minnesota, Twin Cities Campus	M,D
University of Nebraska–Lincoln	M,D
University of Nevada, Las Vegas	M,D,O
University of Nevada, Reno	M
University of New Haven	M
University of New Mexico	M,D
The University of North Carolina at Chapel Hill	M,D
University of North Texas	M,D,O
University of Oklahoma	M,D
University of Ottawa	M
University of Portland	M
University of Rhode Island	M,D
University of Rochester	M,D
University of Saskatchewan	M,D
University of Southern California	M,D
University of South Florida	M,D,O
The University of Tennessee	M,D
The University of Tennessee Health Science Center	M,D
The University of Texas at Austin	M,D
The University of Texas at Dallas	M,D
The University of Texas at El Paso	M,D,O
The University of Texas at San Antonio	M,D
The University of Texas Health Science Center at San Antonio	M,D
The University of Texas Southwestern Medical Center	M,D
The University of Toledo	D
University of Toronto	M,D
University of Vermont	D
University of Virginia	M,D
University of Wisconsin–Madison	M,D
University of Wisconsin–Milwaukee	M,D
Vanderbilt University	M,D
Virginia Commonwealth University	M,D
Virginia Polytechnic Institute and State University	M,D
Wake Forest University	M,D
Washington University in St. Louis	M,D
Wayne State University	M,D,O
Wichita State University	M
Widener University	M
Worcester Polytechnic Institute	M,D,O
Wright State University	M
Yale University	M,D

BIOMETRY

Cornell University	M,D
San Diego State University	M
University of Wisconsin–Madison	M

BIOPHYSICS

Albert Einstein College of Medicine	D
Baylor College of Medicine	D
Boston University	M,D
Brandeis University	M,D
California Institute of Technology	D
Carnegie Mellon University	M,D
Case Western Reserve University	M,D
Columbia University	M,D
Cornell University	D
Dalhousie University	M,D
East Carolina University	D
Emory University	D
Harvard University	D

Howard University	D
Illinois State University	M,D
Iowa State University of Science and Technology	M,D
Johns Hopkins University	D
Medical College of Wisconsin	D
Northwestern University	D
The Ohio State University	M,D
Oregon State University	M,D
Purdue University	M,D
Rensselaer Polytechnic Institute	M,D
Rosalind Franklin University of Medicine and Science	M,D
Stanford University	D
Stony Brook University, State University of New York	D
Texas Christian University	M,D
Université de Sherbrooke	M,D
Université du Québec à Trois-Rivières	
University at Buffalo, the State University of New York	M,D
University of California, Berkeley	D
University of California, Davis	M,D
University of California, Irvine	
University of California, San Diego	M,D
University of California, San Francisco	D
University of California, Santa Barbara	D
University of Chicago	D
University of Cincinnati	D
University of Colorado Denver	M,D
University of Connecticut	M,D
University of Guelph	M,D
University of Illinois at Chicago	M,D
University of Illinois at Urbana–Champaign	M,D
The University of Iowa	M,D
The University of Kansas	M,D
University of Louisville	M,D
The University of Manchester	M,D
University of Maryland, College Park	D
University of Miami	D
University of Michigan	D
University of Minnesota, Duluth	M,D
University of Minnesota, Twin Cities Campus	M,D
University of Mississippi Medical Center	D
University of Missouri–Kansas City	D
The University of North Carolina at Chapel Hill	M,D
University of Regina	M,D
University of Rochester	D
University of Southern California	M
The University of Texas Medical Branch	D
University of Toronto	M,D
University of Virginia	M,D
University of Washington	D
The University of Western Ontario	M,D
University of Wisconsin–Madison	D
Vanderbilt University	M,D
Washington State University	M,D
Weill Cornell Medicine	M,D
Yale University	D

BIOPSYCHOLOGY

Adler University	M,D,O
American University	M,D,O
Argosy University, Atlanta	M,D,O
Argosy University, Twin Cities	M,D,O
Binghamton University, State University of New York	D
Boston University	M
Carnegie Mellon University	D
Cornell University	D
Drexel University	M,D
Duke University	D
Florida State University	M,D
The Graduate Center, City University of New York	D
Harvard University	D
Howard University	M,D
Indiana University–Purdue University Indianapolis	M,D
Louisiana State University and Agricultural & Mechanical College	M,D
Memorial University of Newfoundland	M,D
Northwestern University	D
Oregon Health & Science University	D
Palo Alto University	D
Penn State University Park	M,D
Philadelphia College of Osteopathic Medicine	M,D,O
Rutgers University–Newark	D
Rutgers University–New Brunswick	D
The University of British Columbia	M,D
University of Connecticut	M,D
University of Michigan	D
University of Minnesota, Twin Cities Campus	D
University of Nebraska–Lincoln	M,D
The University of North Carolina at Chapel Hill	D
University of Oklahoma Health Sciences Center	M,D
University of Oregon	M,D
The University of Texas at Austin	D
University of Windsor	M,D
University of Wisconsin–Madison	D
Wayne State University	M,D,O

M—masters degree; D—doctorate; O—other advanced degree; *—Close-Up and/or Display

BIOSTATISTICS

American University of Beirut	M
Boston University	M,D
Brown University	M,D
California State University, East Bay	M
Case Western Reserve University	M,D
Columbia University	M,D
Dartmouth College	D
Drexel University	M,D,O
Duke University	M
East Tennessee State University	M,D,O
Emory University	M,D
Florida International University	M,D
Florida State University	M,D
George Mason University	M,D,O
Georgetown University	M,O
The George Washington University	M,D
Georgia Southern University	M,D
Georgia State University	M,D
Grand Valley State University	M
Harvard University	M,D
Indiana University Bloomington	M,D
Indiana University–Purdue University Indianapolis	M,D,O
Iowa State University of Science and Technology	M,D
Johns Hopkins University	M,D
Kent State University	M,D
Loma Linda University	M,D
Louisiana State University Health Sciences Center	M,D
McGill University	M,D,O
Medical College of Wisconsin	D
Medical University of South Carolina	M,D
Middle Tennessee State University	M
Monroe College	M
New Jersey Institute of Technology	M,D,O
New York Medical College	M,D,O
Northwestern University	D
The Ohio State University	M,D
Old Dominion University	M,D
Oregon State University	M,D
Penn State Hershey Medical Center	D
Rice University	M,D
Rutgers University–New Brunswick	M,D,O
San Diego State University	M,D
Stanford University	M,D
Tufts University	M,D,O
Tulane University	M,D
University at Albany, State University of New York	M,D
University at Buffalo, the State University of New York	M,D
The University of Alabama at Birmingham	M,D
University of Alberta	M,D,O
The University of Arizona	M,D
University of Arkansas for Medical Sciences	M,D,O
University of California, Berkeley	M,D
University of California, Davis	M,D
University of California, Los Angeles	M,D
University of California, San Diego	D
University of Cincinnati	M,D
University of Colorado Denver	M,D
University of Florida	M,D,O
University of Illinois at Chicago	M,D
The University of Iowa	M,D,O
The University of Kansas	M,D,O
University of Kentucky	D
University of Louisville	M,D
University of Maryland, Baltimore	M,D
University of Maryland, Baltimore County	M,D
University of Maryland, College Park	M,D
University of Massachusetts Amherst	M,D
University of Memphis	M,D
University of Michigan	M,D
University of Minnesota, Twin Cities Campus	M,D
University of Nebraska Medical Center	D
The University of North Carolina at Chapel Hill	M,D
University of North Texas Health Science Center at Fort Worth	M,D,O
University of Oklahoma Health Sciences Center	M,D
University of Pennsylvania	M,D
University of Pittsburgh	M,D
University of Puerto Rico, Medical Sciences Campus	M
University of Rochester	M
University of South Carolina	M,D
University of Southern California	M,D
University of Southern Mississippi	M
University of South Florida	M,D,O
The University of Toledo	M,O
University of Toronto	M,D
University of Utah	M,D
University of Vermont	M
University of Washington	M,D
University of Waterloo	M,D
The University of Western Ontario	M,D
University of Wisconsin–Milwaukee	M,D,O
Virginia Commonwealth University	M,D,O
Washington University in St. Louis	M,D,O
West Virginia University	M,D
Yale University	M,D

BIOSYSTEMS ENGINEERING

Auburn University	M,D
Clemson University	M,D
Michigan State University	M,D
South Dakota State University	M,D
The University of Arizona	M,D

University of Manitoba	M,D
University of Minnesota, Twin Cities Campus	M,D
The University of Tennessee	M,D

BIOTECHNOLOGY

Adelphi University	M
The American University in Cairo	M,D,O
Arizona State University at the Tempe campus	M,D
Arkansas State University	M,O
Azusa Pacific University	M
Brandeis University	M
Brigham Young University	M,D
Brock University	M,D
Brown University	M,D
California State University Channel Islands	M
California State University, Fullerton	M
Carnegie Mellon University	M,D
The Catholic University of America	M,D
Claflin University	M
Clarkson University	D
Columbia University	M,D
Concordia University (Canada)	M,D,O
Cornell University	M,D
Dartmouth College	M,D
Duquesne University	M
East Carolina University	M
Eastern Virginia Medical School	M
Florida Institute of Technology	M,D
The George Washington University	M,D,O
Harvard University	M,O
Hood College	M
Howard University	M,D
Husson University	M
Illinois State University	M
Indiana University Bloomington	M,D
Instituto Tecnológico y de Estudios Superiores de Monterrey, Campus Monterrey	M,D
Inter American University of Puerto Rico, Bayamón Campus	M
Johns Hopkins University	M
Kean University	M
Long Island University–Hudson	M,O
Marywood University	M
McGill University	M,D,O
Michigan Technological University	M,D
Middle Tennessee State University	M
Mount St. Mary's University (MD)	M
New Mexico State University	M,D
New York University	M
North Carolina State University	M
Northeastern University	M,D
Northwestern University	M,D
Oregon State University	M,D
Penn State University Park	M,D
Pontifical John Paul II Institute for Studies on Marriage and Family	M,D,O
Purdue University	D
Purdue University Northwest	M
Regis College (MA)	M
Roosevelt University	M
St. John's University (NY)	M
San Francisco State University	M
San Jose State University	M,O
Simon Fraser University	M,D,O
Southeastern Oklahoma State University	M
Stephen F. Austin State University	M
Temple University	M,D
Tennessee State University	M,D
Texas Tech University	M,D
Texas Tech University Health Sciences Center	M
Thomas Jefferson University	M
Tufts University	M,D,O
Universidad de las Américas Puebla	M
University at Buffalo, the State University of New York	M
The University of Alabama at Birmingham	M
The University of Alabama in Huntsville	M,D
University of Alberta	M,D
University of Calgary	M,D
University of California, Irvine	M
University of Central Florida	M,D
University of Delaware	M,D
University of Guelph	M,D
University of Houston–Clear Lake	M
University of Illinois at Chicago	M,D
The University of Kansas	M
The University of Manchester	M,D
University of Maryland, Baltimore County	M,O
University of Maryland University College	M,O
University of Massachusetts Amherst	M
University of Massachusetts Boston	M,D
University of Massachusetts Dartmouth	M,D
University of Minnesota, Twin Cities Campus	M
University of Missouri–St. Louis	M,D
University of Nevada, Reno	M
University of North Texas Health Science Center at Fort Worth	M,D
University of Pennsylvania	M
University of Rhode Island	M,D
University of San Francisco	M
University of Saskatchewan	M
University of Southern California	M
University of South Florida	M,D,O
The University of Texas at Dallas	M,D

The University of Texas at San Antonio	M,D
University of the Sciences	M,D,O
University of Toronto	M
University of Utah	M
University of Washington	D
University of Wyoming	D
Virginia Polytechnic Institute and State University	M,D
Wayne State University	M,D
West Virginia State University	M
William Paterson University of New Jersey	M,D
Worcester Polytechnic Institute	M,D
Worcester State University	M

BOTANY

Auburn University	M,D
Claremont Graduate University	M,D
Colorado State University	M,D
Dalhousie University	M
Eastern New Mexico University	M
Emporia State University	M
Illinois State University	M,D
Kent State University	M,D
North Carolina State University	M,D
North Dakota State University	M,D
Oklahoma State University	M,D
Oregon State University	M,D
Purdue University	M,D
The University of British Columbia	M,D
University of California, Riverside	M,D
University of Connecticut	M,D
University of Florida	M,D
University of Guelph	M,D
University of Hawaii at Manoa	M,D
The University of Kansas	M,D
University of Maine	M,D
University of Manitoba	M,D
The University of North Carolina at Chapel Hill	M,D
University of Wisconsin–Madison	M,D
University of Wisconsin–Milwaukee	M,D
University of Wisconsin–Oshkosh	M
University of Wyoming	M,D

BROADCAST JOURNALISM

The American University in Cairo	M,O
Emerson College	M
Northwestern University	M
Quinnipiac University	M
Syracuse University	M
University of Maryland, College Park	M,D
University of Miami	M,D
University of the Sacred Heart	M,O

BUILDING SCIENCE

Arizona State University at the Tempe campus	M,D
Auburn University	M
Carnegie Mellon University	M,D
Georgia Institute of Technology	M,D
Pontificia Universidad Catolica Madre y Maestra	M
Rensselaer Polytechnic Institute	M,D
University of California, Berkeley	M
Virginia Polytechnic Institute and State University	M,D,O

BUSINESS ADMINISTRATION AND MANAGEMENT—GENERAL

Abilene Christian University	M
Adelphi University	M
Alabama State University	M
Alaska Pacific University	M
Albany State University	M
Albertus Magnus College	M
Alcorn State University	M
Alfred University	M
Alliant International University–Los Angeles	D
Alliant International University–San Diego	M
Alvernia University	M
Alverno College	M
Amberton University	M
American Business & Technology University	M
The American College of Financial Services	M
American College of Thessaloniki	M,O
American Graduate University	M,O
American InterContinental University Houston	M
American InterContinental University Online	M
American International College	M,D,O
American Jewish University	M
American National University	M
American Public University System	M
American Sentinel University	M
The American University in Cairo	M,O
The American University in Dubai	M
American University of Armenia	M
American University of Beirut	M
The American University of Paris	M
American University of Sharjah	M
Anaheim University	M,D,O
Anderson University (IN)	M,D
Anderson University (SC)	M
Angelo State University	M
Anna Maria College	M,O
Antioch University Los Angeles	M
Antioch University Midwest	M
Antioch University New England	M
Antioch University Santa Barbara	M
Appalachian State University	M
Aquinas College (MI)	M
Arcadia University	M
Argosy University, Atlanta	M,D

Argosy University, Chicago	M,D
Argosy University, Dallas	M,D,O
Argosy University, Denver	M,D
Argosy University, Hawai'i	M,D,O
Argosy University, Inland Empire	M,D
Argosy University, Los Angeles	M,D
Argosy University, Nashville	M,D
Argosy University, Northern Virginia	M,D,O
Argosy University, Orange County	M,D,O
Argosy University, Phoenix	M,D
Argosy University, Salt Lake City	M,D
Argosy University, San Diego	M,D
Argosy University, San Francisco Bay Area	M,D
Argosy University, Sarasota	M,D,O
Argosy University, Schaumburg	M,D,O
Argosy University, Seattle	M,D
Argosy University, Tampa	M,D
Argosy University, Twin Cities	M,D
Arizona State University at the Tempe campus	M,D
Arkansas State University	M
Arkansas Tech University	M
Armstrong State University	M,O
Ashland University	M
Ashworth College	M
Aspen University	M,O
Assumption College	M,O
Athabasca University	M,D,O
Auburn University	M,D
Auburn University at Montgomery	M
Augsburg College	M
Augusta University	M
Aurora University	M
Austin Peay State University	M
Averett University	M
Avila University	M
Azusa Pacific University	M
Babson College	M,O
Baker College Center for Graduate Studies–Online	M,D
Baker University	M
Bakke Graduate University	M
Baldwin Wallace University	M,O
Ball State University	M
Barry University	M,O
Baruch College of the City University of New York	M,D,O
Bayamón Central University	M
Baylor University	M
Belhaven University (MS)	M
Bellarmine University	M
Bellevue University	M,D
Belmont University	M
Benedictine College	M
Benedictine University	M,D
Bentley University	M,D,O
Berkeley College–Woodland Park Campus	M
Berry College	M
Bethel College	M
Bethel University (MN)	M,D,O
Bethel University (TN)	M
Binghamton University, State University of New York	M,D
Biola University	M
Black Hills State University	M
Bloomsburg University of Pennsylvania	M,O
Bluffton University	M
Bob Jones University	M,D,O
Boise State University	M
Boston College	M
Boston University	M,D
Bowie State University	M
Bowling Green State University	M
Bradley University	M
Brandeis University	M
Brandman University	M
Brenau University	M
Brescia University	M
Bridgewater State University	M
Briercrest Seminary	M
Brigham Young University	M
Bristol University	M
Broadview University–West Jordan	M
Brock University	M
Brooklyn College of the City University of New York	M
Bryan College	M
Bryant University	M,O
Bryan University	M
Butler University	M
Cairn University	M,O
Caldwell University	M
California Baptist University	M
California Coast University	M
California Intercontinental University	M,D
California International Business University	M,D
California Lutheran University	M,O
California Miramar University	M
California Polytechnic State University, San Luis Obispo	M
California State Polytechnic University, Pomona	M
California State University, Bakersfield	M
California State University Channel Islands	M
California State University, Chico	M
California State University, Dominguez Hills	M
California State University, East Bay	M
California State University, Fullerton	M
California State University, Long Beach	M
California State University, Los Angeles	M,O

California State University, Monterey Bay	M
California State University, Northridge	M
California State University, Sacramento	M
California State University, San Bernardino	M
California State University, San Marcos	M
California State University, Stanislaus	M
California University of Management and Sciences	M,D
California University of Pennsylvania	M
Cambridge College	M
Cameron University	M
Campbellsville University	M
Campbell University	M
Canisius College	M
Cape Breton University	M
Capella University	M,D
Capital University	M
Capitol Technology University	M
Cardinal Stritch University	M
Carleton University	M,D
Carlos Albizu University, Miami Campus	M,D
Carlow University	M
Carnegie Mellon University	M,D
Carroll University	M
Carson-Newman University	M
Case Western Reserve University	M,D
The Catholic University of America	M
Cedar Crest College	M
Cedarville University	M,D
Centenary College of Louisiana	M
Centenary University	M
Central Connecticut State University	M
Central European University	M,D
Central Michigan University	M,O
Chadron State College	M
Chaminade University of Honolulu	M
Champlain College	M
Chapman University	M
Charleston Southern University	M
Chatham University	M
Christian Brothers University	M,O
The Citadel, The Military College of South Carolina	M
City College of the City University of New York	M
City University of Seattle	M,O
Claflin University	M
Claremont Graduate University	M,D,O
Clarion University of Pennsylvania	M
Clark Atlanta University	M
Clarke University	M
Clarkson University	M,O
Clark University	M
Clayton State University	M
Cleary University	M,O
Clemson University	M,D
Cleveland State University	M,D
Coastal Carolina University	M,O
College of Charleston	M
College of Saint Elizabeth	M
College of St. Joseph	M
The College of Saint Rose	M
The College of St. Scholastica	M,O
College of Staten Island of the City University of New York	M
The College of William and Mary	M
Colorado Christian University	M
Colorado Mesa University	M
Colorado State University	M
Colorado State University– Global Campus	M
Colorado State University– Pueblo	M
Colorado Technical University Aurora	M
Colorado Technical University Colorado Springs	M,D
Columbia College (MO)	M
Columbia Southern University	M,D
Columbia University	M,D
Columbus State University	M,O
Concordia University (United States)	M
Concordia University (Canada)	M,D,O
Concordia University Chicago	M
Concordia University Irvine	M
Concordia University, St. Paul	M
Concordia University Wisconsin	M
Copenhagen Business School	M,D
Corban University	M
Cornell University	M,D
Cornerstone University	M,O
Creighton University	M
Culver-Stockton College	M
Cumberland University	M
Curry College	M,O
Daemen College	M
Dakota State University	M,D,O
Dalhousie University	M,O
Dallas Baptist University	M,D
Dartmouth College	M
Davenport University	M
Defiance College	M
Delaware State University	M
Delaware Valley University	M
Delta State University	M
DePaul University	M
DeSales University	M
DeVry College of New York– Midtown Manhattan Campus	M
DeVry University (GA)	M,O

DeVry University–Alpharetta Campus	M
DeVry University–Arlington Campus	M
DeVry University–Charlotte Campus	M
DeVry University–Chesapeake Campus	M
DeVry University–Chicago Campus	M
DeVry University–Chicago Loop Campus	M
DeVry University–Cincinnati Campus	M
DeVry University–Columbus Campus	M
DeVry University–Decatur Campus	M
DeVry University–Folsom Campus	M
DeVry University–Fremont Campus	M
DeVry University–Ft. Washington Campus	M
DeVry University–Henderson Campus	M
DeVry University–Irving Campus	M
DeVry University– Jacksonville Campus	M
DeVry University–Long Beach Campus	M
DeVry University–Miramar Campus	M
DeVry University–Morrisville Campus	M
DeVry University–Nashville Campus	M
DeVry University–North Brunswick Campus	M
DeVry University Online	M
DeVry University–Orlando Campus	M
DeVry University–Phoenix Campus	M
DeVry University–Pomona Campus	M
DeVry University–San Diego Campus	M,O
DeVry University–Seven Hills Campus	M,O
DeVry University–Tinley Park Campus	M
Doane University	M
Dominican College	M
Dominican University	M
Dominican University of California	M
Drake University	M
Drexel University	M,D,O
Drury University	M
Duke University	M,D,O
Duquesne University	M
D'Youville College	M
East Carolina University	M,D,O
Eastern Illinois University	M
Eastern Kentucky University	M
Eastern Mennonite University	M
Eastern Michigan University	M,O
Eastern Nazarene College	M
Eastern New Mexico University	M
Eastern Oregon University	M
Eastern University	M,D
Eastern Washington University	M
East Tennessee State University	M,O
East Texas Baptist University	M
Edgewood College	M
Elmhurst College	M
Elms College	M
Elon University	M
Embry-Riddle Aeronautical University–Daytona	M
Embry-Riddle Aeronautical University–Worldwide	M
Emmanuel College (United States)	M,O
Emory University	M,D
Emporia State University	M
Endicott College	M
ESSEC Business School	M,D
Everest University	M
Everglades University	M
Excelsior College	M,O
Fairfield University	M,O
Fairleigh Dickinson University, College at Florham	M,O
Fairleigh Dickinson University, Metropolitan Campus	M,O
Fairmont State University	M
Fashion Institute of Technology	M
Faulkner University	M
Fayetteville State University	M
Felician University	M,D
Ferris State University	M
Fisher College	M
Fitchburg State University	M
Florida Agricultural and Mechanical University	M
Florida Atlantic University	M
Florida Gulf Coast University	M
Florida Institute of Technology	M,D
Florida Memorial University	M
Florida National University	M
Florida Southern College	M
Florida State University	M,D
Fontbonne University	M
Fordham University	M
Fort Hays State University	M
Framingham State University	M
Franciscan University of Steubenville	M
Francis Marion University	M
Franklin Pierce University	M,D,O

Franklin University	M
Freed-Hardeman University	M
Fresno Pacific University	M
Frostburg State University	M
Full Sail University	M
Gannon University	M
Gardner-Webb University	M
Geneva College	M
George Fox University	M,D
George Mason University	M
Georgetown University	M
The George Washington University	M,D,O
Georgia Christian University	M
Georgia College & State University	M
Georgia Institute of Technology	M,D
Georgian Court University	M,O
Georgia Southern University	M
Georgia Southwestern State University	M
Georgia State University	M,D
Goddard College	M
Golden Gate University	M,D,O
Goldey-Beacom College	M
Gonzaga University	M
Goucher College	M
Governors State University	M
The Graduate Center, City University of New York	D
Grand Canyon University	M,D
Grand Valley State University	M
Granite State College	M
Grantham University	M,O
Green Mountain College	M
Gwynedd Mercy University	M
Hallmark University	M
Hamline University	M,D
Hampton University	M,D
Harding University	M
Hardin-Simmons University	M
Harvard University	M,D,O
Hawai`i Pacific University	M
HEC Montreal	M,D,O
Heidelberg University	M
Henderson State University	M
Herzing University Online	M
High Point University	M
Hodges University	M
Hofstra University	M,O
Holy Family University	M
Holy Names University	M
Hood College	M
Houston Baptist University	M
Howard Payne University	M
Howard University	M
Hult International Business School (United States)	M
Humboldt State University	M
Husson University	M
Idaho State University	M,O
IGlobal University	M
Illinois Institute of Technology	M,D
Illinois State University	M
IMCA–International Management Centres Association	M
Independence University	M
Indiana State University	M
Indiana Tech	M
Indiana University Bloomington	M,D
Indiana University Kokomo	M,O
Indiana University Northwest	M,O
Indiana University of Pennsylvania	M
Indiana University–Purdue University Fort Wayne	M
Indiana University–Purdue University Indianapolis	M
Indiana University South Bend	M,O
Indiana University Southeast	M
Indiana Wesleyan University	M,O
Instituto Centroamericano de Administración de Empresas	M
Instituto Tecnologico de Santo Domingo	M,O
Instituto Tecnológico y de Estudios Superiores de Monterrey, Campus Central de Veracruz	M
Instituto Tecnológico y de Estudios Superiores de Monterrey, Campus Ciudad de México	M,D
Instituto Tecnológico y de Estudios Superiores de Monterrey, Campus Ciudad Juárez	M
Instituto Tecnológico y de Estudios Superiores de Monterrey, Campus Ciudad Obregón	M
Instituto Tecnológico y de Estudios Superiores de Monterrey, Campus Cuernavaca	M
Instituto Tecnológico y de Estudios Superiores de Monterrey, Campus Estado de México	M,D
Instituto Tecnológico y de Estudios Superiores de Monterrey, Campus Guadalajara	M
Instituto Tecnológico y de Estudios Superiores de Monterrey, Campus Irapuato	M,D
Instituto Tecnológico y de Estudios Superiores de Monterrey, Campus Laguna	M
Instituto Tecnológico y de Estudios Superiores de Monterrey, Campus León	M
Instituto Tecnológico y de Estudios Superiores de Monterrey, Campus Monterrey	M,D
Instituto Tecnológico y de Estudios Superiores de Monterrey, Campus Querétaro	M
Instituto Tecnológico y de Estudios Superiores de Monterrey, Campus Sonora Norte	M

Instituto Tecnológico y de Estudios Superiores de Monterrey, Campus Toluca	M
Inter American University of Puerto Rico, Aguadilla Campus	M
Inter American University of Puerto Rico, Arecibo Campus	M
Inter American University of Puerto Rico, Barranquitas Campus	M
Inter American University of Puerto Rico, Fajardo Campus	M
Inter American University of Puerto Rico, Guayama Campus	M
Inter American University of Puerto Rico, Metropolitan Campus	M
Inter American University of Puerto Rico, San Germán Campus	M,D
International College of the Cayman Islands	M
International Technological University	M,D
International University in Geneva	M,D
The International University of Monaco	M
Iona College	M,O
Iowa State University of Science and Technology	M
Ithaca College	M
Jackson State University	M,D
Jacksonville State University	M
Jacksonville University	M,D
James Madison University	M
John Brown University	M
John Carroll University	M
John F. Kennedy University	M,O
Johns Hopkins University	M,O
Johnson & Wales University	M
Judson University	M
Kansas State University	M,O
Kansas Wesleyan University	M
Kaplan University, Davenport Campus	M
Kean University	M
Keiser University	M,D
Kennesaw State University	M,D
Kent State University	M
Kent State University at Stark	M
Kentucky State University	M
Kettering University	M
Keuka College	M
King University	M
Kutztown University of Pennsylvania	M
Lake Erie College	M
Lake Forest Graduate School of Management	M
Lakeland University	M
Lamar University	M
La Salle University	M,O
Lasell College	M
La Sierra University	M,O
Laurentian University	M
Lawrence Technological University	M,O
Lebanese American University	M
Lebanon Valley College	M
Lee University	M
Lehigh University	M
Le Moyne College	M
Lenoir-Rhyne University	M
LeTourneau University	M
Lewis University	M
Liberty University	M,D,O
LIM College	M
Limestone College	M
Lincoln Memorial University	M
Lincoln University (CA)	M,D
Lincoln University (MO)	M
Lindenwood University	M,O
Lindenwood University– Belleville	M
Lipscomb University	M,O
Long Island University– Hudson	M,O
Long Island University–LIU Brooklyn	M,O
Long Island University–LIU Post	M
Longwood University	M
Louisiana State University and Agricultural & Mechanical College	M,D
Louisiana State University in Shreveport	M
Louisiana Tech University	M,D
Lourdes University	M
Loyola Marymount University	M
Loyola University Chicago	M,O
Loyola University Maryland	M
Loyola University New Orleans	M
Lynchburg College	M
Lynn University	M
Maastricht School of Management	M,D
Madonna University	M
Maharishi University of Management	M,D
Malone University	M
Manhattan College	M
Marconi International University	M
Marian University (WI)	M
Marist College	M
Marlboro College	M,O
Marquette University	M
Marshall University	M
Maryland Institute College of Art	M
Marylhurst University	M
Marymount California University	M
Marymount University	M,O
Maryville University of Saint Louis	M,O
Marywood University	M
Massachusetts College of Liberal Arts	M,O

M—masters degree; D—doctorate; O—other advanced degree; *—Close-Up and/or Display

Institution	Degree
Massachusetts Institute of Technology	M,D
McGill University	M,D,O
McKendree University	M
McMaster University	M,D
McNeese State University	M
Medaille College	M
Melbourne Business School	M,D,O
Memorial University of Newfoundland	M
Mercer University	M
Mercer University	M
Mercy College	M
Meredith College	M
Merrimack College	M
Messiah College	M
Methodist University	M
Metropolitan College of New York	M
Metropolitan State University	M,D,O
Miami University	M
Michigan State University	M,D
Michigan Technological University	M
Mid-America Christian University	M
MidAmerica Nazarene University	M
Middlebury Institute of International Studies at Monterey	M
Middle Tennessee State University	M
Midway University	M
Midwestern State University	M
Millennia Atlantic University	M
Milligan College	M,O
Millikin University	M
Millsaps College	M
Mills College	M
Milwaukee School of Engineering	M
Minnesota State University Mankato	M
Minnesota State University Moorhead	M
Minot State University	M
Misericordia University	M
Mississippi College	M,O
Mississippi State University	M,D
Missouri Baptist University	M,O
Missouri Southern State University	M
Missouri State University	M
Missouri University of Science and Technology	M
Missouri Western State University	M
Molloy College	M,O
Monmouth University	M,O
Monroe College	M
Montclair State University	M,O
Moravian College	M
Morehead State University	M
Morgan State University	D
Mount Aloysius College	M
Mount Ida College	M
Mount Marty College	M
Mount Mary University	M
Mount Mercy University	M
Mount St. Joseph University	M
Mount Saint Mary College	M
Mount Saint Mary's University (CA)	M,D,O
Mount St. Mary's University (MD)	M
Mount Vernon Nazarene University	M
Murray State University	M
National American University	M
National Louis University	M
National University	M
National University College	M
Naval Postgraduate School	M
Nazareth College of Rochester	M
Neumann University	M
New Charter University	M
New England College	M
New Jersey City University	M,O
New Jersey Institute of Technology	M,D,O
Newman University	M
New Mexico Highlands University	M
New Mexico State University	M,D
New York Institute of Technology	M
New York Medical College	M,D,O
New York University	M,D,O
Niagara University	M
Nicholls State University	M
Nichols College	M
North Carolina Agricultural and Technical State University	M
North Carolina Central University	M
North Carolina State University	M
North Central College	M
Northcentral University	M,D,O
North Dakota State University	M
Northeastern Illinois University	M
Northeastern State University	M
Northeastern University	M,D,O
Northern Arizona University	M
Northern Illinois University	M
Northern Kentucky University	M,O
Northern Michigan University	M
North Park University	M
Northwest Christian University	M
Northwestern Polytechnic University	M,D
Northwestern University	M,D
Northwest Missouri State University	M
Northwest Nazarene University	M
Northwest University	M
Northwood University, Michigan Campus	M
Norwich University	M
Notre Dame de Namur University	M
Notre Dame of Maryland University	M
Nova Southeastern University	M
Nyack College	M
Oakland City University	M
Oakland University	M,O
Oglala Lakota College	M
Ohio Christian University	M
Ohio Dominican University	M
The Ohio State University	M,D
Ohio University	M
Oklahoma Baptist University	M
Oklahoma Christian University	M
Oklahoma City University	M
Oklahoma State University	M,D
Old Dominion University	M,D
Olivet Nazarene University	M
Open University	M
Oral Roberts University	M
Oregon State University	M,D
Ottawa University	M
Otterbein University	M
Our Lady of the Lake University	M
Pace University	M,D,O
Pacific Lutheran University	M
Pacific States University	M,D
Pacific University	M
Palm Beach Atlantic University	M
Park University	M,O
Penn State Erie, The Behrend College	M
Penn State Great Valley	M,O
Penn State Harrisburg	M,O
Penn State University Park	M,D
Pensacola Christian College	M,D,O
Pepperdine University	M
Pfeiffer University	M
Philadelphia University	M
Phillips Theological Seminary	M,D
Piedmont College	M
Pittsburg State University	M
Plymouth State University	M
Point Loma Nazarene University	M
Point Park University	M
Polytechnic University of Puerto Rico	M
Polytechnic University of Puerto Rico, Miami Campus	M
Polytechnic University of Puerto Rico, Orlando Campus	M
Pontifical Catholic University of Puerto Rico	M,D,O
Pontificia Universidad Catolica Madre y Maestra	M
Portland State University	M,D,O
Post University	M
Prairie View A&M University	M
Presidio Graduate School (CA)	M,O
Providence College	M
Purdue University	M,D
Purdue University Northwest	M
Queen's University at Kingston	M
Queens University of Charlotte	M
Quincy University	M
Quinnipiac University	M
Radford University	M
Ramapo College of New Jersey	M
Regent's University London	M
Regent University	M,D,O
Reinhardt University	M
Rensselaer at Hartford	M
Rensselaer Polytechnic Institute	M,D
Rice University	M
Rider University	M
Rivier University	M
Robert Morris University	M
Robert Morris University Illinois	M
Roberts Wesleyan College	M
Rochester Institute of Technology	M
Rockford University	M
Rockhurst University	M,O
Rogers State University	M
Rollins College	M,D
Roosevelt University	M
Roseman University of Health Sciences	M,O
Rosemont College	M
Rowan University	M,O
Royal Military College of Canada	M
Royal Roads University	M,O
Rutgers University–Camden	M
Rutgers University–Newark	M,D
Ryerson University	M
Sage Graduate School	M
Saginaw Valley State University	M
St. Ambrose University	M,D
St. Bonaventure University	M
St. Catherine University	M
St. Cloud State University	M
St. Edward's University	M,O
Saint Francis University	M
St. John Fisher College	M
St. John's University (NY)	M
St. Joseph's College, Long Island Campus	M
St. Joseph's College, New York	M
Saint Joseph's College of Maine	M
Saint Joseph's University	M,O
Saint Leo University	M,D,O
Saint Louis University	M
Saint Martin's University	M
Saint Mary's College of California	M
Saint Mary's University (Canada)	M,D
St. Mary's University (United States)	M
Saint Mary's University of Minnesota	M,D
St. Norbert College	M
Saint Peter's University	M
St. Thomas Aquinas College	M
St. Thomas University	M,O
Saint Vincent College	M
Saint Xavier University	M,O
Salem International University	M
Salem State University	M
Salisbury University	M
Salve Regina University	M,O
Samford University	M
Sam Houston State University	M
San Diego State University	M
San Francisco State University	M
Santa Clara University	M
Savannah State University	M
Schiller International University (United States)	M
Schiller International University (Germany)	M
Schiller International University (Spain)	M
Schreiner University	M
Seattle Pacific University	M
Seattle University	M,O
Seton Hall University	M,O
Seton Hill University	M,O
Shenandoah University	M,O
Shippensburg University of Pennsylvania	M,O
Shorter University	M
Siena College	M
Silicon Valley University	M
Silver Lake College of the Holy Family	M
Simmons College	M
Simon Fraser University	M,D,O
SIT Graduate Institute	M
Slippery Rock University of Pennsylvania	M
Sonoma State University	M
South Carolina State University	M
Southeastern Louisiana University	M
Southeastern Oklahoma State University	M
Southeastern University (FL)	M
Southeast Missouri State University	M
Southern Adventist University	M
Southern Arkansas University–Magnolia	M
Southern Connecticut State University	M
Southern Illinois University Carbondale	M,D
Southern Illinois University Edwardsville	M
Southern Methodist University	M
Southern Nazarene University	M
Southern New Hampshire University	M,O
Southern Oregon University	M,O
Southern University and Agricultural and Mechanical College	M
Southern Utah University	M
Southern Wesleyan University	M
South University	M
South University	M
South University (TX)	M
South University (MI)	M
South University (OH)	M
South University (NC)	M
South University (SC)	M
South University (GA)	M
South University (AL)	M
South University	M
Southwest Baptist University	M
Southwestern Adventist University	M
Southwestern College (KS)	M
Southwestern College (KS)	M
Southwestern Oklahoma State University	M
Southwest Minnesota State University	M
Southwest University	M
Spring Arbor University	M
Springfield College	M
Spring Hill College	M
Stanford University	M,D
State University of New York at New Paltz	M
State University of New York at Oswego	M
State University of New York College at Geneseo	M
State University of New York College at Old Westbury	M
State University of New York Empire State College	M
State University of New York Polytechnic Institute	M
Stephen F. Austin State University	M
Stetson University	M
Stevens Institute of Technology	M,O
Stockton University	M
Stony Brook University, State University of New York	M,O
Stratford University (VA)	M
Strayer University	M
Suffolk University	M
Sullivan University	M,D
Sul Ross State University	M
Syracuse University	M,D
Tabor College	M
Tarleton State University	M
Taylor University	M
Temple University	M,D
Tennessee State University	M
Tennessee Technological University	M
Tennessee Wesleyan University	M
Texas A&M International University	M,D
Texas A&M University	M
Texas A&M University–Central Texas	M,O
Texas A&M University–Commerce	M
Texas A&M University–Corpus Christi	M
Texas A&M University–Kingsville	M
Texas A&M University–San Antonio	M
Texas A&M University–Texarkana	M
Texas Christian University	M
Texas Health and Science University	M,D
Texas Southern University	M
Texas State University	M
Texas Tech University	M,D
Texas Wesleyan University	M
Texas Woman's University	M
Thomas College	M
Thomas Edison State University	M
Thomas More College	M
Thomas University	M
Thompson Rivers University	M
Tiffin University	M
Trevecca Nazarene University	M
Trident University International	M,D
Trinity International University	M,D,O
Trinity University	M
Trinity Washington University	M
Trinity Western University	M
Troy University	M
Tulane University	M,D
Tusculum College	M
Union University	M
United States International University–Africa	M
Universidad Autonoma de Guadalajara	M,D
Universidad de las Americas, A.C.	M
Universidad de las Américas Puebla	M
Universidad del Este	M
Universidad del Turabo	M,D
Universidad Iberoamericana	M,D
Universidad Metropolitana	M
Université de Moncton	M
Université de Sherbrooke	M,D,O
Université du Québec à Chicoutimi	M
Université du Québec à Montréal	M,D,O
Université du Québec à Rimouski	M,O
Université du Québec à Trois-Rivières	M,D
Université du Québec en Abitibi-Témiscamingue	M
Université Laval	M,D,O
University at Albany, State University of New York	M
University at Buffalo, the State University of New York	M,D
The University of Akron	M
The University of Alabama	M,D
The University of Alabama at Birmingham	M
The University of Alabama in Huntsville	M,O
University of Alaska Anchorage	M
University of Alaska Fairbanks	M
University of Alberta	M,D
University of Antelope Valley	M
The University of Arizona	M,D,O
University of Arkansas	M,D
University of Arkansas at Little Rock	M,O
University of Baltimore	M,O
University of Bridgeport	M
The University of British Columbia	M,D
University of Calgary	M,D
University of California, Berkeley	M,D,O
University of California, Davis	M
University of California, Irvine	M,D
University of California, Los Angeles	M,D
University of California, Riverside	M,D
University of California, San Diego	M,D
University of Central Arkansas	M
University of Central Florida	M,D,O
University of Central Missouri	M,D,O
University of Charleston	M
University of Chicago	M,D,O
University of Cincinnati	M,D
University of Colorado Boulder	M
University of Colorado Colorado Springs	M
University of Colorado Denver	M
University of Connecticut	M,D
University of Dallas	M,D
University of Dayton	M
University of Delaware	M,D
University of Denver	M
University of Detroit Mercy	M,O
University of Dubuque	M
The University of Findlay	M,D
University of Florida	M,D
University of Georgia	M
University of Guam	M
University of Guelph	M,D
University of Hartford	M
University of Hawaii at Manoa	M
University of Houston	M,D
University of Houston–Clear Lake	M
University of Houston–Downtown	M
University of Houston–Victoria	M
University of Idaho	M,D
University of Illinois at Chicago	M,D
University of Illinois at Springfield	M
University of Illinois at Urbana–Champaign	M,D
University of Indianapolis	M,O
The University of Iowa	M,D
The University of Kansas	M
University of Kentucky	M,D
University of La Verne	M,D,O
University of Lethbridge	M,D
University of Louisiana at Lafayette	M
University of Louisiana at Monroe	M

Institution	Degree
University of Louisville	M
University of Maine	M,O
University of Management and Technology	M,D,O
The University of Manchester	M
University of Manitoba	M,D
University of Mary	M
University of Mary Hardin-Baylor	M
University of Maryland, College Park	M,D
University of Maryland University College	M,D,O
University of Mary Washington	M
University of Massachusetts Amherst	M,D
University of Massachusetts Boston	M
University of Massachusetts Dartmouth	M,O
University of Massachusetts Lowell	M,D
University of Memphis	M,D
University of Miami	M,D
University of Michigan	M,D
University of Michigan–Dearborn	M
University of Michigan–Flint	M,O
University of Minnesota, Duluth	M
University of Minnesota Rochester	M,D
University of Minnesota, Twin Cities Campus	M,D
University of Mississippi	M,D
University of Missouri	M,D
University of Missouri–Kansas City	M,D
University of Missouri–St. Louis	M,D,O
University of Mobile	M
University of Montana	M
University of Montevallo	M
University of Mount Olive	M
University of Nebraska at Kearney	M
University of Nebraska at Omaha	M,O
University of Nebraska–Lincoln	M,D
University of Nevada, Las Vegas	M,O
University of Nevada, Reno	M
University of New Brunswick Fredericton	M
University of New Brunswick Saint John	M
University of New Hampshire	M,O
University of New Haven	M,O
University of New Mexico	M
University of New Orleans	M
University of North Alabama	M
The University of North Carolina at Chapel Hill	M,D
The University of North Carolina at Charlotte	M,D,O
The University of North Carolina at Greensboro	M,O
The University of North Carolina at Pembroke	M
The University of North Carolina Wilmington	M
University of North Dakota	M
University of Northern Colorado	M
University of Northern Iowa	M
University of North Florida	M
University of North Georgia	M
University of North Texas	M,D,O
University of North Texas at Dallas	M
University of Northwestern–St. Paul	M
University of Notre Dame	M
University of Oklahoma	M,D
University of Oregon	M,D
University of Ottawa	M
University of Pennsylvania	M,D
University of Phoenix–Atlanta Campus	M
University of Phoenix–Augusta Campus	M
University of Phoenix–Bay Area Campus	M,D
University of Phoenix–Central Valley Campus	M
University of Phoenix–Charlotte Campus	M
University of Phoenix–Colorado Campus	M
University of Phoenix–Colorado Springs Downtown Campus	M
University of Phoenix–Columbus Georgia Campus	M
University of Phoenix–Dallas Campus	M
University of Phoenix–Hawaii Campus	M
University of Phoenix–Houston Campus	M
University of Phoenix–Jersey City Campus	M
University of Phoenix–Las Vegas Campus	M
University of Phoenix–New Mexico Campus	M
University of Phoenix–North Florida Campus	M
University of Phoenix–Online Campus	M,D,O
University of Phoenix–Phoenix Campus	M,O
University of Phoenix–Sacramento Valley Campus	M
University of Phoenix–San Antonio Campus	M
University of Phoenix–San Diego Campus	M
University of Phoenix–Southern Arizona Campus	M
University of Phoenix–Southern California Campus	M
University of Phoenix–South Florida Campus	M
University of Phoenix–Utah Campus	M
University of Phoenix–Washington D.C. Campus	M,D
University of Phoenix–Western Washington Campus	M
University of Pikeville	M
University of Pittsburgh	M,D
University of Portland	M
University of Puerto Rico, Mayagüez Campus	M
University of Puerto Rico, Río Piedras Campus	M,D
University of Redlands	M
University of Regina	M,O
University of Rhode Island	M,D
University of Richmond	M
University of Rochester	M,D
University of St. Francis (IL)	M,O
University of Saint Francis (IN)	M
University of Saint Joseph	M
University of Saint Mary	M
University of St. Thomas (TX)	M
University of St. Thomas (MN)	M
University of San Diego	M
University of San Francisco	M
University of Saskatchewan	M
The University of Scranton	M
University of Sioux Falls	M
University of South Africa	M,D
University of South Alabama	M,D
University of South Carolina	M,D
University of South Carolina Aiken	M
The University of South Dakota	M
University of Southern California	M,D
University of Southern Indiana	M
University of Southern Maine	M,O
University of Southern Mississippi	M,D
University of South Florida	M,D
University of South Florida, St. Petersburg	M
University of South Florida Sarasota-Manatee	M
The University of Tampa	M
The University of Tennessee	M,D
The University of Tennessee at Chattanooga	M
The University of Tennessee at Martin	M
The University of Texas at Austin	M,D
The University of Texas at Dallas	M,D
The University of Texas at El Paso	M,D,O
The University of Texas at San Antonio	M,D,O
The University of Texas at Tyler	M
The University of Texas of the Permian Basin	M
The University of Texas Rio Grande Valley	M,D
University of the Cumberlands	M
University of the District of Columbia	M
University of the Pacific	M
University of the Potomac	M
University of the Sacred Heart	M
University of the Southwest	M
University of the Virgin Islands	M
University of the West	M
The University of Toledo	M
University of Toronto	M,D
The University of Tulsa	M
University of Utah	M,D,O
University of Vermont	M
University of Victoria	M
University of Virginia	M,D,O
University of Washington	M,D
University of Washington, Bothell	M
University of Washington, Tacoma	M
University of Waterloo	M
The University of West Alabama	M
The University of Western Ontario	M,D
University of West Florida	M
University of West Georgia	M
University of Windsor	M
University of Wisconsin–Eau Claire	M
University of Wisconsin–Green Bay	M
University of Wisconsin–La Crosse	M
University of Wisconsin–Madison	M
University of Wisconsin–Milwaukee	M,O
University of Wisconsin–Oshkosh	M
University of Wisconsin–Parkside	M
University of Wisconsin–River Falls	M
University of Wisconsin–Stevens Point	M
University of Wisconsin–Whitewater	M
University of Wyoming	M
Upper Iowa University	M
Urbana University	M
Ursuline College	M
Utah State University	M
Utah Valley University	M
Valdosta State University	M
Valparaiso University	M,O
Vancouver Island University	M
Vanderbilt University	M
Villanova University	M

Institution	Degree
Virginia College in Birmingham	M
Virginia Commonwealth University	M,D
Virginia International University	M,O
Virginia Polytechnic Institute and State University	M,D
Viterbo University	M
Wagner College	M
Wake Forest University	M
Walden University	M,D,O
Walsh College of Accountancy and Business Administration	M
Walsh University	M
Warner University	M
Washburn University	M
Washington Adventist University	M
Washington State University	M,D
Washington University in St. Louis	M,D
Wayland Baptist University	M,D
Waynesburg University	M,D
Wayne State College	M
Wayne State University	M,D,O
Webber International University	M
Weber State University	M
Webster University	M,D,O
Wesleyan College	M
Wesley College	M
West Chester University of Pennsylvania	M,O
Western Carolina University	M
Western Connecticut State University	M
Western Governors University	M
Western Illinois University	M,O
Western Kentucky University	M
Western Michigan University	M
Western New England University	M
Western New Mexico University	M
Western Washington University	M
Westminster College (UT)	M,O
West Texas A&M University	M
West Virginia University	M
West Virginia Wesleyan College	M
Wheeling Jesuit University	M
Whitworth University	M
WHU - Otto Beisheim School of Management	M
Wichita State University	M
Widener University	M
Wilfrid Laurier University	M,D
Wilkes University	M
Willamette University	M
William Carey University	M
William Paterson University of New Jersey	M
William Woods University	M,D,O
Wilmington University	M,D
Wilson College	M
Wingate University	M
Winston-Salem State University	M
Winthrop University	M
Woodbury University	M
Worcester Polytechnic Institute	M,D,O
Worcester State University	M
Wright State University	M
Xavier University	M
Yale University	M,D
Yeshiva University	M
York College of Pennsylvania	M
York University	M,D
Youngstown State University	M,O

BUSINESS EDUCATION

Institution	Degree
Alabama Agricultural and Mechanical University	M,O
Arkansas State University	O
Ball State University	M,O
Bloomsburg University of Pennsylvania	M
Bowling Green State University	M
Buffalo State College, State University of New York	M
Canisius College	M,O
Capella University	D
Chadron State College	M,O
Clemson University	M,D
Colorado Christian University	M
East Carolina University	M
Eastern Kentucky University	M
Emporia State University	M
Florida Agricultural and Mechanical University	M
Hofstra University	M,D,O
Indiana University of Pennsylvania	M
Inter American University of Puerto Rico, Metropolitan Campus	M
Inter American University of Puerto Rico, San Germán Campus	M
International College of the Cayman Islands	M
Johnson & Wales University	M
Lehman College of the City University of New York	M
Lock Haven University of Pennsylvania	M
Louisiana State University and Agricultural & Mechanical College	M,D
Manhattanville College	M
Maryville University of Saint Louis	M,O
Middle Tennessee State University	M
Milwaukee School of Engineering	M
Mississippi College	M,D,O
Morehead State University	M,O
New York University	M,O
North Carolina Agricultural and Technical State University	M
North Carolina State University	M
Nova Southeastern University	M
Old Dominion University	M
Pace University	M,O
Pepperdine University	M

Institution	Degree
Pontifical Catholic University of Puerto Rico	M,D
Regis University	M,O
Rider University	O
Robert Morris University	M,D,O
Salve Regina University	M,O
South Carolina State University	M
Southern New Hampshire University	M,D,O
Spalding University	M
State University of New York at Oswego	M
Temple University	M
Thomas College	M
University of Delaware	M,D
University of Georgia	M,D,O
University of Missouri	M,D,O
The University of North Carolina at Charlotte	D
University of St. Francis (IL)	M,O
University of South Carolina	M,D
University of the Cumberlands	M,D,O
The University of Toledo	M,D,O
University of Washington	M,D
University of West Georgia	M,D,O
University of Wisconsin–Whitewater	M
Utah State University	M,D
Washington State University	M,D
Wayne State College	M
West Chester University of Pennsylvania	M,O

CANADIAN STUDIES

Institution	Degree
Carleton University	M,D
Queen's University at Kingston	M,D
Saint Mary's University (Canada)	M,O
Trent University	M,D
Université de Saint-Boniface	M
Université de Sherbrooke	M,D
Université du Québec à Chicoutimi	M
University at Buffalo, the State University of New York	M,D,O
University of Lethbridge	M,D
University of Manitoba	M
University of Ottawa	D
University of Regina	M,D
University of Saskatchewan	M,D
Wilfrid Laurier University	M,D

CANCER BIOLOGY/ONCOLOGY

Institution	Degree
Augusta University	D
Baylor College of Medicine	D
Case Western Reserve University	D
Colorado State University	M,D
Duke University	D
Emory University	D
Gerstner Sloan Kettering Graduate School of Biomedical Sciences	D
Grand Valley State University	M
Irell & Manella Graduate School of Biological Sciences	D*
Mayo Clinic Graduate School of Biomedical Sciences	D
McMaster University	M,D
Medical University of South Carolina	D
Meharry Medical College	D
Memorial University of Newfoundland	M,D
New York University	D
Oregon Health & Science University	D
Purdue University	D
Queen's University at Kingston	M,D
Rutgers University–Newark	D,O
Rutgers University–New Brunswick	M,D
Thomas Jefferson University	D
Tufts University	D
Université Laval	O
University at Buffalo, the State University of New York	M
The University of Alabama at Birmingham	D
University of Alberta	M,D
The University of Arizona	D
University of Calgary	M,D
University of Chicago	D
University of Cincinnati	D
University of Colorado Denver	D
University of Delaware	M,D
The University of Kansas	M,D
The University of Manchester	M,D
University of Manitoba	D
University of Maryland, Baltimore	D
University of Massachusetts Medical School	M,D
University of Miami	D
University of Michigan	M,D
University of Minnesota, Twin Cities Campus	D
University of Nebraska Medical Center	D
University of North Texas Health Science Center at Fort Worth	M,D
University of Pennsylvania	D
University of Regina	M,D
University of Southern California	D
University of South Florida	M,D
The University of Texas Health Science Center at Houston	M,D
The University of Texas Southwestern Medical Center	D
University of the District of Columbia	M,D
The University of Toledo	M,D
University of Utah	M,D

*M—masters degree; D—doctorate; O—other advanced degree; *—Close-Up and/or Display*

University of Wisconsin–La Crosse — M
University of Wisconsin–Madison — D
Vanderbilt University — M,D
Wake Forest University — D
Wayne State University — M,D,O
West Virginia University — M,D
Yale University — D

CARDIOVASCULAR SCIENCES

Albany Medical College — M,D
Augusta University — D
Baylor College of Medicine — D
Johns Hopkins University — M,D
Marquette University — M
McMaster University — M,D
Medical University of South Carolina — D
Memorial University of Newfoundland — M,D
Midwestern University, Glendale Campus — M
Milwaukee School of Engineering — M
Queen's University at Kingston — M,D
Quinnipiac University — M
Université Laval — O
University of Calgary — M,D
University of Guelph — M,D,O
University of Mary — M
The University of South Dakota — M,D
University of South Florida — O
The University of Toledo — M,D

CELL BIOLOGY

Albany College of Pharmacy and Health Sciences — M
Albany Medical College — M,D
Albert Einstein College of Medicine — D
American University of Beirut — M
Appalachian State University — M
Arizona State University at the Tempe campus — M,D
Auburn University — M,D
Augusta University — D
Baylor College of Medicine — D
Boston University — M,D
Brandeis University — M,D
Brown University — M,D
California Institute of Technology — D
California State University, Sacramento — M
Carnegie Mellon University — M,D
Case Western Reserve University — D
The Catholic University of America — M,D
Colorado State University — M,D
Columbia University — M,D
Cornell University — D
Dartmouth College — M,D
Drexel University — M,D
Duke University — D,O
East Carolina University — D
Eastern Michigan University — M
Eastern New Mexico University — M
Emory University — D
Emporia State University — M
Florida Institute of Technology — M,D
Florida State University — M,D
Georgia State University — M,D
Grand Valley State University — M
Harvard University — D
Illinois Institute of Technology — M,D
Illinois State University — M,D
Indiana State University — M,D
Indiana University Bloomington — M,D
Indiana University–Purdue University Indianapolis — M,D
Iowa State University of Science and Technology — M,D
Irell & Manella Graduate School of Biological Sciences — D*
Johns Hopkins University — D
Kent State University — M,D
Lehigh University — M,D
Louisiana State University Health Sciences Center — D
Louisiana State University Health Sciences Center at Shreveport — M,D
Loyola University Chicago — M,D
Marquette University — M,D
Massachusetts Institute of Technology — D
Mayo Clinic Graduate School of Biomedical Sciences — D
McGill University — M,D
McMaster University — M,D
Medical University of South Carolina — D
Michigan State University — M,D
Missouri State University — M
New York Medical College — M,D
New York University — D
North Carolina State University — M,D
North Dakota State University — M,D
Northwestern University — D
The Ohio State University — M,D
Ohio University — M,D
Oregon Health & Science University — D
Oregon State University — M,D
Penn State Hershey Medical Center — D
Penn State University Park — M,D
Purdue University — D
Queen's University at Kingston — M,D
Quinnipiac University — M
Rice University — M,D
Rosalind Franklin University of Medicine and Science — D
Rush University — M,D
Rutgers University–Newark — D
Rutgers University–New Brunswick — M,D
San Diego State University — M,D

San Francisco State University — M
Sonoma State University — M
Southern Methodist University — M,D
State University of New York Downstate Medical Center — D
State University of New York Upstate Medical University — M,D
Stony Brook University, State University of New York — M,D
Texas Tech University Health Sciences Center — M,D
Thomas Jefferson University — M,D
Tufts University — D
Tulane University — M,D
Uniformed Services University of the Health Sciences — M,D
Universidad Central del Caribe — M,D
Université de Montréal — M,D
Université de Sherbrooke — M,D
Université Laval — M,D
University at Buffalo, the State University of New York — D
The University of Alabama at Birmingham — D
University of Alberta — M,D
The University of Arizona — D
University of Arkansas — M,D
The University of British Columbia — M,D
University of California, Berkeley — D
University of California, Davis — M,D
University of California, Irvine — M,D
University of California, Los Angeles — M,D
University of California, Riverside — M,D
University of California, San Francisco — D
University of California, Santa Barbara — M,D
University of California, Santa Cruz — M,D
University of Chicago — D
University of Cincinnati — D
University of Colorado Boulder — M,D
University of Colorado Denver — M,D
University of Connecticut — M,D
University of Connecticut Health Center — D
University of Delaware — M,D
University of Denver — M,D
University of Florida — M,D
University of Georgia — M,D
University of Guelph — M,D
University of Illinois at Chicago — M,D
University of Illinois at Urbana–Champaign — D
The University of Iowa — M,D
The University of Kansas — M,D
The University of Manchester — M,D
University of Maryland, Baltimore — M,D
University of Maryland, Baltimore County — D
University of Maryland, College Park — M,D
University of Massachusetts Amherst — M,D
University of Massachusetts Medical School — M,D
University of Miami — D
University of Michigan — M,D
University of Minnesota, Twin Cities Campus — M,D
University of Missouri–Kansas City — D
University of Montana — D
University of Nebraska Medical Center — M,D
University of Nevada, Reno — M,D
University of New Haven — M,O
University of New Mexico — M,D
The University of North Carolina at Chapel Hill — M,D
University of Notre Dame — M,D
University of Oklahoma Health Sciences Center — M,D
University of Ottawa — M,D
University of Pennsylvania — D
University of Pittsburgh — D
University of Puerto Rico, Río Piedras Campus — M,D
University of Rhode Island — M,D
University of Saskatchewan — M,D
University of South Carolina — M,D
The University of South Dakota — M,D
University of Southern California — M,D
University of South Florida — M,D
The University of Texas at Austin — D
The University of Texas at Dallas — M,D
The University of Texas at San Antonio — M,D
The University of Texas Health Science Center at Houston — M,D
The University of Texas Health Science Center at San Antonio — M,D
The University of Texas Medical Branch — M,D
The University of Texas Southwestern Medical Center — D
University of the Sciences — M
University of Toronto — M,D
University of Vermont — D
University of Virginia — D
University of Washington — D
The University of Western Ontario — M,D
University of Wisconsin–La Crosse — M
University of Wisconsin–Madison — D
University of Wisconsin–Milwaukee — M,D
University of Wyoming — D
Vanderbilt University — M,D
Washington University in St. Louis — M,D,O
Wayne State University — M,D,O
Weill Cornell Medicine — M,D
Wesleyan University — D

West Virginia University — M,D
Yale University — D

CELTIC LANGUAGES

Harvard University — D

CERAMIC SCIENCES AND ENGINEERING

Alfred University — M,D
Missouri University of Science and Technology — M,D

CHEMICAL ENGINEERING

American University of Sharjah — M
Arizona State University at the Tempe campus — M,D
Auburn University — M,D
Brigham Young University — M,D
Brown University — M,D
Bucknell University — M
California Institute of Technology — M,D
Carnegie Mellon University — M,D
Case Western Reserve University — M,D
City College of the City University of New York — M,D
Clarkson University — M,D
Clemson University — M,D
Cleveland State University — M,D
Colorado School of Mines — M,D
Colorado State University — M,D
Columbia University — M,D
Cooper Union for the Advancement of Science and Art — M
Cornell University — M,D
Dalhousie University — M,D
Drexel University — M,D
École Polytechnique de Montréal — M,D,O
Fairleigh Dickinson University, College at Florham — M,O
Florida Agricultural and Mechanical University — M,D
Florida Institute of Technology — M,D
Florida State University — M,D
Georgia Institute of Technology — M,D
The Graduate Center, City University of New York — D
Howard University — M
Illinois Institute of Technology — M,D
Instituto Tecnológico y de Estudios Superiores de Monterrey, Campus Monterrey — M,D
Iowa State University of Science and Technology — M,D
Johns Hopkins University — M,D
Kansas State University — M,D,O
Lamar University — M,D
Lehigh University — M,D
Louisiana State University and Agricultural & Mechanical College — M,D
Louisiana Tech University — M
Manhattan College — M
Massachusetts Institute of Technology — M,D
McGill University — M,D
McMaster University — M,D
McNeese State University — M
Miami University — M
Michigan State University — M,D
Michigan Technological University — M,D
Mississippi State University — M,D
Missouri University of Science and Technology — M,D
Montana State University — M,D
New Jersey Institute of Technology — M,D
New Mexico State University — M,D
New York University — M,D
North Carolina Agricultural and Technical State University — M
North Carolina State University — M,D
Northeastern University — M,D,O
Northwestern University — M,D
The Ohio State University — M,D
Ohio University — M,D
Oklahoma State University — M,D
Oregon State University — M,D
Penn State University Park — M,D
Princeton University — M,D
Purdue University — M,D
Queen's University at Kingston — M,D
Rensselaer Polytechnic Institute — M,D
Rice University — M,D
Rose-Hulman Institute of Technology — M
Rowan University — M
Royal Military College of Canada — M,D
Rutgers University–New Brunswick — M,D
South Dakota School of Mines and Technology — M,D
Stanford University — M,D
Stevens Institute of Technology — M,D,O
Syracuse University — M,D
Tennessee Technological University — M
Texas A&M University — M,D
Texas A&M University–Kingsville — M
Texas Tech University — M,D
Tufts University — M,D
Tulane University — M,D
Universidad de las Américas Puebla — M
Université de Sherbrooke — M,D
Université Laval — M,D
University at Buffalo, the State University of New York — M,D
The University of Akron — M,D
The University of Alabama — M,D
The University of Alabama in Huntsville — M,D
University of Alberta — M,D
The University of Arizona — M,D
University of Arkansas — M,D
The University of British Columbia — M,D

University of Calgary — M,D
University of California, Berkeley — M,D
University of California, Davis — M,D
University of California, Irvine — M,D
University of California, Los Angeles — M,D
University of California, Riverside — M,D
University of California, San Diego — M,D
University of California, Santa Barbara — M,D
University of Cincinnati — M,D
University of Colorado Boulder — M,D
University of Connecticut — M,D
University of Dayton — M
University of Delaware — M,D
University of Florida — M,D,O
University of Houston — M,D
University of Idaho — M,D
University of Illinois at Chicago — M,D
University of Illinois at Urbana–Champaign — M,D
The University of Iowa — M,D
The University of Kansas — M,D,O
University of Kentucky — M,D
University of Louisiana at Lafayette — M
University of Louisville — M,D
University of Maine — M,D
The University of Manchester — M,D
University of Maryland, Baltimore County — M,D
University of Maryland, College Park — M,D
University of Massachusetts Amherst — M,D
University of Massachusetts Lowell — M,D
University of Michigan — M,D,O
University of Minnesota, Twin Cities Campus — M,D
University of Missouri — M,D
University of Nebraska–Lincoln — M,D
University of Nevada, Reno — M,D
University of New Brunswick Fredericton — M,D
University of New Hampshire — M,D
University of New Mexico — M,D
University of North Dakota — M,D
University of Notre Dame — M,D
University of Oklahoma — M,D
University of Ottawa — M,D
University of Pennsylvania — M,D
University of Pittsburgh — M,D
University of Puerto Rico, Mayagüez Campus — M,D
University of Rhode Island — M,D,O
University of Rochester — M,D
University of Saskatchewan — M
University of South Africa — M
University of South Alabama — M
University of South Carolina — M,D
University of Southern California — M,D,O
University of South Florida — M,D
The University of Tennessee — M,D
The University of Tennessee at Chattanooga — M
The University of Texas at Austin — M,D
The University of Toledo — M,D
University of Toronto — M,D
The University of Tulsa — M,D
University of Utah — M,D
University of Virginia — M,D
University of Washington — M,D
University of Waterloo — M,D
The University of Western Ontario — M,D
University of Wisconsin–Madison — D
University of Wyoming — M,D
Vanderbilt University — M,D
Villanova University — M,O
Virginia Polytechnic Institute and State University — M,D
Washington State University — M,D
Washington University in St. Louis — M,D
Wayne State University — M,D,O
Western Michigan University — M
Widener University — M
Worcester Polytechnic Institute — M,D
Yale University — M,D

CHEMICAL PHYSICS

Columbia University — M,D
Cornell University — D
Harvard University — D
Kent State University — M,D
Marquette University — M,D
McMaster University — M,D
Michigan State University — M,D
The Ohio State University — M,D
Tufts University — M,D
University of Illinois at Urbana–Champaign — M,D
University of Louisville — M,D
University of Maryland, College Park — M,D
University of Minnesota, Twin Cities Campus — M,D
University of Nevada, Reno — D
The University of Tennessee — M,D
University of Utah — M,D
Virginia Commonwealth University — D
Wesleyan University — D
West Virginia University — M,D

CHEMISTRY

Acadia University — M
American University — M
The American University in Cairo — M,D,O
American University of Beirut — M,D
Arizona State University at the Tempe campus — M,D
Arkansas State University — M,O
Auburn University — M,D

Ball State University — M,D
Baylor University — M,D
Binghamton University, State University of New York — M,D
Boise State University — M
Boston College — M,D
Boston University — M,D
Bowling Green State University — M,D
Bradley University — M
Brandeis University — M,D
Brigham Young University — M,D
Brock University — M,D
Brooklyn College of the City University of New York — M,D
Brown University — D
Bryn Mawr College — M,D
Bucknell University — M
Buffalo State College, State University of New York — M
California Institute of Technology — M,D
California Polytechnic State University, San Luis Obispo — M
California State Polytechnic University, Pomona — M
California State University, East Bay — M
California State University, Fresno — M
California State University, Fullerton — M
California State University, Long Beach — M
California State University, Los Angeles — M
California State University, Northridge — M
California State University, Sacramento — M,D
Carleton University — M,D
Carnegie Mellon University — D
Case Western Reserve University — M,D
Central Michigan University — M
Central Washington University — M
City College of the City University of New York — M,D
Clark Atlanta University — M,D
Clarkson University — M,D
Clark University — D
Clemson University — M,D
Cleveland State University — M,D
The College at Brockport, State University of New York — M,O
The College of William and Mary — M
Colorado School of Mines — M,D
Colorado State University — M,D
Colorado State University–Pueblo — M
Columbia University — M,D
Columbus State University — M,O
Concordia University (Canada) — M,D
Cornell University — D
Dalhousie University — M,D
Dartmouth College — M,D
Delaware State University — M,D
DePaul University — M,D
Drew University — M,D,O
Drexel University — M,D
Duke University — D
Duquesne University — D
East Carolina University — M
Eastern Illinois University — M
Eastern Kentucky University — M
Eastern Michigan University — M
Eastern New Mexico University — M
East Tennessee State University — M
Emory University — D
Fairleigh Dickinson University, College at Florham — M
Fairleigh Dickinson University, Metropolitan Campus — M
Fisk University — M
Florida Agricultural and Mechanical University — M
Florida Atlantic University — M,D
Florida Institute of Technology — M,D
Florida International University — M,D
Florida State University — M,D
Furman University — M
George Mason University — M,D
Georgetown University — D
The George Washington University — M,D
Georgia Institute of Technology — M,D
Georgia State University — M,D
The Graduate Center, City University of New York — D
Hampton University — M
Harvard University — D
Howard University — M,D
Hunter College of the City University of New York — M,D
Idaho State University — M
Illinois Institute of Technology — M,D
Illinois State University — M
Indiana University Bloomington — M,D
Indiana University of Pennsylvania — M
Indiana University–Purdue University Indianapolis — M,D
Instituto Tecnológico y de Estudios Superiores de Monterrey, Campus Monterrey — M,D
Iowa State University of Science and Technology — M,D
Ithaca College — M
Jackson State University — M,D
Johns Hopkins University — M,D
Kansas State University — M,D
Kennesaw State University — M
Kent State University — M,D
Lakehead University — M
Lamar University — M
Laurentian University — M

Lehigh University — M,D
Long Island University–LIU Brooklyn — M,D,O
Louisiana State University and Agricultural & Mechanical College — M,D
Louisiana Tech University — M,D
Loyola University Chicago — M,D
Marquette University — M,D
Marshall University — M
Massachusetts Institute of Technology — D
McGill University — M,D
McMaster University — M,D
McNeese State University — M
MCPHS University — M,D
Memorial University of Newfoundland — M,D
Miami University — M,D
Michigan State University — M,D
Michigan Technological University — M,D
Middle Tennessee State University — M
Mississippi College — M
Mississippi State University — M,D
Missouri State University — M
Missouri University of Science and Technology — M,D
Missouri Western State University — M
Montana State University — M,D
Montclair State University — M
Morgan State University — M
Mount Allison University — M
Murray State University — M
New Jersey Institute of Technology — M,D,O
New Mexico Highlands University — M
New Mexico Institute of Mining and Technology — M,D
New Mexico State University — M,D
New York University — M,D,O
North Carolina Agricultural and Technical State University — M,D
North Carolina Central University — M
North Carolina State University — M,D
North Dakota State University — M
Northeastern Illinois University — M
Northeastern University — M,D
Northern Arizona University — M
Northwestern University — D
Oakland University — M,D
The Ohio State University — M,D
Oklahoma State University — M,D
Old Dominion University — M,D
Oregon State University — M,D
Pace University — M,O
Penn State University Park — M,D
Pittsburg State University — M
Pontifical Catholic University of Puerto Rico — M
Portland State University — M,D
Prairie View A&M University — M
Princeton University — M,D
Purdue University — M,D
Queens College of the City University of New York — M
Queen's University at Kingston — M,D
Rensselaer Polytechnic Institute — M,D
Rice University — M,D
Rochester Institute of Technology — M
Roosevelt University — M
Royal Military College of Canada — M,D
Rutgers University–Camden — M
Rutgers University–Newark — M,D
Rutgers University–New Brunswick — M,D
Sacred Heart University — M
St. Francis Xavier University — M
St. John Fisher College — M
St. John's University (NY) — M
Saint Louis University — M,D
Sam Houston State University — M
San Diego State University — M,D
San Francisco State University — M
San Jose State University — M,O
The Scripps Research Institute — D
Seton Hall University — M,D
Simon Fraser University — M,D
Smith College — M
South Dakota State University — M,D
Southeast Missouri State University — M
Southern Connecticut State University — M
Southern Illinois University Carbondale — M,D
Southern Illinois University Edwardsville — M
Southern Methodist University — M,D
Southern University and Agricultural and Mechanical College — M
Stanford University — D
State University of New York at New Paltz — M,O
State University of New York at Oswego — M
State University of New York College of Environmental Science and Forestry — M,D
Stephen F. Austin State University — M
Stevens Institute of Technology — M,D,O
Stevenson University — M
Stony Brook University, State University of New York — M,D
Syracuse University — M,D
Teachers College, Columbia University — M,D
Temple University — M,D
Tennessee State University — M
Tennessee Technological University — M,D
Texas A&M University — M,D

Texas A&M University–Commerce — M,O
Texas A&M University–Kingsville — M
Texas Christian University — M,D
Texas Southern University — M
Texas State University — M
Texas Tech University — M,D
Texas Woman's University — M
Trent University — M
Tufts University — M,D
Tulane University — M,D
Tuskegee University — M
Universidad del Turabo — M
Université de Moncton — M
Université de Montréal — M,D
Université de Sherbrooke — M,D,O
Université du Québec à Montréal — M
Université du Québec à Trois-Rivières — M
Université Laval — M,D
University at Albany, State University of New York — M,D
University at Buffalo, the State University of New York — M,D
The University of Akron — M,D
The University of Alabama — M,D
The University of Alabama at Birmingham — M,D
The University of Alabama in Huntsville — M,D
University of Alaska Fairbanks — M,D
University of Alberta — M,D
The University of Arizona — M,D
University of Arkansas — M,D
University of Arkansas at Little Rock — M
The University of British Columbia — M,D
University of Calgary — M,D
University of California, Berkeley — D
University of California, Davis — M,D
University of California, Irvine — M,D
University of California, Los Angeles — M,D
University of California, Merced — M,D
University of California, Riverside — M,D
University of California, San Diego — M,D
University of California, San Francisco — D
University of California, Santa Barbara — M,D
University of California, Santa Cruz — M,D
University of Central Florida — M,D,O
University of Chicago — D
University of Cincinnati — M,D
University of Colorado Boulder — M,D
University of Colorado Denver — M
University of Connecticut — M,D
University of Dayton — M
University of Delaware — M,D
University of Detroit Mercy — M,D
University of Florida — M,D
University of Georgia — M,D
University of Guelph — M,D
University of Hawaii at Manoa — M,D
University of Houston — M,D
University of Houston–Clear Lake — M
University of Idaho — M,D
University of Illinois at Chicago — M,D
University of Illinois at Urbana–Champaign — M,D
The University of Iowa — D
The University of Kansas — M,D
University of Kentucky — M,D
University of Lethbridge — M,D
University of Louisville — M,D
University of Maine — M,D
The University of Manchester — M,D
University of Manitoba — M,D
University of Maryland, Baltimore County — M,D,O
University of Maryland, College Park — M,D
University of Maryland Eastern Shore — M,D
University of Massachusetts Amherst — M,D
University of Massachusetts Boston — M,D
University of Massachusetts Dartmouth — M,D
University of Massachusetts Lowell — M,D
University of Memphis — M,D
University of Miami — M,D
University of Michigan — D
University of Minnesota, Duluth — M
University of Minnesota, Twin Cities Campus — M,D
University of Mississippi — M,D
University of Missouri — M,D
University of Missouri–Kansas City — M,D
University of Missouri–St. Louis — M,D
University of Montana — M,D
University of Nebraska–Lincoln — M,D
University of Nevada, Las Vegas — M,D
University of Nevada, Reno — M,D
University of New Brunswick Fredericton — M,D
University of New Hampshire — M,D
University of New Mexico — M,D
University of New Orleans — M,D
The University of North Carolina at Chapel Hill — M,D

The University of North Carolina at Charlotte — M,D
The University of North Carolina at Greensboro — M
The University of North Carolina Wilmington — M
University of North Dakota — M,D
University of Northern Colorado — M,D
University of North Texas — M,D,O
University of Notre Dame — M,D
University of Oklahoma — M,D
University of Oregon — M,D
University of Ottawa — M,D
University of Pennsylvania — M,D
University of Pittsburgh — M,D
University of Prince Edward Island — M,D
University of Puerto Rico, Mayagüez Campus — M,D
University of Puerto Rico, Río Piedras Campus — M,D
University of Regina — M,D
University of Rhode Island — M,D
University of Rochester — D
University of Saint Joseph — M
University of San Francisco — M
University of Saskatchewan — M,D
The University of Scranton — M
University of South Carolina — M,D
The University of South Dakota — M,D
University of Southern California — D
University of Southern Mississippi — M,D
University of South Florida — M,D
The University of Tennessee — M,D
The University of Texas at Arlington — M,D
The University of Texas at Austin — D
The University of Texas at Dallas — M,D
The University of Texas at El Paso — M,D
The University of Texas at San Antonio — M,D
The University of Texas Rio Grande Valley — M
University of the Sciences — M,D
The University of Toledo — M,D
University of Toronto — M,D
The University of Tulsa — M,D
University of Utah — M,D
University of Vermont — M,D
University of Victoria — M,D
University of Virginia — M,D
University of Washington — M,D
University of Waterloo — M,D
The University of Western Ontario — M,D
University of Windsor — M,D
University of Wisconsin–Madison — M,D
University of Wisconsin–Milwaukee — M,D
University of Wyoming — M,D
Utah State University — M,D
Vanderbilt University — M,D
Villanova University — M
Virginia Commonwealth University — M,D
Virginia Polytechnic Institute and State University — M,D
Wake Forest University — M,D
Washington State University — M,D
Washington University in St. Louis — D
Wayne State University — M,D
Wesleyan University — D
West Chester University of Pennsylvania — O
Western Carolina University — M
Western Illinois University — M
Western Kentucky University — M
Western Michigan University — M,D,O
Western Washington University — M
West Texas A&M University — M
West Virginia University — M,D
Wichita State University — M,D
Wilfrid Laurier University — M
Worcester Polytechnic Institute — M,D
Wright State University — M
Yale University — D
York University — M,D
Youngstown State University — M

CHILD AND FAMILY STUDIES

Alabama Agricultural and Mechanical University — M
Amberton University — M
Arizona State University at the Tempe campus — M,D
Astbury University — M
Assumption College — M,O
Auburn University — M,D
Bank Street College of Education — M
Brandeis University — M,D
Brigham Young University — M,D
Brock University — M
California State University, East Bay — M
California State University, Los Angeles — M
California State University, San Marcos — M
Capella University — M
Central Michigan University — M,O
Central Washington University — M
Colorado State University — M,D
Concordia University (Canada) — M,D
Concordia University, St. Paul — M,D
Concordia University Wisconsin — M
Cornell University — M,D
Dallas Theological Seminary — M,D,O
East Carolina University — M,D
Eastern University — D
Fairfield University — M,O
Florida State University — M,D
Indiana University–Purdue University Indianapolis — M

---

*M—masters degree; D—doctorate; O—other advanced degree; *—Close-Up and/or Display*

Iowa State University of Science and Technology	M,D
Kansas State University	M,D,O
Kean University	M
Kent State University	M
Liberty University	M,D,O
Loma Linda University	M,D,O
London Metropolitan University	M,D
Miami University	M,D
Michigan State University	M,D
Mississippi State University	M,D
Missouri State University	M
Montclair State University	M,D,O
Mount Saint Vincent University	M
North Carolina Agricultural and Technical State University	M
North Dakota State University	M,D,O
Northern Illinois University	M
The Ohio State University	M
Ohio University	M
Oklahoma State University	M,D
Oregon State University	M,D
Oxford Graduate School	M,D
Penn State University Park	M,D
Purdue University	M,D
Purdue University Northwest	M
Queens College of the City University of New York	M,O
Roberts Wesleyan College	M
St. Cloud State University	M
San Diego State University	M
South Carolina State University	M
Spring Arbor University	M
State University of New York at Oswego	M
Syracuse University	M
Texas State University	M
Texas Tech University	M
Texas Woman's University	M,D
Towson University	M,O
Tufts University	M,D
The University of Akron	M
The University of Alabama	M
The University of Arizona	M,D,O
University of Central Oklahoma	M
University of Connecticut	M,D
University of Delaware	M,D
University of Denver	M,D,O
University of Georgia	M
University of Guelph	M,D
University of Illinois at Springfield	M,O
University of Kentucky	M
University of La Verne	M
University of Manitoba	M
University of Maryland, College Park	M,D
University of Massachusetts Amherst	M,D,O
University of Minnesota, Twin Cities Campus	M,D
University of Missouri	M
University of Montana	M,D,O
University of Nebraska–Lincoln	M,D
University of Nevada, Reno	M,O
University of New Hampshire	M
University of New Mexico	M
University of North Alabama	M
The University of North Carolina at Charlotte	M,D,O
The University of North Carolina at Greensboro	M,D
University of North Texas	M,D,O
University of Rhode Island	M
University of Southern California	M
University of Southern Mississippi	M
University of South Florida	M,D,O
The University of Tennessee	M,D
The University of Tennessee at Martin	M
The University of Texas at Austin	M,D
The University of Texas at Dallas	M,D
University of Utah	M
University of Victoria	M,D
University of Wisconsin–Madison	M,D
Utah State University	M,D
Vanderbilt University	M
Walden University	M,D
Washington University in St. Louis	M,D
Wheelock College	M

CHILD DEVELOPMENT

California State University, Los Angeles	M
California State University, Sacramento	M,D
California State University, San Bernardino	M
Chaminade University of Honolulu	M
East Carolina University	M,D
Erikson Institute	M
Fielding Graduate University	D,O
Kansas State University	M,D,O
Lee University	M
Michigan State University	M,D
Montclair State University	M,D
Mount Saint Mary College	M,O
North Carolina Agricultural and Technical State University	M
North Dakota State University	M
Ohio University	M
Purdue University	M
Purdue University Northwest	M
Rutgers University–Camden	M
San Diego State University	M
San Jose State University	M,D,O
Sarah Lawrence College	M
Southern New Hampshire University	M,D,O
Texas Woman's University	M
Tufts University	M,D
The University of Akron	M
University of California, Davis	M

University of Central Florida	M,O
University of Florida	M
University of La Verne	M
University of Minnesota, Twin Cities Campus	M,D
University of Nebraska–Lincoln	M,D
The University of North Carolina at Charlotte	M,D,O
The University of Tennessee at Martin	M
The University of Texas at Austin	M,D
The University of West Alabama	M,O
University of Wyoming	M
Whittier College	M

CHINESE

Arizona State University at the Tempe campus	M,D
DePaul University	M
Harvard University	D
Hunter College of the City University of New York	M
Indiana University Bloomington	M,D
Middlebury College	M
New York University	M,D,O
The Ohio State University	M,D
Saginaw Valley State University	M
San Francisco State University	M
Stanford University	M,D
University of Alberta	M
University of California, Berkeley	D
University of California, Irvine	M,D
University of Colorado Boulder	M,D
University of Delaware	M
University of Hawaii at Manoa	M,D,O
The University of Iowa	M
The University of Manchester	M,D
University of Massachusetts Amherst	M
University of Oregon	M,D
University of Pittsburgh	M
University of Washington	M,D
University of Wisconsin–Madison	M,D
Valparaiso University	M
Washington University in St. Louis	M,D

CHIROPRACTIC

Canadian Memorial Chiropractic College	D,O
Cleveland University–Kansas City	D
D'Youville College	D
Institut Franco-Européen de Chiropraxie	D
Life Chiropractic College West	D
Life University	D
Logan University	M,D
National University of Health Sciences	M,D
New York Chiropractic College	D
Northwestern Health Sciences University	D
Palmer College of Chiropractic	D
Parker University	D
Sherman College of Chiropractic	D
Southern California University of Health Sciences	D
Texas Chiropractic College	D
Université du Québec à Trois-Rivières	D
University of Bridgeport	D
University of Western States	D

CIVIL ENGINEERING

American University of Beirut	M,D
American University of Sharjah	M
Arizona State University at the Tempe campus	M,D
Auburn University	M,D
Boise State University	M
Bradley University	M
Brigham Young University	M
Bucknell University	M
California Baptist University	M
California Institute of Technology	M,D,O
California Polytechnic State University, San Luis Obispo	M
California State Polytechnic University, Pomona	M
California State University, Fresno	M
California State University, Fullerton	M
California State University, Long Beach	M
California State University, Los Angeles	M
California State University, Northridge	M
California State University, Sacramento	M
Carleton University	M,D
Carnegie Mellon University	M,D
Case Western Reserve University	M,D
The Catholic University of America	M,D,O
The Citadel, The Military College of South Carolina	M,O
City College of the City University of New York	M,D
Clarkson University	M,D
Clemson University	M,D
Cleveland State University	M,D
Colorado School of Mines	M,D
Colorado State University	M,D
Columbia University	M,D
Concordia University (Canada)	M,D,O
Cooper Union for the Advancement of Science and Art	M
Cornell University	M,D
Dalhousie University	M,D
Drexel University	M,D
Duke University	M,D

École Polytechnique de Montréal	M,D,O
Embry-Riddle Aeronautical University–Daytona	M
Florida Agricultural and Mechanical University	M,D
Florida Atlantic University	M,D
Florida Institute of Technology	M,D
Florida International University	M,D
Florida State University	M,D
George Mason University	M,D
The George Washington University	M,D,O
Georgia Institute of Technology	M,D
Georgia Southern University	M
The Graduate Center, City University of New York	D
Howard University	M
Idaho State University	M
Illinois Institute of Technology	M,D
Indiana University–Purdue University Fort Wayne	M
Instituto Tecnológico y de Estudios Superiores de Monterrey, Campus Monterrey	M,D
Iowa State University of Science and Technology	M,D
Jackson State University	M,D
Johns Hopkins University	M,D,O
Kansas State University	M,D
Lawrence Technological University	M,D
Lehigh University	M,D
Louisiana State University and Agricultural & Mechanical College	M,D
Louisiana Tech University	M
Loyola Marymount University	M
Manhattan College	M
Marquette University	M,D,O
Massachusetts Institute of Technology	M,D,O
McGill University	M,D
McMaster University	M,D
McNeese State University	M
Memorial University of Newfoundland	M,D
Merrimack College	M
Michigan State University	M,D
Milwaukee School of Engineering	M
Mississippi State University	M,D
Missouri University of Science and Technology	M,D
Montana State University	M,D
Morgan State University	M,D
New Mexico State University	M,D
New York University	M,D
North Carolina Agricultural and Technical State University	M
North Carolina State University	M,D
North Dakota State University	M,D
Northeastern University	M,D,O
Northern Arizona University	M
Northwestern University	M,D
Norwich University	M
The Ohio State University	M,D
Oklahoma State University	M,D
Old Dominion University	M,D
Oregon State University	M,D
Penn State University Park	M,D
Polytechnic University of Puerto Rico	M
Portland State University	M,D,O
Princeton University	M,D
Purdue University	M,D
Queen's University at Kingston	M,D
Rensselaer Polytechnic Institute	M,D
Rice University	M,D
Rose-Hulman Institute of Technology	M
Rowan University	M
Royal Military College of Canada	M,D
Rutgers University–New Brunswick	M,D
Saint Martin's University	M
San Diego State University	M
Santa Clara University	M,D,O
South Carolina State University	M
South Dakota School of Mines and Technology	M,D
South Dakota State University	M
Southern Illinois University Carbondale	M,D
Southern Illinois University Edwardsville	M
Southern Methodist University	M,D
Stanford University	M,D,O
Stevens Institute of Technology	M,D,O
Stony Brook University, State University of New York	M,D,O
Syracuse University	M,D
Temple University	M,D,O
Tennessee State University	M,D
Tennessee Technological University	M
Texas A&M University	M,D
Texas A&M University–Kingsville	M
Texas Tech University	M,D
Tufts University	M,D
United States Merchant Marine Academy	M
Université de Moncton	M
Université de Sherbrooke	M,D
Université Laval	M,D,O
University at Buffalo, the State University of New York	M,D
The University of Akron	M,D
The University of Alabama	M,D
The University of Alabama at Birmingham	M,D
The University of Alabama in Huntsville	M,D
University of Alaska Anchorage	M,O
University of Alaska Fairbanks	M,D,O
University of Alberta	M,D

University of Arkansas	M,D
The University of British Columbia	M,D
University of Calgary	M,D
University of California, Berkeley	M,D
University of California, Davis	M,D,O
University of California, Irvine	M,D
University of California, Los Angeles	M,D
University of Central Florida	M,D,O
University of Cincinnati	M,D
University of Colorado Boulder	M,D
University of Colorado Denver	M,D
University of Connecticut	M,D
University of Dayton	M
University of Delaware	M,D
University of Detroit Mercy	M,D
University of Florida	M,D
University of Hawaii at Manoa	M,D
University of Houston	M,D
University of Idaho	M,D
University of Illinois at Chicago	M,D
University of Illinois at Urbana–Champaign	M,D
The University of Iowa	M,D
The University of Kansas	M,D
University of Kentucky	M,D
University of Louisiana at Lafayette	M
University of Louisville	M,D,O
University of Maine	M,D
The University of Manchester	M,D
University of Manitoba	M,D
University of Maryland, College Park	M,D
University of Massachusetts Amherst	M,D
University of Massachusetts Dartmouth	M,D
University of Massachusetts Lowell	M
University of Memphis	M,D,O
University of Miami	M,D
University of Michigan	M,D,O
University of Minnesota, Twin Cities Campus	M,D,O
University of Missouri	M,D
University of Missouri–Kansas City	M,D,O
University of Nebraska–Lincoln	M,D
University of Nevada, Las Vegas	M,D
University of Nevada, Reno	M,D
University of New Brunswick Fredericton	M,D
University of New Hampshire	M,D
University of New Mexico	M,D
The University of North Carolina at Charlotte	M,D
University of North Dakota	M,D
University of North Florida	M
University of Notre Dame	M,D
University of Oklahoma	M,D
University of Ottawa	M,D
University of Pittsburgh	M,D
University of Portland	M
University of Puerto Rico, Mayagüez Campus	M,D
University of Rhode Island	M,D
University of Saskatchewan	M,D
University of South Alabama	M
University of South Carolina	M,D
University of Southern California	M,D,O
University of South Florida	M,D,O
The University of Tennessee	M,D
The University of Tennessee at Chattanooga	M
The University of Texas at Arlington	M,D
The University of Texas at Austin	M,D
The University of Texas at El Paso	M,D,O
The University of Texas at San Antonio	M,D
The University of Texas at Tyler	M
The University of Toledo	M,D
University of Toronto	M,D
University of Utah	M,D
University of Vermont	M,D
University of Virginia	M,D
University of Washington	M,D
University of Waterloo	M,D
The University of Western Ontario	M,D
University of Windsor	M,D
University of Wisconsin–Madison	M,D
University of Wisconsin–Milwaukee	M,D
University of Wyoming	M,D
Utah State University	M,D,O
Vanderbilt University	M,D
Villanova University	M
Virginia Polytechnic Institute and State University	M,D,O
Washington State University	M,D
Wayne State University	M,D
Wentworth Institute of Technology	M
Western Michigan University	M
Western New England University	M
Widener University	M
Worcester Polytechnic Institute	M,D,O
Youngstown State University	M

CLASSICS

American Public University System	M
Asbury University	M
Bethel Seminary	M,D,O
Boston College	M
Boston University	M,D
Brandeis University	M
Brigham Young University	M
Brock University	M
Brown University	M,D
Bryn Mawr College	M,D
The Catholic University of America	M,D,O
City College of the City University of New York	M

Columbia University	M,D
Cornell University	D
Dalhousie University	M,D
Duke University	D
Duquesne University	M
Florida State University	M,D
Fordham University	M,D
The Graduate Center, City University of New York	M,D
Harvard University	D
Heritage Christian University	M
Hunter College of the City University of New York	M
Indiana University Bloomington	M,D
Johns Hopkins University	D
Knox Theological Seminary	M
Marshall University	M,O
McMaster University	M,D
Memorial University of Newfoundland	M
New York University	M,D,O
The Ohio State University	M,D
Princeton University	D
Queen's University at Kingston	M
Rutgers University–New Brunswick	M
San Francisco State University	M
Stanford University	M,D
Texas Tech University	M,D
Tufts University	M
Tulane University	M
Université de Montréal	M
University at Buffalo, the State University of New York	M,D,O
University of Alberta	M,D
The University of Arizona	M
The University of British Columbia	M,D
University of Calgary	M,D
University of California, Berkeley	M,D
University of California, Irvine	M,D
University of California, Los Angeles	M,D
University of California, Riverside	D
University of California, Santa Barbara	M,D
University of Chicago	M,D
University of Cincinnati	M,D
University of Colorado Boulder	M,D
University of Dallas	M
University of Florida	M,D
University of Georgia	M
University of Illinois at Urbana–Champaign	M,D
The University of Iowa	M,D
The University of Kansas	M
University of Kentucky	M
The University of Manchester	D
University of Manitoba	M
University of Maryland, College Park	M
University of Massachusetts Amherst	M
University of Massachusetts Boston	M
University of Michigan	M,D,O
University of Minnesota, Twin Cities Campus	M,D
University of Missouri	M,D
University of Nebraska–Lincoln	M
University of New Brunswick Fredericton	M
The University of North Carolina at Chapel Hill	M,D
The University of North Carolina at Greensboro	M
University of Oregon	M
University of Ottawa	M,D
University of Pennsylvania	M,D
University of South Africa	M,D
University of Southern California	M,D
The University of Texas at Austin	M,D
University of Toronto	M,D
University of Victoria	M,D
University of Virginia	M,D
University of Washington	M,D
The University of Western Ontario	M
University of Wisconsin–Madison	M,D
University of Wisconsin–Milwaukee	M,O
Vanderbilt University	M
Villanova University	M
Washington University in St. Louis	M
Yale University	M,D

CLINICAL LABORATORY SCIENCES/MEDICAL TECHNOLOGY

Albany College of Pharmacy and Health Sciences	M
Austin Peay State University	M
Baylor College of Medicine	M
The Catholic University of America	M,D
The College of William and Mary	M
Dominican University of California	M
Duke University	M
Fairleigh Dickinson University, Metropolitan Campus	M
Inter American University of Puerto Rico, Metropolitan Campus	M
Medical College of Wisconsin	M
Michigan State University	M
Milwaukee School of Engineering	M
Northern Michigan University	M
Northwestern University	M
Pontifical Catholic University of Puerto Rico	O
Quinnipiac University	M
Rush University	M
Rutgers University–Newark	M

Rutgers University–New Brunswick	M
State University of New York Upstate Medical University	M
Tarleton State University	M
Thomas Jefferson University	M
Universidad de las Américas Puebla	M
Université de Sherbrooke	M,D
University at Buffalo, the State University of New York	M
The University of Alabama at Birmingham	M,D
University of Alberta	M,D
University of California, San Diego	M,D
University of Colorado Denver	M,D
University of Florida	M,D
University of Maryland, Baltimore	M
University of Massachusetts Dartmouth	M,D
University of Massachusetts Lowell	M
University of Minnesota, Twin Cities Campus	M
University of Nebraska Medical Center	M,O
University of New Mexico	M,D
University of Pennsylvania	M
University of Pittsburgh	D
University of Puerto Rico, Medical Sciences Campus	M,O
University of Rhode Island	M
University of Southern Mississippi	M
The University of Tennessee Health Science Center	M,D
The University of Texas at Austin	M,D
The University of Texas Health Science Center at San Antonio	D
The University of Texas Medical Branch	M,D
The University of Texas Rio Grande Valley	M
University of Utah	M
University of Vermont	M,D,O
University of Washington	M
Virginia Commonwealth University	M,D

CLINICAL PSYCHOLOGY

Abilene Christian University	M
Acadia University	M
Adelphi University	D
Adler Graduate School	M
Adler University	M,D,O
Alabama Agricultural and Mechanical University	M,O
Alliant International University–Fresno	D
Alliant International University–Los Angeles	D
Alliant International University–Sacramento	D
Alliant International University–San Diego	M,D
Alliant International University–San Francisco	M,D,O
American International College	M,D,O
American University	M,D,O
American University of Beirut	M,D
Andrews University	M
Antioch University Los Angeles	M,D
Antioch University New England	M,D
Antioch University Santa Barbara	M,D
Antioch University Seattle	D
Appalachian State University	M
Argosy University, Atlanta	M,D,O
Argosy University, Chicago	M,D
Argosy University, Dallas	M,D
Argosy University, Denver	M,D
Argosy University, Hawai'i	M,D,O
Argosy University, Inland Empire	M,D
Argosy University, Los Angeles	M,D
Argosy University, Northern Virginia	M,D
Argosy University, Orange County	M,D
Argosy University, Phoenix	M,D
Argosy University, San Diego	M,D
Argosy University, San Francisco Bay Area	M,D
Argosy University, Schaumburg	M,D
Argosy University, Seattle	M,D,O
Argosy University, Tampa	M,D
Argosy University, Twin Cities	M,D,O
Arizona State University at the Tempe campus	M,D
Arkansas State University	M,O
Ashland Theological Seminary	M,O
Auburn University at Montgomery	M,O
Augusta University	M,O
Austin Peay State University	M
Azusa Pacific University	D
Ball State University	M,D
Barry University	M,O
Baylor University	D
Bay Path University	M
Benedictine University	M
Bethel Seminary	M,D,O
Binghamton University, State University of New York	D
Biola University	D
Bowling Green State University	M,D
Bradley University	M
Brigham Young University	D
Butler University	M,O
California Institute of Integral Studies	M,D
California Lutheran University	M,D
California State University, Dominguez Hills	M
California State University, Fullerton	M

California State University, Northridge	M
California State University, San Bernardino	M
California University of Pennsylvania	M
Capella University	M,D
Cardinal Stritch University	M
Carlos Albizu University	M,D
Carlos Albizu University, Miami Campus	M,D
Case Western Reserve University	D
The Catholic University of America	M,D
Central Michigan University	D
Chestnut Hill College	M,D,O
The Chicago School of Professional Psychology	M,D
The Chicago School of Professional Psychology at Downtown Los Angeles	M,D
The Chicago School of Professional Psychology at Irvine	D
City College of the City University of New York	M,D
Clarion University of Pennsylvania	M
Clark University	D
Clayton State University	M
College of St. Joseph	M
College of Staten Island of the City University of New York	M
Columbus State University	M,D,O
Concordia University (Canada)	D,O
Dalhousie University	M,D
DePaul University	M,D
Drexel University	D
Duke University	D
Duquesne University	M,D,O
East Carolina University	M,D
Eastern Illinois University	M,O
Eastern Kentucky University	M,O
Eastern Michigan University	M,D
Eastern Virginia Medical School	D
Eastern Washington University	M
East Tennessee State University	M,D
Edinboro University of Pennsylvania	M,O
Emory University	D
Emporia State University	M
Evangel University	M
Fairfield University	M,O
Fairleigh Dickinson University, College at Florham	M
Fairleigh Dickinson University, Metropolitan Campus	M,D
Fielding Graduate University	D,O
Fisk University	M
Florida Institute of Technology	D
Florida International University	M,D,O
Florida State University	D
Fordham University	D
Franciscan University of Steubenville	M
Francis Marion University	M,O
Fuller Theological Seminary	M,D,O
Gallaudet University	M,D,O
Gannon University	M
Geneva College	M
George Fox University	M,D
The George Washington University	M,D
Georgian Court University	M,O
Georgia Southern University	M,D
Georgia State University	D
Goddard College	M
Grace College	M
The Graduate Center, City University of New York	D
Hawai'i Pacific University	M
Heidelberg University	M
Hodges University	M
Hofstra University	M,D
Hood College	M
Howard University	M,D
Husson University	M
Idaho State University	D
Illinois Institute of Technology	M,D
Illinois State University	M,D,O
Immaculata University	M,D,O
Indiana State University	M,D,O
Indiana University of Pennsylvania	M,D
Indiana University–Purdue University Indianapolis	M,D
Indiana University South Bend	M,O
The Institute for the Psychological Sciences	M,D
Jackson State University	M,D
James Madison University	D
John Brown University	M,O
Johns Hopkins University	M,D
Johnson & Wales University	M
Johnson University	M,D,O
Judson University	M
Kean University	M,D
Kent State University	M,D
Kutztown University of Pennsylvania	M
LaGrange College	M
Lakehead University	M,D
Lamar University	M
La Salle University	M,D
Lenoir-Rhyne University	M
Lesley University	M,D,O
Lewis University	M
Liberty University	M,D,O
Lipscomb University	M,O
Lock Haven University of Pennsylvania	M
Loma Linda University	D
London Metropolitan University	M,D
Long Island University–Brentwood Campus	M,O

Long Island University–LIU Brooklyn	M,D,O
Long Island University–LIU Post	M,D,O
Louisiana State University and Agricultural & Mechanical College	M,D
Loyola University Chicago	M,D
Loyola University Maryland	M,D,O
Loyola University New Orleans	M
Lynchburg College	M
Madonna University	M
Marquette University	M,D
Marshall University	M,D,O
Marymount University	M
Marywood University	M,D
McGill University	M,D
McKendree University	M
Medaille College	M,D
Memorial University of Newfoundland	M,D
Mercer University	M,D
Merrimack College	M
Messiah College	M,O
Michigan School of Professional Psychology	M,D
MidAmerica Nazarene University	M
Middle Tennessee State University	M,O
Midwestern State University	M
Midwestern University, Downers Grove Campus	M,D
Midwestern University, Glendale Campus	D
Millersville University of Pennsylvania	M
Milligan College	M,O
Minnesota State University Mankato	M,D
Mississippi State University	M,D,O
Missouri State University	M,O
Molloy College	M
Montclair State University	M
Morehead State University	M
Mount Mary University	M,O
Murray State University	M
National University	M,O
Neumann University	M,D,O
New Mexico Highlands University	M
The New School	M,D
Nicholls State University	M,O
Norfolk State University	M
North Dakota State University	M,D
Northern Arizona University	M
Northern Kentucky University	M
Northern State University	M
Northwestern State University of Louisiana	M
Northwestern University	D
Northwest Nazarene University	M
Notre Dame de Namur University	M
Nova Southeastern University	M,D,O
The Ohio State University	D
Ohio University	D
Oklahoma State University	M,D
Old Dominion University	D
Oregon State University	M,D
Pace University	M,D
Pacifica Graduate Institute	M,D
Pacific University	M,D
Palo Alto University	M,D
Penn State Harrisburg	M,D,O
Pepperdine University	M,D
Philadelphia College of Osteopathic Medicine	M,D,O
Pittsburg State University	M
Plymouth State University	M,O
Point Loma Nazarene University	M
Point Park University	M,D
Ponce Health Sciences University	D
Pontifical Catholic University of Puerto Rico	D
Pontificia Universidad Catolica Madre y Maestra	M
Prairie View A&M University	M,D
Purdue University	D
Queen's University at Kingston	M,D
Regent University	M,D,O
Richmont Graduate University	M
Rivier University	M
Roberts Wesleyan College	M,D
Roger Williams University	M
Roosevelt University	M,D
Rosalind Franklin University of Medicine and Science	M,D
Rowan University	M,O
Rutgers University–New Brunswick	M,D
St. John's University (NY)	M,D,O
Saint Louis University	M,D
Saint Michael's College	M
Sam Houston State University	M,D,O
San Diego State University	M,D
San Francisco State University	M,O
San Jose State University	M,O
Saybrook University	M
Seattle Pacific University	D
Shippensburg University of Pennsylvania	M,D
Siena Heights University	M,O
Slippery Rock University of Pennsylvania	M
Sofia University	M,D
Sonoma State University	M
Southeastern Oklahoma State University	M
Southern Illinois University Carbondale	M,D
Southern Illinois University Edwardsville	M
Southern Methodist University	D
South University (OH)	M
Spalding University	M,D

*M—masters degree; D—doctorate; O—other advanced degree; *—Close-Up and/or Display*

Springfield College	M,D,O
State University of New York at Plattsburgh	M,O
Stephens College	M,O
Stony Brook University, State University of New York	D
Suffolk University	M,D,O
Syracuse University	M,D
Teachers College, Columbia University	M,D
Texas A&M University	M,D
Texas A&M University–Central Texas	M,O
Texas A&M University–Corpus Christi	M
Texas Tech University	M,D
Trinity Washington University	M
Uniformed Services University of the Health Sciences	D
Union College (KY)	M
Union Institute & University	M
Universidad de Iberoamerica	M,D
Université Laval	D
University of Albany, State University of New York	M,D
The University of Akron	M
The University of Alabama	D
The University of Alabama at Birmingham	M,D
University of Alaska Anchorage	M,D
University of Alaska Fairbanks	M
University of Bridgeport	M
The University of British Columbia	M,D
University of Calgary	M,D
University of California, San Diego	D
University of California, Santa Barbara	M,D,O
University of Central Florida	M,D
University of Cincinnati	D
University of Colorado Denver	M,D
University of Connecticut	M,D
University of Dayton	M,O
University of Delaware	D
University of Denver	M,D
University of Detroit Mercy	M,D,O
University of Florida	M,D
University of Guelph	M,D
University of Hartford	M,D
University of Hawaii at Manoa	M,D,O
University of Houston	M,D
University of Houston–Clear Lake	M
University of Indianapolis	M,D
The University of Kansas	M,D
University of La Verne	M
University of Louisiana at Monroe	M
University of Louisville	D
The University of Manchester	M,D
University of Manitoba	M,D
University of Mary Hardin-Baylor	M
University of Maryland, Baltimore County	M,D
University of Maryland, College Park	M,D
University of Massachusetts Amherst	M,D
University of Massachusetts Boston	D
University of Massachusetts Dartmouth	M,O
University of Memphis	M,D,O
University of Miami	M,D
University of Michigan	D
University of Michigan–Dearborn	M
University of Minnesota, Twin Cities Campus	D
University of Missouri–St. Louis	M,D,O
University of Montana	M,D,O
University of Nebraska–Lincoln	M,D
University of Nevada, Las Vegas	M,D,O
University of Nevada, Reno	D
University of New Brunswick Saint John	M,D
University of New Mexico	D
University of North Alabama	M
The University of North Carolina at Chapel Hill	D
The University of North Carolina at Greensboro	M,D
University of North Dakota	M,D
University of Northern Colorado	M
University of North Georgia	M
University of North Texas	M,D,O
University of North Texas at Dallas	M
University of Oklahoma	M,O
University of Oregon	D
University of Phoenix–Phoenix Campus	M
University of Pittsburgh	D
University of Puerto Rico, Río Piedras Campus	M,D
University of Regina	M,D
University of Rhode Island	M,D
University of Rochester	D
University of Saint Francis (IN)	M,O
University of Saint Joseph	M,O
University of San Francisco	M
The University of Scranton	M
University of South Africa	M,D
University of South Alabama	M,D
University of South Carolina	M,D
University of South Carolina Aiken	M
The University of South Dakota	M,D
University of Southern California	M,D
University of Southern Mississippi	M,D
University of South Florida	D
The University of Tennessee	M,D
The University of Texas at Austin	D
The University of Texas at El Paso	M,D
The University of Texas at Tyler	M

The University of Texas of the Permian Basin	M
The University of Texas Rio Grande Valley	M
The University of Texas Southwestern Medical Center	D
University of the Cumberlands	D
The University of Toledo	M,D
The University of Tulsa	M,D
University of Utah	M,D,O
University of Vermont	D
University of Victoria	M,D
University of Virginia	D
University of Washington	D
University of Windsor	M,D
University of Wisconsin–Madison	D
University of Wisconsin–Milwaukee	M,D
University of Wisconsin–Stout	M
Utah State University	M,D
Valparaiso University	M
Vanguard University of Southern California	M
Virginia Commonwealth University	D
Virginia State University	M,D
Walden University	M,D,O
Washburn University	M
Washington State University	M,D
Waynesburg University	M
Wayne State University	M,D
West Chester University of Pennsylvania	M,D,O
Western Connecticut State University	M
Western Illinois University	M,O
Western Kentucky University	M,O
Western Michigan University	M,D
West Virginia University	M,D
Wheaton College	M,D
Wichita State University	D
Widener University	D
William James College	M,D,O
William Paterson University of New Jersey	M,D
Wilmington University	M
Winona State University	M,O
Wisconsin School of Professional Psychology	M,D
Wright Institute	D
Wright State University	D
Xavier University	M,D
Yale University	D
Yeshiva University	D

CLINICAL RESEARCH

Albert Einstein College of Medicine	D
American University of Health Sciences	M
Augusta University	M
Boston University	M
Case Western Reserve University	M,D
Clemson University	M,D,O
Duke University	M
Eastern Michigan University	M,O
Emory University	M
Icahn School of Medicine at Mount Sinai	M,D
Johns Hopkins University	M,D
Loyola University Chicago	M
Medical College of Wisconsin	
Medical University of South Carolina	M
Memorial University of Newfoundland	M,D
Morehouse School of Medicine	M
New York University	M,O
Northwestern University	M,O
Oregon Health & Science University	M
Palmer College of Chiropractic	M
Stanford University	M,D
Thomas Jefferson University	M,O
Trident University International	M,D,O
Tufts University	M,D,O
University of California, Berkeley	O
University of California, Davis	M
University of California, Los Angeles	M
University of California, San Diego	M
University of Colorado Denver	M,D
University of Connecticut Health Center	M
University of Florida	M,D,O
The University of Iowa	M,D
The University of Kansas	M
University of Kentucky	M
University of Maryland, Baltimore	M,D,O
University of Massachusetts Medical School	M,D
University of Michigan	D
University of Minnesota, Twin Cities Campus	M
The University of North Carolina at Chapel Hill	M,D
The University of North Carolina Wilmington	M,D,O
University of Pittsburgh	M,O
University of Puerto Rico, Medical Sciences Campus	M,O
University of Rochester	M
University of Southern California	M,D,O
University of South Florida	M,D,O
The University of Texas Health Science Center at San Antonio	M
University of Virginia	M
University of Washington	M,D
University of Wisconsin–Madison	M,D
Vanderbilt University	M
Walden University	M,D,O
Washington University in St. Louis	M

CLOTHING AND TEXTILES

Alabama Agricultural and Mechanical University	M
Auburn University	M,O
Central Michigan University	M,O
Cornell University	M,D
Eastern Michigan University	M
Fashion Institute of Technology	M
Georgia State University	M
Iowa State University of Science and Technology	M,D
Kansas State University	M,D
LIM College	M
New Mexico State University	M
The New School	M
North Carolina State University	D
North Dakota State University	M,O
Oklahoma State University	M,D
Oregon State University	M,D
Philadelphia University	M
Rutgers University–Newark	M
Savannah College of Art and Design	M
The University of Akron	M
The University of Alabama	M
University of Alberta	M,D
University of California, Davis	M
University of Delaware	M
University of Georgia	M,D
The University of Manchester	M,D
University of Manitoba	M
University of Minnesota, Twin Cities Campus	M,D,O
University of Missouri	M,D
University of Nebraska–Lincoln	M,D
The University of Tennessee	M,D
University of the Incarnate Word	M
Washington State University	M

COGNITIVE SCIENCES

American University	M,D,O
Arizona State University at the Tempe campus	M,D
Ball State University	M
Binghamton University, State University of New York	D
Brandeis University	M,D
Brigham Young University	D
Brown University	M,D
Carleton University	D
Carnegie Mellon University	D
Case Western Reserve University	M
Central European University	D
Claremont Graduate University	M,D,O
Cornell University	D
Dartmouth College	D
Duke University	D
Emory University	D
Florida International University	M,D
Florida State University	D
George Mason University	M,D,O
The George Washington University	D
Georgia State University	D
The Graduate Center, City University of New York	D
Grand Canyon University	D
Harvard University	M,D
Illinois State University	M,D,O
Indiana University Bloomington	D
Iowa State University of Science and Technology	M,D
Johns Hopkins University	D
Louisiana State University and Agricultural & Mechanical College	M,D
Massachusetts Institute of Technology	D
Michigan Technological University	M,D,O
Mississippi State University	M,D
The New School	M,D
New York University	M,D,O
North Dakota State University	M,D
Northwestern University	D
The Ohio State University	D
Oregon State University	M,D
Purdue University	D
Queen's University at Kingston	M,D
Rensselaer Polytechnic Institute	D
Rice University	M,D
Rutgers University–Newark	D
Rutgers University–New Brunswick	
Stony Brook University, State University of New York	D
Syracuse University	D
Texas Christian University	M,D
Tufts University	M,D
University at Albany, State University of New York	M,D
The University of British Columbia	M,D
University of California, Merced	M,D
University of California, San Diego	D
University of California, Santa Barbara	M,D
University of Connecticut	M,D
University of Delaware	M,D
University of Denver	D
University of Guelph	M,D
The University of Kansas	M,D
University of Louisiana at Lafayette	D
University of Louisville	D
University of Maryland, Baltimore County	D
University of Maryland, College Park	D
University of Massachusetts Amherst	M,D
University of Massachusetts Boston	M
University of Michigan	D
University of Minnesota, Twin Cities Campus	D

University of Nebraska–Lincoln	M,D,O
University of Nevada, Reno	M,D
University of New Mexico	D
The University of North Carolina at Chapel Hill	D
The University of North Carolina at Charlotte	M,D,O
The University of North Carolina at Greensboro	M,D
University of Notre Dame	D
University of Oregon	M,D
University of Rochester	D
University of Southern California	M,D
University of South Florida	D
The University of Texas at Dallas	M,D
University of Washington	D
University of Wisconsin–Madison	D
Wayne State University	M,D
Wilfrid Laurier University	M,D
Yale University	D

COMMUNICATION—GENERAL

Abilene Christian University	M
American University	M,D
The American University in Cairo	M,D,O
The American University of Paris	M
Andrews University	M
Angelo State University	M
Arizona State University at the Tempe campus	M,D
Arkansas State University	M,O
Auburn University	M,O
Austin Peay State University	M
Ball State University	M,O
Barry University	M,O
Baylor University	M
Bellarmine University	M
Boise State University	M,D
Boston University	M,D
Bowling Green State University	M,D
Brigham Young University	M
Bryant University	M,O
California Baptist University	M
California State University, Chico	M
California State University, East Bay	M
California State University, Fresno	M
California State University, Fullerton	M
California State University, Long Beach	M
California State University, Los Angeles	M
California State University, Northridge	M
California State University, Sacramento	M
California State University, San Bernardino	M
Carleton University	M,D
Carnegie Mellon University	M,D
Central Connecticut State University	M,O
Central Michigan University	M
Chatham University	M
Clarion University of Pennsylvania	M
Clarks Summit University	M,D
Clark University	M
Clemson University	M,D
Cleveland State University	M,D,O
The College at Brockport, State University of New York	M
The College of New Rochelle	M,O
Columbia University	M,D
Concordia University (Canada)	M,D,O
Cornell University	M,D
Dallas Baptist University	M
DePaul University	M
DEREE - The American College of Greece	M
Drake University	M
Drexel University	M
Drury University	M
Duquesne University	M,D
Eastern Michigan University	M
Eastern New Mexico University	M
Eastern University	M,D,O
Eastern Washington University	M
East Tennessee State University	M
Edinboro University of Pennsylvania	M
Emerson College	M
Fairfield University	M
Fairleigh Dickinson University, Metropolitan Campus	M
Fitchburg State University	M,O
Florida Atlantic University	M,O
Florida Institute of Technology	M
Florida International University	M
Florida State University	M,D
Fordham University	M
Fort Hays State University	M
George Mason University	M,D,O
Georgetown University	M
The George Washington University	M
Georgia State University	M,D
Governors State University	M
Grand Valley State University	M
Harvard University	M,O
Hawai'i Pacific University	M
Howard University	M,D
Illinois Institute of Technology	M,D
Illinois State University	M
Indiana State University	D
Indiana University of Pennsylvania	D
Indiana University–Purdue University Fort Wayne	M
Indiana University–Purdue University Indianapolis	M,D
Indiana University South Bend	M,D

Institution	Degree
Instituto Tecnologico de Santo Domingo	M,O
Instituto Tecnológico y de Estudios Superiores de Monterrey, Campus Ciudad Obregón	M
Instituto Tecnológico y de Estudios Superiores de Monterrey, Campus Monterrey	M,D
International University in Geneva	M,D
James Madison University	M
Johns Hopkins University	M,O
Kansas State University	M,D,O
Kean University	M
Kennesaw State University	M
Kent State University	M
La Salle University	M,O
Lasell College	M,O
La Sierra University	M
Lawrence Technological University	M,O
Liberty University	M
Lindenwood University	M,O
Lindenwood University–Belleville	M
Louisiana State University and Agricultural & Mechanical College	M,D
Loyola University Chicago	M,O
Lynn University	M,O
Marist College	M,O
Marquette University	M,O
Marshall University	M
Marywood University	M,D
McGill University	M,D
Michigan State University	M,D
Minnesota State University Mankato	M,O
Mississippi College	M
Missouri State University	M,O
Monmouth University	M,O
Montana State University Billings	M
Moore College of Art & Design	M
Morehead State University	M
New Mexico State University	M
New York Institute of Technology	M
New York University	M,D
Norfolk State University	M
North Carolina State University	M
North Dakota State University	M,D
Northeastern State University	M
Northern Arizona University	M
Northern Illinois University	M
Northern Kentucky University	M,O
Northwestern University	M,D
Notre Dame of Maryland University	M
The Ohio State University	M,D
Ohio University	M,D
Penn State Harrisburg	M,D,O
Penn State University Park	M,D
Pepperdine University	M
Pittsburg State University	M
Point Park University	M
Purdue University	M,D
Purdue University Northwest	M
Queen's University at Kingston	M,D
Queens University of Charlotte	M
Quincy University	M
Quinnipiac University	M
Regent University	M,D
Rochester Institute of Technology	M
Roosevelt University	M
Rutgers University–New Brunswick	D
Sacred Heart University	M
Saginaw Valley State University	M
Saint Louis University	M
St. Mary's University (United States)	M,O
St. Thomas University	M,D,O
Sam Houston State University	M
San Diego State University	M
San Jose State University	M,O
Seton Hall University	M
Shippensburg University of Pennsylvania	M
Simmons College	M
Simon Fraser University	M,D
South Dakota State University	M
Southeastern Louisiana University	M
Southern Illinois University Carbondale	M,D
Southern Utah University	M
Spring Arbor University	M
Stanford University	M,D
State University of New York at Oswego	M
State University of New York College at Potsdam	M
Stephen F. Austin State University	M,D,O
Stevens Institute of Technology	M,D,O
Stevenson University	M
Syracuse University	M,D
Tarleton State University	M
Teachers College, Columbia University	M,D
Temple University	M,D
Texas A&M University	M,D
Texas A&M University–Corpus Christi	M
Texas Christian University	M
Texas Southern University	M
Texas State University	M
Texas Tech University	M
Tiffin University	M
Towson University	M
Trinity Washington University	M
Troy University	M,D
Université de Montréal	M
Université du Québec à Montréal	M,D
Université du Québec à Trois-Rivières	M,O
University at Albany, State University of New York	M,D
University at Buffalo, the State University of New York	M,D
The University of Akron	M
The University of Alabama	M,D
The University of Alabama at Birmingham	M
University of Alaska Fairbanks	M
University of Alberta	M
The University of Arizona	M,D
University of Arkansas	M
University of Bridgeport	M
University of Calgary	M,D
University of California, Davis	M
University of California, San Diego	D
University of California, Santa Barbara	D
University of California, Santa Cruz	O
University of Central Florida	M,O
University of Central Missouri	M,D,O
University of Cincinnati	M,D
University of Colorado Boulder	M,D
University of Colorado Colorado Springs	M
University of Colorado Denver	M
University of Connecticut	M
University of Dayton	M
University of Delaware	M
University of Denver	M,D,O
University of Dubuque	M
University of Florida	M,D
University of Georgia	M,D
University of Hartford	M
University of Hawaii at Manoa	M,O
University of Houston	M
University of Illinois at Chicago	M,D
University of Illinois at Springfield	M
University of Illinois at Urbana–Champaign	M,D
The University of Iowa	M,D
The University of Kansas	M,D,O
University of Kentucky	M,D
University of Louisiana at Lafayette	M
University of Louisiana at Monroe	M
University of Louisville	M
University of Maine	M,D
University of Maryland, Baltimore County	M
University of Maryland, College Park	M,D
University of Massachusetts Amherst	M,D
University of Memphis	M,D
University of Miami	M,D
University of Michigan	D
University of Michigan–Flint	M
University of Minnesota, Twin Cities Campus	M,D,O
University of Missouri	M,D
University of Missouri–St. Louis	M
University of Montana	M
University of Nebraska at Omaha	M,O
University of Nebraska–Lincoln	M,D
University of Nevada, Las Vegas	M
University of New Mexico	M,D
The University of North Carolina at Chapel Hill	D
The University of North Carolina at Charlotte	M
The University of North Carolina at Greensboro	M
University of North Dakota	D
University of Northern Colorado	M
University of Northern Iowa	M
University of North Texas	M,D,O
University of Oklahoma	M,D
University of Oregon	M,D
University of Ottawa	M
University of Pennsylvania	D
University of Pittsburgh	M,D
University of Portland	M
University of Puerto Rico, Río Piedras Campus	M
University of Rhode Island	M
University of San Francisco	M
University of South Africa	M,D
University of South Alabama	M
The University of South Dakota	M
University of Southern California	M,D
University of Southern Indiana	M
University of South Florida	M,D
The University of Tennessee	M,D
The University of Tennessee at Martin	M
The University of Texas at Arlington	M
The University of Texas at Austin	M,D
The University of Texas at Dallas	M,D
The University of Texas at El Paso	M
The University of Texas at San Antonio	M
The University of Texas at Tyler	M
The University of Texas Rio Grande Valley	M,O
University of the Incarnate Word	M
University of the Pacific	M
University of the Sacred Heart	M
University of Toledo	O
University of Utah	M,D
University of Vermont	M
University of Washington	M,D
University of West Florida	M
University of Windsor	M
University of Wisconsin–Madison	M,D
University of Wisconsin–Milwaukee	M,D,O
University of Wisconsin–Stevens Point	M
University of Wisconsin–Superior	M
University of Wisconsin–Whitewater	M
University of Wyoming	M
Utah State University	M
Valparaiso University	M,O
Villanova University	M
Virginia Commonwealth University	D
Virginia Polytechnic Institute and State University	M,D,O
Wake Forest University	M
Walden University	M,D
Washington State University	M,D
Wayne State College	M
Wayne State University	M,D,O
Weber State University	M
Webster University	M,O
West Chester University of Pennsylvania	M
Western Illinois University	M
Western Kentucky University	M,O
Western Michigan University	M
Western New England University	M
Westminster College (UT)	M
West Texas A&M University	M
West Virginia University	M,D
Wichita State University	M
Wilfrid Laurier University	M
York University	M,D

COMMUNICATION DISORDERS

Institution	Degree
Abilene Christian University	M
Adelphi University	M,D
Alabama Agricultural and Mechanical University	M
Andrews University	M
Appalachian State University	M
Arizona State University at the Tempe campus	M,D
Arkansas State University	M,O
Armstrong State University	M
A.T. Still University	M,D,O
Auburn University	M,D
Baldwin Wallace University	M
Ball State University	M,D
Barry University	M
Baylor University	M
Biola University	M,O
Bloomsburg University of Pennsylvania	M,D
Boston University	M,D
Bowling Green State University	M,D
Bridgewater State University	M
Brigham Young University	M
Brooklyn College of the City University of New York	M,D
Buffalo State College, State University of New York	M
California Baptist University	M
California State University, Chico	M
California State University, East Bay	M
California State University, Fresno	M
California State University, Fullerton	M
California State University, Los Angeles	M
California State University, Northridge	M
California State University, Sacramento	M
California State University, San Marcos	M
California University of Pennsylvania	M
Canisius College	M,O
Carlos Albizu University	M,D
Carlos Albizu University, Miami Campus	M,D
Case Western Reserve University	M,D
Central Michigan University	M,D
Chapman University	M
Clarion University of Pennsylvania	M,D
Cleveland State University	M
The College of Saint Rose	M
Dalhousie University	M,D
Duquesne University	M,D,O
East Carolina University	M,D,O
Eastern Illinois University	M
Eastern Kentucky University	M
Eastern Michigan University	M
Eastern New Mexico University	M
Eastern Washington University	M
East Stroudsburg University of Pennsylvania	M
East Tennessee State University	M,D
Edinboro University of Pennsylvania	M
Elmhurst College	M
Elms College	M,O
Emerson College	M,O
Florida Atlantic University	M
Florida International University	M
Florida State University	M,D
Fontbonne University	M
Fort Hays State University	M
Gallaudet University	M,D,O
The George Washington University	M
Georgia State University	M,D
Governors State University	M
The Graduate Center, City University of New York	D
Grand Valley State University	M
Hampton University	M
Harding University	M
Hofstra University	M,D,O
Howard University	M,D
Hunter College of the City University of New York	M
Idaho State University	M,D,O
Illinois State University	M
Indiana State University	M,D,O
Indiana University Bloomington	M,D
Indiana University of Pennsylvania	M
Iona College	M
Ithaca College	M
Jackson State University	M
Jacksonville University	M
James Madison University	M,D
Kansas State University	M,D,O
Kean University	M
Kent State University	M,D,O
Lamar University	M,D
La Salle University	M
Lehman College of the City University of New York	M
Lewis & Clark College	M
Lindenwood University	M,D,O
Loma Linda University	M,D
Long Island University–LIU Brooklyn	M,D,O
Long Island University–LIU Post	M,D,O
Longwood University	M
Louisiana State University and Agricultural & Mechanical College	M,D
Louisiana State University Health Sciences Center	M,D
Louisiana Tech University	M,D
Loyola University Maryland	M
Marquette University	M,O
Marshall University	M
Maryville University of Saint Louis	M
Marywood University	M
Massachusetts Institute of Technology	M,D
McGill University	M,D
Mercy College	M
MGH Institute of Health Professions	M,O
Miami University	M
Michigan State University	M,D
Midwestern University, Downers Grove Campus	M
Midwestern University, Glendale Campus	M
Minnesota State University Mankato	M
Minnesota State University Moorhead	M,O
Minot State University	M
Misericordia University	M
Mississippi University for Women	M,O
Missouri State University	M,D
Molloy College	M
Monmouth University	M,D,O
Montclair State University	M,D
Murray State University	M
Nazareth College of Rochester	M
New Mexico State University	M,D,O
New York Medical College	M,D,O
New York University	M,D
North Carolina Central University	M
Northeastern State University	M
Northern Arizona University	M
Northern Illinois University	M,D
Northwestern University	M,D
Nova Southeastern University	M,D
The Ohio State University	M,D
Ohio University	M,D
Oklahoma State University	M
Old Dominion University	M
Our Lady of the Lake University	M,D
Pacific University	M,D
Penn State University Park	M,D,O
Portland State University	M
Purdue University	M,D
Queens College of the City University of New York	M,O
Radford University	M
Rockhurst University	M
Rocky Mountain University of Health Professions	D
Rush University	M,D
Sacred Heart University	M
St. Ambrose University	M
St. Cloud State University	M
St. John's University (NY)	M,D
Saint Joseph's University	M,D,O
Saint Louis University	M
Saint Mary's College	M
Saint Xavier University	M
Salus University	D
Samford University	M
San Diego State University	M,D
San Francisco State University	M
San Jose State University	M,D,O
Seton Hall University	M
South Carolina State University	M
Southeastern Louisiana University	M
Southeast Missouri State University	M
Southern Connecticut State University	M
Southern Illinois University Carbondale	M
Southern Illinois University Edwardsville	M
Southern University and Agricultural and Mechanical College	M
State University of New York at Fredonia	M
State University of New York at New Paltz	M

*M—masters degree; D—doctorate; O—other advanced degree; *—Close-Up and/or Display*

State University of New York at Plattsburgh	M
State University of New York College at Cortland	M
Stephen F. Austin State University	M
Stockton University	M,D
Syracuse University	M,D
Teachers College, Columbia University	M,D,O
Temple University	M,D
Tennessee State University	M
Texas A&M University–Kingsville	M
Texas Christian University	M
Texas State University	M
Texas Tech University Health Sciences Center	M
Texas Woman's University	M
Touro College	M,D
Towson University	M,D
Truman State University	M
Universidad del Turabo	M
Université de Montréal	M,O
Université Laval	M
University at Buffalo, the State University of New York	M,D
The University of Akron	M,D
The University of Alabama	M
University of Alberta	M,D
The University of Arizona	M,D,O
University of Arkansas	M
University of Arkansas for Medical Sciences	M,D
The University of British Columbia	M,D
University of California, San Diego	D
University of Central Arkansas	M,D
University of Central Florida	M,D,O
University of Central Missouri	M,D,O
University of Central Oklahoma	M
University of Cincinnati	M,D,O
University of Colorado Boulder	M,D
University of Connecticut	M,D
University of Delaware	M
University of Florida	M,D
University of Georgia	M,D,O
University of Hawaii at Manoa	M
University of Houston	M
University of Illinois at Urbana–Champaign	M,D
The University of Iowa	M,D
The University of Kansas	M,D
University of Kentucky	M
University of Louisiana at Lafayette	M,D
University of Louisiana at Monroe	M
University of Louisville	M,D
University of Maine	M
The University of Manchester	M,D
University of Maryland, College Park	M,D
University of Massachusetts Amherst	M,D
University of Memphis	M,D
University of Minnesota, Duluth	M
University of Minnesota, Twin Cities Campus	M,D
University of Mississippi	M,D
University of Missouri	M,D
University of Montana	M,O
University of Montevallo	M
University of Nebraska at Kearney	M
University of Nebraska at Omaha	M
University of Nebraska–Lincoln	M,D
University of Nevada, Reno	M,D
University of New Hampshire	M
University of New Mexico	M
The University of North Carolina at Chapel Hill	M,D
The University of North Carolina at Greensboro	M,D
University of North Dakota	M
University of Northern Colorado	M,D
University of Northern Iowa	M
University of North Florida	M
University of North Texas	M,D,O
University of Oklahoma Health Sciences Center	M,D,O
University of Ottawa	M
University of Pittsburgh	M,D
University of Puerto Rico, Medical Sciences Campus	M,D
University of Redlands	M
University of Rhode Island	M
University of San Diego	M
University of South Alabama	M,D
University of South Carolina	M
The University of South Dakota	M,D
University of Southern Mississippi	M
University of South Florida	M,D,O
The University of Tennessee	M,D,O
The University of Tennessee Health Science Center	M,D
The University of Texas at Austin	M,D
The University of Texas at Dallas	M,D
The University of Texas at El Paso	M
The University of Texas Health Science Center at San Antonio	M,D
The University of Texas Rio Grande Valley	M
University of the District of Columbia	M
University of the Pacific	M
The University of Toledo	M
University of Toronto	M,D
The University of Tulsa	M
University of Utah	M,D
University of Vermont	M
University of Virginia	M
University of Washington	M
The University of Western Ontario	M
University of West Georgia	M,D,O

University of Wisconsin–Eau Claire	M
University of Wisconsin–Madison	M,D
University of Wisconsin–Milwaukee	M
University of Wisconsin–River Falls	M
University of Wisconsin–Stevens Point	M,D
University of Wisconsin–Whitewater	M
University of Wyoming	M
Utah State University	M,D,O
Valdosta State University	M,D
Vanderbilt University	M,D
Washington State University	M
Washington University in St. Louis	M,D
Wayne State University	M,D
Webster University	M
West Chester University of Pennsylvania	M
Western Carolina University	M
Western Illinois University	M
Western Kentucky University	M
Western Michigan University	M,D
Western Washington University	M
West Texas A&M University	M
West Virginia University	D
Wichita State University	M,D
William Paterson University of New Jersey	M,D
Worcester State University	M
Yeshiva University	M

COMMUNITY COLLEGE EDUCATION

Argosy University, Chicago	M,D,O
Argosy University, Denver	M,D
Argosy University, Inland Empire	M,D
Argosy University, Los Angeles	M,D
Argosy University, Northern Virginia	M,D,O
Argosy University, Orange County	M,D
Argosy University, Phoenix	M,D,O
Argosy University, San Diego	M,D
Argosy University, San Francisco Bay Area	M,D
Argosy University, Seattle	M,D
Argosy University, Tampa	M,D,O
Arkansas State University	M,D,O
California State University, San Bernardino	M
California State University, Stanislaus	D
Central Michigan University	M,D,O
Drew University	M,D,O
East Carolina University	M,D,O
Eastern Illinois University	M
Eastern Michigan University	M,D,O
Elizabeth City State University	M
Ferris State University	D
Florida State University	M
George Mason University	M,D,O
Lenoir-Rhyne University	M
Marymount University	M,O
Mississippi State University	M,D,O
Morgan State University	D
North Carolina State University	M,D
Northern Arizona University	M,D,O
Old Dominion University	M,D
University of Arkansas at Little Rock	M,D
University of Central Florida	M,D,O
University of Memphis	M,D,O
University of Northern Iowa	M
University of South Florida	M,D,O
Wingate University	M,D,O

COMMUNITY HEALTH

Adelphi University	M,O
American University of Beirut	M
Arizona State University at the Tempe campus	M,D,O
Bloomsburg University of Pennsylvania	M
Boston University	M,D
Brooklyn College of the City University of New York	M
Brown University	M,D
Canisius College	M,O
Clark University	M
Columbia University	M,D
Daemen College	M
Dalhousie University	M
East Carolina University	M,O
Eastern Kentucky University	M
East Tennessee State University	M,D,O
George Mason University	M,O
The George Washington University	M,D
Georgia Southern University	M,D
Icahn School of Medicine at Mount Sinai	M,D
Idaho State University	O
Independence University	M
Indiana University Bloomington	M,D
Indiana University–Purdue University Indianapolis	M,D,O
Johns Hopkins University	M,D
Long Island University–LIU Brooklyn	M,D,O
Louisiana State University Health Sciences Center	M,D
McGill University	M,D,O
Medical College of Wisconsin	D
Memorial University of Newfoundland	M,D,O
Merrimack College	M
Midwestern State University	M,O
Minnesota State University Mankato	M
Monroe College	M
New Jersey City University	M
New York University	M,D
Old Dominion University	M
Quinnipiac University	D
Saint Louis University	M

Southern Illinois University Carbondale	M
Southern New Hampshire University	M,O
State University of New York College at Cortland	M
State University of New York College at Potsdam	M
State University of New York Downstate Medical Center	M
Stony Brook University, State University of New York	M,D,O
Suffolk University	M
Teachers College, Columbia University	M,D,O
Texas A&M University	M,D
Tulane University	M,D
Universidad de Ciencias Medicas	M,D,O
Université de Montréal	M,D,O
Université Laval	M,D,O
University at Buffalo, the State University of New York	M,D
The University of Alabama	M
The University of Alabama at Birmingham	M
University of Alberta	M,D
University of Arkansas	M,D
University of Calgary	M,D
University of California, Los Angeles	M,D
University of Colorado Denver	M,D
University of Illinois at Chicago	M,D
University of Illinois at Springfield	M,O
University of Illinois at Urbana–Champaign	M,D
The University of Iowa	M,D
The University of Kansas	M,D,O
University of Louisville	M
University of Manitoba	M,D,O
University of Massachusetts Amherst	M,D
University of Massachusetts Dartmouth	M,D,O
University of Massachusetts Medical School	M,D,O
University of Miami	D
University of Minnesota, Twin Cities Campus	M
University of Missouri	M,D
University of Montana	M,D
University of Nevada, Las Vegas	M,D,O
University of New Mexico	M
The University of North Carolina at Charlotte	M,D,O
The University of North Carolina at Greensboro	M,D
University of Northern British Columbia	M,D,O
University of Northern Colorado	M
University of Northern Iowa	M
University of North Florida	M,O
University of Ottawa	M,D,O
University of Phoenix–Central Valley Campus	M
University of Phoenix–Hawaii Campus	M
University of Pittsburgh	M,D,O
University of Saskatchewan	M,D
University of South Florida	M,D,O
The University of Tennessee	M,D
University of Toronto	M,D
University of Virginia	M,D
University of Washington	M,D
University of Wisconsin–La Crosse	M
University of Wisconsin–Madison	M,D
University of Wisconsin–Milwaukee	D
University of Wyoming	M,D
Virginia State University	M,D
Walden University	M,D,O
Washington State University	M,D,O
West Virginia University	M,D
William James College	M,D

COMMUNITY HEALTH NURSING

Allen College	M,D
American University of Beirut	M
Hampton University	M,D
Hunter College of the City University of New York	M
Husson University	M,O
Independence University	M
Johns Hopkins University	M
Kean University	M
La Salle University	M,D
Louisiana State University Health Sciences Center	M,D,O
New Mexico State University	M,D,O
Oregon Health & Science University	M,O
Rush University	D
San Francisco State University	M,O
Seattle University	M
University of Cincinnati	M,D
University of Hartford	M
University of Hawaii at Manoa	M,D,O
University of Illinois at Chicago	M,O
The University of Kansas	M,D,O
University of Maryland, Baltimore	M
University of Massachusetts Amherst	M,D
University of Massachusetts Dartmouth	M,D,O
University of North Dakota	M,D,O
University of Puerto Rico, Medical Sciences Campus	M
University of South Carolina	M
The University of Texas at Austin	M,D
The University of Texas Health Science Center at San Antonio	M,D,O
The University of Toledo	M,O
University of Washington, Tacoma	M
Worcester State University	M

COMPARATIVE AND INTERDISCIPLINARY ARTS

Brigham Young University	M
Columbia College Chicago	M
Florida Atlantic University	M,D
Goddard College	M
John F. Kennedy University	M
Ohio University	D
Simon Fraser University	M

COMPARATIVE LITERATURE

American University	M
The American University in Cairo	M,O
Arizona State University at the Tempe campus	M,D,O
Binghamton University, State University of New York	M,D
Brigham Young University	M
Brock University	M
Brown University	D
California State University, Northridge	M
Carleton University	D
Carnegie Mellon University	M,D
Case Western Reserve University	M
Claremont Graduate University	M,D
Columbia University	M,D
Cornell University	D
Dartmouth College	M
Duke University	D
East Carolina University	M,D,O
Emory University	D,O
Fairleigh Dickinson University, Metropolitan Campus	M
Florida Atlantic University	M
Georgetown University	M,D
The Graduate Center, City University of New York	M,D
Harrison Middleton University	M,D
Harvard University	D
Hunter College of the City University of New York	M
Indiana University Bloomington	M,D
Johns Hopkins University	D
Louisiana State University and Agricultural & Mechanical College	M,D
New York University	M,D
Northwestern University	M,D
Penn State University Park	M,D
Princeton University	D
Purdue University	M,D
Rutgers University–New Brunswick	M,D
San Francisco State University	M
Stanford University	D
Stony Brook University, State University of New York	M,D,O
Université de Montréal	M,D
Université de Sherbrooke	M,D
Université du Québec à Chicoutimi	M
Université du Québec à Montréal	M,D
Université du Québec à Rimouski	M,D
Université du Québec à Trois-Rivières	M
Université Laval	M,D
University at Buffalo, the State University of New York	M,D
University of Arkansas	M,D
University of California, Berkeley	D
University of California, Davis	D
University of California, Irvine	M,D
University of California, Los Angeles	M,D
University of California, Riverside	M,D
University of California, Santa Barbara	D
University of California, Santa Cruz	M,D
University of Chicago	M,D
University of Colorado Boulder	M,D
University of Dallas	D
University of Georgia	M,D
University of Guelph	D
University of Houston	M
University of Illinois at Urbana–Champaign	M,D
University of Maryland, College Park	M,D
University of Massachusetts Amherst	M,D
University of Memphis	M,D,O
University of Michigan	D
University of Minnesota, Twin Cities Campus	D
University of Missouri	M,D
University of Nebraska–Lincoln	M,D
University of New Mexico	M,D
University of Notre Dame	D
University of Oregon	M,D
University of Pennsylvania	M,D
University of Puerto Rico, Río Piedras Campus	M
University of South Carolina	M,D
University of Southern California	M,D
University of South Florida	O
The University of Texas at Austin	M,D
The University of Texas at Dallas	M,D
University of Toronto	M,D
University of Utah	M,D
University of Washington	M,D
The University of Western Ontario	M,D
University of Wisconsin–Madison	M,D
University of Wisconsin–Milwaukee	M,O
Washington University in St. Louis	M,D
Western Kentucky University	M
Yale University	D

COMPUTATIONAL BIOLOGY

Albert Einstein College of Medicine	D
Baylor College of Medicine	D
Carnegie Mellon University	M,D
Claremont Graduate University	M,D
The College of William and Mary	M,D
Cornell University	D
Duke University	D,O
George Mason University	M,D,O
Harvard University	M
Iowa State University of Science and Technology	M,D
Massachusetts Institute of Technology	D
New Jersey Institute of Technology	M,D,O
New York University	D
Oregon State University	M,D
Princeton University	D
Rutgers University–Camden	M,D
Rutgers University–Newark	M
Rutgers University–New Brunswick	D
University of California, Irvine	D
University of Colorado Denver	M,D
University of Idaho	M,D
University of Illinois at Urbana–Champaign	M,D
The University of Iowa	M,D,O
The University of Kansas	D
University of Maryland, College Park	D
University of Massachusetts Medical School	M,D
University of Minnesota Rochester	M,D
The University of North Carolina at Chapel Hill	D
University of Pennsylvania	D
University of Pittsburgh	D
University of Rochester	D
University of Southern California	D
University of South Florida	M,D
The University of Texas Medical Branch	D
University of Wyoming	D
Washington University in St. Louis	D
Wayne State University	M,D
Weill Cornell Medicine	D
Worcester Polytechnic Institute	M,D
Yale University	D

COMPUTATIONAL SCIENCES

American University of Beirut	M,D
California Institute of Technology	M,D
Chapman University	M,D
Claremont Graduate University	M,D
The College of William and Mary	M
Cornell University	M,D
Emory University	D
Florida State University	M,D
Georgia Institute of Technology	M,D
Hampton University	M
Harvard University	M,D
Lehigh University	M,D
Marquette University	M,D
Massachusetts Institute of Technology	M
McGill University	M,D
Memorial University of Newfoundland	M
Michigan Technological University	M,D,O
Middle Tennessee State University	D
North Carolina Agricultural and Technical State University	M
The Ohio State University	M,D
Oregon State University	M,D
Princeton University	D
Purdue University	D
Rice University	M,D
St. John's University (NY)	M
Sam Houston State University	M,D
San Diego State University	M,D
San Jose State University	M,O
Simon Fraser University	M,D
South Dakota State University	M,D
Southern Illinois University Edwardsville	M
Southern Methodist University	M,D
Stanford University	M,D
Stockton University	M
University at Buffalo, the State University of New York	O
The University of Alabama at Birmingham	D
University of Alaska Fairbanks	M,D
University of California, San Diego	M,D
University of California, Santa Barbara	M,D
University of Chicago	M
University of Colorado Denver	M,D
The University of Iowa	D
University of Lethbridge	M,D
University of Manitoba	M
University of Massachusetts Dartmouth	D
University of Memphis	M
University of Michigan–Dearborn	M
University of Minnesota, Duluth	M
University of Minnesota, Twin Cities Campus	M,D
University of Notre Dame	M,D
University of Pennsylvania	M,D
University of Puerto Rico, Mayagüez Campus	M
University of Southern Mississippi	M,D
The University of Tennessee at Chattanooga	M,D
The University of Texas at Austin	M,D
The University of Texas at El Paso	M,D

COMPUTER AND INFORMATION SYSTEMS SECURITY

American InterContinental University Online	M
American Public University System	M
Armstrong State University	M,O
Auburn University at Montgomery	M
Augusta University	M
Bay Path University	M
Benedictine University	M
Boston University	M,D,O
Brandeis University	M
California State University, San Bernardino	M
Capella University	M,D
Capitol Technology University	M
Carlow University	M
Carnegie Mellon University	M
Central Michigan University	O
Champlain College	M
City University of Seattle	M,O
Claremont Graduate University	M,D,O
Colorado Christian University	M
Colorado Technical University Aurora	M
Colorado Technical University Colorado Springs	M,D
Columbus State University	M,O
Concordia University (Canada)	M,D,O
Concordia University, Nebraska	M
Concordia University of Edmonton	M
Concordia University, St. Paul	M
Dakota State University	M,D,O
Davenport University	M
DePaul University	M,D
DeSales University	M,O
Drury University	O
East Carolina University	M,D,O
Eastern Illinois University	M,O
Eastern Michigan University	O
EC-Council University	M
Embry-Riddle Aeronautical University–Daytona	M,D
Embry-Riddle Aeronautical University–Worldwide	M
Fairfield University	M,O
Ferris State University	M
Florida Institute of Technology	M
Florida International University	M,D
Florida State University	M,D
Fordham University	M
George Mason University	M
The George Washington University	M,D,O
Georgia Institute of Technology	M
Hampton University	M
Harrisburg University of Science and Technology	M
Hofstra University	M
Hood College	M,O
Illinois Institute of Technology	M,D
Indiana University Bloomington	M,D
Indiana University–Purdue University Indianapolis	M,D,O
Inter American University of Puerto Rico, Guayama Campus	M
Iona College	M,O
James Madison University	M
Johns Hopkins University	M,O
Johnson & Wales University	M
Kaplan University, Davenport Campus	M
Keiser University	M
Kennesaw State University	M,O
Kent State University	M
Lawrence Technological University	M,O
Lewis University	M
Liberty University	M,D,O
Lindenwood University	M,O
Lipscomb University	M,O
London Metropolitan University	M,D
Marymount University	M,O
Maryville University of Saint Louis	M,O
Marywood University	M
Mercy College	M
Mercyhurst University	M
Metropolitan State University	M,D,O
Michigan Technological University	M,D
Middle Georgia State University	M
Missouri State University	M
Missouri Western State University	M
Naval Postgraduate School	M,D
New Jersey City University	M,D,O
New Jersey Institute of Technology	M,D,O
New York Institute of Technology	M
New York University	O
Northeastern University	M,D,O
Northern Kentucky University	M,O
Northwestern University	M
Norwich University	M
Nova Southeastern University	M,D
Our Lady of the Lake University	M
Pace University	M,O
Penn State Great Valley	M,O
Purdue University	M
Regis University	M,O
Robert Morris University	M,D
Robert Morris University Illinois	M
Rochester Institute of Technology	M,O
Roger Williams University	M
Rowan University	O
Sacred Heart University	M
St. Cloud State University	M,D,O
Saint Leo University	M
St. Mary's University (United States)	M
Salem International University	M
Salve Regina University	M,O
Sam Houston State University	M,D
San Jose State University	M,O
Shippensburg University of Pennsylvania	M,O
Southern Arkansas University–Magnolia	M
Southern Utah University	M
State University of New York Polytechnic Institute	M
Stevens Institute of Technology	M,D,O
Stevenson University	M
Stratford University (VA)	M
Strayer University	M
Syracuse University	M,O
Texas A&M University–San Antonio	M
Thomas Edison State University	M
Towson University	M,D,O
Trident University International	M
Tuskegee University	M
Universidad del Este	M
Université de Sherbrooke	M
University at Albany, State University of New York	M,O
University of Advancing Technology	M
The University of Alabama at Birmingham	M
The University of Alabama in Huntsville	M,D,O
University of Colorado Colorado Springs	M,D
University of Dallas	M,D
University of Dayton	M
University of Denver	M
University of Detroit Mercy	M,D,O
University of Houston	M
University of Louisville	M,D,O
University of Maryland, Baltimore County	M
University of Maryland University College	M,O
University of Michigan–Dearborn	D
University of Minnesota, Twin Cities Campus	M
University of Missouri–St. Louis	M,D,O
University of Nebraska at Omaha	M,D,O
University of New Haven	M,D,O
University of New Mexico	M
The University of North Carolina at Charlotte	M,D,O
University of Pittsburgh	M,D,O
University of San Diego	M
University of Southern California	M,D
University of South Florida	M
The University of Texas at Austin	M,D
The University of Texas at San Antonio	M,D,O
The University of Texas at Tyler	M
The University of Tulsa	M,D
University of Utah	M,O
University of Washington	M,D
University of West Florida	M
University of Wisconsin–Madison	M
Utah Valley University	O
Utica College	M
Valparaiso University	M
Villanova University	M
Virginia International University	M,O
Virginia Polytechnic Institute and State University	M,O
Walden University	M,D,O
Walsh College of Accountancy and Business Administration	M
Webster University	M
West Chester University of Pennsylvania	M
Western Governors University	M
Wilmington University	M

COMPUTER ART AND DESIGN

Academy of Art University	M
Alfred University	M
ArtCenter College of Design	M
The Art Institute of California–San Francisco, a campus of Argosy University	M
Bowling Green State University	M
California College of the Arts	M
Carnegie Mellon University	M
Chatham University	M
City College of the City University of New York	M
Claremont Graduate University	M
Clemson University	M
Concordia University (Canada)	M,O
Cornell University	M,D
DePaul University	M,D
DigiPen Institute of Technology	M
Digital Media Arts College	M
Drexel University	M
East Tennessee State University	M
Emily Carr University of Art + Design	M
Full Sail University	M
Georgia Institute of Technology	M
Georgian Court University	M,O
Goucher College	M
Indiana University–Purdue University Indianapolis	M
International Technological University	M
Johnson State College	M
Lindenwood University–Belleville	M

COMPUTER EDUCATION

Arcadia University	M,D,O
Ball State University	M,D,O
Eastern Washington University	M
Florida Institute of Technology	M
Illinois Institute of Technology	M,D
Kent State University	M,D
Lesley University	M,D,O
Marlboro College	M,O
Mississippi College	M
Ohio University	M,D
Stony Brook University, State University of New York	M
Teachers College, Columbia University	M,D
Thomas College	M,D,O
University of Bridgeport	M,D,O
University of Illinois at Chicago	D
University of Phoenix–Central Valley Campus	M
University of Phoenix–North Florida Campus	M
University of Phoenix–Online Campus	M,O
University of Phoenix–San Diego Campus	M
University of Phoenix–South Florida Campus	M
University of Phoenix–Washington D.C. Campus	M,D,O

COMPUTER ENGINEERING

Air Force Institute of Technology	M,D
American University of Beirut	M,D
American University of Sharjah	M
Arizona State University at the Tempe campus	M,D
Auburn University	M,D
Baylor University	M,D
Boise State University	M,D
Boston University	M,D,O
Brigham Young University	M,D
Brown University	M,D
Bucknell University	M
California State University, Chico	M
California State University, Fresno	M
California State University, Fullerton	M
California State University, Long Beach	M
Carnegie Mellon University	M,D
Case Western Reserve University	M,D
The Citadel, The Military College of South Carolina	M,O
Clarkson University	M,D
Clemson University	M,D
Colorado Technical University Aurora	M
Colorado Technical University Colorado Springs	M
Columbia University	M,D
Concordia University (Canada)	M,D
Cornell University	M,D
Dalhousie University	M,D
Dartmouth College	M,D
Drexel University	M,D
Duke University	M,D
East Carolina University	M,D,O
École Polytechnique de Montréal	M,O
Fairfield University	M,O
Fairleigh Dickinson University, Metropolitan Campus	M

COMPUTATIONAL SCIENCES (continued — top of column)

University of Utah	M
University of Washington	M,D
Valparaiso University	M
Western Kentucky University	M
Western Michigan University	M,D

---

*M—masters degree; D—doctorate; O—other advanced degree; *—Close-Up and/or Display*

Institution	Degrees
Florida Atlantic University	M,D
Florida Institute of Technology	M,D
Florida International University	M,D
George Mason University	M,D,O
The George Washington University	M,D,O
Georgia Institute of Technology	M,D
Grand Valley State University	M
Illinois Institute of Technology	M,D
Indiana State University	M
Indiana University–Purdue University Fort Wayne	M
Indiana University–Purdue University Indianapolis	M,D
Instituto Tecnológico y de Estudios Superiores de Monterrey, Campus Chihuahua	M,O
International Technological University	M
Iowa State University of Science and Technology	M,D
Johns Hopkins University	M,D,O
Kansas State University	M,D
Kennesaw State University	M
Lakehead University	M
Lawrence Technological University	M,D
Lehigh University	M,D
Louisiana State University and Agricultural & Mechanical College	M,D
Manhattan College	M
Marquette University	M,D,O
Massachusetts Institute of Technology	M,D,O
McGill University	M,D
Memorial University of Newfoundland	M,D
Mercer University	M
Miami University	M
Michigan Technological University	M,D,O
Mississippi State University	M,D
Missouri University of Science and Technology	M,D
Montana State University	M,D
Naval Postgraduate School	M,D,O
New Jersey Institute of Technology	M,D
New Mexico State University	M,D,O
New York Institute of Technology	M
New York University	M,O
Norfolk State University	M
North Carolina Agricultural and Technical State University	M,D
North Carolina State University	M,D
North Dakota State University	M,D
Northeastern University	M,D,O
Northern Arizona University	M
Northwestern Polytechnic University	M,D
Northwestern University	M,D
Oakland University	M,D
The Ohio State University	M,D
Oklahoma Christian University	M
Oklahoma State University	M,D
Old Dominion University	M,D
Oregon Health & Science University	M,D
Oregon State University	M,D
Polytechnic University of Puerto Rico	M
Portland State University	M,D
Purdue University	M,D
Purdue University Northwest	M
Queen's University at Kingston	M,D
Rensselaer at Hartford	M
Rensselaer Polytechnic Institute	M,D
Rice University	M,D
Rochester Institute of Technology	M
Rose-Hulman Institute of Technology	M
Royal Military College of Canada	M,D
Rutgers University–New Brunswick	M,D
St. Mary's University (United States)	M
Santa Clara University	M,D,O
Silicon Valley University	M
Southern Illinois University Carbondale	M,D
Southern Methodist University	M,D
Stevens Institute of Technology	M,D,O
Stony Brook University, State University of New York	M,D
Syracuse University	M,D
Tennessee State University	M,D
Texas A&M University	M,D
Universidad del Turabo	M
The University of Akron	M,D
The University of Alabama	M,D
The University of Alabama at Birmingham	M,D
The University of Alabama in Huntsville	M,D
University of Alberta	M,D
The University of Arizona	M,D
University of Arkansas	M,D
University of Bridgeport	M,D
The University of British Columbia	M,D
University of Calgary	M,D
University of California, Davis	M,D
University of California, Riverside	M
University of California, San Diego	M,D
University of California, Santa Barbara	M,D
University of California, Santa Cruz	M,D
University of Central Florida	M,D
University of Cincinnati	M,D
University of Colorado Boulder	M,D
University of Dayton	M,D
University of Delaware	M,D
University of Denver	M,D
University of Detroit Mercy	M,D
University of Florida	M,D
University of Houston–Clear Lake	M
University of Idaho	M,D
University of Illinois at Chicago	M,D
University of Illinois at Urbana–Champaign	M,D
The University of Iowa	M,D
The University of Kansas	M
University of Louisiana at Lafayette	M,D
University of Louisville	M,D,O
University of Maine	M,D
University of Manitoba	M,D
University of Maryland, Baltimore County	M,D
University of Maryland, College Park	M,D
University of Massachusetts Amherst	M,D
University of Massachusetts Dartmouth	M,D,O
University of Massachusetts Lowell	M,D
University of Memphis	M,D,O
University of Miami	M,D
University of Michigan	M,D
University of Michigan–Dearborn	M,D
University of Minnesota, Duluth	M
University of Minnesota, Twin Cities Campus	M,D
University of Missouri–Kansas City	M,D,O
University of Nebraska–Lincoln	M,D
University of Nevada, Las Vegas	M,D
University of Nevada, Reno	M,D
University of New Brunswick Fredericton	M,D
University of New Haven	M
University of New Mexico	M,D
The University of North Carolina at Charlotte	M,D
University of North Texas	M,D,O
University of Notre Dame	M,D
University of Oklahoma	M,D
University of Ottawa	M,D
University of Pittsburgh	M,D
University of Puerto Rico, Mayagüez Campus	M,D
University of Regina	M,D
University of Rhode Island	M,D
University of Rochester	M,D
University of San Diego	M
University of South Alabama	M
University of South Carolina	M,D
University of Southern California	M,D,O
University of South Florida	M,D
The University of Tennessee	M,D
The University of Texas at Arlington	M,D
The University of Texas at Austin	M,D
The University of Texas at Dallas	M,D
The University of Texas at El Paso	M,D
The University of Texas at San Antonio	M,D
University of Toronto	M,D
University of Victoria	M,D
University of Virginia	M,D
University of Washington, Bothell	M
University of Washington, Tacoma	M
University of Waterloo	M,D
The University of Western Ontario	M,D
University of Wisconsin–Milwaukee	M,D
Villanova University	M,O
Virginia Polytechnic Institute and State University	M,D,O
Washington State University	M,D
Washington University in St. Louis	M,D
Wayne State University	M,D
Weber State University	M
Western Michigan University	M,D
West Virginia University	D
Wichita State University	M,D
Worcester Polytechnic Institute	M,D,O
Wright State University	M,D
Youngstown State University	M

COMPUTER SCIENCE

Institution	Degrees
Acadia University	M
Air Force Institute of Technology	M,D
Alabama Agricultural and Mechanical University	M
Alcorn State University	M
American Sentinel University	M
The American University in Cairo	M,D,O
American University of Armenia	M
American University of Beirut	M,D
Appalachian State University	M
Arizona State University at the Tempe campus	M,D
Arkansas State University	M
Armstrong State University	M
Auburn University	M,D
Ball State University	M
Baylor University	M,D
Binghamton University, State University of New York	M,D
Boise State University	M,O
Boston University	M,D,O
Bowie State University	M,D
Bowling Green State University	M.
Bradley University	M
Brandeis University	M,D
Bridgewater State University	M
Brigham Young University	M,D
Brock University	M,D
Brooklyn College of the City University of New York	M,O
Brown University	M,D
California Institute of Technology	M,D
California Polytechnic State University, San Luis Obispo	M
California State Polytechnic University, Pomona	M
California State University Channel Islands	M
California State University, Chico	M
California State University, Dominguez Hills	M
California State University, East Bay	M
California State University, Fresno	M
California State University, Fullerton	M
California State University, Long Beach	M
California State University, Los Angeles	M
California State University, Northridge	M
California State University, Sacramento	M
California State University, San Bernardino	M
California State University, San Marcos	M
Capitol Technology University	M
Carleton University	M,D
Carnegie Mellon University	M,D
Case Western Reserve University	M,D
The Catholic University of America	M,D
Central Connecticut State University	M,O
Central Michigan University	M
Chicago State University	M
Christopher Newport University	M
City College of the City University of New York	M,D
City University of Seattle	M,O
Clark Atlanta University	M
Clarkson University	M,D
Clemson University	M,D
Coastal Carolina University	M,D,O
College of Charleston	M
The College of Saint Rose	M,O
College of Staten Island of the City University of New York	M
The College of William and Mary	M,D
Colorado School of Mines	M,D
Colorado State University	M,D
Colorado Technical University Aurora	M
Colorado Technical University Colorado Springs	M,D
Columbia University	M,D
Columbus State University	M,O
Concordia University (Canada)	M,D,O
Concordia University, Nebraska	M
Cornell University	M,D
Dakota State University	M,D,O
Dalhousie University	M,D
Dartmouth College	M,D
DePaul University	M,D
DigiPen Institute of Technology	M
Drexel University	M,D,O
Duke University	M,D
East Carolina University	M,D,O
Eastern Illinois University	M
Eastern Michigan University	M,O
Eastern Washington University	M
East Stroudsburg University of Pennsylvania	M
East Tennessee State University	M
École Polytechnique de Montréal	M,D,O
Embry-Riddle Aeronautical University–Daytona	M,D
Emory University	M,D
Fairleigh Dickinson University, College at Florham	M
Fairleigh Dickinson University, Metropolitan Campus	M
Fitchburg State University	M
Florida Atlantic University	M,D
Florida Institute of Technology	M,D
Florida International University	M,D
Florida State University	M,D
Fontbonne University	M
Fordham University	M
Franklin University	M
Frostburg State University	M
Gannon University	M
George Mason University	M,D,O
Georgetown University	M,D
The George Washington University	M,D,O
Georgia Institute of Technology	M,D
Georgia Southern University	M
Georgia Southwestern State University	M,O
Georgia State University	M,D
Governors State University	M
The Graduate Center, City University of New York	D
Grand Valley State University	M
Hampton University	M
Harvard University	M,D
Hood College	M,O
Howard University	M
Illinois Institute of Technology	M,D
Indiana State University	M
Indiana University Bloomington	M,D,O
Indiana University–Purdue University Fort Wayne	M
Indiana University–Purdue University Indianapolis	M,D,O
Indiana University South Bend	M,O
Instituto Tecnológico y de Estudios Superiores de Monterrey, Campus Central de Veracruz	M
Instituto Tecnológico y de Estudios Superiores de Monterrey, Campus Ciudad de México	M,D
Instituto Tecnológico y de Estudios Superiores de Monterrey, Campus Cuernavaca	M,D
Instituto Tecnológico y de Estudios Superiores de Monterrey, Campus Estado de México	M,D
Instituto Tecnológico y de Estudios Superiores de Monterrey, Campus Irapuato	M,D
Instituto Tecnológico y de Estudios Superiores de Monterrey, Campus Monterrey	M,D
Inter American University of Puerto Rico, Fajardo Campus	M
Inter American University of Puerto Rico, Guayama Campus	M
Inter American University of Puerto Rico, Metropolitan Campus	M
Iona College	M
Iowa State University of Science and Technology	M,D
Jackson State University	M
Jacksonville State University	M
James Madison University	M
Johns Hopkins University	M,D,O
Kansas State University	M,D
Kennesaw State University	M
Kent State University	M,D
Kentucky State University	M
Knowledge Systems Institute	M
Kutztown University of Pennsylvania	M
Lakehead University	M
Lamar University	M
La Salle University	M,O
Lawrence Technological University	M,O
Lebanese American University	M
Lehigh University	M,D
Lehman College of the City University of New York	M
Long Island University–LIU Brooklyn	M,O
Louisiana State University and Agricultural & Mechanical College	M,D
Louisiana State University in Shreveport	M
Louisiana Tech University	M,D
Loyola University Chicago	M
Maharishi University of Management	M
Marist College	M,O
Marquette University	M,D
Marshall University	M
Massachusetts Institute of Technology	M,D,O
McGill University	M,D
McMaster University	M,D
McNeese State University	M
Memorial University of Newfoundland	M,D
Merrimack College	M
Metropolitan State University	M
Michigan State University	M,D
Michigan Technological University	M,D
Middle Tennessee State University	M
Midwestern State University	M
Mills College	M,O
Minnesota State University Mankato	M,O
Mississippi College	M
Mississippi State University	M
Missouri State University	M
Missouri University of Science and Technology	M,D
Monmouth University	M
Monroe College	M
Montana State University	M,O
Montclair State University	M,O
National University	M
Naval Postgraduate School	M,D,O
New Jersey Institute of Technology	M,D,O
New Mexico Highlands University	M
New Mexico Institute of Mining and Technology	M,D
New Mexico State University	M,D
New York Institute of Technology	M,D
New York University	M,D
Norfolk State University	M
North Carolina Agricultural and Technical State University	M
North Carolina State University	M,D
North Central College	M
North Dakota State University	M,D,O
Northeastern Illinois University	M
Northeastern University	M
Northern Arizona University	M
Northern Illinois University	M
Northern Kentucky University	M
Northwestern Polytechnic University	M,D
Northwestern University	M,D
Northwest Missouri State University	M
Notre Dame College (OH)	M,O
Nova Southeastern University	M,D
Oakland University	M,D
The Ohio State University	M,D
Ohio University	M,D
Oklahoma Christian University	M
Oklahoma City University	M
Oklahoma State University	M,D
Old Dominion University	M,D
Oregon Health & Science University	M,D
Oregon State University	M,D
Pace University	M,D,O
Pacific States University	M
Penn State Harrisburg	M,O
Penn State University Park	M,D
Polytechnic University of Puerto Rico	M
Portland State University	M,D
Prairie View A&M University	M,D
Princeton University	M,D
Purdue University	M,D
Purdue University Northwest	M
Queens College of the City University of New York	M
Queen's University at Kingston	M,D

Regis University	M,O
Rensselaer at Hartford	M
Rensselaer Polytechnic Institute	M,D
Rice University	M,D
Rivier University	M
Rochester Institute of Technology	M,D
Roosevelt University	M
Rowan University	M
Royal Military College of Canada	M
Rutgers University–Camden	M
Rutgers University–New Brunswick	M,D
Sacred Heart University	M
St. Cloud State University	M
St. Francis Xavier University	M
Saint Joseph's University	M,O
St. Mary's University (United States)	M
Saint Xavier University	M
Sam Houston State University	M,D
San Diego State University	M
San Francisco State University	M
San Jose State University	M,O
Santa Clara University	M,D,O
Seattle University	M
Shippensburg University of Pennsylvania	M,O
Silicon Valley University	M
Simon Fraser University	M,D
Sofia University	M,D
Southern Arkansas University–Magnolia	M
Southern Connecticut State University	M
Southern Illinois University Carbondale	M,D
Southern Illinois University Edwardsville	M
Southern Methodist University	M,D
Southern Oregon University	M
Southern University and Agricultural and Mechanical College	M
Stanford University	M,D
State University of New York at New Paltz	M
State University of New York Polytechnic Institute	M
Stephen F. Austin State University	M
Stevens Institute of Technology	M,D,O
Stony Brook University, State University of New York	M,D,O
Stratford University (VA)	M
Syracuse University	M
Télé-université	M
Tennessee Technological University	M
Texas A&M University	M,D
Texas A&M University–Corpus Christi	M
Texas A&M University–Kingsville	M
Texas Southern University	M
Texas State University	M,D
Texas Tech University	M,D
Towson University	M
Toyota Technological Institute at Chicago	D
Trent University	M
Troy University	M
Tufts University	M,D,O
Universidad Autonoma de Guadalajara	M,D
Universidad de las Américas Puebla	M,D
Université de Moncton	M,O
Université de Montréal	M,D
Université du Québec à Trois-Rivières	M
Université du Québec en Outaouais	M,D,O
Université Laval	M,D
University at Albany, State University of New York	M,D
University at Buffalo, the State University of New York	M,D,O
University of Advancing Technology	M
The University of Akron	M
The University of Alabama	M,D
The University of Alabama at Birmingham	M,D
The University of Alabama in Huntsville	M,D,O
University of Alaska Fairbanks	M
University of Alberta	M,D
The University of Arizona	M,D
University of Arkansas	M,D
University of Arkansas at Little Rock	M,D
University of Bridgeport	M,D
The University of British Columbia	M,D
University of Calgary	M,D
University of California, Berkeley	M,D
University of California, Davis	M,D
University of California, Irvine	M,D
University of California, Los Angeles	M,D
University of California, Merced	M,D
University of California, Riverside	M,D
University of California, San Diego	M,D
University of California, Santa Barbara	M,D
University of California, Santa Cruz	M,D
University of Central Arkansas	M
University of Central Florida	M,D
University of Central Missouri	M,D,O
University of Central Oklahoma	M
University of Chicago	M,D
University of Cincinnati	M,D
University of Colorado Boulder	M,D
University of Colorado Colorado Springs	M
University of Colorado Denver	M,D
University of Connecticut	M,D
University of Dayton	M
University of Delaware	M,D
University of Denver	M
University of Detroit Mercy	M,D,O
University of Florida	M,D
University of Georgia	M,D
University of Guelph	M,D
University of Hawaii at Manoa	M,D,O
University of Houston	M,D
University of Houston–Clear Lake	M
University of Houston–Victoria	M
University of Idaho	M,D
University of Illinois at Chicago	M,D
University of Illinois at Springfield	M
University of Illinois at Urbana–Champaign	M,D
The University of Iowa	M,D
The University of Kansas	M,D
University of Kentucky	M,D
University of Lethbridge	M,D
University of Louisiana at Lafayette	M,D
University of Louisville	M,D,O
University of Maine	M,D,O
University of Management and Technology	M,O
The University of Manchester	M,D
University of Manitoba	M,D
University of Maryland, Baltimore County	M,D
University of Maryland, College Park	M,D
University of Maryland Eastern Shore	M
University of Massachusetts Amherst	M,D
University of Massachusetts Boston	M,D
University of Massachusetts Dartmouth	M,D,O
University of Massachusetts Lowell	M,D
University of Memphis	M,D
University of Miami	M,D
University of Michigan	M,D
University of Michigan–Dearborn	D
University of Michigan–Flint	M
University of Minnesota, Duluth	M
University of Minnesota, Twin Cities Campus	M,D
University of Missouri	M,D
University of Missouri–Kansas City	M,D,O
University of Missouri–St. Louis	M,D
University of Montana	M
University of Nebraska at Omaha	M,O
University of Nebraska–Lincoln	M,D
University of Nevada, Las Vegas	M,D
University of Nevada, Reno	M,D
University of New Brunswick Fredericton	M,D
University of New Hampshire	M,D
University of New Haven	M,D,O
University of New Mexico	M,D
University of New Orleans	M
The University of North Carolina at Chapel Hill	M,D
The University of North Carolina at Charlotte	M,D,O
The University of North Carolina at Greensboro	M
The University of North Carolina Wilmington	M
University of North Dakota	M
University of Northern British Columbia	M,D,O
University of North Florida	M
University of North Texas	M,D,O
University of Notre Dame	M,D
University of Oklahoma	M,D
University of Oregon	M,D
University of Ottawa	M,D
University of Pennsylvania	M,D
University of Pittsburgh	M,D
University of Portland	M
University of Puerto Rico, Mayagüez Campus	M,D
University of Regina	M,D
University of Rhode Island	M,D,O
University of Rochester	M,D
University of San Francisco	M
University of Saskatchewan	M,D
University of South Alabama	M,D
University of South Carolina	M,D
The University of South Dakota	M
University of Southern California	M,D
University of Southern Maine	M,O
University of Southern Mississippi	M,D
University of South Florida	M,D
The University of Tennessee	M,D
The University of Tennessee at Chattanooga	M
The University of Texas at Arlington	M,D
The University of Texas at Austin	M,D
The University of Texas at Dallas	M,D
The University of Texas at El Paso	M,D
The University of Texas at San Antonio	M,D
The University of Texas at Tyler	M
The University of Texas of the Permian Basin	M
The University of Texas Rio Grande Valley	M
University of the District of Columbia	M
The University of Toledo	M,D
The University of Tulsa	M,D
University of Utah	M,D
University of Vermont	M,D
University of Victoria	M,D
University of Virginia	M,D
University of Waterloo	M,D
The University of Western Ontario	M,D
University of West Florida	M
University of West Georgia	M,O
University of Windsor	M,D
University of Wisconsin–Madison	M,D
University of Wisconsin–Milwaukee	M,D
University of Wisconsin–Parkside	M
University of Wisconsin–Platteville	M
University of Wyoming	M,D
Utah State University	M,D
Vanderbilt University	M,D
Villanova University	M,D
Virginia Commonwealth University	M,D
Virginia International University	M,O
Virginia Polytechnic Institute and State University	M,D,O
Virginia State University	M
Wake Forest University	M
Washington State University	M,D
Washington University in St. Louis	M,D
Wayne State University	M,D
Webster University	M
Wesleyan University	M,D
West Chester University of Pennsylvania	M,O
Western Illinois University	M
Western Kentucky University	M
Western Michigan University	M,D
Western Washington University	M
West Virginia University	M,D
Wichita State University	M,D
Winston-Salem State University	M
Worcester Polytechnic Institute	M,D,O
Wright State University	M,D
Yale University	M,D
York University	M,D
Youngstown State University	M

CONDENSED MATTER PHYSICS

Iowa State University of Science and Technology	M,D
Memorial University of Newfoundland	M,D
Rutgers University–New Brunswick	M,D
University of Alberta	M,D
The University of Manchester	M,D
University of Victoria	M,D
West Virginia University	M,D

CONFLICT RESOLUTION AND MEDIATION/PEACE STUDIES

Abilene Christian University	M,O
American Public University System	M
American University	M,D,O
The American University of Paris	M
Anabaptist Mennonite Biblical Seminary	M,O
Antioch University Midwest	M
Arcadia University	M
Bethany Theological Seminary	M,O
Bethel University (TN)	M
Brandeis University	M
California State University, Dominguez Hills	M
Cambridge College	M
Carleton University	M,O
Champlain College	M
Colgate Rochester Crozer Divinity School	M,D,O
Colorado Technical University Aurora	M
Colorado Technical University Colorado Springs	M,D
Columbia College (SC)	M
Columbia University	M
Cornell University	M,D
Creighton University	M,O
Dallas Baptist University	M
Dominican University	M
Drew University	M,D,O
Eastern Mennonite University	M,O
Excelsior College	M,O
Fresno Pacific University	M,O
George Mason University	M,D,O
Georgetown University	M
Henley-Putnam University	M
Kansas State University	M,D,O
Kennesaw State University	M,D
Kent State University	M,D
Lesley University	M,D,O
Lipscomb University	M,O
London Metropolitan University	M,D
Middlebury Institute of International Studies at Monterey	M
Montclair State University	M,O
Naval Postgraduate School	M,D
New York University	M,O
Norwich University	M
Nova Southeastern University	M,D,O
Old Dominion University	M,D
Pepperdine University	M
Portland State University	M
Regent University	M,D
Royal Roads University	M,O
Saint Mary's College of California	M
St. Mary's University (United States)	M,O
Saint Paul University	M
Salisbury University	M
Salve Regina University	M,D
SIT Graduate Institute	M
Southern Methodist University	M
Southern New Hampshire University	M,O
Syracuse University	O
Trident University International	M,D
Tufts University	M,D
United States International University–Africa	M
United Theological Seminary of the Twin Cities	M,D,O
Universidad del Turabo	M
Université de Sherbrooke	M,D,O
University of Arkansas at Little Rock	O
University of Baltimore	M
University of Bridgeport	M
University of Denver	M
University of Hawaii at Manoa	M,O
University of Idaho	D
The University of Manchester	D
University of Massachusetts Amherst	M,D
University of Massachusetts Boston	M,O
University of Massachusetts Lowell	M
University of Missouri	M,D,O
University of New Brunswick Fredericton	M
University of New Haven	M,O
The University of North Carolina at Greensboro	M,O
The University of North Carolina Wilmington	M
University of Notre Dame	M,D
University of Phoenix–Online Campus	M,O
University of San Diego	M
University of the Sacred Heart	M
University of Victoria	M,D
University of Wisconsin–Milwaukee	M,D,O
Walden University	M,D,O
Wayne State University	M,D,O
Wilfrid Laurier University	D
Willamette University	M,D
Yeshiva University	M,D

CONSERVATION BIOLOGY

Antioch University New England	M
Arizona State University at the Tempe campus	M,D
California State University, Sacramento	M
California State University, Stanislaus	M
Central Michigan University	M
Colorado State University	M,D
Columbia University	M,D
Cornell University	M,D
Florida Institute of Technology	M
Fordham University	M,D,O
Frostburg State University	M
Illinois State University	M,D
Oregon State University	M,D
State University of New York College of Environmental Science and Forestry	M,D
Texas State University	M
Tropical Agriculture Research and Higher Education Center	M,D
University of Alberta	M,D
University of Central Florida	M,D,O
University of Hawaii at Hilo	M
University of Illinois at Urbana–Champaign	M,D
University of Maryland, College Park	M
University of Minnesota, Twin Cities Campus	M,D
University of Missouri	M,D,O
University of Nevada, Reno	D
University of New Hampshire	M,D
The University of West Alabama	M
University of Wisconsin–Madison	M
University of Wisconsin–Milwaukee	M,D
University of Wisconsin–Stout	M

CONSTRUCTION ENGINEERING

The American University in Cairo	M,D,O
Arizona State University at the Tempe campus	M,D
Auburn University	M
Bradley University	M
Colorado School of Mines	M,D
Columbia University	M,D
Concordia University (Canada)	M,D,O
George Mason University	M,D
Illinois Institute of Technology	M,D
Iowa State University of Science and Technology	M,D
Lawrence Technological University	M,D
Marquette University	M,D
Massachusetts Institute of Technology	M,D,O
Missouri University of Science and Technology	M,D
Montana State University	M,D
Ohio University	M,D
Oregon State University	M,D
Pittsburg State University	M
Stanford University	M,D,O
Stevens Institute of Technology	M,O

Texas Tech University	M,D
The University of Alabama	M,D
The University of Alabama at Birmingham	M,D
University of Alberta	M,D
University of Central Florida	M,D,O
University of Michigan	M,D,O
University of Missouri–Kansas City	M,D,O
University of New Brunswick Fredericton	M,D
University of Puerto Rico, Mayagüez Campus	M,D
University of Southern Mississippi	M
University of Virginia	D
University of Washington	M,D
Virginia Polytechnic Institute and State University	M,D,O
Wentworth Institute of Technology	

CONSTRUCTION MANAGEMENT

The American University in Dubai	M
Arizona State University at the Tempe campus	M,D
Brigham Young University	M
California Baptist University	M
California State University, Chico	M
California State University, East Bay	M
California State University, Northridge	M
Carnegie Mellon University	M,D
Central Connecticut State University	M,O
Clemson University	M
Colorado State University	M
Columbia University	M,D
Drexel University	M
East Carolina University	M
Eastern Michigan University	M,O
Florida International University	M
Georgia Southern University	M
Illinois Institute of Technology	M,D
Indiana University–Purdue University Fort Wayne	M
Instituto Tecnologico de Santo Domingo	M,O
Kennesaw State University	M
Louisiana State University and Agricultural & Mechanical College	M,D
Marquette University	M,D,O
Michigan State University	M,D
Milwaukee School of Engineering	M
Missouri State University	M
New England Institute of Technology	M
NewSchool of Architecture and Design	
New York University	M,D,O
North Carolina Agricultural and Technical State University	M
North Dakota State University	M,O
Norwich University	M
Philadelphia University	M
Pittsburg State University	M,O
Polytechnic University of Puerto Rico, Miami Campus	M
Polytechnic University of Puerto Rico, Orlando Campus	M
Purdue University	M
South Dakota School of Mines and Technology	M
State University of New York College of Environmental Science and Forestry	M,D
Stevens Institute of Technology	M,O
Texas A&M University	M
Universidad de las Américas Puebla	M,D,O
University of Alaska Fairbanks	M
University of Arkansas at Little Rock	M,O
University of California, Berkeley	O
University of Denver	M
University of Florida	M,D
University of Houston	M
The University of Kansas	M
University of Nevada, Las Vegas	M,O
University of New Mexico	M,D
The University of North Carolina at Charlotte	M,O
University of North Florida	M
University of Oklahoma	M,D
University of Southern California	M,D,O
The University of Tennessee at Chattanooga	M,O
The University of Texas at Arlington	M,D
The University of Texas at El Paso	M,D,O
University of Washington	M
University of Wisconsin–Stout	M
Virginia Polytechnic Institute and State University	M,D,O
Wentworth Institute of Technology	M
Western Carolina University	M
Worcester Polytechnic Institute	M,D,O

CONSUMER ECONOMICS

Colorado State University	M
Cornell University	M,D
Kansas State University	M,D,O
North Carolina Agricultural and Technical State University	M
North Dakota State University	M,O
Ohio University	M
Oklahoma State University	M,D
Purdue University	M
South Dakota State University	M
State University of New York at Oswego	M,D
Texas Tech University	M,D
Université Laval	O
The University of Alabama	M
University of Guelph	M

University of Idaho	M
University of Illinois at Urbana–Champaign	M,D
University of Missouri	M,D,O
University of Nebraska–Lincoln	M,D
University of South Carolina	M
The University of Tennessee	M,D
University of Utah	M
University of Wisconsin–Madison	M,D
University of Wyoming	M
Utah State University	M

CORPORATE AND ORGANIZATIONAL COMMUNICATION

Argosy University, Schaumburg	M,D,O
Armstrong State University	M,O
Ashland University	M
Barry University	M,O
Baruch College of the City University of New York	M
Bellevue University	M
Boston University	M
Bowie State University	M,O
Bryant University	M,O
California State University, San Bernardino	M
Canisius College	M
Carnegie Mellon University	M
City College of the City University of New York	M
Columbia University	M
Concordia University, St. Paul	M
Concordia University Wisconsin	M
Cornell University	M,D
Dallas Baptist University	M
DePaul University	M
Drexel University	M
Eastern Michigan University	M,O
East Tennessee State University	M
Emerson College	M
Fairleigh Dickinson University, College at Florham	M
Florida State University	M,D
Franklin University	M
Golden Gate University	M,D,O
HEC Montreal	O
High Point University	M
Howard University	M,D
Illinois Institute of Technology	M
Iowa State University of Science and Technology	M,D
La Salle University	M,O
Lasell College	M,O
Loyola University Chicago	M
Manhattanville College	M
Marist College	M
Minnesota State University Mankato	M,O
Mississippi College	M
Monmouth University	M,O
Montclair State University	M
Murray State University	M
New Mexico State University	M,D
New York University	M
Northeastern University	M
Northwestern University	M,D
Ohio University	M,D
Radford University	M
Regent University	M,D,O
Regis College (MA)	M
Rider University	M
Roosevelt University	M
Rowan University	O
St. Bonaventure University	M
Seton Hall University	M
Southern Illinois University Edwardsville	M
Spalding University	M
State University of New York at Oswego	M
Stevens Institute of Technology	O
Suffolk University	M
Temple University	M,D
Texas Christian University	M
Towson University	M
Troy University	M
Universidad Autonoma de Guadalajara	M,D
Universidad Iberoamericana	M,D
Université de Sherbrooke	M
University of Alaska Fairbanks	M
University of Central Florida	M,O
University of Colorado Denver	M
University of Nebraska–Lincoln	M,D
University of Oklahoma	M,D
University of Portland	M
University of Southern California	M
University of South Florida	M,O
University of Wisconsin–Milwaukee	M,D,O
University of Wisconsin–Stevens Point	M
University of Wisconsin–Whitewater	M
Washington State University	M,D
Webster University	M
Western Kentucky University	M,O
West Virginia University	M,D,O

COUNSELING PSYCHOLOGY

Abilene Christian University	M
Adelphi University	M
Adler Graduate School	M
Adler University	M,D,O
Alabama Agricultural and Mechanical University	M,O
Alaska Pacific University	M
Alfred University	M,D,O
Amberton University	M
American International College	M,D
Amridge University	M,D
Andrews University	M,D
Angelo State University	M

Anna Maria College	M
Antioch University New England	M
Appalachian State University	M
Arcadia University	M
Argosy University, Chicago	D
Argosy University, Denver	M,D
Argosy University, Hawai`i	D
Argosy University, Inland Empire	M,D
Argosy University, Los Angeles	M,D
Argosy University, Nashville	M,D
Argosy University, Northern Virginia	M,D
Argosy University, Orange County	M,D
Argosy University, Phoenix	M
Argosy University, Salt Lake City	M,D
Argosy University, San Diego	M,D
Argosy University, San Francisco Bay Area	M,D
Argosy University, Sarasota	M,D
Argosy University, Schaumburg	M,O
Argosy University, Seattle	M,D
Argosy University, Tampa	M,D
Arizona State University at the Tempe campus	D
Assumption College	M,O
Athabasca University	M,O
Austin Peay State University	M
Avila University	M
Ball State University	M,D
Bastyr University	M,O
Becker College	M
Bethel University (MN)	M,D,O
Boston College	M,D
Boston Graduate School of Psychoanalysis	M
Boston University	M
Bowie State University	M
Bradley University	M
Brandman University	M
Brigham Young University	M,D,O
Brooklyn College of the City University of New York	M,D,O
Caldwell University	M,O
California Baptist University	M
California Institute of Integral Studies	M,D
California State University, Bakersfield	M
California State University, Fresno	M
California State University, Sacramento	M
California State University, San Bernardino	M
California State University, Stanislaus	M
California University of Pennsylvania	M
Cambridge College	M,O
Capella University	M
Carlos Albizu University, Miami Campus	M,D
Carlow University	M,D,O
Centenary University	M
Central Michigan University	M,D,O
Central Washington University	M
Chaminade University of Honolulu	M
Chatham University	M,D
Chestnut Hill College	M,O
City University of Seattle	M
Clemson University	M,O
Cleveland State University	M,D,O
The College at Brockport, State University of New York	M,O
The College of New Rochelle	M,O
College of Saint Elizabeth	M,D,O
College of St. Joseph	M
The College of Saint Rose	M,O
College of Staten Island of the City University of New York	M
Colorado Christian University	M
Concordia University Chicago	M
Dallas Baptist University	M
Delaware Valley University	M
DePaul University	M,D
Dominican University of California	M
Duquesne University	M,D,O
Eastern Nazarene College	M
Eastern University	M,O
Eastern Washington University	M
East Texas Baptist University	M
Edinboro University of Pennsylvania	M
Emporia State University	M
Evangel University	M
Fairfield University	M,O
Fairleigh Dickinson University, College at Florham	M
Felician University	M
Fitchburg State University	M
Florida International University	M,D,O
Florida State University	D
Fordham University	M
Fort Valley State University	M
Franciscan University of Steubenville	M
Francis Marion University	M,O
Frostburg State University	M
Gallaudet University	M,D,O
Gannon University	M
Gardner-Webb University	M
Geneva College	M
George Fox University	M,O
Georgian Court University	M,O
Georgia State University	M,O
Governors State University	M
Grace University	M
Harding University	M
Hardin-Simmons University	M
Heidelberg University	M
Henderson State University	M,O
Hodges University	M

Hofstra University	M,O
Holy Family University	M,D
Holy Names University	M
Houston Baptist University	M
Howard University	D
Humboldt State University	M
Husson University	M
Idaho State University	M,D,O
Illinois State University	M,D,O
Immaculata University	M,D,O
Indiana University Northwest	M,O
Indiana University South Bend	M,O
Indiana Wesleyan University	M
Instituto Tecnologico de Santo Domingo	M,O
Inter American University of Puerto Rico, Aguadilla Campus	M
Inter American University of Puerto Rico, Metropolitan Campus	M,D
Inter American University of Puerto Rico, San Germán Campus	M
Iona College	M,O
Iowa State University of Science and Technology	M,D
Jacksonville University	M
James Madison University	D
John Brown University	M,O
John Carroll University	M,O
John F. Kennedy University	M
Johns Hopkins University	M,D,O
Kean University	M
Kent State University	M
Kutztown University of Pennsylvania	M
Lamar University	M
Lancaster Bible College	M,D
La Salle University	M
Lee University	M
Lehigh University	M,D,O
Lenoir-Rhyne University	M
Lesley University	M,D,O
LeTourneau University	M
Lewis & Clark College	M
Lewis University	M
Liberty University	M,D,O
Lindenwood University	M,D,O
Lindsey Wilson College	M,D
Lipscomb University	M,O
Lock Haven University of Pennsylvania	M
London Metropolitan University	M,D
Long Island University–Brentwood Campus	M,O
Long Island University–Hudson	M,O
Long Island University–LIU Brooklyn	M,O
Long Island University–LIU Post	M,D,O
Louisiana Tech University	M,D
Loyola Marymount University	M
Loyola University Chicago	D
Loyola University Maryland	M,O
Lynchburg College	M
Lynn University	M
Marist College	M,O
Marquette University	M,D
Marymount University	M
Marywood University	M
McGill University	M,D,O
McKendree University	M
McNeese State University	M
Medaille College	M,D
Mercy College	M,O
Messiah College	M,O
Mid-America Christian University	M
Middle Tennessee State University	M
Midwestern State University	M
Minnesota State University Mankato	M,D
Mississippi College	M,O
Missouri State University	M
Monmouth University	M,O
Montana State University Billings	M
Moody Theological Seminary–Michigan	M,O
Morehead State University	M,O
Mount Mary University	M,O
Mount Saint Mary's University (CA)	M,D,O
Naropa University	M
National University	M
New England College	M
New Mexico Highlands University	M
New Mexico State University	M,D,O
New York University	M,D,O
Niagara University	M,O
North Dakota State University	M,D
Northeastern State University	M
Northeastern University	M,D,O
Northern Arizona University	M
Northern Kentucky University	M
Northern State University	M
Northwest Christian University	M
Northwestern Oklahoma State University	M
Northwest University	M,D
Nova Southeastern University	M,D,O
Nyack College	M
Oakland University	M,D,O
Old Dominion University	M,D,O
Ottawa University	M
Our Lady of the Lake University	D
Pace University	M,D
Pacifica Graduate Institute	M,D
Palm Beach Atlantic University	M
Palo Alto University	M
Philadelphia College of Osteopathic Medicine	M,D,O
Phoenix Seminary	M,D,O
Prescott College	M
Providence University College & Theological Seminary	M,D,O
Purdue University Northwest	M

Queens College of the City University of New York — M,O
Radford University — D
Regent University — M,D,O
Regis College (MA) — M,D,O
Rhode Island College — M,O
Rivier University — M,D,O
Robert Morris University — M,D,O
Rosemont College — M
Rutgers University–New Brunswick — M
Sage Graduate School — M,O
St. Bonaventure University — M,O
St. Edward's University — M
St. John Fisher College — M
St. John's University (NY) — M,O
Saint Martin's University — M
St. Mary's University (United States) — M
Saint Mary's University of Minnesota — M,D,O
Saint Paul University — M
St. Thomas University — M
Salem State University — M,O
Salve Regina University — M,O
San Francisco State University — M,O
Santa Clara University — M
Saybrook University — M
The Seattle School of Theology and Psychology — M
Seton Hall University — M,D
Siena Heights University — M,O
Simpson University — M
Slippery Rock University of Pennsylvania — M
Sofia University — M,D
Sonoma State University — M
Southeastern Oklahoma State University — M
Southeastern University (FL) — M
Southeast Missouri State University — M,O
Southern Adventist University — M
Southern California Seminary — M,D
Southern Illinois University Carbondale — M,D
Southern Nazarene University — M
Southern Oregon University — M
South University — M
South University (TX) — M
South University (MI) — M
South University (OH) — M
South University (NC) — M
South University (SC) — M
South University (GA) — M
South University (AL) — M
South University — M
Southwestern Assemblies of God University — M
Southwestern College (NM) — M,O
Spring Arbor University — M
Springfield College — M,D,O
State University of New York at New Paltz — M,O
State University of New York at Oswego — M
State University of New York at Plattsburgh — M,O
State University of New York College at Old Westbury — M
Stetson University — M,D,O
Tarleton State University — M
Teachers College, Columbia University — M,D
Temple University — M,D,O
Tennessee State University — M
Texas A&M International University — M,D
Texas A&M University–Texarkana —
Texas Tech University — M,D
Texas Wesleyan University — M,D
Texas Woman's University — M,D,O
Touro College — M,D
Towson University — M
Trinity Christian College — M
Trinity International University — M,D,O
Trinity International University Florida — M
Trinity Washington University — M
Trinity Western University — M
Union College (KY) — M
United States International University–Africa — M
Universidad del Turabo — M,D,O
Universidad Metropolitana — M
University at Albany, State University of New York — M,D
University at Buffalo, the State University of New York — M,D,O
The University of Akron — M,D
University of Alberta — M,D
The University of Arizona — M
University of Baltimore — M
University of Bridgeport — M
The University of British Columbia — M,D,O
University of Calgary — M
University of California, Berkeley — O
University of California, Santa Barbara — M,D,O
University of Central Arkansas — M
University of Central Missouri — M,D,O
University of Central Oklahoma — M
University of Colorado Denver — M
University of Connecticut — M,D
University of Dayton — M,O
University of Denver — M,D,O
University of Florida — M,D
University of Great Falls — M

University of Hawaii at Hilo — M
University of Houston — M,D
University of Houston–Victoria — M
University of Indianapolis — M,D
The University of Iowa — M,D,O
The University of Kansas — M,D
University of Kentucky — M,D,O
University of Lethbridge — M
University of Louisiana at Monroe — M
University of Louisville — M,D
The University of Manchester — M,D
University of Mary Hardin-Baylor — M
University of Maryland, College Park — M,D,O
University of Massachusetts Boston — M,D
University of Memphis — M,D
University of Miami — D
University of Minnesota, Twin Cities Campus — D
University of Missouri — M,D,O
University of Missouri–Kansas City — M,D,O
University of Missouri–St. Louis — M,D
University of Montana — M
University of Nebraska at Kearney — M,O
University of Nebraska–Lincoln — M,D,O
University of Nevada, Las Vegas — M,D,O
The University of North Carolina at Greensboro — M,D
The University of North Carolina at Pembroke — M
University of North Dakota — M,D
University of Northern Colorado — M,D
University of Northern Iowa — M
University of North Florida — M,O
University of North Texas — M,D,O
University of Notre Dame — D
University of Oklahoma — M,D
University of Pennsylvania — M
University of Phoenix–Las Vegas Campus — M
University of Phoenix–Phoenix Campus — M
University of Puget Sound — M
University of Rhode Island — M
University of Saint Francis (IN) — M,O
University of Saint Joseph — M,O
University of Saint Mary — M
University of St. Thomas (MN) — M,D
University of San Diego — M
University of San Francisco — M
The University of Scranton — M
University of South Africa — M,D
University of South Alabama — M,D
University of Southern Maine — M
University of Southern Mississippi — M,D
University of South Florida — M,D,O
The University of Tennessee — M,D
The University of Texas at Austin — M,D
The University of Texas at Tyler — M
University of the Cumberlands — M
University of the District of Columbia — M
University of the Southwest — M
University of Utah — M,D,O
University of Vermont — M,D
University of Victoria — M
The University of Western Ontario — M
University of West Florida — M
University of Wisconsin–Madison — D
University of Wisconsin–Milwaukee — M,D,O
University of Wisconsin–Stout — M
Utah State University — M,D
Virginia Commonwealth University — M,D
Viterbo University — M
Walden University — M,D,O
Walsh University — M
Washington Adventist University — M
Washington State University — M,D
Wayland Baptist University — M
Waynesburg University — M,D
Wayne State University — M,D,O
Webster University — M
Western Kentucky University — M
Western Michigan University — M,D
Western Washington University — M
Westfield State University — M
Westminster College (UT) — M
West Virginia University — D
Wheaton College — M
William Carey University — M
William James College — M,D,O
William Paterson University of New Jersey — M
Wilmington University — M
Winebrenner Theological Seminary — M,D
Wright Institute — M
Xavier University — M
Yeshiva University — M
Youngstown State University — M

COUNSELOR EDUCATION

Acadia University — M
Adams State University — M
Adler Graduate School — M
Adler University — M,D,O
Alabama Agricultural and Mechanical University — M,O
Alabama State University — M,D,O
Albany State University — M,O
Alcorn State University — M
Alfred University — M,D,O
Alliant International University–San Francisco — M
American International College — M

Amridge University — M,D
Angelo State University — M
Appalachian State University — M
Argosy University, Atlanta — M,D,O
Argosy University, Chicago — D
Argosy University, Dallas — D
Argosy University, Denver — M
Argosy University, Nashville — D
Argosy University, Northern Virginia — M,D
Argosy University, Salt Lake City — M,D
Argosy University, Sarasota — M,D,O
Argosy University, Tampa — M,D,O
Arizona State University at the Tempe campus — M
Arkansas State University — M,O
Arkansas Tech University — M,D,O
Ashland Theological Seminary — M,D
Athabasca University — M,O
Auburn University at Montgomery — M,O
Augusta University — M,O
Austin Peay State University — M
Azusa Pacific University — M
Ball State University — M,D
Barry University — M,D,O
Bayamón Central University — M
Becker College — M
Bellevue University — M
Bloomsburg University of Pennsylvania — M
Bob Jones University — M,D,O
Boise State University — M,O
Bowie State University — M
Bowling Green State University — M
Bradley University — M
Brandman University — M,D
Brandon University — M,O
Bridgewater State University — M,O
Brooklyn College of the City University of New York — M
Buena Vista University — M
Butler University — M,O
Caldwell University — M,O
California Baptist University — M
California Lutheran University — M,D
California State University, Bakersfield — M
California State University, Dominguez Hills — M
California State University, East Bay — M
California State University, Fresno — M
California State University, Fullerton — M
California State University, Long Beach — M,D
California State University, Los Angeles — M,D
California State University, Northridge — M
California State University, Sacramento — M,D
California State University, San Bernardino — M
California State University, Stanislaus — M
California University of Pennsylvania — M
Cambridge College — M,D,O
Campbell University — M
Canisius College — M
Capella University — M,D
Carlow University — M,O
Carson-Newman University — M
Carthage College — M,O
Central Connecticut State University — M,O
Central Methodist University — M
Central Michigan University — M
Central Washington University — M
Chadron State College — M,O
Chapman University — M,D,O
Chicago State University — M
The Citadel, The Military College of South Carolina — M,O
City University of Seattle — M,O
Clark Atlanta University — M
Clarks Summit University — M
Clemson University — M,O
Cleveland State University — M,D,O
The College at Brockport, State University of New York — M,O
The College of New Jersey — M
College of St. Joseph — M
The College of Saint Rose — M,O
The College of William and Mary — M,D
Colorado State University — M,D
Columbia International University — M,D,O
Columbus State University — M,D,O
Concordia University Chicago — M,O
Concordia University Irvine — M
Concordia University Wisconsin — M
Creighton University — M
Dallas Baptist University — M,O
Delta State University — M,D,O
DePaul University — M,D
Doane University — M
Duquesne University — M,D,O
East Carolina University — M,D,O
East Central University — M
Eastern Illinois University — M
Eastern Kentucky University — M
Eastern Mennonite University — M
Eastern Michigan University — M,O
Eastern New Mexico University — M
Eastern University — M,O
Eastern Washington University — M
East Tennessee State University — M
Edinboro University of Pennsylvania — M,O

Emporia State University — M
Evangel University — M
Fairfield University — M,O
Faulkner University — M
Fitchburg State University — M,O
Florida Agricultural and Mechanical University — M,D
Florida Atlantic University — M,D
Florida International University — M,D,O
Fordham University — M,D
Fort Hays State University — M
Fort Valley State University — M,O
Freed-Hardeman University — M
Fresno Pacific University — M
Frostburg State University — M
Gallaudet University — M,D,O
Geneva College — M
George Fox University — M
George Mason University — M
The George Washington University — M,D,O
Georgian Court University — M
Georgia Southern University — M,O
Georgia State University — M,O
Grambling State University — M,D,O
Gwynedd Mercy University — M
Hampton University — M,D,O
Harding University — M
Hardin-Simmons University — M
Henderson State University — M,O
Heritage University — M
Hofstra University — M,O
Houston Baptist University — M,D
Howard University — M
Hunter College of the City University of New York — M
Husson University — M
Idaho State University — M,D,O
Indiana State University — M,D,O
Indiana University Bloomington — M,D,O
Indiana University of Pennsylvania — M
Indiana University–Purdue University Fort Wayne — M,O
Indiana University–Purdue University Indianapolis — M,O
Indiana University South Bend — M,O
Indiana University Southeast — M
Indiana Wesleyan University — M
Inter American University of Puerto Rico, Arecibo Campus — M
Inter American University of Puerto Rico, Metropolitan Campus — M,D
Inter American University of Puerto Rico, San Germán Campus — M,D
Iowa State University of Science and Technology — M,D
Jackson State University — M
Jacksonville State University — M
John Brown University — M,O
John Carroll University — M,O
Johns Hopkins University — M,O
Johnson State College — M
Johnson University — M,D,O
Kansas State University — M,D,O
Kean University — M
Keene State College — M,O
Kent State University — M,D,O
Kutztown University of Pennsylvania — M
Lakeland University — M
Lamar University — M
Lancaster Bible College — M,D
La Sierra University — M,O
Lee University — M
Lehigh University — M,D,O
Lehman College of the City University of New York — M
Lenoir-Rhyne University — M
Lewis University — M
Liberty University — M,D,O
Lincoln Memorial University — M,D,O
Lincoln University (MO) — M
Lindenwood University–Belleville — M
Lindsey Wilson College — M,D
Loma Linda University — M,D,O
Long Island University–Brentwood Campus — M,O
Long Island University–Hudson — M,O
Long Island University–LIU Brooklyn — M,O
Longwood University — M
Louisiana State University and Agricultural & Mechanical College — M,D,O
Louisiana State University in Shreveport — M
Louisiana Tech University — M,D
Loyola Marymount University — M
Loyola University Chicago — M,O
Loyola University Maryland — M,O
Lynchburg College — M
Lyndon State College — M
Malone University — M
Manhattan College — M
Marquette University — M,D
Marshall University — M,O
Marymount University — M
Marywood University — M
McDaniel College — M
McNeese State University — M,O
Mercer University — M,D
Mercy College — M,O
Messiah College — M
Michigan State University — M,D,O
Middle Tennessee State University — M,O
Midwestern State University — M
Milligan College — M
Minnesota State University Mankato — M,D
Minnesota State University Moorhead — M,O
Mississippi College — M,O

---

*M—masters degree; D—doctorate; O—other advanced degree; *—Close-Up and/or Display*

Mississippi State University	M,D,O
Missouri Baptist University	M,O
Missouri State University	M
Montana State University Billings	M
Montana State University–Northern	M
Montclair State University	M,D
Morehead State University	M,O
Mount Mary University	M,O
Murray State University	M,O
Naropa University	M
National Louis University	M,D,O
New Jersey City University	M
New Mexico Highlands University	M
New Mexico State University	M,D,O
New York Institute of Technology	M,O
New York University	M,D,O
Niagara University	M,O
Nicholls State University	M,O
North Carolina Agricultural and Technical State University	M
North Carolina Central University	M
North Carolina State University	M,D
North Dakota State University	M,D
Northeastern Illinois University	M
Northeastern State University	M
Northern Arizona University	M,D,O
Northern Illinois University	M,D
Northern Kentucky University	M
Northern State University	M
Northwest Christian University	M
Northwestern Oklahoma State University	M
Northwestern State University of Louisiana	M,O
Northwest Nazarene University	M
Nova Southeastern University	M,D,O
Nyack College	M
Ohio University	M,D
Oklahoma City University	M
Old Dominion University	M,D,O
Oregon State University	M,D
Ottawa University	M
Our Lady of the Lake University	M
Palm Beach Atlantic University	M
Penn State University Park	M,D,O
Phillips Graduate University	M
Pittsburg State University	M
Plymouth State University	M
Point Loma Nazarene University	M
Pontifical Catholic University of Puerto Rico	M
Prairie View A&M University	M,D
Prescott College	M,D
Providence College	M
Purdue University	M,D,O
Purdue University Northwest	M
Queens College of the City University of New York	M,O
Quincy University	M
Radford University	M
Regent University	M,D,O
Regis University	M,D,O
Rhode Island College	M,O
Richmont Graduate University	M
Rider University	M,O
Rivier University	M,D,O
Roberts Wesleyan College	M,D
Rollins College	M
Roosevelt University	M
Rosemont College	M
Rowan University	M
Rutgers University–New Brunswick	M
Sage Graduate School	M,O
St. Bonaventure University	M,O
St. Cloud State University	M
St. Edward's University	M,O
St. John's University (NY)	M,O
St. Lawrence University	M,O
Saint Louis University	M,D,O
Saint Mary's College of California	M,O
St. Mary's University (United States)	D
Saint Peter's University	M
St. Thomas University	M,O
Saint Xavier University	M
Salem College	M
Salem State University	M
Sam Houston State University	M,D
San Diego State University	M
San Francisco State University	M,O
San Jose State University	M,D,O
Santa Clara University	M
Seattle Pacific University	M,D,O
Seattle University	M,O
Seton Hall University	M,D
Shippensburg University of Pennsylvania	M,D,O
Simon Fraser University	M
Slippery Rock University of Pennsylvania	M
South Carolina State University	M
South Dakota State University	M
Southeastern Louisiana University	M
Southeastern Oklahoma State University	M
Southeastern University (FL)	M
Southeast Missouri State University	M,O
Southern Adventist University	M
Southern Arkansas University–Magnolia	M
Southern Connecticut State University	M,O
Southern Methodist University	M
Southern University and Agricultural and Mechanical College	M
Southwestern Oklahoma State University	M
Spalding University	M
Springfield College	M,D,O

State University of New York at New Paltz	M,O
State University of New York at Plattsburgh	M,O
State University of New York College at Oneonta	M,O
Stephen F. Austin State University	M
Stephens College	M,O
Stetson University	M
Suffolk University	M,D,O
Sul Ross State University	M
Syracuse University	M,D
Texas A&M International University	M
Texas A&M University–Central Texas	M,O
Texas A&M University–Commerce	M,D,O
Texas A&M University–Corpus Christi	M
Texas A&M University–Kingsville	M,D
Texas A&M University–San Antonio	M
Texas Christian University	M,D,O
Texas Southern University	M,D
Texas State University	M
Texas Tech University	M,D
Texas Wesleyan University	M,D
Texas Woman's University	M,D
Trevecca Nazarene University	M,D
Trinity Washington University	M
Troy University	M,O
Universidad del Turabo	M
Université de Moncton	M
Université Laval	M,D
University at Buffalo, the State University of New York	M,D,O
The University of Akron	M,D
The University of Alabama	M,D,O
The University of Alabama at Birmingham	M
University of Alaska Anchorage	M
University of Alaska Fairbanks	M,O
University of Alberta	M,D
The University of Arizona	M
University of Arkansas	M,D,O
University of Arkansas at Little Rock	M
University of Central Arkansas	M
University of Central Florida	M,O
University of Central Missouri	M,D,O
University of Central Oklahoma	M
University of Cincinnati	M,D,O
University of Colorado Colorado Springs	M,D
University of Colorado Denver	M,D
University of Connecticut	M,D
University of Dayton	M,O
University of Florida	M,D,O
University of Georgia	M,D,O
University of Guam	M
University of Hartford	M,O
University of Holy Cross	M
University of Houston–Clear Lake	M
University of Houston–Victoria	M
University of Idaho	M,O
University of Illinois at Urbana–Champaign	M,D,O
The University of Iowa	M,D
University of La Verne	M,D,O
University of Lethbridge	M,D
University of Louisiana at Lafayette	M
University of Louisiana at Monroe	M
University of Louisville	M,D
University of Manitoba	M
University of Mary Hardin-Baylor	M
University of Maryland, College Park	M,D,O
University of Maryland Eastern Shore	M
University of Massachusetts Amherst	M,D,O
University of Massachusetts Boston	M
University of Memphis	M,D
University of Miami	M,O
University of Minnesota, Twin Cities Campus	M
University of Missouri–Kansas City	M,D,O
University of Missouri–St. Louis	M,D
University of Montana	M,D,O
University of Montevallo	M
University of Nebraska at Kearney	M,O
University of Nebraska at Omaha	M
University of Nevada, Las Vegas	M,D,O
University of Nevada, Reno	M,D,O
University of New Mexico	M,D
University of New Orleans	M,D
University of North Alabama	M
The University of North Carolina at Chapel Hill	M
The University of North Carolina at Charlotte	M,D,O
The University of North Carolina at Greensboro	M,D,O
The University of North Carolina at Pembroke	M
University of Northern Colorado	M
University of Northern Iowa	M
University of North Florida	M,D
University of North Texas	M,D,O
University of North Texas at Dallas	M
University of Pennsylvania	M
University of Phoenix–Las Vegas Campus	M
University of Phoenix–New Mexico Campus	M
University of Phoenix–Phoenix Campus	M

University of Phoenix–Southern Arizona Campus	M,O
University of Phoenix–Southern California Campus	M
University of Puerto Rico, Río Piedras Campus	M,D
University of Puget Sound	M
University of Rochester	M,D
University of Saint Francis (IN)	M,O
University of Saint Joseph	M,O
University of St. Thomas (TX)	M,D
University of San Diego	M
University of San Francisco	M
The University of Scranton	M
University of South Africa	M,D
University of South Alabama	M,D
University of South Carolina	D,O
The University of South Dakota	M,D,O
University of Southern California	M
University of Southern Maine	M,O
University of South Florida	M,D,O
The University of Tennessee	M,D,O
The University of Tennessee at Chattanooga	M,D,O
The University of Tennessee at Martin	M
The University of Texas at Austin	M,D
The University of Texas at El Paso	M
The University of Texas at San Antonio	M,D
The University of Texas of the Permian Basin	M
The University of Texas Rio Grande Valley	M
University of the Cumberlands	M,D,O
University of the Southwest	M
The University of Toledo	M,D,O
University of Utah	M,D,O
University of Vermont	M
University of Victoria	M,D
University of Virginia	M,D,O
The University of West Alabama	M,O
University of West Georgia	M,D,O
University of Wisconsin–Madison	M
University of Wisconsin–Milwaukee	M,D,O
University of Wisconsin–Oshkosh	M
University of Wisconsin–Platteville	M
University of Wisconsin–River Falls	M,O
University of Wisconsin–Stevens Point	M
University of Wisconsin–Superior	M
University of Wyoming	M,D
Utah State University	M,D
Valdosta State University	M,O
Vanderbilt University	M
Villanova University	M
Virginia Commonwealth University	M,D
Virginia Polytechnic Institute and State University	M,D,O
Virginia State University	M
Wake Forest University	M
Walden University	M,D
Walsh University	M
Waynesburg University	M,D
Wayne State College	M
Wayne State University	M,D,O
West Chester University of Pennsylvania	M,O
Western Connecticut State University	M
Western Illinois University	M
Western Kentucky University	M
Western Michigan University	M,D
Western Washington University	M
Westfield State University	M
Westminster College (PA)	M,O
West Texas A&M University	M
West Virginia University	M
Whitworth University	M
Wichita State University	M,D,O
Widener University	M,D
William Paterson University of New Jersey	M
Wilmington University	M,D
Winona State University	M,O
Winthrop University	M
Wright State University	M
Xavier University	M
Xavier University of Louisiana	M
Youngstown State University	M

CRIMINAL JUSTICE AND CRIMINOLOGY

Adler University	M,D,O
Adrian College	M
Albany State University	M
Albertus Magnus College	M
Alliant International University–San Francisco	M
American Public University System	M
American University	M,D
American University of Puerto Rico	M
Anderson University (SC)	M
Angelo State University	M
Anna Maria College	M
Arizona State University at the Tempe campus	M,D,O
Arkansas State University	M,O
Armstrong State University	M,O
Ashworth College	M
Auburn University at Montgomery	M
Ball State University	M,O
Bellevue University	M
Boise State University	M
Boston University	M
Bowling Green State University	M
Bridgewater State University	M
Buffalo State College, State University of New York	M

California Coast University	M
California State University, Chico	M
California State University, Fresno	M
California State University, Long Beach	M
California State University, Los Angeles	M
California State University, Sacramento	M
California State University, San Bernardino	M
California State University, Stanislaus	M
California University of Pennsylvania	M
Calumet College of Saint Joseph	M
Capella University	M,D
Caribbean University	M,D
Carnegie Mellon University	M
The Catholic University of America	M
Central Connecticut State University	M
Chaminade University of Honolulu	M
Charleston Southern University	M
Chicago State University	M
Clark Atlanta University	M
Clayton State University	M
College of Saint Elizabeth	M
Colorado State University–Global Campus	M
Colorado Technical University Aurora	M
Colorado Technical University Colorado Springs	M
Columbia College (MO)	M
Columbia Southern University	M
Columbus State University	M
Concordia University, St. Paul	M,D
Coppin State University	M
Curry College	M
Dallas Baptist University	M
Delta State University	M
DeSales University	M,O
East Carolina University	M
East Central University	M
Eastern Kentucky University	M
Eastern Michigan University	M
East Tennessee State University	M,O
Excelsior College	M
Fairleigh Dickinson University, Metropolitan Campus	M
Fairmont State University	M
Faulkner University	M
Fayetteville State University	M
Ferris State University	M
Florida Agricultural and Mechanical University	M
Florida Atlantic University	M
Florida Gulf Coast University	M
Florida International University	M,D
Florida State University	M,D
Gannon University	M
George Mason University	M,D
The George Washington University	M,O
Georgia College & State University	M
Georgia State University	M,D,O
Governors State University	M
The Graduate Center, City University of New York	D
Grambling State University	M
Grand Valley State University	M
Hilbert College	M
Holy Family University	M,D
Howard Payne University	M
Husson University	M
Illinois State University	M
Indiana State University	M
Indiana University Bloomington	M,D
Indiana University Northwest	M,O
Indiana University of Pennsylvania	M,D
Indiana University–Purdue University Indianapolis	M,O
Inter American University of Puerto Rico, Aguadilla Campus	M
Inter American University of Puerto Rico, Metropolitan Campus	M
Inter American University of Puerto Rico, Ponce Campus	M,O
Iona College	M,O
Jackson State University	M
Jacksonville State University	M
John Jay College of Criminal Justice of the City University of New York	M,D
Johnson & Wales University	M
Kaplan University, Davenport Campus	M
Kean University	M
Keiser University	M
Kennesaw State University	M
Kent State University	M,D
Keuka College	M
Lamar University	M
Lasell College	M,O
Lewis University	M
Liberty University	M,D,O
Lincoln University (MO)	M
Lindenwood University	M,O
Lindenwood University–Belleville	M
Loma Linda University	M,D
London Metropolitan University	M,D
Long Island University–LIU Post	M,O
Loyola University Chicago	M
Loyola University New Orleans	M
Lynn University	M
Madonna University	M
Marshall University	M
Marywood University	M
McNeese State University	M
Mercer University	M,D
Mercyhurst University	M,O

Merrimack College	M,O
Methodist University	M
Metropolitan State University	M
Michigan State University	M,D
Middle Tennessee State University	M,O
Midwestern State University	M,O
Minnesota State University Mankato	M
Mississippi College	M,O
Mississippi Valley State University	M
Missouri Southern State University	M
Missouri State University	M,O
Molloy College	M
Monmouth University	M,O
Monroe College	M
Morehead State University	M
Mount Mercy University	M
National University	M
New Charter University	M
New Jersey City University	M,D,O
New Mexico State University	M
Niagara University	M
Norfolk State University	M
North Carolina Central University	M
North Dakota State University	M,D
Northeastern State University	M
Northeastern University	M,D
Northern Arizona University	M
Northern Michigan University	M
Norwich University	M
Oklahoma City University	M
Old Dominion University	M,D
Penn State Harrisburg	M,D,O
Penn State University Park	M,D
Point Park University	M
Pontifical Catholic University of Puerto Rico	M
Pontificia Universidad Catolica Madre y Maestra	M
Portland State University	M,D
Radford University	M,O
Regent University	M,D
Regis University	M,O
Robert Morris University Illinois	M
Rochester Institute of Technology	M
Roger Williams University	M
Rowan University	M
Rutgers University–Camden	M
Rutgers University–Newark	M,D
Sacred Heart University	M
St. Ambrose University	M
St. Cloud State University	M
St. John's University (NY)	M
Saint Joseph's University	M
Saint Leo University	M
Saint Mary's University (Canada)	M
Saint Peter's University	M
St. Thomas University	M,O
Salem State University	M
Salve Regina University	M,O
Sam Houston State University	M,D
San Diego State University	M
San Francisco State University	M
Seattle University	M,O
Shippensburg University of Pennsylvania	M
Simon Fraser University	M,D
Simpson College	M
Slippery Rock University of Pennsylvania	M
Southeast Missouri State University	M
Southern Illinois University Carbondale	M,D
Southern University and Agricultural and Mechanical College	M
Southern University at New Orleans	M
South University	M
South University (SC)	M
South University (GA)	M
South University (AL)	M
South University	M
Southwestern College (KS)	M
Southwest University	M
Stockton University	M
Suffolk University	M
Sul Ross State University	M
Tarleton State University	M
Temple University	M,D
Tennessee State University	M
Texas A&M International University	M
Texas A&M University–Central Texas	M,O
Texas A&M University–Commerce	M,D,O
Texas A&M University–Kingsville	M
Texas Christian University	M
Texas Southern University	M,D
Texas State University	M,D
Tiffin University	M
Trident University International	M,D
Trine University	M
Troy University	M
Universidad del Este	M
Universidad del Turabo	M
Université de Montréal	M,D
University at Albany, State University of New York	M,D
The University of Alabama	M
The University of Alabama at Birmingham	M
University of Alaska Fairbanks	M
University of Alberta	M,D
University of Antelope Valley	M
University of Arkansas at Little Rock	M,D
University of Baltimore	M
University of California, Irvine	M,D
University of Central Florida	M,D,O
University of Central Missouri	M,D,O
University of Central Oklahoma	M
University of Cincinnati	M,D
University of Colorado Colorado Springs	M
University of Colorado Denver	M,D
University of Delaware	M,D
University of Denver	M,O
University of Detroit Mercy	M,D,O
University of Florida	M,D
University of Great Falls	M
University of Guelph	M,D
University of Houston–Clear Lake	M
University of Houston–Downtown	M
University of Illinois at Chicago	M,D
University of Louisiana at Monroe	M
University of Louisville	M,D
University of Management and Technology	M,O
The University of Manchester	M,D
University of Maryland, College Park	M,D
University of Maryland Eastern Shore	M
University of Massachusetts Lowell	M
University of Memphis	M
University of Michigan–Dearborn	M
University of Michigan–Flint	M
University of Minnesota, Duluth	M
University of Missouri–Kansas City	M
University of Missouri–St. Louis	M,D
University of Montana	M
University of Nebraska at Omaha	M,D,O
University of Nevada, Las Vegas	M,D
University of Nevada, Reno	M
University of New Haven	M,D,O
University of North Alabama	M
The University of North Carolina at Charlotte	M
The University of North Carolina at Greensboro	M
The University of North Carolina Wilmington	M
University of North Dakota	D
University of Northern Colorado	M
University of North Florida	M
University of North Georgia	M
University of North Texas	M,D,O
University of North Texas at Dallas	M
University of Oklahoma	M,O
University of Ottawa	M,D
University of Pennsylvania	M,D
University of Phoenix–Augusta Campus	M
University of Phoenix–Bay Area Campus	M
University of Phoenix–Dallas Campus	M
University of Phoenix–Jersey City Campus	M
University of Phoenix–Online Campus	M
University of Phoenix–Phoenix Campus	M
University of Phoenix–San Antonio Campus	M
University of Phoenix–Southern California Campus	M
University of Phoenix–Washington D.C. Campus	M
University of Phoenix–Western Washington Campus	M
University of Pittsburgh	M
University of Regina	M
University of St. Thomas (MN)	M,D
University of San Diego	M
University of South Africa	M,D
University of South Carolina	M,D
The University of South Dakota	M
University of Southern Mississippi	M,D
University of South Florida	M,D,O
University of South Florida Sarasota-Manatee	M
The University of Tennessee	M,D
The University of Tennessee at Chattanooga	M
The University of Texas at Arlington	M
The University of Texas at Dallas	M
The University of Texas at San Antonio	M
The University of Texas at Tyler	M
The University of Texas of the Permian Basin	M
The University of Texas Rio Grande Valley	M
University of the Fraser Valley	M
The University of Toledo	M,O
University of Toronto	M,D
University of West Florida	M
University of West Georgia	M,D,O
University of Windsor	M,D
University of Wisconsin–Milwaukee	M,O
University of Wisconsin–Platteville	M
Urbana University	M
Utica College	M
Virginia College in Birmingham	M
Virginia Commonwealth University	M,O
Virginia State University	M
Walden University	M,D
Waldorf University	M
Washburn University	M
Washington State University	M
Wayland Baptist University	M
Waynesburg University	M,D
Wayne State University	M,D
Webber International University	M
Webster University	M,D,O
West Chester University of Pennsylvania	M
Western Connecticut State University	M
Western Illinois University	M,O
Western Kentucky University	M
Western Oregon University	M
Westfield State University	M
West Liberty University	M
West Texas A&M University	M
West Virginia State University	M
Wichita State University	M
Widener University	M
Wilfrid Laurier University	M
Wilmington University	M
Wright State University	M
Xavier University	M
Youngstown State University	M

CULTURAL ANTHROPOLOGY

California Institute of Integral Studies	M
Concordia University (Canada)	M,D
Cornell University	D
Duke University	D
Eastern University	M
The Graduate Center, City University of New York	D
Memorial University of Newfoundland	M,D
North Carolina State University	M
Northern Arizona University	M
Rice University	M,D
San Francisco State University	M
Southern Illinois University Edwardsville	M
University of California, Santa Barbara	M,D
University of California, Santa Cruz	D
University of Denver	M
University of Michigan	D
The University of Tennessee	M,D
University of Wisconsin–Madison	D
University of Wisconsin–Milwaukee	M,D,O
Washington State University	M,D

CULTURAL STUDIES

American University	M,D,O
The American University of Paris	M
Appalachian State University	M
Arizona State University at the Tempe campus	M,D
Assemblies of God Theological Seminary	M,D
Athabasca University	M,O
Baptist Bible College	M
Binghamton University, State University of New York	M,D
Biola University	M,D,O
Boston University	M
Brock University	M
Carnegie Mellon University	D
Central Michigan University	M
Chapman University	M,D,O
Charlotte Christian College and Theological Seminary	M
Claremont Graduate University	M,D,O
Clarks Summit University	M
Columbia International University	M,D,O
Concordia University Irvine	M
Cornell University	M,D
Drew University	M,D,O
Eastern Michigan University	O
Florida State University	M,D
Gardner-Webb University	M,D
George Fox University	M,D,O
George Mason University	D
Georgia State University	M,O
Goucher College	M
Grace Theological Seminary	M,D,O
Graduate Theological Union	M,D,O
Johnson University	M,D,O
Lincoln Christian University	M
Maranatha Baptist University	M
McMaster University	M,D
Michigan Technological University	M,D
Nazarene Theological Seminary	M,D
New Mexico State University	M,D,O
New York University	M,D,O
North Central College	M
Northern Kentucky University	M,O
Northwest University	M
Old Dominion University	M,D
Pacific Northwest College of Art	M
Plymouth State University	M
Regent University	M,D
Regis College (MA)	M
St. Francis Xavier University	M
San Francisco State University	M
School of Visual Arts (NY)	M
Simmons College	M
Simon Fraser University	D
Southern Illinois University Carbondale	M
Stanford University	M,D
Stony Brook University, State University of New York	M,D,O
Taylor College and Seminary	M,O
Texas A&M University	M
Texas A&M University–Kingsville	M
Texas Tech University	M,D
Trent University	D

Trinity College (United States)	M
Union Institute & University	M
Union University	M
University of Alaska Fairbanks	M
University of California, Davis	M,D
University of California, Irvine	D
University of California, Riverside	D
University of California, Santa Barbara	M,D
University of Dayton	M
University of Denver	M,O
University of Hawaii at Hilo	M,D
University of Hawaii at Manoa	O
University of Houston	M
University of Houston–Clear Lake	M
The University of Kansas	M,D
University of Louisville	M,D
The University of Manchester	M,D
University of Massachusetts Boston	M
University of Minnesota, Twin Cities Campus	D
University of Montana	M,D,O
University of New Mexico	M,D
University of North Carolina at Asheville	M,O
The University of North Carolina at Charlotte	M,O
University of Oklahoma	M,D
University of Pittsburgh	O
University of Southern California	D
University of Southern Indiana	M
University of Southern Maine	M
The University of Texas at Austin	M,D
The University of Texas at San Antonio	M,D
University of the Sacred Heart	M
University of Washington, Bothell	M
Washington State University	M
West Chester University of Pennsylvania	M,O
Wheaton College	M,O
Wilfrid Laurier University	M
Wilson College	M

CURRICULUM AND INSTRUCTION

Acadia University	M
American College of Education	M
American InterContinental University Online	M
American Public University System	M
Andrews University	M,D,O
Angelo State University	M
Appalachian State University	M
Arcadia University	M,D,O
Arizona State University at the Tempe campus	M
Arkansas Tech University	M,D,O
Arlington Baptist College	M
Armstrong State University	M,O
Auburn University	M,D,O
Augusta University	M,O
Aurora University	M,D
Austin Peay State University	M,O
Averett University	M
Azusa Pacific University	M
Ball State University	M,D
Barry University	D,O
Baylor University	M,D
Bay Path University	M
Benedictine University	M
Berry College	M,O
Biola University	M,O
Black Hills State University	M
Bloomsburg University of Pennsylvania	M,O
Bluffton University	M
Bob Jones University	M,D,O
Boise State University	M,D,O
Boston College	M,D,O
Bowling Green State University	M
Bradley University	M
Brandon University	M,O
Brescia University	M
Buena Vista University	M
Caldwell University	M,D,O
California Baptist University	M
California Coast University	M,D
California State Polytechnic University, Pomona	M
California State University, Chico	M
California State University, Fresno	M
California State University, Los Angeles	M
California State University, Northridge	M
California State University, Sacramento	M,D
California State University, Stanislaus	M
Calvary University	M
Calvin College	M
Cambridge College	M,D,O
Capella University	M,D
Caribbean University	M,D
Carson-Newman University	M
Castleton University	M
Central Michigan University	M,D,O
Central Washington University	M
Chapman University	M,D,O
City University of Seattle	M,O
Clarion University of Pennsylvania	M
Clark Atlanta University	M
Clarks Summit University	M
Clemson University	D
The College at Brockport, State University of New York	M
The College of Idaho	M
The College of Saint Rose	M,O

M—masters degree; D—doctorate; O—other advanced degree; *—Close-Up and/or Display

Curriculum and Instruction (continued)

Institution	Degree
The College of William and Mary	M,D
Colorado Christian University	M
Columbia International University	M,D,O
Columbus State University	M,D,O
Concordia University (United States)	M,D
Concordia University Ann Arbor	M
Concordia University Chicago	M
Concordia University Irvine	M
Concordia University, St. Paul	M,D,O
Coppin State University	M
Cornell University	M,D
Dakota Wesleyan University	M
Dallas Baptist University	M
Delaware State University	M
Delaware Valley University	M
DePaul University	M,D
DeVry University—Folsom Campus	M
Doane University	M
Drexel University	M,D
Drury University	M,O
Duquesne University	M,O
East Carolina University	M,O
Eastern Kentucky University	M
Eastern Michigan University	M,O
Eastern New Mexico University	M
Eastern Washington University	M
East Tennessee State University	M,O
East Texas Baptist University	M
Emporia State University	M
Evangel University	M,D
Fairleigh Dickinson University, Metropolitan Campus	M,O
Ferris State University	M
Fitchburg State University	M
Florida Atlantic University	M,D,O
Florida Gulf Coast University	M
Florida International University	M,D,O
Florida State University	M,D,O
Fontbonne University	M
Fordham University	M,O
Framingham State University	M
Franciscan University of Steubenville	M
Franklin Pierce University	M,D,O
Freed-Hardeman University	M,O
Fresno Pacific University	M
Frostburg State University	M
Furman University	M,O
Gannon University	M,O
Gardner-Webb University	D
George Mason University	M
The George Washington University	M,D,O
Georgia Southern University	M,D
Georgia State University	M,D
Graceland University (IA)	M
Grambling State University	M,D,O
Grand Canyon University	M,D,O
Grand Valley State University	M
Harvard University	M
Henderson State University	M,O
Hood College	M,O
Houston Baptist University	M,D
Idaho State University	M,O
Illinois State University	M,D
Indiana State University	M,D
Indiana University Bloomington	M,D,O
Indiana University of Pennsylvania	D
Indiana University–Purdue University Indianapolis	M,O
Inter American University of Puerto Rico, Arecibo Campus	M
Inter American University of Puerto Rico, Barranquitas Campus	M
Inter American University of Puerto Rico, Metropolitan Campus	M,D
Inter American University of Puerto Rico, San Germán Campus	D
Iowa State University of Science and Technology	M,D
John Brown University	M
Johnson State College	M
Kansas State University	M,D,O
Kean University	M
Keene State College	M,O
Kent State University	M,D,O
Kent State University at Stark	M
Kutztown University of Pennsylvania	M
LaGrange College	M,O
La Sierra University	M,D,O
Lee University	M,O
Lesley University	M,D,O
LeTourneau University	M
Lewis & Clark College	M
Lincoln Memorial University	M,D,O
Louisiana State University in Shreveport	M,D
Louisiana Tech University	M,D
Lourdes University	M
Loyola University Chicago	M,D
Loyola University Maryland	M
Lynchburg College	M
Lyndon State College	M
Malone University	M
Marian University (WI)	M,D
Marquette University	M,D,O
Martin Luther College	M
Massachusetts College of Liberal Arts	M,O
McDaniel College	M
McGill University	M,D,O
McKendree University	M,D,O
McNeese State University	M
Medaille College	M
Memorial University of Newfoundland	M,D,O
Mercer University	M,D,O
Meredith College	M,O
Merrimack College	M,O
Messiah College	M
Michigan State University	M,D,O
Middle Tennessee State University	M,O

Institution	Degree
Midwestern State University	M
Minnesota State University Moorhead	M,O
Mississippi College	M,D,O
Mississippi State University	M,D,O
Mississippi University for Women	M
Montana State University	M,D,O
Montana State University Billings	M
Montclair State University	M
Moravian College	M
Morehead State University	M,O
Mount Saint Vincent University	M
National Louis University	M,D,O
Newman University	M
New Mexico Highlands University	M
New Mexico State University	M,D,O
Nicholls State University	M
North Carolina State University	M,D
North Dakota State University	M
Northern Arizona University	M,D
Northern Illinois University	M,D
Northern Michigan University	M
Northern State University	M
Northwestern Oklahoma State University	M
Northwestern State University of Louisiana	M
Northwest Nazarene University	M,D,O
Notre Dame de Namur University	M
Ohio Dominican University	M
Ohio University	M,D
Ohio Valley University	M
Oklahoma State University	M,D
Old Dominion University	M,D
Olivet Nazarene University	M
Oral Roberts University	M,D
Ottawa University	M
Our Lady of the Lake University	M
Pacific Lutheran University	M
Park University	M,O
Penn State Harrisburg	M,D,O
Penn State University Park	M,D,O
Penn State York	M,O
Pensacola Christian College	M,D,O
Peru State College	M
Piedmont College	M,O
Piedmont International University	M,D
Plymouth State University	M
Point Park University	M,D
Pontifical Catholic University of Puerto Rico	M,D
Prairie View A&M University	M
Purdue University	M,D,O
Quincy University	M
Randolph College	M
Regent University	M,D,O
Regis University	M,O
Rider University	M,O
Rivier University	M,D,O
St. Catherine University	M
St. Cloud State University	M
St. Francis Xavier University	M
Saint Joseph's University	M,D,O
Saint Louis University	M,D
Saint Vincent College	M
Saint Xavier University	M
Salem International University	M
Salisbury University	M
Sam Houston State University	M,D
San Diego State University	M
San Jose State University	M,D,O
Shawnee State University	M
Shaw University	M
Shepherd University (WV)	M
Shippensburg University of Pennsylvania	M,O
Simon Fraser University	M,D
Simpson University	M
Sonoma State University	M,O
South Dakota State University	M
Southeastern Louisiana University	M
Southeastern University (FL)	M,D
Southern Arkansas University–Magnolia	M
Southern Illinois University Carbondale	M,D
Southern Illinois University Edwardsville	M
Southern New Hampshire University	M,D,O
Southwestern Adventist University	M
Southwestern Assemblies of God University	M
Southwestern College (KS)	M,D
Stanford University	M
State University of New York at Fredonia	M
State University of New York at Oswego	M
State University of New York at Plattsburgh	M
State University of New York College at Potsdam	M
Syracuse University	M,D,O
Tarleton State University	M
Teachers College, Columbia University	M,D
Tennessee State University	M,D
Tennessee Technological University	M,O
Texas A&M International University	M
Texas A&M University	M,D
Texas A&M University–Central Texas	M,O
Texas A&M University–Commerce	M,D,O
Texas A&M University–Corpus Christi	M,D
Texas A&M University–Texarkana	M
Texas Christian University	M,D,O
Texas Southern University	M,D
Texas Tech University	M,D
Texas Woman's University	M,D
Trevecca Nazarene University	M,O
Trinity Washington University	M

Institution	Degree
Tusculum College	M
Universidad Adventista de las Antillas	M
Universidad del Turabo	M,D
Universidad Metropolitana	M
Université de Montréal	M,D,O
Université Laval	M,D
University at Albany, State University of New York	M,D,O
University at Buffalo, the State University of New York	M,D,O
The University of Akron	M
The University of Alabama at Birmingham	O
University of Arkansas	M,D,O
University of Arkansas at Little Rock	M
The University of British Columbia	M,D
University of Calgary	M,D
University of California, Davis	M,D
University of California, San Diego	M,D
University of Central Arkansas	M,O
University of Central Florida	D
University of Cincinnati	M,D
University of Colorado Boulder	M,D
University of Colorado Colorado Springs	M,D
University of Connecticut	M,D
University of Delaware	M,D,O
University of Denver	M,D,O
University of Detroit Mercy	M,D,O
University of Florida	M,D,O
University of Hawaii at Manoa	M,D
University of Holy Cross	M
University of Houston	M,D
University of Houston–Clear Lake	M
University of Houston–Downtown	M
University of Houston–Victoria	M
University of Idaho	M,O
University of Illinois at Chicago	M,D
University of Illinois at Urbana–Champaign	M,D,O
University of Indianapolis	M
University of Jamestown	M
The University of Kansas	M,D
University of Kentucky	M,D
University of Louisiana at Lafayette	M
University of Louisiana at Monroe	M,D
University of Louisville	M,D,O
University of Manitoba	M,D
University of Mary	M,D
University of Mary Hardin-Baylor	M,D
University of Maryland, College Park	M,D,O
University of Massachusetts Lowell	M
University of Memphis	M,D,O
University of Michigan–Dearborn	D,O
University of Michigan–Flint	M,D,O
University of Minnesota, Twin Cities Campus	M,D
University of Missouri	M,D,O
University of Missouri–Kansas City	M,D,O
University of Missouri–St. Louis	M
University of Montana	M,D
University of Nebraska at Kearney	M
University of Nebraska–Lincoln	M,D,O
University of Nevada, Las Vegas	M,D,O
University of Nevada, Reno	D
University of New England	M,D,O
University of New Hampshire	D,O
University of New Orleans	M,D
The University of North Carolina at Chapel Hill	M,D
The University of North Carolina at Charlotte	M,D,O
The University of North Carolina at Greensboro	M,D,O
The University of North Carolina Wilmington	M,D
University of Northern Colorado	M,D
University of Northern Iowa	D
University of North Texas	M,D,O
University of North Texas at Dallas	M
University of Oklahoma	M,D
University of Phoenix–Central Valley Campus	M
University of Phoenix–Colorado Campus	M
University of Phoenix–Colorado Springs Downtown Campus	M,O
University of Phoenix–Dallas Campus	M
University of Phoenix–Hawaii Campus	M
University of Phoenix–Houston Campus	M
University of Phoenix–Las Vegas Campus	M
University of Phoenix–New Mexico Campus	M
University of Phoenix–North Florida Campus	M
University of Phoenix–Online Campus	M,D,O
University of Phoenix–Phoenix Campus	M
University of Phoenix–Sacramento Valley Campus	M,O
University of Phoenix–San Antonio Campus	M
University of Phoenix–San Diego Campus	M

Institution	Degree
University of Phoenix–Southern Arizona Campus	M,O
University of Phoenix–South Florida Campus	M
University of Phoenix–Utah Campus	M
University of Phoenix–Washington D.C. Campus	M,D,O
University of Puerto Rico, Río Piedras Campus	M,D
University of Regina	M
University of Rochester	M,D
University of St. Francis (IL)	M,D,O
University of Saint Joseph	M
University of St. Thomas (TX)	M,D
University of San Diego	M
University of San Francisco	M,D
University of Saskatchewan	M,D,O
The University of Scranton	M
University of South Africa	M,D
University of South Carolina	D
The University of South Dakota	M,D,O
University of Southern Mississippi	M,D
University of South Florida Sarasota-Manatee	M
The University of Tampa	M
The University of Tennessee	M,D,O
The University of Tennessee at Martin	M
The University of Texas at Arlington	M
The University of Texas at Austin	M,D
The University of Texas at El Paso	M,D
The University of Texas at San Antonio	M,D
The University of Texas Rio Grande Valley	M,D
University of the Pacific	M
University of the Southwest	M
The University of Toledo	M
University of Vermont	M
University of Victoria	M,D
University of Virginia	M,D,O
University of Washington	M,D
The University of West Alabama	M
The University of Western Ontario	M
University of West Florida	M,O
University of Wisconsin–Madison	M,D
University of Wisconsin–Milwaukee	M,D,O
University of Wisconsin–Oshkosh	M
University of Wisconsin–Superior	M
University of Wyoming	M,D
Utah State University	D
Virginia Commonwealth University	D
Virginia Polytechnic Institute and State University	M,D,O
Virginia Union University	M
Walden University	M,D,O
Walla Walla University	M
Warner University	M
Washburn University	M
Washington State University	M,D
Waynesburg University	M,D
Wayne State College	M
Wayne State University	M,D,O
Weber State University	M
Western Connecticut State University	M
Western Illinois University	M
Western New England University	M
West Texas A&M University	M
West Virginia University	M,D
Wichita State University	M
Wilkes University	M,D
William Woods University	M,D,O
Wisconsin Lutheran College	M
Wright State University	O
Xavier University of Louisiana	M
Youngstown State University	M

DANCE

Institution	Degree
Arizona State University at the Tempe campus	M
Bennington College	M
California Institute of the Arts	M,O
California State University, Long Beach	M
Case Western Reserve University	M
The College at Brockport, State University of New York	M
Eastern Michigan University	M
Florida State University	M
The George Washington University	M,O
Hollins University	M
Jacksonville University	M
Mills College	M
New York University	M,D,O
Northern Illinois University	M
The Ohio State University	M,D
Saint Mary's College of California	M
Sam Houston State University	M
Sarah Lawrence College	M
Smith College	M
Temple University	M,D
Texas Woman's University	M,D
Tulane University	M
Université du Québec à Montréal	M
The University of Arizona	M
University of California, Irvine	M
University of California, Los Angeles	M,D
University of California, Riverside	M
University of California, San Diego	M,D
University of Colorado Boulder	M,D
University of Hawaii at Manoa	M,D

University of Illinois at
  Urbana–Champaign — M
The University of Iowa — M
University of Maryland, Baltimore
  County — M
University of Maryland, College
  Park — M
University of Michigan — M
University of New Mexico — M
The University of North Carolina
  at Greensboro — M
University of Oklahoma — M
University of Oregon — M
The University of Texas at Austin — M,D
University of Utah — M,O
University of Washington — M
Washington University in St. Louis — M
Wayne State University — M,D,O
Wilson College — M
York University — M,D

DATABASE SYSTEMS

Austin Peay State University — M
Boston University — M,O
California Polytechnic State
  University, San Luis Obispo — M
California State University, East
  Bay — M
Case Western Reserve University — M
Central European University — M,D
Claremont Graduate University — M,D,O
Clark University — M
College of Staten Island of the
  City University of New York — O
Colorado Technical University
  Aurora — M
Colorado Technical University
  Colorado Springs — M,D
Columbia University — M
DeSales University — M,O
Elmhurst College — M,O
Fairfield University — M,O
Ferris State University — M,D
Florida International University — M,D
Fordham University — M
Grand Canyon University — D
IGlobal University — M
Illinois Institute of Technology — M,D
Indiana University Bloomington — M,O
Indiana University–Purdue
  University Indianapolis — M,D,O
Iowa State University of Science
  and Technology — M
Kansas State University — M,O
Lawrence Technological University — M,O
Lewis University — M
Lipscomb University — M
London Metropolitan University — M,D
Manhattan College — M
Merrimack College — M
Metropolitan State University — M,D,O
Michigan Technological University — M,D
Montclair State University — O
New College of Florida — M
New Jersey Institute of Technology — M,D,O
The New School — M
New York University — M,O
Northeastern University — M,D
Northwestern University — M
Ohio Dominican University — M
Penn State Great Valley — M,O
Queens College of the City
  University of New York — M
Radford University — M
Regis University — M,O
Robert Morris University — M,D
Rochester Institute of Technology — O
Rockhurst University — M,O
St. John's University (NY) — M
Saint Mary's College — M
Saint Mary's College of
  California — M
Saint Peter's University — M
Seattle University — M,O
Slippery Rock University of
  Pennsylvania — M
Southern Arkansas University–
  Magnolia — M
Southern Methodist University — M
Stevens Institute of Technology — M,D,O
Syracuse University — M
Texas Tech University — M,D
Towson University — M,D,O
University of California, Berkeley — M
University of California, San
  Diego — M
University of Houston–
  Downtown — M
University of Illinois at
  Springfield — M
The University of Iowa — M
University of Maryland University
  College — M
University of Massachusetts
  Dartmouth — M
University of Michigan — M,D,O
University of Michigan–
  Dearborn — M,D
University of Minnesota, Twin
  Cities Campus — M
University of Nebraska at Omaha — M,D,O
University of Nevada, Las Vegas — M,O
University of New Haven — M
The University of North Carolina
  at Charlotte — M,O
University of Notre Dame — M
University of Oklahoma — M,D
University of Rochester — M
University of St. Thomas (MN) — M,O
University of San Francisco — M
The University of South Dakota — M

University of Southern Indiana — M
University of South Florida — M,D
The University of Texas at Dallas — M,D
University of Virginia — M
University of Washington — M,D
University of West Florida — M
University of Wisconsin–La
  Crosse — M
Villanova University — M
Virginia International University — M,O
Wake Forest University — M
Washington University in St. Louis — M
Wayne State University — M,D,O
Western Governors University — M
Worcester Polytechnic Institute — M,D,O

DECORATIVE ARTS

Bard Graduate Center — M,D
Sotheby's Institute of
  Art–London — M
Sotheby's Institute of
  Art–New York — M

DEMOGRAPHY AND POPULATION STUDIES

Bowling Green State University — M,D
Cornell University — M,D
Florida State University — M,D
Harvard University — M,D
Johns Hopkins University — M,D
Miami University — M,D
New York University — D,O
Princeton University — M,D
Université de Montréal — M,D
Université du Québec,
  Institut National de la Recherche
  Scientifique — M,D,O
University at Albany, State
  University of New York — M,D,O
University of Alberta — M,D
University of California, Berkeley — M,D
University of California, Irvine — M,D
University of Guelph — M,D
University of Hawaii at Manoa — O
University of Pennsylvania — M,D
University of Puerto Rico, Medical
  Sciences Campus — M
The University of Texas at San
  Antonio — D
The University of Texas Medical
  Branch — D
University of Wisconsin–
  Madison — M,D

DENTAL HYGIENE

Eastern Washington University — M
Idaho State University — M
Missouri Southern State University — M
The Ohio State University — M,D
Old Dominion University — M
Texas A&M University — M,D,O
Université de Montréal — O
University of Alberta — O
University of Bridgeport — M
University of Michigan — M
University of Missouri–
  Kansas City — M,D,O
University of New Mexico — M
The University of North Carolina
  at Chapel Hill — M,D

DENTISTRY

A.T. Still University — D,O
Augusta University — D
Boston University — M,D,O
Case Western Reserve University — D
Columbia University — D
Creighton University — D
East Carolina University — D
Harvard University — M,D,O
Howard University — D,O
Idaho State University — O
Indiana University–Purdue
  University Indianapolis — M,D,O
Jacksonville University — M,O
Loma Linda University — M,D,O
Louisiana State University Health
  Sciences Center — D
Marquette University — D
McGill University — M,D,O
Medical University of South
  Carolina — D
Meharry Medical College — D
Midwestern University, Downers
  Grove Campus — D
Midwestern University, Glendale
  Campus — D
New York University — D
Nova Southeastern University — M,D
The Ohio State University — M,D
Oregon Health & Science University — D,O
Roseman University of Health
  Sciences — M,D,O
Rutgers University–Newark — M,D,O
Saint Louis University — M
Southern Illinois University
  Edwardsville — D
Stony Brook University, State
  University of New York — D,O
Temple University — D
Texas A&M University — M,D,O
Tufts University — D
Universidad Central del Este — D
Universidad Iberoamericana — M,D
Universidad Nacional Pedro
  Henriquez Urena — D
Université Laval — D
University at Buffalo, the State
  University of New York — D
The University of Alabama at
  Birmingham — D
University of Alberta — D

The University of British Columbia — D
University of California, Los
  Angeles — D,O
University of California, San
  Francisco — D
University of Colorado Denver — M,D
University of Connecticut Health
  Center — D,O
University of Detroit Mercy — M,D,O
University of Florida — D,O
University of Illinois at Chicago — D
The University of Iowa — M,D,O
University of Kentucky — D
University of Louisville — M,D
The University of Manchester — M,D
University of Manitoba — D
University of Maryland, Baltimore — D,O
University of Michigan — D
University of Minnesota, Twin
  Cities Campus — D
University of Mississippi Medical
  Center — M,D
University of Missouri–
  Kansas City — M,D,O
University of Nebraska Medical
  Center — M,D,O
University of Nevada, Las Vegas — M,D
University of New England — D
The University of North Carolina
  at Chapel Hill — D
University of Oklahoma Health
  Sciences Center — D,O
University of Pennsylvania — D
University of Pittsburgh — D,O
University of Puerto Rico, Medical
  Sciences Campus — D
University of Saskatchewan — D
University of Southern California — D
The University of Tennessee Health
  Science Center — D
The University of Texas Health
  Science Center at Houston — M,D
The University of Texas Health
  Science Center at San Antonio — M,D,O
University of the Pacific — M,D,O
University of Toronto — D
University of Utah — D
University of Washington — D
The University of Western Ontario — D
Virginia Commonwealth University — M,D
Western University of Health
  Sciences — D
West Virginia University — D

DEVELOPMENTAL BIOLOGY

Albert Einstein College of
  Medicine — D
Baylor College of Medicine — D
Brigham Young University — M,D
California Institute of Technology — D
California State University,
  Sacramento — M
Carnegie Mellon University — M,D
Columbia University — M,D
Cornell University — M,D
Duke University — O
Emory University — D
Illinois State University — M,D
Iowa State University of Science
  and Technology — M,D
Irell & Manella Graduate School of
  Biological Sciences — D*
Johns Hopkins University — D
Louisiana State University Health
  Sciences Center — D
Marquette University — M,D
Massachusetts Institute of
  Technology — D
Medical University of South
  Carolina — D
New York University — M,D
Northwestern University — D
The Ohio State University — M,D
Oregon Health & Science University — D
Oregon State University — M,D
Penn State Hershey Medical Center — D
Purdue University — M,D
Rutgers University–Newark — D,O
Rutgers University–New
  Brunswick — M,D
San Francisco State University — M
Stanford University — M,D
Stony Brook University, State
  University of New York — M,D
Thomas Jefferson University — M,D
Tufts University — D
The University of Alabama at
  Birmingham — D
The University of British Columbia — M,D
University of California, Davis — M,D
University of California, Irvine — M,D
University of California, Los
  Angeles — M,D
University of California,
  Riverside — M,D
University of California, San
  Francisco — D
University of California, Santa
  Barbara — M,D
University of California, Santa
  Cruz — M,D
University of Chicago — D
University of Cincinnati — D
University of Colorado Boulder — M,D
University of Colorado Denver — M,D
University of Connecticut — M,D
University of Connecticut Health
  Center — D
University of Delaware — M,D
University of Hawaii at Manoa — M,D

University of Illinois at
  Urbana–Champaign — D
The University of Kansas — D
The University of Manchester — M,D
University of Massachusetts
  Amherst — D
University of Miami — D
University of Michigan — M,D
University of Minnesota, Twin
  Cities Campus — M,D
University of Montana — D
The University of North Carolina
  at Chapel Hill — M,D
University of Pennsylvania — D
University of Pittsburgh — D
University of South Carolina — M,D
University of Southern California — D
The University of Texas
  Southwestern Medical Center — D
Vanderbilt University — D
Washington University in St. Louis — D
Wesleyan University — D
West Virginia University — M,D
Yale University — D

DEVELOPMENTAL EDUCATION

Austin Peay State University — M
East Tennessee State University — M,O
Ferris State University — M
Grambling State University — M,D,O
Instituto Tecnológico y de
  Estudios Superiores de Monterrey,
  Campus Ciudad Obregón — M
National Louis University — M,D,O
North Carolina State University — M,D,O
Penn State Harrisburg — M,D,O
Rutgers University–New
  Brunswick — M
Sam Houston State University — M,D
Texas State University — M,D
The University of Iowa — M,D
University of St. Francis (IL) — M,O
Walden University — M,D,O
Wayne State University — M,D

DEVELOPMENTAL PSYCHOLOGY

Andrews University — M,D
Arizona State University at the
  Tempe campus — M,D
Bay Path University — M
Boston College — M,D
Boston Graduate School of
  Psychoanalysis — O
Bowling Green State University — M,D
Brandeis University — M,D
Brigham Young University — D
Capella University — M
Carnegie Mellon University — D
Chatham University — M,D
Claremont Graduate University — M,D,O
Clark University — M
Clayton State University — M
Cornell University — M,D
Delaware Valley University — M
Duke University — D
Emory University — D
Erikson Institute — M,O
Florida International University — M,D
Florida State University — M,D
Fordham University — M,D
George Mason University — M,D,O
Georgia State University — D
The Graduate Center, City
  University of New York — D
Harvard University — D
Howard University — M,D
Humboldt State University — M
Illinois State University — M,D,O
Indiana University Bloomington — D
La Salle University — M,D
Louisiana State University and
  Agricultural & Mechanical College — M,D
Loyola University Chicago — M,D
McGill University — M,D,O
New York University — M,D
North Carolina State University — M,D
North Dakota State University — M,D
The Ohio State University — D
Pace University — M,D
Pontificia Universidad Catolica
  Madre y Maestra — M
Queens College of the City
  University of New York — M,O
Queen's University at
  Kingston — M,D
Regis University — M,D,O
San Francisco State University — M,O
Teachers College, Columbia
  University — M,D
Texas Christian University — M,D
Université de Montréal — M,D
The University of Alabama at
  Birmingham — M,D
The University of British Columbia — M,D
University of Connecticut — M,D
University of Denver — D
University of Houston — M,D
University of Illinois at Chicago — M,D
The University of Kansas — D
University of Louisville — D
The University of Manchester — M,D
University of Maryland, Baltimore
  County — D
University of Maryland, College
  Park — M,D
University of Massachusetts
  Amherst — M,D
University of Miami — M,D
University of Michigan — D
University of Montana — M,D,O

---

*M—masters degree; D—doctorate; O—other advanced degree; *—Close-Up and/or Display*

University of Nebraska–Lincoln	M,D,O
University of New Mexico	D
The University of North Carolina at Chapel Hill	D
The University of North Carolina at Greensboro	M,D
University of Notre Dame	D
University of Oregon	M,D
University of Pittsburgh	M,D
University of Rochester	D
University of Southern California	D
The University of Texas at Austin	D
University of Victoria	M,D
University of Washington	D
University of Wisconsin–Madison	D
University of Wisconsin–Milwaukee	M,D,O
Viterbo University	M
Washington University in St. Louis	D
Wayne State University	M,D
Wilfrid Laurier University	M,D
Yale University	D

DISABILITY STUDIES

Brandeis University	D
Brock University	M,O
California Baptist University	M
Chapman University	M,D,O
Montclair State University	M,O
Syracuse University	O
University of Hawaii at Manoa	O
University of Illinois at Chicago	M,D
University of Manitoba	M
University of Northern British Columbia	M,D,O
University of Pittsburgh	O
Utah State University	M
York University	M,D

DISTANCE EDUCATION DEVELOPMENT

American Public University System	M
Athabasca University	M,D,O
Barry University	O
Boise State University	M,D,O
Brandeis University	M
California Baptist University	M
Capella University	M,D
Clemson University	M,D,O
Coastal Carolina University	M,O
Colorado Christian University	M
Dallas Baptist University	M
Drury University	M
Eastern Michigan University	M,O
Endicott College	M
The George Washington University	O
Kansas State University	M,D,O
Keiser University	M
Lenoir-Rhyne University	M
Lesley University	M,D,O
Millersville University of Pennsylvania	M
Mississippi State University	M,D,O
National University	M,O
New Mexico State University	O
New York Institute of Technology	M,O
Nova Southeastern University	M,D,O
Post University	M
Regent University	M,D,O
Saginaw Valley State University	M
Shippensburg University of Pennsylvania	M,O
Télé-université	M,D
Texas Tech University	M
Thomas Edison State University	M,O
University at Buffalo, the State University of New York	M,D,O
University of Colorado Denver	M
University of Illinois at Springfield	M,O
The University of Kansas	M,D
University of Maryland, Baltimore County	
University of Maryland University College	M
University of Nevada, Las Vegas	M,D,O
University of South Florida	O
Virginia Polytechnic Institute and State University	M,O
Walden University	M,D,O
Waynesburg University	M,D
Wayne State University	M,D,O
Western Illinois University	M,O
Wilkes University	M,O

EARLY CHILDHOOD EDUCATION

Alabama Agricultural and Mechanical University	M,D,O
Alabama State University	M,O
Albany State University	M,O
Albright College	M
American International College	M,O
Anna Maria College	M,O
Antioch University Midwest	M
Antioch University New England	M
Arcadia University	M,D,O
Arkansas State University	M,D,O
Armstrong State University	M,O
Auburn University at Montgomery	M,O
Bank Street College of Education	
Barry University	M,D,O
Bayamón Central University	M
Berry College	M
Binghamton University, State University of New York	M
Biola University	M,O
Bloomsburg University of Pennsylvania	M
Boise State University	M
Brenau University	M,O
Bridgewater State University	M
Brooklyn College of the City University of New York	

Buffalo State College, State University of New York	M
California State University, Dominguez Hills	M
California State University, East Bay	M
California State University, Fresno	M
California State University, Northridge	M
Cambridge College	M,D,O
Canisius College	M
Capella University	M
Caribbean University	M,D
Carlow University	M
Carroll University	M
The Catholic University of America	M,O
Central Connecticut State University	M,O
Central Michigan University	M
Chaminade University of Honolulu	M
Champlain College	M
Chatham University	M
Chestnut Hill College	M
Chicago State University	M
The Citadel, The Military College of South Carolina	M,O
City College of the City University of New York	M
Clarion University of Pennsylvania	M
Clarkson University	M
Clemson University	M,O
Cleveland State University	M
The College at Brockport, State University of New York	M
College of Charleston	M
The College of New Jersey	M
The College of New Rochelle	M
The College of Saint Rose	M,O
Colorado Christian University	M
Columbia International University	M,D,O
Columbus State University	M,O
Concordia University (United States)	M,D
Concordia University Chicago	M,D
Concordia University, Nebraska	M
Concordia University Wisconsin	M
Daemen College	M
Dallas Baptist University	M,D
DePaul University	M,D
Dominican University	M
Duquesne University	M
East Carolina University	M,D
Eastern Connecticut State University	M
Eastern Illinois University	M
Eastern Michigan University	M
Eastern Nazarene College	M
Eastern New Mexico University	M
Eastern University	M,D,O
Eastern Washington University	M
East Stroudsburg University of Pennsylvania	M
East Tennessee State University	M,O
Edinboro University of Pennsylvania	M,O
Elms College	M,O
Emporia State University	M
Endicott College	M
Erikson Institute	M,D
Fairleigh Dickinson University, College at Florham	M,O
Fairleigh Dickinson University, Metropolitan Campus	M
Fitchburg State University	M
Five Towns College	M,D
Florida Atlantic University	M,D,O
Florida International University	M,D,O
Florida State University	M,D,O
Fontbonne University	M
Fordham University	M,O
Framingham State University	M
Furman University	M,O
Gallaudet University	M,D,O
Gateway Seminary	M,D,O
George Mason University	M
The George Washington University	M
Georgia College & State University	M
Georgia Southern University	M,O
Georgia Southwestern State University	M,O
Georgia State University	M,D,O
Gordon College	M,O
Governors State University	M
Grand Canyon University	M,D,O
Grand Valley State University	M
Harding University	M,O
Hebrew College	M,O
Henderson State University	M,O
Hofstra University	M,D,O
Holy Family University	M
Hunter College of the City University of New York	M,D,O
Indiana University–Purdue University Indianapolis	M,O
Inter American University of Puerto Rico, Guayama Campus	M
Iona College	M
Jackson State University	M,D,O
Jacksonville State University	M
James Madison University	M
Johns Hopkins University	M
Jose Maria Vargas University	M
Kansas State University	M,D,O
Kean University	M
Kennesaw State University	M
Kent State University	M,D,O
Keuka College	M
Keystone College	M
Lander University	M
La Salle University	M,O
Lee University	M,O
Lehman College of the City University of New York	M

Le Moyne College	M,O
Lesley University	M,D,O
Lincoln University (PA)	M
London Metropolitan University	M,D
Long Island University–Brentwood Campus	M,O
Long Island University–Hudson	M,O
Long Island University–LIU Brooklyn	M,O
Long Island University–LIU Post	M,O
Long Island University–Riverhead	M,O
Louisiana Tech University	M,D
Loyola University Maryland	M,O
Lynn University	M,D
Manhattan College	M,O
Manhattanville College	M,O
Marshall University	M
Martin Luther College	M
Maryville University of Saint Louis	M,D
Marywood University	M
McNeese State University	M,O
Mercer University	M,D,O
Mercy College	M
Merrimack College	M,O
Middle Tennessee State University	M,O
Millersville University of Pennsylvania	M
Milligan College	M,D,O
Mills College	M
Mississippi State University	M,D,O
Missouri Southern State University	M
Missouri State University	M
Molloy College	M,O
Monmouth University	M,D,O
Mount St. Joseph University	M,O
Murray State University	M
National Louis University	M,D,O
Nazareth College of Rochester	M
New Jersey City University	M
New Mexico State University	M,D,O
New York Institute of Technology	M
New York University	M
Niagara University	M,O
Norfolk State University	M
North Carolina Agricultural and Technical State University	M
Northeastern Illinois University	M
Northeastern State University	M
Northern Arizona University	M,D
Northern Illinois University	M,D
Northwestern College	M,O
Northwestern State University of Louisiana	M
Northwest Missouri State University	M,D,O
Oakland University	M,D,O
Oklahoma City University	M
Old Dominion University	M,D
Oregon State University	M,D
Ottawa University	M
Pace University	M,O
Pacific Oaks College	M
Pacific University	M
Piedmont College	M,O
Pontificia Universidad Catolica Madre y Maestra	M
Prescott College	M,D
Queens College of the City University of New York	M,O
Radford University	M
Regent University	M,D,O
Reinhardt University	M
Rhode Island College	M
Rivier University	M,D,O
Roberts Wesleyan College	M
Rockford University	M
Roosevelt University	M
Rudolf Steiner College	M
Rutgers University–New Brunswick	M,D
Saginaw Valley State University	M
St. Bonaventure University	M
St. Catherine University	M
St. John's University (NY)	M,O
St. Joseph's College, Long Island Campus	M
Saint Joseph's University	M,D,O
Saint Mary's College of California	M
Saint Xavier University	M
Salem State University	M
Samford University	M,D,O
San Francisco State University	M,D,O
San Jose State University	M,D,O
Shaw University	M
Shippensburg University of Pennsylvania	M,O
Siena Heights University	M,O
Sonoma State University	M,O
South Carolina State University	M
Southern Oregon University	M
Southwestern College (KS)	M,D
Southwestern Oklahoma State University	M
Southwest Minnesota State University	M
Spring Hill College	M
State University of New York at Fredonia	M
State University of New York at New Paltz	M
State University of New York at Oswego	M
State University of New York at Plattsburgh	O
State University of New York College at Cortland	M
State University of New York College at Geneseo	M

State University of New York College at Potsdam	M
Stephen F. Austin State University	M
Syracuse University	M
Teachers College, Columbia University	M,D
Tennessee Technological University	M,O
Texas A&M University–Commerce	M,D,O
Texas A&M University–Corpus Christi	M,D
Texas A&M University–Kingsville	M
Texas A&M University–San Antonio	M
Texas Woman's University	M,D
Theological University of the Caribbean	M,D
Towson University	M,O
Trident University International	M
Trinity Washington University	M
Troy University	M,O
Tufts University	M,D
Universidad del Turabo	M
University at Buffalo, the State University of New York	M,D,O
The University of Alabama at Birmingham	M,D
University of Alaska Anchorage	M,O
University of Arkansas	
University of Bridgeport	M
University of Central Florida	D
University of Central Missouri	M,D,O
University of Central Oklahoma	M
University of Cincinnati	M
University of Colorado Denver	M,D
University of Dayton	M
University of Denver	M,D,O
University of Florida	M,D,O
University of Hartford	M
University of Hawaii at Manoa	M
University of Houston–Clear Lake	M
University of Illinois at Chicago	M,D
The University of Kansas	M,D,O
University of Kentucky	M,D
University of Louisiana at Monroe	M,D
University of Louisville	M,D,O
University of Maine	M,D,O
University of Maine at Farmington	M
University of Maryland, Baltimore County	M
University of Massachusetts Amherst	M,D,O
University of Massachusetts Boston	D
University of Massachusetts Dartmouth	M,D,O
University of Memphis	M,D,O
University of Miami	M,O
University of Michigan–Dearborn	M,D,O
University of Michigan–Flint	M,D,O
University of Minnesota, Twin Cities Campus	M,D,O
University of Missouri	M,D,O
University of Missouri–St. Louis	M
University of Montana	M,D
University of Nebraska at Kearney	M
University of Nebraska–Lincoln	M,D
University of Nevada, Las Vegas	M,D,O
University of New England	M,D,O
University of New Hampshire	M,D,O
University of New Mexico	D
The University of North Carolina at Chapel Hill	M,D
The University of North Carolina at Charlotte	M,D,O
The University of North Carolina at Greensboro	M,D,O
The University of North Carolina Wilmington	M
University of North Dakota	M
University of Northern Iowa	M
University of North Georgia	M,O
University of North Texas	M,D,O
University of Oklahoma	M,D
University of Phoenix–Bay Area Campus	M,D,O
University of Phoenix–North Florida Campus	M
University of Phoenix–Online Campus	M,O
University of Phoenix–Phoenix Campus	M
University of Phoenix–South Florida Campus	M
University of Phoenix–Washington D.C. Campus	M,D,O
University of Pittsburgh	M
University of Puerto Rico, Río Piedras Campus	M
University of South Alabama	M,D
University of South Carolina	M,D
University of South Carolina Upstate	M
The University of South Dakota	M,D,O
University of South Florida	M,D,O
The University of Tennessee	M,D,O
The University of Texas at Austin	M,D
The University of Texas at San Antonio	M,D
The University of Texas at Tyler	M
The University of Texas of the Permian Basin	M
The University of Texas Rio Grande Valley	M
University of the District of Columbia	
University of the Sacred Heart	M,O
University of the Southwest	M
The University of Toledo	M,D,O
University of Utah	M,D

University of Victoria	M,D
University of Virginia	M,D
The University of West Alabama	M,O
University of West Georgia	M,D,O
University of Wisconsin–Milwaukee	M
University of Wisconsin–Oshkosh	M
Upper Iowa University	M
Ursuline College	M
Valdosta State University	M,O
Virginia Commonwealth University	M
Viterbo University	M,O
Wagner College	M
Walden University	M,D,O
Wayne State College	M
Wayne State University	M,D,O
Webster University	M,O
Wesleyan College	M
West Chester University of Pennsylvania	M,O
Western Kentucky University	M,O
Western Oregon University	M
Westfield State University	M
Westminster College (PA)	M,O
West Virginia University	M,D
Wheelock College	M
Wichita State University	M
Widener University	M,D
Wilkes University	M,D
Worcester State University	M
Xavier University	M
Youngstown State University	M

EAST EUROPEAN AND RUSSIAN STUDIES

Boston College	M
Brown University	M,D
Carleton University	M,O
Columbia University	M,D
Cornell University	M,D
Florida State University	M
Georgetown University	M
The George Washington University	M
Harvard University	M
Indiana University Bloomington	M,O
The Ohio State University	M,D
Stanford University	M
University of Alberta	M,D
The University of British Columbia	M,D
University of Illinois at Chicago	M,D
University of Illinois at Urbana–Champaign	M
The University of Kansas	M,O
University of Michigan	M,O
The University of North Carolina at Chapel Hill	M
University of Pittsburgh	O
University of Saskatchewan	M
The University of Texas at Austin	M
University of Toronto	M
University of Washington	M
Yale University	M,D

ECOLOGY

Baylor University	D
Brown University	D
California Institute of Integral Studies	M,D
California State University, Stanislaus	M
Colorado State University	M,D
Columbia University	M,D
Cornell University	M,D
Dalhousie University	M
Dartmouth College	D
Duke University	D,O
Eastern Kentucky University	M
Eastern Michigan University	M
Eastern New Mexico University	M
Emory University	D
Florida Institute of Technology	M,D
Florida State University	M,D
Frostburg State University	M
George Mason University	M,D
Illinois State University	M,D
Indiana State University	M,D
Indiana University Bloomington	M,D,O
Inter American University of Puerto Rico, Bayamón Campus	M
Iowa State University of Science and Technology	M,D
Kent State University	M,D
Laurentian University	M,D
Lesley University	M,D,O
Marquette University	M,D
Michigan State University	D
Michigan Technological University	M,D
Montana State University	M,D
Montclair State University	M
North Dakota State University	M,D
Northeastern University	M,D
The Ohio State University	M,D
Ohio University	M,D
Oklahoma State University	M,D
Old Dominion University	D
Oregon State University	M,D
Penn State University Park	M,D
Princeton University	D
Purdue University	M,D
Rice University	M,D
Rutgers University–New Brunswick	M,D
San Diego State University	M,D
San Francisco State University	M
San Jose State University	M,O
Sonoma State University	M
Stanford University	M,D
State University of New York College of Environmental Science and Forestry	M,D

Stony Brook University, State University of New York	M,D
Tulane University	M,D
Universidad Nacional Pedro Henríquez Ureña	M
University at Buffalo, the State University of New York	M,D,O
University of Alberta	M,D
The University of Arizona	M,D
University of California, Davis	M,D
University of California, Irvine	M,D
University of California, Los Angeles	M,D
University of California, Santa Barbara	M,D
University of California, Santa Cruz	M,D
University of Chicago	D
University of Colorado Boulder	M,D
University of Colorado Denver	M,D
University of Connecticut	M,D
University of Delaware	M,D
University of Denver	M,D
University of Florida	M,D,O
University of Georgia	M,D
University of Guelph	M,D
University of Illinois at Urbana–Champaign	M,D
The University of Kansas	M,D
The University of Manchester	M,D
University of Manitoba	M,D
University of Maryland, College Park	M,D
University of Michigan	M,D
University of Minnesota, Twin Cities Campus	M,D
University of Missouri	M,D
University of Montana	M,D
University of Nevada, Reno	D
University of New Haven	M,O
The University of North Carolina at Chapel Hill	M,D
University of Notre Dame	M,D
University of Oklahoma	D
University of Oregon	M,D
University of Pittsburgh	D
University of Puerto Rico, Río Piedras Campus	M,D
University of South Carolina	M,D
University of South Florida	M,D
The University of Tennessee	M,D
The University of Texas at Austin	D
The University of Toledo	M,D
University of Toronto	M,D
University of Washington	M,D
University of Wisconsin–Madison	M
University of Wisconsin–Milwaukee	M,D
University of Wyoming	M,D
Utah State University	M,D
Washington University in St. Louis	D
Western Illinois University	D
Yale University	D

ECONOMIC DEVELOPMENT

Albany State University	M
The American University in Cairo	M,O
Ball State University	M,O
Boston University	M
The Catholic University of America	M
Claremont Graduate University	M,D,O
Cleveland State University	M,O
Concordia University (Canada)	O
Cornell University	M,D
East Carolina University	M,O
Eastern University	M
East Tennessee State University	M
Fordham University	M,O
Georgetown University	D
Georgia Institute of Technology	M,D
Georgia State University	M,D,O
Indiana University Bloomington	M,D,O
New Mexico State University	M,D,O
Northeastern University	M
Oregon State University	M,D
Penn State University Park	M,D,O
State University of New York Empire State College	M
Thomas Edison State University	M
Troy University	M
Université de Sherbrooke	D
University of Central Arkansas	M,O
University of Colorado Denver	M
University of Houston–Victoria	M
University of Massachusetts Lowell	M,O
University of North Alabama	M
The University of North Carolina at Greensboro	M,D,O
University of Oklahoma	M,D
University of Pennsylvania	M,O
University of Puerto Rico, Río Piedras Campus	M
University of Southern California	M
University of Southern Mississippi	M
University of Waterloo	M
Vanderbilt University	M,D
Wayne State University	M,D,O
Western Illinois University	M
West Virginia University	M
Williams College	M
Yale University	M

ECONOMICS

Albany State University	M
American University	M,D,O
The American University in Cairo	M,O
American University of Armenia	M
American University of Beirut	M,D

Andrews University	M
Arizona State University at the Tempe campus	D
Assumption College	M,O
Auburn University	M
Bard College	M
Baruch College of the City University of New York	M
Baylor University	M
Binghamton University, State University of New York	M,D
Boston College	D
Boston University	M,D
Bowling Green State University	M
Brandeis University	M,D
Brock University	M
Brooklyn College of the City University of New York	M
Brown University	D
Buffalo State College, State University of New York	M
California Lutheran University	M,O
California Polytechnic State University, San Luis Obispo	M
California State Polytechnic University, Pomona	M
California State University, East Bay	M
California State University, Fullerton	M
California State University, Long Beach	M
California State University, Los Angeles	M
California University of Management and Sciences	M,D
Carleton University	M,D
Carnegie Mellon University	D
Central European University	M,D
Central Michigan University	M
City College of the City University of New York	M
Claremont Graduate University	M,D,O
Clark Atlanta University	M
Clark University	D
Clemson University	M,D
Cleveland State University	M,O
Colorado State University	M,D
Columbia University	M,D
Concordia University (Canada)	M,D,O
Copenhagen Business School	M,D
Cornell University	M,D
Dalhousie University	M,D
DePaul University	M
Drexel University	M,D,O
Duke University	M,D
Eastern Illinois University	M
Eastern Michigan University	M,O
Emory University	D
Florida Atlantic University	M
Florida International University	M,D
Florida State University	M,D
Fordham University	M,D,O
George Mason University	M,D
Georgetown University	D
The George Washington University	M,D
Georgia Institute of Technology	M,D
Georgia State University	M,D
The Graduate Center, City University of New York	D
Harvard University	D
Hawai'i Pacific University	M
Howard University	M,D
Hunter College of the City University of New York	M
Illinois State University	M
Indiana University Bloomington	M,D
Indiana University–Purdue University Indianapolis	M
Instituto Tecnológico de Santo Domingo	M,O
Instituto Tecnológico y de Estudios Superiores de Monterrey, Campus Ciudad de México	M,D
Iowa State University of Science and Technology	M,D
Johns Hopkins University	D
Kansas State University	M,D
Kent State University	M
Lakehead University	M
Lee University	M,O
Lehigh University	M,D
Louisiana State University and Agricultural & Mechanical College	M,D
Louisiana Tech University	M
Loyola University Chicago	M
Marquette University	M,O
Massachusetts Institute of Technology	M,D
McGill University	M,D
McMaster University	M,D
Memorial University of Newfoundland	M
Miami University	M
Michigan State University	M,D
Middle Tennessee State University	M,D
Mississippi State University	M,D
Morgan State University	M
Murray State University	M
New Mexico State University	M,D,O
The New School	M,D
New York University	M,D,O
North Carolina State University	M,D
Northeastern University	M,D
Northern Illinois University	M,D
Northwestern University	D
Oakland University	M,O
The Ohio State University	M,D
Ohio University	M
Oklahoma State University	M,D
Old Dominion University	M

Oregon State University	M,D
Pace University	O
Penn State University Park	M,D
Pepperdine University	M
Peru State College	M
Portland State University	M,D,O
Princeton University	D,O
Purdue University	D
Queens College of the City University of New York	M
Regis University	M,O
Rice University	M,D
Roosevelt University	M
Rutgers University–Newark	M,D
Rutgers University–New Brunswick	M,D
St. Cloud State University	M
San Diego State University	M
San Francisco State University	M
San Jose State University	M
Simon Fraser University	M,D
South Dakota State University	M
Southern Illinois University Carbondale	M,D
Southern Illinois University Edwardsville	M
Southern Methodist University	M,D
Stanford University	D
State University of New York College of Environmental Science and Forestry	M,D
Stony Brook University, State University of New York	M,D
Syracuse University	M,D
Teachers College, Columbia University	M,D
Temple University	M,D
Texas A&M University	M,D
Texas Tech University	M,D
Troy University	M
Tufts University	M,D
Tulane University	M,D
Universidad de las Américas Puebla	M
Université de Moncton	M
Université de Montréal	M,D,O
Université de Sherbrooke à Montréal	M,D
Université Laval	M,D
University at Albany, State University of New York	M,D,O
University at Buffalo, the State University of New York	M,D,O
The University of Akron	M
The University of Alabama	M,D
University of Alaska Fairbanks	M
University of Alberta	M,D
The University of Arizona	M,D
University of Arkansas	M,D
The University of British Columbia	M,D
University of Calgary	M,D
University of California, Berkeley	D
University of California, Davis	M,D
University of California, Irvine	M,D
University of California, Los Angeles	M,D
University of California, Riverside	M,D
University of California, San Diego	D
University of California, Santa Barbara	M,D
University of California, Santa Cruz	D
University of Central Arkansas	M,O
University of Chicago	M,D,O
University of Cincinnati	D
University of Colorado Boulder	M,D
University of Colorado Denver	M
University of Connecticut	M,D
University of Delaware	M,D
University of Denver	M
University of Detroit Mercy	M,D,O
University of Florida	M,D
University of Georgia	M,D
University of Guelph	M,D
University of Hawaii at Manoa	M,D
University of Houston	M,D
University of Illinois at Chicago	M,D
University of Illinois at Urbana–Champaign	M,D
The University of Iowa	D
The University of Kansas	M,D
University of Kentucky	M,D
University of Lethbridge	M,D
University of Maine	M
The University of Manchester	D
University of Manitoba	M,D
University of Maryland, Baltimore County	M,D
University of Maryland, College Park	M,D
University of Massachusetts Amherst	M,D
University of Massachusetts Lowell	M,O
University of Memphis	M,D
University of Michigan	M,D
University of Minnesota, Twin Cities Campus	M,D
University of Mississippi	M,D
University of Missouri	M,D
University of Missouri–Kansas City	M,D
University of Missouri–St. Louis	M
University of Montana	M
University of Nebraska at Omaha	M
University of Nebraska–Lincoln	M,D
University of Nevada, Las Vegas	M

M—masters degree; D—doctorate; O—other advanced degree; *—Close-Up and/or Display

Institution	Degree
University of Nevada, Reno	M
University of New Brunswick Fredericton	M
University of New Hampshire	M,D
University of New Mexico	M,D
University of New Orleans	D
The University of North Carolina at Chapel Hill	M,D
The University of North Carolina at Charlotte	M,O
The University of North Carolina at Greensboro	D
University of North Florida	M
University of North Texas	M,D,O
University of Notre Dame	M,D
University of Oklahoma	M,D
University of Oregon	M,D
University of Ottawa	M,D
University of Pennsylvania	M,D
University of Pittsburgh	M,D
University of Puerto Rico, Río Piedras Campus	M
University of Regina	M,D,O
University of Rhode Island	M,D
University of Rochester	D
University of San Francisco	M
University of Saskatchewan	M,O
University of South Africa	M,D
University of South Carolina	M,D
University of Southern California	M,D
University of Southern Mississippi	M
University of South Florida	M,D
The University of Tennessee	M,D
The University of Texas at Arlington	M
The University of Texas at Austin	M,D
The University of Texas at Dallas	M,D
The University of Texas at El Paso	M
The University of Texas at San Antonio	M
The University of Toledo	M,D,O
University of Toronto	M,D
University of Utah	M,D
University of Victoria	M,D
University of Virginia	M,D
University of Washington	D
University of Waterloo	M,D
The University of Western Ontario	M,D
University of Windsor	M
University of Wisconsin–Madison	D
University of Wisconsin–Milwaukee	M,D
University of Wyoming	M,D
Utah State University	M,D
Vanderbilt University	M,D
Virginia Commonwealth University	M
Virginia Polytechnic Institute and State University	M,D
Virginia State University	M
Washington State University	M,D,O
Washington University in St. Louis	D
Wayne State University	M,D
Western Illinois University	M
Western Michigan University	M,D
West Texas A&M University	M
West Virginia University	M,D
Wichita State University	M
Wilfrid Laurier University	M,D
Wright State University	M
Yale University	M,D
Yeshiva University	M,D
York University	M,D
Youngstown State University	M

EDUCATION—GENERAL

Institution	Degree
Abilene Christian University	M,O
Acacia University	M
Acadia University	M,D
Adams State University	M
Adelphi University	M,D,O
Alabama Agricultural and Mechanical University	M,D,O
Alabama State University	M,D,O
Alaska Pacific University	M
Albany State University	M,O
Albertus Magnus College	M
Albright College	M
Alcorn State University	M,O
Alfred University	M
Alliant International University–Los Angeles	M,O
Alliant International University–Sacramento	M,O
Alliant International University–San Diego	M,O
Alliant International University–San Francisco	M,O
Alvernia University	M
Alverno College	M
American College of Education	M
American InterContinental University Online	M,D,O
American International College	M,D,O
American Jewish University	M
American University	M
The American University in Cairo	M
The American University in Dubai	M,D
American University of Beirut	M,D
American University of Puerto Rico	M
Anderson University (IN)	M
Anderson University (SC)	M
Andrews University	M,D,O
Anna Maria College	M
Antioch University Los Angeles	M
Antioch University Midwest	M
Antioch University New England	M,O
Antioch University Santa Barbara	M
Antioch University Seattle	M
Aquinas College (MI)	M
Aquinas College (TN)	M
Arcadia University	M,D,O
Argosy University, Atlanta	M,D,O
Argosy University, Chicago	M,D,O

Institution	Degree
Argosy University, Dallas	M,D
Argosy University, Denver	M,D
Argosy University, Hawai`i	M,D
Argosy University, Inland Empire	M,D
Argosy University, Los Angeles	M,D
Argosy University, Nashville	M,D,O
Argosy University, Northern Virginia	M,D,O
Argosy University, Orange County	M,D
Argosy University, Phoenix	M,D,O
Argosy University, Salt Lake City	M,D
Argosy University, San Diego	M,D
Argosy University, San Francisco Bay Area	M,D
Argosy University, Sarasota	M,D,O
Argosy University, Seattle	M,D
Argosy University, Tampa	M,D,O
Argosy University, Twin Cities	M,D,O
Arizona State University at the Tempe campus	M,D,O
Arkansas State University	M,D,O
Arkansas Tech University	M,D,O
Arlington Baptist University	M
Armstrong State University	M,O
Ashland University	M,D
Athabasca University	M,D,O
Auburn University	M,D,O
Auburn University at Montgomery	M,O
Augsburg College	M
Augustana University	M
Aurora University	M,D
Austin College	M
Austin Peay State University	M,O
Averett University	M
Avila University	M,O
Azusa Pacific University	M,D
Baker University	M,D
Baldwin Wallace University	M
Ball State University	M,D,O
Bank Street College of Education	M
Bard College	M
Barry University	M,D,O
Bayamón Central University	M,O
Baylor University	M,D,O
Belhaven University (MS)	M
Bellarmine University	M,D
Bemidji State University	M
Benedictine College	M
Benedictine University	M
Berry College	M,O
Bethany College	M
Bethel College	M
Bethel University (MN)	M,D,O
Binghamton University, State University of New York	M,D,O
Biola University	M,O
Bishop's University	M,O
Bloomsburg University of Pennsylvania	M,O
Bluefield College	M
Bluffton University	M
Boise State University	M,D,O
Boston College	M,D,O
Boston University	M,D,O
Bowie State University	M
Bradley University	M,D,O
Brandman University	M,D
Brandon University	M,O
Brenau University	M,O
Bridgewater State University	M,O
Brigham Young University	M,D,O
Brock University	M,D
Brooklyn College of the City University of New York	M,O
Brown University	M
Bucknell University	M
Buena Vista University	M
Butler University	M,O
Cabrini University	M
Cairn University	M,O
Caldwell University	M,D,O
California Baptist University	M
California Coast University	M,D
California Lutheran University	M,D
California Polytechnic State University, San Luis Obispo	M
California State University, Dominguez Hills	M
California State University, East Bay	M
California State University, Fresno	M,D
California State University, Long Beach	M,D
California State University, Los Angeles	M,D,O
California State University, Monterey Bay	M
California State University, Northridge	M,D
California State University, Sacramento	M,D
California State University, San Bernardino	M
California State University, San Marcos	M,D
California State University, Stanislaus	M,D
California University of Pennsylvania	M
Calvary University	M
Calvin College	M
Cambridge College	M,D,O
Cameron University	M
Campbellsville University	M
Campbell University	M
Canisius College	M
Capella University	M,D
Cardinal Stritch University	M,D
Caribbean University	M,D
Carlow University	M,O
Carroll University	M
Carson-Newman University	M
Carthage College	M,O

Institution	Degree
Castleton University	M,O
The Catholic University of America	M,O
Cedar Crest College	M
Cedarville University	M,D
Centenary College of Louisiana	M
Centenary University	M,D
Central Connecticut State University	M,D,O
Central Methodist University	M
Central Michigan University	M,D,O
Central Washington University	M
Chadron State College	M,O
Chaminade University of Honolulu	M
Chapman University	M,D,O
Charleston Southern University	M
Chatham University	M
Chestnut Hill College	M
Cheyney University of Pennsylvania	M,O
Chicago State University	M,D
Chowan University	M
Christian Brothers University	M
Christopher Newport University	M
The Citadel, The Military College of South Carolina	M,O
City College of the City University of New York	M,O
City University of Seattle	M,O
Claremont Graduate University	M,D,O
Clarion University of Pennsylvania	M
Clark Atlanta University	M,D,O
Clarke University	M
Clarkson University	M
Clark University	M
Clayton State University	M
Clemson University	M,D,O
Cleveland State University	M,D,O
Coastal Carolina University	M,O
The College at Brockport, State University of New York	M,O
College of Charleston	M,O
The College of Idaho	M
College of Mount Saint Vincent	M,O
The College of New Jersey	M,O
The College of New Rochelle	M,O
College of Saint Elizabeth	M,D,O
College of St. Joseph	M
College of Saint Mary	M
College of the Saint Rose	M,O
The College of St. Scholastica	M,D
College of Staten Island of the City University of New York	M,O
The College of William and Mary	M,D,O
Colorado Christian University	M
The Colorado College	M
Colorado Mesa University	M,O
Colorado State University	M,D
Colorado State University–Global Campus	M
Colorado State University–Pueblo	M
Columbia College (MO)	M
Columbia College (SC)	M
Columbia International University	M,D,O
Columbus State University	M,D,O
Concordia College	M
Concordia University (United States)	M,D
Concordia University (Canada)	M,O
Concordia University Chicago	M
Concordia University Irvine	M
Concordia University, Nebraska	M
Concordia University, St. Paul	M,D,O
Concordia University Texas	M
Concordia University Wisconsin	M
Concord University	M
Converse College	M,O
Coppin State University	M
Corban University	M
Cornell University	M,D
Cornerstone University	M,O
Covenant College	M
Crandall University	M
Creighton University	M
Cumberland University	M
Curry College	M
Daemen College	M
Dakota State University	M
Dakota Wesleyan University	M
Dallas Baptist University	M
Defiance College	M
Delaware State University	M,D
Delta State University	M,D,O
DePaul University	M,D
DeSales University	M,O
Doane University	M
Dominican College	M
Dominican University	M
Dominican University of California	M
Dordt College	M
Drake University	M,D,O
Drexel University	M,D
Drury University	M
Duke University	M
Duquesne University	M,D,O
D'Youville College	M,D
Earlham College	M
East Carolina University	M,D,O
East Central University	M
Eastern Connecticut State University	M
Eastern Illinois University	M,O
Eastern Kentucky University	M
Eastern Mennonite University	M
Eastern Michigan University	M,D,O
Eastern Nazarene College	M,O
Eastern New Mexico University	M
Eastern Oregon University	M
Eastern University	M,D,O
Eastern Washington University	M
East Stroudsburg University of Pennsylvania	M,D
East Tennessee State University	M,D,O
East Texas Baptist University	M
Edgewood College	M,D,O

Institution	Degree
Elizabeth City State University	M
Elms College	M,O
Elon University	M
Embry-Riddle Aeronautical University–Worldwide	M
Emmanuel College (United States)	M
Emory & Henry College	M
Emory University	M,D
Emporia State University	M
Evangel University	M
The Evergreen State College	M
Fairfield University	M,O
Fairleigh Dickinson University, College at Florham	M,O
Fairleigh Dickinson University, Metropolitan Campus	M,O
Fairmont State University	M
Faulkner University	M
Felician University	M,O
Ferris State University	M
Fielding Graduate University	M,D,O
Florida Agricultural and Mechanical University	M,D
Florida Atlantic University	M,D
Florida Gulf Coast University	M
Florida Institute of Technology	M
Florida Memorial University	M
Florida Southern College	M,D
Florida State University	M,D,O
Fontbonne University	M
Fordham University	M,D,O
Fort Hays State University	M,O
Franciscan University of Steubenville	M
Francis Marion University	M
Freed-Hardeman University	M,O
Fresno Pacific University	M
Frostburg State University	M
Furman University	M
Gallaudet University	M,D,O
Gannon University	M,O
Gardner-Webb University	M,D,O
Geneva College	M
George Fox University	M,D,O
George Mason University	M,D,O
Georgetown College	M
The George Washington University	M,D,O
Georgia College & State University	M,O
Georgian Court University	M,O
Georgia Southern University	M,D,O
Georgia Southwestern State University	M
Georgia State University	M,D,O
Goddard College	M
Gonzaga University	M
Gordon College	M,O
Goucher College	M,O
Governors State University	M
Graceland University (IA)	M
Grambling State University	M,D,O
Grand Canyon University	M,D,O
Grand Valley State University	M
Gratz College	M
Greensboro College	M
Greenville College	M
Gwynedd Mercy University	M
Hamline University	M
Hampton University	M,D,O
Hannibal-LaGrange University	M
Harding University	M
Hardin-Simmons University	M,D
Harrison Middleton University	M,D
Harvard University	M,D
Hastings College	M
Hebrew College	M,O
Hebrew Union College–Jewish Institute of Religion (NY)	M
Heidelberg University	M
Henderson State University	M,O
Heritage University	M
High Point University	M
Hofstra University	M,D,O
Hollins University	M
Holy Family University	M,D
Holy Names University	M,O
Hood College	M,O
Hope International University	M
Houston Baptist University	M,D
Howard University	M,D,O
Humboldt State University	M
Hunter College of the City University of New York	M,D,O
Huntington University	M,D
Idaho State University	M,D,O
Illinois College	M
Illinois State University	M,D,O
Indiana State University	M,D,O
Indiana University Bloomington	M,D,O
Indiana University East	M
Indiana University Northwest	M,O
Indiana University of Pennsylvania	M,D,O
Indiana University–Purdue University Fort Wayne	M,O
Indiana University–Purdue University Indianapolis	M,O
Indiana University South Bend	M,O
Indiana University Southeast	M
Institute for Christian Studies	M,D
Instituto Tecnologico de Santo Domingo	M,O
Instituto Tecnológico y de Estudios Superiores de Monterrey, Campus Central de Veracruz	M
Instituto Tecnológico y de Estudios Superiores de Monterrey, Campus Ciudad de México	M,D
Instituto Tecnológico y de Estudios Superiores de Monterrey, Campus Ciudad Juárez	M
Instituto Tecnológico y de Estudios Superiores de Monterrey, Campus Ciudad Obregón	M

Instituto Tecnológico y de Estudios Superiores de Monterrey, Campus Estado de México — M,D
Instituto Tecnológico y de Estudios Superiores de Monterrey, Campus Irapuato — M,D
Instituto Tecnológico y de Estudios Superiores de Monterrey, Campus Sonora Norte — M
Inter American University of Puerto Rico, Arecibo Campus — M
Inter American University of Puerto Rico, Barranquitas Campus — M
Inter American University of Puerto Rico, Metropolitan Campus — M,D
International Baptist College and Seminary — M
Iona College — M
Iowa State University of Science and Technology — M,D
Jackson State University — M,D,O
Jacksonville State University — M,O
John Brown University — M
John F. Kennedy University — M
Johns Hopkins University — M,D,O
Johnson & Wales University — M
Johnson State College — M
Johnson University — M,D,O
Kansas State University — M,D,O
Kaplan University, Davenport Campus — M
Kean University — M
Keene State College — M,O
Keiser University — M
Kennesaw State University — M,D,O
Kent State University — M,D,O
Kent State University at Stark — M
King's College — M
Kutztown University of Pennsylvania — M
LaGrange College — M,O
Lake Erie College — M
Lake Forest College — M
Lakehead University — M,D
Lakeland University — M
Lamar University — M,D,O
Lander University — M
Langston University — M
La Salle University — M,O
Lasell College — M
La Sierra University — M,D,O
Lee University — M,O
Lehigh University — M,D,O
Lehman College of the City University of New York — M
Le Moyne College — M,O
Lenoir-Rhyne University — M
Lesley University — M,D,O
Lewis University — M,D
Liberty University — M,D,O
Lincoln Memorial University — M,D,O
Lindenwood University — M,D,O
Lindenwood University–Belleville — M
Lipscomb University — M,D,O
Lock Haven University of Pennsylvania — M
London Metropolitan University — M,D
Long Island University–LIU Brooklyn — M,O
Long Island University–LIU Post — M,D,O
Longwood University — M
Louisiana College — M
Louisiana State University and Agricultural & Mechanical College — M,D,O
Louisiana State University in Shreveport — M,D
Louisiana Tech University — M,D
Loyola Marymount University — M,D
Loyola University Chicago — M,D,O
Loyola University Maryland — M,O
Loyola University New Orleans — M
Lyndon State College — M
Lynn University — M,D
Madonna University — M
Malone University — M
Manhattan College — M,O
Manhattanville College — M,D,O
Mansfield University of Pennsylvania — M
Maranatha Baptist University — M
Marian University (WI) — M,D
Marist College — M,O
Marlboro College — M,O
Marquette University — M,D,O
Marshall University — M,D,O
Martin Luther College — M
Mary Baldwin University — M
Marygrove College — M
Marylhurst University — M
Marymount University — M
Maryville University of Saint Louis — M,D
Marywood University — M
Massachusetts College of Liberal Arts — M,O
McGill University — M,D,O
McKendree University — M,D,O
McNeese State University — O
McPherson College — M
Medaille College — M
Memorial University of Newfoundland — M,D,O
Mercer University — M,D,O
Mercy College — M,O
Meredith College — M,O
Merrimack College — M,O
Metropolitan State University of Denver — M
Miami University — M,D,O

Michigan State University — M,D,O
MidAmerica Nazarene University — M
Middle Tennessee State University — M,D,O
Midway University — M
Midwestern State University — M
Millersville University of Pennsylvania — M,D,O
Milligan College — M,D,O
Mills College — M,D,O
Minnesota State University Mankato — M,D,O
Minnesota State University Moorhead — M,O
Mississippi College — M,D,O
Mississippi State University — M,D,O
Mississippi University for Women — M
Mississippi Valley State University — M
Missouri Baptist University — M,O
Missouri Southern State University — M
Molloy College — M,O
Monmouth University — M,D,O
Montana State University — M,D,O
Montana State University Billings — M,O
Montana State University–Northern — M
Montclair State University — M,D,O
Moravian College — M
Morehead State University — M,O
Morgan State University — M,D
Morningside College — M
Mount Mary University — M
Mount Mercy University — M
Mount St. Joseph University — M,O
Mount Saint Mary College — M,O
Mount Saint Mary's University (CA) — M,D,O
Mount St. Mary's University (MD) — M
Mount Saint Vincent University — M
Mount Vernon Nazarene University — M
Multnomah University — M
Murray State University — M,D,O
Muskingum University — M
Naropa University — M
National Louis University — M,D,O
National University — M,O
Nazareth College of Rochester — M
Neumann University — M
New England College — M,D
New Jersey City University — M,D
Newman University — M
New Mexico Highlands University — M
New Mexico State University — M,D,O
New York Institute of Technology — M,O
New York University — M,D,O
Niagara University — M,O
Nicholls State University — M
Nipissing University — M,O
Norfolk State University — M
North Carolina Agricultural and Technical State University — M
North Carolina Central University — M
North Carolina State University — M,D,O
North Central College — M
Northcentral University — M,D,O
North Dakota State University — M,D,O
Northeastern Illinois University — M
Northeastern State University — M
Northern Arizona University — M,D,O
Northern Illinois University — M,D,O
Northern Kentucky University — M,D,O
Northern Michigan University — M
Northern State University — M
North Greenville University — M,D
North Park University — M
Northwest Christian University — M
Northwestern College — M,O
Northwestern Oklahoma State University — M
Northwestern State University of Louisiana — M,O
Northwestern University — M,D
Northwest Missouri State University — M,D,O
Northwest Nazarene University — M,D,O
Northwest University — M
Notre Dame de Namur University — M,D
Notre Dame of Maryland University — M
Nova Southeastern University — M,D,O
Oakland City University — M,D
Oakland University — M,D,O
Ohio Dominican University — M
The Ohio State University — M,D,O
The Ohio State University at Marion — M
The Ohio State University–Mansfield Campus — M
The Ohio State University–Newark Campus — M
Ohio University — M,D
Ohio Valley University — M
Oklahoma State University — M,D,O
Old Dominion University — M,D,O
Olivet Nazarene University — M
Open University — M
Oral Roberts University — M,D
Oregon State University — M,D
Oregon State University–Cascades — M
Ottawa University — M
Otterbein University — M
Pace University — M,O
Pacific Lutheran University — M
Pacific Oaks College — M
Pacific Union College — M
Pacific University — M
Palm Beach Atlantic University — M
Park University — M,O
Penn State Harrisburg — M,D,O
Penn State University Park — M,D,O
Penn State York — M

Peru State College — M
Piedmont College — M,O
Pittsburg State University — M,O
Plymouth State University — O
Point Loma Nazarene University — M
Point Park University — M,D
Pontifical Catholic University of Puerto Rico — M,D
Portland State University — M,D
Post University — M
Prairie View A&M University — M,D
Prescott College — M,D
Purdue University — M,D,O
Purdue University Northwest — M
Queens College of the City University of New York — M,O
Queen's University at Kingston — M,D
Queens University of Charlotte — M
Quincy University — M
Quinnipiac University — M,O
Randolph College — M
Regent University — M,D,O
Regis College (MA) — M,D
Regis University — M
Reinhardt University — M
Relay Graduate School of Education — M
Rhode Island College — D
Rice University — M,O
Rider University — M,O
Rivier University — M,D,O
Robert Morris University — M,D,O
Roberts Wesleyan College — M
Rockford University — M
Rockhurst University — M
Roger Williams University — M
Rollins College — M
Roosevelt University — M
Rosemont College — M
Rowan University — M,D,O
Rudolf Steiner College — M
Rutgers University–New Brunswick — M,D
Sacred Heart University — M,O
Sage Graduate School — M,D,O
Saginaw Valley State University — M,O
St. Ambrose University — M
St. Bonaventure University — M,O
St. Catherine University — M
St. Cloud State University — M,D
St. Edward's University — M
Saint Francis University — M
St. Francis Xavier University — M
St. John Fisher College — M,D,O
St. John's University (NY) — M,D,O
St. Joseph's College, New York — M
Saint Joseph's College of Maine — M
Saint Joseph's University — M,D,O
St. Lawrence University — M,O
Saint Leo University — M
Saint Louis University — M,D
Saint Martin's University — M
Saint Mary's College of California — M,D,O
St. Mary's College of Maryland — M
Saint Mary's University of Minnesota — M,O
Saint Michael's College — M
Saint Peter's University — M,D,O
St. Thomas Aquinas College — M,O
St. Thomas University — M,D,O
Saint Vincent College — M
Saint Xavier University — M
Salem College — M
Salem International University — M
Samford University — M,D
Sam Houston State University — M,D
San Diego Christian College — M
San Diego State University — M,D
San Francisco State University — M,D,O
San Jose State University — M,D,O
Santa Clara University — M
Sarah Lawrence College — M
Schreiner University — M,O
Seattle Pacific University — D
Seattle University — M,D,O
Seton Hall University — M,D,O
Shawnee State University — M
Shenandoah University — M,D,O
Shippensburg University of Pennsylvania — M
Siena Heights University — M,O
Sierra Nevada College — M
Silver Lake College of the Holy Family — M
Simmons College — M,D,O
Simon Fraser University — M,D
Simpson College — M
Simpson University — M
Sinte Gleska University — M
Slippery Rock University of Pennsylvania — M,D
Smith College — M
Sonoma State University — M
South Carolina State University — M
South Dakota State University — M,D
Southeastern Louisiana University — M,D
Southeastern Oklahoma State University — M
Southeastern University (FL) — M,O
Southern Adventist University — M
Southern Arkansas University–Magnolia — M
Southern Connecticut State University — M,D,O
Southern Illinois University Carbondale — M,D

Southern Illinois University Edwardsville — M,D,O
Southern Methodist University — M,D
Southern New Hampshire University — M,D,O
Southern Oregon University — M
Southern University and Agricultural and Mechanical College — M,D
Southern Utah University — M,O
Southern Wesleyan University — M
Southwest Baptist University — M,O
Southwestern Adventist University — M
Southwestern Assemblies of God University — M,D
Southwestern College (KS) — M,D
Southwestern Oklahoma State University — M
Southwest Minnesota State University — M
Spalding University — M
Spring Arbor University — M
Springfield College — M
Spring Hill College — M
Stanford University — M,D
State University of New York at Fredonia — M
State University of New York at New Paltz — M,O
State University of New York at Oswego — M,O
State University of New York College at Cortland — M,O
State University of New York College at Geneseo — M
State University of New York College at Old Westbury — M
State University of New York College at Oneonta — M,O
State University of New York Empire State College — M
Stephen F. Austin State University — M,D
Stetson University — M
Stevenson University — M
Stockton University — M
Strayer University — M
Sul Ross State University — M,O
Sweet Briar College — M
Syracuse University — M,D,O
Taft University System — M
Tarleton State University — M,D,O
Teachers College, Columbia University — M,D
Temple University — M,D,O
Tennessee State University — M,D,O
Tennessee Technological University — M,D,O
Texas A&M International University — M
Texas A&M University — M,D
Texas A&M University–Commerce — M,D,O
Texas A&M University–Corpus Christi — M,D
Texas A&M University–Kingsville — M,D,O
Texas A&M University–Texarkana — M
Texas Christian University — M
Texas Southern University — M,D
Texas State University — M,D,O
Texas Tech University — M,D
Texas Wesleyan University — M,D
Texas Woman's University — M,D
Thomas More College — M
Thomas University — M
Thompson Rivers University — M
Tiffin University — M
Touro College — M
Touro University California — M,D
Towson University — M
Trevecca Nazarene University — M,O
Trident University International — M,D
Trinity International University — M
Trinity University — M
Trinity Washington University — M
Troy University — M,O
Truman State University — M
Tufts University — M,D,O
Tusculum College — M
Union College (KY) — M
Union Institute & University — D
Union University — M,D,O
Universidad Autonoma de Guadalajara — M,D
Universidad de las Americas, A.C. — M
Universidad de las Américas Puebla — M
Universidad del Turabo — M
Universidad Metropolitana — M
Université de Moncton — M
Université de Montréal — M,D,O
Université de Saint-Boniface — M
Université de Sherbrooke — M,O
Université du Québec à Chicoutimi — M,D
Université du Québec à Montréal — M,D,O
Université du Québec à Rimouski — M,D,O
Université du Québec à Trois-Rivières — M,D
Université du Québec en Abitibi-Témiscamingue — M,D,O
Université du Québec en Outaouais — M,D,O
Université Laval — M,D,O
Université Sainte-Anne — M
University at Albany, State University of New York — M,D,O
University at Buffalo, the State University of New York — M,D,O
The University of Akron — M
The University of Alabama at Birmingham — M,D,O

---

*M—masters degree; D—doctorate; O—other advanced degree; *—Close-Up and/or Display*

The University of Alabama in Huntsville — M,O
University of Alaska Anchorage — M,O
University of Alaska Fairbanks — M,O
University of Alaska Southeast — M
The University of Arizona — M,D,O
University of Arkansas — M,D,O
University of Arkansas at Little Rock — M,D,O
University of Arkansas at Monticello — M
University of Arkansas at Pine Bluff — M
University of Bridgeport — M,D,O
The University of British Columbia — M,D,O
University of California, Berkeley — M,D,O
University of California, Davis — M,D
University of California, Irvine — M,D
University of California, Los Angeles — M,D
University of California, Riverside — M,D,O
University of California, San Diego — M,D
University of California, Santa Barbara — M,D,O
University of California, Santa Cruz — M,D
University of Central Arkansas — M,O
University of Central Florida — M,O
University of Central Missouri — M,D,O
University of Central Oklahoma — M
University of Cincinnati — M,D,O
University of Colorado Boulder — M,D
University of Colorado Colorado Springs — M,D
University of Colorado Denver — M,D,O
University of Connecticut — M,D
University of Delaware — M,D,O
University of Denver — M,D,O
The University of Findlay — M,D
University of Florida — M,D,O
University of Georgia — M,D,O
University of Guam — M
University of Hartford — M,D,O
University of Hawaii at Hilo — M
University of Hawaii at Manoa — M,D,O
University of Holy Cross — M
University of Houston — M,D
University of Houston–Clear Lake — M,D
University of Houston–Victoria — M
University of Idaho — M,D,O
University of Illinois at Chicago — M,D
University of Illinois at Springfield — M,O
University of Illinois at Urbana–Champaign — M,D,O
University of Indianapolis — M
The University of Iowa — M,D,O
University of Jamestown — M
The University of Kansas — M,D,O
University of Kentucky — M,D,O
University of La Verne — M,O
University of Lethbridge — M,D
University of Louisiana at Lafayette — M,D
University of Louisiana at Monroe — M,D
University of Louisville — M,D,O
University of Maine — M,D,O
University of Maine at Farmington — M
The University of Manchester — M,D
University of Manitoba — M,D
University of Mary — M,D
University of Mary Hardin-Baylor — M,D
University of Maryland, Baltimore County — M,O
University of Maryland, College Park — M,D,O
University of Maryland Eastern Shore — M
University of Maryland University College — M
University of Mary Washington — M
University of Massachusetts Amherst — M,D,O
University of Massachusetts Boston — M,D
University of Massachusetts Dartmouth — M,D,O
University of Massachusetts Lowell — M
University of Memphis — M,D,O
University of Miami — M,D,O
University of Michigan — M,D
University of Michigan–Dearborn — M
University of Michigan–Flint — M,D,O
University of Minnesota, Duluth — M,D
University of Minnesota, Twin Cities Campus — M,D,O
University of Mississippi — M,D,O
University of Missouri — M,D,O
University of Missouri–Kansas City — M,D,O
University of Missouri–St. Louis — M,D,O
University of Mobile — M
University of Montana — M,D,O
University of Montevallo — M,O
University of Nebraska at Kearney — M,O
University of Nebraska at Omaha — M,D,O
University of Nevada, Las Vegas — M,D,O
University of Nevada, Reno — M,D,O
University of New Brunswick Fredericton — M,D
University of New England — M,D,O
University of New Hampshire — M,D,O
University of New Mexico — M,D,O
University of New Orleans — M,D
University of North Alabama — M,O
The University of North Carolina at Chapel Hill — M,D
The University of North Carolina at Charlotte — M,D,O

The University of North Carolina at Greensboro — M,D,O
The University of North Carolina at Pembroke — M
The University of North Carolina Wilmington — M,D
University of North Dakota — M,D,O
University of Northern British Columbia — M,D,O
University of Northern Colorado — M,D,O
University of Northern Iowa — M,D,O
University of North Florida — M,D
University of North Georgia — M,O
University of North Texas — M,D,O
University of Northwestern–St. Paul — M
University of Notre Dame — M,D
University of Oklahoma — M,D,O
University of Oregon — M,D
University of Ottawa — M,D,O
University of Pennsylvania — M,D,O
University of Phoenix–Bay Area Campus — M,D,O
University of Phoenix–Central Valley Campus — M
University of Phoenix–Colorado Campus — M
University of Phoenix–Colorado Springs Downtown Campus — M,O
University of Phoenix–Dallas Campus — M
University of Phoenix–Hawaii Campus — M
University of Phoenix–Houston Campus — M
University of Phoenix–Las Vegas Campus — M
University of Phoenix–New Mexico Campus — M
University of Phoenix–North Florida Campus — M
University of Phoenix–Online Campus — M
University of Phoenix–Phoenix Campus — M
University of Phoenix–Sacramento Valley Campus — M,O
University of Phoenix–San Diego Campus — M
University of Phoenix–Southern Arizona Campus — M,O
University of Phoenix–Southern California Campus — M,O
University of Phoenix–South Florida Campus — M
University of Phoenix–Utah Campus — M
University of Phoenix–Washington D.C. Campus — M,D,O
University of Pikeville — M
University of Pittsburgh — M,D
University of Portland — M,D
University of Prince Edward Island — M,D
University of Puerto Rico, Río Piedras Campus — M,D
University of Puget Sound — M
University of Redlands — M,D,O
University of Regina — M,D,O
University of Rhode Island — M,D
University of Rio Grande — M
University of Rochester — M,D
University of St. Francis (IL) — M,D,O
University of Saint Francis (IN) — M
University of Saint Joseph — M
University of Saint Mary — M
University of St. Thomas (MN) — M,D,O
University of St. Thomas (TX) — M,D
University of San Diego — M,D,O
University of San Francisco — M,D
University of Saskatchewan — M,D,O
The University of Scranton — M
University of Sioux Falls — M,O
University of South Africa — M,D
University of South Alabama — M,D
University of South Carolina — M,D,O
University of South Carolina Upstate — M
The University of South Dakota — M,D,O
University of Southern California — M,D
University of Southern Indiana — M
University of Southern Maine — M,D,O
University of Southern Mississippi — M,D,O
University of South Florida — M,D,O
University of South Florida, St. Petersburg — M
The University of Tampa — M
The University of Tennessee — M,D,O
The University of Tennessee at Chattanooga — M,D,O
The University of Tennessee at Martin — M
The University of Texas at Arlington — M,D
The University of Texas at Austin — M,D
The University of Texas at El Paso — M,D
The University of Texas of the Permian Basin — M
The University of Texas Rio Grande Valley — M,D
University of the Cumberlands — M,D,O
University of the Pacific — M,D,O
University of the Sacred Heart — M,O
University of the Southwest — M
University of the Virgin Islands — M,D,O
The University of Toledo — M,D,O
The University of Toronto — M,D
The University of Tulsa — M,D
University of Utah — M,D,O
University of Vermont — M,D
University of Victoria — M,D
University of Virginia — M,D,O
University of Washington — M,D
University of Washington, Bothell — M

University of Washington, Tacoma — M
The University of West Alabama — M,O
The University of Western Ontario — M,D
University of West Georgia — M,D,O
University of Windsor — M,D
University of Wisconsin–Eau Claire — M
University of Wisconsin–Green Bay — M
University of Wisconsin–La Crosse — M,O
University of Wisconsin–Madison — M,D,O
University of Wisconsin–Milwaukee — M,D,O
University of Wisconsin–Oshkosh — M
University of Wisconsin–Platteville — M
University of Wisconsin–River Falls — M
University of Wisconsin–Stevens Point — M
University of Wisconsin–Stout — M,D,O
University of Wisconsin–Superior — M
University of Wisconsin–Whitewater — M,O
Upper Iowa University — M
Urbana University — M
Utah State University — M,D,O
Utah Valley University — M
Utica College — M,O
Valley City State University — M
Vanderbilt University — M,D
Vanguard University of Southern California — M
Villanova University — M
Virginia Commonwealth University — M,D,O
Virginia International University — M
Virginia Polytechnic Institute and State University — M,O
Virginia State University — M,D
Virginia Union University — M
Viterbo University — M,O
Wagner College — M,O
Wake Forest University — M
Walden University — M,D,O
Walla Walla University — M
Walsh University — M
Warner Pacific College — M
Warner University — M
Washburn University — M
Washington State University — M,D
Washington University in St. Louis — M,D
Wayland Baptist University — M
Wayne State College — M,O
Wayne State University — M,D,O
Weber State University — M
Webster University — M,O
Wesleyan College — M
Wesley College — M
West Chester University of Pennsylvania — M,D,O
Western Carolina University — M
Western Connecticut State University — M,D
Western Governors University — M,O
Western Illinois University — M,D,O
Western Michigan University — M,D,O
Western New Mexico University — M
Western Oregon University — M
Western State Colorado University — M
Western Washington University — M
Westfield State University — M
West Liberty University — M
Westminster College (UT) — M
West Texas A&M University — M
West Virginia University — M,D
West Virginia Wesleyan College — M
Wheaton College — M
Wheelock College — M
Whittier College — M
Whitworth University — M
Wichita State University — M,D,O
Widener University — M,D
Wilkes University — M,D
William Carey University — M,O
William Jessup University — M
William Jewell College — M
William Paterson University of New Jersey — M
Wilmington College — M
Wilmington University — M,D
Wilson College — M
Wingate University — M,D,O
Winona State University — O
Winston-Salem State University — M
Winthrop University — M
Wittenberg University — M
Worcester State University — M,O
Wright State University — M,D
Xavier University — M,D
Xavier University of Louisiana — M
York College of Pennsylvania — M
York University — M,D
Youngstown State University — M,D

EDUCATIONAL LEADERSHIP AND ADMINISTRATION

Abilene Christian University — M,D,O
Acacia University — M
Acadia University — M
Adelphi University — M,D,O
Alabama State University — M,D,O
Albany State University — M,O
Alliant International University–San Diego — M,D,O
Alliant International University–San Francisco — M,D,O
Alverno College — M
American College of Education — M

American InterContinental University Online — M
American International College — M,D,O
American Public University System — M
The American University in Cairo — M
Anderson University (SC) — M,D,O
Andrews University — M
Angelo State University — M
Antioch University Midwest — M,O
Antioch University New England — M,O
Appalachian State University — M,D,O
Arcadia University — M,D,O
Argosy University, Atlanta — M,D,O
Argosy University, Chicago — M,D,O
Argosy University, Dallas — M,D
Argosy University, Denver — M,D
Argosy University, Hawai`i — M,D
Argosy University, Inland Empire — M,D
Argosy University, Los Angeles — M,D
Argosy University, Nashville — M,D,O
Argosy University, Northern Virginia — M,D,O
Argosy University, Orange County — M,D,O
Argosy University, Phoenix — M,D,O
Argosy University, Salt Lake City — M,D
Argosy University, San Diego — M,D
Argosy University, San Francisco Bay Area — M,D
Argosy University, Sarasota — M,D,O
Argosy University, Seattle — M,D
Argosy University, Tampa — M,D
Argosy University, Twin Cities — M,D,O
Arizona State University at the Tempe campus — M,D
Arkansas State University — M,D,O
Arkansas Tech University — M,D,O
Arlington Baptist College — M
Asbury University — M
Ashland University — M,D
Auburn University — M,D,O
Auburn University at Montgomery — M,O
Augusta University — M,O
Aurora University — M,D
Austin Peay State University — M
Averett University — M
Azusa Pacific University — M,D
Baldwin Wallace University — M
Ball State University — M,D,O
Bank Street College of Education — M
Barry University — M,D,O
Baruch College of the City University of New York — M,O
Bayamón Central University — M,O
Baylor University — M
Bay Path University — M
Bellarmine University — M,D,O
Benedictine College — M
Benedictine University — M,D
Berry College — O
Bethel University (MN) — M,D,O
Bethel University (TN) — M
Binghamton University, State University of New York — M,D,O
Bloomsburg University of Pennsylvania — M
Bob Jones University — M,D,O
Boise State University — M,D,O
Boston College — M,D,O
Bowie State University — M,D
Bowling Green State University — M,D,O
Bradley University — M
Brandeis University — M,O
Brandman University — M,D
Brandon University — M,O
Bridgewater State University — M,O
Brigham Young University — M,D
Brooklyn College of the City University of New York — M
Buffalo State College, State University of New York — O
Butler University — M,O
Cairn University — M,O
Caldwell University — M,D,O
California Baptist University — M
California Coast University — M,D
California Lutheran University — M,D
California State Polytechnic University, Pomona — D
California State University, Bakersfield — M,D
California State University, East Bay — M,D
California State University, Fresno — M,D
California State University, Fullerton — M,D
California State University, Long Beach — M,D
California State University, Northridge — M,D
California State University, Sacramento — M,D
California State University, San Bernardino — M,D
California State University, San Marcos — M,D
California State University, Stanislaus — M,D
California University of Pennsylvania — M
Calumet College of Saint Joseph — M
Calvary University — M
Cambridge College — M,D,O
Cameron University — M
Campbell University — M
Canisius College — M
Capella University — M,D,O
Cardinal Stritch University — M,D
Caribbean University — M
Carlow University — M
Carroll University — M
Carson-Newman University — M
Carthage College — M,O
Castleton University — M,O

Institution	Degree
The Catholic University of America	M,O
Centenary University	M,D
Central Connecticut State University	M,D,O
Central Michigan University	M,O
Central Washington University	M
Chadron State College	M
Chaminade University of Honolulu	M
Chapman University	M,D,O
Charleston Southern University	M
Chestnut Hill College	M
Cheyney University of Pennsylvania	M,O
Chicago State University	M,D
Christian Brothers University	M
The Citadel, The Military College of South Carolina	M,O
City College of the City University of New York	M,O
City University of Seattle	M,D,O
Claremont Graduate University	M,D,O
Clark Atlanta University	M,D,O
Clarke University	M
Clarks Summit University	M
Clemson University	M,D,O
Cleveland State University	M,D,O
Coastal Carolina University	M,O
The College at Brockport, State University of New York	M,O
The College of New Jersey	M,O
The College of New Rochelle	M,O
College of Saint Elizabeth	M,D,O
College of Saint Mary	M
The College of Saint Rose	M,O
College of Staten Island of the City University of New York	O
The College of William and Mary	M,D
Colorado Mesa University	M,O
Colorado State University	M,D
Colorado State University–Global Campus	M
Columbia College (MO)	M
Columbia College (SC)	M
Columbia International University	M,D,O
Columbus State University	M
Concordia University (United States)	M,D
Concordia University Ann Arbor	M
Concordia University Chicago	M,D,O
Concordia University Irvine	M
Concordia University, Nebraska	M
Concordia University, St. Paul	M,D,O
Concordia University Wisconsin	M
Concord University	M
Converse College	M,O
Creighton University	M,D
Dakota Wesleyan University	M
Dallas Baptist University	M,D
Dallas Theological Seminary	M,D,O
Delaware State University	M,D
Delaware Valley University	M
Delta State University	M,D
DePaul University	M,D
DeVry University–Folsom Campus	M
Doane University	M
Drexel University	M,D
Drury University	M
Duquesne University	M,D,O
D'Youville College	M,D
East Carolina University	M,D,O
Eastern Illinois University	M,O
Eastern Kentucky University	M,D
Eastern Michigan University	M,D,O
Eastern Nazarene College	M,O
Eastern New Mexico University	M
Eastern University	M,D,O
East Tennessee State University	M,D,O
East Texas Baptist University	M
Edgewood College	M,D,O
Edinboro University of Pennsylvania	M
Elizabeth City State University	M
Elmhurst College	M
Emporia State University	M
Endicott College	M,D
Evangel University	M,D
Fairleigh Dickinson University, College at Florham	M
Fairleigh Dickinson University, Metropolitan Campus	M
Fayetteville State University	M,D
Felician University	M,O
Ferris State University	M,D
Fielding Graduate University	M,D,O
Fitchburg State University	M,O
Florida Agricultural and Mechanical University	M,D
Florida Atlantic University	M,D,O
Florida Gulf Coast University	M
Florida International University	M,D,O
Florida Southern College	M,D
Florida State University	M,D,O
Fordham University	M,D,O
Fort Hays State University	M,O
Fort Lewis College	M,O
Framingham State University	M
Franciscan University of Steubenville	M
Freed-Hardeman University	M,O
Fresno Pacific University	M
Frostburg State University	M
Furman University	M
Gannon University	D,O
Gardner-Webb University	M,D,O
Gateway Seminary	M,D,O
Geneva College	M
George Fox University	M,D,O
George Mason University	M,O
The George Washington University	M,D,O
Georgia College & State University	O
Georgian Court University	M,O
Georgia Southern University	M,D,O
Georgia State University	M,D,O
Gordon College	M,O
Goucher College	M,O
Governors State University	M,D
Graceland University (IA)	M
Grambling State University	M,D,O
Grand Canyon University	M,D,O
Grand Valley State University	M,O
Grand View University	M,O
Gratz College	M,D
Gwynedd Mercy University	M
Hampton University	M,D
Harding University	M,O
Hardin-Simmons University	D
Harvard University	M,D
Henderson State University	M,O
Heritage University	M
High Point University	M
Hofstra University	M,D,O
Holy Family University	M,D
Hood College	M
Hope International University	M
Houston Baptist University	M,D
Howard Payne University	M
Howard University	M,D,O
Hunter College of the City University of New York	D,O
Huston-Tillotson University	M
Idaho State University	M,D,O
Illinois State University	M,D
Immaculata University	M,D
Indiana State University	M,D,O
Indiana University Bloomington	M,D,O
Indiana University Northwest	M,O
Indiana University of Pennsylvania	D,O
Indiana University–Purdue University Fort Wayne	M,O
Indiana University–Purdue University Indianapolis	M,O
Indiana University South Bend	M,O
Indiana Wesleyan University	M,O
Instituto Tecnologico de Santo Domingo	M,O
Instituto Tecnológico y de Estudios Superiores de Monterrey, Campus Central de Veracruz	M
Instituto Tecnológico y de Estudios Superiores de Monterrey, Campus Ciudad Juárez	M
Instituto Tecnológico y de Estudios Superiores de Monterrey, Campus Estado de México	M,D
Instituto Tecnológico y de Estudios Superiores de Monterrey, Campus Irapuato	M,D
Inter American University of Puerto Rico, Aguadilla Campus	M
Inter American University of Puerto Rico, Arecibo Campus	M
Inter American University of Puerto Rico, Barranquitas Campus	M
Inter American University of Puerto Rico, Fajardo Campus	M
Inter American University of Puerto Rico, Metropolitan Campus	M,D
Iona College	M
Iowa State University of Science and Technology	M,D
Jackson State University	M,D,O
Jacksonville State University	M,O
Jacksonville University	M
James Madison University	M,D,O
Johns Hopkins University	M,D,O
Johnson & Wales University	D
Kansas State University	M,D,O
Kaplan University, Davenport Campus	M
Kean University	M,D
Keene State College	M,O
Keiser University	M,D,O
Kennesaw State University	M,D,O
Kent State University	M,D,O
Keystone College	M
Kutztown University of Pennsylvania	M
Lamar University	M,D
La Salle University	M,O
La Sierra University	M,D,O
Lee University	M,O
Lehigh University	M,D,O
Le Moyne College	M,O
Lenoir-Rhyne University	M
Lesley University	M,D,O
LeTourneau University	M
Lewis & Clark College	M,D,O
Lewis University	M,D
Liberty University	M,D,O
Lincoln Memorial University	M,D
Lincoln University (PA)	M
Lindenwood University	M,D,O
Lindenwood University–Belleville	M
Lindsey Wilson College	M
Lipscomb University	M,D,O
Lock Haven University of Pennsylvania	M
Long Island University–Hudson	M,O
Long Island University–LIU Brooklyn	M,O
Long Island University–LIU Post	M,D,O
Loras College	M
Louisiana State University and Agricultural & Mechanical College	M,D,O
Louisiana State University in Shreveport	M
Louisiana Tech University	M,D
Lourdes University	M
Loyola Marymount University	M,D
Loyola University Chicago	M,D,O
Loyola University Maryland	M,O
Lynchburg College	M,D
Lynn University	M,D
Madonna University	M
Malone University	M
Manhattan College	M,O
Manhattanville College	M,D,O
Marconi International University	M,D
Marian University (WI)	M
Marquette University	M,D,O
Marshall University	M,D,O
Martin Luther College	M
Marygrove College	M
Maryville University of Saint Louis	M,D
Marywood University	M,D
Massachusetts College of Liberal Arts	M,O
McDaniel College	M
McGill University	M,D,O
McKendree University	M,D,O
McNeese State University	M,O
Memorial University of Newfoundland	M,D,O
Mercer University	M,D,O
Mercy College	M
Mercyhurst University	M,O
Merrimack College	M,O
Michigan State University	M,D,O
Middle Tennessee State University	M,O
Midwestern State University	M
Millersville University of Pennsylvania	M,D
Milligan College	M,D,O
Mills College	M
Minnesota State University Mankato	M
Minnesota State University Moorhead	M,O
Mississippi College	M,D,O
Mississippi State University	M,D,O
Mississippi University for Women	M
Missouri Baptist University	M,O
Missouri State University	M,O
Monmouth University	M,D,O
Montana State University	M,D,O
Montclair State University	M,O
Morehead State University	M,O
Morgan State University	M,D
Mount Holyoke College	M
Mount Mercy University	M
Murray State University	M
National Louis University	M,D,O
National University	M,O
Neumann University	M,D
New England College	M,D
New Jersey City University	M
Newman University	M
New Mexico Highlands University	M
New Mexico State University	M
New York University	M,D,O
Niagara University	M
Nicholls State University	M
Norfolk State University	M
North American University	M
North Carolina Agricultural and Technical State University	M
North Carolina Central University	M
North Carolina State University	M,D
North Central College	M
North Dakota State University	M,O
Northeastern Illinois University	M
Northeastern State University	M
Northeastern University	M
Northern Arizona University	M,D,O
Northern Illinois University	M,D,O
Northern Kentucky University	M,O
Northern Michigan University	M
Northern State University	M
Northwestern College	M,O
Northwestern Oklahoma State University	M
Northwestern State University of Louisiana	M,O
Northwestern University	M,D
Northwest Missouri State University	M,D,O
Northwest Nazarene University	M,D,O
Notre Dame de Namur University	M
Notre Dame of Maryland University	M,D
Oakland City University	M,D
Oakland University	M,D,O
Oglala Lakota College	M
Ohio Dominican University	M
The Ohio State University	M,D,O
Ohio University	M,D
Oklahoma State University	M,D,O
Old Dominion University	M,D,O
Olivet Nazarene University	M
Oral Roberts University	M,D
Oregon State University	M,D
Ottawa University	M
Park University	M,O
Penn State University Park	M,D,O
Pensacola Christian College	M,D,O
Pepperdine University	M,D
Piedmont International University	M,D
Pittsburg State University	M,O
Plymouth State University	M,O
Point Loma Nazarene University	M
Point Park University	M,D
Pontifical Catholic University of Puerto Rico	D
Post University	M
Prairie View A&M University	M,D
Prescott College	M,D
Providence College	M
Purdue University	M,D,O
Purdue University Northwest	M
Queens College of the City University of New York	M,O
Queens University of Charlotte	M
Quincy University	M
Quinnipiac University	M,O
Radford University	M
Ramapo College of New Jersey	M
Regent University	M,D,O
Regis College (MA)	M,D
Regis University	M,D,O
Rhode Island College	M,O
Rider University	M,O
Rivier University	M,D,O
Robert Morris University	M,D,O
Robert Morris University Illinois	M
Rocky Mountain College	M
Rowan University	M,D,O
Rutgers University–Camden	O
Rutgers University–New Brunswick	M,D
Sacred Heart University	O
Sage Graduate School	D
Saginaw Valley State University	M,O
St. Ambrose University	M
St. Bonaventure University	M,O
St. Cloud State University	M,D
Saint Francis University	M
St. Francis Xavier University	M
St. John Fisher College	M,D
St. John's University (NY)	M,D,O
St. Joseph's College, Long Island Campus	M
St. Joseph's College, New York	M
Saint Joseph's College of Maine	M
Saint Joseph's University	M,D,O
St. Lawrence University	M,O
Saint Leo University	M,O
Saint Louis University	M,D,O
Saint Mary's College of California	M,D,O
St. Mary's University (United States)	M
Saint Mary's University of Minnesota	M,D,O
Saint Michael's College	M,D
Saint Peter's University	M,D
St. Thomas Aquinas College	M
St. Thomas University	M,D,O
Saint Vincent College	M
Saint Xavier University	M
Salem International University	M
Salem State University	M
Salisbury University	M
Samford University	M,D
Sam Houston State University	M,D
San Diego State University	M
San Francisco State University	M,D,O
San Jose State University	M
Santa Clara University	M
Schreiner University	M,D,O
Seattle Pacific University	M,D,O
Seattle University	D,O
Seton Hall University	M,D,O
Shenandoah University	M,D
Shippensburg University of Pennsylvania	M,D
Siena Heights University	M
Sierra Nevada College	M
Silver Lake College of the Holy Family	M
Simon Fraser University	M
Simpson University	M
SIT Graduate Institute	M
Slippery Rock University of Pennsylvania	M,D
Soka University of America	M
Sonoma State University	M,O
South Carolina State University	D,O
South Dakota State University	M
Southeastern Louisiana University	M,D
Southeastern Oklahoma State University	M
Southeastern University (FL)	M,D
Southeast Missouri State University	M,D,O
Southern Adventist University	M
Southern Arkansas University–Magnolia	M
Southern Connecticut State University	M,D,O
Southern Illinois University Carbondale	M,D
Southern Illinois University Edwardsville	M,D,O
Southern New Hampshire University	M,D,O
Southern Oregon University	M
Southern University and Agricultural and Mechanical College	M
Southwest Baptist University	M,O
Southwestern Adventist University	M
Southwestern Assemblies of God University	M
Southwestern College (KS)	M,D
Southwestern Oklahoma State University	M
Southwest Minnesota State University	M
Spalding University	M,D
Stanford University	M,D
State University of New York at New Paltz	M,O
State University of New York at Oswego	O
State University of New York at Plattsburgh	O
State University of New York College at Cortland	O
Stephen F. Austin State University	M,D
Stetson University	M

*M—masters degree; D—doctorate; O—other advanced degree; *—Close-Up and/or Display*

Stony Brook University, State University of New York	M,O
Suffolk University	M,O
Sul Ross State University	M
Syracuse University	M,D,O
Tarleton State University	M,D,O
Teachers College, Columbia University	M,D
Tennessee Technological University	M,O
Texas A&M International University	M
Texas A&M University–Central Texas	M,O
Texas A&M University–Commerce	M,D,O
Texas A&M University–Corpus Christi	M,D
Texas A&M University–Kingsville	M,D
Texas A&M University–San Antonio	M
Texas A&M University–Texarkana	M
Texas Christian University	M,D,O
Texas Southern University	M,D
Texas State University	M,D
Texas Tech University	M,D
Texas Woman's University	M,D
Thomas Edison State University	M,O
Thomas More College	M
Tiffin University	M
Touro College	M
Towson University	M,O
Trevecca Nazarene University	M,D,O
Trident University International	M,D
Trinity Baptist College	M
Trinity University	M
Trinity Washington University	M
Trinity Western University	M,O
Troy University	M,O
Union College (KY)	M
Union University	M,D,O
Universidad Adventista de las Antillas	M
Universidad del Turabo	M,D
Universidad Iberoamericana	M,D
Universidad Metropolitana	M
Université de Moncton	M
Université de Montréal	M,D,O
Université de Sherbrooke	M
Université du Québec à Trois-Rivières	O
Université Laval	M,D,O
University at Albany, State University of New York	M,D,O
University at Buffalo, the State University of New York	M,D,O
The University of Akron	M
The University of Alabama	M,D,O
The University of Alabama at Birmingham	M,D,O
University of Alaska Anchorage	M,O
University of Alaska Southeast	M
University of Alberta	M,D,O
The University of Arizona	M,D,O
University of Arkansas	M,D,O
University of Arkansas at Little Rock	M,D,O
University of Arkansas at Monticello	M
University of Bridgeport	M,D
The University of British Columbia	M,D
University of Calgary	M,D
University of California, Berkeley	M,D
University of California, Irvine	M,D
University of California, Los Angeles	D
University of California, Riverside	M,D,O
University of California, San Diego	M,D
University of Central Arkansas	M,O
University of Central Florida	M,D,O
University of Central Missouri	M,D,O
University of Central Oklahoma	M
University of Cincinnati	M,D,O
University of Colorado Colorado Springs	M,D
University of Colorado Denver	M,D,O
University of Connecticut	M
University of Dayton	M,D,O
University of Delaware	M,D,O
University of Denver	M,D,O
University of Detroit Mercy	M,D,O
The University of Findlay	M,D
University of Florida	M,D,O
University of Georgia	D,O
University of Guam	M
University of Hartford	D,O
University of Hawaii at Manoa	M,D
University of Holy Cross	M
University of Houston	M,D
University of Houston–Clear Lake	M,D
University of Houston–Victoria	M
University of Idaho	M,O
University of Illinois at Chicago	M,D
University of Illinois at Springfield	M,O
University of Illinois at Urbana–Champaign	M,D,O
University of Indianapolis	M
The University of Iowa	M,D,O
The University of Kansas	M,D,O
University of Kentucky	M,D,O
University of La Verne	M,D,O
University of Lethbridge	M,D
University of Louisiana at Lafayette	M,D
University of Louisiana at Monroe	M,D
University of Louisville	M,D,O
University of Maine	M,D
University of Maine at Farmington	M
University of Manitoba	M

University of Mary	M,D
University of Mary Hardin-Baylor	M,D
University of Maryland, College Park	M,D,O
University of Maryland Eastern Shore	D
University of Massachusetts Amherst	M,D
University of Massachusetts Boston	D
University of Massachusetts Dartmouth	D
University of Memphis	M,D,O
University of Michigan–Dearborn	M,D,O
University of Michigan–Flint	M,D,O
University of Minnesota, Twin Cities Campus	M,D
University of Missouri	M,D,O
University of Missouri–Kansas City	M,D,O
University of Missouri–St. Louis	M,D,O
University of Montana	M,D,O
University of Montevallo	M,O
University of Mount Union	M
University of Nebraska at Kearney	M,O
University of Nebraska at Omaha	M,D,O
University of Nebraska–Lincoln	M,D,O
University of Nevada, Las Vegas	M,D,O
University of Nevada, Reno	M,D,O
University of New England	M,D,O
University of New Hampshire	M,O
University of New Mexico	M,D,O
University of New Orleans	M,D
University of North Alabama	M
The University of North Carolina at Chapel Hill	M,D
The University of North Carolina at Charlotte	M,D,O
The University of North Carolina at Greensboro	M,D,O
The University of North Carolina at Pembroke	M
The University of North Carolina Wilmington	M,D
University of North Dakota	M,D,O
University of Northern Colorado	M,D,O
University of Northern Iowa	M,D
University of North Florida	M,D
University of North Georgia	M,O
University of North Texas	M,D,O
University of North Texas at Dallas	M
University of Oklahoma	M,D
University of Pennsylvania	M,D
University of Phoenix–Bay Area Campus	M,D,O
University of Phoenix–Colorado Campus	M
University of Phoenix–Colorado Springs Downtown Campus	M,O
University of Phoenix–Hawaii Campus	M
University of Phoenix–Las Vegas Campus	M
University of Phoenix–New Mexico Campus	M
University of Phoenix–North Florida Campus	M
University of Phoenix–Online Campus	M,D,O
University of Phoenix–Phoenix Campus	M
University of Phoenix–Southern Arizona Campus	M,O
University of Phoenix–Southern California Campus	M,O
University of Phoenix–South Florida Campus	M
University of Phoenix–Utah Campus	M
University of Phoenix–Washington D.C. Campus	M,D,O
University of Pikeville	M
University of Pittsburgh	M,D
University of Portland	M,D
University of Prince Edward Island	M,D
University of Puerto Rico, Río Piedras Campus	M,D
University of Regina	M
University of Rio Grande	M
University of Rochester	M,D
University of St. Francis (IL)	M,D,O
University of St. Thomas (MN)	M,D,O
University of St. Thomas (TX)	M,D
University of San Diego	M,D,O
University of San Francisco	M,D
University of Saskatchewan	M,D,O
The University of Scranton	M
University of Sioux Falls	M,O
University of South Africa	M,D
University of South Alabama	M,D
University of South Carolina	M,D,O
The University of South Dakota	M,D,O
University of Southern California	D
University of Southern Indiana	M
University of Southern Maine	M,O
University of Southern Mississippi	M,D,O
University of South Florida	M,D,O
University of South Florida, St. Petersburg	M
University of South Florida Sarasota-Manatee	M
The University of Tennessee	M,D,O
The University of Tennessee at Chattanooga	M,D,O
The University of Tennessee at Martin	M
The University of Texas at Arlington	M,D
The University of Texas at Austin	M,D
The University of Texas at El Paso	M,D

The University of Texas at San Antonio	M,D
The University of Texas at Tyler	M
The University of Texas of the Permian Basin	M
The University of Texas Rio Grande Valley	M,D
University of the Cumberlands	M,D,O
University of the Pacific	M,D
University of the Southwest	M
University of the Virgin Islands	M,D,O
The University of Toledo	M,D,O
University of Utah	M,D
University of Vermont	M,D
University of Victoria	M,D
University of Virginia	M,D,O
University of Washington	M,D
University of Washington, Bothell	M
University of Washington, Tacoma	M
The University of West Alabama	M,O
University of West Florida	M,D
University of West Georgia	M,D,O
University of Wisconsin–Madison	M,D,O
University of Wisconsin–Milwaukee	M,D,O
University of Wisconsin–Oshkosh	M
University of Wisconsin–Stevens Point	M
University of Wisconsin–Superior	M,O
University of Wisconsin–Whitewater	M
University of Wyoming	M,D,O
Upper Iowa University	M
Ursuline College	M
Utah Valley University	M
Valdosta State University	M,D
Valparaiso University	M,O
Vanderbilt University	M,D
Villanova University	M
Virginia Commonwealth University	M,D
Virginia Polytechnic Institute and State University	M,D,O
Virginia State University	M,D
Virginia Theological Seminary	M,D
Viterbo University	M,O
Wagner College	M,O
Walden University	M,D,O
Waldorf University	M
Walla Walla University	M
Washburn University	M
Washington State University	M,D
Wayland Baptist University	M
Waynesburg University	M,D
Wayne State College	M,O
Wayne State University	M,D,O
West Chester University of Pennsylvania	M,D,O
Western Connecticut State University	D
Western Governors University	M,O
Western Illinois University	M,D,O
Western Kentucky University	M,D,O
Western Michigan University	M,D,O
Western New Mexico University	M
Western State Colorado University	M
Western Washington University	M
Westminster College (PA)	M,O
West Texas A&M University	M
West Virginia University	D
Wheeling Jesuit University	M
Wheelock College	M
Whittier College	M
Whitworth University	M
Wichita State University	M,D,O
Widener University	M,D
Wilkes University	M,D
William Paterson University of New Jersey	M
William Woods University	M,D,O
Wilmington University	M,D
Wingate University	M,D,O
Winona State University	M,O
Winthrop University	M
Wisconsin Lutheran College	M
Worcester State University	M,O
Wright State University	O
Xavier University	M,D
Xavier University of Louisiana	M
Yeshiva University	M,D,O
York College of Pennsylvania	M
Youngstown State University	M,D

EDUCATIONAL MEASUREMENT AND EVALUATION

American InterContinental University Online	M
American University	M,O
Arizona State University at the Tempe campus	D
Ball State University	M,D,O
Baylor University	M,D,O
Boston College	M
Brandeis University	O
Brigham Young University	D
Cambridge College	M,D,O
Claremont Graduate University	M,D,O
Clemson University	D
College of Saint Mary	M
Duquesne University	M
Eastern Michigan University	M,O
Florida State University	M,D,O
Georgia Southern University	M,D,O
Georgia State University	M,D
Houston Baptist University	M,D
Indiana University Bloomington	M,D,O
Iowa State University of Science and Technology	M,D
James Madison University	M,D
Kent State University	M,D
Louisiana State University and Agricultural & Mechanical College	M,D,O

Loyola University Chicago	M,D
McNeese State University	M,O
Michigan State University	M,D,O
Missouri State University	O
Missouri Western State University	M,O
Montclair State University	O
New Mexico State University	M,D,O
North Carolina State University	D
Ohio University	M,D
Old Dominion University	D
Rutgers University–New Brunswick	M
Seton Hall University	M,D,O
Southern Connecticut State University	M,D,O
Southwestern Oklahoma State University	M
Sul Ross State University	M,O
Syracuse University	M,D,O
Teachers College, Columbia University	M,D
Tennessee Technological University	D
Texas A&M University–San Antonio	M
Université Laval	M,D,O
University at Albany, State University of New York	M,D,O
The University of Akron	M,O
University of Arkansas	M,D
The University of British Columbia	M,D,O
University of Calgary	M,D
University of Colorado Boulder	D
University of Colorado Denver	M,D,O
University of Denver	M,D
University of Florida	M,D,O
University of Illinois at Chicago	M,D
The University of Iowa	M,D,O
The University of Kansas	M,D
University of Kentucky	M,D
University of Louisiana at Monroe	M,D
University of Louisville	M,D
University of Maryland, College Park	M,D
University of Massachusetts Amherst	M,D,O
University of Memphis	M,D
University of Miami	M,D
University of Michigan–Dearborn	M
University of Minnesota, Twin Cities Campus	M,D
University of Missouri–St. Louis	M,D,O
University of Nebraska–Lincoln	M,D,O
The University of North Carolina at Chapel Hill	M,D
The University of North Carolina at Greensboro	D
University of Northern Colorado	M,D
University of Northern Iowa	M
University of North Texas	M,D,O
University of Pennsylvania	M,D
University of Pittsburgh	M,D
University of Puerto Rico, Río Piedras Campus	M
University of St. Thomas (TX)	M,D
University of South Carolina	M,D
University of Southern Mississippi	M,D,O
University of South Florida	O
The University of Tennessee	M,D,O
The University of Texas at El Paso	M
The University of Texas Rio Grande Valley	M
The University of Toledo	M,D,O
University of Victoria	M,D
University of Virginia	M,D,O
University of Washington	M,D
University of Wisconsin–Milwaukee	M,D,O
Utah State University	M,D
Virginia Commonwealth University	D
Virginia Polytechnic Institute and State University	M,D,O
Walden University	M,D,O
Washington University in St. Louis	D
Wayland Baptist University	M
Wayne State University	M,D,O
Western Governors University	M,O
Western Michigan University	M,D,O
West Texas A&M University	M
Wilkes University	M,D

EDUCATIONAL MEDIA/INSTRUCTIONAL TECHNOLOGY

Abilene Christian University	M,O
Acadia University	M
Adelphi University	M
Alabama Agricultural and Mechanical University	M,O
Alabama State University	M,D,O
Alverno College	M
American College of Education	M
American InterContinental University Online	M
Antioch University New England	M,O
Appalachian State University	M,O
Arcadia University	M,D,O
Argosy University, Atlanta	M,D,O
Argosy University, Denver	M,D,O
Argosy University, Nashville	M,D,O
Argosy University, Orange County	M,D,O
Argosy University, Phoenix	M,D,O
Argosy University, San Francisco Bay Area	M,D
Argosy University, Sarasota	M,D,O
Argosy University, Seattle	M,D,O
Argosy University, Twin Cities	M,D,O
Arizona State University at the Tempe campus	M,D,O
Arkansas Tech University	M
Ashland University	M
Auburn University	M,D,O
Auburn University at Montgomery	M,O

Augustana University — M
Augusta University — D
Aurora University — M,D
Avila University — M
Azusa Pacific University — M
Baldwin Wallace University — M
Ball State University — M,D
Barry University — M,D,O
Bay Path University — M
Belhaven University (MS) — M
Bellevue University — M
Bloomsburg University of Pennsylvania — M,O
Boise State University — M,D,O
Bowling Green State University — M
Bridgewater State University — M
Brigham Young University — M,D
Buffalo State College, State University of New York — M
California Baptist University — M
California State University, East Bay — M
California State University, Fullerton — M
California State University, Northridge — M
California State University, Sacramento — M,D
California State University, Stanislaus — M
Cambridge College — M,D,O
Canisius College — M,O
Capella University — M,D
Caribbean University — M,D
Central Michigan University — M,D,O
Chestnut Hill College — M,O
Chicago State University — M
Cleary University — M,O
Cleveland State University — D
Coastal Carolina University — M,O
College of Mount Saint Vincent — M,O
College of Saint Elizabeth — M,D,O
The College of William and Mary — M,D
Colorado Christian University — M
Colorado State University–Pueblo — M
Concordia University (United States) — M,D
Concordia University (Canada) — M,O
Concordia University Chicago — M
Concordia University Irvine — M
Concordia University, St. Paul — M,D,O
Dakota State University — M
Dallas Baptist University — M
Delaware Valley University — M
DeSales University — M,O
DeVry University–Folsom Campus — M
Drexel University — M,D
Drury University — M
Duquesne University — M,D,O
East Carolina University — M,O
Eastern Connecticut State University — M
Eastern Michigan University — M,O
Eastern New Mexico University — M
East Stroudsburg University of Pennsylvania — M
East Tennessee State University — M,O
Emporia State University — M
Fairfield University — M,O
Fairleigh Dickinson University, College at Florham — M,O
Fairleigh Dickinson University, Metropolitan Campus — M,O
Fairmont State University — M
Florida Atlantic University — M
Florida Institute of Technology — M
Florida International University — M,D,O
Florida State University — M,D,O
Fontbonne University — M
Fort Hays State University — M
Framingham State University — M
Franklin University — M
Fresno Pacific University — M
Frostburg State University — M
Full Sail University — M,O
George Fox University — M,O
George Mason University — M
The George Washington University — M,O
Georgia College & State University — M
Georgian Court University — M,O
Georgia Southern University — M,O
Georgia State University — M,D
Goucher College — M,O
Graceland University (IA) — M
Grambling State University — M,D,O
Grand Canyon University — M,D,O
Grand Valley State University — M
Harrisburg University of Science and Technology — M
Harvard University — M,O
Hofstra University — M,D,O
Idaho State University — M,D,O
Indiana State University — M,D
Indiana University Bloomington — M,D
Indiana University of Pennsylvania — M,D
Indiana University South Bend — M,O
Instituto Tecnológico y de Estudios Superiores de Monterrey, Campus Central de Veracruz — M
Instituto Tecnológico y de Estudios Superiores de Monterrey, Campus Ciudad de México — M,D
Instituto Tecnológico y de Estudios Superiores de Monterrey, Campus Ciudad Juárez — M,D
Instituto Tecnológico y de Estudios Superiores de Monterrey, Campus Estado de México — M,D

Instituto Tecnológico y de Estudios Superiores de Monterrey, Campus Irapuato — M,D
Inter American University of Puerto Rico, Metropolitan Campus — M
Iowa State University of Science and Technology — M,D
Jacksonville State University — M
James Madison University — M
Johns Hopkins University — M
Johnson University — M,D,O
Kansas State University — M,D,O
Kaplan University, Davenport Campus — M
Keiser University — D,O
Kennesaw State University — M
Kent State University — M,D
Kutztown University of Pennsylvania — M
Lamar University — M,D
La Salle University — M,O
Lawrence Technological University — M,O
Lehigh University — M,D,O
Lenoir-Rhyne University — M
Lesley University — M,D,O
Lewis University — M
Lindenwood University — M,D,O
Lipscomb University — M,D,O
Long Island University–LIU Post — M
Longwood University — M
Louisiana State University and Agricultural & Mechanical College — M,D,O
Loyola University Maryland — M
Manhattan College — M
Marconi International University — M,D
Marian University (WI) — M,D
Marlboro College — M,O
Martin Luther College — M
Marygrove College — M
Massachusetts College of Liberal Arts — M,O
McDaniel College — M
McNeese State University — M,O
Memorial University of Newfoundland — M,D,O
Michigan State University — M,D,O
MidAmerica Nazarene University — M
Middle Tennessee State University — M,O
Midwestern State University — M
Misericordia University — M
Mississippi State University — M,D,O
Missouri Southern State University — M
Missouri State University — M,O
Molloy College — M,O
Montana State University Billings — M
Morehead State University — M,O
National Louis University — M,D,O
Nazareth College of Rochester — M
New Jersey City University — M,D
New York Institute of Technology — M,O
New York University — M,D,O
North Carolina Agricultural and Technical State University — M
North Carolina Central University — M
North Carolina State University — M,D
Northeastern State University — M
Northern Arizona University — M,O
Northern Illinois University — M,D
Northern State University — M
Northwestern State University of Louisiana — M,O
Northwestern University — M,D
Northwest Missouri State University — M
Nova Southeastern University — M,D,O
Ohio University — M,D
Old Dominion University — M,D,O
Ottawa University — M
Pace University — M,O
Penn State University Park — M,D,O
Pepperdine University — M,D
Piedmont College — M,O
Pittsburg State University — M
Plymouth State University — M
Post University — M
Purdue University — M,D,O
Purdue University Northwest — M
Quinnipiac University — M
Ramapo College of New Jersey — M
Regent University — M,D,O
Robert Morris University Illinois — M
Rockford University — M
Saginaw Valley State University — M
St. Cloud State University — M
Saint Joseph's University — M,D,O
Saint Leo University — M,O
Saint Mary's University of Minnesota — M,D,O
St. Thomas University — M,D,O
Saint Vincent College — M
Saint Xavier University — M
Salem State University — M
Samford University — M,D,O
San Diego State University — M,D
San Francisco State University — M
Seattle Pacific University — M
Seton Hall University — M
Simon Fraser University — M,D
Slippery Rock University of Pennsylvania — M,D
Southern Illinois University Edwardsville — M,O
Southern New Hampshire University — M,D,O
Southern University and Agricultural and Mechanical College — M
Stanford University — M
State University of New York College at Potsdam — M
State University of New York Empire State College — M

Stockton University — M
Stony Brook University, State University of New York — M,O
Strayer University — M
Syracuse University — M,O
Tarleton State University — M
Teachers College, Columbia University — M,D
Tennessee Technological University — M,O
Texas A&M University — M,D
Texas A&M University–Commerce — M,D,O
Texas A&M University–Corpus Christi — M,D
Texas A&M University–Kingsville — M
Texas A&M University–Texarkana — M
Texas State University — M
Texas Tech University — M,D
Thomas Edison State University — M,O
Tiffin University — M
Touro College — M
Towson University — M,D
Trevecca Nazarene University — M
Trident University International — M,D
Université Laval — M,D
University at Albany, State University of New York — M,D,O
University at Buffalo, the State University of New York — M,D,O
The University of Akron — M
University of Alaska Southeast — M
University of Alberta — M,D
University of Arkansas — M
University of Arkansas at Little Rock — M
University of California, Irvine — M
University of Central Arkansas — M
University of Central Florida — M,D,O
University of Central Missouri — M,D,O
University of Central Oklahoma — M
University of Colorado Denver — M
University of Connecticut — M,D
University of Dayton — M
The University of Findlay — M,D
University of Georgia — M,D,O
University of Hartford — M
University of Hawaii at Manoa — M,D
University of Houston–Clear Lake — M
University of Houston–Victoria — M
University of Illinois at Springfield — M,O
The University of Kansas — M,O
University of Kentucky — M,D
University of Maine — M,D,O
University of Maine at Farmington — M
University of Maryland, Baltimore County — M,O
University of Maryland, College Park — M,D,O
University of Maryland University College — M
University of Massachusetts Amherst — M,D,O
University of Massachusetts Boston — M,O
University of Memphis — M,D,O
University of Michigan–Dearborn — M
University of Michigan–Flint — M,D,O
University of Minnesota, Twin Cities Campus — M,D,O
University of Missouri — M,D
University of Nebraska at Kearney — M
University of Nevada, Las Vegas — M,D,O
University of New Hampshire — M,O
University of New Mexico — M,D,O
The University of North Carolina at Charlotte — M,D,O
The University of North Carolina at Greensboro — M,D,O
The University of North Carolina Wilmington — M
University of North Dakota — M
University of Northern Iowa — M
University of North Florida — M,D
University of Oklahoma — M,D
University of Pennsylvania — M
University of Phoenix–Online Campus — D,O
University of Phoenix–Washington D.C. Campus — M,D,O
University of St. Francis (IL) — M,D
University of Saint Joseph — M
University of San Francisco — M,D
University of Sioux Falls — M,O
University of South Africa — M,D
University of South Alabama — M,D
University of South Carolina — M
University of South Carolina Aiken — M
The University of South Dakota — M
University of Southern Mississippi — M,D
University of South Florida — O
The University of Tampa — M
The University of Tennessee — M,D,O
The University of Tennessee at Chattanooga — M,D,O
The University of Texas at Austin — M,D
The University of Texas at San Antonio — M,D,O
The University of Texas Rio Grande Valley — M,D
University of the Sacred Heart — M
The University of Toledo — M,D,O
University of Utah — M,D,O
University of Virginia — M,D,O
University of Washington — M,O
The University of West Alabama — M,O
University of West Florida — M

University of West Georgia — M,D,O
University of Wisconsin–Milwaukee — M,O
University of Wyoming — M,D
Utah State University — M,D,O
Utah Valley University — M
Valley City State University — M
Virginia Commonwealth University — M
Virginia Polytechnic Institute and State University — M,O
Walden University — M,D,O
Warner University — M
Wayland Baptist University — M
Waynesburg University — M,D
Wayne State University — M,D,O
Webster University — M,O
West Chester University of Pennsylvania — M,O
Western Connecticut State University — M
Western Governors University — M,O
Western Illinois University — M,O
Western Kentucky University — M,O
Western Michigan University — M,D,O
Western Oregon University — M
West Texas A&M University — M
West Virginia University — M,D
Widener University — M,D
Wilkes University — M,D
William Woods University — M,D,O
Wilmington University — M,D
Wisconsin Lutheran College — M
Worcester Polytechnic Institute — M,D
York College of Pennsylvania — M
Youngstown State University — M

EDUCATIONAL POLICY

Alabama State University — M,D,O
American University — M,O
Arizona State University at the Tempe campus — D
Ball State University — D
Brigham Young University — M,D
California State University, Sacramento — M,D
Cleveland State University — D
The College of William and Mary — M,D
Cornell University — M,D
Eastern Michigan University — M
Florida State University — M,D,O
The George Washington University — M,D,O
Georgia State University — M,D,O
Harvard University — M
Howard University — M,D,O
Illinois State University — M,D
Indiana University Bloomington — M,D,O
Johns Hopkins University — D
Loyola University Chicago — M,D,O
Marquette University — M
Michigan State University — D
New York University — M,D
Northwest Missouri State University — M,D,O
The Ohio State University — M,D,O
Oregon State University — M,D
Penn State University Park — M,D,O
Rutgers University–Camden — M
Rutgers University–New Brunswick — D
Stanford University — M
Syracuse University — O
Teachers College, Columbia University — M,D
University at Albany, State University of New York — M,D,O
University of Alberta — M,D,O
University of Arkansas — D
The University of British Columbia — M,D
University of Colorado Boulder — M
University of Colorado Denver — D
University of Denver — M,D,O
University of Florida — M,D,O
University of Georgia — D,O
University of Hawaii at Manoa — D
University of Illinois at Chicago — M,D
University of Illinois at Urbana–Champaign — M,D,O
The University of Iowa — M,D,O
The University of Kansas — M,D
University of Kentucky — M,D
University of Maryland, Baltimore County — M,D
University of Massachusetts Amherst — M,D,O
University of Massachusetts Boston — D
University of Massachusetts Dartmouth — M,D,O
University of Minnesota, Twin Cities Campus — M,D
University of Missouri–St. Louis — M,D,O
The University of North Carolina Wilmington — M
University of Northern Colorado — M,D,O
University of Oklahoma — M,D
University of Pennsylvania — M,D
University of Pittsburgh — D
University of Rochester — M,D
University of Southern California — D
The University of Texas at Arlington — M,D
University of Virginia — D
University of Washington — M
The University of Western Ontario — M
University of Wisconsin–Madison — M,D,O
University of Wisconsin–Milwaukee — M,O
Vanderbilt University — M,D
Virginia Polytechnic Institute and State University — M,D,O

M—masters degree; D—doctorate; O—other advanced degree; *—Close-Up and/or Display

Institution	Degrees
Wayne State University	M,D,O
West Chester University of Pennsylvania	D

EDUCATIONAL PSYCHOLOGY

Institution	Degrees
Alliant International University–Irvine	M,D,O
Alliant International University–Los Angeles	M,D,O
Alliant International University–San Diego	M,D,O
Alliant International University–San Francisco	M,D,O
American International College	M,D,O
Andrews University	M,D
Ball State University	M,D
Baylor University	M,D,O
Boston College	M,D
Brigham Young University	M,D
California Coast University	M,D
California State University, Long Beach	M,D
California State University, Northridge	M
Capella University	M,D
Chapman University	M,D,O
Clark Atlanta University	M
The College of Saint Rose	M,O
Eastern Michigan University	M,O
Edinboro University of Pennsylvania	M,O
Florida Atlantic University	M
Florida State University	M,D
Fordham University	M,D
George Mason University	M,O
Georgia State University	M,D
The Graduate Center, City University of New York	D
Harvard University	M
Holy Names University	M,O
Howard University	D
Immaculata University	M,D,O
Indiana University Bloomington	M,D,O
Indiana University of Pennsylvania	M,O
Instituto Tecnologico de Santo Domingo	M,O
John Carroll University	M,O
Kent State University	M
La Sierra University	M,O
McGill University	M,D,O
Memorial University of Newfoundland	M,D,O
Miami University	M,O
Michigan School of Professional Psychology	M,D
Michigan State University	M,D,O
Mississippi State University	M,D,O
Mount Saint Vincent University	M
National Louis University	M,D,O
New York University	M,D
Northern Arizona University	M,D,O
Northern Illinois University	M,D,O
Oklahoma State University	M,D,O
Old Dominion University	D
Penn State University Park	M,D,O
Pontifical Catholic University of Puerto Rico	M
Purdue University	M,D,O
Regent University	M,D,O
Rutgers University–New Brunswick	M,D
Simon Fraser University	M,D
Southern Illinois University Carbondale	M,D
State University of New York College at Oneonta	M,O
Teachers College, Columbia University	M,D,O
Temple University	M,D,O
Tennessee Technological University	M,O
Texas A&M University	M,D
Texas A&M University–Central Texas	M,O
Texas A&M University–Commerce	M,D,O
Texas Tech University	M,D
Universidad de Iberoamerica	M,D
Université de Moncton	M
Université de Montréal	M,D,O
Université du Québec à Trois-Rivières	M,D
Université du Québec en Outaouais	M
Université Laval	M,D
University at Albany, State University of New York	M,D,O
University at Buffalo, the State University of New York	M,D,O
University of Alberta	M,D
The University of Arizona	M,D,O
University of California, Davis	M,D
University of California, Riverside	M,D,O
University of Colorado Boulder	M,D
University of Colorado Denver	M,D,O
University of Connecticut	M,D,O
University of Georgia	O
University of Hawaii at Manoa	M,D
University of Houston	M,D
University of Illinois at Chicago	M,D
University of Illinois at Urbana–Champaign	M,D,O
The University of Iowa	M,D,O
The University of Kansas	M,D
University of Kentucky	M,D,O
University of Louisville	M,D
The University of Manchester	M,D
University of Manitoba	M
University of Memphis	M,D
University of Minnesota, Twin Cities Campus	M,D,O
University of Missouri	M,D,O
University of Missouri–St. Louis	D
University of Nebraska–Lincoln	M,D,O
University of Nevada, Reno	M,D,O
University of New Mexico	M,D
The University of North Carolina at Chapel Hill	M,D
University of Northern Colorado	M,D
University of Northern Iowa	M
University of North Texas	M,D,O
University of Oklahoma	M,D
University of Phoenix–Southern Arizona Campus	M,O
University of Regina	M,D,O
University of Saskatchewan	M,D,O
University of South Africa	M,D
University of South Carolina	M,D
The University of South Dakota	M,D
University of Southern California	D
University of Southern Maine	M,O
University of South Florida	M,D,O
The University of Tennessee	M,D,O
The University of Texas at Austin	M,D
The University of Texas at El Paso	M
The University of Texas Rio Grande Valley	M
University of the Pacific	M,D,O
The University of Toledo	M,D,O
University of Utah	M,D,O
University of Victoria	M,D
University of Virginia	M,D,O
University of Washington	M,D
The University of Western Ontario	M
University of Wisconsin–Madison	M,D
University of Wisconsin–Milwaukee	M,D,O
Virginia Commonwealth University	D
Walden University	M,D,O
Washington State University	M,D
Wayne State University	M,D,O
Webster University	M,O
West Virginia University	M
Wichita State University	M,D,O
Widener University	M

EDUCATION OF STUDENTS WITH SEVERE/MULTIPLE DISABILITIES

Institution	Degrees
Cleveland State University	M
Georgia State University	M
Hunter College of the City University of New York	M
Norfolk State University	M
Syracuse University	M
Teachers College, Columbia University	M,D,O
University of Illinois at Urbana–Champaign	M,D,O
West Virginia University	M,D

EDUCATION OF THE GIFTED

Institution	Degrees
Arkansas State University	M,D,O
Ashland University	M
Ball State University	M,D,O
Barry University	M,D,O
Canisius College	M,O
Carlos Albizu University, Miami Campus	M,D
Carthage College	M,O
The College of New Rochelle	O
The College of William and Mary	M
Colorado Mesa University	M,O
Converse College	M
Drury University	M
Elon University	M
Emporia State University	M
Florida Gulf Coast University	M
George Mason University	M
Grand Canyon University	M,D,O
Hardin-Simmons University	M
Hofstra University	M,D,O
James Madison University	M
Johns Hopkins University	M,O
Kent State University	M,D,O
Liberty University	M,D,O
Lindenwood University	M,D,O
Lynn University	M,D
Maryville University of Saint Louis	M,D
Meredith College	M,O
Millersville University of Pennsylvania	M,O
Mississippi University for Women	M
Morehead State University	M,O
Northeastern Illinois University	M
Pacific University	M
Purdue University	M,D,O
Regent University	M,D,O
St. Bonaventure University	M,O
St. John's University (NY)	D,O
Saint Leo University	M,O
Saint Mary's University of Minnesota	M,O
St. Thomas University	M,D,O
Samford University	M,D,O
Southeastern University (FL)	M,D
Southern Arkansas University–Magnolia	M
Southern Methodist University	M,D
Teachers College, Columbia University	M,D
Tennessee Technological University	D
University at Buffalo, the State University of New York	M,D,O
The University of Alabama	M,D,O
University of Arkansas at Little Rock	M,O
University of Central Arkansas	M,O
University of Connecticut	O
University of Louisiana at Lafayette	M
University of Louisiana at Monroe	M,D
University of Minnesota, Twin Cities Campus	M,D,O
University of Missouri	M,D
University of Nebraska at Kearney	M

Institution	Degrees
The University of North Carolina at Charlotte	M,D,O
The University of North Carolina Wilmington	M
University of Northern Colorado	M,D
University of North Texas	M,D,O
University of Southern Maine	M,O
The University of Toledo	M,D,O
University of Virginia	M,D,O
Viterbo University	M,O
Western Washington University	M
West Virginia University	M,D
Whitworth University	M
Wichita State University	M,O
William Carey University	M,O
Wilmington University	M,D
Youngstown State University	M

ELECTRICAL ENGINEERING

Institution	Degrees
Air Force Institute of Technology	M,D
Alfred University	M,D
The American University in Cairo	M,D,O
American University of Beirut	M,D
American University of Sharjah	M
Arizona State University at the Tempe campus	M,D,O
Auburn University	M,D
Baylor University	M,D
Binghamton University, State University of New York	M,D
Boise State University	M,D
Boston University	M,D
Bradley University	M
Brigham Young University	M,D
Brown University	M,D
Bucknell University	M
California Institute of Technology	M,D,O
California Polytechnic State University, San Luis Obispo	M
California State Polytechnic University, Pomona	M
California State University, Chico	M
California State University, Fresno	M
California State University, Fullerton	M
California State University, Long Beach	M
California State University, Los Angeles	M
California State University, Northridge	M
California State University, Sacramento	M
Capitol Technology University	M
Carleton University	M,D
Carnegie Mellon University	M,D
Case Western Reserve University	M,D
The Catholic University of America	M,D
The Citadel, The Military College of South Carolina	M,O
City College of the City University of New York	M,D
Clarkson University	M,D,O
Clemson University	M,D
Cleveland State University	M,D
Colorado School of Mines	M,D
Colorado State University	M,D
Colorado Technical University Aurora	M
Colorado Technical University Colorado Springs	M
Columbia University	M,D
Concordia University (Canada)	M,D
Cooper Union for the Advancement of Science and Art	M
Cornell University	M,D
Dalhousie University	M,D
Drexel University	M
Duke University	M,D
École Polytechnique de Montréal	M,D,O
Embry-Riddle Aeronautical University–Daytona	M,D
Fairfield University	M,O
Fairleigh Dickinson University, Metropolitan Campus	M
Florida Agricultural and Mechanical University	M,D
Florida Atlantic University	M,D
Florida Institute of Technology	M,D
Florida International University	M,D
Florida State University	M,D
Gannon University	M
George Mason University	M,D,O
The George Washington University	M,D,O
Georgia Institute of Technology	M,D
Georgia Southern University	M
The Graduate Center, City University of New York	D
Grand Valley State University	M
Harvard University	M,D
Howard University	M,D
Illinois Institute of Technology	M,D
Indiana University–Purdue University Fort Wayne	M
Indiana University–Purdue University Indianapolis	M,D
Instituto Tecnológico y de Estudios Superiores de Monterrey, Campus Chihuahua	M,O
Instituto Tecnológico y de Estudios Superiores de Monterrey, Campus Monterrey	M,D
Inter American University of Puerto Rico, Bayamón Campus	M
International Technological University	M,D
Iowa State University of Science and Technology	M,D
Johns Hopkins University	M,D,O
Kansas State University	M,D
Kennesaw State University	M
Kettering University	M

Institution	Degrees
Lakehead University	M
Lamar University	M,D
Lawrence Technological University	M,D
Lehigh University	M,D
Louisiana State University and Agricultural & Mechanical College	M,D
Louisiana Tech University	M,D
Loyola Marymount University	M
Manhattan College	M
Marquette University	M,D,O
Massachusetts Institute of Technology	M,D,O
McGill University	M,D
McMaster University	M,D
McNeese State University	M
Memorial University of Newfoundland	M
Mercer University	M
Miami University	M
Michigan State University	M,D
Michigan Technological University	M,D,O
Mississippi State University	M,D
Missouri University of Science and Technology	M,D
Montana State University	M,D
Montana Tech of The University of Montana	M
Morgan State University	M,D
Naval Postgraduate School	M,D,O
New Jersey Institute of Technology	M,D
New Mexico Institute of Mining and Technology	M
New Mexico State University	M,D,O
New York Institute of Technology	M
New York University	M,D
Norfolk State University	M
North Carolina Agricultural and Technical State University	M,D
North Carolina State University	M,D
North Dakota State University	M,D
Northeastern University	M,D,O
Northern Arizona University	M
Northern Illinois University	M
Northwestern Polytechnic University	M,D
Northwestern University	M,D
Oakland University	M,D
The Ohio State University	M,D
Ohio University	M,D
Oklahoma Christian University	M
Oklahoma State University	M,D
Old Dominion University	M,D
Oregon Health & Science University	M,D
Oregon State University	M,D
Penn State Harrisburg	M,O
Penn State University Park	M,D
Pittsburg State University	M
Polytechnic University of Puerto Rico	M
Portland State University	M,D
Prairie View A&M University	M,D
Princeton University	M,D
Purdue University	M,D
Purdue University Northwest	M
Queen's University at Kingston	M,D
Rensselaer at Hartford	M
Rensselaer Polytechnic Institute	M,D
Rice University	M,D
Rochester Institute of Technology	M
Rose-Hulman Institute of Technology	M
Rowan University	M
Royal Military College of Canada	M,D
Rutgers University–New Brunswick	M,D
St. Cloud State University	M
St. Mary's University (United States)	M
San Diego State University	M
San Francisco State University	M
Santa Clara University	M,D,O
South Dakota School of Mines and Technology	M
South Dakota State University	M,D
Southern Illinois University Carbondale	M,D
Southern Illinois University Edwardsville	M
Southern Methodist University	M,D
Stanford University	M,D
State University of New York at New Paltz	M
Stevens Institute of Technology	M,D,O
Stony Brook University, State University of New York	M,D
Syracuse University	M,D,O
Temple University	M
Tennessee State University	M,D
Tennessee Technological University	M,D
Texas A&M University	M,D
Texas A&M University–Kingsville	M
Texas State University	M
Texas Tech University	M,D
Tufts University	M,D,O
Tuskegee University	M
Universidad de las Américas Puebla	M
Universidad del Turabo	M
Université de Moncton	M
Université de Sherbrooke	M,D
Université du Québec à Trois-Rivières	M
Université Laval	M,D
University at Buffalo, the State University of New York	M,D
The University of Akron	M,D
The University of Alabama	M,D
The University of Alabama at Birmingham	M,D
The University of Alabama in Huntsville	M,D
University of Alaska Fairbanks	M

Institution	Degree
University of Alberta	M,D
The University of Arizona	M,D
University of Arkansas	M,D
University of Bridgeport	M
The University of British Columbia	M,D
University of Calgary	M,D
University of California, Berkeley	M,D
University of California, Davis	M,D
University of California, Irvine	M,D
University of California, Los Angeles	M,D
University of California, Merced	M,D
University of California, Riverside	M,D
University of California, San Diego	M,D
University of California, Santa Barbara	M,D
University of California, Santa Cruz	M,D
University of Central Florida	M,D
University of Central Oklahoma	M
University of Cincinnati	M,D
University of Colorado Boulder	M,D
University of Colorado Colorado Springs	M
University of Colorado Denver	M,D
University of Connecticut	M,D
University of Dayton	M,D
University of Delaware	M,D
University of Denver	M,D
University of Detroit Mercy	M,D
University of Florida	M,D
University of Hawaii at Manoa	M,D
University of Houston	M,D
University of Idaho	M,D
University of Illinois at Chicago	M,D
University of Illinois at Urbana–Champaign	M,D
The University of Iowa	M,D
The University of Kansas	M,D
University of Kentucky	M,D
University of Louisville	M,D
University of Maine	M,D
The University of Manchester	M,D
University of Manitoba	M,D
University of Maryland, Baltimore County	M,D
University of Maryland, College Park	M,D
University of Massachusetts Amherst	M,D
University of Massachusetts Dartmouth	M,D,O
University of Massachusetts Lowell	M,D
University of Memphis	M,D,O
University of Miami	M,D
University of Michigan	M,D
University of Michigan–Dearborn	M,D
University of Minnesota, Duluth	M
University of Minnesota, Twin Cities Campus	M,D
University of Missouri	M,D
University of Missouri–Kansas City	M,D,O
University of Nebraska–Lincoln	M,D
University of Nevada, Las Vegas	M,D
University of Nevada, Reno	M,D
University of New Brunswick Fredericton	M,D
University of New Haven	M
University of New Mexico	M,D
The University of North Carolina at Charlotte	M,D
University of North Dakota	M,D
University of North Florida	M
University of North Texas	M,D,O
University of Notre Dame	M,D
University of Oklahoma	M,D
University of Ottawa	M,D
University of Pennsylvania	M,D
University of Pittsburgh	M,D
University of Portland	M
University of Puerto Rico, Mayagüez Campus	M,D
University of Rhode Island	M,D
University of Rochester	M,D
University of St. Thomas (MN)	M,O
University of Saskatchewan	M,D,O
University of South Alabama	M
University of South Carolina	M,D
University of Southern California	M,D,O
University of South Florida	M,D
The University of Tennessee	M,D
The University of Tennessee at Chattanooga	M
The University of Texas at Arlington	M,D
The University of Texas at Austin	M,D
The University of Texas at Dallas	M,D
The University of Texas at El Paso	M,D
The University of Texas at San Antonio	M,D
The University of Texas at Tyler	M
The University of Texas Rio Grande Valley	M
University of the District of Columbia	M
The University of Toledo	M,D
University of Toronto	M,D
The University of Tulsa	M,D
University of Utah	M,D
University of Vermont	M,D
University of Victoria	M,D
University of Virginia	M,D
University of Washington	M,D
University of Waterloo	M,D
The University of Western Ontario	M,D
University of Windsor	M,D
University of Wisconsin–Madison	M,D
University of Wisconsin–Milwaukee	M,D
University of Wyoming	M,D
Utah State University	M,D
Vanderbilt University	M,D
Villanova University	M,O
Virginia Polytechnic Institute and State University	M,D,O
Washington State University	M,D
Wayne State University	M,D
Western Michigan University	M,D
Western New England University	M
West Virginia University	M,D
Wichita State University	M,D
Widener University	M
Wilkes University	M
Worcester Polytechnic Institute	M,D,O
Wright State University	M
Yale University	M,D
Youngstown State University	M

ELECTRONIC COMMERCE

Institution	Degree
California State University, Fullerton	M
Claremont Graduate University	M,D,O
Dalhousie University	M,D
DePaul University	M,D
Eastern Michigan University	M,O
Fairleigh Dickinson University, Metropolitan Campus	M
Florida Institute of Technology	M,D
Fordham University	M
HEC Montreal	M,O
Instituto Tecnológico y de Estudios Superiores de Monterrey, Campus Central de Veracruz	M
Instituto Tecnológico y de Estudios Superiores de Monterrey, Campus Ciudad Juárez	M
Instituto Tecnológico y de Estudios Superiores de Monterrey, Campus Estado de México	M,D
Instituto Tecnológico y de Estudios Superiores de Monterrey, Campus Irapuato	M,D
Lewis University	M
New York University	M,D,O
Northwestern University	M
Pace University	O
Stevens Institute of Technology	M,O
Towson University	M,O
Universidad del Este	M
Université de Montréal	M,D
Université de Sherbrooke	M
Université Laval	M
University at Buffalo, the State University of New York	M,D,O
University of New Brunswick Saint John	M
University of North Florida	M
University of Ottawa	M,D,O
University of Phoenix–Colorado Campus	M
University of Phoenix–Columbus Georgia Campus	M
University of Phoenix–Dallas Campus	M
University of Phoenix–Houston Campus	M
University of Phoenix–New Mexico Campus	M
University of Phoenix–San Antonio Campus	M

ELECTRONIC MATERIALS

Institution	Degree
Colorado School of Mines	M,D
Princeton University	D
University of Arkansas	M,D

ELEMENTARY EDUCATION

Institution	Degree
Acacia University	M
Adelphi University	M
Alabama Agricultural and Mechanical University	M,D,O
Alabama State University	M,O
Alaska Pacific University	M
Albright College	M
Alcorn State University	M,O
American International College	M,O
American Public University System	M
American University of Puerto Rico	M
Anderson University (SC)	M
Andrews University	M,D,O
Anna Maria College	M,O
Antioch University New England	M,O
Appalachian State University	M
Aquinas College (TN)	M
Arcadia University	M,D,O
Argosy University, Atlanta	M,D,O
Argosy University, Chicago	M,D,O
Argosy University, Denver	M,D
Argosy University, Hawai`i	M,D
Argosy University, Inland Empire	M,D
Argosy University, Los Angeles	M,D
Argosy University, Nashville	M,D,O
Argosy University, Northern Virginia	M,D,O
Argosy University, Orange County	M,D
Argosy University, Phoenix	M,D,O
Argosy University, San Diego	M,D
Argosy University, San Francisco Bay Area	M,D
Argosy University, Sarasota	M,D
Argosy University, Seattle	M,D
Argosy University, Tampa	M,D
Argosy University, Twin Cities	M,D,O
Arizona State University at the Tempe campus	M
Arkansas State University	M,D,O
Arkansas Tech University	M
Auburn University	M,D,O
Auburn University at Montgomery	M,O
Augusta University	M,O
Austin Peay State University	M,O
Ball State University	M,D,O
Bank Street College of Education	M
Barry University	M,D,O
Barton College	M
Bayamón Central University	M
Belhaven University (MS)	M
Bellarmine University	M,D,O
Benedictine University	M
Bethel University (MN)	M,D,O
Blue Mountain College	M
Bob Jones University	M,D,O
Boston College	M
Bowie State University	M
Brandeis University	M,O
Brandman University	M,D
Bridgewater State University	M
Brooklyn College of the City University of New York	M,O
Brown University	M
Buffalo State College, State University of New York	M
California Lutheran University	M,D
California State University, Fullerton	M
California State University, Long Beach	M
California State University, Los Angeles	M
California State University, Northridge	M
California State University, Stanislaus	M
California University of Pennsylvania	M
Calvary University	M
Cambridge College	M,D,O
Campbell University	M
Canisius College	M,O
Capella University	M,D
Caribbean University	M,D
Carroll University	M
Carson-Newman University	M
Catawba College	M
Centenary College of Louisiana	M
Central Connecticut State University	M,O
Central Michigan University	M,O
Chadron State College	M,O
Chaminade University of Honolulu	M
Chapman University	M,D,O
Charleston Southern University	M
Chatham University	M
Chestnut Hill College	M
Cheyney University of Pennsylvania	M
Chicago State University	M
City University of Seattle	M,O
College of Charleston	M
The College of New Jersey	M
The College of New Rochelle	M
College of St. Joseph	M
College of Staten Island of the City University of New York	M
The College of William and Mary	M
Colorado Christian University	M
The Colorado College	M
Columbia College (SC)	M
Columbia International University	M,D,O
Concordia University (United States)	M,D
Concordia University Chicago	M
Concordia University, Nebraska	M
Converse College	M
Creighton University	M
Curry College	M,O
Dallas Baptist University	M
Delta State University	M,D,O
DePaul University	M,D
Dominican College	M
Dominican University	M
Drew University	M,D,O
Drury University	M
Duquesne University	M,D
D'Youville College	M,O
East Carolina University	M,O
Eastern Connecticut State University	M
Eastern Illinois University	M
Eastern Kentucky University	M
Eastern Nazarene College	M
Eastern New Mexico University	M
Eastern Oregon University	M
Eastern University	M,D,O
Eastern Washington University	M
East Stroudsburg University of Pennsylvania	M
East Tennessee State University	M,O
Elizabeth City State University	M
Elms College	M
Elon University	M
Emporia State University	M
Endicott College	M
Fairfield University	M,O
Fayetteville State University	M
Fitchburg State University	M
Florida Agricultural and Mechanical University	M
Florida Atlantic University	M
Florida Gulf Coast University	M
Florida Institute of Technology	M
Florida International University	M,D,O
Florida Memorial University	M
Florida State University	M,D,O
Fontbonne University	M
Fordham University	M,O
Framingham State University	M
Franklin Pierce University	M,D,O
Frostburg State University	M
Gallaudet University	M,D,O
George Mason University	M
The George Washington University	M
Georgia State University	M,D,O
Gonzaga University	M
Gordon College	M
Goucher College	M,O
Grand Canyon University	M,D,O
Grand Valley State University	M
Greensboro College	M
Greenville College	M
Hampton University	M
Harding University	M,O
Hawai`i Pacific University	M
High Point University	M
Hofstra University	M,D,O
Holy Family University	M
Hood College	M,O
Hope International University	M
Howard University	M
Hunter College of the City University of New York	M
Idaho State University	M,O
Indiana University Bloomington	M,D,O
Indiana University Northwest	M,O
Indiana University–Purdue University Fort Wayne	M
Indiana University South Bend	M,O
Indiana University Southeast	M
Inter American University of Puerto Rico, Aguadilla Campus	M
Inter American University of Puerto Rico, Arecibo Campus	M
Inter American University of Puerto Rico, Barranquitas Campus	M
Inter American University of Puerto Rico, Fajardo Campus	M
Inter American University of Puerto Rico, Guayama Campus	M
Inter American University of Puerto Rico, Metropolitan Campus	M
Inter American University of Puerto Rico, Ponce Campus	M
Inter American University of Puerto Rico, San Germán Campus	M
Iowa State University of Science and Technology	M,D
Ithaca College	M
Jackson State University	M,D,O
Jacksonville State University	M
James Madison University	M
Johns Hopkins University	M
Johnson & Wales University	M
Kansas State University	M,D,O
Kennesaw State University	M
Keuka College	M
Kutztown University of Pennsylvania	M
Lake Forest College	M
Lancaster Bible College	M,D
Langston University	M
Lasell College	M
Lee University	M,O
Lehigh University	M,D,O
Lehman College of the City University of New York	M
Le Moyne College	M,O
Lesley University	M,D,O
Lewis & Clark College	M
Lewis University	M
Lincoln University (MO)	M
Lock Haven University of Pennsylvania	M
Long Island University–Brentwood Campus	M,O
Long Island University–Hudson	M,O
Long Island University–Riverhead	M,O
Longwood University	M
Louisiana State University and Agricultural & Mechanical College	M,D,O
Loyola Marymount University	M
Loyola University Chicago	M,O
Loyola University Maryland	M,O
Manhattan College	M,O
Manhattanville College	M,O
Mansfield University of Pennsylvania	M
Marquette University	M,D,O
Marshall University	M,O
Mars Hill University	M
Mary Baldwin University	M
Marygrove College	M
Marylhurst University	M
Marymount University	M
Maryville University of Saint Louis	M,D
Marywood University	M
McDaniel College	M,O
McNeese State University	M,O
Medaille College	M
Mercy College	M
Meredith College	M
Merrimack College	M,O
Metropolitan College of New York	M
Metropolitan State University of Denver	M
Middle Tennessee State University	M,O
Milligan College	M,D,O
Minot State University	M
Mississippi College	M,D,O
Mississippi State University	M,D,O
Missouri State University	M,O
Monmouth University	M,O
Montana State University Billings	M
Morehead State University	M,O
Morgan State University	M,D
Mount Saint Vincent University	M
Murray State University	M,O
National Louis University	M,D,O

*M—masters degree; D—doctorate; O—other advanced degree; *—Close-Up and/or Display*

Elementary Education (continued)

Institution	Degree
Nazareth College of Rochester	M
Neumann University	M
New Jersey City University	M
New York Institute of Technology	M
New York University	M
Niagara University	M,O
Nicholls State University	M
North Carolina Agricultural and Technical State University	M
North Carolina State University	M
Northeastern Illinois University	M
Northeastern University	M
Northern Arizona University	M,D
Northern Illinois University	M
Northern Michigan University	M
Northwest Christian University	M
Northwestern Oklahoma State University	M
Northwestern State University of Louisiana	M,O
Northwestern University	M
Northwest Missouri State University	M,D,O
Nyack College	M
Oakland University	M,O
Oklahoma City University	M,O
Old Dominion University	M,O
Olivet Nazarene University	M
Oregon State University	M
Ottawa University	M,O
Pace University	M,O
Pacific Union College	M
Pacific University	M
Pfeiffer University	M
Plymouth State University	M
Point Park University	M,D
Prescott College	M,D
Providence College	M
Purdue University	M,D,O
Queens College of the City University of New York	M,O
Queens University of Charlotte	M
Quinnipiac University	M
Regent University	M,D,O
Regis College (MA)	M,D
Regis University	M,O
Rhode Island College	M
Rider University	O
Rivier University	M,D,O
Rockford University	M
Rollins College	M
Roosevelt University	M
Rosemont College	M
Rudolf Steiner College	M
Rutgers University–New Brunswick	M,D
Sage Graduate School	M
Saginaw Valley State University	M
St. John Fisher College	M,O
St. John's University (NY)	M,O
Saint Joseph's University	M,D,O
Saint Mary's University of Minnesota	M
Saint Peter's University	M,O
St. Thomas Aquinas College	M,O
St. Thomas University	M,D,O
Saint Xavier University	M
Salem College	M
Salem State University	M
Samford University	M,D,O
San Diego State University	M
San Francisco State University	M
San Jose State University	M,D,O
Seton Hill University	M,O
Shippensburg University of Pennsylvania	M,O
Siena Heights University	M,O
Sierra Nevada College	M
Simmons College	M,D,O
Sinte Gleska University	M
Slippery Rock University of Pennsylvania	M
Smith College	M
South Carolina State University	M
Southeastern Louisiana University	M
Southeastern University (FL)	M,D
Southeast Missouri State University	M,D,O
Southern Connecticut State University	M,O
Southern New Hampshire University	M,D,O
Southern Oregon University	M
Southern University and Agricultural and Mechanical College	M
Southwestern Oklahoma State University	M
Spalding University	M
Spring Hill College	M
Stanford University	M
State University of New York at New Paltz	M
State University of New York at Oswego	M
State University of New York at Plattsburgh	M,O
State University of New York College at Oneonta	M
State University of New York College at Potsdam	M
Stephen F. Austin State University	M
Sul Ross State University	M
Tarleton State University	M
Teachers College, Columbia University	M,D
Tennessee State University	M,D
Tennessee Technological University	M,O
Texas A&M University–Commerce	M,D,O
Texas A&M University–Corpus Christi	M
Texas State University	M
Texas Tech University	M,D
Towson University	M
Trevecca Nazarene University	M,O

Institution	Degree
Trinity Washington University	M
Troy University	M,O
Tufts University	M,D
Union College (KY)	M
Universidad del Este	M
Universidad Metropolitana	M
Université de Sherbrooke	M,O
University at Buffalo, the State University of New York	M,D,O
The University of Akron	M
The University of Alabama	M,D,O
The University of Alabama at Birmingham	M
University of Alaska Southeast	M
University of Alberta	M,D
The University of Arizona	M,D
University of Arkansas at Pine Bluff	M
University of Bridgeport	M,D,O
University of California, Irvine	M,D
University of Central Florida	M
University of Central Missouri	M,D,O
University of Central Oklahoma	M
University of Cincinnati	M
University of Colorado Denver	M
University of Connecticut	M,D
University of Florida	M,D,O
University of Hartford	M
University of Illinois at Chicago	M,D
University of Indianapolis	M
The University of Iowa	M,D
University of Kentucky	M
University of La Verne	M,D,O
University of Louisiana at Monroe	M,D
University of Louisville	M,D,O
University of Mary Hardin-Baylor	M,D
University of Maryland, Baltimore County	M
University of Mary Washington	M
University of Massachusetts Amherst	M,D,O
University of Memphis	M,D,O
University of Minnesota, Twin Cities Campus	M
University of Missouri	M,D,O
University of Missouri–St. Louis	M,D
University of Montevallo	M
University of Nebraska at Kearney	M
University of Nebraska at Omaha	M
University of Nevada, Las Vegas	M,D,O
University of Nevada, Reno	M
University of New Hampshire	M,O
University of New Mexico	M
University of North Alabama	M,O
The University of North Carolina at Charlotte	M,O
The University of North Carolina at Greensboro	D
The University of North Carolina at Pembroke	M
The University of North Carolina Wilmington	M
University of North Dakota	M
University of Northern Colorado	M,D
University of Northern Iowa	M
University of North Florida	M
University of Oklahoma	M,D
University of Pennsylvania	M
University of Phoenix–Bay Area Campus	M,D,O
University of Phoenix–Central Valley Campus	M
University of Phoenix–Colorado Campus	M
University of Phoenix–Colorado Springs Downtown Campus	M,O
University of Phoenix–Hawaii Campus	M
University of Phoenix–Las Vegas Campus	M
University of Phoenix–New Mexico Campus	M
University of Phoenix–North Florida Campus	M
University of Phoenix–Online Campus	M,O
University of Phoenix–Phoenix Campus	M
University of Phoenix–Sacramento Valley Campus	M,O
University of Phoenix–San Diego Campus	M
University of Phoenix–Southern Arizona Campus	M,O
University of Phoenix–Southern California Campus	M,O
University of Phoenix–South Florida Campus	M
University of Phoenix–Utah Campus	M
University of Phoenix–Washington D.C. Campus	M,D,O
University of Pittsburgh	M
University of Puget Sound	M
University of St. Francis (IL)	M,D,O
University of Saint Mary	M
University of St. Thomas (TX)	M,D
University of South Alabama	M,D
University of South Carolina	M,D
University of South Carolina Upstate	M
The University of South Dakota	M
University of Southern Indiana	M
University of Southern Mississippi	M,D
University of South Florida	M,D,O
University of South Florida, St. Petersburg	M
University of South Florida Sarasota-Manatee	M
The University of Tennessee	M,D,O
The University of Tennessee at Chattanooga	M,D,O

Institution	Degree
The University of Tennessee at Martin	M
The University of Texas Rio Grande Valley	M,D
University of the Cumberlands	M,D,O
University of the District of Columbia	M
The University of Toledo	M,D,O
The University of Tulsa	M
University of Utah	M,D,O
University of Virginia	M,D,O
University of Washington, Tacoma	M
The University of West Alabama	M
University of West Florida	M
University of Wisconsin–Milwaukee	M
University of Wisconsin–River Falls	M
University of Wisconsin–Stevens Point	M
Utah State University	M
Utah Valley University	M
Valley City State University	M
Valparaiso University	M
Vanderbilt University	M
Virginia Commonwealth University	M
Wagner College	M
Walden University	M,D,O
Warner University	M
Washington State University	M,D
Washington University in St. Louis	M
Wayland Baptist University	M
Wayne State College	M
Wayne State University	M,D,O
Webster University	M
Western Governors University	M,O
Western Kentucky University	M,O
Western New Mexico University	M
Western Washington University	M
Westfield State University	M
West Virginia University	M
Wheaton College	M
Wheelock College	M
Whittier College	M
Whitworth University	M
Widener University	M,D
William Carey University	M,O
William Paterson University of New Jersey	M
Wilmington University	M,D
Wilson College	M
Wingate University	M,D,O
Worcester State University	M
Wright State University	M
Xavier University	M

EMERGENCY MANAGEMENT

Institution	Degree
Adelphi University	O
Adler University	M,D,O
American Public University System	M
Anna Maria College	M,O
Arizona State University at the Tempe campus	M,D
Arkansas State University	M
Arkansas Tech University	M
Auburn University at Montgomery	M
Ball State University	M
Benedictine University	M
Boston University	M
California State University, Long Beach	M
California State University Maritime Academy	M
Capella University	M,D
Clemson University	M,O
Columbia Southern University	M
Drexel University	M
Excelsior College	M
Florida Institute of Technology	M,D
Florida International University	M
Fordham University	M
Georgetown University	M
The George Washington University	M,D,O
Georgia State University	M,D,O
Grand Canyon University	M
Indiana University–Purdue University Indianapolis	M,O
Jacksonville State University	M,D
Lander University	M
Lasell College	M,O
Liberty University	M,D,O
London Metropolitan University	M,D
Massachusetts Maritime Academy	M
Metropolitan College of New York	M
Millersville University of Pennsylvania	M
New Jersey Institute of Technology	M,D,O
New York Medical College	M
Norwich University	M
Nova Southeastern University	M,D,O
Oklahoma State University	M,D
Pace University	M,O
Park University	M,O
Philadelphia University	M
Regent University	M
Royal Roads University	M,O
Rutgers University–New Brunswick	M,D,O
Saint Leo University	M
San Diego State University	M
Sul Ross State University	M
Syracuse University	O
Trident University International	M,D,O
Trine University	M
Tulane University	M,D
Université de Montréal	O
University at Albany, State University of New York	O
University of Alaska Fairbanks	M
University of Central Florida	M
University of Chicago	M
University of Colorado Denver	M,D
University of Delaware	M,D
University of Denver	M,O

Institution	Degree
University of Florida	M
University of Hawaii at Manoa	O
University of Illinois at Springfield	M,D,O
University of Maryland, Baltimore County	M,D,O
University of Nebraska Medical Center	M
University of Nevada, Las Vegas	M,D,O
University of New Haven	M,O
The University of North Carolina at Charlotte	M,O
University of North Texas	M,D,O
University of South Florida	O
The University of Toledo	M,O
Upper Iowa University	M
Virginia Commonwealth University	M,D,O
Walden University	M,D,O
Waldorf University	M
West Chester University of Pennsylvania	M,O
York University	M

EMERGENCY MEDICAL SERVICES

Institution	Degree
Baylor University	D
Creighton University	M
Drexel University	M
San Diego State University	M,D
Université Laval	O
University of Guelph	M,D,O

ENERGY AND POWER ENGINEERING

Institution	Degree
Appalachian State University	M
Arizona State University at the Tempe campus	M,D
Carnegie Mellon University	M,D
The Catholic University of America	M,D
Clarkson University	M,D
Cornell University	M,D
Florida State University	M,D
Georgia Southern University	M
Instituto Tecnologico de Santo Domingo	M,D,O
Inter American University of Puerto Rico, Bayamón Campus	M
Kansas State University	M
Lehigh University	M
New Jersey Institute of Technology	M,D
New York Institute of Technology	M,O
North Carolina Agricultural and Technical State University	M,D
Northeastern University	M,D,O
San Francisco State University	M
Santa Clara University	M,D,O
Southern Illinois University Carbondale	D
Stanford University	M,D,O
Syracuse University	M
Texas A&M University–Kingsville	D
Texas Tech University	M,D
Universidad Autonoma de Guadalajara	M,D
University of Alberta	M,D
University of Calgary	M,D
University of Colorado Colorado Springs	M,D
University of Illinois at Urbana–Champaign	M,D
The University of Iowa	M,D
University of Massachusetts Lowell	M,D
University of Memphis	M,D
University of Michigan	M,D
University of Michigan–Dearborn	M
The University of North Carolina at Charlotte	M,O
University of North Texas	M,D,O
University of Puerto Rico, Mayagüez Campus	M,D
University of Rochester	M
The University of Tennessee	D
The University of Tennessee at Chattanooga	M,D
Washington State University	M,D
Wayne State University	M,D
Worcester Polytechnic Institute	M,D

ENERGY MANAGEMENT AND POLICY

Institution	Degree
American University of Armenia	M
Boston University	M,D
Colorado State University	M
Duke University	M,O
Eastern Illinois University	M
Franklin Pierce University	M,D,O
Indiana University Bloomington	M,D,O
Instituto Tecnologico de Santo Domingo	M,D,O
Johns Hopkins University	M,O
Kansas State University	M,D
Michigan Technological University	M,D
New York Institute of Technology	M,O
New York University	M
Norwich University	M
Oklahoma Baptist University	M
Oklahoma City University	M
Rice University	M
Samford University	M
Tulane University	M,D
Université du Québec, Institut National de la Recherche Scientifique	M,D
University of Calgary	M,D
University of California, Berkeley	M,D
University of California, San Diego	M
University of Colorado Denver	M
University of Delaware	M,D
University of Illinois at Urbana–Champaign	M
University of Mary	M
University of Phoenix–Bay Area Campus	M,D
University of Phoenix–Online Campus	M,O

University of Phoenix–Phoenix Campus	M,O
University of Phoenix–Southern California Campus	M
University of Pittsburgh	M
University of Rochester	M
University of San Francisco	M
The University of Texas at Tyler	M
The University of Tulsa	M
Vermont Law School	M
Waynesburg University	M,D

ENGINEERING AND APPLIED SCIENCES—GENERAL

Air Force Institute of Technology	M,D
Alabama Agricultural and Mechanical University	M,D
Alfred University	M,D
The American University in Cairo	M,D,O
American University of Beirut	M,D
Arizona State University at the Tempe campus	M,D
Arkansas State University	M
Arkansas Tech University	M
Auburn University	M,D,O
Austin Peay State University	M
Binghamton University, State University of New York	M,D
Boise State University	M,D,O
Boston University	M,D
Bradley University	M
Brigham Young University	M,D
Brown University	M,D
Bucknell University	M
California Institute of Technology	M,D,O
California Polytechnic State University, San Luis Obispo	M
California State University, Chico	M
California State University, East Bay	M
California State University, Fresno	M
California State University, Fullerton	M
California State University, Los Angeles	M
California State University, Northridge	M
California State University, Sacramento	M
Carleton University	M,D
Case Western Reserve University	M,D
The Catholic University of America	M,D,O
Central Connecticut State University	M
Central Michigan University	M
Central Washington University	M
Christian Brothers University	M
The Citadel, The Military College of South Carolina	M,O
City College of the City University of New York	M,D
Clarkson University	M,D,O
Clemson University	M,D,O
Cleveland State University	M,D
Colorado School of Mines	M,D,O
Colorado State University	M,D
Colorado State University–Pueblo	M
Columbia University	M,D
Concordia University (Canada)	M,D,O
Cooper Union for the Advancement of Science and Art	M
Cornell University	M,D
Dalhousie University	M,D
Dartmouth College	M,D
Drexel University	M,D,O
Duke University	M
Eastern Illinois University	M,O
Eastern Michigan University	M
École Polytechnique de Montréal	M,D,O
Fairfield University	M,O
Fairleigh Dickinson University, Metropolitan Campus	M
Florida Agricultural and Mechanical University	M,D
Florida Atlantic University	M,D
Florida Institute of Technology	M,D
Florida International University	M,D
Florida State University	M,D,O
George Mason University	M,D,O
The George Washington University	M,D,O
Georgia Institute of Technology	M,D
Georgia Southern University	M,O
Gonzaga University	M,O
The Graduate Center, City University of New York	D
Grand Valley State University	M
Grantham University	M,D
Harvard University	M,D
Hofstra University	M
Howard University	M,D
Idaho State University	M,D,O
Illinois Institute of Technology	M,D
Indiana State University	M
Indiana University–Purdue University Fort Wayne	M,O
Instituto Tecnológico de Santo Domingo	M,O
Instituto Tecnológico y de Estudios Superiores de Monterrey, Campus Ciudad Obregón	M
Instituto Tecnológico y de Estudios Superiores de Monterrey, Campus Monterrey	M,D
James Madison University	M
Johns Hopkins University	M,D,O
Kansas State University	M,D,O
Kennesaw State University	M,O
Kent State University	M

Lakehead University	M
Lamar University	M,D
Laurentian University	M,D
Lawrence Technological University	M,D
Lehigh University	M,D
LeTourneau University	M
Liberty University	M
Louisiana State University and Agricultural & Mechanical College	M,D
Louisiana Tech University	M,D
Manhattan College	M
Marquette University	M,D,O
Marshall University	M
Massachusetts Institute of Technology	M,D,O
McGill University	M,D
McMaster University	M,D
McNeese State University	M,O
Memorial University of Newfoundland	M,D
Mercer University	M
Merrimack College	M
Miami University	M
Michigan State University	M,D
Michigan Technological University	M,D,O
Milwaukee School of Engineering	M
Mississippi State University	M,D
Missouri Western State University	M
Montana State University	M,D
Montana Tech of The University of Montana	M
Morgan State University	M,D
New Jersey Institute of Technology	M,D
New Mexico State University	M,D,O
New York Institute of Technology	M,O
New York University	M,D,O
North Carolina Agricultural and Technical State University	M,D
North Carolina State University	M,D
North Dakota State University	M,D,O
Northeastern University	M,D,O
Northern Arizona University	M,D,O
Northern Illinois University	M
Northwestern Polytechnic University	M,D
Northwestern University	M,D,O
Oakland University	M,D,O
The Ohio State University	M,D
Ohio University	M,D
Oklahoma Christian University	M
Oklahoma State University	M,D
Old Dominion University	M,D
Open University	M
Oregon State University	M,D
Penn State Erie, The Behrend College	M
Penn State Great Valley	M,O
Penn State Harrisburg	M,O
Penn State University Park	M,D
Pontificia Universidad Catolica Madre y Maestra	M
Portland State University	M,D,O
Prairie View A&M University	M,D
Princeton University	M,D
Purdue University	M,D
Purdue University Northwest	M
Queen's University at Kingston	M,D
Rensselaer at Hartford	M
Rensselaer Polytechnic Institute	M,D
Rice University	M,D
Robert Morris University	M
Rochester Institute of Technology	M,D,O
Rose-Hulman Institute of Technology	M
Rowan University	M
Royal Military College of Canada	M,D
Saginaw Valley State University	M
St. Cloud State University	M
San Diego State University	M,D
San Francisco State University	M
Santa Clara University	M,D,O
Seattle University	M
Simon Fraser University	M,D
South Dakota School of Mines and Technology	M,D
South Dakota State University	M,D
Southern Illinois University Carbondale	M,D
Southern Illinois University Edwardsville	M
Southern Methodist University	M,D
Southern University and Agricultural and Mechanical College	M
Stanford University	M,D,O
Stevens Institute of Technology	M,D,O
Stony Brook University, State University of New York	M,D,O
Syracuse University	M,D,O
Temple University	D
Tennessee State University	M,D
Tennessee Technological University	M,D
Texas A&M University–Kingsville	M,D
Texas State University	M
Texas Tech University	M,D
Tufts University	M,D
Tuskegee University	M,D
Universidad de las Américas Puebla	M
Universidad del Turabo	M
Université de Moncton	M
Université de Sherbrooke	M,D,O
Université du Québec à Chicoutimi	M,D
Université du Québec à Rimouski	M
Université du Québec, École de technologie supérieure	M,D,O
Université du Québec en Abitibi-Témiscamingue	M,O

Université Laval	M,D,O
University at Albany, State University of New York	M,D,O
University at Buffalo, the State University of New York	M,D,O
The University of Akron	M,D
The University of Alabama	M,D
The University of Alabama at Birmingham	M,D
The University of Alabama in Huntsville	M,D
University of Alaska Anchorage	M,O
University of Alaska Fairbanks	D
The University of Arizona	M,D,O
University of Arkansas	M,D
University of Bridgeport	M,D
The University of British Columbia	M,D
University of Calgary	M,D
University of California, Berkeley	M,D,O
University of California, Davis	M,D,O
University of California, Irvine	M,D
University of California, Los Angeles	M,D
University of California, Merced	M,D
University of California, Santa Barbara	M,D
University of California, Santa Cruz	M,D
University of Central Florida	M,D,O
University of Central Oklahoma	M
University of Cincinnati	M,D
University of Colorado Boulder	M,D
University of Colorado Colorado Springs	M,D
University of Colorado Denver	M,D
University of Connecticut	M,D
University of Delaware	M,D
University of Denver	M,D
University of Detroit Mercy	M,D
University of Florida	M,D,O
University of Guelph	M,D
University of Hartford	M
University of Hawaii at Manoa	M,D
University of Houston	M,D
University of Idaho	M,D
University of Illinois at Chicago	M,D
University of Illinois at Urbana–Champaign	M,D
The University of Iowa	M,D
The University of Kansas	M,D,O
University of Kentucky	M,D
University of Louisville	M,D,O
University of Maine	M,D
University of Manitoba	M,D
University of Maryland, Baltimore County	M,D,O
University of Maryland, College Park	M
University of Massachusetts Amherst	M,D
University of Massachusetts Dartmouth	D
University of Massachusetts Lowell	M,D
University of Memphis	M,D,O
University of Miami	M,D
University of Michigan	M,D,O
University of Michigan–Dearborn	M,D
University of Minnesota, Twin Cities Campus	M,D,O
University of Mississippi	M,D
University of Missouri	M,D,O
University of Missouri–Kansas City	M,D,O
University of Nebraska–Lincoln	M,D
University of Nevada, Las Vegas	M,D,O
University of Nevada, Reno	M,D
University of New Brunswick Fredericton	M,D,O
University of New Haven	M,O
University of New Mexico	M,D
University of New Orleans	M,D
The University of North Carolina at Charlotte	M,D
University of North Dakota	D
University of North Texas	M,D,O
University of Notre Dame	M,D
University of Oklahoma	M,D
University of Ottawa	M,D,O
University of Pennsylvania	M,D
University of Pittsburgh	M,D
University of Portland	M
University of Puerto Rico, Mayagüez Campus	M
University of Regina	M,D
University of Rhode Island	M,D
University of Rochester	M,D
University of St. Thomas (MN)	M,D
University of Saskatchewan	M,D,O
University of South Africa	M,D
University of South Alabama	M,D
University of South Carolina	M,D
University of Southern California	M,D,O
University of Southern Indiana	M
University of South Florida	M,D,O
The University of Tennessee	M,D
The University of Texas at Arlington	M,D
The University of Texas at Austin	M,D
The University of Texas at Dallas	M,D
The University of Texas at El Paso	M,D,O
The University of Texas at San Antonio	M,D
University of the District of Columbia	M
University of the Pacific	M
The University of Toledo	M
University of Toronto	M,D
The University of Tulsa	M,D
University of Utah	M,D

University of Vermont	M,D
University of Victoria	M,D
University of Virginia	M,D
University of Washington	M,D,O
University of Waterloo	M,D
The University of Western Ontario	M,D
University of Windsor	M,D
University of Wisconsin–Madison	M,D
University of Wisconsin–Milwaukee	M,D
University of Wisconsin–Platteville	M
University of Wyoming	M,D
Utah State University	M,D,O
Vanderbilt University	M,D
Villanova University	M,D,O
Virginia Commonwealth University	M,D
Virginia Polytechnic Institute and State University	M,D
Washington State University	M,D,O
Washington University in St. Louis	M,D
Wayne State University	M,D,O
Western Michigan University	M,D
Western New England University	M,D
West Texas A&M University	M
West Virginia University	M,D
Wichita State University	M,D
Widener University	M
Wilkes University	M
Worcester Polytechnic Institute	M,D,O
Yale University	M,D
Youngstown State University	M

ENGINEERING DESIGN

Harvard University	M,D
Northwestern University	M
Ohio Dominican University	M
Penn State University Park	M
Rochester Institute of Technology	M
San Diego State University	M,D
Stanford University	M
Stevens Institute of Technology	M
University of Michigan	M,D
Worcester Polytechnic Institute	M,D,O

ENGINEERING MANAGEMENT

Air Force Institute of Technology	M
American University of Beirut	M
American University of Sharjah	M
Arkansas State University	M
California State Polytechnic University, Pomona	M
California State University, East Bay	M
California State University, Long Beach	M,D
California State University Maritime Academy	M
California State University, Northridge	M
Case Western Reserve University	M
The Catholic University of America	M,O
Central Michigan University	M,O
The Citadel, The Military College of South Carolina	M,O
Clarkson University	M
Colorado School of Mines	M,D
Cornell University	M,D
Dallas Baptist University	M
Dartmouth College	M
Drexel University	M,O
Duke University	M
Eastern Michigan University	M
Embry-Riddle Aeronautical University–Worldwide	M
Florida Institute of Technology	M
Florida International University	M
Gannon University	M
The George Washington University	M,D,O
Georgia Southern University	M
Indiana Tech	M
Instituto Tecnológico y de Estudios Superiores de Monterrey, Campus Chihuahua	M,O
International Technological University	M
Johns Hopkins University	M
Kansas State University	M
Kettering University	M
Lamar University	M,D
Lawrence Technological University	M
LeTourneau University	M
Long Island University–LIU Post	M
Loyola Marymount University	M
Marquette University	M,D,O
Marshall University	M
Massachusetts Institute of Technology	M
McNeese State University	M
Mercer University	M
Merrimack College	M
Middle Tennessee State University	M
Milwaukee School of Engineering	M
Missouri University of Science and Technology	M,D
Naval Postgraduate School	M,D,O
New Jersey Institute of Technology	M,D
New Mexico Institute of Mining and Technology	M
Northeastern University	M
Northwestern University	M
Oakland University	M,D,O
Oklahoma Christian University	M
Old Dominion University	D
Oregon State University	M,D
Penn State Great Valley	M,O
Penn State Harrisburg	M,O
Point Park University	M

*M—masters degree; D—doctorate; O—other advanced degree; *—Close-Up and/or Display*

Polytechnic University of Puerto Rico	M
Polytechnic University of Puerto Rico, Orlando Campus	
Portland State University	M,D,O
Rensselaer Polytechnic Institute	M,D
Robert Morris University	M
Rochester Institute of Technology	M
Rose-Hulman Institute of Technology	M
St. Cloud State University	M
Saint Martin's University	M
St. Mary's University (United States)	M
Santa Clara University	M,D,O
South Dakota School of Mines and Technology	M
Southern Illinois University Carbondale	M
Southern Methodist University	M,D
Stanford University	M,D
Stevens Institute of Technology	M,D,O
Syracuse University	M
Tarleton State University	M
Temple University	M,O
Texas A&M University	M,D
Texas Tech University	M,D
Tufts University	M
Université de Sherbrooke	M,O
The University of Alabama at Birmingham	M
University of Alaska Anchorage	M
University of Alberta	M,D
The University of Arizona	M,D,O
University of California, Berkeley	M,D
University of California, Irvine	M
University of Colorado Boulder	M
University of Colorado Colorado Springs	M,D
University of Dayton	M
University of Denver	M,D
University of Detroit Mercy	M,D
University of Idaho	M,D
The University of Kansas	M,O
University of Louisiana at Lafayette	M
University of Louisville	M,D,O
University of Management and Technology	M
The University of Manchester	M,D
University of Maryland, Baltimore County	M,O
University of Michigan–Dearborn	M
University of Minnesota, Duluth	M
University of Missouri–Kansas City	M,D,O
University of Nebraska–Lincoln	M,D
University of New Brunswick Fredericton	M
University of New Haven	M,O
University of New Orleans	M
The University of North Carolina at Charlotte	M,O
University of Ottawa	M,O
University of Puerto Rico, Mayagüez Campus	M,D
University of Regina	M,O
University of St. Thomas (MN)	M,O
University of Southern California	M,D,O
University of Southern Indiana	M
University of South Florida	M,D
The University of Tennessee	M,D
The University of Tennessee at Chattanooga	M,O
The University of Texas at Arlington	M
The University of Texas at Tyler	M
The University of Texas Rio Grande Valley	M
University of Waterloo	M,D
Valparaiso University	M,O
Virginia Polytechnic Institute and State University	M,O
Washington State University	M,O
Wayne State University	M,D,O
Western Michigan University	M,D
Western New England University	M,D
Wichita State University	M,D
Widener University	M
Wilkes University	M

ENGINEERING PHYSICS

Air Force Institute of Technology	M,D
Cornell University	M,D
École Polytechnique de Montréal	M,D,O
Embry-Riddle Aeronautical University–Daytona	M,D
George Mason University	M,D
McMaster University	M,D
Rensselaer Polytechnic Institute	M,D
Stanford University	M,D
University of California, San Diego	M,D
University of Central Oklahoma	M
University of Oklahoma	M,D
University of Saskatchewan	M,D
The University of Tulsa	M
University of Virginia	M,D
University of Wisconsin–Madison	M,D
Yale University	M,D

ENGLISH

Abilene Christian University	M
Acadia University	M
The American University in Cairo	M,O
American University of Beirut	M
Andrews University	M
Angelo State University	M
Appalachian State University	M
Arcadia University	M
Arizona State University at the Tempe campus	M,D,O
Arkansas State University	M,O
Arkansas Tech University	M
Asbury University	M
Auburn University	M,D,O
Austin Peay State University	M
Ball State University	M,D
Bard College	M
Baylor University	M,D
Bemidji State University	M
Binghamton University, State University of New York	M,D
Bob Jones University	M,D,O
Boston College	M,D
Boston University	M,D
Bowie State University	M
Bowling Green State University	M,D
Bradley University	M
Brandeis University	M,D
Bridgewater State University	M
Brigham Young University	M
Brock University	M
Brooklyn College of the City University of New York	M
Brown University	M,D
Bucknell University	M
Buffalo State College, State University of New York	M
Butler University	M
California Baptist University	M
California Polytechnic State University, San Luis Obispo	M
California State Polytechnic University, Pomona	M
California State University, Bakersfield	M
California State University, Chico	M
California State University, Dominguez Hills	M,O
California State University, East Bay	M
California State University, Fresno	M
California State University, Fullerton	M
California State University, Long Beach	M
California State University, Los Angeles	M,O
California State University, Northridge	M
California State University, Sacramento	M
California State University, San Bernardino	M
California State University, San Marcos	M
California State University, Stanislaus	M,O
Carleton University	M,D
Carnegie Mellon University	M,D
Case Western Reserve University	M,D
The Catholic University of America	M,D,O
Central Michigan University	M
Central Washington University	M
Chapman University	M
Chicago State University	M
The Citadel, The Military College of South Carolina	M
City College of the City University of New York	M
Claremont Graduate University	M,D
Clark Atlanta University	M,D
Clarks Summit University	M
Clark University	M
Clemson University	M
Cleveland State University	M
The College at Brockport, State University of New York	M,O
College of Charleston	M
The College of New Jersey	M
College of Staten Island of the City University of New York	M
The College of William and Mary	M
Colorado State University	M
Columbia University	M,D
Concordia University (Canada)	M,D
Converse College	M
Cornell University	M,D
Creighton University	M
Dalhousie University	M,D
DePaul University	M
Dominican University of California	M
Drew University	M,D,O
Duke University	D
Duquesne University	M,D
East Carolina University	M,D,O
Eastern Illinois University	M
Eastern Kentucky University	M
Eastern Michigan University	M
Eastern New Mexico University	M
Eastern Washington University	M
East Tennessee State University	M,O
Emory University	D,O
Emporia State University	M
Fairleigh Dickinson University, Metropolitan Campus	M
Fitchburg State University	M,O
Florida Atlantic University	M
Florida Gulf Coast University	M
Florida International University	M
Florida State University	M,D
Fordham University	M,D
Fort Hays State University	M
Gannon University	M
Gardner-Webb University	M
George Mason University	M,D,O
Georgetown University	M
The George Washington University	M
Georgia College & State University	M
Georgia Southern University	M
Georgia State University	M,D
Governors State University	M
The Graduate Center, City University of New York	D
Grambling State University	M,D,O
Grand Valley State University	M
Hardin-Simmons University	M
Harvard University	M,D,O
Heritage University	M
Hofstra University	M
Hollins University	M
Howard University	M,D
Humboldt State University	M
Idaho State University	M,D,O
Illinois State University	M,D,O
Indiana State University	M
Indiana University Bloomington	M,D
Indiana University of Pennsylvania	M,D
Indiana University–Purdue University Fort Wayne	M,O
Indiana University–Purdue University Indianapolis	M,O
Indiana University South Bend	M
Inter American University of Puerto Rico, Metropolitan Campus	M
Iona College	M
Iowa State University of Science and Technology	M,D
Jackson State University	M
Jacksonville State University	M
James Madison University	M
John Carroll University	M
Johns Hopkins University	M,D
Kansas State University	M,O
Kent State University	M,D
Kutztown University of Pennsylvania	M
Lakehead University	M
Lamar University	M
La Salle University	M,O
La Sierra University	M
Lee University	M
Lehigh University	M,D
Lehman College of the City University of New York	M
Liberty University	M
Lipscomb University	M,D,O
Long Island University–LIU Brooklyn	M,D,O
Long Island University–LIU Post	M,O
Louisiana State University and Agricultural & Mechanical College	M,D
Louisiana Tech University	M,O
Loyola Marymount University	M
Loyola University Chicago	M,D
Manhattan College	M,O
Marquette University	M,D
Marshall University	M,O
Mary Baldwin University	M
Marygrove College	M
Marymount University	M,O
McGill University	M,D
McMaster University	M,D
McNeese State University	M
Memorial University of Newfoundland	M,D
Mercy College	M
Miami University	M,D
Michigan State University	M,D
Middlebury College	M
Middle Tennessee State University	M,D
Midwestern State University	M,D
Millersville University of Pennsylvania	M,O
Mills College	M,O
Minnesota State University Mankato	M,O
Mississippi College	M
Mississippi State University	M,D
Missouri State University	M,O
Molloy College	M,O
Monmouth University	M
Montana State University	M
Montclair State University	M
Morehead State University	M
Morgan State University	M,D
Mount Mary University	M
Mount Saint Mary's University (CA)	M,D,O
Murray State University	M
New Mexico Highlands University	M
New Mexico State University	M,D
New York University	M,D
North Carolina Agricultural and Technical State University	M
North Carolina Central University	M
North Carolina State University	M
North Dakota State University	M,D
Northeastern Illinois University	M
Northeastern State University	M
Northeastern University	M,D
Northern Arizona University	M,D,O
Northern Illinois University	M,D
Northern Kentucky University	M,O
Northern Michigan University	M,O
Northwestern State University of Louisiana	M
Northwestern University	M,D
Northwest Missouri State University	M,O
Notre Dame de Namur University	M
Oakland University	M
Ohio Dominican University	M
The Ohio State University	M,D
Ohio University	M,D
Oklahoma State University	M,D
Old Dominion University	M,D
Oregon State University	M
Our Lady of the Lake University	M
Pace University	M,O
Penn State University Park	M,D
Pittsburg State University	M
Portland State University	M
Princeton University	D
Purdue University	M,D
Purdue University Northwest	M
Queens College of the City University of New York	M,O
Queen's University at Kingston	M,D
Radford University	M
Rhode Island College	M,O
Rice University	M,D
Rivier University	M
Rutgers University–Camden	M
Rutgers University–Newark	M
Rutgers University–New Brunswick	D
St. Cloud State University	M
St. John's University (NY)	M,D
Saint Louis University	M,D
Saint Louis University–Madrid Campus	M
St. Mary's University (United States)	M
Salem State University	M
Salisbury University	M
Sam Houston State University	M
San Diego State University	M
San Francisco State University	M,O
San Jose State University	M,O
Seton Hall University	M
Sewanee: The University of the South	M
Simmons College	M
Simon Fraser University	M,D
Slippery Rock University of Pennsylvania	M
Sonoma State University	M
South Carolina State University	M
South Dakota State University	M
Southeastern Louisiana University	M
Southeast Missouri State University	M
Southern Connecticut State University	M
Southern Illinois University Carbondale	M,D
Southern Illinois University Edwardsville	M,O
Southern Methodist University	M,D
Spring Hill College	M,O
Stanford University	M,D
State University of New York at New Paltz	M
State University of New York at Oswego	M
State University of New York College at Cortland	M
State University of New York College at Potsdam	M
Stephen F. Austin State University	M
Stony Brook University, State University of New York	M,D,O
Sul Ross State University	M
Syracuse University	M,D
Tarleton State University	M
Temple University	M,D
Tennessee Technological University	M
Texas A&M International University	M,D
Texas A&M University	M,D
Texas A&M University–Commerce	M,D,O
Texas A&M University–Corpus Christi	M
Texas A&M University–Kingsville	M
Texas A&M University–San Antonio	M
Texas A&M University–Texarkana	M
Texas Christian University	M,D
Texas Southern University	M
Texas State University	M
Texas Tech University	M,D
Texas Woman's University	M,D
Tiffin University	M
Trinity College (United States)	M
Trinity Western University	M
Truman State University	M
Tufts University	M,D
Tulane University	M
Universidad de las Américas Puebla	M
Université de Montréal	M,D
Université Laval	M,D
University at Albany, State University of New York	M,D
University at Buffalo, the State University of New York	M,D,O
The University of Akron	M
The University of Alabama	M,D
The University of Alabama at Birmingham	M
The University of Alabama in Huntsville	M,O
University of Alaska Anchorage	M
University of Alaska Fairbanks	M
University of Alberta	M,D
The University of Arizona	M,D
University of Arkansas	M,D
The University of British Columbia	M,D
University of Calgary	M,D
University of California, Berkeley	D
University of California, Davis	M,D
University of California, Irvine	M,D
University of California, Los Angeles	M,D
University of California, Riverside	M,D
University of California, San Diego	M,D
University of California, Santa Barbara	D
University of California, Santa Cruz	M,D
University of Central Arkansas	M,D
University of Central Florida	M,D
University of Central Missouri	M,D,O
University of Central Oklahoma	M

University of Chicago	M,D	The University of Toledo	M,D	Cleveland State University	M	Missouri State University	M,O
University of Cincinnati	M,D	University of Toronto	M,D	Coastal Carolina University	M,O	Missouri Western State University	M,O
University of Colorado Boulder	M,D	The University of Tulsa	M,D	College of Charleston	O	Molloy College	M,O
University of Colorado Denver	M	University of Utah	M,D	College of Mount Saint Vincent	M,O	Monmouth University	M,D,O
University of Connecticut	M,D	University of Vermont	M	The College of New Jersey	M,O	Montclair State University	M,O
University of Dallas	M	University of Victoria	M,D	The College of New Rochelle	M,O	Mount Saint Vincent University	M
University of Dayton	M	University of Virginia	M,D	College of Saint Mary	M	Multnomah University	M
University of Delaware	M,D	University of Washington	M,D	College of Staten Island of the		Murray State University	M
University of Denver	M,D	University of Waterloo	M,D	City University of New York	M,O	Nazareth College of Rochester	M
University of Florida	M,D	The University of Western Ontario	M,D	Colorado Mesa University	M	New Jersey City University	M
University of Georgia	M,D	University of West Florida	M	Colorado State University	M	Newman University	M
University of Guam	M	University of West Georgia	M,O	Columbia International University	M,D,O	New Mexico State University	M,D,O
University of Guelph	M	University of Windsor	M	Columbus State University	O	The New School	M
University of Hawaii at Manoa	M,D	University of Wisconsin–Eau		Concordia University (United		New York University	M,D,O
University of Houston–Clear		Claire	M	States)	M,D	Niagara University	M,O
Lake	M	University of Wisconsin–		Concordia University (Canada)	M,O	Northeastern Illinois University	M
University of Houston–		Madison	M,D	Cornerstone University	M,O	Northern Arizona University	M,D,O
Downtown	M	University of Wisconsin–		Dallas Baptist University	M	Northern Michigan University	M
University of Idaho	M	Milwaukee	M,D	DeSales University	M,O	Northwest Christian University	M
University of Illinois at Chicago	M,D	University of Wisconsin–		Dominican University	M	Northwest Missouri State	
University of Illinois at		Oshkosh	M	Duquesne University	M	University	M,D,O
Springfield	M,O	University of Wisconsin–		East Carolina University	M,D,O	Notre Dame of Maryland University	M
University of Illinois at		Stevens Point	M	Eastern Michigan University	M,O	Nyack College	M
Urbana–Champaign	M,D	University of Wyoming	M	Eastern Nazarene College	M,O	Oakland University	M,O
University of Indianapolis	M	Utah State University	M	Eastern New Mexico University	M	Ohio Dominican University	M
The University of Iowa	M,D	Valdosta State University	M	Eastern University	M,D,O	Oklahoma City University	M
The University of Kansas	M,D	Valparaiso University	M	Eastern Washington University	M	Old Dominion University	M
University of Kentucky	M,D	Vanderbilt University	M,D	East Tennessee State University	M,O	Oregon State University	M,D
University of La Verne	M,O	Villanova University	M	Elms College	M,O	Pacific University	M
University of Lethbridge	M,D	Virginia Commonwealth University	M	Emporia State University	M	Penn State Harrisburg	M,D,O
University of Louisiana at		Virginia Polytechnic Institute and		Erikson Institute	M,O	Penn State University Park	M,D
Lafayette	M,D	State University	M,D,O	Fairfield University	M,O	Penn State York	M,O
University of Louisiana at Monroe	M	Wake Forest University	M	Florida Atlantic University	M,D,O	Pontifical Catholic University of	
University of Louisville	M,D	Washington State University	M,D	Florida International University	M,D,O	Puerto Rico	M
University of Maine	M	Washington University in St. Louis	M,D	Fordham University	M,O	Portland State University	M
The University of Manchester	D	Wayne State University	M,D	Framingham State University	M	Post University	M
University of Manitoba	M,D	Weber State University	M	Fresno Pacific University	M,O	Providence University College &	
University of Maryland, Baltimore		West Chester University of		Furman University	M,O	Theological Seminary	M,D,O
County	M	Pennsylvania	M,O	Gannon University	O	Queens College of the City	
University of Maryland, College		Western Carolina University	M	George Fox University	M,O	University of New York	M,O
Park	M,D	Western Connecticut State		George Mason University	M	Quincy University	M
University of Massachusetts		University	M	Gonzaga University	M	Regent University	M,D,O
Amherst	M,D	Western Illinois University	M,O	Gordon College	M,O	Rhode Island College	M
University of Massachusetts Boston	M	Western Kentucky University	M	Grand Canyon University	M,D,O	Rider University	O
University of Memphis	M,D,O	Western Michigan University	M,D	Grand Valley State University	M	Rowan University	O
University of Miami	M,D	Western Washington University	M	Greensboro College	M	Rutgers University–New	
University of Michigan	M,D,O	Westfield State University	M	Hamline University	M,D	Brunswick	M,D
University of Michigan–Flint	M	West Texas A&M University	M	Harding University	M,O	Sacred Heart University	M,O
University of Minnesota, Duluth	M	West Virginia University	M,D	Hawai'i Pacific University	M,O	St. Cloud State University	M
University of Minnesota, Twin		Wichita State University	M	Henderson State University	M,O	St. John's University (NY)	M,D,O
Cities Campus	M,D	Wilfrid Laurier University	M,D	Heritage University	M	Saint Michael's College	M,O
University of Mississippi	M,D	William Paterson University of New		Hofstra University	M,D,O	St. Thomas University	M,D,O
University of Missouri	M,D	Jersey	M,D	Holy Family University	M,O	Saint Xavier University	M
University of Missouri–		Wilson College	M	Houston Baptist University	M,D	Salem College	M
Kansas City	M,D	Winona State University	M	Humboldt State University		Salem State University	M
University of Missouri–St.		Winthrop University	M	Hunter College of the City		Salisbury University	M
Louis	M	Wright State University	M	University of New York	M	San Diego State University	M,O
University of Montana	M	Xavier University	M	Huntington University	M,D	San Francisco State University	M
University of Montevallo	M	Yale University	M,D	Idaho State University	M,D,O	San Jose State University	M,O
University of Nebraska at Kearney	M	York University	M,D	Immaculata University	M	Seattle Pacific University	M
University of Nebraska at Omaha	M,O	Youngstown State University	M	Indiana State University	M,D,O	Seattle University	M,O
University of Nebraska–				Indiana University Bloomington	M,D	Shippensburg University of	
Lincoln	M,D	**ENGLISH AS A SECOND LANGUAGE**		Indiana University of Pennsylvania	M,D	Pennsylvania	M,O
University of Nevada, Las Vegas	M,D	Acacia University	M	Indiana University–Purdue		Simon Fraser University	M
University of Nevada, Reno	M,D	Adelphi University	M,O	University Fort Wayne	M,O	SIT Graduate Institute	M
University of New Brunswick		Albright College	M	Indiana University–Purdue		Slippery Rock University of	
Fredericton	M,D	Alliant International		University Indianapolis	M,O	Pennsylvania	M
University of New Hampshire	M,D	University–San Diego	M,D,O	Inter American University of		Southeastern University (FL)	M,D
University of New Mexico	M,D	Alliant International		Puerto Rico, Arecibo Campus	M	Southeast Missouri State	
University of New Orleans	M	University–San Francisco	M,O	Inter American University of		University	M
University of North Alabama	M	American College of Education	M	Puerto Rico, Barranquitas Campus	M	Southern Connecticut State	
The University of North Carolina		American Public University System	M	Inter American University of		University	M
at Chapel Hill	M,D	American University	M,O	Puerto Rico, Metropolitan Campus	M	Southern Illinois University	
The University of North Carolina		The American University in Cairo	M,O	Inter American University of		Carbondale	M
at Charlotte	M,O	American University of Armenia	M	Puerto Rico, Ponce Campus	M	Southern Illinois University	
The University of North Carolina		American University of Sharjah	M	Inter American University of		Edwardsville	M,O
at Greensboro	M,D	Anaheim University	M,D,O	Puerto Rico, San Germán Campus	M	Southern New Hampshire University	M,D,O
The University of North Carolina		Andrews University	M,D,O	Iowa State University of Science		Southwest Minnesota State	
Wilmington	M	Angelo State University	M	and Technology	M	University	M
University of North Dakota	M,D	Arizona State University at the		James Madison University	M	State University of New York at	
University of Northern Colorado	M	Tempe campus	M,D,O	Kansas State University	M,D,O	Fredonia	M
University of Northern Iowa	M	Arkansas Tech University	M	Kean University	M	State University of New York at	
University of North Florida	M	Asbury University	M	Kennesaw State University	M	New Paltz	M,O
University of North Texas	M,D,O	Aurora University	M,D	Kent State University	M,D	State University of New York	
University of Notre Dame	M,D	Avila University	M,O	Langston University	M	College at Cortland	M
University of Oklahoma	M,D	Azusa Pacific University	M	La Salle University	M,O	Stony Brook University, State	
University of Oregon	M,D	Ball State University	M	Lee University	M,O	University of New York	M
University of Ottawa	M,D	Barry University	M,D,O	Lehman College of the City		Syracuse University	M,O
University of Pennsylvania	M,D	Binghamton University, State		University of New York	M	Taylor College and Seminary	M,O
University of Pittsburgh	M,D	University of New York	M	Le Moyne College	M,O	Teachers College, Columbia	
University of Puerto Rico,		Biola University	M,D,O	Lesley University	M,D,O	University	M,D,O
Mayagüez Campus	M	Bishop's University	M,O	Lewis University	M	Temple University	M
University of Puerto Rico,		Boise State University	M	Lindenwood University	M,D,O	Texas A&M University–	
Río Piedras Campus	M,D	Boricua College	M	Long Island University–		Commerce	M,D,O
University of Regina	M,D	Brigham Young University	M	Hudson	M,O	Texas A&M University–	
University of Rhode Island	M,D	Brock University	M	Long Island University–LIU		Kingsville	M,D
University of Rochester	M,D	Brown University	M,D	Brooklyn	M,O	Touro College	M
University of St. Thomas (MN)	M	Buena Vista University	M	Long Island University–LIU		Trevecca Nazarene University	M,O
University of Saskatchewan	M,D	California Baptist University	M	Post	M,D,O	Trinity Western University	M
University of South Africa	M,D	California State University,		Long Island University–		Troy University	M
University of South Alabama	M	Dominguez Hills	M,O	Riverhead	M,O	Universidad del Este	M
University of South Carolina	M,D	California State University, East		Madonna University	M	Universidad del Turabo	M
The University of South Dakota	M,D	Bay	M	Manhattanville College	M,O	University at Buffalo, the State	
University of Southern California	M,D	California State University,		Marlboro College	M	University of New York	M,D,O
University of Southern Indiana	M	Fresno	M	Marymount University	M	The University of Alabama	M,D
University of Southern Mississippi	M,D	California State University, Long		McDaniel College	M	The University of Alabama at	
University of South Florida	M,D,O	Beach	M,O	Mercy College	M,O	Birmingham	M,O
The University of Tennessee	M,D	California State University,		Meredith College	M,O	The University of Alabama in	
The University of Tennessee at		Sacramento	M	Merrimack College	M	Huntsville	M,O
Chattanooga	M	California State University,		Messiah College	M	University of Alberta	M,D
The University of Texas at		Stanislaus	M	Michigan State University	M,D	The University of Arizona	M,D
Arlington	M,D	Cambridge College	M,D,O	MidAmerica Nazarene University	M	University of Arkansas at Little	
The University of Texas at Austin	M,D	Canisius College	M,O	Middlebury Institute of		Rock	M
The University of Texas at El Paso	M,D,O	Carlos Albizu University, Miami		International Studies at Monterey	M	The University of British Columbia	M,D
The University of Texas at San		Campus	M	Middle Tennessee State University	M,O	University of California, Berkeley	O
Antonio	M,D	Carson-Newman University	M	Millersville University of		University of California, Los	
The University of Texas at Tyler	M	Central Michigan University	M	Pennsylvania	M	Angeles	M,D,O
The University of Texas of the		Central Washington University	M	Minnesota State University Mankato	M,O	University of California,	
Permian Basin	M	City College of the City		Minnesota State University		Riverside	M,D,O
The University of Texas Rio Grande		University of New York	M	Moorhead	M	University of Central Florida	M,D,O
Valley	M	Clarks Summit University	M	Mississippi College	M	University of Central Missouri	M,D,O

M—masters degree; D—doctorate; O—other advanced degree; *—Close-Up and/or Display

University of Central Oklahoma	M
University of Cincinnati	M,D,O
University of Colorado Colorado Springs	M,D
University of Dayton	M
University of Delaware	M,D,O
The University of Findlay	M,D
University of Florida	M,D,O
University of Guam	M
University of Hawaii at Manoa	M,D,O
University of Idaho	M
University of Illinois at Chicago	M,D
University of Illinois at Springfield	M,O
University of Illinois at Urbana–Champaign	M,D
The University of Iowa	M,D
University of Louisiana at Monroe	M,D
The University of Manchester	M,D
University of Manitoba	M
University of Maryland, Baltimore County	M,O
University of Maryland, College Park	M,D,O
University of Massachusetts Amherst	M,D,O
University of Massachusetts Dartmouth	M,D,O
University of Memphis	M,D,O
University of Minnesota, Twin Cities Campus	M,D,O
University of Missouri–St. Louis	M
University of Nebraska at Kearney	M
University of Nebraska at Omaha	M,O
University of Nevada, Las Vegas	M,D,O
University of Nevada, Reno	M
University of New Mexico	M,D
The University of North Carolina at Chapel Hill	M
The University of North Carolina at Charlotte	M,D,O
The University of North Carolina at Greensboro	M,D,O
The University of North Carolina Wilmington	M,D,O
University of Northern Colorado	M,D
University of Northern Iowa	M
University of North Florida	M
University of North Texas	M,D,O
University of Pennsylvania	M
University of Phoenix–Online Campus	M,O
University of Phoenix–San Diego Campus	M
University of Phoenix–Southern California Campus	M,O
University of Phoenix–Washington D.C. Campus	M,D,O
University of Pittsburgh	M,D,O
University of Portland	M,D
University of Puerto Rico, Río Piedras Campus	M,D,O
University of St. Francis (IL)	M,D,O
University of St. Thomas (TX)	M,D
University of San Diego	M
University of South Africa	M,D
University of South Carolina	M,D,O
University of Southern California	M
University of Southern Indiana	M
University of Southern Maine	M,O
University of South Florida	M,D,O
The University of Tennessee	M,D,O
The University of Texas at Arlington	M
The University of Texas at El Paso	M,O
The University of Texas at San Antonio	M,D,O
The University of Texas of the Permian Basin	M
The University of Texas Rio Grande Valley	M
University of the Southwest	M
The University of Toledo	M,D,O
University of Washington	M,D
University of Wisconsin–Milwaukee	M,D,O
University of Wisconsin–River Falls	M
Upper Iowa University	M
Utah Valley University	M
Valley City State University	M
Valparaiso University	M,O
Virginia International University	M
Walden University	M,D,O
Washington State University	M,D
Wayland Baptist University	M
Wayne State College	M
Wayne State University	M,D,O
Webster University	M,O
West Chester University of Pennsylvania	M,O
Western Carolina University	M
Western Illinois University	M,O
Western Kentucky University	M
Western New Mexico University	M
West Virginia University	M
Wheaton College	M,O
Wilkes University	M,D
Wilmington University	M,D
Winona State University	M
Worcester State University	M,O

ENGLISH EDUCATION

Alabama Agricultural and Mechanical University	M,O
Alabama State University	M,O
Albany State University	M
Andrews University	M,D,O
Anna Maria College	M
Appalachian State University	M
Arcadia University	M,D,O
Arkansas State University	M,O
Arkansas Tech University	M

Binghamton University, State University of New York	M
Bloomsburg University of Pennsylvania	M
Bob Jones University	M,D,O
Boise State University	M
Brooklyn College of the City University of New York	M
Brown University	M
Buffalo State College, State University of New York	M
California Baptist University	M
California State University, Northridge	M
Caribbean University	M,D
Carthage College	M,O
Chadron State College	M,O
Chatham University	M
The Citadel, The Military College of South Carolina	M,O
City College of the City University of New York	M,O
Clayton State University	M
The College at Brockport, State University of New York	M,O
College of St. Joseph	M
College of Staten Island of the City University of New York	M
The Colorado College	M
Columbus State University	M,O
Converse College	M
Delta State University	M
Duquesne University	M
East Carolina University	M,D,O
Eastern Kentucky University	M
Eastern Michigan University	M
Eastern University	M,D,O
Elms College	M,O
Fitchburg State University	M,O
Florida Agricultural and Mechanical University	M
Florida Atlantic University	M
Florida Gulf Coast University	M
Florida International University	M,D,O
Florida State University	M,D,O
Framingham State University	M
Gardner-Webb University	M
George Mason University	M
Georgia Southern University	M
Georgia Southwestern State University	M,O
Georgia State University	M,D
Grand Valley State University	M
Harding University	M
Hofstra University	M,D,O
Houston Baptist University	M
Hunter College of the City University of New York	M
Indiana University of Pennsylvania	M,D
Indiana University–Purdue University Fort Wayne	M,O
Iona College	M
Ithaca College	M
Jackson State University	M
Kansas State University	M,D,O
Kennesaw State University	M
Kent State University	M,D
Kutztown University of Pennsylvania	M
Lake Forest College	M
Lehman College of the City University of New York	M
Le Moyne College	M
Lewis University	M
Lincoln Memorial University	M,D,O
Lipscomb University	M,D,O
London Metropolitan University	M,D
Manhattanville College	M
Marymount University	M,O
Mississippi College	M,D,O
Missouri State University	M,O
Montclair State University	M,O
Morehead State University	M,O
National Louis University	M,D,O
New Mexico State University	M,D
New York University	M,D,O
North Carolina Agricultural and Technical State University	M
North Carolina State University	M
Northern Arizona University	M,D,O
Northwest Missouri State University	M,O
Oregon State University	M
Plymouth State University	M
Purdue University	M,D,O
Queens College of the City University of New York	M,O
Quinnipiac University	M
Rhode Island College	M
Rider University	O
Rowan University	O
Rutgers University–New Brunswick	M
St. John Fisher College	M
San Francisco State University	M
Simon Fraser University	M,D
Slippery Rock University of Pennsylvania	M
Smith College	M
South Carolina State University	M
Southeastern Louisiana University	M
Southern Illinois University Edwardsville	M,O
Southern New Hampshire University	M,D,O
Southwestern Oklahoma State University	M
State University of New York at New Paltz	M,O
State University of New York at Plattsburgh	M
State University of New York College at Cortland	M
State University of New York College at Geneseo	M

State University of New York College at Old Westbury	M
State University of New York College at Potsdam	M
Stony Brook University, State University of New York	M,D,O
Syracuse University	M
Teachers College, Columbia University	M,D,O
Temple University	M
Trinity Washington University	M
University at Buffalo, the State University of New York	M,D,O
The University of Akron	M
The University of Alabama in Huntsville	M,O
The University of Arizona	M,D
University of Arkansas at Pine Bluff	M
University of Central Florida	M
University of Colorado Denver	M
University of Connecticut	M,D
University of Florida	M,D,O
University of Georgia	M,D
University of Illinois at Springfield	M,O
University of Indianapolis	M
The University of Iowa	M,D
University of Louisiana at Monroe	M,D
University of Manitoba	M
University of Maryland, Baltimore County	M
University of Michigan	D
University of Minnesota, Twin Cities Campus	M
University of Missouri	M,D,O
University of Montana	M
University of New Mexico	M,D
The University of North Carolina at Chapel Hill	M
The University of North Carolina at Greensboro	M,D
The University of North Carolina at Pembroke	M
University of Northern Colorado	M,D
University of Northern Iowa	M
University of North Georgia	M,O
University of Oklahoma	M,D
University of Pennsylvania	M,D
University of Phoenix–Online Campus	M,O
University of Phoenix–Washington D.C. Campus	M,D,O
University of Pittsburgh	M,D
University of Puerto Rico, Mayagüez Campus	M
University of St. Francis (IL)	M,D,O
University of South Carolina	M,D
University of Southern Mississippi	M,D
University of South Florida, St. Petersburg	M
University of South Florida Sarasota-Manatee	M
The University of Tennessee	M,D,O
The University of Texas at El Paso	M,D,O
University of the District of Columbia	M
University of the Sacred Heart	M,O
The University of Toledo	M,D,O
The University of Tulsa	M
University of Victoria	M,D
University of Virginia	M,D,O
University of Washington	M,D
The University of West Alabama	M
University of Wisconsin–La Crosse	M,O
University of Wisconsin–Milwaukee	M
Valdosta State University	M
Valley City State University	M
Vanderbilt University	M
Wagner College	M
Wayland Baptist University	M
Wayne State College	M
Wayne State University	M,D,O
West Chester University of Pennsylvania	M,O
Western Governors University	M,O
Western Kentucky University	M
Western Michigan University	M,D
Western New England University	M
Widener University	M,D
William Carey University	M,O
William Jessup University	M
Worcester State University	M

ENTERTAINMENT MANAGEMENT

Berklee College of Music	M
California Intercontinental University	M
California State University, Northridge	M,O
Carnegie Mellon University	M
Columbia College Chicago	M
Full Sail University	M
Hofstra University	M,O
New York Institute of Technology	M,O
Point Park University	M
Syracuse University	M
Universidad Autonoma de Guadalajara	M,D
University of Colorado Denver	M
University of Dallas	M
University of Massachusetts Amherst	M
University of South Carolina	M
Valparaiso University	M

ENTOMOLOGY

Auburn University	M,D
Clemson University	M,D
Colorado State University	M,D
Cornell University	M,D
Illinois State University	M
Iowa State University of Science and Technology	M,D

Kansas State University	M,D
Louisiana State University and Agricultural & Mechanical College	M,D
McGill University	M,D
Michigan State University	M,D
New Mexico State University	M
North Carolina State University	M,D
North Dakota State University	M,D
The Ohio State University	M,D
Oklahoma State University	M,D
Penn State University Park	M,D
Purdue University	M,D
Rutgers University–New Brunswick	M,D
Simon Fraser University	M,D,O
State University of New York College of Environmental Science and Forestry	M,D
Texas A&M University	M,D
The University of Arizona	M,D
University of Arkansas	M,D
University of California, Davis	M,D
University of California, Riverside	M,D
University of Delaware	M,D
University of Georgia	M,D
University of Guelph	M,D
University of Hawaii at Manoa	M,D
University of Idaho	M,D
University of Illinois at Urbana–Champaign	M,D
The University of Kansas	M,D
University of Kentucky	M,D
University of Maine	M,D
University of Manitoba	M,D
University of Maryland, College Park	M,D
University of Minnesota, Twin Cities Campus	M,D
University of Missouri	M,D
University of Nebraska–Lincoln	M,D
The University of Tennessee	M,D
University of Wisconsin–Madison	M,D
University of Wyoming	M,D
Virginia Polytechnic Institute and State University	M,D
Washington State University	M,D
West Virginia University	M

ENTREPRENEURSHIP

American College of Thessaloniki	M,O
American Public University System	M
American University	M,D,O
Anaheim University	M,D,O
Arizona State University at the Tempe campus	M,D
Azusa Pacific University	M
Babson College	M,O
Bakke Graduate University	M,D
Baldwin Wallace University	M
Baruch College of the City University of New York	M,D
Baylor University	D
Bay Path University	M
Benedictine University	M
Brandeis University	M
Brandman University	M
Brigham Young University	M
Cairn University	M,O
California Baptist University	M
California Intercontinental University	M,D
California Lutheran University	M,O
California State University, East Bay	M
California State University, Fullerton	M
California State University, San Bernardino	M
California University of Pennsylvania	M
Cambridge College	M
Cameron University	M
Capella University	M,D
Carlos Albizu University, Miami Campus	M,D
Carnegie Mellon University	D
City Vision University	M
Clarion University of Pennsylvania	M
Clemson University	M
Cogswell Polytechnical College	M
Columbia University	M
Dallas Baptist University	M
Dartmouth College	D
Delaware Valley University	M
DePaul University	M
Drexel University	M
Duke University	M,O
Eastern Michigan University	M,O
East Tennessee State University	M,O
East Texas Baptist University	M
Emory University	M
Everglades University	M
Fairfield University	M,O
Fairleigh Dickinson University, College at Florham	M,O
Fairleigh Dickinson University, Metropolitan Campus	M,O
Felician University	M,D
Florida Institute of Technology	M
Fordham University	M
Georgia State University	M,D
Grand Canyon University	M
Harrisburg University of Science and Technology	M
Hult International Business School (United States)	M
IGlobal University	M
Illinois Institute of Technology	M
Indiana University–Purdue University Indianapolis	M
International University in Geneva	M,D

The International University of Monaco	M
James Madison University	M
Kansas State University	M,O
Kaplan University, Davenport Campus	M
Lamar University	M
Lehigh University	M
Lenoir-Rhyne University	M
LIM College	M
Lindenwood University	M
Loyola University Chicago	M
Loyola University New Orleans	M
Manhattanville College	M
Marlboro College	M
Marquette University	M,O
McGill University	M,D,O
Mercer University	M
Mercyhurst University	M,O
Monroe College	M
New York University	M,D,O
North Carolina State University	M
Northeastern University	M
Northwestern University	M,D
Notre Dame de Namur University	M
Nova Southeastern University	M,O
Oakland University	M,D
Oklahoma State University	M
Oral Roberts University	M,D
Oregon State University	M
Pace University	M,O
Penn State Great Valley	M
Peru State College	M
Point Loma Nazarene University	M
Pontificia Universidad Catolica Madre y Maestra	
Post University	M
Queen's University at Kingston	M
Regent University	M,D,O
Rensselaer Polytechnic Institute	M
Rochester Institute of Technology	M
Rockhurst University	M,O
Rollins College	M,D
Salve Regina University	M
Samford University	M
San Diego State University	M
San Francisco State University	M
Seton Hall University	M,O
Seton Hill University	M,O
Sonoma State University	M
South Carolina State University	M
Southeastern University (FL)	M
Southeast Missouri State University	M
Southern Methodist University	M
Southern New Hampshire University	M,O
South University (GA)	M
Stevens Institute of Technology	M,O
Stratford University (VA)	M
Suffolk University	M
Syracuse University	M
Temple University	M,D
Texas A&M University	M
Tufts University	M
Tulane University	M,D
United States International University–Africa	M
Université Laval	M,O
University at Albany, State University of New York	M
The University of Alabama in Huntsville	M,O
University of Arkansas at Little Rock	O
University of Baltimore	M
University of Bridgeport	M
University of Central Florida	M,O
University of Chicago	M,O
University of Colorado Denver	M
University of Delaware	M,D
University of Florida	M,D,O
University of Hawaii at Manoa	M,O
University of Houston–Victoria	M
University of Idaho	D
University of Louisville	M,D
The University of Manchester	M
University of Massachusetts Amherst	M,D
University of Massachusetts Lowell	M,D
University of Minnesota, Twin Cities Campus	D
University of New Brunswick Fredericton	M
University of New Mexico	M
University of Notre Dame	M
University of Oklahoma	M,D
University of Pennsylvania	M
University of Portland	M
University of Rhode Island	M,D
University of Rochester	M
University of San Francisco	M
University of Sioux Falls	M
University of Southern California	M
University of South Florida	M,O
The University of Tampa	M
The University of Texas at Austin	M
The University of Texas at Dallas	M,D
University of Washington	M,D
University of Waterloo	M,D
The University of Western Ontario	M,D
Ursuline College	M
Virginia International University	M,O
Walden University	M,D,O
Washington University in St. Louis	M
Wayne State University	M,D,O
West Chester University of Pennsylvania	M,O
Western Carolina University	M
Wichita State University	M
Wilkes University	M
Wingate University	M

ENVIRONMENTAL AND OCCUPATIONAL HEALTH

American University of Beirut	M
Augusta University	M
Boise State University	M,O
Boston University	M,D
California State University, Northridge	M
Capella University	M,D
Clemson University	M
Colorado State University	M,D
Columbia Southern University	M
Columbia University	M,D
Duke University	O
East Carolina University	M,D
Eastern Kentucky University	M
East Tennessee State University	M,D,O
Embry-Riddle Aeronautical University–Worldwide	M
Emory University	M,D
Florida International University	M,D
Fort Valley State University	M
Gannon University	M
The George Washington University	D
Georgia Southern University	M,D,O
Harvard University	M,D
Indiana State University	M
Indiana University Bloomington	M,D
Indiana University of Pennsylvania	M,D
Indiana University–Purdue University Indianapolis	M,D,O
Keene State College	M,O
Kent State University	M,D
Lewis University	M
Loma Linda University	M
Louisiana State University Health Sciences Center	M,D
McGill University	M,D,O
Meharry Medical College	M
Mercer University	M,D
Murray State University	M
New York Medical College	M,D,O
New York University	M,D
North Carolina Agricultural and Technical State University	M
Northeastern State University	M
Oakland University	M
Old Dominion University	M
Oregon State University	M,D
Purdue University	M,D
Rochester Institute of Technology	M
Rutgers University–New Brunswick	M,D,O
San Diego State University	M,D
Southeastern Oklahoma State University	M
Syracuse University	O
Temple University	M,D
Towson University	D
Trident University International	M,D,O
Tufts University	M,D
Tulane University	M,D
Uniformed Services University of the Health Sciences	M,D
Universidad Autonoma de Guadalajara	M,D
Universidad de Ciencias Medicas	M,D,O
Université de Montréal	M
Université du Québec à Montréal	O
Université Laval	O
University at Albany, State University of New York	M,D
The University of Alabama at Birmingham	M,D
University of Alberta	M,D
University of Arkansas for Medical Sciences	M,D,O
University of California, Berkeley	M,D
University of California, Irvine	M,D
University of California, Los Angeles	M,D
University of Central Missouri	M,D,O
University of Cincinnati	M,D
University of Colorado Denver	M,D
University of Connecticut	O
University of Florida	M,D,O
University of Georgia	M,D
University of Illinois at Chicago	M,D
University of Illinois at Springfield	M,O
The University of Iowa	M,D,O
University of Maryland, College Park	M
University of Massachusetts Amherst	M,D
University of Memphis	M,D
University of Miami	M
University of Michigan	M,D
University of Minnesota, Twin Cities Campus	M,D,O
University of Nebraska Medical Center	D
University of Nevada, Reno	M,D
University of New Haven	M,O
The University of North Carolina at Chapel Hill	M,D
University of Oklahoma Health Sciences Center	M,D
University of Pennsylvania	M
University of Pittsburgh	M,D
University of Puerto Rico, Medical Sciences Campus	M,D
University of Saint Francis (IN)	M
University of South Alabama	M
University of South Carolina	M,D
University of Southern California	M
University of South Florida	M,D,O
The University of Texas at Tyler	M
University of the Sacred Heart	M
The University of Toledo	M,O
University of Toronto	M,D
University of Washington	M,D
University of Wisconsin–Milwaukee	M,D,O
University of Wisconsin–Whitewater	M
West Virginia University	D
Yale University	M,D

ENVIRONMENTAL BIOLOGY

Baylor University	M,D
Chatham University	M
Dalhousie University	M
Emporia State University	M
Georgia State University	M,D
Hampton University	M
Hood College	M
Massachusetts Institute of Technology	M,D,O
Missouri University of Science and Technology	M
Morgan State University	D
Nicholls State University	M
Ohio University	M,D
Oregon State University	M,D
Regis University	M
Rutgers University–New Brunswick	M,D
Sonoma State University	M
State University of New York College of Environmental Science and Forestry	M,D
Universidad del Turabo	M,D
University of Alberta	M,D
University of California, Santa Cruz	M,D
University of Guelph	M,D
University of Louisiana at Lafayette	M,D
University of Louisville	M,D
The University of Manchester	M,D
University of Massachusetts Amherst	M,D
University of Southern California	M,D
University of Southern Mississippi	M,D
University of South Florida	M,D
University of Wisconsin–Madison	M,D
Washington University in St. Louis	D
West Virginia University	M,D
Youngstown State University	M

ENVIRONMENTAL DESIGN

Arizona State University at the Tempe campus	D
ArtCenter College of Design	M
Bastyr University	M,O
Clemson University	D
Columbia University	M
Cornell University	M
Kansas State University	D
Kent State University	M
Michigan State University	M,D
San Diego State University	M
Texas Tech University	M,D
Université de Montréal	M,D,O
University of Calgary	M,D
University of California, Berkeley	M,D
University of California, Irvine	D
University of Georgia	M
The University of Manchester	M,D
Virginia Polytechnic Institute and State University	M,D,O
Yale University	M,D

ENVIRONMENTAL EDUCATION

Alaska Pacific University	M
Antioch University New England	M
Arcadia University	M,D,O
Ball State University	M,O
Brooklyn College of the City University of New York	M
Chatham University	M
Concordia University (United States)	M,D
Concordia University Wisconsin	M
Florida Atlantic University	M
Florida Institute of Technology	M
Goshen College	M
Hamline University	M,D
Instituto Tecnologico de Santo Domingo	M,D,O
Montclair State University	M
New York University	M
Oregon State University	M,D
Prescott College	M,D
Royal Roads University	M,O
Slippery Rock University of Pennsylvania	M
Southern Connecticut State University	M,O
Southern Oregon University	M
State University of New York College at Cortland	M
Université du Québec à Montréal	M,D,O
University of Colorado Denver	M
University of Florida	M,D,O
University of South Africa	M,D
University of Victoria	M,D
Western Washington University	M
West Virginia University	M,D

ENVIRONMENTAL ENGINEERING

Air Force Institute of Technology	M,D
The American University in Cairo	M,D,O
Arizona State University at the Tempe campus	M,D
California Institute of Technology	M,D
California Polytechnic State University, San Luis Obispo	M
California State University, Fullerton	M
Carleton University	M,D
Carnegie Mellon University	M,D
The Catholic University of America	M,D
Clarkson University	M,D
Clemson University	M,D
Cleveland State University	M,D
Colorado School of Mines	M,D
Columbia University	M,D
Concordia University (Canada)	M,D,O
Cornell University	M,D
Dalhousie University	M,D
Dartmouth College	M,D
Drexel University	M,D
Duke University	M,D
École Polytechnique de Montréal	M,D,O
Florida Atlantic University	M
Florida International University	M,D
Florida State University	M,D
Gannon University	M
The George Washington University	M,D,O
Georgia Institute of Technology	M
Harvard University	M,D
Idaho State University	M
Illinois Institute of Technology	M,D
Instituto Tecnologico de Santo Domingo	M,O
Instituto Tecnológico y de Estudios Superiores de Monterrey, Campus Ciudad de México	M,D
Instituto Tecnológico y de Estudios Superiores de Monterrey, Campus Monterrey	M,D
Iowa State University of Science and Technology	M,D
Jackson State University	M,D
Johns Hopkins University	M,O
Kansas State University	M,D
Lakehead University	M
Lamar University	M,D
Lehigh University	M,D
Louisiana State University and Agricultural & Mechanical College	M
Manhattan College	M
Marquette University	M,D,O
Marshall University	M
Massachusetts Institute of Technology	M,D,O
McGill University	M,D
Memorial University of Newfoundland	M
Mercer University	M
Michigan State University	M,D
Michigan Technological University	M,D,O
Missouri University of Science and Technology	M,D
Montana State University	M
Montana Tech of The University of Montana	M
New Jersey Institute of Technology	M,D
New Mexico Institute of Mining and Technology	M
New Mexico State University	M,D
New York Institute of Technology	M
New York University	M
North Dakota State University	M,D
Northeastern University	M,D,O
Northern Arizona University	M
Northwestern University	M,D
Norwich University	M
Ohio University	M,D
Oklahoma State University	M,D
Old Dominion University	M,D
Oregon Health & Science University	M,D
Oregon State University	M,D
Penn State Harrisburg	M,O
Penn State University Park	M,D
Polytechnic University of Puerto Rico, Miami Campus	M
Polytechnic University of Puerto Rico, Orlando Campus	
Portland State University	M,D
Princeton University	M,D
Purdue University	M,D
Rensselaer Polytechnic Institute	M,D
Rice University	M,D
Rose-Hulman Institute of Technology	M
Royal Military College of Canada	M,D
Rutgers University–New Brunswick	M,D
Southern Illinois University Carbondale	D
Southern Illinois University Edwardsville	M
Southern Methodist University	M,D
Stanford University	M,D,O
State University of New York College of Environmental Science and Forestry	M,D
Stevens Institute of Technology	M,D,O
Syracuse University	M
Temple University	M,D,O
Tennessee State University	M,D
Texas A&M University–Kingsville	M,D
Texas Tech University	M,D
Tufts University	M,D
Universidad Central del Este	M
Universidad Nacional Pedro Henriquez Urena	M
Université de Sherbrooke	M
Université Laval	M,D
University at Buffalo, the State University of New York	M,D
The University of Alabama	M,D

M—masters degree; D—doctorate; O—other advanced degree; *—Close-Up and/or Display

The University of Alabama in Huntsville	M,D	Baylor University	M	Tropical Agriculture Research and Higher Education Center	M,D	California State University, Northridge	M
University of Alaska Anchorage	M	Bemidji State University	M	Troy University	M	California State University, San Bernardino	M
University of Alaska Fairbanks	M,D,O	Binghamton University, State University of New York	M,D	Tufts University	M,D,O	Carnegie Mellon University	D
University of Alberta	M,D	Boston University	M	Universidad Autonoma de Guadalajara	M,D	Christopher Newport University	M
The University of Arizona	M,D	California State University, Fullerton	M	Universidad del Turabo	M,D	Clarkson University	M
University of Arkansas	M	Central European University	M,D	Universidad Metropolitana	M	Clark University	M
University of Calgary	M,D	The Citadel, The Military College of South Carolina	M,O	Université de Montréal	O	Clemson University	M,D
University of California, Berkeley	M,D	Clarkson University	M	Université du Québec à Chicoutimi	M	Cleveland State University	M,D
University of California, Davis	M,D,O	Clark University	M	Université du Québec, Institut National de la Recherche Scientifique	M,D	The College at Brockport, State University of New York	M
University of California, Irvine	M,D	Clemson University	M,D	Université Laval	M,D,O	College of Charleston	M
University of California, Los Angeles	M,D	Cleveland State University	M,O	University of Alaska Fairbanks	M	College of Staten Island of the City University of New York	M,D
University of California, Merced	M,D	College of the Atlantic	M	University of Alberta	M,D	The College of William and Mary	M,D
University of California, Riverside	M,D	Colorado State University	M,D	The University of Arizona	M,D	Columbia University	M,D
University of Central Florida	M,D	Columbia University	M	The University of British Columbia	M,D	Columbus State University	M,O
University of Cincinnati	M,D	Columbus State University	M	University of Calgary	M,D,O	Cornell University	M,D
University of Colorado Boulder	M,D	Concordia University (Canada)	M,D,O	University of California, Berkeley	M,D,O	Dalhousie University	M
University of Colorado Denver	M,D	Cornell University	M,D	University of California, San Diego	M	Drexel University	M,D
University of Connecticut	M,D	Dalhousie University	M	University of California, Santa Barbara	M,D	Duke University	M,D
University of Dayton	M	Drexel University	M,D	University of California, Santa Cruz	D	Duquesne University	M,O
University of Delaware	M,D	Duke University	M,D	University of Central Missouri	M,D,O	Florida Agricultural and Mechanical University	M,D
University of Detroit Mercy	M,D	Duquesne University	M,O	University of Chicago	M	Florida Gulf Coast University	M
University of Florida	M,D,O	The Evergreen State College	M	University of Colorado Boulder	M,D	Florida Institute of Technology	M,D
University of Georgia	M	Florida Gulf Coast University	M	University of Colorado Denver	M,D	Florida State University	M,D
University of Guelph	M,D	Florida Institute of Technology	M	University of Dayton	M,D	Gannon University	M
University of Hawaii at Manoa	M,D	Florida International University	M,D	University of Delaware	M,D	George Mason University	M,D
University of Illinois at Urbana–Champaign	M,D	Florida State University	M,D	University of Denver	M,O	Georgia Southern University	O
The University of Iowa	M,D	George Mason University	M,D	The University of Findlay	M,D	The Graduate Center, City University of New York	D
The University of Kansas	M,D	The George Washington University	M	University of Guelph	M,D	Harvard University	M,D
University of Louisville	M,D,O	Georgia Institute of Technology	M,D	University of Hawaii at Manoa	M,D,O	Howard University	M,D
The University of Manchester	M	Georgia State University	M,D,O	University of Houston–Clear Lake	M	Humboldt State University	M
University of Maryland, Baltimore County	M,D	Goucher College	M	University of Illinois at Springfield	M	Idaho State University	M,O
University of Maryland, College Park	M,D	Green Mountain College	M	University of Maine	D	Indiana University Bloomington	M,D,O
University of Massachusetts Amherst	M,D	Hardin-Simmons University	M	The University of Manchester	M,D	Instituto Tecnologico de Santo Domingo	M,D,O
University of Massachusetts Lowell	M,D	Harvard University	M,O	University of Maryland, Baltimore County	M,D	Instituto Tecnológico y de Estudios Superiores de Monterrey, Campus Ciudad de México	M,D
University of Memphis	M,D,O	Humboldt State University	M	University of Maryland Eastern Shore	M,D	Inter American University of Puerto Rico, San Germán Campus	M
University of Michigan	M,D,O	Idaho State University	M	University of Maryland University College	M	Iowa State University of Science and Technology	M,D
University of Missouri	M,D	Illinois Institute of Technology	M	University of Massachusetts Amherst	M,D	Jackson State University	M
University of Nebraska–Lincoln	M,D	Indiana University Bloomington	M,D,O	University of Massachusetts Dartmouth	M,O	Johns Hopkins University	M,O
University of Nevada, Las Vegas	M,D	Indiana University Northwest	M,O	University of Michigan	M,D	Kansas State University	M,D,O
University of New Brunswick Fredericton	M,D	Indiana University of Pennsylvania	M	University of Minnesota, Twin Cities Campus	M	Laurentian University	M
University of New Hampshire	M,D	Instituto Tecnologico de Santo Domingo	M,D,O	University of Montana	M	Lehigh University	M
University of New Haven	M	Instituto Tecnológico y de Estudios Superiores de Monterrey, Campus Estado de México	M,D	University of Nevada, Reno	M	Lincoln University (MO)	M
The University of North Carolina at Chapel Hill	M,D	Instituto Tecnológico y de Estudios Superiores de Monterrey, Campus Irapuato	M,D	University of New Brunswick Fredericton	M,D	Louisiana State University and Agricultural & Mechanical College	M,D
The University of North Carolina at Charlotte	M,D	Inter American University of Puerto Rico, Metropolitan Campus	M	University of New Hampshire	M,D	Loyola Marymount University	M
University of North Dakota	M,D	James Madison University	M	University of New Haven	M,O	Marshall University	M
University of Notre Dame	M,D	Johns Hopkins University	M,O	University of New Mexico	M	Massachusetts Institute of Technology	M,D,O
University of Oklahoma	M,D	Kentucky State University	M	The University of North Carolina Wilmington	M	McNeese State University	M
University of Pittsburgh	M,D	Lake Forest College	M	University of Northern British Columbia	M,D,O	Memorial University of Newfoundland	M,D
University of Puerto Rico, Mayagüez Campus	M,D	Lamar University	M,D	University of Oregon	M,D	Mercer University	M
University of Regina	M,D	Lehigh University	M,O	University of Pennsylvania	M	Miami University	M
University of Rhode Island	M,D	Long Island University–LIU Post	M,O	University of Puerto Rico, Río Piedras Campus	M	Michigan State University	M,D
University of South Alabama	M	Louisiana State University and Agricultural & Mechanical College	M,D	University of Rhode Island	M,D	Minnesota State University Mankato	M
University of Southern California	M,D,O	McGill University	M	University of Rochester	M	Montana State University	M,D
University of South Florida	M,D	Michigan Technological University	M,D	University of South Africa	M,D	Montclair State University	M
The University of Tennessee	M	Middlebury Institute of International Studies at Monterey	M	University of South Alabama	M,D	Murray State University	M
The University of Texas at Austin	M,D	Millersville University of Pennsylvania	M	University of South Carolina	M	New Jersey Institute of Technology	M,D,O
The University of Texas at El Paso	M,D,O	Missouri State University	M,O	University of South Florida	M,D,O	New Mexico State University	M,D
The University of Texas at San Antonio	M,D	Montclair State University	M,D	University of South Florida, St. Petersburg	M	New York University	M
The University of Texas at Tyler	M	Morehead State University	M	The University of Tennessee	M,D	North Carolina Agricultural and Technical State University	M
University of Utah	M,D	New Jersey Institute of Technology	M,D,O	The University of Texas at Austin	M	North Dakota State University	M,D
University of Vermont	M,D	The New School	M,O	University of Washington	M,D	Northern Arizona University	M,D
University of Washington	M,D	New York Institute of Technology	M,O	University of Waterloo	M,D	Nova Southeastern University	M,D
University of Waterloo	M,D	New York University	M,O	University of Wisconsin–Green Bay	M	Oakland University	M,D
The University of Western Ontario	M,D	Northeastern Illinois University	M	Utah State University	M,D	The Ohio State University	M,D
University of Windsor	M,D	Northeastern State University	M	Vanderbilt University	M,D	Oklahoma State University	M,D,O
University of Wisconsin–Madison	M,D	Northern Arizona University	M,D	Vermont Law School	M	Old Dominion University	M,D
University of Wyoming	M	The Ohio State University	M,D	Virginia Commonwealth University	M	Oregon Health & Science University	M,D
Utah State University	M,D,O	Ohio University	M,O	Virginia Polytechnic Institute and State University	M,D,O	Oregon State University	M,D
Vanderbilt University	M,D	Oregon State University	M,D	Webster University	M	Pace University	M
Villanova University	M,O	Pace University	M	Wesley College	M	Penn State Harrisburg	M,O
Virginia Polytechnic Institute and State University	M,D,O	Penn State University Park	M	Western State Colorado University	M	Penn State University Park	M
Washington State University	M	Plymouth State University	M	West Virginia University	M,D	Pontifical Catholic University of Puerto Rico	M
Washington University in St. Louis	M,D	Point Park University	M	Wilfrid Laurier University	M,D	Portland State University	M,D
Worcester Polytechnic Institute	M,D,O	Polytechnic University of Puerto Rico	M	Wilmington University	M,D	Queens College of the City University of New York	M
Yale University	M,D	Polytechnic University of Puerto Rico, Miami Campus	M	Yale University	M,D	Rice University	M,D
Youngstown State University	M	Polytechnic University of Puerto Rico, Orlando Campus	M	York University	M,D	Rochester Institute of Technology	M
		Portland State University	M,D	Youngstown State University	M,O	Royal Military College of Canada	M,D
ENVIRONMENTAL LAW		Prescott College	M			Rutgers University–Newark	M,D
Chapman University	M,D	Purdue University	M,D	**ENVIRONMENTAL SCIENCES**		Rutgers University–New Brunswick	M,D
Florida State University	M,D	Rice University	M	Adelphi University	M	Sitting Bull College	M
Georgetown University	M,D	Royal Roads University	M,O	Alaska Pacific University	M	South Dakota School of Mines and Technology	D
Golden Gate University	M,D	St. Cloud State University	M	American University	M,O	Southeast Missouri State University	M
Lehigh University	M,O	St. Edward's University	M	American University of Beirut	M,D	Southern Connecticut State University	M,O
Lewis & Clark College	M,D	Samford University	M	Antioch University New England	M,D	Southern Illinois University Carbondale	D
Montclair State University	O	San Francisco State University	M	Arizona State University at the Tempe campus	M,D,O	Southern Illinois University Edwardsville	M
Pace University	M,D	San Jose State University	M,O	Arkansas State University	M,D	Southern Methodist University	M,D
Stanford University	M,D	Shippensburg University of Pennsylvania	M	Ball State University	D	Southern University and Agricultural and Mechanical College	M
University of Calgary	M,O	Simon Fraser University	M,D,O	Baylor University	D	Stanford University	M,D,O
University of Colorado Denver	M,D	Slippery Rock University of Pennsylvania	M	Binghamton University, State University of New York	M,D	State University of New York College of Environmental Science and Forestry	M,D
University of Florida	M,D	Southeast Missouri State University	M	Boston University	M,D	Stephen F. Austin State University	M
University of Houston	M,D	Southern Illinois University Carbondale	M,D	Brigham Young University	M,D	Stockton University	M
University of Idaho	D	Southern Illinois University Edwardsville	M	Bryant University	M,O	Tarleton State University	M
University of Pittsburgh	M	Southern New Hampshire University	M,O	California Institute of Technology	M,D	Tennessee Technological University	D
The University of Tulsa	M,D,O	State University of New York College of Environmental Science and Forestry	M,D	California State Polytechnic University, Pomona	M	Texas A&M University–Commerce	M,O
Vermont Law School	M	Stony Brook University, State University of New York	M,O	California State University, Chico	M	Texas A&M University–Corpus Christi	M
Western Michigan University Thomas M. Cooley Law School	M,D	Tennessee Technological University	M	California State University, East Bay	M	Texas Christian University	M
		Texas Southern University	M,D			Texas Tech University	M,D
ENVIRONMENTAL MANAGEMENT AND POLICY		Texas Tech University	M,D				
Adelphi University	M	Thomas Edison State University	M				
Air Force Institute of Technology	M	Towson University	M				
American Public University System	M	Trent University	M,D				
American University	M,D,O						
American University of Beirut	M,D						
Antioch University New England	M,D						
Arizona State University at the Tempe campus	M						
Ball State University	M,O						
Bard College	M,O						

Thompson Rivers University	M,O
Towson University	M,D
Tufts University	M
Tuskegee University	M,D
Universidad del Turabo	
Universidad Nacional Pedro Henriquez Urena	M
Université de Sherbrooke	M,O
Université du Québec à Montréal	M,D,O
Université du Québec à Trois-Rivières	M,D
Université du Québec en Abitibi-Témiscamingue	M,D
Université Laval	M,D
University at Buffalo, the State University of New York	M,D
University of Alaska Anchorage	M
University of Alberta	M,D,O
The University of Arizona	M,D,O
University of California, Berkeley	M,D
University of California, Davis	M,D
University of California, Los Angeles	M,D
University of California, Riverside	M
University of California, Santa Barbara	M,D
University of Chicago	M
University of Cincinnati	M,D
University of Colorado Colorado Springs	M
University of Colorado Denver	M
University of Guam	M,D
University of Guelph	M,D
University of Hawaii at Hilo	M
University of Houston–Clear Lake	M
University of Idaho	M,D
University of Illinois at Springfield	M
University of Illinois at Urbana–Champaign	M,D
The University of Kansas	M,D
University of Lethbridge	M,D
The University of Manchester	M,D
University of Manitoba	M,D
University of Maryland, Baltimore	M,D
University of Maryland, Baltimore County	M,D
University of Maryland, College Park	M,D
University of Maryland Eastern Shore	M,D
University of Massachusetts Boston	M,D
University of Massachusetts Lowell	M,D
University of Michigan	M,D
University of Michigan–Dearborn	
University of Missouri	M,D,O
University of Montana	M
University of Nevada, Reno	M,D
University of New Hampshire	D,O
University of New Haven	M,O
University of New Orleans	M
The University of North Carolina at Chapel Hill	M,D
University of North Texas	M,D,O
University of Oklahoma	M,D
University of Pennsylvania	M,D
University of Pittsburgh	M,D
University of Prince Edward Island	M,D
University of Puerto Rico, Mayagüez Campus	M,D
University of Puerto Rico, Río Piedras Campus	M,D
University of Rhode Island	M,D
University of Saskatchewan	M
University of South Africa	M,D
University of South Florida	M,D
University of South Florida, St. Petersburg	M
The University of Tennessee at Chattanooga	M
The University of Texas at Arlington	M,D
The University of Texas at El Paso	M,D
The University of Texas at San Antonio	M,D
University of the Virgin Islands	M
The University of Toledo	M,D
University of Toronto	M,D
University of Utah	M
University of Virginia	M,D
University of Waterloo	M,D
The University of Western Ontario	M,D
University of West Florida	M
University of Windsor	M,D
University of Wisconsin–Green Bay	M
University of Wisconsin–Milwaukee	M,D
Vanderbilt University	M
Virginia Polytechnic Institute and State University	M,D,O
Washington State University	M,D
Wesleyan University	M
Western Connecticut State University	M
Western Illinois University	D
Western Washington University	M
West Texas A&M University	M
Wichita State University	M
Wilfrid Laurier University	M
Wright State University	D
Yale University	M,D

EPIDEMIOLOGY

American University of Beirut	M
Boston University	M,D
Brown University	M,D
Capella University	D
Case Western Reserve University	M,D
Colorado State University	M,D
Columbia University	M,D
Cornell University	M,D
Daemen College	M
Dalhousie University	M
Drexel University	M,D,O
East Tennessee State University	M,D
Emory University	M,D
Florida International University	M,O
George Mason University	M,O
Georgetown University	M
The George Washington University	M
Georgia Southern University	M,D
Harvard University	M,D
Indiana University Bloomington	M,D
Indiana University–Purdue University Indianapolis	M,D,O
Johns Hopkins University	M,D
Kent State University	M,D
Loma Linda University	M,D
Louisiana State University Health Sciences Center	M,D
McGill University	M,D,O
Medical University of South Carolina	M,D
Memorial University of Newfoundland	M,D
Michigan State University	M,D
Monroe College	M
New York Medical College	M,D,O
New York University	M,D
North Carolina State University	M,D
Northwestern University	D
Oregon State University	M,D
Ponce Health Sciences University	M,D
Purdue University	M,D
Queen's University at Kingston	M,D
Rutgers University–Newark	M,O
Rutgers University–New Brunswick	M,D,O
San Diego State University	M,D
Stanford University	M,D
Temple University	M,D
Tufts University	M,D,O
Tulane University	M,D
Université Laval	M,D
University at Albany, State University of New York	M,D
University at Buffalo, the State University of New York	M,D
The University of Alabama at Birmingham	M,D
University of Alberta	M,D
The University of Arizona	M,D
University of Arkansas for Medical Sciences	M,D,O
University of California, Berkeley	M,D
University of California, Davis	M,D
University of California, Irvine	M,D
University of California, Los Angeles	M,D
University of California, San Diego	D
University of Cincinnati	M,D
University of Colorado Denver	M,D
University of Florida	M,D,O
University of Guelph	M,D
University of Hawaii at Manoa	D
University of Illinois at Chicago	M,D
University of Illinois at Springfield	M,O
The University of Iowa	M,D
The University of Kansas	M
University of Kentucky	D
University of Louisville	M,D
University of Maryland, Baltimore	M,D,O
University of Maryland, Baltimore County	M,D,O
University of Maryland, College Park	M,D
University of Massachusetts Amherst	M,D
University of Memphis	M,D
University of Miami	M,D
University of Michigan	M,D
University of Minnesota, Twin Cities Campus	M,D
University of Nebraska Medical Center	D
University of New Mexico	M
The University of North Carolina at Chapel Hill	M,D
University of North Texas Health Science Center at Fort Worth	M,D,O
University of Oklahoma Health Sciences Center	M
University of Ottawa	M
University of Pennsylvania	M
University of Pittsburgh	M,D
University of Prince Edward Island	M,D
University of Puerto Rico, Medical Sciences Campus	M
University of Rochester	D
University of Saskatchewan	M
University of South Carolina	M,D
University of Southern California	M,D
University of Southern Mississippi	M
University of South Florida	M,D,O
The University of Tennessee Health Science Center	M,D
The University of Toledo	M,O
University of Toronto	M,D
University of Washington	M,D
The University of Western Ontario	M,D
University of Wisconsin–Madison	M,D
University of Wisconsin–Milwaukee	M,D
Walden University	M,D,O
Washington University in St. Louis	M,D
Weill Cornell Medicine	M
Yale University	M

ERGONOMICS AND HUMAN FACTORS

Arizona State University at the Tempe campus	M
Bentley University	M
California State University, Long Beach	M
The Catholic University of America	D
Clemson University	D
Colorado State University	M
Cornell University	M
Embry-Riddle Aeronautical University–Daytona	M,D
Florida Institute of Technology	M,D
Georgia Institute of Technology	M,D
Indiana University Bloomington	M,D
Michigan Technological University	M,D,O
Mississippi State University	M,D
Missouri Western State University	M
New York University	M,D
North Carolina State University	D
Old Dominion University	D
Purdue University	M,D
Tufts University	M,D
Université de Montréal	O
Université du Québec à Montréal	O
The University of Alabama	M
University of Cincinnati	M,D
The University of Iowa	M,D,O
University of Miami	M
University of Wisconsin–Madison	M,D
University of Wisconsin–Milwaukee	M
Wright State University	M,D

ETHICS

American University	M,D,O
Anabaptist Mennonite Biblical Seminary	M,O
Arizona State University at the Tempe campus	M,D
Azusa Pacific University	M
Boston University	M,D
Chicago Theological Seminary	M,D
Claremont Graduate University	M,D
Claremont Lincoln University	M
Claremont School of Theology	M,D
Columbia University	M,D
Duke University	M,O
Emory University	M,D
Fordham University	M,D
Freed-Hardeman University	M
George Mason University	M
Georgetown University	M,D
Graduate Theological Union	M,D,O
John Brown University	M
Kennesaw State University	O
Lancaster Theological Seminary	M,D,O
Lebanon Valley College	M
Lee University	M
Loyola University Chicago	M
Lutheran Theological Seminary Saskatoon	M,D
Marquette University	M,D
New England College of Business and Finance	M
Northwestern University	M
Oregon State University	M
Phillips Theological Seminary	M,D
Pontifical John Paul II Institute for Studies on Marriage and Family	M,D,O
Santa Clara University	M,D,O
Schreiner University	M
Southeastern Baptist Theological Seminary	M,D
Southern Methodist University	M,O
Southern New Hampshire University	M,O
Spring Hill College	M,O
Stevens Institute of Technology	M,O
Suffolk University	M,O
Texas State University	M
Université de Sherbrooke	M,D,O
Université du Québec à Chicoutimi	O
Université du Québec à Rimouski	M,O
Université Laval	O
University of Baltimore	M
University of Chicago	D
University of Detroit Mercy	M
University of Maryland, Baltimore	O
The University of North Carolina at Charlotte	M,O
University of North Florida	M,O
University of Pennsylvania	M,D
University of St. Thomas (MN)	M,D
University of South Africa	M,D
The University of Tennessee at Chattanooga	M,D
Valparaiso University	M,O
Viterbo University	M,O
West Chester University of Pennsylvania	M
Xavier University	M

ETHNIC STUDIES

Colorado State University	M
Cornell University	M,D
Minnesota State University Mankato	M
Northern Arizona University	O
San Francisco State University	M
United Theological Seminary of the Twin Cities	M,D,O
Université Laval	M,D
The University of British Columbia	M,D
University of California, Berkeley	D
University of California, Riverside	D
University of California, San Diego	D
University of Colorado Boulder	D
University of New Mexico	M,D

EVOLUTIONARY BIOLOGY

Arizona State University at the Tempe campus	M,D
Brown University	D
Columbia University	M,D
Cornell University	D
Dartmouth College	D
Emory University	D
Florida State University	M,D
Harvard University	D
Illinois State University	M,D
Indiana State University	M,D
Indiana University Bloomington	M,D
Iowa State University of Science and Technology	M,D
Johns Hopkins University	D
Michigan State University	D
Montclair State University	M
Northeastern University	M,D
The Ohio State University	M,D
Ohio University	M,D
Oklahoma State University	M,D
Oregon State University	M,D
Princeton University	D
Purdue University	M,D
Rice University	M,D
Rutgers University–New Brunswick	M,D
Sonoma State University	M
Stony Brook University, State University of New York	M,D
Tulane University	M,D
University at Buffalo, the State University of New York	M,D,O
University of Alberta	M,D
The University of Arizona	M,D
University of California, Davis	D
University of California, Irvine	M,D
University of California, Los Angeles	M,D
University of California, Riverside	M,D
University of California, Santa Barbara	M,D
University of California, Santa Cruz	M,D
University of Chicago	D
University of Colorado Boulder	M,D
University of Colorado Denver	M,D
University of Delaware	M,D
University of Denver	M,D
University of Guelph	M,D
University of Illinois at Urbana–Champaign	M,D
The University of Iowa	M,D
The University of Kansas	M,D
University of Louisiana at Lafayette	M,D
The University of Manchester	M,D
University of Maryland, College Park	M,D
University of Massachusetts Amherst	M,D
University of Miami	M,D
University of Michigan	M,D
University of Minnesota, Twin Cities Campus	M,D
University of Missouri	M,D
University of Nevada, Reno	D
University of New Hampshire	D
The University of North Carolina at Chapel Hill	M,D
University of Notre Dame	M,D
University of Oklahoma	D
University of Oregon	M,D
University of Pittsburgh	D
University of Puerto Rico, Río Piedras Campus	M,D
University of South Carolina	M,D
University of Southern California	D
University of South Florida	M,D
The University of Tennessee	M,D
The University of Texas at Austin	D
University of Toronto	M,D
University of Wisconsin–Milwaukee	M,D
Washington University in St. Louis	M,D
Wayne State University	M,D
Wesleyan University	M,D
West Virginia University	M,D
Yale University	M,D

EXERCISE AND SPORTS SCIENCE

American International College	M,D
American Public University System	M
Appalachian State University	M
Arizona State University at the Tempe campus	M,D
Arkansas State University	M,O
Armstrong State University	M,O
Ashland University	M
Auburn University	M,D,O
Auburn University at Montgomery	M,O
Austin Peay State University	M
Ball State University	M,D
Barry University	M
Benedictine University	M
Bloomsburg University of Pennsylvania	M
Brigham Young University	M
Brooklyn College of the City University of New York	M
California Baptist University	M

*M—masters degree; D—doctorate; O—other advanced degree; *—Close-Up and/or Display*

California State University, Fresno — M
California State University, Long Beach — M
California University of Pennsylvania — M
Central Connecticut State University — M,O
Central Michigan University — M,D
Central Washington University — M
The Citadel, The Military College of South Carolina — M,O
College of Saint Elizabeth — M,O
The College of St. Scholastica — M
Colorado State University — M,D
Columbus State University — M
Concordia University (Canada) — M
Concordia University Chicago — M
Concordia University, St. Paul — M,D
Delaware State University — M
Delta State University — M
East Carolina University — M,D,O
Eastern Illinois University — M
Eastern Kentucky University — M
Eastern Michigan University — M
Eastern New Mexico University — M
Eastern Washington University — M
East Tennessee State University — M,D
Fairmont State University — M
Florida Atlantic University — M
Florida State University — M,D
Gannon University — M
Gardner-Webb University — M
George Mason University — M,O
The George Washington University — M
Georgia College & State University — M
Georgia State University — M
Hofstra University — M
Howard University — M
Indiana University Bloomington — M,D
Indiana University of Pennsylvania — M
Inter American University of Puerto Rico, Metropolitan Campus — M
Iowa State University of Science and Technology — M
Ithaca College — M
James Madison University — M
Kean University — M
Kennesaw State University — M
Kent State University — M,D
Lakehead University — M
Life University — M
Lipscomb University — M
Logan University — M,D
Long Island University–LIU Brooklyn — M,D,O
Louisiana Tech University — M
Manhattanville College — M,O
Marshall University — M
Marywood University — M
McDaniel College — M
McNeese State University — M
Memorial University of Newfoundland — M
Merrimack College — M
Miami University — M
Middle Tennessee State University — M,D
Midwestern State University — M
Mississippi State University — M,D
Montclair State University — M,O
Morehead State University — M
Murray State University — M
New Mexico Highlands University — M
North Dakota State University — M,D
Northeastern Illinois University — M
Northeastern University — M,D,O
Northern Michigan University — M
Northwest Missouri State University — M
Oakland University — M,D,O
Ohio University — M,D
Old Dominion University — M
Pittsburg State University — M
Point Loma Nazarene University — M
Purdue University — M,D
Queens College of the City University of New York — M,O
Queen's University at Kingston — M,D
Rowan University — M
Sacred Heart University — M
St. Cloud State University — M
Saint Mary's College of California — M
San Diego State University — M
San Jose State University — M,O
Smith College — M
South Dakota State University — M,D
Southeastern Louisiana University — M
Southeast Missouri State University — M
Southern Connecticut State University — M
Southern Illinois University Edwardsville — M
Southern Utah University — M
Springfield College — M,D
Syracuse University — M
Tennessee State University — M
Texas A&M University– Commerce — M,D,O
Texas Tech University — M
Texas Woman's University — M,D
United States Sports Academy — M
University at Buffalo, the State University of New York — M,D,O
The University of Akron — M
The University of Alabama — M,D
University of Alberta — M,D
University of Arkansas at Little Rock — M
University of California, Davis — M
University of Central Florida — M,D
University of Central Oklahoma — M

University of Connecticut — M,D
University of Dayton — M
University of Florida — M,D
University of Houston — M,D
University of Houston–Clear Lake — M
The University of Iowa — M,D
The University of Kansas — M,D
University of Kentucky — M,D
University of Lethbridge — M,D
University of Louisiana at Monroe — M
University of Louisville — M,D,O
University of Maine — M
University of Mary — M
University of Mary Hardin-Baylor — M
University of Massachusetts Boston — M,D
University of Memphis — M,O
University of Miami — M,D
University of Minnesota, Twin Cities Campus — M,D
University of Mississippi — M
University of Montana — M
University of Nebraska at Kearney — M
University of Nebraska at Omaha — M,D
University of Nebraska– Lincoln — M,D
University of Nevada, Las Vegas — M,D
University of New Brunswick Fredericton — M
University of New Mexico — D
University of North Alabama — M
The University of North Carolina at Chapel Hill — M
The University of North Carolina at Pembroke — M
University of Northern Colorado — M,D
University of North Florida — M,D
University of Oklahoma — M,D
University of Pittsburgh — M,D
University of Puerto Rico, Mayagüez Campus — M
University of Puerto Rico, Río Piedras Campus — M
University of Rhode Island — M
University of South Alabama — M
University of South Carolina — M,D
The University of South Dakota — M
University of Southern Mississippi — M,D
The University of Tampa — M
The University of Tennessee — M,D,O
The University of Texas at Arlington — M,D
The University of Texas at Austin — M,D
The University of Texas Rio Grande Valley — M
University of the Pacific — M
The University of Toledo — M,D
University of West Florida — M
University of Wisconsin–La Crosse — M
University of Wisconsin–Milwaukee — M,D
University of Wyoming — M
Virginia Commonwealth University — M
Virginia Polytechnic Institute and State University — M
Wake Forest University — M
Washington State University — M
Wayne State College — M
Wayne State University — M,D
West Chester University of Pennsylvania — M,O
Western Michigan University — M
Western Washington University — M
West Texas A&M University — M
West Virginia University — M,D
Wichita State University — M
William Paterson University of New Jersey — M,D

EXPERIMENTAL PSYCHOLOGY

Bowling Green State University — M,D
Brooklyn College of the City University of New York — M,D
California State University, Fresno — M,O
California State University, Northridge — M
California State University, San Bernardino — M
Case Western Reserve University — D
The Catholic University of America — M,D
Central Michigan University — M
Central Washington University — M
Cornell University — D
Duke University — D
Eastern Washington University — M
East Tennessee State University — D
Fairleigh Dickinson University, Metropolitan Campus — M,O
The Graduate Center, City University of New York — D
Harvard University — D
Howard University — D
Idaho State University — D
Iona College — M,O
James Madison University — M
Kent State University — M,D
Lakehead University — M,D
Laurentian University — M
McGill University — M,D
McNeese State University — M
Memorial University of Newfoundland — M,D
Middle Tennessee State University — M,O
Missouri State University — M
Morehead State University — M
North Carolina State University — D
Nova Southeastern University — M,D,O
Ohio University — D
Rivier University — M
Rochester Institute of Technology — M
Saint Louis University — M
San Jose State University — M,O
Seton Hall University — M

Southern Illinois University Carbondale — M,D
Southern Methodist University — M,D
Texas A&M University–Central Texas — M,O
Texas Christian University — M,D
Texas Tech University — M,D
Towson University — M
The University of Alabama — D
University of Central Florida — M
University of Central Oklahoma — M
University of Cincinnati — D
University of Connecticut — M,D
University of Hartford — M
University of Idaho — M,D
University of Louisville — D
University of Maryland, College Park — M,D
University of Massachusetts Dartmouth — M,O
University of Memphis — M,D,O
University of Mississippi — M,D
University of Montana — M,D,O
University of New Brunswick Saint John — M
University of Regina — M,D
University of South Carolina — M,D
The University of Tennessee — M,D
The University of Tennessee at Chattanooga — M
The University of Texas at Arlington — M,D
The University of Texas at El Paso — M,D
The University of Texas of the Permian Basin — M
The University of Texas Rio Grande Valley — M
The University of Toledo — M,D
University of Victoria — M
The University of West Alabama — M
University of West Florida — M
University of Wisconsin– Milwaukee — M,D
University of Wisconsin– Oshkosh — M
Washington State University — M
Western Illinois University — M,O
Western Kentucky University — M
Western Washington University — M

FACILITIES MANAGEMENT

Cornell University — M
Indiana University–Purdue University Fort Wayne — M
Maastricht School of Management — M,D
Massachusetts Maritime Academy — M
Pratt Institute — M
Université Laval — M,O
University of California, Berkeley — O
University of New Haven — M,O
The University of North Carolina at Charlotte — M
Wentworth Institute of Technology — M

FAMILY AND CONSUMER SCIENCES-GENERAL

Alabama Agricultural and Mechanical University — M
Ball State University — M
California State University, Northridge — M
Central Michigan University — M,O
Central Washington University — M
Clemson University — D,O
East Carolina University — M
Eastern Illinois University — M
Florida State University — M,D
Fontbonne University — M
Hofstra University — M,D,O
Illinois State University — M
Iowa State University of Science and Technology — M
Kansas State University — M,D,O
Lamar University — M
Louisiana State University and Agricultural & Mechanical College — M,D
Louisiana Tech University — M
New Mexico State University — M
North Dakota State University — M
The Ohio State University — M,D
Oklahoma State University — M,D
Queens College of the City University of New York — M,O
Sam Houston State University — M
San Francisco State University — M
South Carolina State University — M
South Dakota State University — M
Stephen F. Austin State University — M
Tennessee State University — M,D
Texas A&M University– Kingsville — M
Texas Southern University — M
Texas State University — M
Texas Tech University — M,D
Tufts University — M
The University of Alabama — M,D
University of Alberta — M,D
The University of Arizona — D
University of Arkansas — M
University of Central Arkansas — M
University of Central Oklahoma — M
University of Florida — M
University of Georgia — M,D
University of Houston — M
University of Louisiana at Monroe — M
University of Manitoba — M
University of Maryland, College Park — M,D
University of Missouri — M,D,O
University of Nebraska– Lincoln — M,D
University of Puerto Rico, Río Piedras Campus — M
University of South Africa — M,D
The University of Tennessee — D

The University of Tennessee at Martin — M
The University of Texas at Austin — M,D
University of Wisconsin– Madison — M,D
University of Wisconsin– Stevens Point — M
Utah State University — M,D
Western Michigan University — M

FAMILY NURSE PRACTITIONER STUDIES

Albany State University — M
Allen College — M,D
Alvernia University — M,D,O
Alverno College — M,D
American International College — M,D
Angelo State University — M
Arizona State University at the Tempe campus — M,D,O
Armstrong State University — M,O
Ashland University — D
Augsburg College — M
Augusta University — D
Austin Peay State University — M
Ball State University — M,D,O
Barry University — M,O
Baylor University — M,D
Bellarmine University — M,D
Bellin College — M
Bloomsburg University of Pennsylvania — M
Bowie State University — M
Bradley University — M,D,O
Brenau University — M
Brigham Young University — M
California Baptist University — M
California State University, San Marcos — M
Carlow University — M,O
Carson-Newman University — M
Case Western Reserve University — M
Cedarville University — M,D
Clarion University of Pennsylvania — M,D,O
Clarke University — D
Clarkson College — M,O
Clayton State University — M
Clemson University — M,D,O
College of Mount Saint Vincent — M,O
The College of New Rochelle — M,O
College of Staten Island of the City University of New York — D
Colorado Mesa University — M,D,O
Columbia University — M,O
Columbus State University — M
Concordia University Wisconsin — M,D
Coppin State University — M
Cox College — M
Creighton University — M,D,O
Delta State University — M,D
DePaul University — M,D
DeSales University — M,D,O
Dominican College — M,D
Drexel University — M
Duke University — M,D,O
Duquesne University — M,O
D'Youville College — M,D,O
Eastern Kentucky University — M
East Tennessee State University — M,D,O
Edinboro University of Pennsylvania — M,D
Emory University — M
Fairfield University — M,D
Felician University — M
Florida National University — M
Florida Southern College — M
Florida State University — M,D,O
Francis Marion University — M
Fresno Pacific University — M
Frontier Nursing University — M,D,O
Gannon University — M,O
Gardner-Webb University — M,D
Georgetown University — M,D
The George Washington University — M,D,O
Georgia Southern University — M
Georgia Southwestern State University — M,O
Georgia State University — M,D,O
Goshen College — M
Graceland University (IA) — M,D,O
Grambling State University — M,O
Grand Canyon University — M,D,O
Gwynedd Mercy University — M,D
Hardin-Simmons University — M
Hofstra University — M
Holy Names University — M,O
Howard University — M
Husson University — M,O
Illinois State University — M,D,O
Indiana State University — M,D
Indiana University Kokomo — M
Indiana University–Purdue University Fort Wayne — M,O
Indiana University–Purdue University Indianapolis — M
Indiana University South Bend — M
Jacksonville University — M
James Madison University — M,D
Johns Hopkins University — D
Kent State University — M,D
King University — M,D
La Salle University — M,D,O
Le Moyne College — M,O
Lewis University — M,D
Liberty University — M,D
Lincoln Memorial University — M
Long Island University–LIU Brooklyn — M,O
Long Island University–LIU Post — M,O
Louisiana State University Health Sciences Center — M,D,O
Loyola University New Orleans — M,D
Malone University — M

Marquette University	M,D,O
Marymount University	M,D,O
Maryville University of Saint Louis	M,D
McGill University	M,D,O
McMurry University	M
McNeese State University	M,O
Medical University of South Carolina	M,D
Middle Tennessee State University	M,O
Midwestern State University	M
Millersville University of Pennsylvania	M,O
Minnesota State University Mankato	M,D
Missouri State University	M,D
Molloy College	M,D,O
Monmouth University	M,D,O
Montana State University	M,D,O
Mount Carmel College of Nursing	M,D
Mount Saint Mary College	M,O
Murray State University	M
New Mexico State University	M,D,O
New York University	M,D,O
Nicholls State University	M
Northeastern University	M,D,O
Northern Arizona University	M,D,O
Northern Michigan University	M,D
Oakland University	M,O
Ohio University	M,D
Old Dominion University	M,D
Olivet Nazarene University	M
Oregon Health & Science University	M
Otterbein University	M,D,O
Pace University	M,D,O
Pacific Lutheran University	D
Palm Beach Atlantic University	M,D
Point Loma Nazarene University	M,O
Purdue University	M,D,O
Purdue University Northwest	M
Queen's University at Kingston	M,D,O
Quinnipiac University	D
Ramapo College of New Jersey	M
Regis College (MA)	M,D,O
Research College of Nursing	M
Rivier University	M,D
Rocky Mountain University of Health Professions	D
Rush University	D
Rutgers University–Camden	D
Rutgers University–Newark	M,D,O
Sacred Heart University	M,D,O
Sage Graduate School	M
Saginaw Valley State University	M,D
Saint Francis Medical Center College of Nursing	M,D,O
Saint Joseph's College of Maine	M,O
Salisbury University	D
Samford University	M,D
Samuel Merritt University	M,D,O
San Francisco State University	M,O
Seattle Pacific University	M,O
Seattle University	M
Shenandoah University	M,D,O
Simmons College	M,D,O
Sonoma State University	M
Southeastern Louisiana University	M,D
Southern Adventist University	M
Southern Connecticut State University	M,D
Southern Illinois University Edwardsville	M,D,O
Southern University and Agricultural and Mechanical College	M,D,O
South University	M
South University	M
South University	M
Spalding University	M,D,O
State University of New York Downstate Medical Center	M,O
State University of New York Polytechnic Institute	M,O
State University of New York Upstate Medical University	M,O
Stony Brook University, State University of New York	M,D,O
Temple University	D
Tennessee State University	M,O
Tennessee Technological University	M
Texas A&M International University	M
Texas A&M University	M
Texas A&M University–Corpus Christi	M
Texas Christian University	D
Texas State University	M
Texas Tech University Health Sciences Center	M,D,O
Texas Woman's University	M,D
Troy University	M,D
Uniformed Services University of the Health Sciences	M,D
Union University	M,D,O
United States University	M
Universidad del Turabo	M,O
University at Buffalo, the State University of New York	M,D,O
The University of Alabama at Birmingham	M,D
The University of Alabama in Huntsville	M,D,O
The University of Arizona	M,D,O
University of Central Arkansas	M,O
University of Colorado Denver	M,D
University of Delaware	M,O
University of Detroit Mercy	M,D,O
University of Hawaii at Manoa	M,D,O
University of Houston	M
University of Illinois at Chicago	M,O
University of Indianapolis	M,D

University of Louisiana at Lafayette	M
University of Louisville	M,D
University of Maine	M,O
University of Mary	M,D
University of Mary Hardin-Baylor	M,D,O
University of Massachusetts Amherst	M
University of Massachusetts Lowell	M
University of Massachusetts Medical School	M,D,O
University of Memphis	M,O
University of Miami	M,D
University of Michigan–Flint	M,D,O
University of Minnesota, Twin Cities Campus	M,D
University of Missouri	M,D,O
University of Missouri–Kansas City	M,D
University of Missouri–St. Louis	D,O
University of Nevada, Las Vegas	M,D,O
University of New Hampshire	M,D,O
The University of North Carolina at Chapel Hill	M,D,O
The University of North Carolina at Charlotte	M,D,O
The University of North Carolina Wilmington	M,D,O
University of North Dakota	M,D,O
University of Northern Colorado	M,D
University of North Florida	M,D,O
University of North Georgia	M,O
University of Pennsylvania	M,O
University of Phoenix–Hawaii Campus	M
University of Phoenix–Online Campus	M,O
University of Phoenix–Phoenix Campus	M,O
University of Phoenix–Sacramento Valley Campus	M
University of Phoenix–Southern California Campus	M,O
University of Pittsburgh	M,D
University of Portland	M,D
University of Puerto Rico, Medical Sciences Campus	M
University of Rhode Island	M,D
University of Rochester	M,D
University of St. Francis (IL)	M,D,O
University of Saint Francis (IN)	M,D,O
University of Saint Joseph	M,D
University of San Diego	M,D
The University of Scranton	M,D,O
University of South Carolina	M
University of Southern Indiana	M,D,O
University of Southern Maine	M,D,O
University of Southern Mississippi	M,D,O
University of South Florida	M,D,O
The University of Tampa	M
The University of Tennessee at Chattanooga	M,D,O
The University of Texas at Arlington	M,D
The University of Texas at Austin	M,D
The University of Texas at El Paso	M,D
The University of Texas at Tyler	M,D
The University of Texas Health Science Center at San Antonio	M,D,O
The University of Texas Rio Grande Valley	M
The University of Toledo	M,O
The University of Tulsa	D
University of Victoria	M,D
University of Wisconsin–Eau Claire	M,D
University of Wisconsin–Oshkosh	M
Ursuline College	M,D
Valdosta State University	M
Vanderbilt University	M,D,O
Villanova University	M,D,O
Virginia Commonwealth University	M
Walden University	M,D,O
Washington State University	M,D,O
West Coast University	M,D
Westminster College (UT)	M
West Texas A&M University	M
West Virginia Wesleyan College	M,O
Wilmington University	M,D
Winona State University	M,D,O
Winston-Salem State University	M,D
Wright State University	M

FILM, TELEVISION, AND VIDEO PRODUCTION

Academy of Art University	M
American Film Institute Conservatory	M
American University	M
Arizona State University at the Tempe campus	M
ArtCenter College of Design	M
The Art Institute of California–San Francisco, a campus of Argosy University	M
Bard College	M
Bob Jones University	M,D,O
Boston University	M
Bowling Green State University	M,D
Brigham Young University	M
Brooklyn College of the City University of New York	M
California College of the Arts	M
California Institute of the Arts	M,O
California State University, Fullerton	M
California State University, Northridge	M
Carleton University	M

Carnegie Mellon University	M
Central Michigan University	M
Chapman University	M
Chatham University	M
Columbia College Chicago	M
Columbia University	M
Concordia University (Canada)	M,D
DePaul University	M,D
Drexel University	M
Emerson College	M
Florida Atlantic University	M,O
Florida State University	M
Georgia State University	M,D
Governors State University	M
Hollins University	M
Howard University	M
Johns Hopkins University	M
Lindenwood University	M
Lipscomb University	M
Loyola Marymount University	M
Maryland Institute College of Art	M
Massachusetts College of Art and Design	M,O
Miami International University of Art & Design	M
Minneapolis College of Art and Design	M
Missouri State University	M,O
Montana State University	M
Mount Saint Mary's University (CA)	M,D,O
National University	M
New York Film Academy	M
New York University	M
Northwestern University	M,D
Ohio University	M
Quinnipiac University	M
Regent University	M,D
Rochester Institute of Technology	M
Sacred Heart University	M
St. Thomas University	M
San Diego State University	M
San Francisco State University	M
Savannah College of Art and Design	M
School of the Art Institute of Chicago	M
School of Visual Arts (NY)	M
Stanford University	M,D
Stevens Institute of Technology	M
Stony Brook University, State University of New York	M
Syracuse University	M
Temple University	M
Universidad Autonoma de Guadalajara	M,D
The University of British Columbia	M
University of California, Los Angeles	M,D
University of California, Santa Barbara	D
University of Central Arkansas	M
University of Central Florida	M
University of Colorado Boulder	M
The University of Iowa	M
University of Memphis	M,D
University of Miami	M,D
University of Montana	M
University of Nevada, Las Vegas	M,O
University of New Orleans	M
The University of North Carolina at Greensboro	M
University of North Carolina School of the Arts	M
University of North Texas	M,D,O
University of Regina	M
University of Southern California	M
The University of Texas at Arlington	M
The University of Texas at Austin	M,D
University of the Sacred Heart	M,O
University of Utah	M
University of Victoria	M
Vermont College of Fine Arts	M
Virginia Commonwealth University	M,D
Western State Colorado University	M
York University	M,D

FILM, TELEVISION, AND VIDEO THEORY AND CRITICISM

Brooklyn College of the City University of New York	M
California College of the Arts	M
Central Michigan University	M
Claremont Graduate University	M,D
College of Staten Island of the City University of New York	M
Concordia University (Canada)	M,D
DePaul University	M
Emory University	M,D,O
Hollins University	M
Ohio University	M
Salisbury University	M
San Francisco State University	M
Savannah College of Art and Design	M
Syracuse University	M
Texas A&M University–Commerce	M,D,O
Tiffin University	M
Université de Montréal	M,D
Université Laval	M,D
University at Buffalo, the State University of New York	M,D,O
The University of Arizona	M
The University of British Columbia	M
University of California, Berkeley	D
University of California, Santa Cruz	D
University of Chicago	D
The University of Iowa	M,D
The University of Kansas	M,D
University of Miami	M,D

University of Michigan	D,O
University of Pittsburgh	M,D,O
University of Southern California	M,D
University of South Florida	M
University of Toronto	M,D
University of Wisconsin–Madison	M,D
University of Wisconsin–Milwaukee	M,D
Wayne State University	M,D
Wilfrid Laurier University	M,D
Yale University	D

FINANCE AND BANKING

Adelphi University	M
American Business & Technology University	M
The American College of Financial Services	M,O
American College of Thessaloniki	M,O
American InterContinental University Online	M
American Public University System	M
American University	M
The American University in Cairo	M
The American University in Dubai	M
American University of Beirut	M
Andrews University	M
Argosy University, Atlanta	M,D
Argosy University, Chicago	M,D
Argosy University, Dallas	M,D,O
Argosy University, Denver	M,D
Argosy University, Hawai'i	M,D,O
Argosy University, Inland Empire	M,D
Argosy University, Los Angeles	M,D
Argosy University, Nashville	M,D
Argosy University, Northern Virginia	M,D,O
Argosy University, Orange County	M,D,O
Argosy University, Phoenix	M,D
Argosy University, Salt Lake City	M,D
Argosy University, San Diego	M,D
Argosy University, San Francisco Bay Area	M,D
Argosy University, Sarasota	M,D,O
Argosy University, Schaumburg	M,D,O
Argosy University, Seattle	M,D
Argosy University, Tampa	M,D
Argosy University, Twin Cities	M,D
Arizona State University at the Tempe campus	M,D
Aspen University	M,O
Assumption College	M,O
Auburn University	M
Avila University	M
Azusa Pacific University	M
Baker College Center for Graduate Studies–Online	M,D
Barry University	O
Baruch College of the City University of New York	M,D
Bayamón Central University	M
Bellevue University	M,D
Benedictine University	M
Bentley University	M
Bluffton University	M
Boston College	M,D
Boston University	M
Brandeis University	M,D
Brandman University	M
Bridgewater State University	M
Brigham Young University	M
Brooklyn College of the City University of New York	M
Bryant University	M,O
Butler University	M
California College of the Arts	M
California Intercontinental University	M,D
California Lutheran University	M,O
California State University, East Bay	M
California State University, Fullerton	M
California State University, Los Angeles	M
California State University, San Bernardino	M
Capella University	M,D
Carnegie Mellon University	D
Case Western Reserve University	M
Central European University	M,D
Central Michigan University	M
Charleston Southern University	M
City University of Seattle	M,O
Claremont McKenna College	M
Clarion University of Pennsylvania	M
Clark University	M
Cleary University	M,O
College for Financial Planning	M
The College of Saint Rose	O
Colorado State University	M
Colorado State University–Global Campus	M
Colorado Technical University Aurora	M
Colorado Technical University Colorado Springs	M,D
Columbia Southern University	M
Columbia University	M,D
Concordia University (Canada)	M,D,O
Concordia University Wisconsin	M
Cornell University	D
Creighton University	M
Culver-Stockton College	M
Curry College	M,O
Dalhousie University	M
Dallas Baptist University	M
Davenport University	M
Delaware Valley University	M
DePaul University	M

M—masters degree; D—doctorate; O—other advanced degree; *—Close-Up and/or Display

Institution	Degree
DeSales University	M
DeVry University–Folsom Campus	M
Drexel University	M,D,O
Duke University	M,D,O
Duquesne University	M
Eastern Michigan University	M,O
Elms College	M
Embry-Riddle Aeronautical University–Daytona	M
Embry-Riddle Aeronautical University–Worldwide	M
Emory University	M,D
Fairfield University	M,O
Fairleigh Dickinson University, College at Florham	M,O
Fairleigh Dickinson University, Metropolitan Campus	M,O
Florida Agricultural and Mechanical University	M
Florida Atlantic University	M
Florida International University	M
Florida National University	M
Florida State University	M,D
Fordham University	M
Gannon University	M
Geneva College	M
George Fox University	M,D
Georgetown University	M,D
The George Washington University	M,D
Georgia State University	M,D,O
Golden Gate University	M,D,O
Goldey-Beacom College	M
The Graduate Center, City University of New York	D
Grand Canyon University	M
Hawai`i Pacific University	M
HEC Montreal	M,O
Hofstra University	M,O
Holy Family University	M
Holy Names University	M
Hood College	M
Howard University	M
Hult International Business School (United States)	M
IGlobal University	M
Illinois Institute of Technology	M,D
Indiana University Bloomington	M,D,O
Indiana University–Purdue University Indianapolis	M
Indiana University South Bend	M,O
Indiana University Southeast	M
Instituto Centroamericano de Administración de Empresas	M
Instituto Tecnologico de Santo Domingo	M,O
Instituto Tecnológico y de Estudios Superiores de Monterrey, Campus Central de Veracruz	M
Instituto Tecnológico y de Estudios Superiores de Monterrey, Campus Ciudad de México	M,D
Instituto Tecnológico y de Estudios Superiores de Monterrey, Campus Ciudad Obregón	M
Instituto Tecnológico y de Estudios Superiores de Monterrey, Campus Cuernavaca	M
Instituto Tecnológico y de Estudios Superiores de Monterrey, Campus Estado de México	M,D
Instituto Tecnológico y de Estudios Superiores de Monterrey, Campus Guadalajara	M
Instituto Tecnológico y de Estudios Superiores de Monterrey, Campus Irapuato	M,D
Instituto Tecnológico y de Estudios Superiores de Monterrey, Campus Monterrey	M
Inter American University of Puerto Rico, Aguadilla Campus	M
Inter American University of Puerto Rico, Arecibo Campus	M
Inter American University of Puerto Rico, Barranquitas Campus	M
Inter American University of Puerto Rico, Metropolitan Campus	M
Inter American University of Puerto Rico, Ponce Campus	M
Inter American University of Puerto Rico, San Germán Campus	M,D
The International University of Monaco	M
Iona College	M,O
Iowa State University of Science and Technology	M
Jacksonville University	M
Johns Hopkins University	M,D,O
Johnson & Wales University	M
Kansas State University	M,D,O
Kaplan University, Davenport Campus	M
Kent State University	D
King University	M
Lake Forest Graduate School of Management	M
Lakeland University	M
La Salle University	M,O
La Sierra University	M,O
Lawrence Technological University	M,O
Lehigh University	M
Lewis University	M
Lincoln University (CA)	M,D
Lincoln University (PA)	M
Lindenwood University	M
Lipscomb University	M,O
Long Island University–Hudson	M,O
Long Island University–LIU Post	M
Louisiana State University and Agricultural & Mechanical College	M,D
Louisiana Tech University	M,D

Institution	Degree
Loyola University Chicago	M
Loyola University Maryland	M
Manhattanville College	M
Marquette University	M,O
Maryville University of Saint Louis	M,O
Marywood University	M
McGill University	M,D,O
Metropolitan College of New York	M
Michigan State University	M,D
Minnesota State University Moorhead	M
Mississippi College	M,O
Mississippi State University	M,D
Molloy College	M,O
Monmouth University	M
Monroe College	M
Mount Saint Mary College	M
Naval Postgraduate School	M
New Charter University	M
New England College of Business and Finance	M
New Jersey City University	M,O
Newman University	M
New Mexico State University	M
The New School	M,D
New York Institute of Technology	M
New York University	M,D,O
Niagara University	M
North Central College	M
Northeastern Illinois University	M
Northeastern State University	M
Northeastern University	M
Northern State University	M
North Greenville University	M,D
Northwestern University	M,D
Norwich University	M
Notre Dame de Namur University	M
Nova Southeastern University	M
Oakland University	M,O
Ohio Christian University	M
Ohio Dominican University	M
The Ohio State University	M
Ohio University	M
Oklahoma Christian University	M
Oklahoma State University	M
Old Dominion University	D
Oral Roberts University	M
Oregon State University	M,D
Ottawa University	M
Our Lady of the Lake University	M
Pace University	M,D,O
Pacific Lutheran University	M
Pacific States University	M,D
Pacific University	M
Park University	M,O
Penn State Great Valley	M,O
Penn State Harrisburg	M,D,O
Pepperdine University	M
Polytechnic University of Puerto Rico, Miami Campus	M
Polytechnic University of Puerto Rico, Orlando Campus	M
Pontifical Catholic University of Puerto Rico	M
Pontificia Universidad Catolica Madre y Maestra	M
Portland State University	M
Post University	M
Princeton University	M
Providence College	M
Purdue University	M
Queens College of the City University of New York	M
Queen's University at Kingston	M
Regent's University London	M
Regent University	M,D,O
Regis University	M,O
Rhode Island College	M,O
Robert Morris University Illinois	M
Rochester Institute of Technology	M
Rockhurst University	M,O
Rollins College	M,D
Rutgers University–Newark	M,D
Sacred Heart University	M,D
St. John's University (NY)	M
Saint Joseph's University	M,O
Saint Louis University	M
Saint Mary's College of California	M
Saint Peter's University	M
St. Thomas Aquinas College	M,O
Saint Xavier University	M,O
Samford University	M
Sam Houston State University	M
San Diego State University	M
San Francisco State University	M
Santa Clara University	M
Schiller International University (United States)	M
Seattle University	M,O
Seton Hall University	M,O
Shippensburg University of Pennsylvania	M
Simon Fraser University	M,D,O
Slippery Rock University of Pennsylvania	M
Southeast Missouri State University	M
Southern Adventist University	M
Southern Illinois University Edwardsville	M
Southern Methodist University	M
Southern New Hampshire University	M,O
Southwestern Adventist University	M
State University of New York Polytechnic Institute	M
Stevens Institute of Technology	M,O
Stony Brook University, State University of New York	M,O
Strayer University	M
Suffolk University	M
Syracuse University	M,D

Institution	Degree
Télé-université	M,D
Temple University	M
Tennessee Technological University	M
Texas A&M International University	M
Texas A&M University	M
Texas A&M University–Commerce	M
Texas A&M University–Corpus Christi	M
Texas A&M University–San Antonio	M
Texas Christian University	M
Texas Tech University	M,D
Tiffin University	M
Trident University International	M,D
Troy University	M
Tulane University	M,D
United States International University–Africa	M
Universidad Central del Este	M
Universidad de las Americas, A.C.	M
Universidad de las Américas Puebla	M
Universidad Metropolitana	M
Université de Sherbrooke	M
Université du Québec à Montréal	O
Université du Québec à Trois-Rivières	O
Université du Québec en Outaouais	M,O
Université Laval	M,O
University at Albany, State University of New York	M,D,O
University at Buffalo, the State University of New York	M,D
The University of Akron	M
The University of Alabama	M,D
The University of Alabama at Birmingham	M
The University of Alabama in Huntsville	M,O
University of Alaska Fairbanks	M
University of Alberta	M,D
The University of Arizona	M
University of Baltimore	M
University of Bridgeport	M
The University of British Columbia	M
University of California, Berkeley	D,O
University of California, Los Angeles	M,D
University of California, San Diego	M,D
University of California, Santa Barbara	M,D
University of California, Santa Cruz	M
University of Central Missouri	M,D,O
University of Chicago	M,O
University of Cincinnati	M,D
University of Colorado Denver	M
University of Connecticut	M,D,O
University of Dallas	M
University of Dayton	M
University of Delaware	M
University of Denver	M
University of Detroit Mercy	M,D,O
University of Florida	M,D,O
University of Hawaii at Manoa	M
University of Houston	M
University of Houston–Clear Lake	M
University of Houston–Downtown	M
University of Houston–Victoria	M
University of Illinois at Chicago	M
University of Illinois at Urbana–Champaign	M,D
The University of Iowa	D
The University of Kansas	M,D
University of La Verne	M
University of Lethbridge	M
University of Maine	M
The University of Manchester	M
University of Maryland University College	M
University of Massachusetts Amherst	M,D
University of Massachusetts Boston	M
University of Massachusetts Dartmouth	M,O
University of Memphis	M
University of Michigan–Dearborn	M
University of Michigan–Flint	M,O
University of Minnesota, Twin Cities Campus	M,D
University of Missouri	M,D
University of Missouri–Kansas City	M
University of Missouri–St. Louis	M,D,O
University of Nebraska–Lincoln	M
University of Nevada, Reno	M
University of New Haven	M,O
University of New Mexico	M
University of New Orleans	M
University of North Alabama	M
The University of North Carolina at Chapel Hill	D
The University of North Carolina at Charlotte	M,O
The University of North Carolina at Greensboro	M,O
University of North Florida	M
University of North Texas	M,D,O
University of Notre Dame	M
University of Oklahoma	M
University of Oregon	D
University of Ottawa	D,O
University of Pennsylvania	M,D
University of Pittsburgh	M,D

Institution	Degree
University of Portland	M
University of Puerto Rico, Mayagüez Campus	M
University of Puerto Rico, Río Piedras Campus	M,D
University of Rhode Island	M,D
University of Rochester	M,D
University of St. Francis (IL)	M,O
University of Saint Mary	M
University of St. Thomas (TX)	M
University of San Diego	M
University of San Francisco	M
University of Saskatchewan	M
The University of Scranton	M
University of Southern Maine	M
University of South Florida	M
The University of Tampa	M
The University of Tennessee	M,D
The University of Tennessee at Martin	M
The University of Texas at Arlington	M,D
The University of Texas at Austin	M
The University of Texas at Dallas	M
The University of Texas at San Antonio	M,D
The University of Texas Rio Grande Valley	M,D
University of the West	M
The University of Toledo	M
University of Toronto	M
The University of Tulsa	M
University of Utah	M
University of Virginia	M
University of Washington, Tacoma	M
University of Waterloo	M,D
The University of West Alabama	M
The University of Western Ontario	M,D
University of Wisconsin–Madison	M,D
University of Wisconsin–Whitewater	M
University of Wyoming	M
Upper Iowa University	M
Ursuline College	M
Valparaiso University	M,O
Vancouver Island University	M
Vanderbilt University	M
Villanova University	M
Virginia Commonwealth University	M
Virginia International University	M,O
Wagner College	M
Walden University	M,D,O
Walsh College of Accountancy and Business Administration	M
Washington University in St. Louis	M,D
Waynesburg University	M
Wayne State University	M,D,O
Webster University	M
Western Michigan University Thomas M. Cooley Law School	M,D
West Texas A&M University	M
Wilfrid Laurier University	M
Wilkes University	M
Wilmington University	M
Wingate University	M
Xavier University	M
Yale University	D
York College of Pennsylvania	M
York University	M,D
Youngstown State University	M

FINANCIAL ENGINEERING

Institution	Degree
Baruch College of the City University of New York	M
Claremont Graduate University	M
Columbia University	M,D
HEC Montreal	M
The International University of Monaco	M
New York University	M,O
North Carolina State University	M,D
Princeton University	M,D
Rensselaer Polytechnic Institute	M
Stevens Institute of Technology	M,D,O
Temple University	M
University of California, Berkeley	M
University of California, Los Angeles	M,D
University of Illinois at Urbana–Champaign	M
The University of Tulsa	M

FIRE PROTECTION ENGINEERING

Institution	Degree
Oklahoma State University	M,D
University of Maryland, College Park	M
University of New Haven	M,O
The University of North Carolina at Charlotte	M
Worcester Polytechnic Institute	M,D,O

FISH, GAME, AND WILDLIFE MANAGEMENT

Institution	Degree
American Public University System	M
Arkansas Tech University	M
Auburn University	M,D
Brigham Young University	M,D
Clemson University	M,D
Colorado State University	M,D
Cornell University	M
Frostburg State University	M
Humboldt State University	M
Iowa State University of Science and Technology	M,D
Louisiana State University and Agricultural & Mechanical College	M,D
McGill University	M,D
Memorial University of Newfoundland	M,O
Michigan State University	M,D
Mississippi State University	M,D
Montana State University	M
New Mexico State University	M
North Carolina State University	M,D

The Ohio State University — M,D
Oregon State University — M,D
Penn State University Park — M,D
Purdue University — M,D
Simon Fraser University — M,D,O
South Dakota State University — M,D
State University of New York
   College of Environmental Science
   and Forestry — M,D
Sul Ross State University — M
Tarleton State University — M
Tennessee Technological University — M
Texas A&M University — M,D
Texas A&M University–
   Kingsville — M,D
Texas State University — M
Texas Tech University — M,D
Université du Québec
   à Rimouski — M,D,O
University of Arkansas at Pine
   Bluff — M,D
University of Delaware — M,D
University of Florida — M,D,O
University of Maine — M,D
University of Maryland Eastern
   Shore — M,D
University of Massachusetts
   Amherst — M,D
University of Miami — M,D
University of Minnesota, Twin
   Cities Campus — M,D,O
University of Missouri — M,D,O
University of Montana — M,D
University of New Hampshire — M,D
University of North Dakota — M,D
University of Rhode Island — M,D
The University of Tennessee — M
University of Washington — M,D
University of Wisconsin–
   Madison — M,D
Utah State University — M,D
Virginia Polytechnic Institute and
   State University — M,D
West Virginia University — M

FOLKLORE
The George Washington University — M,D
Indiana University Bloomington — M,D
Memorial University of
   Newfoundland — M,D
Penn State Harrisburg — M,D,O
University of Alberta — M,D
University of California, Berkeley — M
University of Louisiana at
   Lafayette — M,D
The University of North Carolina
   at Chapel Hill — M
University of Oregon — M
The University of Texas at Austin — M,D
University of Wisconsin–
   Madison — M,D
Utah State University — M

FOOD SCIENCE AND TECHNOLOGY
Alabama Agricultural and
   Mechanical University — M,D
American University of Beirut — M
Auburn University — M,D,O
Boston University — M
Brigham Young University — M
California Polytechnic State
   University, San Luis Obispo — M
Chapman University — M
Clemson University — M,D
Colorado State University — M,D
Cornell University — M,D
Dalhousie University — M,D
Drexel University — M
Florida State University — M,D
Framingham State University — M
Illinois Institute of Technology — M
Iowa State University of Science
   and Technology — M,D
Kansas State University — M,D
London Metropolitan University — M,D
Louisiana State University and
   Agricultural & Mechanical College — M,D
Marlboro College — M
McGill University — M,D
Memorial University of
   Newfoundland — M,D
Michigan State University — M,D
Mississippi State University — M,D
New Mexico State University — M
New York University — M,D
North Carolina State University — M,D
North Dakota State University — M,D,O
The Ohio State University — M,D
Oklahoma State University — M,D
Oregon State University — M,D
Penn State University Park — M,D
Purdue University — M,D
Rutgers University–New
   Brunswick — M,D
Texas A&M University — M,D
Texas Tech University — M,D
Texas Woman's University — M,D
Tuskegee University — M
Universidad de las Américas
   Puebla — M
Université de Moncton — M
Université Laval — M,D
University of Arkansas — M,D
The University of British Columbia — M,D
University of California, Davis — M,D
University of Delaware — M,D
University of Florida — M,D
University of Georgia — M,D
University of Guelph — M,D
University of Hawaii at Manoa — M
University of Idaho — M,D

University of Illinois at
   Urbana–Champaign — M,D
University of Kentucky — M,D
University of Manitoba — M,D
University of Maryland, College
   Park — M,D
University of Maryland Eastern
   Shore — M,D
University of Massachusetts
   Amherst — M,D
University of Minnesota, Twin
   Cities Campus — M,D
University of Mississippi — M,D
University of Missouri — M,D
University of Nebraska–
   Lincoln — M,D
University of Puerto Rico,
   Mayagüez Campus — M
University of Rhode Island — M,D
University of Saskatchewan — M,D
University of Southern California — M,D,O
University of Southern Mississippi — M,D
The University of Tennessee — M,D
The University of Tennessee at
   Martin — M
University of Vermont — M,D
University of Wisconsin–
   Madison — M,D
University of Wisconsin–
   Stout — M
University of Wyoming — M
Utah State University — M,D
Washington State University — M,D
Wayne State University — M,D,O

FOREIGN LANGUAGES EDUCATION
Andrews University — M,D,O
Appalachian State University — M
Arizona State University at the
   Tempe campus — M,D
Augusta University — M,O
Binghamton University, State
   University of New York — M
Brigham Young University — M
Brooklyn College of the City
   University of New York — M
California State University,
   Sacramento — M
Caribbean University — M,D
Central Connecticut State
   University — M,O
City College of the City
   University of New York — M
Cleveland State University — M
College of Charleston — M
The College of William and Mary — M
The Colorado College — M
Colorado State University–
   Pueblo — M
Columbia University — M,D
Concordia College — M
Cornell University — M,D
Delaware State University — M
DePaul University — M,D
Duquesne University — M
East Carolina University — M
Eastern Michigan University — M,O
Eastern University — M,D,O
Elms College — M,O
Florida International University — M,D,O
Florida State University — M,D,O
Framingham State University — M
George Mason University — M
The George Washington University — M
Georgia Southern University — M
Georgia State University — M,O
Harding University — M,O
Hofstra University — M,D,O
Hunter College of the City
   University of New York — M
Indiana State University — M,D,O
Indiana University Bloomington — M,D
Indiana University of Pennsylvania — M
Indiana University–Purdue
   University Indianapolis — M,O
Inter American University of
   Puerto Rico, Arecibo Campus — M
Inter American University of
   Puerto Rico, Barranquitas Campus — M
Inter American University of
   Puerto Rico, Metropolitan Campus — M
Iona College — M
Ithaca College — M
James Madison University — M
Kean University — M
Kennesaw State University — M
Lamar University — M
Le Moyne College — M,O
London Metropolitan University — M,D
Manhattanville College — M
Marquette University — M
McGill University — M,D,O
Michigan State University — D
Middlebury Institute of
   International Studies at Monterey — M
Middle Tennessee State University — M
Minnesota State University Mankato — M
Mississippi State University — M
Morehead State University — M
New Mexico State University — M,D,O
New York University — M,D,O
Northern Arizona University — M
Pace University — M
Plymouth State University — M
Portland State University — M
Purdue University — M,D,O
Queens College of the City
   University of New York — M,O
Quinnipiac University — M
Rhode Island College — M
Rider University — O

Rivier University — M
Rutgers University–New
   Brunswick — M,D
Saginaw Valley State University — M
St. John Fisher College — M
Saint Xavier University — M
Shippensburg University of
   Pennsylvania — M,O
Smith College — M
Southern Connecticut State
   University — M
Southern Oregon University — M
Spalding University — M
State University of New York at
   Plattsburgh — M
State University of New York
   College at Geneseo — M
State University of New York
   College at Old Westbury — M
Stony Brook University, State
   University of New York — M,O
Texas A&M International University — M,D
Texas A&M University–
   Kingsville — M
Universidad del Este — M
Université du Québec
   en Outaouais — O
University at Buffalo, the State
   University of New York — M,D,O
University of Arkansas at Little
   Rock — M
University of California, Irvine — M,D
University of Central Arkansas — M
University of Connecticut — M
University of Delaware — M
University of Florida — M
University of Hawaii at Hilo — M,D
University of Hawaii at Manoa — M,D,O
University of Illinois at Chicago — M,D
University of Illinois at
   Urbana–Champaign — M,D
University of Indianapolis — M
The University of Iowa — M,D
University of Kentucky — M,D
University of Louisiana at Monroe — M,D
University of Maine — M
University of Maryland, Baltimore
   County — M
University of Maryland, College
   Park — D
University of Massachusetts
   Amherst — M
University of Michigan — M,D
University of Minnesota, Twin
   Cities Campus — M
University of Mississippi — M,D
University of Missouri — M,D,O
University of Nebraska at Kearney — M
University of Nebraska at Omaha — M
University of Nevada, Reno — M
The University of North Carolina
   at Chapel Hill — M
The University of North Carolina
   at Charlotte — M,D,O
The University of North Carolina
   at Greensboro — M,D,O
The University of North Carolina
   Wilmington — M
University of Northern Colorado — M,D
University of Northern Iowa — M
University of Oklahoma — M,D
University of Pittsburgh — M,D
University of Puerto Rico,
   Río Piedras Campus — M,D
University of South Carolina — M,D
University of Southern Mississippi — M
University of South Florida — O
The University of Tennessee — M,D,O
University of the Sacred Heart — M,O
The University of Toledo — M,D,O
University of Utah — M,D
University of Victoria — M
University of Virginia — M,D,O
University of Wisconsin–Madison — M,D
University of Wisconsin–Milwaukee — M,O
Valparaiso University — M
Vanderbilt University — M,D
Virginia Polytechnic Institute and
   State University — M,D
Wagner College — M
Washington State University — M
Wayne State University — M,D,O
West Chester University of
   Pennsylvania — M,O
Western Kentucky University — M
Worcester State University — M

FORENSIC NURSING
Aspen University — M
Boston College — M,D
Duquesne University — M,O
Fitchburg State University — M,O
Monmouth University — M,D,O

FORENSIC PSYCHOLOGY
Adler University — M,D,O
Alliant International
   University–Fresno — D
Alliant International
   University–Irvine — D
Alliant International
   University–Los Angeles — D
Alliant International
   University–Sacramento — D
Alliant International
   University–San Diego — D
Alliant International
   University–San Francisco — M,D
American International College — M,D,O
Argosy University, Atlanta — M,D,O
Argosy University, Chicago — D

Argosy University, Dallas — M
Argosy University, Denver — M,D
Argosy University, Hawai'i — M
Argosy University, Inland Empire — M,D
Argosy University, Los Angeles — M,D
Argosy University, Northern
   Virginia — M,D
Argosy University, Orange County — M
Argosy University, Phoenix — M
Argosy University, Salt Lake City — M,D
Argosy University, San Diego — M,D
Argosy University, San Francisco
   Bay Area — M
Argosy University, Sarasota — M,D
Argosy University, Schaumburg — M,O
Argosy University, Twin Cities — M,D,O
California Baptist University — M
Cambridge College — M,O
Castleton University — M
The Chicago School of Professional
   Psychology — M,D
The Chicago School of Professional
   Psychology at Downtown
   Los Angeles — D
The Chicago School of Professional
   Psychology at Irvine — D
The Chicago School of Professional
   Psychology: Online — M,O
College of Saint Elizabeth — M,D,O
Drexel University — D
Fairleigh Dickinson University,
   Metropolitan Campus — M
Fielding Graduate University — D,O
The George Washington University — O
Holy Names University — M
Immaculata University — M,D,O
John Jay College of Criminal
   Justice of the City University of
   New York — M
Kean University — M
London Metropolitan University — M,D
Marymount University — M
Montclair State University — O
Nova Southeastern University — M,D,O
Pontificia Universidad Catolica
   Madre y Maestra — M
Prairie View A&M University — M,D
Roger Williams University — M,D
Sage Graduate School — M,O
Tiffin University — M
Trine University — M
Universidad de Iberoamerica — M,D
Universidad del Turabo — M,D,O
University of Central Oklahoma — M
University of Denver — M,D
University of Houston–
   Victoria — M
University of Louisiana at Monroe — M
University of New Haven — M,D,O
University of North Dakota — M,D
Walden University — M,D,O
Westfield State University — M
William James College — M,D,O

FORENSIC SCIENCES
Alabama State University — M
Alliant International
   University–Irvine — D
American Public University System — M
Arcadia University — M
Boston University — M
Carlow University — M
Cedar Crest College — M
Champlain College — M
The College at Brockport, State
   University of New York — M,O
DeSales University — M,O
Duquesne University — M
Emporia State University — M,O
Florida Gulf Coast University — M
Florida International University — M,D
George Mason University — M
The George Washington University — M,O
Georgia State University — M,O
Golden Gate University — M,O
Indiana University–Purdue
   University Indianapolis — M
Iona College — M,O
James Madison University — M
John Jay College of Criminal
   Justice of the City University of
   New York — M,D
La Salle University — M,O
Long Island University–LIU
   Brooklyn — M,D,O
Marshall University — M,O
McGill University — M,D,O
Mercyhurst University — M
Michigan State University — M,D
Middle Georgia State University — M
Missouri Western State University — M,O
Nebraska Wesleyan University — M
Oklahoma State University Center
   for Health Sciences — M
Pace University — M
Penn State University Park — M
Philadelphia College of
   Osteopathic Medicine — M
St. Joseph's College, New
   York — M
Saint Leo University — M
Salve Regina University — M,O
Sam Houston State University — M,D
Seattle University — M,O
Stevenson University — M
Stratford University (VA) — M
Syracuse University — M,O
Texas Tech University — M
Towson University — M
Universidad del Turabo — M

M—masters degree; D—doctorate; O—other advanced degree; *—Close-Up and/or Display

University at Albany, State University of New York	M
The University of Alabama at Birmingham	M
University of California, Davis	M
University of Central Florida	M,D
University of Central Oklahoma	M
University of Charleston	M
University of Colorado Denver	M
University of Detroit Mercy	M,O
University of Florida	M,O
University of Houston–Victoria	M
University of Illinois at Chicago	M
University of New Haven	M,D,O
University of North Texas Health Science Center at Fort Worth	M,D,O
University of Rhode Island	M,D,O
University of St. Francis (IL)	M
University of Southern Mississippi	M,D
University of South Florida	M,D,O
Utica College	M
Virginia Commonwealth University	M
Webster University	M
West Virginia University	M,D

FORESTRY

Auburn University	M,D
California Polytechnic State University, San Luis Obispo	M
Clemson University	M,D
Cornell University	M,D
Duke University	M,D
Harvard University	M
Humboldt State University	M
Iowa State University of Science and Technology	M,D
Lakehead University	M,D
Louisiana State University and Agricultural & Mechanical College	M,D
McGill University	M,D
Michigan State University	M,D
Michigan Technological University	M,D
Mississippi State University	M,D
North Carolina State University	M,D
Northern Arizona University	M,D
The Ohio State University	M,D
Oklahoma State University	M,D
Oregon State University	M,D
Penn State University Park	M,D
Purdue University	M,D
Southern Illinois University Carbondale	M
Southern University and Agricultural and Mechanical College	M
State University of New York College of Environmental Science and Forestry	M,D
Stephen F. Austin State University	M,D
Texas A&M University	M,D
Tropical Agriculture Research and Higher Education Center	M,D
Université du Québec en Abitibi-Témiscamingue	M,D
Université Laval	M,D
University of Alberta	M,D
The University of Arizona	M,D
University of Arkansas at Monticello	M
The University of British Columbia	M,D
University of California, Berkeley	M,D
University of Florida	M,D
University of Georgia	M,D
University of Kentucky	M
University of Maine	M,D
University of Massachusetts Amherst	M,D
University of Minnesota, Twin Cities Campus	M,D
University of Missouri	M,D,O
University of Montana	M,D
University of New Brunswick Fredericton	M,D
University of New Hampshire	M,D
The University of Tennessee	M
University of Toronto	M,D
University of Vermont	M,D
University of Washington	M,D
University of Wisconsin–Madison	M,D
Utah State University	M,D
Virginia Polytechnic Institute and State University	M,D
West Virginia University	M,D
Yale University	M,D

FOUNDATIONS AND PHILOSOPHY OF EDUCATION

Antioch University New England	M
Arkansas State University	M,D,O
Ashland University	M
Azusa Pacific University	M
Ball State University	D
Bank Street College of Education	M
Binghamton University, State University of New York	M,D,O
Brigham Young University	M,D
Central Washington University	M
Chicago State University	M
College of Staten Island of the City University of New York	M
Columbia University	M,D
Curry College	M,O
DePaul University	M,D
Duquesne University	M
Eastern Michigan University	M
Eastern Washington University	M
East Tennessee State University	M
Fairfield University	M,O
Fairleigh Dickinson University, Metropolitan Campus	M
Florida Atlantic University	M
Florida State University	M,D
Georgia State University	M,D

Harvard University	M,O
Indiana University Bloomington	M,D,O
Iowa State University of Science and Technology	M,D
Johnson State College	M
Kent State University	M,D
Marquette University	M,D,O
McGill University	M,D,O
Mount Saint Vincent University	M
New York University	M,D
Northern Arizona University	M,D,O
Northern Illinois University	M,D,O
Penn State University Park	M,D,O
Purdue University	M,D,O
Rutgers University–New Brunswick	M,D
Saint Louis University	M,D
Simon Fraser University	M,D
Southern Illinois University Edwardsville	M
Spring Hill College	M
Syracuse University	M,D,O
Teachers College, Columbia University	M,D,O
University at Buffalo, the State University of New York	M,D,O
The University of British Columbia	M,D
University of California, Riverside	M,D,O
University of Cincinnati	M,D
University of Hawaii at Manoa	M,D
University of Houston	M,D
University of Houston–Clear Lake	M
The University of Iowa	M,D,O
University of Manitoba	M
University of Maryland, College Park	M,D,O
University of Minnesota, Twin Cities Campus	M,D
University of New Mexico	M,D
University of Pennsylvania	M,D
University of Pittsburgh	M,D
University of Rochester	D
University of Saskatchewan	M,D,O
University of South Africa	M,D
University of South Carolina	D
The University of Tennessee	M,D,O
The University of Texas of the Permian Basin	M
The University of Toledo	M,D,O
University of Utah	M,D
University of Victoria	M,D
University of Washington	M,D
University of Wisconsin–Milwaukee	M,D,O
Wayne State University	M,D,O
Western Illinois University	M,O
Widener University	M,D
William Paterson University of New Jersey	M,D

FRENCH

American University	M,O
Arizona State University at the Tempe campus	M
Asbury University	M
Binghamton University, State University of New York	M
Boston College	M
Boston University	M,D
Bowling Green State University	M
Brigham Young University	M
Brooklyn College of the City University of New York	M
Brown University	D
California State University, Long Beach	M
California State University, Los Angeles	M
Carleton University	M
Case Western Reserve University	M
Central Connecticut State University	M,O
Colorado State University	M
Columbia University	M,D
Concordia University (Canada)	M
Cornell University	D
Dalhousie University	M,D
DePaul University	M
Drew University	M,D,O
Duke University	D
Eastern Michigan University	M,D,O
Emory University	D
Florida Atlantic University	M
Florida State University	M,D
George Mason University	M
Georgia State University	M,O
The Graduate Center, City University of New York	D
Harvard University	M,D
Howard University	M
Hunter College of the City University of New York	M
Illinois State University	M
Indiana University Bloomington	M,D
Johns Hopkins University	D
Kent State University	M,D
Lake Forest College	M
Louisiana State University and Agricultural & Mechanical College	M,D
McGill University	M,D
McMaster University	M
Memorial University of Newfoundland	M
Miami University	M
Michigan State University	M,D
Middlebury College	M
Middle Tennessee State University	M
Millersville University of Pennsylvania	M
Minnesota State University Mankato	M
Montclair State University	M
New York University	M,D,O

North Carolina State University	M
Northern Illinois University	M
Northwestern University	D,O
The Ohio State University	M,D
Ohio University	M
Penn State University Park	M,D
Portland State University	M
Princeton University	D
Purdue University	M,D
Queens College of the City University of New York	M
Queen's University at Kingston	M,D
Rider University	O
Rutgers University–New Brunswick	M,D
St. John Fisher College	M
Saint Louis University	M
San Francisco State University	M
San Jose State University	M,O
Simon Fraser University	M
Smith College	M
Southern Oregon University	M
Stanford University	M,D
State University of New York at New Paltz	M,O
Stony Brook University, State University of New York	M
Syracuse University	M
Tufts University	M
Tulane University	M,D
Université de Moncton	M,D
Université de Montréal	M,D
Université de Sherbrooke	M,D
Université du Québec à Chicoutimi	O
University at Buffalo, the State University of New York	M,D,O
The University of Alabama	M,D
University of Alberta	M,D
The University of Arizona	M,D
University of Arkansas	M
The University of British Columbia	M,D
University of Calgary	M,D
University of California, Berkeley	D
University of California, Davis	D
University of California, Irvine	M,D
University of California, Los Angeles	M,D
University of California, Santa Barbara	D
University of Chicago	D
University of Cincinnati	M,D
University of Colorado Boulder	M,D
University of Delaware	M
University of Florida	M,D
University of Georgia	M,D
University of Guelph	M,D
University of Hawaii at Manoa	M
University of Illinois at Chicago	M
University of Illinois at Urbana–Champaign	M,D
The University of Iowa	M,D
The University of Kansas	M,D
University of Lethbridge	M,D
University of Louisiana at Lafayette	M,D
University of Louisville	M,O
University of Maine	M
The University of Manchester	M,D
University of Manitoba	M,D
University of Maryland, College Park	M,D
University of Massachusetts Amherst	M
University of Memphis	M
University of Miami	D
University of Michigan	D
University of Minnesota, Twin Cities Campus	M,D
University of Missouri	M,D
University of Missouri–Kansas City	M
University of Montana	M
University of Nebraska–Lincoln	M,D
University of Nevada, Reno	M
University of New Mexico	M,D
The University of North Carolina at Chapel Hill	M,D
The University of North Carolina at Greensboro	M
University of North Texas	M,D,O
University of Notre Dame	M,D
University of Oklahoma	M
University of Oregon	M
University of Ottawa	M,D
University of Pennsylvania	M,D
University of Pittsburgh	M,D
University of Regina	M
University of Saskatchewan	M
University of South Africa	M,D
University of South Carolina	M
University of South Florida	M
The University of Tennessee	M,D
The University of Texas at Arlington	M
The University of Texas at Austin	M,D
The University of Toledo	M
University of Toronto	M,D
University of Utah	M
University of Victoria	M
University of Virginia	M,D
University of Washington	M,D
University of Waterloo	M,D
The University of Western Ontario	M,D
University of Wisconsin–Madison	M,D,O
University of Wisconsin–Milwaukee	M,O
University of Wyoming	M
Vanderbilt University	M,D
Washington University in St. Louis	D
Wayne State University	M,D

West Chester University of Pennsylvania	M,O
Western Kentucky University	M
West Virginia University	M
Yale University	M
York University	M,D

GAME DESIGN AND DEVELOPMENT

Academy of Art University	M
Concordia University (Canada)	M,D,O
DePaul University	M,D
Full Sail University	M
Iona College	M
Long Island University–LIU Post	M
Michigan State University	M
New York University	M
Rochester Institute of Technology	M
Sacred Heart University	M
Savannah College of Art and Design	M
Shepherd University (CA)	M
University of Advancing Technology	M
University of Central Florida	M
The University of North Carolina at Charlotte	M,O
University of Southern California	M,D
University of Utah	M
Virginia International University	M,O
Worcester Polytechnic Institute	M

GENDER STUDIES

American University	M,D,O
The American University in Cairo	M,O
Arizona State University at the Tempe campus	M,D,O
Brandeis University	M,D
Carnegie Mellon University	D
Central European University	M,D
Central Michigan University	M
The College of New Jersey	O
Cornell University	M,D
Delta State University	M
Dominican University of California	M
Eastern Michigan University	M,O
George Mason University	M
The George Washington University	O
Indiana University Bloomington	M,O
Indiana University Northwest	
Indiana University–Purdue University Indianapolis	M
Instituto Tecnologico de Santo Domingo	M,O
Kansas State University	O
Memorial University of Newfoundland	M,D
Middle Tennessee State University	O
Minnesota State University Mankato	M
Northern Arizona University	O
Northwestern University	O
The Ohio State University	M,D
Oregon State University	M,D
Queen's University at Kingston	M,D
Rutgers University–New Brunswick	M,D
Saint Mary's University (Canada)	M
San Diego State University	O
Simmons College	M
Simon Fraser University	M,D
Stony Brook University, State University of New York	O
Texas Woman's University	M,D
University at Buffalo, the State University of New York	M,D,O
The University of Arizona	M,D,O
The University of British Columbia	M,D
University of California, Los Angeles	M,D
University of Chicago	M
University of Colorado Denver	M
University of Florida	M,O
University of Lethbridge	M,D
University of Memphis	O
University of Michigan–Flint	M
The University of North Carolina at Charlotte	M,D,O
The University of North Carolina at Greensboro	M,O
University of Northern British Columbia	M
University of Northern Iowa	M
University of Oklahoma	O
University of Rhode Island	M,D,O
University of Saskatchewan	M,D
University of South Florida	M,O
The University of Toledo	O
University of Toronto	M,D
University of Wisconsin–Milwaukee	M,O
Wayne State University	M,D,O
Wilfrid Laurier University	M
York University	M,D

GENETIC COUNSELING

Arcadia University	M
Boston University	M
Brandeis University	M
California State University, Stanislaus	M
Case Western Reserve University	M,D
Emory University	M
Icahn School of Medicine at Mount Sinai	M
Johns Hopkins University	M,D
Long Island University–LIU Post	M,O
McGill University	M,D
Northwestern University	M
Sarah Lawrence College	M
Thomas Jefferson University	M
Université de Montréal	O
The University of Alabama at Birmingham	M

University of Arkansas for Medical
 Sciences — M,D
The University of British Columbia — M
University of California, Irvine — M
University of Cincinnati — M
University of Colorado Denver — M,D
University of Maryland, Baltimore — M
University of Michigan — M,D
University of Minnesota, Twin
 Cities Campus — M,D
The University of North Carolina
 at Greensboro — M
University of Oklahoma Health
 Sciences Center — M
University of Pittsburgh — M,D,O
University of South Carolina — M
The University of Texas Health
 Science Center at Houston — M,D
University of Toronto — M,D
University of Wisconsin–
 Madison — M,D
Wayne State University — M,D,O

GENETICS

Albert Einstein College of
 Medicine — D
Baylor College of Medicine — D
Boston University — D
Brandeis University — M,D
California Institute of Technology — D
Carnegie Mellon University — M,D
Clemson University — M,D,O
Columbia University — M,D
Cornell University — D
Dartmouth College — D
Drexel University — M,D
Duke University — D
Emory University — D
Harvard University — D
Illinois State University — M,D
Indiana University Bloomington — M,D
Iowa State University of Science
 and Technology — M,D
Irell & Manella Graduate School of
 Biological Sciences — D*
Johns Hopkins University — M,D
Kansas State University — M,D
Kent State University — M,D
Marquette University — M,D
Massachusetts Institute of
 Technology — D
Mayo Clinic Graduate School of
 Biomedical Sciences — D
McMaster University — M,D
Medical University of South
 Carolina — D
Michigan State University — M,D
Mississippi State University — M,D
New York University — M,D
North Carolina State University — M,D
The Ohio State University — M,D
Oregon Health & Science University — D
Oregon State University — M,D
Purdue University — M,D
Rutgers University–New
 Brunswick — M,D
Stanford University — D
Stony Brook University, State
 University of New York — D
Thomas Jefferson University — D
Tufts University — D
Université de Montréal — O
Université du Québec
 à Chicoutimi — M
University at Buffalo, the State
 University of New York — M,D
The University of Alabama at
 Birmingham — D
University of Alberta — M,D
The University of Arizona — M,D
The University of British Columbia — M,D
University of Calgary — M,D
University of California, Davis — M,D
University of California, Irvine — D
University of California,
 Riverside — D
University of California, San
 Francisco — D
University of Chicago — D
University of Colorado Denver — M,D
University of Connecticut — M,D
University of Connecticut Health
 Center — D
University of Delaware — M,D
University of Florida — D
University of Georgia — M,D
University of Hawaii at Manoa — M,D
University of Illinois at Chicago — D
The University of Iowa — M,D
The University of Manchester — M,D
University of Massachusetts
 Amherst — M,D
University of Miami — M,D
University of Minnesota, Twin
 Cities Campus — M,D
University of Missouri — D
University of Nebraska Medical
 Center — M,D
University of New Hampshire — M,D
University of New Mexico — M,D
The University of North Carolina
 at Chapel Hill — M,D
University of North Dakota — M,D
University of North Texas Health
 Science Center at Fort Worth — M,D
University of Notre Dame — M,D
University of Oregon — M,D
University of Pennsylvania — D
University of Puerto Rico,
 Río Piedras Campus — M,D
University of Rochester — D

The University of Tennessee — M,D
The University of Texas Health
 Science Center at Houston — M,D
The University of Texas MD
 Anderson Cancer Center — M
The University of Texas Medical
 Branch — D
The University of Texas
 Southwestern Medical Center — D
University of Washington — M,D,O
University of Wisconsin–
 Madison — M,D
University of Wisconsin–
 Milwaukee — M,D
University of Wyoming — D
Van Andel Institute Graduate
 School — D
Virginia Polytechnic Institute and
 State University — M,D
Washington State University — M,D
Washington University in St. Louis — M,D
Wesleyan University — D
West Virginia University — M,D
Yale University — D

GENOMIC SCIENCES

Albert Einstein College of
 Medicine — D
Augusta University — D
Black Hills State University — M
Boston University — D
Case Western Reserve University — M,D
Concordia University (Canada) — M,D,O
Cornell University — D
Duke University — D
Harvard University — D
Manchester University — M
Massachusetts Institute of
 Technology — D
New York University — M,D
North Carolina State University — M,D
North Dakota State University — M,D
Oregon State University — M,D
Purdue University — D
Thomas Jefferson University — D
University at Buffalo, the State
 University of New York — M,D
The University of Alabama at
 Birmingham — D
University of California,
 Riverside — D
University of California, San
 Francisco — D
University of Chicago — D
University of Cincinnati — M,D
University of Connecticut — M,D
University of Georgia — M,D
University of Maryland, Baltimore — M,D
University of Maryland, College
 Park — D
University of Pennsylvania — D
University of Rochester — D
University of Southern California — D
The University of Tennessee — M,D
The University of Tennessee–
 Oak Ridge National Laboratory — M,D
The University of Toledo — M,O
University of Washington — D
Wake Forest University — D
Washington University in St. Louis — M
Wayne State University — M,D,O
Wesleyan University — D
West Virginia University — M,D
Yale University — D

GEOCHEMISTRY

California Institute of Technology — M,D
Colorado School of Mines — M,D
Cornell University — M,D
Georgia State University — M,D
Indiana University Bloomington — M,D
Massachusetts Institute of
 Technology — M,D
McMaster University — M,D
Missouri University of Science and
 Technology — M,D
Montana Tech of The University of
 Montana — M
New Mexico Institute of Mining and
 Technology — M,D
Ohio University — M
Oregon State University — M,D
University of California, Los
 Angeles — M,D
University of Hawaii at Manoa — M,D
The University of Manchester — M,D
University of Nevada, Reno — M,D
The University of Texas at Dallas — M,D
Yale University — D

GEODETIC SCIENCES

The Ohio State University — M,D
Université Laval — M,D
University of New Brunswick
 Fredericton — M,D

GEOGRAPHIC INFORMATION SYSTEMS

Acadia University — M
Appalachian State University — M
Arizona State University at the
 Tempe campus — M,D,O
Auburn University at Montgomery — M
Ball State University — M,O
Boston University — M,D
Central Michigan University — M
Chicago State University — M
Claremont Graduate University — M,D,O
Clark University — M
The College of William and Mary — M
East Carolina University — M,O
Eastern Illinois University — M
Eastern Michigan University — M,O

Elizabeth City State University — M
Elmhurst College — M
Florida State University — M,D
George Mason University — M,D,O
Georgia Institute of Technology — M,D
Georgia State University — O
Hunter College of the City
 University of New York — M,O
Idaho State University — M,O
Indiana University of Pennsylvania — M,O
Indiana University–Purdue
 University Indianapolis — M,O
Johns Hopkins University — M,O
Kansas State University — M,D,O
Kent State University — M,D
Long Island University–LIU
 Post — M,O
Michigan Technological University — M
Millersville University of
 Pennsylvania — M
Montclair State University — O
Naval Postgraduate School — M,D,O
North Carolina State University — M,D
Northeastern University — M
Northern Arizona University — M,O
Northern Kentucky University — M,O
Northwest Missouri State
 University — M,O
Oregon State University — M
Penn State University Park — M,D
Saint Louis University — M,D,O
Saint Mary's University of
 Minnesota — M,O
Salisbury University — M,O
Sam Houston State University — M,O
San Francisco State University — M
State University of New York
 College of Environmental Science
 and Forestry — M,D
Stony Brook University, State
 University of New York — O
Temple University — M,D,O
Texas State University — M,D
Université du Québec
 à Montréal — O
Université Laval — M,O
University at Albany, State
 University of New York — M,O
University at Buffalo, the State
 University of New York — M,D
The University of Alabama — M,D
University of Alaska Fairbanks — M
The University of Arizona — M,D,O
University of Central Arkansas — M,O
University of Central Florida — M,O
University of Colorado Denver — M,O
University of Denver — M,O
University of Florida — M,O
The University of Iowa — M,D,O
The University of Kansas — M,D
University of Lethbridge — M,D
University of Maryland, Baltimore
 County — M,O
University of Memphis — M,D,O
University of Minnesota, Twin
 Cities Campus — M,D
University of Missouri — M,D,O
University of Nebraska at Omaha — M,O
University of New Hampshire — O
University of New Haven — M,O
University of North Alabama — M
The University of North Carolina
 at Charlotte — M,D
The University of North Carolina
 at Greensboro — M,D,O
University of North Dakota — M
University of North Texas Health
 Science Center at Fort Worth — M,D,O
University of Pennsylvania — M,D,O
University of Pittsburgh — M,D
University of Redlands — M,D
University of Southern California — M,O
University of South Florida — M,D,O
The University of Texas at Dallas — M,D,O
The University of Toledo — M,D,O
University of Utah — M,D
University of West Florida — M
University of West Georgia — M,O
University of Wisconsin–
 Madison — M,D,O
University of Wisconsin–
 Milwaukee — M,D,O
Virginia Commonwealth University — O
Virginia Polytechnic Institute and
 State University — M,D
West Chester University of
 Pennsylvania — M,O
Western Illinois University — M,O
Western Michigan University — M,O
West Virginia University — M,O
Wilmington University — M

GEOGRAPHY

Appalachian State University — M
Arizona State University at the
 Tempe campus — M,D,O
Auburn University — M,O
Ball State University — M,O
Binghamton University, State
 University of New York — M
Boston University — M
Brock University — M
California State University, East
 Bay — M
California State University,
 Fullerton — M
California State University, Long
 Beach — M
California State University, Los
 Angeles — M

California State University,
 Northridge — M
Carleton University — M,D
Central Connecticut State
 University — M
Chicago State University — M
Clark University — D
Concordia University (Canada) — M,D,O
East Carolina University — M,O
East Stroudsburg University of
 Pennsylvania — M
Florida State University — M,D
Fort Hays State University — M
George Mason University — M,D,O
The George Washington University — M
Georgia State University — M,D
Hunter College of the City
 University of New York — M,O
Indiana University Bloomington — D
Indiana University of Pennsylvania — M
Kansas State University — M,D,O
Kent State University — M,D
Louisiana State University and
 Agricultural & Mechanical College — M,D
Marshall University — M,O
McGill University — M,D
McMaster University — M,D
Memorial University of
 Newfoundland — M
Miami University — M
Michigan State University — M,D
Minnesota State University Mankato — M
Mississippi State University — M
Missouri State University — M
New Mexico State University — M
Northeastern Illinois University — M
Northern Arizona University — M,O
Northern Illinois University — M,D
The Ohio State University — M,D
Ohio University — M
Oklahoma State University — M,D
Oregon State University — M,D
Penn State University Park — M,D
Philadelphia University — M
Portland State University — M,D
Queen's University at
 Kingston — M,D
Rutgers University–New
 Brunswick — M,D
St. Cloud State University — M
Salem State University — M
San Diego State University — M
San Francisco State University — M
San Jose State University — M,O
Shippensburg University of
 Pennsylvania — M,O
Simon Fraser University — M,D
South Dakota State University — M
Southern Illinois University
 Carbondale — M,D
Southern Illinois University
 Edwardsville — M
Syracuse University — M,D
Temple University — M,D,O
Texas A&M University — M,D
Texas State University — M,D
Texas Tech University — M,D
Towson University — M
Trent University — M
Université de Montréal — M,D,O
Université de Sherbrooke — M,D
Université du Québec
 à Montréal — M
Université Laval — M
University at Albany, State
 University of New York — M
University at Buffalo, the State
 University of New York — M,D
The University of Alabama — M,D
The University of Arizona — M,D,O
University of Arkansas — M
The University of British Columbia — M,D
University of Calgary — M,D
University of California, Berkeley — D
University of California, Davis — M,D
University of California, Los
 Angeles — M,D
University of California, Santa
 Barbara — M,D
University of Central Arkansas — M,O
University of Cincinnati — M
University of Colorado Boulder — M,D
University of Colorado Colorado
 Springs — M
University of Connecticut — M,D
University of Delaware — M,D
University of Florida — M,D
University of Georgia — M,D
University of Guelph — M,D
University of Hawaii at Manoa — M,D,O
University of Idaho — M,D
University of Illinois at Chicago — M
University of Illinois at
 Urbana–Champaign — M,D
The University of Iowa — M,D,O
The University of Kansas — M,D,O
University of Kentucky — M,D
University of Lethbridge — M,D
University of Louisville — M
The University of Manchester — M,D
University of Manitoba — M
University of Maryland, Baltimore
 County — M,D
University of Maryland, College
 Park — M,D
University of Massachusetts
 Amherst — M
University of Memphis — M,D,O
University of Miami — M
University of Minnesota, Twin
 Cities Campus — M,D

M—masters degree; D—doctorate; O—other advanced degree; *—Close-Up and/or Display

University of Missouri	M,O
University of Montana	M,O
University of Nebraska at Omaha	M,O
University of Nebraska–Lincoln	M,D
University of Nevada, Reno	M,D
University of New Mexico	M
University of New Orleans	M
The University of North Carolina at Chapel Hill	M,D
The University of North Carolina at Charlotte	M,D
The University of North Carolina at Greensboro	M,D,O
University of North Dakota	M
University of Northern Iowa	M
University of North Texas	M,D,O
University of Oklahoma	M,D
University of Oregon	M,D
University of Ottawa	M,D
University of Prince Edward Island	M
University of Regina	M,D
University of Saskatchewan	M,D
University of South Africa	M,D
University of South Carolina	M,D
University of Southern California	M,O
University of Southern Mississippi	M,D
University of South Florida	O
The University of Tennessee	M,D
The University of Texas at Austin	M,D
The University of Texas at Dallas	M,D
The University of Toledo	M,D,O
University of Toronto	M,D
University of Utah	M,D
University of Victoria	M,D
University of Washington	M,D
University of Waterloo	M,D
The University of Western Ontario	M,D
University of Wisconsin–Madison	M,D,O
University of Wisconsin–Milwaukee	M,D
University of Wyoming	M
Utah State University	M,D
Virginia Polytechnic Institute and State University	M,D
West Chester University of Pennsylvania	M,O
Western Illinois University	M,O
Western Michigan University	M,D,O
Western Washington University	M
West Virginia University	M,D
Wilfrid Laurier University	M,D
York University	M,D

GEOLOGICAL ENGINEERING

Arizona State University at the Tempe campus	M,D
Colorado School of Mines	M,D
Missouri University of Science and Technology	M,D
Montana Tech of The University of Montana	M
New Mexico Institute of Mining and Technology	M
New Mexico State University	M,D
South Dakota School of Mines and Technology	M,D
The University of Akron	M
University of Alaska Anchorage	M
University of Alaska Fairbanks	M
The University of Arizona	M,D,O
The University of British Columbia	M,D
University of Hawaii at Manoa	M,D
University of Idaho	M,D
University of Minnesota, Twin Cities Campus	M,D,O
University of Nevada, Reno	M,D
University of North Dakota	M,D
University of Oklahoma	M,D
University of Saskatchewan	M,D
University of Utah	M,D
University of Wisconsin–Madison	M,D

GEOLOGY

Acadia University	M
American University of Beirut	M,D
Arizona State University at the Tempe campus	M,D
Auburn University	M
Ball State University	M,D
Binghamton University, State University of New York	M,D
Boston College	M
Bowling Green State University	M
Brigham Young University	M
Brooklyn College of the City University of New York	M,D
California Institute of Technology	M,D
California State Polytechnic University, Pomona	M
California State University, Bakersfield	M
California State University, Chico	M
California State University, East Bay	M
California State University, Fresno	M
California State University, Fullerton	M
California State University, Long Beach	M
California State University, Los Angeles	M
California State University, Northridge	M
Case Western Reserve University	M,D
Central Washington University	M
City College of the City University of New York	M
Colorado School of Mines	M,D
Cornell University	M,D
Duke University	M,D
East Carolina University	M,O

Eastern Kentucky University	M,D
Florida Atlantic University	M,D
Florida State University	M,D
Fort Hays State University	M
Georgia State University	M
Humboldt State University	M
Idaho State University	M,O
Indiana University Bloomington	M,D
Indiana University–Purdue University Indianapolis	M,D
Iowa State University of Science and Technology	M,D
Kansas State University	M
Kent State University	M,D
Lakehead University	M
Laurentian University	M,D
Lehigh University	M,D
Louisiana State University and Agricultural & Mechanical College	M,D
Massachusetts Institute of Technology	M,D
McMaster University	M,D
Memorial University of Newfoundland	M,D
Miami University	M,D
Mississippi State University	M,D
Missouri State University	M
Missouri University of Science and Technology	M,D
Montana Tech of The University of Montana	M
New Mexico Institute of Mining and Technology	M,D
New Mexico State University	M
Northern Arizona University	M,D
Northern Illinois University	M,D
Northwestern University	D
The Ohio State University	M,D
Ohio University	M
Oklahoma State University	M,D
Oregon State University	M,D
Portland State University	M,D
Queens College of the City University of New York	M
Queen's University at Kingston	M,D
Rensselaer Polytechnic Institute	M,D
Rutgers University–Newark	M
Rutgers University–New Brunswick	M,D
St. Francis Xavier University	M
San Diego State University	M
San Jose State University	M,O
South Dakota School of Mines and Technology	M,D
Southern Illinois University Carbondale	M,D
Southern Methodist University	M,D
Stephen F. Austin State University	M
Sul Ross State University	M
Syracuse University	M,D
Temple University	M,D
Texas A&M University	M,D
Texas Christian University	M
Université du Québec à Montréal	M,D,O
Université Laval	M,D
University at Buffalo, the State University of New York	M,D
The University of Akron	M
The University of Alabama	M,D
The University of Arkansas	M
The University of British Columbia	M,D
University of Calgary	M,D
University of California, Berkeley	M,D
University of California, Davis	M,D
University of California, Los Angeles	M,D
University of California, Riverside	M,D
University of Cincinnati	M,D
University of Colorado Boulder	M,D
University of Connecticut	M,D
University of Delaware	M,D
University of Florida	M,D
University of Georgia	M,D
University of Hawaii at Manoa	M,D
University of Houston	M,D
University of Idaho	M,D
University of Illinois at Chicago	M,D
University of Illinois at Urbana–Champaign	M,D
The University of Kansas	M,D
University of Kentucky	M,D
University of Louisiana at Lafayette	M
University of Maine	M,O
University of Manitoba	M,D
University of Maryland, College Park	M,D
University of Memphis	M,D,O
University of Minnesota, Duluth	M
University of Minnesota, Twin Cities Campus	M,D
University of Missouri	M,D
University of Montana	M,D
University of Nevada, Reno	M,D
University of New Brunswick Fredericton	M,D
University of New Hampshire	M
The University of North Carolina at Chapel Hill	M,D
University of North Dakota	M,D
University of Oklahoma	M,D
University of Oregon	M,D
University of Pittsburgh	M,D
University of Puerto Rico, Mayagüez Campus	M
University of Regina	M,D
University of Rochester	M,D
University of Saskatchewan	M,D,O
University of South Carolina	M,D
University of Southern Mississippi	M,D
University of South Florida	M,D,O

The University of Tennessee	M,D
The University of Texas at Arlington	M,D
The University of Texas at Austin	M,D
The University of Texas at El Paso	M,D
The University of Texas at San Antonio	M
The University of Texas of the Permian Basin	M
The University of Toledo	M,D
University of Toronto	M,D
University of Utah	M,D
University of Vermont	M
University of Washington	M,D
The University of Western Ontario	M,D
University of Wisconsin–Madison	M,D
University of Wisconsin–Milwaukee	M,D
University of Wyoming	M,D
Utah State University	M
Vanderbilt University	M,D
Washington State University	M,D
Wayne State University	M
Western Kentucky University	M
Western Washington University	M
West Virginia University	M
Wichita State University	M
Wright State University	O
Yale University	D

GEOPHYSICS

Boise State University	M,D
Boston College	M
Bowling Green State University	M
California Institute of Technology	M,D
Colorado School of Mines	M,D
Cornell University	M,D
Florida State University	D
Idaho State University	M,O
Indiana University Bloomington	M,D
Louisiana State University and Agricultural & Mechanical College	M,D
Massachusetts Institute of Technology	M,D
Memorial University of Newfoundland	M,D
Michigan Technological University	M,D
Missouri University of Science and Technology	M,D
New Mexico Institute of Mining and Technology	M,D
Oregon State University	M,D
Rice University	M
Saint Louis University	M,D
Southern Methodist University	M,D
Stanford University	M,D
Texas A&M University	M,D
University of Alaska Fairbanks	M
University of Alberta	M,D
The University of British Columbia	M,D
University of Calgary	M,D
University of California, Berkeley	M,D
University of California, Los Angeles	M,D
University of California, San Diego	M,D
University of Chicago	D
University of Colorado Boulder	M,D
University of Hawaii at Manoa	M,D
University of Houston	M,D
University of Manitoba	M,D
University of Memphis	M,D,O
University of Miami	M,D
University of Minnesota, Twin Cities Campus	M,D
University of Nevada, Reno	M,D
University of Oklahoma	M,D
The University of Texas at Dallas	M,D
The University of Texas at El Paso	M
The University of Tulsa	M,D
University of Utah	M,D
University of Washington	M,D
The University of Western Ontario	M,D
University of Wisconsin–Madison	M,D
University of Wyoming	M,D
West Virginia University	M,D
Wright State University	M
Yale University	D

GEOSCIENCES

Arizona State University at the Tempe campus	M,D
Ball State University	M
Baylor University	M,D
Boston University	M,D
Brock University	M
Brooklyn College of the City University of New York	M
Brown University	D
California State University, Chico	M
California State University, San Bernardino	M
Carleton University	M,D
Case Western Reserve University	M,D
City College of the City University of New York	M
Colorado State University	M,D
Columbia University	M,D
Cornell University	M,D
Dalhousie University	M,D
Dartmouth College	M,D
East Tennessee State University	M
Emporia State University	M,O
Florida Atlantic University	M,D
Florida Institute of Technology	M,D
Florida International University	M,D
Florida State University	M,D
Fort Hays State University	M
George Mason University	M,D,O
Georgia Institute of Technology	M,D
Georgia State University	M,D,O
The Graduate Center, City University of New York	D

Harvard University	M,D
Hunter College of the City University of New York	M
Idaho State University	M,O
Indiana University Bloomington	M
Indiana University–Purdue University Indianapolis	M,D
Iowa State University of Science and Technology	M,D
Ithaca College	M
Jackson State University	M
Johns Hopkins University	M,D
Lehigh University	M,D
Long Island University–LIU Post	M,O
Massachusetts Institute of Technology	M,D
McGill University	M,D
McMaster University	M,D
Memorial University of Newfoundland	M,D
Michigan State University	M,D
Middle Tennessee State University	O
Mississippi State University	M,D
Missouri State University	M
Montana State University	M,D
Montana Tech of The University of Montana	M
Montclair State University	M
Murray State University	M
New Mexico Institute of Mining and Technology	M,D
North Carolina Central University	M
North Carolina State University	M,D
Northwestern University	D
The Ohio State University	M,D
Pace University	M,O
Penn State University Park	M,D
Princeton University	D
Purdue University	M,D
Queens College of the City University of New York	M
Rice University	M
St. Francis Xavier University	M
Saint Louis University	M,D
St. Thomas University	M,D,O
San Francisco State University	M
Simon Fraser University	M,D
South Dakota State University	D
Southern Illinois University Carbondale	M,D
Stanford University	M,D,O
State University of New York at New Paltz	M,O
Stony Brook University, State University of New York	M,D
Teachers College, Columbia University	M,D
Temple University	M,D
Texas Tech University	M,D
Université du Québec à Chicoutimi	M
Université du Québec à Montréal	M,D,O
Université du Québec, Institut National de la Recherche Scientifique	M,D
Université Laval	M,D
University at Buffalo, the State University of New York	M,D
The University of Akron	M
The University of Alabama	M,D
The University of Alabama in Huntsville	M,D
University of Alberta	M,D
The University of Arizona	M,D
University of Arkansas at Little Rock	O
University of Calgary	M,D
University of California, Irvine	M,D
University of California, Los Angeles	M,D
University of California, San Diego	M,D
University of California, Santa Barbara	M,D
University of California, Santa Cruz	M,D
University of Chicago	D
University of Florida	M,D
University of Illinois at Chicago	M,D
University of Illinois at Urbana–Champaign	M,D
The University of Iowa	M,D
University of Maine	M,D
The University of Manchester	M,D
University of Massachusetts Amherst	M,D
University of Michigan	M,D
University of Missouri–Kansas City	M,D
University of Montana	M,D
University of Nebraska–Lincoln	M,D
University of Nevada, Las Vegas	M,D
University of New Hampshire	M,D,O
University of New Haven	M,O
University of New Mexico	M,D
University of New Orleans	M
The University of North Carolina at Charlotte	M,D
The University of North Carolina Wilmington	M
University of North Dakota	M,D
University of Northern Colorado	M
University of Northern Iowa	M
University of Notre Dame	M,D
University of Ottawa	M,D
University of Pennsylvania	M,D
University of Rhode Island	M,D
University of Rochester	M,D
University of South Carolina	M,D
University of Southern California	M,D
University of South Florida	M,D

The University of Texas at Austin — M,D
The University of Texas at Dallas — M,D
The University of Tulsa — M,D
University of Victoria — M,D
University of Waterloo — M,D
The University of Western Ontario — M,D
University of Windsor — M,D
Virginia Polytechnic Institute and State University — M,D
Washington University in St. Louis — D
Wesleyan University — M
West Chester University of Pennsylvania — M,O
Western Connecticut State University — M
Western Kentucky University
Western Michigan University — M,D,O
Yale University — D
York University — M,D

GEOTECHNICAL ENGINEERING
The Citadel, The Military College of South Carolina — M,O
Cornell University — M,D
Drexel University — M,D
École Polytechnique de Montréal — M,D,O
Illinois Institute of Technology — M,D
Iowa State University of Science and Technology — M,D
Kansas State University — M,D
Louisiana State University and Agricultural & Mechanical College — M,D
Massachusetts Institute of Technology — M,D,O
McGill University — M,D
Missouri University of Science and Technology — M,D
Northwestern University — M,D
Norwich University — M
Ohio State University — M,D
Old Dominion University — M
Oregon State University — M,D
Penn State University Park — M,D
Southern Illinois University Edwardsville — M
Stanford University — M,D,O
Tufts University — M,D
University of Alberta — M,D
University of Calgary — M,D
University of California, Berkeley — M,D
University of Colorado Denver — M,D
University of Dayton — M
University of Delaware — M,D
University of Massachusetts Amherst — M,D
University of Memphis — M,D,O
University of Missouri — M,D
University of New Brunswick Fredericton — M,D
University of Puerto Rico, Mayagüez Campus — M,D
University of Southern California — M,D,O
University of South Florida — M,D
The University of Texas at Austin — M,D
University of Washington — M,D

GERMAN
Arizona State University at the Tempe campus — M
Bowling Green State University — M
Brown University — D
California State University, Long Beach — M
Central Connecticut State University — M,O
Colorado State University — M
Columbia University — M,D
Cornell University — M,D
Dalhousie University — M
DePaul University — M
Duke University — D
Florida Atlantic University — M
Florida State University — M
Georgetown University — M,D
Georgia State University — O
The Graduate Center, City University of New York — M,D
Harvard University — D
Illinois State University — M
Indiana University Bloomington — M,D
Johns Hopkins University — D
Kent State University — M,D
McGill University — M,D
Memorial University of Newfoundland — M
Michigan State University — M,D
Middlebury College — M,D
Middle Tennessee State University — M
Millersville University of Pennsylvania — M
New York University — M,D
Northwestern University — D
The Ohio State University — M,D
Penn State University Park — M,D
Portland State University — M
Princeton University — D
Purdue University — M,D
Queen's University at Kingston — M,D
Rider University — O
Rutgers University–New Brunswick — M,D
San Francisco State University — M
Stanford University — M,D
Texas Tech University — M,D
Tufts University — M
Université de Montréal — M
University at Buffalo, the State University of New York — M,D,O
The University of Alabama — M,D

University of Alberta — M,D
The University of Arizona — M,D
University of Arkansas — M
The University of British Columbia — M,D
University of Calgary — M,D
University of California, Berkeley — D
University of California, Davis — M,D
University of California, Irvine — M,D
University of California, Los Angeles — M,D
University of Chicago — M,D
University of Cincinnati — M,D
University of Colorado Boulder — M
University of Delaware — M
University of Florida — M,D
University of Georgia — M
University of Illinois at Chicago — M,D
University of Illinois at Urbana–Champaign — M,D
The University of Kansas — M,D
University of Kentucky — M,D
University of Lethbridge — M,D
The University of Manchester — M,D
University of Manitoba — M
University of Maryland, College Park — M,D
University of Massachusetts Amherst — M,D
University of Michigan — M,D,O
University of Minnesota, Twin Cities Campus — M,D
University of Missouri — M
University of Montana — M
University of Nebraska–Lincoln — M,D
University of Nevada, Reno — M
University of New Mexico — M,D
The University of North Carolina at Chapel Hill — D
University of Oklahoma — M
University of Oregon — M,D
University of Pennsylvania — M,D
University of Saskatchewan — M
University of South Africa — M,D
University of South Carolina — M,D
The University of Tennessee — M,D
The University of Texas at Austin — M,D
The University of Toledo — M
University of Toronto — M,D
University of Vermont — M
University of Victoria — M
University of Virginia — M
University of Washington — M,D
University of Waterloo — M,D
University of Wisconsin–Madison — M,D
University of Wisconsin–Milwaukee — M,O
University of Wyoming — M
Vanderbilt University — M,D
Washington University in St. Louis — D
Wayne State University — M,D
West Chester University of Pennsylvania — M,O
Western Kentucky University — M
Yale University — D

GERONTOLOGICAL NURSING
Allen College — M,D
Alvernia University — M,D,O
American University of Beirut — M
Arizona State University at the Tempe campus — M,D,O
Armstrong State University — M,O
Augusta University — D
Ball State University — M,D,O
Boise State University — M,D,O
Boston College — M,D
California State University, Stanislaus — M
Capella University — M
Caribbean University — M,D
Case Western Reserve University — M
Clemson University — M,D,O
College of Staten Island of the City University of New York — M,O
Columbia University — M,O
Creighton University — M,D,O
Duke University — M,D,O
East Tennessee State University — M,D,O
Fairleigh Dickinson University, College at Florham — M
Felician University — M
Florida Southern College — M
Goldfarb School of Nursing at Barnes-Jewish College — M
Graceland University (IA) — M,D,O
Gwynedd Mercy University — M,D
Hampton University — M,D
Hofstra University — M
Hunter College of the City University of New York — M
Independence University — M
Indiana University–Purdue University Fort Wayne — M,O
Indiana University–Purdue University Indianapolis — M
James Madison University — M,D
Johns Hopkins University — D
Kent State University — M,D
Keuka College — M
La Salle University — M,D,O
Lehman College of the City University of New York — M
Loma Linda University — M
Louisiana State University Health Sciences Center — M,D,O
Marquette University — M,D
Maryville University of Saint Louis — M,D

Medical University of South Carolina — M,D
Mercer University — M,D,O
MGH Institute of Health Professions — M,D,O
Middle Georgia State University — M
Molloy College — M,D,O
Monmouth University — M,D
Mount Carmel College of Nursing — M,D
Neumann University — M,O
New Mexico State University — M,D,O
New York University — M,D,O
Northeastern University — M,D,O
Oakland University — M,O
Old Dominion University — M
Oregon Health & Science University — M
Point Loma Nazarene University — M,O
Purdue University — M,D,O
Research College of Nursing — M
Rush University — M
Rutgers University–Camden — D
Sage Graduate School — M,O
St. Catherine University — M,D
Saint Francis Medical Center College of Nursing — M,D,O
Salem State University — M
Seattle Pacific University — M,O
Seattle University — M
Seton Hall University — M,D
Shenandoah University — M,D,O
Southern University and Agricultural and Mechanical College — M,D,O
Stony Brook University, State University of New York — M,D,O
Texas Christian University — M,O
Texas Tech University Health Sciences Center — M,D,O
Uniformed Services University of the Health Sciences — M,D
University at Buffalo, the State University of New York — M,D,O
The University of Alabama at Birmingham — M,D
The University of Alabama in Huntsville — M,D,O
University of Colorado Colorado Springs — M,D
University of Delaware — M
University of Illinois at Chicago — M,O
The University of Kansas — M,D,O
University of Louisville — M,D
University of Massachusetts Amherst — M,D
University of Massachusetts Dartmouth — M,D,O
University of Massachusetts Lowell — M
University of Massachusetts Medical School — M,D,O
University of Minnesota, Twin Cities Campus — M,D,O
University of Missouri — M,D,O
University of Missouri–Kansas City — M,D
University of Missouri–St. Louis — D,O
The University of North Carolina at Chapel Hill — M,D,O
The University of North Carolina at Charlotte — M,D,O
The University of North Carolina at Greensboro — M,D,O
University of North Dakota — M,D,O
University of Pennsylvania — M
University of Phoenix–Bay Area Campus — M,D
University of Phoenix–Phoenix Campus — M,O
University of Pittsburgh — M,D
University of Puerto Rico, Medical Sciences Campus — M
University of Rhode Island — M,D
University of Rochester — M,D
University of San Diego — M,D
University of Southern Maine — M,D
University of South Florida — M,D,O
The University of Tennessee Health Science Center — D,O
The University of Texas at Austin — M,D
The University of Texas Health Science Center at San Antonio — M,D,O
The University of Tulsa — D
University of Utah — M,O
University of Wisconsin–Eau Claire — M,D
University of Wisconsin–Madison — D
Ursuline College — M,D
Valdosta State University — M
Vanderbilt University — M,D,O
Walden University — M,D,O
West Chester University of Pennsylvania — M,D
Western Connecticut State University — M,D
Wilmington University — M,D
Winona State University — M,D,O
Wright State University — M
York College of Pennsylvania — M,D,O

GERONTOLOGY
Adelphi University — M,O
Alliant International University–Los Angeles — M
Arizona State University at the Tempe campus — M,D,O
Arkansas State University — M,D,O
California State University, Fullerton — M
California State University, Long Beach — M
Capella University — M

Central Michigan University — M,O
The College at Brockport, State University of New York — M,O
Concordia University Chicago — M
DeSales University — M,D,O
Duke University — M,O
East Carolina University — M,O
Eastern Illinois University — M
Eastern Michigan University — O
East Tennessee State University — M,D,O
Georgia State University — M,O
Kansas State University — M,O
Kent State University — M,D
Lakehead University — M,D
La Salle University — M,D,O
Loma Linda University — M,D
Long Island University–LIU Brooklyn — M,O
Long Island University–LIU Post — M
Marywood University — M
McDaniel College — M,O
Mercer University — M,D
Miami University — M,D
Middle Tennessee State University — O
Minnesota State University Mankato — M
Morehead State University — M
Mount Saint Vincent University — M
North Dakota State University — M,D
Northeastern Illinois University — M
Oregon Health & Science University — M,O
Sage Graduate School — M
St. Cloud State University — M
San Diego State University — M
San Francisco State University — M
Simon Fraser University — M,D
Temple University — D
Texas Christian University — D
Texas State University — M
Texas Tech University — M,D
Université de Sherbrooke — O
Université Laval — O
The University of Akron — D
University of Arkansas at Little Rock — O
University of Central Missouri — M,D,O
University of Central Oklahoma — M
University of Georgia — O
University of Illinois at Springfield — M,O
University of Indianapolis — M,D,O
The University of Kansas — D
University of Kentucky — D,O
University of La Verne — M
University of Louisiana at Monroe — M,O
University of Louisville — M,D,O
University of Maryland, Baltimore — M,D
University of Maryland, Baltimore County — M,D
University of Massachusetts Boston — M,D,O
University of Michigan–Flint — M,D,O
University of Missouri — M,D,O
University of Missouri–St. Louis — M,O
University of Nebraska at Omaha — M,O
University of Nebraska–Lincoln — M,D
The University of North Carolina at Charlotte — M,D,O
The University of North Carolina at Greensboro — M,O
The University of North Carolina Wilmington — M,O
University of Northern Colorado — M,D
University of North Texas — M,D,O
University of Phoenix–Central Valley Campus — M
University of Phoenix–Charlotte Campus — M
University of Phoenix–Colorado Springs Downtown Campus — M
University of Phoenix–Hawaii Campus — M
University of Phoenix–Washington D.C. Campus — M,D
University of Puerto Rico, Medical Sciences Campus — M,O
University of Regina — M
University of Saint Joseph — O
University of South Carolina — O
University of Southern California — M,D,O
University of Southern Indiana — M,D,O
University of South Florida — M,D,O
The University of Tennessee — M
The University of Toledo — M,O
University of Utah — M,O
University of Wisconsin–Milwaukee — M,D,O
Virginia Commonwealth University — M,D
Walden University — M,D
Washington University in St. Louis — M,D
Wayne State University — M,D,O
Webster University — M
West Chester University of Pennsylvania — M,O
Wichita State University — M
Youngstown State University — M

GRAPHIC DESIGN
Academy of Art University — M
ArtCenter College of Design — M
Atlantic University College — M
Bob Jones University — M,D,O
Boston University — M
Bowling Green State University — M
Bradley University — M
California College of the Arts — M
California Institute of the Arts — M
California State University, Los Angeles — M

M—masters degree; D—doctorate; O—other advanced degree; *—Close-Up and/or Display

Graphic Design (continued)

Central Connecticut State University	M
City College of the City University of New York	M
Digital Media Arts College	M
East Carolina University	M
Florida Atlantic University	M
Full Sail University	M
George Mason University	M
Georgia Southern University	M
Georgia State University	M
Illinois State University	M
Indiana State University	M
Indiana University–Purdue University Indianapolis	M
Inter American University of Puerto Rico, San Germán Campus	M
Iowa State University of Science and Technology	M
Kent State University	M
Louisiana State University and Agricultural & Mechanical College	M
Louisiana Tech University	M
Maryland Institute College of Art	M
Marywood University	M
Minneapolis College of Art and Design	M,O
Morehead State University	M
New York Institute of Technology	M
New York University	M
North Carolina Agricultural and Technical State University	M
North Carolina State University	M
Ohio University	M
Oklahoma State University	M
Otis College of Art and Design	M
Pensacola Christian College	M,D,O
Pittsburg State University	M,O
Pratt Institute	M
Rhode Island School of Design	M
Rochester Institute of Technology	M
San Diego State University	M
Savannah College of Art and Design	M
School of the Art Institute of Chicago	M
School of Visual Arts (NY)	M
State University of New York at Oswego	M
Suffolk University	M
Temple University	M
Texas State University	M
Université Laval	M
University of Baltimore	M,D
University of Cincinnati	M
University of Guam	M
University of Illinois at Chicago	M
University of Illinois at Urbana–Champaign	M
University of Memphis	M,O
University of Miami	M
University of Minnesota, Duluth	M
University of Notre Dame	M
University of Pennsylvania	M,O
The University of South Dakota	M
The University of Tennessee	M
University of Utah	M
Vermont College of Fine Arts	M
Wayne State University	M
West Virginia University	M
Yale University	M

HAZARDOUS MATERIALS MANAGEMENT

Humboldt State University	M
Idaho State University	M
Marquette University	M,D,O
New Mexico Institute of Mining and Technology	M
Rutgers University–New Brunswick	M,D
Tufts University	M,D
The University of Manchester	M,D
University of New Haven	M
University of South Carolina	M,D
University of Southern California	M,D,O

HEALTH COMMUNICATION

Arkansas State University	M,O
Boston University	M
Chapman University	M
Chatham University	M
Cornell University	M,D
DePaul University	M
East Carolina University	M
Fontbonne University	M
Gannon University	M
The George Washington University	M,D
Indiana University–Purdue University Indianapolis	M,D
Johns Hopkins University	M,D
Kansas State University	M
Lasell College	M,O
Marquette University	M,O
Michigan State University	M
Ohio University	M,D
Southern Illinois University Edwardsville	M
State University of New York at Oswego	M
Stony Brook University, State University of New York	M,O
Tufts University	M,D,O
University of Florida	M,D,O
University of Houston	M
University of Missouri	M,D
University of Oklahoma	M,D
University of Southern California	M
Wayne State University	M,D,O

HEALTH EDUCATION

Adelphi University	M,O
Alabama State University	M
Albany State University	M,O
Alcorn State University	M
Allen College	M,D

American University	M,O
Arcadia University	M
Arizona State University at the Tempe campus	D
Arkansas State University	M,D,O
Auburn University	M,D,O
Austin Peay State University	M
Baldwin Wallace University	M
Baylor University	M,D
Benedictine University	M
Brandeis University	D
California Baptist University	M
California Institute of Integral Studies	M,D
California State University, Long Beach	M
California State University, Northridge	M,O
California State University, San Marcos	M,D,O
Cambridge College	M
Central Washington University	M
Clark University	M
Cleveland State University	M
The College at Brockport, State University of New York	M
The College of New Jersey	M
College of Saint Mary	D
Colorado State University–Pueblo	M
Columbus State University	M,D
Concordia University Wisconsin	M,D
Daemen College	M
Dalhousie University	M
Delta State University	M
Drew University	M,D,O
East Carolina University	M
Eastern Kentucky University	M
Eastern Michigan University	M,O
Eastern University	M,D,O
East Stroudsburg University of Pennsylvania	M
Emory University	M,D
Excelsior College	M,O
Fairfield University	M,D
Florida State University	M,D
Fort Hays State University	M
Framingham State University	M
Georgia College & State University	M
Georgia Southern University	M,D
Georgia State University	M
Harding University	M,O
Hofstra University	M,D,O
Howard University	M
Idaho State University	M
Illinois State University	M
Indiana State University	M,D
Indiana University Bloomington	M,D
Indiana University of Pennsylvania	M
Indiana University–Purdue University Indianapolis	M,D
Inter American University of Puerto Rico, Metropolitan Campus	M
Inter American University of Puerto Rico, San Germán Campus	M
Ithaca College	M
Jackson State University	M
James Madison University	M
John F. Kennedy University	M
Johns Hopkins University	M,D
Kansas State University	M,D
Keiser University	M,D
Kent State University	M,D
Lake Erie College of Osteopathic Medicine	M,D,O
Lehman College of the City University of New York	M
Lock Haven University of Pennsylvania	M
Logan University	M,D
Loma Linda University	M,D
Longwood University	M
Marshall University	M
Marymount University	M
Marywood University	D
Massachusetts College of Liberal Arts	M,O
Meredith College	M,O
Middle Tennessee State University	M
Minnesota State University Mankato	M,O
Mississippi University for Women	M
Montana State University	M
Montclair State University	M
Morehead State University	M
New Jersey City University	M
New Mexico Highlands University	M
New York Medical College	M,D,O
Nicholls State University	M
North Carolina Agricultural and Technical State University	M
Northeastern State University	M
Northwestern State University of Louisiana	M
Northwest Missouri State University	M
Nova Southeastern University	M,D,O
Oklahoma State University	M,D,O
Old Dominion University	M,D
Penn State Harrisburg	M,D,O
Pennsylvania College of Health Sciences	M
Pittsburg State University	M
Plymouth State University	M
Prairie View A&M University	M
Purdue University	M,D
Rhode Island College	M,O
Rosalind Franklin University of Medicine and Science	M
Rutgers University–Newark	M,D
Rutgers University–New Brunswick	M,D,O
Sage Graduate School	M
Saint Francis University	M

Saint Joseph's College of Maine	M
Saint Joseph's University	M
San Francisco State University	M
Shenandoah University	M,D,O
Simmons College	M,D,O
Southeastern Louisiana University	M
Southern Connecticut State University	M
Southern Illinois University Carbondale	M,D
Southern Illinois University Edwardsville	M,D,O
State University of New York College at Cortland	M
Teachers College, Columbia University	M,D,O
Tennessee Technological University	M
Texas A&M University	M,D
Texas A&M University–Kingsville	M
Texas Southern University	M
Texas State University	M
Texas Woman's University	M,D
Thomas Jefferson University	M,D
Trident University International	M,D,O
Union College (KY)	M
The University of Alabama	M,D
The University of Alabama at Birmingham	D
University of Arkansas	M,D
University of Arkansas at Little Rock	M,D
University of Arkansas for Medical Sciences	M,D,O
University of Central Arkansas	M
University of Cincinnati	M,D
University of Colorado Denver	M,D
University of Florida	M,D,O
University of Georgia	M,D
University of Houston	M,D
University of Illinois at Chicago	M
University of Illinois at Springfield	M,O
The University of Kansas	M,D,O
University of Louisville	M,D,O
University of Maryland, Baltimore County	M
University of Maryland, College Park	M,D
University of Massachusetts Amherst	M,D
University of Michigan	M,D
University of Michigan–Flint	M
University of Missouri	M,D,O
University of Missouri–Kansas City	M,D
University of Montana	M
University of Nebraska at Omaha	M,D
University of New Mexico	M
The University of North Carolina Wilmington	M
University of Northern Colorado	M
University of Northern Iowa	M
University of Oklahoma Health Sciences Center	D
University of Phoenix–Charlotte Campus	M
University of Phoenix–Colorado Springs Downtown Campus	M
University of Phoenix–Online Campus	M,O
University of Phoenix–Washington D.C. Campus	M,D
University of Pittsburgh	M,D
University of Puerto Rico, Medical Sciences Campus	M
University of Rhode Island	M
University of St. Augustine for Health Sciences	M,D
University of South Africa	M,D
University of South Alabama	M
University of South Carolina	M,D,O
University of Southern California	M
University of Southern Mississippi	M
University of South Florida	M
The University of Tennessee	M
The University of Texas at Austin	M,D
The University of Texas at San Antonio	M
The University of Texas at Tyler	M
The University of Toledo	M,D,O
University of Utah	M,D
University of Waterloo	M,D
University of Wisconsin–La Crosse	M
University of Wyoming	M
Utah State University	M
Virginia State University	M,D
Walden University	M,D,O
Washburn University	M
Wayne State University	M,D,O
West Chester University of Pennsylvania	M
Western Illinois University	M,O
Western Michigan University	D,O
Western Oregon University	M
Western University of Health Sciences	M
Widener University	M,D
Worcester State University	M
Wright State University	M

HEALTH INFORMATICS

Adelphi University	M,O
American Public University System	M
American Sentinel University	M
Arkansas Tech University	M
Augusta University	M
Barry University	O
Benedictine University	M
Boston University	M,O
Brandeis University	M

Brooklyn College of the City University of New York	M,O
Canisius College	M,O
Capella University	M
Chatham University	M
Claremont Graduate University	M,D,O
Clarkson University	M
The College of St. Scholastica	M,O
Colorado Mesa University	M,D,O
Dakota State University	M,D,O
DePaul University	M,D
DeSales University	M,O
Duke University	M
East Carolina University	M
Emory University	M,D
Excelsior College	M,O
Georgia Southwestern State University	M,O
Georgia State University	M,D,O
Golden Gate University	M,D,O
Grand Canyon University	M,D,O
Hofstra University	M
Indiana University Bloomington	M,D
Indiana University–Purdue University Indianapolis	M,D
Jacksonville University	M
Johns Hopkins University	M,D,O
Kennesaw State University	M,O
Kent State University	M
Lipscomb University	M,D,O
Logan University	M
Louisiana Tech University	M
Marshall University	M
Marymount University	M,O
Mercer University	M,D
Metropolitan State University	M,D,O
Middle Georgia State University	M
Midwestern State University	M,O
Millennia Atlantic University	M
Montana Tech of The University of Montana	O
Northeastern University	M,D
Northern Kentucky University	M,O
Northwestern University	D
Nova Southeastern University	M,D,O
Oregon Health & Science University	M,D,O
Regis University	M,O
Roberts Wesleyan College	M
Sacred Heart University	M
St. Joseph's College, Long Island Campus	M
St. Joseph's College, New York	M
Saint Joseph's University	M
Slippery Rock University of Pennsylvania	M
Southern Illinois University Edwardsville	M
Southern New Hampshire University	M,O
Stephens College	M,O
Stevens Institute of Technology	M,D,O
Stony Brook University, State University of New York	M,D
Temple University	M,D
Texas State University	M
Trident University International	M,D,O
The University of Alabama at Birmingham	M
University of Central Florida	M,O
University of Cincinnati	M
The University of Findlay	M,D
University of Illinois at Chicago	M,O
University of Illinois at Urbana–Champaign	M,D,O
The University of Iowa	M,D,O
The University of Kansas	M,O
University of Maryland, Baltimore County	M
University of Maryland University College	M
University of Michigan	M,D
University of Michigan–Dearborn	M
University of Michigan–Flint	M
University of Minnesota, Twin Cities Campus	M,D
University of Missouri	M,O
University of New England	M,D,O
The University of North Carolina at Charlotte	M,O
University of Phoenix–Charlotte Campus	M
University of Phoenix–Online Campus	M,O
University of Phoenix–Washington D.C. Campus	M,D
University of Pittsburgh	M
University of Puerto Rico, Medical Sciences Campus	M
University of St. Augustine for Health Sciences	M
University of San Diego	M,D
University of San Francisco	M
University of South Carolina Upstate	M
University of Southern Indiana	M
University of South Florida	M,D,O
The University of Tennessee Health Science Center	M,D
University of Toronto	M
University of Victoria	M
University of Virginia	M
University of Washington	M,D
University of Waterloo	M,D
University of Wisconsin–Milwaukee	M,D
Virginia International University	M,O
Walden University	M,D,O
Weill Cornell Medicine	M

HEALTH LAW

Case Western Reserve University	M,D
DePaul University	M,D
Georgetown University	M,D

Hofstra University	M,D
Indiana University–Purdue University Indianapolis	M,D,O
Nova Southeastern University	M,D
Seton Hall University	M,D
Southern Illinois University Carbondale	M
Suffolk University	M,D
Université de Sherbrooke	M,D,O
University of California, San Diego	M
University of California, San Francisco	M
University of Houston	M,D
The University of Manchester	M,D
University of Pittsburgh	M
The University of Tulsa	M,D
Widener University	M,D

HEALTH PHYSICS/RADIOLOGICAL HEALTH

Colorado State University	M,D
East Carolina University	M,D
Georgetown University	M
Georgia Institute of Technology	M,D
Idaho State University	M,D
Illinois Institute of Technology	M,D
McMaster University	M,D
Midwestern State University	M
Northwestern State University of Louisiana	M
Oregon State University	M,D
Purdue University	M,D
Quinnipiac University	M
Rutgers University–Newark	M
San Diego State University	M
Texas A&M University	M,D
Thomas Jefferson University	M
Université Laval	O
University of Alberta	M,D
University of Arkansas for Medical Sciences	M,D
University of Cincinnati	M
University of Kentucky	M
University of Massachusetts Lowell	M
University of Michigan	M,D,O
University of Missouri	M
University of Nevada, Las Vegas	M,D,O
University of Oklahoma Health Sciences Center	M,D
University of Toronto	M,D
Vanderbilt University	M,D
Virginia Commonwealth University	D
Weber State University	M

HEALTH PROMOTION

American College of Healthcare Sciences	M,O
American University	M
American University of Beirut	M
Arizona State University at the Tempe campus	M,D
Ball State University	M
Benedictine University	M
Boise State University	M,O
Bridgewater State University	M
Brigham Young University	M,D
California Baptist University	M
California State University, Fresno	M
Claremont Graduate University	M,D
Cleveland University–Kansas City	M
Concord University	M
East Carolina University	M
Eastern Kentucky University	M
Eastern Michigan University	M,O
Emory University	M
Fairmont State University	M
Florida Atlantic University	M,D
Florida International University	M,D
George Mason University	M,O
Georgetown University	M,D
Georgia College & State University	M
Goddard College	M
Harvard University	M,D
Immaculata University	M
Independence University	M
Indiana University Bloomington	M,D
Instituto Tecnológico de Santo Domingo	M,O
Kent State University	M,D
Lehman College of the City University of New York	M
Liberty University	M,D,O
Lindenwood University	M
Lock Haven University of Pennsylvania	M
Manhattanville College	M,O
Maryland University of Integrative Health	M,O
Marymount University	M
McNeese State University	M
Merrimack College	M
Mount St. Joseph University	M,O
Nebraska Methodist College	M
New York University	M,D,O
North Dakota State University	M,D
Old Dominion University	M
Oregon State University	M,D
Plymouth State University	M
Portland State University	M,D
Rosalind Franklin University of Medicine and Science	M
Rowan University	M
San Diego State University	M,D
Simmons College	M,D,O
Sonoma State University	M
Southeastern Louisiana University	M
Springfield College	M,D
Tennessee Technological University	M

Texas A&M University	M,D
Union Institute & University	M
Universidad del Turabo	M
The University of Alabama	M,D
The University of Alabama at Birmingham	D
University of Alberta	M,O
University of Arkansas	M,D
University of Arkansas for Medical Sciences	M,D,O
University of Central Oklahoma	M
University of Chicago	M,D
University of Cincinnati	M
University of Delaware	M
University of Georgia	M,D
The University of Kansas	M,D,O
University of Kentucky	M
University of Massachusetts Lowell	D
University of Memphis	M,O
University of Michigan	M,D
University of Mississippi	M,O
University of Missouri	M,O
University of Nebraska–Lincoln	M,D
University of Nebraska Medical Center	D
University of North Alabama	M
The University of North Carolina at Chapel Hill	M
University of Northern Iowa	M
University of Oklahoma	M,D
University of Oklahoma Health Sciences Center	M,D
University of Puerto Rico, Medical Sciences Campus	O
University of South Carolina	M,D,O
University of Southern California	M
The University of Tennessee	M
The University of Toledo	M,D,O
University of Toronto	M,D
University of Utah	M,D
University of West Florida	M
University of Wisconsin–Milwaukee	M,D,O
University of Wisconsin–Stevens Point	M
University of Wyoming	M
Walden University	M,D,O
Wilfrid Laurier University	M
Wright State University	M

HEALTH PSYCHOLOGY

Adler University	M,D,O
Alliant International University–Los Angeles	D
Appalachian State University	M
Argosy University, Atlanta	M,D,O
Argosy University, Chicago	D
Argosy University, Northern Virginia	M,D
Argosy University, Twin Cities	M,D,O
Bastyr University	M,O
California Institute of Integral Studies	M,D
California State University, Dominguez Hills	M
Central Michigan University	M,D
Chatham University	M,D
Claremont Graduate University	M,D,O
Drexel University	D
Duke University	D
East Carolina University	M
Fielding Graduate University	D,O
Georgian Court University	M,O
John F. Kennedy University	M
La Salle University	M,D,O
Lesley University	M,D,O
North Dakota State University	M
Northern Kentucky University	M,O
Oklahoma State University	M,D,O
Oregon State University	M
Penn State Harrisburg	M,D,O
Prescott College	M
Rhode Island College	M,O
Rutgers University–New Brunswick	D
San Diego State University	M,D
Saybrook University	M,D
Southwestern College (NM)	O
Stony Brook University, State University of New York	D
United States International University–Africa	M
The University of Alabama at Birmingham	M,D
The University of British Columbia	M,D
University of Colorado Denver	M,D
University of Florida	M,D
University of Michigan–Dearborn	M
University of New Mexico	D
The University of North Carolina at Chapel Hill	M,D
The University of North Carolina at Charlotte	M,D,O
The University of Texas at Arlington	M,D
University of the Sciences	M
University of Wisconsin–Milwaukee	M,D
Virginia Commonwealth University	D
Virginia State University	M
Viterbo University	M
Walden University	M,D,O
Yeshiva University	D

HEALTH SERVICES MANAGEMENT AND HOSPITAL ADMINISTRATION

Adelphi University	M
Adventist University of Health Sciences	M

Alaska Pacific University	M
Albany State University	M
American InterContinental University Online	M
American Public University System	M
American Sentinel University	M
American University	M,O
American University of Beirut	M
Anderson University (SC)	M
Aquinas Institute of Theology	M,D,O
Argosy University, Atlanta	M,D
Argosy University, Chicago	M,D
Argosy University, Dallas	M,D,O
Argosy University, Denver	M,D,O
Argosy University, Hawai`i	M,D,O
Argosy University, Inland Empire	M,D
Argosy University, Los Angeles	M,D
Argosy University, Nashville	M,D
Argosy University, Northern Virginia	M,D,O
Argosy University, Orange County	M,D,O
Argosy University, Phoenix	M,D
Argosy University, Salt Lake City	M,D
Argosy University, San Francisco Bay Area	M,D
Argosy University, Sarasota	M,D,O
Argosy University, Schaumburg	M,D,O
Argosy University, Seattle	M,D
Argosy University, Tampa	M,D
Argosy University, Twin Cities	M,D
Arizona State University at the Tempe campus	M,D
Arkansas State University	M,D,O
Armstrong State University	M
Ashworth College	M
Assumption College	M,O
A.T. Still University	M,D,O
Avila University	M
Baker College Center for Graduate Studies–Online	M,D
Baldwin Wallace University	M
Barry University	M,O
Baruch College of the City University of New York	M
Baylor University	M
Belhaven University (MS)	M
Bellevue University	M
Belmont University	M
Benedictine University	M
Binghamton University, State University of New York	M,D
Bluffton University	M
Boston University	M,D
Bradley University	M,D,O
Brandeis University	M
Brandman University	M,D
Brenau University	M
Brigham Young University	M
Broadview University–West Jordan	M
Brooklyn College of the City University of New York	M
California Baptist University	M
California Coast University	M
California Intercontinental University	M,D
California State University, Bakersfield	M
California State University, Chico	M
California State University, East Bay	M
California State University, Fresno	M
California State University, Long Beach	M
California State University, Los Angeles	M,O
California State University, Northridge	M
California State University, San Bernardino	M
Cambridge College	M
Capella University	M,D
Cardinal Stritch University	M
Carlow University	M
Carnegie Mellon University	M
Case Western Reserve University	M
The Catholic University of America	M
Cedarville University	M,D
Central Michigan University	M,D,O
Champlain College	M
Clarion University of Pennsylvania	M
Clarkson University	M,O
Cleary University	M,O
Cleveland State University	M
The College at Brockport, State University of New York	M,O
College of Saint Elizabeth	M
Colorado State University–Global Campus	M
Columbia Southern University	M
Columbia University	M
Columbus State University	M
Concordia University Irvine	M
Concordia University, St. Paul	M
Concordia University Wisconsin	M
Copenhagen Business School	M,D
Cornell University	M,D
Creighton University	M
Daemen College	M
Dalhousie University	M,D
Dallas Baptist University	M
Dartmouth College	M,D
Davenport University	M
Delta State University	M,D
DePaul University	M
DeSales University	M
Des Moines University	M
Dominican College	M
Drew University	M,D,O
Duke University	M,O

Duquesne University	M,D
D'Youville College	M,D,O
Eastern Kentucky University	M
Eastern Mennonite University	M
Eastern Michigan University	M,O
Eastern University	M
East Tennessee State University	M,D,O
Elmhurst College	M
Elms College	M
Emory University	M,D
Excelsior College	M,O
Fairleigh Dickinson University, College at Florham	M
Fairleigh Dickinson University, Metropolitan Campus	M
Felician University	M
Florida Institute of Technology	M
Florida International University	M,D
Florida National University	M
Fordham University	M
Framingham State University	M
Francis Marion University	M
Franklin Pierce University	M,D,O
Friends University	M
George Mason University	M,D,O
The George Washington University	M,D,O
Georgia Institute of Technology	M
Georgia Southern University	M,D
Georgia State University	M,D,O
Goldey-Beacom College	M
Governors State University	M
Grambling State University	M
Grand Canyon University	M,D,O
Grand Valley State University	M,D
Gwynedd Mercy University	M
Harvard University	M
Herzing University Online	M
Hilbert College	M
Hodges University	M
Hofstra University	M,O
Holy Family University	M
Husson University	M
IGlobal University	M
Independence University	M
Indiana Tech	M
Indiana University Bloomington	M,D
Indiana University Kokomo	M,O
Indiana University Northwest	M,O
Indiana University of Pennsylvania	M,D
Indiana University–Purdue University Indianapolis	M,D,O
Indiana University South Bend	M,O
Indiana Wesleyan University	M,O
Institute of Public Administration	M
Iona College	M,O
Johns Hopkins University	M,D
Kaplan University, Davenport Campus	M,O
Kean University	M
Keiser University	M
Kennesaw State University	M
Kent State University	M,D
King's College	M
King University	M
Lake Erie College	M
Lake Forest Graduate School of Management	M
Lakeland University	M
Lamar University	M
Lasell College	M,O
Lebanon Valley College	M
Lehigh University	M,O
Lenoir-Rhyne University	M
LeTourneau University	M
Lewis University	M
Lindenwood University	M,O
Lindenwood University–Belleville	M
Lipscomb University	M,O
Lock Haven University of Pennsylvania	M
Loma Linda University	M,D
London Metropolitan University	M,D
Long Island University–Hudson	M,O
Long Island University–LIU Brooklyn	M,O
Long Island University–LIU Post	M,O
Louisiana State University Health Sciences Center	M,D
Louisiana State University in Shreveport	M
Loyola University Chicago	M
Loyola University New Orleans	M,D
Madonna University	M
Marshall University	M
Maryhurst University	M
Marymount University	M
Maryville University of Saint Louis	M,O
Marywood University	M
McGill University	M,D,O
MCPHS University	M
Medical University of South Carolina	M,D
Meharry Medical College	M
Mercy College	M
Metropolitan College of New York	M
Midwestern State University	M,O
Milligan College	M,O
Milwaukee School of Engineering	M
Minnesota State University Moorhead	M,O
Misericordia University	M
Mississippi College	M
Missouri State University	M
Molloy College	M,D,O
Monroe College	M
Montana State University Billings	M
Moravian College	M

M—masters degree; D—doctorate; O—other advanced degree; *—Close-Up and/or Display

Mount Aloysius College	M
Mount Ida College	M
Mount St. Joseph University	D
Mount Saint Mary College	M
Mount Saint Mary's University (CA)	M,D,O
Mount St. Mary's University (MD)	M
National University	M,D,O
Nebraska Methodist College	M
New Charter University	M
New England College	M
New Jersey City University	M
New Jersey Institute of Technology	M,D
New York Medical College	M,D,O
New York University	M,D,O
Niagara University	M
Northeast Ohio Medical University	M,D,O
Northwestern University	M,D
Ohio Christian University	M
Ohio Dominican University	M
The Ohio State University	M,D
Ohio University	M
Oklahoma Christian University	M
Oklahoma State University Center for Health Sciences	M
Oregon Health & Science University	M,O
Oregon State University	M,D
Our Lady of the Lake College	M
Our Lady of the Lake University	M
Pace University	M
Pacific University	M
Park University	M,O
Penn State Great Valley	M,O
Penn State Harrisburg	M,D,O
Penn State University Park	M,D
Pennsylvania College of Health Sciences	M
Pfeiffer University	M
Point Loma Nazarene University	M
Point Park University	M
Portland State University	M,D
Post University	M
Queen's University at Kingston	M,D
Quinnipiac University	M
Regent University	M,D,O
Regis College (MA)	M,D,O
Regis University	M,D,O
Rhode Island College	M
Rice University	M
Robert Morris University Illinois	M
Roberts Wesleyan College	M
Rochester Institute of Technology	M,O
Rockhurst University	M
Roger Williams University	M
Rollins College	M
Rosalind Franklin University of Medicine and Science	M,O
Royal Roads University	O
Rush University	M,D
Rutgers University–Camden	M,O
Rutgers University–Newark	M,D,O
Rutgers University–New Brunswick	M,D,O
Sage Graduate School	M
Saginaw Valley State University	M
St. Ambrose University	M,D
St. Catherine University	M
St. Joseph's College, Long Island Campus	M
St. Joseph's College, New York	M
Saint Joseph's College of Maine	M
Saint Joseph's University	M,O
Saint Leo University	M,D,O
Saint Louis University	M,D
Saint Mary's University of Minnesota	M
St. Norbert College	M
Saint Peter's University	M
St. Thomas University	M,O
Saint Xavier University	M,O
Salve Regina University	M,O
Samford University	M,D
San Diego State University	M
San Francisco State University	M
Seton Hall University	M
Shenandoah University	M,O
Shippensburg University of Pennsylvania	M,O
Siena Heights University	M,O
Simmons College	M
South Carolina State University	M
Southern Adventist University	M
Southern Illinois University Carbondale	M
Southern Nazarene University	M
Southern New Hampshire University	M,O
South University	M
South University (SC)	M
South University (GA)	M
South University (AL)	M
South University	M
Southwest Baptist University	M
Stevenson University	M
Stony Brook University, State University of New York	M,D,O
Stratford University (VA)	M
Strayer University	M
Suffolk University	M
Syracuse University	O
Temple University	M
Texas A&M University	M,D
Texas A&M University–Corpus Christi	M
Texas A&M University–San Antonio	M
Texas Health and Science University	M,D
Texas Southern University	M
Texas State University	M
Texas Tech University	M,D

Texas Tech University Health Sciences Center	M
Texas Woman's University	M,D
Thomas Jefferson University	M,D,U
Tiffin University	M,O
Towson University	M,O
Trident University International	M,D,O
Trinity University	M
Trinity Western University	M,O
Troy University	M
Tufts University	M,D,O
Tulane University	M,D
Tusculum College	M
Uniformed Services University of the Health Sciences	M,D
Universidad de Ciencias Medicas	M,D,O
Universidad de Iberoamerica	M,D
Université de Montréal	M,O
University at Albany, State University of New York	M,D,O
University at Buffalo, the State University of New York	M,D,O
The University of Akron	M
The University of Alabama at Birmingham	M,D
The University of Alabama in Huntsville	M,D,O
University of Alberta	M,D
University of Arkansas for Medical Sciences	M,D,O
University of Arkansas–Fort Smith	M
University of Baltimore	M
The University of British Columbia	M,D
University of California, Berkeley	D
University of California, Irvine	M
University of California, Los Angeles	M,D
University of California, San Diego	M
University of Central Florida	M,O
University of Chicago	M,O
University of Colorado Denver	M,D
University of Connecticut	M,D
University of Dallas	M,D
University of Denver	M,O
University of Detroit Mercy	M,D,O
University of Evansville	M
The University of Findlay	M,D
University of Florida	M,D
University of Houston–Clear Lake	M
University of Illinois at Chicago	M,D
University of Illinois at Urbana–Champaign	M
The University of Iowa	M,D
The University of Kansas	M,D
University of Kentucky	M
University of La Verne	M,D,O
University of Louisville	M
University of Management and Technology	M
University of Mary	M
University of Maryland, Baltimore County	M,D,O
University of Maryland, College Park	M,D
University of Maryland University College	M
University of Massachusetts Amherst	M,D
University of Massachusetts Dartmouth	M
University of Memphis	M,D
University of Michigan	M,D
University of Michigan–Flint	M,O
University of Minnesota, Twin Cities Campus	M,D
University of Missouri	M,D,O
University of Nevada, Las Vegas	M,O
University of New Haven	M,O
University of New Mexico	M
University of New Orleans	M
University of North Alabama	M
The University of North Carolina at Chapel Hill	M,D
The University of North Carolina at Charlotte	M,D,O
University of Northern Colorado	M
University of North Texas	M,D,O
University of North Texas Health Science Center at Fort Worth	M,D,O
University of Oklahoma	M,O
University of Oklahoma Health Sciences Center	M
University of Ottawa	M
University of Pennsylvania	M,D
University of Phoenix–Atlanta Campus	M
University of Phoenix–Augusta Campus	M
University of Phoenix–Bay Area Campus	M,D
University of Phoenix–Central Valley Campus	M
University of Phoenix–Charlotte Campus	M
University of Phoenix–Colorado Campus	M
University of Phoenix–Colorado Springs Downtown Campus	M
University of Phoenix–Hawaii Campus	M
University of Phoenix–Houston Campus	M
University of Phoenix–New Mexico Campus	M
University of Phoenix–North Florida Campus	M
University of Phoenix–Online Campus	M,D,O
University of Phoenix–Phoenix Campus	M,O

University of Phoenix–Sacramento Valley Campus	M
University of Phoenix–San Antonio Campus	M
University of Phoenix–Southern California Campus	M
University of Phoenix–South Florida Campus	M
University of Phoenix–Washington D.C. Campus	M,D
University of Pittsburgh	M,D,O
University of Portland	M
University of Puerto Rico, Medical Sciences Campus	M
University of Regina	M,D,O
University of Rhode Island	M,D
University of Rochester	M,D
University of St. Augustine for Health Sciences	M
University of St. Francis (IL)	M,O
University of Saint Francis (IN)	M
University of Saint Mary	M
University of St. Thomas (MN)	M
University of San Francisco	M
University of Saskatchewan	M
The University of Scranton	M
University of Sioux Falls	M
University of South Africa	M,D
University of South Carolina	M,D
The University of South Dakota	M
University of Southern California	M,O
University of Southern Indiana	M
University of Southern Maine	M
University of Southern Mississippi	M
University of South Florida	M,D,O
The University of Tennessee	M
The University of Texas at Arlington	M
The University of Texas at Dallas	M,D
The University of Texas at El Paso	M,D
The University of Texas at Tyler	M
The University of Texas Rio Grande Valley	M
University of the Sciences	M,D
The University of Toledo	M,D
University of Toronto	M,D
University of Utah	M,D
University of Virginia	M
University of Washington	M,D
The University of Western Ontario	M,D
University of West Florida	M
University of West Georgia	M,D,O
University of Wisconsin–Milwaukee	M,D
University of Wisconsin–Oshkosh	M
University of Wyoming	M,D
Ursuline College	M
Utica College	M
Valdosta State University	M
Valparaiso University	M
Vanderbilt University	M
Villanova University	M
Virginia College in Birmingham	M
Virginia Commonwealth University	M,D
Virginia International University	M,O
Viterbo University	M
Wagner College	M
Walden University	M,D,O
Walsh University	M
Washington Adventist University	M
Washington State University	M
Wayland Baptist University	M,D
Waynesburg University	M,D
Wayne State University	M,D
Weber State University	M
Webster University	M,D,O
West Chester University of Pennsylvania	M,O
West Coast University	M,D
Western Carolina University	M
Western Connecticut State University	M
Western Governors University	M
Western Illinois University	M
Western Kentucky University	M
Western Michigan University	M,D,O
Widener University	M
Wilkes University	M
William Woods University	M,D,O
Wilmington University	M
Wilson College	M
Wingate University	M
Winston-Salem State University	M
Worcester State University	M
Xavier University	M
Yale University	M,D
York College of Pennsylvania	M
Youngstown State University	M

HEALTH SERVICES RESEARCH

Albany College of Pharmacy and Health Sciences	M,D
Brown University	D
Clarkson University	M
Dartmouth College	M,D
Emory University	M,D
Florida Agricultural and Mechanical University	M,D
The George Washington University	M,D,O
Lakehead University	M
McMaster University	M,D
Northwestern University	D
Old Dominion University	M
Penn State Hershey Medical Center	M
Stanford University	M
Texas A&M University	M,D
Thomas Jefferson University	M,D,O
The University of Alabama at Birmingham	M,D
University of Alberta	M,D
University of Arkansas for Medical Sciences	M,D,O
University of Cincinnati	M

University of Colorado Denver	M,D
University of Florida	D
University of Illinois at Chicago	M,D
University of La Verne	M
University of Maryland, Baltimore	M,D
University of Massachusetts Medical School	M,D
University of Minnesota, Twin Cities Campus	M,D
University of Nebraska Medical Center	D
University of New Brunswick Fredericton	M
The University of North Carolina at Charlotte	D
University of North Texas Health Science Center at Fort Worth	M,D,O
University of Ottawa	D,O
University of Pennsylvania	M
University of Puerto Rico, Medical Sciences Campus	M
University of Rochester	M,D
University of Southern California	D
The University of Tennessee Health Science Center	M
University of Utah	M,D
University of Virginia	M
University of Washington	M
Virginia Commonwealth University	D
Wake Forest University	M
Washington University in St. Louis	M,O
Weill Cornell Medicine	M

HIGHER EDUCATION

Abilene Christian University	M
Alliant International University–San Diego	M,D,O
Alliant International University–San Francisco	M,D,O
Andrews University	M,D,O
Angelo State University	M
Appalachian State University	M,O
Argosy University, Atlanta	M,D,O
Argosy University, Chicago	M,D,O
Argosy University, Dallas	M,D
Argosy University, Denver	M,D
Argosy University, Hawai`i	M,D
Argosy University, Inland Empire	M,D
Argosy University, Los Angeles	M,D
Argosy University, Nashville	M,D,O
Argosy University, Northern Virginia	M,D,O
Argosy University, Orange County	M,D
Argosy University, Phoenix	M,D,O
Argosy University, San Diego	M,D
Argosy University, San Francisco Bay Area	M,D
Argosy University, Sarasota	M,D,O
Argosy University, Seattle	M,D
Argosy University, Tampa	M,D,O
Argosy University, Twin Cities	M,D
Arizona State University at the Tempe campus	M
Auburn University	M,D,O
Aurora University	M,D
Azusa Pacific University	M,D
Ball State University	M,D
Barry University	M
Baruch College of the City University of New York	M,D
Bay Path University	M
Bellarmine University	M,D
Benedictine University	D
Boston College	M,D
Bowling Green State University	D
California Baptist University	M
California Lutheran University	M,D
California State University, Long Beach	M,D
California State University, Sacramento	M,D
Capella University	M,D
Cardinal Stritch University	M,D
Central Michigan University	M,D,O
Chicago State University	M,D
Claremont Graduate University	M,D,O
Clemson University	D
Cleveland State University	M,D
College of Saint Elizabeth	M,D,O
The College of Saint Rose	M,O
Colorado State University	M,D
Columbia College (SC)	M
Columbus State University	M,D,O
Dallas Baptist University	M,D
Delta State University	D
DeVry University–FolsomCampus	M
Drexel University	M,D
Eastern Kentucky University	M
Eastern Michigan University	M,D,O
Florida Atlantic University	M,D,O
Florida International University	M,D,O
Florida State University	M,D
Geneva College	M
George Mason University	D,O
The George Washington University	M,D,O
Georgia Southern University	M
Grambling State University	M,D,O
Grand Valley State University	M
Illinois State University	M,D
Indiana State University	M,D,O
Indiana University Bloomington	M,D
Indiana University of Pennsylvania	M,D
Indiana Wesleyan University	M
Inter American University of Puerto Rico, Metropolitan Campus	M
Iowa State University of Science and Technology	M,D,O
Jackson State University	M,D,O
James Madison University	M
Johnson State University	M,D,O
Kaplan University, Davenport Campus	M
Kent State University	M,D,O

Lee University	M,O
Lewis University	M
Lincoln Memorial University	M,D,O
Lincoln University (MO)	M
London Metropolitan University	M,D
Louisiana State University and Agricultural & Mechanical College	M,D,O
Louisiana Tech University	M,D
Loyola Marymount University	M
Loyola University Chicago	M,D
Lynchburg College	M
Maryville University of Saint Louis	M,D
Marywood University	M,D
McKendree University	M
Mercer University	M,D,O
Mercyhurst University	M,O
Merrimack College	M,O
Messiah College	M
Michigan State University	M,D,O
Minnesota State University Mankato	M
Mississippi College	M,D,O
Missouri State University	M
Montana State University	M,D,O
Morehead State University	M,O
Morgan State University	M,D
New England College	M,D
New Mexico State University	M,D
North Carolina State University	M,D
North Dakota State University	O
Northeastern University	M
Northern Arizona University	M,D,O
Northern Illinois University	M,D
Northern Michigan University	M
Northwest Missouri State University	M,D,O
Oakland University	M,D,O
Ohio University	M,D
Oklahoma State University	M,D
Old Dominion University	M,D,O
Oral Roberts University	M,D
Oregon State University	M,D
Penn State University Park	M,D,O
Phillips Theological Seminary	M,D
Plymouth State University	D,O
Purdue University	M,D,O
Regent University	M,D
Regis College (MA)	M,D
Robert Morris University	M,D,O
Robert Morris University Illinois	M
Rowan University	M
St. Cloud State University	M,D
Saint Louis University	M,D,O
Saint Peter's University	D
Salem State University	M
Sam Houston State University	M,D
San Diego State University	M
San Jose State University	M,D,O
Seton Hall University	D
Shippensburg University of Pennsylvania	M
Siena Heights University	M,O
Southeast Missouri State University	M,D,O
Southern Arkansas University–Magnolia	M
Southern Illinois University Carbondale	M
Southern Illinois University Edwardsville	M
Stony Brook University, State University of New York	M,O
Syracuse University	M,D
Taylor University	M
Teachers College, Columbia University	M,D
Texas A&M University–Commerce	M,D,O
Texas Southern University	M,D
Texas State University	M
Texas Tech University	M,D
Tiffin University	M
Trident University International	M,D
Union University	M,D,O
Universidad Central del Este	M
Université de Sherbrooke	M,O
University at Albany, State University of New York	M,D,O
University at Buffalo, the State University of New York	M,D,O
The University of Akron	M
The University of Alabama	M,D
The University of Arizona	M,D
University of Arkansas	M,D,O
University of Arkansas at Little Rock	M,D
The University of British Columbia	M,D
University of California, Riverside	
University of Central Florida	M,D,O
University of Central Oklahoma	M
University of Connecticut	D
University of Dayton	M
University of Delaware	M,D,O
University of Denver	M,D,O
University of Florida	M,D,O
University of Georgia	M,D
University of Houston	M,D
University of Houston–Victoria	M
University of Illinois at Springfield	M,O
The University of Iowa	M,D
The University of Kansas	M,D
University of Kentucky	M,D
University of Louisville	M,D,O
University of Maine	M,D,O
University of Manitoba	M
University of Mary Hardin-Baylor	M,D

University of Massachusetts Amherst	M,D,O
University of Massachusetts Boston	D
University of Memphis	M,D
University of Miami	M,D,O
University of Minnesota, Twin Cities Campus	M,D
University of Missouri	M,D,O
University of Missouri–Kansas City	M,D
University of Missouri–St. Louis	M,D,O
University of Nevada, Las Vegas	M,D,O
University of New Hampshire	O
University of New Mexico	O
The University of North Carolina at Greensboro	D
The University of North Carolina Wilmington	M,D
University of Northern Colorado	M,D
University of Northern Iowa	M
University of North Texas	M,D,O
University of Oklahoma	M,D,O
University of Pennsylvania	M,D
University of Phoenix–Bay Area Campus	M,D,O
University of Phoenix–Online Campus	D,O
University of Phoenix–Washington D.C. Campus	M,D,O
University of Pittsburgh	M,D
University of Puerto Rico, Mayagüez Campus	M
University of Rochester	M,D
University of San Diego	M,D,O
University of South Carolina	M
The University of South Dakota	M,D,O
University of Southern California	D
University of Southern Maine	M,O
University of Southern Mississippi	M,D
University of South Florida	M,D,O
The University of Texas at Arlington	M,D
The University of Texas at San Antonio	M,D
The University of Toledo	M,D,O
University of Utah	M,D
University of Virginia	M,D,O
University of Washington	M,D
The University of West Alabama	M
University of Wisconsin–La Crosse	M
University of Wisconsin–Madison	M,D,O
University of Wisconsin–Milwaukee	M,O
Upper Iowa University	M
Vanderbilt University	M,D
Virginia Polytechnic Institute and State University	M,D,O
Walden University	M,D,O
Walsh University	M
Wayland Baptist University	M
Wayne State University	M,D,O
West Chester University of Pennsylvania	M,O
Western Governors University	M,O
Western Illinois University	M
Western Kentucky University	M
Western Michigan University	M,D
Western Washington University	M
West Virginia University	M,D
Wilmington University	M,D

HISPANIC AND LATIN AMERICAN LANGUAGES

Boston University	M,D
Brigham Young University	M
California State University, San Marcos	M
Cornell University	D
The Graduate Center, City University of New York	D
Indiana University Bloomington	M,D
Indiana University of Pennsylvania	M
Michigan State University	M,D
Queens College of the City University of New York	M
Stony Brook University, State University of New York	M,D
Université de Montréal	M,D
University of California, Berkeley	D
University of California, Los Angeles	D
University of California, Santa Barbara	M,D
University of Colorado Boulder	M,D
University of Illinois at Chicago	M,D
University of Massachusetts Amherst	M,D
University of Minnesota, Twin Cities Campus	M,D
The University of North Carolina at Greensboro	M,O
University of Pittsburgh	M,D
The University of Texas at Austin	M,D
University of Washington	M

HISPANIC STUDIES

Brown University	D
California State University, Los Angeles	M
California State University, Northridge	M
California State University, San Marcos	M
The Catholic University of America	M,D
The Citadel, The Military College of South Carolina	O
Columbia University	M,D
La Salle University	M,D

Louisiana State University and Agricultural & Mechanical College	M
McGill University	M,D
Michigan State University	M,D
Oregon State University	M
Pontifical Catholic University of Puerto Rico	M,O
Queen's University at Kingston	M
St. Thomas University	M,O
San Jose State University	M,O
Texas A&M International University	M,D
Texas A&M University–Kingsville	D
University of Alberta	M,D
The University of British Columbia	M,D
University of California, Riverside	M,D
University of California, Santa Barbara	M,D
University of Houston	M,D
University of Illinois at Chicago	M,D
University of Kentucky	M,D
The University of Manchester	M,D
University of Nevada, Las Vegas	M
The University of North Carolina at Greensboro	M,O
University of Puerto Rico, Mayagüez Campus	M
University of Puerto Rico, Río Piedras Campus	M,D
The University of Texas at Austin	M
University of Victoria	M
Villanova University	M

HISTORIC PRESERVATION

The American University of Rome	M
Arkansas State University	M
Ball State University	M
Boston Architectural College	M
Boston University	M
Buffalo State College, State University of New York	M,O
Clemson University	M,O
College of Charleston	M
Colorado State University	M
Columbia University	M,O
Cornell University	M,D
Delaware State University	M
Eastern Michigan University	M,D
The George Washington University	M,O
Georgia State University	M,D
Goucher College	M
Morgan State University	M,D
New York University	M
Penn State Harrisburg	M,D,O
Plymouth State University	M
Pratt Institute	M
Roger Williams University	M
Rutgers University–New Brunswick	M,D,O
St. Cloud State University	M
Savannah College of Art and Design	M
School of the Art Institute of Chicago	M
Southeast Missouri State University	M,O
Universidad Nacional Pedro Henríquez Ureña	M
University at Buffalo, the State University of New York	M,D,O
University of California, Los Angeles	M
University of Colorado Denver	M
University of Delaware	M,D
University of Florida	M,D
University of Georgia	M
University of Hawaii at Manoa	O
The University of Kansas	M,D,O
University of Kentucky	M
University of Maryland, College Park	M,O
University of Massachusetts Amherst	M
University of New Mexico	O
The University of North Carolina at Greensboro	M,O
University of Oregon	M
University of Pennsylvania	M,O
University of Rochester	M
University of South Carolina	M,O
The University of Texas at Austin	M
University of Vermont	M
University of Washington	O
Ursuline College	M

HISTORY

Adams State University	M
Alabama State University	M
American Public University System	M
American University	M,D
American University of Beirut	M,D
Appalachian State University	M
Arizona State University at the Tempe campus	M,D,O
Arkansas State University	M,O
Arkansas Tech University	M
Armstrong State University	M
Ashland University	M
Auburn University	M,D,O
Ball State University	M
Bard College	M
Baylor University	M,D
Binghamton University, State University of New York	M,D
Bob Jones University	M,D,O
Boise State University	M
Boston College	M,D
Boston University	M,D
Bowling Green State University	M,D
Brandeis University	M,D

Brock University	M
Brooklyn College of the City University of New York	M
Brown University	M,D
Buffalo State College, State University of New York	M
Butler University	M
California Polytechnic State University, San Luis Obispo	M
California State Polytechnic University, Pomona	M
California State University, Bakersfield	M
California State University, Chico	M
California State University, East Bay	M
California State University, Fresno	M
California State University, Fullerton	M
California State University, Long Beach	M
California State University, Los Angeles	M
California State University, Northridge	M
California State University, San Marcos	M
California State University, Stanislaus	M
Carleton University	M,D
Carnegie Mellon University	D
Case Western Reserve University	M,D
The Catholic University of America	M,D
Central Connecticut State University	M,O
Central European University	M,D
Central Michigan University	M,O
Central Washington University	M
Centro de Estudios Avanzados de Puerto Rico y el Caribe	M,D
Chicago State University	M
The Citadel, The Military College of South Carolina	M,O
City College of the City University of New York	M
Claremont Graduate University	M,D,O
Clark Atlanta University	M,D
Clark University	D
Clayton State University	M
Clemson University	M
Cleveland State University	M
The College at Brockport, State University of New York	M
College of Charleston	M
College of Staten Island of the City University of New York	M
The College of William and Mary	M,D
Colorado State University	M
Columbia University	M,D
Columbus State University	M,O
Concordia University (Canada)	M,D
Converse College	M
Cornell University	M,D
Dalhousie University	M,D
DePaul University	M
Dominican University of California	M
Drew University	M,D,O
Duke University	M,D
Duquesne University	M
East Carolina University	M
Eastern Illinois University	M
Eastern Kentucky University	M
Eastern Michigan University	M
Eastern Washington University	M
East Stroudsburg University of Pennsylvania	M
East Tennessee State University	M,O
Edinboro University of Pennsylvania	M
Emory & Henry College	M
Emory University	D
Emporia State University	M
Fairleigh Dickinson University, Metropolitan Campus	M
Faulkner University	M
Fitchburg State University	M,O
Florida Agricultural and Mechanical University	M
Florida Atlantic University	M
Florida Gulf Coast University	M
Florida International University	M,D
Florida State University	M,D
Fordham University	M,D
Fort Hays State University	M
George Mason University	M,D
Georgetown University	M,D
The George Washington University	M,D
Georgia College & State University	M
Georgia Southern University	M,O
Georgia State University	M,D
The Graduate Center, City University of New York	D
Hardin-Simmons University	M
Harvard University	D
High Point University	M
Howard University	M,D
Hunter College of the City University of New York	M
Idaho State University	M
Illinois State University	M
Indiana State University	M
Indiana University Bloomington	M,D,O
Indiana University of Pennsylvania	M
Indiana University–Purdue University Indianapolis	M
Inter American University of Puerto Rico, Metropolitan Campus	M,D
Iona College	M
Iowa State University of Science and Technology	M,D

M—masters degree; D—doctorate; O—other advanced degree; *—Close-Up and/or Display

Jackson State University — M
Jacksonville State University — M
James Madison University — M
Johns Hopkins University — D
Kansas State University — M,D
Kent State University — M,D
Lake Forest College — M
Lakehead University — M
Lamar University — M
La Salle University — M,O
Laurentian University — M
Lee University — M,O
Lehigh University — M,D
Lehman College of the City University of New York — M
Liberty University — M
Lincoln University (MO) — M
Long Island University–LIU Post — M,O
Louisiana State University and Agricultural & Mechanical College — M,D
Louisiana Tech University — M
Loyola University Chicago — M,D
Marquette University — M
Marshall University — M,D
McGill University — M,D
McMaster University — M,D
Memorial University of Newfoundland — M,D
Miami University — M
Michigan State University — M
Middle Tennessee State University — M
Midwestern State University — M
Millersville University of Pennsylvania — M
Minnesota State University Mankato — M
Mississippi College — M,O
Mississippi State University — M,D
Missouri State University — M,O
Monmouth University — M
Montana State University — M,D
Morgan State University — M,D
Murray State University — M
Nebraska Wesleyan University — M
New Jersey Institute of Technology — M,D,O
New Mexico Highlands University — M
New Mexico State University — M
The New School — M,D
New York University — M,D,O
North Carolina Central University — M
North Carolina State University — M
North Dakota State University — M,D
Northeastern Illinois University — M
Northeastern University — M,D
Northern Arizona University — M
Northern Illinois University — M,D
Northwestern University — M,D
Norwich University — M
Oakland University — M
The Ohio State University — M,D
Ohio University — M,D
Oklahoma State University — M,D
Old Dominion University — M
Open University — M
Penn State University Park — M,D
Pittsburg State University — M
Pontifical Catholic University of Puerto Rico — M
Portland State University — M
Princeton University — D
Providence College — M
Purdue University — M,D
Purdue University Northwest — M
Queens College of the City University of New York — M,O
Regent University — M,D
Rhode Island College — M
Rice University — M,D
Roosevelt University — M
Rowan University — M,O
Rutgers University–Camden — M
Rutgers University–Newark — M
Rutgers University–New Brunswick — D
St. Cloud State University — M
St. John's University (NY) — M,D
Saint Louis University — M,D
Saint Mary's University (Canada) — M
Salem State University — M
Salisbury University — M
Sam Houston State University — M
San Diego State University — M
San Francisco State University — M
San Jose State University — M,O
Sarah Lawrence College — M
Seton Hall University — M
Shippensburg University of Pennsylvania — M,O
Simmons College — M
Simon Fraser University — M,D
Slippery Rock University of Pennsylvania — M
Smith College — M
Sonoma State University — M
Southeastern Louisiana University — M
Southeast Missouri State University — M,O
Southern Connecticut State University — M
Southern Illinois University Carbondale — M,D
Southern Illinois University Edwardsville — M
Southern Methodist University — M,D
Southern University and Agricultural and Mechanical College — M
Southwestern Assemblies of God University — M
Spring Hill College — M,O
Stanford University — M,D
State University of New York at Oswego — M

State University of New York College at Cortland — M
Stephen F. Austin State University — M
Stony Brook University, State University of New York — M,D
Sul Ross State University — M
Syracuse University — M,D
Tarleton State University — M
Temple University — M,D
Texas A&M International University — M,D
Texas A&M University — M,D
Texas A&M University–Central Texas — M
Texas A&M University–Commerce — M,D,O
Texas A&M University–Corpus Christi — M
Texas Christian University — M,D
Texas Southern University — M
Texas State University — M
Texas Tech University — M,D
Texas Woman's University — M
Trinity Western University — M
Troy University — M
Tufts University — M,D
Tulane University — M,D
Union Institute & University — M
Université de Moncton — M
Université de Montréal — M,D
Université de Sherbrooke — M
Université du Québec à Montréal — M,D
Université Laval — M,D
University at Albany, State University of New York — M,D,O
University at Buffalo, the State University of New York — M,D,O
The University of Akron — M,D
The University of Alabama — M,D
The University of Alabama at Birmingham — M
The University of Alabama in Huntsville — M
University of Alaska Fairbanks — M
University of Alberta — M,D
The University of Arizona — M,D,O
University of Arkansas — M,D
The University of British Columbia — M,D
University of Calgary — M,D
University of California, Berkeley — M,D
University of California, Davis — M,D
University of California, Irvine — M,D
University of California, Los Angeles — M,D
University of California, Riverside — M,D
University of California, San Diego — M,D
University of California, Santa Barbara — D
University of California, Santa Cruz — M,D
University of Central Arkansas — M
University of Central Florida — M
University of Central Missouri — M,D,O
University of Central Oklahoma — M
University of Chicago — D
University of Cincinnati — M,D
University of Colorado Boulder — M,D
University of Colorado Colorado Springs — M
University of Colorado Denver — M
University of Connecticut — M,D
University of Delaware — M,D
University of Denver — M,O
University of Florida — M,D
University of Georgia — M,D
University of Guelph — M,D
University of Hawaii at Manoa — M,D
University of Houston — M,D
University of Houston–Clear Lake — M
University of Idaho — M,D
University of Illinois at Chicago — M,D
University of Illinois at Springfield — M
University of Illinois at Urbana–Champaign — M,D
University of Indianapolis — M
The University of Iowa — M,D
The University of Kansas — M,D
University of Kentucky — M,D
University of Louisiana at Lafayette — M
University of Louisiana at Monroe — M
University of Louisville — M,O
University of Maine — M
The University of Manchester — D
University of Manitoba — M,D
University of Maryland, Baltimore County — M
University of Maryland, College Park — M,D
University of Massachusetts Amherst — M
University of Massachusetts Boston — M
University of Memphis — M,D
University of Miami — M,D
University of Michigan — D,O
University of Minnesota, Twin Cities Campus — M,D
University of Mississippi — M,D
University of Missouri — M,D
University of Missouri–Kansas City — M,D
University of Montana — M,D
University of Nebraska at Kearney — M
University of Nebraska at Omaha — M
University of Nebraska–Lincoln — M,D
University of Nevada, Las Vegas — M,D
University of Nevada, Reno — M,D
University of New Brunswick Fredericton — M,D

University of New Hampshire — M,D
University of New Mexico — M,D
University of New Orleans — M
University of North Alabama — M
The University of North Carolina at Chapel Hill — M,D
The University of North Carolina at Charlotte — M
The University of North Carolina at Greensboro — M,D,O
The University of North Carolina Wilmington — M
University of North Dakota — M,D
University of Northern British Columbia — M,D,O
University of Northern Colorado — M
University of Northern Iowa — M
University of North Florida — M
University of North Georgia — M
University of North Texas — M,D,O
University of Notre Dame — M,D
University of Oklahoma — M,D
University of Oregon — M,D
University of Ottawa — M,D
University of Pennsylvania — M,D
University of Pittsburgh — M,D
University of Puerto Rico, Río Piedras Campus — M,D
University of Regina — M
University of Rhode Island — M
University of Rochester — M,D
University of Saskatchewan — M,D
University of South Africa — M,D
University of South Alabama — M
University of South Carolina — M,D,O
The University of South Dakota — M
University of Southern California — D
University of Southern Mississippi — M,D
University of South Florida — M,D
The University of Tennessee — M,D
The University of Texas at Arlington — M,D
The University of Texas at Austin — M,D
The University of Texas at Dallas — M,D
The University of Texas at El Paso — M,D
The University of Texas at San Antonio — M
The University of Texas at Tyler — M
The University of Texas of the Permian Basin — M
The University of Texas Rio Grande Valley — M
The University of Toledo — M,D
University of Toronto — M,D
The University of Tulsa — M
University of Utah — M,D
University of Vermont — M
University of Victoria — M,D
University of Virginia — M,D
University of Washington — M,D
University of Waterloo — M,D
The University of West Alabama — M
The University of Western Ontario — M,D
University of West Florida — M
University of West Georgia — M,O
University of Windsor — M
The University of Winnipeg — M
University of Wisconsin–Eau Claire — M
University of Wisconsin–Madison — M,D
University of Wisconsin–Milwaukee — M,D
University of Wisconsin–Stevens Point — M
University of Wyoming — M
Utah State University — M
Valparaiso University — M,O
Vanderbilt University — M,D
Villanova University — M
Virginia Commonwealth University — M
Virginia Polytechnic Institute and State University — M,D,O
Washington State University — M
Washington University in St. Louis — D
Wayland Baptist University — M
Wayne State University — M,D,O
West Chester University of Pennsylvania — M
Western Carolina University — M
Western Connecticut State University — M
Western Illinois University — M
Western Kentucky University — M
Western Michigan University — M,D
Western Washington University — M
West Texas A&M University — M
West Virginia University — M,D
Wichita State University — M
Wilfrid Laurier University — M,D
William Paterson University of New Jersey — M,D
Winthrop University — M
Worcester State University — M
Wright State University — M
Yale University — M,D
York University — M,D
Youngstown State University — M

HISTORY OF MEDICINE
The College at Brockport, State University of New York — M,O
McGill University — M,D
Oregon State University — M,D
Rutgers University–New Brunswick — D
The University of Manchester — M,D
University of Minnesota, Twin Cities Campus — M,D
Yale University — M,D

HISTORY OF SCIENCE AND TECHNOLOGY
Arizona State University at the Tempe campus — M,D

Brown University — D
Carnegie Mellon University — D
Cornell University — M,D
Drexel University — M
Georgia Institute of Technology — M
Harvard University — M,D
Indiana University Bloomington — M,D
Johns Hopkins University — M,D
Massachusetts Institute of Technology — D
Oregon State University — M,D
Princeton University — D
Rensselaer Polytechnic Institute — M,D
Rutgers University–New Brunswick — D
University of California, Berkeley — D
University of California, San Diego — D
University of California, San Francisco — M,D
University of Delaware — M,D
The University of Manchester — M,D
University of Minnesota, Twin Cities Campus — M,D
University of Notre Dame — M,D
University of Oklahoma — M,D
University of Pennsylvania — M,D
University of Pittsburgh — D
University of Toronto — M,D
University of Wisconsin–Madison — M,D
Virginia Polytechnic Institute and State University — M,D,O
Wayne State University — M,D
West Virginia University — M,D
Yale University — M,D

HIV/AIDS NURSING
University of Delaware — M,O

HOLOCAUST AND GENOCIDE STUDIES
Chapman University — M
Clark University — D
Gratz College — M,D
Kean University — M
Seton Hill University — M,O
Stockton University — M
West Chester University of Pennsylvania — M,O

HOME ECONOMICS EDUCATION
Alabama Agricultural and Mechanical University — M,O
Cambridge College — M,D,O
Central Washington University — M
Eastern Kentucky University — M
Louisiana State University and Agricultural & Mechanical College — M,D
Montana State University — M
Purdue University — M,D,O
South Carolina State University — M
Texas Tech University — M,D
The University of British Columbia — M,D
University of Nebraska–Lincoln — M,D
Utah State University — M
Wayne State College — M

HOMELAND SECURITY
American Public University System — M
Angelo State University — M
Arizona State University at the Tempe campus — M,D
Auburn University at Montgomery — M
Aurora University — M
Ball State University — M,O
Capella University — M
The Citadel, The Military College of South Carolina — M,O
Clemson University — M,O
Columbus State University — M
Drexel University — M
Endicott College — M
Excelsior College — M
Fairleigh Dickinson University, Metropolitan Campus — M
Georgian Court University — M
Henley-Putnam University — M
Indiana University–Purdue University Indianapolis — M,O
Johns Hopkins University — M
Keiser University — M
Lasell College — M,O
London Metropolitan University — M,D
Missouri State University — M,O
Monmouth University — M
National Defense University — M
The National Graduate School of Quality Management — M,D
Naval Postgraduate School — M,D
Northeastern University — M,D
Northwestern State University of Louisiana — M
Notre Dame College (OH) — M,O
Pace University — M
Penn State Harrisburg — M,D,O
Regent University — M
St. Mary's University (United States) — M,O
Salve Regina University — M,D
Sam Houston State University — M
Southern Illinois University Carbondale — M
Texas A&M University — M,O
Thomas Edison State University — M
Tiffin University — M
Towson University — M
University at Albany, State University of New York — M,D,O
University of Alaska Fairbanks — M
University of Central Florida — M,O
University of Colorado Denver — M,D,O
University of Denver — M
University of Illinois at Springfield — M,O

University of Management and Technology	M
University of Oklahoma Health Sciences Center	M
University of Phoenix–Online Campus	M
University of Phoenix–Phoenix Campus	M
University of Phoenix–Southern California Campus	M
University of Southern California	M,O
University of the District of Columbia	M
Upper Iowa University	M
Virginia Commonwealth University	M,O
Walden University	M,D,O
Wayland Baptist University	M
Western Kentucky University	M
Western Michigan University Thomas M. Cooley Law School	M,D
Wilmington University	M,D

HORTICULTURE

Auburn University	M,D
Colorado State University	M,D
Cornell University	M,D
Dalhousie University	M
Iowa State University of Science and Technology	M,D
Kansas State University	M,D
Michigan State University	M,D
Mississippi State University	M,D
New Mexico State University	M,D
North Carolina State University	M,D,O
The Ohio State University	M,D
Oklahoma State University	M,D
Oregon State University	M,D
Penn State University Park	M,D
Purdue University	M,D
Rutgers University–New Brunswick	M,D
Texas A&M University	M,D
Texas A&M University–Kingsville	M,D
Texas Tech University	M,D
Universidad Nacional Pedro Henriquez Urena	M
University of Arkansas	M
University of California, Davis	M
University of Delaware	M
University of Florida	M,D
University of Georgia	M,D
University of Guelph	M,D
University of Hawaii at Manoa	M,D,O
University of Maine	M,D,O
University of Manitoba	M,D
University of Maryland, College Park	M,D
University of Missouri	M,D
University of Nebraska–Lincoln	M,D
University of Puerto Rico, Mayagüez Campus	M
University of South Africa	M,D
University of Vermont	M,D
University of Washington	M,D
University of Wisconsin–Madison	M,D
Virginia Polytechnic Institute and State University	M,D
Washington State University	M,D
West Virginia University	M

HOSPICE NURSING

Madonna University	M

HOSPITALITY MANAGEMENT

Alabama Agricultural and Mechanical University	M
American International College	M,D,O
California State Polytechnic University, Pomona	M
California State University, Northridge	M,O
Cornell University	M,D
DePaul University	M
Drexel University	M
East Carolina University	M
Eastern Michigan University	M,O
Ecole Hôtelière de Lausanne	M
ESSEC Business School	M,D
Fairleigh Dickinson University, College at Florham	M
Fairleigh Dickinson University, Metropolitan Campus	M
Florida International University	M
Georgetown University	M,D
The George Washington University	M,O
Glion Institute of Higher Education	M
Hawai'i Pacific University	M
Husson University	M
IGlobal University	M
Johnson & Wales University	M
Kansas State University	M,D
Kent State University	M
Lasell College	M,O
Les Roches International School of Hotel Management	M
Lynn University	M
Marylhurst University	M
Michigan State University	M
Monroe College	M
New York University	M,D,O
Oklahoma State University	M,D
Penn State University Park	M,D
Pontificia Universidad Catolica Madre y Maestra	M
Purdue University	M,D
Rochester Institute of Technology	M
Roosevelt University	M

Royal Roads University	M,O
San Francisco State University	M
Schiller International University (United States)	M
South University (GA)	M
Stratford University (VA)	M
Stratford University (MD)	M
Strayer University	M
Syracuse University	M,O
Temple University	M,D
Texas Tech University	M,D
The University of Alabama	M
University of Central Florida	M,D,O
University of Delaware	M
The University of Findlay	M,D
University of Guelph	M
University of Houston	M
University of Kentucky	M
University of Massachusetts Amherst	M,D
University of Memphis	M,D
University of Missouri	M,D
University of Nevada, Las Vegas	M,D
University of New Orleans	M
University of North Texas	M,D,O
University of South Carolina	M
University of South Florida Sarasota-Manatee	M
The University of Tennessee	M
University of the Pacific	M
Virginia International University	M,O
Virginia Polytechnic Institute and State University	M,D
Widener University	M,D

HUMAN-COMPUTER INTERACTION

Brandeis University	M
Carnegie Mellon University	M,D
Clemson University	D
Cornell University	M,D
Dalhousie University	M
DePaul University	M,D
Florida Institute of Technology	M
Georgia Institute of Technology	M
Indiana University Bloomington	M,D
Indiana University–Purdue University Indianapolis	M,D
Iowa State University of Science and Technology	M,D
Rochester Institute of Technology	M
State University of New York at Oswego	M
Tufts University	O
University of Baltimore	M
University of Illinois at Urbana–Champaign	M,D,O

HUMAN DEVELOPMENT

Alabama Agricultural and Mechanical University	M
Argosy University, Chicago	D
Arizona State University at the Tempe campus	M,D
Auburn University	M,D
Ball State University	M,D,O
Bradley University	M
Brigham Young University	M,D
Brock University	M,D
California State University, Fresno	M,D
Central Michigan University	M,O
Claremont Graduate University	M,D,O
Clemson University	M,O
Colorado State University	M,D
Cornell University	M,D
Duke University	D
East Tennessee State University	M
Erikson Institute	M,O
Fielding Graduate University	M,D,O
Georgetown University	M
The George Washington University	M
Georgia State University	M,D,O
Harvard University	M
Hofstra University	M,D,O
Hood College	M
Iowa State University of Science and Technology	M,D
Kansas State University	M,D
Kent State University	M,D
Laurentian University	M
Lindsey Wilson College	M,D
Marywood University	D
Mississippi State University	M,D
Montana State University	M
National Louis University	M,D,O
New York University	M,D,O
Northern Arizona University	O
Northwestern University	D
The Ohio State University	M,D
Oklahoma State University	M,D
Oregon State University	M,D
Pacific Oaks College	M
Penn State University Park	M,D
Purdue University	M,D
St. Lawrence University	M,O
Saint Louis University	M,D,O
Saint Mary's University of Minnesota	M
Texas Tech University	M,D
Tufts University	M,D
The University of Alabama	M
The University of Arizona	M,D,O
The University of British Columbia	M,D,O
University of California, Berkeley	M,D
University of California, Davis	D
University of Central Oklahoma	M
University of Chicago	D
University of Colorado Denver	M,D,O
University of Connecticut	M,D
University of Dayton	M
University of Delaware	M,D

University of Guelph	M,D
University of Illinois at Chicago	M,D
University of Illinois at Springfield	M
University of Illinois at Urbana–Champaign	M,D
University of Maine	M,D,O
University of Maryland, College Park	M,D
University of Missouri	M,D
University of Nebraska–Lincoln	M,D,O
University of Nevada, Reno	M
University of New Mexico	M,D
The University of North Carolina at Greensboro	M,D
University of North Texas	M,D,O
University of Pennsylvania	M,D
University of Rhode Island	M
University of Rochester	M
University of St. Thomas (MN)	M,D
University of South Africa	M,D
The University of South Dakota	M,D,O
The University of Texas at Austin	M,D
University of Utah	M,D
University of Victoria	M
University of Washington	M,D
University of Wisconsin–Madison	M,D
University of Wisconsin–Stevens Point	M
Utah State University	M,D
Vanderbilt University	M
Virginia Polytechnic Institute and State University	M,D,O
Washington State University	D
West Virginia University	M
Wheelock College	M

HUMAN GENETICS

Baylor College of Medicine	D
Case Western Reserve University	M,D
Emory University	M
Louisiana State University Health Sciences Center	D
McGill University	M,D
Memorial University of Newfoundland	M,D
Sarah Lawrence College	M
Thomas Jefferson University	M
Tulane University	M
University of California, Los Angeles	M,D
University of Chicago	D
University of Manitoba	M,D
University of Maryland, Baltimore	M,D
University of Michigan	M,D
University of Pennsylvania	M
University of Pittsburgh	M,D,O
University of Utah	M,D
Vanderbilt University	D
Virginia Commonwealth University	M,D
Wake Forest University	D
Washington University in St. Louis	D
West Virginia University	M,D

HUMANITIES

American Public University System	M
Antioch University New England	M
Arcadia University	M
Brandeis University	M
Brigham Young University	M
California Institute of Integral Studies	M,D
California State University, Dominguez Hills	M
Central Michigan University	M
Claremont Graduate University	M,D,O
The Colorado College	M
Concordia University (Canada)	D
Dominican University of California	M
Duke University	M
Georgetown University	M,D
Harrison Middleton University	M,D
Hofstra University	M,D,O
Hollins University	M
Hood College	M
Illinois Institute of Technology	M,D
Instituto Tecnologico de Santo Domingo	M
Instituto Tecnológico y de Estudios Superiores de Monterrey, Campus Central de Veracruz	M
Instituto Tecnológico y de Estudios Superiores de Monterrey, Campus Ciudad de México	M,D
Instituto Tecnológico y de Estudios Superiores de Monterrey, Campus Ciudad Juárez	M
Instituto Tecnológico y de Estudios Superiores de Monterrey, Campus Estado de México	M,D
Instituto Tecnológico y de Estudios Superiores de Monterrey, Campus Irapuato	M,D
John Carroll University	M
Laurentian University	M
Loyola University Chicago	M
Marshall University	M,O
Memorial University of Newfoundland	M
Mount Saint Mary's University (CA)	M,D
New York University	M,D,O
Nova Southeastern University	M,D,O
Old Dominion University	M
Penn State Harrisburg	M,D,O
Pepperdine University	M
Prescott College	M
St. Edward's University	M,O
Salve Regina University	M,D

Sam Houston State University	M,D,O
San Francisco State University	M
Simon Fraser University	M
Tiffin University	M
Trinity Western University	M
United Theological Seminary of the Twin Cities	M,D,O
University at Buffalo, the State University of New York	M
University of California, Santa Cruz	D
University of Chicago	M
University of Colorado Denver	M
University of Dallas	M
University of Houston–Clear Lake	M
University of Louisville	M,D
University of South Florida	M
The University of Texas at Dallas	M,D
The University of Texas Medical Branch	M,D
University of Utah	M
Virginia Polytechnic Institute and State University	M,D,O
Wayland Baptist University	M
West Chester University of Pennsylvania	M,O
Wilson College	M
Wright State University	M
York University	M,D

HUMAN RESOURCES DEVELOPMENT

Abilene Christian University	M
Amberton University	M
Antioch University Los Angeles	M
Azusa Pacific University	M
Barry University	M,D
Bowie State University	M
California State University, Sacramento	M
Claremont Graduate University	M,D,O
Clemson University	M,D,O
The College of New Rochelle	M,O
Drexel University	M
Florida International University	M,D,O
The George Washington University	M,D,O
Grantham University	M,O
Illinois Institute of Technology	M
Indiana State University	M
Indiana Tech	M
Indiana University of Pennsylvania	M
Inter American University of Puerto Rico, Metropolitan Campus	M
Inter American University of Puerto Rico, San Germán Campus	M,D
Iowa State University of Science and Technology	M,D
John F. Kennedy University	M,O
Kentucky State University	M,O
La Salle University	M,O
Lawrence Technological University	M,O
Lincoln Memorial University	M,D,O
Louisiana State University and Agricultural & Mechanical College	M,D
Marquette University	M
McDaniel College	M
Midwestern State University	M
Mississippi State University	M,D,O
Moravian College	M
National Louis University	M
New York University	M,O
North Carolina State University	M
Northeastern Illinois University	M
Ottawa University	M
Penn State Great Valley	M,O
Penn State University Park	M
Pittsburg State University	M
Regent University	M,D,O
Rochester Institute of Technology	M
Rockhurst University	M,O
Rollins College	M
Roosevelt University	M
South Dakota State University	M
Texas A&M University	M
Towson University	M
Universidad Central del Este	M
Universidad Iberoamericana	M,D
University of Arkansas	M
University of Bridgeport	M
University of Houston	M
University of Louisville	M,D,O
University of Minnesota, Twin Cities Campus	M,D,O
University of Nebraska at Omaha	M,D,O
University of Regina	M
The University of Scranton	M
University of South Africa	M,D
University of South Florida	O
The University of Tennessee	M
The University of Texas at Tyler	M,D
University of Wisconsin–Stout	M
Villanova University	M
Virginia Commonwealth University	M
Waldorf University	M
Webster University	M,D,O
Western Seminary	M
William Woods University	M,D,O
Xavier University	M,D

HUMAN RESOURCES MANAGEMENT

Adelphi University	M,O
Albany State University	M
Amberton University	M
American InterContinental University Online	M
American Public University System	M
American University	M,O
American University of Beirut	M
Anderson University (SC)	M
Argosy University, Schaumburg	M,D,O

*M—masters degree; D—doctorate; O—other advanced degree; *—Close-Up and/or Display*

Human Resources Management (continued)

Institution	Degree
Ashworth College	M,O
Assumption College	M,O
Austin Peay State University	M
Averett University	M
Avila University	M
Azusa Pacific University	M
Baker College Center for Graduate Studies–Online	M,D
Baldwin Wallace University	M
Barry University	O
Baruch College of the City University of New York	M,D
Belhaven University (MS)	M
Bellevue University	M,D
Benedictine University	M
Brandman University	M
Brigham Young University	M
Buffalo State College, State University of New York	M,O
California Coast University	M
California Intercontinental University	M,D
California State University, East Bay	M
California State University, Sacramento	M
Capella University	M,D
Caribbean University	M,D
Carlow University	M
The Catholic University of America	M
Central Michigan University	M,O
Charleston Southern University	M
City University of Seattle	M
Claremont Graduate University	M
Clarkson University	M
Clayton State University	M
Clemson University	M,D,O
Cleveland State University	M
College of Saint Elizabeth	M
Colorado State University–Global Campus	M
Colorado Technical University Aurora	M
Colorado Technical University Colorado Springs	M,D
Columbia College (MO)	M
Columbia Southern University	M
Columbia University	M
Columbus State University	M,O
Concordia University, St. Paul	M
Concordia University Wisconsin	M
Cornell University	M,D
Dallas Baptist University	M
Davenport University	M
Delaware Valley University	M
DePaul University	M
DeSales University	M
DeVry University–Folsom Campus	M
East Central University	M
Eastern Michigan University	M,O
Embry-Riddle Aeronautical University–Daytona	M
Embry-Riddle Aeronautical University–Worldwide	M
Emmanuel College (United States)	M,O
Everest University	M
Everglades University	M
Excelsior College	M,O
Fairfield University	M,O
Fairleigh Dickinson University, College at Florham	M
Fairleigh Dickinson University, Metropolitan Campus	M,O
Fitchburg State University	M
Florida Institute of Technology	M,D
Florida International University	M,D
Florida State University	M,D
Framingham State University	M
Franklin Pierce University	M,D,O
Gannon University	M
George Fox University	M,D
George Mason University	M
Georgetown University	M
The George Washington University	M,O
Georgia State University	M,D
Golden Gate University	M,D,O
Goldey-Beacom College	M
Grambling State University	M
Grand Canyon University	M
Grantham University	M,O
Hawai`i Pacific University	M
HEC Montreal	M
Herzing University Online	M
Hofstra University	M,O
Holy Family University	M
Hood College	M
Houston Baptist University	M
Howard University	M
IGlobal University	M
Indiana Tech	M
Indiana University South Bend	M,O
Indiana Wesleyan University	M,O
Instituto Tecnologico de Santo Domingo	M,O
Instituto Tecnológico y de Estudios Superiores de Monterrey, Campus Cuernavaca	M
Inter American University of Puerto Rico, Aguadilla Campus	M
Inter American University of Puerto Rico, Arecibo Campus	M
Inter American University of Puerto Rico, Bayamón Campus	M
Inter American University of Puerto Rico, Metropolitan Campus	M
Inter American University of Puerto Rico, Ponce Campus	M
Inter American University of Puerto Rico, San Germán Campus	M,D
International College of the Cayman Islands	M
Iona College	M,O
James Madison University	M
Johnson & Wales University	M
Kaplan University, Davenport Campus	M
King University	M
La Roche College	M,O
La Salle University	M,O
Lasell College	M,O
La Sierra University	M,O
Lewis University	M
Lincoln University (CA)	M,D
Lincoln University (PA)	M,D
Lindenwood University	M,O
Lindenwood University–Belleville	M
Lipscomb University	M,O
London Metropolitan University	M,D
Long Island University–LIU Brooklyn	M,O
Loyola University Chicago	M
Lynn University	M
Manhattanville College	M
Marquette University	M,O
Marshall University	M
Marygrove College	M
Marymount University	M,O
Maryville University of Saint Louis	M,O
McKendree University	M
McMaster University	M,D
Mercy College	M
Mercyhurst University	M,O
Michigan State University	M,D
Middle Tennessee State University	M
Millennia Atlantic University	M
Misericordia University	M
Monmouth University	M,O
Monroe College	M
Moravian College	M
Mount Ida College	M
Mount Mercy University	M
National Louis University	M
National University	M
Nazareth College of Rochester	M
New Mexico Highlands University	M
New York Institute of Technology	M,O
New York University	M,D,O
Niagara University	M
North Carolina Agricultural and Technical State University	M
North Central College	M
Northern Michigan University	M
North Greenville University	M,D
Northwestern University	M,D
Northwest Missouri State University	M
Norwich University	M
Notre Dame de Namur University	M
Nova Southeastern University	M
Oakland University	M,O
Ohio Christian University	M
The Ohio State University	M,D
Oklahoma Christian University	M
Ottawa University	M
Pace University	M
Penn State Great Valley	M,O
Penn State Harrisburg	M,D,O
Penn State University Park	M
Pepperdine University	M
Polytechnic University of Puerto Rico, Miami Campus	M
Polytechnic University of Puerto Rico, Orlando Campus	M
Pontifical Catholic University of Puerto Rico	M,O
Pontificia Universidad Catolica Madre y Maestra	M
Purdue University	M,D
Regent's University London	M
Regent University	M,D,O
Regis University	M,O
Robert Morris University	M
Robert Morris University Illinois	M
Rollins College	M
Roosevelt University	M
Royal Roads University	M,O
Rutgers University–Newark	M,D
Rutgers University–New Brunswick	M,D
Sacred Heart University	M
St. Ambrose University	M,D
Saint Francis University	M
St. Joseph's College, Long Island Campus	M
St. Joseph's College, New York	M
Saint Joseph's University	M,O
Saint Leo University	M,D,O
Saint Mary's University of Minnesota	M
Saint Peter's University	M
St. Thomas University	M,O
Salve Regina University	M,O
San Diego State University	M
Savannah State University	M
Seattle Pacific University	M
Southern New Hampshire University	M,O
State University of New York Polytechnic Institute	M
Stevens Institute of Technology	M
Stony Brook University, State University of New York	M,O
Strayer University	M
Tarleton State University	M
Temple University	M,D
Tennessee State University	M,D
Tennessee Technological University	M
Texas A&M University	M
Texas A&M University–Central Texas	M,O
Texas A&M University–San Antonio	M
Texas State University	M
Thomas College	M
Thomas Edison State University	M
Tiffin University	M
Trident University International	M,D
Trinity International University	M,D
Trinity Washington University	M
Troy University	M
Tusculum College	M
United States International University–Africa	M
Universidad del Este	M
Universidad del Turabo	M
Universidad Metropolitana	M
University at Albany, State University of New York	M,D,O
University at Buffalo, the State University of New York	M,D,O
The University of Alabama in Huntsville	M,O
University of Bridgeport	M
University of California, Berkeley	O
University of Colorado Denver	M
University of Connecticut	M
University of Dallas	M,D
University of Denver	M,O
University of Florida	M,D
University of Hawaii at Manoa	M
University of Houston–Clear Lake	M
University of Houston–Downtown	M
University of Illinois at Urbana–Champaign	M,D,O
The University of Kansas	M,D
University of La Verne	M,O
University of Lethbridge	M,D
University of Louisville	M,D,O
The University of Manchester	M
University of Mary	M
University of Memphis	M,O
University of Minnesota, Twin Cities Campus	M
University of Missouri–St. Louis	M,D,O
University of Nebraska at Kearney	M
University of New Haven	M,O
University of New Mexico	M
University of Northern Colorado	M
University of North Florida	M
University of North Texas	M,D,O
University of North Texas at Dallas	M
University of Oklahoma	M,O
University of Phoenix–Atlanta Campus	M
University of Phoenix–Augusta Campus	M
University of Phoenix–Bay Area Campus	M,D
University of Phoenix–Central Valley Campus	M
University of Phoenix–Colorado Campus	M
University of Phoenix–Colorado Springs Downtown Campus	M
University of Phoenix–Columbus Georgia Campus	M
University of Phoenix–Dallas Campus	M
University of Phoenix–Hawaii Campus	M
University of Phoenix–Houston Campus	M
University of Phoenix–Jersey City Campus	M
University of Phoenix–Las Vegas Campus	M
University of Phoenix–New Mexico Campus	M
University of Phoenix–North Florida Campus	M
University of Phoenix–Online Campus	M,O
University of Phoenix–Phoenix Campus	M,O
University of Phoenix–Sacramento Valley Campus	M
University of Phoenix–San Antonio Campus	M
University of Phoenix–San Diego Campus	M
University of Phoenix–Southern Arizona Campus	M
University of Phoenix–Southern California Campus	M
University of Phoenix–South Florida Campus	M
University of Phoenix–Utah Campus	M
University of Phoenix–Washington D.C. Campus	M,D
University of Pittsburgh	M,D
University of Puerto Rico, Mayagüez Campus	M
University of Puerto Rico, Río Piedras Campus	M,D
University of Regina	M,O
University of Rhode Island	M,O
University of St. Francis (IL)	M,O
University of Saint Mary	M
University of South Carolina	M
The University of South Dakota	M
University of Southern Indiana	M
University of South Florida	M
The University of Texas at Arlington	M
University of the Sacred Heart	M
University of Toronto	M,D
University of Wisconsin–Madison	M,D
University of Wisconsin–Platteville	M
Upper Iowa University	M
Utah State University	M
Virginia International University	M,O
Walden University	M,D,O
Walsh College of Accountancy and Business Administration	M
Warner University	M
Wayland Baptist University	M,D
Waynesburg University	M,D
Wayne State University	M,D
Webster University	M,D,O
West Chester University of Pennsylvania	M,O
Wilfrid Laurier University	M,D
Wilkes University	M
Wilmington University	M,D
York University	M,D

HUMAN SERVICES

Institution	Degree
Abilene Christian University	M,O
Albertus Magnus College	M
Amridge University	M,D
Bellevue University	M
Boricua College	M
Brandeis University	M
California State University, Sacramento	M
Capella University	M,D
Carlos Albizu University, Miami Campus	M,D
Chestnut Hill College	M,O
Concordia University Chicago	M
Concordia University, St. Paul	M,D
Coppin State University	M
East Central University	M
Eastern Michigan University	O
Eastern New Mexico University	M
Ferris State University	M
Georgia State University	M,O
Governors State University	M
Judson University	M
Kansas State University	M,D,O
Kent State University	M,D,O
Lehigh University	M,D,O
Lenoir-Rhyne University	M
Liberty University	M,D,O
Lincoln University (PA)	M
Lock Haven University of Pennsylvania	M
McDaniel College	M
Mercer University	M,D
Minnesota State University Mankato	M
Minnesota State University Moorhead	M,O
Murray State University	M
National Louis University	M,D,O
National University	M,D,O
New England College	M
Northeastern University	M
Pontifical Catholic University of Puerto Rico	M,D
Post University	M
Purdue University Northwest	M
Roberts Wesleyan College	M
Rosemont College	M
St. Joseph's College, Long Island Campus	M
St. Joseph's College, New York	M
Saint Leo University	M
South Carolina State University	M
Southeastern University (FL)	M
Springfield College	M
Texas Southern University	M
Thomas University	M
Universidad del Turabo	M
Université de Montréal	D
University of Baltimore	M
University of Bridgeport	M
University of Central Missouri	M,D,O
University of Colorado Colorado Springs	M,D
University of Great Falls	M
University of Idaho	M,O
University of Illinois at Springfield	M,O
University of Illinois at Urbana–Champaign	M,D
University of Maryland, Baltimore County	M,D
University of Massachusetts Boston	M
University of Nebraska at Kearney	M
University of Northern Iowa	M
University of Northwestern–St. Paul	M
University of Oklahoma	M,O
Upper Iowa University	M
Walden University	M,D
Warner Pacific College	M
Washburn University	M
Webster University	M
Western Michigan University	D,O
West Virginia University	M,D
Wichita State University	M
Wilmington University	M
Winona State University	M
Youngstown State University	M

HYDRAULICS

Institution	Degree
Drexel University	M,D
École Polytechnique de Montréal	M,D,O
McGill University	M,D
Missouri University of Science and Technology	M,D
Old Dominion University	M
University of Colorado Denver	M,D

HYDROGEOLOGY

Institution	Degree
Clemson University	M
East Carolina University	M,O
Illinois State University	O
Indiana University Bloomington	M
Montana Tech of The University of Montana	M
University of Hawaii at Manoa	M,D
University of Nevada, Reno	M,D
University of South Florida	O

The University of Texas at Dallas	M,D
West Virginia University	M,D

HYDROLOGY

Boise State University	M,D
California State University, Bakersfield	M
Colorado School of Mines	M,D
Cornell University	M,D
Drexel University	M,D
Idaho State University	M,O
Illinois State University	O
Massachusetts Institute of Technology	M,D,O
Missouri University of Science and Technology	M,D
Murray State University	M
New Mexico Institute of Mining and Technology	M,D
New Mexico State University	M,D
Stanford University	M,D,O
Stevens Institute of Technology	M,D,O
Temple University	M,O
Université du Québec, Institut National de la Recherche Scientifique	M,D
The University of Arizona	D,O
University of Calgary	M,D
University of California, Davis	M,D
University of Colorado Denver	M,D
University of Florida	M,D
University of Minnesota, Twin Cities Campus	M,D
University of Nevada, Reno	M,D
University of New Brunswick Fredericton	M
University of New Hampshire	M
University of Southern Mississippi	M,D
University of Washington	M,D

ILLUSTRATION

Academy of Art University	M
Bob Jones University	M,D,O
East Carolina University	M
Fashion Institute of Technology	M
Hollins University	M
Kent State University	M
Maryland Institute College of Art	M
Marywood University	M
Memphis College of Art	M,O
Mills College	
Minneapolis College of Art and Design	M
Savannah College of Art and Design	M
School of Visual Arts (NY)	M
Syracuse University	M
University of Massachusetts Dartmouth	M
Western Connecticut State University	M

IMMUNOLOGY

Albany Medical College	M,D
Albert Einstein College of Medicine	D
American University of Beirut	M,D
Baylor College of Medicine	D
Boston University	D
California Institute of Technology	D
Case Western Reserve University	D
Colorado State University	M,D
Cornell University	M,D
Creighton University	M,D
Dalhousie University	M,D
Dartmouth College	D
Drexel University	M,D
Duke University	D
East Carolina University	M,D
Emory University	D
Georgetown University	M,D
The George Washington University	D
Hood College	M
Illinois State University	M,D
Indiana University–Purdue University Indianapolis	M,D
Iowa State University of Science and Technology	M,D
Irell & Manella Graduate School of Biological Sciences	D*
Johns Hopkins University	M,D
London Metropolitan University	M,D
Louisiana State University Health Sciences Center	D
Louisiana State University Health Sciences Center at Shreveport	M,D
Loyola University Chicago	M,D
Massachusetts Institute of Technology	D
Mayo Clinic Graduate School of Biomedical Sciences	D
McGill University	M,D
McMaster University	M,D
Medical University of South Carolina	M,D
Meharry Medical College	D
Memorial University of Newfoundland	M,D
Montana State University	M,D
New York Medical College	M,D
New York University	M,D
Oregon Health & Science University	D
Oregon State University	M,D
Penn State Hershey Medical Center	M,D
Purdue University	M,D
Queen's University at Kingston	M,D
Rosalind Franklin University of Medicine and Science	D
Rush University	M,D
Rutgers University–Newark	D
Rutgers University–New Brunswick	M,D

Saint Louis University	D
Stanford University	D
State University of New York Upstate Medical University	M,D
Stony Brook University, State University of New York	M,D
Thomas Jefferson University	D
Tufts University	D
Tulane University	M
Uniformed Services University of the Health Sciences	
Universidad Central del Caribe	M,D
Université de Montréal	M,D
Université de Sherbrooke	M,D
Université du Québec, Institut National de la Recherche Scientifique	M,D
Université Laval	M,D
University at Buffalo, the State University of New York	M,D
University of Alberta	M,D
The University of Arizona	D
University of Arkansas for Medical Sciences	M,D,O
The University of British Columbia	M,D
University of Calgary	M,D
University of California, Berkeley	D
University of California, Davis	M,D
University of California, Los Angeles	D
University of Chicago	D
University of Cincinnati	M,D
University of Colorado Denver	D
University of Connecticut Health Center	D
University of Florida	M,D
University of Guelph	M,D,O
University of Illinois at Chicago	D
The University of Iowa	M,D
University of Kentucky	D
University of Louisville	M,D
The University of Manchester	M,D
University of Manitoba	M,D
University of Maryland, Baltimore	D
University of Massachusetts Medical School	M,D
University of Miami	D
University of Michigan	M,D
University of Minnesota, Duluth	M,D
University of Minnesota, Twin Cities Campus	D
University of Missouri	D
University of Montana	D
University of Nebraska Medical Center	D
The University of North Carolina at Chapel Hill	M,D
University of North Texas Health Science Center at Fort Worth	M,D
University of Oklahoma Health Sciences Center	M,D
University of Ottawa	M,D
University of Pennsylvania	D
University of Pittsburgh	D
University of Prince Edward Island	M,D
University of Rochester	M,D
University of Saskatchewan	M,D
The University of South Dakota	M,D
University of Southern California	M
University of Southern Maine	M
University of South Florida	M,D
The University of Texas Health Science Center at Houston	M,D
The University of Texas Health Science Center at San Antonio	M,D
The University of Texas Medical Branch	M,D
The University of Texas Southwestern Medical Center	D
The University of Toledo	M,D
University of Toronto	D
The University of Western Ontario	M,D
Vanderbilt University	M,D
Virginia Commonwealth University	M,D
Wake Forest University	M,D
Washington State University	M,D
Washington University in St. Louis	M,D,O
Wayne State University	M,D
Weill Cornell Medicine	M,D
West Virginia University	M,D
Wright State University	M
Yale University	D

INDUSTRIAL/MANAGEMENT ENGINEERING

American University of Armenia	M
Arizona State University at the Tempe campus	M,D
Auburn University	M,D,O
Binghamton University, State University of New York	M,D
Bradley University	M
Buffalo State College, State University of New York	M
California Polytechnic State University, San Luis Obispo	M
California State University, East Bay	M
California State University, Fresno	M
California State University, Northridge	M
Central Washington University	M
Clemson University	M,D
Cleveland State University	M,D
Colorado State University	M,D
Colorado State University–Pueblo	M
Columbia University	M,D
Concordia University (Canada)	M,D,O

Cornell University	M,D
Dalhousie University	M,D
Eastern Kentucky University	M
École Polytechnique de Montréal	M,D,O
Florida Agricultural and Mechanical University	M,D
Florida State University	M,D
Georgia Institute of Technology	M,D
Illinois State University	M
Indiana University–Purdue University Fort Wayne	M
Instituto Tecnologico de Santo Domingo	M,O
Instituto Tecnológico y de Estudios Superiores de Monterrey, Campus Chihuahua	M,O
Instituto Tecnológico y de Estudios Superiores de Monterrey, Campus Ciudad de México	M,D
Instituto Tecnológico y de Estudios Superiores de Monterrey, Campus Laguna	M
Instituto Tecnológico y de Estudios Superiores de Monterrey, Campus Monterrey	M,D
Iowa State University of Science and Technology	M,D
Kansas State University	M,D
Lamar University	M,D
Lawrence Technological University	M,D
Louisiana Tech University	M
Mississippi State University	M,D
Montana State University	M,D
Montana Tech of The University of Montana	M
Morehead State University	M
Morgan State University	M,D
New Jersey Institute of Technology	M,D
New Mexico State University	M,D,O
New York University	M
North Carolina Agricultural and Technical State University	M,D
North Carolina State University	M,D
North Dakota State University	M,D
Northeastern University	M,D,O
Northern Illinois University	M,D
Northwestern University	M,D
The Ohio State University	M,D
Ohio University	M,D
Oklahoma State University	M,D
Oregon State University	M,D
Penn State University Park	M,D
Purdue University	M,D
Rensselaer Polytechnic Institute	M,D
Rochester Institute of Technology	M
Rutgers University–New Brunswick	M,D
St. Mary's University (United States)	M
South Dakota State University	M
Southern Illinois University Edwardsville	M
Stanford University	M,D
Texas A&M University	M,D
Texas A&M University–Kingsville	M
Texas Southern University	M
Texas State University	M
Texas Tech University	M,D
Universidad de las Américas Puebla	M
Université de Moncton	M
Université du Québec à Trois-Rivières	M,O
Université Laval	O
University at Buffalo, the State University of New York	M,D
The University of Alabama in Huntsville	M,D
The University of Arizona	M,D,O
University of Arkansas	M,D
University of California, Berkeley	M,D
University of Central Florida	M,D,O
University of Cincinnati	M,D
University of Florida	M,D,O
University of Houston	M,D
University of Illinois at Chicago	M,D
University of Illinois at Urbana–Champaign	M,D
The University of Iowa	M,D
University of Louisville	M,D,O
University of Manitoba	M,D
University of Massachusetts Amherst	M,D
University of Massachusetts Dartmouth	M,D
University of Massachusetts Lowell	D
University of Miami	M,D
University of Michigan	M,D
University of Michigan–Dearborn	M,D
University of Minnesota, Twin Cities Campus	M,D
University of Missouri	M,D
University of Nebraska–Lincoln	M,D
University of New Haven	M,O
University of Oklahoma	M,D
University of Pittsburgh	M,D
University of Puerto Rico, Mayagüez Campus	M
University of Regina	M
University of Southern California	M,D,O
University of South Florida	M,D,O
The University of Tennessee	M,D
The University of Tennessee at Chattanooga	M
The University of Texas at Arlington	M,D
The University of Texas at Austin	M,D

The University of Texas at El Paso	M,O
The University of Toledo	M,D
University of Toronto	M,D
University of Washington	M,D
University of Windsor	M,D
University of Wisconsin–Madison	M,D
University of Wisconsin–Milwaukee	M,D
University of Wisconsin–Stout	M
Virginia Polytechnic Institute and State University	M,D,O
Wayne State University	M,D,O
Western Michigan University	M,D
Western New England University	M
West Virginia University	M,D
Wichita State University	M,D
Wright State University	M
Youngstown State University	M

INDUSTRIAL AND LABOR RELATIONS

Baruch College of the City University of New York	M
Carnegie Mellon University	D
Cleveland State University	M
Cornell University	M,D
Georgetown University	D
Georgia State University	M,D
Indiana University of Pennsylvania	M
Inter American University of Puerto Rico, Metropolitan Campus	M,D
McMaster University	M
Memorial University of Newfoundland	M
Michigan State University	M,D
New York Institute of Technology	M,O
The Ohio State University	M,D
Penn State University Park	M,D
Queen's University at Kingston	M
Rutgers University–New Brunswick	M,D
Southern New Hampshire University	M,O
State University of New York Empire State College	M
Université de Montréal	M,D,O
Université du Québec à Trois-Rivières	O
Université du Québec en Outaouais	M,D,O
Université Laval	M,D
University of Alberta	D
University of California, Berkeley	D
University of Cincinnati	M
University of Illinois at Urbana–Champaign	M,D
The University of Manchester	M
University of Massachusetts Amherst	M
University of Minnesota, Twin Cities Campus	M
University of New Haven	M,O
University of Rhode Island	M,O
University of Toronto	M,D
Wayne State University	M,D
West Virginia University	M,D

INDUSTRIAL AND MANUFACTURING MANAGEMENT

American InterContinental University Online	M
Baruch College of the City University of New York	M,D
Bluffton University	M
California State University, East Bay	M
Carnegie Mellon University	M,D
Case Western Reserve University	M,D
Cedarville University	M,D
Central Connecticut State University	M,O
Central Michigan University	M
Colorado Technical University Aurora	M
Colorado Technical University Colorado Springs	M,D
DePaul University	M
Duke University	M,D,O
East Carolina University	M,D,O
Embry-Riddle Aeronautical University–Worldwide	M
Emory University	M
Everglades University	M
Georgetown University	D
Harvard University	D
HEC Montreal	M
Illinois Institute of Technology	M
Instituto Tecnologico de Santo Domingo	M,O
Instituto Tecnológico y de Estudios Superiores de Monterrey, Campus Estado de México	M,D
Instituto Tecnológico y de Estudios Superiores de Monterrey, Campus Irapuato	M,D
Inter American University of Puerto Rico, Metropolitan Campus	M
Inter American University of Puerto Rico, San Germán Campus	M,D
Lawrence Technological University	M,D
Marquette University	M,O
McGill University	M,D,O
Milligan College	M,O
Milwaukee School of Engineering	M
Mississippi State University	M,D
Northern Illinois University	M,D
Northwestern University	M,D
Notre Dame de Namur University	M
Oakland University	M,O

Penn State Erie, The Behrend
 College — M
Polytechnic University of Puerto
 Rico — M
Polytechnic University of Puerto
 Rico, Miami Campus — M
Polytechnic University of Puerto
 Rico, Orlando Campus — M
Portland State University — M,D
Regis University — M,O
Rochester Institute of Technology — M
San Francisco State University — M
Southern New Hampshire University — M,O
Stevens Institute of Technology — M
Stony Brook University, State
 University of New York — M,O
Texas A&M University–
 Commerce — M,D,O
Texas A&M University–
 Kingsville — M
Universidad de las Américas
 Puebla — M
The University of Alabama — M,D
University of Arkansas — M
University of Bridgeport — M
University of Central Missouri — M,D,O
University of Chicago — M,O
University of Cincinnati — D
The University of Manchester — M,D
University of Michigan–Flint — M,O
University of Minnesota, Twin
 Cities Campus — M
University of Missouri–St.
 Louis — M
University of New Haven — M,O
The University of North Carolina
 at Charlotte — M,D,O
University of North Texas — M,D,O
University of Pittsburgh — M
University of Portland — M
University of Puerto Rico,
 Mayagüez Campus — M
University of Puerto Rico,
 Río Piedras Campus — M,D
University of Rochester — D
University of Southern Indiana — M
The University of Tennessee — M
The University of Texas at Austin — M,D
The University of Texas at Dallas — M,D
The University of Texas at Tyler — M
University of Utah — M,D,O
Wayne State University — M,D
Wilkes University — M

INDUSTRIAL AND ORGANIZATIONAL PSYCHOLOGY

Adler University — M,D,O
Alliant International
 University–Fresno — M,D
Alliant International
 University–Los Angeles — M,D
Alliant International
 University–San Diego — M,D
Alliant International
 University–San Francisco — M,D
American InterContinental
 University Online — M
Angelo State University — M
Anna Maria College — M
Argosy University, Atlanta — M,D,O
Argosy University, Chicago — M,D
Argosy University, Dallas — M
Argosy University, Denver — M,D
Argosy University, Inland Empire — M,D
Argosy University, Phoenix — M
Argosy University, Schaumburg — M,O
Argosy University, Tampa — M,D
Argosy University, Twin Cities — M,D,O
Austin Peay State University — M
Baruch College of the City
 University of New York — M,D
Bayamón Central University — M
Bowling Green State University — M,D
Brooklyn College of the City
 University of New York — M,D
California State University, Long
 Beach — M
California State University,
 Sacramento — M
California State University, San
 Bernardino — M
Capella University — M,D
Carlos Albizu University — M,D
Carlos Albizu University, Miami
 Campus — M,D
Central Michigan University — M,D
Chatham University — M,D
The Chicago School of Professional
 Psychology — M,D
The Chicago School of Professional
 Psychology at Downtown
 Los Angeles — M
The Chicago School of Professional
 Psychology: Online — M,D,O
Claremont Graduate University — M,D,O
Clemson University — D
East Carolina University — M
Eastern Kentucky University — M,O
Elmhurst College — M
Emporia State University — M
Fairleigh Dickinson University,
 College at Florham — M
Florida Institute of Technology — M,D
Florida International University — M,D
George Mason University — M,D,O
The Graduate Center, City
 University of New York — D
Grand Canyon University — D
Hofstra University — M
Illinois Institute of Technology — M,D
Illinois State University — M,D,O
Indiana University–Purdue
 University Indianapolis — M,D

Inter American University of
 Puerto Rico, Metropolitan Campus — M,D
Iona College — M,O
John F. Kennedy University — M,O
Kean University — M,D
Keiser University — M
Lamar University — M,D
London Metropolitan University — M,D
Louisiana Tech University — M,O
Middle Tennessee State University — M,O
Minnesota State University Mankato — M,O
Missouri State University — M,O
Montclair State University — M
New York University — M,D,O
North Carolina State University — D
Northern Kentucky University — M,O
Ohio University — D
Old Dominion University — D
Philadelphia College of
 Osteopathic Medicine — M,D,O
Pontifical Catholic University of
 Puerto Rico — D
Purdue University — D
Rice University — M,D
Roosevelt University — M,D
Sacred Heart University — M
St. Cloud State University — M
Saint Louis University — M,D
Saint Mary's University
 (Canada) — M,D
St. Mary's University
 (United States) — M
San Diego State University — M
San Francisco State University — M,O
San Jose State University — M,O
Seattle Pacific University — M,D
South Dakota State University — M
Southeastern Louisiana University — M
Southern Illinois University
 Edwardsville — M
Springfield College — M,D,O
Teachers College, Columbia
 University — M,D
Texas A&M University — M,D
Thomas Edison State University — M,O
Touro College — M,D
University at Albany, State
 University of New York — M,D
The University of Akron — M,D
The University of Alabama in
 Huntsville — M
University of Central Florida — M,D
University of Connecticut — M,D
University of Detroit Mercy — M,D,O
University of Guelph — M,D
University of Houston — M,D
The University of Manchester — M
University of Maryland, Baltimore
 County — M
University of Maryland, College
 Park — M,D
University of Minnesota, Twin
 Cities Campus — D
University of Missouri–St.
 Louis — M,D,O
University of Nebraska at Omaha — M,D,O
University of New Haven — M,O
The University of North Carolina
 at Charlotte — M,D,O
University of Oklahoma — M,D
University of Phoenix–Online
 Campus — M,D,O
University of Phoenix–
 Washington D.C. Campus — M,D
University of Puerto Rico,
 Río Piedras Campus — M,D
University of South Africa — M,D
University of South Florida — D
The University of Tennessee — D
The University of Tennessee at
 Chattanooga — M
The University of Texas at
 Arlington — M,D
The University of Tulsa — M,D
University of West Florida — M
University of Wisconsin–
 Oshkosh — M
Walden University — M,D,O
Wayne State University — M,D
West Chester University of
 Pennsylvania — M,D,O
Western Kentucky University — M,O
Western Michigan University — M,D
William James College — M,D,O
Wright State University — M,D
Xavier University — M,D

INDUSTRIAL DESIGN

Academy of Art University — M
ArtCenter College of Design — M
Auburn University — M
California College of the Arts — M
Carleton University — M
Florida State University — M
Georgia Institute of Technology — M
Iowa State University of Science
 and Technology — M
The New School — M
North Carolina State University — M
The Ohio State University — M
Philadelphia University — M
Pratt Institute — M
Purdue University — M,D
Rhode Island School of Design — M
Rochester Institute of Technology — M
Savannah College of Art and Design — M
University of Cincinnati — M
University of Detroit Mercy — M,D
University of Illinois at
 Urbana–Champaign — M
University of Notre Dame — M
The University of the Arts — M
University of Washington — M
Wayne State University — M

INDUSTRIAL HYGIENE

California State University,
 Northridge — M
Colorado State University — M,D
Eastern Kentucky University — M
Montana Tech of The University of
 Montana — M
Murray State University — M
New York Medical College — M,D,O
Old Dominion University — M
The University of Alabama at
 Birmingham — M,D
University of Central Missouri — M,D,O
University of Cincinnati — M,D
The University of Iowa — M,D
University of Michigan — M,D
University of Minnesota, Twin
 Cities Campus — M,D
University of Puerto Rico, Medical
 Sciences Campus — M
University of South Carolina — M,D
The University of Toledo — M,O
University of Wisconsin–
 Stout — M
West Virginia University — M

INFECTIOUS DISEASES

Cornell University — M,D
Georgetown University — M,D
The George Washington University — M,D,O
Johns Hopkins University — M,D
Loyola University Chicago — M,D
Montana State University — M,D
North Carolina State University — M,D
North Dakota State University — M
Rutgers University–Newark — D,O
Thomas Jefferson University — O
Tufts University — M,D
Uniformed Services University of
 the Health Sciences — D
Université Laval — O
The University of British Columbia — M,D
University of Calgary — M,D
University of California, Berkeley — M,D
University of Georgia — D
University of Guelph — M,D,O
University of Minnesota, Twin
 Cities Campus — M,D
University of Nebraska Medical
 Center — D
University of Pittsburgh — M,D
The University of Texas Health
 Science Center at Houston — M,D
Washington State University — M,D
Yale University — D

INFORMATION SCIENCE

Alcorn State University — M
American InterContinental
 University Atlanta — M
American InterContinental
 University Online — M
American University of Armenia — M
Arizona State University at the
 Tempe campus — M
Arkansas Tech University — M
Armstrong State University — M
Aspen University — M,O
Auburn University at Montgomery — M
Ball State University — M,O
Barry University — M
Bellevue University — M
Bentley University — M
Bradley University — M
Brigham Young University — M
Brooklyn College of the City
 University of New York — M,O
California State University,
 Fullerton — M
Capitol Technology University — M
Carleton University — M,D
Carnegie Mellon University — M,D
Case Western Reserve University — M,D
The Citadel, The Military College
 of South Carolina — M
Claremont Graduate University — M,D,O
Clark Atlanta University — M
Clarkson University — M
Clark University — M
Coleman University — M
The College of Saint Rose — M,O
Cornell University — D
Dakota State University — M,D,O
DePaul University — M,D
Drexel University — M,D,O
East Tennessee State University — M
Florida Institute of Technology — M
Florida International University — M,D
Gannon University — M
George Mason University — M,D,O
Georgia State University — M,D,O
Grand Valley State University — M
Harvard University — M,D,O
Hood College — M,O
Indiana University Bloomington — M,D,O
Indiana University–Purdue
 University Fort Wayne — M
Indiana University–Purdue
 University Indianapolis — M
Instituto Tecnologico de Santo
 Domingo — M,O
Instituto Tecnológico y de
 Estudios Superiores de Monterrey,
 Campus Cuernavaca — M,D
Instituto Tecnológico y de
 Estudios Superiores de Monterrey,
 Campus Estado de México — M,D
Instituto Tecnológico y de
 Estudios Superiores de Monterrey,
 Campus Irapuato — M,D
Instituto Tecnológico y de
 Estudios Superiores de Monterrey,
 Campus Monterrey — M,D

Instituto Tecnológico y de
 Estudios Superiores de Monterrey,
 Campus Sonora Norte — M
Iowa State University of Science
 and Technology — M
Kennesaw State University — M,O
Kent State University — M
Knowledge Systems Institute — M
Lawrence Technological University — M,O
Lehigh University — M
Loyola University Chicago — M
Marshall University — M
Maryville University of Saint
 Louis — M,O
Massachusetts Institute of
 Technology — M,D,O
Minnesota State University Mankato — M,O
Missouri University of Science and
 Technology — M
Monroe College — M
Naval Postgraduate School — M,D,O
New Jersey Institute of Technology — M,D,O
Northern Kentucky University — M,O
Northwestern University — M,D
Nova Southeastern University — M,D
Oklahoma State University — M
Old Dominion University — D
Pace University — M,D,O
Penn State Great Valley — M,O
Penn State University Park — M,D
Regis University — M,O
Rensselaer at Hartford — M
Rensselaer Polytechnic Institute — M
Robert Morris University — M
Rochester Institute of Technology — M,D
Roosevelt University — M
Rutgers University–New
 Brunswick — M
Sacred Heart University — M
St. John's University (NY)
St. Mary's University
 (United States)
Sam Houston State University — M,D
Shippensburg University of
 Pennsylvania — M,O
Simmons College — M,D,O
Southern Arkansas University–
 Magnolia — M
Southern Methodist University — M
State University of New York
 Polytechnic Institute — M
Stevens Institute of Technology — M,O
Strayer University — M
Syracuse University — M,D
Texas Woman's University — M
Thomas Edison State University — M,O
Towson University — M,D,O
Trevecca Nazarene University — M,O
Université de Sherbrooke — M,D
University at Albany, State
 University of New York — D
The University of Alabama at
 Birmingham — M,D
University of Arkansas at Little
 Rock — M,D,O
University of California, Irvine — M,D
University of California, Merced — M,D
University of Central Missouri — M
University of Colorado Boulder — D
University of Colorado Denver — M,D
University of Delaware — M,D
University of Denver — M,O
University of Florida — M,D
University of Hawaii at Manoa — M,D
University of Houston — M,D
University of Houston–Clear
 Lake — M
University of Illinois at
 Urbana–Champaign — M,D,O
The University of Iowa — M,D,O
University of Kentucky — M
University of Maine — M,D,O
University of Maryland, Baltimore
 County — M,D
University of Maryland University
 College — M
University of Massachusetts
 Dartmouth — D
University of Michigan — M,D
University of Michigan–
 Dearborn — M,D
University of Michigan–Flint — M
University of Nebraska at Omaha — M,D,O
University of Nebraska–
 Lincoln — M,D
University of North Alabama — M
The University of North Carolina
 at Charlotte — M,O
University of North Texas — M,D,O
University of Oregon — M,D
University of Ottawa — M,O
University of Pennsylvania — M,D
University of Pittsburgh — M,D,O
University of Puerto Rico,
 Mayagüez Campus — M,D
University of Puerto Rico,
 Río Piedras Campus — M,O
University of St. Thomas (MN) — M,O
University of South Africa — M,O
University of South Carolina
 Upstate — M
University of Southern Mississippi — M,O
University of South Florida — M
The University of Tennessee — M
The University of Texas at El Paso — M,D
The University of Texas at San
 Antonio — M,D,O
University of the Sacred Heart — O
University of Washington — M
University of Waterloo — M,D
University of Wisconsin–Parkside — M
University of Wisconsin–Stout — M
Western Governors University — M
Youngstown State University — M

INFORMATION STUDIES

The Catholic University of America	M,O
Central Connecticut State University	M
Columbia University	M
Cornell University	D
Dalhousie University	M
Dominican University	M,D,O
Emporia State University	M
Florida State University	M,D,O
Lock Haven University of Pennsylvania	M
Louisiana State University and Agricultural & Mechanical College	M
Loyola University Chicago	M,O
Mansfield University of Pennsylvania	M
McGill University	M,D,O
Metropolitan State University	M,D,O
Missouri Western State University	M
Neumann University	M
North Carolina Central University	M
Pratt Institute	M,O
Queens College of the City University of New York	M,O
Queen's University at Kingston	M,D
Rutgers University–New Brunswick	M,D
St. Catherine University	M
St. John's University (NY)	M,O
Southern Connecticut State University	M,O
Syracuse University	M
Universidad del Turabo	M
Université de Montréal	M,D
University at Albany, State University of New York	M,O
University at Buffalo, the State University of New York	M,D
The University of Alabama	M
University of Alberta	M
The University of Arizona	M,D
The University of British Columbia	M,D
University of California, Berkeley	M,D
University of California, Los Angeles	M,D,O
University of Hawaii at Manoa	M,O
University of Illinois at Urbana–Champaign	M,D,O
The University of Iowa	M,D
University of Maryland, College Park	M,D
University of Michigan	M,D
University of Missouri	M,D,O
The University of North Carolina at Chapel Hill	M,D,O
The University of North Carolina at Greensboro	M
University of Oklahoma	M
University of Pittsburgh	M,D
University of Puerto Rico, Río Piedras Campus	M,O
University of Rhode Island	M
University of South Carolina	M,D,O
University of South Florida	M,O
The University of Texas at Austin	M,D
University of Toronto	M,D
The University of Western Ontario	M,D
University of Wisconsin–Madison	M,D
University of Wisconsin–Milwaukee	M,D,O
Valdosta State University	M
Wayne State University	M,O

INORGANIC CHEMISTRY

Auburn University	M,D
Binghamton University, State University of New York	M,D
Boston College	M,D
Brandeis University	M,D
Cornell University	D
Eastern New Mexico University	M
Florida State University	M,D
Georgetown University	D
The George Washington University	M,D
Harvard University	D
Howard University	M,D
Illinois Institute of Technology	M,D
Indiana University Bloomington	M,D
Iowa State University of Science and Technology	M,D
Marquette University	M,D
Massachusetts Institute of Technology	D
McMaster University	M,D
Old Dominion University	M,D
Oregon State University	M,D
Purdue University	M,D
Rice University	M,D
Rutgers University–Newark	M,D
Rutgers University–New Brunswick	M,D
Seton Hall University	M,D
Southern University and Agricultural and Mechanical College	M
University of Calgary	M,D
University of Cincinnati	M,D
University of Louisville	M,D
The University of Manchester	M,D
University of Maryland, College Park	M,D
University of Massachusetts Lowell	M,D
University of Memphis	M,D
University of Miami	M,D
University of Michigan	D
University of Missouri–Kansas City	M,D
University of Montana	M,D
University of Nebraska–Lincoln	M,D
University of Notre Dame	M,D
University of Oklahoma	M,D
University of Regina	M,D

INSURANCE

Florida State University	M,D
Georgia State University	M,D,O
Olivet College	M
Pontificia Universidad Catolica Madre y Maestra	M
St. John's University (NY)	M
Temple University	D
University of Colorado Denver	M
University of Florida	M,D,O
University of Pennsylvania	M,D
University of Wisconsin–Madison	M,D
Western Michigan University Thomas M. Cooley Law School	M,D

INTELLECTUAL PROPERTY LAW

Case Western Reserve University	M,D
DePaul University	M,D
Fordham University	M,D
Golden Gate University	M,D
Indiana University–Purdue University Indianapolis	M,D,O
Michigan State University College of Law	M,D
Montclair State University	M,O
Santa Clara University	M,D
Suffolk University	M,D
University of Baltimore	M,D
University of Houston	M,D
University of New Hampshire	M,D,O
University of Pittsburgh	M
University of San Francisco	M
University of Washington	M,D
Western Michigan University Thomas M. Cooley Law School	M,D
Yeshiva University	M,D

INTERDISCIPLINARY STUDIES

Alaska Pacific University	M
Amberton University	M
Antioch University Midwest	M
Antioch University New England	M
Arizona State University at the Tempe campus	M
Athabasca University	M,O
Baylor University	D
Boise State University	M
Bowling Green State University	M,D
Buffalo State College, State University of New York	M
California College of the Arts	M
California Institute of Integral Studies	M,D
California State University, Bakersfield	M
California State University, East Bay	M
California State University, San Bernardino	M
California State University, Stanislaus	M
Cambridge College	M,D,O
Campbell University	M
Central Washington University	M
The Citadel, The Military College of South Carolina	M,O
Clarkson University	M,D
Concordia University (Canada)	M,D
Dalhousie University	D
Dallas Baptist University	M
DePaul University	M
Eastern Washington University	M
Emory University	D
Fitchburg State University	O
Florida Gulf Coast University	M
Florida Institute of Technology	M
Fresno Pacific University	M
Frostburg State University	M
George Mason University	M
Georgetown University	M,D
Goddard College	M
The Graduate Center, City University of New York	M,D
Harrison Middleton University	M,D
Hiram College	M
Hollins University	M
Idaho State University	M
Indiana University Southeast	M,O
Iowa State University of Science and Technology	M
Kansas State University	M,O
Lehigh University	M,D
Lesley University	M,D,O
Long Island University– LIU Post	M,D,O
Marquette University	M
Marylhurst University	M
Marywood University	D
Massachusetts College of Art and Design	M,O
Michigan Technological University	M,D,O
Mills College	M,O
Minnesota State University Mankato	M
Montana State University Billings	M
Montana Tech of The University of Montana	M
New Mexico State University	M,D
New York Institute of Technology	M
New York University	M

Niagara University	M
Northeastern University	M,D,O
Nova Southeastern University	M,D,O
The Ohio State University	M,D
Oregon State University	M
Regent University	M,D,O
Rochester Institute of Technology	M
Rosalind Franklin University of Medicine and Science	D
Rutgers University– New Brunswick	D
San Diego State University	M
Sonoma State University	M
Southern Illinois University Edwardsville	M
Southern Oregon University	M
State University of New York at Fredonia	M
Stephen F. Austin State University	M
Teachers College, Columbia University	M,D
Texas A&M University– Texarkana	M
Texas State University	M
Texas Tech University	M,D
Trinity Western University	M
Tufts University	D
Tulane University	D
Union Institute & University	M,D
University at Buffalo, the State University of New York	M
The University of Alabama	D
The University of Alabama at Birmingham	D
University of Alaska Anchorage	M
University of Alaska Fairbanks	M,D
The University of Arizona	M,D
University of Arkansas	M,D
University of Arkansas at Little Rock	M
University of California, Santa Barbara	D
University of California, Santa Cruz	M,D
University of Central Florida	M,O
University of Central Oklahoma	M
University of Cincinnati	D
University of Colorado Colorado Springs	M
University of Florida	M,D
University of Houston–Victoria	M
University of Idaho	M
University of Illinois at Chicago	D
University of Illinois at Springfield	M
University of Illinois at Urbana–Champaign	D
The University of Kansas	D
University of Louisville	M,D
University of Maine	M,D
University of Manitoba	M,D
University of Massachusetts Medical School	M,D
University of Memphis	M,D,O
University of Minnesota, Twin Cities Campus	D
University of Missouri– Kansas City	D
University of Montana	M,D
University of New Brunswick Fredericton	M,D
University of North Alabama	M
The University of North Carolina at Charlotte	M,D,O
University of Northern British Columbia	M,D,O
University of North Texas	M,D,O
University of Oklahoma	M,D
University of Oregon	M
University of Ottawa	D,O
University of Pittsburgh	D
University of Regina	M
University of South Alabama	M,D
The University of South Dakota	M
University of South Florida	M,D
The University of Tennessee at Martin	M
The University of Texas at Dallas	M
The University of Texas at El Paso	M
The University of Texas at San Antonio	M,D
The University of Texas at Tyler	M
The University of Texas Health Science Center at San Antonio	D
The University of Texas Rio Grande Valley	M
University of Vermont	M
University of Virginia	M,D
University of Washington, Tacoma	M
The University of Western Ontario	M,D
Virginia Commonwealth University	M
Virginia Polytechnic Institute and State University	M,D
Virginia State University	M
Walden University	M,D,O
Washington State University	D
Wayland Baptist University	M
Western Kentucky University	M,O
Western New Mexico University	M
West Texas A&M University	M
Worcester Polytechnic Institute	M,D,O
York University	M

INTERIOR DESIGN

Academy of Art University	M
Ball State University	M
Boston Architectural College	M
Brenau University	M
California State Polytechnic University, Pomona	M
Chatham University	M

Colorado State University	M
Cornell University	M
Drexel University	M
Eastern Michigan University	M
Endicott College	M
Florida International University	M,O
Florida State University	M
The George Washington University	M
Georgia State University	M
Interior Designers Institute	M
Iowa State University of Science and Technology	M
Lawrence Technological University	M,O
Marymount University	M
Marywood University	M
Miami University	M
Michigan State University	M,D
Moore College of Art & Design	M
The New School	M
New York School of Interior Design	M
The Ohio State University	M
Paris College of Art	M
Philadelphia University	M
Pontificia Universidad Catolica Madre y Maestra	M
Pratt Institute	M
Purdue University	M
Queens University of Charlotte	M
Rhode Island School of Design	M
San Diego State University	M
Savannah College of Art and Design	M
School of the Art Institute of Chicago	M
Suffolk University	M
Texas Tech University	M,D
University of California, Berkeley	O
University of Cincinnati	M
University of Florida	M,D
University of Georgia	M,D
University of Kentucky	M
University of Manitoba	M
University of Massachusetts Amherst	M
University of Minnesota, Twin Cities Campus	M,D,O
University of Nebraska–Lincoln	M,D
The University of North Carolina at Greensboro	M,O
University of North Texas	M,D,O
University of Oklahoma	M,D,O
University of Oregon	M
The University of Texas at Austin	M
Utah State University	M
Virginia Commonwealth University	M,D
Washington State University	M
Wayne State University	M

INTERNATIONAL AFFAIRS

American Graduate School in Paris	M,D
American Public University System	M
American University	M,D,O
American University of Armenia	M
American University of Beirut	M
The American University of Paris	M
Anabaptist Mennonite Biblical Seminary	M,O
Arcadia University	M
Azusa Pacific University	M
Baruch College of the City University of New York	M
Baylor University	M,D
Boston University	M
Brandeis University	M
Brigham Young University	M
Brock University	M
Brooklyn College of the City University of New York	M
California State University, Stanislaus	M
Carleton University	M,D
The Catholic University of America	M,D
Central Connecticut State University	M
Central European University	M,D
Central Michigan University	M,O
Chapman University	M
City College of the City University of New York	M
Claremont Graduate University	M,D
Cleveland State University	M
Colorado School of Mines	O
Columbia University	M,D
Concordia University Irvine	M
Cornell University	D
Creighton University	M
Dallas Baptist University	M
DePaul University	M
East Carolina University	M
Embry-Riddle Aeronautical University–Worldwide	M
Fairleigh Dickinson University, Metropolitan Campus	M
Florida International University	M,D
Florida State University	M
Fordham University	M,O
George Mason University	M
Georgetown University	M,D
The George Washington University	M,D
Georgia Institute of Technology	M
Harvard University	D
Indiana University South Bend	M,O
Instituto Tecnologico de Santo Domingo	M,O
Instituto Tecnológico y de Estudios Superiores de Monterrey, Campus Ciudad Obregón	M
International University in Geneva	M,D
Johns Hopkins University	M,D,O
Kennesaw State University	M
Lebanese American University	M
Lesley University	M,D,O

M—masters degree; D—doctorate; O—other advanced degree; *—Close-Up and/or Display

Liberty University	M,D,O
London Metropolitan University	M,D
Marquette University	M,D
McMaster University	M,D
Middlebury Institute of International Studies at Monterey	M
Middle Tennessee State University	M
Missouri State University	M
Morgan State University	M
New England College	M
The New School	M
New York University	M,D,O
North Carolina State University	M
Northeastern University	M,D
Northwestern University	M,D,O
Norwich University	M
Ohio University	M
Oklahoma State University	M,D,O
Old Dominion University	M,D
Penn State University Park	M
Pepperdine University	M,D
Pepperdine University	M,D
Pontificia Universidad Catolica Madre y Maestra	M
Princeton University	M,D
Queen's University at Kingston	M,D
Regent's University London	M
Regent University	M
Richmond, The American International University in London	M
Rutgers University–Camden	M
Rutgers University–Newark	M,D
Rutgers University–New Brunswick	M,D
St. John's University (NY)	M
St. Mary's University (United States)	M,O
Salve Regina University	M
San Francisco State University	M
Schiller International University	M
Seton Hall University	M,O
Simon Fraser University	M
SIT Graduate Institute	M
Syracuse University	M
Teachers College, Columbia University	M,D,O
Texas A&M University	M,O
Texas State University	M
Troy University	M
Tufts University	M,D
United States International University–Africa	M
Universidad de las Americas, A.C.	M
Universidad Nacional Pedro Henriquez Urena	M
Université de Montréal	M,D
Université Laval	M,D
University of Bridgeport	M
The University of British Columbia	M
University of California, Berkeley	M
University of California, San Diego	M,D
University of California, Santa Barbara	M
University of California, Santa Cruz	D
University of Central Oklahoma	M
University of Chicago	M
University of Colorado Denver	M
University of Connecticut	M
University of Delaware	M,D
University of Denver	M,D,O
University of Florida	M
University of Georgia	M,D
University of Hawaii at Manoa	O
University of Indianapolis	M
The University of Kansas	M
University of Kentucky	M
University of Maine	M
The University of Manchester	D
University of Massachusetts Boston	M
University of Miami	M,D
University of Michigan–Flint	M
The University of North Carolina at Chapel Hill	M
University of Northern British Columbia	M,D,O
University of North Georgia	M
University of North Texas	M,D,O
University of Notre Dame	M
University of Oklahoma	M
University of Oregon	M
University of Pennsylvania	M
University of Pittsburgh	M,D,O
University of Rhode Island	M
University of Rochester	M,D
University of San Diego	M
University of San Francisco	M
University of South Carolina	M,D
University of Southern California	M,D
University of South Florida	M,D,O
University of the Pacific	M
University of Toronto	M
University of Utah	M,D
University of Virginia	M,D
University of Washington	D
University of Waterloo	M,D
University of Wyoming	M
Virginia International University	M
Virginia Polytechnic Institute and State University	M,D,O
Walden University	M,D,O
Webster University	M
Western Michigan University	M,D
West Virginia University	M,D
Wilfrid Laurier University	M,D
Yale University	M
York University	M

INTERNATIONAL AND COMPARATIVE EDUCATION

American University	M
The American University in Cairo	M

Andrews University	M
Avila University	M,O
Boston College	M
Bowling Green State University	M
California Baptist University	M
California State University, Dominguez Hills	M
The College of New Jersey	M,O
Drexel University	M,D
Florida International University	M,D,O
Florida State University	M,D
Gallaudet University	M,D,O
George Mason University	M
The George Washington University	M,D,O
Harvard University	M,D
Indiana University Bloomington	M,D,O
Lehigh University	M,D,O
Louisiana State University and Agricultural & Mechanical College	M,D
Middlebury Institute of International Studies at Monterey	M
Morehead State University	M,O
New York University	M,D,O
SIT Graduate Institute	M
Stanford University	M,D
Teachers College, Columbia University	M,D
University at Albany, State University of New York	M,D,O
University of Bridgeport	M,D,O
University of Massachusetts Amherst	M,D,O
University of Minnesota, Twin Cities Campus	M,D
University of Pennsylvania	M
University of Pittsburgh	M,D
University of San Francisco	M,D
University of South Africa	M,D
University of Wisconsin–Madison	M,D,O
Vanderbilt University	M,D
Walden University	M,D,O
Wilkes University	M,D

INTERNATIONAL BUSINESS

American Business & Technology University	M
American InterContinental University Atlanta	M
American InterContinental University Online	M
The American University in Dubai	M
The American University of Paris	M
Anaheim University	M,D,O
Argosy University, Atlanta	M,D
Argosy University, Chicago	M,D
Argosy University, Dallas	M,D,O
Argosy University, Denver	M,D
Argosy University, Hawai'i	M,D,O
Argosy University, Inland Empire	M,D
Argosy University, Los Angeles	M,D
Argosy University, Nashville	M,D
Argosy University, Northern Virginia	M,D,O
Argosy University, Orange County	M,D,O
Argosy University, Phoenix	M,D
Argosy University, Salt Lake City	M,D
Argosy University, San Diego	M,D
Argosy University, San Francisco Bay Area	M,D
Argosy University, Sarasota	M,D,O
Argosy University, Schaumburg	M,D,O
Argosy University, Seattle	M,D
Argosy University, Tampa	M,D
Argosy University, Twin Cities	M,D
Arizona State University at the Tempe campus	M,D
Ashworth College	M
Assumption College	M,O
Avila University	M
Azusa Pacific University	M
Baldwin Wallace University	M
Barry University	O
Baruch College of the City University of New York	M,D
Benedictine University	M
Boston University	M
Brandeis University	M,D
Brandman University	M
Bristol University	M
Brooklyn College of the City University of New York	M
Bryant University	M,O
Butler University	M
California Intercontinental University	M,D
California Lutheran University	M,O
California State University, East Bay	M
California State University, Fullerton	M
California State University, Los Angeles	M
California State University, San Bernardino	M
California University of Management and Sciences	M
Canisius College	M
Central European University	M,D
Central Michigan University	M,O
Christian Brothers University	M,O
City University of Seattle	M,O
Clarkson University	M,O
Clayton State University	M
Colorado State University–Global Campus	M
Columbia University	M
Concordia University Wisconsin	M
Copenhagen Business School	M,D
Daemen College	M
Dallas Baptist University	M
Delaware Valley University	M
Dominican University of California	M
Duke University	M,O

D'Youville College	M
Eastern Michigan University	M,O
Embry-Riddle Aeronautical University–Worldwide	M
Emerson College	M
Emory University	M
ESSEC Business School	M,D
Everest University	M
Fairfield University	M,O
Fairleigh Dickinson University, College at Florham	M,O
Fairleigh Dickinson University, Metropolitan Campus	M
Florida International University	M,D
Florida State University	M
Franklin University Switzerland	M
George Mason University	M
Georgetown University	M,D
The George Washington University	M,D
Georgia Institute of Technology	M
Georgia State University	M
Golden Gate University	M,D,O
Goldey-Beacom College	M
Hallmark University	M
Harding University	M
Hawai'i Pacific University	M
HEC Montreal	M
Hofstra University	M,O
Hope International University	M
Houston Baptist University	M
Howard University	M
Hult International Business School (United States)	M
IGlobal University	M
Indiana Tech	D
Instituto Tecnologico de Santo Domingo	M,O
Instituto Tecnológico y de Estudios Superiores de Monterrey, Campus Central de Veracruz	M
Instituto Tecnológico y de Estudios Superiores de Monterrey, Campus Chihuahua	M,O
Instituto Tecnológico y de Estudios Superiores de Monterrey, Campus Ciudad de México	M,D
Instituto Tecnológico y de Estudios Superiores de Monterrey, Campus Cuernavaca	M
Instituto Tecnológico y de Estudios Superiores de Monterrey, Campus Irapuato	M,D
Instituto Tecnológico y de Estudios Superiores de Monterrey, Campus Monterrey	M
Inter American University of Puerto Rico, Metropolitan Campus	M,D
Inter American University of Puerto Rico, San Germán Campus	M,D
International University in Geneva	M,D
The International University of Monaco	M
Iona College	M,O
John Brown University	M
Kaplan University, Davenport Campus	M
Kean University	M
Keiser University	M,D
Lake Forest Graduate School of Management	M
La Salle University	M,O
Lenoir-Rhyne University	M
Lewis University	M
Liberty University	M,D,O
Lincoln University (CA)	M,D
Lindenwood University	M
Long Island University–LIU Post	M
Loyola University Chicago	M
Lynn University	M
Madonna University	M
Maine Maritime Academy	M
Manhattanville College	M
Marconi International University	M,D
Marquette University	M,O
McGill University	M,D,O
McKendree University	M
Middlebury Institute of International Studies at Monterey	M
Milwaukee School of Engineering	M
New Jersey Institute of Technology	M,D,O
Newman University	M
New Mexico Highlands University	M
New York University	M,D
Niagara University	M
Northeastern University	M
Northern Arizona University	M
Northwestern University	M,D
Northwest University	M
Norwich University	M
Nova Southeastern University	M
Oakland University	M,O
Oklahoma Christian University	M
Old Dominion University	M
Oral Roberts University	M
Pace University	M,O
Pacific States University	M,D
Park University	M,O
Pepperdine University	M
Pittsburg State University	M
Point Park University	M
Polytechnic University of Puerto Rico	M
Polytechnic University of Puerto Rico, Miami Campus	M
Polytechnic University of Puerto Rico, Orlando Campus	M
Pontifical Catholic University of Puerto Rico	M
Pontificia Universidad Catolica Madre y Maestra	M
Portland State University	M
Providence College	M
Purdue University	M

Regent's University London	M
Rochester Institute of Technology	M
Rockhurst University	M,O
Rollins College	M,D
Rutgers University–Newark	D
St. John's University (NY)	M
Saint Joseph's University	M,O
Saint Louis University	M,D
Saint Mary's University of Minnesota	M
Saint Peter's University	M
St. Thomas University	M,O
Salem International University	M
San Francisco State University	M
Schiller International University (United States)	M
Schiller International University (Germany)	M
Schiller International University (Spain)	M
Seton Hall University	M,O
SIT Graduate Institute	M
Sonoma State University	M
Southern New Hampshire University	M,O
Southern Oregon University	M,O
State University of New York Empire State College	M
Stevens Institute of Technology	M
Stratford University (VA)	M
Suffolk University	M
Taylor University	M
Temple University	M,D
Tennessee Technological University	M
Texas A&M International University	M,D
Texas A&M University–Corpus Christi	M
Texas A&M University–San Antonio	M
Tiffin University	M
Trident University International	M,D
Trinity Western University	M
Tufts University	M,D
Tulane University	M,D
United States International University–Africa	M
Universidad Autonoma de Guadalajara	M,D
Universidad Metropolitana	M
Université de Sherbrooke	M
Université du Québec, Ecole nationale d'administration publique	M,O
Université Laval	M
University at Buffalo, the State University of New York	M,D
The University of Akron	M
University of Alberta	M
University of Baltimore	M
University of Bridgeport	M
University of California, Berkeley	O
University of California, San Diego	M
University of Chicago	M,O
University of Colorado Denver	M
University of Dallas	M
University of Florida	M,D
University of Hawaii at Manoa	M,D
University of Houston–Victoria	M
University of Kentucky	M
University of La Verne	M
University of Lethbridge	M,D
University of Louisville	M
The University of Manchester	M
University of Mary Hardin-Baylor	M
University of Massachusetts Boston	M
University of Massachusetts Dartmouth	M,O
University of Michigan–Flint	M,O
University of Missouri–St. Louis	M,D,O
University of New Brunswick Saint John	M
University of New Haven	M,O
University of New Mexico	M
University of North Alabama	M
The University of North Carolina Wilmington	M
University of North Florida	M
University of Oklahoma	M,D
University of Pennsylvania	M
University of Phoenix–Atlanta Campus	M
University of Phoenix–Augusta Campus	M
University of Phoenix–Bay Area Campus	M,D
University of Phoenix–Central Valley Campus	M
University of Phoenix–Charlotte Campus	M
University of Phoenix–Colorado Campus	M
University of Phoenix–Colorado Springs Downtown Campus	M
University of Phoenix–Columbus Georgia Campus	M
University of Phoenix–Dallas Campus	M
University of Phoenix–Hawaii Campus	M
University of Phoenix–Houston Campus	M
University of Phoenix–Jersey City Campus	M
University of Phoenix–Las Vegas Campus	M
University of Phoenix–New Mexico Campus	M
University of Phoenix–North Florida Campus	M

University of Phoenix–
  Online Campus — M,O
University of Phoenix–
  Phoenix Campus — M,O
University of Phoenix–
  Sacramento Valley Campus — M
University of Phoenix–
  San Antonio Campus — M
University of Phoenix–
  San Diego Campus — M
University of Phoenix–
  Southern Arizona Campus — M
University of Phoenix–
  Southern California Campus — M
University of Phoenix–South
  Florida Campus — M
University of Phoenix–Utah
  Campus — M
University of Pittsburgh — O
University of Puerto Rico,
  Río Piedras Campus — M,D
University of Regina — M,O
University of St. Thomas (TX) — M
University of San Diego — M
University of San Francisco — M
University of Saskatchewan — M,D
The University of Scranton — M
University of South Carolina — M
The University of Tampa — M
The University of Texas at Dallas — M,D
The University of Texas at El Paso — M,D,O
University of the West — M
The University of Toledo — M
University of Virginia — M,O
University of Washington — M,D,O
The University of Western Ontario — M,D
University of Wisconsin–Milwaukee — M,O
University of Wisconsin–Oshkosh — M
Vancouver Island University — M
Villanova University — M
Virginia International University — M,O
Viterbo University — M
Wagner College — M
Walden University — M,D,O
Walsh College of Accountancy and
  Business Administration — M
Warner University — M
Wayland Baptist University — M,D
Webber International University — M
Webster University — M
Wilkes University — M
Xavier University — M
York University — M,D

INTERNATIONAL DEVELOPMENT

American University — M,D,O
Andrews University — M
Athabasca University — M,O
Clark University — M
Colorado State University — M
Dalhousie University — M
Duke University — M
Eastern University — M
Fordham University — M,O
Georgetown University — M
The George Washington University — M,D
Harvard University — M
Hope International University — M
Indiana University Bloomington — M,D,O
Johns Hopkins University — M,D,O
Lehigh University — M,D,O
Marymount California University — M
McGill University — M,D,O
Middlebury Institute of
  International Studies at Monterey — M
New York University — M,O
Norwich University — M
Ohio University — M
Old Dominion University — M,D
Rutgers University–Camden — M
Saint Mary's University
  (Canada) — M,O
St. Mary's University
  (United States) — M,O
Saint Mary's University of
  Minnesota — M
Tufts University — M,D
Tulane University — M,D
University of California,
  San Diego — M
University of Denver — M,D,O
University of Florida — M,D,O
University of Guelph — M,D
University of Hawaii at Manoa — M,D,O
The University of Manchester — M,D
University of Massachusetts Boston — M,D
University of Minnesota, Twin
  Cities Campus — M
University of New Brunswick
  Fredericton — M
University of New Mexico — M,D
University of Ottawa — M
University of Pittsburgh — M
University of San Francisco — M
University of Southern Mississippi — M,D
Walden University — M,D,O

INTERNATIONAL ECONOMICS

American University — M,D,O
Baruch College of the City
  University of New York — M
Bryant University — M,O
Claremont Graduate University — M,D,O
Cleveland State University — M
Fordham University — M,O
Johns Hopkins University — M,D,O
The New School — M,D
Pace University — O
University of California,
  San Diego — M
University of New Mexico — M,D

University of Wisconsin–Milwaukee — M,D
Valparaiso University — M
Wayne State University — M,D
West Virginia University — M,D
Wichita State University — M
Wilfrid Laurier University — M
Yale University — M

INTERNATIONAL HEALTH

Arizona State University at the
  Tempe campus — M,D,O
A.T. Still University — M,D,O
Boston University — M,D
Brandeis University — M,D
Cedarville University — M,D
Central Michigan University — M,D,O
Clark University — M
Clemson University — M,D,O
Duke University — M
Emory University — M
George Mason University — M,O
Georgetown University — M,D
The George Washington University — M,D
Harvard University — M,D
Johns Hopkins University — M,D
Liberty University — M
Loma Linda University — M
Medical University of South
  Carolina — M
New York Medical College — M,D,O
New York University — M,D
Northwestern University — M
Oregon State University — M,D
Park University — M,O
San Diego State University — M,D
Seton Hall University — M,O
Simon Fraser University — M,D,O
Syracuse University — M
Trident University International — M,D,O
Tufts University — M,D
Tulane University — M,D
Uniformed Services University of
  the Health Sciences — M,D
University of Alberta — M,D
University of California,
  Riverside — M,D
University of California,
  San Diego — D
University of Colorado Denver — M
University of Denver — M,D,O
University of Florida — M,D
University of Massachusetts
  Dartmouth — M,D,O
University of Michigan — M,D
University of Minnesota, Twin
  Cities Campus — M,D
University of Missouri — M,O
University of Northern Colorado — M
University of North Texas Health
  Science Center at Fort Worth — M,D,O
University of Pennsylvania — M
University of Southern California — M,O
University of South Florida — M,D,O
The University of Toledo — M,O
University of Washington — M,D
Walden University — M,D,O
William James College — M,D,O
Yale University — M,D

INTERNATIONAL TRADE POLICY

Baruch College of the City
  University of New York — M
The George Washington University — M
Middlebury Institute of
  International Studies at Monterey — M
Valparaiso University — M

INTERNET AND INTERACTIVE MULTIMEDIA

Academy of Art University — M
Alfred University — M
Ball State University — M
Boston University — M,O
Brandeis University — M
Brooklyn College of the City
  University of New York — M
California State University, East
  Bay — M
Champlain College — M
Concordia University (Canada) — M,D,O
DePaul University — M,D
Elon University — M
Excelsior College — M,O
Fairfield University — M,O
Full Sail University — M
Georgetown University — M
Georgia Institute of Technology — M,D
Indiana University–Purdue
  University Indianapolis — M,D,O
Ithaca College — M
Kutztown University of
  Pennsylvania — M
Lindenwood University–Belleville — M
Lindsey Wilson College — M
London Metropolitan University — M,D
Long Island University–
  LIU Post — M
Louisiana State University and
  Agricultural & Mechanical College — M
Lynn University — M,O
Marlboro College — M,O
Mississippi State University — M,D,O
Mount Mary University — M
National University — M
New Mexico Highlands University — M
New York University — M,O
Northeastern University — M
Northwestern University — M
The Ohio State University — M
Pace University — M,D,O
Philadelphia University — M
Pratt Institute — M

Quinnipiac University — M
Robert Morris University — M,D
Rochester Institute of Technology — O
Rocky Mountain College of
  Art + Design — M
Sam Houston State University — M
San Diego State University — M
Savannah College of Art and Design — M
School of Visual Arts (NY) — M
Southern New Hampshire University — M,O
State University of New York at
  Oswego — M
Stevens Institute of Technology — M,D,O
Tennessee Technological University — M
Touro College — M
Towson University — M,D,O
Universidad Autonoma de
  Guadalajara — M,D
University of Advancing Technology — M
University of Colorado Boulder — D
University of Massachusetts
  Dartmouth — M
University of Miami — M
University of Montana — M
University of North Texas — M,D,O
University of Pennsylvania — M,O
University of Southern California — M,D,O
University of South Florida — M,O
The University of Texas at Dallas — M,D
University of the Sacred Heart — M,O
University of Utah — M
Virginia Polytechnic Institute and
  State University — M,D,O
Webster University — M
Wilmington University — M
Worcester Polytechnic Institute — M

INTERNET ENGINEERING

Hofstra University — M
New Jersey Institute of Technology — M,D
Wilmington University — M

INVESTMENT MANAGEMENT

Alaska Pacific University — M,O
DePaul University — M
Fordham University — M
The George Washington University — M,D
Hofstra University — M,O
Johns Hopkins University — M,O
Lincoln University (CA) — M,D
Lynn University — M
Manhattanville College — M
Marywood University — M
New York University — M,O
Pace University — M,O
Regent University — M,D,O
Sacred Heart University — M,D
St. John's University (NY) — M
Saint Mary's College of
  California — M
Southern New Hampshire University — M,O
University of Colorado Denver — M
University of Houston–
  Downtown — M
University of Notre Dame — M
The University of Texas at Dallas — M
The University of Tulsa — M
University of Wisconsin–
  Madison — D
University of Wisconsin–
  Milwaukee — M,O

ITALIAN

Binghamton University, State
  University of New York — M
Boston College — M
Brown University — D
Central Connecticut State
  University — M,O
Columbia University — M,D
Cornell University — D
DePaul University — M
Drew University — M,D,O
Duke University — D
Florida State University — M
The Graduate Center, City
  University of New York — M,D
Harvard University — M,D
Hunter College of the City
  University of New York — M
Indiana University Bloomington — M,D
Johns Hopkins University — D
McGill University — M,D
Middlebury College — M,D
New York University — M,D,O
Northwestern University — D,O
The Ohio State University — M,D
Queens College of the City
  University of New York — M
Rutgers University–New
  Brunswick — M,D
San Francisco State University — M
Stanford University — M,D
Stony Brook University, State
  University of New York — M
University of Alberta — M,D
University of California, Berkeley — D
University of California, Los
  Angeles — M,D
University of Chicago — D
University of Georgia — M,D
University of Illinois at
  Urbana–Champaign — M,D
The University of Manchester — M,D
University of Massachusetts
  Amherst — M
University of Michigan — D
The University of North Carolina
  at Chapel Hill — M,D
University of Notre Dame — M
University of Oregon — M
University of Pennsylvania — M,D

University of Pittsburgh — M,D
University of South Africa — M,D
The University of Tennessee — D
The University of Texas at Austin — M,D
University of Toronto — M,D
University of Victoria — M
University of Washington — M,D
University of Wisconsin–Madison — M,D
Wayne State University — M,D
Yale University — D

JAPANESE

Arizona State University at the
  Tempe campus — M
Columbia University — M,D
DePaul University — M
Harvard University — D
Indiana University Bloomington — M,D
Kent State University — M,D
New York University — M,D,O
The Ohio State University — M,D
Portland State University — M
Purdue University — M,D
San Francisco State University — M
Stanford University — M,D
University of Alberta — M
University of California, Berkeley — D
University of California, Irvine — M,D
University of Colorado Boulder — M,D
University of Hawaii at Manoa — M,D,O
The University of Manchester — M,D
University of Massachusetts
  Amherst — M
University of Oregon — M,D
University of Pittsburgh — M
University of Washington — M,D
University of Wisconsin–Madison — M,D
Washington University in St. Louis — M,D

JEWISH STUDIES

American Jewish University — M
Biola University — M,D,O
Brandeis University — M,D
Brooklyn College of the City
  University of New York — M
Central Yeshiva Tomchei
  Tmimim-Lubavitch — M
Columbia University — M,D
Concordia University (Canada) — M
Cornell University — M,D
Criswell College — M
Dallas Theological Seminary — M,D,O
Graduate Theological Union — M,D,O
Gratz College — M,O
Harvard University — M,D
Hebrew College — M,O
Hebrew Union College–Jewish
  Institute of Religion (NY) — M
Indiana University Bloomington — M
The Jewish Theological Seminary — M
McGill University — M
New York University — M,D,O
Reconstructionist Rabbinical
  College — M,D,O
Rice University — D
Rutgers University–
  New Brunswick — M,O
Seton Hall University — M,O
Southern Evangelical Seminary — M,D,O
Spertus Institute for Jewish
  Learning and Leadership — M,D
Telshe Yeshiva–Chicago — O
Touro College — M
Towson University — M,O
University of California,
  San Diego — M,D
University of Connecticut — M
University of Florida — M,D
University of Maryland,
  College Park — M
University of Michigan — M,D,O
University of St. Michael's
  College — M,D,O
University of Wisconsin–Madison — M
Washington University in St. Louis — M
Yeshiva University — M,D

JOURNALISM

American University — M
The American University in Cairo — M,O
Arizona State University at the
  Tempe campus — M,D
Arkansas State University — M
Arkansas Tech University — M
Ball State University — M
Baylor University — M
Bob Jones University — M,D,O
Boston University — M
California State University,
  Northridge — M
Carleton University — M,D
Columbia College Chicago — M
Columbia University — M,D
Concordia University (Canada) — M,O
CUNY Graduate School of Journalism — M
DePaul University — M
Emerson College — M
Florida Agricultural and
  Mechanical University — M
Florida International University — M
Full Sail University — M
Georgetown University — M,D
Harvard University — M,O
Hofstra University — M
Iowa State University of Science
  and Technology — M
Kansas State University — M
Kent State University — M
Marquette University — M,O
Marshall University — M
Michigan State University — M
National University — M

*M—masters degree; D—doctorate; O—other advanced degree; *—Close-Up and/or Display*

New York University	M,D,O
Northeastern University	M
Northwestern University	M
Ohio University	M,D
Point Park University	M
Quinnipiac University	M
Regent University	M,D
Sacred Heart University	M
School of the Art Institute of Chicago	M
South Dakota State University	M
Stony Brook University, State University of New York	M,O
Syracuse University	M
Temple University	M
Université Laval	O
The University of Alabama	M
The University of Arizona	M
University of Arkansas	M
The University of British Columbia	M
University of California, Berkeley	M
University of Colorado Boulder	M,D
University of Florida	M
University of Georgia	M,D
University of Illinois at Springfield	M
University of Illinois at Urbana–Champaign	M
The University of Iowa	M,D
The University of Kansas	M,D
University of King's College	M
University of Maryland, College Park	M,D
University of Memphis	M,O
University of Miami	M,D
University of Mississippi	M
University of Missouri	M,D
University of Montana	M
University of Nebraska–Lincoln	M
University of Nevada, Las Vegas	M
University of Nevada, Reno	M
University of North Texas	M,D,O
University of Oklahoma	M,D
University of Oregon	M,D
University of Puerto Rico, Río Piedras Campus	M
University of Regina	M
University of South Carolina	M,D
University of Southern California	M
University of South Florida	M,O
University of South Florida, St. Petersburg	M
The University of Tennessee	M,D
The University of Texas at Austin	M,D
The University of Western Ontario	M
University of Wisconsin–Madison	M,D
Virginia Commonwealth University	M
Wayne State University	M
West Virginia University	M,O

KINESIOLOGY AND MOVEMENT STUDIES

Alabama Agricultural and Mechanical University	M
A.T. Still University	M,D,O
Ball State University	M,D,O
Barry University	M
Boise State University	M
Bowling Green State University	M
Brooklyn College of the City University of New York	M
California Polytechnic State University, San Luis Obispo	M
California State Polytechnic University, Pomona	M
California State University, Chico	M
California State University, Fresno	M
California State University, Long Beach	M
California State University, Los Angeles	M,O
California State University, Northridge	M
Canisius College	M
Columbia University	M,D
Dalhousie University	M
Dallas Baptist University	M
East Carolina University	M,D,O
Eastern Illinois University	M
Eastern Michigan University	M
East Tennessee State University	M,D
East Texas Baptist University	M
Fresno Pacific University	M
Georgia College & State University	M
Georgia Southern University	M
Georgia State University	D
Hardin-Simmons University	M
Humboldt State University	M
Indiana University Bloomington	M,D
Indiana University–Purdue University Indianapolis	M,O
Inter American University of Puerto Rico, San Germán Campus	M
Iowa State University of Science and Technology	M,D
Jacksonville University	M
James Madison University	M
Kansas State University	M
Lakehead University	M
Lamar University	M
Louisiana State University and Agricultural & Mechanical College	M
McGill University	M,D,O
McMaster University	M,D
Memorial University of Newfoundland	M
Michigan State University	M,D
Michigan Technological University	M
Mississippi College	M
Mississippi State University	M,D
Missouri State University	M
New Mexico State University	D

New York University	M,D,O
Northeastern State University	M
Northwestern University	D
The Ohio State University	M,D
Old Dominion University	M,D
Oregon State University	M
Penn State University Park	M,D,O
Point Loma Nazarene University	M
Prairie View A&M University	M
Purdue University	M,D
Saint Mary's College of California	M
Sam Houston State University	M
San Diego State University	M
San Francisco State University	M
San Jose State University	M,O
Sarah Lawrence College	M
Simon Fraser University	M,D
Sonoma State University	M
Southeastern Louisiana University	M
Southern Arkansas University–Magnolia	M
Southern Illinois University Carbondale	M
Southern Illinois University Edwardsville	M
Southwestern Oklahoma State University	M
Stephen F. Austin State University	M
Syracuse University	M,D,O
Tarleton State University	M
Teachers College, Columbia University	M,D
Temple University	M
Tennessee Technological University	M
Texas A&M University	M,D
Texas A&M University–Commerce	M,D,O
Texas A&M University–Corpus Christi	M,D
Texas A&M University–Kingsville	M
Texas A&M University–San Antonio	M
Texas Christian University	M
Texas Tech University	M
Texas Woman's University	M,D
Université de Montréal	M,D,O
Université de Sherbrooke	M,O
Université du Québec à Montréal	M
Université Laval	M,D
The University of Alabama	M,D
University of Arkansas	M,D
The University of British Columbia	M,D
University of Calgary	M,D
University of Central Arkansas	M
University of Central Missouri	M,D,O
University of Colorado Boulder	M,D
University of Delaware	M,D
University of Florida	M,D
University of Georgia	M,D
University of Hawaii at Manoa	M,D
University of Houston	M,D
University of Illinois at Chicago	M,D
University of Illinois at Urbana–Champaign	M,D
University of Kentucky	M,D
University of Lethbridge	M,D
University of Maine	M,D,O
University of Manitoba	M
University of Mary	M
University of Maryland, College Park	M,D
University of Massachusetts Amherst	M
University of Michigan	M,D
University of Minnesota, Twin Cities Campus	M,D
University of Mississippi	M,D
University of Nebraska at Omaha	M,D
University of Nevada, Las Vegas	M,D
University of New Hampshire	M,O
University of North Alabama	M
The University of North Carolina at Chapel Hill	M,D
The University of North Carolina at Charlotte	M
The University of North Carolina at Greensboro	M,D
University of North Dakota	M
University of Northern Iowa	M
University of North Texas	M,D,O
University of Ottawa	M
University of Puerto Rico, Mayagüez Campus	M
University of Regina	M,D
University of Saskatchewan	M,D,O
University of South Alabama	M
The University of South Dakota	M
University of Southern California	M,D
The University of Tennessee	M,D
The University of Texas at Arlington	M,D
The University of Texas at Austin	M,D
The University of Texas at El Paso	M
The University of Texas at San Antonio	M
The University of Texas at Tyler	M
The University of Texas of the Permian Basin	M
The University of Texas Rio Grande Valley	M
University of Toronto	M
The University of Tulsa	M
University of Utah	M,D
University of Victoria	M
University of Virginia	M,D
University of Waterloo	M,D
The University of Western Ontario	M,D
University of Windsor	M
University of Wisconsin–Madison	M,D
University of Wisconsin–Milwaukee	M,D
University of Wyoming	M

Washington University in St. Louis	D
Wayne State University	M,D,O
West Chester University of Pennsylvania	M,O
Western Illinois University	M
Wilfrid Laurier University	M
York University	M,D

LANDSCAPE ARCHITECTURE

Academy of Art University	M
Arizona State University at the Tempe campus	M,D
Auburn University	M
Ball State University	M
Bastyr University	M,O
Boston Architectural College	M
California State Polytechnic University, Pomona	M
Chatham University	M
City College of the City University of New York	M
Clemson University	M
Colorado State University	M,D
Columbia University	M
Cornell University	M
Florida Agricultural and Mechanical University	M
Florida International University	M
Harvard University	M,D
Illinois Institute of Technology	M,D
Iowa State University of Science and Technology	M
Kansas State University	M
Kent State University	M
Louisiana State University and Agricultural & Mechanical College	M
Mississippi State University	M
Morgan State University	M
North Carolina State University	M
The Ohio State University	M,D
Oklahoma State University	M,D
Penn State University Park	M,D
Polytechnic University of Puerto Rico	M
Pontificia Universidad Catolica Madre y Maestra	M
Rhode Island School of Design	M
State University of New York College of Environmental Science and Forestry	M
Temple University	M
Texas A&M University	M,D
Texas Tech University	M
The University of Arizona	M
The University of British Columbia	M
University of California, Berkeley	M,D,O
University of Colorado Denver	M
University of Florida	M,D
University of Georgia	M
University of Guelph	M
University of Idaho	M
University of Illinois at Urbana–Champaign	M,D
The University of Manchester	M,D
University of Manitoba	M
University of Maryland, College Park	M
University of Massachusetts Amherst	M
University of Michigan	M
University of Minnesota, Twin Cities Campus	M
University of New Mexico	M
University of Oklahoma	M
University of Oregon	M
University of Pennsylvania	M,O
The University of Tennessee	M
The University of Texas at Arlington	M
The University of Texas at Austin	M
University of Toronto	M
University of Virginia	M
University of Washington	M
University of Wisconsin–Madison	M
Utah State University	M
Virginia Polytechnic Institute and State University	M,D,O
Washington State University	M

LATIN AMERICAN STUDIES

American University	M,O
Boricua College	M
Brown University	M,D
California State University, Los Angeles	M
The Catholic University of America	M,D
Centro de Estudios Avanzados de Puerto Rico y el Caribe	M,D
College of Staten Island of the City University of New York	M
Columbia University	M,D
Cornell University	M,D
Duke University	M,D
Florida International University	M
Georgetown University	M
The George Washington University	M
Georgia State University	M,O
Indiana University Bloomington	M
La Salle University	M,O
Michigan State University	D
New York University	M,O
Northeastern Illinois University	M
The Ohio State University	M
Ohio University	M
San Diego State University	M
Simon Fraser University	M,O
Texas Christian University	M
Tulane University	M,D
University at Albany, State University of New York	M,D,O
University at Buffalo, the State University of New York	M,D,O
The University of Arizona	M
University of California, Los Angeles	M

University of California, San Diego	M
University of California, Santa Barbara	M
University of Chicago	M
University of Connecticut	M
University of Florida	M,O
University of Illinois at Chicago	M
University of Illinois at Urbana–Champaign	M
The University of Kansas	M,O
The University of Manchester	M,D
University of Massachusetts Dartmouth	M,D
University of Miami	M
University of New Mexico	M,D
The University of North Carolina at Chapel Hill	M,D,O
The University of North Carolina at Charlotte	M,D,O
University of Notre Dame	M
University of Pittsburgh	O
University of Southern California	D
University of South Florida	M,D,O
The University of Texas at Austin	M
The University of Texas at Dallas	M,D
University of Utah	M
University of Wisconsin–Madison	M,D
Vanderbilt University	M
West Virginia University	M
Yale University	D

LAW

Albany Law School	M,D
Alliant International University–San Francisco	D
The American University in Cairo	M,O
American University of Armenia	M
The American University of Paris	M
Appalachian School of Law	D
Arizona State University at the Tempe campus	M,D
Arizona Summit Law School	D
Atlanta's John Marshall Law School	M,D
Ave Maria School of Law	D
Barry University	D
Baylor University	D
Belmont University	D
Boston College	D
Boston University	M,D
Brigham Young University	M,D
Brooklyn Law School	M,D
California Western School of Law	M,D
Campbell University	D
Capital University	M,D
Case Western Reserve University	M,D
The Catholic University of America	M,D
Central European University	M,D
Champlain College	M
Chapman University	M,D
Charleston School of Law	M,D
City University of New York School of Law	D
Cleveland State University	M,D,O
The College of William and Mary	M,D
Columbia University	M,D
Concord Law School	D
Cornell University	M,D
Creighton University	M,D,O
Dalhousie University	M,D
DePaul University	M,D
Drake University	M,D
Duke University	M,D
Dunlap-Stone University	M
Duquesne University	M,D
Elon University	D
Emory University	M,D,O
Empire College	M,D
Faulkner University	D
Florida Agricultural and Mechanical University	D
Florida Coastal School of Law	D
Florida International University	M,D
Florida State University	M,D
Fordham University	M,D
Friends University	M
George Mason University	M,D
Georgetown University	M,D
The George Washington University	M,D
Georgia State University	D
Golden Gate University	M,D
Gonzaga University	D
Harvard University	M,D
Hofstra University	M,D
Howard University	M,D
Humphreys University	D
Illinois Institute of Technology	M,D
Indiana University Bloomington	M,D,O
Indiana University–Purdue University Indianapolis	M,D,O
Instituto Tecnológico y de Estudios Superiores de Monterrey, Campus Ciudad de México	O
Inter American University of Puerto Rico School of Law	D
John F. Kennedy University	D
The John Marshall Law School	M,D
The Judge Advocate General's School, U.S. Army	M
Kaplan University, Davenport Campus	M
Lewis & Clark College	M,D
Liberty University	D
Lincoln Memorial University	D
London Metropolitan University	M
Louisiana State University and Agricultural & Mechanical College	M,D
Loyola Marymount University	M,D
Loyola University Chicago	M,D
Loyola University New Orleans	D
Marquette University	M
Massachusetts School of Law at Andover	D

McGill University	M,D,O
Mercer University	D
Michigan State University College of Law	M,D
Mississippi College	D,O
Mitchell Hamline School of Law	M,D
Montclair State University	M,O
New York Law School	M,D
New York University	M,D,O
North Carolina Central University	D
Northeastern University	M,D
Northern Illinois University	D
Northern Kentucky University	D
Northwestern University	M,D
Nova Southeastern University	M,D
Ohio Northern University	M,D
The Ohio State University	M,D
Oklahoma City University	M,D
Pace University	M,D
Penn State University–Dickinson Law	M,D
Penn State University Park	M,D
Pepperdine University	D
Pontifical Catholic University of Puerto Rico	D
Pontificia Universidad Catolica Madre y Maestra	M
Queen's University at Kingston	M,D
Quinnipiac University	M,D
Regent University	M,D
Roger Williams University	M,D
Rutgers University–Camden	D
Rutgers University–Newark	D
St. John's University (NY)	D
Saint Joseph's University	M,O
Saint Louis University	M,D
St. Mary's University (United States)	M,D
St. Thomas University	M,D
Samford University	M,D
San Joaquin College of Law	D
The Santa Barbara and Ventura Colleges of Law–Santa Barbara	M,D
The Santa Barbara and Ventura Colleges of Law–Ventura	M,D
Santa Clara University	M,D
Savannah Law School	D
Seattle University	D
Seton Hall University	M,D
Southern Illinois University Carbondale	M,D
Southern Methodist University	M,D
Southern University and Agricultural and Mechanical College	D
South Texas College of Law Houston	D
Southwestern Law School	M,D
Stanford University	M,D
Stetson University	M,D
Suffolk University	M,D
Syracuse University	M,D
Taft University System	M,D
Temple University	M,D
Texas A&M University	M,D
Texas Southern University	D
Texas Tech University	M,D
Thomas Jefferson School of Law	D
Touro College	M,D
Trine University	M
Trinity International University	M,D
Tufts University	M,D
Tulane University	M,D
Universidad Autonoma de Guadalajara	M,D
Universidad Central del Este	D
Universidad Iberoamericana	M,D
Université de Montréal	M,D,O
Université de Sherbrooke	M,D,O
Université du Québec à Montréal	O
Université Laval	M,D,O
University at Albany, State University of New York	M
University at Buffalo, the State University of New York	M,D
The University of Akron	M,D
The University of Alabama	M,D
University of Alberta	M,D
The University of Arizona	M,D
University of Arkansas	M,D
University of Arkansas at Little Rock	D
University of Baltimore	M,D
The University of British Columbia	M,D
University of Calgary	M,D,O
University of California, Berkeley	M,D
University of California, Davis	M,D
University of California, Hastings College of the Law	M,D
University of California, Irvine	D
University of California, Los Angeles	M,D
University of California, San Diego	M
University of Chicago	M,D
University of Cincinnati	M,D
University of Colorado Boulder	D
University of Connecticut	D
University of Dayton	M,D
University of Denver	M,D,O
University of Detroit Mercy	D
University of Florida	M,D
University of Georgia	M,D
University of Hawaii at Manoa	M,D,O
University of Houston	M,D
University of Idaho	D
University of Illinois at Urbana–Champaign	M,D
The University of Iowa	M,D
The University of Kansas	D
University of Kentucky	D
University of La Verne	D

University of Louisville	D
University of Maine	D
The University of Manchester	M,D
University of Manitoba	M
University of Maryland, Baltimore	M,D
University of Maryland, College Park	M,D
University of Massachusetts Dartmouth	D
University of Memphis	D
University of Miami	M,D
University of Michigan	M,D
University of Minnesota, Twin Cities Campus	M,D
University of Mississippi	M,D
University of Missouri	M,D
University of Missouri–Kansas City	M,D
University of Montana	D
University of Nebraska–Lincoln	M,D
University of Nevada, Las Vegas	M,D
University of New Hampshire	M,D,O
University of New Mexico	D
University of North Alabama	M
The University of North Carolina at Chapel Hill	M,D
University of Notre Dame	M,D
University of Oklahoma	M,D
University of Oregon	M,D
University of Ottawa	M,D
University of Pennsylvania	M,D
University of Pittsburgh	M
University of Puerto Rico, Río Piedras Campus	M,D
University of Richmond	D
University of St. Thomas (MN)	M,D
University of San Diego	M,D,O
University of San Francisco	D
University of Saskatchewan	M,D
University of South Africa	M,D
University of South Carolina	D
The University of South Dakota	D
University of Southern California	M,D
The University of Tennessee	D
The University of Texas at Austin	M,D
The University of Texas at Dallas	M,D
University of the District of Columbia	M,D
University of the Pacific	M,D
The University of Toledo	M,D,O
University of Toronto	M,D
The University of Tulsa	M,D,O
University of Utah	M,D
University of Victoria	M,D
University of Virginia	M,D
University of Washington	M,D
The University of Western Ontario	M,D,O
University of Wisconsin–Madison	M,D
University of Wyoming	D
Valparaiso University	M,D
Vanderbilt University	M,D
Vermont Law School	D
Villanova University	D
Wake Forest University	M,D
Walden University	M,D,O
Washburn University	M,D
Washington and Lee University	D
Washington University in St. Louis	M,D
Wayne State University	M,D
Western Michigan University Thomas M. Cooley Law School	M,D
Western New England University	M,D
Western State College of Law at Argosy University	D
West Virginia University	D
Widener University	M,D
Willamette University	M,D
Yale University	M,D
Yeshiva University	M,D
York University	M,D

LEGAL AND JUSTICE STUDIES

American Public University System	M
Arizona State University at the Tempe campus	M,D,O
Auburn University at Montgomery	M
Binghamton University, State University of New York	M,D
Brock University	M
California University of Pennsylvania	M
Capital University	M
Carleton University	M,O
Case Western Reserve University	M,D
The Catholic University of America	M,D,O
Central European University	M,D
Columbia University	M,D
The George Washington University	M,D,O
Golden Gate University	M
Governors State University	M
Harrison Middleton University	M,D
Harvard University	D
Hodges University	M
Hofstra University	M,D
Illinois Institute of Technology	M,D
Indiana University South Bend	M,O
John Jay College of Criminal Justice of the City University of New York	M,D
Kaplan University, Davenport Campus	M,O
Loyola University Chicago	M,O
Marlboro College	M
Marygrove College	M
Michigan State University College of Law	M,D
Mississippi College	M,O
Montclair State University	O
National Paralegal College	M
National University	M
New York University	M,D,O

Northeastern University	M,D
Nova Southeastern University	M,D
Oregon State University	M,D
Pace University	M,D
Prairie View A&M University	M
Prescott College	M
Queen's University at Kingston	M,D
Regent University	M,D
Rutgers University–New Brunswick	M,D
St. John's University (NY)	M
Saint Leo University	M
St. Mary's University (United States)	M
San Francisco State University	M
San Jose State University	M,O
The Santa Barbara and Ventura Colleges of Law–Santa Barbara	M,D
The Santa Barbara and Ventura Colleges of Law–Ventura	M,D
Simon Fraser University	M,D
Southern Illinois University Carbondale	M
Southern New Hampshire University	M,O
Stanford University	M,D
Stetson University	M
Taft University System	M,D
Temple University	M,D
Texas State University	M,D
Texas Tech University	M,D
Touro College	M,D
Trident University International	M,D,O
Universidad Autonoma de Guadalajara	M,D
Université Laval	O
University of Baltimore	M,D
University of Calgary	M,O
University of California, Berkeley	M,D
University of California, San Diego	M
University of Charleston	M
University of Denver	M,D
University of Illinois at Springfield	M
University of Massachusetts Lowell	M
University of Montana	M
University of Nebraska–Lincoln	M
University of Nevada, Reno	M,D
University of New Hampshire	M,D,O
University of Pennsylvania	M,D
University of Pittsburgh	M
University of San Diego	M,D,O
University of South Florida	O
University of the District of Columbia	M,D
University of the Sacred Heart	M
University of Washington	M,D
University of Windsor	M
Vermont Law School	M
Washburn University	M,D
Weber State University	M
Webster University	M,O
Western Michigan University Thomas M. Cooley Law School	M,D
Wilfrid Laurier University	D

LEISURE STUDIES

Bowling Green State University	M
California State University, Long Beach	M
Dalhousie University	M
East Carolina University	M,O
Howard University	M
Indiana University Bloomington	M,D
Murray State University	M
Penn State University Park	M
Prescott College	M
San Francisco State University	M
Southeast Missouri State University	M
Southern Connecticut State University	M
Texas State University	M
Universidad Metropolitana	M
Université du Québec à Trois-Rivières	M,O
University of Illinois at Urbana–Champaign	M,D
The University of Iowa	M,D
University of Nebraska at Kearney	M
The University of Tennessee	M,D
The University of Toledo	M,D
University of Utah	M,D
University of Victoria	M
University of Waterloo	M,D
University of West Florida	M

LIBERAL STUDIES

Abilene Christian University	M
Alaska Pacific University	M
Albertus Magnus College	M
Alvernia University	M
Arizona State University at the Tempe campus	M
Arkansas Tech University	M
Auburn University at Montgomery	M,D
Baker University	M
Barry University	M
Brooklyn College of the City University of New York	M
Cardinal Stritch University	M
Clayton State University	M
Coastal Carolina University	M
The College at Brockport, State University of New York	M
College of Staten Island of the City University of New York	M
The Colorado College	M
Colorado State University	M

Concordia University Chicago	M
Converse College	M
Dallas Baptist University	M
Dartmouth College	M
Delta State University	M
DePaul University	M
Drew University	M,D,O
Duke University	M
East Tennessee State University	M,O
Excelsior College	M
Faulkner University	M
Florida International University	M
Fort Hays State University	M
Georgetown University	M,D
The Graduate Center, City University of New York	M
Harvard University	M,O
Hawai`i Pacific University	M
Henderson State University	M
Hollins University	M
Houston Baptist University	M
Indiana University Northwest	M,O
Indiana University–Purdue University Indianapolis	M,D,O
Indiana University South Bend	M,O
Jacksonville State University	M
Johns Hopkins University	M,O
Kean University	M,O
Kent State University	M
Lake Forest College	M
Louisiana State University and Agricultural & Mechanical College	M
Louisiana State University in Shreveport	M
Loyola University Maryland	M
Madonna University	M
McDaniel College	M,O
Metropolitan State University	M
Mississippi College	M
The New School	M
North Carolina State University	M
North Central College	M
Northern Arizona University	M
Northern Kentucky University	M
Northwestern University	M
Notre Dame of Maryland University	M
Oakland University	M
Queens College of the City University of New York	M
Reed College	M
Rice University	M
Rollins College	M
Rutgers University–Camden	M
St. Edward's University	M,O
St. John's College (MD)	M
St. John's College (NM)	M
St. John's University (NY)	M
St. Norbert College	M
San Diego State University	M
San Francisco State University	M
Simon Fraser University	M
Southern Methodist University	M
Spring Hill College	M,O
State University of New York College at Old Westbury	M
State University of New York Empire State College	M
Stony Brook University, State University of New York	M,O
Texas A&M University–Central Texas	M,O
Texas Christian University	M
Thomas Edison State University	M,O
Towson University	M
Tulane University	M
University at Albany, State University of New York	M
University of Chicago	M
University of Delaware	M
University of Detroit Mercy	M,D,O
University of Memphis	M,O
University of Miami	M
University of Minnesota, Duluth	M
University of New Hampshire	M
University of North Carolina at Asheville	M,O
The University of North Carolina at Charlotte	M,D,O
The University of North Carolina at Greensboro	M
The University of North Carolina Wilmington	M
University of Oklahoma	M,O
University of Pennsylvania	M
University of St. Thomas (TX)	M
University of Southern Indiana	M
University of South Florida	M
University of South Florida, St. Petersburg	M
University of South Florida Sarasota-Manatee	M
The University of Texas at El Paso	M
University of the Virgin Islands	M
The University of Toledo	M
University of Wisconsin–Milwaukee	M
Ursuline College	M
Utica College	M
Valparaiso University	M
Vanderbilt University	M
Villanova University	M
Virginia Polytechnic Institute and State University	M,O
Wake Forest University	M
Washburn University	M
Wesleyan University	M,O
Western Illinois University	M
Wichita State University	M
Widener University	M
Winthrop University	M

*M—masters degree; D—doctorate; O—other advanced degree; *—Close-Up and/or Display*

LIBRARY SCIENCE

Appalachian State University	M,O
Azusa Pacific University	M,O
The Catholic University of America	M,O
Chicago State University	M
Clarion University of Pennsylvania	M,O
Dalhousie University	M
Drexel University	M,D,O
East Carolina University	M
Eastern Kentucky University	M
East Tennessee State University	M,O
Emporia State University	M,D,O
Florida State University	M,D,O
Indiana University Bloomington	M,D,O
Indiana University–Purdue University Indianapolis	M,O
Instituto Tecnológico y de Estudios Superiores de Monterrey, Campus Irapuato	M,D
Inter American University of Puerto Rico, Barranquitas Campus	M
Inter American University of Puerto Rico, San Germán Campus	M
Kent State University	M
Kutztown University of Pennsylvania	M
Louisiana State University and Agricultural & Mechanical College	M
Mansfield University of Pennsylvania	M
McDaniel College	M
McGill University	M,D,O
McNeese State University	O
North Carolina Central University	M
Old Dominion University	M,O
Olivet Nazarene University	M
Pratt Institute	M,O
Queens College of the City University of New York	M,O
Rowan University	M,D,O
Rutgers University–New Brunswick	D
St. Catherine University	M
St. John's University (NY)	M,O
Sam Houston State University	M
San Jose State University	M,O
Simmons College	M,D,O
Southern Arkansas University–Magnolia	M
Southern Connecticut State University	M,O
Syracuse University	M
Tennessee Technological University	M,O
Texas A&M University–Commerce	M,D,O
Texas Woman's University	M,D
Trevecca Nazarene University	M,O
Universidad del Turabo	M
Université de Montréal	M,D
University at Albany, State University of New York	M,O
University at Buffalo, the State University of New York	M,O
The University of Alabama	M,D
University of Alberta	M
The University of Arizona	M,D
The University of British Columbia	M,D
University of California, Los Angeles	M,D,O
University of Central Arkansas	M
University of Central Missouri	M,D,O
University of Central Oklahoma	M
University of Denver	M,D,O
University of Hawaii at Manoa	M,O
University of Houston–Clear Lake	M
University of Illinois at Urbana–Champaign	M,D,O
The University of Iowa	M,D
University of Kentucky	M
University of Maryland, College Park	M,D,O
University of Missouri	M,D,O
University of Nebraska at Kearney	M
The University of North Carolina at Chapel Hill	M,D,O
The University of North Carolina at Greensboro	M
University of Oklahoma	M
University of Pittsburgh	M,D
University of Puerto Rico, Río Piedras Campus	M,O
University of Rhode Island	M
University of South Carolina	M,D,O
University of Southern Mississippi	M,O
University of South Florida	M
University of Washington	M,D
The University of Western Ontario	M,D
University of Wisconsin–Eau Claire	M
University of Wisconsin–Madison	M,D
University of Wisconsin–Milwaukee	M,D,O
Valdosta State University	M
Valley City State University	M
Wayne State University	M,O

LIGHTING DESIGN

The New School	M
New York School of Interior Design	M
Rensselaer Polytechnic Institute	M,D
University of Washington	M,D,O

LIMNOLOGY

Baylor University	M,D
Cornell University	D
Oregon State University	M,D
University of Alaska Fairbanks	M,D
University of Florida	M,D

LINGUISTICS

Arizona State University at the Tempe campus	M,D,O
Ball State University	M
Biola University	M,D,O
Boston College	M
Boston University	M,D
Brandeis University	M
Brigham Young University	M
Brown University	M,D
California State University, Fresno	M
California State University, Fullerton	M
California State University, Long Beach	M,O
California State University, Northridge	M
Carleton University	M
Carnegie Mellon University	M,D
Case Western Reserve University	M
Concordia University (Canada)	M,O
Cornell University	M,D
East Carolina University	M,D,O
Eastern Michigan University	M
Florida Atlantic University	M
Florida International University	M
Gallaudet University	M,D,O
George Mason University	M,D,O
Georgetown University	M,D
Georgia State University	M,D
The Graduate Center, City University of New York	M,D
Graduate Institute of Applied Linguistics	M,O
Grand Valley State University	M
Harvard University	D
Hofstra University	M,D,O
Indiana State University	M,D,O
Indiana University Bloomington	M,D
Instituto Tecnologico de Santo Domingo	M,O
Iowa State University of Science and Technology	M,D
Kent State University	M,D
Massachusetts Institute of Technology	D
McGill University	M,D
Memorial University of Newfoundland	M,D
Michigan State University	M,D
Montclair State University	M,O
New York University	M,D
Northeastern Illinois University	M
Northern Arizona University	M,D,O
Northwestern University	D
Oakland University	M,O
The Ohio State University	M,D
Ohio University	M
Old Dominion University	M
Penn State University Park	M,D
Purdue University	M,D
Queens College of the City University of New York	M,O
Rice University	M,D
Rutgers University–New Brunswick	D
San Diego State University	M,O
San Francisco State University	M,O
San Jose State University	M,O
Simon Fraser University	M,D
Southern Illinois University Carbondale	M
Stanford University	M,D
Stony Brook University, State University of New York	M,D
Syracuse University	M
Teachers College, Columbia University	M,D,O
Texas A&M University–Commerce	M,D,O
Texas Tech University	M,D
Trinity Western University	M
Universidad de las Américas Puebla	M
Université de Montréal	M,D,O
Université de Sherbrooke	M,D
Université du Québec à Chicoutimi	M
Université du Québec à Montréal	M,D
Université Laval	M,D
University at Buffalo, the State University of New York	M,D
University of Alaska Fairbanks	M
University of Alberta	M,D
The University of Arizona	M,D
The University of British Columbia	M,D
University of Calgary	M,D
University of California, Berkeley	D
University of California, Davis	M,D
University of California, Los Angeles	M,D
University of California, San Diego	D
University of California, Santa Barbara	M,D
University of California, Santa Cruz	M,D
University of Chicago	M,D
University of Colorado Boulder	M,D
University of Colorado Denver	M
University of Connecticut	M,D
University of Delaware	M,D
University of Florida	M,D,O
University of Georgia	M,D
University of Hawaii at Manoa	M,D
University of Houston	M,D
University of Illinois at Chicago	M
University of Illinois at Urbana–Champaign	M,D
The University of Iowa	M,D
The University of Kansas	M,D
University of Louisville	M,D
The University of Manchester	M,D
University of Manitoba	M,D
University of Maryland, Baltimore County	M
University of Maryland, College Park	M,D
University of Massachusetts Amherst	M,D
University of Massachusetts Boston	M,D
University of Memphis	M,D,O
University of Michigan	D
University of Minnesota, Twin Cities Campus	M,D
University of Montana	M,D
University of New Hampshire	M,D
University of New Mexico	M,D
The University of North Carolina at Chapel Hill	M
The University of North Carolina at Charlotte	M,O
University of North Dakota	M
University of North Texas	M,D,O
University of Oregon	M,D
University of Ottawa	M,D
University of Pennsylvania	M,D
University of Puerto Rico, Río Piedras Campus	M
University of Regina	M
University of Rochester	M,D
University of South Africa	M,D,O
University of South Carolina	M,D
University of Southern California	M,D
University of South Florida	M,D
The University of Tennessee	D
The University of Texas at Arlington	M,D
The University of Texas at Austin	M,D
The University of Texas at El Paso	M,O
University of Toronto	M,D
University of Utah	M,D
University of Victoria	M,D
University of Virginia	M
University of Washington	M,D
University of Wisconsin–Madison	M,D
University of Wisconsin–Milwaukee	M,D,O
Virginia International University	M
Wayne State University	M
Wesley Biblical Seminary	M
West Virginia University	M
Yale University	D
York University	M,D

LOGISTICS

Air Force Institute of Technology	M,D
Albany State University	M
American Public University System	M
Benedictine University	M
Case Western Reserve University	M,D
Central Connecticut State University	M,O
Central Michigan University	M,O
Colorado Technical University Colorado Springs	M,D
Copenhagen Business School	M,D
East Carolina University	M,D,O
Embry-Riddle Aeronautical University–Worldwide	M
Florida Institute of Technology	M,D
Friends University	M
George Mason University	M,O
Georgia College & State University	M
Georgia Institute of Technology	M
Georgia Southern University	D
HEC Montreal	M
Kaplan University, Davenport Campus	M
Maryville University of Saint Louis	M,O
Massachusetts Institute of Technology	M
Michigan State University	M,D
Naval Postgraduate School	M
North Dakota State University	M,D
Norwich University	M
The Ohio State University	M
Polytechnic University of Puerto Rico, Miami Campus	M
Pontifical Catholic University of Puerto Rico	O
Pontificia Universidad Catolica Madre y Maestra	M
Rutgers University–Newark	M
Shippensburg University of Pennsylvania	M,O
Stevens Institute of Technology	O
Trident University International	M,D
Universidad del Turabo	M
University at Buffalo, the State University of New York	M,D
The University of Alabama in Huntsville	M,O
University of Alaska Anchorage	M,O
University of Dallas	M,D
University of Houston	M
The University of Kansas	M,D
University of Louisville	M,D,O
University of Missouri–St. Louis	M,D,O
The University of North Carolina at Charlotte	M,O
University of North Florida	M
University of North Texas	M,D,O
University of St. Francis (IL)	M,O
University of South Africa	M,D
University of Southern Mississippi	M
The University of Tennessee	M
The University of Tennessee at Chattanooga	M,O
The University of Texas at Arlington	M
University of Washington	O
Virginia International University	M,O
Wright State University	M

MANAGEMENT INFORMATION SYSTEMS

Adelphi University	M
Air Force Institute of Technology	M
American Business & Technology University	M
American InterContinental University Atlanta	M
American Public University System	M
American Sentinel University	M
American University	M,D,O
American University of Armenia	M
Argosy University, Atlanta	M,D
Argosy University, Chicago	M,D
Argosy University, Dallas	M,D,O
Argosy University, Denver	M,D
Argosy University, Hawai`i	M,D,O
Argosy University, Inland Empire	M,D
Argosy University, Los Angeles	M,D
Argosy University, Nashville	M,D
Argosy University, Northern Virginia	M,D,O
Argosy University, Orange County	M,D
Argosy University, Phoenix	M,D
Argosy University, Salt Lake City	M,D
Argosy University, San Diego	M,D
Argosy University, San Francisco Bay Area	M,D
Argosy University, Sarasota	M,D,O
Argosy University, Schaumburg	M,D,O
Argosy University, Seattle	M,D
Argosy University, Tampa	M,D
Argosy University, Twin Cities	M,D
Arizona State University at the Tempe campus	M,D
Arkansas State University	O
Aspen University	M
Auburn University at Montgomery	M
Avila University	M
Baker College Center for Graduate Studies–Online	M,D
Ball State University	M,O
Barry University	O
Baruch College of the City University of New York	M,D
Baylor University	M,D
Bay Path University	M
Bellevue University	M
Benedictine University	M
Boston University	M,O
Bowie State University	M,O
Brandeis University	M
Broadview University–West Jordan	M
California Intercontinental University	M,D
California Lutheran University	M,O
California State Polytechnic University, Pomona	M
California State University, East Bay	M
California State University, Fullerton	M
California State University, Los Angeles	M
California State University, Monterey Bay	M
California State University, San Bernardino	M
California University of Management and Sciences	M,D
Capella University	M,D
Capitol Technology University	M,D
Carnegie Mellon University	M,D
The Catholic University of America	M,O
Central European University	M,O
Central Michigan University	M
Central Penn College	M
Charleston Southern University	M
City College of the City University of New York	M,D
City University of Seattle	M,O
Claremont Graduate University	M,D,O
Clark University	M
Clemson University	M,D
Cleveland State University	D
Coastal Carolina University	M,D,O
College of Charleston	M
The College of St. Scholastica	M,O
Colorado State University	M
Colorado State University–Global Campus	M
Concordia University Wisconsin	M
Copenhagen Business School	M,D
Daemen College	M
Dakota State University	M,D,O
Dalhousie University	M
Dallas Baptist University	M
DePaul University	M,D
DeSales University	M,O
DeVry University–Folsom Campus	M
Dominican University	M,D,O
Drexel University	M,D,O
Duquesne University	M
East Carolina University	M,D,O
Eastern Michigan University	M,O
Elmhurst College	M
Embry-Riddle Aeronautical University–Worldwide	M
Emory University	M
Endicott College	M
Fairfield University	M,O
Fairleigh Dickinson University, Metropolitan Campus	M,O
Ferris State University	M
Florida Agricultural and Mechanical University	M
Florida Atlantic University	M
Florida Institute of Technology	M,D
Florida International University	M,D,O
Florida State University	M,D,O
Fordham University	M
Franklin Pierce University	M,D,O
Friends University	M
George Mason University	M
The George Washington University	M,D

Georgia College & State University	M
Georgia Institute of Technology	M
Georgia Southern University	M,O
Georgia Southwestern State University	M,D,O
Georgia State University	M,D,O
Golden Gate University	M,D,O
Goldey-Beacom College	M
Governors State University	M
The Graduate Center, City University of New York	D
Grand Valley State University	M
Grantham University	M,O
Harrisburg University of Science and Technology	M
Hawai'i Pacific University	M
HEC Montreal	M
Hodges University	M
Hofstra University	M,O
Holy Family University	M
Hood College	M
Howard University	M
Idaho State University	M,O
IGlobal University	M
Illinois Institute of Technology	M,D
Illinois State University	M
Indiana University Bloomington	M,D,O
Indiana University Northwest	M,O
Instituto Tecnológico y de Estudios Superiores de Monterrey, Campus Central de Veracruz	M
Instituto Tecnológico y de Estudios Superiores de Monterrey, Campus Ciudad de México	M,D
Instituto Tecnológico y de Estudios Superiores de Monterrey, Campus Ciudad Juárez	M
Instituto Tecnológico y de Estudios Superiores de Monterrey, Campus Ciudad Obregón	M
Instituto Tecnológico y de Estudios Superiores de Monterrey, Campus Estado de México	M,D
Instituto Tecnológico y de Estudios Superiores de Monterrey, Campus Irapuato	M,D
Instituto Tecnológico y de Estudios Superiores de Monterrey, Campus Laguna	M
Inter American University of Puerto Rico, Aguadilla Campus	M
Inter American University of Puerto Rico, Fajardo Campus	M
Inter American University of Puerto Rico, Metropolitan Campus	M
Inter American University of Puerto Rico, San Germán Campus	M,D
Iowa State University of Science and Technology	M,D
James Madison University	M
Johns Hopkins University	M,O
Johnson & Wales University	M
Kaplan University, Davenport Campus	M
Kean University	M
Keiser University	M
Kent State University	M,D
Lake Erie College	M
Le Moyne College	M
Lenoir-Rhyne University	M
Lewis University	M
Liberty University	M,D,O
Lincoln University (CA)	M,D
Lincoln University (MO)	M
Lindenwood University	M,O
Lipscomb University	M
London Metropolitan University	M,D
Long Island University–LIU Post	M
Louisiana State University and Agricultural & Mechanical College	M,D
Loyola University Maryland	M
Marist College	M,O
Marquette University	M,O
Marymount University	M,O
Marywood University	M
McGill University	M,D,O
McMaster University	D
Metropolitan State University	M,D,O
Michigan State University	M,D
Middle Georgia State University	M
Middle Tennessee State University	M
Minot State University	M
Mississippi State University	M,D
Missouri State University	M
Morehead State University	M
Naval Postgraduate School	M,D,O
New England Institute of Technology	M
New Jersey Institute of Technology	M,D,O
Newman University	M
New Mexico State University	M
New York University	M,D,O
North Carolina Agricultural and Technical State University	M,D,O
Northeastern University	M
Northwestern University	M
Northwest Missouri State University	M
Nova Southeastern University	M,D
Oakland University	M,D,O
The Ohio State University	M,D
Oklahoma State University	M,D
Old Dominion University	M,D
Our Lady of the Lake University	M,D,O
Pace University	M,D
Pacific States University	M,O
Park University	M,O
Penn State Harrisburg	M,D
Penn State University Park	M
Point Park University	

Polytechnic University of Puerto Rico	M
Pontifical Catholic University of Puerto Rico	M,O
Prairie View A&M University	M,D
Purdue University	M
Radford University	M
Regent's University London	M
Regis University	M,O
Rensselaer Polytechnic Institute	M
Rivier University	M
Robert Morris University	M,D
Robert Morris University Illinois	M
Rochester Institute of Technology	O
Rose-Hulman Institute of Technology	M
Rutgers University–Newark	M,D
St. John's University (NY)	M
Saint Joseph's University	M
Saint Peter's University	M
San Diego State University	M
San Francisco State University	M
Santa Clara University	M
Schiller International University (United States)	M
Schiller International University (Germany)	M
Seattle Pacific University	M
Shepherd University (CA)	M
Shippensburg University of Pennsylvania	M,O
Southeastern Oklahoma State University	M
Southern Illinois University Edwardsville	M
Southern Methodist University	M
Southern New Hampshire University	M,O
Southern University at New Orleans	M
South University	M
South University (TX)	M
South University (AL)	M
South University	M
Stevens Institute of Technology	M,D,O
Stony Brook University, State University of New York	M,D,O
Stratford University (VA)	M
Strayer University	M
Suffolk University	M
Syracuse University	M,D,O
Tarleton State University	M
Temple University	M,D
Tennessee Technological University	M
Texas A&M International University	M,D
Texas A&M University	M,O
Texas A&M University–Central Texas	M,O
Texas A&M University–San Antonio	M
Texas Southern University	M
Texas State University	M
Texas Tech University	M
Touro College	M
Towson University	M,D,O
Trident University International	M,D,O
Troy University	M
Tuskegee University	M
United States International University–Africa	M
Universidad del Este	M
Universidad del Turabo	D
Universidad Metropolitana	M
Université de Sherbrooke	M,O
Université du Québec à Montréal	M
Université Laval	M,O
University at Albany, State University of New York	M,D,O
University at Buffalo, the State University of New York	M,D,O
The University of Akron	M
The University of Alabama at Birmingham	M
The University of Alabama in Huntsville	M,O
The University of Arizona	M,O
University of Arkansas	M
University of Arkansas at Little Rock	M,O
University of Baltimore	M,O
University of Bridgeport	M
The University of British Columbia	D
University of California, Berkeley	M,D,O
University of California, Santa Cruz	D
University of Central Missouri	M,D,O
University of Cincinnati	M,D
University of Colorado Denver	M,D
University of Dallas	M,D
University of Delaware	M
University of Detroit Mercy	M,D,O
University of Florida	M,D,O
University of Hawaii at Manoa	M,D
University of Houston–Clear Lake	M
University of Houston–Victoria	M
University of Illinois at Chicago	M,D
University of Illinois at Springfield	M
University of Illinois at Urbana–Champaign	M,D,O
The University of Kansas	M
University of La Verne	M,O
University of Lethbridge	M,D
University of Management and Technology	M
University of Mary Hardin-Baylor	M
University of Massachusetts Boston	M
University of Massachusetts Dartmouth	M,O

University of Memphis	M,D,O
University of Michigan–Dearborn	M
University of Michigan–Flint	M,O
University of Minnesota, Twin Cities Campus	M,D
University of Mississippi	M,D
University of Missouri–St. Louis	M,D,O
University of Nebraska at Kearney	M
University of Nebraska at Omaha	M,D,O
University of Nebraska–Lincoln	M
University of Nevada, Las Vegas	M,O
University of Nevada, Reno	M
University of New Hampshire	M,O
University of New Mexico	M,O
University of North Alabama	M
The University of North Carolina at Chapel Hill	D
The University of North Carolina at Charlotte	M,D,O
The University of North Carolina at Greensboro	M,D,O
The University of North Carolina Wilmington	M
University of North Florida	M
University of North Texas	M,D,O
University of Oklahoma	M,D,O
University of Oregon	M
University of Pennsylvania	M,D
University of Phoenix–Atlanta Campus	M
University of Phoenix–Augusta Campus	M
University of Phoenix–Bay Area Campus	M,D
University of Phoenix–Central Valley Campus	M
University of Phoenix–Charlotte Campus	M
University of Phoenix–Colorado Campus	M
University of Phoenix–Colorado Springs Downtown Campus	M
University of Phoenix–Columbus Georgia Campus	M
University of Phoenix–Dallas Campus	M
University of Phoenix–Hawaii Campus	M
University of Phoenix–Houston Campus	M
University of Phoenix–Jersey City Campus	M
University of Phoenix–Las Vegas Campus	M
University of Phoenix–New Mexico Campus	M
University of Phoenix–North Florida Campus	M
University of Phoenix–Online Campus	M
University of Phoenix–Sacramento Valley Campus	M
University of Phoenix–San Antonio Campus	M
University of Phoenix–San Diego Campus	M
University of Phoenix–Southern Arizona Campus	M
University of Phoenix–South Florida Campus	M
University of Phoenix–Utah Campus	M
University of Phoenix–Washington D.C. Campus	M,D
University of Pittsburgh	M,D
University of Redlands	M
University of Rochester	M,D
University of San Francisco	M
The University of Scranton	M
University of South Africa	M
University of South Alabama	M,D
University of South Florida	M,D,O
The University of Tampa	M
The University of Texas at Arlington	M,D
The University of Texas at Austin	M,D
The University of Texas at Dallas	M,D
The University of Texas Rio Grande Valley	M
University of the Sacred Heart	M
University of the West	M
University of Utah	M,D,O
University of Washington	M,D
University of Wisconsin–Madison	D
Utah State University	M,D
Valparaiso University	M
Villanova University	M
Virginia Commonwealth University	M,O
Virginia International University	M
Virginia Polytechnic Institute and State University	M,D,O
Walden University	M,D,O
Walsh College of Accountancy and Business Administration	M
Wayland Baptist University	M
Wayne State University	M,D
Webster University	M,D
West Chester University of Pennsylvania	M
Western Governors University	M
Wichita State University	M
Wilmington University	M,D
Winston-Salem State University	M
Worcester Polytechnic Institute	M,D,O
Wright State University	M

MANAGEMENT OF TECHNOLOGY

Air Force Institute of Technology	M,D
Arizona State University at the Tempe campus	M
Athabasca University	M,D,O
Boston University	M
California Lutheran University	M,O
California State University, Los Angeles	M
Cambridge College	M
Capella University	M
Carleton University	M
The Catholic University of America	M,O
Central Connecticut State University	M,O
Champlain College	M
City University of Seattle	M,O
Coleman University	M
Colorado School of Mines	M,D
Colorado Technical University Aurora	M
Colorado Technical University Colorado Springs	M,D
Columbia University	M
Dallas Baptist University	M
DePaul University	M,D
East Carolina University	M,D,O
Eastern Michigan University	D
École Polytechnique de Montréal	M,D,O
Embry-Riddle Aeronautical University–Worldwide	M
Excelsior College	M,O
Fairfield University	M,O
Fairleigh Dickinson University, College at Florham	M,O
Florida Institute of Technology	M,D
George Mason University	M
Georgetown University	M,D
The George Washington University	M,D
Golden Gate University	M,D,O
Grand Canyon University	M
Harrisburg University of Science and Technology	M
Harvard University	D
Herzing University Online	M
Idaho State University	M
Illinois State University	M
Indiana State University	M,D
Indiana University–Purdue University Indianapolis	M
Instituto Centroamericano de Administración de Empresas	M
Instituto Tecnológico y de Estudios Superiores de Monterrey, Campus Cuernavaca	M,D
Instituto Tecnológico y de Estudios Superiores de Monterrey, Campus Irapuato	M,D
Iona College	M,O
Johns Hopkins University	M,O
Kansas State University	M
La Salle University	M,O
Lewis University	M
Liberty University	M,D,O
Lipscomb University	M
London Metropolitan University	M,D
Marist College	M,O
Marquette University	M,D
Marshall University	M
Mercer University	M
Murray State University	M
New Jersey Institute of Technology	M,D,O
New York University	M,D,O
North Carolina Agricultural and Technical State University	M
North Carolina State University	D
Northern Kentucky University	M
Notre Dame de Namur University	M
Pacific States University	M,D
Pittsburg State University	M,O
Polytechnic University of Puerto Rico	M
Polytechnic University of Puerto Rico, Orlando Campus	M
Portland State University	M,D
Purdue University	M,D
Rensselaer Polytechnic Institute	M,D
Rollins College	M,D
Rutgers University–Newark	D
Ryerson University	M
St. Ambrose University	M
Seton Hall University	M,O
Simon Fraser University	M,D,O
South Dakota School of Mines and Technology	M
Southeast Missouri State University	M
State University of New York Polytechnic Institute	M
Stevens Institute of Technology	M,D,O
Stevenson University	M
Stony Brook University, State University of New York	M
Texas A&M University	M
Texas A&M University–Commerce	M,O
Texas State University	M
Towson University	M,O
University at Albany, State University of New York	M
University of Advancing Technology	M
The University of Alabama in Huntsville	M,O
University of Bridgeport	M,D
University of California, Los Angeles	M,D
University of California, Santa Barbara	M
University of California, Santa Cruz	D

M—masters degree; D—doctorate; O—other advanced degree; *—Close-Up and/or Display

University of Central Missouri	M,D,O
University of Colorado Denver	M
University of Dallas	M,D
University of Delaware	M
University of Idaho	M,D
University of Illinois at Urbana–Champaign	M,D
University of Massachusetts Dartmouth	M
University of Miami	M,D
University of Minnesota, Twin Cities Campus	M
University of New Mexico	M
University of Phoenix–Atlanta Campus	M
University of Phoenix–Augusta Campus	M
University of Phoenix–Bay Area Campus	M,D
University of Phoenix–Central Valley Campus	M
University of Phoenix–Charlotte Campus	M
University of Phoenix–Colorado Campus	M
University of Phoenix–Colorado Springs Downtown Campus	M
University of Phoenix–Columbus Georgia Campus	M
University of Phoenix–Dallas Campus	M
University of Phoenix–Hawaii Campus	M
University of Phoenix–Houston Campus	M
University of Phoenix–Jersey City Campus	M
University of Phoenix–Las Vegas Campus	M
University of Phoenix–New Mexico Campus	M
University of Phoenix–Online Campus	M,O
University of Phoenix–Phoenix Campus	M,O
University of Phoenix–Sacramento Valley Campus	M
University of Phoenix–San Antonio Campus	M
University of Phoenix–San Diego Campus	M
University of Phoenix–Southern Arizona Campus	M
University of Phoenix–Southern California Campus	M
University of Phoenix–Utah Campus	M
University of Portland	M
University of St. Thomas (MN)	M,O
University of South Florida	O
The University of Texas at Dallas	M
The University of Texas at San Antonio	M,D,O
University of Toronto	M
University of Virginia	M
University of Washington	M,D
University of Waterloo	M,D
University of Wisconsin–Madison	M
University of Wisconsin–Milwaukee	M,O
Walsh College of Accountancy and Business Administration	M
Washington State University	M,O
Webster University	M,D,O
Wentworth Institute of Technology	M
Western Kentucky University	M
Wilfrid Laurier University	M,D

MANAGEMENT STRATEGY AND POLICY

Amberton University	M
American Public University System	M
Antioch University Midwest	M
Antioch University Santa Barbara	M
Arizona State University at the Tempe campus	M,D
Austin Peay State University	M
Azusa Pacific University	M
Baldwin Wallace University	M
Bay Path University	M
Bellarmine University	M
Bentley University	O
Black Hills State University	M
Boston University	M,O
Brandeis University	M
Bryant University	M,O
California Miramar University	M
California State University, East Bay	M
California State University, Fullerton	M
California University of Pennsylvania	M
Capella University	M,D
Claremont Graduate University	M,D,O
Cleary University	M,O
Clemson University	M
The College of Saint Rose	M,O
Dakota State University	M,D,O
Davenport University	M
Defiance College	M
DePaul University	M
Dominican University of California	M
Drexel University	M,D,O
Duke University	M,D,O
East Tennessee State University	M,O
Embry-Riddle Aeronautical University–Worldwide	M
Fairfield University	M,O
Fisher College	M
Florida State University	M,D
Fordham University	M
Freed-Hardeman University	M
Friends University	M
The George Washington University	M,D,O

Georgia State University	M,D
Golden Gate University	M,D,O
Grantham University	M,O
Gwynedd Mercy University	M
Harrisburg University of Science and Technology	M
Harvard University	D
HEC Montreal	M
Hofstra University	M,O
Hult International Business School (United States)	M
James Madison University	D
Lawrence Technological University	M,O
Lenoir-Rhyne University	M
LeTourneau University	M
Manhattanville College	M
McGill University	M,D,O
Mercer University	M
Mercyhurst University	M,O
Merrimack College	M
Messiah College	M,O
Michigan State University	M,D
Middlebury Institute of International Studies at Monterey	M
Middle Tennessee State University	M
Mount Mercy University	M
Neumann University	M
New England College	M
The New School	M,O
New York University	M,D,O
Niagara University	M
North Central College	M
Northwestern University	M,D
Norwich University	M
Nova Southeastern University	M
Ohio Dominican University	M
Oklahoma Wesleyan University	M
Oregon State University	M,D
Pace University	M
Philadelphia University	M
Pontificia Universidad Catolica Madre y Maestra	M
Regent University	M,D,O
Regis University	M,O
Robert Morris University Illinois	M
Roberts Wesleyan College	M
Rockhurst University	M,O
St. John's University (NY)	M
Saint Joseph's University	M
Saint Mary-of-the-Woods College	M
Salve Regina University	M,O
San Jose State University	M,O
Southern Illinois University Edwardsville	M
Southern Methodist University	M
Stevens Institute of Technology	M
Suffolk University	M
Syracuse University	M
Taylor University	M
Temple University	D
Tennessee State University	M,D
Tennessee Technological University	M
Tufts University	O
Tulane University	M,D
United States International University–Africa	M
Universidad del Este	M
University at Buffalo, the State University of New York	M,D
The University of Arizona	M,D
The University of British Columbia	D
University of Calgary	M,D
University of California, Los Angeles	M,D
University of California, San Diego	M,D
University of Charleston	M
University of Chicago	M,O
University of Colorado Denver	M
University of Dallas	M,D
University of Denver	M
University of Detroit Mercy	M,O
University of Illinois at Urbana–Champaign	M,D,O
The University of Kansas	M,D
University of Lethbridge	M,D
The University of Manchester	M
University of Massachusetts Amherst	M,D
University of Massachusetts Dartmouth	M,O
University of Memphis	M,O
University of Michigan–Dearborn	M
University of Minnesota, Twin Cities Campus	D
University of Missouri–St. Louis	M,D,O
University of New Haven	M,O
University of New Mexico	M
The University of North Carolina at Chapel Hill	D
University of North Texas	M,D,O
University of North Texas at Dallas	M
University of Notre Dame	M
University of Pittsburgh	M,D
University of Rhode Island	M,D
University of Rochester	M
University of St. Francis (IL)	M,O
University of South Florida	M,D,O
The University of Texas at Dallas	M
University of Utah	M,D,O
University of Virginia	M
The University of Western Ontario	M,D
University of Wisconsin–Madison	M,D
University of Wisconsin–Milwaukee	M,O
Valparaiso University	M,O
Vanderbilt University	M
Villanova University	M
Walsh College of Accountancy and Business Administration	M

Wayne State University	M,D,O
West Chester University of Pennsylvania	M,O
Western Governors University	M
Xavier University	M

MANUFACTURING ENGINEERING

American University of Armenia	
Arizona State University at the Tempe campus	M
Boston University	M,D
Bradley University	M
Brigham Young University	M
California State University, Northridge	M
The Citadel, The Military College of South Carolina	M,O
Clemson University	M
Cornell University	M,D
Eastern Kentucky University	M
East Tennessee State University	M
Florida State University	M,D
Georgia Southern University	M,O
Grand Valley State University	M
Illinois Institute of Technology	M,D
Instituto Tecnológico y de Estudios Superiores de Monterrey, Campus Monterrey	M,D
Kansas State University	M,D
Kettering University	M
Lawrence Technological University	M,D
Lehigh University	M
Massachusetts Institute of Technology	M,D,O
Michigan State University	M,D
Minnesota State University Mankato	M
Missouri University of Science and Technology	M,D
New Jersey Institute of Technology	M,D
New York University	M,D
North Carolina State University	M
North Dakota State University	M,D
Oregon Institute of Technology	M
Oregon State University	M,D
Pittsburg State University	M
Polytechnic University of Puerto Rico	M
Portland State University	M,D
Rochester Institute of Technology	M,D
Southern Methodist University	M,D
Stevens Institute of Technology	M,D
Tennessee State University	M,D
Texas A&M University	M
Texas State University	M
Texas Tech University	M,D
Tufts University	O
Universidad Autonoma de Guadalajara	M,D
Universidad de las Américas Puebla	M
University of Calgary	M,D
University of California, Irvine	M,D
University of California, Los Angeles	M
The University of Iowa	M,D
University of Kentucky	M
University of Manitoba	M,D
University of Maryland, College Park	M,D
University of Michigan	M,D
University of Michigan–Dearborn	M
University of Missouri	M,D
University of Nebraska–Lincoln	M,D
University of New Mexico	M
University of Puerto Rico, Mayagüez Campus	M,D
University of St. Thomas (MN)	M,O
University of Southern California	M,D,O
The University of Texas at El Paso	M,O
The University of Texas at San Antonio	M,D
The University of Texas Rio Grande Valley	M
University of Toronto	M
University of Windsor	M,D
University of Wisconsin–Madison	M,D
University of Wisconsin–Milwaukee	M,D
University of Wisconsin–Stout	M
Villanova University	M,O
Wayne State University	M,D,O
Western Illinois University	M
Western Michigan University	M
Western New England University	M
Wichita State University	M,D
Worcester Polytechnic Institute	M,D

MARINE AFFAIRS

Dalhousie University	M
Louisiana State University and Agricultural & Mechanical College	M,D
Memorial University of Newfoundland	M,D,O
Nova Southeastern University	M,D
Oregon State University	M
Stevens Institute of Technology	M
Stony Brook University, State University of New York	M
Université du Québec à Rimouski	M,O
University of Delaware	M,D
University of Massachusetts Dartmouth	M,D
University of Miami	M
University of Rhode Island	M,D
University of San Diego	M
University of Washington	M,O

MARINE BIOLOGY

College of Charleston	M
Florida Institute of Technology	M,D
Montclair State University	M
Nicholls State University	M
Northeastern University	M,D

Nova Southeastern University	M,D
Princeton University	D
Rutgers University–New Brunswick	M,D
San Francisco State University	M
Texas A&M University	M,D
Texas A&M University–Corpus Christi	M,D
Texas State University	M,D
University of Alaska Fairbanks	M,D
University of California, San Diego	M,D
University of California, Santa Barbara	M,D
University of Guam	M
University of Hawaii at Hilo	M
University of Hawaii at Manoa	M,D
University of Massachusetts Dartmouth	M
University of Miami	M,D
University of New Hampshire	M,D
The University of North Carolina Wilmington	M,D
University of Oregon	M,D
University of Southern California	M,D
University of Southern Mississippi	M,D
Western Illinois University	M,O
Woods Hole Oceanographic Institution	D

MARINE GEOLOGY

Cornell University	M,D
Massachusetts Institute of Technology	M,D
University of Delaware	M,D
University of Hawaii at Manoa	M,D
University of Miami	M,D
University of Washington	M,D
Woods Hole Oceanographic Institution	D

MARINE SCIENCES

California State University, East Bay	M
California State University, Fresno	M
California State University, Monterey Bay	M
Coastal Carolina University	M,D,O
College of Charleston	M
The College of William and Mary	M,D
Cornell University	M,D
Duke University	D
Florida Institute of Technology	M,D
Florida State University	M,D
Hawai'i Pacific University	M
Instituto Tecnologico de Santo Domingo	M,D,O
Jacksonville University	M
Medical University of South Carolina	D
Memorial University of Newfoundland	M,O
North Carolina State University	M,D
Nova Southeastern University	M,D
Oregon State University	M
San Francisco State University	M
San Jose State University	M,O
Savannah State University	M
Southern Connecticut State University	M,O
Stony Brook University, State University of New York	M,D
Texas A&M University	M
Texas A&M University–Corpus Christi	M,D
University of Alaska Fairbanks	M,D
The University of British Columbia	M,D
University of California, San Diego	M
University of California, Santa Barbara	M,D
University of California, Santa Cruz	M,D
University of Delaware	M,D
University of Florida	M,D
University of Georgia	M,D
University of Hawaii at Manoa	O
University of Maine	M,D
University of Maryland, Baltimore	M,D
University of Maryland, Baltimore County	M,D
University of Maryland, College Park	M,D
University of Maryland Eastern Shore	M,D
University of Massachusetts Amherst	M,D
University of Massachusetts Boston	M,D
University of Massachusetts Dartmouth	M,D
University of Miami	M,D
University of New England	M
The University of North Carolina at Chapel Hill	M,D
The University of North Carolina Wilmington	M,D
University of Puerto Rico, Mayagüez Campus	M,D
University of Rhode Island	M,D
University of San Diego	M,D
University of South Alabama	M,D
University of South Carolina	M,D
University of Southern California	M,D
University of Southern Mississippi	M,D
University of South Florida	M,D
The University of Texas at Austin	M,D
University of the Virgin Islands	M
University of Wisconsin–La Crosse	M
University of Wisconsin–Madison	M,D
Western Washington University	M

MARKETING

Adelphi University	M
American Business & Technology University	M
American College of Thessaloniki	M,O
American InterContinental University Online	M
American Public University System	M
American University	M
The American University in Dubai	M
Anderson University (SC)	M
Aquinas College (MI)	M,D
Argosy University, Atlanta	M,D
Argosy University, Chicago	M,D
Argosy University, Dallas	M,D,O
Argosy University, Denver	M,D
Argosy University, Hawai`i	M,D,O
Argosy University, Inland Empire	M,D
Argosy University, Los Angeles	M,D
Argosy University, Nashville	M,D
Argosy University, Northern Virginia	M,D,O
Argosy University, Orange County	M,D,O
Argosy University, Phoenix	M,D
Argosy University, Salt Lake City	M,D
Argosy University, San Diego	M,D
Argosy University, San Francisco Bay Area	M,D
Argosy University, Sarasota	M,D,O
Argosy University, Schaumburg	M,D,O
Argosy University, Seattle	M,D
Argosy University, Tampa	M,D
Argosy University, Twin Cities	M,D
Arizona State University at the Tempe campus	M,D
Ashworth College	M
Assumption College	M,O
Averett University	M
Avila University	M
Azusa Pacific University	M
Baker College Center for Graduate Studies–Online	M,D
Barry University	O
Baruch College of the City University of New York	M,D
Bayamón Central University	M
Benedictine University	M
Bentley University	M
Brandeis University	M
Brandman University	M
Brigham Young University	M
Bristol University	M
Butler University	M
California Coast University	M
California Intercontinental University	M,D
California Lutheran University	M,O
California State University, East Bay	M
California State University, Fullerton	M
California State University, Los Angeles	M
California State University, San Bernardino	M
Capella University	M,D
Carnegie Mellon University	D
Central Michigan University	M,O
City College of the City University of New York	M
City University of Seattle	M,O
Clark University	M
Cleveland State University	D
Colorado Technical University Aurora	M
Colorado Technical University Colorado Springs	M,D
Columbia Southern University	M
Columbia University	M,D
Concordia University (Canada)	M,D,O
Concordia University Wisconsin	M
Cornell University	D
Daemen College	M
Dallas Baptist University	M
DePaul University	M
DEREE - The American College of Greece	M
DeSales University	M
Drexel University	M,D,O
Duke University	M,D,O
Duquesne University	M
Eastern Michigan University	M,O
East Tennessee State University	M,O
Emerson College	M
Emory University	M,D
Fairfield University	M,O
Fairleigh Dickinson University, College at Florham	M,O
Fairleigh Dickinson University, Metropolitan Campus	M,O
Fashion Institute of Technology	M
Florida Agricultural and Mechanical University	M
Florida Atlantic University	M
Florida International University	M
Florida National University	M
Florida State University	M,D
Fordham University	M
Franklin University	M
Full Sail University	M
Gannon University	M
Geneva College	M
George Fox University	M,D
The George Washington University	M,D
Georgia State University	M,D
Golden Gate University	M,D,O
Goldey-Beacom College	M
Grand Canyon University	M,D
Harvard University	D
Hawai`i Pacific University	M
HEC Montreal	M

Herzing University Online	M
Hofstra University	M,O
Holy Names University	M
Hood College	M
Hope International University	M
Howard University	M
Hult International Business School (United States)	M
Illinois Institute of Technology	M
Indiana Tech	M
Indiana University–Purdue University Indianapolis	M
Indiana University South Bend	M,O
Instituto Tecnologico de Santo Domingo	M,O
Instituto Tecnológico y de Estudios Superiores de Monterrey, Campus Central de Veracruz	M
Instituto Tecnológico y de Estudios Superiores de Monterrey, Campus Ciudad Obregón	M
Instituto Tecnológico y de Estudios Superiores de Monterrey, Campus Cuernavaca	M
Instituto Tecnológico y de Estudios Superiores de Monterrey, Campus Estado de México	M,D
Instituto Tecnológico y de Estudios Superiores de Monterrey, Campus Monterrey	M
Inter American University of Puerto Rico, Aguadilla Campus	M
Inter American University of Puerto Rico, Fajardo Campus	M
Inter American University of Puerto Rico, Guayama Campus	M
Inter American University of Puerto Rico, Metropolitan Campus	M
Inter American University of Puerto Rico, Ponce Campus	M
Inter American University of Puerto Rico, San Germán Campus	M,D
International University in Geneva	M,D
The International University of Monaco	M
Iona College	M,O
Jacksonville University	M
Johns Hopkins University	M
Kansas State University	M,O
Kaplan University, Davenport Campus	M
Keiser University	M,D
Kent State University	D
King University	M
Lake Forest Graduate School of Management	M
La Salle University	M,O
Lasell College	M,O
La Sierra University	M,O
Lawrence Technological University	M,O
Lewis University	M
Liberty University	M,D,O
LIM College	M
Lindenwood University	M,O
Long Island University–LIU Post	M
Loyola University Chicago	M
Loyola University New Orleans	M
Lynn University	M
Manhattanville College	M
Marist College	M
Marquette University	M,O
Maryville University of Saint Louis	M,O
McGill University	M,D,O
Melbourne Business School	M,D,O
Michigan State University	M,D
Milwaukee School of Engineering	M
Mississippi State University	D
Molloy College	M,O
Monmouth University	M,O
Monroe College	M
National University College	M
New England College	M
New Jersey City University	M
New Mexico State University	D
New York Institute of Technology	M
New York University	M,D,O
Niagara University	M
Northeastern Illinois University	M
Northwestern University	M,D
Northwest Missouri State University	M
Notre Dame de Namur University	M
Nova Southeastern University	M
Oakland University	M,O
Ohio Christian University	M
Oklahoma Christian University	M
Oklahoma State University	M,D
Old Dominion University	D
Oral Roberts University	M
Ottawa University	M
Pace University	M,D,O
Philadelphia University	M
Polytechnic University of Puerto Rico, Miami Campus	M
Pontifical Catholic University of Puerto Rico	M
Pontificia Universidad Catolica Madre y Maestra	M
Post University	M
Providence College	M
Queen's University at Kingston	M
Regent's University London	M
Regis University	M,O
Roberts Wesleyan College	M
Rollins College	M,D
Roosevelt University	M
Rowan University	O
Rutgers University–Newark	D

Sacred Heart University	M,O
St. Bonaventure University	M
St. Catherine University	M
St. John's University (NY)	M
Saint Joseph's University	M,O
Saint Leo University	M,D,O
Saint Peter's University	M
St. Thomas Aquinas College	M
Saint Xavier University	M,O
Samford University	M
San Diego State University	M
San Francisco State University	M
Seton Hall University	M,O
Slippery Rock University of Pennsylvania	M
Southern Adventist University	M
Southern Methodist University	M
Southern New Hampshire University	M,O
Southwest Minnesota State University	M
State University of New York Polytechnic Institute	M
Stephen F. Austin State University	M
Stevens Institute of Technology	M,O
Stony Brook University, State University of New York	M,O
Strayer University	M
Suffolk University	M
Syracuse University	M
Tarleton State University	M
Temple University	M
Texas A&M University	M,D
Texas A&M University–Commerce	M
Texas Christian University	M
Texas Tech University	M,D
Tiffin University	M
Trident University International	M,D
United States International University–Africa	M
Universidad del Turabo	M
Universidad Iberoamericana	M,D
Universidad Metropolitana	M
Université de Sherbrooke	M
Université Laval	M,O
University at Albany, State University of New York	M
University at Buffalo, the State University of New York	M,D
The University of Akron	M
The University of Alabama	M,D
The University of Alabama at Birmingham	M
The University of Alabama in Huntsville	M,O
University of Alberta	D
The University of Arizona	M,D
University of Baltimore	M
University of Bridgeport	M
The University of British Columbia	D
University of California, Berkeley	D,O
University of California, Los Angeles	M,D
University of Central Missouri	M,D,O
University of Chicago	M,O
University of Cincinnati	M,D
University of Colorado Denver	M
University of Connecticut	M,D
University of Dallas	M,D
University of Dayton	M
University of Denver	M
University of Florida	M,D
University of Hawaii at Manoa	M,D
University of Houston	D
University of Houston–Victoria	M
The University of Iowa	D
The University of Kansas	M,D
University of La Verne	M
University of Lethbridge	M,D
The University of Manchester	M
University of Massachusetts Amherst	M,D
University of Massachusetts Dartmouth	M,O
University of Memphis	M,D
University of Michigan–Flint	M,O
University of Minnesota, Twin Cities Campus	M,D
University of Missouri	M,D
University of Missouri–St. Louis	M,D,O
University of Nebraska at Kearney	M
University of Nebraska–Lincoln	M,D
University of New Brunswick Fredericton	M,D
University of New Haven	M,O
University of New Mexico	M
The University of North Carolina at Chapel Hill	D
The University of North Carolina at Greensboro	M,D
University of North Texas	M,D,O
University of Notre Dame	M
University of Oklahoma	M,D
University of Oregon	D
University of Pennsylvania	M,D
University of Phoenix–Atlanta Campus	M
University of Phoenix–Augusta Campus	M
University of Phoenix–Bay Area Campus	M,D
University of Phoenix–Central Valley Campus	M
University of Phoenix–Colorado Campus	M
University of Phoenix–Colorado Springs Downtown Campus	M

University of Phoenix–Columbus Georgia Campus	M
University of Phoenix–Dallas Campus	M
University of Phoenix–Hawaii Campus	M
University of Phoenix–Houston Campus	M
University of Phoenix–Jersey City Campus	M
University of Phoenix–Las Vegas Campus	M
University of Phoenix–New Mexico Campus	M
University of Phoenix–North Florida Campus	M
University of Phoenix–Online Campus	M,O
University of Phoenix–Phoenix Campus	M,O
University of Phoenix–Sacramento Valley Campus	M
University of Phoenix–San Antonio Campus	M
University of Phoenix–San Diego Campus	M
University of Phoenix–Southern Arizona Campus	M
University of Phoenix–Southern California Campus	M
University of Phoenix–South Florida Campus	M
University of Phoenix–Utah Campus	M
University of Pittsburgh	M,D
University of Portland	M
University of Puerto Rico, Río Piedras Campus	M,D
University of Rhode Island	M,D
University of Rochester	M,D
University of Saint Mary	M
University of San Francisco	M
University of Saskatchewan	M
The University of Scranton	M
University of Sioux Falls	M
University of South Africa	M,D
University of South Florida	M,D
The University of Tampa	M
The University of Tennessee	M,D
The University of Texas at Arlington	M
The University of Texas at Austin	M,D
The University of Texas at Dallas	M
The University of Texas at San Antonio	M
The University of Texas at Tyler	M
The University of Texas Rio Grande Valley	M,D
University of the Cumberlands	M,D,O
University of the Sacred Heart	M
The University of Toledo	M
University of Utah	M,D
University of Virginia	M
The University of Western Ontario	M,D
University of Wisconsin–Madison	D
University of Wisconsin–Whitewater	M
Ursuline College	M
Vancouver Island University	M
Vanderbilt University	M
Villanova University	M
Virginia International University	M,O
Wagner College	M
Walden University	M,D,O
Walsh College of Accountancy and Business Administration	M
Walsh University	M
Webster University	M,D,O
West Virginia University	M,O
Wilfrid Laurier University	M,D
William Woods University	M,D,O
Wilmington University	M,D
Wingate University	M
Worcester Polytechnic Institute	M,D,O
Xavier University	M
Yale University	D
Yeshiva University	M
York College of Pennsylvania	M
Youngstown State University	M

MARKETING RESEARCH

Baldwin Wallace University	M
Hofstra University	M,O
Instituto Tecnológico y de Estudios Superiores de Monterrey, Campus Irapuato	M,D
Marquette University	M
Michigan State University	M,D
Pacific Lutheran University	M
Saint Leo University	M,D,O
Southern Illinois University Edwardsville	M
Towson University	M
Universidad Autonoma de Guadalajara	M,D
Universidad de las Americas, A.C.	M
University of Colorado Denver	M
University of Rochester	M
The University of Texas at Arlington	M
University of Wisconsin–Madison	M

MARRIAGE AND FAMILY THERAPY

Abilene Christian University	M
Adler Graduate School	M
Adler University	M,D,O
Alliant International University–Irvine	M,D

M—masters degree; D—doctorate; O—other advanced degree; *—Close-Up and/or Display

Institution	Degrees
Alliant International University–Los Angeles	M,D
Alliant International University–Sacramento	M,D
Alliant International University–San Diego	M,D
Amridge University	M,D
Antioch University New England	M,D,O
Appalachian State University	M
Arcadia University	M
Argosy University, Atlanta	M,D,O
Argosy University, Chicago	D
Argosy University, Denver	M,D
Argosy University, Hawai'i	M
Argosy University, Inland Empire	M,D
Argosy University, Los Angeles	M,D
Argosy University, Northern Virginia	M,D
Argosy University, Orange County	M,D
Argosy University, Salt Lake City	M,D
Argosy University, San Diego	M,D
Argosy University, Sarasota	M,D
Argosy University, Tampa	M,D
Argosy University, Twin Cities	M,D,O
Arizona State University at the Tempe campus	M,D
Azusa Pacific University	D
Barry University	M,O
Bayamón Central University	M,O
Bethel Seminary	M,D,O
Brandman University	M
Briercrest Seminary	M
Brigham Young University	M,D
California Lutheran University	M
California State University, Chico	M
California State University, Dominguez Hills	M
California State University, East Bay	M
California State University, Fresno	M
California State University, Long Beach	M,D
California State University, Northridge	M
Cambridge College	M,O
Campbellsville University	M
Capella University	M
Carlos Albizu University, Miami Campus	M,D
Central Connecticut State University	M,O
Chaminade University of Honolulu	M
Chapman University	M
Chatham University	M,D
Chestnut Hill College	M,D,O
The Chicago School of Professional Psychology at Downtown Los Angeles	M,D
The Chicago School of Professional Psychology at Irvine	M,D
Christian Theological Seminary	M,D
The College of New Jersey	O
The College of New Rochelle	M
The College of William and Mary	M,D
Colorado State University	M,D
Converse College	M
Denver Seminary	M,D,O
Dominican University of California	M
Drexel University	M,D
Duquesne University	M,D,O
East Carolina University	M,D
Eastern Nazarene College	M
Eastern University	D
East Tennessee State University	M
Edgewood College	M
Evangelical Seminary	M
Fairfield University	M,O
Florida State University	M,D
Fresno Pacific University	M
Friends University	M
Fuller Theological Seminary	M,D,O
Geneva College	M
George Fox University	M,O
Gonzaga University	M
Harding University	M
Hardin-Simmons University	M
Hofstra University	M,O
Hope International University	M
Idaho State University	M,D,O
Indiana University–Purdue University Fort Wayne	M,O
Indiana University South Bend	M
Indiana Wesleyan University	M
Instituto Tecnologico de Santo Domingo	M,O
Iona College	M
John Brown University	M,O
Kansas State University	M
Kean University	M,O
Kutztown University of Pennsylvania	M
Lancaster Bible College	M,D
La Salle University	M
Lee University	M
LeTourneau University	M
Lewis & Clark College	M
Liberty University	M,D,O
Lipscomb University	M,O
Loma Linda University	M,D,O
Long Island University–Hudson	M,O
Long Island University–LIU Brooklyn	M
Loyola Marymount University	M
Maryville University of Saint Louis	M
Medaille College	M
Mercy College	M,O
Messiah College	M
Michigan State University	M,D
Mid-America Christian University	M
MidAmerica Nazarene University	M
Mississippi College	M,O
Mount Mercy University	M
Northcentral University	M,D,O
North Dakota State University	D
Northeastern Illinois University	M
Northern Kentucky University	M,O
Northwestern University	M
Northwest Nazarene University	M
Notre Dame de Namur University	M
Nova Southeastern University	M,D,O
Nyack College	M
Oklahoma Baptist University	M
Oklahoma State University	M,D
Oral Roberts University	M,D
Ottawa University	M
Our Lady of the Lake University	M,D
Pacific Lutheran University	M
Pacific Oaks College	M
Palm Beach Atlantic University	M
Palo Alto University	M
Pepperdine University	M,D
Phillips Graduate University	M
Pontifical John Paul II Institute for Studies on Marriage and Family	M,D,O
Purdue University	M,D
Purdue University Northwest	M
Reformed Theological Seminary–Jackson Campus	M,D,O
Regent University	M,D,O
Regis University	M,D,O
Richmont Graduate University	M
St. Cloud State University	M
Saint Louis University	M,D,O
Saint Mary's College of California	M,O
St. Mary's University (United States)	M,D
Saint Mary's University of Minnesota	M
Saint Paul University	M
St. Thomas University	M,O
San Francisco State University	M,O
Saybrook University	M,D
Seattle Pacific University	M,O
Seattle University	M
Seton Hall University	M
Seton Hill University	M
Shippensburg University of Pennsylvania	M,D,O
Sioux Falls Seminary	M
Southeastern University (FL)	M
Southern California Seminary	M,D
Southern Nazarene University	M
Stetson University	M
Syracuse University	M,D
Texas A&M University–Central Texas	M,O
Texas State University	M
Texas Tech University	M,D
Texas Wesleyan University	M,D
Texas Woman's University	M,D
Thomas Jefferson University	M
Trevecca Nazarene University	M
Universidad de las Americas, A.C.	M
The University of Akron	M
The University of Alabama	M
University of Central Florida	M,O
University of Central Oklahoma	M
University of Colorado Denver	M
University of Denver	M,D,O
University of Florida	M,D,O
University of Guelph	M,D
University of Holy Cross	M
University of Houston–Clear Lake	M
The University of Iowa	M,D
University of La Verne	M
University of Louisiana at Monroe	M,D
University of Louisville	M,D,O
University of Mary Hardin-Baylor	M
University of Maryland, College Park	M,D
University of Massachusetts Boston	M
University of Miami	M,O
University of Minnesota, Twin Cities Campus	M,D
University of Missouri–St. Louis	M,D
University of Mobile	M
University of Nebraska–Lincoln	M,D
University of Nevada, Las Vegas	M
University of New Hampshire	M,O
The University of North Carolina at Greensboro	M,D,O
University of Phoenix–Bay Area Campus	M
University of Phoenix–Central Valley Campus	M
University of Phoenix–Las Vegas Campus	M
University of Phoenix–Phoenix Campus	M
University of Phoenix–Southern California Campus	M
University of Rhode Island	M
University of Rochester	M
University of Saint Joseph	M
University of San Diego	M
University of San Francisco	M
University of Southern California	M
University of Southern Mississippi	M
University of South Florida	M,D,O
The University of Texas at Tyler	M
The University of West Alabama	M
The University of Winnipeg	M,O
University of Wisconsin–Stout	M
Utah State University	M,D
Valdosta State University	M,O
Walden University	M,D
Western Kentucky University	M
Western Seminary–Sacramento Campus	M
Western Seminary–San Jose Campus	M,D
Wheaton College	M,D

MASS COMMUNICATION

Institution	Degrees
American University	M,D,O
The American University in Cairo	M,O
Arizona State University at the Tempe campus	M,D
Arkansas State University	M
Boston University	M
Brigham Young University	M
Bryant University	M,O
California State University, Fullerton	M
California State University, Northridge	M
Drexel University	M
Florida International University	M
The George Washington University	M,O
Georgia State University	M,D
Grambling State University	M
Howard University	M,D
Iona College	M,O
Iowa State University of Science and Technology	M
Kansas State University	M
Kent State University	M
Louisiana State University and Agricultural & Mechanical College	M,D
Lynn University	M,O
Marquette University	M,O
Middle Tennessee State University	M
Murray State University	M
North Dakota State University	M,D
Oklahoma State University	M
Penn State University Park	M,D
Point Park University	M
St. Cloud State University	M
San Jose State University	M,O
Southern Illinois University Carbondale	M,D
Southern Illinois University Edwardsville	M,O
Southern University and Agricultural and Mechanical College	M
Stephen F. Austin State University	M
Syracuse University	M,D
Texas Christian University	M
Texas State University	M
Texas Tech University	M,D
Université Laval	M,D
The University of Alabama	D
University of Arkansas at Little Rock	M
University of Colorado Boulder	M,D
University of Denver	M
University of Florida	M,D
University of Georgia	M,D
University of Houston	M
The University of Iowa	M,D
University of Louisiana at Lafayette	M
University of Michigan	D
University of Minnesota, Twin Cities Campus	M,D
University of Nebraska–Lincoln	M
The University of North Carolina at Chapel Hill	M,D,O
University of Oklahoma	M,D
University of Puerto Rico, Río Piedras Campus	M
University of Southern Mississippi	M,D
University of South Florida	M,O
University of Wisconsin–Madison	M,D
University of Wisconsin–Milwaukee	M,D,O
University of Wisconsin–Superior	M
University of Wisconsin–Whitewater	M
Virginia Commonwealth University	M

MATERIALS ENGINEERING

Institution	Degrees
Alabama Agricultural and Mechanical University	M
Arizona State University at the Tempe campus	M,D
Auburn University	M,D
Binghamton University, State University of New York	M,D
Boise State University	M,D
Boston University	M
California State University, Northridge	M
Carleton University	M,D
Carnegie Mellon University	M,D
Case Western Reserve University	M,D
The Catholic University of America	M
Clarkson University	D
Clemson University	M,D
The College of William and Mary	M,D
Colorado School of Mines	M,D
Columbia University	M,D
Cornell University	M,D
Dalhousie University	M,D
Dartmouth College	M,D
Drexel University	M,D
Duke University	M
Florida International University	M,D
Florida State University	M,D
Georgia Institute of Technology	M,D
Illinois Institute of Technology	M,D
Instituto Tecnológico y de Estudios Superiores de Monterrey, Campus Estado de México	M,D
Iowa State University of Science and Technology	M,D
Johns Hopkins University	M,D
Lehigh University	M,D
Massachusetts Institute of Technology	M,D,O
McGill University	M,D,O
McMaster University	M,D
Michigan State University	M,D
Michigan Technological University	M
New Jersey Institute of Technology	M,D,O
New Mexico Institute of Mining and Technology	M
North Carolina State University	M,D
Northwestern University	M,D,O
The Ohio State University	M,D
Oklahoma State University	M,D
Penn State University Park	M,D
Purdue University	M,D
Rensselaer Polytechnic Institute	M,D
Rochester Institute of Technology	M
Rutgers University–New Brunswick	M,D
South Dakota School of Mines and Technology	M,D
Southern Methodist University	M,D
Stanford University	M,D,O
Stevens Institute of Technology	M,D
Stony Brook University, State University of New York	M,D
Texas A&M University	M,D
Texas State University	D
Tuskegee University	D
The University of Alabama	M,D
The University of Alabama at Birmingham	M,D
University of Alberta	M,D
The University of Arizona	M,D
The University of British Columbia	M,D
University of California, Berkeley	M,D
University of California, Davis	M,D
University of California, Irvine	M,D
University of California, Los Angeles	M,D
University of California, Riverside	M
University of California, Santa Barbara	M,D
University of Central Florida	M,D
University of Cincinnati	M,D
University of Connecticut	M
University of Dayton	M,D
University of Delaware	M,D
University of Denver	M,D
University of Florida	M,D
University of Illinois at Chicago	M,D
University of Illinois at Urbana–Champaign	M,D
The University of Iowa	M,D
University of Kentucky	M,D
University of Maryland, College Park	M,D
University of Michigan	M,D
University of Minnesota, Twin Cities Campus	M,D
University of Nebraska–Lincoln	M,D
University of Nevada, Las Vegas	M,D,O
University of Nevada, Reno	M,D
University of New Hampshire	M,D
University of Pennsylvania	M,D
University of Puerto Rico, Mayagüez Campus	M,D
University of Southern California	M,D,O
University of South Florida	M,D,O
The University of Tennessee	M,D
The University of Texas at Arlington	M,D
The University of Texas at Austin	M,D
The University of Texas at Dallas	M,D
The University of Texas at El Paso	M,D
The University of Texas at San Antonio	M,D
University of Toronto	M,D
University of Utah	M,D
University of Washington	M,D
The University of Western Ontario	M,D
University of Windsor	M,D
University of Wisconsin–Madison	M,D
University of Wisconsin–Milwaukee	M,D
Virginia Polytechnic Institute and State University	M,D
Washington State University	M,D
Worcester Polytechnic Institute	M,D
Wright State University	M

MATERIALS SCIENCES

Institution	Degrees
Air Force Institute of Technology	M,D
Alabama Agricultural and Mechanical University	M,D
Alfred University	M,D
Arizona State University at the Tempe campus	M,D
Binghamton University, State University of New York	M,D
Boston University	M,D
Brown University	M,D
California Institute of Technology	M,D
Carnegie Mellon University	M,D
Case Western Reserve University	M,D
The Catholic University of America	M
Central Michigan University	D
Clarkson University	D
Clemson University	M,D
The College of William and Mary	M,D
Colorado School of Mines	M,D
Columbia University	M,D
Cornell University	M,D
Dartmouth College	M,D
Duke University	M,D
Florida International University	M,D
Florida State University	M,D
Georgetown University	D
The George Washington University	M,D
Harvard University	M,D
Illinois Institute of Technology	M,D
Indiana University Bloomington	M,D

Instituto Tecnológico y de Estudios Superiores de Monterrey, Campus Estado de México	M,D
Iowa State University of Science and Technology	M,D
Jackson State University	M,D
Johns Hopkins University	M,D
Lehigh University	M,D
Massachusetts Institute of Technology	M,D,O
McMaster University	M,D
Michigan State University	M,D
Missouri State University	M
Montana Tech of The University of Montana	D
New Jersey Institute of Technology	M,D,O
Norfolk State University	M
North Carolina State University	M,D
North Dakota State University	M,D
Northwestern University	M,D,O
The Ohio State University	M,D
Oklahoma State University	M,D
Oregon State University	M,D
Penn State University Park	M,D
Princeton University	D
Rensselaer Polytechnic Institute	M,D
Rice University	M,D
Rochester Institute of Technology	M
Royal Military College of Canada	M,D
Rutgers University–New Brunswick	M,D
School of the Art Institute of Chicago	M
South Dakota School of Mines and Technology	M,D
Southern Methodist University	M,D
Stanford University	M,D,O
State University of New York College of Environmental Science and Forestry	M,D,O
Stevens Institute of Technology	M,D
Stony Brook University, State University of New York	M,D
Texas A&M University	M,D
Texas State University	M,D
Trent University	M
Université du Québec, Institut National de la Recherche Scientifique	M,D
The University of Alabama	D
The University of Alabama in Huntsville	M,D
The University of Arizona	M,D
University of Calgary	M,D
University of California, Berkeley	M,D
University of California, Davis	M,D
University of California, Irvine	M,D
University of California, Los Angeles	M,D
University of California, Riverside	M
University of California, San Diego	M,D
University of California, Santa Barbara	M,D
University of Central Florida	M,D
University of Cincinnati	M,D
University of Connecticut	M,D
University of Delaware	M,D
University of Denver	M,D
University of Florida	M,D
University of Idaho	M,D
University of Illinois at Urbana–Champaign	M,D
University of Kentucky	M,D
The University of Manchester	M,D
University of Maryland, College Park	M,D
University of Michigan	M,D
University of Minnesota, Twin Cities Campus	M,D
University of Mississippi Medical Center	M,D
University of Nebraska–Lincoln	M,D
University of New Brunswick Fredericton	M,D
University of New Hampshire	M,D
University of Pennsylvania	M,D
University of Pittsburgh	M,D
University of Puerto Rico, Mayagüez Campus	M,D
University of Rochester	M,D
University of Southern California	M,D,O
University of South Florida	O
The University of Tennessee	M,D
The University of Texas at Arlington	M,D
The University of Texas at Austin	M,D
The University of Texas at Dallas	M,D
The University of Texas at El Paso	M,D
The University of Toledo	M,D
University of Toronto	M,D
University of Utah	M,D
University of Vermont	M,D
University of Virginia	M,D
University of Washington	M,D
Vanderbilt University	M,D
Virginia Polytechnic Institute and State University	M,D
Washington State University	M,D
Washington University in St. Louis	M,D
Wayne State University	M,D,O
Worcester Polytechnic Institute	M,D
Wright State University	M

MATERNAL AND CHILD/NEONATAL NURSING

Baylor University	M,D
Boston College	M,D
Case Western Reserve University	M

Creighton University	M,D,O
Duke University	M,D,O
Hardin-Simmons University	M
Lehman College of the City University of New York	M
Louisiana State University Health Sciences Center	M,D,O
Medical University of South Carolina	M,D
Northeastern University	M,D,O
Old Dominion University	M,D
Point Loma Nazarene University	M,O
Regis University	M,D,O
Rush University	D,O
St. Catherine University	M,D
Saint Francis Medical Center College of Nursing	M,D,O
Stony Brook University, State University of New York	M,D
University of Alberta	D
University of Cincinnati	M,D
University of Delaware	M,O
University of Illinois at Chicago	M,O
University of Indianapolis	M,D
University of Louisville	M,D
University of Maryland, Baltimore	M
University of Missouri–Kansas City	M,D
University of Pennsylvania	M
University of Pittsburgh	M,D
University of Puerto Rico, Medical Sciences Campus	M
University of Rochester	M,D
University of South Africa	M,D
University of Southern Mississippi	M,D,O
The University of Texas at Austin	M,D
Vanderbilt University	M,D,O
Wright State University	M

MATERNAL AND CHILD HEALTH

Bank Street College of Education	M
Columbia University	M,D
East Carolina University	M,D
Instituto Tecnologico de Santo Domingo	M,O
Oakland University	D,O
Troy University	M,D
The University of Alabama at Birmingham	M,D
University of California, Davis	M
University of Maryland, College Park	M,D
University of Minnesota, Twin Cities Campus	M
The University of North Carolina at Chapel Hill	M,D
University of Puerto Rico, Medical Sciences Campus	M
University of South Florida	O
University of Washington	M,D

MATHEMATICAL AND COMPUTATIONAL FINANCE

Boston University	M,D
Carnegie Mellon University	M,D
DePaul University	M,D
Florida State University	M,D
The George Washington University	M,D,O
Georgia Institute of Technology	M
Illinois Institute of Technology	M,D
Johns Hopkins University	M,D,O
New Jersey Institute of Technology	M,D,O
New York University	M,D,O
North Carolina State University	M
Oregon State University	M,D
Rice University	M,D
Rochester Institute of Technology	M
Université de Montréal	M,D,O
University of Alberta	M,D,O
University of California, Santa Barbara	M,D
University of Chicago	M
University of Connecticut	M
University of Dayton	M
The University of Manchester	M,D
University of Miami	M,D
The University of North Carolina at Charlotte	M,O
University of Notre Dame	M,D
University of Southern California	M,D
University of Toronto	M

MATHEMATICAL PHYSICS

Indiana University Bloomington	M,D
New Mexico Institute of Mining and Technology	M,D
University of Alberta	M,D,O
University of Colorado Boulder	M,D

MATHEMATICS

Alabama State University	M
American University	M,O
American University of Beirut	M
American University of Sharjah	M
Appalachian State University	M
Arizona State University at the Tempe campus	M,D,O
Arkansas State University	M
Auburn University	M,D
Augustana University	M
Aurora University	M
Ball State University	M
Baylor University	M,D
Bemidji State University	M
Binghamton University, State University of New York	M,D
Boise State University	M
Boston College	D
Boston University	M,D
Bowling Green State University	M,D
Brandeis University	M,D
Brigham Young University	M,D

Brock University	M
Brooklyn College of the City University of New York	M
Brown University	D
Bryn Mawr College	M,D
Bucknell University	M
California Institute of Technology	D
California Polytechnic State University, San Luis Obispo	M
California State Polytechnic University, Pomona	M
California State University Channel Islands	M
California State University, East Bay	M
California State University, Fresno	M
California State University, Fullerton	M
California State University, Long Beach	M
California State University, Los Angeles	M
California State University, Northridge	M
California State University, Sacramento	M
California State University, San Bernardino	M
California State University, San Marcos	M
Carleton University	M,D
Carnegie Mellon University	M,D
Case Western Reserve University	M,D
Central Connecticut State University	M,O
Central European University	M,D
Central Michigan University	M,D
Central Washington University	M
Chicago State University	M
City College of the City University of New York	M
Claremont Graduate University	M
Clark Atlanta University	M
Clarkson University	M,D
Clemson University	M,D
Cleveland State University	M
The College at Brockport, State University of New York	M,O
College of Charleston	M
The College of William and Mary	M
Colorado State University	M,D
Columbia University	M,D
Columbus State University	M,O
Concordia University (Canada)	M,D
Cornell University	D
Dalhousie University	M,D
Dartmouth College	M,D
Delaware State University	M
DePaul University	M,D
Drew University	M,D,O
Duke University	D
Duquesne University	M
East Carolina University	M,O
Eastern Illinois University	M
Eastern Kentucky University	M
Eastern Michigan University	M
East Tennessee State University	M,O
Elizabeth City State University	M
Emory University	M,D
Emporia State University	M
Fairfield University	M
Fairleigh Dickinson University, Metropolitan Campus	M
Fayetteville State University	M
Florida Atlantic University	M,D
Florida International University	M
Florida State University	M,D
George Mason University	M,D
Georgetown University	M
The George Washington University	M,D,O
Georgia Institute of Technology	M,D
Georgia Southern University	M
Georgia State University	M,D
The Graduate Center, City University of New York	D
Hardin-Simmons University	M
Harvard University	D
Howard University	M,D
Hunter College of the City University of New York	M
Idaho State University	M,D
Illinois State University	M
Indiana State University	M
Indiana University Bloomington	M,D
Indiana University of Pennsylvania	M
Indiana University–Purdue University Fort Wayne	M,O
Indiana University–Purdue University Indianapolis	M,D
Instituto Tecnologico de Santo Domingo	M,D,O
Iowa State University of Science and Technology	M,D
Jackson State University	M
Jacksonville State University	M
Jacksonville University	M
John Carroll University	M
Johns Hopkins University	D
Kansas State University	M,D,O
Kent State University	M,D
Kutztown University of Pennsylvania	M
Lakehead University	M
Lamar University	M
Lee University	M,O
Lehigh University	M,D
Lehman College of the City University of New York	M
Long Island University–LIU Post	M,O

Louisiana State University and Agricultural & Mechanical College	M,D
Louisiana Tech University	M,D
Loyola University Chicago	M
Manhattan College	M,O
Marquette University	M,D
Marshall University	M
Massachusetts Institute of Technology	D
McGill University	M,D
McMaster University	M,D
McNeese State University	M
Memorial University of Newfoundland	M,D
Miami University	M,D
Michigan State University	M,D
Michigan Technological University	M,D
Middle Tennessee State University	M
Minnesota State University Mankato	M
Mississippi College	M
Mississippi State University	M,D
Missouri State University	M
Missouri University of Science and Technology	M,D
Molloy College	M,O
Montana State University	M,D
Montclair State University	M
Morgan State University	M
Murray State University	M
New Jersey Institute of Technology	M,D,O
New Mexico Institute of Mining and Technology	M,D
New Mexico State University	M,D
New York Institute of Technology	M
New York University	M,D
North Carolina Agricultural and Technical State University	M
North Carolina Central University	M
North Carolina State University	M,D
North Dakota State University	M,D
Northeastern Illinois University	M
Northeastern University	M,D
Northern Arizona University	M,O
Northern Illinois University	M,D
Northwestern University	D
Northwest Missouri State University	M,O
Oakland University	M
The Ohio State University	M,D
Ohio University	M,D
Oklahoma State University	M,D
Old Dominion University	M,D
Oregon State University	M,D
Pace University	M,O
Penn State University Park	M,D
Pepperdine University	M,D
Pittsburg State University	M
Portland State University	M,D,O
Princeton University	D
Purdue University	M,D
Purdue University Northwest	M
Queens College of the City University of New York	M
Queen's University at Kingston	M,D
Rensselaer Polytechnic Institute	M,D
Rhode Island College	M,O
Rice University	D
Rivier University	M
Rochester Institute of Technology	M,D,O
Roosevelt University	M
Rowan University	M
Royal Military College of Canada	M
Rutgers University–Camden	M
Rutgers University–Newark	D
Rutgers University–New Brunswick	M,D
St. Cloud State University	M
St. John's University (NY)	M
Saint Joseph's University	M,O
Saint Louis University	M
Salem State University	M
Sam Houston State University	M
San Diego State University	M,D
San Francisco State University	M
San Jose State University	M,D,O
Simon Fraser University	M,D
Smith College	O
South Carolina State University	M
South Dakota State University	M,D
Southeast Missouri State University	M
Southern Connecticut State University	M
Southern Illinois University Carbondale	M,D
Southern Illinois University Edwardsville	M
Southern Methodist University	M,D
Southern University and Agricultural and Mechanical College	M
Stanford University	M,D
State University of New York College at Cortland	M
State University of New York College at Potsdam	M
Stephen F. Austin State University	M
Stevens Institute of Technology	M,D
Stony Brook University, State University of New York	M,D
Syracuse University	M,D
Tarleton State University	M
Temple University	M,D
Tennessee State University	M,D
Tennessee Technological University	M
Texas A&M International University	M
Texas A&M University	M,D
Texas A&M University–Central Texas	M,O
Texas A&M University–Commerce	M,O

M—masters degree; D—doctorate; O—other advanced degree; *—Close-Up and/or Display

Institution	Degrees
Texas A&M University–Corpus Christi	M
Texas A&M University–Kingsville	M
Texas Christian University	M,D
Texas Southern University	M
Texas State University	M,D
Texas Tech University	M,D
Texas Woman's University	M
Tufts University	M,D
Tulane University	M,D
Université de Moncton	M
Université de Montréal	M,D,O
Université de Sherbrooke	M,D
Université du Québec à Montréal	M,D
Université du Québec à Trois-Rivières	M
Université Laval	M,D
University at Albany, State University of New York	M,D
University at Buffalo, the State University of New York	M,D
The University of Akron	M
The University of Alabama	M,D
The University of Alabama at Birmingham	M
The University of Alabama in Huntsville	M,D
University of Alaska Fairbanks	M,D,O
University of Alberta	M,D,O
The University of Arizona	M,D
University of Arkansas	M,D
University of Arkansas at Little Rock	M,O
The University of British Columbia	M,D
University of Calgary	M,D
University of California, Berkeley	M,D
University of California, Davis	M,D
University of California, Irvine	M,D
University of California, Los Angeles	M,D
University of California, Riverside	M,D
University of California, San Diego	M,D
University of California, Santa Barbara	M,D
University of California, Santa Cruz	M,D
University of Central Arkansas	M
University of Central Florida	M,D,O
University of Central Missouri	M,D,O
University of Central Oklahoma	M
University of Chicago	D
University of Cincinnati	M,D
University of Colorado Boulder	M,D
University of Colorado Colorado Springs	D
University of Colorado Denver	M,D
University of Delaware	M,D
University of Denver	M,D
University of Florida	M,D
University of Georgia	M,D
University of Guelph	M,D
University of Hawaii at Manoa	M,D
University of Houston	M,D
University of Houston–Clear Lake	M
University of Idaho	M,D
University of Illinois at Chicago	M,D
University of Illinois at Urbana–Champaign	M,D
The University of Iowa	M,D
The University of Kansas	M,D,O
University of Kentucky	M,D
University of Lethbridge	M,D
University of Louisiana at Lafayette	M,D
University of Louisville	M,D
University of Maine	M
The University of Manchester	M,D
University of Manitoba	M,D
University of Maryland, College Park	M,D
University of Massachusetts Amherst	M,D
University of Massachusetts Lowell	D
University of Memphis	M,D,O
University of Miami	M,D
University of Michigan	M,D
University of Michigan–Flint	M
University of Minnesota, Twin Cities Campus	M,D,O
University of Mississippi	M,D
University of Missouri	M,D
University of Missouri–Kansas City	M,D
University of Missouri–St. Louis	M,D
University of Montana	M,D
University of Nebraska at Omaha	M
University of Nebraska–Lincoln	M,D
University of Nevada, Las Vegas	M,D
University of Nevada, Reno	M
University of New Brunswick Fredericton	M,D
University of New Mexico	M,D
University of New Orleans	M
The University of North Carolina at Chapel Hill	M,D
The University of North Carolina at Charlotte	M,D,O
The University of North Carolina at Greensboro	M,D
The University of North Carolina at Wilmington	M
University of North Dakota	M
University of Northern British Columbia	M,D,O
University of Northern Colorado	M,D
University of Northern Iowa	M
University of North Florida	M
University of North Texas	M,D,O
University of Notre Dame	M,D
University of Oklahoma	M,D
University of Oregon	M,D
University of Ottawa	M,D
University of Pennsylvania	M,D
University of Pittsburgh	M,D
University of Puerto Rico, Mayagüez Campus	M
University of Puerto Rico, Río Piedras Campus	M,D
University of Regina	M,D
University of Rhode Island	M,D
University of Rochester	D
University of San Diego	M
University of Saskatchewan	M,D
University of South Alabama	M
University of South Carolina	M,D
The University of South Dakota	M
University of Southern California	M,D
University of Southern Mississippi	M,D
University of South Florida	M,D,O
The University of Tennessee	M,D
The University of Tennessee at Chattanooga	M
The University of Texas at Arlington	M,D
The University of Texas at Austin	M,D
The University of Texas at Dallas	M,D
The University of Texas at El Paso	M
The University of Texas at San Antonio	M
The University of Texas at Tyler	M
The University of Texas Rio Grande Valley	M
University of the Incarnate Word	M
University of the Virgin Islands	M
The University of Toledo	M,D
The University of Toronto	M,D
The University of Tulsa	M,D
University of Utah	M,D
University of Vermont	M
University of Victoria	M,D
University of Virginia	M,D
University of Washington	M,D
University of Waterloo	M,D
The University of Western Ontario	M,D
University of West Florida	M
University of West Georgia	M,O
University of Windsor	M,D
University of Wisconsin–Madison	D
University of Wisconsin–Milwaukee	M,D
University of Wyoming	M,D
Utah State University	M,D
Vanderbilt University	M,D
Villanova University	M
Virginia Commonwealth University	M
Virginia Polytechnic Institute and State University	M,D
Virginia State University	M
Wake Forest University	M
Washington State University	M,D
Washington University in St. Louis	M,D
Wayne State University	M,D
Wesleyan University	M,D
West Chester University of Pennsylvania	M,O
Western Connecticut State University	M
Western Illinois University	M
Western Kentucky University	M
Western Michigan University	M,D
Western Washington University	M
West Texas A&M University	M
West Virginia University	M,D
Wichita State University	M,D
Wilfrid Laurier University	M
Wilkes University	M
Worcester Polytechnic Institute	M,D,O
Wright State University	M
Yale University	M,D
Yeshiva University	M,D
York University	M,D
Youngstown State University	M

MATHEMATICS EDUCATION

Institution	Degrees
Acadia University	M
Alabama Agricultural and Mechanical University	M,O
Alabama State University	M,O
Appalachian State University	M
Arcadia University	M,D,O
Arizona State University at the Tempe campus	M,D,O
Arkansas State University	M
Asbury University	M
Ball State University	M
Bank Street College of Education	M
Bard College	M
Bemidji State University	M
Binghamton University, State University of New York	M
Bloomsburg University of Pennsylvania	M
Bob Jones University	M,D,O
Boise State University	M
Bowling Green State University	M,D
Bridgewater State University	M
Brigham Young University	M
Brooklyn College of the City University of New York	M
Buffalo State College, State University of New York	M
California State University, Bakersfield	M
California State University, Chico	M
California State University, East Bay	M
California State University, Fresno	M
California State University, Fullerton	M
California State University, Long Beach	M
California State University, Northridge	M
California State University, San Bernardino	M
Cambridge College	M,D,O
Caribbean University	M,D
Central Michigan University	M,D
Chatham University	M
The Citadel, The Military College of South Carolina	M,O
City College of the City University of New York	M,O
Clarion University of Pennsylvania	M
Clark Atlanta University	M
Clayton State University	M
Clemson University	M,O
Cleveland State University	M
The College at Brockport, State University of New York	M
College of Charleston	M
College of Staten Island of the City University of New York	M
The College of William and Mary	M
The Colorado College	M
Columbus State University	M,O
Concordia University (United States)	M,D
Concordia University (Canada)	M,D
Converse College	M
Cornell University	M,D
Delaware State University	M
DePaul University	M,D
Duquesne University	M
East Carolina University	M,O
Eastern Illinois University	M
Eastern Kentucky University	M
Eastern University	M,D,O
Elizabeth City State University	M
Florida Agricultural and Mechanical University	M
Florida Atlantic University	M
Florida Gulf Coast University	M
Florida Institute of Technology	M,D,O
Florida International University	M,D
Florida State University	M,D,O
Framingham State University	M
Fresno Pacific University	M
George Mason University	M
The George Washington University	M
Georgia Southwestern State University	M,O
Georgia State University	M,D,O
Gordon College	M,O
Grambling State University	M,D,O
Harding University	M,O
Harvard University	M,O
High Point University	M
Hofstra University	M,D,O
Hood College	M
Hunter College of the City University of New York	M,D
Idaho State University	M,D
Illinois Institute of Technology	M,D
Illinois State University	M,D
Indiana University Bloomington	M,D,O
Indiana University of Pennsylvania	M
Indiana University–Purdue University Fort Wayne	M,O
Indiana University–Purdue University Indianapolis	M,D
Instituto Tecnológico y de Estudios Superiores de Monterrey, Campus Ciudad Obregón	M
Inter American University of Puerto Rico, Arecibo Campus	M
Inter American University of Puerto Rico, Barranquitas Campus	M
Inter American University of Puerto Rico, Metropolitan Campus	M
Inter American University of Puerto Rico, Ponce Campus	M
Inter American University of Puerto Rico, San Germán Campus	M
Iona College	M
Iowa State University of Science and Technology	M,D
Ithaca College	M
Jackson State University	M
James Madison University	M
Kaplan University, Davenport Campus	M
Kennesaw State University	M
Kent State University	M
Lake Forest College	M
Lebanon Valley College	M,O
Lee University	M,O
Lehman College of the City University of New York	M
Lesley University	M,D,O
Lewis University	M,D,O
Liberty University	M,D,O
Longwood University	M
Loyola Marymount University	M
Manhattanville College	M
Marquette University	M,D
McDaniel College	M,O
Miami University	M,D
Michigan State University	M,D
Middle Tennessee State University	M,D
Millersville University of Pennsylvania	M
Minnesota State University Mankato	M
Minot State University	M
Mississippi College	M,D,O
Missouri State University	M
Missouri University of Science and Technology	M,D
Montana State University	M,D
Montclair State University	M,D,O
Morehead State University	M
Morgan State University	M,D
Mount Holyoke College	M
National Louis University	M,D,O
New Jersey City University	M
New York Institute of Technology	M,O
New York University	M
North Carolina Central University	M
North Carolina State University	M
North Dakota State University	M,D,O
Northeastern Illinois University	M
Northeastern State University	M
Northern Arizona University	M,O
Northwest Missouri State University	M,D,O
The Ohio State University	M,D
Oklahoma State University	M,D
Oregon State University	M
Plymouth State University	M
Portland State University	M
Providence College	M
Purdue University	M,D
Purdue University Northwest	M
Queens College of the City University of New York	M,O
Quinnipiac University	M
Radford University	M
Regent University	M
Rhode Island College	M
Rider University	O
Rowan University	M
Rutgers University–Camden	M
Rutgers University–New Brunswick	M,D
St. John Fisher College	M
St. Joseph's College, Long Island Campus	M
Saint Peter's University	M,D,O
Salem State University	M
Salisbury University	M
San Diego State University	M,D
San Francisco State University	M,O
San Jose State University	M,O
Seattle Pacific University	M
Shippensburg University of Pennsylvania	M,O
Simon Fraser University	M,D
Slippery Rock University of Pennsylvania	M
Smith College	M
South Carolina State University	M
Southeastern Oklahoma State University	M
Southern Illinois University Edwardsville	M
Southern University and Agricultural and Mechanical College	D
Southwestern Oklahoma State University	M
Southwest Minnesota State University	M
State University of New York at New Paltz	M
State University of New York at Plattsburgh	M
State University of New York College at Cortland	M
State University of New York College at Old Westbury	M
State University of New York College at Potsdam	M
Stephen F. Austin State University	M
Stevenson University	M
Stony Brook University, State University of New York	M,O
Syracuse University	M,D
Teachers College, Columbia University	M,D
Temple University	M
Tennessee Technological University	M,O
Texas Christian University	M,O
Texas State University	M,D
Texas Woman's University	M
Touro College	M
Towson University	M
Tufts University	M,D
Tusculum College	M
Universidad Autonoma de Guadalajara	M,D
University at Buffalo, the State University of New York	M,D,O
The University of Akron	M
The University of Alabama in Huntsville	M,D,O
University of Alaska Southeast	M
The University of Arizona	M
University of Arkansas	M
University of Arkansas at Pine Bluff	M
The University of British Columbia	M,D
University of California, Berkeley	M,D
University of California, San Diego	D
University of Central Arkansas	M
University of Central Florida	M,D,O
University of Cincinnati	M,D
University of Colorado Denver	M,D
University of Connecticut	M,D
University of Dayton	M
University of Detroit Mercy	M,D
University of Florida	M,D,O
University of Georgia	M,D,O
University of Illinois at Chicago	M,D
University of Illinois at Urbana–Champaign	M
University of Indianapolis	M
The University of Iowa	M
University of Louisiana at Monroe	M,D
University of Maryland, Baltimore County	M
University of Massachusetts Dartmouth	M,D,O
University of Memphis	M
University of Miami	D
University of Minnesota, Twin Cities Campus	M,D,O
University of Missouri	M,D,O

University of Montana	M,D
University of Nebraska at Kearney	M
University of Nevada, Reno	M
University of New Hampshire	M,D,O
The University of North Carolina at Chapel Hill	M
The University of North Carolina at Greensboro	M,D,O
The University of North Carolina at Pembroke	M
University of Northern Colorado	M,D
University of Northern Iowa	M
University of North Georgia	M,O
University of Oklahoma	M,D
University of Phoenix–North Florida Campus	M
University of Phoenix–Online Campus	M,O
University of Phoenix–South Florida Campus	M
University of Phoenix–Washington D.C. Campus	M,D,O
University of Pittsburgh	M,D
University of Puerto Rico, Mayagüez Campus	M
University of Puerto Rico, Río Piedras Campus	M,D
University of St. Francis (IL)	M,D,O
University of South Africa	M,D
University of South Carolina	M,D
University of Southern Indiana	M
University of Southern Mississippi	M,D
University of South Florida, St. Petersburg	M
The University of Tennessee	M,D,O
The University of Tennessee at Chattanooga	M
The University of Texas at Arlington	M,D
The University of Texas at Dallas	M,D
The University of Texas at El Paso	M
The University of Texas at San Antonio	M
University of the District of Columbia	M
University of the Incarnate Word	M
University of the Sacred Heart	M,O
University of the Virgin Islands	M
The University of Toledo	M,D,O
The University of Tulsa	M
University of Utah	M,D
University of Vermont	M
University of Victoria	M,D
University of Virginia	M,D,O
University of Washington	M,D
University of Washington, Tacoma	M
The University of West Alabama	M
University of Wisconsin–Madison	M,D
University of Wisconsin–Milwaukee	M,D,O
University of Wisconsin–Oshkosh	M
University of Wisconsin–River Falls	M
University of Wyoming	M,D
Utah Valley University	M
Virginia Polytechnic Institute and State University	M,D
Virginia State University	M
Wagner College	M
Walden University	M,D,O
Washington State University	M,D
Wayne State College	M
Wayne State University	M,D,O
Webster University	M,O
West Chester University of Pennsylvania	M,O
Western Governors University	M,O
Western Michigan University	M,D
Western New England University	M
Western Oregon University	M
Westfield State University	M
West Virginia University	M,D
Widener University	M,D
William Jessup University	M
Wright State University	D
Youngstown State University	M

MECHANICAL ENGINEERING

Alfred University	M,D
The American University in Cairo	M,D,O
American University of Beirut	M,D
American University of Sharjah	M
Arizona State University at the Tempe campus	M,D
Auburn University	M,D
Baylor University	M,D
Binghamton University, State University of New York	M,D
Boise State University	M
Boston University	M
Bradley University	M
Brigham Young University	M,D
Brown University	M,D
Bucknell University	M
California Baptist University	M
California Institute of Technology	M,D,O
California Polytechnic State University, San Luis Obispo	M
California State Polytechnic University, Pomona	M
California State University, Fresno	M
California State University, Fullerton	M
California State University, Long Beach	M,D
California State University, Los Angeles	M

California State University, Northridge	M
California State University, Sacramento	M
Carleton University	M,D
Carnegie Mellon University	M,D
Case Western Reserve University	M,D
The Catholic University of America	M,D
The Citadel, The Military College of South Carolina	M,O
City College of the City University of New York	M,D
Clarkson University	M,D
Clemson University	M,D
Cleveland State University	M,D
Colorado School of Mines	M,D
Colorado State University	M,D
Columbia University	M,D
Concordia University (Canada)	M,D,O
Cooper Union for the Advancement of Science and Art	M
Cornell University	M,D
Dalhousie University	M,D
Dartmouth College	M,D
Drexel University	M,D
Duke University	M,D
École Polytechnique de Montréal	M,D,O
Embry-Riddle Aeronautical University–Daytona	M,D
Fairfield University	M,O
Florida Agricultural and Mechanical University	M,D
Florida Atlantic University	M,D
Florida Institute of Technology	M,D
Florida International University	M,D
Florida State University	M,D
Gannon University	M
The George Washington University	M,D,O
Georgia Institute of Technology	M,D
Georgia Southern University	M
The Graduate Center, City University of New York	D
Grand Valley State University	M
Harvard University	M,D
Howard University	M
Idaho State University	M
Illinois Institute of Technology	M,D
Indiana University–Purdue University Fort Wayne	M
Indiana University–Purdue University Indianapolis	M,D
Instituto Tecnológico y de Estudios Superiores de Monterrey, Campus Chihuahua	M,O
Instituto Tecnológico y de Estudios Superiores de Monterrey, Campus Monterrey	M,D
Inter American University of Puerto Rico, Bayamón Campus	M
Iowa State University of Science and Technology	M,D
Johns Hopkins University	M,D,O
Kansas State University	M,D
Kettering University	M
Lamar University	M,D
Lawrence Technological University	M,D
Lehigh University	M,D
Louisiana State University and Agricultural & Mechanical College	M,D
Loyola Marymount University	M
Manhattan College	M
Marquette University	M,D
Massachusetts Institute of Technology	M,D,O
McGill University	M,D
McMaster University	M,D
McNeese State University	M,O
Memorial University of Newfoundland	M,D
Mercer University	M
Merrimack College	M
Miami University	M
Michigan State University	M,D
Michigan Technological University	M,D,O
Mississippi State University	M,D
Missouri University of Science and Technology	M,D
Montana State University	M,D
Naval Postgraduate School	M,D,O
New Jersey Institute of Technology	M,D
New Mexico Institute of Mining and Technology	M
New Mexico State University	M,D
New York University	M,D
North Carolina Agricultural and Technical State University	M,D
North Carolina State University	M,D
North Dakota State University	M,D
Northeastern University	M,D,O
Northern Arizona University	M
Northern Illinois University	M
Northwestern University	M,D
Oakland University	M,D
The Ohio State University	M,D
Ohio University	M
Oklahoma Christian University	M
Oklahoma State University	M,D
Old Dominion University	M,D
Oregon State University	M,D
Penn State University Park	M,D
Pittsburg State University	M
Polytechnic University of Puerto Rico	M
Portland State University	M,D
Princeton University	M,D
Purdue University	M,D,O
Purdue University Northwest	M
Queen's University at Kingston	M,D
Rensselaer at Hartford	M

Rensselaer Polytechnic Institute	M,D
Rice University	M,D
Rochester Institute of Technology	M
Rose-Hulman Institute of Technology	M
Rowan University	M
Royal Military College of Canada	M,D
Rutgers University–New Brunswick	M,D
St. Cloud State University	M
Saint Martin's University	M
San Diego State University	M,D
Santa Clara University	M,D,O
Simon Fraser University	M,D
South Carolina State University	M
South Dakota School of Mines and Technology	M,D
South Dakota State University	M,D
Southern Illinois University Carbondale	M,D
Southern Illinois University Edwardsville	M
Southern Methodist University	M,D
Stanford University	M,D,O
Stevens Institute of Technology	M,D,O
Stony Brook University, State University of New York	M,D
Syracuse University	M,D
Temple University	M,D
Tennessee State University	M,D
Tennessee Technological University	M
Texas A&M University	M,D
Texas A&M University–Kingsville	M
Texas Tech University	M,D
Tufts University	M,D
Tuskegee University	M
Universidad del Turabo	M
Université de Moncton	M
Université de Sherbrooke	M,D
Université Laval	M,D
University at Buffalo, the State University of New York	M,D
The University of Akron	M,D
The University of Alabama	M,D
The University of Alabama at Birmingham	M
The University of Alabama in Huntsville	M,D
University of Alaska Fairbanks	M
University of Alberta	M,D
The University of Arizona	M,D
University of Arkansas	M,D
University of Bridgeport	M
The University of British Columbia	M,D
University of Calgary	M,D
University of California, Berkeley	M,D
University of California, Davis	M,D,O
University of California, Irvine	M,D
University of California, Los Angeles	M,D
University of California, Merced	M,D
University of California, Riverside	M,D
University of California, San Diego	M,D
University of California, Santa Barbara	M,D
University of Central Florida	M,D
University of Central Oklahoma	M
University of Cincinnati	M,D
University of Colorado Boulder	M,D
University of Colorado Colorado Springs	M
University of Colorado Denver	M
University of Connecticut	M,D
University of Dayton	M,D
University of Delaware	M,D
University of Denver	M,D
University of Detroit Mercy	M
University of Florida	M,D
University of Hawaii at Manoa	M,D
University of Houston	M,D
University of Idaho	M
University of Illinois at Chicago	M,D
University of Illinois at Urbana–Champaign	M,D
The University of Iowa	M,D
The University of Kansas	M,D
University of Kentucky	M,D
University of Louisiana at Lafayette	M
University of Louisville	M,D
University of Maine	M,D
The University of Manchester	M,D
University of Manitoba	M,D
University of Maryland, Baltimore County	M,D,O
University of Maryland, College Park	M,D
University of Massachusetts Amherst	M,D
University of Massachusetts Dartmouth	M,D
University of Massachusetts Lowell	M,D
University of Memphis	M,D,O
University of Miami	M,D
University of Michigan	M,D
University of Michigan–Dearborn	M,D
University of Michigan–Flint	M
University of Minnesota, Twin Cities Campus	M,D
University of Missouri	M,D
University of Missouri–Kansas City	M,D,O
University of Nebraska–Lincoln	M,D
University of Nevada, Las Vegas	M,D,O
University of Nevada, Reno	M,D

University of New Brunswick Fredericton	M,D
University of New Hampshire	M,D
University of New Haven	M
University of New Mexico	M,D
University of New Orleans	M
The University of North Carolina at Charlotte	M,D
University of North Dakota	M,D
University of North Florida	M
University of North Texas	M,D,O
University of Notre Dame	M,D
University of Oklahoma	M,D
University of Ottawa	M,D
University of Pennsylvania	M,D
University of Pittsburgh	M,D
University of Portland	M
University of Puerto Rico, Mayagüez Campus	M,D
University of Rochester	M,D
University of St. Thomas (MN)	M,O
University of Saskatchewan	M,D
University of South Alabama	M
University of South Carolina	M,D
University of Southern California	M,D,O
University of South Florida	M,D
The University of Tennessee	M,D
The University of Tennessee at Chattanooga	M
The University of Texas at Arlington	M,D
The University of Texas at Austin	M,D
The University of Texas at Dallas	M,D
The University of Texas at El Paso	M,D
The University of Texas at San Antonio	M
The University of Texas at Tyler	M
The University of Texas Rio Grande Valley	M
The University of Toledo	M,D
University of Toronto	M,D
The University of Tulsa	M,D
University of Utah	M,D
University of Vermont	M,D
University of Victoria	M,D
University of Virginia	M,D
University of Washington	M,D
University of Waterloo	M,D
The University of Western Ontario	M,D
University of Windsor	M,D
University of Wisconsin–Madison	M,D
University of Wisconsin–Milwaukee	M,D
University of Wyoming	M,D
Utah State University	M,D
Vanderbilt University	M,D
Villanova University	M,O
Virginia Commonwealth University	M,D
Virginia Polytechnic Institute and State University	M,D
Washington State University	M,D
Washington University in St. Louis	M,D
Wayne State University	M,D
Western Michigan University	M,D
Western New England University	M
West Virginia University	M,D
Wichita State University	M,D
Widener University	M
Wilkes University	M
Worcester Polytechnic Institute	M,D,O
Wright State University	M
Yale University	M,D
Youngstown State University	M

MECHANICS

Brown University	M,D
California Institute of Technology	M,D
Carnegie Mellon University	M,D
Columbia University	M,D
Cornell University	M,D
Drexel University	M,D
École Polytechnique de Montréal	M,D,O
Georgia Institute of Technology	M
Iowa State University of Science and Technology	M,D
Johns Hopkins University	M,D
Lehigh University	M,D
Louisiana State University and Agricultural & Mechanical College	M,D
McGill University	M,D
Michigan State University	M,D
Michigan Technological University	M,D,O
Missouri University of Science and Technology	M,D
Montana State University	M,D
New Mexico Institute of Mining and Technology	M
Northwestern University	M,D
Ohio University	M,D
Penn State University Park	M,D
Rutgers University–New Brunswick	M,D
San Diego State University	M,D
Southern Illinois University Carbondale	M
Stanford University	M,D,O
The University of Alabama	M,D
University of Calgary	M,D
University of California, Berkeley	M,D
University of California, Merced	M,D
University of California, San Diego	M,D
University of Cincinnati	M,D
University of Colorado Denver	M,D
University of Dayton	M
University of Illinois at Urbana–Champaign	M,D
University of Maryland, College Park	M,D

M—masters degree; D—doctorate; O—other advanced degree; *—Close-Up and/or Display

University of Massachusetts Amherst	M,D
University of Massachusetts Dartmouth	D
University of Minnesota, Twin Cities Campus	M,D
University of Nebraska–Lincoln	M,D
University of New Brunswick Fredericton	M,D
University of Pennsylvania	M,D
University of Southern California	M,D,O
The University of Texas at Austin	M,D
University of Washington	M,D
University of Wisconsin–Madison	M,D
University of Wisconsin–Milwaukee	M,D
Virginia Polytechnic Institute and State University	M,D

MEDIA STUDIES

American University	M,D
American University of Beirut	M,D
Angelo State University	M
Arizona State University at the Tempe campus	M,D
Arkansas State University	M
Bob Jones University	M,D,O
Boston University	M,D
Bowling Green State University	M,D
Brooklyn College of the City University of New York	M
California College of the Arts	M
Carnegie Mellon University	M
Central Michigan University	M
Champlain College	M
City College of the City University of New York	M
Claremont Graduate University	M,D,O
College of Staten Island of the City University of New York	M
Colorado State University	M,D
Concordia University (Canada)	M,D,O
Cornell University	M,D
Dallas Theological Seminary	M,D,O
DePaul University	M
Digital Media Arts College	M
Drexel University	M
Duke University	M
Emerson College	M
Fairleigh Dickinson University, Metropolitan Campus	M
Fielding Graduate University	M,D,O
Florida Atlantic University	M,O
Florida State University	M,D
Fordham University	M
Full Sail University	M
Georgetown University	M,D
Georgia State University	M,D
Governors State University	M
Howard University	M,D
Hunter College of the City University of New York	M
Indiana State University	M
Indiana University Bloomington	M,D
Indiana University of Pennsylvania	D
International University in Geneva	M,D
Johns Hopkins University	M
Kent State University	M
La Salle University	M,O
Lindenwood University	M,O
Lindenwood University–Belleville	M
Long Island University–LIU Brooklyn	M,D,O
Louisiana State University and Agricultural & Mechanical College	M,D
Loyola University Maryland	M
Lynn University	M,O
Massachusetts College of Art and Design	M,O
Massachusetts Institute of Technology	M,D
Metropolitan College of New York	M
Michigan State University	M,D
Missouri Western State University	M
Monmouth University	M,O
New Mexico Highlands University	M
The New School	M,O
New York University	M,D,O
Norfolk State University	M
Northern Kentucky University	M,D
Northwestern University	M,D
Ohio University	M
Pace University	M
Paris College of Art	M
Penn State University Park	M,D
Pepperdine University	M
Point Park University	M
Pratt Institute	M
Queens College of the City University of New York	M
Rhode Island School of Design	M
Robert Morris University Illinois	M
Rochester Institute of Technology	M
Rowan University	O
Sacred Heart University	M
Saginaw Valley State University	M
San Diego State University	M
San Francisco State University	M
San Jose State University	M,O
Savannah College of Art and Design	M
Southern Illinois University Carbondale	M,D
Southern Illinois University Edwardsville	O
Stevens Institute of Technology	M
Syracuse University	M
Temple University	M
Texas Tech University	M,D
Trinity College (United States)	M
University at Buffalo, the State University of New York	M,D,O

University of Bridgeport	M
University of California, Los Angeles	M
University of California, Santa Barbara	M,D
University of Chicago	M,D
University of Colorado Boulder	M,D
University of Denver	M
University of Illinois at Urbana–Champaign	M,D
The University of Iowa	M,D
The University of Kansas	M,D
University of Lethbridge	M,D
University of Maryland, College Park	M,D
University of Michigan	M
University of Missouri–St. Louis	M
University of Nevada, Las Vegas	M
The University of North Carolina at Greensboro	M
University of Oregon	M,D
University of South Carolina	M
University of Southern California	M,D
University of South Florida	M
University of South Florida, St. Petersburg	M
The University of Tennessee	M,D
The University of Texas at Austin	M,D
The University of Western Ontario	M,D
University of Wisconsin–Madison	M,D
University of Wisconsin–Milwaukee	M,D
University of Wisconsin–Stevens Point	M
Valparaiso University	M,O
Virginia Commonwealth University	M,O
Virginia State University	M
Wayne State University	M,D,O
Webster University	M
West Virginia State University	M
Wilfrid Laurier University	M

MEDICAL/SURGICAL NURSING

Case Western Reserve University	M
Daemen College	M,D,O
Eastern Virginia Medical School	M
Inter American University of Puerto Rico, Arecibo Campus	M
Pontifical Catholic University of Puerto Rico	M
Saint Francis Medical Center College of Nursing	M,D,O
State University of New York Downstate Medical Center	M,O
Universidad Adventista de las Antillas	M
University of South Africa	M,D
University of South Carolina	M
Ursuline College	M,D

MEDICAL ILLUSTRATION

Augusta University	M
Johns Hopkins University	M
Rochester Institute of Technology	M
University of Illinois at Chicago	M

MEDICAL IMAGING

Boston University	M
Illinois Institute of Technology	M,D
Medical University of South Carolina	D
National University of Health Sciences	M,D
New York University	D
Oregon State University	M,D
Rutgers University–Newark	M
University of California, San Francisco	M
University of Cincinnati	M,D
University of Guelph	M,D,O
University of Southern California	M,D
University of Wisconsin–Milwaukee	D
Wayne State University	M,D,O

MEDICAL INFORMATICS

Arizona State University at the Tempe campus	M,D
Brandeis University	M
Cambridge College	M
Columbia University	M,D,O
Dalhousie University	M,D
Excelsior College	M,O
Grand Valley State University	M
Johns Hopkins University	M,D,O
Michigan Technological University	M
Middle Tennessee State University	M
Milwaukee School of Engineering	M
Northwestern University	M
Nova Southeastern University	M,D,O
Oregon Health & Science University	M,D,O
Regis University	M,O
Rutgers University–Newark	M,D,O
Stanford University	M,D
University at Buffalo, the State University of New York	M,D
The University of Arizona	M,D,O
University of California, Davis	M
University of Colorado Denver	M,D
University of Illinois at Urbana–Champaign	M,D,O
The University of Kansas	M,D,O
University of Phoenix–Phoenix Campus	M,O
The University of Tennessee at Chattanooga	M,D
University of Washington	M,D
University of Wisconsin–Milwaukee	M

MEDICAL MICROBIOLOGY

The Citadel, The Military College of South Carolina	M,O
Creighton University	M,D

Idaho State University	M,D
Rutgers University–New Brunswick	M,D
Université du Québec, Institut National de la Recherche Scientifique	M,D
University of Alberta	M,D
University of Hawaii at Manoa	M,D
University of Manitoba	M,D
University of Minnesota, Duluth	M,D
University of Southern California	D
University of South Florida	M,D
University of Wisconsin–La Crosse	M
University of Wisconsin–Madison	D

MEDICAL PHYSICS

The College of William and Mary	M,D
Columbia University	M,D
Duke University	M,D
East Carolina University	M,D
Hampton University	M,D
Harvard University	D
Hofstra University	M
Indiana University Bloomington	M,D
Louisiana State University and Agricultural & Mechanical College	M,D
Massachusetts Institute of Technology	M,D
McGill University	M,D
McMaster University	M,D
Oakland University	M,D
Oregon State University	M,D
Purdue University	M,D
Rush University	M,D
Southern Illinois University Carbondale	M
Stony Brook University, State University of New York	M,D
University at Buffalo, the State University of New York	M,D
University of Alberta	M,D
The University of Arizona	M
University of California, Los Angeles	M,D
University of Chicago	D
University of Cincinnati	M
University of Florida	M,D,O
University of Kentucky	M
University of Minnesota, Twin Cities Campus	M,D
University of Oklahoma Health Sciences Center	M,D
University of Pennsylvania	M,D
The University of Texas Health Science Center at Houston	M,D
The University of Texas Health Science Center at San Antonio	D
The University of Toledo	M,D
University of Utah	M,D
University of Victoria	M,D
University of Wisconsin–Madison	M,D
Virginia Commonwealth University	M,D
Wayne State University	M,D,O

MEDICINAL AND PHARMACEUTICAL CHEMISTRY

Duquesne University	M,D
Florida Agricultural and Mechanical University	M,D
Idaho State University	M,D
Medical University of South Carolina	D
New Jersey Institute of Technology	M,D,O
Oregon State University	M,D
Purdue University	D
Rutgers University–New Brunswick	M,D
Temple University	M,D
University at Buffalo, the State University of New York	M,D
University of California, Irvine	D
University of California, San Francisco	D
University of Connecticut	M,D
University of Florida	M,D
The University of Iowa	M,D
The University of Kansas	M,D
University of Michigan	D
University of Minnesota, Twin Cities Campus	M,D
University of Montana	M,D
University of Rhode Island	M,D
The University of Texas at Austin	M,D
University of the Sciences	M,D
The University of Toledo	M,D
University of Utah	M,D
University of Washington	D
Virginia Commonwealth University	M,D
Wayne State University	M,D
West Virginia University	M,D

MEDIEVAL AND RENAISSANCE STUDIES

Arizona State University at the Tempe campus	M,D,O
The Catholic University of America	M,D,O
Central European University	M,D
Columbia University	M,D
Cornell University	M,D
Fordham University	M,O
Georgetown University	M,D
The Graduate Center, City University of New York	M,D
Harvard University	M,D
Indiana University Bloomington	M,D
Rutgers University–New Brunswick	D
Southern Methodist University	M
University of California, Santa Barbara	M,D
University of Chicago	D
University of Connecticut	M,D

University of Guelph	D
University of Minnesota, Twin Cities Campus	M,D
University of Notre Dame	M,D
University of Pittsburgh	O
University of Toronto	M,D
Yale University	M,D

METALLURGICAL ENGINEERING AND METALLURGY

Colorado School of Mines	M,D
Michigan Technological University	M,D
Missouri University of Science and Technology	M,D
Montana Tech of The University of Montana	M
The Ohio State University	M,D
Université Laval	M,D
The University of Alabama	M,D
University of Connecticut	M
University of Idaho	M,D
The University of Manchester	M,D
University of Nebraska–Lincoln	M,D
University of Nevada, Reno	M,D
The University of Texas at El Paso	M,D
University of Utah	M,D

METEOROLOGY

Ball State University	M,O
Florida Institute of Technology	M
Florida State University	M,D
Iowa State University of Science and Technology	M,D
McGill University	M,D
Millersville University of Pennsylvania	M
Mississippi State University	M,D
Naval Postgraduate School	M,D
North Carolina State University	M,D
Northern Arizona University	M,D
Penn State University Park	M,D
Plymouth State University	M
Saint Louis University	M,D
San Jose State University	M,O
Texas A&M University	M,D
Université du Québec à Montréal	M,D,O
University of California, San Diego	M
University of Hawaii at Manoa	M,D
University of Maryland, College Park	M,D
University of Miami	M,D
University of Oklahoma	M,D
Utah State University	M,D
Yale University	D

MICROBIOLOGY

Albany Medical College	M,D
Albert Einstein College of Medicine	D
American University of Beirut	M,D
Arizona State University at the Tempe campus	M,D
Baylor College of Medicine	D
Brandeis University	M,D
Brigham Young University	M,D
California State University, Long Beach	M
Case Western Reserve University	D
The Catholic University of America	M,D
Clemson University	M,D
Colorado State University	M,D
Columbia University	M,D
Cornell University	D
Dalhousie University	M,D
Dartmouth College	D
Drexel University	M,D
Duke University	D
East Carolina University	M,D
Eastern New Mexico University	M
East Tennessee State University	D
Emory University	D
Emporia State University	M
Georgetown University	M,D
The George Washington University	M,D,O
Georgia State University	M,D
Harvard University	D
Hood College	M
Howard University	D
Idaho State University	M,D
Illinois Institute of Technology	M,D
Illinois State University	M,D
Indiana University Bloomington	M,D
Indiana University–Purdue University Indianapolis	M,D
Inter American University of Puerto Rico, Metropolitan Campus	M
Iowa State University of Science and Technology	M,D
Johns Hopkins University	M,D
Loma Linda University	M,D
Louisiana State University Health Sciences Center	D
Louisiana State University Health Sciences Center at Shreveport	M,D
Loyola University Chicago	M,D
Marquette University	M,D
Massachusetts Institute of Technology	D
McGill University	M,D
Medical College of Wisconsin	M,D
Medical University of South Carolina	M,D
Meharry Medical College	D
Miami University	M,D
Michigan State University	M,D
Montana State University	M,D
New York Medical College	M,D
New York University	M,D
North Carolina State University	M,D
North Dakota State University	M,D
The Ohio State University	M,D
Ohio University	M,D

Oklahoma State University	M,D
Oregon Health & Science University	D
Oregon State University	M,D
Purdue University	M,D
Queen's University at Kingston	M,D
Rosalind Franklin University of Medicine and Science	D
Rush University	M,D
Rutgers University–Newark	D
Rutgers University–New Brunswick	M,D
Saint Louis University	D
San Diego State University	M
San Francisco State University	M
Seton Hall University	M,D
South Dakota State University	M,D
Southern Illinois University Carbondale	M,D
Southwestern Oklahoma State University	M
Stanford University	D
State University of New York Upstate Medical University	M,D
Stony Brook University, State University of New York	D
Texas A&M University	M,D
Texas Tech University	M,D
Thomas Jefferson University	D
Tufts University	M
Tulane University	M
Universidad Central del Caribe	M,D
Université de Montréal	M,D
Université de Sherbrooke	M,D
Université du Québec, Institut National de la Recherche Scientifique	M,D
Université Laval	M,D
University at Buffalo, the State University of New York	M,D
The University of Alabama at Birmingham	D
University of Alberta	M,D
The University of Arizona	D
University of Arkansas for Medical Sciences	M,D,O
The University of British Columbia	M,D
University of Calgary	M,D
University of California, Berkeley	D
University of California, Davis	M,D
University of California, Irvine	M,D
University of California, Los Angeles	M,D
University of California, Riverside	M,D
University of Chicago	D
University of Cincinnati	M,D
University of Colorado Denver	M,D
University of Connecticut	M,D
University of Delaware	M,D
University of Florida	M,D
University of Georgia	M,D
University of Guelph	M,D
University of Hawaii at Manoa	M,D
University of Idaho	M,D
University of Illinois at Chicago	D
University of Illinois at Urbana–Champaign	M,D
The University of Iowa	M,D
The University of Kansas	M,D
University of Kentucky	D
University of Louisville	M,D
University of Maine	M,D
The University of Manchester	M,D
University of Manitoba	M,D
University of Maryland, Baltimore	D
University of Massachusetts Amherst	M,D
University of Massachusetts Medical School	M,D
University of Miami	D
University of Michigan	M,D
University of Minnesota, Twin Cities Campus	D
University of Mississippi Medical Center	D
University of Missouri	D
University of Montana	D
University of Nebraska Medical Center	M,D
University of New Hampshire	M,D
University of New Mexico	M,D
The University of North Carolina at Chapel Hill	M,D
University of North Texas Health Science Center at Fort Worth	M,D
University of Oklahoma	M,D
University of Oklahoma Health Sciences Center	M,D
University of Ottawa	M,D
University of Pennsylvania	D
University of Pittsburgh	M,D
University of Puerto Rico, Medical Sciences Campus	M,D
University of Rhode Island	M,D
University of Rochester	M,D
University of Saskatchewan	M,D
The University of South Dakota	M,D
University of Southern California	M
University of Southern Mississippi	M,D
University of South Florida	M,D
The University of Tennessee	M,D
The University of Texas at Austin	D
The University of Texas Health Science Center at Houston	D
The University of Texas Health Science Center at San Antonio	M,D
The University of Texas Medical Branch	M,D
The University of Texas Southwestern Medical Center	D

University of Victoria	M,D
University of Virginia	D
University of Washington	D
The University of Western Ontario	M,D
University of Wisconsin–La Crosse	M
University of Wisconsin–Madison	D
University of Wisconsin–Milwaukee	M,D
University of Wisconsin–Oshkosh	M
University of Wyoming	D
Vanderbilt University	M,D
Virginia Commonwealth University	M
Wagner College	M
Wake Forest University	D
Washington University in St. Louis	D
Wayne State University	M,D,O
West Virginia University	D
Wright State University	M
Yale University	D
Youngstown State University	M

MIDDLE SCHOOL EDUCATION

Alaska Pacific University	M
Albany State University	M,O
American International College	M,O
Antioch University Midwest	M
Appalachian State University	M
Arkansas State University	M,D,O
Augusta University	M,O
Ball State University	M,O
Bellarmine University	M
Berry College	M
Bloomsburg University of Pennsylvania	M
Brenau University	M,O
Brooklyn College of the City University of New York	M,O
California Lutheran University	M,D
California State University, Bakersfield	M
Cambridge College	M
Campbell University	M
Canisius College	M
Capella University	M,D
Chestnut Hill College	M
Chicago State University	M
The Citadel, The Military College of South Carolina	M,O
City College of the City University of New York	M,O
Clarkson University	M
Clemson University	M,D,O
The College at Brockport, State University of New York	M
College of Mount Saint Vincent	M,O
The College of Saint Rose	M,O
Columbus State University	M,O
Converse College	M
Daemen College	M
Drury University	M
Duquesne University	M
East Carolina University	M
Eastern Illinois University	M
Eastern Michigan University	M
Eastern Nazarene College	M,O
Eastern University	M,D,O
East Tennessee State University	M,O
Edinboro University of Pennsylvania	M
Emory University	M,D
Fayetteville State University	M
Fitchburg State University	M
Florida Gulf Coast University	M
Fontbonne University	M
Georgia Southern University	M,O
Georgia Southwestern State University	M,O
Georgia State University	M,D
Gordon College	M,O
Goucher College	M,O
Grand Valley State University	M
Hebrew College	M,O
Henderson State University	M
Hofstra University	M,D,O
Huntington University	M,D
James Madison University	M
Kansas State University	M,D,O
Kennesaw State University	M
Kent State University	M
Kutztown University of Pennsylvania	M
LaGrange College	M,O
La Salle University	M,O
Lee University	M,O
Le Moyne College	M
Lesley University	M,D,O
Liberty University	M,D,O
Lincoln University (MO)	M
Long Island University–Hudson	M,O
Long Island University–LIU Post	M,D,O
Long Island University–Riverhead	M,O
Longwood University	M
Louisiana Tech University	M,D
Lynn University	M,D
Manhattanville College	M
Mary Baldwin University	M
Maryville University of Saint Louis	M,D
McNeese State University	O
Mercer University	M,D,O
Mercy College	M,O
Merrimack College	M,O
Middle Tennessee State University	M,O
Milligan College	M,D,O
Minot State University	M

Mississippi State University	M,D,O
Morehead State University	M,O
Morgan State University	M
Mount St. Joseph University	M,O
Mount Saint Mary College	M,O
Mount Saint Vincent University	M
Murray State University	M,O
National Louis University	M,D,O
Nazareth College of Rochester	M
New York Institute of Technology	M
New York University	M,D,O
Niagara University	M,O
Nicholls State University	M
North Carolina State University	M
Northwestern State University of Louisiana	M
Northwest Missouri State University	M,D,O
Ohio University	M,D
Old Dominion University	M,O
Pacific University	M
Piedmont College	M,O
Point Park University	M,D
Queens College of the City University of New York	M,O
Quinnipiac University	M
Roberts Wesleyan College	M
Saginaw Valley State University	M,O
St. Bonaventure University	M
St. John Fisher College	M
St. John's University (NY)	M,O
Saint Joseph's University	M,D,O
Saint Peter's University	M,O
St. Thomas Aquinas College	M,O
Salem College	M
Salem State University	M
Salisbury University	M
Seton Hill University	M,O
Shenandoah University	M,D,O
Shippensburg University of Pennsylvania	M,O
Smith College	M
Southeast Missouri State University	M
Spalding University	M
State University of New York at Fredonia	M
State University of New York at Oswego	M
State University of New York College at Potsdam	M
Temple University	M
Tennessee Technological University	M
Theological University of the Caribbean	M,D
Tufts University	M,D
Union College (KY)	M
University of Arkansas	M,D,O
University of Arkansas at Little Rock	M
University of Bridgeport	M,D,O
University of Central Florida	M
University of Dayton	M
University of Houston–Downtown	M
University of Kentucky	M,D
University of Louisiana at Monroe	M,D
University of Louisville	M,D,O
University of Massachusetts Dartmouth	M,D,O
University of Missouri–St. Louis	M
The University of North Carolina at Charlotte	M,D,O
The University of North Carolina at Greensboro	M,D,O
The University of North Carolina Wilmington	M
University of Northern Iowa	M
University of North Georgia	M,O
University of Phoenix–Online Campus	M,O
University of South Florida, St. Petersburg	M
University of the Cumberlands	M,D,O
University of the District of Columbia	M
The University of Toledo	M
University of Washington, Bothell	M
University of West Florida	M
University of Wisconsin–Milwaukee	M
Ursuline College	M
Wagner College	M
Webster University	M,O
Western Kentucky University	M,O
Wichita State University	M
Widener University	M,D
Wilkes University	M,D
Winston-Salem State University	M
Worcester State University	M,O
Youngstown State University	M

MILITARY AND DEFENSE STUDIES

American Public University System	M
Austin Peay State University	M
Bellevue University	M
The Citadel, The Military College of South Carolina	M,O
East Carolina University	M
Embry-Riddle Aeronautical University–Prescott	M
The George Washington University	M
Hawai'i Pacific University	M
Henley-Putnam University	M
The Institute of World Politics	M,O
Johns Hopkins University	M
The Judge Advocate General's School, U.S. Army	M
Liberty University	M,D,O
London Metropolitan University	M,D

Missouri State University	M,O
National Defense University	M
National Intelligence University	M
Naval Postgraduate School	M,D
Norwich University	M
Royal Military College of Canada	M,D
School of Advanced Air and Space Studies	M
United States Army Command and General Staff College	M
University of Calgary	M,D
University of Colorado Denver	M,D
University of Pittsburgh	M

MINERAL/MINING ENGINEERING

Colorado School of Mines	M,D
Dalhousie University	M,D
Laurentian University	M,D
McGill University	M,D,O
Missouri University of Science and Technology	M,D
Montana Tech of The University of Montana	M
New Mexico Institute of Mining and Technology	M
Penn State University Park	M,D
Queen's University at Kingston	M,D
South Dakota School of Mines and Technology	M
Southern Illinois University Carbondale	M
Université du Québec en Abitibi-Témiscamingue	M,D
Université Laval	M,D
University of Alaska Fairbanks	M
University of Alberta	M,D
The University of Arizona	M,D,O
The University of British Columbia	M,D
University of Kentucky	M,D
University of Nevada, Reno	M
The University of Texas at Austin	M
University of Utah	M,D
Virginia Polytechnic Institute and State University	M,D

MINERAL ECONOMICS

Colorado School of Mines	M,D
Michigan Technological University	M
The University of Texas at Austin	M

MINERALOGY

Cornell University	M,D
Indiana University Bloomington	M,D
Université du Québec à Chicoutimi	D
Université du Québec à Montréal	M,D,O

MISSIONS AND MISSIOLOGY

Abilene Christian University	M
Anderson University (IN)	M,D
Asbury Theological Seminary	M,D,O
Assemblies of God Theological Seminary	M,D
Bethel Seminary	M,D,O
Biblical Theological Seminary	M,D,O
Biola University	M,D,O
Boston University	M
Briercrest Seminary	M
Calvin Theological Seminary	M,D
Catholic Theological Union	M,D,O
Cedarville University	M,D
Central Baptist Theological Seminary	M,O
Charlotte Christian College and Theological Seminary	M
Clarks Summit University	M,D
Columbia International University	M,D,O
Dallas Baptist University	M
Dallas Theological Seminary	M,D,O
Evangelical Seminary	M
Faulkner University	M
Fresno Pacific University	M
Fuller Theological Seminary	M,D,O
Gardner-Webb University	M,D
Georgia Christian University	M,D
Global University	M,D
Gordon-Conwell Theological Seminary	M,D
Grace Mission University	M,D
Grace Theological Seminary	M,D,O
Grand Rapids Theological Seminary of Cornerstone University	M
Hope International University	M
Huntington University	M,D
Liberty University	M,D,O
Luther Seminary	M,D
Milligan College	M,D,O
Northwest Nazarene University	M
Northwest University	M
Nyack College	M,D
Oral Roberts University	M,D
Phillips Theological Seminary	M,D
Providence University College & Theological Seminary	M
Reformed Theological Seminary–Jackson Campus	M,D,O
Regent University	M,D
Rochester College	M
Saint Paul University	M
Simpson University	M
Southeastern Baptist Theological Seminary	M,D
Southern Adventist University	M
The Southern Baptist Theological Seminary	M,D
Southern Evangelical Seminary	M,D,O
Southwestern Assemblies of God University	M
Southwestern Baptist Theological Seminary	M,D

M—masters degree; D—doctorate; O—other advanced degree; *—Close-Up and/or Display

Southwestern Christian University — M
Taylor College and Seminary — M,O
Theological University of the Caribbean — M
Trinity Bible College and Graduate School — M
Trinity International University — M,D,O
Trinity Lutheran Seminary — M
Trinity School for Ministry — M,D,O
Tyndale University College & Seminary — M,O
University of South Africa — M,D
Villanova University — M
Wesley Biblical Seminary — M
Westminster Theological Seminary — M,D,O
Wheaton College — M,O

MODELING AND SIMULATION

Arizona State University at the Tempe campus — M,D
Carnegie Mellon University — M,D
Columbus State University — M,O
Naval Postgraduate School — M,D
Old Dominion University — M,D
Oregon State University — M,D
Philadelphia University — M
Portland State University — M,D,O
Rochester Institute of Technology — D
Stevens Institute of Technology — M,D,O
Trent University — M,D
Université Laval — M,O
University at Buffalo, the State University of New York — M,D
The University of Alabama in Huntsville — M,D,O
University of California, San Diego — M,D
University of Central Florida — M,D,O
The University of Manchester — M,D
University of Pittsburgh — D
University of Southern California — M,D
Worcester Polytechnic Institute — M,D

MOLECULAR BIOLOGY

Albany College of Pharmacy and Health Sciences — M
Albany Medical College — M,D
Albert Einstein College of Medicine — D
American University of Beirut — M,D
Appalachian State University — M
Arizona State University at the Tempe campus — M,D
Arkansas State University — M,D
Auburn University — M,D
Baylor College of Medicine — D
Boise State University — M,D
Boston University — M,D
Brandeis University — M,D
Brigham Young University — M,D
Brown University — M,D
California Institute of Technology — D
California State University, Sacramento — M
Carnegie Mellon University — M,D
Case Western Reserve University — D
Central Connecticut State University — M,O
Clemson University — D
Colorado State University — M,D
Columbia University — D
Cornell University — M,D
Dartmouth College — D
Drexel University — M,D
Duke University — D,O
East Carolina University — M,D
Eastern Michigan University — M
Eastern New Mexico University — M
Emory University — D
Florida Institute of Technology — M,D
Florida State University — M,D
Georgetown University — M,D
Georgia State University — M,D
Grand Valley State University — M
Harvard University — D
Hood College — M
Howard University — M,D
Illinois Institute of Technology — M,D
Illinois State University — M,D
Indiana State University — M,D
Indiana University Bloomington — M,D
Indiana University–Purdue University Indianapolis — M,D
Inter American University of Puerto Rico, Metropolitan Campus — M
Iowa State University of Science and Technology — M,D
Irell & Manella Graduate School of Biological Sciences — D*
Johns Hopkins University — M,D
Kent State University — M,D
Lehigh University — M,D
Lipscomb University — M
Louisiana State University Health Sciences Center at Shreveport — M,D
Louisiana Tech University — M
Loyola University Chicago — M,D
Marquette University — M,D
Massachusetts Institute of Technology — M,D,O
Mayo Clinic Graduate School of Biomedical Sciences — D
McMaster University — M,D
Medical University of South Carolina — M,D
Michigan State University — M,D
Michigan Technological University — M,D
Middle Tennessee State University — D
Mississippi State University — M,D
Missouri State University — M
Montclair State University — M,O
New Mexico State University — M,D
New York Medical College — M,D
New York University — M,D
North Dakota State University — M,D

Northwestern University — D
The Ohio State University — M,D
Ohio University — D
Oklahoma State University — M,D
Oregon Health & Science University — M,D
Oregon State University — M,D
Pace University — M
Penn State University Park — M,D
Princeton University — D
Purdue University — M,D
Queen's University at Kingston — M,D
Quinnipiac University — M
Rosalind Franklin University of Medicine and Science — D
Rutgers University–Newark — M,D
Rutgers University–New Brunswick — M,D
Sacred Heart University — M
Saint Louis University — M,D
San Diego State University — M,D
San Francisco State University — M
San Jose State University — M,O
Seton Hall University — M,D
Simon Fraser University — M,D,O
Sonoma State University — M
Southern Illinois University Carbondale — M,D
Southern Methodist University — M,D
State University of New York Downstate Medical Center — D
State University of New York Upstate Medical University — M,D
Stony Brook University, State University of New York — M,D
Texas Woman's University — D
Tufts University — M,D
Tulane University — M,D
Uniformed Services University of the Health Sciences — M,D
Universidad Central del Caribe — M,D
Université de Montréal — M,D
Université Laval — M,D
University at Buffalo, the State University of New York — D
The University of Alabama at Birmingham — D
University of Alberta — M,D
The University of Arizona — D
University of Arkansas — M,D
University of Arkansas for Medical Sciences — M,D,O
The University of British Columbia — M,D
University of Calgary — M,D
University of California, Berkeley — D
University of California, Davis — M,D
University of California, Irvine — M,D
University of California, Los Angeles — M,D
University of California, Riverside — M,D
University of California, San Francisco — D
University of California, Santa Barbara — M,D
University of California, Santa Cruz — M,D
University of Chicago — D
University of Cincinnati — M,D
University of Colorado Boulder — M,D
University of Colorado Denver — M,D
University of Connecticut — M,D
University of Connecticut Health Center — D
University of Delaware — M,D
University of Denver — M,D
University of Florida — M,D
University of Georgia — M,D
University of Guelph — M,D
University of Hawaii at Manoa — M,D
University of Illinois at Chicago — D
The University of Iowa — D
The University of Kansas — D
University of Lethbridge — M,D
University of Louisville — M,D
University of Maine — M,D
The University of Manchester — M,D
University of Maryland, Baltimore — M,D
University of Maryland, Baltimore County — M,D
University of Maryland, College Park — D
University of Miami — D
University of Michigan — M,D
University of Minnesota, Duluth — M,D
University of Minnesota, Twin Cities Campus — M,D
University of Missouri–Kansas City — D
University of Montana — D
University of Nebraska Medical Center — M,D
University of Nevada, Reno — M,D
University of New Haven — M,O
University of New Mexico — M,D
The University of North Carolina at Chapel Hill — M,D
University of North Texas — M,D,O
University of Notre Dame — M,D
University of Oklahoma Health Sciences Center — M,D
University of Oregon — M,D
University of Ottawa — M,D
University of Pennsylvania — D
University of Pittsburgh — D
University of Puerto Rico, Río Piedras Campus — M,D
University of Rhode Island — M,D
University of Rochester — D
University of South Carolina — M,D
The University of South Dakota — M,D
University of Southern California — M,D
University of Southern Maine — M
University of Southern Mississippi — M,D

University of South Florida — M,D
The University of Texas at Austin — D
The University of Texas at Dallas — M,D
The University of Texas at San Antonio — M,D
University of Utah — D
University of Vermont — D
University of Washington — D
University of Wisconsin–La Crosse — M
University of Wisconsin–Madison — D
University of Wisconsin–Milwaukee — M,D
University of Wisconsin–Parkside — M
University of Wyoming — M,D
Vanderbilt University — M,D
Virginia Commonwealth University — M,D
Wake Forest University — D
Washington University in St. Louis — D
Wayne State University — M,D,O
Weill Cornell Medicine — D
Wesleyan University — D
West Virginia University — M,D
Wright State University — M
Yale University — D
Youngstown State University — M

MOLECULAR BIOPHYSICS

Baylor College of Medicine — D
California Institute of Technology — M,D
Carnegie Mellon University — D
Duke University — O
Florida State University — D
Illinois Institute of Technology — M,D
Johns Hopkins University — D
New York University — D
Rutgers University–New Brunswick — D
University at Buffalo, the State University of New York — M,D
University of Arkansas for Medical Sciences — D
University of Chicago — D
University of Massachusetts Amherst — D
University of Pennsylvania — D
University of Pittsburgh — D
The University of Texas Medical Branch — D
The University of Texas Southwestern Medical Center — D
Washington University in St. Louis — D
Wesleyan University — D
Yale University — D

MOLECULAR GENETICS

Albert Einstein College of Medicine — D
Duke University — D
Emory University — D
Georgia State University — M,D
Harvard University — D
Illinois State University — M,D
Indiana University–Purdue University Indianapolis — M,D
Iowa State University of Science and Technology — M,D
Medical College of Wisconsin — M,D
Michigan State University — M,D
New York University — M,D
Northern Michigan University — M
The Ohio State University — M,D
Oklahoma State University — M,D
Penn State Hershey Medical Center — M,D
Rutgers University–Newark — D
Rutgers University–New Brunswick — M,D
Stony Brook University, State University of New York — D
University of Calgary — M,D
University of California, Irvine — M,D
University of California, Los Angeles — M,D
University of Cincinnati — D
University of Colorado Denver — D
University of Florida — M
University of Guelph — M,D
University of Illinois at Chicago — D
The University of Manchester — M,D
University of Maryland, College Park — M,D
University of Nebraska Medical Center — M,D
University of Pittsburgh — D
University of Rhode Island — M,D
University of Toronto — M,D
University of Virginia — D
Van Andel Institute Graduate School — D
Virginia Commonwealth University — M,D
Wake Forest University — D
Washington University in St. Louis — D
Wayne State University — M,D,O
Wesleyan University — D

MOLECULAR MEDICINE

Augusta University — D
Baylor College of Medicine — D
Boston University — D
Case Western Reserve University — D
Cleveland State University — M,D
Cornell University — M,D
Dartmouth College — M
Drexel University — M
Elmezzi Graduate School of Molecular Medicine — D
The George Washington University — D
Hofstra University — D
Johns Hopkins University — D
Penn State Hershey Medical Center — D
Queen's University at Kingston — M,D
Rutgers University–Newark — D

Tufts University — D
The University of Alabama at Birmingham — D
The University of Arizona — M,D
University of Cincinnati — D
University of Maryland, Baltimore — D
University of Nebraska Medical Center — D
University of South Florida — M,D
The University of Texas Health Science Center at San Antonio — M,D
Wake Forest University — M,D
Wayne State University — M,D,O
Yale University — D

MOLECULAR PATHOGENESIS

Dartmouth College — D
Emory University — D
North Dakota State University — M,D
Oregon State University — D
Washington University in St. Louis — D

MOLECULAR PATHOLOGY

Rutgers University–Newark — D
Texas Tech University Health Sciences Center — M
University of Michigan — D
University of Pittsburgh — D
University of Wisconsin–Madison — D
Yale University — D

MOLECULAR PHARMACOLOGY

Albert Einstein College of Medicine — D
Brown University — M,D
Harvard University — D
Loyola University Chicago — M,D
Mayo Clinic Graduate School of Biomedical Sciences — D
Medical University of South Carolina — M,D
New York University — D
Purdue University — D
Rosalind Franklin University of Medicine and Science — M,D
Rutgers University–New Brunswick — M,D
Thomas Jefferson University — D
University at Buffalo, the State University of New York — D
University of Massachusetts Medical School — M,D
University of Nevada, Reno — D
University of Pittsburgh — D
University of Southern California — M,D
University of South Florida — M,D

MOLECULAR PHYSIOLOGY

Baylor College of Medicine — D
Loyola University Chicago — M,D
Rutgers University–New Brunswick — M,D
Stony Brook University, State University of New York — D
University of California, Los Angeles — D
University of Illinois at Urbana–Champaign — M,D
The University of North Carolina at Chapel Hill — D
University of Pittsburgh — D
University of Virginia — M,D
Vanderbilt University — M,D
Yale University — D

MOLECULAR TOXICOLOGY

Massachusetts Institute of Technology — D
New York University — M,D
North Carolina State University — M,D
Oregon State University — M,D
Penn State Hershey Medical Center — D
University of California, Berkeley — D
University of California, Los Angeles — D
University of Cincinnati — M,D

MULTILINGUAL AND MULTICULTURAL EDUCATION

Alliant International University–San Francisco — M,O
American College of Education — M
American University — M,O
Azusa Pacific University — M
Bank Street College of Education — M
Belhaven University (MS) — M
Boise State University — M
Brooklyn College of the City University of New York — M
Brown University — M,D
Buffalo State College, State University of New York — M
California State University, Fullerton — M
California State University, Northridge — M
California State University, Sacramento — M,D
California State University, Stanislaus — M
Chicago State University — M
City College of the City University of New York — M
The College at Brockport, State University of New York — M,O
College of Mount Saint Vincent — M,O
The College of New Rochelle — M,O
Columbia International University — M,D,O
Dallas Baptist University — M
DePaul University — M,D
Eastern New Mexico University — M
Eastern University — M,D,O
Fairfield University — M,O
Fairleigh Dickinson University, Metropolitan Campus — M

Florida Atlantic University	M,D,O
Florida International University	M,D,O
Gallaudet University	M,D,O
George Mason University	M
The George Washington University	M,D,O
Georgia Southern University	D
Graduate Institute of Applied Linguistics	M,O
Heritage University	M
Hofstra University	M,D,O
Howard University	M,D
Hunter College of the City University of New York	M
Immaculata University	M
Indiana State University	M,D,O
Indiana University Bloomington	M,D
James Madison University	M
Kean University	M
Langston University	M
La Salle University	M,O
Lehman College of the City University of New York	M
Long Island University–Hudson	M,O
Long Island University–LIU Brooklyn	M,O
Loyola Marymount University	M
Manhattan College	M,O
Molloy College	M,O
Mount St. Joseph University	M,O
New Jersey City University	M
New Mexico State University	M,D,O
New York University	M,D,O
Northeastern Illinois University	M
Northern Arizona University	M,O
Queens College of the City University of New York	M,O
Quincy University	M
Rutgers University–New Brunswick	M,D
St. John's University (NY)	M,O
Saint Mary's University of Minnesota	M,O
San Diego State University	M,D
Southern Connecticut State University	M
Southern Methodist University	M,D
State University of New York at New Paltz	M,O
State University of New York College at Geneseo	M
Sul Ross State University	M
Teachers College, Columbia University	M,D,O
Texas A&M University	M,D
Texas A&M University–Kingsville	M,D
Texas A&M University–San Antonio	M
Texas Southern University	M
Texas State University	M
Texas Tech University	M,D
University at Buffalo, the State University of New York	M,D,O
University of Alaska Fairbanks	M
University of Alberta	M
University of Calgary	M,D
University of California, Riverside	M,D,O
University of California, San Diego	M,D
University of Colorado Boulder	M,D
University of Colorado Denver	M
University of Connecticut	M,D
University of Delaware	M,D,O
The University of Findlay	M,D
University of Houston–Clear Lake	M
University of Maryland, Baltimore County	M,D
University of Massachusetts Amherst	M,D,O
University of Miami	D
University of Minnesota, Twin Cities Campus	M,D,O
University of New Mexico	M,D
The University of North Carolina at Greensboro	M,D,O
University of Northern Colorado	M,D
University of Pennsylvania	M
University of St. Thomas (TX)	M,D
University of San Francisco	M,D
University of Southern California	D
The University of Tennessee	M,D,O
The University of Texas at Austin	M,D
The University of Texas at El Paso	M,D,O
The University of Texas at San Antonio	M,D
The University of Texas Rio Grande Valley	M
University of the Southwest	M
University of Washington	M,D
University of Wisconsin–Milwaukee	M,D,O
Utah State University	M
Vanderbilt University	M,D
Walden University	M,D,O
Wayne State University	M,D,O
Western New Mexico University	M
Western Oregon University	M
Winona State University	O
Xavier University	M

MUSEUM EDUCATION

Bank Street College of Education	M
Eastern Michigan University	O
The George Washington University	M
Seton Hall University	M
Tufts University	M,D
The University of the Arts	M

MUSEUM STUDIES

American Museum of Natural History–Richard Gilder Graduate School	D
Arizona State University at the Tempe campus	M,D,O
Bard College	M
Baylor University	M
Boston University	M,D,O
California College of the Arts	M
California State University, Chico	M,D
Caribbean University	M
Case Western Reserve University	M
Christie's Education	M
City College of the City University of New York	M
Claremont Graduate University	M,D,O
Cleveland State University	M
Colorado State University	M
Columbia University	M,D
Eastern Michigan University	M,O
Fashion Institute of Technology	M
Florida International University	M,O
Florida State University	M,D
The George Washington University	M,D,O
Harvard University	M,O
Indiana University–Purdue University Indianapolis	M,O
John F. Kennedy University	M,O
Johns Hopkins University	M,O
Marist College	M
Maryland Institute College of Art	M
Morgan State University	M,D
New Mexico State University	M,O
The New School	M
New York University	M,O
Penn State Harrisburg	M,D,O
St. John's University (NY)	M
San Francisco Art Institute	M
San Francisco State University	M
Seton Hall University	M
Southern Illinois University Edwardsville	O
Southern University at New Orleans	M
State University of New York College at Oneonta	M
Syracuse University	M
Texas Tech University	M,D
Trinity College (United States)	M
Tufts University	M,D,O
Université de Montréal	M
Université du Québec à Montréal	M
Université Laval	O
University at Buffalo, the State University of New York	M,D
The University of British Columbia	M,D
University of Central Oklahoma	M
University of Colorado Boulder	M
University of Denver	M
University of Florida	M,D
University of Hawaii at Manoa	O
University of Illinois at Chicago	M,D
The University of Kansas	M,O
University of Louisville	M,D
The University of Manchester	D
University of Memphis	M,O
University of Michigan–Flint	M
University of Missouri–St. Louis	M,O
University of New Hampshire	M,D
The University of North Carolina at Greensboro	M,D,O
University of North Texas	M,D,O
University of San Francisco	M
University of South Carolina	M,D
University of South Florida	O
The University of the Arts	M
University of Toronto	M
The University of Tulsa	M
University of Washington	M
University of West Georgia	M,O
University of Wisconsin–Milwaukee	M,D,O
Virginia Commonwealth University	M,D
Western Illinois University	M,O

MUSIC

Academy of Art University	M
American University	M,O
Andrews University	M
Appalachian State University	M
Aquinas Institute of Theology	M,D,O
Arizona State University at the Tempe campus	M,D
Arkansas State University	M,O
Austin Peay State University	M
Azusa Pacific University	M
Ball State University	M,D,O
The Baptist College of Florida	M
Bard College	M,O
Baylor University	M,D
Bennington College	M
Berklee College of Music	M,O
Bethesda University	M
Binghamton University, State University of New York	M
Bob Jones University	M,D,O
Boise State University	M
Boston University	M,D,O
Bowling Green State University	M,D
Brandeis University	M,D
Brandon University	M
Brigham Young University	M
Brooklyn College of the City University of New York	M,D
Brown University	D
Butler University	M
California Baptist University	M
California Institute of Integral Studies	M,D
California Institute of the Arts	M,O
California State University, East Bay	M
California State University, Fresno	M
California State University, Fullerton	M
California State University, Long Beach	M
California State University, Los Angeles	M
California State University, Northridge	M
California State University, Sacramento	M
California State University, San Bernardino	M
Campbellsville University	M
Capital University	M
Carleton University	M
Carnegie Mellon University	M
Case Western Reserve University	M,D
The Catholic University of America	M,D,O
Central Michigan University	M
Central Washington University	M
Charlotte Christian College and Theological Seminary	M
Claremont Graduate University	M,D
Cleveland Institute of Music	M,D,O
Cleveland State University	M
The Colburn School Conservatory of Music	M,O
Colorado State University	M,D
Columbia College Chicago	M
Columbia University	M,D
Columbus State University	M,O
Concordia University (Canada)	O
Concordia University Chicago	M
Concordia University Wisconsin	M
Conservatorio de Musica de Puerto Rico	O
Converse College	M
Cornell University	M,D
Curtis Institute of Music	M
Dalhousie University	M
Dartmouth College	M
DePaul University	M,O
Dominican University of California	M
Duke University	D
Duquesne University	M,O
East Carolina University	M
Eastern Illinois University	M
Eastern Kentucky University	M
Eastern Michigan University	M
Eastern Washington University	M
Emory University	M
Emporia State University	M
Five Towns College	M,D
Florida Atlantic University	M
Florida International University	M
Florida State University	M,D
Fuller Theological Seminary	M,D,O
Garrett-Evangelical Theological Seminary	M,D
George Mason University	M,D
Georgia Christian University	M
Georgia Institute of Technology	M,D
Georgia Southern University	M
Georgia State University	M,D,O
The Graduate Center, City University of New York	D
Hardin-Simmons University	M
Harvard University	M,D
Hebrew College	M,O
Hebrew Union College–Jewish Institute of Religion (NY)	M
Hollins University	M
Holy Names University	M,O
Hope International University	M
Houghton College	M
Howard University	M
Hunter College of the City University of New York	M
Illinois State University	M
Indiana State University	M
Indiana University Bloomington	M,D,O
Indiana University of Pennsylvania	M
Indiana University–Purdue University Indianapolis	M,D
Indiana University South Bend	M,D
Inter American University of Puerto Rico, San Germán Campus	M
Ithaca College	M
Jacksonville State University	M
James Madison University	M
The Jewish Theological Seminary	M
Johns Hopkins University	M,D,O
The Juilliard School	M,D,O
Kansas State University	M
Kent State University	M,D
Lamar University	M
Lee University	M
Liberty University	M,D
Long Island University–LIU Post	M
Louisiana State University and Agricultural & Mechanical College	M,D
Loyola University New Orleans	M
Lynchburg College	M
Lynn University	M,O
Manhattan School of Music	M,D,O
Mansfield University of Pennsylvania	M
Marshall University	M
McGill University	M,D
McNally Smith College of Music	M
Memorial University of Newfoundland	M
Mercer University	M
Messiah College	M
Miami University	M
Michigan State University	M,D
Middle Tennessee State University	M
Midwestern Baptist Theological Seminary	M,D,O
Mills College	M
Minnesota State University Mankato	M,O
Mississippi College	M
Missouri State University	M
Montclair State University	M,O
Morehead State University	M
Morgan State University	M
Murray State University	M
Nazareth College of Rochester	M
New England Conservatory of Music	M,D,O
New Jersey City University	M
New Mexico State University	M
New Orleans Baptist Theological Seminary	M,D
The New School	M,O
New York University	M,D,O
Norfolk State University	M
North Carolina Central University	M
North Dakota State University	M
Northeastern Illinois University	M
Northern Arizona University	M,O
Northern Illinois University	M,O
Northern Kentucky University	M,O
North Park University	M
Northwestern State University of Louisiana	M
Northwestern University	M,D
Notre Dame de Namur University	M,O
Oakland University	M,O
Oberlin College	M,O
The Ohio State University	M,D
Ohio University	M,O
Oklahoma City University	M
Oklahoma State University	M
Open University	M
Park University	M,O
Penn State University Park	M,D,O
Pensacola Christian College	M,D,O
Phillips Theological Seminary	M
Pittsburg State University	M
Point Park University	M
Portland State University	M
Pratt Institute	M
Princeton University	D
Purchase College, State University of New York	M
Queens College of the City University of New York	M,O
Radford University	M
Rice University	M,D
Rider University	M
Roosevelt University	M
Rowan University	M
Rutgers University–Newark	M
Rutgers University–New Brunswick	M,D,O
St. Cloud State University	M
Saint John's University (MN)	M
Samford University	M
Sam Houston State University	M
San Diego State University	M
San Francisco Conservatory of Music	M,O
San Francisco State University	M
San Jose State University	M,O
Savannah College of Art and Design	M
School of the Art Institute of Chicago	M
Shenandoah University	M,D,O
Shepherd University (CA)	M
Silver Lake College of the Holy Family	M
Southeastern Baptist Theological Seminary	M,D
Southeastern Louisiana University	M
Southern Illinois University Carbondale	M
Southern Illinois University Edwardsville	M
Southern Methodist University	M
Southern Oregon University	M
Southern Utah University	M
Southwestern Baptist Theological Seminary	M,D
Southwestern Oklahoma State University	M
Stanford University	M,D
State University of New York at Fredonia	M
State University of New York at New Paltz	M
State University of New York College at Potsdam	M
Stephen F. Austin State University	M
Stony Brook University, State University of New York	M,D
Syracuse University	M
Temple University	M,D
Texas A&M University	M
Texas A&M University–Commerce	M,D,O
Texas A&M University–Kingsville	M
Texas Christian University	M,D
Texas Southern University	M
Texas State University	M
Texas Tech University	M,D
Texas Woman's University	M
Towson University	M
Trinity College (Canada)	M,D,O
Trinity Lutheran Seminary	M
Truman State University	M
Tufts University	M
Tulane University	M
Université de Montréal	M,D,O
Université Laval	M,D

*M—masters degree; D—doctorate; O—other advanced degree; *—Close-Up and/or Display*

University at Buffalo, the State University of New York	M,D,O
The University of Akron	M
The University of Alabama	M,D
The University of Alabama at Birmingham	M
University of Alaska Fairbanks	M
University of Alberta	M,D
The University of Arizona	M,D
University of Arkansas	M
The University of British Columbia	M,D
University of Calgary	M,D
University of California, Berkeley	D
University of California, Davis	M,D
University of California, Irvine	M
University of California, Los Angeles	M,D
University of California, Riverside	M,D
University of California, San Diego	M,D
University of California, Santa Barbara	M,D
University of California, Santa Cruz	M,D
University of Central Arkansas	M,O
University of Central Florida	M
University of Central Missouri	M,D,O
University of Central Oklahoma	M
University of Chicago	M,D
University of Cincinnati	M,D,O
University of Colorado Boulder	M,D
University of Colorado Denver	M
University of Connecticut	M
University of Delaware	M
University of Denver	M,O
University of Florida	M,D
University of Georgia	M,D
University of Hartford	M,D,O
University of Hawaii at Manoa	M,D
University of Houston	M,D
University of Idaho	M
University of Illinois at Urbana–Champaign	M,D
The University of Iowa	M,D
The University of Kansas	M,D
University of Kentucky	M,D
University of Lethbridge	M,D
University of Louisiana at Lafayette	M
University of Louisville	M
University of Maine	M
The University of Manchester	D
University of Manitoba	M
University of Maryland, Baltimore County	O
University of Maryland, College Park	M,D
University of Massachusetts Amherst	M,D
University of Massachusetts Lowell	M
University of Memphis	M,D
University of Miami	M,D,O
University of Michigan	M,D,O
University of Michigan–Flint	M
University of Minnesota, Duluth	M
University of Minnesota, Twin Cities Campus	M,D
University of Mississippi	M,D
University of Missouri	M
University of Missouri–Kansas City	M,D
University of Montana	M
University of Nebraska at Omaha	M
University of Nebraska–Lincoln	M,D
University of Nevada, Las Vegas	M,D,O
University of Nevada, Reno	M
University of New Hampshire	M
University of New Mexico	M
University of New Orleans	M
The University of North Carolina at Chapel Hill	M,D
The University of North Carolina at Charlotte	O
The University of North Carolina at Greensboro	M,D
University of North Carolina School of the Arts	M,O
University of North Dakota	M,D
University of Northern Colorado	M,D
University of Northern Iowa	M
University of North Texas	M,D,O
University of Oklahoma	M,D,O
University of Oregon	M,D
University of Ottawa	M,O
University of Pennsylvania	M,D
University of Pittsburgh	M,D
University of Redlands	M
University of Regina	M
University of Rhode Island	M
University of Rochester	M,D
University of St. Thomas (MN)	M,D
University of St. Thomas (TX)	M
University of Saskatchewan	M
University of South Africa	M,D
University of South Alabama	M
University of South Carolina	M,D,O
The University of South Dakota	M
University of Southern California	M,D,O
University of Southern Maine	M
University of Southern Mississippi	M,D
University of South Florida	M,D
The University of Tennessee	M
The University of Tennessee at Chattanooga	M
The University of Texas at Arlington	M,D
The University of Texas at Austin	M,D
The University of Texas at El Paso	M
The University of Texas at San Antonio	M
The University of Texas Rio Grande Valley	M
The University of the Arts	M
University of the Pacific	M
The University of Toledo	M,O
University of Toronto	M,D
University of Utah	M,D
University of Valley Forge	M,D
University of Victoria	M,D
University of Virginia	M,D
University of Washington	M,D
The University of Western Ontario	M,D
University of West Georgia	M,O
University of Wisconsin–Madison	M,D
University of Wyoming	M
Valdosta State University	M
Vermont College of Fine Arts	M
Virginia Commonwealth University	M
Washington State University	M
Washington University in St. Louis	M,D
Wayne State University	M,D,O
Webster University	M
Wesleyan University	M,D
West Chester University of Pennsylvania	M,O
Western Illinois University	M
Western Michigan University	M,O
Western Oregon University	M
Western Washington University	M
West Texas A&M University	M
West Virginia University	M,D
Wichita State University	M
William Paterson University of New Jersey	M
Winthrop University	M
Yale University	M,D,O
York University	M,D
Youngstown State University	M

MUSIC EDUCATION

Alabama Agricultural and Mechanical University	M
Alabama State University	M,O
Arcadia University	M,D,O
Arizona State University at the Tempe campus	M,D
Arkansas State University	M,O
Augusta University	M,O
Austin Peay State University	M
Azusa Pacific University	M
Ball State University	M,D,O
Bob Jones University	M,D,O
Boise State University	M
Boston University	M,D
Bowling Green State University	M,D
Brandon University	M
Brigham Young University	M
Brooklyn College of the City University of New York	M
Butler University	M
California Baptist University	M
California State University, Fresno	M
California State University, Fullerton	M
California State University, Los Angeles	M
California State University, Northridge	M
Campbellsville University	M
Capital University	M
Carnegie Mellon University	M
Case Western Reserve University	M,D
The Catholic University of America	M,D,O
Central Connecticut State University	M,O
Central Methodist University	M
Central Michigan University	M
Cleveland State University	M
College of Charleston	M
College of Staten Island of the City University of New York	M
The Colorado College	M
Colorado State University	M
Colorado State University–Pueblo	M
Columbus State University	M,O
Conservatorio de Musica de Puerto Rico	M
Converse College	M
DePaul University	M,O
Duquesne University	M,O
East Carolina University	M,O
Eastern Kentucky University	M
Eastern Washington University	M
Five Towns College	M,D
Florida Atlantic University	M
Florida International University	M
George Mason University	M
Georgia College & State University	M
Georgia Southern University	M
Georgia State University	M,D,O
Gordon College	M
Hampton University	M
Hardin-Simmons University	M
Hebrew College	M,O
Heidelberg University	M
Hofstra University	M,D,O
Holy Names University	M,O
Howard University	M
Hunter College of the City University of New York	M
Indiana State University	M
Indiana University of Pennsylvania	M
Inter American University of Puerto Rico, Metropolitan Campus	M
Inter American University of Puerto Rico, San Germán Campus	M
Ithaca College	M
Jackson State University	M
James Madison University	M
Kent State University	M,D
Lake Forest College	M
Lebanon Valley College	M
Lee University	M
Lehman College of the City University of New York	M
Liberty University	M,D
Long Island University–LIU Post	M,D,O
Louisiana State University and Agricultural & Mechanical College	M,D
Loyola University Maryland	M
Manhattanville College	M
Marywood University	M
McGill University	M,D
McKendree University	M,D,O
McNeese State University	O
Miami University	M
Michigan State University	M,D
Minnesota State University Mankato	M
Mississippi College	M
Montclair State University	M
Morehead State University	M
Murray State University	M
Nazareth College of Rochester	M
New Jersey City University	M
New Mexico State University	M
New York University	M,D,O
Norfolk State University	M
North Dakota State University	M,D,O
Northern State University	M
Northwestern University	M,D
Oakland University	M,D
Ohio University	M,O
Oklahoma State University	M
Old Dominion University	M
Oregon State University	M
Penn State University Park	M,O
Piedmont College	M,O
Pittsburg State University	M
Plymouth State University	M
Portland State University	M
Queens College of the City University of New York	M,O
Rhode Island College	M
Rider University	M
Rutgers University–New Brunswick	M,D,O
St. Cloud State University	M
Saint Xavier University	M
Samford University	M
San Diego State University	M
San Francisco Conservatory of Music	M,O
San Francisco State University	M
Shenandoah University	M,D,O
Southern Illinois University Edwardsville	M,O
Southern Methodist University	M
Southern Utah University	M
Southwestern Oklahoma State University	M
State University of New York at Fredonia	M
State University of New York College at Potsdam	M
Syracuse University	M
Tarleton State University	M
Teachers College, Columbia University	M,D,O
Temple University	M,D
Tennessee Technological University	M
Texas A&M University–Kingsville	M
Texas Christian University	M,D
Texas State University	M
Texas Tech University	M,D
Texas Woman's University	M
Towson University	M,O
Union College (KY)	M
Université Laval	M,D
University at Buffalo, the State University of New York	M,D,O
The University of Akron	M
The University of Alabama	M,D,O
The University of Arizona	M,D
University of Bridgeport	M,D,O
The University of British Columbia	M,D
University of Central Arkansas	M,O
University of Cincinnati	M
University of Colorado Boulder	M,D
University of Connecticut	M,D
University of Dayton	M
University of Delaware	M
University of Denver	M,D
University of Florida	M,D
University of Georgia	M,D
University of Hartford	M,D,O
University of Houston	M,D
University of Illinois at Urbana–Champaign	M,D
The University of Iowa	M,D
The University of Kansas	M,D
University of Kentucky	M,D
University of Louisiana at Lafayette	M
University of Louisiana at Monroe	M
University of Louisville	M,D,O
University of Maryland, Baltimore County	M
University of Maryland, College Park	M,D
University of Massachusetts Amherst	M,D
University of Massachusetts Lowell	M
University of Memphis	M
University of Miami	M,D,O
University of Michigan	M,D,O
University of Minnesota, Duluth	M
University of Missouri	M,D,O
University of Missouri–Kansas City	M,D
University of Missouri–St. Louis	M
University of Nebraska at Kearney	M
University of Nebraska–Lincoln	M,D
University of New Mexico	M
The University of North Carolina at Chapel Hill	M
The University of North Carolina at Greensboro	M,D
University of North Dakota	M,D
University of Northern Colorado	M,D
University of Northern Iowa	M
University of North Texas	M,D,O
University of Oklahoma	M,D,O
University of Oregon	M,D
University of Ottawa	M,O
University of Rhode Island	M
University of Rochester	M,D
University of St. Thomas (MN)	M,D
University of South Alabama	M
University of South Carolina	M,D,O
The University of South Dakota	M
University of Southern California	M,D,O
University of Southern Maine	M
University of Southern Mississippi	M,D
University of South Florida	M,D
The University of Tennessee	M
The University of Tennessee at Chattanooga	M
The University of Texas at Arlington	M
The University of Texas at Austin	M
The University of Texas at El Paso	M
The University of Texas Rio Grande Valley	M
The University of the Arts	M
University of the Pacific	M
The University of Toledo	M,O
University of Toronto	M,D
University of Utah	M,D
University of Victoria	M,D
University of Washington	M,D
University of West Georgia	M,O
University of Wisconsin–Madison	M
University of Wisconsin–Stevens Point	M
University of Wyoming	M
VanderCook College of Music	M
Virginia Commonwealth University	M
Wayne State College	M
Wayne State University	M,O
Webster University	M
West Chester University of Pennsylvania	M,O
Western Connecticut State University	M
Western Kentucky University	M
Western Michigan University	M,O
West Virginia University	M,D
Wichita State University	M
Winthrop University	M
Wright State University	M
Youngstown State University	M

NANOTECHNOLOGY

The American University in Cairo	M,D,O
Arizona State University at the Tempe campus	M,D
Carnegie Mellon University	D
The College of William and Mary	M,D
Cornell University	M,D
Indiana University of Pennsylvania	M
Johns Hopkins University	M
Louisiana Tech University	M,D
Michigan Technological University	M,D,O
North Dakota State University	M,D
South Dakota School of Mines and Technology	D
State University of New York Polytechnic Institute	M,D
Stevens Institute of Technology	D
University of Alberta	M,D
University of California, Riverside	M
University of California, San Diego	M,D
University of Central Florida	M
University of New Mexico	M,D
University of Pennsylvania	M
University of South Florida	M,D
University of Washington	M,D
Virginia Commonwealth University	M,D

NATIONAL SECURITY

American Public University System	M
Angelo State University	M
Bellevue University	M
California State University, San Bernardino	M
The Citadel, The Military College of South Carolina	M,O
George Mason University	M,D,O
The George Washington University	M,D
Henley-Putnam University	D
The Institute of World Politics	M,O
Kansas State University	M,D
National Defense University	M
Naval Postgraduate School	M,D,O
Naval War College	M
New Jersey City University	M,D,O
New York University	M,O
Regent University	M,O
Texas A&M University	M
Trinity Washington University	M
University of Central Florida	M,D,O
University of Nebraska at Omaha	M,O
University of New Haven	M
Virginia Polytechnic Institute and State University	M,O
Western Michigan University Thomas M. Cooley Law School	M,D

NATURAL RESOURCES

American University	M,D,O
Auburn University	M,D
Ball State University	M,D,O
Boise State University	M
California Polytechnic State University, San Luis Obispo	M

Institution	Degree
Central Washington University	M
Colorado State University	M,D
Cornell University	M,D
Dalhousie University	M
Delaware State University	M
Duke University	M,D
Florida International University	M,D
Humboldt State University	M
Indiana University–Purdue University Indianapolis	M,D,O
Instituto Tecnologico de Santo Domingo	M,D,O
Iowa State University of Science and Technology	M,D
Kansas State University	M,D
Laurentian University	M,D
Louisiana State University and Agricultural & Mechanical College	M,D
McGill University	M,D
Michigan State University	M,D
Montana State University	M
New Mexico Highlands University	M
North Carolina State University	M,D
North Dakota State University	M,D
Northeastern State University	M
The Ohio State University	M,D
Oklahoma State University	M,D
Oregon State University	M,D
Purdue University	M,D
State University of New York College of Environmental Science and Forestry	M,D
Sul Ross State University	M
Tarleton State University	M
Texas A&M University	M,D
Texas Tech University	M,D
Unity College	M
Universidad Metropolitana	M
Universidad Nacional Pedro Henriquez Urena	M
Université du Québec à Montréal	M,D,O
Université du Québec en Abitibi-Témiscamingue	M,D
University of Alaska Fairbanks	M,D
University of Alberta	M,D
The University of Arizona	M,D
University of Arkansas at Monticello	M
The University of British Columbia	M,D
University of California, Berkeley	M,D
University of Connecticut	M,D
University of Delaware	M
University of Florida	M,D
University of Georgia	M,D
University of Guelph	M,D
University of Hawaii at Manoa	M,D
University of Idaho	M,D
University of Illinois at Urbana–Champaign	M,D
The University of Manchester	M,D
University of Manitoba	M,D
University of Maryland, College Park	M,D
University of Michigan	M,D
University of Minnesota, Twin Cities Campus	M,D
University of Montana	M,D
University of Nebraska–Lincoln	M,D
University of New Brunswick Saint John	M
University of New Hampshire	M,D,O
University of New Mexico	M,D
University of Northern British Columbia	M,D,O
University of Rhode Island	M,D
University of San Francisco	M
University of South Africa	M,D
The University of Texas at Austin	M
University of Vermont	M,D
University of Washington	M,D
University of Wisconsin–Madison	M,D
University of Wisconsin–Stevens Point	M
University of Wyoming	M,D
Utah State University	M
Virginia Polytechnic Institute and State University	M,D,O
Washington State University	M,D
West Virginia University	M,D

NATUROPATHIC MEDICINE

Institution	Degree
Bastyr University	D
Canadian College of Naturopathic Medicine	O
National University of Natural Medicine	M,D
Southwest College of Naturopathic Medicine and Health Sciences	D
Universidad del Turabo	D
University of Bridgeport	D

NEAR AND MIDDLE EASTERN LANGUAGES

Institution	Degree
The American University in Cairo	M,O
American University of Beirut	M,D
Bethel Seminary	M,D,O
Brandeis University	M,D
The Catholic University of America	M,D
DePaul University	M
Georgetown University	M,O
Harvard University	M,D
Hebrew Union College–Jewish Institute of Religion (NY)	D
Houston Baptist University	M
Indiana University Bloomington	M,D
Johns Hopkins University	D
Kent State University	M,D
London Metropolitan University	M,D
Middlebury College	M
The Ohio State University	M,D
Oral Roberts University	M,D
University of California, Los Angeles	M,D
University of Chicago	D
The University of Manchester	M,D
University of Michigan	M,D
University of South Africa	M,D
The University of Texas at Austin	M,D
University of Utah	M,D
University of Wisconsin–Madison	M,D
Wayne State University	M,D
Yale University	M,D

NEAR AND MIDDLE EASTERN STUDIES

Institution	Degree
The American University in Cairo	M,O
American University of Beirut	M,D
The American University of Paris	M
Brandeis University	M,D
Brown University	D
California State University, Long Beach	M
The Catholic University of America	M,D,O
College of Staten Island of the City University of New York	M
Columbia University	M,D
Cornell University	M,D
George Mason University	M,O
Georgetown University	M,O
The George Washington University	M
Harvard University	M,D
Johns Hopkins University	D
McGill University	M,D,O
New York University	M,D,O
Princeton University	M,D
Rice University	D
Southern Evangelical Seminary	M,D,O
Southwestern Baptist Theological Seminary	M,D
The University of Arizona	M,D,O
University of California, Berkeley	M,D
University of California, Los Angeles	M,D
University of Chicago	M,D
University of Illinois at Urbana–Champaign	M
The University of Kansas	M,O
The University of Manchester	M,D
University of Memphis	M,D
University of Michigan	M,D
University of Pennsylvania	M,D
University of South Africa	M,D
The University of Texas at Austin	M,D
University of Toronto	M,D
University of Utah	M,D
University of Virginia	M
University of Washington	M,D
University of Waterloo	M
University of Wisconsin–Madison	M,D
Washington University in St. Louis	M
Wayne State University	M,D
Yale University	M,D

NEUROBIOLOGY

Institution	Degree
Albert Einstein College of Medicine	D
Boston University	M,D
Brandeis University	M,D
California Institute of Technology	D
Carnegie Mellon University	M,D
Columbia University	D
Cornell University	D
Dalhousie University	M,D
Duke University	D
Georgia State University	M,D
Harvard University	D
Illinois State University	M,D
Indiana University–Purdue University Indianapolis	D
Louisiana State University Health Sciences Center	D
Massachusetts Institute of Technology	D
New York University	M,D
Northwestern University	M,D
Penn State Hershey Medical Center	D
Purdue University	M,D
Queen's University at Kingston	M,D
Université Laval	M,D
The University of Alabama at Birmingham	D
University of Arkansas for Medical Sciences	M,D,O
University of California, Irvine	M,D
University of California, Los Angeles	M,D
University of Chicago	D
University of Colorado Denver	M,D
University of Connecticut	M,D
The University of Iowa	M,D
University of Kentucky	D
University of Louisville	M,D
The University of Manchester	M,D
University of Maryland, Baltimore	D
University of Minnesota, Twin Cities Campus	M,D
The University of North Carolina at Chapel Hill	D
University of Oklahoma	D
University of Pittsburgh	D
University of Rochester	D
University of Southern California	D
The University of Texas at Austin	D
The University of Texas at San Antonio	M,D
University of Utah	D
University of Washington	D
Virginia Commonwealth University	M
Wake Forest University	D
Wayne State University	M,D
Wesleyan University	D
West Virginia University	M,D
Yale University	D

NEUROSCIENCE

Institution	Degree
Albany Medical College	M,D
Alliant International University–San Diego	M,D,O
American University	M,D,O
American University of Beirut	M,D
Argosy University, Chicago	D
Argosy University, Phoenix	M,D
Argosy University, Tampa	M,D
Arizona State University at the Tempe campus	M,D
Augusta University	M,D
Ball State University	M,D,O
Baylor College of Medicine	D
Boston University	D
Brandeis University	M,D
Brigham Young University	M,D
Brock University	M,D
Brown University	D
California Institute of Technology	M,D
Carleton University	M,D
Carnegie Mellon University	M,D
Case Western Reserve University	D
Central Michigan University	M,D
College of Staten Island of the City University of New York	M
The College of William and Mary	M,D
Colorado State University	D
Dalhousie University	M,D
Dartmouth College	D
Delaware State University	M,D
Drexel University	M,D
Duke University	D,O
Emory University	D
Fielding Graduate University	D,O
Florida Atlantic University	D
Florida International University	M,D
Florida State University	M,D
Gallaudet University	M,D,O
George Mason University	M,D,O
Georgetown University	D
Georgia State University	D
The Graduate Center, City University of New York	D
Harvard University	D
Icahn School of Medicine at Mount Sinai	M,D
Illinois State University	M,D
Immaculata University	M,D,O
Indiana University Bloomington	M,D
Iowa State University of Science and Technology	M,D
Irell & Manella Graduate School of Biological Sciences	D*
Johns Hopkins University	D
Kent State University	M,D
Louisiana State University Health Sciences Center	D
Loyola University Chicago	M,D
Marquette University	M,D
Massachusetts Institute of Technology	D
Mayo Clinic Graduate School of Biomedical Sciences	D
McGill University	M,D
McMaster University	M,D
Medical College of Wisconsin	D
Medical University of South Carolina	M,D
Meharry Medical College	D
Memorial University of Newfoundland	M,D
Michigan State University	M,D
Montana State University	M,D
New York University	D
Northwestern University	D
The Ohio State University	D
Ohio University	M,D
Oregon Health & Science University	D
Penn State Hershey Medical Center	D
Princeton University	D
Purdue University	D
Queens College of the City University of New York	M,O
Queen's University at Kingston	M,D
Rosalind Franklin University of Medicine and Science	D
Rush University	M,D
Rutgers University–Newark	D
Rutgers University–New Brunswick	M,D
Seton Hall University	M,D
State University of New York Downstate Medical Center	D
State University of New York Upstate Medical University	D
Stony Brook University, State University of New York	M,D
Syracuse University	M,D
Teachers College, Columbia University	M,D
Texas Christian University	M,D
Thomas Jefferson University	D
Tufts University	M,D
Tulane University	M,D
Uniformed Services University of the Health Sciences	D
Universidad de Iberoamerica	M,D
Université de Montréal	M,D
University at Albany, State University of New York	M,D
University at Buffalo, the State University of New York	M,D
The University of Alabama at Birmingham	M,D
University of Alaska Fairbanks	M,D
University of Alberta	M,D
The University of Arizona	D
The University of British Columbia	M,D
University of Calgary	M,D
University of California, Berkeley	D
University of California, Davis	D
University of California, Irvine	D
University of California, Los Angeles	D
University of California, Riverside	D
University of California, San Diego	M,D
University of California, San Francisco	D
University of California, Santa Barbara	D
University of Chicago	D
University of Cincinnati	D
University of Colorado Denver	D
University of Connecticut	M,D
University of Connecticut Health Center	D
University of Delaware	D
University of Florida	D
University of Georgia	D
University of Guelph	M,D,O
University of Hartford	M
University of Illinois at Chicago	M,D
University of Illinois at Urbana–Champaign	D
The University of Iowa	D
The University of Kansas	M,D
University of Lethbridge	M,D
The University of Manchester	M,D
University of Maryland, Baltimore	D
University of Maryland, Baltimore County	D
University of Maryland, College Park	M,D
University of Massachusetts Amherst	M,D
University of Massachusetts Medical School	M,D
University of Miami	M,D
University of Michigan	D
University of Michigan–Flint	D,O
University of Minnesota, Twin Cities Campus	M,D
University of Mississippi Medical Center	D
University of Missouri	M,D,O
University of Missouri–St. Louis	M,D,O
University of Montana	M,D
University of Nebraska Medical Center	D
University of New Mexico	M,D
The University of North Carolina at Chapel Hill	D
University of North Texas Health Science Center at Fort Worth	M,D
University of Oklahoma Health Sciences Center	M,D
University of Oregon	M,D
University of Pennsylvania	D
University of Pittsburgh	D
University of Puerto Rico, Río Piedras Campus	M,D
University of Rochester	D
The University of South Dakota	M,D
University of Southern California	M,D
University of South Florida	M,D,O
The University of Texas at Austin	D
The University of Texas at Dallas	M,D
The University of Texas Health Science Center at Houston	M,D
The University of Texas Health Science Center at San Antonio	D
The University of Texas Medical Branch	D
The University of Texas Southwestern Medical Center	D
The University of Toledo	M,D
University of Utah	D
University of Vermont	D
University of Virginia	D
The University of Western Ontario	M,D
University of Wisconsin–Madison	D
University of Wisconsin–Milwaukee	M,D
Virginia Commonwealth University	M,D,O
Wake Forest University	D
Washington State University	M,D
Washington University in St. Louis	D
Wayne State University	M,D,O
Weill Cornell Medicine	M,D
West Virginia University	M,D
Wilfrid Laurier University	M,D
Wright State University	M
Yale University	D

NONPROFIT MANAGEMENT

Institution	Degree
Adler University	M,D,O
American Jewish University	M
American Public University System	M
American University	M,D,O
Antioch University Los Angeles	M
Antioch University Santa Barbara	M
Arizona State University at the Tempe campus	M,D,O
Assumption College	M,O
Azusa Pacific University	M
Baruch College of the City University of New York	M
Bay Path University	M
Bradley University	M

*M—masters degree; D—doctorate; O—other advanced degree; *—Close-Up and/or Display*

Nonprofit Management (continued)

Brandeis University	M
Brigham Young University	M
Cairn University	M,O
California Baptist University	M
California Lutheran University	M,O
California State University, Northridge	O
Cambridge College	M
Capella University	D
Carlos Albizu University, Miami Campus	M,D
Case Western Reserve University	M,D,O
Central Michigan University	M,O
Chaminade University of Honolulu	M
Clemson University	M,O
Cleveland State University	M,O
The College at Brockport, State University of New York	M,O
Columbia University	M
Corban University	M
Daemen College	M
Dallas Baptist University	M
DePaul University	M
Drury University	M
Eastern Mennonite University	M
Eastern Michigan University	M,O
Eastern University	M,D
East Tennessee State University	M
Fairleigh Dickinson University, Metropolitan Campus	M,O
Fielding Graduate University	M,D,O
Florida Atlantic University	M,D
Fordham University	M,D
Geneva College	M
The George Washington University	M,O
Georgian Court University	M,O
Georgia Southern University	O
Georgia State University	M,D,O
Grand Valley State University	M
Gratz College	M
Hamline University	M,D
Hebrew Union College–Jewish Institute of Religion (NY)	M
High Point University	M
Hope International University	M
Indiana University Bloomington	M,D,O
Indiana University Northwest	M,O
Indiana University of Pennsylvania	D
Indiana University–Purdue University Indianapolis	M,O
Indiana University South Bend	M,O
Iona College	M,O
James Madison University	M,D
John Carroll University	M
Johns Hopkins University	M,O
Johnson & Wales University	M
Johnson University	M,D,O
Kean University	M
La Salle University	M
Lasell College	M,O
Lewis University	M
Lindenwood University	M
Lipscomb University	M,O
Long Island University–LIU Brooklyn	M,O
Long Island University–LIU Post	M,O
Louisiana State University in Shreveport	M
Marymount University	M,O
Metropolitan State University	M,D,O
Minnesota State University Mankato	M,O
Mount Aloysius College	M
New England College	M
The New School	M
New York University	M,D,O
North Carolina State University	M,D,O
Northeastern University	M
Northern Kentucky University	M,O
North Park University	M
Norwich University	M
Notre Dame of Maryland University	M
Oakland University	M
Oklahoma Christian University	M
Oklahoma State University	M,D,O
Oral Roberts University	M
Our Lady of the Lake University	M
Pace University	M
Park University	M,O
Penn State Harrisburg	M,D,O
Post University	M
Regent University	M,D,O
Regis University	M,O
Rockhurst University	M
St. Cloud State University	M
Saint Mary-of-the-Woods College	M
Salve Regina University	M,O
San Francisco State University	M
Seton Hall University	M,O
Simmons College	M
Sonoma State University	M,O
Southern Adventist University	M
Southern New Hampshire University	M,O
Suffolk University	M,O
Texas A&M University	M,O
Thomas Edison State University	M
Tiffin University	M
Trinity Washington University	M
Trinity Western University	M,O
Tufts University	O
Tusculum College	M
Unification Theological Seminary	M,D
University at Albany, State University of New York	M,D,O
University of Arkansas at Little Rock	O
University of California, San Diego	M
University of Central Florida	M,O
University of Colorado Denver	M,D
University of Connecticut	M,O
University of Florida	M
University of Georgia	M

University of Houston–Downtown	M
University of La Verne	M,O
University of Louisville	M,D
University of Maryland, Baltimore County	M,O
University of Memphis	M,O
University of Michigan–Flint	M
University of Missouri	M,D,O
University of Missouri–St. Louis	M,O
University of Nevada, Las Vegas	M,O
The University of North Carolina at Charlotte	M
The University of North Carolina at Greensboro	M,O
University of Northern Iowa	M
University of North Florida	M,O
University of North Texas	M,D,O
University of Notre Dame	M
University of Oklahoma	M,O
University of Pennsylvania	M,O
University of Pittsburgh	M
University of Portland	M
University of San Diego	M,D,O
University of San Francisco	M
University of Southern California	M,O
University of Southern Indiana	M
University of South Florida	O
The University of Tampa	M
The University of Tennessee at Chattanooga	M,O
The University of Texas at Dallas	M,D
University of the Sacred Heart	M
University of the West	M
The University of Toledo	M,O
University of West Georgia	M,D,O
University of Wisconsin–Milwaukee	M,D,O
Upper Iowa University	M
Villanova University	M,O
Virginia Commonwealth University	O
Virginia Polytechnic Institute and State University	M,O
Walden University	M,D,O
Warner Pacific College	M
Wayne State University	M,D
Webster University	M,D,O
West Chester University of Pennsylvania	M,O
Western Michigan University	M,D,O
Westfield State University	M
Worcester State University	M

NORTHERN STUDIES

University of Alaska Fairbanks	M
University of Manitoba	M

NUCLEAR ENGINEERING

Air Force Institute of Technology	M,D
Arizona State University at the Tempe campus	M,D,O
Colorado School of Mines	M,D
École Polytechnique de Montréal	M,D,O
Georgia Institute of Technology	M,D
Idaho State University	M,D
Kansas State University	M,D
Massachusetts Institute of Technology	M,D,O
McMaster University	M,D
Missouri University of Science and Technology	M,D
North Carolina State University	M,D
The Ohio State University	M,D
Oregon State University	M,D
Penn State University Park	M,D
Purdue University	M,D
Rensselaer Polytechnic Institute	M,D
Royal Military College of Canada	M,D
Stevens Institute of Technology	M,D,O
Texas A&M University	M,D
University of California, Berkeley	M,D
University of Cincinnati	M,D
University of Florida	M,D
University of Idaho	M,D
University of Illinois at Urbana–Champaign	M,D
The University of Manchester	M,D
University of Maryland, College Park	M,D
University of Massachusetts Lowell	M,D
University of Michigan	M,D,O
University of Missouri	M,D,O
University of Nevada, Las Vegas	M,D,O
University of New Mexico	M,D
University of South Carolina	M,D
The University of Tennessee	M,D
University of Utah	M,D
University of Wisconsin–Madison	M,D
Virginia Commonwealth University	M,D
Virginia Polytechnic Institute and State University	M,D

NURSE ANESTHESIA

Adventist University of Health Sciences	M
Albany Medical College	M
Arkansas State University	M,D,O
Augusta University	D
Barry University	M
Baylor College of Medicine	D
Bloomsburg University of Pennsylvania	M
Boston College	M
Bryan College of Health Sciences	M
California State University, Fullerton	M,D
Case Western Reserve University	M
Columbia University	M,O
DeSales University	M,D,O
Drexel University	M
Duke University	M,D,O
Fairfield University	M,D

Florida Gulf Coast University	M
Florida International University	M,O
Gannon University	M,O
Georgetown University	M,D
Goldfarb School of Nursing at Barnes-Jewish College	M
Inter American University of Puerto Rico, Arecibo Campus	M
La Roche College	M,D
La Salle University	M,D,O
Lincoln Memorial University	M
Louisiana State University Health Sciences Center	M,D,O
Lourdes University	M
Marshall University	D
Mayo Clinic School of Health Sciences	D
Medical University of South Carolina	M
Middle Tennessee School of Anesthesia	M,D
Midwestern University, Glendale Campus	M
Millikin University	M,D
Missouri State University	D
Mount Marty College	M
Murray State University	M
Newman University	M
Oakland University	M,O
Old Dominion University	D
Oregon Health & Science University	M
Otterbein University	M,D,O
Our Lady of the Lake College	M
Quinnipiac University	D
Rosalind Franklin University of Medicine and Science	D
Rush University	D
Rutgers University–Newark	M,D,O
Saint Mary's University of Minnesota	M
Saint Vincent College	M,D
Samford University	M,D
Samuel Merritt University	M,D,O
Southern Illinois University Edwardsville	D
State University of New York Downstate Medical Center	M
Texas Christian University	D
Texas Wesleyan University	M,D
Uniformed Services University of the Health Sciences	M,D
Union University	M,D,O
University at Buffalo, the State University of New York	M,D,O
The University of Alabama at Birmingham	M,D
University of Cincinnati	M,O
University of Detroit Mercy	M,D,O
The University of Kansas	D
University of Maryland, Baltimore	M
University of Miami	M,D
University of Michigan–Flint	M,D
University of Minnesota, Twin Cities Campus	M,D
University of New England	M,D
The University of North Carolina at Charlotte	M,D,O
The University of North Carolina at Greensboro	M,D,O
University of North Dakota	M,D,O
University of North Florida	M,D,O
University of Pennsylvania	M
University of Pittsburgh	D
University of Saint Francis (IN)	M,D,O
The University of Scranton	M,D,O
University of South Carolina	M
University of South Florida	M,D,O
The University of Tennessee at Chattanooga	M,D,O
University of Wisconsin–La Crosse	M
Villanova University	M,D,O
Virginia Commonwealth University	M,D
Wayne State University	M,O
Webster University	D
Westminster College (UT)	M
Wolford College	M,D
York College of Pennsylvania	M,D,O

NURSE MIDWIFERY

Bastyr University	M,O
Baylor University	M,D
Bethel University (MN)	M,D,O
Case Western Reserve University	M
Columbia University	M,D,O
DeSales University	M,D,O
Emory University	M
Frontier Nursing University	M,D,O
Georgetown University	M,D
James Madison University	M,D
Marquette University	M,D,O
Midwives College of Utah	M
National College of Midwifery	M,D
New York University	M,D,O
Old Dominion University	M,D
Oregon Health & Science University	M
Philadelphia University	M,O
Seattle University	M
Shenandoah University	M,D,O
State University of New York Downstate Medical Center	M,O
Stony Brook University, State University of New York	M,D,O
University of Cincinnati	M,D
University of Colorado Denver	M,D
University of Illinois at Chicago	M,D
University of Indianapolis	M,D
The University of Kansas	M,D,O
The University of Manchester	M,D
University of Maryland, Baltimore	M
University of Miami	M,D
University of Minnesota, Twin Cities Campus	M,D
University of Pennsylvania	M

University of Pittsburgh	D
University of Puerto Rico, Medical Sciences Campus	M,O
University of South Africa	M,D
Vanderbilt University	M,D,O
West Virginia Wesleyan College	M,O

NURSING—GENERAL

Abilene Christian University	D
Adelphi University	D
Albany State University	M
Alcorn State University	M
Allen College	M,D
Alvernia University	M,D,O
Alverno College	M,D
American Sentinel University	M
American University of Beirut	M
Andrews University	M
Angelo State University	M
Arizona State University at the Tempe campus	M,D,O
Arkansas State University	M,D,O
Arkansas Tech University	M
Armstrong State University	M
Ashland University	D
Aspen University	M
Athabasca University	M,O
Auburn University	M
Auburn University at Montgomery	M
Augsburg College	M,D
Augusta University	D
Aurora University	M
Austin Peay State University	M
Azusa Pacific University	M,D
Ball State University	M,D,O
Barry University	M,D
Baylor University	M,D
Bellarmine University	M,D
Bellin College	M
Belmont University	M,D
Benedictine University	M
Bethel College	M
Binghamton University, State University of New York	M,D,O
Blessing-Rieman College of Nursing & Health Sciences	M
Bloomsburg University of Pennsylvania	M
Boise State University	M,D,O
Boston College	M,D
Bowie State University	M
Bradley University	M,D,O
Brandman University	D
Briar Cliff University	M,D,O
Brigham Young University	M
Brookline College	M
California Baptist University	M,D
California State University, Chico	M
California State University, Dominguez Hills	M
California State University, Fresno	M,D
California State University, Fullerton	M,D
California State University, Long Beach	M,D,O
California State University, Los Angeles	M,O
California State University, Sacramento	M
California State University, San Bernardino	M
California State University, San Marcos	M
California State University, Stanislaus	M
Capella University	M,D
Capital University	M
Cardinal Stritch University	M
Carlow University	D
Carson-Newman University	M
Case Western Reserve University	M,D
The Catholic University of America	M,D,O
Cedar Crest College	M
Central Methodist University	M
Chatham University	M,D
Chicago State University	M
Clarion University of Pennsylvania	M
Clarke University	D
Clarkson College	M,O
Clayton State University	M
Clemson University	M,D,O
Cleveland State University	M,D
College of Mount Saint Vincent	M,O
The College of New Jersey	M,O
The College of New Rochelle	M,O
College of Saint Elizabeth	M
College of Saint Mary	M
The College of St. Scholastica	M,O
College of Staten Island of the City University of New York	M,D,O
Colorado Mesa University	M,D,O
Colorado State University–Pueblo	M
Columbia College of Nursing	M
Columbia University	M,D,O
Columbus State University	M
Concordia University Irvine	M
Concordia University Wisconsin	M,D
Coppin State University	M,O
Cox College	M
Creighton University	M,D,O
Curry College	M
Daemen College	M,D,O
Dalhousie University	M,D
Delaware State University	M
Delta State University	M,D
DePaul University	M,D
DeSales University	M,D,O
Drexel University	M,D
Duke University	D
Duquesne University	M,D,O
D'Youville College	M,D,O
East Carolina University	M,D,O

Institution	Degree
Eastern Kentucky University	M
Eastern Mennonite University	M
Eastern New Mexico University	M
East Tennessee State University	M,D,O
Edgewood College	M,D
Edinboro University of Pennsylvania	M,D
EDP University of Puerto Rico–San Sebastian	M
Elmhurst College	M
Elms College	M
Emmanuel College (United States)	M,O
Emory University	M,D
Endicott College	M,D
Excelsior College	M
Fairfield University	M,D
Fairleigh Dickinson University, College at Florham	M
Fairleigh Dickinson University, Metropolitan Campus	M,D,O
Felician University	M,D,O
Ferris State University	M
Florida Agricultural and Mechanical University	M,D
Florida Atlantic University	M,D,O
Florida International University	M,D
Florida National University	M
Florida Southern College	M
Florida State University	M,D,O
Fort Hays State University	M
Framingham State University	M
Franciscan University of Steubenville	M
Francis Marion University	M
Fresno Pacific University	M
Frontier Nursing University	M,D,O
Frostburg State University	M
Gannon University	M,D
Gardner-Webb University	M,D
George Mason University	M,D,O
Georgetown University	M,D
The George Washington University	M,D,O
Georgia College & State University	M,D
Georgia Southern University	D
Georgia Southwestern State University	M,O
Georgia State University	M,D,O
Goldfarb School of Nursing at Barnes-Jewish College	M
Gonzaga University	M,D
Goshen College	M
Governors State University	M
Graceland University (IA)	M,D,O
The Graduate Center, City University of New York	D
Grambling State University	M,O
Grand Canyon University	M,D,O
Grand Valley State University	M,D
Gwynedd Mercy University	M,D
Hampton University	M,D
Hardin-Simmons University	M
Hawai`i Pacific University	M
Herzing University Online	M
Hofstra University	M
Holy Family University	M
Holy Names University	M,O
Howard University	M
Hunter College of the City University of New York	M,O
Husson University	M,O
Idaho State University	M,O
Illinois State University	M,D,O
Immaculata University	M
Independence University	M
Indiana State University	M,D
Indiana University East	M
Indiana University Kokomo	M
Indiana University of Pennsylvania	D
Indiana University–Purdue University Fort Wayne	M,O
Indiana University–Purdue University Indianapolis	M,D
Indiana University South Bend	M
Indiana Wesleyan University	M
Inter American University of Puerto Rico, Arecibo Campus	M
Jacksonville State University	M
Jacksonville University	M,D
James Madison University	M,D
Jefferson College of Health Sciences	M
Johns Hopkins University	M,D,O
Kaplan University, Davenport Campus	M
Kean University	M
Keiser University	M
Kennesaw State University	M,D
Kent State University	M,D
Kentucky State University	M,D
Keuka College	M
King University	M,D
Lamar University	M
Lander University	M
La Roche College	M
La Salle University	M,D,O
Laurentian University	M
Lehman College of the City University of New York	M
Le Moyne College	M,O
Lenoir-Rhyne University	M
Lewis University	M,D
Liberty University	M,D
Lincoln Memorial University	M
Lindenwood University	M
Loma Linda University	D
Long Island University–LIU Brooklyn	M,O
Louisiana State University Health Sciences Center	M,D,O
Loyola University Chicago	M,D,O
Loyola University New Orleans	M,D

Institution	Degree
Lynchburg College	M
Madonna University	M
Malone University	M
Mansfield University of Pennsylvania	M
Marian University (WI)	M
Marquette University	M,D,O
Marshall University	M
Marymount University	M,D,O
Maryville University of Saint Louis	M,D,O
McGill University	M,D,O
McKendree University	M
McMaster University	M,D
McMurry University	M
McNeese State University	M,O
MCPHS University	M
Medical University of South Carolina	D
Memorial University of Newfoundland	M,D
Mercer University	M,D,O
Mercy College	M
Metropolitan State University	M
MGH Institute of Health Professions	M,D,O
Miami Regional University	M
Michigan State University	M,D
MidAmerica Nazarene University	M
Middle Tennessee State University	M,O
Midwestern State University	M
Millersville University of Pennsylvania	D
Millikin University	M
Minnesota State University Mankato	M,D
Minnesota State University Moorhead	M,O
Misericordia University	M
Mississippi University for Women	M,O
Missouri Southern State University	M
Missouri State University	M,D
Missouri Western State University	M
Molloy College	M,D,O
Monmouth University	M,D,O
Montana State University	M,D,O
Moravian College	M
Morgan State University	M
Mount Carmel College of Nursing	M
Mount Marty College	M
Mount Mercy University	M
Mount St. Joseph University	M,D
Mount Saint Mary College	M,O
Mount Saint Mary's University (CA)	M,D,O
Murray State University	M
National University	M,D,O
Nebraska Methodist College	M
Nebraska Wesleyan University	M
Neumann University	M,O
New Mexico State University	M,D,O
New York University	M,D,O
Nicholls State University	M
North Dakota State University	M,D
Northeastern University	M,D,O
Northern Arizona University	M,D,O
Northern Illinois University	M
Northern Kentucky University	M,D,O
Northern Michigan University	M,D
North Park University	M
Northwestern State University of Louisiana	M
Norwich University	M
Nova Southeastern University	M,D
Oakland University	M,D,O
The Ohio State University	M,D
Ohio University	M,D
Oklahoma Baptist University	M
Oklahoma City University	M,D
Old Dominion University	M,D
Olivet Nazarene University	M
Oregon Health & Science University	M,D,O
Otterbein University	M,D,O
Our Lady of the Lake College	M
Pace University	M,D,O
Pacific Lutheran University	M,D
Palm Beach Atlantic University	M,D
Penn State University Park	M,D
Pensacola Christian College	M,D,O
Pittsburg State University	M
Point Loma Nazarene University	M,O
Pontifical Catholic University of Puerto Rico	M
Prairie View A&M University	M,D
Purdue University	M,D,O
Purdue University Northwest	M
Queen's University at Kingston	M,D,O
Queens University of Charlotte	D
Quinnipiac University	D
Radford University	D
Ramapo College of New Jersey	M
Regis College (MA)	M,D,O
Research College of Nursing	M
Resurrection University	M
Rhode Island College	M,D
Rivier University	M,D
Robert Morris University	M,D
Roberts Wesleyan College	M
Rowan University	M
Rush University	M,D,O
Rutgers University–Camden	D
Rutgers University–Newark	M,D,O
Sacred Heart University	M,D,O
Sage Graduate School	M,D,O
Saginaw Valley State University	M
St. Ambrose University	M
Saint Anthony College of Nursing	M
St. Catherine University	M,D
Saint Francis Medical Center College of Nursing	M,D,O
St. John Fisher College	M,D,O

Institution	Degree
St. Joseph's College, Long Island Campus	M
St. Joseph's College, New York	M
Saint Joseph's College of Maine	M,O
Saint Louis University	M,D,O
Saint Mary's College	D
Saint Peter's University	M,D,O
Saint Xavier University	M,O
Salem State University	M
Salisbury University	M,D
Salve Regina University	D
Samford University	M,D
Samuel Merritt University	M,D,O
San Diego State University	M
San Francisco State University	M,O
Seattle Pacific University	M,O
Seattle University	M,D
Seton Hall University	M,D
Shenandoah University	M,D,O
Simmons College	M,D,O
Sonoma State University	M
South Dakota State University	M,D
Southeastern Louisiana University	M,D
Southeast Missouri State University	M
Southern Adventist University	M
Southern Connecticut State University	M,D
Southern Illinois University Edwardsville	M,D,O
Southern Nazarene University	M
Southern New Hampshire University	M,O
Southern University and Agricultural and Mechanical College	M,D,O
South University	M
South University	M
South University (MI)	M
South University (SC)	M
South University (GA)	M
South University (AL)	M
South University	M
Spalding University	M,D,O
Spring Arbor University	M
Spring Hill College	M,O
Stanbridge University	M
State University of New York Downstate Medical Center	M,O
State University of New York Upstate Medical University	M,O
Stevenson University	M
Stockton University	M
Stony Brook University, State University of New York	M,D,O
Tarleton State University	M
Temple University	D
Tennessee State University	M,O
Tennessee Technological University	M
Texas A&M International University	M
Texas A&M University	M,D
Texas A&M University–Corpus Christi	M
Texas Christian University	M,D,O
Texas Tech University Health Sciences Center	M,D,O
Texas Woman's University	M,D
Thomas Edison State University	M,D
Thomas Jefferson University	M,D
Thomas University	M
Towson University	M,O
Trinity Western University	M
Troy University	M,D
Uniformed Services University of the Health Sciences	M,D
Union University	M,D,O
Universidad Metropolitana	M,O
Université de Montréal	M,D,O
Université du Québec à Rimouski	M,O
Université du Québec à Trois-Rivières	M,O
Université du Québec en Outaouais	M,O
Université Laval	M,D,O
University at Buffalo, the State University of New York	M,D,O
The University of Akron	M,D
The University of Alabama	M,D
The University of Alabama at Birmingham	M,D
The University of Alabama in Huntsville	M,D,O
University of Alaska Anchorage	M
University of Alberta	M,D
The University of Arizona	M,D,O
University of Arkansas	M
University of Arkansas for Medical Sciences	D
The University of British Columbia	M,D
University of Calgary	M,D,O
University of California, Irvine	M
University of California, Los Angeles	M,D
University of California, San Francisco	M,D
University of Central Arkansas	M,D
University of Central Florida	M,D,O
University of Central Missouri	M,D,O
University of Central Oklahoma	M
University of Cincinnati	M,D
University of Colorado Colorado Springs	M,D
University of Colorado Denver	M,D
University of Connecticut	M,D,O
University of Delaware	M,O
University of Detroit Mercy	M,D,O
University of Florida	M,D
University of Hartford	M
University of Hawaii at Hilo	D

Institution	Degree
University of Hawaii at Manoa	M,D,O
University of Houston	M
University of Illinois at Chicago	M,D,O
University of Indianapolis	M,D
The University of Iowa	M,D
The University of Kansas	M,D,O
University of Kentucky	D
University of Lethbridge	M,D
University of Louisiana at Lafayette	M
University of Louisville	M,D
University of Maine	M,O
The University of Manchester	M,D
University of Manitoba	M
University of Mary	M
University of Mary Hardin-Baylor	M,D
University of Maryland, Baltimore	M,D,O
University of Massachusetts Amherst	M,D
University of Massachusetts Boston	M,D
University of Massachusetts Dartmouth	M,D
University of Massachusetts Lowell	M,D
University of Massachusetts Medical School	M,D,O
University of Memphis	M,O
University of Miami	M,D
University of Michigan	M,D,O
University of Michigan–Flint	M,D,O
University of Minnesota, Twin Cities Campus	M,D
University of Mississippi Medical Center	M,D
University of Missouri	M,D,O
University of Missouri–Kansas City	M,D
University of Missouri–St. Louis	D,O
University of Mobile	M
University of Mount Olive	M
University of Nebraska Medical Center	D
University of Nevada, Las Vegas	M,D,O
University of Nevada, Reno	M,D
University of New Brunswick Fredericton	M
University of New Hampshire	M,D,O
University of New Mexico	M,D
University of North Alabama	M
The University of North Carolina at Chapel Hill	M,D,O
The University of North Carolina at Charlotte	M,D,O
The University of North Carolina at Greensboro	M,D,O
The University of North Carolina at Pembroke	M
The University of North Carolina Wilmington	M,D,O
University of North Dakota	M,D,O
University of Northern Colorado	M,D
University of North Florida	M,D,O
University of Oklahoma Health Sciences Center	M
University of Ottawa	M,D,O
University of Pennsylvania	M,D,O
University of Phoenix–Atlanta Campus	M
University of Phoenix–Augusta Campus	M
University of Phoenix–Bay Area Campus	M,D
University of Phoenix–Central Valley Campus	M
University of Phoenix–Charlotte Campus	M
University of Phoenix–Colorado Campus	M
University of Phoenix–Colorado Springs Downtown Campus	M
University of Phoenix–Columbus Georgia Campus	M
University of Phoenix–Hawaii Campus	M
University of Phoenix–Houston Campus	M
University of Phoenix–New Mexico Campus	M
University of Phoenix–North Florida Campus	M
University of Phoenix–Online Campus	M,D,O
University of Phoenix–Phoenix Campus	M,O
University of Phoenix–Sacramento Valley Campus	M
University of Phoenix–San Antonio Campus	M
University of Phoenix–San Diego Campus	M
University of Phoenix–Southern California Campus	M,O
University of Phoenix–South Florida Campus	M
University of Phoenix–Utah Campus	M
University of Phoenix–Washington D.C. Campus	M,D
University of Pittsburgh	D
University of Portland	M,D
University of Puerto Rico, Medical Sciences Campus	M
University of Regina	M
University of Rhode Island	M,D
University of Rochester	M,D
University of St. Augustine for Health Sciences	M,D
University of St. Francis (IL)	M,D,O
University of Saint Francis (IN)	M,D,O
University of Saint Joseph	M,D

*M—masters degree; D—doctorate; O—other advanced degree; *—Close-Up and/or Display*

University	Degrees
University of Saint Mary	M
University of San Diego	M,D
University of San Francisco	D
University of Saskatchewan	M
The University of Scranton	M,D,O
University of South Alabama	M,D,O
University of South Carolina	M,O
University of Southern Indiana	M,D,O
University of Southern Maine	M,D,O
University of Southern Mississippi	M,D,O
University of South Florida	M,D,O
The University of Tampa	M
The University of Tennessee	M,D
The University of Tennessee at Chattanooga	M,D,O
The University of Tennessee Health Science Center	M,D,O
The University of Texas at Arlington	M,D
The University of Texas at Austin	M,D
The University of Texas at El Paso	M,D
The University of Texas at Tyler	M,D
The University of Texas Health Science Center at Houston	M,D
The University of Texas Health Science Center at San Antonio	M,D,O
The University of Texas Medical Branch	M,D
The University of Texas Rio Grande Valley	M
The University of Toledo	M,D,O
University of Toronto	M,D
The University of Tulsa	D
University of Utah	M,D
University of Vermont	M,D
University of Victoria	M,D
University of Virginia	M,D
University of Washington	M,D,O
University of Washington, Bothell	M
University of Washington, Tacoma	M
The University of Western Ontario	M,D
University of West Florida	M
University of West Georgia	M,D,O
University of Windsor	M
University of Wisconsin–Eau Claire	M,D
University of Wisconsin–Madison	D
University of Wisconsin–Milwaukee	M,D,O
University of Wisconsin–Oshkosh	M
University of Wyoming	M
Urbana University	M
Ursuline College	M,D
Utah Valley University	M
Valdosta State University	M
Vanderbilt University	M,D,O
Vanguard University of Southern California	M
Villanova University	M,D,O
Virginia Commonwealth University	M,D,O
Viterbo University	D
Walden University	M,D,O
Walsh University	M,D
Washburn University	M,D,O
Washington Adventist University	M
Washington State University	M,D,O
Waynesburg University	M,D
Weber State University	M
Webster University	M
Wesley College	M
West Chester University of Pennsylvania	M,D,O
West Coast University	M,D
Western Carolina University	M,D,O
Western Connecticut State University	M,D
Western Kentucky University	M
Western Michigan University	M
Western University of Health Sciences	M,D
Westminster College (UT)	M
West Texas A&M University	M
West Virginia University	M,D,O
West Virginia Wesleyan College	M,O
Wheeling Jesuit University	M
Wichita State University	M,D
Widener University	M,D,O
Wilkes University	M,D
William Carey University	M
William Paterson University of New Jersey	M,D
Wilmington University	M,D
Wilson College	M
Winona State University	M,D,O
Winston-Salem State University	M,D
Wright State University	M

NURSING AND HEALTHCARE ADMINISTRATION

University	Degrees
Abilene Christian University	D
Adelphi University	M,O
Allen College	M,D
Alvernia University	M,D,O
American International College	M,D
American University of Beirut	M
Arizona State University at the Tempe campus	M,D,O
Aspen University	M
Athabasca University	M,O
Augusta University	M,D
Austin Peay State University	M,D,O
Barry University	M,D,O
Bellarmine University	M,D
Blessing-Rieman College of Nursing & Health Sciences	M
Bloomsburg University of Pennsylvania	M

University	Degrees
Bowie State University	M
Bradley University	M,D,O
Brenau University	M
Brookline College	M
California State University, Fullerton	M,D
California State University, San Marcos	M
California University of Pennsylvania	M
Capella University	M
Capital University	M
Carlow University	M
Cedar Crest College	M
Central Methodist University	M
Chatham University	M,D
Clarkson College	M,O
Clarkson University	M,O
College of Mount Saint Vincent	M,O
Columbus State University	M
Cox College	M
Creighton University	M,D,O
Daemen College	M,D,O
DeSales University	M,D,O
Drexel University	M,D,O
Duke University	M,D,O
Eastern Mennonite University	M
Eastern Michigan University	M,O
East Tennessee State University	M,D,O
Elms College	M,D
Emmanuel College (United States)	M,O
Emory University	M
Excelsior College	M
Fairfield University	M,D
Felician University	M,D,O
Ferris State University	M
Florida Agricultural and Mechanical University	M,D
Florida Atlantic University	M,D,O
Florida National University	M
Florida Southern College	M
Florida State University	M,D,O
Framingham State University	M
Franklin Pierce University	M,D,O
Frostburg State University	M
Gannon University	M,D
The George Washington University	M,D,O
Georgia Southwestern State University	M,O
Georgia State University	M,D,O
Goldfarb School of Nursing at Barnes-Jewish College	M
Grand Valley State University	M,D
Grand View University	M,O
Grantham University	M
Herzing University Online	M
Holy Family University	M,D
Holy Names University	M,O
Immaculata University	M
Independence University	M
Indiana State University	M,D
Indiana University Kokomo	M
Indiana University of Pennsylvania	M
Indiana University–Purdue University Fort Wayne	M,O
Indiana University–Purdue University Indianapolis	M,D
Indiana Wesleyan University	M,O
Jacksonville University	M
James Madison University	M,D
Jefferson College of Health Sciences	M
Johns Hopkins University	M,D
Kaplan University, Davenport Campus	M
Kean University	M,D
Kent State University	M,D
King University	M,D
Lamar University	M
La Roche College	M
La Salle University	M,D,O
Le Moyne College	M,O
Lenoir-Rhyne University	M
Lewis University	M,D
Liberty University	M,D
Loma Linda University	M
Louisiana State University Health Sciences Center	M,D,O
Lourdes University	M
Lynchburg College	M
Madonna University	M
Marquette University	M,D,O
McKendree University	M
McNeese State University	M,O
Medical University of South Carolina	M
Mercy College	M
Metropolitan State University	M,D
Miami Regional University	M
MidAmerica Nazarene University	M
Middle Tennessee State University	M
Milwaukee School of Engineering	M
Missouri Western State University	M,O
Monmouth University	M,D,O
Montana State University	M,D,O
Moravian College	M
Mount Mary University	M
Mount Mercy University	M
Mount St. Joseph University	M
Mount Saint Mary College	M,O
Nebraska Methodist College	M
New Mexico State University	M,D,O
New York University	M,O
Nicholls State University	M
Northeastern University	M,D,O
North Park University	M
Northwest Nazarene University	M
Norwich University	M
Ohio University	M,D
Oklahoma Wesleyan University	M
Old Dominion University	M,D
Otterbein University	M,D,O
Our Lady of the Lake College	M

University	Degrees
Pace University	M,D,O
Palm Beach Atlantic University	M,D
Pennsylvania College of Health Sciences	M
Purdue University Northwest	M
Queens University of Charlotte	M
Quinnipiac University	D
Ramapo College of New Jersey	M
Regis University	M,D,O
Research College of Nursing	M
Rivier University	M,D
Roberts Wesleyan College	M
Rush University	M
Sacred Heart University	M,D,O
Saginaw Valley State University	M
Saint Francis Medical Center College of Nursing	M,D,O
Saint Joseph's College of Maine	M,O
Saint Peter's University	M,D,O
Salem State University	M
Salisbury University	M,D
Samford University	M,D
Samuel Merritt University	M,D,O
San Francisco State University	M,O
Seattle Pacific University	M,O
Seton Hall University	M,D
Shenandoah University	M,D,O
Southern Adventist University	M
Southern Illinois University Edwardsville	M
Southern Nazarene University	M
Southern New Hampshire University	M,O
Southern University and Agricultural and Mechanical College	M,D,O
Spalding University	M,D,O
Spring Hill College	M,O
State University of New York Polytechnic Institute	M
Stevenson University	M
Stony Brook University, State University of New York	M,D,O
Tarleton State University	M
Teachers College, Columbia University	M,D
Tennessee Technological University	M
Texas A&M University–Corpus Christi	M
Texas Christian University	M,D,O
Texas Tech University Health Sciences Center	M,D,O
Texas Woman's University	M,D
Thomas Edison State University	M
Union University	M,D,O
Universidad Metropolitana	M,O
University at Buffalo, the State University of New York	M,D,O
The University of Alabama at Birmingham	M,D
University of Central Arkansas	M,O
University of Cincinnati	M,D
University of Colorado Denver	M,D
University of Delaware	M,O
University of Hawaii at Manoa	M,D,O
University of Houston	M
University of Illinois at Chicago	M,O
University of Indianapolis	M,D
University of Louisville	M,O
University of Mary	M,D
University of Maryland, Baltimore	M
University of Massachusetts Amherst	M,D
University of Massachusetts Medical School	M,D
University of Memphis	M,O
University of Minnesota, Twin Cities Campus	M,D
University of Missouri	M,D
University of Missouri–Kansas City	M,D
University of New England	M,D,O
The University of North Carolina at Chapel Hill	M,D,O
The University of North Carolina at Charlotte	M,D,O
The University of North Carolina at Greensboro	M,D,O
The University of North Carolina at Pembroke	M
University of Pennsylvania	M,D
University of Phoenix–Bay Area Campus	M,D
University of Phoenix–Washington D.C. Campus	M,D
University of Pittsburgh	M,D
University of Rochester	M,D
University of St. Augustine for Health Sciences	M
University of St. Francis (IL)	M,D,O
University of Saint Mary	M,D
University of San Diego	M,D
The University of Scranton	M,D,O
University of South Alabama	M,D,O
University of South Carolina	M
University of Southern Indiana	M,D,O
University of Southern Maine	M,D,O
The University of Tennessee at Chattanooga	M,D,O
The University of Texas at Arlington	M,D
The University of Texas at Austin	M,D
The University of Texas at El Paso	M,D,O
The University of Texas at Tyler	M,D
The University of Texas Health Science Center at San Antonio	M,D,O
The University of Toledo	M,O
University of Victoria	M,D
University of Virginia	M,D
University of Washington, Tacoma	M
University of Wisconsin–Eau Claire	M,D
University of Wisconsin–Green Bay	M
Vanderbilt University	M,D,O

University	Degrees
Virginia Commonwealth University	M,D,O
Walden University	M,D,O
Walsh University	M,D
Washburn University	M,D,O
Washington Adventist University	M
Waynesburg University	M,D
Western Governors University	M
Western University of Health Sciences	M
West Virginia Wesleyan College	M,O
Wilmington University	M,D
Wilson College	M
Winona State University	M,D,O
Wright State University	M

NURSING EDUCATION

University	Degrees
Albany State University	M
Alvernia University	M,D,O
American International College	M,D
Angelo State University	M
Arizona State University at the Tempe campus	M,D,O
Aspen University	M
Auburn University	M
Auburn University at Montgomery	M
Austin Peay State University	M
Azusa Pacific University	M,D
Ball State University	M,D,O
Barry University	M,D
Bellarmine University	M,D
Bellin College	M
Bethel University (MN)	M,D,O
Blessing-Rieman College of Nursing & Health Sciences	M
Bowie State University	M
Bradley University	M,D,O
Brenau University	M
California Baptist University	M
California State University, Fullerton	M,D
California State University, San Marcos	M
California State University, Stanislaus	M
Capella University	M,D
Carlow University	M
Carson-Newman University	M
Case Western Reserve University	M
Cedar Crest College	M
Cedarville University	M
Central Methodist University	M
Chatham University	M,D
Clarion University of Pennsylvania	M,D,O
Clarkson College	M,O
Cleveland State University	D
College of Mount Saint Vincent	M,O
The College of New Rochelle	M,O
Colorado Mesa University	M,D,O
Columbus State University	M
Cox College	M
Daemen College	M,D
Delta State University	M,D
DeSales University	M,D
Drexel University	M
Duke University	M,D,O
Duquesne University	M,O
Eastern Michigan University	M
East Tennessee State University	M,D,O
Edinboro University of Pennsylvania	M,D
Elms College	M,D
Emmanuel College (United States)	M
Excelsior College	M
Felician University	M,O
Ferris State University	M
Florida National University	M
Florida Southern College	M
Florida State University	M,D,O
Framingham State University	M
Francis Marion University	M
Franklin Pierce University	M,D,O
Frostburg State University	M
Georgetown University	M,D
The George Washington University	M,D,O
Georgia Southern University	O
Georgia Southwestern State University	M,O
Goldfarb School of Nursing at Barnes-Jewish College	M
Graceland University (IA)	M,D,O
Grand Canyon University	M,D,O
Grand Valley State University	M,D
Grand View University	M,O
Gwynedd Mercy University	M,D
Herzing University Online	M
Holy Family University	M
Howard University	M
Immaculata University	M
Indiana State University	M
Indiana University Kokomo	M
Indiana University of Pennsylvania	M
Indiana University–Purdue University Fort Wayne	M,O
Indiana University–Purdue University Indianapolis	M
Indiana Wesleyan University	M
Jacksonville University	M
Jefferson College of Health Sciences	M
Kaplan University, Davenport Campus	M
Kent State University	M
Keuka College	M
King University	M,D
Lamar University	M
La Roche College	M
La Salle University	M,D,O
Le Moyne College	M
Lenoir-Rhyne University	M
Lewis University	M,D
Liberty University	M,D
Loma Linda University	M
Long Island University–LIU Brooklyn	M,O

Long Island University–LIU Post — M,O
Louisiana State University Health Sciences Center — M,D,O
Lourdes University — M
Loyola University New Orleans — M,D
Marian University (WI) — M
McKendree University — M
McMurry University — M
McNeese State University — M
Medical University of South Carolina — M
Mercy College — M
Messiah College — M
Metropolitan State University — M,D
MGH Institute of Health Professions — M,D,O
Miami Regional University — M
MidAmerica Nazarene University — M
Middle Tennessee State University — M
Midwestern State University — M
Millersville University of Pennsylvania — M,O
Millikin University — M,D
Minnesota State University Mankato — M,D
Missouri State University — M,D
Missouri Western State University — M,O
Molloy College — M,D,O
Monmouth University — M,D,O
Montana State University — M,D,O
Moravian College — M
Mount Mercy University — M
Mount St. Joseph University — M
Mount Saint Mary College — M,O
Nebraska Methodist College — M
New York University — M,O
Nicholls State University — M
Northeastern State University — M
Norwich University — M
Ohio University — M,D
Oklahoma Baptist University — M
Oklahoma City University — M,D
Oklahoma Wesleyan University — M
Old Dominion University — M,D
Oregon Health & Science University — M,O
Otterbein University — M,D,O
Our Lady of the Lake College — M
Pennsylvania College of Health Sciences — M
Queens University of Charlotte — M
Ramapo College of New Jersey — M
Regis College (MA) — M,D,O
Regis University — M,D
Rivier University — M,D
Roberts Wesleyan College — M
Sacred Heart University — M,D,O
Sage Graduate School — D
St. Catherine University — M,D
Saint Francis Medical Center College of Nursing — M,D,O
Saint Joseph's College of Maine — M,O
Salem State University — M
Salisbury University — M
Seattle Pacific University — M,O
Seton Hall University — M,D
Shenandoah University — M,D,O
Southeastern Louisiana University — M,D
Southern Connecticut State University — M,D
Southern Illinois University Edwardsville — M,O
Southern Nazarene University — M
Southern New Hampshire University — M,O
Southern University and Agricultural and Mechanical College — M,D,O
South University — M
South University (GA) — M
Spalding University — M,D,O
State University of New York College of Technology at Delhi — M
State University of New York Empire State College — M
State University of New York Polytechnic Institute — M,O
Stevenson University — M
Stony Brook University, State University of New York — M,O
Tarleton State University — M
Teachers College, Columbia University — M,D,O
Tennessee Technological University — M
Texas A&M University — M
Texas A&M University–Corpus Christi — M,O
Texas Christian University — M
Texas Tech University Health Sciences Center — M,D,O
Texas Woman's University — M,D
Thomas Edison State University — M
Towson University — M,O
Union University — M,D,O
The University of Alabama in Huntsville — M,D,O
University of Central Arkansas — M,O
University of Detroit Mercy — M,D,O
University of Hartford — M
University of Houston — M
University of Indianapolis — M,D
University of Louisiana at Lafayette — M
University of Louisville — M,D
University of Maine — M,O
University of Mary — M,D
University of Mary Hardin-Baylor — M,D,O
University of Maryland, Baltimore — M
University of Massachusetts Medical School — M,D,O
University of Memphis — M,O

University of Missouri–Kansas City — M,D
University of Nevada, Las Vegas — M,D,O
University of New Brunswick Fredericton — M
The University of North Carolina at Chapel Hill — M,D,O
The University of North Carolina at Charlotte — M,D,O
The University of North Carolina at Greensboro — M,D,O
The University of North Carolina at Pembroke — M
The University of North Carolina Wilmington — M,D,O
University of North Dakota — M,D,O
University of Northern Colorado — M,D
University of Phoenix–Atlanta Campus — M
University of Phoenix–Augusta Campus — M
University of Phoenix–Bay Area Campus — M,D
University of Phoenix–Charlotte Campus — M
University of Phoenix–Hawaii Campus — M
University of Phoenix–New Mexico Campus — M
University of Phoenix–North Florida Campus — M
University of Phoenix–Online Campus — M,O
University of Phoenix–Phoenix Campus — M,O
University of Phoenix–Sacramento Valley Campus — M
University of Phoenix–San Diego Campus — M
University of Phoenix–Southern California Campus — M,O
University of Phoenix–South Florida Campus — M
University of Phoenix–Utah Campus — M
University of Phoenix–Washington D.C. Campus — M,D
University of Portland — M,D
University of Rhode Island — M,D
University of Rochester — M,D
University of St. Augustine for Health Sciences — M
University of St. Francis (IL) — M,D,O
University of Saint Joseph — M,D
University of Saint Mary — M
University of South Alabama — M,D,O
University of Southern Indiana — M,D,O
University of Southern Maine — M,D,O
University of South Florida — M,D,O
The University of Tennessee at Chattanooga — M,D,O
The University of Texas at Arlington — M,D
The University of Texas at Austin — M,D
The University of Texas at El Paso — M,D,O
The University of Texas at Tyler — M,D
The University of Texas Health Science Center at San Antonio — M,D,O
The University of Toledo — M,O
University of Victoria — M,D
University of Washington, Tacoma — M
University of West Georgia — M,D,O
University of Wisconsin–Eau Claire — M,D
Ursuline College — M,D
Valparaiso University — M,D,O
Villanova University — M,D,O
Virginia Commonwealth University — M,D,O
Walden University — M,D,O
Walsh University — M,D
Washington Adventist University — M
Waynesburg University — M,D
Webster University — M
West Chester University of Pennsylvania — M,D,O
Western Connecticut State University — D
Western Governors University — M
West Virginia Wesleyan College — M,O
Wilson College — M
Winona State University — M,D,O
Winston-Salem State University — M,D
Worcester State University — M
York College of Pennsylvania — M,D,O

NURSING INFORMATICS

Aspen University — M
Austin Peay State University — M
Columbus State University — M
Duke University — M,D,O
Emporia State University — M
Excelsior College — M
Ferris State University — M
Georgia Southwestern State University — M,O
Georgia State University — M,D,O
Holy Names University — M,O
Jacksonville University — M
Le Moyne College — M,O
National University — M,O
New York University — M,O
Rutgers University–Newark — M,D
Samford University — M,D
Seattle Pacific University — M,O
Tennessee Technological University — M
Thomas Edison State University — M
Troy University — M,D
The University of Alabama at Birmingham — M,D
University of Minnesota, Twin Cities Campus — M,D

The University of North Carolina at Chapel Hill — M,D,O
University of Phoenix–Bay Area Campus — M,D
University of Phoenix–Charlotte Campus — M
University of Phoenix–Phoenix Campus — M,O
University of Phoenix–Southern California Campus — M,O
University of Phoenix–Washington D.C. Campus — M,D
University of Pittsburgh — M,D
University of St. Augustine for Health Sciences — M
Vanderbilt University — M,D,O
Walden University — M,D,O
Waynesburg University — M,D

NUTRITION

Abilene Christian University — O
Adelphi University — M,D,O
Alabama Agricultural and Mechanical University — M
American College of Healthcare Sciences — M,O
American University — M,O
American University of Beirut — M,O
Andrews University — M
Appalachian State University — M
Arizona State University at the Tempe campus — M,D
Auburn University — M,D,O
Ball State University — M
Bastyr University — M,O
Baylor University — M
Benedictine University — M
Boston University — M,D
Bradley University — M
Brigham Young University — M
Brooklyn College of the City University of New York — M
California Polytechnic State University, San Luis Obispo — M
California State University, Chico — M
California State University, Long Beach — M
California State University, Los Angeles — M,O
Canisius College — M
Case Western Reserve University — M,D
Cedar Crest College — O
Central Michigan University — M,D,O
Central Washington University — M
Chapman University — M
Clemson University — M
College of Saint Elizabeth — M,O
Colorado State University — M,D
Columbia University — M,D
Cornell University — M,D
D'Youville College — M
East Carolina University — M
Eastern Illinois University — M
Eastern Kentucky University — M
Eastern Michigan University — M
East Tennessee State University — M
Emory University — M,D
Florida International University — M,D
Florida State University — M,D
Framingham State University — M
George Mason University — M,O
Georgia Southern University — O
Georgia State University — M
Grand Valley State University — M
Harvard University — D
Howard University — M,D
Hunter College of the City University of New York — M
Huntington College of Health Sciences — M,O
Idaho State University — M,O
Immaculata University — M
Indiana University Bloomington — M,D
Indiana University of Pennsylvania — M
Indiana University–Purdue University Indianapolis — M,D
Instituto Tecnologico de Santo Domingo — M,O
Iowa State University of Science and Technology — M,D
James Madison University — M
Johns Hopkins University — M,D
Kansas State University — M,D
Kent State University — M
Lehman College of the City University of New York — M
Liberty University — M
Life University — M
Lipscomb University — M
Logan University — M,D
Loma Linda University — M,D
London Metropolitan University — M,D
Long Island University–LIU Post — M,O
Louisiana Tech University — M
Marshall University — M
Maryland University of Integrative Health — M,D,O
Marywood University — M,O
McGill University — M,D,O
McMaster University — M,D
McNeese State University — M
Meredith College — M,O
Michigan State University — M,D
Mississippi State University — M,D
Missouri State University — M,O
Montclair State University — M,D
Mount Mary University — M
Mount Saint Vincent University — M
New York Chiropractic College — M
New York Institute of Technology — M

New York University — M,D
North Carolina Agricultural and Technical State University — M
North Carolina State University — M,D
North Dakota State University — M,D
Northeastern University — M
Northern Illinois University — M
Nova Southeastern University — M,D,O
The Ohio State University — M,D
Ohio University — M
Oklahoma State University — M,D
Oregon Health & Science University — M,O
Oregon State University — M,D
Penn State University Park — M,D
Purdue University — M,D
Queens College of the City University of New York — M,O
Rosalind Franklin University of Medicine and Science — M
Rush University — M
Rutgers University–Newark — M,D,O
Rutgers University–New Brunswick — M,D
Sacred Heart University — M
Sage Graduate School — M,O
Saint Louis University — M
Sam Houston State University — M
San Diego State University — M
San Jose State University — M,O
Saybrook University — M,D,O
Simmons College — M,D,O
South Carolina State University — M
South Dakota State University — M,D
Southern Illinois University Carbondale — M
State University of New York College at Oneonta — M
Stony Brook University, State University of New York — M,O
Syracuse University — M,D
Teachers College, Columbia University — M,D,O
Texas A&M University — M
Texas State University — M
Texas Tech University — M,D
Texas Woman's University — M,D
Tufts University — M,D,O
Tuskegee University — M
Université de Moncton — M
Université de Montréal — M,D,O
Université Laval — M,D
University at Buffalo, the State University of New York — M,D,O
The University of Alabama — M
The University of Alabama at Birmingham — M,D
The University of Arizona — M,D
University of Arkansas for Medical Sciences — M,D,O
University of Bridgeport — M
The University of British Columbia — M
University of California, Berkeley — M,D
University of California, Davis — M,D
University of Central Oklahoma — M
University of Chicago — D
University of Cincinnati — M
University of Connecticut — M,D
University of Delaware — M,D
University of Florida — M,D
University of Georgia — M,D
University of Guelph — M,D
University of Hawaii at Manoa — M,D
University of Houston — M
University of Illinois at Chicago — M,D
University of Illinois at Urbana–Champaign — M,D
The University of Kansas — M,D,O
University of Kentucky — M,D
University of Manitoba — M,D
University of Maryland, College Park — M,D
University of Massachusetts Amherst — M,D
University of Memphis — M,O
University of Miami — M
University of Michigan — M
University of Minnesota, Twin Cities Campus — M,D
University of Mississippi — M,D
University of Missouri — M,D
University of Nebraska–Lincoln — M,D
University of Nebraska Medical Center — O
University of Nevada, Las Vegas — M
University of Nevada, Reno — M
University of New England — M,D,O
University of New Hampshire — M
University of New Haven — M
University of New Mexico — M
The University of North Carolina at Chapel Hill — M,D
The University of North Carolina at Greensboro — M,D
University of North Florida — M
University of Oklahoma Health Sciences Center — M
University of Pittsburgh — M
University of Puerto Rico, Medical Sciences Campus — M,D,O
University of Puerto Rico, Río Piedras Campus — M
University of Rhode Island — M,D
University of Saint Joseph — M
University of Southern Mississippi — M
University of South Florida — M,D,O
The University of Tampa — M
The University of Tennessee — M
The University of Tennessee at Martin — M
The University of Texas at Austin — M,D

The University of Texas Rio Grande Valley — M
The University of Texas Southwestern Medical Center — M
University of the District of Columbia — M
University of the Incarnate Word — M
The University of Toledo — M,O
University of Toronto — M,D
University of Utah — M,D
University of Vermont — M
University of Washington — M,D
University of Wisconsin–Madison — M,D
University of Wisconsin–Milwaukee — M,D
University of Wisconsin–Stevens Point — M
University of Wisconsin–Stout — M
University of Wyoming — M
Utah State University — M,D
Virginia Polytechnic Institute and State University — M,D
Washington State University — M
Wayne State University — M,D,O
West Chester University of Pennsylvania — M
Winthrop University — M,O

OCCUPATIONAL HEALTH NURSING

Rutgers University–Newark — M
University of Cincinnati — M,D
University of Illinois at Chicago — M,O
University of Minnesota, Twin Cities Campus — M,D
The University of North Carolina at Chapel Hill — M
University of South Florida — M,D,O
University of the Sacred Heart — M

OCCUPATIONAL THERAPY

Abilene Christian University — M
Adventist University of Health Sciences — M
Alabama State University — M
Allen College — M,D
Alvernia University — M
American International College — M,D
Arkansas State University — D
A.T. Still University — M,D,O
Augusta University — M
Barry University — M
Bay Path University — M
Belmont University — M,D
Boston University — D
Brenau University — M
Cabarrus College of Health Sciences — M
California State University, Dominguez Hills — M
Chatham University — M,D
Chicago State University — M
Clarkson University — M
Cleveland State University — M
College of Saint Mary — M
The College of St. Scholastica — M
Colorado State University — M,D
Columbia University — M,D
Concordia University Wisconsin — M
Creighton University — D
Dalhousie University — M
Dominican College — M
Dominican University of California — M
Duquesne University — M,D
D'Youville College — M
East Carolina University — M,D,O
Eastern Kentucky University — M
Eastern Michigan University — M
Eastern Washington University — M
Elizabethtown College — M
Elmhurst College — M
Florida Agricultural and Mechanical University — M
Florida Gulf Coast University — M
Florida International University — M
Gannon University — M,D
Governors State University — M
Grand Valley State University — M
Hofstra University — M
Idaho State University — M
Indiana State University — M,D
Indiana University–Purdue University Indianapolis — M,D
Ithaca College — M
James Madison University — M
Jefferson College of Health Sciences — M
Kean University — M
Keuka College — M
Le Moyne College — M
Lenoir-Rhyne University — M
Loma Linda University — M,D
Long Island University–LIU Brooklyn — M,D,O
Louisiana State University Health Sciences Center — M
Mary Baldwin University — D
Maryville University of Saint Louis — M
McMaster University — M
Medical University of South Carolina — M
Mercy College — M
MGH Institute of Health Professions — D
Midwestern University, Downers Grove Campus — M
Midwestern University, Glendale Campus — M
Milligan College — M
Misericordia University — M,D
Missouri State University — M
Mount Mary University — M,D

New England Institute of Technology — M
New York Institute of Technology — M
New York University — M,D
Northeastern State University — M
Northern Arizona University — D
Nova Southeastern University — M,D
The Ohio State University — M
Pacific University — D
Philadelphia University — M,D
Queen's University at Kingston — M,D
Radford University — M
Regis College (MA) — M,D,O
Regis University — M,D,O
Rochester Institute of Technology — M
Rockhurst University — M
Rocky Mountain University of Health Professions — D
Rush University — M
Sacred Heart University — M
Sage Graduate School — M
Saginaw Valley State University — M
St. Ambrose University — M
St. Catherine University — M
Saint Francis University — M
Saint Louis University — M
Salem State University — M
Samuel Merritt University — D
San Jose State University — M,O
Seton Hall University — M
Shawnee State University — M
Shenandoah University — M,D,O
Sonoma State University — M
South University — D
Spalding University — M
Springfield College — M
Stanbridge University — M
State University of New York Downstate Medical Center — M
Stockton University — M
Stony Brook University, State University of New York — M,D,O
Temple University — M,D
Tennessee State University — M
Texas Tech University Health Sciences Center — M
Texas Woman's University — M,D
Thomas Jefferson University — M,D
Touro College — M,D
Towson University — M
Tufts University — M,D,O
Tuskegee University — M
Université de Montréal — O
University at Buffalo, the State University of New York — M
The University of Alabama at Birmingham — M,O
University of Alberta — M,D
The University of British Columbia — M
University of Central Arkansas — M
The University of Findlay — M,D
University of Florida — M
University of Illinois at Chicago — M,D
University of Indianapolis — M,D
The University of Kansas — M,D
University of Louisiana at Monroe — M
University of Manitoba — M,D
University of Mary — M
University of Minnesota Rochester — M,D
University of Mississippi Medical Center — M
University of Missouri — M
University of New England — M,D
University of New Hampshire — M,O
University of New Mexico — M
The University of North Carolina at Chapel Hill — M,D
University of North Dakota — M
University of Oklahoma Health Sciences Center — M
University of Pittsburgh — M,D
University of Puerto Rico, Medical Sciences Campus — M
University of Puget Sound — M,D
University of St. Augustine for Health Sciences — M
The University of Scranton — M
University of South Alabama — M
The University of South Dakota — M,D
University of Southern California — M
University of Southern Indiana — M
University of Southern Maine — M
The University of Tennessee at Chattanooga — D
The University of Tennessee Health Science Center — M,D
The University of Texas at El Paso — M
The University of Texas Health Science Center at San Antonio — M,D
The University of Texas Medical Branch — M
The University of Texas Rio Grande Valley — M
University of the Sciences — M,D
The University of Toledo — M
University of Toronto — M
University of Utah — M,D
University of Washington — M,D
The University of Western Ontario — M
University of Wisconsin–La Crosse — M
University of Wisconsin–Madison — M
University of Wisconsin–Milwaukee — M
Utica College — M
Virginia Commonwealth University — M,D
Washington University in St. Louis — M,D
Wayne State University — M
West Coast University — M,D
Western Michigan University — M
Western New England University — D
Western New Mexico University — M

West Virginia University — M
Winston-Salem State University — M
Worcester State University — M
Xavier University — M

OCEAN ENGINEERING

Florida Atlantic University — M,D
Florida Institute of Technology — M,D
Massachusetts Institute of Technology — M,D,O
Memorial University of Newfoundland — M,D
Oregon State University — M,D
Princeton University — D
Stevens Institute of Technology — M,D
University of Alaska Anchorage — M,O
University of California, San Diego — M,D
University of Delaware — M,D
University of Florida — M,D
University of Hawaii at Manoa — M,D
University of Michigan — M,D,O
University of New Hampshire — M,D,O
University of Rhode Island — M,D
Virginia Polytechnic Institute and State University — M,D,O
Woods Hole Oceanographic Institution — D

OCEANOGRAPHY

Cornell University — D
Dalhousie University — M,D
Florida Institute of Technology — M,D
Florida State University — M,D
Louisiana State University and Agricultural & Mechanical College — M,D
Massachusetts Institute of Technology — M,D,O
McGill University — M,D
Memorial University of Newfoundland — M,D
Naval Postgraduate School — M,D
North Carolina State University — M,D
Nova Southeastern University — M,D
Old Dominion University — M,D
Oregon State University — M,D
Princeton University — D
Rutgers University–New Brunswick — M,D
Texas A&M University — M,D
Université du Québec à Rimouski — M,D
Université Laval — D
University of Alaska Fairbanks — M,D
The University of British Columbia — M,D
University of California, Los Angeles — M
University of California, San Diego — M,D
University of Colorado Boulder — M,D
University of Delaware — M,D
University of Hawaii at Manoa — M,D
University of Maryland, College Park — M,D
University of Miami — M,D
University of New Hampshire — M,D,O
University of Rhode Island — M,D
University of Southern California — M,D
University of South Florida — M,D
University of Victoria — M,D
University of Washington — M,D
University of Wisconsin–Madison — M,D
Woods Hole Oceanographic Institution — D
Yale University — D

ONCOLOGY NURSING

Gwynedd Mercy University — M,D
Universidad Metropolitana — M,O
University of Delaware — M,O
University of South Florida — M,D,O

OPERATIONS RESEARCH

Air Force Institute of Technology — M,D
Bowling Green State University — M
Capella University — M
Carnegie Mellon University — D
Case Western Reserve University — M,D
Claremont Graduate University — M,D
The College of William and Mary — M
Colorado School of Mines — M,D
Columbia University — M,D
Cornell University — M,D
École Polytechnique de Montréal — M,D,O
Florida Institute of Technology — M,D
George Mason University — M,D,O
Georgia Institute of Technology — M,D
Georgia State University — M,D
HEC Montreal — M
Idaho State University — M
Indiana University–Purdue University Fort Wayne — M,O
Iowa State University of Science and Technology — M,D
Johns Hopkins University — M,D
Kansas State University — M,D
Massachusetts Institute of Technology — M,D
Mississippi State University — M,D
Naval Postgraduate School — M,D
New Mexico Institute of Mining and Technology — M,D
North Carolina State University — M,D
Northeastern University — M
The Ohio State University — M
Princeton University — M,D
Rutgers University–New Brunswick — M,D
Simon Fraser University — M,D
Southern Illinois University Edwardsville — M
Southern Methodist University — M,D

The University of Alabama in Huntsville — M,D
University of Arkansas — M,D
The University of British Columbia — M
University of California, Berkeley — M,D
University of Colorado Denver — M,D
University of Delaware — M
University of Illinois at Chicago — M,D
The University of Iowa — M,D
University of Massachusetts Amherst — M,D
University of Michigan — M,D
The University of North Carolina at Chapel Hill — M,D
University of Southern California — M,D,O
The University of Texas at Austin — M,D
University of Waterloo — M,D

OPTICAL SCIENCES

Air Force Institute of Technology — M,D
Alabama Agricultural and Mechanical University — M,D
The College of William and Mary — M,D
Delaware State University — M,D
Duke University — M
École Polytechnique de Montréal — M,D,O
Norfolk State University — M
North Carolina Agricultural and Technical State University — M,D
The Ohio State University — M,D
Rochester Institute of Technology — M,D
Rose-Hulman Institute of Technology — M
The University of Alabama in Huntsville — M,D
The University of Arizona — M,D,O
University of Central Florida — M,D
University of Dayton — M,D
University of New Mexico — M,D
The University of North Carolina at Charlotte — M,D
University of Rochester — M,D

OPTOMETRY

Ferris State University — D
Illinois College of Optometry — D
Indiana University Bloomington — M,D
Inter American University of Puerto Rico School of Optometry — D
Marshall B. Ketchum University — M,D
MCPHS University — D
Midwestern University, Downers Grove Campus — D
Midwestern University, Glendale Campus — D
New England College of Optometry — M,D
Northeastern State University — D
Nova Southeastern University — M,D
The Ohio State University — M,D
Pacific University — M,D
Salus University — D
Southern College of Optometry — D
State University of New York College of Optometry — D
Université de Montréal — D
The University of Alabama at Birmingham — D
University of California, Berkeley — D,O
University of Houston — D
The University of Manchester — M,D
University of Missouri–St. Louis — D
University of Pikeville — D
University of the Incarnate Word — D
University of Waterloo — M,D
Western University of Health Sciences — D

ORAL AND DENTAL SCIENCES

American University of Beirut — M,D
A.T. Still University — M,D,O
Augusta University — M,D
Boston University — M,D
Case Western Reserve University — M,O
Columbia University — M,D,O
Dalhousie University — M
Harvard University — M,D,O
Howard University — D,O
Idaho State University — O
Jacksonville University — M,O
Loma Linda University — M,O
Marquette University — M,O
McGill University — M,D,O
Metropolitan State University — M,D
New York University — M,D,O
The Ohio State University — M,D
Oregon Health & Science University — M,D,O
Rutgers University–Newark — M,D,O
Saint Louis University — M
Seton Hill University — M,O
Stony Brook University, State University of New York — M,D,O
Temple University — M,O
Texas A&M University — M,D,O
Tufts University — M,O
Université de Montréal — M,O
Université Laval — M,O
University at Buffalo, the State University of New York — M,D,O
The University of Alabama at Birmingham — M
University of Alberta — M,D
The University of British Columbia — M,D
University of California, Los Angeles — M,D
University of California, San Francisco — M,D
University of Colorado Denver — M,D
University of Connecticut Health Center — M
University of Detroit Mercy — M,D,O
University of Florida — M,D,O
University of Illinois at Chicago — M,D
The University of Iowa — M,D,O

University of Kentucky	M
University of Louisville	M,D
The University of Manchester	M,D
University of Manitoba	M,D
University of Maryland, Baltimore	M,D,O
University of Michigan	M,D
University of Minnesota, Twin Cities Campus	M,D,O
University of Mississippi Medical Center	M,D
University of Missouri–Kansas City	M,D,O
University of Nebraska Medical Center	M,D
University of Nevada, Las Vegas	M,D
The University of North Carolina at Chapel Hill	M,D
University of Oklahoma Health Sciences Center	M
University of Pittsburgh	M,D,O
University of Puerto Rico, Medical Sciences Campus	O
University of Rochester	M
University of Southern California	M,D,O
The University of Tennessee Health Science Center	M,D
The University of Toledo	M
University of Toronto	M,D
University of Washington	M,D,O
The University of Western Ontario	M

ORGANIC CHEMISTRY

Auburn University	M,D
Binghamton University, State University of New York	M,D
Boston College	M,D
Brandeis University	M,D
Cleveland State University	M,D
Cornell University	D
Eastern New Mexico University	M
Florida State University	M,D
Georgetown University	D
The George Washington University	M,D
Georgia State University	M,D
Harvard University	D
Howard University	M,D
Indiana University Bloomington	M,D
Instituto Tecnológico y de Estudios Superiores de Monterrey, Campus Monterrey	M,D
Iowa State University of Science and Technology	M,D
Laurentian University	M
Marquette University	M,D
Massachusetts Institute of Technology	M,D,O
McMaster University	M,D
Old Dominion University	M,D
Oregon State University	M,D
Purdue University	M,D
Rice University	M,D
Rutgers University–Newark	M,D
Rutgers University–New Brunswick	M,D
Seton Hall University	M,D
Southern University and Agricultural and Mechanical College	M
State University of New York College of Environmental Science and Forestry	M,D
University of Calgary	M,D
University of Cincinnati	M,D
University of Louisville	M,D
The University of Manchester	M,D
University of Maryland, College Park	M,D
University of Massachusetts Lowell	M,D
University of Memphis	M,D
University of Miami	M,D
University of Michigan	D
University of Missouri–Kansas City	M,D
University of Montana	M,D
University of Nebraska–Lincoln	M,D
University of Notre Dame	M,D
University of Oklahoma	M,D
University of Regina	M,D
University of Southern Mississippi	M,D
The University of Tennessee	M,D
The University of Texas at Austin	D
The University of Toledo	M,D
University of Wisconsin–Milwaukee	M,D
Vanderbilt University	M,D
Virginia Commonwealth University	M,D
Wake Forest University	M,D
Wayne State University	M,D
Wesleyan University	D
West Virginia University	M,D
Yale University	D
Youngstown State University	M

ORGANIZATIONAL BEHAVIOR

Argosy University, Chicago	D
Arizona State University at the Tempe campus	M,D
A.T. Still University	M,D,O
Baruch College of the City University of New York	M,D
Benedictine University	M,D
Boston College	D
Brooklyn College of the City University of New York	M,D
California Lutheran University	M,O
Carnegie Mellon University	D
Case Western Reserve University	M,D
Cornell University	M,D
Drexel University	M,D,O

Fairleigh Dickinson University, College at Florham	M,O
Florida Institute of Technology	M
Florida State University	M,D
The Graduate Center, City University of New York	D
Harvard University	D
International Institute for Restorative Practices	M,O
John Jay College of Criminal Justice of the City University of New York	M,D
Lake Forest Graduate School of Management	M
New York University	M,D,O
Northwestern University	M
Phillips Graduate University	D
Purdue University	D
Saybrook University	M,D
Suffolk University	M
Towson University	O
Universidad de las Américas, A.C.	M
Université de Sherbrooke	M
University at Albany, State University of New York	M,D,O
The University of British Columbia	D
University of California, Berkeley	D
University of Chicago	M,O
University of Hartford	M
University of Hawaii at Manoa	M
The University of Kansas	M,D
University of New Mexico	M
The University of North Carolina at Chapel Hill	D
University of North Texas at Dallas	M
University of Oklahoma	M,O
University of Pittsburgh	M,D
The University of Texas at Austin	M
University of Utah	M,D
Wayne State University	M,D
Wilfrid Laurier University	M,D

ORGANIZATIONAL MANAGEMENT

Albertus Magnus College	M
Alvernia University	D
The American College of Financial Services	M
American Public University System	M
American University	M,O
Antioch University Los Angeles	M
Aquinas College (MI)	M
Argosy University, Chicago	D
Argosy University, Denver	M,D
Argosy University, Hawai'i	D
Argosy University, Inland Empire	M,D
Argosy University, Los Angeles	M,D
Argosy University, Northern Virginia	M,D,O
Argosy University, Orange County	D
Argosy University, San Diego	M,D
Argosy University, San Francisco Bay Area	M,D
Argosy University, Sarasota	M,D,O
Argosy University, Schaumburg	M,D,O
Argosy University, Seattle	M,D
Argosy University, Tampa	M,D
Argosy University, Twin Cities	M,D
Athabasca University	M,O
Auburn University at Montgomery	M
Augsburg College	M
Avila University	M
Azusa Pacific University	M
Baker University	M
Bellevue University	M
Benedictine University	M,D
Bethel University (MN)	M,D,O
Bluffton University	M
Boise State University	M
Boston College	D
Boston University	M
Bowling Green State University	M
Brandman University	M
Brenau University	M
Briercrest Seminary	M
Cabrini University	M
Cairn University	M,O
California Baptist University	M
California Coast University	M,D
California College of the Arts	M
California Intercontinental University	M,D
California State University, East Bay	M
California State University, Fullerton	M
Calvary University	M
Cambridge College	M
Capella University	M,D
Carlos Albizu University, Miami Campus	M,D
Carlow University	M,D,O
Carson-Newman University	M
Central Penn College	M
Charleston Southern University	M
The Chicago School of Professional Psychology	M,D
City University of Seattle	M,O
Clarks Summit University	M,D
Clemson University	M,D,O
College of Saint Elizabeth	M
College of Saint Mary	M
The College of Saint Rose	O
Colorado State University–Global Campus	M
Columbia Southern University	M
Columbus State University	M
Concordia College–New York	M
Concordia University (Canada)	M,O
Concordia University Ann Arbor	M
Concordia University, St. Paul	M

Concordia University Wisconsin	M
Crandall University	M
Creighton University	M
Dallas Baptist University	M,D
DePaul University	M
Drury University	M
Duke University	M,D,O
Duquesne University	M
Eastern Connecticut State University	M
Eastern Mennonite University	M
Eastern Michigan University	M,O
Eastern University	M,D
Embry-Riddle Aeronautical University–Worldwide	M
Emory & Henry College	M
Emory University	M
Endicott College	M
Evangel University	M
Excelsior College	M,O
Fairleigh Dickinson University, College at Florham	M,O
Fielding Graduate University	O
Florida Institute of Technology	M
Gannon University	D
Gardner-Webb University	D
Geneva College	M
George Fox University	M,D
George Mason University	M
The George Washington University	M,O
Georgia State University	M,D
Gonzaga University	M,D
Graceland University (IA)	M,D,O
Grand Canyon University	M,D
Grand View University	M,O
Granite State College	M
Harding University	M
Hawai'i Pacific University	M
HEC Montreal	D
Hood College	D
Husson University	M
Immaculata University	M
Indiana Tech	M
Indiana University Bloomington	M,D,O
Indiana University–Purdue University Fort Wayne	M,O
Indiana University–Purdue University Indianapolis	M,O
Indiana Wesleyan University	M,D,O
Instituto Tecnologico de Santo Domingo	M,O
Jacksonville University	M
James Madison University	D
John F. Kennedy University	M
Johns Hopkins University	M
John Wesley University	M,D
Judson University	M
Kaplan University, Davenport Campus	M
Keiser University	D
LaGrange College	M
Lenoir-Rhyne University	M
Lewis University	M
Lincoln Christian University	M
Lipscomb University	M
Lourdes University	M
Loyola University New Orleans	M
Malone University	M
Manhattan College	M
Manhattanville College	M
Mansfield University of Pennsylvania	M
Marian University (WI)	M
Marlboro College	M
Maryville University of Saint Louis	M
Medaille College	M
Mercer University	M,D
Mercy College	M
Mercyhurst University	M,O
Messiah College	M,O
Mid-America Christian University	M
Midway University	M
Misericordia University	M
Mount St. Joseph University	M
Neumann University	M
New Jersey City University	M
Newman University	M
The New School	M,O
New York University	M,D,O
Nichols College	M
Northern Kentucky University	M,D
Northwestern University	M
Northwest University	M
Norwich University	M
Nyack College	M
Oakland University	M,D,O
Ohio Christian University	M
Oklahoma Christian University	M
Olivet Nazarene University	M
Oregon State University	M,D
Our Lady of the Lake University	M,D
Oxford Graduate School	M
Palm Beach Atlantic University	M
Peirce College	M
Penn State University Park	M,D
Pepperdine University	M,D
Peru State College	M
Pfeiffer University	M
Point Loma Nazarene University	M
Point Park University	M
Queens University of Charlotte	M
Quinnipiac University	M
Regent University	M,D,O
Regis University	M
Rider University	M
Robert Morris University	M
Rochester Institute of Technology	O
Roosevelt University	M
Rutgers University–Newark	D
Sage Graduate School	M

St. Ambrose University	M
St. Catherine University	M
St. Edward's University	M
St. Joseph's College, Long Island Campus	M
St. Joseph's College, New York	M
Saint Louis University	M,D,O
Saint Mary-of-the-Woods College	M
Saint Mary's College of California	M
Saint Mary's University of Minnesota	M
Salve Regina University	M,O
San Diego Christian College	M
Saybrook University	M,D
Seattle University	M,O
Shippensburg University of Pennsylvania	M
Siena Heights University	M,O
Simpson University	M
SIT Graduate Institute	M
Southeastern University (FL)	M,D
Southern Arkansas University–Magnolia	M
Southern New Hampshire University	M,O
South University	M
South University (MI)	M
South University (SC)	M
South University (GA)	M
Southwest University	M
State University of New York College at Potsdam	M
Stockton University	D
Syracuse University	O
Thomas Edison State University	M
Trevecca Nazarene University	M,D
Trinity Washington University	M
Trinity Western University	M,O
Union Institute & University	M
United States International University–Africa	M
Université Laval	M,O
University of Alberta	D
The University of Arizona	M,D
University of Central Arkansas	D
University of Charleston	D
University of Cincinnati	M
University of Dallas	M,D
University of Denver	M,O
University of Guelph	M
University of Hawaii at Manoa	M,D
The University of Kansas	M,D,O
University of La Verne	M,D,O
University of Maryland Eastern Shore	D
University of Massachusetts Amherst	M,D
University of Massachusetts Dartmouth	M,O
University of Michigan–Flint	M,O
University of Missouri	M,D,O
University of Nebraska at Omaha	M
University of New Haven	M,O
University of New Mexico	M
University of Northwestern–St. Paul	M
University of Oklahoma	M,O
University of Pennsylvania	M,O
University of Phoenix–Bay Area Campus	M,D
University of Phoenix–Online Campus	D,O
University of Phoenix–Washington D.C. Campus	M,D
University of Portland	M,D
University of Regina	M,O
University of Saint Francis (IN)	M
University of St. Thomas (MN)	M
University of San Francisco	M
The University of South Dakota	M
University of Southern California	M
University of Southern Indiana	M,D,O
The University of Texas at San Antonio	D
The University of Texas at Tyler	M
University of Wisconsin–Platteville	M
Upper Iowa University	M
Vanderbilt University	M,D
Viterbo University	M,O
Walden University	M,D,O
Waldorf University	M
Warner Pacific College	M
Washington University in St. Louis	M
Wayland Baptist University	M,D
Waynesburg University	M
Wayne State College	M
Wayne State University	M,D
Western New England University	M
West Liberty University	M
Wheeling Jesuit University	M
Wilfrid Laurier University	M,D
Wilkes University	M
William Penn University	M
Williamson College	M
Wilmington University	M,D
Winona State University	M,D,O
Woodbury University	M
Worcester Polytechnic Institute	M,D,O
Worcester State University	M
Yale University	D

OSTEOPATHIC MEDICINE

Alabama College of Osteopathic Medicine	D
A.T. Still University	M,D
Campbell University	D
Des Moines University	D
Edward Via College of Osteopathic Medicine–Carolinas Campus	D

Edward Via College of Osteopathic Medicine–Virginia Campus	D
Georgia Campus–Philadelphia College of Osteopathic Medicine	D
Kansas City University of Medicine and Biosciences	D
Lake Erie College of Osteopathic Medicine	M,D,O
Liberty University	D
Lincoln Memorial University	D
Marian University (IN)	M,D
Michigan State University	D
Midwestern University, Downers Grove Campus	D
Midwestern University, Glendale Campus	D
New York Institute of Technology	M,D
Nova Southeastern University	M,D,O
Ohio University	D
Oklahoma State University Center for Health Sciences	D
Pacific Northwest University of Health Sciences	D
Philadelphia College of Osteopathic Medicine	D
Rocky Vista University	D
Rowan University	D
Touro University California	M,D
University of New England	D
University of North Texas Health Science Center at Fort Worth	D
University of Pikeville	D
University of the Incarnate Word	M,D
Western University of Health Sciences	D
West Virginia School of Osteopathic Medicine	D
William Carey University	D

PACIFIC AREA/PACIFIC RIM STUDIES

The University of British Columbia	M
University of Guam	M
University of Hawaii at Manoa	M,O
University of San Francisco	M
University of Victoria	M

PALEONTOLOGY

Cornell University	M,D
Duke University	D
East Tennessee State University	M
South Dakota School of Mines and Technology	M,D
University of Chicago	D
The University of Manchester	M,D
The University of Texas at Dallas	M,D
West Virginia University	M,D
Yale University	D

PAPER AND PULP ENGINEERING

Georgia Institute of Technology	M,D
North Carolina State University	M,D
State University of New York College of Environmental Science and Forestry	M,D,O
The University of Manchester	M,D
University of Minnesota, Twin Cities Campus	M,D
Western Michigan University	M,D

PARASITOLOGY

Illinois State University	M,D
Louisiana State University Health Sciences Center	D
McGill University	M,D,O
Oregon State University	M,D
Tulane University	M,D,O
University of Notre Dame	M,D
University of Prince Edward Island	M,D

PASTORAL MINISTRY AND COUNSELING

Abilene Christian University	M,D
Ambrose University	M,O
American Baptist Seminary of the West	M
Amridge University	M,D
Anabaptist Mennonite Biblical Seminary	M,O
Anderson University (SC)	M,D
Andrews University	M,D,O
Appalachian Bible College	M
Aquinas Institute of Theology	M,D,O
Argosy University, Sarasota	M,D
Asbury Theological Seminary	M,D,O
Ashland Theological Seminary	M,D
Assemblies of God Theological Seminary	M,D
Atlantic School of Theology	M,O
Atlantic University	O
Austin Presbyterian Theological Seminary	M,D
Ave Maria University	M,D
Azusa Pacific University	M
Bakke Graduate University	M,D
Baptist Bible College	M
The Baptist College of Florida	M
Baptist Theological Seminary at Richmond	M,D,O
Barry University	M,D
Bethany Global University	M
Bethany Theological Seminary	M,O
Bethel College	M
Bethel Seminary	M,D,O
Biblical Theological Seminary	M,D,O
Biola University	M,D,O
Bob Jones University	M,D,O
Boston College	M,D,O
Boston University	M,D
Briercrest Seminary	M
Brite Divinity School	M,D,O
Cairn University	M
California Baptist University	M
Calvary University	M
Calvin Theological Seminary	M,D
Campbell University	M,D
Canadian Southern Baptist Seminary	M

Cardinal Stritch University	M
Carolina Christian College	M
Catholic Theological Union	M,D,O
The Catholic University of America	M,D,O
Cedarville University	M,D
Chaminade University of Honolulu	M
Charlotte Christian College and Theological Seminary	M
Chicago Theological Seminary	M,D
Christian Theological Seminary	M,D
Christ the King Seminary	M
Cincinnati Christian University	M
City Vision University	M
Claremont Lincoln University	M
Claremont School of Theology	M,D
Clarks Summit University	M,D
Columbia International University	M,D,O
Concordia University, Nebraska	M
Corban University	M,D,O
Covenant Theological Seminary	M,D
Criswell College	M
Dallas Baptist University	M,D
Dallas Theological Seminary	M,D,O
Denver Seminary	M,D,O
Eastern Mennonite University	M,O
Eastern University	M,D
East Texas Baptist University	M
Ecumenical Theological Seminary	D
Emory University	M,D
Evangelical Seminary	M
Fairfield University	M
Faith Baptist Bible College and Theological Seminary	M
Faulkner University	M
Fordham University	M,D,O
Freed-Hardeman University	M,D
Fresno Pacific University	M
Fuller Theological Seminary	M,D,O
Gannon University	M,O
Gardner-Webb University	M,D
Garrett-Evangelical Theological Seminary	M,D
Gateway Seminary	M,D,O
General Theological Seminary	M,D,O
Geneva College	M
George Fox University	M,D,O
Georgia Christian University	M,D
Global University	M,D
Gordon-Conwell Theological Seminary	M,D
Grace Theological Seminary	M,D,O
Grace University	M
Grand Canyon University	D
Grand Rapids Theological Seminary of Cornerstone University	M
Greenville College	M
Hampton University	M,D,O
Harding School of Theology	M,D
Harding University	M
Hardin-Simmons University	M,D
Hartford Seminary	M,D,O
Heritage Christian University	M
Holmes Institute	M
Holy Names University	M
Houston Baptist University	M
Houston Graduate School of Theology	M,D
Howard Payne University	M
Huntington University	M,D
Iliff School of Theology	M,D
Indiana Wesleyan University	M
Inter American University of Puerto Rico, Metropolitan Campus	D
Interdenominational Theological Center	M,D
International Baptist College and Seminary	M,D
Johnson University	M,D,O
John Wesley University	M,D
Judson University	M
The King's University	M,D,O
Kingswood University	M
Knox Theological Seminary	D
Lancaster Bible College	M,D,O
La Salle University	M
La Sierra University	M
Lee University	M
Liberty University	M,D,O
Lincoln Christian Seminary	M,D
Lincoln Christian University	M
Lipscomb University	M,D,O
Loras College	M
Louisiana College	M
Loyola Marymount University	M
Loyola University Chicago	M,O
Lutheran School of Theology at Chicago	M,D
Lutheran Theological Seminary at Gettysburg	M,D
The Lutheran Theological Seminary at Philadelphia	M,D,O
Lutheran Theological Seminary Saskatoon	M,D
Luther Rice College & Seminary	M,D
Luther Seminary	M,D
Madonna University	M
Maple Springs Baptist Bible College and Seminary	M,D,O
Maranatha Baptist University	M
Martin University	M
Marymount University	M
The Master's University	M
McCormick Theological Seminary	M,D,O
McMaster University	M,D,O
Meadville Lombard Theological School	M,D
Mercer University	M,D
Mid-America Christian University	M
Midwestern Baptist Theological Seminary	M,D,O
Milligan College	M,D
Missouri Baptist University	M,O
Moody Bible Institute	M,O
Moravian Theological Seminary	M,O

Mount Marty College	M
Mount St. Joseph University	M,O
Nashotah House Theological Seminary	M,D,O
Neumann University	M,D
New Brunswick Theological Seminary	M,D
New Orleans Baptist Theological Seminary	M,D
Northern Seminary	M,D
North Greenville University	M,D
North Park Theological Seminary	M,O
Northwest Nazarene University	M
Northwest University	M
Nyack College	M,D
Oakwood University	M
Oblate School of Theology	M,D,O
Ohio Christian University	M
Oral Roberts University	M
Ottawa University	M
Pacific Rim Christian University	M
Pentecostal Theological Seminary	M
Pepperdine University	M
Phillips Theological Seminary	M,D,O
Phoenix Seminary	M,D
Piedmont International University	M,D
Pittsburgh Theological Seminary	M,D
Point Loma Nazarene University	M
Providence University College & Theological Seminary	M,D
Randall University	M
Reformed Theological Seminary–Charlotte Campus	M,D
Reformed Theological Seminary–Jackson Campus	M,D,O
Reformed Theological Seminary–Orlando Campus	M,D,O
Regent University	M,D,O
Regis College (Canada)	M,D,O
Richmont Graduate University	M,O
Sacred Heart Major Seminary	M
St. Ambrose University	M
St. Augustine's Seminary of Toronto	M,O
St. Bernard's School of Theology and Ministry	M,O
St. Catherine University	M,O
St. John's Seminary (CA)	M,O
Saint John's University (MN)	M
Saint Joseph's College of Maine	M
St. Joseph's Seminary	M,D
Saint Paul University	M,D,O
Saints Cyril and Methodius Seminary	M
St. Stephen's College	M
St. Thomas University	M,D,O
Saint Vincent Seminary	M
Santa Clara University	M,D,O
Seattle University	M
Selma University	M
Seton Hall University	M,O
Shasta Bible College	M
Shepherds Theological Seminary	M
Shiloh University	M,D
Simpson University	M
Sioux Falls Seminary	M
Southeastern University (FL)	M,D
The Southern Baptist Theological Seminary	M,D
Southern Evangelical Seminary	M
Southern Wesleyan University	M
South University (MI)	D
South University (GA)	D
Southwestern Assemblies of God University	M
Southwestern Baptist Theological Seminary	M,D,O
Southwestern Christian University	M
Spring Arbor University	M
Spring Hill College	M,O
SUM Bible College & Theological Seminary	M
Theological University of the Caribbean	M,D
Trevecca Nazarene University	M
Trinity College (Canada)	M,D,O
Trinity International University	M,D,O
Trinity Lutheran Seminary	M
Trinity School for Ministry	M,D,O
Trinity Western University	M,D
Tyndale University College & Seminary	M,O
Unification Theological Seminary	M,D
Union University	M,D
United Theological Seminary	M,D
United Theological Seminary of the Twin Cities	M,D,O
University of Chicago	M
University of Dallas	M,D
University of Dayton	M,D
University of Fort Lauderdale	M
University of Northwestern–St. Paul	M
University of Portland	M
University of Saint Mary of the Lake–Mundelein Seminary	M,D
University of St. Michael's College	M,D,O
University of St. Thomas (MN)	M
University of St. Thomas (TX)	M
University of South Africa	M,D
University of the Incarnate Word	M
Ursuline College	M
Virginia Beach Theological Seminary	M
Virginia University of Lynchburg	M,D
Viterbo University	M,O
Walsh University	M
Wayland Baptist University	M
Wesley Biblical Seminary	M
Western Seminary	M,D,O
Western Seminary–Sacramento Campus	M,O

Western Seminary–San Jose Campus	M,O
Western Theological Seminary	M,D,O
Westminster Theological Seminary	M,D,O
Wheaton College	M,D
Wilfrid Laurier University	M,D,O
Xavier University	M
Xavier University of Louisiana	M

PATHOBIOLOGY

Brown University	M,D
Columbia University	M,D
Drexel University	M,D
Johns Hopkins University	D
Kansas State University	M,D
Medical University of South Carolina	D
Michigan State University	M,D
New York University	D
Penn State University Park	M,D
Purdue University	M,D
The University of Alabama at Birmingham	D
University of Cincinnati	D
University of Connecticut	M,D
University of Illinois at Urbana–Champaign	M,D
University of Missouri	M,D
University of Toronto	M,D
University of Washington	D
University of Wyoming	M
Wake Forest University	M,D
Yale University	D

PATHOLOGY

Albert Einstein College of Medicine	D
Baylor College of Medicine	D
Boston University	D
Case Western Reserve University	M,D
Colorado State University	M,D
Columbia University	M,D
Dalhousie University	M,D
Duke University	M,D
Harvard University	D
Indiana University–Purdue University Indianapolis	M,D
Iowa State University of Science and Technology	M,D
Johns Hopkins University	D
Loma Linda University	D
McGill University	M,D
Medical University of South Carolina	M,D
Michigan State University	M,D
New York Medical College	M,D
North Carolina State University	M,D
North Dakota State University	M,D
Purdue University	M,D
Queen's University at Kingston	M,D
Quinnipiac University	M
Rosalind Franklin University of Medicine and Science	M
Rutgers University–Newark	D
Saint Louis University	D
Stony Brook University, State University of New York	M,D
Tufts University	M,D
Université de Montréal	M,D
Université Laval	O
University at Buffalo, the State University of New York	M,D
University of Alberta	M,D
The University of British Columbia	M,D
University of Calgary	M,D
University of California, Davis	M,D
University of California, Irvine	D
University of California, Los Angeles	M,D
University of Cincinnati	D
University of Georgia	M,D
University of Guelph	M,D,O
The University of Iowa	M
The University of Kansas	M,D
University of Manitoba	M
University of Maryland, Baltimore	M
University of Michigan	D
University of Mississippi Medical Center	D
University of Missouri	M
University of Nebraska Medical Center	M,D
University of New Mexico	M,D
The University of North Carolina at Chapel Hill	D
University of Oklahoma Health Sciences Center	D
University of Pittsburgh	D
University of Prince Edward Island	M,D
University of Rochester	D
University of Saskatchewan	M,D
University of Southern California	M
University of South Florida	M,D
The University of Tennessee Health Science Center	M,D
The University of Texas Medical Branch	D
The University of Toledo	M,O
University of Utah	M,D
University of Vermont	D
University of Virginia	D
University of Washington	D
The University of Western Ontario	M,D
University of Wisconsin–Madison	D
Vanderbilt University	D
Wayne State University	M,D,O
Yale University	M,D

PEDIATRIC NURSING

Augusta University	D
Boston College	M,D
Caribbean University	M,D
Case Western Reserve University	M

Columbia University	M,O
Creighton University	M,D,O
Drexel University	M
Duke University	M,D,O
Emory University	M
Florida International University	M,D
Georgia State University	M,D,O
Gwynedd Mercy University	M,D
Hampton University	M,D
Indiana University–Purdue University Indianapolis	M
Johns Hopkins University	D
Kent State University	M,D
King University	M,D
Lehman College of the City University of New York	M
Loma Linda University	M
Marquette University	M,D,O
Maryville University of Saint Louis	M,D
MGH Institute of Health Professions	M,D,O
Molloy College	M,D,O
New York University	M,D,O
Northeastern University	M,D,O
Old Dominion University	M,D
Oregon Health & Science University	M
Purdue University	M,D,O
Queen's University at Kingston	M,D,O
Rush University	D,O
St. Catherine University	M,D
San Francisco State University	M,O
Seton Hall University	M,D
Spalding University	M,D,O
Stony Brook University, State University of New York	M,D,O
Texas Christian University	M,D,O
Texas Tech University Health Sciences Center	M,D,O
Texas Woman's University	M,D
The University of Alabama at Birmingham	M,D
University of Cincinnati	M,D
University of Colorado Denver	M,D
University of Delaware	M,O
University of Illinois at Chicago	M,O
University of Maryland, Baltimore	M
University of Michigan	M,D,O
University of Minnesota, Twin Cities Campus	M,D
University of Missouri	M,D,O
University of Missouri–Kansas City	M,D
University of Missouri–St. Louis	D,O
The University of North Carolina at Chapel Hill	M,D,O
University of Pennsylvania	M
University of Pittsburgh	M,D
University of Puerto Rico, Medical Sciences Campus	M
University of Rochester	M,D
University of South Carolina	M
University of South Florida	M,D,O
The University of Texas at Austin	M,D
The University of Texas Health Science Center at San Antonio	M,D,O
The University of Toledo	M,O
University of Wisconsin–Madison	D
Vanderbilt University	M,D,O
Villanova University	M,D,O
Virginia Commonwealth University	M,D,O
Wayne State University	M,O
Wright State University	M

PERFUSION

Milwaukee School of Engineering	M
Quinnipiac University	M
Rush University	M
The University of Arizona	M,D
University of Nebraska Medical Center	M

PETROLEUM ENGINEERING

Colorado School of Mines	M,D
Louisiana State University and Agricultural & Mechanical College	M,D
Missouri University of Science and Technology	M,D
Montana Tech of The University of Montana	M
New Mexico Institute of Mining and Technology	M,D
Texas A&M University	M,D
Texas A&M University–Kingsville	M
Texas Tech University	M,D
University of Alaska Fairbanks	M
University of Alberta	M,D
University of Calgary	M,D
University of Houston	M,D
The University of Kansas	M,D,O
University of Louisiana at Lafayette	M
University of Oklahoma	M,D,O
University of Pittsburgh	M,D
University of Regina	M,D
University of Southern California	M,D,O
The University of Texas at Austin	M,D
The University of Tulsa	M,D
University of Utah	M,D
University of Wyoming	M,D

PHARMACEUTICAL ADMINISTRATION

Columbia University	M
Duquesne University	M
Fairleigh Dickinson University, Metropolitan Campus	M,D
Florida Agricultural and Mechanical University	M,D

Idaho State University	M,D
New Jersey Institute of Technology	M,D
Northeast Ohio Medical University	M,D,O
The Ohio State University	M,D
Purdue University	M,D,O
Rutgers University–Newark	M
St. John's University (NY)	M
San Diego State University	M
Temple University	M
University of Florida	M,D
University of Georgia	D
University of Houston	M,D
University of Illinois at Chicago	M,D
University of Maryland, Baltimore	M,D
University of Michigan	D
University of Minnesota, Twin Cities Campus	M,D
The University of North Carolina at Chapel Hill	M,D
University of Pittsburgh	M
University of Southern California	M
University of the Sciences	M
The University of Toledo	M
University of Utah	M,D
University of Wisconsin–Madison	M,D
Virginia Commonwealth University	M,D
West Virginia University	M,D

PHARMACEUTICAL ENGINEERING

New Jersey Institute of Technology	M,D
University of Michigan	M,D

PHARMACEUTICAL SCIENCES

Albany College of Pharmacy and Health Sciences	M,D
Auburn University	M,D
Boston University	M,D
Butler University	M,D
Campbell University	M,D
Chapman University	M,D
Creighton University	M,D
Drexel University	M
Duquesne University	M,D
East Tennessee State University	D
Florida Agricultural and Mechanical University	M,D
Idaho State University	M,D
Irell & Manella Graduate School of Biological Sciences	D*
Johns Hopkins University	M
Long Island University–Hudson	M,O
Long Island University–LIU Brooklyn	M,D
MCPHS University	M,D
Memorial University of Newfoundland	M,D
Mercer University	D
Northeastern University	M,D,O
Northeast Ohio Medical University	M,D,O
Oregon State University	M,D
Purdue University	M,D
Queen's University at Kingston	M,D
Rowan University	M
Rush University	M,D
Rutgers University–New Brunswick	M,D
St. John's University (NY)	M,D
South Dakota State University	M,D
Stevens Institute of Technology	M,O
Temple University	M,D
Texas Southern University	M,D
Texas Tech University Health Sciences Center	M,D
Université de Montréal	M,D,O
Université Laval	M,D,O
University at Buffalo, the State University of New York	M,D
University of Alberta	M,D
The University of Arizona	M,D
The University of British Columbia	M,D
University of California, Irvine	D
University of California, San Francisco	D
University of Cincinnati	M,D
University of Colorado Denver	D
University of Connecticut	M,D
University of Florida	M,D
University of Georgia	M,D
University of Hawaii at Hilo	D
University of Houston	M,D
University of Illinois at Chicago	M,D
The University of Iowa	M,D
University of Kentucky	M,D
The University of Manchester	M,D
University of Manitoba	M,D
University of Maryland, Baltimore	D
University of Maryland Eastern Shore	M,D
University of Michigan	D
University of Minnesota, Twin Cities Campus	M,D
University of Montana	M,D
University of Nebraska Medical Center	M,D
University of New Mexico	M,D
The University of North Carolina at Chapel Hill	M,D
University of North Texas Health Science Center at Fort Worth	M,D
University of Oklahoma Health Sciences Center	M,D
University of Pittsburgh	M,D
University of Puerto Rico, Medical Sciences Campus	M,D
University of Rhode Island	M,D
University of Saskatchewan	M,D
University of South Carolina	M,D
University of Southern California	M,D,O
University of South Florida	M,D

The University of Tennessee Health Science Center	M,D
The University of Texas at Austin	M,D
University of the Pacific	M,D
University of the Sciences	M,D
The University of Toledo	M
University of Toronto	M,D
University of Utah	M,D
University of Washington	M,D
University of Wisconsin–Madison	M,D
Virginia Commonwealth University	M,D
Wayne State University	M,D
Western University of Health Sciences	M
West Virginia University	D

PHARMACOLOGY

Albany College of Pharmacy and Health Sciences	M,D
Albany Medical College	M,D
Alliant International University–San Francisco	M
American University of Beirut	M,D
Argosy University, Hawai`i	M,O
Augusta University	M,D
Baylor College of Medicine	D
Boston University	D
Case Western Reserve University	D
Columbia University	M,D
Cornell University	M,D
Creighton University	M,D
Dalhousie University	M,D
Drexel University	M,D
Duke University	D
Duquesne University	M,D
East Carolina University	D
East Tennessee State University	D
Emory University	D
Fairleigh Dickinson University, College at Florham	M,O
Florida Agricultural and Mechanical University	M,D
Georgetown University	M,D
Howard University	M,D
Husson University	M,D
Idaho State University	M,D
Indiana University–Purdue University Indianapolis	M,D
Johns Hopkins University	D
Kent State University	M,D
Loma Linda University	D
London Metropolitan University	M,D
Long Island University–LIU Brooklyn	M,D
Louisiana State University Health Sciences Center	D
Louisiana State University Health Sciences Center at Shreveport	M,D
McGill University	M,D
McMaster University	M,D
MCPHS University	M,D
Medical College of Wisconsin	D
Meharry Medical College	D
Michigan State University	M,D
Montclair State University	M
New Jersey Institute of Technology	M,D
New York Medical College	M,D
North Carolina State University	M,D
Northeastern University	M,D,O
The Ohio State University	M,D
Oregon Health & Science University	D
Oregon State University	M,D
Purdue University	M,D
Queen's University at Kingston	M,D
Rush University	M,D
Rutgers University–Newark	D
Saint Louis University	M,D
Southern Illinois University Carbondale	M,D
State University of New York Upstate Medical University	D
Stony Brook University, State University of New York	
Thomas Jefferson University	M
Tulane University	M
Universidad Central del Caribe	M,D
Université de Montréal	M,D
Université de Sherbrooke	M,D
University at Buffalo, the State University of New York	M,D
The University of Alabama at Birmingham	D
University of Alberta	M,D
The University of Arizona	M,D
University of Arkansas for Medical Sciences	M,D,O
The University of British Columbia	M,D
University of California, Davis	M,D
University of California, Los Angeles	M,D
University of California, San Francisco	D
University of Cincinnati	D
University of Colorado Denver	D
University of Connecticut	M,D
University of Florida	M,D
University of Georgia	M,D
University of Guelph	M,D
University of Hawaii at Hilo	M
University of Houston	M,D
University of Illinois at Chicago	D
The University of Iowa	M,D
The University of Kansas	M,D
University of Kentucky	D
University of Louisville	M,D
The University of Manchester	M,D
University of Manitoba	M,D
University of Maryland, Baltimore	M,D
University of Miami	D

University of Michigan	M,D
University of Minnesota, Duluth	M,D
University of Minnesota, Twin Cities Campus	M,D
University of Mississippi Medical Center	D
University of Missouri	M,D
University of Nebraska Medical Center	M,D
The University of North Carolina at Chapel Hill	D
University of North Texas Health Science Center at Fort Worth	M,D
University of Pennsylvania	D
University of Prince Edward Island	M,D
University of Puerto Rico, Medical Sciences Campus	M,D
University of Rhode Island	M,D
University of Rochester	M,D
University of Saskatchewan	M,D
The University of South Dakota	M,D
The University of Tennessee Health Science Center	M,D
The University of Texas at Austin	M,D
The University of Texas Health Science Center at Houston	M,D
The University of Texas Health Science Center at San Antonio	D
The University of Texas Medical Branch	M,D
University of the Sciences	M,D
The University of Toledo	M,D
University of Toronto	M,D
University of Utah	D
University of Vermont	D
University of Virginia	D
University of Washington	D
University of Wisconsin–Madison	D
Vanderbilt University	D
Virginia Commonwealth University	M,D,O
Wake Forest University	D
Wayne State University	M,D,O
Weill Cornell Medicine	M,D
West Virginia University	D
Wright State University	M
Yale University	D

PHARMACY

Albany College of Pharmacy and Health Sciences	M,D
Appalachian College of Pharmacy	D
Auburn University	D
Belmont University	D
Butler University	M,D
Campbell University	M,D
Cedarville University	M,D
Chapman University	D
Chicago State University	D
Concordia University Wisconsin	D
Creighton University	D
Drake University	D
Duquesne University	D
D'Youville College	D
East Tennessee State University	D
Fairleigh Dickinson University, College at Florham	D
Ferris State University	D
Florida Agricultural and Mechanical University	D
Georgia Campus–Philadelphia College of Osteopathic Medicine	D
Hampton University	D
Harding University	D
Howard University	D
Husson University	M,D
Idaho State University	M,D
Keck Graduate Institute	D
Lake Erie College of Osteopathic Medicine	M,D,O
Lebanese American University	D
Lipscomb University	M,D
Loma Linda University	D
Long Island University–Hudson	M,O
Long Island University–LIU Brooklyn	M,D
Manchester University	D
Marshall University	D
MCPHS University	D
Medical University of South Carolina	D
Mercer University	D
Midwestern University, Downers Grove Campus	D
Midwestern University, Glendale Campus	D
North Dakota State University	D
Northeastern University	M,D,O
Northeast Ohio Medical University	D
Notre Dame of Maryland University	D
Nova Southeastern University	M,D
Ohio Northern University	D
The Ohio State University	M,D
Oregon State University	D
Pacific University	D
Palm Beach Atlantic University	D
Purdue University	D
Regis University	D
Roosevelt University	D
Rosalind Franklin University of Medicine and Science	D
Roseman University of Health Sciences	D
Rutgers University–New Brunswick	M,D
St. John Fisher College	D
St. Louis College of Pharmacy	D
Samford University	D
Shenandoah University	D
South College	D

M—masters degree; D—doctorate; O—other advanced degree; *—Close-Up and/or Display

Institution	Degree
South Dakota State University	D
Southern Illinois University Edwardsville	D
South University (SC)	D
South University (GA)	D
Southwestern Oklahoma State University	D
Sullivan University	D
Temple University	M,D
Texas A&M University	D
Texas Southern University	D
Thomas Jefferson University	D
Touro University California	M,D
Union University	D
Universidad de Ciencias Medicas	M,D,O
University at Buffalo, the State University of New York	D
University of Alberta	M,D
University of Arizona	D
University of Arkansas for Medical Sciences	M,D
The University of British Columbia	M,D
University of California, San Diego	D
University of California, San Francisco	D
University of Charleston	D
University of Cincinnati	D
University of Colorado Denver	D
University of Connecticut	D
The University of Findlay	M,D
University of Florida	M,D
University of Georgia	M,D,O
University of Hawaii at Hilo	D
University of Houston	M,D
University of Illinois at Chicago	M,D
The University of Iowa	M,D
University of Kentucky	D
University of Louisiana at Monroe	D
The University of Manchester	M,D
University of Maryland, Baltimore	M,D
University of Maryland Eastern Shore	M,D
University of Michigan	D
University of Minnesota, Duluth	M,D
University of Minnesota, Twin Cities Campus	D
University of Mississippi	M,D
University of Missouri–Kansas City	D
University of Montana	M,D
University of Nebraska Medical Center	D
University of New England	D
University of New Mexico	D
The University of North Carolina at Chapel Hill	M,D
University of Oklahoma Health Sciences Center	D
University of Pittsburgh	D
University of Puerto Rico, Medical Sciences Campus	M,D
University of Rhode Island	M,D
University of Saint Joseph	D
University of South Carolina	D
University of Southern California	D
University of South Florida	M,D,O
The University of Tennessee Health Science Center	M,D
The University of Texas at Austin	D
The University of Texas at Tyler	D
University of the Incarnate Word	D
University of the Pacific	D
University of the Sciences	D
University of Utah	D
University of Washington	M,D
University of Wisconsin–Madison	D
University of Wyoming	M,D
Virginia Commonwealth University	D
Washington State University	M,D
Wayne State University	D
West Coast University	M,D
Western New England University	D
Western University of Health Sciences	D
West Virginia University	M,D
Wilkes University	D
Wingate University	D
Xavier University of Louisiana	D

PHILANTHROPIC STUDIES

Institution	Degree
Indiana University–Purdue University Indianapolis	M,D
Saint Mary's University of Minnesota	M

PHILOSOPHY

Institution	Degree
Acadia University	M
American University	M
The American University in Cairo	M,O
Arizona State University at the Tempe campus	M,D,O
Baylor University	M,D
Binghamton University, State University of New York	M,D
Boston College	M,D
Boston University	M,D
Bowling Green State University	M,D
Brandeis University	M
Brock University	M
Brown University	D
California Institute of Integral Studies	M,D
California State University, Long Beach	M
California State University, Los Angeles	M,O
Carleton University	M
Carnegie Mellon University	M,D
The Catholic University of America	M,D,O
Central European University	M,D
Claremont Graduate University	M,D
Clarks Summit University	M
Cleveland State University	M,O
Collège Dominicain de Philosophie et de Théologie	M,D
Colorado State University	M,D
Columbia University	M,D
Concordia University (Canada)	M
Cornell University	D
Dalhousie University	M,D
Dallas Theological Seminary	M,D,O
Delta State University	M
Dominican School of Philosophy and Theology	M,O
Dominican University of California	M
Duke University	D
Duquesne University	M,D
Eastern Michigan University	M
Emory University	D,O
Florida State University	M,D
Fordham University	M,D
Franciscan University of Steubenville	M
George Mason University	M,D
Georgetown University	M,D
The George Washington University	M
Georgia State University	M
Gonzaga University	M
The Graduate Center, City University of New York	D
Harrison Middleton University	M,D
Harvard University	D
Houston Baptist University	M
Howard University	M
Indiana University Bloomington	M,D,O
Indiana University–Purdue University Indianapolis	M,O
Institute for Christian Studies	M,D
Institute for Doctoral Studies in the Visual Arts	D
Johns Hopkins University	M,D
Kent State University	M
Lake Forest College	M
Lincoln Christian University	M
Louisiana State University and Agricultural & Mechanical College	M
Loyola Marymount University	M
Loyola University Chicago	M,D
Marquette University	M,D
Massachusetts Institute of Technology	D
McGill University	M,D
McMaster University	M,D
Memorial University of Newfoundland	M,D
Miami University	M
Michigan State University	M,D
Midwestern State University	M
Mount St. Mary's University (MD)	M
The New School	M,D
New York University	M,D
Northern Illinois University	M
Northwestern University	D
The Ohio State University	M,D
Ohio University	M
Oklahoma State University	M
Open University	M
Penn State University Park	M,D
Princeton University	D
Purdue University	M,D
Queen's University at Kingston	M,D
Regis College (Canada)	M,D,O
Rice University	M,D
Roosevelt University	M
Rutgers University–New Brunswick	D
Saint Louis University	M,D
Saint Mary's University (Canada)	M
San Diego State University	M
San Francisco State University	M
San Jose State University	M,O
Simon Fraser University	M,D
Southeastern Baptist Theological Seminary	M,D
The Southern Baptist Theological Seminary	M,D
Southern Evangelical Seminary	M,D,O
Southern Illinois University Carbondale	M,D
Stanford University	M,D
Stony Brook University, State University of New York	M,D,O
Syracuse University	M,D
Teachers College, Columbia University	M,D,O
Temple University	M,D
Texas A&M University	M,D
Texas State University	M
Texas Tech University	M
Trinity Western University	M
Tufts University	M
Tulane University	M,D
Universidad Autonoma de Guadalajara	M,D
Université de Montréal	M,D
Université de Sherbrooke	M,D,O
Université du Québec à Montréal	M,D
Université du Québec à Trois-Rivières	M,D
Université Laval	M,D
University at Albany, State University of New York	M,D
University at Buffalo, the State University of New York	M,D
University of Alberta	M,D
The University of Arizona	M,D
University of Arkansas	M,D
The University of British Columbia	M,D
University of Calgary	M,D
University of California, Berkeley	D
University of California, Davis	M,D
University of California, Irvine	M,D
University of California, Los Angeles	M,D
University of California, Riverside	M,D
University of California, San Diego	D
University of California, Santa Barbara	M
University of California, Santa Cruz	M
University of Chicago	M,D
University of Cincinnati	M,D
University of Colorado Boulder	M,D
University of Connecticut	M,D
University of Dallas	M,D
University of Florida	M,D
University of Georgia	M,D
University of Guelph	M,D
University of Hawaii at Manoa	M,D
University of Houston	M
University of Idaho	M
University of Illinois at Chicago	M,D
University of Illinois at Urbana–Champaign	M,D
The University of Iowa	D
The University of Kansas	M,D
University of Kentucky	M,D
University of Lethbridge	M,D
University of Louisville	M,D
The University of Manchester	M,D
University of Manitoba	M
University of Maryland, College Park	M,D
University of Massachusetts Amherst	M,D
University of Memphis	M,D
University of Miami	M
University of Michigan	M,D
University of Minnesota, Twin Cities Campus	M,D
University of Mississippi	M,D
University of Missouri	D
University of Missouri–St. Louis	M
University of Montana	M
University of Nebraska–Lincoln	M,D
University of Nevada, Reno	M
University of New Mexico	M,D
The University of North Carolina at Chapel Hill	M,D
The University of North Carolina at Charlotte	M,O
University of North Florida	M
University of North Georgia	M
University of North Texas	M,D,O
University of Notre Dame	D
University of Oklahoma	M,D
University of Oregon	M,D
University of Ottawa	M,D
University of Pennsylvania	M,D
University of Pittsburgh	D
University of Puerto Rico, Río Piedras Campus	M
University of Regina	M
University of Rochester	D
University of St. Thomas (TX)	M,D
University of Saskatchewan	M
University of South Africa	M,D
University of South Carolina	M,D
University of Southern California	M,D
University of South Florida	M,D
The University of Tennessee	M,D
The University of Texas at Austin	D
The University of Texas at El Paso	M
The University of Texas at San Antonio	M
The University of Toledo	M,D
University of Toronto	M,D
University of Utah	M,D
University of Victoria	M,D
University of Virginia	M,D
University of Washington	M,D
University of Waterloo	M,D
The University of Western Ontario	M,D
University of Windsor	M
University of Wisconsin–Madison	M,D
University of Wisconsin–Milwaukee	M
University of Wyoming	M,D
Vanderbilt University	M,D
Villanova University	D
Virginia Polytechnic Institute and State University	M,D,O
Washington University in St. Louis	D
Wayne State University	M,D
West Chester University of Pennsylvania	M,O
Western Michigan University	M
Wilfrid Laurier University	M
Yale University	D
York University	M,D

PHOTOGRAPHY

Institution	Degree
Academy of Art University	M
Ball State University	M
Bard College	M
Barry University	M
Bradley University	M
Brooklyn College of the City University of New York	M
California College of the Arts	M
California Institute of the Arts	M,O
California State University, Los Angeles	M
Claremont Graduate University	M
Columbia College Chicago	M
Columbia University	M
Cornell University	M,D
Cranbrook Academy of Art	M
East Carolina University	M
Ferris State University	M
George Mason University	M
The George Washington University	M,O
Georgia State University	M,D
Governors State University	M
Howard University	M
Illinois State University	M
Indiana State University	M
Indiana University–Purdue University Indianapolis	M
Inter American University of Puerto Rico, San Germán Campus	M
Ithaca College	M
James Madison University	M
Johnson State College	M
Lesley University	M
Louisiana State University and Agricultural & Mechanical College	M
Louisiana Tech University	M
Maryland Institute College of Art	M
Marywood University	M
Massachusetts College of Art and Design	M,O
Memphis College of Art	M
Mills College	M
Minneapolis College of Art and Design	M
New Hampshire Institute of Art	M
The New School	M
New York Film Academy	M
Ohio University	M
Oklahoma City University	M
Otis College of Art and Design	M
Paris College of Art	M
Purdue University	M,D
Rhode Island School of Design	M
Rochester Institute of Technology	M
San Jose State University	M,O
Savannah College of Art and Design	M
School of the Art Institute of Chicago	M
School of Visual Arts (NY)	M
Southern Methodist University	M
Southwest University of Visual Arts	M
Syracuse University	M
Temple University	M
The University of Alabama	M
University of Alaska Fairbanks	M
University of Colorado Boulder	M
University of Illinois at Urbana–Champaign	M
University of Massachusetts Dartmouth	M
University of Memphis	M,O
University of Miami	M
University of Montana	M
University of New Mexico	M,D
University of Notre Dame	M
University of Rochester	M
The University of South Dakota	M
University of Southern California	M
The University of Tennessee	M
University of Utah	M
University of Victoria	M
University of Washington	M
Virginia Commonwealth University	M,D
Wayne State University	M
Wichita State University	M
Yale University	M

PHOTONICS

Institution	Degree
Duke University	M
Johns Hopkins University	M,O
Lehigh University	M,D
Oklahoma State University	M,D
Princeton University	D
Queens College of the City University of New York	M
Stevens Institute of Technology	M,D,O
The University of Alabama in Huntsville	M,D
University of Arkansas	M,D
University of California, San Diego	M,D
University of California, Santa Barbara	M,D
University of Central Florida	M,D
University of Dayton	M,D
University of New Mexico	M,D

PHYSICAL CHEMISTRY

Institution	Degree
Auburn University	M,D
Binghamton University, State University of New York	M,D
Boston College	M,D
Brandeis University	M,D
Cleveland State University	M,D
Cornell University	D
Dartmouth College	M,D
Eastern New Mexico University	M
Florida State University	M,D
The George Washington University	M,D
Georgia State University	M,D
Harvard University	D
Howard University	M,D
Indiana University Bloomington	M,D
Iowa State University of Science and Technology	M,D
Laurentian University	M
Marquette University	M,D
Massachusetts Institute of Technology	D
McMaster University	M,D
Old Dominion University	M,D
Oregon State University	M,D
Purdue University	M,D
Rice University	M,D
Rutgers University–Newark	M,D
Rutgers University–New Brunswick	M,D
Seton Hall University	M,D
Southern University and Agricultural and Mechanical College	M
University of Calgary	M,D
University of Cincinnati	M,D
University of Louisville	M,D

The University of Manchester — M,D
University of Maryland, College Park — M,D
University of Memphis — M,D
University of Miami — M,D
University of Michigan — D
University of Missouri–Kansas City — M,D
University of Montana — M,D
University of Nebraska–Lincoln — M,D
University of Notre Dame — M,D
University of Oklahoma — M,D
University of Puerto Rico, Mayagüez Campus — M,D
University of Southern California — D
University of Southern Mississippi — M,D
The University of Tennessee — M,D
The University of Texas at Austin — D
The University of Toledo — M,D
University of Wisconsin–Milwaukee — M,D
Vanderbilt University — M,D
Virginia Commonwealth University — M,D
Wake Forest University — M,D
Wayne State University — M,D
West Virginia University — M,D
Yale University — D
Youngstown State University — M

PHYSICAL EDUCATION

Adams State University — M
Adelphi University — M,O
Alabama Agricultural and Mechanical University — M
Alabama State University — M
Albany State University — M,O
Alcorn State University — M,O
American University of Puerto Rico — M
Arizona State University at the Tempe campus — M
Arkansas State University — M,O
Armstrong State University — M,O
Auburn University — M,D,O
Auburn University at Montgomery — M,O
Azusa Pacific University — M
Ball State University — M
Baylor University — M,D
Bridgewater State University — M
Brigham Young University — M
Brooklyn College of the City University of New York — M
California Baptist University — M
California State University, East Bay — M
California State University, Fullerton — M
California State University, Long Beach — M
California State University, Los Angeles — M,O
California State University, Sacramento — M
California State University, Stanislaus — M
Campbell University — M
Canisius College — M,D
Caribbean University — M,D
Central Connecticut State University — M,O
Central Washington University — M
Chicago State University — M
The Citadel, The Military College of South Carolina — M,O
Clemson University — M
Cleveland State University — M
The College at Brockport, State University of New York — M,O
The College of New Jersey — M
Colorado State University–Pueblo — M
Columbus State University — M
Concordia University Irvine — M
Delta State University — M
East Carolina University — M,D,O
Eastern Kentucky University — M
Eastern Michigan University — M
Eastern New Mexico University — M
Eastern University — M,D,O
Eastern Washington University — M
East Stroudsburg University of Pennsylvania — M
East Texas Baptist University — M
Emporia State University — M
Florida Agricultural and Mechanical University — M
Florida International University — M,D,O
Fort Hays State University — M
Gardner-Webb University — M
George Mason University — M
Georgia College & State University — M
Georgia State University — M
Goucher College — M,O
Henderson State University — M
Hofstra University — M,D,O
Howard University — M
Idaho State University — M
Illinois State University — M
Indiana State University — M,D
Indiana University Bloomington — M,D
Indiana University of Pennsylvania — M
Indiana University–Purdue University Indianapolis — M,O
Inter American University of Puerto Rico, Metropolitan Campus — M
Inter American University of Puerto Rico, San Germán Campus — M
Ithaca College — M
Jackson State University — M
Jacksonville State University — M,O
James Madison University — M

Longwood University — M
Louisiana Tech University — M
Massachusetts College of Liberal Arts — M
McDaniel College — M
McGill University — M,D,O
Memorial University of Newfoundland — M
Meredith College — M,O
Middle Tennessee State University — M
Millersville University of Pennsylvania — M,O
Minnesota State University Mankato — M
Mississippi State University — M,D
Missouri State University — M
Montclair State University — M
Morehead State University — M
Murray State University — M,O
North Carolina Agricultural and Technical State University — M
North Carolina Central University — M
Northern Illinois University — M
Northwest Missouri State University — M
The Ohio State University — M,D
Ohio University — M
Old Dominion University — M
Pittsburg State University — M
Plymouth State University — M
Purdue University — M,D
Queens College of the City University of New York — M,O
Rhode Island College — M
Salem State University — M
Shenandoah University — M,D,O
Slippery Rock University of Pennsylvania — M
Sonoma State University — M
Southern Connecticut State University — M
Southern Illinois University Carbondale — M
Southern Illinois University Edwardsville — M
Springfield College — M,D,O
State University of New York College at Cortland — M
Stony Brook University, State University of New York — M,O
Sul Ross State University — M
Teachers College, Columbia University — M,D
Temple University — M
Tennessee State University — M
Tennessee Technological University — M
Texas Southern University — M
Texas State University — M,D
Texas Woman's University — M,D
Union College (KY) — M
United States Sports Academy — M
Universidad del Turabo — M
Universidad Metropolitana — M
Université de Montréal — M,D,O
Université de Sherbrooke — M,O
Université du Québec à Trois-Rivières — M
The University of Akron — M
The University of Alabama — M,D
University of Alberta — M,D
University of Arkansas — M
The University of British Columbia — M,D
University of Dayton — M
University of Florida — M,D
University of Georgia — M,D
University of Houston — M,D
University of Idaho — M,D
University of Indianapolis — M
The University of Kansas — M,D
University of Kentucky — M,D
University of Louisville — M,D,O
University of Maine — M,D,O
University of Manitoba — M
University of Mary — M
University of Memphis — M,O
University of Montana — M
University of Nebraska at Kearney — M
University of New Brunswick Fredericton — M
University of New Hampshire — M,O
University of New Mexico — D
University of North Alabama — M
The University of North Carolina at Chapel Hill — M
The University of North Carolina at Pembroke — M
The University of North Carolina Wilmington — M
University of Northern Colorado — M,D
University of Northern Iowa — M
University of North Georgia — M,O
University of Rhode Island — M
University of Rio Grande — M
University of South Alabama — M
University of South Carolina — M,D
University of Southern Mississippi — M,D
The University of Tennessee at Chattanooga — M
The University of Tennessee at Martin — M
The University of Texas at Austin — M,D
The University of Toledo — M
University of Toronto — M,D
University of Victoria — M
University of Virginia — M,D
University of Washington — M,D
The University of West Alabama — M
University of West Florida — M,D
University of Wisconsin–La Crosse — M
University of Wyoming — M
Utah State University — M

Wayne State College — M
Wayne State University — M,D
West Chester University of Pennsylvania — M,O
Western Kentucky University — M
Western Michigan University — M
Western Washington University — M
Westfield State University — M
West Virginia University — M,D
Wilfrid Laurier University — M
William Woods University — M,D,O
Winthrop University — M

PHYSICAL THERAPY

Adventist University of Health Sciences — D
Alabama State University — D
American International College — M,D
Andrews University — D
Angelo State University — D
Arcadia University — D
Arkansas State University — D
Armstrong State University — D
A.T. Still University — M,D,O
Augusta University — D
Azusa Pacific University — D
Baylor University — D
Bellarmine University — M,D
Belmont University — M,D
Boston University — D
Bradley University — D
California State University, Fresno — D
California State University, Long Beach — D
California State University, Northridge — M
California State University, Sacramento — D
Campbell University — M,D
Carroll University — D
Central Michigan University — M,D
Chapman University — D
Chatham University — D
Clarke University — D
Clarkson University — D
Cleveland State University — D
The College of St. Scholastica — D
College of Staten Island of the City University of New York — D
Columbia University — D
Concordia University, St. Paul — M,D
Concordia University Wisconsin — D
Creighton University — D
Daemen College — D,O
Dalhousie University — M
Des Moines University — D
Dominican College — M,D
Drexel University — M,D,O
Duke University — D
Duquesne University — M,D
D'Youville College — D,O
East Carolina University — D
Eastern Washington University — D
East Tennessee State University — D
Elon University — D
Emory University — D
Florida Agricultural and Mechanical University — D
Florida Gulf Coast University — D
Florida International University — D
Franklin Pierce University — M,D,O
Gannon University — D
George Fox University — D
The George Washington University — D
Georgia State University — D
Governors State University — D
The Graduate Center, City University of New York — D
Grand Valley State University — D
Hampton University — D
Harding University — D
Hardin-Simmons University — D
Hunter College of the City University of New York — D
Husson University — D
Idaho State University — D
Indiana State University — M,D
Indiana University–Purdue University Indianapolis — M,D
Ithaca College — D
Kean University — D
Langston University — D
Lebanon Valley College — D
Loma Linda University — M,D
Long Island University–LIU Brooklyn — M,D,O
Louisiana State University Health Sciences Center — D
Lynchburg College — D
Marquette University — D
Marshall University — D
Marymount University — D
Maryville University of Saint Louis — D
Mayo Clinic School of Health Sciences — D
McMaster University — M
MCPHS University — D
Medical University of South Carolina — D
Mercer University — M,D
Mercy College — D
MGH Institute of Health Professions — M,D,O
Midwestern University, Downers Grove Campus — D
Midwestern University, Glendale Campus — D
Misericordia University — D
Missouri State University — D

Mount St. Joseph University — D
Mount Saint Mary's University (CA) — M,D,O
Nazareth College of Rochester — D
Neumann University — D
New York Institute of Technology — D
New York Medical College — M,D,O
New York University — M,D,O
Northern Arizona University — D
Northern Illinois University — M,D
Northwestern University — D
Nova Southeastern University — M,D
Oakland University — D,O
The Ohio State University — D
Ohio University — D
Old Dominion University — M,D
Pacific University — M,D
Queen's University at Kingston — M,D
Radford University — D
Regis University — M,D,O
Rockhurst University — D
Rocky Mountain University of Health Professions — D
Rosalind Franklin University of Medicine and Science — M,D
Rush University — M
Rutgers University–Camden — D
Rutgers University–Newark — D
Sacred Heart University — D
Sage Graduate School — D
St. Ambrose University — D
St. Catherine University — D
Saint Francis University — D
Saint Louis University — M,D
Samford University — M,D
Samuel Merritt University — D
San Diego State University — D
San Francisco State University — D
Seton Hall University — D
Shenandoah University — M,D,O
Simmons College — M,D,O
Slippery Rock University of Pennsylvania — D
Sonoma State University — M
Southwest Baptist University — D
Springfield College — D
State University of New York Upstate Medical University — D
Stockton University — D
Stony Brook University, State University of New York — M,D,O
Temple University — D
Tennessee State University — D
Texas State University — D
Texas Tech University Health Sciences Center — D
Texas Woman's University — D
Thomas Jefferson University — D
Touro College — M,D
Trine University — D
University at Buffalo, the State University of New York — D
The University of Alabama at Birmingham — D
University of Alberta — M,D
University of California, San Francisco — D
University of Central Arkansas — D
University of Central Florida — D
University of Cincinnati — D
University of Colorado Denver — D
University of Connecticut — D
University of Dayton — D
University of Delaware — D
University of Evansville — D
The University of Findlay — M,D
University of Florida — D
University of Hartford — M,D
University of Illinois at Chicago — M,D
University of Indianapolis — M,D
The University of Iowa — M,D
University of Jamestown — D
The University of Kansas — D
University of Kentucky — D
University of Manitoba — M,D
University of Mary — D
University of Mary Hardin-Baylor — D
University of Maryland, Baltimore — D
University of Maryland Eastern Shore — D
University of Massachusetts Lowell — D
University of Miami — D
University of Michigan–Flint — D,O
University of Minnesota, Twin Cities Campus — M,D
University of Mississippi Medical Center — M
University of Missouri — D
University of Montana — D
University of Nebraska Medical Center — D
University of Nevada, Las Vegas — D
University of New England — M,D
University of New Mexico — D
The University of North Carolina at Chapel Hill — M,D
University of North Dakota — D
University of North Florida — M,D
University of North Georgia — D
University of North Texas Health Science Center at Fort Worth — M,D
University of Oklahoma Health Sciences Center — M
University of Pittsburgh — M,D
University of Puerto Rico, Medical Sciences Campus — M
University of Puget Sound — D
University of Rhode Island — D
University of St. Augustine for Health Sciences — D

*M—masters degree; D—doctorate; O—other advanced degree; *—Close-Up and/or Display*

University	Degree
University of Saint Mary	D
The University of Scranton	D
University of South Alabama	D
The University of South Dakota	D
University of Southern California	M,D
University of South Florida	D
The University of Tennessee at Chattanooga	D
The University of Tennessee Health Science Center	M,D
The University of Texas at El Paso	D
The University of Texas Health Science Center at San Antonio	M,D
The University of Texas Medical Branch	M,D
The University of Texas Southwestern Medical Center	D
University of the Incarnate Word	D
University of the Pacific	M,D
University of the Sciences	D
The University of Toledo	M,D
University of Toronto	M
University of Utah	D
University of Vermont	D
University of Washington	M,D
The University of Western Ontario	M,O
University of Wisconsin–La Crosse	D
University of Wisconsin–Madison	D
University of Wisconsin–Milwaukee	M,D
Utica College	D
Virginia Commonwealth University	M,D
Walsh University	D
Washington University in St. Louis	D
Wayne State University	D
West Coast University	M,D
Western Carolina University	D
Western Kentucky University	D
Western University of Health Sciences	D
West Virginia University	D
Wheeling Jesuit University	D
Wichita State University	D
Widener University	M,D
Wingate University	D
Winston-Salem State University	D
Youngstown State University	D

PHYSICIAN ASSISTANT STUDIES

University	Degree
Adventist University of Health Sciences	M
Albany Medical College	M
Alderson Broaddus University	M
Arcadia University	M
A.T. Still University	M,D,O
Augsburg College	M
Augusta University	M
Baldwin Wallace University	M
Barry University	M
Baylor College of Medicine	M
Bay Path University	M
Bethel University (MN)	M,D,O
Bethel University (TN)	M
Boston University	M
Bryant University	M
Butler University	M,D
California Baptist University	M
Campbell University	M,D
Carroll University	M
Case Western Reserve University	M
Central Michigan University	M,D
Chapman University	M
Chatham University	M
Christian Brothers University	M
Clarkson University	M
Cleveland State University	M
Daemen College	M
Des Moines University	M
Drexel University	M
Duke University	M
Duquesne University	M,D
D'Youville College	M
East Carolina University	M
Eastern Michigan University	M
Eastern Virginia Medical School	M
Elon University	M
Emory University	M
Florida International University	M,D
Francis Marion University	M
Franklin Pierce University	M,D,O
Gannon University	M
Gardner-Webb University	M
The George Washington University	M
Grand Valley State University	M
Harding University	M
Hofstra University	M
Idaho State University	M
Indiana State University	M,D
James Madison University	M
Jefferson College of Health Sciences	M
Johnson & Wales University	M
Keiser University	M
Kettering College	M
King's College	M
Le Moyne College	M
Lenoir-Rhyne University	M
Lock Haven University of Pennsylvania	M
Loma Linda University	M
Long Island University–LIU Brooklyn	M,D,O
Louisiana State University Health Sciences Center	M
Marietta College	M
Marquette University	M
Marywood University	M
MCPHS University	M
Medical University of South Carolina	M
Mercer University	M,D
Mercy College	M

University	Degree
Mercyhurst University	M
Methodist University	M
MGH Institute of Health Professions	M
Midwestern University, Downers Grove Campus	M
Midwestern University, Glendale Campus	M
Milligan College	M
Missouri State University	M
Monmouth University	M,D,O
New York Institute of Technology	M
Northern Arizona University	M
Nova Southeastern University	M,D
Ohio Dominican University	M
Oregon Health & Science University	M
Our Lady of the Lake College	M
Pace University	M
Pacific University	M
Philadelphia College of Osteopathic Medicine	M
Philadelphia University	M
Quinnipiac University	M
Rocky Mountain College	M
Rocky Mountain University of Health Professions	M
Rosalind Franklin University of Medicine and Science	M
Rush University	M
Rutgers University–Newark	M
Sacred Heart University	M
St. Catherine University	M
Saint Francis University	M
Saint Louis University	M
Salus University	M
Samuel Merritt University	M
Seton Hall University	M
Seton Hill University	M
Shenandoah University	M,D,O
Slippery Rock University of Pennsylvania	M
South College	M
Southern Illinois University Carbondale	M
South University	M
South University (GA)	M
Springfield College	M
Stephens College	M,O
Stony Brook University, State University of New York	M,D,O
Texas Tech University Health Sciences Center	M
Thomas Jefferson University	M
Touro College	M,D
Towson University	M
Trevecca Nazarene University	M
Trine University	M
Tufts University	M,D,O
Union College (NE)	M
The University of Alabama at Birmingham	M
University of Arkansas for Medical Sciences	M,D
University of Bridgeport	M
University of Charleston	M
University of Colorado Denver	M
University of Dayton	M
University of Detroit Mercy	M,D,O
The University of Findlay	M,D
University of Florida	M
The University of Iowa	M
University of Kentucky	M
University of Mount Union	M
University of Nebraska Medical Center	M
University of New England	M,D
University of New Mexico	M
University of North Dakota	M
University of North Texas Health Science Center at Fort Worth	M,D
University of Oklahoma Health Sciences Center	M
University of Pittsburgh	M
University of St. Francis (IL)	M,O
University of Saint Francis (IN)	M
University of South Alabama	M
The University of South Dakota	M
University of Southern California	M
The University of Tennessee Health Science Center	M,D
The University of Texas Health Science Center at San Antonio	M,D
The University of Texas Medical Branch	M
The University of Texas Rio Grande Valley	M
The University of Texas Southwestern Medical Center	M
University of the Cumberlands	M
University of the Sciences	M
The University of Toledo	M
University of Utah	M
University of Wisconsin–La Crosse	M
University of Wisconsin–Madison	M
Valparaiso University	M,D,O
Wayne State University	M
Weill Cornell Medicine	M
Western Michigan University	M
Western University of Health Sciences	M
Wichita State University	M
Wingate University	M
Yale University	M

PHYSICS

University	Degree
Alabama Agricultural and Mechanical University	M,D
The American University in Cairo	M,D,O
American University of Beirut	M,D
Arizona State University at the Tempe campus	M,D
Auburn University	M,D

University	Degree
Ball State University	M
Baylor University	M,D
Binghamton University, State University of New York	M,D
Boston College	D
Boston University	M,D
Bowling Green State University	M
Brandeis University	M,D
Brigham Young University	M,D
Brock University	M
Brooklyn College of the City University of New York	M
Brown University	M,D
Bryn Mawr College	M,D
California Institute of Technology	D
California State University, Fresno	M
California State University, Fullerton	M
California State University, Long Beach	M
California State University, Los Angeles	M
California State University, Northridge	M
Carleton University	M,D
Carnegie Mellon University	M,D
Case Western Reserve University	M,D
The Catholic University of America	M,D
Central Michigan University	M,D
Christopher Newport University	M
City College of the City University of New York	M,D
Clark Atlanta University	M
Clarkson University	M,D
Clark University	D
Clemson University	M,D
Cleveland State University	M
The College of William and Mary	M,D
Colorado School of Mines	M,D
Colorado State University	M,D
Columbia University	M,D
Concordia University (Canada)	M,D
Cornell University	M,D
Creighton University	M
Dalhousie University	M,D
Dartmouth College	D
Delaware State University	M,D
DePaul University	M,D
Drexel University	M,D
Duke University	M,D
East Carolina University	M,D
Eastern Michigan University	M
Emory University	D
Fisk University	M
Florida Agricultural and Mechanical University	M,D
Florida Atlantic University	M,D
Florida Institute of Technology	M,D
Florida International University	M,D
Florida State University	M,D
George Mason University	M,D
The George Washington University	M,D
Georgia Institute of Technology	M,D
Georgia State University	M,D
The Graduate Center, City University of New York	D
Hampton University	M,D
Harvard University	D
Howard University	M,D
Hunter College of the City University of New York	M
Idaho State University	M,D
Illinois Institute of Technology	M,D
Indiana University Bloomington	M,D
Indiana University of Pennsylvania	M
Indiana University–Purdue University Indianapolis	M,D
Iowa State University of Science and Technology	M,D
Ithaca College	M
Jackson State University	M,D
Johns Hopkins University	M,D
Kansas State University	M,D
Kennesaw State University	M
Kent State University	M,D
Lakehead University	M
Lehigh University	M,D
Louisiana State University and Agricultural & Mechanical College	M,D
Louisiana Tech University	M
Marshall University	M
Massachusetts Institute of Technology	M,D
McGill University	M,D
McMaster University	D
Memorial University of Newfoundland	M,D
Miami University	M
Michigan State University	M,D
Michigan Technological University	M,D
Minnesota State University Mankato	M
Mississippi State University	M,D
Missouri State University	M
Missouri University of Science and Technology	M,D
Montana State University	M,D
Naval Postgraduate School	M,D
New Mexico Institute of Mining and Technology	M,D
New Mexico State University	M,D
New York University	M,D,O
North Carolina Agricultural and Technical State University	M
North Carolina Central University	M
North Carolina State University	M,D
North Dakota State University	M,D
Northeastern University	M,D
Northern Arizona University	M,D
Northern Illinois University	M,D
Northwestern University	D
Oakland University	M,D
The Ohio State University	M,D
Ohio University	M,D

University	Degree
Oklahoma State University	M,D
Old Dominion University	M,D
Oregon State University	M,O
Pace University	M,O
Penn State University Park	M
Pittsburg State University	M
Portland State University	M,D
Princeton University	D
Purdue University	M,D
Queens College of the City University of New York	M
Queen's University at Kingston	M,D
Rensselaer Polytechnic Institute	M,D
Rice University	M,D
Royal Military College of Canada	M
Rutgers University–New Brunswick	M,D
St. John Fisher College	M
San Diego State University	M
San Francisco State University	M
San Jose State University	M,O
Simon Fraser University	M,D
South Dakota School of Mines and Technology	M,D
South Dakota State University	M,D
Southern Illinois University Carbondale	M,D
Southern Methodist University	M,D
Southern University and Agricultural and Mechanical College	M
Stanford University	D
State University of New York College at Cortland	M
Stephen F. Austin State University	M
Stevens Institute of Technology	M,D,O
Stony Brook University, State University of New York	M,D
Syracuse University	M,D
Teachers College, Columbia University	M,D
Temple University	M,D
Texas A&M University	M,D
Texas A&M University–Commerce	M,O
Texas Christian University	M,D
Texas State University	M
Texas Tech University	M,D
Trent University	M
Tufts University	M,D
Tulane University	M,D
Université de Moncton	M
Université de Montréal	M,D
Université de Sherbrooke	M,D
Université du Québec à Trois-Rivières	M,D
Université Laval	M,D
University at Albany, State University of New York	M,D
University at Buffalo, the State University of New York	M,D
The University of Akron	M
The University of Alabama	M,D
The University of Alabama at Birmingham	M,D
The University of Alabama in Huntsville	M,D
University of Alaska Fairbanks	M,D
University of Alberta	M,D
The University of Arizona	M,D
University of Arkansas	M,D
The University of British Columbia	M,D
University of Calgary	M,D
University of California, Berkeley	D
University of California, Davis	M,D
University of California, Irvine	M,D
University of California, Los Angeles	M,D
University of California, Merced	M,D
University of California, Riverside	M,D
University of California, San Diego	M,D
University of California, Santa Barbara	D
University of California, Santa Cruz	M,D
University of Central Florida	M,D
University of Chicago	M,D
University of Cincinnati	M,D
University of Colorado Boulder	M,D
University of Colorado Colorado Springs	D
University of Connecticut	M,D
University of Delaware	M,D
University of Denver	M,D
University of Florida	M,D
University of Georgia	M,D
University of Guelph	M,D
University of Hawaii at Manoa	M,D
University of Houston	M,D
University of Houston–Clear Lake	M
University of Idaho	M,D
University of Illinois at Chicago	M,D
University of Illinois at Urbana–Champaign	M,D
The University of Iowa	M,D
The University of Kansas	M,D
University of Kentucky	M,D
University of Lethbridge	M,D
University of Louisiana at Lafayette	M
University of Louisville	M,D
University of Maine	M,D
The University of Manchester	M,D
University of Manitoba	M,D
University of Maryland, Baltimore County	M,D
University of Maryland, College Park	M,D
University of Massachusetts Amherst	M,D

University of Massachusetts Dartmouth	M
University of Massachusetts Lowell	M,D
University of Memphis	M
University of Miami	M,D
University of Michigan	D
University of Minnesota, Duluth	M
University of Minnesota, Twin Cities Campus	M,D
University of Mississippi	M,D
University of Missouri	M,D
University of Missouri–Kansas City	M,D
University of Missouri–St. Louis	M,D
University of Nebraska–Lincoln	M,D
University of Nevada, Las Vegas	M,D
University of Nevada, Reno	M,D
University of New Brunswick Fredericton	M,D
University of New Hampshire	M,D
University of New Mexico	M,D
University of New Orleans	M,D
The University of North Carolina at Chapel Hill	M,D
University of North Dakota	M,D
University of Northern Iowa	M
University of Notre Dame	M,D
University of Oklahoma	M,D
University of Oregon	M,D
University of Ottawa	M,D
University of Pennsylvania	M,D
University of Pittsburgh	M,D
University of Puerto Rico, Mayagüez Campus	M
University of Puerto Rico, Río Piedras Campus	M,D
University of Regina	M,D
University of Rhode Island	M,D
University of Rochester	M,D
University of Saskatchewan	M,D
University of South Carolina	M,D
The University of South Dakota	M,D
University of Southern California	M,D
University of Southern Mississippi	M,D
University of South Florida	M,D
The University of Tennessee	M,D
The University of Texas at Arlington	M,D
The University of Texas at Austin	M,D
The University of Texas at Dallas	M,D
The University of Texas at El Paso	M
The University of Texas at San Antonio	M,D
The University of Texas Rio Grande Valley	M
The University of Toledo	M,D
University of Toronto	M,D
The University of Tulsa	M,D
University of Utah	M,D
University of Vermont	M
University of Victoria	M,D
University of Virginia	M,D
University of Washington	M,D
University of Waterloo	M,D
The University of Western Ontario	M,D
University of Windsor	M,D
University of Wisconsin–Madison	M,D
University of Wisconsin–Milwaukee	M,D
Utah State University	M,D
Vanderbilt University	M,D
Virginia Commonwealth University	M
Virginia Polytechnic Institute and State University	M,D
Wake Forest University	M,D
Washington State University	M,D
Washington University in St. Louis	D
Wayne State University	M,D
Wesleyan University	D
Western Illinois University	M
Western Kentucky University	M
Western Michigan University	M,D,O
West Virginia University	M,D
Wichita State University	M,D
Worcester Polytechnic Institute	M,D
Wright State University	M
Yale University	D
York University	M,D

PHYSIOLOGY

Albert Einstein College of Medicine	D
American College of Healthcare Sciences	M,O
American University of Beirut	M,D
Augusta University	D
Ball State University	M
Boston University	M,D
Brigham Young University	M,D
Brown University	M,D
Case Western Reserve University	M,D
Columbia University	M,D
Cornell University	M,D
Dalhousie University	M,D
East Carolina University	D
Eastern Michigan University	M
East Tennessee State University	D
Georgetown University	M,D
Georgia Institute of Technology	M,D
Georgia State University	M,D
Gonzaga University	M,D
Harvard University	M,D
Howard University	M,D
Illinois State University	M,D
Indiana State University	M,D
James Madison University	M
Johns Hopkins University	D
Kansas State University	M,D

Kent State University	M,D
Loma Linda University	D
Louisiana State University Health Sciences Center	D
Louisiana State University Health Sciences Center at Shreveport	M,D
Loyola University Chicago	M,D
Maharishi University of Management	D
Marquette University	M,D
McGill University	M,D
McMaster University	M,D
Medical College of Wisconsin	D
Michigan State University	M,D
Montclair State University	M
New York Medical College	M,D
New York University	D
North Carolina State University	M,D
Northwestern University	M
Ohio University	M,D
Oregon Health & Science University	D
Oregon State University	M,D
Penn State University Park	M,D
Purdue University	M,D
Queen's University at Kingston	M,D
Rocky Mountain University of Health Professions	D
Rosalind Franklin University of Medicine and Science	M,D
Rush University	D
Rutgers University–Newark	D
Rutgers University–New Brunswick	M,D
Saint Louis University	D
Salisbury University	M
San Francisco State University	M
San Jose State University	M,O
Southern Illinois University Carbondale	M,D
Southern Methodist University	M
Stanford University	D
State University of New York Upstate Medical University	M,D
Stony Brook University, State University of New York	D
Teachers College, Columbia University	M,D
Tulane University	M,D
Universidad Central del Caribe	M,D
Université de Montréal	M,D
Université de Sherbrooke	M,D
Université Laval	M,D
University at Buffalo, the State University of New York	M,D
University of Alberta	M,D
The University of Arizona	M,D
University of Arkansas for Medical Sciences	M,D,O
University of Calgary	M,D
University of California, Berkeley	M,D
University of California, Davis	M,D
University of California, Irvine	D
University of California, Los Angeles	M,D
University of Central Florida	M
University of Colorado Boulder	M,D
University of Colorado Denver	M,D
University of Connecticut	M,D
University of Delaware	M,D
University of Florida	M,D
University of Georgia	M,D
University of Guelph	M,D
University of Hawaii at Manoa	M,D
University of Illinois at Chicago	M,D
University of Illinois at Urbana–Champaign	M,D
The University of Iowa	M,D
The University of Kansas	D
University of Kentucky	D
University of Louisville	M,D
The University of Manchester	M,D
University of Manitoba	M,D
University of Massachusetts Amherst	M,D
University of Miami	D
University of Michigan	M,D
University of Minnesota, Duluth	M,D
University of Minnesota, Twin Cities Campus	D
University of Mississippi Medical Center	D
University of Missouri	M,D
University of Nebraska Medical Center	D
University of Nevada, Reno	D
University of New Mexico	M,D
University of North Texas Health Science Center at Fort Worth	M,D
University of Notre Dame	M,D
University of Oklahoma Health Sciences Center	M,D
University of Oregon	M,D
University of Pennsylvania	D
University of Prince Edward Island	M,D
University of Puerto Rico, Medical Sciences Campus	M,D
University of Rochester	M,D
University of Saskatchewan	M,D
The University of South Dakota	M,D
University of Southern California	M
University of South Florida	M,D
The University of Tennessee	M,D
The University of Texas Medical Branch	M,D
University of Toronto	M,D
University of Utah	M,D
University of Virginia	D
University of Washington	M,D
The University of Western Ontario	M,D
University of Wisconsin–La Crosse	M

University of Wisconsin–Madison	M,D
University of Wyoming	M,D
Virginia Commonwealth University	M,D
Wake Forest University	D
Wayne State University	M,D,O
Weill Cornell Medicine	M,D
Western Michigan University	M
West Virginia University	M,D
Wright State University	M
Yale University	D
Youngstown State University	M

PLANETARY AND SPACE SCIENCES

Air Force Institute of Technology	M,D
Alabama Agricultural and Mechanical University	M,D
American Public University System	M
Arizona State University at the Tempe campus	M,D
California Institute of Technology	M,D
Cornell University	D
Florida Institute of Technology	M,D
Hampton University	M,D
Harvard University	M,D
Massachusetts Institute of Technology	M,D
McGill University	M,D
St. Thomas University	M,D,O
The University of Arizona	M,D
University of Arkansas	M,D
University of California, Los Angeles	M,D
University of California, Santa Cruz	M,D
University of Chicago	D
University of Hawaii at Manoa	M,D
University of Houston	M,D
University of Maryland, Baltimore County	M
University of Michigan	M,D
University of New Mexico	M,D
University of North Dakota	M
Washington University in St. Louis	D
Western Connecticut State University	M
Yale University	M,D
York University	M,D

PLANT BIOLOGY

Arizona State University at the Tempe campus	M,D
Clemson University	M,D
Cornell University	M,D
Illinois State University	M,D
Indiana University Bloomington	M,D
Iowa State University of Science and Technology	M,D
Michigan State University	M,D
New York University	M,D
North Carolina State University	M,D
Northwestern University	M,D
Ohio University	M,D
Oklahoma State University	M,D
Penn State University Park	M,D
Rutgers University–New Brunswick	M,D
Southern Illinois University Carbondale	M,D
Université Laval	M,D
University of Alberta	D
University of California, Berkeley	D
University of California, Davis	M,D
University of California, Riverside	M,D
University of Florida	M,D
University of Georgia	M,D
University of Illinois at Urbana–Champaign	M,D
University of Maryland, College Park	M,D
University of Massachusetts Amherst	M,D
University of Minnesota, Twin Cities Campus	M,D
University of Missouri	M,D
University of Oklahoma	M,D
The University of Texas at Austin	M,D
University of Vermont	M,D
Washington University in St. Louis	D
Yale University	D

PLANT MOLECULAR BIOLOGY

Cornell University	M,D
Illinois State University	M,D
Oregon State University	D
Rutgers University–New Brunswick	M,D
University of California, Riverside	M,D
University of Florida	M,D
University of Massachusetts Amherst	M,D

PLANT PATHOLOGY

Auburn University	M,D
Colorado State University	M,D
Cornell University	M,D
Dalhousie University	M
Iowa State University of Science and Technology	M,D
Kansas State University	M,D
Louisiana State University and Agricultural & Mechanical College	M,D
Michigan State University	M,D
Montana State University	M,D
New Mexico State University	M
North Carolina State University	M,D
North Dakota State University	M,D
The Ohio State University	M,D
Oklahoma State University	M,D
Oregon State University	M,D

Penn State University Park	M,D
Purdue University	M,D
Rutgers University–New Brunswick	M,D
State University of New York College of Environmental Science and Forestry	M,D
Texas A&M University	M,D
The University of Arizona	M,D
University of Arkansas	M
University of California, Davis	M,D
University of California, Riverside	M,D
University of Florida	M,D
University of Georgia	M,D
University of Guelph	M,D
University of Hawaii at Manoa	M,D
University of Kentucky	M,D
University of Maine	M,D
University of Minnesota, Twin Cities Campus	M,D
The University of Tennessee	M,D
University of Wisconsin–Madison	M,D
Virginia Polytechnic Institute and State University	M,D
Washington State University	M,D
West Virginia University	M

PLANT PHYSIOLOGY

Cornell University	M,D
Dalhousie University	M
Oregon State University	M,D
Purdue University	M,D
University of Manitoba	M,D
University of Massachusetts Amherst	M,D
The University of Tennessee	M,D
Virginia Polytechnic Institute and State University	M,D

PLANT SCIENCES

Alabama Agricultural and Mechanical University	M,D
American University of Beirut	M
Brigham Young University	M,D
California State University, Fresno	M
Clemson University	M,D
Colorado State University	M,D
Cornell University	M,D
Delaware State University	M
Illinois State University	M,D
Iowa State University of Science and Technology	M,D
Kansas State University	M,D,O
Lehman College of the City University of New York	D
McGill University	M,D,O
Michigan State University	M,D
Mississippi State University	M,D
Missouri State University	M
Montana State University	M,D
New Mexico State University	M
North Carolina Agricultural and Technical State University	M
North Dakota State University	M,D
The Ohio State University	D
Oklahoma State University	M,D
Penn State University Park	M,D
Purdue University	D
South Dakota State University	M,D
Southern Illinois University Carbondale	M
State University of New York College of Environmental Science and Forestry	M,D
Tennessee State University	M,D
Texas A&M University–Kingsville	M
Texas Tech University	M,D
Tuskegee University	M
The University of Arizona	M,D
University of Arkansas	D
The University of British Columbia	M,D
University of California, Riverside	M,D
University of Connecticut	M,D
University of Delaware	M,D
University of Florida	D
University of Georgia	M,D
University of Hawaii at Manoa	M,D
University of Idaho	M,D
University of Kentucky	M,D
The University of Manchester	M,D
University of Manitoba	M,D
University of Massachusetts Amherst	M,D
University of Minnesota, Twin Cities Campus	M,D
University of Missouri	M,D
University of Saskatchewan	M,D
The University of Tennessee	M
University of Vermont	M,D
University of Wisconsin–Madison	M,D
Utah State University	M,D
West Texas A&M University	M

PLASMA PHYSICS

Princeton University	D
University of Colorado Boulder	M,D
West Virginia University	M,D

PODIATRIC MEDICINE

Barry University	D
Des Moines University	D
Kent State University	
Midwestern University, Glendale Campus	D
New York College of Podiatric Medicine	D

*M—masters degree; D—doctorate; O—other advanced degree; *—Close-Up and/or Display*

Rosalind Franklin University of Medicine and Science — D
Samuel Merritt University — D
Temple University — D
Western University of Health Sciences — D

POLITICAL SCIENCE

Acadia University — M
American Public University System — M
American University — M,D,O
American University of Armenia — M
American University of Beirut — M,D
Appalachian State University — M
Arizona State University at the Tempe campus — M,D
Arkansas State University — M,O
Ashland University — M
Auburn University — M,D,O
Auburn University at Montgomery — M,D
Ball State University — M
Baylor University — M,D
Binghamton University, State University of New York — M,D
Boise State University — M
Boston College — M,D
Boston University — D
Brandeis University — M,D
Brigham Young University — M
Brock University — M
Brooklyn College of the City University of New York — M
Brown University — D
California Polytechnic State University, San Luis Obispo — M
California State University, Chico — M
California State University, Fullerton — M
California State University, Long Beach — M
California State University, Los Angeles — M
California State University, Northridge — M
California State University, Sacramento — M
Carleton University — M,D
Case Western Reserve University — M,D
The Catholic University of America — M,D
Central European University — M,D
Central Michigan University — M,O
The Citadel, The Military College of South Carolina — M
Claremont Graduate University — M,D
Clark Atlanta University — M,D
Clemson University — M,O
Colorado State University — M,D
Columbia University — M,D
Columbus State University — M
Concordia University (Canada) — M,D
Converse College — M
Cornell University — D
Dalhousie University — M
Dominican University of California — M
Duke University — M,D
East Carolina University — M,O
Eastern Illinois University — M
Eastern Kentucky University — M
East Stroudsburg University of Pennsylvania — M
East Tennessee State University — M
Edinboro University of Pennsylvania — M
Emory University — D
Fairleigh Dickinson University, Metropolitan Campus — M
Florida Agricultural and Mechanical University — M
Florida Atlantic University — M
Florida International University — M,D
Florida State University — M,D
Fordham University — M
George Mason University — M,D
Georgetown University — M,D
The George Washington University — M,D
Georgia State University — M,D
Governors State University — M
The Graduate Center, City University of New York — M,D
Grambling State University — M
Harvard University — M,D
Hillsdale College — M,D
Howard University — M,D
Idaho State University — M,D
Illinois State University — M
Indiana University Bloomington — M,D
Indiana University–Purdue University Indianapolis — M
Institute for Christian Studies — M,D
The Institute of World Politics — M,O
Iowa State University of Science and Technology — M
Jackson State University — M
Jacksonville State University — M
James Madison University — M
Johns Hopkins University — M,D,O
Kansas State University — M
Kaplan University, Davenport Campus — M,O
Kent State University — M,D
Lamar University — M
Lehigh University — M
Long Island University–LIU Brooklyn — M,D,O
Long Island University–LIU Post — M,O
Louisiana State University and Agricultural & Mechanical College — M,D
Loyola University Chicago — M,D
Marquette University — M
Marshall University — M
Massachusetts Institute of Technology — M,D
McGill University — M,D

McMaster University — M,D
Memorial University of Newfoundland — M
Miami University — M,D
Michigan State University — M,D
Middle Tennessee State University — M
Midwestern State University — M,O
Mississippi College — M,O
Mississippi State University — M,O
Missouri State University — M,O
Montclair State University — M,O
New Mexico Highlands University — M
New Mexico State University — M
The New School — M,D
New York University — M,D
Northeastern Illinois University — M
Northeastern University — M,D
Northern Arizona University — M,D,O
Northern Illinois University — M,D
Northwestern University — D
The Ohio State University — D
Ohio University — M
Oklahoma State University — M,D
Penn State University Park — M,D
Pepperdine University — M
Portland State University — M,D
Princeton University — D
Purdue University — M,D
Queen's University at Kingston — M,D
Regent University — M
Rice University — D
Rutgers University–Newark — M
Rutgers University–New Brunswick — M,D
St. John's University (NY) — M,O
Saint Louis University — M
Sam Houston State University — M
San Diego State University — M
San Francisco State University — M
Simon Fraser University — M,D
Sonoma State University — M,O
Southern Connecticut State University — M
Southern Illinois University Carbondale — M,D
Southern University and Agricultural and Mechanical College — M
Stanford University — M,D
Stony Brook University, State University of New York — M,D
Suffolk University — M,O
Sul Ross State University — M
Syracuse University — M,D,O
Tarleton State University — M
Teachers College, Columbia University — M,D
Temple University — M,D
Texas A&M International University — M,D
Texas A&M University — M,D
Texas A&M University–Central Texas — M,O
Texas A&M University–Commerce — M,D,O
Texas State University — M
Texas Tech University — M,D
Texas Woman's University — M
Tulane University — D
Universidad Nacional Pedro Henriquez Urena — M
Université de Montréal — M,D
Université du Québec à Montréal — M,D
Université Laval — M,D
University at Albany, State University of New York — M,D
University at Buffalo, the State University of New York — M,D
The University of Akron — M
The University of Alabama — M,D
University of Alberta — M,D
The University of Arizona — M,D
University of Arkansas — M
The University of British Columbia — M,D
University of Calgary — M,D
University of California, Berkeley — D
University of California, Davis — M,D
University of California, Irvine — D
University of California, Los Angeles — M,D
University of California, Riverside — M,D
University of California, San Diego — M,D
University of California, Santa Barbara — M,D
University of California, Santa Cruz — D
University of Central Florida — M,D,O
University of Central Oklahoma — M
University of Chicago — D
University of Cincinnati — M,D
University of Colorado Boulder — M,D
University of Colorado Denver — M,D
University of Connecticut — M,D
University of Dallas — M,D
University of Delaware — M,D
University of Florida — M,D,O
University of Georgia — M,D
University of Guelph — M
University of Hawaii at Manoa — M,D
University of Houston — M,D
University of Idaho — M,D
University of Illinois at Chicago — M,D
University of Illinois at Springfield — M
University of Illinois at Urbana–Champaign — M,D
The University of Iowa — D
The University of Kansas — M,D
University of Kentucky — M,D
University of Lethbridge — M,D
University of Louisville — M,D
The University of Manchester — M,D

University of Manitoba — M
University of Maryland, College Park — D
University of Massachusetts Amherst — M,D
University of Memphis — M
University of Miami — M
University of Michigan — D
University of Michigan–Flint — M
University of Minnesota, Twin Cities Campus — D
University of Mississippi — M
University of Missouri — M,D
University of Missouri–Kansas City — M
University of Missouri–St. Louis — M,D
University of Montana — M
University of Nebraska at Omaha — M,O
University of Nebraska–Lincoln — M,D,O
University of Nevada, Las Vegas — M,D
University of Nevada, Reno — M,O
University of New Brunswick Fredericton — M
University of New Hampshire — M,O
University of New Mexico — M,D
University of New Orleans — M,D
University of North Alabama — M
The University of North Carolina at Chapel Hill — M,D,O
The University of North Carolina at Greensboro — M,O
University of Northern British Columbia — M,D,O
University of North Texas — M,D,O
University of Notre Dame — D
University of Oklahoma — M,D
University of Oregon — M,D
University of Ottawa — M
University of Pennsylvania — M,D,O
University of Pittsburgh — M,D
University of Regina — M
University of Rhode Island — M
University of Rochester — D
University of Saskatchewan — M
University of South Africa — M,D
University of South Carolina — M,D
The University of South Dakota — M,D
University of Southern California — M,D
University of Southern Mississippi — M,D
University of South Florida — M,D,O
The University of Tennessee — M,D
The University of Tennessee at Chattanooga — M,O
The University of Texas at Arlington — M
The University of Texas at Austin — M,D
The University of Texas at Dallas — M,D
The University of Texas at El Paso — M
The University of Texas at San Antonio — M
The University of Texas at Tyler — M
The University of Texas of the Permian Basin — M
The University of Toledo — M,O
University of Toronto — M,D
University of Utah — M,D
University of Victoria — M,D
University of Virginia — M,D
University of Washington — M,D
University of Waterloo — M,D
The University of Western Ontario — M,D
University of West Florida — M
University of Windsor — M
University of Wisconsin–Madison — D
University of Wisconsin–Milwaukee — M,D
University of Wyoming — M
Utah State University — M
Vanderbilt University — M,D
Villanova University — M
Virginia Commonwealth University — M,D,O
Virginia Polytechnic Institute and State University — M,D,O
Walden University — M,D,O
Washington State University — M,D,O
Washington University in St. Louis — D
Wayne State University — M,D
Western Illinois University — M
Western Kentucky University — M
Western Michigan University — M
Western Washington University — M
West Virginia University — M,D
Wilfrid Laurier University — M,D
Yale University — D
York University — M,D

POLYMER SCIENCE AND ENGINEERING

Auburn University — M,D
California Polytechnic State University, San Luis Obispo — M
Carnegie Mellon University — M
Case Western Reserve University — M,D
The College of William and Mary — M,D
Cornell University — M,D
Eastern Michigan University — M,O
Lehigh University — M,D
North Carolina State University — D
North Dakota State University — M,D
Pittsburg State University — M
Stevens Institute of Technology — M,D,O
The University of Akron — M,D
University of Connecticut — M,D
The University of Manchester — M,D
University of Massachusetts Amherst — M,D
University of Massachusetts Lowell — M,D
University of Missouri–Kansas City — M,D
University of Southern Mississippi — M,D
The University of Tennessee — M,D
Wayne State University — M,D,O

PORTUGUESE

Brigham Young University — M
Emory University — D,O
Harvard University — M,D
Indiana University Bloomington — M,D
Michigan State University — M,D
New York University — M,D
Northwestern University — D
The Ohio State University — M,D
Princeton University — D
Tulane University — M,D
University of California, Los Angeles — M
University of California, Santa Barbara — M,D
University of Georgia — M,D
University of Illinois at Urbana–Champaign — M,D
University of Maryland, College Park — M,D
University of Massachusetts Amherst — M,D
University of Massachusetts Dartmouth — M,D
University of Minnesota, Twin Cities Campus — M,D
University of New Mexico — M,D
The University of North Carolina at Chapel Hill — M,D
University of South Africa — M,D
The University of Tennessee — D
The University of Texas at Austin — M,D
University of Toronto — M,D
University of Washington — M
University of Wisconsin–Madison — M,D
University of Wisconsin–Milwaukee — M
Vanderbilt University — M,D
Yale University — D

PROJECT MANAGEMENT

Amberton University — M
American Business & Technology University — M
American InterContinental University Online — M
American Public University System — M
American University — M,O
Aspen University — M,O
Athabasca University — M,D,O
Avila University — M
Bellevue University — M
Boston University — M,O
Brandeis University — M
Brenau University — M
California Intercontinental University — M,D
Capella University — M,D
Carlow University — M
The Catholic University of America — M,O
Christian Brothers University — M
The Citadel, The Military College of South Carolina — M,O
City University of Seattle — M,D
Colorado Christian University — M
Colorado State University–Global Campus — M
Colorado Technical University Aurora — M
Colorado Technical University Colorado Springs — M,D
Dallas Baptist University — M
DeSales University — M,O
DeVry University–Folsom Campus — M
Drexel University — M
Elmhurst College — M
Embry-Riddle Aeronautical University–Worldwide — M
Everglades University — M
Ferris State University — M
Florida Institute of Technology — M,D
Geneva College — M
George Mason University — M
The George Washington University — M,D,O
Grand Canyon University — M
Granite State College — M
Grantham University — M,O
Harrisburg University of Science and Technology — M
Herzing University Online — M
Hult International Business School (United States) — M
IGlobal University — M
Iona College — M,O
Kaplan University, Davenport Campus — M
King University — M
Lakeland University — M
Lasell College — M,O
Lawrence Technological University — M,O
Lehigh University — M
Lewis University — M
Liberty University — M,D,O
Lindenwood University — M,O
Marlboro College — M
Marymount University — M,O
Maryville University of Saint Louis — M
Metropolitan State University — M,D,O
Mississippi State University — M,D
Missouri State University — M
Montana Tech of The University of Montana — M
Mount Aloysius College — M
New England College — M
New York University — M,D,O
Northeastern University — M
Northwestern University — M
Northwest University — M
Norwich University — M
Oklahoma Christian University — M

Penn State Erie, The Behrend
  College — M
Point Loma Nazarene University — M
Polytechnic University of Puerto
  Rico, Miami Campus — M
Post University — M
Queen's University at
  Kingston — M
Regis University — M,O
Robert Morris University — M,D
Rochester Institute of Technology — O
Royal Roads University — O
Saint Leo University — M,D,O
Saint Mary's University of
  Minnesota — M,O
Saint Xavier University — M,O
Sam Houston State University — M
Southern Illinois University
  Edwardsville — M
Southern New Hampshire University — M,O
Stevens Institute of Technology — M,O
Stevenson University — M
Texas A&M University–San
  Antonio — M
Thomas Edison State University — M
Trident University International — M,D
Universidad del Turabo — M
Universidad Nacional Pedro
  Henriquez Urena — M
Université du Québec
  à Chicoutimi — M
Université du Québec
  à Montréal — M,O
Université du Québec
  à Rimouski — M,O
Université du Québec
  en Abitibi-Témiscamingue — M,O
Université du Québec
  en Outaouais — M,O
The University of Alabama in
  Huntsville — M,O
University of Alaska Anchorage — M
University of Calgary — M,D
University of California, Berkeley — O
University of Dallas — M,D
University of Denver — M,O
University of Houston — M
The University of Kansas — M
University of Management and
  Technology — M,D,O
The University of Manchester — M
University of Mary — M
University of Michigan–
  Dearborn — M
University of Nebraska at Omaha — M,D,O
University of North Alabama — M
University of Oklahoma — M,O
University of Ottawa — M,O
University of Phoenix–Bay
  Area Campus — M,D
University of Phoenix–Online
  Campus — M,O
University of Phoenix–
  Phoenix Campus — M,O
University of Phoenix–
  Southern California Campus — M
University of Regina — M,O
The University of Tennessee at
  Chattanooga — M,O
The University of Texas at Dallas — M,D
University of Wisconsin–
  Platteville — M
University of Wisconsin–
  Stout — M
Virginia International University — M,O
Viterbo University — M
Walden University — M,D,O
Wayland Baptist University — M,D
West Chester University of
  Pennsylvania — M,O
Western Carolina University — M,O
Wingate University — M

PSYCHIATRIC NURSING

Alverno College — M,D
American University of Beirut — M
Arizona State University at the
  Tempe campus — M,D,O
Augusta University — D
Boston College — M,D
California State University, San
  Marcos — M
Case Western Reserve University — M
Columbia University — M,D,O
Creighton University — M,D,O
Drexel University — M
East Tennessee State University — M,D,O
Fairfield University — M,D
Fairleigh Dickinson University,
  College at Florham — M
Florida International University — M,D
Florida State University — M,D,O
Georgia Southern University — M
Georgia State University — M,D,O
Hampton University — M,D
Hofstra University — M
Hunter College of the City
  University of New York — M,O
Jacksonville University — M
James Madison University — M,D
Kent State University — M
Lincoln Memorial University — M
McNeese State University — M,O
MGH Institute of Health
  Professions — M,D
Midwestern State University — M
Monmouth University — M,D,O
Montana State University — M,D,O
New Mexico State University — M,D,O
New York University — M,D,O
Nicholls State University — M

Northeastern University — M,D,O
Oregon Health & Science University — M
Pontifical Catholic University of
  Puerto Rico — M,D
Rivier University — M,D
Rush University — D
Sage Graduate School — M,O
Saint Francis Medical Center
  College of Nursing — M,D,O
Seattle University — M
Shenandoah University — M,D,O
Southeastern Louisiana University — M,D
Southern Arkansas University–
  Magnolia — M
Stony Brook University, State
  University of New York — M,D,O
Uniformed Services University of
  the Health Sciences — M,D
University at Buffalo, the State
  University of New York — M,D,O
The University of Alabama at
  Birmingham — M,D
University of Cincinnati — M,D
University of Colorado Denver — M,D
University of Delaware — M,O
The University of Kansas — M,D,O
University of Louisville — M
University of Maryland, Baltimore — M
University of Massachusetts
  Dartmouth — M,D,O
University of Michigan–Flint — M,D,O
University of Minnesota, Twin
  Cities Campus — M,D
University of Missouri — M,D,O
University of Missouri–St.
  Louis — D,O
University of New Hampshire — M,D,O
The University of North Carolina
  at Chapel Hill — M,D,O
University of North Dakota — M,D,O
University of Pennsylvania — M
University of Pittsburgh — M,D
University of Puerto Rico, Medical
  Sciences Campus — M
University of Rochester — M,D
University of St. Francis (IL) — M,D
University of Saint Joseph — M,D
University of San Diego — M,D
University of South Carolina — M,O
University of Southern Indiana — M,D,O
University of Southern Maine — M,D,O
University of Southern Mississippi — M,D,O
The University of Texas at Austin — M,D
The University of Texas Health
  Science Center at San Antonio — M,D,O
University of Virginia — M,D
University of Wisconsin–
  Madison — D
Valdosta State University — M
Vanderbilt University — M,D,O
Virginia Commonwealth University — M,D,O
Washington State University — M,D,O
West Virginia Wesleyan College — M,O
Wright State University — M

PSYCHOANALYSIS AND PSYCHOTHERAPY

Adler Graduate School — M
Adler University — M,D,O
Argosy University, Chicago — D
Atlantic University — O
Boston Graduate School of
  Psychoanalysis — M,D,O
Immaculata University — M,D,O
Naropa University — M
The New School — M,D
New York University — M,D,O
Prescott College — M
Regent University — M,D

PSYCHOLOGY—GENERAL

Abilene Christian University — M
Acadia University — M
Adelphi University — M
Adler University — M,D,O
Alabama Agricultural and
  Mechanical University — M,O
Alliant International
  University–Fresno — M,D
Alliant International
  University–Los Angeles — M,D
Alliant International
  University–Sacramento — M,D
Alliant International
  University–San Diego — M,D
Alliant International
  University–San Francisco — M,D,O
American International College — M,D,O
American Public University System — M
American University — M,D,O
The American University in Cairo — M,O
American University of Beirut — M,D
Andrews University — M
Angelo State University — M
Antioch University Los Angeles — M,D
Appalachian State University — M
Arcadia University — M,D,O
Argosy University, Atlanta — M,D,O
Argosy University, Chicago — M,D
Argosy University, Dallas — M,D
Argosy University, Denver — M,D
Argosy University, Hawai'i — M,D,O
Argosy University, Inland Empire — M,D
Argosy University, Los Angeles — M,D
Argosy University, Nashville — M,D
Argosy University, Northern
  Virginia — M,D
Argosy University, Orange County — M,D
Argosy University, Phoenix — M,D
Argosy University, Salt Lake City — M,D
Argosy University, San Diego — M,D

Argosy University, San Francisco
  Bay Area — M,D
Argosy University, Sarasota — M,D
Argosy University, Schaumburg — M,O
Argosy University, Seattle — M,D,O
Argosy University, Tampa — M,D
Argosy University, Twin Cities — M,D,O
Arizona State University at the
  Tempe campus — M,D
Arkansas Tech University — M
Auburn University — M,D
Auburn University at Montgomery — M
Augusta University — M
Austin Peay State University — M
Avila University — M
Azusa Pacific University — M
Ball State University — M
Barry University — M
Baylor University — M,D
Binghamton University, State
  University of New York — D
Biola University — D
Boston College — D
Boston Graduate School of
  Psychoanalysis — M,D
Boston University — M,D
Bowling Green State University — M,D
Brandeis University — M,D
Brandman University — M
Brenau University — M
Bridgewater State University — M
Brigham Young University — D
Brock University — M,D
Brooklyn College of the City
  University of New York — M,D
Brown University — M,D
Bucknell University — M,D
California Coast University — M
California Institute of Integral
  Studies — M,D
California Lutheran University — M,D
California Polytechnic State
  University, San Luis Obispo — M
California State Polytechnic
  University, Pomona — M
California State University, Chico — M
California State University,
  Dominguez Hills — M
California State University,
  Fresno — M,O
California State University,
  Fullerton — M
California State University, Long
  Beach — M
California State University, Los
  Angeles — M
California State University,
  Northridge — M
California State University,
  Sacramento — M
California State University, San
  Bernardino — M
California State University, San
  Marcos — M
California State University,
  Stanislaus — M
Cambridge College — M,O
Cameron University — M
Capella University — M,D
Cardinal Stritch University — M
Carleton University — M,D
Carlos Albizu University — M,D
Carlos Albizu University, Miami
  Campus — M,D
Carnegie Mellon University — D
Case Western Reserve University — M,D
Castleton University — M
The Catholic University of America — M,D
Central Connecticut State
  University — M
Central Michigan University — M,D,O
Central Washington University — M
Chestnut Hill College — M,D,O
The Chicago School of Professional
  Psychology — M,D
The Chicago School of Professional
  Psychology at Irvine — D
The Chicago School of Professional
  Psychology: Online — M,D
The Citadel, The Military College
  of South Carolina — M,O
City College of the City
  University of New York — M,D
Claremont Graduate University — M,D,O
Clayton State University — M
Clemson University — D
Cleveland State University — M,D,O
The College at Brockport, State
  University of New York — M
College of Saint Elizabeth — M,D,O
College of St. Joseph — M
The College of William and Mary — M
Colorado State University — M,D
Columbia University — M,D
Concordia University (Canada) — M,D
Concordia University Chicago — M
Cornell University — D
Dalhousie University — M,D
Dartmouth College — D
DePaul University — M,D
Drexel University — M,D
Duke University — D
Duquesne University — D
East Central University — M
Eastern Illinois University — M,O
Eastern Kentucky University — M,O
Eastern Michigan University — M,D
Eastern Washington University — M,O
East Tennessee State University — D
Emory University — D
Emporia State University — M

Evangel University — M
Fairleigh Dickinson University,
  College at Florham — M,O
Fairleigh Dickinson University,
  Metropolitan Campus — M,D,O
Fayetteville State University — M
Fielding Graduate University — M,D,O
Fisk University — M
Fitchburg State University — O
Florida Agricultural and
  Mechanical University — M
Florida Atlantic University — M
Florida Institute of Technology — M,D
Florida International University — M,D
Florida State University — M,D
Fordham University — M,D
Fort Hays State University — M,O
Framingham State University — M
Francis Marion University — M,O
Frostburg State University — M
Gardner-Webb University — M
Geneva College — M
George Mason University — M,D,O
Georgetown University — D
The George Washington University — M,D,O
Georgia Institute of Technology — M,D
Georgia Southern University — M,D
Georgia State University — D
Goddard College — M
Golden Gate University — M,D,O
Governors State University — M
The Graduate Center, City
  University of New York — D
Grand Canyon University — D
Hardin-Simmons University — M
Harvard University — D
Hofstra University — M,D
Hood College — M
Houston Baptist University — M
Howard University — M,D
Humboldt State University — M
Hunter College of the City
  University of New York — M,O
Idaho State University — D
Illinois Institute of Technology — M,D
Illinois State University — M,D,O
Immaculata University — M,D,O
Indiana State University — M,D
Indiana Tech — M
Indiana University Bloomington — D
Indiana University of Pennsylvania — M,D
Indiana University–Purdue
  University Indianapolis — M,D
Inter American University of
  Puerto Rico, Metropolitan Campus — M,D
Inter American University of
  Puerto Rico, San Germán Campus — M,D
Iona College — M,O
Iowa State University of Science
  and Technology — M,D
Jackson State University — D
Jacksonville State University — M
James Madison University — M
John F. Kennedy University — M,D,O
Johns Hopkins University — D
Kansas State University — M,D
Kean University — M
Keiser University — M,D
Kent State University — M,D
Kentucky State University — M
Lakehead University — M,D
Lamar University — M
La Salle University — M,D
Laurentian University — M
Lehigh University — M,D
Lesley University — M,D,O
LeTourneau University — M
Lipscomb University — M,O
Loma Linda University — D
Long Island University–LIU
  Brooklyn — M,D,O
Long Island University–LIU
  Post — M,O
Louisiana State University and
  Agricultural & Mechanical College — M,D
Louisiana Tech University — M,D
Loyola University Chicago — M,D
Loyola University Maryland — M,D,O
Madonna University — M
Mansfield University of
  Pennsylvania — M
Marietta College — M
Marist College — M,O
Marquette University — D
Marshall University — M,D,O
Martin University — M
Marywood University — M
McGill University — M,D
McMaster University — M,D
McNeese State University — M
Medaille College — M
Memorial University of
  Newfoundland — M,D
Mercy College — M
Metropolitan State University — M,D
Miami University — M,D
Michigan School of Professional
  Psychology — M,D
Michigan State University — M,D
Middle Tennessee State University — M,O
Millersville University of
  Pennsylvania — M
Minnesota State University Mankato — M,D
Mississippi State University — M,D
Missouri State University — M,O
Monmouth University — M,O
Montana State University — M
Montana State University Billings — M
Montclair State University — M
Morehead State University — M
Morgan State University — M,D

---

*M—masters degree; D—doctorate; O—other advanced degree; *—Close-Up and/or Display*

Psychology—General (continued)

Institution	Degrees
Mount Aloysius College	M
Murray State University	M
National Louis University	M,D,O
New Mexico Highlands University	M
New Mexico State University	M,D
The New School	M,D
New York Medical College	M,D,O
New York University	M,D,O
Norfolk State University	M,D
North Carolina Central University	M
North Carolina State University	D
Northcentral University	M,D,O
North Dakota State University	M,D
Northeastern State University	M
Northeastern University	M,D
Northern Arizona University	M
Northern Illinois University	M,D
Northern Michigan University	M,O
Northwestern State University of Louisiana	M
Northwestern University	D
Northwest University	M,D
Notre Dame de Namur University	M
Nova Southeastern University	M,D,O
The Ohio State University	D
Ohio University	D
Oklahoma State University	M,D
Old Dominion University	M,D
Oregon State University	M,D
Our Lady of the Lake University	M
Pace University	M
Pacifica Graduate Institute	M,D
Pacific University	M,D
Palo Alto University	M,D
Penn State Harrisburg	M,D,O
Penn State University Park	M,D
Pepperdine University	M,D
Philadelphia College of Osteopathic Medicine	M,D,O
Pittsburg State University	M
Pontifical Catholic University of Puerto Rico	M,D
Pontificia Universidad Catolica Madre y Maestra	M
Portland State University	M,D,O
Princeton University	D
Purdue University	D
Queens College of the City University of New York	M,O
Queen's University at Kingston	M,D
Rhode Island College	M,O
Rice University	M,D
Rivier University	M
Roberts Wesleyan College	M,D
Rochester Institute of Technology	M,O
Roosevelt University	M,D
Rosalind Franklin University of Medicine and Science	M,D
Rowan University	M,O
Rutgers University–Camden	M
Rutgers University–Newark	D
Rutgers University–New Brunswick	D
Sage Graduate School	M,O
St. Cloud State University	M,D
St. John's University (NY)	M
Saint Joseph's University	M,O
Saint Louis University	M,D
Saint Mary's University (Canada)	M,D
Salem State University	M,O
Sam Houston State University	M,D,O
San Diego State University	M,D
San Francisco State University	M,O
San Jose State University	M,O
Saybrook University	M,D
The Seattle School of Theology and Psychology	M
Seattle University	M
Seton Hall University	M,D
Shippensburg University of Pennsylvania	M
Simon Fraser University	M,D
Sofia University	M,D
Southeastern Baptist Theological Seminary	M,D
Southeastern Louisiana University	M
Southern Adventist University	M
Southern California Seminary	M,D
Southern Connecticut State University	M
Southern Illinois University Carbondale	M,D
Southern Illinois University Edwardsville	M,O
Southern Methodist University	D
Southern Nazarene University	M
Southern New Hampshire University	M,O
Southern Oregon University	M
Southern University and Agricultural and Mechanical College	M
Southwestern College (NM)	O
Spalding University	M,D
Stanford University	D
State University of New York at New Paltz	M,O
State University of New York at Plattsburgh	M,O
Stephen F. Austin State University	M
Stony Brook University, State University of New York	M,D
Suffolk University	M,D,O
Sul Ross State University	M
Teachers College, Columbia University	M,D
Temple University	M,D
Tennessee State University	M
Texas A&M International University	M
Texas A&M University	M,D
Texas A&M University–Commerce	M,D,O
Texas A&M University–Corpus Christi	M
Texas A&M University–Kingsville	M
Texas A&M University–Texarkana	M
Texas Christian University	M,D
Texas Southern University	M
Texas State University	M
Texas Tech University	M,D
Texas Woman's University	M,D,O
Tiffin University	M
Towson University	M
Tufts University	M,D
Tulane University	M,D
Uniformed Services University of the Health Sciences	D
Union College (KY)	M
Universidad de las Americas, A.C.	M
Universidad de las Américas Puebla	M
Université de Montréal	M,D
Université de Sherbrooke	M
Université du Québec à Montréal	D
Université du Québec à Trois-Rivières	D,O
Université Laval	D
University at Albany, State University of New York	M,D
University at Buffalo, the State University of New York	M,D
The University of Akron	M,D
The University of Alabama	D
The University of Alabama at Birmingham	M,D
The University of Alabama in Huntsville	M
University of Alaska Anchorage	M,D
University of Alaska Fairbanks	D
University of Alberta	M,D
The University of Arizona	M,D
University of Arkansas	M,D
University of Arkansas at Little Rock	M
The University of British Columbia	M,D
University of Calgary	M,D
University of California, Berkeley	D
University of California, Davis	D
University of California, Irvine	D
University of California, Los Angeles	M,D
University of California, Merced	M,D
University of California, Riverside	D
University of California, San Diego	D
University of California, Santa Barbara	D
University of California, Santa Cruz	D
University of Central Arkansas	M,D,O
University of Central Florida	M,D
University of Central Missouri	M,D,O
University of Central Oklahoma	M
University of Chicago	D
University of Cincinnati	D
University of Colorado Boulder	M,D
University of Colorado Colorado Springs	M,D
University of Connecticut	M,D
University of Dallas	M
University of Dayton	M
University of Delaware	D
University of Denver	M,D
University of Florida	M,D
University of Georgia	D
University of Guelph	M,D
University of Hartford	M,D
University of Hawaii at Manoa	M,D,O
University of Houston	M,D
University of Houston–Clear Lake	M
University of Houston–Victoria	M
University of Idaho	M,D
University of Illinois at Chicago	M,D
University of Illinois at Urbana–Champaign	M,D
University of Indianapolis	M,D
The University of Iowa	M,D,O
The University of Kansas	M,D,O
University of Kentucky	M,D
University of La Verne	M,D
University of Lethbridge	M,D
University of Louisiana at Lafayette	M
University of Louisiana at Monroe	M
University of Louisville	D
University of Maine	M,D
The University of Manchester	M,D
University of Manitoba	M,D
University of Maryland, Baltimore County	M,D
University of Maryland, College Park	M,D
University of Massachusetts Amherst	M,D
University of Massachusetts Dartmouth	M,O
University of Massachusetts Lowell	M
University of Memphis	M,D,O
University of Miami	M,D
University of Michigan	D,O
University of Minnesota, Twin Cities Campus	D
University of Missouri	M,D
University of Missouri–Kansas City	M,D
University of Missouri–St. Louis	M,D,O
University of Montana	M,D,O
University of Nebraska at Omaha	M,D,O
University of Nebraska–Lincoln	M,D
University of Nevada, Las Vegas	M,D,O
University of Nevada, Reno	M,D
University of New Brunswick Fredericton	M,D
University of New Brunswick Saint John	M,D
University of New Hampshire	D
University of New Mexico	D
University of New Orleans	M,D
The University of North Carolina at Chapel Hill	D
The University of North Carolina at Charlotte	M,D,O
The University of North Carolina at Greensboro	M,D
The University of North Carolina Wilmington	M
University of North Dakota	M,D
University of Northern British Columbia	M,D,O
University of Northern Iowa	M
University of North Florida	M
University of North Texas	M,D,O
University of Notre Dame	D
University of Oklahoma	M,D,O
University of Oregon	D
University of Ottawa	D
University of Pennsylvania	D
University of Philosophical Research	M
University of Phoenix–Jersey City Campus	M
University of Phoenix–Online Campus	M,O
University of Phoenix–Phoenix Campus	M
University of Phoenix–Southern Arizona Campus	M
University of Phoenix–Southern California Campus	M
University of Phoenix–Washington D.C. Campus	M
University of Pittsburgh	D
University of Puerto Rico, Río Piedras Campus	M,D
University of Regina	M,D
University of Rhode Island	M,D
University of Rochester	D
University of Saint Mary	M
University of Saskatchewan	M
University of South Africa	M,D
University of South Alabama	M,D
University of South Carolina	M,D
The University of South Dakota	M,D
University of Southern California	M,D
University of Southern Mississippi	M,D
University of South Florida	D
University of South Florida, St. Petersburg	M
The University of Tennessee	M,D
The University of Tennessee at Chattanooga	M
The University of Texas at Arlington	M,D
The University of Texas at Austin	D
The University of Texas at Dallas	M,D
The University of Texas at El Paso	M,D
The University of Texas at San Antonio	M,D
The University of Texas at Tyler	M
The University of Texas of the Permian Basin	M
The University of Texas Rio Grande Valley	M
University of the Pacific	M
University of the Rockies	M,D
University of the West	M
The University of Toledo	M,D
University of Toronto	M,D
The University of Tulsa	M,D
University of Utah	D
University of Vermont	D
University of Victoria	M,D
University of Virginia	M,D
University of Washington	D
University of Waterloo	M,D
The University of Western Ontario	M,D
University of West Florida	M
University of West Georgia	M,D,O
University of Windsor	M,D
University of Wisconsin–Eau Claire	M,O
University of Wisconsin–La Crosse	M,O
University of Wisconsin–Madison	D
University of Wisconsin–Milwaukee	M,D
University of Wisconsin–Oshkosh	M
University of Wisconsin–Whitewater	M,O
University of Wyoming	M,D
Utah State University	M,D
Valdosta State University	M,O
Vanderbilt University	D
Villanova University	M
Virginia Polytechnic Institute and State University	M,D
Virginia State University	M,D
Wake Forest University	M
Walden University	M,D,O
Washburn University	M
Washington State University	M,D
Washington University in St. Louis	D
Wayne State University	M,D
Webster University	M
West Chester University of Pennsylvania	M,D,O
Western Carolina University	M
Western Illinois University	M,O
Western Kentucky University	M,O
Western Michigan University	M,D
Western Washington University	M
Westfield State University	M
West Texas A&M University	M
West Virginia University	M,D
Wheaton College	M,D
Wichita State University	D
Widener University	
Wilfrid Laurier University	M,D
William Carey University	M
William James College	M,D,O
Winthrop University	M,O
Wisconsin School of Professional Psychology	M,D
Wright Institute	D
Wright State University	M,D
Xavier University	M,D
Yale University	D
Yeshiva University	M,D
York University	M,D
Youngstown State University	M

PUBLIC ADMINISTRATION

Institution	Degrees
Adelphi University	O
Adler University	M,D,O
Albany State University	M
Alfred University	M
American Public University System	M
American University	M,D,O
The American University in Cairo	M,O
American University of Beirut	M,D
Anabaptist Mennonite Biblical Seminary	M,O
Anna Maria College	M
Appalachian State University	M
Argosy University, Chicago	M,D
Argosy University, Dallas	M,D,O
Argosy University, Denver	M,D
Argosy University, Inland Empire	M,D
Argosy University, Los Angeles	M,D
Argosy University, Northern Virginia	M,D,O
Argosy University, Orange County	M,D
Argosy University, Phoenix	M,D
Argosy University, Salt Lake City	M,D
Argosy University, San Diego	M,D
Argosy University, San Francisco Bay Area	M,D
Argosy University, Sarasota	M,D,O
Argosy University, Schaumburg	M,D,O
Argosy University, Seattle	M,D
Argosy University, Tampa	M,D
Argosy University, Twin Cities	M,D
Arizona State University at the Tempe campus	M,D
Arkansas State University	M,O
Auburn University	M,D,O
Auburn University at Montgomery	M,D
Azusa Pacific University	M
Ball State University	M,O
Barry University	M
Baruch College of the City University of New York	M
Baylor University	M
Belhaven University (MS)	M
Bellevue University	M
Binghamton University, State University of New York	M
Boise State University	M,D,O
Bowie State University	M
Bowling Green State University	M
Brandman University	M
Bridgewater State University	M
Brigham Young University	M
California Baptist University	M
California State Polytechnic University, Pomona	M
California State University, Bakersfield	M
California State University, Chico	M
California State University, Dominguez Hills	M
California State University, East Bay	M
California State University, Fresno	M
California State University, Fullerton	M
California State University, Long Beach	M,O
California State University, Los Angeles	M
California State University, Northridge	M,O
California State University, Sacramento	M
California State University, San Bernardino	M
California State University, Stanislaus	M
Capella University	M,D
Carleton University	M,D
Carnegie Mellon University	M
Central European University	M,O
Central Michigan University	M,O
Cheyney University of Pennsylvania	M
City College of the City University of New York	M
Clark Atlanta University	M
Clark University	M,O
Clemson University	M,D,O
Cleveland State University	M,D,O
The College at Brockport, State University of New York	M
College of Charleston	M
The College of New Rochelle	M
College of Saint Elizabeth	M
Columbia University	M
Columbus State University	M
Concordia University (Canada)	M,D
Concordia University Wisconsin	M
Copenhagen Business School	M,D,O
Cumberland University	M
Dalhousie University	M
DePaul University	M
DeVry University–Folsom Campus	M

Drake University	M	Pontifical Catholic University of		University of Missouri–St.		Wayne State University	M,D
East Carolina University	M,O	Puerto Rico	M	Louis	M,D,O	Webster University	M,D,O
Eastern Kentucky University	M	Portland State University	M,D	University of Montana	M	West Chester University of
Eastern Michigan University	M,O	Post University	M	University of Nebraska at Omaha	M,D,O	Pennsylvania	M,O
Eastern Washington University	M	Regent University	M	University of Nevada, Las Vegas	M,D,O	Western Kentucky University	M
East Stroudsburg University of		Rhode Island College	M	University of Nevada, Reno	M	Western Michigan University	M,D,O
Pennsylvania	M	Roger Williams University	M	University of New Brunswick		Westfield State University	M
East Tennessee State University	M	Roosevelt University	M	Fredericton	M	West Virginia University	M
The Evergreen State College	M	Rutgers University–Camden	M	University of New Hampshire	M,O	Wichita State University	M
Excelsior College	M	Rutgers University–Newark	M,D	University of New Haven	M,O	Widener University	M
Fairfield University	M	Saginaw Valley State University	M	University of New Mexico	M	Wilmington University	M,D
Fairleigh Dickinson University,		St. John's University (NY)	M,O	University of New Orleans	M	Wright State University	M
College at Florham	M	Saint Louis University	M,D,O	The University of North Carolina		York University	M
Fairleigh Dickinson University,		St. Mary's University		at Chapel Hill	M	
Metropolitan Campus	M,O	(United States)	M,O	The University of North Carolina		**PUBLIC AFFAIRS**
Florida Agricultural and		Saint Peter's University	M	at Charlotte	M,O	American University	M
Mechanical University	M	St. Thomas University	M,O	The University of North Carolina		Arizona State University at the
Florida Atlantic University	M,D	Sam Houston State University	M	at Pembroke	M	Tempe campus	M,D
Florida Gulf Coast University	M	San Diego State University	M	The University of North Carolina		Cleveland State University	D
Florida Institute of Technology	M,D	San Francisco State University	M	Wilmington	M	Concordia University (Canada)	O
Florida International University	M,D	San Jose State University	M,O	University of North Dakota	M	Cornell University	M
Florida National University	M	Savannah State University	M	University of North Florida	M,O	Florida International University	M,D
Florida State University	M,D,O	Seattle University	M	University of North Georgia	M	George Mason University	M
Framingham State University	M	Seton Hall University	M,O	University of North Texas	M,D,O	The George Washington University	M,O
Gallaudet University	M,D,O	Shippensburg University of		University of North Texas at		Indiana University Bloomington	M,D,O
Gannon University	M	Pennsylvania	M	Dallas	M	Indiana University Northwest	M,O
George Mason University	M	Sonoma State University	M,O	University of Oklahoma	M	Indiana University of Pennsylvania	M
The George Washington University	M,D	Southeast Missouri State		University of Ottawa	D,O	Indiana University–Purdue
Georgia College & State University	M	University	M	University of Pennsylvania	M,O	University Indianapolis	M,O
Georgia Southern University	M	Southern Arkansas University–		University of Phoenix–		Indiana University South Bend	M,O
Georgia State University	M,D	Magnolia	M	Atlanta Campus	M	The Institute of World Politics	M,O
Golden Gate University	M,D,O	Southern Illinois University		University of Phoenix–		Jackson State University	M,D
Governors State University	M	Carbondale	M	Augusta Campus	M	McMaster University	M,D
Grambling State University	M	Southern Illinois University		University of Phoenix–Bay		Merrimack College	M
Grand Valley State University	M	Edwardsville	M	Area Campus	M,D	Metropolitan College of New York	M
Hamline University	M,D	Southern University and		University of Phoenix–		Murray State University	M
Harvard University	M	Agricultural and Mechanical College	M	Central Valley Campus	M	New Mexico Highlands University	M
Hilbert College	M	Southern Utah University	M	University of Phoenix–		Notre Dame de Namur University	M
Hood College	M	South University (GA)	M	Colorado Campus	M	The Ohio State University	M,D
Howard University	M	South University (AL)	M	University of Phoenix–		Park University	M,O
Idaho State University	M	South University	M	Colorado Springs		Penn State Harrisburg	M,D,O
IGlobal University	M	Stephen F. Austin State University	M	Downtown Campus	M	Portland State University	M,D
Illinois Institute of Technology	M	Strayer University	M	University of Phoenix–		Princeton University	M,D,O
Indiana State University	M	Suffolk University	M	Columbus Georgia Campus	M	Regis College (MA)	M
Indiana University Bloomington	M,D,O	Syracuse University	M,D	University of Phoenix–Dallas		Syracuse University	
Indiana University Kokomo	M,O	Tarleton State University	M	Campus	M	Texas A&M University	M,O
Indiana University Northwest	M,O	Tennessee State University	M,D	University of Phoenix–Hawaii		The University of Alabama in
Indiana University–Purdue		Texas A&M International University	M	Campus	M	Huntsville	M
University Indianapolis	M,O	Texas A&M University	M,O	University of Phoenix–		University of Arkansas at Little
Indiana University South Bend	M,O	Texas A&M University–Corpus		Houston Campus	M	Rock	M,O
Institute of Public Administration	M	Christi	M	University of Phoenix–Jersey		University of Baltimore	M,D
Instituto Tecnológico y de		Texas Southern University	M	City Campus	M	University of California, Berkeley	M
Estudios Superiores de Monterrey,		Texas State University	M	University of Phoenix–Las		University of Central Florida	M,D,O
Campus Ciudad Juárez	M	Texas Tech University	M,D	Vegas Campus	M	University of Colorado Colorado
International University in Geneva	M,D	Thomas Edison State University	M	University of Phoenix–North		Springs	M
Iowa State University of Science		Trident University International	M,D	Florida Campus	M	University of Colorado Denver	M,D
and Technology	M	Trine University	M	University of Phoenix–Online		University of Florida	M,D,O
Jackson State University	M,D	Troy University	O	Campus	M,O	University of Louisville	M,D
James Madison University	M	Tufts University	M	University of Phoenix–		University of Minnesota, Twin
John Jay College of Criminal		Université de Moncton	M	Phoenix Campus	M	Cities Campus	M,D
Justice of the City University of		Université de Sherbrooke	M	University of Phoenix–		University of Missouri	M,D,O
New York	M	Université du Québec		Sacramento Valley Campus	M	University of Missouri–
Johns Hopkins University	M,O	à Montréal	M	University of Phoenix–		Kansas City	M,D
Kansas State University	M	Université du Québec,		San Antonio Campus	M	University of Nevada, Las Vegas	M,D,O
Kean University	M	École nationale d'administration		University of Phoenix–		The University of North Carolina
Kennesaw State University	M	publique	D,O	San Diego Campus	M	at Greensboro	M,O
Kent State University	M,D	University at Albany, State		University of Phoenix–		University of San Francisco	M
Kentucky State University	M,D	University of New York	M,D,O	Southern California Campus	M	University of Saskatchewan	M,D
Kutztown University of		The University of Akron	M	University of Phoenix–South		University of South Florida	O
Pennsylvania	M	The University of Alabama	M,D	Florida Campus	M	The University of Texas at Austin	M,D
Lamar University	M	The University of Alabama at		University of Phoenix–		The University of Texas Rio Grande
Liberty University	M,D,O	Birmingham	M	Washington D.C. Campus	M,D	Valley	M
Lincoln University (MO)	M	University of Alaska Anchorage	M	University of Pittsburgh	M,D	University of Washington	M,D
Lindenwood University	M	University of Alaska Southeast	M	University of Puerto Rico,		University of Waterloo	M
Lipscomb University	M	The University of Arizona	M,D,O	Río Piedras Campus	M	University of Wisconsin–
London Metropolitan University	M,D	University of Arkansas	M	University of Regina	M,D,O	Madison	M
Long Island University–		University of Arkansas at Little		University of Rhode Island	M	Virginia Commonwealth University	M,D,O
Hudson	M,O	Rock	M	University of St. Thomas (TX)	M	Virginia Polytechnic Institute and
Long Island University–LIU		University of Baltimore	M,D	University of San Francisco	M	State University	M,D,O
Brooklyn	M,O	University of Central Florida	M,O	University of South Africa	M,D	Washington State University	M,D,O
Long Island University–LIU		University of Central Oklahoma	M	University of South Alabama	M	West Chester University of
Post	M,O	University of Colorado Colorado		University of South Carolina	M	Pennsylvania	M,O
Louisiana State University and		Springs	M	The University of South Dakota	M,D	Western Carolina University	M
Agricultural & Mechanical College	M,D	University of Colorado Denver	M,D	University of Southern California	M,O	Western Michigan University	M,D,O
Marist College	M	University of Connecticut	M	University of Southern Indiana	M	York University	M
Marshall University	M	University of Dayton	M	University of South Florida	M,D,O	
Marywood University	M	University of Delaware	M	The University of Tennessee	M	**PUBLIC HEALTH—GENERAL**
McMaster University	M,D	University of Evansville	M	The University of Tennessee at		Adelphi University	M,O
Metropolitan College of New York	M	The University of Findlay	M,D	Chattanooga	M,O	Allen College	M,D
Metropolitan State University	M,D,O	University of Georgia	M,D	The University of Texas at		American Public University System	M
Mid-America Christian University	M	University of Guam	M	Arlington	M	American University of Armenia	M
Middlebury Institute of		University of Guelph	M	The University of Texas at Austin	M,D	Andrews University	M,O
International Studies at Monterey	M	University of Hawaii at Manoa	M,O	The University of Texas at Dallas	M,D	Arcadia University	M
Minnesota State University Mankato	M	University of Houston	M,D	The University of Texas at San		Argosy University, Atlanta	M
Mississippi State University	M,D	University of Idaho	M,D	Antonio	M	Argosy University, Chicago	M
Missouri State University	M,O	University of Illinois at Chicago	M,D	The University of Texas at Tyler	M	Argosy University, Dallas	M
Montana State University	M	University of Illinois at		The University of Texas Rio Grande		Argosy University, Denver	M
Morehead State University	M	Springfield	M,D,O	Valley	M	Argosy University, Hawai`i	M
National University	M	The University of Kansas	M,D,O	University of the District of		Argosy University, Inland Empire	M
New Charter University	M	University of Kentucky	M,D,O	Columbia	M	Argosy University, Los Angeles	M
New Mexico State University	M	University of La Verne	M,D	The University of Toledo	M,O	Argosy University, Nashville	M
New York University	M,D,O	University of Louisiana at Monroe	M	University of Utah	M,D	Argosy University, Northern
North Carolina Central University	M	University of Louisville	M,D	University of Vermont	M	Virginia	M
North Carolina State University	M,D	University of Management and		University of Victoria	M,D	Argosy University, Orange County	M
Northeastern University	M,D	Technology	M,O	University of Washington	M,D	Argosy University, Phoenix	M
Northern Arizona University	M,D,O	University of Manitoba	M	University of West Georgia	M,D,O	Argosy University, Salt Lake City	M
Northern Illinois University	M	University of Maryland, College		The University of Winnipeg	M	Argosy University, San Diego	M
Northern Kentucky University	M,O	Park	M	University of Wisconsin–		Argosy University, San Francisco
Northern Michigan University	M	University of Massachusetts		Milwaukee	M	Bay Area	M
Northwestern University	M	Amherst	M	University of Wisconsin–		Argosy University, Sarasota	M
Norwich University	M	University of Massachusetts Boston	M	Oshkosh	M	Argosy University, Schaumburg	M
Notre Dame de Namur University	M	University of Massachusetts		University of Wyoming	M	Argosy University, Seattle	M
Nova Southeastern University	M	Dartmouth	M,O	Upper Iowa University	M	Argosy University, Tampa	M
Oakland University	M,O	University of Memphis	M,O	Villanova University	M,O	Argosy University, Twin Cities	M
The Ohio State University	M,D	University of Michigan–		Virginia Commonwealth University	M	Arizona State University at the
Ohio University	M,O	Dearborn	M	Virginia International University	M	Tempe campus	M,D,O
Old Dominion University	M,D	University of Michigan–Flint	M	Virginia Polytechnic Institute and		Armstrong State University	M
Pace University	M	University of Missouri	M,D,O	State University	M,D,O	A.T. Still University	M,D,O
Park University	M	University of Missouri–		Walden University	M,D,O	Augusta University	M
Penn State Harrisburg	M,D,O	Kansas City	M,D	Waldorf University	M	Austin Peay State University	M
				Washington Adventist University	M	Baldwin Wallace University	M

M—masters degree; D—doctorate; O—other advanced degree; *—Close-Up and/or Display

Public Health—General

Institution	Degrees
Barry University	
Benedictine University	M
Boise State University	M,D,O
Boston University	M,D
Bowling Green State University	M
Brigham Young University	M
Brooklyn College of the City University of New York	M
Brown University	M
California Baptist University	M
California State University, Fresno	M
California State University, Long Beach	M
California State University, Northridge	M
California State University, San Bernardino	M
Case Western Reserve University	M
Charles R. Drew University of Medicine and Science	M
Chicago State University	M
Claremont Graduate University	M,D,O
Clemson University	M,D,O
Cleveland State University	M
The College at Brockport, State University of New York	M
Columbia University	M,D
Daemen College	M
Dartmouth College	M
Davenport University	M
DePaul University	M
Des Moines University	M
Drexel University	M,D,O
East Carolina University	M
Eastern Virginia Medical School	M
Eastern Washington University	M
East Stroudsburg University of Pennsylvania	M
East Tennessee State University	M,D,O
Elmhurst College	M
Emory University	M,D
Everglades University	M
Excelsior College	M,O
Florida Agricultural and Mechanical University	M,D
Florida International University	M,D
Florida State University	M,D
Fort Valley State University	M
George Mason University	M,O
Georgetown University	M,D
The George Washington University	M,D
Georgia Southern University	M,D
Georgia State University	M,D,O
The Graduate Center, City University of New York	D
Grand Canyon University	M,D,O
Grand Valley State University	M
Harvard University	M,D
Hawai`i Pacific University	M
Hofstra University	M
Howard University	M
Hunter College of the City University of New York	M
Icahn School of Medicine at Mount Sinai	M,D
Idaho State University	M,O
Independence University	M
Indiana University Bloomington	M,D
Indiana University–Purdue University Indianapolis	M,D,O
Jackson State University	M,D
Johns Hopkins University	M,D
Kansas State University	M,D,O
Kent State University	M,D
Lamar University	M
La Salle University	M
Laurentian University	D
Lenoir-Rhyne University	M
Loma Linda University	M,D
London Metropolitan University	M,D
Long Island University–LIU Brooklyn	M,D,O
Louisiana State University Health Sciences Center	M,D
Louisiana State University in Shreveport	M
Loyola University Chicago	M,O
Marshall University	M
Medical College of Wisconsin	M,D,O
Meharry Medical College	M
Mercer University	M,D
Michigan State University	M
MidAmerica Nazarene University	M
Missouri State University	M
Monroe College	M
Montclair State University	M
Morehouse School of Medicine	M
Morgan State University	M,D
National University	M,D,O
New England Institute of Technology	M
New Mexico State University	M,O
New York Medical College	M,D,O
New York University	M,D
North Dakota State University	M
Northeast Ohio Medical University	M,D,O
Northwestern University	M
Nova Southeastern University	M,D,O
The Ohio State University	M,D
Ohio University	M
Oregon State University	M
Penn State Hershey Medical Center	M,D
Ponce Health Sciences University	M,D
Portland State University	M,D
Purdue University	M,D
Queen's University at Kingston	M,D
Rivier University	M,D
Rutgers University–Camden	M,O
Rutgers University–Newark	M,O
Rutgers University–New Brunswick	M,D
St. Catherine University	M
St. John's University (NY)	M
Saint Louis University	M
Salus University	M
Samford University	M
San Diego State University	M,D
San Francisco State University	M
San Jose State University	M,D
Sarah Lawrence College	M
Simmons College	M
Simon Fraser University	M,D,O
Slippery Rock University of Pennsylvania	M
Southern Connecticut State University	M
State University of New York Downstate Medical Center	M
Stony Brook University, State University of New York	M,O
Syracuse University	M
Tarleton State University	M
Temple University	M,D
Tennessee State University	M
Texas A&M University	M,D,O
Thomas Edison State University	M
Thomas Jefferson University	M,O
Touro University California	M,D
Trident University International	M,D,O
Trinity Washington University	M
Tufts University	M,D,O
Tulane University	M,D
Uniformed Services University of the Health Sciences	M,D
Université de Montréal	M,D,O
University at Albany, State University of New York	M,D
University at Buffalo, the State University of New York	M,D
The University of Akron	M,D
The University of Alabama at Birmingham	M,D
University of Alaska Anchorage	M
University of Alberta	M,D
The University of Arizona	M,D
University of Arkansas for Medical Sciences	M,D,O
The University of British Columbia	M,D
University of California, Berkeley	M,D
University of California, Irvine	M,D
University of California, Los Angeles	M,D
University of California, San Diego	D
University of Cincinnati	M,D
University of Colorado Denver	M,D
University of Connecticut Health Center	M
University of Florida	M,D,O
University of Georgia	D
University of Hawaii at Manoa	M,D,O
University of Illinois at Chicago	M,D
University of Illinois at Springfield	M,O
University of Illinois at Urbana–Champaign	M,D
University of Indianapolis	M
The University of Iowa	M,D,O
The University of Kansas	M
University of Kentucky	M,D
University of Louisville	M,D
The University of Manchester	M,D
University of Maryland, College Park	M,D
University of Massachusetts Amherst	M,D
University of Memphis	M,D
University of Miami	M,D
University of Michigan	M,D
University of Michigan–Flint	M
University of Minnesota, Twin Cities Campus	M,D,O
University of Missouri	M,O
University of Montana	M,O
University of Nebraska Medical Center	M
University of Nevada, Las Vegas	M,D,O
University of Nevada, Reno	M,D
University of New England	M,D,O
University of New Hampshire	M,O
University of New Mexico	M
The University of North Carolina at Chapel Hill	M,D
The University of North Carolina at Charlotte	M,D,O
University of North Dakota	M
University of Northern Colorado	M
University of North Florida	M,O
University of North Texas Health Science Center at Fort Worth	M,D,O
University of Oklahoma Health Sciences Center	M,D
University of Ottawa	D
University of Pennsylvania	M
University of Pittsburgh	M,D,O
University of Rochester	M
University of San Francisco	M
University of South Africa	M,D
University of South Carolina	M,D
The University of South Dakota	M
University of Southern California	M,D
University of Southern Maine	M
University of Southern Mississippi	M,D
University of South Florida	M,D,O
The University of Tennessee	M
The University of Texas at El Paso	M,O
The University of Texas Health Science Center at Houston	M,D
The University of Texas Medical Branch	M
University of the Sciences	M
The University of Toledo	M,O
University of Toronto	M,D
University of Utah	M,D
University of Virginia	M,D
University of Washington	M
University of Waterloo	M,D
University of West Florida	M
University of Wisconsin–Madison	M
University of Wisconsin–Milwaukee	M,D,O
Valparaiso University	M,D,O
Vanderbilt University	M
Virginia Polytechnic Institute and State University	M,D
Walden University	M,D,O
Washington University in St. Louis	M,D
Wayne State University	M,D,O
West Chester University of Pennsylvania	M,O
Western Kentucky University	M
Westminster College (UT)	M
West Virginia University	M,D
Wright State University	M
Yale University	M,D

PUBLIC HISTORY

Institution	Degrees
American Public University System	M
Arizona State University at the Tempe campus	M,D,O
Armstrong State University	M
California State University, East Bay	M
California State University, Sacramento	M,D
The College at Brockport, State University of New York	M
Colorado State University	M
Drew University	M,D,O
Duquesne University	M
East Carolina University	M
Eastern Illinois University	M
Florida State University	M,D
Georgia Southern University	M,O
Georgia State University	M,D
Indiana University of Pennsylvania	M
Indiana University–Purdue University Indianapolis	M
James Madison University	M
La Salle University	M,O
Lehigh University	M,D
Loyola University Chicago	M,D
Middle Tennessee State University	D
New York University	M,D,O
North Carolina State University	M
Northeastern University	M,D
Northern Kentucky University	M
Rutgers University–Camden	M
St. John's University (NY)	M,D
Shippensburg University of Pennsylvania	M
Sonoma State University	M
Southeast Missouri State University	M,O
Texas A&M University–Commerce	M,D,O
University at Albany, State University of New York	M,D,O
University at Buffalo, the State University of New York	M,D,O
University of Arkansas at Little Rock	M
University of California, Santa Barbara	D
University of Colorado Denver	M
University of Illinois at Springfield	M
University of Louisville	M,O
University of Maryland, Baltimore County	M,D
University of Missouri–St. Louis	M,O
University of North Alabama	M
University of Northern Iowa	M
University of South Carolina	M,O
The University of Texas at Austin	M,D
University of West Florida	M
University of West Georgia	M,O
University of Wisconsin–Milwaukee	M,D
Wayne State University	M,D,O

PUBLIC POLICY

Institution	Degrees
Adler University	M,D,O
Albany State University	M
American Public University System	M,O
American University	M,O
American University of Beirut	M,D
The American University of Paris	M
Arizona State University at the Tempe campus	M,D
Auburn University at Montgomery	M,D
Aurora University	M
Baruch College of the City University of New York	M
Baylor University	M,D
Boise State University	M,D,O
Brandeis University	M
Brock University	M
Brooklyn College of the City University of New York	M
Brown University	M
California Lutheran University	M,O
California State University, East Bay	M
California State University, Long Beach	M,O
California State University, Sacramento	M
Carleton University	M,D
Carnegie Mellon University	M,D
The Catholic University of America	M
Central European University	M,D
Claremont Graduate University	M,D,O
Clemson University	D,O
The College of William and Mary	M
Columbia University	M
Concordia University (Canada)	M,D
Cornell University	M,D
DePaul University	M
Duke University	M,D
Eastern Michigan University	M,O
Eastern University	M,D
Florida State University	M,D,O
Frederick S. Pardee RAND Graduate School	D
George Mason University	M,D
Georgetown University	M,D
The George Washington University	M,D
Georgia Institute of Technology	M
Georgia State University	M,D,O
The Graduate Center, City University of New York	M,D
Harvard University	M,D
Indiana University Bloomington	M,D,O
Indiana University Kokomo	M,O
Indiana University–Purdue University Fort Wayne	M,O
The Institute of World Politics	M,D
Jackson State University	M,D
Jacksonville University	M
John Jay College of Criminal Justice of the City University of New York	M,D
Johns Hopkins University	M,D
Liberty University	M
Lincoln University (MO)	M
Lipscomb University	M
London Metropolitan University	M,D
Loyola University Chicago	M,D
McMaster University	M,D
Mills College	M
Mississippi State University	M,D
Monmouth University	M
Morehead State University	M
National Louis University	M,D,O
New England College	M
The New School	D
New York University	M,D
Northeastern University	M,D,O
Northwestern University	M,D
Norwich University	M
The Ohio State University	M,D
Oregon State University	M,D
Pepperdine University	M
Portland State University	M,D
Princeton University	M,D
Queen's University at Kingston	M
Regent University	M
Rochester Institute of Technology	M
Rutgers University–Camden	M
Rutgers University–Newark	M,D,O
Rutgers University–New Brunswick	M,D
Saint Louis University	M,D,O
St. Mary's University (United States)	M,O
San Francisco State University	M
Seton Hall University	M,O
Simmons College	M
Simon Fraser University	M
Southern University and Agricultural and Mechanical College	D
State University of New York Empire State College	M
Stony Brook University, State University of New York	M
Suffolk University	M,O
Trinity College (United States)	M
Tufts University	M
Union Institute & University	M
Universidad Autonoma de Guadalajara	M,D
Universidad del Este	M
Université de Montréal	O
University at Albany, State University of New York	M,D,O
The University of Arizona	M,D,O
University of Arkansas	D
The University of British Columbia	M
University of California, Berkeley	M,D
University of California, Los Angeles	M
University of California, Riverside	M,D
University of California, San Diego	M
University of Chicago	M,D
University of Delaware	M,D
University of Denver	M
University of Georgia	M,D
University of Guelph	M
University of Hawaii at Manoa	O
University of Houston	M
University of Kentucky	M,D,O
University of Louisville	M,D
University of Maryland, Baltimore County	M,D,O
University of Maryland, College Park	M,D
University of Massachusetts Amherst	M
University of Massachusetts Boston	M,D
University of Massachusetts Dartmouth	M,O
University of Memphis	M,O
University of Michigan	M,D
University of Minnesota, Twin Cities Campus	M,D,O
University of Missouri	M,D,O
University of Missouri–St. Louis	M,D,O
University of Nebraska–Lincoln	M,D,O
University of Nevada, Las Vegas	M,D,O
University of New Brunswick Fredericton	M
University of New Hampshire	M
The University of North Carolina at Chapel Hill	D
The University of North Carolina at Charlotte	M,D,O
University of Northern Iowa	M

University of Oregon	M
University of Pennsylvania	M,D
University of Pittsburgh	M,D
University of Puerto Rico, Río Piedras Campus	M
University of Regina	M,D,O
University of Rhode Island	M
University of St. Thomas (TX)	M
University of Saskatchewan	M,D
The University of South Dakota	M,D
University of Southern California	M,D,O
University of Southern Maine	M
The University of Texas at Arlington	M,D
The University of Texas at Austin	M,D
The University of Texas at Dallas	M,D
The University of Texas Rio Grande Valley	M
University of the Pacific	M,D
University of Utah	M
University of Virginia	M
University of Washington	M,D
University of Washington, Bothell	M
Vanderbilt University	D
Virginia Commonwealth University	D
Virginia Polytechnic Institute and State University	M,D
Walden University	M,D,O
Wayne State University	M,D
West Virginia University	M,D
Wilfrid Laurier University	M
William Paterson University of New Jersey	M,D
York University	M

PUBLISHING

Arizona State University at the Tempe campus	M,D,O
Brown University	M,D
Carnegie Mellon University	M
DePaul University	M
Emerson College	M
The George Washington University	M
New York University	M
Northwestern University	M
Pace University	M
Rosemont College	O
Rowan University	M
Sam Houston State University	M
Simon Fraser University	M
University of Baltimore	M
University of Houston–Victoria	M
Vermont College of Fine Arts	M

QUALITY MANAGEMENT

California Intercontinental University	M,D
California State University, Dominguez Hills	M
Calumet College of Saint Joseph	M
East Carolina University	M,D,O
Eastern Michigan University	M,O
Florida Institute of Technology	M,D
Hofstra University	M,O
Instituto Tecnologico de Santo Domingo	M,O
Instituto Tecnológico y de Estudios Superiores de Monterrey, Campus Ciudad de México	M,D
Instituto Tecnológico y de Estudios Superiores de Monterrey, Campus Ciudad Juárez	M
Instituto Tecnológico y de Estudios Superiores de Monterrey, Campus Estado de México	M,D
Instituto Tecnológico y de Estudios Superiores de Monterrey, Campus Irapuato	M,D
Madonna University	M
Mount Mercy University	M
The National Graduate School of Quality Management	M,D
Northwestern University	M
Penn State Erie, The Behrend College	M
Regis College (MA)	M
Rutgers University–New Brunswick	M,D
Southern New Hampshire University	M,O
Stevens Institute of Technology	M,O
Stevenson University	M
Trident University International	M,D,O
Universidad de las Americas, A.C.	M
Universidad del Turabo	M
The University of Alabama	M
University of Massachusetts Boston	M,O
The University of Tennessee at Chattanooga	M,O
The University of Texas at Tyler	M
University of Wisconsin–Stout	M

QUANTITATIVE ANALYSIS

Ball State University	M
Baruch College of the City University of New York	M
Columbia University	M,D
Cornell University	M,D
Drexel University	M,D,O
Duke University	M,D,O
Fordham University	M
Hofstra University	M,O
Instituto Tecnologico de Santo Domingo	M,O
La Salle University	M,O
Lehigh University	M
Northwestern University	M,D
Purdue University	M,D
Rutgers University–Newark	M,O
St. John's University (NY)	M
San Francisco State University	M

University at Buffalo, the State University of New York	M,D
The University of Alabama at Birmingham	M,D
The University of British Columbia	M,D
University of California, Santa Barbara	M,D
University of Cincinnati	M
University of Colorado Denver	M
University of Connecticut	M,O
University of Florida	M,D,O
The University of Iowa	M,D,O
University of Maryland, College Park	M,D
University of Minnesota, Twin Cities Campus	M,D,O
University of New Mexico	D
University of North Texas	M,D,O
University of Oregon	M
University of Puerto Rico, Río Piedras Campus	M,D
University of South Africa	M,D
University of Southern California	M,D
The University of Texas at Arlington	M,D
The University of Texas at Austin	M,D
The University of Texas Health Science Center at Houston	M,D
Vanderbilt University	M
Virginia Polytechnic Institute and State University	M,O

RADIATION BIOLOGY

Colorado State University	M,D
Georgetown University	M
Université de Sherbrooke	M,D
The University of Iowa	M
University of Oklahoma Health Sciences Center	M,D

RANGE SCIENCE

Kansas State University	M,D,O
Montana State University	M,D
New Mexico State University	M,D
Oregon State University	M,D
Sul Ross State University	M
Texas A&M University–Kingsville	M
The University of Arizona	M
University of California, Berkeley	M
University of Wyoming	M,D
Utah State University	M,D

READING EDUCATION

Adelphi University	M
Alabama Agricultural and Mechanical University	M,D,O
Alabama State University	M,O
Alfred University	M
Alverno College	M
American International College	M,O
American Public University System	M
Appalachian State University	M
Arcadia University	M,D,O
Arkansas State University	M,D,O
Armstrong State University	M,O
Asbury University	M
Ashland University	M
Augustana University	M
Aurora University	M,D
Austin Peay State University	M,O
Avila University	M,O
Baldwin Wallace University	M
Ball State University	M,D,O
Bank Street College of Education	M
Barry University	M,D,O
Belhaven University (MS)	M
Bellarmine University	M,D,O
Benedictine University	M
Berry College	M
Binghamton University, State University of New York	M
Bloomsburg University of Pennsylvania	M
Blue Mountain College	M
Bluffton University	M
Boise State University	M
Boston College	M,O
Bowie State University	M
Bowling Green State University	M,O
Bridgewater State University	M,O
Brigham Young University	M
Buffalo State College, State University of New York	M
Caldwell University	M,D,O
California Baptist University	M
California State Polytechnic University, Pomona	M
California State University, East Bay	M
California State University, Fresno	M
California State University, Northridge	M
California State University, Sacramento	M,D
California State University, San Marcos	M,D
California State University, Stanislaus	M
California University of Pennsylvania	M
Cambridge College	M,D,O
Canisius College	M,O
Capella University	M,D
Cardinal Stritch University	M,O
Carthage College	M,O
Castleton University	M,O
Centenary University	M,D
Central Connecticut State University	M
Central Michigan University	M,D,O

Central Washington University	M
Chestnut Hill College	M
Chicago State University	M
The Citadel, The Military College of South Carolina	M,O
City College of the City University of New York	M
City University of Seattle	M,O
Clarion University of Pennsylvania	M
Clarks Summit University	M
Clemson University	M,D
Coker College	M
The College at Brockport, State University of New York	M
The College of New Jersey	M,O
The College of New Rochelle	M
College of St. Joseph	M
The College of Saint Rose	M,O
College of Staten Island of the City University of New York	M
The College of William and Mary	M
Concordia University (United States)	M,D
Concordia University Chicago	M
Concordia University, Nebraska	M
Concordia University, St. Paul	M,D,O
Concordia University Wisconsin	M
Concord University	M
Converse College	O
Coppin State University	M
Crandall University	M
Curry College	M,O
Dallas Baptist University	M
Delaware State University	M
DePaul University	M
Dominican University	M
Drury University	M
Duquesne University	M
East Carolina University	M
Eastern Connecticut State University	M
Eastern Michigan University	M,O
Eastern Nazarene College	M,O
Eastern New Mexico University	M
Eastern University	M,D,O
Eastern Washington University	M
East Stroudsburg University of Pennsylvania	M
East Tennessee State University	M,O
Edinboro University of Pennsylvania	M,O
Elms College	M,O
Emory & Henry College	M
Emporia State University	M
Endicott College	M
Evangel University	M
Fairleigh Dickinson University, College at Florham	M,O
Fairleigh Dickinson University, Metropolitan Campus	M,O
Fairmont State University	M
Fitchburg State University	O
Florida Atlantic University	M
Florida International University	M,D,O
Florida Memorial University	M
Florida State University	M,D,O
Fontbonne University	M
Framingham State University	M
Fresno Pacific University	M,O
Frostburg State University	M
Furman University	M,O
Gannon University	M,O
George Fox University	M,O
George Mason University	M
Georgetown College	M
Georgia College & State University	M
Georgia Southern University	M,O
Georgia State University	M,D
Gordon College	M,O
Goucher College	M,O
Governors State University	M
Graceland University (IA)	M
Grambling State University	M,D,O
Grand Canyon University	M,D,O
Grand Valley State University	M
Hamline University	M,D
Hannibal-LaGrange University	M
Harding University	M,O
Hardin-Simmons University	M
Harvard University	M
Heritage University	M
Hofstra University	M,D,O
Holy Family University	M
Hood College	M,O
Houston Baptist University	M,D
Idaho State University	M,O
Illinois State University	M
Indiana University Bloomington	M,D,O
Indiana University of Pennsylvania	M,O
Indiana University–Purdue University Indianapolis	M,O
Jackson State University	M,D,O
Jacksonville State University	M
James Madison University	M
Johns Hopkins University	M
Judson University	M,D
Kansas State University	M,D,O
Kaplan University, Davenport Campus	M
Kean University	M
Kennesaw State University	M
Kent State University	M
Kutztown University of Pennsylvania	M
La Salle University	M,O
Lehman College of the City University of New York	M
Le Moyne College	M,O
Lesley University	M,D,O
Lewis University	M
Liberty University	M,D,O

Lipscomb University	M,D,O
Long Island University–Brentwood Campus	M,O
Long Island University–Hudson	M,O
Long Island University–LIU Post	M,D,O
Long Island University–Riverhead	M,O
Longwood University	M
Lourdes University	M
Loyola Marymount University	M
Loyola University Maryland	M
Lynchburg College	M
Lyndon State College	M
Madonna University	M
Manhattanville College	M
Marquette University	M,D,O
Marshall University	M,O
Marygrove College	M
Maryville University of Saint Louis	M,D
Marywood University	M
Massachusetts College of Liberal Arts	M,O
McDaniel College	M
McKendree University	M,D,O
McNeese State University	M,O
Medaille College	M
Mercer University	M,D,O
Mercy College	M
Meredith College	M,O
MGH Institute of Health Professions	M,O
Michigan State University	M
MidAmerica Nazarene University	M
Middle Tennessee State University	M,D
Midwestern State University	M
Millersville University of Pennsylvania	M
Misericordia University	M
Mississippi State University	M,D,O
Mississippi University for Women	M
Missouri State University	M
Monmouth University	M,D,O
Montana State University Billings	M
Montclair State University	M
Morehead State University	M
Mount Mercy University	M
Mount St. Joseph University	M,O
Mount Saint Mary College	M,O
Mount Saint Vincent University	M
Murray State University	M,O
National Louis University	M,D,O
Nazareth College of Rochester	M
Newman University	M
New Mexico State University	M,D,O
New York University	M
Niagara University	M
North Carolina Agricultural and Technical State University	M
Northeastern Illinois University	M
Northeastern State University	M
Northern Illinois University	M,D
Northern Michigan University	M
Northwestern Oklahoma State University	M
Northwestern State University of Louisiana	M,O
Northwest Missouri State University	M,D,O
Notre Dame College (OH)	M,O
Oakland University	M,D,O
Ohio University	M,O
Old Dominion University	M,D
Olivet Nazarene University	M
Pace University	M,O
Park University	M,O
Penn State Harrisburg	M,D,O
Plymouth State University	M
Providence College	M
Purdue University	M,D
Queens College of the City University of New York	M,O
Queens University of Charlotte	M
Quincy University	M
Radford University	M
Regent University	M,D,O
Regis College (MA)	M,D
Regis University	M,O
Rhode Island College	M
Rider University	M,O
Rivier University	M,D,O
Robert Morris University	M,D,O
Roberts Wesleyan College	M
Rockford University	M
Roger Williams University	M
Roosevelt University	M
Rowan University	M,O
Rutgers University–New Brunswick	M,D
Sacred Heart University	O
Sage Graduate School	M
Saginaw Valley State University	M
St. Bonaventure University	M
Saint Francis University	M
St. John Fisher College	M
St. John's University (NY)	M,D,O
St. Joseph's College, Long Island Campus	M
St. Joseph's College, New York	M
Saint Joseph's University	M,D,O
Saint Leo University	M,O
Saint Mary's University of Minnesota	M,O
Saint Michael's College	M,O
Saint Peter's University	M,O
St. Thomas Aquinas College	M,O
St. Thomas University	M,D,O
Saint Xavier University	M

M—masters degree; D—doctorate; O—other advanced degree; *—Close-Up and/or Display

Institution	Degree
Salem College	M
Salem State University	M
Salisbury University	M,D
Sam Houston State University	M,D
San Diego State University	M
San Francisco State University	M,O
Seattle Pacific University	M
Shenandoah University	M,D,O
Shippensburg University of Pennsylvania	M,O
Siena Heights University	M,O
Simmons College	M,D,O
Simon Fraser University	D
Slippery Rock University of Pennsylvania	M
Sonoma State University	M
Southeastern Louisiana University	M
Southeastern Oklahoma State University	M
Southeastern University (FL)	M,D
Southern Adventist University	M
Southern Connecticut State University	M,O
Southern Illinois University Edwardsville	M,O
Southern Methodist University	M,D
Southern New Hampshire University	M,D,O
Southern Oregon University	M
Southwestern Adventist University	M
Southwest Minnesota State University	M
Spring Arbor University	M
State University of New York at Fredonia	M
State University of New York at New Paltz	M
State University of New York at Oswego	M
State University of New York at Plattsburgh	M
State University of New York College at Cortland	M
State University of New York College at Geneseo	M
State University of New York College at Oneonta	M
State University of New York College at Potsdam	M
Sul Ross State University	M,O
Syracuse University	M,D
Tarleton State University	M
Teachers College, Columbia University	M,D,O
Tennessee Technological University	M,D,O
Texas A&M University–Commerce	M,D,O
Texas A&M University–Corpus Christi	M,D
Texas A&M University–Kingsville	M
Texas A&M University–San Antonio	M
Texas Christian University	M,O
Texas State University	M
Texas Tech University	M,D
Texas Woman's University	M,D
Touro College	M
Towson University	M,O
Trident University International	M
Trinity Washington University	M
Union College (KY)	M
University at Albany, State University of New York	M,D,O
University at Buffalo, the State University of New York	M,D,O
The University of Akron	M
The University of Alabama at Birmingham	M
The University of Alabama in Huntsville	M,O
University of Alaska Southeast	M
The University of Arizona	M,D,O
University of Arkansas at Little Rock	M,D,O
University of Bridgeport	M,D,O
The University of British Columbia	M,D
University of California, Riverside	M,D,O
University of Central Arkansas	M
University of Central Florida	M,D,O
University of Central Missouri	M,D,O
University of Central Oklahoma	M
University of Cincinnati	M,D
University of Colorado Denver	M
University of Connecticut	M,D
University of Dayton	M
The University of Findlay	M,D
University of Florida	M,D,O
University of Georgia	M
University of Guam	M
University of Houston–Clear Lake	M
University of Kentucky	M,D
University of La Verne	M,O
University of Louisiana at Monroe	M,O
University of Maine	M,D,O
University of Mary	M,D
University of Maryland, College Park	M,D,O
University of Massachusetts Amherst	M,D,O
University of Memphis	M,D,O
University of Miami	D
University of Michigan–Flint	M,D,O
University of Minnesota, Twin Cities Campus	M,D,O
University of Missouri	M,D,O
University of Missouri–Kansas City	M,D,O
University of Missouri–St. Louis	M
University of Nebraska at Kearney	M
University of Nevada, Reno	M,D
University of New England	M,D,O
University of New Mexico	M,D
The University of North Carolina at Chapel Hill	M,D
The University of North Carolina at Charlotte	M,O
The University of North Carolina at Greensboro	M,D,O
The University of North Carolina at Pembroke	M
The University of North Carolina Wilmington	M
University of North Dakota	M
University of Northern Colorado	M
University of Northern Iowa	M
University of North Florida	M
University of Oklahoma	M,D
University of Oklahoma Health Sciences Center	M,D,O
University of Pennsylvania	M
University of Phoenix–Online Campus	M,O
University of Phoenix–Phoenix Campus	M
University of Pittsburgh	M,D
University of Portland	M,D
University of Rhode Island	M,D
University of St. Francis (IL)	M,D,O
University of Saint Joseph	M
University of St. Thomas (TX)	M,D
University of San Diego	M
University of San Francisco	M,D
The University of Scranton	M
University of Sioux Falls	M,O
University of South Alabama	M,D
University of South Carolina	M,D
The University of South Dakota	M
University of Southern Maine	M,O
University of South Florida	M,D,O
University of South Florida, St. Petersburg	M
The University of Tennessee	M,D,O
The University of Texas at Arlington	M
The University of Texas at Austin	M,D
The University of Texas at El Paso	M,D
The University of Texas at San Antonio	M,D
The University of Texas at Tyler	M
The University of Texas of the Permian Basin	M
The University of Texas Rio Grande Valley	M,D,O
University of the Cumberlands	M,D,O
University of Utah	M,D,O
University of Victoria	M,D
University of Virginia	M,D
University of Washington	M,D
University of West Florida	M
University of West Georgia	M,D,O
University of Wisconsin–Eau Claire	M
University of Wisconsin–La Crosse	M,O
University of Wisconsin–Milwaukee	M
University of Wisconsin–Oshkosh	M
University of Wisconsin–River Falls	M
University of Wisconsin–Stevens Point	M
University of Wisconsin–Superior	M
Upper Iowa University	M
Utah Valley University	M
Vanderbilt University	M
Virginia Commonwealth University	M,O
Viterbo University	M,O
Wagner College	M
Walden University	M,D,O
Walla Walla University	M
Walsh University	M
Washburn University	M
Washington State University	M,D
Wayne State University	M,D,O
Webster University	M,O
West Chester University of Pennsylvania	M,O
Western Connecticut State University	M
Western Illinois University	M
Western Kentucky University	M,O
Western Michigan University	M,D
Western New Mexico University	M
Western State Colorado University	M
Westfield State University	M
Westminster College (PA)	M,O
West Texas A&M University	M
Wheelock College	M
Widener University	M,D
Wilkes University	M,D
William Paterson University of New Jersey	M
Wilmington College	M
Wilmington University	M,D
Worcester State University	M,O
Xavier University	M
York College of Pennsylvania	M
Youngstown State University	M

REAL ESTATE

Institution	Degree
American University	M,O
Arizona State University at the Tempe campus	M,D
Auburn University	M
Baruch College of the City University of New York	M
Brandeis University	M
California State University, Sacramento	M
Clemson University	M
Columbia University	M
Cornell University	M
DePaul University	M
Drexel University	M
Emory University	M
Florida International University	M
Georgetown University	M
The George Washington University	O
Georgia State University	M,D,O
Instituto Centroamericano de Administración de Empresas	M
Johns Hopkins University	M
Longwood University	M
Marquette University	M
Marylhurst University	M
Massachusetts Institute of Technology	M
Monmouth University	M,O
New York University	M,O
Northwestern University	M,D
Pacific States University	M,D
Philadelphia University	M
Pontificia Universidad Catolica Madre y Maestra	M
Portland State University	M
Pratt Institute	M
Roosevelt University	M,O
Rutgers University–Newark	M
San Jose State University	M,O
Southern Methodist University	M
Syracuse University	M
Texas A&M University	M
Universidad Iberoamericana	M,D
University at Buffalo, the State University of New York	M
University of California, Berkeley	D
University of Denver	M
University of Florida	M,D,O
University of Hawaii at Manoa	M
University of Illinois at Chicago	M
University of Maryland, College Park	M
University of Memphis	M,D
University of Miami	M,D
The University of North Carolina at Charlotte	M,O
University of Pennsylvania	M,D
University of San Diego	M
University of South Africa	M,D
University of Southern California	M
University of South Florida	M,D
The University of Texas at Arlington	M,D
The University of Texas at Dallas	M
University of Utah	M
University of Wisconsin–Madison	M,D
Villanova University	M
Virginia Commonwealth University	O

RECREATION AND PARK MANAGEMENT

Institution	Degree
Acadia University	M
Bowling Green State University	M
California State University, Chico	M
California State University, East Bay	M
California State University, Long Beach	M
California State University, Northridge	M,O
California State University, Sacramento	M
Central Michigan University	M
Clemson University	M,D,O
Colorado State University	M,D
Delta State University	M
East Carolina University	M,O
Eastern Kentucky University	M
Eastern Washington University	M
Florida International University	M,D,O
Frostburg State University	M
Hardin-Simmons University	M
Indiana State University	M,D
Indiana University Bloomington	M,D
Iona College	M,O
Kent State University	M
Lehman College of the City University of New York	M
Liberty University	M,D,O
Loyola Marymount University	M
Michigan State University	M,D
Middle Tennessee State University	M
Naropa University	M
New England College	M
North Carolina Central University	M
North Carolina State University	M,D
Northwest Missouri State University	M
Ohio University	M
Penn State University Park	M,D
Purdue University	M,D
San Francisco State University	M
San Jose State University	M,O
Slippery Rock University of Pennsylvania	M
South Dakota State University	M,D
Southern Adventist University	M
Southern Connecticut State University	M
Southern Illinois University Carbondale	M
Southern University and Agricultural and Mechanical College	M
Southwestern Oklahoma State University	M
Springfield College	M
State University of New York College at Cortland	M
Temple University	M,D
Texas A&M University	M,D
Texas State University	M
Universidad Metropolitana	M
University of Alberta	M,D
University of Arkansas	M,D
University of Florida	M,D
University of Idaho	M,D
The University of Iowa	M,D
University of Louisiana at Monroe	M
University of Manitoba	M
University of Mississippi	M,D
University of Montana	M
University of Nebraska at Kearney	M
University of New Brunswick Fredericton	M
University of New Hampshire	M
The University of North Carolina at Greensboro	M
University of Rhode Island	M
The University of Tennessee	M
The University of Toledo	M,D
University of Utah	M
University of Waterloo	M,D
University of Wisconsin–La Crosse	M
Utah State University	M
Virginia Commonwealth University	M
Western Illinois University	M
Western Kentucky University	M
West Virginia University	M

REHABILITATION COUNSELING

Institution	Degree
Adler University	M,D,O
Alabama Agricultural and Mechanical University	M,O
Alabama State University	M
Arkansas State University	M,O
Assumption College	M,O
Ball State University	M,O
Barry University	M,O
Bayamón Central University	M
California State University, Fresno	M
California State University, Los Angeles	M,D
California State University, San Bernardino	M
Central Connecticut State University	M
Coppin State University	M
East Carolina University	M,D,O
East Central University	M
Edinboro University of Pennsylvania	M,O
Emporia State University	M
Florida International University	M,D,O
Fort Valley State University	M
The George Washington University	M
Georgia State University	M
Hofstra University	M,O
Hunter College of the City University of New York	M
Illinois Institute of Technology	M,D
Kent State University	M
Langston University	M
Louisiana State University Health Sciences Center	M
Maryville University of Saint Louis	M
Mercer University	M
Michigan State University	M,D,O
Minnesota State University Mankato	M
Mississippi State University	M,D,O
Montana State University Billings	M
Mount Mary University	M
Northeastern Illinois University	M
Ohio University	M,D
Pontifical Catholic University of Puerto Rico	M
Rutgers University–Newark	M,D
St. Bonaventure University	M,O
St. Cloud State University	M
Salve Regina University	M,O
San Diego State University	M
San Francisco State University	M
South Carolina State University	M
Southern University and Agricultural and Mechanical College	M
Springfield College	M
Texas Tech University Health Sciences Center	M
Thomas University	M
University at Buffalo, the State University of New York	M,D,O
The University of Arizona	M,D
University of Arkansas	M,D
University of Arkansas at Little Rock	M,O
University of Idaho	M,O
The University of Iowa	M,D
University of Kentucky	M,D
University of Louisiana at Lafayette	M
University of Maryland, College Park	M,D,O
University of Maryland Eastern Shore	M
University of Massachusetts Boston	M
University of Memphis	M,D
The University of North Carolina at Chapel Hill	M,D
University of Northern Colorado	M,D,O
University of North Texas	M,D,O
University of Puerto Rico, Río Piedras Campus	M
The University of Scranton	M
University of South Carolina	M
University of Southern Maine	M,O
University of South Florida	M,D,O
The University of Tennessee	M
The University of Texas at Austin	M,D
The University of Texas at El Paso	M
The University of Texas Rio Grande Valley	M,D
The University of Texas Southwestern Medical Center	M
University of the District of Columbia	M
University of Wisconsin–Madison	M,D

University of Wisconsin–Stout — M
Utah State University — M
Virginia Commonwealth University — M
Wayne State University — M,D,O
Western Michigan University — M
Western Oregon University — M
Western Washington University — M
Wilberforce University — M
Winston-Salem State University — M
Wright State University — M

REHABILITATION SCIENCES

Alabama State University — M
Augusta University — D
Boston University — D
California University of Pennsylvania — M
Central Michigan University — M,D
Concordia University Wisconsin — M
Duquesne University — M,D
East Carolina University — M,D,O
East Stroudsburg University of Pennsylvania — M
George Mason University — D,O
Indiana University–Purdue University Indianapolis — M
Jackson State University — M
Lasell College — M
Logan University — M,D
Loma Linda University — M,D
Marquette University — M,D
McGill University — M,D,O
McMaster University — M,D
Medical University of South Carolina — D
New York University — M,D
Northwestern University — D
The Ohio State University — D
Old Dominion University — D
Queen's University at Kingston — M,D
Salus University — M,O
Stony Brook University, State University of New York — M,D,O
Temple University — M,D
Texas Tech University Health Sciences Center — D
Université de Montréal — O
University at Buffalo, the State University of New York — M,D,O
The University of Alabama at Birmingham — D
University of Alberta — D
The University of British Columbia — M,D
University of Colorado Denver — D
University of Florida — D
University of Illinois at Urbana–Champaign — M,D
The University of Iowa — M,D
The University of Kansas — M,D
University of Kentucky — D
University of Manitoba — M
University of Maryland, Baltimore — D
University of Maryland Eastern Shore — M
University of Northern Colorado — M,D
University of North Texas Health Science Center at Fort Worth — M,D
University of Oklahoma Health Sciences Center — M
University of Ottawa — M
University of Pittsburgh — M,D
University of South Carolina — M,O
University of South Florida — D
The University of Texas Medical Branch — D
University of Toronto — M,D
The University of Tulsa — M
University of Utah — D
University of Washington — M,D
University of Wisconsin–La Crosse — M
University of Wisconsin–Milwaukee — D
Virginia Commonwealth University — D
Washington University in St. Louis — D
Western Michigan University — M

RELIABILITY ENGINEERING

Arizona State University at the Tempe campus — M
University of Maryland, College Park — M,D
The University of Tennessee — M,D

RELIGION

Abilene Christian University — M
Ambrose University — M,O
The American University of Rome — M
Amridge University — M,D
Arizona State University at the Tempe campus — M,D,O
The Baptist College of Florida — M
Baptist Theological Seminary at Richmond — M,D,O
Baylor University — M,D
Bethany Theological Seminary — M,O
Bethel Seminary — M,D,O
Bethesda University — M
Beulah Heights University — M
Biola University — M,D,O
Bob Jones University — M,D,O
Boston University — M,D
Briercrest Seminary — M
Brown University — D
Bryn Athyn College of the New Church — M
Cairn University — M
California Institute of Integral Studies — M,D

California State University, Long Beach — M
Calvin Theological Seminary — M,D
Canadian Southern Baptist Seminary — M
Cardinal Stritch University — M
The Catholic University of America — M,D,O
Charlotte Christian College and Theological Seminary — M
Chicago Theological Seminary — M,D
Christian Brothers University — M
Christian Theological Seminary — M,D
Cincinnati Christian University — M
Claremont Graduate University — M,D
Claremont Lincoln University — M
Claremont School of Theology — M,D
Clarks Summit University — M,D
Columbia University — M,D
Concordia University (Canada) — M,D
Concordia University Chicago — M
Concordia University Irvine — M
Concordia University of Edmonton — M
Cornell University — M,D
Dallas Baptist University — M
Dallas Theological Seminary — M,D,O
Delta State University — M
Denver Seminary — M,D,O
Dominican University of California — M
Drew University — M,D
Duke University — M,D
Earlham School of Religion — M
Eastern Mennonite University — M,D
East Texas Baptist University — M
Elms College — M
Emory University — D
Faith Baptist Bible College and Theological Seminary — M
Florida International University — M
Florida State University — M,D
Fordham University — M,D,O
General Theological Seminary — M,D,O
George Mason University — M
Georgetown University — M
The George Washington University — M
Georgia State University — M
Gordon-Conwell Theological Seminary — M,D
Grace College of Divinity — M
Graceland University (IA) — M
Graduate Theological Union — M,D,O
Grand Rapids Theological Seminary of Cornerstone University — M
Harding School of Theology — M,D
Hardin-Simmons University — M
Harrison Middleton University — M,D
Hartford Seminary — M,D,O
Harvard University — D
Heritage Christian University — M
Hope International University — M
Iliff School of Theology — M,D
Indiana University Bloomington — M,D
The Jewish Theological Seminary — M,D
John Carroll University — M
Kentucky Christian University — M
Knox Theological Seminary — M
Lancaster Theological Seminary — M,D,O
La Sierra University — M
Lee University — M
Liberty University — M,D,O
Lincoln Christian University — M
Loma Linda University — M
Louisville Presbyterian Theological Seminary — M,D
Lutheran Theological Seminary at Gettysburg — M,D
The Lutheran Theological Seminary at Philadelphia — M,D,O
Lutheran Theological Seminary Saskatoon — M,D
Luther Rice College & Seminary — M,D
Maranatha Baptist University — M
McGill University — M,D
McMaster University — M,D
Memorial University of Newfoundland — M
Milligan College — M,D,O
Missouri State University — M,O
Moody Theological Seminary—Michigan — M,O
Mount St. Joseph University — M
Mount Saint Mary's University (CA) — M,D,O
Naropa University — M
Nashotah House Theological Seminary — M,D,O
New Saint Andrews College — M,O
New York University — M,O
Northern Seminary — M,D
Northwestern University — M
Northwest Nazarene University — M
Nyack College — M
Oblate School of Theology — M,D,O
Olivet Nazarene University — M
Oregon State University — M
Oxford Graduate School — M,D
Pacific School of Religion — M,D,O
Pepperdine University — M
Princeton Theological Seminary — M,D
Princeton University — D
Queen's University at Kingston — M
Reformed Theological Seminary—Charlotte Campus — M,D
Reformed Theological Seminary—Houston Campus — M
Reformed Theological Seminary–Jackson Campus — M,D,O
Reformed Theological Seminary–Washington D.C. — M
Regent University — M,D
Rice University — D

The Robert E. Webber Institute for Worship Studies — M,D
Rutgers University–New Brunswick — M,O
St. Bonaventure University — M,O
Saint Charles Borromeo Seminary, Overbrook — M
Saint John's Seminary (MA) — M
St. Joseph's Seminary — M
Saint Mary's University (Canada) — M
Salve Regina University — M,D
Santa Clara University — M,D,O
Seattle Pacific University — M,O
The Seattle School of Theology and Psychology — M
Selma University — M
Seton Hall University — M,O
Sioux Falls Seminary — M
Southern Adventist University — M
The Southern Baptist Theological Seminary — M,D
Southern California Seminary — M,D
Southern Evangelical Seminary — M,D,O
Southern Methodist University — M,D
Southwestern Assemblies of God University — M
Stanford University — D
SUM Bible College & Theological Seminary — M
Syracuse University — M,D
Temple University — M,D
Trevecca Nazarene University — M
Trinity International University Florida — M,O
Trinity School for Ministry — M,D,O
Unification Theological Seminary — M,D
Union University — M,D
United Theological Seminary of the Twin Cities — M,D,O
Université de Montréal — M,D,O
Université de Sherbrooke — M,D,O
Université du Québec à Montréal — M,D
Université Laval — M,D
The University of British Columbia — M,D
University of Calgary — M,D
University of California, Berkeley — D
University of California, Riverside — M,D
University of California, Santa Barbara — M,D
University of Chicago — M,D
University of Colorado Boulder — M
University of Denver — M,D,O
University of Florida — M,D
University of Georgia — M
University of Hawaii at Manoa — M
University of Illinois at Urbana–Champaign — M
The University of Iowa — M,D
The University of Kansas — M,O
University of Lethbridge — M,D
The University of Manchester — D
University of Manitoba — M,D
University of Michigan — M,D
University of Minnesota, Twin Cities Campus — M,D
University of Missouri — M
The University of North Carolina at Chapel Hill — M,D
The University of North Carolina at Charlotte — M
University of Notre Dame — M
University of Ottawa — M,D
University of Pennsylvania — D
University of Regina — M
University of St. Thomas (MN) — M
University of St. Thomas (TX) — M
University of Saskatchewan — M
University of South Africa — M,D
University of South Carolina — M
University of South Florida — M,D
The University of Tennessee — M,D
University of the Cumberlands — M
University of the West — M,D
University of Toronto — M,D
University of Valley Forge — M
University of Virginia — M,D
University of Washington — M,D
University of Waterloo — D
The University of Winnipeg — M
Vancouver School of Theology — M,O
Vanderbilt University — M,D
Vanguard University of Southern California — M
Virginia University of Lynchburg — M,D
Wake Forest University — M
Washington Adventist University — M
Washington University in St. Louis — M
Wayland Baptist University — M
Wesley Biblical Seminary — M
Western Michigan University — M,O
Western Seminary — M,O
Westminster Seminary California — M
Westminster Theological Seminary — M,D,O
Wilfrid Laurier University — M
WON Institute of Graduate Studies — M
Wycliffe College — M,D,O
Yale University — D
Yeshiva Derech Chaim — D

RELIGIOUS EDUCATION

Andrews University — M,D,O
Asbury Theological Seminary — M,D,O
Azusa Pacific University — M
Baptist Theological Seminary at Richmond — M,D,O
Biola University — M,D,O
Boston College — M,D,O
Boston University — M,D

Brandeis University — M,O
Brigham Young University — M
Calvary University — M
Calvin Theological Seminary — M,D
Carolina Christian College — M
Claremont School of Theology — M,D
Clarks Summit University — M
Columbia International University — M,D,O
Concordia University Chicago — M
Concordia University, Nebraska — M
Dallas Baptist University — M
Dallas Theological Seminary — M,D,O
Felician University — M,O
Fordham University — M,D,O
Gardner-Webb University — M,D
Garrett-Evangelical Theological Seminary — M,D
Global University — M,D
Grand Rapids Theological Seminary of Cornerstone University — M
Gratz College — M,D
Hebrew College — M,O
Hebrew Union College–Jewish Institute of Religion (NY) — M
Inter American University of Puerto Rico, Metropolitan Campus — D
Interdenominational Theological Center — M,D
The Jewish Theological Seminary — M,D
Lancaster Theological Seminary — M,D,O
La Sierra University — M
Liberty University — M,D,O
Lincoln Christian Seminary — M,D
Loyola Marymount University — M
Loyola University Chicago — M,O
Maple Springs Baptist Bible College and Seminary — M,D,O
Midwestern Baptist Theological Seminary — M,D,O
Milligan College — M,D,O
Moody Theological Seminary—Michigan — M,O
Newman Theological College — M,O
New Orleans Baptist Theological Seminary — M,D
Oral Roberts University — M,D
Palm Beach Atlantic University — M
Pfeiffer University — M
Phillips Theological Seminary — M,D
Pontifical Catholic University of Puerto Rico — M
Providence University College & Theological Seminary — M,D,O
Reformed Theological Seminary–Jackson Campus — M,D,O
Regent University — M,D,O
Rochester College — M
St. Augustine's Seminary of Toronto — M,O
Saint Mary's University of Minnesota — M
Saints Cyril and Methodius Seminary — M
Selma University — M
Shasta Bible College — M
Southeastern Baptist Theological Seminary — M,D
Southern Adventist University — M
Southern Evangelical Seminary — M,D,O
Southwestern Assemblies of God University — M
Southwestern Baptist Theological Seminary — M,D
Towson University — M,O
Trinity International University — M,D,O
Trinity Lutheran Seminary — M
Unification Theological Seminary — M,D
Union Presbyterian Seminary — M,D
University of Detroit Mercy — M,D,O
University of St. Michael's College — M,D
University of St. Thomas (TX) — M,D
University of St. Thomas (MN) — M,D
University of San Francisco — M,D
Walsh University — M
Wesley Biblical Seminary — M
Wheaton College — M
Xavier University — M
Yeshiva University — M,D,O

REPRODUCTIVE BIOLOGY

Cornell University — M,D
Eastern Virginia Medical School — M
Oregon State University — M,D
Queen's University at Kingston — M,D
Rutgers University–New Brunswick — M,D
Tufts University — M,D
The University of British Columbia — M,D
University of Hawaii at Manoa — M,D
University of Saskatchewan — M,D
University of Wyoming — M,D
West Virginia University — M,D

RHETORIC

Abilene Christian University — M
Arizona State University at the Tempe campus — M,D,O
Ball State University — M,D
Bob Jones University — M,D,O
Boise State University — M
Bowling Green State University — M,D
Brigham Young University — M
California State University, Dominguez Hills — M,O
California State University, Fresno — M
California State University, Northridge — M

---

*M—masters degree; D—doctorate; O—other advanced degree; *—Close-Up and/or Display*

California State University, Stanislaus — M,O
Carnegie Mellon University — M,D
The Catholic University of America — M,D,O
Clemson University — D
Colorado State University — M
DePaul University — M,D
Duquesne University — M,D
East Carolina University — M,D,O
Eastern Washington University — M
Florida State University — M,D
Georgia State University — M,D
Idaho State University — M
Indiana University Bloomington — M,D
Iowa State University of Science and Technology — M,D
James Madison University — M
Kent State University — M,D
Michigan State University — M,D
Michigan Technological University — M,D
Missouri Western State University — M,O
Monmouth University — M
New Mexico Highlands University — M
New Mexico State University — M,D
North Carolina State University — D
North Dakota State University — M,D
Northern Arizona University — M,D,O
Northern Kentucky University — M,O
Northwestern University — M,D
Ohio University — M,D
Rensselaer Polytechnic Institute — O
Rowan University — O
Salisbury University — M
San Diego State University — M
Southern Illinois University Carbondale — M,D
Syracuse University — M,D
Texas Christian University — M,D
Texas State University — M
Texas Tech University — M,D
Texas Woman's University — M,D
The University of Alabama — M,D
The University of Alabama at Birmingham — M
The University of Arizona — M,D
University of Arkansas at Little Rock — M
University of California, Berkeley — D
University of Colorado Denver — M
University of Dayton — M
University of Denver — M,D
The University of Findlay — M,D
University of Houston–Downtown — M
The University of Iowa — M,D
University of Louisiana at Lafayette — M,D
University of Louisville — M,D
University of Massachusetts Amherst — M,D
University of Michigan–Flint — M
University of Nebraska–Lincoln — M,D
The University of North Carolina at Greensboro — M,D
University of Oklahoma — M,D
University of Southern California — D
University of South Florida — M,D
The University of Tennessee at Chattanooga — M
The University of Texas at El Paso — M,D,O
The University of Texas Rio Grande Valley — M
University of Utah — M,D
University of Wisconsin–Madison — M,D
University of Wisconsin–Milwaukee — M,D,O
Valdosta State University — M
Virginia Polytechnic Institute and State University — M,D,O
Wayne State University — M,D

ROMANCE LANGUAGES
Boston University — M,D
Clark Atlanta University — M,D
Columbia University — M,D
Cornell University — M,D
Hunter College of the City University of New York — M
Johns Hopkins University — D
Michigan State University — M,D
New York University — M,D
Northern Illinois University — M
Queens College of the City University of New York — M
San Diego State University — M
Stony Brook University, State University of New York — M
Texas Tech University — M,D
University at Buffalo, the State University of New York — M,D
The University of Alabama — M,D
University of California, Berkeley — D
University of Chicago — M,D
University of Cincinnati — M,D
University of Illinois at Urbana–Champaign — D
University of Miami — D
University of Missouri — M,D
University of Missouri–Kansas City — M
University of New Orleans — M
The University of North Carolina at Chapel Hill — M,D
University of Notre Dame — M
University of Oregon — M,D
University of Pennsylvania — M,D
University of South Africa — M,D
The University of Texas at Austin — M,D
Washington University in St. Louis — D
Wayne State University — M,D

RURAL PLANNING AND STUDIES
Brandon University — M,O

Dalhousie University — M
East Carolina University — M,O
Iowa State University of Science and Technology — D
Université Laval — O
University of Alaska Fairbanks — M
University of Guelph — M,D
University of Montana — M
University of Wyoming — M

RURAL SOCIOLOGY
Cornell University — M,D
Iowa State University of Science and Technology — M,D
The Ohio State University — M,D
Penn State University Park — M,D,O
University of Alberta — M,D
University of Missouri — M,D
University of Montana — M
University of Puerto Rico, Mayagüez Campus — M
University of Wisconsin–Madison — M,D

RUSSIAN
American University — M,O
Boston College — M
Brown University — M,D
Columbia University — M,D
Harvard University — D
Kent State University — M,D
McGill University — M,D
Middlebury College — M
New York University — M,D
Penn State University Park — M,D
Princeton University — D
The University of Arizona — M
University of California, Berkeley — D
The University of Manchester — M,D
University of Missouri — M
University of Oregon — M
University of South Africa — M,D
The University of Tennessee — D
University of Washington — M,D
University of Waterloo — M,D
Yale University — D

SAFETY ENGINEERING
Embry-Riddle Aeronautical University–Prescott — M
Florida Institute of Technology — M
Indiana University Bloomington — M,D
Murray State University — M
New Jersey Institute of Technology — M,D
Rochester Institute of Technology — M
University of Minnesota, Duluth — M
University of Southern California — M,D,O
West Virginia University — M

SCANDINAVIAN LANGUAGES
Cornell University — M,D
Harvard University — D
University of California, Berkeley — D
University of California, Los Angeles — M
University of Massachusetts Amherst — M,D
University of Minnesota, Twin Cities Campus — M,D
University of Washington — M,D
University of Wisconsin–Madison — M,D

SCHOOL NURSING
California State University, Fullerton — M,D,O
Cambridge College — M,D,O
Eastern Mennonite University — M
Eastern University — M,D,O
La Salle University — M,D,O
Lewis University — M,D
Monmouth University — M,D,O
Rowan University — M,D,O
Seton Hall University — M,D
University of Illinois at Chicago — M,O
West Chester University of Pennsylvania — M,D,O
Wright State University — M

SCHOOL PSYCHOLOGY
Abilene Christian University — O
Adelphi University — M
Alabama Agricultural and Mechanical University — M,O
Alfred University — M,D,O
Alliant International University–Irvine — M,D,O
Alliant International University–Los Angeles — M,D,O
Alliant International University–San Diego — M,D,O
Alliant International University–San Francisco — M,D,O
Andrews University — M,O
Appalachian State University — M,O
Argosy University, Dallas — M,D
Argosy University, Hawai'i — M
Argosy University, Phoenix — M,D
Argosy University, Sarasota — M,D,O
Arkansas State University — M,O
Assumption College — M,O
Auburn University at Montgomery — M,O
Augusta University — M,O
Azusa Pacific University — M
Ball State University — M,D,O
Barry University — M,O
Baylor University — M,D,O
Brigham Young University — M,D,O
Brooklyn College of the City University of New York — M,O
Caldwell University — M
California Baptist University — M
California State University, Chico — M
California State University, Dominguez Hills — M
California State University, East Bay — M

California State University, Fresno — M,O
California State University, Los Angeles — M,D
California State University, Northridge — M
California State University, Sacramento — M
California University of Pennsylvania — M
Cambridge College — M,D,O
Canisius College — M
Capella University — M,D
Carlos Albizu University, Miami Campus — M,D
Central Connecticut State University — M,O
Central Michigan University — D,O
Central Washington University — M
Chaminade University of Honolulu — M
Chapman University — M,D,O
The Chicago School of Professional Psychology — D,O
The Citadel, The Military College of South Carolina — M,O
Clemson University — M,D
The College of New Rochelle — M
College of St. Joseph — M
The College of Saint Rose — M
The College of William and Mary — M,O
Creighton University — M
DePaul University — M,D
Duquesne University — M,D
Eastern Illinois University — M,O
Eastern Kentucky University — M,O
Eastern University — M,O
Eastern Washington University — O
East Tennessee State University — M
Edinboro University of Pennsylvania — M,O
Emporia State University — M,O
Evangel University — M
Fairfield University — M,O
Fairleigh Dickinson University, Metropolitan Campus — M,D
Florida International University — M,D,O
Florida State University — D
Fordham University — M,D
Fort Hays State University — O
Francis Marion University — M
Fresno Pacific University — M
Gallaudet University — M,D,O
Gardner-Webb University — M
George Fox University — M,O
Georgian Court University — M,O
Georgia Southern University — M,O
Georgia State University — M,D,O
Grand Valley State University — M,O
Heidelberg University — M
Hofstra University — M,D
Hood College — M
Houston Baptist University — M
Howard University — M,D
Humboldt State University — M
Husson University — M
Idaho State University — M,D,O
Illinois State University — D,O
Immaculata University — M,D,O
Indiana State University — M,D,O
Indiana University Bloomington — M,D,O
Indiana University of Pennsylvania — D,O
Indiana University South Bend — M,O
Inter American University of Puerto Rico, Metropolitan Campus — M,D
Inter American University of Puerto Rico, San Germán Campus — M,D
Iona College — M
Jackson State University — M
James Madison University — M,D,O
Johnson State College — M
Kean University — D,O
Keene State College — M,O
Kent State University — M,D,O
La Sierra University — M,O
Lehigh University — D,O
Lesley University — M,O
LeTourneau University — M
Lewis & Clark College — M,O
Lindenwood University — M,D,O
Long Island University–Hudson — M,O
Long Island University–LIU Post — M,D,O
Louisiana State University and Agricultural & Mechanical College — M,D
Louisiana State University in Shreveport — O
Loyola Marymount University — M
Loyola University Chicago — D,O
Lynchburg College — M
Marist College — M
Marshall University — O
McGill University — M,D,O
McNeese State University — M
Mercer University — M
Mercy College — M
Merrimack College — M,O
Michigan State University — M,D,O
MidAmerica Nazarene University — M
Middle Tennessee State University — M
Millersville University of Pennsylvania — M
Minnesota State University Mankato — M,D
Minnesota State University Moorhead — M,O
Minot State University — O
Mississippi State University — M,D,O
Monmouth University — M,D,O
Montana State University — M,D,O
Mount Saint Vincent University — M,O
National Louis University — M,D,O
New Mexico State University — M,D,O
Niagara University — M
Nicholls State University — M,O

North Carolina State University — D
North Dakota State University — M,D
Northeastern University — M,D,O
Northern Arizona University — M,D,O
Northwest Nazarene University — M
Nova Southeastern University — M,D,O
Old Dominion University — M,D
Oregon State University — M,D
Oregon State University–Cascades — M
Ottawa University — M
Our Lady of the Lake University — M
Pace University — M,D
Penn State University Park — M,D,O
Philadelphia College of Osteopathic Medicine — M
Pittsburg State University — O
Plymouth State University — M,O
Purdue University Northwest — M
Queens College of the City University of New York — M,O
Quincy University — O
Radford University — O
Rhode Island College — M,D
Rider University — O
Roberts Wesleyan College — M,D
Rochester Institute of Technology — M
Roosevelt University — M
Rowan University — M,O
Rutgers University–New Brunswick — M,D
St. John's University (NY) — M,D
Saint Mary's College of California — M,O
Sam Houston State University — M,D,O
San Diego State University — M
San Francisco State University — M,O
San Jose State University — M,O
Seattle University — M,O
Seton Hall University — M
Slippery Rock University of Pennsylvania — M
Sonoma State University — M
Southern Connecticut State University — M,O
Southern Illinois University Edwardsville — O
Southwestern Oklahoma State University — M
State University of New York at Plattsburgh — M,O
Stephen F. Austin State University — M
Suffolk University — M,D,O
Syracuse University — M,D,O
Teachers College, Columbia University — M,D,O
Temple University — M,D
Texas A&M University — M,D
Texas A&M University–Central Texas — M,O
Texas A&M University–Commerce — M,D,O
Texas State University — O
Texas Woman's University — M,D,O
Towson University — M
Trinity University — M
Tufts University — M
Union College (KY) — M
The University of Akron — M,D
University of Alberta — M,D
The University of Arizona — D,O
The University of British Columbia — M,D
University of Calgary — M,D
University of California, Riverside — M,D,O
University of California, Santa Barbara — M,D,O
University of Central Arkansas — M,D,O
University of Central Florida — O
University of Central Oklahoma — M
University of Cincinnati — D,O
University of Colorado Denver — M,D,O
University of Dayton — M,O
University of Delaware — M,D,O
University of Denver — M,D,O
University of Detroit Mercy — M,D,O
University of Florida — M
University of Hartford — M
University of Houston–Clear Lake — M
University of Houston–Victoria — M
The University of Iowa — M,D,O
The University of Kansas — D,O
University of Kentucky — M,D,O
University of La Verne — M,D
University of Louisville — M,D
University of Manitoba — M,D
University of Maryland, College Park — M,D,O
University of Massachusetts Amherst — M,D,O
University of Massachusetts Boston — M,D
University of Memphis — M,D,O
University of Minnesota, Twin Cities Campus — M,D,O
University of Missouri — M,D,O
University of Missouri–St. Louis — M,D,O
University of Montana — M,D,O
University of Nebraska at Kearney — M,D,O
University of Nebraska at Omaha — M,D,O
University of Nebraska–Lincoln — M,D,O
The University of North Carolina at Chapel Hill — M,D
The University of North Carolina at Greensboro — M,D
University of Northern Colorado — O
University of Northern Iowa — M,O
University of Oklahoma — M
University of Phoenix–Colorado Campus — M

University of Phoenix– Colorado Springs Downtown Campus	M,O
University of Phoenix– Las Vegas Campus	M
University of Phoenix–Utah Campus	M
University of Rhode Island	M,D
University of South Carolina	D
The University of South Dakota	M,D,O
University of Southern Maine	M,D
University of Southern Mississippi	M,D
University of South Florida	M,D,O
The University of Tennessee	M,D,O
The University of Tennessee at Chattanooga	M,D,O
The University of Texas at Austin	M,D
The University of Texas at San Antonio	M,O
The University of Texas at Tyler	M
The University of Texas Rio Grande Valley	M,D,O
University of the Pacific	M,D,O
University of the Virgin Islands	M,D,O
The University of Toledo	M,D,O
University of Utah	M,D,O
University of Virginia	M,D
University of Washington	M,D
The University of West Alabama	M,O
University of Wisconsin–Eau Claire	M,O
University of Wisconsin–La Crosse	M,O
University of Wisconsin– Milwaukee	M,D,O
University of Wisconsin– River Falls	M,O
University of Wisconsin– Stout	M,O
University of Wisconsin– Superior	M
University of Wisconsin– Whitewater	M,O
Utah State University	M,D
Valparaiso University	M,O
Wayne State University	M,D,O
Western Illinois University	M,O
Western Kentucky University	M,O
Wichita State University	M,D,O
William James College	M,D,O
Worcester State University	O
Yeshiva University	D
Youngstown State University	M

SCIENCE EDUCATION

Acadia University	M
Alabama Agricultural and Mechanical University	M,O
Alabama State University	M,O
Alverno College	M
American University of Puerto Rico	M
Andrews University	M,D,O
Angelo State University	M
Antioch University New England	M
Appalachian State University	M
Arcadia University	M,D,O
Arkansas State University	M,O
Asbury University	M
Athabasca University	M,O
Augustana University	M
Bard College	M
Benedictine University	M
Binghamton University, State University of New York	M
Biola University	M,O
Bloomsburg University of Pennsylvania	M
Boise State University	M,D
Boston College	M,D
Bowling Green State University	M
Bridgewater State University	M
Brigham Young University	M,D
Brooklyn College of the City University of New York	M
Brown University	M
Buffalo State College, State University of New York	M
California Baptist University	M
California State University, Bakersfield	M
California State University, Fullerton	M
California State University, Long Beach	M
California State University, Northridge	M
Cambridge College	M,D,O
Caribbean University	M,O
Carthage College	M,O
Catawba College	M
Central Connecticut State University	M
Central Michigan University	M
Chatham University	M
The Citadel, The Military College of South Carolina	M,O
City College of the City University of New York	M
Clarion University of Pennsylvania	M
Clark Atlanta University	M
Clemson University	M,D,O
Cleveland State University	M
The College at Brockport, State University of New York	M,O
College of Charleston	M
College of Staten Island of the City University of New York	M
The College of William and Mary	M
The Colorado College	M
Columbia University	M,D,O
Columbus State University	M,O

Concordia University (United States)	M,D
Converse College	M
Delaware State University	M,D
DePaul University	M,D
Duquesne University	M,O
East Carolina University	M,O
Eastern Kentucky University	M
Eastern Michigan University	M
Eastern University	M,D,O
Elizabeth City State University	M
Elms College	M,O
Fairleigh Dickinson University, Metropolitan Campus	M
Fitchburg State University	M,O
Florida Agricultural and Mechanical University	M
Florida Atlantic University	M,D
Florida Gulf Coast University	M
Florida Institute of Technology	M,D,O
Florida International University	M,D,O
Florida State University	M,D,O
Fresno Pacific University	M
George Mason University	M
The George Washington University	M
Georgia State University	M,D
Grambling State University	M,D,O
Grand Canyon University	M,D,O
Hamline University	M,D
Hardin-Simmons University	M,D
Harrison Middleton University	M,D
Heritage University	M
Hofstra University	M,D,O
Hood College	M,O
Hunter College of the City University of New York	M
Illinois Institute of Technology	M,D
Indiana State University	M,D
Indiana University Bloomington	M,D,O
Instituto Tecnológico y de Estudios Superiores de Monterrey, Campus Monterrey	M,D
Inter American University of Puerto Rico, Arecibo Campus	M
Inter American University of Puerto Rico, Barranquitas Campus	M
Inter American University of Puerto Rico, Metropolitan Campus	M
Inter American University of Puerto Rico, Ponce Campus	M
Inter American University of Puerto Rico, San Germán Campus	M
Iona College	M
Iowa State University of Science and Technology	M
Jackson State University	M,D
Kaplan University, Davenport Campus	M
Lake Forest College	M
Laurentian University	O
Lebanon Valley College	M,O
Lehman College of the City University of New York	M
Lesley University	M,D,O
Lewis University	M
Lynchburg College	M
Lyndon State College	M
Manhattanville College	M
McDaniel College	M,O
McNeese State University	M
Michigan State University	M,D
Michigan Technological University	M,D,O
Middle Tennessee State University	M,D
Millersville University of Pennsylvania	M,D
Minnesota State University Mankato	M
Minot State University	M
Mississippi College	M,D,O
Missouri State University	M
Montclair State University	M
Morehead State University	M
Morgan State University	M,D
National Louis University	M,D,O
New Mexico Institute of Mining and Technology	M
New York Institute of Technology	M
New York University	M,D,O
North Carolina Agricultural and Technical State University	M
North Carolina State University	M,D
North Dakota State University	M,D,O
Northeastern State University	M,O
Northern Arizona University	M
Northern Michigan University	M
Northwest Missouri State University	M,O
Oregon State University	M,D
Our Lady of the Lake University	M
Pacific University	M
Pepperdine University	M
Plymouth State University	M
Portland State University	M,D
Purdue University	M,D,O
Purdue University Northwest	M
Queens College of the City University of New York	M,O
Quinnipiac University	M
Regent University	M,D,O
Rice University	M,D
Rider University	O
Rowan University	M
Rutgers University–New Brunswick	M,D
Saginaw Valley State University	M
Saint Xavier University	M
Salem State University	M
San Diego State University	M,D
San Jose State University	M
Seattle Pacific University	M
Shippensburg University of Pennsylvania	M,O

Slippery Rock University of Pennsylvania	M
Smith College	M
South Carolina State University	M
Southern Connecticut State University	M,O
Southern University and Agricultural and Mechanical College	D
Southwestern Oklahoma State University	M
State University of New York at New Paltz	M,O
State University of New York at Plattsburgh	M
State University of New York College at Cortland	M
State University of New York College at Geneseo	M
State University of New York College at Old Westbury	M
State University of New York College at Potsdam	M
Stevenson University	M
Stony Brook University, State University of New York	M,D,O
Syracuse University	M,D
Teachers College, Columbia University	M,D
Temple University	M
Tennessee Technological University	M,O
Texas Christian University	M,D,O
Texas Tech University	M,D
Touro College	M
Tufts University	M,D
Universidad Nacional Pedro Henriquez Urena	M
University at Buffalo, the State University of New York	M,D
The University of Akron	M
The University of Alabama in Huntsville	M
University of Arkansas at Pine Bluff	M
The University of British Columbia	M,D
University of California, Berkeley	M,D
University of California, San Diego	D
University of Central Florida	M,D,O
University of Chicago	D
University of Cincinnati	M,D
University of Colorado Denver	M,D
University of Connecticut	M,D
The University of Findlay	M,D
University of Florida	M,D,O
University of Georgia	M,D,O
University of Illinois at Chicago	D
University of Illinois at Urbana–Champaign	M,D
University of Indianapolis	M
The University of Iowa	M,D
University of Louisiana at Monroe	M,D
University of Maryland, Baltimore County	M
University of Massachusetts Amherst	M,D,O
University of Massachusetts Dartmouth	M,D,O
University of Memphis	M,D,O
University of Miami	D
University of Michigan–Dearborn	M
University of Minnesota, Twin Cities Campus	M
University of Missouri	M,D,O
University of Missouri–St. Louis	M,D,O
University of Nebraska at Kearney	M
University of Nebraska at Omaha	M,O
University of New Hampshire	M,D
University of New Haven	M
University of New Mexico	O
The University of North Carolina at Chapel Hill	M
The University of North Carolina at Greensboro	M,D,O
The University of North Carolina at Pembroke	M
University of Northern Colorado	M,D
University of Northern Iowa	M
University of Oklahoma	M,D
University of Pennsylvania	M,O
University of Phoenix–Online Campus	M,O
University of Pittsburgh	M,D
University of Puerto Rico, Río Piedras Campus	M,D
University of St. Francis (IL)	M,D,O
University of San Diego	M
University of South Africa	M,D
University of South Alabama	M,D
University of South Carolina	M,D
University of Southern Mississippi	M,D
University of South Florida, St. Petersburg	M
The University of Tennessee	M,D,O
The University of Texas at Arlington	M
The University of Texas at Dallas	M
The University of Texas at El Paso	M
The University of Texas at Toledo	M,D,O
The University of Tulsa	M
University of Utah	M,D
University of Vermont	M
University of Victoria	M,D
University of Virginia	M,D,O
University of Washington	M,D
University of Washington, Tacoma	M
The University of West Alabama	M
University of Wisconsin–Madison	M,D

University of Wisconsin–Milwaukee	M
University of Wisconsin–River Falls	M
University of Wisconsin–Stevens Point	M
University of Wyoming	M
Vanderbilt University	M,D
Wagner College	M
Walden University	M,D,O
Warner University	M
Wayland Baptist University	M
Wayne State College	M
Wayne State University	M,D,O
West Chester University of Pennsylvania	M,O
Western Governors University	M,O
Western Michigan University	M,D,O
Western Oregon University	M
Western Washington University	M
Westfield State University	M
Widener University	M,D
Wilkes University	M,D
Wisconsin Lutheran College	M,D
Wright State University	M,D
Youngstown State University	M

SECONDARY EDUCATION

Acacia University	M
Adelphi University	M
Alabama Agricultural and Mechanical University	M,O
Alabama State University	M,O
Alcorn State University	M,O
American International College	M,O
American Public University System	M
Andrews University	M,D,O
Aquinas College (TN)	M
Arcadia University	M,D,O
Argosy University, Atlanta	M,D,O
Argosy University, Chicago	M,D,O
Argosy University, Hawai'i	M,D
Argosy University, Inland Empire	M,D
Argosy University, Los Angeles	M,D
Argosy University, Nashville	M,D,O
Argosy University, Northern Virginia	M,D,O
Argosy University, Orange County	M,D
Argosy University, Phoenix	M,D,O
Argosy University, San Diego	M,D
Argosy University, San Francisco Bay Area	M,D
Argosy University, Sarasota	M,D,O
Argosy University, Seattle	M,D
Argosy University, Tampa	M,D,O
Argosy University, Twin Cities	M,D,O
Arizona State University at the Tempe campus	M
Armstrong State University	M,O
Auburn University at Montgomery	M,O
Augusta University	M,O
Austin Peay State University	M,O
Ball State University	M
Bard College	M
Belhaven University (MS)	M
Bellarmine University	M,D,O
Benedictine University	M
Berry College	M
Bethel University (MN)	M,D,O
Binghamton University, State University of New York	M
Bob Jones University	M,D,O
Boston College	M
Bowie State University	M
Brandeis University	M,O
Brandman University	M,D
Brenau University	M,O
Bridgewater State University	M
Brooklyn College of the City University of New York	M
Brown University	M
California State University, Bakersfield	M
California State University, Fullerton	M
California State University, Long Beach	M
California State University, Northridge	M
California State University, Stanislaus	M
California University of Pennsylvania	M
Campbell University	M
Canisius College	M,O
Carroll University	M
Carson-Newman University	M,O
The Catholic University of America	M,O
Centenary College of Louisiana	M
Central Connecticut State University	M,O
Central Michigan University	M,D,O
Chadron State College	M,O
Chaminade University of Honolulu	M
Chapman University	M,D,O
Chatham University	M
Chestnut Hill College	M
Chicago State University	M
The Citadel, The Military College of South Carolina	M,O
City College of the City University of New York	M,O
Clarkson University	M
Clemson University	M
Colgate University	M
The College of New Jersey	M
College of St. Joseph	M
The College of Saint Rose	M,O
College of Staten Island of the City University of New York	M
The College of William and Mary	M

---

*M—masters degree; D—doctorate; O—other advanced degree; *—Close-Up and/or Display*

The Colorado College	M
Columbus State University	M,O
Concordia University (United States)	M,D
Concordia University Chicago	M
Concordia University, Nebraska	M
Converse College	M
Cornell University	M,D
Creighton University	M
Dakota Wesleyan University	M
Dallas Baptist University	M
Delta State University	M,D,O
DePaul University	M,O
DeSales University	M,O
Drew University	M,D,O
Drury University	M
Duquesne University	M
D'Youville College	M,D
Eastern Connecticut State University	M
Eastern Kentucky University	M
Eastern Michigan University	M
Eastern Nazarene College	M,O
Eastern New Mexico University	M
Eastern Oregon University	M
Eastern University	M,D,O
Eastern Washington University	M
East Stroudsburg University of Pennsylvania	M
East Tennessee State University	M,O
Edinboro University of Pennsylvania	M
Elms College	M,O
Emory University	M,D
Endicott College	M
Evangel University	M
Fairfield University	M,O
Fayetteville State University	M
Florida Agricultural and Mechanical University	M
Fontbonne University	M
Frostburg State University	M
Gallaudet University	M,D,O
George Mason University	M
The George Washington University	M
Georgia College & State University	M
Georgia Southern University	M,O
Georgia State University	M,D
Gonzaga University	M
Gordon College	M,O
Goucher College	M,O
Grand Canyon University	M,D,O
Grand Valley State University	M
Greenville College	M
Hampton University	M
Harding University	M,O
Hawai'i Pacific University	M
High Point University	M
Hofstra University	M,D,O
Hood College	M,O
Hope International University	M
Howard University	M
Hunter College of the City University of New York	M
Idaho State University	M,O
Immaculata University	M,D,O
Indiana University Bloomington	M,D,O
Indiana University Northwest	M,O
Indiana University–Purdue University Fort Wayne	M
Indiana University South Bend	M,O
Indiana University Southeast	M
Instituto Tecnologico de Santo Domingo	M,O
Ithaca College	M
Jacksonville State University	M
James Madison University	M
John Brown University	M
John Carroll University	M
Johns Hopkins University	M
Johnson & Wales University	M
Kaplan University, Davenport Campus	M
Kennesaw State University	M
Kent State University	M,D
Keuka College	M
Kutztown University of Pennsylvania	M
LaGrange College	M,O
Lake Forest College	M
Lancaster Bible College	M,D
La Salle University	M,O
Lee University	M,O
Le Moyne College	M,O
Lenoir-Rhyne University	M
Lesley University	M,D,O
Lewis & Clark College	M
Lewis University	M
Liberty University	M,D,O
Lincoln University (MO)	M
Long Island University–LIU Post	M,D,O
Long Island University–Riverhead	M,O
Louisiana State University and Agricultural & Mechanical College	M,D,O
Loyola Marymount University	M
Loyola University Chicago	M
Loyola University Maryland	M
Loyola University New Orleans	M
Manhattanville College	M,O
Mansfield University of Pennsylvania	M
Marquette University	M
Marshall University	M
Marygrove College	M
Marymount University	M
Maryville University of Saint Louis	M,D
Marywood University	M,O
McDaniel College	M,O
McNeese State University	M
Medaille College	M
Mercer University	M,D,O

Mercy College	M,O
Mercyhurst University	M
Merrimack College	M,O
Middle Tennessee State University	M
Milligan College	M,D,O
Mississippi College	M,D,O
Mississippi State University	M,D,O
Missouri State University	M,O
Monmouth University	M,D,O
Montana State University Billings	M
Morehead State University	M,O
Morgan State University	M
Mount St. Joseph University	M,O
Murray State University	M,O
National Louis University	M,D,O
Neumann University	M
New Jersey City University	M
New York Institute of Technology	M
New York University	M,D,O
Niagara University	M,O
Nicholls State University	M
Norfolk State University	M
North Carolina Agricultural and Technical State University	
North Carolina State University	M
Northeastern Illinois University	M
Northern Arizona University	M,D
Northern Illinois University	M,D
Northern Michigan University	M
Northwest Christian University	M
Northwestern Oklahoma State University	M
Northwestern State University of Louisiana	M,O
Northwestern University	M
Oakland University	M,O
Ohio University	M,D
Old Dominion University	M
Olivet Nazarene University	M
Pacific Union College	M
Pacific University	M
Piedmont College	M,O
Plymouth State University	M
Point Park University	M,D
Prescott College	M,D
Providence College	M
Queens College of the City University of New York	M,O
Quinnipiac University	M
Regis University	M,O
Rhode Island College	M
Roberts Wesleyan College	M
Rochester Institute of Technology	M
Rockford University	M
Roosevelt University	M
Saginaw Valley State University	M
St. Bonaventure University	M
St. John's University (NY)	M
Saint Joseph's University	M,D,O
Saint Mary's University of Minnesota	M
Saint Peter's University	M,O
St. Thomas Aquinas College	M,O
Saint Xavier University	M
Salem College	M
Salem State University	M
Salisbury University	M
San Diego State University	M
San Francisco State University	M,O
Seattle Pacific University	M
Shenandoah University	M,D,O
Siena Heights University	M,O
Sierra Nevada College	M
Simpson College	M
Slippery Rock University of Pennsylvania	M
Smith College	M
South Carolina State University	M
Southeast Missouri State University	M,D,O
Southern New Hampshire University	M,D,O
Southern Oregon University	M
Southern University and Agricultural and Mechanical College	M
Southwestern Assemblies of God University	M
Southwestern Oklahoma State University	M
Spalding University	M
Springfield College	M
Spring Hill College	M
Stanford University	M
State University of New York at Fredonia	M
State University of New York at New Paltz	M,O
State University of New York at Oswego	M
State University of New York at Plattsburgh	M
State University of New York College at Cortland	M
State University of New York College at Geneseo	M
State University of New York College at Potsdam	M
Stephen F. Austin State University	M,D
Sul Ross State University	M
Tarleton State University	M
Teachers College, Columbia University	M,D
Temple University	M,D
Tennessee Technological University	M,O
Texas A&M University–Commerce	M,D,O
Texas A&M University–Corpus Christi	M
Texas A&M University–Kingsville	M
Texas Southern University	M,D
Texas State University	M
Texas Tech University	M,D
Towson University	M
Trevecca Nazarene University	M,O

Trinity Washington University	M
Troy University	M
Tufts University	M,D
Union College (KY)	M
Universidad Metropolitana	M
The University of Akron	M
The University of Alabama	M,D,O
The University of Alabama at Birmingham	M
The University of Alabama in Huntsville	M,O
University of Alaska Southeast	M
University of Alberta	M,D
The University of Arizona	M,D
University of Arkansas	M,O
University of Arkansas at Little Rock	M
University of Arkansas at Pine Bluff	M
University of Bridgeport	M,D,O
University of California, Irvine	M,D
University of Central Oklahoma	M
University of Cincinnati	M
University of Colorado Denver	M
University of Connecticut	M,D
University of Dayton	M
University of Guam	M
University of Houston–Downtown	M
University of Illinois at Chicago	M,D
University of Indianapolis	M
The University of Iowa	M,D
University of Kentucky	M,D
University of La Verne	M,D,O
University of Louisiana at Monroe	M
University of Louisville	M,D,O
University of Mary Hardin-Baylor	M,D
University of Maryland, College Park	M,D,O
University of Massachusetts Amherst	M,D,O
University of Massachusetts Dartmouth	M,D,O
University of Memphis	M,D,O
University of Michigan–Flint	M,D,O
University of Missouri–St. Louis	M,D
University of Montevallo	M
University of Nebraska at Kearney	M
University of Nebraska at Omaha	M,O
University of Nevada, Las Vegas	M,D,O
University of Nevada, Reno	M
University of New Hampshire	M,O
University of New Mexico	M
University of North Alabama	M
The University of North Carolina at Chapel Hill	M
The University of North Carolina at Charlotte	M,D,O
The University of North Carolina at Wilmington	M
University of Northern Iowa	M
University of North Florida	M
University of North Georgia	M,O
University of Pennsylvania	M
University of Phoenix–Bay Area Campus	M,D,O
University of Phoenix–Central Valley Campus	M
University of Phoenix–Colorado Campus	M
University of Phoenix–Colorado Springs Downtown Campus	M,O
University of Phoenix–Hawaii Campus	M
University of Phoenix–New Mexico Campus	M
University of Phoenix–North Florida Campus	M,D,O
University of Phoenix–Online Campus	M,O
University of Phoenix–Phoenix Campus	M
University of Phoenix–Sacramento Valley Campus	M,O
University of Phoenix–San Diego Campus	M
University of Phoenix–Southern Arizona Campus	M,O
University of Phoenix–Southern California Campus	M,O
University of Phoenix–South Florida Campus	M
University of Phoenix–Utah Campus	M
University of Phoenix–Washington D.C. Campus	M,D,O
University of Pittsburgh	M,D
University of Puget Sound	M
University of St. Francis (IL)	M,D,O
University of Saint Francis (IN)	M
University of St. Thomas (TX)	M,D
The University of Scranton	M
University of South Alabama	M,D
University of South Carolina	M,D
The University of South Dakota	M
University of Southern Indiana	M
University of Southern Mississippi	M,D
University of South Florida	O
The University of Tennessee	M,D,O
The University of Tennessee at Chattanooga	M,D,O
The University of Tennessee at Martin	M
The University of Texas Rio Grande Valley	M,D
University of the Cumberlands	M,D,O
University of the District of Columbia	M
University of the Virgin Islands	M
The University of Toledo	M,D,O
The University of Tulsa	M
University of Utah	M,D

University of Washington, Bothell	M
The University of West Alabama	M
University of West Florida	M
University of West Georgia	M,D,O
University of Wisconsin–Eau Claire	M
University of Wisconsin–Stevens Point	M
Ursuline College	M
Utah State University	M
Valparaiso University	M,O
Vanderbilt University	M
Villanova University	M
Wagner College	M
Wake Forest University	M
Washington State University	M,D
Washington University in St. Louis	M
Wayland Baptist University	M
Wayne State University	M,D,O
Webster University	M,O
West Chester University of Pennsylvania	M,O
Western Kentucky University	M,O
Western New Mexico University	M
Western Oregon University	M
Western Washington University	M
Westfield State University	M
West Virginia University	M,D
Wheaton College	M
Whittier College	M
Whitworth University	M
Wichita State University	M
William Carey University	M,O
William Paterson University of New Jersey	M
Wilmington University	M,D
Wilson College	M
Winthrop University	M
Worcester State University	M,O
Wright State University	M
Xavier University	M
Youngstown State University	M

SLAVIC LANGUAGES

Brown University	M,D
Columbia University	M,D
Cornell University	M,D
Duke University	M,O
Florida State University	M
Harvard University	D
Indiana University Bloomington	M,D
New York University	M
Northwestern University	D
The Ohio State University	M,D
Princeton University	D
Stanford University	D
University of Alberta	M,D
University of California, Berkeley	D
University of California, Los Angeles	M,D
University of Chicago	M
University of Illinois at Chicago	M,D
University of Illinois at Urbana–Champaign	M,D
The University of Kansas	M,D
The University of Manchester	M,D
University of Manitoba	M
University of Michigan	M,D
The University of North Carolina at Chapel Hill	D
University of Pittsburgh	M,D
University of Southern California	M,D
The University of Texas at Austin	M,D
University of Toronto	M,D
University of Virginia	M,D
University of Washington	M,D
University of Wisconsin–Madison	M,D
Yale University	D

SOCIAL PSYCHOLOGY

Adler University	M,D,O
Alliant International University–Los Angeles	D
Alvernia University	M
Alverno College	M
Andrews University	M
Argosy University, Atlanta	M,D,O
Argosy University, Chicago	M,D
Argosy University, Dallas	M
Argosy University, Northern Virginia	M,D
Argosy University, Sarasota	M,D
Arizona State University at the Tempe campus	M,D
Ball State University	M
Becker College	M
Bowling Green State University	M,D
Brandeis University	M,D
Brock University	M,D
Brooklyn College of the City University of New York	M,D
California Institute of Integral Studies	M,D
California State University, East Bay	M
California State University, Fullerton	M
Canisius College	M
Carnegie Mellon University	D
Claremont Graduate University	M,D,O
Clark University	M,D
College of St. Joseph	M
Cornell University	M,D
Delaware Valley University	M
Florida Agricultural and Mechanical University	M
Florida State University	D
Future Generations Graduate School	M
The George Washington University	D
Georgia State University	M
The Graduate Center, City University of New York	D
Harvard University	D
Hofstra University	M,D

Howard University	M,D
Humboldt State University	M
Husson University	M
Indiana University Bloomington	D
Indiana University of Pennsylvania	M
Indiana Wesleyan University	M
Iowa State University of Science and Technology	M,D
Lesley University	M,D,O
Loyola University Chicago	M,O
Marquette University	M,D
Martin University	M
Marymount California University	M
Missouri Valley College	M
Mount Aloysius College	M
The New School	M,D
New York University	M,D,O
Norfolk State University	M
North Carolina State University	M
North Dakota State University	M,D
Northeastern Illinois University	M
Northwestern University	D
The Ohio State University	D
Oregon State University–Cascades	M,D,O
Penn State Harrisburg	M,D,O
Philadelphia University	M
Queen's University at Kingston	M,D
Rutgers University–Newark	D
Rutgers University–New Brunswick	D
Sacred Heart University	M
Sage Graduate School	M
St. Bonaventure University	M,O
St. Cloud State University	M
Saint Martin's University	M
San Francisco State University	M,O
Southwestern College (NM)	O
Stony Brook University, State University of New York	D
Syracuse University	D
Teachers College, Columbia University	M,D
Temple University	M,D,O
Texas Christian University	M
Texas State University	M
Thomas University	M
Université du Québec à Rimouski	M
Université Laval	D
University at Albany, State University of New York	M,D
University of Alaska Anchorage	M,D
University of Alaska Fairbanks	M,D,O
University of Bridgeport	M,D
The University of British Columbia	M,D
University of Central Arkansas	M
University of Connecticut	M
University of Delaware	D
University of Denver	D
University of Guelph	M,D
University of Hawaii at Manoa	M,D,O
University of Houston	M,D
The University of Kansas	M,D
University of Maryland, Baltimore County	M,D
University of Maryland, College Park	M,D
University of Massachusetts Amherst	M,D
University of Massachusetts Lowell	M
University of Michigan	D
University of Minnesota, Twin Cities Campus	D
University of Missouri–Kansas City	M,D
University of Nebraska–Lincoln	M,D
University of Nevada, Reno	D
University of New Haven	M,O
The University of North Carolina at Chapel Hill	D
The University of North Carolina at Greensboro	M,D
University of Oregon	M,D
University of Phoenix–Phoenix Campus	M
University of Puerto Rico, Río Piedras Campus	M,D
University of Rochester	M,D
University of South Carolina	M,D
University of Southern California	M,D
The University of Tennessee at Chattanooga	M,D,O
The University of Tennessee at Martin	M
University of Victoria	M,D
University of Washington	D
University of Windsor	M,D
University of Wisconsin–Madison	D
University of Wisconsin–Milwaukee	M,D,O
University of Wisconsin–Superior	M
Walden University	M,D,O
Wayne State University	M
Western Illinois University	M,O
Wichita State University	D
Wilfrid Laurier University	M,D
Yale University	D

SOCIAL SCIENCES

Antioch University Midwest	M
Assumption College	O
Augusta University	M
California Institute of Technology	M
California State University, Chico	M
California State University, San Bernardino	M

Campbellsville University	M
Carnegie Mellon University	D
The Citadel, The Military College of South Carolina	M
Columbia University	M,D
Eastern Michigan University	M
Florida Agricultural and Mechanical University	M
Graduate Theological Union	M,D,O
Harrison Middleton University	M,D
Hollins University	M
Humboldt State University	M
Indiana University Bloomington	M,D,O
Indiana University–Purdue University Indianapolis	M,D
Johns Hopkins University	M,D
Massachusetts Institute of Technology	D
Mississippi College	M,O
Montclair State University	M
The New School	M,D
New York University	M,D
North Dakota State University	M
Nova Southeastern University	M,D,O
The Ohio State University	M,D
Ohio University	M
Oregon State University	M,D
Southern University and Agricultural and Mechanical College	M
Syracuse University	M
Texas A&M International University	M
Towson University	M
Troy University	M
University at Buffalo, the State University of New York	M
University of California, Merced	M,D
University of California, Santa Barbara	D
University of California, Santa Cruz	D
University of Chicago	M,D
University of Florida	M,D,O
University of Illinois at Springfield	M,O
The University of Manchester	M,D
University of Maryland, Baltimore County	D
University of Memphis	M,D
University of Michigan	D
University of Michigan–Flint	M
University of Northern Iowa	M
University of Regina	M
University of South Florida Sarasota-Manatee	M
The University of Texas at Tyler	M
University of the Virgin Islands	M
University of Toronto	M,D
University of Washington	M,D
Wilfrid Laurier University	M
Worcester Polytechnic Institute	M,D,O
Yale University	M,D

SOCIAL SCIENCES EDUCATION

Acadia University	M
Alabama Agricultural and Mechanical University	M,O
Alabama State University	M,O
American Public University System	M
Andrews University	M,D,O
Appalachian State University	M
Arkansas State University	M,D,O
Asbury University	M
Binghamton University, State University of New York	M
Bloomsburg University of Pennsylvania	M
Bob Jones University	M,D,O
Bridgewater State University	M
Brooklyn College of the City University of New York	M
Brown University	M
Buffalo State College, State University of New York	M
California State University, East Bay	M
California State University, Fresno	M
Cambridge College	M,D,O
Caribbean University	M,D
Carthage College	M,O
Chadron State College	M,O
Chatham University	M
The Citadel, The Military College of South Carolina	M,O
City College of the City University of New York	M,O
The College at Brockport, State University of New York	M,O
College of St. Joseph	M
College of Staten Island of the City University of New York	M
The Colorado College	M
Columbus State University	M,O
Converse College	M
Delta State University	M
Duquesne University	M
East Carolina University	M
Eastern Kentucky University	M
Eastern University	M,D,O
Fayetteville State University	M
Fitchburg State University	M,O
Florida Agricultural and Mechanical University	M
Florida Atlantic University	M
Florida Gulf Coast University	M
Florida International University	M,D,O
Florida State University	M,D,O
Framingham State University	M
George Mason University	M
Georgia State University	M,D
Grambling State University	M

Harding University	M
Hofstra University	M,D,O
Hunter College of the City University of New York	M
Indiana University Bloomington	M,D,O
Instituto Tecnologico de Santo Domingo	M,O
Inter American University of Puerto Rico, Arecibo Campus	M
Inter American University of Puerto Rico, Barranquitas Campus	M
Inter American University of Puerto Rico, Metropolitan Campus	M
Inter American University of Puerto Rico, Ponce Campus	M
Iona College	M
Ithaca College	M
Johns Hopkins University	M
Kent State University	M,D
Kutztown University of Pennsylvania	M
Lake Forest College	M
La Salle University	M,O
Lebanon Valley College	M,O
Lee University	M,O
Lehman College of the City University of New York	M
Le Moyne College	M,O
Lewis University	M
Long Island University–LIU Brooklyn	M,D,O
Manhattanville College	M
Michigan State University	M,D
Minnesota State University Mankato	M
Mississippi College	M,D,O
Missouri State University	M,O
Molloy College	M,O
Morehead State University	M,O
New York University	M,D,O
North Carolina State University	M
North Dakota State University	M,D,O
Northwest Missouri State University	M,O
Oregon State University	M,D
Pace University	M,O
Plymouth State University	M
Portland State University	M
Purdue University	M,D,O
Queens College of the City University of New York	M,O
Quinnipiac University	M
Regis College (MA)	M
Rhode Island College	M
Rider University	O
Rivier University	M
Rutgers University–New Brunswick	M,D
St. John Fisher College	M
Slippery Rock University of Pennsylvania	M
Smith College	M
South Carolina State University	M
Southwestern Oklahoma State University	M
Spring Hill College	M,O
State University of New York at New Paltz	M,O
State University of New York at Plattsburgh	M
State University of New York College at Old Westbury	M
State University of New York College at Potsdam	M
Stony Brook University, State University of New York	M,O
Syracuse University	M
Teachers College, Columbia University	M,D,O
Temple University	M
Trinity Washington University	M
University at Buffalo, the State University of New York	M,D,O
The University of Akron	M
The University of Alabama in Huntsville	M,O
University of Arkansas at Pine Bluff	M
The University of British Columbia	M,D
University of California, Santa Cruz	M
University of Central Florida	M,D
University of Cincinnati	M,D,O
University of Connecticut	M,D
University of Florida	M,D,O
University of Illinois at Chicago	D
University of Indianapolis	M
The University of Iowa	M
University of Louisiana at Monroe	M,D
University of Maine	M,D,O
University of Maryland, Baltimore County	M
University of Minnesota, Twin Cities Campus	M
University of Missouri	M,D,O
The University of North Carolina at Chapel Hill	M
The University of North Carolina at Greensboro	M,D,O
The University of North Carolina at Pembroke	M
University of North Georgia	M,O
University of Oklahoma	M,D
University of Pittsburgh	M,D
University of Puerto Rico, Río Piedras Campus	M,D
University of St. Francis (IL)	M,D,O
University of South Carolina	M,D
University of South Florida	M,D,O
The University of Tennessee	M,D,O
University of the District of Columbia	M

The University of Toledo	M,D,O
University of Victoria	M,D
University of Virginia	M,D,O
University of Washington	M
The University of West Alabama	M
University of Wisconsin–Milwaukee	M
University of Wisconsin–River Falls	M
Virginia Polytechnic Institute and State University	M,D,O
Wagner College	M
Wayland Baptist University	M
Wayne State College	M
Wayne State University	M,D,O
Western Governors University	M,O
Western Oregon University	M
Westfield State University	M
Widener University	M,D
William Carey University	M,O
Worcester State University	M

SOCIAL WORK

Abilene Christian University	M
Adelphi University	M,D
Alabama Agricultural and Mechanical University	M,O
Alabama State University	M
Albany State University	M
American Jewish University	M
Andrews University	M
Anna Maria College	M
Appalachian State University	M
Arizona State University at the Tempe campus	M,D,O
Arkansas State University	M,O
Asbury University	M
Augsburg College	M
Aurora University	M,D
Austin Peay State University	M
Azusa Pacific University	M
Barry University	M,D
Baylor University	M,D
Binghamton University, State University of New York	M
Boise State University	M
Boston College	M,D
Boston University	M,D
Brescia University	M
Bridgewater State University	M
Brigham Young University	M
Bryn Mawr College	M,D
California Baptist University	M
California State University, Bakersfield	M
California State University, Chico	M
California State University, Dominguez Hills	M
California State University, East Bay	M
California State University, Fresno	M
California State University, Fullerton	M
California State University, Long Beach	M
California State University, Los Angeles	M
California State University, Monterey Bay	M
California State University, Northridge	M,O
California State University, Sacramento	M
California State University, San Bernardino	M
California State University, San Marcos	M
California State University, Stanislaus	M
California University of Pennsylvania	M
Campbellsville University	M
Capella University	D
Carleton University	M
Case Western Reserve University	M,D
The Catholic University of America	M,D
Chicago State University	M
Clark Atlanta University	M,D
Clarke University	M
Cleveland State University	M
The College at Brockport, State University of New York	M,O
The College of Saint Rose	M
The College of St. Scholastica	M
College of Staten Island of the City University of New York	M
Colorado State University	M,D
Columbia University	M,D
Concord University	M
Cornell University	M,D
Daemen College	M
Dalhousie University	M
Delaware State University	M
DePaul University	M
Dominican University	M
East Carolina University	M,O
Eastern Michigan University	M
Eastern Washington University	M
East Tennessee State University	M
Edinboro University of Pennsylvania	M
Fayetteville State University	M
Florida Agricultural and Mechanical University	M
Florida Atlantic University	M,D
Florida Gulf Coast University	M
Florida International University	M,D
Florida State University	M,D
Fordham University	M,D
Gallaudet University	M,D,O

---

*M—masters degree; D—doctorate; O—other advanced degree; *—Close-Up and/or Display*

George Fox University	M
George Mason University	M
Georgia State University	M,O
Governors State University	M
The Graduate Center, City University of New York	D
Grambling State University	M
Grand Valley State University	M
Gratz College	M,O
Hawai'i Pacific University	M
Howard University	M,D
Humboldt State University	M
Hunter College of the City University of New York	M
Illinois State University	M
Indiana State University	M
Indiana University East	M
Indiana University Northwest	M
Indiana University–Purdue University Indianapolis	M,D,O
Indiana University South Bend	M
Institute for Clinical Social Work	D
Inter American University of Puerto Rico, Metropolitan Campus	M
Jackson State University	M,D
Johnson C. Smith University	M
Kean University	M
Kennesaw State University	M
Keuka College	M
Kutztown University of Pennsylvania	M,D
Lakehead University	M
Laurentian University	M
Loma Linda University	M,D
London Metropolitan University	M
Long Island University–LIU Brooklyn	M,D,O
Long Island University–LIU Post	M,O
Louisiana State University and Agricultural & Mechanical College	M,D
Loyola University Chicago	M,D,O
Marshall University	M
Marywood University	M,D
McGill University	M,D,O
McMaster University	M
Memorial University of Newfoundland	M,D
Metropolitan State University of Denver	M
Michigan State University	M,D
Middle Tennessee State University	M
Millersville University of Pennsylvania	M
Minnesota State University Mankato	M
Missouri State University	M
Monmouth University	M,O
Morgan State University	M,D
Nazareth College of Rochester	M
Newman University	M
New Mexico Highlands University	M
New Mexico State University	M
New York University	M,D
Norfolk State University	M,D
North Carolina Agricultural and Technical State University	M
North Carolina State University	M
Northern Kentucky University	M
Northwest Nazarene University	M
Nyack College	M
The Ohio State University	M
The Ohio State University at Lima	M
The Ohio State University–Mansfield Campus	M
The Ohio State University–Newark Campus	M
Ohio University	M
Our Lady of the Lake University	M
Pacific University	M
Park University	M,O
Phillips Theological Seminary	M,D
Pontifical Catholic University of Puerto Rico	M
Portland State University	M,D
Quinnipiac University	M
Radford University	M
Ramapo College of New Jersey	M
Rhode Island College	M
Roberts Wesleyan College	M
Rutgers University–New Brunswick	M,D
Sacred Heart University	M
St. Ambrose University	M
St. Catherine University	M,D
St. Cloud State University	M
Saint Leo University	M
Saint Louis University	M
Salem State University	M
Salisbury University	M
Samford University	M
San Diego State University	M
San Francisco State University	M
San Jose State University	M
Savannah State University	M
Seattle University	M
Seton Hall University	M
Shippensburg University of Pennsylvania	M
Simmons College	M,D,O
Smith College	M,D
Southeastern University (FL)	M
Southern Adventist University	M
Southern Connecticut State University	M
Southern Illinois University Carbondale	M
Southern Illinois University Edwardsville	M
Southern University at New Orleans	M
Spalding University	M
Springfield College	M,O
Stephen F. Austin State University	M
Stockton University	M
Stony Brook University, State University of New York	M,D
Syracuse University	M
Tarleton State University	M
Temple University	M
Tennessee State University	M,D
Texas A&M University–Commerce	M,D,O
Texas Christian University	M
Texas State University	M
Texas Tech University	M
Thompson Rivers University	M
Touro College	M
Troy University	M
Tulane University	M,D
Union University	M
Universidad del Este	M
Université de Moncton	O
Université de Montréal	O
Université de Sherbrooke	M
Université du Québec à Montréal	M
Université du Québec en Abitibi-Témiscamingue	M
Université du Québec en Outaouais	M
Université Laval	M,D
University at Albany, State University of New York	M,D
University at Buffalo, the State University of New York	M,D
The University of Akron	M
The University of Alabama	M,D
University of Alaska Anchorage	M,O
University of Arkansas	M
University of Arkansas at Little Rock	M
The University of British Columbia	M,D
University of Calgary	M,D,O
University of California, Berkeley	M,D
University of California, Los Angeles	M,D
University of Central Florida	M,O
University of Chicago	M,D
University of Cincinnati	M
University of Denver	M,D,O
University of Georgia	M,D,O
University of Guam	M
University of Hawaii at Manoa	M,D
University of Houston	M,D
University of Houston–Downtown	M
University of Illinois at Chicago	M,D,O
University of Illinois at Urbana–Champaign	M,D
The University of Iowa	M,D
The University of Kansas	M,D
University of Kentucky	M,D
University of Louisville	M,D,O
University of Maine	M,O
The University of Manchester	M,D
University of Manitoba	M,D
University of Maryland, Baltimore	M,D
University of Maryland, College Park	M
University of Memphis	M
University of Michigan	M,D
University of Minnesota, Duluth	M
University of Minnesota, Twin Cities Campus	M,D
University of Mississippi	M,D
University of Missouri	M,D,O
University of Missouri–Kansas City	M
University of Missouri–St. Louis	M
University of Montana	M
University of Nebraska at Omaha	M
University of Nevada, Las Vegas	M
University of Nevada, Reno	M
University of New England	M,D,O
University of New Hampshire	M,O
The University of North Carolina at Chapel Hill	M,D
The University of North Carolina at Charlotte	M
The University of North Carolina at Greensboro	M
The University of North Carolina at Pembroke	M
The University of North Carolina Wilmington	M
University of North Dakota	M
University of Northern British Columbia	M,D,O
University of Northern Iowa	M
University of Oklahoma	M
University of Ottawa	M
University of Pennsylvania	M,D
University of Pittsburgh	M,D,O
University of Puerto Rico, Río Piedras Campus	M,D
University of Regina	M,D
University of St. Francis (IL)	M,O
University of St. Thomas (MN)	M
University of South Africa	M,D
University of South Carolina	M,D
The University of South Dakota	M
University of Southern California	M,D
University of Southern Indiana	M
University of Southern Maine	M
University of Southern Mississippi	M
University of South Florida	M,D,O
University of South Florida Sarasota-Manatee	M
The University of Tennessee	M,D
The University of Texas at Arlington	M,D
The University of Texas at Austin	M,D
The University of Texas at El Paso	M
The University of Texas at San Antonio	M
The University of Texas Rio Grande Valley	M
University of the Fraser Valley	M
The University of Toledo	M,O
University of Toronto	M,D
University of Utah	M,D
University of Vermont	M
University of Victoria	M
University of Washington	M,D
University of Washington, Tacoma	M
University of West Florida	M
University of Windsor	M
University of Wisconsin–Green Bay	M
University of Wisconsin–Madison	M
University of Wisconsin–Milwaukee	M,D,O
University of Wisconsin–Oshkosh	M
University of Wyoming	M
Valdosta State University	M
Virginia Commonwealth University	M,D
Walden University	M,D
Walla Walla University	M
Washburn University	M
Washington University in St. Louis	M,D
Wayne State University	M,D,O
West Chester University of Pennsylvania	M
Western Carolina University	M
Western Kentucky University	M
Western Michigan University	M
Western New Mexico University	M
Westfield State University	M
West Texas A&M University	M
West Virginia University	M
Wheelock College	M
Wichita State University	M
Widener University	M,D
Wilfrid Laurier University	M,D
Winthrop University	M
Yeshiva University	M,D
York University	M,D

SOCIOLOGY

Acadia University	M
American University	M,O
American University of Beirut	M,D
Arizona State University at the Tempe campus	M,D
Arkansas State University	M,O
Arkansas Tech University	M
Auburn University	M
Ball State University	M
Baylor University	M,D
Binghamton University, State University of New York	M,D
Boston College	M,D
Boston University	M,D
Bowling Green State University	M,D
Brandeis University	M,D
Brigham Young University	M
Brock University	M
Brooklyn College of the City University of New York	M,D
Brown University	M,D
California State University, Bakersfield	M
California State University, Dominguez Hills	M
California State University, Fullerton	M
California State University, Los Angeles	M
California State University, Northridge	M
California State University, Sacramento	M
California State University, San Marcos	M
Carleton University	M,D
Case Western Reserve University	M,D
The Catholic University of America	M
Central European University	M,D
City College of the City University of New York	M
Clark Atlanta University	M
Clemson University	M
Colorado State University	M,D
Columbia University	M,D
Concordia University (Canada)	M,D
Cornell University	M,D
Dalhousie University	M,D
DePaul University	M
Duke University	M,D
East Carolina University	M
Eastern Michigan University	M
East Tennessee State University	M
Emory University	D
Fayetteville State University	M
Florida Atlantic University	M
Florida International University	M,D
Florida State University	M,D
George Mason University	M,D
The George Washington University	M,D
Georgia Southern University	M
Georgia State University	M,D
The Graduate Center, City University of New York	D
Harvard University	D
Howard University	M,D
Humboldt State University	M
Hunter College of the City University of New York	M
Idaho State University	M
Illinois State University	M
Indiana University Bloomington	M,D
Indiana University of Pennsylvania	M
Indiana University–Purdue University Indianapolis	M
Iowa State University of Science and Technology	M,D
Jackson State University	M
Johns Hopkins University	M,D
Kansas State University	M,D
Kent State University	M,D
Lakehead University	M
Laurentian University	M
Lehigh University	M
Lincoln University (MO)	M
Long Island University–LIU Brooklyn	M,D,O
Louisiana State University and Agricultural & Mechanical College	M,D
Loyola University Chicago	M,D
Marshall University	M
McGill University	M,D,O
McMaster University	M,D
Memorial University of Newfoundland	M,D
Michigan State University	M,D
Middle Tennessee State University	M
Minnesota State University Mankato	M
Mississippi State University	M,D
Morehead State University	M
Morgan State University	M
New Mexico Highlands University	M
New Mexico State University	M
The New School	M,D
New York University	M,D
North Carolina State University	M
North Dakota State University	M
Northeastern University	M,D
Northern Arizona University	M
Northern Illinois University	M
Northwestern University	M,D
The Ohio State University	D
Ohio University	M
Oklahoma City University	M
Oklahoma State University	M
Old Dominion University	M
Our Lady of the Lake University	M
Oxford Graduate School	D
Penn State University Park	M,D
Portland State University	M,D
Prairie View A&M University	M
Princeton University	D,O
Purdue University	M,D
Queens College of the City University of New York	M
Queen's University at Kingston	M,D
Rice University	D
Rutgers University–New Brunswick	M,D
St. John's University (NY)	M
Sam Houston State University	M
San Diego State University	M
San Jose State University	M,O
Shippensburg University of Pennsylvania	M
Simon Fraser University	M,D
South Dakota State University	M,D
Southeastern Louisiana University	M
Southern Connecticut State University	M
Southern Illinois University Carbondale	M,D
Southern Illinois University Edwardsville	M
Stanford University	D
Stony Brook University, State University of New York	M,D
Syracuse University	M,D
Teachers College, Columbia University	M,D
Temple University	M,D
Texas A&M University	M,D
Texas A&M University–Commerce	M,D,O
Texas A&M University–Kingsville	M
Texas Southern University	M
Texas State University	M
Texas Tech University	M
Texas Woman's University	M
Tulane University	M
Université de Montréal	M,D
Université du Québec à Montréal	M,D
Université Laval	M,D
University at Albany, State University of New York	M,D,O
University at Buffalo, the State University of New York	M,D
The University of Akron	M,D
The University of Alabama at Birmingham	D
University of Alberta	M,D
The University of Arizona	M,D
University of Arkansas	M
The University of British Columbia	M,D
University of Calgary	M,D
University of California, Berkeley	D
University of California, Davis	M,D
University of California, Irvine	D
University of California, Los Angeles	M,D
University of California, Merced	M,D
University of California, Riverside	M,D
University of California, San Diego	D
University of California, San Francisco	D
University of California, Santa Barbara	D
University of California, Santa Cruz	D
University of Central Florida	M
University of Central Missouri	M,D,O
University of Central Oklahoma	M
University of Chicago	D
University of Cincinnati	D
University of Colorado Boulder	M,D
University of Colorado Colorado Springs	M
University of Colorado Denver	M,D
University of Connecticut	M,D
University of Delaware	M,D
University of Florida	M,D
University of Georgia	M,D
University of Guelph	M,D
University of Hawaii at Manoa	M,D
University of Houston	M

University of Houston–Clear Lake	M
University of Illinois at Chicago	M,D
University of Illinois at Urbana–Champaign	M,D
University of Indianapolis	M
The University of Iowa	M,D
The University of Kansas	D
University of Kentucky	M,D
University of Lethbridge	M,D
University of Louisville	M,D
The University of Manchester	M,D
University of Manitoba	M,D
University of Maryland, Baltimore County	M
University of Maryland, College Park	M,D
University of Massachusetts Amherst	M,D
University of Massachusetts Boston	M,D
University of Massachusetts Lowell	M,O
University of Memphis	M
University of Miami	M,D
University of Michigan	D
University of Minnesota, Duluth	M
University of Minnesota, Twin Cities Campus	M,D
University of Missouri	D
University of Missouri–Kansas City	M
University of Montana	M
University of Nebraska at Omaha	M
University of Nebraska–Lincoln	M,D
University of Nevada, Las Vegas	M,D
University of Nevada, Reno	M
University of New Brunswick Fredericton	M,D
University of New Hampshire	M,D
University of New Mexico	M,D
University of New Orleans	M
The University of North Carolina at Chapel Hill	M,D
The University of North Carolina at Charlotte	M
The University of North Carolina at Greensboro	M
The University of North Carolina Wilmington	M
University of North Dakota	M
University of Northern Colorado	M
University of North Texas	M,D,O
University of Notre Dame	D
University of Oklahoma	M,D
University of Oregon	M,D
University of Ottawa	M
University of Pennsylvania	M,D
University of Pittsburgh	M,D
University of Puerto Rico, Río Piedras Campus	M
University of Regina	M
University of Saskatchewan	M,D
University of South Africa	M,D
University of South Alabama	M
University of South Carolina	M,D
University of Southern California	D
University of South Florida	M,D
The University of Tennessee	M,D
The University of Texas at Arlington	M
The University of Texas at Austin	M,D
The University of Texas at El Paso	M,O
The University of Texas at San Antonio	M
The University of Texas at Tyler	M
The University of Texas Rio Grande Valley	M
The University of Toledo	M
University of Toronto	M,D
University of Utah	M,D
University of Victoria	M,D
University of Virginia	M,D
University of Washington	M,D
University of Waterloo	M,D
The University of Western Ontario	M,D
University of West Georgia	M,D,O
University of Windsor	M,D
University of Wisconsin–Madison	M,D
University of Wisconsin–Milwaukee	M,D
University of Wyoming	M
Utah State University	M,D
Vanderbilt University	M,D
Virginia Commonwealth University	M
Virginia Polytechnic Institute and State University	M,D,O
Washington State University	M,D
Wayne State University	M,D
Western Illinois University	M
Western Kentucky University	M
Western Michigan University	M,D
West Virginia University	M,D
Wichita State University	M
Wilfrid Laurier University	M
William Paterson University of New Jersey	M,D
Yale University	D
York University	M,D

SOFTWARE ENGINEERING

American Public University System	M
Arizona State University at the Tempe campus	M,D
Auburn University	M,D
Boston University	M,O
Bowling Green State University	M
Brandeis University	M
California Baptist University	M
California State University, Fullerton	M
California State University, Northridge	M
California State University, Sacramento	M

Carnegie Mellon University	M
Carroll University	M
Cleveland State University	M,D
Colorado Technical University Aurora	M
Colorado Technical University Colorado Springs	M,D
Concordia University (Canada)	M,D,O
DePaul University	M,D
Drexel University	M,D,O
East Carolina University	M
Embry-Riddle Aeronautical University–Daytona	M,D
Fairfield University	M,O
Florida Agricultural and Mechanical University	M
Florida Institute of Technology	M,D
Gannon University	M
Grand Valley State University	M
Harrisburg University of Science and Technology	M
Illinois Institute of Technology	M
Indiana University–Purdue University Indianapolis	M,D,O
Instituto Tecnologico de Santo Domingo	M,O
International Technological University	M
Jacksonville State University	M
Kennesaw State University	M,O
Lipscomb University	M
Loyola University Chicago	M
Marist College	M,O
Marymount University	M,O
McMaster University	M,D
Mercer University	M
Monmouth University	M
Naval Postgraduate School	M,D
New Jersey Institute of Technology	M,D,O
New York University	O
North Dakota State University	M,D,O
Northern Kentucky University	M,O
Northwestern University	M
Oakland University	M,D
Oklahoma Christian University	M
Oregon State University	M,D
Pace University	M,D,O
Penn State Great Valley	M,O
Portland State University	M,D
Regis University	M
Rochester Institute of Technology	M
Rose-Hulman Institute of Technology	M
Royal Military College of Canada	M,D
St. Mary's University (United States)	M,O
Santa Clara University	M,D,O
Seattle University	M
Shippensburg University of Pennsylvania	M,O
Southern Methodist University	M,O
Stevens Institute of Technology	M,O
Stony Brook University, State University of New York	M,D,O
Stratford University (VA)	M
Strayer University	M
Tennessee Technological University	M
Texas State University	M
Texas Tech University	M
Towson University	M,D,O
Université Laval	O
The University of Alabama in Huntsville	M,D,O
University of Calgary	M,D
University of Colorado Colorado Springs	M,D
University of Connecticut	M,D
University of Detroit Mercy	M,D
University of Houston–Clear Lake	M
University of Management and Technology	M,O
University of Massachusetts Dartmouth	M,O
University of Michigan–Dearborn	M,D
University of Minnesota, Twin Cities Campus	M
University of Missouri–Kansas City	M,D,O
University of Nebraska at Omaha	M,O
University of New Haven	M
University of North Florida	M
University of Regina	M,D
University of St. Thomas (MN)	M,O
The University of Scranton	M
University of South Carolina	M,D
University of Southern California	M,D
University of Southern Maine	M,O
The University of Texas at Arlington	M,D
The University of Texas at Dallas	M,D
The University of Texas at El Paso	M,D,O
University of Utah	M,O
University of Washington, Bothell	M
University of Washington, Tacoma	M
University of Waterloo	M,D
University of West Florida	M
University of Wisconsin–La Crosse	M
Villanova University	M
Virginia International University	M,O
Virginia Polytechnic Institute and State University	M,O
West Virginia University	M

SPANISH

American University	M,O
Arizona State University at the Tempe campus	M,D
Asbury University	M

Auburn University	M
Bard College	M
Baylor University	M
Binghamton University, State University of New York	M
Boston College	M
Bowling Green State University	M
Brigham Young University	M
Brooklyn College of the City University of New York	M
California State University, Bakersfield	M
California State University, Fresno	M
California State University, Fullerton	M
California State University, Long Beach	M
California State University, Los Angeles	M
California State University, Northridge	M
California State University, San Bernardino	M
California State University, San Marcos	M
The Catholic University of America	M,D
Central Connecticut State University	M,O
Central Michigan University	M
City College of the City University of New York	M
Cleveland State University	M
Colorado State University	M
Columbia University	M,D
Cornell University	D
DePaul University	M
Duke University	D
Eastern University	M,D,O
Emory University	D,O
Florida Atlantic University	M
Florida International University	M,D
Florida State University	M,D
Framingham State University	M
Georgetown University	M,D
Georgia Southern University	M
Georgia State University	M,O
Harvard University	M,D
Howard University	M
Hunter College of the City University of New York	M
Illinois State University	M
Indiana State University	M,D,O
Indiana University Bloomington	M,D
Inter American University of Puerto Rico, Metropolitan Campus	M
Inter American University of Puerto Rico, Ponce Campus	M
Iona College	M
Ithaca College	M
Johns Hopkins University	D
Kent State University	M,D
Lake Forest College	M
Lamar University	M
Lee University	M,O
Lehman College of the City University of New York	M
Loyola University Chicago	M
Marquette University	M
Michigan State University	M,D
Middlebury College	M,D
Middle Tennessee State University	M
Millersville University of Pennsylvania	M
Minnesota State University Mankato	M
Molloy College	M,O
Montclair State University	M
New Mexico State University	M,D,O
New York University	M,D,O
North Carolina State University	M
Northern Arizona University	M
Northern Illinois University	M
Northwestern University	D
The Ohio State University	M,D
Ohio University	M
Penn State University Park	M,D
Pontifical Catholic University of Puerto Rico	M,O
Portland State University	M
Princeton University	D
Purdue University	M,D
Queens College of the City University of New York	M
Queen's University at Kingston	M
Rider University	O
Rutgers University–New Brunswick	M,D
St. John's University (NY)	M
Saint Louis University	M
Saint Louis University–Madrid Campus	M
Saint Xavier University	M
Salem State University	M
Sam Houston State University	M
San Diego State University	M
San Francisco State University	M
San Jose State University	M
Smith College	M
Southern Oregon University	M
Stanford University	M,D
State University of New York at New Paltz	M,O
Syracuse University	M
Temple University	M,D
Texas A&M University	M,D
Texas A&M University–Commerce	M,D,O
Texas A&M University–Kingsville	M
Texas State University	M
Texas Tech University	M,D

Tulane University	M,D
Universidad Autonoma de Guadalajara	M,D
Université de Montréal	M
Université Laval	M,D
University at Albany, State University of New York	M,D
University at Buffalo, the State University of New York	M,D,O
The University of Akron	M
The University of Alabama	M,D
The University of Arizona	M,D
University of Arkansas	M
University of Calgary	M
University of California, Berkeley	D
University of California, Davis	M,D
University of California, Irvine	M,D
University of California, Los Angeles	M
University of California, Riverside	M,D
University of California, Santa Barbara	M,D
University of Central Florida	M
University of Chicago	D
University of Cincinnati	M,D
University of Colorado Boulder	M,D
University of Colorado Denver	M
University of Delaware	M
University of Florida	M,D
University of Georgia	M,D
University of Hawaii at Manoa	M
University of Houston	M,D
University of Illinois at Chicago	M,D
University of Illinois at Urbana–Champaign	M,D
The University of Iowa	M,D
The University of Kansas	M,D
University of Lethbridge	M,D
University of Louisville	M,O
The University of Manchester	M,D
University of Maryland, College Park	M,D
University of Massachusetts Amherst	M,D
University of Memphis	M
University of Miami	M,D
University of Michigan	D
University of Minnesota, Twin Cities Campus	M,D
University of Missouri	M,D
University of Missouri–Kansas City	M
University of Montana	M
University of Nebraska–Lincoln	M,D
University of Nevada, Reno	M
University of New Hampshire	M,O
University of New Mexico	M,D
The University of North Carolina at Chapel Hill	M,D
The University of North Carolina at Charlotte	M,O
The University of North Carolina at Greensboro	M,O
The University of North Carolina Wilmington	M
University of Northern Iowa	M
University of North Texas	M,D,O
University of Notre Dame	M
University of Oklahoma	M,D
University of Oregon	M
University of Ottawa	M,D
University of Pennsylvania	M,D
University of Pittsburgh	M,D
University of Rhode Island	M
University of South Africa	M
University of South Carolina	M,D
University of Southern California	D
University of South Florida	M,D
The University of Tennessee	M,D
The University of Texas at Arlington	M
The University of Texas at Austin	M,D
The University of Texas at El Paso	M,O
The University of Texas at San Antonio	M
The University of Texas of the Permian Basin	M
The University of Texas Rio Grande Valley	M
The University of Toledo	M
University of Toronto	M,D
University of Utah	M,D
University of Virginia	M,D
University of Washington	M
The University of Western Ontario	M,D
University of Wisconsin–Madison	M,D
University of Wisconsin–Milwaukee	M
University of Wyoming	M
Vanderbilt University	M
Washington University in St. Louis	D
Wayne State University	M,D
West Chester University of Pennsylvania	M,O
Western Kentucky University	M
Western Michigan University	M
West Virginia University	M
Wichita State University	M
Worcester State University	M
Yale University	D

SPECIAL EDUCATION

Acacia University	M
Acadia University	M
Adams State University	M
Adelphi University	M
Alabama Agricultural and Mechanical University	M,D,O
Alabama State University	M,O
Albany State University	M
Albright College	M
Alcorn State University	M,O

Alliant International University–San Francisco — M,O
Alverno College — M
American International College — M,O
American Public University System — M
American University — M
American University of Puerto Rico — M
Andrews University — M
Antioch University Midwest — M
Antioch University New England — M,O
Appalachian State University — M
Arcadia University — M,D,O
Arizona State University at the Tempe campus — M,O
Arkansas State University — M,D,O
Armstrong State University — M,O
Asbury University — M
Ashland University — M
Assumption College — M,O
Auburn University — M,O
Auburn University at Montgomery — M,O
Augustana University — M
Augusta University — M,O
Aurora University — M
Austin Peay State University — M
Averett University — M
Azusa Pacific University — M
Baldwin Wallace University — M
Ball State University — M,D,O
Bank Street College of Education — M
Barry University — M,D,O
Bayamón Central University — M,O
Baylor University — M,D,O
Bay Path University — M
Bellarmine University — M
Bemidji State University — M
Benedictine University — M
Bethel University (MN) — M,D,O
Binghamton University, State University of New York — M
Biola University — M,O
Bloomsburg University of Pennsylvania — M,O
Bluffton University — M
Bob Jones University — M,D,O
Boise State University — M
Boston College — M,O
Bowie State University — M
Bowling Green State University — M
Brandman University — M,D
Brandon University — M,O
Brenau University — M,O
Bridgewater State University — M
Brigham Young University — M,D,O
Brooklyn College of the City University of New York — M,O
Buffalo State College, State University of New York — M
Butler University — M,O
Caldwell University — M,D,O
California Baptist University — M
California Lutheran University — M,D
California State University, Bakersfield — M
California State University, Chico — M
California State University, Dominguez Hills — M
California State University, East Bay — M
California State University, Fresno — M
California State University, Fullerton — M
California State University, Long Beach — M,D
California State University, Los Angeles — M,D
California State University, Northridge — M
California State University, Sacramento — M,D
California State University, San Marcos — M,D
California State University, Stanislaus — M
California University of Pennsylvania — M
Cambridge College — M,D,O
Campbellsville University — M
Canisius College — M,O
Capella University — M,D
Cardinal Stritch University — M,D
Caribbean University — M,D
Carlos Albizu University, Miami Campus — M,D
Carlow University — M
Castleton University — M,O
The Catholic University of America — M,O
Centenary University — M,D
Central Connecticut State University — M,O
Central Michigan University — M,O
Central Washington University — M
Chaminade University of Honolulu — M
Chapman University — M,D,O
Chatham University — M
Chestnut Hill College — M,O
Cheyney University of Pennsylvania — M
Chicago State University — M
City College of the City University of New York — M,O
City University of Seattle — M,O
Claremont Graduate University — M,D,O
Clarion University of Pennsylvania — M
Clark Atlanta University — M
Clemson University — M,D
Cleveland State University — M
Coastal Carolina University — M,O
College of Charleston — M
The College of New Jersey — M,O
The College of New Rochelle — M
College of St. Joseph — M
The College of Saint Rose — M,O

College of Staten Island of the City University of New York — M,O
The College of William and Mary — M
Colorado Christian University — M
Colorado Mesa University — M,O
Colorado State University–Pueblo — M,O
Columbus State University — M,O
Concordia College–New York — M
Concordia University (United States) — M,D
Concordia University, St. Paul — M,D,O
Concordia University Wisconsin — M
Concord University — M
Converse College — M
Coppin State University — M
Curry College — M,O
Daemen College — M
Dallas Baptist University — M
Delaware State University — M
Delta State University — M
DePaul University — M,D
DeSales University — M,O
Dominican College — M
Dominican University — M
Dominican University of California — M
Drew University — M,D,O
Drexel University — M,D
Drury University — M
Duquesne University — M,D
D'Youville College — M,D
East Carolina University — M,O
Eastern Illinois University — M
Eastern Kentucky University — M
Eastern Michigan University — M,O
Eastern Nazarene College — M,O
Eastern New Mexico University — M
Eastern University — M,D,O
East Stroudsburg University of Pennsylvania — M
East Tennessee State University — M,O
Edgewood College — M,D,O
Edinboro University of Pennsylvania — M,O
Elmhurst College — M
Elms College — M,O
Elon University — M
Emporia State University — M
Endicott College — M,D
Fairfield University — M,O
Fairleigh Dickinson University, Metropolitan Campus — M
Fairmont State University — M
Ferris State University — M
Fitchburg State University — M
Florida Atlantic University — M,D
Florida Gulf Coast University — M
Florida International University — M,D,O
Florida Memorial University — M
Florida State University — M,D,O
Fontbonne University — M
Fordham University — M,O
Fort Hays State University — M
Framingham State University — M
Francis Marion University — M
Franklin Pierce University — M,D,O
Freed-Hardeman University — M,O
Fresno Pacific University — M
Frostburg State University — M
Furman University — M,O
Gallaudet University — M,D,O
George Fox University — M,O
George Mason University — M,D,O
Georgetown College — M
The George Washington University — M,D,O
Georgia College & State University — M,O
Georgian Court University — M,O
Georgia Southern University — M
Georgia Southwestern State University — M,O
Georgia State University — M,D
Gonzaga University — M
Gordon College — M,O
Goucher College — M,O
Governors State University — M
Graceland University (IA) — M
Grambling State University — M
Grand Canyon University — M,D,O
Grand Valley State University — M
Greensboro College — M
Gwynedd Mercy University — M
Harding University — M,O
Hebrew College — M,O
Henderson State University — M,O
Heritage University — M
High Point University — M
Hofstra University — M,D,O
Holy Family University — M
Holy Names University — M,O
Hood College — M,O
Howard University — M
Hunter College of the City University of New York — M
Idaho State University — M,D,O
Illinois State University — M,D,O
Immaculata University — M,D,O
Indiana University Bloomington — M,D,O
Indiana University of Pennsylvania — M
Indiana University–Purdue University Fort Wayne — M,O
Indiana University–Purdue University Indianapolis — M,O
Indiana University South Bend — M,O
Inter American University of Puerto Rico, Barranquitas Campus — M
Inter American University of Puerto Rico, Fajardo Campus — M
Inter American University of Puerto Rico, Metropolitan Campus — M
Inter American University of Puerto Rico, San Germán Campus — M
Iona College — M
Iowa State University of Science and Technology — M,D
Jackson State University — M,O

Jacksonville State University — M
James Madison University — M
Johns Hopkins University — M,O
Johnson & Wales University — M
Johnson State College — M
Kansas State University — M,D,O
Kaplan University, Davenport Campus — M
Kean University — M
Keene State College — M
Kennesaw State University — M
Kent State University — M
Kentucky State University — M,D
Lamar University — M,D
Lancaster Bible College — M,D
La Salle University — M,O
Lasell College — M
Lee University — M,O
Lehigh University — M,D
Lehman College of the City University of New York — M
Le Moyne College — M,O
Lesley University — M,D,O
Lewis & Clark College — M
Lewis University — M
Lincoln University (PA) — M
Lipscomb University — M,D,O
London Metropolitan University — M,D
Long Island University–Brentwood Campus — M,O
Long Island University–Hudson — M,O
Long Island University–LIU Brooklyn — M,O
Long Island University–LIU Post — M,D,O
Long Island University–Riverhead — M,O
Longwood University — M
Loras College — M
Loyola Marymount University — M
Loyola University Chicago — M,O
Lynchburg College — M
Lyndon State College — M
Lynn University — M,D
Madonna University — M
Malone University — M
Manhattan College — M,O
Manhattanville College — M,O
Mansfield University of Pennsylvania — M
Marian University (WI) — M,D
Marshall University — M
Martin Luther College — M
Marymount University — M
Marywood University — M
Massachusetts College of Liberal Arts — M,O
McDaniel College — M
McKendree University — M,D,O
McNeese State University — M
Medaille College — M
Mercyhurst University — M
Meredith College — M,O
Merrimack College — M,O
Messiah College — M
Metropolitan College of New York — M
Metropolitan State University of Denver — M
Michigan State University — M,D,O
Middle Tennessee State University — M
Midwestern State University — M
Millersville University of Pennsylvania — M
Milligan College — M,D,O
Minnesota State University Mankato — M,O
Minnesota State University Moorhead — M,O
Minot State University — M
Misericordia University — M
Mississippi College — M,D,O
Mississippi State University — M,D,O
Missouri State University — M
Missouri Western State University — M,O
Molloy College — M,O
Monmouth University — M,D,O
Montana State University Billings — M
Montclair State University — M
Morehead State University — M,O
Morningside College — M
Mount Mercy University — M
Mount St. Joseph University — M,O
Mount Saint Mary College — M
Mount Saint Vincent University — M
Murray State University — M
National Louis University — M,D,O
National University College — M
Neumann University — M
New England College — M,D
New Jersey City University — M
New Mexico Highlands University — M
New Mexico State University — M,D,O
New York University — M,D,O
Niagara University — M,O
Norfolk State University — M
North Carolina Central University — M
North Carolina State University — M
Northeastern Illinois University — M
Northeastern State University — M
Northeastern University — M
Northern Arizona University — M,O
Northern Illinois University — M,D
Northern Kentucky University — M,O
Northern Michigan University — M
Northwestern State University of Louisiana — M,O
Northwest Missouri State University — M,D,O
Northwest Nazarene University — M,D,O
Notre Dame College (OH) — M,O
Notre Dame de Namur University — M
Nyack College — M
Oakland University — M
The Ohio State University — D
Ohio University — M,D
Old Dominion University — M,D
Ottawa University — M
Pace University — M,O

Pacific Oaks College — M
Pacific University — M
Penn State University Park — M,D,O
Piedmont College — M,O
Pittsburg State University — M,O
Plymouth State University — M
Point Loma Nazarene University — M
Point Park University — M,D
Prescott College — M,D
Providence College — M
Purdue University — M,D,O
Purdue University Northwest — M
Queens College of the City University of New York — M,O
Quincy University — M
Radford University — M,O
Ramapo College of New Jersey — M
Randolph College — M
Regent University — M,D,O
Regis College (MA) — M,D
Regis University — M,O
Rhode Island College — M,O
Rider University — M,O
Rivier University — M,D,O
Robert Morris University — M,O
Roberts Wesleyan College — M
Rochester Institute of Technology — M
Rockford University — M
Roosevelt University — M
Rowan University — M,O
Rutgers University–New Brunswick — M,D
Sage Graduate School — M
Saginaw Valley State University — M
St. Ambrose University — M
St. Bonaventure University — M
St. Cloud State University — M
St. John Fisher College — M,O
St. John's University (NY) — M,D,O
St. Joseph's College, Long Island Campus — M
St. Joseph's College, New York — M
Saint Joseph's University — M,D,O
Saint Louis University — M,D
Saint Mary's College of California — M
Saint Mary's University of Minnesota — M,O
Saint Michael's College — M,O
Saint Peter's University — M,O
St. Thomas Aquinas College — M
St. Thomas University — M,D,O
Saint Vincent College — M
Saint Xavier University — M
Salem College — M
Salem State University — M
Salus University — M,O
Samford University — M,D,O
Sam Houston State University — M,D
San Diego State University — M
San Francisco State University — M,O
Seattle University — M,O
Seton Hall University — M
Seton Hill University — M
Shenandoah University — M,D,O
Shippensburg University of Pennsylvania — M,D
Siena Heights University — M,O
Simmons College — M,D,O
Slippery Rock University of Pennsylvania — M,D
Sonoma State University — M,O
South Carolina State University — M
Southeastern Louisiana University — M
Southeast Missouri State University — M
Southern Connecticut State University — M
Southern Illinois University Carbondale — M,D
Southern Illinois University Edwardsville — M,O
Southern Methodist University — M,D,O
Southern New Hampshire University — M,O
Southern Oregon University — M
Southern University and Agricultural and Mechanical College — M,D
Southwestern College (KS) — M,D
Southwestern Oklahoma State University — M
Southwest Minnesota State University — M
Spalding University — M
Spring Arbor University — M
Springfield College — M
State University of New York at New Paltz — M
State University of New York at Oswego — M
State University of New York at Plattsburgh — M
State University of New York College at Cortland — M
State University of New York College at Oneonta — M,O
State University of New York College at Potsdam — M
Stephen F. Austin State University — M,D
Syracuse University — M,D
Tarleton State University — M
Teachers College, Columbia University — M,D,O
Tennessee State University — M,D
Tennessee Technological University — M,O
Texas A&M International University — M
Texas A&M University — M
Texas A&M University–Commerce — M,D,O
Texas A&M University–Corpus Christi — M
Texas A&M University–Kingsville — M
Texas A&M University–San Antonio — M
Texas A&M University–Texarkana — M

Texas Christian University	M,O
Texas State University	M
Texas Tech University	M,D
Texas Woman's University	M,D
Touro College	M
Towson University	M,O
Trevecca Nazarene University	M,O
Trinity Baptist College	M
Trinity Christian College	M
Trinity Washington University	M
Tusculum College	M
Union College (KY)	M
Universidad del Este	M
Universidad del Turabo	M
Universidad Iberoamericana	M,D
Universidad Metropolitana	M
Université de Sherbrooke	M,O
University at Albany, State University of New York	M
University at Buffalo, the State University of New York	M,D,O
The University of Akron	M
The University of Alabama	M,D,O
The University of Alabama at Birmingham	M
The University of Alabama in Huntsville	M,O
University of Alaska Anchorage	M,O
University of Alaska Fairbanks	M
University of Alaska Southeast	M
University of Alberta	M,D
The University of Arizona	M,D
University of Arkansas	M
University of Arkansas at Little Rock	M,O
The University of British Columbia	M,D,O
University of California, Berkeley	M,D
University of California, Los Angeles	D
University of California, Riverside	M,D,O
University of Central Arkansas	M,O
University of Central Florida	M,D,O
University of Central Missouri	M,D,O
University of Central Oklahoma	M
University of Cincinnati	M,D
University of Colorado Colorado Springs	M,D
University of Colorado Denver	M,D
University of Denver	M,D,O
University of Detroit Mercy	M,D,O
University of Florida	M,D,O
University of Georgia	M,D,O
University of Guam	M
University of Hawaii at Manoa	M,D
University of Houston	M
University of Houston–Victoria	M
University of Idaho	M
University of Illinois at Chicago	M,D
University of Illinois at Urbana–Champaign	M,D,O
The University of Iowa	M,D
The University of Kansas	M,D,O
University of Kentucky	M,D
University of La Verne	M,D,O
University of Louisiana at Monroe	M,D
University of Louisville	M,D,O
University of Maine	M,D,O
University of Manitoba	M
University of Mary	M,D
University of Maryland Eastern Shore	M
University of Massachusetts Amherst	M,D,O
University of Massachusetts Boston	M
University of Massachusetts Dartmouth	M,O
University of Memphis	M,D
University of Miami	M,D,O
University of Michigan–Dearborn	M
University of Minnesota, Twin Cities Campus	M,D
University of Missouri	M,D
University of Missouri–Kansas City	M,D,O
University of Missouri–St. Louis	M
University of Nebraska at Kearney	M,O
University of Nebraska at Omaha	M
University of Nebraska–Lincoln	M,D,O
University of Nevada, Las Vegas	M,D,O
University of Nevada, Reno	M,D
University of New Hampshire	M
University of New Mexico	M,D,O
University of New Orleans	M,D
University of North Alabama	M
The University of North Carolina at Charlotte	M,D,O
The University of North Carolina at Greensboro	M,D,O
The University of North Carolina Wilmington	M
University of North Dakota	M,D
University of Northern Colorado	M,D
University of Northern Iowa	M
University of North Florida	M
University of North Texas	M,D,O
University of Oklahoma	M,D
University of Oklahoma Health Sciences Center	M,D,O
University of Phoenix–Bay Area Campus	M,D,O
University of Phoenix–Hawaii Campus	M
University of Phoenix–Online Campus	M,O
University of Phoenix–Phoenix Campus	M
University of Phoenix–Southern Arizona Campus	M,O
University of Phoenix–Utah Campus	M
University of Phoenix–Washington D.C. Campus	M,D,O
University of Pittsburgh	M,D
University of Portland	M,D
University of Puerto Rico, Medical Sciences Campus	O
University of Puerto Rico, Río Piedras Campus	M
University of Rhode Island	M,D
University of Rio Grande	M
University of St. Francis (IL)	M,D,O
University of Saint Francis (IN)	M
University of Saint Joseph	M
University of Saint Mary	M
University of St. Thomas (MN)	M,O
University of St. Thomas (TX)	M,D
University of San Diego	M
University of San Francisco	M,D
University of Saskatchewan	M,D,O
The University of Scranton	M
University of South Alabama	M,D
University of South Carolina	M,D
University of South Carolina Upstate	M
The University of South Dakota	M,D,O
University of Southern Maine	M,O
University of Southern Mississippi	M,D
University of South Florida	O
The University of Tennessee	M,D,O
The University of Tennessee at Chattanooga	M,D,O
The University of Tennessee at Martin	M
The University of Texas at Austin	M
The University of Texas at El Paso	M
The University of Texas at San Antonio	M,D
The University of Texas at Tyler	M
The University of Texas Health Science Center at San Antonio	M,D
The University of Texas of the Permian Basin	M,D
The University of Texas Rio Grande Valley	M
University of the Cumberlands	M
University of the Pacific	M,D
University of the Southwest	M
The University of Toledo	M,D,O
University of Utah	M,D
University of Vermont	M
University of Victoria	M
University of Virginia	M,D,O
University of Washington	M,D
University of Washington, Tacoma	M
The University of West Alabama	M,O
The University of Western Ontario	M
University of West Florida	M
University of West Georgia	M,D,O
University of Wisconsin–Eau Claire	M
University of Wisconsin–La Crosse	M,O
University of Wisconsin–Madison	M,D
University of Wisconsin–Milwaukee	M,D,O
University of Wisconsin–Oshkosh	M
University of Wisconsin–Stevens Point	M
University of Wisconsin–Superior	M
University of Wisconsin–Whitewater	M,O
University of Wyoming	M,D,O
Ursuline College	M
Utah State University	M,D,O
Valdosta State University	M,O
Vanderbilt University	M,D
Virginia Commonwealth University	M,D
Viterbo University	M,O
Wagner College	M
Walden University	M,D,O
Walla Walla University	M
Washburn University	M
Washington State University	M,D
Washington University in St. Louis	M,D
Wayland Baptist University	M
Waynesburg University	M,D
Wayne State College	M
Wayne State University	M,D,O
Webster University	M,O
West Chester University of Pennsylvania	M,O
Western Connecticut State University	M
Western Governors University	M,O
Western Illinois University	M
Western Kentucky University	M,O
Western Michigan University	M
Western New Mexico University	M
Western Oregon University	M
Westfield State University	M
Westminster College (PA)	M,O
West Virginia University	M,D
Wheelock College	M
Whitworth University	M
Wichita State University	M
Widener University	M,D
Wilkes University	M
William Carey University	M,O
William Paterson University of New Jersey	M
Wilmington College	M
Wilmington University	M,D
Winona State University	M
Winston-Salem State University	M
Winthrop University	M
Worcester State University	M,O
Wright State University	M
Xavier University	M
Youngstown State University	M

SPEECH AND INTERPERSONAL COMMUNICATION

Ball State University	M
Bob Jones University	M,D,O
Brooklyn College of the City University of New York	M,D
California State University, Fullerton	M
California State University, Northridge	M
Colorado State University	M,D
Eastern Illinois University	M
Georgia State University	M
Idaho State University	M
Marquette University	M,O
New York University	M,D
North Dakota State University	M,D
Northeastern Illinois University	M
Northwestern University	M,D
Ohio University	M,D
Old Dominion University	M
Portland State University	M,O
Rensselaer Polytechnic Institute	M,D
San Francisco State University	M
Seton Hall University	M
Southern Illinois University Carbondale	M,D
Southern Illinois University Edwardsville	M
Texas Christian University	M
The University of Alabama	M
University of Arkansas at Little Rock	M
University of California, Santa Barbara	D
University of Denver	M
University of Hawaii at Manoa	M
University of Houston	M
The University of Iowa	M
University of Louisiana at Monroe	M,D
University of Maryland, College Park	M,D
University of Nebraska–Lincoln	M,D
University of Nevada, Reno	M
University of South Carolina	M,D
University of Southern Mississippi	M,D
The University of Tennessee	M,D
University of Wisconsin–Madison	M
University of Wisconsin–Stevens Point	M
University of Wisconsin–Superior	M
Wake Forest University	M
Washington University in St. Louis	M,D

SPORT PSYCHOLOGY

Adler University	M,D,O
Argosy University, Atlanta	M,D,O
Argosy University, Inland Empire	M,D
Argosy University, Orange County	M
Argosy University, Phoenix	M,D
Argosy University, San Francisco Bay Area	M,D
Argosy University, Schaumburg	M,O
A.T. Still University	M,D,O
Ball State University	M
Barry University	M
California State University, Fresno	M
California State University, Long Beach	M
California University of Pennsylvania	M
Capella University	M
Chatham University	M,D
Florida State University	M,D
John F. Kennedy University	M
Lock Haven University of Pennsylvania	M
Purdue University	M,D
Queen's University at Kingston	M,D
Seton Hall University	M
Southern Illinois University Edwardsville	M
Springfield College	M,D,O
University of Denver	M,D
University of Rhode Island	M,D
The University of Texas at Austin	M,D
West Virginia University	M,D

SPORTS MANAGEMENT

Adelphi University	M
American Public University System	M
American University	M,O
Angelo State University	M
Arkansas State University	M,O
Auburn University at Montgomery	M,O
Augustana University	M
Austin Peay State University	M
Ball State University	M
Barry University	M
Belhaven University (MS)	M
Boise State University	M
Bowling Green State University	M
Bristol University	M
Brooklyn College of the City University of New York	M
California Baptist University	M
California State University, Fresno	M
California State University, Long Beach	M
California University of Management and Sciences	M,D
California University of Pennsylvania	M
Canisius College	M
Cardinal Stritch University	M
Central Michigan University	M,O
Central Washington University	M
The Citadel, The Military College of South Carolina	M,O
Clayton State University	M
Clemson University	M,D,O
Coastal Carolina University	M,D,O
Coker College	M
The College at Brockport, State University of New York	M,O
Columbia University	M
Concordia University Irvine	M
Concordia University, St. Paul	M
Dallas Baptist University	M
DePaul University	M
Drexel University	M
Duquesne University	M
East Carolina University	M,D,O
Eastern Kentucky University	M
Eastern Michigan University	M
Eastern New Mexico University	M
Eastern Washington University	M
East Stroudsburg University of Pennsylvania	M
Endicott College	M
Fairleigh Dickinson University, College at Florham	M
Fairleigh Dickinson University, Metropolitan Campus	M
Florida Agricultural and Mechanical University	M
Florida International University	M,D,O
Florida State University	M,D,O
Franklin Pierce University	M,D,O
Georgetown University	M,D
The George Washington University	M,O
Georgia Southern University	M
Georgia State University	M
Gonzaga University	M
Grambling State University	M
Grand Canyon University	M
Grand View University	M,O
Hampton University	M
Hardin-Simmons University	M
Henderson State University	M
Hofstra University	M,O
Howard Payne University	M
Howard University	M
Husson University	M
Indiana State University	M
Indiana University Bloomington	M,D
Indiana University of Pennsylvania	M
Iona College	M,O
Ithaca College	M
Jackson State University	M
Jacksonville State University	M
Kansas Wesleyan University	M
Kent State University	M
Keystone College	M
Lasell College	M,O
Lewis University	M
Liberty University	M,D,O
Lindenwood University	M
Lipscomb University	M,O
Lock Haven University of Pennsylvania	M
Lynn University	M
Manhattanville College	M
Marquette University	M,O
Marshall University	M
Maryville University of Saint Louis	M,O
Mercyhurst University	M,O
Messiah College	M
Midwestern State University	M
Millersville University of Pennsylvania	M,O
Misericordia University	M
Mississippi State University	M,D
Missouri State University	M,O
Missouri Western State University	M
Montclair State University	M
Morehead State University	M
Mount Ida College	M
Mount St. Mary's University (MD)	M
Neumann University	M
New England College	M
New Mexico Highlands University	M
New York University	M,O
North Carolina Central University	M
North Carolina State University	M,D
Northeastern University	M
Northern State University	M
Northwestern University	M
Ohio Dominican University	M
Ohio University	M
Old Dominion University	M
Pittsburg State University	M
Point Loma Nazarene University	M
Point Park University	M
Purdue University	M,D
Robert Morris University Illinois	M
St. Cloud State University	M
St. John's University (NY)	M
Saint Mary's College of California	M
St. Thomas University	M,O
Sam Houston State University	M,O
San Diego State University	M
San Jose State University	M,O
Seattle University	M
Seton Hall University	M,O
Sonoma State University	M
Southeastern University (FL)	M
Southeast Missouri State University	M
Southern Methodist University	M
Southern Nazarene University	M
Southern New Hampshire University	M
Springfield College	M,D,O
State University of New York College at Cortland	M

M—masters degree; D—doctorate; O—other advanced degree; *—Close-Up and/or Display

Syracuse University M
Temple University M,D
Tennessee State University M
Tennessee Technological University M,D
Texas A&M University M,D
Texas Tech University M
Texas Woman's University M,D
Tiffin University M
Troy University M
United States Sports Academy M,D
The University of Alabama M
University of Alberta M
University of Arkansas M,D
University of Arkansas at Little Rock M
University of Central Florida M
University of Cincinnati M
University of Colorado Denver M
University of Connecticut M
University of Dallas M,D
University of Florida M
University of Indianapolis M
The University of Iowa M
The University of Kansas M,D
University of Louisiana at Monroe M
University of Louisville M,D,O
University of Mary M
University of Mary Hardin-Baylor M
University of Massachusetts Amherst M,D
University of Miami M
University of Michigan M,D
University of Minnesota, Twin Cities Campus M,D
University of Nebraska at Kearney M
University of New Brunswick Fredericton M
University of New Haven M,O
University of New Mexico D
The University of North Carolina at Chapel Hill M
University of Northern Colorado M
University of Northern Iowa M
University of North Florida M
University of Oregon M
University of San Francisco M
University of South Alabama M
University of South Carolina M
University of Southern Indiana M
University of Southern Mississippi M,D
The University of Tennessee M
University of the Southwest M
Upper Iowa University M
Valparaiso University M
Waldorf University M
Washington State University M,D
Wayland Baptist University M
Wayne State College M
Wayne State University M
Webber International University M
West Chester University of Pennsylvania M,O
Western Illinois University M
Western Kentucky University M
Western Michigan University M
Western New England University M
West Texas A&M University M
West Virginia University M,D
Wichita State University M
Wingate University M
Winona State University M,O
Xavier University M

STATISTICS

Acadia University M
American University M,O
American University of Beirut M,D
Arizona State University at the Tempe campus M,D,O
Auburn University M,D
Ball State University M
Baruch College of the City University of New York M
Baylor University M,D
Bowling Green State University M,D
Brigham Young University M
Brock University M
California State University, East Bay M
Carnegie Mellon University M,D
Central Connecticut State University M,O
Claremont Graduate University M,D
Clemson University M,D
Colorado State University M,D
Columbia University M,D
Concordia University (Canada) M,D
Cornell University M,D
Dalhousie University M,D
Duke University M,D
East Carolina University M,O
Florida Atlantic University M
Florida International University M
Florida State University M,D,O
George Mason University M,D,O
Georgetown University M
The George Washington University M,D,O
Georgia Institute of Technology M
Georgia State University M,D
Hampton University M
Harvard University M,D
Hunter College of the City University of New York M
Indiana University Bloomington M,D
Indiana University–Purdue University Indianapolis M
Iowa State University of Science and Technology M,D
Jackson State University M
Johns Hopkins University M,D
Kansas State University M,D,O
Lehigh University M,D
Louisiana State University and Agricultural & Mechanical College M

Louisiana Tech University M,D
Loyola University Chicago M
McGill University M,D,O
McMaster University M
McNeese State University M
Memorial University of Newfoundland M,D
Miami University M
Michigan State University M,D
Michigan Technological University M,D
Minnesota State University Mankato M
Mississippi State University M,D
Missouri University of Science and Technology M,D
Montana State University M,D
Montclair State University M
Murray State University M
New Jersey Institute of Technology M,D,O
New Mexico Institute of Mining and Technology M,D
New York University M,D
North Carolina State University M,D
North Dakota State University M,D,O
Northern Arizona University M,O
Northern Illinois University M
Northwestern University M,D
Oakland University O
The Ohio State University M,D
Oklahoma State University M,D
Old Dominion University M,D
Oregon State University M,D
Penn State University Park M,D
Portland State University M,D
Purdue University M,D
Queen's University at Kingston M,D
Rice University M,D
Rochester Institute of Technology O
Rutgers University–New Brunswick M,D
St. John's University (NY) M
Sam Houston State University M
San Diego State University M
San Jose State University M,O
Simon Fraser University M,D
South Dakota State University M,D
Southern Illinois University Edwardsville M
Southern Methodist University M,D
Stanford University M,D
Stephen F. Austin State University M
Stevens Institute of Technology M,O
Stony Brook University, State University of New York M,D,O
Temple University M,D
Texas A&M University M,D
Texas A&M University–Kingsville M
Texas Tech University M,D
Université de Montréal M,D,O
Université Laval M
The University of Akron M
University of Alaska Fairbanks M,D,O
University of Alberta M,D,O
The University of Arizona M,D
University of Arkansas M
The University of British Columbia M,D
University of Calgary M,D
University of California, Berkeley M,D
University of California, Davis M,D
University of California, Irvine M,D
University of California, Los Angeles M,D
University of California, Riverside M
University of California, San Diego M,D
University of California, Santa Barbara M,D
University of California, Santa Cruz M,D
University of Central Florida M,O
University of Central Oklahoma M
University of Chicago M,D,O
University of Cincinnati M,D
University of Colorado Denver M,D
University of Connecticut M,D
University of Delaware M
University of Denver M
University of Florida M,D
University of Georgia M,D
University of Guelph M,D
University of Houston–Clear Lake M
University of Idaho M
University of Illinois at Chicago M,D
University of Illinois at Urbana–Champaign M,D
The University of Iowa M,D,O
The University of Kansas M,D,O
University of Kentucky M,D
The University of Manchester M,D
University of Manitoba M,D
University of Maryland, Baltimore County M,D
University of Maryland, College Park M,D
University of Massachusetts Amherst M,D
University of Memphis M,D
University of Michigan M,D,O
University of Minnesota, Twin Cities Campus M,D
University of Missouri M,D
University of Missouri–Kansas City M,D
University of Nebraska–Lincoln M,D
University of New Brunswick Fredericton M,D
University of New Mexico M,D
The University of North Carolina at Chapel Hill M,D

The University of North Carolina at Charlotte M,O
The University of North Carolina Wilmington M
University of North Florida M
University of Notre Dame M,D
University of Ottawa M,D
University of Pennsylvania M,D
University of Pittsburgh M,D
University of Regina M,D
University of Rhode Island M,D,O
University of Rochester M,D
University of Saskatchewan M,D
University of South Africa M,D
University of South Carolina M,D,O
University of Southern California M,D
University of Southern Maine M,O
University of South Florida M,D
The University of Tennessee M,D
The University of Texas at Austin M,D
The University of Texas at Dallas M,D
The University of Texas at El Paso M
The University of Texas at San Antonio M,D
The University of Texas Rio Grande Valley M
The University of Toledo M,D
University of Toronto M,D
University of Utah M,D,O
University of Vermont M
University of Victoria M,D
University of Virginia M,D
University of Washington M,D
University of Waterloo M,D
The University of Western Ontario M,D
University of Windsor M,D
University of Wisconsin–Madison M,D
University of Wisconsin–Milwaukee M,D
University of Wyoming M,D
Utah State University M,D
Virginia Polytechnic Institute and State University M,D
Washington University in St. Louis M,D
Wayne State University M,D
Western Michigan University M,D,O
West Virginia University M,D
Yale University M,D
York University M,D
Youngstown State University M

STRUCTURAL BIOLOGY

Baylor College of Medicine D
Carnegie Mellon University D
Columbia University D
Cornell University O
Duke University D
Harvard University D
Illinois State University M,D
Iowa State University of Science and Technology M,D
Massachusetts Institute of Technology D
Mayo Clinic Graduate School of Biomedical Sciences D
Michigan State University D
New York University D
Northwestern University D
Oregon State University D
Stanford University D
Stony Brook University, State University of New York D
Tufts University M,D
Tulane University D
University at Buffalo, the State University of New York M,D
The University of Alabama at Birmingham D
University of Connecticut M,D
The University of Manchester M,D
University of Minnesota, Twin Cities Campus D
University of Pittsburgh D
University of Rochester D
The University of Texas Health Science Center at San Antonio M,D
The University of Texas Medical Branch D
University of Washington D
Weill Cornell Medicine M,D

STRUCTURAL ENGINEERING

California State University, Northridge M
The Citadel, The Military College of South Carolina M,O
Cornell University M,D
Drexel University M,D
Ecole Polytechnique de Montréal M,D,O
George Mason University M,D
Illinois Institute of Technology M,D
Instituto Tecnologico de Santo Domingo M,O
Iowa State University of Science and Technology M,D
Kansas State University M,D
Louisiana State University and Agricultural & Mechanical College M,D
Marquette University M,D,O
Massachusetts Institute of Technology M,D,O
McGill University M,D
Northwestern University M,D
Norwich University M
Ohio University M,D
Old Dominion University M
Oregon State University M,D
Penn State Harrisburg M,O
Pontificia Universidad Catolica Madre y Maestra M
Southern Illinois University Edwardsville M
Southern Methodist University M,D

Stanford University M,D,O
Stevens Institute of Technology M,D,O
Tufts University M,D
University at Buffalo, the State University of New York M,D
The University of Alabama at Birmingham M,D
University of Alberta M,D
University of Calgary M,D
University of California, Berkeley M,D
University of California, San Diego M,D
University of Central Florida M,D,O
University of Colorado Denver M,D
University of Dayton M
University of Delaware M,D
The University of Manchester M,D
University of Massachusetts Amherst M,D
University of Memphis M,D,O
University of Michigan M,D,O
University of Missouri M,D
University of New Brunswick Fredericton M,D
University of Puerto Rico, Mayagüez Campus M
University of South Florida M,D
The University of Texas at Tyler M
University of Washington M,D

STUDENT AFFAIRS

Alfred University M
Alliant International University–Los Angeles M,D,O
Alliant International University–San Diego M,D,O
Appalachian State University M
Arkansas State University M,O
Arkansas Tech University M,D,O
Azusa Pacific University M
Binghamton University, State University of New York M
Bloomsburg University of Pennsylvania M
Bob Jones University M,D,O
Bowling Green State University M
Bucknell University M
Buffalo State College, State University of New York M
California State University, Bakersfield M
California State University, Fresno M
California State University, Long Beach M,D
Canisius College M,O
Cardinal Stritch University M,D
Central Michigan University M,D,O
The Citadel, The Military College of South Carolina M,O
Claremont Graduate University M,D,O
Clemson University M,D,O
College of Saint Elizabeth M,D,O
The College of Saint Rose M
Colorado State University M,D
Dallas Baptist University M
DePaul University M,D
Eastern Illinois University M
Eastern Michigan University M,D,O
Fresno Pacific University M,O
The George Washington University M,D,O
Grambling State University M,D,O
Hampton University M,D,O
Illinois State University M
Indiana State University M,D,O
Indiana University Bloomington M,D,O
Indiana University of Pennsylvania M
Iowa State University of Science and Technology M,D
Kansas State University M,D,O
Kaplan University, Davenport Campus M
Kent State University M
Lewis & Clark College M,D,O
Lewis University M
Manhattan College M,O
Marquette University M,D,O
Merrimack College M,O
Messiah College M
Minnesota State University Mankato M,D
Mississippi State University M,D,O
Missouri State University M
Monmouth University M,D,O
New York University M,D
Northern Arizona University M,D,O
Northern Michigan University M
Northwestern State University of Louisiana M
Nova Southeastern University M,D,O
Ohio University M,D
Oregon State University M
Providence University College & Theological Seminary M,D,O
Regent University M,D,O
Rutgers University–New Brunswick M
St. Cloud State University M
St. Edward's University M
Saint Louis University M,D,O
Seton Hall University M
Shippensburg University of Pennsylvania M,D,O
Slippery Rock University of Pennsylvania M
Southern Arkansas University–Magnolia M
Southern Illinois University Edwardsville M
Springfield College M,D,O
State University of New York at Plattsburgh M,O
Syracuse University M
Texas State University M

University of Arkansas at Little Rock	M,D
University of Bridgeport	M
University of Central Arkansas	M
University of Central Florida	M,D,O
University of Central Missouri	M,D,O
University of Central Oklahoma	M
University of Dayton	M,O
University of Florida	M,D,O
University of Georgia	M,D,O
The University of Iowa	M,D
University of Louisville	M,D
University of Maryland, College Park	M,D,O
University of Minnesota, Twin Cities Campus	M
University of Nebraska at Kearney	M
University of Northern Colorado	M,D
University of Northern Iowa	M
University of Oklahoma	M
University of Rhode Island	M
University of Rochester	M
University of St. Thomas (MN)	M
University of South Carolina	M
University of Southern California	M
University of Southern Mississippi	M,D,O
University of South Florida	M,D,O
The University of Tennessee	M
The University of Tennessee at Martin	M
University of the Cumberlands	M,D,O
University of Utah	M,D
University of Virginia	M,D,O
University of West Florida	M
University of Wisconsin–La Crosse	M,D
University of Wyoming	M
Virginia Commonwealth University	M
Virginia Polytechnic Institute and State University	M,D,O
Walsh University	M
West Chester University of Pennsylvania	M,O
Western Illinois University	M
Western Kentucky University	M
William James College	M,D,O

SUPPLY CHAIN MANAGEMENT

Adelphi University	M
Albany State University	M
American Graduate University	M,O
Anderson University (SC)	M
Arizona State University at the Tempe campus	M,D
Boston University	M
Brigham Young University	M
Bryant University	M,O
California State University, East Bay	M
California State University, San Bernardino	M
Capella University	M,D
Case Western Reserve University	M,D
Central Connecticut State University	M,O
Clarkson University	M,O
Clayton State University	M
Clemson University	M,D
Concordia University (Canada)	M,D,O
Delaware Valley University	M
DeSales University	M
Eastern Michigan University	M,O
Elmhurst College	M
Embry-Riddle Aeronautical University–Worldwide	M
Fairleigh Dickinson University, College at Florham	M
Ferris State University	M
Florida Institute of Technology	M,D
Fontbonne University	M
Friends University	M
Georgia Southern University	D
Golden Gate University	M,D,O
HEC Montreal	M,O
Howard University	M
Indiana University–Purdue University Indianapolis	M
Johnson & Wales University	M
Kaplan University, Davenport Campus	M
Lindenwood University	M
Loyola University Chicago	M,O
Maine Maritime Academy	M
Marquette University	M,O
Maryville University of Saint Louis	M,O
Michigan State University	M,D
Moravian College	M
Naval Postgraduate School	M
New York Institute of Technology	M
Niagara University	M
North Carolina Agricultural and Technical State University	M
North Carolina State University	M
Norwich University	M
Nova Southeastern University	M
Old Dominion University	M
Oregon State University	M,D
Penn State Harrisburg	M,O
Penn State University Park	M,D
Polytechnic University of Puerto Rico, Miami Campus	M
Portland State University	M
Quinnipiac University	M
Rensselaer Polytechnic Institute	M
Rutgers University–Newark	D
Saint Leo University	M,D,O
St. Norbert College	M
Santa Clara University	M
Seton Hall University	M,O

Shippensburg University of Pennsylvania	M,O
Southern Arkansas University–Magnolia	M,O
Southern New Hampshire University	M,O
Strayer University	M
Suffolk University	M
Syracuse University	M
Temple University	M,D
Texas A&M University–San Antonio	M
Texas Christian University	M
Towson University	M,O
University at Buffalo, the State University of New York	M,D
The University of Akron	M
The University of Alabama in Huntsville	M,O
University of Dallas	M,D
University of Florida	M,D,O
University of Houston	M
University of Houston–Downtown	M
The University of Kansas	M,D
University of La Verne	M
University of Louisville	M,D,O
The University of Manchester	M
University of Massachusetts Dartmouth	M,O
University of Memphis	M,D
University of Michigan	M,D
University of Michigan–Dearborn	M
University of Minnesota, Twin Cities Campus	M,D
University of Missouri–St. Louis	M,D,O
The University of North Carolina at Charlotte	M,O
The University of North Carolina at Greensboro	M,D,O
University of North Texas	M,D,O
University of Oklahoma	M,D
University of Pittsburgh	M
University of Rhode Island	M,D
University of San Diego	M,O
University of Southern California	M,D,O
The University of Tennessee at Chattanooga	M,O
The University of Texas at Austin	M,D
The University of Texas at Dallas	M
University of Washington	M,D
University of Wisconsin–Madison	M
University of Wisconsin–Platteville	M
University of Wisconsin–Stout	M
Walden University	M,D,O
Washington University in St. Louis	M
Western Illinois University	M,O
Wilfrid Laurier University	M,D
Wright State University	M

SURVEYING SCIENCE AND ENGINEERING

University of New Brunswick Fredericton	M,D

SURVEY METHODOLOGY

University of Maryland, College Park	M,D
University of Michigan	M,D,O
University of Nebraska–Lincoln	M,D

SUSTAINABILITY MANAGEMENT

American University	M
Anaheim University	M,D,O
Antioch University New England	M
Aquinas College (MI)	M
Argosy University, Chicago	M,D
Argosy University, Dallas	M,D,O
Argosy University, Denver	M,D
Argosy University, Hawai'i	M,D,O
Argosy University, Inland Empire	M,D
Argosy University, Los Angeles	M,D
Argosy University, Northern Virginia	M,D,O
Argosy University, Orange County	M,D,O
Argosy University, Phoenix	M,D
Argosy University, Salt Lake City	M,D
Argosy University, San Francisco Bay Area	M,D
Argosy University, Sarasota	M,D,O
Argosy University, Schaumburg	M,D,O
Argosy University, Seattle	M,D
Argosy University, Tampa	M,D
Argosy University, Twin Cities	M,D
Baldwin Wallace University	M
Bard College	M,O
Baruch College of the City University of New York	M,D
Case Western Reserve University	D
Chatham University	M
City University of Seattle	M,O
Clark University	M
Colorado State University	M
Columbia University	M
DePaul University	M
Dominican University of California	M
Duquesne University	M
Edgewood College	M
Fairleigh Dickinson University, College at Florham	O
Franklin Pierce University	M,D,O
Goddard College	M
Illinois Institute of Technology	M
Indiana University Bloomington	M,D,O
James Madison University	M
Lipscomb University	M,O
Maastricht School of Management	M,D
Maharishi University of Management	M
Michigan Technological University	M,D,O
The New School	M,O
Oklahoma State University	M,D,O

Oregon State University	M,O
Penn State Great Valley	M,O
Presidio Graduate School (CA)	M,O
Rochester Institute of Technology	M,D
San Francisco State University	M
Seattle Pacific University	M
Southern New Hampshire University	M,O
South University (GA)	M
State University of New York College of Environmental Science and Forestry	M,D,O
Syracuse University	O
The University of British Columbia	M,D
University of California, Berkeley	O
University of Colorado Denver	M
University of Louisville	M,D
University of New Hampshire	M,O
University of Portland	M
University of Saint Francis (IN)	M
University of Saskatchewan	M
University of Southern Maine	M
University of South Florida	M,O
University of Wisconsin–Green Bay	M
University of Wisconsin–Stout	M
University of Wisconsin–Superior	M

SUSTAINABLE DEVELOPMENT

Acadia University	M
American University	M,D,O
The American University in Cairo	M,D,O
Antioch University Los Angeles	M
Antioch University New England	M,O
Arizona State University at the Tempe campus	M,D,O
Baruch College of the City University of New York	M
Binghamton University, State University of New York	M
Boston Architectural College	M
Brandeis University	M
California State University, Stanislaus	M
Carnegie Mellon University	M,D
The Catholic University of America	M,O
City College of the City University of New York	M
Clarkson University	M,D
Clark University	M
Clemson University	M,O
Cleveland State University	M,O
Colorado State University	M
Columbia University	M,D
Cornell University	M,D
DePaul University	M
Eastern Illinois University	M
Eastern Michigan University	M,O
Emory University	M
Future Generations Graduate School	M
Hawai'i Pacific University	M
HEC Montreal	O
Hofstra University	M
Hunter College of the City University of New York	M,O
Instituto Centroamericano de Administración de Empresas	M
Instituto Tecnologico de Santo Domingo	M,O
Iowa State University of Science and Technology	M,D
Judson University	M
Lehigh University	M,O
Lenoir-Rhyne University	M
Lesley University	M,D,O
Lipscomb University	M,O
Long Island University–LIU Post	M,O
Minneapolis College of Art and Design	O
Mississippi State University	M,D
Montclair State University	M
New Jersey Institute of Technology	M,D,O
New York School of Interior Design	M
New York University	M
Northern Arizona University	M
Pace University	M,D
Penn State University Park	M
Philadelphia University	M
Pratt Institute	M
Rochester Institute of Technology	M,D
St. Edward's University	M
San Jose State University	M,O
Savannah College of Art and Design	M
Saybrook University	M,D
SIT Graduate Institute	M
Southern Illinois University Edwardsville	M
Southern Methodist University	M,D
Stanford University	M,D,O
State University of New York College of Environmental Science and Forestry	M,D,O
Temple University	M,O
Texas A&M University–Kingsville	D
Texas State University	M
Texas Tech University	M,D
Unity College	M
University of Alaska Fairbanks	M,D
University of Calgary	M,D
University of California, Berkeley	M,O
University of California, Santa Barbara	M,D
University of Colorado Denver	M,D
University of Florida	M,O
University of Georgia	M,D
University of Hawaii at Manoa	M,D,O
University of Maryland, College Park	M
University of Massachusetts Amherst	M
University of Michigan	M,D

University of New Brunswick Fredericton	M
University of North Carolina at Asheville	M,O
University of Notre Dame	M
University of Oklahoma	M,D
University of Southern California	M,D,O
University of South Florida	M,O
The University of Texas at Austin	M
University of Washington	M,D
The University of Western Ontario	M,D
University of Wisconsin–Madison	M
Walden University	M,D,O
West Chester University of Pennsylvania	M,O
Western Illinois University	M,O
Xavier University	M

SYSTEMS BIOLOGY

Albert Einstein College of Medicine	D
George Mason University	M,D,O
The George Washington University	D
Harvard University	D
Massachusetts Institute of Technology	D
Michigan State University	D
Northwestern University	D
Purdue University	D
Rutgers University–New Brunswick	D
Stanford University	D
University of California, Irvine	D
University of California, Merced	M,D
University of California, San Diego	D
University of Chicago	D
University of Cincinnati	D
University of Pittsburgh	D
University of Toronto	M,D
Virginia Commonwealth University	D
Washington University in St. Louis	D
Weill Cornell Medicine	M,D

SYSTEMS ENGINEERING

Air Force Institute of Technology	M,D
Arizona State University at the Tempe campus	M
Auburn University	M,D,O
Boston University	M,D
California Institute of Technology	M,D
California State Polytechnic University, Pomona	M
California State University, Fullerton	M
California State University, Northridge	M
Carleton University	M,D
Carnegie Mellon University	M
Case Western Reserve University	M,D
The Catholic University of America	M,O
The Citadel, The Military College of South Carolina	M,O
Clarkson University	M,O
Colorado State University	M,D
Colorado State University–Pueblo	M
Colorado Technical University Aurora	M
Colorado Technical University Colorado Springs	M
Concordia University (Canada)	M,D,O
Cornell University	M,D
Embry-Riddle Aeronautical University–Daytona	M,D
Embry-Riddle Aeronautical University–Worldwide	M
Florida Institute of Technology	M,D
George Mason University	M,D,O
Georgetown University	M,D
The George Washington University	M,D,O
Georgia Institute of Technology	M
Georgia Southern University	M
Harrisburg University of Science and Technology	M
Indiana University Bloomington	D
Indiana University–Purdue University Fort Wayne	M
Instituto Tecnológico y de Estudios Superiores de Monterrey, Campus Chihuahua	M,O
Instituto Tecnológico y de Estudios Superiores de Monterrey, Campus Monterrey	M,D
Iowa State University of Science and Technology	M
Johns Hopkins University	M,O
Kennesaw State University	M,O
Lehigh University	M
Loyola Marymount University	M
Massachusetts Institute of Technology	M,D
Mississippi State University	M,D
Missouri University of Science and Technology	M,D
Naval Postgraduate School	M,D,O
New Mexico Institute of Mining and Technology	M
New Mexico State University	M,D,O
New York University	M
North Carolina Agricultural and Technical State University	M,D
Northeastern University	M,D,O
Oakland University	M,D,O
The Ohio State University	M,D
Ohio University	M
Old Dominion University	M,D
Oregon State University	M,D
Penn State Great Valley	M,O
Regis University	M
Rensselaer Polytechnic Institute	M,D,O

Rochester Institute of Technology	M,D
Rose-Hulman Institute of Technology	M
Rutgers University–New Brunswick	M,D
Simon Fraser University	M,D
Southern Methodist University	M,D
Stevens Institute of Technology	M,D,O
Stony Brook University, State University of New York	M
Tennessee State University	M,D
Texas A&M University–Kingsville	D
Texas Tech University	M,D
The University of Alabama in Huntsville	M,D
University of Alberta	M,D
The University of Arizona	M,D,O
University of Arkansas at Little Rock	M,D
University of California, Merced	M,D
University of Colorado Colorado Springs	M,D
University of Florida	M,D,O
University of Houston–Clear Lake	M
University of Illinois at Urbana–Champaign	M,D
University of Maryland, Baltimore County	M,O
University of Maryland, College Park	M
University of Massachusetts Dartmouth	M,D
University of Michigan	M,D
University of Michigan–Dearborn	M,D
University of Nebraska at Omaha	M,O
University of New Mexico	M,D
The University of North Carolina at Charlotte	M,D,O
University of Pennsylvania	M,D
University of Regina	M,D
University of St. Thomas (MN)	M,O
University of South Alabama	D
University of Southern California	M,D,O
University of South Florida	O
The University of Texas at Arlington	M
The University of Texas at Dallas	M,D
The University of Texas at El Paso	M,O
The University of Texas Rio Grande Valley	M
University of Utah	M,O
University of Virginia	M,D
University of Waterloo	M,D
University of Wisconsin–Madison	M,D
Virginia Polytechnic Institute and State University	M,D,O
Wayne State University	M,D,O
Worcester Polytechnic Institute	M,O

SYSTEMS SCIENCE

Arizona State University at the Tempe campus	M,D
Binghamton University, State University of New York	M,D
Carleton University	M,D
Claremont Graduate University	M,D,O
Eastern Illinois University	M,O
Fairleigh Dickinson University, Metropolitan Campus	M
Harrisburg University of Science and Technology	M
Hood College	M
Louisiana State University and Agricultural & Mechanical College	M,D
Louisiana State University in Shreveport	M
Miami University	M
New Jersey Institute of Technology	M,D,O
Oakland University	M,D
Portland State University	M,D,O
Rensselaer at Hartford	M
Southern Methodist University	M,D
Stevens Institute of Technology	M,D,O
Strayer University	M
Universidad Autonoma de Guadalajara	M,D
University of Michigan	M,D
University of Ottawa	M,D,O
Worcester Polytechnic Institute	M,D,O

TAXATION

American International College	M,D,O
American University	M,O
Appalachian State University	M
Baruch College of the City University of New York	M
Bentley University	M
Boise State University	M
Bryant University	M,O
California Miramar University	M
California Polytechnic State University, San Luis Obispo	M
California State University, Fullerton	M
California State University, Northridge	M,O
Capital University	M
Chapman University	M,D
Colorado State University	M
DePaul University	M,D
Fairfield University	M,O
Fairleigh Dickinson University, College at Florham	M,O
Fairleigh Dickinson University, Metropolitan Campus	M
Florida Gulf Coast University	M
Florida State University	M,D
Fordham University	M
Georgetown University	M,D
Georgia Southern University	M
Georgia State University	M
Golden Gate University	M,D,O
Goldey-Beacom College	M

Gonzaga University	M
Grand Valley State University	M
HEC Montreal	M,O
Hofstra University	M,O
Illinois Institute of Technology	M,D
Instituto Tecnologico de Santo Domingo	M,O
James Madison University	M
Long Island University–LIU Brooklyn	M,O
Long Island University–LIU Post	M
Metropolitan State University of Denver	M
Michigan State University	M,D
Mississippi State University	M
National Paralegal College	M
New York University	M,D,O
Northeastern University	M
Northern Illinois University	M
Northern Kentucky University	M,O
Northwestern University	M,D
Nova Southeastern University	M
Pace University	M
Philadelphia University	M
Robert Morris University	M
St. John's University (NY)	M
St. Thomas University	M,D
San Jose State University	M
Seton Hall University	O
Southern Illinois University Edwardsville	M
Southern Methodist University	M,D
Southern New Hampshire University	M,O
State University of New York College at Old Westbury	M
Strayer University	M
Suffolk University	M,O
Taft University System	M,D
Temple University	M,D
Texas Christian University	M
Texas Tech University	M,D
Troy University	M,O
Université de Montréal	M,D,O
Université de Sherbrooke	M,O
University at Albany, State University of New York	M
The University of Akron	M
The University of Alabama	M,D
The University of Alabama in Huntsville	M
University of Baltimore	M,D
The University of British Columbia	M,D
University of Cincinnati	M
University of Colorado Denver	M
University of Denver	M
University of Florida	M,D
University of Hartford	M,O
University of Hawaii at Manoa	M
University of Houston	M,D
University of Illinois at Urbana–Champaign	M,D
University of Miami	M,D
University of Michigan	M,D
University of Minnesota, Twin Cities Campus	M
University of Mississippi	M,D
University of Missouri	M,D,O
University of New Haven	M,O
University of New Mexico	M
University of New Orleans	M
University of Notre Dame	M
University of San Diego	M,D,O
University of Southern California	M
University of South Florida	M,D
The University of Texas at Arlington	M,D
University of the Sacred Heart	M
University of Washington	M,D
University of Waterloo	M,D
University of Wisconsin–Madison	M
University of Wisconsin–Milwaukee	M,O
Villanova University	M
Wake Forest University	M
Walsh College of Accountancy and Business Administration	M
Wayne State University	M,D,O
Weber State University	M
Western Michigan University Thomas M. Cooley Law School	M,D
Wichita State University	M
Widener University	M

TECHNICAL COMMUNICATION

Auburn University	M,D,O
Boise State University	M
Bowling Green State University	M,D
Drexel University	M
East Carolina University	M,D,O
Eastern Michigan University	M,O
Eastern Washington University	M
Harvard University	M
Indiana University–Purdue University Indianapolis	M
Lawrence Technological University	M,O
Minnesota State University Mankato	M,O
Missouri Western State University	M,O
Montana Tech of The University of Montana	M
New Jersey Institute of Technology	M,D,O
North Carolina State University	M
Northeastern University	M
Texas State University	M
University of Houston–Downtown	M
University of Nebraska at Omaha	M,O
University of South Florida	O
University of Washington	M,D,O
University of Wisconsin–Stout	M

TECHNICAL WRITING

Carnegie Mellon University	M
Drexel University	M
Illinois Institute of Technology	M,D
James Madison University	M

Johns Hopkins University	M,O
Laurentian University	O
Louisiana Tech University	M,O
Massachusetts Institute of Technology	M
Metropolitan State University	M
Texas Tech University	M,D
The University of Alabama in Huntsville	M,O
University of Arkansas at Little Rock	M
The University of North Carolina at Charlotte	M,O
The University of North Carolina at Greensboro	M,D,O
University of the Sciences	M,O
University of Waterloo	M,D

TECHNOLOGY AND PUBLIC POLICY

Arizona State University at the Tempe campus	M
Carnegie Mellon University	M,D
Eastern Michigan University	M
The George Washington University	M,O
Massachusetts Institute of Technology	M,D
Rensselaer Polytechnic Institute	M,D
Rochester Institute of Technology	M
St. Cloud State University	M
Stony Brook University, State University of New York	D
University of Minnesota, Twin Cities Campus	M
University of South Africa	M,D
The University of Texas at Austin	M

TELECOMMUNICATIONS

Ball State University	M
Boston University	M,O
California Miramar University	M
Claremont Graduate University	M,D,O
Drexel University	M
Fairfield University	M,O
Florida International University	M,D
Franklin Pierce University	M,D,O
The George Washington University	M,D,O
Illinois Institute of Technology	M,D
Instituto Tecnologico de Santo Domingo	M,O
Michigan State University	M
New Jersey Institute of Technology	M,D
Northeastern University	M,D,O
Ohio University	M
Pace University	M,D,O
Rochester Institute of Technology	M
Saint Mary's University of Minnesota	M
Southern Methodist University	M,D
State University of New York Polytechnic Institute	M,D,O
Stevens Institute of Technology	M,D,O
Stratford University (VA)	M
Universidad del Turabo	M
Université du Québec, Institut National de la Recherche Scientifique	M,D
University of Alberta	M,D
University of Arkansas	M,D
University of California, San Diego	M,D
University of Colorado Boulder	M
University of Florida	M
University of Hawaii at Manoa	O
University of Houston	M
University of Louisiana at Lafayette	M
University of Maryland, College Park	M
University of Massachusetts Dartmouth	M,D,O
University of Missouri–Kansas City	M,D,O
The University of North Carolina at Chapel Hill	M,D,O
University of Oklahoma	M
University of Pittsburgh	M,D,O
University of Southern California	M,D,O
The University of Texas at Dallas	M,D

TELECOMMUNICATIONS MANAGEMENT

Alaska Pacific University	M
Boston University	M,O
California Miramar University	M
Capitol Technology University	M
Carnegie Mellon University	M
Concordia University (Canada)	M,D,O
East Carolina University	M,D,O
Instituto Tecnológico y de Estudios Superiores de Monterrey, Campus Ciudad de México	M
Instituto Tecnológico y de Estudios Superiores de Monterrey, Campus Ciudad Obregón	M
Instituto Tecnológico y de Estudios Superiores de Monterrey, Campus Estado de México	M,D
Instituto Tecnológico y de Estudios Superiores de Monterrey, Campus Irapuato	M
Murray State University	M
New York University	M,D,O
Oklahoma State University	M,D,O
San Diego State University	M
Stevens Institute of Technology	M,D,O
Strayer University	M
University of Colorado Boulder	M
University of South Africa	M,D
University of Wisconsin–Stout	M

TERATOLOGY

West Virginia University	M,D

TEXTILE DESIGN

Academy of Art University	M
Arizona State University at the Tempe campus	M,D

California College of the Arts	M
California State University, Los Angeles	M
Concordia University (Canada)	M
Cornell University	M,D
Cranbrook Academy of Art	M
Drexel University	M
East Carolina University	M
Illinois State University	M
LIM College	M
Massachusetts College of Art and Design	M,O
The New School	M
Paris College of Art	M
Philadelphia University	M
Rhode Island School of Design	M
Savannah College of Art and Design	M
School of the Art Institute of Chicago	M,O
Temple University	M
University of California, Davis	M
University of Cincinnati	M
The University of Kansas	M
The University of Manchester	M,D
University of Minnesota, Twin Cities Campus	M,D,O
The University of North Carolina at Greensboro	M,D
University of North Texas	M,D,O
Wayne State University	M

TEXTILE SCIENCES AND ENGINEERING

Cornell University	M,D
North Carolina State University	M,D
Philadelphia University	M,D
The University of Texas at Austin	M

THANATOLOGY

Brooklyn College of the City University of New York	M
The College of New Rochelle	M,O
Marian University (WI)	M
Southwestern College (NM)	M,O
University of Maryland, Baltimore	O
Washington & Jefferson College	M,O

THEATER

Academy of Art University	M
American Conservatory Theater	M,O
Arcadia University	M,D,O
Arizona State University at the Tempe campus	M,D
Baylor University	M
Berklee College of Music	M,O
Binghamton University, State University of New York	M
Bob Jones University	M,D,O
Boston University	M,O
Bowling Green State University	M,D
Brandeis University	M
Brigham Young University	M
Brooklyn College of the City University of New York	M
Brown University	M,D
California Institute of Integral Studies	M,D
California Institute of the Arts	M,O
California State University, Fullerton	M
California State University, Long Beach	M
California State University, Los Angeles	M
California State University, Northridge	M
Carnegie Mellon University	M
Case Western Reserve University	M
The Catholic University of America	M,O
Central Washington University	M
Columbia University	M
Columbus State University	M
Cornell University	D
Dell'Arte International School of Physical Theatre	M
DePaul University	M
Eastern Michigan University	M
Emerson College	M
Florida Atlantic University	M
Florida State University	M,D
Fontbonne University	M
Fordham University	M
The George Washington University	M,O
The Graduate Center, City University of New York	D
Hollins University	M,O
Hunter College of the City University of New York	M
Idaho State University	M
Illinois State University	M
Indiana University Bloomington	M,D
The Juilliard School	M,D,O
Kansas State University	M
Kent State University	M
Long Island University–LIU Post	M
Louisiana State University and Agricultural & Mechanical College	M,D
Louisiana Tech University	M
Mary Baldwin University	M
Miami University	M
Michigan State University	M
Minnesota State University Mankato	M
Missouri State University	M
Montclair State University	M
Naropa University	M
The New School	M
New York University	M,D,O
Northern Illinois University	M
Northern Michigan University	M,O
Northwestern University	M,D
The Ohio State University	M,D
Ohio University	M
Oklahoma State University	M
Pace University	M
Penn State University Park	M

Pensacola Christian College	M,D,O
Point Park University	M
Portland State University	M
Purdue University	M
Regent University	M,D
Roosevelt University	M
Rowan University	M
Rutgers University–New Brunswick	M
San Diego State University	M
San Francisco State University	M
San Jose State University	M,O
Sarah Lawrence College	M
Savannah College of Art and Design	M
Smith College	M
Southern Illinois University Carbondale	M,D
Southern Methodist University	M
Southern Oregon University	M
Stanford University	D
Stony Brook University, State University of New York	M
Temple University	M
Texas A&M University–Commerce	M,D,O
Texas State University	M
Texas Tech University	M
Texas Woman's University	M
Towson University	M
Tufts University	M,D
Tulane University	M
Université de Sherbrooke	M,D
Université Laval	M,D
University at Buffalo, the State University of New York	M,D
The University of Akron	M
The University of Alabama	M
University of Alberta	M
The University of Arizona	M
University of Arkansas	M
The University of British Columbia	M,D
University of Calgary	M
University of California, Berkeley	D
University of California, Davis	M
University of California, Irvine	M,D
University of California, Los Angeles	M,D
University of California, San Diego	M,D
University of California, Santa Barbara	M,D
University of California, Santa Cruz	O
University of Central Florida	M
University of Central Missouri	M,D,O
University of Chicago	M
University of Cincinnati	M
University of Colorado Boulder	M,D
University of Connecticut	M
University of Delaware	M
University of Florida	M
University of Georgia	M,D
University of Guelph	M
University of Hawaii at Manoa	M,D
University of Houston	M
University of Idaho	M
University of Illinois at Urbana–Champaign	M,D
The University of Iowa	M
The University of Kansas	M,D
University of Lethbridge	M,D
University of Louisville	M
The University of Manchester	D
University of Maryland, Baltimore County	M
University of Maryland, College Park	M,D
University of Massachusetts Amherst	M
University of Memphis	M
University of Minnesota, Twin Cities Campus	M,D
University of Missouri	M,D
University of Missouri–Kansas City	M
University of Montana	M
University of Nebraska–Lincoln	M
University of Nevada, Las Vegas	M
University of New Mexico	M
University of New Orleans	M
The University of North Carolina at Chapel Hill	M
The University of North Carolina at Charlotte	M,D,O
The University of North Carolina at Greensboro	M
University of North Carolina School of the Arts	M
University of Oklahoma	M
University of Oregon	M,D
University of Ottawa	M
University of Pittsburgh	M,D
University of Portland	M
University of San Diego	M
University of Saskatchewan	M
University of South Carolina	M
The University of South Dakota	M
University of Southern California	M
University of Southern Mississippi	M
The University of Tennessee	M
The University of Texas at Austin	M,D
The University of Texas Rio Grande Valley	M,O
University of the Cumberlands	M,D,O
University of Toronto	M
University of Victoria	M
University of Virginia	M
University of Washington	M,D
University of Wisconsin–Madison	M
University of Wisconsin–Superior	M
Utah State University	M
Villanova University	M

Virginia Commonwealth University	M
Virginia Polytechnic Institute and State University	M,D,O
Washington University in St. Louis	M
Wayne State University	M
Western Illinois University	M
Yale University	M,D,O
York University	M,D

THEOLOGY

Abilene Christian University	M
Acadia University	M,D
Ambrose University	M,O
American Baptist Seminary of the West	M
American Jewish University	M
Amridge University	M,D
Anabaptist Mennonite Biblical Seminary	M,O
Anderson University (IN)	M,D
Andrews University	M,D,O
Apex School of Theology	M,D
Aquinas Institute of Theology	M,D,O
Arlington Baptist College	M
Asbury Theological Seminary	M,D,O
Ashland Theological Seminary	M,D
Assemblies of God Theological Seminary	M,O
The Athenaeum of Ohio	M,O
Atlantic School of Theology	M,O
Austin Graduate School of Theology	M
Austin Presbyterian Theological Seminary	M,D
Ave Maria University	M,D
Azusa Pacific University	M,D
Bakke Graduate University	M,D
Baptist Bible College	M
The Baptist College of Florida	M
Baptist Missionary Association Theological Seminary	M
Baptist Theological Seminary at Richmond	M,D
Barclay College	M
Barry University	M
Baylor University	M,D
Bethany Theological Seminary	M,O
Bethel College	M
Bethel Seminary	M,D,O
Bethesda University	M
Beth HaMedrash Shaarei Yosher Institute	
Beth Hatalmud Rabbinical College	
Beth Medrash Govoha	
Bethune-Cookman University	M
Bexley Seabury Seminary	M,D,O
Biblical Theological Seminary	M,D,O
Biola University	M,D,O
Bob Jones University	M,D,O
Boston College	M,D,O
Boston University	M,D,O
Briercrest Seminary	M
Brite Divinity School	M,D,O
Bryn Athyn College of the New Church	M
Byzantine Catholic Seminary of Saints Cyril and Methodius	M
Cairn University	M
California Institute of Integral Studies	M,D
California Lutheran University	M,D
Calvary University	M
Calvin Theological Seminary	M,D
Campbellsville University	M
Campbell University	M,D
Canadian Southern Baptist Seminary	M
Carey Theological College	M,D
Carson-Newman University	M
Catholic Distance University	M
Catholic Theological Union	M,D,O
The Catholic University of America	M,D,O
Central Baptist Theological Seminary	M,O
Central Yeshiva Tomchei Tmimim-Lubavitch	M
Chaminade University of Honolulu	M
Charlotte Christian College and Theological Seminary	M
Chicago Theological Seminary	M,D
Christendom College	M
Christian Theological Seminary	M,D
Christ the King Seminary	M
Church Divinity School of the Pacific	M,D,O
Cincinnati Christian University	M
Claremont Graduate University	M,D
Claremont School of Theology	M,D
Clarks Summit University	M,D
Colgate Rochester Crozer Divinity School	M,D,O
Collège Dominicain de Philosophie et de Théologie	M,D,O
College of Emmanuel and St. Chad	M,D,O
College of Saint Elizabeth	M
Columbia International University	M,D,O
Columbia Theological Seminary	M,D
Concordia Lutheran Seminary	M
Concordia Seminary	M,D,O
Concordia Theological Seminary	M,D
Concordia University (Canada)	M
Concordia University Irvine	M
Concordia University of Edmonton	M
Corban University	M
Covenant Theological Seminary	M,D,O
Creighton University	M
Criswell College	M
Crown College	M
Dallas Baptist University	M
Dallas Theological Seminary	M,D,O
Denver Seminary	M

Dominican House of Studies, Pontifical Faculty of the Immaculate Conception	M,D,O
Dominican School of Philosophy and Theology	M,O
Drew University	M,D,O
Duke University	M,D
Duquesne University	M,D
Earlham School of Religion	M
Eastern Mennonite University	M,O
Eastern University	M,D
Ecumenical Theological Seminary	M
Eden Theological Seminary	M,D
Emory University	M,D
Episcopal Divinity School	M,D,O
Erskine Theological Seminary	M,D
Evangelical Seminary	M
Evangelical Seminary of Puerto Rico	M,D
Faith Baptist Bible College and Theological Seminary	M
Faith Evangelical College & Seminary	M,D
Faith Theological Seminary	M
Faulkner University	M
Fordham University	M,D
Franciscan School of Theology	M
Franciscan University of Steubenville	M
Freed-Hardeman University	M,O
Fresno Pacific University	M
Fuller Theological Seminary	M,D,O
Gannon University	M,O
Gardner-Webb University	M,D
Garrett-Evangelical Theological Seminary	M,D
Gateway Seminary	M,D,O
General Theological Seminary	M,D,O
George Fox University	M,D,O
Georgetown University	D
Georgia Christian University	M,D
Georgian Court University	M,O
Global University	M,D
Gonzaga University	M
Gordon-Conwell Theological Seminary	M,D
Graceland University (IA)	M
Grace School of Theology	M
Grace Theological Seminary	M,D,O
Grace University	M
Graduate Theological Union	M,D,O
Grand Rapids Theological Seminary of Cornerstone University	M
Harding School of Theology	M
Hardin-Simmons University	M,D
Hartford Seminary	M,D,O
Harvard University	M
Hebrew College	M
Hebrew Union College–Jewish Institute of Religion (NY)	M,D
Heritage College and Seminary	M,O
Holy Apostles College and Seminary	M,O
Holy Cross Greek Orthodox School of Theology	M
Hood Theological Seminary	M,D
Houston Baptist University	M
Houston Graduate School of Theology	M,D
Howard Payne University	M
Howard University	M,D
Iliff School of Theology	M,D
Indiana Wesleyan University	M
Institute for Christian Studies	M,D
Inter American University of Puerto Rico, Metropolitan Campus	D
Interdenominational Theological Center	M,D
International Baptist College and Seminary	M
The Jewish Theological Seminary	M,D,O
John Carroll University	M
John Paul the Great Catholic University	M
Johnson University	M,D,O
John Wesley University	M,D
Kehilath Yakov Rabbinical Seminary	
Kenrick-Glennon Seminary	M
Kentucky Christian University	M
The King's University	M,D,O
Kingswood University	M
Knox College	M,D
Knox Theological Seminary	M
Lakeland University	M
Lancaster Bible College	M,D,O
Lancaster Theological Seminary	M,D,O
Lee University	M
Lenoir-Rhyne University	M
Lexington Theological Seminary	M,D
Liberty University	M,D,O
Lincoln Christian Seminary	M,D
Lincoln Christian University	M
Lipscomb University	M,D,O
Logos Evangelical Seminary	M,D,O
Loras College	M
Louisiana College	M
Louisville Presbyterian Theological Seminary	M,D
Lourdes University	M
Loyola Marymount University	M
Loyola University Chicago	M,D,O
Loyola University Maryland	M
Loyola University New Orleans	M,O
Lubbock Christian University	M
Lutheran School of Theology at Chicago	M,D
Lutheran Theological Seminary at Gettysburg	M,D
The Lutheran Theological Seminary at Philadelphia	M,D,O
Lutheran Theological Seminary Saskatoon	M,D

Luther Rice College & Seminary	M,D
Luther Seminary	M,D
Machzikei Hadath Rabbinical College	O
Madonna University	M
Malone University	M
Maple Springs Baptist Bible College and Seminary	M,D,O
Maranatha Baptist University	M
Marquette University	M,D
Marylhurst University	M
The Master's University	M,D
McCormick Theological Seminary	M,D,O
McGill University	M,D
McMaster University	M,D,O
Meadville Lombard Theological School	M
Memphis Theological Seminary	M,D
Mercer University	M,D
Mesivta of Eastern Parkway–Yeshiva Zichron Meilech	
Mesivta Torah Vodaath Rabbinical Seminary	
Mesivtha Tifereth Jerusalem of America	
Methodist Theological School in Ohio	M,D
Mid-America Baptist Theological Seminary	M,D
Mid-America Baptist Theological Seminary Northeast Branch	M
Mid-America Reformed Seminary	M
Midwestern Baptist Theological Seminary	M,D,O
Milligan College	M,D,O
Mirrer Yeshiva	
Moody Bible Institute	M,O
Moody Theological Seminary—Michigan	M,O
Moravian Theological Seminary	M,O
Mount Angel Seminary	M
Mount St. Joseph University	M,O
Mount St. Mary's University (MD)	M
Mount Vernon Nazarene University	M
Multnomah University	M,D
Naropa University	M
Nashotah House Theological Seminary	M,D,O
Nazarene Theological Seminary	M,D
Ner Israel Rabbinical College	M,D,O
Ner Israel Yeshiva College of Toronto	
New Brunswick Theological Seminary	M,D
Newman Theological College	M
Newman University	M
New Orleans Baptist Theological Seminary	M,D
New Saint Andrews College	M,O
New York Theological Seminary	M,D
Northeastern Seminary at Roberts Wesleyan College	M,D
Northern Seminary	M,D
North Park Theological Seminary	M,D
Northwest Nazarene University	M
Northwest University	M
Notre Dame Seminary	M
Nyack College	M,D
Oakland City University	M,D
Oblate School of Theology	M,D,O
Ohio Christian University	M
Ohio Dominican University	M
Ohr Hameir Theological Seminary	
Oklahoma Christian University	M
Oklahoma Wesleyan University	M
Olivet Nazarene University	M
Oral Roberts University	M,D
Pacific School of Religion	M,D,O
Palm Beach Atlantic University	M
Payne Theological Seminary	M
Pentecostal Theological Seminary	M,D
Pfeiffer University	M
Phillips Theological Seminary	M,D
Phoenix Seminary	M,D,O
Piedmont International University	M,D
Pittsburgh Theological Seminary	M,D
Point Loma Nazarene University	M
Pontifical Catholic University of Puerto Rico	M
Pontifical College Josephinum	M
Pontifical John Paul II Institute for Studies on Marriage and Family	M,D,O
Pope St. John XXIII National Seminary	M
Princeton Theological Seminary	M,D
Providence College	M
Providence University College & Theological Seminary	M,D,O
Queen's University at Kingston	M,O
Rabbinical Academy Mesivta Rabbi Chaim Berlin	O
Rabbinical College Beth Shraga	
Rabbinical College Bobover Yeshiva B'nei Zion	
Rabbinical College of Long Island	
Rabbinical Seminary of America	
Reconstructionist Rabbinical College	M,D,O
Reformed Episcopal Seminary	M
Reformed Presbyterian Theological Seminary	M
Reformed Theological Seminary–Atlanta Campus	M,D,O
Reformed Theological Seminary–Charlotte Campus	M,D
Reformed Theological Seminary–Jackson Campus	M,D,O
Reformed Theological Seminary–Orlando Campus	M,D,O

M—masters degree; D—doctorate; O—other advanced degree; *—Close-Up and/or Display

Reformed Theological Seminary–Washington D.C.	M,O
Regent College	M
Regent University	M,D,O
Regis College (Canada)	M,D,O
Sacred Heart Major Seminary	M
Sacred Heart School of Theology	M,O
St. Andrew's College	M,D,O
St. Andrew's College in Winnipeg	M
St. Augustine's Seminary of Toronto	M,O
St. Bernard's School of Theology and Ministry	M,O
St. Catherine University	M,O
Saint Charles Borromeo Seminary, Overbrook	
St. John's Seminary (CA)	M
Saint John's Seminary (MA)	M
Saint John's University (MN)	M
St. John's University (NY)	M,O
St. Joseph's Seminary	M
Saint Leo University	M,O
Saint Louis University	M,D
Saint Mary Seminary and Graduate School of Theology	M,D
St. Mary's Seminary and University	M,D,O
Saint Mary's University (Canada)	M
St. Mary's University (United States)	M
Saint Meinrad School of Theology	M
St. Norbert College	M
St. Patrick's Seminary & University	M,O
Saint Paul School of Theology	M,D
Saint Paul University	M,D,O
St. Peter's Seminary	M
Saints Cyril and Methodius Seminary	M
St. Stephen's College	M
St. Thomas University	M,D,O
St. Tikhon's Orthodox Theological Seminary	M
St. Vincent de Paul Regional Seminary	M
Saint Vincent Seminary	M
St. Vladimir's Orthodox Theological Seminary	M,D
Samford University	M,D
San Francisco Theological Seminary	M,D
Santa Clara University	M,D,O
Seattle Pacific University	M,O
The Seattle School of Theology and Psychology	M
Seattle University	M,D,O
Seminary of the Southwest	M,O
Seton Hall University	M,O
Sewanee: The University of the South	M
Shaw University	M
Shepherds Theological Seminary	M
Shepherd University (CA)	M,D
Shiloh University	M,D
Sh'or Yoshuv Rabbinical College	
Sioux Falls Seminary	M,D,O
Southeastern Baptist Theological Seminary	M,D
Southeastern University (FL)	M,D
Southern Adventist University	M
The Southern Baptist Theological Seminary	M,D
Southern California Seminary	M,D
Southern Evangelical Seminary	M,D,O
Southern Methodist University	M,D
South Florida Bible College and Theological Seminary	M
Southwestern Assemblies of God University	M
Southwestern Baptist Theological Seminary	M,D
Spring Arbor University	M
Spring Hill College	M,O
Starr King School for the Ministry	M
SUM Bible College & Theological Seminary	M
Talmudic University	M
Taylor College and Seminary	M,O
Toronto School of Theology	M,D
Trinity Bible College and Graduate School	M
Trinity College (Canada)	M,D,O
Trinity International University	M,D,O
Trinity Lutheran Seminary	M
Trinity School for Ministry	M,D,O
Trinity Western University	M
Tri-State Bible College	M
Truett McConnell University	M
Tyndale University College & Seminary	M,O
Unification Theological Seminary	M,D
Union Theological Seminary in the City of New York	M,D
United Talmudical Seminary	
United Theological Seminary	M,D
United Theological Seminary of the Twin Cities	M,D,O
Université de Montréal	M,D,O
Université de Sherbrooke	M,D,O
Université du Québec à Chicoutimi	M,D
Université Laval	M,D
University of Chicago	D
University of Dallas	M
University of Dayton	M,D
University of Dubuque	M
The University of Manchester	D
University of Northwestern–St. Paul	M
University of Notre Dame	M,D
University of Philosophical Research	M

University of Saint Mary of the Lake–Mundelein Seminary	M,D
University of St. Michael's College	M,D,O
University of St. Thomas (MN)	M
University of St. Thomas (TX)	M
The University of Scranton	M
University of South Africa	M,D
University of the West	M
University of Valley Forge	M
The University of Winnipeg	M
Urshan Graduate School of Theology	M
Ursuline College	M
Valparaiso University	M,O
Vancouver School of Theology	M,O
Vanderbilt University	M
Vanguard University of Southern California	M
Victoria University	M,D,O
Villanova University	M,D
Virginia Baptist College	M
Virginia Beach Theological Seminary	M
Virginia Theological Seminary	M,D
Virginia Union University	M,D
Walsh University	M
Wartburg Theological Seminary	M
Wayland Baptist University	M
Wesley Biblical Seminary	M
Wesley Theological Seminary	M,D
Western Seminary	M,O
Western Seminary–Sacramento Campus	M,O
Western Seminary–San Jose Campus	M,O
Western Theological Seminary	M,D,O
Westminster Seminary California	M
Westminster Theological Seminary	M,D
Wheaton College	M,D
Whitworth University	M
Wilfrid Laurier University	M,D,O
Winebrenner Theological Seminary	M
Wycliffe College	M,D,O
Xavier University	M
Xavier University of Louisiana	M
Yale University	M
Yeshiva Beth Moshe	O
Yeshiva Karlin Stolin Rabbinical Institute	O
Yeshiva of Nitra Rabbinical College	
Yeshiva Shaar Hatorah Talmudic Research Institute	
Yeshivath Zichron Moshe	O

THEORETICAL CHEMISTRY

Carnegie Mellon University	D
Cornell University	D
Georgetown University	D
Laurentian University	M
University of Calgary	M,D
The University of Manchester	M,D
University of Regina	M,D
The University of Tennessee	M,D
Vanderbilt University	M,D
Wesleyan University	D
West Virginia University	M,D
Yale University	D

THEORETICAL PHYSICS

American University of Beirut	M,D
Cornell University	M,D
Delaware State University	D
Emory University	D
Harvard University	D
Rutgers University–New Brunswick	M,D
The University of Manchester	M,D
University of Victoria	M,D
West Virginia University	M,D

THERAPIES—DANCE, DRAMA, AND MUSIC

Antioch University New England	M,O
Antioch University Seattle	M
Appalachian State University	M
Arizona State University at the Tempe campus	M,D
Berklee College of Music	M
California Institute of Integral Studies	M,D
Colorado State University	M
Columbia College Chicago	M,O
Concordia University (Canada)	M
Drexel University	M,O
East Carolina University	M
Florida State University	M,D
Georgia College & State University	M
Immaculata University	M,D
Indiana University–Purdue University Indianapolis	M,D
Lesley University	M,D,O
Loyola University New Orleans	M
Maryville University of Saint Louis	M
Michigan State University	M,D
Molloy College	M
Montclair State University	M,O
Naropa University	M
Nazareth College of Rochester	M
New York University	M,O
Ohio University	M,O
Pratt Institute	M
Saint Mary-of-the-Woods College	M
Shenandoah University	M,D,O
Slippery Rock University of Pennsylvania	M
State University of New York at New Paltz	M,D
Temple University	M,D
The University of Kansas	M,D
University of Kentucky	M,D
University of Miami	M,D,O
University of Missouri–Kansas City	M,D

University of the Pacific	M
Western Michigan University	M,O
Wilfrid Laurier University	M

TOXICOLOGY

Colorado State University	M,D
Columbia University	M,D
Cornell University	M,D
Duke University	O
Florida Agricultural and Mechanical University	M,D
The George Washington University	M,O
Indiana University Bloomington	M,D,O
Indiana University–Purdue University Indianapolis	M,D
Iowa State University of Science and Technology	M,D
Long Island University–LIU Brooklyn	M,D
Louisiana State University and Agricultural & Mechanical College	M,D
Massachusetts Institute of Technology	M,D
Medical College of Wisconsin	D
Medical University of South Carolina	D
Michigan State University	M,D
New York University	M,D
North Carolina State University	M,D
Oklahoma State University Center for Health Sciences	M
Oregon State University	M,D
Purdue University	M,D
Queen's University at Kingston	M,D
Rutgers University–New Brunswick	M,D
St. John's University (NY)	M
San Diego State University	M,D
Simon Fraser University	M,D,O
Texas Southern University	M,D
Texas Tech University	M,D
Thomas Jefferson University	M
Université de Montréal	O
University at Albany, State University of New York	M,D
University at Buffalo, the State University of New York	M,D
The University of Alabama at Birmingham	M,D
University of Arkansas for Medical Sciences	M,D,O
University of California, Davis	M,D
University of California, Irvine	M,D
University of California, Los Angeles	D
University of California, Riverside	M,D
University of California, Santa Cruz	M,D
University of Colorado Denver	D
University of Connecticut	M,D
University of Florida	M,D,O
University of Guelph	M,D
University of Illinois at Chicago	M
The University of Iowa	M,D
The University of Kansas	M,D
University of Kentucky	M,D
University of Louisiana at Monroe	D
University of Louisville	M,D
The University of Manchester	M,D
University of Maryland, Baltimore	M,D
University of Maryland Eastern Shore	M,D
University of Michigan	M,D
University of Minnesota, Duluth	M,D
University of Minnesota, Twin Cities Campus	M,D
University of Mississippi Medical Center	D
University of Montana	M,D
University of Nebraska–Lincoln	M,D
University of Nebraska Medical Center	D
University of New Mexico	M,D
The University of North Carolina at Chapel Hill	M,D
University of Prince Edward Island	M,D
University of Puerto Rico, Medical Sciences Campus	M,D
University of Rhode Island	M,D
University of Rochester	D
University of Saskatchewan	M,D,O
University of South Alabama	M
University of Southern California	M,D
The University of Texas at Austin	M,D
The University of Texas Health Science Center at San Antonio	M
The University of Texas Medical Branch	M,D
University of the Sciences	M,D
University of Utah	D
University of Washington	M,D
University of Wisconsin–Madison	M,D
Utah State University	M,D
Virginia Commonwealth University	M,D,O
Wayne State University	M,D
West Virginia University	M,D
Wright State University	M

TRANSCULTURAL NURSING

Augsburg College	M,D
Rutgers University–Newark	M,D,O

TRANSLATIONAL BIOLOGY

Baylor College of Medicine	D
Cedars-Sinai Medical Center	M
Rutgers University–New Brunswick	M
University of California, Irvine	M
The University of Iowa	M
University of Massachusetts Medical School	M,D

The University of Texas at San Antonio	D
The University of Texas Medical Branch	M,D

TRANSLATION AND INTERPRETATION

American University of Sharjah	M
Arizona State University at the Tempe campus	M,D,O
Babel University Professional School of Translation	M
Binghamton University, State University of New York	D,O
Columbia University	M,D
Concordia University (Canada)	M,O
Gallaudet University	M,D,O
Georgia State University	O
Kent State University	M,D
La Salle University	M
London Metropolitan University	M,D
Marygrove College	O
Middlebury Institute of International Studies at Monterey	M
Mills College	M,O
Montclair State University	O
New York University	M
Rochester Institute of Technology	M
Rutgers University–New Brunswick	M,D
Texas A&M International University	M,D
Universidad Autonoma de Guadalajara	M,D
Université de Montréal	M,D,O
Université Laval	M,D
University of California, Santa Barbara	M
University of Delaware	M
University of Denver	M,O
University of Illinois at Urbana–Champaign	M
The University of Manchester	M,D
The University of North Carolina at Charlotte	M,O
University of North Florida	M
University of Ottawa	M,D
University of Puerto Rico, Río Piedras Campus	M,O
University of Rochester	M,O
University of Wisconsin–Milwaukee	M,O
Wesley Biblical Seminary	M
York University	M

TRANSPERSONAL AND HUMANISTIC PSYCHOLOGY

Atlantic University	M
California Institute of Integral Studies	M,D
John F. Kennedy University	M
Michigan School of Professional Psychology	M,D
Saybrook University	M,D
Seattle University	M
Sofia University	M,D

TRANSPORTATION AND HIGHWAY ENGINEERING

Arizona State University at the Tempe campus	M,D,O
ArtCenter College of Design	M
The Catholic University of America	M,D,O
The Citadel, The Military College of South Carolina	M,O
College for Creative Studies	M
Cornell University	M,D
École Polytechnique de Montréal	M,D,O
George Mason University	M,D
Illinois Institute of Technology	M,D
Iowa State University of Science and Technology	M,D
Kansas State University	M,D
Louisiana State University and Agricultural & Mechanical College	M
Marquette University	M,D,O
Marshall University	M
Massachusetts Institute of Technology	M,D,O
Morgan State University	M
New Jersey Institute of Technology	M,D
New York University	M
North Dakota State University	D
Northwestern University	M,D
Ohio University	M,D
Old Dominion University	M
Oregon State University	M,D
Rensselaer Polytechnic Institute	M,D
South Carolina State University	M
Southern Illinois University Edwardsville	M
Stevens Institute of Technology	M,D,O
Texas Southern University	M
University of Arkansas	M,D
University of Calgary	M,D
University of California, Berkeley	M,D
University of California, Davis	M,D
University of California, Irvine	M,D
University of Central Florida	M,D,O
University of Colorado Denver	M,D
University of Dayton	M
University of Delaware	M,D
University of Massachusetts Amherst	M,D
University of Memphis	M,D,O
University of Missouri	M,D
University of Nevada, Las Vegas	M,D
University of New Brunswick Fredericton	M,D
University of Puerto Rico, Mayagüez Campus	M
University of Southern California	M,D,O
University of South Florida	M,D,O
The University of Texas at Tyler	M
University of Washington	M,D

Virginia Polytechnic Institute and State University — M,O
Wentworth Institute of Technology — M

TRANSPORTATION MANAGEMENT
American Public University System — M
California State University Maritime Academy
Florida Institute of Technology — M,D
George Mason University — M,O
Instituto Tecnologico de Santo Domingo — M,O
Iowa State University of Science and Technology — M
Maine Maritime Academy — M
McGill University — M,D
Morgan State University — M
Naval Postgraduate School — M
New Jersey Institute of Technology — M,D
New York University — M
North Dakota State University — M,D
Pontifical Catholic University of Puerto Rico — O
San Jose State University — M
State University of New York Maritime College — M
Temple University — M,O
Texas A&M University — M
Texas Southern University — M
The University of British Columbia — D
University of California, Davis — M,D
University of California, Santa Barbara — M,D
University of Hawaii at Manoa — M,D,O
University of New Orleans — M
The University of Tennessee — M,D
University of Washington — O

TRAVEL AND TOURISM
Arizona State University at the Tempe campus — M,D,O
Boston University — M
California State University, Chico — M
California State University, East Bay — M
California State University, Fullerton — M
California State University, Northridge — M
Clemson University — M,D,O
Colorado State University — M,D
The George Washington University — M,O
IGlobal University — M
Indiana University Bloomington — M,D
Kent State University — M
Lasell College — M,O
Liberty University — M,D,O
New Mexico State University — M
New York University — M,O
North Carolina State University — M,D
Penn State University Park — M,D
Pontificia Universidad Catolica Madre y Maestra — M
Purdue University — M,D
Rochester Institute of Technology — M
Royal Roads University — M,O
San Francisco State University — M
Savannah College of Art and Design — M
Schiller International University (United States) — M
Strayer University — M
Syracuse University — M
Temple University — M,D
Tropical Agriculture Research and Higher Education Center — M,D
Université du Québec à Trois-Rivières — M,O
University of Central Florida — M,D,O
University of Florida — M,D
University of Hawaii at Manoa — M
University of Massachusetts Amherst — M,D
University of Minnesota, Twin Cities Campus — M,D
University of New Orleans — M
University of North Texas — M,D,O
University of South Africa — M,D
University of South Carolina — M
University of South Florida — M,O
The University of Tennessee — M
Virginia Polytechnic Institute and State University — M,D
Western Illinois University — M

URBAN AND REGIONAL PLANNING
Alabama Agricultural and Mechanical University — M
American University of Beirut — M,D
American University of Sharjah — M
Andrews University — M
Arizona State University at the Tempe campus — M,D,O
Auburn University — M
Ball State University — M,O
Boston University — M
California Polytechnic State University, San Luis Obispo — M
California State Polytechnic University, Pomona — M
The Catholic University of America — M,O
Clark University — M
Clemson University — M
Cleveland State University — M,O
College of Charleston — O
Columbia University — M,D
Concordia University (Canada) — O
Cornell University — M
Dalhousie University — M
Delta State University — M
East Carolina University — M,O
Eastern Kentucky University — M
Eastern Michigan University — M,O

Eastern University — M
Eastern Washington University — M
Florida Atlantic University — M
Florida State University — M,D
Future Generations Graduate School — M
Georgetown University — M,D
Georgia Institute of Technology — M,D
Georgia State University — M,D,O
Harvard University — M,D
Hunter College of the City University of New York — M
Indiana University of Pennsylvania — M
Iowa State University of Science and Technology — M
Jackson State University — M,D
Kansas State University — M
Lesley University — M,D,O
Massachusetts Institute of Technology — M,D
McGill University — M,D
Michigan State University — M,D
Minnesota State University Mankato — M,O
Missouri State University — M
Morgan State University — M
New York University — M
North Dakota State University — M
Northern Arizona University — M,O
Northwest University — M
The Ohio State University — M,D
Penn State University Park — M,D,O
Philadelphia University — M
Portland State University — M
Pratt Institute — M
Queen's University at Kingston — M
Rutgers University–New Brunswick — M,D
St. Francis Xavier University — M
San Diego State University — M
Savannah State University — M
Southeastern University (FL) — M
State University of New York College of Environmental Science and Forestry — M,D
Syracuse University — O
Temple University — M,O
Texas A&M University — M,D
Texas Southern University — M
Thomas Edison State University — M
Tufts University — M
Université de Montréal — M,D,O
Université du Québec à Rimouski — M,D,O
Université du Québec en Outaouais — M
Université Laval — M,D
University at Albany, State University of New York — M
University at Buffalo, the State University of New York — M,D,O
The University of Arizona — M
The University of British Columbia — M,D
University of California, Berkeley — M,D
University of California, Davis — M
University of California, Irvine — M,D
University of California, Los Angeles — M,D
University of Central Arkansas — M,O
University of Central Florida — M,O
University of Cincinnati — M
University of Colorado Denver — M,D
University of Detroit Mercy — M
University of Florida — M,D
University of Hawaii at Manoa — M,D,O
University of Idaho — M
University of Illinois at Chicago — M,D
University of Illinois at Urbana–Champaign — M,D
The University of Iowa — M
The University of Kansas — M,D
University of Louisville — M
University of Manitoba — M
University of Maryland, College Park — M,D
University of Massachusetts Amherst — M,D
University of Massachusetts Boston — M,D
University of Massachusetts Lowell — M,O
University of Memphis — M
University of Michigan — D,O
University of Minnesota, Twin Cities Campus — M,D
University of Nebraska–Lincoln — M,D
University of New Brunswick Fredericton — M
University of New Haven — M,O
University of New Mexico — M
University of New Orleans — M
The University of North Carolina at Chapel Hill — M,D
The University of North Carolina at Charlotte — M,O
University of Oklahoma — M
University of Oregon — M
University of Pennsylvania — M,D,O
University of Pittsburgh — M
University of Puerto Rico, Río Piedras Campus — M
University of Southern California — M,D,O
University of Southern Maine — M,O
University of South Florida — M,D,O
The University of Texas at Arlington — D
The University of Texas at Austin — M,D
The University of Texas at San Antonio — M
The University of Toledo — M,D,O
University of Toronto — M,D
University of Utah — M,D
University of Virginia — M

University of Washington — M,D
University of Waterloo — M,D
University of West Georgia — M,D,O
University of Wisconsin–Madison — M,D
University of Wisconsin–Milwaukee — M
Utah State University — M,D
Vanderbilt University — M
Virginia Commonwealth University — M
Virginia Polytechnic Institute and State University — M,D,O
Wayne State University — M,O
West Chester University of Pennsylvania — M,O
West Virginia University — M,D

URBAN DESIGN
American University of Beirut — M,D
Arizona State University at the Tempe campus — M,D
Ball State University — M
Carnegie Mellon University — M,D
City College of the City University of New York — M
Cornell University — M,D
DePaul University — M
Georgia Institute of Technology — M,D
Harvard University — M
Hofstra University — M
Judson University — M
Kent State University — M
Lawrence Technological University — M,O
London Metropolitan University — M,D
The New School — M
New York Institute of Technology — M
Pratt Institute — M
Rice University — M
Savannah College of Art and Design — M
State University of New York College of Environmental Science and Forestry — M
University at Buffalo, the State University of New York — M,D,O
The University of British Columbia — M
University of California, Berkeley — M,D
University of California, Los Angeles — M,D
University of Colorado Denver — M,D
The University of Kansas — M,D,O
University of Miami — M
University of Michigan — M
The University of North Carolina at Charlotte — M
University of Pennsylvania — M,D,O
University of South Florida — M
The University of Texas at Austin — M
University of Toronto — M,D
University of Utah — M,D
University of Washington — M,D,O
Washington University in St. Louis — M

URBAN EDUCATION
Alvernia University — M
Bakke Graduate University — M,D
Brown University — M
Cardinal Stritch University — M,D
Cheyney University of Pennsylvania — M
Claremont Graduate University — M,D,O
Cleveland State University — D
College of Mount Saint Vincent — M,O
Eastern Michigan University — M,O
Florida International University — M,D,O
Georgia State University — M,D,O
The Graduate Center, City University of New York — D
Grand View University — M,O
Holy Names University — M,O
Johns Hopkins University — O
Langston University — M
Long Island University–LIU Brooklyn — M,O
Loyola Marymount University — M
Manhattanville College — M,O
Marygrove College — M
Morgan State University — D
New Jersey City University — M
Norfolk State University — M
Northeastern Illinois University — M
Providence College — M
Teachers College, Columbia University — M,D
Temple University — M
University of Chicago — M
University of Houston–Downtown — M
University of Illinois at Chicago — M,D
University of Massachusetts Boston — D
University of Memphis — M,D,O
University of Michigan–Dearborn — M,D
University of Nebraska at Omaha — M,O
University of Pennsylvania — M
University of San Francisco — M
University of Southern California — M
University of Wisconsin–Milwaukee — M,D,O
Vanderbilt University — M
Virginia Commonwealth University — D

URBAN STUDIES
Arizona State University at the Tempe campus — M,D,O
Azusa Pacific University — M
Boston University — M
Brooklyn College of the City University of New York — M
Cleveland State University — M,D,O
Columbus State University — M
Concordia University (Canada) — M,D,O
Eastern University — M
Fordham University — M
Fresno Pacific University — M

The Graduate Center, City University of New York — M,D
Hunter College of the City University of New York — M
Indiana University Northwest — M,O
Le Moyne College — M,O
Long Island University–LIU Brooklyn — M,D,O
Loyola University Chicago — M
Massachusetts Institute of Technology — M,D
Minnesota State University Mankato — M,O
Moody Bible Institute — M,O
New Jersey City University — M
New Jersey Institute of Technology — M
The New School — M
New York University — M
Norfolk State University — M
North Dakota State University — M,D
Northeastern University — M,D
Old Dominion University — D
Portland State University — M,D
Queens College of the City University of New York — M
Rutgers University–Newark — M,D
Saint Louis University — M,D,O
Savannah State University — M
Simon Fraser University — M,O
Temple University — M,D,O
Tufts University — M
Université du Québec à Montréal — M,D
Université du Québec, École nationale d'administration publique — M
Université du Québec, Institut National de la Recherche Scientifique — M,D,O
University at Albany, State University of New York — M,D,O
University of California, Irvine — M,D
University of Delaware — M,D
University of Lethbridge — M,D
University of Louisville — M,D
University of Maryland, Baltimore County — M,D
University of New Orleans — M,D
University of San Francisco — M
Virginia Polytechnic Institute and State University — M,D,O
Wayne State University — M,D
Wright State University — M

VETERINARY MEDICINE
Auburn University — D
Colorado State University — D
Cornell University — D
Iowa State University of Science and Technology — M
Kansas State University — D
Louisiana State University and Agricultural & Mechanical College — D
Michigan State University — D
Mississippi State University — D
North Carolina State University — M,D
Oklahoma State University — D
Oregon State University — D
Purdue University — D
Texas A&M University — M,D
Tufts University — M,D
Tuskegee University — M,D
Université de Montréal — D
University of California, Davis — D
University of Florida — D
University of Georgia — M,D
University of Guelph — M,D,O
University of Illinois at Urbana–Champaign — D
University of Maryland, College Park — D
University of Minnesota, Twin Cities Campus — D
University of Missouri — M,D
University of Pennsylvania — D
University of Prince Edward Island — D
University of Saskatchewan — M,D
The University of Tennessee — D
University of Wisconsin–Madison — M,D
Virginia Polytechnic Institute and State University — M,D
Washington State University — D
Western University of Health Sciences — D

VETERINARY SCIENCES
Colorado State University — M,D
Drexel University — M
Iowa State University of Science and Technology — M,D
Kansas State University — M,O
Louisiana State University and Agricultural & Mechanical College — M,D
Michigan State University — M,D
Mississippi State University — M,D
North Carolina State University — M,D
The Ohio State University — M,D
Oklahoma State University — M,D
Penn State Hershey Medical Center — M
Purdue University — M,D
South Dakota State University — M,D
Texas A&M University — M,D
Tuskegee University — M,D
Université de Montréal — M,D
University of California, Davis — M,O
University of Florida — M,D,O
University of Guelph — M,D,O
University of Idaho — M,D
University of Illinois at Urbana–Champaign — M,D
University of Kentucky — M,D

M—masters degree; D—doctorate; O—other advanced degree; *—Close-Up and/or Display

University of Maryland, College Park	M,D
University of Minnesota, Twin Cities Campus	M,D
University of Missouri	M
University of Nebraska–Lincoln	M,D
University of Prince Edward Island	M,D
University of Saskatchewan	M,D
University of Washington	M
University of Wisconsin–Madison	M,D
Utah State University	M,D
Virginia Polytechnic Institute and State University	M,D
Washington State University	M,D

VIROLOGY

Baylor College of Medicine	D
Case Western Reserve University	D
Mayo Clinic Graduate School of Biomedical Sciences	D
McMaster University	M,D
Oregon State University	M,D
Penn State Hershey Medical Center	M,D
Purdue University	M,D
Rush University	M,D
Rutgers University–New Brunswick	M,D
Université de Montréal	D
Université du Québec, Institut National de la Recherche Scientifique	M,D
The University of Iowa	M,D
University of Minnesota, Twin Cities Campus	D
University of Pennsylvania	D
University of Pittsburgh	D
University of Prince Edward Island	M,D
Yale University	D

VISION SCIENCES

Eastern Virginia Medical School	O
Marshall B. Ketchum University	M,D
New England College of Optometry	M,D
Pacific University	M,D
Salus University	M,O
State University of New York College of Optometry	D
Université de Montréal	M,O
The University of Alabama at Birmingham	M,D
University of Alberta	M,D
University of California, Berkeley	M,D
University of Guelph	M,D,O
University of Houston	M,D
The University of Manchester	M,D
University of Massachusetts Boston	M
University of Nebraska Medical Center	M,D
University of Pittsburgh	M,D
University of Waterloo	M,D

VITICULTURE AND ENOLOGY

California State University, Fresno	M
University of California, Davis	M,D

VOCATIONAL AND TECHNICAL EDUCATION

Alcorn State University	M,O
Appalachian State University	M
Bowling Green State University	M
Buffalo State College, State University of New York	M
California Baptist University	M
California University of Pennsylvania	M
Capella University	D
Central Connecticut State University	M
Central Washington University	M
Chicago State University	M
Clarion University of Pennsylvania	M
Clarkson University	M
Concordia University (United States)	M,D
East Carolina University	M
Eastern Kentucky University	M
Eastern New Mexico University	M
Fitchburg State University	M
Florida Agricultural and Mechanical University	M
The George Washington University	O
Idaho State University	M
Indiana State University	M
Indiana University of Pennsylvania	M
Inter American University of Puerto Rico, Metropolitan Campus	M
Iowa State University of Science and Technology	M,D
Jackson State University	M,D
James Madison University	M
Kent State University	M
Louisiana State University and Agricultural & Mechanical College	M,D
Marshall University	M
Middle Tennessee State University	M
Millersville University of Pennsylvania	M
Mississippi State University	M,D,O
Montana State University	M,D,O
Morehead State University	M
Murray State University	M
North Carolina Agricultural and Technical State University	M
North Dakota State University	M,D,O
Northern Arizona University	M,O
Old Dominion University	M
Penn State University Park	M,D,O
Pittsburg State University	M,O
Purdue University	M,D,O
South Carolina State University	M
Southern Illinois University Carbondale	M,D

State University of New York at Oswego	M
Temple University	M
Texas State University	M
University of Arkansas	M,D,O
The University of British Columbia	M,D
University of Central Florida	M,D,O
University of Central Missouri	M,D,O
University of Georgia	M,D
University of Idaho	M,O
University of Maryland Eastern Shore	M
University of Minnesota, Twin Cities Campus	M,D
University of Missouri	M,D,O
University of Nebraska–Lincoln	M,D,O
University of New England	M,D,O
University of Northern Iowa	M,D
University of North Texas	M,D,O
University of Phoenix–Phoenix Campus	M
University of South Africa	M,D
University of South Florida	M,D,O
The University of Toledo	M,D,O
University of Victoria	M,D
University of Wisconsin–Stout	M,D,O
Utah State University	M
Valley City State University	M
Virginia Polytechnic Institute and State University	M,D,O
Washington State University	M,D
Wayne State College	M
Wayne State University	M,D,O
Western Michigan University	M
Westfield State University	M
Wilmington University	M,D

WATER RESOURCES

Albany State University	M
California State University, Monterey Bay	M
Colorado State University	M,D
Cornell University	M,D
Dalhousie University	M
Eastern Michigan University	M
Humboldt State University	M
Marquette University	M,D,O
Michigan Technological University	M,D,O
Missouri University of Science and Technology	M,D
Montclair State University	O
New Mexico State University	M,D
Old Dominion University	M
Oregon State University	M,D
Rutgers University–New Brunswick	M,D
State University of New York College of Environmental Science and Forestry	M,D
Tropical Agriculture Research and Higher Education Center	M,D
The University of Arizona	M,D,O
University of Calgary	M,D
University of California, Riverside	M,D
University of Colorado Denver	M
University of Florida	M,D
University of Idaho	M,D
University of Maine	M,D
University of Massachusetts Amherst	M,D
University of Minnesota, Twin Cities Campus	M,D
University of Missouri	M,D,O
University of Nevada, Las Vegas	M
University of New Brunswick Fredericton	M,D
University of New Hampshire	M,D
University of New Mexico	M
University of Southern California	M,D,O
University of the District of Columbia	M
University of the Pacific	M,D
University of Wisconsin–Madison	M,D
University of Wisconsin–Milwaukee	M,D
University of Wyoming	M,D
Utah State University	M,D

WATER RESOURCES ENGINEERING

American University of Beirut	M,D
Carnegie Mellon University	M,D
Cornell University	M,D
Indiana University Bloomington	M,D,O
Kansas State University	M,D
Lawrence Technological University	M,D
Louisiana State University and Agricultural & Mechanical College	M,D
Marquette University	M,D,O
McGill University	M,D
New Mexico Institute of Mining and Technology	M
Ohio University	M,D
Oregon State University	M,D
Southern Methodist University	M,D
State University of New York College of Environmental Science and Forestry	M,D
Stevens Institute of Technology	M,D,O
Tufts University	M,D
University of Alberta	M,D
University of California, Berkeley	M,D
University of Dayton	M
University of Delaware	M,D
University of Guelph	M,D
University of Idaho	M,D
University of Massachusetts Amherst	M,D
University of Memphis	M,D,O
University of Missouri	M,D
University of New Haven	M
University of South Florida	M,D,O
The University of Texas at Austin	M,D
The University of Texas at Tyler	M

Utah State University	M,D
Villanova University	M,O

WESTERN EUROPEAN STUDIES

American Public University System	M
American University	M,D,O
Armstrong State University	M
Boston College	M,D
Brown University	M,D
Carleton University	M,O
The Catholic University of America	M,D
Central Michigan University	M,O
Claremont Graduate University	M,D,O
College of Staten Island of the City University of New York	M
Columbia University	M,D
Cornell University	M,D
Creighton University	M
Dallas Baptist University	M
Drew University	M,D,O
East Carolina University	M
Georgetown University	M
The George Washington University	M
Indiana University Bloomington	M
La Salle University	M,O
Mississippi State University	M,D
Monmouth University	M
New York University	M
San Diego State University	M
University of Colorado Denver	M
University of Connecticut	M
University of Guelph	M
University of Illinois at Urbana–Champaign	M
University of Nevada, Reno	D
University of Pittsburgh	O
University of Rochester	M,D
University of South Florida	M,D
Wayne State University	M,D,O

WOMEN'S HEALTH NURSING

Boston College	M,D
California State University, Fullerton	M,D
Case Western Reserve University	M
Drexel University	M
Duke University	M,D,O
Emory University	M
Frontier Nursing University	M,D,O
Georgia State University	M,D,O
Hampton University	M,D
Kent State University	M,D
MGH Institute of Health Professions	M,D,O
Queen's University at Kingston	M,D,O
Rutgers University–Newark	M,D,O
San Francisco State University	M,O
Stony Brook University, State University of New York	M,D,O
Texas Woman's University	M,D
Uniformed Services University of the Health Sciences	M,D
The University of Alabama at Birmingham	M,D
University of Cincinnati	M,D
University of Colorado Denver	M,D
University of Delaware	M,O
University of Illinois at Chicago	M,O
University of Indianapolis	M,D
University of Louisville	M,D
University of Minnesota, Twin Cities Campus	M,D
University of Missouri–Kansas City	M,D
University of Missouri–St. Louis	D,O
University of Pennsylvania	M
University of South Carolina	M
Vanderbilt University	M,D,O
Virginia Commonwealth University	M,D,O

WOMEN'S STUDIES

American University	O
The American University in Cairo	M,O
Benedictine University	M
Brandeis University	M,D
California Institute of Integral Studies	M,D
Carnegie Mellon University	D
Chatham University	M
Claremont Graduate University	M,D
Clark Atlanta University	M,D
Cornell University	M,D
DePaul University	M
Eastern Michigan University	M,O
Emory University	D,O
Florida Atlantic University	M
George Mason University	M
The George Washington University	M,O
Georgia State University	M,D,O
Grace Theological Seminary	M,D,O
The Graduate Center, City University of New York	M,D
Inter American University of Puerto Rico, Metropolitan Campus	M
The Jewish Theological Seminary	M
Kansas State University	O
Lakehead University	M,D
Lesley University	M,D,O
London Metropolitan University	M,D
Middle Tennessee State University	O
Minnesota State University Mankato	M
Mount Saint Vincent University	M
Northern Arizona University	O
The Ohio State University	M,D
Old Dominion University	M
Oregon State University	M,D
Queen's University at Kingston	M,D
Reconstructionist Rabbinical College	M,D,O
Rutgers University–New Brunswick	M,D
Saint Mary's University (Canada)	M
San Diego State University	M
San Francisco State University	M
Sarah Lawrence College	M
Simon Fraser University	M,D

Smith College	O
Southeastern Baptist Theological Seminary	M,D
Southern Connecticut State University	M
Stony Brook University, State University of New York	O
Texas Woman's University	M,D
Towson University	M,O
United Theological Seminary of the Twin Cities	M,D,O
Université Laval	O
University at Albany, State University of New York	M
The University of Alabama	M
The University of Arizona	M,D,O
University of California, Santa Barbara	M,D
University of Cincinnati	M,O
University of Colorado Denver	M
University of Florida	M,O
University of Georgia	O
University of Hawaii at Manoa	O
The University of Iowa	O
University of Lethbridge	M,D
University of Louisville	M,O
University of Maryland, College Park	M,D
University of Michigan	D,O
University of Minnesota, Twin Cities Campus	D
The University of North Carolina at Charlotte	M,D,O
The University of North Carolina at Greensboro	M,D,O
University of Northern Iowa	M
University of Oklahoma	O
University of Ottawa	M
University of Pittsburgh	O
University of Regina	O
University of Rhode Island	O
University of Saskatchewan	M,D
University of South Carolina	O
University of South Florida	M
The University of Toledo	O
University of Toronto	M,D
University of Washington	D
University of Wisconsin–Madison	M,D
University of Wisconsin–Milwaukee	M,O
Western Seminary	M
Western Seminary–Sacramento Campus	O
Western Seminary–San Jose Campus	M,O
Wilson College	M
York University	M,D

WRITING

Abilene Christian University	M
Academy of Art University	M
Adelphi University	M
Albertus Magnus College	M
American University	M
Antioch University Los Angeles	M,O
Antioch University Santa Barbara	M
Arcadia University	M
Arizona State University at the Tempe campus	M,D
Armstrong State University	M
Asbury University	M
Ashland University	M
Auburn University at Montgomery	M
Ball State University	M,D
Bard College	M
Bay Path University	M
Bennington College	M
Binghamton University, State University of New York	M,D
Boise State University	M
Boston University	M
Bowling Green State University	M,D
Brigham Young University	M
Brooklyn College of the City University of New York	M
Brown University	M,D
Butler University	M
California College of the Arts	M
California Institute of Integral Studies	M,D
California Institute of the Arts	M,O
California State University, East Bay	M
California State University, Fresno	M
California State University, Long Beach	M
California State University, Northridge	M
California State University, Sacramento	M
California State University, San Bernardino	M
California State University, San Marcos	M
California State University, Stanislaus	M,O
Carlow University	M
Carnegie Mellon University	M
Cedar Crest College	M
Central Michigan University	M
Chapman University	M
Chatham University	M
Chicago State University	M
City University of the City University of New York	M
Claremont Graduate University	M,D
Clemson University	M
Cleveland State University	M
Coastal Carolina University	M
The College at Brockport, State University of New York	M,O
College of Charleston	M
Colorado State University	M
Columbia College Chicago	M

Institution	Degree
Columbia University	M
Concordia University (Canada)	M
Cornell University	M,D
Creighton University	M
DePaul University	M
Dominican University of California	M
Drew University	M,D,O
East Carolina University	M,D,O
Eastern Kentucky University	M
Eastern Michigan University	M,O
Eastern Oregon University	M
Eastern Washington University	M
Emerson College	M
Fairfield University	M
Fairleigh Dickinson University, College at Florham	M
Florida International University	M
Florida State University	M,D
Full Sail University	M
George Mason University	M
Georgia College & State University	M
Georgia State University	M,D
Goddard College	M
Goucher College	M
Hamline University	M
Hofstra University	M
Hollins University	M,O
Holy Names University	M
Hunter College of the City University of New York	M
Illinois State University	O
Indiana State University	M
Indiana University Bloomington	M,D
Indiana University–Purdue University Indianapolis	M,O
Indiana University South Bend	M,O
Institute of American Indian Arts	M
Iowa State University of Science and Technology	M,D
Ithaca College	M
James Madison University	M
Johns Hopkins University	M,O
Kean University	M
Kennesaw State University	M
Kent State University	M
Lake Forest College	M
La Sierra University	M
Lenoir-Rhyne University	M
Lesley University	M,D,O
Lindenwood University	M,O
Lipscomb University	M
London Metropolitan University	M,D
Long Island University–LIU Brooklyn	M,D,O
Louisiana State University and Agricultural & Mechanical College	M,D
Loyola Marymount University	M
Maharishi University of Management	M
Manhattanville College	M
Massachusetts Institute of Technology	M
McDaniel College	M,O
McNeese State University	M
Michigan State University	M,D
Millersville University of Pennsylvania	M,O
Mills College	M,O
Minnesota State University Mankato	M,O
Missouri State University	M,O
Missouri Western State University	M,O
Monmouth University	M
Montclair State University	O
Mount Mary University	M
Mount Saint Mary's University (CA)	M,D,O
Murray State University	M
Naropa University	M
National Louis University	M,D,O
National University	M,O
New England College	M
New Hampshire Institute of Art	M
New Mexico Highlands University	M
New Mexico State University	M,D
The New School	M
New York University	M
North Carolina State University	M
North Dakota State University	M,D
Northeastern Illinois University	M
Northern Arizona University	M,D,O
Northern Kentucky University	M,O
Northern Michigan University	M,O
Northwestern University	M
Oklahoma City University	M
Oklahoma State University	M,D
Old Dominion University	M
Oregon State University	M
Otis College of Art and Design	M
Our Lady of the Lake University	M
Pacific Lutheran University	M
Pacific University	M
Park University	M,O
Penn State Harrisburg	M,D,O
Pepperdine University	M
Pittsburg State University	M
Pratt Institute	M
Purdue University	M,D
Queens College of the City University of New York	M,O
Queens University of Charlotte	M
Regent University	M,D
Regis University	M,O
Rhode Island College	M,O
Rivier University	M
Roosevelt University	M
Rosemont College	M
Rowan University	M,O
Rutgers University–Camden	M
Rutgers University–Newark	M
Rutgers University–New Brunswick	M
St. Joseph's College, New York	M
Saint Joseph's University	M
Saint Leo University	M
Saint Mary's College of California	M
Salisbury University	M
Sam Houston State University	M
San Diego State University	M
San Francisco State University	M
San Jose State University	M,O
Sarah Lawrence College	M
Savannah College of Art and Design	M
School of the Art Institute of Chicago	M,O
School of Visual Arts (NY)	M
Seattle Pacific University	M
Seton Hall University	M
Sewanee: The University of the South	M
Simmons College	M,D,O
Sonoma State University	M
Southeastern Louisiana University	M
Southern Illinois University Carbondale	M
Southern Illinois University Edwardsville	M
Southern New Hampshire University	M
Spalding University	M
Stephens College	M,O
Stetson University	M
Stony Brook University, State University of New York	M,O
Syracuse University	M,D
Temple University	M,D
Texas A&M University–Commerce	M,D,O
Texas State University	M
Tiffin University	M
Towson University	M
Trinity College (United States)	M
Union Institute & University	M
The University of Akron	M
The University of Alabama	M,D
The University of Alabama at Birmingham	M
University of Alaska Anchorage	M
University of Alaska Fairbanks	M
The University of Arizona	M
University of Arkansas	M
University of Arkansas at Little Rock	M
University of Baltimore	M
The University of British Columbia	M,D
University of California, Berkeley	O
University of California, Davis	M,D
University of California, Irvine	M
University of California, Riverside	M
University of California, San Diego	M,D
University of California, Santa Barbara	D
University of California, Santa Cruz	M
University of Central Arkansas	M
University of Central Florida	M,D,O
University of Central Oklahoma	M
University of Chicago	M
University of Colorado Boulder	M,D
University of Colorado Denver	M
University of Dayton	M
University of Denver	M,D,O
The University of Findlay	M,D
University of Florida	M,D
University of Houston	M,D
University of Houston–Victoria	M
University of Idaho	M
University of Illinois at Urbana–Champaign	M,D
The University of Iowa	M,D
The University of Kansas	M,D
University of King's College	M
University of Louisiana at Lafayette	M,D
University of Louisville	M,D
The University of Manchester	D
University of Maryland, College Park	M,D
University of Massachusetts Amherst	M
University of Massachusetts Boston	M
University of Massachusetts Dartmouth	M,O
University of Memphis	M,D,O
University of Miami	M,D
University of Michigan	M
University of Michigan–Flint	M
University of Missouri–St. Louis	M
University of Montana	M
University of Nebraska at Kearney	M
University of Nebraska at Omaha	M,O
University of Nebraska–Lincoln	M,D
University of Nevada, Las Vegas	M,D,O
University of New Hampshire	M,D
University of New Mexico	M
The University of North Carolina at Charlotte	M,O
The University of North Carolina at Greensboro	M
The University of North Carolina Wilmington	M
University of Northern Iowa	M
University of North Florida	M
University of North Texas	M,D,O
University of Notre Dame	M
University of Oklahoma	M
University of Oregon	M
University of Pittsburgh	M,D
University of Regina	M,D
University of San Francisco	M
University of South Alabama	M
University of South Carolina	M,D
University of Southern California	M,D
University of Southern Maine	M
University of Southern Mississippi	M,D
University of South Florida	M,D,O
The University of Tampa	M
The University of Tennessee at Chattanooga	M
The University of Texas at Austin	M,D
The University of Texas at El Paso	M,D,O
The University of Texas Rio Grande Valley	M
University of the Sacred Heart	M,O
The University of Toledo	M,O
University of Toronto	M,D
University of Utah	M,D
University of Victoria	M
University of Virginia	M
University of Washington	M
University of Washington, Bothell	M
University of West Florida	M
University of Windsor	M
University of Wisconsin–Eau Claire	M
University of Wisconsin–Madison	M,D
University of Wisconsin–Milwaukee	M,D
University of Wyoming	M
Utah State University	M
Vanderbilt University	M
Vermont College of Fine Arts	M
Virginia Commonwealth University	M
Virginia Polytechnic Institute and State University	M,D,O
Warren Wilson College	M
Washington & Jefferson College	M,O
Washington University in St. Louis	M
Wayne State University	M,D
Wesleyan University	M,O
West Chester University of Pennsylvania	M,O
Western Connecticut State University	M
Western Illinois University	M,O
Western Kentucky University	M
Western Michigan University	M,D
Western New England University	M
Western State Colorado University	M
Westminster College (UT)	M
West Virginia University	M
West Virginia Wesleyan College	M
Wichita State University	M
Wilkes University	M
William Paterson University of New Jersey	M,D
Yale University	M,D,O

ZOOLOGY

Institution	Degree
Auburn University	M,D
Canisius College	M
Colorado State University	M,D
Cornell University	D
Eastern New Mexico University	M
Emporia State University	M
Illinois State University	M,D
Indiana University Bloomington	M,D
Michigan State University	M,D
North Carolina State University	M,D
North Dakota State University	M,D
Southern Illinois University Carbondale	M,D
Texas Tech University	M,D
Uniformed Services University of the Health Sciences	M,D
The University of British Columbia	M,D
University of California, Davis	M
University of Chicago	D
University of Florida	M,D
University of Guelph	M
University of Hawaii at Manoa	M,D
University of Illinois at Urbana–Champaign	M,D
University of Maine	M,D
University of Manitoba	M,D
University of Montana	M,D
University of North Dakota	M,D
University of Wisconsin–Madison	M,D
University of Wisconsin–Oshkosh	M
University of Wyoming	M,D
Western Illinois University	M,O

M—masters degree; D—doctorate; O—other advanced degree; *—Close-Up and/or Display

DIRECTORY OF INSTITUTIONS AND THEIR OFFERINGS

ABILENE CHRISTIAN UNIVERSITY

Accounting	M
Business Administration and Management—General	M
Clinical Psychology	M
Communication Disorders	M
Communication—General	M
Conflict Resolution and Mediation/Peace Studies	M,O
Counseling Psychology	M
Education—General	M,O
Educational Leadership and Administration	M,D,O
Educational Media/Instructional Technology	M,O
English	M
Higher Education	M
Human Resources Development	M
Human Services	M,O
Liberal Studies	M
Marriage and Family Therapy	M
Missions and Missiology	M
Nursing and Healthcare Administration	D
Nursing—General	M
Nutrition	O
Occupational Therapy	M
Pastoral Ministry and Counseling	M,D
Psychology—General	M
Religion	M
Rhetoric	M
School Psychology	O
Social Work	M
Theology	M
Writing	M

ACACIA UNIVERSITY

Education—General	M
Educational Leadership and Administration	M
Elementary Education	M
English as a Second Language	M
Secondary Education	M
Special Education	M

ACADEMY FOR FIVE ELEMENT ACUPUNCTURE

Acupuncture and Oriental Medicine	M

ACADEMY OF ART UNIVERSITY

Advertising and Public Relations	M
Applied Arts and Design—General	M
Architecture	M
Art Education	M
Art History	M
Art/Fine Arts	M
Arts Journalism	M
Computer Art and Design	M
Film, Television, and Video Production	M
Game Design and Development	M
Graphic Design	M
Illustration	M
Industrial Design	M
Interior Design	M
Internet and Interactive Multimedia	M
Landscape Architecture	M
Music	M
Photography	M
Textile Design	M
Theater	M
Writing	M

ACADEMY OF CHINESE CULTURE AND HEALTH SCIENCES

Acupuncture and Oriental Medicine	M

ACADIA UNIVERSITY

Applied Mathematics	M
Biological and Biomedical Sciences—General	M
Chemistry	M
Clinical Psychology	M
Computer Science	M
Counselor Education	M
Curriculum and Instruction	M
Education—General	M,D
Educational Leadership and Administration	M
Educational Media/Instructional Technology	M
English	M
Geographic Information Systems	M
Geology	M
Mathematics Education	M
Philosophy	M
Political Science	M
Psychology—General	M
Recreation and Park Management	M
Science Education	M
Social Sciences Education	M
Sociology	M
Special Education	M
Statistics	M
Sustainable Development	M
Theology	M,D

ACUPUNCTURE & INTEGRATIVE MEDICINE COLLEGE, BERKELEY

Acupuncture and Oriental Medicine	M

ACUPUNCTURE AND MASSAGE COLLEGE

Acupuncture and Oriental Medicine	M

ADAMS STATE UNIVERSITY

Art/Fine Arts	M
Counselor Education	M
Education—General	M
History	M
Physical Education	M
Special Education	M

ADELPHI UNIVERSITY

Accounting	M
Adult Nursing	M
Art Education	M
Art/Fine Arts	M
Biological and Biomedical Sciences—General	M
Biotechnology	M
Business Administration and Management—General	M
Clinical Psychology	D
Communication Disorders	M,D
Community Health	M,O
Counseling Psychology	M
Education—General	M,D,O
Educational Leadership and Administration	M,O
Educational Media/Instructional Technology	M
Elementary Education	M
Emergency Management	O
English as a Second Language	M,O
Environmental Management and Policy	M
Environmental Sciences	M
Finance and Banking	M
Gerontology	M,O
Health Education	M,O
Health Informatics	M,O
Health Services Management and Hospital Administration	M
Human Resources Management	M,O
Management Information Systems	M
Marketing	M
Nursing and Healthcare Administration	M,O
Nursing—General	D
Nutrition	M,D,O
Physical Education	M,O
Psychology—General	M
Public Administration	O
Public Health—General	M,O
Reading Education	M
School Psychology	M
Secondary Education	M
Social Work	M,D
Special Education	M,O
Sports Management	M
Supply Chain Management	M
Writing	M

ADLER GRADUATE SCHOOL

Addictions/Substance Abuse Counseling	M
Art Therapy	M
Clinical Psychology	M
Counseling Psychology	M
Counselor Education	M
Marriage and Family Therapy	M
Psychoanalysis and Psychotherapy	M

ADLER UNIVERSITY

Addictions/Substance Abuse Counseling	M,D,O
Art Therapy	M,D,O
Biopsychology	M,D,O
Clinical Psychology	M,D,O
Counseling Psychology	M,D,O
Counselor Education	M,D,O
Criminal Justice and Criminology	M,D,O
Emergency Management	M,D,O
Forensic Psychology	M,D,O
Health Psychology	M,D,O
Industrial and Organizational Psychology	M,D,O
Marriage and Family Therapy	M,D,O
Nonprofit Management	M,D,O
Psychoanalysis and Psychotherapy	M,D,O
Psychology—General	M,D,O*
Public Administration	M,D,O
Public Policy	M,D,O
Rehabilitation Counseling	M,D,O
Social Psychology	M,D,O
Sport Psychology	M,D,O

ADRIAN COLLEGE

Accounting	M
Athletic Training and Sports Medicine	M
Criminal Justice and Criminology	M

ADVENTIST UNIVERSITY OF HEALTH SCIENCES

Health Services Management and Hospital Administration	M
Nurse Anesthesia	M
Occupational Therapy	M
Physical Therapy	D
Physician Assistant Studies	M

AIR FORCE INSTITUTE OF TECHNOLOGY

Aerospace/Aeronautical Engineering	M,D
Applied Mathematics	M,D
Applied Physics	M,D
Astrophysics	M,D
Computer Engineering	M,D
Computer Science	M,D
Electrical Engineering	M,D
Engineering and Applied Sciences—General	M,D
Engineering Management	M
Engineering Physics	M,D
Environmental Engineering	M
Environmental Management and Policy	M
Logistics	M,D
Management Information Systems	M
Management of Technology	M,D
Materials Sciences	M,D
Nuclear Engineering	M,D
Operations Research	M,D
Optical Sciences	M,D
Planetary and Space Sciences	M,D
Systems Engineering	M,D

ALABAMA AGRICULTURAL AND MECHANICAL UNIVERSITY

Agricultural Sciences—General	M,D
Agronomy and Soil Sciences	M,D
Art Education	M
Biological and Biomedical Sciences—General	M,D
Business Administration	M,O
Child and Family Studies	M
Clinical Psychology	M
Clothing and Textiles	M
Communication Disorders	M
Computer Science	M
Counseling Psychology	M,O
Counselor Education	M,O
Early Childhood Education	M,D,O
Education—General	M,D,O
Educational Media/Instructional Technology	M,O
Elementary Education	M,D,O
Engineering and Applied Sciences—General	M,D
English Education	M,O
Family and Consumer Sciences-General	M
Food Science and Technology	M,D
Home Economics Education	M,O
Hospitality Management	M
Human Development	M
Kinesiology and Movement Studies	M
Materials Engineering	M
Materials Sciences	M,D
Mathematics Education	M,O
Music Education	M
Nutrition	M
Optical Sciences	M,D
Physical Education	M
Physics	M,D
Planetary and Space Sciences	M,D
Plant Sciences	M,D
Psychology—General	M,O
Reading Education	M,D,O
Rehabilitation Counseling	M,O
School Psychology	M,O
Science Education	M,O
Secondary Education	M,O
Social Sciences Education	M,O
Social Work	M
Special Education	M,D,O
Urban and Regional Planning	M

ALABAMA COLLEGE OF OSTEOPATHIC MEDICINE

Osteopathic Medicine	D

ALABAMA STATE UNIVERSITY

Accounting	M
Allied Health—General	M,D
Biological and Biomedical Sciences—General	M,D
Business Administration and Management—General	M
Counselor Education	M,D,O
Early Childhood Education	M,O
Education—General	M,D,O
Educational Leadership and Administration	M,D,O
Educational Media/Instructional Technology	M,D,O
Educational Policy	M,D,O
Elementary Education	M,O
English Education	M,O
Forensic Sciences	M
Health Education	M
History	M
Mathematics Education	M,O
Mathematics	M
Music Education	M,O
Occupational Therapy	M
Physical Education	M
Physical Therapy	D
Reading Education	M,O
Rehabilitation Counseling	M
Rehabilitation Sciences	M
Science Education	M,O
Secondary Education	M,O
Social Sciences Education	M,O
Social Work	M
Special Education	M,O

ALASKA PACIFIC UNIVERSITY

Business Administration and Management—General	M
Counseling Psychology	M
Education—General	M
Elementary Education	M
Environmental Education	M
Environmental Sciences	M
Health Services Management and Hospital Administration	M
Interdisciplinary Studies	M
Investment Management	M,O
Liberal Studies	M
Middle School Education	M
Telecommunications Management	M

ALBANY COLLEGE OF PHARMACY AND HEALTH SCIENCES

Cell Biology	M
Clinical Laboratory Sciences/Medical Technology	M
Health Services Research	M,D
Molecular Biology	M
Pharmaceutical Sciences	M,D
Pharmacology	M,D
Pharmacy	M,D

ALBANY LAW SCHOOL

Law	M,D

ALBANY MEDICAL COLLEGE

Allopathic Medicine	D
Bioethics	M,D,O
Cardiovascular Sciences	M,D
Cell Biology	M,D
Immunology	M,D
Microbiology	M,D
Molecular Biology	M,D
Neuroscience	M,D
Nurse Anesthesia	M
Pharmacology	M,D
Physician Assistant Studies	M

ALBANY STATE UNIVERSITY

Accounting	M
Business Administration and Management—General	M
Counselor Education	M,O
Criminal Justice and Criminology	M
Early Childhood Education	M,O
Economic Development	M
Economics	M
Education—General	M,O
Educational Leadership and Administration	M
English Education	M
Family Nurse Practitioner Studies	M
Health Education	M,O
Health Services Management and Hospital Administration	M
Human Resources Management	M
Logistics	M
Middle School Education	M
Nursing Education	M
Nursing—General	M
Physical Education	M,O
Public Administration	M
Public Policy	M
Social Work	M
Special Education	M,O
Supply Chain Management	M
Water Resources	M

ALBERT EINSTEIN COLLEGE OF MEDICINE

Allopathic Medicine	D
Anatomy	D
Biochemistry	D
Biological and Biomedical Sciences—General	D
Biophysics	D
Cell Biology	D
Clinical Research	D
Computational Biology	D
Developmental Biology	D
Genetics	D
Genomic Sciences	D
Immunology	D
Microbiology	D
Molecular Biology	D
Molecular Genetics	D
Molecular Pharmacology	D
Neurobiology	D
Pathology	D
Physiology	D
Systems Biology	D

ALBERTUS MAGNUS COLLEGE

Accounting	M
Art Therapy	M
Business Administration and Management—General	M
Criminal Justice and Criminology	M
Education—General	M
Human Services	M
Liberal Studies	M
Organizational Management	M
Writing	M

ALBRIGHT COLLEGE

Early Childhood Education	M
Education—General	M
Elementary Education	M
English as a Second Language	M
Special Education	M

ALCORN STATE UNIVERSITY

Agricultural Economics and Agribusiness	M
Agricultural Education	M,O
Agricultural Sciences—General	M
Agronomy and Soil Sciences	M
Animal Sciences	M
Biological and Biomedical Sciences—General	M
Business Administration and Management—General	M
Computer Science	M
Counselor Education	M,O
Education—General	M,O
Elementary Education	M,O
Health Education	M,O
Information Science	M
Nursing—General	M
Physical Education	M,O
Secondary Education	M,O
Special Education	M,O
Vocational and Technical Education	M,O

ALDERSON BROADDUS UNIVERSITY

Physician Assistant Studies	M

ALFRED UNIVERSITY

Accounting	M
Applied Arts and Design—General	M
Art/Fine Arts	M,D
Bioengineering	M,D
Business Administration and Management—General	M
Ceramic Sciences and Engineering	M,D
Computer Art and Design	M
Counseling Psychology	M,D,O
Counselor Education	M,D,O
Education—General	M
Electrical Engineering	M,D

Engineering and Applied Sciences—General M,D
Internet and Interactive Multimedia M
Materials Sciences M,D
Mechanical Engineering M,D
Public Administration M
Reading Education M
School Psychology M,D,O
Student Affairs M

ALLEN COLLEGE
Adult Nursing M,D
Community Health Nursing M,D
Family Nurse Practitioner Studies M,D
Gerontological Nursing M,D
Health Education M,D
Nursing and Healthcare Administration M,D
Nursing—General M,D
Occupational Therapy M,D
Public Health—General M,D

ALLIANT INTERNATIONAL UNIVERSITY–FRESNO
Clinical Psychology D
Forensic Psychology D
Industrial and Organizational Psychology M,D
Psychology—General M,D

ALLIANT INTERNATIONAL UNIVERSITY–IRVINE
Educational Psychology M,D,O
Forensic Psychology D
Forensic Sciences D
Marriage and Family Therapy M,D
School Psychology M,D,O

ALLIANT INTERNATIONAL UNIVERSITY–LOS ANGELES
Addictions/Substance Abuse Counseling M
Business Administration and Management—General D
Clinical Psychology D
Education—General M,O
Educational Psychology M,D,O
Forensic Psychology D
Gerontology M
Health Psychology D
Industrial and Organizational Psychology M,D
Marriage and Family Therapy M,D
Psychology—General M,D
School Psychology M,D,O
Social Psychology D
Student Affairs M,D,O

ALLIANT INTERNATIONAL UNIVERSITY–SACRAMENTO
Clinical Psychology D
Education—General M,O
Forensic Psychology D
Marriage and Family Therapy M,D
Psychology—General M,D

ALLIANT INTERNATIONAL UNIVERSITY–SAN DIEGO
Business Administration and Management—General M
Clinical Psychology M,D
Education—General M,O
Educational Leadership and Administration M,D,O
Educational Psychology M,D,O
English as a Second Language M,D,O
Forensic Psychology D
Higher Education M,D,O
Industrial and Organizational Psychology M,D
Marriage and Family Therapy M,D
Neuroscience M,D,O
Psychology—General M,D
School Psychology M,D,O
Student Affairs M,D,O

ALLIANT INTERNATIONAL UNIVERSITY–SAN FRANCISCO
Clinical Psychology M,D,O
Counselor Education M
Criminal Justice and Criminology M
Education—General M,O
Educational Leadership and Administration M,D,O
Educational Psychology M,D,O
English as a Second Language M,O
Forensic Psychology M,D
Higher Education M,D,O
Industrial and Organizational Psychology M,D
Law D
Multilingual and Multicultural Education M,O
Pharmacology M
Psychology—General M,D,O
School Psychology M,D,O
Special Education M,O

ALVERNIA UNIVERSITY
Business Administration and Management—General M
Education—General M
Family Nurse Practitioner Studies M,D,O
Gerontological Nursing M,D,O
Liberal Studies M
Nursing and Healthcare Administration M,D,O
Nursing Education M,D,O
Nursing—General M,D,O
Occupational Therapy M
Organizational Management D
Social Psychology M

Urban Education M

ALVERNO COLLEGE
Adult Education M
Business Administration and Management—General M
Education—General M
Educational Leadership and Administration M
Educational Media/Instructional Technology M
Family Nurse Practitioner Studies M,D
Nursing—General M,D
Psychiatric Nursing M,D
Reading Education M
Science Education M
Social Psychology M
Special Education M

AMBERTON UNIVERSITY
Business Administration and Management—General M
Child and Family Studies M
Counseling Psychology M
Human Resources Development M
Human Resources Management M
Interdisciplinary Studies M
Management Strategy and Policy M
Project Management M

AMBROSE UNIVERSITY
Pastoral Ministry and Counseling M,O
Religion M,O
Theology M,O

AMERICAN ACADEMY OF ACUPUNCTURE AND ORIENTAL MEDICINE
Acupuncture and Oriental Medicine M,D

AMERICAN BAPTIST SEMINARY OF THE WEST
Pastoral Ministry and Counseling M
Theology M

AMERICAN BUSINESS & TECHNOLOGY UNIVERSITY
Accounting M
Business Administration and Management—General M
Finance and Banking M
International Business M
Management Information Systems M
Marketing M
Project Management M

AMERICAN COLLEGE OF ACUPUNCTURE AND ORIENTAL MEDICINE
Acupuncture and Oriental Medicine M

AMERICAN COLLEGE OF EDUCATION
Curriculum and Instruction M
Education—General M
Educational Leadership and Administration M
Educational Media/Instructional Technology M
English as a Second Language M
Multilingual and Multicultural Education M

THE AMERICAN COLLEGE OF FINANCIAL SERVICES
Business Administration and Management—General M
Finance and Banking M
Organizational Management M

AMERICAN COLLEGE OF HEALTHCARE SCIENCES
Allied Health—General M,O
Health Promotion M,O
Nutrition M,O
Physiology M,O

AMERICAN COLLEGE OF THESSALONIKI
Business Administration and Management—General M,O
Entrepreneurship M,O
Finance and Banking M,O
Marketing M,O

AMERICAN CONSERVATORY THEATER
Theater M,O

AMERICAN FILM INSTITUTE CONSERVATORY
Film, Television, and Video Production M

AMERICAN GRADUATE SCHOOL IN PARIS
International Affairs M,D

AMERICAN GRADUATE UNIVERSITY
Business Administration and Management—General M,O
Supply Chain Management M,O

AMERICAN INTERCONTINENTAL UNIVERSITY ATLANTA
Information Science M
International Business M
Management Information Systems M

AMERICAN INTERCONTINENTAL UNIVERSITY HOUSTON
Business Administration and Management—General M

AMERICAN INTERCONTINENTAL UNIVERSITY ONLINE
Accounting M

Business Administration and Management—General M
Computer and Information Systems Security M
Curriculum and Instruction M
Education—General M
Educational Leadership and Administration M
Educational Measurement and Evaluation M
Educational Media/Instructional Technology M
Finance and Banking M
Health Services Management and Hospital Administration M
Human Resources Management M
Industrial and Manufacturing Management M
Industrial and Organizational Psychology M
Information Science M
International Business M
Marketing M
Project Management M

AMERICAN INTERNATIONAL COLLEGE
Accounting M,D,O
Business Administration and Management—General M,D,O
Clinical Psychology M,D
Counseling Psychology M,D
Counselor Education M,O
Early Childhood Education M,O
Education—General M,D,O
Educational Leadership and Administration M,D,O
Educational Psychology M,D,O
Elementary Education M,O
Exercise and Sports Science M,O
Family Nurse Practitioner Studies M,D
Forensic Psychology M,D,O
Hospitality Management M,D,O
Middle School Education M,O
Nursing and Healthcare Administration M,D
Nursing Education M,D
Occupational Therapy M,D
Physical Therapy M,D
Psychology—General M,D,O
Reading Education M,O
Secondary Education M,O
Special Education M,O
Taxation M,D,O

AMERICAN JEWISH UNIVERSITY
Business Administration and Management—General M
Education—General M
Jewish Studies M
Nonprofit Management M
Social Work M
Theology M

AMERICAN MUSEUM OF NATURAL HISTORY–RICHARD GILDER GRADUATE SCHOOL
Biological and Biomedical Sciences—General D
Museum Studies D

AMERICAN NATIONAL UNIVERSITY
Business Administration and Management—General M

AMERICAN PUBLIC UNIVERSITY SYSTEM
Accounting M
Aerospace/Aeronautical Engineering M
American Studies M
Business Administration and Management—General M
Classics M
Computer and Information Systems Security M
Conflict Resolution and Mediation/Peace Studies M
Criminal Justice and Criminology M
Curriculum and Instruction M
Distance Education Development M
Educational Leadership and Administration M
Elementary Education M
Emergency Management M
English as a Second Language M
Entrepreneurship M
Environmental Management and Policy M
Exercise and Sports Science M
Finance and Banking M
Fish, Game, and Wildlife Management M
Forensic Sciences M
Health Informatics M
Health Services Management and Hospital Administration M
History M
Homeland Security M
Human Resources Management M
Humanities M
International Affairs M
Legal and Justice Studies M
Logistics M
Management Information Systems M
Management Strategy and Policy M
Marketing M
Military and Defense Studies M
National Security M
Nonprofit Management M
Organizational Management M
Planetary and Space Sciences M

Political Science M
Project Management M
Psychology—General M
Public Administration M
Public Health—General M
Public History M
Public Policy M
Reading Education M
Secondary Education M
Social Sciences Education M
Software Engineering M
Special Education M
Sports Management M
Transportation Management M
Western European Studies M

AMERICAN SENTINEL UNIVERSITY
Business Administration and Management—General M
Computer Science M
Health Informatics M
Health Services Management and Hospital Administration M
Management Information Systems M
Nursing—General M

AMERICAN UNIVERSITY
Accounting M,O
American Studies M,D,O
Anthropology M,D,O
Applied Social Research M,O
Applied Statistics M,O
Art History M
Arts Administration M,O
Asian Studies O
Biopsychology M,D,O
Chemistry M
Clinical Psychology M,D,O
Cognitive Sciences M,D,O
Communication—General M
Comparative Literature M
Conflict Resolution and Mediation/Peace Studies M,D,O
Criminal Justice and Criminology M,D
Cultural Studies M,D,O
Economics M,D,O
Education—General M,O
Educational Measurement and Evaluation M,O
Educational Policy M,O
English as a Second Language M,O
Entrepreneurship M,D,O
Environmental Management and Policy M,D,O
Environmental Sciences M,D,O
Ethics M,D,O
Film, Television, and Video Production M
Finance and Banking M
French M,O
Gender Studies M,D,O
Health Education M,O
Health Promotion M
Health Services Management and Hospital Administration M,O
History M,D
Human Resources Management M,O
International Affairs M,D,O
International and Comparative Education M
International Development M,D,O
International Economics M,D,O
Journalism M
Latin American Studies M,O
Management Information Systems M,D,O
Marketing M
Mass Communication M,D,O
Mathematics M
Media Studies M,D
Multilingual and Multicultural Education M,O
Music M,O
Natural Resources M,D,O
Neuroscience M,D,O
Nonprofit Management M,D,O
Nutrition M,O
Organizational Management M,O
Philosophy M
Political Science M,D,O
Project Management M,O
Psychology—General M,D,O
Public Administration M,D,O
Public Affairs M
Public Policy M
Real Estate M,O
Russian M,O
Sociology M,O
Spanish M,O
Special Education M
Sports Management M,O
Statistics M,O
Sustainability Management M
Sustainable Development M,D,O
Taxation M,O
Western European Studies M,D,O
Women's Studies O
Writing M

THE AMERICAN UNIVERSITY IN CAIRO
Artificial Intelligence/Robotics M,D,O
Biotechnology M,D,O
Broadcast Journalism M,O
Business Administration and Management—General M,O
Chemistry M,D,O
Communication—General M,D,O
Comparative Literature M,O
Computer Science M,D,O
Construction Engineering M,D,O
Economic Development M,O
Economics M,O
Education—General M

M—masters degree; D—doctorate; O—other advanced degree; *—Close-Up and/or Display

Educational Leadership and Administration — M
Electrical Engineering — M,D,O
Engineering and Applied Sciences—General — M,D,O
English as a Second Language — M,O
English — M,O
Environmental Engineering — M,D,O
Finance and Banking — M,O
Gender Studies — M,O
International and Comparative Education — M
Journalism — M,O
Law — M,O
Mass Communication — M,O
Mechanical Engineering — M,D,O
Nanotechnology — M,D,O
Near and Middle Eastern Languages — M,O
Near and Middle Eastern Studies — M,O
Philosophy — M,O
Physics — M,D,O
Psychology—General — M,O
Public Administration — M,O
Sustainable Development — M,D,O
Women's Studies — M

THE AMERICAN UNIVERSITY IN DUBAI
Business Administration and Management—General — M
Construction Management — M
Education—General — M
Finance and Banking — M
International Business — M
Marketing — M

AMERICAN UNIVERSITY OF ARMENIA
Business Administration and Management—General — M
Computer Science — M
Economics — M
Energy Management and Policy — M
English as a Second Language — M
Industrial/Management Engineering — M
Information Science — M
International Affairs — M
Law — M
Management Information Systems — M
Manufacturing Engineering — M
Political Science — M
Public Health—General — M

AMERICAN UNIVERSITY OF BEIRUT
Agricultural Economics and Agribusiness — M
Allopathic Medicine — M,D
American Studies — M,D
Animal Sciences — M
Anthropology — M,D
Aquaculture — M
Archaeology — M,D
Art History — M,D
Biochemistry — M,D
Biological and Biomedical Sciences—General — M,D
Biomedical Engineering — M,D
Biostatistics — M
Business Administration and Management—General — M
Cell Biology — M,D
Chemistry — M,D
Civil Engineering — M,D
Clinical Psychology — M,D
Community Health Nursing — M
Community Health — M
Computational Sciences — M,D
Computer Engineering — M,D
Computer Science — M,D
Economics — M,D
Education—General — M,D
Electrical Engineering — M,D
Engineering and Applied Sciences—General — M,D
Engineering Management — M,D
English — M,D
Environmental and Occupational Health — M
Environmental Management and Policy — M,D
Environmental Sciences — M,D
Epidemiology — M
Finance and Banking — M,D
Food Science and Technology — M
Geology — M,D
Gerontological Nursing — M
Health Promotion — M
Health Services Management and Hospital Administration — M
History — M,D
Human Resources Management — M
Immunology — M,D
International Affairs — M,D
Mathematics — M,D
Mechanical Engineering — M,D
Media Studies — M,D
Microbiology — M,D
Molecular Biology — M,D
Near and Middle Eastern Languages — M,D
Near and Middle Eastern Studies — M,D
Neuroscience — M,D
Nursing and Healthcare Administration — M
Nursing—General — M
Nutrition — M
Oral and Dental Sciences — M,D
Pharmacology — M,D
Physics — M,D
Physiology — M,D
Plant Sciences — M
Political Science — M,D
Psychiatric Nursing — M
Psychology—General — M,D
Public Administration — M,D

Public Policy — M,D
Sociology — M,D
Statistics — M,D
Theoretical Physics — M,D
Urban and Regional Planning — M,D
Urban Design — M,D
Water Resources Engineering — M,D

AMERICAN UNIVERSITY OF HEALTH SCIENCES
Clinical Research — M

THE AMERICAN UNIVERSITY OF PARIS
Business Administration and Management—General — M
Communication—General — M
Conflict Resolution and Mediation/Peace Studies — M
Cultural Studies — M
International Affairs — M
International Business — M
Law — M
Near and Middle Eastern Studies — M
Public Policy — M

AMERICAN UNIVERSITY OF PUERTO RICO
Art Education — M
Criminal Justice and Criminology — M
Education—General — M
Elementary Education — M
Physical Education — M
Science Education — M
Special Education — M

THE AMERICAN UNIVERSITY OF ROME
Historic Preservation — M
Religion — M

AMERICAN UNIVERSITY OF SHARJAH
Accounting — M
Biomedical Engineering — M
Business Administration and Management—General — M
Chemical Engineering — M
Civil Engineering — M
Computer Engineering — M
Electrical Engineering — M
Engineering Management — M
English as a Second Language — M
Mathematics — M
Mechanical Engineering — M
Translation and Interpretation — M
Urban and Regional Planning — M

AMRIDGE UNIVERSITY
Counseling Psychology — M,D
Counselor Education — M,D
Human Services — M,D
Marriage and Family Therapy — M,D
Pastoral Ministry and Counseling — M,D
Religion — M,D
Theology — M,D

ANABAPTIST MENNONITE BIBLICAL SEMINARY
Conflict Resolution and Mediation/Peace Studies — M,O
Ethics — M,O
International Affairs — M,O
Pastoral Ministry and Counseling — M,O
Public Administration — M,O
Theology — M,O

ANAHEIM UNIVERSITY
Business Administration and Management—General — M,D,O
English as a Second Language — M,D,O
Entrepreneurship — M,D,O
International Business — M,D,O
Sustainability Management — M,D,O

ANDERSON UNIVERSITY (IN)
Accounting — M,D
Business Administration and Management—General — M,D
Education—General — M
Missions and Missiology — M,D
Theology — M,D

ANDERSON UNIVERSITY (SC)
Business Administration and Management—General — M
Criminal Justice and Criminology — M
Education—General — M
Educational Leadership and Administration — M
Elementary Education — M
Health Services Management and Hospital Administration — M
Human Resources Management — M
Marketing — M
Pastoral Ministry and Counseling — M,D
Supply Chain Management — M

ANDREWS UNIVERSITY
Accounting — M
Allied Health—General — M
Architecture — M
Biological and Biomedical Sciences—General — M
Clinical Psychology — M
Communication Disorders — M
Communication—General — M
Counseling Psychology — M,D
Curriculum and Instruction — M,D,O
Developmental Psychology — M,D
Economics — M
Education—General — M,D,O
Educational Leadership and Administration — M,D,O
Educational Psychology — M,D
Elementary Education — M,D,O
English as a Second Language — M,D,O
English Education — M,D,O
English — M
Finance and Banking — M
Foreign Languages Education — M

Higher Education — M,D,O
International and Comparative Education — M
International Development — M
Music — M
Nursing—General — M,D
Nutrition — M,O
Pastoral Ministry and Counseling — M,D,O
Physical Therapy — D
Psychology—General — M,D,O
Public Health—General — M,O
Religious Education — M,D,O
School Psychology — M,O
Science Education — M,D,O
Secondary Education — M,D,O
Social Psychology — M
Social Sciences Education — M,D,O
Social Work — M
Special Education — M
Theology — M,D,O
Urban and Regional Planning — M

ANGELO STATE UNIVERSITY
Accounting — M
Agricultural Sciences—General — M
Animal Sciences — M
Applied Psychology — M
Biological and Biomedical Sciences—General — M
Business Administration and Management—General — M
Communication—General — M
Counseling Psychology — M
Counselor Education — M
Criminal Justice and Criminology — M
Curriculum and Instruction — M
Educational Leadership and Administration — M
English as a Second Language — M
English — M
Family Nurse Practitioner Studies — M
Higher Education — M
Homeland Security — M
Industrial and Organizational Psychology — M
Media Studies — M
National Security — M
Nursing Education — M
Nursing—General — M
Physical Therapy — D
Psychology—General — M
Science Education — M
Sports Management — M

ANNA MARIA COLLEGE
Art/Fine Arts — M,O
Business Administration and Management—General — M,O
Counseling Psychology — M
Criminal Justice and Criminology — M
Early Childhood Education — M,O
Education—General — M,O
Elementary Education — M,O
Emergency Management — M,O
English Education — M,O
Industrial and Organizational Psychology — M
Public Administration — M
Social Work — M

ANTIOCH UNIVERSITY LOS ANGELES
Business Administration and Management—General — M
Clinical Psychology — M
Education—General — M
Human Resources Development — M
Nonprofit Management — M
Organizational Management — M
Psychology—General — M
Sustainable Development — M
Writing — M,O

ANTIOCH UNIVERSITY MIDWEST
Applied Psychology — M
Business Administration and Management—General — M
Conflict Resolution and Mediation/Peace Studies — M
Early Childhood Education — M
Education—General — M
Educational Leadership and Administration — M
Interdisciplinary Studies — M
Management Strategy and Policy — M
Middle School Education — M
Social Sciences — M
Special Education — M

ANTIOCH UNIVERSITY NEW ENGLAND
Addictions/Substance Abuse Counseling — M
Applied Behavior Analysis — M
Applied Psychology — M,D,O
Business Administration and Management—General — M
Clinical Psychology — M,D
Conservation Biology — M
Counseling Psychology — M
Early Childhood Education — M
Education—General — M,O
Educational Leadership and Administration — M,O
Educational Media/Instructional Technology — M,O
Elementary Education — M
Environmental Education — M
Environmental Management and Policy — M,D
Environmental Sciences — M,D
Foundations and Philosophy of Education — M
Humanities — M
Interdisciplinary Studies — M
Marriage and Family Therapy — M,D,O
Science Education — M

Special Education — M,O
Sustainability Management — M
Sustainable Development — M,O
Therapies—Dance, Drama, and Music — M,O

ANTIOCH UNIVERSITY SANTA BARBARA
Business Administration and Management—General — M
Clinical Psychology — M,D
Education—General — M
Management Strategy and Policy — M
Nonprofit Management — M
Writing — M

ANTIOCH UNIVERSITY SEATTLE
Adult Education — M
Clinical Psychology — D
Education—General — M
Therapies—Dance, Drama, and Music — M

AOMA GRADUATE SCHOOL OF INTEGRATIVE MEDICINE
Acupuncture and Oriental Medicine — M,D

APEX SCHOOL OF THEOLOGY
Theology — M,D

APPALACHIAN BIBLE COLLEGE
Pastoral Ministry and Counseling — M

APPALACHIAN COLLEGE OF PHARMACY
Pharmacy — D

APPALACHIAN SCHOOL OF LAW
Law — D

APPALACHIAN STATE UNIVERSITY
Accounting — M
American Studies — M
Biological and Biomedical Sciences—General — M
Business Administration and Management—General — M
Cell Biology — M
Clinical Psychology — M
Communication Disorders — M
Computer Science — M
Counseling Psychology — M
Counselor Education — M
Cultural Studies — M
Curriculum and Instruction — M
Educational Leadership and Administration — M,O
Educational Media/Instructional Technology — M,O
Elementary Education — M
Energy and Power Engineering — M
English Education — M
English — M
Exercise and Sports Science — M
Foreign Languages Education — M
Geographic Information Systems — M
Geography — M
Health Psychology — M
Higher Education — M,O
History — M
Library Science — M,O
Marriage and Family Therapy — M
Mathematics Education — M
Mathematics — M
Middle School Education — M
Molecular Biology — M
Music — M
Nutrition — M
Political Science — M
Psychology—General — M
Public Administration — M
Reading Education — M
School Psychology — M
Science Education — M
Social Sciences Education — M
Social Work — M
Special Education — M
Student Affairs — M
Taxation — M
Therapies—Dance, Drama, and Music — M
Vocational and Technical Education — M

AQUINAS COLLEGE (MI)
Business Administration and Management—General — M
Education—General — M
Marketing — M
Organizational Management — M
Sustainability Management — M

AQUINAS COLLEGE (TN)
Education—General — M
Elementary Education — M
Secondary Education — M

AQUINAS INSTITUTE OF THEOLOGY
Health Services Management and Hospital Administration — M,D,O
Music — M,D,O
Pastoral Ministry and Counseling — M,D,O
Theology — M,D,O

ARCADIA UNIVERSITY
Advertising and Public Relations — M
Applied Behavior Analysis — M
Art Education — M,D,O
Business Administration and Management—General — M
Computer Education — M,D,O
Conflict Resolution and Mediation/Peace Studies — M
Counseling Psychology — M
Curriculum and Instruction — M,D,O
Early Childhood Education — M
Education—General — M,D,O

Educational Leadership and Administration	M,D,O
Educational Media/Instructional Technology	M,D,O
Elementary Education	M,D,O
English Education	M,D,O
English	M
Environmental Education	M,D,O
Forensic Sciences	M
Genetic Counseling	M
Health Education	M
Humanities	M
International Affairs	M
Marriage and Family Therapy	M
Mathematics Education	M,D,O
Music Education	D
Physical Therapy	D
Physician Assistant Studies	M
Psychology—General	M,D,O
Public Health—General	M
Reading Education	M,D,O
Science Education	M,D,O
Secondary Education	M,D,O
Special Education	M,D,O
Theater	M,D,O
Writing	M

ARGOSY UNIVERSITY, ATLANTA

Accounting	M,D
Biopsychology	M,D,O
Business Administration and Management—General	M,D
Clinical Psychology	M,D,O
Counselor Education	M,D,O
Education—General	M,D
Educational Leadership and Administration	M,D,O
Educational Media/Instructional Technology	M,D,O
Elementary Education	M,D,O
Finance and Banking	M,D
Forensic Psychology	M,D,O
Health Psychology	M,D,O
Health Services Management and Hospital Administration	M,D
Higher Education	M,D,O
Industrial and Organizational Psychology	M,D,O
International Business	M,D
Management Information Systems	M,D
Marketing	M,D
Marriage and Family Therapy	M,D,O
Psychology—General	M,D,O
Public Health—General	M
Secondary Education	M,D,O
Social Psychology	M,D,O
Sport Psychology	M,D,O

ARGOSY UNIVERSITY, CHICAGO

Accounting	M,D
Adult Education	M,D,O
Business Administration and Management—General	M,D
Clinical Psychology	M,D
Community College Education	M,D,O
Counseling Psychology	D
Counselor Education	D
Education—General	M,D,O
Educational Leadership and Administration	M,D,O
Elementary Education	M,D,O
Finance and Banking	M,D
Forensic Psychology	D
Health Psychology	D
Health Services Management and Hospital Administration	M,D
Higher Education	M,D,O
Human Development	D
Industrial and Organizational Psychology	M,D
International Business	M,D
Management Information Systems	M,D
Marketing	M,D
Marriage and Family Therapy	D
Neuroscience	D
Organizational Behavior	D
Organizational Management	D
Psychoanalysis and Psychotherapy	D
Psychology—General	M,D
Public Administration	M,D
Public Health—General	M
Secondary Education	M,D,O
Social Psychology	M,D
Sustainability Management	M,D

ARGOSY UNIVERSITY, DALLAS

Accounting	M,D,O
Business Administration and Management—General	M,D,O
Clinical Psychology	M,D
Counselor Education	D
Education—General	M,D
Educational Leadership and Administration	M,D
Finance and Banking	M,D,O
Forensic Psychology	M
Health Services Management and Hospital Administration	M,D,O
Higher Education	M,D
Industrial and Organizational Psychology	M
International Business	M,D,O
Management Information Systems	M,D,O
Marketing	M,D,O
Psychology—General	M,D
Public Administration	M,D,O
Public Health—General	M
School Psychology	M,D
Social Psychology	M
Sustainability Management	M,D,O

ARGOSY UNIVERSITY, DENVER

Accounting	M,D
Business Administration and Management—General	M,D
Clinical Psychology	M,D
Community College Education	M,D
Counseling Psychology	M,D
Counselor Education	M,D
Education—General	M,D
Educational Leadership and Administration	M,D
Educational Media/Instructional Technology	M,D
Elementary Education	M,D
Finance and Banking	M,D
Forensic Psychology	M,D
Health Services Management and Hospital Administration	M,D
Higher Education	M,D
Industrial and Organizational Psychology	M,D
International Business	M,D
Management Information Systems	M,D
Marketing	M,D
Marriage and Family Therapy	M,D
Organizational Management	M,D
Psychology—General	M,D
Public Administration	M,D
Public Health—General	M
Sustainability Management	M,D

ARGOSY UNIVERSITY, HAWAI'I

Accounting	M,D,O
Addictions/Substance Abuse Counseling	O
Adult Education	M,D
Business Administration and Management—General	M,D,O
Clinical Psychology	M,D,O
Counseling Psychology	D
Education—General	M,D
Educational Leadership and Administration	M,D
Elementary Education	M,D
Finance and Banking	M,D,O
Forensic Psychology	M
Health Services Management and Hospital Administration	M,D,O
Higher Education	M,D
International Business	M,D,O
Management Information Systems	M,D,O
Marketing	M,D,O
Marriage and Family Therapy	M
Organizational Management	D
Pharmacology	M,O
Psychology—General	M,D,O
Public Health—General	M
School Psychology	M,D
Secondary Education	M
Sustainability Management	M,D,O

ARGOSY UNIVERSITY, INLAND EMPIRE

Accounting	M,D
Business Administration and Management—General	M,D
Clinical Psychology	M,D
Community College Education	M,D
Counseling Psychology	M,D
Education—General	M,D
Educational Leadership and Administration	M,D
Elementary Education	M,D
Finance and Banking	M,D
Forensic Psychology	M,D
Health Services Management and Hospital Administration	M,D
Higher Education	M,D
Industrial and Organizational Psychology	M,D
International Business	M,D
Management Information Systems	M,D
Marketing	M,D
Marriage and Family Therapy	M,D
Organizational Management	M,D
Psychology—General	M,D
Public Administration	M,D
Public Health—General	M
Secondary Education	M,D
Sport Psychology	M,D
Sustainability Management	M,D

ARGOSY UNIVERSITY, LOS ANGELES

Accounting	M,D
Business Administration and Management—General	M,D
Clinical Psychology	M,D
Community College Education	M,D
Counseling Psychology	M,D
Education—General	M,D
Educational Leadership and Administration	M,D
Elementary Education	M,D
Finance and Banking	M,D
Forensic Psychology	M,D
Health Services Management and Hospital Administration	M,D
Higher Education	M,D
International Business	M,D
Management Information Systems	M,D
Marketing	M,D
Marriage and Family Therapy	M,D
Organizational Management	M,D
Psychology—General	M,D
Public Administration	M,D
Public Health—General	M
Secondary Education	M,D
Sustainability Management	M,D

ARGOSY UNIVERSITY, NASHVILLE

Accounting	M,D
Business Administration and Management—General	M,D

ARGOSY UNIVERSITY, NORTHERN VIRGINIA

Counseling Psychology	M,D
Counselor Education	D
Education—General	M,D,O
Educational Leadership and Administration	M,D,O
Educational Media/Instructional Technology	M,D,O
Elementary Education	M,D,O
Finance and Banking	M,D
Health Services Management and Hospital Administration	M,D
Higher Education	M,D,O
International Business	M,D,O
Management Information Systems	M,D
Marketing	M,D
Psychology—General	M,D
Public Health—General	M
Secondary Education	M,D,O
Accounting	M,D,O
Business Administration and Management—General	M,D,O
Clinical Psychology	M,D
Community College Education	M,D
Counseling Psychology	M,D
Counselor Education	M,D
Education—General	M,D,O
Educational Leadership and Administration	M,D,O
Elementary Education	M,D,O
Finance and Banking	M,D
Forensic Psychology	M,D
Health Psychology	M,D
Health Services Management and Hospital Administration	M,D,O
Higher Education	M,D,O
International Business	M,D,O
Management Information Systems	M,D,O
Marketing	M,D,O
Marriage and Family Therapy	M,D
Organizational Management	M,D,O
Psychology—General	M,D
Public Administration	M,D,O
Public Health—General	M
Secondary Education	M,D,O
Social Psychology	M,D
Sustainability Management	M,D,O

ARGOSY UNIVERSITY, ORANGE COUNTY

Accounting	M,D,O
Business Administration and Management—General	M,D,O
Clinical Psychology	M,D
Community College Education	M,D
Counseling Psychology	M,D
Education—General	M,D
Educational Leadership and Administration	M,D
Educational Media/Instructional Technology	M,D
Elementary Education	M,D
Finance and Banking	M,D,O
Forensic Psychology	M,D
Health Services Management and Hospital Administration	M,D,O
Higher Education	M,D
International Business	M,D,O
Management Information Systems	M,D,O
Marketing	M,D,O
Marriage and Family Therapy	M,D
Organizational Management	D
Psychology—General	M,D
Public Administration	M,D,O
Public Health—General	M
Secondary Education	M,D
Sport Psychology	M
Sustainability Management	M,D,O

ARGOSY UNIVERSITY, PHOENIX

Accounting	M,D
Adult Education	M,D,O
Business Administration and Management—General	M,D
Clinical Psychology	M,D
Community College Education	M,D,O
Counseling Psychology	M
Education—General	M,D,O
Educational Leadership and Administration	M,D,O
Educational Media/Instructional Technology	M,D,O
Elementary Education	M,D
Finance and Banking	M,D
Forensic Psychology	M,D
Health Services Management and Hospital Administration	M,D
Higher Education	M,D,O
Industrial and Organizational Psychology	M
International Business	M,D
Management Information Systems	M,D
Marketing	M,D
Neuroscience	M,D
Psychology—General	M,D
Public Administration	M,D
Public Health—General	M
School Psychology	M,D
Secondary Education	M,D,O
Sport Psychology	M,D
Sustainability Management	M,D

ARGOSY UNIVERSITY, SALT LAKE CITY

Accounting	M,D
Business Administration and Management—General	M,D
Counseling Psychology	M,D
Counselor Education	M,D
Education—General	M,D

Educational Leadership and Administration	M,D
Finance and Banking	M,D
Forensic Psychology	M,D
Health Services Management and Hospital Administration	M,D
International Business	M,D
Management Information Systems	M,D
Marketing	M,D
Marriage and Family Therapy	M,D
Psychology—General	M,D
Public Administration	M,D
Public Health—General	M
Sustainability Management	M,D

ARGOSY UNIVERSITY, SAN DIEGO

Accounting	M,D
Business Administration and Management—General	M,D
Clinical Psychology	M,D
Community College Education	M,D
Counseling Psychology	M,D
Education—General	M,D
Educational Leadership and Administration	M,D
Elementary Education	M,D
Finance and Banking	M,D
Forensic Psychology	M,D
Higher Education	M,D
International Business	M,D
Management Information Systems	M,D
Marketing	M,D
Marriage and Family Therapy	M,D
Organizational Management	M,D
Psychology—General	M,D
Public Administration	M,D
Public Health—General	M
Secondary Education	M,D

ARGOSY UNIVERSITY, SAN FRANCISCO BAY AREA

Accounting	M,D
Business Administration and Management—General	M,D
Clinical Psychology	M,D
Community College Education	M,D
Counseling Psychology	M,D
Education—General	M,D
Educational Leadership and Administration	M,D
Educational Media/Instructional Technology	M,D
Elementary Education	M,D
Finance and Banking	M,D
Forensic Psychology	M
Health Services Management and Hospital Administration	M,D
Higher Education	M,D
International Business	M,D
Management Information Systems	M,D
Marketing	M,D
Organizational Management	M,D
Psychology—General	M,D
Public Administration	M,D
Public Health—General	M
Secondary Education	M,D
Sport Psychology	M,D
Sustainability Management	M,D

ARGOSY UNIVERSITY, SARASOTA

Accounting	M,D,O
Business Administration and Management—General	M,D,O
Counseling Psychology	M,D
Counselor Education	M,D,O
Education—General	M,D,O
Educational Leadership and Administration	M,D,O
Educational Media/Instructional Technology	M,D,O
Elementary Education	M,D,O
Finance and Banking	M,D
Forensic Psychology	M,D
Health Services Management and Hospital Administration	M,D,O
Higher Education	M,D,O
International Business	M,D,O
Management Information Systems	M,D,O
Marketing	M,D,O
Marriage and Family Therapy	M,D
Organizational Management	M,D,O
Pastoral Ministry and Counseling	M,D
Psychology—General	M,D
Public Administration	M,D,O
Public Health—General	M
School Psychology	M,D,O
Secondary Education	M,D
Social Psychology	M,D
Sustainability Management	M,D,O

ARGOSY UNIVERSITY, SCHAUMBURG

Accounting	M,D,O
Business Administration and Management—General	M,D,O
Clinical Psychology	M,D
Corporate and Organizational Communication	M,D,O
Counseling Psychology	M,O
Finance and Banking	M,D,O
Forensic Psychology	M,O
Health Services Management and Hospital Administration	M,D,O
Human Resources Management	M,D,O
Industrial and Organizational Psychology	M,O
International Business	M,D,O
Management Information Systems	M,D,O
Marketing	M,D,O
Organizational Management	M,D,O
Psychology—General	M,O
Public Administration	M,D,O
Public Health—General	M

*M—masters degree; D—doctorate; O—other advanced degree; *—Close-Up and/or Display*

Sport Psychology	M,O
Sustainability Management	M,D,O

ARGOSY UNIVERSITY, SEATTLE

Accounting	M,D
Adult Education	M,D
Business Administration and Management—General	M,D
Clinical Psychology	M,D,O
Community College Education	M,D
Counseling Psychology	M,D
Education—General	M,D
Educational Leadership and Administration	M,D
Educational Media/Instructional Technology	M,D
Elementary Education	M,D
Finance and Banking	M,D
Health Services Management and Hospital Administration	M,D
Higher Education	M,D
International Business	M,D
Management Information Systems	M,D
Marketing	M,D
Organizational Management	M,D
Psychology—General	M,D,O
Public Administration	M,D
Public Health—General	M
Secondary Education	M,D
Sustainability Management	M,D

ARGOSY UNIVERSITY, TAMPA

Accounting	M,D
Business Administration and Management—General	M,D
Clinical Psychology	M,D
Community College Education	M,D,O
Counseling Psychology	M,D
Counselor Education	M,D,O
Education—General	M,D,O
Educational Leadership and Administration	M,D,O
Elementary Education	M,D,O
Finance and Banking	M,D
Health Services Management and Hospital Administration	M,D
Higher Education	M,D,O
Industrial and Organizational Psychology	M,D
International Business	M,D
Management Information Systems	M,D
Marketing	M,D
Marriage and Family Therapy	M,D
Neuroscience	M,D
Organizational Management	M,D
Psychology—General	M,D
Public Administration	M,D
Public Health—General	M
Secondary Education	M,D,O
Sustainability Management	M,D

ARGOSY UNIVERSITY, TWIN CITIES

Accounting	M,D
Biopsychology	M,D,O
Business Administration and Management—General	M,D
Clinical Psychology	M,D,O
Education—General	M,D,O
Educational Leadership and Administration	M,D,O
Educational Media/Instructional Technology	M,D,O
Elementary Education	M,D,O
Finance and Banking	M,D
Forensic Psychology	M,D,O
Health Psychology	M,D,O
Health Services Management and Hospital Administration	M,D
Higher Education	M,D,O
Industrial and Organizational Psychology	M,D,O
International Business	M,D
Management Information Systems	M,D
Marketing	M,D
Marriage and Family Therapy	M,D,O
Organizational Management	M,D
Psychology—General	M,D,O
Public Administration	M,D
Public Health—General	M
Secondary Education	M,D,O
Sustainability Management	M,D

ARIZONA SCHOOL OF ACUPUNCTURE AND ORIENTAL MEDICINE

Acupuncture and Oriental Medicine	M

ARIZONA STATE UNIVERSITY AT THE TEMPE CAMPUS

Accounting	M,D
Aerospace/Aeronautical Engineering	M,D
African Studies	M,D,O
Agricultural Economics and Agribusiness	D
Animal Behavior	M,D
Anthropology	M,D,O
Applied Arts and Design—General	M,D
Applied Behavior Analysis	M,D
Applied Mathematics	M,D,O
Applied Psychology	M
Archaeology	M,D,O
Architectural History	D
Architecture	M,D
Art Education	M,D
Art History	M,D
Art/Fine Arts	M,D
Arts Administration	M,D
Astrophysics	M,D
Aviation Management	M
Biochemistry	M,D
Bioinformatics	M,D
Biological and Biomedical Sciences—General	M,D
Biomedical Engineering	M,D
Biotechnology	M,D
Building Science	M,D

Business Administration and Management—General	M,D
Cell Biology	M,D
Chemical Engineering	M,D
Chemistry	M,D
Child and Family Studies	M,D
Chinese	M,D
Civil Engineering	M,D
Clinical Psychology	M,D
Cognitive Sciences	M,D
Communication Disorders	M,D
Communication—General	M,D
Community Health	M,D,O
Comparative Literature	M,D,O
Computer Engineering	M,D
Computer Science	M,D
Conservation Biology	M,D
Construction Engineering	M,D
Construction Management	M,D
Counseling Psychology	D
Counselor Education	M
Criminal Justice and Criminology	M,D,O
Cultural Studies	M,D
Curriculum and Instruction	M
Dance	M
Developmental Psychology	M,D
Economics	D
Education—General	M,D,O
Educational Leadership and Administration	M,D
Educational Measurement and Evaluation	D
Educational Media/Instructional Technology	M,O
Educational Policy	D
Electrical Engineering	M,D,O
Elementary Education	M
Emergency Management	M,D
Energy and Power Engineering	M,D
Engineering and Applied Sciences—General	M,D
English as a Second Language	M,D,O
English	M,D,O
Entrepreneurship	M,D
Environmental Design	D
Environmental Engineering	M,D
Environmental Management and Policy	M
Environmental Sciences	M,D,O
Ergonomics and Human Factors	M
Ethics	M,D
Evolutionary Biology	M,D
Exercise and Sports Science	M,D
Family Nurse Practitioner Studies	M,D,O
Film, Television, and Video Production	M
Finance and Banking	M,D
Foreign Languages Education	M,D
French	M
Gender Studies	M,D,O
Geographic Information Systems	M,D,O
Geography	M,D,O
Geological Engineering	M,D
Geology	M,D
Geosciences	M,D
German	M
Gerontological Nursing	M,D,O
Gerontology	M,D,O
Health Education	D
Health Promotion	M,D
Health Services Management and Hospital Administration	M,D
Higher Education	M
History of Science and Technology	M,D
History	M,D,O
Homeland Security	M,D
Human Development	M,D
Industrial/Management Engineering	M,D
Information Science	M
Interdisciplinary Studies	M
International Business	M,D
International Health	M,D,O
Japanese	M
Journalism	M,D
Landscape Architecture	M,D
Law	M,D
Legal and Justice Studies	M,D,O
Liberal Studies	M
Linguistics	M,D,O
Management Information Systems	M,D
Management of Technology	M
Management Strategy and Policy	M,D
Manufacturing Engineering	M
Marketing	M,D
Marriage and Family Therapy	M,D
Mass Communication	M,D
Materials Engineering	M,D
Materials Sciences	M,D
Mathematics Education	M,D,O
Mathematics	M,D,O
Mechanical Engineering	M,D
Media Studies	M,D
Medical Informatics	M,D
Medieval and Renaissance Studies	M,D
Microbiology	M,D
Modeling and Simulation	M,D
Molecular Biology	M,D
Museum Studies	M,D,O
Music Education	M,D
Music	M,D
Nanotechnology	M,D
Neuroscience	M,D
Nonprofit Management	M,D
Nuclear Engineering	M,D,O
Nursing and Healthcare Administration	M,D,O
Nursing Education	M,D,O
Nursing—General	M,D,O
Nutrition	M,D
Organizational Behavior	M,D
Philosophy	M,D,O

Physical Education	M
Physics	M,D
Planetary and Space Sciences	M,D
Plant Biology	M,D
Political Science	M,D
Psychiatric Nursing	M,D,O
Psychology—General	M,D
Public Administration	M,D
Public Affairs	M,D
Public Health—General	M,D,O
Public History	M,D,O
Public Policy	M,D
Publishing	M,D,O
Real Estate	M,D
Reliability Engineering	M
Religion	M,D,O
Rhetoric	M,D,O
Secondary Education	M
Social Psychology	M,D
Social Work	M,D,O
Sociology	M,D
Software Engineering	M,D
Spanish	M,D
Special Education	M,O
Statistics	M,D,O
Supply Chain Management	M,D
Sustainable Development	M,D,O
Systems Engineering	M
Systems Science	M,D
Technology and Public Policy	M
Textile Design	M,D
Theater	M,D
Therapies—Dance, Drama, and Music	M,D
Translation and Interpretation	M,D,O
Transportation and Highway Engineering	M,D,O
Travel and Tourism	M,D,O
Urban and Regional Planning	M,D,O
Urban Design	M,D
Urban Studies	M,D,O
Writing	M,D

ARIZONA SUMMIT LAW SCHOOL

Law	D

ARKANSAS STATE UNIVERSITY

Accounting	M
Addictions/Substance Abuse Counseling	M,O
Agricultural Education	M,O
Agricultural Sciences—General	M,O
Biological and Biomedical Sciences—General	M,O
Biotechnology	M,O
Business Administration and Management—General	M
Business Education	O
Chemistry	M,O
Clinical Psychology	M,O
Communication Disorders	M,O
Communication—General	M,O
Community College Education	M,D,O
Computer Science	M
Counselor Education	M,O
Criminal Justice and Criminology	M,O
Early Childhood Education	M,D,O
Education of the Gifted	M,D,O
Education—General	M,D,O
Educational Leadership and Administration	M,D,O
Elementary Education	M,D,O
Emergency Management	M,O
Engineering and Applied Sciences—General	M
Engineering Management	M
English Education	M,O
English	M,O
Environmental Sciences	M,D
Exercise and Sports Science	M,O
Foundations and Philosophy of Education	M,D,O
Gerontology	M,D,O
Health Communication	M,O
Health Education	M,D,O
Health Services Management and Hospital Administration	M,D,O
Historic Preservation	M,D
History	M,O
Journalism	M
Management Information Systems	O
Mass Communication	M
Mathematics Education	M
Mathematics	M
Media Studies	M
Middle School Education	M,D,O
Molecular Biology	M,D
Music Education	M,O
Music	M,O
Nurse Anesthesia	M,D,O
Nursing—General	M,D,O
Occupational Therapy	D
Physical Education	M,O
Physical Therapy	D
Political Science	M,O
Public Administration	M,O
Reading Education	M,D,O
Rehabilitation Counseling	M,O
School Psychology	M,O
Science Education	M,O
Social Sciences Education	M,D,O
Social Work	M,O
Sociology	M,O
Special Education	M,D,O
Sports Management	M,O
Student Affairs	M,O

ARKANSAS TECH UNIVERSITY

Business Administration and Management—General	M
Counselor Education	M,D,O
Curriculum and Instruction	M,D,O
Education—General	M,D,O

Physical Education	M
Educational Leadership and Administration	M,D,O
Educational Media/Instructional Technology	M,D,O
Elementary Education	M,D,O
Emergency Management	M
Engineering and Applied Sciences—General	M
English as a Second Language	M
English Education	M
English	M
Fish, Game, and Wildlife Management	M
Health Informatics	M
History	M
Information Science	M
Journalism	M
Liberal Studies	M
Nursing—General	M
Psychology—General	M
Sociology	M
Student Affairs	M,D,O

ARLINGTON BAPTIST COLLEGE

Curriculum and Instruction	M
Education—General	M
Educational Leadership and Administration	M
Theology	M

ARMSTRONG STATE UNIVERSITY

Adult Education	M,O
Adult Nursing	M,O
American Studies	M
Athletic Training and Sports Medicine	M,O
Business Administration and Management—General	M,O
Communication Disorders	M
Computer and Information Systems Security	M,O
Computer Science	M
Corporate and Organizational Communication	M,O
Criminal Justice and Criminology	M,O
Curriculum and Instruction	M,O
Early Childhood Education	M,O
Education—General	M,O
Exercise and Sports Science	M,O
Family Nurse Practitioner Studies	M,O
Gerontological Nursing	M,O
Health Services Management and Hospital Administration	M
History	M
Information Science	M
Nursing—General	M,O
Physical Education	M,O
Physical Therapy	D
Public Health—General	M
Public History	M
Reading Education	M,O
Secondary Education	M,O
Special Education	M,O
Western European Studies	M,O
Writing	M,O

ART ACADEMY OF CINCINNATI

Art Education	M

ARTCENTER COLLEGE OF DESIGN

Art/Fine Arts	M
Computer Art and Design	M
Environmental Design	M
Film, Television, and Video Production	M
Graphic Design	M
Industrial Design	M
Transportation and Highway Engineering	M

THE ART INSTITUTE OF CALIFORNIA–SAN FRANCISCO, A CAMPUS OF ARGOSY UNIVERSITY

Computer Art and Design	M
Film, Television, and Video Production	M

THE ART INSTITUTE OF DALLAS, A BRANCH OF MIAMI INTERNATIONAL UNIVERSITY OF ART & DESIGN

Applied Arts and Design—General	M

ASBURY THEOLOGICAL SEMINARY

Missions and Missiology	M,D,O
Pastoral Ministry and Counseling	M,D,O
Religious Education	M,D,O
Theology	M,D,O

ASBURY UNIVERSITY

Child and Family Studies	M
Classics	M
Educational Leadership and Administration	M
English as a Second Language	M
English	M
French	M
Mathematics Education	M
Reading Education	M
Science Education	M
Social Sciences Education	M
Social Work	M
Spanish	M
Special Education	M
Writing	M

ASHLAND THEOLOGICAL SEMINARY

Clinical Psychology	M,D
Counselor Education	M,D
Pastoral Ministry and Counseling	M,D
Theology	M,D

ASHLAND UNIVERSITY

Business Administration and Management—General	M
Corporate and Organizational Communication	M
Education of the Gifted	M

Education—General | M,D
Educational Leadership and Administration | M,D
Educational Media/Instructional Technology | M
Exercise and Sports Science | M
Family Nurse Practitioner Studies | D
Foundations and Philosophy of Education | M
History | M
Nursing—General | D
Political Science | M
Reading Education | M
Special Education | M
Writing | M

ASHWORTH COLLEGE

Business Administration and Management—General | M
Criminal Justice and Criminology | M
Health Services Management and Hospital Administration | M
Human Resources Management | M
International Business | M
Marketing | M

ASPEN UNIVERSITY

Business Administration and Management—General | M,O
Finance and Banking | M,O
Forensic Nursing | M
Information Science | M,O
Management Information Systems | M,O
Nursing and Healthcare Administration | M
Nursing Education | M
Nursing Informatics | M
Nursing—General | M
Project Management | M,O

ASSEMBLIES OF GOD THEOLOGICAL SEMINARY

Cultural Studies | M,D
Missions and Missiology | M,D
Pastoral Ministry and Counseling | M,D
Theology | M,D

ASSUMPTION COLLEGE

Accounting | M,O
Addictions/Substance Abuse Counseling | O
Applied Behavior Analysis | M,O
Business Administration and Management—General | M,O
Child and Family Studies | M,O
Counseling Psychology | M,O
Economics | M,O
Finance and Banking | M,O
Health Services Management and Hospital Administration | M,O
Human Resources Management | M,O
International Business | M,O
Marketing | M,O
Nonprofit Management | M,O
Rehabilitation Counseling | M,O
School Psychology | M,O
Social Sciences | O
Special Education | M,O

ATHABASCA UNIVERSITY

Adult Education | M,O
Allied Health—General | M,O
Applied Psychology | M,O
Architecture | M,O
Art Therapy | M,O
Business Administration and Management—General | M,D,O
Counseling Psychology | M,O
Counselor Education | M,O
Cultural Studies | M,O
Distance Education Development | M,D,O
Education—General | M,D,O
Interdisciplinary Studies | M,O
International Development | M,O
Management of Technology | M,D,O
Nursing and Healthcare Administration | M,O
Nursing—General | M,O
Organizational Management | M,O
Project Management | M,D,O
Science Education | M,O

THE ATHENAEUM OF OHIO

Theology | M,O

ATLANTA'S JOHN MARSHALL LAW SCHOOL

Law | M,D

ATLANTIC INSTITUTE OF ORIENTAL MEDICINE

Acupuncture and Oriental Medicine | M,D

ATLANTIC SCHOOL OF THEOLOGY

Pastoral Ministry and Counseling | M,O
Theology | M,O

ATLANTIC UNIVERSITY

Pastoral Ministry and Counseling | O
Psychoanalysis and Psychotherapy | O
Transpersonal and Humanistic Psychology | M

ATLANTIC UNIVERSITY COLLEGE

Graphic Design | M

A.T. STILL UNIVERSITY

Allied Health—General | M,D,O
Athletic Training and Sports Medicine | M,D,O
Biological and Biomedical Sciences—General | M,D
Communication Disorders | M,D,O
Dentistry | D,O

Health Services Management and Hospital Administration | M,D,O
International Health | M,D,O
Kinesiology and Movement Studies | M,D,O
Occupational Therapy | M,D,O
Oral and Dental Sciences | M,D,O
Organizational Behavior | M,D,O
Osteopathic Medicine | M,D
Physical Therapy | M,D,O
Physician Assistant Studies | M,D,O
Public Health—General | M,D,O
Sport Psychology | M,D,O

AUBURN UNIVERSITY

Accounting | M
Adult Education | M,D,O
Aerospace/Aeronautical Engineering | M,D
Agricultural Economics and Agribusiness | M
Agricultural Sciences—General | M,D
Agronomy and Soil Sciences | M,D
Analytical Chemistry | M,D
Animal Sciences | M,D
Applied Economics | D
Applied Mathematics | M,D
Aquaculture | M,D
Architecture | M,D
Biochemistry | M,D
Biological and Biomedical Sciences—General | M,D
Biosystems Engineering | M,D
Botany | M,D
Building Science | M
Business Administration and Management—General | M,D
Cell Biology | M,D
Chemical Engineering | M,D
Chemistry | M,D
Child and Family Studies | M,D
Civil Engineering | M,D
Clothing and Textiles | M,D
Communication Disorders | M,D
Communication—General | M,O
Computer Engineering | M,D
Computer Science | M,D
Construction Engineering | M
Curriculum and Instruction | M,D,O
Economics | M
Education—General | M,D,O
Educational Leadership and Administration | M,D,O
Educational Media/Instructional Technology | M,D,O
Electrical Engineering | M,D
Elementary Education | M,D,O
Engineering and Applied Sciences—General | M,D,O
English | M,D,O
Entomology | M,D
Exercise and Sports Science | M,D,O
Finance and Banking | M
Fish, Game, and Wildlife Management | M,D
Food Science and Technology | M,D,O
Forestry | M,D
Geography | M
Geology | M
Health Education | M,D,O
Higher Education | M,D,O
History | M,D,O
Horticulture | M,D
Human Development | M,D
Industrial Design | M
Industrial/Management Engineering | M,D,O
Inorganic Chemistry | M,D
Landscape Architecture | M
Materials Engineering | M,D
Mathematics | M,D
Mechanical Engineering | M,D
Molecular Biology | M,D
Natural Resources | M,D
Nursing Education | M
Nursing—General | M
Nutrition | M,D,O
Organic Chemistry | M,D
Pharmaceutical Sciences | M,D
Pharmacy | D
Physical Chemistry | M,D
Physical Education | M,D,O
Physics | M,D
Plant Pathology | M,D
Political Science | M,D,O
Polymer Science and Engineering | M,D
Psychology—General | M,D
Public Administration | M,D,O
Real Estate | M
Sociology | M
Software Engineering | M,D
Spanish | M
Special Education | M,D
Statistics | M,D
Systems Engineering | M,D,O
Technical Communication | M,D,O
Urban and Regional Planning | M
Veterinary Medicine | D
Zoology | M,D

AUBURN UNIVERSITY AT MONTGOMERY

Accounting | M
Business Administration and Management—General | M
Clinical Psychology | M,O
Computer and Information Systems Security | M
Counselor Education | M,O

Criminal Justice and Criminology | M
Early Childhood Education | M,O
Education—General | M,O
Educational Leadership and Administration | M,O
Educational Media/Instructional Technology | M,O
Elementary Education | M,O
Emergency Management | M
Exercise and Sports Science | M
Geographic Information Systems | M
Homeland Security | M
Information Science | M
Legal and Justice Studies | M
Liberal Studies | M,D
Management Information Systems | M
Nursing Education | M
Nursing—General | M
Organizational Management | M
Physical Education | M,O
Political Science | M,D
Psychology—General | M
Public Administration | M,D
Public Policy | M,D
School Psychology | M,O
Secondary Education | M,O
Special Education | M,O
Sports Management | M,O
Writing | M

AUGSBURG COLLEGE

Business Administration and Management—General | M
Education—General | M
Family Nurse Practitioner Studies | M,D
Nursing—General | M,D
Organizational Management | M
Physician Assistant Studies | M
Social Work | M
Transcultural Nursing | M,D

AUGUSTANA UNIVERSITY

Education—General | M
Educational Media/Instructional Technology | M
Mathematics | M
Reading Education | M
Science Education | M
Special Education | M
Sports Management | M

AUGUSTA UNIVERSITY

Acute Care/Critical Care Nursing | D
Allied Health—General | D
Allopathic Medicine | D
Anatomy | D
Biochemistry | D
Business Administration and Management—General | M
Cancer Biology/Oncology | D
Cardiovascular Sciences | D
Cell Biology | D
Clinical Psychology | M,O
Clinical Research | M
Computer and Information Systems Security | M
Counselor Education | M,O
Curriculum and Instruction | M,O
Dentistry | D
Educational Leadership and Administration | M,O
Educational Media/Instructional Technology | D
Elementary Education | M,O
Environmental and Occupational Health | M
Family Nurse Practitioner Studies | M
Foreign Languages Education | M,O
Genomic Sciences | D
Gerontological Nursing | D
Health Informatics | M
Medical Illustration | M
Middle School Education | M,O
Molecular Medicine | D
Music Education | M,O
Neuroscience | D
Nurse Anesthesia | D
Nursing and Healthcare Administration | M,D
Nursing—General | D
Occupational Therapy | M
Oral and Dental Sciences | M,D
Pediatric Nursing | D
Pharmacology | D
Physical Therapy | D
Physician Assistant Studies | M
Physiology | D
Psychiatric Nursing | D
Psychology—General | M
Public Health—General | M
Rehabilitation Sciences | D
School Psychology | M,O
Secondary Education | M,O
Social Sciences | M
Special Education | M,O

AURORA UNIVERSITY

Accounting | M
Adult Education | M,D
Applied Behavior Analysis | M
Business Administration and Management—General | M
Curriculum and Instruction | M,D
Education—General | M,D
Educational Leadership and Administration | M,D
Educational Media/Instructional Technology | M,D
English as a Second Language | M,D
Higher Education | M,D
Homeland Security | M
Mathematics | M

Nursing—General | M
Public Policy | M
Reading Education | M,D
Social Work | M,D
Special Education | M,D

AUSTIN COLLEGE

Education—General | M

AUSTIN GRADUATE SCHOOL OF THEOLOGY

Theology | M

AUSTIN PEAY STATE UNIVERSITY

Biological and Biomedical Sciences—General | M
Business Administration and Management—General | M
Clinical Laboratory Sciences/Medical Technology | M
Clinical Psychology | M
Communication—General | M
Counseling Psychology | M
Counselor Education | M,O
Curriculum and Instruction | M,O
Database Systems | M
Developmental Education | M
Education—General | M,O
Educational Leadership and Administration | M,O
Elementary Education | M,O
Engineering and Applied Sciences—General | M
English | M
Exercise and Sports Science | M
Family Nurse Practitioner Studies | M
Health Education | M
Human Resources Management | M
Industrial and Organizational Psychology | M
Management Strategy and Policy | M
Military and Defense Studies | M
Music Education | M
Music | M
Nursing and Healthcare Administration | M
Nursing Education | M
Nursing Informatics | M
Nursing—General | M
Psychology—General | M
Public Health—General | M
Reading Education | M,O
Secondary Education | M,O
Social Work | M
Special Education | M
Sports Management | M

AUSTIN PRESBYTERIAN THEOLOGICAL SEMINARY

Pastoral Ministry and Counseling | M,D
Theology | M,D

AVE MARIA SCHOOL OF LAW

Law | D

AVE MARIA UNIVERSITY

Pastoral Ministry and Counseling | M,D
Theology | M,D

AVERETT UNIVERSITY

Accounting | M
Business Administration and Management—General | M
Curriculum and Instruction | M
Education—General | M
Educational Leadership and Administration | M
Human Resources Management | M
Marketing | M
Special Education | M

AVILA UNIVERSITY

Accounting | M
Business Administration and Management—General | M
Counseling Psychology | M
Education—General | M,O
Educational Media/Instructional Technology | M
English as a Second Language | M,O
Finance and Banking | M
Health Services Management and Hospital Administration | M
Human Resources Management | M
International and Comparative Education | M,O
International Business | M
Management Information Systems | M
Marketing | M
Organizational Management | M
Project Management | M
Psychology—General | M
Reading Education | M,O

AZUSA PACIFIC UNIVERSITY

Art/Fine Arts | M
Athletic Training and Sports Medicine | M
Biotechnology | M
Business Administration and Management—General | D
Clinical Psychology | D
Counselor Education | M
Curriculum and Instruction | M
Education—General | M,D
Educational Leadership and Administration | M,D
Educational Media/Instructional Technology | M
English as a Second Language | M
Entrepreneurship | M
Ethics | M
Finance and Banking | M

Foundations and Philosophy of
  Education — M
Higher Education — M,D
Human Resources Development — M
Human Resources Management — M
International Affairs — M
International Business — M
Library Science — M,O
Management Strategy and Policy — M
Marketing — M
Marriage and Family Therapy — D
Multilingual and Multicultural
  Education — M
Music Education — M
Music — M
Nonprofit Management — M
Nursing Education — M,D
Nursing—General — M,D
Organizational Management — M
Pastoral Ministry and Counseling — M
Physical Education — M
Physical Therapy — D
Psychology—General — M,D
Public Administration — M
Religious Education — M
School Psychology — M
Social Work — M
Special Education — M
Student Affairs — M
Theology — M,D
Urban Studies — M

BABEL UNIVERSITY PROFESSIONAL SCHOOL OF TRANSLATION
Translation and Interpretation — M

BABSON COLLEGE
Accounting — M,O
Business Administration and
  Management—General — M,O
Entrepreneurship — M,O

BAKER COLLEGE CENTER FOR GRADUATE STUDIES–ONLINE
Accounting — M,D
Business Administration and
  Management—General — M,D
Finance and Banking — M,D
Health Services Management and
  Hospital Administration — M,D
Human Resources Management — M,D
Management Information Systems — M,D
Marketing — M,D

BAKER UNIVERSITY
Business Administration and
  Management—General — M
Education—General — M,D
Liberal Studies — M
Organizational Management — M

BAKKE GRADUATE UNIVERSITY
Business Administration and
  Management—General — M,D
Entrepreneurship — M,D
Pastoral Ministry and Counseling — M,D
Theology — M,D
Urban Education — M,D

BALDWIN WALLACE UNIVERSITY
Accounting — M
Business Administration and
  Management—General — M
Communication Disorders — M
Education—General — M
Educational Leadership and
  Administration — M
Educational Media/Instructional
  Technology — M
Entrepreneurship — M
Health Education — M
Health Services Management and
  Hospital Administration — M
Human Resources Management — M
International Business — M
Management Strategy and Policy — M
Marketing Research — M
Physician Assistant Studies — M
Public Health—General — M
Reading Education — M
Special Education — M
Sustainability Management — M

BALL STATE UNIVERSITY
Accounting — M
Actuarial Science — M
Adult Education — M,D
Advertising and Public Relations — M
Anthropology — M,O
Applied Behavior Analysis — M
Architecture — M
Art/Fine Arts — M
Biological and Biomedical
  Sciences—General — M,D
Business Administration and
  Management—General — M,O
Business Education — M,O
Chemistry — M,D
Clinical Psychology — M,D
Cognitive Sciences — M
Communication Disorders — M,D
Communication—General — M,O
Computer Education — M,D,O
Computer Science — M
Counseling Psychology — M,D
Counselor Education — M,D
Criminal Justice and Criminology — M,O
Curriculum and Instruction — M,D
Economic Development — M,O
Education of the Gifted — M,D,O
Education—General — M,D,O
Educational Leadership and
  Administration — M,D,O
Educational Measurement and
  Evaluation — M,D,O

Educational Media/Instructional
  Technology — M,D
Educational Policy — D
Educational Psychology — M,D
Elementary Education — M,D,O
Emergency Management — M,O
English as a Second Language — M
English — M,D
Environmental Education — M,O
Environmental Management
  and Policy — M,O
Environmental Sciences — D
Exercise and Sports Science — M,D
Family and Consumer
  Sciences–General — M
Family Nurse Practitioner Studies — M,D,O
Foundations and Philosophy of
  Education — D
Geographic Information Systems — M,O
Geography — M,O
Geology — M,D
Geosciences — M
Gerontological Nursing — M,D,O
Health Promotion — M
Higher Education — M,D
Historic Preservation — M
History — M
Homeland Security — M,O
Human Development — M,D,O
Information Science — M,O
Interior Design — M
Internet and Interactive
  Multimedia — M
Journalism — M
Kinesiology and Movement Studies — M,D,O
Landscape Architecture — M
Linguistics — M
Management Information Systems — M,O
Mathematics Education — M
Mathematics — M
Meteorology — M,O
Middle School Education — M,O
Music Education — M,D,O
Music — M,D,O
Natural Resources — M,O
Neuroscience — M
Nursing Education — M,D,O
Nursing—General — M,D,O
Nutrition — M
Photography — M
Physical Education — M
Physics — M
Physiology — M
Political Science — M
Psychology—General — M
Public Administration — M,O
Quantitative Analysis — M
Reading Education — M,D,O
Rehabilitation Counseling — M,D
Rhetoric — M,D
School Psychology — M,D,O
Secondary Education — M
Social Psychology — M
Sociology — M
Special Education — M,D,O
Speech and Interpersonal
  Communication — M
Sport Psychology — M
Sports Management — M
Statistics — M
Telecommunications — M
Urban and Regional Planning — M,O
Urban Design — M
Writing — M,D

BANK STREET COLLEGE OF EDUCATION
Child and Family Studies — M
Early Childhood Education — M
Education—General — M
Educational Leadership and
  Administration — M
Elementary Education — M
Foundations and Philosophy of
  Education — M
Maternal and Child Health — M
Mathematics Education — M
Multilingual and Multicultural
  Education — M
Museum Education — M
Reading Education — M
Special Education — M

BAPTIST BIBLE COLLEGE
Cultural Studies — M
Pastoral Ministry and Counseling — M
Theology — M

THE BAPTIST COLLEGE OF FLORIDA
Music — M
Pastoral Ministry and Counseling — M
Religion — M
Theology — M

BAPTIST MISSIONARY ASSOCIATION THEOLOGICAL SEMINARY
Theology — M

BAPTIST THEOLOGICAL SEMINARY AT RICHMOND
Pastoral Ministry and Counseling — M,D,O
Religion — M,D,O
Religious Education — M,D,O
Theology — M,D,O

BARCLAY COLLEGE
Theology — M

BARD COLLEGE
Art/Fine Arts — M
Atmospheric Sciences — M,O
Economics — M
Education—General — M
English — M
Environmental Management
  and Policy — M,O

Film, Television, and Video
  Production — M
History — M
Mathematics Education — M
Museum Studies — M
Music — M,O
Photography — M
Science Education — M
Secondary Education — M
Spanish — M
Sustainability Management — M
Writing — M

BARD GRADUATE CENTER
Art History — M,D*
Decorative Arts — M,D

BARRY UNIVERSITY
Accounting — M
Acute Care/Critical Care Nursing — M,O
Anatomy — M
Art/Fine Arts — M
Athletic Training and Sports
  Medicine — M
Biological and Biomedical
  Sciences—General — M
Business Administration and
  Management—General — M,O
Clinical Psychology — M,O
Communication Disorders — M
Communication—General — M
Corporate and Organizational
  Communication — M,O
Counselor Education — M,D,O
Curriculum and Instruction — D,O
Distance Education Development — O
Early Childhood Education — M,D,O
Education of the Gifted — M,D,O
Education—General — M,D,O
Educational Leadership and
  Administration — M,D,O
Educational Media/Instructional
  Technology — M,D,O
Elementary Education — M,D,O
English as a Second Language — M,D,O
Exercise and Sports Science — M
Family Nurse Practitioner Studies — M,O
Finance and Banking — O
Health Informatics — O
Health Services Management and
  Hospital Administration — M,O
Higher Education — M,D
Human Resources Development — M,D
Human Resources Management — O
Information Science — M
International Business — O
Kinesiology and Movement Studies — M
Law — D
Liberal Studies — M
Management Information Systems — O
Marketing — O
Marriage and Family Therapy — M,O
Nurse Anesthesia — M
Nursing and Healthcare
  Administration — M,D,O
Nursing Education — M,O
Nursing—General — M,D,O
Occupational Therapy — M
Pastoral Ministry and Counseling — M,D
Photography — M
Physician Assistant Studies — M
Podiatric Medicine — D
Psychology—General — M,O
Public Administration — M
Public Health—General — M
Reading Education — M,D,O
Rehabilitation Counseling — M,O
School Psychology — M
Social Work — M,D
Special Education — M,D,O
Sport Psychology — M
Sports Management — M
Theology — M,D

BARTON COLLEGE
Elementary Education — M

BARUCH COLLEGE OF THE CITY UNIVERSITY OF NEW YORK
Accounting — M,D
Arts Administration — M
Business Administration and
  Management—General — M,D,O
Corporate and Organizational
  Communication — M
Counseling Psychology — M
Economics — M
Educational Leadership and
  Administration — M,O
Entrepreneurship — M,D
Finance and Banking — M,D
Financial Engineering — M
Health Services Management and
  Hospital Administration — M
Higher Education — M
Human Resources Management — M,D
Industrial and Labor Relations — M
Industrial and Manufacturing
  Management — M,D
Industrial and Organizational
  Psychology — M,D
International Affairs — M*
International Business — M,D
International Economics — M
International Trade Policy — M
Management Information Systems — M,D
Marketing — M
Nonprofit Management — M
Organizational Behavior — M,D
Public Administration — M
Public Policy — M
Quantitative Analysis — M
Real Estate — M
Statistics — M
Sustainability Management — M,D

Sustainable Development — M
Taxation — M

BASTYR UNIVERSITY
Acupuncture and Oriental Medicine — M,D,O
Counseling Psychology — M,O
Environmental Design — M
Health Psychology — M,O
Landscape Architecture — M,O
Naturopathic Medicine — D
Nurse Midwifery — M,O
Nutrition — M,O

BAYAMÓN CENTRAL UNIVERSITY
Accounting — M
Business Administration and
  Management—General — M
Counselor Education — M,O
Early Childhood Education — M,O
Education—General — M,O
Educational Leadership and
  Administration — M,O
Elementary Education — M,O
Finance and Banking — M
Industrial and Organizational
  Psychology — M
Marketing — M
Marriage and Family Therapy — M,O
Rehabilitation Counseling — M,O
Special Education — M,O

BAYLOR COLLEGE OF MEDICINE
Allopathic Medicine — M
Biochemistry — D
Bioengineering — D
Biological and Biomedical
  Sciences—General — M,D
Biomedical Engineering — D
Biophysics — D
Cancer Biology/Oncology — D
Cardiovascular Sciences — D
Cell Biology — D
Clinical Laboratory
  Sciences/Medical Technology — M,D
Computational Biology — D
Developmental Biology — D
Genetics — D
Human Genetics — D
Immunology — D
Microbiology — D
Molecular Biology — D
Molecular Biophysics — D
Molecular Medicine — D
Molecular Physiology — D
Neuroscience — D
Nurse Anesthesia — D
Pathology — D
Pharmacology — D
Physician Assistant Studies — M
Structural Biology — D
Translational Biology — D
Virology — D

BAYLOR UNIVERSITY
Accounting — M
Allied Health—General — M,D
American Studies — M
Applied Behavior Analysis — M,D,O
Biochemistry — M,D
Biological and Biomedical
  Sciences—General — M,D
Biomedical Engineering — M,D
Business Administration and
  Management—General — M
Chemistry — M,D
Clinical Psychology — D
Communication Disorders — M
Communication—General — M
Computer Engineering — M,D
Computer Science — M,D
Curriculum and Instruction — M,D
Ecology — D
Economics — M
Education—General — M,D,O
Educational Leadership and
  Administration — M,O
Educational Measurement and
  Evaluation — M,D,O
Educational Psychology — M,D,O
Electrical Engineering — M,D
Emergency Medical Services — D
English — M,D
Entrepreneurship — D
Environmental Biology — M,D
Environmental Management
  and Policy — M
Environmental Sciences — D
Family Nurse Practitioner Studies — M,D
Geosciences — M,D
Health Education — M,D
Health Services Management and
  Hospital Administration — M
History — M,D
Interdisciplinary Studies — D
International Affairs — M,D
Journalism — M
Law — D
Limnology — M,D
Management Information Systems — M,D
Maternal and Child/Neonatal
  Nursing — M,D
Mathematics — M,D
Mechanical Engineering — M,D
Museum Studies — M
Music — M,D
Nurse Midwifery — M,D
Nursing—General — M
Nutrition — M
Philosophy — M,D
Physical Education — M,D
Physical Therapy — D
Physics — M,D
Political Science — M,D
Psychology—General — M,D
Public Administration — M,D

Public Policy — M,D
Religion — M,D
School Psychology — M,D,O
Social Work — M,D
Sociology — M,D
Spanish — M
Special Education — M,D,O
Statistics — M,D
Theater — M,D
Theology — M,D

BAY PATH UNIVERSITY
Accounting — M
Addictions/Substance Abuse Counseling — M
Applied Behavior Analysis — M
Applied Statistics — M
Clinical Psychology — M
Computer and Information Systems Security — M
Curriculum and Instruction — M
Developmental Psychology — M
Educational Leadership and Administration — M
Educational Media/Instructional Technology — M
Entrepreneurship — M
Higher Education — M
Management Information Systems — M
Management Strategy and Policy — M
Nonprofit Management — M
Occupational Therapy — M
Physician Assistant Studies — M
Special Education — M
Writing — M

BECKER COLLEGE
Counseling Psychology — M
Counselor Education — M
Social Psychology — M

BELHAVEN UNIVERSITY (MS)
Business Administration and Management—General — M
Education—General — M
Educational Media/Instructional Technology — M
Elementary Education — M
Health Services Management and Hospital Administration — M
Human Resources Management — M
Multilingual and Multicultural Education — M
Public Administration — M
Reading Education — M
Secondary Education — M
Sports Management — M

BELLARMINE UNIVERSITY
Business Administration and Management—General — M
Communication—General — M
Education—General — M,D,O
Educational Leadership and Administration — M,D,O
Elementary Education — M,D,O
Family Nurse Practitioner Studies — M,D
Higher Education — M,D,O
Management Strategy and Policy — M
Middle School Education — M,D,O
Nursing and Healthcare Administration — M,D
Nursing Education — M,D
Nursing—General — M,D
Physical Therapy — M,D
Reading Education — M,D,O
Secondary Education — M,D,O
Special Education — M,D,O

BELLEVUE UNIVERSITY
Business Administration and Management—General — M,D
Corporate and Organizational Communication — M
Counselor Education — M
Criminal Justice and Criminology — M
Educational Media/Instructional Technology — M
Finance and Banking — M,D
Health Services Management and Hospital Administration — M
Human Resources Management — M,D
Human Services — M
Information Science — M
Management Information Systems — M
Military and Defense Studies — M
National Security — M
Organizational Management — M
Project Management — M
Public Administration — M

BELLIN COLLEGE
Family Nurse Practitioner Studies — M
Nursing Education — M
Nursing—General — M

BELMONT UNIVERSITY
Accounting — M
Allied Health—General — M,D
Business Administration and Management—General — M
Health Services Management and Hospital Administration — M
Law — D
Nursing—General — M,D
Occupational Therapy — M,D
Pharmacy — D
Physical Therapy — M,D

BEMIDJI STATE UNIVERSITY
Biological and Biomedical Sciences—General — M
Education—General — M
English — M

Environmental Management and Policy — M
Mathematics Education — M
Mathematics — M
Special Education — M

BENEDICTINE COLLEGE
Business Administration and Management—General — M
Education—General — M
Educational Leadership and Administration — M

BENEDICTINE UNIVERSITY
Accounting — M
Business Administration and Management—General — M,D
Clinical Psychology — M
Computer and Information Systems Security — M
Curriculum and Instruction — M
Education—General — M
Educational Leadership and Administration — M,D
Elementary Education — M
Emergency Management — M
Entrepreneurship — M
Exercise and Sports Science — M
Finance and Banking — M
Health Education — M
Health Informatics — M
Health Promotion — M
Health Services Management and Hospital Administration — M
Higher Education — D
Human Resources Management — M
International Business — M
Logistics — M
Management Information Systems — M
Marketing — M
Nursing—General — M
Nutrition — M
Organizational Behavior — M,D
Organizational Management — M,D
Public Health—General — M
Reading Education — M
Science Education — M
Secondary Education — M
Special Education — M
Women's Studies — M

BENNINGTON COLLEGE
Allied Health—General — O
Dance — M
Music — M
Writing — M

BENTLEY UNIVERSITY
Accounting — M,D
Business Administration and Management—General — M,D,O
Ergonomics and Human Factors — M
Finance and Banking — M
Information Science — M
Management Strategy and Policy — O
Marketing — M
Taxation — M

BERGIN UNIVERSITY OF CANINE STUDIES
Animal Sciences — M

BERKELEY COLLEGE–WOODLAND PARK CAMPUS
Business Administration and Management—General — M

BERKLEE COLLEGE OF MUSIC
Entertainment Management — M
Music — M,O
Theater — M,O
Therapies—Dance, Drama, and Music — M

BERRY COLLEGE
Business Administration and Management—General — M
Curriculum and Instruction — M,O
Early Childhood Education — M
Education—General — M,O
Educational Leadership and Administration — O
Middle School Education — M
Reading Education — M
Secondary Education — M

BETHANY COLLEGE
Education—General — M

BETHANY GLOBAL UNIVERSITY
Pastoral Ministry and Counseling — M

BETHANY THEOLOGICAL SEMINARY
Conflict Resolution and Mediation/Peace Studies — M,O
Pastoral Ministry and Counseling — M,O
Religion — M,O
Theology — M,O

BETHEL COLLEGE
Business Administration and Management—General — M
Education—General — M
Nursing—General — M
Pastoral Ministry and Counseling — M
Theology — M

BETHEL SEMINARY
Classics — M,D,O
Clinical Psychology — M,D,O
Marriage and Family Therapy — M,D,O
Missions and Missiology — M,D,O
Near and Middle Eastern Languages — M,D,O
Pastoral Ministry and Counseling — M,D,O

Religion — M,D,O
Theology — M,D,O

BETHEL UNIVERSITY (MN)
Business Administration and Management—General — M,D,O
Counseling Psychology — M,D,O
Education—General — M,D,O
Educational Leadership and Administration — M,D,O
Elementary Education — M,D,O
Nurse Midwifery — M,D,O
Nursing Education — M,D,O
Organizational Management — M,D,O
Physician Assistant Studies — M,D,O
Secondary Education — M,D,O
Special Education — M,D,O

BETHEL UNIVERSITY (TN)
Business Administration and Management—General — M
Conflict Resolution and Mediation/Peace Studies — M
Educational Leadership and Administration — M
Physician Assistant Studies — M

BETHESDA UNIVERSITY
Music — M
Religion — M
Theology — M

BETH HAMEDRASH SHAAREI YOSHER INSTITUTE
Theology

BETH HATALMUD RABBINICAL COLLEGE
Theology

BETH MEDRASH GOVOHA
Theology

BETHUNE-COOKMAN UNIVERSITY
Theology — M

BEULAH HEIGHTS UNIVERSITY
Religion — M

BEXLEY SEABURY SEMINARY
Theology — M,D,O

BIBLICAL THEOLOGICAL SEMINARY
Missions and Missiology — M,D,O
Pastoral Ministry and Counseling — M,D,O
Theology — M,D,O

BINGHAMTON UNIVERSITY, STATE UNIVERSITY OF NEW YORK
Accounting — M
Analytical Chemistry — M,D
Anthropology — M,D
Applied Physics — M,D
Applied Statistics — M,D
Art History — M,D
Asian Studies — M,O
Asian-American Studies — M,O
Biological and Biomedical Sciences—General — M,D
Biomedical Engineering — M,D
Biopsychology — D
Business Administration and Management—General — M,D
Chemistry — M,D
Clinical Psychology — D
Cognitive Sciences — D
Comparative Literature — M,D
Computer Science — M,D
Cultural Studies — M,D
Early Childhood Education — M
Economics — M,D
Education—General — M,D,O
Educational Leadership and Administration — M,D,O
Electrical Engineering — M,D
Engineering and Applied Sciences—General — M,D*
English as a Second Language — M
English Education — M
English — M,D
Environmental Management and Policy — M,D
Environmental Sciences — M,D
Foreign Languages Education — M
Foundations and Philosophy of Education — M,D,O
French — M
Geography — M
Geology — M,D
Health Services Management and Hospital Administration — M,D
History — M,D
Industrial/Management Engineering — M,D
Inorganic Chemistry — M,D
Italian — M
Legal and Justice Studies — M,D
Materials Engineering — M,D
Materials Sciences — M,D
Mathematics Education — M
Mathematics — M,D
Mechanical Engineering — M,D
Music — M
Nursing—General — M,D,O
Organic Chemistry — M,D
Philosophy — M,D
Physical Chemistry — M,D
Physics — M,D
Political Science — M,D
Psychology—General — D
Public Administration — M
Reading Education — M
Science Education — M
Secondary Education — M

Social Sciences Education — M
Social Work — M
Sociology — M,D
Spanish — M
Special Education — M
Student Affairs — M
Sustainable Development — M
Systems Science — M,D
Theater — M
Translation and Interpretation — D,O
Writing — M,D

BIOLA UNIVERSITY
Anthropology — M,D,O
Business Administration and Management—General — M
Clinical Psychology — D
Communication Disorders — M,O
Cultural Studies — M,D,O
Curriculum and Instruction — M,O
Early Childhood Education — M,O
Education—General — M,O
English as a Second Language — M,D,O
Jewish Studies — M,D,O
Linguistics — M,D,O
Missions and Missiology — M,D,O
Pastoral Ministry and Counseling — M,D,O
Psychology—General — D
Religion — M,D,O
Religious Education — M,D,O
Science Education — M,O
Special Education — M,O
Theology — M,D,O

BISHOP'S UNIVERSITY
Education—General — M,O
English as a Second Language — M,O

BLACK HILLS STATE UNIVERSITY
Business Administration and Management—General — M
Curriculum and Instruction — M
Genomic Sciences — M
Management Strategy and Policy — M

BLESSING-RIEMAN COLLEGE OF NURSING & HEALTH SCIENCES
Nursing and Healthcare Administration — M
Nursing Education — M
Nursing—General — M

BLOOMFIELD COLLEGE
Accounting — M

BLOOMSBURG UNIVERSITY OF PENNSYLVANIA
Accounting — M
Adult Nursing — M
Athletic Training and Sports Medicine — M
Biological and Biomedical Sciences—General — M
Business Administration and Management—General — M,O
Business Education — M
Communication Disorders — M,D
Community Health — M
Counselor Education — M
Curriculum and Instruction — M,O
Early Childhood Education — M
Education—General — M,O
Educational Leadership and Administration — M
Educational Media/Instructional Technology — M
English Education — M
Exercise and Sports Science — M
Family Nurse Practitioner Studies — M
Mathematics Education — M
Middle School Education — M
Nurse Anesthesia — M
Nursing and Healthcare Administration — M
Nursing—General — M
Reading Education — M
Science Education — M
Social Sciences Education — M
Special Education — M,O
Student Affairs — M

BLUEFIELD COLLEGE
Education—General — M

BLUE MOUNTAIN COLLEGE
Elementary Education — M
Reading Education — M

BLUFFTON UNIVERSITY
Accounting — M
Business Administration and Management—General — M
Curriculum and Instruction — M
Education—General — M
Finance and Banking — M
Health Services Management and Hospital Administration — M
Industrial and Manufacturing Management — M
Organizational Management — M
Reading Education — M
Special Education — M

BOB JONES UNIVERSITY
Accounting — M,D,O
Art/Fine Arts — M,D,O
Business Administration and Management—General — M,D,O
Counselor Education — M,D,O
Curriculum and Instruction — M,D,O
Educational Leadership and Administration — M,D,O
Elementary Education — M,D,O
English Education — M,D,O

---

*M—masters degree; D—doctorate; O—other advanced degree; *—Close-Up and/or Display*

English	M,D,O
Film, Television, and Video Production	M,D,O
Graphic Design	M,D,O
History	M,D,O
Illustration	M,D,O
Journalism	M,D,O
Mathematics Education	M,D,O
Media Studies	M,D,O
Music Education	M,D,O
Music	M,D,O
Pastoral Ministry and Counseling	M,D,O
Religion	M,D,O
Rhetoric	M,D,O
Secondary Education	M,D,O
Social Sciences Education	M,D,O
Special Education	M,D,O
Speech and Interpersonal Communication	M,D,O
Student Affairs	M,D,O
Theater	M,D,O
Theology	M,D,O

BOISE STATE UNIVERSITY

Accounting	M
Animal Sciences	M,D
Anthropology	M
Art Education	M
Art/Fine Arts	M
Biological and Biomedical Sciences—General	M,D
Business Administration and Management—General	M
Chemistry	M
Civil Engineering	M
Communication—General	M
Computer Engineering	M,D
Computer Science	M,O
Counselor Education	M,O
Criminal Justice and Criminology	M
Curriculum and Instruction	M,D,O
Distance Education Development	M,D,O
Early Childhood Education	M
Education—General	M,D,O
Educational Leadership and Administration	M,D,O
Educational Media/Instructional Technology	M,D,O
Electrical Engineering	M,D
Engineering and Applied Sciences—General	M,D,O
English as a Second Language	M
English Education	M
Environmental and Occupational Health	M,O
Geophysics	M,D
Gerontological Nursing	M,D,O
Health Promotion	M,O
History	M
Hydrology	M,D
Interdisciplinary Studies	M
Kinesiology and Movement Studies	M
Materials Engineering	M,D
Mathematics Education	M
Mathematics	M
Mechanical Engineering	M
Molecular Biology	M,D
Multilingual and Multicultural Education	M
Music Education	M
Music	M
Natural Resources	M,D,O
Nursing—General	M,D,O
Organizational Management	M,O
Political Science	M
Public Administration	M,D,O
Public Health—General	M,D,O
Public Policy	M,D,O
Reading Education	M
Rhetoric	M
Science Education	M,D
Social Work	M
Special Education	M
Sports Management	M
Taxation	M
Technical Communication	M
Writing	M

BORICUA COLLEGE

English as a Second Language	M
Human Services	M
Latin American Studies	M

BOSTON ARCHITECTURAL COLLEGE

Architecture	M
Historic Preservation	M
Interior Design	M
Landscape Architecture	M
Sustainable Development	M

BOSTON COLLEGE

Accounting	M
Adult Nursing	M,D
Applied Psychology	M
Biochemistry	M,D
Biological and Biomedical Sciences—General	D
Business Administration and Management—General	M
Chemistry	M,D
Classics	M
Counseling Psychology	M,D
Curriculum and Instruction	M,D,O
Developmental Psychology	M,D
East European and Russian Studies	M
Economics	D
Education—General	M,D,O
Educational Leadership and Administration	M,D,O
Educational Measurement and Evaluation	M,D
Educational Psychology	M,D
Elementary Education	M
English	M,D
Finance and Banking	M,D

Forensic Nursing	M,D
French	M
Geology	M
Geophysics	M
Gerontological Nursing	M,D
Higher Education	M,D
History	M,D
Inorganic Chemistry	M,D
International and Comparative Education	M
Italian	M
Law	D
Linguistics	M
Maternal and Child/Neonatal Nursing	M,D
Mathematics	D
Nurse Anesthesia	M,D
Nursing—General	M,D
Organic Chemistry	M,D
Organizational Behavior	D
Organizational Management	M
Pastoral Ministry and Counseling	M,D,O
Pediatric Nursing	M,D
Philosophy	M,D
Physical Chemistry	M,D
Physics	M,D
Political Science	M,D
Psychiatric Nursing	M,D
Psychology—General	D
Reading Education	M,O
Religious Education	M,D,O
Russian	M
Science Education	M,D
Secondary Education	M
Social Work	M,D
Sociology	M,D
Spanish	M
Special Education	M,O
Theology	M,D,O
Western European Studies	M,D
Women's Health Nursing	M,D

BOSTON GRADUATE SCHOOL OF PSYCHOANALYSIS

Counseling Psychology	M
Developmental Psychology	O
Psychoanalysis and Psychotherapy	M,D,O
Psychology—General	M

BOSTON UNIVERSITY

Actuarial Science	M
Advertising and Public Relations	M
African-American Studies	M
Allied Health—General	M,D
Allopathic Medicine	D
American Studies	D
Anatomy	M,D
Anthropology	M,D
Archaeology	M,D
Art Education	M
Art History	M,D,O
Art/Fine Arts	M
Arts Administration	M,O
Astronomy	M,D
Athletic Training and Sports Medicine	D
Biochemistry	M,D
Bioinformatics	M,D
Biological and Biomedical Sciences—General	M,D
Biomedical Engineering	M,D
Biophysics	M,D
Biopsychology	M
Biostatistics	M,D
Business Administration and Management—General	M,D
Cell Biology	M,D
Chemistry	M,D
Classics	M,D
Clinical Research	M
Communication Disorders	M,D
Communication—General	M,D
Community Health	M,D
Computer and Information Systems Security	M,D,O
Computer Engineering	M,D,O
Computer Science	M,D,O
Corporate and Organizational Communication	M
Counseling Psychology	M
Criminal Justice and Criminology	M
Cultural Studies	M
Database Systems	M,O
Dentistry	M,D,O
Economic Development	M
Economics	M,D
Education—General	M,D,O
Electrical Engineering	M,D
Emergency Management	M
Energy Management and Policy	M,D
Engineering and Applied Sciences—General	M,D
English	M,D
Environmental and Occupational Health	M,D
Environmental Management and Policy	M,D
Environmental Sciences	M,D
Epidemiology	M,D
Ethics	M,D
Film, Television, and Video Production	M
Finance and Banking	M
Food Science and Technology	M
Forensic Sciences	M
French	M,D
Genetic Counseling	M
Genetics	D
Genomic Sciences	D
Geographic Information Systems	M,D
Geography	M,D
Geosciences	M,D
Graphic Design	M

Health Communication	M
Health Informatics	M,O
Health Services Management and Hospital Administration	M,D
Hispanic and Latin American Languages	M,D
Historic Preservation	M
History	M,D
Immunology	D
International Affairs	M*
International Business	M
International Health	M,D
Internet and Interactive Multimedia	M,O
Journalism	M
Law	M,D
Linguistics	M,D
Management Information Systems	M,O
Management of Technology	M
Management Strategy and Policy	M,O
Manufacturing Engineering	M,D
Mass Communication	M
Materials Engineering	M,D
Materials Sciences	M,D
Mathematical and Computational Finance	M,D
Mathematics	M,D
Mechanical Engineering	M,D
Media Studies	M
Medical Imaging	M
Missions and Missiology	M,D
Molecular Biology	M,D
Molecular Medicine	D
Museum Studies	M,D,O
Music Education	M,D,O
Music	M,D,O
Neurobiology	M,D
Neuroscience	D
Nutrition	M,D
Occupational Therapy	D
Oral and Dental Sciences	M,D
Organizational Management	M
Pastoral Ministry and Counseling	M,D
Pathology	D
Pharmaceutical Sciences	M,D
Pharmacology	M,D
Philosophy	M,D
Physical Therapy	D
Physician Assistant Studies	M
Physics	D
Physiology	M,D
Political Science	D
Project Management	M,O
Psychology—General	M,D
Public Health—General	M,D
Rehabilitation Sciences	D
Religion	M,D
Religious Education	M,D
Romance Languages	M,D
Social Work	M,D
Sociology	M,D
Software Engineering	M,O
Supply Chain Management	M
Systems Engineering	M,D
Telecommunications Management	M,O
Telecommunications	M,O
Theater	M,O
Theology	M,D
Travel and Tourism	M
Urban and Regional Planning	M
Urban Studies	M
Writing	M

BOWIE STATE UNIVERSITY

Applied Mathematics	M
Business Administration and Management—General	M
Computer Science	M,D
Corporate and Organizational Communication	M,O
Counseling Psychology	M
Counselor Education	M
Education—General	M
Educational Leadership and Administration	M,D
Elementary Education	M
English	M
Family Nurse Practitioner Studies	M
Human Resources Development	M
Management Information Systems	M,O
Nursing and Healthcare Administration	M
Nursing Education	M
Nursing—General	M
Public Administration	M
Reading Education	M
Secondary Education	M
Special Education	M

BOWLING GREEN STATE UNIVERSITY

Accounting	M
American Studies	M,D
Applied Arts and Design—General	M
Applied Statistics	M
Art Education	M
Art History	M
Art/Fine Arts	M
Biological and Biomedical Sciences—General	M,D
Business Administration and Management—General	M
Business Education	M
Chemistry	M,D
Clinical Psychology	M,D
Communication Disorders	M,D
Communication—General	M,D
Computer Art and Design	M
Computer Science	M
Counselor Education	M
Criminal Justice and Criminology	M
Curriculum and Instruction	M
Demography and Population Studies	M,D
Developmental Psychology	M,D
Economics	M

Educational Leadership and Administration	M,D,O
Educational Media/Instructional Technology	M
English	M,D
Experimental Psychology	M,D
Film, Television, and Video Production	M,D
French	M
Geology	M
Geophysics	M
German	M
Graphic Design	M
Higher Education	D
History	M,D
Industrial and Organizational Psychology	M,D
Interdisciplinary Studies	M,D
International and Comparative Education	M
Kinesiology and Movement Studies	M
Leisure Studies	M
Mathematics Education	M,D
Mathematics	M,D
Media Studies	M,D
Music Education	M,D
Music	M,D
Operations Research	M
Organizational Management	M
Philosophy	M,D
Physics	M
Psychology—General	M,D
Public Administration	M
Public Health—General	M
Reading Education	M,O
Recreation and Park Management	M
Rhetoric	M,D
Science Education	M
Social Psychology	M,D
Sociology	M,D
Software Engineering	M
Spanish	M
Special Education	M
Sports Management	M
Statistics	M,D
Student Affairs	M
Technical Communication	M,D
Theater	M
Vocational and Technical Education	M
Writing	M,D

BRADLEY UNIVERSITY

Accounting	M
Art/Fine Arts	M
Biochemistry	M
Biological and Biomedical Sciences—General	M
Business Administration and Management—General	M
Chemistry	M
Civil Engineering	M
Clinical Psychology	M
Computer Science	M
Construction Engineering	M
Counseling Psychology	M
Counselor Education	M
Curriculum and Instruction	M
Education—General	M,D,O
Educational Leadership and Administration	M
Electrical Engineering	M
Engineering and Applied Sciences—General	M
English	M
Family Nurse Practitioner Studies	M,D,O
Graphic Design	M
Health Services Management and Hospital Administration	M,D,O
Human Development	M
Industrial/Management Engineering	M
Information Science	M
Manufacturing Engineering	M
Mechanical Engineering	M
Nonprofit Management	M
Nursing and Healthcare Administration	M,D,O
Nursing Education	M,D,O
Nursing—General	M,D,O
Nutrition	M
Photography	M
Physical Therapy	D

BRANDEIS UNIVERSITY

Anthropology	M,D
Art/Fine Arts	O
Biochemistry	M,D
Bioinformatics	M
Biological and Biomedical Sciences—General	M,D,O
Biophysics	M,D
Biotechnology	M
Business Administration and Management—General	M
Cell Biology	M,D
Chemistry	M,D
Child and Family Studies	M,D
Classics	M
Cognitive Sciences	M,D
Computer and Information Systems Security	M
Computer Science	M,D
Conflict Resolution and Mediation/Peace Studies	M
Developmental Psychology	M,D
Disability Studies	D
Distance Education Development	M,D
Economics	M,D
Educational Leadership and Administration	M,O
Educational Measurement and Evaluation	O
Elementary Education	M,O
English	M,D
Entrepreneurship	M

Finance and Banking	M,D
Gender Studies	M,D
Genetic Counseling	M
Genetics	M,D
Health Education	D
Health Informatics	M
Health Services Management and Hospital Administration	M
History	M,D
Human Services	M
Human-Computer Interaction	M
Humanities	M
Inorganic Chemistry	M,D
International Affairs	M
International Business	M,D
International Health	M,D
Internet and Interactive Multimedia	M
Jewish Studies	M,D
Linguistics	M
Management Information Systems	M
Management Strategy and Policy	M
Marketing	M
Mathematics	M,D,O
Medical Informatics	M
Microbiology	M,D
Molecular Biology	M,D
Music	M,D
Near and Middle Eastern Languages	M,D
Near and Middle Eastern Studies	M,D
Neurobiology	M,D
Neuroscience	M,D
Nonprofit Management	M
Organic Chemistry	M,D
Philosophy	M
Physical Chemistry	M,D
Physics	M,D
Political Science	M,D
Project Management	M
Psychology—General	M,D
Public Policy	M
Real Estate	M
Religious Education	M,O
Secondary Education	M,O
Social Psychology	M,D
Sociology	M,D
Software Engineering	M
Sustainable Development	M
Theater	M
Women's Studies	M

BRANDMAN UNIVERSITY

Accounting	M
Business Administration and Management—General	M
Counseling Psychology	M
Counselor Education	M,D
Education—General	M,D
Educational Leadership and Administration	M,D
Elementary Education	M,D
Entrepreneurship	M
Finance and Banking	M
Health Services Management and Hospital Administration	M,D
Human Resources Management	M
International Business	M
Marketing	M
Marriage and Family Therapy	M
Nursing—General	D
Organizational Management	M
Psychology—General	M
Public Administration	M
Secondary Education	M,D
Special Education	M,D

BRANDON UNIVERSITY

Counselor Education	M,O
Curriculum and Instruction	M,O
Education—General	M,O
Educational Leadership and Administration	M,O
Music Education	M
Music	M
Rural Planning and Studies	M,O
Special Education	M,O

BRENAU UNIVERSITY

Accounting	M
Business Administration and Management—General	M
Early Childhood Education	M,O
Education—General	M,O
Family Nurse Practitioner Studies	M
Health Services Management and Hospital Administration	M
Interior Design	M
Middle School Education	M,O
Nursing and Healthcare Administration	M
Nursing Education	M
Occupational Therapy	M
Organizational Management	M
Project Management	M
Psychology—General	M
Secondary Education	M,O
Special Education	M,O

BRESCIA UNIVERSITY

Business Administration and Management—General	M
Curriculum and Instruction	M
Social Work	M

BRIAR CLIFF UNIVERSITY

Nursing—General	M,D,O

BRIDGEWATER COLLEGE

Athletic Training and Sports Medicine	M

BRIDGEWATER STATE UNIVERSITY

Accounting	M

Art Education	M
Business Administration and Management—General	M
Communication Disorders	M
Computer Science	M
Counselor Education	M,O
Criminal Justice and Criminology	M
Early Childhood Education	M
Education—General	M,O
Educational Leadership and Administration	M,O
Educational Media/Instructional Technology	M
Elementary Education	M
English	M
Finance and Banking	M
Health Promotion	M
Mathematics Education	M
Physical Education	M
Psychology—General	M
Public Administration	M
Reading Education	M,O
Science Education	M
Secondary Education	M
Social Sciences Education	M
Social Work	M
Special Education	M

BRIERCREST SEMINARY

Business Administration and Management—General	M
Marriage and Family Therapy	M
Missions and Missiology	M
Organizational Management	M
Pastoral Ministry and Counseling	M
Religion	M
Theology	M

BRIGHAM YOUNG UNIVERSITY

Agricultural Sciences—General	M,D
Analytical Chemistry	M,D
Animal Sciences	M,D
Anthropology	M
Applied Psychology	D
Applied Statistics	M
Art Education	M
Art/Fine Arts	M
Astronomy	M,D
Athletic Training and Sports Medicine	M,D
Biochemistry	M,D
Biological and Biomedical Sciences—General	M,D
Biotechnology	M,D
Business Administration and Management—General	M
Chemical Engineering	M,D
Chemistry	M,D
Child and Family Studies	M,D
Civil Engineering	M,D
Classics	M
Clinical Psychology	D
Cognitive Sciences	D
Communication Disorders	M
Communication—General	M
Comparative and Interdisciplinary Arts	M
Comparative Literature	M
Computer Engineering	M,D
Computer Science	M,D
Construction Management	M
Counseling Psychology	M,D,O
Developmental Biology	M,D
Developmental Psychology	D
Education—General	M,D,O
Educational Leadership and Administration	M,D
Educational Measurement and Evaluation	D
Educational Media/Instructional Technology	M,D
Educational Policy	M,D
Educational Psychology	M,D
Electrical Engineering	M,D
Engineering and Applied Sciences—General	M,D
English as a Second Language	M
English	M
Entrepreneurship	M
Environmental Sciences	M,D
Exercise and Sports Science	M,D
Family Nurse Practitioner Studies	M
Film, Television, and Video Production	M
Finance and Banking	M
Fish, Game, and Wildlife Management	M,D
Food Science and Technology	M
Foreign Languages Education	M
Foundations and Philosophy of Education	M,D
French	M
Geology	M
Health Promotion	M,D
Health Services Management and Hospital Administration	M
Hispanic and Latin American Languages	M
Human Development	M,D
Human Resources Management	M
Humanities	M
Information Science	M
International Affairs	M
Law	M,D
Linguistics	M
Manufacturing Engineering	M
Marketing	M
Marriage and Family Therapy	M,D
Mass Communication	M

Mathematics Education	M
Mathematics	M,D
Mechanical Engineering	M,D
Microbiology	M,D
Molecular Biology	M,D
Music Education	M
Music	M
Neuroscience	M,D
Nonprofit Management	M
Nursing—General	M
Nutrition	M
Physical Education	M
Physics	M,D
Physiology	M,D
Plant Sciences	M,D
Political Science	M
Portuguese	M
Psychology—General	D
Public Administration	M
Public Health—General	M
Reading Education	M
Religious Education	M
Rhetoric	M
School Psychology	M,D,O
Science Education	M,D
Social Work	M
Sociology	M
Spanish	M
Special Education	M,D,O
Statistics	M
Supply Chain Management	M
Theater	M
Writing	M

BRISTOL UNIVERSITY

Business Administration and Management—General	M
International Business	M
Marketing	M
Sports Management	M

BRITE DIVINITY SCHOOL

Pastoral Ministry and Counseling	M,D,O
Theology	M,D,O

BROADVIEW UNIVERSITY–WEST JORDAN

Business Administration and Management—General	M
Health Services Management and Hospital Administration	M
Management Information Systems	M

BROCK UNIVERSITY

Accounting	M
Allied Health—General	M,D
Biological and Biomedical Sciences—General	M,D
Biotechnology	M,D
Business Administration and Management—General	M
Chemistry	M,D
Child and Family Studies	M
Classics	M
Comparative Literature	M
Computer Science	M
Cultural Studies	M
Disability Studies	M,O
Economics	M
Education—General	M,D
English as a Second Language	M
English	M
Geography	M
Geosciences	M
History	M
Human Development	M,D
International Affairs	M
Legal and Justice Studies	M
Mathematics	M
Neuroscience	M,D
Philosophy	M
Physics	M
Political Science	M
Psychology—General	M,D
Public Health	M
Social Psychology	M,D
Sociology	M
Statistics	M

BROOKLINE COLLEGE

Nursing and Healthcare Administration	M
Nursing—General	M

BROOKLYN COLLEGE OF THE CITY UNIVERSITY OF NEW YORK

Accounting	M
Art Education	M
Art History	M
Art/Fine Arts	M
Arts Administration	M
Biological and Biomedical Sciences—General	M
Business Administration and Management—General	M
Chemistry	M,D
Communication Disorders	M,D
Community Health	M
Computer Science	M,O
Counseling Psychology	M,D,O
Counselor Education	M
Early Childhood Education	M,O
Economics	M
Education—General	M,O
Educational Leadership and Administration	M
Elementary Education	M,O
English Education	M
English	M
Environmental Education	M
Exercise and Sports Science	M
Experimental Psychology	M,D

Film, Television, and Video Production	M
Film, Television, and Video Theory and Criticism	M
Finance and Banking	M
Foreign Languages Education	M
French	M
Geology	M,D
Geosciences	M
Health Informatics	M,O
Health Services Management and Hospital Administration	M
History	M
Industrial and Organizational Psychology	M,D
Information Science	M,O
International Affairs	M
International Business	M
Internet and Interactive Multimedia	M
Jewish Studies	M
Kinesiology and Movement Studies	M
Liberal Studies	M
Mathematics Education	M
Mathematics	M
Media Studies	M
Middle School Education	M,O
Multilingual and Multicultural Education	M
Music Education	M
Music	M
Nutrition	M
Organizational Behavior	M,D
Photography	M
Physical Education	M
Physics	M
Political Science	M
Psychology—General	M,D
Public Health—General	M
Public Policy	M
School Psychology	M,O
Science Education	M
Secondary Education	M
Social Psychology	M,D
Social Sciences Education	M
Sociology	M,D
Spanish	M
Special Education	M,O
Speech and Interpersonal Communication	M,D
Sports Management	M
Thanatology	M
Theater	M
Urban Studies	M
Writing	M

BROOKLYN LAW SCHOOL

Law	M,D

BROWN UNIVERSITY

Allopathic Medicine	D
American Studies	M,D
Anthropology	M,D
Applied Mathematics	M,D
Archaeology	D
Art History	D
Asian Studies	D
Biochemical Engineering	M,D
Biochemistry	M,D
Biological and Biomedical Sciences—General	M,D
Biomedical Engineering	M,D
Biostatistics	M,D
Biotechnology	M,D
Cell Biology	M,D
Chemical Engineering	M,D
Chemistry	D
Classics	M,D
Cognitive Sciences	M,D
Community Health	M,D
Comparative Literature	D
Computer Engineering	M,D
Computer Science	M,D
East European and Russian Studies	M,D
Ecology	D
Economics	D
Education—General	M
Electrical Engineering	M,D
Elementary Education	M
Engineering and Applied Sciences—General	M,D
English as a Second Language	M,D
English Education	M
English	M,D
Epidemiology	M,D
Evolutionary Biology	D
French	D
Geosciences	D
German	D
Health Services Research	M,D
Hispanic Studies	D
History of Science and Technology	D
History	M,D
Italian	M
Latin American Studies	M,D
Linguistics	M,D
Materials Sciences	M,D
Mathematics	D
Mechanical Engineering	M,D
Mechanics	M,D
Molecular Biology	M,D
Molecular Pharmacology	M,D
Multilingual and Multicultural Education	M,D
Music	D
Near and Middle Eastern Studies	M,D
Neuroscience	D
Pathobiology	M,D
Philosophy	D
Physics	M,D
Physiology	M,D

Political Science — D
Psychology—General — M,D
Public Health—General — M
Public Policy — M
Publishing — M,D
Religion — D
Russian — M,D
Science Education — M
Secondary Education — M
Slavic Languages — M,D
Social Sciences Education — M
Sociology — M,D
Theater — M,D
Urban Education — M
Western European Studies — M,D
Writing — M,D

BRYAN COLLEGE

Business Administration and
  Management—General — M

BRYAN COLLEGE OF HEALTH SCIENCES

Nurse Anesthesia — M

BRYANT UNIVERSITY

Accounting — M,O
Business Administration and
  Management—General — M,O
Communication—General — M,O
Corporate and Organizational
  Communication — M,O
Environmental Sciences — M,O
Finance and Banking — M,O
International Business — M,O
International Economics — M,O
Management Strategy and Policy — M,O
Mass Communication — M,O
Physician Assistant Studies — M
Supply Chain Management — M,O
Taxation — M,O

BRYAN UNIVERSITY

Business Administration and
  Management—General — M

BRYN ATHYN COLLEGE OF THE NEW CHURCH

Religion — M
Theology — M

BRYN MAWR COLLEGE

Archaeology — M,D
Art History — M,D
Chemistry — M,D
Classics — M,D
Mathematics — M,D
Physics — M,D
Social Work — M,D

BUCKNELL UNIVERSITY

Animal Behavior — M
Biological and Biomedical
  Sciences—General — M
Chemical Engineering — M
Chemistry — M
Civil Engineering — M
Computer Engineering — M
Education—General — M
Electrical Engineering — M
Engineering and Applied
  Sciences—General — M
English — M
Mathematics — M
Mechanical Engineering — M
Psychology—General — M
Student Affairs — M

BUENA VISTA UNIVERSITY

Counselor Education — M
Curriculum and Instruction — M
Education—General — M
English as a Second Language — M

BUFFALO STATE COLLEGE, STATE UNIVERSITY OF NEW YORK

Adult Education — M,O
Applied Economics — M
Art Education — M
Biological and Biomedical
  Sciences—General — M
Business Education — M
Chemistry — M
Communication Disorders — M
Criminal Justice and Criminology — M
Early Childhood Education — M
Economics — M
Educational Leadership and
  Administration — O
Educational Media/Instructional
  Technology — M
Elementary Education — M
English Education — M
English — M,O
Historic Preservation — M
History — M
Human Resources Management — M,O
Industrial/Management
  Engineering — M
Interdisciplinary Studies — M
Mathematics Education — M
Multilingual and Multicultural
  Education — M
Reading Education — M
Science Education — M
Social Sciences Education — M
Special Education — M
Student Affairs — M
Vocational and Technical Education — M

BUTLER UNIVERSITY

Accounting — M
Art/Fine Arts — M
Business Administration and
  Management—General — M
Clinical Psychology — M,O
Counselor Education — M,O

Education—General — M,O
Educational Leadership and
  Administration — M,O
English — M
Finance and Banking — M
History — M
International Business — M
Marketing — M
Music Education — M
Music — M
Pharmaceutical Sciences — M,D
Pharmacy — M,D
Physician Assistant Studies — M,D
Special Education — M,O
Writing — M

BYZANTINE CATHOLIC SEMINARY OF SAINTS CYRIL AND METHODIUS

Theology — M

CABARRUS COLLEGE OF HEALTH SCIENCES

Occupational Therapy — M

CABRINI UNIVERSITY

Accounting — M
Education—General — M
Organizational Management — M

CAIRN UNIVERSITY

Accounting — M,O
Applied Behavior Analysis — M,O
Business Administration and
  Management—General — M,O
Education—General — M,O
Educational Leadership and
  Administration — M,O
Entrepreneurship — M,O
Nonprofit Management — M,O
Organizational Management — M,O
Pastoral Ministry and Counseling — M
Religion — M
Theology — M

CALDWELL UNIVERSITY

Accounting — M
Applied Behavior Analysis — M,D,O
Art Therapy — M,O
Business Administration and
  Management—General — M
Counseling Psychology — M,O
Counselor Education — M,O
Curriculum and Instruction — M,D,O
Education—General — M,D,O
Educational Leadership and
  Administration — M,D,O
Reading Education — M,D,O
School Psychology — M,O
Special Education — M,D,O

CALIFORNIA BAPTIST UNIVERSITY

Accounting — M
Adult Education — M
Adult Nursing — M
Advertising and Public Relations — M
Applied Mathematics — M
Architecture — M
Athletic Training and Sports
  Medicine — M
Business Administration and
  Management—General — M
Civil Engineering — M
Communication Disorders — M
Communication—General — M
Construction Management — M
Counseling Psychology — M
Counselor Education — M
Curriculum and Instruction — M
Disability Studies — M
Distance Education Development — M
Education—General — M
Educational Leadership and
  Administration — M
Educational Media/Instructional
  Technology — M
English as a Second Language — M
English Education — M
English — M
Entrepreneurship — M
Exercise and Sports Science — M
Family Nurse Practitioner Studies — M
Forensic Psychology — M
Health Education — M
Health Promotion — M
Health Services Management and
  Hospital Administration — M
Higher Education — M
International and Comparative
  Education — M
Mechanical Engineering — M
Music Education — M
Music — M
Nonprofit Management — M
Nursing Education — M
Nursing—General — M,D
Organizational Management — M
Pastoral Ministry and Counseling — M
Physical Education — M
Physician Assistant Studies — M
Public Administration — M
Public Health—General — M
Reading Education — M
School Psychology — M
Science Education — M
Social Work — M
Software Engineering — M
Special Education — M
Sports Management — M
Vocational and Technical Education — M

CALIFORNIA COAST UNIVERSITY

Business Administration and
  Management—General — M
Criminal Justice and Criminology — M
Curriculum and Instruction — M,D
Education—General — M,D

Educational Leadership and
  Administration — M,D
Educational Psychology — M,D
Health Services Management and
  Hospital Administration — M
Human Resources Management — M
Marketing — M
Organizational Management — M,D
Psychology—General — M

CALIFORNIA COLLEGE OF THE ARTS

Applied Arts and Design—General — M
Architecture — M
Art/Fine Arts — M
Computer Art and Design — M
Film, Television, and Video
  Production — M
Film, Television, and Video
  Theory and Criticism — M
Finance and Banking — M
Graphic Design — M
Industrial Design — M
Interdisciplinary Studies — M
Media Studies — M
Museum Studies — M
Organizational Management — M
Photography — M
Textile Design — M
Writing — M

CALIFORNIA INSTITUTE OF INTEGRAL STUDIES

Acupuncture and Oriental Medicine — M,D
Art Therapy — M,D
Asian Studies — M,D
Clinical Psychology — M,D
Counseling Psychology — M,D
Cultural Anthropology — M,D
Ecology — M,D
Health Education — M,D
Health Psychology — M,D
Humanities — M,D
Interdisciplinary Studies — M,D
Music — M,D
Philosophy — M,D
Psychology—General — M,D
Religion — M,D
Social Psychology — M,D
Theater — M,D
Theology — M,D
Therapies—Dance, Drama, and
  Music — M,D
Transpersonal and Humanistic
  Psychology — M,D
Women's Studies — M,D
Writing — M,D

CALIFORNIA INSTITUTE OF TECHNOLOGY

Aerospace/Aeronautical
  Engineering — M,D,O
Applied Mathematics — M,D
Applied Physics — M,D
Astronomy — D
Biochemistry — M,D
Bioengineering — M,D
Biological and Biomedical
  Sciences—General — D
Biophysics — D
Cell Biology — D
Chemical Engineering — M,D
Chemistry — M,D
Civil Engineering — M,D,O
Computational Sciences — M,D
Computer Science — M,D
Developmental Biology — D
Electrical Engineering — M,D,O
Engineering and Applied
  Sciences—General — M,D,O
Environmental Engineering — M,D
Environmental Sciences — M,D
Genetics — D
Geochemistry — M,D
Geology — M,D
Geophysics — M,D
Immunology — D
Materials Sciences — M,D
Mathematics — D
Mechanical Engineering — M,D,O
Mechanics — M,D
Molecular Biology — D
Molecular Biophysics — M,D
Neurobiology — D
Neuroscience — M,D
Physics — D
Planetary and Space
  Sciences — M,D
Social Sciences — M,D
Systems Engineering — M,D

CALIFORNIA INSTITUTE OF THE ARTS

Applied Arts and Design—General — M,O
Art/Fine Arts — M,O
Dance — M,O
Film, Television, and Video
  Production — M,O
Graphic Design — M,O
Music — M,O
Photography — M,O
Theater — M,O
Writing — M,O

CALIFORNIA INTERCONTINENTAL UNIVERSITY

Business Administration and
  Management—General — M,D
Entertainment Management — M
Entrepreneurship — M,D
Finance and Banking — M
Health Services Management and
  Hospital Administration — M,D
Human Resources Management — M,D
International Business — M,D
Management Information Systems — M,D
Marketing — M,D

Organizational Management — M,D
Project Management — M,D
Quality Management — M,D

CALIFORNIA INTERNATIONAL BUSINESS UNIVERSITY

Business Administration and
  Management—General — M,D

CALIFORNIA LUTHERAN UNIVERSITY

Business Administration and
  Management—General — M,O
Clinical Psychology — M,D
Counselor Education — M,D
Economics — M,O
Education—General — M,D
Educational Leadership and
  Administration — M,D
Elementary Education — M,D
Entrepreneurship — M,O
Finance and Banking — M,O
Higher Education — M,D
International Business — M,O
Management Information Systems — M,O
Management of Technology — M,O
Marketing — M,O
Marriage and Family Therapy — M,D
Middle School Education — M,D
Nonprofit Management — M,O
Organizational Behavior — M,O
Psychology—General — M,D
Public Policy — M,D
Special Education — M,D
Theology — M,D,O

CALIFORNIA MIRAMAR UNIVERSITY

Business Administration and
  Management—General — M
Management Strategy and Policy — M
Taxation — M
Telecommunications
  Management — M
Telecommunications — M

CALIFORNIA POLYTECHNIC STATE UNIVERSITY, SAN LUIS OBISPO

Accounting — M
Aerospace/Aeronautical
  Engineering — M
Agricultural Economics and
  Agribusiness — M
Agricultural Education — M
Agricultural Sciences—
  General — M
Architectural Engineering — M*
Architecture — M
Biochemistry — M
Biological and Biomedical
  Sciences—General — M*
Business Administration and
  Management—General — M
Chemistry — M
Civil Engineering — M
Computer Science — M
Database Systems — M
Economics — M
Education—General — M
Electrical Engineering — M
Engineering and Applied
  Sciences—General — M
English — M
Environmental Engineering — M
Food Science and
  Technology — M
Forestry — M
History — M
Industrial/Management
  Engineering — M
Kinesiology and Movement Studies — M
Mathematics — M
Mechanical Engineering — M
Natural Resources — M
Nutrition — M*
Political Science — M
Polymer Science and
  Engineering — M
Psychology—General — M
Taxation — M
Urban and Regional Planning — M

CALIFORNIA STATE POLYTECHNIC UNIVERSITY, POMONA

Accounting — M
Aerospace/Aeronautical
  Engineering — M
Agricultural Sciences—
  General — M
Applied Mathematics — M
Architecture — M
Biological and Biomedical
  Sciences—General — M
Business Administration and
  Management—General — M
Chemistry — M
Civil Engineering — M
Computer Science — M
Curriculum and Instruction — M
Economics — M
Educational Leadership and
  Administration — D
Electrical Engineering — M
Engineering Management — M
English — M
Environmental Sciences — M
Geology — M
History — M
Hospitality Management — M
Interior Design — M
Kinesiology and Movement Studies — M
Landscape Architecture — M
Management Information Systems — M
Mathematics — M
Mechanical Engineering — M
Psychology—General — M
Public Administration — M

Reading Education — M
Systems Engineering — M
Urban and Regional Planning — M

CALIFORNIA STATE UNIVERSITY, BAKERSFIELD

Anthropology — M
Biological and Biomedical Sciences—General — M
Business Administration and Management—General — M
Counseling Psychology — M
Counselor Education — M
Educational Leadership and Administration — M,D
English — M
Geology — M
Health Services Management and Hospital Administration — M
History — M
Hydrology — M
Interdisciplinary Studies — M
Mathematics Education — M
Middle School Education — M
Public Administration — M
Science Education — M
Secondary Education — M
Social Work — M
Sociology — M
Spanish — M
Special Education — M
Student Affairs — M

CALIFORNIA STATE UNIVERSITY CHANNEL ISLANDS

Bioinformatics — M
Biotechnology — M
Business Administration and Management—General — M
Computer Science — M
Mathematics — M

CALIFORNIA STATE UNIVERSITY, CHICO

Agricultural Education — M
Agricultural Sciences—General — M
Anthropology — M
Applied Psychology — M
Art History — M
Art/Fine Arts — M
Biological and Biomedical Sciences—General — M
Business Administration and Management—General — M
Communication Disorders — M
Communication—General — M
Computer Engineering — M
Computer Science — M
Construction Management — M
Criminal Justice and Criminology — M
Curriculum and Instruction — M
Electrical Engineering — M
Engineering and Applied Sciences—General — M
English — M
Environmental Sciences — M
Geology — M
Geosciences — M
Health Services Management and Hospital Administration — M
History — M
Kinesiology and Movement Studies — M
Marriage and Family Therapy — M
Mathematics Education — M
Museum Studies — M
Nursing—General — M
Nutrition — M
Political Science — M
Psychology—General — M
Public Administration — M
Recreation and Park Management — M
School Psychology — M
Social Sciences — M
Social Work — M
Special Education — M
Travel and Tourism — M

CALIFORNIA STATE UNIVERSITY, DOMINGUEZ HILLS

Applied Social Research — M
Bioinformatics — M
Biological and Biomedical Sciences—General — M
Business Administration and Management—General — M
Clinical Psychology — M
Computer Science — M
Conflict Resolution and Mediation/Peace Studies — M
Counselor Education — M
Early Childhood Education — M
Education—General — M
English as a Second Language — M,O
English — M,O
Health Psychology — M
Humanities — M
International and Comparative Education — M
Marriage and Family Therapy — M
Nursing—General — M
Occupational Therapy — M
Psychology—General — M
Public Administration — M
Quality Management — M
Rhetoric — M,O
School Psychology — M
Social Work — M
Sociology — M
Special Education — M

CALIFORNIA STATE UNIVERSITY, EAST BAY

Accounting — M
Actuarial Science — M
Anthropology — M
Applied Mathematics — M
Applied Statistics — M
Biochemistry — M
Biological and Biomedical Sciences—General — M
Biostatistics — M
Business Administration and Management—General — M
Chemistry — M
Child and Family Studies — M
Communication Disorders — M
Communication—General — M
Computer Science — M
Construction Management — M
Counselor Education — M
Database Systems — M
Early Childhood Education — M
Economics — M
Education—General — M
Educational Leadership and Administration — M,D
Educational Media/Instructional Technology — M
Engineering and Applied Sciences—General — M
Engineering Management — M
English as a Second Language — M
English — M
Entrepreneurship — M
Environmental Sciences — M
Finance and Banking — M
Geography — M
Geology — M
Health Services Management and Hospital Administration — M
History — M
Human Resources Management — M
Industrial and Manufacturing Management — M
Industrial/Management Engineering — M
Interdisciplinary Studies — M
International Business — M
Internet and Interactive Multimedia — M
Management Information Systems — M
Management Strategy and Policy — M
Marine Sciences — M
Marketing — M
Marriage and Family Therapy — M
Mathematics Education — M
Mathematics — M
Music — M
Organizational Management — M
Physical Education — M
Public Administration — M
Public History — M
Public Policy — M
Reading Education — M
Recreation and Park Management — M
School Psychology — M
Social Psychology — M
Social Sciences Education — M
Social Work — M
Special Education — M
Statistics — M
Supply Chain Management — M
Travel and Tourism — M
Writing — M

CALIFORNIA STATE UNIVERSITY, FRESNO

Animal Sciences — M
Applied Arts and Design—General — M
Applied Behavior Analysis — M,O
Art/Fine Arts — M
Biological and Biomedical Sciences—General — M
Chemistry — M
Civil Engineering — M
Communication Disorders — M
Communication—General — M
Computer Engineering — M
Computer Science — M
Counseling Psychology — M
Counselor Education — M
Criminal Justice and Criminology — M
Curriculum and Instruction — M
Early Childhood Education — M
Education—General — M,D
Educational Leadership and Administration — M,D
Electrical Engineering — M
Engineering and Applied Sciences—General — M
English as a Second Language — M
English — M
Exercise and Sports Science — M
Experimental Psychology — M,O
Geology — M
Health Promotion — M
Health Services Management and Hospital Administration — M
History — M
Human Development — M,D
Industrial/Management Engineering — M
Kinesiology and Movement Studies — M
Linguistics — M
Marine Sciences — M
Marriage and Family Therapy — M
Mathematics Education — M
Mathematics — M
Mechanical Engineering — M
Music Education — M
Music — M

Nursing—General — M,D
Physical Therapy — D
Physics — M
Plant Sciences — M
Psychology—General — M,O
Public Administration — M
Public Health—General — M
Reading Education — M
Rehabilitation Counseling — M
Rhetoric — M
School Psychology — M,O
Social Sciences Education — M
Social Work — M
Spanish — M
Special Education — M
Sport Psychology — M
Sports Management — M
Student Affairs — M
Viticulture and Enology — M
Writing — M

CALIFORNIA STATE UNIVERSITY, FULLERTON

Accounting — M
American Studies — M
Anthropology — M
Applied Mathematics — M
Architectural Engineering — M
Biological and Biomedical Sciences—General — M
Biotechnology — M
Business Administration and Management—General — M
Chemistry — M
Civil Engineering — M
Clinical Psychology — M
Communication Disorders — M
Communication—General — M
Computer Engineering — M
Computer Science — M
Counselor Education — M
Economics — M
Educational Leadership and Administration — M,D
Educational Media/Instructional Technology — M
Electrical Engineering — M
Electronic Commerce — M
Elementary Education — M
Engineering and Applied Sciences—General — M
English — M
Entrepreneurship — M
Environmental Engineering — M
Environmental Management and Policy — M
Film, Television, and Video Production — M
Finance and Banking — M
Geography — M
Geology — M
Gerontology — M
History — M
Information Science — M
International Business — M
Linguistics — M
Management Information Systems — M
Management Strategy and Policy — M
Marketing — M
Mass Communication — M
Mathematics Education — M
Mathematics — M
Mechanical Engineering — M
Multilingual and Multicultural Education — M
Music Education — M
Music — M
Nurse Anesthesia — M,D
Nursing and Healthcare Administration — M,D
Nursing Education — M,D
Nursing—General — M,D
Organizational Management — M
Physical Education — M
Physics — M
Political Science — M
Psychology—General — M
Public Administration — M
School Nursing — M,D
Science Education — M
Secondary Education — M
Social Psychology — M
Social Work — M
Sociology — M
Software Engineering — M
Spanish — M
Special Education — M
Speech and Interpersonal Communication — M
Systems Engineering — M
Taxation — M
Theater — M
Travel and Tourism — M
Women's Health Nursing — M,D

CALIFORNIA STATE UNIVERSITY, LONG BEACH

African Studies — M
Anthropology — M
Applied Mathematics — M,D
Applied Statistics — M
Art Education — M
Art/Fine Arts — M
Asian Studies — M
Asian-American Studies — M
Athletic Training and Sports Medicine — M
Biochemistry — M
Biological and Biomedical Sciences—General — M

Business Administration and Management—General — M
Chemistry — M
Civil Engineering — M
Communication—General — M
Computer Engineering — M
Computer Science — M
Counselor Education — M,D
Criminal Justice and Criminology — M
Dance — M
Economics — M
Education—General — M,D
Educational Leadership and Administration — M,D
Educational Psychology — M,D
Electrical Engineering — M
Elementary Education — M
Emergency Management — M
Engineering Management — M,D
English as a Second Language — M,O
English — M
Ergonomics and Human Factors — M
Exercise and Sports Science — M
French — M
Geography — M
Geology — M
German — M
Gerontology — M
Health Education — M
Health Services Management and Hospital Administration — M
Higher Education — M,D
History — M
Industrial and Organizational Psychology — M
Kinesiology and Movement Studies — M
Leisure Studies — M
Linguistics — M,O
Marriage and Family Therapy — M,D
Mathematics Education — M
Mathematics — M
Mechanical Engineering — M,D
Microbiology — M
Music — M
Near and Middle Eastern Studies — M
Nursing—General — M,D,O
Nutrition — M
Philosophy — M
Physical Education — M
Physical Therapy — D
Physics — M
Political Science — M
Psychology—General — M
Public Administration — M,O
Public Health—General — M
Public Policy — M,O
Recreation and Park Management — M
Religion — M
Science Education — M
Secondary Education — M
Social Work — M
Spanish — M
Special Education — M,D
Sport Psychology — M
Sports Management — M
Student Affairs — M,D
Theater — M
Writing — M

CALIFORNIA STATE UNIVERSITY, LOS ANGELES

Accounting — M
Analytical Chemistry — M
Anthropology — M
Applied Arts and Design—General — M
Applied Mathematics — M
Art Education — M
Art History — M
Art Therapy — M
Art/Fine Arts — M
Biochemistry — M
Biological and Biomedical Sciences—General — M
Business Administration and Management—General — M,O
Chemistry — M
Child and Family Studies — M
Child Development — M
Civil Engineering — M
Communication Disorders — M
Communication—General — M
Computer Science — M
Counselor Education — M,D
Criminal Justice and Criminology — M
Curriculum and Instruction — M
Economics — M
Education—General — M,D,O
Electrical Engineering — M
Elementary Education — M
Engineering and Applied Sciences—General — M
English — M,O
Finance and Banking — M
French — M
Geography — M
Geology — M
Graphic Design — M
Health Services Management and Hospital Administration — M,O
Hispanic Studies — M
History — M
International Business — M
Kinesiology and Movement Studies — M,O
Latin American Studies — M
Management Information Systems — M
Management of Technology — M
Marketing — M
Mathematics — M
Mechanical Engineering — M
Music Education — M

Music	M,O
Nursing—General	M,O
Nutrition	M,O
Philosophy	M
Photography	M
Physical Education	M,O
Physics	M
Political Science	M
Psychology—General	M
Public Administration	M
Rehabilitation Counseling	M,D
School Psychology	M,D
Social Work	M
Sociology	M
Spanish	M
Special Education	M,D
Textile Design	M
Theater	M

CALIFORNIA STATE UNIVERSITY MARITIME ACADEMY

Emergency Management	M
Engineering Management	M
Transportation Management	M

CALIFORNIA STATE UNIVERSITY, MONTEREY BAY

Business Administration and Management—General	M
Education—General	M
Management Information Systems	M
Marine Sciences	M
Social Work	M
Water Resources	M

CALIFORNIA STATE UNIVERSITY, NORTHRIDGE

Anthropology	M
Applied Mathematics	M
Archaeology	M
Art Education	M
Art History	M
Art/Fine Arts	M
Artificial Intelligence/Robotics	M
Biochemistry	M
Biological and Biomedical Sciences—General	M
Business Administration and Management—General	M
Chemistry	M
Civil Engineering	M
Clinical Psychology	M
Communication Disorders	M
Communication—General	M
Comparative Literature	M
Computer Science	M
Construction Management	M
Counselor Education	M
Curriculum and Instruction	M
Early Childhood Education	M
Education—General	M,D
Educational Leadership and Administration	M,D
Educational Media/Instructional Technology	M
Educational Psychology	M
Electrical Engineering	M
Elementary Education	M
Engineering and Applied Sciences—General	M
Engineering Management	M
English Education	M
English	M
Entertainment Management	M,O
Environmental and Occupational Health	M
Environmental Sciences	M
Experimental Psychology	M
Family and Consumer Sciences-General	M
Film, Television, and Video Production	M
Geography	M
Geology	M
Health Education	M,O
Health Services Management and Hospital Administration	M*
Hispanic Studies	M
History	M
Hospitality Management	M,O
Industrial Hygiene	M
Industrial/Management Engineering	M
Journalism	M
Kinesiology and Movement Studies	M
Linguistics	M
Manufacturing Engineering	M
Marriage and Family Therapy	M
Mass Communication	M
Materials Engineering	M
Mathematics Education	M
Mathematics	M
Mechanical Engineering	M
Multilingual and Multicultural Education	M
Music Education	M
Music	O
Nonprofit Management	O
Physical Therapy	M
Physics	M
Political Science	M
Psychology—General	M,O*
Public Administration	M,O*
Public Health—General	M*
Reading Education	M
Recreation and Park Management	M,O
Rhetoric	M
School Psychology	M
Science Education	M
Secondary Education	M
Social Work	M,O*
Sociology	M
Software Engineering	M
Spanish	M
Special Education	M

Speech and Interpersonal Communication	M
Structural Engineering	M
Systems Engineering	M
Taxation	M,O
Theater	M
Travel and Tourism	M
Writing	M

CALIFORNIA STATE UNIVERSITY, SACRAMENTO

Accounting	M
Anthropology	M
Applied Behavior Analysis	M
Art/Fine Arts	M
Biochemistry	M
Biological and Biomedical Sciences—General	M
Business Administration and Management—General	M
Cell Biology	M
Chemistry	M
Child Development	M,D
Civil Engineering	M
Communication Disorders	M
Communication—General	M
Computer Science	M
Conservation Biology	M
Counseling Psychology	M
Counselor Education	M,D
Criminal Justice and Criminology	M
Curriculum and Instruction	M,D
Developmental Biology	M
Education—General	M,D
Educational Leadership and Administration	M,D
Educational Media/Instructional Technology	M,D
Educational Policy	M,D
Electrical Engineering	M
Engineering and Applied Sciences—General	M
English as a Second Language	M
English	M
Foreign Languages Education	M
Higher Education	M,D
Human Resources Development	M
Human Resources Management	M
Human Services	M
Industrial and Organizational Psychology	M
Mathematics	M
Mechanical Engineering	M
Molecular Biology	M
Multilingual and Multicultural Education	M,D
Music	M
Nursing—General	M
Physical Education	M
Physical Therapy	D
Political Science	M
Psychology—General	M
Public Administration	M
Public History	M,D
Public Policy	M
Reading Education	M,D
Real Estate	M
Recreation and Park Management	M
School Psychology	M,D
Social Work	M
Sociology	M
Software Engineering	M
Special Education	M,D
Writing	M

CALIFORNIA STATE UNIVERSITY, SAN BERNARDINO

Accounting	M
Archaeology	M
Art/Fine Arts	M
Biological and Biomedical Sciences—General	M
Business Administration and Management—General	M
Child Development	M
Clinical Psychology	M
Communication—General	M
Community College Education	M
Computer and Information Systems Security	M
Computer Science	M
Corporate and Organizational Communication	M
Counseling Psychology	M
Counselor Education	M
Criminal Justice and Criminology	M
Education—General	M
Educational Leadership and Administration	M,D
English	M
Entrepreneurship	M
Environmental Sciences	M
Experimental Psychology	M
Finance and Banking	M
Geosciences	M
Health Services Management and Hospital Administration	M
Industrial and Organizational Psychology	M
Interdisciplinary Studies	M
International Business	M
Management Information Systems	M
Marketing	M
Mathematics Education	M
Mathematics	M
Music	M
National Security	M
Nursing—General	M
Psychology—General	M
Public Administration	M
Public Health—General	M
Rehabilitation Counseling	M
Social Sciences	M
Social Work	M

Spanish	M
Supply Chain Management	M
Writing	M

CALIFORNIA STATE UNIVERSITY, SAN MARCOS

Biological and Biomedical Sciences—General	M
Business Administration and Management—General	M
Child and Family Studies	M
Communication Disorders	M
Computer Science	M
Education—General	M,D
Educational Leadership and Administration	M,D
English	M
Family Nurse Practitioner Studies	M
Health Education	M
Hispanic and Latin American Languages	M
Hispanic Studies	M
History	M
Mathematics	M
Nursing and Healthcare Administration	M
Nursing Education	M
Nursing—General	M
Psychiatric Nursing	M
Psychology—General	M
Reading Education	M,D
Social Work	M
Sociology	M
Spanish	M
Special Education	M,D
Writing	M

CALIFORNIA STATE UNIVERSITY, STANISLAUS

Applied Behavior Analysis	M
Business Administration and Management—General	M
Community College Education	D
Conservation Biology	M
Counseling Psychology	M
Counselor Education	M
Criminal Justice and Criminology	M
Curriculum and Instruction	M
Ecology	M
Education—General	M,D
Educational Leadership and Administration	M,D
Educational Media/Instructional Technology	M
Elementary Education	M
English as a Second Language	M,O
English	M,O
Genetic Counseling	M
Gerontological Nursing	M
History	M
Interdisciplinary Studies	M
International Affairs	M
Multilingual and Multicultural Education	M
Nursing Education	M
Nursing—General	M
Physical Education	M
Psychology—General	M
Public Administration	M
Reading Education	M
Rhetoric	M,O
Secondary Education	M
Social Work	M
Special Education	M
Sustainable Development	M
Writing	M,O

CALIFORNIA UNIVERSITY OF MANAGEMENT AND SCIENCES

Business Administration and Management—General	M,D
Economics	M,D
International Business	M,D
Management Information Systems	M,D
Sports Management	M,D

CALIFORNIA UNIVERSITY OF PENNSYLVANIA

Athletic Training and Sports Medicine	M
Business Administration and Management—General	M
Clinical Psychology	M
Communication Disorders	M
Counseling Psychology	M
Counselor Education	M
Criminal Justice and Criminology	M
Education—General	M
Educational Leadership and Administration	M
Elementary Education	M
Entrepreneurship	M
Exercise and Sports Science	M
Legal and Justice Studies	M
Management Strategy and Policy	M
Nursing and Healthcare Administration	M
Reading Education	M
Rehabilitation Sciences	M
School Psychology	M
Secondary Education	M
Social Work	M
Special Education	M
Sport Psychology	M
Sports Management	M
Vocational and Technical Education	M

CALIFORNIA WESTERN SCHOOL OF LAW

Accounting	M,D
Law	M,D

CALUMET COLLEGE OF SAINT JOSEPH

Criminal Justice and Criminology	M
Educational Leadership and Administration	M

Quality Management	M

CALVARY UNIVERSITY

Curriculum and Instruction	M
Education—General	M
Educational Leadership and Administration	M
Elementary Education	M
Organizational Management	M
Pastoral Ministry and Counseling	M
Religious Education	M
Theology	M

CALVIN COLLEGE

Curriculum and Instruction	M
Education—General	M

CALVIN THEOLOGICAL SEMINARY

Missions and Missiology	M,D
Pastoral Ministry and Counseling	M,D
Religion	M,D
Religious Education	M,D
Theology	M,D

CAMBRIDGE COLLEGE

Addictions/Substance Abuse Counseling	M,O
Business Administration and Management—General	M
Conflict Resolution and Mediation/Peace Studies	M
Counseling Psychology	M,O
Counselor Education	M,D,O
Curriculum and Instruction	M,D,O
Early Childhood Education	M,D,O
Education—General	M,D,O
Educational Leadership and Administration	M,D,O
Educational Measurement and Evaluation	M,D,O
Educational Media/Instructional Technology	M,D,O
Elementary Education	M,D,O
English as a Second Language	M,D,O
Entrepreneurship	M
Forensic Psychology	M,O
Health Education	M,D,O
Health Services Management and Hospital Administration	M,D,O
Home Economics Education	M,D,O
Interdisciplinary Studies	M,D,O
Management of Technology	M
Marriage and Family Therapy	M,O
Mathematics Education	M,D,O
Medical Informatics	M
Middle School Education	M,D,O
Nonprofit Management	M
Organizational Management	M
Psychology—General	M,O
Reading Education	M,D,O
School Nursing	M,D,O
School Psychology	M,D,O
Science Education	M,D,O
Social Sciences Education	M,D,O
Special Education	M,D,O

CAMERON UNIVERSITY

Business Administration and Management—General	M
Education—General	M
Educational Leadership and Administration	M
Entrepreneurship	M
Psychology—General	M

CAMPBELLSVILLE UNIVERSITY

Business Administration and Management—General	M
Education—General	M
Marriage and Family Therapy	M
Music Education	M
Music	M
Social Sciences	M
Social Work	M
Special Education	M
Theology	M

CAMPBELL UNIVERSITY

Business Administration and Management—General	M
Counselor Education	M
Education—General	M
Educational Leadership and Administration	M
Elementary Education	M
Interdisciplinary Studies	M
Law	D
Middle School Education	M
Osteopathic Medicine	D
Pastoral Ministry and Counseling	M,D
Pharmaceutical Sciences	M,D
Pharmacy	M,D
Physical Education	M
Physical Therapy	M,D
Physician Assistant Studies	M,D
Secondary Education	M
Theology	M,D

CANADIAN COLLEGE OF NATUROPATHIC MEDICINE

Naturopathic Medicine	O*

CANADIAN MEMORIAL CHIROPRACTIC COLLEGE

Acupuncture and Oriental Medicine	O
Chiropractic	D,O

CANADIAN SOUTHERN BAPTIST SEMINARY

Pastoral Ministry and Counseling	M
Religion	M
Theology	M

CANISIUS COLLEGE

Accounting	M
Allied Health—General	M,O
Anthropology	M

Business Administration and Management—General	M
Business Education	M,O
Communication Disorders	M,O
Community Health	M,O
Corporate and Organizational Communication	M
Counselor Education	M
Early Childhood Education	M,O
Education of the Gifted	M,O
Education—General	M,O
Educational Leadership and Administration	M,O
Educational Media/Instructional Technology	M,O
Elementary Education	M,O
English as a Second Language	M,O
Health Informatics	M,O
International Business	M
Kinesiology and Movement Studies	M
Middle School Education	M
Nutrition	M,O
Physical Education	M
Reading Education	M,O
School Psychology	M
Secondary Education	M,O
Social Psychology	M
Special Education	M,O
Sports Management	M
Student Affairs	M,O
Zoology	M

CAPE BRETON UNIVERSITY

Business Administration and Management—General	M

CAPELLA UNIVERSITY

Accounting	M,D
Addictions/Substance Abuse Counseling	M,D
Adult Education	M,D
Applied Behavior Analysis	M
Business Administration and Management—General	M,D
Business Education	D
Child and Family Studies	M
Clinical Psychology	M,D
Computer and Information Systems Security	M,D
Counseling Psychology	M
Counselor Education	M,D
Criminal Justice and Criminology	M,D
Curriculum and Instruction	M,D
Developmental Psychology	M
Distance Education Development	M,D
Early Childhood Education	M
Education—General	M,D
Educational Leadership and Administration	M,D
Educational Media/Instructional Technology	M,D
Educational Psychology	M,D
Elementary Education	M,D
Emergency Management	M,D
Entrepreneurship	M,D
Environmental and Occupational Health	M,D
Epidemiology	D
Finance and Banking	M,D
Gerontological Nursing	M
Gerontology	M
Health Informatics	M
Health Services Management and Hospital Administration	M,D
Higher Education	M,D
Homeland Security	M
Human Resources Management	M,D
Human Services	M,D
Industrial and Organizational Psychology	M,D
Management Information Systems	M,D
Management of Technology	M,D
Management Strategy and Policy	M,D
Marketing	M,D
Marriage and Family Therapy	M
Middle School Education	M,D
Nonprofit Management	D
Nursing and Healthcare Administration	M
Nursing Education	M,D
Nursing—General	M,D
Operations Research	M
Organizational Management	M,D
Project Management	M,D
Psychology—General	M,D
Public Administration	M,D
Reading Education	M,D
School Psychology	M,D
Social Work	D
Special Education	M,D
Sport Psychology	M
Supply Chain Management	M,D
Vocational and Technical Education	D

CAPITAL UNIVERSITY

Business Administration and Management—General	M
Law	M,D
Legal and Justice Studies	M
Music Education	M
Music	M
Nursing and Healthcare Administration	M
Nursing—General	M
Taxation	M

CAPITOL TECHNOLOGY UNIVERSITY

Business Administration and Management—General	M
Computer and Information Systems Security	M
Computer Science	M

Electrical Engineering	M
Information Science	M
Management Information Systems	M
Telecommunications Management	M

CARDINAL STRITCH UNIVERSITY

Business Administration and Management—General	M
Clinical Psychology	M
Education—General	M,D
Educational Leadership and Administration	M,D
Health Services Management and Hospital Administration	M
Higher Education	M,D
Liberal Studies	M
Nursing—General	M
Pastoral Ministry and Counseling	M
Psychology—General	M
Reading Education	M,D
Religion	M
Special Education	M,D
Sports Management	M
Student Affairs	M
Urban Education	M,D

CAREY THEOLOGICAL COLLEGE

Theology	M,D

CARIBBEAN UNIVERSITY

Art History	M,D
Criminal Justice and Criminology	M,D
Curriculum and Instruction	M,D
Early Childhood Education	M,D
Education—General	M,D
Educational Leadership and Administration	M,D
Educational Media/Instructional Technology	M,D
Elementary Education	M,D
English Education	M,D
Foreign Languages Education	M,D
Gerontological Nursing	M,D
Human Resources Management	M,D
Mathematics Education	M,D
Museum Studies	M,D
Pediatric Nursing	M,D
Physical Education	M,D
Science Education	M,D
Social Sciences Education	M,D
Special Education	M,D

CARLETON UNIVERSITY

Aerospace/Aeronautical Engineering	M,D
Anthropology	M
Architecture	M
Art History	M
Biological and Biomedical Sciences—General	M,D
Biomedical Engineering	M
Business Administration and Management—General	M,D
Canadian Studies	M,D
Chemistry	M,D
Civil Engineering	M,D
Cognitive Sciences	D
Communication—General	M,D
Comparative Literature	D
Computer Science	M,D
Conflict Resolution and Mediation/Peace Studies	M,O
East European and Russian Studies	M,O
Economics	M,D
Electrical Engineering	M,D
Engineering and Applied Sciences—General	M,D
English	M,D
Environmental Engineering	M,D
Film, Television, and Video Production	M
French	M
Geography	M,D
Geosciences	M,D
History	M,D
Industrial Design	M
Information Science	M,D
International Affairs	M,D
Journalism	M,D
Legal and Justice Studies	M,D
Linguistics	M
Management of Technology	M
Materials Engineering	M,D
Mathematics	M,D
Mechanical Engineering	M,D
Music	M
Neuroscience	M,D
Philosophy	M
Physics	M,D
Political Science	M,D
Psychology—General	M,D
Public Administration	M,D
Public Policy	M
Social Work	M
Sociology	M,D
Systems Engineering	M,D
Systems Science	M,D
Western European Studies	M,O

CARLOS ALBIZU UNIVERSITY

Clinical Psychology	M,D
Communication Disorders	M,D
Industrial and Organizational Psychology	M,D
Psychology—General	M,D

CARLOS ALBIZU UNIVERSITY, MIAMI CAMPUS

Business Administration and Management—General	M,D
Clinical Psychology	M,D
Communication Disorders	M,D

Counseling Psychology	M,D
Education of the Gifted	M,D
English as a Second Language	M,D
Entrepreneurship	M,D
Human Services	M,D
Industrial and Organizational Psychology	M,D
Marriage and Family Therapy	M,D
Nonprofit Management	M,D
Organizational Management	M,D
Psychology—General	M,D
School Psychology	M,D
Special Education	M,D

CARLOW UNIVERSITY

Addictions/Substance Abuse Counseling	M,O
Business Administration and Management—General	M
Computer and Information Systems Security	M
Counseling Psychology	M,D,O
Counselor Education	M,O
Early Childhood Education	M
Education—General	M,O
Educational Leadership and Administration	M
Family Nurse Practitioner Studies	M,O
Forensic Sciences	M
Health Services Management and Hospital Administration	M
Human Resources Management	M
Nursing and Healthcare Administration	M
Nursing Education	M
Nursing—General	D
Organizational Management	M,D,O
Project Management	M
Special Education	M
Writing	M

CARNEGIE MELLON UNIVERSITY

Accounting	D
African Studies	M
African-American Studies	D
Applied Arts and Design—General	M,D
Applied Physics	M,D
Architectural Engineering	M
Architecture	M,D
Art/Fine Arts	M
Artificial Intelligence/Robotics	M,D
Arts Administration	M
Atmospheric Sciences	D
Biochemistry	M,D
Bioengineering	M
Biological and Biomedical Sciences—General	M,D
Biomedical Engineering	M,D
Biophysics	M,D
Biopsychology	D
Biotechnology	M
Building Science	M,D
Business Administration and Management—General	M,D
Cell Biology	M
Chemical Engineering	M,D
Chemistry	D
Civil Engineering	M,D
Cognitive Sciences	D
Communication—General	M,D
Comparative Literature	M,D
Computational Biology	M,D
Computer and Information Systems Security	M
Computer Art and Design	M
Computer Engineering	M,D
Computer Science	M,D
Construction Management	M,D
Corporate and Organizational Communication	M
Criminal Justice and Criminology	M
Cultural Studies	D
Developmental Biology	M,D
Developmental Psychology	D
Economics	D
Electrical Engineering	M,D
Energy and Power Engineering	M,D
English	M,D
Entertainment Management	M
Entrepreneurship	D
Environmental Engineering	M,D
Environmental Sciences	D
Film, Television, and Video Production	M
Finance and Banking	D
Gender Studies	D
Genetics	M,D
Health Services Management and Hospital Administration	M
History of Science and Technology	D
History	D
Human-Computer Interaction	M,D
Industrial and Labor Relations	D
Industrial and Manufacturing Management	M,D
Information Science	M,D
Linguistics	M,D
Management Information Systems	M,D
Marketing	D
Materials Engineering	M,D
Materials Sciences	M,D
Mathematical and Computational Finance	M,D
Mathematics	M,D
Mechanical Engineering	M,D
Mechanics	M,D
Media Studies	M
Modeling and Simulation	M,D
Molecular Biology	M,D
Molecular Biophysics	D

Music Education	M
Music	M
Nanotechnology	D
Neurobiology	M,D
Neuroscience	D
Operations Research	D
Organizational Behavior	D
Philosophy	M,D
Physics	M,D
Polymer Science and Engineering	M
Psychology—General	D
Public Administration	M
Public Policy	M,D
Publishing	M
Rhetoric	M,D
Social Psychology	D
Social Sciences	D
Software Engineering	M,D
Statistics	M,D
Structural Biology	M,D
Sustainable Development	M,D
Systems Engineering	M
Technical Writing	M
Technology and Public Policy	M,D
Telecommunications Management	M
Theater	M
Theoretical Chemistry	D
Urban Design	M,D
Water Resources Engineering	M,D
Women's Studies	D
Writing	M

CAROLINA CHRISTIAN COLLEGE

Pastoral Ministry and Counseling	M
Religious Education	M

CARROLL UNIVERSITY

Adult Education	M
Business Administration and Management—General	M
Early Childhood Education	M
Education—General	M
Educational Leadership and Administration	M
Elementary Education	M
Physical Therapy	D
Physician Assistant Studies	M
Secondary Education	M
Software Engineering	M

CARSON-NEWMAN UNIVERSITY

Business Administration and Management—General	M
Counselor Education	M
Curriculum and Instruction	M
Education—General	M
Educational Leadership and Administration	M
Elementary Education	M
English as a Second Language	M
Family Nurse Practitioner Studies	M
Nursing Education	M
Nursing—General	M
Organizational Management	M
Secondary Education	M
Theology	M

CARTHAGE COLLEGE

Art Education	M,O
Counselor Education	M,O
Education of the Gifted	M,O
Education—General	M,O
Educational Leadership and Administration	M,O
English Education	M,O
Reading Education	M,O
Science Education	M,O
Social Sciences Education	M,O

CASE WESTERN RESERVE UNIVERSITY

Accounting	M,D
Acute Care/Critical Care Nursing	M
Aerospace/Aeronautical Engineering	M,D
Allopathic Medicine	D
Anatomy	M
Anesthesiologist Assistant Studies	M
Anthropology	M,D
Applied Mathematics	M,D
Art Education	M
Art History	M,D
Astronomy	M,D
Biochemistry	M,D
Bioethics	M
Biological and Biomedical Sciences—General	M,D
Biomedical Engineering	M,D*
Biophysics	M,D
Biostatistics	M,D
Business Administration and Management—General	M,D
Cancer Biology/Oncology	D
Cell Biology	D
Chemical Engineering	M,D
Chemistry	M,D
Civil Engineering	M,D
Clinical Psychology	D
Clinical Research	M,D
Cognitive Sciences	M
Communication Disorders	M,D
Comparative Literature	M
Computer Engineering	M,D
Computer Science	M,D
Dance	M
Database Systems	M
Dentistry	D
Electrical Engineering	M,D
Engineering and Applied Sciences—General	M,D
Engineering Management	M

English — M,D
Epidemiology — D
Experimental Psychology — M
Family Nurse Practitioner Studies — M
Finance and Banking — M
French — M
Genetic Counseling — M,D
Genomic Sciences — M,D
Geology — M,D
Geosciences — M,D
Gerontological Nursing — M
Health Law — M,D
Health Services Management and Hospital Administration — M
History — M,D
Human Genetics — M,D
Immunology — D
Industrial and Manufacturing Management — M,D
Information Science — M,D
Intellectual Property Law — M,D
Law — M,D
Legal and Justice Studies — M,D
Linguistics — M,D
Logistics — M
Materials Engineering — M,D
Materials Sciences — M,D
Maternal and Child/Neonatal Nursing — M
Mathematics — M,D
Mechanical Engineering — M,D
Medical/Surgical Nursing — M
Microbiology — D
Molecular Biology — M
Molecular Medicine — D
Museum Studies — M
Music Education — M,D
Music — M
Neuroscience — D
Nonprofit Management — M,D,O
Nurse Anesthesia — M
Nurse Midwifery — M
Nursing Education — M
Nursing—General — M,D
Nutrition — M,D
Operations Research — M,D
Oral and Dental Sciences — M,O
Organizational Behavior — M,D
Pathology — M,D
Pediatric Nursing — M
Pharmacology — D
Physician Assistant Studies — M
Physics — M,D
Physiology — M,D
Political Science — M,D
Polymer Science and Engineering — M,D
Psychiatric Nursing — M
Psychology—General — M,D
Public Health—General — M
Social Work — M,D
Sociology — M,D
Supply Chain Management — M,D
Sustainability Management — D
Systems Engineering — M,D
Theater — M
Virology — D
Women's Health Nursing — M

CASTLETON UNIVERSITY
Curriculum and Instruction — M
Education—General — M,O
Educational Leadership and Administration — M,O
Forensic Psychology — M
Psychology—General — M
Reading Education — M,O
Special Education — M,O

CATAWBA COLLEGE
Elementary Education — M
Science Education — M

CATHOLIC DISTANCE UNIVERSITY
Theology — M

CATHOLIC THEOLOGICAL UNION
Missions and Missiology — M,D,O
Pastoral Ministry and Counseling — M,D,O
Theology — M,D,O

THE CATHOLIC UNIVERSITY OF AMERICA
Accounting — M
American Studies — M,D
Anthropology — M
Applied Psychology — M,D
Architecture — M,O
Biological and Biomedical Sciences—General — M,D
Biomedical Engineering — M,D
Biotechnology — M,D
Business Administration and Management—General — M
Cell Biology — M,D
Civil Engineering — M,D,O
Classics — M,D,O
Clinical Laboratory Sciences/Medical Technology — M,D
Clinical Psychology — M,D
Computer Science — M,D
Criminal Justice and Criminology — M
Early Childhood Education — M,O
Economic Development — M
Education—General — M,O
Educational Leadership and Administration — M,O
Electrical Engineering — M,D
Energy and Power Engineering — M,D
Engineering and Applied Sciences—General — M,D,O
Engineering Management — M,O
English — M,D,O
Environmental Engineering — M,D

Ergonomics and Human Factors — M,D
Experimental Psychology — M,D
Health Services Management and Hospital Administration
Hispanic Studies — M,D
History — M,D
Human Resources Management — M
Information Studies — M,O
International Affairs — M,D
Latin American Studies — M,D
Law — M,D
Legal and Justice Studies — M,D,O
Library Science — M,O
Management Information Systems — M,O
Management of Technology — M,O
Materials Engineering — M,D
Materials Sciences — M
Mechanical Engineering — M,D
Medieval and Renaissance Studies — M,D,O
Microbiology — M,D
Music Education — M,D,O
Music — M,D,O
Near and Middle Eastern Languages — M,D
Near and Middle Eastern Studies — M,D,O
Nursing—General — M,D,O
Pastoral Ministry and Counseling — M,D,O
Philosophy — M,D
Physics — M,D
Political Science — M,D
Project Management — M,O
Psychology—General — M,D
Public Policy — M
Religion — M,D,O
Rhetoric — M,D,O
Secondary Education — M,O
Social Work — M,D
Sociology — M
Spanish — M,D
Special Education — M,O
Sustainable Development — M,O
Systems Engineering — M,O
Theater — M
Theology — M,D,O
Transportation and Highway Engineering — M,D,O
Urban and Regional Planning — M,O
Western European Studies — M,D

CEDAR CREST COLLEGE
Art Therapy — M
Business Administration and Management—General — M
Education—General — M
Forensic Sciences — M
Nursing and Healthcare Administration — M
Nursing Education — M
Nursing—General — M
Nutrition — O
Writing — M

CEDARS-SINAI MEDICAL CENTER
Biological and Biomedical Sciences—General — D
Translational Biology — D

CEDARVILLE UNIVERSITY
Business Administration and Management—General — M,D
Education—General — M,D
Family Nurse Practitioner Studies — M,D
Health Services Management and Hospital Administration — M,D
Industrial and Manufacturing Management — M,D
International Health — M,D
Missions and Missiology — M,D
Nursing Education — M,D
Pastoral Ministry and Counseling — M,D
Pharmacy — M,D

CENTENARY COLLEGE OF LOUISIANA
Business Administration and Management—General — M
Education—General — M
Elementary Education — M
Secondary Education — M

CENTENARY UNIVERSITY
Accounting — M
Business Administration and Management—General — M
Counseling Psychology — M
Education—General — M,D
Educational Leadership and Administration — M,D
Reading Education — M,D
Special Education — M,D

CENTRAL BAPTIST THEOLOGICAL SEMINARY
Missions and Missiology — M,O
Theology — M,O

CENTRAL CONNECTICUT STATE UNIVERSITY
Accounting — M
Actuarial Science — M,O
Art Education — M,O
Biological and Biomedical Sciences—General — M,O
Business Administration and Management—General — M
Communication—General — M,O
Computer Science — M,O
Construction Management — M,O
Counselor Education — M,O
Criminal Justice and Criminology — M
Early Childhood Education — M,O
Education—General — M,D,O
Educational Leadership and Administration — M,D,O
Elementary Education — M,O
Engineering and Applied Sciences—General — M

Exercise and Sports Science — M,O
Foreign Languages Education — M,O
French — M
Geography — M,O
German — M
Graphic Design — M
History — M,O
Industrial and Manufacturing Management — M,O
Information Studies — M
International Affairs — M
Italian — M
Logistics — M,O
Management of Technology — M
Marriage and Family Therapy — M,O
Mathematics — M,O
Molecular Biology — M
Music Education — M,O
Physical Education — M,O
Psychology—General — M
Reading Education — M,O
Rehabilitation Counseling — M,O
School Psychology — M,O
Science Education — M
Secondary Education — M,O
Spanish — M
Special Education — M,O
Statistics — M,O
Supply Chain Management — M,O
Vocational and Technical Education — M

CENTRAL EUROPEAN UNIVERSITY
Anthropology — M,D
Applied Mathematics — M,D
Business Administration and Management—General — M,D
Cognitive Sciences — D
Database Systems — M,D
Economics — M,D
Environmental Management and Policy — M,D
Finance and Banking — M,D
Gender Studies — M,D
History — M,D
International Affairs — M,D
International Business — M,D
Law — M,D
Legal and Justice Studies — M,D
Management Information Systems — M,D
Mathematics — M,D
Medieval and Renaissance Studies — M,D
Philosophy — M,D
Political Science — M,D
Public Administration — M,D
Public Policy — M,D
Sociology — M,D

CENTRAL METHODIST UNIVERSITY
Counselor Education — M
Education—General — M
Music Education — M
Nursing and Healthcare Administration — M
Nursing Education — M
Nursing—General — M

CENTRAL MICHIGAN UNIVERSITY
Accounting — M,O
American Indian/Native American Studies — M
American Studies — M,O
Applied Psychology — M,D
Biological and Biomedical Sciences—General — M
Business Administration and Management—General — M,O
Chemistry — M
Child and Family Studies — M,O
Clinical Psychology — D
Clothing and Textiles — M,O
Communication Disorders — M,D
Communication—General — M
Community College Education — M,D,O
Computer and Information Systems Security — O
Computer Science — M
Conservation Biology — M
Counseling Psychology — M,D,O
Counselor Education — M
Cultural Studies — M
Curriculum and Instruction — M,D,O
Early Childhood Education — M,O
Economics — M
Education—General — M,D,O
Educational Leadership and Administration — M,D,O
Educational Media/Instructional Technology — M,D,O
Elementary Education — M,D,O
Engineering and Applied Sciences—General — M
Engineering Management — M,O
English as a Second Language — M
English — M
Exercise and Sports Science — M,D
Experimental Psychology — M,D
Family and Consumer Sciences—General — M,O
Film, Television, and Video Production — M
Film, Television, and Video Theory and Criticism — M
Finance and Banking — M
Gender Studies — M
Geographic Information Systems — M
Gerontology — M,D
Health Psychology — M,D
Health Services Management and Hospital Administration — M,D,O
Higher Education — M,O
History — M,O
Human Development — M,O
Human Resources Management — M,O
Humanities — M

Industrial and Manufacturing Management — M
Industrial and Organizational Psychology — M,D
International Affairs — M,O
International Business — M,O
International Health — M,D,O
Logistics — M,O
Management Information Systems — M,O
Marketing — M,O
Materials Sciences — D
Mathematics Education — M,D
Mathematics — M,D
Media Studies — M
Music Education — M
Music — M
Neuroscience — M,D
Nonprofit Management — M,O
Nutrition — M,D,O
Physical Therapy — M,D
Physician Assistant Studies — M,D
Physics — M,D
Political Science — M,O
Psychology—General — M,D,O
Public Administration — M,O
Reading Education — M,D,O
Recreation and Park Management — M,O
Rehabilitation Sciences — M,D
School Psychology — D,O
Science Education — M
Secondary Education — M,D,O
Spanish — M
Special Education — M,O
Sports Management — M,O
Student Affairs — M,D,O
Western European Studies — M,O
Writing — M

CENTRAL PENN COLLEGE
Management Information Systems — M
Organizational Management — M

CENTRAL WASHINGTON UNIVERSITY
Accounting — M
Art/Fine Arts — M
Biological and Biomedical Sciences—General — M
Chemistry — M
Child and Family Studies — M
Counseling Psychology — M
Counselor Education — M
Curriculum and Instruction — M
Education—General — M
Educational Leadership and Administration — M
Engineering and Applied Sciences—General — M
English as a Second Language — M
English — M
Exercise and Sports Science — M
Experimental Psychology — M
Family and Consumer Sciences-General — M
Foundations and Philosophy of Education — M
Geology — M
Health Education — M
History — M
Home Economics Education — M
Industrial/Management Engineering — M
Interdisciplinary Studies — M
Mathematics — M
Music — M
Natural Resources — M
Nutrition — M
Physical Education — M
Psychology—General — M
Reading Education — M
School Psychology — M
Special Education — M
Sports Management — M
Theater — M
Vocational and Technical Education — M

CENTRAL YESHIVA TOMCHEI TMIMIM-LUBAVITCH
Jewish Studies — M
Theology — M

CENTRO DE ESTUDIOS AVANZADOS DE PUERTO RICO Y EL CARIBE
History — M,D
Latin American Studies — M,D

CHADRON STATE COLLEGE
Business Administration and Management—General — M
Business Education — M,O
Counselor Education — M,O
Education—General — M,O
Educational Leadership and Administration — M,O
Elementary Education — M,O
English Education — M,O
Secondary Education — M,O
Social Sciences Education — M,O

CHAMINADE UNIVERSITY OF HONOLULU
Accounting — M
Business Administration and Management—General — M
Child Development — M
Counseling Psychology — M
Criminal Justice and Criminology — M
Early Childhood Education — M
Education—General — M
Educational Leadership and Administration — M
Elementary Education — M
Marriage and Family Therapy — M
Nonprofit Management — M
Pastoral Ministry and Counseling — M
School Psychology — M
Secondary Education — M

Special Education — M
Theology — M

CHAMPLAIN COLLEGE
Business Administration and Management—General — M
Computer and Information Systems Security — M
Conflict Resolution and Mediation/Peace Studies — M
Early Childhood Education — M
Forensic Sciences — M
Health Services Management and Hospital Administration — M
Internet and Interactive Multimedia — M
Law — M
Management of Technology — M
Media Studies — M

CHAPMAN UNIVERSITY
Accounting — M
Athletic Training and Sports Medicine — M
Business Administration and Management—General — M
Communication Disorders — M
Computational Sciences — M,D*
Counselor Education — M,D,O
Cultural Studies — M,D,O
Curriculum and Instruction — M,D,O
Disability Studies — M,D,O
Education—General — M,D,O
Educational Leadership and Administration — M,D,O
Educational Psychology — M,D,O
Elementary Education — M,D,O
English — M
Environmental Law — M,D
Film, Television, and Video Production — M
Food Science and Technology — M*
Health Communication — M
Holocaust and Genocide Studies — M
International Affairs — M
Law — M,D
Marriage and Family Therapy — M
Nutrition — M
Pharmaceutical Sciences — M,D
Pharmacy — M,D
Physical Therapy — D
Physician Assistant Studies — M
School Psychology — M,D,O
Secondary Education — M,D,O
Special Education — M,D,O
Taxation — M,D
Writing — M

CHARLES R. DREW UNIVERSITY OF MEDICINE AND SCIENCE
Allopathic Medicine — D
Public Health—General — M

CHARLESTON SCHOOL OF LAW
Law — M,D

CHARLESTON SOUTHERN UNIVERSITY
Accounting — M
Business Administration and Management—General — M
Criminal Justice and Criminology — M
Education—General — M
Educational Leadership and Administration — M
Elementary Education — M
Finance and Banking — M
Human Resources Management — M
Management Information Systems — M
Organizational Management — M

CHARLOTTE CHRISTIAN COLLEGE AND THEOLOGICAL SEMINARY
Cultural Studies — M
Missions and Missiology — M
Music — M
Pastoral Ministry and Counseling — M
Religion — M
Theology — M

CHATHAM UNIVERSITY
Accounting — M
Art Education — M
Biological and Biomedical Sciences—General — M
Business Administration and Management—General — M
Communication—General — M
Computer Art and Design — M
Counseling Psychology — M,D
Developmental Psychology — M,D
Early Childhood Education — M
Education—General — M
Elementary Education — M
English Education — M
Environmental Biology — M
Environmental Education — M
Film, Television, and Video Production — M
Health Communication — M
Health Informatics — M
Health Psychology — M,D
Industrial and Organizational Psychology — M,D
Interior Design — M
Landscape Architecture — M
Marriage and Family Therapy — M
Mathematics Education — M
Nursing and Healthcare Administration — M,D
Nursing Education — M,D
Nursing—General — M,D
Occupational Therapy — M,D

Physical Therapy — D
Physician Assistant Studies — M
Science Education — M
Secondary Education — M
Social Sciences Education — M
Special Education — M
Sport Psychology — M,D
Sustainability Management — M
Women's Studies — M
Writing — M

CHESTNUT HILL COLLEGE
Clinical Psychology — M,D,O
Counseling Psychology — M,O
Early Childhood Education — M
Education—General — M
Educational Leadership and Administration — M
Educational Media/Instructional Technology — M,O
Elementary Education — M
Human Services — M,O
Marriage and Family Therapy — M,D,O
Middle School Education — M
Psychology—General — M,D,O
Reading Education — M
Secondary Education — M
Special Education — M,O

CHEYNEY UNIVERSITY OF PENNSYLVANIA
Education—General — M,O
Educational Leadership and Administration — M,O
Elementary Education — M
Public Administration — M
Special Education — M
Urban Education — M

THE CHICAGO SCHOOL OF PROFESSIONAL PSYCHOLOGY
Applied Behavior Analysis — M,D
Clinical Psychology — M,D
Forensic Psychology — M,D
Industrial and Organizational Psychology — M,D
Organizational Management — M,D
Psychology—General — M
School Psychology — D,O

THE CHICAGO SCHOOL OF PROFESSIONAL PSYCHOLOGY AT DOWNTOWN LOS ANGELES
Applied Behavior Analysis — M,D
Clinical Psychology — M,D
Forensic Psychology — D
Industrial and Organizational Psychology — M
Marriage and Family Therapy — M,D

THE CHICAGO SCHOOL OF PROFESSIONAL PSYCHOLOGY AT IRVINE
Clinical Psychology — D
Forensic Psychology — D
Marriage and Family Therapy — M,D
Psychology—General — D

THE CHICAGO SCHOOL OF PROFESSIONAL PSYCHOLOGY: ONLINE
Applied Psychology — M,O
Forensic Psychology — M,O
Industrial and Organizational Psychology — M,D,O
Psychology—General — M,D

CHICAGO STATE UNIVERSITY
Biological and Biomedical Sciences—General — M
Computer Science — M
Counselor Education — M
Criminal Justice and Criminology — M
Early Childhood Education — M
Education—General — M,D
Educational Leadership and Administration — M,D
Educational Media/Instructional Technology — M
Elementary Education — M
English — M
Foundations and Philosophy of Education — M
Geographic Information Systems — M
Geography — M
Higher Education — M,D
History — M
Library Science — M
Mathematics — M
Middle School Education — M
Multilingual and Multicultural Education — M
Nursing—General — M
Occupational Therapy — M
Pharmacy — D
Physical Education — M
Public Health—General — M
Reading Education — M
Secondary Education — M
Social Work — M
Special Education — M
Vocational and Technical Education — M
Writing — M

CHICAGO THEOLOGICAL SEMINARY
Ethics — M,D
Pastoral Ministry and Counseling — M,D
Religion — M,D
Theology — M,D

CHOWAN UNIVERSITY
Education—General — M

CHRISTENDOM COLLEGE
Theology — M

CHRISTIAN BROTHERS UNIVERSITY
Accounting — M,O
Business Administration and Management—General — M,O
Education—General — M,O
Educational Leadership and Administration — M,O
Engineering and Applied Sciences—General — M
International Business — M,O
Physician Assistant Studies — M
Project Management — M,O
Religion — M

CHRISTIAN THEOLOGICAL SEMINARY
Marriage and Family Therapy — M,D
Pastoral Ministry and Counseling — M,D
Religion — M,D
Theology — M,D

CHRISTIE'S EDUCATION
Art History — M
Art/Fine Arts — O
Arts Administration — M,O
Museum Studies — M

CHRISTOPHER NEWPORT UNIVERSITY
Applied Physics — M
Computer Science — M
Education—General — M
Environmental Sciences — M
Physics — M

CHRIST THE KING SEMINARY
Pastoral Ministry and Counseling — M
Theology — M

CHURCH DIVINITY SCHOOL OF THE PACIFIC
Theology — M,D,O

CINCINNATI CHRISTIAN UNIVERSITY
Pastoral Ministry and Counseling — M
Religion — M
Theology — M

THE CITADEL, THE MILITARY COLLEGE OF SOUTH CAROLINA
Aerospace/Aeronautical Engineering — M,O
Biological and Biomedical Sciences—General — M,O
Business Administration and Management—General — M
Civil Engineering — M,O
Computer Engineering — M,O
Counselor Education — M,O
Early Childhood Education — M,O
Education—General — M,O
Educational Leadership and Administration — M,O
Electrical Engineering — M,O
Engineering and Applied Sciences—General — M,O
Engineering Management — M,O
English Education — M,O
English — M
Environmental Management and Policy — M,O
Exercise and Sports Science — M,O
Geotechnical Engineering — M,O
Hispanic Studies — O
History — M,O
Homeland Security — M,O
Information Science — M
Interdisciplinary Studies — M,O
Manufacturing Engineering — M,O
Mathematics Education — M,O
Mechanical Engineering — M,O
Medical Microbiology — M,O
Middle School Education — M,O
Military and Defense Studies — M,O
National Security — M,O
Physical Education — M,O
Political Science — M
Project Management — M,O
Psychology—General — M,O
Reading Education — M,O
School Psychology — M,O
Science Education — M,O
Secondary Education — M,O
Social Sciences Education — M,O
Social Sciences — M
Sports Management — M,O
Structural Engineering — M,O
Student Affairs — M,O
Systems Engineering — M,O
Transportation and Highway Engineering — M,O

CITY COLLEGE OF THE CITY UNIVERSITY OF NEW YORK
Architecture — M
Art History — M
Art/Fine Arts — M
Atmospheric Sciences — M
Biochemistry — M,D
Biological and Biomedical Sciences—General — M,D
Biomedical Engineering — M,D
Business Administration and Management—General — M
Chemical Engineering — M,D
Chemistry — M,D
Civil Engineering — M,D
Classics — M
Clinical Psychology — M,D
Computer Art and Design — M
Computer Science — M,D
Corporate and Organizational Communication — M

Early Childhood Education — M
Economics — M
Education—General — M,O
Educational Leadership and Administration — M,O
Electrical Engineering — M,D
Engineering and Applied Sciences—General — M,D
English as a Second Language — M
English Education — M,O
English — M
Foreign Languages Education — M
Geology — M
Geosciences — M
Graphic Design — M
History — M
International Affairs — M
Landscape Architecture — M
Management Information Systems — M,D
Marketing — M
Mathematics Education — M,O
Mathematics — M
Mechanical Engineering — M,D
Media Studies — M
Middle School Education — M,O
Multilingual and Multicultural Education — M
Museum Studies — M
Physics — M,D
Psychology—General — M,D
Public Administration — M,D
Reading Education — M
Science Education — M
Secondary Education — M,O
Social Sciences Education — M,O
Sociology — M
Spanish — M
Special Education — M
Sustainable Development — M
Urban Design — M
Writing — M

CITY UNIVERSITY OF NEW YORK SCHOOL OF LAW
Law — D

CITY UNIVERSITY OF SEATTLE
Accounting — M,O
Business Administration and Management—General — M,O
Computer and Information Systems Security — M,O
Computer Science — M,O
Counseling Psychology — M
Counselor Education — M,O
Curriculum and Instruction — M,O
Education—General — M,O
Educational Leadership and Administration — M,D,O
Elementary Education — M,O
Finance and Banking — M,O
Human Resources Management — M,O
International Business — M
Management Information Systems — M,O
Management of Technology — M,O
Marketing — M,O
Organizational Management — M,O
Project Management — M,O
Reading Education — M,O
Special Education — M,O
Sustainability Management — M,O

CITY VISION UNIVERSITY
Entrepreneurship — M
Pastoral Ministry and Counseling — M

CLAFLIN UNIVERSITY
Biotechnology — M
Business Administration and Management—General — M

CLAREMONT GRADUATE UNIVERSITY
African Studies — M,D,O
American Studies — M,D,O
Applied Mathematics — M,D
Archives/Archival Administration — M,D,O
Art/Fine Arts — M
Arts Administration — M
Botany — M,D
Business Administration and Management—General — M,D,O
Cognitive Sciences — M,D,O
Comparative Literature — M,D
Computational Biology — M,D
Computational Sciences — M,D
Computer and Information Systems Security — M,D,O
Computer Art and Design — M
Cultural Studies — M,D,O
Database Systems — M,D,O
Developmental Psychology — M,D,O
Economic Development — M,D,O
Economics — M,D,O
Education—General — M,D,O
Educational Leadership and Administration — M,D,O
Educational Measurement and Evaluation — M,D,O
Electronic Commerce — M,D,O
English — M,D
Ethics — M,D
Film, Television, and Video Theory and Criticism — M,D
Financial Engineering — M
Geographic Information Systems — M,D,O
Health Informatics — M,D,O
Health Promotion — M,D
Health Psychology — M,D,O
Higher Education — M,D,O
History — M,D,O
Human Development — M,D,O
Human Resources Development — M,D,O

*M—masters degree; D—doctorate; O—other advanced degree; *—Close-Up and/or Display*

Human Resources Management — M
Humanities — M,D,O
Industrial and Organizational Psychology — M,D,O
Information Science — M,D,O
International Affairs — M,D
International Economics — M,D,O
Management Information Systems — M,D,O
Management Strategy and Policy — M,D
Mathematics — M,D
Media Studies — M,D,O
Museum Studies — M,D,O
Music — M,D
Operations Research — M,D
Philosophy — M,D
Photography — M
Political Science — M,D
Psychology—General — M,D,O
Public Health—General — M,D
Public Policy — M,D,O
Religion — M,D
Social Psychology — M,D,O
Special Education — M,D,O
Statistics — M,D
Student Affairs — M,D,O
Systems Science — M,D,O
Telecommunications — M,D,O
Theology — M,D
Urban Education — M,D,O
Western European Studies — M,D,O
Women's Studies — M,D
Writing — M

CLAREMONT LINCOLN UNIVERSITY
Ethics — M
Pastoral Ministry and Counseling — M
Religion — M

CLAREMONT MCKENNA COLLEGE
Finance and Banking — M

CLAREMONT SCHOOL OF THEOLOGY
Ethics — M,D
Pastoral Ministry and Counseling — M,D
Religion — M,D
Religious Education — M,D
Theology — M,D

CLARION UNIVERSITY OF PENNSYLVANIA
Accounting — M
Advertising and Public Relations — O
Business Administration and Management—General — M
Clinical Psychology — M
Communication Disorders — M
Communication—General — M
Curriculum and Instruction — M
Early Childhood Education — M
Education—General — M
Entrepreneurship — M
Family Nurse Practitioner Studies — M,D,O
Finance and Banking — M
Health Services Management and Hospital Administration — M
Library Science — M,O
Mathematics Education — M
Nursing Education — M,D,O
Nursing—General — M,D
Reading Education — M
Science Education — M
Special Education — M
Vocational and Technical Education — M

CLARK ATLANTA UNIVERSITY
Accounting — M
African-American Studies — M,D
Biological and Biomedical Sciences—General — M,D
Business Administration and Management—General — M
Chemistry — M,D
Computer Science — M
Counselor Education — M
Criminal Justice and Criminology — M
Curriculum and Instruction — M
Economics — M
Education—General — M,D,O
Educational Leadership and Administration — M,D,O
Educational Psychology — M
English — M,D
History — M,D
Information Science — M
Mathematics Education — M
Mathematics — M
Physics — M
Political Science — M,D
Public Administration — M
Romance Languages — M,D
Science Education — M
Social Work — M,D
Sociology — M
Special Education — M
Women's Studies — M,D

CLARKE UNIVERSITY
Business Administration and Management—General — M
Education—General — M
Educational Leadership and Administration — M
Family Nurse Practitioner Studies — D
Nursing—General — D
Physical Therapy — D
Social Work — M

CLARKSON COLLEGE
Adult Nursing — M,O
Family Nurse Practitioner Studies — M,O
Nursing and Healthcare Administration — M,O
Nursing Education — M,O
Nursing—General — M,O

CLARKSON UNIVERSITY
Bioethics — M,O
Biological and Biomedical Sciences—General — M,O
Biotechnology — D
Business Administration and Management—General — M,O
Chemical Engineering — M,D
Chemistry — M,D
Civil Engineering — M,D
Computer Engineering — M,D
Computer Science — M,D
Early Childhood Education — M
Education—General — M
Electrical Engineering — M,D,O
Energy and Power Engineering — M,O
Engineering and Applied Sciences—General — M,D,O
Engineering Management — M
Environmental Engineering — M,D
Environmental Management and Policy — M
Environmental Sciences — M,D
Health Informatics — M
Health Services Management and Hospital Administration — M,O
Health Services Research — M,O
Human Resources Management — M,O
Information Science — M,D
Interdisciplinary Studies — M,D
International Business — M,O
Materials Engineering — D
Materials Sciences — D
Mathematics — M,D
Mechanical Engineering — M,D
Middle School Education — M
Nursing and Healthcare Administration — M,O
Occupational Therapy — M
Physical Therapy — D
Physician Assistant Studies — M
Physics — M,D
Secondary Education — M
Supply Chain Management — M,O
Sustainable Development — M,D
Systems Engineering — M,O
Vocational and Technical Education — M

CLARKS SUMMIT UNIVERSITY
Communication—General — M,D
Counselor Education — M
Cultural Studies — M
Curriculum and Instruction — M
Educational Leadership and Administration — M
English as a Second Language — M
English — M
Missions and Missiology — M,D
Organizational Management — M,D
Pastoral Ministry and Counseling — M,D
Philosophy — M
Reading Education — M
Religion — M,D
Religious Education — M,D
Theology — M,D

CLARK UNIVERSITY
Accounting — M
American Studies — D
Biochemistry — D
Biological and Biomedical Sciences—General — D
Business Administration and Management—General — M
Chemistry — D
Clinical Psychology — D
Communication—General — M
Community Health — M
Database Systems — M
Developmental Psychology — D
Economics — D
Education—General — M
English — M
Environmental Management and Policy — M
Environmental Sciences — M
Finance and Banking — M
Geographic Information Systems — M
Geography — D
Health Education — M
History — D
Holocaust and Genocide Studies — D
Information Science — M
International Development — M
International Health — M
Management Information Systems — M
Marketing — M
Physics — D
Public Administration — M,O
Social Psychology — D
Sustainability Management — M
Sustainable Development — M
Urban and Regional Planning — M

CLAYTON STATE UNIVERSITY
Accounting — M
Applied Psychology — M
Archives/Archival Administration — M
Biological and Biomedical Sciences—General — M
Business Administration and Management—General — M
Clinical Psychology — M
Criminal Justice and Criminology — M
Developmental Psychology — M
Education—General — M
English Education — M
Family Nurse Practitioner Studies — M
History — M
Human Resources Management — M
International Business — M
Liberal Studies — M
Mathematics Education — M
Nursing—General — M

Psychology—General — M
Sports Management — M
Supply Chain Management — M

CLEARY UNIVERSITY
Business Administration and Management—General — M,O
Educational Media/Instructional Technology — M,O
Finance and Banking — M,O
Health Services Management and Hospital Administration — M,O
Management Strategy and Policy — M,O

CLEMSON UNIVERSITY
Accounting — M
Agricultural Education — M
Agricultural Sciences—General — M,D
Applied Economics — M,D
Applied Psychology — M
Architecture — M,O
Automotive Engineering — M,D
Biochemistry — D
Bioengineering — M,D,O
Biological and Biomedical Sciences—General — M
Biomedical Engineering — M,D
Biosystems Engineering — M,D
Business Administration and Management—General — M,D
Business Education — M,D
Chemical Engineering — M,D
Chemistry — M,D
Civil Engineering — M,D
Clinical Research — M,D,O
Communication—General — M,D
Computer Art and Design — M
Computer Engineering — M,D
Computer Science — M,D
Construction Management — M,O
Counseling Psychology — M,O
Counselor Education — M,O
Curriculum and Instruction — D
Distance Education Development — M,D,O
Early Childhood Education — M,O
Economics — M,D
Education—General — M,D,O
Educational Leadership and Administration — M,D,O
Educational Measurement and Evaluation — D
Electrical Engineering — M,D
Emergency Management — M,O
Engineering and Applied Sciences—General — M,D,O
English — M
Entomology — M,D
Entrepreneurship — M
Environmental and Occupational Health — M
Environmental Design — D
Environmental Engineering — M,D
Environmental Management and Policy — M,D
Environmental Sciences — M,D
Ergonomics and Human Factors — D
Family and Consumer Sciences-General — D,O
Family Nurse Practitioner Studies — M,D,O
Fish, Game, and Wildlife Management — M,D
Food Science and Technology — M,D
Forestry — M,D
Genetics — M,D,O
Gerontological Nursing — M,D,O
Higher Education — D
Historic Preservation — M,O
History — M
Homeland Security — M,O
Human Development — M,O
Human Resources Development — M,D,O
Human Resources Management — M,D,O
Human-Computer Interaction — D
Hydrogeology — M
Industrial and Organizational Psychology — D
Industrial/Management Engineering — M,D
International Health — M,D,O
Landscape Architecture — M
Management Information Systems — M,D
Management Strategy and Policy — M
Manufacturing Engineering — M
Materials Engineering — M,D
Materials Sciences — M,D
Mathematics Education — M,O
Mathematics — M,D
Mechanical Engineering — M,D
Microbiology — M,D
Middle School Education — M,D,O
Molecular Biology — D
Nonprofit Management — M,O
Nursing—General — M,D,O
Nutrition — M
Organizational Management — M,D,O
Physical Education — M
Physics — M,D
Plant Biology — M,D
Plant Sciences — M,D
Political Science — M,O
Psychology—General — M
Public Administration — M,D,O
Public Health—General — M,D,O
Public Policy — D,O
Reading Education — M,D
Real Estate — M
Recreation and Park Management — M,D,O
Rhetoric — D
School Psychology — M,O
Science Education — M,D,O
Secondary Education — M

Sociology — M
Special Education — M,D
Sports Management — M,D,O
Statistics — M,D
Student Affairs — M,D,O
Supply Chain Management — M,D
Sustainable Development — M,O
Travel and Tourism — M,D,O
Urban and Regional Planning — M
Writing — M

CLEVELAND INSTITUTE OF MUSIC
Music — M,D,O

CLEVELAND STATE UNIVERSITY
Accounting — M
Adult Education — M,D,O
Allied Health—General — M
Applied Statistics — M
Art Education — M
Art History — M
Bioethics — M
Biological and Biomedical Sciences—General — M,D
Biomedical Engineering — D
Business Administration and Management—General — M,D
Chemical Engineering — M,D
Chemistry — M,D
Civil Engineering — M,D
Communication Disorders — M
Communication—General — M,D,O
Counseling Psychology — M,D,O
Counselor Education — M,D,O
Early Childhood Education — M
Economic Development — M,O
Economics — M,O
Education of Students with Severe/Multiple Disabilities — M
Education—General — M,D,O
Educational Leadership and Administration — M,D,O
Educational Media/Instructional Technology — D
Educational Policy — D
Electrical Engineering — M,D
Engineering and Applied Sciences—General — M,D
English as a Second Language — M
English — M
Environmental Engineering — M,D
Environmental Management and Policy — M,O
Environmental Sciences — M,D
Foreign Languages Education — M
Health Education — M
Health Services Management and Hospital Administration — M
Higher Education — D
History — M
Human Resources Management — M
Industrial and Labor Relations — M
Industrial/Management Engineering — M,D
International Affairs — M
International Economics — M
Law — M,D,O
Management Information Systems — D
Marketing — D
Mathematics Education — M
Mathematics — M
Mechanical Engineering — M,D
Molecular Medicine — M,D
Museum Studies — M
Music Education — M
Music — M
Nonprofit Management — M,O
Nursing Education — D
Nursing—General — M
Occupational Therapy — M
Organic Chemistry — M,D
Philosophy — M,O
Physical Chemistry — M,D
Physical Education — M
Physical Therapy — D
Physician Assistant Studies — M
Physics — M
Psychology—General — M,D,O
Public Administration — M,D,O
Public Affairs — D
Public Health—General — M
Science Education — M
Social Work — M
Software Engineering — M,D
Spanish — M
Special Education — M
Sustainable Development — M,O
Urban and Regional Planning — M,O
Urban Education — M
Urban Studies — M,D,O
Writing — M

CLEVELAND UNIVERSITY–KANSAS CITY
Chiropractic — D
Health Promotion — M

COASTAL CAROLINA UNIVERSITY
Accounting — M,O
Business Administration and Management—General — M,O
Computer Science — M,D,O
Distance Education Development — M,O
Education—General — M,O
Educational Leadership and Administration — M,O
Educational Media/Instructional Technology — M,O
English as a Second Language — M
Liberal Studies — M
Management Information Systems — M,D,O
Marine Sciences — M,D,O
Special Education — M,O
Sports Management — M,D,O
Writing — M

COGSWELL POLYTECHNICAL COLLEGE
Entrepreneurship — M

COKER COLLEGE
Reading Education — M
Sports Management — M

THE COLBURN SCHOOL CONSERVATORY OF MUSIC
Music — M,O

COLD SPRING HARBOR LABORATORY
Biological and Biomedical Sciences—General — D

COLEMAN UNIVERSITY
Information Science — M
Management of Technology — M

COLGATE ROCHESTER CROZER DIVINITY SCHOOL
Conflict Resolution and Mediation/Peace Studies — M,D,O
Theology — M,D,O

COLGATE UNIVERSITY
Secondary Education — M

THE COLLEGE AT BROCKPORT, STATE UNIVERSITY OF NEW YORK
Accounting — M,O
American Studies — M
Art/Fine Arts — M
Arts Administration — M,O
Biological and Biomedical Sciences—General — M,O
Chemistry — M,O
Communication—General — M
Counseling Psychology — M,O
Counselor Education — M,O
Curriculum and Instruction — M
Dance — M
Early Childhood Education — M
Education—General — M,O
Educational Leadership and Administration — M,O
English Education — M,O
English — M,O
Environmental Sciences — M,O
Forensic Sciences — M,O
Gerontology — M,O
Health Education — M
Health Services Management and Hospital Administration — M,O
History of Medicine — M,O
History — M
Liberal Studies — M
Mathematics Education — M,O
Mathematics — M,O
Middle School Education — M
Multilingual and Multicultural Education — M,O
Nonprofit Management — M,O
Physical Education — M,O
Psychology—General — M
Public Administration — M,O
Public Health—General — M
Public History — M
Reading Education — M
Science Education — M,O
Social Sciences Education — M,O
Social Work — M,O
Sports Management — M,O
Writing — M,O

COLLÈGE DOMINICAIN DE PHILOSOPHIE ET DE THÉOLOGIE
Philosophy — M,D
Theology — M,D,O

COLLEGE FOR CREATIVE STUDIES
Applied Arts and Design—General — M
Art/Fine Arts — M
Automotive Engineering — M
Transportation and Highway Engineering — M

COLLEGE FOR FINANCIAL PLANNING
Finance and Banking — M

COLLEGE OF CHARLESTON
Accounting — M
Arts Administration — O
Business Administration and Management—General — M
Computer Science — M
Early Childhood Education — M
Education—General — M,O
Elementary Education — M
English as a Second Language — O
English — M
Environmental Sciences — M
Foreign Languages Education — M
Historic Preservation — M
History — M
Management Information Systems — M
Marine Biology — M
Marine Sciences — M
Mathematics Education — M
Mathematics — M
Music Education — M
Public Administration — M
Science Education — M
Special Education — M
Urban and Regional Planning — O
Writing — M

COLLEGE OF EMMANUEL AND ST. CHAD
Theology — M,D,O

THE COLLEGE OF IDAHO
Curriculum and Instruction — M
Education—General — M

COLLEGE OF MOUNT SAINT VINCENT
Education—General — M,O
Educational Media/Instructional Technology — M,O
English as a Second Language — M,O
Family Nurse Practitioner Studies — M,O
Middle School Education — M,O
Multilingual and Multicultural Education — M,O
Nursing and Healthcare Administration — M,O
Nursing Education — M,O
Nursing—General — M,O
Urban Education — M,O

THE COLLEGE OF NEW JERSEY
Addictions/Substance Abuse Counseling — M
Counselor Education — M
Early Childhood Education — M
Education—General — M,O
Educational Leadership and Administration — M,O
Elementary Education — M
English as a Second Language — M,O
English — M
Gender Studies — O
Health Education — M
International and Comparative Education — M,O
Marriage and Family Therapy — O
Nursing—General — M,O
Physical Education — M
Reading Education — M,O
Secondary Education — M
Special Education — M,O

THE COLLEGE OF NEW ROCHELLE
Acute Care/Critical Care Nursing — M,O
Art Education — M
Art Therapy — M
Communication—General — M,O
Counseling Psychology — M,O
Early Childhood Education — M
Education of the Gifted — O
Education—General — M,O
Educational Leadership and Administration — M,O
Elementary Education — M
English as a Second Language — M,O
Family Nurse Practitioner Studies — M,O
Human Resources Development — M,O
Marriage and Family Therapy — M
Multilingual and Multicultural Education — M,O
Nursing and Healthcare Administration — M,O
Nursing Education — M,O
Nursing—General — M,O
Public Administration — M
Reading Education — M
School Psychology — M
Special Education — M
Thanatology — M,O

COLLEGE OF SAINT ELIZABETH
Business Administration and Management—General — M
Counseling Psychology — M,D,O
Criminal Justice and Criminology — M
Education—General — M,D,O
Educational Leadership and Administration — M,D,O
Educational Media/Instructional Technology — M,D,O
Exercise and Sports Science — M,O
Forensic Psychology — M,D,O
Health Services Management and Hospital Administration — M,D,O
Higher Education — M,D,O
Human Resources Management — M
Nursing—General — M
Nutrition — M,O
Organizational Management — M
Psychology—General — M,D,O
Public Administration — M
Student Affairs — M,D,O
Theology — M

COLLEGE OF ST. JOSEPH
Addictions/Substance Abuse Counseling — M
Business Administration and Management—General — M
Clinical Psychology — M
Counseling Psychology — M
Counselor Education — M
Education—General — M
Elementary Education — M
English Education — M
Psychology—General — M
Reading Education — M
School Psychology — M
Secondary Education — M
Social Psychology — M
Social Sciences Education — M
Special Education — M

COLLEGE OF SAINT MARY
Education—General — M
Educational Leadership and Administration — M
Educational Measurement and Evaluation — M
English as a Second Language — M
Health Education — D
Nursing—General — M
Occupational Therapy — M
Organizational Management — M

THE COLLEGE OF SAINT ROSE
Accounting — M

Business Administration and Management—General — M
Communication Disorders — M
Computer Science — M,O
Counseling Psychology — M,O
Counselor Education — M,O
Curriculum and Instruction — M
Early Childhood Education — M,O
Education—General — M,O
Educational Leadership and Administration — M,O
Educational Psychology — M,O
Finance and Banking — O
Higher Education — M,O
Information Science — M,O
Management Strategy and Policy — M,O
Middle School Education — M,O
Organizational Management — O
Reading Education — M,O
School Psychology — M,O
Secondary Education — M,O
Social Work — M,O
Special Education — M,O
Student Affairs — M

THE COLLEGE OF ST. SCHOLASTICA
Athletic Training and Sports Medicine — M
Business Administration and Management—General — M,O
Education—General — M,O
Exercise and Sports Science — M
Health Informatics — M,O
Management Information Systems — M,O
Nursing—General — M,O
Occupational Therapy — M
Physical Therapy — D
Social Work — M

COLLEGE OF STATEN ISLAND OF THE CITY UNIVERSITY OF NEW YORK
Accounting — M
Adult Nursing — M,O
African Studies — M
American Studies — M
Biological and Biomedical Sciences—General — M
Business Administration and Management—General — M
Clinical Psychology — M
Computer Science — M
Counseling Psychology — M
Database Systems — O
Education—General — M,O
Educational Leadership and Administration — O
Elementary Education — M
English as a Second Language — M,O
English Education — M
English — M
Environmental Sciences — M
Family Nurse Practitioner Studies — D
Film, Television, and Video Theory and Criticism — M
Foundations and Philosophy of Education — M
Gerontological Nursing — M,O
History — M
Latin American Studies — M
Liberal Studies — M
Mathematics Education — M
Media Studies — M
Music Education — M
Near and Middle Eastern Studies — M
Neuroscience — M
Nursing—General — M,D,O
Physical Therapy — D
Reading Education — M
Science Education — M
Secondary Education — M
Social Sciences Education — M
Social Work — M
Special Education — M,O
Western European Studies — M

COLLEGE OF THE ATLANTIC
Environmental Management and Policy — M

THE COLLEGE OF WILLIAM AND MARY
Accounting — M
Addictions/Substance Abuse Counseling — M,D
American Studies — M,D
Anthropology — M,D
Applied Mathematics — M,D
Applied Physics — M,D
Applied Science and Technology — M,D
Artificial Intelligence/Robotics — M,D
Atmospheric Sciences — M,D
Biological and Biomedical Sciences—General — M
Biomathematics — M,D
Business Administration and Management—General — M
Chemistry — M
Clinical Laboratory Sciences/Medical Technology — M,D
Computational Biology — M,D
Computational Sciences — M
Computer Science — M,D
Counselor Education — M,D
Curriculum and Instruction — M,D
Education of the Gifted — M
Education—General — M,D,O*
Educational Leadership and Administration — M,D
Educational Media/Instructional Technology — M,D
Educational Policy — M,D
Elementary Education — M

English — M
Environmental Sciences — M,D
Foreign Languages Education — M,D
Geographic Information Systems — M,D
History — M,D
Law — M,D
Marine Sciences — M,D
Marriage and Family Therapy — M,D
Materials Engineering — M,D
Materials Sciences — M,D
Mathematics Education — M
Mathematics — M
Medical Physics — M,D
Nanotechnology — M,D
Neuroscience — M,D
Operations Research — M,D
Optical Sciences — M,D
Physics — M,D
Polymer Science and Engineering — M,D
Psychology—General — M
Public Policy — M
Reading Education — M
School Psychology — M,O
Science Education — M
Secondary Education — M
Special Education — M

COLORADO CHRISTIAN UNIVERSITY
Business Administration and Management—General — M
Business Education — M
Computer and Information Systems Security — M
Counseling Psychology — M
Curriculum and Instruction — M
Distance Learning Development — M
Early Childhood Education — M
Education—General — M
Educational Media/Instructional Technology — M
Elementary Education — M
Project Management — M
Special Education — M

THE COLORADO COLLEGE
American Studies — M
Art Education — M
Education—General — M
Elementary Education — M
English Education — M
Foreign Languages Education — M
Humanities — M
Liberal Studies — M
Mathematics Education — M
Music Education — M
Science Education — M
Secondary Education — M
Social Sciences Education — M

COLORADO MESA UNIVERSITY
Business Administration and Management—General — M
Education of the Gifted — M,O
Education—General — M,O
Educational Leadership and Administration — M,O
English as a Second Language — M,O
Family Nurse Practitioner Studies — M,D,O
Health Informatics — M,D,O
Nursing Education — M,D,O
Nursing—General — M,D,O
Special Education — M,O

COLORADO SCHOOL OF MINES
Applied Mathematics — M,D
Applied Physics — M,D
Applied Statistics — M,D
Bioengineering — M,D
Chemical Engineering — M,D
Chemistry — M,D
Civil Engineering — M,D
Computer Science — M,D
Construction Engineering — M,D
Electrical Engineering — M,D
Electronic Materials — M,D
Engineering and Applied Sciences—General — M,D,O
Engineering Management — M,D
Environmental Engineering — M,D
Geochemistry — M,D
Geological Engineering — M,D
Geology — M,D
Geophysics — M,D
Hydrology — M,D
International Affairs — O
Management of Technology — M,D
Materials Engineering — M,D
Materials Sciences — M,D
Mechanical Engineering — M,D
Metallurgical Engineering and Metallurgy — M,D
Mineral Economics — M,D
Mineral/Mining Engineering — M,D
Nuclear Engineering — M,D
Operations Research — M,D
Petroleum Engineering — M,D
Physics — M,D

COLORADO SCHOOL OF TRADITIONAL CHINESE MEDICINE
Acupuncture and Oriental Medicine — M

COLORADO STATE UNIVERSITY
Accounting — M
Adult Education — M,D
Advertising and Public Relations — M,D
Agricultural Economics and Agribusiness — M,D
Agricultural Sciences—General — M,D
Agronomy and Soil Sciences — M,D
Animal Sciences — M,D

---

*M—masters degree; D—doctorate; O—other advanced degree; *—Close-Up and/or Display*

Anthropology	M
Art History	M
Art/Fine Arts	M
Arts Administration	M
Atmospheric Sciences	M,D
Biochemistry	M,D
Bioengineering	M,D
Biological and Biomedical Sciences—General	M,D
Biomedical Engineering	M,D
Botany	M,D
Business Administration and Management—General	M
Cancer Biology/Oncology	M,D
Cell Biology	M,D
Chemical Engineering	M,D
Chemistry	M,D
Child and Family Studies	M,D
Civil Engineering	M,D
Computer Science	M,D
Conservation Biology	M,D
Construction Management	M
Consumer Economics	M
Counselor Education	M,D
Ecology	M,D
Economics	M,D
Education—General	M,D
Educational Leadership and Administration	M,D
Electrical Engineering	M,D
Energy Management and Policy	M
Engineering and Applied Sciences—General	M,D
English as a Second Language	M
English	M
Entomology	M,D
Environmental and Occupational Health	M,D
Environmental Management and Policy	M,D
Epidemiology	M,D
Ergonomics and Human Factors	M,D
Ethnic Studies	M
Exercise and Sports Science	M
Finance and Banking	M
Fish, Game, and Wildlife Management	M,D
Food Science and Technology	M,D
French	M
Geosciences	M,D
German	M
Health Physics/Radiological Health	M,D
Higher Education	M,D
Historic Preservation	M
History	M
Horticulture	M,D
Human Development	M,D
Immunology	M,D
Industrial Hygiene	M,D
Industrial/Management Engineering	M,D
Interior Design	M
International Development	M
Landscape Architecture	M,D
Liberal Studies	M
Management Information Systems	M
Marriage and Family Therapy	M,D
Mathematics	M,D
Mechanical Engineering	M,D
Media Studies	M,D
Microbiology	M,D
Molecular Biology	M,D
Museum Studies	M
Music Education	M,D
Music	M,D
Natural Resources	M,D
Neuroscience	D
Nutrition	M,D
Occupational Therapy	M,D
Pathology	M,D
Philosophy	M
Physics	M,D
Plant Pathology	M,D
Plant Sciences	M,D
Political Science	M,D
Psychology—General	M,D
Public History	M
Radiation Biology	M,D
Recreation and Park Management	M,D
Rhetoric	M
Social Work	M,D
Sociology	M
Spanish	M
Speech and Interpersonal Communication	M,D
Statistics	M,D
Student Affairs	M,D
Sustainability Management	M
Sustainable Development	M
Systems Engineering	M,D
Taxation	M
Therapies—Dance, Drama, and Music	M
Toxicology	M,D
Travel and Tourism	M,D
Veterinary Medicine	D
Veterinary Sciences	M,D
Water Resources	M,D
Writing	M
Zoology	M,D

COLORADO STATE UNIVERSITY–GLOBAL CAMPUS

Accounting	M
Business Administration and Management—General	M
Criminal Justice and Criminology	M
Education—General	M
Educational Leadership and Administration	M
Finance and Banking	M
Health Services Management and Hospital Administration	M
Human Resources Management	M
International Business	M
Management Information Systems	M
Organizational Management	M
Project Management	M

COLORADO STATE UNIVERSITY–PUEBLO

Applied Science and Technology	M
Art Education	M
Biochemistry	M
Biological and Biomedical Sciences—General	M
Business Administration and Management—General	M
Chemistry	M
Education—General	M
Educational Media/Instructional Technology	M
Engineering and Applied Sciences—General	M
Foreign Languages Education	M
Health Education	M
Industrial/Management Engineering	M
Music Education	M
Nursing—General	M
Physical Education	M
Special Education	M
Systems Engineering	M

COLORADO TECHNICAL UNIVERSITY AURORA

Accounting	M
Business Administration and Management—General	M
Computer and Information Systems Security	M
Computer Engineering	M
Computer Science	M
Conflict Resolution and Mediation/Peace Studies	M
Criminal Justice and Criminology	M
Database Systems	M
Electrical Engineering	M
Finance and Banking	M
Human Resources Management	M
Industrial and Manufacturing Management	M
Management of Technology	M
Marketing	M
Project Management	M
Software Engineering	M
Systems Engineering	M

COLORADO TECHNICAL UNIVERSITY COLORADO SPRINGS

Accounting	M,D
Business Administration and Management—General	M,D
Computer and Information Systems Security	M,D
Computer Engineering	M
Computer Science	M,D
Conflict Resolution and Mediation/Peace Studies	M,D
Criminal Justice and Criminology	M
Database Systems	M,D
Electrical Engineering	M
Finance and Banking	M,D
Human Resources Management	M,D
Industrial and Manufacturing Management	M,D
Logistics	M,D
Management of Technology	M,D
Marketing	M,D
Project Management	M,D
Software Engineering	M,D
Systems Engineering	M

COLUMBIA COLLEGE (MO)

Accounting	M
Business Administration and Management—General	M
Criminal Justice and Criminology	M
Education—General	M
Educational Leadership and Administration	M
Human Resources Management	M

COLUMBIA COLLEGE (SC)

Conflict Resolution and Mediation/Peace Studies	M
Education—General	M
Educational Leadership and Administration	M
Elementary Education	M
Higher Education	M

COLUMBIA COLLEGE CHICAGO

Arts Administration	M
Comparative and Interdisciplinary Arts	M
Entertainment Management	M
Film, Television, and Video Production	M
Journalism	M
Music	M
Photography	M
Therapies—Dance, Drama, and Music	M,O
Writing	M

COLUMBIA COLLEGE OF NURSING

Nursing—General	M

COLUMBIA INTERNATIONAL UNIVERSITY

Counselor Education	M,D,O
Cultural Studies	M,D,O
Curriculum and Instruction	M,D,O
Early Childhood Education	M,D,O
Education—General	M,D,O
Educational Leadership and Administration	M,D,O
Elementary Education	M,D,O
English as a Second Language	M,D,O
Missions and Missiology	M,D,O
Multilingual and Multicultural Education	M,D,O
Pastoral Ministry and Counseling	M,D,O
Religious Education	M,D,O
Theology	M,D,O

COLUMBIA SOUTHERN UNIVERSITY

Business Administration and Management—General	M,D
Criminal Justice and Criminology	M
Emergency Management	M
Environmental and Occupational Health	M
Finance and Banking	M
Health Services Management and Hospital Administration	M
Human Resources Management	M
Marketing	M
Organizational Management	M

COLUMBIA THEOLOGICAL SEMINARY

Theology	M,D

COLUMBIA UNIVERSITY

Accounting	M,D
Actuarial Science	M
Acute Care/Critical Care Nursing	M,O
Adult Nursing	M,O
African Studies	M,D
African-American Studies	M,D
Allopathic Medicine	M,D
American Studies	M,D
Anatomy	M,D
Anthropology	M,D
Applied Mathematics	M,D
Applied Physics	M,D
Archaeology	M,D
Architecture	M,D
Archives/Archival Administration	M
Art History	M,D
Art/Fine Arts	M,D*
Asian Studies	M,D,O
Astronomy	M,D
Atmospheric Sciences	M,D
Biochemistry	M,D
Bioethics	M
Biological and Biomedical Sciences—General	M,D,O*
Biomedical Engineering	M,D
Biophysics	M,D
Biostatistics	M,D
Biotechnology	M,D
Business Administration and Management—General	M,D
Cell Biology	M,D
Chemical Engineering	M,D
Chemical Physics	M,D
Chemistry	M,D
Civil Engineering	M,D
Classics	M,D
Communication—General	M,D
Community Health	M,D
Comparative Literature	M,D
Computer Engineering	M,D
Computer Science	M,D
Conflict Resolution and Mediation/Peace Studies	M
Conservation Biology	M,D
Construction Engineering	M,D
Construction Management	M,D
Corporate and Organizational Communication	M
Database Systems	M
Dentistry	D
Developmental Biology	M,D
East European and Russian Studies	M,D
Ecology	M,D
Economics	M,D
Electrical Engineering	M,D
Engineering and Applied Sciences—General	M,D
English	M
Entrepreneurship	M
Environmental and Occupational Health	M,D
Environmental Design	M
Environmental Engineering	M,D
Environmental Management and Policy	M
Environmental Sciences	M,D
Epidemiology	M,D
Ethics	M
Evolutionary Biology	M,D
Family Nurse Practitioner Studies	M,O
Film, Television, and Video Production	M
Finance and Banking	M,D
Financial Engineering	M,D
Foreign Languages Education	M,D
Foundations and Philosophy of Education	M,D
French	M,D
Genetics	M,D
Geosciences	M,D
German	M,D
Gerontological Nursing	M,O
Health Services Management and Hospital Administration	M
Hispanic Studies	M,D
Historic Preservation	M,O
History	M,D
Human Resources Management	M
Industrial/Management Engineering	M,D
Information Studies	M
International Affairs	M
International Business	M
Italian	M,D
Japanese	M,D
Jewish Studies	M,D
Journalism	M,D
Kinesiology and Movement Studies	M,D
Landscape Architecture	M
Latin American Studies	M,D
Law	M,D
Legal and Justice Studies	M,D
Management of Technology	M
Marketing	M,D
Materials Engineering	M,D
Materials Sciences	M,D
Maternal and Child Health	M,D
Mathematics	M,D
Mechanical Engineering	M,D*
Mechanics	M,D
Medical Informatics	M,D,O
Medical Physics	M,D
Medieval and Renaissance Studies	M,D
Microbiology	M,D
Molecular Biology	D
Museum Studies	M,D
Music	M,D
Near and Middle Eastern Studies	M,D
Neurobiology	D
Nonprofit Management	M
Nurse Anesthesia	M,O
Nurse Midwifery	M
Nursing—General	M,D,O
Nutrition	M,D
Occupational Therapy	M,D
Operations Research	M,D
Oral and Dental Sciences	M,D,O
Pathobiology	M,D
Pathology	M,D
Pediatric Nursing	M,O
Pharmaceutical Administration	M
Pharmacology	M,D
Philosophy	M,D
Photography	M
Physical Therapy	D
Physics	M,D
Physiology	M,D
Political Science	M,D
Psychiatric Nursing	M,O
Psychology—General	M,D
Public Administration	M
Public Health—General	M
Public Policy	M
Quantitative Analysis	M,D
Real Estate	M
Religion	M,D
Romance Languages	M,D
Russian	M,D
Science Education	M,D,O
Slavic Languages	M,D
Social Sciences	M,D
Social Work	M,D
Sociology	M,D
Spanish	M,D
Sports Management	M
Statistics	M,D
Structural Biology	D
Sustainability Management	M
Sustainable Development	M,D
Theater	M,D
Toxicology	M,D
Translation and Interpretation	M,D
Urban and Regional Planning	M,D
Western European Studies	M,D
Writing	M

COLUMBUS STATE UNIVERSITY

Art Education	M
Biological and Biomedical Sciences—General	M
Business Administration and Management—General	M,O
Chemistry	M,O
Clinical Psychology	M,D,O
Computer and Information Systems Security	M,O
Computer Science	M,O
Counselor Education	M,D,O
Criminal Justice and Criminology	M
Curriculum and Instruction	M,D,O
Early Childhood Education	M,O
Education—General	M,D,O
Educational Leadership and Administration	M,D,O
English as a Second Language	O
English Education	M,O
Environmental Management and Policy	M
Environmental Sciences	M,O
Exercise and Sports Science	M
Family Nurse Practitioner Studies	M
Health Education	M
Health Services Management and Hospital Administration	M
Higher Education	M,D,O
History	M,O
Homeland Security	M
Human Resources Management	M,O
Mathematics Education	M,O
Mathematics	M,O
Middle School Education	M,O
Modeling and Simulation	M,O
Music Education	M,O
Music	M,O
Nursing and Healthcare Administration	M
Nursing Education	M
Nursing Informatics	M
Nursing—General	M
Organizational Management	M,O
Physical Education	M
Political Science	M
Public Administration	M
Science Education	M,O
Secondary Education	M,O
Social Sciences Education	M,O
Special Education	M,O
Theater	M
Urban Studies	M

CONCORDIA COLLEGE
Education—General	M
Foreign Languages Education	M

CONCORDIA COLLEGE–NEW YORK
Organizational Management	M
Special Education	M

CONCORDIA LUTHERAN SEMINARY
Theology	M,O

CONCORDIA SEMINARY
Theology	M,D,O

CONCORDIA THEOLOGICAL SEMINARY
Theology	M,D

CONCORDIA UNIVERSITY (CANADA)
Adult Education	M,O
Aerospace/Aeronautical Engineering	M
Anthropology	M,D
Applied Arts and Design—General	M,O
Art Education	M,O
Art History	M,D
Art Therapy	M
Art/Fine Arts	M
Biological and Biomedical Sciences—General	M,D,O
Biotechnology	M,D,O
Business Administration and Management—General	M,D,O
Chemistry	M,D
Child and Family Studies	M
Civil Engineering	M,D,O
Clinical Psychology	D,O
Communication—General	M,D,O
Computer and Information Systems Security	M,D,O
Computer Art and Design	M,O
Computer Engineering	M,D
Computer Science	M,D,O
Construction Engineering	M,D,O
Cultural Anthropology	M,D
Economic Development	O
Economics	M,D,O
Education—General	M,O
Educational Media/Instructional Technology	M,O
Electrical Engineering	M,D
Engineering and Applied Sciences—General	M,D,O
English as a Second Language	M,O
English	M,D
Environmental Engineering	M,D,O
Environmental Management and Policy	M,D,O
Exercise and Sports Science	M
Film, Television, and Video Production	M,D
Film, Television, and Video Theory and Criticism	M,D
Finance and Banking	M,D,O
French	M,O
Game Design and Development	M,D,O
Genomic Sciences	M,D,O
Geography	M,D,O
History	M,D
Humanities	D
Industrial/Management Engineering	M,D,O
Interdisciplinary Studies	M,D
Internet and Interactive Multimedia	M,D,O
Jewish Studies	M
Journalism	M,O
Linguistics	M,O
Marketing	M,D,O
Mathematics Education	M,D
Mathematics	M,D
Mechanical Engineering	M,D,O
Media Studies	M,D,O
Music	O
Organizational Management	M,O
Philosophy	M
Physics	M,D
Political Science	M
Psychology—General	M
Public Administration	M,D
Public Affairs	O
Public Policy	M,D
Religion	M,D
Sociology	M,D
Software Engineering	M,D,O
Statistics	M,D
Supply Chain Management	M,D,O
Systems Engineering	M,D,O
Telecommunications Management	M,D,O
Textile Design	M
Theology	M
Therapies—Dance, Drama, and Music	M
Translation and Interpretation	M,O
Urban and Regional Planning	O
Urban Studies	M,D,O
Writing	M

CONCORDIA UNIVERSITY (UNITED STATES)
Business Administration and Management—General	M
Curriculum and Instruction	M,D
Early Childhood Education	M,D
Education—General	M,D
Educational Leadership and Administration	M,D
Educational Media/Instructional Technology	M,D
Elementary Education	M,D
English as a Second Language	M,D
Environmental Education	M,D

Mathematics Education	M,D
Reading Education	M,D
Science Education	M,D
Secondary Education	M,D
Special Education	M,D
Vocational and Technical Education	M,D

CONCORDIA UNIVERSITY ANN ARBOR
Curriculum and Instruction	M
Educational Leadership and Administration	M
Organizational Management	M

CONCORDIA UNIVERSITY CHICAGO
Business Administration and Management—General	M
Counseling Psychology	M
Counselor Education	M,O
Curriculum and Instruction	M
Early Childhood Education	M,D
Education—General	M
Educational Leadership and Administration	M,D,O
Educational Media/Instructional Technology	M
Elementary Education	M
Exercise and Sports Science	M
Gerontology	M
Human Services	M
Liberal Studies	M
Music	M
Psychology—General	M
Reading Education	M
Religion	M
Religious Education	M
Secondary Education	M

CONCORDIA UNIVERSITY IRVINE
Applied Social Research	M
Business Administration and Management—General	M
Counselor Education	M
Cultural Studies	M
Curriculum and Instruction	M
Education—General	M
Educational Leadership and Administration	M
Educational Media/Instructional Technology	M
Health Services Management and Hospital Administration	M
International Affairs	M*
Nursing—General	M
Physical Education	M
Religion	M
Sports Management	M
Theology	M

CONCORDIA UNIVERSITY, NEBRASKA
Computer and Information Systems Security	M
Computer Science	M
Early Childhood Education	M
Education—General	M
Educational Leadership and Administration	M
Elementary Education	M
Pastoral Ministry and Counseling	M
Reading Education	M
Religious Education	M
Secondary Education	M

CONCORDIA UNIVERSITY OF EDMONTON
Computer and Information Systems Security	M
Religion	M
Theology	M

CONCORDIA UNIVERSITY, ST. PAUL
Allied Health—General	M,D
Business Administration and Management—General	M
Child and Family Studies	M,D
Computer and Information Systems Security	M
Corporate and Organizational Communication	M
Criminal Justice and Criminology	M,D
Curriculum and Instruction	M,D,O
Education—General	M,D,O
Educational Leadership and Administration	M,D,O
Educational Media/Instructional Technology	M,D,O
Exercise and Sports Science	M,D
Health Services Management and Hospital Administration	M
Human Resources Management	M
Human Services	M,D
Organizational Management	M
Physical Therapy	M,D
Reading Education	M,D,O
Special Education	M,D,O
Sports Management	M,D

CONCORDIA UNIVERSITY TEXAS
Education—General	M

CONCORDIA UNIVERSITY WISCONSIN
Art Education	M
Business Administration and Management—General	M
Child and Family Studies	M
Corporate and Organizational Communication	M
Counselor Education	M
Early Childhood Education	M
Education—General	M
Educational Leadership and Administration	M,D
Environmental Education	M,D
Family Nurse Practitioner Studies	M,D

Finance and Banking	M
Health Education	M
Health Services Management and Hospital Administration	M
Human Resources Management	M
International Business	M
Management Information Systems	M
Marketing	M
Music	M
Nursing—General	M,D
Occupational Therapy	M
Organizational Management	M
Pharmacy	M,D
Physical Therapy	D
Public Administration	M
Reading Education	M
Rehabilitation Sciences	M
Special Education	M

CONCORD LAW SCHOOL
Law	D

CONCORD UNIVERSITY
Education—General	M
Educational Leadership and Administration	M
Health Promotion	M
Reading Education	M
Social Work	M
Special Education	M

CONSERVATORIO DE MUSICA DE PUERTO RICO
Music Education	M
Music	O

CONVERSE COLLEGE
Art Education	M
Education of the Gifted	M
Education—General	M,O
Educational Leadership and Administration	M,O
Elementary Education	M
English Education	M
English	M
History	M
Liberal Studies	M
Marriage and Family Therapy	M
Mathematics Education	M
Middle School Education	M
Music Education	M
Music	M
Political Science	O
Reading Education	M
Science Education	M
Secondary Education	M
Social Sciences Education	M
Special Education	M

COOPER UNION FOR THE ADVANCEMENT OF SCIENCE AND ART
Architecture	M
Chemical Engineering	M
Civil Engineering	M
Electrical Engineering	M
Engineering and Applied Sciences—General	M
Mechanical Engineering	M

COPENHAGEN BUSINESS SCHOOL
Business Administration and Management—General	M,D
Economics	M,D
Health Services Management and Hospital Administration	M,D
International Business	M,D
Logistics	M,D
Management Information Systems	M,D
Public Administration	M,D

COPPIN STATE UNIVERSITY
Addictions/Substance Abuse Counseling	M
Adult Education	M
Criminal Justice and Criminology	M
Curriculum and Instruction	M
Education—General	M
Family Nurse Practitioner Studies	M,O
Human Services	M
Nursing—General	M,O
Reading Education	M
Rehabilitation Counseling	M
Special Education	M

CORBAN UNIVERSITY
Business Administration and Management—General	M
Education—General	M
Nonprofit Management	M
Pastoral Ministry and Counseling	M,D,O
Theology	M,D,O

CORNELL UNIVERSITY
Accounting	M,D
Adult Education	M,D
Aerospace/Aeronautical Engineering	M,D
African Studies	M,D
African-American Studies	M,D
Agricultural Economics and Agribusiness	M,D
Agricultural Education	M,D
Agricultural Engineering	M,D
Agronomy and Soil Sciences	M,D
American Studies	M,D
Analytical Chemistry	D
Anatomy	M
Animal Behavior	D
Animal Sciences	M,D
Anthropology	D
Applied Economics	M,D
Applied Mathematics	M,D
Applied Physics	M,D
Applied Statistics	M,D

Archaeology	M,D
Architectural History	M,D
Architecture	D
Art History	M
Art/Fine Arts	M
Artificial Intelligence/Robotics	M,D
Asian Languages	M,D
Asian Studies	M,D
Astronomy	D
Astrophysics	D
Atmospheric Sciences	M,D
Biochemical Engineering	M,D
Biochemistry	M,D
Bioengineering	M,D
Biological and Biomedical Sciences—General	M,D
Biomedical Engineering	M,D
Biometry	M,D
Biophysics	D
Biopsychology	D
Biotechnology	M,D
Business Administration and Management—General	M,D
Cell Biology	D
Chemical Engineering	M,D
Chemical Physics	D
Chemistry	D
Child and Family Studies	M,D
Civil Engineering	M,D
Classics	D
Clothing and Textiles	M,D
Cognitive Sciences	D
Communication—General	M,D
Comparative Literature	D
Computational Biology	D
Computational Sciences	M,D
Computer Art and Design	M,D
Computer Engineering	M,D
Computer Science	M,D
Conflict Resolution and Mediation/Peace Studies	M,D
Conservation Biology	M,D
Consumer Economics	M,D
Corporate and Organizational Communication	M,D
Cultural Anthropology	D
Cultural Studies	M,D
Curriculum and Instruction	M,D
Demography and Population Studies	M,D
Developmental Biology	M,D
Developmental Psychology	M,D
East European and Russian Studies	M,D
Ecology	M,D
Economic Development	M,D
Economics	M,D
Education—General	M,D
Educational Policy	M,D
Electrical Engineering	M,D
Energy and Power Engineering	M,D
Engineering and Applied Sciences—General	M,D
Engineering Management	M,D
Engineering Physics	M,D
English	M,D
Entomology	M,D
Environmental Design	M
Environmental Engineering	M,D
Environmental Management and Policy	M,D
Environmental Sciences	M,D
Epidemiology	M,D
Ergonomics and Human Factors	M
Ethnic Studies	M,D
Evolutionary Biology	D
Experimental Psychology	D
Facilities Management	M
Finance and Banking	D
Fish, Game, and Wildlife Management	M,D
Food Science and Technology	M,D
Foreign Languages Education	M,D
Forestry	M,D
French	D
Gender Studies	M,D
Genetics	D
Genomic Sciences	D
Geochemistry	M,D
Geology	M,D
Geophysics	M,D
Geosciences	M,D
Geotechnical Engineering	M,D
German	M,D
Health Communication	M,D
Health Services Management and Hospital Administration	M,D
Hispanic and Latin American Languages	D
Historic Preservation	M,D
History of Science and Technology	M,D
History	M,D
Horticulture	M,D
Hospitality Management	M,D
Human Development	M,D
Human Resources Management	M,D
Human-Computer Interaction	M,D
Hydrology	M,D
Immunology	M,D
Industrial and Labor Relations	M,D
Industrial/Management Engineering	M,D
Infectious Diseases	D
Information Science	D
Information Studies	D
Inorganic Chemistry	D
Interior Design	M
International Affairs	M,D
Italian	D
Jewish Studies	M,D

---

*M—masters degree; D—doctorate; O—other advanced degree; *—Close-Up and/or Display*

Landscape Architecture	M
Latin American Studies	M,D
Law	D
Limnology	D
Linguistics	M,D
Manufacturing Engineering	M,D
Marine Geology	M,D
Marine Sciences	M,D
Marketing	D
Materials Engineering	M,D
Materials Sciences	M,D
Mathematics Education	M,D
Mathematics	D
Mechanical Engineering	M,D
Mechanics	M,D
Media Studies	M,D
Medieval and Renaissance Studies	M,D
Microbiology	D
Mineralogy	M,D
Molecular Biology	M,D
Molecular Medicine	M,D
Music	M,D
Nanotechnology	M,D
Natural Resources	M,D
Near and Middle Eastern Studies	M,D
Neurobiology	D
Nutrition	M,D
Oceanography	D
Operations Research	M,D
Organic Chemistry	D
Organizational Behavior	M,D
Paleontology	M,D
Pharmacology	M,D
Philosophy	D
Photography	M,D
Physical Chemistry	D
Physics	M,D
Physiology	M,D
Planetary and Space Sciences	D
Plant Biology	M,D
Plant Molecular Biology	M,D
Plant Pathology	M,D
Plant Physiology	M,D
Plant Sciences	M,D
Political Science	D
Polymer Science and Engineering	M,D
Psychology—General	D
Public Affairs	M
Public Policy	M,D
Quantitative Analysis	M,D
Real Estate	M
Religion	M,D
Reproductive Biology	M,D
Romance Languages	M,D
Rural Sociology	M,D
Scandinavian Languages	M,D
Secondary Education	M,D
Slavic Languages	M,D
Social Psychology	M,D
Social Work	M,D
Sociology	M,D
Spanish	D
Statistics	M,D
Structural Biology	M,D
Structural Engineering	M,D
Sustainable Development	M,D
Systems Engineering	M,D
Textile Design	M,D
Textile Sciences and Engineering	M,D
Theater	D
Theoretical Chemistry	D
Theoretical Physics	M,D
Toxicology	M,D
Transportation and Highway Engineering	M,D
Urban and Regional Planning	M,D
Urban Design	M,D
Veterinary Medicine	D
Water Resources Engineering	M,D
Water Resources	M,D
Western European Studies	M,D
Women's Studies	M,D
Writing	M,D
Zoology	D

CORNERSTONE UNIVERSITY

Business Administration and Management—General	M,O
Education—General	M,O
English as a Second Language	M,O

COVENANT COLLEGE

Education—General	M

COVENANT THEOLOGICAL SEMINARY

Pastoral Ministry and Counseling	M,D,O
Theology	M,D,O

COX COLLEGE

Family Nurse Practitioner Studies	M
Nursing and Healthcare Administration	M
Nursing Education	M
Nursing—General	M

CRANBROOK ACADEMY OF ART

Architecture	M
Art/Fine Arts	M
Photography	M
Textile Design	M

CRANDALL UNIVERSITY

Education—General	M
Organizational Management	M
Reading Education	M

CREIGHTON UNIVERSITY

Accounting	M
Adult Nursing	M,D,O
Allied Health—General	M,D
Allopathic Medicine	D
Anatomy	M
Anthropology	M

Asian Studies	M
Biological and Biomedical Sciences—General	M,D
Business Administration and Management—General	M
Conflict Resolution and Mediation/Peace Studies	M,O
Counselor Education	M
Dentistry	D
Education—General	M
Educational Leadership and Administration	M,D
Elementary Education	M
Emergency Medical Services	M
English	M
Family Nurse Practitioner Studies	M,D,O
Finance and Banking	M
Gerontological Nursing	M,D,O
Health Services Management and Hospital Administration	M
Immunology	M,D
International Affairs	M
Law	M,D,O
Maternal and Child/Neonatal Nursing	M,D,O
Medical Microbiology	M,D
Nursing and Healthcare Administration	M,D,O
Nursing—General	M,D,O
Occupational Therapy	M
Organizational Management	M
Pediatric Nursing	M,D,O
Pharmaceutical Sciences	M,D
Pharmacology	M,D
Pharmacy	D
Physical Therapy	D
Physics	M
Psychiatric Nursing	M,D,O
School Psychology	M
Secondary Education	M
Theology	M
Western European Studies	M
Writing	M

CRISWELL COLLEGE

Jewish Studies	M
Pastoral Ministry and Counseling	M
Theology	M

CROWN COLLEGE

Theology	M

CULVER-STOCKTON COLLEGE

Accounting	M
Business Administration and Management—General	M
Finance and Banking	M

CUMBERLAND UNIVERSITY

Business Administration and Management—General	M
Education—General	M
Public Administration	M

CUNY GRADUATE SCHOOL OF JOURNALISM

Journalism	M

CURRY COLLEGE

Business Administration and Management—General	M,O
Criminal Justice and Criminology	M
Education—General	M,O
Elementary Education	M,O
Finance and Banking	M,O
Foundations and Philosophy of Education	M,O
Nursing—General	M
Reading Education	M,O
Special Education	M,O

CURTIS INSTITUTE OF MUSIC

Music	M

DAEMEN COLLEGE

Accounting	M
Adult Nursing	M,D,O
Arts Administration	M
Business Administration and Management—General	M
Community Health	M
Early Childhood Education	M
Education—General	M
Epidemiology	M
Health Education	M
Health Services Management and Hospital Administration	M
International Business	M
Management Information Systems	M
Marketing	M
Medical/Surgical Nursing	M,D,O
Middle School Education	M
Nonprofit Management	M
Nursing and Healthcare Administration	M,D,O
Nursing Education	M,D,O
Nursing—General	M,D,O
Physical Therapy	D,O
Physician Assistant Studies	M
Public Health—General	M
Social Work	M
Special Education	M

DAKOTA STATE UNIVERSITY

Business Administration and Management—General	M,D,O
Computer and Information Systems Security	M,D,O
Computer Science	M,D,O
Education—General	M
Educational Media/Instructional Technology	M
Health Informatics	M,D,O
Information Science	M,D,O
Management Information Systems	M,D,O
Management Strategy and Policy	M,D,O

DAKOTA WESLEYAN UNIVERSITY

Curriculum and Instruction	M
Education—General	M
Educational Leadership and Administration	M
Secondary Education	M

DALHOUSIE UNIVERSITY

Agricultural Engineering	M,D
Agricultural Sciences—General	M
Agronomy and Soil Sciences	M
Allopathic Medicine	M,D
Anatomy	M,D
Animal Sciences	M
Anthropology	M,D
Applied Mathematics	M,D
Aquaculture	M
Architecture	M
Biochemistry	M,D
Bioengineering	M,D
Bioinformatics	M,D
Biological and Biomedical Sciences—General	M,D
Biomedical Engineering	M,D
Biophysics	M,D
Botany	M
Business Administration and Management—General	M,O
Chemical Engineering	M,D
Chemistry	M,D
Civil Engineering	M,D
Classics	M,D
Clinical Psychology	M,D
Communication Disorders	M,D
Community Health	M
Computer Engineering	M,D
Computer Science	M,D
Ecology	M
Economics	M,D
Electrical Engineering	M,D
Electronic Commerce	M,D
Engineering and Applied Sciences—General	M,D
English	M,D
Environmental Biology	M
Environmental Engineering	M,D
Environmental Management and Policy	M
Environmental Sciences	M
Epidemiology	M
Finance and Banking	M
Food Science and Technology	M,D
French	M,D
Geosciences	M,D
German	M
Health Education	M
Health Services Management and Hospital Administration	M,D
History	M,D
Horticulture	M
Human-Computer Interaction	M
Immunology	M,D
Industrial/Management Engineering	M,D
Information Studies	M
Interdisciplinary Studies	D
International Development	M
Kinesiology and Movement Studies	M
Law	M,D
Leisure Studies	M
Library Science	M
Management Information Systems	M
Marine Affairs	M
Materials Engineering	M,D
Mathematics	M,D
Mechanical Engineering	M,D
Medical Informatics	M,D
Microbiology	M,D
Mineral/Mining Engineering	M,D
Music	M
Natural Resources	M
Neurobiology	M,D
Neuroscience	M,D
Nursing—General	M,D
Occupational Therapy	M
Oceanography	M,D
Oral and Dental Sciences	M
Pathology	M,D
Pharmacology	M,D
Philosophy	M,D
Physical Therapy	M
Physics	M,D
Physiology	M,D
Plant Pathology	M
Plant Physiology	M
Political Science	M,D
Psychology—General	M,D
Public Administration	M,O
Rural Planning and Studies	M
Social Work	M
Sociology	M,D
Statistics	M,D
Urban and Regional Planning	M
Water Resources	M

DALLAS BAPTIST UNIVERSITY

Accounting	M
Asian Studies	M
Business Administration and Management—General	M,D
Communication—General	M
Conflict Resolution and Mediation/Peace Studies	M
Corporate and Organizational Communication	M
Counseling Psychology	M
Counselor Education	M,O
Criminal Justice and Criminology	M
Curriculum and Instruction	M
Distance Education Development	M
Early Childhood Education	M,D
Education—General	M

Educational Leadership and Administration	M,D
Educational Media/Instructional Technology	M
Elementary Education	M
Engineering Management	M
English as a Second Language	M
Entrepreneurship	M
Finance and Banking	M
Health Services Management and Hospital Administration	M
Higher Education	M,D
Human Resources Management	M
Interdisciplinary Studies	M
International Affairs	M
International Business	M
Kinesiology and Movement Studies	M
Liberal Studies	M
Management Information Systems	M
Management of Technology	M
Marketing	M
Missions and Missiology	M
Multilingual and Multicultural Education	M
Nonprofit Management	M
Organizational Management	M,D
Pastoral Ministry and Counseling	M,D
Project Management	M
Reading Education	M
Religion	M
Religious Education	M
Secondary Education	M
Special Education	M
Sports Management	M
Student Affairs	M
Theology	M
Western European Studies	M

DALLAS THEOLOGICAL SEMINARY

Adult Education	M,D,O
Child and Family Studies	M,D,O
Educational Leadership and Administration	M,D,O
Jewish Studies	M,D,O
Media Studies	M,D,O
Missions and Missiology	M,D,O
Pastoral Ministry and Counseling	M,D,O
Philosophy	M,D,O
Religion	M,D,O
Religious Education	M,D,O
Theology	M,D,O

DARTMOUTH COLLEGE

Allopathic Medicine	D
Astronomy	D
Biochemical Engineering	M,D
Biochemistry	M,D
Biological and Biomedical Sciences—General	D
Biomedical Engineering	M,D
Biostatistics	D
Biotechnology	M,D
Business Administration and Management—General	M
Cell Biology	D
Chemistry	M,D
Cognitive Sciences	D
Comparative Literature	M
Computer Engineering	M,D
Computer Science	M,D
Ecology	D
Engineering and Applied Sciences—General	M,D
Engineering Management	M
Entrepreneurship	D
Environmental Engineering	M,D
Evolutionary Biology	D
Genetics	D
Geosciences	M,D
Health Services Management and Hospital Administration	M,D
Health Services Research	M,D
Immunology	D*
Liberal Studies	M*
Materials Engineering	M,D
Materials Sciences	M,D
Mathematics	M,D
Mechanical Engineering	M,D
Microbiology	D
Molecular Biology	D
Molecular Medicine	
Molecular Pathogenesis	D
Music	M
Neuroscience	D
Physical Chemistry	M,D
Physics	D
Psychology—General	D
Public Health—General	M

DAVENPORT UNIVERSITY

Accounting	M
Business Administration and Management—General	M
Computer and Information Systems Security	M
Finance and Banking	M
Health Services Management and Hospital Administration	M
Human Resources Management	M
Management Strategy and Policy	M
Public Health—General	M

DEFIANCE COLLEGE

Business Administration and Management—General	M
Education—General	M
Management Strategy and Policy	M

DELAWARE STATE UNIVERSITY

Adult Education	M
Applied Mathematics	M,D
Art Education	M
Biological and Biomedical Sciences—General	M
Business Administration and Management—General	M

Chemistry	M,D
Curriculum and Instruction	M
Education—General	M,D
Educational Leadership and Administration	M,D
Exercise and Sports Science	M
Foreign Languages Education	M
Historic Preservation	M
Mathematics Education	M
Mathematics	M
Natural Resources	M
Neuroscience	M,D
Nursing—General	M
Optical Sciences	M,D
Physics	M,D
Plant Sciences	M
Reading Education	M
Science Education	M,D
Social Work	M
Special Education	M
Theoretical Physics	D

DELAWARE VALLEY UNIVERSITY

Accounting	M
Agricultural Economics and Agribusiness	M
Business Administration and Management—General	M
Counseling Psychology	M
Curriculum and Instruction	M
Developmental Psychology	M
Educational Leadership and Administration	M
Educational Media/Instructional Technology	M
Entrepreneurship	M
Finance and Banking	M
Human Resources Management	M
International Business	M
Social Psychology	M
Supply Chain Management	M

DELL'ARTE INTERNATIONAL SCHOOL OF PHYSICAL THEATRE

Theater	M

DELTA STATE UNIVERSITY

Accounting	M
Aviation Management	M
Biological and Biomedical Sciences—General	M
Business Administration and Management—General	M
Counselor Education	M,D,O
Criminal Justice and Criminology	M
Education—General	M,D,O
Educational Leadership and Administration	M,D,O
Elementary Education	M,D,O
English Education	M
Exercise and Sports Science	M
Family Nurse Practitioner Studies	M,D
Gender Studies	M
Health Education	M
Health Services Management and Hospital Administration	M,D
Higher Education	D
Liberal Studies	M
Nursing Education	M,D
Nursing—General	M,D
Philosophy	M
Physical Education	M
Recreation and Park Management	M
Religion	M
Secondary Education	M,D,O
Social Sciences Education	M
Special Education	M
Urban and Regional Planning	M

DENVER SEMINARY

Marriage and Family Therapy	M,D,O
Pastoral Ministry and Counseling	M,D,O
Religion	M,D,O
Theology	M,D,O

DEPAUL UNIVERSITY

Accounting	M
Adult Education	M,D
Advertising and Public Relations	M
Applied Economics	M
Applied Mathematics	M,D
Applied Statistics	M,D
Biological and Biomedical Sciences—General	M,D
Business Administration and Management—General	M
Chemistry	M,D
Chinese	M
Clinical Psychology	M,D
Communication—General	M
Computer and Information Systems Security	M,D
Computer Art and Design	M,D
Computer Science	M,D
Corporate and Organizational Communication	M
Counseling Psychology	M,D
Counselor Education	M,D
Curriculum and Instruction	M,D
Early Childhood Education	M,D
Economics	M
Education—General	M,D
Educational Leadership and Administration	M,D
Electronic Commerce	M,D
Elementary Education	M,D
English	M
Entrepreneurship	M
Family Nurse Practitioner Studies	M,D
Film, Television, and Video Production	M,D

Film, Television, and Video Theory and Criticism	M
Finance and Banking	M
Foreign Languages Education	M,D
Foundations and Philosophy of Education	M,D
French	M
Game Design and Development	M,D
German	M
Health Communication	M
Health Informatics	M,D
Health Law	M,D
Health Services Management and Hospital Administration	M
History	M
Hospitality Management	M
Human Resources Management	M
Human-Computer Interaction	M,D
Industrial and Manufacturing Management	M
Information Science	M,D
Intellectual Property Law	M
Interdisciplinary Studies	M
International Affairs	M
Internet and Interactive Multimedia	M,D
Investment Management	M
Italian	M
Japanese	M
Journalism	M
Law	M,D
Liberal Studies	M
Management Information Systems	M,D
Management of Technology	M,D
Management Strategy and Policy	M
Marketing	M
Mathematical and Computational Finance	M,D
Mathematics Education	M,D
Mathematics	M,D
Media Studies	M
Multilingual and Multicultural Education	M,D
Music Education	M,O
Music	M,O
Near and Middle Eastern Languages	M
Nonprofit Management	M
Nursing—General	M,D
Organizational Management	M
Physics	M,D
Psychology—General	M,D
Public Administration	M
Public Health—General	M
Public Policy	M
Publishing	M
Reading Education	M,D
Real Estate	M
Rhetoric	M
School Psychology	M,D
Science Education	M,D
Secondary Education	M,D
Social Work	M
Sociology	M
Software Engineering	M,D
Spanish	M
Special Education	M,D
Sports Management	M
Student Affairs	M,D
Sustainability Management	M
Sustainable Development	M
Taxation	M,D
Theater	M
Urban Design	M
Women's Studies	M
Writing	M

DEREE - THE AMERICAN COLLEGE OF GREECE

Applied Psychology	M
Communication—General	M
Marketing	M

DESALES UNIVERSITY

Accounting	M
Business Administration and Management—General	M
Computer and Information Systems Security	M,O
Criminal Justice and Criminology	M,O
Database Systems	M,O
Education—General	M,O
Educational Media/Instructional Technology	M,O
English as a Second Language	M,O
Family Nurse Practitioner Studies	M,D,O
Finance and Banking	M
Forensic Sciences	M,O
Gerontology	M,D,O
Health Informatics	M,O
Health Services Management and Hospital Administration	M
Human Resources Management	M
Management Information Systems	M
Marketing	M
Nurse Anesthesia	M,D,O
Nurse Midwifery	M,D,O
Nursing and Healthcare Administration	M,D,O
Nursing Education	M,D,O
Nursing—General	M,D,O
Project Management	M,O
Secondary Education	M,O
Special Education	M,O
Supply Chain Management	M

DES MOINES UNIVERSITY

Anatomy	M
Biological and Biomedical Sciences—General	M

Health Services Management and Hospital Administration	M
Osteopathic Medicine	D
Physical Therapy	D
Physician Assistant Studies	M
Podiatric Medicine	D
Public Health—General	M

DEVRY COLLEGE OF NEW YORK–MIDTOWN MANHATTAN CAMPUS

Business Administration and Management—General	M

DEVRY UNIVERSITY (GA)

Business Administration and Management—General	M,O

DEVRY UNIVERSITY–ALPHARETTA CAMPUS

Business Administration and Management—General	M

DEVRY UNIVERSITY–ARLINGTON CAMPUS

Business Administration and Management—General	M

DEVRY UNIVERSITY–CHARLOTTE CAMPUS

Business Administration and Management—General	M

DEVRY UNIVERSITY–CHESAPEAKE CAMPUS

Business Administration and Management—General	M

DEVRY UNIVERSITY–CHICAGO CAMPUS

Business Administration and Management—General	M

DEVRY UNIVERSITY–CHICAGO LOOP CAMPUS

Business Administration and Management—General	M

DEVRY UNIVERSITY–CINCINNATI CAMPUS

Business Administration and Management—General	M

DEVRY UNIVERSITY–COLUMBUS CAMPUS

Business Administration and Management—General	M

DEVRY UNIVERSITY–DECATUR CAMPUS

Business Administration and Management—General	M

DEVRY UNIVERSITY–FOLSOM CAMPUS

Accounting	M
Business Administration and Management—General	M
Curriculum and Instruction	M
Educational Leadership and Administration	M
Educational Media/Instructional Technology	M
Finance and Banking	M
Higher Education	M
Human Resources Management	M
Management Information Systems	M
Project Management	M
Public Administration	M

DEVRY UNIVERSITY–FREMONT CAMPUS

Business Administration and Management—General	M

DEVRY UNIVERSITY–FT. WASHINGTON CAMPUS

Business Administration and Management—General	M

DEVRY UNIVERSITY–HENDERSON CAMPUS

Business Administration and Management—General	M

DEVRY UNIVERSITY–IRVING CAMPUS

Business Administration and Management—General	M

DEVRY UNIVERSITY–JACKSONVILLE CAMPUS

Business Administration and Management—General	M

DEVRY UNIVERSITY–LONG BEACH CAMPUS

Business Administration and Management—General	M

DEVRY UNIVERSITY–MIRAMAR CAMPUS

Business Administration and Management—General	M

DEVRY UNIVERSITY–MORRISVILLE CAMPUS

Business Administration and Management—General	M

DEVRY UNIVERSITY–NASHVILLE CAMPUS

Business Administration and Management—General	M

DEVRY UNIVERSITY–NORTH BRUNSWICK CAMPUS

Business Administration and Management—General	M

DEVRY UNIVERSITY ONLINE

Business Administration and Management—General	M

DEVRY UNIVERSITY–ORLANDO CAMPUS

Business Administration and Management—General	M

DEVRY UNIVERSITY–PHOENIX CAMPUS

Business Administration and Management—General	M

DEVRY UNIVERSITY–POMONA CAMPUS

Business Administration and Management—General	M

DEVRY UNIVERSITY–SAN DIEGO CAMPUS

Business Administration and Management—General	M,O

DEVRY UNIVERSITY–SEVEN HILLS CAMPUS

Business Administration and Management—General	M,O

DEVRY UNIVERSITY–TINLEY PARK CAMPUS

Business Administration and Management—General	M

DIGIPEN INSTITUTE OF TECHNOLOGY

Computer Art and Design	M
Computer Science	M

DIGITAL MEDIA ARTS COLLEGE

Computer Art and Design	M
Graphic Design	M
Media Studies	M

DOANE UNIVERSITY

Business Administration and Management—General	M
Counselor Education	M
Curriculum and Instruction	M
Education—General	M
Educational Leadership and Administration	M

DOMINICAN COLLEGE

Accounting	M
Allied Health—General	M,D
Business Administration and Management—General	M
Education—General	M
Elementary Education	M
Family Nurse Practitioner Studies	M,D
Health Services Management and Hospital Administration	M
Occupational Therapy	M
Physical Therapy	M,D
Special Education	M

DOMINICAN HOUSE OF STUDIES, PONTIFICAL FACULTY OF THE IMMACULATE CONCEPTION

Theology	M,D,O

DOMINICAN SCHOOL OF PHILOSOPHY AND THEOLOGY

Philosophy	M,O
Theology	M,O

DOMINICAN UNIVERSITY

Accounting	M
Business Administration and Management—General	M
Conflict Resolution and Mediation/Peace Studies	M
Early Childhood Education	M
Education—General	M
Elementary Education	M
English as a Second Language	M
Information Studies	M,D,O
Management Information Systems	M,D,O
Reading Education	M
Social Work	M
Special Education	M

DOMINICAN UNIVERSITY OF CALIFORNIA

Art History	M
Biological and Biomedical Sciences—General	M
Business Administration and Management—General	M
Clinical Laboratory Sciences/Medical Technology	M
Counseling Psychology	M
Education—General	M
English	M
Gender Studies	M
History	M
Humanities	M
International Business	M
Management Strategy and Policy	M
Marriage and Family Therapy	M
Music	M
Occupational Therapy	M
Philosophy	M
Political Science	M
Religion	M
Special Education	M
Sustainability Management	M
Writing	M

DONGGUK UNIVERSITY LOS ANGELES

Acupuncture and Oriental Medicine	M

DORDT COLLEGE

Education—General	M

DRAGON RISES COLLEGE OF ORIENTAL MEDICINE

Acupuncture and Oriental Medicine	M

*M—masters degree; D—doctorate; O—other advanced degree; *—Close-Up and/or Display*

DRAKE UNIVERSITY

Business Administration and Management—General	M
Communication—General	M
Education—General	M,D,O
Law	M,D
Pharmacy	D
Public Administration	M

DREW UNIVERSITY

American Studies	M,D,O
Art/Fine Arts	M,D,O
Biological and Biomedical Sciences—General	M,D,O
Chemistry	M,D,O
Community College Education	M,D,O
Conflict Resolution and Mediation/Peace Studies	M,D,O
Cultural Studies	M,D,O
Elementary Education	M,D,O
English	M,D,O
French	M,D,O
Health Education	M,D,O
Health Services Management and Hospital Administration	M,D,O
History	M,D,O
Italian	M,D,O
Liberal Studies	M,D,O
Mathematics	M,D,O
Public History	M,D,O
Religion	M,D,O
Secondary Education	M,D,O
Special Education	M,D,O
Theology	M,D,O
Western European Studies	M,D,O
Writing	M,D,O

DREXEL UNIVERSITY

Accounting	M,D,O
Acute Care/Critical Care Nursing	M
Allied Health—General	M,D,O
Allopathic Medicine	D
Applied Arts and Design—General	M*
Applied Behavior Analysis	M
Architectural Engineering	M,D
Archives/Archival Administration	M
Art Therapy	M,O
Arts Administration	M
Biochemical Engineering	M
Biochemistry	M,D
Biological and Biomedical Sciences—General	M,D,O
Biomedical Engineering	M,D
Biopsychology	M,D
Biostatistics	M,D,O
Business Administration and Management—General	M,D,O
Cell Biology	M,D
Chemical Engineering	M,D
Chemistry	M,D
Civil Engineering	M,D
Clinical Psychology	D
Communication—General	M
Computer Art and Design	M
Computer Engineering	M
Computer Science	M,D,O*
Construction Management	M
Corporate and Organizational Communication	M
Curriculum and Instruction	M,D
Economics	M,D,O
Education—General	M,D*
Educational Leadership and Administration	M,D
Educational Media/Instructional Technology	M,D
Electrical Engineering	M
Emergency Management	M
Emergency Medical Services	M
Engineering and Applied Sciences—General	M,D,O
Engineering Management	M,O
Entrepreneurship	M
Environmental Engineering	M,D
Environmental Management and Policy	M
Environmental Sciences	M,D
Epidemiology	M,D,O
Family Nurse Practitioner Studies	M
Film, Television, and Video Production	M
Finance and Banking	M,D,O
Food Science and Technology	M
Forensic Psychology	D
Genetics	M,D
Geotechnical Engineering	M,D
Health Psychology	D
Higher Education	M,D
History of Science and Technology	M
Homeland Security	M
Hospitality Management	M
Human Resources Development	M,D
Hydraulics	M,D
Hydrology	M,D
Immunology	M,D
Information Science	M,D,O
Interior Design	M
International and Comparative Education	M,D
Library Science	M,D,O
Management Information Systems	M,D,O
Management Strategy and Policy	M,D,O
Marketing	M,D,O
Marriage and Family Therapy	M,D
Mass Communication	M
Materials Engineering	M
Mechanical Engineering	M,D
Mechanics	M,D
Media Studies	M
Microbiology	M,D
Molecular Biology	M,D
Molecular Medicine	M
Neuroscience	M,D
Nurse Anesthesia	M

Nursing and Healthcare Administration	M
Nursing Education	M
Nursing—General	M,D
Organizational Behavior	M,D,O
Pathobiology	M,D
Pediatric Nursing	M
Pharmaceutical Sciences	M
Pharmacology	M,D
Physical Therapy	M,D,O
Physician Assistant Studies	M
Physics	M
Project Management	M
Psychiatric Nursing	M
Psychology—General	M,D
Public Health—General	M,D,O
Quantitative Analysis	M,D,O
Real Estate	M
Software Engineering	M,D,O
Special Education	M,D
Sports Management	M
Structural Engineering	M,D
Technical Communication	M
Technical Writing	M
Telecommunications	M
Textile Design	M
Therapies—Dance, Drama, and Music	M,O
Veterinary Sciences	M
Women's Health Nursing	M

DRURY UNIVERSITY

Business Administration and Management—General	M
Communication—General	M
Computer and Information Systems Security	O
Curriculum and Instruction	M
Distance Education Development	M
Education of the Gifted	M
Education—General	M
Educational Leadership and Administration	M
Educational Media/Instructional Technology	M
Elementary Education	M
Middle School Education	M
Nonprofit Management	M
Organizational Management	M
Reading Education	M
Secondary Education	M
Special Education	M

DUKE UNIVERSITY

Accounting	D
Acute Care/Critical Care Nursing	M,D,O
Adult Nursing	M,D,O
Allopathic Medicine	D
Anatomy	D
Art History	M,D
Art/Fine Arts	M,D
Asian Studies	M,O
Biochemistry	D
Bioethics	M
Bioinformatics	D,O
Biological and Biomedical Sciences—General	M,D
Biological Anthropology	D
Biomedical Engineering	M,D
Biopsychology	D
Biostatistics	M
Business Administration and Management—General	M,D,O
Cancer Biology/Oncology	D
Cell Biology	D,O
Chemistry	D
Civil Engineering	M,D
Classics	D
Clinical Laboratory Sciences/Medical Technology	M
Clinical Psychology	D
Clinical Research	M
Cognitive Sciences	D
Comparative Literature	D
Computational Biology	D,O
Computer Engineering	M,D
Computer Science	M,D
Cultural Anthropology	D
Developmental Biology	D
Developmental Psychology	D
Ecology	D,O
Economics	M,D
Education—General	M
Electrical Engineering	M,D*
Energy Management and Policy	M,O
Engineering and Applied Sciences—General	M
Engineering Management	M
English	M,D
Entrepreneurship	M,O
Environmental and Occupational Health	O
Environmental Engineering	M,D
Environmental Management and Policy	M,D
Environmental Sciences	M,D
Ethics	M,O
Experimental Psychology	D
Family Nurse Practitioner Studies	M,D,O
Finance and Banking	M,D,O
Forestry	M,D
French	D
Genetics	D
Genomic Sciences	D
Geology	M,D
German	D
Gerontological Nursing	M,D,O
Gerontology	M,D,O
Health Informatics	M
Health Physics/Radiological Health	D
Health Services Management and Hospital Administration	M,O
History	M,D
Human Development	D

Humanities	M
Immunology	D
Industrial and Manufacturing Management	M,D,O
International Business	M,O
International Development	M
International Health	M
Italian	D
Latin American Studies	M,D
Law	M
Liberal Studies	M
Management Strategy and Policy	M,D,O
Marine Sciences	D
Marketing	M,D,O
Materials Engineering	M
Materials Sciences	M,D
Maternal and Child/Neonatal Nursing	M
Mathematics	D
Mechanical Engineering	M,D
Media Studies	M
Medical Physics	M,D
Microbiology	D
Molecular Biology	D,O
Molecular Biophysics	O
Molecular Genetics	D
Music	D
Natural Resources	M,D
Neurobiology	D
Neuroscience	D,O
Nurse Anesthesia	M,D,O
Nursing and Healthcare Administration	M,D,O
Nursing Education	M,D,O
Nursing Informatics	M,D,O
Nursing—General	D
Optical Sciences	M
Organizational Management	M,D,O
Paleontology	D
Pathology	M,D
Pediatric Nursing	M,D,O
Pharmacology	D
Philosophy	D
Photonics	M
Physical Therapy	D
Physician Assistant Studies	M
Physics	D
Political Science	M,D
Psychology—General	D
Public Policy	M,D
Quantitative Analysis	M,D,O
Religion	M,D
Slavic Languages	M,D
Sociology	M,D
Spanish	D
Statistics	M,D
Structural Biology	O
Theology	M,D
Toxicology	O
Women's Health Nursing	M,D,O

DUNLAP-STONE UNIVERSITY

Law	M

DUQUESNE UNIVERSITY

Accounting	M
Allied Health—General	M,D,O
Bioethics	M,D,O
Biological and Biomedical Sciences—General	D
Biotechnology	M
Business Administration and Management—General	M
Chemistry	M
Classics	M
Clinical Psychology	M,D,O
Communication Disorders	M,D
Communication—General	M,D
Counseling Psychology	M,D,O
Counselor Education	M,D,O
Curriculum and Instruction	M,O
Early Childhood Education	M
Education—General	M,D,O
Educational Leadership and Administration	M,D,O
Educational Measurement and Evaluation	M
Educational Media/Instructional Technology	M,D,O
Elementary Education	M
English as a Second Language	M
English Education	M
English	M,D
Environmental Management and Policy	M,O
Environmental Sciences	M,O
Family Nurse Practitioner Studies	M,O
Finance and Banking	M
Foreign Languages Education	M
Forensic Nursing	M
Forensic Sciences	M
Foundations and Philosophy of Education	M
Health Services Management and Hospital Administration	M,D
History	M,D
Law	M,D
Management Information Systems	M
Marketing	M
Marriage and Family Therapy	M,D,O
Mathematics Education	M
Mathematics	M
Medicinal and Pharmaceutical Chemistry	M,D
Middle School Education	M
Music Education	M,O
Music	M,O
Nursing Education	M,O
Nursing—General	M,D,O*
Occupational Therapy	M,D
Organizational Management	M
Pharmaceutical Administration	M
Pharmaceutical Sciences	M,D
Pharmacology	M,D
Pharmacy	D

Philosophy	M,D
Physical Therapy	M,D
Physician Assistant Studies	M,D
Psychology—General	D
Public History	M
Reading Education	M
Rehabilitation Sciences	M,D
Rhetoric	M,D
School Psychology	M,D
Science Education	M
Secondary Education	M
Social Sciences Education	M
Special Education	M,D
Sports Management	M
Sustainability Management	M
Theology	M,D

D'YOUVILLE COLLEGE

Business Administration and Management—General	M
Chiropractic	D
Education—General	M,D
Educational Leadership and Administration	M,D
Elementary Education	M,D
Family Nurse Practitioner Studies	M,D,O
Health Services Management and Hospital Administration	M,D,O
International Business	M
Nursing—General	M,D,O
Nutrition	M
Occupational Therapy	M
Pharmacy	D
Physical Therapy	D,O
Physician Assistant Studies	M
Secondary Education	M,D
Special Education	M,D

EARLHAM COLLEGE

Education—General	M

EARLHAM SCHOOL OF RELIGION

Religion	M
Theology	M

EAST CAROLINA UNIVERSITY

Accounting	M
Addictions/Substance Abuse Counseling	M,D,O
Adult Education	M
Allied Health—General	M,D,O
Allopathic Medicine	D
American Studies	M
Anatomy	D
Anthropology	M
Applied Economics	M
Applied Physics	M,D
Art Education	M
Art/Fine Arts	M
Biochemistry	M,D
Biological and Biomedical Sciences—General	M,D
Biomedical Engineering	M
Biophysics	M,D
Biotechnology	M
Business Administration and Management—General	M,D,O
Business Education	M
Cell Biology	D
Chemistry	M
Child and Family Studies	M,D
Child Development	M,D
Clinical Psychology	M,D
Communication Disorders	M,D,O
Community College Education	M,D,O
Community Health	M,O
Comparative Literature	M,D,O
Computer and Information Systems Security	M,D,O
Computer Engineering	M
Computer Science	M,D,O
Construction Management	M
Counselor Education	M,D,O
Criminal Justice and Criminology	M,O
Curriculum and Instruction	M,O
Dentistry	D
Early Childhood Education	M,D
Economic Development	M,O
Education—General	M,D,O
Educational Leadership and Administration	M,D,O
Educational Media/Instructional Technology	M,O
Elementary Education	M,O
English as a Second Language	M,D,O
English Education	M,D,O
English	M,D,O
Environmental and Occupational Health	M,D
Exercise and Sports Science	M,D,O
Family and Consumer Sciences-General	M
Foreign Languages Education	M
Geographic Information Systems	M,O
Geography	M,O
Geology	M,O
Gerontology	M,O
Graphic Design	M
Health Communication	M
Health Education	M
Health Informatics	M
Health Physics/Radiological Health	M
Health Promotion	M
Health Psychology	M
History	M
Hospitality Management	M
Hydrogeology	M,O
Illustration	M
Immunology	M,D
Industrial and Manufacturing Management	M,D,O
Industrial and Organizational Psychology	M,D
International Affairs	M
Kinesiology and Movement Studies	M,D,O

Leisure Studies — M,O
Library Science — M
Linguistics — M,D,O
Logistics — M,D,O
Management Information Systems — M,D,O
Management of Technology — M,D,O
Marriage and Family Therapy — M,D
Maternal and Child Health — M,D
Mathematics Education — M,O
Mathematics — M,O
Medical Physics — M,D
Microbiology — M,D
Middle School Education — M
Military and Defense Studies — M
Molecular Biology — M,D
Music Education — M,O
Music — M,D,O
Nursing—General — M,D,O
Nutrition — M
Occupational Therapy — M,D,O
Pharmacology — D
Photography — M
Physical Education — M,D,O
Physical Therapy — D
Physician Assistant Studies — M
Physics — M,D
Physiology — D
Political Science — M,O
Public Administration — M,O
Public Health—General — M
Public History — M
Quality Management — M,D,O
Reading Education — M
Recreation and Park Management — M,O
Rehabilitation Counseling — M,D,O
Rehabilitation Sciences — M,D,O
Rhetoric — M,D,O
Rural Planning and Studies — M,O
Science Education — M,O
Social Sciences Education — M
Social Work — M,O
Sociology — M
Software Engineering — M
Special Education — M,O
Sports Management — M,D,O
Statistics — M,O
Technical Communication — M,D,O
Telecommunications Management — M,D,O
Textile Design — M
Therapies—Dance, Drama, and Music — M,O
Urban and Regional Planning — M,O
Vocational and Technical Education — M
Western European Studies — M
Writing — M,D,O

EAST CENTRAL UNIVERSITY
Counselor Education — M
Criminal Justice and Criminology — M
Education—General — M
Human Resources Management — M
Human Services — M
Psychology—General — M
Rehabilitation Counseling — M

EASTERN CONNECTICUT STATE UNIVERSITY
Accounting — M
Early Childhood Education — M
Education—General — M
Educational Media/Instructional Technology — M
Elementary Education — M
Organizational Management — M
Reading Education — M
Secondary Education — M

EASTERN ILLINOIS UNIVERSITY
Accounting — M
Art Education — M
Art/Fine Arts — M
Biological and Biomedical Sciences—General — M
Business Administration and Management—General — M
Chemistry — M
Clinical Psychology — M,O
Communication Disorders — M
Community College Education — M
Computer and Information Systems Security — M,O
Computer Science — M
Counselor Education — M
Early Childhood Education — M
Economics — M
Education—General — M,O
Educational Leadership and Administration — M,O
Elementary Education — M
Energy Management and Policy — M
Engineering and Applied Sciences—General — M,O
English — M
Exercise and Sports Science — M
Family and Consumer Sciences-General — M
Geographic Information Systems — M
Gerontology — M
History — M
Kinesiology and Movement Studies — M
Mathematics Education — M
Mathematics — M
Middle School Education — M
Music — M
Nutrition — M
Political Science — M
Psychology—General — M,O
Public History — M
School Psychology — M,O
Special Education — M

EASTERN KENTUCKY UNIVERSITY
Agricultural Education — M
Allied Health—General — M
Art Education — M
Biological and Biomedical Sciences—General — M
Business Administration and Management—General — M
Business Education — M
Chemistry — M
Clinical Psychology — M,O
Communication Disorders — M
Community Health — M
Counselor Education — M
Criminal Justice and Criminology — M
Curriculum and Instruction — M
Ecology — M
Education—General — M
Educational Leadership and Administration — M
Elementary Education — M
English Education — M
English — M
Environmental and Occupational Health — M
Exercise and Sports Science — M
Family Nurse Practitioner Studies — M,D
Geology — M
Health Education — M
Health Promotion — M
Health Services Management and Hospital Administration — M
Higher Education — M
History — M
Home Economics Education — M
Industrial and Organizational Psychology — M,O
Industrial Hygiene — M
Industrial/Management Engineering — M
Library Science — M
Manufacturing Engineering — M
Mathematics Education — M
Mathematics — M
Music Education — M
Music — M
Nursing—General — M
Nutrition — M
Occupational Therapy — M
Physical Education — M
Political Science — M
Psychology—General — M,O
Public Administration — M
Recreation and Park Management — M
School Psychology — M,O
Science Education — M
Secondary Education — M
Social Sciences Education — M
Special Education — M
Sports Management — M
Urban and Regional Planning — M
Vocational and Technical Education — M
Writing — M

EASTERN MENNONITE UNIVERSITY
Biological and Biomedical Sciences—General — M
Business Administration and Management—General — M
Conflict Resolution and Mediation/Peace Studies — M,O
Counselor Education — M
Education—General — M
Health Services Management and Hospital Administration — M
Nonprofit Management — M
Nursing and Healthcare Administration — M
Nursing—General — M
Organizational Management — M
Pastoral Ministry and Counseling — M,O
Religion — M,O
School Nursing — M
Theology — M,O

EASTERN MICHIGAN UNIVERSITY
Accounting — M,O
Adult Nursing — M,O
African-American Studies — O
Art Education — M
Art/Fine Arts — M
Arts Administration — M
Athletic Training and Sports Medicine — M,O
Biological and Biomedical Sciences—General — M
Business Administration and Management—General — M
Cell Biology — M
Chemistry — M
Clinical Psychology — M,D
Clinical Research — M,O
Clothing and Textiles — M
Communication Disorders — M
Communication—General — M
Community College Education — M,D,O
Computer and Information Systems Security — O
Computer Science — M,O
Construction Management — M,O
Corporate and Organizational Communication — M
Counselor Education — M,O
Criminal Justice and Criminology — M
Cultural Studies — O
Curriculum and Instruction — M,O

Dance — M
Distance Education Development — M,O
Early Childhood Education — M
Ecology — M
Economics — M,O
Education—General — M,D,O
Educational Leadership and Administration — M,D,O
Educational Measurement and Evaluation — M,O
Educational Media/Instructional Technology — M,O
Educational Policy — M
Educational Psychology — M,O
Electronic Commerce — M,O
Engineering and Applied Sciences—General — M
Engineering Management — M
English as a Second Language — M,O
English Education — M
English — M
Entrepreneurship — M,O
Exercise and Sports Science — M
Finance and Banking — M,O
Foreign Languages Education — M,O
Foundations and Philosophy of Education — M
Gender Studies — M,O
Geographic Information Systems — M,O
Gerontology — O
Health Education — M
Health Promotion — M,O
Health Services Management and Hospital Administration — M,O
Higher Education — M,D,O
Historic Preservation — M,O
History — M
Hospitality Management — M
Human Resources Management — M,O
Human Services — O
Interior Design — M
International Business — M
Kinesiology and Movement Studies — M
Linguistics — M
Management Information Systems — M,O
Management of Technology — D
Marketing — M
Mathematics — M
Middle School Education — M
Molecular Biology — M
Museum Education — O
Museum Studies — M,O
Music — M
Nonprofit Management — M,O
Nursing and Healthcare Administration — M,O
Nursing Education — M,O
Nutrition — M
Occupational Therapy — M
Organizational Management — M,O
Philosophy — M
Physical Education — M
Physician Assistant Studies — M
Physics — M
Physiology — M
Polymer Science and Engineering — M,O
Psychology—General — M,D
Public Administration — M,O
Public Policy — M,O
Quality Management — M,O
Reading Education — M,O
Science Education — M
Secondary Education — M
Social Sciences — M
Social Work — M
Sociology — M
Special Education — M,O
Sports Management — M
Student Affairs — M,D,O
Supply Chain Management — M,O
Sustainable Development — M,O
Technical Communication — M,O
Technology and Public Policy — M
Theater — M
Urban and Regional Planning — M,O
Urban Education — M
Water Resources — M
Women's Studies — M,O
Writing — M,O

EASTERN NAZARENE COLLEGE
Business Administration and Management—General — M
Counseling Psychology — M
Early Childhood Education — M,O
Education—General — M,O
Educational Leadership and Administration — M,O
Elementary Education — M,O
English as a Second Language — M,O
Marriage and Family Therapy — M
Middle School Education — M,O
Reading Education — M,O
Secondary Education — M,O
Special Education — M,O

EASTERN NEW MEXICO UNIVERSITY
Analytical Chemistry — M
Anthropology — M
Biochemistry — M
Biological and Biomedical Sciences—General — M
Botany — M
Business Administration and Management—General — M
Cell Biology — M
Chemistry — M
Communication Disorders — M
Communication—General — M
Counselor Education — M

Curriculum and Instruction — M
Early Childhood Education — M
Ecology — M
Education—General — M
Educational Leadership and Administration — M
Educational Media/Instructional Technology — M
Elementary Education — M
English as a Second Language — M
English — M
Exercise and Sports Science — M
Human Services — M
Inorganic Chemistry — M
Microbiology — M
Molecular Biology — M
Multilingual and Multicultural Education — M
Nursing—General — M
Organic Chemistry — M
Physical Chemistry — M
Physical Education — M
Reading Education — M
Secondary Education — M
Special Education — M
Sports Management — M
Vocational and Technical Education — M
Zoology — M

EASTERN OREGON UNIVERSITY
Business Administration and Management—General — M
Education—General — M
Elementary Education — M
Secondary Education — M
Writing — M

EASTERN UNIVERSITY
Applied Behavior Analysis — M,O
Business Administration and Management—General — M,D
Child and Family Studies — D
Communication—General — M,D,O
Counseling Psychology — M,O
Counselor Education — M,O
Cultural Anthropology — M
Early Childhood Education — M,D,O
Economic Development — M
Education—General — M,D,O
Educational Leadership and Administration — M,D,O
Elementary Education — M,D,O
English as a Second Language — M,D,O
English Education — M,D,O
Foreign Languages Education — M,D,O
French — M,D,O
Health Education — M,D,O
Health Services Management and Hospital Administration — M
International Development — M
Marriage and Family Therapy — D
Mathematics Education — M,D,O
Middle School Education — M,D,O
Multilingual and Multicultural Education — M,D,O
Nonprofit Management — M,D
Organizational Management — M,D
Pastoral Ministry and Counseling — M,D
Physical Education — M,D,O
Public Policy — M,D
Reading Education — M,D,O
School Nursing — M,D,O
School Psychology — M,O
Science Education — M,D,O
Secondary Education — M,D,O
Social Sciences Education — M,D,O
Spanish — M,D,O
Special Education — M,D,O
Theology — M,D
Urban and Regional Planning — M
Urban Studies — M

EASTERN VIRGINIA MEDICAL SCHOOL
Allopathic Medicine — D
Art Therapy — M
Biological and Biomedical Sciences—General — M,D
Biotechnology — M
Clinical Psychology — D
Medical/Surgical Nursing — M
Physician Assistant Studies — M
Public Health—General — M
Reproductive Biology — M
Vision Sciences — O

EASTERN WASHINGTON UNIVERSITY
Adult Education — M
Applied Psychology — M
Biological and Biomedical Sciences—General — M
Business Administration and Management—General — M
Clinical Psychology — M
Communication Disorders — M
Communication—General — M
Computer Education — M
Computer Science — M
Counseling Psychology — M
Counselor Education — M
Curriculum and Instruction — M
Dental Hygiene — M
Early Childhood Education — M
Education—General — M
Elementary Education — M
English as a Second Language — M
English — M
Exercise and Sports Science — M
Experimental Psychology — M
Foundations and Philosophy of Education — M
History — M
Interdisciplinary Studies — M

M—masters degree; D—doctorate; O—other advanced degree; *—Close-Up and/or Display

Music Education — M
Music — M
Occupational Therapy — M
Physical Education — M
Physical Therapy — D
Psychology—General — M,O
Public Administration — M
Public Health—General — M
Reading Education — M
Recreation and Park Management — M
Rhetoric — M
School Psychology — O
Secondary Education — M
Social Work — M
Sports Management — M
Technical Communication — M
Urban and Regional Planning — M
Writing — M

EAST STROUDSBURG UNIVERSITY OF PENNSYLVANIA
Athletic Training and Sports Medicine — M
Biological and Biomedical Sciences—General — M
Communication Disorders — M
Computer Science — M
Early Childhood Education — M
Education—General — M,D
Educational Media/Instructional Technology — M
Elementary Education — M
Geography — M
Health Education — M
History — M
Physical Education — M
Political Science — M
Public Administration — M
Public Health—General — M
Reading Education — M
Rehabilitation Sciences — M
Secondary Education — M,D
Special Education — M
Sports Management — M

EAST TENNESSEE STATE UNIVERSITY
Accounting — M
Allied Health—General — M,D,O
Allopathic Medicine — D
Anatomy — D
Archives/Archival Administration — M,O
Art/Fine Arts — M
Biochemistry — D
Biological and Biomedical Sciences—General — M,D
Biostatistics — M,D,O
Business Administration and Management—General — M,O
Chemistry — M
Clinical Psychology — M,D
Communication Disorders — M,D
Communication—General — M
Community Health — M,D,O
Computer Art and Design — M
Computer Science — M
Corporate and Organizational Communication — M
Counselor Education — M
Criminal Justice and Criminology — M,O
Curriculum and Instruction — M,O
Developmental Education — M,O
Early Childhood Education — M,O
Economic Development — M
Education—General — M,D,O
Educational Leadership and Administration — M,D,O
Educational Media/Instructional Technology — M,O
Elementary Education — M,O
English as a Second Language — M,O
English — M,O
Entrepreneurship — M,O
Environmental and Occupational Health — M,D,O
Epidemiology — M,D,O
Exercise and Sports Science — M,D
Experimental Psychology — D
Family Nurse Practitioner Studies — M,D,O
Foundations and Philosophy of Education — M,O
Geosciences — M
Gerontological Nursing — M,D,O
Gerontology — M,D,O
Health Services Management and Hospital Administration — M,D,O
History — M,O
Human Development — M
Information Science — M
Kinesiology and Movement Studies — M,D
Liberal Studies — M,O
Library Science — M,O
Management Strategy and Policy — M,O
Manufacturing Engineering — M
Marketing — M,O
Marriage and Family Therapy — M
Mathematics — M
Microbiology — D
Middle School Education — M,O
Nonprofit Management — M
Nursing and Healthcare Administration — M,D,O
Nursing Education — M,D,O
Nursing—General — M,D,O
Nutrition — M
Paleontology — M
Pharmaceutical Sciences — D
Pharmacology — D
Pharmacy — D
Physical Therapy — D
Physiology — D
Political Science — M
Psychiatric Nursing — M,D,O
Psychology—General — D
Public Administration — M
Public Health—General — M,D,O

Reading Education — M,O
School Psychology — M
Secondary Education — M,O
Social Work — M
Sociology — M
Special Education — M,O

EAST TEXAS BAPTIST UNIVERSITY
Business Administration and Management—General — M
Counseling Psychology — M
Curriculum and Instruction — M
Education—General — M
Educational Leadership and Administration — M
Entrepreneurship — M
Kinesiology and Movement Studies — M
Pastoral Ministry and Counseling — M
Physical Education — M
Religion — M

EAST WEST COLLEGE OF NATURAL MEDICINE
Acupuncture and Oriental Medicine — M

EC-COUNCIL UNIVERSITY
Computer and Information Systems Security — M

ECOLE HÔTELIÈRE DE LAUSANNE
Hospitality Management — M

ÉCOLE POLYTECHNIQUE DE MONTRÉAL
Aerospace/Aeronautical Engineering — M,D,O
Applied Mathematics — M,D,O
Biomedical Engineering — M,D,O
Chemical Engineering — M,D,O
Civil Engineering — M,D,O
Computer Engineering — M,D,O
Computer Science — M,D,O
Electrical Engineering — M,D,O
Engineering and Applied Sciences—General — M,D,O
Engineering Physics — M,D,O
Environmental Engineering — M,D,O
Geotechnical Engineering — M,D,O
Hydraulics — M,D,O
Industrial/Management Engineering — M,D,O
Management of Technology — M,D,O
Mechanical Engineering — M,D,O
Mechanics — M,D,O
Nuclear Engineering — M,D,O
Operations Research — M,D,O
Optical Sciences — M,D,O
Structural Engineering — M,D,O
Transportation and Highway Engineering — M,D,O

ECUMENICAL THEOLOGICAL SEMINARY
Pastoral Ministry and Counseling — D
Theology — M

EDEN THEOLOGICAL SEMINARY
Theology — M,D

EDGEWOOD COLLEGE
Accounting — M
Adult Education — M,D,O
Business Administration and Management—General — M
Education—General — M,D,O
Educational Leadership and Administration — M,D,O
Marriage and Family Therapy — M
Nursing—General — M,D
Special Education — M,D,O
Sustainability Management — M

EDINBORO UNIVERSITY OF PENNSYLVANIA
Anthropology — M
Art Education — M
Art Therapy — M,O
Art/Fine Arts — M
Clinical Psychology — M,O
Communication Disorders — M
Communication—General — M
Counseling Psychology — M,O
Counselor Education — M
Early Childhood Education — M,O
Educational Leadership and Administration — M
Educational Psychology — M
Family Nurse Practitioner Studies — M,D
History — M
Middle School Education — M
Nursing Education — M,D
Nursing—General — M
Political Science — M
Reading Education — M,O
Rehabilitation Counseling — M,O
School Psychology — M
Secondary Education — M
Social Work — M
Special Education — M,O

EDP UNIVERSITY OF PUERTO RICO–SAN SEBASTIAN
Nursing—General — M

EDWARD VIA COLLEGE OF OSTEOPATHIC MEDICINE–CAROLINAS CAMPUS
Osteopathic Medicine — D

EDWARD VIA COLLEGE OF OSTEOPATHIC MEDICINE–VIRGINIA CAMPUS
Osteopathic Medicine — D

ELIZABETH CITY STATE UNIVERSITY
Applied Mathematics — M
Biological and Biomedical Sciences—General — M

Community College Education — M
Education—General — M
Educational Leadership and Administration — M
Elementary Education — M
Geographic Information Systems — M
Mathematics Education — M
Mathematics — M
Science Education — M

ELIZABETHTOWN COLLEGE
Occupational Therapy — M

ELMEZZI GRADUATE SCHOOL OF MOLECULAR MEDICINE
Molecular Medicine — D

ELMHURST COLLEGE
Business Administration and Management—General — M
Communication Disorders — M
Database Systems — M
Educational Leadership and Administration — M
Geographic Information Systems — M
Health Services Management and Hospital Administration — M
Industrial and Organizational Psychology — M
Management Information Systems — M
Nursing—General — M
Occupational Therapy — M
Project Management — M
Public Health—General — M
Special Education — M
Supply Chain Management — M

ELMS COLLEGE
Accounting — M
Business Administration and Management—General — M
Communication Disorders — M,O
Early Childhood Education — M,O
Education—General — M,O
Elementary Education — M,O
English as a Second Language — M,O
English Education — M,O
Finance and Banking — M
Foreign Languages Education — M,O
Health Services Management and Hospital Administration — M
Nursing and Healthcare Administration — M,D
Nursing Education — M,D
Nursing—General — M,D
Reading Education — M,O
Religion — M
Science Education — M,O
Secondary Education — M,O
Special Education — M,O

ELON UNIVERSITY
Business Administration and Management—General — M
Education of the Gifted — M
Education—General — M
Elementary Education — M
Internet and Interactive Multimedia — M
Law — D
Physical Therapy — D
Physician Assistant Studies — M
Special Education — M

EMBRY-RIDDLE AERONAUTICAL UNIVERSITY–DAYTONA
Aerospace/Aeronautical Engineering — M,D
Aviation Management — M*
Business Administration and Management—General — M
Civil Engineering — M
Computer and Information Systems Security — M,D
Computer Science — M,D
Electrical Engineering — M,D
Engineering Physics — M,D
Ergonomics and Human Factors — M,D
Finance and Banking — M
Human Resources Management — M
Mechanical Engineering — M,D
Software Engineering — M,D
Systems Engineering — M,D

EMBRY-RIDDLE AERONAUTICAL UNIVERSITY–PRESCOTT
Aviation — M
Military and Defense Studies — M
Safety Engineering — M

EMBRY-RIDDLE AERONAUTICAL UNIVERSITY–WORLDWIDE
Aerospace/Aeronautical Engineering — M
Aviation Management — M
Business Administration and Management—General — M
Computer and Information Systems Security — M
Education—General — M
Engineering Management — M
Environmental and Occupational Health — M
Finance and Banking — M
Human Resources Management — M
Industrial and Manufacturing Management — M
International Affairs — M
International Business — M
Logistics — M
Management Information Systems — M
Management of Technology — M
Management Strategy and Policy — M
Organizational Management — M
Project Management — M

Supply Chain Management — M
Systems Engineering — M

EMERSON COLLEGE
Advertising and Public Relations — M
Broadcast Journalism — M
Communication Disorders — M
Communication—General — M
Corporate and Organizational Communication — M
Film, Television, and Video Production — M
International Business — M
Journalism — M
Marketing — M
Media Studies — M
Publishing — M
Theater — M
Writing — M

EMILY CARR UNIVERSITY OF ART + DESIGN
Applied Arts and Design—General — M
Art/Fine Arts — M
Computer Art and Design — M

EMMANUEL COLLEGE (UNITED STATES)
Business Administration and Management—General — M,O
Education—General — M
Human Resources Management — M,O
Nursing and Healthcare Administration — M,O
Nursing Education — M,O
Nursing—General — M,O

EMORY & HENRY COLLEGE
American Studies — M
Education—General — M
History — M
Organizational Management — M
Reading Education — M

EMORY UNIVERSITY
Accounting — M,D
Adult Nursing — M
Allied Health—General — M,D
Allopathic Medicine — D
Anesthesiologist Assistant Studies — M
Animal Behavior — D
Anthropology — D
Art History — D
Biochemistry — D
Bioethics — M
Bioinformatics — M,D
Biological and Biomedical Sciences—General — D
Biophysics — D
Biostatistics — M,D
Business Administration and Management—General — M,D
Cancer Biology/Oncology — D
Cell Biology — D
Chemistry — D
Clinical Psychology — D
Clinical Research — M
Cognitive Sciences — D
Comparative Literature — D,O
Computational Sciences — D
Computer Science — M,D
Developmental Biology — D
Developmental Psychology — D
Ecology — D
Economics — D
Education—General — M,D
English — D,O
Entrepreneurship — M
Environmental and Occupational Health — M,D
Epidemiology — M,D
Ethics — M,D
Evolutionary Biology — D
Family Nurse Practitioner Studies — M
Film, Television, and Video Theory and Criticism — M,D,O
Finance and Banking — M,D
French — D
Genetic Counseling — M
Genetics — D
Health Education — M,D
Health Informatics — M,D
Health Promotion — M
Health Services Management and Hospital Administration — M,D
Health Services Research — M,D
History — D
Human Genetics — M
Immunology — D
Industrial and Manufacturing Management — M
Interdisciplinary Studies — D
International Business — M
International Health — M
Law — M,D,O
Management Information Systems — M,D
Marketing — M,D
Mathematics — M,D
Microbiology — D
Middle School Education — M,D
Molecular Biology — D
Molecular Genetics — D
Molecular Pathogenesis — D
Music — M
Neuroscience — D
Nurse Midwifery — M
Nursing and Healthcare Administration — M
Nursing—General — M,D
Nutrition — M,D
Organizational Management — M,D
Pastoral Ministry and Counseling — M,D
Pediatric Nursing — M
Pharmacology — D
Philosophy — D,O
Physical Therapy — D

Physician Assistant Studies — M
Physics — D
Political Science — D
Portuguese — D,O
Psychology—General — D
Public Health—General — M,D
Real Estate — M
Religion — D
Secondary Education — M,D.
Sociology — D
Spanish — D,O
Sustainable Development — M
Theology — M,D
Theoretical Physics — D
Women's Health Nursing — M
Women's Studies — D,O

EMPEROR'S COLLEGE OF TRADITIONAL ORIENTAL MEDICINE
Acupuncture and Oriental Medicine — M,D

EMPIRE COLLEGE
Law — M,D

EMPORIA STATE UNIVERSITY
Accounting — M
Art Therapy — M
Biological and Biomedical
  Sciences—General — M
Botany — M
Business Administration and
  Management—General — M
Business Education — M
Cell Biology — M
Clinical Psychology — M
Counseling Psychology — M
Counselor Education — M
Curriculum and Instruction — M
Early Childhood Education — M
Education of the Gifted — M
Education—General — M
Educational Leadership and
  Administration — M
Educational Media/Instructional
  Technology — M
Elementary Education — M
English as a Second Language — M
English — M
Environmental Biology — M
Forensic Sciences — M,O
Geosciences — M,O
History — M
Industrial and Organizational
  Psychology — M
Information Studies — M
Library Science — M,D,O
Mathematics — M
Microbiology — M
Music — M
Nursing Informatics — M
Physical Education — M
Psychology—General — M
Reading Education — M
Rehabilitation Counseling — M
School Psychology — M,O
Special Education — M
Zoology — M

ENDICOTT COLLEGE
Applied Behavior Analysis — M,D
Business Administration and
  Management—General — M
Distance Education Development — M
Early Childhood Education — M
Educational Leadership and
  Administration — M,D
Elementary Education — M
Homeland Security — M
Interior Design — M
Management Information Systems — M
Nursing—General — M,D
Organizational Management — M
Reading Education — M
Secondary Education — M
Special Education — M,D
Sports Management — M

EPISCOPAL DIVINITY SCHOOL
Theology — M,D,O

ERIKSON INSTITUTE
Child Development — M
Developmental Psychology — M,O
Early Childhood Education — M,D
English as a Second Language — M,O
Human Development — M,O

ERSKINE THEOLOGICAL SEMINARY
Theology — M,D

ESSEC BUSINESS SCHOOL
Business Administration and
  Management—General — M,D
Hospitality Management — M,D
International Business — M,D

EVANGELICAL SEMINARY
Marriage and Family Therapy — M
Missions and Missiology — M
Pastoral Ministry and Counseling — M
Theology — M

EVANGELICAL SEMINARY OF PUERTO RICO
Theology — M,D

EVANGEL UNIVERSITY
Clinical Psychology — M
Counseling Psychology — M
Counselor Education — M
Curriculum and Instruction — M,D
Education—General — M
Educational Leadership and
  Administration — M,D

Organizational Management — M
Psychology—General — M
Reading Education — M
School Psychology — M
Secondary Education — M

EVEREST UNIVERSITY
Accounting — M
Business Administration and
  Management—General — M
Human Resources Management — M
International Business — M

EVERGLADES UNIVERSITY
Accounting — M
Aviation — M
Business Administration and
  Management—General — M
Entrepreneurship — M
Human Resources Management — M
Industrial and Manufacturing
  Management — M
Project Management — M
Public Health—General — M

THE EVERGREEN STATE COLLEGE
Education—General — M
Environmental Management
  and Policy — M
Public Administration — M

EXCELSIOR COLLEGE
Business Administration and
  Management—General — M,O
Conflict Resolution and
  Mediation/Peace Studies — M,O
Criminal Justice and Criminology — M,O
Emergency Management — M
Health Education — M,O
Health Informatics — M,O
Health Services Management and
  Hospital Administration — M,O
Homeland Security — M
Human Resources Management — M,O
Internet and Interactive
  Multimedia — M,O
Liberal Studies — M
Management of Technology — M,O
Medical Informatics — M,O
Nursing and Healthcare
  Administration — M,O
Nursing Education — M
Nursing Informatics — M
Nursing—General — M
Organizational Management — M,O
Public Administration — M
Public Health—General — M,O

FAIRFIELD UNIVERSITY
Accounting — M,O
Addictions/Substance Abuse
  Counseling — M,O
American Studies — M
Applied Behavior Analysis — M,O
Applied Psychology — M,O
Business Administration and
  Management—General — M,O
Child and Family Studies — M,O
Clinical Psychology — M,O
Communication—General — M
Computer and Information
  Systems Security — M,O
Computer Engineering — M,O
Counseling Psychology — M,O
Counselor Education — M,O
Database Systems — M,O
Education—General — M,O
Educational Media/Instructional
  Technology — M,O
Electrical Engineering — M,O
Elementary Education — M,O
Engineering and Applied
  Sciences—General — M,O
English as a Second Language — M,O
Entrepreneurship — M,O
Family Nurse Practitioner Studies — M,D
Finance and Banking — M,O
Foundations and Philosophy of
  Education — M,O
Health Education — M,D
Human Resources Management — M,O
International Business — M,O
Internet and Interactive
  Multimedia — M,O
Management Information Systems — M,O
Management of Technology — M,O
Management Strategy and Policy — M,O
Marketing — M,O
Marriage and Family Therapy — M,O
Mathematics — M
Mechanical Engineering — M,O
Multilingual and Multicultural
  Education — M,O
Nurse Anesthesia — M,D
Nursing and Healthcare
  Administration — M,D
Nursing—General — M,D
Pastoral Ministry and Counseling — M,O
Psychiatric Nursing — M,D
Public Administration — M
School Psychology — M,O
Secondary Education — M,O
Software Engineering — M,O
Special Education — M,O
Taxation — M,O
Telecommunications — M,O
Writing — M

FAIRLEIGH DICKINSON UNIVERSITY, COLLEGE AT FLORHAM
Accounting — M
Biological and Biomedical
  Sciences—General — M

Business Administration and
  Management—General — M,O
Chemical Engineering — M,O
Chemistry — M
Clinical Psychology — M
Computer Science — M
Corporate and Organizational
  Communication — M
Counseling Psychology — M
Early Childhood Education — M,O
Education—General — M,O
Educational Leadership and
  Administration — M
Educational Media/Instructional
  Technology — M,O
Entrepreneurship — M,O
Finance and Banking — M,O
Gerontological Nursing — M
Health Services Management and
  Hospital Administration — M
Hospitality Management — M
Human Resources Management — M
Industrial and Organizational
  Psychology — M
International Business — M,O
Management of Technology — M,O
Marketing — M,O
Nursing—General — M
Organizational Behavior — M
Organizational Management — M,O
Pharmacology — M,O
Pharmacy — D
Psychiatric Nursing — M
Psychology—General — M,O
Public Administration — M
Reading Education — M,O
Sports Management — M
Supply Chain Management — M
Sustainability Management — O
Taxation — M,O
Writing — M

FAIRLEIGH DICKINSON UNIVERSITY, METROPOLITAN CAMPUS
Accounting — M,O
Art/Fine Arts — M
Biological and Biomedical
  Sciences—General — M
Business Administration and
  Management—General — M,O
Chemistry — M
Clinical Laboratory
  Sciences/Medical Technology — M
Clinical Psychology — M,D
Communication—General — M
Comparative Literature — M
Computer Engineering — M
Computer Science — M
Criminal Justice and Criminology — M
Curriculum and Instruction — M,O
Early Childhood Education — M
Education—General — M,O
Educational Leadership and
  Administration — M
Educational Media/Instructional
  Technology — M,O
Electrical Engineering — M
Electronic Commerce — M
Engineering and Applied
  Sciences—General — M
English — M
Entrepreneurship — M,O
Experimental Psychology — M,O
Finance and Banking — M,O
Forensic Psychology — M
Foundations and Philosophy of
  Education — M
Health Services Management and
  Hospital Administration — M
History — M
Homeland Security — M
Hospitality Management — M
Human Resources Management — M,O
International Affairs — M
International Business — M
Management Information Systems — M,O
Marketing — M,O
Mathematics — M
Media Studies — M
Multilingual and Multicultural
  Education — M
Nonprofit Management — M,O
Nursing—General — M,D,O
Pharmaceutical Administration — M,O
Political Science — M
Psychology—General — M,D,O
Public Administration — M,O
Reading Education — M,O
School Psychology — M,D
Science Education — M
Special Education — M
Sports Management — M
Systems Science — M
Taxation — M

FAIRMONT STATE UNIVERSITY
Business Administration and
  Management—General — M
Criminal Justice and Criminology — M
Education—General — M
Educational Media/Instructional
  Technology — M
Exercise and Sports Science — M
Health Promotion — M
Reading Education — M
Special Education — M

FAITH BAPTIST BIBLE COLLEGE AND THEOLOGICAL SEMINARY
Pastoral Ministry and Counseling — M
Religion — M
Theology — M

FAITH EVANGELICAL COLLEGE & SEMINARY
Theology — M,D

FAITH THEOLOGICAL SEMINARY
Theology — M,D

FASHION INSTITUTE OF TECHNOLOGY
Applied Arts and Design—General — M*
Art History — M
Arts Administration — M*
Business Administration and
  Management—General — M*
Clothing and Textiles — M*
Illustration — M*
Marketing — M*
Museum Studies — M*

FAULKNER UNIVERSITY
Business Administration and
  Management—General — M
Counselor Education — M
Criminal Justice and Criminology — M
Education—General — M
History — M
Law — D
Liberal Studies — M
Missions and Missiology — M
Pastoral Ministry and Counseling — M
Theology — M

FAYETTEVILLE STATE UNIVERSITY
Biological and Biomedical
  Sciences—General — M
Business Administration and
  Management—General — M
Criminal Justice and Criminology — M
Educational Leadership and
  Administration — M,D
Elementary Education — M
Mathematics — M
Middle School Education — M
Psychology—General — M
Secondary Education — M
Social Sciences Education — M
Social Work — M
Sociology — M

FELICIAN UNIVERSITY
Adult Nursing — M,O
Business Administration and
  Management—General — M,D
Counseling Psychology — M
Education—General — M,O
Educational Leadership and
  Administration — M,O
Entrepreneurship — M,D
Family Nurse Practitioner Studies — M,O
Gerontological Nursing — M,O
Health Services Management and
  Hospital Administration — M
Nursing and Healthcare
  Administration — M,D,O
Nursing Education — M,O
Nursing—General — M,D,O
Religious Education — M,O

FERRIS STATE UNIVERSITY
Allied Health—General — M
Applied Arts and Design—General — M
Architecture — M
Art Education — M
Art/Fine Arts — M
Business Administration and
  Management—General — M
Community College Education — D
Computer and Information
  Systems Security — M
Criminal Justice and Criminology — M
Curriculum and Instruction — M
Database Systems — M
Developmental Education — M
Education—General — M
Educational Leadership and
  Administration — M,D
Human Services — M
Management Information Systems — M
Nursing and Healthcare
  Administration — M
Nursing Education — M
Nursing Informatics — M
Nursing—General — D
Optometry — D
Pharmacy — D
Photography — M
Project Management — M
Special Education — M
Supply Chain Management — M

FIELDING GRADUATE UNIVERSITY
Child Development — D,O
Clinical Psychology — D,O
Education—General — M,D,O
Educational Leadership and
  Administration — M,D,O
Forensic Psychology — D,O
Health Psychology — D,O
Human Development — M,D,O
Media Studies — M,D,O
Neuroscience — D,O
Nonprofit Management — M,D,O
Organizational Management — O
Psychology—General — M,D,O

FISHER COLLEGE
Business Administration and
  Management—General — M
Management Strategy and Policy — M

FISK UNIVERSITY
Biological and Biomedical
  Sciences—General — M
Chemistry — M
Clinical Psychology — M

*M—masters degree; D—doctorate; O—other advanced degree; *—Close-Up and/or Display*

Physics	M
Psychology—General	M

FITCHBURG STATE UNIVERSITY

Accounting	M
Art Education	M,O
Biological and Biomedical Sciences—General	M,O
Business Administration and Management—General	M
Communication—General	M,O
Computer Science	M
Counseling Psychology	M
Counselor Education	M,O
Curriculum and Instruction	M
Early Childhood Education	M
Educational Leadership and Administration	M,O
Elementary Education	M
English Education	M,O
English	M,O
Forensic Nursing	M,O
History	M,O
Human Resources Management	M
Interdisciplinary Studies	O
Middle School Education	M
Psychology—General	O
Reading Education	O
Science Education	M,O
Social Sciences Education	M,O
Special Education	M
Vocational and Technical Education	M

FIVE BRANCHES UNIVERSITY

Acupuncture and Oriental Medicine	M,D

FIVE TOWNS COLLEGE

Early Childhood Education	M,D
Music Education	M,D
Music	M,D

FLORIDA AGRICULTURAL AND MECHANICAL UNIVERSITY

Accounting	M
Adult Education	M,D
Allied Health—General	M,D
Architecture	M
Biomedical Engineering	M,D
Business Administration and Management—General	M
Business Education	M
Chemical Engineering	M,D
Chemistry	M
Civil Engineering	M,D
Counselor Education	M,D
Criminal Justice and Criminology	M
Education—General	M,D
Educational Leadership and Administration	M,D
Electrical Engineering	M,D
Elementary Education	M
Engineering and Applied Sciences—General	M,D
English Education	M
Environmental Sciences	M,D
Finance and Banking	M
Health Services Research	M,D
History	M
Industrial/Management Engineering	M,D
Journalism	M
Landscape Architecture	M
Law	D
Management Information Systems	M
Marketing	M
Mathematics Education	M
Mechanical Engineering	M,D
Medicinal and Pharmaceutical Chemistry	M,D
Nursing and Healthcare Administration	M,D
Nursing—General	M,D
Occupational Therapy	M
Pharmaceutical Administration	M,D
Pharmaceutical Sciences	M,D
Pharmacology	M,D
Pharmacy	D
Physical Education	M
Physical Therapy	D
Physics	M,D
Political Science	M
Psychology—General	M
Public Administration	M
Public Health—General	M,D
Science Education	M
Secondary Education	M
Social Psychology	M
Social Sciences Education	M
Social Sciences	M
Social Work	M
Software Engineering	M
Sports Management	M
Toxicology	M,D
Vocational and Technical Education	M

FLORIDA ATLANTIC UNIVERSITY

Accounting	M
Adult Education	M,D,O
Anthropology	M
Applied Arts and Design—General	M
Applied Mathematics	M,D
Art Education	M
Art/Fine Arts	M
Bioengineering	M,D
Biological and Biomedical Sciences—General	M
Business Administration and Management—General	M
Chemistry	M,D
Civil Engineering	M
Communication Disorders	M
Communication—General	M,O
Comparative and Interdisciplinary Arts	M,D
Comparative Literature	M
Computer Engineering	M,D

Computer Science	M,D
Counselor Education	M,D
Criminal Justice and Criminology	M
Curriculum and Instruction	M,D,O
Early Childhood Education	M
Economics	M
Education—General	M,D,O
Educational Leadership and Administration	M,D,O
Educational Media/Instructional Technology	M
Educational Psychology	M
Electrical Engineering	M,D
Elementary Education	M
Engineering and Applied Sciences—General	M,D
English as a Second Language	M,D,O
English Education	M
English	M
Environmental Education	M
Environmental Engineering	M
Exercise and Sports Science	M
Film, Television, and Video Production	M,O
Finance and Banking	M
Foundations and Philosophy of Education	M
French	M
Geology	M,D
Geosciences	M,D
German	M
Graphic Design	M
Health Promotion	M
Higher Education	M,D,O
History	M
Linguistics	M
Management Information Systems	M
Marketing	M
Mathematics Education	M
Mathematics	M,D
Mechanical Engineering	M,D
Media Studies	M,O
Multilingual and Multicultural Education	M,D,O
Music Education	M
Music	M
Neuroscience	D
Nonprofit Management	M,D
Nursing and Healthcare Administration	M,D,O
Nursing—General	M,D,O
Ocean Engineering	M,D
Physics	M,D
Political Science	M
Psychology—General	M
Public Administration	M,D
Reading Education	M
Science Education	M,D
Social Sciences Education	M
Social Work	M,D
Sociology	M
Spanish	M
Special Education	M,D
Statistics	M,D
Theater	M
Urban and Regional Planning	M
Women's Studies	M

FLORIDA COASTAL SCHOOL OF LAW

Law	D

FLORIDA COLLEGE OF INTEGRATIVE MEDICINE

Acupuncture and Oriental Medicine	M

FLORIDA GULF COAST UNIVERSITY

Accounting	M
Allied Health—General	M,D
Business Administration and Management—General	M
Criminal Justice and Criminology	M
Curriculum and Instruction	M
Education of the Gifted	M
Education—General	M
Educational Leadership and Administration	M
Elementary Education	M
English Education	M
English	M
Environmental Management and Policy	M
Environmental Sciences	M
Forensic Sciences	M
History	M
Interdisciplinary Studies	M
Mathematics Education	M
Middle School Education	M
Nurse Anesthesia	M
Occupational Therapy	M
Physical Therapy	D
Public Administration	M
Science Education	M
Social Sciences Education	M
Social Work	M
Special Education	M
Taxation	M

FLORIDA INSTITUTE OF TECHNOLOGY

Aerospace/Aeronautical Engineering	M,D
Applied Behavior Analysis	M,D
Applied Mathematics	M,D
Aviation Management	M
Aviation	M,D
Biochemistry	M
Biological and Biomedical Sciences—General	M,D
Biomedical Engineering	M,D
Biotechnology	M,D
Business Administration and Management—General	M,D
Cell Biology	M,D
Chemical Engineering	M,D
Chemistry	M,D
Civil Engineering	M,D

Clinical Psychology	D
Communication—General	M
Computer and Information Systems Security	M
Computer Education	M
Computer Engineering	M,D
Computer Science	M,D
Conservation Biology	M,D
Ecology	M,D
Education—General	M
Educational Media/Instructional Technology	M
Electrical Engineering	M,D
Electronic Commerce	M,D
Elementary Education	M
Emergency Management	M,D
Engineering and Applied Sciences—General	M,D
Engineering Management	M,D
Entrepreneurship	M
Environmental Education	M
Environmental Management and Policy	M
Environmental Sciences	M,D
Ergonomics and Human Factors	M,D
Geosciences	M
Health Services Management and Hospital Administration	M
Human Resources Management	M,D
Human-Computer Interaction	M
Industrial and Organizational Psychology	M,D
Information Science	M
Interdisciplinary Studies	M
Logistics	M,D
Management Information Systems	M,D
Management of Technology	M,D
Marine Biology	M,D
Marine Sciences	M,D
Mathematics Education	M,D,O
Mechanical Engineering	M,D
Meteorology	M
Molecular Biology	M,D
Ocean Engineering	M,D
Oceanography	M,D
Operations Research	M,D
Organizational Behavior	M
Organizational Management	M
Physics	M,D
Planetary and Space Sciences	M,D
Project Management	M,D
Psychology—General	M,D
Public Administration	M,D
Quality Management	M
Safety Engineering	M
Science Education	M,D,O
Software Engineering	M,D
Supply Chain Management	M,D
Systems Engineering	M,D
Transportation Management	M,D

FLORIDA INTERNATIONAL UNIVERSITY

Accounting	M
Adult Education	M,D,O
Adult Nursing	M,D
African Studies	M
Allopathic Medicine	M,D
Applied Behavior Analysis	M,D
Architecture	M
Art Education	M,D,O
Art/Fine Arts	M,O
Asian Studies	M
Athletic Training and Sports Medicine	M
Biological and Biomedical Sciences—General	M,D
Biomedical Engineering	M,D
Biostatistics	M,D
Chemistry	M,D
Civil Engineering	M,D
Clinical Psychology	M,D,O
Cognitive Sciences	M,D
Communication Disorders	M
Communication—General	M
Computer and Information Systems Security	M,D
Computer Engineering	M,D
Computer Science	M,D
Construction Management	M
Counseling Psychology	M,D,O
Counselor Education	M,D,O
Criminal Justice and Criminology	M,D
Curriculum and Instruction	M,D,O
Database Systems	M,D
Developmental Psychology	M
Early Childhood Education	M,D,O
Economics	M,D
Educational Leadership and Administration	M,D,O
Educational Media/Instructional Technology	M,D,O
Electrical Engineering	M,D
Elementary Education	M,D,O
Emergency Management	M
Engineering and Applied Sciences—General	M,D
Engineering Management	M
English as a Second Language	M,D,O
English Education	M,D,O
English	M
Environmental and Occupational Health	M,D
Environmental Engineering	M,D
Environmental Management and Policy	M,D
Epidemiology	M,D
Finance and Banking	M
Foreign Languages Education	M,D,O
Forensic Sciences	M,D
Geosciences	M
Health Promotion	M,D

Health Services Management and Hospital Administration	M,D
Higher Education	M,D,O
History	M,D
Hospitality Management	M
Human Resources Development	M,D,O
Human Resources Management	M
Industrial and Organizational Psychology	M,D
Information Science	M,D
Interior Design	M,O
International Affairs	M,D
International and Comparative Education	M,D,O
International Business	M
Journalism	M
Landscape Architecture	M
Latin American Studies	M
Law	M
Liberal Studies	M
Linguistics	M
Management Information Systems	M,D
Marketing	M
Mass Communication	M
Materials Engineering	M,D
Materials Sciences	M,D
Mathematics Education	M,D,O
Mathematics	M
Mechanical Engineering	M,D
Multilingual and Multicultural Education	M,D,O
Museum Studies	M,O
Music Education	M
Music	M
Natural Resources	M,D
Neuroscience	M,D
Nurse Anesthesia	M,D
Nursing—General	M,D
Nutrition	M,D
Occupational Therapy	M
Pediatric Nursing	M,D
Physical Education	M,D,O
Physical Therapy	D
Physician Assistant Studies	M,D
Physics	M,D
Political Science	M,D
Psychiatric Nursing	M,D
Psychology—General	M,D
Public Administration	M,D
Public Affairs	M,D
Public Health—General	M,D
Reading Education	M,D,O
Real Estate	M
Recreation and Park Management	M,D,O
Rehabilitation Counseling	M,D,O
Religion	M
School Psychology	M,D,O
Science Education	M,D,O
Social Sciences Education	M,D,O
Social Work	M,D
Sociology	M,D
Spanish	M,D
Special Education	M,D,O
Sports Management	M,D,O
Statistics	M
Telecommunications	M,D
Urban Education	M,D,O
Writing	M

FLORIDA MEMORIAL UNIVERSITY

Business Administration and Management—General	M
Education—General	M
Elementary Education	M
Reading Education	M
Special Education	M

FLORIDA NATIONAL UNIVERSITY

Business Administration and Management—General	M
Family Nurse Practitioner Studies	M
Finance and Banking	M
Health Services Management and Hospital Administration	M
Marketing	M
Nursing and Healthcare Administration	M
Nursing Education	M
Nursing—General	M
Public Administration	M

FLORIDA SOUTHERN COLLEGE

Accounting	M
Adult Nursing	M
Business Administration and Management—General	M
Education—General	M,D
Educational Leadership and Administration	M,D
Family Nurse Practitioner Studies	M
Gerontological Nursing	M
Nursing and Healthcare Administration	M
Nursing Education	M
Nursing—General	M

FLORIDA STATE UNIVERSITY

Accounting	M,D
Actuarial Science	M,D
American Studies	M,D
Analytical Chemistry	M,D
Applied Behavior Analysis	M
Applied Economics	M,D
Applied Mathematics	M,D
Applied Social Research	M,D
Applied Statistics	M,D
Archaeology	M
Architecture	M
Art Education	M,D
Art History	M,D
Art/Fine Arts	M
Arts Administration	M,D
Asian Studies	M
Atmospheric Sciences	M,D
Biochemistry	M,D

Biological and Biomedical Sciences—General	M,D
Biomedical Engineering	M,D
Biopsychology	M,D
Biostatistics	M,D
Business Administration and Management—General	M,D
Cell Biology	M,D
Chemical Engineering	M,D
Chemistry	M,D
Child and Family Studies	M,D
Civil Engineering	M,D
Classics	M,D
Clinical Psychology	D
Cognitive Sciences	D
Communication Disorders	M,D
Communication—General	M,D
Community College Education	M
Computational Sciences	M,D
Computer and Information Systems Security	M,D
Computer Science	M,D
Corporate and Organizational Communication	M,D
Counseling Psychology	D
Criminal Justice and Criminology	M,D
Cultural Studies	M,D
Curriculum and Instruction	M,D,O
Dance	M
Demography and Population Studies	M
Developmental Psychology	D
Early Childhood Education	M,D,O
East European and Russian Studies	M
Ecology	M,D
Economics	M,D
Education—General	M,D,O
Educational Leadership and Administration	M,D,O
Educational Measurement and Evaluation	M,D,O
Educational Media/Instructional Technology	M,D,O
Educational Policy	M,D,O
Educational Psychology	M,D
Electrical Engineering	M,D
Elementary Education	M,D,O
Energy and Power Engineering	M,D
Engineering and Applied Sciences—General	M,D
English Education	M,D,O
English	M,D
Environmental Engineering	M,D
Environmental Law	M,D
Environmental Sciences	M,D
Evolutionary Biology	M,D
Exercise and Sports Science	M,D
Family and Consumer Sciences—General	M,D
Family Nurse Practitioner Studies	M,D,O
Film, Television, and Video Production	M*
Finance and Banking	M,D
Food Science and Technology	M,D
Foreign Languages Education	M,D,O
Foundations and Philosophy of Education	M,D
French	M,D
Geographic Information Systems	M,D
Geography	M,D
Geology	M,D
Geophysics	D
Geosciences	M,D
German	M
Health Education	M,D
Higher Education	M,D
History	M,D
Human Resources Management	M,D
Industrial Design	M
Industrial/Management Engineering	M,D
Information Studies	M,D,O
Inorganic Chemistry	M,D
Insurance	M,D
Interior Design	M
International Affairs	M
International and Comparative Education	M,D
International Business	M
Italian	M
Law	M,D
Library Science	M,D,O
Management Information Systems	M,D,O
Management Strategy and Policy	M,D
Manufacturing Engineering	M,D
Marine Sciences	M,D
Marketing	M,D
Marriage and Family Therapy	M,D
Materials Engineering	M,D
Materials Sciences	M,D
Mathematical and Computational Finance	M,D
Mathematics Education	M,D,O
Mathematics	M,D
Mechanical Engineering	M,D
Media Studies	M,D
Meteorology	M,D
Molecular Biology	M,D
Molecular Biophysics	D
Museum Studies	M,D
Music	M,D
Neuroscience	M,D
Nursing and Healthcare Administration	M,D,O
Nursing Education	M,D,O
Nursing—General	M,D,O
Nutrition	M,D
Oceanography	M,D
Organic Chemistry	M,D
Organizational Behavior	M,D
Philosophy	M,D
Physical Chemistry	M,D
Physics	M,D
Political Science	M,D
Psychiatric Nursing	M,D,O
Psychology—General	M,D
Public Administration	M,D,O
Public Health—General	M,D
Public History	M,D
Public Policy	M,D,O
Reading Education	M,D,O
Religion	M,D
Rhetoric	M,D
School Psychology	D
Science Education	M,D,O
Slavic Languages	M
Social Psychology	D
Social Sciences Education	M,D,O
Social Work	M,D
Sociology	M,D
Spanish	M,D
Special Education	M,D,O
Sport Psychology	M,D
Sports Management	M,D,O
Statistics	M,D,O
Taxation	M,D
Theater	M,D
Therapies—Dance, Drama, and Music	M,D
Urban and Regional Planning	M,D
Writing	M,D

FONTBONNE UNIVERSITY

Accounting	M
Art Education	M
Art/Fine Arts	M
Business Administration and Management—General	M
Communication Disorders	M
Computer Science	M
Curriculum and Instruction	M
Early Childhood Education	M
Education—General	M
Educational Media/Instructional Technology	M
Elementary Education	M
Family and Consumer Sciences-General	M
Health Communication	M
Middle School Education	M
Reading Education	M
Secondary Education	M
Special Education	M
Supply Chain Management	M
Theater	M

FORDHAM UNIVERSITY

Accounting	M
Applied Psychology	M,D
Applied Statistics	M
Biological and Biomedical Sciences—General	M,D,O
Business Administration and Management—General	M
Classics	M,D
Clinical Psychology	D
Communication—General	M
Computer and Information Systems Security	M
Computer Science	M
Conservation Biology	M,D,O
Counseling Psychology	M,D
Counselor Education	M,D
Curriculum and Instruction	M,O
Database Systems	M
Developmental Psychology	D
Early Childhood Education	M,O
Economic Development	M
Economics	M,D,O
Education—General	M,D,O
Educational Leadership and Administration	M,D,O
Educational Psychology	M,D
Electronic Commerce	M
Elementary Education	M,O
Emergency Management	M
English as a Second Language	M,O
English	M,D
Entrepreneurship	M
Ethics	M,O
Finance and Banking	M
Health Services Management and Hospital Administration	M
History	M,D
Intellectual Property Law	M,D
International Affairs	M,O
International Development	M,O
International Economics	M,O
Investment Management	M
Law	M,D
Management Information Systems	M
Management Strategy and Policy	M
Marketing	M
Media Studies	M,O
Medieval and Renaissance Studies	M,O
Nonprofit Management	M
Pastoral Ministry and Counseling	M,D,O
Philosophy	M,D
Political Science	M
Psychology—General	M,D
Quantitative Analysis	M
Religion	M
Religious Education	M,D,O
School Psychology	M,D,O
Social Work	M,D
Special Education	M,O
Taxation	M
Theater	M
Theology	M,D
Urban Studies	M

FORT HAYS STATE UNIVERSITY

Art/Fine Arts	M
Biological and Biomedical Sciences—General	M
Business Administration and Management—General	M
Communication Disorders	M
Communication—General	M
Counselor Education	M
Education—General	M,O
Educational Leadership and Administration	M,O
Educational Media/Instructional Technology	M
English	M
Geography	M
Geology	M
Geosciences	M
Health Education	M
History	M
Liberal Studies	M
Nursing—General	M
Physical Education	M
Psychology—General	M,O
School Psychology	O
Special Education	M

FORT LEWIS COLLEGE

Educational Leadership and Administration	M,O

FORT VALLEY STATE UNIVERSITY

Animal Sciences	M
Counseling Psychology	M
Counselor Education	M,O
Environmental and Occupational Health	M
Public Health—General	M
Rehabilitation Counseling	M

FRAMINGHAM STATE UNIVERSITY

Art/Fine Arts	M
Business Administration and Management—General	M
Curriculum and Instruction	M
Early Childhood Education	M
Educational Leadership and Administration	M
Educational Media/Instructional Technology	M
Elementary Education	M
English as a Second Language	M
English Education	M
Food Science and Technology	M
Health Education	M
Health Services Management and Hospital Administration	M
Human Resources Management	M
Mathematics Education	M
Nursing and Healthcare Administration	M
Nursing Education	M
Nursing—General	M
Nutrition	M
Psychology—General	M
Public Administration	M
Reading Education	M
Social Sciences Education	M
Spanish	M
Special Education	M

FRANCISCAN SCHOOL OF THEOLOGY

Theology	M

FRANCISCAN UNIVERSITY OF STEUBENVILLE

Business Administration and Management—General	M
Clinical Psychology	M
Counseling Psychology	M
Curriculum and Instruction	M
Education—General	M
Educational Leadership and Administration	M
Nursing—General	M
Philosophy	M
Theology	M

FRANCIS MARION UNIVERSITY

Applied Psychology	M,O
Business Administration and Management—General	M
Clinical Psychology	M,O
Counseling Psychology	M,O
Education—General	M
Family Nurse Practitioner Studies	M
Health Services Management and Hospital Administration	M
Nursing Education	M
Nursing—General	M
Physician Assistant Studies	M
Psychology—General	M,O
School Psychology	M,O
Special Education	M

FRANKLIN COLLEGE

Athletic Training and Sports Medicine	M

FRANKLIN PIERCE UNIVERSITY

Business Administration and Management—General	M,D,O
Curriculum and Instruction	M,D,O
Elementary Education	M,D,O
Energy Management and Policy	M,D,O
Health Services Management and Hospital Administration	M,D,O
Human Resources Management	M,D,O
Management Information Systems	M,D,O

(continued)

Nursing and Healthcare Administration	M,D,O
Nursing Education	M,D,O
Physical Therapy	M,D,O
Physician Assistant Studies	M,D,O
Special Education	M,D,O
Sports Management	M,D,O
Sustainability Management	M,D,O
Telecommunications	M,D,O

FRANKLIN UNIVERSITY

Accounting	M
Business Administration and Management—General	M
Computer Science	M
Corporate and Organizational Communication	M
Educational Media/Instructional Technology	M
Marketing	M

FRANKLIN UNIVERSITY SWITZERLAND

International Business	M

FREDERICK S. PARDEE RAND GRADUATE SCHOOL

Public Policy	D

FREED-HARDEMAN UNIVERSITY

Accounting	M
Business Administration and Management—General	M
Counselor Education	M,O
Curriculum and Instruction	M,O
Education—General	M,O
Educational Leadership and Administration	M,O
Ethics	M
Management Strategy and Policy	M
Pastoral Ministry and Counseling	M
Special Education	M,O
Theology	M

FRESNO PACIFIC UNIVERSITY

Business Administration and Management—General	M
Conflict Resolution and Mediation/Peace Studies	M,O
Counselor Education	M
Curriculum and Instruction	M
Education—General	M,O
Educational Leadership and Administration	M
Educational Media/Instructional Technology	M
English as a Second Language	M,O
Family Nurse Practitioner Studies	M
Interdisciplinary Studies	M
Kinesiology and Movement Studies	M
Marriage and Family Therapy	M
Mathematics Education	M
Missions and Missiology	M
Nursing—General	M
Pastoral Ministry and Counseling	M
Reading Education	M,O
School Psychology	M
Science Education	M
Special Education	M
Student Affairs	M,O
Theology	M
Urban Studies	M

FRIENDS UNIVERSITY

Accounting	M
Health Services Management and Hospital Administration	M
Law	M
Logistics	M
Management Information Systems	M
Management Strategy and Policy	M
Marriage and Family Therapy	M
Supply Chain Management	M

FRONTIER NURSING UNIVERSITY

Family Nurse Practitioner Studies	M,D,O
Nurse Midwifery	M
Nursing—General	M,D,O*
Women's Health Nursing	M,D,O

FROSTBURG STATE UNIVERSITY

Biological and Biomedical Sciences—General	M
Business Administration and Management—General	M
Computer Science	M
Conservation Biology	M
Counseling Psychology	M
Counselor Education	M
Curriculum and Instruction	M
Ecology	M
Education—General	M
Educational Leadership and Administration	M
Educational Media/Instructional Technology	M
Elementary Education	M
Fish, Game, and Wildlife Management	M
Interdisciplinary Studies	M
Nursing and Healthcare Administration	M
Nursing Education	M
Nursing—General	M
Psychology—General	M
Reading Education	M
Recreation and Park Management	M
Secondary Education	M
Special Education	M

FULLER THEOLOGICAL SEMINARY

Clinical Psychology	M,D,O
Marriage and Family Therapy	M,D,O
Missions and Missiology	M,D,O
Music	M,D,O

*M—masters degree; D—doctorate; O—other advanced degree; *—Close-Up and/or Display*

Pastoral Ministry and Counseling — M,D,O
Theology — M,D,O

FULL SAIL UNIVERSITY
Art/Fine Arts — M
Business Administration and Management—General — M
Computer Art and Design — M
Educational Media/Instructional Technology — M
Entertainment Management — M
Game Design and Development — M
Graphic Design — M
Internet and Interactive Multimedia — M
Journalism — M
Marketing — M
Media Studies — M
Writing — M

FURMAN UNIVERSITY
Chemistry — M
Curriculum and Instruction — M,O
Early Childhood Education — M,O
Education—General — M,O
Educational Leadership and Administration — M,O
English as a Second Language — M,O
Reading Education — M,O
Special Education — M,O

FUTURE GENERATIONS GRADUATE SCHOOL
Social Psychology — M
Sustainable Development — M
Urban and Regional Planning — M

GALLAUDET UNIVERSITY
Clinical Psychology — M,D,O
Communication Disorders — M,D,O
Counseling Psychology — M,D,O
Counselor Education — M,D,O
Early Childhood Education — M,D,O
Education—General — M,D,O
Elementary Education — M,D,O
International and Comparative Education — M,D,O
Linguistics — M,D,O
Multilingual and Multicultural Education — M,D,O
Neuroscience — M,D,O
Public Administration — M,D,O
School Psychology — M,D,O
Secondary Education — M,D,O
Social Work — M,D,O
Special Education — M,D,O
Translation and Interpretation — M,D,O

GANNON UNIVERSITY
Athletic Training and Sports Medicine — M
Business Administration and Management—General — M
Clinical Psychology — M
Computer Science — M
Counseling Psychology — M
Criminal Justice and Criminology — M
Curriculum and Instruction — M,O
Education—General — M,O
Educational Leadership and Administration — D,O
Electrical Engineering — M
Engineering Management — M
English as a Second Language — O
English — M
Environmental and Occupational Health — M
Environmental Engineering — M
Environmental Sciences — M
Exercise and Sports Science — M
Family Nurse Practitioner Studies — M,O
Finance and Banking — M
Health Communication — M
Human Resources Management — M
Information Science — M
Marketing — M
Mechanical Engineering — M
Nurse Anesthesia — M,O
Nursing and Healthcare Administration — M,D
Nursing—General — M,D
Occupational Therapy — M,D
Organizational Management — D
Pastoral Ministry and Counseling — M,O
Physical Therapy — D
Physician Assistant Studies — M
Public Administration — M
Reading Education — M,O
Software Engineering — M
Theology — M,O

GARDNER-WEBB UNIVERSITY
Business Administration and Management—General — M
Counseling Psychology — M
Cultural Studies — M,D
Curriculum and Instruction — D
Education—General — M,D,O
Educational Leadership and Administration — M,D,O
English Education — M
English — M
Exercise and Sports Science — M
Family Nurse Practitioner Studies — M,D
Missions and Missiology — M,D
Nursing—General — M,D
Organizational Management — D
Pastoral Ministry and Counseling — M,D
Physical Education — M
Physician Assistant Studies — M
Psychology—General — M
Religious Education — M,D
School Psychology — M
Theology — M,D

GARRETT-EVANGELICAL THEOLOGICAL SEMINARY
Music — M,D
Pastoral Ministry and Counseling — M,D
Religious Education — M,D
Theology — M,D

GATEWAY SEMINARY
Early Childhood Education — M
Educational Leadership and Administration — M,D,O
Pastoral Ministry and Counseling — M,D,O
Theology — M,D,O

GEISINGER COMMONWEALTH SCHOOL OF MEDICINE
Allied Health—General — D
Biological and Biomedical Sciences—General — M

GENERAL THEOLOGICAL SEMINARY
Pastoral Ministry and Counseling — M
Religion — M,D,O
Theology — M,D,O

GENEVA COLLEGE
Business Administration and Management—General — M
Clinical Psychology — M
Counseling Psychology — M
Counselor Education — M
Education—General — M
Educational Leadership and Administration — M
Finance and Banking — M
Higher Education — M
Marketing — M
Marriage and Family Therapy — M
Nonprofit Management — M
Organizational Management — M
Pastoral Ministry and Counseling — M
Project Management — M
Psychology—General — M

GEORGE FOX UNIVERSITY
Accounting — M,D
Business Administration and Management—General — M
Clinical Psychology — M,D,O
Counseling Psychology — M,O
Counselor Education — M,O
Cultural Studies — M,D,O
Education—General — M,D,O
Educational Leadership and Administration — M,D,O
Educational Media/Instructional Technology — M,O
English as a Second Language — M,O
Finance and Banking — M,D
Human Resources Management — M,D
Marketing — M,D
Marriage and Family Therapy — M,O
Organizational Management — M
Pastoral Ministry and Counseling — M,D,O
Physical Therapy — D
Reading Education — M,O
School Psychology — M,O
Social Work — M
Special Education — M,O
Theology — M,D,O

GEORGE MASON UNIVERSITY
Accounting — M,O
Anthropology — M,D
Applied Physics — M,D
Applied Psychology — M,D,O
Art Education — M
Art History — M
Art/Fine Arts — M
Arts Administration — M,O
Astronomy — D
Atmospheric Sciences — D
Biochemistry — M,D
Bioengineering — M
Bioinformatics — M,D,O
Biological and Biomedical Sciences—General — M,D,O
Biostatistics — M,D,O
Business Administration and Management—General — M
Chemistry — M,D
Civil Engineering — M,D
Cognitive Sciences — M,D,O
Communication—General — M,D,O
Community College Education — M,D,O
Community Health — M,O
Computational Biology — M,D,O
Computer and Information Systems Security — M
Computer Engineering — M,D,O
Computer Science — M,D,O
Conflict Resolution and Mediation/Peace Studies — M,D,O
Construction Engineering — M,D
Counselor Education — M
Criminal Justice and Criminology — M,D
Cultural Studies — D
Curriculum and Instruction — M
Developmental Psychology — M,D,O
Early Childhood Education — M
Ecology — M,D
Economics — M,D
Education of the Gifted — M
Education—General — M,D,O
Educational Leadership and Administration — M,O
Educational Media/Instructional Technology — M
Educational Psychology — M,O
Electrical Engineering — M,D,O
Elementary Education — M
Engineering and Applied Sciences—General — M,D,O
Engineering Physics — M,D
English as a Second Language — M
English Education — M

English — M,D,O
Environmental Management and Policy — M,D
Environmental Sciences — M,D
Epidemiology — M,O
Ethics — M
Exercise and Sports Science — M,O
Foreign Languages Education — M
Forensic Sciences — M
French — M
Gender Studies — M
Geographic Information Systems — M,D,O
Geography — M,D,O
Geosciences — M,D,O
Graphic Design — M
Health Promotion — M,O
Health Services Management and Hospital Administration — M
Higher Education — D,O
History — M,D
Human Resources Management — M
Industrial and Organizational Psychology — M,D,O
Information Science — M,D,O
Interdisciplinary Studies — M
International Affairs — M
International and Comparative Education — M
International Business — M
International Health — M,O
Law — M,D
Linguistics — M,D,O
Logistics — M,O
Management Information Systems — M,D
Management of Technology — M
Mathematics Education — M
Mathematics — M,D
Multilingual and Multicultural Education — M
Music Education — M
Music — M,D
National Security — M,O
Near and Middle Eastern Studies — M,O
Neuroscience — M,D,O
Nursing—General — M,D,O
Nutrition — M,O
Operations Research — M,D,O
Organizational Management — M
Philosophy — M
Photography — M
Physical Education — M
Physics — M,D
Political Science — M
Project Management — M,D
Psychology—General — M,D,O
Public Administration — M
Public Affairs — M
Public Health—General — M,O
Public Policy — M,D
Reading Education — M
Rehabilitation Sciences — D,O
Religion — M
Science Education — M
Secondary Education — M
Social Sciences Education — M
Social Work — M
Sociology — M,D
Special Education — M,D,O
Statistics — M,D,O
Structural Engineering — M,D
Systems Biology — M,D,O
Systems Engineering — M,D,O
Transportation and Highway Engineering — M,D
Transportation Management — M,O
Women's Studies — M
Writing — M

GEORGETOWN COLLEGE
Education—General — M
Reading Education — M
Special Education — M

GEORGETOWN UNIVERSITY
Acute Care/Critical Care Nursing — M,D
Advertising and Public Relations — M
Allopathic Medicine — D
American Studies — M,D
Analytical Chemistry — D
Asian Studies — M
Biochemistry — M,D
Bioinformatics — M,O
Biological and Biomedical Sciences—General — M,D
Biostatistics — M,O
Business Administration and Management—General — M
Chemistry — D
Communication—General — M
Comparative Literature — M,D
Computer Science — M,D
Conflict Resolution and Mediation/Peace Studies — M,D,O
East European and Russian Studies — M
Economic Development — M
Economics — D
Emergency Management — M,D
English — M,D
Environmental Law — M
Epidemiology — M,O
Ethics — M,D
Family Nurse Practitioner Studies — M,D
Finance and Banking — M,D
German — M,D
Health Law — M
Health Physics/Radiological Health — M
Health Promotion — M
History — M,D
Hospitality Management — M
Human Development — M
Human Resources Management — M,D
Humanities — M,D
Immunology — M,D
Industrial and Labor Relations — D

Industrial and Manufacturing Management — D
Infectious Diseases — M,D
Inorganic Chemistry — D
Interdisciplinary Studies — M,D
International Affairs — M,D
International Business — M,D
International Development — M
International Health — M,D
Internet and Interactive Multimedia — M
Journalism — M,D
Latin American Studies — M,D
Law — M,D
Liberal Studies — M,D
Linguistics — M,D
Management of Technology — M,D
Materials Sciences — D
Mathematics — M,D
Media Studies — M,D
Medieval and Renaissance Studies — M,D
Microbiology — M,D
Molecular Biology — M,D
Near and Middle Eastern Languages — M,O
Near and Middle Eastern Studies — M,O
Neuroscience — D
Nurse Anesthesia — M,D
Nurse Midwifery — M,D
Nursing Education — M,D
Nursing—General — M,D
Organic Chemistry — D
Pharmacology — M,D
Philosophy — M,D
Physiology — M,D
Political Science — D
Psychology—General — D
Public Health—General — M,D
Public Policy — M,D
Radiation Biology — M
Real Estate — M
Religion — M,D
Spanish — M,D
Sports Management — M,D
Statistics — M,D
Systems Engineering — M,D
Taxation — M,D
Theology — D
Theoretical Chemistry — D
Urban and Regional Planning — M,D
Western European Studies — M

THE GEORGE WASHINGTON UNIVERSITY
Accounting — M
Addictions/Substance Abuse Counseling — M
Adult Education — O
Adult Nursing — M,D,O
Aerospace/Aeronautical Engineering — M,D,O
Allopathic Medicine — D
American Studies — M,D
Analytical Chemistry — M,D
Anthropology — M,D
Applied Mathematics — M,D,O
Applied Psychology — D
Art Education — M
Art History — M
Art Therapy — M,O
Art/Fine Arts — M,O
Asian Studies — M
Biochemistry — D
Biological and Biomedical Sciences—General — M,D
Biomedical Engineering — M,D
Biostatistics — M,D
Biotechnology — M,D,O
Business Administration and Management—General — M,D,O
Chemistry — M,D
Civil Engineering — M,D,O
Clinical Psychology — M,D
Cognitive Sciences — D
Communication Disorders — M
Communication—General — M
Community Health — M,D
Computer and Information Systems Security — M,D,O
Computer Engineering — M,D,O
Computer Science — M,D,O
Counselor Education — M,D,O
Criminal Justice and Criminology — M,O
Curriculum and Instruction — M,O
Dance — M,O
Distance Education Development — O
Early Childhood Education — M
East European and Russian Studies — M
Economics — M,D
Education—General — M,D,O
Educational Leadership and Administration — M,D,O
Educational Media/Instructional Technology — M,O
Educational Policy — M,D,O
Electrical Engineering — M,D,O
Elementary Education — M
Emergency Management — M,D,O
Engineering and Applied Sciences—General — M,D,O
Engineering Management — M,D
English — M,D
Environmental and Occupational Health — D
Environmental Engineering — M,D,O
Environmental Management and Policy — M
Epidemiology — M
Exercise and Sports Science — M
Family Nurse Practitioner Studies — M,D,O
Finance and Banking — M,D
Folklore — M,D
Foreign Languages Education — M
Forensic Psychology — O
Forensic Sciences — M,O

Gender Studies — O
Geography — M,O
Health Communication — M,D
Health Services Management and Hospital Administration — M,D,O
Health Services Research — M,D,O
Higher Education — M,D,O
Historic Preservation — M,D
History — M,D
Hospitality Management — M,O
Human Development — M
Human Resources Development — M,D,O
Human Resources Management — M,O
Immunology — D
Infectious Diseases — M,D,O
Inorganic Chemistry — M,D
Interior Design — M
International Affairs — M,D
International and Comparative Education — M,D,O
International Business — M,D
International Development — M,D
International Health — M
International Trade Policy — M
Investment Management — M,D
Latin American Studies — M
Law — M,D
Legal and Justice Studies — M,D,O
Management Information Systems — M,D
Management of Technology — M,D
Management Strategy and Policy — M,D,O
Marketing — M,D
Mass Communication — M,O
Materials Sciences — M,D
Mathematical and Computational Finance — M,D,O
Mathematics Education — M
Mathematics — M,D,O
Mechanical Engineering — M,D,O
Microbiology — M,D,O
Military and Defense Studies — M
Molecular Medicine — D
Multilingual and Multicultural Education — M,D,O
Museum Education — M
Museum Studies — M,D,O
National Security — M,D
Near and Middle Eastern Studies — M
Nonprofit Management — M,O
Nursing and Healthcare Administration — M,D,O
Nursing Education — M,D,O
Nursing—General — M,D,O
Organic Chemistry — M,D
Organizational Management — M,O
Philosophy — M
Photography — M
Physical Chemistry — M,D
Physical Therapy — D
Physician Assistant Studies — M
Physics — M,D
Political Science — M,D
Project Management — M,D,O
Psychology—General — M,D,O
Public Administration — M,D
Public Affairs — M,O
Public Health—General — M,D
Public Policy — M,D
Publishing — M
Real Estate — O
Rehabilitation Counseling — M
Religion — M
Science Education — M
Secondary Education — M
Social Psychology — D
Sociology — M
Special Education — M,D,O
Sports Management — M,O
Statistics — M,D,O
Student Affairs — M,D,O
Systems Biology — D
Systems Engineering — M,D,O
Technology and Public Policy — M,O
Telecommunications — M,D,O
Theater — M,O
Toxicology — M,O
Travel and Tourism — M,O
Vocational and Technical Education — O
Western European Studies — M
Women's Studies — M,O

GEORGIA CAMPUS–PHILADELPHIA COLLEGE OF OSTEOPATHIC MEDICINE

Osteopathic Medicine — D
Pharmacy — D*

GEORGIA CHRISTIAN UNIVERSITY

Business Administration and Management—General — M
Missions and Missiology — M,D
Music — M
Pastoral Ministry and Counseling — M,D
Theology — M,D

GEORGIA COLLEGE & STATE UNIVERSITY

Accounting — M
Art Therapy — M
Biological and Biomedical Sciences—General — M
Business Administration and Management—General — M
Criminal Justice and Criminology — M
Early Childhood Education — M
Education—General — M,O
Educational Leadership and Administration — O
Educational Media/Instructional Technology — M
English — M
Exercise and Sports Science — M

Health Education — M
Health Promotion — M
History — M
Kinesiology and Movement Studies — M
Logistics — M
Management Information Systems — M
Music Education — M
Nursing—General — M,D
Physical Education — M
Public Administration — M
Reading Education — M
Secondary Education — M
Special Education — M,O
Therapies—Dance, Drama, and Music — M
Writing — M

GEORGIA INSTITUTE OF TECHNOLOGY

Aerospace/Aeronautical Engineering — M,D
Architecture — M,D
Artificial Intelligence/Robotics — D
Atmospheric Sciences — M,D
Bioengineering — M,D
Bioinformatics — M,D
Biological and Biomedical Sciences—General — M,D
Biomedical Engineering — D
Building Science — M,D
Business Administration and Management—General — M,D
Chemical Engineering — M,D
Chemistry — M,D
Civil Engineering — M,D
Computational Sciences — M,D
Computer and Information Systems Security — M
Computer Art and Design — M,D
Computer Engineering — M,D
Computer Science — M,D
Economic Development — M,D
Economics — M,D
Electrical Engineering — M,D
Engineering and Applied Sciences—General — M,D
Environmental Engineering — M
Environmental Management and Policy — M,D
Ergonomics and Human Factors — M,D
Geographic Information Systems — M,D
Geosciences — M,D
Health Physics/Radiological Health — M,D
Health Services Management and Hospital Administration — M
History of Science and Technology — M
Human-Computer Interaction — M
Industrial Design — M
Industrial/Management Engineering — M,D
International Affairs — M
International Business — M
Internet and Interactive Multimedia — M,D
Logistics — M
Management Information Systems — M
Materials Engineering — M,D
Mathematical and Computational Finance — M
Mathematics — M,D
Mechanical Engineering — M,D
Mechanics — M
Music — M,D
Nuclear Engineering — M,D
Operations Research — M,D
Paper and Pulp Engineering — M,D
Physics — M,D
Physiology — M,D
Psychology—General — M,D
Public Policy — M,D
Statistics — M
Systems Engineering — M,D
Urban and Regional Planning — M,D
Urban Design — M,D

GEORGIAN COURT UNIVERSITY

Applied Behavior Analysis — M,O
Business Administration and Management—General — M,O
Clinical Psychology — M,O
Computer Art and Design — M,O
Counseling Psychology — M,O
Counselor Education — M,O
Education—General — M,O
Educational Leadership and Administration — M,O
Educational Media/Instructional Technology — M,O
Health Psychology — M,O
Homeland Security — M,O
Nonprofit Management — M,O
School Psychology — M,O
Special Education — M,O
Theology — M,O

GEORGIA SOUTHERN UNIVERSITY

Accounting — M
Allied Health—General — M,D,O
Applied Economics — M,O
Applied Physics — M
Art/Fine Arts — M
Biological and Biomedical Sciences—General — M
Biostatistics — M,D
Business Administration and Management—General — M
Civil Engineering — M
Clinical Psychology — M,D
Community Health — M
Computer Science — M
Construction Management — M

Counselor Education — M,D
Curriculum and Instruction — M,D
Early Childhood Education — M,D
Education—General — M,D,O
Educational Leadership and Administration — M,D,O
Educational Measurement and Evaluation — M,D
Educational Media/Instructional Technology — M,O
Electrical Engineering — M
Energy and Power Engineering — M
Engineering and Applied Sciences—General — M,O
Engineering Management — M
English Education — M
English — M
Environmental and Occupational Health — M,D,O
Environmental Sciences — O
Epidemiology — M,D
Family Nurse Practitioner Studies — M
Foreign Languages Education — M
Graphic Design — M
Health Education — M,D
Health Services Management and Hospital Administration — M,D
Higher Education — M
History — M,O
Kinesiology and Movement Studies — M,D
Logistics — D
Management Information Systems — M,O
Manufacturing Engineering — M,O
Mathematics — M
Mechanical Engineering — M
Middle School Education — M,O
Multilingual and Multicultural Education — D
Music Education — M
Music — M
Nonprofit Management — O
Nursing Education — O
Nursing—General — D
Nutrition — O
Psychiatric Nursing — M
Psychology—General — M,D
Public Administration — M
Public Health—General — M,D
Public History — M,O
Reading Education — M,O
School Psychology — M,O
Secondary Education — M,O
Sociology — M
Spanish — M
Special Education — M,O
Sports Management — M
Supply Chain Management — D
Systems Engineering — M
Taxation — M

GEORGIA SOUTHWESTERN STATE UNIVERSITY

Business Administration and Management—General — M
Computer Science — M,O
Early Childhood Education — M,O
Education—General — M,O
English Education — M,O
Family Nurse Practitioner Studies — M,O
Health Informatics — M,O
Management Information Systems — M,O
Mathematics Education — M,O
Middle School Education — M,O
Nursing and Healthcare Administration — M,O
Nursing Education — M,O
Nursing Informatics — M,O
Nursing—General — M,O
Special Education — M,O

GEORGIA STATE UNIVERSITY

Accounting — M
Actuarial Science — M
Adult Nursing — M,D,O
African-American Studies — M
Allied Health—General — M
Analytical Chemistry — M,D
Anthropology — M
Art Education — M
Art History — M
Art/Fine Arts — M
Astronomy — D
Athletic Training and Sports Medicine — M
Biochemistry — M,D
Bioinformatics — M,D
Biological and Biomedical Sciences—General — M,D
Biostatistics — M,D
Business Administration and Management—General — M,D
Cell Biology — M,D
Chemistry — M,D
Clinical Psychology — D
Clothing and Textiles — M
Cognitive Sciences — D
Communication Disorders — M,D
Communication—General — M,D
Computer Science — M,D
Counseling Psychology — M,O
Counselor Education — M,O
Criminal Justice and Criminology — M,D,O
Cultural Studies — M,O
Curriculum and Instruction — M,D
Developmental Psychology — D
Early Childhood Education — M,D,O
Economic Development — M,D,O
Economics — M,D

Education of Students with Severe/Multiple Disabilities — M
Education—General — M,D,O
Educational Leadership and Administration — M,D,O
Educational Measurement and Evaluation — M,D
Educational Media/Instructional Technology — M,D
Educational Policy — M,D,O
Educational Psychology — M,D
Elementary Education — M,D,O
Emergency Management — M,D,O
English Education — M,D
English — M,D
Entrepreneurship — M,D
Environmental Biology — M,D
Environmental Management and Policy — M,D,O
Exercise and Sports Science — M
Family Nurse Practitioner Studies — M,D,O
Film, Television, and Video Production — M,D
Finance and Banking — M,D,O
Foreign Languages Education — M,O
Forensic Sciences — M,O
Foundations and Philosophy of Education — M,D
French — M,O
Geochemistry — M,D
Geographic Information Systems — O
Geography — M,D
Geology — M
Geosciences — M,D,O
German — O
Gerontology — M,O
Graphic Design — M
Health Education — M
Health Informatics — M,D,O
Health Services Management and Hospital Administration — M,D,O
Historic Preservation — M,D
History — M,D
Human Development — M,D,O
Human Resources Management — M,D
Human Services — M,O
Industrial and Labor Relations — M,D
Information Science — M,D,O
Insurance — M,D,O
Interior Design — M
International Business — M
Kinesiology and Movement Studies — D
Latin American Studies — M,O
Law — D
Linguistics — M,D
Management Information Systems — M,D,O
Management Strategy and Policy — M,D
Marketing — M,D
Mass Communication — M,D
Mathematics Education — M,D,O
Mathematics — M,D
Media Studies — M,D
Microbiology — M,D
Middle School Education — M,D
Molecular Biology — M,D
Molecular Genetics — M,D
Music Education — M,D,O
Music — M,D,O
Neurobiology — M,D
Neuroscience — D
Nonprofit Management — M,D,O
Nursing and Healthcare Administration — M,D,O
Nursing Informatics — M,D,O
Nursing—General — M,D,O
Nutrition — M
Operations Research — M,D
Organic Chemistry — M,D
Organizational Management — M,D
Pediatric Nursing — M,D,O
Philosophy — M
Photography — M,D
Physical Chemistry — M,D
Physical Education — M
Physical Therapy — D
Physics — M,D
Physiology — M,D
Political Science — M,D
Psychiatric Nursing — M,D,O
Psychology—General — D
Public Administration — M,D
Public Health—General — M,D,O
Public History — M,D
Public Policy — M,D,O
Reading Education — M,D
Real Estate — M,D,O
Rehabilitation Counseling — M
Religion — M
Rhetoric — M,D
School Psychology — M,D,O
Science Education — M,D
Secondary Education — M,D
Social Psychology — D
Social Sciences Education — M,D
Social Work — M,D
Sociology — M,D
Spanish — M,O
Special Education — M,D
Speech and Interpersonal Communication — M,D
Sports Management — M
Statistics — M,D
Taxation — M
Translation and Interpretation — O
Urban and Regional Planning — M,D,O
Urban Education — M,D,O
Women's Health Nursing — M,D,O
Women's Studies — M,O
Writing — M,D

---

*M—masters degree; D—doctorate; O—other advanced degree; *—Close-Up and/or Display*

GERSTNER SLOAN KETTERING GRADUATE SCHOOL OF BIOMEDICAL SCIENCES
Biological and Biomedical Sciences—General	D
Cancer Biology/Oncology	D*

GLION INSTITUTE OF HIGHER EDUCATION
Hospitality Management	M

GLOBAL UNIVERSITY
Missions and Missiology	M,D
Pastoral Ministry and Counseling	M,D
Religious Education	M,D
Theology	M,D

GODDARD COLLEGE
Art Therapy	M
Business Administration and Management—General	M
Clinical Psychology	M
Comparative and Interdisciplinary Arts	M
Education—General	M
Health Promotion	M
Interdisciplinary Studies	M
Psychology—General	M
Sustainability Management	M
Writing	M

GOLDEN GATE UNIVERSITY
Accounting	M,D,O
Advertising and Public Relations	M,D,O
Business Administration and Management—General	M,D,O
Corporate and Organizational Communication	M,D,O
Environmental Law	M,D
Finance and Banking	M,D,O
Forensic Sciences	M,O
Health Informatics	M,D,O
Human Resources Management	M,D,O
Intellectual Property Law	M,D
International Business	M,D,O
Law	M,D
Legal and Justice Studies	M,D
Management Information Systems	M,D,O
Management of Technology	M,D,O
Management Strategy and Policy	M,D,O
Marketing	M,D,O
Psychology—General	M,D,O
Public Administration	M,D,O
Supply Chain Management	M,D,O
Taxation	M,D,O

GOLDEY-BEACOM COLLEGE
Business Administration and Management—General	M
Finance and Banking	M
Health Services Management and Hospital Administration	M
Human Resources Management	M
International Business	M
Management Information Systems	M
Marketing	M
Taxation	M

GOLDFARB SCHOOL OF NURSING AT BARNES-JEWISH COLLEGE
Acute Care/Critical Care Nursing	M
Gerontological Nursing	M
Nurse Anesthesia	M
Nursing and Healthcare Administration	M
Nursing Education	M
Nursing—General	M

GONZAGA UNIVERSITY
Accounting	M
Business Administration and Management—General	M
Education—General	M
Elementary Education	M
Engineering and Applied Sciences—General	M,O
English as a Second Language	M
Law	D
Marriage and Family Therapy	M
Nursing—General	M,D
Organizational Management	M,D
Philosophy	M
Physiology	M,D
Secondary Education	M
Special Education	M
Sports Management	M
Taxation	M
Theology	M

GORDON COLLEGE
Early Childhood Education	M,O
Education—General	M,O
Educational Leadership and Administration	M,O
Elementary Education	M,O
English as a Second Language	M,O
Mathematics Education	M,O
Middle School Education	M,O
Music Education	M
Reading Education	M,O
Secondary Education	M,O
Special Education	M,O

GORDON-CONWELL THEOLOGICAL SEMINARY
Archaeology	M,D
Missions and Missiology	M,D
Pastoral Ministry and Counseling	M,D
Religion	M,D
Theology	M,D

GOSHEN COLLEGE
Environmental Education	M
Family Nurse Practitioner Studies	M
Nursing—General	M

GOUCHER COLLEGE
Arts Administration	M
Biological and Biomedical Sciences—General	O
Business Administration and Management—General	M
Computer Art and Design	M
Cultural Studies	M
Education—General	M,O
Educational Leadership and Administration	M,O
Educational Media/Instructional Technology	M,O
Elementary Education	M,O
Environmental Management and Policy	M
Historic Preservation	M
Middle School Education	M,O
Physical Education	M,O
Reading Education	M,O
Secondary Education	M,O
Special Education	M
Writing	M

GOVERNORS STATE UNIVERSITY
Accounting	M
Addictions/Substance Abuse Counseling	M
Analytical Chemistry	M
Art/Fine Arts	M
Business Administration and Management—General	M
Communication Disorders	M
Communication—General	M
Computer Science	M
Counseling Psychology	M
Criminal Justice and Criminology	M
Early Childhood Education	M
Education—General	M
Educational Leadership and Administration	M,D
English	M
Environmental Biology	M
Film, Television, and Video Production	M
Health Services Management and Hospital Administration	M
Human Services	M,D
Legal and Justice Studies	M
Management Information Systems	M
Media Studies	M
Nursing—General	M
Occupational Therapy	M
Photography	M
Physical Therapy	D
Political Science	M
Psychology—General	M
Public Administration	M
Reading Education	M
Social Work	M
Special Education	M

GRACE COLLEGE
Clinical Psychology	M

GRACE COLLEGE OF DIVINITY
Religion	M

GRACELAND UNIVERSITY (IA)
Curriculum and Instruction	M
Education—General	M
Educational Leadership and Administration	M
Educational Media/Instructional Technology	M
Family Nurse Practitioner Studies	M,D,O
Gerontological Nursing	M,D,O
Nursing Education	M,D,O
Nursing—General	M,D,O
Organizational Management	M,D,O
Reading Education	M
Religion	M
Special Education	M
Theology	M

GRACE MISSION UNIVERSITY
Missions and Missiology	M,D

GRACE SCHOOL OF THEOLOGY
Theology	M

GRACE THEOLOGICAL SEMINARY
Cultural Studies	M,D,O
Missions and Missiology	M,D,O
Pastoral Ministry and Counseling	M,D,O
Theology	M,D,O
Women's Studies	M,D,O

GRACE UNIVERSITY
Counseling Psychology	M
Pastoral Ministry and Counseling	M
Theology	M

THE GRADUATE CENTER, CITY UNIVERSITY OF NEW YORK
Accounting	D
Anthropology	D
Archaeology	D
Architectural History	D
Art History	D
Biochemistry	D
Biological and Biomedical Sciences—General	D
Biomedical Engineering	D
Biopsychology	D
Business Administration and Management—General	D
Chemical Engineering	D
Chemistry	D
Civil Engineering	D
Classics	M,D
Clinical Psychology	D
Cognitive Sciences	D
Communication Disorders	D
Comparative Literature	M,D
Computer Science	D
Criminal Justice and Criminology	D
Cultural Anthropology	D
Developmental Psychology	D
Economics	D
Educational Psychology	D
Electrical Engineering	D
Engineering and Applied Sciences—General	D
English	D
Environmental Sciences	D
Experimental Psychology	D
Finance and Banking	D
French	D
Geosciences	D
German	M,D
Hispanic and Latin American Languages	D
History	D
Industrial and Organizational Psychology	D
Interdisciplinary Studies	M,D
Italian	M,D
Liberal Studies	M
Linguistics	M,D
Management Information Systems	D
Mathematics	D
Mechanical Engineering	D
Medieval and Renaissance Studies	M,D
Music	D
Neuroscience	D
Nursing—General	D
Organizational Behavior	D
Philosophy	M,D
Physical Therapy	D
Physics	D
Political Science	M,D
Psychology—General	D
Public Health—General	D
Public Policy	M,D
Social Psychology	D
Social Work	D
Sociology	D
Theater	D
Urban Education	D
Urban Studies	M,D
Women's Studies	M,D

GRADUATE INSTITUTE OF APPLIED LINGUISTICS
Linguistics	M,O
Multilingual and Multicultural Education	M,O

GRADUATE THEOLOGICAL UNION
Art History	M,D,O
Cultural Studies	M,D,O
Ethics	M,D,O
Jewish Studies	M,D,O
Religion	M,D,O
Social Sciences	M,D,O
Theology	M,D,O

GRAMBLING STATE UNIVERSITY
Counselor Education	M,D,O
Criminal Justice and Criminology	M,D,O
Curriculum and Instruction	M,D,O
Developmental Education	M,D,O
Education—General	M,D,O
Educational Leadership and Administration	M,D,O
Educational Media/Instructional Technology	M,D,O
English	M,D,O
Family Nurse Practitioner Studies	M,O
Health Services Management and Hospital Administration	M
Higher Education	M,D,O
Human Resources Management	M
Mass Communication	M
Mathematics Education	M,O
Nursing—General	M,O
Political Science	M
Public Administration	M
Reading Education	M,D,O
Science Education	M,D,O
Social Sciences Education	M
Social Work	M
Special Education	M
Sports Management	M
Student Affairs	M,D,O

GRAND CANYON UNIVERSITY
Accounting	M
Acute Care/Critical Care Nursing	M,D,O
Business Administration and Management—General	M,D
Cognitive Sciences	D
Curriculum and Instruction	M,D,O
Database Systems	D
Early Childhood Education	M,D,O
Education of the Gifted	M,D,O
Education—General	M,D,O
Educational Leadership and Administration	M,D,O
Educational Media/Instructional Technology	M,D,O
Elementary Education	M,D,O
Emergency Management	M
English as a Second Language	M
Entrepreneurship	M
Family Nurse Practitioner Studies	M,D,O
Finance and Banking	M
Health Informatics	M,D,O
Health Services Management and Hospital Administration	M
Human Resources Management	M
Industrial and Organizational Psychology	D
Management of Technology	M
Marketing	M
Nursing Education	M,D,O
Nursing—General	M,D,O
Organizational Management	M,D
Pastoral Ministry and Counseling	M
Project Management	M
Psychology—General	D

GRAND RAPIDS THEOLOGICAL SEMINARY OF CORNERSTONE UNIVERSITY
Missions and Missiology	M
Pastoral Ministry and Counseling	M
Religion	M
Religious Education	M
Theology	M

GRAND VALLEY STATE UNIVERSITY
Accounting	M
Adult Education	M
Allied Health—General	M,D
Bioinformatics	M
Biological and Biomedical Sciences—General	M
Biostatistics	M
Business Administration and Management—General	M
Cancer Biology/Oncology	M
Cell Biology	M
Communication Disorders	M
Communication—General	M
Computer Engineering	M
Computer Science	M
Criminal Justice and Criminology	M
Curriculum and Instruction	M
Early Childhood Education	M
Education—General	M
Educational Leadership and Administration	M,O
Educational Media/Instructional Technology	M
Electrical Engineering	M
Elementary Education	M
Engineering and Applied Sciences—General	M
English as a Second Language	M
English Education	M
English	M
Health Services Management and Hospital Administration	M,D
Higher Education	M
Information Science	M
Linguistics	M
Management Information Systems	M
Manufacturing Engineering	M
Mechanical Engineering	M
Medical Informatics	M
Middle School Education	M
Molecular Biology	M
Nonprofit Management	M
Nursing and Healthcare Administration	M,D
Nursing Education	M,D
Nursing—General	M,D
Nutrition	M
Occupational Therapy	M
Physical Therapy	D
Physician Assistant Studies	M
Public Administration	M
Public Health—General	M
Reading Education	M
School Psychology	M,O
Secondary Education	M
Social Work	M
Software Engineering	M
Special Education	M
Taxation	M

GRAND VIEW UNIVERSITY
Athletic Training and Sports Medicine	M,O
Educational Leadership and Administration	M,O
Nursing and Healthcare Administration	M,O
Nursing Education	M,O
Organizational Management	M,O
Sports Management	M,O
Urban Education	M,O

GRANITE STATE COLLEGE
Business Administration and Management—General	M
Organizational Management	M
Project Management	M

GRANTHAM UNIVERSITY
Business Administration and Management—General	M,O
Engineering and Applied Sciences—General	M
Human Resources Development	M,O
Human Resources Management	M,O
Management Information Systems	M,O
Management Strategy and Policy	M,O
Nursing and Healthcare Administration	M
Project Management	M,O

GRATZ COLLEGE
Education—General	M
Educational Leadership and Administration	M,D
Holocaust and Genocide Studies	M,D
Jewish Studies	M,O
Nonprofit Management	M
Religious Education	M,D
Social Work	M,O

GREEN MOUNTAIN COLLEGE
Business Administration and Management—General	M
Environmental Management and Policy	M

GREENSBORO COLLEGE
Education—General	M
Elementary Education	M

English as a Second Language — M
Special Education — M

GREENVILLE COLLEGE
Education—General — M
Elementary Education — M
Pastoral Ministry and Counseling — M
Secondary Education — M

GWYNEDD MERCY UNIVERSITY
Adult Nursing — M,D
Business Administration and
    Management—General — M
Counselor Education — M
Education—General — M
Educational Leadership and
    Administration — M
Family Nurse Practitioner Studies — M,D
Gerontological Nursing — M,D
Health Services Management and
    Hospital Administration — M
Management Strategy and Policy — M
Nursing Education — M,D
Nursing—General — M,D
Oncology Nursing — M,D
Pediatric Nursing — M,D
Special Education — M

HALLMARK UNIVERSITY
Business Administration and
    Management—General — M
International Business — M

HAMLINE UNIVERSITY
Business Administration and
    Management—General — M,D
Education—General — M,D
English as a Second Language — M,D
Environmental Education — M,D
Nonprofit Management — M,D
Public Administration — M,D
Reading Education — M,D
Science Education — M,D
Writing — M

HAMPTON UNIVERSITY
Adult Nursing — M,D
Allied Health—General — M
Applied Mathematics — M
Architecture — M
Atmospheric Sciences — M,D
Biological and Biomedical
    Sciences—General — M
Business Administration and
    Management—General — M,D
Chemistry — M
Communication Disorders — M
Community Health Nursing — M,D
Computational Sciences — M
Computer and Information
    Systems Security — M
Computer Science — M
Counselor Education — M,D,O
Education—General — M,D,O
Educational Leadership and
    Administration — M,D
Elementary Education — M
Environmental Biology — M
Gerontological Nursing — M,D
Medical Physics — M,D
Music Education — M
Nursing—General — M,D
Pastoral Ministry and Counseling — M,D,O
Pediatric Nursing — M,D
Pharmacy — D
Physical Therapy — D
Physics — M,D
Planetary and Space
    Sciences — M,D
Psychiatric Nursing — M,D
Secondary Education — M
Sports Management — M
Statistics — M
Student Affairs — M,D,O
Women's Health Nursing — M,D

HANNIBAL-LAGRANGE UNIVERSITY
Education—General — M
Reading Education — M

HARDING SCHOOL OF THEOLOGY
Pastoral Ministry and Counseling — M,D
Religion — M,D
Theology — M,D

HARDING UNIVERSITY
Allied Health—General — M,D
Art Education — M,O
Business Administration and
    Management—General — M
Communication Disorders — M
Counseling Psychology — M
Counselor Education — M,O
Early Childhood Education — M,O
Education—General — M,O
Educational Leadership and
    Administration — M,O
Elementary Education — M,O
English as a Second Language — M,O
English Education — M,O
Foreign Languages Education — M,O
Health Education — M,O
International Business — M
Marriage and Family Therapy — M
Mathematics Education — M,O
Organizational Management — M
Pastoral Ministry and Counseling — M
Pharmacy — D
Physical Therapy — D
Physician Assistant Studies — M
Reading Education — M,O
Secondary Education — M,O
Social Sciences Education — M,O
Special Education — M,O

HARDIN-SIMMONS UNIVERSITY
Business Administration and
    Management—General — M
Counseling Psychology — M
Counselor Education — M
Education of the Gifted — M
Education—General — M,D
Educational Leadership and
    Administration — D
English — M
Environmental Management
    and Policy — M
Family Nurse Practitioner Studies — M
History — M
Kinesiology and Movement Studies — M
Marriage and Family Therapy — M
Maternal and Child/Neonatal
    Nursing — M
Mathematics — M
Music Education — M
Music — M
Nursing—General — M
Pastoral Ministry and Counseling — M,D
Physical Therapy — D
Psychology—General — M
Reading Education — M
Recreation and Park Management — M
Religion — M
Science Education — M,D
Sports Management — M
Theology — M,D

HARRISBURG UNIVERSITY OF SCIENCE AND TECHNOLOGY
Computer and Information
    Systems Security — M
Educational Media/Instructional
    Technology — M
Entrepreneurship — M
Management Information Systems — M
Management of Technology — M
Management Strategy and Policy — M
Project Management — M
Software Engineering — M
Systems Engineering — M
Systems Science — M

HARRISON MIDDLETON UNIVERSITY
Comparative Literature — M,D
Education—General — M,D
Humanities — M,D
Interdisciplinary Studies — M,D
Legal and Justice Studies — M,D
Philosophy — M,D
Religion — M,D
Science Education — M,D
Social Sciences — M,D

HARTFORD SEMINARY
Pastoral Ministry and Counseling — M,D,O
Religion — M,D,O
Theology — M,D,O

HARVARD UNIVERSITY
Accounting — D
African Studies — D
African-American Studies — D
Allopathic Medicine — D
American Studies — D
Anthropology — M,D
Applied Mathematics — M,D
Applied Physics — M,D
Applied Science and
    Technology — M,O
Archaeology — M,D
Architectural History — D
Architecture — M,D
Art Education — M
Art History — D
Asian Languages — M,D
Asian Studies — M,D
Astronomy — D
Astrophysics — D
Biochemistry — D
Bioengineering — M,D
Biological and Biomedical
    Sciences—General — M,D,O
Biomedical Engineering — D
Biophysics — D*
Biopsychology — D
Biostatistics — M,D
Biotechnology — M,O
Business Administration and
    Management—General — M,D,O
Cell Biology — D
Celtic Languages — D
Chemical Physics — D
Chemistry — D
Chinese — D
Classics — D
Cognitive Sciences — M,D
Communication—General — M,O
Comparative Literature — D
Computational Biology — M
Computational Sciences — M,D
Computer Science — M,D
Curriculum and Instruction — M
Demography and Population Studies — M,D
Dentistry — M,D,O
Developmental Psychology — D
East European and Russian Studies — M
Economics — D
Education—General — M,D
Educational Leadership and
    Administration — M,D
Educational Media/Instructional
    Technology — M,O
Educational Policy — M
Educational Psychology — M
Electrical Engineering — M,D
Engineering and Applied
    Sciences—General — M,D

Engineering Design — M,D
English — M,D,O
Environmental and Occupational
    Health — M,D
Environmental Engineering — M,D
Environmental Management
    and Policy — M,O
Environmental Sciences — M,D
Epidemiology — M,D
Evolutionary Biology — D
Experimental Psychology — D
Forestry — M
Foundations and Philosophy of
    Education — M,O
French — M,D
Genetics — D
Genomic Sciences — D
Geosciences — M,D
German — D
Health Promotion — M,D
Health Services Management and
    Hospital Administration — M,D
History of Science and Technology — M,D
History — D
Human Development — M
Industrial and Manufacturing
    Management — D
Information Science — M,D,O
Inorganic Chemistry — D
International Affairs — D
International and Comparative
    Education — M
International Development — M
International Health — M,D
Italian — M,D
Japanese — D
Jewish Studies — M,D
Journalism — M,O
Landscape Architecture — M,D
Law — M,D
Legal and Justice Studies — D
Liberal Studies — M,O
Linguistics — D
Management of Technology — D
Management Strategy and Policy — D
Marketing — D
Materials Sciences — M,D
Mathematics Education — M,O
Mathematics — D
Mechanical Engineering — M,D
Medical Physics — D
Medieval and Renaissance Studies — D
Microbiology — D
Molecular Biology — D
Molecular Genetics — D
Molecular Pharmacology — D
Museum Studies — M,O
Music — M,D
Near and Middle Eastern Languages — M,D
Near and Middle Eastern Studies — M,D
Neurobiology — D
Neuroscience — D
Nutrition — D
Oral and Dental Sciences — M,D,O
Organic Chemistry — D
Organizational Behavior — D
Pathology — D
Philosophy — M,D
Physical Chemistry — D
Physics — D
Physiology — M,D
Planetary and Space
    Sciences — M,D
Political Science — M,D
Portuguese — M,D
Psychology—General — D
Public Administration — M
Public Health—General — M,D*
Public Policy — M
Reading Education — M
Religion — D
Russian — D
Scandinavian Languages — D
Slavic Languages — D
Social Psychology — D
Sociology — D
Spanish — M,D
Statistics — M,D
Structural Biology — D
Systems Biology — D
Technical Communication — M
Theology — M
Theoretical Physics — D
Urban and Regional Planning — M,D
Urban Design — M

HASTINGS COLLEGE
Education—General — M

HAWAI'I PACIFIC UNIVERSITY
Accounting — M
Business Administration and
    Management—General — M
Clinical Psychology — M
Communication—General — M
Economics — M
Elementary Education — M
English as a Second Language — M
Finance and Banking — M
Hospitality Management — M
Human Resources Management — M
International Business — M
Liberal Studies — M
Management Information Systems — M
Marine Sciences — M
Marketing — M
Military and Defense Studies — M
Nursing—General — M
Organizational Management — M
Public Health—General — M
Secondary Education — M

Social Work — M
Sustainable Development — M

HAZELDEN GRADUATE SCHOOL OF ADDICTION STUDIES
Addictions/Substance Abuse
    Counseling — M,O

HEBREW COLLEGE
Early Childhood Education — M,O
Education—General — M,O
Jewish Studies — M,O
Middle School Education — M,O
Music Education — M,O
Music — M,O
Religious Education — M,O
Special Education — M,O
Theology — M

HEBREW UNION COLLEGE–JEWISH INSTITUTE OF RELIGION (NY)
Education—General — M
Jewish Studies — M
Music — M
Near and Middle Eastern Languages — D
Nonprofit Management — M
Religious Education — M
Theology — M,D

HEC MONTREAL
Accounting — M,O
Applied Economics — M
Arts Administration — O
Business Administration and
    Management—General — M,D,O
Corporate and Organizational
    Communication — O
Electronic Commerce — M,O
Finance and Banking — M,O
Financial Engineering — M
Human Resources Management — M
Industrial and Manufacturing
    Management — M
International Business — M
Logistics — M
Management Information Systems — M
Management Strategy and Policy — M
Marketing — M
Operations Research — M
Organizational Management — M
Supply Chain Management — M,O
Sustainable Development — O
Taxation — M,O

HEIDELBERG UNIVERSITY
Business Administration and
    Management—General — M
Clinical Psychology — M
Counseling Psychology — M
Education—General — M
Music Education — M
School Psychology — M

HENDERSON STATE UNIVERSITY
Business Administration and
    Management—General — M
Counseling Psychology — M,O
Counselor Education — M,O
Curriculum and Instruction — M,O
Early Childhood Education — M,O
Education—General — M,O
Educational Leadership and
    Administration — M,O
English as a Second Language — M,O
Liberal Studies — M
Middle School Education — M,O
Physical Education — M
Special Education — M,O
Sports Management — M

HENDRIX COLLEGE
Accounting — M

HENLEY-PUTNAM UNIVERSITY
Conflict Resolution and
    Mediation/Peace Studies — M
Homeland Security — M
Military and Defense Studies — M
National Security — D

HERITAGE CHRISTIAN UNIVERSITY
Classics — M
Pastoral Ministry and Counseling — M
Religion — M

HERITAGE COLLEGE AND SEMINARY
Theology — M,O

HERITAGE UNIVERSITY
Counselor Education — M
Education—General — M
Educational Leadership and
    Administration — M
English as a Second Language — M
English — M
Multilingual and Multicultural
    Education — M
Reading Education — M
Science Education — M
Special Education — M

HERZING UNIVERSITY ONLINE
Accounting — M
Business Administration and
    Management—General — M
Health Services Management and
    Hospital Administration — M
Human Resources Management — M
Management of Technology — M
Marketing — M
Nursing and Healthcare
    Administration — M
Nursing Education — M
Nursing—General — M
Project Management — M

M—masters degree; D—doctorate; O—other advanced degree; *—Close-Up and/or Display

HIGH POINT UNIVERSITY
Business Administration and Management—General	M
Corporate and Organizational Communication	M
Education—General	M
Educational Leadership and Administration	M
Elementary Education	M
History	M
Mathematics Education	M
Nonprofit Management	M
Secondary Education	M
Special Education	M

HILBERT COLLEGE
Criminal Justice and Criminology	M
Health Services Management and Hospital Administration	M
Public Administration	M

HILLSDALE COLLEGE
Political Science	M,D

HIRAM COLLEGE
Interdisciplinary Studies	M

HODGES UNIVERSITY
Accounting	M
Business Administration and Management—General	M
Clinical Psychology	M
Counseling Psychology	M
Health Services Management and Hospital Administration	M
Legal and Justice Studies	M
Management Information Systems	M

HOFSTRA UNIVERSITY
Accounting	M,O
Addictions/Substance Abuse Counseling	M,O
Advertising and Public Relations	M
Allopathic Medicine	D
Applied Behavior Analysis	M,D,O
Art Education	M,D,O
Art Therapy	M,O
Biological and Biomedical Sciences—General	M
Business Administration and Management—General	M,O
Business Education	M,D,O
Clinical Psychology	M,D
Communication Disorders	M,D,O
Computer and Information Systems Security	M
Counseling Psychology	M,O
Counselor Education	M,O
Early Childhood Education	M,D,O
Education of the Gifted	M,D,O
Education—General	M,D,O
Educational Leadership and Administration	M,D,O
Educational Media/Instructional Technology	M,D,O
Elementary Education	M,D,O
Engineering and Applied Sciences—General	M
English as a Second Language	M,D,O
English Education	M,D,O
English	M
Entertainment Management	M,O
Exercise and Sports Science	M
Family and Consumer Sciences-General	M,D,O
Family Nurse Practitioner Studies	M
Finance and Banking	M,O
Foreign Languages Education	M,D,O
Gerontological Nursing	M
Health Education	M,D,O
Health Informatics	M
Health Law	M,D
Health Services Management and Hospital Administration	M,O
Human Development	M,D,O
Human Resources Management	M,O
Humanities	M,D,O
Industrial and Organizational Psychology	M,D
International Business	M,O
Internet Engineering	M
Investment Management	M,O
Journalism	M
Law	M,D
Legal and Justice Studies	M,D
Linguistics	M,D,O
Management Information Systems	M,O
Management Strategy and Policy	M,O
Marketing Research	M,O
Marketing	M,O
Marriage and Family Therapy	M,O
Mathematics Education	M,D,O
Medical Physics	M
Middle School Education	M,D,O
Molecular Medicine	D
Multilingual and Multicultural Education	M,D,O
Music Education	M,D,O
Nursing—General	M
Occupational Therapy	M
Physical Education	M,D,O
Physician Assistant Studies	M
Psychiatric Nursing	M
Psychology—General	M,D
Public Health—General	M
Quality Management	M,O
Quantitative Analysis	M,O
Reading Education	M,D,O
Rehabilitation Counseling	M,O
School Psychology	M,D
Science Education	M,D,O
Secondary Education	M,D,O
Social Psychology	M,D
Social Sciences Education	M,D,O
Special Education	M,D,O
Sports Management	M,O

HOLLINS UNIVERSITY
Art/Fine Arts	M
Dance	M
Education—General	M
English	M
Film, Television, and Video Production	M
Film, Television, and Video Theory and Criticism	M
Humanities	M
Illustration	M
Interdisciplinary Studies	M
Liberal Studies	M
Music	M
Social Sciences	M
Theater	M,O
Writing	M,O

HOLMES INSTITUTE
Pastoral Ministry and Counseling	M

HOLY APOSTLES COLLEGE AND SEMINARY
Theology	M,O

HOLY CROSS GREEK ORTHODOX SCHOOL OF THEOLOGY
Theology	M

HOLY FAMILY UNIVERSITY
Accounting	M,D
Business Administration and Management—General	M
Counseling Psychology	M,D
Criminal Justice and Criminology	M,D
Early Childhood Education	M
Education—General	M,D
Educational Leadership and Administration	M,D
Elementary Education	M
English as a Second Language	M
Finance and Banking	M
Health Services Management and Hospital Administration	M
Human Resources Management	M
Management Information Systems	M
Nursing and Healthcare Administration	M,D
Nursing Education	M
Nursing—General	M
Reading Education	M
Special Education	M

HOLY NAMES UNIVERSITY
Business Administration and Management—General	M
Counseling Psychology	M
Education—General	M,O
Educational Psychology	M,O
Family Nurse Practitioner Studies	M,O
Finance and Banking	M
Forensic Psychology	M
Marketing	M
Music Education	M,O
Music	M,O
Nursing and Healthcare Administration	M,O
Nursing Informatics	M,O
Nursing—General	M,O
Pastoral Ministry and Counseling	M
Special Education	M,O
Urban Education	M,O
Writing	M

HOOD COLLEGE
Accounting	M
Art/Fine Arts	M,O
Bioinformatics	M,O
Biological and Biomedical Sciences—General	M
Biotechnology	M
Business Administration and Management—General	M
Clinical Psychology	M
Computer and Information Systems Security	M,O
Computer Science	M,O
Curriculum and Instruction	M,O
Education—General	M,O
Educational Leadership and Administration	M,O
Elementary Education	M,O
Environmental Biology	M
Finance and Banking	M
Human Development	M
Human Resources Management	M
Humanities	M
Immunology	M
Information Science	M,O
Management Information Systems	M
Marketing	M
Mathematics Education	M,O
Microbiology	M
Molecular Biology	M
Organizational Management	D
Psychology—General	M
Public Administration	M
Reading Education	M,O
School Psychology	M
Science Education	M,O
Secondary Education	M,O
Special Education	M,O
Systems Science	M

HOOD THEOLOGICAL SEMINARY
Theology	M,D

HOPE INTERNATIONAL UNIVERSITY
Education—General	M
Educational Leadership and Administration	M
Elementary Education	M

International Business	M
International Development	M
Marketing	M
Marriage and Family Therapy	M
Missions and Missiology	M
Music	M
Nonprofit Management	M
Religion	M
Secondary Education	M

HOUGHTON COLLEGE
Music	M

HOUSTON BAPTIST UNIVERSITY
Art/Fine Arts	M
Business Administration and Management—General	M
Counseling Psychology	M
Counselor Education	M,D
Curriculum and Instruction	M,D
Education—General	M,D
Educational Leadership and Administration	M,D
Educational Measurement and Evaluation	M,D
English as a Second Language	M,D
English Education	M
Human Resources Management	M
International Business	M
Liberal Studies	M
Near and Middle Eastern Languages	M
Pastoral Ministry and Counseling	M
Philosophy	M
Psychology—General	M
Reading Education	M,D
School Psychology	M
Theology	M

HOUSTON GRADUATE SCHOOL OF THEOLOGY
Pastoral Ministry and Counseling	M
Theology	M,D

HOWARD PAYNE UNIVERSITY
Business Administration and Management—General	M
Criminal Justice and Criminology	M
Educational Leadership and Administration	M
Pastoral Ministry and Counseling	M
Sports Management	M
Theology	M

HOWARD UNIVERSITY
Accounting	M
African Studies	M,D
Allopathic Medicine	D
Analytical Chemistry	M,D
Anatomy	M,D
Applied Arts and Design—General	M
Applied Mathematics	M,D
Art History	M
Art/Fine Arts	M
Atmospheric Sciences	M,D
Biochemistry	M,D
Biological and Biomedical Sciences—General	M,D
Biophysics	D
Biopsychology	M,D
Biotechnology	M,D
Business Administration and Management—General	M
Chemical Engineering	M
Chemistry	M,D
Civil Engineering	M
Clinical Psychology	M,D
Communication Disorders	M,D
Communication—General	M,D
Computer Science	M
Corporate and Organizational Communication	M,D
Counseling Psychology	D
Counselor Education	M
Dentistry	D,O
Developmental Psychology	M,D
Economics	M,D
Education—General	M,D,O
Educational Leadership and Administration	M,D,O
Educational Policy	M,D,O
Educational Psychology	D
Electrical Engineering	M,D
Elementary Education	M
Engineering and Applied Sciences—General	M,D
English	M,D
Environmental Sciences	M,D
Exercise and Sports Science	M
Experimental Psychology	M,D
Family Nurse Practitioner Studies	M
Film, Television, and Video Production	M
Finance and Banking	M
French	M
Health Education	M
History	M,D
Human Resources Management	M
Inorganic Chemistry	M,D
International Business	M
Law	M,D
Leisure Studies	M
Management Information Systems	M
Marketing	M
Mass Communication	M,D
Mathematics	M,D
Mechanical Engineering	M,D
Media Studies	M,D
Microbiology	D
Molecular Biology	M,D
Multilingual and Multicultural Education	M,D
Music Education	M
Music	M
Nursing Education	M
Nursing—General	M
Nutrition	M,D

Oral and Dental Sciences	D,O
Organic Chemistry	M,D
Pharmacology	M,D
Pharmacy	D
Philosophy	M
Photography	M
Physical Chemistry	M,D
Physical Education	M
Physics	M,D
Physiology	D
Political Science	M,D
Psychology—General	M,D
Public Administration	M
Public Health—General	M
School Psychology	M,D
Secondary Education	M
Social Psychology	M,D
Social Work	M,D
Sociology	M,D
Spanish	M
Special Education	M
Sports Management	M
Supply Chain Management	M
Theology	M,D

HULT INTERNATIONAL BUSINESS SCHOOL (UNITED STATES)
Business Administration and Management—General	M
Entrepreneurship	M
Finance and Banking	M
International Business	M
Management Strategy and Policy	M
Marketing	M
Project Management	M

HUMBOLDT STATE UNIVERSITY
Anthropology	M
Biological and Biomedical Sciences—General	M
Business Administration and Management—General	M
Counseling Psychology	M
Developmental Psychology	M
Education—General	M
English as a Second Language	M
English	M
Environmental Management and Policy	M
Environmental Sciences	M
Fish, Game, and Wildlife Management	M
Forestry	M
Geology	M
Hazardous Materials Management	M
Kinesiology and Movement Studies	M
Natural Resources	M
Psychology—General	M
School Psychology	M
Social Psychology	M
Social Sciences	M
Social Work	M
Sociology	M
Water Resources	M

HUMPHREYS UNIVERSITY
Law	D

HUNTER COLLEGE OF THE CITY UNIVERSITY OF NEW YORK
Accounting	M
Adult Nursing	M
Animal Behavior	M,O
Anthropology	M
Applied Mathematics	M
Applied Social Research	M
Art History	M
Art/Fine Arts	M
Astronomy	M,D
Biochemistry	M,D
Bioinformatics	M
Biological and Biomedical Sciences—General	M,D
Chemistry	M,D
Chinese	M
Classics	M
Communication Disorders	M
Community Health Nursing	M
Comparative Literature	M
Counselor Education	M
Early Childhood Education	M,D,O
Economics	M
Education of Students with Severe/Multiple Disabilities	M
Education—General	M,D,O
Educational Leadership and Administration	D,O
Elementary Education	M
English as a Second Language	M
English Education	M
Foreign Languages Education	M
French	M
Geographic Information Systems	M,O
Geography	M,O
Geosciences	M
Gerontological Nursing	M
History	M
Italian	M
Mathematics Education	M
Mathematics	M
Media Studies	M
Multilingual and Multicultural Education	M
Music Education	M
Music	M
Nursing—General	M,O
Nutrition	M
Physical Therapy	D
Physics	M,D
Psychiatric Nursing	M
Psychology—General	M,O
Public Health—General	M
Rehabilitation Counseling	M
Romance Languages	M

Science Education M
Secondary Education M
Social Sciences Education M
Social Work M
Sociology M
Spanish M
Special Education M
Statistics M
Sustainable Development M,O
Theater M
Urban and Regional Planning M
Urban Studies M
Writing M

HUNTINGTON COLLEGE OF HEALTH SCIENCES
Nutrition M,D

HUNTINGTON UNIVERSITY
Education—General M,D
English as a Second Language M,D
Middle School Education M,D
Missions and Missiology M,D
Pastoral Ministry and Counseling M,D

HUSSON UNIVERSITY
Biotechnology M
Business Administration and Management—General M
Clinical Psychology M
Community Health Nursing M,O
Counseling Psychology M
Counselor Education M
Criminal Justice and Criminology M
Family Nurse Practitioner Studies M,O
Health Services Management and Hospital Administration M
Hospitality Management M
Nursing—General M,O
Organizational Management M
Pharmacology M,D
Pharmacy M,D
Physical Therapy D
School Psychology M
Social Psychology M
Sports Management M

HUSTON-TILLOTSON UNIVERSITY
Educational Leadership and Administration M

ICAHN SCHOOL OF MEDICINE AT MOUNT SINAI
Allopathic Medicine D
Bioethics M
Biological and Biomedical Sciences—General M,D
Clinical Research M,D
Community Health M,D
Genetic Counseling M,D
Neuroscience M,D
Public Health—General M,D

IDAHO STATE UNIVERSITY
Allied Health—General M,D,O
Anthropology M
Applied Physics M,D
Art/Fine Arts M
Biological and Biomedical Sciences—General M,D
Business Administration and Management—General M,O
Chemistry M
Civil Engineering M
Clinical Psychology D
Communication Disorders M,D,O
Community Health O
Counseling Psychology M,D,O
Counselor Education M,D,O
Curriculum and Instruction M,O
Dental Hygiene M
Dentistry O
Education—General M,D,O
Educational Leadership and Administration M,D,O
Educational Media/Instructional Technology M,D,O
Elementary Education M,O
Engineering and Applied Sciences—General M,D
English as a Second Language M,D,O
English M,D,O
Environmental Engineering M
Environmental Management and Policy M
Environmental Sciences M,O
Experimental Psychology D
Geographic Information Systems M,O
Geology M,O
Geophysics M,O
Geosciences M,O
Hazardous Materials Management M
Health Education M
Health Physics/Radiological Health M,D
History M
Hydrology M,O
Interdisciplinary Studies M
Management Information Systems M,O
Management of Technology M
Marriage and Family Therapy M,D,O
Mathematics Education M
Mathematics M
Mechanical Engineering M
Medical Microbiology M,D
Medicinal and Pharmaceutical Chemistry M,D
Microbiology M,D
Nuclear Engineering M,D
Nursing—General M,D
Nutrition M,O
Occupational Therapy M
Operations Research M

Oral and Dental Sciences O
Pharmaceutical Administration M,D
Pharmaceutical Sciences M,D
Pharmacology M,D
Pharmacy M,D
Physical Education M
Physical Therapy D
Physician Assistant Studies M
Physics M,D
Political Science M,D
Psychology—General D
Public Administration M
Public Health—General M,O
Reading Education M,O
Rhetoric M
School Psychology M,D,O
Secondary Education M,O
Sociology M
Special Education M,D,O
Speech and Interpersonal Communication M
Theater M
Vocational and Technical Education M

IGLOBAL UNIVERSITY
Accounting M
Business Administration and Management—General M
Database Systems M
Entrepreneurship M
Finance and Banking M
Health Services Management and Hospital Administration M
Hospitality Management M
Human Resources Management M
International Business M
Management Information Systems M
Project Management M
Public Administration M
Travel and Tourism M

ILIFF SCHOOL OF THEOLOGY
Pastoral Ministry and Counseling M,D
Religion M,D
Theology M,D

ILLINOIS COLLEGE
Education—General M

ILLINOIS COLLEGE OF OPTOMETRY
Optometry D

ILLINOIS INSTITUTE OF TECHNOLOGY
Aerospace/Aeronautical Engineering M,D
Agricultural Engineering M
Analytical Chemistry M,D
Applied Arts and Design—General M,D
Applied Mathematics M,D
Applied Physics M,D
Architectural Engineering M,D
Architecture M,D
Artificial Intelligence/Robotics M,D
Biochemistry M,D
Bioengineering M,D
Biological and Biomedical Sciences—General M,D
Biomedical Engineering M,D
Business Administration and Management—General M,D
Cell Biology M,D
Chemical Engineering M,D
Chemistry M,D
Civil Engineering M,D
Clinical Psychology M,D
Communication—General M,D
Computer and Information Systems Security M,D
Computer Education M,D
Computer Engineering M,D
Computer Science M,D
Construction Engineering M,D
Construction Management M,D
Corporate and Organizational Communication M
Database Systems M,D
Electrical Engineering M,D
Engineering and Applied Sciences—General M,D
Entrepreneurship M
Environmental Engineering M,D
Environmental Management and Policy M
Finance and Banking M,D
Food Science and Technology M
Geotechnical Engineering M,D
Health Physics/Radiological Health M,D
Human Resources Development M,D
Humanities M,D
Industrial and Manufacturing Management M
Industrial and Organizational Psychology M,D
Inorganic Chemistry M,D
Landscape Architecture M,D
Law M,D
Legal and Justice Studies M,D
Management Information Systems M,D
Manufacturing Engineering M,D
Marketing M
Materials Engineering M,D
Materials Sciences M,D
Mathematical and Computational Finance M,D
Mathematics Education M,D
Mechanical Engineering M,D
Medical Imaging M,D
Microbiology M,D
Molecular Biology M,D
Molecular Biophysics M,D
Physics M,D

Psychology—General M,D
Public Administration M
Rehabilitation Counseling M,D
Science Education M,D
Software Engineering M,D
Structural Engineering M,D
Sustainability Management M
Taxation M,D
Technical Writing M,D
Telecommunications M,D
Transportation and Highway Engineering M,D

ILLINOIS STATE UNIVERSITY
Accounting M
Agricultural Economics and Agribusiness M
Agricultural Sciences—General M
Animal Behavior M,D
Archaeology M
Art History M
Art/Fine Arts M
Bacteriology M,D
Biochemistry M,D
Biological and Biomedical Sciences—General M,D
Biophysics M,D
Biotechnology M
Botany M,D
Business Administration and Management—General M
Cell Biology M,D
Chemistry M
Clinical Psychology M,D,O
Cognitive Sciences M,D,O
Communication Disorders M
Communication—General M
Conservation Biology M,D
Counseling Psychology M,D,O
Criminal Justice and Criminology M,D
Curriculum and Instruction M,D
Developmental Biology M,D
Developmental Psychology M,D,O
Ecology M,D
Economics M
Education—General M,D,O
Educational Leadership and Administration M,D
Educational Policy M,D
English M,D,O
Entomology M,D
Evolutionary Biology M,D
Family and Consumer Sciences-General M
Family Nurse Practitioner Studies M,D,O
French M
Genetics M,D
German M
Graphic Design M
Health Education M
Higher Education M,D
History M
Hydrogeology O
Hydrology O
Immunology M,D
Industrial and Organizational Psychology M,D,O
Industrial/Management Engineering M
Management Information Systems M
Management of Technology M
Mathematics Education M,D
Mathematics M
Microbiology M,D
Molecular Biology M,D
Molecular Genetics M,D
Music M
Neurobiology M,D
Neuroscience M,D
Nursing—General M,D,O
Parasitology M,D
Photography M
Physical Education M
Physiology M,D
Plant Biology M,D
Plant Molecular Biology M,D
Plant Sciences M,D
Political Science M
Psychology—General M,D,O
Reading Education M
School Psychology D,O
Social Work M
Sociology M
Spanish M
Special Education M,D,O
Structural Biology M,D
Student Affairs M
Textile Design M
Theater M
Writing O
Zoology M,D

IMCA–INTERNATIONAL MANAGEMENT CENTRES ASSOCIATION
Business Administration and Management—General M

IMMACULATA UNIVERSITY
Clinical Psychology M,D,O
Counseling Psychology M,D,O
Educational Leadership and Administration M,D,O
Educational Psychology M,D,O
English as a Second Language M
Forensic Psychology M,D,O
Health Promotion M
Multilingual and Multicultural Education M
Neuroscience M,D,O
Nursing and Healthcare Administration M

Nursing Education M
Nursing—General M
Nutrition M
Organizational Management M
Psychoanalysis and Psychotherapy M,D,O
Psychology—General M,D,O
School Psychology M,D,O
Secondary Education M,D,O
Special Education M,D,O
Therapies—Dance, Drama, and Music M

INDEPENDENCE UNIVERSITY
Business Administration and Management—General M
Community Health Nursing M
Community Health M
Gerontological Nursing M
Health Promotion M
Health Services Management and Hospital Administration M
Nursing and Healthcare Administration M
Nursing—General M
Public Health—General M

INDIANA STATE UNIVERSITY
Art/Fine Arts M
Athletic Training and Sports Medicine M,D
Biological and Biomedical Sciences—General M,D
Business Administration and Management—General M
Cell Biology M,D
Clinical Psychology M,D,O
Communication Disorders M,D,O
Communication—General M
Computer Engineering M
Computer Science M
Counselor Education M,D,O
Criminal Justice and Criminology M
Curriculum and Instruction M,D
Ecology M,D
Education—General M,D,O
Educational Leadership and Administration M,D,O
Educational Media/Instructional Technology M,D
Engineering and Applied Sciences—General M
English as a Second Language M,D,O
English M
Environmental and Occupational Health M
Evolutionary Biology M,D
Family Nurse Practitioner Studies M,D
Foreign Languages Education M,D,O
Graphic Design M
Health Education M,D
Higher Education M,D,O
History M
Human Resources Development M
Linguistics M,D,O
Management of Technology M,D
Mathematics M
Media Studies M
Molecular Biology M,D
Multilingual and Multicultural Education M,D,O
Music Education M
Music M
Nursing and Healthcare Administration M,D
Nursing Education M,D
Nursing—General M,D
Occupational Therapy M,D
Photography M
Physical Education M,D
Physical Therapy M,D
Physician Assistant Studies M,D
Physiology M,D
Psychology—General M,D
Public Administration M
Recreation and Park Management M,D
School Psychology M,D,O
Science Education M,D
Social Work M
Spanish M,D,O
Sports Management M,D
Student Affairs M,D,O
Vocational and Technical Education M
Writing M

INDIANA TECH
Accounting M
Business Administration and Management—General M
Engineering Management M
Health Services Management and Hospital Administration M
Human Resources Development M
Human Resources Management M
International Business D
Marketing M
Organizational Management M
Psychology—General M

INDIANA UNIVERSITY BLOOMINGTON
African Studies M
African-American Studies M,D
Analytical Chemistry M,D
Anthropology M,D
Applied Arts and Design—General M,D
Applied Mathematics M,D
Applied Statistics M,D
Archaeology M,D
Art Education M,D,O
Art/Fine Arts M
Artificial Intelligence/Robotics D
Arts Administration M
Asian Languages M,D

*M—masters degree; D—doctorate; O—other advanced degree; *—Close-Up and/or Display*

Program	Degrees
Asian Studies	M,D
Astronomy	M,D
Astrophysics	M,D
Athletic Training and Sports Medicine	M,D
Biochemistry	M,D
Bioinformatics	M,D,O
Biological and Biomedical Sciences—General	M,D
Biostatistics	M,D
Biotechnology	M,D
Business Administration and Management—General	M,D
Cell Biology	M,D
Chemistry	M,D
Chinese	M,D
Classics	M,D
Cognitive Sciences	D
Communication Disorders	M,D
Community Health	M,D
Comparative Literature	M,D
Computer and Information Systems Security	M,D
Computer Science	M,D,O
Counselor Education	M,D,O
Criminal Justice and Criminology	M,D
Curriculum and Instruction	M,D,O
Database Systems	M,O
Developmental Psychology	M,D
East European and Russian Studies	M,O
Ecology	M,D,O
Economic Development	M,D,O
Economics	M,D
Education—General	M,D,O
Educational Leadership and Administration	M,D,O
Educational Measurement and Evaluation	M,D,O
Educational Media/Instructional Technology	M,D
Educational Policy	M,D,O
Educational Psychology	M,D,O
Elementary Education	M,D,O
Energy Management and Policy	M,D,O
English as a Second Language	M,D
English	M,D
Environmental and Occupational Health	M,D
Environmental Management and Policy	M,D,O
Environmental Sciences	M,D,O
Epidemiology	M,D
Ergonomics and Human Factors	M,D
Evolutionary Biology	M,D
Exercise and Sports Science	M,D
Finance and Banking	M,D,O
Folklore	M,D
Foreign Languages Education	M,D
Foundations and Philosophy of Education	M,D,O
French	M,D
Gender Studies	D
Genetics	M,D
Geochemistry	M,D
Geography	D
Geology	M,D
Geophysics	M,D
Geosciences	M,D
German	M,D
Health Education	M,D
Health Informatics	M,D
Health Promotion	M,D
Health Services Management and Hospital Administration	M,D
Higher Education	M,D,O
Hispanic and Latin American Languages	M,D
History of Science and Technology	M,D
History	M,D,O
Human-Computer Interaction	M,D
Hydrogeology	M,D
Information Science	M,D,O
Inorganic Chemistry	M,D
International and Comparative Education	M,D,O
International Development	M,D,O
Italian	M,D
Japanese	M,D
Jewish Studies	M
Kinesiology and Movement Studies	M,D
Latin American Studies	M
Law	M,D,O
Leisure Studies	M,D
Library Science	M,D,O
Linguistics	M,D
Management Information Systems	M,D
Materials Sciences	M,D
Mathematical Physics	M,D
Mathematics Education	M,D,O
Mathematics	M,D
Media Studies	M,D
Medical Physics	M,D
Medieval and Renaissance Studies	M,D
Microbiology	M,D
Mineralogy	M,D
Molecular Biology	M,D
Multilingual and Multicultural Education	M,D
Music	M,D,O
Near and Middle Eastern Languages	M,D
Neuroscience	D
Nonprofit Management	M,D,O
Nutrition	M,D
Optometry	M,D
Organic Chemistry	M,D
Organizational Management	M,D,O
Philosophy	M,D,O
Physical Chemistry	M,D
Physical Education	M,D
Physics	M,D
Plant Biology	M,D
Political Science	M,D
Portuguese	M,D
Psychology—General	D
Public Administration	M,D,O
Public Affairs	M,D,O
Public Health—General	M,D
Public Policy	M,D,O
Reading Education	M,D,O
Recreation and Park Management	M,D
Religion	M,D
Rhetoric	M,D
Safety Engineering	M,D
School Psychology	M,D,O
Science Education	M,D,O
Secondary Education	M,D,O
Slavic Languages	M,D
Social Psychology	D
Social Sciences Education	M,D,O
Social Sciences	M,D,O
Sociology	M,D
Spanish	M,D
Special Education	M,D,O
Sports Management	M,D
Statistics	M,D
Student Affairs	M,D,O
Sustainability Management	M,D,O
Systems Engineering	D
Theater	M,D,O
Toxicology	M,D,O
Travel and Tourism	M,D
Water Resources Engineering	M,D,O
Western European Studies	M
Writing	M,D
Zoology	M,D

INDIANA UNIVERSITY EAST

Program	Degrees
Education—General	M
Nursing—General	M
Social Work	M

INDIANA UNIVERSITY KOKOMO

Program	Degrees
Accounting	M,O
Business Administration and Management—General	M,O
Family Nurse Practitioner Studies	M
Health Services Management and Hospital Administration	M,O
Nursing and Healthcare Administration	M
Nursing Education	M
Nursing—General	M
Public Administration	M,O
Public Policy	M,O

INDIANA UNIVERSITY NORTHWEST

Program	Degrees
Accounting	M,O
Addictions/Substance Abuse Counseling	M,O
Business Administration and Management—General	M,O
Counseling Psychology	M,O
Criminal Justice and Criminology	M,O
Education—General	M,O
Educational Leadership and Administration	M,O
Elementary Education	M,O
Environmental Management and Policy	M,O
Gender Studies	M,O
Health Services Management and Hospital Administration	M,O
Liberal Studies	M,O
Management Information Systems	M,O
Nonprofit Management	M,O
Public Administration	M,O
Public Affairs	M,O
Secondary Education	M,O
Social Work	M
Urban Studies	M,O

INDIANA UNIVERSITY OF PENNSYLVANIA

Program	Degrees
Adult Education	M
Applied Mathematics	M
Archaeology	M
Art/Fine Arts	M
Biological and Biomedical Sciences—General	M
Business Administration and Management—General	M
Business Education	M
Chemistry	M
Clinical Psychology	M,D
Communication Disorders	M
Communication—General	D
Counselor Education	M
Criminal Justice and Criminology	M,D
Curriculum and Instruction	D
Education—General	M,D,O
Educational Leadership and Administration	D,O
Educational Media/Instructional Technology	M,D
Educational Psychology	M,O
English as a Second Language	M,D
English Education	M,D
English	M,D
Environmental and Occupational Health	M,D
Environmental Management and Policy	M,D
Exercise and Sports Science	M
Foreign Languages Education	M
Geographic Information Systems	M
Geography	M
Health Education	M
Health Services Management and Hospital Administration	M,D
Higher Education	M
Hispanic and Latin American Languages	M
History	M
Human Resources Development	M
Industrial and Labor Relations	M
Mathematics Education	M
Mathematics	M

INDIANA UNIVERSITY–PURDUE UNIVERSITY FORT WAYNE

Program	Degrees
Adult Nursing	M,O
Applied Mathematics	M,O
Applied Statistics	M,O
Biological and Biomedical Sciences—General	M
Business Administration and Management—General	M
Civil Engineering	M
Communication—General	M
Computer Engineering	M
Computer Science	M
Construction Management	M
Counselor Education	M,O
Education—General	M,O
Educational Leadership and Administration	M,O
Electrical Engineering	M
Elementary Education	M
Engineering and Applied Sciences—General	M,O
English as a Second Language	M,O
English Education	M,O
English	M
Facilities Management	M
Family Nurse Practitioner Studies	M,O
Gerontological Nursing	M,O
Industrial/Management Engineering	M
Information Science	M
Marriage and Family Therapy	M,O
Mathematics Education	M,O
Mathematics	M,O
Mechanical Engineering	M
Nursing and Healthcare Administration	M,O
Nursing Education	M,O
Nursing—General	M,O
Operations Research	M,O
Organizational Management	M,O
Public Policy	M,O
Secondary Education	M
Special Education	M
Systems Engineering	M

INDIANA UNIVERSITY–PURDUE UNIVERSITY INDIANAPOLIS

Program	Degrees
Accounting	M
Acute Care/Critical Care Nursing	M
Addictions/Substance Abuse Counseling	M,D
Allopathic Medicine	M,D
Anatomy	M,D
Applied Mathematics	M,D
Applied Statistics	M,D
Art Therapy	M
Art/Fine Arts	M
Biochemistry	M,D
Bioethics	M,D,O
Bioinformatics	M,D
Biological and Biomedical Sciences—General	M,D
Biomedical Engineering	M,D
Biopsychology	M,D
Biostatistics	M,D,O
Business Administration and Management—General	M
Cell Biology	M,D
Chemistry	M,D
Child and Family Studies	M
Clinical Psychology	M,D
Communication—General	M,D
Community Health	M,D,O
Computer and Information Systems Security	M,D,O
Computer Art and Design	M
Computer Engineering	M,D
Computer Science	M,D,O
Counselor Education	M,O
Criminal Justice and Criminology	M,D
Curriculum and Instruction	M,D,O
Database Systems	M,D,O
Dentistry	M,D,O
Early Childhood Education	M,O
Economics	M
Education—General	M,O
Educational Leadership and Administration	M,O
Electrical Engineering	M,D
Emergency Management	M
English as a Second Language	M
English	M,O
Entrepreneurship	M
Environmental and Occupational Health	M,D,O
Epidemiology	M,D,O
Family Nurse Practitioner Studies	M
Finance and Banking	M

INDIANA UNIVERSITY SOUTH BEND

Program	Degrees
Foreign Languages Education	M,O
Forensic Sciences	M
Gender Studies	M
Geographic Information Systems	M,O
Geology	M,D
Geosciences	M,D
Gerontological Nursing	M
Graphic Design	M
Health Communication	M,D
Health Education	M,D
Health Informatics	M,D
Health Law	M,D,O
Health Services Management and Hospital Administration	M,D,O
History	M
Homeland Security	M
Human-Computer Interaction	M
Immunology	M,D
Industrial and Organizational Psychology	M,D
Information Science	M
Intellectual Property Law	M,D,O
Internet and Interactive Multimedia	M,D,O
Kinesiology and Movement Studies	M,O
Law	M,D,O
Liberal Studies	M,D,O
Library Science	M,D,O
Management of Technology	M
Marketing	M
Mathematics Education	M,D
Mathematics	M,D
Mechanical Engineering	M,D
Microbiology	M,D
Molecular Biology	M,D
Molecular Genetics	M,D
Museum Studies	M,D
Music	M,D
Natural Resources	M,D,O
Neurobiology	D
Nonprofit Management	M,O
Nursing and Healthcare Administration	M,D
Nursing Education	M,D
Nursing—General	M,D
Nutrition	M,D
Occupational Therapy	M,D
Organizational Management	M,D
Pathology	M,D
Pediatric Nursing	M
Pharmacology	M,D
Philanthropic Studies	M,D,O
Philosophy	M,D
Photography	M
Physical Education	M,D
Physical Therapy	M,D
Physics	M,D
Political Science	M
Psychology—General	M,D
Public Administration	M,D
Public Affairs	M,O
Public Health—General	M,D,O
Public History	M
Reading Education	M,O
Rehabilitation Sciences	M,D
Social Sciences	M,D,O
Social Work	M,D,O
Sociology	M
Software Engineering	M,D,O
Special Education	M,O
Statistics	M,D
Supply Chain Management	M
Technical Communication	M
Therapies—Dance, Drama, and Music	M,D
Toxicology	M,D
Writing	M,D

INDIANA UNIVERSITY SOUTH BEND

Program	Degrees
Accounting	M,O
Addictions/Substance Abuse Counseling	M,O
Applied Mathematics	M,O
Business Administration and Management—General	M,O
Clinical Psychology	M,D
Communication—General	M,D
Computer Science	M,O
Counseling Psychology	M,O
Counselor Education	M,O
Education—General	M,O
Educational Leadership and Administration	M,O
Educational Media/Instructional Technology	M,O
Elementary Education	M,O
English	M,O
Family Nurse Practitioner Studies	M
Finance and Banking	M,O
Health Services Management and Hospital Administration	M,O
Human Resources Management	M,O
International Affairs	M,O
Legal and Justice Studies	M,O
Liberal Studies	M,O
Marketing	M,O
Marriage and Family Therapy	M,O
Music	M,O
Nonprofit Management	M,O
Nursing—General	M
Public Administration	M,O
Public Affairs	M,O
School Psychology	M,O
Secondary Education	M,O
Social Work	M
Special Education	M,O
Writing	M,O

INDIANA UNIVERSITY SOUTHEAST

Program	Degrees
Business Administration and Management—General	M
Counselor Education	M
Education—General	M
Elementary Education	M
Finance and Banking	M

Interdisciplinary Studies M,O
Secondary Education M

INDIANA WESLEYAN UNIVERSITY
Accounting M,O
Addictions/Substance Abuse
 Counseling M
Business Administration and
 Management—General M,O
Counseling Psychology M
Counselor Education M
Educational Leadership and
 Administration M,O
Health Services Management and
 Hospital Administration M,O
Higher Education M,O
Human Resources Management M,O
Marriage and Family Therapy M
Nursing and Healthcare
 Administration M
Nursing Education M
Nursing—General M
Organizational Management M,D,O
Pastoral Ministry and Counseling M
Social Psychology M
Theology M

INSTITUTE FOR CHRISTIAN STUDIES
Education—General M,D
Philosophy M,D
Political Science M,D
Theology M,D

INSTITUTE FOR CLINICAL SOCIAL WORK
Social Work D

INSTITUTE FOR DOCTORAL STUDIES IN THE VISUAL ARTS
Art/Fine Arts D
Philosophy D

THE INSTITUTE FOR THE PSYCHOLOGICAL SCIENCES
Clinical Psychology M,D

INSTITUTE OF AMERICAN INDIAN ARTS
Writing M

INSTITUTE OF CLINICAL ACUPUNCTURE AND ORIENTAL MEDICINE
Acupuncture and Oriental Medicine M

INSTITUTE OF PUBLIC ADMINISTRATION
Health Services Management and
 Hospital Administration M,O
Public Administration M,O

INSTITUTE OF TAOIST EDUCATION AND ACUPUNCTURE
Acupuncture and Oriental Medicine M

THE INSTITUTE OF WORLD POLITICS
Military and Defense Studies M,O
National Security M,O
Political Science M,O
Public Affairs M,O
Public Policy M,O

INSTITUT FRANCO-EUROPÉEN DE CHIROPRAXIE
Chiropractic D

INSTITUTO CENTROAMERICANO DE ADMINISTRACIÓN DE EMPRESAS
Agricultural Economics and
 Agribusiness M
Business Administration and
 Management—General M
Finance and Banking M
Management of Technology M
Real Estate M
Sustainable Development M

INSTITUTO TECNOLOGICO DE SANTO DOMINGO
Accounting M,O
Adult Education M,O
Allopathic Medicine M,D
Bioethics M,O
Business Administration and
 Management—General M,O
Communication—General M,O
Construction Management M,O
Counseling Psychology M,O
Economics M,O
Education—General M,O
Educational Leadership and
 Administration M,O
Educational Psychology M,O
Energy and Power
 Engineering M,D,O
Energy Management and
 Policy M,D,O
Engineering and Applied
 Sciences—General M,O
Environmental Education M,D,O
Environmental Engineering M,O
Environmental Management
 and Policy M,D,O
Environmental Sciences M,D,O
Finance and Banking M,O
Gender Studies M,O
Health Promotion M,O
Human Resources Management M,O
Humanities M,O
Industrial and Manufacturing
 Management M,O
Industrial/Management
 Engineering M,O
Information Science M,O
International Affairs M,O

International Business M,O
Linguistics M,O
Marine Sciences M,D,O
Marketing M,O
Marriage and Family Therapy M,O
Maternal and Child Health M,O
Mathematics M,D,O
Natural Resources M,D,O
Nutrition M,O
Organizational Management M,O
Quality Management M,O
Quantitative Analysis M,O
Secondary Education M,O
Social Sciences Education M,O
Software Engineering M,O
Structural Engineering M,O
Sustainable Development M,O
Taxation M,O
Telecommunications M,O
Transportation Management M,O

INSTITUTO TECNOLÓGICO Y DE ESTUDIOS SUPERIORES DE MONTERREY, CAMPUS CENTRAL DE VERACRUZ
Business Administration and
 Management—General M
Computer Science M
Education—General M
Educational Leadership and
 Administration M
Educational Media/Instructional
 Technology M
Electronic Commerce M
Finance and Banking M
Humanities M
International Business M
Management Information Systems M
Marketing M

INSTITUTO TECNOLÓGICO Y DE ESTUDIOS SUPERIORES DE MONTERREY, CAMPUS CHIHUAHUA
Computer Engineering M,O
Electrical Engineering M,O
Engineering Management M,O
Industrial/Management
 Engineering M,O
International Business M,O
Mechanical Engineering M,O
Systems Engineering M,O

INSTITUTO TECNOLÓGICO Y DE ESTUDIOS SUPERIORES DE MONTERREY, CAMPUS CIUDAD DE MÉXICO
Business Administration and
 Management—General M,D
Computer Science M,D
Economics M,D
Education—General M,D
Educational Media/Instructional
 Technology M,D
Environmental Engineering M,D
Environmental Sciences M,D
Finance and Banking M,D
Humanities M,D
Industrial/Management
 Engineering M,D
International Business M,D
Law O
Management Information Systems M,D
Quality Management M,D
Telecommunications
 Management M,D

INSTITUTO TECNOLÓGICO Y DE ESTUDIOS SUPERIORES DE MONTERREY, CAMPUS CIUDAD JUÁREZ
Business Administration and
 Management—General M
Education—General M
Educational Leadership and
 Administration M
Educational Media/Instructional
 Technology M,D
Electronic Commerce M
Humanities M
Management Information Systems M
Public Administration M
Quality Management M

INSTITUTO TECNOLÓGICO Y DE ESTUDIOS SUPERIORES DE MONTERREY, CAMPUS CIUDAD OBREGÓN
Business Administration and
 Management—General M
Communication—General M
Developmental Education M
Education—General M
Engineering and Applied
 Sciences—General M
Finance and Banking M
International Affairs M
Management Information Systems M
Marketing M
Mathematics Education M
Telecommunications
 Management M

INSTITUTO TECNOLÓGICO Y DE ESTUDIOS SUPERIORES DE MONTERREY, CAMPUS CUERNAVACA
Business Administration and
 Management—General M
Computer Science M,D
Finance and Banking M
Human Resources Management M
Information Science M,D

International Business M
Management of Technology M,D
Marketing M

INSTITUTO TECNOLÓGICO Y DE ESTUDIOS SUPERIORES DE MONTERREY, CAMPUS ESTADO DE MÉXICO
Architecture M,D
Business Administration and
 Management—General M,D
Computer Science M,D
Education—General M,D
Educational Leadership and
 Administration M,D
Educational Media/Instructional
 Technology M,D
Electronic Commerce M,D
Environmental Management
 and Policy M,D
Finance and Banking M,D
Humanities M,D
Industrial and Manufacturing
 Management M,D
Information Science M,D
Management Information Systems M,D
Marketing M,D
Materials Engineering M,D
Materials Sciences M,D
Quality Management M,D
Telecommunications
 Management M,D

INSTITUTO TECNOLÓGICO Y DE ESTUDIOS SUPERIORES DE MONTERREY, CAMPUS GUADALAJARA
Business Administration and
 Management—General M
Finance and Banking M

INSTITUTO TECNOLÓGICO Y DE ESTUDIOS SUPERIORES DE MONTERREY, CAMPUS IRAPUATO
Architecture M,D
Business Administration and
 Management—General M,D
Computer Science M,D
Education—General M,D
Educational Leadership and
 Administration M,D
Educational Media/Instructional
 Technology M,D
Electronic Commerce M,D
Environmental Management
 and Policy M,D
Finance and Banking M,D
Humanities M,D
Industrial and Manufacturing
 Management M,D
Information Science M,D
International Business M,D
Library Science M,D
Management Information Systems M,D
Management of Technology M,D
Marketing Research M,D
Quality Management M,D
Telecommunications
 Management M,D

INSTITUTO TECNOLÓGICO Y DE ESTUDIOS SUPERIORES DE MONTERREY, CAMPUS LAGUNA
Business Administration and
 Management—General M
Industrial/Management
 Engineering M
Management Information Systems M

INSTITUTO TECNOLÓGICO Y DE ESTUDIOS SUPERIORES DE MONTERREY, CAMPUS LEÓN
Business Administration and
 Management—General M

INSTITUTO TECNOLÓGICO Y DE ESTUDIOS SUPERIORES DE MONTERREY, CAMPUS MONTERREY
Agricultural Engineering M,D
Agricultural Sciences—
 General M,D
Applied Statistics M,D
Artificial Intelligence/Robotics M,D
Biotechnology M,D
Business Administration and
 Management—General M,D
Chemical Engineering M,D
Chemistry M,D
Civil Engineering M,D
Communication—General M
Computer Science M,D
Electrical Engineering M,D
Engineering and Applied
 Sciences—General M,D
Environmental Engineering M,D
Finance and Banking M
Industrial/Management
 Engineering M,D
Information Science M,D
International Business M
Manufacturing Engineering M,D
Marketing M
Mechanical Engineering M,D
Organic Chemistry M,D
Science Education M,D
Systems Engineering M,D

INSTITUTO TECNOLÓGICO Y DE ESTUDIOS SUPERIORES DE MONTERREY, CAMPUS QUERÉTARO
Business Administration and
 Management—General M

INSTITUTO TECNOLÓGICO Y DE ESTUDIOS SUPERIORES DE MONTERREY, CAMPUS SONORA NORTE
Business Administration and
 Management—General M
Education—General M
Information Science M

INSTITUTO TECNOLÓGICO Y DE ESTUDIOS SUPERIORES DE MONTERREY, CAMPUS TOLUCA
Business Administration and
 Management—General M

INTER AMERICAN UNIVERSITY OF PUERTO RICO, AGUADILLA CAMPUS
Accounting M
Business Administration and
 Management—General M
Counseling Psychology M
Criminal Justice and Criminology M
Educational Leadership and
 Administration M
Elementary Education M
Finance and Banking M
Human Resources Management M
Management Information Systems M
Marketing M

INTER AMERICAN UNIVERSITY OF PUERTO RICO, ARECIBO CAMPUS
Accounting M
Acute Care/Critical Care Nursing M
Business Administration and
 Management—General M
Counselor Education M
Curriculum and Instruction M
Education—General M
Educational Leadership and
 Administration M
Elementary Education M
English as a Second Language M
Finance and Banking M
Foreign Languages Education M
Human Resources Management M
Mathematics Education M
Medical/Surgical Nursing M
Nurse Anesthesia M
Nursing—General M
Science Education M
Social Sciences Education M

INTER AMERICAN UNIVERSITY OF PUERTO RICO, BARRANQUITAS CAMPUS
Accounting M
Business Administration and
 Management—General M
Curriculum and Instruction M
Education—General M
Educational Leadership and
 Administration M
Elementary Education M
English as a Second Language M
Finance and Banking M
Foreign Languages Education M
Library Science M
Mathematics Education M
Science Education M
Social Sciences Education M
Special Education M

INTER AMERICAN UNIVERSITY OF PUERTO RICO, BAYAMÓN CAMPUS
Aerospace/Aeronautical
 Engineering M
Biotechnology M
Ecology M
Electrical Engineering M
Energy and Power
 Engineering M
Human Resources Management M
Mechanical Engineering M

INTER AMERICAN UNIVERSITY OF PUERTO RICO, FAJARDO CAMPUS
Business Administration and
 Management—General M
Computer Science M
Educational Leadership and
 Administration M
Elementary Education M
Management Information Systems M
Marketing M
Special Education M

INTER AMERICAN UNIVERSITY OF PUERTO RICO, GUAYAMA CAMPUS
Business Administration and
 Management—General M
Computer and Information
 Systems Security M
Computer Science M
Early Childhood Education M
Elementary Education M
Marketing M

INTER AMERICAN UNIVERSITY OF PUERTO RICO, METROPOLITAN CAMPUS
Accounting M
American Studies M,D
Athletic Training and Sports
 Medicine M
Business Administration and
 Management—General M
Business Education M
Clinical Laboratory
 Sciences/Medical Technology M
Computer Science M
Counseling Psychology M,D

---

*M—masters degree; D—doctorate; O—other advanced degree; *—Close-Up and/or Display*

Counselor Education	M,D
Criminal Justice and Criminology	M
Curriculum and Instruction	M,D
Education—General	M,D
Educational Leadership and Administration	M,D
Educational Media/Instructional Technology	M
Elementary Education	M
English as a Second Language	M
English	M
Environmental Management and Policy	M
Exercise and Sports Science	M
Finance and Banking	M
Foreign Languages Education	M
Health Education	M
Higher Education	M
History	M,D
Human Resources Development	M
Human Resources Management	M
Industrial and Labor Relations	M,D
Industrial and Manufacturing Management	M
Industrial and Organizational Psychology	M,D
International Business	M,D
Management Information Systems	M
Marketing	M
Mathematics Education	M
Microbiology	M
Molecular Biology	M
Music Education	M
Pastoral Ministry and Counseling	D
Physical Education	M
Psychology—General	M,D
Religious Education	D
School Psychology	M,D
Science Education	M
Social Sciences Education	M
Social Work	M
Spanish	M
Special Education	M
Theology	D
Vocational and Technical Education	M
Women's Studies	M

INTER AMERICAN UNIVERSITY OF PUERTO RICO, PONCE CAMPUS

Accounting	M
Criminal Justice and Criminology	M
Elementary Education	M
English as a Second Language	M
Finance and Banking	M
Human Resources Management	M
Marketing	M
Mathematics Education	M
Science Education	M
Social Sciences Education	M
Spanish	M

INTER AMERICAN UNIVERSITY OF PUERTO RICO, SAN GERMÁN CAMPUS

Accounting	M
Applied Mathematics	M
Art/Fine Arts	M
Business Administration and Management—General	M,D
Business Education	M
Counseling Psychology	M,D
Counselor Education	M,D
Curriculum and Instruction	D
Elementary Education	M
English as a Second Language	M
Environmental Sciences	M
Finance and Banking	M,D
Graphic Design	M
Health Education	M
Human Resources Development	M,D
Human Resources Management	M,D
Industrial and Manufacturing Management	M,D
International Business	M,D
Kinesiology and Movement Studies	M
Library Science	M
Management Information Systems	M,D
Marketing	M,D
Mathematics Education	M
Music Education	M
Music	M
Photography	M
Physical Education	M
Psychology—General	M,D
School Psychology	M,D
Science Education	M
Special Education	M

INTER AMERICAN UNIVERSITY OF PUERTO RICO SCHOOL OF LAW

Law	D

INTER AMERICAN UNIVERSITY OF PUERTO RICO SCHOOL OF OPTOMETRY

Optometry	D

INTERDENOMINATIONAL THEOLOGICAL CENTER

Pastoral Ministry and Counseling	M,D
Religious Education	M,D
Theology	M,D

INTERIOR DESIGNERS INSTITUTE

Interior Design	M

INTERNATIONAL BAPTIST COLLEGE AND SEMINARY

Education—General	M
Pastoral Ministry and Counseling	M,D
Theology	M

INTERNATIONAL COLLEGE OF THE CAYMAN ISLANDS

Business Administration and Management—General	M
Business Education	M

Human Resources Management	M

INTERNATIONAL INSTITUTE FOR RESTORATIVE PRACTICES

Organizational Behavior	M,O

INTERNATIONAL TECHNOLOGICAL UNIVERSITY

Business Administration and Management—General	M,D
Computer Art and Design	M
Computer Engineering	M
Electrical Engineering	M,D
Engineering Management	M
Software Engineering	M

INTERNATIONAL UNIVERSITY IN GENEVA

Business Administration and Management—General	M,D
Communication—General	M,D
Entrepreneurship	M,D
International Affairs	M,D
International Business	M,D
Marketing	M,D
Media Studies	M,D
Public Administration	M,D

THE INTERNATIONAL UNIVERSITY OF MONACO

Business Administration and Management—General	M
Entrepreneurship	M
Finance and Banking	M
Financial Engineering	M
International Business	M
Marketing	M

IONA COLLEGE

Accounting	M,O
Advertising and Public Relations	M,O
Business Administration and Management—General	M,O
Communication Disorders	M
Computer and Information Systems Security	M,O
Computer Science	M
Counseling Psychology	M,O
Criminal Justice and Criminology	M,O
Early Childhood Education	M
Education—General	M
Educational Leadership and Administration	M
English Education	M
English	M
Experimental Psychology	M,O
Finance and Banking	M,O
Foreign Languages Education	M
Forensic Sciences	M,O
Game Design and Development	M
Health Services Management and Hospital Administration	M,O
History	M,O
Human Resources Management	M,O
Industrial and Organizational Psychology	M,O
International Business	M,O
Management of Technology	M,O
Marketing	M,O
Marriage and Family Therapy	M
Mass Communication	M,O
Mathematics Education	M
Nonprofit Management	M,O
Project Management	M,O
Psychology—General	M,O
Recreation and Park Management	M,O
School Psychology	M,O
Science Education	M
Social Sciences Education	M
Spanish	M
Special Education	M
Sports Management	M,O

IOWA STATE UNIVERSITY OF SCIENCE AND TECHNOLOGY

Accounting	M
Aerospace/Aeronautical Engineering	M,D
Agricultural Economics and Agribusiness	M,D
Agricultural Education	M,D
Agricultural Engineering	M,D
Agricultural Sciences—General	M,D
Agronomy and Soil Sciences	M,D
Analytical Chemistry	M,D
Animal Sciences	M,D
Anthropology	M
Applied Arts and Design—General	M,D
Applied Mathematics	M,D
Applied Physics	M,D
Architecture	M
Art/Fine Arts	M
Astrophysics	M,D
Bioinformatics	M,D
Biological and Biomedical Sciences—General	M,D
Biophysics	M,D
Biostatistics	M,D
Business Administration and Management—General	M
Cell Biology	M,D
Chemical Engineering	M,D
Chemistry	M,D
Child and Family Studies	M,D
Civil Engineering	M,D
Clothing and Textiles	M,D
Cognitive Sciences	M,D
Computational Biology	M,D
Computer Engineering	M,D
Computer Science	M,D
Condensed Matter Physics	M,D
Construction Engineering	M,D
Corporate and Organizational Communication	M,D

Counseling Psychology	M,D
Counselor Education	M,D
Curriculum and Instruction	M,D
Database Systems	M,D
Developmental Biology	M,D
Ecology	M,D
Economics	M,D
Education—General	M,D
Educational Leadership and Administration	M,D
Educational Measurement and Evaluation	M,D
Educational Media/Instructional Technology	M,D
Electrical Engineering	M,D
Elementary Education	M,D
English as a Second Language	M
English	M,D
Entomology	M,D
Environmental Engineering	M,D
Environmental Sciences	M,D
Evolutionary Biology	M,D
Exercise and Sports Science	M
Family and Consumer Sciences-General	M
Finance and Banking	M
Fish, Game, and Wildlife Management	M,D
Food Science and Technology	M,D
Forestry	M,D
Foundations and Philosophy of Education	M,D
Genetics	M,D
Geology	M,D
Geosciences	M,D
Geotechnical Engineering	M,D
Graphic Design	M
Higher Education	M,D
History	M,D
Horticulture	M,D
Human Development	M,D
Human Resources Development	M,D
Human-Computer Interaction	M,D
Immunology	M,D
Industrial Design	M
Industrial/Management Engineering	M,D
Information Science	M
Inorganic Chemistry	M,D
Interdisciplinary Studies	M
Interior Design	M
Journalism	M
Kinesiology and Movement Studies	M,D
Landscape Architecture	M
Linguistics	M,D
Management Information Systems	M,D
Mass Communication	M
Materials Engineering	M,D
Materials Sciences	M,D
Mathematics Education	M,D
Mathematics	M,D
Mechanical Engineering	M,D
Mechanics	M,D
Meteorology	M,D
Microbiology	M,D
Molecular Biology	M,D
Molecular Genetics	M,D
Natural Resources	M,D
Neuroscience	M,D
Nutrition	M,D
Operations Research	M,D
Organic Chemistry	M,D
Pathology	M,D
Physical Chemistry	M,D
Physics	M,D
Plant Biology	M,D
Plant Pathology	M,D
Plant Sciences	M,D
Political Science	M
Psychology—General	M,D
Public Administration	M
Rhetoric	M,D
Rural Planning and Studies	D
Rural Sociology	M,D
Science Education	M
Social Psychology	M,D
Sociology	M,D
Special Education	M,D
Statistics	M,D
Structural Biology	M,D
Structural Engineering	M,D
Student Affairs	M,D
Sustainable Development	M,D
Systems Engineering	M
Toxicology	M,D
Transportation and Highway Engineering	M,D
Transportation Management	M
Urban and Regional Planning	M
Veterinary Medicine	M
Veterinary Sciences	M,D
Vocational and Technical Education	M,D
Writing	M,D

IRELL & MANELLA GRADUATE SCHOOL OF BIOLOGICAL SCIENCES

Biochemistry	D
Biological and Biomedical Sciences—General	D*
Cancer Biology/Oncology	D
Cell Biology	D
Developmental Biology	D
Genetics	D
Immunology	D
Molecular Biology	D
Neuroscience	D
Pharmaceutical Sciences	D

ITHACA COLLEGE

Accounting	M
Agricultural Education	M
Allied Health—General	M,D
Art/Fine Arts	M

Biological and Biomedical Sciences—General	M
Business Administration and Management—General	M
Chemistry	M
Communication Disorders	M
Elementary Education	M
English Education	M
Exercise and Sports Science	M
Foreign Languages Education	M
Geosciences	M
Health Education	M
Internet and Interactive Multimedia	M
Mathematics Education	M
Music Education	M
Music	M
Occupational Therapy	M
Photography	M
Physical Education	M
Physical Therapy	D
Physics	M
Secondary Education	M
Social Sciences Education	M
Spanish	M
Sports Management	M
Writing	M

JACKSON STATE UNIVERSITY

Accounting	M
Applied Mathematics	M
Atmospheric Sciences	M,D
Biological and Biomedical Sciences—General	M
Business Administration and Management—General	M,D
Chemistry	M,D
Civil Engineering	M,D
Clinical Psychology	M,D
Communication Disorders	M
Computer Science	M
Counselor Education	M
Criminal Justice and Criminology	M
Early Childhood Education	M,D,O
Education—General	M,D,O
Educational Leadership and Administration	M,D,O
Elementary Education	M,D,O
English Education	M
English	M
Environmental Engineering	M,D
Environmental Sciences	M
Geosciences	M,D
Health Education	M
Higher Education	M,D,O
History	M
Materials Sciences	M,D
Mathematics Education	M
Mathematics	M
Music Education	M
Physical Education	M
Physics	M,D
Political Science	M
Psychology—General	D
Public Administration	M,D
Public Affairs	M,D
Public Health—General	M,D
Public Policy	M,D
Reading Education	M,D,O
Rehabilitation Sciences	M
School Psychology	M
Science Education	M,D
Social Work	M,D
Sociology	M
Special Education	M,O
Sports Management	M
Statistics	M
Urban and Regional Planning	M,D
Vocational and Technical Education	M,D

JACKSONVILLE STATE UNIVERSITY

Biological and Biomedical Sciences—General	M
Business Administration and Management—General	M
Computer Science	M
Counselor Education	M
Criminal Justice and Criminology	M
Early Childhood Education	M
Education—General	M,O
Educational Leadership and Administration	M,O
Educational Media/Instructional Technology	M
Elementary Education	M
Emergency Management	M,D
English	M
History	M
Liberal Studies	M
Mathematics	M
Music	M
Nursing—General	M
Physical Education	M,O
Political Science	M
Psychology—General	M
Reading Education	M
Secondary Education	M
Software Engineering	M
Special Education	M

JACKSONVILLE UNIVERSITY

Accounting	M
Allied Health—General	M
Art/Fine Arts	M
Business Administration and Management—General	M,D*
Communication Disorders	M
Counseling Psychology	M
Dance	M
Dentistry	M,O
Educational Leadership and Administration	M
Family Nurse Practitioner Studies	M
Finance and Banking	M
Health Informatics	M

Kinesiology and Movement Studies	M
Marine Sciences	M
Marketing	M
Mathematics	M
Nursing and Healthcare Administration	M
Nursing Education	M
Nursing Informatics	M
Nursing—General	M,D
Oral and Dental Sciences	M,O
Organizational Management	M
Psychiatric Nursing	M
Public Policy	M
Sports Management	M

JAMES MADISON UNIVERSITY

Accounting	M
American Studies	M
Applied Behavior Analysis	M
Art Education	M
Art History	M
Art/Fine Arts	M
Biological and Biomedical Sciences—General	M
Business Administration and Management—General	M
Clinical Psychology	D
Communication Disorders	M,D
Communication—General	M
Computer and Information Systems Security	M
Computer Science	M
Counseling Psychology	D
Early Childhood Education	M
Education of the Gifted	M
Educational Leadership and Administration	M
Educational Measurement and Evaluation	M,D
Educational Media/Instructional Technology	M
Elementary Education	M
Engineering and Applied Sciences—General	M
English as a Second Language	M
English	M
Entrepreneurship	M
Environmental Management and Policy	M
Exercise and Sports Science	M
Experimental Psychology	M
Family Nurse Practitioner Studies	M,D
Foreign Languages Education	M
Forensic Sciences	M
Gerontological Nursing	M,D
Health Education	M
Higher Education	M
History	M
Human Resources Management	M
Kinesiology and Movement Studies	M
Management Information Systems	M
Management Strategy and Policy	D
Mathematics Education	M
Middle School Education	M
Multilingual and Multicultural Education	M
Music Education	M
Music	M,D
Nonprofit Management	M,D
Nurse Midwifery	M,D
Nursing and Healthcare Administration	M,D
Nursing—General	M,D
Nutrition	M
Occupational Therapy	M
Organizational Management	D
Photography	M
Physical Education	M
Physician Assistant Studies	M
Physiology	M
Political Science	M
Psychiatric Nursing	M,D
Psychology—General	M
Public Administration	M
Public History	M
Reading Education	M
Rhetoric	M
School Psychology	M,D,O
Secondary Education	M
Special Education	M
Sustainability Management	M
Taxation	M
Technical Writing	M
Vocational and Technical Education	M
Writing	M

JEFFERSON COLLEGE OF HEALTH SCIENCES

Nursing and Healthcare Administration	M
Nursing Education	M
Nursing—General	M
Occupational Therapy	M
Physician Assistant Studies	M

THE JEWISH THEOLOGICAL SEMINARY

Jewish Studies	M,D
Music	M
Religion	M,D
Religious Education	M,D
Theology	M,D,O
Women's Studies	M,D

JOHN BROWN UNIVERSITY

Business Administration and Management—General	M
Clinical Psychology	M,O
Counseling Psychology	M,O
Counselor Education	M,O
Curriculum and Instruction	M
Education—General	M
Ethics	M

International Business	M
Marriage and Family Therapy	M,O
Secondary Education	M

JOHN CARROLL UNIVERSITY

Accounting	M
Biological and Biomedical Sciences—General	M
Business Administration and Management—General	M
Counseling Psychology	M,O
Counselor Education	M,O
Educational Psychology	M,O
English	M
Humanities	M
Mathematics	M
Nonprofit Management	M
Religion	M
Secondary Education	M
Theology	M

JOHN F. KENNEDY UNIVERSITY

Art/Fine Arts	M
Business Administration and Management—General	M,O
Comparative and Interdisciplinary Arts	M
Counseling Psychology	M
Education—General	M
Health Education	M
Health Psychology	M
Human Resources Development	M,O
Industrial and Organizational Psychology	M,O
Law	D
Museum Studies	M,O
Organizational Management	M,O
Psychology—General	M,D,O
Sport Psychology	M
Transpersonal and Humanistic Psychology	M

JOHN JAY COLLEGE OF CRIMINAL JUSTICE OF THE CITY UNIVERSITY OF NEW YORK

Criminal Justice and Criminology	M,D
Forensic Psychology	M,D
Forensic Sciences	M,D
Legal and Justice Studies	M,D
Organizational Behavior	M,D
Public Administration	M
Public Policy	M,D

THE JOHN MARSHALL LAW SCHOOL

Law	M,D

JOHN PAUL THE GREAT CATHOLIC UNIVERSITY

Theology	M

JOHNS HOPKINS UNIVERSITY

Aerospace/Aeronautical Engineering	M
Allopathic Medicine	D
Anatomy	D
Anthropology	D
Applied Behavior Analysis	O
Applied Economics	M
Applied Mathematics	M,D,O
Applied Physics	M,O
Archaeology	D
Art History	M,D
Artificial Intelligence/Robotics	M
Asian Studies	M,D,O
Astronomy	D
Biochemistry	M,D
Bioengineering	M,D
Bioethics	M,D
Bioinformatics	M
Biological and Biomedical Sciences—General	M,D
Biomedical Engineering	M,D,O
Biophysics	D
Biostatistics	M,D
Biotechnology	M
Business Administration and Management—General	M,O
Cardiovascular Sciences	M,D
Cell Biology	D
Chemical Engineering	M,D
Chemistry	M,D
Civil Engineering	M,D,O
Classics	D
Clinical Psychology	M,D
Clinical Research	M,D
Cognitive Sciences	D
Communication—General	M,O
Community Health Nursing	M
Community Health	M,D
Comparative Literature	D
Computer and Information Systems Security	M,O
Computer Engineering	M,D,O
Computer Science	M,D,O
Counseling Psychology	M,O
Counselor Education	M,O
Demography and Population Studies	M,D
Developmental Biology	D
Early Childhood Education	M
Economics	D
Education of the Gifted	M,O
Education—General	M,D,O
Educational Leadership and Administration	M,D,O
Educational Media/Instructional Technology	M
Educational Policy	D
Electrical Engineering	M,D,O
Elementary Education	M
Energy Management and Policy	M,O
Engineering and Applied Sciences—General	M,D,O

Engineering Management	M
English	M,D
Environmental Engineering	M,O
Environmental Management and Policy	M,O
Environmental Sciences	M,O
Epidemiology	M,D
Evolutionary Biology	D
Family Nurse Practitioner Studies	D
Film, Television, and Video Production	M
Finance and Banking	M,D,O
French	D
Genetic Counseling	M,D
Genetics	M,D
Geographic Information Systems	M,O
Geosciences	M,D
German	D
Gerontological Nursing	D
Health Communication	M,D
Health Education	M,D
Health Informatics	M,D,O
Health Services Management and Hospital Administration	M,D
History of Science and Technology	M,D
History	D
Homeland Security	M,O
Immunology	M,D
Infectious Diseases	M,D
International Affairs	M,D,O
International Development	M,D,O
International Economics	M,D,O
International Health	M,D
Investment Management	M,O
Italian	M,O
Liberal Studies	M,O
Management Information Systems	M,O
Management of Technology	M,O
Marketing	M
Materials Engineering	M,D
Materials Sciences	M,D
Mathematical and Computational Finance	M,D,O
Mathematics	D
Mechanical Engineering	M,D,O
Mechanics	M,D
Media Studies	M
Medical Illustration	M
Medical Informatics	M,D,O
Microbiology	M,D
Military and Defense Studies	M
Molecular Biology	M,D
Molecular Biophysics	D
Molecular Medicine	D
Museum Studies	M,O
Music	M,D,O
Nanotechnology	M
Near and Middle Eastern Languages	D
Near and Middle Eastern Studies	D
Neuroscience	D
Nonprofit Management	M,O
Nursing and Healthcare Administration	M,D
Nursing—General	M,D,O*
Nutrition	M,D
Operations Research	M,D
Organizational Management	M
Pathobiology	D
Pathology	D
Pediatric Nursing	D
Pharmaceutical Sciences	M
Pharmacology	D
Philosophy	M,D
Photonics	M,O
Physics	M,D
Physiology	D
Political Science	M,D,O
Psychology—General	D
Public Administration	M,O
Public Health—General	M,D
Public Policy	M,D
Reading Education	M
Real Estate	M
Romance Languages	D
Secondary Education	M
Social Sciences Education	M
Social Sciences	M,D
Sociology	M,D
Spanish	D
Special Education	M,O
Statistics	M,D
Systems Engineering	M,O
Technical Writing	M,O
Urban Education	O
Writing	M,O

JOHNSON & WALES UNIVERSITY

Accounting	M
Addictions/Substance Abuse Counseling	M
Business Administration and Management—General	M
Business Education	M
Clinical Psychology	M
Computer and Information Systems Security	M
Criminal Justice and Criminology	M
Education—General	M
Educational Leadership and Administration	D
Elementary Education	M
Finance and Banking	M
Hospitality Management	M
Human Resources Management	M
Management Information Systems	M
Nonprofit Management	M
Physician Assistant Studies	M
Secondary Education	M
Special Education	M
Supply Chain Management	M

JOHNSON C. SMITH UNIVERSITY

Social Work	M

JOHNSON STATE COLLEGE

Addictions/Substance Abuse Counseling	M
Applied Behavior Analysis	M
Art/Fine Arts	M
Computer Art and Design	M
Counselor Education	M
Curriculum and Instruction	M
Education—General	M
Foundations and Philosophy of Education	M
Photography	M
School Psychology	M
Special Education	M

JOHNSON UNIVERSITY

Clinical Psychology	M,D,O
Counselor Education	M,D,O
Cultural Studies	M,D,O
Education—General	M,D,O
Educational Media/Instructional Technology	M,D,O
Higher Education	M,D,O
Nonprofit Management	M,D,O
Pastoral Ministry and Counseling	M,D,O
Theology	M,D,O

JOHN WESLEY UNIVERSITY

Organizational Management	M,D
Pastoral Ministry and Counseling	M,D
Theology	M,D

JOSE MARIA VARGAS UNIVERSITY

Early Childhood Education	M

THE JUDGE ADVOCATE GENERAL'S SCHOOL, U.S. ARMY

Law	M
Military and Defense Studies	M

JUDSON UNIVERSITY

Architecture	M
Business Administration and Management—General	M
Clinical Psychology	M
Human Services	M
Organizational Management	M
Pastoral Ministry and Counseling	M
Reading Education	M,D
Sustainable Development	M
Urban Design	M

THE JUILLIARD SCHOOL

Music	M,D,O
Theater	M,D,O

JUNIATA COLLEGE

Accounting	M

KANSAS CITY UNIVERSITY OF MEDICINE AND BIOSCIENCES

Bioethics	M
Biological and Biomedical Sciences—General	M
Osteopathic Medicine	D

KANSAS STATE UNIVERSITY

Accounting	M
Adult Education	M,D,O
Advertising and Public Relations	M
Agricultural Economics and Agribusiness	M,D
Agricultural Education	M
Agricultural Engineering	M,D
Agricultural Sciences—General	M,D,O
Agronomy and Soil Sciences	M,D,O
Animal Sciences	M,D
Applied Science and Technology	M,O
Architectural Engineering	M
Architecture	M
Art/Fine Arts	M
Biochemistry	M,D
Bioengineering	M,D
Biological and Biomedical Sciences—General	M,D
Business Administration and Management—General	M,O
Chemical Engineering	M,D,O
Chemistry	M,D
Child and Family Studies	M,D,O
Child Development	M,D,O
Civil Engineering	M,D
Clothing and Textiles	M,D
Communication Disorders	M,D,O
Communication—General	M,D,O
Computer Engineering	M,D
Computer Science	M,D
Conflict Resolution and Mediation/Peace Studies	M,D
Consumer Economics	M,D,O
Counselor Education	M,D,O
Curriculum and Instruction	M,D,O
Database Systems	M,O
Distance Education Development	M,D,O
Early Childhood Education	M,D,O
Economics	M,D
Education—General	M,D,O
Educational Leadership and Administration	M,D,O
Educational Media/Instructional Technology	M,D,O
Electrical Engineering	M,D
Elementary Education	M,D,O
Energy and Power Engineering	M,D
Energy Management and Policy	M,D
Engineering and Applied Sciences—General	M,D,O

Engineering Management	M,D,O
English as a Second Language	M,D,O
English Education	M,D,O
English	M,O
Entomology	M,D
Entrepreneurship	M,O
Environmental Design	D
Environmental Engineering	M,D
Environmental Sciences	M,D,O
Family and Consumer Sciences-General	M,D,O
Finance and Banking	M,D,O
Food Science and Technology	M,D
Gender Studies	O
Genetics	M,D
Geographic Information Systems	M,D,O
Geography	M,D,O
Geology	M
Geotechnical Engineering	M,D
Gerontology	M,O
Health Communication	M
Health Education	M,D
History	M,D
Horticulture	M,D
Hospitality Management	M,D
Human Development	M,D,O
Human Services	M,D,O
Industrial/Management Engineering	M,D
Interdisciplinary Studies	M,O
Journalism	M
Kinesiology and Movement Studies	M
Landscape Architecture	M
Management of Technology	M
Manufacturing Engineering	M,D
Marketing	M,O
Marriage and Family Therapy	M,D,O
Mass Communication	M
Mathematics	M,D,O
Mechanical Engineering	M,D
Middle School Education	M,D
Music	M
National Security	M,D
Natural Resources	M,D
Nuclear Engineering	M
Nutrition	M,D
Operations Research	M,D
Pathobiology	M,D
Physics	M,D
Physiology	M,D
Plant Pathology	M,D
Plant Sciences	M,D,O
Political Science	M
Psychology—General	M,D
Public Administration	M
Public Health—General	M,D,O
Range Science	M,D,O
Reading Education	M,D,O
Sociology	M,D
Special Education	M,D,O
Statistics	M,D,O
Structural Engineering	M,D
Student Affairs	M,D,O
Theater	M
Transportation and Highway Engineering	M,D
Urban and Regional Planning	M
Veterinary Medicine	D
Veterinary Sciences	M,O
Water Resources Engineering	M,D
Women's Studies	O

KANSAS WESLEYAN UNIVERSITY

Business Administration and Management—General	M
Sports Management	M

KAPLAN UNIVERSITY, DAVENPORT CAMPUS

Business Administration and Management—General	M
Computer and Information Systems Security	M
Criminal Justice and Criminology	M
Education—General	M
Educational Leadership and Administration	M
Educational Media/Instructional Technology	M
Entrepreneurship	M
Finance and Banking	M
Health Services Management and Hospital Administration	M,O
Higher Education	M
Human Resources Management	M
International Business	M
Law	M
Legal and Justice Studies	M,O
Logistics	M
Management Information Systems	M
Marketing	M
Mathematics Education	M
Nursing and Healthcare Administration	M
Nursing Education	M
Nursing—General	M
Organizational Management	M
Political Science	M,O
Project Management	M
Reading Education	M
Science Education	M
Secondary Education	M
Special Education	M
Student Affairs	M
Supply Chain Management	M

KEAN UNIVERSITY

Accounting	M
Addictions/Substance Abuse Counseling	M
Art Education	M
Biotechnology	M
Business Administration and Management—General	M

Child and Family Studies	M
Clinical Psychology	M,D
Communication Disorders	M
Communication—General	M
Community Health Nursing	M
Counseling Psychology	M
Counselor Education	M
Criminal Justice and Criminology	M
Curriculum and Instruction	M
Early Childhood Education	M
Education—General	M
Educational Leadership and Administration	M,D
English as a Second Language	M
Exercise and Sports Science	M
Foreign Languages Education	M
Forensic Psychology	M
Health Services Management and Hospital Administration	M
Holocaust and Genocide Studies	M
Industrial and Organizational Psychology	M
International Business	M
Liberal Studies	M,O
Management Information Systems	M
Marriage and Family Therapy	M,O
Multilingual and Multicultural Education	M
Nonprofit Management	M
Nursing and Healthcare Administration	M,D
Nursing—General	M
Occupational Therapy	M
Physical Therapy	D
Psychology—General	M
Public Administration	M
Reading Education	M
School Psychology	D,O
Social Work	M
Special Education	M
Writing	M

KECK GRADUATE INSTITUTE

Biological and Biomedical Sciences—General	M,D,O
Pharmacy	D

KEENE STATE COLLEGE

Counselor Education	M,O
Curriculum and Instruction	M,O
Education—General	M,O
Educational Leadership and Administration	M,O
Environmental and Occupational Health	M,O
School Psychology	M,O
Special Education	M,O

KEHILATH YAKOV RABBINICAL SEMINARY

Theology	M

KEISER UNIVERSITY

Accounting	M
Business Administration and Management—General	M,D
Computer and Information Systems Security	M
Criminal Justice and Criminology	M
Distance Education Development	M
Education—General	M
Educational Leadership and Administration	M,D,O
Educational Media/Instructional Technology	D,O
Health Education	M
Health Services Management and Hospital Administration	M
Homeland Security	M
Industrial and Organizational Psychology	M,D
International Business	M,D
Management Information Systems	M
Marketing	M,D
Nursing—General	M
Organizational Management	D
Physician Assistant Studies	M
Psychology—General	M,D

KENNESAW STATE UNIVERSITY

Accounting	M
American Studies	M
Applied Statistics	M
Architecture	M
Art Education	M
Biochemistry	M
Biological and Biomedical Sciences—General	M
Business Administration and Management—General	M,D
Chemistry	M
Communication—General	M
Computer and Information Systems Security	M,O
Computer Engineering	M
Computer Science	M
Conflict Resolution and Mediation/Peace Studies	M,D
Construction Management	M
Criminal Justice and Criminology	M
Early Childhood Education	M
Education—General	M,D,O
Educational Leadership and Administration	M,D
Educational Media/Instructional Technology	M
Electrical Engineering	M
Elementary Education	M
Engineering and Applied Sciences—General	M
English as a Second Language	M
English Education	M
Ethics	O
Exercise and Sports Science	M
Foreign Languages Education	M
Health Informatics	M,O

Health Services Management and Hospital Administration	M
Information Science	M,O
International Affairs	M
Mathematics Education	M
Middle School Education	M
Nursing—General	M,D
Physics	M
Public Administration	M
Reading Education	M
Secondary Education	M
Social Work	M
Software Engineering	M,O
Special Education	M
Systems Engineering	M,O
Writing	M

KENRICK-GLENNON SEMINARY

Theology	M

KENT STATE UNIVERSITY

Accounting	M,D
Adult Nursing	M,D
Advertising and Public Relations	M
Anthropology	M
Applied Mathematics	M,D
Architecture	M
Art Education	M
Art History	M
Art/Fine Arts	M
Athletic Training and Sports Medicine	M,D
Biological and Biomedical Sciences—General	M,D
Biological Anthropology	M,D
Biostatistics	M,D
Botany	M,D
Business Administration and Management—General	M
Cell Biology	M,D
Chemical Physics	M,D
Chemistry	M,D
Child and Family Studies	M
Clinical Psychology	M,D
Communication Disorders	M,D,O
Communication—General	M
Computer and Information Systems Security	M
Computer Education	M,D
Computer Science	M,D
Conflict Resolution and Mediation/Peace Studies	M
Counseling Psychology	M
Counselor Education	M,D,O
Criminal Justice and Criminology	M,D
Curriculum and Instruction	M,D,O
Early Childhood Education	M,D,O
Ecology	M,D
Economics	M
Education of the Gifted	M,D,O
Education—General	M,D,O
Educational Leadership and Administration	M,D,O
Educational Measurement and Evaluation	M,D
Educational Media/Instructional Technology	M,D
Educational Psychology	M
Engineering and Applied Sciences—General	M
English as a Second Language	M,D
English Education	M,D
English	M,D
Environmental and Occupational Health	M,D
Environmental Design	M
Epidemiology	M,D
Exercise and Sports Science	M,D
Experimental Psychology	M,D
Family Nurse Practitioner Studies	M,D
Finance and Banking	D
Foundations and Philosophy of Education	M,D
French	M,D
Genetics	M,D
Geographic Information Systems	M,D
Geography	M,D
Geology	M,D
German	M,D
Gerontological Nursing	M,D
Gerontology	M,D
Graphic Design	M
Health Education	M,D
Health Informatics	M
Health Promotion	M,D
Health Services Management and Hospital Administration	M,D
Higher Education	M,D,O
History	M,D
Hospitality Management	M
Human Development	M,D
Human Services	M,D,O
Illustration	M
Information Science	M
Japanese	M,D
Journalism	M
Landscape Architecture	M
Liberal Studies	M
Library Science	M
Linguistics	M,D
Management Information Systems	M,D
Marketing	D
Mass Communication	M
Mathematics Education	M,D
Mathematics	M
Media Studies	M
Middle School Education	M
Molecular Biology	M,D
Music Education	M,D
Music	M,D
Near and Middle Eastern Languages	M,D
Neuroscience	M,D
Nursing and Healthcare Administration	M,D
Nursing Education	M,D

Nursing—General	M,D
Nutrition	M
Pediatric Nursing	M,D
Pharmacology	M,D
Philosophy	M
Physics	M,D
Physiology	M
Podiatric Medicine	D
Political Science	M,D
Psychiatric Nursing	M,D
Psychology—General	M,D
Public Administration	M,D
Public Health—General	M,D
Reading Education	M,D
Recreation and Park Management	M
Rehabilitation Counseling	M
Rhetoric	M,D
Russian	M,D
School Psychology	M,D,O
Secondary Education	M,D
Social Sciences Education	M,D
Sociology	M,D
Spanish	M,D
Special Education	M,D,O
Sports Management	M
Student Affairs	M
Theater	M
Translation and Interpretation	M,D
Travel and Tourism	M
Urban Design	M
Vocational and Technical Education	M
Women's Health Nursing	M,D
Writing	M,D

KENT STATE UNIVERSITY AT STARK

Business Administration and Management—General	M
Curriculum and Instruction	M
Education—General	M

KENTUCKY CHRISTIAN UNIVERSITY

Religion	M
Theology	M

KENTUCKY STATE UNIVERSITY

Aquaculture	M
Business Administration and Management—General	M
Computer Science	M
Environmental Management and Policy	M
Human Resources Development	M,D
Nursing—General	M,D
Psychology—General	M
Public Administration	M,D
Special Education	M,D

KETTERING COLLEGE

Physician Assistant Studies	M

KETTERING UNIVERSITY

Business Administration and Management—General	M
Electrical Engineering	M
Engineering Management	M
Manufacturing Engineering	M
Mechanical Engineering	M

KEUKA COLLEGE

Business Administration and Management—General	M
Criminal Justice and Criminology	M
Early Childhood Education	M
Elementary Education	M
Gerontological Nursing	M
Nursing Education	M
Nursing—General	M
Occupational Therapy	M
Secondary Education	M
Social Work	M

KEYSTONE COLLEGE

Accounting	M
Early Childhood Education	M
Educational Leadership and Administration	M
Sports Management	M

KING'S COLLEGE

Education—General	M
Health Services Management and Hospital Administration	M
Physician Assistant Studies	M

THE KING'S UNIVERSITY

Pastoral Ministry and Counseling	M,D,O
Theology	M,D,O

KINGSWOOD UNIVERSITY

Pastoral Ministry and Counseling	M
Theology	M

KING UNIVERSITY

Accounting	M
Business Administration and Management—General	M
Family Nurse Practitioner Studies	M,D
Finance and Banking	M
Health Services Management and Hospital Administration	M
Human Resources Management	M
Marketing	M
Nursing and Healthcare Administration	M,D
Nursing Education	M,D
Nursing—General	M,D
Pediatric Nursing	M,D
Project Management	M

KNOWLEDGE SYSTEMS INSTITUTE

Computer Science	M
Information Science	M

KNOX COLLEGE

Theology	M,D

KNOX THEOLOGICAL SEMINARY

Classics	M
Pastoral Ministry and Counseling	D

Religion — M
Theology — M

KUTZTOWN UNIVERSITY OF PENNSYLVANIA
Art Education — M
Biological and Biomedical
  Sciences—General — M
Business Administration and
  Management—General — M
Clinical Psychology — M
Computer Science — M
Counseling Psychology — M
Counselor Education — M
Curriculum and Instruction — M
Education—General — M
Educational Leadership and
  Administration — M
Educational Media/Instructional
  Technology — M
Elementary Education — M
English Education — M
English — M
Internet and Interactive
  Multimedia — M
Library Science — M
Marriage and Family Therapy — M
Mathematics — M
Middle School Education — M
Public Administration — M
Reading Education — M
Secondary Education — M
Social Sciences Education — M
Social Work — M,D

LAGRANGE COLLEGE
Clinical Psychology — M
Curriculum and Instruction — M,O
Education—General — M,O
Middle School Education — M,O
Organizational Management — M
Secondary Education — M,O

LAGUNA COLLEGE OF ART & DESIGN
Art/Fine Arts — M

LAKE ERIE COLLEGE
Business Administration and
  Management—General — M
Education—General — M
Health Services Management and
  Hospital Administration — M
Management Information Systems — M

LAKE ERIE COLLEGE OF OSTEOPATHIC MEDICINE
Biological and Biomedical
  Sciences—General — M,D,O
Health Education — M,D,O
Osteopathic Medicine — M,D,O
Pharmacy — M,D,O

LAKE FOREST COLLEGE
American Studies — M
Art Education — M
Art/Fine Arts — M
Education—General — M
Elementary Education — M
English Education — M
Environmental Management
  and Policy — M
French — M
History — M
Liberal Studies — M
Mathematics Education — M
Music Education — M
Philosophy — M
Science Education — M
Secondary Education — M
Social Sciences Education — M
Spanish — M
Writing — M

LAKE FOREST GRADUATE SCHOOL OF MANAGEMENT
Business Administration and
  Management—General — M
Finance and Banking — M
Health Services Management and
  Hospital Administration — M
International Business — M
Marketing — M
Organizational Behavior — M

LAKEHEAD UNIVERSITY
Biological and Biomedical
  Sciences—General — M
Chemistry — M
Clinical Psychology — M,D
Computer Engineering — M
Computer Science — M
Economics — M
Education—General — M,D
Electrical Engineering — M
Engineering and Applied
  Sciences—General — M
English — M
Environmental Engineering — M
Exercise and Sports Science — M
Experimental Psychology — M
Forestry — M,D
Geology — M
Gerontology — M,D
Health Services Research — M
History — M
Kinesiology and Movement Studies — M
Mathematics — M
Physics — M
Psychology—General — M,D
Social Work — M
Sociology — M
Women's Studies — M,D

LAKELAND UNIVERSITY
Accounting — M
Business Administration and
  Management—General — M
Counselor Education — M
Education—General — M
Finance and Banking — M
Health Services Management and
  Hospital Administration — M
Project Management — M
Theology — M

LAMAR UNIVERSITY
Accounting — M
Biological and Biomedical
  Sciences—General — M
Business Administration and
  Management—General — M
Chemical Engineering — M,D
Chemistry — M
Clinical Psychology — M
Communication Disorders — M,D
Computer Science — M
Counseling Psychology — M
Counselor Education — M
Criminal Justice and Criminology — M
Education—General — M,D,O
Educational Leadership and
  Administration — M,D
Educational Media/Instructional
  Technology — M,D
Electrical Engineering — M,D
Engineering and Applied
  Sciences—General — M,D
Engineering Management — M,D
English — M
Entrepreneurship — M
Environmental Engineering — M,D
Environmental Management
  and Policy — M,D
Family and Consumer
  Sciences-General — M
Foreign Languages Education — M
Health Services Management and
  Hospital Administration — M
History — M
Industrial and Organizational
  Psychology — M
Industrial/Management
  Engineering — M,D
Kinesiology and Movement Studies — M
Mathematics — M
Mechanical Engineering — M,D
Music — M
Nursing and Healthcare
  Administration — M
Nursing Education — M
Nursing—General — M
Political Science — M
Psychology—General — M
Public Administration — M
Public Health—General — M
Spanish — M
Special Education — M,D

LANCASTER BIBLE COLLEGE
Counseling Psychology — M,D
Counselor Education — M,D
Elementary Education — M,D
Marriage and Family Therapy — M,D
Pastoral Ministry and Counseling — M,D,O
Secondary Education — M,D
Special Education — M,D
Theology — M,D,O

LANCASTER THEOLOGICAL SEMINARY
Art History — M,D,O
Ethics — M,D,O
Religion — M,D,O
Religious Education — M,D,O
Theology — M,D,O

LANDER UNIVERSITY
Early Childhood Education — M
Education—General — M
Emergency Management — M
Nursing—General — M

LANGSTON UNIVERSITY
Education—General — M
Elementary Education — M
English as a Second Language — M
Multilingual and Multicultural
  Education — M
Physical Therapy — D
Rehabilitation Counseling — M
Urban Education — M

LA ROCHE COLLEGE
Accounting — M
Human Resources Management — M,O
Nurse Anesthesia — M,D
Nursing and Healthcare
  Administration — M
Nursing Education — M
Nursing—General — M

LA SALLE UNIVERSITY
Accounting — M,O
Adult Nursing — M,D,O
Advertising and Public Relations — M,O
American Studies — M,O
Business Administration and
  Management—General — M,O
Clinical Psychology — M
Communication Disorders — M
Communication—General — M,O
Community Health Nursing — M,D,O
Computer Science — M,O
Corporate and Organizational
  Communication — M,O
Counseling Psychology — M
Developmental Psychology — M,D

Early Childhood Education — M,O
Education—General — M,O
Educational Leadership and
  Administration — M
Educational Media/Instructional
  Technology — M,O
English as a Second Language — M,O
English — M,O
Family Nurse Practitioner Studies — M,D,O
Finance and Banking — M,O
Forensic Sciences — M,O
Gerontological Nursing — M,D,O
Gerontology — M,D,O
Health Psychology — M,D
Hispanic Studies — M,O
History — M,O
Human Resources Development — M,O
Human Resources Management — M,O
International Business — M,O
Latin American Studies — M,O
Management of Technology — M,O
Marketing — M,O
Marriage and Family Therapy — M
Media Studies — M,O
Middle School Education — M,O
Multilingual and Multicultural
  Education — M,O
Nonprofit Management — M
Nurse Anesthesia — M,D,O
Nursing and Healthcare
  Administration — M,D,O
Nursing Education — M,D,O
Nursing—General — M,D,O
Pastoral Ministry and Counseling — M
Psychology—General — M,D
Public Health—General — M
Public History — M
Quantitative Analysis — M,O
Reading Education — M,O
School Nursing — M,D,O
Secondary Education — M,O
Social Sciences Education — M,O
Special Education — M,O
Translation and Interpretation — M,O
Western European Studies — M,O

LASELL COLLEGE
Advertising and Public Relations — M,O
Business Administration and
  Management—General — M,O
Communication—General — M,O
Corporate and Organizational
  Communication — M,O
Criminal Justice and Criminology — M,O
Education—General — M
Elementary Education — M
Emergency Management — M,O
Health Communication — M,O
Health Services Management and
  Hospital Administration — M,O
Homeland Security — M,O
Hospitality Management — M,O
Human Resources Management — M,O
Marketing — M,O
Nonprofit Management — M,O
Project Management — M,O
Rehabilitation Sciences — M
Special Education — M
Sports Management — M,O
Travel and Tourism — M,O

LA SIERRA UNIVERSITY
Accounting — M,O
Advertising and Public Relations — M
Business Administration and
  Management—General — M,O
Communication—General — M
Counselor Education — M,O
Curriculum and Instruction — M,D,O
Education—General — M,D,O
Educational Leadership and
  Administration — M,D,O
Educational Psychology — M,O
English — M
Finance and Banking — M,O
Human Resources Management — M,O
Marketing — M,O
Pastoral Ministry and Counseling — M
Religion — M
Religious Education — M
School Psychology — M,O
Writing — M

LAURENTIAN UNIVERSITY
Analytical Chemistry — M
Applied Physics — M
Applied Psychology — M
Applied Social Research — M
Biochemistry — M
Biological and Biomedical
  Sciences—General — M,D
Business Administration and
  Management—General — M
Chemistry — M
Ecology — M,D
Engineering and Applied
  Sciences—General — M,D
Environmental Sciences — M
Experimental Psychology — M
Geology — M,D
History — M
Human Development — M
Humanities — M
Mineral/Mining Engineering — M,D
Natural Resources — M
Nursing—General — M
Organic Chemistry — M
Physical Chemistry — M
Psychology—General — M
Public Health—General — D
Science Education — O
Social Work — M

Sociology — M
Technical Writing — O
Theoretical Chemistry — M

LAWRENCE TECHNOLOGICAL UNIVERSITY
Architectural Engineering — M,D
Architecture — M,O
Automotive Engineering — M,D
Bioinformatics — M,O
Biomedical Engineering — M,D
Business Administration and
  Management—General — M,O
Civil Engineering — M,D
Communication—General — M,O
Computer and Information
  Systems Security — M,O
Computer Engineering — M,D
Computer Science — M,O
Construction Engineering — M,D
Database Systems — M,O
Educational Media/Instructional
  Technology — M,O
Electrical Engineering — M,D
Engineering and Applied
  Sciences—General — M,D
Engineering Management — M,D
Finance and Banking — M,O
Human Resources Development — M,O
Industrial and Manufacturing
  Management — M,D
Industrial/Management
  Engineering — M,D
Information Science — M,O
Interior Design — M,O
Management Strategy and Policy — M,O
Manufacturing Engineering — M,D
Marketing — M,O
Mechanical Engineering — M,D
Project Management — M,O
Technical Communication — M,O
Urban Design — M,O
Water Resources Engineering — M,D

LEBANESE AMERICAN UNIVERSITY
Business Administration and
  Management—General — M
Computer Science — M
International Affairs — M
Pharmacy — D

LEBANON VALLEY COLLEGE
Athletic Training and Sports
  Medicine — M
Business Administration and
  Management—General — M
Ethics — M
Health Services Management and
  Hospital Administration — M
Mathematics Education — M,O
Music Education — M
Physical Therapy — D
Science Education — M,O
Social Sciences Education — M,O

LEE UNIVERSITY
Art/Fine Arts — M,O
Biological and Biomedical
  Sciences—General — M,O
Business Administration and
  Management—General — M
Child Development — M
Counseling Psychology — M
Counselor Education — M
Curriculum and Instruction — M,O
Early Childhood Education — M,O
Economics — M,O
Education—General — M,O
Educational Leadership and
  Administration — M,O
Elementary Education — M,O
English as a Second Language — M,O
English — M,O
Ethics — M
Higher Education — M,O
History — M,O
Marriage and Family Therapy — M
Mathematics Education — M,O
Mathematics — M,O
Middle School Education — M,O
Music Education — M
Music — M
Pastoral Ministry and Counseling — M
Religion — M
Secondary Education — M,O
Social Sciences Education — M,O
Spanish — M,O
Special Education — M,O
Theology — M

LEHIGH UNIVERSITY
Accounting — M
American Studies — M,D,O
Applied Mathematics — M,D
Biochemical Engineering — M,D
Biochemistry — M,D
Bioengineering — M,D
Biological and Biomedical
  Sciences—General — M,D
Business Administration and
  Management—General — M
Cell Biology — M,D
Chemical Engineering — M,D
Chemistry — M,D
Civil Engineering — M,D
Computational Sciences — M,D
Computer Engineering — M,D
Computer Science — M,D
Counseling Psychology — M,D,O
Counselor Education — M,D,O
Economics — M,D
Education—General — M,D,O

Educational Leadership and Administration	M,D,O
Educational Media/Instructional Technology	M,D,O
Electrical Engineering	M,D
Elementary Education	M,D,O
Energy and Power Engineering	M
Engineering and Applied Sciences—General	M,D
Engineering Management	M,D,O
English	M,D
Entrepreneurship	M
Environmental Engineering	M,D
Environmental Law	M,O
Environmental Management and Policy	M,O
Environmental Sciences	M,D
Finance and Banking	M
Geology	M,D
Geosciences	M,D
Health Services Management and Hospital Administration	M,O
History	M,D
Human Services	M,D,O
Information Science	M
Interdisciplinary Studies	M,D
International and Comparative Education	M,D,O
International Development	M,D,O
Manufacturing Engineering	M
Materials Engineering	M,D
Materials Sciences	M,D
Mathematics	M,D
Mechanical Engineering	M,D
Mechanics	M,D
Molecular Biology	M,D
Photonics	M,D
Physics	M,D
Political Science	M
Polymer Science and Engineering	M,D
Project Management	M
Psychology—General	M,D
Public History	M,D
Quantitative Analysis	M
School Psychology	D,O
Sociology	M
Special Education	M,D
Statistics	M,D
Sustainable Development	M,O
Systems Engineering	M

LEHMAN COLLEGE OF THE CITY UNIVERSITY OF NEW YORK

Accounting	M
Adult Nursing	M
Art/Fine Arts	M
Biological and Biomedical Sciences—General	M
Business Education	M
Communication Disorders	M
Computer Science	M
Counselor Education	M
Early Childhood Education	M
Education—General	M
Elementary Education	M
English as a Second Language	M
English Education	M
English	M
Gerontological Nursing	M
Health Education	M
Health Promotion	M
History	M
Maternal and Child/Neonatal Nursing	M
Mathematics Education	M
Mathematics	M
Multilingual and Multicultural Education	M
Music Education	M
Nursing—General	M
Nutrition	M
Pediatric Nursing	M
Plant Sciences	D
Reading Education	M
Recreation and Park Management	M
Science Education	M
Social Sciences Education	M
Spanish	M
Special Education	M

LE MOYNE COLLEGE

Arts Administration	M
Business Administration and Management—General	M
Early Childhood Education	M,O
Education—General	M,O
Educational Leadership and Administration	M,O
Elementary Education	M,O
English as a Second Language	M,O
English Education	M,O
Family Nurse Practitioner Studies	M,O
Foreign Languages Education	M,O
Management Information Systems	M
Middle School Education	M,O
Nursing and Healthcare Administration	M,O
Nursing Education	M,O
Nursing Informatics	M,O
Nursing—General	M,O
Occupational Therapy	M
Physician Assistant Studies	M
Reading Education	M,O
Secondary Education	M,O
Social Sciences Education	M,O
Special Education	M,O
Urban Studies	M,O

LENOIR-RHYNE UNIVERSITY

Accounting	M
Addictions/Substance Abuse Counseling	M

Athletic Training and Sports Medicine	M
Business Administration and Management—General	M
Clinical Psychology	M
Community College Education	M
Counseling Psychology	M
Counselor Education	M
Distance Education Development	M
Education—General	M
Educational Leadership and Administration	M
Educational Media/Instructional Technology	M
Entrepreneurship	M
Health Services Management and Hospital Administration	M
Human Services	M
International Business	M
Management Information Systems	M
Management Strategy and Policy	M
Nursing and Healthcare Administration	M
Nursing Education	M
Nursing—General	M
Occupational Therapy	M
Organizational Management	M
Physician Assistant Studies	M
Public Health—General	M
Secondary Education	M
Sustainable Development	M
Theology	M
Writing	M

LESLEY UNIVERSITY

Adult Education	M,D,O
Art Education	M,D,O
Art Therapy	M,D,O
Art/Fine Arts	M,D,O
Clinical Psychology	M,D,O
Computer Education	M,D,O
Conflict Resolution and Mediation/Peace Studies	M,D,O
Counseling Psychology	M,D,O
Curriculum and Instruction	M,D,O
Distance Education Development	M,D,O
Early Childhood Education	M,D,O
Ecology	M,D,O
Education—General	M,D,O
Educational Leadership and Administration	M,D,O
Educational Media/Instructional Technology	M,D,O
Elementary Education	M,D,O
English as a Second Language	M,D,O
Health Education	M,D,O
Interdisciplinary Studies	M,D,O
International Affairs	M,D,O
Mathematics Education	M,D,O
Middle School Education	M,D,O
Photography	M
Psychology—General	M,D,O
Reading Education	M,D,O
School Psychology	M,D,O
Science Education	M,D,O
Secondary Education	M,D,O
Social Psychology	M,D,O
Special Education	M,D,O
Sustainable Development	M,D,O
Therapies—Dance, Drama, and Music	M,D,O
Urban and Regional Planning	M,D,O
Women's Studies	M,D,O
Writing	M,D,O

LES ROCHES INTERNATIONAL SCHOOL OF HOTEL MANAGEMENT

Hospitality Management	M

LETOURNEAU UNIVERSITY

Business Administration and Management—General	M
Counseling Psychology	M
Curriculum and Instruction	M
Educational Leadership and Administration	M
Engineering and Applied Sciences—General	M
Engineering Management	M
Health Services Management and Hospital Administration	M
Management Strategy and Policy	M
Marriage and Family Therapy	M
Psychology—General	M
School Psychology	M

LEWIS & CLARK COLLEGE

Addictions/Substance Abuse Counseling	M
Communication Disorders	M
Counseling Psychology	M
Curriculum and Instruction	M
Educational Leadership and Administration	M,D,O
Elementary Education	M
Environmental Law	M,D
Law	M,D
Marriage and Family Therapy	M
School Psychology	M,O
Secondary Education	M
Special Education	M
Student Affairs	M,D,O

LEWIS UNIVERSITY

Accounting	M
Adult Nursing	M,D
Aviation Management	M
Aviation	M
Business Administration and Management—General	M
Clinical Psychology	M
Computer and Information Systems Security	M
Counseling Psychology	M
Counselor Education	M
Criminal Justice and Criminology	M

Database Systems	M
Education—General	M,D
Educational Leadership and Administration	M,D
Educational Media/Instructional Technology	M
Electronic Commerce	M
Elementary Education	M
English as a Second Language	M
English Education	M
Environmental and Occupational Health	M
Family Nurse Practitioner Studies	M,D
Finance and Banking	M
Health Services Management and Hospital Administration	M
Higher Education	M
Human Resources Management	M
International Business	M
Management Information Systems	M
Management of Technology	M
Marketing	M
Mathematics Education	M
Nonprofit Management	M
Nursing and Healthcare Administration	M,D
Nursing Education	M,D
Nursing—General	M,D
Organizational Management	M
Project Management	M
Reading Education	M
School Nursing	M,D
Science Education	M
Secondary Education	M
Social Sciences Education	M
Special Education	M
Sports Management	M
Student Affairs	M

LEXINGTON THEOLOGICAL SEMINARY

Theology	M,D

LIBERTY UNIVERSITY

Accounting	M,D,O
Addictions/Substance Abuse Counseling	M,D,O
Advertising and Public Relations	M,D,O
Art/Fine Arts	M
Biological and Biomedical Sciences—General	M
Business Administration and Management—General	M,D,O
Child and Family Studies	M,D,O
Clinical Psychology	M,D,O
Communication—General	M
Computer and Information Systems Security	M,D,O
Counseling Psychology	M,D,O
Counselor Education	M,D,O
Criminal Justice and Criminology	M,D,O
Education of the Gifted	M,D,O
Education—General	M,D,O
Educational Leadership and Administration	M,D,O
Emergency Management	M,D,O
Engineering and Applied Sciences—General	M
English	M
Family Nurse Practitioner Studies	M,D
Health Promotion	M,D,O
History	M
Human Services	M,D,O
International Affairs	M,D,O
International Business	M,D,O
International Health	M
Law	D
Management Information Systems	M,D,O
Management of Technology	M,D,O
Marketing	M,D,O
Marriage and Family Therapy	M,D,O
Mathematics Education	M,D,O
Middle School Education	M,D,O
Military and Defense Studies	M,D,O
Missions and Missiology	M,D,O
Music Education	M,D
Music	M,D
Nursing and Healthcare Administration	M,D
Nursing Education	M,D
Nursing—General	M,D
Nutrition	M
Osteopathic Medicine	D
Pastoral Ministry and Counseling	M,D,O
Project Management	M,D,O
Public Administration	M,D,O
Public Policy	M
Reading Education	M,D,O
Recreation and Park Management	M,D,O
Religion	M,D,O
Religious Education	M,D,O
Secondary Education	M,D,O
Sports Management	M,D,O
Theology	M,D,O
Travel and Tourism	M,D,O

LIFE CHIROPRACTIC COLLEGE WEST

Chiropractic	D

LIFE UNIVERSITY

Athletic Training and Sports Medicine	M
Chiropractic	D
Exercise and Sports Science	M
Nutrition	M

LIM COLLEGE

Business Administration and Management—General	M
Clothing and Textiles	M
Entrepreneurship	M
Marketing	M
Textile Design	M

LIMESTONE COLLEGE

Business Administration and Management—General	M

LINCOLN CHRISTIAN SEMINARY

Pastoral Ministry and Counseling	M,D
Religious Education	M,D
Theology	M,D

LINCOLN CHRISTIAN UNIVERSITY

Cultural Studies	M
Organizational Management	M
Pastoral Ministry and Counseling	M
Philosophy	M
Religion	M
Theology	M

LINCOLN MEMORIAL UNIVERSITY

Business Administration and Management—General	M
Counselor Education	M,D,O
Curriculum and Instruction	M,D,O
Education—General	M,D,O
Educational Leadership and Administration	M,D,O
English Education	M,D,O
Family Nurse Practitioner Studies	M
Higher Education	M,D,O
Human Resources Development	M,D,O
Law	D
Nurse Anesthesia	M
Nursing—General	M
Osteopathic Medicine	D
Psychiatric Nursing	M

LINCOLN UNIVERSITY (CA)

Business Administration and Management—General	M,D
Finance and Banking	M,D
Human Resources Management	M,D
International Business	M,D
Investment Management	M,D
Management Information Systems	M,D

LINCOLN UNIVERSITY (MO)

Accounting	M
Business Administration and Management—General	M
Counselor Education	M
Criminal Justice and Criminology	M
Elementary Education	M
Environmental Sciences	M
Higher Education	M
History	M
Management Information Systems	M
Middle School Education	M
Public Administration	M
Public Policy	M
Secondary Education	M
Sociology	M

LINCOLN UNIVERSITY (PA)

Early Childhood Education	M
Educational Leadership and Administration	M
Finance and Banking	M
Human Resources Management	M
Human Services	M
Special Education	M

LINDENWOOD UNIVERSITY

Accounting	M
Business Administration and Management—General	M,O
Communication Disorders	M,D,O
Communication—General	M,O
Computer and Information Systems Security	M,O
Counseling Psychology	M,D,O
Criminal Justice and Criminology	M,O
Education of the Gifted	M,D,O
Education—General	M,D,O
Educational Leadership and Administration	M,D,O
Educational Media/Instructional Technology	M,D,O
English as a Second Language	M,D,O
Entrepreneurship	M
Film, Television, and Video Production	M
Finance and Banking	M
Health Promotion	M
Health Services Management and Hospital Administration	M,O
Human Resources Management	M,O
International Business	M
Management Information Systems	M,O
Marketing	M,O
Media Studies	M,O
Nonprofit Management	M
Nursing—General	M,O
Project Management	M,O
Public Administration	M
School Psychology	M,D,O
Sports Management	M
Supply Chain Management	M
Writing	M,O

LINDENWOOD UNIVERSITY–BELLEVILLE

Business Administration and Management—General	M
Communication—General	M
Computer Art and Design	M
Counselor Education	M
Criminal Justice and Criminology	M
Education—General	M
Educational Leadership and Administration	M
Health Services Management and Hospital Administration	M
Human Resources Management	M
Internet and Interactive Multimedia	M
Media Studies	M

LINDSEY WILSON COLLEGE

Counseling Psychology	M,D
Counselor Education	M,D
Educational Leadership and Administration	M

Human Development — M,D
Internet and Interactive Multimedia — M

LIPSCOMB UNIVERSITY

Accounting — M,O
Applied Behavior Analysis — M,D,O
Business Administration and Management—General — M,O
Clinical Psychology — M,O
Computer and Information Systems Security — M,O
Conflict Resolution and Mediation/Peace Studies — M,O
Counseling Psychology — M,O
Database Systems — M
Education—General — M,D,O
Educational Leadership and Administration — M,D,O
Educational Media/Instructional Technology — M,D,O
English Education — M,D,O
English — M,D,O
Exercise and Sports Science — M
Film, Television, and Video Production — M
Finance and Banking — M,O
Health Informatics — M,D,O
Health Services Management and Hospital Administration — M,O
Human Resources Management — M,O
Management Information Systems — M
Management of Technology — M
Marriage and Family Therapy — M,O
Molecular Biology — M
Nonprofit Management — M,O
Nutrition — M
Organizational Management — M
Pastoral Ministry and Counseling — M,D,O
Pharmacy — M,D
Psychology—General — M,O
Public Administration — M
Public Policy — M
Reading Education — M,D,O
Software Engineering — M
Special Education — M,D,O
Sports Management — M,O
Sustainability Management — M,O
Sustainable Development — M,O
Theology — M,D,O
Writing — M

LOCK HAVEN UNIVERSITY OF PENNSYLVANIA

Actuarial Science — M
Athletic Training and Sports Medicine — M
Business Education — M
Clinical Psychology — M
Counseling Psychology — M
Education—General — M
Educational Leadership and Administration — M
Elementary Education — M
Health Education — M
Health Promotion — M
Health Services Management and Hospital Administration — M
Human Services — M
Information Studies — M
Physician Assistant Studies — M
Sport Psychology — M
Sports Management — M

LOGAN UNIVERSITY

Chiropractic — M,D
Exercise and Sports Science — M,D
Health Education — M,D
Health Informatics — M,D
Nutrition — M,D
Rehabilitation Sciences — M,D

LOGOS EVANGELICAL SEMINARY

Theology — M,D,O

LOMA LINDA UNIVERSITY

Addictions/Substance Abuse Counseling — M,D,O
Adult Nursing — M
Allied Health—General — M,D
Allopathic Medicine — M,D
Anatomy — D
Applied Social Research — M,D
Biochemistry — M,D
Bioethics — M,O
Biostatistics — M,D
Child and Family Studies — M,D,O
Clinical Psychology — D
Communication Disorders — M,D
Counselor Education — M,D,O
Criminal Justice and Criminology — M,D
Dentistry — M,D
Environmental and Occupational Health — M
Epidemiology — M,D
Gerontological Nursing — M
Gerontology — M,D
Health Education — M,D
Health Services Management and Hospital Administration — M
International Health — M
Marriage and Family Therapy — M,D,O
Microbiology — M,D
Nursing and Healthcare Administration — M
Nursing Education — M
Nursing—General — D
Nutrition — M,D
Occupational Therapy — M,O
Oral and Dental Sciences — M,O
Pathology — D
Pediatric Nursing — M

Pharmacology — D
Pharmacy — D
Physical Therapy — M,D
Physician Assistant Studies — M
Physiology — D
Psychology—General — D
Public Health—General — M,D
Rehabilitation Sciences — M,D
Religion — M
Social Work — M,D

LONDON METROPOLITAN UNIVERSITY

Applied Psychology — M,D
Architecture — M,D
Arts Administration — M,D
Athletic Training and Sports Medicine — M,D
Biological and Biomedical Sciences—General — M,D
Child and Family Studies — M,D
Clinical Psychology — M,D
Computer and Information Systems Security — M,D
Conflict Resolution and Mediation/Peace Studies — M,D
Counseling Psychology — M,D
Criminal Justice and Criminology — M,D
Database Systems — M,D
Early Childhood Education — M,D
Education—General — M,D
Emergency Management — M,D
English Education — M,D
Food Science and Technology — M,D
Foreign Languages Education — M,D
Forensic Psychology — M,D
Health Services Management and Hospital Administration — M,D
Higher Education — M,D
Homeland Security — M,D
Human Resources Management — M,D
Immunology — M,D
Industrial and Organizational Psychology — M,D
International Affairs — M,D
Internet and Interactive Multimedia — M,D
Law — M,D
Management Information Systems — M,D
Management of Technology — M,D
Military and Defense Studies — M,D
Near and Middle Eastern Languages — M,D
Nutrition — M,D
Pharmacology — M,D
Public Administration — M,D
Public Health—General — M,D
Public Policy — M,D
Social Work — M,D
Special Education — M,D
Translation and Interpretation — M,D
Urban Design — M,D
Women's Studies — M,D
Writing — M,D

LONG ISLAND UNIVERSITY–BRENTWOOD CAMPUS

Clinical Psychology — M,O
Counseling Psychology — M,O
Counselor Education — M,O
Early Childhood Education — M,O
Elementary Education — M,O
Reading Education — M,O
Special Education — M,O

LONG ISLAND UNIVERSITY–HUDSON

Addictions/Substance Abuse Counseling — M,O
Biotechnology — M,O
Business Administration and Management—General — M,O
Counseling Psychology — M,O
Counselor Education — M,O
Early Childhood Education — M,O
Educational Leadership and Administration — M,O
Elementary Education — M,O
English as a Second Language — M,O
Finance and Banking — M,O
Health Services Management and Hospital Administration — M,O
Marriage and Family Therapy — M,O
Middle School Education — M,O
Multilingual and Multicultural Education — M,O
Pharmaceutical Sciences — M,O
Pharmacy — M,O
Public Administration — M,O
Reading Education — M,O
School Psychology — M,O
Special Education — M,O

LONG ISLAND UNIVERSITY–LIU BROOKLYN

Accounting — M,O
Adult Nursing — M,O
Applied Behavior Analysis — M,O
Athletic Training and Sports Medicine — M,D,O
Biological and Biomedical Sciences—General — M,D,O
Business Administration and Management—General — M,O
Chemistry — M,D,O
Clinical Psychology — M,D,O
Communication Disorders — M,D,O
Community Health — M,D,O
Computer Science — M,O
Counseling Psychology — M,O
Counselor Education — M,O
Early Childhood Education — M,O
Education—General — M,O

Educational Leadership and Administration — M,O
English as a Second Language — M,O
English — M,D,O
Exercise and Sports Science — M,D,O
Family Nurse Practitioner Studies — M,O
Forensic Sciences — M,D,O
Gerontology — M,O
Health Services Management and Hospital Administration — M,O
Human Resources Management — M,O
Marriage and Family Therapy — M,O
Media Studies — M,D,O
Multilingual and Multicultural Education — M,O
Nonprofit Management — M,O
Nursing Education — M,O
Nursing—General — M,O
Occupational Therapy — M,D,O
Pharmaceutical Sciences — M,D
Pharmacology — M,D
Pharmacy — M,D
Physical Therapy — M,D,O
Physician Assistant Studies — M,D,O
Political Science — M,D,O
Psychology—General — M,D,O
Public Administration — M,O
Public Health—General — M,D,O
Social Sciences Education — M,D,O
Social Work — M,D,O
Sociology — M,D,O
Special Education — M,O
Taxation — M,O
Toxicology — M,D
Urban Education — M,O
Urban Studies — M,D,O
Writing — M,D

LONG ISLAND UNIVERSITY–LIU POST

Accounting — M
Allied Health—General — M,O
Applied Behavior Analysis — M,O
Applied Mathematics — M,O
Art Education — M,D,O
Art Therapy — M
Art/Fine Arts — M
Biological and Biomedical Sciences—General — M,O
Business Administration and Management—General — M
Clinical Psychology — M,D,O
Communication Disorders — M,D,O
Counseling Psychology — M,D,O
Criminal Justice and Criminology — M,O
Early Childhood Education — M,D,O
Education—General — M,D,O
Educational Leadership and Administration — M,D,O
Educational Media/Instructional Technology — M,D,O
Engineering Management — M
English as a Second Language — M,D,O
English — M,O
Environmental Management and Policy — M,O
Family Nurse Practitioner Studies — M,O
Finance and Banking — M
Game Design and Development — M
Genetic Counseling — M,O
Geographic Information Systems — M,O
Geosciences — M,O
Gerontology — M,O
Health Services Management and Hospital Administration — M,O
History — M,O
Interdisciplinary Studies — M,D,O
International Business — M
Internet and Interactive Multimedia — M
Management Information Systems — M
Marketing — M
Mathematics — M,O
Middle School Education — M,D,O
Music Education — M,D,O
Music — M
Nonprofit Management — M,O
Nursing Education — M,O
Nutrition — M,O
Political Science — M,O
Psychology—General — M,O
Public Administration — M,O
Reading Education — M,D,O
School Psychology — M,D,O
Secondary Education — M,D,O
Social Work — M,O
Special Education — M,D,O
Sustainable Development — M,O
Taxation — M
Theater — M

LONG ISLAND UNIVERSITY–RIVERHEAD

Early Childhood Education — M,O
Elementary Education — M,O
English as a Second Language — M,O
Middle School Education — M,O
Reading Education — M,O
Secondary Education — M,O
Special Education — M,O

LONGWOOD UNIVERSITY

Business Administration and Management—General — M
Communication Disorders — M
Counselor Education — M
Education—General — M
Educational Media/Instructional Technology — M
Elementary Education — M
Health Education — M
Mathematics Education — M

Middle School Education — M
Physical Education — M
Reading Education — M
Real Estate — M
Special Education — M

LORAS COLLEGE

Applied Psychology — M
Educational Leadership and Administration — M
Pastoral Ministry and Counseling — M
Special Education — M
Theology — M

LOUISIANA COLLEGE

Education—General — M
Pastoral Ministry and Counseling — M
Theology — M

LOUISIANA STATE UNIVERSITY AND AGRICULTURAL & MECHANICAL COLLEGE

Accounting — M,D
Agricultural Economics and Agribusiness — M,D
Agricultural Education — M,D
Agricultural Engineering — M,D
Agricultural Sciences—General — M,D
Animal Sciences — M,D
Anthropology — M,D
Applied Arts and Design—General — M
Applied Science and Technology — M
Applied Statistics — M
Architecture — M
Art History — M
Art/Fine Arts — M
Astronomy — M,D
Astrophysics — M,D
Biochemistry — M,D
Bioengineering — M,D
Biological and Biomedical Sciences—General — M,D
Biopsychology — M,D
Business Administration and Management—General — M,D
Business Education — M,D
Chemical Engineering — M,D
Chemistry — M,D
Civil Engineering — M,D
Clinical Psychology — M,D
Cognitive Sciences — M,D
Communication Disorders — M,D
Communication—General — M,D
Comparative Literature — M,D
Computer Engineering — M,D
Computer Science — M,D
Construction Management — M,D
Counselor Education — M,D,O
Developmental Psychology — M,D
Economics — M,D
Education—General — M,D,O
Educational Leadership and Administration — M,D,O
Educational Measurement and Evaluation — M,D,O
Educational Media/Instructional Technology — M,D,O
Electrical Engineering — M,D
Elementary Education — M,D,O
Engineering and Applied Sciences—General — M,D
English — M,D
Entomology — M,D
Environmental Engineering — M,D
Environmental Management and Policy — M,D
Environmental Sciences — M,D
Family and Consumer Sciences-General — M,D
Finance and Banking — M,D
Fish, Game, and Wildlife Management — M,D
Food Science and Technology — M,D
Forestry — M,D
French — M,D
Geography — M,D
Geology — M,D
Geophysics — M,D
Geotechnical Engineering — M,D
Graphic Design — M
Higher Education — M,D,O
Hispanic Studies — M
History — M,D
Home Economics Education — M,D
Human Resources Development — M,D
Information Studies — M
International and Comparative Education — M,D
Internet and Interactive Multimedia — M
Kinesiology and Movement Studies — M,D
Landscape Architecture — M
Law — M,D
Liberal Studies — M
Library Science — M
Management Information Systems — M,D
Marine Affairs — M,D
Mass Communication — M,D
Mathematics — M,D
Mechanical Engineering — M,D
Mechanics — M,D
Media Studies — M,D
Medical Physics — M,D
Music Education — M,D
Music — M,D
Natural Resources — M,D
Oceanography — M,D
Petroleum Engineering — M,D
Philosophy — M

Photography	M
Physics	M,D
Plant Pathology	M,D
Political Science	M,D
Psychology—General	M,D
Public Administration	M,D
School Psychology	M,D
Secondary Education	M,D,O
Social Work	M,D
Sociology	M,D
Statistics	M
Structural Engineering	M,D
Systems Science	M,D
Theater	M,D
Toxicology	M,D
Transportation and Highway Engineering	M,D
Veterinary Medicine	D
Veterinary Sciences	M,D
Vocational and Technical Education	M,D
Water Resources Engineering	M,D
Writing	M,D

LOUISIANA STATE UNIVERSITY HEALTH SCIENCES CENTER

Allopathic Medicine	M,D
Anatomy	D
Biological and Biomedical Sciences—General	D
Biostatistics	M,D
Cell Biology	D
Communication Disorders	M,D
Community Health Nursing	M,D,O
Community Health	M,D
Dentistry	D
Developmental Biology	D
Environmental and Occupational Health	M,D
Epidemiology	M,D
Family Nurse Practitioner Studies	M,D,O
Gerontological Nursing	M,D,O
Health Services Management and Hospital Administration	M,D
Human Genetics	D
Immunology	D
Maternal and Child/Neonatal Nursing	M,D,O
Microbiology	D
Neurobiology	D
Neuroscience	D
Nurse Anesthesia	M,D,O
Nursing and Healthcare Administration	M,D,O
Nursing Education	M,D,O
Nursing—General	M,D,O
Occupational Therapy	M
Parasitology	D
Pharmacology	D
Physical Therapy	D
Physician Assistant Studies	M
Physiology	D
Public Health—General	M,D
Rehabilitation Counseling	M

LOUISIANA STATE UNIVERSITY HEALTH SCIENCES CENTER AT SHREVEPORT

Allopathic Medicine	D
Anatomy	M,D
Biochemistry	M,D
Biological and Biomedical Sciences—General	M
Cell Biology	M,D
Immunology	M,D
Microbiology	M,D
Molecular Biology	M,D
Pharmacology	M,D
Physiology	M,D

LOUISIANA STATE UNIVERSITY IN SHREVEPORT

Biological and Biomedical Sciences—General	M
Business Administration and Management—General	M
Computer Science	M
Counselor Education	M
Curriculum and Instruction	M,D
Education—General	M,D
Educational Leadership and Administration	M,D
Health Services Management and Hospital Administration	M
Liberal Studies	M
Nonprofit Management	M
Public Health—General	M
School Psychology	O
Systems Science	M

LOUISIANA TECH UNIVERSITY

Accounting	M
Applied Arts and Design—General	M
Applied Physics	M
Architecture	M
Art/Fine Arts	M
Biological and Biomedical Sciences—General	M
Biomedical Engineering	D
Business Administration and Management—General	M,D
Chemical Engineering	M
Chemistry	M,D
Civil Engineering	M
Communication Disorders	M,D
Computer Science	M,D
Counseling Psychology	M,D
Counselor Education	M,D
Curriculum and Instruction	M,D
Early Childhood Education	M,D
Economics	M
Education—General	M,D
Educational Leadership and Administration	M,D
Electrical Engineering	M,D

Engineering and Applied Sciences—General	M,D
English	M,O
Exercise and Sports Science	M
Family and Consumer Sciences—General	M
Finance and Banking	M,D
Graphic Design	M
Health Informatics	M
Higher Education	M,D
History	M
Industrial and Organizational Psychology	M,D
Industrial/Management Engineering	M
Mathematics	M,D
Middle School Education	M,D
Molecular Biology	M
Nanotechnology	M,D
Nutrition	M
Photography	M
Physical Education	M
Physics	M
Psychology—General	M,D
Statistics	M,D
Technical Writing	M,O
Theater	M

LOUISVILLE PRESBYTERIAN THEOLOGICAL SEMINARY

Religion	M,D
Theology	M,D

LOURDES UNIVERSITY

Business Administration and Management—General	M
Curriculum and Instruction	M
Educational Leadership and Administration	M
Nurse Anesthesia	M
Nursing and Healthcare Administration	M
Nursing Education	M
Organizational Management	M
Reading Education	M
Theology	M

LOYOLA MARYMOUNT UNIVERSITY

Accounting	M
Bioethics	M
Business Administration and Management—General	M
Civil Engineering	M
Counseling Psychology	M
Counselor Education	M
Education—General	M,D
Educational Leadership and Administration	M,D
Electrical Engineering	M
Elementary Education	M
Engineering Management	M
English	M
Environmental Sciences	M
Film, Television, and Video Production	M
Higher Education	M
Law	M,D
Marriage and Family Therapy	M
Mathematics Education	M
Mechanical Engineering	M
Multilingual and Multicultural Education	M
Pastoral Ministry and Counseling	M
Philosophy	M
Reading Education	M
Recreation and Park Management	M
Religious Education	M
School Psychology	M
Secondary Education	M
Special Education	M
Systems Engineering	M
Theology	M
Urban Education	M
Writing	M

LOYOLA UNIVERSITY CHICAGO

Accounting	M
Applied Statistics	M
Biochemistry	M,D
Bioethics	M,D,O
Biological and Biomedical Sciences—General	M,D
Business Administration and Management—General	M,O
Cell Biology	M,D
Chemistry	M,D
Clinical Psychology	M,D
Clinical Research	M
Communication—General	M
Computer Science	M
Corporate and Organizational Communication	M
Counseling Psychology	D
Counselor Education	M,O
Criminal Justice and Criminology	M
Curriculum and Instruction	M,D
Developmental Psychology	M,D
Economics	M
Education—General	M,D,O
Educational Leadership and Administration	M,D,O
Educational Measurement and Evaluation	M,D
Educational Policy	M,D
Elementary Education	M,O
English	M,D
Entrepreneurship	M
Ethics	M
Finance and Banking	M
Health Services Management and Hospital Administration	M
Higher Education	M,D
History	M,D
Human Resources Management	M
Humanities	M

Immunology	M,D
Infectious Diseases	M,D
Information Science	M
Information Studies	M,O
International Business	M
Law	M,D
Legal and Justice Studies	M,O
Marketing	M
Mathematics	M
Microbiology	M,D
Molecular Biology	M,D
Molecular Pharmacology	M,D
Molecular Physiology	M,D
Neuroscience	M,D
Nursing—General	M,D,O
Pastoral Ministry and Counseling	M,O
Philosophy	M,D
Physiology	M,D
Political Science	M,D
Psychology—General	M,O
Public Health—General	M,O
Public History	M,D
Public Policy	M
Religious Education	M,O
School Psychology	D,O
Secondary Education	M,O
Social Psychology	M,O
Social Work	M,D,O
Sociology	M,D
Software Engineering	M
Spanish	M
Special Education	M
Statistics	M
Supply Chain Management	M,O
Theology	M,D,O
Urban Studies	M

LOYOLA UNIVERSITY MARYLAND

Accounting	M
Business Administration and Management—General	M
Clinical Psychology	M,D,O
Communication Disorders	M
Counseling Psychology	M,O
Counselor Education	M,O
Curriculum and Instruction	M
Early Childhood Education	M,O
Education—General	M,O
Educational Leadership and Administration	M,O
Educational Media/Instructional Technology	M
Elementary Education	M,O
Finance and Banking	M
Liberal Studies	M
Management Information Systems	M
Media Studies	M
Music Education	M
Psychology—General	M,D,O
Reading Education	M
Secondary Education	M
Theology	M

LOYOLA UNIVERSITY NEW ORLEANS

Business Administration and Management—General	M
Clinical Psychology	M
Criminal Justice and Criminology	M
Education—General	M
Entrepreneurship	M
Family Nurse Practitioner Studies	M,D
Health Services Management and Hospital Administration	M,D
Law	M,D
Marketing	M
Music	M
Nursing Education	M,D
Nursing—General	M,D
Organizational Management	M
Secondary Education	M
Theology	M,O
Therapies—Dance, Drama, and Music	M

LUBBOCK CHRISTIAN UNIVERSITY

Theology	M

LUTHERAN SCHOOL OF THEOLOGY AT CHICAGO

Pastoral Ministry and Counseling	M,D
Theology	M,D

LUTHERAN THEOLOGICAL SEMINARY AT GETTYSBURG

Pastoral Ministry and Counseling	M,D
Religion	M,D
Theology	M,D

THE LUTHERAN THEOLOGICAL SEMINARY AT PHILADELPHIA

Pastoral Ministry and Counseling	M,D,O
Religion	M,D,O
Theology	M,D,O

LUTHERAN THEOLOGICAL SEMINARY SASKATOON

Ethics	M,D
Pastoral Ministry and Counseling	M,D
Religion	M,D
Theology	M,D

LUTHER RICE COLLEGE & SEMINARY

Pastoral Ministry and Counseling	M,D
Religion	M,D
Theology	M,D

LUTHER SEMINARY

Missions and Missiology	M,D
Pastoral Ministry and Counseling	M,D
Theology	M,D

LYNCHBURG COLLEGE

Business Administration and Management—General	M
Clinical Psychology	M
Counseling Psychology	M
Counselor Education	M

Curriculum and Instruction	M
Educational Leadership and Administration	M,D
Higher Education	M
Music	M
Nursing and Healthcare Administration	M
Nursing—General	M
Physical Therapy	D
Reading Education	M
School Psychology	M
Science Education	M
Special Education	M

LYNDON STATE COLLEGE

Counselor Education	M
Curriculum and Instruction	M
Education—General	M
Reading Education	M
Science Education	M
Special Education	M

LYNN UNIVERSITY

Applied Psychology	M
Aviation Management	M
Business Administration and Management—General	M
Communication—General	M,O
Computer Art and Design	M,O
Counseling Psychology	M
Criminal Justice and Criminology	M
Early Childhood Education	M,D
Education of the Gifted	M,D
Education—General	M,D
Educational Leadership and Administration	M,D
Hospitality Management	M
Human Resources Management	M
International Business	M
Internet and Interactive Multimedia	M,O
Investment Management	M
Marketing	M
Mass Communication	M,O
Media Studies	M,O
Middle School Education	M,D
Music	M,O
Special Education	M,D
Sports Management	M

MAASTRICHT SCHOOL OF MANAGEMENT

Business Administration and Management—General	M,D
Facilities Management	M,D
Sustainability Management	M,D

MACHZIKEI HADATH RABBINICAL COLLEGE

Theology	O

MADONNA UNIVERSITY

Adult Nursing	M
Business Administration and Management—General	M
Clinical Psychology	M
Criminal Justice and Criminology	M
Education—General	M
Educational Leadership and Administration	M
English as a Second Language	M
Health Services Management and Hospital Administration	M
Hospice Nursing	M
International Business	M
Liberal Studies	M
Nursing and Healthcare Administration	M
Nursing—General	M
Pastoral Ministry and Counseling	M
Psychology—General	M
Quality Management	M
Reading Education	M
Special Education	M
Theology	M

MAHARISHI UNIVERSITY OF MANAGEMENT

Accounting	M,D
Asian Studies	M,D
Business Administration and Management—General	M,D
Computer Science	M
Physiology	D
Sustainability Management	M,D
Writing	M

MAINE COLLEGE OF ART

Art/Fine Arts	M

MAINE MARITIME ACADEMY

International Business	M
Supply Chain Management	M
Transportation Management	M

MALONE UNIVERSITY

Business Administration and Management—General	M
Counselor Education	M
Curriculum and Instruction	M
Education—General	M
Educational Leadership and Administration	M
Family Nurse Practitioner Studies	M
Nursing—General	M
Organizational Management	M
Special Education	M
Theology	M

MANCHESTER UNIVERSITY

Athletic Training and Sports Medicine	M
Genomic Sciences	M
Pharmacy	D

MANHATTAN COLLEGE

Applied Mathematics	M

Business Administration and
Management—General M
Chemical Engineering M
Civil Engineering M
Computer Engineering M
Counselor Education M,O
Database Systems M
Early Childhood Education M,O
Education—General M,O
Educational Leadership and
Administration M,O
Educational Media/Instructional
Technology M
Electrical Engineering M
Elementary Education M,O
Engineering and Applied
Sciences—General M
English M,O
Environmental Engineering M
Mathematics M,O
Mechanical Engineering M
Multilingual and Multicultural
Education M,O
Organizational Management M
Special Education M,O
Student Affairs M,O

MANHATTAN SCHOOL OF MUSIC
Music M,D,O

MANHATTANVILLE COLLEGE
Accounting M
Art Education M
Business Education M
Corporate and Organizational
Communication M
Early Childhood Education M,O
Education—General M,D,O*
Educational Leadership and
Administration M,D,O
Elementary Education M,O
English as a Second Language M,O
English Education M
Entrepreneurship M
Exercise and Sports Science M,O
Finance and Banking M
Foreign Languages Education M
Health Promotion M,O
Human Resources Management M
International Business M
Investment Management M
Management Strategy and Policy M
Marketing M
Mathematics Education M
Middle School Education M
Music Education M
Organizational Management M
Reading Education M
Science Education M
Secondary Education M,O
Social Sciences Education M,O
Special Education M,O
Sports Management M
Urban Education M,O
Writing M

MANSFIELD UNIVERSITY OF PENNSYLVANIA
Art Education M
Education—General M
Elementary Education M
Information Studies M
Library Science M
Music M
Nursing—General M
Organizational Management M
Psychology—General M
Secondary Education M
Special Education M

MAPLE SPRINGS BAPTIST BIBLE COLLEGE AND SEMINARY
Pastoral Ministry and Counseling M,D,O
Religious Education M,D,O
Theology M,D,O

MARANATHA BAPTIST UNIVERSITY
Cultural Studies M
Education—General M
Pastoral Ministry and Counseling M
Religion M
Theology M

MARCONI INTERNATIONAL UNIVERSITY
Business Administration and
Management—General M,D
Educational Leadership and
Administration M,D
Educational Media/Instructional
Technology M,D
International Business M,D

MARIAN UNIVERSITY (IN)
Osteopathic Medicine M,D

MARIAN UNIVERSITY (WI)
Adult Nursing M
Business Administration and
Management—General M
Curriculum and Instruction M,D
Education—General M,D
Educational Leadership and
Administration M,D
Educational Media/Instructional
Technology M,D
Nursing Education M
Nursing—General M
Organizational Management M
Special Education M,D
Thanatology M

MARIETTA COLLEGE
Physician Assistant Studies M
Psychology—General M

MARIST COLLEGE
Business Administration and
Management—General M,O
Communication—General M
Computer Science M,O
Corporate and Organizational
Communication M
Counseling Psychology M,O
Education—General M,O
Management Information Systems M,O
Management of Technology M,O
Marketing M
Museum Studies M
Psychology—General M,O
Public Administration M,O
School Psychology M,O
Software Engineering M,O

MARLBORO COLLEGE
Business Administration and
Management—General M
Computer Education M,O
Education—General M,O
Educational Media/Instructional
Technology M,O
English as a Second Language M
Entrepreneurship M
Food Science and
Technology M
Internet and Interactive
Multimedia M
Legal and Justice Studies M
Organizational Management M
Project Management M

MARQUETTE UNIVERSITY
Accounting M
Acute Care/Critical Care Nursing M,D,O
Adult Nursing M,D,O
Advertising and Public Relations M,O
Analytical Chemistry M,D
Bioinformatics M,D
Biological and Biomedical
Sciences—General M,D
Biomedical Engineering M,D
Business Administration and
Management—General M,O
Cardiovascular Sciences M,D
Cell Biology M,D
Chemical Physics M,D
Chemistry M,D
Civil Engineering M,D,O
Clinical Psychology M,D
Communication Disorders M,O
Communication—General M,O
Computational Sciences M,D
Computer Engineering M,D,O
Computer Science M,D
Construction Engineering M,D,O
Construction Management M,D
Counseling Psychology M,D
Counselor Education M,D
Curriculum and Instruction M,D,O
Dentistry D
Developmental Biology M,D
Ecology M,D
Economics M
Education—General M,D,O
Educational Leadership and
Administration M,D,O
Educational Policy M,D,O
Electrical Engineering M,D,O
Elementary Education M,D,O
Engineering and Applied
Sciences—General M,D,O
Engineering Management M,D,O
English M,D
Entrepreneurship M,O
Environmental Engineering M,D,O
Ethics M,D
Family Nurse Practitioner Studies M,D,O
Finance and Banking M,O
Foreign Languages Education M
Foundations and Philosophy of
Education M,D,O
Genetics M,D
Gerontological Nursing M,D,O
Hazardous Materials
Management M,D,O
Health Communication M,O
History M,D
Human Resources Development M
Human Resources Management M,O
Industrial and Manufacturing
Management M,O
Inorganic Chemistry M,D
Interdisciplinary Studies D
International Affairs M,D
International Business M,O
Journalism M,O
Law D
Management Information Systems M,O
Management of Technology M,D
Marketing Research M
Marketing M,O
Mass Communication M,O
Mathematics Education M,D
Mathematics M,D
Mechanical Engineering M,D,O
Microbiology M,D
Molecular Biology M,D
Neuroscience M,D
Nurse Midwifery M,D,O
Nursing and Healthcare
Administration M,D,O
Nursing—General M,D,O
Oral and Dental Sciences M,O
Organic Chemistry M,D
Pediatric Nursing M,D,O
Philosophy M,D
Physical Chemistry M,D

Physical Therapy D
Physician Assistant Studies M
Physiology M,D
Political Science M
Psychology—General D
Reading Education M,D,O
Real Estate M
Rehabilitation Sciences M,D
Secondary Education M,D,O
Social Psychology M,D
Spanish M
Speech and Interpersonal
Communication M
Sports Management M,O
Structural Engineering M,D,O
Student Affairs M,D,O
Supply Chain Management M,O
Theology M,D
Transportation and Highway
Engineering M,D,O
Water Resources Engineering M,D,O
Water Resources M,D,O

MARSHALL B. KETCHUM UNIVERSITY
Optometry M,D
Vision Sciences M,D

MARSHALL UNIVERSITY
Accounting M
Adult Education M
Advertising and Public Relations M
Allopathic Medicine D
Athletic Training and Sports
Medicine M
Biological and Biomedical
Sciences—General M,D
Business Administration and
Management—General M
Chemistry M
Classics M,O
Clinical Psychology M,D,O
Communication Disorders M
Communication—General M
Computer Science M
Counselor Education M,O
Criminal Justice and Criminology M
Early Childhood Education M
Education—General M,D,O
Educational Leadership and
Administration M,D,O
Elementary Education M,O
Engineering and Applied
Sciences—General M
Engineering Management M
English M,O
Environmental Engineering M
Environmental Sciences M
Exercise and Sports Science M
Forensic Sciences M,O
Geography M,O
Health Education M
Health Informatics M
Health Services Management and
Hospital Administration M
History M,O
Human Resources Management M
Humanities M,O
Information Science M
Journalism M
Management of Technology M
Mathematics M
Music M
Nurse Anesthesia D
Nursing—General M
Nutrition M
Pharmacy D
Physical Therapy D
Physics M
Political Science M
Psychology—General M,D,O
Public Administration M
Public Health—General M
Reading Education M,O
School Psychology O
Secondary Education M
Social Work M
Sociology M
Special Education M
Sports Management M
Transportation and Highway
Engineering M
Vocational and Technical Education M

MARS HILL UNIVERSITY
Elementary Education M

MARTIN LUTHER COLLEGE
Curriculum and Instruction M
Early Childhood Education M
Education—General M
Educational Leadership and
Administration M
Educational Media/Instructional
Technology M
Special Education M

MARTIN UNIVERSITY
Pastoral Ministry and Counseling M
Psychology—General M
Social Psychology M

MARY BALDWIN UNIVERSITY
Education—General M
Elementary Education M
English M
Middle School Education M
Occupational Therapy D
Theater M

MARYGROVE COLLEGE
Education—General M
Educational Leadership and
Administration M

Educational Media/Instructional
Technology M
Elementary Education M
English M
Human Resources Management M
Legal and Justice Studies M
Reading Education M
Secondary Education M
Translation and Interpretation O
Urban Education M

MARYLAND INSTITUTE COLLEGE OF ART
Applied Arts and Design—General M
Art Education M
Art/Fine Arts M,O
Business Administration and
Management—General M
Film, Television, and Video
Production M
Graphic Design M
Illustration M
Museum Studies M
Photography M

MARYLAND UNIVERSITY OF INTEGRATIVE HEALTH
Acupuncture and Oriental Medicine M,D,O
Health Promotion M,O
Nutrition M,D,O

MARYLHURST UNIVERSITY
Art Therapy M,O
Business Administration and
Management—General M
Education—General M
Elementary Education M
Health Services Management and
Hospital Administration M
Hospitality Management M
Interdisciplinary Studies M
Real Estate M
Theology M

MARYMOUNT CALIFORNIA UNIVERSITY
Business Administration and
Management—General M
International Development M
Social Psychology M

MARYMOUNT UNIVERSITY
Allied Health—General M,D,O
Business Administration and
Management—General M,O
Clinical Psychology M
Community College Education M,O
Computer and Information
Systems Security M,O
Counseling Psychology M
Counselor Education M
Education—General M
Elementary Education M
English as a Second Language M
English Education M,O
English M,O
Family Nurse Practitioner Studies M,D,O
Forensic Psychology M
Health Education M
Health Informatics M,O
Health Promotion M
Health Services Management and
Hospital Administration M
Human Resources Management M,O
Interior Design M
Management Information Systems M,O
Nonprofit Management M,O
Nursing—General M,D,O
Pastoral Ministry and Counseling M
Physical Therapy D
Project Management M,O
Secondary Education M
Software Engineering M,O
Special Education M

MARYVILLE UNIVERSITY OF SAINT LOUIS
Accounting M,O
Actuarial Science M
Acute Care/Critical Care Nursing M,D
Addictions/Substance Abuse
Counseling M
Adult Nursing M,D
Allied Health—General M,D
Business Administration and
Management—General M,O
Business Education M,O
Communication Disorders M
Computer and Information
Systems Security M,O
Early Childhood Education M,D
Education of the Gifted M,D
Education—General M,D
Educational Leadership and
Administration M,D
Elementary Education M,D
Family Nurse Practitioner Studies M,D
Finance and Banking M,O
Gerontological Nursing M,D
Health Services Management and
Hospital Administration M,O
Higher Education M,D
Human Resources Management M,O
Information Science M,O
Logistics M,O
Marketing M,O
Marriage and Family Therapy M
Middle School Education M,D
Nursing—General M,D
Occupational Therapy M
Organizational Management M
Pediatric Nursing M,D
Physical Therapy D
Project Management M,O

M—masters degree; D—doctorate; O—other advanced degree; *—Close-Up and/or Display

Reading Education — M,D
Rehabilitation Counseling — M
Secondary Education — M,D
Sports Management — M,O
Supply Chain Management — M,O
Therapies—Dance, Drama, and Music — M

MARYWOOD UNIVERSITY

Architecture — M
Art Education — M
Art Therapy — M,O
Art/Fine Arts — M
Biotechnology — M
Business Administration and Management—General — M
Clinical Psychology — M,D
Communication Disorders — M
Communication—General — M
Computer and Information Systems Security — M
Counseling Psychology — M
Counselor Education — M
Criminal Justice and Criminology — M
Early Childhood Education — M
Education—General — M
Educational Leadership and Administration — M,D
Elementary Education — M
Exercise and Sports Science — M
Finance and Banking — M
Gerontology — M
Graphic Design — M
Health Education — D
Health Services Management and Hospital Administration — M
Higher Education — M,D
Human Development — D
Illustration — M
Interdisciplinary Studies — D
Interior Design — M
Investment Management — M
Management Information Systems — M
Music Education — M
Nutrition — M,O
Photography — M
Physician Assistant Studies — M
Psychology—General — M
Public Administration — M
Reading Education — M
Secondary Education — M
Social Work — M,D
Special Education — M

MASSACHUSETTS COLLEGE OF ART AND DESIGN

Applied Arts and Design—General — M,O
Architecture — M
Art Education — M,O
Art/Fine Arts — M,O
Film, Television, and Video Production — M,O
Interdisciplinary Studies — M,O
Media Studies — M,O
Photography — M,O
Textile Design — M,O

MASSACHUSETTS COLLEGE OF LIBERAL ARTS

Business Administration and Management—General — M,O
Curriculum and Instruction — M,O
Education—General — M,O
Educational Leadership and Administration — M,O
Educational Media/Instructional Technology — M,O
Health Education — M,O
Physical Education — M,O
Reading Education — M,O
Special Education — M,O

MASSACHUSETTS INSTITUTE OF TECHNOLOGY

Aerospace/Aeronautical Engineering — M,D,O
Archaeology — M,D,O
Architectural History — M,D
Architecture — M,D
Art History — M,D
Atmospheric Sciences — M,D
Biochemistry — D
Bioengineering — M,D
Bioinformatics — M,D
Biological and Biomedical Sciences—General — M,D
Biomedical Engineering — M,D
Business Administration and Management—General — M,D
Cell Biology — D
Chemical Engineering — M,D
Chemistry — D
Civil Engineering — M,D,O
Cognitive Sciences — D
Communication Disorders — M,D
Computational Biology — D
Computational Sciences — M
Computer Engineering — M,D,O
Computer Science — M,D,O
Construction Engineering — M,D,O
Developmental Biology — D
Economics — M,D
Electrical Engineering — M,D,O
Engineering and Applied Sciences—General — M,D,O
Engineering Management — M
Environmental Biology — M,D,O
Environmental Engineering — M,D,O
Environmental Sciences — M,D,O
Genetics — D
Genomic Sciences — M,D
Geochemistry — M,D
Geology — M,D
Geophysics — M,D
Geosciences — M,D

Geotechnical Engineering — M,D,O
History of Science and Technology — D
Hydrology — M,D,O
Immunology — D
Information Science — M,D,O
Inorganic Chemistry — D
Linguistics — D
Logistics — M
Manufacturing Engineering — M,D,O
Marine Geology — M,D
Materials Engineering — M,D,O
Materials Sciences — M,D,O
Mathematics — D
Mechanical Engineering — M,D,O
Media Studies — M,D
Medical Physics — M,D
Microbiology — D
Molecular Biology — M,D,O
Molecular Toxicology — D
Neurobiology — D
Neuroscience — D
Nuclear Engineering — M,D,O
Ocean Engineering — M,D,O
Oceanography — M,D,O
Operations Research — M,D
Organic Chemistry — M,D,O
Philosophy — D
Physical Chemistry — D
Physics — M,D
Planetary and Space Sciences — M,D
Political Science — M,D
Real Estate — M
Social Sciences — D
Structural Biology — D
Structural Engineering — M,D,O
Systems Biology — D
Systems Engineering — M,D
Technical Writing — M
Technology and Public Policy — M,D
Toxicology — M,D
Transportation and Highway Engineering — M,D,O
Urban and Regional Planning — M,D
Urban Studies — M
Writing — M

MASSACHUSETTS MARITIME ACADEMY

Emergency Management — M
Facilities Management — M

MASSACHUSETTS SCHOOL OF LAW AT ANDOVER

Law — D

THE MASTER'S UNIVERSITY

Pastoral Ministry and Counseling — M,D
Theology — M,D

MAYO CLINIC GRADUATE SCHOOL OF BIOMEDICAL SCIENCES

Biochemistry — D
Biological and Biomedical Sciences—General — D
Biomedical Engineering — D
Cancer Biology/Oncology — D
Cell Biology — D
Genetics — D
Immunology — D
Molecular Biology — D
Molecular Pharmacology — D
Neuroscience — D
Structural Biology — D
Virology — D

MAYO CLINIC SCHOOL OF HEALTH SCIENCES

Nurse Anesthesia — D
Physical Therapy — D

MAYO CLINIC SCHOOL OF MEDICINE

Allopathic Medicine — D

MCCORMICK THEOLOGICAL SEMINARY

Pastoral Ministry and Counseling — M,D,O
Theology — M,D,O

MCDANIEL COLLEGE

Counselor Education — M
Curriculum and Instruction — M
Educational Leadership and Administration — M
Educational Media/Instructional Technology — M
Elementary Education — M,O
English as a Second Language — M
Exercise and Sports Science — M
Gerontology — M,O
Human Resources Development — M
Human Services — M
Liberal Studies — M,O
Library Science — M
Mathematics Education — M,O
Physical Education — M
Reading Education — M
Science Education — M,O
Secondary Education — M,O
Special Education — M
Writing — M,O

MCGILL UNIVERSITY

Accounting — M,D,O
Aerospace/Aeronautical Engineering — M,D
Agricultural Economics and Agribusiness — M
Agricultural Engineering — M
Agricultural Sciences—General — M,D,O
Agronomy and Soil Sciences — M,D
Allopathic Medicine — M,D
Anatomy — M,D
Animal Sciences — M,D
Anthropology — M,D
Applied Mathematics — M,D
Architecture — M,D,O
Art History — M,D

Asian Studies — M,D
Atmospheric Sciences — M,D
Biochemistry — M,D
Bioengineering — M,D
Bioethics — M,D,O
Bioinformatics — M,D
Biological and Biomedical Sciences—General — M,D
Biomedical Engineering — M,D
Biostatistics — M,D,O
Biotechnology — M,D,O
Business Administration and Management—General — M,D
Cell Biology — M,D
Chemical Engineering — M,D
Chemistry — M,D
Civil Engineering — M,D
Clinical Psychology — M,D
Communication Disorders — M,D
Communication—General — M,D
Community Health — M,D,O
Computational Sciences — M,D
Computer Engineering — M,D
Computer Science — M,D
Counseling Psychology — M,D,O
Curriculum and Instruction — M,D,O
Dentistry — M,D,O
Developmental Psychology — M,D
Economics — M,D
Education—General — M,D,O
Educational Leadership and Administration — M,D,O
Educational Psychology — M,D,O
Electrical Engineering — M,D
Engineering and Applied Sciences—General — M,D,O
English — M,D
Entomology — M,D
Entrepreneurship — M,D,O
Environmental and Occupational Health — M,D,O
Environmental Engineering — M,D
Environmental Management and Policy — M,D
Epidemiology — M,D
Experimental Psychology — M,D
Family Nurse Practitioner Studies — M,D
Finance and Banking — M,D,O
Fish, Game, and Wildlife Management — M,D
Food Science and Technology — M,D
Foreign Languages Education — M,D,O
Forensic Sciences — M,D,O
Forestry — M,D
Foundations and Philosophy of Education — M,D,O
French — M,D
Genetic Counseling — M,D
Geography — M,D
Geosciences — M,D
Geotechnical Engineering — M,D
German — M,D
Health Services Management and Hospital Administration — M,D,O
Hispanic Studies — M,D
History of Medicine — M,D
History — M,D
Human Genetics — M,D
Hydraulics — M,D
Immunology — M,D
Industrial and Manufacturing Management — M,D,O
Information Studies — M,D,O
International Business — M,D,O
International Development — M,D,O
Italian — M,D
Jewish Studies — M
Kinesiology and Movement Studies — M,D,O
Law — M,D,O
Library Science — M,D,O
Linguistics — M,D
Management Information Systems — M,D,O
Management Strategy and Policy — M,D,O
Marketing — M,D,O
Materials Engineering — M,D,O
Mathematics — M,D
Mechanical Engineering — M,D
Mechanics — M,D
Medical Physics — M,D
Meteorology — M,D
Microbiology — M,D
Mineral/Mining Engineering — M,D,O
Music Education — M,D
Music — M,D
Natural Resources — M,D
Near and Middle Eastern Studies — M,D,O
Neuroscience — M,D
Nursing—General — M,D,O
Nutrition — M,D,O
Oceanography — M,D
Oral and Dental Sciences — M,D,O
Parasitology — M,D,O
Pathology — M,D
Pharmacology — M,D
Philosophy — M,D
Physical Education — M,D,O
Physics — M,D
Physiology — M,D
Planetary and Space Sciences — M,D
Plant Sciences — M,D,O
Political Science — M,D
Psychology—General — M,D
Rehabilitation Sciences — M,D,O
Religion — M,D
Russian — M,D
School Psychology — M,D,O
Social Work — M,D,O
Sociology — M,D,O
Statistics — M,D,O
Structural Engineering — M,D
Theology — M,D
Transportation Management — M,D

Urban and Regional Planning — M,D
Water Resources Engineering — M,D

MCKENDREE UNIVERSITY

Business Administration and Management—General — M
Clinical Psychology — M
Counseling Psychology — M
Curriculum and Instruction — M,D,O
Education—General — M,D,O
Educational Leadership and Administration — M,D,O
Higher Education — M,D,O
Human Resources Management — M
International Business — M
Music Education — M,D,O
Nursing and Healthcare Administration — M
Nursing Education — M
Nursing—General — M
Reading Education — M
Special Education — M,D,O

MCMASTER UNIVERSITY

Analytical Chemistry — M,D
Anthropology — M,D
Applied Statistics — M
Astrophysics — D
Biochemistry — M,D
Biological and Biomedical Sciences—General — M,D
Business Administration and Management—General — M,D
Cancer Biology/Oncology — M,D
Cardiovascular Sciences — M,D
Cell Biology — M,D
Chemical Engineering — M,D
Chemical Physics — M,D
Chemistry — M,D
Civil Engineering — M,D
Classics — M,D
Computer Science — M,D
Cultural Studies — M,D
Economics — M,D
Electrical Engineering — M,D
Engineering and Applied Sciences—General — M,D
Engineering Physics — M,D
English — M,D
French — M
Genetics — M,D
Geochemistry — M,D
Geography — M,D
Geology — M,D
Geosciences — M,D
Health Physics/Radiological Health — M,D
Health Services Research — M,D
History — M,D
Human Resources Management — M,D
Immunology — M,D
Industrial and Labor Relations — M
Inorganic Chemistry — M,D
International Affairs — M,D
Kinesiology and Movement Studies — M,D
Management Information Systems — D
Materials Engineering — M,D
Materials Sciences — M,D
Mathematics — M,D
Mechanical Engineering — M,D
Medical Physics — M,D
Molecular Biology — M,D
Neuroscience — M,D
Nuclear Engineering — M,D
Nursing—General — M,D
Nutrition — M,D
Occupational Therapy — M
Organic Chemistry — M,D
Pastoral Ministry and Counseling — M,D,O
Pharmacology — M,D
Philosophy — M,D
Physical Chemistry — M,D
Physical Therapy — M
Physics — D
Physiology — M,D
Political Science — M,D
Psychology—General — M,D
Public Administration — M,D
Public Affairs — M,D
Public Policy — M,D
Rehabilitation Sciences — M,D
Religion — M,D
Social Work — M
Sociology — M,D
Software Engineering — M,D
Statistics — M
Theology — M,D,O
Virology — M,D

MCMURRY UNIVERSITY

Family Nurse Practitioner Studies — M
Nursing Education — M
Nursing—General — M

MCNALLY SMITH COLLEGE OF MUSIC

Music — M

MCNEESE STATE UNIVERSITY

Addictions/Substance Abuse Counseling — M
Agricultural Sciences—General — M
Applied Behavior Analysis — M
Business Administration and Management—General — M
Chemical Engineering — M
Chemistry — M
Civil Engineering — M
Computer Science — M
Counseling Psychology — M
Counselor Education — M,O
Criminal Justice and Criminology — M
Curriculum and Instruction — M
Early Childhood Education — M,O
Education—General — O
Educational Leadership and Administration — M,O

Educational Measurement and Evaluation	M,O
Educational Media/Instructional Technology	M,O
Electrical Engineering	M
Elementary Education	M
Engineering and Applied Sciences—General	M,O
Engineering Management	M
English	M
Environmental Sciences	M
Exercise and Sports Science	M
Experimental Psychology	M
Family Nurse Practitioner Studies	M,O
Health Promotion	M
Library Science	O
Mathematics	M
Mechanical Engineering	M,O
Middle School Education	O
Music Education	O
Nursing and Healthcare Administration	M,O
Nursing Education	M
Nursing—General	M,O
Nutrition	M
Psychiatric Nursing	M,O
Psychology—General	M
Reading Education	M,O
School Psychology	M
Science Education	M
Secondary Education	M,O
Special Education	M,O
Statistics	M
Writing	M

MCPHERSON COLLEGE
Education—General	M

MCPHS UNIVERSITY
Acupuncture and Oriental Medicine	M
Chemistry	M,D
Health Services Management and Hospital Administration	M
Nursing—General	M
Optometry	D
Pharmaceutical Sciences	M,D
Pharmacology	M,D
Pharmacy	D
Physical Therapy	D
Physician Assistant Studies	M

MEADVILLE LOMBARD THEOLOGICAL SCHOOL
Pastoral Ministry and Counseling	M,D
Theology	M,D

MEDAILLE COLLEGE
Business Administration and Management—General	M
Clinical Psychology	M,D
Counseling Psychology	M,D
Curriculum and Instruction	M
Education—General	M
Elementary Education	M
Marriage and Family Therapy	M,D
Organizational Management	M
Psychology—General	M,D
Reading Education	M
Secondary Education	M
Special Education	M

MEDICAL COLLEGE OF WISCONSIN
Allopathic Medicine	D
Biochemistry	D
Bioethics	M,O
Biological and Biomedical Sciences—General	M,D,O
Biophysics	D
Biostatistics	D
Clinical Laboratory Sciences/Medical Technology	M
Clinical Research	
Community Health	D
Microbiology	M,D
Molecular Genetics	M,D
Neuroscience	D
Pharmacology	D
Physiology	D
Public Health—General	M,D,O
Toxicology	D

MEDICAL UNIVERSITY OF SOUTH CAROLINA
Adult Nursing	M,D
Allied Health—General	M,D
Allopathic Medicine	D
Biochemistry	M,D
Biological and Biomedical Sciences—General	M,D
Biostatistics	M,D
Cancer Biology/Oncology	D
Cardiovascular Sciences	D
Cell Biology	D
Clinical Research	M
Dentistry	D
Developmental Biology	D
Epidemiology	M,D
Family Nurse Practitioner Studies	M,D
Genetics	D
Gerontological Nursing	M,D
Health Services Management and Hospital Administration	M,D
Immunology	M,D
International Health	M
Marine Sciences	D
Maternal and Child/Neonatal Nursing	M,D
Medical Imaging	D
Medicinal and Pharmaceutical Chemistry	D
Microbiology	M,D
Molecular Biology	M,D
Molecular Pharmacology	M,D

Neuroscience	M,D
Nurse Anesthesia	M
Nursing and Healthcare Administration	M
Nursing Education	M
Nursing—General	D
Occupational Therapy	M
Pathobiology	D
Pathology	M,D
Pharmacy	D
Physical Therapy	D
Physician Assistant Studies	M
Rehabilitation Sciences	D
Toxicology	D

MEHARRY MEDICAL COLLEGE
Allopathic Medicine	D
Biochemistry	D
Biological and Biomedical Sciences—General	D
Cancer Biology/Oncology	D
Dentistry	D
Environmental and Occupational Health	M
Health Services Management and Hospital Administration	M
Immunology	D
Microbiology	D
Neuroscience	D
Pharmacology	D
Public Health—General	M

MELBOURNE BUSINESS SCHOOL
Business Administration and Management—General	M,D,O
Marketing	M,D,O

MEMORIAL UNIVERSITY OF NEWFOUNDLAND
Adult Education	M,D,O
Anthropology	M,D
Aquaculture	M
Archaeology	M,D
Biochemistry	M,D
Biological and Biomedical Sciences—General	M,D,O
Biopsychology	M,D
Business Administration and Management—General	M
Cancer Biology/Oncology	M,D
Cardiovascular Sciences	M,D
Chemistry	M,D
Civil Engineering	M,D
Classics	M
Clinical Psychology	M,D
Clinical Research	M
Community Health	M,D,O
Computational Sciences	M
Computer Engineering	M,D
Computer Science	M,D
Condensed Matter Physics	M,D
Cultural Anthropology	M,D
Curriculum and Instruction	M,D,O
Economics	M
Education—General	M,D,O
Educational Leadership and Administration	M,D,O
Educational Media/Instructional Technology	M,D,O
Educational Psychology	M,D,O
Electrical Engineering	M,D
Engineering and Applied Sciences—General	M,D
English	M,D
Environmental Engineering	M
Environmental Sciences	M,D
Epidemiology	M,D,O
Exercise and Sports Science	M
Experimental Psychology	M,D
Fish, Game, and Wildlife Management	M,O
Folklore	M,D
Food Science and Technology	M,D
French	M
Gender Studies	M,D
Geography	M,D
Geology	M,D
Geophysics	M,D
Geosciences	M,D
German	M
History	M,D
Human Genetics	M,D
Humanities	M
Immunology	M,D
Industrial and Labor Relations	M
Kinesiology and Movement Studies	M
Linguistics	M,D
Marine Affairs	M,D,O
Marine Sciences	M,O
Mathematics	M,D
Mechanical Engineering	M,D
Music	M,D
Neuroscience	M,D
Nursing—General	M,D
Ocean Engineering	M,D
Oceanography	M,D
Pharmaceutical Sciences	M,D
Philosophy	M,D
Physical Education	M
Physics	M,D
Political Science	M
Psychology—General	M,D
Religion	M
Social Work	M,D
Sociology	M,D
Statistics	M,D

MEMPHIS COLLEGE OF ART
Applied Arts and Design—General	M
Art Education	M
Art/Fine Arts	M

Illustration	M
Photography	M

MEMPHIS THEOLOGICAL SEMINARY
Theology	M,D

MERCER UNIVERSITY
Accounting	M
Allopathic Medicine	M,D
Biomedical Engineering	M
Business Administration and Management—General	M
Clinical Psychology	M,D
Computer Engineering	M
Counselor Education	M,D
Criminal Justice and Criminology	M,D
Curriculum and Instruction	M,D,O
Early Childhood Education	M,D,O
Education—General	M,D,O
Educational Leadership and Administration	M,D,O
Electrical Engineering	M
Engineering and Applied Sciences—General	M
Engineering Management	M
Entrepreneurship	M
Environmental and Occupational Health	M,D
Environmental Engineering	M
Environmental Sciences	M
Gerontological Nursing	M,D,O
Gerontology	M,D
Health Informatics	M,D
Higher Education	M,D,O
Human Services	M,D
Law	D
Management of Technology	M
Management Strategy and Policy	M
Mechanical Engineering	M
Middle School Education	M,D,O
Music	M
Nursing—General	M,D,O
Organizational Management	M,D
Pastoral Ministry and Counseling	M,D
Pharmaceutical Sciences	D
Pharmacy	D
Physical Therapy	M,D
Physician Assistant Studies	M,D
Public Health—General	M,D
Reading Education	M,D,O
Rehabilitation Counseling	M,D
School Psychology	M,D
Secondary Education	M,D,O
Software Engineering	M
Theology	M,D

MERCY COLLEGE
Accounting	M
Allied Health—General	M,D
Business Administration and Management—General	M
Communication Disorders	M
Computer and Information Systems Security	M
Counseling Psychology	M,O
Counselor Education	M,O
Early Childhood Education	M
Education—General	M,O
Educational Leadership and Administration	M,O
Elementary Education	M
English as a Second Language	M,O
English	M
Health Services Management and Hospital Administration	M
Human Resources Management	M
Marriage and Family Therapy	M,O
Middle School Education	M,O
Nursing and Healthcare Administration	M
Nursing Education	M
Nursing—General	M
Occupational Therapy	M
Organizational Management	M
Physical Therapy	D
Physician Assistant Studies	M
Psychology—General	M
Reading Education	M,O
School Psychology	M
Secondary Education	M,O

MERCYHURST UNIVERSITY
Accounting	M,O
Anthropology	M
Applied Behavior Analysis	M
Archaeology	M
Biological Anthropology	M
Computer and Information Systems Security	M
Criminal Justice and Criminology	M,O
Educational Leadership and Administration	M,O
Entrepreneurship	M,O
Forensic Sciences	M
Higher Education	M,O
Human Resources Management	M,O
Management Strategy and Policy	M,O
Organizational Management	M,O
Physician Assistant Studies	M
Secondary Education	M
Special Education	M
Sports Management	M,O

MEREDITH COLLEGE
Business Administration and Management—General	M
Curriculum and Instruction	M,O
Education of the Gifted	M,O
Education—General	M,O
Elementary Education	M,O
English as a Second Language	M,O
Health Education	M,O

Nutrition	M,O
Physical Education	M,O
Reading Education	M,O
Special Education	M,O

MERRIMACK COLLEGE
Accounting	M
Adult Education	M,O
Athletic Training and Sports Medicine	M
Business Administration and Management—General	M
Civil Engineering	M
Clinical Psychology	M
Community Health	M
Computer Science	M
Criminal Justice and Criminology	M,O
Curriculum and Instruction	M,O
Database Systems	M
Early Childhood Education	M,O
Education—General	M,O
Educational Leadership and Administration	M,O
Elementary Education	M,O
Engineering and Applied Sciences—General	M
Engineering Management	M
English as a Second Language	M,O
Exercise and Sports Science	M
Health Promotion	M
Higher Education	M
Management Strategy and Policy	M
Mechanical Engineering	M
Middle School Education	M,O
Public Affairs	M
School Psychology	M,O
Secondary Education	M,O
Special Education	M,O
Student Affairs	M,O

MESIVTA OF EASTERN PARKWAY–YESHIVA ZICHRON MEILECH
Theology	

MESIVTA TORAH VODAATH RABBINICAL SEMINARY
Theology	

MESIVTHA TIFERETH JERUSALEM OF AMERICA
Theology	

MESSIAH COLLEGE
Business Administration and Management—General	M,O
Clinical Psychology	M,O
Counseling Psychology	M,O
Counselor Education	M,O
Curriculum and Instruction	M
English as a Second Language	M
Higher Education	M
Management Strategy and Policy	M,O
Marriage and Family Therapy	M,O
Music	M
Nursing Education	M
Organizational Management	M,O
Special Education	M
Sports Management	M
Student Affairs	M

METHODIST THEOLOGICAL SCHOOL IN OHIO
Theology	M,D

METHODIST UNIVERSITY
Business Administration and Management—General	M
Criminal Justice and Criminology	M
Physician Assistant Studies	M

METROPOLITAN COLLEGE OF NEW YORK
Business Administration and Management—General	M
Elementary Education	M
Emergency Management	M
Finance and Banking	M
Health Services Management and Hospital Administration	M
Media Studies	M
Public Administration	M
Public Affairs	M
Special Education	M

METROPOLITAN STATE UNIVERSITY
Business Administration and Management—General	M,D,O
Computer and Information Systems Security	M,D,O
Computer Science	M
Criminal Justice and Criminology	M
Database Systems	M,D,O
Health Informatics	M,D,O
Information Studies	M,D,O
Liberal Studies	M
Management Information Systems	M,D,O
Nonprofit Management	M,D,O
Nursing and Healthcare Administration	M,D
Nursing Education	M,D
Nursing—General	M,D
Oral and Dental Sciences	M,D
Project Management	M,D,O
Psychology—General	M,D
Public Administration	M,D,O
Technical Writing	M

METROPOLITAN STATE UNIVERSITY OF DENVER
Accounting	M
Education—General	M
Elementary Education	M
Social Work	M
Special Education	M

---

*M—masters degree; D—doctorate; O—other advanced degree; *—Close-Up and/or Display*

Taxation — M

MGH INSTITUTE OF HEALTH PROFESSIONS
Communication Disorders — M,O
Gerontological Nursing — M,D,O
Nursing Education — M,D,O
Nursing—General — M,D,O
Occupational Therapy — D
Pediatric Nursing — M,D,O
Physical Therapy — M,D,O
Physician Assistant Studies — M
Psychiatric Nursing — M,D,O
Reading Education — M,O
Women's Health Nursing — M,D,O

MIAMI INTERNATIONAL UNIVERSITY OF ART & DESIGN
Applied Arts and Design—General — M
Film, Television, and Video Production — M

MIAMI REGIONAL UNIVERSITY
Nursing and Healthcare Administration — M
Nursing Education — M
Nursing—General — M

MIAMI UNIVERSITY
Accounting — M
Architecture — M
Art Education — M
Art/Fine Arts — M
Biochemistry — M,D
Biological and Biomedical Sciences—General — M,D
Business Administration and Management—General — M
Chemical Engineering — M
Chemistry — M,D
Child and Family Studies — M
Communication Disorders — M
Computer Engineering — M
Demography and Population Studies — M,D
Economics — M
Education—General — M,D,O
Educational Psychology — M,O
Electrical Engineering — M
Engineering and Applied Sciences—General — M
English — M,D
Environmental Sciences — M
Exercise and Sports Science — M
French — M
Geography — M
Geology — M,D
Gerontology — M,D
History — M
Interior Design — M
Mathematics Education — M
Mathematics — M
Mechanical Engineering — M
Microbiology — M,D
Music Education — M
Music — M
Philosophy — M
Physics — M
Political Science — M
Psychology—General — M,D
Statistics — M
Systems Science — M
Theater — M

MICHIGAN SCHOOL OF PROFESSIONAL PSYCHOLOGY
Clinical Psychology — M,D
Educational Psychology — M,D
Psychology—General — M,D
Transpersonal and Humanistic Psychology — M,D

MICHIGAN STATE UNIVERSITY
Accounting — M,D
Adult Education — M,D,O
Advertising and Public Relations — M,D
African Studies — M,D
African-American Studies — M,D
Agricultural Economics and Agribusiness — M,D
Agricultural Sciences—General — M,D
Agronomy and Soil Sciences — M,D
Allopathic Medicine — D
American Studies — M,D
Animal Sciences — M,D
Anthropology — M,D
Applied Mathematics — M,D
Applied Statistics — M,D
Art/Fine Arts — M
Astronomy — M,D
Astrophysics — M,D
Biochemistry — M,D
Biological and Biomedical Sciences—General — M,D
Biosystems Engineering — M,D
Business Administration and Management—General — M,D
Cell Biology — M,D
Chemical Engineering — M,D
Chemical Physics — M,D
Chemistry — M,D
Child and Family Studies — M,D
Child Development — M,D
Civil Engineering — M,D
Clinical Laboratory Sciences/Medical Technology — M
Communication Disorders — M,D
Communication—General — M,D
Computer Art and Design — M
Computer Science — M,D
Construction Management — M,D
Counselor Education — M,D,O
Criminal Justice and Criminology — M,D
Curriculum and Instruction — M,D,O
Ecology — D
Economics — M,D

Education—General — M,D,O
Educational Leadership and Administration — M,D,O
Educational Measurement and Evaluation — M,D,O
Educational Media/Instructional Technology — M,D,O
Educational Policy — D
Educational Psychology — M,D,O
Electrical Engineering — M,D
Engineering and Applied Sciences—General — M,D
English as a Second Language — M,D
English — M,D
Entomology — M,D
Environmental Design — M,D
Environmental Engineering — M,D
Environmental Sciences — M,D
Epidemiology — M,D
Evolutionary Biology — D
Finance and Banking — M,D
Fish, Game, and Wildlife Management — M,D
Food Science and Technology — M,D
Foreign Languages Education — D
Forensic Sciences — M,D
Forestry — M,D
French — M,D
Game Design and Development — M
Genetics — M,D
Geography — M,D
Geosciences — M,D
German — M,D
Health Communication — M
Higher Education — M,D,O
Hispanic and Latin American Languages — M,D
Hispanic Studies — M,D
History — M,D
Horticulture — M,D
Hospitality Management — M
Human Resources Management — M,D
Industrial and Labor Relations — M,D
Interior Design — M,D
Journalism — M
Kinesiology and Movement Studies — M,D
Latin American Studies — D
Linguistics — M,D
Logistics — M,D
Management Information Systems — M,D
Management Strategy and Policy — M,D
Manufacturing Engineering — M,D
Marketing Research — M,D
Marketing — M,D
Marriage and Family Therapy — M,D
Materials Engineering — M,D
Materials Sciences — M,D
Mathematics Education — M,D
Mathematics — M,D
Mechanical Engineering — M,D
Mechanics — M,D
Media Studies — M,D
Microbiology — M,D
Molecular Biology — M,D
Molecular Genetics — M,D
Music Education — M,D
Music — M,D
Natural Resources — M,D
Neuroscience — M,D
Nursing—General — M,D
Nutrition — M,D
Osteopathic Medicine — D
Pathobiology — M,D
Pathology — M,D
Pharmacology — M,D
Philosophy — M,D
Physics — M,D
Physiology — M,D
Plant Biology — M,D
Plant Pathology — M,D
Plant Sciences — M,D
Political Science — M,D
Portuguese — M,D
Psychology—General — M,D
Public Health—General — M
Reading Education — M
Recreation and Park Management — M,D
Rehabilitation Counseling — M,D,O
Rhetoric — M,D
Romance Languages — M,D
School Psychology — M,D,O
Science Education — M,D
Social Sciences Education — M,D
Social Work — M,D
Sociology — M,D
Spanish — M,D
Special Education — M,D,O
Statistics — M,D
Structural Biology — D
Supply Chain Management — M,D
Systems Biology — D
Taxation — M,D
Telecommunications — M
Theater — M
Therapies—Dance, Drama, and Music — M,D
Toxicology — M,D
Urban and Regional Planning — M,D
Veterinary Medicine — D
Veterinary Sciences — M,D
Writing — M,D
Zoology — M,D

MICHIGAN STATE UNIVERSITY COLLEGE OF LAW
Intellectual Property Law — M,D
Law — M,D
Legal and Justice Studies — M,D

MICHIGAN TECHNOLOGICAL UNIVERSITY
Accounting — M

Applied Mathematics — M,D
Applied Physics — M,D
Archaeology — M,D
Atmospheric Sciences — M,D,O
Automotive Engineering — M,D,O
Biochemistry — M,D,O
Biological and Biomedical Sciences—General — M,D
Biomedical Engineering — M,D
Biotechnology — M,D
Business Administration and Management—General — M
Chemical Engineering — M,D
Chemistry — M,D
Cognitive Sciences — M,D
Computational Sciences — M,D,O
Computer and Information Systems Security — M,D
Computer Engineering — M,D,O
Computer Science — M,D
Cultural Studies — M,D
Database Systems — M,D,O
Ecology — M,D
Electrical Engineering — M,D,O
Energy Management and Policy — M,D
Engineering and Applied Sciences—General — M,D,O
Environmental Engineering — M,D,O
Environmental Management and Policy — M,D
Ergonomics and Human Factors — M,D,O
Forestry — M,D
Geographic Information Systems — M,D
Geophysics — M,D
Interdisciplinary Studies — M,D,O
Kinesiology and Movement Studies — M
Materials Engineering — M,D
Mathematics — M,D
Mechanical Engineering — M,D,O
Mechanics — M,D,O
Medical Informatics — M
Metallurgical Engineering and Metallurgy — M,D
Mineral Economics — M
Molecular Biology — M,D,O
Nanotechnology — M,D,O
Physics — M,D
Rhetoric — M,D
Science Education — M,D,O
Statistics — M,D
Sustainability Management — M,D,O
Water Resources — M,D,O

MID-AMERICA BAPTIST THEOLOGICAL SEMINARY
Theology — M,D

MID-AMERICA BAPTIST THEOLOGICAL SEMINARY NORTHEAST BRANCH
Theology — M

MID-AMERICA CHRISTIAN UNIVERSITY
Business Administration and Management—General — M
Counseling Psychology — M
Marriage and Family Therapy — M
Organizational Management — M
Pastoral Ministry and Counseling — M
Public Administration — M

MIDAMERICA NAZARENE UNIVERSITY
Business Administration and Management—General — M
Clinical Psychology — M
Education—General — M
Educational Media/Instructional Technology — M
English as a Second Language — M
Marriage and Family Therapy — M
Nursing and Healthcare Administration — M
Nursing Education — M
Nursing—General — M
Public Health—General — M
Reading Education — M
School Psychology — M

MID-AMERICA REFORMED SEMINARY
Theology — M

MIDDLEBURY COLLEGE
Chinese — M
English — M
French — M,D
German — M,D
Italian — M,D
Near and Middle Eastern Languages — M
Russian — M,D
Spanish — M,D

MIDDLEBURY INSTITUTE OF INTERNATIONAL STUDIES AT MONTEREY
Business Administration and Management—General — M
Conflict Resolution and Mediation/Peace Studies — M
English as a Second Language — M
Environmental Management and Policy — M
Foreign Languages Education — M
International Affairs — M
International and Comparative Education — M
International Business — M
International Development — M
International Trade Policy — M
Management Strategy and Policy — M
Public Administration — M
Translation and Interpretation — M

MIDDLE GEORGIA STATE UNIVERSITY
Computer and Information Systems Security — M

Forensic Sciences — M
Gerontological Nursing — M
Health Informatics — M
Management Information Systems — M

MIDDLE TENNESSEE SCHOOL OF ANESTHESIA
Nurse Anesthesia — M,D

MIDDLE TENNESSEE STATE UNIVERSITY
Accounting — M
Actuarial Science — M
Aerospace/Aeronautical Engineering — M
Archives/Archival Administration — M,D,O
Aviation Management — M
Biological and Biomedical Sciences—General — M
Biostatistics — M
Biotechnology — M
Business Administration and Management—General — M
Business Education — M
Chemistry — M
Clinical Psychology — M,O
Computational Sciences — D
Computer Science — M
Counseling Psychology — M
Counselor Education — M
Criminal Justice and Criminology — M
Curriculum and Instruction — M,O
Early Childhood Education — M
Economics — M,D
Education—General — M,D,O
Educational Leadership and Administration — M,O
Educational Media/Instructional Technology — M,O
Elementary Education — M,O
Engineering Management — M
English as a Second Language — M,O
English — M,D
Exercise and Sports Science — M,D
Experimental Psychology — M,O
Family Nurse Practitioner Studies — M,O
Foreign Languages Education — M
French — M
Gender Studies — O
Geosciences — O
German — M
Gerontology — O
Health Education — M
History — M
Human Resources Management — M
Industrial and Organizational Psychology — M,O
International Affairs — M
Management Information Systems — M
Management Strategy and Policy — M
Mass Communication — M
Mathematics Education — M,D
Mathematics — M
Medical Informatics — M
Middle School Education — M,O
Molecular Biology — D
Music — M
Nursing and Healthcare Administration — M
Nursing Education — M
Nursing—General — M,O
Physical Education — M
Political Science — M
Psychology—General — M,O
Public History — D
Reading Education — M,D
Recreation and Park Management — M
School Psychology — M,O
Science Education — M,D
Secondary Education — M,O
Social Work — M
Sociology — M
Spanish — M
Special Education — M
Vocational and Technical Education — M,O
Women's Studies — O

MIDWAY UNIVERSITY
Business Administration and Management—General — M
Education—General — M
Organizational Management — M

MIDWEST COLLEGE OF ORIENTAL MEDICINE
Acupuncture and Oriental Medicine — M,O

MIDWESTERN BAPTIST THEOLOGICAL SEMINARY
Music — M,D,O
Pastoral Ministry and Counseling — M,D,O
Religious Education — M,D,O
Theology — M,D,O

MIDWESTERN STATE UNIVERSITY
Biological and Biomedical Sciences—General — M
Business Administration and Management—General — M
Clinical Psychology — M
Community Health — M,O
Computer Science — M
Counseling Psychology — M
Counselor Education — M
Criminal Justice and Criminology — M,O
Curriculum and Instruction — M
Education—General — M
Educational Leadership and Administration — M
Educational Media/Instructional Technology — M
English — M,D
Exercise and Sports Science — M
Family Nurse Practitioner Studies — M
Health Informatics — M,O
Health Physics/Radiological Health — M

Health Services Management and
  Hospital Administration — M,O
History — M
Human Resources Development — M
Nursing Education — M
Nursing—General — M
Philosophy — M,D
Political Science — M
Psychiatric Nursing — M
Reading Education — M
Special Education — M
Sports Management — M

MIDWESTERN UNIVERSITY, DOWNERS GROVE CAMPUS
Allied Health—General — D
Biological and Biomedical
  Sciences—General — M
Clinical Psychology — M,D
Communication Disorders — M
Dentistry — D
Occupational Therapy — M
Optometry — D
Osteopathic Medicine — D
Pharmacy — D
Physical Therapy — D
Physician Assistant Studies — M

MIDWESTERN UNIVERSITY, GLENDALE CAMPUS
Allied Health—General — M,D
Biological and Biomedical
  Sciences—General — M
Cardiovascular Sciences — M
Clinical Psychology — D
Communication Disorders — M
Dentistry — D
Nurse Anesthesia — M
Occupational Therapy — M
Optometry — D
Osteopathic Medicine — D
Pharmacy — D
Physical Therapy — D
Physician Assistant Studies — M
Podiatric Medicine — D

MIDWIVES COLLEGE OF UTAH
Nurse Midwifery — M

MILLENNIA ATLANTIC UNIVERSITY
Accounting — M
Business Administration and
  Management—General — M
Health Informatics — M
Human Resources Management — M

MILLERSVILLE UNIVERSITY OF PENNSYLVANIA
Applied Arts and Design—General — M
Art Education — M
Art/Fine Arts — M
Atmospheric Sciences — M
Clinical Psychology — M
Distance Education Development — M
Early Childhood Education — M
Education of the Gifted — M,O
Education—General — M,D,O
Educational Leadership and
  Administration — M,D
Emergency Management — M
English as a Second Language — M
English — M,O
Environmental Management
  and Policy — M
Family Nurse Practitioner Studies — M,O
French — M
Geographic Information Systems — M
German — M
History — M
Mathematics Education — M
Meteorology — M
Nursing Education — M,O
Nursing—General — D
Physical Education — M
Psychology—General — M
Reading Education — M
School Psychology — M
Science Education — M,D
Social Work — M,D
Spanish — M
Special Education — M
Sports Management — M,O
Vocational and Technical Education — M
Writing — M,O

MILLIGAN COLLEGE
Business Administration and
  Management—General — M,O
Clinical Psychology — M,O
Counselor Education — M,O
Early Childhood Education — M,D,O
Education—General — M,D,O
Educational Leadership and
  Administration — M,D,O
Elementary Education — M,D,O
Health Services Management and
  Hospital Administration — M,O
Industrial and Manufacturing
  Management — M,O
Middle School Education — M,D,O
Missions and Missiology — M,D,O
Occupational Therapy — M
Pastoral Ministry and Counseling — M,D,O
Physician Assistant Studies — M
Religion — M,D,O
Religious Education — M,D,O
Secondary Education — M,D,O
Special Education — M,D,O
Theology — M,D,O

MILLIKIN UNIVERSITY
Business Administration and
  Management—General — M

Nurse Anesthesia — M,D
Nursing Education — M,D
Nursing—General — M,D

MILLSAPS COLLEGE
Accounting — M
Business Administration and
  Management—General — M

MILLS COLLEGE
Applied Economics — M
Art/Fine Arts — M
Biological and Biomedical
  Sciences—General — O
Business Administration and
  Management—General — M
Computer Science — M,O
Dance — M
Early Childhood Education — M
Education—General — M,D,O
Educational Leadership and
  Administration — M
English — M,O
Illustration — M,O
Interdisciplinary Studies — M,O
Music — M
Photography — M
Public Policy — M
Translation and Interpretation — M,O
Writing — M,O

MILWAUKEE SCHOOL OF ENGINEERING
Architectural Engineering — M
Business Administration and
  Management—General — M
Business Education — M
Cardiovascular Sciences — M
Civil Engineering — M
Clinical Laboratory
  Sciences/Medical Technology — M
Construction Management — M
Engineering and Applied
  Sciences—General — M
Engineering Management — M
Health Services Management and
  Hospital Administration — M
Industrial and Manufacturing
  Management — M
International Business — M
Marketing — M
Medical Informatics — M
Nursing and Healthcare
  Administration — M
Perfusion — M

MINNEAPOLIS COLLEGE OF ART AND DESIGN
Applied Arts and Design—General — M
Art/Fine Arts — M,O
Computer Art and Design — O
Film, Television, and Video
  Production — M
Graphic Design — M,O
Illustration — M
Photography — M
Sustainable Development — O

MINNESOTA STATE UNIVERSITY MANKATO
Accounting — M
Allied Health—General — M,D,O
Anthropology — M
Applied Statistics — M
Art Education — M
Art/Fine Arts — M
Astronomy — M
Automotive Engineering — M
Biological and Biomedical
  Sciences—General — M
Business Administration and
  Management—General — M
Clinical Psychology — M,D
Communication Disorders — M
Communication—General — M,O
Community Health — M,O
Computer Science — M,O
Corporate and Organizational
  Communication — M,O
Counseling Psychology — M,D
Counselor Education — M,D
Criminal Justice and Criminology — M
Education—General — M,D,O
Educational Leadership and
  Administration — M
English as a Second Language — M,O
English — M,O
Environmental Sciences — M
Ethnic Studies — M
Family Nurse Practitioner Studies — M,D
Foreign Languages Education — M
French — M
Gender Studies — M
Geography — M
Gerontology — M
Health Education — M,O
Higher Education — M
History — M
Human Services — M
Industrial and Organizational
  Psychology — M,D
Information Science — M,O
Interdisciplinary Studies — M
Manufacturing Engineering — M
Mathematics Education — M
Mathematics — M
Music Education — M
Music — M,O
Nonprofit Management — M,O
Nursing Education — M,D
Nursing—General — M,D
Physical Education — M

Physics — M,D
Psychology—General — M,D
Public Administration — M
Rehabilitation Counseling — M
School Psychology — M,D
Science Education — M
Social Sciences Education — M
Social Work — M
Sociology — M
Spanish — M
Special Education — M,O
Statistics — M
Student Affairs — M,D
Technical Communication — M,O
Theater — M
Urban and Regional Planning — M,O
Urban Studies — M,O
Women's Studies — M
Writing — M,O

MINNESOTA STATE UNIVERSITY MOORHEAD
Accounting — M
Business Administration and
  Management—General — M
Communication Disorders — M,O
Counselor Education — M,O
Curriculum and Instruction — M,O
Education—General — M,O
Educational Leadership and
  Administration — M,O
English as a Second Language — M
Finance and Banking — M
Health Services Management and
  Hospital Administration — M,O
Human Services — M,O
Nursing—General — M,O
School Psychology — M,O
Special Education — M,O

MINOT STATE UNIVERSITY
Business Administration and
  Management—General — M
Communication Disorders — M
Elementary Education — M
Management Information Systems — M
Mathematics Education — M
Middle School Education — M
School Psychology — O
Science Education — M
Special Education — M

MIRRER YESHIVA
Theology

MISERICORDIA UNIVERSITY
Accounting — M
Allied Health—General — M,D
Business Administration and
  Management—General — M
Communication Disorders — M
Educational Media/Instructional
  Technology — M
Health Services Management and
  Hospital Administration — M
Human Resources Management — M
Nursing—General — M,D
Occupational Therapy — M,D
Organizational Management — M
Physical Therapy — D
Reading Education — M
Special Education — M
Sports Management — M

MISSISSIPPI COLLEGE
Accounting — M,O
Advertising and Public Relations — M
Art Education — M,D,O
Art/Fine Arts — M
Biochemistry — M
Biological and Biomedical
  Sciences—General — M
Business Administration and
  Management—General — M,O
Business Education — M,D,O
Chemistry — M
Communication—General — M
Computer Education — M,D,O
Computer Science — M
Corporate and Organizational
  Communication — M
Counseling Psychology — M,O
Counselor Education — M,O
Criminal Justice and Criminology — M,O
Curriculum and Instruction — M,D,O
Education—General — M,D,O
Educational Leadership and
  Administration — M,D,O
Elementary Education — M,D,O
English as a Second Language — M
English Education — M,D,O
English — M
Finance and Banking — M,O
Health Services Management and
  Hospital Administration — M
Higher Education — M,D,O
History — M,O
Kinesiology and Movement Studies — M
Law — D,O
Legal and Justice Studies — M,O
Liberal Studies — M
Marriage and Family Therapy — M,O
Mathematics Education — M,D,O
Mathematics — M
Music Education — M
Music — M
Political Science — M,O
Science Education — M,D,O
Secondary Education — M,D,O
Social Sciences Education — M,D,O
Social Sciences — M,O
Special Education — M,D,O

MISSISSIPPI STATE UNIVERSITY
Accounting — M
Aerospace/Aeronautical
  Engineering — M,D
Agricultural Economics and
  Agribusiness — M
Agricultural Education — M,D
Agricultural Sciences—
  General — M,D
Agronomy and Soil Sciences — M,D
American Studies — M,D
Animal Sciences — M,D
Anthropology — M
Atmospheric Sciences — M,D
Biochemistry — M,D
Bioengineering — M,D
Biological and Biomedical
  Sciences—General — M,D
Biomedical Engineering — M,D
Business Administration and
  Management—General — M,D
Chemical Engineering — M,D
Chemistry — M,D
Child and Family Studies — M,D
Civil Engineering — M,D
Clinical Psychology — M,D,O
Cognitive Sciences — M,D
Community College Education — M,D,O
Computer Engineering — M,D
Computer Science — M,D
Counselor Education — M,D,O
Curriculum and Instruction — M,D,O
Distance Education Development — M,D,O
Early Childhood Education — M,D,O
Economics — M,D
Education—General — M,D,O
Educational Leadership and
  Administration — M,D,O
Educational Media/Instructional
  Technology — M,D,O
Educational Psychology — M,D,O
Electrical Engineering — M,D
Elementary Education — M,D,O
Engineering and Applied
  Sciences—General — M,D
English — M
Ergonomics and Human
  Factors — M,D
Exercise and Sports Science — M,D
Finance and Banking — M,D
Fish, Game, and Wildlife
  Management — M,D
Food Science and
  Technology — M,D
Foreign Languages Education — M
Forestry — M,D
Genetics — M,D
Geography — M,D
Geology — M,D
Geosciences — M,D
History — M,D
Horticulture — M,D
Human Development — M,D
Human Resources Development — M,D,O
Industrial and Manufacturing
  Management — M,D
Industrial/Management
  Engineering — M,D
Internet and Interactive
  Multimedia — M,D,O
Kinesiology and Movement Studies — M,D
Landscape Architecture — M
Management Information Systems — M,D
Marketing — D
Mathematics — M,D
Mechanical Engineering — M,D
Meteorology — M,D
Middle School Education — M,D,O
Molecular Biology — M,D
Nutrition — M,D
Operations Research — M,D
Physical Education — M,D
Physics — M,D
Plant Sciences — M,D
Political Science — M,D
Project Management — M,D
Psychology—General — M,D
Public Administration — M,D
Public Policy — M,D
Reading Education — M,D,O
Rehabilitation Counseling — M,D,O
School Psychology — M,D,O
Secondary Education — M,D,O
Sociology — M,D
Special Education — M,D,O
Sports Management — M,D
Statistics — M,D
Student Affairs — M,D,O
Sustainable Development — M,D
Systems Engineering — M,D
Taxation — M
Veterinary Medicine — D
Veterinary Sciences — M,D
Vocational and Technical Education — M,D,O
Western European Studies — M,D

MISSISSIPPI UNIVERSITY FOR WOMEN
Communication Disorders — M,O
Curriculum and Instruction — M
Education of the Gifted — M
Education—General — M
Educational Leadership and
  Administration — M
Health Education — M
Nursing—General — M,O
Reading Education — M

MISSISSIPPI VALLEY STATE UNIVERSITY
Criminal Justice and Criminology — M
Education—General — M

MISSOURI BAPTIST UNIVERSITY

Business Administration and Management—General	M,O
Counselor Education	M,O
Education—General	M,O
Educational Leadership and Administration	M,O
Pastoral Ministry and Counseling	M,O

MISSOURI SOUTHERN STATE UNIVERSITY

Business Administration and Management—General	M
Criminal Justice and Criminology	M
Dental Hygiene	M
Early Childhood Education	M
Education—General	M
Educational Media/Instructional Technology	M
Nursing—General	M

MISSOURI STATE UNIVERSITY

Accounting	M
Agricultural Sciences—General	M
Applied Behavior Analysis	M,O
Applied Science and Technology	M
Art/Fine Arts	M
Athletic Training and Sports Medicine	M
Biological and Biomedical Sciences—General	M
Business Administration and Management—General	M
Cell Biology	M
Chemistry	M
Child and Family Studies	M
Clinical Psychology	M,O
Communication Disorders	M,D
Communication—General	M,O
Computer and Information Systems Security	M
Computer Science	M
Construction Management	M
Counseling Psychology	M
Counselor Education	M
Criminal Justice and Criminology	M,O
Early Childhood Education	M
Educational Leadership and Administration	M,O
Educational Measurement and Evaluation	O
Educational Media/Instructional Technology	M
Elementary Education	M,O
English as a Second Language	M,O
English Education	M,O
English	M,O
Environmental Management and Policy	M,O
Experimental Psychology	M,O
Family Nurse Practitioner Studies	M,D
Film, Television, and Video Production	M,O
Geography	M
Geology	M
Geosciences	M
Health Services Management and Hospital Administration	M
Higher Education	M
History	M,O
Homeland Security	M,O
Industrial and Organizational Psychology	M,O
International Affairs	M
Kinesiology and Movement Studies	M
Management Information Systems	M
Materials Sciences	M
Mathematics Education	M
Mathematics	M
Military and Defense Studies	M,O
Molecular Biology	M
Music	M
Nurse Anesthesia	D
Nursing Education	M,D
Nursing—General	M,D
Nutrition	M,D,O
Occupational Therapy	M
Physical Education	M
Physical Therapy	D
Physician Assistant Studies	M
Physics	M
Plant Sciences	M
Political Science	M,O
Project Management	M
Psychology—General	M,O
Public Administration	M,O
Public Health—General	M
Reading Education	M
Religion	M,O
Science Education	M
Secondary Education	M,O
Social Sciences Education	M,O
Social Work	M
Special Education	M
Sports Management	M,O
Student Affairs	M
Theater	M
Urban and Regional Planning	M
Writing	M

MISSOURI UNIVERSITY OF SCIENCE AND TECHNOLOGY

Aerospace/Aeronautical Engineering	M,D
Applied Mathematics	M,D
Biological and Biomedical Sciences—General	M
Business Administration and Management—General	M
Ceramic Sciences and Engineering	M,D
Chemical Engineering	M,D
Chemistry	M,D
Civil Engineering	M,D
Computer Engineering	M,D
Computer Science	M,D
Construction Engineering	M,D
Electrical Engineering	M,D
Engineering Management	M,D
Environmental Biology	M
Environmental Engineering	M,D
Geochemistry	M,D
Geological Engineering	M,D
Geology	M,D
Geophysics	M,D
Geotechnical Engineering	M,D
Hydraulics	M,D
Hydrology	M,D
Information Science	M
Manufacturing Engineering	M,D
Mathematics Education	M,D
Mathematics	M,D
Mechanical Engineering	M,D
Mechanics	M,D
Metallurgical Engineering and Metallurgy	M,D
Mineral/Mining Engineering	M,D
Nuclear Engineering	M,D
Petroleum Engineering	M,D
Physics	M,D
Statistics	M,D
Systems Engineering	M,D
Water Resources	M,D

MISSOURI VALLEY COLLEGE

Social Psychology	M

MISSOURI WESTERN STATE UNIVERSITY

Accounting	M
Animal Sciences	M
Biological and Biomedical Sciences—General	M
Business Administration and Management—General	M
Chemistry	M
Computer and Information Systems Security	M
Educational Measurement and Evaluation	M,O
Engineering and Applied Sciences—General	M
English as a Second Language	M,O
Ergonomics and Human Factors	M
Forensic Sciences	M,O
Information Studies	M
Media Studies	M
Nursing and Healthcare Administration	M,O
Nursing Education	M,O
Nursing—General	M,O
Rhetoric	M,O
Special Education	M,O
Sports Management	M
Technical Communication	M,O
Writing	M,O

MITCHELL HAMLINE SCHOOL OF LAW

Law	M,D

MOLLOY COLLEGE

Accounting	M,O
Biological and Biomedical Sciences—General	M,O
Business Administration and Management—General	M,O
Clinical Psychology	M
Communication Disorders	M
Criminal Justice and Criminology	M
Early Childhood Education	M,O
Education—General	M,O
Educational Media/Instructional Technology	M,O
English as a Second Language	M,O
English	M,O
Family Nurse Practitioner Studies	M,D,O
Finance and Banking	M,O
Gerontological Nursing	M,D,O
Health Services Management and Hospital Administration	M,D,O
Marketing	M,O
Mathematics	M,O
Multilingual and Multicultural Education	M,O
Nursing Education	M,D,O
Nursing—General	M,D,O
Pediatric Nursing	M,D,O
Social Sciences Education	M,O
Spanish	M,O
Special Education	M,O
Therapies—Dance, Drama, and Music	M

MONMOUTH UNIVERSITY

Accounting	M,O
Addictions/Substance Abuse Counseling	M,O
Adult Nursing	M,D,O
Advertising and Public Relations	M,O
American Studies	M
Anthropology	M
Applied Behavior Analysis	M,D,O
Business Administration and Management—General	M,O*
Communication Disorders	M,D,O
Communication—General	M,O
Computer Science	M
Corporate and Organizational Communication	M,O
Counseling Psychology	M,O
Criminal Justice and Criminology	M,O
Early Childhood Education	M,D,O
Education—General	M,D,O
Educational Leadership and Administration	M,D,O
Elementary Education	M,D,O
English as a Second Language	M,D,O
English	M

MONROE COLLEGE

Accounting	M
Biostatistics	M
Business Administration and Management—General	M
Community Health	M
Computer Science	M
Criminal Justice and Criminology	M
Entrepreneurship	M
Epidemiology	M
Finance and Banking	M
Health Services Management and Hospital Administration	M
Hospitality Management	M
Human Resources Management	M
Information Science	M
Marketing	M
Public Health—General	M

MONTANA STATE UNIVERSITY

Accounting	M
Adult Education	M,D,O
Agricultural Education	M
Agricultural Sciences—General	M,D
American Indian/Native American Studies	M
Animal Sciences	M,D
Architecture	M
Art History	M
Art/Fine Arts	M
Biochemistry	M,D
Biological and Biomedical Sciences—General	M,D
Chemical Engineering	M,D
Chemistry	M,D
Civil Engineering	M,D
Computer Engineering	M,D
Computer Science	M,D
Construction Engineering	M,D
Curriculum and Instruction	M,D,O
Ecology	M,D
Education—General	M,D,O
Educational Leadership and Administration	M,D,O
Electrical Engineering	M,D
Engineering and Applied Sciences—General	M,D
English	M
Environmental Engineering	M,D
Environmental Sciences	M,D
Family Nurse Practitioner Studies	M,D,O
Film, Television, and Video Production	M
Fish, Game, and Wildlife Management	M,D
Geosciences	M,D
Health Education	M
Higher Education	M,D,O
History	M,D
Home Economics Education	M
Human Development	M
Immunology	M,D
Industrial/Management Engineering	M,D
Infectious Diseases	M,D
Mathematics Education	M,D
Mathematics	M,D
Mechanical Engineering	M,D
Mechanics	M,D
Microbiology	M,D
Natural Resources	M
Neuroscience	M,D
Nursing and Healthcare Administration	M,D,O
Nursing Education	M,D,O
Nursing—General	M,D,O
Physics	M,D
Plant Pathology	M,D
Plant Sciences	M,D
Psychiatric Nursing	M,D,O
Psychology—General	M
Public Administration	M
Range Science	M,D
School Psychology	M,D,O
Statistics	M,D
Vocational and Technical Education	M,D,O

MONTANA STATE UNIVERSITY BILLINGS

Advertising and Public Relations	M
Applied Behavior Analysis	M
Athletic Training and Sports Medicine	M
Communication—General	M

Family Nurse Practitioner Studies	M,D,O
Finance and Banking	M,O
Forensic Nursing	M,D,O
Gerontological Nursing	M,D,O
History	M
Homeland Security	M,O
Human Resources Management	M,O
Marketing	M,O
Media Studies	M
Nursing and Healthcare Administration	M,D,O
Nursing Education	M,D,O
Nursing—General	M,D,O
Physician Assistant Studies	M,D,O
Psychiatric Nursing	M,D,O
Psychology—General	M,O
Public Policy	M
Reading Education	M,D,O
Real Estate	M,O
Rhetoric	M
School Nursing	M,D,O
School Psychology	M,D,O
Secondary Education	M,D,O
Social Work	M,O
Software Engineering	M,O
Special Education	M,D,O
Student Affairs	M,D,O
Western European Studies	M
Writing	M

MONTANA STATE UNIVERSITY–NORTHERN

Counselor Education	M
Education—General	M

MONTANA TECH OF THE UNIVERSITY OF MONTANA

Electrical Engineering	M
Engineering and Applied Sciences—General	M
Environmental Engineering	M
Geochemistry	M
Geological Engineering	M
Geology	M
Geosciences	M
Health Informatics	O
Hydrogeology	M
Industrial Hygiene	M
Industrial/Management Engineering	M
Interdisciplinary Studies	M
Materials Sciences	D
Metallurgical Engineering and Metallurgy	M
Mineral/Mining Engineering	M
Petroleum Engineering	M
Project Management	M
Technical Communication	M

MONTCLAIR STATE UNIVERSITY

Accounting	M,O
Addictions/Substance Abuse Counseling	O
Advertising and Public Relations	M
Applied Mathematics	M
Archives/Archival Administration	M
Art Education	M
Art/Fine Arts	M
Arts Administration	M
Biochemistry	M
Biological and Biomedical Sciences—General	M
Business Administration and Management—General	M,O
Chemistry	M
Child and Family Studies	M,D,O
Child Development	M
Clinical Psychology	M
Communication Disorders	M,D
Computer Science	M,O
Conflict Resolution and Mediation/Peace Studies	M,O
Corporate and Organizational Communication	M
Counselor Education	M,D
Curriculum and Instruction	M
Database Systems	O
Disability Studies	M,O
Ecology	M
Education—General	M,D,O
Educational Leadership and Administration	M,D
Educational Measurement and Evaluation	O
English as a Second Language	M,O
English Education	M,O
English	M
Environmental Education	M
Environmental Law	O
Environmental Management and Policy	M,D
Environmental Sciences	M
Evolutionary Biology	M
Exercise and Sports Science	M,O
Forensic Psychology	O
French	M
Geographic Information Systems	O
Geosciences	M
Health Education	M
Industrial and Organizational Psychology	M
Intellectual Property Law	M,O
Law	M,O
Legal and Justice Studies	O
Linguistics	M,O
Marine Biology	M
Mathematics Education	M,D,O
Mathematics	M
Molecular Biology	M,O
Music Education	M
Music	M,O
Nutrition	M,O
Pharmacology	M
Physical Education	M
Physiology	M
Political Science	M,O
Psychology—General	M
Public Health—General	M
Reading Education	M
Science Education	M
Social Sciences	M
Spanish	M
Special Education	M
Sports Management	M
Statistics	M
Sustainable Development	M
Theater	M
Therapies—Dance, Drama, and Music	M,O

MONTCLAIR STATE UNIVERSITY (continued)

(Montana State University — continued from prior columns)

COUNSELING / EDUCATION (Montana State University Billings continued)

Counseling Psychology	M
Counselor Education	M
Curriculum and Instruction	M
Education—General	M,O
Educational Media/Instructional Technology	M
Elementary Education	M
Health Services Management and Hospital Administration	M
Interdisciplinary Studies	M
Psychology—General	M
Reading Education	M
Rehabilitation Counseling	M
Secondary Education	M
Special Education	M

Translation and Interpretation — O
Water Resources — O
Writing — O

MOODY BIBLE INSTITUTE
Pastoral Ministry and Counseling — M,O
Theology — M,O
Urban Studies — M,O

MOODY THEOLOGICAL SEMINARY—MICHIGAN
Counseling Psychology — M,O
Religion — M,O
Religious Education — M,O
Theology — M,O

MOORE COLLEGE OF ART & DESIGN
Art Education — M
Art/Fine Arts — M
Arts Administration — M
Communication—General — M
Interior Design — M

MORAVIAN COLLEGE
Accounting — M
Acute Care/Critical Care Nursing — M
Allied Health—General — M
Athletic Training and Sports Medicine — M
Business Administration and Management—General — M
Curriculum and Instruction — M
Education—General — M
Health Services Management and Hospital Administration — M
Human Resources Development — M
Human Resources Management — M
Nursing and Healthcare Administration — M
Nursing Education — M
Nursing—General — M
Supply Chain Management — M

MORAVIAN THEOLOGICAL SEMINARY
Pastoral Ministry and Counseling — M,O
Theology — M,O

MOREHEAD STATE UNIVERSITY
Adult Education — M,O
Agricultural Sciences—General — M
Art Education — M
Art/Fine Arts — M
Biological and Biomedical Sciences—General — M
Business Administration and Management—General — M
Business Education — M,O
Clinical Psychology — M
Communication—General — M
Counseling Psychology — M
Counselor Education — M,O
Criminal Justice and Criminology — M
Curriculum and Instruction — M
Education of the Gifted — M,O
Education—General — M,O
Educational Leadership and Administration — M,O
Educational Media/Instructional Technology — M,O
Elementary Education — M,O
English Education — M,O
English — M
Environmental Management and Policy — M
Exercise and Sports Science — M
Experimental Psychology — M
Foreign Languages Education — M
Gerontology — M
Graphic Design — M
Health Education — M
Higher Education — M,O
Industrial/Management Engineering — M
International and Comparative Education — M,O
Management Information Systems — M
Mathematics Education — M
Middle School Education — M
Music Education — M
Music — M
Physical Education — M
Psychology—General — M
Public Administration — M
Public Policy — M
Reading Education — M,O
Science Education — M
Secondary Education — M,O
Social Sciences Education — M,O
Sociology — M
Special Education — M,O
Sports Management — M
Vocational and Technical Education — M

MOREHOUSE SCHOOL OF MEDICINE
Allopathic Medicine — D
Biological and Biomedical Sciences—General — M,D
Clinical Research — M
Public Health—General — M

MORGAN STATE UNIVERSITY
African-American Studies — M,D
Architecture — M
Bioinformatics — M
Biological and Biomedical Sciences—General — M,D
Business Administration and Management—General — D
Chemistry — M
Civil Engineering — M,D
Community College Education — D
Economics — M

Education—General — M,D
Educational Leadership and Administration — M,D
Electrical Engineering — M,D
Elementary Education — M
Engineering and Applied Sciences—General — M,D
English — M,D
Environmental Biology — D
Higher Education — M,D
Historic Preservation — M,D
History — M,D
Industrial/Management Engineering — M,D
International Affairs — M
Landscape Architecture — M
Mathematics Education — M,D
Mathematics — M
Middle School Education — M
Museum Studies — M,D
Music — M
Nursing—General — M
Psychology—General — M
Public Health—General — M,D
Science Education — M,D
Secondary Education — M,D
Social Work — M,D
Sociology — M
Transportation and Highway Engineering — M
Transportation Management — M
Urban and Regional Planning — M
Urban Education — D

MORNINGSIDE COLLEGE
Education—General — M
Special Education — M

MOUNT ALLISON UNIVERSITY
Biological and Biomedical Sciences—General — M
Chemistry — M

MOUNT ALOYSIUS COLLEGE
Accounting — M
Business Administration and Management—General — M
Health Services Management and Hospital Administration — M
Nonprofit Management — M
Project Management — M
Psychology—General — M
Social Psychology — M

MOUNT ANGEL SEMINARY
Theology — M

MOUNT CARMEL COLLEGE OF NURSING
Acute Care/Critical Care Nursing — M,D
Adult Nursing — M,D
Family Nurse Practitioner Studies — M,D
Gerontological Nursing — M,D
Nursing—General — M,D

MOUNT HOLYOKE COLLEGE
Educational Leadership and Administration — M
Mathematics Education — M

MOUNT IDA COLLEGE
Business Administration and Management—General — M
Health Services Management and Hospital Administration — M
Human Resources Management — M
Sports Management — M

MOUNT MARTY COLLEGE
Business Administration and Management—General — M
Nurse Anesthesia — M
Nursing—General — M
Pastoral Ministry and Counseling — M

MOUNT MARY UNIVERSITY
Art Therapy — M,D
Business Administration and Management—General — M
Clinical Psychology — M,O
Counseling Psychology — M,O
Counselor Education — M,O
Education—General — M
English — M
Internet and Interactive Multimedia — M
Nursing and Healthcare Administration — M
Nutrition — M
Occupational Therapy — M,D
Rehabilitation Counseling — M,O
Writing — M

MOUNT MERCY UNIVERSITY
Business Administration and Management—General — M
Criminal Justice and Criminology — M
Education—General — M
Educational Leadership and Administration — M
Human Resources Management — M
Management Strategy and Policy — M
Marriage and Family Therapy — M
Nursing and Healthcare Administration — M
Nursing Education — M
Nursing—General — M
Quality Management — M
Reading Education — M
Special Education — M

MOUNT ST. JOSEPH UNIVERSITY
Business Administration and Management—General — M,O
Early Childhood Education — M,O

Education—General — M,D
Health Promotion — M,O
Health Services Management and Hospital Administration — D
Middle School Education — M
Multilingual and Multicultural Education — M,O
Nursing and Healthcare Administration — M
Nursing Education — M
Nursing—General — M,D
Organizational Management — M
Pastoral Ministry and Counseling — M,O
Physical Therapy — D
Reading Education — M,O
Religion — M,O
Secondary Education — M,O
Special Education — M,O
Theology — M,O

MOUNT SAINT MARY COLLEGE
Adult Nursing — M,O
Business Administration and Management—General — M
Child Development — M,O
Education—General — M,O
Family Nurse Practitioner Studies — M
Finance and Banking — M
Health Services Management and Hospital Administration — M
Middle School Education — M,O
Nursing and Healthcare Administration — M,O
Nursing Education — M,O
Nursing—General — M,O
Reading Education — M,O
Special Education — M,O

MOUNT SAINT MARY'S UNIVERSITY (CA)
Business Administration and Management—General — M,D,O
Counseling Psychology — M,D,O
Education—General — M,D,O
English — M,D,O
Film, Television, and Video Production — M,D,O
Health Services Management and Hospital Administration — M,D,O
Humanities — M,D,O
Nursing—General — M,D,O
Physical Therapy — M,D,O
Religion — M,D,O
Writing — M,D,O

MOUNT ST. MARY'S UNIVERSITY (MD)
Biotechnology — M
Business Administration and Management—General — M
Education—General — M
Health Services Management and Hospital Administration — M
Philosophy — M
Sports Management — M
Theology — M

MOUNT SAINT VINCENT UNIVERSITY
Adult Education — M
Child and Family Studies — M
Curriculum and Instruction — M
Education—General — M
Educational Psychology — M
Elementary Education — M
English as a Second Language — M
Foundations and Philosophy of Education — M
Gerontology — M
Middle School Education — M
Nutrition — M
Reading Education — M
School Psychology — M
Special Education — M
Women's Studies — M

MOUNT VERNON NAZARENE UNIVERSITY
Business Administration and Management—General — M
Education—General — M
Theology — M

MULTNOMAH UNIVERSITY
Education—General — M
English as a Second Language — M
Theology — M,D

MURRAY STATE UNIVERSITY
Accounting — M
Agricultural Education — M
Agricultural Sciences—General — M
Biological and Biomedical Sciences—General — M,D
Business Administration and Management—General — M
Chemistry — M
Clinical Psychology — M
Communication Disorders — M
Corporate and Organizational Communication — M
Counselor Education — M,O
Early Childhood Education — M
Economics — M
Education—General — M,D,O
Educational Leadership and Administration — M,O
Elementary Education — M,O
English as a Second Language — M
English — M
Environmental and Occupational Health — M
Environmental Sciences — M
Exercise and Sports Science — M

Family Nurse Practitioner Studies — M
Geosciences — M
History — M
Human Services — M
Hydrology — M
Industrial Hygiene — M
Leisure Studies — M
Management of Technology — M
Mass Communication — M
Mathematics — M
Middle School Education — M,O
Music Education — M
Music — M
Nurse Anesthesia — M
Nursing—General — M
Physical Education — M,O
Psychology—General — M
Public Affairs — M
Reading Education — M
Safety Engineering — M
Secondary Education — M,O
Special Education — M
Statistics — M
Telecommunications Management — M
Vocational and Technical Education — M
Writing — M

MUSKINGUM UNIVERSITY
Education—General — M

NAROPA UNIVERSITY
Art Therapy — M
Counseling Psychology — M
Counselor Education — M
Education—General — M
Psychoanalysis and Psychotherapy — M
Recreation and Park Management — M
Religion — M
Theater — M
Theology — M
Therapies—Dance, Drama, and Music — M
Writing — M

NASHOTAH HOUSE THEOLOGICAL SEMINARY
Pastoral Ministry and Counseling — M,D,O
Religion — M,D,O
Theology — M,D,O

NATIONAL AMERICAN UNIVERSITY
Business Administration and Management—General — M

NATIONAL COLLEGE OF MIDWIFERY
Nurse Midwifery — M,D

NATIONAL DEFENSE UNIVERSITY
Homeland Security — M
Military and Defense Studies — M
National Security — M

THE NATIONAL GRADUATE SCHOOL OF QUALITY MANAGEMENT
Homeland Security — M,D
Quality Management — M,D

NATIONAL INTELLIGENCE UNIVERSITY
Military and Defense Studies — M

NATIONAL LOUIS UNIVERSITY
Adult Education — M,D,O
Business Administration and Management—General — M
Counselor Education — M,D,O
Curriculum and Instruction — M,D,O
Developmental Education — M,D,O
Early Childhood Education — M,D,O
Education—General — M,D,O
Educational Leadership and Administration — M,D,O
Educational Media/Instructional Technology — M,D,O
Educational Psychology — M,D,O
Elementary Education — M,D,O
English Education — M,D,O
Human Development — M,D,O
Human Resources Development — M
Human Resources Management — M
Human Services — M,D,O
Mathematics Education — M,D,O
Middle School Education — M,D,O
Psychology—General — M,D,O
Public Policy — M,D,O
Reading Education — M,D,O
School Psychology — M,D,O
Science Education — M,D,O
Secondary Education — M,D,O
Special Education — M,D,O
Writing — M,D,O

NATIONAL PARALEGAL COLLEGE
Legal and Justice Studies — M
Taxation — M

NATIONAL TEST PILOT SCHOOL
Aviation — M

NATIONAL UNIVERSITY
Biological and Biomedical Sciences—General — M,O
Business Administration and Management—General — M,O
Clinical Psychology — M,O
Computer Science — M
Counseling Psychology — M,O
Criminal Justice and Criminology — M
Distance Education Development — M,O
Education—General — M,O
Educational Leadership and Administration — M,O
Film, Television, and Video Production — M

M—masters degree; D—doctorate; O—other advanced degree; *—Close-Up and/or Display

Health Services Management and Hospital Administration	M,D,O
Human Resources Management	M
Human Services	M,D,O
Internet and Interactive Multimedia	M
Journalism	M
Legal and Justice Studies	M
Nursing Informatics	M,D,O
Nursing—General	M,D,O
Public Administration	M
Public Health—General	M,D,O
Writing	M

NATIONAL UNIVERSITY COLLEGE

Business Administration and Management—General	M
Marketing	M
Special Education	M

NATIONAL UNIVERSITY OF HEALTH SCIENCES

Acupuncture and Oriental Medicine	M,D
Chiropractic	M,D
Medical Imaging	M,D

NATIONAL UNIVERSITY OF NATURAL MEDICINE

Acupuncture and Oriental Medicine	M
Naturopathic Medicine	M,D

NAVAJO TECHNICAL UNIVERSITY

American Indian/Native American Studies	M

NAVAL POSTGRADUATE SCHOOL

Acoustics	M,D
Aerospace/Aeronautical Engineering	M,D,O
Applied Mathematics	M,D
Applied Physics	M,D,O
Applied Science and Technology	M,D
Business Administration and Management—General	M
Computer and Information Systems Security	M,D
Computer Engineering	M,D,O
Computer Science	M,D,O
Conflict Resolution and Mediation/Peace Studies	M,D
Electrical Engineering	M,D,O
Engineering Management	M,D,O
Finance and Banking	M
Geographic Information Systems	M,D,O
Homeland Security	M,D
Information Science	M,D,O
Logistics	M
Management Information Systems	M,D,O
Mechanical Engineering	M,D,O
Meteorology	M,D
Military and Defense Studies	M,D
Modeling and Simulation	M,D
National Security	M,D,O
Oceanography	M,D
Operations Research	M,D
Physics	M,D
Software Engineering	M,D
Supply Chain Management	M
Systems Engineering	M,D,O
Transportation Management	M

NAVAL WAR COLLEGE

National Security	M

NAZARENE THEOLOGICAL SEMINARY

Cultural Studies	M,D
Theology	M

NAZARETH COLLEGE OF ROCHESTER

Art Education	M
Art Therapy	M
Business Administration and Management—General	M
Communication Disorders	M
Early Childhood Education	M
Education—General	M
Educational Media/Instructional Technology	M
Elementary Education	M
English as a Second Language	M
Human Resources Management	M
Middle School Education	M
Music Education	M
Music	M
Physical Therapy	D
Reading Education	M
Social Work	M
Therapies—Dance, Drama, and Music	M

NEBRASKA METHODIST COLLEGE

Health Promotion	M
Health Services Management and Hospital Administration	M
Nursing and Healthcare Administration	M
Nursing Education	M
Nursing—General	M

NEBRASKA WESLEYAN UNIVERSITY

Forensic Sciences	M
History	M
Nursing—General	M

NER ISRAEL RABBINICAL COLLEGE

Theology	M,D,O

NER ISRAEL YESHIVA COLLEGE OF TORONTO

Theology	M

NEUMANN UNIVERSITY

Accounting	M
Adult Nursing	M,O
Business Administration and Management—General	M
Clinical Psychology	M,D,O

Education—General	M
Educational Leadership and Administration	M,D
Elementary Education	M
Gerontological Nursing	M,O
Information Studies	M
Management Strategy and Policy	M
Nursing—General	M,O
Organizational Management	M
Pastoral Ministry and Counseling	M,D,O
Physical Therapy	D
Secondary Education	M
Special Education	M
Sports Management	M

NEW BRUNSWICK THEOLOGICAL SEMINARY

Pastoral Ministry and Counseling	M,D
Theology	M,D

NEW CHARTER UNIVERSITY

Business Administration and Management—General	M
Criminal Justice and Criminology	M
Finance and Banking	M
Health Services Management and Hospital Administration	M
Public Administration	M

NEW COLLEGE OF FLORIDA

Database Systems	M

NEW ENGLAND COLLEGE

Accounting	M
Business Administration and Management—General	M
Counseling Psychology	M
Education—General	M,D
Educational Leadership and Administration	M,D
Health Services Management and Hospital Administration	M
Higher Education	M
Human Services	M
International Affairs	M
Management Strategy and Policy	M
Marketing	M
Nonprofit Management	M
Project Management	M
Public Policy	M
Recreation and Park Management	M
Special Education	M,D
Sports Management	M
Writing	M

NEW ENGLAND COLLEGE OF BUSINESS AND FINANCE

Ethics	M
Finance and Banking	M

NEW ENGLAND COLLEGE OF OPTOMETRY

Optometry	M,D
Vision Sciences	M,D

NEW ENGLAND CONSERVATORY OF MUSIC

Music	M,D,O

NEW ENGLAND INSTITUTE OF TECHNOLOGY

Construction Management	M
Management Information Systems	M
Occupational Therapy	M
Public Health—General	M

NEW HAMPSHIRE INSTITUTE OF ART

Art Education	M
Art/Fine Arts	M
Photography	M
Writing	M

NEW JERSEY CITY UNIVERSITY

Accounting	M,O
Allied Health—General	M
Art Education	M
Art/Fine Arts	M
Business Administration and Management—General	M,O
Community Health	M
Computer and Information Systems Security	M,D,O
Counselor Education	M
Criminal Justice and Criminology	M,D,O
Early Childhood Education	M
Education—General	M,D
Educational Leadership and Administration	M
Educational Media/Instructional Technology	M,D
Elementary Education	M
English as a Second Language	M
Finance and Banking	M,O
Health Education	M
Health Services Management and Hospital Administration	M
Marketing	M
Mathematics Education	M
Multilingual and Multicultural Education	M
Music Education	M
Music	M
National Security	M,D,O
Organizational Management	M
Secondary Education	M
Special Education	M
Urban Education	M
Urban Studies	M

NEW JERSEY INSTITUTE OF TECHNOLOGY

Applied Mathematics	M,D,O
Applied Physics	M,D,O
Applied Statistics	M,D,O
Architecture	M,D
Bioinformatics	M,D,O

Biological and Biomedical Sciences—General	M,D,O
Biomedical Engineering	M,D
Biostatistics	M
Business Administration and Management—General	M,D,O
Chemical Engineering	M,D
Chemistry	M,D,O
Computational Biology	M,D,O
Computer and Information Systems Security	M,D,O
Computer Engineering	M,D
Computer Science	M,D,O
Database Systems	M,D,O
Electrical Engineering	M,D
Emergency Management	M,D,O
Energy and Power Engineering	M,D
Engineering and Applied Sciences—General	M,D
Engineering Management	M,D
Environmental Engineering	M,D
Environmental Management and Policy	M,D,O
Environmental Sciences	M,D,O
Health Services Management and Hospital Administration	M,D
History	M,D,O
Industrial/Management Engineering	M,D
Information Science	M,D,O
International Business	M,D,O
Internet Engineering	M,D,O
Management Information Systems	M,D,O
Management of Technology	M,D,O
Manufacturing Engineering	M,D
Materials Engineering	M,D,O
Materials Sciences	M,D,O
Mathematical and Computational Finance	M,D
Mathematics	M,D,O
Mechanical Engineering	M,D
Medicinal and Pharmaceutical Chemistry	M,D,O
Pharmaceutical Administration	M,D
Pharmaceutical Engineering	M,D
Pharmacology	M,D
Safety Engineering	M,D
Software Engineering	M,D,O
Statistics	M,D
Sustainable Development	M,D,O
Systems Science	M,D,O
Technical Communication	M,D
Telecommunications	M,D
Transportation and Highway Engineering	M,D
Transportation Management	M,D
Urban Studies	M,D

NEWMAN THEOLOGICAL COLLEGE

Religious Education	M,O
Theology	M

NEWMAN UNIVERSITY

Business Administration and Management—General	M
Curriculum and Instruction	M
Education—General	M
Educational Leadership and Administration	M
English as a Second Language	M
Finance and Banking	M
International Business	M
Management Information Systems	M
Nurse Anesthesia	M
Organizational Management	M
Reading Education	M
Social Work	M
Theology	M

NEW MEXICO HIGHLANDS UNIVERSITY

American Studies	M
Anthropology	M
Business Administration and Management—General	M
Chemistry	M
Clinical Psychology	M
Computer Art and Design	M
Computer Science	M
Counseling Psychology	M
Counselor Education	M
Curriculum and Instruction	M
Education—General	M
Educational Leadership and Administration	M
English	M
Exercise and Sports Science	M
Health Education	M
History	M
Human Resources Management	M
International Business	M
Internet and Interactive Multimedia	M
Media Studies	M
Natural Resources	M
Political Science	M
Psychology—General	M
Public Affairs	M
Rhetoric	M
Social Work	M
Sociology	M
Special Education	M
Sports Management	M
Writing	M

NEW MEXICO INSTITUTE OF MINING AND TECHNOLOGY

Applied Mathematics	M,D
Astrophysics	M,D
Atmospheric Sciences	M,D
Biological and Biomedical Sciences—General	M,D
Chemistry	M,D
Computer Science	M,D
Electrical Engineering	M

Engineering Management	M
Environmental Engineering	M,D
Geochemistry	M,D
Geological Engineering	M
Geology	M,D
Geophysics	M,D
Geosciences	M,D
Hazardous Materials Management	M
Hydrology	M,D
Materials Engineering	M,D
Mathematical Physics	M,D
Mathematics	M,D
Mechanical Engineering	M
Mechanics	M
Mineral/Mining Engineering	M
Operations Research	M,D
Petroleum Engineering	M
Physics	M,D
Science Education	M
Statistics	M
Systems Engineering	M
Water Resources Engineering	M

NEW MEXICO STATE UNIVERSITY

Accounting	M
Aerospace/Aeronautical Engineering	M,D
Agricultural Economics and Agribusiness	M,D
Agricultural Education	M
Agricultural Sciences—General	M,D
Animal Sciences	M,D
Anthropology	M,O
Applied Statistics	M,D,O
Art History	M
Art/Fine Arts	M
Astronomy	M,D
Astrophysics	M,D
Bioinformatics	M,D
Biological and Biomedical Sciences—General	M,D
Biotechnology	M,D
Business Administration and Management—General	M,D
Chemical Engineering	M,D
Chemistry	M,D
Civil Engineering	M,D
Clothing and Textiles	M
Communication Disorders	M,D,O
Communication—General	M
Community Health Nursing	M,D,O
Computer Engineering	M,D,O
Computer Science	M,D
Corporate and Organizational Communication	M,D
Counseling Psychology	M,D,O
Counselor Education	M,D,O
Criminal Justice and Criminology	M
Cultural Studies	M,D,O
Curriculum and Instruction	M,D,O
Distance Education Development	O
Early Childhood Education	M,D,O
Economic Development	M,D,O
Economics	M,D
Education—General	M,D,O
Educational Leadership and Administration	M,D
Educational Measurement and Evaluation	M,D,O
Electrical Engineering	M,D,O
Engineering and Applied Sciences—General	M,D,O
English as a Second Language	M,D,O
English Education	M,D
English	M,D
Entomology	M
Environmental Engineering	M,D
Environmental Sciences	M,D
Family and Consumer Sciences-General	M
Family Nurse Practitioner Studies	M,D,O
Finance and Banking	M,O
Fish, Game, and Wildlife Management	M
Food Science and Technology	M
Foreign Languages Education	M,D,O
Geography	M
Geological Engineering	M,D
Geology	M
Gerontological Nursing	M,D,O
Higher Education	M,D
History	M,D
Horticulture	M,D
Hydrology	M,D
Industrial/Management Engineering	M,D,O
Interdisciplinary Studies	M
Kinesiology and Movement Studies	D
Management Information Systems	M
Marketing	D
Mathematics	M,D
Mechanical Engineering	M,D
Molecular Biology	M,D
Multilingual and Multicultural Education	M,D,O
Museum Studies	M,O
Music Education	M
Music	M
Nursing and Healthcare Administration	M,D,O
Nursing—General	M,D,O
Physics	M,D
Plant Pathology	M
Plant Sciences	M
Political Science	M
Psychiatric Nursing	M,D,O
Psychology—General	M,D
Public Administration	M
Public Health—General	M,O
Range Science	M
Reading Education	M,D,O

Rhetoric M,D
School Psychology M,D,O
Social Work M
Sociology M
Spanish M,D,O
Special Education M,D,O
Systems Engineering M,D,O
Travel and Tourism M
Water Resources M,D
Writing M,D

NEW ORLEANS BAPTIST THEOLOGICAL SEMINARY
Music M,D
Pastoral Ministry and Counseling M,D
Religious Education M,D
Theology M,D

NEW SAINT ANDREWS COLLEGE
Religion M,O
Theology M,O

THE NEW SCHOOL
Anthropology M,D
Applied Arts and Design—General M
Applied Social Research M,D
Architecture M
Art/Fine Arts M
Clinical Psychology M,D
Clothing and Textiles M
Cognitive Sciences M,D
Computer Art and Design M
Database Systems M
Economics M,D
English as a Second Language M
Environmental Management and Policy M,O
Finance and Banking M,D
History M,D
Industrial Design M
Interior Design M
International Affairs M
International Economics M,D
Liberal Studies M
Lighting Design M
Management Strategy and Policy M,O
Media Studies M,O
Museum Studies M
Music M,O
Nonprofit Management M
Organizational Management M,O
Philosophy M,D
Photography M
Political Science M,D
Psychoanalysis and Psychotherapy M,D
Psychology—General M,D
Public Policy D
Social Psychology M,D
Social Sciences M,D
Sociology M,D
Sustainability Management M,O
Textile Design M
Theater M
Urban Design M
Urban Studies M
Writing M

NEWSCHOOL OF ARCHITECTURE AND DESIGN
Architecture M
Construction Management M

NEW YORK ACADEMY OF ART
Anatomy M
Art/Fine Arts M

NEW YORK CHIROPRACTIC COLLEGE
Acupuncture and Oriental Medicine M
Anatomy M
Chiropractic D*
Nutrition M

NEW YORK COLLEGE OF HEALTH PROFESSIONS
Acupuncture and Oriental Medicine M

NEW YORK COLLEGE OF PODIATRIC MEDICINE
Podiatric Medicine D

NEW YORK COLLEGE OF TRADITIONAL CHINESE MEDICINE
Acupuncture and Oriental Medicine M

NEW YORK FILM ACADEMY
Film, Television, and Video Production M
Photography M

NEW YORK INSTITUTE OF TECHNOLOGY
Accounting M
Applied Arts and Design—General M
Architecture M
Art/Fine Arts M
Arts Administration M,O
Business Administration and Management—General M
Communication—General M
Computer and Information Systems Security M
Computer Art and Design M
Computer Engineering M
Computer Science M
Counselor Education M,O
Distance Education Development M,O
Early Childhood Education M
Education—General M,O
Educational Media/Instructional Technology M,O
Electrical Engineering M
Elementary Education M
Energy and Power Engineering M,O

Energy Management and Policy M,O
Engineering and Applied Sciences—General M,O
Entertainment Management M,O
Environmental Engineering M
Environmental Management and Policy M,O
Finance and Banking M
Graphic Design M
Human Resources Management M,O
Industrial and Labor Relations M,O
Interdisciplinary Studies M,O
Marketing M
Mathematics Education M,O
Mathematics M
Middle School Education M
Nutrition M
Occupational Therapy M
Osteopathic Medicine M,D
Physical Therapy D
Physician Assistant Studies M
Science Education M,O
Secondary Education M
Supply Chain Management M
Urban Design M

NEW YORK LAW SCHOOL
Law M,D

NEW YORK MEDICAL COLLEGE
Allopathic Medicine D
Biochemistry M,D
Biological and Biomedical Sciences—General M,D
Biostatistics M,D,O
Business Administration and Management—General M,D,O
Cell Biology M,D
Communication Disorders M,D,O
Emergency Management M,D,O
Environmental and Occupational Health M,D,O
Epidemiology M,D,O
Health Education M,D,O
Health Services Management and Hospital Administration M,D,O
Immunology M,D
Industrial Hygiene M,D,O
International Health M,D,O
Microbiology M,D
Molecular Biology M,D
Pathology M,D
Pharmacology M,D
Physical Therapy M,D,O
Physiology M,D
Psychology—General M,D,O
Public Health—General M,D,O

NEW YORK SCHOOL OF INTERIOR DESIGN
Interior Design M
Lighting Design M
Sustainable Development M

NEW YORK STUDIO SCHOOL OF DRAWING, PAINTING AND SCULPTURE
Art/Fine Arts M,O*

NEW YORK THEOLOGICAL SEMINARY
Theology M,D

NEW YORK UNIVERSITY
Accounting M,D
Acute Care/Critical Care Nursing M,D,O
Adult Nursing M,D,O
Advertising and Public Relations M
African Studies M,D,O
Agricultural Engineering M,D
Allopathic Medicine M,D
American Studies M,D
Anthropology M,D
Applied Arts and Design—General M
Applied Economics M,D,O
Applied Physics M,D
Applied Psychology M,D,O
Applied Social Research M
Applied Statistics M
Archaeology M,D
Architectural History M
Archives/Archival Administration M,D,O
Art Education M,O
Art History M,D
Art Therapy M
Art/Fine Arts M,D,O
Arts Administration M
Asian Studies M,D
Bioethics M
Bioinformatics M,D
Biological and Biomedical Sciences—General M,D,O
Biomedical Engineering M,D
Biotechnology M
Business Administration and Management—General M,D,O
Business Education M,O
Cancer Biology/Oncology M,D
Cell Biology D
Chemical Engineering M,D
Chemistry M,D,O
Chinese M,D,O
Civil Engineering M,D
Classics M,D,O
Clinical Research M
Cognitive Sciences M,D,O
Communication Disorders M,D
Communication—General M,D
Community Health M
Comparative Literature M,D
Computational Biology D
Computer and Information Systems Security O
Computer Art and Design M

Computer Engineering M,O
Computer Science M,D
Conflict Resolution and Mediation/Peace Studies M,O
Construction Management M,D,O
Corporate and Organizational Communication M
Counseling Psychology M,D,O
Counselor Education M,D,O
Cultural Studies M,D,O
Dance M,D,O
Database Systems M,O
Demography and Population Studies M,D
Dentistry D
Developmental Biology M,D
Developmental Psychology M,D
Early Childhood Education M
Economics M,D,O
Education—General M,D,O
Educational Leadership and Administration M,D,O
Educational Media/Instructional Technology M,D,O
Educational Policy M,D
Educational Psychology M,D
Electrical Engineering M,D
Electronic Commerce M,D,O
Elementary Education M
Energy Management and Policy M,O
Engineering and Applied Sciences—General M,D,O
English as a Second Language M,D,O
English Education M,D,O
English M,D
Entrepreneurship M,D,O
Environmental and Occupational Health M,D*
Environmental Education M
Environmental Engineering M
Environmental Management and Policy M
Environmental Sciences M
Epidemiology M,D
Ergonomics and Human Factors M,D
Family Nurse Practitioner Studies M,D,O
Film, Television, and Video Production M
Finance and Banking M,D,O
Financial Engineering M,O
Food Science and Technology M,D
Foreign Languages Education M,D,O
Foundations and Philosophy of Education M,D
French M,D,O
Game Design and Development M
Genetics M,D
Genomic Sciences D
German M,D
Gerontological Nursing M,D,O
Graphic Design M
Health Promotion M,D,O
Health Services Management and Hospital Administration M,D,O
Higher Education M,D
Historic Preservation M
History M,D,O
Hospitality Management M,D,O
Human Development M,D,O
Human Resources Development M,O
Human Resources Management M,D,O
Humanities M,O
Immunology M,D
Industrial and Organizational Psychology M,D,O
Industrial/Management Engineering M
Interdisciplinary Studies M
International Affairs M,D,O
International and Comparative Education M,D,O
International Business M,D
International Development M,O
International Health M,D
Internet and Interactive Multimedia M,O
Investment Management M,O
Italian M,D,O
Japanese M,D,O
Jewish Studies M,D,O
Journalism M,D,O
Kinesiology and Movement Studies M,D,O
Latin American Studies M,O
Law M,D,O
Legal and Justice Studies M,D,O
Linguistics M,D
Management Information Systems M,D,O
Management of Technology M,D,O
Management Strategy and Policy M,D,O
Manufacturing Engineering M
Marketing M,D,O
Mathematical and Computational Finance M,D,O
Mathematics Education M
Mathematics M,D*
Mechanical Engineering M,D
Media Studies M,D,O
Medical Imaging D
Microbiology M,D
Middle School Education M,D,O
Molecular Biology M,D
Molecular Biophysics D
Molecular Genetics M,D
Molecular Pharmacology D
Molecular Toxicology M,D
Multilingual and Multicultural Education M,D,O
Museum Studies M,O

Music Education M,D,O
Music M,D,O
National Security M,O
Near and Middle Eastern Studies M,D,O
Neurobiology M,D
Neuroscience D
Nonprofit Management M,D,O
Nurse Midwifery M,D,O
Nursing and Healthcare Administration M,O
Nursing Education M,O
Nursing Informatics M,O
Nursing—General M,D,O
Nutrition M,D
Occupational Therapy M,D
Oral and Dental Sciences M,D,O
Organizational Behavior M,D,O
Organizational Management M,D,O
Pathobiology D
Pediatric Nursing M,D,O
Philosophy M,D
Physical Therapy M,D,O
Physics M,D,O
Physiology D
Plant Biology M,D
Political Science M,D
Portuguese M,D
Project Management M,D,O
Psychiatric Nursing M,D,O
Psychoanalysis and Psychotherapy M,D,O
Psychology—General M,D,O
Public Administration M,D
Public Health—General M,D
Public History M,D,O
Public Policy M,D
Publishing M
Reading Education M
Real Estate M,O
Rehabilitation Sciences M,D
Religion M,O
Romance Languages M,D
Russian M
Science Education M,D,O
Secondary Education M,D,O
Slavic Languages M
Social Psychology M,D,O
Social Sciences Education M,D
Social Sciences M,D
Social Work M
Sociology M,D
Software Engineering O
Spanish M,D,O
Special Education M
Speech and Interpersonal Communication M,D
Sports Management M,O
Statistics M,D
Structural Biology D
Student Affairs M,D
Sustainable Development M
Systems Engineering M
Taxation M,D,O
Telecommunications Management M,D,O
Theater M,D,O
Therapies—Dance, Drama, and Music M
Toxicology M,D
Translation and Interpretation M
Transportation and Highway Engineering M,D
Transportation Management M
Travel and Tourism M,O
Urban and Regional Planning M
Urban Studies M
Western European Studies M
Writing M

NIAGARA UNIVERSITY
Accounting M
Business Administration and Management—General M
Counseling Psychology M,O
Counselor Education M,O
Criminal Justice and Criminology M
Early Childhood Education M,O
Education—General M,O
Educational Leadership and Administration M,O
Elementary Education M,O
English as a Second Language M,O
Finance and Banking M
Health Services Management and Hospital Administration M
Human Resources Management M
Interdisciplinary Studies M
International Business M
Management Strategy and Policy M
Marketing M
Middle School Education M,O
Reading Education M
School Psychology M
Secondary Education M,O
Special Education M,O
Supply Chain Management M

NICHOLLS STATE UNIVERSITY
Business Administration and Management—General M
Clinical Psychology M,O
Counselor Education M,O
Curriculum and Instruction M
Education—General M
Educational Leadership and Administration M
Elementary Education M
Environmental Biology M
Family Nurse Practitioner Studies M
Health Education M
Marine Biology M
Middle School Education M

M—masters degree; D—doctorate; O—other advanced degree; *—Close-Up and/or Display

Nursing and Healthcare
  Administration — M
Nursing Education — M
Nursing—General — M
Psychiatric Nursing — M
School Psychology — M,O
Secondary Education — M

NICHOLS COLLEGE
Business Administration and
  Management—General — M
Organizational Management — M

NIPISSING UNIVERSITY
Education—General — M,O

NORFOLK STATE UNIVERSITY
Art/Fine Arts — M
Clinical Psychology — M
Communication—General — M
Computer Engineering — M
Computer Science — M
Criminal Justice and Criminology — M
Early Childhood Education — M
Education of Students with
  Severe/Multiple Disabilities — M
Education—General — M
Educational Leadership and
  Administration — M
Electrical Engineering — M
Materials Sciences — M
Media Studies — M
Music Education — M
Music — M
Optical Sciences — M
Psychology—General — M,D
Secondary Education — M
Social Psychology — M
Social Work — M,D
Special Education — M
Urban Education — M
Urban Studies — M

NORTH AMERICAN UNIVERSITY
Educational Leadership and
  Administration — M

NORTH CAROLINA AGRICULTURAL AND TECHNICAL STATE UNIVERSITY
Accounting — M
Adult Education — M
African-American Studies — M
Agricultural Economics and
  Agribusiness — M
Agricultural Education — M
Agricultural Sciences—
  General — M
Agronomy and Soil Sciences — M
Animal Sciences — M
Applied Economics — M
Applied Mathematics — M
Bioengineering — M
Biological and Biomedical
  Sciences—General — M
Business Administration and
  Management—General — M
Business Education — M
Chemical Engineering — M
Chemistry — M,D
Child and Family Studies — M
Child Development — M
Civil Engineering — M
Computational Sciences — M
Computer Art and Design — M
Computer Engineering — M,D
Computer Science — M
Construction Management — M
Consumer Economics — M
Counselor Education — M
Early Childhood Education — M
Education—General — M
Educational Leadership and
  Administration — M
Educational Media/Instructional
  Technology — M
Electrical Engineering — M,D
Elementary Education — M
Energy and Power
  Engineering — M,D
Engineering and Applied
  Sciences—General — M,D
English Education — M
English — M
Environmental and Occupational
  Health — M
Environmental Sciences — M
Graphic Design — M
Health Education — M
Human Resources Management — M
Industrial/Management
  Engineering — M,D
Management Information Systems — M
Management of Technology — M
Mathematics — M
Mechanical Engineering — M,D
Nutrition — M
Optical Sciences — M,D
Physical Education — M
Physics — M
Plant Sciences — M
Reading Education — M
Science Education — M
Secondary Education — M
Social Work — M
Supply Chain Management — M
Systems Engineering — M
Vocational and Technical Education — M

NORTH CAROLINA CENTRAL UNIVERSITY
Applied Mathematics — M
Biological and Biomedical
  Sciences—General — M
Business Administration and
  Management—General — M
Chemistry — M

Communication Disorders — M
Counselor Education — M
Criminal Justice and Criminology — M
Education—General — M
Educational Leadership and
  Administration — M
Educational Media/Instructional
  Technology — M
English — M
Geosciences — M
History — M
Information Studies — M
Law — D
Library Science — M
Mathematics Education — M
Mathematics — M
Music — M
Physical Education — M
Physics — M
Psychology—General — M
Public Administration — M
Recreation and Park Management — M
Special Education — M
Sports Management — M

NORTH CAROLINA STATE UNIVERSITY
Accounting — M
Adult Education — M,D
Aerospace/Aeronautical
  Engineering — M,D
Agricultural Economics and
  Agribusiness — M
Agricultural Education — M,O
Agricultural Engineering — M,D,O
Agricultural Sciences—
  General — M,D,O
Agronomy and Soil Sciences — M,D
Animal Sciences — M,D
Anthropology — M
Applied Arts and Design—General — M,D
Applied Mathematics — M,D
Architecture — M
Atmospheric Sciences — M,D
Biochemistry — D
Bioengineering — M,D,O
Bioinformatics — M,D
Biological and Biomedical
  Sciences—General — M,D,O
Biomathematics — M,D
Biomedical Engineering — M,D
Biotechnology — M
Botany — M,D
Business Administration and
  Management—General — M
Business Education — M
Cell Biology — M,D
Chemical Engineering — M,D
Chemistry — M,D
Civil Engineering — M,D
Clothing and Textiles — D
Communication—General — M
Community College Education — M,D
Computer Art and Design — D
Computer Engineering — M,D
Computer Science — M,D
Counselor Education — M,D
Cultural Anthropology — M
Curriculum and Instruction — M,D
Developmental Education — M,D,O
Developmental Psychology — D
Economics — M,D
Education—General — M,D,O
Educational Leadership and
  Administration — M,D
Educational Measurement and
  Evaluation — D
Educational Media/Instructional
  Technology — M,D
Electrical Engineering — M,D
Elementary Education — M
Engineering and Applied
  Sciences—General — M,D
English Education — M
English — M
Entomology — M,D
Entrepreneurship — M
Epidemiology — M,D
Ergonomics and Human
  Factors — D
Experimental Psychology — D
Financial Engineering — M
Fish, Game, and Wildlife
  Management — M,D
Food Science and
  Technology — M,D
Forestry — M,D
French — M
Genetics — M,D
Genomic Sciences — M,D
Geographic Information Systems — M,D
Geosciences — M,D
Graphic Design — M
Higher Education — M,D
History — M
Horticulture — M,D,O
Human Resources Development — M
Industrial and Organizational
  Psychology — D
Industrial Design — M
Industrial/Management
  Engineering — M,D
Infectious Diseases — M,D
International Affairs — M
Landscape Architecture — M
Liberal Studies — M
Management of Technology — D
Manufacturing Engineering — M
Marine Sciences — M,D
Materials Engineering — M,D
Materials Sciences — M,D
Mathematical and
  Computational Finance — M
Mathematics Education — M,D
Mathematics — M,D

Mechanical Engineering — M,D
Meteorology — M,D
Microbiology — M,D
Middle School Education — M
Molecular Toxicology — M,D
Natural Resources — M
Nonprofit Management — M,D,O
Nuclear Engineering — M,D
Nutrition — M,D
Oceanography — M,D
Operations Research — M,D
Paper and Pulp Engineering — M,D
Pathology — M,D
Pharmacology — M,D
Physics — M,D
Physiology — M,D
Plant Biology — M,D
Plant Pathology — M,D
Polymer Science and
  Engineering — D
Psychology—General — D
Public Administration — M,D
Public History — M
Recreation and Park Management — M,D
Rhetoric — M
School Psychology — D
Science Education — M,D
Secondary Education — M
Social Psychology — M
Social Sciences Education — M
Social Work — M
Sociology — M,D
Spanish — M
Special Education — M
Sports Management — M,D
Statistics — M,D
Supply Chain Management — M
Technical Communication — M
Textile Sciences and
  Engineering — M,D
Toxicology — M,D
Travel and Tourism — M,D
Veterinary Medicine — M,D
Veterinary Sciences — M,D
Writing — M
Zoology — M,D

NORTH CENTRAL COLLEGE
Business Administration and
  Management—General — M
Computer Science — M
Cultural Studies — M
Education—General — M
Educational Leadership and
  Administration — M
Finance and Banking — M
Human Resources Management — M
Liberal Studies — M
Management Strategy and Policy — M

NORTHCENTRAL UNIVERSITY
Business Administration and
  Management—General — M,D,O
Education—General — M,D,O
Marriage and Family Therapy — M,D,O
Psychology—General — M,D,O

NORTH DAKOTA STATE UNIVERSITY
Accounting — M
Adult Education — M,D,O
Agricultural Economics and
  Agribusiness — M
Agricultural Education — M
Agricultural Sciences—
  General — M,D*
Agronomy and Soil Sciences — M,D
Animal Sciences — M,D
Anthropology — M
Applied Mathematics — M,D
Architecture — M
Athletic Training and Sports
  Medicine — M,D
Biochemistry — M,D
Bioinformatics — M,D
Biological and Biomedical
  Sciences—General — M,D
Botany — M,D
Business Administration and
  Management—General — M*
Cell Biology — M,D
Chemistry — M,D
Child and Family Studies — M,D,O*
Child Development — M
Civil Engineering — M,D
Clinical Psychology — M,D
Clothing and Textiles — M,O
Cognitive Sciences — M,D
Communication—General — M,D
Computer Engineering — M,D
Computer Science — M,D,O
Construction Management — M,O
Consumer Economics — M,O
Counseling Psychology — M,D
Counselor Education — M,D
Criminal Justice and Criminology — M,D
Curriculum and Instruction — M
Developmental Psychology — D
Ecology — M,D
Education—General — M,D,O
Educational Leadership and
  Administration — M,O
Electrical Engineering — M,D
Engineering and Applied
  Sciences—General — M,D,O*
English — M,D
Entomology — M,D
Environmental Engineering — M,D
Environmental Sciences — M,D
Exercise and Sports Science — M,D
Family and Consumer
  Sciences—General — M
Food Science and
  Technology — M,D,O
Genomic Sciences — M,D
Gerontology — M,O

Health Promotion — M,D
Health Psychology — M,D
Higher Education — O
History — M,D
Industrial/Management
  Engineering — M,D
Infectious Diseases — M,D
Logistics — M,D
Manufacturing Engineering — M,D
Marriage and Family Therapy — D
Mass Communication — M,D
Materials Sciences — M,D
Mathematics Education — M,D,O
Mathematics — M,D*
Mechanical Engineering — M,D
Microbiology — M,D
Molecular Biology — M,D
Molecular Pathogenesis — M,D
Music Education — M,D,O
Music — M,D
Nanotechnology — M,D
Natural Resources — M,D
Nursing—General — M,D
Nutrition — M,D
Pathology — M,D
Pharmacy — M,D
Physics — M,D
Plant Pathology — M,D
Plant Sciences — M,D
Polymer Science and
  Engineering — M,D
Psychology—General — M,D
Public Health—General — M*
Rhetoric — M,D*
School Psychology — M,D
Science Education — M,D,O
Social Psychology — M,D
Social Sciences Education — M,D,O
Social Sciences — M
Sociology — M
Software Engineering — M,D,O
Speech and Interpersonal
  Communication — M,D
Statistics — M,D,O
Transportation and Highway
  Engineering — D
Transportation Management — M,D
Urban and Regional Planning — M
Urban Studies — M,D
Vocational and Technical Education — M,D,O
Writing — M,D
Zoology — M,D

NORTHEASTERN ILLINOIS UNIVERSITY
Accounting — M
Applied Mathematics — M
Biological and Biomedical
  Sciences—General — M
Business Administration and
  Management—General — M
Chemistry — M
Computer Science — M
Counselor Education — M
Early Childhood Education — M
Education of the Gifted — M
Education—General — M
Educational Leadership and
  Administration — M
Elementary Education — M
English as a Second Language — M
English — M
Environmental Management
  and Policy — M
Exercise and Sports Science — M
Finance and Banking — M
Geography — M
Gerontology — M
History — M
Human Resources Development — M
Latin American Studies — M
Linguistics — M
Marketing — M
Marriage and Family Therapy — M
Mathematics Education — M
Mathematics — M
Multilingual and Multicultural
  Education — M
Music — M
Political Science — M
Reading Education — M
Rehabilitation Counseling — M
Secondary Education — M
Social Psychology — M
Special Education — M
Speech and Interpersonal
  Communication — M
Urban Education — M
Writing — M

NORTHEASTERN SEMINARY AT ROBERTS WESLEYAN COLLEGE
Theology — M,D

NORTHEASTERN STATE UNIVERSITY
Accounting — M
Addictions/Substance Abuse
  Counseling — M
American Indian/Native American
  Studies — M
Business Administration and
  Management—General — M
Communication Disorders — M
Communication—General — M
Counseling Psychology — M
Counselor Education — M
Criminal Justice and Criminology — M
Early Childhood Education — M
Education—General — M
Educational Leadership and
  Administration — M
Educational Media/Instructional
  Technology — M
English — M
Environmental and Occupational
  Health — M

Environmental Management
and Policy — M
Finance and Banking — M
Health Education — M
Kinesiology and Movement Studies — M
Mathematics Education — M
Natural Resources — M
Nursing Education — M
Occupational Therapy — M
Optometry — D
Psychology—General — M
Reading Education — M
Science Education — M
Special Education — M

NORTHEASTERN UNIVERSITY
Accounting — M
Acute Care/Critical Care Nursing — M,D,O
Allied Health—General — M
Applied Arts and Design—General — M
Applied Behavior Analysis — M,D,O
Applied Mathematics — M,D
Architecture — M
Art/Fine Arts — M
Bioengineering — M,D,O
Bioinformatics — M,D
Biological and Biomedical
Sciences—General — M,D
Biotechnology — M,D
Business Administration and
Management—General — M,D,O
Chemical Engineering — M,D,O
Chemistry — M,D
Civil Engineering — M,D,O
Computer and Information
Systems Security — M,D
Computer Engineering — M,D,O
Computer Science — M,D
Corporate and Organizational
Communication — M
Counseling Psychology — M,D,O
Criminal Justice and Criminology — M,D
Database Systems — M,D
Ecology — M,D
Economic Development — M
Economics — M,D
Educational Leadership and
Administration — M
Electrical Engineering — M,D,O
Elementary Education — M
Energy and Power
Engineering — M,D,O
Engineering and Applied
Sciences—General — M,D,O
Engineering Management — M,D,O
English — M,D
Entrepreneurship — M
Environmental Engineering — M,D,O
Evolutionary Biology — M,D
Exercise and Sports Science — M,D,O
Family Nurse Practitioner Studies — M,D,O
Finance and Banking — M
Geographic Information Systems — M
Gerontological Nursing — M,D,O
Health Informatics — M,D
Higher Education — M
History — M,D
Homeland Security — M,D
Human Services — M
Industrial/Management
Engineering — M,D,O
Interdisciplinary Studies — M,D,O
International Affairs — M,D
International Business — M
Internet and Interactive
Multimedia — M
Journalism — M
Law — M,D
Legal and Justice Studies — M
Management Information Systems — M,D,O
Marine Biology — M,D
Maternal and Child/Neonatal
Nursing — M,D,O
Mathematics — M,D
Mechanical Engineering — M,D,O
Nonprofit Management — M
Nursing and Healthcare
Administration — M,D,O
Nursing—General — M,D,O
Nutrition — M
Operations Research — M,D,O
Pediatric Nursing — M,D,O
Pharmaceutical Sciences — M,D,O
Pharmacology — M,D,O
Pharmacy — M,D,O
Physics — M,D
Political Science — M,D
Project Management — M
Psychiatric Nursing — M,D,O
Psychology—General — M,D
Public Administration — M,D
Public History — M,D
Public Policy — M,D,O
School Psychology — M,D,O
Sociology — M,D
Special Education — M
Sports Management — M
Systems Engineering — M,D,O
Taxation — M
Technical Communication — M
Telecommunications — M,D,O
Urban Studies — M,D

NORTHEAST OHIO MEDICAL UNIVERSITY
Allopathic Medicine — D
Bioethics — M,D,O
Health Services Management and
Hospital Administration — M,D,O
Pharmaceutical Administration — M,D,O
Pharmaceutical Sciences — M,D,O

Pharmacy — D
Public Health—General — M,D,O

NORTHERN ARIZONA UNIVERSITY
Allied Health—General — M,D,O
Anthropology — M
Applied Physics — M,D
Applied Statistics — M,O
Archaeology — M
Atmospheric Sciences — M,D
Biological and Biomedical
Sciences—General — M,D
Business Administration and
Management—General — M
Chemistry — M
Civil Engineering — M
Clinical Psychology — M
Communication Disorders — M
Communication—General — M
Community College Education — M,D,O
Computer Engineering — M
Computer Science — M
Counseling Psychology — M,D,O
Counselor Education — M,D,O
Criminal Justice and Criminology — M
Cultural Anthropology — M
Curriculum and Instruction — M,D
Early Childhood Education — M,D
Education—General — M,D,O
Educational Leadership and
Administration — M,D,O
Educational Media/Instructional
Technology — M,O
Educational Psychology — M,D,O
Electrical Engineering — M
Elementary Education — M,D
Engineering and Applied
Sciences—General — M,D,O
English as a Second Language — M,D,O
English Education — M,D,O
English — M,D,O
Environmental Engineering — M
Environmental Management
and Policy — M,D
Environmental Sciences — M,D
Ethnic Studies — O
Family Nurse Practitioner Studies — M,D,O
Foreign Languages Education — M
Forestry — M,D
Foundations and Philosophy of
Education — M,D,O
Gender Studies — O
Geographic Information Systems — M,O
Geography — M,D
Geology — M,D
Higher Education — M,D,O
History — M
Human Development — O
International Business — M
Liberal Studies — M
Linguistics — M,D,O
Mathematics Education — M,O
Mathematics — M,O
Mechanical Engineering — M
Meteorology — M,D
Multilingual and Multicultural
Education — M,O
Music — M,O
Nursing—General — M,D,O
Occupational Therapy — D
Physical Therapy — D
Physician Assistant Studies — M
Physics — M,D
Political Science — M,D,O
Psychology—General — M
Public Administration — M,D,O
Rhetoric — M,D,O
School Psychology — M,D,O
Science Education — M,O
Secondary Education — M,D
Sociology — M
Spanish — M
Special Education — M,O
Statistics — M,O
Student Affairs — M,D,O
Sustainable Development — M
Urban and Regional Planning — M,O
Vocational and Technical Education — M,O
Women's Studies — O
Writing — M,D,O

NORTHERN ILLINOIS UNIVERSITY
Accounting — M
Adult Education — M,D
Anthropology — M
Art/Fine Arts — M
Biological and Biomedical
Sciences—General — M,D
Business Administration and
Management—General — M
Child and Family Studies — M
Communication Disorders — M,D
Communication—General — M
Computer Science — M
Counselor Education — M,D
Curriculum and Instruction — M,D
Dance — M
Early Childhood Education — M,D
Economics — M,D
Education—General — M,D,O
Educational Leadership and
Administration — M,D,O
Educational Media/Instructional
Technology — M,D
Educational Psychology — M,D,O
Electrical Engineering — M
Elementary Education — M,D
Engineering and Applied
Sciences—General — M
English — M,D

Foundations and Philosophy of
Education — M,D,O
French — M
Geography — M,D
Geology — M,D
Higher Education — M,D
History — M,D
Industrial and Manufacturing
Management — M
Industrial/Management
Engineering — M
Law — D
Mathematics — M,D
Mechanical Engineering — M
Music — M,O
Nursing—General — M
Nutrition — M
Philosophy — M
Physical Education — M
Physical Therapy — M,D
Physics — M,D
Political Science — M,D
Psychology—General — M,D
Public Administration — M
Reading Education — M,D
Romance Languages — M
Secondary Education — M,D
Sociology — M
Spanish — M
Special Education — M,D
Statistics — M
Taxation — M
Theater — M

NORTHERN KENTUCKY UNIVERSITY
Accounting — M,O
Advertising and Public Relations — M,O
Allied Health—General — M
Business Administration and
Management—General — M,O
Clinical Psychology — M
Communication—General — M,O
Computer and Information
Systems Security — M,O
Computer Science — M,O
Counseling Psychology — M
Counselor Education — M
Cultural Studies — M,O
Education—General — M,D,O
Educational Leadership and
Administration — M,D,O
English — M,O
Geographic Information Systems — M,O
Health Informatics — M,O
Health Psychology — M,O
Industrial and Organizational
Psychology — M,O
Information Science — M,O
Law — D
Liberal Studies — M
Management of Technology — M
Marriage and Family Therapy — M,O
Media Studies — M,O
Music — M,O
Nonprofit Management — M,O
Nursing—General — M,D,O
Organizational Management — M
Public Administration — M,O
Public History — M
Rhetoric — M,O
Social Work — M
Software Engineering — M,O
Special Education — M,O
Taxation — M,O
Writing — M,O

NORTHERN MICHIGAN UNIVERSITY
Applied Behavior Analysis — M,O
Biochemistry — M
Biological and Biomedical
Sciences—General — M
Business Administration and
Management—General — M
Clinical Laboratory
Sciences/Medical Technology — M
Criminal Justice and Criminology — M
Curriculum and Instruction — M
Education—General — M
Educational Leadership and
Administration — M
Elementary Education — M
English as a Second Language — M,O
English — M,O
Exercise and Sports Science — M
Family Nurse Practitioner Studies — M,D
Higher Education — M
Human Resources Management — M
Molecular Genetics — M
Nursing—General — M,D
Psychology—General — M,O
Public Administration — M
Reading Education — M
Science Education — M
Secondary Education — M
Special Education — M
Student Affairs — M
Theater — M,O
Writing — M,O

NORTHERN SEMINARY
Pastoral Ministry and Counseling — M,D
Religion — M,D
Theology — M,D

NORTHERN STATE UNIVERSITY
Clinical Psychology — M
Counseling Psychology — M
Counselor Education — M
Curriculum and Instruction — M
Education—General — M
Educational Leadership and
Administration — M

Educational Media/Instructional
Technology — M
Finance and Banking — M
Music Education — M
Sports Management — M

NORTH GREENVILLE UNIVERSITY
Education—General — M,D
Finance and Banking — M,D
Human Resources Management — M,D
Pastoral Ministry and Counseling — M,D

NORTH PARK THEOLOGICAL SEMINARY
Pastoral Ministry and Counseling — M,O
Theology — M,D

NORTH PARK UNIVERSITY
Adult Nursing — M
Business Administration and
Management—General — M
Education—General — M
Music — M
Nonprofit Management — M
Nursing and Healthcare
Administration — M
Nursing—General — M

NORTHWEST CHRISTIAN UNIVERSITY
Accounting — M
Business Administration and
Management—General — M
Counseling Psychology — M
Counselor Education — M
Education—General — M
Elementary Education — M
English as a Second Language — M
Secondary Education — M

NORTHWESTERN COLLEGE
Early Childhood Education — M,O
Education—General — M,O
Educational Leadership and
Administration — M,O

NORTHWESTERN HEALTH SCIENCES UNIVERSITY
Acupuncture and Oriental Medicine — M
Chiropractic — D

NORTHWESTERN OKLAHOMA STATE UNIVERSITY
Adult Education — M
American Studies — M
Counseling Psychology — M
Counselor Education — M
Curriculum and Instruction — M
Education—General — M
Educational Leadership and
Administration — M
Elementary Education — M
Reading Education — M
Secondary Education — M

NORTHWESTERN POLYTECHNIC UNIVERSITY
Business Administration and
Management—General — M,D
Computer Engineering — M,D
Computer Science — M,D
Electrical Engineering — M,D
Engineering and Applied
Sciences—General — M,D

NORTHWESTERN STATE UNIVERSITY OF LOUISIANA
Adult Education — M
Art/Fine Arts — M
Clinical Psychology — M
Counselor Education — M,O
Curriculum and Instruction — M
Early Childhood Education — M
Education—General — M,O
Educational Leadership and
Administration — M,O
Educational Media/Instructional
Technology — M,O
Elementary Education — M,O
English — M
Health Education — M
Health Physics/Radiological Health — M
Homeland Security — M
Middle School Education — M
Music — M
Nursing—General — M
Psychology—General — M
Reading Education — M,O
Secondary Education — M,O
Special Education — M,O
Student Affairs — M

NORTHWESTERN UNIVERSITY
Accounting — M,D
African Studies — O
African-American Studies — D
Allopathic Medicine —
American Studies — M
Anthropology — D
Applied Mathematics — M,D
Applied Physics — D
Art History — D
Art/Fine Arts — M
Artificial Intelligence/Robotics — M
Arts Administration — M
Astronomy — D
Biochemistry — D
Bioengineering — D
Biological and Biomedical
Sciences—General — D
Biomedical Engineering — M,D
Biophysics — D
Biopsychology — D
Biostatistics — D
Biotechnology — M,D

Broadcast Journalism	M
Business Administration and Management—General	M,D
Cell Biology	D
Chemical Engineering	M,D
Chemistry	D
Civil Engineering	M,D
Clinical Laboratory Sciences/Medical Technology	M
Clinical Psychology	D
Clinical Research	M,O
Cognitive Sciences	D
Communication Disorders	M,D
Communication—General	M,D
Comparative Literature	M,D
Computer and Information Systems Security	M
Computer Engineering	M,D
Computer Science	M,D
Corporate and Organizational Communication	M,D
Database Systems	M
Developmental Biology	D
Economics	D
Education—General	M,D*
Educational Leadership and Administration	M
Educational Media/Instructional Technology	M,D
Electrical Engineering	M,D
Electronic Commerce	M
Elementary Education	M
Engineering and Applied Sciences—General	M,D,O
Engineering Design	M
Engineering Management	M
English	M,D
Entrepreneurship	M,D
Environmental Engineering	M,D
Epidemiology	D
Ethics	M
Film, Television, and Video Production	M,D
Finance and Banking	M,D
French	D,O
Gender Studies	O
Genetic Counseling	M
Geology	D
Geosciences	D
Geotechnical Engineering	M,D
German	D
Health Informatics	D
Health Services Management and Hospital Administration	M,D
Health Services Research	D
History	M,D
Human Development	D
Human Resources Management	M,D
Industrial and Manufacturing Management	M,D
Industrial/Management Engineering	M,D
Information Science	M
International Affairs	M,D,O
International Business	M,D
International Health	M
Internet and Interactive Multimedia	M
Italian	D,O
Journalism	M
Kinesiology and Movement Studies	D
Law	M,D
Liberal Studies	M
Linguistics	D
Management Information Systems	M
Management Strategy and Policy	M,D
Marketing	M,D
Marriage and Family Therapy	M
Materials Engineering	M,D,O
Materials Sciences	M,D,O
Mathematics	D
Mechanical Engineering	M,D
Mechanics	M,D
Media Studies	M,D
Medical Informatics	M,D
Molecular Biology	D
Music Education	M,D
Music	M,D
Neurobiology	M,D
Neuroscience	D
Organizational Behavior	M
Organizational Management	M,D
Philosophy	D
Physical Therapy	D
Physics	D
Physiology	M
Plant Biology	M,D
Political Science	D
Portuguese	D
Project Management	M
Psychology—General	D
Public Administration	M
Public Health—General	M
Public Policy	M,D
Publishing	M
Quality Management	M
Quantitative Analysis	M,D
Real Estate	M,D
Rehabilitation Sciences	D
Religion	M,D
Rhetoric	M
Secondary Education	M
Slavic Languages	D
Social Psychology	D
Sociology	M,D
Software Engineering	M
Spanish	D
Speech and Interpersonal Communication	M,D
Sports Management	M
Statistics	M,D
Structural Biology	D
Structural Engineering	M,D
Systems Biology	D
Taxation	M,D
Theater	M,D
Transportation and Highway Engineering	M,D
Writing	M

NORTHWEST MISSOURI STATE UNIVERSITY

Agricultural Economics and Agribusiness	M
Agricultural Education	M
Agricultural Sciences—General	M
Biological and Biomedical Sciences—General	M,O
Business Administration and Management—General	M
Computer Science	M
Early Childhood Education	M,D,O
Education—General	M,D,O
Educational Leadership and Administration	M,D,O
Educational Media/Instructional Technology	M
Educational Policy	M,D,O
Elementary Education	M,D,O
English as a Second Language	M,D,O
English Education	M,O
English	M,O
Exercise and Sports Science	M
Geographic Information Systems	M,O
Health Education	M
Higher Education	M,D,O
Human Resources Management	M
Management Information Systems	M
Marketing	M
Mathematics Education	M,D,O
Mathematics	M,O
Middle School Education	M,D,O
Physical Education	M
Reading Education	M,D,O
Recreation and Park Management	M
Science Education	M,O
Social Sciences Education	M,O
Special Education	M,D,O

NORTHWEST NAZARENE UNIVERSITY

Addictions/Substance Abuse Counseling	M
Business Administration and Management—General	M
Clinical Psychology	M
Counselor Education	M
Curriculum and Instruction	M,D,O
Education—General	M,D,O
Educational Leadership and Administration	M,D,O
Marriage and Family Therapy	M
Missions and Missiology	M
Nursing and Healthcare Administration	M
Pastoral Ministry and Counseling	M
Religion	M
School Psychology	M
Social Work	M
Special Education	M,D,O
Theology	M

NORTHWEST UNIVERSITY

Business Administration and Management—General	M
Counseling Psychology	M,D
Cultural Studies	M
Education—General	M
International Business	M
Missions and Missiology	M
Organizational Management	M
Pastoral Ministry and Counseling	M
Project Management	M
Psychology—General	M,D
Theology	M
Urban and Regional Planning	M,D

NORTHWOOD UNIVERSITY, MICHIGAN CAMPUS

Business Administration and Management—General	M

NORWICH UNIVERSITY

Business Administration and Management—General	M
Civil Engineering	M
Computer and Information Systems Security	M
Conflict Resolution and Mediation/Peace Studies	M
Construction Management	M
Criminal Justice and Criminology	M
Emergency Management	M
Energy Management and Policy	M
Environmental Engineering	M
Finance and Banking	M
Geotechnical Engineering	M
History	M
Human Resources Management	M
International Affairs	M
International Business	M
International Development	M
Logistics	M
Management Strategy and Policy	M
Military and Defense Studies	M
Nonprofit Management	M
Nursing and Healthcare Administration	M
Nursing Education	M
Nursing—General	M
Organizational Management	M
Project Management	M
Public Administration	M
Public Policy	M
Structural Engineering	M
Supply Chain Management	M

NOTRE DAME COLLEGE (OH)

Computer Science	M,O

Homeland Security	M,O
Reading Education	M,O
Special Education	M,O

NOTRE DAME DE NAMUR UNIVERSITY

Art Therapy	M
Business Administration and Management—General	M
Clinical Psychology	M
Curriculum and Instruction	M,D
Education—General	M,D
Educational Leadership and Administration	M
English	M
Entrepreneurship	M
Finance and Banking	M
Human Resources Management	M
Industrial and Manufacturing Management	M
Management of Technology	M
Marketing	M
Marriage and Family Therapy	M
Music	M,O
Psychology—General	M
Public Administration	M
Public Affairs	M
Special Education	M

NOTRE DAME OF MARYLAND UNIVERSITY

Business Administration and Management—General	M
Communication—General	M
Education—General	M
Educational Leadership and Administration	M,D
English as a Second Language	M
Liberal Studies	M
Nonprofit Management	M
Pharmacy	D

NOTRE DAME SEMINARY

Theology	M

NOVA SOUTHEASTERN UNIVERSITY

Accounting	M
Allied Health—General	M,D
Anesthesiologist Assistant Studies	M,D
Art/Fine Arts	M,D,O
Bioinformatics	M,D,O
Biological and Biomedical Sciences—General	M,D
Business Administration and Management—General	M
Business Education	M
Clinical Psychology	M,D,O
Communication Disorders	M,D
Computer and Information Systems Security	M,D
Computer Science	M,D
Conflict Resolution and Mediation/Peace Studies	M,D,O
Counseling Psychology	M,D,O
Counselor Education	M,D,O
Dentistry	M,D
Distance Education Development	M,D,O
Education—General	M,D,O
Educational Media/Instructional Technology	M,D,O
Emergency Management	M,D,O
Entrepreneurship	M
Environmental Sciences	M,D
Experimental Psychology	M,D,O
Finance and Banking	M
Forensic Psychology	M,D,O
Health Education	M,D,O
Health Informatics	M,D,O
Health Law	M,D
Human Resources Management	M
Humanities	M,D,O
Information Science	M,D
Interdisciplinary Studies	M,D,O
International Business	M
Law	M,D
Legal and Justice Studies	M,D
Management Information Systems	M,D
Management Strategy and Policy	M
Marine Affairs	M,D
Marine Biology	M,D
Marine Sciences	M,D
Marketing	M
Marriage and Family Therapy	M,D,O
Medical Informatics	M,D,O
Nursing—General	M,D
Nutrition	M,D,O
Occupational Therapy	M,D
Oceanography	M,D
Optometry	M,D
Osteopathic Medicine	M,D,O
Pharmacy	M,D*
Physical Therapy	M,D
Physician Assistant Studies	M,D
Psychology—General	M,D,O
Public Administration	M
Public Health—General	M,D,O
School Psychology	M,D,O
Social Sciences	M,D,O
Student Affairs	M,D,O
Supply Chain Management	M
Taxation	M

NSCAD UNIVERSITY

Applied Arts and Design—General	M
Art/Fine Arts	M

NYACK COLLEGE

Business Administration and Management—General	M
Counseling Psychology	M
Counselor Education	M
Elementary Education	M
English as a Second Language	M
Marriage and Family Therapy	M
Missions and Missiology	M,D
Organizational Management	M
Pastoral Ministry and Counseling	M,D

Religion	M
Social Work	M
Special Education	M
Theology	M,D

OAKLAND CITY UNIVERSITY

Business Administration and Management—General	M
Education—General	M,D
Educational Leadership and Administration	M,D
Theology	M,D

OAKLAND UNIVERSITY

Accounting	M,O
Allied Health—General	M,D,O
Applied Behavior Analysis	M,O
Applied Mathematics	M,O
Applied Statistics	M
Biological and Biomedical Sciences—General	M,D,O
Business Administration and Management—General	M,O
Chemistry	M,D
Computer Engineering	M,D
Computer Science	M,D
Counseling Psychology	M,D,O
Early Childhood Education	M,D,O
Economics	M,O
Education—General	M,D,O
Educational Leadership and Administration	M,D,O
Electrical Engineering	M,D
Elementary Education	M,O
Engineering and Applied Sciences—General	M,D,O
Engineering Management	M,D,O
English as a Second Language	M,O
English	M
Entrepreneurship	M,O
Environmental and Occupational Health	M
Environmental Sciences	M,D
Exercise and Sports Science	M,D,O
Family Nurse Practitioner Studies	M,O
Finance and Banking	M,O
Gerontological Nursing	M,O
Higher Education	M,D,O
History	M
Human Resources Management	M,O
Industrial and Manufacturing Management	M,O
International Business	M
Liberal Studies	M
Linguistics	M,D
Management Information Systems	M,D,O
Marketing	M,O
Maternal and Child Health	D,O
Mathematics	M
Mechanical Engineering	M,D
Medical Physics	M,D
Music Education	M,D
Music	M,D
Nonprofit Management	M,O
Nurse Anesthesia	M
Nursing—General	M,D,O
Organizational Management	M,D,O
Physical Therapy	D,O
Physics	M,D
Public Administration	M,O
Reading Education	M,D,O
Secondary Education	M,O
Software Engineering	M,D
Special Education	M,O
Statistics	O
Systems Engineering	M,D
Systems Science	M,D

OAKWOOD UNIVERSITY

Pastoral Ministry and Counseling	M

OBERLIN COLLEGE

Music	M,O

OBLATE SCHOOL OF THEOLOGY

African-American Studies	M,D,O
Pastoral Ministry and Counseling	M,D,O
Religion	M,D,O
Theology	M,D,O

OCCIDENTAL COLLEGE

Biological and Biomedical Sciences—General	M

OGLALA LAKOTA COLLEGE

Business Administration and Management—General	M
Educational Leadership and Administration	M

OHIO CHRISTIAN UNIVERSITY

Accounting	M
Business Administration and Management—General	M
Finance and Banking	M
Health Services Management and Hospital Administration	M
Human Resources Management	M
Marketing	M
Organizational Management	M
Pastoral Ministry and Counseling	M
Theology	M

OHIO DOMINICAN UNIVERSITY

Accounting	M
Business Administration and Management—General	M
Curriculum and Instruction	M
Database Systems	M
Education—General	M
Educational Leadership and Administration	M
Engineering Design	M
English as a Second Language	M
English	M
Finance and Banking	M

Health Services Management and
  Hospital Administration — M
Management Strategy and Policy — M
Physician Assistant Studies — M
Sports Management — M
Theology — M

OHIO NORTHERN UNIVERSITY
Accounting — M
Law — M,D
Pharmacy — D

THE OHIO STATE UNIVERSITY
Accounting — M,D
Actuarial Science — M,D
Aerospace/Aeronautical
  Engineering — M,D
African Studies — M,D
African-American Studies — M,D
Agricultural Economics and
  Agribusiness — M,D
Agricultural Education — M
Agricultural Engineering — M,D
Agricultural Sciences—
  General — M,D
Agronomy and Soil Sciences — M,D
Allied Health—General — M
Allopathic Medicine — D
Anatomy — M,D
Animal Sciences — M,D
Anthropology — M,D
Architecture — M,D
Art Education — M,D
Art History — M,D
Art/Fine Arts — M
Arts Administration — M
Asian Languages — M,D
Asian Studies — M
Astronomy — M,D
Atmospheric Sciences — M,D
Biochemistry — M,D
Bioengineering — M,D
Biological and Biomedical
  Sciences—General — M,D
Biomedical Engineering — M,D
Biophysics — M,D
Biostatistics — M,D
Business Administration and
  Management—General — M,D
Cell Biology — M,D
Chemical Engineering — M,D
Chemical Physics — M,D
Chemistry — M,D
Child and Family Studies — M,D
Chinese — M,D
Civil Engineering — M,D
Classics — M,D
Clinical Psychology — D
Cognitive Sciences — D
Communication Disorders — M,D
Communication—General — M,D
Computational Sciences — M,D
Computer Art and Design — M
Computer Engineering — M,D
Computer Science — M,D
Dance — M
Dental Hygiene — M,D
Dentistry — M,D
Developmental Biology — M,D
Developmental Psychology — D
East European and Russian Studies — M,D
Ecology — M,D
Economics — M,D
Education—General — M,D,O
Educational Leadership and
  Administration — M,D,O
Educational Policy — M,D,O
Electrical Engineering — M,D
Engineering and Applied
  Sciences—General — M,D
English — M,D
Entomology — M,D
Environmental Management
  and Policy — M,D
Environmental Sciences — M,D
Evolutionary Biology — M,D
Family and Consumer
  Sciences-General — M,D
Finance and Banking — M
Fish, Game, and Wildlife
  Management — M,D
Food Science and
  Technology — M,D
Forestry — M,D
French — M,D
Gender Studies — M,D
Genetics — M,D
Geodetic Sciences — M,D
Geography — M,D
Geology — M,D
Geosciences — M,D
German — M,D
Health Services Management and
  Hospital Administration — M,D
History — M,D
Horticulture — M,D
Human Development — M,D
Human Resources Management — M,D
Industrial and Labor Relations — M,D
Industrial Design — M
Industrial/Management
  Engineering — M,D
Interdisciplinary Studies — M,D
Interior Design — M
Internet and Interactive
  Multimedia — M
Italian — M,D
Japanese — M,D
Kinesiology and Movement Studies — M,D
Landscape Architecture — M,D
Latin American Studies — M

Law — M,D
Linguistics — M,D
Logistics — M,D
Management Information Systems — M,D
Materials Engineering — M,D
Materials Sciences — M,D
Mathematics Education — M,D
Mathematics — M,D
Mechanical Engineering — M,D
Metallurgical Engineering and
  Metallurgy — M,D
Microbiology — M,D
Molecular Biology — M,D
Molecular Genetics — M,D
Music — M,D
Natural Resources — M,D
Near and Middle Eastern Languages — M,D
Neuroscience — D
Nuclear Engineering — M,D
Nursing—General — M,D
Nutrition — M,D
Occupational Therapy — M
Operations Research — M
Optical Sciences — M,D
Optometry — M,D
Oral and Dental Sciences — M,D
Pharmaceutical Administration — M,D
Pharmacology — M,D
Pharmacy — M,D
Philosophy — M,D
Physical Education — M,D
Physical Therapy — D
Physics — M,D
Plant Pathology — M,D
Plant Sciences — D
Political Science — D
Portuguese — M,D
Psychology—General — D
Public Administration — M,D
Public Affairs — M,D
Public Health—General — M,D
Public Policy — M,D
Rehabilitation Sciences — D
Rural Sociology — M,D
Slavic Languages — M,D
Social Psychology — D
Social Sciences — M,D
Social Work — M,D
Sociology — D
Spanish — M,D
Special Education — D
Statistics — M,D
Systems Engineering — M,D
Theater — M,D
Urban and Regional Planning — M,D
Veterinary Sciences — M,D
Women's Studies — M,D

THE OHIO STATE UNIVERSITY AT LIMA
Social Work — M

THE OHIO STATE UNIVERSITY AT MARION
Education—General — M

THE OHIO STATE UNIVERSITY–MANSFIELD CAMPUS
Education—General — M
Social Work — M

THE OHIO STATE UNIVERSITY–NEWARK CAMPUS
Education—General — M
Social Work — M

OHIO UNIVERSITY
African Studies — M
Applied Economics — M
Art History — M
Art/Fine Arts — M
Asian Studies — M
Astronomy — M,D
Athletic Training and Sports
  Medicine — M
Biochemistry — M,D
Biological and Biomedical
  Sciences—General — M,D
Biomedical Engineering — M
Business Administration and
  Management—General — M
Cell Biology — M,D
Chemical Engineering — M,D
Child and Family Studies — M
Child Development — M
Civil Engineering — M,D
Clinical Psychology — D
Communication Disorders — M,D
Communication—General — M,D
Comparative and Interdisciplinary
  Arts — D
Computer Education — M,D
Computer Science — M,D
Construction Engineering — M,D
Consumer Economics — M
Corporate and Organizational
  Communication — M,D
Counselor Education — M,D
Curriculum and Instruction — M,D
Ecology — M,D
Economics — M
Education—General — M,D
Educational Leadership and
  Administration — M,D
Educational Measurement and
  Evaluation — M,D
Educational Media/Instructional
  Technology — M,D
Electrical Engineering — M,D
Engineering and Applied
  Sciences—General — M,D
English — M,D
Environmental Biology — M,D

Environmental Engineering — M,D
Environmental Management
  and Policy — M,O
Evolutionary Biology — M,D
Exercise and Sports Science — M,D
Experimental Psychology — D
Family Nurse Practitioner Studies — M,D
Film, Television, and Video
  Production — M
Film, Television, and Video
  Theory and Criticism — M
Finance and Banking — M
French — M
Geochemistry — M
Geography — M
Geology — M
Geotechnical Engineering — M,D
Graphic Design — M
Health Communication — M,D
Health Services Management and
  Hospital Administration — M
Higher Education — M,D
History — M,D
Industrial and Organizational
  Psychology — D
Industrial/Management
  Engineering — M,D
International Affairs — M
International Development — M
Journalism — M,D
Latin American Studies — M
Linguistics — M
Mathematics — M,D
Mechanical Engineering — M,D
Mechanics — M,D
Media Studies — M,D
Microbiology — M,D
Middle School Education — M,D
Molecular Biology — D
Music Education — M,O
Music — M,O
Neuroscience — M,D
Nursing and Healthcare
  Administration — M,D
Nursing Education — M,D
Nursing—General — M,D
Nutrition — M
Osteopathic Medicine — D
Philosophy — M
Photography — M
Physical Education — M
Physical Therapy — D
Physics — M,D
Physiology — M,D
Plant Biology — M,D
Political Science — M
Psychology—General — D
Public Administration — M,O
Public Health—General — M
Reading Education — M
Recreation and Park Management — M
Rehabilitation Counseling — M,D
Rhetoric — M,D
Secondary Education — M,D
Social Sciences — M
Social Work — M
Sociology — M
Spanish — M
Special Education — M,D
Speech and Interpersonal
  Communication — M,D
Sports Management — M
Structural Engineering — M,D
Student Affairs — M,D
Systems Engineering — M
Telecommunications — M
Theater — M
Therapies—Dance, Drama, and
  Music — M,O
Transportation and Highway
  Engineering — M,D
Water Resources Engineering — M,D

OHIO VALLEY UNIVERSITY
Curriculum and Instruction — M
Education—General — M

OHR HAMEIR THEOLOGICAL SEMINARY
Theology

OKLAHOMA BAPTIST UNIVERSITY
Business Administration and
  Management—General — M
Energy Management and
  Policy — M
Marriage and Family Therapy — M
Nursing Education — M
Nursing—General — M

OKLAHOMA CHRISTIAN UNIVERSITY
Accounting — M
Business Administration and
  Management—General — M
Computer Engineering — M
Computer Science — M
Electrical Engineering — M
Engineering and Applied
  Sciences—General — M
Engineering Management — M
Finance and Banking — M
Health Services Management and
  Hospital Administration — M
Human Resources Management — M
International Business — M
Marketing — M
Mechanical Engineering — M
Nonprofit Management — M
Organizational Management — M
Project Management — M
Software Engineering — M
Theology — M

OKLAHOMA CITY UNIVERSITY
Applied Behavior Analysis — M
Business Administration and
  Management—General — M
Computer Science — M
Counselor Education — M
Criminal Justice and Criminology — M
Early Childhood Education — M
Elementary Education — M
Energy Management and
  Policy — M
English as a Second Language — M
Law — M,D
Music — M
Nursing Education — M,D
Nursing—General — M,D
Photography — M
Sociology — M
Writing — M

OKLAHOMA STATE UNIVERSITY
Accounting — M,D
Agricultural Economics and
  Agribusiness — M,D
Agricultural Education — M,D
Agricultural Engineering — M,D
Agricultural Sciences—
  General — M,D
Agronomy and Soil Sciences — M,D
Animal Sciences — M,D
Applied Arts and Design—General — M,D
Applied Behavior Analysis — M,D,O
Applied Mathematics — M,D
Applied Psychology — M,D,O
Art History — M
Biochemistry — M,D
Bioengineering — M,D
Biological and Biomedical
  Sciences—General — M,D
Botany — M,D
Business Administration and
  Management—General — M,D
Chemical Engineering — M,D
Chemistry — M,D
Child and Family Studies — M,D
Civil Engineering — M,D
Clinical Psychology — M,D
Clothing and Textiles — M,D
Communication Disorders — M
Computer Engineering — M,D
Computer Science — M,D
Consumer Economics — M,D
Curriculum and Instruction — M,D
Ecology — M,D
Economics — M,D
Education—General — M,D,O
Educational Leadership and
  Administration — M,D
Educational Psychology — M,D,O
Electrical Engineering — M,D
Emergency Management — M,D
Engineering and Applied
  Sciences—General — M,D
English — M,D
Entomology — M,D
Entrepreneurship — M,D
Environmental Engineering — M,D
Environmental Sciences — M,D,O
Evolutionary Biology — M,D
Family and Consumer
  Sciences-General — M,D
Finance and Banking — M,D
Fire Protection Engineering — M,D
Food Science and
  Technology — M,D
Forestry — M,D
Geography — M,D
Geology — M,D
Graphic Design — M
Health Education — M,D,O
Health Psychology — M,D,O
Higher Education — M,D
History — M,D
Horticulture — M,D
Hospitality Management — M,D
Human Development — M,D
Industrial/Management
  Engineering — M,D
Information Science — M,D
International Affairs — M,D,O
Landscape Architecture — M,D
Management Information Systems — M,D
Marketing — M,D
Marriage and Family Therapy — M,D
Mass Communication — M
Materials Engineering — M,D
Materials Sciences — M,D
Mathematics Education — M,D
Mathematics — M,D
Mechanical Engineering — M,D
Microbiology — M,D
Molecular Biology — M,D
Molecular Genetics — M,D
Music Education — M
Music — M
Natural Resources — M,D
Nonprofit Management — M,D,O
Nutrition — M,D
Philosophy — M
Photonics — M,D
Physics — M,D
Plant Biology — M,D
Plant Pathology — M,D
Plant Sciences — M,D
Political Science — M,D
Psychology—General — M,D
Sociology — M,D
Statistics — M,D
Sustainability Management — M,D,O
Telecommunications
  Management — M,D,O

---

*M—masters degree; D—doctorate; O—other advanced degree; *—Close-Up and/or Display*

Theater	M
Veterinary Medicine	D
Veterinary Sciences	M,D
Writing	M,D

OKLAHOMA STATE UNIVERSITY CENTER FOR HEALTH SCIENCES

Biological and Biomedical Sciences—General	M,D
Forensic Sciences	M
Health Services Management and Hospital Administration	M
Osteopathic Medicine	D
Toxicology	M

OKLAHOMA WESLEYAN UNIVERSITY

Management Strategy and Policy	M
Nursing and Healthcare Administration	M
Nursing Education	M
Theology	M

OLD DOMINION UNIVERSITY

Accounting	M
Adult Nursing	M,D
Aerospace/Aeronautical Engineering	M,D
Allied Health—General	M,D
Analytical Chemistry	M,D
Applied Mathematics	M,D
Applied Psychology	D
Athletic Training and Sports Medicine	M,D
Biochemistry	M,D
Biological and Biomedical Sciences—General	M,D
Biomedical Engineering	M,D
Biostatistics	M,D
Business Administration and Management—General	M,D
Business Education	M,D
Chemistry	M,D
Civil Engineering	M,D
Clinical Psychology	D
Communication Disorders	M
Community College Education	M,D
Community Health	M
Computer Art and Design	M
Computer Engineering	M,D
Computer Science	M,D
Conflict Resolution and Mediation/Peace Studies	M,D
Counseling Psychology	M,D,O
Counselor Education	M,D,O
Criminal Justice and Criminology	M,D
Cultural Studies	M,D
Curriculum and Instruction	M,D
Dental Hygiene	M
Early Childhood Education	M,D
Ecology	D
Economics	M
Education—General	M,D,O
Educational Leadership and Administration	M,D,O
Educational Measurement and Evaluation	D
Educational Media/Instructional Technology	M,D,O
Educational Psychology	D
Electrical Engineering	M,D
Elementary Education	M,O
Engineering and Applied Sciences—General	M,D
Engineering Management	D
English as a Second Language	M
English	M,D
Environmental and Occupational Health	M
Environmental Engineering	M,D
Environmental Sciences	M,D
Ergonomics and Human Factors	D
Exercise and Sports Science	M
Family Nurse Practitioner Studies	M,D
Finance and Banking	D
Geotechnical Engineering	M
Gerontological Nursing	M,D
Health Education	M,D
Health Promotion	M
Health Services Research	D
Higher Education	M,D,O
History	M
Humanities	M
Hydraulics	M
Industrial and Organizational Psychology	D
Industrial Hygiene	M
Information Science	D
Inorganic Chemistry	M,D
International Affairs	M,D
International Business	M
International Development	M,D
Kinesiology and Movement Studies	M,D
Library Science	M,O
Linguistics	M
Management Information Systems	M,D
Marketing	D
Maternal and Child/Neonatal Nursing	M,D
Mathematics	M,D
Mechanical Engineering	M,D
Middle School Education	M,O
Modeling and Simulation	M,D
Music Education	M
Nurse Anesthesia	D
Nurse Midwifery	M,D
Nursing and Healthcare Administration	M,D
Nursing Education	M,D
Nursing—General	M,D
Oceanography	M,D
Organic Chemistry	M,D
Pediatric Nursing	M
Physical Chemistry	M,D
Physical Education	M,D
Physical Therapy	M,D
Physics	M,D
Psychology—General	M,D
Public Administration	M
Reading Education	M,D
Rehabilitation Sciences	D
School Psychology	M,D,O
Secondary Education	M
Sociology	M
Special Education	M,D
Speech and Interpersonal Communication	M
Sports Management	M
Statistics	M,D
Structural Engineering	M
Supply Chain Management	M
Systems Engineering	M,D
Transportation and Highway Engineering	M
Urban Studies	D
Vocational and Technical Education	M,D
Water Resources	M
Women's Studies	M
Writing	M

OLIVET COLLEGE

Insurance	M

OLIVET NAZARENE UNIVERSITY

Business Administration and Management—General	M
Curriculum and Instruction	M
Education—General	M
Educational Leadership and Administration	M
Elementary Education	M
Family Nurse Practitioner Studies	M
Library Science	M
Nursing—General	M
Organizational Management	M
Reading Education	M
Religion	M
Secondary Education	M
Theology	M

OPEN UNIVERSITY

Business Administration and Management—General	M
Education—General	M
Engineering and Applied Sciences—General	M
History	M
Music	M
Philosophy	M

ORAL ROBERTS UNIVERSITY

Accounting	M
Business Administration and Management—General	M
Curriculum and Instruction	M,D
Education—General	M,D
Educational Leadership and Administration	M,D
Entrepreneurship	M
Finance and Banking	M
Higher Education	M,D
International Business	M
Marketing	M
Marriage and Family Therapy	M,D
Missions and Missiology	M,D
Near and Middle Eastern Languages	M,D
Nonprofit Management	M
Pastoral Ministry and Counseling	M,D
Religious Education	M,D
Theology	M,D

OREGON COLLEGE OF ART AND CRAFT

Art/Fine Arts	M

OREGON COLLEGE OF ORIENTAL MEDICINE

Acupuncture and Oriental Medicine	M,D

OREGON HEALTH & SCIENCE UNIVERSITY

Allopathic Medicine	D
Biochemistry	M,D
Bioinformatics	M,D,O
Biological and Biomedical Sciences—General	M,D,O
Biomedical Engineering	D
Biopsychology	D
Cancer Biology/Oncology	D
Cell Biology	D
Clinical Research	M,O
Community Health Nursing	M,O
Computer Engineering	M,D
Computer Science	M,D
Dentistry	D,O
Developmental Biology	D
Electrical Engineering	M,D
Environmental Engineering	M,D
Environmental Sciences	M,D
Family Nurse Practitioner Studies	M
Genetics	D
Gerontological Nursing	M
Gerontology	M,O
Health Informatics	M,D,O
Health Services Management and Hospital Administration	M,O
Immunology	D
Medical Informatics	M,D,O
Microbiology	D
Molecular Biology	M,D
Neuroscience	D
Nurse Anesthesia	M
Nurse Midwifery	M
Nursing Education	M,O
Nursing—General	M,D,O
Nutrition	M,D,O
Oral and Dental Sciences	M,D,O
Pediatric Nursing	M
Pharmacology	D
Physician Assistant Studies	M
Physiology	D

Psychiatric Nursing	M

OREGON INSTITUTE OF TECHNOLOGY

Manufacturing Engineering	M

OREGON STATE UNIVERSITY

Accounting	M,D
Actuarial Science	M,D
Adult Education	M,D
Agricultural Education	M,D
Agricultural Engineering	M,D
Agronomy and Soil Sciences	M,D
Allied Health—General	M,D
Analytical Chemistry	M,D
Animal Behavior	M,D
Animal Sciences	M,D
Anthropology	M,D
Applied Mathematics	M,D
Applied Statistics	M
Aquaculture	M,D
Artificial Intelligence/Robotics	M,D
Athletic Training and Sports Medicine	M
Atmospheric Sciences	M,D
Biochemistry	M,D
Bioengineering	M,D
Bioinformatics	D
Biological and Biomedical Sciences—General	M,D
Biophysics	M,D
Biostatistics	M,D
Biotechnology	M,D
Botany	M,D
Business Administration and Management—General	M,D
Cell Biology	M,D
Chemical Engineering	M,D
Chemistry	M,D
Child and Family Studies	M,D
Civil Engineering	M,D
Clinical Psychology	M,D
Clothing and Textiles	M,D
Cognitive Sciences	M,D
Computational Biology	M,D
Computational Sciences	M,D
Computer Engineering	M,D
Computer Science	M,D
Conservation Biology	M,D
Construction Engineering	M,D
Counselor Education	M,D
Developmental Biology	M,D
Early Childhood Education	M,D
Ecology	M,D
Economic Development	M,D
Economics	M,D
Education—General	M,D
Educational Leadership and Administration	M,D
Educational Policy	M,D
Electrical Engineering	M,D
Elementary Education	M
Engineering and Applied Sciences—General	M,D
Engineering Management	M,D
English as a Second Language	M,D
English Education	M
English	M
Entrepreneurship	M,D
Environmental and Occupational Health	M,D
Environmental Biology	M,D
Environmental Education	M,D
Environmental Engineering	M,D
Environmental Management and Policy	M,D
Environmental Sciences	M,D
Epidemiology	M,D
Ethics	M
Evolutionary Biology	M,D
Finance and Banking	M,D
Fish, Game, and Wildlife Management	M,D
Food Science and Technology	M,D
Forestry	M,D
Gender Studies	M,D
Genetics	M,D
Genomic Sciences	M,D
Geochemistry	M,D
Geographic Information Systems	M
Geography	M,D
Geology	M,D
Geophysics	M,D
Geotechnical Engineering	M,D
Health Physics/Radiological Health	M,D
Health Promotion	M,D
Health Psychology	M,D
Health Services Management and Hospital Administration	M,D
Higher Education	M,D
Hispanic Studies	M
History of Medicine	M,D
History of Science and Technology	M,D
Horticulture	M,D
Human Development	M,D
Immunology	M,D
Industrial/Management Engineering	M,D
Inorganic Chemistry	M,D
Interdisciplinary Studies	M
International Health	M,D
Kinesiology and Movement Studies	M,D
Legal and Justice Studies	M,D
Limnology	M,D
Management Strategy and Policy	M,D
Manufacturing Engineering	M,D
Marine Affairs	M
Marine Sciences	M
Materials Sciences	M,D
Mathematical and Computational Finance	M,D
Mathematics Education	M,D
Mathematics	M,D
Mechanical Engineering	M,D
Medical Imaging	M,D

Medical Physics	M,D
Medicinal and Pharmaceutical Chemistry	M,D
Microbiology	M,D
Modeling and Simulation	M,D
Molecular Biology	M,D
Molecular Pathogenesis	D
Molecular Toxicology	M,D
Music Education	M
Natural Resources	M,D
Nuclear Engineering	M,D
Nutrition	M,D
Ocean Engineering	M,D
Oceanography	M,D
Organic Chemistry	M,D
Organizational Management	M,D
Parasitology	M,D
Pharmaceutical Sciences	M,D
Pharmacology	M,D
Pharmacy	D
Physical Chemistry	M,D
Physics	M,D
Physiology	M,D
Plant Molecular Biology	D
Plant Pathology	M,D
Plant Physiology	M,D
Psychology—General	M,D
Public Health—General	M,D
Public Policy	M,D
Range Science	M,D
Religion	M
Reproductive Biology	M,D
School Psychology	M,D
Science Education	M,D
Social Sciences Education	M,D
Social Sciences	M,D
Software Engineering	M,D
Statistics	M,D
Structural Biology	D
Structural Engineering	M,D
Student Affairs	M
Supply Chain Management	M,D
Sustainability Management	M,D
Systems Engineering	M,D
Toxicology	M,D
Transportation and Highway Engineering	M,D
Veterinary Medicine	D
Virology	M,D
Water Resources Engineering	M,D
Water Resources	M,D
Women's Studies	M,D
Writing	M

OREGON STATE UNIVERSITY–CASCADES

Education—General	M
School Psychology	M
Social Psychology	M

OTIS COLLEGE OF ART AND DESIGN

Art/Fine Arts	M
Graphic Design	M
Photography	M
Writing	M

OTTAWA UNIVERSITY

Art Therapy	M
Business Administration and Management—General	M
Counseling Psychology	M
Counselor Education	M
Curriculum and Instruction	M
Early Childhood Education	M
Education—General	M
Educational Leadership and Administration	M
Educational Media/Instructional Technology	M
Elementary Education	M
Finance and Banking	M
Human Resources Development	M
Human Resources Management	M
Marketing	M
Marriage and Family Therapy	M
Pastoral Ministry and Counseling	M
School Psychology	M
Special Education	M

OTTERBEIN UNIVERSITY

Business Administration and Management—General	M
Education—General	M
Family Nurse Practitioner Studies	M,D,O
Nurse Anesthesia	M,D,O
Nursing and Healthcare Administration	M,D,O
Nursing Education	M,D,O
Nursing—General	M,D,O

OUR LADY OF THE LAKE COLLEGE

Health Services Management and Hospital Administration	M
Nurse Anesthesia	M
Nursing and Healthcare Administration	M
Nursing Education	M
Nursing—General	M
Physician Assistant Studies	M

OUR LADY OF THE LAKE UNIVERSITY

Accounting	M
Business Administration and Management—General	M
Communication Disorders	M
Computer and Information Systems Security	M
Counseling Psychology	D
Counselor Education	M
Curriculum and Instruction	M
English	M
Finance and Banking	M
Health Services Management and Hospital Administration	M
Management Information Systems	M
Marriage and Family Therapy	M

Nonprofit Management	M
Organizational Management	M,D
Psychology—General	M
School Psychology	M
Science Education	M
Social Work	M
Sociology	M
Writing	M

OXFORD GRADUATE SCHOOL
Child and Family Studies	M,D
Organizational Management	M,D
Religion	M,D
Sociology	M,D

PACE UNIVERSITY
Accounting	M,O
Addictions/Substance Abuse Counseling	M,D
Art/Fine Arts	M,O
Biochemistry	M
Biological and Biomedical Sciences—General	M,O
Business Administration and Management—General	M,D,O
Business Education	M,O
Chemistry	M,O
Clinical Psychology	M,D
Computer and Information Systems Security	M,D,O
Computer Science	M,D,O
Counseling Psychology	M,D
Developmental Psychology	M,D
Early Childhood Education	M,O
Economics	O
Education—General	M,O
Educational Media/Instructional Technology	M,O
Electronic Commerce	O
Elementary Education	M,O
Emergency Management	M
English	M,O
Entrepreneurship	M
Environmental Law	M,D
Environmental Management and Policy	M
Environmental Sciences	M
Family Nurse Practitioner Studies	M,D,O
Finance and Banking	M,D,O
Foreign Languages Education	M,O
Forensic Sciences	M
Geosciences	M,O
Health Services Management and Hospital Administration	M
Homeland Security	M
Human Resources Management	M
Information Science	M,D,O
International Business	M,O
International Economics	O
Internet and Interactive Multimedia	M,D,O
Investment Management	M,O
Law	M,D
Legal and Justice Studies	M,D
Management Information Systems	M,D,O
Management Strategy and Policy	M
Marketing	M,D,O
Mathematics	M,O
Media Studies	M
Molecular Biology	M
Nonprofit Management	M
Nursing and Healthcare Administration	M,D,O
Nursing—General	M,D,O
Physician Assistant Studies	M
Physics	M,O
Psychology—General	M
Public Administration	M
Publishing	M
Reading Education	M,O
School Psychology	M,D
Social Sciences Education	M,O
Software Engineering	M,D,O
Special Education	M,D
Sustainable Development	M,D
Taxation	M
Telecommunications	M,D,O
Theater	M

PACIFICA GRADUATE INSTITUTE
Clinical Psychology	M,D
Counseling Psychology	M,D
Psychology—General	M,D

PACIFIC COLLEGE OF ORIENTAL MEDICINE
Acupuncture and Oriental Medicine	M,D

PACIFIC COLLEGE OF ORIENTAL MEDICINE–CHICAGO
Acupuncture and Oriental Medicine	M

PACIFIC COLLEGE OF ORIENTAL MEDICINE-NEW YORK
Acupuncture and Oriental Medicine	M

PACIFIC LUTHERAN UNIVERSITY
Accounting	M
Business Administration and Management—General	M
Curriculum and Instruction	M
Education—General	M
Family Nurse Practitioner Studies	D
Finance and Banking	M
Marketing Research	M
Marriage and Family Therapy	M
Nursing—General	M,D
Writing	M

PACIFIC NORTHWEST COLLEGE OF ART
Applied Arts and Design—General	M

Art/Fine Arts	M
Cultural Studies	M

PACIFIC NORTHWEST UNIVERSITY OF HEALTH SCIENCES
Osteopathic Medicine	D

PACIFIC OAKS COLLEGE
Early Childhood Education	M
Education—General	M
Human Development	M
Marriage and Family Therapy	M
Special Education	M

PACIFIC RIM CHRISTIAN UNIVERSITY
Pastoral Ministry and Counseling	M

PACIFIC SCHOOL OF RELIGION
Religion	M,D,O
Theology	M,D,O

PACIFIC STATES UNIVERSITY
Accounting	M,D
Business Administration and Management—General	M,D
Computer Science	M
Finance and Banking	M,D
International Business	M,D
Management Information Systems	M,D
Management of Technology	M,D
Real Estate	M,D

PACIFIC UNION COLLEGE
Education—General	M
Elementary Education	M
Secondary Education	M

PACIFIC UNIVERSITY
Athletic Training and Sports Medicine	M,D
Business Administration and Management—General	M
Clinical Psychology	M,D
Communication Disorders	M,D
Early Childhood Education	M
Education of the Gifted	M
Education—General	M
Elementary Education	M
English as a Second Language	M
Finance and Banking	M
Health Services Management and Hospital Administration	M
Middle School Education	M
Occupational Therapy	D
Optometry	M,D
Pharmacy	D
Physical Therapy	M,D
Physician Assistant Studies	M,D
Psychology—General	M,D
Science Education	M
Secondary Education	M
Social Work	M
Special Education	M
Vision Sciences	M,D
Writing	M

PALM BEACH ATLANTIC UNIVERSITY
Addictions/Substance Abuse Counseling	M
Business Administration and Management—General	M
Counseling Psychology	M
Counselor Education	M
Education—General	M
Family Nurse Practitioner Studies	M,D
Marriage and Family Therapy	M
Nursing and Healthcare Administration	M,D
Nursing—General	M,D
Organizational Management	M
Pharmacy	D
Religious Education	M
Theology	M

PALMER COLLEGE OF CHIROPRACTIC
Anatomy	M
Chiropractic	D
Clinical Research	M

PALO ALTO UNIVERSITY
Biopsychology	D
Clinical Psychology	M,D
Counseling Psychology	M
Marriage and Family Therapy	M
Psychology—General	M,D

PARIS COLLEGE OF ART
Art/Fine Arts	M
Interior Design	M
Media Studies	M
Photography	M
Textile Design	M

PARKER UNIVERSITY
Chiropractic	D

PARK UNIVERSITY
Business Administration and Management—General	M,O
Curriculum and Instruction	M,O
Education—General	M,O
Educational Leadership and Administration	M,O
Emergency Management	M,O
Finance and Banking	M,O
Health Services Management and Hospital Administration	M,O
International Business	M,O
International Health	M,O
Management Information Systems	M,O
Music	M,O
Nonprofit Management	M,O
Public Administration	M,O
Public Affairs	M,O
Reading Education	M,O

Social Work	M,O
Writing	M,O

PAYNE THEOLOGICAL SEMINARY
Theology	M

PEIRCE COLLEGE
Organizational Management	M

PENN STATE ERIE, THE BEHREND COLLEGE
Accounting	M
Business Administration and Management—General	M
Engineering and Applied Sciences—General	M
Industrial and Manufacturing Management	M
Project Management	M
Quality Management	M

PENN STATE GREAT VALLEY
Business Administration and Management—General	M,O
Computer and Information Systems Security	M,O
Database Systems	M,O
Engineering and Applied Sciences—General	M,O
Engineering Management	M,O
Entrepreneurship	M,O
Finance and Banking	M,O
Health Services Management and Hospital Administration	M,O
Human Resources Development	M,O
Human Resources Management	M,O
Information Science	M,O
Software Engineering	M,O
Sustainability Management	M,O
Systems Engineering	M,O

PENN STATE HARRISBURG
Accounting	M,O
Adult Education	M,D,O
American Studies	M,D,O
Applied Behavior Analysis	M,D,O
Applied Psychology	M,D,O
Business Administration and Management—General	M,O
Clinical Psychology	M,D,O
Communication—General	M,D,O
Computer Science	M,O
Criminal Justice and Criminology	M,D,O
Curriculum and Instruction	M,D,O
Developmental Education	M,D,O
Education—General	M,D,O
Electrical Engineering	M,O
Engineering and Applied Sciences—General	M,O
Engineering Management	M,O
English as a Second Language	M,D,O
Environmental Engineering	M,O
Environmental Sciences	M,O
Finance and Banking	M,D,O
Folklore	M,D,O
Health Education	M,D,O
Health Psychology	M,D,O
Health Services Management and Hospital Administration	M,D,O
Historic Preservation	M,D,O
Homeland Security	M,D,O
Human Resources Management	M,D,O
Humanities	M,D,O
Management Information Systems	M,O
Museum Studies	M,D,O
Nonprofit Management	M,D,O
Psychology—General	M,D,O
Public Administration	M,D,O
Public Affairs	M,D,O
Reading Education	M,D,O
Social Psychology	M,D,O
Structural Engineering	M,O
Supply Chain Management	M,O
Writing	M,D,O

PENN STATE HERSHEY MEDICAL CENTER
Allopathic Medicine	M,D
Anatomy	M,D
Biochemistry	M,D
Biological and Biomedical Sciences—General	M,D
Biostatistics	D
Cell Biology	D
Developmental Biology	D
Health Services Research	M
Immunology	M,D
Molecular Genetics	M,D
Molecular Medicine	D
Molecular Toxicology	D
Neurobiology	D
Neuroscience	M,D
Public Health—General	M,D
Veterinary Sciences	M
Virology	M,D

PENN STATE UNIVERSITY–DICKINSON LAW
Law	M,D

PENN STATE UNIVERSITY PARK
Accounting	M,D
Acoustics	M,D
Adult Education	M,D,O
Aerospace/Aeronautical Engineering	M,D
Agricultural Economics and Agribusiness	M,D,O
Agricultural Education	M,D,O
Agricultural Engineering	M,D
Agricultural Sciences—General	M,D,O
Agronomy and Soil Sciences	M,D

Animal Sciences	M,D
Anthropology	M,D
Applied Statistics	M,D
Architectural Engineering	M,D
Architecture	M,D
Art Education	M,D,O
Art History	M,D
Art/Fine Arts	M,D,O
Astronomy	M,D
Astrophysics	M,D
Biochemistry	M,D
Bioengineering	M,D
Biological and Biomedical Sciences—General	M,D
Biopsychology	M,D
Biotechnology	M,D
Business Administration and Management—General	M,D
Cell Biology	M,D
Chemical Engineering	M,D
Chemistry	M,D
Child and Family Studies	M,D
Civil Engineering	M,D
Communication Disorders	M,D,O
Communication—General	M,D
Comparative Literature	M,D
Computer Science	M,D
Counselor Education	M,D,O
Criminal Justice and Criminology	M,D
Curriculum and Instruction	M,D,O
Ecology	M,D
Economic Development	M,D,O
Economics	M,D
Education—General	M,D,O
Educational Leadership and Administration	M,D,O
Educational Media/Instructional Technology	M,D,O
Educational Policy	M,D,O
Educational Psychology	M,D,O
Electrical Engineering	M,D
Engineering and Applied Sciences—General	M,D
Engineering Design	M
English as a Second Language	M,D
English	M,D
Entomology	M,D
Environmental Engineering	M,D
Environmental Management and Policy	M
Environmental Sciences	M
Fish, Game, and Wildlife Management	M,D
Food Science and Technology	M,D
Forensic Sciences	M
Forestry	M,D
Foundations and Philosophy of Education	M,D,O
French	M,D
Geographic Information Systems	M,D
Geography	M,D
Geosciences	M,D
Geotechnical Engineering	M,D
German	M,D
Health Services Management and Hospital Administration	M,D
Higher Education	M,D,O
History	M,D
Horticulture	M,D
Hospitality Management	M,D
Human Development	M,D
Human Resources Development	M
Human Resources Management	M
Industrial and Labor Relations	M
Industrial/Management Engineering	M,D
Information Science	M,D
International Affairs	M,D
Kinesiology and Movement Studies	M,D,O
Landscape Architecture	M,D
Law	M,D
Leisure Studies	M,D
Linguistics	M,D
Management Information Systems	M,D
Mass Communication	M,D
Materials Engineering	M,D
Materials Sciences	M,D
Mathematics	M,D
Mechanical Engineering	M,D
Mechanics	M,D
Media Studies	M,D
Meteorology	M,D
Mineral/Mining Engineering	M,D
Molecular Biology	M,D
Music Education	M,D,O
Music	M,D,O
Nuclear Engineering	M,D
Nursing—General	M,D
Nutrition	M,D
Organizational Management	M,D
Pathobiology	M,D
Philosophy	M,D
Physics	M,D
Physiology	M,D
Plant Biology	M,D
Plant Pathology	M,D
Plant Sciences	M,D
Political Science	M,D
Psychology—General	M,D
Recreation and Park Management	M,D
Rural Sociology	M,D,O
Russian	M,D
School Psychology	M,D,O
Sociology	M,D
Spanish	M,D
Special Education	M,D,O
Statistics	M,D
Supply Chain Management	M,D
Sustainable Development	M
Theater	M

M—masters degree; D—doctorate; O—other advanced degree; *—Close-Up and/or Display

Travel and Tourism	M,D
Urban and Regional Planning	M,D,O
Vocational and Technical Education	M,D,O

PENN STATE YORK
Curriculum and Instruction	M,O
Education—General	M,O
English as a Second Language	M,O

PENNSYLVANIA ACADEMY OF THE FINE ARTS
Art/Fine Arts	M,O

PENNSYLVANIA COLLEGE OF HEALTH SCIENCES
Health Education	M
Health Services Management and Hospital Administration	M
Nursing and Healthcare Administration	M
Nursing Education	M

PENSACOLA CHRISTIAN COLLEGE
Art/Fine Arts	M,D,O
Business Administration and Management—General	M,D,O
Curriculum and Instruction	M,D,O
Educational Leadership and Administration	M,D,O
Graphic Design	M,D,O
Music	M,D,O
Nursing—General	M,D,O
Theater	M,D,O

PENTECOSTAL THEOLOGICAL SEMINARY
Pastoral Ministry and Counseling	M,D
Theology	M,D

PEPPERDINE UNIVERSITY
Accounting	M
American Studies	M
Business Administration and Management—General	M
Business Education	M
Clinical Psychology	M,D
Communication—General	M
Conflict Resolution and Mediation/Peace Studies	M
Economics	M
Educational Leadership and Administration	M,D
Educational Media/Instructional Technology	M,D
Finance and Banking	M
Human Resources Management	M
Humanities	M
International Affairs	M,D
International Business	M
Law	D
Marriage and Family Therapy	M,D
Mathematics	M,D
Media Studies	M
Organizational Management	M,D
Pastoral Ministry and Counseling	M
Political Science	M
Psychology—General	M,D
Public Policy	M
Religion	M
Science Education	M,D
Writing	M

PERU STATE COLLEGE
Curriculum and Instruction	M
Economics	M
Education—General	M
Entrepreneurship	M
Organizational Management	M

PFEIFFER UNIVERSITY
Business Administration and Management—General	M
Elementary Education	M
Health Services Management and Hospital Administration	M
Organizational Management	M
Religious Education	M
Theology	M

PHILADELPHIA COLLEGE OF OSTEOPATHIC MEDICINE
Applied Behavior Analysis	M,D,O
Biological and Biomedical Sciences—General	M
Biopsychology	M,D,O
Clinical Psychology	M,D,O
Counseling Psychology	M,D,O
Forensic Sciences	M
Industrial and Organizational Psychology	M,D,O
Osteopathic Medicine	D
Physician Assistant Studies	M*
Psychology—General	M,D,O*
School Psychology	M,D,O

PHILADELPHIA UNIVERSITY
Architecture	M
Art/Fine Arts	M
Athletic Training and Sports Medicine	M
Business Administration and Management—General	M
Clothing and Textiles	M
Construction Management	M
Emergency Management	M
Geography	M
Industrial Design	M
Interior Design	M
Internet and Interactive Multimedia	M
Management Strategy and Policy	M
Marketing	M
Modeling and Simulation	M
Nurse Midwifery	M,O
Occupational Therapy	M,D
Physician Assistant Studies	M
Real Estate	M

Social Psychology	M
Sustainable Development	M
Taxation	M
Textile Design	M
Textile Sciences and Engineering	M,D
Urban and Regional Planning	M

PHILLIPS GRADUATE UNIVERSITY
Art Therapy	M
Counselor Education	M
Marriage and Family Therapy	M
Organizational Behavior	D

PHILLIPS THEOLOGICAL SEMINARY
Business Administration and Management—General	M,D
Ethics	M,D
Higher Education	M,D
Missions and Missiology	M,D
Music	M,D
Pastoral Ministry and Counseling	D
Religious Education	M,D
Social Work	M,D
Theology	M,D

PHOENIX INSTITUTE OF HERBAL MEDICINE & ACUPUNCTURE
Acupuncture and Oriental Medicine	M

PHOENIX SEMINARY
Counseling Psychology	M,D,O
Pastoral Ministry and Counseling	M,D,O
Theology	M,D,O

PIEDMONT COLLEGE
Art Education	M,O
Business Administration and Management—General	M
Curriculum and Instruction	M,O
Early Childhood Education	M,O
Education—General	M,O
Educational Media/Instructional Technology	M,O
Middle School Education	M,O
Music Education	M,O
Secondary Education	M,O
Special Education	M,O

PIEDMONT INTERNATIONAL UNIVERSITY
Curriculum and Instruction	M,D
Educational Leadership and Administration	M,D
Pastoral Ministry and Counseling	M,D
Theology	M,D

PITTSBURGH THEOLOGICAL SEMINARY
Pastoral Ministry and Counseling	M,D
Theology	M,D

PITTSBURG STATE UNIVERSITY
Accounting	M
Biological and Biomedical Sciences—General	M
Business Administration and Management—General	M
Chemistry	M
Clinical Psychology	M
Communication—General	M
Construction Engineering	M
Construction Management	M,O
Counselor Education	M
Education—General	M,O
Educational Leadership and Administration	M,O
Educational Media/Instructional Technology	M
Electrical Engineering	M
English	M
Exercise and Sports Science	M
Graphic Design	M,O
Health Education	M
History	M
Human Resources Development	M
International Business	M
Management of Technology	M,O
Manufacturing Engineering	M
Mathematics	M
Mechanical Engineering	M
Music Education	M
Music	M
Nursing—General	M,D
Physical Education	M
Physics	M
Polymer Science and Engineering	M
Psychology—General	M
School Psychology	O
Special Education	M,O
Sports Management	M
Vocational and Technical Education	M,O
Writing	M

PLYMOUTH STATE UNIVERSITY
Adult Education	D
Art Education	M
Athletic Training and Sports Medicine	M
Biological and Biomedical Sciences—General	M
Business Administration and Management—General	M
Clinical Psychology	M,O
Counselor Education	M
Cultural Studies	M
Curriculum and Instruction	M
Education—General	O
Educational Leadership and Administration	M
Educational Media/Instructional Technology	M
Elementary Education	M
English Education	M
Environmental Management and Policy	M

Foreign Languages Education	M
Health Education	M
Health Promotion	M
Higher Education	D,O
Historic Preservation	M
Mathematics Education	M
Meteorology	M
Music Education	M
Physical Education	M
Reading Education	M
School Psychology	M,O
Science Education	M
Secondary Education	M
Social Sciences Education	M
Special Education	M

POINT LOMA NAZARENE UNIVERSITY
Biological and Biomedical Sciences—General	M
Business Administration and Management—General	M
Clinical Psychology	M
Counselor Education	M
Education—General	M
Educational Leadership and Administration	M
Entrepreneurship	M
Exercise and Sports Science	M
Family Nurse Practitioner Studies	M,O
Gerontological Nursing	M,O
Health Services Management and Hospital Administration	M
Kinesiology and Movement Studies	M
Maternal and Child/Neonatal Nursing	M,O
Nursing—General	M,O
Organizational Management	M
Pastoral Ministry and Counseling	M
Project Management	M
Special Education	M
Sports Management	M
Theology	M

POINT PARK UNIVERSITY
Adult Education	M,D
Business Administration and Management—General	M
Clinical Psychology	M,D
Communication—General	M
Criminal Justice and Criminology	M
Curriculum and Instruction	M,D
Education—General	M,D
Educational Leadership and Administration	M,D
Elementary Education	M,D
Engineering Management	M
Entertainment Management	M
Environmental Management and Policy	M
Health Services Management and Hospital Administration	M
International Business	M
Journalism	M
Management Information Systems	M
Mass Communication	M
Media Studies	M
Middle School Education	M,D
Music	M
Organizational Management	M
Secondary Education	M,D
Special Education	M,D
Sports Management	M
Theater	M

POLYTECHNIC UNIVERSITY OF PUERTO RICO
Business Administration and Management—General	M
Civil Engineering	M
Computer Engineering	M
Computer Science	M
Electrical Engineering	M
Engineering Management	M
Environmental Management and Policy	M
Industrial and Manufacturing Management	M
International Business	M
Landscape Architecture	M
Management Information Systems	M
Management of Technology	M
Manufacturing Engineering	M
Mechanical Engineering	M

POLYTECHNIC UNIVERSITY OF PUERTO RICO, MIAMI CAMPUS
Accounting	M
Business Administration and Management—General	M
Construction Management	M
Environmental Engineering	M
Environmental Management and Policy	M
Finance and Banking	M
Human Resources Management	M
Industrial and Manufacturing Management	M
International Business	M
Logistics	M
Marketing	M
Project Management	M
Supply Chain Management	M

POLYTECHNIC UNIVERSITY OF PUERTO RICO, ORLANDO CAMPUS
Accounting	M
Business Administration and Management—General	M
Construction Management	M
Engineering Management	M
Environmental Engineering	M
Environmental Management and Policy	M
Finance and Banking	M
Human Resources Management	M

Industrial and Manufacturing Management	M
International Business	M
Management of Technology	M

PONCE HEALTH SCIENCES UNIVERSITY
Allopathic Medicine	D
Biological and Biomedical Sciences—General	D
Clinical Psychology	D
Epidemiology	M,D
Public Health—General	M,D

PONTIFICAL CATHOLIC UNIVERSITY OF PUERTO RICO
Accounting	M,O
Art/Fine Arts	M
Biological and Biomedical Sciences—General	M
Business Administration and Management—General	M,D,O
Business Education	M,D
Chemistry	M
Clinical Laboratory Sciences/Medical Technology	O
Clinical Psychology	D
Counselor Education	M
Criminal Justice and Criminology	M
Curriculum and Instruction	M,D
Education—General	M,D
Educational Leadership and Administration	D
Educational Psychology	M
English as a Second Language	M
Environmental Sciences	M
Finance and Banking	M
Hispanic Studies	M,O
History	M
Human Resources Management	M
Human Services	M,D
Industrial and Organizational Psychology	D
International Business	M
Law	D
Logistics	O
Management Information Systems	M,O
Marketing	M
Medical/Surgical Nursing	M
Nursing—General	M
Psychiatric Nursing	M
Psychology—General	M,D
Public Administration	M
Rehabilitation Counseling	M
Religious Education	M
Social Work	M
Spanish	M,O
Theology	M
Transportation Management	O

PONTIFICAL COLLEGE JOSEPHINUM
Theology	M

PONTIFICAL JOHN PAUL II INSTITUTE FOR STUDIES ON MARRIAGE AND FAMILY
Biotechnology	M,D,O
Ethics	M,D,O
Marriage and Family Therapy	M,D,O
Theology	M,D,O

PONTIFICIA UNIVERSIDAD CATOLICA MADRE Y MAESTRA
Allopathic Medicine	D
Architecture	M
Building Science	M
Business Administration and Management—General	M
Clinical Psychology	M
Criminal Justice and Criminology	M
Developmental Psychology	M
Early Childhood Education	M
Engineering and Applied Sciences—General	M
Entrepreneurship	M
Finance and Banking	M
Forensic Psychology	M
Hospitality Management	M
Human Resources Management	M
Insurance	M
Interior Design	M
International Affairs	M
International Business	M
Landscape Architecture	M
Law	M
Logistics	M
Management Strategy and Policy	M
Marketing	M
Psychology—General	M
Real Estate	M
Structural Engineering	M
Travel and Tourism	M

POPE ST. JOHN XXIII NATIONAL SEMINARY
Theology	M

PORTLAND STATE UNIVERSITY
Anthropology	M,D,O
Applied Economics	M,D
Applied Social Research	M,D
Architecture	M
Art/Fine Arts	M
Artificial Intelligence/Robotics	M,D,O
Biological and Biomedical Sciences—General	M,D
Business Administration and Management—General	M,D,O
Chemistry	M,D
Civil Engineering	M,D,O
Communication Disorders	M
Computer Engineering	M,D
Computer Science	M,D
Conflict Resolution and Mediation/Peace Studies	M
Criminal Justice and Criminology	M,D
Economics	M,D,O

Education—General M,D
Electrical Engineering M,D
Engineering and Applied
  Sciences—General M,D,O
Engineering Management M,D,O
English as a Second Language M
English M
Environmental Engineering M,D
Environmental Management
  and Policy M,D
Environmental Sciences M,D
Finance and Banking M
Foreign Languages Education M
French M,D
Geography M,D
Geology M,D
German M,D
Health Promotion M,D
Health Services Management and
  Hospital Administration M
History M
Industrial and Manufacturing
  Management M,D
International Business M
Japanese M
Management of Technology M,D
Manufacturing Engineering M,D
Mathematics Education M,D
Mathematics M,D,O
Mechanical Engineering M,D,O
Modeling and Simulation M,D,O
Music Education M
Music M
Physics M,D
Political Science M,D
Psychology—General M,D,O
Public Administration M,D
Public Affairs M,D
Public Health—General M,D
Public Policy M,D
Real Estate M
Science Education M,D
Social Sciences Education M
Social Work M,D
Sociology M,D,O
Software Engineering M,D
Spanish M
Speech and Interpersonal
  Communication M,O
Statistics M,D
Supply Chain Management M
Systems Science M,D,O
Theater M
Urban and Regional Planning M
Urban Studies M,D

POST UNIVERSITY
Accounting M
Addictions/Substance Abuse
  Counseling M
Business Administration and
  Management—General M
Distance Education Development M
Education—General M
Educational Leadership and
  Administration M
Educational Media/Instructional
  Technology M
English as a Second Language M
Entrepreneurship M
Finance and Banking M
Health Services Management and
  Hospital Administration M
Human Services M
Marketing M
Nonprofit Management M
Project Management M
Public Administration M

PRAIRIE VIEW A&M UNIVERSITY
Accounting M
Agricultural Sciences—
  General M
Architecture M
Business Administration and
  Management—General M
Chemistry M
Clinical Psychology M,D
Computer Science M,D
Counselor Education M,D
Curriculum and Instruction M
Education—General M,D
Educational Leadership and
  Administration M,D
Electrical Engineering M,D
Engineering and Applied
  Sciences—General M,D
Forensic Psychology M,D
Health Education M
Kinesiology and Movement Studies M
Legal and Justice Studies M,D
Management Information Systems M
Nursing—General M,D
Sociology M

PRATT INSTITUTE
Applied Arts and Design—General M,O*
Architecture M*
Art Education M,O
Art History M
Art Therapy M
Art/Fine Arts M*
Arts Administration M
Facilities Management M
Graphic Design M
Historic Preservation M
Industrial Design M
Information Studies M,O*
Interior Design M
Internet and Interactive
  Multimedia M
Library Science M,O

Media Studies M*
Music M
Real Estate M
Sustainable Development M
Therapies—Dance, Drama, and
  Music M
Urban and Regional Planning M
Urban Design M
Writing M

PRESCOTT COLLEGE
Art Therapy M
Art/Fine Arts M
Counseling Psychology M
Counselor Education M,D
Early Childhood Education M,D
Education—General M,D
Educational Leadership and
  Administration M,D
Elementary Education M,D
Environmental Education M,D
Environmental Management
  and Policy M
Health Psychology M
Humanities M
Legal and Justice Studies M
Leisure Studies M
Psychoanalysis and Psychotherapy M
Secondary Education M,D
Special Education M,D

PRESIDIO GRADUATE SCHOOL (CA)
Agricultural Economics and
  Agribusiness M,O
Business Administration and
  Management—General M,O
Sustainability Management M,O

PRINCETON THEOLOGICAL SEMINARY
Religion M,D
Theology M,D

PRINCETON UNIVERSITY
Aerospace/Aeronautical
  Engineering M,D
Anthropology D
Applied Mathematics D
Archaeology D
Architecture M,D
Asian Studies D
Astronomy D
Astrophysics D
Atmospheric Sciences D
Chemical Engineering M,D
Chemistry M,D
Civil Engineering M,D
Classics D
Comparative Literature D
Computational Biology D
Computational Sciences D
Computer Science M,D
Demography and Population Studies D,O
Ecology D
Economics D,O
Electrical Engineering M,D
Electronic Materials D
Engineering and Applied
  Sciences—General M,D
English D
Environmental Engineering M,D
Evolutionary Biology D
Finance and Banking M
Financial Engineering M,D
French D
Geosciences D
German D
History of Science and Technology D
History D
International Affairs M,D
Marine Biology D
Materials Sciences D
Mathematics D
Mechanical Engineering M,D
Molecular Biology D
Music D
Near and Middle Eastern Studies M,D
Neuroscience D
Ocean Engineering D
Oceanography D
Operations Research M,D
Philosophy D
Photonics D
Physics D
Plasma Physics D
Political Science D
Portuguese D
Psychology—General D
Public Affairs M,D,O
Public Policy M,D
Religion D
Russian D
Slavic Languages D
Sociology D,O
Spanish D

PROVIDENCE COLLEGE
Accounting M
American Studies M
Business Administration and
  Management—General M
Counselor Education M
Educational Leadership and
  Administration M
Elementary Education M
Finance and Banking M
History M
International Business M
Marketing M
Mathematics Education M
Reading Education M
Secondary Education M
Special Education M

Theology M
Urban Education M

PROVIDENCE UNIVERSITY COLLEGE & THEOLOGICAL SEMINARY
Counseling Psychology M,D,O
English as a Second Language M,D,O
Missions and Missiology M,D,O
Pastoral Ministry and Counseling M,D,O
Religious Education M,D,O
Student Affairs M,D,O
Theology M,D,O

PURCHASE COLLEGE, STATE UNIVERSITY OF NEW YORK
Art History M
Art/Fine Arts M
Music M

PURDUE UNIVERSITY
Aerospace/Aeronautical
  Engineering D
Agricultural Economics and
  Agribusiness M,D
Agricultural Education M,D,O
Agricultural Engineering M,D
Agricultural Sciences—
  General M,D
Agronomy and Soil Sciences M,D
Allied Health—General M,D
American Studies M,D
Analytical Chemistry M,D
Anatomy M,D
Animal Sciences M,D
Anthropology M,D
Applied Arts and Design—General M,D
Aquaculture M,D
Art Education M,D,O
Art/Fine Arts M,D
Atmospheric Sciences M,D
Aviation Management M
Biochemistry M,D
Biological and Biomedical
  Sciences—General M,D
Biomedical Engineering M,D
Biophysics M,D
Biotechnology D
Botany M,D
Business Administration and
  Management—General M,D*
Cancer Biology/Oncology D
Cell Biology M,D
Chemical Engineering M,D
Chemistry M,D
Child and Family Studies M,D
Child Development M,D
Civil Engineering M,D
Clinical Psychology D
Cognitive Sciences D
Communication Disorders M,D
Communication—General M,D
Comparative Literature M,D
Computational Sciences D
Computer and Information
  Systems Security M
Computer Art and Design M,D
Computer Engineering M,D
Computer Science M,D
Construction Management M
Consumer Economics M,D
Counselor Education M,D,O
Curriculum and Instruction M,D,O
Developmental Biology M,D
Ecology M,D
Economics D
Education of the Gifted M,D,O
Education—General M,D,O
Educational Leadership and
  Administration M,D,O
Educational Media/Instructional
  Technology M,D,O
Educational Psychology M,D,O
Electrical Engineering M,D
Elementary Education M,D,O
Engineering and Applied
  Sciences—General M,D,O
English Education M,D,O
English M,D
Entomology M,D
Environmental and Occupational
  Health M,D
Environmental Engineering M,D
Environmental Management
  and Policy M,D
Epidemiology M,D
Ergonomics and Human
  Factors M,D
Evolutionary Biology M,D
Exercise and Sports Science M,D
Family Nurse Practitioner Studies M,D,O
Finance and Banking M
Fish, Game, and Wildlife
  Management M,D
Food Science and
  Technology M,D
Foreign Languages Education M,D,O
Forestry M,D
Foundations and Philosophy of
  Education M,D,O
French M,D
Genetics M,D
Genomic Sciences D
Geosciences M,D
German M,D
Gerontological Nursing M,D,O
Health Education M,D
Health Physics/Radiological Health M,D
Higher Education M,D,O
History M,D
Home Economics Education M,D,O
Horticulture M,D
Hospitality Management M,D

Human Development M,D
Human Resources Management M,D*
Immunology M,D
Industrial and Organizational
  Psychology D
Industrial Design M,D
Industrial/Management
  Engineering M,D
Inorganic Chemistry M,D
Interior Design M,D
International Business M
Japanese M,D
Kinesiology and Movement Studies M,D
Linguistics M,D
Management Information Systems M
Management of Technology M,D
Marriage and Family Therapy M,D
Materials Engineering M,D
Mathematics Education M,D,O
Mathematics M,D
Mechanical Engineering M,D,O
Medical Physics M,D
Medicinal and Pharmaceutical
  Chemistry D
Microbiology M,D
Molecular Biology M,D
Molecular Pharmacology D
Natural Resources M,D
Neurobiology M,D
Neuroscience D
Nuclear Engineering M,D
Nursing—General M,D,O
Nutrition M,D
Organic Chemistry M,D
Organizational Behavior D
Pathobiology M,D
Pathology M,D
Pediatric Nursing M,D,O
Pharmaceutical Administration M,D,O
Pharmaceutical Sciences M,D
Pharmacology M,D
Pharmacy D
Philosophy M,D
Photography M,D
Physical Chemistry M,D
Physical Education M,D
Physics M,D
Physiology M,D
Plant Pathology M,D
Plant Physiology M,D
Plant Sciences D
Political Science M,D
Psychology—General D
Public Health—General M,D
Quantitative Analysis M,D
Reading Education M,D,O
Recreation and Park Management M,D
Science Education M,D,O
Social Sciences Education M,D,O
Sociology M,D
Spanish M,D
Special Education M,D,O
Sport Psychology M,D
Sports Management M,D
Statistics M,D
Systems Biology D
Theater M
Toxicology M,D
Travel and Tourism M,D
Veterinary Medicine D
Veterinary Sciences M,D
Virology M,D
Vocational and Technical Education M,D,O
Writing M

PURDUE UNIVERSITY NORTHWEST
Accounting M
Acute Care/Critical Care Nursing M
Adult Nursing M
Biological and Biomedical
  Sciences—General M
Biotechnology M
Business Administration and
  Management—General M
Child and Family Studies M
Child Development M
Communication—General M
Computer Engineering M
Computer Science M
Counseling Psychology M
Counselor Education M
Education—General M
Educational Leadership and
  Administration M
Educational Media/Instructional
  Technology M
Electrical Engineering M
Engineering and Applied
  Sciences—General M
English M
Family Nurse Practitioner Studies M
History M
Human Services M
Marriage and Family Therapy M
Mathematics Education M
Mathematics M
Mechanical Engineering M
Nursing and Healthcare
  Administration M
Nursing—General M
School Psychology M
Science Education M
Special Education M

QUEENS COLLEGE OF THE CITY UNIVERSITY OF NEW YORK
Accounting M
Applied Behavior Analysis M,O
Applied Social Research M
Art Education M,O
Art History M

Program	Degree
Art/Fine Arts	M
Biological and Biomedical Sciences—General	M,O
Chemistry	M
Child and Family Studies	M,O
Communication Disorders	M,O
Computer Science	M
Counseling Psychology	M,O
Counselor Education	M,O
Database Systems	M
Developmental Psychology	M,O
Early Childhood Education	M,O
Economics	M
Education—General	M,O
Educational Leadership and Administration	M,O
Elementary Education	M,O
English as a Second Language	M,O
English Education	M,O
English	M,O
Environmental Sciences	M
Exercise and Sports Science	M,O
Family and Consumer Sciences-General	M,O
Finance and Banking	M
Foreign Languages Education	M,O
French	M
Geology	M
Geosciences	M
Hispanic and Latin American Languages	M
History	M,O
Information Studies	M,O
Italian	M
Liberal Studies	M
Library Science	M,O
Linguistics	M,O
Mathematics Education	M,O
Mathematics	M
Media Studies	M
Middle School Education	M,O
Multilingual and Multicultural Education	M,O
Music Education	M,O
Music	M,O
Neuroscience	M,O
Nutrition	M
Photonics	M
Physical Education	M,O
Physics	M
Psychology—General	M,O
Reading Education	M,O
Romance Languages	M
School Psychology	M,O
Science Education	M,O
Secondary Education	M,O
Social Sciences Education	M,O
Sociology	M
Spanish	M
Special Education	M,O
Urban Studies	M
Writing	M,O

QUEEN'S UNIVERSITY AT KINGSTON

Program	Degree
Allopathic Medicine	D
Anatomy	M,D
Biochemistry	M,D
Biological and Biomedical Sciences—General	M,D
Business Administration and Management—General	M
Canadian Studies	M,D
Cancer Biology/Oncology	M,D
Cardiovascular Sciences	M,D
Cell Biology	M,D
Chemical Engineering	M,D
Chemistry	M,D
Civil Engineering	M,D
Classics	M
Clinical Psychology	M,D
Cognitive Sciences	M,D
Communication—General	M,D
Computer Engineering	M,D
Computer Science	M,D
Developmental Psychology	M,D
Education—General	M,D
Electrical Engineering	M,D
Engineering and Applied Sciences—General	M,D
English	M,D
Entrepreneurship	M
Epidemiology	M,D
Exercise and Sports Science	M,D
Family Nurse Practitioner Studies	M,D,O
Finance and Banking	M
French	M,D
Gender Studies	M,D
Geography	M,D
Geology	M,D
German	M,D
Health Services Management and Hospital Administration	M,D
Hispanic Studies	M
Immunology	M,D
Industrial and Labor Relations	M
Information Studies	M,D
International Affairs	M,D
Law	M,D
Legal and Justice Studies	M,D
Marketing	M
Mathematics	M,D
Mechanical Engineering	M,D
Microbiology	M,D
Mineral/Mining Engineering	M,D
Molecular Biology	M,D
Molecular Medicine	M,D
Neurobiology	M,D
Neuroscience	M,D
Nursing—General	M,D,O
Occupational Therapy	M,D
Pathology	M,D
Pediatric Nursing	M,D,O
Pharmaceutical Sciences	M,D
Pharmacology	M,D
Philosophy	M,D
Physical Therapy	M,D
Physics	M,D
Physiology	M,D
Political Science	M,D
Project Management	M
Psychology—General	M,D
Public Health—General	M,D
Public Policy	M,D
Rehabilitation Sciences	M,D
Religion	M,D
Reproductive Biology	M,D
Social Psychology	M,D
Sociology	M,D
Spanish	M,D
Sport Psychology	M,D
Statistics	M,D
Theology	M,O
Toxicology	M,D
Urban and Regional Planning	M
Women's Health Nursing	M,D,O
Women's Studies	M,D

QUEENS UNIVERSITY OF CHARLOTTE

Program	Degree
Business Administration and Management—General	M
Communication—General	M
Education—General	M
Educational Leadership and Administration	M
Elementary Education	M
Interior Design	M
Nursing and Healthcare Administration	M
Nursing Education	M
Nursing—General	M
Organizational Management	M
Reading Education	M
Writing	M

QUINCY UNIVERSITY

Program	Degree
Business Administration and Management—General	M
Communication—General	M
Counselor Education	M
Curriculum and Instruction	M
Education—General	M
Educational Leadership and Administration	M
English as a Second Language	M
Multilingual and Multicultural Education	M
Reading Education	M
School Psychology	M
Special Education	M

QUINNIPIAC UNIVERSITY

Program	Degree
Adult Nursing	D
Advertising and Public Relations	M
Allied Health—General	M
Allopathic Medicine	D
Anesthesiologist Assistant Studies	M
Broadcast Journalism	M
Business Administration and Management—General	M
Cardiovascular Sciences	M
Cell Biology	M
Clinical Laboratory Sciences/Medical Technology	M
Communication—General	M
Community Health	D
Education—General	M,O
Educational Leadership and Administration	M,O
Educational Media/Instructional Technology	M
Elementary Education	M
English Education	M
Family Nurse Practitioner Studies	D
Film, Television, and Video Production	M
Foreign Languages Education	M
Health Physics/Radiological Health	M
Health Services Management and Hospital Administration	M
Internet and Interactive Multimedia	M
Journalism	M
Law	M,D
Mathematics Education	M
Middle School Education	M
Molecular Biology	M
Nurse Anesthesia	D
Nursing and Healthcare Administration	D
Nursing—General	D
Organizational Management	M
Pathology	M
Perfusion	M
Physician Assistant Studies	M
Science Education	M
Secondary Education	M
Social Sciences Education	M
Social Work	M
Supply Chain Management	M

RABBINICAL ACADEMY MESIVTA RABBI CHAIM BERLIN

Program	Degree
Theology	O

RABBINICAL COLLEGE BETH SHRAGA

Program	Degree
Theology	

RABBINICAL COLLEGE BOBOVER YESHIVA B'NEI ZION

Program	Degree
Theology	

RABBINICAL COLLEGE OF LONG ISLAND

Program	Degree
Theology	

RABBINICAL SEMINARY OF AMERICA

Program	Degree
Theology	

RADFORD UNIVERSITY

Program	Degree
Art/Fine Arts	M
Business Administration and Management—General	M
Communication Disorders	M
Corporate and Organizational Communication	M
Counseling Psychology	D
Counselor Education	M
Criminal Justice and Criminology	M,O
Database Systems	M
Early Childhood Education	M
Educational Leadership and Administration	M
English	M
Management Information Systems	M
Mathematics Education	M
Music	M
Nursing—General	D
Occupational Therapy	M
Physical Therapy	D
Reading Education	M
School Psychology	O
Social Work	M
Special Education	M,O

RAMAPO COLLEGE OF NEW JERSEY

Program	Degree
Business Administration and Management—General	M
Educational Leadership and Administration	M
Educational Media/Instructional Technology	M
Family Nurse Practitioner Studies	M
Nursing and Healthcare Administration	M
Nursing Education	M
Nursing—General	M
Social Work	M
Special Education	M

RANDALL UNIVERSITY

Program	Degree
Pastoral Ministry and Counseling	M

RANDOLPH COLLEGE

Program	Degree
Curriculum and Instruction	M
Education—General	M
Special Education	M

RECONSTRUCTIONIST RABBINICAL COLLEGE

Program	Degree
Jewish Studies	M,D,O
Theology	M,D,O
Women's Studies	M,D,O

REED COLLEGE

Program	Degree
Liberal Studies	M

REFORMED EPISCOPAL SEMINARY

Program	Degree
Theology	M

REFORMED PRESBYTERIAN THEOLOGICAL SEMINARY

Program	Degree
Theology	M,D

REFORMED THEOLOGICAL SEMINARY–ATLANTA CAMPUS

Program	Degree
Theology	M,D,O

REFORMED THEOLOGICAL SEMINARY–CHARLOTTE CAMPUS

Program	Degree
Pastoral Ministry and Counseling	M,D
Religion	M,D
Theology	M,D

REFORMED THEOLOGICAL SEMINARY–HOUSTON CAMPUS

Program	Degree
Religion	M

REFORMED THEOLOGICAL SEMINARY–JACKSON CAMPUS

Program	Degree
Marriage and Family Therapy	M,D,O
Missions and Missiology	M,D,O
Pastoral Ministry and Counseling	M,D,O
Religion	M,D,O
Religious Education	M,D,O
Theology	M,D,O

REFORMED THEOLOGICAL SEMINARY–ORLANDO CAMPUS

Program	Degree
Pastoral Ministry and Counseling	M,D,O
Theology	M,D,O

REFORMED THEOLOGICAL SEMINARY–WASHINGTON D.C.

Program	Degree
Religion	M
Theology	M

REGENT COLLEGE

Program	Degree
Theology	M,O

REGENT'S UNIVERSITY LONDON

Program	Degree
Business Administration and Management—General	M
Finance and Banking	M
Human Resources Management	M
International Affairs	M
International Business	M
Management Information Systems	M
Marketing	M

REGENT UNIVERSITY

Program	Degree
Accounting	M,D,O
Adult Education	M,D,O
American Studies	M
Business Administration and Management—General	M,D,O
Clinical Psychology	M,D,O
Communication—General	M,D
Conflict Resolution and Mediation/Peace Studies	M,D
Corporate and Organizational Communication	M
Counseling Psychology	M,D,O
Counselor Education	M,D,O
Criminal Justice and Criminology	M,D
Cultural Studies	M,D,O
Curriculum and Instruction	M,D,O
Distance Education Development	M,D,O
Early Childhood Education	M,D,O
Education of the Gifted	M,D,O
Education—General	M,D,O
Educational Leadership and Administration	M,D,O
Educational Media/Instructional Technology	M,D,O
Educational Psychology	M,D,O
Elementary Education	M,D,O
Emergency Management	M
English as a Second Language	M,D,O
Entrepreneurship	M,D,O
Film, Television, and Video Production	M,D
Finance and Banking	M,D,O
Health Services Management and Hospital Administration	M,D,O
Higher Education	M,D,O
History	M,D
Homeland Security	M
Human Resources Development	M,D,O
Human Resources Management	M,D,O
Interdisciplinary Studies	M,D
International Affairs	M
Investment Management	M,D,O
Journalism	M,D
Law	M,D
Legal and Justice Studies	M,D
Management Strategy and Policy	M,D,O
Marriage and Family Therapy	M,D,O
Mathematics Education	M,D
Missions and Missiology	M,D
National Security	M,D
Nonprofit Management	M,D,O
Organizational Management	M,D,O
Pastoral Ministry and Counseling	M,D,O
Political Science	M
Psychoanalysis and Psychotherapy	M,D
Public Administration	M
Public Policy	M
Reading Education	M,D,O
Religion	M,D
Religious Education	M,D,O
Science Education	M,D,O
Special Education	M,D,O
Student Affairs	M,D,O
Theater	M,D
Theology	M,D
Writing	M,D

REGIS COLLEGE (CANADA)

Program	Degree
Pastoral Ministry and Counseling	M,D,O
Philosophy	M,D,O
Theology	M,D,O

REGIS COLLEGE (MA)

Program	Degree
Applied Behavior Analysis	M,D,O
Biotechnology	M
Corporate and Organizational Communication	M
Counseling Psychology	M,D,O
Cultural Studies	M
Education—General	M,D
Educational Leadership and Administration	M,D
Elementary Education	M,D
Family Nurse Practitioner Studies	M,D,O
Health Services Management and Hospital Administration	M,D,O
Higher Education	M,D
Nursing Education	M,D,O
Nursing—General	M,D,O
Occupational Therapy	M,D,O
Public Affairs	M
Quality Management	M
Reading Education	M,D
Social Sciences Education	M
Special Education	M,D

REGIS UNIVERSITY

Program	Degree
Accounting	M,O
Allied Health—General	M,D,O
Biological and Biomedical Sciences—General	M
Business Education	M,O
Computer and Information Systems Security	M,O
Computer Science	M,O
Counselor Education	M,D,O
Criminal Justice and Criminology	M,O
Curriculum and Instruction	M,O
Database Systems	M,O
Developmental Psychology	M,D,O
Economics	M,O
Education—General	M
Educational Leadership and Administration	M,O
Elementary Education	M,O
Environmental Biology	M
Finance and Banking	M,O
Health Informatics	M,O
Health Services Management and Hospital Administration	M,D,O
Human Resources Management	M,O
Industrial and Manufacturing Management	M,O
Information Science	M,O
Management Information Systems	M,O
Management Strategy and Policy	M,O
Marketing	M,O
Marriage and Family Therapy	M,D,O
Maternal and Child/Neonatal Nursing	M,D,O
Medical Informatics	M,O
Nonprofit Management	M,O
Nursing and Healthcare Administration	M,D,O
Nursing Education	M,D,O
Occupational Therapy	M,D,O
Organizational Management	M,O
Pharmacy	M,D,O
Physical Therapy	M,D,O
Project Management	M,O
Reading Education	M,O
Secondary Education	M,O
Software Engineering	M,O
Special Education	M,O

Systems Engineering — M,O
Writing — M,O

REINHARDT UNIVERSITY
Business Administration and Management—General — M
Early Childhood Education — M
Education—General — M

RELAY GRADUATE SCHOOL OF EDUCATION
Education—General — M

RENSSELAER AT HARTFORD
Business Administration and Management—General — M
Computer Engineering — M
Computer Science — M
Electrical Engineering — M
Engineering and Applied Sciences—General — M
Information Science — M
Mechanical Engineering — M
Systems Science — M

RENSSELAER POLYTECHNIC INSTITUTE
Acoustics — M,D
Aerospace/Aeronautical Engineering — M,D
Applied Mathematics — M
Architecture — M,D
Art/Fine Arts — D
Biochemistry — M,D
Bioengineering — M,D
Biological and Biomedical Sciences—General — M,D
Biomedical Engineering — M,D
Biophysics — M,D
Building Science — M,D
Business Administration and Management—General — M,D
Chemical Engineering — M,D
Chemistry — M,D
Civil Engineering — M,D
Cognitive Sciences — D
Computer Art and Design — D
Computer Engineering — M,D
Computer Science — M,D
Electrical Engineering — M,D
Engineering and Applied Sciences—General — M,D
Engineering Management — M,D
Engineering Physics — M,D
Entrepreneurship — M
Environmental Engineering — M,D
Financial Engineering — M
Geology — M,D
History of Science and Technology — M,D
Industrial/Management Engineering — M,D
Information Science — M
Lighting Design — M,D
Management Information Systems — M
Management of Technology — M,D
Materials Engineering — M,D
Materials Sciences — M,D
Mathematics — M,D
Mechanical Engineering — M,D
Nuclear Engineering — M,D
Physics — M,D
Rhetoric — M,D
Speech and Interpersonal Communication — M,D
Supply Chain Management — M
Systems Engineering — M,D
Technology and Public Policy — M,D
Transportation and Highway Engineering — M,D

RESEARCH COLLEGE OF NURSING
Adult Nursing — M
Family Nurse Practitioner Studies — M
Gerontological Nursing — M
Nursing and Healthcare Administration — M
Nursing—General — M

RESURRECTION UNIVERSITY
Nursing—General — M

RHODE ISLAND COLLEGE
Accounting — M,O
Art Education — M
Art/Fine Arts — M
Arts Administration — M
Biological and Biomedical Sciences—General — M,O
Counseling Psychology — M,O
Counselor Education — M,O
Early Childhood Education — M
Education—General — D
Educational Leadership and Administration — M,O
Elementary Education — M
English as a Second Language — M
English Education — M
English — M,O
Finance and Banking — M,O
Foreign Languages Education — M
Health Education — M,O
Health Psychology — M,O
Health Services Management and Hospital Administration — M
History — M
Mathematics Education — M
Mathematics — M,O
Music Education — M
Nursing—General — M,D
Physical Education — M,O
Psychology—General — M,O
Public Administration — M
Reading Education — M

School Psychology — M,O
Secondary Education — M
Social Sciences Education — M
Social Work — M
Special Education — M,O
Writing — M,O

RHODE ISLAND SCHOOL OF DESIGN
Applied Arts and Design—General — M
Architecture — M
Art Education — M
Art/Fine Arts — M
Computer Art and Design — M
Graphic Design — M
Industrial Design — M
Interior Design — M
Landscape Architecture — M
Media Studies — M
Photography — M
Textile Design — M

RHODES COLLEGE
Accounting — M

RICE UNIVERSITY
African Studies — D
American Studies — D
Anthropology — M,D
Applied Mathematics — M,D
Applied Physics — M,D
Archaeology — M,D
Architecture — M,D
Art History — D
Astronomy — M,D
Biochemistry — M,D
Bioengineering — M,D
Bioinformatics — M,D
Biomedical Engineering — M,D
Biostatistics — M,D
Business Administration and Management—General — M
Cell Biology — M,D
Chemical Engineering — M,D
Chemistry — M,D
Civil Engineering — M,D
Cognitive Sciences — M,D
Computational Sciences — M,D
Computer Engineering — M,D
Computer Science — M,D
Cultural Anthropology — M,D
Ecology — M,D
Economics — M,D
Education—General — M
Electrical Engineering — M,D
Energy Management and Policy — M,D
Engineering and Applied Sciences—General — M,D
English — M,D
Environmental Engineering — M,D
Environmental Management and Policy — M
Environmental Sciences — M,D
Evolutionary Biology — M,D
Geophysics — M,D
Geosciences — M,D
Health Services Management and Hospital Administration — M
History — M,D
Industrial and Organizational Psychology — M,D
Inorganic Chemistry — M,D
Jewish Studies — D
Liberal Studies — M
Linguistics — M,D
Materials Sciences — M,D
Mathematical and Computational Finance — M,D
Mathematics — D
Mechanical Engineering — M,D
Music — M,D
Near and Middle Eastern Studies — D
Organic Chemistry — M,D
Philosophy — M,D
Physical Chemistry — M,D
Physics — M,D
Political Science — D
Psychology—General — M,D
Religion — D
Science Education — M,D
Sociology — D
Statistics — M,D
Urban Design — M,D

RICHMOND, THE AMERICAN INTERNATIONAL UNIVERSITY IN LONDON
Art History — M
International Affairs — M

RICHMONT GRADUATE UNIVERSITY
Clinical Psychology — M
Counselor Education — M
Marriage and Family Therapy — M
Pastoral Ministry and Counseling — M,O

RIDER UNIVERSITY
Accounting — M
Applied Psychology — M
Business Administration and Management—General — M
Business Education — O
Corporate and Organizational Communication — M
Counselor Education — M,O
Curriculum and Instruction — M,O
Education—General — M,O
Educational Leadership and Administration — M,O
Elementary Education — O
English as a Second Language — O
English Education — O
Foreign Languages Education — O

French — O
German — O
Mathematics Education — O
Music Education — M
Music — M
Organizational Management — M
Reading Education — M,O
School Psychology — O
Science Education — O
Social Sciences Education — O
Spanish — O
Special Education — M,O

RIVIER UNIVERSITY
Business Administration and Management—General — M
Clinical Psychology — M
Computer Science — M
Counseling Psychology — M,D,O
Counselor Education — M,D,O
Curriculum and Instruction — M,D,O
Early Childhood Education — M,D,O
Education—General — M,D,O
Educational Leadership and Administration — M,D,O
Elementary Education — M,D,O
English — M
Experimental Psychology — M
Family Nurse Practitioner Studies — M,D
Foreign Languages Education — M
Management Information Systems — M
Mathematics — M
Nursing and Healthcare Administration — M,D
Nursing Education — M,D
Nursing—General — M,D
Psychiatric Nursing — M,D
Psychology—General — M
Public Health—General — M,D
Reading Education — M,D,O
Social Sciences Education — M
Special Education — M,D,O
Writing — M

THE ROBERT E. WEBBER INSTITUTE FOR WORSHIP STUDIES
Religion — M,D

ROBERT MORRIS UNIVERSITY
Business Administration and Management—General — M
Business Education — M,D,O
Computer and Information Systems Security — M,D
Counseling Psychology — M,D,O
Database Systems — M,D
Education—General — M,D,O
Educational Leadership and Administration — M,D,O
Engineering and Applied Sciences—General — M
Engineering Management — M
Higher Education — M,D,O
Human Resources Management — M
Information Science — M,D
Internet and Interactive Multimedia — M,D
Management Information Systems — M,D
Nursing—General — M,D
Organizational Management — M,D
Project Management — M,D
Reading Education — M,D,O
Special Education — M,D,O
Taxation — M

ROBERT MORRIS UNIVERSITY ILLINOIS
Accounting — M
Arts Administration — M
Business Administration and Management—General — M
Computer and Information Systems Security — M
Criminal Justice and Criminology — M
Educational Leadership and Administration — M
Educational Media/Instructional Technology — M
Finance and Banking — M
Health Services Management and Hospital Administration — M
Higher Education — M
Human Resources Management — M
Management Information Systems — M
Management Strategy and Policy — M
Media Studies — M
Sports Management — M

ROBERTS WESLEYAN COLLEGE
Business Administration and Management—General — M
Child and Family Studies — M
Clinical Psychology — M,D
Counselor Education — M,D
Early Childhood Education — M
Education—General — M
Health Informatics — M
Health Services Management and Hospital Administration — M
Human Services — M
Management Strategy and Policy — M
Marketing — M
Middle School Education — M
Nursing and Healthcare Administration — M
Nursing Education — M
Nursing—General — M
Psychology—General — M,D
Reading Education — M
School Psychology — M,D
Secondary Education — M
Social Work — M
Special Education — M

ROCHESTER COLLEGE
Missions and Missiology — M
Religious Education — M

ROCHESTER INSTITUTE OF TECHNOLOGY
Accounting — M
Applied Mathematics — M
Applied Statistics — M,O
Architecture — M
Art Education — M
Art/Fine Arts — M
Astrophysics — M,D
Bioinformatics — M
Biological and Biomedical Sciences—General — M
Business Administration and Management—General — M
Chemistry — M
Communication—General — M
Computer and Information Systems Security — M,O
Computer Art and Design — M
Computer Engineering — M
Computer Science — M,D
Criminal Justice and Criminology — M
Database Systems — O
Electrical Engineering — M
Engineering and Applied Sciences—General — M,D,O
Engineering Design — M
Engineering Management — M
Entrepreneurship — M
Environmental and Occupational Health — M
Environmental Sciences — M
Experimental Psychology — M
Film, Television, and Video Production — M
Finance and Banking — M
Game Design and Development — M
Graphic Design — M
Health Services Management and Hospital Administration — M,O
Hospitality Management — M
Human Resources Development — M
Human-Computer Interaction — M
Industrial and Manufacturing Management — M
Industrial Design — M
Industrial/Management Engineering — M
Information Science — M,D
Interdisciplinary Studies — M
International Business — M
Internet and Interactive Multimedia — O
Management Information Systems — O
Manufacturing Engineering — M
Materials Engineering — M
Materials Sciences — M
Mathematical and Computational Finance — M
Mathematics — M,D,O
Mechanical Engineering — M
Media Studies — M
Medical Illustration — M
Modeling and Simulation — D
Occupational Therapy — M
Optical Sciences — M,D
Organizational Management — O
Photography — M
Project Management — O
Psychology—General — M,O
Public Policy — M
Safety Engineering — M
School Psychology — M,O
Secondary Education — M
Software Engineering — M
Special Education — M
Statistics — O
Sustainability Management — M,D
Sustainable Development — M,D
Systems Engineering — M,D
Technology and Public Policy — M
Telecommunications — M
Translation and Interpretation — M
Travel and Tourism — M

THE ROCKEFELLER UNIVERSITY
Biological and Biomedical Sciences—General — M,D*

ROCKFORD UNIVERSITY
Business Administration and Management—General — M
Early Childhood Education — M
Education—General — M
Educational Media/Instructional Technology — M
Elementary Education — M
Reading Education — M
Secondary Education — M
Special Education — M

ROCKHURST UNIVERSITY
Accounting — M,O
Business Administration and Management—General — M,O
Communication Disorders — M
Database Systems — M,O
Education—General — M
Entrepreneurship — M,O
Finance and Banking — M,O
Health Services Management and Hospital Administration — M,O
Human Resources Development — M,O
International Business — M,O
Management Strategy and Policy — M,O
Nonprofit Management — M,O
Occupational Therapy — M

*M—masters degree; D—doctorate; O—other advanced degree; *—Close-Up and/or Display*

Physical Therapy — D

ROCKY MOUNTAIN COLLEGE
Accounting — M
Educational Leadership and
　Administration — M
Physician Assistant Studies — M

ROCKY MOUNTAIN COLLEGE OF ART + DESIGN
Art Education — M
Arts Administration — M
Internet and Interactive
　Multimedia — M

ROCKY MOUNTAIN UNIVERSITY OF HEALTH PROFESSIONS
Communication Disorders — D
Family Nurse Practitioner Studies — D
Occupational Therapy — D
Physical Therapy — D
Physician Assistant Studies — M
Physiology — D

ROCKY VISTA UNIVERSITY
Biological and Biomedical
　Sciences—General — M
Osteopathic Medicine — D

ROGERS STATE UNIVERSITY
Business Administration and
　Management—General — M

ROGER WILLIAMS UNIVERSITY
Architectural History — M
Architecture — M
Art History — M
Clinical Psychology — M
Computer and Information
　Systems Security — M
Criminal Justice and Criminology — M
Education—General — M
Forensic Psychology — M
Health Services Management and
　Hospital Administration — M
Historic Preservation — M
Law — M,D
Public Administration — M
Reading Education — M

ROLLINS COLLEGE
Applied Behavior Analysis — M
Business Administration and
　Management—General — M,D
Counselor Education — M
Education—General — M
Elementary Education — M
Entrepreneurship — M,D
Finance and Banking — M,D
Health Services Management and
　Hospital Administration — M
Human Resources Development — M
Human Resources Management — M
International Business — M,D
Liberal Studies — M
Management of Technology — M,D
Marketing — M,D

ROOSEVELT UNIVERSITY
Accounting — M
Actuarial Science — M
Arts Administration — M,O
Biotechnology — M
Business Administration and
　Management—General — M
Chemistry — M
Clinical Psychology — M,D
Communication—General — M
Computer Science — M
Corporate and Organizational
　Communication — M
Counselor Education — M
Early Childhood Education — M
Economics — M
Education—General — M
Elementary Education — M
History — M
Hospitality Management — M
Human Resources Development — M
Human Resources Management — M
Industrial and Organizational
　Psychology — M,D
Information Science — M
Marketing — M
Mathematics — M
Music — M,O
Organizational Management — M
Pharmacy — D
Philosophy — M
Psychology—General — M,D
Public Administration — M
Reading Education — M
Real Estate — M,O
School Psychology — M
Secondary Education — M
Special Education — M
Theater — M
Writing — M

ROSALIND FRANKLIN UNIVERSITY OF MEDICINE AND SCIENCE
Allied Health—General — M,D,O
Allopathic Medicine — D
Anatomy — D
Biochemistry — D
Biological and Biomedical
　Sciences—General — M
Biophysics — M,D
Cell Biology — D
Clinical Psychology — M,D
Health Education — M
Health Promotion — M
Health Services Management and
　Hospital Administration — M,O
Immunology — D
Interdisciplinary Studies — D
Microbiology — D

Molecular Biology — D
Molecular Pharmacology — M,D
Neuroscience — D
Nurse Anesthesia — D
Nutrition — M
Pathology — M
Pharmacy — D
Physical Therapy — M,D
Physician Assistant Studies — M
Physiology — M,D
Podiatric Medicine — D
Psychology—General — M,D

ROSE-HULMAN INSTITUTE OF TECHNOLOGY
Biomedical Engineering — M
Chemical Engineering — M
Civil Engineering — M
Computer Engineering — M
Electrical Engineering — M
Engineering and Applied
　Sciences—General — M
Engineering Management — M
Environmental Engineering — M
Management Information Systems — M
Mechanical Engineering — M
Optical Sciences — M
Software Engineering — M
Systems Engineering — M

ROSEMAN UNIVERSITY OF HEALTH SCIENCES
Business Administration and
　Management—General — M,O
Dentistry — M,D,O
Pharmacy — D

ROSEMONT COLLEGE
Business Administration and
　Management—General — M
Counseling Psychology — M
Counselor Education — M
Education—General — M
Elementary Education — M
Human Services — M
Publishing — M
Writing — M

ROWAN UNIVERSITY
Advertising and Public Relations — M
Applied Behavior Analysis — M,O
Arts Administration — M
Bioinformatics — M
Biological and Biomedical
　Sciences—General — M
Business Administration and
　Management—General — M,O
Chemical Engineering — M
Civil Engineering — M
Clinical Psychology — M,O
Computer and Information
　Systems Security — O
Computer Science — M
Corporate and Organizational
　Communication — O
Counselor Education — M
Criminal Justice and Criminology — M
Education—General — M,D,O
Educational Leadership and
　Administration — M,D,O
Electrical Engineering — M
Engineering and Applied
　Sciences—General — M
English as a Second Language — O
English Education — O
Exercise and Sports Science — M
Health Promotion — M
Higher Education — M
History — M,O
Library Science — M,D,O
Marketing — O
Mathematics Education — M
Mathematics — M
Mechanical Engineering — M
Media Studies — O
Music — M
Nursing—General — M
Osteopathic Medicine — D
Pharmaceutical Sciences — M
Psychology—General — M,O
Publishing — O
Reading Education — M,O
Rhetoric — O
School Nursing — M,D,O
School Psychology — M,O
Science Education — M
Special Education — M,O
Theater — M
Writing — M,O

ROYAL MILITARY COLLEGE OF CANADA
Business Administration and
　Management—General — M
Chemical Engineering — M,D
Chemistry — M,D
Civil Engineering — M,D
Computer Engineering — M
Computer Science — M
Electrical Engineering — M,D
Engineering and Applied
　Sciences—General — M,D
Environmental Engineering — M,D
Environmental Sciences — M,D
Materials Sciences — M,D
Mathematics — M,D
Mechanical Engineering — M,D
Military and Defense Studies — M,D
Nuclear Engineering — M,D
Physics — M
Software Engineering — M,D

ROYAL ROADS UNIVERSITY
Advertising and Public Relations — O
Business Administration and
　Management—General — M,O

Conflict Resolution and
　Mediation/Peace Studies — M,O
Emergency Management — M,O
Environmental Education — M,O
Environmental Management
　and Policy — M,O
Health Services Management and
　Hospital Administration — O
Hospitality Management — M,O
Human Resources Management — M,O
Project Management — O
Travel and Tourism — M,O

RUDOLF STEINER COLLEGE
Early Childhood Education — M
Education—General — M
Elementary Education — M

RUSH UNIVERSITY
Adult Nursing — D
Allopathic Medicine — D
Anatomy — M
Biochemistry — M,D
Cell Biology — M,D
Clinical Laboratory
　Sciences/Medical Technology — M
Communication Disorders — M,D
Community Health Nursing — D
Family Nurse Practitioner Studies — D
Gerontological Nursing — D
Health Services Management and
　Hospital Administration — M,D
Immunology — M,D
Maternal and Child/Neonatal
　Nursing — D,O
Medical Physics — M
Microbiology — M,D
Neuroscience — M,D
Nurse Anesthesia — D
Nursing and Healthcare
　Administration — M
Nursing—General — M,D,O
Nutrition — M
Occupational Therapy — M
Pediatric Nursing — D,O
Perfusion — M
Pharmaceutical Sciences — M,D
Pharmacology — M,D
Physical Therapy — M
Physician Assistant Studies — M
Physiology — D
Psychiatric Nursing — M
Virology — M,D

RUTGERS UNIVERSITY–CAMDEN
Applied Mathematics — M
Biological and Biomedical
　Sciences—General — M
Business Administration and
　Management—General — M
Chemistry — M
Child Development — M,D
Computational Biology — M,D
Computer Science — M
Criminal Justice and Criminology — M
Educational Leadership and
　Administration — M
Educational Policy — M
English — M
Family Nurse Practitioner Studies — D
Gerontological Nursing — D
Health Services Management and
　Hospital Administration — M,O
History — M
International Affairs — M
International Development — M
Law — D
Liberal Studies — M
Mathematics Education — M
Mathematics — M
Nursing—General — D
Physical Therapy — D
Psychology—General — M
Public Administration — M
Public Health—General — M,O
Public History — M
Public Policy — M
Writing — M

RUTGERS UNIVERSITY–NEWARK
Accounting — M,D
Adult Nursing — M,D,O
Allied Health—General — M,D,O
Allopathic Medicine — D
American Studies — M,D
Analytical Chemistry — M,D
Applied Physics — M,D
Biochemistry — M,D
Bioinformatics — M,D
Biological and Biomedical
　Sciences—General — M,D,O
Biomedical Engineering — O
Biopsychology — D
Business Administration and
　Management—General — M,D
Cancer Biology/Oncology — D,O
Cell Biology — D
Chemistry — M,D
Clinical Laboratory
　Sciences/Medical Technology — M
Clothing and Textiles — M
Cognitive Sciences — D
Computational Biology — M
Criminal Justice and Criminology — M,D
Dentistry — M,D,O
Developmental Biology — D,O
Economics — M,D
English — M
Environmental Sciences — M,D
Epidemiology — M,O
Family Nurse Practitioner Studies — M,D,O
Finance and Banking — M,D
Geology — M
Health Education — M
Health Physics/Radiological Health — M

Health Services Management and
　Hospital Administration — M,D,O
History — M
Human Resources Management — M,D
Immunology — D
Infectious Diseases — D,O
Inorganic Chemistry — M,D
International Affairs — M,D
International Business — D
Law — D
Logistics — M
Management Information Systems — M,D
Management of Technology — D
Marketing — D
Mathematics — D
Medical Imaging — M
Medical Informatics — M,D,O
Microbiology — D
Molecular Biology — M,D
Molecular Genetics — D
Molecular Medicine — M
Molecular Pathology — D
Music — M
Neuroscience — D
Nurse Anesthesia — M,D,O
Nursing Informatics — M
Nursing—General — M,D,O
Nutrition — M,D,O
Occupational Health Nursing — M,D,O
Oral and Dental Sciences — M,D,O
Organic Chemistry — M,D
Organizational Management — D
Pathology — D
Pharmaceutical Administration — M
Pharmacology — D
Physical Chemistry — M,D
Physical Therapy — D
Physician Assistant Studies — M
Physiology — D
Political Science — M
Psychology—General — D
Public Administration — M,D
Public Health—General — M,O
Public Policy — M,D,O
Quantitative Analysis — M,O
Real Estate — M
Rehabilitation Counseling — M,D
Social Psychology — D
Supply Chain Management — D
Transcultural Nursing — M,D,O
Urban Studies — M,D
Women's Health Nursing — M,D,O
Writing — M

RUTGERS UNIVERSITY–NEW BRUNSWICK
Aerospace/Aeronautical
　Engineering — M,D
African Studies — D
African-American Studies — D
Agricultural Economics and
　Agribusiness — M
Allopathic Medicine — D
Animal Sciences — M,D
Anthropology — M,D
Applied Arts and Design—General — M
Applied Mathematics — M,D
Applied Psychology — M,D
Applied Statistics — M,D
Art History — M,D,O
Art/Fine Arts — M
Asian Studies — M,D
Astronomy — M,D
Atmospheric Sciences — M,D
Biochemical Engineering — M,D
Biochemistry — M,D
Biological and Biomedical
　Sciences—General — M,D
Biomedical Engineering — M,D
Biopsychology — D
Biostatistics — M,D,O
Cancer Biology/Oncology — M,D
Cell Biology — M,D
Chemical Engineering — M,D
Chemistry — M,D
Civil Engineering — M,D
Classics — M,D
Clinical Laboratory
　Sciences/Medical Technology — M
Clinical Psychology — M,D
Cognitive Sciences — D
Communication—General — D
Comparative Literature — M,D
Computational Biology — D
Computer Engineering — M,D
Computer Science — M,D
Condensed Matter Physics — M,D
Counseling Psychology — M
Counselor Education — M
Developmental Biology — M,D
Developmental Education — M,D
Early Childhood Education — M,D
Ecology — M,D
Economics — M,D
Education—General — M,D
Educational Leadership and
　Administration — M,D
Educational Measurement and
　Evaluation — M
Educational Policy — D
Educational Psychology — M,D
Electrical Engineering — M,D
Elementary Education — M,D
Emergency Management — M,D,O
English as a Second Language — M,D
English Education — M
English — D
Entomology — M,D
Environmental and Occupational
　Health — M,D,O
Environmental Biology — M,D
Environmental Engineering — M,D
Environmental Sciences — M,D
Epidemiology — M,D,O

Evolutionary Biology	M,D
Food Science and	
Technology	M,D
Foreign Languages Education	M,D
Foundations and Philosophy of	
Education	M,D
French	M,D
Gender Studies	M,D
Genetics	M,D
Geography	M,D
Geology	M,D
German	M,D
Hazardous Materials	
Management	M,D
Health Education	M,D,O
Health Psychology	D
Health Services Management and	
Hospital Administration	M,D,O
Historic Preservation	M,D,O
History of Medicine	D
History of Science and Technology	D
History	D
Horticulture	M,D
Human Resources Management	M,D
Immunology	M,D
Industrial and Labor Relations	M,D
Industrial/Management	
Engineering	M,D
Information Science	M
Information Studies	M,D
Inorganic Chemistry	M,D
Interdisciplinary Studies	D
International Affairs	M,D
Italian	M,O
Jewish Studies	M
Legal and Justice Studies	M
Library Science	D
Linguistics	D
Marine Biology	M,D
Materials Engineering	M,D
Materials Sciences	M,D
Mathematics Education	M,D
Mathematics	M,D
Mechanical Engineering	M,D
Mechanics	M,D
Medical Microbiology	M,D
Medicinal and Pharmaceutical	
Chemistry	M,D
Medieval and Renaissance Studies	D
Microbiology	M,D
Molecular Biology	M,D
Molecular Biophysics	D
Molecular Genetics	M,D
Molecular Pharmacology	M,D
Molecular Physiology	M,D
Multilingual and Multicultural	
Education	M,D
Music Education	M,D,O
Music	M,D,O
Neuroscience	M,D
Nutrition	M,D
Oceanography	M,D
Operations Research	D
Organic Chemistry	M,D
Pharmaceutical Sciences	M,D
Pharmacy	M,D
Philosophy	D
Physical Chemistry	M,D
Physics	M,D
Physiology	M,D
Plant Biology	M,D
Plant Molecular Biology	M,D
Plant Pathology	M,D
Political Science	M,D
Psychology—General	D
Public Health—General	M,D
Public Policy	M,D
Quality Management	M,D
Reading Education	M,D
Religion	M,O
Reproductive Biology	M,D
School Psychology	M,D
Science Education	M,D
Social Psychology	D
Social Sciences Education	M,D
Social Work	M,D*
Sociology	M,D
Spanish	M,D
Special Education	M,D
Statistics	M,D
Student Affairs	M
Systems Biology	D
Systems Engineering	M,D
Theater	M
Theoretical Physics	M,D
Toxicology	M,D
Translation and Interpretation	M,D
Translational Biology	M
Urban and Regional Planning	M,D
Virology	M,D
Water Resources	M,D
Women's Studies	M,D
Writing	M

RYERSON UNIVERSITY

Arts Administration	M
Business Administration and	
Management—General	M
Management of Technology	M

SACRED HEART MAJOR SEMINARY

Pastoral Ministry and Counseling	M
Theology	M

SACRED HEART SCHOOL OF THEOLOGY

Theology	M,O

SACRED HEART UNIVERSITY

Accounting	M
Applied Psychology	M

Biological and Biomedical	
Sciences—General	M,D
Chemistry	M
Communication Disorders	M
Communication—General	M
Computer and Information	
Systems Security	M
Computer Science	M
Criminal Justice and Criminology	M
Education—General	M,O
Educational Leadership and	
Administration	O
English as a Second Language	M,O
Exercise and Sports Science	M
Family Nurse Practitioner Studies	M,D,O
Film, Television, and Video	
Production	M
Finance and Banking	M,D
Game Design and	
Development	M
Health Informatics	M
Human Resources Management	M
Industrial and Organizational	
Psychology	M
Information Science	M
Investment Management	M,D
Journalism	M
Marketing	M,O
Media Studies	M
Molecular Biology	M
Nursing and Healthcare	
Administration	M,D,O
Nursing Education	M,D,O
Nursing—General	M,D,O
Nutrition	M
Occupational Therapy	M
Physical Therapy	D
Physician Assistant Studies	M
Reading Education	O
Social Psychology	M
Social Work	M

SAGE GRADUATE SCHOOL

Applied Behavior Analysis	M,O
Business Administration and	
Management—General	M
Counseling Psychology	M
Counselor Education	M,O
Education—General	M,D,O
Educational Leadership and	
Administration	D
Elementary Education	M
Family Nurse Practitioner Studies	M
Forensic Psychology	M,O
Gerontological Nursing	M,O
Gerontology	M
Health Education	M
Health Services Management and	
Hospital Administration	M
Nursing Education	D
Nursing—General	M,D,O
Nutrition	M,O
Occupational Therapy	M
Organizational Management	M
Physical Therapy	D
Psychiatric Nursing	M,O
Psychology—General	M,O
Reading Education	M
Social Psychology	M
Special Education	M

SAGINAW VALLEY STATE UNIVERSITY

Business Administration and	
Management—General	M
Chinese	M
Communication—General	M
Distance Education Development	M
Early Childhood Education	M
Education—General	M,O
Educational Leadership and	
Administration	M,O
Educational Media/Instructional	
Technology	M
Elementary Education	M
Engineering and Applied	
Sciences—General	M
Family Nurse Practitioner Studies	M,D
Foreign Languages Education	M
Health Services Management and	
Hospital Administration	M
Media Studies	M
Middle School Education	M
Nursing and Healthcare	
Administration	M
Nursing—General	M
Occupational Therapy	M
Public Administration	M
Reading Education	M
Science Education	M
Secondary Education	M
Special Education	M

ST. AMBROSE UNIVERSITY

Accounting	M
Business Administration and	
Management—General	M,D
Communication Disorders	M
Criminal Justice and Criminology	M
Education—General	M
Educational Leadership and	
Administration	M
Health Services Management and	
Hospital Administration	M,D
Human Resources Management	M,D
Management of Technology	M
Nursing—General	M
Occupational Therapy	M
Organizational Management	M
Pastoral Ministry and Counseling	M
Physical Therapy	D
Social Work	M
Special Education	M

ST. ANDREW'S COLLEGE

Theology	M,D,O

ST. ANDREW'S COLLEGE IN WINNIPEG

Theology	M

SAINT ANTHONY COLLEGE OF NURSING

Nursing—General	M

ST. AUGUSTINE'S SEMINARY OF TORONTO

Pastoral Ministry and Counseling	M,O
Religious Education	M,O
Theology	M,O

ST. BERNARD'S SCHOOL OF THEOLOGY AND MINISTRY

Pastoral Ministry and Counseling	M,O
Theology	M,O

ST. BONAVENTURE UNIVERSITY

Accounting	M
Business Administration and	
Management—General	M
Corporate and Organizational	
Communication	M
Counseling Psychology	M,O
Counselor Education	M,O
Early Childhood Education	M
Education of the Gifted	M,O
Education—General	M,O
Educational Leadership and	
Administration	M,O
Marketing	M
Middle School Education	M
Reading Education	M
Rehabilitation Counseling	M,O
Religion	M,O
Secondary Education	M
Social Psychology	M,O
Special Education	M,O

ST. CATHERINE UNIVERSITY

Adult Nursing	M,D
Business Administration and	
Management—General	M
Curriculum and Instruction	M
Early Childhood Education	M
Education—General	M
Gerontological Nursing	M,D
Health Services Management and	
Hospital Administration	M
Information Studies	M
Library Science	M
Marketing	M
Maternal and Child/Neonatal	
Nursing	M,D
Nursing Education	M,D
Nursing—General	M,D
Occupational Therapy	M,D
Organizational Management	M
Pastoral Ministry and Counseling	M,O
Pediatric Nursing	M,D
Physical Therapy	D
Physician Assistant Studies	M
Public Health—General	M
Social Work	M,D
Theology	M,O

SAINT CHARLES BORROMEO SEMINARY, OVERBROOK

Religion	M
Theology	M

ST. CLOUD STATE UNIVERSITY

Applied Behavior Analysis	M
Applied Economics	M
Applied Statistics	M
Archaeology	M
Biological and Biomedical	
Sciences—General	M
Biomedical Engineering	M
Business Administration and	
Management—General	M
Child and Family Studies	M
Communication Disorders	M
Computer and Information	
Systems Security	M
Computer Science	M
Counselor Education	M
Criminal Justice and Criminology	M
Curriculum and Instruction	M
Economics	M
Education—General	M,D
Educational Leadership and	
Administration	M,D
Educational Media/Instructional	
Technology	M
Electrical Engineering	M
Engineering and Applied	
Sciences—General	M
Engineering Management	M
English as a Second Language	M
English	M
Environmental Management	
and Policy	M
Exercise and Sports Science	M
Geography	M
Gerontology	M
Higher Education	M,D
Historic Preservation	M
History	M
Industrial and Organizational	
Psychology	M
Marriage and Family Therapy	M
Mass Communication	M
Mathematics	M
Mechanical Engineering	M
Music Education	M
Music	M
Nonprofit Management	M
Psychology—General	M,D

Rehabilitation Counseling	M
Social Psychology	M
Social Work	M
Special Education	M
Sports Management	M
Student Affairs	M
Technology and Public Policy	M

ST. EDWARD'S UNIVERSITY

Accounting	M,O
Business Administration and	
Management—General	M,O
Counseling Psychology	M
Counselor Education	M,O
Education—General	M,O
Environmental Management	
and Policy	M
Humanities	M,O
Liberal Studies	M,O
Organizational Management	M
Student Affairs	M
Sustainable Development	M

ST. FRANCIS COLLEGE

Accounting	M

SAINT FRANCIS MEDICAL CENTER COLLEGE OF NURSING

Family Nurse Practitioner Studies	M,D,O
Gerontological Nursing	M,D,O
Maternal and Child/Neonatal	
Nursing	M,D,O
Medical/Surgical Nursing	M,D,O
Nursing and Healthcare	
Administration	M,D,O
Nursing Education	M,D,O
Nursing—General	M,D,O
Psychiatric Nursing	M,D,O

SAINT FRANCIS UNIVERSITY

Biological and Biomedical	
Sciences—General	M
Business Administration and	
Management—General	M
Education—General	M
Educational Leadership and	
Administration	M
Health Education	M
Human Resources Management	M
Occupational Therapy	M
Physical Therapy	D
Physician Assistant Studies	M
Reading Education	M

ST. FRANCIS XAVIER UNIVERSITY

Adult Education	M
Biological and Biomedical	
Sciences—General	M
Chemistry	M
Computer Science	M
Cultural Studies	M
Curriculum and Instruction	M
Education—General	M
Educational Leadership and	
Administration	M
Geology	M
Geosciences	M
Urban and Regional Planning	M

ST. JOHN FISHER COLLEGE

Biological and Biomedical	
Sciences—General	M
Business Administration and	
Management—General	M
Chemistry	M
Counseling Psychology	M
Education—General	M,D,O
Educational Leadership and	
Administration	M,D
Elementary Education	M,O
English Education	M
Foreign Languages Education	M
French	M
Mathematics Education	M
Middle School Education	M
Nursing—General	M,D,O
Pharmacy	D
Physics	M
Reading Education	M
Social Sciences Education	M
Special Education	M,O

ST. JOHN'S COLLEGE (MD)

Liberal Studies	M

ST. JOHN'S COLLEGE (NM)

Asian Languages	M
Asian Studies	M
Liberal Studies	M

ST. JOHN'S SEMINARY (CA)

Pastoral Ministry and Counseling	M
Theology	M

SAINT JOHN'S SEMINARY (MA)

Religion	M
Theology	M

SAINT JOHN'S UNIVERSITY (MN)

Music	M
Pastoral Ministry and Counseling	M
Theology	M

ST. JOHN'S UNIVERSITY (NY)

Accounting	M
Actuarial Science	M
Applied Mathematics	M
Asian Studies	M
Biological and Biomedical	
Sciences—General	M,D
Biotechnology	M
Business Administration and	
Management—General	M
Chemistry	M
Clinical Psychology	M,D,O

Communication Disorders	M,D
Computational Sciences	M
Counseling Psychology	M,O
Counselor Education	M,O
Criminal Justice and Criminology	M
Database Systems	M
Early Childhood Education	M,O
Education of the Gifted	D,O
Education—General	M,D,O
Educational Leadership and Administration	M,D,O
Elementary Education	M,O
English as a Second Language	M,D,O
English	M,D
Finance and Banking	M
History	M,D
Information Science	M
Information Studies	M,O
Insurance	M
International Affairs	M
International Business	M
Investment Management	M
Law	D
Legal and Justice Studies	M
Liberal Studies	M
Library Science	M,O
Management Information Systems	M
Management Strategy and Policy	M
Marketing	M
Mathematics	M
Middle School Education	M,O
Multilingual and Multicultural Education	M,O
Museum Studies	M
Pharmaceutical Administration	M
Pharmaceutical Sciences	M,D
Political Science	M,O
Psychology—General	M
Public Administration	M,O
Public Health—General	M
Public History	M,D
Quantitative Analysis	M
Reading Education	M,D,O
School Psychology	M,D
Secondary Education	M
Sociology	M
Spanish	M
Special Education	M,D,O
Sports Management	M
Statistics	M
Taxation	M
Theology	M,O
Toxicology	M

ST. JOSEPH'S COLLEGE, LONG ISLAND CAMPUS

Accounting	M
Business Administration and Management—General	M
Early Childhood Education	M
Educational Leadership and Administration	M
Health Informatics	M
Health Services Management and Hospital Administration	M
Human Resources Management	M
Human Services	M
Mathematics Education	M
Nursing—General	M
Organizational Management	M
Reading Education	M
Special Education	M

ST. JOSEPH'S COLLEGE, NEW YORK

Accounting	M
Business Administration and Management—General	M
Education—General	M
Educational Leadership and Administration	M
Forensic Sciences	M
Health Informatics	M
Health Services Management and Hospital Administration	M
Human Resources Management	M
Human Services	M
Nursing—General	M
Organizational Management	M
Reading Education	M
Special Education	M
Writing	M

SAINT JOSEPH'S COLLEGE OF MAINE

Accounting	M
Adult Education	M
Business Administration and Management—General	M
Education—General	M
Educational Leadership and Administration	M
Family Nurse Practitioner Studies	M,O
Health Education	M
Health Services Management and Hospital Administration	M
Nursing and Healthcare Administration	M,O
Nursing Education	M,O
Nursing—General	M,O
Pastoral Ministry and Counseling	M

ST. JOSEPH'S SEMINARY

Pastoral Ministry and Counseling	M
Religion	M
Theology	M

SAINT JOSEPH'S UNIVERSITY

Accounting	M,O
Biological and Biomedical Sciences—General	M
Business Administration and Management—General	M,O
Communication Disorders	M,D,O
Computer Science	M,O
Criminal Justice and Criminology	M
Curriculum and Instruction	M,D,O
Early Childhood Education	M,D,O

Education—General	M,D,O
Educational Leadership and Administration	M,D,O
Educational Media/Instructional Technology	M,D,O
Elementary Education	M,D,O
Finance and Banking	M,O
Health Education	M
Health Informatics	M
Health Services Management and Hospital Administration	M,O
Human Resources Management	M,O
International Business	M,O
Law	M,O
Management Information Systems	M
Management Strategy and Policy	M
Marketing	M
Mathematics	M,O
Middle School Education	M,D,O
Psychology—General	M,O
Reading Education	M,D,O
Secondary Education	M,D,O
Special Education	M,D,O
Writing	M

ST. LAWRENCE UNIVERSITY

Counselor Education	M,O
Education—General	M,O
Educational Leadership and Administration	M,O
Human Development	M,O

SAINT LEO UNIVERSITY

Accounting	M,D,O
Agricultural Education	M
Business Administration and Management—General	M,D,O
Computer and Information Systems Security	M,D,O
Criminal Justice and Criminology	M
Education of the Gifted	M,O
Education—General	M,O
Educational Leadership and Administration	M,O
Educational Media/Instructional Technology	M,O
Emergency Management	M
Forensic Sciences	M
Health Services Management and Hospital Administration	M,D,O
Human Resources Management	M,D,O
Human Services	M
Legal and Justice Studies	M
Marketing Research	M,D,O
Marketing	M,D,O
Project Management	M,D,O
Reading Education	M,O
Social Work	M
Supply Chain Management	M,D,O
Theology	M,O
Writing	M

ST. LOUIS COLLEGE OF PHARMACY

Pharmacy	D*

SAINT LOUIS UNIVERSITY

Accounting	M
Allied Health—General	M,D,O
Allopathic Medicine	D
American Studies	M,D
Anatomy	M,D
Athletic Training and Sports Medicine	M,D
Biochemistry	D
Bioethics	D,O
Biological and Biomedical Sciences—General	M,D
Biomedical Engineering	M,D
Business Administration and Management—General	M
Chemistry	M,D
Clinical Psychology	M,D
Communication Disorders	M
Communication—General	M
Community Health	M
Counselor Education	M,D,O
Curriculum and Instruction	M,D
Dentistry	M
Education—General	M,D
Educational Leadership and Administration	M,D,O
English	M,D
Experimental Psychology	M,D
Finance and Banking	M
Foundations and Philosophy of Education	M,D
French	M
Geographic Information Systems	M,D,O
Geophysics	M,D
Geosciences	M,D
Health Services Management and Hospital Administration	M,D
Higher Education	M,D,O
History	M,D
Human Development	M,D,O
Immunology	D
Industrial and Organizational Psychology	M,D
International Business	M,D
Law	M,D
Marriage and Family Therapy	M,D,O
Mathematics	M,D
Meteorology	M,D
Microbiology	D
Molecular Biology	D
Nursing—General	M,D,O
Nutrition	M
Occupational Therapy	M
Oral and Dental Sciences	M
Organizational Management	M,D,O
Pathology	D
Pharmacology	D
Philosophy	M,D
Physical Therapy	M,D
Physician Assistant Studies	M

Physiology	D
Political Science	M
Psychology—General	M,D
Public Administration	M,D,O
Public Health—General	M,D
Public Policy	M,D,O
Social Work	M
Spanish	M
Special Education	M,D
Student Affairs	M,D,O
Theology	M,D
Urban Studies	M,D,O

SAINT LOUIS UNIVERSITY—MADRID CAMPUS

English	M
Spanish	M

SAINT MARTIN'S UNIVERSITY

Business Administration and Management—General	M
Civil Engineering	M
Counseling Psychology	M
Education—General	M
Engineering Management	M
Mechanical Engineering	M
Social Psychology	M

SAINT MARY-OF-THE-WOODS COLLEGE

Art Therapy	M,O
Management Strategy and Policy	M
Nonprofit Management	M
Organizational Management	M
Therapies—Dance, Drama, and Music	M

SAINT MARY'S COLLEGE

Communication Disorders	M
Database Systems	M
Nursing—General	D

SAINT MARY'S COLLEGE OF CALIFORNIA

Accounting	M
Business Administration and Management—General	M
Conflict Resolution and Mediation/Peace Studies	M
Counselor Education	M,O
Dance	M
Database Systems	M
Early Childhood Education	M
Education—General	M,D,O
Educational Leadership and Administration	M,D,O
Exercise and Sports Science	M
Finance and Banking	M
Investment Management	M
Kinesiology and Movement Studies	M
Marriage and Family Therapy	M,O
Organizational Management	M
School Psychology	M,O
Special Education	M
Sports Management	M
Writing	M

ST. MARY'S COLLEGE OF MARYLAND

Education—General	M

SAINT MARY SEMINARY AND GRADUATE SCHOOL OF THEOLOGY

Theology	M,D

ST. MARY'S SEMINARY AND UNIVERSITY

Theology	M,D,O

SAINT MARY'S UNIVERSITY (CANADA)

Applied Psychology	M,D
Applied Science and Technology	M
Astronomy	M,D
Business Administration and Management—General	M,D
Canadian Studies	M,O
Criminal Justice and Criminology	M
Gender Studies	M
History	M
Industrial and Organizational Psychology	M,D
International Development	M,O
Philosophy	M
Psychology—General	M,D
Religion	M
Theology	M
Women's Studies	M

ST. MARY'S UNIVERSITY (UNITED STATES)

Accounting	M
Business Administration and Management—General	M
Communication—General	M,O
Computer and Information Systems Security	M
Computer Engineering	M
Computer Science	M
Conflict Resolution and Mediation/Peace Studies	M,O
Counseling Psychology	M
Counselor Education	D
Educational Leadership and Administration	M
Electrical Engineering	M
Engineering Management	M
English	M
Homeland Security	M,O
Industrial and Organizational Psychology	M
Industrial/Management Engineering	M
Information Science	M
International Affairs	M,O
International Development	M,O
Law	M,D
Legal and Justice Studies	M

Marriage and Family Therapy	M,D
Public Administration	M,O
Public Policy	M,O
Software Engineering	M,O
Theology	M

SAINT MARY'S UNIVERSITY OF MINNESOTA

Accounting	M
Addictions/Substance Abuse Counseling	M,O
Arts Administration	M
Business Administration and Management—General	M,D
Counseling Psychology	M,D,O
Education of the Gifted	M,O
Education—General	M,O
Educational Leadership and Administration	M,D,O
Educational Media/Instructional Technology	M
Elementary Education	M
Geographic Information Systems	M,O
Health Services Management and Hospital Administration	M
Human Development	M
Human Resources Management	M
International Business	M
International Development	M
Marriage and Family Therapy	M
Multilingual and Multicultural Education	M,O
Nurse Anesthesia	M
Organizational Management	M
Philanthropic Studies	M
Project Management	M,O
Reading Education	M
Religious Education	M
Secondary Education	M
Special Education	M,O
Telecommunications	M

SAINT MEINRAD SCHOOL OF THEOLOGY

Theology	M

SAINT MICHAEL'S COLLEGE

Art Education	M,O
Clinical Psychology	M
Education—General	M,O
Educational Leadership and Administration	M,O
English as a Second Language	M,O
Reading Education	M,O
Special Education	M,O

ST. NORBERT COLLEGE

Business Administration and Management—General	M
Health Services Management and Hospital Administration	M
Liberal Studies	M
Supply Chain Management	M
Theology	M

ST. PATRICK'S SEMINARY & UNIVERSITY

Theology	M,O

SAINT PAUL SCHOOL OF THEOLOGY

Theology	M,D

SAINT PAUL UNIVERSITY

Conflict Resolution and Mediation/Peace Studies	M
Counseling Psychology	M
Marriage and Family Therapy	M
Missions and Missiology	M
Pastoral Ministry and Counseling	M,D,O
Theology	M,D,O

ST. PETER'S SEMINARY

Theology	M

SAINT PETER'S UNIVERSITY

Accounting	M
Adult Nursing	M,D,O
Applied Behavior Analysis	M,D,O
Business Administration and Management—General	M
Counselor Education	M,O
Criminal Justice and Criminology	M
Database Systems	M
Education—General	M,D,O
Educational Leadership and Administration	M,D
Elementary Education	M,O
Finance and Banking	M
Health Services Management and Hospital Administration	D
Higher Education	D
Human Resources Management	M
International Business	M
Management Information Systems	M
Marketing	M
Mathematics Education	M,D,O
Middle School Education	M,O
Nursing and Healthcare Administration	M,D,O
Nursing—General	M,D,O
Public Administration	M
Reading Education	M,O
Secondary Education	M,O
Special Education	M,O

SAINTS CYRIL AND METHODIUS SEMINARY

Pastoral Ministry and Counseling	M
Religious Education	M
Theology	M

ST. STEPHEN'S COLLEGE

Pastoral Ministry and Counseling	M,D
Theology	M,D

ST. THOMAS AQUINAS COLLEGE

Business Administration and Management—General	M

Education—General M,O
Educational Leadership and Administration M,O
Elementary Education M,O
Finance and Banking M
Marketing M
Middle School Education M,O
Reading Education M,O
Secondary Education M,O
Special Education M,O

ST. THOMAS UNIVERSITY
Accounting M,O
Arts Administration M
Business Administration and Management—General M,O
Communication—General M,D,O
Counseling Psychology M
Counselor Education M,O
Criminal Justice and Criminology M,O
Education of the Gifted M,D,O
Education—General M,D,O
Educational Leadership and Administration M,D,O
Educational Media/Instructional Technology M,D,O
Elementary Education M,D,O
English as a Second Language M,D,O
Film, Television, and Video Production M
Geosciences M,D,O
Health Services Management and Hospital Administration M,O
Hispanic Studies M,O
Human Resources Management M,O
International Business M,O
Law M,D
Marriage and Family Therapy M,O
Pastoral Ministry and Counseling M,D,O
Planetary and Space Sciences M,D,O
Public Administration M,O
Reading Education M,D,O
Special Education M,D,O
Sports Management M,O
Taxation M,D
Theology M,D,O

ST. TIKHON'S ORTHODOX THEOLOGICAL SEMINARY
Theology M

SAINT VINCENT COLLEGE
Business Administration and Management—General M
Curriculum and Instruction M
Education—General M
Educational Leadership and Administration M
Educational Media/Instructional Technology M
Nurse Anesthesia M,D
Special Education M

ST. VINCENT DE PAUL REGIONAL SEMINARY
Theology M

SAINT VINCENT SEMINARY
Pastoral Ministry and Counseling M
Theology M

ST. VLADIMIR'S ORTHODOX THEOLOGICAL SEMINARY
Theology M,D

SAINT XAVIER UNIVERSITY
Business Administration and Management—General M,O
Communication Disorders M
Computer Science M
Counselor Education M
Curriculum and Instruction M
Early Childhood Education M
Education—General M
Educational Leadership and Administration M
Educational Media/Instructional Technology M
Elementary Education M
English as a Second Language M
Finance and Banking M,O
Foreign Languages Education M
Health Services Management and Hospital Administration M,O
Marketing M,O
Music Education M,O
Nursing—General M,O
Project Management M
Reading Education M
Science Education M
Secondary Education M
Spanish M
Special Education M

SALEM COLLEGE
Art Education M
Counselor Education M
Education—General M
Elementary Education M
English as a Second Language M
Middle School Education M
Reading Education M
Secondary Education M
Special Education M

SALEM INTERNATIONAL UNIVERSITY
Business Administration and Management—General M
Computer and Information Systems Security M
Curriculum and Instruction M
Education—General M

Educational Leadership and Administration M
International Business M

SALEM STATE UNIVERSITY
Art Education M
Business Administration and Management—General M
Counseling Psychology M,O
Counselor Education M
Criminal Justice and Criminology M
Early Childhood Education M
Educational Leadership and Administration M
Educational Media/Instructional Technology M
Elementary Education M
English as a Second Language M
English M
Geography M
Gerontological Nursing M
Higher Education M
History M
Mathematics Education M
Mathematics M
Middle School Education M
Nursing and Healthcare Administration M
Nursing Education M
Nursing—General M
Occupational Therapy M
Physical Education M
Psychology—General M,O
Reading Education M
Science Education M
Secondary Education M
Social Work M
Spanish M
Special Education M

SALISBURY UNIVERSITY
American Studies M
Athletic Training and Sports Medicine M
Biological and Biomedical Sciences—General M
Business Administration and Management—General M
Conflict Resolution and Mediation/Peace Studies M
Curriculum and Instruction M
Educational Leadership and Administration M
English as a Second Language M
English M
Family Nurse Practitioner Studies D
Film, Television, and Video Theory and Criticism M
Geographic Information Systems M
History M
Mathematics Education M
Middle School Education M
Nursing and Healthcare Administration M,D
Nursing Education M
Nursing—General M,D
Physiology M
Reading Education M,D
Rhetoric M
Secondary Education M
Social Work M
Writing M

SALUS UNIVERSITY
Communication Disorders D
Optometry D
Physician Assistant Studies M
Public Health—General M
Rehabilitation Sciences M,O
Special Education M,O
Vision Sciences M,O

SALVE REGINA UNIVERSITY
Addictions/Substance Abuse Counseling M,O
Business Administration and Management—General M,O
Business Education M,O
Computer and Information Systems Security M,O
Conflict Resolution and Mediation/Peace Studies M,D
Counseling Psychology M,O
Criminal Justice and Criminology M,O
Entrepreneurship M
Forensic Sciences M,O
Health Services Management and Hospital Administration M,O
Homeland Security M,O
Human Resources Management M,O
Humanities M,D
International Affairs M,O
Management Strategy and Policy M,O
Nonprofit Management M,O
Nursing—General D
Organizational Management M,O
Rehabilitation Counseling M,O
Religion M,D

SAMFORD UNIVERSITY
Accounting M
Applied Arts and Design—General M
Athletic Training and Sports Medicine M,D
Business Administration and Management—General M
Communication Disorders M,D
Early Childhood Education M,D,O
Education of the Gifted M,D,O
Education—General M,D,O
Educational Leadership and Administration M,D,O

Educational Media/Instructional Technology M,D,O
Elementary Education M,D,O
Energy Management and Policy M
Entrepreneurship M
Environmental Management and Policy M
Family Nurse Practitioner Studies M,D
Finance and Banking M
Health Services Management and Hospital Administration M,D
Law M,D
Marketing M
Music Education M
Music M
Nurse Anesthesia M,D
Nursing and Healthcare Administration M,D
Nursing Informatics M,D
Nursing—General M,D
Pharmacy D
Physical Therapy M,D
Public Health—General M
Social Work M
Special Education M,D,O
Theology M

SAM HOUSTON STATE UNIVERSITY
Accounting M
Agricultural Sciences—General M
Allied Health—General M
Biological and Biomedical Sciences—General M
Business Administration and Management—General M
Chemistry M
Clinical Psychology M,D,O
Communication—General M
Computational Sciences M,D
Computer and Information Systems Security M,D
Computer Science M,D
Counselor Education M,D
Criminal Justice and Criminology M,D
Curriculum and Instruction M,D
Dance M
Developmental Education M,D
Education—General M,D
Educational Leadership and Administration M,D
English M
Family and Consumer Sciences—General M
Finance and Banking M
Forensic Sciences M,D
Geographic Information Systems M,O
Higher Education M,D
History M
Homeland Security M
Humanities M,D,O
Information Science M,D
Internet and Interactive Multimedia M
Kinesiology and Movement Studies M
Library Science M
Mathematics M
Music M
Nutrition M
Political Science M
Project Management M
Psychology—General M,D,O
Public Administration M
Publishing M
Reading Education M,D
School Psychology M,D,O
Sociology M
Spanish M
Special Education M,D
Sports Management M
Statistics M
Writing M

SAMUEL MERRITT UNIVERSITY
Family Nurse Practitioner Studies M,D,O
Nurse Anesthesia M,D,O
Nursing and Healthcare Administration M,D,O
Nursing—General M,D,O
Occupational Therapy D
Physical Therapy D
Physician Assistant Studies M
Podiatric Medicine D

SAN DIEGO CHRISTIAN COLLEGE
Education—General M
Organizational Management M

SAN DIEGO STATE UNIVERSITY
Accounting M
Advertising and Public Relations M
Aerospace/Aeronautical Engineering M,D
Anthropology M
Applied Arts and Design—General M
Applied Mathematics M
Art History M
Art/Fine Arts M
Asian Studies M
Astronomy M
Biochemistry M,D
Biological and Biomedical Sciences—General M,D
Biometry M
Biostatistics M,D
Business Administration and Management—General M
Cell Biology M,D
Chemistry M,D
Child and Family Studies M
Child Development M

Civil Engineering M
Clinical Psychology M,D
Communication Disorders M,D
Communication—General M
Computational Sciences M,D
Computer Science M
Counselor Education M
Criminal Justice and Criminology M
Curriculum and Instruction M
Ecology M,D
Economics M
Education—General M,D
Educational Leadership and Administration M
Educational Media/Instructional Technology M,D
Electrical Engineering M
Elementary Education M
Emergency Management M,D
Emergency Medical Services M,D
Engineering and Applied Sciences—General M,D
Engineering Design M,D
English as a Second Language M,O
English M
Entrepreneurship M
Environmental and Occupational Health M,D
Environmental Design M
Epidemiology M,D
Exercise and Sports Science M
Film, Television, and Video Production M
Finance and Banking M
Gender Studies O
Geography M,D
Geology M
Gerontology M
Graphic Design M
Health Physics/Radiological Health M
Health Promotion M,D
Health Psychology M,D
Health Services Management and Hospital Administration M
Higher Education M
History M
Human Resources Management M
Industrial and Organizational Psychology M,D
Interdisciplinary Studies M
Interior Design M
International Health M,D
Internet and Interactive Multimedia M
Kinesiology and Movement Studies M
Latin American Studies M
Liberal Studies M
Linguistics M,O
Management Information Systems M
Marketing M
Mathematics Education M,D
Mathematics M,D
Mechanical Engineering M,D
Mechanics M,D
Media Studies M
Microbiology M
Molecular Biology M,D
Multilingual and Multicultural Education M,D
Music Education M
Music M
Nursing—General M
Nutrition M
Pharmaceutical Administration M
Philosophy M
Physical Therapy D
Physics M
Political Science M
Psychology—General M,D
Public Administration M
Public Health—General M,D
Reading Education M
Rehabilitation Counseling M
Rhetoric M
Romance Languages M
School Psychology M
Science Education M,D
Secondary Education M
Social Work M
Sociology M
Spanish M
Special Education M
Sports Management M
Statistics M
Telecommunications Management M
Theater M
Toxicology M,D
Urban and Regional Planning M
Western European Studies M
Women's Studies M
Writing M

SANFORD BURNHAM PREBYS MEDICAL DISCOVERY INSTITUTE
Biological and Biomedical Sciences—General D

SAN FRANCISCO ART INSTITUTE
Art History M
Art/Fine Arts M,O
Museum Studies M

SAN FRANCISCO CONSERVATORY OF MUSIC
Music Education M,O
Music M,O

SAN FRANCISCO STATE UNIVERSITY
Accounting M
Acute Care/Critical Care Nursing M,O
Adult Education M

---

*M—masters degree; D—doctorate; O—other advanced degree; *—Close-Up and/or Display*

Anthropology	M
Applied Arts and Design—General	M
Archaeology	M
Art History	M
Art/Fine Arts	M
Asian-American Studies	M
Astronomy	M
Biochemistry	M
Biological and Biomedical Sciences—General	M
Biotechnology	M
Business Administration and Management—General	M
Cell Biology	M
Chemistry	M
Chinese	M
Classics	M
Clinical Psychology	M,O
Communication Disorders	M
Community Health Nursing	M,O
Comparative Literature	M
Computer Science	M
Counseling Psychology	M,O
Counselor Education	M,O
Criminal Justice and Criminology	M
Cultural Anthropology	M
Cultural Studies	M
Developmental Biology	M
Developmental Psychology	M,O
Early Childhood Education	M,D,O
Ecology	M
Economics	M
Education—General	M,D,O
Educational Leadership and Administration	M,D,O
Educational Media/Instructional Technology	M
Electrical Engineering	M
Elementary Education	M
Energy and Power Engineering	M
Engineering and Applied Sciences—General	M
English as a Second Language	M
English Education	M,O
English	M,O
Entrepreneurship	M
Environmental Management and Policy	M
Ethnic Studies	M
Family and Consumer Sciences-General	M
Family Nurse Practitioner Studies	M,O
Film, Television, and Video Production	M
Film, Television, and Video Theory and Criticism	M
Finance and Banking	M
French	M
Geographic Information Systems	M
Geography	M
Geosciences	M
German	M
Gerontology	M
Health Education	M
Health Services Management and Hospital Administration	M
History	M
Hospitality Management	M
Humanities	M
Industrial and Manufacturing Management	M
Industrial and Organizational Psychology	M,O
International Affairs	M
International Business	M
Italian	M
Japanese	M
Kinesiology and Movement Studies	M
Legal and Justice Studies	M
Leisure Studies	M
Liberal Studies	M
Linguistics	M
Management Information Systems	M
Marine Biology	M
Marine Sciences	M
Marketing	M
Marriage and Family Therapy	M,O
Mathematics Education	M,O
Mathematics	M
Media Studies	M
Microbiology	M
Molecular Biology	M
Museum Studies	M
Music Education	M
Music	M
Nonprofit Management	M
Nursing and Healthcare Administration	M,O
Nursing—General	M,O
Pediatric Nursing	M
Philosophy	M
Physical Therapy	D
Physics	M
Physiology	M
Political Science	M
Psychology—General	M
Public Administration	M
Public Health—General	M
Public Policy	M
Quantitative Analysis	M
Reading Education	M,O
Recreation and Park Management	M,O
Rehabilitation Counseling	M
School Psychology	M,O
Secondary Education	M,O
Social Psychology	M,O
Social Work	M
Spanish	M
Special Education	M,O
Speech and Interpersonal Communication	M
Sustainability Management	M
Theater	M

Travel and Tourism	M
Women's Health Nursing	M,O
Women's Studies	M
Writing	M

SAN FRANCISCO THEOLOGICAL SEMINARY

Theology	M,D

SAN JOAQUIN COLLEGE OF LAW

Law	D

SAN JOSE STATE UNIVERSITY

Accounting	M
Anthropology	M,O
Art History	M,O
Athletic Training and Sports Medicine	M,O
Biological and Biomedical Sciences—General	M,O
Biotechnology	M,O
Chemistry	M,O
Child Development	M,D,O
Clinical Psychology	M,O
Communication Disorders	M,D,O
Communication—General	M,O
Computational Sciences	M,O
Computer and Information Systems Security	M,O
Computer Science	M,O
Counselor Education	M,D,O
Curriculum and Instruction	M,D,O
Early Childhood Education	M,D,O
Ecology	M,O
Economics	M,O
Education—General	M,D,O
Educational Leadership and Administration	M,D,O
Elementary Education	M,D,O
English as a Second Language	M,O
English	M,O
Environmental Management and Policy	M,O
Exercise and Sports Science	M,O
Experimental Psychology	M,O
French	M,O
Geography	M,O
Geology	M,O
Higher Education	M,D,O
Hispanic Studies	M,O
History	M,O
Industrial and Organizational Psychology	M,O
Kinesiology and Movement Studies	M,O
Legal and Justice Studies	M,O
Library Science	M,O
Linguistics	M,O
Management Strategy and Policy	M,O
Marine Sciences	M,O
Mass Communication	M,O
Mathematics Education	M,O
Mathematics	M,D,O
Media Studies	M,O
Meteorology	M,O
Molecular Biology	M,O
Music	M,O
Nutrition	M,O
Occupational Therapy	M,O
Philosophy	M,O
Photography	M,O
Physics	M,O
Physiology	M,O
Psychology—General	M,O
Public Administration	M,O
Public Health—General	M,O
Real Estate	M,O
Recreation and Park Management	M,O
School Psychology	M,D,O
Science Education	M,O
Social Work	M,O
Sociology	M,O
Spanish	M,O
Sports Management	M,O
Statistics	M,O
Sustainable Development	M,O
Taxation	M
Theater	M,O
Transportation Management	M
Writing	M

THE SANTA BARBARA AND VENTURA COLLEGES OF LAW–SANTA BARBARA

Law	M,D
Legal and Justice Studies	M,D

THE SANTA BARBARA AND VENTURA COLLEGES OF LAW–VENTURA

Law	M,D
Legal and Justice Studies	M,D

SANTA CLARA UNIVERSITY

Applied Mathematics	M,D,O
Bioengineering	M,D,O
Business Administration and Management—General	M
Civil Engineering	M,D,O
Computer Engineering	M,D,O
Computer Science	M,D,O
Counseling Psychology	M
Counselor Education	M
Education—General	M
Educational Leadership and Administration	M
Electrical Engineering	M,D,O
Energy and Power Engineering	M,D,O
Engineering and Applied Sciences—General	M,D,O
Engineering Management	M,D,O
Ethics	M
Finance and Banking	M
Intellectual Property Law	M,D
Law	M,D
Management Information Systems	M
Mechanical Engineering	M,D,O
Pastoral Ministry and Counseling	M,D,O

Religion	M,D,O
Software Engineering	M,D,O
Supply Chain Management	M
Theology	M,D,O

SARAH LAWRENCE COLLEGE

Child Development	M
Dance	M
Education—General	M
Genetic Counseling	M
History	M
Human Genetics	M
Kinesiology and Movement Studies	M
Public Health—General	M
Theater	M
Women's Studies	M
Writing	M

SAVANNAH COLLEGE OF ART AND DESIGN

Advertising and Public Relations	M
Applied Arts and Design—General	M
Architectural History	M
Architecture	M
Art History	M
Art/Fine Arts	M
Arts Administration	M
Clothing and Textiles	M
Computer Art and Design	M
Film, Television, and Video Production	M
Film, Television, and Video Theory and Criticism	M
Game Design and Development	M
Graphic Design	M
Historic Preservation	M
Illustration	M
Industrial Design	M
Interior Design	M
Internet and Interactive Multimedia	M
Media Studies	M
Music	M
Photography	M
Sustainable Development	M
Textile Design	M
Theater	M
Travel and Tourism	M
Urban Design	M
Writing	M

SAVANNAH LAW SCHOOL

Law	D

SAVANNAH STATE UNIVERSITY

Business Administration and Management—General	M
Human Resources Management	M
Marine Sciences	M
Public Administration	M
Social Work	M
Urban and Regional Planning	M
Urban Studies	M

SAYBROOK UNIVERSITY

Clinical Psychology	M
Counseling Psychology	M
Health Psychology	M,D
Marriage and Family Therapy	M,D
Nutrition	M,D,O
Organizational Behavior	M,D
Organizational Management	M,D
Psychology—General	M,D
Sustainable Development	M,D
Transpersonal and Humanistic Psychology	M,D

SCHILLER INTERNATIONAL UNIVERSITY (GERMANY)

Business Administration and Management—General	M
International Business	M
Management Information Systems	M

SCHILLER INTERNATIONAL UNIVERSITY

Business Administration and Management—General	M
International Affairs	M
International Business	M

SCHILLER INTERNATIONAL UNIVERSITY (SPAIN)

Business Administration and Management—General	M
International Business	M

SCHILLER INTERNATIONAL UNIVERSITY (UNITED STATES)

Business Administration and Management—General	M
Finance and Banking	M
Hospitality Management	M
International Business	M
Management Information Systems	M
Travel and Tourism	M

SCHOOL OF ADVANCED AIR AND SPACE STUDIES

Military and Defense Studies	M

SCHOOL OF ARCHITECTURE AT TALIESIN

Architecture	M*

SCHOOL OF THE ART INSTITUTE OF CHICAGO

Applied Arts and Design—General	M
Architecture	M
Art Education	M
Art History	M
Art Therapy	M
Art/Fine Arts	M
Arts Administration	M
Arts Journalism	M
Film, Television, and Video Production	M

Graphic Design	M
Historic Preservation	M
Interior Design	M
Journalism	M
Materials Sciences	M
Music	M
Photography	M
Textile Design	M,O
Writing	M,O

SCHOOL OF VISUAL ARTS (NY)

Applied Arts and Design—General	M
Art Education	M
Art History	M
Art Therapy	M
Art/Fine Arts	M
Computer Art and Design	M
Cultural Studies	M
Film, Television, and Video Production	M
Graphic Design	M
Illustration	M
Internet and Interactive Multimedia	M
Photography	M
Writing	M

SCHREINER UNIVERSITY

Business Administration and Management—General	M
Education—General	M,O
Educational Leadership and Administration	M,O
Ethics	M

THE SCRIPPS RESEARCH INSTITUTE

Biological and Biomedical Sciences—General	D
Chemistry	D

SEATTLE INSTITUTE OF ORIENTAL MEDICINE

Acupuncture and Oriental Medicine	M

SEATTLE PACIFIC UNIVERSITY

Adult Nursing	M,O
Business Administration and Management—General	M
Clinical Psychology	D
Counselor Education	M,D,O
Education—General	D
Educational Leadership and Administration	M,D,O
Educational Media/Instructional Technology	M
English as a Second Language	M
Family Nurse Practitioner Studies	M,O
Gerontological Nursing	M,O
Human Resources Management	M
Industrial and Organizational Psychology	M,D
Management Information Systems	M
Marriage and Family Therapy	M,O
Mathematics Education	M
Nursing and Healthcare Administration	M,O
Nursing Education	M,O
Nursing Informatics	M,O
Nursing—General	M,O
Reading Education	M
Religion	M,O
Science Education	M
Secondary Education	M
Sustainability Management	M
Theology	M,O
Writing	M

THE SEATTLE SCHOOL OF THEOLOGY AND PSYCHOLOGY

Counseling Psychology	M
Psychology—General	M
Religion	M
Theology	M

SEATTLE UNIVERSITY

Accounting	M
Adult Education	M,O
Adult Nursing	M
Arts Administration	M
Business Administration and Management—General	M,O
Community Health Nursing	M
Computer Science	M
Counselor Education	M,O
Criminal Justice and Criminology	M,O
Database Systems	M,O
Education—General	M,D,O
Educational Leadership and Administration	M,D,O
Engineering and Applied Sciences—General	M
English as a Second Language	M,O
Family Nurse Practitioner Studies	M
Finance and Banking	M,O
Forensic Sciences	M,O
Gerontological Nursing	M
Law	D
Marriage and Family Therapy	M
Nurse Midwifery	M
Nursing—General	M,D
Organizational Management	M,O
Pastoral Ministry and Counseling	M
Psychiatric Nursing	M
Psychology—General	M
Public Administration	M
School Psychology	M,O
Social Work	M
Software Engineering	M
Special Education	M,O
Sports Management	M
Theology	M,D,O
Transpersonal and Humanistic Psychology	M

SELMA UNIVERSITY

Pastoral Ministry and Counseling	M

Religion | M

SEMINARY OF THE SOUTHWEST
Theology | M,O

SETON HALL UNIVERSITY
Accounting | M,O
Adult Nursing | M,D
Advertising and Public Relations | M
Allied Health—General | D
Analytical Chemistry | M
Asian Studies | M
Athletic Training and Sports Medicine | M
Biochemistry | M,D
Biological and Biomedical Sciences—General | M,D
Business Administration and Management—General | M,D
Chemistry | M,D
Communication Disorders | M
Communication—General | M
Corporate and Organizational Communication | M
Counseling Psychology | M,D
Counselor Education | M,D
Education—General | M,D,O
Educational Leadership and Administration | D,O
Educational Measurement and Evaluation | M,D,O
Educational Media/Instructional Technology | M
English | M
Entrepreneurship | M,O
Experimental Psychology | M
Finance and Banking | M,O
Gerontological Nursing | M,D
Health Law | M,D
Health Services Management and Hospital Administration | M,D
Higher Education | D
History | M
Inorganic Chemistry | M,D
International Affairs | M,O
International Business | M,O
International Health | M,O
Jewish Studies | M,O
Law | M,D
Management of Technology | M,O
Marketing | M
Marriage and Family Therapy | M
Microbiology | M,D
Molecular Biology | M,D
Museum Education | M
Museum Studies | M
Neuroscience | M,D
Nonprofit Management | M,O
Nursing and Healthcare Administration | M,D
Nursing Education | M,D
Nursing—General | M,D
Occupational Therapy | M
Organic Chemistry | M,D
Pastoral Ministry and Counseling | M,O
Pediatric Nursing | M,D
Physical Chemistry | M,D
Physical Therapy | D
Physician Assistant Studies | M
Psychology—General | M,D
Public Administration | M,O
Public Policy | M,O
Religion | M,O
School Nursing | M
School Psychology | M
Social Work | M
Special Education | M
Speech and Interpersonal Communication | M
Sport Psychology | M
Sports Management | M,O
Student Affairs | M
Supply Chain Management | M,O
Taxation | O
Theology | M,O

SETON HILL UNIVERSITY
Accounting | M,O
Art Therapy | M
Business Administration and Management—General | M,O
Elementary Education | M,O
Entrepreneurship | M,O
Holocaust and Genocide Studies | O
Marriage and Family Therapy | M
Middle School Education | M,O
Oral and Dental Sciences | M,O
Physician Assistant Studies | M
Special Education | M
Writing | M,O

SEWANEE: THE UNIVERSITY OF THE SOUTH
English | M
Theology | M,D
Writing | M

SHASTA BIBLE COLLEGE
Educational Leadership and Administration | M
Pastoral Ministry and Counseling | M
Religious Education | M

SHAWNEE STATE UNIVERSITY
Curriculum and Instruction | M
Education—General | M
Occupational Therapy | M

SHAW UNIVERSITY
Curriculum and Instruction | M
Early Childhood Education | M
Theology | M

SHENANDOAH UNIVERSITY
Adult Nursing | M,D,O
Allied Health—General | M,D,O
Applied Behavior Analysis | M
Athletic Training and Sports Medicine | M
Business Administration and Management—General | M,O
Education—General | M,D,O
Educational Leadership and Administration | M,D,O
Family Nurse Practitioner Studies | M,D,O
Gerontological Nursing | M,D,O
Health Education | M,D,O
Health Services Management and Hospital Administration | M,O
Middle School Education | M,D,O
Music Education | M,D,O
Music | M,D,O
Nurse Midwifery | M,D,O
Nursing and Healthcare Administration | M,D,O
Nursing Education | M,D,O
Nursing—General | M,D,O
Occupational Therapy | M,D,O
Pharmacy | D
Physical Education | M,D,O
Physical Therapy | M,D,O
Physician Assistant Studies | M,D,O
Psychiatric Nursing | M,D,O
Reading Education | M,D,O
Secondary Education | M,D,O
Special Education | M,D,O
Therapies—Dance, Drama, and Music | M,D,O

SHEPHERDS THEOLOGICAL SEMINARY
Pastoral Ministry and Counseling | M
Theology | M

SHEPHERD UNIVERSITY (CA)
Computer Art and Design | M
Game Design and Development | M
Management Information Systems | M
Music | M
Theology | M,D

SHEPHERD UNIVERSITY (WV)
Curriculum and Instruction | M

SHERMAN COLLEGE OF CHIROPRACTIC
Chiropractic | D

SHILOH UNIVERSITY
Pastoral Ministry and Counseling | M,D
Theology | M,D

SHIPPENSBURG UNIVERSITY OF PENNSYLVANIA
Biological and Biomedical Sciences—General | M
Business Administration and Management—General | M,O
Clinical Psychology | M,D,O
Communication—General | M
Computer and Information Systems Security | M,O
Computer Science | M,O
Counselor Education | M,D,O
Criminal Justice and Criminology | M
Curriculum and Instruction | M,O
Distance Education Development | M,O
Early Childhood Education | M,O
Education—General | M,D,O
Educational Leadership and Administration | M,D
Elementary Education | M,O
English as a Second Language | M,O
Environmental Management and Policy | M
Finance and Banking | M,O
Foreign Languages Education | M,O
Geography | M,O
Health Services Management and Hospital Administration | M,O
Higher Education | M
History | M,O
Information Science | M,O
Logistics | M,O
Management Information Systems | M,O
Marriage and Family Therapy | M,D,O
Mathematics Education | M,O
Middle School Education | M,O
Organizational Management | M
Psychology—General | M
Public Administration | M
Public History | M
Reading Education | M,O
Science Education | M,O
Social Work | M
Sociology | M
Software Engineering | M,O
Special Education | M,D
Student Affairs | M,D,O
Supply Chain Management | M,O

SHORTER UNIVERSITY
Accounting | M
Business Administration and Management—General | M

SH'OR YOSHUV RABBINICAL COLLEGE
Theology | M

SIENA COLLEGE
Accounting | M
Business Administration and Management—General | M

SIENA HEIGHTS UNIVERSITY
Clinical Psychology | M,O
Counseling Psychology | M,O

Early Childhood Education | M,O
Education—General | M,O
Educational Leadership and Administration | M,O
Elementary Education | M,O
Health Services Management and Hospital Administration | M,O
Higher Education | M,O
Organizational Management | M,O
Reading Education | M,O
Secondary Education | M,O
Special Education | M,O

SIERRA NEVADA COLLEGE
Education—General | M
Educational Leadership and Administration | M
Elementary Education | M
Secondary Education | M

SILICON VALLEY UNIVERSITY
Business Administration and Management—General | M
Computer Engineering | M
Computer Science | M

SILVER LAKE COLLEGE OF THE HOLY FAMILY
Business Administration and Management—General | M
Education—General | M
Educational Leadership and Administration | M
Music | M

SIMMONS COLLEGE
Applied Behavior Analysis | M,D,O
Business Administration and Management—General | M
Communication—General | M
Cultural Studies | M
Education—General | M,D,O
Elementary Education | M,D,O
English | M
Family Nurse Practitioner Studies | M,D,O
Gender Studies | M
Health Education | M,D,O
Health Promotion | M,D,O
Health Services Management and Hospital Administration | M
History | M
Information Science | M,D,O
Library Science | M,D,O
Nonprofit Management | M
Nursing—General | M,D,O
Nutrition | M,D,O
Physical Therapy | M,D,O
Public Health—General | M
Public Policy | M
Reading Education | M,D,O
Social Work | M,D,O
Special Education | M,D,O
Writing | M,D,O

SIMON FRASER UNIVERSITY
Actuarial Science | M,D
Anthropology | M,D
Applied Mathematics | M,D
Archaeology | M,D
Art Education | M,D
Biochemistry | M,D,O
Bioinformatics | M,D,O
Biological and Biomedical Sciences—General | M,D,O
Biotechnology | M,D,O
Business Administration and Management—General | M,D,O
Chemistry | M,D
Communication—General | M,D
Comparative and Interdisciplinary Arts | M
Computational Sciences | M,D
Computer Science | M,D
Counselor Education | M
Criminal Justice and Criminology | M,D
Cultural Studies | D
Curriculum and Instruction | M,D
Economics | M,D
Education—General | M,D,O
Educational Leadership and Administration | M,D
Educational Media/Instructional Technology | M,D
Educational Psychology | M,D
Engineering and Applied Sciences—General | M,D
English as a Second Language | M
English Education | M,D
English | M,D
Entomology | M,D,O
Environmental Management and Policy | M,D,O
Finance and Banking | M,D,O
Fish, Game, and Wildlife Management | M,D,O
Foundations and Philosophy of Education | M,D
French | M
Gender Studies | M,D
Geography | M,D
Geosciences | M,D
Gerontology | M,D
History | M,D
Humanities | M
International Affairs | M
International Health | M,D,O
Kinesiology and Movement Studies | M,D
Latin American Studies | M,O
Legal and Justice Studies | M,D
Liberal Studies | M
Linguistics | M,D
Management of Technology | M,D,O

Mathematics Education | M,D
Mathematics | M,D
Mechanical Engineering | M,D
Molecular Biology | M,D,O
Operations Research | M,D
Philosophy | M,D
Physics | M,D
Political Science | M,D
Psychology—General | M,D
Public Health—General | M,D,O
Public Policy | M
Publishing | M
Reading Education | D
Sociology | M,D
Statistics | M,D
Systems Engineering | M,D
Toxicology | M,D,O
Urban Studies | M,O
Women's Studies | M,D

SIMPSON COLLEGE
Criminal Justice and Criminology | M
Education—General | M
Secondary Education | M

SIMPSON UNIVERSITY
Counseling Psychology | M
Curriculum and Instruction | M
Education—General | M
Educational Leadership and Administration | M
Missions and Missiology | M
Organizational Management | M
Pastoral Ministry and Counseling | M

SINTE GLESKA UNIVERSITY
Education—General | M
Elementary Education | M

SIOUX FALLS SEMINARY
Marriage and Family Therapy | M
Pastoral Ministry and Counseling | M
Religion | M
Theology | M,D,O

SIT GRADUATE INSTITUTE
Business Administration and Management—General | M
Conflict Resolution and Mediation/Peace Studies | M
Educational Leadership and Administration | M
English as a Second Language | M
International Affairs | M
International and Comparative Education | M
International Business | M
Organizational Management | M
Sustainable Development | M

SITTING BULL COLLEGE
Environmental Sciences | M

SLIPPERY ROCK UNIVERSITY OF PENNSYLVANIA
Accounting | M
Business Administration and Management—General | M
Clinical Psychology | M
Counseling Psychology | M
Counselor Education | M
Criminal Justice and Criminology | M
Database Systems | M
Education—General | M,D
Educational Leadership and Administration | M,D
Educational Media/Instructional Technology | M,D
Elementary Education | M
English as a Second Language | M
English Education | M
English | M
Environmental Education | M
Environmental Management and Policy | M
Finance and Banking | M
Health Informatics | M
History | M
Marketing | M
Mathematics Education | M
Physical Education | M
Physical Therapy | D
Physician Assistant Studies | M
Public Health—General | M
Reading Education | M
Recreation and Park Management | M
School Psychology | M
Science Education | M
Secondary Education | M
Social Sciences Education | M
Special Education | M,D
Student Affairs | M
Therapies—Dance, Drama, and Music | M

SMITH COLLEGE
Biological and Biomedical Sciences—General | M
Chemistry | M
Dance | M
Education—General | M
Elementary Education | M
English Education | M
Exercise and Sports Science | M
Foreign Languages Education | M
French | M
History | M
Mathematics Education | M
Mathematics | O
Middle School Education | M
Science Education | M
Secondary Education | M
Social Sciences Education | M

---

*M—masters degree; D—doctorate; O—other advanced degree; *—Close-Up and/or Display*

Social Work M,D
Spanish M
Theater M
Women's Studies O

SOFIA UNIVERSITY
Clinical Psychology M,D
Computer Science M,D
Counseling Psychology M,D
Psychology—General M,D
Transpersonal and Humanistic
 Psychology M,D

SOKA UNIVERSITY OF AMERICA
Educational Leadership and
 Administration M*

SONOMA STATE UNIVERSITY
Anthropology M
Biochemistry M
Biological and Biomedical
 Sciences—General M
Business Administration and
 Management—General M
Cell Biology M
Clinical Psychology M
Counseling Psychology M
Curriculum and Instruction M,O
Early Childhood Education M,O
Ecology M
Education—General M,O
Educational Leadership and
 Administration M,O
English M
Entrepreneurship M
Environmental Biology M
Evolutionary Biology M
Family Nurse Practitioner Studies M
Health Promotion M
History M
Interdisciplinary Studies M
International Business M
Kinesiology and Movement Studies M
Molecular Biology M
Nonprofit Management M,O
Nursing—General M
Occupational Therapy M
Physical Education M
Physical Therapy M
Political Science M,O
Public Administration M,O
Public History M
Reading Education M,O
School Psychology M
Special Education M,O
Sports Management M
Writing M

SOTHEBY'S INSTITUTE OF ART–LONDON
Art/Fine Arts M
Arts Administration M
Decorative Arts M

SOTHEBY'S INSTITUTE OF ART–NEW YORK
Art/Fine Arts M
Arts Administration M
Decorative Arts M

SOUTH BAYLO UNIVERSITY
Acupuncture and Oriental Medicine M

SOUTH CAROLINA STATE UNIVERSITY
Agricultural Economics and
 Agribusiness M
Allied Health—General M
Biological and Biomedical
 Sciences—General M
Business Administration and
 Management—General M
Business Education M
Child and Family Studies M
Civil Engineering M
Communication Disorders M
Counselor Education M
Early Childhood Education M
Education—General M
Educational Leadership and
 Administration D,O
Elementary Education M
English Education M
English M
Entrepreneurship M
Family and Consumer
 Sciences-General M
Health Services Management and
 Hospital Administration M
Home Economics Education M
Human Services M
Mathematics Education M
Mathematics M
Mechanical Engineering M
Nutrition M
Rehabilitation Counseling M
Science Education M
Secondary Education M
Social Sciences Education M
Special Education M
Transportation and Highway
 Engineering M
Vocational and Technical Education M

SOUTH COLLEGE
Pharmacy D
Physician Assistant Studies M

SOUTH DAKOTA SCHOOL OF MINES AND TECHNOLOGY
Artificial Intelligence/Robotics M
Atmospheric Sciences M,D
Bioengineering D
Biomedical Engineering M,D
Chemical Engineering M,D
Civil Engineering M,D
Construction Management M
Electrical Engineering M

Engineering and Applied
 Sciences—General M,D
Engineering Management M
Environmental Sciences D
Geological Engineering M,D
Geology M,D
Management of Technology M
Materials Engineering M,D
Materials Sciences M,D
Mechanical Engineering M,D
Mineral/Mining Engineering M,D
Nanotechnology D
Paleontology M,D
Physics M,D

SOUTH DAKOTA STATE UNIVERSITY
Agricultural Education M
Agricultural Engineering M,D
Agricultural Sciences—
 General M,D
Agronomy and Soil Sciences M,D
Animal Sciences M,D
Athletic Training and Sports
 Medicine M,D
Biological and Biomedical
 Sciences—General M,D
Biosystems Engineering M,D
Chemistry M,D
Civil Engineering M
Communication—General M
Computational Sciences M,D
Consumer Economics M
Counselor Education M
Curriculum and Instruction M
Economics M
Education—General M,D
Educational Leadership and
 Administration M,D
Electrical Engineering M,D
Engineering and Applied
 Sciences—General M,D
English M
Exercise and Sports Science M,D
Family and Consumer
 Sciences-General M
Fish, Game, and Wildlife
 Management M,D
Geography M
Geosciences D
Human Resources Development M
Industrial and Organizational
 Psychology M
Industrial/Management
 Engineering M
Journalism M
Mathematics M,D
Mechanical Engineering M,D
Microbiology M,D
Nursing—General M,D
Nutrition M,D
Pharmaceutical Sciences M,D
Pharmacy D
Physics M
Plant Sciences M,D
Recreation and Park Management M,D
Sociology M,D
Statistics M,D
Veterinary Sciences M,D

SOUTHEASTERN BAPTIST THEOLOGICAL SEMINARY
Ethics M,D
Missions and Missiology M,D
Music M,D
Philosophy M,D
Psychology—General M,D
Religious Education M,D
Theology M,D
Women's Studies M,D

SOUTHEASTERN LOUISIANA UNIVERSITY
Applied Science and
 Technology M
Biological and Biomedical
 Sciences—General M
Business Administration and
 Management—General M
Communication Disorders M
Communication—General M
Counselor Education M
Curriculum and Instruction M
Education—General M,D
Educational Leadership and
 Administration M,D
Elementary Education M
English Education M
English M
Exercise and Sports Science M
Family Nurse Practitioner Studies M,D
Health Education M
Health Promotion M
History M
Industrial and Organizational
 Psychology M
Kinesiology and Movement Studies M
Music M
Nursing Education M,D
Nursing—General M,D
Psychiatric Nursing M,D
Psychology—General M
Reading Education M
Sociology M
Special Education M
Writing M

SOUTHEASTERN OKLAHOMA STATE UNIVERSITY
Aviation Management M
Aviation M
Biotechnology M
Business Administration and
 Management—General M
Clinical Psychology M
Counseling Psychology M

Counselor Education M
Education—General M
Educational Leadership and
 Administration M
Environmental and Occupational
 Health M
Management Information Systems M
Mathematics Education M
Reading Education M

SOUTHEASTERN UNIVERSITY (FL)
Business Administration and
 Management—General M
Counseling Psychology M
Counselor Education M
Curriculum and Instruction M
Education of the Gifted M,D
Education—General M,D
Educational Leadership and
 Administration M,D
Elementary Education M,D
English as a Second Language M,D
Entrepreneurship M
Human Services M
Marriage and Family Therapy M
Organizational Management M,D
Pastoral Ministry and Counseling M,D
Reading Education M,D
Social Work M
Sports Management M
Theology M,D
Urban and Regional Planning M

SOUTHEAST MISSOURI STATE UNIVERSITY
Accounting M
Biological and Biomedical
 Sciences—General M
Business Administration and
 Management—General M
Chemistry M
Communication Disorders M
Counseling Psychology M,O
Counselor Education M
Criminal Justice and Criminology M
Educational Leadership and
 Administration M,D,O
Elementary Education M,D,O
English as a Second Language M
English M
Entrepreneurship M
Environmental Management
 and Policy M
Environmental Sciences M
Exercise and Sports Science M
Finance and Banking M
Higher Education M,D,O
Historic Preservation M,O
History M,O
Leisure Studies M
Management of Technology M
Mathematics M
Middle School Education M
Nursing—General M
Public Administration M
Public History M,O
Secondary Education M,D,O
Special Education M
Sports Management M

SOUTHERN ADVENTIST UNIVERSITY
Accounting M
Acute Care/Critical Care Nursing M
Adult Nursing M
Business Administration and
 Management—General M
Counseling Psychology M
Counselor Education M
Education—General M
Educational Leadership and
 Administration M
Family Nurse Practitioner Studies M
Finance and Banking M
Health Services Management and
 Hospital Administration M
Marketing M
Missions and Missiology M
Nonprofit Management M
Nursing and Healthcare
 Administration M
Nursing—General M
Psychology—General M
Reading Education M
Recreation and Park Management M
Religion M
Religious Education M
Social Work M
Theology M

SOUTHERN ARKANSAS UNIVERSITY–MAGNOLIA
Adult Education M
Agricultural Sciences—
 General M
Business Administration and
 Management—General M
Computer and Information
 Systems Security M
Computer Science M
Counselor Education M
Curriculum and Instruction M
Database Systems M
Education of the Gifted M
Education—General M
Educational Leadership and
 Administration M
Higher Education M
Information Science M
Kinesiology and Movement Studies M
Library Science M
Organizational Management M
Psychiatric Nursing M
Public Administration M
Student Affairs M
Supply Chain Management M

THE SOUTHERN BAPTIST THEOLOGICAL SEMINARY
Missions and Missiology M,D
Pastoral Ministry and Counseling M,D
Philosophy M,D
Religion M,D
Theology M,D

SOUTHERN CALIFORNIA INSTITUTE OF ARCHITECTURE
Architecture M*

SOUTHERN CALIFORNIA SEMINARY
Counseling Psychology M,D
Marriage and Family Therapy M,D
Psychology—General M,D
Religion M,D
Theology M,D

SOUTHERN CALIFORNIA UNIVERSITY OF HEALTH SCIENCES
Acupuncture and Oriental Medicine M,D
Chiropractic D

SOUTHERN COLLEGE OF OPTOMETRY
Optometry D

SOUTHERN CONNECTICUT STATE UNIVERSITY
Art Education M
Biological and Biomedical
 Sciences—General M
Business Administration and
 Management—General M
Chemistry M
Communication Disorders M
Computer Science M
Counselor Education M,O
Education—General M,D,O
Educational Leadership and
 Administration M,D,O
Educational Measurement and
 Evaluation M,D,O
Elementary Education M,O
English as a Second Language M
English M
Environmental Education M,O
Environmental Sciences M,O
Exercise and Sports Science M
Family Nurse Practitioner Studies M
Foreign Languages Education M
Health Education M
History M
Information Studies M,O
Leisure Studies M
Library Science M,O
Marine Sciences M,O
Mathematics M
Multilingual and Multicultural
 Education M
Nursing Education M,D
Nursing—General M,D
Physical Education M
Political Science M
Psychology—General M
Public Health—General M
Reading Education M
Recreation and Park Management M
School Psychology M,O
Science Education M,O
Social Work M
Sociology M
Special Education M
Women's Studies M

SOUTHERN EVANGELICAL SEMINARY
Jewish Studies M,D,O
Missions and Missiology M,D,O
Near and Middle Eastern Studies M,D,O
Pastoral Ministry and Counseling M,D,O
Philosophy M,D,O
Religion M,D,O
Religious Education M,D,O
Theology M,D,O

SOUTHERN ILLINOIS UNIVERSITY CARBONDALE
Accounting M,D
Agricultural Economics and
 Agribusiness M
Agricultural Sciences—
 General M
Agronomy and Soil Sciences M
Animal Sciences M
Anthropology M,D
Applied Arts and Design—General M
Applied Physics M,D
Architecture M
Art/Fine Arts M
Biochemistry M,D
Biological and Biomedical
 Sciences—General M,D
Biomedical Engineering M
Business Administration and
 Management—General M,D
Chemistry M,D
Civil Engineering M,D
Clinical Psychology M,D
Communication Disorders M
Communication—General M,D
Community Health M
Computer Engineering M,D
Computer Science M,D
Counseling Psychology M,D
Criminal Justice and Criminology M
Cultural Studies M
Curriculum and Instruction M,D
Economics M,D
Education—General M,D
Educational Leadership and
 Administration M,D
Educational Psychology M,D
Electrical Engineering M,D
Energy and Power
 Engineering D

Engineering and Applied
Sciences—General — M,D
Engineering Management — M
English as a Second Language — M
English — M,D
Environmental Engineering — D
Environmental Management
and Policy — M,D
Environmental Sciences — D
Experimental Psychology — M,D
Forestry — M
Geography — M,D
Geology — M,D
Geosciences — M,D
Health Education — M,D
Health Law — M
Health Services Management and
Hospital Administration — M
Higher Education — M,D
History — M,D
Homeland Security — M
Kinesiology and Movement Studies — M
Law — M
Legal and Justice Studies — M
Linguistics — M
Mass Communication — M,D
Mathematics — M,D
Mechanical Engineering — M,D
Mechanics — M
Media Studies — M,D
Medical Physics — M
Microbiology — M,D
Mineral/Mining Engineering — M
Molecular Biology — M,D
Music — M
Nutrition — M
Pharmacology — M,D
Philosophy — M,D
Physical Education — M
Physician Assistant Studies — M
Physics — M,D
Physiology — M,D
Plant Biology — M,D
Plant Sciences — M
Political Science — M,D
Psychology—General — M,D
Public Administration — M
Recreation and Park Management — M
Rhetoric — M,D
Social Work — M
Sociology — M,D
Special Education — M,D
Speech and Interpersonal
Communication — M,D
Theater — M
Vocational and Technical Education — M,D
Writing — M
Zoology — M,D

SOUTHERN ILLINOIS UNIVERSITY EDWARDSVILLE
Accounting — M
Advertising and Public Relations — M
Applied Mathematics — M
Art Therapy — M
Art/Fine Arts — M
Biological and Biomedical
Sciences—General — M
Business Administration and
Management—General — M
Chemistry — M
Civil Engineering — M
Clinical Psychology — M
Communication Disorders — M
Computational Sciences — M
Computer Science — M
Corporate and Organizational
Communication — M
Cultural Anthropology — M
Curriculum and Instruction — M
Dentistry — D
Economics — M
Education—General — M,D,O
Educational Leadership and
Administration — M,D,O
Educational Media/Instructional
Technology — M,O
Electrical Engineering — M
Engineering and Applied
Sciences—General — M
English as a Second Language — M,O
English Education — M,O
English — M,O
Environmental Engineering — M
Environmental Management
and Policy — M
Environmental Sciences — M
Exercise and Sports Science — M
Family Nurse Practitioner Studies — M,D,O
Finance and Banking — M
Foundations and Philosophy of
Education — M
Geography — M
Geotechnical Engineering — M
Health Communication — M
Health Education — M,D,O
Health Informatics — M
Higher Education — M
History — M
Industrial and Organizational
Psychology — M
Industrial/Management
Engineering — M
Interdisciplinary Studies — M
Kinesiology and Movement Studies — M
Management Information Systems — M
Management Strategy and Policy — M
Marketing Research — M
Mass Communication — M
Mathematics Education — M
Mathematics — M

Mechanical Engineering — M
Media Studies — O
Museum Studies — M
Music Education — M,O
Music — M
Nurse Anesthesia — D
Nursing and Healthcare
Administration — M,O
Nursing Education — M,O
Nursing—General — M,D,O
Operations Research — M
Pharmacy — D
Physical Education — M
Project Management — M
Psychology—General — M,O
Public Administration — M
Reading Education — M,O
School Psychology — O
Social Work — M
Sociology — M
Special Education — M,O
Speech and Interpersonal
Communication — M
Sport Psychology — M
Statistics — M
Structural Engineering — M
Student Affairs — M
Sustainable Development — M
Taxation — M
Transportation and Highway
Engineering — M
Writing — M

SOUTHERN METHODIST UNIVERSITY
Accounting — M
Advertising and Public Relations — M
Anthropology — M,D
Applied Economics — M,D
Applied Mathematics — M,D
Applied Science and
Technology — M,D
Art History — M,D
Art/Fine Arts — M
Arts Administration — M
Atmospheric Sciences — M,D
Biological and Biomedical
Sciences—General — M,D
Business Administration and
Management—General — M
Cell Biology — M,D
Chemistry — M,D
Civil Engineering — M,D
Clinical Psychology — D
Computational Sciences — M,D
Computer Engineering — M,D
Computer Science — M,D
Conflict Resolution and
Mediation/Peace Studies — M
Counselor Education — M
Database Systems — M
Economics — M,D
Education of the Gifted — M,D
Education—General — M,D
Electrical Engineering — M,D
Engineering and Applied
Sciences—General — M,D
Engineering Management — M,D
English — M,D
Entrepreneurship — M
Environmental Engineering — M,D
Environmental Sciences — M,D
Ethics — M,D
Experimental Psychology — M,D
Finance and Banking — M
Geology — M,D
Geophysics — M,D
History — M,D
Information Science — M,D
Law — M,D
Liberal Studies — M
Management Information Systems — M
Management Strategy and Policy — M
Manufacturing Engineering — M,D
Marketing — M
Materials Engineering — M,D
Materials Sciences — M,D
Mathematics — M,D
Mechanical Engineering — M,D
Medieval and Renaissance Studies — M
Molecular Biology — M,D
Multilingual and Multicultural
Education — M,D
Music Education — M
Music — M
Operations Research — M,D
Photography — M
Physics — M,D
Physiology — M
Psychology—General — D
Reading Education — M,D
Real Estate — M
Religion — M,D
Software Engineering — M,D
Special Education — M,D
Sports Management — M
Statistics — M,D
Structural Engineering — M,D
Sustainable Development — M,D
Systems Engineering — M,D
Systems Science — M,D
Taxation — M,D
Telecommunications — M,D
Theater — M
Theology — M,D
Water Resources Engineering — M,D

SOUTHERN NAZARENE UNIVERSITY
Business Administration and
Management—General — M
Counseling Psychology — M

Health Services Management and
Hospital Administration — M
Marriage and Family Therapy — M
Nursing and Healthcare
Administration — M
Nursing Education — M
Nursing—General — M
Psychology—General — M
Sports Management — M

SOUTHERN NEW HAMPSHIRE UNIVERSITY
Accounting — M,O
Business Administration and
Management—General — M,O
Business Education — M,D,O
Child Development — M,D,O
Community Health — M,O
Conflict Resolution and
Mediation/Peace Studies — M,O
Curriculum and Instruction — M,D,O
Education—General — M,D,O
Educational Leadership and
Administration — M,D,O
Educational Media/Instructional
Technology — M,D,O
Elementary Education — M,D,O
English as a Second Language — M,D,O
English Education — M,D,O
Entrepreneurship — M,O
Environmental Management
and Policy — M,O
Ethics — M,O
Finance and Banking — M,O
Health Informatics — M,O
Health Services Management and
Hospital Administration — M,O
Human Resources Management — M,O
Industrial and Labor Relations — M,O
Industrial and Manufacturing
Management — M,O
International Business — M,O
Internet and Interactive
Multimedia — M,O
Investment Management — M,O
Legal and Justice Studies — M,O
Management Information Systems — M,O
Marketing — M,O
Nonprofit Management — M,O
Nursing and Healthcare
Administration — M,O
Nursing Education — M,O
Nursing—General — M,O
Organizational Management — M,O
Project Management — M,O
Psychology—General — M,O
Quality Management — M,O
Reading Education — M,D,O
Secondary Education — M,D,O
Special Education — M,D,O
Sports Management — M,O
Supply Chain Management — M,O
Sustainability Management — M,O
Taxation — M,O
Writing — M,O

SOUTHERN OREGON UNIVERSITY
Accounting — M,O
Business Administration and
Management—General — M,O
Computer Science — M
Counseling Psychology — M
Early Childhood Education — M
Education—General — M
Educational Leadership and
Administration — M
Elementary Education — M
Environmental Education — M
Foreign Languages Education — M
French — M
Interdisciplinary Studies — M
International Business — M,O
Music — M
Psychology—General — M
Reading Education — M
Secondary Education — M
Spanish — M
Special Education — M
Theater — M

SOUTHERN UNIVERSITY AND AGRICULTURAL AND MECHANICAL COLLEGE
Agricultural Sciences—
General — M
Analytical Chemistry — M
Biochemistry — M
Biological and Biomedical
Sciences—General — M
Business Administration and
Management—General — M
Chemistry — M
Communication Disorders — M
Computer Science — M
Counselor Education — M
Criminal Justice and Criminology — M
Education—General — M,D
Educational Leadership and
Administration — M
Educational Media/Instructional
Technology — M
Elementary Education — M
Engineering and Applied
Sciences—General — M
Environmental Sciences — M
Family Nurse Practitioner Studies — M,D,O
Forestry — M
Gerontological Nursing — M,D,O
History — M
Inorganic Chemistry — M
Law — D

Mass Communication — M
Mathematics Education — D
Mathematics — M
Nursing and Healthcare
Administration — M,D,O
Nursing Education — M,D,O
Nursing—General — M,D,O
Organic Chemistry — M
Physical Chemistry — M
Physics — M
Political Science — M
Psychology—General — M
Public Administration — M
Public Policy — D
Recreation and Park Management — M
Rehabilitation Counseling — M
Science Education — D
Secondary Education — M
Social Sciences — M
Special Education — M,D

SOUTHERN UNIVERSITY AT NEW ORLEANS
Criminal Justice and Criminology — M
Management Information Systems — M
Museum Studies — M
Social Work — M

SOUTHERN UTAH UNIVERSITY
Accounting — M
Arts Administration — M
Business Administration and
Management—General — M
Communication—General — M
Computer and Information
Systems Security — M
Education—General — M,O
Exercise and Sports Science — M
Music Education — M
Music — M
Public Administration — M

SOUTHERN WESLEYAN UNIVERSITY
Business Administration and
Management—General — M
Education—General — M
Pastoral Ministry and Counseling — M

SOUTH FLORIDA BIBLE COLLEGE AND THEOLOGICAL SEMINARY
Theology — M

SOUTH TEXAS COLLEGE OF LAW HOUSTON
Law — D

SOUTH UNIVERSITY (AL)
Business Administration and
Management—General — M
Counseling Psychology — M
Criminal Justice and Criminology — M
Health Services Management and
Hospital Administration — M
Management Information Systems — M
Nursing—General — M
Public Administration — M

SOUTH UNIVERSITY
Business Administration and
Management—General — M
Counseling Psychology — M
Criminal Justice and Criminology — M
Family Nurse Practitioner Studies — M
Health Services Management and
Hospital Administration — M
Management Information Systems — M
Nursing—General — M
Occupational Therapy — D
Public Administration — M

SOUTH UNIVERSITY
Adult Nursing — M
Business Administration and
Management—General — M
Criminal Justice and Criminology — M
Family Nurse Practitioner Studies — M
Health Services Management and
Hospital Administration — M
Management Information Systems — M
Nursing Education — M
Nursing—General — M
Physician Assistant Studies — M

SOUTH UNIVERSITY (GA)
Anesthesiologist Assistant Studies — M
Business Administration and
Management—General — M
Counseling Psychology — M
Criminal Justice and Criminology — M
Entrepreneurship — M
Health Services Management and
Hospital Administration — M
Hospitality Management — M
Nursing Education — M
Nursing—General — M
Organizational Management — M
Pastoral Ministry and Counseling — D
Pharmacy
Physician Assistant Studies — M
Public Administration — M
Sustainability Management — M

SOUTH UNIVERSITY (MI)
Business Administration and
Management—General — M
Counseling Psychology — M
Nursing—General — M
Organizational Management — M
Pastoral Ministry and Counseling — D

SOUTH UNIVERSITY (NC)
Business Administration and
Management—General — M
Counseling Psychology — M

---

*M—masters degree; D—doctorate; O—other advanced degree; *—Close-Up and/or Display*

SOUTH UNIVERSITY (OH)
Business Administration and Management—General	M
Clinical Psychology	M
Counseling Psychology	M

SOUTH UNIVERSITY (SC)
Business Administration and Management—General	M
Counseling Psychology	M
Criminal Justice and Criminology	M
Health Services Management and Hospital Administration	M
Nursing—General	M
Organizational Management	M
Pharmacy	D

SOUTH UNIVERSITY (TX)
Business Administration and Management—General	M
Counseling Psychology	M
Management Information Systems	M

SOUTH UNIVERSITY
Business Administration and Management—General	M
Counseling Psychology	M
Nursing—General	M

SOUTH UNIVERSITY
Business Administration and Management—General	M
Counseling Psychology	M
Family Nurse Practitioner Studies	M
Management Information Systems	M
Nursing—General	M
Organizational Management	M

SOUTHWEST ACUPUNCTURE COLLEGE
Acupuncture and Oriental Medicine	M

SOUTHWEST BAPTIST UNIVERSITY
Business Administration and Management—General	M
Education—General	M,O
Educational Leadership and Administration	M,O
Health Services Management and Hospital Administration	M
Physical Therapy	D

SOUTHWEST COLLEGE OF NATUROPATHIC MEDICINE AND HEALTH SCIENCES
Naturopathic Medicine	D

SOUTHWESTERN ADVENTIST UNIVERSITY
Accounting	M
Business Administration and Management—General	M
Curriculum and Instruction	M
Education—General	M
Educational Leadership and Administration	M
Finance and Banking	M
Reading Education	M

SOUTHWESTERN ASSEMBLIES OF GOD UNIVERSITY
Counseling Psychology	M
Curriculum and Instruction	M
Education—General	M
Educational Leadership and Administration	M
History	M
Missions and Missiology	M
Pastoral Ministry and Counseling	M
Religion	M
Religious Education	M
Secondary Education	M
Theology	M

SOUTHWESTERN BAPTIST THEOLOGICAL SEMINARY
Missions and Missiology	M,D
Music	M,D
Near and Middle Eastern Studies	M,D
Pastoral Ministry and Counseling	M,D,O
Religious Education	M,D
Theology	M,D

SOUTHWESTERN CHRISTIAN UNIVERSITY
Missions and Missiology	M
Pastoral Ministry and Counseling	M

SOUTHWESTERN COLLEGE (KS)
Business Administration and Management—General	M
Criminal Justice and Criminology	M
Curriculum and Instruction	M,D
Early Childhood Education	M,D
Education—General	M,D
Educational Leadership and Administration	M,D
Special Education	M,D

SOUTHWESTERN COLLEGE (NM)
Art Therapy	M
Counseling Psychology	M,O
Health Psychology	O
Psychology—General	O
Social Psychology	O
Thanatology	M,O

SOUTHWESTERN LAW SCHOOL
Law	M,D

SOUTHWESTERN OKLAHOMA STATE UNIVERSITY
Allied Health—General	M
Art Education	M
Business Administration and Management—General	M
Counselor Education	M
Early Childhood Education	M
Education—General	M

Educational Leadership and Administration	M
Educational Measurement and Evaluation	M
Elementary Education	M
English Education	M
Kinesiology and Movement Studies	M
Mathematics Education	M
Microbiology	M
Music Education	M
Music	M
Pharmacy	D
Recreation and Park Management	M
School Psychology	M
Science Education	M
Secondary Education	M
Social Sciences Education	M
Special Education	M

SOUTHWEST MINNESOTA STATE UNIVERSITY
Business Administration and Management—General	M
Early Childhood Education	M
Education—General	M
Educational Leadership and Administration	M
English as a Second Language	M
Marketing	M
Mathematics Education	M
Reading Education	M
Special Education	M

SOUTHWEST UNIVERSITY
Business Administration and Management—General	M
Criminal Justice and Criminology	M
Organizational Management	M

SOUTHWEST UNIVERSITY OF VISUAL ARTS
Art/Fine Arts	M
Photography	M

SPALDING UNIVERSITY
Adult Nursing	M,D,O
Art Education	M
Athletic Training and Sports Medicine	M
Business Education	M
Clinical Psychology	M,D
Corporate and Organizational Communication	M
Counselor Education	M
Education—General	M,D
Educational Leadership and Administration	M,D
Elementary Education	M
Family Nurse Practitioner Studies	M,D,O
Foreign Languages Education	M
Middle School Education	M
Nursing and Healthcare Administration	M,D,O
Nursing Education	M,D,O
Nursing—General	M,D,O
Occupational Therapy	M
Pediatric Nursing	M,D,O
Psychology—General	M,D
Secondary Education	M
Social Work	M
Special Education	M
Writing	M

SPERTUS INSTITUTE FOR JEWISH LEARNING AND LEADERSHIP
Jewish Studies	M,D

SPRING ARBOR UNIVERSITY
Business Administration and Management—General	M
Child and Family Studies	M
Communication—General	M
Counseling Psychology	M
Education—General	M
Nursing—General	M
Pastoral Ministry and Counseling	M
Reading Education	M
Special Education	M
Theology	M

SPRINGFIELD COLLEGE
Addictions/Substance Abuse Counseling	M
Art Therapy	M,O
Athletic Training and Sports Medicine	M,D
Business Administration and Management—General	M
Clinical Psychology	M,D,O
Counseling Psychology	M,D,O
Counselor Education	M,D,O
Education—General	M
Exercise and Sports Science	M,D
Health Promotion	M,D
Human Services	M
Industrial and Organizational Psychology	M,D,O
Occupational Therapy	M
Physical Education	M,D,O
Physical Therapy	D
Physician Assistant Studies	M
Recreation and Park Management	M
Rehabilitation Counseling	M
Secondary Education	M
Social Work	M,O
Special Education	M
Sport Psychology	M
Sports Management	M,D,O
Student Affairs	M,D,O

SPRING HILL COLLEGE
Art/Fine Arts	M,O
Business Administration and Management—General	M
Early Childhood Education	M
Education—General	M
Elementary Education	M

English	M,O
Ethics	M,O
Foundations and Philosophy of Education	M
History	M,O
Liberal Studies	M,O
Nursing and Healthcare Administration	M,O
Nursing—General	M,O
Pastoral Ministry and Counseling	M
Secondary Education	M
Social Sciences Education	M
Theology	M,O

STANBRIDGE UNIVERSITY
Nursing—General	M
Occupational Therapy	M

STANFORD UNIVERSITY
Aerospace/Aeronautical Engineering	M,D,O
Allopathic Medicine	D
Anthropology	M,D
Applied Arts and Design—General	M,D,O
Applied Physics	M,D
Archaeology	M,D
Art/Fine Arts	M,D
Asian Languages	M,D
Asian Studies	M
Biochemistry	D
Bioengineering	M,D
Biological and Biomedical Sciences—General	M,D
Biomedical Engineering	M,D,O
Biophysics	D
Biostatistics	M,D
Business Administration and Management—General	M,D
Chemical Engineering	M,D
Chemistry	D
Chinese	M,D
Civil Engineering	M,D,O
Classics	M,D
Clinical Research	M,D
Communication—General	M,D
Comparative Literature	D
Computational Sciences	M,D
Computer Science	M,D
Construction Engineering	M,D,O
Cultural Studies	M,D
Curriculum and Instruction	M,D
Developmental Biology	M,D
East European and Russian Studies	M
Ecology	M,D
Economics	D
Education—General	M,D
Educational Leadership and Administration	M
Educational Media/Instructional Technology	M
Educational Policy	M
Electrical Engineering	M,D
Elementary Education	M
Energy and Power Engineering	M,D,O
Engineering and Applied Sciences—General	M,D,O
Engineering Design	M
Engineering Management	M,D
Engineering Physics	M,D
English	M,D
Environmental Engineering	M,D,O
Environmental Law	M,D
Environmental Sciences	M,D,O
Epidemiology	M,D
Film, Television, and Video Production	M,D
French	M,D
Genetics	D
Geophysics	M,D
Geosciences	M,D,O
Geotechnical Engineering	M,D,O
German	M,D
Health Services Research	M,D
History	M,D
Hydrology	M,D,O
Immunology	D
Industrial/Management Engineering	M,D
International and Comparative Education	M,D
Italian	M,D
Japanese	M,D
Law	M,D
Legal and Justice Studies	M,D
Linguistics	M,D
Materials Engineering	M,D,O
Materials Sciences	M,D,O
Mathematics	M,D
Mechanical Engineering	M,D,O
Mechanics	M,D
Medical Informatics	M,D
Microbiology	D
Music	M,D
Philosophy	M,D
Physics	D
Physiology	D
Political Science	M,D
Psychology—General	D
Religion	D
Secondary Education	M
Slavic Languages	M,D
Sociology	D
Spanish	M,D
Statistics	M,D
Structural Biology	D
Structural Engineering	M,D,O
Sustainable Development	M,D,O
Systems Biology	D
Theater	D

STARR KING SCHOOL FOR THE MINISTRY
Theology	M

STATE UNIVERSITY OF NEW YORK AT FREDONIA
Biological and Biomedical Sciences—General	M
Communication Disorders	M
Curriculum and Instruction	M
Early Childhood Education	M
Education—General	M
English as a Second Language	M
Interdisciplinary Studies	M
Middle School Education	M
Music Education	M
Music	M
Reading Education	M
Secondary Education	M

STATE UNIVERSITY OF NEW YORK AT NEW PALTZ
Accounting	M
Art Education	M
Art/Fine Arts	M
Business Administration and Management—General	M
Chemistry	M,O
Communication Disorders	M
Computer Science	M
Counseling Psychology	M,O
Counselor Education	M,O
Early Childhood Education	M
Education—General	M,O
Educational Leadership and Administration	M,O
Electrical Engineering	M
Elementary Education	M
English as a Second Language	M,O
English Education	M,O
English	M,O
French	M,O
Geosciences	M,O
Mathematics Education	M
Multilingual and Multicultural Education	M,O
Music	M
Psychology—General	M,O
Reading Education	M
Science Education	M,O
Secondary Education	M,O
Social Sciences Education	M,O
Spanish	M,O
Special Education	M
Therapies—Dance, Drama, and Music	M

STATE UNIVERSITY OF NEW YORK AT OSWEGO
Agricultural Education	M
Art Education	M
Art/Fine Arts	M
Business Administration and Management—General	M
Business Education	M
Chemistry	M
Child and Family Studies	M
Communication—General	M
Consumer Economics	M
Corporate and Organizational Communication	M
Counseling Psychology	M
Curriculum and Instruction	M
Early Childhood Education	M
Education—General	M,O
Educational Leadership and Administration	O
Elementary Education	M
English	M
Graphic Design	M
Health Communication	M
History	M
Human-Computer Interaction	M
Internet and Interactive Multimedia	M
Middle School Education	M
Reading Education	M
Secondary Education	M
Special Education	M
Vocational and Technical Education	M

STATE UNIVERSITY OF NEW YORK AT PLATTSBURGH
Clinical Psychology	M,O
Communication Disorders	M
Counseling Psychology	M,O
Counselor Education	M,O
Curriculum and Instruction	M
Early Childhood Education	O
Educational Leadership and Administration	O
Elementary Education	M,O
English Education	M
Foreign Languages Education	M
Mathematics Education	M
Psychology—General	M,O
Reading Education	M
School Psychology	M,O
Science Education	M
Secondary Education	M
Social Sciences Education	M
Special Education	M
Student Affairs	M,O

STATE UNIVERSITY OF NEW YORK COLLEGE AT CORTLAND
Communication Disorders	M
Community Health	M
Early Childhood Education	M
Education—General	M,O
Educational Leadership and Administration	O
English as a Second Language	M
English Education	M
English	M
Environmental Education	M
Health Education	M
History	M
Mathematics Education	M

Mathematics	M
Physical Education	M
Physics	M
Reading Education	M
Recreation and Park Management	M
Science Education	M
Secondary Education	M
Special Education	M
Sports Management	M

STATE UNIVERSITY OF NEW YORK COLLEGE AT GENESEO

Accounting	M
Business Administration and Management—General	M
Early Childhood Education	M
Education—General	M
English Education	M
Foreign Languages Education	M
Multilingual and Multicultural Education	M
Reading Education	M
Science Education	M
Secondary Education	M

STATE UNIVERSITY OF NEW YORK COLLEGE AT OLD WESTBURY

Accounting	M
Business Administration and Management—General	M
Counseling Psychology	M
Education—General	M
English Education	M
Foreign Languages Education	M
Liberal Studies	M
Mathematics Education	M
Science Education	M
Social Sciences Education	M
Taxation	M

STATE UNIVERSITY OF NEW YORK COLLEGE AT ONEONTA

Biological and Biomedical Sciences—General	M
Counselor Education	M,O
Education—General	M,O
Educational Psychology	M,O
Elementary Education	M
Museum Studies	M
Nutrition	M
Reading Education	M
Special Education	M,O

STATE UNIVERSITY OF NEW YORK COLLEGE AT POTSDAM

Communication—General	M
Community Health	M
Curriculum and Instruction	M
Early Childhood Education	M
Educational Media/Instructional Technology	M
Elementary Education	M
English Education	M
English	M
Mathematics Education	M
Mathematics	M
Middle School Education	M
Music Education	M
Music	M
Organizational Management	M
Reading Education	M
Science Education	M
Secondary Education	M
Social Sciences Education	M
Special Education	M

STATE UNIVERSITY OF NEW YORK COLLEGE OF ENVIRONMENTAL SCIENCE AND FORESTRY

Biochemistry	M,D
Chemistry	M,D
Conservation Biology	M,D
Construction Management	M,D
Ecology	M,D
Economics	M,D
Entomology	M,D
Environmental Biology	M,D
Environmental Engineering	M,D
Environmental Management and Policy	M,D
Environmental Sciences	M,D
Fish, Game, and Wildlife Management	M,D
Forestry	M,D
Geographic Information Systems	M,D
Landscape Architecture	M
Materials Sciences	M,D,O
Natural Resources	M,D
Organic Chemistry	M,D
Paper and Pulp Engineering	M,D,O
Plant Pathology	M,D
Plant Sciences	M,D
Sustainability Management	M,D,O
Sustainable Development	M,D
Urban and Regional Planning	M,D
Urban Design	M
Water Resources Engineering	M,D
Water Resources	M

STATE UNIVERSITY OF NEW YORK COLLEGE OF OPTOMETRY

Optometry	D
Vision Sciences	D

STATE UNIVERSITY OF NEW YORK COLLEGE OF TECHNOLOGY AT DELHI

Nursing Education	M

STATE UNIVERSITY OF NEW YORK DOWNSTATE MEDICAL CENTER

Allopathic Medicine	M,D
Biological and Biomedical Sciences—General	M,D

Biomedical Engineering	M,D
Cell Biology	D
Community Health	M
Family Nurse Practitioner Studies	M,O
Medical/Surgical Nursing	M,O
Molecular Biology	D
Neuroscience	D
Nurse Anesthesia	M
Nurse Midwifery	M,O
Nursing—General	M,O
Occupational Therapy	M
Public Health—General	M

STATE UNIVERSITY OF NEW YORK EMPIRE STATE COLLEGE

Adult Education	M
Business Administration and Management—General	M
Economic Development	M
Education—General	M
Educational Media/Instructional Technology	M
Industrial and Labor Relations	M
International Business	M
Liberal Studies	M
Nursing Education	M
Public Policy	M

STATE UNIVERSITY OF NEW YORK MARITIME COLLEGE

Transportation Management	M

STATE UNIVERSITY OF NEW YORK POLYTECHNIC INSTITUTE

Accounting	M
Business Administration and Management—General	M
Computer and Information Systems Security	M
Computer Science	M
Family Nurse Practitioner Studies	M,O
Finance and Banking	M
Human Resources Management	M
Information Science	M
Management of Technology	M
Marketing	M
Nanotechnology	M,D
Nursing and Healthcare Administration	M
Nursing Education	M,O
Telecommunications	M

STATE UNIVERSITY OF NEW YORK UPSTATE MEDICAL UNIVERSITY

Allopathic Medicine	D
Anatomy	M,D
Biochemistry	M,D
Biological and Biomedical Sciences—General	M,D
Cell Biology	M,D
Clinical Laboratory Sciences/Medical Technology	M
Family Nurse Practitioner Studies	M,O
Immunology	M,D
Microbiology	M,D
Molecular Biology	M,D
Neuroscience	D
Nursing—General	M,O
Pharmacology	D
Physical Therapy	D
Physiology	M,D

STEPHEN F. AUSTIN STATE UNIVERSITY

Accounting	M
Agricultural Education	M
Applied Arts and Design—General	M
Art/Fine Arts	M
Athletic Training and Sports Medicine	M
Biological and Biomedical Sciences—General	M
Biotechnology	M
Business Administration and Management—General	M
Chemistry	M
Communication Disorders	M
Communication—General	M
Computer Science	M
Counselor Education	M
Early Childhood Education	M
Education—General	M,D
Educational Leadership and Administration	M,D
Elementary Education	M
English	M
Environmental Sciences	M
Family and Consumer Sciences-General	M
Forestry	M,D
Geology	M
History	M
Interdisciplinary Studies	M
Kinesiology and Movement Studies	M
Marketing	M
Mass Communication	M
Mathematics Education	M
Mathematics	M
Music	M
Physics	M
Psychology—General	M
Public Administration	M
School Psychology	M
Secondary Education	M,D
Social Work	M
Special Education	M
Statistics	M

STEPHENS COLLEGE

Addictions/Substance Abuse Counseling	M,O
Clinical Psychology	M,O
Counselor Education	M,O

Health Informatics	M,O
Physician Assistant Studies	M,O
Writing	M,O

STETSON UNIVERSITY

Accounting	M
Business Administration and Management—General	M
Counseling Psychology	M
Counselor Education	M
Education—General	M
Educational Leadership and Administration	M
Law	M,D
Legal and Justice Studies	M
Marriage and Family Therapy	M
Writing	M

STEVENS INSTITUTE OF TECHNOLOGY

Aerospace/Aeronautical Engineering	M,O
Analytical Chemistry	M,D,O
Applied Mathematics	M
Applied Statistics	O
Artificial Intelligence/Robotics	M,D,O
Atmospheric Sciences	M,D,O
Biochemistry	M,D,O
Bioinformatics	M,D,O
Biomedical Engineering	M,D,O
Business Administration and Management—General	M,O
Chemical Engineering	M,D,O
Chemistry	M,D,O
Civil Engineering	M,D,O
Communication—General	M,D,O
Computer and Information Systems Security	M,D,O
Computer Art and Design	M,D,O
Computer Engineering	M,D,O
Computer Science	M,D,O
Construction Engineering	M,O
Construction Management	M,O
Corporate and Organizational Communication	O
Database Systems	M,D,O
Electrical Engineering	M,D,O
Electronic Commerce	M,O
Engineering and Applied Sciences—General	M,D,O
Engineering Design	M
Engineering Management	M,D,O
Entrepreneurship	M,O
Environmental Engineering	M,D,O
Ethics	M,O
Film, Television, and Video Production	M
Finance and Banking	M,O
Financial Engineering	M,D,O
Health Informatics	M,D,O
Human Resources Management	M
Hydrology	M,D,O
Industrial and Manufacturing Management	M
Information Science	M,O
International Business	M
Internet and Interactive Multimedia	M,D,O
Logistics	O
Management Information Systems	M,D,O
Management of Technology	M,D,O
Management Strategy and Policy	M
Manufacturing Engineering	M,D,O
Marine Affairs	M
Marketing	M,O
Materials Engineering	M,D
Materials Sciences	M,D
Mathematics	M,D
Mechanical Engineering	M,D,O
Media Studies	M
Modeling and Simulation	M,D,O
Nanotechnology	D
Nuclear Engineering	M,D,O
Ocean Engineering	M,D
Pharmaceutical Sciences	M,O
Photonics	M,D,O
Physics	M,D,O
Polymer Science and Engineering	M,D,O
Project Management	M,O
Quality Management	M,O
Software Engineering	M,O
Statistics	M,O
Structural Engineering	M,D,O
Systems Engineering	M,D,O
Systems Science	M,D,O
Telecommunications Management	M,D,O
Telecommunications	M,D,O
Transportation and Highway Engineering	M,D,O
Water Resources Engineering	M,D,O

STEVENSON UNIVERSITY

Biological and Biomedical Sciences—General	M
Chemistry	M
Communication—General	M
Computer and Information Systems Security	M
Education—General	M
Forensic Sciences	M
Health Services Management and Hospital Administration	M
Management of Technology	M
Mathematics Education	M
Nursing and Healthcare Administration	M
Nursing Education	M
Nursing—General	M
Project Management	M
Quality Management	M
Science Education	M

STOCKTON UNIVERSITY

American Studies	M,O
Business Administration and Management—General	M
Communication Disorders	M
Computational Sciences	M
Criminal Justice and Criminology	M
Education—General	M
Educational Media/Instructional Technology	M
Environmental Sciences	M
Holocaust and Genocide Studies	M
Nursing—General	M
Occupational Therapy	M
Organizational Management	D
Physical Therapy	D
Social Work	M

STONY BROOK UNIVERSITY, STATE UNIVERSITY OF NEW YORK

Accounting	M,O
Addictions/Substance Abuse Counseling	M,D,O
Adult Nursing	M,D,O
African Studies	M,O
Allopathic Medicine	D
Anatomy	D
Anthropology	M,D
Applied Mathematics	M,D,O
Art History	M,D
Art/Fine Arts	M
Asian Studies	M
Asian-American Studies	M
Astronomy	D
Atmospheric Sciences	M,D
Biochemistry	M,D
Bioethics	M
Bioinformatics	M,D,O
Biological and Biomedical Sciences—General	M,D,O
Biomedical Engineering	M,D,O
Biophysics	D
Business Administration and Management—General	M,O
Cell Biology	M,D
Chemistry	M,D
Civil Engineering	M,D,O
Clinical Psychology	D
Cognitive Sciences	D
Community Health	M,D,O
Comparative Literature	M,D,O
Computer Education	M
Computer Engineering	M,D
Computer Science	M,D,O
Cultural Studies	M,D,O
Dentistry	D,O
Developmental Biology	M,D
Ecology	M,D
Economics	M,D
Educational Leadership and Administration	M,O
Educational Media/Instructional Technology	M,O
Electrical Engineering	M,D
Engineering and Applied Sciences—General	M,D,O
English as a Second Language	M
English Education	M,D,O
English	M,D,O
Environmental Management and Policy	M,O
Evolutionary Biology	M,D
Family Nurse Practitioner Studies	M,D,O
Film, Television, and Video Production	M
Finance and Banking	M,O
Foreign Languages Education	M,O
French	M
Gender Studies	O
Genetics	D
Geographic Information Systems	O
Geosciences	M,D
Gerontological Nursing	M,D,O
Health Communication	M,O
Health Informatics	M,D,O
Health Psychology	D
Health Services Management and Hospital Administration	M,D,O
Higher Education	M,O
Hispanic and Latin American Languages	M,D
History	M,D
Human Resources Management	M,O
Immunology	M,D
Industrial and Manufacturing Management	M,O
Italian	M
Journalism	M,O
Liberal Studies	M,O
Linguistics	M,D
Management Information Systems	M,D,O
Management of Technology	M
Marine Affairs	M
Marine Sciences	M,D
Marketing	M,O
Materials Engineering	M,D
Materials Sciences	M,D
Maternal and Child/Neonatal Nursing	M,D,O
Mathematics Education	M,O
Mathematics	M,D
Mechanical Engineering	M,D
Medical Physics	M,D
Microbiology	D
Molecular Biology	M,D
Molecular Genetics	D
Molecular Physiology	D
Music	M,D
Neuroscience	M,D
Nurse Midwifery	M,D,O

M—masters degree; D—doctorate; O—other advanced degree; *—Close-Up and/or Display

Nursing and Healthcare Administration	M,O
Nursing Education	M,O
Nursing—General	M,D,O
Nutrition	M
Occupational Therapy	M,D,O
Oral and Dental Sciences	M,D
Pathology	M,D
Pediatric Nursing	M,D,O
Pharmacology	M,D
Philosophy	M,D,O
Physical Education	M,O
Physical Therapy	M,D,O
Physician Assistant Studies	M,D,O
Physics	D
Physiology	D
Political Science	M,D
Psychiatric Nursing	M,D,O
Psychology—General	M,D
Public Health—General	M,O
Public Policy	M
Rehabilitation Sciences	M,D,O
Romance Languages	M
Science Education	M,D,O
Social Psychology	D
Social Sciences Education	M,O
Social Work	M,D
Sociology	M,D
Software Engineering	M,D,O
Statistics	M,D,O
Structural Biology	D
Systems Engineering	M
Technology and Public Policy	D
Theater	M
Women's Health Nursing	M,D,O
Women's Studies	O
Writing	M,O

STRATFORD UNIVERSITY (MD)
Hospitality Management	M

STRATFORD UNIVERSITY (VA)
Accounting	M
Business Administration and Management—General	M
Computer and Information Systems Security	M
Computer Science	M
Entrepreneurship	M
Forensic Sciences	M
Health Services Management and Hospital Administration	M
Hospitality Management	M
International Business	M
Management Information Systems	M
Software Engineering	M
Telecommunications	M

STRAYER UNIVERSITY
Accounting	M
Business Administration and Management—General	M
Computer and Information Systems Security	M
Education—General	M
Educational Media/Instructional Technology	M
Finance and Banking	M
Health Services Management and Hospital Administration	M
Hospitality Management	M
Human Resources Management	M
Information Science	M
Management Information Systems	M
Marketing	M
Public Administration	M
Software Engineering	M
Supply Chain Management	M
Systems Science	M
Taxation	M
Telecommunications Management	M
Travel and Tourism	M

SUFFOLK UNIVERSITY
Accounting	M,O
Advertising and Public Relations	M
Applied Arts and Design—General	M
Business Administration and Management—General	M
Clinical Psychology	M,D,O
Community Health	M
Corporate and Organizational Communication	M
Counseling Psychology	M,D,O
Counselor Education	M,D,O
Criminal Justice and Criminology	M
Educational Leadership and Administration	M,O
Entrepreneurship	M
Ethics	M,O
Finance and Banking	M
Graphic Design	M
Health Law	M,D
Health Services Management and Hospital Administration	M
Intellectual Property Law	M,D
Interior Design	M
International Business	M
Law	M,D
Management Information Systems	M
Management Strategy and Policy	M
Marketing	M
Nonprofit Management	M
Organizational Behavior	M
Political Science	M,O
Psychology—General	M,D,O
Public Administration	M
Public Policy	M,O
School Psychology	M,D,O
Supply Chain Management	M
Taxation	M,O

SULLIVAN UNIVERSITY
Business Administration and Management—General	M,D
Pharmacy	D

SUL ROSS STATE UNIVERSITY
Animal Sciences	M
Art Education	M
Art History	M
Art/Fine Arts	M
Biological and Biomedical Sciences—General	M
Business Administration and Management—General	M
Counselor Education	M
Criminal Justice and Criminology	M
Education—General	M,O
Educational Leadership and Administration	M
Educational Measurement and Evaluation	M,O
Elementary Education	M
Emergency Management	M
English	M
Fish, Game, and Wildlife Management	M
Geology	M
History	M
Multilingual and Multicultural Education	M
Natural Resources	M
Physical Education	M
Political Science	M
Psychology—General	M
Range Science	M
Reading Education	M,O
Secondary Education	M

SUM BIBLE COLLEGE & THEOLOGICAL SEMINARY
Pastoral Ministry and Counseling	M
Religion	M
Theology	M

SWEDISH INSTITUTE, COLLEGE OF HEALTH SCIENCES
Acupuncture and Oriental Medicine	M

SWEET BRIAR COLLEGE
Education—General	M

SYRACUSE UNIVERSITY
Accounting	M
Addictions/Substance Abuse Counseling	M,O
Advertising and Public Relations	M
Aerospace/Aeronautical Engineering	M,D
African Studies	M
African-American Studies	M
Anthropology	M,D
Applied Arts and Design—General	M
Applied Statistics	M
Architecture	M
Art Education	M
Art History	M
Art/Fine Arts	M
Arts Journalism	M
Bioengineering	M,D
Biological and Biomedical Sciences—General	M,D
Broadcast Journalism	M
Business Administration and Management—General	M,D
Chemical Engineering	M,D
Chemistry	M,D
Child and Family Studies	M,D
Civil Engineering	M,D
Clinical Psychology	M,D
Cognitive Sciences	D
Communication Disorders	M,D
Communication—General	M,D
Computer and Information Systems Security	M,O
Computer Art and Design	M
Computer Engineering	M,D
Computer Science	M
Conflict Resolution and Mediation/Peace Studies	O
Counselor Education	M,D
Curriculum and Instruction	M,D,O
Database Systems	M
Disability Studies	O
Early Childhood Education	M
Economics	M,D
Education of Students with Severe/Multiple Disabilities	M
Education—General	M,D,O
Educational Leadership and Administration	M,D,O
Educational Measurement and Evaluation	M,D,O
Educational Media/Instructional Technology	M,O
Educational Policy	O
Electrical Engineering	M,D,O
Emergency Management	O
Energy and Power Engineering	M
Engineering and Applied Sciences—General	M,D,O
Engineering Management	M,O
English as a Second Language	M,O
English Education	M,D
English	M
Entertainment Management	M
Entrepreneurship	M
Environmental and Occupational Health	O
Environmental Engineering	M
Exercise and Sports Science	M
Film, Television, and Video Production	M
Film, Television, and Video Theory and Criticism	M

Finance and Banking	M,D
Forensic Sciences	M
Foundations and Philosophy of Education	M,D,O
French	M
Geography	M,D
Geology	M,D
Health Services Management and Hospital Administration	O
Higher Education	M,D
History	M,D
Hospitality Management	M,O
Illustration	M
Information Science	M
Information Studies	M
International Affairs	M
International Health	M
Journalism	M
Kinesiology and Movement Studies	M,D
Law	M,D
Library Science	M*
Linguistics	M
Management Information Systems	M,D,O
Management Strategy and Policy	M
Marketing	M
Marriage and Family Therapy	M,D
Mass Communication	M,D
Mathematics Education	M,D
Mathematics	M,D
Mechanical Engineering	M,D
Media Studies	M
Museum Studies	M
Music Education	M
Music	M
Neuroscience	M,D
Nutrition	M,D
Organizational Management	O
Philosophy	M,D
Photography	M
Physics	M,D
Political Science	M,D,O
Public Administration	M,D
Public Affairs	M
Public Health—General	M
Reading Education	M
Real Estate	M
Religion	M,D
Rhetoric	M
School Psychology	M,D,O
Science Education	M,D
Social Psychology	D
Social Sciences Education	M
Social Sciences	M,D
Social Work	M
Sociology	M,D
Spanish	M
Special Education	M,D
Sports Management	M
Student Affairs	M
Supply Chain Management	M
Sustainability Management	O
Travel and Tourism	M
Urban and Regional Planning	O
Writing	M,D

TABOR COLLEGE
Accounting	M
Business Administration and Management—General	M

TAFT UNIVERSITY SYSTEM
Education—General	M
Law	M,D
Legal and Justice Studies	M,D
Taxation	M,D

TALMUDIC UNIVERSITY
Theology	M

TARLETON STATE UNIVERSITY
Accounting	M
Agricultural Sciences—General	M
Applied Psychology	M
Athletic Training and Sports Medicine	M
Biological and Biomedical Sciences—General	M
Business Administration and Management—General	M
Clinical Laboratory Sciences/Medical Technology	M
Communication—General	M
Counseling Psychology	M
Criminal Justice and Criminology	M
Curriculum and Instruction	M
Education—General	M,D,O
Educational Leadership and Administration	M,D,O
Educational Media/Instructional Technology	M
Elementary Education	M
Engineering Management	M
English	M
Environmental Sciences	M
Fish, Game, and Wildlife Management	M
History	M
Human Resources Management	M
Kinesiology and Movement Studies	M
Management Information Systems	M
Marketing	M
Mathematics	M
Music Education	M
Natural Resources	M
Nursing and Healthcare Administration	M
Nursing Education	M
Nursing—General	M
Political Science	M
Public Administration	M
Public Health—General	M
Reading Education	M
Secondary Education	M

Social Work	M
Special Education	M

TAYLOR COLLEGE AND SEMINARY
Cultural Studies	M,O
English as a Second Language	M,O
Missions and Missiology	M,O
Theology	M,O

TAYLOR UNIVERSITY
Business Administration and Management—General	M
Higher Education	M
International Business	M
Management Strategy and Policy	M

TEACHERS COLLEGE, COLUMBIA UNIVERSITY
Adult Education	M,D
Anthropology	M,D
Applied Behavior Analysis	M,D,O
Applied Psychology	M,D
Applied Statistics	M,D
Art Education	M,D,O
Arts Administration	M,D,O
Biological and Biomedical Sciences—General	M,D
Chemistry	M,D
Clinical Psychology	M,D
Communication Disorders	M,D,O
Communication—General	M,D,O
Community Health	M,D,O
Computer Education	M,D
Counseling Psychology	M,D
Curriculum and Instruction	M,D
Developmental Psychology	M,D
Early Childhood Education	M,D
Economics	M,D
Education of Students with Severe/Multiple Disabilities	M,D,O
Education of the Gifted	M,D
Education—General	M,D
Educational Leadership and Administration	M,D
Educational Measurement and Evaluation	M,D
Educational Media/Instructional Technology	M,D
Educational Policy	M,D
Educational Psychology	M,D,O
Elementary Education	M,D
English as a Second Language	M,D,O
English Education	M,D,O
Foundations and Philosophy of Education	M,D,O
Geosciences	M,D
Health Education	M,D,O
Higher Education	M,D
Industrial and Organizational Psychology	M,D
Interdisciplinary Studies	M,D
International Affairs	M,D,O
International and Comparative Education	M,D
Kinesiology and Movement Studies	M,D
Linguistics	M,D,O
Mathematics Education	M,D
Multilingual and Multicultural Education	M,D,O
Music Education	M,D,O
Neuroscience	M,D
Nursing and Healthcare Administration	M,D
Nursing Education	M,D,O
Nutrition	M,D,O
Philosophy	M,D
Physical Education	M,D
Physics	M,D
Physiology	M,D
Political Science	M,D
Psychology—General	M,D
Reading Education	M,D,O
School Psychology	M,D,O
Science Education	M,D
Secondary Education	M,D
Social Psychology	M,D
Social Sciences Education	M,D,O
Sociology	M,D
Special Education	M,D,O
Urban Education	M,D

TÉLÉ-UNIVERSITÉ
Computer Science	M,D
Distance Education Development	M,D
Finance and Banking	M,D

TELSHE YESHIVA–CHICAGO
Jewish Studies	O

TEMPLE UNIVERSITY
Accounting	M,D
Actuarial Science	M
Adult Nursing	D
African-American Studies	M,D
Allied Health—General	M,D
Allopathic Medicine	D
Anthropology	D
Applied Behavior Analysis	M,D,O
Applied Mathematics	M,D
Architecture	M
Art Education	M
Art History	M
Art/Fine Arts	M
Artificial Intelligence/Robotics	M,D
Arts Administration	M,D
Athletic Training and Sports Medicine	M,D
Bioengineering	M,D
Biological and Biomedical Sciences—General	M,D
Biotechnology	M,D
Business Administration and Management—General	M,D
Business Education	M
Chemistry	M,D
Civil Engineering	M,D,O

Communication Disorders — M,D
Communication—General — M,D
Corporate and Organizational
  Communication — M,D
Counseling Psychology — M,D,O
Criminal Justice and Criminology — M,D
Dance — M
Dentistry — D
Economics — M,D
Education—General — M,D,O
Educational Psychology — M,D,O
Electrical Engineering — M,D
Engineering and Applied
  Sciences—General — D*
Engineering Management — M,O
English as a Second Language — M
English Education — M
English — M,D
Entrepreneurship — M,D
Environmental and Occupational
  Health — M,D
Environmental Engineering — M,D,O
Epidemiology — M,D
Family Nurse Practitioner Studies — D
Film, Television, and Video
  Production — M
Finance and Banking — M,D
Financial Engineering — M
Geographic Information Systems — M,D,O
Geography — M,D,O
Geology — M,D
Geosciences — M,D
Gerontology — D
Graphic Design — M
Health Informatics — M,D
Health Services Management and
  Hospital Administration — M
History — M,D
Hospitality Management — M,D*
Human Resources Management — M
Hydrology — M,O
Insurance — D
International Business — M,D
Journalism — M
Kinesiology and Movement Studies — M,D
Landscape Architecture — M
Law — M,D
Legal and Justice Studies — M
Management Information Systems — M,D
Management Strategy and Policy — D
Marketing — M,D
Mathematics Education — M
Mathematics — M,D
Mechanical Engineering — M,D
Media Studies — M
Medicinal and Pharmaceutical
  Chemistry — M,D
Middle School Education — M
Music Education — M,D
Music — M,D
Nursing—General — D
Occupational Therapy — M,D
Oral and Dental Sciences — M,D
Pharmaceutical Administration — M
Pharmaceutical Sciences — M,D
Pharmacy — M,D
Philosophy — M,D
Photography — M
Physical Education — M,D
Physical Therapy — D
Physics — M,D
Podiatric Medicine — D
Political Science — M,D
Psychology—General — M,D
Public Health—General — M,D
Recreation and Park Management — M,D
Rehabilitation Sciences — M,D
Religion — M,D
School Psychology — M,D,O
Science Education — M
Secondary Education — M
Social Psychology — M,D,O
Social Sciences Education — M
Social Work — M
Sociology — M,D
Spanish — M,D
Sports Management — M,D*
Statistics — M,D
Supply Chain Management — M,D
Sustainable Development — M,O
Taxation — M
Textile Design — M
Theater — M
Therapies—Dance, Drama, and
  Music — M
Transportation Management — M,O
Travel and Tourism — M,D
Urban and Regional Planning — M,O
Urban Education — M
Urban Studies — M,D,O
Vocational and Technical Education — M
Writing — M,D

TENNESSEE STATE UNIVERSITY

Agricultural Education — M,D
Agricultural Sciences—
  General — M,D
Agronomy and Soil Sciences — M,D
Allied Health—General — M,D,O
Biological and Biomedical
  Sciences—General — D
Biomedical Engineering — M,D
Biotechnology — M,D
Business Administration and
  Management—General — M
Chemistry — M
Civil Engineering — M,D
Communication Disorders — M
Computer Engineering — M,D
Counseling Psychology — M
Criminal Justice and Criminology — M

Curriculum and Instruction — M,D
Education—General — M,D,O
Electrical Engineering — M,D
Elementary Education — M,D
Engineering and Applied
  Sciences—General — M,D
Environmental Engineering — M,D
Exercise and Sports Science — M
Family and Consumer
  Sciences—General — M
Family Nurse Practitioner Studies — M,O
Human Resources Management — M,D
Management Strategy and Policy — M,D
Manufacturing Engineering — M,D
Mathematics — M,D
Mechanical Engineering — M,D
Nursing—General — M,O
Occupational Therapy — M
Physical Education — M
Physical Therapy — D
Plant Sciences — M,D
Psychology—General — M
Public Administration — M,D
Public Health—General — M
Social Work — M,D
Special Education — M,D
Sports Management — M,D
Systems Engineering — M,D

**TENNESSEE TECHNOLOGICAL
UNIVERSITY**

Accounting — M
Applied Behavior Analysis — D
Biological and Biomedical
  Sciences—General — M,D
Business Administration and
  Management—General — M
Chemical Engineering — M
Chemistry — M,D
Civil Engineering — M
Computer Science — M
Curriculum and Instruction — M,O
Early Childhood Education — M,O
Education of the Gifted — D
Education—General — M,D,O
Educational Leadership and
  Administration — M,O
Educational Measurement and
  Evaluation — D
Educational Media/Instructional
  Technology — M,O
Educational Psychology — M,O
Electrical Engineering — M
Elementary Education — M,O
Engineering and Applied
  Sciences—General — M,D
English — M
Environmental Management
  and Policy — M
Environmental Sciences — D
Family Nurse Practitioner Studies — M
Finance and Banking — M
Fish, Game, and Wildlife
  Management — M
Health Education — M
Health Promotion — M
Human Resources Management — M
International Business — M
Internet and Interactive
  Multimedia — M
Kinesiology and Movement Studies — M
Library Science — M,O
Management Information Systems — M
Management Strategy and Policy — M
Mathematics Education — M,O
Mathematics — M
Mechanical Engineering — M
Middle School Education — M
Music Education — M
Nursing and Healthcare
  Administration — M
Nursing Education — M
Nursing Informatics — M
Nursing—General — M
Physical Education — M
Reading Education — M,D,O
Science Education — M,O
Secondary Education — M,O
Software Engineering — M
Special Education — M,O
Sports Management — M

TENNESSEE WESLEYAN UNIVERSITY

Accounting — M
Business Administration and
  Management—General — M

**TEXAS A&M INTERNATIONAL
UNIVERSITY**

Accounting — M
Biological and Biomedical
  Sciences—General — M
Business Administration and
  Management—General — M,D
Counseling Psychology — M
Counselor Education — M
Criminal Justice and Criminology — M
Curriculum and Instruction — M
Education—General — M
Educational Leadership and
  Administration — M
English — M,D
Family Nurse Practitioner Studies — M
Finance and Banking — M
Foreign Languages Education — M,D
Hispanic Studies — M,D
History — M,D
International Business — M,D
Management Information Systems — M,D
Mathematics — M
Nursing—General — M
Political Science — M,D

Psychology—General — M
Public Administration — M
Social Sciences — M
Special Education — M
Translation and Interpretation — M,D

TEXAS A&M UNIVERSITY

Accounting — M
Aerospace/Aeronautical
  Engineering — M,D
Agricultural Economics and
  Agribusiness — M,D
Agricultural Education — M,D
Agricultural Engineering — M,D
Agricultural Sciences—
  General — M,D
Agronomy and Soil Sciences — M,D
Allied Health—General — M,D
Animal Sciences — M,D
Anthropology — M,D
Applied Physics — M,D
Architecture — M,D
Art/Fine Arts — M
Astronomy — M,D
Athletic Training and Sports
  Medicine — M,D
Biochemistry — M,D
Bioengineering — M,D
Biological and Biomedical
  Sciences—General — M,D,O
Biomedical Engineering — M,D
Business Administration and
  Management—General — M
Chemical Engineering — M,D
Chemistry — M,D
Civil Engineering — M,D
Clinical Psychology — M,D
Communication—General — M,D
Community Health — M
Computer Engineering — M,D
Computer Science — M,D
Construction Management — M
Counseling Psychology — M,D
Cultural Studies — M
Curriculum and Instruction — M,D
Dental Hygiene — M,D,O
Dentistry — M,D,O
Economics — M,D
Education—General — M,D
Educational Leadership and
  Administration — M,D
Educational Media/Instructional
  Technology — M,D
Educational Psychology — M,D
Electrical Engineering — M,D
Engineering Management — M,D
English — M,D
Entomology — M,D
Entrepreneurship — M
Family Nurse Practitioner Studies — M
Finance and Banking — M
Fish, Game, and Wildlife
  Management — M,D
Food Science and
  Technology — M,D
Forestry — M,D
Geography — M,D
Geology — M,D
Geophysics — M,D
Health Education — M,D
Health Physics/Radiological Health — M,D
Health Promotion — M,D
Health Services Management and
  Hospital Administration — M,D
Health Services Research — M,D
History — M,D
Homeland Security — M,O
Horticulture — M,D
Human Resources Development — M,D
Human Resources Management — M
Industrial and Organizational
  Psychology — M,D
Industrial/Management
  Engineering — M,D
International Affairs — M,O
Kinesiology and Movement Studies — M,D
Landscape Architecture — M,D
Law — M,D
Management Information Systems — M
Management of Technology — M
Manufacturing Engineering — M
Marine Biology — M,D
Marine Sciences — M
Marketing — M
Materials Engineering — M,D
Materials Sciences — M,D
Mathematics — M,D
Mechanical Engineering — M,D
Meteorology — M,D
Microbiology — M,D
Multilingual and Multicultural
  Education — M,D
Music — M
National Security — M,O
Natural Resources — M,D
Nonprofit Management — M,O
Nuclear Engineering — M,D
Nursing Education — M
Nursing—General — M
Nutrition — M,D
Oceanography — M,D
Oral and Dental Sciences — M,D,O
Petroleum Engineering — M,D
Pharmacy — D
Philosophy — M,D
Physics — M,D
Plant Pathology — M,D
Political Science — M,D
Psychology—General — M,D
Public Administration — M,O
Public Affairs — M,D

Psychology—General — M
Public Administration — M
Social Sciences — M
Special Education — M
Translation and Interpretation — M,D

Public Health—General — M,D,O
Real Estate — M
Recreation and Park Management — M,D
School Psychology — M,D
Sociology — M,D
Spanish — M,D
Special Education — M,D
Sports Management — M,D
Statistics — M,D
Transportation Management — M
Urban and Regional Planning — M,D
Veterinary Medicine — M,D
Veterinary Sciences — M,D

**TEXAS A&M UNIVERSITY–CENTRAL
TEXAS**

Accounting — M,O
Business Administration and
  Management—General — M,O
Clinical Psychology — M,O
Counselor Education — M,O
Criminal Justice and Criminology — M,O
Curriculum and Instruction — M,O
Educational Leadership and
  Administration — M,O
Educational Psychology — M,O
Experimental Psychology — M,O
History — M,O
Human Resources Management — M,O
Liberal Studies — M,O
Management Information Systems — M,O
Marriage and Family Therapy — M,O
Mathematics — M,O
Political Science — M,O
School Psychology — M,O

TEXAS A&M UNIVERSITY–COMMERCE

Accounting — M
Agricultural Sciences—
  General — M
Art/Fine Arts — M,D,O
Biological and Biomedical
  Sciences—General — M,O
Business Administration and
  Management—General — M
Chemistry — M,O
Counselor Education — M,D,O
Criminal Justice and Criminology — M,D,O
Curriculum and Instruction — M,D,O
Early Childhood Education — M,D,O
Education—General — M,D,O
Educational Leadership and
  Administration — M,D,O
Educational Media/Instructional
  Technology — M,D,O
Educational Psychology — M,D,O
Elementary Education — M,D,O
English as a Second Language — M,D,O
English — M,D,O
Environmental Sciences — M,O
Exercise and Sports Science — M,D,O
Film, Television, and Video
  Theory and Criticism — M,D,O
Finance and Banking — M
Higher Education — M,D,O
History — M,D,O
Industrial and Manufacturing
  Management — M,D,O
Kinesiology and Movement Studies — M,D,O
Library Science — M,D,O
Linguistics — M,D,O
Management of Technology — M,O
Marketing — M
Mathematics — M,O
Music — M,D,O
Physics — M,O
Political Science — M,D,O
Psychology—General — M,D,O
Public History — M,D,O
Reading Education — M,D,O
School Psychology — M,D,O
Secondary Education — M,D,O
Social Work — M,D,O
Sociology — M,D,O
Spanish — M,D,O
Special Education — M,D,O
Theater — M,D,O
Writing — M,D,O

**TEXAS A&M UNIVERSITY–CORPUS
CHRISTI**

Accounting — M
Aquaculture — M
Art/Fine Arts — M
Biological and Biomedical
  Sciences—General — M
Business Administration and
  Management—General — M
Clinical Psychology — M
Communication—General — M
Computer Science — M
Counselor Education — M,D
Curriculum and Instruction — M,D
Early Childhood Education — M,D
Education—General — M,D
Educational Leadership and
  Administration — M,D
Educational Media/Instructional
  Technology — M,D
Elementary Education — M,D
English — M
Environmental Sciences — M
Family Nurse Practitioner Studies — M
Finance and Banking — M
Health Services Management and
  Hospital Administration — M
History — M
International Business — M
Kinesiology and Movement Studies — M,D
Marine Biology — M,D
Marine Sciences — M,D
Mathematics — M

M—masters degree; D—doctorate; O—other advanced degree; *—Close-Up and/or Display

Nursing and Healthcare
  Administration M
Nursing Education M
Nursing—General M
Psychology—General M
Public Administration M
Reading Education M,D
Secondary Education M
Special Education M

TEXAS A&M UNIVERSITY–KINGSVILLE
Adult Education M,D
Agricultural Economics and
  Agribusiness M,D
Agricultural Sciences—
  General M,D
Agronomy and Soil Sciences M
Animal Sciences M
Biological and Biomedical
  Sciences—General M
Business Administration and
  Management—General M
Chemical Engineering M
Chemistry M
Civil Engineering M
Communication Disorders M
Computer Science M
Counselor Education M,D
Criminal Justice and Criminology M
Cultural Studies M
Early Childhood Education M
Education—General M,D,O
Educational Leadership and
  Administration M,D
Educational Media/Instructional
  Technology M
Electrical Engineering M
Energy and Power
  Engineering D
Engineering and Applied
  Sciences—General M,D
English as a Second Language M,D
English M
Environmental Engineering M,D
Family and Consumer
  Sciences—General M
Fish, Game, and Wildlife
  Management M,D
Foreign Languages Education M
Health Education M
Hispanic Studies D
Horticulture M,D
Industrial and Manufacturing
  Management M
Industrial/Management
  Engineering M
Kinesiology and Movement Studies M
Mathematics M
Mechanical Engineering M
Multilingual and Multicultural
  Education M,D
Music Education M
Music M
Petroleum Engineering M
Plant Sciences M
Psychology—General M
Range Science M
Reading Education M
Secondary Education M
Sociology M
Spanish M
Special Education M
Statistics M
Sustainable Development D
Systems Engineering D

TEXAS A&M UNIVERSITY–SAN ANTONIO
Accounting M
Business Administration and
  Management—General M
Computer and Information
  Systems Security M
Counselor Education M
Early Childhood Education M
Educational Leadership and
  Administration M
Educational Measurement and
  Evaluation M
English M
Finance and Banking M
Health Services Management and
  Hospital Administration M
Human Resources Management M
International Business M
Kinesiology and Movement Studies M
Management Information Systems M
Multilingual and Multicultural
  Education M
Project Management M
Reading Education M
Special Education M
Supply Chain Management M

TEXAS A&M UNIVERSITY–TEXARKANA
Accounting M
Adult Education M
Business Administration and
  Management—General M
Counseling Psychology M
Curriculum and Instruction M
Education—General M
Educational Leadership and
  Administration M
Educational Media/Instructional
  Technology M
English M
Interdisciplinary Studies M
Psychology—General M
Special Education M

TEXAS CHIROPRACTIC COLLEGE
Chiropractic D

TEXAS CHRISTIAN UNIVERSITY
Accounting M

Adult Nursing M,O
Allied Health—General M,D,O
American Studies M
Applied Mathematics M,D
Art History M
Art/Fine Arts M
Astrophysics M,D
Biochemistry M,D
Biological and Biomedical
  Sciences—General M
Biophysics M,D
Business Administration and
  Management—General M
Chemistry M,D
Cognitive Sciences M,D
Communication Disorders M
Communication—General M
Corporate and Organizational
  Communication M
Counselor Education M,D,O
Criminal Justice and Criminology M
Curriculum and Instruction M,D,O
Developmental Psychology M,D
Education—General M,D,O
Educational Leadership and
  Administration M,D,O
English M,D
Environmental Sciences M
Experimental Psychology M,D
Family Nurse Practitioner Studies D
Finance and Banking M
Geology M
Gerontological Nursing M,O
Gerontology D
History M,D
Kinesiology and Movement Studies M
Latin American Studies M,D
Liberal Studies M
Marketing M
Mass Communication M
Mathematics Education M,O
Mathematics M,D
Music Education M,D
Music M,D
Neuroscience D
Nurse Anesthesia D
Nursing and Healthcare
  Administration M,D,O
Nursing Education M,O
Nursing—General M,D,O
Pediatric Nursing M,D,O
Physics M,D
Psychology—General M,D
Reading Education M,O
Rhetoric M,D
Science Education M,D,O
Social Psychology M,D
Social Work M
Special Education M,O
Speech and Interpersonal
  Communication M
Supply Chain Management M
Taxation M

TEXAS HEALTH AND SCIENCE UNIVERSITY
Business Administration and
  Management—General M,D
Health Services Management and
  Hospital Administration M,D

TEXAS LUTHERAN UNIVERSITY
Accounting M

TEXAS SOUTHERN UNIVERSITY
Art/Fine Arts M
Biological and Biomedical
  Sciences—General M
Business Administration and
  Management—General M
Chemistry M
Communication—General M
Computer Science M
Counselor Education M,D
Criminal Justice and Criminology M,D
Curriculum and Instruction M,D
Education—General M,D
Educational Leadership and
  Administration M,D
English M
Environmental Management
  and Policy M,D
Family and Consumer
  Sciences-General M
Health Education M
Health Services Management and
  Hospital Administration M
Higher Education M,D
History M
Human Services M
Industrial/Management
  Engineering M
Law D
Management Information Systems M
Mathematics M
Multilingual and Multicultural
  Education M,D
Music M
Pharmaceutical Sciences M,D
Pharmacy D
Physical Education M
Psychology—General M
Public Administration M
Secondary Education M,D
Sociology M
Toxicology M,D
Transportation and Highway
  Engineering M
Transportation Management M
Urban and Regional Planning M,D

TEXAS STATE UNIVERSITY
Accounting M
Adult Education M,D
Agricultural Education M

Allied Health—General M,D
Anthropology M
Applied Arts and Design—General M
Applied Mathematics M
Athletic Training and Sports
  Medicine M
Biochemistry M
Biological and Biomedical
  Sciences—General M
Business Administration and
  Management—General M
Chemistry M
Child and Family Studies M
Communication Disorders M
Communication—General M
Computer Art and Design M
Computer Science M,D
Conservation Biology M
Counselor Education M
Criminal Justice and Criminology M,D
Developmental Education M
Education—General M,D,O
Educational Leadership and
  Administration M,D
Educational Media/Instructional
  Technology M
Electrical Engineering M
Elementary Education M
Engineering and Applied
  Sciences—General M
English M
Ethics M
Family and Consumer
  Sciences-General M
Family Nurse Practitioner Studies M
Fish, Game, and Wildlife
  Management M
Geographic Information Systems D
Geography M,D
Gerontology M
Graphic Design M
Health Education M
Health Informatics M
Health Services Management and
  Hospital Administration M
Higher Education M
History M
Human Resources Management M
Industrial/Management
  Engineering M
Interdisciplinary Studies M
International Affairs M
Legal and Justice Studies M
Leisure Studies M
Management Information Systems M
Management of Technology M
Manufacturing Engineering M
Marine Biology M,D
Marriage and Family Therapy M
Mass Communication M
Materials Engineering D
Materials Sciences M,D
Mathematics Education M,D
Mathematics M
Multilingual and Multicultural
  Education M
Music Education M
Music M
Nutrition M
Philosophy M
Physical Education M
Physical Therapy D
Physics M
Political Science M
Psychology—General M
Public Administration M
Reading Education M
Recreation and Park Management M
Rhetoric M
School Psychology O
Secondary Education M
Social Psychology M
Social Work M
Sociology M
Software Engineering M
Spanish M
Special Education M
Student Affairs M
Sustainable Development M
Technical Communication M
Theater M
Vocational and Technical Education M
Writing M

TEXAS TECH UNIVERSITY
Accounting M,D
Agricultural Economics and
  Agribusiness M,D
Agricultural Education M,D
Agricultural Sciences—
  General M,D
Agronomy and Soil Sciences M,D
Animal Sciences M,D
Anthropology M
Applied Economics M,D
Architecture M,D
Art Education M
Art History M
Art/Fine Arts M,D
Astronomy M,D
Atmospheric Sciences M,D
Bioengineering M
Biological and Biomedical
  Sciences—General M,D
Biotechnology M,D
Business Administration and
  Management—General M,D
Chemical Engineering M,D
Chemistry M,D
Child and Family Studies M,D
Civil Engineering M,D
Classics M
Clinical Psychology M,D
Communication—General M

Computer Science M,D
Construction Engineering M,D
Consumer Economics M,D
Counseling Psychology M,D
Counselor Education M,D
Cultural Studies M,D
Curriculum and Instruction M,D
Database Systems M,D
Distance Education Development M,D
Economics M,D
Education—General M,D
Educational Leadership and
  Administration M,D
Educational Media/Instructional
  Technology M,D
Educational Psychology M,D
Electrical Engineering M,D
Elementary Education M,D
Energy and Power
  Engineering M,D
Engineering and Applied
  Sciences—General M,D
Engineering Management M,D
English M,D
Environmental Design M,D
Environmental Engineering M,D
Environmental Management
  and Policy M,D
Environmental Sciences M,D
Exercise and Sports Science M
Experimental Psychology M,D
Family and Consumer
  Sciences-General M,D
Finance and Banking M,D
Fish, Game, and Wildlife
  Management M,D
Food Science and
  Technology M,D
Forensic Sciences M
Geography M,D
Geosciences M,D
German M,D
Gerontology M,D
Health Services Management and
  Hospital Administration M,D
Higher Education M,D
History M,D
Home Economics Education M,D
Horticulture M,D
Hospitality Management M,D
Human Development M,D
Industrial/Management
  Engineering M,D
Interdisciplinary Studies M,D
Interior Design M,D
Kinesiology and Movement Studies M
Landscape Architecture M
Law M,D
Legal and Justice Studies M,D
Linguistics M,D
Management Information Systems M,D
Manufacturing Engineering M,D
Marketing M,D
Marriage and Family Therapy M,D
Mass Communication M,D
Mathematics M,D
Mechanical Engineering M,D
Media Studies M,D
Microbiology M,D
Multilingual and Multicultural
  Education M,D
Museum Studies M,D
Music Education M,D
Music M,D
Natural Resources M,D
Nutrition M,D
Petroleum Engineering M,D
Philosophy M
Physics M,D
Plant Sciences M,D
Political Science M,D
Psychology—General M,D
Public Administration M,D
Reading Education M,D
Rhetoric M,D
Romance Languages M,D
Science Education M,D
Secondary Education M,D
Social Work M
Sociology M,D
Software Engineering M,D
Spanish M,D
Special Education M,D
Sports Management M,D
Statistics M,D
Sustainable Development M,D
Systems Engineering M,D
Taxation M,D
Technical Writing M,D
Theater M
Toxicology M,D
Zoology M,D

TEXAS TECH UNIVERSITY HEALTH SCIENCES CENTER
Acute Care/Critical Care Nursing M,D,O
Allopathic Medicine D
Athletic Training and Sports
  Medicine M
Biological and Biomedical
  Sciences—General M,D
Biotechnology M
Cell Biology M,D
Communication Disorders M,D
Family Nurse Practitioner Studies M,D,O
Gerontological Nursing M,D,O
Health Services Management and
  Hospital Administration M
Molecular Pathology M
Nursing and Healthcare
  Administration M,D,O
Nursing Education M,D,O
Nursing—General M,D,O
Occupational Therapy M

Pediatric Nursing M,D,O
Pharmaceutical Sciences M,D
Physical Therapy D
Physician Assistant Studies M
Rehabilitation Counseling M
Rehabilitation Sciences D

TEXAS WESLEYAN UNIVERSITY
Business Administration and
  Management—General M
Counseling Psychology M,D
Counselor Education M,D
Education—General M,D
Marriage and Family Therapy M,D
Nurse Anesthesia M,D

TEXAS WOMAN'S UNIVERSITY
Accounting M
Acute Care/Critical Care Nursing M,D
Adult Nursing M,D
Allied Health—General M,D
Art/Fine Arts M
Biological and Biomedical
  Sciences—General M,D
Business Administration and
  Management—General M
Chemistry M
Child and Family Studies M,D
Child Development M,D
Communication Disorders M
Counseling Psychology M,D,O
Counselor Education M,D
Curriculum and Instruction M,D
Dance M,D
Early Childhood Education M,D
Education—General M,D
Educational Leadership and
  Administration M,D
English M,D
Exercise and Sports Science M,D
Family Nurse Practitioner Studies M,D
Food Science and
  Technology M,D
Gender Studies M,D
Health Education M,D
Health Services Management and
  Hospital Administration M,D
History M
Information Science M
Kinesiology and Movement Studies M,D
Library Science M,D
Marriage and Family Therapy M,D
Mathematics Education M
Mathematics M
Molecular Biology M,D
Music Education M
Music M
Nursing and Healthcare
  Administration M,D
Nursing Education M,D
Nursing—General M,D
Nutrition M,D
Occupational Therapy M,D
Pediatric Nursing M,D
Physical Education M,D
Physical Therapy D
Political Science M
Psychology—General M,D,O
Reading Education M,D
Rhetoric M,D
School Psychology M,D,O
Sociology M,D
Special Education M,D
Sports Management M,D
Theater M
Women's Health Nursing M,D
Women's Studies M,D

THEOLOGICAL UNIVERSITY OF THE CARIBBEAN
Early Childhood Education M,D
Middle School Education M,D
Missions and Missiology M,D
Pastoral Ministry and Counseling M,D

THOMAS COLLEGE
Business Administration and
  Management—General M
Business Education M
Computer Education M
Human Resources Management M

THOMAS EDISON STATE UNIVERSITY
Accounting M
Applied Science and
  Technology M,O
Business Administration and
  Management—General M
Computer and Information
  Systems Security M,O
Distance Education Development M,O
Economic Development M
Educational Leadership and
  Administration M,O
Educational Media/Instructional
  Technology M,O
Environmental Management
  and Policy M
Homeland Security M
Human Resources Management M
Industrial and Organizational
  Psychology M,O
Information Science M,O
Liberal Studies M,O
Nonprofit Management M
Nursing and Healthcare
  Administration M,D
Nursing Education M
Nursing Informatics M
Nursing—General M,D
Organizational Management M
Project Management M

Public Administration M
Public Health—General M
Urban and Regional Planning M

THOMAS JEFFERSON SCHOOL OF LAW
Law D

THOMAS JEFFERSON UNIVERSITY
Allopathic Medicine D
Applied Economics M,D,O
Biochemistry D
Biological and Biomedical
  Sciences—General M,D,O
Biotechnology M
Cancer Biology/Oncology D
Cell Biology M,D
Clinical Laboratory
  Sciences/Medical Technology M
Clinical Research M,O
Developmental Biology M,D
Genetic Counseling M
Genetics D
Genomic Sciences D
Health Education M,D,O
Health Physics/Radiological Health M
Health Services Management and
  Hospital Administration M,D,O
Health Services Research M,D,O
Human Genetics M
Immunology D
Infectious Diseases O
Marriage and Family Therapy M
Microbiology M,D
Molecular Pharmacology M
Neuroscience D
Nursing—General M,D
Occupational Therapy M,D
Pharmacology M
Pharmacy D
Physical Therapy D
Physician Assistant Studies M
Public Health—General M,O
Toxicology M

THOMAS MORE COLLEGE
Business Administration and
  Management—General M
Education—General M
Educational Leadership and
  Administration M

THOMAS UNIVERSITY
Business Administration and
  Management—General M
Education—General M
Human Services M
Nursing—General M
Rehabilitation Counseling M
Social Psychology M

THOMPSON RIVERS UNIVERSITY
Business Administration and
  Management—General M
Education—General M
Environmental Sciences M
Social Work M

TIFFIN UNIVERSITY
Art/Fine Arts M
Business Administration and
  Management—General M
Communication—General M
Criminal Justice and Criminology M
Education—General M
Educational Leadership and
  Administration M
Educational Media/Instructional
  Technology M
English M
Film, Television, and Video
  Theory and Criticism M
Finance and Banking M
Forensic Psychology M
Health Services Management and
  Hospital Administration M
Higher Education M
Homeland Security M
Human Resources Management M
Humanities M
International Business M
Marketing M
Nonprofit Management M
Psychology—General M
Sports Management M
Writing M

TORONTO SCHOOL OF THEOLOGY
Theology M,D

TOURO COLLEGE
Communication Disorders M,D
Counseling Psychology M,D
Education—General M
Educational Leadership and
  Administration M
Educational Media/Instructional
  Technology M
English as a Second Language M
Industrial and Organizational
  Psychology M,D
Internet and Interactive
  Multimedia M
Jewish Studies M
Law M,D
Legal and Justice Studies M,D
Management Information Systems M
Mathematics Education M
Occupational Therapy M,D
Physical Therapy M,D
Physician Assistant Studies M,D
Reading Education M
Science Education M
Social Work M
Special Education M

TOURO UNIVERSITY CALIFORNIA
Education—General M,D
Osteopathic Medicine M,D
Pharmacy M,D
Public Health—General M,D

TOWSON UNIVERSITY
Accounting M
Allied Health—General M
Applied Mathematics M
Applied Physics M
Art Education M,O
Art History M
Art/Fine Arts M
Biological and Biomedical
  Sciences—General M
Child and Family Studies M,O
Communication Disorders M,D
Communication—General M
Computer and Information
  Systems Security M,D,O
Computer Science M
Corporate and Organizational
  Communication M
Counseling Psychology M
Database Systems M,D,O
Early Childhood Education M,O
Education—General M
Educational Leadership and
  Administration M,O
Educational Media/Instructional
  Technology M,D
Electronic Commerce M,O
Elementary Education M
Environmental and Occupational
  Health D
Environmental Management
  and Policy M
Environmental Sciences M,O
Experimental Psychology M
Forensic Sciences M
Geography M
Health Services Management and
  Hospital Administration M,O
Homeland Security M,O
Human Resources Development M
Information Science M,D,O
Internet and Interactive
  Multimedia M,D,O
Jewish Studies M,O
Liberal Studies M
Management Information Systems M,D,O
Management of Technology M
Marketing Research M
Mathematics Education M
Music Education M,O
Music M
Nursing Education M,O
Nursing—General M,O
Occupational Therapy M
Organizational Behavior O
Physician Assistant Studies M
Psychology—General M
Reading Education M,O
Religious Education M,O
School Psychology M
Secondary Education M
Social Sciences M
Software Engineering M,D,O
Special Education M,O
Supply Chain Management M,O
Theater M
Women's Studies M,O
Writing M

TOYOTA TECHNOLOGICAL INSTITUTE AT CHICAGO
Computer Science D

TRENT UNIVERSITY
American Indian/Native American
  Studies M,D
Anthropology M
Biological and Biomedical
  Sciences—General M,D
Canadian Studies M,D
Chemistry M
Computer Science M
Cultural Studies D
Environmental Management
  and Policy M,D
Geography M,D
Materials Sciences M
Modeling and Simulation M,D
Physics M

TREVECCA NAZARENE UNIVERSITY
Business Administration and
  Management—General M
Counselor Education M,D
Curriculum and Instruction M,O
Education—General M,O
Educational Leadership and
  Administration M,D,O
Educational Media/Instructional
  Technology M
Elementary Education M,O
English as a Second Language M,O
Information Science M,O
Library Science M,O
Marriage and Family Therapy M,D
Organizational Management M,D
Pastoral Ministry and Counseling M
Physician Assistant Studies M
Religion M
Secondary Education M,O
Special Education M,O

TRIDENT UNIVERSITY INTERNATIONAL
Adult Education M
Business Administration and
  Management—General M,D

Clinical Research M,D,O
Computer and Information
  Systems Security M,D
Conflict Resolution and
  Mediation/Peace Studies M,D
Criminal Justice and Criminology M,D
Early Childhood Education M,D
Education—General M,D
Educational Leadership and
  Administration M,D
Educational Media/Instructional
  Technology M,D
Emergency Management M,D,O
Environmental and Occupational
  Health M,D,O
Finance and Banking M,D
Health Education M,D,O
Health Informatics M,D,O
Health Services Management and
  Hospital Administration M,D
Higher Education M,D
Human Resources Management M,D
International Business M,D
International Health M,D,O
Legal and Justice Studies M,D,O
Logistics M,D
Management Information Systems M,D
Marketing M,D
Project Management M,D
Public Administration M,D
Public Health—General M,D,O
Quality Management M,D,O
Reading Education M

TRINE UNIVERSITY
Criminal Justice and Criminology M
Emergency Management M
Forensic Psychology M
Law M
Physical Therapy D
Physician Assistant Studies M
Public Administration M

TRINITY BAPTIST COLLEGE
Educational Leadership and
  Administration M
Special Education M

TRINITY BIBLE COLLEGE AND GRADUATE SCHOOL
Missions and Missiology M
Theology M

TRINITY CHRISTIAN COLLEGE
Counseling Psychology M
Special Education M

TRINITY COLLEGE (CANADA)
Music M,D,O
Pastoral Ministry and Counseling M,D,O
Theology M,D,O

TRINITY COLLEGE (UNITED STATES)
American Studies M
Cultural Studies M
English M
Media Studies M
Museum Studies M
Public Policy M
Writing M

TRINITY INTERNATIONAL UNIVERSITY
Archaeology M,D,O
Athletic Training and Sports
  Medicine M
Bioethics M,D
Business Administration and
  Management—General M,D,O
Counseling Psychology M,D,O
Education—General M
Human Resources Management M,D
Law M,D
Missions and Missiology M,D,O
Pastoral Ministry and Counseling M,D,O
Religious Education M,D,O
Theology M,D,O

TRINITY INTERNATIONAL UNIVERSITY FLORIDA
Counseling Psychology M
Religion M,O

TRINITY LUTHERAN SEMINARY
African-American Studies M
Missions and Missiology M
Music M
Pastoral Ministry and Counseling M
Religious Education M
Theology M

TRINITY SCHOOL FOR MINISTRY
Missions and Missiology M,D,O
Pastoral Ministry and Counseling M,D,O
Religion M,D,O
Theology M,D,O

TRINITY UNIVERSITY
Accounting M
Business Administration and
  Management—General M
Education—General M
Educational Leadership and
  Administration M
Health Services Management and
  Hospital Administration M
School Psychology M

TRINITY WASHINGTON UNIVERSITY
Business Administration and
  Management—General M
Clinical Psychology M
Communication—General M
Counseling Psychology M
Counselor Education M
Curriculum and Instruction M

---

*M—masters degree; D—doctorate; O—other advanced degree; *—Close-Up and/or Display*

Early Childhood Education — M
Education—General — M
Educational Leadership and
   Administration — M
Elementary Education — M
English Education — M
Human Resources Management — M
National Security — M
Nonprofit Management — M
Organizational Management — M
Public Health—General — M
Reading Education — M
Secondary Education — M
Social Sciences Education — M
Special Education — M

TRINITY WESTERN UNIVERSITY
Business Administration and
   Management—General — M
Counseling Psychology — M
Educational Leadership and
   Administration — M,O
English as a Second Language — M
English — M
Health Services Management and
   Hospital Administration — M,O
History — M
Humanities — M
Interdisciplinary Studies — M
International Business — M
Linguistics — M
Nonprofit Management — M,O
Nursing—General — M
Organizational Management — M,O
Pastoral Ministry and Counseling — M,D
Philosophy — M
Theology — M,D

TRI-STATE BIBLE COLLEGE
Theology — M

TRI-STATE COLLEGE OF ACUPUNCTURE
Acupuncture and Oriental Medicine — M,O

TROPICAL AGRICULTURE RESEARCH AND HIGHER EDUCATION CENTER
Agricultural Economics and
   Agribusiness — M,D
Agricultural Sciences—
   General — M,D
Conservation Biology — M,D
Environmental Management
   and Policy — M,D
Forestry — M,D
Travel and Tourism — M,D
Water Resources — M,D

TROY UNIVERSITY
Accounting — M
Adult Education — M
Adult Nursing — M,D
Biological and Biomedical
   Sciences—General — M,O
Business Administration and
   Management—General — M
Communication—General — M
Computer Science — M
Corporate and Organizational
   Communication — M
Counselor Education — M,O
Criminal Justice and Criminology — M
Early Childhood Education — M,O
Economic Development — M
Economics — M
Education—General — M,O
Educational Leadership and
   Administration — M,O
Elementary Education — M,O
English as a Second Language — M
Environmental Management
   and Policy — M
Family Nurse Practitioner Studies — M,D
Finance and Banking — M
Health Services Management and
   Hospital Administration — M
History — M
Human Resources Management — M
International Affairs — M
Management Information Systems — M
Maternal and Child Health — M,D
Nursing Informatics — M,D
Nursing—General — M,D
Public Administration — M
Secondary Education — M
Social Sciences — M
Social Work — M
Sports Management — M
Taxation — M,O

TRUETT MCCONNELL UNIVERSITY
Theology — M

TRUMAN STATE UNIVERSITY
Accounting — M
Biological and Biomedical
   Sciences—General — M
Communication Disorders — M
Education—General — M
English — M
Music — M

TUFTS UNIVERSITY
Allopathic Medicine — D
Animal Sciences — M
Archaeology — M
Art Education — M,D,O
Art History — M
Art/Fine Arts — M,O
Astrophysics — M,D
Biochemistry — D
Bioengineering — M,D,O
Bioinformatics — M,D
Biological and Biomedical
   Sciences—General — M,D,O
Biomedical Engineering — M,D
Biostatistics — M,D,O

Biotechnology — M,D,O
Cancer Biology/Oncology — D
Cell Biology — D
Chemical Engineering — M,D
Chemical Physics — M,D
Chemistry — M,D
Child and Family Studies — M,D
Child Development — M,D
Civil Engineering — M,D
Classics — M
Clinical Research — M,D,O
Cognitive Sciences — M,D
Computer Science — M,D,O
Conflict Resolution and
   Mediation/Peace Studies — M,D
Dentistry — D
Developmental Biology — D
Early Childhood Education — M,D
Economics — M
Education—General — M,D,O
Electrical Engineering — M,D,O
Elementary Education — M,D
Engineering and Applied
   Sciences—General — M,D*
Engineering Management — M
English — M,D
Entrepreneurship — M
Environmental and Occupational
   Health — M,D
Environmental Engineering — M,D
Environmental Management
   and Policy — M,D,O
Environmental Sciences — M,D
Epidemiology — M,D,O
Ergonomics and Human
   Factors — M,D
Family and Consumer
   Sciences-General — M,D
French — M
Genetics — D
Geotechnical Engineering — M,D
German — M
Hazardous Materials
   Management — M,D
Health Communication — M,D,O
Health Services Management and
   Hospital Administration — M,D,O
History — M,D
Human Development — M,D
Human-Computer Interaction — O
Immunology — D
Infectious Diseases — M,D
Interdisciplinary Studies — D
International Affairs — M,D
International Business — M,D
International Development — M,D
International Health — M,D
Law — M,D
Management Strategy and Policy — O
Manufacturing Engineering — O
Mathematics Education — M,D
Mathematics — M,D
Mechanical Engineering — M,D
Microbiology — D
Middle School Education — M,D
Molecular Biology — D
Molecular Medicine — D
Museum Education — M,D
Museum Studies — M,D,O
Music — M
Neuroscience — M,D
Nonprofit Management — O
Nutrition — M,D,O
Occupational Therapy — M,D,O
Oral and Dental Sciences — M,O
Pathology — M,D
Philosophy — M
Physician Assistant Studies — M,D,O
Physics — M,D
Psychology—General — M,D
Public Administration — O
Public Health—General — M,D,O
Public Policy — M
Reproductive Biology — M,D
School Psychology — M,O
Science Education — M,D
Secondary Education — M,D
Structural Biology — D
Structural Engineering — M,D
Theater — M,D
Urban and Regional Planning — M
Urban Studies — M
Veterinary Medicine — M,D
Water Resources Engineering — M,D

TULANE UNIVERSITY
Accounting — M,D
Allopathic Medicine — D
Anthropology — D
Architecture — M
Art History — M
Art/Fine Arts — M
Biochemistry — M
Biological and Biomedical
   Sciences—General — M,D
Biomedical Engineering — M,D
Biostatistics — M,D
Business Administration and
   Management—General — M,D
Cell Biology — M,D
Chemical Engineering — M,D
Chemistry — M,D
Classics — M
Community Health — M,D
Dance — M
Ecology — M,D
Economics — M,D
Emergency Management — M,D
Energy Management and
   Policy — M
English — M
Entrepreneurship — M,D
Environmental and Occupational
   Health — M,D

Epidemiology — M,D
Evolutionary Biology — M,D
Finance and Banking — M,D
French — M,D
Health Services Management and
   Hospital Administration — M
History — M,D
Human Genetics — M
Immunology — M
Interdisciplinary Studies — D
International Business — M,D
International Development — M,D
International Health — M,D
Latin American Studies — M,D
Law — M,D
Liberal Studies — M
Management Strategy and Policy — M,D
Mathematics — M,D
Microbiology — M,D
Molecular Biology — M,D
Music — M,D
Neuroscience — M,D
Parasitology — M,D,O
Pharmacology — M
Philosophy — M,D
Physics — M,D
Physiology — M
Political Science — D
Portuguese — M,D
Psychology—General — M,D
Public Health—General — M,D
Social Work — M,D
Sociology — M,D
Spanish — M,D
Structural Biology — M,D
Theater — M

TUSCULUM COLLEGE
Business Administration and
   Management—General — M
Curriculum and Instruction — M
Education—General — M
Health Services Management and
   Hospital Administration — M
Human Resources Management — M
Mathematics Education — M
Nonprofit Management — M
Special Education — M

TUSKEGEE UNIVERSITY
Agricultural Economics and
   Agribusiness — M
Agronomy and Soil Sciences — M
Animal Sciences — M
Biological and Biomedical
   Sciences—General — M,D
Chemistry — M
Computer and Information
   Systems Security — M
Electrical Engineering — M
Engineering and Applied
   Sciences—General — M
Environmental Sciences — M
Food Science and
   Technology — M
Management Information Systems — M
Materials Engineering — D
Mechanical Engineering — M
Nutrition — M
Occupational Therapy — M
Plant Sciences — M
Veterinary Medicine — M,D
Veterinary Sciences — M,D

TYNDALE UNIVERSITY COLLEGE & SEMINARY
Missions and Missiology — M,O
Pastoral Ministry and Counseling — M,O
Theology — M,O

UNIFICATION THEOLOGICAL SEMINARY
Nonprofit Management — M,D
Pastoral Ministry and Counseling — M,D
Religion — M,D
Religious Education — M,D
Theology — M,D

UNIFORMED SERVICES UNIVERSITY OF THE HEALTH SCIENCES
Biological and Biomedical
   Sciences—General — M,D
Cell Biology — M,D
Clinical Psychology — D
Environmental and Occupational
   Health — M,D
Family Nurse Practitioner Studies — M,D
Gerontological Nursing — M,D
Health Services Management and
   Hospital Administration — M,D
Immunology — D
Infectious Diseases — D*
International Health — M,D
Molecular Biology — M,D*
Neuroscience — D*
Nurse Anesthesia — M,D
Nursing—General — M,D
Psychiatric Nursing — M,D
Psychology—General — D
Public Health—General — M,D
Women's Health Nursing — M,D
Zoology — M,D

UNION COLLEGE (KY)
Clinical Psychology — M
Counseling Psychology — M
Education—General — M
Educational Leadership and
   Administration — M
Elementary Education — M
Health Education — M
Middle School Education — M
Music Education — M
Physical Education — M
Psychology—General — M
Reading Education — M

School Psychology — M
Secondary Education — M
Special Education — M

UNION COLLEGE (NE)
Physician Assistant Studies — M

UNION INSTITUTE & UNIVERSITY
Clinical Psychology — M
Cultural Studies — M
Education—General — D
Health Promotion — M
History — M
Interdisciplinary Studies — M,D
Organizational Management — M
Public Policy — M
Writing — M

UNION PRESBYTERIAN SEMINARY
Religious Education — M,D

UNION THEOLOGICAL SEMINARY IN THE CITY OF NEW YORK
Theology — M,D

UNION UNIVERSITY
Accounting — M
Business Administration and
   Management—General — M
Cultural Studies — M
Education—General — M,D,O
Educational Leadership and
   Administration — M,D,O
Family Nurse Practitioner Studies — M,D,O
Higher Education — M,D,O
Nurse Anesthesia — M,D,O
Nursing and Healthcare
   Administration — M,D,O
Nursing Education — M,D,O
Nursing—General — M,D,O
Pastoral Ministry and Counseling — M,D
Pharmacy — D
Religion — M,D
Social Work — M

UNITED STATES ARMY COMMAND AND GENERAL STAFF COLLEGE
Military and Defense Studies — M

UNITED STATES INTERNATIONAL UNIVERSITY–AFRICA
Addictions/Substance Abuse
   Counseling — M
Business Administration and
   Management—General — M
Conflict Resolution and
   Mediation/Peace Studies — M
Counseling Psychology — M
Entrepreneurship — M
Finance and Banking — M
Health Psychology — M
Human Resources Management — M
International Affairs — M
International Business — M
Management Information Systems — M
Management Strategy and Policy — M
Marketing — M
Organizational Management — M

UNITED STATES MERCHANT MARINE ACADEMY
Civil Engineering — M

UNITED STATES SPORTS ACADEMY
Athletic Training and Sports
   Medicine — M
Exercise and Sports Science — M
Physical Education — M
Sports Management — M,D

UNITED STATES UNIVERSITY
Family Nurse Practitioner Studies — M

UNITED TALMUDICAL SEMINARY
Theology

UNITED THEOLOGICAL SEMINARY
Pastoral Ministry and Counseling — M,D
Theology — M,D

UNITED THEOLOGICAL SEMINARY OF THE TWIN CITIES
Art/Fine Arts — M,D,O
Asian Studies — M,D,O
Conflict Resolution and
   Mediation/Peace Studies — M,D,O
Ethnic Studies — M,D,O
Humanities — M,D,O
Pastoral Ministry and Counseling — M,D,O
Religion — M,D,O
Theology — M,D,O
Women's Studies — M,D,O

UNITY COLLEGE
Natural Resources — M
Sustainable Development — M

UNIVERSIDAD ADVENTISTA DE LAS ANTILLAS
Curriculum and Instruction — M
Educational Leadership and
   Administration — M
Medical/Surgical Nursing — M

UNIVERSIDAD AUTONOMA DE GUADALAJARA
Advertising and Public Relations — M,D
Allopathic Medicine — D
Architecture — M,D
Business Administration and
   Management—General — M,D
Computer Art and Design — M,D
Computer Science — M,D
Corporate and Organizational
   Communication — M,D
Education—General — M,D
Energy and Power
   Engineering — M,D
Entertainment Management — M,D

Environmental and Occupational Health — M,D
Environmental Management and Policy — M,D
Film, Television, and Video Production — M,D
International Business — M,D
Internet and Interactive Multimedia — M,D
Law — M,D
Legal and Justice Studies — M,D
Manufacturing Engineering — M,D
Marketing Research — M,D
Mathematics Education — M,D
Philosophy — M,D
Public Policy — M,D
Spanish — M,D
Systems Science — M,D
Translation and Interpretation — M,D

UNIVERSIDAD CENTRAL DEL CARIBE
Addictions/Substance Abuse Counseling — M
Allopathic Medicine — M,D
Anatomy — M,D
Biochemistry — M,D
Biological and Biomedical Sciences—General — M,D
Cell Biology — M,D
Immunology — M,D
Microbiology — M,D
Molecular Biology — M,D
Pharmacology — M,D
Physiology — M,D

UNIVERSIDAD CENTRAL DEL ESTE
Allopathic Medicine — D
Dentistry — D
Environmental Engineering — M
Finance and Banking — M
Higher Education — M
Human Resources Development — M
Law — D

UNIVERSIDAD DE CIENCIAS MEDICAS
Allopathic Medicine — M,D,O
Anatomy — M,D,O
Biological and Biomedical Sciences—General — M,D,O
Community Health — M,D,O
Environmental and Occupational Health — M,D,O
Health Services Management and Hospital Administration — M,D,O
Pharmacy — M,D,O

UNIVERSIDAD DE IBEROAMERICA
Acute Care/Critical Care Nursing — M,D
Allopathic Medicine — M,D
Clinical Psychology — M,D
Educational Psychology — M,D
Forensic Psychology — M,D
Health Services Management and Hospital Administration — M,D
Neuroscience — M,D

UNIVERSIDAD DE LAS AMERICAS, A.C.
Business Administration and Management—General — M
Education—General — M
Finance and Banking — M
International Affairs — M
Marketing Research — M
Marriage and Family Therapy — M
Organizational Behavior — M
Psychology—General — M
Quality Management — M

UNIVERSIDAD DE LAS AMÉRICAS PUEBLA
American Studies — M
Anthropology — M
Archaeology — M
Biotechnology — M
Business Administration and Management—General — M
Chemical Engineering — M
Clinical Laboratory Sciences/Medical Technology — M
Computer Art and Design — M
Computer Science — M,D
Construction Management — M
Economics — M
Education—General — M
Electrical Engineering — M
Engineering and Applied Sciences—General — M,D
English — M
Finance and Banking — M
Food Science and Technology — M
Industrial and Manufacturing Management — M
Industrial/Management Engineering — M
Linguistics — M
Manufacturing Engineering — M
Psychology—General — M

UNIVERSIDAD DEL ESTE
Accounting — M
Adult Education — M
Agricultural Economics and Agribusiness — M
Business Administration and Management—General — M
Computer and Information Systems Security — M
Criminal Justice and Criminology — M
Electronic Commerce — M
Elementary Education — M
English as a Second Language — M
Foreign Languages Education — M

Human Resources Management — M
Management Information Systems — M
Management Strategy and Policy — M
Public Policy — M
Social Work — M
Special Education — M

UNIVERSIDAD DEL TURABO
Accounting — M
Adult Nursing — M,O
Art/Fine Arts — M
Arts Administration — M
Athletic Training and Sports Medicine — M
Business Administration and Management—General — M,D
Chemistry — M,D
Communication Disorders — M
Computer Engineering — M
Conflict Resolution and Mediation/Peace Studies — M
Counseling Psychology — M,D,O
Counselor Education — M
Criminal Justice and Criminology — M
Curriculum and Instruction — M,D
Early Childhood Education — M
Education—General — M,D
Educational Leadership and Administration — M,D
Electrical Engineering — M
Engineering and Applied Sciences—General — M
English as a Second Language — M
Environmental Biology — M,D
Environmental Management and Policy — M,D
Environmental Sciences — M,D
Family Nurse Practitioner Studies — M,O
Forensic Psychology — M,D,O
Forensic Sciences — M
Health Promotion — M
Human Resources Management — M
Human Services — M
Information Studies — M
Library Science — M
Logistics — M
Management Information Systems — D
Marketing — M
Mechanical Engineering — M
Naturopathic Medicine — D
Physical Education — M
Project Management — M
Quality Management — M
Special Education — M
Telecommunications — M

UNIVERSIDAD IBEROAMERICANA
Allopathic Medicine — D
Business Administration and Management—General — M,D
Corporate and Organizational Communication — M,D
Dentistry — M,D
Educational Leadership and Administration — M,D
Human Resources Development — M,D
Law — M,D
Marketing — M,D
Real Estate — M,D
Special Education — M,D

UNIVERSIDAD METROPOLITANA
Accounting — M
Adult Education — M
Business Administration and Management—General — M
Counseling Psychology — M
Curriculum and Instruction — M
Education—General — M
Educational Leadership and Administration — M
Elementary Education — M
Environmental Management and Policy — M
Finance and Banking — M
Human Resources Management — M
International Business — M
Leisure Studies — M
Management Information Systems — M
Marketing — M
Natural Resources — M
Nursing and Healthcare Administration — M,O
Nursing—General — M,O
Oncology Nursing — M,O
Physical Education — M
Recreation and Park Management — M
Secondary Education — M
Special Education — M

UNIVERSIDAD NACIONAL PEDRO HENRIQUEZ URENA
Agricultural Sciences—General — M
Allopathic Medicine — D
Animal Sciences — M
Architecture — M
Dentistry — D
Ecology — M
Environmental Engineering — M
Environmental Sciences — M
Historic Preservation — M
Horticulture — M
International Affairs — M
Natural Resources — M
Political Science — M
Project Management — M
Science Education — M

UNIVERSITÉ DE MONCTON
Astronomy — M
Biochemistry — M

Biological and Biomedical Sciences—General — M
Business Administration and Management—General — M
Chemistry — M
Civil Engineering — M
Computer Science — M,O
Counselor Education — M
Economics — M
Education—General — M
Educational Leadership and Administration — M
Educational Psychology — M
Electrical Engineering — M
Engineering and Applied Sciences—General — M
Food Science and Technology — M
French — M,D
History — M
Industrial/Management Engineering — M
Mathematics — M
Mechanical Engineering — M
Nutrition — M
Physics — M
Public Administration — M
Social Work — M

UNIVERSITÉ DE MONTRÉAL
Allopathic Medicine — D
Anthropology — M,D
Art History — M,D
Biochemistry — M,D,O
Bioethics — M,D,O
Bioinformatics — M,D
Biological and Biomedical Sciences—General — M,D
Biomedical Engineering — M,D,O
Cell Biology — M,D
Chemistry — M,D
Classics — M
Communication Disorders — M,O
Communication—General — M,D
Community Health — M,D,O
Comparative Literature — M,D
Computer Science — M,D
Criminal Justice and Criminology — M,D
Curriculum and Instruction — M,D,O
Demography and Population Studies — M,D
Dental Hygiene — O
Developmental Psychology — M,D
Economics — M,D,O
Education—General — M,D,O
Educational Leadership and Administration — M,D,O
Educational Psychology — M,D,O
Electronic Commerce — M,D
Emergency Management — O
English — M,D
Environmental and Occupational Health — M
Environmental Design — M,D,O
Environmental Management and Policy — O
Ergonomics and Human Factors — O
Film, Television, and Video Theory and Criticism — M,D
French — M,D
Genetic Counseling — O
Genetics — O
Geography — M,D,O
German — M
Health Services Management and Hospital Administration — M,O
Hispanic and Latin American Languages — M,D
History — M,D
Human Services — D
Immunology — M,D
Industrial and Labor Relations — M,D,O
Information Studies — M,D
International Affairs — M,O
Kinesiology and Movement Studies — M,D,O
Law — M,D,O
Library Science — M,D
Linguistics — M,D,O
Mathematical and Computational Finance — M,D,O
Mathematics — M,D,O
Microbiology — M,D
Molecular Biology — M,D
Museum Studies — M
Music — M,D,O
Neuroscience — M,D
Nursing—General — M,D
Nutrition — M,D,O
Occupational Therapy — O
Optometry — D
Oral and Dental Sciences — M,O
Pathology — M,D
Pharmaceutical Sciences — M,D,O
Pharmacology — M,D
Philosophy — M,D
Physical Education — M,D,O
Physics — M,D
Physiology — M,D
Political Science — M,D
Psychology—General — M,D
Public Health—General — M,D,O
Public Policy — O
Rehabilitation Sciences — O
Religion — M,D,O
Social Work — O
Sociology — M,D
Spanish — M
Statistics — M,D,O
Taxation — M,D,O
Theology — M,D,O
Toxicology — O

Translation and Interpretation — M,D,O
Urban and Regional Planning — M,D,O
Veterinary Medicine — D
Veterinary Sciences — M,D
Virology — D
Vision Sciences — M

UNIVERSITÉ DE SAINT-BONIFACE
Canadian Studies — M
Education—General — M

UNIVERSITÉ DE SHERBROOKE
Accounting — M
Allopathic Medicine — D
Biochemistry — M,D
Biological and Biomedical Sciences—General — M,D,O
Biophysics — M,D
Business Administration and Management—General — M,D,O
Canadian Studies — M,D
Cell Biology — M,D
Chemical Engineering — M,D
Chemistry — M,D,O
Civil Engineering — M,D
Clinical Laboratory Sciences/Medical Technology — M,D
Comparative Literature — M,D
Computer and Information Systems Security — M
Conflict Resolution and Mediation/Peace Studies — M,D,O
Corporate and Organizational Communication — M
Economic Development — D
Economics — M
Education—General — M,O
Educational Leadership and Administration — M
Electrical Engineering — M,D
Electronic Commerce — M
Elementary Education — M,O
Engineering and Applied Sciences—General — M,D,O
Engineering Management — M,O
Environmental Engineering — M
Environmental Sciences — M,O
Ethics — M,D,O
Finance and Banking — M,D
French — M,D
Geography — M,D
Gerontology — M
Health Law — M,D,O
Higher Education — M,O
History — M
Immunology — M,D
Information Science — M,D
International Business — M
Kinesiology and Movement Studies — M,O
Law — M,D,O
Linguistics — M,D
Management Information Systems — M
Marketing — M
Mathematics — M,D
Mechanical Engineering — M,D
Microbiology — M,D
Organizational Behavior — M
Pharmacology — M,D
Philosophy — M,D,O
Physical Education — M,O
Physics — M,D
Physiology — M,D
Psychology—General — M
Public Administration — M
Radiation Biology — M,D
Religion — M,D,O
Social Work — M
Special Education — M,O
Taxation — M,O
Theater — M,D
Theology — M,D

UNIVERSITÉ DU QUÉBEC À CHICOUTIMI
Art/Fine Arts — M
Business Administration and Management—General — M
Canadian Studies — M
Comparative Literature — M
Education—General — M,D
Engineering and Applied Sciences—General — M,D
Environmental Management and Policy — M
Ethics — O
French — M
Genetics — M
Geosciences — M
Linguistics — M
Mineralogy — D
Project Management — M
Theology — M,D

UNIVERSITÉ DU QUÉBEC À MONTRÉAL
Accounting — M,O
Actuarial Science — O
Art History — M,D
Art/Fine Arts — M
Atmospheric Sciences — M,D,O
Biological and Biomedical Sciences—General — M,D
Business Administration and Management—General — M,D,O
Chemistry — M,D
Communication—General — M,D
Comparative Literature — M,D
Dance — M
Economics — M,D
Education—General — M,D,O
Environmental and Occupational Health — O
Environmental Education — M,D,O
Environmental Sciences — M,D,O

M—masters degree; D—doctorate; O—other advanced degree; *—Close-Up and/or Display

Ergonomics and Human Factors	O
Finance and Banking	O
Geographic Information Systems	O
Geography	M
Geology	M,D,O
Geosciences	M,D,O
History	M,D
Kinesiology and Movement Studies	M
Law	O
Linguistics	M,D
Management Information Systems	M
Mathematics	M,D
Meteorology	M,D,O
Mineralogy	M,D,O
Museum Studies	M
Natural Resources	M,D,O
Philosophy	M,D
Political Science	M,D
Project Management	M,O
Psychology—General	D
Public Administration	M
Religion	M
Social Work	M
Sociology	M,D
Urban Studies	M,D

UNIVERSITÉ DU QUÉBEC À RIMOUSKI

Business Administration and Management—General	M,O
Comparative Literature	M,D
Education—General	M,D,O
Engineering and Applied Sciences—General	M
Ethics	M,O
Fish, Game, and Wildlife Management	M,D,O
Marine Affairs	M
Nursing—General	M,O
Oceanography	M,D
Project Management	M,O
Social Psychology	M
Urban and Regional Planning	M,D,O

UNIVERSITÉ DU QUÉBEC À TROIS-RIVIÈRES

Accounting	M
Biophysics	M,D
Business Administration and Management—General	M,D
Chemistry	M
Chiropractic	D
Communication—General	M,O
Comparative Literature	M
Computer Science	M
Education—General	M,D
Educational Leadership and Administration	O
Educational Psychology	M,D
Electrical Engineering	M,D
Environmental Sciences	M,D
Finance and Banking	O
Industrial and Labor Relations	O
Industrial/Management Engineering	M,O
Leisure Studies	M,O
Mathematics	M
Nursing—General	M,O
Philosophy	M,D
Physical Education	M
Physics	M,D
Psychology—General	D,O
Travel and Tourism	M,O

UNIVERSITÉ DU QUÉBEC, ÉCOLE DE TECHNOLOGIE SUPÉRIEURE

Engineering and Applied Sciences—General	M,D,O

UNIVERSITÉ DU QUÉBEC, ÉCOLE NATIONALE D'ADMINISTRATION PUBLIQUE

International Business	M,O
Public Administration	D,O
Urban Studies	M

UNIVERSITÉ DU QUÉBEC EN ABITIBI-TÉMISCAMINGUE

Biological and Biomedical Sciences—General	M,D
Business Administration and Management—General	M
Education—General	M,D,O
Engineering and Applied Sciences—General	M,O
Environmental Sciences	M,D
Forestry	M,D
Mineral/Mining Engineering	M,O
Natural Resources	M,D
Project Management	M,O
Social Work	M

UNIVERSITÉ DU QUÉBEC EN OUTAOUAIS

Accounting	M,O
Computer Science	M,D,O
Education—General	M,D,O
Educational Psychology	M
Finance and Banking	M,O
Foreign Languages Education	O
Industrial and Labor Relations	M,D,O
Nursing—General	M,O
Project Management	M,O
Social Work	M
Urban and Regional Planning	M

UNIVERSITÉ DU QUÉBEC, INSTITUT NATIONAL DE LA RECHERCHE SCIENTIFIQUE

Biological and Biomedical Sciences—General	M,D
Demography and Population Studies	M,D,O
Energy Management and Policy	M,D
Environmental Management and Policy	M,D

Geosciences	M,D
Hydrology	M,D
Immunology	M,D
Materials Sciences	M,D
Medical Microbiology	M,D
Microbiology	M,D
Telecommunications	M,D
Urban Studies	M,D
Virology	M,D

UNIVERSITÉ LAVAL

Accounting	M,O
Advertising and Public Relations	O
Aerospace/Aeronautical Engineering	M
Agricultural Economics and Agribusiness	M
Agricultural Engineering	M
Agricultural Sciences—General	M,D,O
Agronomy and Soil Sciences	M,D
Allopathic Medicine	D,O
Anatomy	O
Anesthesiologist Assistant Studies	O
Animal Sciences	M,D
Anthropology	M,D
Archaeology	M,D
Architecture	M
Art History	M
Art/Fine Arts	M
Biochemistry	M,D,O
Biological and Biomedical Sciences—General	M,D,O
Business Administration and Management—General	M,D
Cancer Biology/Oncology	O
Cardiovascular Sciences	O
Cell Biology	M,D
Chemical Engineering	M,D
Chemistry	M,D
Civil Engineering	M,D,O
Clinical Psychology	D
Communication Disorders	M
Community Health	M,D,O
Comparative Literature	M,D
Computer Science	M,D
Consumer Economics	O
Counselor Education	M,D
Curriculum and Instruction	M,D
Dentistry	D
Economics	M,D
Education—General	M,D,O
Educational Leadership and Administration	M,D,O
Educational Measurement and Evaluation	M,D,O
Educational Media/Instructional Technology	M,D
Educational Psychology	M,D
Electrical Engineering	M,D
Electronic Commerce	M,O
Emergency Medical Services	O
Engineering and Applied Sciences—General	M,D,O
English	M,D
Entrepreneurship	M,O
Environmental and Occupational Health	O
Environmental Engineering	M,D
Environmental Management and Policy	M,D,O
Environmental Sciences	M,D
Epidemiology	M,D
Ethics	O
Ethnic Studies	M,D
Facilities Management	M,O
Film, Television, and Video Theory and Criticism	M,D
Finance and Banking	M,O
Food Science and Technology	M,D
Forestry	M,D
Geodetic Sciences	M,D
Geographic Information Systems	M,O
Geography	M,D
Geology	M,D
Geosciences	M,D
Gerontology	O
Graphic Design	M
Health Physics/Radiological Health	O
History	M,D
Immunology	M,D
Industrial and Labor Relations	M,D
Industrial/Management Engineering	O
Infectious Diseases	O
International Affairs	M,D
International Business	M,O
Journalism	O
Kinesiology and Movement Studies	M,D
Law	M,D,O
Legal and Justice Studies	M,D
Linguistics	M,D
Management Information Systems	M,O
Marketing	M,O
Mass Communication	M,D
Mathematics	M,D
Mechanical Engineering	M,D
Metallurgical Engineering and Metallurgy	M,D
Microbiology	M,D
Mineral/Mining Engineering	M,D
Modeling and Simulation	M,O
Molecular Biology	M,D
Museum Studies	O
Music Education	M,D
Music	M,D
Neurobiology	M,D
Nursing—General	M,D,O
Nutrition	M,D
Oceanography	D
Oral and Dental Sciences	M,D
Organizational Management	M,O
Pathology	O

Pharmaceutical Sciences	M,D,O
Philosophy	M,D
Physics	M,D
Physiology	M,D
Plant Biology	M,D
Political Science	M,D
Psychology—General	D
Religion	M,D
Rural Planning and Studies	O
Social Psychology	D
Social Work	M,D
Sociology	M,D
Software Engineering	O
Spanish	M,D
Statistics	M
Theater	M,D
Theology	M,D
Translation and Interpretation	M,D
Urban and Regional Planning	M,O
Women's Studies	O

UNIVERSITÉ SAINTE-ANNE

Education—General	M

UNIVERSITY AT ALBANY, STATE UNIVERSITY OF NEW YORK

Accounting	M
African Studies	M
African-American Studies	M
Anthropology	M,D
Art/Fine Arts	M
Atmospheric Sciences	M,D
Biological and Biomedical Sciences—General	M,D
Biostatistics	M,D
Business Administration and Management—General	M
Chemistry	M,D
Clinical Psychology	M,D
Cognitive Sciences	M,D
Communication—General	M,D
Computer and Information Systems Security	M,O
Computer Science	M,D
Counseling Psychology	M,D
Criminal Justice and Criminology	M,D
Curriculum and Instruction	M,D,O
Demography and Population Studies	M,D,O
Economics	M,D,O
Education—General	M,D,O
Educational Leadership and Administration	M,D,O
Educational Measurement and Evaluation	M,D,O
Educational Media/Instructional Technology	M,D,O
Educational Policy	M,D,O
Educational Psychology	M,D,O
Emergency Management	O
Engineering and Applied Sciences—General	M,D,O
English	M,D
Entrepreneurship	M
Environmental and Occupational Health	M,D
Epidemiology	M,D
Finance and Banking	M,D,O
Forensic Sciences	M
Geographic Information Systems	M,O
Geography	M
Health Services Management and Hospital Administration	M,D,O
Higher Education	M,D,O
History	M,D,O
Homeland Security	M,O
Human Resources Management	M,D,O
Industrial and Organizational Psychology	M,D
Information Science	D
Information Studies	M,O
International and Comparative Education	M,D,O
Latin American Studies	M,D,O
Law	M
Liberal Studies	M
Library Science	M,O
Management Information Systems	M,D,O
Management of Technology	M
Marketing	M
Mathematics	M,D
Neuroscience	M,D
Nonprofit Management	M,D,O
Organizational Behavior	M,D,O
Philosophy	M,D
Physics	M,D
Political Science	M,D
Psychology—General	M,D
Public Administration	M,D
Public Health—General	M,D
Public History	M,D,O
Public Policy	M,D,O
Reading Education	M,D,O
Social Psychology	M,D
Social Work	M,D,O
Sociology	M,D,O
Spanish	M,D
Special Education	M
Taxation	M
Toxicology	M,D
Urban and Regional Planning	M,D
Urban Studies	M,D,O
Women's Studies	M

UNIVERSITY AT BUFFALO, THE STATE UNIVERSITY OF NEW YORK

Accounting	M,D
Adult Nursing	M,D,O
Aerospace/Aeronautical Engineering	M,D
Allied Health—General	M,D
Allopathic Medicine	D
American Studies	M,D
Anatomy	M,D
Anthropology	M,D
Architecture	M

Art History	M,D
Art/Fine Arts	M,D
Arts Administration	M
Biochemistry	M,D
Bioengineering	M,D
Bioinformatics	M
Biological and Biomedical Sciences—General	M,D
Biomedical Engineering	M,D
Biophysics	M,D
Biostatistics	M,D
Biotechnology	M
Business Administration and Management—General	M,D
Canadian Studies	M,D,O
Cancer Biology/Oncology	M
Cell Biology	D
Chemical Engineering	M,D
Chemistry	M,D
Civil Engineering	M,D
Classics	M,D,O
Clinical Laboratory Sciences/Medical Technology	M
Communication Disorders	M,D
Communication—General	M,D
Community Health	M,D
Comparative Literature	M,D
Computational Sciences	O
Computer Science	M,D,O
Counseling Psychology	M,D,O
Counselor Education	M,D,O
Curriculum and Instruction	M,D,O
Dentistry	D
Distance Education Development	M,D,O
Early Childhood Education	M,D,O
Ecology	M,D,O
Economics	M,D,O
Education of the Gifted	M,D,O
Education—General	M,D,O
Educational Leadership and Administration	M,D,O
Educational Media/Instructional Technology	M,D,O
Educational Psychology	M,D,O
Electrical Engineering	M,D*
Electronic Commerce	M,D,O
Elementary Education	M,D,O
Engineering and Applied Sciences—General	M,D,O
English as a Second Language	M,D,O
English Education	M,D,O
English	M,D,O
Environmental Engineering	M,D
Environmental Sciences	M,D
Epidemiology	M,D
Evolutionary Biology	M,D,O
Exercise and Sports Science	M,D
Family Nurse Practitioner Studies	M,D,O
Film, Television, and Video Theory and Criticism	M,D,O
Finance and Banking	M,D
Foreign Languages Education	M,D,O
Foundations and Philosophy of Education	M,D,O
French	M,D,O
Gender Studies	M,D,O
Genetics	M,D
Genomic Sciences	M,D
Geographic Information Systems	M,D
Geography	M,D
Geology	M,D
Geosciences	M,D
German	M,D
Gerontological Nursing	M,D,O
Health Services Management and Hospital Administration	M,D,O
Higher Education	M,D,O
Historic Preservation	M,D,O
History	M,D,O
Human Resources Management	M,D,O
Humanities	M
Immunology	M,D
Industrial/Management Engineering	M,D
Information Studies	M,O
Interdisciplinary Studies	M
International Business	M,D
Latin American Studies	M,D,O
Law	M,D
Library Science	M,O
Linguistics	M,D
Logistics	M,D
Management Information Systems	M,D,O
Management Strategy and Policy	M,D
Marketing	M,D
Mathematics Education	M,D,O
Mathematics	M,D
Mechanical Engineering	M,D
Media Studies	M,D
Medical Informatics	M,D
Medical Physics	M,D
Medicinal and Pharmaceutical Chemistry	M,D
Microbiology	M,D
Modeling and Simulation	M,D
Molecular Biology	D
Molecular Biophysics	M,D
Molecular Pharmacology	D
Multilingual and Multicultural Education	M,D,O
Museum Studies	M,D,O
Music Education	M,D,O
Music	M,D,O
Neuroscience	M,D
Nurse Anesthesia	M,D,O
Nursing and Healthcare Administration	M,D,O
Nursing—General	M,D,O
Nutrition	M,D,O
Occupational Therapy	M
Oral and Dental Sciences	M,D,O
Pathology	M,D
Pharmaceutical Sciences	M,D
Pharmacology	M,D

Pharmacy	D
Philosophy	M,D
Physical Therapy	D
Physics	M,D
Physiology	M,D
Political Science	M,D
Psychiatric Nursing	M,D,O
Psychology—General	M,D
Public Health—General	M,D
Public History	M,D,O
Quantitative Analysis	M,D
Reading Education	M,D,O
Real Estate	M
Rehabilitation Counseling	M,D,O
Rehabilitation Sciences	M,D,O
Romance Languages	M,D
Science Education	M,D,O
Social Sciences Education	M,D,O
Social Sciences	M
Social Work	M,D
Sociology	M,D
Spanish	M,D,O
Special Education	M,D,O
Structural Biology	M,D
Structural Engineering	M,D
Supply Chain Management	M,D
Theater	M,D
Toxicology	M,D
Urban and Regional Planning	M,D,O
Urban Design	M,D,O

UNIVERSITY OF ADVANCING TECHNOLOGY

Computer and Information Systems Security	M
Computer Science	M
Game Design and Development	M
Internet and Interactive Multimedia	M
Management of Technology	M

THE UNIVERSITY OF AKRON

Accounting	M
Applied Mathematics	M
Art Education	M
Arts Administration	M
Biological and Biomedical Sciences—General	M,D
Biomedical Engineering	M,D
Business Administration and Management—General	M
Chemical Engineering	M,D
Chemistry	M,D
Child and Family Studies	M
Child Development	M
Civil Engineering	M,D
Clinical Psychology	M
Clothing and Textiles	M
Communication Disorders	M,D
Communication—General	M
Computer Engineering	M,D
Computer Science	M
Counseling Psychology	M,D
Counselor Education	M,D
Curriculum and Instruction	M
Economics	M
Education—General	M
Educational Leadership and Administration	M
Educational Measurement and Evaluation	M,O
Educational Media/Instructional Technology	M
Electrical Engineering	M,D
Elementary Education	M
Engineering and Applied Sciences—General	M,D
English Education	M
English	M
Exercise and Sports Science	M
Finance and Banking	M
Geological Engineering	M
Geology	M
Geosciences	M
Gerontology	D
Health Services Management and Hospital Administration	M
Higher Education	M
History	M,D
Industrial and Organizational Psychology	M,D
International Business	M
Law	M,D
Management Information Systems	M
Marketing	M
Marriage and Family Therapy	M
Mathematics Education	M
Mathematics	M
Mechanical Engineering	M,D
Music Education	M
Music	M
Nursing—General	M,D
Physical Education	M
Physics	M
Political Science	M
Polymer Science and Engineering	M,D
Psychology—General	M,D
Public Administration	M
Public Health—General	M,D
Reading Education	M
School Psychology	M,D
Science Education	M
Secondary Education	M
Social Sciences Education	M
Social Work	M,D
Sociology	M,D
Spanish	M
Special Education	M
Statistics	M
Supply Chain Management	M
Taxation	M
Theater	M
Writing	M

THE UNIVERSITY OF ALABAMA

Accounting	M,D
Advertising and Public Relations	M
Aerospace/Aeronautical Engineering	M,D
American Studies	M
Anthropology	M,D
Applied Mathematics	M,D
Applied Statistics	M,D
Art History	M
Art/Fine Arts	M
Astronomy	M,D
Biological and Biomedical Sciences—General	M,D
Business Administration and Management—General	M,D
Chemical Engineering	M,D
Chemistry	M,D
Child and Family Studies	M
Civil Engineering	M,D
Clinical Psychology	D
Clothing and Textiles	M
Communication Disorders	M
Communication—General	M,D
Community Health	M
Computer Engineering	M,D
Computer Science	M,D
Construction Engineering	M,D
Consumer Economics	M
Counselor Education	M,D,O
Criminal Justice and Criminology	M
Economics	M,D
Education of the Gifted	M,D,O
Educational Leadership and Administration	M,D,O
Electrical Engineering	M,D
Elementary Education	M,D,O
Engineering and Applied Sciences—General	M,D
English as a Second Language	M
English	M,D
Environmental Engineering	M,D
Ergonomics and Human Factors	M
Exercise and Sports Science	M,D
Experimental Psychology	D
Family and Consumer Sciences-General	M,D
Finance and Banking	M,D
French	M,D
Geographic Information Systems	M,D
Geography	M,D
Geology	M,D
Geosciences	M,D
German	M,D
Health Education	M,D
Health Promotion	M,D
Higher Education	M,D
History	M,D
Hospitality Management	M
Human Development	M
Industrial and Manufacturing Management	M,D
Information Studies	M,D
Interdisciplinary Studies	D
Journalism	M
Kinesiology and Movement Studies	M,D
Law	M,D
Library Science	M,D
Marketing	M,D
Marriage and Family Therapy	M
Mass Communication	D
Materials Engineering	M,D
Materials Sciences	D
Mathematics	M,D
Mechanical Engineering	M,D
Mechanics	M,D
Metallurgical Engineering and Metallurgy	M,D
Music Education	M,D,O
Music	M,D
Nursing—General	M,D
Nutrition	M
Photography	M
Physical Education	M,D
Physics	M,D
Political Science	M,D
Psychology—General	D
Public Administration	M,D
Quality Management	M
Rhetoric	M,D
Romance Languages	M,D
Secondary Education	M,D,O
Social Work	M,D
Spanish	M,D
Special Education	M,D,O
Speech and Interpersonal Communication	M
Sports Management	M
Taxation	M,D
Theater	M
Women's Studies	M
Writing	M,D

THE UNIVERSITY OF ALABAMA AT BIRMINGHAM

Accounting	M
Adult Nursing	M,D
Allied Health—General	M,D,O
Allopathic Medicine	D
Anthropology	M
Applied Mathematics	D
Art Education	M
Art History	M
Biochemistry	D
Bioinformatics	D
Biological and Biomedical Sciences—General	M,D
Biomedical Engineering	M,D
Biostatistics	M,D
Biotechnology	M
Business Administration and Management—General	M
Cancer Biology/Oncology	D
Cell Biology	D
Chemistry	M,D
Civil Engineering	M,D
Clinical Laboratory Sciences/Medical Technology	M,D
Clinical Psychology	M,D
Communication—General	M
Community Health	M
Computational Sciences	D
Computer and Information Systems Security	M
Computer Engineering	M,D
Computer Science	M,D
Construction Engineering	M,D
Counselor Education	M
Criminal Justice and Criminology	M
Curriculum and Instruction	O
Dentistry	D
Developmental Biology	D
Developmental Psychology	M,D
Early Childhood Education	M,D
Education—General	M,D,O
Educational Leadership and Administration	M,D,O
Electrical Engineering	M,D
Elementary Education	M
Engineering and Applied Sciences—General	M,D
Engineering Management	M
English as a Second Language	M,O
English	M
Environmental and Occupational Health	M,D
Epidemiology	M,D
Family Nurse Practitioner Studies	M,D
Finance and Banking	M
Forensic Sciences	M
Genetic Counseling	M
Genetics	D
Genomic Sciences	D
Gerontological Nursing	M,D
Health Education	D
Health Informatics	M
Health Promotion	D
Health Psychology	M,D
Health Services Management and Hospital Administration	M,D
Health Services Research	M,D
History	M
Industrial Hygiene	M,D
Information Science	M,D
Interdisciplinary Studies	D
Management Information Systems	M
Marketing	M
Materials Engineering	M,D
Maternal and Child Health	M,D
Mathematics	M
Mechanical Engineering	M
Microbiology	D
Molecular Biology	D
Molecular Medicine	D
Music	M
Neurobiology	D
Neuroscience	M,D
Nurse Anesthesia	M,D
Nursing and Healthcare Administration	M,D
Nursing Informatics	M,D
Nursing—General	M,D
Nutrition	M,D
Occupational Therapy	M,O
Optometry	D
Oral and Dental Sciences	M
Pathobiology	D
Pediatric Nursing	M,D
Pharmacology	D
Physical Therapy	D
Physician Assistant Studies	M
Physics	M,D
Psychiatric Nursing	M,D
Psychology—General	M,D
Public Administration	M
Public Health—General	M,D
Quantitative Analysis	M,D
Reading Education	M
Rehabilitation Sciences	D
Rhetoric	M
Secondary Education	M
Sociology	D
Special Education	M
Structural Biology	D
Structural Engineering	M,D
Toxicology	M,D
Vision Sciences	M,D
Women's Health Nursing	M,D
Writing	M

THE UNIVERSITY OF ALABAMA IN HUNTSVILLE

Accounting	M,O
Acute Care/Critical Care Nursing	M,D,O
Aerospace/Aeronautical Engineering	M,D
Applied Mathematics	M,D
Astronomy	M,D
Atmospheric Sciences	M,D
Biological and Biomedical Sciences—General	M,D
Biotechnology	M,D
Business Administration and Management—General	M,O
Chemical Engineering	M,D
Chemistry	M,D
Civil Engineering	M,D
Computer and Information Systems Security	M,D,O
Computer Engineering	M,D
Computer Science	M,D,O
Education—General	M,O
Electrical Engineering	M,D
Engineering and Applied Sciences—General	M,D
English as a Second Language	M,O
English Education	M,O
English	M,O
Entrepreneurship	M,O
Environmental Engineering	M,D
Family Nurse Practitioner Studies	M,D,O
Finance and Banking	M,O
Geosciences	M,D
Gerontological Nursing	M,D,O
Health Services Management and Hospital Administration	M,D,O
History	M
Human Resources Management	M,O
Industrial and Organizational Psychology	M
Industrial/Management Engineering	M,D
Logistics	M,O
Management Information Systems	M,O
Management of Technology	M,O
Marketing	M,O
Materials Sciences	M,D
Mathematics Education	M,D,O
Mathematics	M,D
Mechanical Engineering	M,D
Modeling and Simulation	M,D,O
Nursing Education	M,D,O
Nursing—General	M,D,O
Operations Research	M,D
Optical Sciences	M,D
Photonics	M,D
Physics	M,D
Project Management	M,O
Psychology—General	M
Public Affairs	M
Reading Education	M,O
Science Education	M,D,O
Secondary Education	M,O
Social Sciences Education	M,O
Software Engineering	M,D,O
Special Education	M,O
Supply Chain Management	M,O
Systems Engineering	M,D
Taxation	M
Technical Writing	M,O

UNIVERSITY OF ALASKA ANCHORAGE

Anthropology	M
Biological and Biomedical Sciences—General	M
Business Administration and Management—General	M
Civil Engineering	M,O
Clinical Psychology	M,D
Counselor Education	M
Early Childhood Education	M,O
Education—General	M,O
Educational Leadership and Administration	M,O
Engineering and Applied Sciences—General	M,O
Engineering Management	M
English	M
Environmental Engineering	M
Environmental Sciences	M
Geological Engineering	M
Interdisciplinary Studies	M
Logistics	M,O
Nursing—General	M
Ocean Engineering	M,O
Project Management	M
Psychology—General	M,D
Public Administration	M
Public Health—General	M
Social Psychology	M,D
Social Work	M,O
Special Education	M,O
Writing	M

UNIVERSITY OF ALASKA FAIRBANKS

Anthropology	M,D
Art/Fine Arts	M
Astrophysics	M,D
Atmospheric Sciences	M,D
Biochemistry	M,D
Business Administration and Management—General	M
Chemistry	M,D
Civil Engineering	M,D,O
Clinical Psychology	D
Communication—General	M
Computational Sciences	M,D
Computer Art and Design	M
Computer Science	M
Construction Management	M,D,O
Corporate and Organizational Communication	M
Counselor Education	M,O
Criminal Justice and Criminology	M
Cultural Studies	M
Economics	M
Education—General	M,O
Electrical Engineering	M
Emergency Management	M
Engineering and Applied Sciences—General	D
English	M
Environmental Engineering	M,D,O
Environmental Management and Policy	M
Finance and Banking	M
Geographic Information Systems	M

*M—masters degree; D—doctorate; O—other advanced degree; *—Close-Up and/or Display*

Geological Engineering — M
Geophysics — M
History — M
Homeland Security — M
Interdisciplinary Studies — M,D
Limnology — M,D
Linguistics — M
Marine Biology — M,D
Marine Sciences — M,D
Mathematics — M,D,O
Mechanical Engineering — M
Mineral/Mining Engineering — M
Multilingual and Multicultural Education — M
Music — M
Natural Resources — M,D
Neuroscience — M,D
Northern Studies — M
Oceanography — M,D
Petroleum Engineering — M
Photography — M
Physics — M,D
Psychology—General — D
Rural Planning and Studies — M
Social Psychology — M,D,O
Special Education — M
Statistics — M,D,O
Sustainable Development — M,D
Writing — M

UNIVERSITY OF ALASKA SOUTHEAST
Education—General — M
Educational Leadership and Administration — M
Educational Media/Instructional Technology — M
Elementary Education — M
Mathematics Education — M
Public Administration — M
Reading Education — M
Secondary Education — M
Special Education — M

UNIVERSITY OF ALBERTA
Accounting — D
Adult Education — M,D,O
Agricultural Economics and Agribusiness — M,D
Agricultural Sciences—General — M,D
Agronomy and Soil Sciences — M,D
Anthropology — M,D
Applied Arts and Design—General — M
Applied Mathematics — M,D,O
Archaeology — M,D
Art History — M
Art/Fine Arts — M
Asian Studies — M
Astrophysics — M,D
Biochemistry — M,D
Biological and Biomedical Sciences—General — M,D
Biomedical Engineering — M,D
Biostatistics — M,D,O
Biotechnology — M,D
Business Administration and Management—General — M,D
Cancer Biology/Oncology — M,D
Cell Biology — M,D
Chemical Engineering — M,D
Chemistry — M,D
Chinese — M
Civil Engineering — M,D
Classics — M,D
Clinical Laboratory Sciences/Medical Technology — M,D
Clothing and Textiles — M,D
Communication Disorders — M,D
Communication—General — M
Community Health — M,D
Computer Engineering — M,D
Computer Science — M,D
Condensed Matter Physics — M,D
Conservation Biology — M,D
Construction Engineering — M,D
Counseling Psychology — M,D
Counselor Education — M,D
Criminal Justice and Criminology — M,D
Demography and Population Studies — M,D
Dental Hygiene — O
Dentistry — D
East European and Russian Studies — M,D
Ecology — M,D
Economics — M,D
Educational Leadership and Administration — M,D,O
Educational Media/Instructional Technology — M,D
Educational Policy — M,D,O
Educational Psychology — M,D
Electrical Engineering — M,D
Elementary Education — M,D
Energy and Power Engineering — M,D
Engineering Management — M,D
English as a Second Language — M,D
English — M,D
Environmental and Occupational Health — M,D
Environmental Biology — M,D
Environmental Engineering — M,D
Environmental Management and Policy — M,D
Environmental Sciences — M,D
Epidemiology — M,D
Evolutionary Biology — M,D
Exercise and Sports Science — M,D
Family and Consumer Sciences-General — M,D
Finance and Banking — M,D
Folklore — M,D
Forestry — M,D
French — M,D
Genetics — M,D
Geophysics — M,D

Geosciences — M,D
Geotechnical Engineering — M,D
German — M,D
Health Physics/Radiological Health — M,D
Health Promotion — M,O
Health Services Management and Hospital Administration — M,D
Health Services Research — M,D
Hispanic Studies — M,D
History — M,D
Immunology — M,D
Industrial and Labor Relations — D
Information Studies — M
International Business — M
International Health — M,D
Italian — M,D
Japanese — M
Law — M,D
Library Science — M
Linguistics — M,D
Marketing — D
Materials Engineering — M,D
Maternal and Child/Neonatal Nursing — D
Mathematical and Computational Finance — M,D,O
Mathematical Physics — M,D,O
Mathematics — M,D,O
Mechanical Engineering — M,D
Medical Microbiology — M,D
Medical Physics — M,D
Microbiology — M,D
Mineral/Mining Engineering — M,D
Molecular Biology — M,D
Multilingual and Multicultural Education — M
Music — M,D
Nanotechnology — M,D
Natural Resources — M,D
Neuroscience — M,D
Nursing—General — M,D
Occupational Therapy — M,D
Oral and Dental Sciences — M,D
Organizational Management — D
Pathology — M,D
Petroleum Engineering — M,D
Pharmaceutical Sciences — M,D
Pharmacology — M,D
Pharmacy — M,D
Philosophy — M,D
Physical Education — M,D
Physical Therapy — M,D
Physics — M,D
Physiology — M,D
Plant Biology — M,D
Political Science — M,D
Psychology—General — M,D
Public Health—General — M,D
Recreation and Park Management — M,D
Rehabilitation Sciences — D
Rural Sociology — M,D
School Psychology — M,D
Secondary Education — M,D
Slavic Languages — M,D
Sociology — M,D
Special Education — M,D
Sports Management — M
Statistics — M,D,O
Structural Engineering — M,D
Systems Engineering — M,D
Telecommunications — M,D
Theater — M
Vision Sciences — M,D
Water Resources Engineering — M,D

UNIVERSITY OF ANTELOPE VALLEY
Business Administration and Management—General — M
Criminal Justice and Criminology — M

THE UNIVERSITY OF ARIZONA
Accounting — M
Aerospace/Aeronautical Engineering — M,D
African Studies — M,D,O
Agricultural Economics and Agribusiness — M
Agricultural Education — M,O
Agricultural Engineering — M,D
Agricultural Sciences—General — M,D,O
Agronomy and Soil Sciences — M,D,O
Allopathic Medicine — M,D
American Indian/Native American Studies — M,D
Animal Sciences — M,D
Anthropology — M,D,O
Applied Mathematics — M,D
Architecture — M
Art Education — M,D
Art History — M,D
Art/Fine Arts — M
Asian Studies — M,D
Astronomy — D
Atmospheric Sciences — M,D
Biochemistry — M,D
Biological and Biomedical Sciences—General — M,D
Biomedical Engineering — M,D
Biostatistics — M,D
Biosystems Engineering — M,D
Business Administration and Management—General — M,D,O
Cancer Biology/Oncology — D
Cell Biology — D
Chemical Engineering — M,D
Chemistry — M,D
Child and Family Studies — M,D,O
Classics — M
Communication Disorders — M,D,O
Communication—General — M,D
Computer Engineering — M,D
Computer Science — M,D
Counseling Psychology — M
Counselor Education — M

Dance — M
Ecology — M,D
Economics — M,D
Education—General — M,D,O
Educational Leadership and Administration — M,D,O
Educational Psychology — M,D,O
Electrical Engineering — M,D
Elementary Education — M,D
Engineering and Applied Sciences—General — M,D,O
Engineering Management — M,D,O
English as a Second Language — M,D
English Education — M,D
English — M,D
Entomology — M,D
Environmental Engineering — M,D
Environmental Management and Policy — M,D
Environmental Sciences — M,D,O
Epidemiology — M,D
Evolutionary Biology — M,D
Family and Consumer Sciences-General — M,D,O
Family Nurse Practitioner Studies — M,D,O
Film, Television, and Video Theory and Criticism — M
Finance and Banking — M
Forestry — M,D
French — M
Gender Studies — M,D,O
Genetics — M,D
Geographic Information Systems — M,D,O
Geography — M,D,O
Geological Engineering — M,D
Geosciences — M,D
German — M,D
Higher Education — M,D
History — M,D,O
Human Development — M,D,O
Hydrology — D,O
Immunology — D
Industrial/Management Engineering — M,D,O
Information Studies — M,D
Interdisciplinary Studies — M,D
Journalism — M
Landscape Architecture — M
Latin American Studies — M
Law — M,D
Library Science — M,D
Linguistics — M,D
Management Information Systems — M,O
Management Strategy and Policy — M,D
Marketing — M,D
Materials Engineering — M,D
Materials Sciences — M,D
Mathematics Education — M
Mathematics — M,D
Mechanical Engineering — M,D
Medical Informatics — M,D,O
Medical Physics — M
Microbiology — D
Mineral/Mining Engineering — M,D,O
Molecular Biology — D
Molecular Medicine — M,D
Music Education — M,D
Music — M,D
Natural Resources — M,D
Near and Middle Eastern Studies — M,D,O
Neuroscience — D
Nursing—General — M,D,O
Nutrition — M,D
Optical Sciences — M,D,O
Organizational Management — M,D
Perfusion — M
Pharmaceutical Sciences — M,D
Pharmacology — M,D
Pharmacy — D
Philosophy — M,D
Physics — M,D
Physiology — M,D
Planetary and Space Sciences — M,D
Plant Pathology — M,D
Plant Sciences — M,D
Political Science — M,D
Psychology—General — M,D
Public Administration — M,D,O
Public Health—General — M,D
Public Policy — M,D,O
Range Science — M,D
Reading Education — M,D,O
Rehabilitation Counseling — M,D
Rhetoric — M,D
Russian — M
School Psychology — D,O
Secondary Education — M,D
Sociology — M,D
Spanish — M,D
Special Education — M,D
Statistics — M,D
Systems Engineering — M,D,O
Theater — M
Urban and Regional Planning — M
Water Resources — M,D,O
Women's Studies — M,D,O
Writing — M

UNIVERSITY OF ARKANSAS
Accounting — M
Adult Education — M,D
Agricultural Economics and Agribusiness — M
Agricultural Education — M
Agricultural Engineering — M,D
Agricultural Sciences—General — M,D
Agronomy and Soil Sciences — M,D
Animal Sciences — M,D
Anthropology — M,D
Applied Physics — M,D
Art/Fine Arts — M

Athletic Training and Sports Medicine — M
Bioengineering — M
Biological and Biomedical Sciences—General — M,D
Biomedical Engineering — M,D
Business Administration and Management—General — M,D
Cell Biology — M,D
Chemical Engineering — M,D
Chemistry — M,D
Civil Engineering — M,D
Communication Disorders — M
Communication—General — M
Community Health — M,D
Comparative Literature — M,D
Computer Engineering — M,D
Computer Science — M,D
Counselor Education — M,D,O
Curriculum and Instruction — M,D,O
Early Childhood Education — M
Economics — M,D,O
Education—General — M,D,O
Educational Leadership and Administration — M,D,O
Educational Measurement and Evaluation — M,D
Educational Media/Instructional Technology — M
Educational Policy — D
Electrical Engineering — M,D
Electronic Materials — M,D
Engineering and Applied Sciences—General — M,D
English — M,D
Entomology — M,D
Environmental Engineering — M
Family and Consumer Sciences-General — M
Food Science and Technology — M,D
French — M
Geography — M
Geology — M
German — M
Health Education — M,D
Health Promotion — M,D
Higher Education — M,D,O
History — M,D
Horticulture — M
Human Resources Development — M,D,O
Industrial and Manufacturing Management — M
Industrial/Management Engineering — M,D
Interdisciplinary Studies — M
Journalism — M
Kinesiology and Movement Studies — M,D
Law — M,D
Management Information Systems — M
Mathematics Education — M
Mathematics — M,D
Mechanical Engineering — M,D
Middle School Education — M,D,O
Molecular Biology — M
Music — M
Nursing—General — M
Operations Research — M,D
Philosophy — M,D
Photonics — M,D
Physical Education — M
Physics — M,D
Planetary and Space Sciences — M,D
Plant Pathology — M
Plant Sciences — D
Political Science — M
Psychology—General — M,D
Public Administration — M
Public Policy — D
Recreation and Park Management — M,D
Rehabilitation Counseling — M,D
Secondary Education — M,O
Social Work — M
Sociology — M
Spanish — M
Special Education — M
Sports Management — M
Statistics — M
Telecommunications — M
Theater — M
Transportation and Highway Engineering — M,D
Vocational and Technical Education — M,D,O
Writing — M

UNIVERSITY OF ARKANSAS AT LITTLE ROCK
Adult Education — M
Applied Mathematics — M,O
Applied Psychology — M
Applied Science and Technology — M,D
Applied Statistics — M,O
Art Education — M
Art History — M
Art/Fine Arts — M
Bioinformatics — M,D
Biological and Biomedical Sciences—General — M
Business Administration and Management—General — M,O
Chemistry — M
Community College Education — M,D
Computer Science — M,D
Conflict Resolution and Mediation/Peace Studies — O
Construction Management — M
Counselor Education — M
Criminal Justice and Criminology — M
Curriculum and Instruction — M
Education of the Gifted — M
Education—General — M,D,O

Educational Leadership and Administration	M,D,O
Educational Media/Instructional Technology	M
English as a Second Language	O
Entrepreneurship	M
Exercise and Sports Science	M
Foreign Languages Education	O
Geosciences	O
Gerontology	O
Health Education	M,D
Higher Education	M
Information Science	M,D,O
Interdisciplinary Studies	M
Law	D
Management Information Systems	M,O
Mass Communication	M
Mathematics	M,O
Middle School Education	M
Nonprofit Management	O
Psychology—General	M
Public Administration	M
Public Affairs	M,O
Public History	M
Reading Education	M,D,O
Rehabilitation Counseling	M,O
Rhetoric	M
Secondary Education	M
Social Work	M
Special Education	M,O
Speech and Interpersonal Communication	M
Sports Management	M
Student Affairs	M,D
Systems Engineering	M,D,O
Technical Writing	M
Writing	M

UNIVERSITY OF ARKANSAS AT MONTICELLO

Education—General	M
Educational Leadership and Administration	M
Forestry	M
Natural Resources	M

UNIVERSITY OF ARKANSAS AT PINE BLUFF

Aquaculture	M,D
Education—General	M
Elementary Education	M
English Education	M
Fish, Game, and Wildlife Management	M,D
Mathematics Education	M
Science Education	M
Secondary Education	M
Social Sciences Education	M

UNIVERSITY OF ARKANSAS FOR MEDICAL SCIENCES

Allopathic Medicine	D
Biochemistry	M,D,O
Bioinformatics	M,D,O
Biological and Biomedical Sciences—General	M,D,O
Biostatistics	M,D,O
Communication Disorders	M,D
Environmental and Occupational Health	M,D,O
Epidemiology	M,D,O
Genetic Counseling	M,D
Health Education	M,D,O
Health Physics/Radiological Health	M,D
Health Promotion	M,D,O
Health Services Management and Hospital Administration	M,D,O
Health Services Research	M,D,O
Immunology	M,D,O
Microbiology	M,D,O
Molecular Biology	M,D,O
Molecular Biophysics	M,D,O
Neurobiology	M,D,O
Nursing—General	D
Nutrition	M,D,O
Pharmacology	M,D,O
Pharmacy	M,D
Physician Assistant Studies	M,D
Physiology	M,D,O
Public Health—General	M,D,O
Toxicology	M,D,O

UNIVERSITY OF ARKANSAS—FORT SMITH

Health Services Management and Hospital Administration	M

UNIVERSITY OF BALTIMORE

Accounting	M,O
Applied Arts and Design—General	M
Applied Psychology	M
Business Administration and Management—General	M,O
Conflict Resolution and Mediation/Peace Studies	M
Counseling Psychology	M
Criminal Justice and Criminology	M
Entrepreneurship	M
Ethics	M
Finance and Banking	M
Graphic Design	M,D
Health Services Management and Hospital Administration	M
Human Services	M
Human-Computer Interaction	M
Intellectual Property Law	M,D
International Business	M
Law	M,D
Legal and Justice Studies	M
Management Information Systems	M,O
Marketing	M
Public Administration	M,D

Public Affairs	M,D
Publishing	M
Taxation	M,D
Writing	M

UNIVERSITY OF BRIDGEPORT

Accounting	M
Acupuncture and Oriental Medicine	M
Applied Arts and Design—General	M
Asian Studies	M
Biomedical Engineering	M
Business Administration and Management—General	M
Chiropractic	D
Clinical Psychology	M
Communication—General	M
Computer Education	M,D,O
Computer Engineering	M,D
Computer Science	M,D
Conflict Resolution and Mediation/Peace Studies	M
Counseling Psychology	M
Dental Hygiene	M
Early Childhood Education	M,D,O
Education—General	M,D,O
Educational Leadership and Administration	M,D,O
Electrical Engineering	M
Elementary Education	M,D,O
Engineering and Applied Sciences—General	M,D
Entrepreneurship	M
Finance and Banking	M
Human Resources Development	M
Human Resources Management	M
Human Services	M
Industrial and Manufacturing Management	M
International Affairs	M
International and Comparative Education	M,D,O
International Business	M
Management Information Systems	M
Management of Technology	M,D
Marketing	M
Mechanical Engineering	M
Media Studies	M
Middle School Education	M,D,O
Music Education	M,D,O
Naturopathic Medicine	D
Nutrition	M
Physician Assistant Studies	M
Reading Education	M,D,O
Secondary Education	M,D,O
Social Psychology	M
Student Affairs	M

THE UNIVERSITY OF BRITISH COLUMBIA

Accounting	D
Adult Education	M,D
Agricultural Sciences—General	M,D
Agronomy and Soil Sciences	M,D
Allopathic Medicine	M,D
Animal Sciences	M,D
Anthropology	M,D
Archaeology	M,D
Architecture	M
Archives/Archival Administration	M,D
Art Education	M,D
Art History	M,D
Art/Fine Arts	M,D
Asian Studies	M,D
Astronomy	M,D
Atmospheric Sciences	M,D
Biochemistry	M,D
Bioengineering	M,D
Bioinformatics	M,D
Biopsychology	M,D
Botany	M,D
Business Administration and Management—General	M,D
Cell Biology	M,D
Chemical Engineering	M,D
Chemistry	M,D
Civil Engineering	M,D
Classics	M,D
Clinical Psychology	M,D
Cognitive Sciences	M,D
Communication Disorders	M,D
Computer Engineering	M,D
Computer Science	M,D
Counseling Psychology	M,D,O
Curriculum and Instruction	M,D
Dentistry	D
Developmental Biology	M,D
Developmental Psychology	M,D
East European and Russian Studies	M,D
Economics	M,D
Education—General	M,D,O
Educational Leadership and Administration	M,D
Educational Measurement and Evaluation	M,D,O
Educational Policy	M,D
Electrical Engineering	M,D
Engineering and Applied Sciences—General	M,D
English as a Second Language	M,D
English	M,D
Environmental Management and Policy	M,D
Ethnic Studies	M,D
Film, Television, and Video Production	M
Film, Television, and Video Theory and Criticism	M
Finance and Banking	D
Food Science and Technology	M,D

Forestry	M,D
Foundations and Philosophy of Education	M,D
French	M,D
Gender Studies	M,D
Genetic Counseling	M
Genetics	M,D
Geography	M,D
Geological Engineering	M,D
Geology	M,D
Geophysics	M,D
German	M,D
Health Psychology	M,D
Health Services Management and Hospital Administration	M,D
Higher Education	M,D
Hispanic Studies	M,D
History	M,D
Home Economics Education	M,D
Human Development	M,D,O
Immunology	M,D
Infectious Diseases	M,D
Information Studies	M,D
International Affairs	M
Journalism	M
Kinesiology and Movement Studies	M,D
Landscape Architecture	M
Law	M,D
Library Science	M,D
Linguistics	M,D
Management Information Systems	D
Management Strategy and Policy	D
Marine Sciences	M,D
Marketing	D
Materials Engineering	M,D
Mathematics Education	M,D
Mathematics	M,D
Mechanical Engineering	M,D
Microbiology	M,D
Mineral/Mining Engineering	M,D
Molecular Biology	M,D
Museum Studies	M,D
Music Education	M,D
Music	M,D
Natural Resources	M,D
Neuroscience	M,D
Nursing—General	M,D
Nutrition	M,D
Occupational Therapy	M
Oceanography	M,D
Operations Research	M
Oral and Dental Sciences	M,D
Organizational Behavior	D
Pacific Area/Pacific Rim Studies	M
Pathology	M,D
Pharmaceutical Sciences	M,D
Pharmacology	M,D
Pharmacy	M,D
Philosophy	M,D
Physical Education	M,D
Physics	M,D
Plant Sciences	M,D
Political Science	M,D
Psychology—General	M,D
Public Health—General	M,D
Public Policy	M
Quantitative Analysis	M,D
Reading Education	M,D
Rehabilitation Sciences	M,D
Religion	M,D
Reproductive Biology	M,D
School Psychology	M,D,O
Science Education	M,D
Social Psychology	M,D
Social Sciences Education	M,D
Social Work	M,D
Sociology	M,D
Special Education	M,D,O
Statistics	M,D
Sustainability Management	M
Taxation	M,D
Theater	M,D
Transportation Management	D
Urban and Regional Planning	M,D
Urban Design	M
Vocational and Technical Education	M,D
Writing	M,D
Zoology	M,D

UNIVERSITY OF CALGARY

Adult Education	M,D
Allopathic Medicine	D
Analytical Chemistry	M,D
Anthropology	M,D
Applied Psychology	M,D
Archaeology	M
Architecture	M,D
Art/Fine Arts	M
Astronomy	M,D
Biochemistry	M,D
Biological and Biomedical Sciences—General	M,D
Biomedical Engineering	M,D
Biotechnology	M
Business Administration and Management—General	M,D
Cancer Biology/Oncology	M,D
Cardiovascular Sciences	M,D
Chemical Engineering	M,D
Chemistry	M,D
Civil Engineering	M,D
Classics	M,D
Clinical Psychology	M,D
Communication—General	M,D
Community Health	M,D
Computer Engineering	M,D
Computer Science	M,D
Counseling Psychology	M,D
Curriculum and Instruction	M,D
Economics	M,D

Educational Leadership and Administration	M,D
Educational Measurement and Evaluation	M,D
Electrical Engineering	M,D
Energy and Power Engineering	M,D
Energy Management and Policy	M,D
Engineering and Applied Sciences—General	M,D
English	M,D
Environmental Design	M,D
Environmental Engineering	M,D
Environmental Law	M,O
Environmental Management and Policy	M,D,O
French	M,D
Genetics	M,D
Geography	M,D
Geology	M,D
Geophysics	M,D
Geosciences	M,D
Geotechnical Engineering	M,D
German	M,D
History	M,D
Hydrology	M,D
Immunology	M,D
Infectious Diseases	M,D
Inorganic Chemistry	M,D
Kinesiology and Movement Studies	M,D
Law	M,D,O
Legal and Justice Studies	M,O
Linguistics	M,D
Management Strategy and Policy	M,D
Manufacturing Engineering	M,D
Materials Sciences	M,D
Mathematics	M,D
Mechanical Engineering	M,D
Mechanics	M,D
Microbiology	M,D
Military and Defense Studies	M,D
Molecular Biology	M,D
Molecular Genetics	M,D
Multilingual and Multicultural Education	M,D
Music	M,D
Neuroscience	M,D
Nursing—General	M,D,O
Organic Chemistry	M,D
Pathology	M,D
Petroleum Engineering	M,D
Philosophy	M,D
Physical Chemistry	M,D
Physics	M,D
Physiology	M,D
Political Science	M,D
Project Management	M,D
Psychology—General	M,D
Religion	M,D
School Psychology	M,D
Social Work	M,D,O
Sociology	M,D
Software Engineering	M,D
Spanish	M,D
Statistics	M,D
Structural Engineering	M,D
Sustainable Development	M,D
Theater	M
Theoretical Chemistry	M,D
Transportation and Highway Engineering	M,D
Water Resources	M,D

UNIVERSITY OF CALIFORNIA, BERKELEY

Accounting	D,O
Addictions/Substance Abuse Counseling	O
African-American Studies	D
Agricultural Economics and Agribusiness	D
Allopathic Medicine	D
Anthropology	D
Applied Arts and Design—General	O
Applied Mathematics	M,D
Applied Science and Technology	D
Archaeology	M,D
Architectural History	M,D
Architecture	M,D
Art History	D
Art/Fine Arts	M,O
Asian Languages	M,D
Asian Studies	M,D
Astrophysics	D
Biochemistry	D
Bioengineering	M,D
Biological and Biomedical Sciences—General	D
Biophysics	D
Biostatistics	M,D
Building Science	M,D
Business Administration and Management—General	M,D,O
Cell Biology	D
Chemical Engineering	M,D
Chemistry	D
Chinese	D
Civil Engineering	M,D
Classics	M,D
Clinical Research	O
Comparative Literature	D
Computer Science	M,D
Construction Management	O
Counseling Psychology	O
Database Systems	M
Demography and Population Studies	M,D
Economics	D
Education—General	M,D,O

*M—masters degree; D—doctorate; O—other advanced degree; *—Close-Up and/or Display*

Educational Leadership and
  Administration — M,D
Electrical Engineering — M,D
Energy Management and
  Policy — M,D
Engineering and Applied
  Sciences—General — M,D,O
Engineering Management — M,D
English as a Second Language — O
English — D
Environmental and Occupational
  Health — M,D
Environmental Design — M,D
Environmental Engineering — M,D
Environmental Management
  and Policy — M,D,O
Environmental Sciences — M,D
Epidemiology — M,D
Ethnic Studies — D
Facilities Management — O
Film, Television, and Video
  Theory and Criticism — D
Finance and Banking — D,O
Financial Engineering — M
Folklore — M
Forestry — M,D
French — D
Geography — D
Geology — M,D
Geophysics — M,D
Geotechnical Engineering — M,D
German — D
Health Services Management and
  Hospital Administration — D
Hispanic and Latin American
  Languages — D
History of Science and Technology — D
History — M,D
Human Development — M,D
Human Resources Management — O
Immunology — D
Industrial and Labor Relations — D
Industrial/Management
  Engineering — M,D
Infectious Diseases — M,D
Information Studies — O
Interior Design — O
International Affairs — M
International Business — O
Italian — D
Japanese — D
Journalism — M
Landscape Architecture — M,D,O
Law — M,D
Legal and Justice Studies — D
Linguistics — D
Management Information Systems — M,D,O
Marketing — D,O
Materials Engineering — M,D
Materials Sciences — M,D
Mathematics Education — M,D
Mathematics — M,D
Mechanical Engineering — M,D
Mechanics — M,D
Microbiology — D
Molecular Biology — D
Molecular Toxicology — D
Music — D
Natural Resources — M,D
Near and Middle Eastern Studies — M,D
Neuroscience — D
Nuclear Engineering — M,D
Nutrition — M,D
Operations Research — M,D
Optometry — D,O
Organizational Behavior — D
Philosophy — D
Physics — D
Physiology — M,D
Plant Biology — D
Political Science — D
Project Management — O
Psychology—General — D
Public Affairs — M
Public Health—General — M,D
Public Policy — M,D
Range Science — M
Real Estate — D
Religion — D
Rhetoric — D
Romance Languages — D
Russian — D
Scandinavian Languages — D
Science Education — M,D
Slavic Languages — D
Social Work — M,D
Sociology — D
Spanish — D
Special Education — M,D
Statistics — M,D
Structural Engineering — M,D
Sustainability Management — O
Sustainable Development — M,O
Theater — D
Transportation and Highway
  Engineering — M,D
Urban and Regional Planning — M,D
Urban Design — M,D
Vision Sciences — M,D
Water Resources Engineering — M,D
Writing — D

UNIVERSITY OF CALIFORNIA, DAVIS

Accounting — M
Aerospace/Aeronautical
  Engineering — M,D,O
Agricultural Economics and
  Agribusiness — M,D
Agricultural Sciences—
  General — M
Agronomy and Soil Sciences — M,D
Allopathic Medicine — D
American Indian/Native American
  Studies — M,D

Animal Behavior — D
Animal Sciences — M,D
Anthropology — M,D
Applied Mathematics — M,D
Applied Science and
  Technology — M,D
Art History — M
Art/Fine Arts — M
Atmospheric Sciences — M,D
Biochemistry — M,D
Bioengineering — M,D
Biomedical Engineering — M,D
Biophysics — M,D
Biostatistics — M,D
Business Administration and
  Management—General — M
Cell Biology — M,D
Chemical Engineering — M,D
Chemistry — M,D
Child Development — M
Civil Engineering — M,D,O
Clinical Research — M
Clothing and Textiles — M
Communication—General — M
Comparative Literature — D
Computer Engineering — M,D
Computer Science — M,D
Cultural Studies — M,D
Curriculum and Instruction — M,D
Developmental Biology — M,D
Ecology — M,D
Economics — M,D
Education—General — M,D
Educational Psychology — M,D
Electrical Engineering — M,D
Engineering and Applied
  Sciences—General — M,D,O
English — M,D
Entomology — M,D
Environmental Engineering — M,D,O
Environmental Sciences — M,D
Epidemiology — M,D
Evolutionary Biology — D
Exercise and Sports Science — M
Food Science and
  Technology — M,D
Forensic Sciences — M
French — D
Genetics — M,D
Geography — M,D
Geology — M,D
German — M,D
History — M,D
Horticulture — M
Human Development — D
Hydrology — M,D
Immunology — M,D
Law — M,D
Linguistics — M,D
Materials Engineering — M,D
Materials Sciences — M,D
Maternal and Child Health — M
Mathematics — M,D
Mechanical Engineering — M,D,O
Medical Informatics — M
Microbiology — M,D
Molecular Biology — M,D
Music — M,D
Neuroscience — D
Nutrition — M,D
Pathology — M,D
Pharmacology — M,D
Philosophy — M,D
Physics — M,D
Physiology — M,D
Plant Biology — M,D
Plant Pathology — M,D
Political Science — M,D
Psychology—General — D
Sociology — M,D
Spanish — M,D
Statistics — M,D
Textile Design — M
Theater — M,D
Toxicology — M,D
Transportation and Highway
  Engineering — M,D
Transportation Management — M,D
Urban and Regional Planning — M
Veterinary Medicine — D
Veterinary Sciences — M,O
Viticulture and Enology — M,D
Writing — M,D
Zoology — M,D

UNIVERSITY OF CALIFORNIA, HASTINGS COLLEGE OF THE LAW

Law — M,D

UNIVERSITY OF CALIFORNIA, IRVINE

Accounting — M
Aerospace/Aeronautical
  Engineering — M,D
Allopathic Medicine — D
Anatomy — M,D
Anthropology — M,D
Applied Mathematics — M,D
Art/Fine Arts — M,D
Asian Languages — M,D
Biochemical Engineering — M,D
Biochemistry — M,D
Biological and Biomedical
  Sciences—General — M,D
Biomedical Engineering — M,D
Biophysics — D
Biotechnology — M
Business Administration and
  Management—General — M,D
Cell Biology — M,D
Chemical Engineering — M,D
Chemistry — M,D
Chinese — M,D
Civil Engineering — M,D
Classics — M,D
Comparative Literature — M,D

Computational Biology — D
Computer Science — M,D
Criminal Justice and Criminology — M,D
Cultural Studies — D
Dance — M
Demography and Population Studies — M
Developmental Biology — M,D
Ecology — M,D
Economics — M,D
Education—General — M,D
Educational Leadership and
  Administration — M,D
Educational Media/Instructional
  Technology — M
Electrical Engineering — M,D
Elementary Education — M,D
Engineering and Applied
  Sciences—General — M,D
Engineering Management — M
English — M,D
Environmental and Occupational
  Health — M,D
Environmental Design — D
Environmental Engineering — M,D
Epidemiology — M,D
Evolutionary Biology — M,D
Foreign Languages Education — M,D
French — M,D
Genetic Counseling — M
Genetics — D
Geosciences — M,D
German — M,D
Health Services Management and
  Hospital Administration — M
History — M,D
Information Science — M,D
Japanese — M,D
Law — D
Manufacturing Engineering — M,D
Materials Engineering — M,D
Materials Sciences — M,D
Mathematics — M,D
Mechanical Engineering — M,D
Medicinal and Pharmaceutical
  Chemistry — D
Microbiology — M,D
Molecular Biology — M,D
Molecular Genetics — M,D
Music — M
Neurobiology — M,D
Neuroscience — D
Nursing—General — M
Pathology — D
Pharmaceutical Sciences — M,D
Philosophy — M,D
Physics — M,D
Physiology — D
Political Science — D
Psychology—General — D
Public Health—General — M,D
Secondary Education — M,D
Sociology — D
Spanish — M,D
Statistics — M,D
Systems Biology — D
Theater — M,D
Toxicology — M,D
Translational Biology — M
Transportation and Highway
  Engineering — M,D
Urban and Regional Planning — M,D
Urban Studies — M,D
Writing — M

UNIVERSITY OF CALIFORNIA, LOS ANGELES

Accounting — M,D
Aerospace/Aeronautical
  Engineering — M,D
African Studies — M
African-American Studies — M
Allopathic Medicine — D
American Indian/Native American
  Studies — M
Anatomy — M,D
Anthropology — M,D
Applied Arts and Design—General — M
Applied Social Research — M,D
Archaeology — M,D
Architecture — M,D
Archives/Archival Administration — M,D,O
Art History — M,D
Art/Fine Arts — M
Asian Languages — M,D
Asian Studies — M,D
Asian-American Studies — M
Astronomy — M,D
Astrophysics — M,D
Atmospheric Sciences — M,D
Biochemistry — M,D
Bioengineering — M,D
Bioinformatics — M,D
Biological and Biomedical
  Sciences—General — M,D
Biomathematics — M,D
Biomedical Engineering — M,D
Biostatistics — M,D
Business Administration and
  Management—General — M,D
Cell Biology — M,D
Chemical Engineering — M,D
Chemistry — M,D
Civil Engineering — M,D
Classics — M,D
Clinical Research — M
Community Health — M,D
Comparative Literature — M,D
Computer Science — M,D
Dance — M,D
Dentistry — D,O
Developmental Biology — M,D
Ecology — M,D
Economics — M,D
Education—General — M,D

Educational Leadership and
  Administration — D
Electrical Engineering — M,D
Engineering and Applied
  Sciences—General — M,D
English as a Second Language — M,D,O
English — M,D
Environmental and Occupational
  Health — M,D
Environmental Engineering — M,D
Environmental Sciences — M,D
Epidemiology — M,D
Evolutionary Biology — M,D
Film, Television, and Video
  Production — M,D
Finance and Banking — M,D
Financial Engineering — M,D
French — M,D
Gender Studies — M,D
Geochemistry — M,D
Geography — M,D
Geology — M,D
Geophysics — M,D
Geosciences — M,D
German — M,D
Health Services Management and
  Hospital Administration — M,D
Hispanic and Latin American
  Languages — D
Historic Preservation — M
History — M,D
Human Genetics — M,D
Immunology — M,D
Information Studies — M,D,O
Italian — M,D
Latin American Studies — M
Law — M,D,O
Library Science — M,D,O
Linguistics — M,D
Management of Technology — M,D
Management Strategy and Policy — M,D
Manufacturing Engineering — M
Marketing — M,D
Materials Engineering — M,D
Materials Sciences — M,D
Mathematics — M,D
Mechanical Engineering — M,D
Media Studies — M,D
Medical Physics — M,D
Microbiology — M,D
Molecular Biology — M,D
Molecular Genetics — M,D
Molecular Physiology — D
Molecular Toxicology — D
Music — M,D
Near and Middle Eastern Languages — M,D
Near and Middle Eastern Studies — M,D
Neurobiology — M,D
Neuroscience — D
Nursing—General — M,D
Oceanography — M,D
Oral and Dental Sciences — M,D
Pathology — M,D
Pharmacology — M,D
Philosophy — M,D
Physics — M,D
Physiology — M,D
Planetary and Space
  Sciences — M,D
Political Science — M
Portuguese — M
Psychology—General — M,D
Public Health—General — M,D
Public Policy — M
Scandinavian Languages — M
Slavic Languages — M,D
Social Work — M,D
Sociology — M,D
Spanish — M
Special Education — D
Statistics — M,D
Theater — M,D
Toxicology — D
Urban and Regional Planning — M,D
Urban Design — M,D

UNIVERSITY OF CALIFORNIA, MERCED

Applied Mathematics — M,D
Biochemistry — M,D
Bioengineering — M,D
Biological and Biomedical
  Sciences—General — M,D
Chemistry — M,D
Cognitive Sciences — M,D
Computer Science — M,D
Electrical Engineering — M,D
Engineering and Applied
  Sciences—General — M,D
Environmental Engineering — M,D
Information Science — M,D
Mechanical Engineering — M,D
Mechanics — M,D
Physics — M,D
Psychology—General — M,D
Social Sciences — M,D
Sociology — M,D
Systems Biology — M,D
Systems Engineering — M,D

UNIVERSITY OF CALIFORNIA, RIVERSIDE

Agronomy and Soil Sciences — M,D
Anthropology — M,D
Archives/Archival Administration — M,D
Art History — M,D
Art/Fine Arts — M
Artificial Intelligence/Robotics — M,D
Asian Studies — M
Biochemistry — M,D
Bioengineering — M,D
Bioinformatics — D
Biological and Biomedical
  Sciences—General — M,D
Botany — M,D

Business Administration and Management—General	M,D
Cell Biology	M,D
Chemical Engineering	M,D
Chemistry	M,D
Classics	D
Comparative Literature	M,D
Computer Engineering	M,D
Computer Science	M,D*
Cultural Studies	D
Dance	M
Developmental Biology	M,D
Economics	M,D
Education—General	M,D,O
Educational Leadership and Administration	M,D,O
Educational Psychology	M,D,O
Electrical Engineering	M,D
English as a Second Language	M,D,O
English	M,D
Entomology	M,D
Environmental Engineering	M,D
Environmental Sciences	M
Ethnic Studies	D
Evolutionary Biology	M,D
Foundations and Philosophy of Education	M,D,O
Genetics	D
Genomic Sciences	D
Geology	M,D
Higher Education	M,D,O
Hispanic Studies	M,D
History	M,D
International Health	M,D
Materials Engineering	M
Materials Sciences	M
Mathematics	M,D
Mechanical Engineering	M,D
Microbiology	M,D
Molecular Biology	M,D
Multilingual and Multicultural Education	M,D,O
Music	M,D
Nanotechnology	M,D
Neuroscience	D
Philosophy	M,D
Physics	M,D
Plant Biology	M,D
Plant Molecular Biology	M,D
Plant Pathology	M,D
Plant Sciences	M,D
Political Science	M,D
Psychology—General	D
Public Policy	M,D
Reading Education	M,D,O
Religion	M,D
School Psychology	M,D,O
Sociology	M,D
Spanish	M,D
Special Education	M,D,O
Statistics	M
Toxicology	M,D
Water Resources	M,D
Writing	M

UNIVERSITY OF CALIFORNIA, SAN DIEGO

Aerospace/Aeronautical Engineering	M,D
Allopathic Medicine	D
Anthropology	D
Applied Mathematics	M,D
Applied Physics	M,D
Architectural Engineering	M
Art History	M,D
Art/Fine Arts	M,D
Artificial Intelligence/Robotics	M,D
Biochemistry	M,D
Bioengineering	M,D*
Bioinformatics	D
Biological and Biomedical Sciences—General	M,D*
Biophysics	M,D
Biostatistics	D
Business Administration and Management—General	M,D
Chemical Engineering	M,D
Chemistry	M,D
Clinical Laboratory Sciences/Medical Technology	M,D
Clinical Psychology	D
Clinical Research	M
Cognitive Sciences	D
Communication Disorders	D
Communication—General	D
Computational Sciences	M,D
Computer Engineering	M,D
Computer Science	M,D
Curriculum and Instruction	M,D
Dance	M,D
Database Systems	M
Economics	D
Education—General	M,D
Educational Leadership and Administration	M,D
Electrical Engineering	M,D
Energy Management and Policy	M
Engineering Physics	M,D
English	M,D
Environmental Management and Policy	M
Epidemiology	D
Ethnic Studies	D
Finance and Banking	M,D
Geophysics	M,D
Geosciences	M,D
Health Law	M
Health Services Management and Hospital Administration	M
History of Science and Technology	D

History	M,D
International Affairs	M,D
International Business	M
International Development	M
International Economics	M
International Health	D
Jewish Studies	M,D
Latin American Studies	M
Law	M
Legal and Justice Studies	M
Linguistics	D
Management Strategy and Policy	M,D
Marine Biology	M,D
Marine Sciences	M
Materials Sciences	M,D
Mathematics Education	D
Mathematics	M,D
Mechanical Engineering	M,D
Mechanics	M,D
Meteorology	M,D
Modeling and Simulation	M,D
Multilingual and Multicultural Education	M,D
Music	M,D
Nanotechnology	M,D
Neuroscience	M,D
Nonprofit Management	M
Ocean Engineering	M,D
Oceanography	M,D
Pharmacy	D
Philosophy	D
Photonics	M,D
Physics	M,D
Political Science	M,D
Psychology—General	D
Public Health—General	D
Public Policy	M
Science Education	D
Sociology	M,D
Statistics	M,D
Structural Engineering	M,D
Systems Biology	D*
Telecommunications	M,D
Theater	M,D
Writing	M,D

UNIVERSITY OF CALIFORNIA, SAN FRANCISCO

Allopathic Medicine	D
Anthropology	D
Biochemistry	D
Bioengineering	D
Bioinformatics	D
Biological and Biomedical Sciences—General	D
Biophysics	D
Cell Biology	D
Chemistry	D
Dentistry	D
Developmental Biology	D
Genetics	D
Genomic Sciences	D
Health Law	M
History of Science and Technology	M,D
Medical Imaging	M
Medicinal and Pharmaceutical Chemistry	D
Molecular Biology	D
Neuroscience	D
Nursing—General	M,D
Oral and Dental Sciences	M,D
Pharmaceutical Sciences	D
Pharmacology	D
Pharmacy	D
Physical Therapy	D
Sociology	D

UNIVERSITY OF CALIFORNIA, SANTA BARBARA

African-American Studies	D
Agricultural Economics and Agribusiness	M,D
Anthropology	M,D
Applied Mathematics	M,D
Applied Statistics	M,D
Art History	D
Art/Fine Arts	M
Asian Languages	M,D
Asian Studies	M,D
Biochemistry	D
Bioengineering	M,D
Biophysics	D
Cell Biology	M,D
Chemical Engineering	M,D
Chemistry	M,D
Classics	M,D
Clinical Psychology	M,D,O
Cognitive Sciences	M,D
Communication—General	D
Comparative Literature	D
Computational Sciences	M,D
Computer Engineering	M,D
Computer Science	M,D
Counseling Psychology	M,D,O
Cultural Anthropology	M,D
Cultural Studies	M,D
Developmental Biology	M,D
Ecology	M,D
Economics	M,D
Education—General	M,D,O
Electrical Engineering	M,D
Engineering and Applied Sciences—General	M,D
English	D
Environmental Management and Policy	M,D
Environmental Sciences	M,D
Evolutionary Biology	M,D
Film, Television, and Video Production	D
Finance and Banking	M,D

French	D
Geography	M,D
Geosciences	M,D
Hispanic and Latin American Languages	M,D
Hispanic Studies	M,D
History	D
Interdisciplinary Studies	D
International Affairs	M,D
Latin American Studies	M
Linguistics	M,D
Management of Technology	M
Marine Biology	M,D
Marine Sciences	M,D
Materials Engineering	M,D
Materials Sciences	M,D
Mathematical and Computational Finance	M,D
Mathematics	M,D
Mechanical Engineering	M,D
Media Studies	M,D
Medieval and Renaissance Studies	M,D
Molecular Biology	M,D
Music	M,D
Neuroscience	D
Philosophy	D
Photonics	M,D
Physics	D
Political Science	M,D
Portuguese	M,D
Psychology—General	D
Public History	D
Quantitative Analysis	M,D
Religion	M,D
School Psychology	M,D,O
Social Sciences	D
Sociology	D
Spanish	M,D
Speech and Interpersonal Communication	D
Statistics	M,D
Sustainable Development	M,D
Theater	M,D
Translation and Interpretation	M,D
Transportation Management	M,D
Women's Studies	M,D
Writing	D

UNIVERSITY OF CALIFORNIA, SANTA CRUZ

Anthropology	D
Applied Economics	M
Applied Mathematics	M,D
Art/Fine Arts	M,D
Astronomy	D
Astrophysics	D
Biochemistry	M,D
Bioinformatics	M,D
Cell Biology	M,D
Chemistry	M,D
Communication—General	O
Comparative Literature	M,D
Computer Art and Design	M,D
Computer Engineering	M,D
Computer Science	M,D
Cultural Anthropology	D
Developmental Biology	M,D
Ecology	M,D
Economics	D
Education—General	M,D
Electrical Engineering	M,D
Engineering and Applied Sciences—General	M,D
English	M,D
Environmental Biology	M,D
Environmental Management and Policy	D
Evolutionary Biology	M,D
Film, Television, and Video Theory and Criticism	D
Finance and Banking	M
Geosciences	M,D
History	M,D
Humanities	D
Interdisciplinary Studies	M,D
International Affairs	D
Linguistics	M,D
Management Information Systems	M,D
Management of Technology	D
Marine Sciences	M,D
Mathematics	M,D
Molecular Biology	M,D
Music	M,D
Philosophy	M,D
Physics	M,D
Planetary and Space Sciences	M,D
Political Science	D
Psychology—General	D
Social Sciences Education	M
Social Sciences	D
Sociology	D
Statistics	M,D
Theater	O
Toxicology	M,D
Writing	M

UNIVERSITY OF CENTRAL ARKANSAS

Accounting	M
Adult Education	M,O
Adult Nursing	M,O
Applied Mathematics	M
Biological and Biomedical Sciences—General	M
Business Administration and Management—General	M
Communication Disorders	M,D
Computer Art and Design	M
Computer Science	M
Counseling Psychology	M
Counselor Education	M

UNIVERSITY OF CENTRAL FLORIDA

Accounting	M
Aerospace/Aeronautical Engineering	M
Allopathic Medicine	M,D
Anthropology	M,O
Applied Psychology	M,D
Art Education	M
Art/Fine Arts	M
Biological and Biomedical Sciences—General	M,D
Biotechnology	M,D
Business Administration and Management—General	M,D,O
Chemistry	M,D
Child Development	M,O
Civil Engineering	M,D,O
Clinical Psychology	M,D
Communication Disorders	M,D,O
Communication—General	M,O
Community College Education	M,D,O
Computer Art and Design	M
Computer Engineering	M,D
Computer Science	M,D
Conservation Biology	M,D,O
Construction Engineering	M,D,O
Corporate and Organizational Communication	M,O
Counselor Education	M,O
Criminal Justice and Criminology	M,D,O
Curriculum and Instruction	D
Early Childhood Education	D
Education—General	M,O
Educational Leadership and Administration	M,D,O
Educational Media/Instructional Technology	M,D,O
Electrical Engineering	M,D
Elementary Education	M,D
Emergency Management	M,O
Engineering and Applied Sciences—General	M,D,O
English as a Second Language	M,D,O
English Education	M
English	M,D,O
Entrepreneurship	M,O
Environmental Engineering	M,D
Exercise and Sports Science	M,D
Experimental Psychology	M,D
Film, Television, and Video Production	M
Forensic Sciences	M,D
Game Design and Development	M
Geographic Information Systems	M,O
Health Informatics	M,O
Health Services Management and Hospital Administration	M,O
Higher Education	M,D,O
History	M
Homeland Security	M,O
Hospitality Management	M,D,O
Industrial and Organizational Psychology	M,D
Industrial/Management Engineering	M,D,O
Interdisciplinary Studies	M,O
Marriage and Family Therapy	M,O
Materials Engineering	M,D
Materials Sciences	M,D
Mathematics Education	M,D,O
Mathematics	M,D,O
Mechanical Engineering	M,D
Middle School Education	M
Modeling and Simulation	M,D,O
Music	M
Nanotechnology	M
National Security	M,D,O
Nonprofit Management	M,O

(continued from left) UNIVERSITY OF CENTRAL FLORIDA

Curriculum and Instruction	M,O
Economic Development	M,O
Economics	M,O
Education of the Gifted	M,O
Education—General	M,O
Educational Leadership and Administration	M,O
Educational Media/Instructional Technology	M
English	M
Family and Consumer Sciences-General	M
Family Nurse Practitioner Studies	M,O
Film, Television, and Video Production	M
Foreign Languages Education	M
Geographic Information Systems	M,O
Geography	M,O
Health Education	M
History	M
Kinesiology and Movement Studies	M
Library Science	M
Mathematics Education	M
Mathematics	M
Music Education	M,O
Music	M,O
Nursing and Healthcare Administration	M,O
Nursing Education	M,O
Nursing—General	M,O
Occupational Therapy	M
Organizational Management	D
Physical Therapy	D
Psychology—General	M,D,O
Reading Education	M
School Psychology	M,D,O
Social Psychology	M
Special Education	M,O
Student Affairs	M
Urban and Regional Planning	M,O
Writing	M

Nursing—General	M,D,O
Optical Sciences	M,D
Photonics	M,D
Physical Therapy	D
Physics	M,D
Physiology	M
Political Science	M,D,O
Psychology—General	M,D
Public Administration	M,O
Public Affairs	M,D,O
Reading Education	M,D,O
School Psychology	O
Science Education	M,D,O
Social Sciences Education	M,D
Social Work	M,O
Sociology	M,D
Spanish	M
Special Education	M,D,O
Sports Management	M
Statistics	M,O
Structural Engineering	M,D,O
Student Affairs	M,D,O
Theater	M
Transportation and Highway Engineering	M,D,O
Travel and Tourism	M,D,O
Urban and Regional Planning	M,O
Vocational and Technical Education	M,D,O
Writing	M

UNIVERSITY OF CENTRAL MISSOURI

Accounting	M,D,O
Aerospace/Aeronautical Engineering	M,D,O
Applied Mathematics	M,D,O
Biological and Biomedical Sciences—General	M,D,O
Business Administration and Management—General	M,D,O
Communication Disorders	M,D,O
Communication—General	M,D,O
Computer Science	M,D,O
Counseling Psychology	M,D,O
Counselor Education	M,D,O
Criminal Justice and Criminology	M,D,O
Early Childhood Education	M,D,O
Education—General	M,D,O
Educational Leadership and Administration	M,D,O
Educational Media/Instructional Technology	M,D,O
Elementary Education	M,D,O
English as a Second Language	M,D,O
English	M,D,O
Environmental and Occupational Health	M,D,O
Environmental Management and Policy	M,D,O
Finance and Banking	M,D,O
Gerontology	M,D,O
History	M,D,O
Human Services	M,D,O
Industrial and Manufacturing Management	M,D,O
Industrial Hygiene	M,D,O
Information Science	M,D,O
Kinesiology and Movement Studies	M,D,O
Library Science	M,D,O
Management Information Systems	M,D,O
Management of Technology	M,D,O
Marketing	M,D,O
Mathematics	M,D,O
Music	M,D,O
Nursing—General	M,D,O
Psychology—General	M,D,O
Reading Education	M,D,O
Sociology	M,D,O
Special Education	M,D,O
Student Affairs	M,D,O
Theater	M,D,O
Vocational and Technical Education	M,D,O

UNIVERSITY OF CENTRAL OKLAHOMA

Accounting	M
Addictions/Substance Abuse Counseling	M
Adult Education	M
Applied Arts and Design—General	M
Applied Mathematics	M
Athletic Training and Sports Medicine	M
Biological and Biomedical Sciences—General	M
Biomedical Engineering	M
Child and Family Studies	M
Communication Disorders	M
Computer Science	M
Counseling Psychology	M
Counselor Education	M
Criminal Justice and Criminology	M
Early Childhood Education	M
Education—General	M
Educational Leadership and Administration	M
Educational Media/Instructional Technology	M
Electrical Engineering	M
Elementary Education	M
Engineering and Applied Sciences—General	M
Engineering Physics	M
English as a Second Language	M
English	M
Exercise and Sports Science	M
Experimental Psychology	M
Family and Consumer Sciences-General	M
Forensic Psychology	M
Forensic Sciences	M
Gerontology	M
Health Promotion	M
Higher Education	M
History	M
Human Development	M
Interdisciplinary Studies	M

International Affairs	M
Library Science	M
Marriage and Family Therapy	M
Mathematics	M
Mechanical Engineering	M
Museum Studies	M
Music	M
Nursing—General	M
Nutrition	M
Political Science	M
Psychology—General	M
Public Administration	M
Reading Education	M
School Psychology	M
Secondary Education	M
Sociology	M
Special Education	M
Statistics	M
Student Affairs	M
Writing	M

UNIVERSITY OF CHARLESTON

Accounting	M
Business Administration and Management—General	M
Forensic Sciences	M
Legal and Justice Studies	M
Management Strategy and Policy	M
Organizational Management	D
Pharmacy	D
Physician Assistant Studies	M

UNIVERSITY OF CHICAGO

Accounting	M,O
Allopathic Medicine	D
Anatomy	D
Anthropology	D
Applied Statistics	M
Archaeology	D
Art History	M,D
Art/Fine Arts	M
Asian Languages	D
Asian Studies	M,D
Astronomy	D
Astrophysics	D
Atmospheric Sciences	D
Bioengineering	M,D
Biological and Biomedical Sciences—General	D
Biophysics	D
Business Administration and Management—General	M,D,O
Cancer Biology/Oncology	D
Cell Biology	D
Chemistry	D
Classics	M,D
Comparative Literature	D
Computational Sciences	M
Computer Science	M,D
Developmental Biology	D
Ecology	D
Economics	M,D,O
Emergency Management	M
English	M,D
Entrepreneurship	M,O
Environmental Management and Policy	M
Environmental Sciences	M
Ethics	D
Evolutionary Biology	D
Film, Television, and Video Theory and Criticism	D
Finance and Banking	M,O
French	D
Gender Studies	M
Genetics	D
Genomic Sciences	D
Geophysics	D
Geosciences	D
German	M,D
Health Promotion	M,D
Health Services Management and Hospital Administration	M,O
History	D
Human Development	D
Human Genetics	D
Humanities	M
Immunology	D
Industrial and Manufacturing Management	M,O
International Affairs	M
International Business	M,O
Italian	D
Latin American Studies	M
Law	M,D
Liberal Studies	M
Linguistics	M,D
Management Strategy and Policy	M,O
Marketing	M,O
Mathematical and Computational Finance	M
Mathematics	D
Media Studies	M,D
Medical Physics	D
Medieval and Renaissance Studies	D
Microbiology	D
Molecular Biology	D
Molecular Biophysics	D
Music	M,D
Near and Middle Eastern Languages	D
Near and Middle Eastern Studies	M,D
Neurobiology	D
Neuroscience	D
Nutrition	D
Organizational Behavior	M,O
Paleontology	D
Pastoral Ministry and Counseling	M
Philosophy	M,D
Physics	M,D
Planetary and Space Sciences	D
Political Science	D
Psychology—General	D
Public Policy	M,D
Religion	M,D

Romance Languages	M,D
Science Education	M
Slavic Languages	M
Social Sciences	M
Social Work	M,D
Sociology	D
Spanish	D
Statistics	M,D,O
Systems Biology	D
Theater	M
Theology	D
Urban Education	M
Writing	M
Zoology	D

UNIVERSITY OF CINCINNATI

Accounting	M,D
Acute Care/Critical Care Nursing	M,D
Addictions/Substance Abuse Counseling	M,D,O
Adult Education	M,D,O
Adult Nursing	M,D
Aerospace/Aeronautical Engineering	M,D
Allopathic Medicine	D
Analytical Chemistry	M,D
Anthropology	M
Applied Arts and Design—General	M
Applied Economics	M
Applied Mathematics	M,D
Architecture	M
Art Education	M
Art History	M
Art/Fine Arts	M
Arts Administration	M
Biochemistry	M,D
Bioinformatics	D,O
Biological and Biomedical Sciences—General	M,D,O
Biomedical Engineering	M,D
Biophysics	D
Biostatistics	M,D
Business Administration and Management—General	M,D
Cancer Biology/Oncology	D
Cell Biology	D
Chemical Engineering	M,D
Chemistry	M,D
Civil Engineering	M,D
Classics	M,D
Clinical Psychology	D
Communication Disorders	M,D,O
Communication—General	M
Community Health Nursing	M,D
Computer Engineering	M,D
Computer Science	M,D
Counselor Education	M,D,O
Criminal Justice and Criminology	M,D
Curriculum and Instruction	M,D
Developmental Biology	D
Early Childhood Education	M
Economics	D
Education—General	M,D,O
Educational Leadership and Administration	M,D,O
Electrical Engineering	M,D
Elementary Education	M
Engineering and Applied Sciences—General	M,D
English as a Second Language	M,D,O
English	M,D
Environmental and Occupational Health	M,D
Environmental Engineering	M,D
Environmental Sciences	M,D
Epidemiology	M,D
Ergonomics and Human Factors	M,D
Experimental Psychology	D
Finance and Banking	M,D
Foundations and Philosophy of Education	M,D
French	M,D
Genetic Counseling	M
Genomic Sciences	M,D
Geography	M,D
Geology	M,D
German	M,D
Graphic Design	M
Health Education	M,D
Health Informatics	M
Health Physics/Radiological Health	M
Health Promotion	M,D
Health Services Research	M
History	M,D
Immunology	M,D
Industrial and Labor Relations	M
Industrial and Manufacturing Management	D
Industrial Design	M
Industrial Hygiene	M,D
Industrial/Management Engineering	M,D
Inorganic Chemistry	M,D
Interdisciplinary Studies	M,D
Interior Design	M
Law	M,D
Management Information Systems	M,D
Marketing	M,D
Materials Engineering	M,D
Materials Sciences	M,D
Maternal and Child/Neonatal Nursing	M,D
Mathematics Education	M,D
Mathematics	M,D
Mechanical Engineering	M,D
Mechanics	M,D
Medical Imaging	M,D
Medical Physics	M
Microbiology	M,D
Molecular Biology	M,D
Molecular Genetics	M,D
Molecular Medicine	D
Molecular Toxicology	M,D

Music Education	M
Music	M,D,O
Neuroscience	D
Nuclear Engineering	M,D
Nurse Anesthesia	M,D
Nurse Midwifery	M,D
Nursing and Healthcare Administration	M,D
Nursing—General	M,D
Nutrition	M
Occupational Health Nursing	M,D
Organic Chemistry	M,D
Organizational Management	M
Pathobiology	D
Pathology	D
Pediatric Nursing	M,D
Pharmaceutical Sciences	M,D
Pharmacology	D
Pharmacy	D
Philosophy	M,D
Physical Chemistry	M,D
Physical Therapy	D
Physics	M,D
Political Science	M,D
Psychiatric Nursing	M,D
Psychology—General	D
Public Health—General	M,D
Quantitative Analysis	M,D
Reading Education	M,D
Romance Languages	M,D
School Psychology	D,O
Science Education	M,D,O
Secondary Education	M
Social Sciences Education	M,D,O
Social Work	M
Sociology	M,D
Spanish	M,D
Special Education	M
Sports Management	M
Statistics	M,D
Systems Biology	D
Taxation	M
Textile Design	M
Theater	M
Urban and Regional Planning	M
Women's Health Nursing	M,D
Women's Studies	M,O

UNIVERSITY OF COLORADO BOULDER

Advertising and Public Relations	M,D
Aerospace/Aeronautical Engineering	M,D
Anthropology	M,D
Applied Mathematics	M,D
Architectural Engineering	M,D
Art History	M
Art/Fine Arts	M
Asian Studies	M,D
Astrophysics	M,D
Atmospheric Sciences	M,D
Biochemistry	M,D
Business Administration and Management—General	M
Cell Biology	M,D
Chemical Engineering	M,D
Chemistry	M,D
Chinese	M,D
Civil Engineering	M,D
Classics	M,D
Communication Disorders	M,D
Communication—General	M,D
Comparative Literature	M,D
Computer Engineering	M,D
Computer Science	M,D
Curriculum and Instruction	M,D
Dance	M,D
Developmental Biology	M,D
Ecology	M,D
Economics	M,D
Education—General	M,D
Educational Measurement and Evaluation	D
Educational Policy	M,D
Educational Psychology	M,D
Electrical Engineering	M,D
Engineering and Applied Sciences—General	M,D
Engineering Management	M
English	M,D
Environmental Engineering	M,D
Environmental Management and Policy	M,D
Ethnic Studies	D
Evolutionary Biology	M,D
Film, Television, and Video Production	M
French	M,D
Geography	M,D
Geology	M,D
Geophysics	M,D
German	M
Hispanic and Latin American Languages	M,D
History	M,D
Information Science	D
Internet and Interactive Multimedia	D
Japanese	M,D
Journalism	M,D
Kinesiology and Movement Studies	M,D
Law	D
Linguistics	M,D
Mass Communication	M,D
Mathematical Physics	M,D
Mathematics	M,D
Mechanical Engineering	M,D
Media Studies	M,D
Molecular Biology	M,D
Multilingual and Multicultural Education	M,D
Museum Studies	M
Music Education	M,D
Music	M,D
Oceanography	M,D

Philosophy	M,D
Photography	M
Physics	M,D
Physiology	M,D
Plasma Physics	M,D
Political Science	M,D
Psychology—General	M,D
Religion	M
Sociology	D
Spanish	M,D
Telecommunications Management	M
Telecommunications	M
Theater	M,D
Writing	M,D

UNIVERSITY OF COLORADO COLORADO SPRINGS

Adult Nursing	M,D
Aerospace/Aeronautical Engineering	M,D
Applied Mathematics	M
Business Administration and Management—General	M
Communication—General	M
Computer and Information Systems Security	M,D
Computer Science	M
Counselor Education	M,D
Criminal Justice and Criminology	M
Curriculum and Instruction	M,D
Education—General	M,D
Educational Leadership and Administration	M,D
Electrical Engineering	M
Energy and Power Engineering	M,D
Engineering and Applied Sciences—General	M,D
Engineering Management	M,D
English as a Second Language	M,D
Environmental Sciences	M
Geography	M
Gerontological Nursing	M,D
History	M
Human Services	M,D
Interdisciplinary Studies	M
Mathematics	D
Mechanical Engineering	M
Nursing—General	M,D
Physics	D
Psychology—General	M,D
Public Administration	M
Public Affairs	M
Sociology	M
Software Engineering	M,D
Special Education	M,D
Systems Engineering	M,D

UNIVERSITY OF COLORADO DENVER

Accounting	M
Adult Education	M
Adult Nursing	M,D
Allopathic Medicine	D
American Studies	M
Anatomy	M,D
Anesthesiologist Assistant Studies	M
Animal Behavior	M,D
Anthropology	M
Applied Mathematics	M,D
Applied Science and Technology	M
Applied Statistics	M,D
Archaeology	M
Architectural History	D
Architecture	M
Art/Fine Arts	M
Biochemistry	D
Bioengineering	M,D
Bioinformatics	D
Biological and Biomedical Sciences—General	M,D
Biophysics	M,D
Biostatistics	M,D
Business Administration and Management—General	M
Cancer Biology/Oncology	D
Cell Biology	M,D
Chemistry	M
Civil Engineering	M,D
Clinical Laboratory Sciences/Medical Technology	M,D
Clinical Psychology	M,D
Clinical Research	M,D
Communication—General	M
Community Health	M,D
Computational Biology	M,D
Computational Sciences	M,D
Computer Science	M,D
Corporate and Organizational Communication	M
Counseling Psychology	M
Counselor Education	M
Criminal Justice and Criminology	M,D
Dentistry	M,D
Developmental Biology	M,D
Distance Education Development	M
Early Childhood Education	M,D
Ecology	M,D
Economic Development	M
Economics	M
Education—General	M,D,O
Educational Leadership and Administration	M,D,O
Educational Measurement and Evaluation	M,D,O
Educational Media/Instructional Technology	M
Educational Policy	D
Educational Psychology	M,D,O
Electrical Engineering	M,D

Elementary Education	M
Emergency Management	M,D
Energy Management and Policy	M
Engineering and Applied Sciences—General	M,D
English Education	M
English	M
Entertainment Management	M
Entrepreneurship	M
Environmental and Occupational Health	M,D
Environmental Education	M
Environmental Engineering	M,D
Environmental Law	M,D
Environmental Management and Policy	M,D
Environmental Sciences	M
Epidemiology	M,D
Evolutionary Biology	M,D
Family Nurse Practitioner Studies	M,D
Finance and Banking	M
Forensic Sciences	M
Gender Studies	M
Genetic Counseling	M,D
Genetics	M,D
Geographic Information Systems	M,D
Geotechnical Engineering	M,D
Health Education	M,D
Health Psychology	M,D
Health Services Management and Hospital Administration	M,D
Health Services Research	M,D
Historic Preservation	M
History	M
Homeland Security	M,D
Human Development	M,D,O
Human Resources Management	M
Humanities	M
Hydraulics	M,D
Hydrology	M,D
Immunology	D
Information Science	M,D
Insurance	M
International Affairs	M
International Business	M
International Health	M
Investment Management	M
Landscape Architecture	M
Linguistics	M
Management Information Systems	M,D
Management of Technology	M
Management Strategy and Policy	M
Marketing Research	M
Marketing	M
Marriage and Family Therapy	M
Mathematics Education	M,D
Mathematics	M,D
Mechanical Engineering	M
Mechanics	M
Medical Informatics	M,D
Microbiology	M,D
Military and Defense Studies	M,D
Molecular Biology	M,D
Molecular Genetics	D
Multilingual and Multicultural Education	M
Music	M
Neurobiology	M,D
Neuroscience	D
Nonprofit Management	M,D
Nurse Midwifery	M,D
Nursing and Healthcare Administration	M,D
Nursing—General	M,D
Operations Research	M,D
Oral and Dental Sciences	M,D
Pediatric Nursing	M,D
Pharmaceutical Sciences	D
Pharmacology	D
Pharmacy	D
Physical Therapy	D
Physician Assistant Studies	M
Physiology	M,D
Political Science	M,D
Psychiatric Nursing	M,D
Public Administration	M,D
Public Affairs	M,D
Public Health—General	M,D
Public History	M
Quantitative Analysis	M
Reading Education	M
Rehabilitation Sciences	D
Rhetoric	M
School Psychology	M,D,O
Science Education	M,D
Secondary Education	M
Sociology	M
Spanish	M
Special Education	M,D
Sports Management	M
Statistics	M,D
Structural Engineering	M,D
Sustainability Management	M
Sustainable Development	M,D
Taxation	M
Toxicology	D
Transportation and Highway Engineering	M,D
Urban and Regional Planning	M,D
Urban Design	M,D
Water Resources	M
Western European Studies	M,D
Women's Health Nursing	M,D
Women's Studies	M
Writing	M

UNIVERSITY OF CONNECTICUT

Accounting	M
Adult Education	M,O

Agricultural Economics and Agribusiness	M,D
Agricultural Education	M,D
Agricultural Sciences—General	M,D
Agronomy and Soil Sciences	M,D
Animal Sciences	M,D
Anthropology	M,D
Applied Arts and Design—General	M
Applied Mathematics	M
Biomedical Engineering	M,D
Biophysics	M,D
Biopsychology	M,D
Botany	M,D
Business Administration and Management—General	M,D
Cell Biology	M,D
Chemical Engineering	M,D
Chemistry	M,D
Child and Family Studies	M,D
Civil Engineering	M,D
Clinical Psychology	M,D
Cognitive Sciences	M,D
Communication Disorders	M,D
Communication—General	M
Computer Science	M,D
Counseling Psychology	M,D
Counselor Education	M,D
Curriculum and Instruction	M,D
Developmental Biology	M,D
Developmental Psychology	M,D
Ecology	M,D
Economics	M,D
Education of the Gifted	O
Education—General	M,D
Educational Leadership and Administration	M
Educational Media/Instructional Technology	M,D
Educational Psychology	M,D,O
Electrical Engineering	M,D
Elementary Education	M,D
Engineering and Applied Sciences—General	M,D
English Education	M,D
English	M,D
Environmental and Occupational Health	O
Environmental Engineering	M,D
Exercise and Sports Science	M,D
Experimental Psychology	M,D
Finance and Banking	M,D,O
Foreign Languages Education	M,D
Genetics	M,D
Genomic Sciences	M,D
Geography	M,D
Geology	M,D
Health Services Management and Hospital Administration	M,D
Higher Education	M
History	M,D
Human Development	M,D
Human Resources Management	M
Industrial and Organizational Psychology	M,D
International Affairs	M
Jewish Studies	M
Latin American Studies	M
Law	D
Linguistics	M,D
Marketing	M,D
Materials Engineering	M
Materials Sciences	M,D
Mathematical and Computational Finance	M
Mathematics Education	M,D
Mechanical Engineering	M,D
Medicinal and Pharmaceutical Chemistry	M,D
Medieval and Renaissance Studies	M,D
Metallurgical Engineering and Metallurgy	M
Microbiology	M,D
Molecular Biology	M,D
Multilingual and Multicultural Education	M,D
Music Education	M,D
Music	M,D
Natural Resources	M,D
Neurobiology	M,D
Neuroscience	M,D
Nonprofit Management	M,O
Nursing—General	M,D,O
Nutrition	M,D
Pathobiology	M,D
Pharmaceutical Sciences	M,D
Pharmacology	M,D
Pharmacy	D
Philosophy	M,D
Physical Therapy	D
Physics	M,D
Physiology	M,D
Plant Sciences	M,D
Political Science	M,D
Polymer Science and Engineering	M,D
Psychology—General	M,D
Public Administration	M
Quantitative Analysis	M,O
Reading Education	M,D
Science Education	M,D
Secondary Education	M,D
Social Psychology	M,D
Social Sciences Education	M,D
Sociology	M,D
Software Engineering	M
Sports Management	M
Statistics	M,D
Structural Biology	M,D
Theater	M
Toxicology	M,D

Western European Studies	M

UNIVERSITY OF CONNECTICUT HEALTH CENTER

Allopathic Medicine	D
Anatomy	D
Biochemistry	D
Biological and Biomedical Sciences—General	D
Cell Biology	D
Clinical Research	M
Dentistry	D,O
Developmental Biology	D
Genetics	D
Immunology	D
Molecular Biology	D
Neuroscience	D
Oral and Dental Sciences	M
Public Health—General	M

UNIVERSITY OF DALLAS

Accounting	M,D
American Studies	M
Art/Fine Arts	M
Business Administration and Management—General	M,D
Classics	M
Comparative Literature	D
Computer and Information Systems Security	M,D
English	M
Entertainment Management	M,D
Finance and Banking	M,D
Health Services Management and Hospital Administration	M,D
Human Resources Management	M,D
Humanities	M
International Business	M,D
Logistics	M,D
Management Information Systems	M,D
Management of Technology	M,D
Management Strategy and Policy	M,D
Marketing	M,D
Organizational Management	M,D
Pastoral Ministry and Counseling	M
Philosophy	M,D
Political Science	M,D
Project Management	M,D
Psychology—General	M
Sports Management	M,D
Supply Chain Management	M,D
Theology	M

UNIVERSITY OF DAYTON

Accounting	M
Aerospace/Aeronautical Engineering	M,D
Applied Mathematics	M
Bioengineering	M
Biological and Biomedical Sciences—General	M,D
Business Administration and Management—General	M
Chemical Engineering	M
Chemistry	M
Civil Engineering	M
Clinical Psychology	M,O
Communication—General	M
Computer and Information Systems Security	M
Computer Engineering	M,D
Computer Science	M
Counseling Psychology	M,O
Counselor Education	M,O
Cultural Studies	M
Early Childhood Education	M
Educational Leadership and Administration	M,D,O
Educational Media/Instructional Technology	M
Electrical Engineering	M,D
Engineering Management	M
English as a Second Language	M
English	M
Environmental Engineering	M
Environmental Management and Policy	M,D
Exercise and Sports Science	M
Finance and Banking	M
Geotechnical Engineering	M
Higher Education	D
Human Development	M,O
Law	M,D
Marketing	M
Materials Engineering	M,D
Mathematical and Computational Finance	M
Mathematics Education	M
Mechanical Engineering	M,D
Mechanics	M
Middle School Education	M
Music Education	M
Optical Sciences	M,D
Pastoral Ministry and Counseling	M,D
Photonics	M,D
Physical Education	M
Physical Therapy	D
Physician Assistant Studies	M
Psychology—General	M
Public Administration	M
Reading Education	M
Rhetoric	M
School Psychology	M,O
Secondary Education	M
Structural Engineering	M
Student Affairs	M,O
Theology	M,D
Transportation and Highway Engineering	M
Water Resources Engineering	M
Writing	M

*M—masters degree; D—doctorate; O—other advanced degree; *—Close-Up and/or Display*

UNIVERSITY OF DELAWARE

Accounting	M
Adult Nursing	M,O
Agricultural Economics and Agribusiness	M
Agricultural Education	M
Agricultural Sciences—General	M,D
Agronomy and Soil Sciences	M,D
American Studies	M
Animal Sciences	M,D
Applied Arts and Design—General	M
Applied Mathematics	M,D
Art History	M,D
Art/Fine Arts	M
Astronomy	M,D
Biochemistry	M,D
Biological and Biomedical Sciences—General	M,D
Biotechnology	M,D
Business Administration and Management—General	M,D
Business Education	M,D
Cancer Biology/Oncology	M,D
Cell Biology	M,D
Chemical Engineering	M,D
Chemistry	M,D
Child and Family Studies	M
Chinese	M
Civil Engineering	M,D
Clinical Psychology	D
Clothing and Textiles	M
Cognitive Sciences	M,D
Communication Disorders	M
Communication—General	M
Computer Engineering	M,D
Computer Science	M,D
Criminal Justice and Criminology	M,D
Curriculum and Instruction	M,D,O
Developmental Biology	M,D
Ecology	M,D
Economics	M,D
Education—General	M,D,O
Educational Leadership and Administration	M,D,O
Electrical Engineering	M,D
Emergency Management	M,D
Energy Management and Policy	M,D
Engineering and Applied Sciences—General	M,D
English as a Second Language	M,D,O
English	M,D
Entomology	M,D
Entrepreneurship	M,D
Environmental Engineering	M,D
Environmental Management and Policy	M,D
Evolutionary Biology	M,D
Family Nurse Practitioner Studies	M,O
Finance and Banking	M
Fish, Game, and Wildlife Management	M,D
Food Science and Technology	M,D
Foreign Languages Education	M
French	M
Genetics	M,D
Geography	M,D
Geology	M,D
Geotechnical Engineering	M,D
German	M
Gerontological Nursing	M,O
Health Promotion	M
Higher Education	M,D,O
Historic Preservation	M,D
History of Science and Technology	M,D
History	M,D
HIV/AIDS Nursing	M,O
Horticulture	M
Hospitality Management	M
Human Development	M,D
Information Science	M,D
International Affairs	M,D
Kinesiology and Movement Studies	M,D
Liberal Studies	M
Linguistics	M,D
Management Information Systems	M,D
Management of Technology	M
Marine Affairs	M,D
Marine Geology	M,D
Marine Sciences	M,D
Materials Engineering	M,D
Materials Sciences	M,D
Maternal and Child/Neonatal Nursing	M,O
Mathematics	M,D
Mechanical Engineering	M,D
Microbiology	M,D
Molecular Biology	M,D
Multilingual and Multicultural Education	M,D,O
Music Education	M
Music	M
Natural Resources	M
Neuroscience	D
Nursing and Healthcare Administration	M,O
Nursing—General	M,O
Nutrition	M
Ocean Engineering	M,D
Oceanography	M,D
Oncology Nursing	M,O
Operations Research	M
Pediatric Nursing	M,O
Physical Therapy	D
Physics	M,D
Physiology	M,D
Plant Sciences	M,D
Political Science	M,D
Psychiatric Nursing	M,O
Psychology—General	D
Public Administration	M*
Public Policy	M,D
School Psychology	M,D,O
Social Psychology	D
Sociology	M,D
Spanish	M
Statistics	M
Structural Engineering	M,D
Theater	M
Translation and Interpretation	M
Transportation and Highway Engineering	M,D
Urban Studies	M,D
Water Resources Engineering	M,D
Women's Health Nursing	M,O

UNIVERSITY OF DENVER

Accounting	M
Anthropology	M
Archaeology	M
Art Education	M,O
Art History	M
Art/Fine Arts	M
Bioengineering	M,D
Biological and Biomedical Sciences—General	M,D
Business Administration and Management—General	M
Cell Biology	M,D
Child and Family Studies	M,D,O
Clinical Psychology	M,D
Cognitive Sciences	D
Communication—General	M,D,O
Computer and Information Systems Security	M,D
Computer Art and Design	M
Computer Engineering	M,D
Computer Science	M,D
Conflict Resolution and Mediation/Peace Studies	M
Construction Management	M
Counseling Psychology	M,D,O
Criminal Justice and Criminology	M,O
Cultural Anthropology	M
Cultural Studies	M,O
Curriculum and Instruction	M,D,O
Developmental Psychology	D
Early Childhood Education	M,D,O
Ecology	M,D
Economics	M
Education—General	M,D,O
Educational Leadership and Administration	M,D,O
Educational Measurement and Evaluation	M,D,O
Educational Policy	M,D,O
Electrical Engineering	M,D
Emergency Management	M,O
Engineering and Applied Sciences—General	M,D
Engineering Management	M,D
English	M,D
Environmental Management and Policy	M,O
Evolutionary Biology	M,D
Finance and Banking	M
Forensic Psychology	M,D
Geographic Information Systems	M,O
Health Services Management and Hospital Administration	M,O
Higher Education	M,D,O
History	M,O
Homeland Security	M,D,O
Human Resources Management	M,O
Information Science	M,O
International Affairs	M,D,O
International Development	M,D,O
International Health	M,D,O
Law	M,D,O
Legal and Justice Studies	M,O
Library Science	M,D,O
Management Strategy and Policy	M
Marketing	M
Marriage and Family Therapy	M,D,O
Mass Communication	M
Materials Engineering	M,D
Materials Sciences	M,D
Mathematics	M,D
Mechanical Engineering	M,D
Media Studies	M
Molecular Biology	M,D
Museum Studies	M
Music Education	M,O
Music	M,O
Organizational Management	M,O
Physics	M,D
Project Management	M,O
Psychology—General	M,D
Public Policy	M
Real Estate	M
Religion	M,D,O
Rhetoric	M,D
School Psychology	M,D,O
Social Psychology	D
Social Work	M,D,O
Special Education	M,D,O
Speech and Interpersonal Communication	M,D
Sport Psychology	M,D
Statistics	M
Taxation	M
Translation and Interpretation	M,O
Writing	M,D,O

UNIVERSITY OF DETROIT MERCY

Accounting	M,O
Addictions/Substance Abuse Counseling	M,D,O
Allied Health—General	M
Architectural Engineering	M
Business Administration and Management—General	M,O
Chemistry	M,D
Civil Engineering	M,D
Clinical Psychology	M,D,O
Computer and Information Systems Security	M,D,O

Computer Engineering	M,D
Computer Science	M,D,O
Criminal Justice and Criminology	M,D,O
Curriculum and Instruction	M,D,O
Dentistry	M,D,O
Economics	M,D,O
Educational Leadership and Administration	M,D,O
Electrical Engineering	M,D
Engineering and Applied Sciences—General	M,D
Engineering Management	M,D
Environmental Engineering	M,D
Ethics	M,O
Family Nurse Practitioner Studies	M,D,O
Finance and Banking	M,D,O
Forensic Sciences	M,O
Health Services Management and Hospital Administration	M,D,O
Industrial and Organizational Psychology	M,D,O
Industrial Design	M,D
Law	D
Liberal Studies	M,D,O
Management Information Systems	M,D,O
Management Strategy and Policy	M,O
Mathematics Education	M,D
Mechanical Engineering	M,D
Nurse Anesthesia	M,D,O
Nursing Education	M,D,O
Nursing—General	M,D,O
Oral and Dental Sciences	M,D,O
Physician Assistant Studies	M,D,O
Religious Education	M,D,O
School Psychology	M,D,O
Software Engineering	M,D
Special Education	M,D,O
Urban and Regional Planning	M

UNIVERSITY OF DUBUQUE

Business Administration and Management—General	M
Communication—General	M
Theology	M,D

UNIVERSITY OF EAST-WEST MEDICINE

Acupuncture and Oriental Medicine	M,D

UNIVERSITY OF EVANSVILLE

Athletic Training and Sports Medicine	M
Health Services Management and Hospital Administration	M
Physical Therapy	D
Public Administration	M

THE UNIVERSITY OF FINDLAY

Accounting	M,D
Athletic Training and Sports Medicine	M,D
Business Administration and Management—General	M,D
Education—General	M,D
Educational Leadership and Administration	M,D
Educational Media/Instructional Technology	M,D
English as a Second Language	M,D
Environmental Management and Policy	M,D
Health Informatics	M,D
Health Services Management and Hospital Administration	M,D
Hospitality Management	M,D
Multilingual and Multicultural Education	M,D
Occupational Therapy	M,D
Pharmacy	M,D
Physical Therapy	M,D
Physician Assistant Studies	M,D
Public Administration	M,D
Reading Education	M,D
Rhetoric	M,D
Science Education	M,D
Writing	M,D

UNIVERSITY OF FLORIDA

Accounting	M,D
Advertising and Public Relations	M,D
Aerospace/Aeronautical Engineering	M,D
Agricultural Economics and Agribusiness	M,D
Agricultural Education	M,D
Agricultural Engineering	M,D,O
Agricultural Sciences—General	M,D,O
Agronomy and Soil Sciences	M,D
Allied Health—General	M,D,O
Allopathic Medicine	D
Animal Sciences	M,D
Anthropology	M,D
Aquaculture	M,D
Architecture	M,D
Art Education	M,D
Art History	M,D
Art/Fine Arts	M,D
Astronomy	M,D
Athletic Training and Sports Medicine	M,D
Biochemistry	D
Bioengineering	M,D,O
Biological and Biomedical Sciences—General	M,D
Biomedical Engineering	M,D,O
Biostatistics	M,D,O
Botany	M,D
Business Administration and Management—General	M,D
Cell Biology	M,D
Chemical Engineering	M,D,O
Chemistry	M,D
Child Development	M
Civil Engineering	M,D
Classics	M,D

Clinical Laboratory Sciences/Medical Technology	M,D
Clinical Psychology	M,D
Clinical Research	M,D,O
Communication Disorders	M,D
Communication—General	M,D
Computer Art and Design	M,D
Computer Engineering	M,D
Computer Science	M,D
Construction Management	M,D
Counseling Psychology	M,D
Counselor Education	M,D,O
Criminal Justice and Criminology	M,D
Curriculum and Instruction	M,D,O
Dentistry	D,O
Early Childhood Education	M,D
Ecology	M,D,O
Economics	M,D
Education—General	M,D,O
Educational Leadership and Administration	M,D,O
Educational Measurement and Evaluation	M,D,O
Educational Policy	M,D
Electrical Engineering	M,D
Elementary Education	M,D
Emergency Management	M
Engineering and Applied Sciences—General	M,D,O
English as a Second Language	M,D,O
English Education	M,D,O
English	M,D
Entrepreneurship	M,D,O
Environmental and Occupational Health	M,D,O
Environmental Education	M,D,O
Environmental Engineering	M,D,O
Environmental Law	M,D
Epidemiology	M,D,O
Exercise and Sports Science	M,D
Family and Consumer Sciences-General	M
Finance and Banking	M,D,O
Fish, Game, and Wildlife Management	M,D,O
Food Science and Technology	M,D
Foreign Languages Education	M,D
Forensic Sciences	M,O
Forestry	M,D
French	M,D
Gender Studies	M,O
Genetics	D
Geographic Information Systems	M,D
Geography	M,D
Geology	M,D
Geosciences	M,D
German	M,D
Health Communication	M,D,O
Health Education	M,D,O
Health Psychology	M,D
Health Services Management and Hospital Administration	M,D
Health Services Research	M,D
Higher Education	M,D,O
Historic Preservation	M,D
History	M,D
Horticulture	M,D
Human Resources Management	M,D
Hydrology	M,D
Immunology	D
Industrial/Management Engineering	M,D,O
Information Science	M,D
Insurance	M,D,O
Interdisciplinary Studies	M,D
Interior Design	M,D
International Affairs	M
International Business	M,D
International Development	M,D,O
International Health	M,D
Jewish Studies	M,D
Journalism	M,D
Kinesiology and Movement Studies	M,D
Landscape Architecture	M,D
Latin American Studies	M,O
Law	M,D
Limnology	M,D
Linguistics	M,D
Management Information Systems	M,D,O
Marine Sciences	M,D
Marketing	M,D
Marriage and Family Therapy	M,D,O
Mass Communication	M,D
Materials Engineering	M,D
Materials Sciences	M,D
Mathematics Education	M,D,O
Mathematics	M,D
Mechanical Engineering	M,D
Medical Physics	M,D,O
Medicinal and Pharmaceutical Chemistry	M,D
Microbiology	M,D
Molecular Biology	M,D
Molecular Genetics	M
Museum Studies	M,D
Music Education	M,D
Music	M,D
Natural Resources	M,D
Neuroscience	D
Nonprofit Management	M
Nuclear Engineering	M,D
Nursing—General	M,D
Nutrition	M,D
Occupational Therapy	M
Ocean Engineering	M,D
Oral and Dental Sciences	M,D,O
Pharmaceutical Administration	M,D
Pharmaceutical Sciences	M,D
Pharmacology	M,D
Pharmacy	M,D
Philosophy	M,D
Physical Education	M,D
Physical Therapy	D

Physician Assistant Studies	M
Physics	M,D
Physiology	M,D
Plant Biology	M,D
Plant Molecular Biology	M,D
Plant Pathology	M,D
Plant Sciences	D
Political Science	M,D,O
Psychology—General	M,D
Public Affairs	M,D,O
Public Health—General	M,D,O
Quantitative Analysis	M,D,O
Reading Education	M,D,O
Real Estate	M,D
Recreation and Park Management	M,D
Rehabilitation Sciences	D
Religion	M
School Psychology	M,D,O
Science Education	M,D,O
Social Sciences Education	M,D,O
Social Sciences	M,D,O
Sociology	M,D
Spanish	M,D
Special Education	M,D,O
Sports Management	M
Statistics	M,D
Student Affairs	M,D,O
Supply Chain Management	M,D,O
Sustainable Development	M,O
Systems Engineering	M,D
Taxation	M,D
Telecommunications	M,D
Theater	M
Toxicology	M,D,O
Travel and Tourism	M,D
Urban and Regional Planning	M,D
Veterinary Medicine	D
Veterinary Sciences	M,D,O
Water Resources	M,D
Women's Studies	M,O
Writing	M,D
Zoology	M,D

UNIVERSITY OF FORT LAUDERDALE

Pastoral Ministry and Counseling	M

UNIVERSITY OF GEORGIA

Accounting	M
Adult Education	D,O
Agricultural Economics and Agribusiness	M,D
Agricultural Sciences—General	M,D
Agronomy and Soil Sciences	M,D
Analytical Chemistry	M,D
Animal Sciences	M,D
Anthropology	M,D
Applied Economics	M,D
Applied Mathematics	M,D
Art History	M,D
Art/Fine Arts	M,D
Artificial Intelligence/Robotics	M
Biochemical Engineering	M
Biochemistry	M,D
Bioinformatics	M,D
Biological and Biomedical Sciences—General	D
Business Administration and Management—General	M
Business Education	M,D,O
Cell Biology	M,D
Chemistry	M,D
Child and Family Studies	M
Classics	M
Clothing and Textiles	M,D
Communication Disorders	M,D,O
Communication—General	M,D
Comparative Literature	M,D
Computer Science	M,D
Counselor Education	M,D,O
Ecology	M,D
Economics	M,D
Education—General	M,D,O
Educational Leadership and Administration	D,O
Educational Media/Instructional Technology	M,D,O
Educational Policy	D,O
Educational Psychology	O
English Education	M,D
English	M,D
Entomology	M,D
Environmental and Occupational Health	M,D
Environmental Design	M
Environmental Engineering	M
Family and Consumer Sciences-General	M,D
Food Science and Technology	M,D
Forestry	M,D
French	M,D
Genetics	M,D
Genomic Sciences	M,D
Geography	M,D
Geology	M,D
German	M,D
Gerontology	O
Health Education	M,D
Health Promotion	M,D
Higher Education	M,D
Historic Preservation	M
History	M,D
Horticulture	M,D
Infectious Diseases	D
Interior Design	M,D
International Affairs	M,D
Italian	M,D
Journalism	M,D
Kinesiology and Movement Studies	M,D
Landscape Architecture	M

Law	M,D
Linguistics	M,D
Marine Sciences	M,D
Mass Communication	M,D
Mathematics Education	M,D,O
Mathematics	M,D
Microbiology	M,D
Molecular Biology	M,D
Music Education	M,D
Music	M,D
Natural Resources	M,D
Neuroscience	D
Nonprofit Management	M,D,O
Nutrition	M,D
Pathology	M,D
Pharmaceutical Administration	D
Pharmaceutical Sciences	M,D
Pharmacology	M,D
Pharmacy	M,D,O
Philosophy	M,D
Physical Education	M,D
Physics	M,D
Physiology	M,D
Plant Biology	M,D
Plant Pathology	M,D
Plant Sciences	M,D
Political Science	M,D
Portuguese	M,D
Psychology—General	D
Public Administration	M,D
Public Health—General	D
Public Policy	M,D
Reading Education	M,D
Religion	M
Science Education	M,D,O
Social Work	M,D,O
Sociology	M,D
Spanish	M,D
Special Education	M,D,O
Statistics	M,D
Student Affairs	M,D,O
Sustainable Development	M,D
Theater	M,D
Veterinary Medicine	M,D
Vocational and Technical Education	M,D,O
Women's Studies	O

UNIVERSITY OF GREAT FALLS

Counseling Psychology	M
Criminal Justice and Criminology	M
Human Services	M

UNIVERSITY OF GUAM

Art/Fine Arts	M
Biological and Biomedical Sciences—General	M
Business Administration and Management—General	M
Counselor Education	M
Education—General	M
Educational Leadership and Administration	M
English as a Second Language	M
English	M
Environmental Sciences	M
Graphic Design	M
Marine Biology	M
Pacific Area/Pacific Rim Studies	M
Public Administration	M
Reading Education	M
Secondary Education	M
Social Work	M
Special Education	M

UNIVERSITY OF GUELPH

Acute Care/Critical Care Nursing	M,D,O
Agricultural Economics and Agribusiness	M,D
Agricultural Sciences—General	M,D,O
Agronomy and Soil Sciences	M,D
Anatomy	M,D
Anesthesiologist Assistant Studies	M,D,O
Animal Sciences	M,D
Anthropology	M,D
Applied Mathematics	M,D
Applied Psychology	M,D
Applied Statistics	M,D
Aquaculture	M
Art/Fine Arts	M
Atmospheric Sciences	M,D
Biochemistry	M,D
Bioengineering	M,D
Biological and Biomedical Sciences—General	M,D
Biophysics	M,D
Biotechnology	M,D
Botany	M,D
Business Administration and Management—General	M,D
Cardiovascular Sciences	M,D,O
Cell Biology	M,D
Chemistry	M,D
Child and Family Studies	M,D
Clinical Psychology	M,D
Cognitive Sciences	M,D
Comparative Literature	D
Computer Science	M,D
Consumer Economics	M
Criminal Justice and Criminology	M,D
Demography and Population Studies	M,D
Ecology	M,D
Economics	M,D
Emergency Medical Services	M,D,O
Engineering and Applied Sciences—General	M,D
English	M
Entomology	M,D
Environmental Biology	M,D
Environmental Engineering	M,D
Environmental Management and Policy	M,D

Environmental Sciences	M,D
Epidemiology	M,D
Evolutionary Biology	M,D
Food Science and Technology	M,D
French	M
Geography	M,D
History	M,D
Horticulture	M,D
Hospitality Management	M
Human Development	M,D
Immunology	M,D,O
Industrial and Organizational Psychology	M,D
Infectious Diseases	M,D,O
International Development	M,D
Landscape Architecture	M
Marriage and Family Therapy	M,D
Mathematics	M,D
Medical Imaging	M,D,O
Medieval and Renaissance Studies	D
Microbiology	M,D
Molecular Biology	M,D
Molecular Genetics	M,D
Natural Resources	M,D
Neuroscience	M,D,O
Nutrition	M,D
Organizational Management	M
Pathology	M,D,O
Pharmacology	M,D
Philosophy	M,D
Physics	M,D
Physiology	M,D
Plant Pathology	M,D
Political Science	M
Psychology—General	M,D
Public Administration	M
Public Policy	M
Rural Planning and Studies	M,D
Social Psychology	M,D
Sociology	M,D
Statistics	M,D
Theater	M
Toxicology	M,D
Veterinary Medicine	M,D,O
Veterinary Sciences	M,D,O
Vision Sciences	M,D,O
Water Resources Engineering	M,D
Western European Studies	M
Zoology	M,D

UNIVERSITY OF HARTFORD

Accounting	M,O
Architecture	M
Art/Fine Arts	M
Biological and Biomedical Sciences—General	M
Business Administration and Management—General	M
Clinical Psychology	M,D
Communication—General	M
Community Health Nursing	M
Counselor Education	M,O
Early Childhood Education	M
Education—General	M,D,O
Educational Leadership and Administration	D,O
Educational Media/Instructional Technology	M
Elementary Education	M
Engineering and Applied Sciences—General	M
Experimental Psychology	M
Music Education	M,D,O
Music	M,D,O
Neuroscience	M
Nursing Education	M
Nursing—General	M
Organizational Behavior	M
Physical Therapy	M,D
Psychology—General	M,D
School Psychology	M
Taxation	M,O

UNIVERSITY OF HAWAII AT HILO

Conservation Biology	M
Counseling Psychology	M
Cultural Studies	M
Education—General	M
Environmental Sciences	M
Foreign Languages Education	M,D
Marine Biology	M
Nursing—General	D
Pharmaceutical Sciences	D*
Pharmacology	M
Pharmacy	M

UNIVERSITY OF HAWAII AT MANOA

Accounting	M,D
Adult Nursing	M,D,O
Agricultural Sciences—General	M,D
Allopathic Medicine	D
American Studies	M,D,O
Animal Sciences	M
Anthropology	M,D
Architecture	D
Art History	M
Art/Fine Arts	M
Asian Languages	M,D
Asian Studies	O
Astronomy	M,D
Bioengineering	M
Biological and Biomedical Sciences—General	M,D
Botany	M,D
Business Administration and Management—General	M
Chemistry	M,D
Chinese	M,D,O
Civil Engineering	M,D
Clinical Psychology	M,D,O

Communication Disorders	M
Communication—General	M,O
Community Health Nursing	M,D,O
Computer Science	M,D,O
Conflict Resolution and Mediation/Peace Studies	M,O
Cultural Studies	O
Curriculum and Instruction	M,D
Dance	M,D
Demography and Population Studies	O
Developmental Biology	M,D
Disability Studies	O
Early Childhood Education	M
Economics	M,D
Education—General	M,D,O
Educational Leadership and Administration	M,D
Educational Media/Instructional Technology	M,D
Educational Policy	D
Educational Psychology	M,D
Electrical Engineering	M,D
Emergency Management	O
Engineering and Applied Sciences—General	M,D
English as a Second Language	M,D,O
English	M,D
Entomology	M,D
Entrepreneurship	M,O
Environmental Engineering	M,D
Environmental Management and Policy	M,D,O
Epidemiology	D
Family Nurse Practitioner Studies	M,D,O
Finance and Banking	M,D
Food Science and Technology	M
Foreign Languages Education	M,D,O
Foundations and Philosophy of Education	M,D
French	M
Genetics	M,D
Geochemistry	M,D
Geography	M,D,O
Geological Engineering	M,D
Geology	M,D
Geophysics	M,D
Historic Preservation	O
History	M,D
Horticulture	M,D
Human Resources Management	M
Hydrogeology	M,D
Information Science	M,D
Information Studies	M,O
International Affairs	M
International Business	M,D
International Development	M,D,O
Japanese	M,D,O
Kinesiology and Movement Studies	M,D
Law	M,D,O
Library Science	M,O
Linguistics	M,D
Management Information Systems	M,D,O
Marine Biology	M,D
Marine Geology	M,D
Marine Sciences	O
Marketing	M,D
Mathematics	M,D
Mechanical Engineering	M,D
Medical Microbiology	M,D
Meteorology	M,D
Microbiology	M,D
Molecular Biology	M,D
Museum Studies	O
Music	M,D
Natural Resources	M,D
Nursing and Healthcare Administration	M,D,O
Nursing—General	M,D,O
Nutrition	M,D
Ocean Engineering	M,D
Oceanography	M,D
Organizational Behavior	M
Organizational Management	M,D
Pacific Area/Pacific Rim Studies	M,O
Philosophy	M,D
Physics	M,D
Physiology	M,D
Planetary and Space Sciences	M,D
Plant Pathology	M,D
Plant Sciences	M,D
Political Science	M,D
Psychology—General	M,D,O
Public Administration	M,O
Public Health—General	M,D,O
Public Policy	O
Real Estate	M
Religion	M
Reproductive Biology	M,D
Social Psychology	M,D,O
Social Work	M,D
Sociology	M,D
Spanish	M
Special Education	M,D
Speech and Interpersonal Communication	M
Sustainable Development	M,D,O
Taxation	M
Telecommunications	O
Theater	M,D
Transportation Management	M,D,O
Travel and Tourism	M
Urban and Regional Planning	M,D,O
Women's Studies	O
Zoology	M,D

UNIVERSITY OF HOLY CROSS

Counselor Education	M
Curriculum and Instruction	M
Education—General	M

M—masters degree; D—doctorate; O—other advanced degree; *—Close-Up and/or Display

Educational Leadership and
  Administration — M
Marriage and Family Therapy — M

UNIVERSITY OF HOUSTON

Accounting — M,D
Advertising and Public Relations — M
Anthropology — M
Applied Economics — M,D
Applied Mathematics — M,D
Architecture — M
Art History — M
Art/Fine Arts — M
Atmospheric Sciences — M,D
Biochemistry — M,D
Biological and Biomedical
  Sciences—General — M,D
Biomedical Engineering — D
Business Administration and
  Management—General — M,D
Chemical Engineering — M,D
Chemistry — M,D
Civil Engineering — M,D
Clinical Psychology — M,D
Communication Disorders — M
Communication—General — M
Comparative Literature — M
Computer and Information
  Systems Security — M
Computer Science — M,D
Construction Management — M
Counseling Psychology — M
Cultural Studies — M
Curriculum and Instruction — M,D
Developmental Psychology — M,D
Economics — M,D
Education—General — M,D
Educational Leadership and
  Administration — M,D
Educational Psychology — M,D
Electrical Engineering — M,D
Engineering and Applied
  Sciences—General — M,D
Environmental Law — M,D
Exercise and Sports Science — M,D
Family and Consumer
  Sciences-General — M
Family Nurse Practitioner Studies — M
Finance and Banking — M
Foundations and Philosophy of
  Education — M,D
Geology — M,D
Geophysics — M,D
Health Communication — M
Health Education — M,D
Health Law — M,D
Higher Education — M,D
Hispanic Studies — M,D
History — M,D
Hospitality Management — M
Human Resources Development — M
Industrial and Organizational
  Psychology — M,D
Industrial/Management
  Engineering — M,D
Information Science — M,D
Intellectual Property Law — M,D
Kinesiology and Movement Studies — M,D
Law — M,D
Linguistics — M,D
Logistics — M
Marketing — D
Mass Communication — M
Mathematics — M,D
Mechanical Engineering — M,D
Music Education — M,D
Music — M,D
Nursing and Healthcare
  Administration — M
Nursing Education — M
Nursing—General — M
Nutrition — M,D
Optometry — D
Petroleum Engineering — M,D
Pharmaceutical Administration — M,D
Pharmaceutical Sciences — M,D
Pharmacology — M,D
Pharmacy — M,D
Philosophy — M
Physical Education — M,D
Physics — M,D
Planetary and Space
  Sciences — M,D
Political Science — M,D
Project Management — M
Psychology—General — M,D
Public Administration — M,D
Public Policy — M
Social Psychology — M,D
Social Work — M,D
Sociology — M
Spanish — M,D
Special Education — M,D
Speech and Interpersonal
  Communication — M
Supply Chain Management — M
Taxation — M,D
Telecommunications — M
Theater — M
Vision Sciences — M,D
Writing — M,D

UNIVERSITY OF HOUSTON–CLEAR LAKE

Accounting — M
Biological and Biomedical
  Sciences—General — M
Biotechnology — M
Business Administration and
  Management—General — M
Chemistry — M
Clinical Psychology — M
Computer Engineering — M
Computer Science — M
Counselor Education — M

Criminal Justice and Criminology — M
Cultural Studies — M
Curriculum and Instruction — M
Early Childhood Education — M
Education—General — M,D
Educational Leadership and
  Administration — M,D
Educational Media/Instructional
  Technology — M
English — M
Environmental Management
  and Policy — M
Environmental Sciences — M
Exercise and Sports Science — M
Finance and Banking — M
Foundations and Philosophy of
  Education — M
Health Services Management and
  Hospital Administration — M
History — M
Human Resources Management — M
Humanities — M
Information Science — M
Library Science — M
Management Information Systems — M
Marriage and Family Therapy — M
Mathematics — M
Multilingual and Multicultural
  Education — M
Physics — M
Psychology—General — M
Reading Education — M
School Psychology — M
Sociology — M
Software Engineering — M
Statistics — M
Systems Engineering — M

UNIVERSITY OF HOUSTON–DOWNTOWN

Business Administration and
  Management—General — M
Criminal Justice and Criminology — M
Curriculum and Instruction — M
Database Systems — M
English — M
Finance and Banking — M
Human Resources Management — M
Investment Management — M
Middle School Education — M
Nonprofit Management — M
Rhetoric — M
Secondary Education — M
Social Work — M
Supply Chain Management — M
Technical Communication — M
Urban Education — M

UNIVERSITY OF HOUSTON–VICTORIA

Accounting — M
Adult Education — M
Biological and Biomedical
  Sciences—General — M
Business Administration and
  Management—General — M
Computer Science — M
Counseling Psychology — M
Counselor Education — M
Curriculum and Instruction — M
Economic Development — M
Education—General — M
Educational Leadership and
  Administration — M
Educational Media/Instructional
  Technology — M
Entrepreneurship — M
Finance and Banking — M
Forensic Psychology — M
Forensic Sciences — M
Higher Education — M
Interdisciplinary Studies — M
International Business — M
Management Information Systems — M
Marketing — M
Psychology—General — M
Publishing — M
School Psychology — M
Special Education — M
Writing — M

UNIVERSITY OF IDAHO

Accounting — M
Agricultural Economics and
  Agribusiness — M
Agronomy and Soil Sciences — M,D
American Indian/Native American
  Studies — D
Animal Sciences — M,D
Anthropology — M
Applied Economics — M
Architecture — M
Art/Fine Arts — M
Athletic Training and Sports
  Medicine — M,D
Biochemistry — M,D
Bioengineering — M,D
Bioinformatics — M,D
Biological and Biomedical
  Sciences—General — M,D
Business Administration and
  Management—General — M,D
Chemical Engineering — M,D
Chemistry — M,D
Civil Engineering — M,D
Computational Biology — M,D
Computer Engineering — M,D
Computer Science — M,D
Conflict Resolution and
  Mediation/Peace Studies — D
Consumer Economics — M
Counselor Education — M,O
Curriculum and Instruction — M,O
Education—General — M,D,O
Educational Leadership and
  Administration — M,O

Electrical Engineering — M,D
Engineering and Applied
  Sciences—General — M,D
Engineering Management — M,D
English as a Second Language — M
English — M,D
Entomology — M,D
Entrepreneurship — D
Environmental Law — D
Environmental Sciences — M,D
Experimental Psychology — M,D
Food Science and
  Technology — M,D
Geography — M,D
Geological Engineering — M,D
Geology — M,D
History — M,D
Human Services — M,O
Interdisciplinary Studies — M
Landscape Architecture — M
Law — D
Management of Technology — M,D
Materials Sciences — M,D
Mathematics — M,D
Mechanical Engineering — M,D
Metallurgical Engineering and
  Metallurgy — M,D
Microbiology — M,D
Music — M
Natural Resources — M,D
Nuclear Engineering — M,D
Philosophy — M
Physical Education — M,D
Physics — M,D
Plant Sciences — M,D
Political Science — M
Psychology—General — M,D
Public Administration — M,D
Recreation and Park Management — M,D
Rehabilitation Counseling — M,O
Special Education — M,O
Statistics — M
Theater — M
Urban and Regional Planning — M
Veterinary Sciences — M,D
Vocational and Technical Education — M,O
Water Resources Engineering — M,D
Water Resources — M,D
Writing — M

UNIVERSITY OF ILLINOIS AT CHICAGO

Accounting — M
Acute Care/Critical Care Nursing — M,O
Adult Nursing — M,O
Allied Health—General — M,D,O
Allopathic Medicine — D
Anatomy — M
Anthropology — M,D
Applied Arts and Design—General — M
Architecture — M
Art History — M,D
Art/Fine Arts — M,D
Biochemistry — D
Bioengineering — M,D
Bioinformatics — M,D
Biological and Biomedical
  Sciences—General — M,D
Biophysics — M,D
Biostatistics — M,D
Biotechnology — M,D
Business Administration and
  Management—General — M,D
Cell Biology — M,D
Chemical Engineering — M,D
Chemistry — M,D
Civil Engineering — M,D
Communication—General — M,D
Community Health Nursing — M,O
Community Health — M,D
Computer Education — D
Computer Engineering — M,D
Computer Science — M,D
Criminal Justice and Criminology — M,D
Curriculum and Instruction — M,D
Dentistry — D
Developmental Psychology — M,D
Disability Studies — M,D
Early Childhood Education — M,D
East European and Russian Studies — M,D
Economics — M,D
Education—General — M,D
Educational Leadership and
  Administration — M,D
Educational Measurement and
  Evaluation — M,D
Educational Policy — M,D
Educational Psychology — M,D
Electrical Engineering — M,D
Elementary Education — M,D
Engineering and Applied
  Sciences—General — M,D
English as a Second Language — M,D
English — M,D
Environmental and Occupational
  Health — M,D
Epidemiology — M,D
Family Nurse Practitioner Studies — M,O
Finance and Banking — M
Foreign Languages Education — M,D
Forensic Sciences — M
French — M
Genetics — D
Geography — M
Geology — M,D
Geosciences — M,D
German — M,D
Gerontological Nursing — M,O
Graphic Design — M
Health Education — M
Health Informatics — M,O
Health Services Management and
  Hospital Administration — M,D
Health Services Research — M,D

Hispanic and Latin American
  Languages — M,D
Hispanic Studies — M,D
History — M,D
Human Development — M,D
Immunology — D
Industrial/Management
  Engineering — M,D
Interdisciplinary Studies — D
Kinesiology and Movement Studies — M,D
Latin American Studies — M
Linguistics — M
Management Information Systems — M,D
Materials Engineering — M,D
Maternal and Child/Neonatal
  Nursing — M,O
Mathematics Education — M,D
Mathematics — M,D
Mechanical Engineering — M,D
Medical Illustration — M
Microbiology — D
Molecular Biology — D
Molecular Genetics — D
Museum Studies — M,D
Neuroscience — D
Nurse Midwifery — M,O
Nursing and Healthcare
  Administration — M,O
Nursing—General — M,D,O
Nutrition — M,O
Occupational Health Nursing — M,O
Occupational Therapy — M,O
Operations Research — M,D
Oral and Dental Sciences — M,D
Pediatric Nursing — M,O
Pharmaceutical Administration — M,D
Pharmaceutical Sciences — M,D
Pharmacology — D
Pharmacy — M,D
Philosophy — M,D
Physical Therapy — M,D
Physics — M,D
Physiology — M,D
Political Science — M,D
Psychology—General — M,D
Public Administration — M,D
Public Health—General — M,D
Real Estate — M
School Nursing — M,O
Science Education — D
Secondary Education — M,D
Slavic Languages — M,D
Social Sciences Education — D
Social Work — M,D,O
Sociology — M,D
Spanish — M,D
Special Education — M,D
Statistics — M,D
Toxicology — M
Urban and Regional Planning — M,D
Urban Education — M,D
Women's Health Nursing — M,O

UNIVERSITY OF ILLINOIS AT SPRINGFIELD

Accounting — M
Addictions/Substance Abuse
  Counseling — M,O
Biological and Biomedical
  Sciences—General — M
Business Administration and
  Management—General — M
Child and Family Studies — M,O
Communication—General — M,O
Community Health — M,O
Computer Science — M
Database Systems — M
Distance Education Development — M,O
Education—General — M,O
Educational Leadership and
  Administration — M,O
Educational Media/Instructional
  Technology — M,O
Emergency Management — M,O
English as a Second Language — M,O
English Education — M,O
English — M,O
Environmental and Occupational
  Health — M,O
Environmental Management
  and Policy — M
Environmental Sciences — M
Epidemiology — M,O
Gerontology — M,O
Health Education — M,O
Higher Education — M,O
History — M
Homeland Security — M,O
Human Development — M,O
Human Services — M,O
Interdisciplinary Studies — M
Journalism — M
Legal and Justice Studies — M
Management Information Systems — M
Political Science — M
Public Administration — M,D,O
Public Health—General — M,O
Public History — M
Social Sciences — M,O

UNIVERSITY OF ILLINOIS AT URBANA–CHAMPAIGN

Accounting — M,D
Actuarial Science — M,D
Advertising and Public Relations — M
Aerospace/Aeronautical
  Engineering — M,D
African Studies — M
Agricultural Economics and
  Agribusiness — M,D
Agricultural Education — M,D
Agricultural Engineering — M,D
Agricultural Sciences—
  General — M

Agronomy and Soil Sciences	M,D
Allopathic Medicine	
Animal Sciences	M,D
Anthropology	M,D
Applied Arts and Design—General	M,D
Applied Economics	M,D
Applied Mathematics	M,D
Applied Statistics	M,D
Architecture	M,D
Art Education	M,D
Art History	M,D
Art/Fine Arts	M
Asian Languages	M,D
Asian Studies	M,D
Astronomy	M,D
Atmospheric Sciences	M,D
Biochemistry	M,D
Bioengineering	M,D
Bioinformatics	M,D,O
Biological and Biomedical Sciences—General	M,D
Biophysics	M,D
Business Administration and Management—General	M,D
Cell Biology	D
Chemical Engineering	M,D
Chemical Physics	M,D
Chemistry	M,D
Civil Engineering	M,D
Classics	M,D
Communication Disorders	M,D
Communication—General	M,D
Community Health	M,D
Comparative Literature	M,D
Computational Biology	M,D
Computer Engineering	M,D
Computer Science	M,D
Conservation Biology	M,D
Consumer Economics	M,D
Counselor Education	M,D,O
Curriculum and Instruction	M,D,O
Dance	M
Developmental Biology	D
East European and Russian Studies	M
Ecology	M,D
Economics	M,D
Education of Students with Severe/Multiple Disabilities	M,D,O
Education—General	M,D,O
Educational Leadership and Administration	M,D,O
Educational Policy	M,D,O
Educational Psychology	M,D,O
Electrical Engineering	M,D
Energy and Power Engineering	M,D
Energy Management and Policy	M
Engineering and Applied Sciences—General	M,D
English as a Second Language	M,D
English	M,D
Entomology	M,D
Environmental Engineering	M,D
Environmental Sciences	M,D
Evolutionary Biology	M,D
Finance and Banking	M,D
Financial Engineering	M
Food Science and Technology	M,D
Foreign Languages Education	M,D
French	M,D
Geography	M,D
Geology	M,D
Geosciences	M,D
German	M,D
Graphic Design	M
Health Informatics	M,D,O
Health Services Management and Hospital Administration	M,D
History	M,D
Human Development	M,D
Human Resources Management	M,D,O
Human Services	M,D
Human-Computer Interaction	M,D,O
Industrial and Labor Relations	M,D
Industrial Design	M
Industrial/Management Engineering	M,D
Information Science	M,D,O
Information Studies	M,D,O
Interdisciplinary Studies	D
Italian	M,D
Journalism	M
Kinesiology and Movement Studies	M,D
Landscape Architecture	M,D
Latin American Studies	M
Law	M,D
Leisure Studies	M,D
Library Science	M,D,O
Linguistics	M,D
Management Information Systems	M,D,O
Management of Technology	M,D
Management Strategy and Policy	M,D,O
Materials Engineering	M,D
Materials Sciences	M,D
Mathematics Education	M,D
Mathematics	M,D
Mechanical Engineering	M,D
Mechanics	M,D
Media Studies	M,D
Medical Informatics	M,D,O
Microbiology	M,D
Molecular Physiology	M,D
Music Education	M,D
Music	M,D
Natural Resources	M
Near and Middle Eastern Studies	M
Neuroscience	D
Nuclear Engineering	M,D
Nutrition	M,D

Pathobiology	M,D
Philosophy	M,D
Photography	M
Physics	M,D
Physiology	M,D
Plant Biology	M,D
Political Science	M,D
Portuguese	M,D
Psychology—General	M,D
Public Health—General	M,D
Rehabilitation Sciences	M,D
Religion	M
Romance Languages	D
Science Education	M,D
Slavic Languages	M,D
Social Work	M,D
Sociology	M,D
Spanish	M,D
Special Education	M,D,O
Statistics	M,D
Systems Engineering	M,D
Taxation	M,D
Theater	M,D
Translation and Interpretation	M
Urban and Regional Planning	M,D
Veterinary Medicine	D
Veterinary Sciences	M,D
Western European Studies	M
Writing	M,D
Zoology	M,D

UNIVERSITY OF INDIANAPOLIS

Anthropology	M
Art Education	M
Art/Fine Arts	M
Biological and Biomedical Sciences—General	M
Business Administration and Management—General	M,O
Clinical Psychology	M,D
Counseling Psychology	M,D
Curriculum and Instruction	M
Education—General	M
Educational Leadership and Administration	M
Elementary Education	M
English Education	M
English	M
Family Nurse Practitioner Studies	M
Foreign Languages Education	M
Gerontology	M,D,O
History	M
International Affairs	M
Maternal and Child/Neonatal Nursing	M,D
Mathematics Education	M
Nurse Midwifery	M,D
Nursing and Healthcare Administration	M,D
Nursing Education	M,D
Nursing—General	M,D
Occupational Therapy	M,D
Physical Education	M
Physical Therapy	M,D
Psychology—General	M,D
Public Health—General	M
Science Education	M
Secondary Education	M
Social Sciences Education	M
Sociology	M
Sports Management	M
Women's Health Nursing	M,D

THE UNIVERSITY OF IOWA

Accounting	M,D
Actuarial Science	M,D
Agricultural Sciences—General	M,D,O
Allopathic Medicine	D
American Studies	M,D
Anatomy	D
Anthropology	M,D
Applied Mathematics	D
Art Education	M,D
Art History	M,D
Art/Fine Arts	M
Asian Languages	M
Asian Studies	M
Astronomy	M
Athletic Training and Sports Medicine	M,D
Bacteriology	M,D
Biochemical Engineering	M,D
Biochemistry	M,D
Bioinformatics	M,D,O
Biological and Biomedical Sciences—General	M,D
Biomedical Engineering	M,D
Biophysics	M,D
Biostatistics	M,D,O
Business Administration and Management—General	M,D
Cell Biology	M,D
Chemical Engineering	M,D
Chemistry	D
Chinese	M
Civil Engineering	M,D
Classics	M,D
Clinical Research	M,D
Communication Disorders	M,D
Communication—General	M,D
Community Health	M,D
Computational Biology	M,D,O
Computational Sciences	D
Computer Engineering	M,D
Computer Science	M,D
Counseling Psychology	M,D,O
Counselor Education	M,D
Dance	M
Database Systems	M
Dentistry	M,D,O

Developmental Education	M,D
Economics	D
Education—General	M,D,O
Educational Leadership and Administration	M,D,O
Educational Measurement and Evaluation	M,D,O
Educational Policy	M,D,O
Educational Psychology	M,D,O
Electrical Engineering	M,D
Elementary Education	M,D
Energy and Power Engineering	M,D
Engineering and Applied Sciences—General	M,D*
English as a Second Language	M,D
English Education	M,D
English	M,D
Environmental and Occupational Health	M,D,O
Environmental Engineering	M,D
Epidemiology	M,D
Ergonomics and Human Factors	M,D,O
Evolutionary Biology	M,D
Exercise and Sports Science	M,D
Film, Television, and Video Production	M
Film, Television, and Video Theory and Criticism	M,D
Finance and Banking	D
Foreign Languages Education	M,D
Foundations and Philosophy of Education	M,D,O
French	M,D
Genetics	M,D
Geographic Information Systems	M,D,O
Geography	M,D,O
Geosciences	M,D
Health Informatics	M,D,O
Health Services Management and Hospital Administration	M,D
Higher Education	M,D
History	M,D
Immunology	M,D
Industrial Hygiene	M,D,O
Industrial/Management Engineering	M,D
Information Science	M,D,O
Information Studies	M,D
Journalism	M,D
Law	M,D
Leisure Studies	M,D
Library Science	M,D
Linguistics	M,D
Manufacturing Engineering	M,D
Marketing	D
Marriage and Family Therapy	M,D
Mass Communication	M,D
Materials Engineering	M,D
Mathematics Education	M,D
Mathematics	M,D
Mechanical Engineering	M,D
Media Studies	M,D
Medicinal and Pharmaceutical Chemistry	M,D
Microbiology	M,D
Molecular Biology	D
Music Education	M,D
Music	M,D
Neurobiology	M,D
Neuroscience	D
Nursing—General	M,D
Operations Research	M,D
Oral and Dental Sciences	M,D,O
Pathology	M
Pharmaceutical Sciences	M,D
Pharmacology	M,D
Pharmacy	M,D
Philosophy	D
Physical Therapy	M,D
Physician Assistant Studies	M
Physics	M,D
Physiology	M,D
Political Science	D
Psychology—General	M,D,O
Public Health—General	M,D,O
Quantitative Analysis	M,D,O
Radiation Biology	M
Recreation and Park Management	M,D
Rehabilitation Counseling	M,D
Rehabilitation Sciences	M,D
Religion	M,D
Rhetoric	M,D
School Psychology	M,D,O
Science Education	M,D
Secondary Education	M,D
Social Sciences Education	M,D
Social Work	M,D
Sociology	M,D
Spanish	M,D
Special Education	M,D
Speech and Interpersonal Communication	M,D
Sports Management	M,D
Statistics	M,D,O
Student Affairs	M,D
Theater	M
Toxicology	M,D
Translational Biology	M,D
Urban and Regional Planning	M
Virology	M,D
Women's Studies	O
Writing	M,D

UNIVERSITY OF JAMESTOWN

Curriculum and Instruction	M
Education—General	M
Physical Therapy	D

THE UNIVERSITY OF KANSAS

Accounting	M,D
Acoustics	M,D,O
Adult Nursing	M,D,O
Aerospace/Aeronautical Engineering	M,D
African Studies	M,O
African-American Studies	M,O
Allied Health—General	M,D,O
Allopathic Medicine	D
American Indian/Native American Studies	M,O
American Studies	M,D
Anatomy	M,D
Anthropology	M
Applied Arts and Design—General	M
Applied Behavior Analysis	M,D,O
Applied Mathematics	M,D,O
Applied Statistics	M,D,O
Architectural Engineering	M
Architecture	M,D,O
Art Education	M
Art History	M,D
Art/Fine Arts	M,D
Asian Languages	M,O
Asian Studies	M,O
Astronomy	M,D
Atmospheric Sciences	M,D,O
Biochemistry	D
Bioengineering	M,D
Biological and Biomedical Sciences—General	D*
Biophysics	D
Biostatistics	M,D,O
Biotechnology	M
Botany	M,D
Business Administration and Management—General	M,D
Cancer Biology/Oncology	M,D
Cell Biology	M,D
Chemical Engineering	M,D,O
Chemistry	M,D
Civil Engineering	M,D
Classics	M
Clinical Psychology	M,D
Clinical Research	M
Cognitive Sciences	M,D
Communication Disorders	M,D
Communication—General	M,D,O
Community Health Nursing	M,D,O
Community Health	M,D,O
Computational Biology	D
Computer Engineering	M
Computer Science	M,D
Construction Management	M
Counseling Psychology	M,D
Cultural Studies	M,D
Curriculum and Instruction	M,D
Developmental Biology	D
Developmental Psychology	M,D
Distance Education Development	M,D
Early Childhood Education	M,D,O
East European and Russian Studies	M,O
Ecology	M,D
Economics	M,D
Education—General	M,D,O
Educational Leadership and Administration	M,D,O
Educational Measurement and Evaluation	M,D
Educational Media/Instructional Technology	M,D
Educational Policy	M,D
Educational Psychology	M,D
Electrical Engineering	M,D
Engineering and Applied Sciences—General	M,D,O
Engineering Management	M,O
English	M,D
Entomology	M,D
Environmental Engineering	M,D
Environmental Sciences	M,D
Epidemiology	M
Evolutionary Biology	M,D
Exercise and Sports Science	M,D
Film, Television, and Video Theory and Criticism	M,D
Finance and Banking	M,D
French	M,D
Geographic Information Systems	M,D,O
Geography	M,D,O
Geology	M,D
German	M,D
Gerontological Nursing	M,D,O
Gerontology	D
Health Education	M,D,O
Health Informatics	M,O
Health Promotion	M,D,O
Health Services Management and Hospital Administration	M,D
Higher Education	M,D
Historic Preservation	M,D,O
History	M,D
Human Resources Management	M,D
Interdisciplinary Studies	D
International Affairs	M
Journalism	M,D
Latin American Studies	M,O
Law	D
Linguistics	M,D
Logistics	M,D
Management Information Systems	M
Management Strategy and Policy	M,D
Marketing	M,D
Mathematics	M,D,O
Mechanical Engineering	M,D
Media Studies	M,D
Medical Informatics	M,D,O
Medicinal and Pharmaceutical Chemistry	M,D
Microbiology	M,D

M—masters degree; D—doctorate; O—other advanced degree; *—Close-Up and/or Display

Molecular Biology — D
Museum Studies — M,O
Music Education — M,D
Music — M,D
Near and Middle Eastern Studies — M,O
Neuroscience — M,D
Nurse Anesthesia — D
Nurse Midwifery — M,D,O
Nursing—General — M,D,O
Nutrition — M,D,O
Occupational Therapy — M,D
Organizational Behavior — M,D
Organizational Management — M,D,O
Pathology — M,D
Petroleum Engineering — M,D,O
Pharmacology — M,D
Philosophy — M,D
Physical Education — M,D
Physical Therapy — D
Physics — M,D
Physiology — D
Political Science — M,D
Project Management — M
Psychiatric Nursing — M,D,O
Psychology—General — M,D,O
Public Administration — M,D,O
Public Health—General — M
Rehabilitation Sciences — M,O
Religion — M,D
School Psychology — D,O
Slavic Languages — M,D
Social Psychology — M,D
Social Work — M,D
Sociology — D
Spanish — M,D
Special Education — M,D,O
Sports Management — M,D
Statistics — M,D,O
Supply Chain Management — M,D
Textile Design — M
Theater — M,D
Therapies—Dance, Drama, and Music — M,D
Toxicology — M,D
Urban and Regional Planning — M
Urban Design — M,D,O
Writing — M,D

UNIVERSITY OF KENTUCKY

Accounting — M
Agricultural Economics and Agribusiness — M,D
Agricultural Engineering — M,D
Agricultural Sciences—General — M,D
Agronomy and Soil Sciences — M,D
Allied Health—General — M,D
Allopathic Medicine — D
Anatomy — D
Animal Sciences — M,D
Anthropology — M
Applied Arts and Design—General — M
Applied Mathematics — M,D
Architecture — M
Art Education — M
Art History — M
Art/Fine Arts — M
Arts Administration — M
Astronomy — M,D
Athletic Training and Sports Medicine — M
Biochemistry — D
Biological and Biomedical Sciences—General — M,D
Biomedical Engineering — M,D
Biostatistics — D
Business Administration and Management—General — M,D
Chemical Engineering — M,D
Chemistry — M,D
Child and Family Studies — M,D
Civil Engineering — M,D
Classics — M
Clinical Research — M
Communication Disorders — M
Communication—General — M,D
Computer Science — M,D
Counseling Psychology — M,D,O
Curriculum and Instruction — M,D
Dentistry — D
Early Childhood Education — M,D
Economics — M,D
Education—General — M,D,O
Educational Leadership and Administration — M,D,O
Educational Measurement and Evaluation — M,D
Educational Media/Instructional Technology — M,D
Educational Policy — M,D
Educational Psychology — M,D,O
Electrical Engineering — M,D
Elementary Education — M,D
Engineering and Applied Sciences—General — M,D
English — M,D
Entomology — M,D
Epidemiology — D
Exercise and Sports Science — M,D
Food Science and Technology — M,D
Foreign Languages Education — M
Forestry — M
Geography — M,D
Geology — M,D
German — M,D
Gerontology — D,O
Health Physics/Radiological Health — M,D
Health Promotion — M,D
Health Services Management and Hospital Administration — M
Higher Education — M,D
Hispanic Studies — M,D
Historic Preservation — M

History — M,D
Hospitality Management — M
Immunology — D
Information Science — M
Interior Design — M
International Affairs — M
International Business — M
Kinesiology and Movement Studies — M,D
Law — D
Library Science — M
Manufacturing Engineering — M
Materials Engineering — M,D
Materials Sciences — M,D
Mathematics — M,D
Mechanical Engineering — M,D
Medical Physics — M
Microbiology — D
Middle School Education — M,D
Mineral/Mining Engineering — M,D
Music Education — M,D
Music — M,D
Neurobiology — D
Nursing—General — D
Nutrition — M,D
Oral and Dental Sciences — M
Pharmaceutical Sciences — M,D
Pharmacology — D
Pharmacy — D
Philosophy — M,D
Physical Education — M,D
Physical Therapy — D
Physician Assistant Studies — M
Physics — M,D
Physiology — D
Plant Pathology — M,D
Plant Sciences — M,D
Political Science — M,D
Psychology—General — M,D
Public Administration — M,D,O
Public Health—General — M,D
Public Policy — M,D,O
Reading Education — M,D
Rehabilitation Counseling — M,D
Rehabilitation Sciences — D
School Psychology — M,D,O
Secondary Education — M,D
Social Work — M,D
Sociology — M,D
Special Education — M,D
Statistics — M,D
Therapies—Dance, Drama, and Music — M,D
Toxicology — M,D
Veterinary Sciences — M,D

UNIVERSITY OF KING'S COLLEGE

Journalism — M
Writing — M

UNIVERSITY OF LA VERNE

Accounting — M
Business Administration and Management—General — M,D,O
Child and Family Studies — M
Child Development — M
Clinical Psychology — D
Counselor Education — M,D,O
Education—General — M,O
Educational Leadership and Administration — M,D,O
Elementary Education — M,D,O
English — M,O
Finance and Banking — M
Gerontology — M,O
Health Services Management and Hospital Administration — M,D,O
Health Services Research — M
Human Resources Management — M,O
International Business — M
Law — D
Management Information Systems — M,O
Marketing — M
Marriage and Family Therapy — M
Nonprofit Management — M,O
Organizational Management — M,D,O
Psychology—General — M,D
Public Administration — M,D
Reading Education — M,O
School Psychology — M,O
Secondary Education — M,D,O
Special Education — M,D,O
Supply Chain Management — M

UNIVERSITY OF LETHBRIDGE

Accounting — M,D
Addictions/Substance Abuse Counseling — M,D
Agricultural Sciences—General — M,D
American Indian/Native American Studies — M,D
Anthropology — M,D
Archaeology — M,D
Art/Fine Arts — M,D
Biochemistry — M,D
Biological and Biomedical Sciences—General — M,D
Business Administration and Management—General — M,D
Canadian Studies — M,D
Chemistry — M,D
Computational Sciences — M,D
Computer Science — M,D
Counseling Psychology — M,D
Counselor Education — M,D
Economics — M,D
Education—General — M,D
Educational Leadership and Administration — M,D
English — M,D
Environmental Sciences — M,D
Exercise and Sports Science — M,D
Finance and Banking — M,D
French — M,D
Gender Studies — M,D

Geographic Information Systems — M,D
Geography — M,D
German — M,D
Human Resources Management — M,D
International Business — M,D
Kinesiology and Movement Studies — M,D
Management Information Systems — M,D
Management Strategy and Policy — M,D
Marketing — M,D
Mathematics — M,D
Media Studies — M,D
Molecular Biology — M,D
Music — M,D
Neuroscience — M,D
Nursing—General — M,D
Philosophy — M,D
Physics — M,D
Political Science — M,D
Psychology—General — M,D
Religion — M,D
Sociology — M,D
Spanish — M,D
Theater — M,D
Urban Studies — M,D
Women's Studies — M,D

UNIVERSITY OF LOUISIANA AT LAFAYETTE

American Studies — D
Architectural Engineering — M
Biological and Biomedical Sciences—General — M,D
Business Administration and Management—General — M
Chemical Engineering — M
Civil Engineering — M
Cognitive Sciences — D
Communication Disorders — M,D
Communication—General — M
Computer Engineering — M,D
Computer Science — M,D
Counselor Education — M
Curriculum and Instruction — M
Education of the Gifted — M
Education—General — M,D
Educational Leadership and Administration — M,D
Engineering Management — M
English — M,D
Environmental Biology — M,D
Evolutionary Biology — M,D
Family Nurse Practitioner Studies — M
Folklore — M,D
French — M,D
Geology — M
History — M
Mass Communication — M
Mathematics — M,D
Mechanical Engineering — M
Music Education — M
Music — M
Nursing Education — M
Nursing—General — M
Petroleum Engineering — M
Physics — M
Psychology—General — M
Rehabilitation Counseling — M
Rhetoric — M,D
Telecommunications — M
Writing — M,D

UNIVERSITY OF LOUISIANA AT MONROE

Art Education — M,D
Biological and Biomedical Sciences—General — M
Business Administration and Management—General — M
Clinical Psychology — M
Communication Disorders — M
Communication—General — M
Counseling Psychology — M
Counselor Education — M
Criminal Justice and Criminology — M
Curriculum and Instruction — M,D
Early Childhood Education — M,D
Education of the Gifted — M,D
Education—General — M,D
Educational Leadership and Administration — M,D
Educational Measurement and Evaluation — M,D
Elementary Education — M,D
English as a Second Language — M,D
English Education — M,D
English — M
Exercise and Sports Science — M
Family and Consumer Sciences-General — M,D
Foreign Languages Education — M,D
Forensic Psychology — M
Gerontology — M,O
History — M
Marriage and Family Therapy — M,D
Mathematics Education — M,D
Middle School Education — M,D
Music Education — M,D
Occupational Therapy — M
Pharmacy — D
Psychology—General — M
Public Administration — M
Reading Education — M,D
Recreation and Park Management — M
Science Education — M,D
Secondary Education — M
Social Sciences Education — M,D
Special Education — M,D
Speech and Interpersonal Communication — M,D
Sports Management — M
Toxicology — D

UNIVERSITY OF LOUISVILLE

Accounting — M

Addictions/Substance Abuse Counseling — M,D,O
African Studies — M
African-American Studies — M
Allopathic Medicine — D
Analytical Chemistry — M,D
Anatomy — M,D
Anthropology — M
Applied Arts and Design—General — M,D
Applied Behavior Analysis — M,D,O
Applied Mathematics — M,D
Art Education — M,D,O
Art History — M,D
Art Therapy — M,D
Biochemistry — M,D
Bioengineering — M
Bioethics — M
Bioinformatics — M,D
Biological and Biomedical Sciences—General — M,D
Biophysics — M,D
Biostatistics — M,D
Business Administration and Management—General — M
Chemical Engineering — M,D
Chemical Physics — M,D
Chemistry — M,D,O
Civil Engineering — M,D,O
Clinical Psychology — D
Cognitive Sciences — D
Communication Disorders — M,D
Communication—General — M
Community Health — M
Computer and Information Systems Security — M,D,O
Computer Engineering — M,D,O
Computer Science — M,D,O
Counseling Psychology — M,D
Counselor Education — M,D
Criminal Justice and Criminology — M,D
Cultural Studies — M,D
Curriculum and Instruction — M,D,O
Dentistry — M,D
Developmental Psychology — D
Early Childhood Education — M,D,O
Education—General — M,D,O
Educational Leadership and Administration — M,D,O
Educational Measurement and Evaluation — M,D
Educational Psychology — M,D
Electrical Engineering — M,D
Elementary Education — M,D,O
Engineering and Applied Sciences—General — M,D,O
Engineering Management — M,D,O
English — M,D
Entrepreneurship — M,D
Environmental Biology — M,D
Environmental Engineering — M,D,O
Epidemiology — M,D
Exercise and Sports Science — M,D,O
Experimental Psychology — D
Family Nurse Practitioner Studies — M,D
French — M,O
Geography — M
Gerontological Nursing — M,D
Gerontology — M,D,O
Health Education — M,D,O
Health Services Management and Hospital Administration — M
Higher Education — M,D,O
History — M,O
Human Resources Development — M,D,O
Human Resources Management — M,D,O
Humanities — M,D
Immunology — M,D
Industrial/Management Engineering — M,D,O
Inorganic Chemistry — M,D
Interdisciplinary Studies — M,D
International Business — M
Law — D
Linguistics — M,D
Logistics — M,D,O
Marriage and Family Therapy — M,D,O
Maternal and Child/Neonatal Nursing — M,D
Mathematics — M,D
Mechanical Engineering — M,D
Microbiology — M,D
Middle School Education — M,D,O
Molecular Biology — M,D
Museum Studies — M,D
Music Education — M,D,O
Music — M
Neurobiology — M,D
Nonprofit Management — M,D
Nursing and Healthcare Administration — M,D
Nursing Education — M,D
Nursing—General — M,D
Oral and Dental Sciences — M,D
Organic Chemistry — M,D
Pharmacology — M,D
Philosophy — M,D
Physical Chemistry — M,D
Physical Education — M,D,O
Physics — M,D
Physiology — M,D
Political Science — M
Psychiatric Nursing — D
Psychology—General — M,D
Public Administration — M,D
Public Affairs — M,D
Public Health—General — M,D
Public History — M,O
Public Policy — M,D
Rhetoric — M,D
School Psychology — M,D
Secondary Education — M,D,O
Social Work — M,D,O
Sociology — M,D
Spanish — M,O

Special Education	M,D,O
Sports Management	M,D,O
Student Affairs	M,D
Supply Chain Management	M,D,O
Sustainability Management	M
Theater	M
Toxicology	M,D
Urban and Regional Planning	M,D
Urban Studies	M,D
Women's Health Nursing	M,D
Women's Studies	M,O
Writing	M,D

UNIVERSITY OF MAINE

Agricultural Economics and Agribusiness	M
Agricultural Sciences—General	M,D,O
Anthropology	D
Art/Fine Arts	M
Bioinformatics	M,D
Biological and Biomedical Sciences—General	M,D
Biomedical Engineering	M,D
Botany	M,D
Business Administration and Management—General	M,O
Chemical Engineering	M,D
Chemistry	M,D
Civil Engineering	M,D
Communication Disorders	M
Communication—General	M,D
Computer Engineering	M,D
Computer Science	M,D,O
Early Childhood Education	M,D,O
Economics	M
Education—General	M,D,O
Educational Leadership and Administration	M,D,O
Educational Media/Instructional Technology	M,D,O
Electrical Engineering	M,D
Engineering and Applied Sciences—General	M,D
English	M
Entomology	M,D
Environmental Management and Policy	D
Exercise and Sports Science	M,D,O
Family Nurse Practitioner Studies	M,O
Finance and Banking	M
Fish, Game, and Wildlife Management	M,D
Foreign Languages Education	M
Forestry	M,D
French	M
Geology	M,O
Geosciences	M,D
Higher Education	M,D,O
History	M,D
Horticulture	M,D,O
Human Development	M,D,O
Information Science	M,D,O
Interdisciplinary Studies	M,D
International Affairs	M
Kinesiology and Movement Studies	M,D,O
Law	D
Marine Sciences	M,D
Mathematics	M
Mechanical Engineering	M,D
Microbiology	M,D
Molecular Biology	M,D
Music	M
Nursing Education	M,O
Nursing—General	M,O
Physical Education	M,D,O
Physics	M,D
Plant Pathology	M,D
Psychology—General	M,D
Reading Education	M,D,O
Social Sciences Education	M,D,O
Social Work	M,O
Special Education	M,D,O
Water Resources	M,D
Zoology	M,D

UNIVERSITY OF MAINE AT FARMINGTON

Early Childhood Education	M
Education—General	M
Educational Leadership and Administration	M
Educational Media/Instructional Technology	M

UNIVERSITY OF MANAGEMENT AND TECHNOLOGY

Business Administration and Management—General	M,D,O
Computer Science	M,O
Criminal Justice and Criminology	M,O
Engineering Management	M
Health Services Management and Hospital Administration	M
Homeland Security	M
Management Information Systems	M,O
Project Management	M,D,O
Public Administration	M,O
Software Engineering	M,O

THE UNIVERSITY OF MANCHESTER

Accounting	M
Actuarial Science	M,D
Aerospace/Aeronautical Engineering	M,D
Analytical Chemistry	M,D
Anthropology	M,D
Applied Mathematics	M,D
Archaeology	M,D
Architecture	M,D
Art History	D
Art/Fine Arts	M,D

Arts Administration	D
Asian Studies	M,D
Astronomy	M,D
Astrophysics	M,D
Atmospheric Sciences	M,D
Biochemical Engineering	M,D
Biochemistry	M,D
Bioinformatics	M,D
Biological and Biomedical Sciences—General	M,D
Biophysics	M,D
Biotechnology	M,D
Business Administration and Management—General	M
Cancer Biology/Oncology	M,D
Cell Biology	M,D
Chemical Engineering	M,D
Chemistry	M,D
Chinese	M,D
Civil Engineering	M,D
Classics	D
Clinical Psychology	M,D
Clothing and Textiles	M,D
Communication Disorders	M,D
Computer Science	M,D
Condensed Matter Physics	M,D
Conflict Resolution and Mediation/Peace Studies	D
Counseling Psychology	M,D
Criminal Justice and Criminology	M,D
Cultural Studies	M,D
Dentistry	M,D
Developmental Biology	M,D
Developmental Psychology	M,D
Ecology	M,D
Economics	D
Education—General	M,D
Educational Psychology	M,D
Electrical Engineering	M,D
Engineering Management	M,D
English as a Second Language	M,D
English	D
Entrepreneurship	M
Environmental Biology	M,D
Environmental Design	M,D
Environmental Engineering	M,D
Environmental Management and Policy	M,D
Environmental Sciences	M,D
Evolutionary Biology	M,D
Finance and Banking	M
French	M,D
Genetics	M,D
Geochemistry	M,D
Geography	M,D
Geosciences	M,D
German	M,D
Hazardous Materials Management	M,D
Health Law	M,D
Hispanic Studies	M,D
History of Medicine	M,D
History of Science and Technology	M,D
History	D
Human Resources Management	M
Immunology	M,D
Industrial and Labor Relations	M
Industrial and Manufacturing Management	M,D
Industrial and Organizational Psychology	M
Inorganic Chemistry	M,D
International Affairs	D
International Business	M
International Development	M,D
Italian	M,D
Japanese	M,D
Landscape Architecture	M,D
Latin American Studies	M,D
Law	M,D
Linguistics	M,D
Management Strategy and Policy	M
Marketing	M
Materials Sciences	M,D
Mathematical and Computational Finance	M,D
Mathematics	M,D
Mechanical Engineering	M,D
Metallurgical Engineering and Metallurgy	M,D
Microbiology	M,D
Modeling and Simulation	M,D
Molecular Biology	M,D
Molecular Genetics	M,D
Museum Studies	D
Music	D
Natural Resources	M,D
Near and Middle Eastern Languages	M,D
Near and Middle Eastern Studies	M,D
Neurobiology	M,D
Neuroscience	M,D
Nuclear Engineering	M,D
Nurse Midwifery	M,D
Nursing—General	M,D
Optometry	M,D
Oral and Dental Sciences	M,D
Organic Chemistry	M,D
Paleontology	M,D
Paper and Pulp Engineering	M,D
Pharmaceutical Sciences	M,D
Pharmacology	M,D
Pharmacy	M,D
Philosophy	M,D
Physical Chemistry	M,D
Physics	M,D
Physiology	M,D
Plant Sciences	M,D
Political Science	M,D
Polymer Science and Engineering	M,D
Project Management	M

Psychology—General	M,D
Public Health—General	M,D
Religion	D
Russian	M,D
Slavic Languages	M,D
Social Sciences	M,D
Social Work	M,D
Sociology	M,D
Spanish	M,D
Statistics	M,D
Structural Biology	M,D
Structural Engineering	M,D
Supply Chain Management	M
Textile Design	M,D
Theater	D
Theology	D
Theoretical Chemistry	M,D
Theoretical Physics	M,D
Toxicology	M,D
Translation and Interpretation	M,D
Vision Sciences	M,D
Writing	D

UNIVERSITY OF MANITOBA

Adult Education	M
Agricultural Economics and Agribusiness	M,D
Agricultural Sciences—General	M,D
Agronomy and Soil Sciences	M,D
American Indian/Native American Studies	M
Anatomy	M,D
Animal Sciences	M,D
Anthropology	M,D
Architecture	M
Archives/Archival Administration	M,D
Biochemistry	M,D
Biological and Biomedical Sciences—General	M,D,O
Biosystems Engineering	M,D
Botany	M,D
Business Administration and Management—General	M,D
Canadian Studies	M
Cancer Biology/Oncology	M,D
Chemistry	M,D
Child and Family Studies	M
Civil Engineering	M,D
Classics	M
Clinical Psychology	M,D
Clothing and Textiles	M
Community Health	M,D,O
Computational Sciences	M
Computer Engineering	M,D
Computer Science	M,D
Counselor Education	M
Curriculum and Instruction	M
Dentistry	D
Disability Studies	M
Ecology	M,D
Economics	M,D
Education—General	M,D
Educational Leadership and Administration	M
Educational Psychology	M
Electrical Engineering	M,D
Engineering and Applied Sciences—General	M,D
English as a Second Language	M
English Education	M
English	M,D
Entomology	M,D
Environmental Sciences	M,D
Family and Consumer Sciences-General	M
Food Science and Technology	M,D
Foundations and Philosophy of Education	M
French	M,D
Geography	M,D
Geology	M,D
Geophysics	M,D
German	M
Higher Education	M
History	M,D
Horticulture	M,D
Human Genetics	M,D
Immunology	M,D
Industrial/Management Engineering	M,D
Interdisciplinary Studies	M,D
Interior Design	M
Kinesiology and Movement Studies	M,D
Landscape Architecture	M
Law	M
Linguistics	M,D
Manufacturing Engineering	M,D
Mathematics	M,D
Mechanical Engineering	M,D
Medical Microbiology	M,D
Microbiology	M,D
Music	M
Natural Resources	M,D
Northern Studies	M
Nursing—General	M
Nutrition	M,D
Occupational Therapy	M,D
Oral and Dental Sciences	M,D
Pathology	M
Pharmaceutical Sciences	M,D
Pharmacology	M,D
Philosophy	M
Physical Education	M
Physical Therapy	M,D
Physics	M,D
Physiology	M,D
Plant Physiology	M,D
Plant Sciences	M,D
Political Science	M

Psychology—General	M,D
Public Administration	M
Recreation and Park Management	M
Rehabilitation Sciences	M,D
Religion	M,D
School Psychology	M,D
Slavic Languages	M
Social Work	M,D
Sociology	M,D
Special Education	M
Statistics	M,D
Urban and Regional Planning	M
Zoology	M,D

UNIVERSITY OF MARY

Bioethics	M
Business Administration and Management—General	M
Cardiovascular Sciences	M
Curriculum and Instruction	M,D
Education—General	M,D
Educational Leadership and Administration	M,D
Energy Management and Policy	M
Exercise and Sports Science	M
Family Nurse Practitioner Studies	M,D
Health Services Management and Hospital Administration	M
Human Resources Management	M
Kinesiology and Movement Studies	M
Nursing and Healthcare Administration	M,D
Nursing Education	M,D
Nursing—General	M,D
Occupational Therapy	M
Physical Education	M
Physical Therapy	D
Project Management	M
Reading Education	M,D
Special Education	M,D
Sports Management	M

UNIVERSITY OF MARY HARDIN-BAYLOR

Accounting	M
Business Administration and Management—General	M
Clinical Psychology	M
Counseling Psychology	M
Counselor Education	M
Curriculum and Instruction	M,D
Education—General	M,D
Educational Leadership and Administration	M,D
Elementary Education	M,D
Exercise and Sports Science	M
Family Nurse Practitioner Studies	M,D,O
Higher Education	M,D
International Business	M
Management Information Systems	M
Marriage and Family Therapy	M
Nursing Education	M,D,O
Nursing—General	M,D,O
Physical Therapy	D
Secondary Education	M,D
Sports Management	M

UNIVERSITY OF MARYLAND, BALTIMORE

Allopathic Medicine	D
Biochemistry	M,D
Biological and Biomedical Sciences—General	M,D,O
Biostatistics	M,D
Cancer Biology/Oncology	D
Cell Biology	M,D
Clinical Laboratory Sciences/Medical Technology	M
Clinical Research	M,D,O
Community Health Nursing	M
Dentistry	D,O
Environmental Sciences	M,D
Epidemiology	M,D,O
Ethics	O
Genetic Counseling	M
Genomic Sciences	M,D
Gerontology	M,D
Health Services Research	M,D
Human Genetics	M,D
Immunology	D
Law	M,D
Marine Sciences	M,D
Maternal and Child/Neonatal Nursing	M
Microbiology	D
Molecular Biology	M,D
Molecular Medicine	D
Neurobiology	D
Neuroscience	D
Nurse Anesthesia	M
Nurse Midwifery	M
Nursing and Healthcare Administration	M
Nursing Education	M
Nursing—General	M,D,O
Oral and Dental Sciences	M,D,O
Pathology	M
Pediatric Nursing	M
Pharmaceutical Administration	M,D
Pharmaceutical Sciences	D
Pharmacology	M,D
Pharmacy	M,D
Physical Therapy	D
Psychiatric Nursing	M
Rehabilitation Sciences	D
Social Work	M,D
Thanatology	O
Toxicology	M,D

UNIVERSITY OF MARYLAND, BALTIMORE COUNTY

Applied Mathematics	M,D

---

*M—masters degree; D—doctorate; O—other advanced degree; *—Close-Up and/or Display*

Applied Psychology	D
Art Education	M
Atmospheric Sciences	M,D
Biochemical Engineering	M,D,O
Biochemistry	M,D,O
Biological and Biomedical Sciences—General	M,D,O
Biostatistics	M,D
Biotechnology	M,O
Cell Biology	D
Chemical Engineering	M,D
Chemistry	M,D,O
Clinical Psychology	M,D
Cognitive Sciences	D
Communication—General	M
Computer and Information Systems Security	M,O
Computer Art and Design	M
Computer Engineering	M,D
Computer Science	M,D
Dance	M
Developmental Psychology	D
Distance Education Development	M,O
Early Childhood Education	M
Economics	M,D
Education—General	M,O
Educational Media/Instructional Technology	M,D
Educational Policy	M,D
Electrical Engineering	M,D
Elementary Education	M
Emergency Management	M,D,O
Engineering and Applied Sciences—General	M,D,O
Engineering Management	M,O
English as a Second Language	M,O
English Education	M
English	M
Environmental Engineering	M,D
Environmental Management and Policy	M,D
Environmental Sciences	M,D
Epidemiology	M,D,O
Foreign Languages Education	M
Geographic Information Systems	M,O
Geography	M,D
Gerontology	M,D
Health Education	M,D,O
Health Informatics	M
Health Services Management and Hospital Administration	M,D,O
History	M
Human Services	M,D
Industrial and Organizational Psychology	M
Information Science	M,D
Linguistics	M
Marine Sciences	M,D
Mathematics Education	M
Mechanical Engineering	M,D,O
Molecular Biology	M,D
Multilingual and Multicultural Education	M,D
Music Education	M
Music	O
Neuroscience	D
Nonprofit Management	M,O
Physics	M,D
Planetary and Space Sciences	M
Psychology—General	M,D
Public History	M,D
Public Policy	M,D,O
Science Education	M
Social Psychology	M,D
Social Sciences Education	M
Social Sciences	D
Sociology	M
Statistics	M,D
Systems Engineering	M,O
Theater	M
Urban Studies	M,D

UNIVERSITY OF MARYLAND, COLLEGE PARK

Advertising and Public Relations	M,D
Aerospace/Aeronautical Engineering	M,D
Agricultural Economics and Agribusiness	M,D
Agricultural Sciences—General	M,D
American Studies	M,D
Analytical Chemistry	M,D
Animal Sciences	M,D
Anthropology	M
Applied Mathematics	M,D
Architecture	M
Art History	M,D
Art Therapy	M,D,O
Art/Fine Arts	M
Astronomy	M,D
Biochemistry	M,D
Bioengineering	M,D
Bioinformatics	D
Biological and Biomedical Sciences—General	M,D
Biophysics	D
Biostatistics	M,D
Broadcast Journalism	M,D
Business Administration and Management—General	M,D
Cell Biology	M,D
Chemical Engineering	M,D
Chemical Physics	M,D
Chemistry	M,D
Child and Family Studies	M,D
Civil Engineering	M,D
Classics	M
Clinical Psychology	M,D
Cognitive Sciences	D
Communication Disorders	B,M,D
Communication—General	M,D
Comparative Literature	M,D

Computational Biology	D
Computer Engineering	M,D
Computer Science	M,D
Conservation Biology	M,D
Counseling Psychology	M,D,O
Counselor Education	M,D,O
Criminal Justice and Criminology	M,D
Curriculum and Instruction	M,D,O
Dance	M
Developmental Psychology	M,D
Ecology	M,D
Economics	M,D
Education—General	M,D,O
Educational Leadership and Administration	M,D,O
Educational Measurement and Evaluation	M,D
Educational Media/Instructional Technology	M,D,O
Electrical Engineering	M,D*
Engineering and Applied Sciences—General	M
English as a Second Language	M,D,O
English	M,D
Entomology	M,D
Environmental and Occupational Health	M
Environmental Engineering	M,D
Environmental Sciences	M,D
Epidemiology	M,D
Evolutionary Biology	M,D
Experimental Psychology	M,D
Family and Consumer Sciences-General	M,D
Fire Protection Engineering	M
Food Science and Technology	M,D
Foreign Languages Education	D
Foundations and Philosophy of Education	M,D,O
French	M,D
Genomic Sciences	D
Geography	M,D
Geology	M,D
German	M,D
Health Education	M,D
Health Services Management and Hospital Administration	M,D
Historic Preservation	M,O
History	M,D
Horticulture	M,D
Human Development	M,D
Industrial and Organizational Psychology	M,D
Information Studies	M,D
Inorganic Chemistry	M,D
Jewish Studies	M
Journalism	M,D
Kinesiology and Movement Studies	M,D
Landscape Architecture	M
Law	
Library Science	
Linguistics	M,D
Manufacturing Engineering	M,D
Marine Sciences	M,D
Marriage and Family Therapy	M,D
Materials Engineering	M,D
Materials Sciences	M,D
Maternal and Child Health	M,D
Mathematics	M,D
Mechanical Engineering	M,D
Mechanics	M,D
Media Studies	M,D
Meteorology	M,D
Molecular Biology	D
Molecular Genetics	M,D
Music Education	M,D
Music	M,D
Natural Resources	M,D
Neuroscience	M,D
Nuclear Engineering	M,D
Nutrition	M,D
Oceanography	M,D
Organic Chemistry	M,D
Philosophy	M,D
Physical Chemistry	M,D
Physics	M,D
Plant Biology	M,D
Political Science	D
Portuguese	M,D
Psychology—General	M,D
Public Administration	M
Public Health—General	M,D
Public Policy	M,D
Quantitative Analysis	M,D,O
Reading Education	M
Real Estate	M,D,O
Rehabilitation Counseling	M,D
Reliability Engineering	M,D,O
School Psychology	M,D,O
Secondary Education	M,D
Social Psychology	
Social Work	
Sociology	M,D
Spanish	M,D
Speech and Interpersonal Communication	M,D
Statistics	M,D
Student Affairs	M,D,O
Survey Methodology	M,D
Sustainable Development	M
Systems Engineering	M
Telecommunications	M,D
Theater	M,D
Urban and Regional Planning	D
Veterinary Medicine	M,D
Veterinary Sciences	M,D
Women's Studies	M,D
Writing	

UNIVERSITY OF MARYLAND EASTERN SHORE

Agricultural Sciences—General	M,D

Chemistry	M,D
Computer Science	M
Counselor Education	M
Criminal Justice and Criminology	M
Education—General	M
Educational Leadership and Administration	D
Environmental Management and Policy	M,D
Environmental Sciences	
Fish, Game, and Wildlife Management	M,D
Food Science and Technology	M,D
Marine Sciences	M,D
Organizational Management	D
Pharmaceutical Sciences	M,D
Pharmacy	M,D
Physical Therapy	D
Rehabilitation Counseling	M
Rehabilitation Sciences	M
Special Education	M
Toxicology	M
Vocational and Technical Education	M

UNIVERSITY OF MARYLAND UNIVERSITY COLLEGE

Accounting	M
Biotechnology	M,O
Business Administration and Management—General	M,D,O
Computer and Information Systems Security	M,O
Database Systems	M,O
Distance Education Development	M
Education—General	M,D
Educational Media/Instructional Technology	M
Environmental Management and Policy	M
Finance and Banking	M
Health Informatics	M
Health Services Management and Hospital Administration	M
Information Science	M

UNIVERSITY OF MARY WASHINGTON

Business Administration and Management—General	M
Education—General	M
Elementary Education	M

UNIVERSITY OF MASSACHUSETTS AMHERST

Accounting	M,D
Adult Nursing	M,D
African-American Studies	M,D
Agricultural Economics and Agribusiness	M,D
American Studies	M,D
Animal Behavior	M,D
Animal Sciences	M,D
Anthropology	M,D
Applied Mathematics	M,D
Architectural Engineering	M,D
Architecture	M
Art Education	M
Art History	M
Art/Fine Arts	M
Astronomy	M,D
Biochemistry	M,D
Biological and Biomedical Sciences—General	M,D
Biostatistics	M,D
Biotechnology	M,D
Business Administration and Management—General	M,D
Cell Biology	M,D
Chemical Engineering	M,D
Chemistry	M,D
Child and Family Studies	M,D,O
Chinese	M
Civil Engineering	M,D
Classics	M
Clinical Psychology	M,D
Cognitive Sciences	M,D
Communication Disorders	M,D
Communication—General	M,D
Community Health Nursing	M,D
Community Health	M,D
Comparative Literature	M,D
Computer Engineering	M,D
Computer Science	M,D
Conflict Resolution and Mediation/Peace Studies	M,D
Counselor Education	M,D,O
Developmental Biology	D
Developmental Psychology	M,D
Early Childhood Education	M,D,O
Economics	M,D
Education—General	M,D,O
Educational Leadership and Administration	M,D,O
Educational Measurement and Evaluation	M,D,O
Educational Media/Instructional Technology	M,D,O
Educational Policy	M,D,O
Electrical Engineering	M,D
Elementary Education	M,D,O
Engineering and Applied Sciences—General	M,D
English as a Second Language	M,D,O
English	M,D
Entertainment Management	
Entrepreneurship	M,D
Environmental and Occupational Health	M,D
Environmental Biology	M,D
Environmental Engineering	M,D
Environmental Management and Policy	M,D
Epidemiology	M,D
Evolutionary Biology	M,D
Family Nurse Practitioner Studies	M,D

Finance and Banking	M,D
Fish, Game, and Wildlife Management	M,D
Food Science and Technology	M,D
Foreign Languages Education	M
Forestry	M,D
French	M
Genetics	M,D
Geography	M,D
Geosciences	M,D
Geotechnical Engineering	M,D
German	M,D
Gerontological Nursing	M,D
Health Education	M,D
Health Services Management and Hospital Administration	
Higher Education	M,D,O
Hispanic and Latin American Languages	M,D
Historic Preservation	M
History	M,D
Hospitality Management	M,D
Industrial and Labor Relations	M
Industrial/Management Engineering	M,D
Interior Design	M
International and Comparative Education	M,D,O
Italian	M
Japanese	M
Kinesiology and Movement Studies	M,D
Landscape Architecture	M
Linguistics	M,D
Management Strategy and Policy	M,D
Marine Sciences	M,D
Marketing	M,D
Mathematics	M,D
Mechanical Engineering	M,D
Mechanics	M,D
Microbiology	M,D*
Molecular Biophysics	D
Multilingual and Multicultural Education	M,D,O
Music Education	M,D
Music	M,D
Neuroscience	M,D
Nursing and Healthcare Administration	M,D
Nursing—General	M,D
Nutrition	M,D
Operations Research	M,D
Organizational Management	M,D
Philosophy	M,D
Physics	M,D
Physiology	M,D
Plant Biology	M,D
Plant Molecular Biology	M,D
Plant Physiology	M,D
Plant Sciences	M,D
Political Science	M,D
Polymer Science and Engineering	M,D
Portuguese	M,D
Psychology—General	M,D
Public Administration	M
Public Health—General	M,D
Public Policy	M
Reading Education	M,D,O
Rhetoric	M,D
Scandinavian Languages	M,D
School Psychology	M,D,O
Science Education	M,D,O
Secondary Education	M,D,O
Social Psychology	M,D
Sociology	M,D
Spanish	M,D
Special Education	M,D,O
Sports Management	M,D
Statistics	M,D
Structural Engineering	M,D
Sustainable Development	M
Theater	M
Transportation and Highway Engineering	M,D
Travel and Tourism	M,D
Urban and Regional Planning	M,D
Water Resources Engineering	M,D
Water Resources	M,D
Writing	M,D

UNIVERSITY OF MASSACHUSETTS BOSTON

Accounting	M
American Studies	M
Applied Economics	M
Applied Physics	M
Archaeology	M
Archives/Archival Administration	M
Biological and Biomedical Sciences—General	M,D
Biomedical Engineering	D
Biotechnology	M,D
Business Administration and Management—General	M
Chemistry	M,D
Classics	M
Clinical Psychology	D
Cognitive Sciences	M
Computer Science	M
Conflict Resolution and Mediation/Peace Studies	M,O
Counseling Psychology	M,D
Counselor Education	M
Cultural Studies	M
Early Childhood Education	D
Education—General	M,D
Educational Leadership and Administration	D
Educational Media/Instructional Technology	M,O
Educational Policy	D
English	M
Environmental Sciences	M,D

Exercise and Sports Science — M,D
Finance and Banking — M
Gerontology — M,D,O
Higher Education — D
History — M
Human Services — M
International Affairs — M
International Business — M
International Development — M,D
Linguistics — M
Management Information Systems — M
Marine Sciences — M,D
Marriage and Family Therapy — M
Nursing—General — M,D
Public Administration — M
Public Policy — M,D
Quality Management — M,O
Rehabilitation Counseling — M
School Psychology — M,D
Sociology — M,D
Special Education — M
Urban and Regional Planning — M
Urban Education — D
Vision Sciences — M
Writing — M

UNIVERSITY OF MASSACHUSETTS DARTMOUTH
Accounting — M,O
Acoustics — M,D,O
Adult Nursing — M,D,O
Applied Arts and Design—General — M
Applied Behavior Analysis — M,O
Art Education — M
Art/Fine Arts — M,O
Biochemistry — M,D
Biological and Biomedical
　Sciences—General — M
Biomedical Engineering — M,D
Biotechnology — M,D
Business Administration and
　Management—General — M,O
Chemistry — M,D
Civil Engineering — M
Clinical Laboratory
　Sciences/Medical Technology — M,D
Clinical Psychology — M,O
Community Health Nursing — M,D,O
Community Health — M,D,O
Computational Sciences — D
Computer Art and Design — M
Computer Engineering — M,D,O
Computer Science — M,D,O
Database Systems — M
Early Childhood Education — M,D,O
Education—General — M,D,O
Educational Leadership and
　Administration — D
Educational Policy — M,D,O
Electrical Engineering — M,D,O
Engineering and Applied
　Sciences—General — D
English as a Second Language — M,D,O
Environmental Management
　and Policy — M,O
Experimental Psychology — M,O
Finance and Banking — M,O
Gerontological Nursing — M,D,O
Health Services Management and
　Hospital Administration — M
Illustration — M
Industrial/Management
　Engineering — M,D
Information Science — D
International Business — M,O
International Health — M,D,O
Internet and Interactive
　Multimedia — M
Latin American Studies — M,D
Law — D
Management Information Systems — M,O
Management of Technology — M
Management Strategy and Policy — M,O
Marine Affairs — M,D
Marine Biology — M
Marine Sciences — M,D
Marketing — M,O
Mathematics Education — M,D,O
Mechanical Engineering — M
Mechanics — D
Middle School Education — M,D,O
Nursing—General — M,D,O
Organizational Management — M,O
Photography — M
Physics — M
Portuguese — M,D
Psychiatric Nursing — M,D,O
Psychology—General — M,O
Public Administration — M,O
Public Policy — M,O
Science Education — M,D,O
Secondary Education — M,D,O
Software Engineering — M,O
Special Education — M,O
Supply Chain Management — M,O
Systems Engineering — M,D
Telecommunications — M,D,O
Writing — M,O

UNIVERSITY OF MASSACHUSETTS LOWELL
Allied Health—General — M,D
Analytical Chemistry — M,D
Biochemistry — M,D
Biological and Biomedical
　Sciences—General — M
Business Administration and
　Management—General — M,D
Chemical Engineering — M,D
Chemistry — M,D
Civil Engineering — M,D

Clinical Laboratory
　Sciences/Medical Technology — M
Computer Engineering — M,D
Computer Science — M,D
Conflict Resolution and
　Mediation/Peace Studies — M
Criminal Justice and Criminology — M
Curriculum and Instruction — M
Economic Development — M,O
Economics — M,O
Education—General — M
Electrical Engineering — M,D
Energy and Power
　Engineering — M,D
Engineering and Applied
　Sciences—General — M,D
Entrepreneurship — M,D
Environmental Engineering — M,D
Environmental Sciences — M,D
Family Nurse Practitioner Studies — M
Gerontological Nursing — M
Health Physics/Radiological Health — M
Health Promotion — D
Industrial/Management
　Engineering — D
Inorganic Chemistry — M,D
Legal and Justice Studies — M
Mathematics — D
Mechanical Engineering — M,D
Music Education — M
Music — M
Nuclear Engineering — M,D
Nursing—General — M,D
Organic Chemistry — M,D
Physical Therapy — D
Physics — M,D
Polymer Science and
　Engineering — M,D
Psychology—General — M
Social Psychology — M
Sociology — M,O
Urban and Regional Planning — M

UNIVERSITY OF MASSACHUSETTS MEDICAL SCHOOL
Adult Nursing — M,D,O
Allopathic Medicine — D
Biochemistry — M,D
Bioinformatics — M,D
Biological and Biomedical
　Sciences—General — M,D
Cancer Biology/Oncology — M,D
Cell Biology — M,D
Clinical Research — M,D
Community Health — M,D,O
Computational Biology — M,D
Family Nurse Practitioner Studies — M,D,O
Gerontological Nursing — M,D,O
Health Services Research — M,D
Immunology — M,D
Interdisciplinary Studies — M,D
Microbiology — M,D
Molecular Pharmacology — M,D
Neuroscience — M,D
Nursing and Healthcare
　Administration — M,D,O
Nursing Education — M,D,O
Nursing—General — M,D,O
Translational Biology — M,D

UNIVERSITY OF MEMPHIS
Accounting — M,D
Adult Education — M,D,O
African-American Studies — M,D,O
Allied Health—General — M,O
Analytical Chemistry — M,D
Anthropology — M
Applied Behavior Analysis — M,D,O
Applied Mathematics — M,D
Applied Statistics — M,D
Archaeology — M,D,O
Architecture — M
Art History — M,O
Art/Fine Arts — M,O
Bioinformatics — M,D
Biological and Biomedical
　Sciences—General — M,D
Biomedical Engineering — M,D
Biostatistics — M,D
Business Administration and
　Management—General — M,D
Chemistry — M,D
Civil Engineering — M,D,O
Clinical Psychology — M,D,O
Communication Disorders — M,D
Communication—General — M,D
Community College Education — M,D,O
Comparative Literature — M,D,O
Computational Sciences — M
Computer Engineering — M,D,O
Computer Science — M,D
Counseling Psychology — M,D
Counselor Education — M,D
Criminal Justice and Criminology — M
Curriculum and Instruction — M,D,O
Early Childhood Education — M,D,O
Economics — M,D
Education—General — M,D,O
Educational Leadership and
　Administration — M,D,O
Educational Measurement and
　Evaluation — M,D
Educational Media/Instructional
　Technology — M,D,O
Educational Psychology — M,D
Electrical Engineering — M,D,O
Elementary Education — M,D,O
Energy and Power
　Engineering — M,D
Engineering and Applied
　Sciences—General — M,D,O

English as a Second Language — M,D,O
English — M,D,O
Environmental and Occupational
　Health — M,D
Environmental Engineering — M,D,O
Epidemiology — M,D
Exercise and Sports Science — M,O
Experimental Psychology — M,D,O
Family Nurse Practitioner Studies — M,O
Film, Television, and Video
　Production — M,D
Finance and Banking — M,D
French — M
Gender Studies — O
Geographic Information Systems — M,D,O
Geography — M,D,O
Geology — M,D,O
Geophysics — M,D,O
Geotechnical Engineering — M,D,O
Graphic Design — M,O
Health Promotion — M,O
Health Services Management and
　Hospital Administration — M,D
Higher Education — M,D,O
History — M,D
Hospitality Management — M,O
Human Resources Management — M,O
Inorganic Chemistry — M,D
Interdisciplinary Studies — M,D,O
Journalism — M,O
Law — D
Liberal Studies — M,O
Linguistics — M,D,O
Management Information Systems — M,D,O
Management Strategy and Policy — M,O
Marketing — M,D
Mathematics Education — M,D
Mathematics — M,D,O
Mechanical Engineering — M,D
Museum Studies — M,O
Music Education — M,D
Music — M,D
Near and Middle Eastern Studies — M,D
Nonprofit Management — M,O
Nursing and Healthcare
　Administration — M,O
Nursing Education — M,O
Nursing—General — M,O
Nutrition — M,O
Organic Chemistry — M,D
Philosophy — M,D
Photography — M,O
Physical Chemistry — M,D
Physical Education — M,O
Physics — M
Political Science — M
Psychology—General — M,D,O
Public Administration — M,O
Public Health—General — M,D
Public Policy — M,O
Reading Education — M,D,O
Real Estate — M,D
Rehabilitation Counseling — M,D
School Psychology — M,D,O
Science Education — M,D,O
Secondary Education — M,D,O
Social Sciences — M,D
Social Work — M
Sociology — M
Spanish — M
Special Education — M,D,O
Statistics — M,D
Structural Engineering — M,D,O
Supply Chain Management — M
Theater — M
Transportation and Highway
　Engineering — M,D,O
Urban and Regional Planning — M
Urban Education — M,D,O
Water Resources Engineering — M,D,O
Writing — M,D,O

UNIVERSITY OF MIAMI
Acute Care/Critical Care Nursing — M,D
Adult Nursing — M,D
Advertising and Public Relations — M,D
Aerospace/Aeronautical
　Engineering — M,D
Allopathic Medicine — D
Architectural Engineering — M,D
Architecture — M
Art History — M
Art/Fine Arts — M
Athletic Training and Sports
　Medicine — M,D
Biochemistry — D
Biological and Biomedical
　Sciences—General — M,D
Biomedical Engineering — M,D
Biophysics — D
Broadcast Journalism — M,D
Business Administration and
　Management—General — M,D
Cancer Biology/Oncology — D
Cell Biology — D
Chemistry — M,D
Civil Engineering — M,D
Clinical Psychology — M,D
Communication—General — M,D
Community Health — D
Computer Engineering — M,D
Computer Science — M,D
Counseling Psychology — D
Counselor Education — M,O
Developmental Biology — D
Developmental Psychology — M,D
Early Childhood Education — M,O
Education—General — M,D
Educational Measurement and
　Evaluation — M,D
Electrical Engineering — M,D

Engineering and Applied
　Sciences—General — M,D
English — M,D
Environmental and Occupational
　Health — M
Epidemiology — M,D
Ergonomics and Human
　Factors — M
Evolutionary Biology — M,D
Exercise and Sports Science — M,D
Family Nurse Practitioner Studies — M,D
Film, Television, and Video
　Production — M,D
Film, Television, and Video
　Theory and Criticism — M,D
Fish, Game, and Wildlife
　Management — M,D
French — D
Genetics — M,D
Geography — M,D
Geophysics — M,D
Graphic Design — M
Higher Education — M,D,O
History — M,D
Immunology — D
Industrial/Management
　Engineering — M,D
Inorganic Chemistry — M,D
International Affairs — M
Internet and Interactive
　Multimedia — M
Journalism — M,D
Latin American Studies — M
Law — M,D
Liberal Studies — M
Management of Technology — M
Marine Affairs — M
Marine Biology — M,D
Marine Geology — M,D
Marine Sciences — M,D
Marriage and Family Therapy — M,O
Mathematical and
　Computational Finance — M,D
Mathematics Education — D
Mathematics — M,D
Mechanical Engineering — M,D
Meteorology — M,D
Microbiology — D
Molecular Biology — D
Multilingual and Multicultural
　Education — D
Music Education — M,D,O
Music — M,D,O
Neuroscience — M,D
Nurse Anesthesia — M,D
Nurse Midwifery — M,D
Nursing—General — M,D
Nutrition — M
Oceanography — M,D
Organic Chemistry — M,D
Pharmacology — D
Philosophy — M,D
Photography — M
Physical Chemistry — M,D
Physical Therapy — D
Physics — M,D
Physiology — D
Political Science — M
Psychology—General — M,D
Public Health—General — M,D
Reading Education — D
Real Estate — M,D
Romance Languages — D
Science Education — M,D
Sociology — M,D
Spanish — M,D
Special Education — M,D,O
Sports Management — M
Taxation — M,D
Therapies—Dance, Drama, and
　Music — M,D,O
Urban Design — M
Writing — M,D

UNIVERSITY OF MICHIGAN
Accounting — M,D
Aerospace/Aeronautical
　Engineering — M,D
Allopathic Medicine — D
American Studies — D
Analytical Chemistry — D
Anthropology — D
Applied Arts and Design—General — M,D
Applied Economics — M
Applied Physics — D
Applied Statistics — M,D
Archaeology — M,D
Architecture — M
Art History — M,D
Art/Fine Arts — M
Artificial Intelligence/Robotics — M,D
Asian Languages — D
Asian Studies — M,D,O
Astronomy — D
Astrophysics — D
Atmospheric Sciences — M,D
Automotive Engineering — M,D
Biochemistry — M,D
Bioinformatics — M,D
Biological and Biomedical
　Sciences—General — M,D
Biomedical Engineering — M,D
Biophysics — D
Biopsychology — D
Biostatistics — M,D
Business Administration and
　Management—General — M,D
Cancer Biology/Oncology — M,D
Cell Biology — M,D
Chemical Engineering — M,D,O
Chemistry — D

M—masters degree; D—doctorate; O—other advanced degree; *—Close-Up and/or Display

Civil Engineering M,D,O
Classics M,D,O
Clinical Psychology D
Clinical Research M
Cognitive Sciences D
Communication—General D
Comparative Literature D
Computer Engineering M,D
Computer Science M,D
Construction Engineering M,D,O
Cultural Anthropology D
Dance M
Database Systems M,D,O
Dental Hygiene M
Dentistry D
Developmental Biology M,D
Developmental Psychology D
East European and Russian Studies M,O
Ecology M,D
Economics M,D
Education—General M,D
Electrical Engineering M,D
Energy and Power
   Engineering M,D
Engineering and Applied
   Sciences—General M,D,O
Engineering Design M,D
English Education D
English M,D,O
Environmental and Occupational
   Health M,D
Environmental Engineering M,D,O
Environmental Management
   and Policy M,D
Environmental Sciences M,D
Epidemiology M,D
Evolutionary Biology M,D
Film, Television, and Video
   Theory and Criticism D,O
Foreign Languages Education M,D
French D
Genetic Counseling M,D
Geosciences M,D
German M,D,O
Health Education M,D
Health Informatics M,D
Health Physics/Radiological Health M,D,O
Health Promotion M,D
Health Services Management and
   Hospital Administration M,D
History D,O
Human Genetics M,D
Immunology M,D
Industrial Hygiene M,D
Industrial/Management
   Engineering M,D
Information Science M,D*
Information Studies M,D
Inorganic Chemistry D
International Health M,D
Italian D
Jewish Studies M,D,O
Kinesiology and Movement Studies M,D
Landscape Architecture M
Law M,D
Linguistics D
Manufacturing Engineering M,D
Mass Communication D
Materials Engineering M,D
Materials Sciences M,D
Mathematics M,D
Mechanical Engineering M,D
Media Studies M
Medicinal and Pharmaceutical
   Chemistry D
Microbiology M,D
Molecular Biology M,D
Molecular Pathology D
Music Education M,D,O
Music M,D,O
Natural Resources M,D
Near and Middle Eastern Languages M,D
Near and Middle Eastern Studies M,D
Neuroscience D
Nuclear Engineering M,D,O
Nursing—General M,D,O
Nutrition M,D
Ocean Engineering M,D,O
Operations Research M,D
Oral and Dental Sciences M,D
Organic Chemistry D
Pathology D
Pediatric Nursing M,D,O
Pharmaceutical Administration D
Pharmaceutical Engineering M,D
Pharmaceutical Sciences D
Pharmacology M,D
Pharmacy D
Philosophy M,D
Physical Chemistry D
Physics D
Physiology M,D
Planetary and Space
   Sciences M,D
Political Science D
Psychology—General D,O
Public Health—General M,D
Public Policy M,D
Religion M,D
Slavic Languages D
Social Psychology D
Social Sciences D
Social Work M,D
Sociology D
Spanish D
Sports Management M,D
Statistics M,D,O
Structural Engineering M,D,O
Supply Chain Management M,D
Survey Methodology M,D,O
Sustainable Development M,D
Systems Engineering M,D
Systems Science M,D
Taxation M

Toxicology M,D
Urban and Regional Planning D,O
Urban Design M
Women's Studies D,O
Writing M

UNIVERSITY OF MICHIGAN–DEARBORN

Accounting M
Applied Mathematics M
Automotive Engineering M,D
Bioengineering M
Business Administration and
   Management—General M
Clinical Psychology M
Computational Sciences M
Computer and Information
   Systems Security D
Computer Engineering M,D
Computer Science D
Criminal Justice and Criminology M
Curriculum and Instruction D,O
Database Systems M,D
Early Childhood Education M
Education—General M
Educational Leadership and
   Administration M,D,O
Educational Measurement and
   Evaluation M
Educational Media/Instructional
   Technology M
Electrical Engineering M,D
Energy and Power
   Engineering M
Engineering and Applied
   Sciences—General M,D
Engineering Management M
Environmental Sciences M
Finance and Banking M
Health Informatics M
Health Psychology M
Industrial/Management
   Engineering M,D
Information Science M,D
Management Information Systems M,D
Management Strategy and Policy M
Manufacturing Engineering M
Mechanical Engineering M,D
Project Management M
Public Administration M
Science Education M
Software Engineering M
Special Education M
Supply Chain Management M
Systems Engineering M,D
Urban Education M,D

UNIVERSITY OF MICHIGAN–FLINT

Accounting M,O
American Studies M
Art/Fine Arts M
Arts Administration M
Biological and Biomedical
   Sciences—General M
Business Administration and
   Management—General M,O
Communication—General M
Computer Science M
Criminal Justice and Criminology M
Curriculum and Instruction M,D,O
Early Childhood Education M,D,O
Education—General M,D,O
Educational Leadership and
   Administration M,D,O
Educational Media/Instructional
   Technology M,D,O
English M
Family Nurse Practitioner Studies M,D,O
Finance and Banking M,O
Gender Studies M
Gerontology M,D,O
Health Education M
Health Informatics M
Health Services Management and
   Hospital Administration M,O
Industrial and Manufacturing
   Management M,O
Information Science M
International Affairs M
International Business M,O
Management Information Systems M,O
Marketing M,O
Mathematics M
Mechanical Engineering M
Museum Studies M
Music M
Neuroscience D,O
Nonprofit Management M
Nurse Anesthesia M,D
Nursing—General M,D,O
Organizational Management M,O
Physical Therapy D,O
Political Science M
Psychiatric Nursing M,D,O
Public Administration M
Public Health—General M
Reading Education M,D,O
Rhetoric M
Secondary Education M,D,O
Social Sciences M
Writing M

UNIVERSITY OF MINNESOTA, DULUTH

Allopathic Medicine D
Anthropology M
Applied Mathematics M
Art/Fine Arts M
Biochemistry M,D
Biological and Biomedical
   Sciences—General M,D
Biophysics M,D
Business Administration and
   Management—General M
Chemistry M
Communication Disorders M
Computational Sciences M

Computer Engineering M
Computer Science M
Criminal Justice and Criminology M
Education—General M,D
Electrical Engineering M
Engineering Management M
English M
Geology M,D
Graphic Design M
Immunology M,D
Liberal Studies M
Medical Microbiology M,D
Molecular Biology M,D
Music Education M
Music M
Pharmacology M,D
Pharmacy M,D
Physics M
Physiology M,D
Safety Engineering M
Social Work M
Sociology M
Toxicology M,D

UNIVERSITY OF MINNESOTA ROCHESTER

Bioinformatics M,D
Business Administration and
   Management—General M,D
Computational Biology M,D
Occupational Therapy M,D

UNIVERSITY OF MINNESOTA, TWIN CITIES CAMPUS

Accounting M,D
Adult Education M,O
Aerospace/Aeronautical
   Engineering M,D
Agricultural Sciences—
   General M,D
Agronomy and Soil Sciences M,D
Allopathic Medicine M,D
American Studies D
Animal Behavior M,D
Animal Sciences M,D
Anthropology M,D
Applied Arts and Design—General M,D,O
Applied Economics M,D
Archaeology M,D
Architecture M
Art Education M
Art History M,D
Art/Fine Arts M
Asian Languages D
Asian Studies D
Astrophysics M,D
Biochemistry D
Biological and Biomedical
   Sciences—General M
Biomedical Engineering M,D
Biophysics M,D
Biopsychology D
Biostatistics M,D
Biosystems Engineering M,D
Biotechnology M
Business Administration and
   Management—General M,D
Cancer Biology/Oncology D
Cell Biology M,D
Chemical Engineering M,D
Chemical Physics M,D
Chemistry M,D
Child and Family Studies M,D
Child Development M,D
Civil Engineering M,D,O
Classics M,D
Clinical Laboratory
   Sciences/Medical Technology M
Clinical Psychology D
Clinical Research M
Clothing and Textiles M,D,O
Cognitive Sciences D
Communication Disorders M,D
Communication—General M,D,O
Community Health M
Comparative Literature D
Computational Sciences M,D
Computer and Information
   Systems Security M
Computer Engineering M,D
Computer Science M,D
Conservation Biology M,D
Counseling Psychology D
Counselor Education M
Cultural Studies D
Curriculum and Instruction M,D,O
Database Systems M
Dentistry D
Developmental Biology M,D
Early Childhood Education M,D,O
Ecology M,D
Economics M,D
Education of the Gifted M,D,O
Education—General M,D,O
Educational Leadership and
   Administration M,D
Educational Measurement and
   Evaluation M,D
Educational Media/Instructional
   Technology M,D,O
Educational Policy M,D
Educational Psychology M,D,O
Electrical Engineering M,D
Elementary Education M
Engineering and Applied
   Sciences—General M,D
English as a Second Language M,D,O
English Education M
English M,D
Entomology M,D
Entrepreneurship D
Environmental and Occupational
   Health M,D,O

Environmental Management
   and Policy M,D
Epidemiology M,D
Evolutionary Biology M,D
Exercise and Sports Science M,D
Family Nurse Practitioner Studies M,D
Finance and Banking M,D
Fish, Game, and Wildlife
   Management M,D
Food Science and
   Technology M,D
Foreign Languages Education M
Forestry M,D
Foundations and Philosophy of
   Education M,D
French M,D
Genetic Counseling M,D
Genetics M,D
Geographic Information Systems M,D
Geography M,D
Geological Engineering M,D,O
Geology M,D
Geophysics M,D
German M,D
Gerontological Nursing M,D
Health Informatics M,D
Health Services Management and
   Hospital Administration M,D
Health Services Research M,D
Higher Education M,D
Hispanic and Latin American
   Languages M,D
History of Medicine M,D
History of Science and Technology M,D
History M,D
Human Resources Development M,D,O
Human Resources Management M
Hydrology M,D
Immunology D
Industrial and Labor Relations M
Industrial and Manufacturing
   Management M
Industrial and Organizational
   Psychology D
Industrial Hygiene M,D
Industrial/Management
   Engineering M,D
Infectious Diseases M,D
Interdisciplinary Studies D
Interior Design M,D,O
International and Comparative
   Education M,D
International Development M
International Health M,D
Kinesiology and Movement Studies M,D
Landscape Architecture M
Law M,D
Linguistics M,D
Management Information Systems M,D
Management of Technology M
Management Strategy and Policy D
Marketing M,D
Marriage and Family Therapy M,D
Mass Communication M,D
Materials Engineering M,D
Materials Sciences M,D
Maternal and Child Health M
Mathematics Education M,D,O
Mathematics M,D,O
Mechanical Engineering M,D
Mechanics M,D
Medical Physics M,D
Medicinal and Pharmaceutical
   Chemistry M,D
Medieval and Renaissance Studies M,D
Microbiology D
Molecular Biology M,D
Multilingual and Multicultural
   Education M,D,O
Music M,D
Natural Resources M,D
Neurobiology M,D
Neuroscience M,D
Nurse Anesthesia M,D
Nurse Midwifery M,D
Nursing and Healthcare
   Administration M,D
Nursing Informatics M,D
Nursing—General M,D
Nutrition M,D
Occupational Health Nursing M,D
Oral and Dental Sciences M,D,O
Paper and Pulp Engineering M,D
Pediatric Nursing M,D
Pharmaceutical Administration M,D
Pharmaceutical Sciences M,D
Pharmacology M,D
Pharmacy D
Philosophy M,D
Physical Therapy M,D
Physics M,D
Physiology D
Plant Biology M,D
Plant Pathology M,D
Plant Sciences M,D
Political Science D
Portuguese M,D
Psychiatric Nursing M,D
Psychology—General D
Public Affairs M,D
Public Health—General M,D,O
Public Policy M,D
Quantitative Analysis M,D,O
Reading Education M,D,O
Religion M,D
Scandinavian Languages M,D
School Psychology M,D,O
Science Education M
Social Psychology D
Social Sciences Education M
Social Work M,D
Sociology M,D
Software Engineering M
Spanish M,D

Special Education	M,D
Sports Management	M,D
Statistics	M,D
Structural Biology	D
Student Affairs	M
Supply Chain Management	M,D
Taxation	M
Technology and Public Policy	M
Textile Design	M,D,O
Theater	M,D
Toxicology	M,D
Travel and Tourism	M,D
Urban and Regional Planning	M,D
Veterinary Medicine	D
Veterinary Sciences	M,D
Virology	D
Vocational and Technical Education	M,D,O
Water Resources	M,D
Women's Health Nursing	M,D
Women's Studies	D

UNIVERSITY OF MISSISSIPPI

Accounting	M,D
Anthropology	M,D
Applied Science and Technology	M,D
Art/Fine Arts	M,D
Biological and Biomedical Sciences—General	M,D
Business Administration and Management—General	M,D
Chemistry	M,D
Communication Disorders	M,D
Economics	M,D
Education—General	M,D,O
Engineering and Applied Sciences—General	M,D
English	M,D
Exercise and Sports Science	M,D
Experimental Psychology	M,D
Food Science and Technology	M,D
Foreign Languages Education	M,D
Health Promotion	M,D
History	M,D
Journalism	M
Kinesiology and Movement Studies	M,D
Law	M,D
Management Information Systems	M,D
Mathematics	M,D
Music	M,D
Nutrition	M,D
Pharmacy	M,D
Philosophy	M,D
Physics	M,D
Political Science	M,D
Recreation and Park Management	M,D
Social Work	M,D
Taxation	M,D

UNIVERSITY OF MISSISSIPPI MEDICAL CENTER

Allied Health—General	M
Allopathic Medicine	D
Anatomy	M,D
Biochemistry	D
Biological and Biomedical Sciences—General	M,D
Biophysics	D
Dentistry	M,D
Materials Sciences	M,D
Microbiology	D
Neuroscience	D
Nursing—General	M,D
Occupational Therapy	M
Oral and Dental Sciences	M,D
Pathology	D
Pharmacology	D
Physical Therapy	M
Physiology	D
Toxicology	D

UNIVERSITY OF MISSOURI

Accounting	M,D,O
Adult Education	M,D,O
Adult Nursing	M,D,O
Aerospace/Aeronautical Engineering	M,D
Agricultural Economics and Agribusiness	M,D,O
Agricultural Education	M,D,O
Agricultural Engineering	M,D
Agricultural Sciences—General	M,D,O
Agronomy and Soil Sciences	M,D,O
Allopathic Medicine	D
Analytical Chemistry	M,D
Anatomy	M
Animal Sciences	M,D
Anthropology	M,D
Applied Mathematics	M,D
Archaeology	M,D
Architecture	M,D
Art Education	M,D,O
Art History	M,D
Art/Fine Arts	M
Astronomy	M,D
Biochemistry	M,D
Bioengineering	M,D
Bioinformatics	D
Biological and Biomedical Sciences—General	M,D
Business Administration and Management—General	M,D
Business Education	M,D,O
Chemical Engineering	M,D
Chemistry	M,D
Child and Family Studies	M,D
Civil Engineering	M,D
Classics	M,D
Clothing and Textiles	M,D
Communication Disorders	M,D

Communication—General	M,D
Community Health	M,D
Comparative Literature	M,D
Computer Science	M,D
Conflict Resolution and Mediation/Peace Studies	M,D,O
Conservation Biology	M,D,O
Consumer Economics	M,D
Counseling Psychology	M,D,O
Curriculum and Instruction	M,D,O
Early Childhood Education	M,D,O
Ecology	M,D
Economics	M,D
Education of the Gifted	M,D
Education—General	M,D,O
Educational Leadership and Administration	M,D,O
Educational Media/Instructional Technology	M,D,O
Educational Psychology	M,D,O
Elementary Education	M,D,O
Engineering and Applied Sciences—General	M,D,O
English Education	M,D,O
English	M,D
Entomology	M,D
Environmental Engineering	M,D
Environmental Sciences	M,D,O
Evolutionary Biology	M,D
Family and Consumer Sciences-General	M,D,O
Family Nurse Practitioner Studies	M,D,O
Finance and Banking	M,D
Fish, Game, and Wildlife Management	M,D,O
Food Science and Technology	M,D
Foreign Languages Education	M,D,O
Forestry	M,D,O
French	M,D
Genetics	D
Geographic Information Systems	M,D,O
Geography	M,O
Geology	M,D
Geotechnical Engineering	M,D
German	M
Gerontological Nursing	M,D,O
Gerontology	M,D,O
Health Communication	M,D
Health Education	M,D,O
Health Informatics	M,O
Health Physics/Radiological Health	M
Health Promotion	M,O
Health Services Management and Hospital Administration	M,D,O
Higher Education	M,D,O
History	M,D
Horticulture	M,D
Hospitality Management	M,D
Human Development	M,D
Immunology	D
Industrial/Management Engineering	M,D
Information Studies	M,D,O
International Health	M,O
Journalism	M,D
Law	M,D
Library Science	M,D,O
Manufacturing Engineering	M,D
Marketing	M,D
Mathematics Education	M,D,O
Mathematics	M,D
Mechanical Engineering	M,D
Microbiology	D
Music Education	M,D,O
Music	M
Neuroscience	M,D,O
Nonprofit Management	M,D,O
Nuclear Engineering	M,D,O
Nursing and Healthcare Administration	M,D,O
Nursing—General	M,D,O
Nutrition	M,D
Occupational Therapy	M
Organizational Management	M,D,O
Pathobiology	M,D
Pathology	M
Pediatric Nursing	M,D,O
Pharmacology	M,D
Philosophy	D
Physical Therapy	D
Physics	M,D
Physiology	M,D
Plant Biology	M,D
Plant Sciences	M,D
Political Science	M,D
Psychiatric Nursing	M,D,O
Psychology—General	M,D
Public Administration	M,D,O
Public Affairs	M,D,O
Public Health—General	M,O
Public Policy	M,D,O
Reading Education	M,D,O
Religion	M
Romance Languages	M,D
Rural Sociology	M,D
Russian	M
School Psychology	M,D,O
Science Education	M,D,O
Social Sciences Education	M,D,O
Social Work	M,D,O
Sociology	D
Spanish	M,D
Special Education	M,D
Statistics	M,D
Structural Engineering	M,D
Taxation	M,D,O
Theater	M,D
Transportation and Highway Engineering	M,D

Veterinary Medicine	M,D
Veterinary Sciences	M
Vocational and Technical Education	M,D,O
Water Resources Engineering	M,D
Water Resources	M,D,O

UNIVERSITY OF MISSOURI–KANSAS CITY

Accounting	M,D
Adult Nursing	M,D
Allopathic Medicine	M,D
Analytical Chemistry	M,D
Art/Fine Arts	M,D
Biochemistry	D
Bioinformatics	M,D,O
Biological and Biomedical Sciences—General	M,D
Biophysics	D
Business Administration and Management—General	M,D
Cell Biology	D
Chemistry	M,D
Civil Engineering	M,D,O
Computer Engineering	M,D,O
Computer Science	M,D,O
Construction Engineering	M,D,O
Counseling Psychology	M,D,O
Counselor Education	M,D,O
Criminal Justice and Criminology	M
Curriculum and Instruction	M,D,O
Dental Hygiene	M,D,O
Dentistry	M,D,O
Economics	M,D
Education—General	M,D,O
Educational Leadership and Administration	M,D,O
Electrical Engineering	M,D,O
Engineering and Applied Sciences—General	M,D,O
Engineering Management	M,D,O
English	M,D
Family Nurse Practitioner Studies	M,D
Finance and Banking	M,D
French	M
Geosciences	M,D
Gerontological Nursing	M,D
Health Education	M,D
Higher Education	M,D,O
History	M,D
Inorganic Chemistry	M,D
Interdisciplinary Studies	D
Law	M,D
Maternal and Child/Neonatal Nursing	M,D
Mathematics	M,D
Mechanical Engineering	M,D,O
Molecular Biology	D
Music Education	M,D
Music	M,D
Nursing and Healthcare Administration	M,D
Nursing Education	M,D
Nursing—General	M,D
Oral and Dental Sciences	M,D,O
Organic Chemistry	M,D
Pediatric Nursing	M,D
Pharmacy	D
Physical Chemistry	M,D
Physics	M,D
Political Science	M
Polymer Science and Engineering	M,D
Psychology—General	M,D
Public Administration	M,D
Public Affairs	M,D
Reading Education	M,D,O
Romance Languages	M
Social Psychology	M,D
Social Work	M
Sociology	M
Software Engineering	M,D,O
Spanish	M
Special Education	M,D,O
Statistics	M,D
Telecommunications	M,D,O
Theater	M
Therapies—Dance, Drama, and Music	M,D
Women's Health Nursing	M,D

UNIVERSITY OF MISSOURI–ST. LOUIS

Accounting	M,D,O
Adult Education	M,D,O
Adult Nursing	D,O
American Studies	M,D
Applied Physics	M,D
Astrophysics	M,D
Biochemistry	M,D
Biological and Biomedical Sciences—General	M,D,O
Biotechnology	M,D
Business Administration and Management—General	M,D,O
Chemistry	M,D
Clinical Psychology	M,D,O
Communication—General	M
Computer and Information Systems Security	M,D,O
Computer Science	M,D
Counseling Psychology	M,D
Counselor Education	M,D
Criminal Justice and Criminology	M,D
Curriculum and Instruction	M
Early Childhood Education	M
Economics	M
Education—General	M,D,O
Educational Leadership and Administration	M,D,O
Educational Measurement and Evaluation	M,D,O
Educational Policy	M,D,O

Educational Psychology	D
Elementary Education	M,D
English as a Second Language	M
English	M
Family Nurse Practitioner Studies	D,O
Finance and Banking	M,D,O
Gerontological Nursing	D,O
Gerontology	M,O
Higher Education	M,D,O
Human Resources Management	M,D,O
Industrial and Manufacturing Management	M,D,O
Industrial and Organizational Psychology	M,D,O
International Business	M,D,O
Logistics	M,D,O
Management Information Systems	M,D,O
Management Strategy and Policy	M,D,O
Marketing	M,D,O
Marriage and Family Therapy	M,D
Mathematics	M,D
Media Studies	M
Middle School Education	M
Museum Studies	M,O
Music Education	M
Neuroscience	M,D,O
Nonprofit Management	M,O
Nursing—General	D,O
Optometry	D
Pediatric Nursing	D,O
Philosophy	M
Physics	M,D
Political Science	M,D
Psychiatric Nursing	D,O
Psychology—General	M,D,O
Public Administration	M,D,O
Public History	M,O
Public Policy	M,D,O
Reading Education	M
School Psychology	M,D,O
Science Education	M,D,O
Secondary Education	M,D,O
Social Work	M
Special Education	M
Supply Chain Management	M,D,O
Women's Health Nursing	D,O
Writing	M

UNIVERSITY OF MOBILE

Business Administration and Management—General	M
Education—General	M
Marriage and Family Therapy	M
Nursing—General	M

UNIVERSITY OF MONTANA

Accounting	M
Analytical Chemistry	M,D
Animal Behavior	M,D,O
Anthropology	M,D
Art Education	M
Art History	M
Art/Fine Arts	M
Biochemistry	D
Biological and Biomedical Sciences—General	M,D
Business Administration and Management—General	M
Cell Biology	D
Chemistry	M,D
Child and Family Studies	M,D,O
Clinical Psychology	M,D,O
Communication Disorders	M,O
Communication—General	M
Community Health	M
Computer Art and Design	M
Computer Science	M
Counseling Psychology	M,D,O
Counselor Education	M,D,O
Criminal Justice and Criminology	M
Cultural Studies	M,D,O
Curriculum and Instruction	M,D
Developmental Biology	D
Developmental Psychology	M,D,O
Early Childhood Education	M,D
Ecology	M,D
Economics	M
Education—General	M,D,O
Educational Leadership and Administration	M,D,O
English Education	M
English	M
Environmental Management and Policy	M
Environmental Sciences	M
Exercise and Sports Science	M
Experimental Psychology	M,D,O
Film, Television, and Video Production	M
Fish, Game, and Wildlife Management	M,D
Forestry	M,D
French	M
Geography	M
Geology	M,D
Geosciences	M,D
German	M
Health Education	M
History	M,D
Immunology	D
Inorganic Chemistry	M,D
Interdisciplinary Studies	M,D
Internet and Interactive Multimedia	M
Journalism	M
Law	D
Legal and Justice Studies	M
Linguistics	M,D
Mathematics Education	M,D
Mathematics	M

*M—masters degree; D—doctorate; O—other advanced degree; *—Close-Up and/or Display*

Medicinal and Pharmaceutical
Chemistry — M,D
Microbiology — D
Molecular Biology — D
Music — M
Natural Resources — M,D
Neuroscience — M,D
Organic Chemistry — M,D
Pharmaceutical Sciences — M,D
Pharmacy — M,D
Philosophy — M
Photography — M
Physical Chemistry — M,D
Physical Education — M
Physical Therapy — D
Political Science — M
Psychology—General — M,D,O
Public Administration — M
Public Health—General — M
Recreation and Park Management — M,D
Rural Planning and Studies — M
Rural Sociology — M
School Psychology — M,D,O
Social Work — M
Sociology — M
Spanish — M
Theater — M
Toxicology — M,D
Writing — M
Zoology — M,D

UNIVERSITY OF MONTEVALLO
Business Administration and
Management—General — M
Communication Disorders — M
Counselor Education — M
Education—General — M,O
Educational Leadership and
Administration — M,O
Elementary Education — M
English — M
Secondary Education — M

UNIVERSITY OF MOUNT OLIVE
Business Administration and
Management—General — M
Nursing—General — M

UNIVERSITY OF MOUNT UNION
Educational Leadership and
Administration — M
Physician Assistant Studies — M

UNIVERSITY OF NEBRASKA AT KEARNEY
Accounting — M
Art Education — M
Biological and Biomedical
Sciences—General — M
Business Administration and
Management—General — M
Communication Disorders — M
Counseling Psychology — M,O
Counselor Education — M,O
Curriculum and Instruction — M
Early Childhood Education — M
Education of the Gifted — M
Education—General — M,O
Educational Leadership and
Administration — M,O
Educational Media/Instructional
Technology — M
Elementary Education — M
English as a Second Language — M
English — M
Exercise and Sports Science — M
Foreign Languages Education — M
History — M
Human Resources Management — M
Human Services — M
Leisure Studies — M
Library Science — M
Management Information Systems — M
Marketing — M
Mathematics Education — M
Music Education — M
Physical Education — M
Reading Education — M
Recreation and Park Management — M
School Psychology — M,O
Science Education — M
Secondary Education — M
Special Education — M,O
Sports Management — M
Student Affairs — M,O
Writing — M

UNIVERSITY OF NEBRASKA AT OMAHA
Accounting — M
Applied Behavior Analysis — M,D,O
Art/Fine Arts — M
Artificial Intelligence/Robotics — M,O
Athletic Training and Sports
Medicine — M,D
Bioinformatics — M,D
Biological and Biomedical
Sciences—General — M,O
Business Administration and
Management—General — M,O
Communication Disorders — M
Communication—General — M,O
Computer and Information
Systems Security — M,D,O
Computer Science — M,O
Counselor Education — M
Criminal Justice and Criminology — M,D,O
Database Systems — M,D,O
Economics — M
Education—General — M,D,O
Educational Leadership and
Administration — M,D,O
Elementary Education — M,O
English as a Second Language — M,O
English — M,O
Exercise and Sports Science — M,D
Foreign Languages Education — M

Geographic Information Systems — M,O
Geography — M,O
Gerontology — M,D,O
Health Education — M,D
History — M
Human Resources Development — M,D,O
Industrial and Organizational
Psychology — M,D,O
Information Science — M,D,O
Kinesiology and Movement Studies — M,D
Management Information Systems — M,D,O
Mathematics — M
Music — M
National Security — M,O
Organizational Management — M
Political Science — M,O
Project Management — M,D,O
Psychology—General — M,D,O
Public Administration — M,D,O
School Psychology — M,O
Science Education — M,O
Secondary Education — M,O
Social Work — M
Sociology — M
Software Engineering — M,O
Special Education — M
Systems Engineering — M,O
Technical Communication — M,O
Urban Education — M,O
Writing — M

UNIVERSITY OF NEBRASKA–LINCOLN
Accounting — M,D
Actuarial Science — M
Adult Education — M,D,O
Advertising and Public Relations — M,D
Agricultural Economics and
Agribusiness — M,D
Agricultural Education — M
Agricultural Engineering — M,D
Agricultural Sciences—
General — M,D
Agronomy and Soil Sciences — M,D
Analytical Chemistry — M,D
Animal Sciences — M,D
Anthropology — M
Archaeology — M,D
Architectural Engineering — M,D
Architecture — M,D
Art History — M
Art/Fine Arts — M
Astronomy — M,D
Biochemistry — M,D
Bioengineering — M,D
Bioinformatics — M,D
Biological and Biomedical
Sciences—General — M,D
Biomedical Engineering — M,D
Biopsychology — M,D
Business Administration and
Management—General — M,D
Chemical Engineering — M,D
Chemistry — M,D
Child and Family Studies — M,D
Child Development — M,D
Civil Engineering — M,D
Classics — M
Clinical Psychology — M,D
Clothing and Textiles — M,D
Cognitive Sciences — M,D,O
Communication Disorders — M,D
Communication—General — M,D
Comparative Literature — M,D
Computer Engineering — M,D
Computer Science — M,D
Consumer Economics — M,D
Corporate and Organizational
Communication — M,D
Counseling Psychology — M,D,O
Curriculum and Instruction — M,D,O
Developmental Psychology — M,D,O
Early Childhood Education — M,D
Economics — M,D
Educational Leadership and
Administration — M,D,O
Educational Measurement and
Evaluation — M,D,O
Educational Psychology — M,D,O
Electrical Engineering — M,D
Engineering and Applied
Sciences—General — M,D
Engineering Management — M,D
English — M,D
Entomology — M,D
Environmental Engineering — M,D
Exercise and Sports Science — M,D
Family and Consumer
Sciences—General — M,D
Finance and Banking — M,D
Food Science and
Technology — M,D
French — M,D
Geography — M,D
Geosciences — M,D
German — M,D
Gerontology — M,D
Health Promotion — M,D
History — M,D
Home Economics Education — M,D
Horticulture — M,D
Human Development — M,D,O
Industrial/Management
Engineering — M,D
Information Science — M,D
Inorganic Chemistry — M,D
Interior Design — M,D
Journalism — M
Law — M,D
Legal and Justice Studies — M
Management Information Systems — M,D
Manufacturing Engineering — M,D
Marketing — M
Marriage and Family Therapy — M,D
Mass Communication — M

Materials Engineering — M,D
Materials Sciences — M,D
Mathematics — M,D
Mechanical Engineering — M,D
Mechanics — M,D
Metallurgical Engineering and
Metallurgy — M,D
Music Education — M,D
Music — M,D
Natural Resources — M,D
Nutrition — M,D
Organic Chemistry — M,D
Philosophy — M,D
Physical Chemistry — M,D
Physics — M,D,O
Political Science — M,D,O
Psychology—General — M,D
Public Policy — M,D,O
Rhetoric — M,D
School Psychology — M,D,O
Social Psychology — M,D
Sociology — M,D
Spanish — M,D
Special Education — M,D,O
Speech and Interpersonal
Communication — M,D
Statistics — M,D
Survey Methodology — M,D
Theater — M
Toxicology — M,D
Urban and Regional Planning — M,D
Veterinary Sciences — M,D
Vocational and Technical Education — M,D,O
Writing — M,D

UNIVERSITY OF NEBRASKA MEDICAL CENTER
Allied Health—General — M,D,O
Allopathic Medicine — D,O
Anatomy — M,D
Applied Behavior Analysis — M,D
Biochemistry — M,D
Bioinformatics — M,D
Biological and Biomedical
Sciences—General — M,D
Biostatistics — M,D
Cancer Biology/Oncology — D
Cell Biology — M,D
Clinical Laboratory
Sciences/Medical Technology — M,O
Dentistry — M,D,O
Emergency Management — M
Environmental and Occupational
Health — D
Epidemiology — D
Genetics — M,D
Health Promotion — D
Health Services Research — D
Immunology — D
Infectious Diseases — D
Microbiology — M,D
Molecular Biology — M,D
Molecular Genetics — M,D
Molecular Medicine — D
Neuroscience — D
Nursing—General — D
Nutrition — O
Oral and Dental Sciences — M,D
Pathology — M,D
Perfusion — M
Pharmaceutical Sciences — M,D
Pharmacology — M,D
Pharmacy — D
Physical Therapy — D
Physician Assistant Studies — M
Physiology — D
Public Health—General — M
Toxicology — D
Vision Sciences — M,D

UNIVERSITY OF NEVADA, LAS VEGAS
Accounting — M,O
Addictions/Substance Abuse
Counseling — M,D,O
Aerospace/Aeronautical
Engineering — M,D,O
Allied Health—General — M,D,O
Anthropology — M,D
Applied Economics — M,O
Architecture — M,O
Art/Fine Arts — M
Astronomy — M,D
Biochemistry — M,D
Biological and Biomedical
Sciences—General — M,D
Biomedical Engineering — M,D,O
Business Administration and
Management—General — M,O
Chemistry — M,D
Civil Engineering — M,D
Clinical Psychology — M,D
Communication—General — M
Community Health — M,D,O
Computer Engineering — M,D
Computer Science — M,D
Construction Management — M,O
Counseling Psychology — M,D,O
Counselor Education — M,D,O
Criminal Justice and Criminology — M,D
Curriculum and Instruction — M,D,O
Database Systems — M,O
Dentistry — M,D
Distance Education Development — M,D,O
Early Childhood Education — M,D,O
Economics — M
Education—General — M,D,O
Educational Leadership and
Administration — M,D,O
Educational Media/Instructional
Technology — M,D,O
Electrical Engineering — M,D
Elementary Education — M,D,O
Emergency Management — M,D,O
Engineering and Applied
Sciences—General — M,D,O

English as a Second Language — M,D,O
English — M,D
Environmental Engineering — M,D
Exercise and Sports Science — M,D
Family Nurse Practitioner Studies — M,D,O
Film, Television, and Video
Production — M,O
Geosciences — M,D
Health Physics/Radiological Health — M,D
Health Services Management and
Hospital Administration — M
Higher Education — M,D,O
Hispanic Studies — M
History — M
Hospitality Management — M
Journalism — M
Kinesiology and Movement Studies — M,D
Law — M,D
Management Information Systems — M
Marriage and Family Therapy — M
Materials Engineering — M,D,O
Mathematics — M,D
Mechanical Engineering — M,D
Media Studies — M
Music — M,D,O
Nonprofit Management — M
Nuclear Engineering — M,D,O
Nursing Education — M,D,O
Nursing—General — M,D,O
Nutrition — M,D
Oral and Dental Sciences — M,D
Physical Therapy — D
Physics — M,D
Political Science — M,D
Psychology—General — M,D,O
Public Administration — M,D,O
Public Affairs — M,D,O
Public Health—General — M,D,O
Public Policy — M,D,O
Secondary Education — M,D,O
Social Work — M
Sociology — M,D
Special Education — M,D,O
Theater — M
Transportation and Highway
Engineering — M,D
Water Resources — M,D
Writing — M,D,O

UNIVERSITY OF NEVADA, RENO
Accounting — M
Agricultural Economics and
Agribusiness — M,D
Agricultural Sciences—
General — M,D
Animal Sciences — M
Anthropology — M,D
Applied Economics — M,D
Art/Fine Arts — M
Atmospheric Sciences — M,D
Biochemistry — M,D
Biological and Biomedical
Sciences—General — M
Biomedical Engineering — M,D
Biotechnology — M
Business Administration and
Management—General — M
Cell Biology — M,D
Chemical Engineering — M,D
Chemical Physics — D
Chemistry — M,D
Child and Family Studies — M
Civil Engineering — M,D
Clinical Psychology — D
Cognitive Sciences — M,D
Communication Disorders — M,D
Computer Engineering — M,D
Computer Science — M,D
Conservation Biology — D
Counselor Education — M,D,O
Criminal Justice and Criminology — M
Curriculum and Instruction — M
Ecology — D
Economics — M
Education—General — M,D,O
Educational Leadership and
Administration — M,D,O
Educational Psychology — M,D,O
Electrical Engineering — M,D
Elementary Education — M
Engineering and Applied
Sciences—General — M,D
English as a Second Language — M
English — M,D
Environmental and Occupational
Health — M,D
Environmental Management
and Policy — M
Environmental Sciences — M,D
Evolutionary Biology — D
Finance and Banking — M
Foreign Languages Education — M
French — M
Geochemistry — M,D
Geography — M,D
Geological Engineering — M,D
Geology — M,D
Geophysics — M,D
German — M
History — M,D
Human Development — M,D
Hydrogeology — M,D
Hydrology — M,D
Journalism — M
Legal and Justice Studies — M,D
Management Information Systems — M
Materials Engineering — M,D
Mathematics Education — M
Mathematics — M
Mechanical Engineering — M,D
Metallurgical Engineering and
Metallurgy — M,D
Mineral/Mining Engineering — M
Molecular Biology — M,D

Molecular Pharmacology	D
Music	M
Nursing—General	M,D
Nutrition	M
Philosophy	M
Physics	M,D
Physiology	D
Political Science	M,D
Psychology—General	M,D
Public Administration	M
Public Health—General	M,D
Reading Education	M,D
Secondary Education	M
Social Psychology	D
Social Work	M
Sociology	M
Spanish	M
Special Education	M,D
Speech and Interpersonal Communication	M
Western European Studies	D

UNIVERSITY OF NEW BRUNSWICK FREDERICTON

Anthropology	M
Applied Economics	M
Biological and Biomedical Sciences—General	M,D
Business Administration and Management—General	M
Chemical Engineering	M,D
Chemistry	M,D
Civil Engineering	M,D
Classics	M
Computer Engineering	M,D
Computer Science	M,D
Conflict Resolution and Mediation/Peace Studies	M
Construction Engineering	M,D
Economics	M
Education—General	M,D
Electrical Engineering	M,D
Engineering and Applied Sciences—General	M,D,O
Engineering Management	M
English	M,D
Entrepreneurship	M
Environmental Engineering	M,D
Environmental Management and Policy	M,D
Exercise and Sports Science	M
Forestry	M,D
Geodetic Sciences	M,D
Geology	M,D
Geotechnical Engineering	M
Health Services Research	M
History	M,D
Hydrology	M,D
Interdisciplinary Studies	M,D
International Development	M
Marketing	M,D
Materials Sciences	M,D
Mathematics	M,D
Mechanical Engineering	M,D
Mechanics	M,D
Nursing Education	M
Nursing—General	M
Physical Education	M
Physics	M,D
Political Science	M
Psychology—General	M,D
Public Administration	M
Public Policy	M
Recreation and Park Management	M
Sociology	M,D
Sports Management	M
Statistics	M,D
Structural Engineering	M,D
Surveying Science and Engineering	M,D
Sustainable Development	M
Transportation and Highway Engineering	M,D
Urban and Regional Planning	M
Water Resources	M,D

UNIVERSITY OF NEW BRUNSWICK SAINT JOHN

Biological and Biomedical Sciences—General	M,D
Business Administration and Management—General	M
Clinical Psychology	M,D
Electronic Commerce	M
Experimental Psychology	M,D
International Business	M
Natural Resources	M
Psychology—General	M,D

UNIVERSITY OF NEW ENGLAND

Biological and Biomedical Sciences—General	M
Curriculum and Instruction	M,D,O
Dentistry	D
Early Childhood Education	M,D,O
Education—General	M,D,O
Educational Leadership and Administration	M,D,O
Health Informatics	M,D,O
Marine Sciences	M
Nurse Anesthesia	M,D
Nursing and Healthcare Administration	M,D,O
Nutrition	M,D,O
Occupational Therapy	M,D
Osteopathic Medicine	D
Pharmacy	D
Physical Therapy	M,D
Physician Assistant Studies	M,D
Public Health—General	M,D,O
Reading Education	M,D,O

Social Work	M,D,O
Vocational and Technical Education	M,D,O

UNIVERSITY OF NEW HAMPSHIRE

Accounting	M
Addictions/Substance Abuse Counseling	M,O
Animal Sciences	D
Applied Mathematics	M,D,O
Biochemistry	M,D
Biological and Biomedical Sciences—General	M,D
Business Administration and Management—General	M,O
Chemical Engineering	M,D
Chemistry	M,D
Child and Family Studies	M,O
Civil Engineering	M,D
Communication Disorders	M
Computer Science	M,D
Conservation Biology	M,D
Curriculum and Instruction	D,O
Early Childhood Education	M,D,O
Economics	M,D
Education—General	M,D,O
Educational Leadership and Administration	M,O
Educational Media/Instructional Technology	M,O
Elementary Education	M,O
English	M,D
Environmental Engineering	M,D
Environmental Management and Policy	M,D
Environmental Sciences	D,O
Evolutionary Biology	D
Family Nurse Practitioner Studies	M,D,O
Fish, Game, and Wildlife Management	M,D
Forestry	M,D
Genetics	M,D
Geographic Information Systems	O
Geology	M
Geosciences	M,D,O
Higher Education	O
History	M,D
Hydrology	M
Intellectual Property Law	M,D,O
Kinesiology and Movement Studies	M,O
Law	M,D,O
Legal and Justice Studies	M,D,O
Liberal Studies	M
Linguistics	M,D
Management Information Systems	M,O
Marine Biology	M,D
Marriage and Family Therapy	M,O
Materials Engineering	M,D
Materials Sciences	M,D
Mathematics Education	M,D,O
Mechanical Engineering	M,D
Microbiology	M,D
Museum Studies	M,D
Music	M
Natural Resources	M,D
Nursing—General	M,D,O
Nutrition	M,D
Occupational Therapy	M,O
Ocean Engineering	M,D,O
Oceanography	M,D,O
Physical Education	M,O
Physics	M,D
Political Science	M,O
Psychiatric Nursing	M,D,O
Psychology—General	D
Public Administration	M,O
Public Health—General	M,O
Public Policy	M
Recreation and Park Management	M
Science Education	M,D
Secondary Education	M,O
Social Work	M,O
Sociology	M,D
Spanish	M,O
Special Education	M
Sustainability Management	M,O
Water Resources	M,D
Writing	M

UNIVERSITY OF NEW HAVEN

Accounting	M,O
Biomedical Engineering	M
Business Administration and Management—General	M,O
Cell Biology	M,O
Computer and Information Systems Security	M,D,O
Computer Engineering	M
Computer Science	M,D,O
Conflict Resolution and Mediation/Peace Studies	M,O
Criminal Justice and Criminology	M,D,O
Database Systems	M
Ecology	M,O
Electrical Engineering	M
Emergency Management	M,O
Engineering and Applied Sciences—General	M,O
Engineering Management	M,O
Environmental and Occupational Health	M,O
Environmental Engineering	M
Environmental Management and Policy	M,O
Environmental Sciences	M,O
Facilities Management	M,O
Finance and Banking	M,O
Fire Protection Engineering	M,O
Forensic Psychology	M
Forensic Sciences	M,D,O
Geographic Information Systems	M,O
Geosciences	M,O

Hazardous Materials Management	M
Health Services Management and Hospital Administration	M,O
Human Resources Management	M,O
Industrial and Labor Relations	M,O
Industrial and Manufacturing Management	M,O
Industrial and Organizational Psychology	M,O
Industrial/Management Engineering	M,O
International Business	M,O
Management Strategy and Policy	M,O
Marketing	M,O
Mechanical Engineering	M
Molecular Biology	M,O
National Security	M,O
Nutrition	M,O
Organizational Management	M,O
Public Administration	M,O
Science Education	M,O
Social Psychology	M,O
Software Engineering	M,O
Sports Management	M,O
Taxation	M,O
Urban and Regional Planning	M,O
Water Resources Engineering	M

UNIVERSITY OF NEW MEXICO

Accounting	M,D
Allied Health—General	M,D,O
Allopathic Medicine	D
American Indian/Native American Studies	M,D
American Studies	M,D
Anthropology	M,D
Archaeology	M,D
Architecture	M,D
Art Education	M
Art History	M,D
Art/Fine Arts	M
Biochemistry	M,D
Biological and Biomedical Sciences—General	M,D
Biomedical Engineering	M,D
Business Administration and Management—General	M
Cell Biology	M,D
Chemical Engineering	M,D
Chemistry	M,D
Child and Family Studies	M,D
Civil Engineering	M,D
Clinical Laboratory Sciences/Medical Technology	M,O
Clinical Psychology	D
Cognitive Sciences	D
Communication Disorders	M
Communication—General	M
Community Health	M
Comparative Literature	M,D
Computer and Information Systems Security	M
Computer Engineering	M,D
Computer Science	M,D
Construction Management	M,D
Counselor Education	M,D
Cultural Studies	M,D
Dance	M
Dental Hygiene	M
Developmental Psychology	D
Early Childhood Education	D
Economics	M,D
Education—General	M,D,O
Educational Leadership and Administration	M,D,O
Educational Media/Instructional Technology	M,D,O
Educational Psychology	M,D
Electrical Engineering	M,D
Elementary Education	M
Engineering and Applied Sciences—General	M,D
English as a Second Language	M,D
English Education	M,D
English	M,D
Entrepreneurship	M
Environmental Management and Policy	M
Epidemiology	M
Ethnic Studies	M,D
Exercise and Sports Science	D
Finance and Banking	M
Foundations and Philosophy of Education	M,D
French	M,D
Genetics	M,D
Geography	M
Geosciences	M,D
German	M,D
Health Education	M
Health Psychology	D
Health Services Management and Hospital Administration	M
Higher Education	O
Historic Preservation	O
History	M,D
Human Development	M,D
Human Resources Management	M
International Business	M
International Development	M,D
International Economics	M,D
Landscape Architecture	M
Latin American Studies	M,D
Law	D
Linguistics	M,D
Management Information Systems	M
Management of Technology	M
Management Strategy and Policy	M
Manufacturing Engineering	M
Marketing	M

Mathematics	M,D
Mechanical Engineering	M,D
Microbiology	M,D
Molecular Biology	M,D
Multilingual and Multicultural Education	M,D
Music Education	M
Music	M
Nanotechnology	M,D
Natural Resources	M,D
Neuroscience	M,D
Nuclear Engineering	M,D
Nursing—General	M,D
Nutrition	M
Occupational Therapy	M
Optical Sciences	M,D
Organizational Behavior	M
Organizational Management	M
Pathology	M,D
Pharmaceutical Sciences	M,D
Pharmacy	D
Philosophy	M,D
Photography	M,D
Photonics	M,D
Physical Education	D
Physical Therapy	D
Physician Assistant Studies	M
Physics	M,D
Physiology	M,D
Planetary and Space Sciences	M,D
Political Science	M,D
Portuguese	M,D
Psychology—General	D
Public Administration	M
Public Health—General	M
Quantitative Analysis	D
Reading Education	M,D
Science Education	O
Secondary Education	M
Sociology	M,D
Spanish	M,D
Special Education	M,D,O
Sports Management	D
Statistics	M,D
Systems Engineering	M,D
Taxation	M
Theater	M
Toxicology	M,D
Urban and Regional Planning	M
Water Resources	M
Writing	M

UNIVERSITY OF NEW ORLEANS

Accounting	M
Art/Fine Arts	M
Arts Administration	M
Biological and Biomedical Sciences—General	M,D
Business Administration and Management—General	M
Chemistry	M,D
Computer Science	M
Counselor Education	M,D
Curriculum and Instruction	M,D
Economics	D
Education—General	M,D
Educational Leadership and Administration	M,D
Engineering and Applied Sciences—General	M,D
Engineering Management	M
English	M
Environmental Sciences	M
Film, Television, and Video Production	M
Finance and Banking	M,D
Geography	M
Geosciences	M
Health Services Management and Hospital Administration	M
History	M
Hospitality Management	M
Mathematics	M
Mechanical Engineering	M
Music	M
Physics	M,D
Political Science	M,D
Psychology—General	M,D
Public Administration	M
Romance Languages	M
Sociology	M
Special Education	M
Taxation	M
Theater	M
Transportation Management	M
Travel and Tourism	M
Urban and Regional Planning	M
Urban Studies	M,D

UNIVERSITY OF NORTH ALABAMA

Accounting	M
Business Administration and Management—General	M
Child and Family Studies	M
Clinical Psychology	M
Counselor Education	M
Criminal Justice and Criminology	M
Economic Development	M
Education—General	M,O
Educational Leadership and Administration	M
Elementary Education	M,O
English	M
Exercise and Sports Science	M
Finance and Banking	M
Geographic Information Systems	M
Health Promotion	M
Health Services Management and Hospital Administration	M
History	M

M—masters degree; D—doctorate; O—other advanced degree; *—Close-Up and/or Display

Information Science — M
Interdisciplinary Studies — M
International Business — M
Kinesiology and Movement Studies — M
Law — M
Management Information Systems — M
Nursing—General — M
Physical Education — M
Political Science — M
Project Management — M
Public History — M
Secondary Education — M
Special Education — M

UNIVERSITY OF NORTH CAROLINA AT ASHEVILLE

Cultural Studies — M,O
Liberal Studies — M,O
Sustainable Development — M,O

THE UNIVERSITY OF NORTH CAROLINA AT CHAPEL HILL

Accounting — M,D
Adult Nursing — M,D,O
Allied Health—General — M,D
Allopathic Medicine — D
Anthropology — M,D
Archaeology — M,D
Art History — M,D
Art/Fine Arts — M
Astronomy — M,D
Astrophysics — M,D
Athletic Training and Sports Medicine — M
Biochemistry — M,D
Bioinformatics — D
Biological and Biomedical Sciences—General — M,D
Biomedical Engineering — M,D
Biophysics — M,D
Biopsychology — D
Biostatistics — M,D
Botany — M,D
Business Administration and Management—General — M,D
Cell Biology — M,D
Chemistry — M,D
Classics — M,D
Clinical Psychology — D
Clinical Research — M,D
Cognitive Sciences — D
Communication Disorders — M,D
Communication—General — M
Computational Biology — D
Computer Science — M,D
Counselor Education — M
Curriculum and Instruction — M,D
Dental Hygiene — M,D
Dentistry — D
Developmental Biology — M,D
Developmental Psychology — D
Early Childhood Education — M,D
East European and Russian Studies — M
Ecology — M,D
Economics — M,D
Education—General — M,D
Educational Leadership and Administration — M,D
Educational Measurement and Evaluation — M,D
Educational Psychology — M,D
English as a Second Language — M
English Education — M
English — M,D
Environmental and Occupational Health — M,D
Environmental Engineering — M,D
Environmental Sciences — M,D
Epidemiology — M,D
Evolutionary Biology — M,D
Exercise and Sports Science — M
Family Nurse Practitioner Studies — M,D,O
Finance and Banking — D
Folklore — M
Foreign Languages Education — M
French — M,D
Genetics — M,D
Geography — M,D
Geology — D
German — D
Gerontological Nursing — M,D,O
Health Promotion — M
Health Psychology — M,D
Health Services Management and Hospital Administration — M,D
History — M,D
Immunology — M,D
Information Studies — M,D,O
International Affairs — M
Italian — M,D
Kinesiology and Movement Studies — M,D
Latin American Studies — M,D,O
Law — M,D
Library Science — M,D,O
Linguistics — M
Management Information Systems — D
Management Strategy and Policy — D
Marine Sciences — M,D
Marketing — D
Mass Communication — M,D,O
Maternal and Child Health — M,D
Mathematics Education — M
Mathematics — M,D
Microbiology — M,D
Molecular Biology — M,D
Molecular Physiology — D
Music Education — M
Music — M,D
Neurobiology — D
Neuroscience — D
Nursing and Healthcare Administration — M,D,O
Nursing Education — M,D,O
Nursing Informatics — M,D,O

Nursing—General — M,D,O
Nutrition — M,D
Occupational Health Nursing — M
Occupational Therapy — M,D
Operations Research — M,D
Oral and Dental Sciences — M,D
Organizational Behavior — D
Pathology — D
Pediatric Nursing — M,D,O
Pharmaceutical Administration — M,D
Pharmaceutical Sciences — M,D
Pharmacology — D
Pharmacy — M,D
Philosophy — M,D
Physical Education — M
Physical Therapy — M,D
Physics — M,D
Political Science — M,D,O
Portuguese — M,D
Psychiatric Nursing — M,D,O
Psychology—General — D
Public Administration — M
Public Health—General — M,D
Public Policy — D
Reading Education — M,D
Rehabilitation Counseling — M,D
Religion — M,D
Romance Languages — M,D
School Psychology — M,D
Science Education — M
Secondary Education — M
Slavic Languages — D
Social Psychology — D
Social Sciences Education — M
Social Work — M,D
Sociology — M,D
Spanish — M,D
Sports Management — M
Statistics — M,D
Telecommunications — M,D,O
Theater — M
Toxicology — M,D
Urban and Regional Planning — M,D

THE UNIVERSITY OF NORTH CAROLINA AT CHARLOTTE

Accounting — M
Acute Care/Critical Care Nursing — M,D,O
Addictions/Substance Abuse Counseling — M,D,O
African Studies — O
Anthropology — M
Applied Economics — M,O
Applied Mathematics — M,D
Applied Physics — M,D
Architecture — M
Art Education — M,D,O
Arts Administration — M,O
Bioinformatics — M,D,O
Biological and Biomedical Sciences—General — M,D
Business Administration and Management—General — M,D,O
Business Education — D
Chemistry — M,D
Child and Family Studies — M,D,O
Child Development — M,D,O
Civil Engineering — M,D
Cognitive Sciences — M,D,O
Communication—General — M
Community Health — M,D,O
Computer and Information Systems Security — M,D,O
Computer Engineering — M,D
Computer Science — M,D,O
Construction Management — M,O
Counselor Education — M,D,O
Criminal Justice and Criminology — M
Cultural Studies — M,O
Curriculum and Instruction — M,D,O
Database Systems — M,O
Early Childhood Education — M,D,O
Economics — M,O
Education of the Gifted — M,D,O
Education—General — M,D,O
Educational Leadership and Administration — M,D,O
Educational Media/Instructional Technology — M,D,O
Electrical Engineering — M,D
Elementary Education — M,O
Emergency Management — M,O
Energy and Power Engineering — M,O
Engineering and Applied Sciences—General — M,D,O
Engineering Management — M,O
English as a Second Language — M,D,O
English — M,O
Environmental Engineering — M,D
Ethics — M,O
Facilities Management — M,O
Family Nurse Practitioner Studies — M,D,O
Finance and Banking — M,O
Fire Protection Engineering — M,O
Foreign Languages Education — M,D,O
Game Design and Development — M,O
Gender Studies — M,D,O
Geographic Information Systems — M,D
Geography — M,D
Geosciences — M,D
Gerontological Nursing — M,D,O
Gerontology — M,O
Health Informatics — M,O
Health Psychology — M,D,O
Health Services Management and Hospital Administration — M
Health Services Research — D
History — M
Industrial and Manufacturing Management — M
Industrial and Organizational Psychology — M,D,O

Information Science — M,O
Interdisciplinary Studies — M
Kinesiology and Movement Studies — M
Latin American Studies — M,D,O
Liberal Studies — M,O
Linguistics — M,O
Logistics — M,O
Management Information Systems — M,D,O
Mathematical and Computational Finance — M,O
Mathematics — M,D,O
Mechanical Engineering — M,D
Middle School Education — M,D,O
Music — O
Nonprofit Management — M,O
Nurse Anesthesia — M,D,O
Nursing and Healthcare Administration — M,D,O
Nursing Education — M,D,O
Nursing—General — M,D,O
Optical Sciences — M,D
Philosophy — M,O
Psychology—General — M,O
Public Administration — M,O
Public Health—General — M,D,O
Public Policy — M,D,O
Reading Education — M,D
Real Estate — M,O
Religion — M
Secondary Education — M,D,O
Social Work — M
Sociology — M
Spanish — M,O
Special Education — M,D,O
Statistics — M,O
Supply Chain Management — M,O
Systems Engineering — M,D,O
Technical Writing — M,O
Theater — M,D,O
Translation and Interpretation — M,O
Urban and Regional Planning — M,O
Urban Design — M
Women's Studies — M,D,O
Writing — M,O

THE UNIVERSITY OF NORTH CAROLINA AT GREENSBORO

Accounting — M
Adult Education — M,D,O
Adult Nursing — M,D,O
Applied Economics — M
Architecture — M,O
Art/Fine Arts — M
Athletic Training and Sports Medicine — M,D
Biochemistry — M
Biological and Biomedical Sciences—General — M
Business Administration and Management—General — M,O
Chemistry — M,D
Child and Family Studies — M,D
Classics — M
Clinical Psychology — M,D
Cognitive Sciences — M,D
Communication Disorders — M,D
Communication—General — M
Community Health — M,D
Computer Science — M
Conflict Resolution and Mediation/Peace Studies — M,O
Counseling Psychology — M,D,O
Counselor Education — M,D,O
Criminal Justice and Criminology — M
Curriculum and Instruction — M,D,O
Dance — M
Developmental Psychology — M,D
Early Childhood Education — M,D,O
Economic Development — M,D,O
Economics — D
Education—General — M,D,O
Educational Leadership and Administration — M,D,O
Educational Measurement and Evaluation — D
Educational Media/Instructional Technology — M,D,O
Elementary Education — D
English as a Second Language — M,D,O
English Education — M,D
English — M,D
Film, Television, and Video Production — M
Finance and Banking — M,O
Foreign Languages Education — M
French — M
Gender Studies — M,O
Genetic Counseling — M
Geographic Information Systems — M,D,O
Geography — M,D,O
Gerontological Nursing — M,D,O
Gerontology — M,O
Higher Education — D
Hispanic and Latin American Languages — M,O
Hispanic Studies — M,O
Historic Preservation — M,O
History — M,D,O
Human Development — M,D
Information Studies — M
Interior Design — M,O
Kinesiology and Movement Studies — M,D,O
Liberal Studies — M
Library Science — M
Management Information Systems — M,D,O
Marketing — M
Marriage and Family Therapy — M,D,O
Mathematics Education — M
Mathematics — M,D
Media Studies — M
Middle School Education — M,D,O
Multilingual and Multicultural Education — M,D,O
Museum Studies — M,D,O

Music Education — M,D
Music — M,D
Nonprofit Management — M,O
Nurse Anesthesia — M,D,O
Nursing and Healthcare Administration — M,D,O
Nursing Education — M,D,O
Nursing—General — M,D,O
Nutrition — M,D
Political Science — M,O
Psychology—General — M,D
Public Affairs — M,O
Reading Education — M,D,O
Recreation and Park Management — M
Rhetoric — M,D
School Psychology — M,D,O
Science Education — M,D,O
Social Psychology — M,D
Social Sciences Education — M,D,O
Social Work — M
Sociology — M
Spanish — M,O
Special Education — M,D,O
Supply Chain Management — M,D,O
Technical Writing — M,D,O
Textile Design — M
Theater — M
Women's Studies — M,D,O
Writing — M

THE UNIVERSITY OF NORTH CAROLINA AT PEMBROKE

Art Education — M
Business Administration and Management—General — M
Counseling Psychology — M
Counselor Education — M
Education—General — M
Educational Leadership and Administration — M
Elementary Education — M
English Education — M
Exercise and Sports Science — M
Mathematics Education — M
Nursing and Healthcare Administration — M
Nursing Education — M
Nursing—General — M
Physical Education — M
Public Administration — M
Reading Education — M
Science Education — M
Social Sciences Education — M
Social Work — M

UNIVERSITY OF NORTH CAROLINA SCHOOL OF THE ARTS

Film, Television, and Video Production — M
Music — M,O
Theater — M

THE UNIVERSITY OF NORTH CAROLINA WILMINGTON

Accounting — M
Applied Behavior Analysis — M
Biological and Biomedical Sciences—General — M,D
Business Administration and Management—General — M
Chemistry — M
Clinical Research — M,D,O
Computer Science — M
Conflict Resolution and Mediation/Peace Studies — M
Criminal Justice and Criminology — M
Curriculum and Instruction — M,D
Early Childhood Education — M
Education of the Gifted — M
Education—General — M,D
Educational Leadership and Administration — M,D
Educational Media/Instructional Technology — M
Educational Policy — M
Elementary Education — M
English as a Second Language — M
English — M
Environmental Management and Policy — M
Family Nurse Practitioner Studies — M,D,O
Foreign Languages Education — M
Geosciences — M
Gerontology — M,O
Health Education — M
Higher Education — M,D
History — M
International Business — M
Liberal Studies — M
Management Information Systems — M
Marine Biology — M,D
Marine Sciences — M,D
Mathematics — M
Middle School Education — M
Nursing Education — M,D,O
Nursing—General — M,D,O
Physical Education — M
Psychology—General — M
Public Administration — M
Reading Education — M
Secondary Education — M
Social Work — M
Sociology — M
Spanish — M
Special Education — M
Statistics — M
Writing — M

UNIVERSITY OF NORTH DAKOTA

Applied Economics — M
Art/Fine Arts — M
Astrophysics — M,D
Atmospheric Sciences — M,D
Aviation — M

Biological and Biomedical Sciences—General — M,D
Business Administration and Management—General — M
Chemical Engineering — M,D
Chemistry — M,D
Civil Engineering — M,D
Clinical Psychology — M,D
Communication Disorders — M
Communication—General — D
Community Health Nursing — M,D,O
Computer Science — M
Counseling Psychology — D
Criminal Justice and Criminology — D
Early Childhood Education — M
Education—General — M,D,O
Educational Leadership and Administration — M,D,O
Educational Media/Instructional Technology — M
Electrical Engineering — M,D
Elementary Education — M
Engineering and Applied Sciences—General — D
English — M,D
Environmental Engineering — M,D
Family Nurse Practitioner Studies — M,D,O
Fish, Game, and Wildlife Management — M,D
Forensic Psychology — M,D
Genetics — M,D
Geographic Information Systems — M
Geography — M
Geological Engineering — M,D
Geology — M,D
Geosciences — M,D
Gerontological Nursing — M,D,O
History — M,D
Kinesiology and Movement Studies — M
Linguistics — M
Mathematics — M
Mechanical Engineering — M,D
Music Education — M,D
Music — M,D
Nurse Anesthesia — M,D,O
Nursing Education — M,D,O
Nursing—General — M,D,O
Occupational Therapy — M
Physical Therapy — D
Physician Assistant Studies — M
Physics — M,D
Planetary and Space Sciences — M
Psychiatric Nursing — M,D,O
Psychology—General — M,D
Public Administration — M
Public Health—General — M
Reading Education — M
Social Work — M
Sociology — M
Special Education — M
Zoology — M,D

UNIVERSITY OF NORTHERN BRITISH COLUMBIA

Community Health — M,D,O
Computer Science — M,D,O
Disability Studies — M,D,O
Education—General — M,D,O
Environmental Management and Policy — M,D,O
Gender Studies — M,D,O
History — M,D,O
Interdisciplinary Studies — M,D,O
International Affairs — M,D,O
Mathematics — M,D,O
Natural Resources — M,D,O
Political Science — M,D,O
Psychology—General — M,D,O
Social Work — M,D,O

UNIVERSITY OF NORTHERN COLORADO

Accounting — M
Acute Care/Critical Care Nursing — M,D
Applied Statistics — M,D
Art Education — M
Art History — M
Art/Fine Arts — M
Biological and Biomedical Sciences—General — M
Business Administration and Management—General — M
Chemistry — M,D
Clinical Psychology — M
Communication Disorders — M,D
Communication—General — M
Community Health — M
Counseling Psychology — M,D
Counselor Education — M
Criminal Justice and Criminology — M
Curriculum and Instruction — M,D
Education of the Gifted — M,D
Education—General — M,D,O
Educational Leadership and Administration — M,D,O
Educational Measurement and Evaluation — M,D
Educational Policy — M,D,O
Educational Psychology — M,D
Elementary Education — M,D
English as a Second Language — M,D
English Education — M,D
English — M
Exercise and Sports Science — M,D
Family Nurse Practitioner Studies — M,D
Foreign Languages Education — M
Geosciences — M
Gerontology — M,D
Health Education — M

Health Services Management and Hospital Administration — M
Higher Education — M,D
History — M
Human Resources Management — M
International Health — M
Mathematics Education — M,D
Mathematics — M,D
Multilingual and Multicultural Education — M,D
Music Education — M,D
Music — M,D
Nursing Education — M,D
Nursing—General — M,D
Physical Education — M,D
Public Health—General — M
Reading Education — M
Rehabilitation Counseling — M,D
Rehabilitation Sciences — M
School Psychology — O
Science Education — M,D
Sociology — M
Special Education — M,D
Sports Management — M,D
Student Affairs — M

UNIVERSITY OF NORTHERN IOWA

Accounting — M
Allied Health—General — M,D
Applied Mathematics — M
Art Education — M
Art/Fine Arts — M
Athletic Training and Sports Medicine — M
Biological and Biomedical Sciences—General — M
Business Administration and Management—General — M
Communication Disorders — M
Communication—General — M
Community College Education — M
Community Health — M
Counseling Psychology — M
Counselor Education — M
Curriculum and Instruction — D
Early Childhood Education — M
Education—General — M,D,O
Educational Leadership and Administration — M,D
Educational Measurement and Evaluation — M
Educational Media/Instructional Technology — M
Educational Psychology — M
Elementary Education — M
English as a Second Language — M
English Education — M
English — M
Foreign Languages Education — M
Gender Studies — M
Geography — M
Geosciences — M
Health Education — M
Health Promotion — M
Higher Education — M
History — M
Human Services — M
Kinesiology and Movement Studies — M
Mathematics Education — M
Mathematics — M
Middle School Education — M
Music Education — M
Music — M
Nonprofit Management — M
Physical Education — M
Physics — M
Psychology—General — M
Public History — M
Public Policy — M
Reading Education — M
School Psychology — M,O
Science Education — M
Secondary Education — M
Social Sciences — M
Social Work — M
Spanish — M
Special Education — M
Sports Management — M
Student Affairs — M
Vocational and Technical Education — M,D
Women's Studies — M
Writing — M

UNIVERSITY OF NORTH FLORIDA

Accounting — M
Adult Education — M
Allied Health—General — M,D,O
Applied Behavior Analysis — M
Biological and Biomedical Sciences—General — M
Business Administration and Management—General — M
Civil Engineering — M
Communication Disorders — M
Community Health — M,O
Computer Science — M
Construction Management — M
Counseling Psychology — M
Counselor Education — M,D
Criminal Justice and Criminology — M
Economics — M
Education—General — M,D
Educational Leadership and Administration — M,D
Educational Media/Instructional Technology — M,D
Electrical Engineering — M
Electronic Commerce — M
Elementary Education — M
English as a Second Language — M
English — M

Ethics — M,O
Exercise and Sports Science — M,D
Family Nurse Practitioner Studies — M,D,O
Finance and Banking — M
History — M
Human Resources Management — M
International Business — M
Logistics — M
Management Information Systems — M
Mathematics — M
Mechanical Engineering — M
Nonprofit Management — M,O
Nurse Anesthesia — M,D,O
Nursing—General — M,D,O
Nutrition — M
Philosophy — M,O
Physical Therapy — M,D
Psychology—General — M
Public Administration — M,O
Public Health—General — M,O
Reading Education — M
Secondary Education — M
Software Engineering — M
Special Education — M
Sports Management — M,D
Statistics — M
Translation and Interpretation — M
Writing — M

UNIVERSITY OF NORTH GEORGIA

Anthropology — M
Business Administration and Management—General — M
Clinical Psychology — M
Criminal Justice and Criminology — M
Early Childhood Education — M,O
Education—General — M,O
Educational Leadership and Administration — M,O
English Education — M,O
Family Nurse Practitioner Studies — M,O
History — M
International Affairs — M
Mathematics Education — M,O
Middle School Education — M,O
Philosophy — M
Physical Education — M,O
Physical Therapy — D
Public Administration — M
Secondary Education — M,O
Social Sciences Education — M,O

UNIVERSITY OF NORTH TEXAS

Accounting — M
Advertising and Public Relations — M,D,O
Anthropology — M,D,O
Applied Arts and Design—General — M,D,O
Applied Behavior Analysis — M,D,O
Art Education — M,D,O
Art History — M,D,O
Art/Fine Arts — M,D,O
Biochemistry — M,D,O
Biological and Biomedical Sciences—General — M,D,O
Biomedical Engineering — M,D,O
Business Administration and Management—General — M,D,O
Chemistry — M,D,O
Child and Family Studies — M,D,O
Clinical Psychology — M,D,O
Communication Disorders — M,D,O
Communication—General — M,D,O
Computer Engineering — M,D,O
Computer Science — M,D,O
Counseling Psychology — M,D,O
Counselor Education — M,D,O
Criminal Justice and Criminology — M,D,O
Curriculum and Instruction — M,D,O
Early Childhood Education — M,D,O
Economics — M,D,O
Education of the Gifted — M,D,O
Education—General — M,D,O
Educational Leadership and Administration — M,D,O
Educational Measurement and Evaluation — M,D,O
Educational Psychology — M,D,O
Electrical Engineering — M,D,O
Emergency Management — M,D,O
Energy and Power Engineering — M,D,O
Engineering and Applied Sciences—General — M,D,O
English as a Second Language — M,D,O
English — M,D,O
Environmental Sciences — M,D,O
Film, Television, and Video Production — M,D,O
Finance and Banking — M,D,O
French — M,D,O
Geography — M,D,O
Gerontology — M,D,O
Health Services Management and Hospital Administration — M,D,O
Higher Education — M,D,O
History — M,D,O
Hospitality Management — M,D,O
Human Development — M,D,O
Human Resources Management — M,D,O
Industrial and Manufacturing Management — M,D,O
Information Science — M,D,O
Interdisciplinary Studies — M,D,O
Interior Design — M,D,O
International Affairs — M,D,O
Internet and Interactive Multimedia — M,D,O
Journalism — M,D,O
Kinesiology and Movement Studies — M,D,O
Linguistics — M,D,O
Logistics — M,D,O

Management Information Systems — M,D,O
Management Strategy and Policy — M,D,O
Marketing — M,D,O
Mathematics — M,D,O
Mechanical Engineering — M,D,O
Molecular Biology — M,D,O
Museum Studies — M,D,O
Music Education — M,D,O
Music — M,D,O
Nonprofit Management — M,D,O
Philosophy — M,D,O
Political Science — M,D,O
Psychology—General — M,D,O
Public Administration — M,D,O
Quantitative Analysis — M,D,O
Rehabilitation Counseling — M,D,O
Sociology — M,D,O
Spanish — M,D,O
Special Education — M,D,O
Supply Chain Management — M,D,O
Textile Design — M,D,O
Travel and Tourism — M,D,O
Vocational and Technical Education — M,D,O
Writing — M,D,O

UNIVERSITY OF NORTH TEXAS AT DALLAS

Accounting — M
Business Administration and Management—General — M
Clinical Psychology — M
Counselor Education — M
Criminal Justice and Criminology — M
Curriculum and Instruction — M
Educational Leadership and Administration — M
Human Resources Management — M
Management Strategy and Policy — M
Organizational Behavior — M
Public Administration — M

UNIVERSITY OF NORTH TEXAS HEALTH SCIENCE CENTER AT FORT WORTH

Anatomy — M,D
Biochemistry — M,D
Biological and Biomedical Sciences—General — M,D
Biostatistics — M,D,O
Biotechnology — M,D
Cancer Biology/Oncology — M,D
Epidemiology — M,D,O
Forensic Sciences — M,D
Genetics — M,D
Geographic Information Systems — M,D,O
Health Services Management and Hospital Administration — M,D,O
Health Services Research — M,D,O
Immunology — M,D
International Health — M,D,O
Microbiology — M,D
Neuroscience — M,D
Osteopathic Medicine — D
Pharmaceutical Sciences — M,D
Pharmacology — M,D
Physical Therapy — M,D
Physician Assistant Studies — M,D
Physiology — M,D
Public Health—General — M,D,O
Rehabilitation Sciences — M,D

UNIVERSITY OF NORTHWESTERN–ST. PAUL

Business Administration and Management—General — M
Education—General — M
Human Services — M
Organizational Management — M
Pastoral Ministry and Counseling — M
Theology — M

UNIVERSITY OF NOTRE DAME

Accounting — M
Aerospace/Aeronautical Engineering — M,D
Applied Arts and Design—General — M
Applied Mathematics — M,D
Applied Statistics — M,D
Architecture — M
Art History — M
Art/Fine Arts — M
Biochemistry — M,D
Bioengineering — M,D
Biological and Biomedical Sciences—General — M,D
Business Administration and Management—General — M
Cell Biology — M,D
Chemical Engineering — M,D
Chemistry — M,D
Civil Engineering — M,D
Cognitive Sciences — D
Comparative Literature — D
Computational Sciences — M,D
Computer Engineering — M,D
Computer Science — M,D
Conflict Resolution and Mediation/Peace Studies — M,D
Counseling Psychology — D
Database Systems — M
Developmental Psychology — D
Ecology — M,D
Economics — M,D
Education—General — M
Electrical Engineering — M,D
Engineering and Applied Sciences—General — M,D
English — M,D
Entrepreneurship — M
Environmental Engineering — M,D
Evolutionary Biology — M,D
Finance and Banking — M
French — M

Genetics — M,D
Geosciences — M,D
Graphic Design — M
History of Science and Technology — M,D
History — M,D
Industrial Design — M
Inorganic Chemistry — M,D
International Affairs — M
Investment Management — M
Italian — M
Latin American Studies — M
Law — M,D
Management Strategy and Policy — M
Marketing — M
Mathematical and Computational Finance — M,D
Mathematics — M,D
Mechanical Engineering — M,D
Medieval and Renaissance Studies — M,D
Molecular Biology — M,D
Nonprofit Management — M
Organic Chemistry — M,D
Parasitology — M,D
Philosophy — D
Photography — M
Physical Chemistry — M,D
Physics — M,D
Physiology — M,D
Political Science — D
Psychology—General — D
Religion — M
Romance Languages — M
Sociology — D
Spanish — M
Statistics — M,D
Sustainable Development — M
Taxation — M
Theology — M,D
Writing — M

UNIVERSITY OF OKLAHOMA
Accounting — M,D
Addictions/Substance Abuse Counseling — M
Adult Education — M
Aerospace/Aeronautical Engineering — M,D
American Indian/Native American Studies — M
Analytical Chemistry — M,D
Anthropology — M,D
Applied Behavior Analysis — M,D
Applied Economics — M,D
Archaeology — M,D
Architecture — M,D
Art History — M,D
Art/Fine Arts — M
Biochemistry — M,D
Biological and Biomedical Sciences—General — D
Biomedical Engineering — M,D
Business Administration and Management—General — M,D
Chemical Engineering — M,D
Chemistry — M,D
Civil Engineering — M,D
Clinical Psychology — M,O
Communication—General — M,D
Computer Engineering — M,D
Computer Science — M,D
Construction Management — M,D
Corporate and Organizational Communication — M,D
Counseling Psychology — M,D
Criminal Justice and Criminology — M,O
Cultural Studies — M,D
Curriculum and Instruction — M,D
Dance — M
Database Systems — M,D
Early Childhood Education — M,D
Ecology — D
Economic Development — M,D
Economics — M,D
Education—General — M,D,O
Educational Leadership and Administration — M,D
Educational Media/Instructional Technology — M,D
Educational Policy — M,D
Educational Psychology — M,D
Electrical Engineering — M,D
Elementary Education — M,D
Engineering and Applied Sciences—General — M,D
Engineering Physics — M,D
English Education — M,D
English — M,D
Entrepreneurship — M,D
Environmental Engineering — M,D
Environmental Sciences — M,D
Evolutionary Biology — D
Exercise and Sports Science — M,D
Finance and Banking — M,D
Foreign Languages Education — M,D
French — M,D
Gender Studies — O
Geography — M,D
Geological Engineering — M,D
Geology — M,D
Geophysics — M,D
German — M
Health Communication — M,D
Health Promotion — M,D
Health Services Management and Hospital Administration — M,O
Higher Education — M,D,O
History of Science and Technology — M,D
History — M,D
Human Resources Management — M,O
Human Services — M,O
Industrial and Organizational Psychology — M,D
Industrial/Management Engineering — M,D

Information Studies — M
Inorganic Chemistry — M,D
Interdisciplinary Studies — M,D
Interior Design — M,D,O
International Affairs — M
International Business — M,D
Journalism — M,D
Landscape Architecture — M
Law — M,D
Liberal Studies — M,O
Library Science — M
Management Information Systems — M,D,O
Marketing — M,D
Mass Communication — M,D
Mathematics Education — M,D
Mathematics — M,D*
Mechanical Engineering — M,D
Meteorology — M,D
Microbiology — M,D
Music Education — M,D,O
Music — M,D,O
Neurobiology — D
Nonprofit Management — M,O
Organic Chemistry — M,D
Organizational Behavior — M,O
Organizational Management — M,O
Petroleum Engineering — M,D,O
Philosophy — M,D
Physical Chemistry — M,D
Physics — M,D
Plant Biology — M,D
Political Science — M,D
Project Management — M,O
Psychology—General — M,D,O
Public Administration — M
Reading Education — M,D
Rhetoric — M,D
School Psychology — M
Science Education — M,D
Social Sciences Education — M,D
Social Work — M
Sociology — M,D
Spanish — M,D
Special Education — M,D
Student Affairs — M
Supply Chain Management — M,D
Sustainable Development — M,D
Telecommunications — M
Theater — M
Urban and Regional Planning — M,D
Women's Studies — O
Writing — M

UNIVERSITY OF OKLAHOMA HEALTH SCIENCES CENTER
Allied Health—General — M,D,O
Allopathic Medicine — D
Biochemistry — M,D
Biological and Biomedical Sciences—General — M,D
Biopsychology — M,D
Biostatistics — M,D
Cell Biology — M,D
Communication Disorders — M,D,O
Dentistry — D,O
Environmental and Occupational Health — M,D
Epidemiology — M,D
Genetic Counseling — M
Health Education — D
Health Physics/Radiological Health — M,D
Health Promotion — M,D
Health Services Management and Hospital Administration — M,D
Homeland Security — M
Immunology — M,D
Medical Physics — M,D
Microbiology — M,D
Molecular Biology — M,D
Neuroscience — M,D
Nursing—General — M,D
Nutrition — M
Occupational Therapy — M
Oral and Dental Sciences — M
Pathology — D
Pharmaceutical Sciences — M,D
Pharmacy — D
Physical Therapy — M
Physician Assistant Studies — M
Physiology — M,D
Public Health—General — M,D
Radiation Biology — M,D
Reading Education — M,D,O
Rehabilitation Sciences — M
Special Education — M,D,O

UNIVERSITY OF OREGON
Accounting — M,D
Anthropology — M,D
Architecture — M
Art History — M,D
Art/Fine Arts — M
Arts Administration — M
Asian Languages — M,D
Asian Studies — M
Biochemistry — M,D
Biological and Biomedical Sciences—General — M,D
Biopsychology — M,D
Business Administration and Management—General — M,D
Chemistry — M,D
Chinese — M,D
Classics — M
Clinical Psychology — M,D
Cognitive Sciences — M,D
Communication—General — M,D
Comparative Literature — M,D
Computer Science — M,D
Dance — M
Developmental Psychology — M,D
Ecology — M,D
Economics — M,D
Education—General — M,D
English — M,D

Environmental Management and Policy — M,D
Evolutionary Biology — M,D
Finance and Banking — D
Folklore — M
French — M
Genetics — M,D
Geography — M,D
Geology — M,D
German — M,D
Historic Preservation — M
History — M,D
Information Science — M,D
Interdisciplinary Studies — M
Interior Design — M
International Affairs — M
Italian — M
Japanese — M,D
Journalism — M,D
Landscape Architecture — M
Law — M,D
Linguistics — M,D
Management Information Systems — M
Marine Biology — M,D
Marketing — D
Mathematics — M,D
Media Studies — M,D
Molecular Biology — M,D
Music Education — M,D
Music — M,D
Neuroscience — M,D
Philosophy — M,D
Physics — M,D
Physiology — M,D
Political Science — M,D
Psychology—General — M,D
Public Policy — M
Quantitative Analysis — M,D
Romance Languages — M,D
Russian — M
Social Psychology — M,D
Sociology — M,D
Spanish — M
Sports Management — M
Theater — M,D
Urban and Regional Planning — M
Writing — M

UNIVERSITY OF OTTAWA
Aerospace/Aeronautical Engineering — M,D
Allopathic Medicine — M,D
Anthropology — M
Biochemistry — M,D
Bioengineering — M,D
Biological and Biomedical Sciences—General — M,D
Biomedical Engineering — M
Business Administration and Management—General — M
Canadian Studies — D
Cell Biology — M,D
Chemical Engineering — M,D
Chemistry — M,D
Civil Engineering — M,D
Classics — M,D
Communication Disorders — M
Communication—General — M
Community Health — M,D,O
Computer Engineering — M,D
Computer Science — M,D
Criminal Justice and Criminology — M,D
Economics — M,D
Education—General — M,D,O
Electrical Engineering — M,D
Electronic Commerce — M,D,O
Engineering and Applied Sciences—General — M,D,O
Engineering Management — M,O
English — M,D
Epidemiology — M
Finance and Banking — D,O
French — M,D
Geography — M,D
Geosciences — M,D
Health Services Management and Hospital Administration — M
Health Services Research — D,O
History — M,D
Immunology — M,D
Information Science — M,O
Interdisciplinary Studies — D,O
International Development — M,D
Kinesiology and Movement Studies — M
Law — M,D
Linguistics — M,D
Mathematics — M,D
Mechanical Engineering — M,D
Microbiology — M,D
Molecular Biology — M,D
Music Education — M,O
Music — M,O
Nursing—General — M,D,O
Philosophy — M,D
Physics — M,D
Political Science — M,D
Project Management — M,O
Psychology—General — D
Public Administration — D,O
Public Health—General — D
Rehabilitation Sciences — M
Religion — M,D
Social Work — M
Sociology — M
Spanish — M,D
Statistics — M,D
Systems Science — M,D,O
Theater — M
Translation and Interpretation — M,D
Women's Studies — M

UNIVERSITY OF PENNSYLVANIA
Accounting — M,D
Acute Care/Critical Care Nursing — M
Adult Nursing — M

African Studies — M,D
Allopathic Medicine — D
Anthropology — M,D
Applied Economics — D
Applied Mathematics — D
Applied Psychology — M
Archaeology — M,D
Architecture — M,D,O
Art History — M,D
Art/Fine Arts — M,O
Artificial Intelligence/Robotics — M
Asian Studies — M
Biochemistry — D
Bioengineering — M,D
Bioethics — M
Biological and Biomedical Sciences—General — M,D
Biostatistics — M,D
Biotechnology — M
Business Administration and Management—General — M,D
Cancer Biology/Oncology — D
Cell Biology — D
Chemical Engineering — M,D
Chemistry — M,D
Classics — M,D
Clinical Laboratory Sciences/Medical Technology — M
Communication—General — D
Comparative Literature — M,D
Computational Biology — D
Computational Sciences — M,D
Computer Art and Design — M,D
Computer Science — M,D
Counseling Psychology — M
Counselor Education — M
Criminal Justice and Criminology — M
Demography and Population Studies — M,D
Dentistry — D
Developmental Biology — D
Economic Development — M,O
Economics — M,D
Education—General — M,D,O
Educational Leadership and Administration — M,D
Educational Measurement and Evaluation — M,D
Educational Media/Instructional Technology — M
Educational Policy — M,D
Electrical Engineering — M,D
Elementary Education — M
Engineering and Applied Sciences—General — M,D*
English as a Second Language — M
English Education — M,D
English — M,D
Entrepreneurship — M
Environmental and Occupational Health — M
Environmental Management and Policy — M
Environmental Sciences — M,D
Epidemiology — M
Ethics — M,D
Family Nurse Practitioner Studies — M,O
Finance and Banking — M,D
Foundations and Philosophy of Education — M,D
French — M,D
Genetics — D
Genomic Sciences — D
Geographic Information Systems — M,D,O
Geosciences — M,D
German — M,D
Gerontological Nursing — M
Graphic Design — M,O
Health Services Management and Hospital Administration — M,D
Health Services Research — M
Higher Education — M,D
Historic Preservation — M,O
History of Science and Technology — M,D
History — M,D
Human Development — M,D
Human Genetics — M
Immunology — D
Information Science — M,D
Insurance — M,D
International Affairs — M
International and Comparative Education — M
International Business — M
International Health — M
Internet and Interactive Multimedia — M,O
Italian — M,D
Landscape Architecture — M,O
Law — M,D
Legal and Justice Studies — M,D
Liberal Studies — M
Linguistics — M,D
Management Information Systems — M,D
Marketing — M,D
Materials Engineering — M,D
Materials Sciences — M,D
Maternal and Child/Neonatal Nursing — M
Mathematics — M,D
Mechanical Engineering — M,D
Mechanics — M,D
Medical Physics — M,D
Microbiology — D
Molecular Biology — D
Molecular Biophysics — D
Multilingual and Multicultural Education — M
Music — M,D
Nanotechnology — M
Near and Middle Eastern Studies — M
Neuroscience — D
Nonprofit Management — M,O
Nurse Anesthesia — M
Nurse Midwifery — M

Nursing and Healthcare Administration	M,D
Nursing—General	M,D,O
Organizational Management	M,O
Pediatric Nursing	M
Pharmacology	D
Philosophy	M,D
Physics	M,D
Physiology	D
Political Science	M,D,O
Psychiatric Nursing	M
Psychology—General	D
Public Administration	M,O
Public Health—General	M
Public Policy	M,D
Reading Education	M
Real Estate	M,D
Religion	D
Romance Languages	M,D
Science Education	M,O
Secondary Education	M
Social Work	M,D
Sociology	M,D
Spanish	M,D
Statistics	M,D
Systems Engineering	M,D
Urban and Regional Planning	M,D,O
Urban Design	M,D,O
Urban Education	M
Veterinary Medicine	D
Virology	D
Women's Health Nursing	M

UNIVERSITY OF PHILOSOPHICAL RESEARCH

Psychology—General	M
Theology	M

UNIVERSITY OF PHOENIX–ATLANTA CAMPUS

Accounting	M
Business Administration and Management—General	M
Health Services Management and Hospital Administration	M
Human Resources Management	M
International Business	M
Management Information Systems	M
Management of Technology	M
Marketing	M
Nursing Education	M
Nursing—General	M
Public Administration	M

UNIVERSITY OF PHOENIX–AUGUSTA CAMPUS

Accounting	M
Business Administration and Management—General	M
Criminal Justice and Criminology	M
Health Services Management and Hospital Administration	M
Human Resources Management	M
International Business	M
Management Information Systems	M
Management of Technology	M
Marketing	M
Nursing Education	M
Nursing—General	M
Public Administration	M

UNIVERSITY OF PHOENIX–BAY AREA CAMPUS

Accounting	M,D
Adult Education	M,D,O
Business Administration and Management—General	M,D
Criminal Justice and Criminology	M
Early Childhood Education	M,D,O
Education—General	M,D,O
Educational Leadership and Administration	M,D,O
Elementary Education	M,D,O
Energy Management and Policy	M,D
Gerontological Nursing	M,D
Health Services Management and Hospital Administration	M,D
Higher Education	M,D,O
Human Resources Management	M,D
International Business	M,D
Management Information Systems	M,D
Management of Technology	M,D
Marketing	M,D
Marriage and Family Therapy	M
Nursing and Healthcare Administration	M,D
Nursing Education	M,D
Nursing Informatics	M,D
Nursing—General	M,D
Organizational Management	M,D
Project Management	M,D
Public Administration	M,D
Secondary Education	M,D,O
Special Education	M,D,O

UNIVERSITY OF PHOENIX–CENTRAL VALLEY CAMPUS

Accounting	M
Business Administration and Management—General	M
Community Health	M
Computer Education	M
Curriculum and Instruction	M
Education—General	M
Elementary Education	M
Gerontology	M
Health Services Management and Hospital Administration	M
Human Resources Management	M
International Business	M
Management Information Systems	M

Management of Technology	M
Marketing	M
Marriage and Family Therapy	M
Nursing—General	M
Public Administration	M
Secondary Education	M

UNIVERSITY OF PHOENIX–CHARLOTTE CAMPUS

Accounting	M
Business Administration and Management—General	M
Gerontology	M
Health Education	M
Health Informatics	M
Health Services Management and Hospital Administration	M
International Business	M
Management Information Systems	M
Management of Technology	M
Nursing Education	M
Nursing Informatics	M
Nursing—General	M

UNIVERSITY OF PHOENIX–COLORADO CAMPUS

Accounting	M
Business Administration and Management—General	M
Curriculum and Instruction	M
Education—General	M
Educational Leadership and Administration	M
Electronic Commerce	M
Elementary Education	M
Health Services Management and Hospital Administration	M
Human Resources Management	M
International Business	M
Management Information Systems	M
Management of Technology	M
Marketing	M
Nursing—General	M
Public Administration	M
School Psychology	M
Secondary Education	M

UNIVERSITY OF PHOENIX–COLORADO SPRINGS DOWNTOWN CAMPUS

Accounting	M
Business Administration and Management—General	M
Curriculum and Instruction	M,O
Education—General	M,O
Educational Leadership and Administration	M,O
Elementary Education	M,O
Gerontology	M
Health Education	M
Health Services Management and Hospital Administration	M
Human Resources Management	M
International Business	M
Management Information Systems	M
Management of Technology	M
Marketing	M
Nursing—General	M
Public Administration	M
School Psychology	M,O
Secondary Education	M,O

UNIVERSITY OF PHOENIX–COLUMBUS GEORGIA CAMPUS

Accounting	M
Business Administration and Management—General	M
Electronic Commerce	M
Human Resources Management	M
International Business	M
Management Information Systems	M
Management of Technology	M
Marketing	M
Nursing—General	M
Public Administration	M

UNIVERSITY OF PHOENIX–DALLAS CAMPUS

Accounting	M
Business Administration and Management—General	M
Criminal Justice and Criminology	M
Curriculum and Instruction	M
Education—General	M
Electronic Commerce	M
Human Resources Management	M
International Business	M
Management Information Systems	M
Management of Technology	M
Marketing	M
Public Administration	M

UNIVERSITY OF PHOENIX–HAWAII CAMPUS

Accounting	M
Business Administration and Management—General	M
Community Health	M
Curriculum and Instruction	M
Education—General	M
Educational Leadership and Administration	M
Elementary Education	M
Family Nurse Practitioner Studies	M
Gerontology	M
Health Services Management and Hospital Administration	M
Human Resources Management	M
International Business	M
Management Information Systems	M
Management of Technology	M
Marketing	M
Nursing Education	M

Nursing—General	M
Public Administration	M
Secondary Education	M
Special Education	M

UNIVERSITY OF PHOENIX–HOUSTON CAMPUS

Accounting	M
Business Administration and Management—General	M
Curriculum and Instruction	M
Education—General	M
Electronic Commerce	M
Health Services Management and Hospital Administration	M
Human Resources Management	M
International Business	M
Management Information Systems	M
Management of Technology	M
Marketing	M
Nursing—General	M
Public Administration	M

UNIVERSITY OF PHOENIX–JERSEY CITY CAMPUS

Accounting	M
Business Administration and Management—General	M
Criminal Justice and Criminology	M
Human Resources Management	M
International Business	M
Management Information Systems	M
Management of Technology	M
Marketing	M
Psychology—General	M
Public Administration	M

UNIVERSITY OF PHOENIX–LAS VEGAS CAMPUS

Accounting	M
Allied Health—General	M
Business Administration and Management—General	M
Counseling Psychology	M
Counselor Education	M
Curriculum and Instruction	M
Education—General	M
Educational Leadership and Administration	M
Elementary Education	M
Human Resources Management	M
International Business	M
Management Information Systems	M
Management of Technology	M
Marketing	M
Marriage and Family Therapy	M
Public Administration	M
School Psychology	M

UNIVERSITY OF PHOENIX–NEW MEXICO CAMPUS

Accounting	M
Business Administration and Management—General	M
Counselor Education	M
Curriculum and Instruction	M
Education—General	M
Educational Leadership and Administration	M
Electronic Commerce	M
Elementary Education	M
Health Services Management and Hospital Administration	M
Human Resources Management	M
International Business	M
Management Information Systems	M
Management of Technology	M
Marketing	M
Nursing Education	M
Nursing—General	M
Secondary Education	M

UNIVERSITY OF PHOENIX–NORTH FLORIDA CAMPUS

Accounting	M
Business Administration and Management—General	M
Computer Education	M
Curriculum and Instruction	M
Early Childhood Education	M
Education—General	M
Educational Leadership and Administration	M
Elementary Education	M
Health Services Management and Hospital Administration	M
Human Resources Management	M
International Business	M
Management Information Systems	M
Marketing	M
Mathematics Education	M
Nursing Education	M
Nursing—General	M
Public Administration	M
Secondary Education	M

UNIVERSITY OF PHOENIX–ONLINE CAMPUS

Accounting	M,O
Adult Education	M,O
Business Administration and Management—General	M,D,O
Computer Education	M,O
Conflict Resolution and Mediation/Peace Studies	M,O
Criminal Justice and Criminology	M
Curriculum and Instruction	M,D,O
Early Childhood Education	M,O
Education—General	M,O
Educational Leadership and Administration	M,D,O

Educational Media/Instructional Technology	D,O
Elementary Education	M,O
Energy Management and Policy	M,O
English as a Second Language	M,O
English Education	M,O
Family Nurse Practitioner Studies	M,O
Health Education	M,O
Health Informatics	M,O
Health Services Management and Hospital Administration	M,D,O
Higher Education	D,O
Homeland Security	M
Human Resources Management	M,O
Industrial and Organizational Psychology	M,D,O
International Business	M,O
Management Information Systems	M
Management of Technology	M,O
Marketing	M,O
Mathematics Education	M,O
Middle School Education	M,O
Nursing Education	M,O
Nursing—General	M,D,O
Organizational Management	D,O
Project Management	M,O
Psychology—General	M,O
Public Administration	M,O
Reading Education	M,O
Science Education	M,O
Secondary Education	M,O
Special Education	M,O

UNIVERSITY OF PHOENIX–PHOENIX CAMPUS

Accounting	M,O
Adult Education	M
Business Administration and Management—General	M,O
Clinical Psychology	M
Counseling Psychology	M
Counselor Education	M
Criminal Justice and Criminology	M
Curriculum and Instruction	M
Early Childhood Education	M
Education—General	M
Educational Leadership and Administration	M
Elementary Education	M
Energy Management and Policy	M,O
Family Nurse Practitioner Studies	M,O
Gerontological Nursing	M,O
Health Services Management and Hospital Administration	M,O
Homeland Security	M
Human Resources Management	M,O
International Business	M,O
Management of Technology	M,O
Marketing	M,O
Marriage and Family Therapy	M
Medical Informatics	M,O
Nursing Education	M,O
Nursing Informatics	M,O
Nursing—General	M,O
Project Management	M,O
Psychology—General	M
Public Administration	M
Reading Education	M
Secondary Education	M
Social Psychology	M
Special Education	M
Vocational and Technical Education	M

UNIVERSITY OF PHOENIX–SACRAMENTO VALLEY CAMPUS

Accounting	M
Adult Education	M,O
Business Administration and Management—General	M
Curriculum and Instruction	M,O
Education—General	M,O
Elementary Education	M,O
Family Nurse Practitioner Studies	M
Health Services Management and Hospital Administration	M
Human Resources Management	M
International Business	M
Management Information Systems	M
Management of Technology	M
Marketing	M
Nursing Education	M
Nursing—General	M
Public Administration	M
Secondary Education	M,O

UNIVERSITY OF PHOENIX–SAN ANTONIO CAMPUS

Accounting	M
Business Administration and Management—General	M
Criminal Justice and Criminology	M
Curriculum and Instruction	M
Electronic Commerce	M
Health Services Management and Hospital Administration	M
Human Resources Management	M
International Business	M
Management Information Systems	M
Management of Technology	M
Marketing	M
Nursing—General	M
Public Administration	M

UNIVERSITY OF PHOENIX–SAN DIEGO CAMPUS

Accounting	M
Business Administration and Management—General	M
Computer Education	M

M—masters degree; D—doctorate; O—other advanced degree; *—Close-Up and/or Display

Curriculum and Instruction — M
Education—General — M
Elementary Education — M
English as a Second Language — M
Human Resources Management — M
International Business — M
Management Information Systems — M
Management of Technology — M
Marketing — M
Nursing Education — M
Nursing—General — M
Public Administration — M
Secondary Education — M

UNIVERSITY OF PHOENIX–SOUTHERN ARIZONA CAMPUS

Accounting — M
Adult Education — M,O
Business Administration and
  Management—General — M
Counselor Education — M,O
Curriculum and Instruction — M,O
Education—General — M,O
Educational Leadership and
  Administration — M,O
Educational Psychology — M,O
Elementary Education — M,O
Human Resources Management — M
International Business — M
Management Information Systems — M
Management of Technology — M
Marketing — M
Psychology—General — M
Secondary Education — M,O
Special Education — M,O

UNIVERSITY OF PHOENIX–SOUTHERN CALIFORNIA CAMPUS

Accounting — M
Adult Education — M,O
Business Administration and
  Management—General — M
Counselor Education — M
Criminal Justice and Criminology — M
Education—General — M,O
Educational Leadership and
  Administration — M,O
Elementary Education — M,O
Energy Management and
  Policy — M
English as a Second Language — M,O
Family Nurse Practitioner Studies — M,O
Health Services Management and
  Hospital Administration — M
Homeland Security — M
Human Resources Management — M
International Business — M
Management of Technology — M
Marketing — M
Marriage and Family Therapy — M
Nursing Education — M,O
Nursing Informatics — M,O
Nursing—General — M,O
Project Management — M
Psychology—General — M
Public Administration — M
Secondary Education — M,O

UNIVERSITY OF PHOENIX–SOUTH FLORIDA CAMPUS

Accounting — M
Business Administration and
  Management—General — M
Computer Education — M
Curriculum and Instruction — M
Early Childhood Education — M
Education—General — M
Educational Leadership and
  Administration — M
Elementary Education — M
Health Services Management and
  Hospital Administration — M
Human Resources Management — M
International Business — M
Management Information Systems — M
Marketing — M
Mathematics Education — M
Nursing Education — M
Nursing—General — M
Public Administration — M
Secondary Education — M

UNIVERSITY OF PHOENIX–UTAH CAMPUS

Accounting — M
Business Administration and
  Management—General — M
Curriculum and Instruction — M
Education—General — M
Educational Leadership and
  Administration — M
Elementary Education — M
Human Resources Management — M
International Business — M
Management Information Systems — M
Management of Technology — M
Marketing — M
Nursing Education — M
Nursing—General — M
School Psychology — M
Secondary Education — M
Special Education — M

UNIVERSITY OF PHOENIX–WASHINGTON D.C. CAMPUS

Accounting — M,D
Adult Education — M,D,O
Business Administration and
  Management—General — M,D
Computer Education — M,D,O
Criminal Justice and Criminology — M
Curriculum and Instruction — M,D,O
Early Childhood Education — M,D,O
Education—General — M,D,O

Educational Leadership and
  Administration — M,D,O
Educational Media/Instructional
  Technology — M,D,O
Elementary Education — M,D,O
English as a Second Language — M,D,O
English Education — M,D,O
Gerontology — M,D
Health Education — M,D
Health Informatics — M,D
Health Services Management and
  Hospital Administration — M,D
Higher Education — M,D,O
Human Resources Management — M,D
Industrial and Organizational
  Psychology — M,D
Management Information Systems — M,D
Mathematics Education — M,D,O
Nursing and Healthcare
  Administration — M,D
Nursing Education — M,D
Nursing Informatics — M,D
Nursing—General — M,D
Organizational Management — M,D
Psychology—General — M,D
Public Administration — M,D
Secondary Education — M,D,O
Special Education — M,D

UNIVERSITY OF PHOENIX–WESTERN WASHINGTON CAMPUS

Business Administration and
  Management—General — M
Criminal Justice and Criminology — M

UNIVERSITY OF PIKEVILLE

Business Administration and
  Management—General — M
Education—General — M
Educational Leadership and
  Administration — M
Optometry — D
Osteopathic Medicine — D

UNIVERSITY OF PITTSBURGH

Accounting — M,D
Acute Care/Critical Care Nursing — M,D
African Studies — O
Allopathic Medicine — D
Anthropology — M,D
Applied Behavior Analysis — M,D
Applied Mathematics — M,D
Applied Psychology — M,D
Applied Statistics — M,D
Architectural History — M,D
Art History — M,D
Artificial Intelligence/Robotics — M,D
Asian Studies — M,O
Astronomy — D
Athletic Training and Sports
  Medicine — M
Bioengineering — M,D
Bioethics — M
Bioinformatics — M,D,O
Biological and Biomedical
  Sciences—General — D
Biostatistics — M,D
Business Administration and
  Management—General — M,D*
Cell Biology — M,D
Chemical Engineering — M,D
Chemistry — M,D
Chinese — M
Civil Engineering — M,D
Clinical Laboratory
  Sciences/Medical Technology — D
Clinical Psychology — D
Clinical Research — M,O
Communication Disorders — M,D
Communication—General — M,D
Community Health — M,D,O
Computational Biology — D
Computer and Information
  Systems Security — M,D,O
Computer Engineering — M,D
Computer Science — M,D
Criminal Justice and Criminology — M
Cultural Studies — O
Dentistry — D,O
Developmental Biology — D
Developmental Psychology — M,D
Disability Studies — O
Early Childhood Education — M
East European and Russian Studies — O
Ecology — D
Economics — M,D
Education—General — M,D*
Educational Leadership and
  Administration — M,D
Educational Measurement and
  Evaluation — M,D
Educational Policy — D
Electrical Engineering — M,D
Elementary Education — M
Energy Management and
  Policy — M
Engineering and Applied
  Sciences—General — M,D
English as a Second Language — M,D,O
English Education — M,D
English — M,D
Environmental and Occupational
  Health — M,D
Environmental Engineering — M,D
Environmental Law — M
Environmental Sciences — M,D
Epidemiology — M,D
Evolutionary Biology — D
Exercise and Sports Science — M,D
Family Nurse Practitioner Studies — M,D
Film, Television, and Video
  Theory and Criticism — M,D,O
Finance and Banking — M,D
Foreign Languages Education — M,D

Foundations and Philosophy of
  Education — M,D
French — M,D
Genetic Counseling — M,D,O
Geographic Information Systems — M,D
Geology — M,D
Gerontological Nursing — M,D
Health Education — M,D
Health Informatics — M,D
Health Law — M
Health Services Management and
  Hospital Administration — M,D,O
Higher Education — M,D
Hispanic and Latin American
  Languages — M,D
History of Science and Technology — D
History — M,D
Human Genetics — M,D,O
Human Resources Management — M,D
Immunology — D
Industrial and Manufacturing
  Management — M
Industrial/Management
  Engineering — M,D
Infectious Diseases — M,D
Information Science — M,D,O
Information Studies — M,D
Intellectual Property Law — M
Interdisciplinary Studies — D
International Affairs — M,D,O
International and Comparative
  Education — O
International Business — O
International Development — M,D
Italian — M,D
Japanese — M
Latin American Studies — O
Law — M
Legal and Justice Studies — M
Library Science — M,D
Management Information Systems — M,D
Management Strategy and Policy — M,D
Marketing — M,D
Materials Sciences — M,D
Maternal and Child/Neonatal
  Nursing — M,D
Mathematics Education — M,D
Mathematics — M,D
Mechanical Engineering — M,D
Medieval and Renaissance Studies — O
Microbiology — M,D
Military and Defense Studies — M
Modeling and Simulation — D
Molecular Biology — D
Molecular Biophysics — D
Molecular Genetics — D
Molecular Pathology — D
Molecular Pharmacology — D
Molecular Physiology — D
Music — M,D
Neurobiology — D
Neuroscience — D
Nonprofit Management — M
Nurse Anesthesia — D
Nurse Midwifery — D
Nursing and Healthcare
  Administration — M,D
Nursing Informatics — M,D
Nursing—General — D
Nutrition — M,D
Occupational Therapy — M,D
Oral and Dental Sciences — M,D,O
Organizational Behavior — M,D
Pathology — D
Pediatric Nursing — M,D
Petroleum Engineering — M,D
Pharmaceutical Administration — M
Pharmaceutical Sciences — M,D
Pharmacy — D
Philosophy — D
Physical Therapy — M,D
Physician Assistant Studies — M
Physics — M,D*
Political Science — M,D
Psychiatric Nursing — M,D
Psychology—General — D
Public Administration — M,D
Public Health—General — M,D,O
Public Policy — M,D
Reading Education — M,D
Rehabilitation Sciences — M,D
Science Education — M,D
Secondary Education — M,D
Slavic Languages — M,D
Social Sciences Education — M,D
Social Work — M,D,O
Sociology — M,D
Spanish — M,D
Special Education — M,D
Statistics — M,D
Structural Biology — D
Supply Chain Management — M
Systems Biology — D
Telecommunications — M,D,O
Theater — M,D
Urban and Regional Planning — M
Virology — D
Vision Sciences — M,D
Western European Studies — O
Women's Studies — O
Writing — M,D

UNIVERSITY OF PORTLAND

Biomedical Engineering — M
Business Administration and
  Management—General — M
Civil Engineering — M
Communication—General — M
Computer Science — M
Corporate and Organizational
  Communication — M
Education—General — M,D
Educational Leadership and
  Administration — M,D

Electrical Engineering — M
Engineering and Applied
  Sciences—General — M
English as a Second Language — M,D
Entrepreneurship — M
Family Nurse Practitioner Studies — M
Finance and Banking — M
Health Services Management and
  Hospital Administration — M
Industrial and Manufacturing
  Management — M
Management of Technology — M
Marketing — M
Mechanical Engineering — M
Nonprofit Management — M
Nursing Education — M,D
Nursing—General — M,D
Organizational Management — M,D
Pastoral Ministry and Counseling — M
Reading Education — M,D
Special Education — M
Sustainability Management — M
Theater — M

UNIVERSITY OF PRINCE EDWARD ISLAND

Anatomy — M,D
Bacteriology — M,D
Biological and Biomedical
  Sciences—General — M,D
Chemistry — M,D
Education—General — M,D
Educational Leadership and
  Administration — M,D
Environmental Sciences — M,D
Epidemiology — M,D
Geography — M
Immunology — M,D
Parasitology — M,D
Pathology — M,D
Pharmacology — M,D
Physiology — M,D
Toxicology — M,D
Veterinary Medicine — D
Veterinary Sciences — M,D
Virology — M,D

UNIVERSITY OF PUERTO RICO, MAYAGÜEZ CAMPUS

Aerospace/Aeronautical
  Engineering — M,D
Agricultural Economics and
  Agribusiness — M
Agricultural Education — M
Agricultural Sciences—
  General — M
Agronomy and Soil Sciences — M
Animal Sciences — M
Applied Mathematics — M
Bioengineering — M,D
Biological and Biomedical
  Sciences—General — M
Business Administration and
  Management—General — M
Chemical Engineering — M,D
Chemistry — M,D
Civil Engineering — M,D
Computational Sciences — M
Computer Engineering — M,D
Computer Science — M,D
Construction Engineering — M,D
Electrical Engineering — M,D
Energy and Power
  Engineering — M,D
Engineering and Applied
  Sciences—General — M,D
Engineering Management — M
English Education — M
English — M
Environmental Engineering — M,D
Environmental Sciences — M,D
Exercise and Sports Science — M
Finance and Banking — M
Food Science and
  Technology — M
Geology — M
Geotechnical Engineering — M,D
Higher Education — M
Hispanic Studies — M
Horticulture — M
Human Resources Management — M
Industrial and Manufacturing
  Management — M
Industrial/Management
  Engineering — M
Information Science — M,D
Kinesiology and Movement Studies — M
Manufacturing Engineering — M,D
Marine Sciences — M,D
Materials Engineering — M,D
Materials Sciences — M,D
Mathematics Education — M
Mathematics — M
Mechanical Engineering — M,D
Physical Chemistry — M,D
Physics — M
Rural Sociology — M
Structural Engineering — M,D
Transportation and Highway
  Engineering — M,D

UNIVERSITY OF PUERTO RICO, MEDICAL SCIENCES CAMPUS

Acute Care/Critical Care Nursing — M
Adult Nursing — M
Allied Health—General — M,D,O
Allopathic Medicine — D
Anatomy — M,D
Biochemistry — M,D
Biological and Biomedical
  Sciences—General — M
Biostatistics — M
Clinical Laboratory
  Sciences/Medical Technology — M,O
Clinical Research — M,O

Communication Disorders	M,D
Community Health Nursing	M
Demography and Population Studies	M
Dentistry	D
Environmental and Occupational Health	M,D
Epidemiology	M
Family Nurse Practitioner Studies	M
Gerontological Nursing	M
Gerontology	M,O
Health Education	M
Health Informatics	M
Health Promotion	O
Health Services Management and Hospital Administration	M
Health Services Research	M
Industrial Hygiene	M
Maternal and Child Health	M
Maternal and Child/Neonatal Nursing	M
Microbiology	M,D
Nurse Midwifery	M,O
Nursing—General	M
Nutrition	M,D,O
Occupational Therapy	M
Oral and Dental Sciences	O
Pediatric Nursing	M
Pharmaceutical Sciences	M,D
Pharmacology	M,D
Pharmacy	M,D
Physical Therapy	M
Physiology	M,D
Psychiatric Nursing	M
Special Education	O
Toxicology	M,D

UNIVERSITY OF PUERTO RICO, RÍO PIEDRAS CAMPUS

Accounting	M,D
Architecture	M
Biological and Biomedical Sciences—General	M,D
Business Administration and Management—General	M,D
Cell Biology	M,D
Chemistry	M,D
Clinical Psychology	M,D
Communication—General	M
Comparative Literature	M
Counselor Education	M,D
Curriculum and Instruction	M,D
Early Childhood Education	M
Ecology	M,D
Economic Development	M
Economics	M,D
Education—General	M,D
Educational Leadership and Administration	M,D
Educational Measurement and Evaluation	M
English as a Second Language	M
English	M,D
Environmental Management and Policy	M
Environmental Sciences	M,D
Evolutionary Biology	M,D
Exercise and Sports Science	M
Family and Consumer Sciences—General	M
Finance and Banking	M,D
Foreign Languages Education	M,D
Genetics	M,D
Hispanic Studies	M,D
History	M,D
Human Resources Management	M,D
Industrial and Manufacturing Management	M,D
Industrial and Organizational Psychology	M,D
Information Science	M,O
Information Studies	M,O
International Business	M,D
Journalism	M
Law	M,D
Library Science	M,O
Linguistics	M,D
Marketing	M,D
Mass Communication	M
Mathematics Education	M,D
Mathematics	M,D
Molecular Biology	M,D
Neuroscience	M,D
Nutrition	M
Philosophy	M
Physics	M,D
Psychology—General	M,D
Public Administration	M
Public Policy	M
Quantitative Analysis	M,D
Rehabilitation Counseling	M
Science Education	M,D
Social Psychology	M,D
Social Sciences Education	M,D
Social Work	M,D
Sociology	M
Special Education	M
Translation and Interpretation	M,O
Urban and Regional Planning	M

UNIVERSITY OF PUGET SOUND

Counseling Psychology	M
Counselor Education	M
Education—General	M
Elementary Education	M
Occupational Therapy	M,D
Physical Therapy	D
Secondary Education	M

UNIVERSITY OF REDLANDS

Business Administration and Management—General	M
Communication Disorders	M

Education—General	M,D,O
Geographic Information Systems	M
Management Information Systems	M
Music	M

UNIVERSITY OF REGINA

Adult Education	M
Analytical Chemistry	M,D
Anthropology	M
Applied Economics	M
Applied Psychology	M,D
Art/Fine Arts	M
Biochemistry	M,D
Biological and Biomedical Sciences—General	M,D
Biophysics	M,D
Business Administration and Management—General	M,O
Canadian Studies	M,D
Cancer Biology/Oncology	M,D
Chemistry	M,D
Clinical Psychology	M,D
Computer Engineering	M,D
Computer Science	M,D
Criminal Justice and Criminology	M
Curriculum and Instruction	M
Economics	M,D,O
Education—General	M,D,O
Educational Leadership and Administration	M
Educational Psychology	M
Engineering and Applied Sciences—General	M,D
Engineering Management	M,O
English	M,D
Environmental Engineering	M,D
Experimental Psychology	M,D
Film, Television, and Video Production	M
French	M
Geography	M,D
Geology	M,D
Gerontology	M
Health Services Management and Hospital Administration	M,D,O
History	M
Human Resources Development	M
Human Resources Management	M,O
Industrial/Management Engineering	M,D
Inorganic Chemistry	M,D
Interdisciplinary Studies	M
International Business	M,O
Journalism	M
Kinesiology and Movement Studies	M,D
Linguistics	M,D
Mathematics	M,D
Music	M
Nursing—General	M
Organic Chemistry	M,D
Organizational Management	M,O
Petroleum Engineering	M,D
Philosophy	M
Physics	M,D
Political Science	M
Project Management	M,O
Psychology—General	M,D
Public Administration	M,D,O
Public Policy	M,D,O
Religion	M
Social Sciences	M
Social Work	M,D
Sociology	M
Software Engineering	M
Statistics	M,D
Systems Engineering	M,D
Theoretical Chemistry	M,D
Women's Studies	M
Writing	M,D

UNIVERSITY OF RHODE ISLAND

Accounting	M,D
Acute Care/Critical Care Nursing	M,D
Animal Sciences	M
Anthropology	M
Applied Mathematics	M,D
Aquaculture	M,D
Archaeology	M
Biochemistry	M,D
Biological and Biomedical Sciences—General	M,D
Biomedical Engineering	M,D
Biotechnology	M,D
Business Administration and Management—General	M,D*
Cell Biology	M,D
Chemical Engineering	M,D,O
Chemistry	M,D
Child and Family Studies	M
Civil Engineering	M,D
Clinical Laboratory Sciences/Medical Technology	M,D
Clinical Psychology	M,D
Communication Disorders	M
Communication—General	M
Computer Art and Design	M
Computer Engineering	M,D
Computer Science	M,D,O
Counseling Psychology	M
Economics	M,D
Education—General	M,D
Electrical Engineering	M,D
Engineering and Applied Sciences—General	M,D,O
English	M,D
Entrepreneurship	M
Environmental Engineering	M,D
Environmental Management and Policy	M,D
Environmental Sciences	M,D
Exercise and Sports Science	M

Family Nurse Practitioner Studies	M,D
Finance and Banking	M,D
Fish, Game, and Wildlife Management	M,D
Food Science and Technology	M,D
Forensic Sciences	M,D,O
Gender Studies	M,D,O
Geosciences	M,D
Gerontological Nursing	M,D
Health Education	M
Health Services Management and Hospital Administration	M,D
History	M
Human Development	M
Human Resources Management	M,O
Industrial and Labor Relations	M,O
Information Studies	M
International Affairs	M
Library Science	M
Management Strategy and Policy	M,D
Marine Affairs	M,D
Marine Sciences	M,D
Marketing	M,D
Marriage and Family Therapy	M
Mathematics	M,D
Medicinal and Pharmaceutical Chemistry	M,D
Microbiology	M,D
Molecular Biology	M,D
Molecular Genetics	M,D
Music Education	M
Music	M
Natural Resources	M,D
Nursing Education	M,D
Nursing—General	M,D
Nutrition	M,D
Ocean Engineering	M,D
Oceanography	M,D
Pharmaceutical Sciences	M,D
Pharmacology	M,D
Pharmacy	M,D
Physical Education	M
Physical Therapy	D
Physics	M,D
Political Science	M
Psychology—General	M,D
Public Administration	M
Public Policy	M
Reading Education	M,D
Recreation and Park Management	M
School Psychology	M,D
Spanish	M
Special Education	M
Sport Psychology	M
Statistics	M,D,O
Student Affairs	M
Supply Chain Management	M,D
Toxicology	M,D
Women's Studies	O

UNIVERSITY OF RICHMOND

Business Administration and Management—General	M
Law	D

UNIVERSITY OF RIO GRANDE

Art Education	M
Education—General	M
Educational Leadership and Administration	M
Physical Education	M
Special Education	M

UNIVERSITY OF ROCHESTER

Accounting	M,D
Acute Care/Critical Care Nursing	M,D
Adult Nursing	M,D
Allopathic Medicine	D
American Studies	M,D
Anatomy	M
Archives/Archival Administration	M
Art History	D
Art/Fine Arts	D
Astronomy	M,D
Biochemistry	D
Biological and Biomedical Sciences—General	M,D
Biomedical Engineering	M,D
Biophysics	D
Biostatistics	M
Business Administration and Management—General	M,D
Chemical Engineering	M,D*
Chemistry	D
Clinical Psychology	D
Clinical Research	M
Cognitive Sciences	D
Computational Biology	D
Computer Engineering	M,D
Computer Science	M,D
Counselor Education	M,D
Curriculum and Instruction	M,D
Database Systems	M
Developmental Psychology	D
Economics	D
Education—General	M,D
Educational Leadership and Administration	M,D
Educational Policy	M,D
Electrical Engineering	M,D
Energy and Power Engineering	M
Energy Management and Policy	M
Engineering and Applied Sciences—General	M,D
English	M,D
Entrepreneurship	M
Environmental Management and Policy	M
Epidemiology	D

Family Nurse Practitioner Studies	M,D
Finance and Banking	M,D
Foundations and Philosophy of Education	D
Genetics	D
Genomic Sciences	D
Geology	M,D
Geosciences	M,D
Gerontological Nursing	M,D
Health Services Management and Hospital Administration	M,D
Health Services Research	M
Higher Education	M
Historic Preservation	M
History	M,D
Human Development	M,D
Immunology	M,D
Industrial and Manufacturing Management	D
International Affairs	M,D
Linguistics	M,D
Management Information Systems	M,D
Management Strategy and Policy	M,D
Marketing Research	M
Marketing	M,D
Marriage and Family Therapy	M
Materials Sciences	M,D
Maternal and Child/Neonatal Nursing	M,D
Mathematics	D
Mechanical Engineering	M,D
Microbiology	M,D
Molecular Biology	D
Music Education	M,D
Music	M,D
Neurobiology	D
Neuroscience	D
Nursing and Healthcare Administration	M,D
Nursing Education	M,D
Nursing—General	M,D
Optical Sciences	M,D
Oral and Dental Sciences	M
Pathology	D
Pediatric Nursing	M,D
Pharmacology	M,D
Philosophy	D
Photography	M
Physics	M,D
Physiology	M,D
Political Science	D
Psychiatric Nursing	M,D
Psychology—General	D
Public Health—General	M
Social Psychology	M,D
Statistics	M,D
Structural Biology	D
Student Affairs	M
Toxicology	D
Translation and Interpretation	M,O
Western European Studies	M,D

UNIVERSITY OF ST. AUGUSTINE FOR HEALTH SCIENCES

Athletic Training and Sports Medicine	M
Health Education	M,D
Health Informatics	M
Health Services Management and Hospital Administration	M
Nursing and Healthcare Administration	M
Nursing Education	M
Nursing Informatics	M
Nursing—General	M,D
Occupational Therapy	M,D
Physical Therapy	D

UNIVERSITY OF ST. FRANCIS (IL)

Accounting	M
Art Education	M,D,O
Business Administration and Management—General	M,O
Business Education	M
Curriculum and Instruction	M,D,O
Developmental Education	M,O
Education—General	M,D,O
Educational Leadership and Administration	M,D,O
Educational Media/Instructional Technology	M,O
Elementary Education	M,D,O
English as a Second Language	M,D,O
English Education	M,D,O
Family Nurse Practitioner Studies	M,D,O
Finance and Banking	M,O
Forensic Sciences	M,O
Health Services Management and Hospital Administration	M,O
Human Resources Management	M,O
Logistics	M,O
Management Strategy and Policy	M,O
Mathematics Education	M,D,O
Nursing and Healthcare Administration	M,D,O
Nursing Education	M,D,O
Nursing—General	M,D,O
Physician Assistant Studies	M,O
Psychiatric Nursing	M,D,O
Reading Education	M,D,O
Science Education	M,D,O
Secondary Education	M,D,O
Social Sciences Education	M,D,O
Social Work	M
Special Education	M,D,O

UNIVERSITY OF SAINT FRANCIS (IN)

Art/Fine Arts	M
Business Administration and Management—General	M
Clinical Psychology	M,O
Counseling Psychology	M,O

Counselor Education	M,O
Education—General	M
Environmental and Occupational Health	M
Family Nurse Practitioner Studies	M,D,O
Health Services Management and Hospital Administration	M
Nurse Anesthesia	M,D,O
Nursing—General	M,D,O
Organizational Management	M
Physician Assistant Studies	M
Secondary Education	M
Special Education	M
Sustainability Management	M

UNIVERSITY OF SAINT JOSEPH

Animal Sciences	M
Applied Behavior Analysis	M,O
Biochemistry	M
Biological and Biomedical Sciences—General	M
Business Administration and Management—General	M
Chemistry	M
Clinical Psychology	M,O
Counseling Psychology	M,O
Counselor Education	M,O
Curriculum and Instruction	M
Education—General	M
Educational Media/Instructional Technology	M
Family Nurse Practitioner Studies	M,D
Gerontology	O
Marriage and Family Therapy	M
Nursing Education	M,D
Nursing—General	M,D
Nutrition	M
Pharmacy	D
Psychiatric Nursing	M,D
Reading Education	M
Special Education	M

UNIVERSITY OF SAINT MARY

Advertising and Public Relations	M
Business Administration and Management—General	M
Counseling Psychology	M
Education—General	M
Elementary Education	M
Finance and Banking	M
Health Services Management and Hospital Administration	M
Human Resources Management	M
Marketing	M
Nursing and Healthcare Administration	M
Nursing Education	M
Nursing—General	M
Physical Therapy	D
Psychology—General	M
Special Education	M

UNIVERSITY OF SAINT MARY OF THE LAKE–MUNDELEIN SEMINARY

Pastoral Ministry and Counseling	M,D
Theology	M,D

UNIVERSITY OF ST. MICHAEL'S COLLEGE

Jewish Studies	M,D,O
Pastoral Ministry and Counseling	M,D,O
Religious Education	M,D,O
Theology	M,D,O

UNIVERSITY OF ST. THOMAS (MN)

Accounting	M
Art History	M
Business Administration and Management—General	M
Counseling Psychology	M,D
Criminal Justice and Criminology	M,D
Database Systems	M,O
Education—General	M,D,O
Educational Leadership and Administration	M,D,O
Electrical Engineering	M,O
Engineering and Applied Sciences—General	M,O
Engineering Management	M,O
English	M
Ethics	M,D
Health Services Management and Hospital Administration	M
Human Development	M,D
Information Science	M,O
Law	M,D
Management of Technology	M,O
Manufacturing Engineering	M,O
Mechanical Engineering	M,O
Music Education	M,D
Music	M,D
Organizational Management	M,D
Pastoral Ministry and Counseling	M
Religion	M
Religious Education	M
Social Work	M
Software Engineering	M,O
Special Education	M,O
Student Affairs	M,D,O
Systems Engineering	M,O
Theology	M

UNIVERSITY OF ST. THOMAS (TX)

Accounting	M
Business Administration and Management—General	M
Counselor Education	M,D
Curriculum and Instruction	M,D
Education—General	M,D
Educational Leadership and Administration	M,D
Educational Measurement and Evaluation	M,D
Elementary Education	M,D
English as a Second Language	M,D
Finance and Banking	M

International Business	M
Liberal Studies	M
Multilingual and Multicultural Education	M
Music	M
Pastoral Ministry and Counseling	M
Philosophy	M
Public Administration	M
Public Policy	M
Reading Education	M
Religion	M
Religious Education	M,D
Secondary Education	M,D
Special Education	M,D
Theology	M

UNIVERSITY OF SAN DIEGO

Accounting	M
Adult Nursing	M,D
Business Administration and Management—General	M
Communication Disorders	M
Computer and Information Systems Security	M
Computer Engineering	M
Conflict Resolution and Mediation/Peace Studies	M
Counseling Psychology	M
Counselor Education	M
Criminal Justice and Criminology	M
Curriculum and Instruction	M
Education—General	M,D,O
Educational Leadership and Administration	M,D,O
English as a Second Language	M
Family Nurse Practitioner Studies	M
Finance and Banking	M
Gerontological Nursing	M,D
Health Informatics	M,D
Higher Education	M,D,O
International Affairs	M
International Business	M
Law	M,D,O
Legal and Justice Studies	M,D,O
Marine Affairs	M
Marine Sciences	M
Marriage and Family Therapy	M
Mathematics	M
Nonprofit Management	M,D,O
Nursing and Healthcare Administration	M,D
Nursing—General	M,D
Psychiatric Nursing	M,D
Reading Education	M
Real Estate	M
Science Education	M
Special Education	M
Supply Chain Management	M,O
Taxation	M,D,O
Theater	M

UNIVERSITY OF SAN FRANCISCO

Applied Behavior Analysis	M
Asian Studies	M
Biological and Biomedical Sciences—General	M
Biotechnology	M
Business Administration and Management—General	M
Chemistry	M
Clinical Psychology	D
Communication—General	M
Computer Science	M
Counseling Psychology	M
Counselor Education	M
Curriculum and Instruction	M,D
Database Systems	M
Economics	M
Education—General	M,D
Educational Leadership and Administration	M,D
Educational Media/Instructional Technology	M,D
Energy Management and Policy	M
Entrepreneurship	M
Finance and Banking	M
Health Informatics	M
Health Services Management and Hospital Administration	M
Intellectual Property Law	M
International Affairs	M
International and Comparative Education	M,D
International Business	M
International Development	M
Law	D
Management Information Systems	M
Marketing	M
Marriage and Family Therapy	M
Multilingual and Multicultural Education	M,D
Museum Studies	M
Natural Resources	M
Nonprofit Management	M
Nursing—General	D
Organizational Management	M
Pacific Area/Pacific Rim Studies	M
Public Administration	M
Public Affairs	M
Public Health—General	M
Reading Education	M,D
Religious Education	M,D
Special Education	M
Sports Management	M
Urban Education	M
Urban Studies	M
Writing	M

UNIVERSITY OF SASKATCHEWAN

Accounting	M
Agricultural Economics and Agribusiness	M,D,O
Agricultural Sciences—General	M,D,O

Agronomy and Soil Sciences	M,D,O
Allopathic Medicine	D
Anatomy	M,D
Animal Sciences	M,D
Anthropology	M
Archaeology	M,D
Art/Fine Arts	M
Biochemistry	M,D
Bioengineering	M,D
Biological and Biomedical Sciences—General	M,D
Biomedical Engineering	M,D
Biotechnology	M
Business Administration and Management—General	M
Canadian Studies	M,D
Cell Biology	M,D
Chemical Engineering	M,D
Chemistry	M,D
Civil Engineering	M,D
Community Health	M
Computer Science	M,D
Curriculum and Instruction	M,D,O
Dentistry	D
East European and Russian Studies	M
Economics	M,O
Education—General	M,D,O
Educational Leadership and Administration	M,D,O
Educational Psychology	M,D,O
Electrical Engineering	M,D,O
Engineering and Applied Sciences—General	M,D,O
Engineering Physics	M,D
English	M,D
Environmental Sciences	M
Epidemiology	M,D
Finance and Banking	M
Food Science and Technology	M,D
Foundations and Philosophy of Education	M,D,O
French	M
Gender Studies	M,D
Geography	M,D
Geological Engineering	M,D
Geology	M,D,O
German	M
Health Services Management and Hospital Administration	M
History	M,D
Immunology	M,D
International Business	M
Kinesiology and Movement Studies	M,D,O
Law	M,D
Marketing	M
Mathematics	M,D
Mechanical Engineering	M,D
Microbiology	M,D
Music	M
Nursing—General	M
Pathology	M,D
Pharmaceutical Sciences	M,D
Pharmacology	M,D
Philosophy	M
Physics	M,D
Physiology	M,D
Plant Sciences	M,D
Political Science	M
Psychology—General	M,D
Public Affairs	M
Public Policy	M
Religion	M
Reproductive Biology	M,D
Sociology	M,D
Special Education	M,D,O
Statistics	M,D
Sustainability Management	M
Theater	M
Toxicology	M,D,O
Veterinary Medicine	M,D
Veterinary Sciences	M,D
Women's Studies	M,D

THE UNIVERSITY OF SCRANTON

Accounting	M
Art/Fine Arts	M
Biochemistry	M
Business Administration and Management—General	M
Chemistry	M
Clinical Psychology	M
Counseling Psychology	M
Counselor Education	M
Curriculum and Instruction	M
Education—General	M
Educational Leadership and Administration	M
Family Nurse Practitioner Studies	M,D,O
Finance and Banking	M
Health Services Management and Hospital Administration	M
Human Resources Development	M
International Business	M
Management Information Systems	M
Marketing	M
Nurse Anesthesia	M,D,O
Nursing and Healthcare Administration	M,D,O
Nursing—General	M,D,O
Occupational Therapy	M
Physical Therapy	D
Reading Education	M
Rehabilitation Counseling	M
Secondary Education	M
Software Engineering	M
Special Education	M
Theology	M

UNIVERSITY OF SIOUX FALLS

Business Administration and Management—General	M
Education—General	M,O
Educational Leadership and Administration	M,O

Educational Media/Instructional Technology	M,O
Entrepreneurship	M
Health Services Management and Hospital Administration	M
Marketing	M
Reading Education	M,O

UNIVERSITY OF SOUTH AFRICA

Accounting	M,D
Acute Care/Critical Care Nursing	M,D
Adult Education	M,D
Agricultural Sciences—General	M,D
Anthropology	M,D
Archaeology	M,D
Art History	M,D
Business Administration and Management—General	M,D
Chemical Engineering	M,D
Classics	M,D
Clinical Psychology	M,D
Communication—General	M,D
Counseling Psychology	M,D
Counselor Education	M,D
Criminal Justice and Criminology	M,D
Curriculum and Instruction	M,D
Economics	M,D
Education—General	M,D
Educational Leadership and Administration	M,D
Educational Media/Instructional Technology	M,D
Educational Psychology	M,D
Engineering and Applied Sciences—General	M
English as a Second Language	M,D
English	M,D
Environmental Education	M,D
Environmental Management and Policy	M,D
Environmental Sciences	M,D
Ethics	M,D
Family and Consumer Sciences—General	M,D
Foundations and Philosophy of Education	M,D
French	M,D
Geography	M,D
German	M,D
Health Education	M,D
Health Services Management and Hospital Administration	M,D
History	M,D
Horticulture	M,D
Human Development	M,D
Human Resources Development	M,D
Industrial and Organizational Psychology	M,D
Information Science	M,D
International and Comparative Education	M,D
Italian	M,D
Law	M,D
Linguistics	M,D
Logistics	M,D
Management Information Systems	M
Marketing	M,D
Maternal and Child/Neonatal Nursing	M,D
Mathematics Education	M,D
Medical/Surgical Nursing	M,D
Missions and Missiology	M,D
Music	M,D
Natural Resources	M,D
Near and Middle Eastern Languages	M,D
Near and Middle Eastern Studies	M,D
Nurse Midwifery	M,D
Pastoral Ministry and Counseling	M,D
Philosophy	M,D
Political Science	M,D
Portuguese	M,D
Psychology—General	M,D
Public Administration	M,D
Public Health—General	M,D
Quantitative Analysis	M,D
Real Estate	M,D
Religion	M,D
Romance Languages	M,D
Russian	M,D
Science Education	M,D
Social Work	M,D
Sociology	M,D
Spanish	M,D
Statistics	M,D
Technology and Public Policy	M,D
Telecommunications Management	M,D
Theology	M,D
Travel and Tourism	M,D
Vocational and Technical Education	M,D

UNIVERSITY OF SOUTH ALABAMA

Accounting	M
Allied Health—General	M,D
Allopathic Medicine	D
Art Education	M,D
Art/Fine Arts	M
Biological and Biomedical Sciences—General	M,D
Business Administration and Management—General	M,D
Chemical Engineering	M
Civil Engineering	M
Clinical Psychology	M,D
Communication Disorders	M,D
Communication—General	M
Computer Engineering	M
Computer Science	M,D
Counseling Psychology	M,D
Counselor Education	M,D
Early Childhood Education	M,D
Education—General	M,D
Educational Leadership and Administration	M,D

Educational Media/Instructional
  Technology — M,D
Electrical Engineering — M
Elementary Education — M,D
Engineering and Applied
  Sciences—General — M,D
English — M
Environmental and Occupational
  Health — M
Environmental Engineering — M
Environmental Management
  and Policy — M,D
Exercise and Sports Science — M
Health Education — M
History — M
Interdisciplinary Studies — M
Kinesiology and Movement Studies — M
Management Information Systems — M,D
Marine Sciences — M,D
Mathematics — M
Mechanical Engineering — M
Music Education — M
Music — M
Nursing and Healthcare
  Administration — M,D,O
Nursing Education — M,D,O
Nursing—General — M,D,O
Occupational Therapy — M
Physical Education — M
Physical Therapy — D
Physician Assistant Studies — M
Psychology—General — M
Public Administration — M
Reading Education — M,D
Science Education — M,D
Secondary Education — M,D
Sociology — M
Special Education — M,D
Sports Management — M
Systems Engineering — D
Toxicology — M
Writing — M

UNIVERSITY OF SOUTH CAROLINA

Accounting — M
Acute Care/Critical Care Nursing — M,O
Adult Nursing — M
Allopathic Medicine — D
Anthropology — M,D
Applied Statistics — M,D,O
Archives/Archival Administration — M,O
Art Education — M
Art History — M
Art/Fine Arts — M
Astronomy — M,D
Biochemistry — M,D
Biological and Biomedical
  Sciences—General — M,D,O
Biostatistics — M,D
Business Administration and
  Management—General — M,D
Business Education — M,D
Cell Biology — M,D
Chemical Engineering — M,D
Chemistry — M,D
Civil Engineering — M,D
Clinical Psychology — M,D
Communication Disorders — M,D
Community Health Nursing — M
Comparative Literature — M,D
Computer Engineering — M,D
Computer Science — M,D
Consumer Economics — M
Counselor Education — D,O
Criminal Justice and Criminology — M,D
Curriculum and Instruction — D
Developmental Biology — M,D
Early Childhood Education — M,D
Ecology — M,D
Economics — M,D
Education—General — M,D,O
Educational Leadership and
  Administration — M,D,O
Educational Measurement and
  Evaluation — M,D
Educational Media/Instructional
  Technology — M
Educational Psychology — M,D
Electrical Engineering — M,D
Elementary Education — M,D
Engineering and Applied
  Sciences—General — M,D
English as a Second Language — M,D,O
English Education — M,D
English — M,D
Entertainment Management — M
Environmental and Occupational
  Health — M,D
Environmental Management
  and Policy — M
Epidemiology — M,D
Evolutionary Biology — M,D
Exercise and Sports Science — M,D
Experimental Psychology — M,D
Family Nurse Practitioner Studies — M
Foreign Languages Education — M,D
Foundations and Philosophy of
  Education — D
French — M,D
Genetic Counseling — M
Geography — M,D
Geology — M,D
Geosciences — M,D
German — M,D
Gerontology — O
Hazardous Materials
  Management — M,D
Health Education — M,D,O
Health Promotion — M,D,O
Health Services Management and
  Hospital Administration — M,D

Higher Education — M
Historic Preservation — M,O
History — M,D,O
Hospitality Management — M
Human Resources Management — M
Industrial Hygiene — M,D
Information Studies — M,D,O
International Affairs — M,D
International Business — M
Journalism — M,D
Law — D
Library Science — M,D,O
Linguistics — M,D
Marine Sciences — M,D
Mathematics Education — M,D
Mathematics — M,D
Mechanical Engineering — M,D
Media Studies — M
Medical/Surgical Nursing — M
Molecular Biology — M,D
Museum Studies — M,O
Music Education — M,D,O
Music — M,D,O
Nuclear Engineering — M,D
Nurse Anesthesia — M
Nursing and Healthcare
  Administration — M
Nursing—General — M,O
Pediatric Nursing — M
Pharmaceutical Sciences — M,D
Pharmacy — D
Philosophy — M,D
Physical Education — M,D
Physics — M,D
Political Science — M,D
Psychiatric Nursing — M,O
Psychology—General — M,D
Public Administration — M
Public Health—General — M
Public History — M,O
Reading Education — M,D
Rehabilitation Counseling — M,O
Rehabilitation Sciences — M,O
Religion — M
School Psychology — D
Science Education — M,D
Secondary Education — M,D
Social Psychology — M,D
Social Sciences Education — M,D
Social Work — M,D
Sociology — M,D
Software Engineering — M,D
Spanish — M,D
Special Education — M,D
Speech and Interpersonal
  Communication — M,D
Sports Management — M
Statistics — M,D,O
Student Affairs — M
Theater — M,D
Travel and Tourism — M
Women's Health Nursing — M
Women's Studies — O
Writing — M,D

**UNIVERSITY OF SOUTH CAROLINA
AIKEN**

Applied Psychology — M
Business Administration and
  Management—General — M
Clinical Psychology — M
Educational Media/Instructional
  Technology — M

**UNIVERSITY OF SOUTH CAROLINA
UPSTATE**

Early Childhood Education — M
Education—General — M
Elementary Education — M
Health Informatics — M
Information Science — M
Special Education — M

THE UNIVERSITY OF SOUTH DAKOTA

Accounting — M
Addictions/Substance Abuse
  Counseling — M
Adult Education — M,D,O
Allied Health—General — M,D,O
Allopathic Medicine — D
Art Education — M
Art/Fine Arts — M
Biological and Biomedical
  Sciences—General — M,D
Business Administration and
  Management—General — M
Cardiovascular Sciences — M,D
Cell Biology — M,D
Chemistry — M,D
Clinical Psychology — M,D
Communication Disorders — M,D
Communication—General — M
Computer Science — M
Counselor Education — M,D,O
Criminal Justice and Criminology — M
Curriculum and Instruction — M,D,O
Database Systems — M
Early Childhood Education — M,D,O
Education—General — M,D,O
Educational Leadership and
  Administration — M,D,O
Educational Media/Instructional
  Technology — M
Educational Psychology — M,D,O
Elementary Education — M
English — M,D
Exercise and Sports Science — M
Graphic Design — M
Health Services Management and
  Hospital Administration — M
Higher Education — M,D,O
History — M

Human Development — M,D,O
Human Resources Management — M
Immunology — M,D
Interdisciplinary Studies — M
Kinesiology and Movement Studies — M
Law — D
Mathematics — M
Microbiology — M,D
Molecular Biology — M,D
Music Education — M
Music — M
Neuroscience — M,D
Occupational Therapy — M,D
Organizational Management — M
Pharmacology — M,D
Photography — M
Physical Therapy — D
Physician Assistant Studies — M
Physics — M,D
Physiology — M,D
Political Science — M,D
Psychology—General — M,D
Public Administration — M,D
Public Health—General — M
Public Policy — M,D
Reading Education — M
School Psychology — M,D,O
Secondary Education — M
Social Work — M
Special Education — M,D,O
Theater — M

**UNIVERSITY OF SOUTHERN
CALIFORNIA**

Accounting — M
Advertising and Public Relations — M
Aerospace/Aeronautical
  Engineering — M,D,O
Allopathic Medicine — D
American Studies — D
Applied Mathematics — M,D
Architecture — M,D
Art History — M,D,O
Art/Fine Arts — M,D,O
Artificial Intelligence/Robotics — M,D
Arts Administration — M
Asian Languages — M,D
Asian Studies — M,D
Biochemistry — M
Bioinformatics — D
Biological and Biomedical
  Sciences—General — M,D,O
Biomedical Engineering — M,D
Biophysics — M
Biostatistics — M,D
Biotechnology — M
Business Administration and
  Management—General — M,D
Cancer Biology/Oncology — D
Cell Biology — M,D
Chemical Engineering — M,D,O
Chemistry — D
Child and Family Studies — M,D
Civil Engineering — M,D,O
Classics — M,D
Clinical Psychology — M,D
Clinical Research — M,D,O
Cognitive Sciences — M,D
Communication—General — M,D
Comparative Literature — D
Computational Biology — D
Computer and Information
  Systems Security — M,D
Computer Art and Design — M
Computer Engineering — M,D,O
Computer Science — M,D
Construction Management — M,D,O
Corporate and Organizational
  Communication — M
Counselor Education — M
Cultural Studies — D
Dentistry — D
Developmental Biology — D
Developmental Psychology — M,D
Economic Development — M,D
Economics — M,D
Education—General — M,D
Educational Leadership and
  Administration — D
Educational Policy — D
Educational Psychology — D
Electrical Engineering — M,D,O
Engineering and Applied
  Sciences—General — M,D,O
Engineering Management — M,D,O
English as a Second Language — M
English — M,D
Entrepreneurship — M
Environmental and Occupational
  Health — M
Environmental Biology — M,D
Environmental Engineering — M,D,O
Epidemiology — M,D
Evolutionary Biology — D
Film, Television, and Video
  Production — M
Film, Television, and Video
  Theory and Criticism — M,D
Food Science and
  Technology — M,D,O
Game Design and
  Development — M,D
Genomic Sciences — D
Geographic Information Systems — M,O
Geography — M,O
Geosciences — M,D
Geotechnical Engineering — M,D,O
Gerontology — M,D,O
Hazardous Materials
  Management — M,D,O
Health Communication — M,D

Health Education — M
Health Promotion — M
Health Services Management and
  Hospital Administration — M,D,O
Health Services Research — D
Higher Education — D
History — D
Homeland Security — M,O
Immunology — M
Industrial/Management
  Engineering — M,D,O
International Affairs — M,D
International Health — M,O
Internet and Interactive
  Multimedia — M,D,O
Journalism — M
Kinesiology and Movement Studies — M,D
Latin American Studies — D
Law — M,D
Linguistics — M,D
Manufacturing Engineering — M,D,O
Marine Biology — M,D
Marine Sciences — M,D
Marriage and Family Therapy — M
Materials Engineering — M,D,O
Materials Sciences — M,D,O
Mathematical and
  Computational Finance — M,D
Mathematics — M,D
Mechanical Engineering — M,D,O
Mechanics — M,D,O
Media Studies — M,D
Medical Imaging — M,D
Medical Microbiology — D
Microbiology — M
Modeling and Simulation — M,D
Molecular Biology — M,D
Molecular Pharmacology — M,D
Multilingual and Multicultural
  Education — D
Music Education — M,D,O
Music — M,D,O
Neurobiology — D
Neuroscience — M,D
Nonprofit Management — M,O
Occupational Therapy — M,D
Oceanography — M,D
Operations Research — M,D,O
Oral and Dental Sciences — M,D,O
Organizational Management — M
Pathology — M
Petroleum Engineering — M,D,O
Pharmaceutical Administration — M
Pharmaceutical Sciences — M,D,O
Pharmacy — D
Philosophy — M,D
Photography — M
Physical Chemistry — D
Physical Therapy — M,D
Physician Assistant Studies — M
Physics — M,D
Physiology — M
Political Science — M,D
Psychology—General — M,D
Public Administration — M,O
Public Health—General — M,D
Public Policy — M,D,O
Quantitative Analysis — M,D
Real Estate — M
Rhetoric — D
Safety Engineering — M,D,O
Slavic Languages — M,D
Social Psychology — M,D
Social Work — M,D
Sociology — D
Software Engineering — M,D
Spanish — D
Statistics — M,D
Student Affairs — M
Supply Chain Management — M,D,O
Sustainable Development — M,D,O
Systems Engineering — M,D,O
Taxation — M
Telecommunications — M,D,O
Theater — M
Toxicology — M,D
Transportation and Highway
  Engineering — M,D,O
Urban and Regional Planning — M,D,O
Urban Education — D
Water Resources — M,D,O
Writing — M,D

UNIVERSITY OF SOUTHERN INDIANA

Accounting — M
Business Administration and
  Management—General — M
Communication—General — M
Cultural Studies — M
Database Systems — M
Education—General — M
Educational Leadership and
  Administration — M
Elementary Education — M
Engineering and Applied
  Sciences—General — M
Engineering Management — M
English as a Second Language — M
English — M
Family Nurse Practitioner Studies — M,D,O
Gerontology — M,D,O
Health Informatics — M
Health Services Management and
  Hospital Administration — M
Human Resources Management — M
Industrial and Manufacturing
  Management — M
Liberal Studies — M
Mathematics Education — M
Nonprofit Management — M

---

*M—masters degree; D—doctorate; O—other advanced degree; *—Close-Up and/or Display*

Nursing and Healthcare Administration	M,D,O
Nursing Education	M,D,O
Nursing—General	M,D,O
Occupational Therapy	M
Organizational Management	M,D,O
Psychiatric Nursing	M,D,O
Public Administration	M
Secondary Education	M
Social Work	M
Sports Management	M

UNIVERSITY OF SOUTHERN MAINE

Accounting	M
Addictions/Substance Abuse Counseling	M,O
Adult Education	M,O
Adult Nursing	M,D,O
American Studies	M,O
Applied Behavior Analysis	M,O
Biological and Biomedical Sciences—General	M
Business Administration and Management—General	M,O
Computer Science	M,O
Counseling Psychology	M,O
Counselor Education	M,O
Cultural Studies	M,O
Education of the Gifted	M,O
Education—General	M,D,O
Educational Leadership and Administration	M,O
Educational Psychology	M,O
English as a Second Language	M,O
Family Nurse Practitioner Studies	M,D,O
Finance and Banking	M
Gerontological Nursing	M,D,O
Health Services Management and Hospital Administration	M,O
Higher Education	M,O
Immunology	M
Molecular Biology	M
Music Education	M
Music	M
Nursing and Healthcare Administration	M,D,O
Nursing Education	M,D,O
Nursing—General	M,D,O
Occupational Therapy	M
Psychiatric Nursing	M,D,O
Public Health—General	M,O
Public Policy	M
Reading Education	M,O
Rehabilitation Counseling	M,O
School Psychology	M,D
Social Work	M
Software Engineering	M,O
Special Education	M,O
Statistics	M,O
Sustainability Management	M
Urban and Regional Planning	M,O
Writing	M

UNIVERSITY OF SOUTHERN MISSISSIPPI

Accounting	M
Advertising and Public Relations	M,D
Anthropology	M
Applied Behavior Analysis	M,D
Biochemistry	M,D
Biological and Biomedical Sciences—General	M,D
Biostatistics	M
Business Administration and Management—General	M
Chemistry	M,D
Child and Family Studies	M
Clinical Laboratory Sciences/Medical Technology	M
Clinical Psychology	M,D
Communication Disorders	M,D
Computational Sciences	M,D
Computer Science	M,D
Construction Engineering	M
Counseling Psychology	M,D
Criminal Justice and Criminology	M,D
Curriculum and Instruction	M,D
Economic Development	M
Economics	M
Education—General	M,D,O
Educational Leadership and Administration	M,D,O
Educational Measurement and Evaluation	M,D,O
Educational Media/Instructional Technology	M,D
Elementary Education	M,D
English Education	M,D
English	M,D
Environmental Biology	M,D
Epidemiology	M,D
Exercise and Sports Science	M,D
Family Nurse Practitioner Studies	M,D,O
Food Science and Technology	M
Foreign Languages Education	M
Forensic Sciences	M,D
Geography	M,D
Geology	M,D
Health Education	M
Health Services Management and Hospital Administration	M
Higher Education	M,D,O
History	M,D
Hydrology	M,D
Information Science	M,D
Inorganic Chemistry	M,D
International Development	M,D
Library Science	M,O
Logistics	M
Marine Biology	M,D
Marine Sciences	M,D
Marriage and Family Therapy	M
Mass Communication	M,D

Maternal and Child/Neonatal Nursing	M,D,O
Mathematics Education	M,D
Mathematics	M,D
Microbiology	M,D
Molecular Biology	M,D
Music Education	M,D
Music	M,D
Nursing—General	M,D,O
Nutrition	M
Organic Chemistry	M,D
Physical Chemistry	M,D
Physical Education	M,D
Physics	M,D
Political Science	M,D
Polymer Science and Engineering	M,D
Psychiatric Nursing	M,D,O
Psychology—General	M,D
Public Health—General	M
School Psychology	M,D
Science Education	M,D
Secondary Education	M,D
Social Work	M
Special Education	M,D
Speech and Interpersonal Communication	M,D
Sports Management	M,D
Student Affairs	M,D,O
Theater	M
Writing	M,D

UNIVERSITY OF SOUTH FLORIDA

Accounting	M
Acute Care/Critical Care Nursing	M,D,O
Addictions/Substance Abuse Counseling	M,D
Adult Education	M,D,O
Adult Nursing	M,D,O
African Studies	M,O
Allopathic Medicine	M,D
American Studies	M,D
Anatomy	M,D
Anthropology	M,D,O
Applied Behavior Analysis	M,D
Applied Physics	M,D
Archaeology	M,D,O
Architecture	M
Art History	M
Art/Fine Arts	M
Athletic Training and Sports Medicine	M,D
Bioethics	O
Bioinformatics	M,D,O
Biological and Biomedical Sciences—General	M,D
Biomedical Engineering	M,D,O
Biostatistics	M,D,O
Biotechnology	M,D,O
Business Administration and Management—General	M,D
Cancer Biology/Oncology	M,D
Cardiovascular Sciences	O
Cell Biology	M,D
Chemical Engineering	M,D,O
Chemistry	M,D
Child and Family Studies	M,D,O
Civil Engineering	M,D,O
Clinical Psychology	D
Clinical Research	M,D,O
Cognitive Sciences	D
Communication Disorders	M,D,O
Communication—General	M,D
Community College Education	M,D,O
Community Health	M,D,O
Comparative Literature	O
Computational Biology	M,D
Computer and Information Systems Security	M
Computer Engineering	M,D
Computer Science	M,D
Corporate and Organizational Communication	M,O
Counseling Psychology	M,D,O
Counselor Education	M,D,O
Criminal Justice and Criminology	M,D,O
Database Systems	M,D
Distance Education Development	O
Early Childhood Education	M,D,O
Ecology	M,D
Economics	M,D
Education—General	M,D,O
Educational Leadership and Administration	M,D,O
Educational Measurement and Evaluation	O
Educational Media/Instructional Technology	O
Educational Psychology	M,D,O
Electrical Engineering	M,D
Elementary Education	M,D,O
Emergency Management	O
Engineering and Applied Sciences—General	M,D,O
Engineering Management	M,D
English as a Second Language	M,D,O
English	M,D,O
Entrepreneurship	M,O
Environmental and Occupational Health	M,D,O
Environmental Biology	M,D
Environmental Engineering	M,D
Environmental Management and Policy	M,D,O
Environmental Sciences	M,D
Epidemiology	M,D
Evolutionary Biology	M,D
Family Nurse Practitioner Studies	M,D
Film, Television, and Video Theory and Criticism	M
Finance and Banking	M,D
Foreign Languages Education	O
Forensic Sciences	M,D,O
French	M,D

Gender Studies	M,O
Geographic Information Systems	M,D,O
Geography	O
Geology	M,D,O
Geosciences	M,D
Geotechnical Engineering	M,D
Gerontological Nursing	M,D,O
Gerontology	M,D,O
Health Education	M,D
Health Informatics	M,D,O
Health Services Management and Hospital Administration	M,D,O
Higher Education	M,D,O
History	M,D
Human Resources Development	O
Human Resources Management	M
Humanities	M
Hydrogeology	O
Immunology	M,D
Industrial and Organizational Psychology	D
Industrial/Management Engineering	M,D,O
Information Science	M
Information Studies	M,O
Interdisciplinary Studies	M,D
International Affairs	M,D,O
International Health	M,D,O
Internet and Interactive Multimedia	M,O
Journalism	M,O
Latin American Studies	M,D,O
Legal and Justice Studies	O
Liberal Studies	M
Library Science	M
Linguistics	M,D
Management Information Systems	M,D,O
Management of Technology	O
Management Strategy and Policy	M,D,O
Marine Sciences	M,D
Marketing	M,D
Marriage and Family Therapy	M,D,O
Mass Communication	M,O
Materials Engineering	M,D,O
Materials Sciences	O
Maternal and Child Health	O
Mathematics	M,D,O
Mechanical Engineering	M,D
Media Studies	M
Medical Microbiology	M,D
Microbiology	M,D
Molecular Biology	M,D
Molecular Medicine	M,D
Molecular Pharmacology	M,D
Museum Studies	O
Music Education	M,D
Music	M,D
Nanotechnology	M,D
Neuroscience	M,D,O
Nonprofit Management	O
Nurse Anesthesia	M,D,O
Nursing Education	M,D,O
Nursing—General	M,D,O
Nutrition	M,D,O
Occupational Health Nursing	M,D,O
Oceanography	M,D
Oncology Nursing	M,D,O
Pathology	M,D
Pediatric Nursing	M,D,O
Pharmaceutical Sciences	M,D
Pharmacy	M,D,O
Philosophy	M,D
Physical Therapy	D
Physics	M,D
Physiology	M,D
Political Science	M,D,O
Psychology—General	D
Public Administration	M,D,O
Public Affairs	O
Public Health—General	M,D,O*
Reading Education	M,D,O
Real Estate	M,D
Rehabilitation Counseling	M,D,O
Rehabilitation Sciences	D
Religion	M,D
Rhetoric	M,D
School Psychology	M,D,O
Secondary Education	O
Social Sciences Education	M,D,O
Social Work	M,D,O
Sociology	M,D
Spanish	M,D
Special Education	O
Statistics	M,D
Structural Engineering	M,D
Student Affairs	M,D,O
Sustainability Management	M,O
Sustainable Development	M,O
Systems Engineering	O
Taxation	M,D
Technical Communication	O
Transportation and Highway Engineering	M,D,O
Travel and Tourism	M,O
Urban and Regional Planning	M,D,O
Urban Design	M
Vocational and Technical Education	M,D,O
Water Resources Engineering	M,D,O
Western European Studies	M,D
Women's Studies	M
Writing	M,D,O

UNIVERSITY OF SOUTH FLORIDA, ST. PETERSBURG

Business Administration and Management—General	M
Computer Art and Design	M
Education—General	M
Educational Leadership and Administration	M
Elementary Education	M
English Education	M
Environmental Management and Policy	M

Environmental Sciences	M
Journalism	M
Liberal Studies	M
Mathematics Education	M
Media Studies	M
Middle School Education	M
Psychology—General	M
Reading Education	M
Science Education	M

UNIVERSITY OF SOUTH FLORIDA SARASOTA-MANATEE

Business Administration and Management—General	M
Criminal Justice and Criminology	M
Curriculum and Instruction	M
Educational Leadership and Administration	M
Elementary Education	M
English Education	M
Hospitality Management	M
Liberal Studies	M
Social Sciences	M
Social Work	M

THE UNIVERSITY OF TAMPA

Accounting	M
Adult Nursing	M
Business Administration and Management—General	M
Curriculum and Instruction	M
Education—General	M
Educational Media/Instructional Technology	M
Entrepreneurship	M
Exercise and Sports Science	M
Family Nurse Practitioner Studies	M
Finance and Banking	M
International Business	M
Management Information Systems	M
Marketing	M
Nonprofit Management	M
Nursing—General	M
Nutrition	M
Writing	M

THE UNIVERSITY OF TENNESSEE

Accounting	M,D
Adult Education	M,D
Advertising and Public Relations	M,D
Aerospace/Aeronautical Engineering	M,D
Agricultural Education	M
Agricultural Engineering	M
Agricultural Sciences—General	M,D
Analytical Chemistry	M,D
Anatomy	M,D
Animal Behavior	M,D
Animal Sciences	M,D
Anthropology	M,D
Applied Mathematics	M,D
Applied Psychology	M,D
Archaeology	M,D
Architecture	M
Art Education	M,D,O
Art/Fine Arts	M
Athletic Training and Sports Medicine	M,D
Aviation	M
Biochemistry	M,D
Bioethics	M,D
Biological and Biomedical Sciences—General	M,D
Biomedical Engineering	M,D
Biosystems Engineering	M,D
Business Administration and Management—General	M,D
Chemical Engineering	M,D
Chemical Physics	M,D
Chemistry	M,D
Child and Family Studies	M,D
Civil Engineering	M,D
Clinical Psychology	M,D
Clothing and Textiles	M,D
Communication Disorders	M,D,O
Communication—General	M,D
Community Health	M,D
Computer Engineering	M,D
Computer Science	M,D
Consumer Economics	M,D
Counseling Psychology	M,D
Counselor Education	M,D,O
Criminal Justice and Criminology	M,D
Cultural Anthropology	M,D
Curriculum and Instruction	M,D,O
Early Childhood Education	M,D,O
Ecology	M,D
Economics	M,D
Education—General	M,D,O
Educational Leadership and Administration	M,D,O
Educational Measurement and Evaluation	M,D,O
Educational Media/Instructional Technology	M,D,O
Educational Psychology	M,D,O
Electrical Engineering	M,D
Elementary Education	M,D,O
Energy and Power Engineering	D
Engineering and Applied Sciences—General	M,D
Engineering Management	M,D
English as a Second Language	M,D,O
English Education	M,D,O
English	M,D
Entomology	M,D
Environmental Engineering	M
Environmental Management and Policy	M,D
Evolutionary Biology	M,D
Exercise and Sports Science	M,D,O
Experimental Psychology	M,D

Family and Consumer
 Sciences—General — D
Finance and Banking — M,D
Fish, Game, and Wildlife
 Management — M
Food Science and
 Technology — M,D
Foreign Languages Education — M,D,O
Forestry — M
Foundations and Philosophy of
 Education — M,D,O
French — M,D
Genetics — M,D
Genomic Sciences — M,D
Geography — M,D
Geology — M,D
German — M,D
Gerontology — M
Graphic Design — M
Health Education — M
Health Promotion — M
Health Services Management and
 Hospital Administration — M
History — M,D
Hospitality Management — M
Human Resources Development — M
Industrial and Manufacturing
 Management — M,D
Industrial and Organizational
 Psychology — D
Industrial/Management
 Engineering — M,D
Information Science — M,D
Inorganic Chemistry — M,D
Italian — D
Journalism — M,D
Kinesiology and Movement Studies — M,D
Landscape Architecture — M
Law — D
Leisure Studies — M,D
Linguistics — D
Logistics — M,D
Marketing — M,D
Materials Engineering — M,D
Materials Sciences — M,D
Mathematics Education — M,D,O
Mathematics — M,D
Mechanical Engineering — M,D
Media Studies — M,D
Microbiology — M,D
Multilingual and Multicultural
 Education — M,D,O
Music Education — M
Music — M
Nuclear Engineering — M,D
Nursing—General — M,D
Nutrition — M
Organic Chemistry — M,D
Philosophy — M,D
Photography — M
Physical Chemistry — M,D
Physics — M,D
Physiology — M,D
Plant Pathology — M,D
Plant Physiology — M,D
Plant Sciences — M
Political Science — M,D
Polymer Science and
 Engineering — M,D
Portuguese — D
Psychology—General — M,D
Public Administration — M
Public Health—General — M
Reading Education — M,D,O
Recreation and Park Management — M,D
Rehabilitation Counseling — M,D
Reliability Engineering — M,D
Religion — M,D
Russian — D
School Psychology — M,D,O
Science Education — M,D,O
Secondary Education — M,D,O
Social Sciences Education — M,D,O
Social Work — M,D
Sociology — M,D
Spanish — M,D
Special Education — M,D,O
Speech and Interpersonal
 Communication — M,D
Sports Management — M
Statistics — M,D
Student Affairs — M
Theater — M
Theoretical Chemistry — M,D
Transportation Management — M,D
Travel and Tourism — M
Veterinary Medicine — D

THE UNIVERSITY OF TENNESSEE AT CHATTANOOGA
Accounting — M
Applied Mathematics — M
Applied Statistics — M
Athletic Training and Sports
 Medicine — M
Automotive Engineering — M
Business Administration and
 Management—General — M
Chemical Engineering — M
Civil Engineering — M
Computational Sciences — M,D
Computer Science — M
Construction Management — M,O
Counselor Education — M,D,O
Criminal Justice and Criminology — M
Education—General — M,D,O
Educational Leadership and
 Administration — M,D,O
Educational Media/Instructional
 Technology — M,D,O
Electrical Engineering — M

Elementary Education — M,D,O
Energy and Power
 Engineering — M,O
Engineering Management — M,O
English — M
Environmental Sciences — M
Ethics — M,O
Experimental Psychology — M
Family Nurse Practitioner Studies — M,D,O
Industrial and Organizational
 Psychology — M
Industrial/Management
 Engineering — M
Logistics — M,O
Mathematics Education — M
Mathematics — M
Mechanical Engineering — M
Medical Informatics — M,D,O
Music Education — M
Music — M
Nonprofit Management — M,O
Nurse Anesthesia — M,D,O
Nursing and Healthcare
 Administration — M,D,O
Nursing Education — M,D,O
Nursing—General — M,D,O
Occupational Therapy — D
Physical Education — M
Physical Therapy — D
Political Science — M,O
Project Management — M,O
Psychology—General — M
Public Administration — M,O
Quality Management — M,O
Rhetoric — M
School Psychology — M,D,O
Secondary Education — M,D,O
Social Psychology — M,D,O
Special Education — M,D,O
Supply Chain Management — M,O
Writing — M

THE UNIVERSITY OF TENNESSEE AT MARTIN
Addictions/Substance Abuse
 Counseling — M
Agricultural Economics and
 Agribusiness — M
Agricultural Sciences—
 General — M
Business Administration and
 Management—General — M
Child and Family Studies — M
Child Development — M
Communication—General — M
Counselor Education — M
Curriculum and Instruction — M
Education—General — M
Educational Leadership and
 Administration — M
Elementary Education — M
Family and Consumer
 Sciences—General — M
Finance and Banking — M
Food Science and
 Technology — M
Interdisciplinary Studies — M
Nutrition — M
Physical Education — M
Secondary Education — M
Social Psychology — M
Special Education — M
Student Affairs — M

THE UNIVERSITY OF TENNESSEE HEALTH SCIENCE CENTER
Allied Health—General — M,D
Allopathic Medicine — D
Biological and Biomedical
 Sciences—General — M,D
Biomedical Engineering — M,D
Clinical Laboratory
 Sciences/Medical Technology — M,D
Communication Disorders — M
Dentistry — D
Epidemiology — M,D
Gerontological Nursing — D,O
Health Informatics — M,D
Health Services Research — M,D
Nursing—General — M,D,O
Occupational Therapy — M,D
Oral and Dental Sciences — M,D
Pathology — M,D
Pharmaceutical Sciences — M,D
Pharmacology — M,D
Pharmacy — M,D
Physical Therapy — M,D
Physician Assistant Studies — M,D

THE UNIVERSITY OF TENNESSEE—OAK RIDGE NATIONAL LABORATORY
Biological and Biomedical
 Sciences—General — M,D
Genomic Sciences — M,D

THE UNIVERSITY OF TEXAS AT ARLINGTON
Accounting — M,D
Aerospace/Aeronautical
 Engineering — M,D
Anthropology — M
Applied Mathematics — M,D
Architecture — M
Art/Fine Arts — M
Athletic Training and Sports
 Medicine — M,D
Bioengineering — M,D
Biological and Biomedical
 Sciences—General — M,D
Chemistry — M,D
Civil Engineering — M,D
Communication—General — M

Computer Engineering — M,D
Computer Science — M,D
Construction Management — M,D
Criminal Justice and Criminology — M
Curriculum and Instruction — M
Economics — M
Education—General — M,D
Educational Leadership and
 Administration — M,D
Educational Policy — M,D
Electrical Engineering — M,D
Engineering and Applied
 Sciences—General — M,D
Engineering Management — M
English as a Second Language — M
English — M,D
Environmental Sciences — M,D
Exercise and Sports Science — M,D
Experimental Psychology — M,D
Family Nurse Practitioner Studies — M,D
Film, Television, and Video
 Production — M
Finance and Banking — M,D
French — M
Geology — M,D
Health Psychology — M,D
Health Services Management and
 Hospital Administration — M
Higher Education — M,D
History — M,D
Human Resources Management — M
Industrial and Organizational
 Psychology — M,D
Industrial/Management
 Engineering — M,D
Kinesiology and Movement Studies — M,D
Landscape Architecture — M
Linguistics — M,D
Logistics — M
Management Information Systems — M,D
Marketing Research — M
Marketing — M
Materials Engineering — M,D
Materials Sciences — M,D
Mathematics Education — M,D
Mathematics — M,D
Mechanical Engineering — M,D
Music Education — M
Music — M
Nursing and Healthcare
 Administration — M,D
Nursing Education — M,D
Nursing—General — M,D
Physics — M,D
Political Science — M
Psychology—General — M,D
Public Administration — M
Public Policy — M,D
Quantitative Analysis — M,D
Reading Education — M
Real Estate — M,D
Science Education — M
Social Work — M,D
Sociology — M
Software Engineering — M,D
Spanish — M
Systems Engineering — M
Taxation — M,D
Urban and Regional Planning — D

THE UNIVERSITY OF TEXAS AT AUSTIN
Accounting — M,D
Actuarial Science — M,D
Adult Nursing — M,D
Advertising and Public Relations — M,D
Aerospace/Aeronautical
 Engineering — M,D
African Studies — M,D
American Studies — M,D
Analytical Chemistry — D
Animal Behavior — D
Anthropology — M,D
Applied Arts and Design—General — M
Applied Mathematics — M,D
Applied Physics — M,D
Archaeology — M,D
Architectural Engineering — M
Architectural History — M,D
Architecture — M
Art Education — M
Art History — M,D
Art/Fine Arts — M
Asian Languages — M,D
Asian Studies — M,D
Astronomy — M,D
Biochemistry — D
Biological and Biomedical
 Sciences—General — M,D
Biomedical Engineering — M,D
Biopsychology — D
Business Administration and
 Management—General — M,D
Cell Biology — D
Chemical Engineering — M,D
Chemistry — D
Child and Family Studies — M,D
Child Development — M,D
Civil Engineering — M,D
Classics — M,D
Clinical Laboratory
 Sciences/Medical Technology — M,D
Clinical Psychology — D
Communication Disorders — M,D
Communication—General — M,D
Community Health Nursing — M,D
Comparative Literature — M,D
Computational Sciences — M,D
Computer and Information
 Systems Security — M,D
Computer Engineering — M,D
Computer Science — M,D

Counseling Psychology — M,D
Counselor Education — M,D
Cultural Studies — M,D
Curriculum and Instruction — M,D
Dance — M
Developmental Psychology — D
Early Childhood Education — M,D
East European and Russian Studies — M
Ecology — D
Economics — M,D
Education—General — M,D
Educational Leadership and
 Administration — M,D
Educational Media/Instructional
 Technology — M,D
Educational Psychology — M,D
Electrical Engineering — M,D
Engineering and Applied
 Sciences—General — M,D
English — M,D
Entrepreneurship — M
Environmental Engineering — M,D
Environmental Management
 and Policy — M
Evolutionary Biology — D
Exercise and Sports Science — M,D
Family and Consumer
 Sciences—General — M,D
Family Nurse Practitioner Studies — M,D
Film, Television, and Video
 Production — M,D
Finance and Banking — M,D
Folklore — M,D
French — M,D
Geography — M,D
Geology — M,D
Geosciences — M,D
Geotechnical Engineering — M,D
German — M,D
Gerontological Nursing — M,D
Health Education — M,D
Hispanic and Latin American
 Languages — M,D
Hispanic Studies — M
Historic Preservation — M
History — M,D
Human Development — M,D
Industrial and Manufacturing
 Management — M,D
Industrial/Management
 Engineering — M,D
Information Studies — M,D
Inorganic Chemistry — D
Interior Design — M
Italian — M
Journalism — M,D
Kinesiology and Movement Studies — M,D
Landscape Architecture — M
Latin American Studies — M
Law — M,D
Linguistics — M,D
Management Information Systems — M,D
Marine Sciences — M,D
Marketing — M,D
Materials Engineering — M,D
Materials Sciences — M,D
Maternal and Child/Neonatal
 Nursing — M,D
Mathematics — M,D
Mechanical Engineering — M,D
Mechanics — M,D
Media Studies — M,D
Medicinal and Pharmaceutical
 Chemistry — M,D
Microbiology — D
Mineral Economics — M
Mineral/Mining Engineering — M
Molecular Biology — D
Multilingual and Multicultural
 Education — M,D
Music Education — M,D
Music — M,D
Natural Resources — M
Near and Middle Eastern Languages — M,D
Near and Middle Eastern Studies — M,D
Neurobiology — D
Neuroscience — D
Nursing and Healthcare
 Administration — M,D
Nursing Education — M,D
Nursing—General — M,D
Nutrition — M,D
Operations Research — M,D
Organic Chemistry — D
Organizational Behavior — M
Pediatric Nursing — M,D
Petroleum Engineering — M,D
Pharmaceutical Sciences — M,D
Pharmacology — M,D
Pharmacy — D
Philosophy — D
Physical Chemistry — D
Physical Education — M,D
Physics — M,D
Plant Biology — M,D
Political Science — M,D
Portuguese — M,D
Psychiatric Nursing — M,D
Psychology—General — D
Public Administration — M,D
Public Affairs — M,D
Public History — M,D
Public Policy — M,D
Quantitative Analysis — M,D
Reading Education — M,D
Rehabilitation Counseling — M,D
Romance Languages — M,D
School Psychology — M,D
Slavic Languages — M,D
Social Work — M,D
Sociology — M,D

M—masters degree; D—doctorate; O—other advanced degree; *—Close-Up and/or Display

Spanish	M,D
Special Education	M,D
Sport Psychology	M,D
Statistics	M,D
Supply Chain Management	M,D
Sustainable Development	M
Technology and Public Policy	M
Textile Sciences and Engineering	M
Theater	M,D
Toxicology	M,D
Urban and Regional Planning	M,D
Urban Design	M
Water Resources Engineering	M,D
Writing	M

THE UNIVERSITY OF TEXAS AT DALLAS

Accounting	M
Actuarial Science	M,D
Applied Mathematics	M,D
Biological and Biomedical Sciences—General	M,D
Biomedical Engineering	M,D
Biotechnology	M,D
Business Administration and Management—General	M,D*
Cell Biology	M,D
Chemistry	M,D
Child and Family Studies	M,D
Cognitive Sciences	M,D
Communication Disorders	M,D
Communication—General	M,D
Comparative Literature	M,D
Computer Engineering	M,D
Computer Science	M,D
Criminal Justice and Criminology	M,D
Database Systems	M,D
Economics	M,D
Electrical Engineering	M,D
Engineering and Applied Sciences—General	M,D
Entrepreneurship	M,D
Finance and Banking	M
Geochemistry	M,D
Geographic Information Systems	M,D
Geography	M,D
Geophysics	M,D
Geosciences	M,D
Health Services Management and Hospital Administration	M,D
History	M,D
Humanities	M,D
Hydrogeology	M,D
Industrial and Manufacturing Management	M,D
Interdisciplinary Studies	M
International Business	M,D
Internet and Interactive Multimedia	M,D
Investment Management	M
Latin American Studies	M,D
Law	M,D
Management Information Systems	M
Management of Technology	M
Management Strategy and Policy	M
Marketing	M
Materials Engineering	M,D
Materials Sciences	M,D
Mathematics Education	M
Mathematics	M,D
Mechanical Engineering	M,D
Molecular Biology	M,D
Neuroscience	M,D
Nonprofit Management	M,D
Paleontology	M,D
Physics	M,D
Political Science	M,D
Project Management	M,D
Psychology—General	M,D
Public Administration	M,D
Public Policy	M,D
Real Estate	M
Science Education	M
Software Engineering	M,D
Statistics	M,D
Supply Chain Management	M
Systems Engineering	M,D
Telecommunications	M,D

THE UNIVERSITY OF TEXAS AT EL PASO

Accounting	M
Allied Health—General	D
Anthropology	M,O
Applied Psychology	M,O
Art Education	M
Art/Fine Arts	M
Bioinformatics	M,D
Biological and Biomedical Sciences—General	M,D
Biomedical Engineering	M,D,O
Business Administration and Management—General	M,D,O
Chemistry	M,D
Civil Engineering	M,D,O
Clinical Psychology	M,D
Communication Disorders	M
Communication—General	M
Computational Sciences	M,D
Computer Engineering	M,D
Computer Science	M,D
Construction Management	M,D,O
Counselor Education	M
Curriculum and Instruction	M,D
Economics	M
Education—General	M,D
Educational Leadership and Administration	M,D
Educational Measurement and Evaluation	M
Educational Psychology	M
Electrical Engineering	M,D
Engineering and Applied Sciences—General	M,D,O
English as a Second Language	M,O

English Education	M,D,O
English	M,D,O
Environmental Engineering	M,D,O
Environmental Sciences	M,D
Experimental Psychology	M,D
Family Nurse Practitioner Studies	M,D,O
Geology	M
Geophysics	M
Health Services Management and Hospital Administration	M,D,O
History	M,D
Industrial/Management Engineering	M,O
Information Science	M,D
Interdisciplinary Studies	M
International Business	M,D,O
Kinesiology and Movement Studies	M
Liberal Studies	M
Linguistics	M,O
Manufacturing Engineering	M,D
Materials Engineering	M,D
Materials Sciences	M,D
Mathematics Education	M
Mathematics	M
Mechanical Engineering	M,D
Metallurgical Engineering and Metallurgy	M,D
Multilingual and Multicultural Education	M,D,O
Music Education	M
Music	M
Nursing and Healthcare Administration	M,D,O
Nursing Education	M,D,O
Nursing—General	M,D,O
Occupational Therapy	M
Philosophy	M
Physical Therapy	D
Physics	M
Political Science	M
Psychology—General	M,D
Public Health—General	M,O
Reading Education	M,D
Rehabilitation Counseling	M
Rhetoric	M,D,O
Science Education	M
Social Work	M
Sociology	M,O
Software Engineering	M,D,O
Spanish	M,O
Special Education	M
Statistics	M
Systems Engineering	M,O
Writing	M,D,O

THE UNIVERSITY OF TEXAS AT SAN ANTONIO

Accounting	M,D
Anthropology	M,D
Applied Behavior Analysis	M,O
Applied Mathematics	M
Applied Statistics	M,D
Architecture	M
Art History	M
Art/Fine Arts	M
Biological and Biomedical Sciences—General	M,D
Biomedical Engineering	M,D
Biotechnology	M,D
Business Administration and Management—General	M,D,O
Cell Biology	M,D
Chemistry	M,D
Civil Engineering	M,D
Communication—General	M
Computer and Information Systems Security	M,D,O
Computer Engineering	M,D
Computer Science	M,D
Counselor Education	M,D
Criminal Justice and Criminology	M
Cultural Studies	M,D
Curriculum and Instruction	M,D
Demography and Population Studies	D
Early Childhood Education	M,D
Economics	M
Educational Leadership and Administration	M,D
Educational Media/Instructional Technology	M,D,O
Electrical Engineering	M,D
Engineering and Applied Sciences—General	M,D
English as a Second Language	M,D,O
English	M,D
Environmental Engineering	M,D
Environmental Sciences	M,D
Finance and Banking	M,D
Geology	M
Health Education	M
Higher Education	M,D
History	M
Information Science	M,D,O
Interdisciplinary Studies	M,D
Kinesiology and Movement Studies	M
Management of Technology	M,D,O
Manufacturing Engineering	M,D
Marketing	M,D
Materials Engineering	M,D
Mathematics Education	M
Mathematics	M
Mechanical Engineering	M,D
Molecular Biology	M,D
Multilingual and Multicultural Education	M,D
Music	M
Neurobiology	M,D
Organizational Management	D
Philosophy	M
Physics	M,D
Political Science	M
Psychology—General	M,D
Public Administration	M
Reading Education	M,D

School Psychology	M,O
Social Work	M
Sociology	M
Spanish	M
Special Education	M,D
Statistics	M,D
Translational Biology	D
Urban and Regional Planning	M

THE UNIVERSITY OF TEXAS AT TYLER

Accounting	M
Art History	M
Art/Fine Arts	M
Biological and Biomedical Sciences—General	M
Business Administration and Management—General	M
Civil Engineering	M
Clinical Psychology	M
Communication—General	M
Computer and Information Systems Security	M
Computer Science	M
Counseling Psychology	M
Criminal Justice and Criminology	M
Early Childhood Education	M
Educational Leadership and Administration	M
Electrical Engineering	M
Energy Management and Policy	M
Engineering Management	M
English	M
Environmental and Occupational Health	M
Environmental Engineering	M
Family Nurse Practitioner Studies	M,D
Health Education	M
Health Services Management and Hospital Administration	M
History	M
Human Resources Development	M,D
Industrial and Manufacturing Management	M
Interdisciplinary Studies	M
Kinesiology and Movement Studies	M
Marketing	M
Marriage and Family Therapy	M
Mathematics	M
Mechanical Engineering	M
Nursing and Healthcare Administration	M,D
Nursing Education	M,D
Nursing—General	M,D
Organizational Management	M
Pharmacy	D
Political Science	M
Psychology—General	M
Public Administration	M
Quality Management	M
Reading Education	M
School Psychology	M
Social Sciences	M
Sociology	M
Special Education	M
Structural Engineering	M
Transportation and Highway Engineering	M
Water Resources Engineering	M

THE UNIVERSITY OF TEXAS HEALTH SCIENCE CENTER AT HOUSTON

Allopathic Medicine	D
Biochemistry	M,D
Bioinformatics	M,D,O
Biological and Biomedical Sciences—General	M,D
Cancer Biology/Oncology	M,D
Cell Biology	M,D
Dentistry	M,D
Genetic Counseling	M,D
Genetics	M,D
Immunology	M,D
Infectious Diseases	M,D
Medical Physics	M,D
Microbiology	M,D
Neuroscience	M,D
Nursing—General	M,D
Pharmacology	M,D
Public Health—General	M,D,O
Quantitative Analysis	M,D

THE UNIVERSITY OF TEXAS HEALTH SCIENCE CENTER AT SAN ANTONIO

Acute Care/Critical Care Nursing	M,D,O
Allopathic Medicine	M,D
Biochemistry	M,D
Biological and Biomedical Sciences—General	D
Biomedical Engineering	M,D
Cell Biology	M,D
Clinical Laboratory Sciences/Medical Technology	D
Clinical Research	M
Communication Disorders	M
Community Health Nursing	M,D,O
Dentistry	M,D,O
Family Nurse Practitioner Studies	M,D,O
Gerontological Nursing	M,D,O
Immunology	M,D
Interdisciplinary Studies	D
Medical Physics	D
Microbiology	M,D
Molecular Medicine	M,D
Neuroscience	D
Nursing and Healthcare Administration	M,D,O
Nursing Education	M,D,O
Nursing—General	M,D,O
Occupational Therapy	M,D
Pediatric Nursing	M,D,O
Pharmacology	D
Physical Therapy	M,D
Physician Assistant Studies	M
Psychiatric Nursing	M,D,O

Special Education	M,D
Structural Biology	M,D
Toxicology	M

THE UNIVERSITY OF TEXAS MD ANDERSON CANCER CENTER

Genetics	M

THE UNIVERSITY OF TEXAS MEDICAL BRANCH

Allied Health—General	M,D
Allopathic Medicine	D
Biochemistry	D
Bioinformatics	D
Biological and Biomedical Sciences—General	M,D
Biophysics	D
Cell Biology	M,D
Clinical Laboratory Sciences/Medical Technology	M,D
Computational Biology	D
Demography and Population Studies	D
Genetics	D
Humanities	M,D
Immunology	M,D
Microbiology	M,D
Molecular Biophysics	D
Neuroscience	D
Nursing—General	M,D
Occupational Therapy	M
Pathology	D
Pharmacology	M,D
Physical Therapy	M,D
Physician Assistant Studies	M
Physiology	M
Public Health—General	M
Rehabilitation Sciences	D
Structural Biology	D
Toxicology	M,D
Translational Biology	M,D

THE UNIVERSITY OF TEXAS OF THE PERMIAN BASIN

Accounting	M
Applied Psychology	M
Biological and Biomedical Sciences—General	M
Business Administration and Management—General	M
Clinical Psychology	M
Computer Science	M
Counselor Education	M
Criminal Justice and Criminology	M
Early Childhood Education	M
Education—General	M
Educational Leadership and Administration	M
English as a Second Language	M
English	M
Experimental Psychology	M
Foundations and Philosophy of Education	M
Geology	M
History	M
Kinesiology and Movement Studies	M
Political Science	M
Psychology—General	M
Reading Education	M
Spanish	M
Special Education	M

THE UNIVERSITY OF TEXAS RIO GRANDE VALLEY

Accounting	M
Adult Nursing	M
Advertising and Public Relations	M,O
Allopathic Medicine	D
Anthropology	M
Art/Fine Arts	M
Biological and Biomedical Sciences—General	M
Business Administration and Management—General	M,D
Chemistry	M
Clinical Laboratory Sciences/Medical Technology	M
Clinical Psychology	M
Communication Disorders	M
Communication—General	M,O
Computer Science	M
Counselor Education	M
Criminal Justice and Criminology	M
Curriculum and Instruction	M,D
Early Childhood Education	M,D
Education—General	M,D
Educational Leadership and Administration	M,D
Educational Measurement and Evaluation	M
Educational Media/Instructional Technology	M,D
Educational Psychology	M
Electrical Engineering	M
Elementary Education	M,D
Engineering Management	M
English as a Second Language	M
English	M
Exercise and Sports Science	M
Experimental Psychology	M
Family Nurse Practitioner Studies	M
Finance and Banking	M,D
Health Services Management and Hospital Administration	M
History	M
Interdisciplinary Studies	M
Kinesiology and Movement Studies	M
Management Information Systems	M
Manufacturing Engineering	M
Marketing	M,D
Mathematics	M
Mechanical Engineering	M
Multilingual and Multicultural Education	M
Music Education	M
Music	M

Nursing—General | M
Nutrition | M
Occupational Therapy | M
Physician Assistant Studies | M
Physics | M
Psychology—General | M
Public Administration | M
Public Affairs | M
Public Policy | M
Reading Education | M
Rehabilitation Counseling | M,D
Rhetoric | M
School Psychology | M
Secondary Education | M,D
Social Work | M
Sociology | M
Spanish | M
Special Education | M
Statistics | M
Systems Engineering | M
Theater | M,O
Writing | M

THE UNIVERSITY OF TEXAS SOUTHWESTERN MEDICAL CENTER
Allopathic Medicine | D
Biochemistry | D
Biological and Biomedical Sciences—General | M,D
Biomedical Engineering | M,D
Cancer Biology/Oncology | D
Cell Biology | D
Clinical Psychology | D
Developmental Biology | D
Genetics | D
Immunology | D
Microbiology | D
Molecular Biophysics | D
Neuroscience | D
Nutrition | M
Physical Therapy | D
Physician Assistant Studies | M
Rehabilitation Counseling | M

THE UNIVERSITY OF THE ARTS
Art Education | M
Art/Fine Arts | M
Industrial Design | M
Museum Education | M
Museum Studies | M
Music Education | M
Music | M

UNIVERSITY OF THE CUMBERLANDS
Accounting | M
Business Administration and Management—General | M
Business Education | M,D,O
Clinical Psychology | D
Counseling Psychology | M
Counselor Education | M,D,O
Education—General | M,D,O
Educational Leadership and Administration | M,D,O
Elementary Education | M,D,O
Marketing | M,D,O
Middle School Education | M,D,O
Physician Assistant Studies | M
Reading Education | M,D,O
Religion | M
Secondary Education | M,D,O
Special Education | M,D,O
Student Affairs | M,D,O
Theater | M,D,O

UNIVERSITY OF THE DISTRICT OF COLUMBIA
Adult Education | O
Architecture | M
Business Administration and Management—General | M
Cancer Biology/Oncology | M
Communication Disorders | M
Computer Science | M
Counseling Psychology | M
Early Childhood Education | M
Electrical Engineering | M
Elementary Education | M
Engineering and Applied Sciences—General | M
English Education | M
Homeland Security | M
Law | M,D
Legal and Justice Studies | M,D
Mathematics Education | M
Middle School Education | M
Nutrition | M
Public Administration | M
Rehabilitation Counseling | M
Secondary Education | M
Social Sciences Education | M
Water Resources | M

UNIVERSITY OF THE FRASER VALLEY
Criminal Justice and Criminology | M
Social Work | M

UNIVERSITY OF THE INCARNATE WORD
Applied Statistics | M
Biological and Biomedical Sciences—General | M
Clothing and Textiles | M
Communication—General | M
Mathematics Education | M
Mathematics | M
Nutrition | M
Optometry | D
Osteopathic Medicine | M,D
Pastoral Ministry and Counseling | M
Pharmacy | D
Physical Therapy | D

UNIVERSITY OF THE PACIFIC
Biological and Biomedical Sciences—General | M
Business Administration and Management—General | M
Communication Disorders | M
Communication—General | M
Curriculum and Instruction | M,D
Dentistry | M,D,O
Education—General | M,D,O
Educational Leadership and Administration | M,D
Educational Psychology | M,D,O
Engineering and Applied Sciences—General | M
Exercise and Sports Science | M
Hospitality Management | M
International Affairs | M,D
Law | M,D
Music Education | M
Music | M
Pharmaceutical Sciences | M,D
Pharmacy | D
Physical Therapy | M,D
Psychology—General | M
Public Policy | M,D
School Psychology | M,D,O
Special Education | M,D
Therapies—Dance, Drama, and Music | M
Water Resources | M,D

UNIVERSITY OF THE POTOMAC
Business Administration and Management—General | M

UNIVERSITY OF THE ROCKIES
Psychology—General | M,D

UNIVERSITY OF THE SACRED HEART
Accounting | M,O
Advertising and Public Relations | M
Broadcast Journalism | M,O
Business Administration and Management—General | M,O
Communication—General | M,O
Conflict Resolution and Mediation/Peace Studies | M
Cultural Studies | M
Early Childhood Education | M,O
Education—General | M,O
Educational Media/Instructional Technology | M
English Education | M,O
Environmental and Occupational Health | M
Film, Television, and Video Production | M,O
Foreign Languages Education | M,O
Human Resources Management | M
Information Science | O
Internet and Interactive Multimedia | M,O
Legal and Justice Studies | M
Management Information Systems | M
Marketing | M
Mathematics Education | M
Nonprofit Management | M
Occupational Health Nursing | M
Taxation | M
Writing | M,O

UNIVERSITY OF THE SCIENCES
Biochemistry | M,D
Bioinformatics | M
Biotechnology | M
Cell Biology | M
Chemistry | M,D
Health Psychology | M
Health Services Management and Hospital Administration | M,D
Medicinal and Pharmaceutical Chemistry | M,D
Occupational Therapy | M,D
Pharmaceutical Administration | M
Pharmaceutical Sciences | M,D
Pharmacology | M,D
Pharmacy | D
Physical Therapy | D
Physician Assistant Studies | M
Public Health—General | M
Technical Writing | M,O
Toxicology | M

UNIVERSITY OF THE SOUTHWEST
Business Administration and Management—General | M
Counseling Psychology | M
Counselor Education | M
Curriculum and Instruction | M
Early Childhood Education | M
Education—General | M
Educational Leadership and Administration | M
English as a Second Language | M
Multilingual and Multicultural Education | M
Special Education | M
Sports Management | M

UNIVERSITY OF THE VIRGIN ISLANDS
Business Administration and Management—General | M
Education—General | M,D,O
Educational Leadership and Administration | M,D,O
Environmental Sciences | M
Liberal Studies | M
Marine Sciences | M
Mathematics Education | M
Mathematics | M
School Psychology | M,D,O

UNIVERSITY OF THE WEST
Business Administration and Management—General | M
Finance and Banking | M
International Business | M
Management Information Systems | M
Nonprofit Management | M
Psychology—General | M
Religion | M,D
Theology | M

THE UNIVERSITY OF TOLEDO
Accounting | M
Analytical Chemistry | M,D
Applied Mathematics | M,D
Art Education | M,D,O
Astrophysics | M,D
Biochemistry | M,D
Bioengineering | M,D
Bioinformatics | M,D
Biological and Biomedical Sciences—General | M,D,O
Biomedical Engineering | D
Biostatistics | M,O
Business Administration and Management—General | M
Business Education | M,D,O
Cancer Biology/Oncology | M,D
Cardiovascular Sciences | M,D
Chemical Engineering | M,D
Chemistry | M,D
Civil Engineering | M,D
Clinical Psychology | M,D
Communication Disorders | M,D
Communication—General | O
Community Health Nursing | M
Computer Science | M,D
Counselor Education | M,D,O
Criminal Justice and Criminology | M,D
Curriculum and Instruction | M,D,O
Early Childhood Education | M,D,O
Ecology | M,D
Economics | M,D,O
Education of the Gifted | M,D,O
Education—General | M,D,O
Educational Leadership and Administration | M,D,O
Educational Measurement and Evaluation | M,D,O
Educational Media/Instructional Technology | M,D,O
Educational Psychology | M,D,O
Electrical Engineering | M,D
Elementary Education | M,D,O
Emergency Management | M,O
Engineering and Applied Sciences—General | M
English as a Second Language | M,D,O
English Education | M,D,O
English | M,O
Environmental and Occupational Health | M,O
Environmental Sciences | M,D
Epidemiology | M,O
Exercise and Sports Science | M,D
Experimental Psychology | M,D
Family Nurse Practitioner Studies | M,O
Finance and Banking | M
Foreign Languages Education | M,D,O
Foundations and Philosophy of Education | M,D,O
French | M
Gender Studies | O
Genomic Sciences | M,O
Geographic Information Systems | M,D,O
Geography | M,D,O
Geology | M,D
German | M
Gerontology | M,O
Health Education | M,D,O
Health Promotion | M,D,O
Health Services Management and Hospital Administration | M,O
Higher Education | M,D,O
History | M,D
Immunology | M,D
Industrial Hygiene | M,O
Industrial/Management Engineering | M,D
Inorganic Chemistry | M,D
International Business | M
International Health | M,O
Law | M,D,O
Leisure Studies | M,D
Liberal Studies | M
Marketing | M
Materials Sciences | M,D
Mathematics Education | M,D,O
Mathematics | M,D
Mechanical Engineering | M,D
Medical Physics | M,D
Medicinal and Pharmaceutical Chemistry | M,D
Middle School Education | M,D,O
Music Education | M,O
Music | M,O
Neuroscience | M,D
Nonprofit Management | M,O
Nursing and Healthcare Administration | M,O
Nursing Education | M,O
Nursing—General | M,D,O
Nutrition | M,O
Occupational Therapy | M,D
Oral and Dental Sciences | M
Organic Chemistry | M,D
Pathology | M,O
Pediatric Nursing | M,O

UNIVERSITY OF TORONTO
Pharmaceutical Administration | M
Pharmaceutical Sciences | M
Pharmacology | M,D
Philosophy | M
Physical Chemistry | M,D
Physical Education | M
Physical Therapy | M,D
Physician Assistant Studies | M
Physics | M,D
Political Science | M,O
Psychology—General | M,D
Public Administration | M,O
Public Health—General | M,O
Recreation and Park Management | M,D
School Psychology | M,D,O
Science Education | M,D,O
Secondary Education | M,D,O
Social Sciences Education | M,D,O
Social Work | M,O
Sociology | M
Spanish | M
Special Education | M,D,O
Statistics | M,D
Urban and Regional Planning | M,D,O
Vocational and Technical Education | M,D,O
Women's Studies | O
Writing | M,O

UNIVERSITY OF TORONTO
Aerospace/Aeronautical Engineering | M,D
Allopathic Medicine | M,D
Anthropology | M,D
Architecture | M
Art History | M,D
Asian Studies | M,D
Astronomy | M,D
Astrophysics | M,D
Biochemistry | M,D
Bioethics | M
Biomedical Engineering | M,D
Biophysics | M,D
Biostatistics | M,D
Biotechnology | M
Business Administration and Management—General | M,D
Cell Biology | M,D
Chemical Engineering | M,D
Chemistry | M,D
Civil Engineering | M,D
Classics | M,D
Communication Disorders | M,D
Community Health | M,D
Comparative Literature | M,D
Computer Engineering | M,D
Computer Science | M,D
Criminal Justice and Criminology | M,D
Dentistry | D
East European and Russian Studies | M
Ecology | M,D
Economics | M,D
Education—General | M,D
Electrical Engineering | M,D
Engineering and Applied Sciences—General | M,D
English | M,D
Environmental and Occupational Health | M,D
Environmental Sciences | M,D
Epidemiology | M,D
Evolutionary Biology | M,D
Film, Television, and Video Theory and Criticism | M,D
Finance and Banking | M
Forestry | M,D
French | M,D
Gender Studies | M,D
Genetic Counseling | M
Geography | M,D
Geology | M,D
German | M,D
Health Informatics | M
Health Physics/Radiological Health | M,D
Health Promotion | M,D
Health Services Management and Hospital Administration | M
History of Science and Technology | M,D
History | M,D
Human Resources Management | M,D
Immunology | M,D
Industrial and Labor Relations | M,D
Industrial/Management Engineering | M,D
Information Studies | M,D
International Affairs | M
Italian | M,D
Kinesiology and Movement Studies | M,D
Landscape Architecture | M
Law | M,D
Linguistics | M,D
Management of Technology | M
Manufacturing Engineering | M
Materials Engineering | M,D
Materials Sciences | M,D
Mathematical and Computational Finance | M
Mathematics | M,D
Mechanical Engineering | M,D
Medieval and Renaissance Studies | M,D
Molecular Genetics | M,D
Museum Studies | M
Music Education | M,D
Music | M,D
Near and Middle Eastern Studies | M,D
Nursing—General | M,D
Nutrition | M
Occupational Therapy | M
Oral and Dental Sciences | M,D
Pathobiology | M,D
Pharmaceutical Sciences | M,D
Pharmacology | M,D

Philosophy	M,D
Physical Education	M,D
Physical Therapy	M
Physics	M,D
Physiology	M,D
Political Science	M,D
Portuguese	M,D
Psychology—General	M,D
Public Health—General	M,D
Rehabilitation Sciences	M,D
Religion	M,D
Slavic Languages	M,D
Social Sciences	M,D
Social Work	M,D
Sociology	M,D
Spanish	M,D
Statistics	M,D
Systems Biology	M,D
Theater	M,D
Urban and Regional Planning	M,D
Urban Design	M,D
Women's Studies	M,D
Writing	M,D

THE UNIVERSITY OF TULSA

Accounting	M
American Indian/Native American Studies	M,D,O
Anthropology	M,D
Applied Mathematics	
Art/Fine Arts	M
Biochemistry	M,D
Biological and Biomedical Sciences—General	M,D
Business Administration and Management—General	M
Chemical Engineering	M,D
Chemistry	M,D
Clinical Psychology	M,D
Communication Disorders	M
Computer and Information Systems Security	M,D
Computer Science	M,D
Education—General	M
Electrical Engineering	M,D
Elementary Education	M
Energy Management and Policy	M
Engineering and Applied Sciences—General	M,D
Engineering Physics	M,D
English Education	M
English	M,D
Environmental Law	M,D,O
Family Nurse Practitioner Studies	D
Finance and Banking	M
Financial Engineering	M
Geophysics	M,D
Geosciences	M,D
Gerontological Nursing	D
Health Law	M,D,O
History	M
Industrial and Organizational Psychology	M,D
Investment Management	M
Kinesiology and Movement Studies	M
Law	M,D,O
Mathematics Education	M
Mathematics	M,D
Mechanical Engineering	M,D
Museum Studies	M
Nursing—General	D
Petroleum Engineering	M,D
Physics	M,D
Psychology—General	M,D
Rehabilitation Sciences	M
Science Education	M
Secondary Education	M

UNIVERSITY OF UTAH

Accounting	M,D
Allopathic Medicine	D
American Studies	M,D
Anatomy	D
Anthropology	M,D
Architecture	M
Art Education	M
Art History	M
Art/Fine Arts	M
Asian Studies	M
Athletic Training and Sports Medicine	D
Atmospheric Sciences	M,D
Biochemistry	M,D
Bioengineering	M,D*
Bioinformatics	M,D,O
Biological and Biomedical Sciences—General	M,D,O
Biostatistics	M,D
Biotechnology	M
Business Administration and Management—General	M,D,O
Cancer Biology/Oncology	M,D
Chemical Engineering	M,D
Chemical Physics	M,D
Chemistry	M,D
Child and Family Studies	M
Civil Engineering	M,D
Clinical Laboratory Sciences/Medical Technology	M
Clinical Psychology	M,D,O
Communication Disorders	M,D
Communication—General	M,D
Comparative Literature	M,D
Computational Sciences	M
Computer and Information Systems Security	M,O
Computer Science	M,D
Consumer Economics	M
Counseling Psychology	M,D,O
Counselor Education	M,D,O
Dance	M,O
Dentistry	D
Early Childhood Education	M,D
Economics	M,D

Education—General	M,D,O
Educational Leadership and Administration	M,D
Educational Media/Instructional Technology	M,D,O
Educational Psychology	M,D,O
Electrical Engineering	M,D
Elementary Education	M,D,O
Engineering and Applied Sciences—General	M,D
English	M,D
Environmental Engineering	M,D
Environmental Sciences	M
Film, Television, and Video Production	M
Finance and Banking	M,D
Foreign Languages Education	M,D
Foundations and Philosophy of Education	M,D
French	M,D
Game Design and Development	M
Geographic Information Systems	M,D
Geography	M,D
Geological Engineering	M,D
Geology	M,D
Geophysics	M,D
Gerontological Nursing	M,O
Gerontology	M,O
Graphic Design	M
Health Education	M,D
Health Promotion	M,D
Health Services Management and Hospital Administration	M,D
Health Services Research	M,D
Higher Education	M,D
History	M,D
Human Development	M
Human Genetics	M,D
Humanities	M
Industrial and Manufacturing Management	M,D,O
International Affairs	M,D
Internet and Interactive Multimedia	M
Kinesiology and Movement Studies	M,D
Latin American Studies	M
Law	M,D
Leisure Studies	M,D
Linguistics	M,D
Management Information Systems	M,D,O
Management Strategy and Policy	M,D,O
Marketing	M,D
Materials Engineering	M,D
Materials Sciences	M,D
Mathematics Education	M,D
Mathematics	M,D
Mechanical Engineering	M,D
Medical Physics	M,D
Medicinal and Pharmaceutical Chemistry	M,D
Metallurgical Engineering and Metallurgy	M,D
Mineral/Mining Engineering	M,D
Molecular Biology	D
Music Education	M,D
Music	M,D
Near and Middle Eastern Languages	M,D
Near and Middle Eastern Studies	M,D
Neurobiology	D
Neuroscience	D
Nuclear Engineering	M,D
Nursing—General	M,D
Nutrition	M,D
Occupational Therapy	M,D
Organizational Behavior	M,D
Pathology	M,D
Petroleum Engineering	M,D
Pharmaceutical Administration	M,D
Pharmaceutical Sciences	M,D
Pharmacology	D
Pharmacy	D
Philosophy	M,D
Photography	M
Physical Therapy	D
Physician Assistant Studies	M
Physics	M,D
Physiology	M,D
Political Science	M,D
Psychology—General	D
Public Administration	M,D
Public Health—General	M,D
Public Policy	M
Reading Education	M,D,O
Real Estate	M
Recreation and Park Management	M,D
Rehabilitation Sciences	D
Rhetoric	M,D
School Psychology	M,D,O
Science Education	M,D
Secondary Education	M,D
Social Work	M,D
Sociology	M,D
Software Engineering	M,O
Spanish	M,D
Special Education	M,D
Statistics	M,D,O
Student Affairs	M,D
Systems Engineering	M,O
Toxicology	D
Urban and Regional Planning	M,D
Urban Design	M,D
Writing	M,D

UNIVERSITY OF VALLEY FORGE

Music	M
Religion	M
Theology	M

UNIVERSITY OF VERMONT

Accounting	M
Agricultural Economics and Agribusiness	M
Agricultural Sciences—General	M,D

Agronomy and Soil Sciences	M,D
Allied Health—General	M,D
Animal Sciences	M,D
Applied Economics	M
Biological and Biomedical Sciences—General	M,D,O
Biomedical Engineering	D
Biostatistics	M
Business Administration and Management—General	M
Cell Biology	D
Chemistry	M,D
Civil Engineering	M,D
Clinical Laboratory Sciences/Medical Technology	M,D,O
Clinical Psychology	D
Communication Disorders	M
Communication—General	M
Computer Science	M,D
Counseling Psychology	M
Counselor Education	M
Curriculum and Instruction	M
Education—General	M,D
Educational Leadership and Administration	M,D
Electrical Engineering	M,D
Engineering and Applied Sciences—General	M
English	M
Environmental Engineering	M,D
Food Science and Technology	M,D
Forestry	M,D
Geology	M
German	M
Historic Preservation	M
History	M
Horticulture	M,D
Interdisciplinary Studies	M
Materials Sciences	M
Mathematics Education	M
Mathematics	M
Mechanical Engineering	M,D
Molecular Biology	D
Natural Resources	M,D
Neuroscience	D
Nursing—General	M,D
Nutrition	M,D
Pathology	M
Pharmacology	M,D
Physical Therapy	D
Physics	M
Plant Biology	M,D
Plant Sciences	M,D
Psychology—General	D
Public Administration	M
Science Education	M,D
Social Work	M
Special Education	M
Statistics	M

UNIVERSITY OF VICTORIA

Anthropology	M
Art Education	M,D
Art History	M,D
Art/Fine Arts	M
Asian Studies	M
Astronomy	M,D
Astrophysics	M,D
Biochemistry	M,D
Biological and Biomedical Sciences—General	M,D
Business Administration and Management—General	M
Chemistry	M,D
Child and Family Studies	M,D
Classics	M,D
Clinical Psychology	M,D
Computer Art and Design	M
Computer Engineering	M,D
Computer Science	M,D
Condensed Matter Physics	M,D
Conflict Resolution and Mediation/Peace Studies	M,D
Counseling Psychology	M,D
Counselor Education	M,D
Curriculum and Instruction	M,D
Developmental Psychology	M,D
Early Childhood Education	M,D
Economics	M,D
Education—General	M,D
Educational Leadership and Administration	M,D
Educational Measurement and Evaluation	M,D
Educational Psychology	M,D
Electrical Engineering	M,D
Engineering and Applied Sciences—General	M,D
English Education	M,D
English	M,D
Environmental Education	M,D
Experimental Psychology	M,D
Family Nurse Practitioner Studies	M,D
Film, Television, and Video Production	M
Foreign Languages Education	M
Foundations and Philosophy of Education	M,D
French	M
Geography	M,D
Geosciences	M,D
German	M
Health Informatics	M
Hispanic Studies	M
History	M,D
Human Development	M,D
Italian	M
Kinesiology and Movement Studies	M
Law	M,D
Leisure Studies	M
Linguistics	M,D
Mathematics Education	M,D
Mathematics	M,D

Mechanical Engineering	M,D
Medical Physics	M,D
Microbiology	M,D
Music Education	M,D
Music	M,D
Nursing and Healthcare Administration	M,D
Nursing Education	M,D
Nursing—General	M,D
Oceanography	M,D
Pacific Area/Pacific Rim Studies	M
Philosophy	M
Photography	M
Physical Education	M
Physics	M,D
Political Science	M,D
Psychology—General	M,D
Public Administration	M,D
Reading Education	M,D
Science Education	M,D
Social Psychology	M,D
Social Sciences Education	M,D
Social Work	M,D
Sociology	M,D
Special Education	M,D
Statistics	M,D
Theater	M,D
Theoretical Physics	M,D
Vocational and Technical Education	M,D
Writing	M

UNIVERSITY OF VIRGINIA

Accounting	M
Acute Care/Critical Care Nursing	M,D
Aerospace/Aeronautical Engineering	M,D
Allopathic Medicine	M,D
Anthropology	M,D
Architectural History	M,D
Art History	M,D
Asian Studies	M
Astronomy	M,D
Biochemistry	D
Biological and Biomedical Sciences—General	M,D
Biomedical Engineering	M,D
Biophysics	M,D
Business Administration and Management—General	M,D,O
Cell Biology	D
Chemical Engineering	M,D
Chemistry	M,D
Civil Engineering	M,D
Classics	M,D
Clinical Psychology	D
Clinical Research	M
Communication Disorders	M
Community Health	M,D
Computer Engineering	M,D
Computer Science	M,D
Construction Engineering	D
Counselor Education	M,D,O
Curriculum and Instruction	M,D,O
Database Systems	M
Early Childhood Education	M,D
Economics	M,D
Education of the Gifted	M,D,O
Education—General	M,D,O
Educational Leadership and Administration	M,D,O
Educational Measurement and Evaluation	M,D,O
Educational Media/Instructional Technology	M,D,O
Educational Policy	D
Educational Psychology	M,D,O
Electrical Engineering	M,D
Elementary Education	M,D,O
Engineering and Applied Sciences—General	M,D
Engineering Physics	M,D
English Education	M,D,O
English	M,D
Environmental Sciences	M,D
Finance and Banking	M
Foreign Languages Education	M,D,O
French	M,D
German	M
Health Informatics	M
Health Services Management and Hospital Administration	M
Health Services Research	M
Higher Education	M,D,O
History	M,D
Interdisciplinary Studies	M,D
International Affairs	M,D
International Business	M,O
Kinesiology and Movement Studies	M,D
Landscape Architecture	M
Law	M,D
Linguistics	M
Management of Technology	M
Management Strategy and Policy	M,O
Marketing	M
Materials Sciences	M,D
Mathematics Education	M,D,O
Mathematics	M,D
Mechanical Engineering	M,D
Microbiology	M,D
Molecular Genetics	D
Molecular Physiology	M,D
Music	M,D
Near and Middle Eastern Studies	M
Neuroscience	D
Nursing and Healthcare Administration	M,D
Nursing—General	M,D
Pathology	D
Pharmacology	M,D
Philosophy	M,D
Physical Education	M,D
Physics	M,D
Physiology	D
Political Science	M,D

Psychiatric Nursing	M,D
Psychology—General	M,D
Public Health—General	M,D
Public Policy	M
Reading Education	M,D
Religion	M,D
School Psychology	M,D
Science Education	M,D,O
Slavic Languages	M,D
Social Sciences Education	M,D,O
Sociology	M,D
Spanish	M,D
Special Education	M,D,O
Statistics	M,D,O
Student Affairs	M,D,O
Systems Engineering	M,D
Theater	M
Urban and Regional Planning	M
Writing	M

UNIVERSITY OF WASHINGTON

Accounting	M,D
Aerospace/Aeronautical Engineering	M,D
Allopathic Medicine	D
Animal Behavior	D
Anthropology	M,D
Applied Arts and Design—General	M
Applied Mathematics	M,D
Applied Physics	M,D
Architecture	M,D,O
Art History	M,D
Art/Fine Arts	M
Asian Languages	M,D
Asian Studies	M,D
Astronomy	M,D
Atmospheric Sciences	M,D
Biochemistry	D
Bioengineering	M,D
Bioethics	M
Bioinformatics	M
Biological and Biomedical Sciences—General	M,D
Biophysics	D
Biostatistics	M,D
Biotechnology	D
Business Administration and Management—General	M,D
Business Education	M,D
Cell Biology	D
Chemical Engineering	M,D
Chemistry	M,D
Chinese	M,D
Civil Engineering	M,D
Classics	M,D
Clinical Laboratory Sciences/Medical Technology	M
Clinical Psychology	D
Clinical Research	M,D
Cognitive Sciences	D
Communication Disorders	M,D
Communication—General	M,D
Community Health	M,D
Comparative Literature	M,D
Computational Sciences	M,D
Computer and Information Systems Security	M,D
Construction Engineering	M,D
Construction Management	M
Curriculum and Instruction	M,D
Dance	M
Database Systems	M,D
Dentistry	D
Developmental Psychology	D
East European and Russian Studies	M
Ecology	M,D
Economics	D
Education—General	M,D
Educational Leadership and Administration	M,D
Educational Measurement and Evaluation	M,D
Educational Media/Instructional Technology	M,D
Educational Policy	M,D
Educational Psychology	M,D
Electrical Engineering	M,D
Engineering and Applied Sciences—General	M,D,O
English as a Second Language	M,D
English Education	M,D
English	M,D
Entrepreneurship	M,D
Environmental and Occupational Health	M,D
Environmental Engineering	M,D
Environmental Management and Policy	M,D
Epidemiology	M,D
Fish, Game, and Wildlife Management	M,D
Forestry	M,D
Foundations and Philosophy of Education	M,D
French	M,D
Genetics	M,D,O
Genomic Sciences	D
Geography	M,D
Geology	M,D
Geophysics	M,D
Geotechnical Engineering	M,D
German	M,D
Health Informatics	M,D
Health Services Management and Hospital Administration	M,D
Health Services Research	M,D
Higher Education	M,D
Hispanic and Latin American Languages	M
Historic Preservation	O
History	M,D

Horticulture	M,D
Human Development	M,D
Hydrology	M,D
Immunology	D
Industrial Design	M
Industrial/Management Engineering	M,D
Information Science	M,D
Intellectual Property Law	M,D
International Affairs	D
International Business	M,D,O
International Health	M,D
Italian	M,D
Japanese	M,D
Landscape Architecture	M
Law	M,D
Legal and Justice Studies	M,D
Library Science	M,D
Lighting Design	M,D,O
Linguistics	M,D
Logistics	O
Management Information Systems	M,D
Management of Technology	M,O
Marine Affairs	M,O
Marine Geology	M,D
Materials Engineering	M,D
Materials Sciences	M,D
Maternal and Child Health	M,D
Mathematics Education	M,D
Mathematics	M,D
Mechanical Engineering	M,D
Mechanics	M,D
Medical Informatics	M,D
Medicinal and Pharmaceutical Chemistry	D
Microbiology	D
Molecular Biology	D
Multilingual and Multicultural Education	M,D
Museum Studies	M
Music Education	M,D
Music	M,D
Nanotechnology	M,D
Natural Resources	M,D
Near and Middle Eastern Studies	M,D
Neurobiology	D
Nursing—General	M,D,O
Nutrition	M,D
Occupational Therapy	M,D
Oceanography	M,D
Oral and Dental Sciences	M,D,O
Pathobiology	D
Pathology	D
Pharmaceutical Sciences	M,D
Pharmacology	D
Pharmacy	M,D
Philosophy	M,D
Photography	M
Physical Education	M,D
Physical Therapy	M,D
Physics	M,D
Physiology	D
Political Science	M,D
Portuguese	M
Psychology—General	D
Public Administration	M,D
Public Affairs	M,D
Public Health—General	M
Public Policy	M,D
Reading Education	M,D
Rehabilitation Sciences	M,D
Religion	M,D
Russian	M,D
Scandinavian Languages	M,D
School Psychology	M,D
Science Education	M,D
Slavic Languages	M,D
Social Psychology	D
Social Sciences Education	M,D
Social Sciences	M,D
Social Work	M,D
Sociology	M,D
Spanish	M
Special Education	M,D
Statistics	M,D
Structural Biology	D
Structural Engineering	M,D
Supply Chain Management	M,D
Sustainable Development	M,D
Taxation	M,D
Technical Communication	M,D,O
Theater	M,D
Toxicology	M,D
Transportation and Highway Engineering	M,D
Transportation Management	O
Urban and Regional Planning	M,D
Urban Design	M,D,O
Veterinary Sciences	M
Women's Studies	D
Writing	M

UNIVERSITY OF WASHINGTON, BOTHELL

Business Administration and Management—General	M
Computer Engineering	M
Cultural Studies	M
Education—General	M
Educational Leadership and Administration	M
Middle School Education	M
Nursing—General	M
Public Policy	M
Secondary Education	M
Software Engineering	M
Writing	M

UNIVERSITY OF WASHINGTON, TACOMA

Accounting	M

Business Administration and Management—General	M
Community Health Nursing	M
Computer Engineering	M
Education—General	M
Educational Leadership and Administration	M
Elementary Education	M
Finance and Banking	M
Interdisciplinary Studies	M
Mathematics Education	M
Nursing and Healthcare Administration	M
Nursing Education	M
Nursing—General	M
Science Education	M
Social Work	M
Software Engineering	M
Special Education	M

UNIVERSITY OF WATERLOO

Accounting	M,D
Actuarial Science	M,D
Anthropology	M
Applied Mathematics	M,D
Architecture	M
Art/Fine Arts	M
Biochemistry	M,D
Biological and Biomedical Sciences—General	M,D
Biostatistics	M,D
Business Administration and Management—General	M
Chemical Engineering	M,D
Chemistry	M,D
Civil Engineering	M,D
Computer Engineering	M,D
Computer Science	M,D
Economic Development	M
Economics	M,D
Electrical Engineering	M,D
Engineering and Applied Sciences—General	M,D
Engineering Management	M
English	M,D
Entrepreneurship	M
Environmental Engineering	M,D
Environmental Management and Policy	M,D
Environmental Sciences	M,D
Finance and Banking	M,D
French	M,D
Geography	M,D
Geosciences	M,D
German	M,D
Health Education	M,D
Health Informatics	M,D
History	M,D
Information Science	M,D
International Affairs	M,D
Kinesiology and Movement Studies	M,D
Leisure Studies	M,D
Management of Technology	M,D
Mathematics	M,D
Mechanical Engineering	M,D
Near and Middle Eastern Studies	M
Operations Research	M,D
Optometry	M,D
Philosophy	M,D
Physics	M,D
Political Science	M,D
Psychology—General	M,D
Public Affairs	M
Public Health—General	M,D
Recreation and Park Management	M,D
Religion	D
Russian	M,D
Sociology	M,D
Software Engineering	M,D
Statistics	M,D
Systems Engineering	M,D
Taxation	M,D
Technical Writing	M,D
Urban and Regional Planning	M,D
Vision Sciences	M,D

THE UNIVERSITY OF WEST ALABAMA

Adult Education	M
Business Administration and Management—General	M
Child Development	M,O
Conservation Biology	M
Counselor Education	M,O
Curriculum and Instruction	M,O
Early Childhood Education	M,O
Education—General	M,O
Educational Leadership and Administration	M,O
Educational Media/Instructional Technology	M,O
Elementary Education	M,O
English Education	M
Experimental Psychology	M
Finance and Banking	M
Higher Education	M
History	M
Marriage and Family Therapy	M
Mathematics Education	M
Physical Education	M
School Psychology	M,O
Science Education	M
Secondary Education	M
Social Sciences Education	M
Special Education	M,O

THE UNIVERSITY OF WESTERN ONTARIO

Allopathic Medicine	M,D
Anatomy	M,D
Anthropology	M,D
Applied Mathematics	M,D
Astronomy	M,D

Biochemical Engineering	M,D
Biochemistry	M,D
Biological and Biomedical Sciences—General	M,D
Biophysics	M,D
Biostatistics	M,D
Business Administration and Management—General	M,D
Cell Biology	M,D
Chemical Engineering	M,D
Chemistry	M,D
Civil Engineering	M,D
Classics	M
Communication Disorders	M,D
Comparative Literature	M,D
Computer Engineering	M,D
Computer Science	M,D
Counseling Psychology	M
Curriculum and Instruction	M
Dentistry	D
Economics	M,D
Education—General	M
Educational Policy	M
Educational Psychology	M
Electrical Engineering	M,D
Engineering and Applied Sciences—General	M,D
English	M,D
Entrepreneurship	M,D
Environmental Engineering	M,D
Environmental Sciences	M,D
Epidemiology	M,D
Finance and Banking	M,D
French	M,D
Geography	M,D
Geology	M,D
Geophysics	M,D
Geosciences	M,D
Health Services Management and Hospital Administration	M,D
History	M,D
Immunology	M,D
Information Studies	M,D
Interdisciplinary Studies	M,D
International Business	M,D
Journalism	M
Kinesiology and Movement Studies	M,D
Law	M,D,O
Library Science	M,D
Management Strategy and Policy	M,D
Marketing	M,D
Materials Engineering	M,D
Mathematics	M,D
Mechanical Engineering	M,D
Media Studies	M,D
Microbiology	M,D
Music	M,D
Neuroscience	M,D
Nursing—General	M,D
Occupational Therapy	M
Oral and Dental Sciences	M
Pathology	M,D
Philosophy	M,D
Physical Therapy	M,O
Physics	M,D
Physiology	M,D
Political Science	M,D
Psychology—General	M,D
Sociology	M,D
Spanish	M,D
Special Education	M
Statistics	M,D
Sustainable Development	M,D

UNIVERSITY OF WESTERN STATES

Chiropractic	D

UNIVERSITY OF WEST FLORIDA

Accounting	M
American Studies	M
Anthropology	M
Applied Behavior Analysis	M
Applied Psychology	M
Archaeology	M
Biological and Biomedical Sciences—General	M
Business Administration and Management—General	M
Communication—General	M
Computer and Information Systems Security	M
Computer Science	M
Counseling Psychology	M
Criminal Justice and Criminology	M
Curriculum and Instruction	M,O
Database Systems	M
Educational Leadership and Administration	M,D
Educational Media/Instructional Technology	M,D
Elementary Education	M
English	M
Environmental Sciences	M
Exercise and Sports Science	M
Experimental Psychology	M
Geographic Information Systems	M
Health Promotion	M
Health Services Management and Hospital Administration	M
History	M
Industrial and Organizational Psychology	M
Leisure Studies	M
Mathematics	M
Middle School Education	M
Nursing—General	M
Physical Education	M,D
Political Science	M
Psychology—General	M
Public Health—General	M
Public History	M

---

*M—masters degree; D—doctorate; O—other advanced degree; *—Close-Up and/or Display*

Reading Education | M
Secondary Education | M
Social Work | M
Software Engineering | M
Special Education | M
Student Affairs | M
Writing | M

UNIVERSITY OF WEST GEORGIA

Accounting | M
Biological and Biomedical Sciences—General | M,O
Business Administration and Management—General | M
Business Education | M,D,O
Communication Disorders | M,D,O
Computer Science | M,O
Counselor Education | M,D,O
Criminal Justice and Criminology | M,D,O
Early Childhood Education | M,D,O
Education—General | M,D,O
Educational Leadership and Administration | M,D,O
Educational Media/Instructional Technology | M,D,O
English | M,O
Geographic Information Systems | M,O
Health Services Management and Hospital Administration | M,D,O
History | M,O
Mathematics | M,O
Museum Studies | M,O
Music Education | M,O
Music | M,O
Nonprofit Management | M,D,O
Nursing Education | M,D,O
Nursing—General | M,D,O
Psychology—General | M,D,O
Public Administration | M,D,O
Public History | M,O
Reading Education | M,D,O
Secondary Education | M,D,O
Sociology | M,D,O
Special Education | M,D,O
Urban and Regional Planning | M,D,O

UNIVERSITY OF WINDSOR

Applied Psychology | M,D
Art/Fine Arts | M
Biochemistry | M,D
Biological and Biomedical Sciences—General | M,D
Biopsychology | M,D
Business Administration and Management—General | M
Chemistry | M,D
Civil Engineering | M,D
Clinical Psychology | M,D
Communication—General | M
Computer Science | M,D
Criminal Justice and Criminology | M,D
Economics | M
Education—General | M,D
Electrical Engineering | M,D
Engineering and Applied Sciences—General | M,D
English | M
Environmental Engineering | M,D
Environmental Sciences | M,D
Geosciences | M,D
History | M
Industrial/Management Engineering | M,D
Kinesiology and Movement Studies | M
Legal and Justice Studies | M
Manufacturing Engineering | M,D
Materials Engineering | M,D
Mathematics | M,D
Mechanical Engineering | M,D
Nursing—General | M
Philosophy | M
Physics | M,D
Political Science | M
Psychology—General | M,D
Social Psychology | M,D
Social Work | M
Sociology | M,D
Statistics | M,D
Writing | M

THE UNIVERSITY OF WINNIPEG

History | M
Marriage and Family Therapy | M,O
Public Administration | M
Religion | M
Theology | M,O

UNIVERSITY OF WISCONSIN–EAU CLAIRE

Adult Nursing | M,D
Business Administration and Management—General | M
Communication Disorders | M
Education—General | M
English | M
Family Nurse Practitioner Studies | M,D
Gerontological Nursing | M,D
History | M
Library Science | M
Nursing and Healthcare Administration | M,D
Nursing Education | M,D
Nursing—General | M,D
Psychology—General | M,O
Reading Education | M
School Psychology | M,O
Secondary Education | M
Special Education | M
Writing | M

DIVERSITY OF WISCONSIN–GREEN BAY

Business Administration and Management—General | M
Education—General | M

Environmental Management and Policy | M
Environmental Sciences | M
Nursing and Healthcare Administration | M
Social Work | M
Sustainability Management | M

UNIVERSITY OF WISCONSIN–LA CROSSE

Athletic Training and Sports Medicine | M
Biological and Biomedical Sciences—General | M
Business Administration and Management—General | M
Cancer Biology/Oncology | M
Cell Biology | M
Community Health | M
Database Systems | M
Education—General | M,O
English Education | M,O
Exercise and Sports Science | M
Health Education | M
Higher Education | M,D
Marine Sciences | M
Medical Microbiology | M
Microbiology | M
Molecular Biology | M
Nurse Anesthesia | M
Occupational Therapy | M
Physical Education | M
Physical Therapy | D
Physician Assistant Studies | M
Physiology | M
Psychology—General | M,O
Reading Education | M,O
Recreation and Park Management | M
Rehabilitation Sciences | M
School Psychology | M,O
Software Engineering | M
Special Education | M,O
Student Affairs | M

UNIVERSITY OF WISCONSIN–MADISON

Accounting | M,D
Adult Nursing | D
African Studies | M,D
African-American Studies | M
Agricultural Economics and Agribusiness | M,D
Agricultural Engineering | M,D
Agricultural Sciences—General | M,D
Agronomy and Soil Sciences | M,D
Allopathic Medicine | D
American Studies | M,D
Animal Sciences | M,D
Anthropology | D
Applied Arts and Design—General | M,D
Applied Economics | M,D
Archaeology | D
Art Education | M,D
Art History | M,D
Art/Fine Arts | M
Arts Administration | M
Asian Languages | M,D
Asian Studies | M,D
Astronomy | D
Atmospheric Sciences | M,D
Automotive Engineering | M,D
Bacteriology | M
Biochemistry | M,D
Bioinformatics | M
Biological and Biomedical Sciences—General | M,D
Biomedical Engineering | M,D
Biometry | M
Biophysics | D
Biopsychology | D
Botany | M,D
Business Administration and Management—General | M
Cancer Biology/Oncology | D
Cell Biology | D
Chemical Engineering | D
Chemistry | M,D
Child and Family Studies | M,D
Chinese | M,D
Civil Engineering | M,D
Classics | M,D
Clinical Psychology | D
Clinical Research | M,D
Cognitive Sciences | D
Communication Disorders | M,D
Communication—General | M,D
Community Health | M,D*
Comparative Literature | M,D
Computer and Information Systems Security | M
Computer Science | M,D
Conservation Biology | M
Consumer Economics | M,D
Counseling Psychology | D
Counselor Education | M
Cultural Anthropology | D
Curriculum and Instruction | M,D
Demography and Population Studies | M,D
Developmental Psychology | D
Ecology | M
Economics | D
Education—General | M,D,O
Educational Leadership and Administration | M,D,O
Educational Policy | M,D,O
Educational Psychology | M,D
Electrical Engineering | M,D
Engineering and Applied Sciences—General | M,D
Engineering Physics | M,D
English | M,D
Entomology | M,D
Environmental Biology | M,D
Environmental Engineering | M,D
Epidemiology | M,D

Ergonomics and Human Factors | M,D
Family and Consumer Sciences—General | M,D
Film, Television, and Video Theory and Criticism | M,D
Finance and Banking | M,D
Fish, Game, and Wildlife Management | M,D
Folklore | M,D
Food Science and Technology | M,D
Foreign Languages Education | M,D
Forestry | M,D
French | M,D,O
Genetic Counseling | M,D
Genetics | M,D
Geographic Information Systems | M,D,O
Geography | M,D,O
Geological Engineering | M,D
Geology | M,D
Geophysics | M,D
German | M,D
Gerontological Nursing | D
Higher Education | M,D,O
History of Science and Technology | M,D
History | M,D
Horticulture | M,D
Human Development | M,D
Human Resources Management | M,D
Industrial/Management Engineering | M,D
Information Studies | M,D
Insurance | M,D
International and Comparative Education | M,D,O
Investment Management | D
Italian | M,D
Japanese | M,D
Jewish Studies | M,D
Journalism | M,D
Kinesiology and Movement Studies | M,D
Landscape Architecture | M
Latin American Studies | M,D
Law | M,D
Library Science | M,D
Linguistics | M,D
Management Information Systems | D
Management of Technology | M,D
Management Strategy and Policy | M,D
Manufacturing Engineering | M
Marine Sciences | M
Marketing Research | M
Marketing | D
Mass Communication | M,D
Materials Engineering | M,D
Mathematics Education | M,D
Mathematics | D
Mechanical Engineering | M,D
Mechanics | M,D
Media Studies | M,D
Medical Microbiology | D
Medical Physics | M,D
Microbiology | D
Molecular Biology | M,D
Molecular Pathology | D
Music Education | M,D
Music | M,D
Natural Resources | M,D
Near and Middle Eastern Languages | M,D
Near and Middle Eastern Studies | M,D
Neuroscience | D
Nuclear Engineering | M,D
Nursing—General | D
Nutrition | M,D
Occupational Therapy | M,D
Oceanography | D
Pathology | D
Pediatric Nursing | D
Pharmaceutical Administration | M,D
Pharmaceutical Sciences | M,D
Pharmacology | D
Pharmacy | D
Philosophy | M,D
Physical Therapy | D
Physician Assistant Studies | M
Physics | M,D
Physiology | M,D
Plant Pathology | M,D
Plant Sciences | M,D
Political Science | D
Portuguese | M,D
Psychiatric Nursing | D
Psychology—General | D
Public Affairs | M
Public Health—General | M
Real Estate | M,D
Rehabilitation Counseling | M,D
Rhetoric | M,D
Rural Sociology | M,D
Scandinavian Languages | M,D
Science Education | M,D
Slavic Languages | M,D
Social Psychology | D
Social Work | M,D
Sociology | M,D
Spanish | M,D
Special Education | M,D
Speech and Interpersonal Communication | M,D
Statistics | M,D
Supply Chain Management | M
Sustainable Development | M
Systems Engineering | M,D
Taxation | M
Theater | M,D
Toxicology | M,D
Urban and Regional Planning | M,D
Veterinary Medicine | M,D
Veterinary Sciences | M,D
Water Resources | M
Women's Studies | M,D
Writing | M,D
Zoology | M,D

UNIVERSITY OF WISCONSIN–MILWAUKEE

Actuarial Science | M,D
Adult Education | M,D,O
African Studies | D
Allied Health—General | M,D,O
Analytical Chemistry | M,D
Anthropology | M,D,O
Applied Arts and Design—General | M
Applied Behavior Analysis | M,D
Applied Mathematics | M,D
Archaeology | M,D,O
Architecture | M,D,O
Art Education | M
Art History | M
Athletic Training and Sports Medicine | M,D
Atmospheric Sciences | M,D
Biochemistry | M,D
Biological and Biomedical Sciences—General | M,D
Biological Anthropology | M,D,O
Biomedical Engineering | M,D
Biostatistics | M,D,O
Botany | M,D
Business Administration and Management—General | M,O
Cell Biology | M,D
Chemistry | M,D
Civil Engineering | M,D
Classics | M,O
Clinical Psychology | M,D
Communication Disorders | M
Communication—General | M,D,O
Community Health | D
Comparative Literature | M,O
Computer Engineering | M,D
Computer Science | M,D
Conflict Resolution and Mediation/Peace Studies | M,D,O
Conservation Biology | M,D
Corporate and Organizational Communication | M,D,O
Counseling Psychology | M,D,O
Counselor Education | M,D,O
Criminal Justice and Criminology | M,O
Cultural Anthropology | M,D,O
Curriculum and Instruction | M,D,O
Developmental Psychology | M,D,O
Early Childhood Education | M
Ecology | M,D
Economics | M,D
Education—General | M,D,O
Educational Leadership and Administration | M,D,O
Educational Measurement and Evaluation | M,D,O
Educational Media/Instructional Technology | M,O
Educational Policy | M,O
Educational Psychology | M,D,O
Electrical Engineering | M,D
Elementary Education | M
Engineering and Applied Sciences—General | M,D
English as a Second Language | M,D,O
English Education | M
English | M,D
Environmental and Occupational Health | M,D,O
Environmental Sciences | M,D
Epidemiology | M,D,O
Ergonomics and Human Factors | M
Evolutionary Biology | M,D
Exercise and Sports Science | M,D
Experimental Psychology | M,D
Film, Television, and Video Theory and Criticism | M,D
Foreign Languages Education | M,O
Foundations and Philosophy of Education | M,D,O
French | M,O
Gender Studies | M,O
Genetics | M,D
Geographic Information Systems | M,D,O
Geography | M,D
Geology | M,D
German | M,D
Gerontology | M,D,O
Health Informatics | M,D
Health Promotion | M,D,O
Health Psychology | M,D
Health Services Management and Hospital Administration | M,D
Higher Education | M,O
History | M,D
Industrial/Management Engineering | M,D
Information Studies | M,D,O
Inorganic Chemistry | M,D
International Business | M,O
International Economics | M,O
Investment Management | M,O
Kinesiology and Movement Studies | M,D
Liberal Studies | M
Library Science | M,D,O
Linguistics | M,D,O
Management of Technology | M,O
Management Strategy and Policy | M,O
Manufacturing Engineering | M,D
Mass Communication | M,D,O
Materials Engineering | M,D
Mathematics Education | M,D
Mathematics | M,D
Mechanical Engineering | M,D
Mechanics | M,D
Media Studies | M,D
Medical Imaging | D
Medical Informatics | M
Microbiology | M,D
Middle School Education | M
Molecular Biology | M,D

Multilingual and Multicultural
Education — M,D,O
Museum Studies — M,D,O
Neuroscience — M,D
Nonprofit Management — M,D,O
Nursing—General — M,D,O*
Nutrition — M,D
Occupational Therapy — M
Organic Chemistry — M,D
Philosophy — M
Physical Chemistry — M,D
Physical Therapy — M,D
Physics — M,D
Political Science — M,D
Portuguese — M
Psychology—General — M,D
Public Administration — M
Public Health—General — M,D,O
Public History — M,D
Reading Education — M
Rehabilitation Sciences — D
Rhetoric — M,D,O
School Psychology — M,D,O
Science Education — M
Social Psychology — M,D,O
Social Sciences Education — M
Social Work — M,D,O
Sociology — M,D
Spanish — M,O
Special Education — M,D,O
Statistics — M,D
Taxation — M,O
Translation and Interpretation — M,O
Urban and Regional Planning — M
Urban Education — M,D,O
Water Resources — M,D
Women's Studies — M,O
Writing — M,D

UNIVERSITY OF WISCONSIN–OSHKOSH
Adult Nursing — M
Biological and Biomedical
Sciences—General — M
Botany — M
Business Administration and
Management—General — M
Counselor Education — M
Curriculum and Instruction — M
Early Childhood Education — M
Education—General — M
Educational Leadership and
Administration — M
English — M
Experimental Psychology — M
Family Nurse Practitioner Studies — M
Health Services Management and
Hospital Administration — M
Industrial and Organizational
Psychology — M
International Business — M
Mathematics Education — M
Microbiology — M
Nursing—General — M
Psychology—General — M
Public Administration — M
Reading Education — M
Social Work — M
Special Education — M
Zoology — M

UNIVERSITY OF WISCONSIN–PARKSIDE
Business Administration and
Management—General — M
Computer Science — M
Information Science — M
Molecular Biology — M

UNIVERSITY OF WISCONSIN–PLATTEVILLE
Adult Education — M
Computer Science — M
Counselor Education — M
Criminal Justice and Criminology — M
Education—General — M
Engineering and Applied
Sciences—General — M
Human Resources Management — M
Organizational Management — M
Project Management — M
Supply Chain Management — M

UNIVERSITY OF WISCONSIN–RIVER FALLS
Agricultural Education — M
Agricultural Sciences—
General — M
Art/Fine Arts — M
Business Administration and
Management—General — M
Communication Disorders — M
Counselor Education — M,O
Education—General — M
Elementary Education — M
English as a Second Language — M
Mathematics Education — M
Reading Education — M
School Psychology — M,O
Science Education — M
Social Sciences Education — M

UNIVERSITY OF WISCONSIN–STEVENS POINT
Advertising and Public Relations — M
Business Administration and
Management—General — M
Communication Disorders — M,D
Communication—General — M
Corporate and Organizational
Communication — M
Counselor Education — M
Education—General — M

Educational Leadership and
Administration — M
Elementary Education — M
English — M
Family and Consumer
Sciences-General — M
Health Promotion — M
History — M
Human Development — M
Media Studies — M
Music Education — M
Natural Resources — M
Nutrition — M
Reading Education — M
Science Education — M
Secondary Education — M
Special Education — M
Speech and Interpersonal
Communication — M

UNIVERSITY OF WISCONSIN–STOUT
Applied Mathematics — M
Applied Psychology — M
Art/Fine Arts — M
Clinical Psychology — M
Conservation Biology — M
Construction Management — M
Counseling Psychology — M
Education—General — M,D,O
Food Science and
Technology — M
Human Resources Development — M
Industrial Hygiene — M
Industrial/Management
Engineering — M
Information Science — M
Manufacturing Engineering — M
Marriage and Family Therapy — M
Nutrition — M
Project Management — M
Quality Management — M
Rehabilitation Counseling — M
School Psychology — M,O
Supply Chain Management — M
Sustainability Management — M
Technical Communication — M
Telecommunications
Management — M
Vocational and Technical Education — M,D,O

UNIVERSITY OF WISCONSIN–SUPERIOR
Art Education — M
Art History — M
Art Therapy — M
Art/Fine Arts — M
Communication—General — M
Counselor Education — M
Curriculum and Instruction — M
Education—General — M
Educational Leadership and
Administration — M,O
Mass Communication — M
Reading Education — M
School Psychology — M
Social Psychology — M
Special Education — M
Speech and Interpersonal
Communication — M
Sustainability Management — M
Theater — M

UNIVERSITY OF WISCONSIN–WHITEWATER
Accounting — M
Business Administration and
Management—General — M
Business Education — M
Communication Disorders — M
Communication—General — M
Corporate and Organizational
Communication — M
Education—General — M,O
Educational Leadership and
Administration — M
Environmental and Occupational
Health — M
Finance and Banking — M
Marketing — M
Mass Communication — M
Psychology—General — M,O
School Psychology — M,O
Special Education — M,O

UNIVERSITY OF WYOMING
Accounting — M
Agricultural Economics and
Agribusiness — M
Agricultural Sciences—
General — M,D
Agronomy and Soil Sciences — M,D
American Studies — M
Animal Sciences — M,D
Anthropology — M,D
Applied Economics — M
Atmospheric Sciences — M,D
Biotechnology — D
Botany — M,D
Business Administration and
Management—General — M
Cell Biology — D
Chemical Engineering — M,D
Chemistry — M,D
Child Development — M
Civil Engineering — M,D
Communication Disorders — M
Communication—General — M
Community Health — M,D
Computational Biology — D
Computer Science — M,D
Consumer Economics — M
Counselor Education — M,D
Curriculum and Instruction — M,D

Ecology — M,D
Economics — M,D
Educational Leadership and
Administration — M,D,O
Educational Media/Instructional
Technology — M,D
Electrical Engineering — M,D
Engineering and Applied
Sciences—General — M,D
English — M
Entomology — M,D
Environmental Engineering — M
Exercise and Sports Science — M
Finance and Banking — M
Food Science and
Technology — M
French — M
Genetics — D
Geography — M
Geology — M,D
Geophysics — M,D
German — M
Health Education — M
Health Promotion — M
Health Services Management and
Hospital Administration — M,D
History — M
International Affairs — M
Kinesiology and Movement Studies — M
Law — D
Mathematics Education — M,D
Mathematics — M,D
Mechanical Engineering — M,D
Microbiology — D
Molecular Biology — M,D
Music Education — M
Music — M
Natural Resources — M,D
Nursing—General — M
Nutrition — M
Pathobiology — M
Petroleum Engineering — M,D
Pharmacy — M,D
Philosophy — M
Physical Education — M
Physiology — M,D
Political Science — M
Psychology—General — M,D
Public Administration — M
Range Science — M,D
Reproductive Biology — M,D
Rural Planning and Studies — M
Science Education — M
Social Work — M
Sociology — M
Spanish — M
Special Education — M,D,O
Statistics — M,D
Student Affairs — M,D
Water Resources — M,D
Writing — M
Zoology — M,D

UPPER IOWA UNIVERSITY
Accounting — M
Business Administration and
Management—General — M
Early Childhood Education — M
Education—General — M
Educational Leadership and
Administration — M
Emergency Management — M
English as a Second Language — M
Finance and Banking — M
Higher Education — M
Homeland Security — M
Human Resources Management — M
Human Services — M
Nonprofit Management — M
Organizational Management — M
Public Administration — M
Reading Education — M
Sports Management — M

URBANA UNIVERSITY
Business Administration and
Management—General — M
Criminal Justice and Criminology — M
Education—General — M
Nursing—General — M

URSHAN GRADUATE SCHOOL OF THEOLOGY
Theology — M

URSULINE COLLEGE
Accounting — M
Adult Nursing — M,D
Art Therapy — M
Business Administration and
Management—General — M
Early Childhood Education — M
Educational Leadership and
Administration — M
Entrepreneurship — M
Family Nurse Practitioner Studies — M,D
Finance and Banking — M
Gerontological Nursing — M,D
Health Services Management and
Hospital Administration — M
Historic Preservation — M
Liberal Studies — M
Marketing — M
Medical/Surgical Nursing — M,D
Middle School Education — M
Nursing Education — M,D
Nursing—General — M,D
Pastoral Ministry and Counseling — M
Secondary Education — M
Special Education — M
Theology — M

UTAH STATE UNIVERSITY
Accounting — M
Aerospace/Aeronautical
Engineering — M,D
Agricultural Education — M
Agricultural Engineering — M,D
Agricultural Sciences—
General — M,D
Agronomy and Soil Sciences — M,D
American Studies — M
Animal Sciences — M,D
Applied Economics — M,D
Applied Mathematics — M,D
Art/Fine Arts — M
Biochemistry — M,D
Biological and Biomedical
Sciences—General — M,D
Business Administration and
Management—General — M
Business Education — M,D
Chemistry — M,D
Child and Family Studies — M,D
Civil Engineering — M,D,O
Clinical Psychology — M,D
Communication Disorders — M,D,O
Communication—General — M
Computer Science — M,D
Consumer Economics — M
Counseling Psychology — M,D
Counselor Education — M,D
Curriculum and Instruction — D
Disability Studies — M,D,O
Ecology — M,D
Economics — M,D
Education—General — M,D,O
Educational Measurement and
Evaluation — M,D
Educational Media/Instructional
Technology — M,D,O
Electrical Engineering — M,D
Elementary Education — M
Engineering and Applied
Sciences—General — M,D,O
English — M
Environmental Engineering — M,D,O
Environmental Management
and Policy — M,D
Family and Consumer
Sciences-General — M,D
Fish, Game, and Wildlife
Management — M,D
Folklore — M
Food Science and
Technology — M,D
Forestry — M,D
Geography — M,D
Geology — M
Health Education — M
History — M
Home Economics Education — M
Human Development — M,D
Human Resources Management — M
Interior Design — M
Landscape Architecture — M
Management Information Systems — M,D
Marriage and Family Therapy — M
Mathematics — M,D
Mechanical Engineering — M,D
Meteorology — M,D
Multilingual and Multicultural
Education — M
Natural Resources — M
Nutrition — M,D
Physical Education — M
Physics — M,D
Plant Sciences — M,D
Political Science — M
Psychology—General — M,D
Range Science — M,D
Recreation and Park Management — M,D
Rehabilitation Counseling — M
School Psychology — M,D
Secondary Education — M
Sociology — M,D
Special Education — M,D,O
Statistics — M,D
Theater — M
Toxicology — M,D
Urban and Regional Planning — M,D
Veterinary Sciences — M,D
Vocational and Technical Education — M
Water Resources Engineering — M,D
Water Resources — M,D
Writing — M

UTAH VALLEY UNIVERSITY
Accounting — M
Business Administration and
Management—General — M
Computer and Information
Systems Security — O
Education—General — M
Educational Leadership and
Administration — M
Educational Media/Instructional
Technology — M
Elementary Education — M
English as a Second Language — M
Mathematics Education — M
Nursing—General — M
Reading Education — M

UTICA COLLEGE
Accounting — M
Computer and Information
Systems Security — M
Criminal Justice and Criminology — M
Education—General — M,O
Forensic Sciences — M
Health Services Management and
Hospital Administration — M

M—masters degree; D—doctorate; O—other advanced degree; *—Close-Up and/or Display

Liberal Studies — M
Occupational Therapy — M
Physical Therapy — D

VALDOSTA STATE UNIVERSITY
Business Administration and
  Management—General — M
Communication Disorders — M,D
Counselor Education — M,O
Early Childhood Education — M,O
Educational Leadership and
  Administration — M
English Education — M
English — M
Family Nurse Practitioner Studies — M
Gerontological Nursing — M
Health Services Management and
  Hospital Administration — M
Information Studies — M
Library Science — M
Marriage and Family Therapy — M,O
Music — M
Nursing—General — M
Psychiatric Nursing — M
Psychology—General — M,O
Rhetoric — M
Social Work — M
Special Education — M,O

VALLEY CITY STATE UNIVERSITY
Education—General — M
Educational Media/Instructional
  Technology — M
Elementary Education — M
English as a Second Language — M
English Education — M
Library Science — M
Vocational and Technical Education — M

VALPARAISO UNIVERSITY
Arts Administration — M
Business Administration and
  Management—General — M
Chinese — M
Clinical Psychology — M
Communication—General — M,O
Computational Sciences — M
Computer and Information
  Systems Security — M
Educational Leadership and
  Administration — M,O
Elementary Education — M,O
Engineering Management — M,O
English as a Second Language — M,O
English — M
Entertainment Management — M
Ethics — M,O
Finance and Banking — M
Foreign Languages Education — M
Health Services Management and
  Hospital Administration — M
History — M,O
International Economics — M
International Trade Policy — M
Law — M,D
Liberal Studies — M
Management Information Systems — M
Management Strategy and Policy — M,O
Media Studies — M,O
Nursing Education — M,D,O
Physician Assistant Studies — M,D,O
Public Health—General — M,D,O
School Psychology — M,O
Secondary Education — M,O
Sports Management — M
Theology — M,O

VAN ANDEL INSTITUTE GRADUATE SCHOOL
Genetics — D
Molecular Genetics — D

VANCOUVER ISLAND UNIVERSITY
Business Administration and
  Management—General — M
Finance and Banking — M
International Business — M
Marketing — M

VANCOUVER SCHOOL OF THEOLOGY
Religion — M,O
Theology — M,O

VANDERBILT UNIVERSITY
Accounting — M
Acute Care/Critical Care Nursing — M,D,O
Adult Nursing — M,D,O
Allopathic Medicine — M,D
Analytical Chemistry — M,D
Anthropology — M,D
Astronomy — M,D
Biochemistry — M,D
Bioinformatics — M,D
Biological and Biomedical
  Sciences—General — M,D
Biomedical Engineering — M,D
Biophysics — M,D
Business Administration and
  Management—General — M
Cancer Biology/Oncology — M,D
Cell Biology — M,D
Chemical Engineering — M,D
Chemistry — M,D
Child and Family Studies — M
Civil Engineering — M,D
Classics — M
Clinical Research — M
Communication Disorders — M,D
Computer Science — M,D
Counselor Education — M
Developmental Biology — M,D
Economic Development — M,D
Economics — M,D
Education—General — M,D*
Educational Leadership and
  Administration — M,D

Educational Policy — M,D
Electrical Engineering — M,D
Elementary Education — M
Engineering and Applied
  Sciences—General — M,D
English Education — M,D
English — M,D
Environmental Engineering — M,D
Environmental Management
  and Policy — M,D
Environmental Sciences — M
Family Nurse Practitioner Studies — M,D,O
Finance and Banking — M
Foreign Languages Education — M,D
French — M,D
Geology — M,D
German — M,D
Gerontological Nursing — M,D,O
Health Physics/Radiological Health — M,D
Health Services Management and
  Hospital Administration — M
Higher Education — M,D
History — M,D
Human Development — M
Human Genetics — D
Immunology — M,D
Inorganic Chemistry — M,D
International and Comparative
  Education — M
Latin American Studies — M
Law — M,D
Liberal Studies — M
Management Strategy and Policy — M
Marketing — M
Materials Sciences — M
Maternal and Child/Neonatal
  Nursing — M,D,O
Mathematics — M,D
Mechanical Engineering — M,D
Microbiology — M,D
Molecular Biology — M,D
Molecular Physiology — M,D
Multilingual and Multicultural
  Education — M,D
Nurse Midwifery — M,D,O
Nursing and Healthcare
  Administration — M,D,O
Nursing Informatics — M,D,O
Nursing—General — M,D,O
Organic Chemistry — M,D
Organizational Management — M,D
Pathology — D
Pediatric Nursing — M,D,O
Pharmacology — D
Philosophy — M,D
Physical Chemistry — M,D
Physics — M,D
Political Science — M,D
Portuguese — M,D
Psychiatric Nursing — M,D,O
Psychology—General — D
Public Health—General — M
Public Policy — D
Quantitative Analysis — M
Reading Education — M
Religion — M,D
Science Education — M,D
Secondary Education — M
Sociology — M,D
Spanish — M,D
Special Education — M
Theology — M
Theoretical Chemistry — M,D
Urban and Regional Planning — M
Urban Education — M
Women's Health Nursing — M,D,O
Writing — M

VANDERCOOK COLLEGE OF MUSIC
Music Education — M

VANGUARD UNIVERSITY OF SOUTHERN CALIFORNIA
Clinical Psychology — M
Education—General — M
Nursing—General — M
Religion — M
Theology — M

VAUGHN COLLEGE OF AERONAUTICS AND TECHNOLOGY
Aviation Management — M

VERMONT COLLEGE OF FINE ARTS
Art Education — M
Art/Fine Arts — M
Film, Television, and Video
  Production — M
Graphic Design — M
Music — M
Publishing — M
Writing — M

VERMONT LAW SCHOOL
Energy Management and
  Policy — M
Environmental Law — M
Environmental Management
  and Policy — M
Law — D
Legal and Justice Studies — M

VICTORIA UNIVERSITY
Theology — M,D,O

VILLANOVA UNIVERSITY
Accounting — M
Adult Nursing — M,D,O
Applied Statistics — M
Artificial Intelligence/Robotics — M,O
Biochemical Engineering — M,O
Biological and Biomedical
  Sciences—General — M
Business Administration and
  Management—General — M
Chemical Engineering — M,O

Chemistry — M
Civil Engineering — M
Classics — M
Communication—General — M
Computer and Information
  Systems Security — M
Computer Engineering — M,O
Computer Science — M,O
Counselor Education — M
Database Systems — M
Education—General — M
Educational Leadership and
  Administration — M
Electrical Engineering — M,O
Engineering and Applied
  Sciences—General — M,D,O
English — M
Environmental Engineering — M
Family Nurse Practitioner Studies — M,D,O
Finance and Banking — M
Health Services Management and
  Hospital Administration — M
Hispanic Studies — M
History — M
Human Resources Development — M
International Business — M
Law — D
Liberal Studies — M
Management Information Systems — M
Management Strategy and Policy — M
Manufacturing Engineering — M,O
Marketing — M
Mathematics — M
Mechanical Engineering — M,O
Missions and Missiology — M
Nonprofit Management — M,O
Nurse Anesthesia — M,D,O
Nursing Education — M,D,O
Nursing—General — M,D,O
Pediatric Nursing — M,D,O
Philosophy — D
Political Science — M
Psychology—General — M
Public Administration — M,O
Real Estate — M
Secondary Education — M
Software Engineering — M
Taxation — M
Theater — M
Theology — M,D
Water Resources Engineering — M,O

VIRGINIA BAPTIST COLLEGE
Theology — M

VIRGINIA BEACH THEOLOGICAL SEMINARY
Pastoral Ministry and Counseling — M
Theology — M

VIRGINIA COLLEGE IN BIRMINGHAM
Business Administration and
  Management—General — M
Criminal Justice and Criminology — M
Health Services Management and
  Hospital Administration — M

VIRGINIA COMMONWEALTH UNIVERSITY
Accounting — M
Adult Education — M
Adult Nursing — M,D,O
Advertising and Public Relations — M
Allied Health—General — D
Allopathic Medicine — D
Analytical Chemistry — M,D
Anatomy — M
Applied Mathematics — M
Applied Physics — M
Art Education — M,D
Art History — M,D
Art/Fine Arts — M,D
Biochemistry — M,D
Biological and Biomedical
  Sciences—General — M,D,O
Biomedical Engineering — M,D
Biostatistics — M,D
Business Administration and
  Management—General — M,D
Chemical Physics — M,D
Chemistry — M,D
Clinical Laboratory
  Sciences/Medical Technology — M
Clinical Psychology — D
Communication—General — D
Computer Science — M,D
Counseling Psychology — M,D
Counselor Education — M,O
Criminal Justice and Criminology — M,O
Curriculum and Instruction — D
Dentistry — M,D
Early Childhood Education — M
Economics — M
Education—General — M,D,O
Educational Leadership and
  Administration — M,D
Educational Measurement and
  Evaluation — D
Educational Media/Instructional
  Technology — M
Educational Psychology — D
Elementary Education — M
Emergency Management — M,O
Engineering and Applied
  Sciences—General — M,D
English — M
Environmental Management
  and Policy — M
Exercise and Sports Science — M
Family Nurse Practitioner Studies — M
Film, Television, and Video
  Production — M,D
Finance and Banking — M
Forensic Sciences — M
Geographic Information Systems — O

Gerontology — M,D
Health Physics/Radiological Health — D
Health Psychology — D
Health Services Management and
  Hospital Administration — M,D
Health Services Research — D
History — M
Homeland Security — M,O
Human Genetics — M,D
Human Resources Development — M
Immunology — M,D
Inorganic Chemistry — M,D
Interdisciplinary Studies — M
Interior Design — M,D
Journalism — M
Management Information Systems — M
Mass Communication — M
Mathematics — M
Mechanical Engineering — M,D
Media Studies — M,D
Medical Physics — M,D
Medicinal and Pharmaceutical
  Chemistry — M,D
Microbiology — M,D
Molecular Biology — M,D
Molecular Genetics — M,D
Museum Studies — M
Music Education — M
Music — M
Nanotechnology — M,D
Neurobiology — M
Neuroscience — M,D,O
Nonprofit Management — O
Nuclear Engineering — M,D
Nurse Anesthesia — M,D
Nursing and Healthcare
  Administration — M,D,O
Nursing Education — M,D,O
Nursing—General — M,D,O
Occupational Therapy — M,D
Organic Chemistry — M,D
Pediatric Nursing — M,D,O
Pharmaceutical Administration — M,D
Pharmaceutical Sciences — M,D
Pharmacology — M,D,O
Pharmacy — D
Photography — M,D
Physical Chemistry — M,D
Physical Therapy — M,D
Physics — M
Physiology — M,D
Political Science — M,D,O
Psychiatric Nursing — M,D,O
Public Administration — M
Public Affairs — M,D,O
Public Policy — D
Reading Education — M,O
Real Estate — O
Recreation and Park Management — M
Rehabilitation Counseling — M
Rehabilitation Sciences — D
Social Work — M,D
Sociology — M
Special Education — M,D
Student Affairs — M
Systems Biology — D
Theater — M
Toxicology — M,D,O
Urban and Regional Planning — M
Urban Education — D
Women's Health Nursing — M,D,O
Writing — M

VIRGINIA INTERNATIONAL UNIVERSITY
Accounting — M,O
Advertising and Public Relations — M,O
Business Administration and
  Management—General — M,O
Computer and Information
  Systems Security — M,O
Computer Art and Design — M,O
Computer Science — M,O
Database Systems — M,O
Education—General — M
English as a Second Language — M
Entrepreneurship — M,O
Finance and Banking — M,O
Game Design and
  Development — M,O
Health Informatics — M,O
Health Services Management and
  Hospital Administration — M,O
Hospitality Management — M,O
Human Resources Management — M,O
International Affairs — M
International Business — M,O
Linguistics — M
Logistics — M,O
Management Information Systems — M,O
Marketing — M,O
Project Management — M,O
Public Administration — M
Software Engineering — M,O

VIRGINIA POLYTECHNIC INSTITUTE AND STATE UNIVERSITY
Accounting — M,D
Aerospace/Aeronautical
  Engineering — M,D,O
Agricultural Economics and
  Agribusiness — M,D
Agricultural Engineering — M,D
Agricultural Sciences—
  General — M,D,O
Agronomy and Soil Sciences — M,D
Animal Sciences — M,D
Applied Economics — M,D
Applied Statistics — M,D
Architecture — M,D,O
Bioengineering — M,D
Bioinformatics — M,D
Biological and Biomedical
  Sciences—General — M,D
Biomedical Engineering — M,D
Biotechnology — M,D

Building Science M,D,O
Business Administration and Management—General M,D
Chemical Engineering M,D
Chemistry M,D
Civil Engineering M,D,O
Communication—General M,D,O
Computer and Information Systems Security M,O
Computer Engineering M,D,O
Computer Science M,D,O
Construction Engineering M,D,O
Construction Management M,D,O
Counselor Education M,D,O
Curriculum and Instruction M,D,O
Distance Education Development M,O
Economics M,D
Education—General M,O
Educational Leadership and Administration M,D,O
Educational Measurement and Evaluation M,D,O
Educational Media/Instructional Technology M,O
Educational Policy M,D,O
Electrical Engineering M,D,O
Engineering and Applied Sciences—General M,D
Engineering Management M,O
English M,D,O
Entomology M,D
Environmental Design M,D,O
Environmental Engineering M,D
Environmental Management and Policy M,D,O
Environmental Sciences M,D,O
Exercise and Sports Science M,D
Fish, Game, and Wildlife Management M,D
Foreign Languages Education M,D,O
Forestry M,D
Genetics M,D
Geographic Information Systems M,D
Geography M,D
Geosciences M,D
Higher Education M,D,O
History of Science and Technology M,D,O
History M,D,O
Horticulture M,D
Hospitality Management M,D
Human Development M,D,O
Humanities M,D,O
Industrial/Management Engineering M,D,O
Interdisciplinary Studies M,D
International Affairs M,D,O
Internet and Interactive Multimedia M,D,O
Landscape Architecture M,D,O
Liberal Studies M,O
Management Information Systems M,D,O
Materials Engineering M,D
Materials Sciences M,D
Mathematics Education M,D
Mathematics M,D
Mechanical Engineering M,D
Mechanics M,D
Mineral/Mining Engineering M,D
National Security M,O
Natural Resources M,D,O
Nonprofit Management M,O
Nuclear Engineering M,D
Nutrition M,D
Ocean Engineering M,D,O
Philosophy M,D,O
Physics M,D
Plant Pathology M,D
Plant Physiology M,D
Political Science M,D,O
Psychology—General M,D
Public Administration M,D,O
Public Affairs M,D,O
Public Health—General M,D
Public Policy M,D
Quantitative Analysis M,O
Rhetoric M,D,O
Social Sciences Education M,D,O
Sociology M,D,O
Software Engineering M,O
Statistics M,D
Student Affairs M,D,O
Systems Engineering M,D,O
Theater M,D,O
Transportation and Highway Engineering M,O
Travel and Tourism M,D
Urban and Regional Planning M,D,O
Urban Studies M,D,O
Veterinary Medicine M,D
Veterinary Sciences M,D
Vocational and Technical Education M,D,O
Writing M,D,O

VIRGINIA STATE UNIVERSITY
Biological and Biomedical Sciences—General M
Clinical Psychology M,D
Community Health M,D
Computer Science M
Counselor Education M
Criminal Justice and Criminology M
Economics M
Education—General M,D
Educational Leadership and Administration M,D
Health Education M,D
Health Psychology M
Interdisciplinary Studies M
Mathematics Education M
Mathematics M
Media Studies M

Psychology—General M,D

VIRGINIA THEOLOGICAL SEMINARY
Educational Leadership and Administration M,D
Theology M,D

VIRGINIA UNION UNIVERSITY
Curriculum and Instruction M
Education—General M
Theology M,D

VIRGINIA UNIVERSITY OF LYNCHBURG
Pastoral Ministry and Counseling M,D
Religion M,D

VITERBO UNIVERSITY
Addictions/Substance Abuse Counseling M
Business Administration and Management—General M
Counseling Psychology M
Developmental Psychology M
Early Childhood Education M,O
Education of the Gifted M,O
Education—General M,O
Educational Leadership and Administration M,O
Ethics M
Health Psychology M
Health Services Management and Hospital Administration M
International Business M
Nursing—General D
Organizational Management M,O
Pastoral Ministry and Counseling M,O
Project Management M
Reading Education M,O
Special Education M,O

WAGNER COLLEGE
Accounting M
Business Administration and Management—General M
Early Childhood Education M
Education—General M,O
Educational Leadership and Administration M,O
Elementary Education M
English Education M
Finance and Banking M
Foreign Languages Education M
Health Services Management and Hospital Administration M
International Business M
Marketing M
Mathematics Education M
Microbiology M
Middle School Education M
Reading Education M
Science Education M
Secondary Education M
Social Sciences Education M
Special Education M

WAKE FOREST UNIVERSITY
Accounting M
Allopathic Medicine D
Analytical Chemistry M,D
Anatomy D
Biochemistry D
Biological and Biomedical Sciences—General M,D
Biomedical Engineering M,D
Business Administration and Management—General M
Cancer Biology/Oncology D
Chemistry M,D
Communication—General M
Computer Science M
Counselor Education M
Database Systems M
Education—General M
English M
Exercise and Sports Science M
Genomic Sciences D
Health Services Research M
Human Genetics D
Immunology D
Inorganic Chemistry M,D
Law M,D
Liberal Studies M
Mathematics M
Microbiology D
Molecular Biology D
Molecular Genetics D
Molecular Medicine M,D
Neurobiology D
Neuroscience D
Organic Chemistry M,D
Pathobiology D
Pharmacology D
Physical Chemistry M,D
Physics M,D
Physiology D
Psychology—General M
Religion M
Secondary Education M
Speech and Interpersonal Communication M
Taxation M

WALDEN UNIVERSITY
Accounting M,D,O
Addictions/Substance Abuse Counseling M,D
Adult Education M,D,O
Adult Nursing M,D,O
Applied Nursing M,D,O
Business Administration and Management—General M,D,O
Child and Family Studies M,D
Clinical Psychology M,D,O

Clinical Research M,D,O
Communication—General M,D,O
Community Health M,D,O
Computer and Information Systems Security M,D,O
Conflict Resolution and Mediation/Peace Studies M,D,O
Counseling Psychology M,D,O
Counselor Education M,D
Criminal Justice and Criminology M,D,O
Curriculum and Instruction M,D,O
Developmental Education M,D,O
Distance Education Development M,D,O
Early Childhood Education M,D,O
Education—General M,D,O
Educational Leadership and Administration M,D,O
Educational Measurement and Evaluation M,D,O
Educational Media/Instructional Technology M,D,O
Educational Psychology M,D,O
Elementary Education M,D,O
Emergency Management M,D,O
English as a Second Language M,D,O
Entrepreneurship M,D,O
Epidemiology M,D,O
Family Nurse Practitioner Studies M,D,O
Finance and Banking M,D,O
Forensic Psychology M,D,O
Gerontological Nursing M,D,O
Gerontology M,D
Health Education M,D,O
Health Informatics M,D,O
Health Promotion M,D,O
Health Services Management and Hospital Administration M,D,O
Higher Education M,D,O
Homeland Security M,D,O
Human Resources Management M,D,O
Human Services M,D
Industrial and Organizational Psychology M,D,O
Interdisciplinary Studies M,D,O
International Affairs M,D,O
International and Comparative Education M,D,O
International Business M,D,O
International Development M,D,O
International Health M,D,O
Law M,D,O
Management Information Systems M,D,O
Marketing M,D,O
Marriage and Family Therapy M,D
Mathematics Education M,D,O
Multilingual and Multicultural Education M,D,O
Nonprofit Management M,D,O
Nursing and Healthcare Administration M,D,O
Nursing Education M,D,O
Nursing Informatics M,D,O
Nursing—General M,D,O
Organizational Management M,D,O
Political Science M,D,O
Project Management M,D,O
Psychology—General M,D,O
Public Administration M,D,O
Public Health—General M,D,O
Public Policy M,D,O
Reading Education M,D,O
Science Education M,D,O
Social Psychology M,D,O
Social Work M,D
Special Education M,D,O
Supply Chain Management M,D,O
Sustainable Development M,D,O

WALDORF UNIVERSITY
Criminal Justice and Criminology M
Educational Leadership and Administration M
Emergency Management M
Human Resources Development M
Organizational Management M
Public Administration M
Sports Management M

WALLA WALLA UNIVERSITY
Biological and Biomedical Sciences—General M
Curriculum and Instruction M
Education—General M
Educational Leadership and Administration M
Reading Education M
Social Work M
Special Education M

WALSH COLLEGE OF ACCOUNTANCY AND BUSINESS ADMINISTRATION
Accounting M
Business Administration and Management—General M
Computer and Information Systems Security M
Finance and Banking M
Human Resources Management M
International Business M
Management Information Systems M
Management of Technology M
Management Strategy and Policy M
Marketing M
Taxation M

WALSH UNIVERSITY
Adult Nursing M,D
Business Administration and Management—General M
Counseling Psychology M
Counselor Education M

Education—General M
Health Services Management and Hospital Administration M
Higher Education M
Marketing M
Nursing and Healthcare Administration M,D
Nursing Education M,D
Nursing—General M,D
Pastoral Ministry and Counseling D
Physical Therapy D
Reading Education M
Religious Education M
Student Affairs M
Theology M

WARNER PACIFIC COLLEGE
Education—General M
Human Services M
Nonprofit Management M
Organizational Management M

WARNER UNIVERSITY
Accounting M
Business Administration and Management—General M
Curriculum and Instruction M
Education—General M
Educational Media/Instructional Technology M
Elementary Education M
Human Resources Management M
International Business M
Science Education M

WARREN WILSON COLLEGE
Writing M

WARTBURG THEOLOGICAL SEMINARY
Theology M

WASHBURN UNIVERSITY
Accounting M
Addictions/Substance Abuse Counseling M
Business Administration and Management—General M
Clinical Psychology M
Criminal Justice and Criminology M
Curriculum and Instruction M
Education—General M
Educational Leadership and Administration M
Health Education M
Human Services M
Law M,D
Legal and Justice Studies M,D
Liberal Studies M
Nursing and Healthcare Administration M,D,O
Nursing—General M,D,O
Psychology—General M
Reading Education M
Social Work M
Special Education M

WASHINGTON ADVENTIST UNIVERSITY
Business Administration and Management—General M
Counseling Psychology M
Health Services Management and Hospital Administration M
Nursing and Healthcare Administration M
Nursing Education M
Nursing—General M
Public Administration M
Religion M

WASHINGTON & JEFFERSON COLLEGE
Accounting M,O
Applied Economics M,O
Thanatology M,O
Writing M,O

WASHINGTON AND LEE UNIVERSITY
Law D

WASHINGTON STATE UNIVERSITY
Accounting M
Agricultural Economics and Agribusiness M,D,O
Agricultural Engineering M,D
Agronomy and Soil Sciences M,D,O
American Studies M,D
Animal Sciences M,D
Anthropology M,D
Applied Mathematics M,D
Archaeology M,D
Architecture M
Art/Fine Arts M
Biochemistry M,D
Bioengineering M,D
Bioethics M,D,O
Biological and Biomedical Sciences—General M,D
Biophysics M,D
Business Administration and Management—General M,D
Business Education M,D
Chemical Engineering M,D
Chemistry M,D
Civil Engineering M,D
Clinical Psychology M,D
Clothing and Textiles M
Communication Disorders M
Communication—General M,D
Community Health M,D,O
Computer Engineering M,D
Computer Science M,D
Corporate and Organizational Communication M,D
Counseling Psychology M,D
Criminal Justice and Criminology M,D

Cultural Anthropology	M,D
Cultural Studies	M,D
Curriculum and Instruction	M,D
Economics	M,D,O
Education—General	M,D
Educational Leadership and Administration	M,D
Educational Psychology	M,D
Electrical Engineering	M,D
Elementary Education	M,D
Energy and Power Engineering	M,D
Engineering and Applied Sciences—General	M,D,O
Engineering Management	M,O
English as a Second Language	M,D
English	M,D
Entomology	M,D
Environmental Engineering	M,D
Environmental Sciences	M,D
Exercise and Sports Science	M
Experimental Psychology	M,D
Family Nurse Practitioner Studies	M,D,O
Food Science and Technology	M,D
Foreign Languages Education	M
Genetics	M,D
Geology	M,D
Health Services Management and Hospital Administration	M
History	M,D
Horticulture	M,D
Human Development	D
Immunology	M,D
Infectious Diseases	M,D
Interdisciplinary Studies	D
Interior Design	M
Landscape Architecture	M
Management of Technology	M,O
Materials Engineering	M,D
Materials Sciences	M,D
Mathematics Education	M,D
Mathematics	M,D
Mechanical Engineering	M,D
Music	M
Natural Resources	M,D
Neuroscience	M,D
Nursing—General	M,D,O
Nutrition	M
Pharmacy	M,D
Physics	M,D
Plant Pathology	M,D
Political Science	M,D,O
Psychiatric Nursing	M,D,O
Psychology—General	M,D
Public Affairs	M,D,O
Reading Education	M,D
Secondary Education	M,D
Sociology	M,D
Special Education	M,D
Sports Management	M,D
Veterinary Medicine	D
Veterinary Sciences	M,D
Vocational and Technical Education	M,D

WASHINGTON UNIVERSITY IN ST. LOUIS

Accounting	M
Aerospace/Aeronautical Engineering	M,D
Allopathic Medicine	D
Anthropology	D
Archaeology	M,D
Architecture	M
Art History	M,D
Art/Fine Arts	M
Asian Languages	M,D
Asian Studies	M,D
Biochemistry	D
Bioethics	M
Biological and Biomedical Sciences—General	D
Biomedical Engineering	M,D
Biostatistics	M,D,O
Business Administration and Management—General	M,D
Cell Biology	D
Chemical Engineering	M,D
Chemistry	D
Child and Family Studies	M,D
Chinese	M,D
Classics	M,D
Clinical Research	M
Communication Disorders	M,D
Comparative Literature	M,D
Computational Biology	D
Computer Engineering	M,D
Computer Science	M,D
Dance	M
Database Systems	M
Developmental Biology	D
Developmental Psychology	D
Ecology	D
Economics	D
Education—General	M,D
Educational Measurement and Evaluation	D
Elementary Education	M
Engineering and Applied Sciences—General	M,D
English	M,D
Entrepreneurship	M
Environmental Biology	D
Environmental Engineering	M,D
Epidemiology	M,D
Evolutionary Biology	D
Finance and Banking	M,D
French	D
Genetics	M,D
Genomic Sciences	M
Geosciences	D
German	D
Gerontology	M,D
Health Services Research	M,O

History	D
Human Genetics	D
Immunology	D
Japanese	M,D
Jewish Studies	M
Kinesiology and Movement Studies	D
Law	M,D
Materials Sciences	M,D
Mathematics	M,D
Mechanical Engineering	M,D
Microbiology	D
Molecular Biology	D
Molecular Biophysics	D
Molecular Genetics	D
Molecular Pathogenesis	D
Music	M,D
Near and Middle Eastern Studies	M
Neuroscience	D
Occupational Therapy	M,D
Organizational Management	M
Philosophy	D
Physical Therapy	D
Physics	D
Planetary and Space Sciences	D
Plant Biology	D
Political Science	D
Psychology—General	D
Public Health—General	M,D
Rehabilitation Sciences	D
Religion	M
Romance Languages	D
Secondary Education	M
Social Work	M,D
Spanish	D
Special Education	M,D
Speech and Interpersonal Communication	M,D
Statistics	M,D
Supply Chain Management	M
Systems Biology	D
Theater	M
Urban Design	M
Writing	M

WAYLAND BAPTIST UNIVERSITY

Accounting	M,D
Business Administration and Management—General	M,D
Counseling Psychology	M
Criminal Justice and Criminology	M
Education—General	M
Educational Leadership and Administration	M
Educational Measurement and Evaluation	M
Educational Media/Instructional Technology	M
Elementary Education	M
English as a Second Language	M
English Education	M
Health Services Management and Hospital Administration	M,D
Higher Education	M
History	M
Homeland Security	M
Human Resources Management	M,D
Humanities	M
Interdisciplinary Studies	M
International Business	M,D
Management Information Systems	M,D
Organizational Management	M,D
Pastoral Ministry and Counseling	M
Project Management	M,D
Religion	M
Science Education	M
Secondary Education	M
Social Sciences Education	M
Special Education	M
Sports Management	M
Theology	M

WAYNESBURG UNIVERSITY

Addictions/Substance Abuse Counseling	M,D
Business Administration and Management—General	M,D
Clinical Psychology	M,D
Counseling Psychology	M,D
Counselor Education	M,D
Criminal Justice and Criminology	M,D
Curriculum and Instruction	M,D
Distance Education Development	M,D
Educational Leadership and Administration	M,D
Educational Media/Instructional Technology	M,D
Energy Management and Policy	M,D
Finance and Banking	M,D
Health Services Management and Hospital Administration	M,D
Human Resources Management	M,D
Nursing and Healthcare Administration	M,D
Nursing Education	M,D
Nursing Informatics	M,D
Nursing—General	M,D
Organizational Management	M,D
Special Education	M,D

WAYNE STATE COLLEGE

Business Administration and Management—General	M
Business Education	M
Communication—General	M
Counselor Education	M
Curriculum and Instruction	M
Early Childhood Education	M
Education—General	M,O
Educational Leadership and Administration	M,O
Elementary Education	M
English as a Second Language	M
English Education	M

WAYNE STATE UNIVERSITY

Accounting	M
Home Economics Education	M
Mathematics Education	M
Music Education	M
Organizational Management	M
Physical Education	M
Science Education	M
Social Sciences Education	M
Special Education	M
Sports Management	M
Vocational and Technical Education	M

WAYNE STATE UNIVERSITY

Accounting	M,D,O
Advertising and Public Relations	M,D,O
African Studies	M,D,O
Allopathic Medicine	D
American Studies	M,D,O
Analytical Chemistry	M,D
Anatomy	M,D,O
Anthropology	M,D,O
Applied Behavior Analysis	M,D,O
Applied Mathematics	M,D
Archives/Archival Administration	M,O
Art Education	M,D,O
Art History	M
Art/Fine Arts	M
Asian Studies	M,D,O
Automotive Engineering	M,O
Biochemistry	M,D
Bioinformatics	M,D
Biological and Biomedical Sciences—General	M,D
Biomedical Engineering	M,D,O
Biopsychology	M,D,O
Biotechnology	M,D
Business Administration and Management—General	M,D,O
Cancer Biology/Oncology	M,D,O
Cell Biology	M,D,O
Chemical Engineering	M,D,O
Chemistry	M,D
Civil Engineering	M,D
Clinical Psychology	M,D
Cognitive Sciences	M,D
Communication Disorders	M,D
Communication—General	M,D,O
Computational Biology	M,D
Computer Engineering	M,D
Computer Science	M,D
Conflict Resolution and Mediation/Peace Studies	M,D,O
Counseling Psychology	M,D,O
Counselor Education	M,D,O
Criminal Justice and Criminology	M
Curriculum and Instruction	M,D,O
Dance	M,D,O
Database Systems	M,D
Developmental Education	M,D,O
Developmental Psychology	M,D
Distance Education Development	M,D,O
Early Childhood Education	M,D,O
Economic Development	M,D,O
Economics	M,D
Education—General	M,D,O
Educational Leadership and Administration	M,D,O
Educational Measurement and Evaluation	M,D,O
Educational Media/Instructional Technology	M,D,O
Educational Policy	M,D,O
Educational Psychology	M,D,O
Electrical Engineering	M,D
Elementary Education	M,D,O
Energy and Power Engineering	M,O
Engineering and Applied Sciences—General	M,D,O
Engineering Management	M,D,O
English as a Second Language	M,D,O
English Education	M,D,O
English	M,D
Entrepreneurship	M,D,O
Evolutionary Biology	M,D
Exercise and Sports Science	M,D
Film, Television, and Video Theory and Criticism	M,D
Finance and Banking	M,D,O
Food Science and Technology	M,D,O
Foreign Languages Education	M,D,O
Foundations and Philosophy of Education	M,D,O
French	M,D
Gender Studies	M,D,O
Genetic Counseling	M,D,O
Genomic Sciences	M,D,O
Geology	M
German	M,D
Gerontology	M,D,O
Graphic Design	M
Health Communication	M,D,O
Health Education	M,D,O
Health Services Management and Hospital Administration	M,D
Higher Education	M,D,O
History of Science and Technology	M,D,O
History	M,D,O
Human Resources Management	M,D
Immunology	M,D,O
Industrial and Labor Relations	M,D
Industrial and Manufacturing Management	M,D
Industrial and Organizational Psychology	M,D
Industrial Design	M
Industrial/Management Engineering	M,D,O
Information Studies	M,O
Inorganic Chemistry	M,D
Interior Design	M
International Economics	M,D
Italian	M

Journalism	M,D,O
Kinesiology and Movement Studies	M,D,O
Law	M,O
Library Science	M,O
Linguistics	M
Management Information Systems	M,D,O
Management Strategy and Policy	M,D,O
Manufacturing Engineering	M,D,O
Materials Sciences	M,D,O
Mathematics Education	M,D,O
Mathematics	M,D
Mechanical Engineering	M,D,O
Media Studies	M,D,O
Medical Imaging	M,D,O
Medical Physics	M,D,O
Medicinal and Pharmaceutical Chemistry	M,D
Microbiology	M,D,O
Molecular Biology	M,D,O
Molecular Genetics	M,D,O
Molecular Medicine	M,D,O
Multilingual and Multicultural Education	M,D,O
Music Education	M,O
Music	M,D,O
Near and Middle Eastern Languages	M,D
Near and Middle Eastern Studies	M,D
Neurobiology	M,D,O
Neuroscience	M,D,O
Nonprofit Management	M,D
Nurse Anesthesia	M,O
Nutrition	M,D,O
Occupational Therapy	M
Organic Chemistry	M,D
Organizational Behavior	M,D
Organizational Management	M,D,O
Pathology	M,D,O
Pediatric Nursing	M,O
Pharmaceutical Sciences	M,D
Pharmacology	M,D,O
Pharmacy	D
Philosophy	M,D
Photography	M
Physical Chemistry	M,D
Physical Education	M,D
Physical Therapy	D
Physician Assistant Studies	M
Physics	M,D
Physiology	M,D,O
Political Science	M,D
Polymer Science and Engineering	M,D,O
Psychology—General	M,D
Public Administration	M,D
Public Health—General	M,D,O
Public History	M,D,O
Public Policy	M,D
Reading Education	M,D,O
Rehabilitation Counseling	M,D,O
Rhetoric	M,D
Romance Languages	M,D
School Psychology	M,D,O
Science Education	M,D,O
Secondary Education	M,D,O
Social Psychology	M,D
Social Sciences Education	M,D,O
Social Work	M,D,O
Sociology	M,D
Spanish	M,D
Special Education	M,D,O
Sports Management	M,D,O
Statistics	M,D
Systems Engineering	M,D,O
Taxation	M,D,O
Textile Design	M
Theater	M
Toxicology	M,D
Urban and Regional Planning	M,O
Urban Studies	M,D
Vocational and Technical Education	M,D,O
Western European Studies	M,D,O
Writing	M,D

WEBBER INTERNATIONAL UNIVERSITY

Accounting	M
Business Administration and Management—General	M
Criminal Justice and Criminology	M
International Business	M
Sports Management	M

WEBER STATE UNIVERSITY

Accounting	M
Athletic Training and Sports Medicine	M
Business Administration and Management—General	M
Communication—General	M
Computer Engineering	M
Curriculum and Instruction	M
Education—General	M
English	M
Health Physics/Radiological Health	M
Health Services Management and Hospital Administration	M
Legal and Justice Studies	M
Nursing—General	M
Taxation	M

WEBSTER UNIVERSITY

Accounting	M
Advertising and Public Relations	M
Aerospace/Aeronautical Engineering	M,D,O
Art History	M
Art/Fine Arts	M
Business Administration and Management—General	M,D,O
Communication Disorders	M
Communication—General	M,O
Computer and Information Systems Security	M
Computer Science	M
Corporate and Organizational Communication	M

Counseling Psychology — M
Criminal Justice and Criminology — M,D,O
Early Childhood Education — M,O
Education—General — M,O
Educational Media/Instructional Technology — M,O
Educational Psychology — M,O
Elementary Education — M,O
English as a Second Language — M,O
Environmental Management and Policy — M
Finance and Banking — M
Forensic Sciences — M
Gerontology — M
Health Services Management and Hospital Administration — M,D,O
Human Resources Development — M,D,O
Human Resources Management — M,D,O
Human Services — M
International Affairs — M
International Business — M
Internet and Interactive Multimedia — M
Legal and Justice Studies — M,O
Management Information Systems — M,D,O
Management of Technology — M,D,O
Marketing — M,D,O
Mathematics Education — M,O
Media Studies — M
Middle School Education — M,O
Music Education — M
Music — M
Nonprofit Management — M,D,O
Nurse Anesthesia — D
Nursing Education — M
Nursing—General — M
Psychology—General — M
Public Administration — M,D,O
Reading Education — M,O
Secondary Education — M,O
Special Education — M,O

WEILL CORNELL MEDICINE
Biochemistry — M,D
Biological and Biomedical Sciences—General — M,D
Biophysics — M,D
Cell Biology — M,D
Computational Biology — D
Epidemiology — M
Health Informatics — M
Health Services Research — M
Immunology — M,D
Molecular Biology — M,D
Neuroscience — M,D
Pharmacology — M,D
Physician Assistant Studies — M
Physiology — M,D
Structural Biology — M,D
Systems Biology — M,D

WENTWORTH INSTITUTE OF TECHNOLOGY
Architecture — M
Civil Engineering — M
Construction Engineering — M
Construction Management — M
Facilities Management — M
Management of Technology — M
Transportation and Highway Engineering — M

WESLEYAN COLLEGE
Business Administration and Management—General — M
Early Childhood Education — M
Education—General — M

WESLEYAN UNIVERSITY
Astronomy — M
Biochemistry — D
Bioinformatics — D
Biological and Biomedical Sciences—General — D
Cell Biology — D
Chemical Physics — D
Chemistry — D
Computer Science — M,D
Developmental Biology — D
Ecology — D
Environmental Sciences — M
Evolutionary Biology — D
Genetics — D
Genomic Sciences — D
Geosciences — M
Inorganic Chemistry — D
Liberal Studies — M,O
Mathematics — M,D
Molecular Biology — D
Molecular Biophysics — D
Molecular Genetics — D
Music — M,D
Neurobiology — D
Organic Chemistry — D
Physics — D
Theoretical Chemistry — D
Writing — M,O

WESLEY BIBLICAL SEMINARY
Linguistics — M
Missions and Missiology — M
Pastoral Ministry and Counseling — M
Religion — M
Religious Education — M
Theology — M
Translation and Interpretation — M

WESLEY COLLEGE
Business Administration and Management—General — M
Education—General — M

Environmental Management and Policy — M
Nursing—General — M

WESLEY THEOLOGICAL SEMINARY
Theology — M,D

WEST CHESTER UNIVERSITY OF PENNSYLVANIA
Applied Mathematics — M,O
Applied Statistics — M,O
Astronomy — M,O
Athletic Training and Sports Medicine — M,O
Biological and Biomedical Sciences—General — M,O
Business Administration and Management—General — M,O
Business Education — M,O
Chemistry — O
Clinical Psychology — M,D,O
Communication Disorders — M,O
Communication—General — M
Computer and Information Systems Security — M,O
Computer Science — M,O
Counselor Education — M,O
Criminal Justice and Criminology — M
Cultural Studies — M,O
Early Childhood Education — M,O
Education—General — M,D,O
Educational Leadership and Administration — M,D,O
Educational Media/Instructional Technology — M,O
Educational Policy — D
Emergency Management — M,O
English as a Second Language — M,O
English Education — M,O
English — M,O
Entrepreneurship — M,O
Ethics — M,O
Exercise and Sports Science — M,O
Foreign Languages Education — M,O
French — M,O
Geographic Information Systems — M,O
Geography — M,O
Geosciences — M,O
German — M,O
Gerontological Nursing — M,D,O
Gerontology — M,O
Health Education — M,O
Health Services Management and Hospital Administration — M,O
Higher Education — M,O
History — M
Holocaust and Genocide Studies — M,O
Human Resources Management — M,O
Humanities — M,O
Industrial and Organizational Psychology — M,D,O
Kinesiology and Movement Studies — M,O
Management Information Systems — M,O
Management Strategy and Policy — M,O
Mathematics Education — M,O
Mathematics — M,O
Music Education — M,O
Music — M,O
Nonprofit Management — M,O
Nursing Education — M,D,O
Nursing—General — M,D,O
Nutrition — M
Philosophy — M,O
Physical Education — M,O
Project Management — M,O
Psychology—General — M,D,O
Public Administration — M,O
Public Affairs — M,O
Public Health—General — M,O
Reading Education — M,O
School Nursing — M,D,O
Science Education — M,O
Secondary Education — M,O
Social Work — M
Spanish — M,O
Special Education — M,O
Sports Management — M,O
Student Affairs — M,O
Sustainable Development — M,O
Urban and Regional Planning — M,O
Writing — M,O

WEST COAST UNIVERSITY
Family Nurse Practitioner Studies — M,D
Health Services Management and Hospital Administration — M,D
Nursing—General — M,D
Occupational Therapy — M,D
Pharmacy — M,D
Physical Therapy — M,D

WESTERN CAROLINA UNIVERSITY
Accounting — M
Applied Arts and Design—General — M
Art/Fine Arts — M
Biological and Biomedical Sciences—General — M
Business Administration and Management—General — M
Chemistry — M
Communication Disorders — M
Construction Management — M
Education—General — M
English as a Second Language — M
English — M
Entrepreneurship — M
Health Services Management and Hospital Administration — M
History — M
Nursing—General — M,D,O
Physical Therapy — D
Project Management — M,O

Psychology—General — M
Public Affairs — M
Social Work — M

WESTERN CONNECTICUT STATE UNIVERSITY
Accounting — M
Adult Nursing — M,D
Art/Fine Arts — M
Biological and Biomedical Sciences—General — M
Business Administration and Management—General — M
Clinical Psychology — M
Counselor Education — M
Criminal Justice and Criminology — M
Curriculum and Instruction — M
Education—General — M,D
Educational Leadership and Administration — D
Educational Media/Instructional Technology — M
English — M
Environmental Sciences — M
Geosciences — M
Gerontological Nursing — M,D
Health Services Management and Hospital Administration — M
History — M
Illustration — M
Mathematics — M
Music Education — M
Nursing Education — D
Nursing—General — M,D
Planetary and Space Sciences — M
Reading Education — M
Special Education — M
Writing — M

WESTERN GOVERNORS UNIVERSITY
Business Administration and Management—General — M
Computer and Information Systems Security — M
Database Systems — M
Education—General — M,O
Educational Leadership and Administration — M,O
Educational Measurement and Evaluation — M,O
Educational Media/Instructional Technology — M,O
Elementary Education — M,O
English Education — M,O
Health Services Management and Hospital Administration — M
Higher Education — M,O
Information Science — M
Management Information Systems — M
Management Strategy and Policy — M
Mathematics Education — M,O
Nursing and Healthcare Administration — M
Nursing Education — M
Science Education — M,O
Social Sciences Education — M,O
Special Education — M,O

WESTERN ILLINOIS UNIVERSITY
Accounting — M
Applied Statistics — M
Biological and Biomedical Sciences—General — M,O
Business Administration and Management—General — M,O
Chemistry — M
Clinical Psychology — M,O
Communication Disorders — M
Communication—General — M
Computer Science — M
Counselor Education — M
Criminal Justice and Criminology — M,O
Curriculum and Instruction — M
Distance Education Development — M,O
Ecology — D
Economic Development — M
Economics — M
Education—General — M,D,O
Educational Leadership and Administration — M,D,O
Educational Media/Instructional Technology — M,O
English as a Second Language — M,O
English — M,O
Environmental Sciences — D
Experimental Psychology — M,O
Foundations and Philosophy of Education — M,O
Geographic Information Systems — M,O
Geography — M,O
Health Education — M,O
Health Services Management and Hospital Administration — M,O
Higher Education — M
History — M
Kinesiology and Movement Studies — M
Liberal Studies — M
Manufacturing Engineering — M
Marine Biology — M,O
Mathematics — M
Museum Studies — M,O
Music — M
Physics — M
Political Science — M
Psychology—General — M,O
Reading Education — M
Recreation and Park Management — M
School Psychology — M,O
Social Psychology — M,O
Sociology — M
Special Education — M

Sports Management — M
Student Affairs — M
Supply Chain Management — M,O
Sustainable Development — M,O
Theater — M
Travel and Tourism — M
Writing — M,O
Zoology — M,O

WESTERN KENTUCKY UNIVERSITY
Adult Education — M,D,O
Agricultural Sciences—General — M
Anthropology — M
Applied Economics — M
Art Education — M
Biological and Biomedical Sciences—General — M
Business Administration and Management—General — M
Chemistry — M
Clinical Psychology — M,O
Communication Disorders — M
Communication—General — M,O
Comparative Literature — M
Computational Sciences — M
Computer Science — M
Corporate and Organizational Communication — M,O
Counseling Psychology — M
Counselor Education — M
Criminal Justice and Criminology — M
Early Childhood Education — M,O
Educational Leadership and Administration — M,D,O
Educational Media/Instructional Technology — M,O
Elementary Education — M
English as a Second Language — M
English Education — M
English — M
Experimental Psychology — M,O
Foreign Languages Education — M
French — M
Geology — M
Geosciences — M
German — M
Health Services Management and Hospital Administration — M
Higher Education — M
History — M
Homeland Security — M
Industrial and Organizational Psychology — M,O
Interdisciplinary Studies — M,O
Management of Technology — M
Marriage and Family Therapy — M
Mathematics — M
Middle School Education — M,O
Music Education — M
Nursing—General — M
Physical Education — M
Physical Therapy — D
Physics — M
Political Science — M
Psychology—General — M,O
Public Administration — M
Public Health—General — M
Reading Education — M,O
Recreation and Park Management — M
School Psychology — M,O
Secondary Education — M,O
Social Work — M
Sociology — M
Spanish — M
Special Education — M,O
Sports Management — M
Student Affairs — M
Writing — M

WESTERN MICHIGAN UNIVERSITY
Accounting — M
Aerospace/Aeronautical Engineering — M,D
Anthropology — M
Applied Arts and Design—General — M
Applied Economics — M,D
Applied Mathematics — M,D
Art Education — M
Athletic Training and Sports Medicine — M
Biological and Biomedical Sciences—General — M,D,O
Business Administration and Management—General — M
Chemical Engineering — M,D
Chemistry — M,D,O
Civil Engineering — M
Clinical Psychology — M,D
Communication Disorders — M,D
Communication—General — M
Computational Sciences — M,D
Computer Engineering — M,D
Computer Science — M,D
Counseling Psychology — M,D
Counselor Education — M,D
Economics — M,D
Education—General — M,D,O
Educational Leadership and Administration — M,D,O
Educational Measurement and Evaluation — M,D,O
Educational Media/Instructional Technology — M,D,O
Electrical Engineering — M,D
Engineering and Applied Sciences—General — M,D
Engineering Management — M,D
English Education — M,D
English — M,D
Exercise and Sports Science — M

Family and Consumer Sciences-General	M
Geographic Information Systems	M
Geography	M,D,O
Geosciences	M,D,O
Health Education	D,O
Health Services Management and Hospital Administration	M,D,O
Higher Education	M,D
History	M,D
Human Services	D,O
Industrial and Organizational Psychology	M
Industrial/Management Engineering	M,D
International Affairs	M,D
Manufacturing Engineering	M
Mathematics Education	M,D
Mathematics	M,D
Mechanical Engineering	M,D
Music Education	M,O
Music	M,O
Nonprofit Management	M,D,O
Nursing—General	M
Occupational Therapy	M
Paper and Pulp Engineering	M,D
Philosophy	M
Physical Education	M
Physician Assistant Studies	M
Physics	M,D,O
Physiology	M
Political Science	M,D
Psychology—General	M,D
Public Administration	M,D,O
Public Affairs	M,D,O
Reading Education	M,D
Rehabilitation Counseling	M
Rehabilitation Sciences	M
Religion	M,O
Science Education	M,D,O
Social Work	M
Sociology	M,D
Spanish	M,D
Special Education	M,D
Sports Management	M
Statistics	M,D,O
Therapies—Dance, Drama, and Music	M,O
Vocational and Technical Education	M
Writing	M,D

WESTERN MICHIGAN UNIVERSITY THOMAS M. COOLEY LAW SCHOOL

Environmental Law	M,D
Finance and Banking	M,D
Homeland Security	M,D
Insurance	M,D
Intellectual Property Law	M,D
Law	M,D
Legal and Justice Studies	M,D
National Security	M,D
Taxation	M,D

WESTERN NEW ENGLAND UNIVERSITY

Accounting	M
Advertising and Public Relations	M
Applied Behavior Analysis	M,D
Business Administration and Management—General	M
Civil Engineering	M
Communication—General	M
Curriculum and Instruction	M
Electrical Engineering	M
Engineering and Applied Sciences—General	M,D
Engineering Management	M,D
English Education	M
Industrial/Management Engineering	M
Law	M,D
Manufacturing Engineering	M
Mathematics Education	M
Mechanical Engineering	M
Occupational Therapy	D
Organizational Management	M
Pharmacy	D
Sports Management	M
Writing	M

WESTERN NEW MEXICO UNIVERSITY

Business Administration and Management—General	M
Education—General	M
Educational Leadership and Administration	M
Elementary Education	M
English as a Second Language	M
Interdisciplinary Studies	M
Multilingual and Multicultural Education	M
Occupational Therapy	M
Reading Education	M
Secondary Education	M
Social Work	M
Special Education	M

WESTERN OREGON UNIVERSITY

Criminal Justice and Criminology	M
Early Childhood Education	M
Education—General	M
Educational Media/Instructional Technology	M
Health Education	M
Mathematics Education	M
Multilingual and Multicultural Education	M
Music	M
Rehabilitation Counseling	M
Science Education	M
Secondary Education	M
Social Sciences Education	M
Special Education	M

WESTERN SEMINARY

Human Resources Development	M
Pastoral Ministry and Counseling	M,D,O

Religion	M,O
Theology	M,O
Women's Studies	M

WESTERN SEMINARY–SACRAMENTO CAMPUS

Marriage and Family Therapy	M
Pastoral Ministry and Counseling	M,O
Theology	M,O
Women's Studies	M

WESTERN SEMINARY–SAN JOSE CAMPUS

Marriage and Family Therapy	M
Pastoral Ministry and Counseling	M,O
Theology	M,O
Women's Studies	M,O

WESTERN STATE COLLEGE OF LAW AT ARGOSY UNIVERSITY

Law	D

WESTERN STATE COLORADO UNIVERSITY

Education—General	M
Educational Leadership and Administration	M
Environmental Management and Policy	M
Film, Television, and Video Production	M
Reading Education	M
Writing	M

WESTERN THEOLOGICAL SEMINARY

Pastoral Ministry and Counseling	M,D,O
Theology	M,D,O

WESTERN UNIVERSITY OF HEALTH SCIENCES

Allied Health—General	M,D
Biological and Biomedical Sciences—General	M
Dentistry	D
Health Education	M
Nursing and Healthcare Administration	M
Nursing—General	M,D
Optometry	D
Osteopathic Medicine	D
Pharmaceutical Sciences	M
Pharmacy	D
Physical Therapy	D
Physician Assistant Studies	M
Podiatric Medicine	D
Veterinary Medicine	D

WESTERN WASHINGTON UNIVERSITY

Adult Education	M
Anthropology	M
Biological and Biomedical Sciences—General	M
Business Administration and Management—General	M
Chemistry	M
Communication Disorders	M
Computer Science	M
Counseling Psychology	M
Counselor Education	M
Education of the Gifted	M
Education—General	M
Educational Leadership and Administration	M
Elementary Education	M
English	M
Environmental Education	M
Environmental Sciences	M
Exercise and Sports Science	M
Experimental Psychology	M
Geography	M
Geology	M
Higher Education	M
History	M
Marine Sciences	M
Mathematics	M
Music	M
Physical Education	M
Political Science	M
Psychology—General	M
Rehabilitation Counseling	M
Science Education	M
Secondary Education	M

WESTFIELD STATE UNIVERSITY

Accounting	M
Applied Behavior Analysis	M
Counseling Psychology	M
Counselor Education	M
Criminal Justice and Criminology	M
Early Childhood Education	M
Education—General	M
Elementary Education	M
English	M
Forensic Psychology	M
Mathematics Education	M
Nonprofit Management	M
Physical Education	M
Psychology—General	M
Public Administration	M
Reading Education	M
Science Education	M
Secondary Education	M
Social Sciences Education	M
Social Work	M
Special Education	M
Vocational and Technical Education	M

WEST LIBERTY UNIVERSITY

Criminal Justice and Criminology	M
Education—General	M
Organizational Management	M

WESTMINSTER COLLEGE (PA)

Counselor Education	M,O
Early Childhood Education	M,O
Educational Leadership and Administration	M,O

Reading Education	M,O
Special Education	M,O

WESTMINSTER COLLEGE (UT)

Accounting	M,O
Business Administration and Management—General	M,O
Communication—General	M
Counseling Psychology	M
Education—General	M
Family Nurse Practitioner Studies	M
Nurse Anesthesia	M
Nursing—General	M
Public Health—General	M
Writing	M

WESTMINSTER SEMINARY CALIFORNIA

Religion	M
Theology	M

WESTMINSTER THEOLOGICAL SEMINARY

Missions and Missiology	M,D,O
Pastoral Ministry and Counseling	M,D,O
Religion	M,D,O
Theology	M,D,O

WEST TEXAS A&M UNIVERSITY

Agricultural Economics and Agribusiness	M
Agricultural Sciences—General	M,D
Animal Sciences	M
Art/Fine Arts	M
Biological and Biomedical Sciences—General	M
Business Administration and Management—General	M
Chemistry	M
Communication Disorders	M
Communication—General	M
Counselor Education	M
Criminal Justice and Criminology	M
Curriculum and Instruction	M
Economics	M
Education—General	M
Educational Leadership and Administration	M
Educational Measurement and Evaluation	M
Educational Media/Instructional Technology	M
Engineering and Applied Sciences—General	M
English	M
Environmental Sciences	M
Exercise and Sports Science	M
Family Nurse Practitioner Studies	M
Finance and Banking	M
History	M
Interdisciplinary Studies	M
Mathematics	M
Music	M
Nursing—General	M
Plant Sciences	M
Psychology—General	M
Reading Education	M
Social Work	M
Sports Management	M

WEST VIRGINIA SCHOOL OF OSTEOPATHIC MEDICINE

Osteopathic Medicine	D

WEST VIRGINIA STATE UNIVERSITY

Biotechnology	M
Criminal Justice and Criminology	M
Media Studies	M

WEST VIRGINIA UNIVERSITY

Accounting	M,D
Aerospace/Aeronautical Engineering	M,D
African Studies	M,D
African-American Studies	M,D
Agricultural Economics and Agribusiness	M
Agricultural Education	M,D
Agricultural Sciences—General	M,D
Agronomy and Soil Sciences	M
Allopathic Medicine	D
American Studies	M,D
Analytical Chemistry	M,D
Applied Mathematics	M,D
Applied Physics	M,D
Art Education	M
Art History	M
Art/Fine Arts	M
Asian Studies	M,D
Athletic Training and Sports Medicine	M,D
Biochemistry	D
Biological and Biomedical Sciences—General	M,D
Biostatistics	M,D
Business Administration and Management—General	M
Cancer Biology/Oncology	M,D
Cell Biology	M,D
Chemical Physics	M,D
Chemistry	M,D
Clinical Psychology	M,D
Communication Disorders	D
Communication—General	M,D
Community Health	M,D
Computer Engineering	D
Computer Science	M
Condensed Matter Physics	M,D
Corporate and Organizational Communication	M,D,O
Counseling Psychology	M
Counselor Education	M
Curriculum and Instruction	M,D
Dentistry	D
Developmental Biology	M,D

Early Childhood Education	M,D
Economic Development	M,D
Economics	M,D
Education of Students with Severe/Multiple Disabilities	M,D
Education of the Gifted	M,D
Education—General	M,D
Educational Leadership and Administration	D
Educational Media/Instructional Technology	M,D
Educational Psychology	M,D
Electrical Engineering	M,D
Elementary Education	M
Engineering and Applied Sciences—General	M,D
English as a Second Language	M
English	M,D
Entomology	M
Environmental and Occupational Health	D
Environmental Biology	M,D
Environmental Education	M,D
Environmental Management and Policy	M,D
Evolutionary Biology	M,D
Exercise and Sports Science	M,D
Fish, Game, and Wildlife Management	M
Forensic Sciences	M,D
Forestry	M,D
French	M
Genetics	M,D
Genomic Sciences	M,D
Geographic Information Systems	M,D
Geography	M,D
Geology	M,D
Geophysics	M,D
Graphic Design	M
Higher Education	M
History of Science and Technology	M,D
History	M,D
Horticulture	M
Human Development	M,D
Human Genetics	M,D
Human Services	M,D
Hydrogeology	M,D
Immunology	M,D
Industrial and Labor Relations	M
Industrial Hygiene	M
Industrial/Management Engineering	M,D
Inorganic Chemistry	M,D
International Affairs	M,D
International Economics	M,D
Journalism	M,O
Latin American Studies	M,D
Law	D
Linguistics	M
Marketing	M,O
Mathematics Education	M,D
Mathematics	M,D
Mechanical Engineering	M,D
Medicinal and Pharmaceutical Chemistry	M,D
Microbiology	D
Molecular Biology	M,D
Music Education	M,D
Music	M,D
Natural Resources	M,D
Neurobiology	M,D
Neuroscience	D
Nursing—General	M,D,O
Occupational Therapy	M
Organic Chemistry	M,D
Paleontology	M,D
Pharmaceutical Administration	M,D
Pharmaceutical Sciences	D
Pharmacology	D
Pharmacy	M,D
Physical Chemistry	M,D
Physical Education	M,D
Physical Therapy	D
Physics	M,D
Physiology	M,D
Plant Pathology	M
Plasma Physics	M,D
Political Science	M,D
Psychology—General	M,D
Public Administration	M
Public Health—General	M,D
Public Policy	M,D
Recreation and Park Management	M
Reproductive Biology	M,D
Safety Engineering	M
Secondary Education	M,D
Social Work	M
Sociology	M,D
Software Engineering	M
Spanish	M
Special Education	M,D
Sport Psychology	M,D
Sports Management	M,D
Statistics	M,D
Teratology	M,D
Theoretical Chemistry	M,D
Theoretical Physics	M,D
Toxicology	M,D
Urban and Regional Planning	M,D
Writing	M

WEST VIRGINIA WESLEYAN COLLEGE

Athletic Training and Sports Medicine	M
Business Administration and Management—General	M
Education—General	M
Family Nurse Practitioner Studies	M,O
Nurse Midwifery	M,O
Nursing and Healthcare Administration	M,O
Nursing Education	M,O
Nursing—General	M,O

Psychiatric Nursing — M,O
Writing — M

WHEATON COLLEGE
Archaeology — M,D
Clinical Psychology — M,D
Counseling Psychology — M,D
Cultural Studies — M,O
Education—General — M
Elementary Education — M
English as a Second Language — M,O
Marriage and Family Therapy — M,D
Missions and Missiology — M,O
Pastoral Ministry and Counseling — M,D
Psychology—General — M,D
Religious Education — M
Secondary Education — M
Theology — M,D

WHEELING JESUIT UNIVERSITY
Accounting — M
Business Administration and
 Management—General — M
Educational Leadership and
 Administration — M
Nursing—General — M
Organizational Management — M
Physical Therapy — D

WHEELOCK COLLEGE
Child and Family Studies — M
Early Childhood Education — M
Education—General — M
Educational Leadership and
 Administration — M
Elementary Education — M
Human Development — M
Reading Education — M
Social Work — M
Special Education — M

WHITTIER COLLEGE
Child Development — M
Education—General — M
Educational Leadership and
 Administration — M
Elementary Education — M
Secondary Education — M

WHITWORTH UNIVERSITY
Business Administration and
 Management—General — M
Counselor Education — M
Education of the Gifted — M
Education—General — M
Educational Leadership and
 Administration — M
Elementary Education — M
Secondary Education — M
Special Education — M
Theology — M

WHU - OTTO BEISHEIM SCHOOL OF MANAGEMENT
Business Administration and
 Management—General — M

WICHITA STATE UNIVERSITY
Accounting — M
Aerospace/Aeronautical
 Engineering — M,D
Allied Health—General — M,D
Anthropology — M
Applied Mathematics — M,D
Art/Fine Arts — M
Biological and Biomedical
 Sciences—General — M
Biomedical Engineering — M
Business Administration and
 Management—General — M
Chemistry — M,D
Clinical Psychology — D
Communication Disorders — M,D
Communication—General — M
Computer Engineering — M,D
Computer Science — M,D
Counselor Education — M,D,O
Criminal Justice and Criminology — M
Curriculum and Instruction — M
Early Childhood Education — M
Economics — M
Education of the Gifted — M
Education—General — M,D,O
Educational Leadership and
 Administration — M,D,O
Educational Psychology — M,D,O
Electrical Engineering — M,D
Engineering and Applied
 Sciences—General — M,D
Engineering Management — M,D
English — M
Entrepreneurship — M
Environmental Sciences — M
Exercise and Sports Science — M
Geology — M
Gerontology — M
History — M
Human Services — M
Industrial/Management
 Engineering — M,D
International Economics — M
Liberal Studies — M
Management Information Systems — M
Manufacturing Engineering — M,D
Mathematics — M,D
Mechanical Engineering — M,D
Middle School Education — M
Music Education — M
Music — M
Nursing—General — M,D
Photography — M
Physical Therapy — D
Physician Assistant Studies — M

Physics — M,D
Psychology—General — D
Public Administration — M
School Psychology — M,D,O
Secondary Education — M
Social Psychology — D
Social Work — M
Sociology — M
Spanish — M
Special Education — M
Sports Management — M
Taxation — M
Writing — M

WIDENER UNIVERSITY
Adult Education — M,D
Biomedical Engineering — M
Business Administration and
 Management—General — M
Chemical Engineering — M
Civil Engineering — M
Clinical Psychology — D
Counselor Education — M,D
Criminal Justice and Criminology — M
Early Childhood Education — M,D
Education—General — M,D
Educational Leadership and
 Administration — M,D
Educational Media/Instructional
 Technology — M,D
Educational Psychology — M,D
Electrical Engineering — M
Elementary Education — M,D
Engineering and Applied
 Sciences—General — M
Engineering Management — M
English Education — M,D
Foundations and Philosophy of
 Education — M
Health Education — M,D
Health Law — M,D
Health Services Management and
 Hospital Administration — M
Hospitality Management — M,D
Law — M,D
Liberal Studies — M
Mathematics Education — M,D
Mechanical Engineering — M
Middle School Education — M,D
Nursing—General — M,D,O
Physical Therapy — M,D
Psychology—General — M
Public Administration — M
Reading Education — M,D
Science Education — M,D
Social Sciences Education — M,D
Social Work — M
Special Education — M,D
Taxation — M

WILBERFORCE UNIVERSITY
Rehabilitation Counseling — M

WILFRID LAURIER UNIVERSITY
Accounting — M,D
American Studies — M,D
Biological and Biomedical
 Sciences—General — M
Business Administration and
 Management—General — M,D
Canadian Studies — M,D
Chemistry — M
Cognitive Sciences — M,D
Communication—General — M
Conflict Resolution and
 Mediation/Peace Studies — D
Criminal Justice and Criminology — M
Cultural Studies — M
Developmental Psychology — M,D
Economics — M,D
English — M,D
Environmental Management
 and Policy — M,D
Environmental Sciences — M,D
Film, Television, and Video
 Theory and Criticism — M,D
Finance and Banking — M,D
Gender Studies — M
Geography — M
Health Promotion — M
History — M,D
Human Resources Management — M,D
International Affairs — M,D
International Economics — M
Kinesiology and Movement Studies — M
Legal and Justice Studies — D
Management of Technology — M,D
Marketing — M,D
Mathematics — M
Media Studies — M
Neuroscience — M,D
Organizational Behavior — M,D
Organizational Management — M
Pastoral Ministry and Counseling — M,D,O
Philosophy — M
Physical Education — M,D
Political Science — M,D
Psychology—General — M,D
Public Policy — M
Religion — M,D
Social Psychology — M,D
Social Sciences — M
Social Work — M,D
Sociology — M
Supply Chain Management — M,D
Theology — M,D,O
Therapies—Dance, Drama, and
 Music — M

WILKES UNIVERSITY
Accounting — M
Art Education — M,D

Bioengineering — M
Business Administration and
 Management—General — M
Curriculum and Instruction — M,D
Distance Education Development — M,D
Early Childhood Education — M,D
Education—General — M,D
Educational Leadership and
 Administration — M,D
Educational Measurement and
 Evaluation — M,D
Educational Media/Instructional
 Technology — M,D
Electrical Engineering — M
Engineering and Applied
 Sciences—General — M
Engineering Management — M
English as a Second Language — M,D
Entrepreneurship — M
Finance and Banking — M
Health Services Management and
 Hospital Administration — M
Human Resources Management — M
Industrial and Manufacturing
 Management — M
International and Comparative
 Education — M,D
International Business — M
Mathematics — M
Mechanical Engineering — M
Middle School Education — M,D
Nursing—General — M,D
Organizational Management — M
Pharmacy — D
Reading Education — M,D
Science Education — M,D
Special Education — M,D
Writing — M

WILLAMETTE UNIVERSITY
Business Administration and
 Management—General — M
Conflict Resolution and
 Mediation/Peace Studies — M,D
Law — M,D

WILLIAM CAREY UNIVERSITY
Art Education — M,O
Business Administration and
 Management—General — M
Counseling Psychology — M
Education of the Gifted — M,O
Education—General — M,O
Elementary Education — M,O
English Education — M,O
Nursing—General — M
Osteopathic Medicine — D
Psychology—General — M
Secondary Education — M,O
Social Sciences Education — M,O
Special Education — M,O

WILLIAM JAMES COLLEGE
Applied Psychology — M,D,O
Clinical Psychology — M,D,O
Community Health — M,D,O
Counseling Psychology — M,D,O
Forensic Psychology — M,D,O
Industrial and Organizational
 Psychology — M,D,O
International Health — M,D,O
Psychology—General — M,D,O
School Psychology — M,D,O
Student Affairs — M,D,O

WILLIAM JESSUP UNIVERSITY
Education—General — M
English Education — M
Mathematics Education — M

WILLIAM JEWELL COLLEGE
Education—General — M

WILLIAM PATERSON UNIVERSITY OF NEW JERSEY
Biological and Biomedical
 Sciences—General — M,D
Biotechnology — M,D
Business Administration and
 Management—General — M
Clinical Psychology — M,D
Communication Disorders — M,D
Counseling Psychology — M,D
Counselor Education — M
Education—General — M
Educational Leadership and
 Administration — M
Elementary Education — M
English — M
Exercise and Sports Science — M,D
Foundations and Philosophy of
 Education — M,D
History — M,D
Music — M
Nursing—General — M,D
Public Policy — M
Reading Education — M
Secondary Education — M
Sociology — M
Special Education — M
Writing — M,D

WILLIAM PENN UNIVERSITY
Organizational Management — M

WILLIAMS COLLEGE
Art History — M
Economic Development — M

WILLIAMSON COLLEGE
Organizational Management — M

WILLIAM WOODS UNIVERSITY
Advertising and Public Relations — M,D,O

Business Administration and
 Management—General — M,D,O
Curriculum and Instruction — M,D,O
Educational Leadership and
 Administration — M,D,O
Educational Media/Instructional
 Technology — M,D,O
Health Services Management and
 Hospital Administration — M,D,O
Human Resources Development — M,D,O
Marketing — M,D,O
Physical Education — M,D,O

WILMINGTON COLLEGE
Education—General — M
Reading Education — M
Special Education — M

WILMINGTON UNIVERSITY
Accounting — M,D
Adult Nursing — M,D
Business Administration and
 Management—General — M,D
Clinical Psychology — M
Computer and Information
 Systems Security — M
Counseling Psychology — M
Counselor Education — M
Criminal Justice and Criminology — M
Education of the Gifted — M,D
Education—General — M,D
Educational Leadership and
 Administration — M,D
Educational Media/Instructional
 Technology — M,D
Elementary Education — M,D
English as a Second Language — M,D
Environmental Management
 and Policy — M,D
Family Nurse Practitioner Studies — M,D
Finance and Banking — M
Geographic Information Systems — M
Gerontological Nursing — M,D
Health Services Management and
 Hospital Administration — M,D
Higher Education — M,D
Homeland Security — M,D
Human Resources Management — M,D
Human Services — M
Internet and Interactive
 Multimedia — M
Internet Engineering — M
Management Information Systems — M
Marketing — M,D
Nursing and Healthcare
 Administration — M,D
Nursing—General — M,D
Organizational Management — M,D
Public Administration — M,D
Reading Education — M,D
Secondary Education — M,D
Special Education — M,D
Vocational and Technical Education — M,D

WILSON COLLEGE
Accounting — M
Art/Fine Arts — M
Business Administration and
 Management—General — M
Cultural Studies — M
Dance — M
Education—General — M
Elementary Education — M
English — M
Health Services Management and
 Hospital Administration — M
Humanities — M
Nursing and Healthcare
 Administration — M
Nursing Education — M
Nursing—General — M
Secondary Education — M
Women's Studies — M

WINEBRENNER THEOLOGICAL SEMINARY
Counseling Psychology — M,D
Theology — M,D

WINGATE UNIVERSITY
Accounting — M
Business Administration and
 Management—General — M
Community College Education — M,D,O
Education—General — M,D,O
Educational Leadership and
 Administration — M,D,O
Elementary Education — M,D,O
Entrepreneurship — M
Finance and Banking — M
Health Services Management and
 Hospital Administration — M
Marketing — M
Pharmacy — D
Physical Therapy — M
Physician Assistant Studies — M
Project Management — M
Sports Management — M

WINONA STATE UNIVERSITY
Acute Care/Critical Care Nursing — M,D,O
Addictions/Substance Abuse
 Counseling — M,O
Adult Nursing — M,D,O
Clinical Psychology — M,O
Counselor Education — M,O
Education—General — O
Educational Leadership and
 Administration — M
English as a Second Language — M
English — M
Family Nurse Practitioner Studies — M,D,O
Gerontological Nursing — M,D,O

---

*M—masters degree; D—doctorate; O—other advanced degree; *—Close-Up and/or Display*

Human Services	M,O
Multilingual and Multicultural Education	O
Nursing and Healthcare Administration	M,D,O
Nursing Education	M,D,O
Nursing—General	M,D,O
Organizational Management	M,D,O
Special Education	M
Sports Management	M,O

WINSTON-SALEM STATE UNIVERSITY

Business Administration and Management—General	M
Computer Science	M
Education—General	M
Family Nurse Practitioner Studies	M,D
Health Services Management and Hospital Administration	M
Management Information Systems	M
Middle School Education	M
Nursing Education	M,D
Nursing—General	M,D
Occupational Therapy	M
Physical Therapy	D
Rehabilitation Counseling	M
Special Education	M

WINTHROP UNIVERSITY

Art Education	M
Art/Fine Arts	M
Arts Administration	M
Biological and Biomedical Sciences—General	M
Business Administration and Management—General	M
Counselor Education	M
Education—General	M
Educational Leadership and Administration	M
English	M
History	M
Liberal Studies	M
Music Education	M
Music	M
Nutrition	M,O
Physical Education	M
Psychology—General	M,O
Secondary Education	M
Social Work	M
Special Education	M

WISCONSIN LUTHERAN COLLEGE

Curriculum and Instruction	M
Educational Leadership and Administration	M
Educational Media/Instructional Technology	M
Science Education	M

WISCONSIN SCHOOL OF PROFESSIONAL PSYCHOLOGY

Clinical Psychology	M,D
Psychology—General	M,D

WITTENBERG UNIVERSITY

Education—General	M

WOLFORD COLLEGE

Nurse Anesthesia	M,D

WON INSTITUTE OF GRADUATE STUDIES

Acupuncture and Oriental Medicine	M,O
Religion	M

WOODBURY UNIVERSITY

Architecture	M
Business Administration and Management—General	M
Organizational Management	M

WOODS HOLE OCEANOGRAPHIC INSTITUTION

Marine Biology	D
Marine Geology	D
Ocean Engineering	D
Oceanography	D

WORCESTER POLYTECHNIC INSTITUTE

Aerospace/Aeronautical Engineering	M,D
Applied Mathematics	M,D,O
Applied Statistics	M,D,O
Artificial Intelligence/Robotics	M,D
Biochemistry	M,D
Bioinformatics	M,D
Biological and Biomedical Sciences—General	M,D
Biomedical Engineering	M,D,O
Biotechnology	M,D
Business Administration and Management—General	M,D,O
Chemical Engineering	M,D
Chemistry	M,D
Civil Engineering	M,D,O
Computational Biology	M,D
Computer Engineering	M,D,O
Computer Science	M,D,O
Construction Management	M,D,O
Database Systems	M,D,O
Educational Media/Instructional Technology	M,D
Electrical Engineering	M,D,O
Energy and Power Engineering	M,D
Engineering and Applied Sciences—General	M,D,O
Engineering Design	M,D,O
Environmental Engineering	M,D,O
Fire Protection Engineering	M,D,O
Game Design and Development	M
Interdisciplinary Studies	M,D,O
Internet and Interactive Multimedia	M
Management Information Systems	M,D,O

Manufacturing Engineering	M,D
Marketing	M,D,O
Materials Engineering	M,D
Materials Sciences	M,D
Mathematics	M,D,O
Mechanical Engineering	M,D,O
Modeling and Simulation	M,D
Organizational Management	M,D,O
Physics	M,D
Social Sciences	M,O
Systems Engineering	M,O
Systems Science	M,D,O

WORCESTER STATE UNIVERSITY

Accounting	M
Biotechnology	M
Business Administration and Management—General	M
Communication Disorders	M
Community Health Nursing	M
Early Childhood Education	M
Education—General	M,O
Educational Leadership and Administration	M,O
Elementary Education	M
English as a Second Language	M
English Education	M
Foreign Languages Education	M
Health Education	M
Health Services Management and Hospital Administration	M
History	M
Middle School Education	M,O
Nonprofit Management	M
Nursing Education	M
Occupational Therapy	M
Organizational Management	M
Reading Education	M,O
School Psychology	O
Secondary Education	M,O
Social Sciences Education	M
Spanish	M
Special Education	M,O

WORLD MEDICINE INSTITUTE

Acupuncture and Oriental Medicine	M

WRIGHT INSTITUTE

Clinical Psychology	D
Counseling Psychology	M
Psychology—General	D

WRIGHT STATE UNIVERSITY

Accounting	M
Acute Care/Critical Care Nursing	M
Adult Nursing	M
Aerospace/Aeronautical Engineering	M
Allopathic Medicine	D
Anatomy	M
Applied Behavior Analysis	M
Applied Economics	M
Applied Mathematics	M
Applied Statistics	M
Biochemistry	M
Biological and Biomedical Sciences—General	M,D
Biomedical Engineering	M
Business Administration and Management—General	M
Chemistry	M
Clinical Psychology	D
Computer Engineering	M,D
Computer Science	M
Counselor Education	M
Criminal Justice and Criminology	M
Curriculum and Instruction	O
Economics	M
Education—General	M,O
Educational Leadership and Administration	O
Electrical Engineering	M
Elementary Education	M
English	M
Environmental Sciences	D
Ergonomics and Human Factors	M,D
Family Nurse Practitioner Studies	M
Geology	O
Geophysics	M
Gerontological Nursing	M
Health Education	M
Health Promotion	M
History	M
Humanities	M
Immunology	M
Industrial and Organizational Psychology	M,D
Industrial/Management Engineering	M
Logistics	M
Management Information Systems	M
Materials Engineering	M
Materials Sciences	M
Maternal and Child/Neonatal Nursing	M
Mathematics Education	D
Mathematics	M
Mechanical Engineering	M
Microbiology	M
Molecular Biology	M
Music Education	M
Neuroscience	M
Nursing and Healthcare Administration	M
Nursing—General	M
Pediatric Nursing	M
Pharmacology	M
Physics	M
Physiology	M
Psychiatric Nursing	M
Psychology—General	M,D
Public Administration	M
Public Health—General	M
Rehabilitation Counseling	M

School Nursing	M
Science Education	M,D
Secondary Education	M
Special Education	M
Supply Chain Management	M
Toxicology	M
Urban Studies	M

WYCLIFFE COLLEGE

Religion	M,D,O
Theology	M,D,O

XAVIER UNIVERSITY

Accounting	M
Athletic Training and Sports Medicine	M
Business Administration and Management—General	M
Clinical Psychology	M,D
Counseling Psychology	M
Counselor Education	M
Criminal Justice and Criminology	M
Early Childhood Education	M
Education—General	M,D
Educational Leadership and Administration	M,D
Elementary Education	M
English	M
Ethics	M
Finance and Banking	M
Health Services Management and Hospital Administration	M*
Human Resources Development	M
Industrial and Organizational Psychology	M,D
International Business	M
Management Strategy and Policy	M
Marketing	M
Multilingual and Multicultural Education	M
Nursing—General	M,D,O
Occupational Therapy	M
Pastoral Ministry and Counseling	M
Psychology—General	M,D
Reading Education	M
Religious Education	M
Secondary Education	M
Special Education	M
Sports Management	M
Sustainable Development	M
Theology	M

XAVIER UNIVERSITY OF LOUISIANA

Counselor Education	M
Curriculum and Instruction	M
Education—General	M
Educational Leadership and Administration	M
Pastoral Ministry and Counseling	M
Pharmacy	D
Theology	M

YALE UNIVERSITY

Accounting	D
African Studies	M
African-American Studies	D
Allopathic Medicine	D
American Studies	D
Anthropology	M,D
Applied Arts and Design—General	M
Applied Mathematics	M,D
Applied Physics	M,D
Archaeology	M,D
Architecture	M,D
Art History	D
Art/Fine Arts	M
Asian Languages	D
Asian Studies	M
Astronomy	M,D
Astrophysics	M,D
Atmospheric Sciences	D
Biochemistry	D
Bioinformatics	D
Biological and Biomedical Sciences—General	D
Biomedical Engineering	M,D
Biophysics	D
Biostatistics	M,D
Business Administration and Management—General	M,D
Cancer Biology/Oncology	D
Cell Biology	D
Chemical Engineering	M,D
Chemistry	D
Classics	M,D
Clinical Psychology	D
Cognitive Sciences	D
Comparative Literature	D
Computational Biology	D
Computer Science	M,D
Developmental Biology	D
Developmental Psychology	D
East European and Russian Studies	M,D
Ecology	M
Economic Development	M
Economics	M,D
Electrical Engineering	M,D
Engineering and Applied Sciences—General	M,D*
Engineering Physics	M,D
English	M,D
Environmental and Occupational Health	M,D
Environmental Design	M,D
Environmental Engineering	M,D
Environmental Management and Policy	M,D
Environmental Sciences	M,D
Epidemiology	M,D
Evolutionary Biology	D
Film, Television, and Video Theory and Criticism	D
Finance and Banking	D
Forestry	M,D
French	M,D

Genetics	D
Genomic Sciences	D
Geochemistry	D
Geology	D
Geophysics	D
Geosciences	D
German	D
Graphic Design	M
Health Services Management and Hospital Administration	M,D
History of Medicine	M,D
History of Science and Technology	M,D
History	M,D
Immunology	D
Infectious Diseases	D
Inorganic Chemistry	D
International Affairs	M
International Economics	M
International Health	M,D
Italian	D
Latin American Studies	M
Law	M,D
Linguistics	D
Marketing	D
Mathematics	M,D
Mechanical Engineering	M,D
Medieval and Renaissance Studies	M,D
Meteorology	D
Microbiology	D
Molecular Biology	D
Molecular Biophysics	D
Molecular Medicine	D
Molecular Pathology	D
Molecular Physiology	D
Music	M,D,O
Near and Middle Eastern Languages	M,D
Near and Middle Eastern Studies	M,D
Neurobiology	D
Neuroscience	D
Nursing—General	M,D,O
Oceanography	D
Organic Chemistry	D
Organizational Management	D
Paleontology	D
Pathobiology	D
Pathology	M,D
Pharmacology	D
Philosophy	D
Photography	M
Physical Chemistry	D
Physician Assistant Studies	M
Physics	D
Physiology	D
Planetary and Space Sciences	M,D
Plant Biology	D
Political Science	D
Portuguese	D
Psychology—General	D
Public Health—General	M,D
Religion	D
Russian	D
Slavic Languages	D
Social Psychology	D
Social Sciences	M,D
Sociology	D
Spanish	D
Statistics	M,D
Theater	M,D,O
Theology	M
Theoretical Chemistry	D
Virology	D
Writing	M,D,O

YESHIVA BETH MOSHE

Theology	O

YESHIVA DERECH CHAIM

Religion	D

YESHIVA KARLIN STOLIN RABBINICAL INSTITUTE

Theology	O

YESHIVA OF NITRA RABBINICAL COLLEGE

Theology	

YESHIVA SHAAR HATORAH TALMUDIC RESEARCH INSTITUTE

Theology	

YESHIVATH ZICHRON MOSHE

Theology	O

YESHIVA UNIVERSITY

Accounting	M
Business Administration and Management—General	M
Clinical Psychology	D
Communication Disorders	M,D
Conflict Resolution and Mediation/Peace Studies	M,D
Counseling Psychology	M
Economics	M,D
Educational Leadership and Administration	M,D,O
Health Psychology	D
Intellectual Property Law	M,D
Jewish Studies	M,D
Law	M,D
Marketing	M
Mathematics	M,D
Psychology—General	M,D
Religious Education	M,D,O
School Psychology	D
Social Work	M,D

YORK COLLEGE OF PENNSYLVANIA

Adult Nursing	M,D,O
Business Administration and Management—General	M
Education—General	M
Educational Leadership and Administration	M
Educational Media/Instructional Technology	M

Finance and Banking	M
Gerontological Nursing	M,D,O
Health Services Management and Hospital Administration	M
Marketing	M
Nurse Anesthesia	M,D,O
Nursing Education	M,D,O
Nursing—General	M,D,O
Reading Education	M

YORK UNIVERSITY

Accounting	M,D
Anthropology	M,D
Applied Arts and Design—General	M
Applied Mathematics	M,D
Art History	M,D
Art/Fine Arts	M,D
Astronomy	M,D
Biological and Biomedical Sciences—General	M,D
Business Administration and Management—General	M,D
Chemistry	M,D
Communication—General	M,D
Computer Science	M,D
Dance	M,D
Disability Studies	M,D
Economics	M,D
Education—General	M,D
Emergency Management	M
English	M,D
Environmental Management and Policy	M,D
Film, Television, and Video Production	M,D

Finance and Banking	M,D
French	M,D
Gender Studies	M,D
Geography	M,D
Geosciences	M,D
History	M,D
Human Resources Management	M,D
Humanities	M,D
Interdisciplinary Studies	M
International Affairs	M
International Business	M,D
Kinesiology and Movement Studies	M,D
Law	M,D
Linguistics	M,D
Mathematics	M,D
Music	M,D
Nursing—General	M
Philosophy	M,D
Physics	M,D
Planetary and Space Sciences	M,D
Political Science	M,D
Psychology—General	M,D
Public Administration	M
Public Affairs	M
Public Policy	M
Social Work	M,D
Sociology	M,D
Statistics	M,D
Theater	M,D
Translation and Interpretation	M
Women's Studies	M,D

YO SAN UNIVERSITY OF TRADITIONAL CHINESE MEDICINE

Acupuncture and Oriental Medicine	M

YOUNGSTOWN STATE UNIVERSITY

Accounting	M
Analytical Chemistry	M
Anatomy	M
Applied Behavior Analysis	M
Applied Mathematics	M
Biochemistry	M
Biological and Biomedical Sciences—General	M
Business Administration and Management—General	M,O
Chemistry	M
Civil Engineering	M
Computer Engineering	M
Computer Science	M
Counseling Psychology	M
Counselor Education	M
Criminal Justice and Criminology	M
Curriculum and Instruction	M
Early Childhood Education	M
Economics	M
Education of the Gifted	M
Education—General	M,D
Educational Leadership and Administration	M,D
Educational Media/Instructional Technology	M
Electrical Engineering	M
Engineering and Applied Sciences—General	M
English	M

Environmental Biology	M
Environmental Engineering	M
Environmental Management and Policy	M,O
Finance and Banking	M
Gerontology	M
Health Services Management and Hospital Administration	M
History	M
Human Services	M
Industrial/Management Engineering	M
Information Science	M
Inorganic Chemistry	M
Marketing	M
Mathematics Education	M
Mathematics	M
Mechanical Engineering	M
Microbiology	M
Middle School Education	M
Molecular Biology	M
Music Education	M
Music	M
Nursing—General	M
Organic Chemistry	M
Physical Chemistry	M
Physical Therapy	D
Physiology	M
Psychology—General	M
Reading Education	M
School Psychology	M
Science Education	M
Secondary Education	M
Special Education	M
Statistics	M

---

*M—masters degree; D—doctorate; O—other advanced degree; *—Close-Up and/or Display*

PROFILES OF INSTITUTIONS OFFERING GRADUATE AND PROFESSIONAL WORK

ABILENE CHRISTIAN UNIVERSITY, Abilene, TX 79699

General Information Independent-religious, coed, university. CGS member. *Enrollment:* 4,910 graduate, professional, and undergraduate students; 798 full-time matriculated graduate/professional students (523 women), 358 part-time matriculated graduate/professional students (208 women). *Enrollment by degree level:* 821 master's, 303 doctoral, 32 other advanced degrees. *Graduate faculty:* 20 full-time (6 women), 70 part-time/adjunct (18 women). *Tuition:* Full-time $19,890; part-time $1105 per credit hour. Tuition and fees vary according to course load and program. *Graduate housing:* On-campus housing not available. *Student services:* Campus employment opportunities, campus safety program, career counseling, exercise/wellness program, grant writing training, international student services, low-cost health insurance, multicultural affairs office, services for students with disabilities, teacher training, writing training. *Library facilities:* Brown Library. *Collection:* Books: 543,851 (physical), 281,582 (digital/electronic); Serial titles: 4,182 (physical), 51,856 (digital/electronic); Databases: 116. Weekly public service hours: 97; students can reserve study rooms. *Research affiliation:* Los Alamos National Laboratory (particle physics), Fermilab (peanut toxins).

Computer facilities: Computer purchase and lease plans are available. 466 computers available on campus for general student use. A campuswide network can be accessed from student residence rooms and from off campus. Online class registration is available. Website: http://www.acu.edu/

General Application Contact: Corey Patterson, Director of Graduate Admission and Recruiting, 325-674-6566, Fax: 325-674-6717, E-mail: gradinfo@acu.edu.

GRADUATE UNITS

College of Graduate and Professional Studies Students: 412 full-time (270 women), 214 part-time (149 women); includes 306 minority (188 Black or African American, non-Hispanic/Latino; 2 American Indian or Alaska Native, non-Hispanic/Latino; 8 Asian, non-Hispanic/Latino; 98 Hispanic/Latino; 10 Two or more races, non-Hispanic/Latino), 7 international. 380 applicants, 93% accepted, 311 enrolled. *Faculty:* 4 full-time (1 woman), 5 part-time/adjunct (3 women). Expenses: Contact institution. *Financial support:* In 2016–17, 3 students received support. Application deadline: 4/1; applicants required to submit FAFSA. In 2016, 66 master's, 50 other advanced degrees awarded. *Program availability:* Part-time, online only. Offers advanced practiced nursing (DNP); child and adolescent therapy (MMFT); executive nursing leadership (DNP); higher education (M Ed); instructional leadership (M Ed); learning with emerging technologies (Certificate); medical family therapy (MMFT); organizational leadership (Ed D); superintendency (Post-Master's Certificate); therapy with military families (MMFT); treatment of trauma (MMFT). *Application deadline:* For fall admission, 8/15 for domestic students; for winter admission, 10/1 for domestic students; for spring admission, 12/15 for domestic students; for summer admission, 4/15 for domestic students. Applications are processed on a rolling basis. *Application fee:* $50. *Application Contact:* Graduate Admissions, 855-219-7000, E-mail: gradonline@acu.edu. *Interim Dean,* Dr. Joe Cope, 214-305-9437, E-mail: graduateonline@acu.edu.

Duncum Center for Conflict Resolution Students: 52 full-time (32 women), 12 part-time (7 women); includes 30 minority (20 Black or African American, non-Hispanic/Latino; 1 Asian, non-Hispanic/Latino; 8 Hispanic/Latino; 1 Two or more races, non-Hispanic/Latino), 1 international. 30 applicants, 83% accepted, 16 enrolled. *Faculty:* 2 full-time (0 women), 4 part-time/adjunct (3 women). Expenses: Contact institution. *Financial support:* In 2016–17, 1 student received support. Available to part-time students. Application deadline: 4/1; applicants required to submit FAFSA. In 2016, 29 master's, 46 other advanced degrees awarded. *Program availability:* Part-time, evening/weekend, online learning. Offers conflict resolution (Certificate); conflict resolution and reconciliation (MA). *Application deadline:* For fall admission, 8/11 for domestic students; for winter admission, 10/1 for domestic students; for spring admission, 12/15 for domestic students; for summer admission, 4/15 for domestic students. Applications are processed on a rolling basis. *Application fee:* $50. Electronic applications accepted. *Application Contact:* Corey Patterson, Director of Graduate Admission and Recruiting, 325-674-6566, Fax: 325-674-6717, E-mail: gradinfo@acu.edu. *Program Director,* Dr. Joe Cope, 325-674-2015, Fax: 325-674-2427, E-mail: conflictresolution@acu.edu.

Graduate Programs Students: 386 full-time (253 women), 144 part-time (59 women); includes 148 minority (74 Black or African American, non-Hispanic/Latino; 2 American Indian or Alaska Native, non-Hispanic/Latino; 4 Asian, non-Hispanic/Latino; 58 Hispanic/Latino; 1 Native Hawaiian or other Pacific Islander, non-Hispanic/Latino; 9 Two or more races, non-Hispanic/Latino), 20 international. 776 applicants, 46% accepted, 223 enrolled. *Faculty:* 16 full-time (5 women), 65 part-time/adjunct (15 women). Expenses: Contact institution. *Financial support:* In 2016–17, 161 students received support, including 39 research assistantships with partial tuition reimbursements available (averaging $5,800 per year), 12 teaching assistantships with partial tuition reimbursements available (averaging $5,800 per year); career-related internships or fieldwork, Federal Work-Study, and scholarships/grants also available. Support available to part-time students. Financial award application deadline: 4/1; financial award applicants required to submit FAFSA. In 2016, 234 master's, 2 doctorates, 10 other advanced degrees awarded. *Program availability:* Part-time, evening/weekend, online learning. *Application deadline:* For fall admission, 4/1 priority date for domestic students; for spring admission, 11/1 priority date for domestic students. Applications are processed on a rolling basis. *Application fee:* $50. Electronic applications accepted. *Application Contact:* Corey Patterson, Director, Graduate Operations and Admissions, 325-674-6566, E-mail: gradinfo@acu.edu. *Assistant Provost for Graduate Programs,* Dr. Lynette Sharp Penya, 325-674-2223, Fax: 325-674-6717, E-mail: gradinfo@acu.edu.

College of Arts and Sciences Students: 116 full-time (86 women), 40 part-time (28 women); includes 54 minority (26 Black or African American, non-Hispanic/Latino; 1 American Indian or Alaska Native, non-Hispanic/Latino; 3 Asian, non-Hispanic/Latino; 20 Hispanic/Latino; 1 Native Hawaiian or other Pacific Islander, non-Hispanic/Latino; 3 Two or more races, non-Hispanic/Latino), 5 international. 129 applicants, 51% accepted, 47 enrolled. *Faculty:* 38 part-time/adjunct (13 women). Expenses: Contact institution. *Financial support:* In 2016–17, 49 students received support, including 21 research assistantships (averaging $5,800 per year), 12 teaching assistantships (averaging $5,800 per year); career-related internships or fieldwork, Federal Work-Study, and scholarships/grants also available. Support available to part-time students. Financial award application deadline: 4/1; financial award applicants required to submit FAFSA. In 2016, 83 master's awarded. *Program availability:* Part-time, online learning. Offers arts and sciences (MA, MLA, MS, Specialist); clinical psychology (MS); communication (MA); composition/rhetoric (MA); counseling psychology (MS); creative writing (MA); liberal arts (MLA); literature (MA); organizational development (MS); psychology (MS, Specialist); school psychology (Specialist). *Application deadline:* For fall admission, 4/1 priority date for domestic students; for spring admission, 11/1 for domestic students. Applications are processed on a rolling basis. *Application fee:* $50. Electronic applications accepted. *Application Contact:* Corey Patterson, Director of Graduate Admission and Recruiting, 325-674-6566, Fax: 325-

674-6717, E-mail: gradinfo@acu.edu. *Dean,* Dr. Greg Straughn, 325-674-2209, Fax: 325-674-6800, E-mail: cas@acu.edu.

College of Biblical Studies Students: 120 full-time (39 women), 84 part-time (16 women); includes 54 minority (40 Black or African American, non-Hispanic/Latino; 1 Asian, non-Hispanic/Latino; 11 Hispanic/Latino; 2 Two or more races, non-Hispanic/Latino), 11 international. 163 applicants, 64% accepted, 73 enrolled. *Faculty:* 13 full-time (2 women), 10 part-time/adjunct (2 women). Expenses: Contact institution. *Financial support:* In 2016–17, 40 students received support. Research assistantships, teaching assistantships, career-related internships or fieldwork, Federal Work-Study, and scholarships/grants available. Support available to part-time students. Financial award application deadline: 4/1; financial award applicants required to submit FAFSA. In 2016, 40 master's, 2 doctorates awarded. *Program availability:* Part-time, evening/weekend, blended/hybrid learning. Offers ancient and Oriental Christianity (MA); Biblical studies (M Div, MA, MACM, MMFT, D Min); Christian ministry (MACM); divinity (M Div); global service (MA); marriage and family therapy (MMFT); ministry (M Div, D Min); missions (M Div); modern and American Christianity (MA); New Testament (MA); Old Testament (MA); theology (M Div, MA, MACM, D Min). *Application deadline:* For fall admission, 4/1 priority date for domestic students; for spring admission, 11/1 for domestic students. Applications are processed on a rolling basis. *Application fee:* $50. Electronic applications accepted. *Application Contact:* Corey Patterson, Director of Graduate Admission and Recruiting, 325-674-6566, Fax: 325-674-6717, E-mail: gradinfo@acu.edu. *Dean,* Dr. Ken Cukrowski, 325-674-3700, Fax: 325-674-6180, E-mail: cukrowski@bible.acu.edu.

College of Business Administration Students: 13 full-time (4 women), 1 (woman) part-time; includes 1 minority (Hispanic/Latino), 2 international. 45 applicants, 40% accepted, 10 enrolled. *Faculty:* 7 part-time/adjunct (0 women). Expenses: Contact institution. *Financial support:* In 2016–17, 11 students received support. Federal Work-Study and scholarships/grants available. Support available to part-time students. Financial award application deadline: 4/1; financial award applicants required to submit FAFSA. In 2016, 28 master's awarded. *Program availability:* Part-time, online learning. Offers accountancy (M Acc); business administration (M Acc, MBA). *Application deadline:* For fall admission, 8/11 for domestic students; for spring admission, 11/1 for domestic students. Applications are processed on a rolling basis. *Application fee:* $50. Electronic applications accepted. *Application Contact:* Corey Patterson, Director of Graduate Admission and Recruiting, 325-674-6566, Fax: 325-674-6717, E-mail: gradinfo@acu.edu. *Dean,* Dr. Brad Crisp, 325-674-2243, Fax: 325-674-2564, E-mail: coba@acu.edu.

College of Education and Human Services Students: 137 full-time (124 women), 19 part-time (14 women); includes 39 minority (8 Black or African American, non-Hispanic/Latino; 1 American Indian or Alaska Native, non-Hispanic/Latino; 26 Hispanic/Latino; 4 Two or more races, non-Hispanic/Latino), 2 international. 439 applicants, 38% accepted, 93 enrolled. *Faculty:* 3 full-time (all women), 26 part-time/adjunct (16 women). Expenses: Contact institution. *Financial support:* In 2016–17, 61 students received support. Career-related internships or fieldwork and scholarships/grants available. Financial award application deadline: 4/1; financial award applicants required to submit FAFSA. In 2016, 83 master's, 10 other advanced degrees awarded. Offers communication sciences and disorders (MS); dietetic internship (Certificate); education and human services (M Ed, MS, Certificate); occupational therapy (MS); social work (MS); teaching and learning (M Ed). *Application deadline:* For fall admission, 8/15 priority date for domestic students; for winter admission, 10/1 priority date for domestic students; for spring admission, 12/15 priority date for domestic students; for summer admission, 4/15 for domestic students. Applications are processed on a rolling basis. *Application fee:* $50. Electronic applications accepted. *Application Contact:* Corey Patterson, Director of Graduate Admission and Recruiting, 325-674-6566, Fax: 325-674-6717, E-mail: gradinfo@acu.edu. *Dean,* Dr. Donnie Snider, 325-674-2700, Fax: 325-674-3707, E-mail: cehs@acu.edu.

ACACIA UNIVERSITY, Tempe, AZ 85284

General Information Private, coed, graduate-only institution.

GRADUATE UNITS

American Graduate School of Education Offers educational administration (M Ed); elementary education (MA); English as a second language (M Ed); secondary education (MA); special education (M Ed).

ACADEMY FOR FIVE ELEMENT ACUPUNCTURE, Gainesville, FL 32601

General Information Independent, coed, graduate-only institution.

GRADUATE UNITS

Graduate Program Offers acupuncture (M Ac).

ACADEMY OF ART UNIVERSITY, San Francisco, CA 94105-3410

General Information Proprietary, coed, comprehensive institution. *Enrollment:* 12,608 graduate, professional, and undergraduate students; 2,653 full-time matriculated graduate/professional students (1,637 women), 1,646 part-time matriculated graduate/professional students (1,071 women). *Enrollment by degree level:* 4,299 master's. *Graduate faculty:* 208 full-time (79 women), 744 part-time/adjunct (307 women). *Tuition:* Part-time $982 per unit. *Graduate housing:* Room and/or apartments guaranteed to single students; on-campus housing not available to married students. *Student services:* Campus employment opportunities, campus safety program, career counseling, international student services, low-cost health insurance, services for students with disabilities, teacher training, writing training. *Library facilities:* Academy of Art University Library. *Collection:* Books: 36,000 (physical), 9,000 (digital/electronic); Serial titles: 197 (physical), 400,000 (digital/electronic); Databases: 20. Weekly public service hours: 83; students can reserve study rooms.

Computer facilities: 900 computers available on campus for general student use. A campuswide network can be accessed. Online class registration, support for students taking online courses are available.
Website: http://www.academyart.edu/

General Application Contact: 800-544-ARTS, E-mail: info@academyart.edu.

GRADUATE UNITS

Graduate Programs Students: 2,653 full-time (1,637 women), 1,646 part-time (1,071 women); includes 740 minority (242 Black or African American, non-Hispanic/Latino; 18 American Indian or Alaska Native, non-Hispanic/Latino; 200 Asian, non-Hispanic/Latino; 216 Hispanic/Latino; 12 Native Hawaiian or other Pacific Islander, non-Hispanic/Latino; 52 Two or more races, non-Hispanic/Latino), 2,341 international. Average age 31. 1,330 applicants, 100% accepted, 835 enrolled. *Faculty:* 208 full-time (79 women), 744 part-time/adjunct (307 women). Expenses: Contact institution. *Financial support:* Career-related internships or fieldwork, Federal Work-Study, and scholarships/grants available.

Financial award application deadline: 8/10; financial award applicants required to submit FAFSA. In 2016, 1,047 master's awarded. *Program availability:* Part-time, 100% online. Offers costume design (MFA); fashion journalism (MA). *Application deadline:* Applications are processed on a rolling basis. *Application fee:* $50. Electronic applications accepted. *Application Contact:* 800-544-ARTS, E-mail: info@academyart.edu.

School of Acting Students: 19 full-time (14 women), 1 part-time (0 women); includes 5 minority (1 Black or African American, non-Hispanic/Latino; 1 Asian, non-Hispanic/Latino; 1 Hispanic/Latino; 2 Two or more races, non-Hispanic/Latino), 10 international. Average age 28. 12 applicants, 100% accepted, 4 enrolled. *Faculty:* 1 (woman) full-time, 17 part-time/adjunct (11 women). Expenses: Contact institution. *Financial support:* Career-related internships or fieldwork, Federal Work-Study, and scholarships/grants available. Financial award application deadline: 8/10; financial award applicants required to submit FAFSA. In 2016, 6 master's awarded. *Program availability:* Part-time. Offers acting (MA, MFA). *Application deadline:* Applications are processed on a rolling basis. *Application fee:* $50. Electronic applications accepted. *Application Contact:* 800-544-ARTS, E-mail: info@academyart.edu.

School of Advertising Students: 85 full-time (56 women), 24 part-time (16 women); includes 16 minority (2 Black or African American, non-Hispanic/Latino; 1 American Indian or Alaska Native, non-Hispanic/Latino; 7 Asian, non-Hispanic/Latino; 6 Hispanic/Latino), 72 international. Average age 28. 32 applicants, 100% accepted, 16 enrolled. *Faculty:* 6 full-time (2 women), 20 part-time/adjunct (6 women). Expenses: Contact institution. *Financial support:* Career-related internships or fieldwork, Federal Work-Study, and scholarships/grants available. Financial award application deadline: 8/10; financial award applicants required to submit FAFSA. In 2016, 47 master's awarded. *Program availability:* Part-time, 100% online. Offers advertising (MFA); advertising and branded media technology (MA). *Application deadline:* Applications are processed on a rolling basis. *Application fee:* $50. Electronic applications accepted. *Application Contact:* 800-544-ARTS, E-mail: info@academyart.edu.

School of Animation and Visual Effects Students: 297 full-time (138 women), 156 part-time (65 women); includes 73 minority (22 Black or African American, non-Hispanic/Latino; 2 American Indian or Alaska Native, non-Hispanic/Latino; 19 Asian, non-Hispanic/Latino; 24 Hispanic/Latino; 1 Native Hawaiian or other Pacific Islander, non-Hispanic/Latino; 5 Two or more races, non-Hispanic/Latino), 276 international. Average age 29. 109 applicants, 100% accepted, 74 enrolled. *Faculty:* 20 full-time (6 women), 64 part-time/adjunct (9 women). Expenses: Contact institution. *Financial support:* Career-related internships or fieldwork, Federal Work-Study, and scholarships/grants available. Financial award application deadline: 8/10; financial award applicants required to submit FAFSA. In 2016, 120 master's awarded. *Program availability:* Part-time, 100% online. Offers 3D animation (MFA). *Application deadline:* Applications are processed on a rolling basis. *Application fee:* $50. Electronic applications accepted. *Application Contact:* 800-544-ARTS, E-mail: info@academyart.edu.

School of Architecture Students: 115 full-time (45 women), 81 part-time (32 women); includes 40 minority (9 Black or African American, non-Hispanic/Latino; 9 Asian, non-Hispanic/Latino; 22 Hispanic/Latino), 65 international. Average age 34. 109 applicants, 100% accepted, 44 enrolled. *Faculty:* 8 full-time (3 women), 32 part-time/adjunct (6 women). Expenses: Contact institution. *Financial support:* Career-related internships or fieldwork, Federal Work-Study, and scholarships/grants available. Financial award application deadline: 8/10; financial award applicants required to submit FAFSA. In 2016, 41 master's awarded. *Program availability:* Part-time, 100% online. Offers advanced architectural design (MA); architecture (M Arch). *Application deadline:* Applications are processed on a rolling basis. *Application fee:* $50. Electronic applications accepted. *Application Contact:* 800-544-ARTS, E-mail: info@academyart.edu.

School of Art Education Students: 33 full-time (30 women), 20 part-time (17 women); includes 8 minority (2 Black or African American, non-Hispanic/Latino; 1 American Indian or Alaska Native, non-Hispanic/Latino; 2 Asian, non-Hispanic/Latino; 2 Hispanic/Latino; 1 Two or more races, non-Hispanic/Latino), 26 international. Average age 33. 30 applicants, 100% accepted, 15 enrolled. *Faculty:* 2 full-time (both women), 10 part-time/adjunct (9 women). Expenses: Contact institution. *Financial support:* Career-related internships or fieldwork, Federal Work-Study, and scholarships/grants available. Financial award application deadline: 8/10; financial award applicants required to submit FAFSA. In 2016, 8 master's awarded. *Program availability:* Part-time, 100% online. Offers art education (MA, MAT). *Application deadline:* Applications are processed on a rolling basis. *Application fee:* $50. Electronic applications accepted. *Application Contact:* 800-544-ARTS, E-mail: info@academyart.edu.

School of Art History Students: 14 full-time (all women), 44 part-time (40 women); includes 9 minority (1 Black or African American, non-Hispanic/Latino; 1 Asian, non-Hispanic/Latino; 7 Hispanic/Latino), 4 international. Average age 34. 24 applicants, 100% accepted, 10 enrolled. *Faculty:* 1 (woman) full-time, 2 part-time/adjunct (1 woman). Expenses: Contact institution. *Financial support:* Career-related internships or fieldwork, Federal Work-Study, and scholarships/grants available. Financial award application deadline: 8/10; financial award applicants required to submit FAFSA. In 2016, 10 master's awarded. *Program availability:* Part-time, 100% online. Offers art history (MA). *Application deadline:* Applications are processed on a rolling basis. *Application fee:* $50. Electronic applications accepted. *Application Contact:* 800-544-ARTS, E-mail: info@academyart.edu.

School of Communications and Media Technologies Students: 60 full-time (40 women), 23 part-time (14 women); includes 7 minority (3 Black or African American, non-Hispanic/Latino; 4 Hispanic/Latino), 60 international. Average age 28. 31 applicants, 100% accepted, 19 enrolled. *Faculty:* 3 full-time (0 women), 11 part-time/adjunct (3 women). Expenses: Contact institution. *Financial support:* Career-related internships or fieldwork, Federal Work-Study, and scholarships/grants available. Financial award application deadline: 8/10; financial award applicants required to submit FAFSA. In 2016, 59 master's awarded. *Program availability:* Part-time, 100% online. Offers communications and media technologies (MA). *Application deadline:* Applications are processed on a rolling basis. *Application fee:* $50. Electronic applications accepted. *Application Contact:* 800-544-ARTS, E-mail: info@academyart.edu.

School of Fashion Students: 376 full-time (335 women), 196 part-time (184 women); includes 154 minority (81 Black or African American, non-Hispanic/Latino; 2 American Indian or Alaska Native, non-Hispanic/Latino; 36 Asian, non-Hispanic/Latino; 25 Hispanic/Latino; 1 Native Hawaiian or other Pacific Islander, non-Hispanic/Latino; 9 Two or more races, non-Hispanic/Latino), 306 international. Average age 29. 190 applicants, 100% accepted, 114 enrolled. *Faculty:* 27 full-time (17 women), 62 part-time/adjunct (47 women). Expenses: Contact institution. *Financial support:* Career-related internships or fieldwork, Federal Work-Study, and scholarships/grants available. Financial award application deadline: 8/10; financial award applicants required to submit FAFSA. In 2016, 137 master's awarded. *Program availability:* Part-

time, 100% online. Offers costume design (MA, MFA); fashion (MA, MFA); fashion journalism (MA); fashion marketing and brand management (MFA); fashion merchandising (MA); fashion merchandising and management (MFA); fashion product development (MFA); textile design (MFA). *Application deadline:* Applications are processed on a rolling basis. *Application fee:* $50. Electronic applications accepted. *Application Contact:* 800-544-ARTS, E-mail: info@academyart.edu.

School of Fine Art Students: 72 full-time (49 women), 162 part-time (123 women); includes 43 minority (9 Black or African American, non-Hispanic/Latino; 2 American Indian or Alaska Native, non-Hispanic/Latino; 11 Asian, non-Hispanic/Latino; 15 Hispanic/Latino; 2 Native Hawaiian or other Pacific Islander, non-Hispanic/Latino; 4 Two or more races, non-Hispanic/Latino), 53 international. Average age 42. 64 applicants, 100% accepted, 34 enrolled. *Faculty:* 18 full-time (8 women), 38 part-time/adjunct (17 women). Expenses: Contact institution. *Financial support:* Career-related internships or fieldwork, Federal Work-Study, and scholarships/grants available. Financial award application deadline: 8/10; financial award applicants required to submit FAFSA. In 2016, 60 master's awarded. *Program availability:* Part-time, 100% online. Offers figurative painting (MFA). *Application deadline:* Applications are processed on a rolling basis. *Application fee:* $50. Electronic applications accepted. *Application Contact:* 800-544-ARTS, E-mail: info@academyart.edu.

School of Game Development Students: 91 full-time (26 women), 35 part-time (8 women); includes 25 minority (5 Black or African American, non-Hispanic/Latino; 5 Asian, non-Hispanic/Latino; 11 Hispanic/Latino; 4 Two or more races, non-Hispanic/Latino), 63 international. Average age 29. 39 applicants, 100% accepted, 33 enrolled. *Faculty:* 11 full-time (0 women), 22 part-time/adjunct (1 woman). Expenses: Contact institution. *Financial support:* Career-related internships or fieldwork, Federal Work-Study, and scholarships/grants available. Financial award application deadline: 8/10; financial award applicants required to submit FAFSA. In 2016, 28 master's awarded. *Program availability:* Part-time, 100% online. Offers game development (MA, MFA). *Application deadline:* Applications are processed on a rolling basis. *Application fee:* $50. Electronic applications accepted. *Application Contact:* 800-544-ARTS, E-mail: info@academyart.edu.

School of Graphic Design Students: 220 full-time (162 women), 145 part-time (103 women); includes 49 minority (14 Black or African American, non-Hispanic/Latino; 1 American Indian or Alaska Native, non-Hispanic/Latino; 16 Asian, non-Hispanic/Latino; 14 Hispanic/Latino; 2 Native Hawaiian or other Pacific Islander, non-Hispanic/Latino; 2 Two or more races, non-Hispanic/Latino), 242 international. Average age 29. 130 applicants, 100% accepted, 80 enrolled. *Faculty:* 7 full-time (1 woman), 33 part-time/adjunct (15 women). Expenses: Contact institution. *Financial support:* Career-related internships or fieldwork, Federal Work-Study, and scholarships/grants available. Financial award application deadline: 8/10; financial award applicants required to submit FAFSA. In 2016, 38 master's awarded. *Program availability:* Part-time, 100% online. Offers graphic design (MFA); graphic design and digital media (MA). *Application deadline:* Applications are processed on a rolling basis. *Application fee:* $50. Electronic applications accepted. *Application Contact:* 800-544-ARTS, E-mail: info@academyart.edu.

School of Illustration Students: 142 full-time (94 women), 98 part-time (67 women); includes 32 minority (9 Black or African American, non-Hispanic/Latino; 5 Asian, non-Hispanic/Latino; 14 Hispanic/Latino; 4 Two or more races, non-Hispanic/Latino), 120 international. Average age 30. 71 applicants, 100% accepted, 46 enrolled. *Faculty:* 9 full-time (2 women), 39 part-time/adjunct (17 women). Expenses: Contact institution. *Financial support:* Career-related internships or fieldwork, Federal Work-Study, and scholarships/grants available. Financial award application deadline: 8/10; financial award applicants required to submit FAFSA. In 2016, 78 master's awarded. *Program availability:* Part-time, 100% online. Offers illustration (MA, MFA). *Application deadline:* Applications are processed on a rolling basis. *Application fee:* $50. Electronic applications accepted. *Application Contact:* 800-544-ARTS, E-mail: info@academyart.edu.

School of Industrial Design Students: 90 full-time (26 women), 56 part-time (23 women); includes 17 minority (3 Black or African American, non-Hispanic/Latino; 7 Asian, non-Hispanic/Latino; 6 Hispanic/Latino; 1 Native Hawaiian or other Pacific Islander, non-Hispanic/Latino), 105 international. Average age 29. 64 applicants, 100% accepted, 27 enrolled. *Faculty:* 4 full-time (0 women), 29 part-time/adjunct (3 women). Expenses: Contact institution. *Financial support:* Career-related internships or fieldwork, Federal Work-Study, and scholarships/grants available. Financial award application deadline: 8/10; financial award applicants required to submit FAFSA. In 2016, 25 master's awarded. *Program availability:* Part-time, 100% online. Offers industrial design (MA, MFA). *Application deadline:* Applications are processed on a rolling basis. *Application fee:* $50. Electronic applications accepted. *Application Contact:* 800-544-ARTS, E-mail: info@academyart.edu.

School of Interior Architecture and Design Students: 137 full-time (100 women), 100 part-time (91 women); includes 39 minority (16 Black or African American, non-Hispanic/Latino; 13 Asian, non-Hispanic/Latino; 7 Hispanic/Latino; 3 Two or more races, non-Hispanic/Latino), 120 international. Average age 32. 96 applicants, 100% accepted, 56 enrolled. *Faculty:* 4 full-time (1 woman), 23 part-time/adjunct (10 women). Expenses: Contact institution. *Financial support:* Career-related internships or fieldwork, Federal Work-Study, and scholarships/grants available. Financial award application deadline: 8/10; financial award applicants required to submit FAFSA. In 2016, 60 master's awarded. *Program availability:* Part-time, 100% online. Offers interior architecture and design (MA, MFA). *Application deadline:* Applications are processed on a rolling basis. *Application fee:* $50. Electronic applications accepted. *Application Contact:* 800-544-ARTS, E-mail: info@academyart.edu.

School of Jewelry and Metal Arts Students: 36 full-time (30 women), 8 part-time (all women); includes 5 minority (1 Black or African American, non-Hispanic/Latino; 3 Asian, non-Hispanic/Latino; 1 Hispanic/Latino), 31 international. Average age 30. 14 applicants, 100% accepted, 12 enrolled. *Faculty:* 2 full-time (both women), 9 part-time/adjunct (5 women). Expenses: Contact institution. *Financial support:* Career-related internships or fieldwork, Federal Work-Study, and scholarships/grants available. Financial award application deadline: 8/10; financial award applicants required to submit FAFSA. In 2016, 8 master's awarded. *Program availability:* Part-time, 100% online. Offers jewelry and metal arts (MA, MFA). *Application deadline:* Applications are processed on a rolling basis. *Application fee:* $50. Electronic applications accepted. *Application Contact:* 800-544-ARTS, E-mail: info@academyart.edu.

School of Landscape Architecture Students: 31 full-time (18 women), 8 part-time (6 women); includes 1 minority (Asian, non-Hispanic/Latino), 34 international. Average age 27. 15 applicants, 100% accepted, 10 enrolled. *Faculty:* 1 (woman) full-time, 14 part-time/adjunct (7 women). Expenses: Contact institution. *Financial support:* Career-related internships or fieldwork, Federal Work-Study, and scholarships/grants available. Financial award application deadline: 8/10; financial award applicants required to submit FAFSA. In 2016, 10 master's awarded. *Program availability:* Part-time, 100% online. Offers landscape architecture (MA, MFA). *Application deadline:* Applications are processed on a rolling basis. *Application fee:* $50. Electronic applications accepted. *Application Contact:* 800-544-ARTS, E-mail: info@academyart.edu.

School of Motion Pictures and Television Students: 185 full-time (87 women), 79 part-time (35 women); includes 41 minority (18 Black or African American, non-Hispanic/Latino; 3 American Indian or Alaska Native, non-Hispanic/Latino; 4 Asian, non-Hispanic/Latino; 11 Hispanic/Latino; 5 Two or more races, non-Hispanic/Latino), 166 international. Average age 30. 58 applicants, 100% accepted, 40 enrolled. *Faculty:* 9 full-time (1 woman), 48 part-time/adjunct (14 women). Expenses: Contact institution. *Financial support:* Career-related internships or fieldwork, Federal Work-Study, and scholarships/grants available. Financial award application deadline: 8/10; financial award applicants required to submit FAFSA. In 2016, 83 master's awarded. *Program availability:* Part-time, 100% online. Offers motion pictures and television (MFA). *Application deadline:* Applications are processed on a rolling basis. *Application fee:* $50. Electronic applications accepted. *Application Contact:* 800-544-ARTS, E-mail: info@academyart.edu.

School of Music Production and Sound Design for Visual Media Students: 97 full-time (46 women), 32 part-time (10 women); includes 21 minority (10 Black or African American, non-Hispanic/Latino; 1 American Indian or Alaska Native, non-Hispanic/Latino; 2 Asian, non-Hispanic/Latino; 6 Hispanic/Latino; 1 Native Hawaiian or other Pacific Islander, non-Hispanic/Latino; 1 Two or more races, non-Hispanic/Latino), 86 international. Average age 29. 31 applicants, 100% accepted, 27 enrolled. *Faculty:* 4 full-time (0 women), 22 part-time/adjunct (3 women). Expenses: Contact institution. *Financial support:* Career-related internships or fieldwork, Federal Work-Study, and scholarships/grants available. Financial award application deadline: 8/10; financial award applicants required to submit FAFSA. In 2016, 38 master's awarded. *Program availability:* Part-time, 100% online. Offers music scoring and composition (MA, MFA); sound design (MA, MFA). *Application deadline:* Applications are processed on a rolling basis. *Application fee:* $50. Electronic applications accepted. *Application Contact:* 800-544-ARTS, E-mail: info@academyart.edu.

School of Photography Students: 117 full-time (59 women), 145 part-time (90 women); includes 48 minority (13 Black or African American, non-Hispanic/Latino; 3 American Indian or Alaska Native, non-Hispanic/Latino; 10 Asian, non-Hispanic/Latino; 16 Hispanic/Latino; 3 Native Hawaiian or other Pacific Islander, non-Hispanic/Latino; 3 Two or more races, non-Hispanic/Latino), 87 international. Average age 36. 75 applicants, 100% accepted, 57 enrolled. *Faculty:* 10 full-time (5 women), 35 part-time/adjunct (14 women). Expenses: Contact institution. *Financial support:* Career-related internships or fieldwork, Federal Work-Study, and scholarships/grants available. Financial award application deadline: 8/10; financial award applicants required to submit FAFSA. In 2016, 54 master's awarded. *Program availability:* Part-time, 100% online. Offers photography (MA, MFA). *Application deadline:* Applications are processed on a rolling basis. *Application fee:* $50. Electronic applications accepted. *Application Contact:* 800-544-ARTS, E-mail: info@academyart.edu.

School of Visual Development Students: 152 full-time (85 women), 80 part-time (44 women); includes 44 minority (8 Black or African American, non-Hispanic/Latino; 1 American Indian or Alaska Native, non-Hispanic/Latino; 16 Asian, non-Hispanic/Latino; 15 Hispanic/Latino; 4 Two or more races, non-Hispanic/Latino), 124 international. Average age 28. 45 applicants, 100% accepted, 36 enrolled. *Faculty:* 5 full-time (0 women), 17 part-time/adjunct (2 women). Expenses: Contact institution.

Financial support: Career-related internships or fieldwork, Federal Work-Study, and scholarships/grants available. Financial award application deadline: 8/10; financial award applicants required to submit FAFSA. In 2016, 33 master's awarded. *Program availability:* Part-time, 100% online. Offers visual development (MA, MFA). *Application deadline:* Applications are processed on a rolling basis. *Application fee:* $50. Electronic applications accepted. *Application Contact:* 800-544-ARTS, E-mail: info@academyart.edu.

School of Web Design and New Media Students: 273 full-time (176 women), 136 part-time (87 women); includes 53 minority (10 Black or African American, non-Hispanic/Latino; 32 Asian, non-Hispanic/Latino; 7 Hispanic/Latino; 1 Native Hawaiian or other Pacific Islander, non-Hispanic/Latino; 3 Two or more races, non-Hispanic/Latino), 287 international. Average age 29. 98 applicants, 100% accepted, 78 enrolled. *Faculty:* 9 full-time (3 women), 49 part-time/adjunct (16 women). Expenses: Contact institution. *Financial support:* Career-related internships or fieldwork, Federal Work-Study, and scholarships/grants available. Financial award application deadline: 8/10; financial award applicants required to submit FAFSA. In 2016, 104 master's awarded. *Program availability:* Part-time, 100% online. Offers Web design and new media (MA, MFA). *Application deadline:* Applications are processed on a rolling basis. *Application fee:* $50. Electronic applications accepted. *Application Contact:* 800-544-ARTS, E-mail: info@academyart.edu.

School of Writing for Film, Television and Digital Media Students: 11 full-time (7 women), 17 part-time (8 women); includes 10 minority (5 Black or African American, non-Hispanic/Latino; 1 American Indian or Alaska Native, non-Hispanic/Latino; 2 Hispanic/Latino; 2 Two or more races, non-Hispanic/Latino), 4 international. Average age 35. 4 applicants, 100% accepted, 3 enrolled. *Faculty:* 2 full-time (1 woman), 9 part-time/adjunct (2 women). Expenses: Contact institution. *Financial support:* Career-related internships or fieldwork, Federal Work-Study, and scholarships/grants available. Financial award application deadline: 8/10; financial award applicants required to submit FAFSA. *Program availability:* Part-time, 100% online. Offers writing for film, television and digital media (MFA). *Application deadline:* Applications are processed on a rolling basis. *Application fee:* $50. Electronic applications accepted. *Application Contact:* 800-544-ARTS, E-mail: info@academyart.edu.

See Display below and Close-Up on page 871.

ACADEMY OF CHINESE CULTURE AND HEALTH SCIENCES, Oakland, CA 94612

General Information Private, coed, graduate-only institution. *Graduate housing:* On-campus housing not available.

GRADUATE UNITS

Program in Traditional Chinese Medicine *Program availability:* Part-time, evening/weekend. Offers traditional Chinese medicine (MS).

ACADIA UNIVERSITY, Wolfville, NS B4P 2R6, Canada

General Information Province-supported, coed, comprehensive institution. *Graduate housing:* Room and/or apartments available on a first-come, first-served basis to single students; on-campus housing not available to married students. Housing application deadline: 5/31. *Research affiliation:* Atlantic Research Laboratory.

GRADUATE UNITS

Divinity College *Program availability:* Part-time. Offers divinity (M Div); theology (MA, D Min).

ACADEMY *of* ART UNIVERSITY®

FOUNDED IN SAN FRANCISCO 1929 BY ARTISTS FOR ARTISTS

If you're looking to refine and enhance your skillset, join our world-class community of artists.

Online or in San Francisco California

Degrees
AA | BA | BS | BFA
MA | MFA | Certificate

Growth
Career or Personal Development

Your Schedule
Flexible Full or Part-time Classes

Academy of Art University | 888.680.8691 | **academyart.edu** | Yellow Ribbon Participant

Visit academyart.edu to learn more about total costs, median student loan debt, potential occupations and other information.
Accredited member WSCUC, NASAD, CIDA (BFA-IAD, MFA-IAD), NAAB (B.ARCH, M.ARCH), CTC (California Teacher Credential).

Faculty of Arts Offers arts (MA); English (MA); political science (MA); social and political thought (MA); sociology (MA).

Faculty of Professional Studies Offers educational studies (PhD).

School of Education Offers counseling (M Ed); cultural and media studies (M Ed); curriculum studies (M Ed); inclusive education (M Ed); leadership (M Ed); learning and technology (M Ed); science, math and technology (M Ed).

School of Recreation Management and Community Development Offers recreation management and community development (MR).

Faculty of Pure and Applied Science Offers applied geomatics (M Sc); applied mathematics and statistics (M Sc); biology (M Sc); chemistry (M Sc); clinical psychology (M Sc); earth and environmental science (M Sc); pure and applied science (M Sc).

Jodrey School of Computer Science Offers computer science (M Sc).

ACUPUNCTURE & INTEGRATIVE MEDICINE COLLEGE, BERKELEY, Berkeley, CA 94704

General Information Independent, coed, graduate-only institution. *Enrollment by degree level:* 86 master's. *Graduate faculty:* 24 part-time/adjunct (15 women). *Tuition:* Full-time $16,949. *Required fees:* $205. *Graduate housing:* On-campus housing not available. *Student services:* Campus employment opportunities, international student services, services for students with disabilities. *Library facilities:* AIMC Berkeley Library plus 1 other. *Collection:* Books: 1,959 (physical). Weekly public service hours: 40.

Computer facilities: 2 computers available on campus for general student use. Website: http://aimc.edu/

General Application Contact: Julie Scheff, Admissions Manager, 510-666-8248 Ext. 121, Fax: 510-666-0111, E-mail: admissions@aimc.edu.

GRADUATE UNITS

Master of Science in Oriental Medicine Program Students: 58 full-time (44 women), 28 part-time (23 women); includes 28 minority (3 Black or African American, non-Hispanic/Latino; 10 Asian, non-Hispanic/Latino; 6 Hispanic/Latino; 1 Native Hawaiian or other Pacific Islander, non-Hispanic/Latino; 8 Two or more races, non-Hispanic/Latino), 3 international. Average age 37. 40 applicants, 85% accepted, 29 enrolled. *Faculty:* 24 part-time/adjunct (15 women). *Expenses:* Contact institution. *Financial support:* Federal Work-Study available. Support available to part-time students. Financial award application deadline: 7/31; financial award applicants required to submit FAFSA. In 2016, 33 master's awarded. *Program availability:* Part-time. Offers Oriental medicine (MS). *Application deadline:* For fall admission, 3/15 priority date for domestic and international students; for winter admission, 7/15 priority date for domestic and international students; for spring admission, 11/15 priority date for domestic and international students. *Application fee:* $100. Electronic applications accepted. *Application Contact:* Julie Scheff, E-mail: admissions@aimc.edu. *President,* Yasou Tanaka, 510-666-8248, Fax: 510-666-0111, E-mail: ytanaka@aimc.edu.

ACUPUNCTURE AND MASSAGE COLLEGE, Miami, FL 33176

General Information Proprietary, coed, graduate-only institution.

GRADUATE UNITS

Program in Oriental Medicine Offers Oriental medicine (MOM).

ADAMS STATE UNIVERSITY, Alamosa, CO 81101

General Information State-supported, coed, comprehensive institution. *Graduate housing:* Rooms and/or apartments available to single and married students. Housing application deadline: 5/15. *Research affiliation:* Sandia National Laboratories (science education).

GRADUATE UNITS

The Graduate School *Program availability:* Part-time, online learning. Offers art (MA); counseling (MA); education (MA); history (MA); human performance and physical education (MA); special education (MA).

ADELPHI UNIVERSITY, Garden City, NY 11530-0701

General Information Independent, coed, university. *Enrollment:* 7,687 graduate, professional, and undergraduate students; 1,407 full-time matriculated graduate/professional students (1,121 women), 1,031 part-time matriculated graduate/professional students (780 women). *Enrollment by degree level:* 2,226 master's, 212 doctoral. *Graduate faculty:* 320 full-time (169 women), 704 part-time/adjunct (470 women). *Tuition:* Full-time $37,623; part-time $1179 per credit hour. *Required fees:* $1335; $405 per semester. Tuition and fees vary according to degree level, campus/location and program. *Graduate housing:* Room and/or apartments available on a first-come, first-served basis to single students; on-campus housing not available to married students. Typical cost: $1080 per year. Room charges vary according to board plan and housing facility selected. Housing application deadline: 5/1. *Student services:* Campus employment opportunities, campus safety program, career counseling, child daycare facilities, exercise/wellness program, free psychological counseling, international student services, low-cost health insurance, multicultural affairs office, services for students with disabilities, teacher training, writing training. *Library facilities:* Swirbul Library. *Collection:* Books: 578,732 (physical), 29,258 (digital/electronic); Serial titles: 660 (physical); Databases: 240. Students can reserve study rooms. *Research affiliation:* The Hagedorn Foundation, North Shore Long Island Jewish Health System (medicine), National Science Foundation, The Research Corporation, Mount Sinai Medical Center, Albert Einstein College of Medicine.

Computer facilities: Computer purchase and lease plans are available. 880 computers available on campus for general student use. A campuswide network can be accessed from student residence rooms and from off campus. Online class registration, payment, drop/add classes, check application status are available. Website: http://www.adelphi.edu/

General Application Contact: Kristen Capezza, Associate Vice President for Enrollment Management, 516-877-3050, Fax: 516-877-3039, E-mail: graduateadmissions@adelphi.edu.

GRADUATE UNITS

College of Arts and Sciences Students: 42 full-time (28 women), 26 part-time (17 women); includes 44 minority (9 Black or African American, non-Hispanic/Latino; 15 Asian, non-Hispanic/Latino; 16 Hispanic/Latino; 4 Two or more races, non-Hispanic/Latino), 12 international. Average age 26. 136 applicants, 58% accepted, 33 enrolled. *Faculty:* 117 full-time (51 women), 192 part-time/adjunct (93 women). *Expenses:* Contact institution. *Financial support:* In 2016–17, 1 fellowship (averaging $20,000 per year), 28 research assistantships with full and partial tuition reimbursements (averaging $15,989 per year) were awarded; teaching assistantships, career-related internships or fieldwork, Federal Work-Study, scholarships/grants, traineeships, tuition waivers (partial), unspecified assistantships, and tuition remission for employees also available. Support available to part-time students. Financial award

application deadline: 2/15; financial award applicants required to submit FAFSA. In 2016, 32 master's awarded. *Program availability:* Part-time. Offers arts and sciences (MA, MFA, MS); biology (MS); biotechnology (MS); creative writing (MFA); environmental studies (MS); studio art (MA). *Application deadline:* For fall admission, 5/1 priority date for international students; for spring admission, 11/1 priority date for international students. Applications are processed on a rolling basis. *Application fee:* $50. Electronic applications accepted. *Application Contact:* Christine Murphy, Director of Admissions, 516-877-3050, Fax: 516-877-3039, E-mail: graduateadmissions@adelphi.edu. *Dean,* Dr. Sam L. Grogg, 516-877-4124, Fax: 516-877-4191, E-mail: sgrogg@adelphi.edu.

College of Nursing and Public Health Students: 26 full-time (18 women), 357 part-time (306 women); includes 63 minority (27 Black or African American, non-Hispanic/Latino; 20 Asian, non-Hispanic/Latino; 13 Hispanic/Latino; 3 Two or more races, non-Hispanic/Latino), 2 international. Average age 37. 315 applicants, 67% accepted, 121 enrolled. *Faculty:* 41 full-time (34 women), 211 part-time/adjunct (189 women). *Expenses:* Contact institution. *Financial support:* In 2016–17, 26 teaching assistantships with full and partial tuition reimbursements (averaging $4,832 per year) were awarded; fellowships, research assistantships, career-related internships or fieldwork, Federal Work-Study, scholarships/grants, traineeships, tuition waivers (partial), unspecified assistantships, and tuition remission for employees also available. Support available to part-time students. Financial award application deadline: 2/15; financial award applicants required to submit FAFSA. In 2016, 69 master's, 2 doctorates awarded. *Program availability:* Part-time, evening/weekend. Offers adult health nurse (MS); health information technology (Advanced Certificate); nurse practitioner in adult health nursing (Certificate); nursing (PhD); nursing administration (MS, Certificate); nursing education (MS, Certificate); nutrition (MS); public health (MPH). *Application deadline:* For fall admission, 3/15 for domestic students, 4/1 for international students; for spring admission, 11/1 for international students. *Application fee:* $50. Electronic applications accepted. *Application Contact:* Christine Murphy, Director of Admissions, 516-877-3050, Fax: 516-877-3039, E-mail: graduateadmissions@adelphi.edu. *Dean,* Dr. Patrick Coonan, 516-877-4511, E-mail: coonan@adelphi.edu.

Gordon F. Derner School of Psychology Students: 201 full-time (162 women), 54 part-time (42 women); includes 32 minority (10 Black or African American, non-Hispanic/Latino; 6 Asian, non-Hispanic/Latino; 13 Hispanic/Latino; 3 Two or more races, non-Hispanic/Latino), 7 international. Average age 27. 495 applicants, 49% accepted, 93 enrolled. *Faculty:* 24 full-time (11 women), 56 part-time/adjunct (32 women). *Expenses:* Contact institution. *Financial support:* In 2016–17, 2 fellowships (averaging $10,000 per year), 126 research assistantships with full and partial tuition reimbursements (averaging $10,078 per year) were awarded; teaching assistantships, career-related internships or fieldwork, Federal Work-Study, scholarships/grants, traineeships, unspecified assistantships, and tuition remission for employees also available. Support available to part-time students. Financial award application deadline: 2/15; financial award applicants required to submit FAFSA. In 2016, 101 master's, 14 doctorates awarded. *Program availability:* Part-time. Offers clinical psychology (PhD); general psychology (MA); mental health counseling (MA); psychology (MA, PhD); school psychology (MA). *Application deadline:* For fall admission, 4/1 priority date for domestic students, 5/1 priority date for international students; for spring admission, 11/1 priority date for international students. *Application fee:* $50. Electronic applications accepted. *Application Contact:* Christine Murphy, Director of Admissions, 516-877-3050, Fax: 516-877-3039, E-mail: graduateadmissions@adelphi.edu. *Dean,* Dr. Jacques P. Barber, 516-877-4803, E-mail: jcmuran@adelphi.edu.

Robert B. Willmstad School of Business Students: 174 full-time (74 women), 134 part-time (70 women); includes 30 minority (9 Black or African American, non-Hispanic/Latino; 11 Asian, non-Hispanic/Latino; 9 Hispanic/Latino; 1 Two or more races, non-Hispanic/Latino), 29 international. Average age 32. 322 applicants, 46% accepted, 81 enrolled. *Faculty:* 42 full-time (12 women), 23 part-time/adjunct (5 women). *Expenses:* Contact institution. *Financial support:* In 2016–17, 35 teaching assistantships with full and partial tuition reimbursements (averaging $9,574 per year) were awarded; fellowships, research assistantships, career-related internships or fieldwork, Federal Work-Study, scholarships/grants, traineeships, tuition waivers (partial), unspecified assistantships, and tuition remission for employees also available. Support available to part-time students. Financial award application deadline: 3/1; financial award applicants required to submit FAFSA. In 2016, 130 master's awarded. *Program availability:* Part-time, evening/weekend. Offers accounting (MBA); business (MBA, MS, Certificate); finance (MBA); health services administration (MBA); human resource management (Certificate); management (MBA); management information systems (MBA); marketing (MBA); sport management (MBA); supply chain management (MS). *Application deadline:* For fall admission, 4/1 for international students; for spring admission, 11/1 for international students. Applications are processed on a rolling basis. *Application fee:* $50. Electronic applications accepted. *Application Contact:* Christine Murphy, Director of Admissions, 516-877-3050, Fax: 516-877-3039, E-mail: graduateadmissions@adelphi.edu. *Dean,* Anthony Libertella, 516-877-4661, E-mail: libertel@adelphi.edu.

Ruth S. Ammon School of Education Students: 448 full-time (378 women), 270 part-time (168 women); includes 29 minority (8 Black or African American, non-Hispanic/Latino; 4 Asian, non-Hispanic/Latino; 15 Hispanic/Latino; 2 Two or more races, non-Hispanic/Latino), 4 international. Average age 27. 1,329 applicants, 47% accepted, 252 enrolled. *Faculty:* 63 full-time (41 women), 101 part-time/adjunct (67 women). *Expenses:* Contact institution. *Financial support:* In 2016–17, 95 teaching assistantships with full and partial tuition reimbursements (averaging $11,059 per year) were awarded; fellowships, research assistantships, career-related internships or fieldwork, Federal Work-Study, scholarships/grants, traineeships, tuition waivers (full and partial), unspecified assistantships, and tuition remission for employees also available. Support available to part-time students. Financial award application deadline: 2/15; financial award applicants required to submit FAFSA. In 2016, 334 master's, 5 doctorates, 82 other advanced degrees awarded. *Program availability:* Part-time, evening/weekend. Offers adolescent education (MA); aging (Certificate); art education (MA); audiology (MS, DA); birth-grade 12 (MS); birth-grade 6 (MS); childhood education (MA); community health education (MA, Certificate); education (MA, MS, DA, Certificate); educational leadership (MA, Certificate); educational technology (MA); grades 5-12 (MS); physical/educational human performance science (MA); school health education (MA); special education (MS, Certificate); speech-language pathology (MS, DA); teaching English to speakers of other languages (MA, Certificate). *Application deadline:* For fall admission, 4/1 for international students; for spring admission, 11/1 for international students. Applications are processed on a rolling basis. *Application fee:* $50. Electronic applications accepted. *Application Contact:* Christine Murphy, Director of Admissions, 516-877-3050, Fax: 516-877-3039, E-mail: graduateadmissions@adelphi.edu. *Dean,* Dr. Jane Ashdown, 516-877-4065, E-mail: jashdown@adelphi.edu.

School of Social Work Students: 370 full-time (317 women), 229 part-time (191 women); includes 51 minority (28 Black or African American, non-Hispanic/Latino; 4 Asian, non-Hispanic/Latino; 17 Hispanic/Latino; 2 Two or more races, non-

Hispanic/Latino), 1 international. Average age 33. 575 applicants, 70% accepted, 225 enrolled. *Faculty:* 27 full-time (17 women), 97 part-time/adjunct (74 women). Expenses: Contact institution. *Financial support:* In 2016–17, 31 teaching assistantships with full and partial tuition reimbursements (averaging $5,801 per year) were awarded; fellowships, research assistantships, career-related internships or fieldwork, Federal Work-Study, scholarships/grants, traineeships, tuition waivers (full and partial), unspecified assistantships, and tuition remission for employees also available. Support available to part-time students. Financial award application deadline: 2/15; financial award applicants required to submit FAFSA. In 2016, 253 master's, 2 doctorates awarded. *Program availability:* Part-time, evening/weekend. Offers social welfare (DSW); social work (MSW, DSW, PhD). *Application deadline:* For fall admission, 4/1 for international students; for spring admission, 12/1 for domestic students, 11/1 for international students. *Application fee:* $50. Electronic applications accepted. *Application Contact:* Christine Murphy, Director of Admissions, 516-877-3050, Fax: 516-877-3039, E-mail: graduateadmissions@adelphi.edu. *Dean*, Dr. Andrew Safyer, 516-877-4300, E-mail: asafyer@adelphi.edu.

University College Students: 3 full-time (1 woman), 15 part-time (6 women); includes 11 minority (7 Black or African American, non-Hispanic/Latino; 3 Hispanic/Latino; 1 Two or more races, non-Hispanic/Latino). Average age 37. 11 applicants, 64% accepted, 4 enrolled. *Faculty:* 22 part-time/adjunct (9 women). Expenses: Contact institution. *Financial support:* In 2016–17, 2 teaching assistantships with full and partial tuition reimbursements (averaging $6,765 per year) were awarded; fellowships, research assistantships, career-related internships or fieldwork, Federal Work-Study, scholarships/grants, traineeships, tuition waivers, unspecified assistantships, and tuition remission for employees also available. Support available to part-time students. In 2016, 12 Certificates awarded. Offers emergency management (Certificate). *Application deadline:* For fall admission, 5/1 for international students; for spring admission, 12/1 for international students. *Application fee:* $50. *Application Contact:* Christine Murphy, Director of Admissions, 516-877-3050, Fax: 516-877-3039, E-mail: graduateadmissions@adelphi.edu. *Dean*, Shawn O'Riley, 516-877-3412, E-mail: ucinfo@adelphi.edu.

ADLER GRADUATE SCHOOL, Richfield, MN 55423

General Information Independent, coed, graduate-only institution. *Enrollment by degree level:* 298 master's, 10 other advanced degrees. *Graduate faculty:* 71 part-time/adjunct (55 women). *Graduate housing:* On-campus housing not available. *Student services:* International student services, services for students with disabilities, writing training. *Library facilities:* Adler Graduate School Library.

Computer facilities: 12 computers available on campus for general student use. A campuswide network can be accessed. Online class registration is available. Website: http://www.alfredadler.edu/

General Application Contact: Evelyn B. Haas, Director of Admissions, 612-767-7044, Fax: 612-861-7559, E-mail: ev@alfredadler.edu.

GRADUATE UNITS

Program in Adlerian Counseling and Psychotherapy Students: 298 part-time (225 women); includes 51 minority (40 Black or African American, non-Hispanic/Latino; 6 American Indian or Alaska Native, non-Hispanic/Latino; 5 Hispanic/Latino). *Faculty:* 71 part-time/adjunct (55 women). Expenses: Contact institution. *Financial support:* Career-related internships or fieldwork and tuition waivers available. Support available to part-time students. Financial award applicants required to submit FAFSA. *Program availability:* Part-time, evening/weekend. Offers Adlerian studies (MA); art therapy (MA); clinical mental health counseling (MA); co-occurring mental health and substance abuse disorders (MA); marriage and family therapy (MA); school counseling (MA). *Application deadline:* Applications are processed on a rolling basis. *Application fee:* $50. Electronic applications accepted. *Application Contact:* Evelyn B. Haas, Director of Admissions, 612-767-7044, Fax: 612-861-7559, E-mail: ev@alfredadler.edu. *President*, Dr. Dan Haugen, 612-767-7048, Fax: 612-861-7559, E-mail: haugen@alfredadler.edu.

ADLER UNIVERSITY, Chicago, IL 60602

General Information Independent, coed, graduate-only institution. *Graduate housing:* On-campus housing not available. *Research affiliation:* LGBTQ Mental Health and Inclusion Center, Adler Child Guidance Center, Adler Institute on Social Exclusion, Adler Institute on Public Safety and Social Justice.

GRADUATE UNITS

Programs in Psychology *Program availability:* Part-time, evening/weekend, online learning. Offers advanced Adlerian psychotherapy (Certificate); art therapy (MA); clinical mental health counseling (MA); clinical neuropsychology (Certificate); clinical psychology (Psy D); community psychology (MA); counseling and organizational psychology (MA); counseling psychology (MA); counselor education and supervision (PhD); couple and family therapy (DCFT); criminology (MA); emergency management (MA); forensic psychology (MA); marriage and family counseling (MA); marriage and family therapy (Certificate); military psychology (MA); nonprofit management (MA); organizational psychology (MA); police psychology (MA); public policy and administration (MA); rehabilitation counseling (MA); sport and health psychology (MA); substance abuse counseling (Certificate). Electronic applications accepted.

ADRIAN COLLEGE, Adrian, MI 49221-2575

General Information Independent-religious, coed, comprehensive institution. *Graduate housing:* On-campus housing not available.

GRADUATE UNITS

Graduate Programs Offers accounting (MS); athletic training (MS); criminal justice (MA).

ADVENTIST UNIVERSITY OF HEALTH SCIENCES, Orlando, FL 32803

General Information Independent, coed, comprehensive institution.

GRADUATE UNITS

Program in Healthcare Administration Offers healthcare administration (MHA).
Program in Nurse Anesthesia Offers nurse anesthesia (MS).
Program in Occupational Therapy Offers occupational therapy (MOT).
Program in Physical Therapy Offers physical therapy (DPT).
Program in Physician Assistant Studies Offers physician assistant studies (MS).

AIR FORCE INSTITUTE OF TECHNOLOGY, Dayton, OH 45433-7765

General Information Federally supported, coed, primarily men, graduate-only institution. *Graduate housing:* On-campus housing not available. *Research affiliation:*

U.S. Air Force Office of Scientific Research, U.S. Air Force Research Laboratory (AFRL), Dayton Area Graduate Studies Institute (aerospace), U.S. Department of Energy, National Security Agency.

GRADUATE UNITS

Graduate School of Engineering and Management *Program availability:* Part-time. Offers aeronautical engineering (MS, PhD); applied mathematics (MS, PhD); applied physics (MS, PhD); astronautical engineering (MS, PhD); computer engineering (MS, PhD); computer systems/science (MS); cost analysis (MS); electrical engineering (MS, PhD); electro-optics (MS, PhD); engineering and management (MS, PhD); environmental and engineering management (MS); environmental engineering science (MS); information resource/systems management (MS); logistics management (MS); materials science (MS, PhD); nuclear engineering (MS, PhD); operations research (MS, PhD); space operations (MS); space physics (MS); systems engineering (MS, PhD).

ALABAMA AGRICULTURAL AND MECHANICAL UNIVERSITY, Huntsville, AL 35811

General Information State-supported, coed, university. CGS member. *Enrollment:* 604 full-time matriculated graduate/professional students (433 women), 404 part-time matriculated graduate/professional students (263 women). *Enrollment by degree level:* 261 master's, 9 doctoral, 738 other advanced degrees. Tuition, nonresident: part-time $826 per credit hour. Full-time tuition and fees vary according to course load and program. *Graduate housing:* Rooms and/or apartments available on a first-come, first-served basis to single and married students. Typical cost: $3530 per year ($7012 including board) for single students. Room and board charges vary according to board plan. Housing application deadline: 5/5. *Student services:* Campus employment opportunities, campus safety program, career counseling, child daycare facilities, exercise/wellness program, free psychological counseling, international student services, low-cost health insurance, services for students with disabilities, writing training. *Library facilities:* J. F. Drake Learning Resources Center. *Research affiliation:* NASA (utilization of space resources), Boeing Defense and Space Group (plant science), Lawrence Livermore National Laboratory (chemistry, physics), Alabama Supercomputer Network (computer services), Nichols Research Corporation (computer science), Hughes Aircraft Corporation (physics).

Computer facilities: 1,000 computers available on campus for general student use. A campuswide network can be accessed from student residence rooms and from off campus.
Website: http://www.aamu.edu/

General Application Contact: Derrek Dunn, Dean, School of Graduate Studies, 256-372-5266, Fax: 256-372-5269.

GRADUATE UNITS

School of Graduate Studies Students: 604 full-time (433 women), 404 part-time (263 women); includes 848 minority (816 Black or African American, non-Hispanic/Latino; 3 American Indian or Alaska Native, non-Hispanic/Latino; 10 Asian, non-Hispanic/Latino; 7 Hispanic/Latino; 1 Native Hawaiian or other Pacific Islander, non-Hispanic/Latino; 11 Two or more races, non-Hispanic/Latino), 27 international. Average age 27. Expenses: Contact institution. *Financial support:* Fellowships with tuition reimbursements, research assistantships with tuition reimbursements, teaching assistantships with tuition reimbursements, career-related internships or fieldwork, Federal Work-Study, and institutionally sponsored loans available. Support available to part-time students. Financial award application deadline: 4/1; financial award applicants required to submit FAFSA. In 2016, 295 master's, 7 doctorates awarded. *Application deadline:* For fall admission, 5/5 priority date for domestic students. Applications are processed on a rolling basis. *Application fee:* $45. Electronic applications accepted. *Application Contact:* Nicole Jackson, Graduate School Administrative Coordinator, 256-372-8747, E-mail: nicole.jackson@aamu.edu. *Dean*, Dr. Derrek Dunn, 256-372-5266, Fax: 256-372-8752, E-mail: derrek.dunn@aamu.edu.

College of Agricultural, Life and Natural Sciences Expenses: Contact institution. *Financial support:* Fellowships, research assistantships, teaching assistantships, career-related internships or fieldwork, and Federal Work-Study available. Support available to part-time students. Financial award application deadline: 4/1. *Program availability:* Part-time, evening/weekend. Offers agricultural, life and natural sciences (MS, MURP, PhD); apparel, merchandising and design (MS); biology (MS); family and consumer sciences (MS); food science (MS, PhD); human development and family studies (MS); nutrition and hospitality management (MS); plant and soil science (MS, PhD); urban and regional planning (MURP). *Application deadline:* For fall admission, 5/1 for domestic students. Applications are processed on a rolling basis. *Application fee:* $25. Electronic applications accepted. *Dean*, Dr. Lloyd T. Walker, 256-372-5783, Fax: 256-372-5906.

College of Business and Public Affairs Expenses: Contact institution. *Financial support:* Research assistantships, teaching assistantships, career-related internships or fieldwork, Federal Work-Study, and institutionally sponsored loans available. Financial award application deadline: 4/1. *Program availability:* Part-time, evening/weekend. Offers business and public affairs (MBA). *Application deadline:* For fall admission, 5/1 for domestic students. Applications are processed on a rolling basis. *Application fee:* $25. Electronic applications accepted. *Dean*, Dr. Delmonize Smith, 256-372-5092, Fax: 256-372-5081.

College of Education, Humanities, and Behavioral Sciences Expenses: Contact institution. *Financial support:* Fellowships, research assistantships, career-related internships or fieldwork, Federal Work-Study, institutionally sponsored loans, and traineeships available. Support available to part-time students. Financial award application deadline: 4/1. *Program availability:* Part-time, evening/weekend. Offers art education (MS); biology (M Ed); business/marketing education (M Ed, Ed S); chemistry (M Ed); collaborative teacher secondary education (M Ed, Ed S); early childhood education (MS Ed); education (M Ed, Ed S); education, humanities, and behavioral sciences (M Ed, MS, MS Ed, PhD, Ed S); elementary education (MS Ed, Ed S); English language arts (M Ed); family/consumer science education (M Ed, Ed S); general science (M Ed); general social science (M Ed); kinesiology (MS); mathematics (M Ed, Ed S); music education (M Ed); physical education (MS); physics (M Ed, Ed S); psychology and counseling (MS, M Ed, Ed S); reading/literacy (PhD); social work (MSW); special education collaborative teacher training (MS Ed, Ed S); speech-language pathology (MS); technology education (M Ed). *Application deadline:* For fall admission, 5/1 for domestic students. Applications are processed on a rolling basis. *Application fee:* $25. Electronic applications accepted. *Interim Dean*, Dr. Rodney Whittle, 256-372-5500.

College of Engineering, Technology, and Physical Sciences Expenses: Contact institution. *Financial support:* Research assistantships with tuition reimbursements and career-related internships or fieldwork available. Financial award application deadline: 4/1. *Program availability:* Part-time, evening/weekend. Offers computer science (MS); engineering, technology, and physical sciences (M Eng, MS, PhD);

material engineering (M Eng); physics (MS, PhD). *Application deadline:* For fall admission, 5/1 for domestic students. Applications are processed on a rolling basis. *Application fee:* $25. Electronic applications accepted. *Dean,* Dr. Chance M. Glenn, Sr., 256-372-5560.

ALABAMA COLLEGE OF OSTEOPATHIC MEDICINE, Dothan, AL 36303

General Information Independent, coed, graduate-only institution.

GRADUATE UNITS

Graduate Program Offers osteophatic medicine (DO).

ALABAMA STATE UNIVERSITY, Montgomery, AL 36101-0271

General Information State-supported, coed, comprehensive institution. CGS member. *Enrollment:* 5,318 graduate, professional, and undergraduate students; 326 full-time matriculated graduate/professional students (228 women), 265 part-time matriculated graduate/professional students (198 women). *Enrollment by degree level:* 425 master's, 146 doctoral, 30 other advanced degrees. *Graduate faculty:* 54 full-time (28 women), 23 part-time/adjunct (14 women). Tuition, state resident: full-time $3087; part-time $2744 per credit. Tuition, nonresident: full-time $6174; part-time $5488 per credit. *Required fees:* $2284; $1142 per credit. $571 per semester. Tuition and fees vary according to class time, course level, course load, degree level, program and student level. *Graduate housing:* On-campus housing not available. *Student services:* Campus employment opportunities, campus safety program, career counseling, child daycare facilities, exercise/wellness program, free psychological counseling, international student services, low-cost health insurance, services for students with disabilities, teacher training, writing training. *Library facilities:* Levi Watkins Learning Center plus 1 other. *Collection:* Books: 435,092 (physical), 69,699 (digital/electronic); Serial titles: 1,607 (physical), 4,986 (digital/electronic); Databases: 171. Weekly public service hours: 50; study areas open 24 hours, 5–7 days a week; students can reserve study rooms.

Computer facilities: 541 computers available on campus for general student use. A campuswide network can be accessed from student residence rooms and from off campus. Online class registration is available. Website: http://www.alasu.edu/

General Application Contact: Dr. William Person, Dean of Graduate Studies, 334-229-4274, Fax: 334-229-4928, E-mail: wperson@alasu.edu.

GRADUATE UNITS

College of Business Administration Students: 9 full-time (7 women), 2 part-time (both women); includes 6 minority (all Black or African American, non-Hispanic/Latino), 4 international. Average age 29. 24 applicants, 33% accepted, 5 enrolled. *Faculty:* 4 full-time (1 woman), 1 part-time/adjunct (0 women). Expenses: Contact institution. *Financial support:* Fellowships and unspecified assistantships available. Financial award application deadline: 6/30; financial award applicants required to submit FAFSA. In 2016, 10 master's awarded. *Program availability:* Part-time. Offers accountancy (M Acc); business administration (M Acc). *Application deadline:* For fall admission, 4/15 for domestic and international students; for spring admission, 11/15 for domestic students, 11/1 for international students; for summer admission, 3/15 for domestic and international students. *Application fee:* $25. Electronic applications accepted. *Application Contact:* Dr. William Person, Dean of Graduate Studies, 334-229-4274, Fax: 334-229-4928, E-mail: wperson@alasu.edu. *Interim Dean,* Dr. Kamal K. Hingorani, 334-229-4124, E-mail: khingorani@alasu.edu.

College of Education Students: 93 full-time (65 women), 221 part-time (168 women); includes 300 minority (297 Black or African American, non-Hispanic/Latino; 3 Two or more races, non-Hispanic/Latino), 3 international. Average age 35. 156 applicants, 55% accepted, 43 enrolled. *Faculty:* 7 full-time (4 women), 7 part-time/adjunct (4 women). Expenses: Contact institution. *Financial support:* In 2016–17, 4 students received support. Research assistantships and unspecified assistantships available. Financial award application deadline: 6/30; financial award applicants required to submit FAFSA. In 2016, 65 master's, 19 doctorates, 10 other advanced degrees awarded. *Program availability:* Part-time. Offers counselor education (M Ed, MS, Ed S); early childhood education (M Ed, Ed S); education (M Ed, MS, Ed D, Ed S); educational administration (M Ed, Ed D, Ed S); elementary education (M Ed, Ed S); health education (M Ed); library education media (M Ed, Ed S); physical education (M Ed); secondary education (M Ed, Ed S); special education (M Ed). *Application deadline:* For fall admission, 4/15 for domestic and international students; for spring admission, 11/15 for domestic and international students; for summer admission, 3/15 for domestic and international students. Applications are processed on a rolling basis. *Application fee:* $25. Electronic applications accepted. *Application Contact:* Dr. William Person, Dean of Graduate Studies, 334-229-4274, Fax: 334-229-4928, E-mail: wperson@alasu.edu. *Interim Dean,* Dr. Doris Screws, 334-229-4250, E-mail: dscrews@alasu.edu.

College of Health Sciences Students: 185 full-time (125 women), 7 part-time (all women); includes 81 minority (64 Black or African American, non-Hispanic/Latino; 13 Asian, non-Hispanic/Latino; 2 Hispanic/Latino; 2 Two or more races, non-Hispanic/Latino), 6 international. Average age 25. 241 applicants, 33% accepted, 64 enrolled. *Faculty:* 19 full-time (16 women), 19 part-time/adjunct (10 women). Expenses: Contact institution. *Financial support:* In 2016–17, 3 students received support. Research assistantships and unspecified assistantships available. Financial award application deadline: 6/30; financial award applicants required to submit FAFSA. In 2016, 45 master's, 39 doctorates awarded. Offers health sciences (MRC, MS, DPT); occupational therapy (MS); physical therapy (DPT); prosthetics and orthotics (MS); rehabilitation counseling (MRC). *Application deadline:* For fall admission, 4/15 for domestic and international students; for spring admission, 11/15 for domestic and international students; for summer admission, 3/15 for domestic and international students. Applications are processed on a rolling basis. *Application fee:* $25. Electronic applications accepted. *Application Contact:* Dr. William Person, Dean of Graduate Studies, 334-229-4274, Fax: 334-229-4928, E-mail: wperson@alasu.edu. *Dean, College of Health Sciences,* Dr. Cheryl E. Easley, 334-229-5053, E-mail: bdawson@alasu.edu.

College of Liberal Arts and Social Sciences Students: 26 full-time (23 women), 6 part-time (all women); all minorities (all Black or African American, non-Hispanic/Latino). Average age 28. 47 applicants, 57% accepted, 22 enrolled. *Faculty:* 16 full-time (4 women). Expenses: Contact institution. *Financial support:* In 2016–17, 2 research assistantships (averaging $9,450 per year) were awarded. In 2016, 1 master's awarded. *Program availability:* Part-time. Offers history (MA); liberal arts and social sciences (MA, MSW); social work (MSW). *Application deadline:* For fall admission, 7/15 for domestic students; for spring admission, 12/15 for domestic students. Applications are processed on a rolling basis. *Application fee:* $25. *Application Contact:* Dr. William Person, Dean of Graduate Studies, 334-229-4274, Fax: 334-229-4928, E-mail: wperson@alasu.edu. *Dean,* Dr. Anthony Troy Adams, 334-229-5176, E-mail: atadams@alasu.edu.

College of Science, Mathematics and Technology Students: 12 full-time (8 women), 26 part-time (14 women); includes 33 minority (30 Black or African American, non-Hispanic/Latino; 1 Asian, non-Hispanic/Latino; 1 Hispanic/Latino; 1 Two or more races, non-Hispanic/Latino), 3 international. Average age 30. 38 applicants, 55% accepted, 8 enrolled. *Faculty:* 11 full-time (4 women). Expenses: Contact institution. *Financial support:* In 2016–17, 22 students received support. Research assistantships and scholarships/grants available. Financial award application deadline: 6/30; financial award applicants required to submit CSS PROFILE or FAFSA. In 2016, 14 master's, 3 doctorates awarded. Offers biological sciences (MS, PhD); forensic science (MS); mathematics (MS); science, mathematics and technology (MS, PhD). *Application deadline:* For fall admission, 4/15 for domestic and international students; for spring admission, 11/15 for domestic and international students; for summer admission, 3/15 for domestic and international students. Applications are processed on a rolling basis. *Application fee:* $25. Electronic applications accepted. *Application Contact:* Dr. William Person, Dean of Graduate Studies, 334-229-4274, Fax: 334-229-4928, E-mail: wperson@alasu.edu. *Dean,* Dr. Kennedy Weskesa, 334-229-4316, Fax: 334-229-4916, E-mail: weskesa@alasu.edu.

ALASKA PACIFIC UNIVERSITY, Anchorage, AK 99508-4672

General Information Independent, coed, comprehensive institution. *Graduate housing:* Room and/or apartments available on a first-come, first-served basis to single students; on-campus housing not available to married students. Housing application deadline: 8/15.

GRADUATE UNITS

Graduate Programs *Program availability:* Part-time, evening/weekend. Offers business administration (MBA); counseling psychology (MSCP); environmental science (MSES, MSOEE); health services administration (MBA); information and communication technology (MBAICT); investment (CGS); outdoor and environmental education (MSOEE); self-designed study (MA); teaching (MAT); teaching (K-8) (MAT). Electronic applications accepted.

ALBANY COLLEGE OF PHARMACY AND HEALTH SCIENCES, Albany, NY 12208

General Information Independent, coed, comprehensive institution. *Enrollment:* 498 full-time matriculated graduate/professional students (290 women), 8 part-time matriculated graduate/professional students (3 women). *Enrollment by degree level:* 44 master's, 462 doctoral. *Graduate faculty:* 85 full-time (38 women), 26 part-time/adjunct (15 women). *Graduate housing:* Room and/or apartments available on a first-come, first-served basis to single students; on-campus housing not available to married students. Housing application deadline: 7/1. *Student services:* Campus employment opportunities, campus safety program, career counseling, exercise/wellness program, free psychological counseling, international student services, low-cost health insurance, services for students with disabilities, writing training. *Library facilities:* George and Leona Lewis Library.

Computer facilities: Computer purchase and lease plans are available. A campuswide network can be accessed from student residence rooms and from off campus. Online class registration is available. Website: http://www.acphs.edu/

General Application Contact: Ann Bruno, Coordinator, Graduate Programs, 518-694-7130, E-mail: graduate@acphs.edu.

GRADUATE UNITS

School of Arts and Sciences Students: 38 full-time (27 women), 5 part-time (3 women); includes 5 minority (2 Black or African American, non-Hispanic/Latino; 2 Asian, non-Hispanic/Latino; 1 Two or more races, non-Hispanic/Latino), 1 international. Average age 25. Expenses: Contact institution. *Financial support:* Research assistantships, teaching assistantships, and scholarships/grants available. Financial award application deadline: 3/1; financial award applicants required to submit FAFSA. In 2016, 12 master's awarded. Offers clinical laboratory sciences (MS); cytotechnology and molecular cytology (MS); health outcomes research (MS); molecular biosciences (MS). *Application deadline:* For fall admission, 6/15 for domestic students, 4/15 for international students. Applications are processed on a rolling basis. *Application fee:* $75. Electronic applications accepted. *Application Contact:* Ann Bruno, Coordinator, Graduate Programs, 518-694-7130, E-mail: graduate@acphs.edu. *Dean of Graduate Studies,* Dr. Martha Hass, 518-694-7238.

School of Pharmacy and Pharmaceutical Sciences Students: 467 full-time (268 women), 7 part-time (2 women); includes 112 minority (14 Black or African American, non-Hispanic/Latino; 4 American Indian or Alaska Native, non-Hispanic/Latino; 69 Asian, non-Hispanic/Latino; 22 Hispanic/Latino; 1 Native Hawaiian or other Pacific Islander, non-Hispanic/Latino; 2 Two or more races, non-Hispanic/Latino), 21 international. Average age 24. Expenses: Contact institution. *Financial support:* Scholarships/grants available. Financial award application deadline: 3/1; financial award applicants required to submit FAFSA. In 2016, 4 master's, 200 doctorates awarded. Offers health outcomes research (MS); pharmaceutical sciences (MS); pharmacy (Pharm D). *Application deadline:* For fall admission, 3/1 for domestic and international students. Applications are processed on a rolling basis. Electronic applications accepted. *Application Contact:* Ann Bruno, Coordinator, Graduate Programs, 518-694-7130, E-mail: graduate@acphs.edu. *Director of Graduate Studies,* Dr. Martha Hass, 518-694-7238.

ALBANY LAW SCHOOL, Albany, NY 12208-3494

General Information Independent, coed, graduate-only institution. *Graduate housing:* On-campus housing not available.

GRADUATE UNITS

Professional Program *Program availability:* Part-time. Offers law (LL M, JD). JD/MBA offered jointly with The College of Saint Rose, The Sage Colleges, Union Graduate College, and University at Albany, State University of New York; JD/MPA, JD/MRP, and JD/MSW offered jointly with University at Albany, State University of New York.

ALBANY MEDICAL COLLEGE, Albany, NY 12208-3479

General Information Independent, coed, graduate-only institution. *Graduate housing:* On-campus housing not available. *Research affiliation:* X-Ray Optical Systems (diagnostic equipment), Integrated Tissue Dynamics INTIGYN (integrated tissue dynamics), Regenerative Research Foundation (biomedical research), Wadsworth Center for Laboratories and Research (biomedical research), ORDWAY Research Institute (biomedical research), General Electric Company (GE) (imaging).

GRADUATE UNITS

Alden March Bioethics Institute *Program availability:* Part-time, evening/weekend, online learning. Offers bioethics (MS, DPS); clinical ethics (Certificate); clinical ethics consultation (Certificate). Electronic applications accepted.

Center for Cardiovascular Sciences *Program availability:* Part-time. Offers cardiovascular sciences (MS, PhD).

Center for Cell Biology and Cancer Research *Program availability:* Part-time. Offers cell biology and cancer research (MS, PhD).

Center for Immunology and Microbial Disease *Program availability:* Part-time. Offers immunology and microbial disease (MS, PhD).

Center for Neuropharmacology and Neuroscience Offers neuropharmacology and neuroscience (MS, PhD).

Center for Nurse Anesthesiology Offers anesthesia (MS). Electronic applications accepted.

Center for Physician Assistant Studies Offers physician assistant studies (MS). Electronic applications accepted.

Professional Program Offers medicine (MD). Electronic applications accepted.

ALBANY STATE UNIVERSITY, Albany, GA 31705-2717

General Information State-supported, coed, comprehensive institution. *Graduate housing:* Room and/or apartments available on a first-come, first-served basis to single students; on-campus housing not available to married students. Housing application deadline: 6/30. *Student services:* Campus employment opportunities, campus safety program, career counseling, child daycare facilities, exercise/wellness program, free psychological counseling, grant writing training, international student services, low-cost health insurance, services for students with disabilities, teacher training, writing training. *Library facilities:* James Pendergrast Memorial Library.

Computer facilities: Computer purchase and lease plans are available. A campuswide network can be accessed from student residence rooms and from off campus. Online class registration, academic advising tools, online payment, and campus one stop portal are available. Website: http://www.asurams.edu/

General Application Contact: Jeffrey Pierce, II, Graduate Admissions Counselor, 229-430-4646, Fax: 229-430-4105, E-mail: jeffrey.pierce@aurams.edu.

GRADUATE UNITS

College of Arts and Humanities Expenses: Contact institution. *Financial support:* Application deadline: 4/15; applicants required to submit FAFSA. *Program availability:* Part-time. Offers criminal justice (MS); English education (M Ed); public administration (MPA); social work (MSW). *Application deadline:* For fall admission, 6/1 for domestic students, 5/1 for international students; for spring admission, 11/1 for domestic students, 10/1 for international students. Applications are processed on a rolling basis. *Application fee:* $20. Electronic applications accepted. *Application Contact:* Jeffrey Pierce, II, Graduate Admissions Counselor, 229-430-4646, Fax: 229-430-4105, E-mail: jeffrey.pierce@asurams.edu. *Dean,* Dr. Rani George, 229-430-1877, Fax: 229-430-4296.

College of Business Expenses: Contact institution. *Financial support:* Application deadline: 4/15; applicants required to submit FAFSA. *Program availability:* Part-time, evening/weekend. Offers accounting (MBA); general business administration (MBA); healthcare (MBA); public administration (MBA); supply chain and logistics (MBA). *Application deadline:* For fall admission, 6/1 for domestic students, 5/1 for international students; for spring admission, 11/1 for domestic students, 10/1 for international students. Applications are processed on a rolling basis. *Application fee:* $20. Electronic applications accepted. *Application Contact:* Jeffrey Pierce, II, Graduate Counselor, 229-430-4646, Fax: 229-430-4105, E-mail: jeffrey.pierce@asurams.edu. *Dean,* Dr. Alicia Jackson, 229-430-7009, Fax: 229-430-5119.

College of Education Expenses: Contact institution. *Financial support:* Scholarships/grants available. Financial award application deadline: 4/15; financial award applicants required to submit FAFSA. *Program availability:* Part-time, evening/weekend, online learning. Offers early childhood education (M Ed); educational leadership (Ed S); health and physical education (M Ed); middle grades education (M Ed); school counseling (M Ed); special education (M Ed). *Application deadline:* For fall admission, 6/1 for domestic students, 5/1 for international students; for spring admission, 11/1 for domestic students, 10/1 for international students. Applications are processed on a rolling basis. *Application fee:* $20. Electronic applications accepted. *Application Contact:* Jeffrey Pierce, II, Graduate Admissions Counselor, 229-430-4646, Fax: 229-430-4105, E-mail: jeffrey.pierce@asurams.edu. *Interim Dean,* Dr. Rhonda C. Porter, 229-430-1718, Fax: 229-430-4993.

Darton College of Health Professions Expenses: Contact institution. *Financial support:* Scholarships/grants and traineeships available. Financial award application deadline: 4/15; financial award applicants required to submit CSS PROFILE or FAFSA. *Program availability:* Part-time, evening/weekend, online learning. Offers nursing (MSN). *Application deadline:* For fall admission, 6/15 for domestic students, 5/1 for international students; for spring admission, 11/1 for domestic students, 10/1 for international students. Applications are processed on a rolling basis. *Application fee:* $20. Electronic applications accepted. *Application Contact:* Jeffrey Pierce, II, Graduate Admissions Counselor, 229-430-4646, Fax: 229-430-4105, E-mail: jeffrey.pierce@asurams.edu.

ALBERT EINSTEIN COLLEGE OF MEDICINE, Bronx, NY 10461

General Information Independent, coed, graduate-only institution.

GRADUATE UNITS

Graduate Division of Biomedical Sciences Offers anatomy (PhD); biochemistry (PhD); biomedical sciences (PhD); cell and developmental biology (PhD); cell biology (PhD); clinical investigation (PhD); computational genetics (PhD); developmental and molecular biology (PhD); microbiology and immunology (PhD); molecular genetics (PhD); molecular pharmacology (PhD); neuroscience (PhD); pathology (PhD); physiology and biophysics (PhD); systems and computational biology (PhD); translational genetics (PhD). Electronic applications accepted.

Medical Scientist Training Program

Professional Program in Medicine Offers medicine (MD).

ALBERTUS MAGNUS COLLEGE, New Haven, CT 06511-1189

General Information Independent-religious, coed, comprehensive institution. *Enrollment:* 1,555 graduate, professional, and undergraduate students; 241 full-time matriculated graduate/professional students (175 women), 94 part-time matriculated graduate/professional students (68 women). *Enrollment by degree level:* 335 master's. *Graduate faculty:* 29 full-time (11 women), 59 part-time/adjunct (27 women). *Tuition:* Full-time $20,112; part-time $2514 per course. *Required fees:* $20. Tuition and fees vary according to course load and program. *Graduate housing:* On-campus housing not available. *Student services:* Campus employment opportunities, career counseling, free psychological counseling, international student services, services for students with

disabilities, teacher training, writing training. *Library facilities:* Rosary Hall. *Collection:* Books: 38,339 (physical), 148,500 (digital/electronic); Databases: 88.

Computer facilities: 117 computers available on campus for general student use. A campuswide network can be accessed from student residence rooms and from off campus. Online class registration, online class sessions are available. Website: http://www.albertus.edu.

General Application Contact: Anthony Reich, Director of Admission, Division of Professional and Graduate Studies, 203-773-5032, E-mail: arreich@albertus.edu.

GRADUATE UNITS

Master of Arts in Art Therapy Program Students: 20 full-time (19 women), 18 part-time (17 women); includes 2 minority (1 Asian, non-Hispanic/Latino; 1 Hispanic/Latino). Average age 28. *Faculty:* 3 full-time (all women), 13 part-time/adjunct (10 women). Expenses: Contact institution. *Financial support:* Federal Work-Study and unspecified assistantships available. Support available to part-time students. Financial award application deadline: 8/15; financial award applicants required to submit FAFSA. In 2016, 15 master's awarded. *Program availability:* Part-time. Offers art therapy (MAAT). *Application deadline:* For fall admission, 5/1 for domestic students; for spring admission, 11/1 for domestic students. Applications are processed on a rolling basis. *Application fee:* $50. Electronic applications accepted. *Application Contact:* Dr. Sean O'Connell, Vice President for Academic Affairs, 203-777-8539, Fax: 203-777-3701, E-mail: soconnell@albertus.edu. *Director,* Abbe Miller, 203-773-8543, Fax: 203-773-3117, E-mail: amiller@albertus.edu.

Master of Arts in Leadership Program Students: 2 full-time (both women), 10 part-time (7 women); includes 4 minority (3 Black or African American, non-Hispanic/Latino; 1 Hispanic/Latino). Average age 39. *Faculty:* 2 full-time (0 women), 4 part-time/adjunct (2 women). Expenses: Contact institution. *Financial support:* Federal Work-Study and unspecified assistantships available. Support available to part-time students. Financial award applicants required to submit FAFSA. In 2016, 8 master's awarded. *Program availability:* Part-time, evening/weekend, blended/hybrid learning. Offers leadership (MA). *Application deadline:* Applications are processed on a rolling basis. *Application fee:* $50. Electronic applications accepted. *Application Contact:* Anthony Reich, Director of Admission, Division of Professional and Graduate Studies, 203-773-5032, Fax: 203-773-5257, E-mail: leadership@albertus.edu. *Director,* Dr. Howard Fero, 203-773-4424, E-mail: hfero@albertus.edu.

Master of Arts in Liberal Studies Program Students: 3 part-time (1 woman); includes 1 minority (Asian, non-Hispanic/Latino). Average age 41. *Faculty:* 10 full-time (3 women). Expenses: Contact institution. *Financial support:* Federal Work-Study and unspecified assistantships available. Support available to part-time students. Financial award application deadline: 8/15; financial award applicants required to submit FAFSA. In 2016, 4 master's awarded. *Program availability:* Part-time, evening/weekend, blended/hybrid learning. Offers liberal studies (MALS). *Application deadline:* For fall admission, 8/31 for domestic students; for spring admission, 1/10 for domestic students. Applications are processed on a rolling basis. *Application fee:* $50. Electronic applications accepted. *Application Contact:* Anthony Reich, Director of Admission, Division of Professional and Graduate Studies, 203-773-5032, Fax: 203-773-5257, E-mail: arreich@albertus.edu. *Director, Liberal Studies Program,* Prof. Julia A. Coash, 203-773-8993, Fax: 203-773-5257, E-mail: jcoash@albertus.edu.

Master of Business Administration Program Students: 82 full-time (53 women), 21 part-time (12 women); includes 61 minority (43 Black or African American, non-Hispanic/Latino; 2 Asian, non-Hispanic/Latino; 13 Hispanic/Latino; 3 Two or more races, non-Hispanic/Latino), 2 international. Average age 34. *Faculty:* 7 full-time (2 women), 24 part-time/adjunct (6 women). *Financial support:* Federal Work-Study and unspecified assistantships available. Support available to part-time students. Financial award applicants required to submit FAFSA. In 2016, 51 master's awarded. *Program availability:* Part-time, evening/weekend, 100% online, blended/hybrid learning. Offers business administration (MBA). Program also offered in East Hartford, CT. *Application deadline:* Applications are processed on a rolling basis. *Application fee:* $50. Electronic applications accepted. *Application Contact:* Anthony Reich, Director of Admission, Division of Professional and Graduate Studies, 203-773-5032, E-mail: arreich@albertus.edu. *Director, MBA Programs,* Dr. Wayne Gineo, 203-672-6670, E-mail: wgineo@albertus.edu.

Master of Fine Arts in Creative Writing Program Students: 5 full-time (3 women), 1 (woman) part-time; includes 3 minority (1 Black or African American, non-Hispanic/Latino; 2 Hispanic/Latino). Average age 35. *Faculty:* 5 full-time (1 woman), 1 part-time/adjunct (0 women). Expenses: Contact institution. *Financial support:* Federal Work-Study and unspecified assistantships available. Support available to part-time students. Financial award applicants required to submit FAFSA. In 2016, 5 master's awarded. *Program availability:* Part-time, evening/weekend, blended/hybrid learning. Offers creative writing (MFA). *Application deadline:* For fall admission, 8/15 for domestic students; for spring admission, 1/15 for domestic students. Applications are processed on a rolling basis. *Application fee:* $50. Electronic applications accepted. *Application Contact:* Prof. Sarah Harris Wallman, Co-Director, 203-777-4473, Fax: 203-777-3701, E-mail: swallman@albertus.edu. *Co-Director,* Charles Rafferty, 203-773-6901, Fax: 203-777-3701, E-mail: crafferty@albertus.edu.

Master of Science in Accounting Program Students: 14 full-time (8 women), 8 part-time (5 women); includes 7 minority (3 Black or African American, non-Hispanic/Latino; 3 Hispanic/Latino; 1 Two or more races, non-Hispanic/Latino). Average age 36. *Faculty:* 7 full-time (2 women), 24 part-time/adjunct (6 women). Expenses: Contact institution. *Financial support:* Federal Work-Study and unspecified assistantships available. Support available to part-time students. Financial award applicants required to submit FAFSA. In 2016, 9 master's awarded. *Program availability:* Part-time, evening/weekend, 100% online, blended/hybrid learning. Offers accounting (MSA). *Application deadline:* Applications are processed on a rolling basis. *Application fee:* $50. Electronic applications accepted. *Application Contact:* Dr. Sean O'Connell, Vice President for Academic Affairs, 203-777-8539, Fax: 203-777-3701, E-mail: soconnell@albertus.edu. *Director of the Business Programs,* Dr. Nancy Fallon, 203-773-8567, E-mail: nfallon@albertus.edu.

Master of Science in Criminal Justice Program Students: 7 full-time (6 women), 7 part-time (5 women); includes 11 minority (8 Black or African American, non-Hispanic/Latino; 1 Hispanic/Latino; 2 Two or more races, non-Hispanic/Latino). Average age 35. Expenses: Contact institution. *Financial support:* Federal Work-Study and unspecified assistantships available. Support available to part-time students. Financial award applicants required to submit FAFSA. *Program availability:* Part-time, evening/weekend, 100% online, blended/hybrid learning. Offers corrections administration (MS); juvenile justice (MS). *Application fee:* $50. *Application Contact:* Dr. Sean O'Connell, Vice President for Academic Affairs, 203-777-8539, Fax: 203-777-3701, E-mail: soconnell@albertus.edu. *Coordinator,* John Lawrie, 203-773-6142, E-mail: jnlawrie@albertus.edu.

Master of Science in Education Program Students: 5 full-time (3 women), 1 part-time (0 women); includes 2 minority (1 Black or African American, non-Hispanic/Latino; 1 Hispanic/Latino). Average age 28. *Faculty:* 3 full-time (1 woman), 9 part-time/adjunct (4 women). Expenses: Contact institution. *Financial support:* Federal Work-Study and unspecified assistantships available. Support available to part-time students. Financial award applicants required to submit FAFSA. In 2016, 7 master's awarded. *Program availability:* Part-time, evening/weekend, blended/hybrid learning. Offers education (MS Ed). *Application deadline:* For fall admission, 8/15 for domestic students; for spring admission, 1/15 for domestic students. *Application fee:* $50. *Application Contact:* Anthony Reich, Director of Admission, Division of Professional and Graduate Studies, 203-773-5032, E-mail: arreich@albertus.edu. *Director, Education Programs,* Dr. Joan Venditto, 203-773-8087, Fax: 203-773-4422, E-mail: jvenditto@albertus.edu.

Master of Science in Human Services Program Students: 49 full-time (41 women), 2 part-time (both women); includes 32 minority (28 Black or African American, non-Hispanic/Latino; 4 Hispanic/Latino; 1 international. Average age 39. *Faculty:* 3 full-time (1 woman), 6 part-time/adjunct (4 women). Expenses: Contact institution. *Financial support:* Federal Work-Study and unspecified assistantships available. Support available to part-time students. Financial award applicants required to submit FAFSA. In 2016, 32 master's awarded. *Program availability:* Part-time, evening/weekend, blended/hybrid learning. Offers human services (MS). *Application deadline:* For fall admission, 8/15 for domestic students; for spring admission, 1/15 for domestic students. Applications are processed on a rolling basis. *Application fee:* $50. Electronic applications accepted. *Application Contact:* Anthony Reich, Director of Admission, Division of Professional and Graduate Studies, 203-773-5032, E-mail: arreich@albertus.edu. *Director,* Ragaa Mazen, 203-773-8574, E-mail: rmazen@albertus.edu.

Program in Management and Organizational Leadership Students: 45 full-time (31 women), 13 part-time (9 women); includes 33 minority (19 Black or African American, non-Hispanic/Latino; 3 American Indian or Alaska Native, non-Hispanic/Latino; 10 Hispanic/Latino; 1 Two or more races, non-Hispanic/Latino). Average age 41. *Faculty:* 8 full-time (2 women), 5 part-time/adjunct (1 woman). Expenses: Contact institution. *Financial support:* Federal Work-Study and unspecified assistantships available. Support available to part-time students. Financial award applicants required to submit FAFSA. In 2016, 24 master's awarded. *Program availability:* Part-time, evening/weekend, blended/hybrid learning. Offers management and organizational leadership (MS). *Application deadline:* For fall admission, 8/14 for domestic students; for spring admission, 1/15 for domestic students. Applications are processed on a rolling basis. *Application fee:* $50. Electronic applications accepted. *Application Contact:* Anthony Reich, Director of Admission, Division of Professional and Graduate Studies, 203-773-5032, E-mail: arreich@albertus.edu. *Director of Leadership Programs,* Dr. Howard Fero, 203-773-4424, E-mail: hfero@albertus.edu.

ALBRIGHT COLLEGE, Reading, PA 19612-5234

General Information Independent-religious, coed, comprehensive institution. *Graduate housing:* On-campus housing not available.

GRADUATE UNITS

Graduate Division *Program availability:* Part-time, evening/weekend. Offers early childhood education (MS); elementary education (MS); English as a second language (MA); general education (MA); special education (MS). Electronic applications accepted.

ALCORN STATE UNIVERSITY, Lorman, MS 39096-7500

General Information State-supported, coed, comprehensive institution. CGS member. *Graduate housing:* Room and/or apartments available on a first-come, first-served basis to single students; on-campus housing not available to married students.

GRADUATE UNITS

School of Graduate Studies *Program availability:* Part-time. Offers workforce education leadership (MS). Electronic applications accepted.

School of Agriculture and Applied Science Offers agricultural economics (MS Ag); agronomy (MS Ag); animal science (MS Ag).

School of Arts and Sciences Offers arts and sciences (MS); biology (MS); computer and information sciences (MS).

School of Business Offers business (MBA).

School of Nursing Offers rural nursing (MSN).

School of Psychology and Education Offers agricultural education (MS Ed); elementary education (MS Ed, Ed S); guidance and counseling (MS Ed); industrial education (MS Ed); secondary education (MS Ed); special education (MS Ed).

ALDERSON BROADDUS UNIVERSITY, Philippi, WV 26416

General Information Independent-religious, coed, comprehensive institution. *Graduate housing:* Rooms and/or apartments available on a first-come, first-served basis to single and married students. Housing application deadline: 8/21.

GRADUATE UNITS

Program in Physician Assistant Studies Offers physician assistant studies (MPAS). Electronic applications accepted.

ALFRED UNIVERSITY, Alfred, NY 14802-1205

General Information Independent, coed, university. *Enrollment:* 2,390 graduate, professional, and undergraduate students. *Graduate faculty:* 81 full-time (30 women). *Tuition:* Full-time $38,020; part-time $810 per credit. *Required fees:* $970; $82 per semester. *Graduate housing:* Room and/or apartments available on a first-come, first-served basis to single students; on-campus housing not available to married students. Typical cost: $12,196 (including board). Room and board charges vary according to board plan, campus/location and housing facility selected. Housing application deadline: 5/1. *Student services:* Campus employment opportunities, campus safety program, career counseling, free psychological counseling, international student services, low-cost health insurance, multicultural affairs office, services for students with disabilities, teacher training, writing tutoring. *Library facilities:* Herrick Memorial Library plus 1 other. *Collection:* Books: 217,226 (physical), 530,999 (digital/electronic); Serial titles: 243 (physical), 114,188 (digital/electronic); Databases: 279. Study areas open 24 hours, 5–7 days a week; students can reserve study rooms. *Research affiliation:* Center for High Temperature Characterization (materials science), New York State Center for Advanced Ceramic Technology (ceramic engineering and materials science), Center for Glass Research (glass engineering and science), National Science Foundation Industry-University Center for Glass Research, Whitewares Research Center (whitewares processing, traditional ceramics), National Science Foundation Industry-University Center for Biosurfaces (bioceramics).

Computer facilities: Computer purchase and lease plans are available. A campuswide network can be accessed from student residence rooms and from off campus. Online class registration, online bill pay are available.
Website: http://www.alfred.edu/

General Application Contact: Sara Love, Coordinator of Graduate Admissions, 607-871-2115, Fax: 607-871-2198, E-mail: gradinquiry@alfred.edu.

GRADUATE UNITS

Graduate School Students: 193 full-time (107 women), 276 part-time (202 women); includes 152 minority (82 Black or African American, non-Hispanic/Latino; 1 American Indian or Alaska Native, non-Hispanic/Latino; 10 Asian, non-Hispanic/Latino; 58 Hispanic/Latino; 1 Two or more races, non-Hispanic/Latino), 23 international. Average age 25. 561 applicants, 50% accepted, 234 enrolled. *Faculty:* 87 full-time (24 women), 7 part-time/adjunct (2 women). Expenses: Contact institution. *Financial support:* In 2016–17, 150 students received support, including 6 fellowships with full tuition reimbursements available (averaging $22,520 per year), 45 research assistantships with partial tuition reimbursements available (averaging $19,010 per year), 36 teaching assistantships with full tuition reimbursements available (averaging $27,270 per year); career-related internships or fieldwork and unspecified assistantships also available. Financial award application deadline: 8/1; financial award applicants required to submit FAFSA. In 2016, 161 master's, 6 doctorates, 68 other advanced degrees awarded. *Program availability:* Part-time. Offers mental health counseling (MS Ed); public administration (MPA); school counseling (MS Ed, CAS); school psychology (MA, Psy D, CAS). *Application deadline:* For fall admission, 8/1 for domestic students, 2/15 for international students; for spring admission, 12/1 for domestic students, 10/1 for international students. Applications are processed on a rolling basis. *Application fee:* $60. Electronic applications accepted. *Application Contact:* Sara Love, Graduate Admissions Coordinator, 607-871-2115, Fax: 607-871-2198, E-mail: gradinquiry@alfred.edu. *Provost and Vice President of Academic Affairs,* Dr. Rick Stephens, 607-871-2967, Fax: 607-871-2198, E-mail: stephens@alfred.edu.

College of Ceramics Expenses: Contact institution. *Financial support:* Fellowships with full tuition reimbursements, research assistantships with full tuition reimbursements, teaching assistantships with full tuition reimbursements, and tuition waivers (full and partial) available. Financial award applicants required to submit FAFSA. Offers biomaterials engineering (MS); ceramic art (MFA); ceramic engineering (MS, PhD); ceramics (MFA, MS, PhD); electrical engineering (MS); electronic integrated arts (MFA); glass science (MS, PhD); materials science and engineering (MS, PhD); mechanical engineering (MS); painting (MFA); sculpture/dimensional studies (MFA). *Application deadline:* For fall admission, 3/1 priority date for domestic students, 3/15 for international students; for spring admission, 12/1 for domestic students, 10/1 for international students. Applications are processed on a rolling basis. *Application fee:* $60. Electronic applications accepted. *Application Contact:* Sara Love, Coordinator of Graduate Admissions, 607-871-2115, Fax: 607-871-2198, E-mail: gradinquiry@alfred.edu. *Vice President,* Dr. Rick Stephens, 607-871-2967, E-mail: stephens@alfred.edu.

Division of Education Students: 50 full-time (38 women), 245 part-time (195 women); includes 169 minority (91 Black or African American, non-Hispanic/Latino; 2 American Indian or Alaska Native, non-Hispanic/Latino; 7 Asian, non-Hispanic/Latino; 69 Hispanic/Latino). Average age 34. *Faculty:* 4 full-time (3 women), 3 part-time/adjunct (2 women). Expenses: Contact institution. *Financial support:* Research assistantships with partial tuition reimbursements, tuition waivers (partial), and unspecified assistantships available. Financial award applicants required to submit FAFSA. In 2016, 21 master's awarded. *Program availability:* Part-time. Offers college student development (MS Ed); literacy (MS Ed). *Application deadline:* For fall admission, 8/1 for domestic students, 3/15 for international students; for spring admission, 12/1 for domestic students, 10/1 for international students. Applications are processed on a rolling basis. *Application fee:* $60. Electronic applications accepted. *Application Contact:* Sara Love, Coordinator of Graduate Admissions, 607-871-2115, Fax: 607-871-2198, E-mail: gradinquiry@alfred.edu. *Program Director,* Kevin Curtin, 607-871-2699.

School of Business Students: 28 full-time (11 women), 20 part-time (8 women); includes 10 minority (7 Black or African American, non-Hispanic/Latino; 1 Asian, non-Hispanic/Latino; 2 Hispanic/Latino), 1 international. Average age 24. Expenses: Contact institution. *Financial support:* Research assistantships with partial tuition reimbursements, tuition waivers (partial), and unspecified assistantships available. Financial award applicants required to submit FAFSA. In 2016, 31 master's awarded. *Program availability:* Part-time. Offers accounting (MBA); business administration (MBA). *Application deadline:* For fall admission, 8/1 for domestic students, 3/15 for international students; for winter admission, 12/1 for domestic students; for spring admission, 10/1 for international students. Applications are processed on a rolling basis. *Application fee:* $60. Electronic applications accepted. *Application Contact:* Sara Love, Coordinator of Graduate Admissions, 607-871-2115, Fax: 607-871-2198, E-mail: gradinquiry@alfred.edu. *Dean of the College of Professional Studies,* Dr. Nancy Evangelista, 607-871-2124, Fax: 607-871-2114, E-mail: fevangel@alfred.edu.

ALLEN COLLEGE, Waterloo, IA 50703

General Information Independent, coed, primarily women, comprehensive institution. *Enrollment:* 620 graduate, professional, and undergraduate students; 71 full-time matriculated graduate/professional students (60 women), 171 part-time matriculated graduate/professional students (148 women). *Enrollment by degree level:* 212 master's, 15 doctoral, 15 other advanced degrees. *Graduate faculty:* 9 full-time (all women), 24 part-time/adjunct (23 women). *Tuition:* Full-time $15,940. *Required fees:* $1240. Tuition and fees vary according to degree level and program. *Graduate housing:* On-campus housing not available. *Student services:* Campus safety program, career counseling, free psychological counseling. *Library facilities:* Barrett Library plus 1 other. *Collection:* Books: 12,926 (physical), 200 (digital/electronic); Serial titles: 218 (physical), 279 (digital/electronic); Databases: 38. Weekly public service hours: 50; study areas open 24 hours, 5–7 days a week.

Computer facilities: 32 computers available on campus for general student use. A campuswide network can be accessed from off campus.
Website: http://www.allencollege.edu/

General Application Contact: Molly Quinn, Director of Admissions, 319-226-2001, Fax: 319-226-2010, E-mail: molly.quinn@allencollege.edu.

GRADUATE UNITS

Graduate Programs Students: 71 full-time (60 women), 171 part-time (148 women); includes 12 minority (6 Black or African American, non-Hispanic/Latino; 1 American Indian or Alaska Native, non-Hispanic/Latino; 2 Hispanic/Latino; 3 Two or more races, non-Hispanic/Latino), 3 international. Average age 34. 291 applicants, 59% accepted, 109 enrolled. *Faculty:* 9 full-time (all women), 24 part-time/adjunct (23 women). Expenses: Contact institution. *Financial support:* In 2016–17, 99 students received support. Institutionally sponsored loans, scholarships/grants, and traineeships available. Support available to part-time students. Financial award application deadline: 8/15; financial award applicants required to submit FAFSA. In 2016, 49 master's, 2 doctorates awarded. *Program availability:* Part-time, blended/hybrid learning. Offers adult-gerontology acute care nurse practitioner (MSN); community/public health nursing (MSN); family nurse practitioner (MSN); health sciences (Ed D); leadership in health care delivery (MSN); nursing (DNP); occupational therapy (MS). *Application deadline:* For fall admission, 2/1 priority date for domestic students; for spring admission, 9/1 priority date for domestic students. Applications are processed on a rolling basis. *Application fee:* $50. Electronic applications accepted. *Application Contact:* Molly Quinn, Director of Admissions, 319-226-2001, Fax: 319-226-2010, E-mail: molly.quinn@allencollege.edu. *Vice Chancellor for Academic Affairs,* Dr. Nancy Kramer, 319-226-2040, Fax: 319-226-2070, E-mail: nancy.kramer@allencollege.edu.

ALLIANT INTERNATIONAL UNIVERSITY–FRESNO, Fresno, CA 93727

General Information Independent, coed, graduate-only institution. *Graduate housing:* On-campus housing not available.

GRADUATE UNITS

California School of Forensic Studies Offers clinical forensic psychology (PhD, Psy D); forensic studies (PhD, Psy D); victimology (Psy D). Electronic applications accepted.

California School of Professional Psychology Offers clinical psychology (PhD, Psy D); organizational behavior (MA); organizational development (Psy D); professional psychology (MA, PhD, Psy D). Electronic applications accepted.

ALLIANT INTERNATIONAL UNIVERSITY–IRVINE, Irvine, CA 92606

General Information Independent, coed, graduate-only institution. *Graduate housing:* On-campus housing not available.

GRADUATE UNITS

California School of Forensic Studies Offers forensic studies (Psy D). Electronic applications accepted.

California School of Professional Psychology *Program availability:* Part-time. Offers couple and family therapy (MA, Psy D); professional psychology (MA, Psy D). Electronic applications accepted.

Shirley M. Hufstedler School of Education *Program availability:* Part-time, evening/weekend, online learning. Offers education (MA, Psy D, Certificate, Credential); educational psychology (Psy D); pupil personnel services (Credential); school psychology (MA). Electronic applications accepted.

ALLIANT INTERNATIONAL UNIVERSITY–LOS ANGELES, Alhambra, CA 91803

General Information Independent, coed, graduate-only institution. *Graduate housing:* Room and/or apartments available to single students; on-campus housing not available to married students.

GRADUATE UNITS

California School of Forensic Studies Offers forensic psychology (Psy D).

California School of Professional Psychology Offers chemical dependency (MA); clinical health psychology (Psy D); clinical psychology (PhD, Psy D); family/child and couple clinical psychology (Psy D); gerontology (MA); Latin American family therapy (MA); multi-interest option (Psy D); multicultural community-clinical psychology (Psy D); professional psychology (MA, PhD, Psy D). Electronic applications accepted.

Organizational Psychology Division *Program availability:* Part-time. Offers organizational psychology (MA, PhD). Electronic applications accepted.

Marshall Goldsmith School of Management Offers management (DBA).

Business Division Offers business (DBA).

Shirley M. Hufstedler School of Education *Program availability:* Part-time, evening/weekend, online learning. Offers education (MA, Psy D, Credential); educational psychology (Psy D); pupil personnel services (Credential); school psychology (MA); teaching (MA, Credential). Electronic applications accepted.

ALLIANT INTERNATIONAL UNIVERSITY–SACRAMENTO, Sacramento, CA 95833

General Information Independent, coed, graduate-only institution. *Graduate housing:* On-campus housing not available.

GRADUATE UNITS

California School of Forensic Studies Offers clinical forensic psychology (Psy D); forensic studies (Psy D). Electronic applications accepted.

California School of Professional Psychology *Program availability:* Part-time. Offers clinical psychology (Psy D); couple and family therapy (MA, Psy D); professional psychology (MA, Psy D). Electronic applications accepted.

Shirley M. Hufstedler School of Education Offers education (MA, Credential); teaching (MA, Credential). Electronic applications accepted.

ALLIANT INTERNATIONAL UNIVERSITY–SAN DIEGO, San Diego, CA 92131

General Information Independent, coed, university. *Graduate housing:* Room and/or apartments available on a first-come, first-served basis to single students; on-campus housing not available to married students.

GRADUATE UNITS

Alliant School of Management *Program availability:* Part-time, evening/weekend. Offers management (MA, MBA). Electronic applications accepted.

Business and Management Division *Program availability:* Part-time, evening/weekend. Offers business administration (MBA). Electronic applications accepted.

California School of Forensic Studies Offers clinical forensic psychology (Psy D); forensic studies (Psy D).

California School of Professional Psychology *Program availability:* Part-time. Offers clinical psychology (PhD, Psy D); marital and family therapy (MA, Psy D); professional psychology (MA, MS, PhD, Psy D).

Organizational Psychology Division *Program availability:* Part-time, evening/weekend. Offers clinical/industrial organizational psychology (PhD); consulting psychology (PhD); industrial/organizational psychology (MA, MS, PhD); leadership (PhD). Electronic applications accepted.

Shirley M. Hufstedler School of Education *Program availability:* Part-time, evening/weekend, online learning. Offers education (MA, Ed D, Psy D, Certificate, Credential); educational administration (MA); educational leadership and management (K-12) (Ed D); educational psychology (Psy D); higher education (Ed D, Certificate); preliminary administrative services (Credential); preliminary single subject (Credential); professional clear multiple subject (Credential); professional clear single subject (Credential); pupil personnel services (Credential); school neuropsychology

(Certificate); school psychology (MA); school-based mental health (Certificate); teacher education (MA); teaching English to speakers of other languages (MA, Ed D, Certificate). Electronic applications accepted.

ALLIANT INTERNATIONAL UNIVERSITY–SAN FRANCISCO, San Francisco, CA 94133

General Information Independent, coed, graduate-only institution. *Graduate housing:* On-campus housing not available.

GRADUATE UNITS

California School of Forensic Studies Offers applied criminology (MS); clinical forensic psychology (PhD, Psy D); victimology (MS).

California School of Professional Psychology Offers clinical counseling (MA); clinical psychology (PhD, Psy D, Certificate); professional psychology (MA, Post-Doctoral MS, PhD, Psy D, Certificate); psychopharmacology (Post-Doctoral MS). Electronic applications accepted.

Organizational Psychology Division *Program availability:* Part-time, evening/weekend. Offers organizational psychology (MA, PhD). Electronic applications accepted.

San Francisco Law School *Program availability:* Part-time, evening/weekend. Offers law (JD). Electronic applications accepted.

Shirley M. Hufstedler School of Education *Program availability:* Part-time, evening/weekend, online learning. Offers auditory oral education (Certificate); CLAD (Certificate); community college administration (Ed D); education (MA, Ed D, Psy D, Certificate, Credential); education specialist: mild/moderate disabilities (Credential); educational administration (MA); educational leadership and management (K-12) (Ed D); educational psychology (Psy D); higher education (Ed D); preliminary administrative services (Credential); preliminary multiple subject (Credential); preliminary single subject (Credential); professional clear multiple subject (Credential); professional clear single subject (Credential); pupil personnel services (Credential); school psychology (MA); special education (MA); teaching (MA); TESOL (Certificate). Electronic applications accepted.

ALVERNIA UNIVERSITY, Reading, PA 19607-1799

General Information Independent-religious, coed, comprehensive institution. *Graduate housing:* On-campus housing not available.

GRADUATE UNITS

School of Graduate Studies *Program availability:* Part-time, evening/weekend. Offers adult gerontology nurse practitioner (DNP); business (MBA); community counseling (MA); family nurse practitioner (DNP); leadership (PhD); liberal studies (MALS); nursing education (MSN); nursing leadership (Graduate Certificate); nursing leadership and healthcare administration (MSN); occupational therapy (MSOT); urban education (M Ed). Electronic applications accepted.

ALVERNO COLLEGE, Milwaukee, WI 53234-3922

General Information Independent-religious, Undergraduate: women only; graduate: coed, comprehensive institution. *Enrollment:* 2,017 graduate, professional, and undergraduate students; 373 full-time matriculated graduate/professional students (341 women), 231 part-time matriculated graduate/professional students (209 women). *Enrollment by degree level:* 604 master's. *Graduate faculty:* 20 full-time (18 women), 41 part-time/adjunct (30 women). Tuition and fees vary according to program. *Graduate housing:* On-campus housing not available. *Student services:* Campus employment opportunities, campus safety program, career counseling, child daycare facilities, exercise/wellness program, free psychological counseling, low-cost health insurance, multicultural affairs office, services for students with disabilities. *Library facilities:* Alverno College Library. *Collection:* Books: 69,144 (physical), 146,724 (digital/electronic); Serial titles: 2,509 (physical), 74,275 (digital/electronic); Databases: 75.

Computer facilities: 735 computers available on campus for general student use. A campuswide network can be accessed from student residence rooms and from off campus. Online class registration is available.
Website: http://www.alverno.edu/

General Application Contact: Janet Stikel, Associate Director of Adult and Graduate Admissions, 414-382-6112, Fax: 414-382-6354, E-mail: janet.stikel@alverno.edu.

GRADUATE UNITS

JoAnn McGrath School of Nursing Students: 94 full-time (88 women), 81 part-time (75 women); includes 38 minority (16 Black or African American, non-Hispanic/Latino; 10 Asian, non-Hispanic/Latino; 7 Hispanic/Latino; 5 Two or more races, non-Hispanic/Latino; 1 international. Average age 36. 67 applicants, 100% accepted, 38 enrolled. *Faculty:* 6 full-time (all women), 8 part-time/adjunct (6 women). Expenses: Contact institution. *Financial support:* In 2016–17, 2 students received support. Federal Work-Study and scholarships/grants available. Support available to part-time students. Financial award applicants required to submit FAFSA. In 2016, 47 master's awarded. *Program availability:* Part-time, evening/weekend. Offers clinical nurse specialist (MSN); family nurse practitioner (MSN); mental health nurse practitioner (MSN); nursing practice (DNP). *Application deadline:* For fall admission, 7/15 priority date for domestic and international students; for spring admission, 12/15 priority date for domestic and international students. Applications are processed on a rolling basis. *Application fee:* $0. Electronic applications accepted. *Application Contact:* Karin Wasiullah, Associate Dean, Master of Science in Nursing, 414-382-6275, Fax: 414-382-6354, E-mail: karin.wasiullah@alverno.edu. *Interim Dean,* Margaret Rauschenberger, 414-382-6276, Fax: 414-382-6354, E-mail: margaret.rauschenberger@alverno.edu.

School of Arts and Sciences Students: 78 full-time (76 women), 12 part-time (all women); includes 37 minority (24 Black or African American, non-Hispanic/Latino; 1 Asian, non-Hispanic/Latino; 11 Hispanic/Latino; 1 Two or more races, non-Hispanic/Latino; 2 international. Average age 34. 27 applicants, 93% accepted, 19 enrolled. *Faculty:* 6 full-time (all women), 7 part-time/adjunct (all women). Expenses: Contact institution. *Financial support:* In 2016–17, 2 students received support. Federal Work-Study and scholarships/grants available. Support available to part-time students. Financial award applicants required to submit FAFSA. In 2016, 19 master's awarded. *Program availability:* Part-time, evening/weekend. Offers community-based research and consultation (MSCP); professional counselor (MSCP). *Application deadline:* For fall admission, 7/15 priority date for domestic and international students; for spring admission, 12/15 priority date for domestic and international students. Applications are processed on a rolling basis. *Application fee:* $0. Electronic applications accepted. *Application Contact:* Katie Kipp, Graduate Admissions Counselor, 414-382-6045, Fax: 414-382-6354, E-mail: katie.kipp@alverno.edu. *Associate Dean, Master of Science in Community Psychology,* Dr. Kimberly Skerven, 414-382-6461, Fax: 414-382-6354, E-mail: kimberly.skerven@alverno.edu.

School of Business Students: 71 full-time (59 women); includes 28 minority (11 Black or African American, non-Hispanic/Latino; 1 American Indian or Alaska Native, non-

Hispanic/Latino; 5 Asian, non-Hispanic/Latino; 8 Hispanic/Latino; 3 Two or more races, non-Hispanic/Latino). Average age 34. 33 applicants, 100% accepted, 29 enrolled. *Faculty:* 4 full-time (3 women), 3 part-time/adjunct (0 women). Expenses: Contact institution. *Financial support:* Federal Work-Study and scholarships/grants available. Support available to part-time students. Financial award applicants required to submit FAFSA. In 2016, 21 master's awarded. *Program availability:* Evening/weekend. Offers business (MBA). *Application deadline:* For fall admission, 7/15 priority date for domestic and international students; for spring admission, 12/15 priority date for domestic and international students. Applications are processed on a rolling basis. *Application fee:* $0. Electronic applications accepted. *Application Contact:* Janet Stikel, Associate Director of Adult and Graduate Admissions, 414-382-6112, Fax: 414-382-6354, E-mail: janet.stikel@alverno.edu. *Dean, School of Business,* Eileen Sherman, 414-382-6503, E-mail: eileen.sherman@alverno.edu.

School of Education Students: 58 full-time (57 women), 62 part-time (54 women); includes 32 minority (22 Black or African American, non-Hispanic/Latino; 2 Asian, non-Hispanic/Latino; 8 Hispanic/Latino), 1 international. Average age 39. 77 applicants, 99% accepted, 61 enrolled. *Faculty:* 4 full-time (3 women), 23 part-time/adjunct (17 women). Expenses: Contact institution. *Financial support:* In 2016–17, 17 students received support. Federal Work-Study and scholarships/grants available. Support available to part-time students. Financial award applicants required to submit FAFSA. In 2016, 85 master's awarded. *Program availability:* Part-time, evening/weekend. Offers adaptive education (MA); administrative leadership (MA); adult education and organizational development (MA); adult educational and instructional design (MA); adult educational and instructional technology (MA); global connections in the humanities (MA); instructional leadership (MA); instructional technology for K-12 settings (MA); professional development (MA); reading education (MA); reading education with adaptive education (MA); science education (MA); special education (MA); teaching in alternative schools (MA). *Application deadline:* For fall admission, 7/15 priority date for domestic and international students; for spring admission, 12/15 priority date for domestic and international students. Applications are processed on a rolling basis. *Application fee:* $0. Electronic applications accepted. *Application Contact:* Katie Kipp, Graduate Admissions Counselor, 414-382-6045, Fax: 414-382-6354, E-mail: katie.kipp@alverno.edu. *Associate Dean, Graduate Program,* Dr. Desiree Pointer Mace, 414-382-6345, Fax: 414-382-6332, E-mail: desiree.pointer-mace@alverno.edu.

AMBERTON UNIVERSITY, Garland, TX 75041-5595

General Information Independent-religious, coed, upper-level institution. *Graduate housing:* On-campus housing not available.

GRADUATE UNITS

Graduate School *Program availability:* Part-time, evening/weekend. Offers counseling (MA); family studies (MS); general business (MBA); human relations and business (MS); human resources training and development (MS); management (MBA); managerial science (MS); professional development (MA); project management (MBA); strategic leadership (MBA).

AMBROSE UNIVERSITY, Calgary, AB T3H 0L5, Canada

General Information Independent-religious, coed, comprehensive institution. *Enrollment:* 920 graduate, professional, and undergraduate students; 55 full-time matriculated graduate/professional students (18 women), 128 part-time matriculated graduate/professional students (64 women). *Enrollment by degree level:* 135 master's, 48 other advanced degrees. *Graduate faculty:* 7 full-time (0 women), 24 part-time/adjunct (2 women). *Tuition:* Full-time $11,850 Canadian dollars; part-time $395 Canadian dollars per credit hour. *Required fees:* $810 Canadian dollars; $27 Canadian dollars per credit hour. $50 Canadian dollars per semester. Tuition and fees vary according to course load and program. *Graduate housing:* Room and/or apartments available on a first-come, first-served basis to single students; on-campus housing not available to married students. Housing application deadline: 8/20. *Student services:* Campus employment opportunities, career counseling, international student services, services for students with disabilities, writing training. *Library facilities:* Archibald Foundation Library. *Collection:* Books: 125,000 (physical), 150,000 (digital/electronic); Serial titles: 185,000 (physical), 65,704 (digital/electronic); Databases: 42. Weekly public service hours: 81; students can reserve study rooms.

Computer facilities: 20 computers available on campus for general student use. A campuswide network can be accessed from student residence rooms. Online class registration is available.
Website: http://www.ambrose.edu/

General Application Contact: Kalie Eeles, Enrollment Advisor, 403-410-2954, Fax: 403-571-2556, E-mail: enrolment@ambrose.edu.

GRADUATE UNITS

Ambrose Seminary 76 applicants, 74% accepted, 35 enrolled. *Faculty:* 14 full-time (3 women), 4 part-time/adjunct (1 woman). Expenses: Contact institution. *Financial support:* Career-related internships or fieldwork and scholarships/grants available. Support available to part-time students. Financial award application deadline: 3/30. In 2016, 21 master's, 1 other advanced degree awarded. *Program availability:* Part-time, blended/hybrid learning. Offers Biblical/theological studies (MA); Christian studies (MCS, Diploma); intercultural ministries (M Div, MA); leadership (Certificate); leadership and ministry (MA); pastoral ministry (M Div). *Application deadline:* For fall admission, 8/1 for domestic students, 4/15 for international students; for winter admission, 12/1 for domestic students, 11/15 for international students. Applications are processed on a rolling basis. *Application fee:* $70 ($100 for international students). Electronic applications accepted. *Application Contact:* Andreas Striefler, Enrollment Advisor, 403-410-2970, Fax: 403-571-2556, E-mail: enrolment@ambrose.edu. *Dean of Theology,* Dr. Jo-Ann Badley, 403-410-2000 Ext. 3994, Fax: 403-571-2556, E-mail: jbadley@ambrose.edu.

AMERICAN ACADEMY OF ACUPUNCTURE AND ORIENTAL MEDICINE, Roseville, MN 55113

General Information Proprietary, coed, graduate-only institution.

GRADUATE UNITS

Graduate Programs Offers acupuncture and Oriental medicine (MAOM, DAOM).

AMERICAN BAPTIST SEMINARY OF THE WEST, Berkeley, CA 94704-3029

General Information Independent-religious, coed, graduate-only institution. *Graduate housing:* Rooms and/or apartments available on a first-come, first-served basis to single and married students. Housing application deadline: 5/1.

GRADUATE UNITS

Graduate and Professional Programs *Program availability:* Part-time, evening/weekend, online learning. Offers community leadership (MA); theology (M Div, MA). MA program in theology offered jointly with Graduate Theological Union. Electronic applications accepted.

AMERICAN BUSINESS & TECHNOLOGY UNIVERSITY, Saint Joseph, MO 64506

General Information Proprietary, coed, comprehensive institution.

GRADUATE UNITS

Programs in Business Administration *Program availability:* Online learning. Offers business administration (MBA); financial management (MBA); global business management (MBA); information systems management (MBA); marketing and social media (MBA); project and operations management (MBA); public accounting (MBA).

AMERICAN COLLEGE OF ACUPUNCTURE AND ORIENTAL MEDICINE, Houston, TX 77063

General Information Proprietary, coed, graduate-only institution. *Research affiliation:* Montrose Clinic (HIV/AIDS research and treatment), Rice University Wellness Center (student and staff care), Baylor College of Medicine (acupuncture for osteoarthritis of the knee), Memorial Herman Healthcare System, Tianjing Hospital, China (traditional Chinese medicine).

GRADUATE UNITS

Graduate Studies *Program availability:* Part-time.

AMERICAN COLLEGE OF EDUCATION, Indianapolis, IN 46204

General Information Proprietary, coed, graduate-only institution.

GRADUATE UNITS

Graduate Programs Offers curriculum and instruction (M Ed); educational leadership (M Ed); educational technology (M Ed).

THE AMERICAN COLLEGE OF FINANCIAL SERVICES, Bryn Mawr, PA 19010-2105

General Information Independent, coed, graduate-only institution. *Graduate housing:* On-campus housing not available.

GRADUATE UNITS

Graduate Programs *Program availability:* Part-time, evening/weekend, online learning. Offers financial services (MSFS); leadership (MSM). Electronic applications accepted.

AMERICAN COLLEGE OF HEALTHCARE SCIENCES, Portland, OR 97239-3719

General Information Independent, coed. *Tuition:* Full-time $8550; part-time $475 per semester hour. *Graduate housing:* On-campus housing not available. *Student services:* Campus safety program, career counseling, international student services, services for students with disabilities, writing training.
Website: http://www.achs.edu/

General Application Contact: Tracey Abell, Chief Operating Officer, 800-487-8839, Fax: 503-244-0727, E-mail: admissions@achs.edu.

GRADUATE UNITS

Graduate Programs Expenses: Contact institution. *Program availability:* Part-time, evening/weekend, online learning. Offers anatomy and physiology (Graduate Certificate); aromatherapy (MS, Graduate Certificate); botanical safety (Graduate Certificate); complementary alternative medicine (MS, Graduate Certificate); health and wellness (MS); herbal medicine (MS, Graduate Certificate); holistic nutrition (MS, Graduate Certificate); wellness coaching (Graduate Certificate). *Application deadline:* For fall admission, 7/15 for domestic and international students; for spring admission, 11/15 for domestic and international students. *Application fee:* $0. *Application Contact:* Tracey Abell, Chief Operating Officer, 800-487-8839, Fax: 503-244-0727, E-mail: admissions@achs.edu.

AMERICAN COLLEGE OF THESSALONIKI, 55535 Pylaia, Greece

General Information Independent, coed, comprehensive institution.

GRADUATE UNITS

Department of Business Administration *Program availability:* Part-time, evening/weekend. Offers banking and finance (MBA); entrepreneurship (MBA, Certificate); finance (Certificate); management (MBA, Certificate); marketing (MBA, Certificate). Electronic applications accepted.

AMERICAN CONSERVATORY THEATER, San Francisco, CA 94108-5800

General Information Independent, coed, graduate-only institution. *Graduate housing:* On-campus housing not available.

GRADUATE UNITS

Program in Acting Offers acting (MFA, Certificate).

AMERICAN FILM INSTITUTE CONSERVATORY, Los Angeles, CA 90027-1657

General Information Independent, coed, graduate-only institution. *Graduate housing:* On-campus housing not available.

GRADUATE UNITS

Graduate Program Offers cinematography (MFA); directing (MFA); editing (MFA); producing (MFA); production design (MFA); screenwriting (MFA). Electronic applications accepted.

AMERICAN GRADUATE SCHOOL IN PARIS, F-75006 Paris, France

General Information Independent, coed, graduate-only institution.

GRADUATE UNITS

Program in International Relations and Diplomacy Offers international relations and diplomacy (MA, PhD).

AMERICAN GRADUATE UNIVERSITY, Covina, CA 91724

General Information Proprietary, coed, graduate-only institution. *Enrollment by degree level:* 922 master's, 38 other advanced degrees. *Graduate faculty:* 15 part-time/adjunct (3 women). *Graduate housing:* On-campus housing not available. *Library facilities:* American Graduate University Library. *Research affiliation:* Library and Information Resources Network.

Computer facilities: Online class registration is available. Website: http://www.agu.edu/

General Application Contact: Debbie McDonald, Registrar, 626-966-4576 Ext. 1001, Fax: 626-915-1709, E-mail: debbiemcdonald@agu.edu.

GRADUATE UNITS

Program in Acquisition Management Expenses: Contact institution. *Program availability:* Part-time, online learning. Offers acquisition management (MAM, Certificate). *Application deadline:* Applications are processed on a rolling basis. *Application fee:* $50. Electronic applications accepted. *Application Contact:* Laurie Mejia, Director of Admissions, 626-966-4576 Ext. 1007, Fax: 626-915-1709, E-mail: lauriemejia@agu.edu. *President*, Paul McDonald, 626-966-4576 Ext. 1006, E-mail: paulmcdonald@agu.edu.

Program in Business Administration Expenses: Contact institution. *Program availability:* Part-time, online learning. Offers acquisition and contracting (MBA); supply chain management (MBA). *Application deadline:* Applications are processed on a rolling basis. *Application fee:* $50. Electronic applications accepted. *Application Contact:* Laurie Mejia, Director of Admissions, 626-966-4576 Ext. 1007, Fax: 626-915-1709, E-mail: lauriemejia@agu.edu. *President*, Paul McDonald, 626-966-4576 Ext. 1006, E-mail: paulmcdonald@agu.edu.

Program in Contract Management Expenses: Contact institution. *Program availability:* Part-time, online learning. Offers contract management (MCM, Certificate). *Application deadline:* Applications are processed on a rolling basis. *Application fee:* $50. Electronic applications accepted. *Application Contact:* Laurie Mejia, Director of Admissions, 626-966-4576 Ext. 1007, Fax: 626-915-1709, E-mail: lauriemejia@agu.edu. *President*, Paul McDonald, 626-966-4576 Ext. 1006, E-mail: paulmcdonald@agu.edu.

Program in Supply Chain Management Expenses: Contact institution. *Program availability:* Part-time, online learning. Offers supply chain management (MSCM, Certificate). *Application fee:* $50. *Application Contact:* Laurie Mejia, Director of Admissions, 626-966-4576 Ext. 1007, Fax: 626-915-1709, E-mail: lauriemejia@agu.edu. *President*, Paul McDonald, 626-966-4576 Ext. 1006, Fax: 626-915-1709, E-mail: paulmcdonald@agu.edu.

AMERICAN INTERCONTINENTAL UNIVERSITY ATLANTA, Atlanta, GA 30328

General Information Proprietary, coed, comprehensive institution. *Graduate housing:* On-campus housing not available.

GRADUATE UNITS

Program in Global Technology Management *Program availability:* Part-time, evening/weekend, online learning. Offers global technology management (MBA). Electronic applications accepted.

Program in Information Technology *Program availability:* Part-time, evening/weekend. Offers information technology (MIT). Electronic applications accepted.

AMERICAN INTERCONTINENTAL UNIVERSITY HOUSTON, Houston, TX 77042

General Information Proprietary, coed, comprehensive institution.

GRADUATE UNITS

School of Business Offers management (MBA).

AMERICAN INTERCONTINENTAL UNIVERSITY ONLINE, Schaumburg, IL 60173

General Information Proprietary, coed, comprehensive institution.

GRADUATE UNITS

Program in Business Administration *Program availability:* Evening/weekend, online learning. Offers accounting and finance (MBA); finance (MBA); healthcare management (MBA); human resource management (MBA); international business (MBA); management (MBA); marketing (MBA); operations management (MBA); organizational psychology and development (MBA); project management (MBA). Electronic applications accepted.

Program in Education *Program availability:* Evening/weekend, online learning. Offers curriculum and instruction (M Ed); educational assessment and evaluation (M Ed); instructional technology (M Ed); leadership of educational organizations (M Ed). Electronic applications accepted.

Program in Information Technology *Program availability:* Evening/weekend, online learning. Offers Internet security (MIT); IT project management (MIT). Electronic applications accepted.

AMERICAN INTERNATIONAL COLLEGE, Springfield, MA 01109-3189

General Information Independent, coed, comprehensive institution. *Enrollment:* 3,387 graduate, professional, and undergraduate students; 1,753 full-time matriculated graduate/professional students (1,374 women), 137 part-time matriculated graduate/professional students (98 women). *Enrollment by degree level:* 1,447 master's, 202 doctoral, 241 other advanced degrees. *Graduate faculty:* 15 full-time (13 women), 111 part-time/adjunct (67 women). *Tuition:* Full-time $7902; part-time $750 per semester hour. *Required fees:* $60; $60 per semester hour. $30 per semester. One-time fee: $100. Tuition and fees vary according to course load, degree level, campus/location and program. *Graduate housing:* Room and/or apartments available on a first-come, first-served basis to single students; on-campus housing not available to married students. Typical cost: $6730 per year ($13,160 including board). Room and board charges vary according to board plan and housing facility selected. Housing application deadline: 8/15. *Student services:* Campus employment opportunities, campus safety program, career counseling, exercise/wellness program, free psychological counseling, international student services, low-cost health insurance, multicultural affairs office, services for students with disabilities, writing training. *Library facilities:* James J. Shea Sr. Library. *Collection:* Books: 56,511 (physical), 179,160 (digital/electronic); Serial titles: 183 (physical), 962 (digital/electronic); Databases: 64. Weekly public service hours: 100; students can reserve study rooms.

Computer facilities: Computer purchase and lease plans are available. 230 computers available on campus for general student use. A campuswide network can be accessed from student residence rooms and from off campus. Online class registration is available. Website: http://www.aic.edu/

General Application Contact: Kerry Barnes, Director of Graduate Admissions, 413-205-3703, Fax: 413-205-3051, E-mail: kerry.barnes@aic.edu.

GRADUATE UNITS

Low Residency Programs Expenses: Contact institution. Offers counseling psychology (MA); educational leadership and supervision (Ed D); individual and institutional development (Ed D); professional counseling and supervision (Ed D); psychology (Ed D); teaching and learning (Ed D). *Application Contact:* Kerry Barnes, Director of Graduate Admissions, 413-205-3703, Fax: 413-205-3051, E-mail: kerry.barnes@aic.edu.

School of Business, Arts and Sciences Expenses: Contact institution. *Financial support:* Career-related internships or fieldwork available. Financial award application deadline: 4/1; financial award applicants required to submit FAFSA. *Program availability:* Part-time, evening/weekend. Offers accounting and taxation (MS); business administration (MBA); clinical psychology (MA); educational psychology (Ed D); forensic psychology (MS); general psychology (MA, CAGS); management (CAGS); resort and casino management (MBA, CAGS). *Application deadline:* For fall admission, 4/1 for domestic and international students; for spring admission, 12/1 for domestic and international students. Applications are processed on a rolling basis. *Application Contact:* Barbara Z. Benoit, Director of Graduate Admissions, 413-205-3700, Fax: 413-205-3051, E-mail: barbara.benoit@aic.edu. *Dean*, Dr. Vickie Hess, 413-205-3216, Fax: 413-205-3943, E-mail: vickie.hess@aic.edu.

School of Education Students: 1,194 full-time (970 women), 118 part-time (83 women); includes 108 minority (15 Black or African American, non-Hispanic/Latino; 4 American Indian or Alaska Native, non-Hispanic/Latino; 12 Asian, non-Hispanic/Latino; 55 Hispanic/Latino; 2 Native Hawaiian or other Pacific Islander, non-Hispanic/Latino; 20 Two or more races, non-Hispanic/Latino). Average age 34. 517 applicants, 417 enrolled. *Faculty:* 1 (woman) full-time, 90 part-time/adjunct (63 women). Expenses: Contact institution. *Financial support:* Applicants required to submit FAFSA. In 2016, 879 master's, 194 CAGSs awarded. *Program availability:* Evening/weekend. Offers early childhood education (M Ed, CAGS); elementary education (M Ed, CAGS); middle education/secondary education (M Ed, CAGS); moderate disabilities (M Ed, CAGS); reading specialist (M Ed, CAGS); school adjustment counseling (MAEP, CAGS); school guidance counseling (MAEP, CAGS); school leadership (M Ed, CAGS). *Application deadline:* Applications are processed on a rolling basis. *Application fee:* $50. Electronic applications accepted. *Application Contact:* Kerry Barnes, Dean of Graduate Admissions, 413-205-3703, Fax: 413-205-3051, E-mail: kerry.barnes@aic.edu. *Dean*, Sylvia Mason, 413-205-1743, Fax: 413-205-3943, E-mail: sylvia.mason@aic.edu.

School of Health Sciences Students: 160 full-time (136 women), 4 part-time (all women); includes 57 minority (24 Black or African American, non-Hispanic/Latino; 13 Asian, non-Hispanic/Latino; 14 Hispanic/Latino; 6 Two or more races, non-Hispanic/Latino), 1 international. Average age 30. 673 applicants, 41% accepted, 100 enrolled. *Faculty:* 25 full-time (22 women), 14 part-time/adjunct (13 women). Expenses: Contact institution. *Financial support:* Application deadline: 4/1; applicants required to submit FAFSA. In 2016, 41 master's, 35 doctorates awarded. *Program availability:* Part-time, 100% online. Offers exercise science (MS); family nurse practitioner (MSN); nursing administrator (MSN); nursing educator (MSN); occupational therapy (MSOT, OTD); physical therapy (DPT). *Application deadline:* For fall admission, 12/1 priority date for domestic and international students. Applications are processed on a rolling basis. *Application fee:* $50. Electronic applications accepted. *Application Contact:* Kerry Barnes, Director of Graduate Admissions, 413-205-3703, Fax: 413-205-3051, E-mail: kerry.barnes@aic.edu. *Dean*, Dr. Cesarina Thompson, 413-205-3056, Fax: 413-654-1430, E-mail: cesarina.thompson@aic.edu.

AMERICAN JEWISH UNIVERSITY, Bel Air, CA 90077-1599

General Information Independent-religious, coed, comprehensive institution. *Graduate housing:* Rooms and/or apartments available on a first-come, first-served basis to single and married students. Housing application deadline: 6/1.

GRADUATE UNITS

Graduate School of Education Offers education (MA Ed); education for working professionals (MA Ed).

Graduate School of Nonprofit Management *Program availability:* Part-time, evening/weekend. Offers general nonprofit administration (MBA); Jewish communal studies (MAJCS); Jewish nonprofit administration (MBA); nonprofit management (MAJCS, MBA).

Ziegler School of Rabbinic Studies Offers rabbinic studies (MARS).

AMERICAN MUSEUM OF NATURAL HISTORY–RICHARD GILDER GRADUATE SCHOOL, New York, NY 10024

General Information Independent, coed, graduate-only institution.

GRADUATE UNITS

Program in Comparative Biology Offers comparative biology (PhD).

AMERICAN NATIONAL UNIVERSITY, Salem, VA 24153

General Information Proprietary, coed, comprehensive institution.

GRADUATE UNITS

Program in Business Administration Offers business administration (MBA).

AMERICAN PUBLIC UNIVERSITY SYSTEM, Charles Town, WV 25414

General Information Proprietary, coed, comprehensive institution. CGS member. *Enrollment:* 48,623 graduate, professional, and undergraduate students; 378 full-time matriculated graduate/professional students (184 women), 8,455 part-time matriculated graduate/professional students (3,484 women). *Enrollment by degree level:* 8,512 master's, 319 other advanced degrees. *Graduate faculty:* 401 full-time (228 women), 1,678 part-time/adjunct (781 women). *Tuition:* Part-time $350 per credit hour. *Required fees:* $50 per course. *Graduate housing:* On-campus housing not available. *Student services:* Career counseling, international student services, services for students with disabilities. *Library facilities:* APUS Online Library.

Computer facilities: Online class registration is available. Website: http://www.apus.edu/

General Application Contact: Terry Grant, Vice President of Enrollment Management, 877-468-6268, Fax: 304-724-3780, E-mail: info@apus.edu.

GRADUATE UNITS

AMU/APU Graduate Programs Students: 378 full-time (184 women), 8,455 part-time (3,484 women); includes 2,972 minority (1,552 Black or African American, non-Hispanic/Latino; 52 American Indian or Alaska Native, non-Hispanic/Latino; 211 Asian, non-Hispanic/Latino; 791 Hispanic/Latino; 70 Native Hawaiian or other Pacific Islander, non-Hispanic/Latino; 296 Two or more races, non-Hispanic/Latino), 109 international. Average age 37. *Faculty:* 401 full-time (228 women), 1,678 part-time/adjunct (781 women). Expenses: Contact institution. *Financial support:* Scholarships/grants available.

Financial award applicants required to submit FAFSA. In 2016, 3,185 master's awarded. *Program availability:* Part-time, evening/weekend, online only, 100% online. Offers accounting (MBA, MS); applied business analytics (MBA, MS); criminal justice (MA); educational leadership (M Ed); emergency and disaster management (MA); entrepreneurship (MBA); environmental policy and management (MS); finance (MBA); general (MBA); government contracting and acquisition (MBA); health care administration (MBA); health information management (MS); history (MA); homeland security (MA); homeland security resource allocation (MBA); humanities (MA); information technology (MS); information technology management (MBA); intelligence studies (MA); international relations and conflict resolution (MA); legal studies (MA); management (MA); marketing (MBA); military history (MA); military studies (MA); national security studies (MA); nonprofit management (MBA); political science (MA); psychology (MA); public administration (MPA); public health (MPH); reverse logistics management (MA); security management (MA); space studies (MS); sports and health sciences (MS); sports management (MBA); teaching (M Ed); transportation and logistics management (MA). *Application deadline:* Applications are processed on a rolling basis. *Application fee:* $0. Electronic applications accepted. *Application Contact:* Terry Grant, Vice President of Enrollment Management, 877-468-6268, Fax: 304-724-3780, E-mail: info@apus.edu. *President,* Dr. Karan Powell, 877-468-6268, Fax: 304-724-3780.

AMERICAN SENTINEL UNIVERSITY, Aurora, CO 80014

General Information Proprietary, coed, comprehensive institution.

GRADUATE UNITS

Graduate Programs *Program availability:* Part-time, evening/weekend, online learning. Electronic applications accepted.

AMERICAN UNIVERSITY, Washington, DC 20016-8001

General Information Independent-religious, coed, university. CGS member. *Enrollment:* 13,347 graduate, professional, and undergraduate students; 3,112 full-time matriculated graduate/professional students (1,937 women), 2,248 part-time matriculated graduate/professional students (1,369 women). *Enrollment by degree level:* 3,588 master's, 1,657 doctoral, 115 other advanced degrees. *Graduate faculty:* 797 full-time (376 women), 701 part-time/adjunct (273 women). *Tuition:* Full-time $28,422; part-time $1579 per credit hour. *Required fees:* $690; $200 per term. Tuition and fees vary according to course load, degree level and program. *Graduate housing:* On-campus housing not available. *Student services:* Campus employment opportunities, campus safety program, career counseling, child daycare facilities, exercise/wellness program, free psychological counseling, grant writing training, international student services, multicultural affairs office, services for students with disabilities, teacher training, writing training. *Library facilities:* Bender Library plus 1 other. *Collection:* Books: 700,000 (physical), 300,000 (digital/electronic); Serial titles: 650 (physical), 125,000 (digital/electronic); Databases: 300. Study areas open 24 hours, 5–7 days a week; students can reserve study rooms.

Computer facilities: 700 computers available on campus for general student use. A campuswide network can be accessed from student residence rooms and from off campus. Online class registration, online e-support through learning management system are available.
Website: http://www.american.edu/

General Application Contact: 202-885-1000.

GRADUATE UNITS

College of Arts and Sciences Students: 528 full-time (348 women), 324 part-time (212 women); includes 165 minority (71 Black or African American, non-Hispanic/Latino; 2 American Indian or Alaska Native, non-Hispanic/Latino; 24 Asian, non-Hispanic/Latino; 46 Hispanic/Latino; 1 Native Hawaiian or other Pacific Islander, non-Hispanic/Latino; 21 Two or more races, non-Hispanic/Latino), 118 international. Average age 30. 1,624 applicants, 58% accepted, 314 enrolled. *Faculty:* 376 full-time (208 women), 233 part-time/adjunct (122 women). Expenses: Contact institution. *Financial support:* Research assistantships, teaching assistantships, institutionally sponsored loans, scholarships/grants, and unspecified assistantships available. Financial award application deadline: 2/1; financial award applicants required to submit FAFSA. In 2016, 422 master's, 36 doctorates, 22 other advanced degrees awarded. *Program availability:* Part-time, evening/weekend, 100% online. Offers addiction and addictive behavior (Certificate); anthropology (MA, PhD, Certificate); applied microeconomics (Certificate); applied statistics (Certificate); art history (MA); art management (MA); arts and sciences (MA, MAT, MFA, MS, PhD, Certificate, Graduate Certificate); audio production (Certificate); audio technology (MA); behavior, cognition, and neuroscience (PhD); biology (MA, MS); chemistry (MS); clinical psychology (PhD); creative writing (MFA); economics (MA, PhD); environmental assessment (Graduate Certificate); environmental science (MS); ethics, peace, and global affairs (MA); gender analysis in economics (Certificate); health promotion management (MS); history (MA, PhD); international arts management (Certificate); international economic relations (Certificate); international economics (MA); literature (MA); mathematics (MA); nutrition education (MS, Certificate); philosophy (MA); professional science: environmental assessment (MS); professional science: quantitative analysis (MS); psychobiology of healing (Certificate); psychology (MA); public sociology (Certificate); social research (Certificate); sociology (MA); Spanish: Latin American studies (MA); statistics (MS); studio art (MFA); teaching English as a foreign language (MA); teaching English to speakers of other languages (MA, Certificate); technology in arts management (Certificate); translation: French (Certificate); translation: Russian (Certificate); translation: Spanish (Certificate). *Application deadline:* Applications are processed on a rolling basis. *Application fee:* $55. Electronic applications accepted. *Application Contact:* Kathleen Clowery, Associate Director, Graduate Enrollment Management, 202-885-3621, Fax: 202-885-2429, E-mail: clowery@american.edu. *Dean,* Dr. Peter Starr, 202-885-2446, Fax: 202-885-2429, E-mail: pstarr@american.edu.

Critical Race, Gender, and Culture Studies Collaborative Offers Asian studies (Graduate Certificate); women's, gender, and sexuality studies (Graduate Certificate).

Kogod School of Business Students: 363 full-time (163 women), 331 part-time (175 women); includes 149 minority (56 Black or African American, non-Hispanic/Latino; 1 American Indian or Alaska Native, non-Hispanic/Latino; 33 Asian, non-Hispanic/Latino; 42 Hispanic/Latino; 17 Two or more races, non-Hispanic/Latino), 96 international. Average age 30. 888 applicants, 75% accepted, 342 enrolled. *Faculty:* 79 full-time (27 women), 68 part-time/adjunct (34 women). Expenses: Contact institution. *Financial support:* Research assistantships, teaching assistantships, institutionally sponsored loans, scholarships/grants, and unspecified assistantships available. Financial award application deadline: 2/1; financial award applicants required to submit FAFSA. In 2016, 207 master's, 29 other advanced degrees awarded. *Program availability:* Part-time, evening/weekend, 100% online. Offers accounting (MS, Certificate); analytics (MS); business (MBA, MS, Certificate); business administration (MBA, Certificate); finance (MS); forensic accounting (Certificate); marketing (MS); real estate (MS, Certificate); sustainability management (MS); taxation (MS, Certificate). *Application deadline:*

Applications are processed on a rolling basis. *Application fee:* $100. Electronic applications accepted. *Application Contact:* Jason Kennedy, Associate Director of Graduate Admissions, 202-885-1968, E-mail: jkennedy@american.edu. *Dean,* John T. Delaney, 202-885-1908, Fax: 202-885-8044.

School of Communication Students: 170 full-time (115 women), 290 part-time (194 women); includes 160 minority (98 Black or African American, non-Hispanic/Latino; 2 American Indian or Alaska Native, non-Hispanic/Latino; 13 Asian, non-Hispanic/Latino; 36 Hispanic/Latino; 11 Two or more races, non-Hispanic/Latino), 45 international. 709 applicants, 33% accepted, 190 enrolled. *Faculty:* 39 full-time (20 women). Expenses: Contact institution. *Financial support:* In 2016–17, 210 students received support, including 3 fellowships with partial tuition reimbursements available (averaging $20,000 per year), 30 research assistantships with partial tuition reimbursements available (averaging $15,000 per year), 30 teaching assistantships with partial tuition reimbursements available (averaging $15,000 per year); career-related internships or fieldwork, Federal Work-Study, institutionally sponsored loans, scholarships/grants, tuition waivers (partial), and unspecified assistantships also available. Support available to part-time students. Financial award application deadline: 2/1; financial award applicants required to submit FAFSA. In 2016, 137 master's, 2 doctorates awarded. *Program availability:* Part-time, evening/weekend, 100% online. Offers broadcast journalism (MA); communication (MA, MFA, PhD); film and electronic media (MFA); film and media arts (MA); global media (MA); international journalism (MA); investigative journalism (MA); journalism and digital storytelling (MA); media industries and institutions (PhD); media, public issues, and engagement (PhD); media, technology, and culture (PhD); political communication (MA); producing film, TV and video (MA); strategic communication (MA). *Application deadline:* For fall admission, 2/1 priority date for domestic and international students; for spring admission, 11/1 for domestic and international students. Applications are processed on a rolling basis. *Application fee:* $55. Electronic applications accepted. *Application Contact:* Christine Rials, Assistant Director for Graduate Admissions, 202-885-2040, Fax: 202-885-2019, E-mail: gradcomm@american.edu. *Dean,* Dr. Jeffrey Rutenbeck, 202-885-2058, Fax: 202-885-2099, E-mail: jeff@american.edu.

School of Education Students: 79 full-time (68 women), 91 part-time (72 women); includes 59 minority (32 Black or African American, non-Hispanic/Latino; 11 Asian, non-Hispanic/Latino; 11 Hispanic/Latino; 5 Two or more races, non-Hispanic/Latino), 7 international. Average age 28. 211 applicants, 89% accepted, 77 enrolled. *Faculty:* 14 full-time (11 women), 27 part-time/adjunct (18 women). Expenses: Contact institution. *Financial support:* Research assistantships, teaching assistantships, institutionally sponsored loans, scholarships/grants, and unspecified assistantships available. Financial award application deadline: 2/1; financial award applicants required to submit FAFSA. In 2016, 139 master's, 10 other advanced degrees awarded. *Program availability:* Part-time, evening/weekend. Offers bilingual education (MA, Certificate); education (M Ed, MA, MAT, Certificate); education policy and leadership (M Ed, Certificate); international training and education (MA); special education: learning disabilities (MA); teacher education (MAT, Certificate). *Application deadline:* Applications are processed on a rolling basis. *Application fee:* $55. Electronic applications accepted. *Application Contact:* Brittney Cosby, Graduate Programs Coordinator, 202-885-8201, E-mail: bcosby@american.edu. *Dean,* Cheryl Holcomb-McCoy, 202-885-3720, E-mail: educate@american.edu.

School of International Service Students: 575 full-time (360 women), 491 part-time (277 women); includes 287 minority (100 Black or African American, non-Hispanic/Latino; 6 American Indian or Alaska Native, non-Hispanic/Latino; 58 Asian, non-Hispanic/Latino; 92 Hispanic/Latino; 1 Native Hawaiian or other Pacific Islander, non-Hispanic/Latino; 30 Two or more races, non-Hispanic/Latino), 151 international. Average age 29. 1,504 applicants, 84% accepted, 403 enrolled. *Faculty:* 116 full-time (53 women), 57 part-time/adjunct (19 women). Expenses: Contact institution. *Financial support:* Research assistantships, teaching assistantships, institutionally sponsored loans, scholarships/grants, and unspecified assistantships available. Financial award application deadline: 1/15; financial award applicants required to submit FAFSA. In 2016, 374 master's, 3 doctorates, 1 other advanced degree awarded. *Program availability:* Part-time, evening/weekend, 100% online. Offers comparative and regional studies (Certificate); cross-cultural communication (Certificate); development management (MS); ethics, peace, and global affairs (MA); European studies (Certificate); global environmental policy (MA, Certificate); global information technology (Certificate); international affairs (MA); international arts management (Certificate); international communication (MA, Certificate); international development (MA); international economic policy (Certificate); international economic relations (Certificate); international economics (MA); international media (MA); international peace and conflict resolution (MA, Certificate); international politics (Certificate); international relations (MA, PhD); international service (MIS); peacebuilding (Certificate); social enterprise (MA); the Americas (Certificate); United States foreign policy (Certificate). *Application fee:* $55. Electronic applications accepted. *Application Contact:* Jia Jiang, Associate Director, Graduate Education Enrollment, 202-885-1689, Fax: 202-885-1109, E-mail: jiang@american.edu. *Dean,* Dr. James Goldgeier, 202-885-1603, Fax: 202-885-2494, E-mail: goldgeier@american.edu.

School of Professional and Extended Studies Students: 26 part-time (22 women); includes 1 minority (American Indian or Alaska Native, non-Hispanic/Latino), 2 international. Average age 38. 37 applicants, 100% accepted, 22 enrolled. *Faculty:* 28 full-time (12 women), 8 part-time/adjunct (4 women). Expenses: Contact institution. *Financial support:* Applicants required to submit FAFSA. *Program availability:* 100% online. Offers healthcare management (MS, Graduate Certificate); human resource analytics and management (Graduate Certificate); measurement and evaluation (MS); project monitoring and evaluation (Graduate Certificate); sports analytics and management (MS, Graduate Certificate). *Application deadline:* Applications are processed on a rolling basis. *Application fee:* $55. Electronic applications accepted. *Application Contact:* Heather Broberg, Assistant Director for Recruitment and Admission, 202-895-4953, E-mail: broberg@american.edu. *Dean,* Carola Weil, 202-885-5990, Fax: 202-895-4960, E-mail: weil@american.edu.

School of Public Affairs Students: 292 full-time (183 women), 339 part-time (208 women); includes 169 minority (92 Black or African American, non-Hispanic/Latino; 4 American Indian or Alaska Native, non-Hispanic/Latino; 36 Asian, non-Hispanic/Latino; 27 Hispanic/Latino; 1 Native Hawaiian or other Pacific Islander, non-Hispanic/Latino; 9 Two or more races, non-Hispanic/Latino), 38 international. Average age 31. 951 applicants, 79% accepted, 260 enrolled. *Faculty:* 82 full-time (37 women), 74 part-time/adjunct (18 women). Expenses: Contact institution. *Financial support:* Research assistantships, teaching assistantships, institutionally sponsored loans, and scholarships/grants available. Financial award application deadline: 2/1; financial award applicants required to submit FAFSA. In 2016, 236 master's, 11 doctorates, 6 other advanced degrees awarded. *Program availability:* Part-time, evening/weekend, 100% online. Offers justice, law and criminology (MS, PhD); leadership for organizational change (Certificate); organization development (MSOD, Certificate); political communication (MA); political science (MA, PhD); public administration (MPA, PhD, Certificate); public administration and policy (MPA, MPAP, MPP, MSOD, PhD, Certificate); public affairs (MA, MPA, MPAP, MPP, MS, MSOD, PhD, Certificate); public policy (MPP); public policy (Certificate); public policy analysis (Certificate); terrorism, homeland security and policy (MS); women, policy and political leadership (Certificate). *Application deadline:* For fall admission, 1/1 for domestic students. *Application fee:* $55. Electronic applications accepted. *Application Contact:* Jennifer Forney, Assistant Dean, Graduate Enrollment, E-mail: forney@american.edu. *Dean,* Dr. Barbara Romzek, 202-885-2940, Fax: 202-885-2353, E-mail: bromzek@american.edu.

Washington College of Law Students: 1,093 full-time (693 women), 367 part-time (217 women); includes 520 minority (126 Black or African American, non-Hispanic/Latino; 2 American Indian or Alaska Native, non-Hispanic/Latino; 121 Asian, non-Hispanic/Latino; 219 Hispanic/Latino; 2 Native Hawaiian or other Pacific Islander, non-Hispanic/Latino; 50 Two or more races, non-Hispanic/Latino), 189 international. Average age 28. 5,236 applicants, 56% accepted, 615 enrolled. *Faculty:* 78 full-time (41 women), 142 part-time/adjunct (48 women). Expenses: Contact institution. *Financial support:* Institutionally sponsored loans and scholarships/grants available. Financial award application deadline: 3/1; financial award applicants required to submit FAFSA. In 2016, 116 master's, 440 doctorates awarded. *Program availability:* Part-time, evening/weekend. Offers law (LL M, JD, SJD). *Application fee:* $70. Electronic applications accepted. *Application Contact:* Hilary Lappin, Associate Director, Graduate Admissions, 202-274-4114, Fax: 202-274-4107, E-mail: hlappin@wcl.american.edu. *Dean,* Camille A. Nelson, 202-274-4004, Fax: 202-274-4005.

THE AMERICAN UNIVERSITY IN CAIRO, 11835 New Cairo, Egypt

General Information Independent, coed, comprehensive institution. CGS member. *Enrollment:* 6,659 graduate, professional, and undergraduate students; 250 full-time matriculated graduate/professional students (143 women), 815 part-time matriculated graduate/professional students (525 women). *Enrollment by degree level:* 1,021 master's, 44 doctoral. *Graduate faculty:* 159 full-time (60 women), 26 part-time/adjunct (8 women). *Tuition:* Full-time $21,834. *Required fees:* $720. Tuition and fees vary according to course load and program. *Graduate housing:* Room and/or apartments available on a first-come, first-served basis to single students; on-campus housing not available to married students. Typical cost: $6360 per year. Room charges vary according to housing facility selected. *Student services:* Campus employment opportunities, campus safety program, career counseling, child daycare facilities, exercise/wellness program, free psychological counseling, grant writing training, international student services, low-cost health insurance, multicultural affairs office, services for students with disabilities, teacher training, writing training. *Library facilities:* American University in Cairo Library plus 1 other. *Collection:* Books: 521,994 (physical), 255,462 (digital/electronic); Databases: 134. Weekly public service hours: 80; students can reserve study rooms.

Computer facilities: 120 computers available on campus for general student use. A campuswide network can be accessed from student residence rooms and from off campus. Online class registration, learning management system, unofficial transcripts, ID creation are available.
Website: http://www.aucegypt.edu/

General Application Contact: Maha Hegazi, Director for Graduate Admissions, 20-2-2615-1462, E-mail: mahahegazi@aucegypt.edu.

GRADUATE UNITS

Graduate School of Education Students: 6 full-time (5 women), 75 part-time (64 women). Average age 33. 60 applicants, 68% accepted, 27 enrolled. *Faculty:* 8 full-time (7 women). Expenses: Contact institution. *Financial support:* Fellowships with partial tuition reimbursements, teaching assistantships, career-related internships or fieldwork, scholarships/grants, tuition waivers (partial), and unspecified assistantships available. Financial award application deadline: 3/10. In 2016, 14 master's awarded. *Program availability:* Part-time, evening/weekend. Offers educational leadership (MA); international and comparative education (MA). *Application deadline:* For fall admission, 2/1 priority date for domestic and international students; for spring admission, 10/15 priority date for domestic and international students. Applications are processed on a rolling basis. *Application fee:* $80. Electronic applications accepted. *Application Contact:* Maha Hegazi, Director for Graduate Admissions, 20-2-2615-1462, E-mail: mahahegazi@aucegypt.edu. *Dean,* Dr. Ted Purinton, 20-2-2615-1490, E-mail: tedpurinton@aucegypt.edu.

School of Business Students: 53 full-time (24 women), 80 part-time (41 women), 1 international. Average age 29. 109 applicants, 45% accepted, 35 enrolled. *Faculty:* 24 full-time (4 women), 5 part-time/adjunct (2 women). Expenses: Contact institution. *Financial support:* Fellowships with partial tuition reimbursements, scholarships/grants, tuition waivers (partial), and unspecified assistantships available. Financial award application deadline: 3/10. In 2016, 49 master's awarded. *Program availability:* Part-time, evening/weekend. Offers business administration (MBA); economics (MA); economics in international development (MA, Diploma); finance (MS). *Application deadline:* For fall admission, 2/1 priority date for domestic and international students; for spring admission, 10/15 priority date for domestic and international students. Applications are processed on a rolling basis. *Application fee:* $80. Electronic applications accepted. *Application Contact:* Maha Hegazi, Director of Graduate Admissions, 20-2-2615-1462, E-mail: mahahegazi@aucegypt.edu. *Interim Dean,* Dr. Nizar Becheikh, 20-2-2615-2120, E-mail: nbecheikh@aucegypt.edu.

School of Global Affairs and Public Policy Students: 69 full-time (40 women), 194 part-time (134 women), 33 international. Average age 29. 322 applicants, 51% accepted, 86 enrolled. *Faculty:* 27 full-time (13 women), 5 part-time/adjunct (3 women). Expenses: Contact institution. *Financial support:* Fellowships with partial tuition reimbursements, scholarships/grants, and unspecified assistantships available. Financial award application deadline: 3/10. In 2016, 112 master's awarded. *Program availability:* Part-time, evening/weekend. Offers gender and women's studies (MA); global affairs (MGA); international and comparative law (LL M); international human rights law (MA); journalism and mass communication (MA); Middle East studies (MA); migration and refugee studies (MA, Diploma); public administration (MPA); public policy (MPP); television and digital journalism (MA). *Application deadline:* For fall admission, 2/1 for domestic and international students; for spring admission, 10/15 for domestic and international students. Applications are processed on a rolling basis. *Application fee:* $80. Electronic applications accepted. *Application Contact:* Maha Hegazi, Director for Graduate Admissions, 20-2-2615-1462, E-mail: mahahegazi@aucegypt.edu. *Dean,* Dr. Nabil Fahmy, 20-2-2615-2671, E-mail: nfahmy@aucegypt.edu.

School of Humanities and Social Sciences Students: 65 full-time (47 women), 179 part-time (138 women), 32 international. Average age 30. 221 applicants, 45% accepted, 54 enrolled. *Faculty:* 51 full-time (29 women), 4 part-time/adjunct (2 women). Expenses: Contact institution. *Financial support:* Fellowships with partial tuition reimbursements, scholarships/grants, tuition waivers (partial), and unspecified

assistantships available. Financial award application deadline: 3/10. In 2016, 95 master's awarded. *Program availability:* Part-time, evening/weekend. Offers Arab and Islamic civilizations (Graduate Diploma); Arabic studies (MA); comparative literary studies (Graduate Diploma); Egyptology and Coptology (MA); English and comparative literature (MA); humanities and social sciences (Graduate Diploma); philosophy (MA); psychology (MA); sociology and anthropology (MA); teaching Arabic as a foreign language (MA); teaching English to speakers of other languages (MA). *Application deadline:* For fall admission, 2/1 priority date for domestic and international students; for spring admission, 10/15 priority date for domestic and international students. Applications are processed on a rolling basis. *Application fee:* $80. Electronic applications accepted. *Application Contact:* Maha Hegazi, Director for Graduate Admissions, 20-2-2615-1462, E-mail: mahahegazi@aucegypt.edu. *Dean,* Dr. Nathaniel Bowditch, 20-2-2615-1788, E-mail: nbowditch@aucegypt.edu.

School of Sciences and Engineering Students: 50 full-time (21 women), 262 part-time (128 women), 13 international. Average age 28. 193 applicants, 46% accepted, 55 enrolled. *Faculty:* 43 full-time (4 women), 12 part-time/adjunct (1 woman). Expenses: Contact institution. *Financial support:* Fellowships with partial tuition reimbursements, scholarships/grants, and unspecified assistantships available. Financial award application deadline: 3/10. In 2016, 71 master's, 5 doctorates awarded. *Program availability:* Part-time, evening/weekend. Offers biotechnology (MS); chemistry (MS); computer science (MS); computing (M Comp); construction engineering (M Eng, MS); electronics and communications engineering (M Eng); environmental engineering (MS); environmental system design (M Eng); mechanical engineering (M Eng, MS); nanotechnology (MS); physics (MS); robotics, control and smart systems (MS); sciences and engineering (PhD); sustainable development (MS, Graduate Diploma). *Application deadline:* For fall admission, 2/1 priority date for domestic and international students; for spring admission, 10/15 priority date for domestic and international students. Applications are processed on a rolling basis. *Application fee:* $80. Electronic applications accepted. *Application Contact:* Maha Hegazi, Director for Graduate Admissions, 20-2-2615-1462, E-mail: mahahegazi@aucegypt.edu. *Dean,* Dr. Hassan El Fawal, 20-2-2615-2926, E-mail: hassan.elfawal@aucegypt.edu.

THE AMERICAN UNIVERSITY IN DUBAI, Dubai, United Arab Emirates

General Information Proprietary, coed, comprehensive institution. *Graduate housing:* Room and/or apartments available on a first-come, first-served basis to single students; on-campus housing not available to married students. Housing application deadline: 7/31.

GRADUATE UNITS

Graduate Programs *Program availability:* Part-time, evening/weekend. Offers construction management (MS); education (M Ed); finance (MBA); generalist (MBA); marketing (MBA). Electronic applications accepted.

AMERICAN UNIVERSITY OF ARMENIA, Yerevan 3750198, Armenia

General Information Independent, coed, graduate-only institution. *Research affiliation:* Samsung (cryptography), Volkswagen Foundation (cryptography), Mentor Graphics (data compression algorithms), IBM (big data and data analytics), Johns Hopkins University Bloomberg School of Public Health (public health), Institut de Medecine Sociale et Preventive, Universite de Geneve (Geneva, Switzerland) (tobacco control/health education).

GRADUATE UNITS

Graduate Programs *Program availability:* Part-time, evening/weekend. Offers business administration (MBA); computer and information science (MS); economics (MS); industrial engineering and systems management (ME); law (LL M); political science and international affairs (MPSIA); public health (MPH); teaching English as a foreign language (MA).

AMERICAN UNIVERSITY OF BEIRUT, 107 2020 Beirut, Lebanon

General Information Independent, coed, university. CGS member. *Enrollment:* 8,851 graduate, professional, and undergraduate students; 1,115 full-time matriculated graduate/professional students (630 women), 706 part-time matriculated graduate/professional students (486 women). *Enrollment by degree level:* 1,267 master's, 142 doctoral, 412 other advanced degrees. *Graduate faculty:* 569 full-time (183 women), 24 part-time/adjunct (5 women). *Tuition:* Full-time $16,740; part-time $930 per credit. *Required fees:* $716. Tuition and fees vary according to course load and program. *Graduate housing:* Room and/or apartments available on a first-come, first-served basis to single students; on-campus housing not available to married students. Typical cost: $2814 per year. Housing application deadline: 6/30. *Student services:* Campus employment opportunities, campus safety program, career counseling, exercise/wellness program, free psychological counseling, grant writing training, international student services, low-cost health insurance, services for students with disabilities, teacher training, writing training. *Library facilities:* Naami Jafet Memorial Library plus 3 others. *Collection:* Books: 425,000 (physical), 1.2 million (digital/electronic); Serial titles: 5,000 (physical), 191,998 (digital/electronic); Databases: 722. Weekly public service hours: 109. *Research affiliation:* LORE Foundation (education), Medical Research Council (MRC) (health management and policy), Supreme Council of Health (SCH), State of Qatar (nutrition and food sciences), U.S. Department of State (gender equality), National Science Foundation (physics), Instituto Affari Internazionali (agriculture).

Computer facilities: 1,476 computers available on campus for general student use. A campuswide network can be accessed from student residence rooms and from off campus. Online class registration is available.
Website: http://www.aub.edu.lb/

General Application Contact: Dr. Salim Kanaan, Director, Admissions Office, 961-1350000 Ext. 2594, Fax: 961-1750775, E-mail: sk00@aub.edu.lb.

GRADUATE UNITS

Graduate Programs Students: 1,115 full-time (630 women), 706 part-time (486 women). Average age 27. 2,045 applicants, 46% accepted, 505 enrolled. *Faculty:* 569 full-time (183 women), 24 part-time/adjunct (5 women). Expenses: Contact institution. *Financial support:* In 2016–17, 384 students received support, including 1,204 research assistantships (averaging $5,458 per year); career-related internships or fieldwork, institutionally sponsored loans, scholarships/grants, health care benefits, and unspecified assistantships also available. Financial award application deadline: 12/20; financial award applicants required to submit CSS PROFILE. In 2016, 413 master's, 103 doctorates awarded. *Program availability:* Part-time, evening/weekend. *Application deadline:* For fall admission, 2/10 priority date for domestic and international students; for spring admission, 11/1 for domestic and international students. *Application fee:* $50. Electronic applications accepted. *Application Contact:* Dr. Salim Kanaan, Director,

Admissions Office, 961-1350000 Ext. 2594, Fax: 961-1750775, E-mail: sk00@aub.edu.lb. *Graduate Council Chairperson,* Dr. Rabih Talhouk, 961-1374374 Ext. 4193, E-mail: rtalhouk@aub.edu.lb.

Faculty of Agricultural and Food Sciences Students: 11 full-time (10 women), 63 part-time (46 women); includes 1 minority (Asian, non-Hispanic/Latino). Average age 26. 108 applicants, 76% accepted, 28 enrolled. *Faculty:* 15 full-time (2 women), 1 part-time/adjunct (0 women). Expenses: Contact institution. *Financial support:* In 2016–17, 5 research assistantships with full and partial tuition reimbursements (averaging $1,800 per year), 58 teaching assistantships with full and partial tuition reimbursements (averaging $1,400 per year) were awarded; scholarships/grants, health care benefits, and unspecified assistantships also available. Financial award application deadline: 2/2. In 2016, 23 master's awarded. *Program availability:* Part-time. Offers agricultural economics (MS); animal science (MS); ecosystem management (MSES); food security (MS); food technology (MS); irrigation (MS); nutrition (MS); plant protection (MS); plant science (MS); poultry science (MS); rural community development (MS). *Application deadline:* For fall admission, 2/10 for domestic and international students; for spring admission, 11/2 for domestic and international students. *Application fee:* $50. Electronic applications accepted. *Application Contact:* Dr. Rabih Talhouk, Director, Graduate Council, 961-1350000 Ext. 4386, Fax: 961-1374374, E-mail: graduate.council@aub.edu.lb. *Dean,* Prof. Nahla Chawkat Hwalla, 961-1350000 Ext. 4400, Fax: 961-1744460, E-mail: nahla@aub.edu.lb.

Faculty of Arts and Sciences Students: 240 full-time (172 women), 227 part-time (166 women). Average age 27. 286 applicants, 67% accepted, 108 enrolled. *Faculty:* 133 full-time (42 women), 6 part-time/adjunct (2 women). Expenses: Contact institution. *Financial support:* In 2016–17, 4 fellowships (averaging $11,200 per year), 18 research assistantships (averaging $5,400 per year) were awarded; teaching assistantships, career-related internships or fieldwork, Federal Work-Study, institutionally sponsored loans, scholarships/grants, traineeships, health care benefits, tuition waivers (full), and unspecified assistantships also available. Support available to part-time students. In 2016, 60 master's, 3 doctorates awarded. *Program availability:* Part-time. Offers anthropology (MA); Arab and Middle Eastern history (PhD); Arabic language and literature (MA, PhD); archaeology (MA); art history and curating (MA); biology (MS); cell and molecular biology (PhD); chemistry (MS); clinical psychology (MA); computational sciences (MS); computer science (MS); economics (MA); education (MA); English language (MA); English literature (MA); environmental policy planning (MS); financial economics (MAFE); geology (MS); history (MA); Islamic studies (MA); mathematics (MS); media studies (MA); Middle Eastern studies (MA); physics (MS); political studies (MA); psychology (MA); public administration (MA); public policy and international affairs (MA); sociology (MA); statistics (MA, MS); theoretical physics (PhD); transnational American studies (MA). *Application deadline:* For fall admission, 4/3 for domestic students; for winter admission, 11/3 for domestic students. *Application fee:* $50. Electronic applications accepted. *Application Contact:* Dr. Salim Kanaan, Director, Admissions Office, 961-1350000 Ext. 2590, Fax: 961-1750775, E-mail: sk00@aub.edu.lb. *Dean, Faculty of Arts and Sciences,* Dr. Nadia Maria El Cheikh, 961-1374374 Ext. 3800, Fax: 961-1744461, E-mail: nmcheikh@aub.edu.lb.

Faculty of Engineering and Architecture Students: 308 full-time (143 women), 86 part-time (39 women). Average age 26. 430 applicants, 69% accepted, 125 enrolled. *Faculty:* 99 full-time (22 women), 1 part-time/adjunct (0 women). Expenses: Contact institution. *Financial support:* In 2016–17, 22 students received support, including 94 fellowships with full tuition reimbursements available (averaging $18,200 per year), 44 research assistantships with full tuition reimbursements available (averaging $7,596 per year), 124 teaching assistantships with full tuition reimbursements available (averaging $1,056 per year); career-related internships or fieldwork, Federal Work-Study, institutionally sponsored loans, scholarships/grants, traineeships, health care benefits, tuition waivers, and unspecified assistantships also available. Support available to part-time students. Financial award application deadline: 12/20. In 2016, 103 master's, 7 doctorates awarded. *Program availability:* Part-time, evening/weekend, 100% online. Offers applied energy (ME); civil engineering (PhD); electrical and computer engineering (PhD); energy studies (MS); engineering management (MEM); environmental and water resources (ME); environmental technology (MSES); mechanical engineering (ME, PhD); urban design (MUD); urban planning and policy (MUPP). *Application deadline:* For fall admission, 2/10 priority date for domestic and international students; for spring admission, 11/2 priority date for domestic students, 11/2 for international students. *Application fee:* $50. Electronic applications accepted. *Application Contact:* Dr. Salim Kanaan, Director, Admissions Office, 961-1350000 Ext. 2594, Fax: 961-1750775, E-mail: sk00@aub.edu.lb. *Interim Dean,* Prof. Alan Shihadeh, 961-1350000 Ext. 3400, Fax: 961-1744462, E-mail: as20@aub.edu.lb.

Faculty of Health Sciences Students: 63 full-time (45 women), 100 part-time (87 women). Average age 27. 212 applicants, 74% accepted, 53 enrolled. *Faculty:* 35 full-time (24 women), 4 part-time/adjunct (1 woman). Expenses: Contact institution. *Financial support:* In 2016–17, 88 students received support. Scholarships/grants and unspecified assistantships available. Financial award application deadline: 4/3. In 2016, 54 master's awarded. *Program availability:* Part-time. Offers environmental sciences (MS); epidemiology (MS); epidemiology and biostatistics (MPH); health care leadership (EMHCL); health management and policy (MPH); health promotion and community health (MPH). *Application deadline:* For fall admission, 2/10 priority date for domestic and international students; for winter admission, 4/3 for domestic and international students; for spring admission, 11/2 for domestic and international students. *Application fee:* $50. Electronic applications accepted. *Application Contact:* Mitra Tauk, Administrative Coordinator, 961-1350000 Ext. 4687, E-mail: mt12@aub.edu.lb. *Dean/Professor,* Prof. Iman Adel Nuwayhid, 961-1759683 Ext. 4600, Fax: 961-1744470, E-mail: nuwayhid@aub.edu.lb.

Faculty of Medicine Students: 491 full-time (248 women). Average age 23. 431 applicants, 50% accepted, 127 enrolled. *Faculty:* 292 full-time (87 women), 58 part-time/adjunct (5 women). Expenses: Contact institution. *Financial support:* In 2016–17, 281 students received support. Institutionally sponsored loans, scholarships/grants, and unspecified assistantships available. In 2016, 18 master's, 88 doctorates awarded. *Program availability:* Part-time. Offers biochemistry (MS); biomedical engineering (MS); biomedical sciences (PhD); human morphology (MS); medicine (MD); microbiology and immunology (MS); neuroscience (MS); orthodontics (MS); pharmacology and therapeutics (MS); physiology (MS). *Application deadline:* For fall admission, 4/3 for domestic and international students. Applications are processed on a rolling basis. *Application fee:* $75. Electronic applications accepted. *Application Contact:* Dr. Salim Kanaan, Director, Admissions Office, 961-1350000 Ext. 2594, Fax: 961-1750775, E-mail: sk00@aub.edu.lb. *Dean,* Dr. Mohamed Sayegh, 961-1350000 Ext. 4700, Fax: 961-1744489, E-mail: msayegh@aub.edu.lb.

Rafic Hariri School of Nursing Students: 6 full-time (all women), 49 part-time (41 women). Average age 28. 38 applicants, 92% accepted, 20 enrolled. *Faculty:* 20 full-time (19 women), 9 part-time/adjunct (7 women). Expenses: Contact institution. *Financial support:* In 2016–17, 13 students received support, including 4 research assistantships (averaging $12,000 per year); teaching assistantships, scholarships/grants, traineeships, health care benefits, and unspecified assistantships also available. Support available to part-time students. Financial award application deadline: 12/20. In 2016, 16 master's awarded. Offers adult gerontology clinical nurse specialist (MSN); community and public health nursing (MSN); nursing administration and management (MSN); psychiatric mental health in nursing (MSN). *Application deadline:* For fall admission, 4/3 priority date for domestic students. *Application fee:* $50. Electronic applications accepted. *Application Contact:* Nisreen Ghalayini, Administrative Assistant, 961-1350000 Ext. 5951, E-mail: ng28@aub.edu.lb. *Director,* Dr. Huda Huijer, 961-1350000 Ext. 5952, Fax: 961-1744476, E-mail: hh35@aub.edu.lb.

Suliman S. Olayan School of Business Students: 58 full-time (34 women), 22 part-time (12 women). Average age 30. 176 applicants, 62% accepted, 67 enrolled. Expenses: Contact institution. *Financial support:* In 2016–17, 25 research assistantships were awarded; scholarships/grants and unspecified assistantships also available. In 2016, 86 master's awarded. *Program availability:* Part-time, evening/weekend, online learning. Offers business (EMBA, M Fin, MBA, MHRM); business administration (MBA); executive business administration (EMBA); finance (M Fin); human resource management (MHRM). *Application fee:* $80. Electronic applications accepted. *Dean,* Dr. Steve Harvey, 961-1350000 Ext. 3934, E-mail: sh146@aub.edu.lb.

AMERICAN UNIVERSITY OF HEALTH SCIENCES, Signal Hill, CA 90755

General Information Proprietary, coed, comprehensive institution.

GRADUATE UNITS

School of Clinical Research Offers clinical research (MSCR).

THE AMERICAN UNIVERSITY OF PARIS, 75007 Paris, France

General Information Independent, coed, comprehensive institution. *Graduate housing:* Room and/or apartments available on a first-come, first-served basis to single students; on-campus housing not available to married students.

GRADUATE UNITS

Graduate Programs Offers cross-cultural and sustainable business management (MA); cultural translation (MA); global communications (MA); global communications and civil society (MA); international affairs (MA); international affairs, conflict resolution and civil society development (MA); Middle East and Islamic studies (MA); Middle East and Islamic studies and international affairs (MA); public policy and international affairs (MA); public policy and international law (MA). Electronic applications accepted.

AMERICAN UNIVERSITY OF PUERTO RICO, Bayamon, PR 00960-2037

General Information Independent, coed, comprehensive institution. *Enrollment:* 23 full-time matriculated graduate/professional students (18 women), 61 part-time matriculated graduate/professional students (45 women). *Enrollment by degree level:* 84 master's, 16 other advanced degrees. *Graduate faculty:* 21 part-time/adjunct (8 women). *Graduate housing:* On-campus housing not available. *Student services:* Services for students with disabilities. *Library facilities:* Loida Figueroa Meacado.

Computer facilities: 359 computers available on campus for general student use. A campuswide network can be accessed.
Website: http://www.aupr.edu/

General Application Contact: Dr. Jose Ramirez-Figueroa, Vice President for Academic and Student Affairs, 787-620-2040 Ext. 2010, Fax: 787-620-2958, E-mail: jramirez@aupr.edu.

GRADUATE UNITS

Program in Criminal Justice Students: 1 full-time (0 women), 8 part-time (3 women); all minorities (all Hispanic/Latino). Average age 32. 2 applicants, 100% accepted, 2 enrolled. *Faculty:* 4 part-time/adjunct (1 woman). Expenses: Contact institution. *Financial support:* In 2016–17, 8 students received support, including 9 fellowships (averaging $500 per year). Financial award applicants required to submit FAFSA. In 2016, 2 master's awarded. *Program availability:* Part-time, evening/weekend. Offers criminal justice (MA). *Application deadline:* For fall admission, 8/1 for domestic students; for winter admission, 10/15 for domestic students; for spring admission, 3/22 for domestic students. Applications are processed on a rolling basis. *Application fee:* $25. *Application Contact:* Keren I. Llanos-Figueroa, Information Contact, 787-620-2040 Ext. 2021, Fax: 787-785-7377, E-mail: kllanos@aupr.edu. *Dean of Faculty,* Prof. Bolivar Ramirez-Carlo, III, 787-620-2040 Ext. 2011, Fax: 787-785-7377, E-mail: bramirez@aupr.edu.

Program in Education Students: 22 full-time (18 women), 54 part-time (42 women); all minorities (all Hispanic/Latino). Average age 33. 22 applicants, 86% accepted, 19 enrolled. *Faculty:* 17 part-time/adjunct (7 women). Expenses: Contact institution. *Financial support:* In 2016–17, 79 students received support, including 76 fellowships (averaging $400 per year), 55 teaching assistantships (averaging $1,741 per year). Financial award applicants required to submit FAFSA. In 2016, 53 master's awarded. *Program availability:* Part-time, evening/weekend. Offers art education (M Ed); elementary education 4-6 (M Ed); elementary education K-3 (M Ed); general science education (M Ed); physical education (M Ed); special education (M Ed). *Application deadline:* For fall admission, 8/1 for domestic students; for winter admission, 10/18 for domestic students; for spring admission, 3/15 for domestic students. Applications are processed on a rolling basis. *Application fee:* $25. *Application Contact:* Keren I. Llanos-Figueroa, Information Contact, 787-620-2040 Ext. 2021, Fax: 787-785-7377, E-mail: oficnaadmissions@aupr.edu. *Dean of Faculty,* Prof. Bolivar Ramirez-Carlo, III, 787-620-2040 Ext. 2010, Fax: 787-620-2958, E-mail: bramirez@aupr.edu.

THE AMERICAN UNIVERSITY OF ROME, 00153 Rome, Italy

General Information Independent, coed, comprehensive institution. *Research affiliation:* ARCA - Association for Research into Crimes against Art (art crime prevention), ENFSI - European Network of Forensic Science Institutes (forensic archaeology), Conservation Science in Cultural Heritage.

GRADUATE UNITS

Graduate School Offers religious studies (MA); sustainable cultural heritage (MA). Electronic applications accepted.

AMERICAN UNIVERSITY OF SHARJAH, Sharjah, United Arab Emirates

General Information Independent, coed, comprehensive institution. *Enrollment:* 123 full-time matriculated graduate/professional students (53 women), 306 part-time matriculated graduate/professional students (151 women). *Enrollment by degree level:* 429 master's. *Graduate faculty:* 59 full-time (4 women), 5 part-time/adjunct (1 woman). *Tuition:* Part-time 4660 United Arab Emirates dirhams per credit hour. *Graduate housing:* Room and/or apartments available on a first-come, first-served basis to single students; on-campus housing not available to married students. Housing application deadline: 7/1. *Student services:* Campus employment opportunities, campus safety program, career counseling, exercise/wellness program, free psychological counseling, international student services, low-cost health insurance. *Library facilities:* University Library. *Research affiliation:* Emirates Foundation (philanthropy), International Atomic Energy Agency (energy), National Research Foundation, Advanced Technology Investment Company (technology and investment), Qatar National Research Foundation.

Computer facilities: 2,400 computers available on campus for general student use. A campuswide network can be accessed from student residence rooms. Online class registration is available.
Website: http://www.aus.edu/

General Application Contact: Mona A. Mabrouk, Graduate Admissions Administrative Assistant, 971-65151012, E-mail: graduateadmission@aus.edu.

GRADUATE UNITS

Graduate Programs Students: 123 full-time (53 women), 306 part-time (151 women). Average age 27. 184 applicants, 83% accepted, 92 enrolled. Expenses: Contact institution. *Financial support:* In 2016–17, 63 students received support, including 28 research assistantships with full and partial tuition reimbursements available, 35 teaching assistantships with full and partial tuition reimbursements available; scholarships/grants also available. In 2016, 97 master's awarded. *Program availability:* Part-time, evening/weekend. Offers accounting (MS); biomedical engineering (MSBME); business (MBA); chemical engineering (MS Ch E); civil engineering (MSCE); computer engineering (MS); electrical engineering (MSEE); engineering systems management (MS); mathematics (MS); mechanical engineering (MSME); mechatronics engineering (MS); teaching English to speakers of other languages (MA); translation and interpreting (MA); urban planning (MUP). *Application deadline:* For fall admission, 8/28 priority date for domestic students, 8/14 priority date for international students; for spring admission, 1/22 priority date for domestic students, 1/8 for international students; for summer admission, 5/21 for domestic and international students. Applications are processed on a rolling basis. *Application fee:* $350. Electronic applications accepted. *Application Contact:* Mona A. Mabrouk, Graduate Admissions/Office of Enrollment Management, 971-65151012, E-mail: graduateadmission@aus.edu. *Executive Director of Enrollment Management*, Ali Shuhaimy, 971-6515-1030.

AMRIDGE UNIVERSITY, Montgomery, AL 36117

General Information Independent-religious, coed, university. *Enrollment:* 636 graduate, professional, and undergraduate students; 81 full-time matriculated graduate/professional students (49 women), 225 part-time matriculated graduate/professional students (137 women). *Enrollment by degree level:* 210 master's, 96 doctoral, 306 other advanced degrees. *Graduate faculty:* 22 full-time (3 women), 10 part-time/adjunct (6 women). *Tuition:* Full-time $12,870; part-time $715 per credit hour. *Required fees:* $1300; $650 per semester. *Graduate housing:* On-campus housing not available. *Student services:* Campus safety program, career counseling, services for students with disabilities. *Library facilities:* Southern Christian University Library.

Computer facilities: 5 computers available on campus for general student use. A campuswide network can be accessed from off campus. Online class registration is available.
Website: http://www.amridgeuniversity.edu/

General Application Contact: Brooks Housley, Student Services Coordinator, 888-790-8080 Ext. 1, Fax: 334-387-3878, E-mail: admissions@amridgeuniversity.edu.

GRADUATE UNITS

Graduate and Professional Programs Students: 81 full-time (49 women), 225 part-time (137 women); includes 81 minority (80 Black or African American, non-Hispanic/Latino; 1 Hispanic/Latino). Average age 41. 122 applicants, 100% accepted, 79 enrolled. *Faculty:* 22 full-time (3 women), 10 part-time/adjunct (6 women). Expenses: Contact institution. *Financial support:* In 2016–17, 45 students received support. Federal Work-Study and scholarships/grants available. Support available to part-time students. Financial award applicants required to submit FAFSA. *Program availability:* Part-time, evening/weekend, online learning. Offers Biblical studies (MA, PhD); Christian ministry (MS); family therapy (D Min); human services (MS); leadership and management (MS); marriage and family therapy (M Div, MA, PhD); ministerial leadership (M Div, MS); New Testament studies (MA); Old Testament studies (MA); professional counseling (M Div, MA, PhD); theology (M Div, D Min). *Application deadline:* Applications are processed on a rolling basis. *Application fee:* $50. Electronic applications accepted. *Application Contact:* Brooks Housley, Student Affairs Coordinator, 888-790-8080 Ext. 1, Fax: 334-387-3878, E-mail: admissions@amridgeuniversity.edu. *Vice President, Student Affairs*, Laina Costanza, 888-790-8080 Ext. 1, Fax: 334-387-3878, E-mail: cc@amridgeuniversity.edu.

ANABAPTIST MENNONITE BIBLICAL SEMINARY, Elkhart, IN 46517-1999

General Information Independent-religious, coed, graduate-only institution. *Enrollment by degree level:* 94 master's, 4 other advanced degrees. *Graduate faculty:* 14 full-time (6 women), 17 part-time/adjunct (8 women). *Tuition:* Full-time $13,950; part-time $5640 per year. *Required fees:* $900; $300 per unit. $50 per term. *Graduate housing:* Rooms and/or apartments available on a first-come, first-served basis to single and married students. Typical cost: $4000 per year for single students; $4000 per year for married students. Room charges vary according to housing facility selected. Housing application deadline: 5/1. *Student services:* Campus employment opportunities, campus safety program, exercise/wellness program, free psychological counseling, international student services, low-cost health insurance, multicultural affairs office, services for students with disabilities, teacher training, writing training. *Library facilities:* AMBS Library. *Collection:* Books: 100,160 (physical), 129,600 (digital/electronic); Serial titles: 1,465 (physical), 7,415 (digital/electronic); Databases: 3. Weekly public service hours: 60; students can reserve study rooms.

Computer facilities: 8 computers available on campus for general student use. A campuswide network can be accessed. Online class registration, X are available.
Website: http://www.ambs.edu/

General Application Contact: Daniel Grimes, Director of Admissions, 574-295-3726, Fax: 574-295-0092, E-mail: admissions@ambs.edu.

GRADUATE UNITS

Graduate and Professional Programs Students: 38 full-time (14 women), 60 part-time (33 women); includes 15 minority (4 Black or African American, non-Hispanic/Latino; 5 Asian, non-Hispanic/Latino; 5 Hispanic/Latino; 1 Two or more races, non-Hispanic/Latino), 15 international. Average age 35. 43 applicants, 70% accepted, 29 enrolled. *Faculty:* 14 full-time (6 women), 17 part-time/adjunct (8 women). Expenses: Contact institution. *Financial support:* In 2016–17, 40 students received support. Career-related internships or fieldwork, scholarships/grants, unspecified assistantships, and church matching grants available. Support available to part-time students. Financial award application deadline: 4/15; financial award applicants required to submit FAFSA. In 2016, 16 master's, 2 other advanced degrees awarded. *Program availability:* Part-time, 100% online, blended/hybrid learning. Offers chaplaincy (M Div); Christian faith formation (M Div); Christian formation (MA); Christian spiritual formation (Certificate); divinity (M Div); pastoral ministry (M Div); pastoral theology for financial professionals (Certificate); peace studies (M Div, Certificate); theological studies (M Div, Certificate); theology and peace studies (MA); United Methodist leadership (M Div). Conflict transformation and environmental sustainability leadership concentrations offered in cooperation with Goshen College; international development administration offered in cooperation with Andrews University. *Application deadline:* For fall admission, 6/1 priority date for domestic students, 5/1 priority date for international students. Applications are processed on a rolling basis. *Application fee:* $25. Electronic applications accepted. *Application Contact:* Daniel Grimes, Director of Admissions, Fax: 574-295-0092, E-mail: admissions@ambs.edu. *President*, Sara Wenger Shenk, 800-964-2627, Fax: 574-295-0092.

ANAHEIM UNIVERSITY, Anaheim, CA 92806-5150

General Information Proprietary, coed, graduate-only institution.
Website: http://www.anaheim.edu/

General Application Contact: Beth Mays, Student Services Coordinator, 714-772-3330, E-mail: admissions@anaheim.edu.

GRADUATE UNITS

Program in Teaching English to Speakers of Other Languages Expenses: Contact institution. In 2016, 1 master's, 1 doctorate awarded. *Program availability:* Part-time, evening/weekend, online only, 100% online. Offers teaching English to speakers of other languages (MA, Ed D, Certificate, Diploma). *Application deadline:* Applications are processed on a rolling basis. *Director, Doctor of Education in TESOL Program*, Hayo Reinders, 714-771-3330, Fax: 714-772-3331, E-mail: admissions@anaheim.edu.

Programs in Business Administration Expenses: Contact institution. In 2016, 3 master's, 4 doctorates awarded. *Program availability:* Part-time, evening/weekend, online only, 100% online. Offers entrepreneurship (ME, DBA); global sustainable management (MBA); international business (MBA, DBA, Certificate, Diploma); management (DBA); sustainable management (DBA, Certificate, Diploma). *Application deadline:* Applications are processed on a rolling basis. Electronic applications accepted. *Dean, Graduate School of Business*, Robert Robertson, 714-772-3330, Fax: 714-772-3331, E-mail: admissions@anaheim.edu.

ANDERSON UNIVERSITY, Anderson, IN 46012-3495

General Information Independent-religious, coed, comprehensive institution. *Graduate housing:* Room and/or apartments available to single students; on-campus housing not available to married students. Housing application deadline: 6/1.

GRADUATE UNITS

Falls School of Business Offers accountancy (MA); business administration (MBA, DBA).

School of Education Offers education (M Ed).

School of Theology *Program availability:* Part-time. Offers missions (MA); theology (M Div, MTS, D Min).

ANDERSON UNIVERSITY, Anderson, SC 29621-4035

General Information Independent-religious, coed, comprehensive institution. *Enrollment:* 3,431 graduate, professional, and undergraduate students; 138 full-time matriculated graduate/professional students (69 women), 19 part-time matriculated graduate/professional students (9 women). *Enrollment by degree level:* 157 master's. *Library facilities:* Thrift Library. *Collection:* Books: 90,729 (physical), 99,204 (digital/electronic); Serial titles: 14,268 (physical), 174,052 (digital/electronic); Databases: 200. Weekly public service hours: 88; students can reserve study rooms.

Computer facilities: 192 computers available on campus for general student use. A campuswide network can be accessed from student residence rooms and from off campus. Online class registration is available.
Website: http://www.andersonuniversity.edu/

General Application Contact: Chris Woodlief, Associate Director of Adult and Graduate Programs, 864-231-5531, E-mail: cwoodlief@andersonuniversity.edu.

GRADUATE UNITS

College of Business Students: 7 full-time (0 women), 1 part-time (0 women). Expenses: Contact institution. *Financial support:* Tuition waivers available. Financial award application deadline: 3/1; financial award applicants required to submit FAFSA. Offers business administration (MBA); healthcare leadership (MBA); human resources (MBA); marketing (MBA); supply chain management (MBA). *Application Contact:* Mallory Knight, Graduate Admission Counselor, 864-231-2182, Fax: 864-231-2115, E-mail: malloryknight@andersonuniversity.edu. *MBA Director/Associate Dean*, Dr. Douglas Goodwin, 864-MBA-6000.

College of Education Expenses: Contact institution. *Financial support:* Tuition waivers available. Financial award application deadline: 3/1; financial award applicants required to submit FAFSA. *Program availability:* 100% online. Offers administration and supervision (M Ed); education (M Ed); elementary education (MAT). *Application Contact:* Mallory Knight, Graduate Admission Counselor, 864-231-2182, Fax: 864-231-2115, E-mail: malloryknight@andersonuniversity.edu. *Dean*, Dr. Mark Butler, 864-231-2042.

Command College of South Carolina Expenses: Contact institution. *Financial support:* Application deadline: 3/1; applicants required to submit FAFSA. *Program availability:* Blended/hybrid learning. Offers criminal justice (MCJ). *Application Contact:* Mallory Knight, Graduate Admission Counselor, 864-231-2182, Fax: 864-231-2115, E-mail: malloryknight@andersonuniversity.edu.

David T. Clamp Graduate School of Christian Ministry Expenses: Contact institution. *Financial support:* Tuition waivers available. Financial award application deadline: 3/1; financial award applicants required to submit FAFSA. *Program availability:* Online learning. Offers Biblical preaching (D Min); ministry (M Min). *Application Contact:*

Mallory Knight, Graduate Admission Counselor, 864-231-2182, Fax: 864-231-2115, E-mail: malloryknight@andersonuniversity.edu. *Dean*, Dr. Michael Duduit, 864-328-1809, E-mail: ministry@andersonuniversity.edu.

ANDREWS UNIVERSITY, Berrien Springs, MI 49104

General Information Independent-religious, coed, university. CGS member. *Enrollment:* 3,349 graduate, professional, and undergraduate students; 833 full-time matriculated graduate/professional students (296 women), 774 part-time matriculated graduate/professional students (240 women). *Enrollment by degree level:* 977 master's, 615 doctoral, 15 other advanced degrees. *Graduate faculty:* 168 full-time (62 women), 32 part-time/adjunct (11 women). *Graduate housing:* Rooms and/or apartments available on a first-come, first-served basis to single and married students. Typical cost: $10,200 (including board) for single students. Room and board charges vary according to board plan and housing facility selected. *Student services:* Campus employment opportunities, campus safety program, career counseling, child daycare facilities, free psychological counseling, international student services, low-cost health insurance. *Library facilities:* James White Library plus 2 others. *Collection:* Books: 895,090 (physical), 449,347 (digital/electronic); Serial titles: 908,572 (physical), 502,424 (digital/electronic); Databases: 185. *Research affiliation:* RAND Corporation (drug abuse), Argonne National Laboratory (physics), Deutches Electronen Synchroton (physics).

Computer facilities: Computer purchase and lease plans are available. 100 computers available on campus for general student use. A campuswide network can be accessed from student residence rooms and from off campus. Online class registration, degree audit are available.
Website: http://www.andrews.edu/

General Application Contact: Justina Clayburn, Supervisor of Graduate Admission, 800-253-2874, Fax: 269-471-3228, E-mail: graduate@andrews.edu.

GRADUATE UNITS

School of Graduate Studies Students: 833 full-time (296 women), 774 part-time (240 women); includes 278,686 minority (352 Black or African American, non-Hispanic/Latino; 4 American Indian or Alaska Native, non-Hispanic/Latino; 89 Asian, non-Hispanic/Latino; 278,224 Hispanic/Latino; 4 Native Hawaiian or other Pacific Islander, non-Hispanic/Latino; 13 Two or more races, non-Hispanic/Latino), 350 international. Average age 38. *Faculty:* 168 full-time (62 women), 32 part-time/adjunct (11 women). *Expenses:* Contact institution. *Financial support:* Fellowships, research assistantships, teaching assistantships, career-related internships or fieldwork, Federal Work-Study, institutionally sponsored loans, scholarships/grants, tuition waivers (partial), and unspecified assistantships available. Support available to part-time students. Financial award applicants required to submit FAFSA. In 2016, 326 master's, 132 doctorates, 2 other advanced degrees awarded. *Program availability:* Part-time, evening/weekend, online learning. *Application deadline:* Applications are processed on a rolling basis. *Application fee:* $40. *Application Contact:* Justina Clayburn, Supervisor of Graduate Admission, 800-253-2874, Fax: 269-471-6321, E-mail: graduate@andrews.edu. *Dean*, Dr. Christon Arthur, 269-471-3405.

College of Arts and Sciences Students: 58 full-time (43 women), 50 part-time (38 women); includes 54 minority (29 Black or African American, non-Hispanic/Latino; 8 Asian, non-Hispanic/Latino; 16 Hispanic/Latino; 1 Native Hawaiian or other Pacific Islander, non-Hispanic/Latino), 26 international. Average age 32. *Faculty:* 76 full-time (31 women), 3 part-time/adjunct (1 woman). *Expenses:* Contact institution. *Financial support:* Fellowships, research assistantships, teaching assistantships, career-related internships or fieldwork, Federal Work-Study, and institutionally sponsored loans available. Financial award applicants required to submit FAFSA. In 2016, 48 master's awarded. *Program availability:* Part-time, evening/weekend. Offers arts and sciences (M Mus, MA, MAT, MS, MSA, MSCID, MSW); biology (MAT, MS); communication (MA); community and international development (MSCID); English (MA, MAT); international development (MSCID); music (M Mus, MA); social work (MSW). *Application deadline:* Applications are processed on a rolling basis. *Application fee:* $40. *Application Contact:* Justina Clayburn, Supervisor of Graduate Admission, 800-253-2874, Fax: 269-471-6321, E-mail: graduate@andrews.edu. *Dean*, Dr. Keith Mattingly, 269-471-3411.

School of Architecture, Art and Design Students: 11 full-time (5 women), 2 part-time (both women); includes 8 minority (1 Black or African American, non-Hispanic/Latino; 1 Asian, non-Hispanic/Latino; 5 Hispanic/Latino; 1 Native Hawaiian or other Pacific Islander, non-Hispanic/Latino), 2 international. Average age 30. *Faculty:* 9 full-time (3 women), 1 (woman) part-time/adjunct. *Expenses:* Contact institution. In 2016, 12 master's awarded. Offers architecture, art and design (M Arch). *Application deadline:* Applications are processed on a rolling basis. *Application fee:* $40. Electronic applications accepted. *Application Contact:* Justina Clayburn, Supervisor of Graduate Admission, 800-253-2874, Fax: 269-471-6321, E-mail: graduate@andrews.edu. *Dean*, Carey Carscallen, 269-471-6003.

School of Business Students: 16 full-time (7 women), 29 part-time (15 women); includes 19 minority (6 Black or African American, non-Hispanic/Latino; 3 Asian, non-Hispanic/Latino; 8 Hispanic/Latino; 2 Two or more races, non-Hispanic/Latino), 12 international. Average age 32. *Faculty:* 8 full-time (3 women). *Expenses:* Contact institution. *Financial support:* Fellowships, research assistantships, teaching assistantships, and Federal Work-Study available. In 2016, 29 master's awarded. *Program availability:* Part-time. Offers business (MBA, MSA). *Application deadline:* For fall admission, 8/15 for domestic students. Applications are processed on a rolling basis. *Application fee:* $40. *Application Contact:* Justina Clayburn, Supervisor of Graduate Admission, 800-253-2874, Fax: 269-471-6321, E-mail: graduate@andrews.edu. *Dean*, Dr. Ralph Trecartin, 269-471-3632.

School of Education Students: 127 full-time (82 women), 76 part-time (49 women); includes 74 minority (42 Black or African American, non-Hispanic/Latino; 3 Asian, non-Hispanic/Latino; 26 Hispanic/Latino; 3 Two or more races, non-Hispanic/Latino), 42 international. Average age 41. *Faculty:* 21 full-time (9 women), 5 part-time/adjunct (2 women). *Expenses:* Contact institution. *Financial support:* Fellowships, research assistantships, teaching assistantships, career-related internships or fieldwork, Federal Work-Study, institutionally sponsored loans, and tuition waivers (partial) available. Support available to part-time students. In 2016, 39 master's, 17 doctorates, 2 other advanced degrees awarded. *Program availability:* Part-time. Offers clinical mental health counseling (MA); community counseling (MA); counseling psychology (PhD); curriculum and instruction (MA, Ed D, PhD, Ed S); education (MA, MAT, MS, Ed D, PhD, Ed S); educational administration and leadership (MA, Ed D, PhD, Ed S); educational and developmental psychology (MA, Ed D, PhD); educational psychology (Ed D, PhD); elementary education (MAT); higher education administration (MA, Ed D, PhD, Ed S); leadership (MA, Ed D, PhD, Ed S); school counseling (MA); school psychology (Ed S); secondary education (MAT); special education (MS); teacher education (MAT). *Application deadline:* Applications are

processed on a rolling basis. *Application fee:* $40. *Application Contact:* Justina Clayburn, Supervisor of Graduate Admission, 800-253-2874, Fax: 269-471-6321, E-mail: graduate@andrews.edu. *Dean*, Dr. Robson Marinho, 269-471-3464.

Seventh-day Adventist Theological Seminary Students: 477 full-time (69 women), 530 part-time (83 women); includes 498 minority (237 Black or African American, non-Hispanic/Latino; 3 American Indian or Alaska Native, non-Hispanic/Latino; 53 Asian, non-Hispanic/Latino; 198 Hispanic/Latino; 2 Native Hawaiian or other Pacific Islander, non-Hispanic/Latino; 5 Two or more races, non-Hispanic/Latino), 234 international. Average age 40. *Faculty:* 40 full-time (5 women), 12 part-time/adjunct (2 women). *Expenses:* Contact institution. *Financial support:* Fellowships, research assistantships, teaching assistantships, career-related internships or fieldwork, Federal Work-Study, and institutionally sponsored loans available. In 2016, 194 master's, 52 doctorates awarded. Offers ministry (M Div, D Min); pastoral ministry (MA); religious education (MA, Ed D, PhD, Ed S); theology (M Th, Th D); youth ministry (MA). *Application deadline:* Applications are processed on a rolling basis. *Application fee:* $40. *Application Contact:* Justina Clayburn, Director, 800-253-2874, Fax: 269-471-6321. *Dean*, Dr. Jiri Moskala, 269-471-3537.

School of Health Professions Students: 144 full-time (90 women), 87 part-time (53 women); includes 87 minority (37 Black or African American, non-Hispanic/Latino; 1 American Indian or Alaska Native, non-Hispanic/Latino; 21 Asian, non-Hispanic/Latino; 25 Hispanic/Latino; 3 Two or more races, non-Hispanic/Latino), 34 international. Average age 32. *Faculty:* 13 full-time (10 women), 11 part-time/adjunct (5 women). *Expenses:* Contact institution. In 2016, 4 master's, 54 doctorates awarded. Offers health professions (MPH, MS, MSMLS, DNP, DPT, Dr Sc PT, TDPT, Certificate); medical laboratory sciences (MSMLS); nursing (MS, DNP); nutrition (MS); nutrition and dietetics (Certificate); physical therapy (DPT, Dr Sc PT, TDPT); public health (MPH); speech-language pathology (MS). *Application fee:* $40. *Application Contact:* Justina Clayburn, Supervisor of Graduate Admission, 800-253-2874, Fax: 269-471-3228, E-mail: graduate@andrews.edu. *Dean*, Dr. Emmanuel Rudatsikira, 269-471-6649, E-mail: rudatsikira@andrews.edu.

ANGELO STATE UNIVERSITY, San Angelo, TX 76909

General Information State-supported, coed, comprehensive institution. *Enrollment:* 9,581 graduate, professional, and undergraduate students; 757 full-time matriculated graduate/professional students (529 women), 730 part-time matriculated graduate/professional students (497 women). *Enrollment by degree level:* 1,409 master's, 78 doctoral. *Graduate faculty:* 126 full-time (52 women). Tuition, state resident: full-time $3726; part-time $2484 per year. Tuition, nonresident: full-time $10,746; part-time $7164 per year. *Required fees:* $2538; $1702 per unit. *Graduate housing:* Room and/or apartments available on a first-come, first-served basis to single students; on-campus housing not available to married students. Typical cost: $7702 (including board). Room and board charges vary according to board plan, campus/location and housing facility selected. Housing application deadline: 7/15. *Student services:* Campus employment opportunities, campus safety program, career counseling, free psychological counseling, grant writing training, international student services, low-cost health insurance, multicultural affairs office, services for students with disabilities, writing training. *Library facilities:* Porter Henderson Library. *Collection:* Books: 484,935 (physical), 85,670 (digital/electronic); Serial titles: 128 (physical), 61,918 (digital/electronic); Databases: 154. Weekly public service hours: 130; study areas open 24 hours, 5–7 days a week; students can reserve study rooms. *Research affiliation:* Purina (animal nutrition), Zinpro Corporation (animal nutrition), Texas Space Consortium (space research and technology), TASCO (animal nutrition), Mannatech, Inc. (nutrition).

Computer facilities: Computer purchase and lease plans are available. 750 computers available on campus for general student use. A campuswide network can be accessed from student residence rooms and from off campus. Online class registration, online courses, tuition payments, book purchase, parking permits, university calendar, discounted hardware and software are available.
Website: http://www.angelo.edu/

General Application Contact: Jennifer McAndrews, Graduate Admissions Assistant, 325-942-2169, Fax: 325-942-2194, E-mail: graduate.studies@angelo.edu.

GRADUATE UNITS

College of Graduate Studies and Research Students: 757 full-time (529 women), 730 part-time (497 women); includes 433 minority (131 Black or African American, non-Hispanic/Latino; 5 American Indian or Alaska Native, non-Hispanic/Latino; 18 Asian, non-Hispanic/Latino; 267 Hispanic/Latino; 12 Two or more races, non-Hispanic/Latino), 19 international. Average age 32. *Expenses:* Contact institution. *Financial support:* Research assistantships, teaching assistantships, career-related internships or fieldwork, Federal Work-Study, scholarships/grants, and unspecified assistantships available. Support available to part-time students. Financial award application deadline: 3/1. *Program availability:* Part-time, evening/weekend, online learning. *Application deadline:* For fall admission, 7/15 priority date for domestic students, 6/10 for international students; for spring admission, 12/1 priority date for domestic students, 11/1 for international students. Applications are processed on a rolling basis. *Application fee:* $40 ($50 for international students). Electronic applications accepted. *Application Contact:* Jennifer Page McAndrews, Graduate Admissions Coordinator, 325-486-6481, Fax: 325-942-2194, E-mail: jennifer.mcandrews@angelo.edu. *Dean*, Dr. Susan E. Keith, 325-942-2169, Fax: 325-942-2194, E-mail: susan.keith@angelo.edu.

Archer College of Health and Human Services Students: 196 full-time (127 women), 136 part-time (93 women); includes 88 minority (20 Black or African American, non-Hispanic/Latino; 1 American Indian or Alaska Native, non-Hispanic/Latino; 5 Asian, non-Hispanic/Latino; 62 Hispanic/Latino), 8 international. Average age 31. *Expenses:* Contact institution. *Financial support:* Research assistantships available. Offers applied psychology (MS); coaching, sport, recreation and fitness administration (M Ed); counseling psychology (MS); family nurse practitioner (MSN); health and human services (M Ed, MS, MSN, DPT); industrial-organizational psychology (MS); nurse educator (MSN); physical therapy (DPT). *Application deadline:* For fall admission, 7/15 priority date for domestic students, 6/10 for international students; for spring admission, 12/1 priority date for domestic students, 11/1 for international students. *Application fee:* $40 ($50 for international students). *Application Contact:* Dr. Leslie M. Mayrand, 325-486-6258, Fax: 325-942-2631, E-mail: leslie.mayrand@angelo.edu. *Dean*, Dr. Leslie M. Mayrand, 325-486-6258, Fax: 325-942-2631, E-mail: leslie.mayrand@angelo.edu.

College of Arts and Humanities Students: 89 full-time (36 women), 127 part-time (49 women); includes 75 minority (26 Black or African American, non-Hispanic/Latino; 1 American Indian or Alaska Native, non-Hispanic/Latino; 7 Asian, non-Hispanic/Latino; 38 Hispanic/Latino; 3 Two or more races, non-Hispanic/Latino), 3 international. Average age 31. *Expenses:* Contact institution. *Financial support:* Research assistantships, teaching assistantships, career-related internships or fieldwork, Federal Work-Study, scholarships/grants, and unspecified assistantships available. Support available to part-time students. Financial award application deadline: 3/1;

financial award applicants required to submit FAFSA. *Program availability:* Part-time, evening/weekend. Offers arts and humanities (MA, MS, MSS); communication (MA); criminal justice (MS); English (MA); homeland security (MA); intelligence, security studies, and analysis (MSS); security studies (MSS); TESOL (MA). *Application deadline:* For fall admission, 7/15 priority date for domestic students, 6/10 for international students; for spring admission, 12/1 priority date for domestic students, 11/1 for international students. Applications are processed on a rolling basis. *Application fee:* $40 ($50 for international students). Electronic applications accepted. *Application Contact:* Dr. Carolyn Gascoigne, Dean, 325-942-2162, E-mail: cgascoigne@angelo.edu. *Dean,* Dr. Carolyn Gascoigne, 325-942-2162, E-mail: cgascoigne@angelo.edu.

College of Business Students: 44 full-time (25 women), 50 part-time (17 women); includes 24 minority (5 Black or African American, non-Hispanic/Latino; 1 American Indian or Alaska Native, non-Hispanic/Latino; 15 Hispanic/Latino; 3 Two or more races, non-Hispanic/Latino), 6 international. Average age 27. Expenses: Contact institution. *Financial support:* Career-related internships or fieldwork, Federal Work-Study, and scholarships/grants available. Support available to part-time students. Financial award application deadline: 3/1; financial award applicants required to submit FAFSA. *Program availability:* Part-time, evening/weekend. Offers business (MBA, MPAC); business administration (MBA); professional accountancy (MPAC). *Application deadline:* For fall admission, 7/15 priority date for domestic students, 6/10 for international students; for spring admission, 12/1 priority date for domestic students, 11/1 for international students. Applications are processed on a rolling basis. *Application fee:* $40 ($50 for international students). Electronic applications accepted. *Application Contact:* Dr. Clifton T. Jones, Dean, 325-942-2337, Fax: 325-942-2718, E-mail: clifton.jones@angelo.edu. *Dean,* Dr. Clifton T. Jones, 325-942-2337, Fax: 325-942-2718, E-mail: clifton.jones@angelo.edu.

College of Education Students: 400 full-time (328 women), 396 part-time (325 women); includes 242 minority (80 Black or African American, non-Hispanic/Latino; 2 American Indian or Alaska Native, non-Hispanic/Latino; 6 Asian, non-Hispanic/Latino; 148 Hispanic/Latino; 6 Two or more races, non-Hispanic/Latino), 1 international. Average age 35. Expenses: Contact institution. *Financial support:* Career-related internships or fieldwork, Federal Work-Study, scholarships/grants, and unspecified assistantships available. Support available to part-time students. Financial award application deadline: 3/1; financial award applicants required to submit FAFSA. *Program availability:* Part-time, evening/weekend. Offers curriculum and instruction (MA); education (M Ed, MA); educational administration (M Ed); guidance and counseling (M Ed); student development and leadership in higher education (M Ed). *Application deadline:* For fall admission, 7/15 priority date for domestic students, 6/10 for international students; for spring admission, 12/1 priority date for domestic students, 11/1 for international students. Applications are processed on a rolling basis. *Application fee:* $40 ($50 for international students). Electronic applications accepted. *Application Contact:* Dr. John J. Miazga, Jr., Dean, 325-942-2212, E-mail: john.miazga@angelo.edu. *Dean,* Dr. John J. Miazga, Jr., 325-942-2212, E-mail: john.miazga@angelo.edu.

College of Science and Engineering Students: 28 full-time (13 women), 21 part-time (13 women); includes 4 minority (all Hispanic/Latino), 1 international. Average age 25. Expenses: Contact institution. *Financial support:* Research assistantships, teaching assistantships, career-related internships or fieldwork, Federal Work-Study, scholarships/grants, and unspecified assistantships available. Support available to part-time students. Financial award application deadline: 8/1; financial award applicants required to submit FAFSA. *Program availability:* Part-time, evening/weekend. Offers agriculture (M Ag); animal science (MS); biology (MS); science and engineering (M Ag, MS); science education (MS). *Application deadline:* For fall admission, 7/15 priority date for domestic students, 6/10 for international students; for spring admission, 12/1 priority date for domestic students, 11/1 for international students. Applications are processed on a rolling basis. *Application fee:* $40 ($50 for international students). Electronic applications accepted. *Application Contact:* Aly Hunter, Graduate Admissions Assistant, 325-942-2169, Fax: 325-942-2194, E-mail: aly.hunter@angelo.edu. *Dean,* Dr. Paul K. Swets, 325-942-2470, Fax: 325-942-2340, E-mail: paul.swets@angelo.edu.

ANNA MARIA COLLEGE, Paxton, MA 01612

General Information Independent-religious, coed, comprehensive institution. *Graduate housing:* On-campus housing not available.

GRADUATE UNITS

Graduate Division *Program availability:* Part-time, evening/weekend. Offers business administration (MBA, AC); counseling psychology (MA); criminal justice (MS); early childhood education (M Ed); education (CAGS); elementary education (M Ed); English language arts (M Ed); health emergency management (MS, Graduate Certificate); industrial/organizational psychology (MS); public administration (MPA); social work (MSW); visual arts (M Ed). Electronic applications accepted.

ANTIOCH UNIVERSITY LOS ANGELES, Culver City, CA 90230

General Information Independent, coed, upper-level institution. *Graduate housing:* On-campus housing not available.

GRADUATE UNITS

Graduate Programs *Program availability:* Part-time, evening/weekend, online learning. Offers clinical psychology (MA); creative writing (MFA); education (MA); human resource development (MA); leadership (MA); nonprofit management (MA); organizational development (MA); pedagogy of creative writing (Certificate); psychology (MA); urban sustainability (MA).

ANTIOCH UNIVERSITY MIDWEST, Yellow Springs, OH 45387-1609

General Information Independent, coed, upper-level institution. *Graduate housing:* On-campus housing not available. *Student services:* International student services, low-cost health insurance, teacher training, writing training. *Library facilities:* Midwest Library.

Computer facilities: 10 computers available on campus for general student use. A campuswide network can be accessed. Online class registration, online bill pay and view/acceptance of financial aid award letter, narrative evaluations are available. Website: http://midwest.antioch.edu/

General Application Contact: Deena Kent-Hummel, Director of Admissions, 937-769-1851, Fax: 937-769-1804, E-mail: dkent@antioch.edu.

GRADUATE UNITS

Graduate Programs Expenses: Contact institution. *Financial support:* Federal Work-Study and scholarships/grants available. Financial award applicants required to submit FAFSA. *Program availability:* Part-time, evening/weekend, online learning. Offers applied psychology (MA); conflict studies (MA); health and human development (MA); integral studies (MA); integrative health studies (MA); management and change leadership

(MA); peace studies (MA); systems and organizations (MA). *Application deadline:* For fall admission, 8/1 for domestic students; for winter admission, 12/1 for domestic students; for spring admission, 3/10 for domestic students. Applications are processed on a rolling basis. *Application fee:* $50. Electronic applications accepted. *Application Contact:* Deena Kent-Hummel, Director of Admissions, 937-769-1800, Fax: 937-769-1804, E-mail: dkent@antioch.edu. *Dean of Students,* Darlene Robertson, 937-769-1820, Fax: 937-769-1804, E-mail: drobertson@antioch.edu.

School of Education Expenses: Contact institution. *Financial support:* Federal Work-Study available. Financial award applicants required to submit FAFSA. *Program availability:* Part-time, evening/weekend. Offers conflict management (M Ed); dyslexia (M Ed); early childhood education (M Ed); educational leadership (M Ed); intervention specialist, mild to moderate (M Ed); middle childhood education (M Ed); trauma informed education (M Ed). *Application deadline:* For fall admission, 9/7 for domestic students; for winter admission, 12/10 for domestic students; for spring admission, 3/10 for domestic students. Applications are processed on a rolling basis. *Application fee:* $50. Electronic applications accepted. *Application Contact:* Deena Kent-Hummel, Director of Admissions, 937-769-1823, Fax: 937-769-1804, E-mail: dkent@antioch.edu. *Director,* Dr. Marian Glancy, 937-769-1880, Fax: 937-769-1805, E-mail: mglancy@antioch.edu.

ANTIOCH UNIVERSITY NEW ENGLAND, Keene, NH 03431-3552

General Information Independent, coed, graduate-only institution. *Graduate housing:* On-campus housing not available. *Research affiliation:* Cheshire Medical Center Cardiac Rehabilitation Program (clinical psychology), Northeast Foundation for Children (education), Pine Hill Waldorf School (education), Harris Center for Conservation Education (environmental studies).

GRADUATE UNITS

Graduate School *Program availability:* Evening/weekend. Offers advocacy for social justice and sustainability (MS); applied behavior analysis (Certificate); applied behavior analysis internship (Certificate); autism spectrum disorders (Certificate); clinical mental health counseling (MA); clinical psychology (Psy D); conservation biology (MS); dance/movement therapy and counseling (M Ed, MA, PMC); early childhood education (M Ed); elementary education (M Ed, Certificate); environmental education (MS); environmental studies (PhD); foundations of education (M Ed); integrated learning (M Ed); marriage and family therapy (MA, PhD, Certificate); principal certification (PMC); resource management and conservation (MS); science teacher certification (MS); self-designed studies (MS); special education (M Ed); substance abuse counseling (MA); sustainability (MBA); sustainable development and climate change (MS); teaching (M Ed, PMC); Waldorf teacher training (M Ed, Certificate). Electronic applications accepted.

ANTIOCH UNIVERSITY SANTA BARBARA, Santa Barbara, CA 93101-1581

General Information Independent, coed, upper-level institution. *Graduate housing:* On-campus housing not available.

GRADUATE UNITS

Program in Business Administration Offers non-profit management (MBA); social business (MBA); strategic leadership (MBA).

Program in Clinical Psychology Offers clinical psychology (MA, Psy D). Electronic applications accepted.

Program in Education/Teacher Credentialing *Program availability:* Part-time. Offers education/teacher credentialing (M Ed, MA). Electronic applications accepted.

Program in Writing and Contemporary Media *Program availability:* Part-time. Offers writing and contemporary media (MFA).

ANTIOCH UNIVERSITY SEATTLE, Seattle, WA 98121-1814

General Information Independent, coed, university. *Enrollment:* 386 full-time matriculated graduate/professional students (313 women), 154 part-time matriculated graduate/professional students (132 women). *Enrollment by degree level:* 439 master's, 100 doctoral, 1 other advanced degree. *Graduate housing:* On-campus housing not available. *Student services:* Campus employment opportunities, career counseling, free psychological counseling, international student services, services for students with disabilities, teacher training, writing training. *Library facilities:* Antioch Seattle Library. *Collection:* Books: 8,425 (physical), 264,631 (digital/electronic); Serial titles: 40,950 (digital/electronic); Databases: 222.
Website: http://www.antiochsea.edu/

General Application Contact: Eileen Knight, Recruitment and Admissions Director, 206-268-4200, Fax: 206-268-4242, E-mail: eknight@antioch.edu.

GRADUATE UNITS

Graduate Programs Expenses: Contact institution. *Financial support:* Fellowships, research assistantships, Federal Work-Study, institutionally sponsored loans, and unspecified assistantships available. Financial award application deadline: 6/15. *Program availability:* Part-time, evening/weekend. Offers adult education (MA); drama therapy (MA); individualized studies (MA); leadership in edible education (MA); psychology (Psy D); teaching (MAT); urban environmental education (MA). *Application deadline:* Applications are processed on a rolling basis. Electronic applications accepted. *Application Contact:* Eileen Knight, Recruitment and Admissions Director, 206-268-4200, E-mail: psmith-mentz@antiochsea.edu. *Vice President of Academic Affairs,* Peter Rojcewicz, 206-268-4108, E-mail: projcewicz@antioch.edu.

AOMA GRADUATE SCHOOL OF INTEGRATIVE MEDICINE, Austin, TX 78757

General Information Proprietary, coed, graduate-only institution. *Enrollment by degree level:* 140 master's, 12 doctoral. *Graduate faculty:* 10 full-time (4 women), 18 part-time/adjunct (10 women). *Tuition:* Full-time $4592; part-time $287 per credit. *Required fees:* $230 per quarter. One-time fee: $240. Tuition and fees vary according to course load. *Graduate housing:* On-campus housing not available. *Student services:* Campus employment opportunities, campus safety program, career counseling, exercise/wellness program, international student services, services for students with disabilities. *Library facilities:* AOMA Library.

Computer facilities: 8 computers available on campus for general student use. Online class registration is available.
Website: http://www.aoma.edu/

General Application Contact: Jessica Du, Associate Director of Admissions, 512-492-3017, Fax: 512-454-7001, E-mail: admissions@aoma.edu.

GRADUATE UNITS

Doctor of Acupuncture and Oriental Medicine Program Students: 10 full-time (4 women), 2 part-time (1 woman); includes 4 minority (2 Black or African American, non-

Hispanic/Latino; 1 Asian, non-Hispanic/Latino; 1 Hispanic/Latino). Average age 39. 20 applicants, 80% accepted, 14 enrolled. *Faculty:* 2 full-time (1 woman), 7 part-time/adjunct (3 women). Expenses: Contact institution. *Financial support:* In 2016–17, 2 students received support. Application deadline: 6/30; applicants required to submit FAFSA. In 2016, 3 doctorates awarded. Offers acupuncture and Oriental medicine (DAOM). *Application deadline:* For fall admission, 5/20 for domestic and international students; for summer admission, 5/15 priority date for domestic and international students. Applications are processed on a rolling basis. *Application fee:* $75. Electronic applications accepted. *Application Contact:* Jessica Du, Associate Director of Admissions, 512-492-3017, Fax: 512-454-7001, E-mail: admissions@aoma.edu. *President,* Dr. John S. Finnell, 512-492-3057, Fax: 512-454-7001, E-mail: jfinnell@aoma.edu.

Master of Acupuncture and Oriental Medicine Program Students: 126 full-time (98 women), 45 part-time (34 women); includes 33 minority (8 Black or African American, non-Hispanic/Latino; 9 Asian, non-Hispanic/Latino; 16 Hispanic/Latino). Average age 35. 42 applicants, 74% accepted, 21 enrolled. *Faculty:* 11 full-time (4 women), 20 part-time/adjunct (12 women). Expenses: Contact institution. *Financial support:* In 2016–17, 24 students received support. Federal Work-Study and scholarships/grants available. Financial award applicants required to submit FAFSA. In 2016, 37 master's awarded. Offers acupuncture and Oriental medicine (MAcOM). *Application deadline:* For fall admission, 8/1 priority date for domestic and international students; for winter admission, 11/6 priority date for domestic and international students; for spring admission, 2/16 priority date for domestic and international students; for summer admission, 5/23 priority date for domestic and international students. Applications are processed on a rolling basis. *Application fee:* $75. Electronic applications accepted. *Application Contact:* Jessica Du, Director of Admissions, 512-492-3017, Fax: 512-454-7001, E-mail: admissions@aoma.edu. *Program Director,* Lesley Hamilton, 512-454-3040, Fax: 512-454-7001, E-mail: admissions@aoma.edu.

APEX SCHOOL OF THEOLOGY, Durham, NC 27703
General Information Independent-religious, coed, comprehensive institution. *Graduate housing:* On-campus housing not available.

GRADUATE UNITS
Graduate Programs

APPALACHIAN BIBLE COLLEGE, Mount Hope, WV 25880
General Information Independent-religious, coed, comprehensive institution. One-time fee: $25 part-time. Tuition and fees vary according to course level, degree level and program. *Graduate housing:* Rooms and/or apartments guaranteed to single students and available on a first-come, first-served basis to married students. Typical cost: $3785 (including board) for single students; $6500 per year for married students. Room and board charges vary according to housing facility selected. Housing application deadline: 9/1. *Student services:* Campus employment opportunities. *Library facilities:* John Van Pufflen Library.

Computer facilities: 30 computers available on campus for general student use. A campuswide network can be accessed from student residence rooms and from off campus.
Website: http://www.abc.edu/

General Application Contact: Benjamin Cale, Director of Admissions, 304-877-6428 Ext. 311, Fax: 304-877-5082, E-mail: benjamin.cale@abc.edu.

GRADUATE UNITS
Graduate Program Expenses: Contact institution. *Program availability:* Part-time, online learning. Offers ministry (MA). *Application fee:* $25. Electronic applications accepted. *Application Contact:* Benjamin Cale, Director of Admissions, 304-877-6428 Ext. 311, Fax: 304-877-5082, E-mail: benjamin.cale@abc.edu. *Dean of Graduate Studies,* Dr. John Rinehart, 304-877-6428.

APPALACHIAN COLLEGE OF PHARMACY, Oakwood, VA 24631
General Information Independent, coed, graduate-only institution.

GRADUATE UNITS
Doctor of Pharmacy Program Offers pharmacy (Pharm D).

APPALACHIAN SCHOOL OF LAW, Grundy, VA 24614
General Information Independent, coed, graduate-only institution. *Graduate housing:* On-campus housing not available.

GRADUATE UNITS
Professional Program in Law Offers law (JD). Electronic applications accepted.

APPALACHIAN STATE UNIVERSITY, Boone, NC 28608
General Information State-supported, coed, comprehensive institution. CGS member. Tuition, state resident: full-time $4744. Tuition, nonresident: full-time $17,913. Full-time tuition and fees vary according to program. *Graduate housing:* On-campus housing not available. *Student services:* Campus employment opportunities, campus safety program, career counseling, child daycare facilities, exercise/wellness program, free psychological counseling, grant writing training, international student services, low-cost health insurance, multicultural affairs office, services for students with disabilities, teacher training, writing training. *Library facilities:* Carol Grotnes Belk Library plus 1 other. *Collection:* Books: 673,768 (physical), 1.2 million (digital/electronic); Serial titles: 14,328 (physical), 117,771 (digital/electronic); Databases: 464. Weekly public service hours: 137; students can reserve study rooms.

Computer facilities: Computer purchase and lease plans are available. 2,280 computers available on campus for general student use. A campuswide network can be accessed from student residence rooms and from off campus. Online class registration is available.
Website: http://www.appstate.edu/

General Application Contact: Dontrell Parson, Director of Graduate Admissions and Recruiting, 828-262-2130, Fax: 828-262-2709, E-mail: parsondo@appstate.edu.

GRADUATE UNITS
Cratis D. Williams Graduate School Expenses: Contact institution. *Financial support:* Fellowships, career-related internships or fieldwork, Federal Work-Study, institutionally sponsored loans, scholarships/grants, and unspecified assistantships available. Financial award application deadline: 4/1; financial award applicants required to submit FAFSA. *Program availability:* Part-time, evening/weekend, online learning. Offers appropriate technology (MS); cell and molecular biology (MS); clinical health psychology (MA); clinical mental health counseling (MA); college student development (MA); computer science (MS); curriculum specialist (MA); educational administration (Ed S); educational media (MA); elementary education (MA); English (MA); exercise science (MS); general history (MA); general management (MBA); geography (MA); higher education (MA, Ed S); library science (MLS); marriage and family therapy (MA);

mathematics (MA); middle grades education (MA); nutrition (MS); political science (MA); public administration (MPA); reading education (MA); renewable energy engineering (MS); romance languages (MA); school administration (MA); school counseling (MA); social work (MSW); special education (MA); speech-language pathology (MS); taxation (MS). *Application deadline:* For fall admission, 2/1 for international students; for spring admission, 7/1 for international students. Applications are processed on a rolling basis. *Application fee:* $55. Electronic applications accepted. *Application Contact:* Sandy Krause, Director of Admissions and Recruiting, 828-262-2130, Fax: 828-262-2709, E-mail: krausesl@appstate.edu. *Dean of Research and Graduate Studies,* Dr. Edelma D. Huntley, 828-262-2130, E-mail: huntleyed@appstate.edu.

Center for Appalachian Studies Expenses: Contact institution. *Financial support:* Fellowships, research assistantships, teaching assistantships, career-related internships or fieldwork, Federal Work-Study, scholarships/grants, and unspecified assistantships available. Financial award application deadline: 4/1; financial award applicants required to submit FAFSA. *Program availability:* Part-time. Offers culture (MA). *Application deadline:* For fall admission, 3/15 priority date for domestic students, 2/1 for international students; for spring admission, 11/1 for domestic students, 7/1 for international students. Applications are processed on a rolling basis. *Application fee:* $55. Electronic applications accepted. *Application Contact:* Dr. Dave Wood, Graduate Program Director, 828-262-7199, E-mail: wooddh@appstate.edu. *Director,* Dr. Pat Beaver, 828-262-2550, E-mail: beaverpd@appstate.edu.

School of Music Expenses: Contact institution. *Financial support:* Fellowships, research assistantships, teaching assistantships, career-related internships or fieldwork, Federal Work-Study, scholarships/grants, tuition waivers (partial), and unspecified assistantships available. Financial award application deadline: 4/1; financial award applicants required to submit FAFSA. *Program availability:* Part-time. Offers music performance (MM); music therapy (MMT). *Application deadline:* For fall admission, 3/15 for domestic students, 2/1 for international students; for spring admission, 11/1 for domestic students, 7/1 for international students. Applications are processed on a rolling basis. *Application fee:* $55. Electronic applications accepted. *Application Contact:* Dr. Jennifer Snodgrass, Graduate Program Director, 828-262-6463, E-mail: snodgrassjs@appstate.edu. *Program Director,* Dr. Kathy McKinney, 828-262-6444, E-mail: mckinneych@appstate.edu.

AQUINAS COLLEGE, Grand Rapids, MI 49506
General Information Independent-religious, coed, comprehensive institution. *Tuition:* Part-time $548 per credit hour. *Required fees:* $120 per credit hour. *Graduate housing:* On-campus housing not available. *Student services:* Campus employment opportunities, campus safety program, career counseling, exercise/wellness program, free psychological counseling, multicultural affairs office, services for students with disabilities, teacher training, writing training. *Library facilities:* Grace Hauenstein Library plus 1 other. *Collection:* Books: 85,348 (physical), 196,003 (digital/electronic); Serial titles: 231 (physical); Databases: 85. Students can reserve study rooms.

Computer facilities: Computer purchase and lease plans are available. 210 computers available on campus for general student use. A campuswide network can be accessed from student residence rooms and from off campus. Online class registration is available.
Website: http://www.aquinas.edu/

General Application Contact: Office of Academic Affairs, 616-632-8900, Fax: 616-732-4465.

GRADUATE UNITS
School of Education Expenses: Contact institution. *Financial support:* Scholarships/grants available. Support available to part-time students. Financial award application deadline: 3/15. *Program availability:* Part-time, evening/weekend. Offers education (M Ed, MAT). *Application deadline:* Applications are processed on a rolling basis. *Application fee:* $0. *Application Contact:* Administrative Assistant, 616-632-2440. *Dean,* Dr. Susan English, 616-632-2800, Fax: 616-732-4465, E-mail: englisus@aquinas.edu.

School of Management Expenses: Contact institution. *Financial support:* Scholarships/grants available. Support available to part-time students. Financial award application deadline: 3/15; financial award applicants required to submit FAFSA. *Program availability:* Part-time, evening/weekend. Offers marketing management (MM); organizational leadership (MM); sustainable business (MM). *Application deadline:* Applications are processed on a rolling basis. *Application fee:* $0. *Application Contact:* Lynn Atkins-Rykert, Program Coordinator, 616-632-2925, Fax: 616-732-4489, E-mail: atkinlyn@aquinas.edu. *Interim Director,* Cynthia G. VanGelderen, 616-632-2922, Fax: 616-732-4489.

AQUINAS COLLEGE, Nashville, TN 37205-2005
General Information Independent-religious, coed, comprehensive institution. *Graduate housing:* On-campus housing not available. *Library facilities:* Aquinas College Library. *Collection:* Books: 55,934 (physical), 71,042 (digital/electronic); Serial titles: 381 (physical), 17,998 (digital/electronic); Databases: 95. Weekly public service hours: 64.

Computer facilities: 59 computers available on campus for general student use. A campuswide network can be accessed. Online class registration is available.
Website: http://www.aquinascollege.edu/

GRADUATE UNITS
School of Education Expenses: Contact institution. Offers elementary education (MAT); secondary education (MAT); teaching and learning (M Ed). *Dean,* Sr. Mary Anne Zuberbueler, OP, 615-297-7545 Ext. 282, Fax: 615-279-3892, E-mail: srmanne@aquinascollege.edu.

AQUINAS INSTITUTE OF THEOLOGY, St. Louis, MO 63108
General Information Independent-religious, coed, graduate-only institution. *Graduate housing:* On-campus housing not available.

GRADUATE UNITS
Graduate and Professional Programs *Program availability:* Part-time, evening/weekend, online learning. Offers biblical studies (Certificate); church music (MM); health care mission (MAHCM); ministry (M Div); pastoral care (Certificate); pastoral ministry (MAPM); pastoral studies (MAPS); preaching (D Min); spiritual direction (Certificate); theology (M Div, MA); Thomistic studies (Certificate).

ARCADIA UNIVERSITY, Glenside, PA 19038-3295
General Information Independent-religious, coed, comprehensive institution. CGS member. *Enrollment:* 3,785 graduate, professional, and undergraduate students; 490 full-time matriculated graduate/professional students (367 women), 719 part-time matriculated graduate/professional students (545 women). *Enrollment by degree level:* 744 master's, 375 doctoral, 90 other advanced degrees. *Graduate faculty:* 106 full-time, 104 part-time/adjunct. *Tuition:* Full-time $28,530; part-time $720 per credit hour. Tuition

and fees vary according to course load and program. *Graduate housing:* On-campus housing not available. *Student services:* Campus safety program, career counseling, international student services, low-cost health insurance, multicultural affairs office, writing training. *Library facilities:* Bette E. Landman Library. *Collection:* Students can reserve study rooms.

Computer facilities: A campuswide network can be accessed from student residence rooms and from off campus. Online class registration is available. Website: http://www.arcadia.edu/

General Application Contact: Information Contact, 215-572-2910, Fax: 215-572-4049, E-mail: admiss@arcadia.edu.

GRADUATE UNITS

College of Arts and Sciences Students: 84 full-time (60 women), 107 part-time (83 women); includes 41 minority (22 Black or African American, non-Hispanic/Latino; 4 Asian, non-Hispanic/Latino; 3 Hispanic/Latino; 12 Two or more races, non-Hispanic/Latino), 14 international. Average age 30. 159 applicants, 66% accepted, 49 enrolled. *Faculty:* 39 full-time (22 women), 34 part-time/adjunct (21 women). Expenses: Contact institution. In 2016, 109 master's awarded. Offers applied behavior analysis (MAC); arts and sciences (MA, MAC, MAH, MFA, MSFS); autism (MAC); child/family therapy (MAC); community public health (MAC); counseling/international peace and conflict resolution dual degree (MAC); creative writing (MFA); English (MA); forensic science (MSFS); humanities (MAH); international peace and conflict resolution (MA); international public relations (MA); mental health counseling (MAC); trauma (MAC). *Application Contact:* Information Contact, 215-572-2910, Fax: 215-572-4049, E-mail: admiss@arcadia.edu. *Interim Dean,* Sandra Crenshaw, 215-572-4009.

College of Health Sciences Students: 384 full-time (291 women), 221 part-time (155 women); includes 103 minority (14 Black or African American, non-Hispanic/Latino; 2 American Indian or Alaska Native, non-Hispanic/Latino; 67 Asian, non-Hispanic/Latino; 14 Hispanic/Latino; 2 Native Hawaiian or other Pacific Islander, non-Hispanic/Latino; 4 Two or more races, non-Hispanic/Latino), 23 international. *Faculty:* 37 full-time (26 women), 46 part-time/adjunct (37 women). Expenses: Contact institution. In 2016, 140 master's, 132 doctorates awarded. Offers genetic counseling (MSGC); health education (MSHE); health sciences (MMS, MPH, MSGC, MSHE, DPT); physical therapy (DPT); physician assistant (MMS); public health (MPH, MSHE). *Application Contact:* Information Contact, 215-572-2910, Fax: 215-572-4049, E-mail: admiss@arcadia.edu. *Dean,* Rebecca Craik, 215-572-2143, E-mail: craikr@arcadia.edu.

Program in Business Administration Students: 35 part-time (23 women); includes 17 minority (11 Black or African American, non-Hispanic/Latino; 2 Asian, non-Hispanic/Latino; 3 Hispanic/Latino; 1 Two or more races, non-Hispanic/Latino), 2 international. Average age 28. 32 applicants, 69% accepted, 18 enrolled. *Faculty:* 11 full-time (5 women), 21 part-time/adjunct (8 women). Expenses: Contact institution. In 2016, 17 master's awarded. Offers business administration (MBA). *Application fee:* $50. *Application Contact:* Office of Enrollment Management, 215-572-2910, Fax: 215-572-4049, E-mail: admiss@arcadia.edu. *Executive Director,* Dr. Thomas M. Brinker, 215-572-4039.

School of Education Students: 22 full-time (16 women), 356 part-time (284 women); includes 84 minority (55 Black or African American, non-Hispanic/Latino; 2 American Indian or Alaska Native, non-Hispanic/Latino; 13 Asian, non-Hispanic/Latino; 11 Hispanic/Latino; 3 Two or more races, non-Hispanic/Latino), 4 international. Average age 34. 145 applicants, 73% accepted, 80 enrolled. *Faculty:* 19 full-time (13 women), 3 part-time/adjunct (all women). Expenses: Contact institution. *Financial support:* Career-related internships or fieldwork, tuition waivers (partial), and unspecified assistantships available. In 2016, 95 master's, 11 doctorates awarded. *Program availability:* Part-time, evening/weekend, online learning. Offers art education (M Ed); computer education (CAS); curriculum (CAS); curriculum studies (M Ed); early childhood education (M Ed); educational leadership (M Ed, Ed D, CAS); elementary education (M Ed); English education (MA Ed); environmental education (MA Ed); instructional technology (M Ed); language arts (M Ed); library science (M Ed); mathematics education (M Ed, MA Ed); music education (MA Ed); psychology (MA Ed); reading (M Ed, CAS); science education (M Ed, CAS); secondary education (M Ed, CAS); special education (M Ed, Ed D, CAS); theater arts (MA Ed); written communication (MA Ed). *Application deadline:* Applications are processed on a rolling basis. *Application fee:* $50. Electronic applications accepted. *Application Contact:* 215-572-2925, Fax: 215-572-2126, E-mail: grad@arcadia.edu. *Interim Dean of the School of Education,* John T Groves, 215-572-2940.

ARGOSY UNIVERSITY, ATLANTA, Atlanta, GA 30328

General Information Proprietary, coed, university.

GRADUATE UNITS

College of Business Offers accounting (DBA); corporate compliance (MBA); customized professional concentration (MBA, DBA); finance (MBA); healthcare administration (MBA); information systems (DBA); information systems management (MBA); international business (MBA, DBA); management (MBA, MSM, DBA); marketing (MBA, DBA).

College of Education Offers educational leadership (MAEd, Ed D, Ed S); teaching and learning (MAEd, Ed D, Ed S).

College of Health Sciences Offers public health (MPH).

Georgia School of Professional Psychology Offers clinical psychology (MA, Psy D, Postdoctoral Respecialization Certificate); community counseling (MA); counselor education and supervision (Ed D); forensic psychology (MA); industrial organizational psychology (MA); marriage and family therapy (Certificate); sport-exercise psychology (MA).

ARGOSY UNIVERSITY, CHICAGO, Chicago, IL 60601

General Information Proprietary, coed, university.

GRADUATE UNITS

College of Business *Program availability:* Online learning. Offers accounting (DBA); customized professional concentration (MBA, DBA); finance (MBA); fraud examination (MBA); global business sustainability (DBA); healthcare administration (MBA); information systems (DBA); information systems management (MBA); international business (MBA, DBA); management (MBA, MSM, DBA); marketing (MBA, DBA); organizational leadership (Ed D); public administration (MBA); sustainable management (MBA).

College of Education *Program availability:* Online learning. Offers adult education and training (MA Ed); community college executive leadership (Ed D); educational leadership (MA Ed, Ed D, Ed S); instructional leadership (Ed D, Ed S).

College of Health Sciences Offers public health (MPH).

Illinois School of Professional Psychology *Program availability:* Online learning. Offers child and adolescent psychology (Psy D); client-centered and experiential psychotherapies (Psy D); clinical psychology (MA, Psy D); community counseling (MA);

counseling psychology (Ed D); counselor education and supervision (Ed D); diversity and multicultural psychology (Psy D); family psychology (Psy D); forensic psychology (Psy D); health psychology (Psy D); industrial organizational psychology (MA); neuropsychology (Psy D); organizational consulting (Psy D); psychoanalytic psychology (Psy D); psychology and spirituality (Psy D).

ARGOSY UNIVERSITY, DALLAS, Farmers Branch, TX 75244

General Information Proprietary, coed, university.

GRADUATE UNITS

College of Business Offers accounting (DBA, AGC); corporate compliance (MBA, Graduate Certificate); customized professional concentration (MBA); finance (MBA, Graduate Certificate); fraud examination (MBA, Graduate Certificate); global business sustainability (DBA, AGC); healthcare administration (Graduate Certificate); healthcare management (MBA); information systems (MBA, DBA, AGC); information systems management (Graduate Certificate); international business (MBA, DBA, AGC, Graduate Certificate); management (MBA, DBA, AGC, Graduate Certificate); marketing (MBA, DBA, AGC, Graduate Certificate); public administration (MBA, Graduate Certificate); sustainable management (MBA, Graduate Certificate).

College of Education Offers educational administration (MA Ed); educational leadership (Ed D); higher and postsecondary education (MA Ed); instructional leadership (MA Ed); school psychology (MA).

College of Health Sciences Offers public health (MPH).

College of Psychology and Behavioral Sciences Offers clinical psychology (MA, Psy D); community counseling (MA); counselor education and supervision (Ed D); forensic psychology (MA); industrial organizational psychology (MA); psychology and behavioral sciences (MA, Ed D, Psy D).

ARGOSY UNIVERSITY, DENVER, Denver, CO 80231

General Information Proprietary, coed, university.

GRADUATE UNITS

College of Business Offers accounting (DBA); corporate compliance (MBA); customized professional concentration (MBA, DBA); finance (MBA); fraud examination (MBA); global business sustainability (DBA); healthcare administration (MBA); information systems (DBA); information systems management (MBA); international business (MBA, DBA); management (MBA, MSM, DBA); marketing (MBA, DBA); organizational leadership (Ed D); public administration (MBA); sustainable management (MBA).

College of Education Offers community college executive leadership (Ed D); educational leadership (MA Ed, Ed D); instructional leadership (MA Ed, Ed D).

College of Health Sciences Offers public health (MPH).

College of Psychology and Behavioral Sciences Offers clinical mental health counseling (MA); clinical psychology (MA, Psy D); counseling psychology (Ed D); counselor education and supervision (Ed D); forensic psychology (MA); industrial organizational psychology (MA); marriage and family therapy (MA, DMFT).

ARGOSY UNIVERSITY, HAWAI`I, Honolulu, HI 96813

General Information Proprietary, coed, university.

GRADUATE UNITS

College of Business Offers accounting (DBA); corporate compliance (MBA); customized professional concentration (MBA, DBA); finance (MBA, Certificate); fraud examination (MBA); global business sustainability (DBA); healthcare administration (MBA, Certificate); information systems (DBA); information systems management (MBA, Certificate); international business (MBA, DBA, Certificate); management (MBA, MSM, DBA); marketing (MBA, DBA, Certificate); organizational leadership (Ed D); public administration (MBA); sustainable management (MBA).

College of Education Offers adult education and training (MAEd); educational leadership (Ed D); instructional leadership (Ed D); school psychology (MA).

College of Health Sciences Offers public health (MPH).

Hawai'i School of Professional Psychology Offers clinical psychology (MA, Psy D, Postdoctoral Respecialization Certificate); counseling psychology (Ed D); forensic psychology (MA); marriage and family therapy (MA); professional psychology (MA, MS, Ed D, Certificate, Postdoctoral Respecialization Certificate); psychopharmacology (MS, Certificate); substance abuse counseling (Certificate).

ARGOSY UNIVERSITY, INLAND EMPIRE, Ontario, CA 91761

General Information Proprietary, coed, university.

GRADUATE UNITS

College of Business Offers accounting (DBA); corporate compliance (MBA); customized professional concentration (MBA, DBA); finance (MBA); fraud examination (MBA); global business sustainability (DBA); healthcare administration (MBA); information systems (DBA); information systems management (MBA); international business (MBA, DBA); management (MBA, MSM, DBA); marketing (MBA, DBA); organizational leadership (Ed D); public administration (MBA); sustainable management (MBA).

College of Education Offers community college executive leadership (Ed D); educational leadership (MA Ed, Ed D); instructional leadership (MA Ed, Ed D).

College of Health Sciences Offers public health (MPH).

College of Psychology and Behavioral Sciences Offers clinical psychology/marriage and family therapy (MA); counseling psychology (Ed D); counseling psychology/marriage and family therapy (MA); forensic psychology (MA); industrial organizational psychology (MA); sport-exercise psychology (MA).

ARGOSY UNIVERSITY, LOS ANGELES, Santa Monica, CA 90045

General Information Proprietary, coed, university.

GRADUATE UNITS

College of Business Offers accounting (DBA); corporate compliance (MBA); customized professional concentration (MBA, DBA); finance (MBA); fraud examination (MBA); global business sustainability (DBA); healthcare administration (MBA); information systems (DBA); information systems management (MBA); international business (MBA, DBA); management (MBA, MSM, DBA); marketing (MBA, DBA); organizational leadership (Ed D); public administration (MBA); sustainable management (MBA).

College of Education Offers community college executive leadership (Ed D); educational leadership (MA Ed, Ed D); instructional leadership (MA Ed, Ed D).

College of Health Sciences Offers public health (MPH).

College of Psychology and Behavioral Sciences Offers clinical psychology/marriage and family therapy (MA); counseling psychology (Ed D); counseling psychology/marriage and family therapy (MA); forensic psychology (MA).

ARGOSY UNIVERSITY, NASHVILLE, Nashville, TN 37214

General Information Proprietary, coed, university.

GRADUATE UNITS

College of Business Offers accounting (DBA); customized professional concentration (MBA, DBA); finance (MBA); healthcare administration (MBA); information systems (MBA, DBA); international business (MBA, DBA); management (MBA, MSM, DBA); marketing (MBA, DBA).

College of Education Offers education (MA Ed, Ed D, Ed S); education technology (Ed D); educational leadership (MA Ed, Ed S); higher education administration (Ed D); instructional leadership (MA Ed, Ed S); K-12 education (Ed D).

College of Health Sciences Offers public health (MPH).

College of Psychology and Behavioral Sciences Offers counselor education and supervision (Ed D); mental health counseling (MA).

ARGOSY UNIVERSITY, NORTHERN VIRGINIA, Arlington, VA 22209

General Information Proprietary, coed, university.

GRADUATE UNITS

American School of Professional Psychology Offers clinical psychology (MA, Psy D); community counseling (MA); counseling psychology (Ed D); counselor education and supervision (Ed D); forensic psychology (MA).

College of Business Offers accounting (DBA); customized professional concentration (MBA, DBA); finance (MBA); fraud examination (MBA); global business sustainability (DBA); healthcare administration (MBA); information systems (DBA); information systems management (MBA); international business (MBA, DBA, Certificate); management (MBA, MSM, DBA); marketing (MBA, DBA, Certificate); organizational leadership (Ed D); public administration (MBA); sustainable management (MBA).

College of Education Offers community college executive leadership (Ed D); educational leadership (MA Ed, Ed D, Ed S); instructional leadership (MA Ed, Ed D, Ed S).

College of Health Sciences Offers public health (MPH).

ARGOSY UNIVERSITY, ORANGE COUNTY, Orange, CA 92868

General Information Proprietary, coed, university.

GRADUATE UNITS

American School of Professional Psychology *Program availability:* Part-time, evening/weekend. Offers child and adolescent psychology (Psy D); counseling psychology (Ed D); forensic psychology (MA); marriage and family therapy (MA); professional psychology (MA, Ed D, Psy D); sport-exercise psychology (MA). Electronic applications accepted.

College of Business Offers accounting (DBA, Adv C); corporate compliance (MBA); customized professional concentration (MBA, DBA); finance (MBA, Certificate); fraud examination (MBA); global business sustainability (DBA); healthcare administration (MBA, Certificate); information systems (DBA, Adv C, Certificate); information systems management (MBA); international business (MBA, DBA, Adv C, Certificate); management (MBA, MSM, DBA, Adv C); marketing (MBA, DBA, Adv C, Certificate); organizational leadership (Ed D); public administration (MBA, Certificate); sustainable management (MBA).

College of Education Offers community college executive leadership (Ed D); educational leadership (MA Ed, Ed D); instructional leadership (MA Ed, Ed D).

College of Health Sciences Offers public health (MPH).

ARGOSY UNIVERSITY, PHOENIX, Phoenix, AZ 85021

General Information Proprietary, coed, university.

GRADUATE UNITS

Arizona School of Professional Psychology Offers clinical psychology (MA); forensic psychology (MA); industrial organizational psychology (MA); mental health counseling (MA); neuropsychology (Psy D); professional psychology (MA, Psy D); sport-exercise psychology (MA); sports-exercise psychology (Psy D).

College of Business Offers accounting (DBA); corporate compliance (MBA); customized professional concentration (MBA, DBA); finance (MBA); fraud examination (MBA); global business sustainability (DBA); healthcare administration (MBA); information systems (DBA); information systems management (MBA); international business (MBA, DBA); management (MBA, DBA); marketing (MBA, DBA); public administration (MBA); sustainable management (MBA).

College of Education Offers adult education and training (MA Ed); advanced educational administration (Ed D, Ed S); community college executive leadership (Ed D); educational administration (MA Ed); educational leadership (MA Ed, Ed D, Ed S); higher and postsecondary education (MA Ed); initial educational administration (Ed D, Ed S); school psychology (MA, Psy D); teaching and learning (MA Ed, Ed D, Ed S).

College of Health Sciences Offers public health (MPH).

ARGOSY UNIVERSITY, SALT LAKE CITY, Draper, UT 84020

General Information Proprietary, coed, university.

GRADUATE UNITS

College of Business Offers accounting (DBA); corporate compliance (MBA); customized professional concentration (MBA, DBA); finance (MBA); fraud examination (MBA); global business sustainability (DBA); healthcare administration (MBA); information systems (DBA); information systems management (MBA); international business (MBA, DBA); management (MBA, DBA); marketing (MBA, DBA); public administration (MBA); sustainable management (MBA).

College of Education Offers educational leadership (MA Ed, Ed D).

College of Health Sciences Offers public health (MPH).

College of Psychology and Behavioral Sciences Offers counseling psychology (Ed D); counselor education and supervision (Ed D); forensic psychology (MA); marriage and family therapy (MA, DMFT); mental health counseling (MA).

ARGOSY UNIVERSITY, SAN DIEGO, San Diego, CA 92108

General Information Proprietary, coed, university.

GRADUATE UNITS

College of Business Offers accounting (DBA); corporate compliance (MBA); customized professional concentration (MBA, DBA); finance (MBA); fraud examination (MBA); global business sustainability (DBA); information systems (DBA); information systems management (MBA); international business (MBA, DBA); management (MBA, MSM, DBA); marketing (MBA, DBA); organizational leadership (Ed D); public administration (MBA).

College of Education Offers community college executive leadership (Ed D); educational leadership (MA Ed, Ed D); instructional leadership (MA Ed, Ed D).

College of Health Sciences Offers public health (MPH).

College of Psychology and Behavioral Sciences Offers clinical psychology/marriage and family therapy (MA); counseling psychology (Ed D); counseling psychology/marriage and family therapy (MA); forensic psychology (MA).

ARGOSY UNIVERSITY, SAN FRANCISCO BAY AREA, Alameda, CA 94501

General Information Proprietary, coed, university.

GRADUATE UNITS

American School of Professional Psychology Offers clinical psychology (MA, Psy D); counseling psychology (MA, Ed D); forensic psychology (MA); sport-exercise psychology (MA).

College of Business Offers accounting (DBA); corporate compliance (MBA); customized professional concentration (MBA, DBA); finance (MBA); fraud examination (MBA); global business sustainability (DBA); healthcare administration (MBA); information systems (DBA); information systems management (MBA); international business (MBA, DBA); management (MBA, MSM, DBA); marketing (MBA, DBA); organizational leadership (Ed D); public administration (MBA); sustainable management (MBA).

College of Education Offers community college executive leadership (Ed D); educational leadership (MA Ed, Ed D); instructional leadership (MA Ed, Ed D).

College of Health Sciences Offers public health (MPH).

ARGOSY UNIVERSITY, SARASOTA, Sarasota, FL 34235

General Information Proprietary, coed, university.

GRADUATE UNITS

College of Business Offers accounting (DBA, Adv C); corporate compliance (MBA, DBA, Certificate); customized professional concentration (MBA, DBA); finance (MBA, Certificate); fraud examination (MBA, Certificate); global business sustainability (DBA, Adv C); healthcare administration (MBA, Certificate); information systems (DBA, Adv C, Certificate); information systems management (MBA); international business (MBA, DBA, Adv C, Certificate); management (MBA, MSM, DBA, Adv C, Certificate); marketing (MBA, DBA, Adv C, Certificate); organizational leadership (Ed D); public administration (MBA, Certificate); sustainable management (MBA, Certificate).

College of Education Offers community college executive leadership (Ed D); educational leadership (MA Ed, Ed D, Ed S); school counseling (MA, Ed S); school psychology (MA); teaching and learning (MA Ed, Ed D, Ed S).

College of Health Sciences Offers public health (MPH).

College of Psychology and Behavioral Sciences Offers community counseling (MA); counseling psychology (Ed D); counselor education and supervision (Ed D); forensic psychology (MA); marriage and family therapy (MA); mental health counseling (MA); pastoral community counseling (Ed D).

ARGOSY UNIVERSITY, SCHAUMBURG, Schaumburg, IL 60173-5403

General Information Proprietary, coed, university.

GRADUATE UNITS

College of Behavioral Sciences Offers clinical mental health counseling (MA); forensic psychology (MA, Post-Graduate Certificate); industrial organizational psychology (MA); sport-exercise psychology (MA).

College of Health Sciences Offers public health (MPH).

Graduate School of Business and Management Offers accounting (DBA, Adv C); customized professional concentration (MBA, DBA); finance (MBA, Certificate); fraud examination (MBA); healthcare administration (MBA, Certificate); human resource management (MS); information systems (Adv C, Certificate); information systems management (MBA); international business (MBA, DBA, Adv C, Certificate); management (MBA, MSM, DBA, Adv C, Certificate); marketing (MBA, DBA, Adv C, Certificate); organizational leadership (MS, Ed D); public administration (MBA); sustainable management (MBA).

Illinois School of Professional Psychology Offers clinical psychology (MA, Psy D).

ARGOSY UNIVERSITY, SEATTLE, Seattle, WA 98121

General Information Proprietary, coed, university.

GRADUATE UNITS

College of Business Offers accounting (DBA); corporate compliance (MBA); customized professional concentration (MBA, DBA); finance (MBA); fraud examination (MBA); global business sustainability (DBA); healthcare administration (MBA); information systems (DBA); information systems management (MBA); international business (MBA, DBA); management (MBA, MSM, DBA); marketing (MBA, DBA); organizational leadership (Ed D); public administration (MBA); sustainable management (MBA).

College of Education Offers adult education and training (MA Ed); community college executive leadership (Ed D); educational leadership (MA Ed, Ed D); higher and postsecondary education (MA Ed); instructional leadership (MA Ed, Ed D).

College of Health Sciences Offers public health (MPH).

College of Psychology and Behavioral Sciences Offers clinical psychology (MA, Psy D, Postdoctoral Respecialization Certificate); counseling psychology (MA, Ed D); psychology and behavioral sciences (MA, Ed D, Psy D, Postdoctoral Respecialization Certificate).

ARGOSY UNIVERSITY, TAMPA, Tampa, FL 33607

General Information Proprietary, coed, university.

GRADUATE UNITS

College of Business Offers accounting (DBA); corporate compliance (MBA); customized professional concentration (MBA, DBA); finance (MBA); fraud examination (MBA); global business sustainability (DBA); healthcare administration (MBA); information systems (DBA); information systems management (MBA); international business (MBA, DBA); management (MBA, MSM, DBA); marketing (MBA, DBA); organizational leadership (Ed D); public administration (MBA); sustainable management (MBA).

College of Education Offers community college executive leadership (Ed D); educational leadership (MA Ed, Ed D, Ed S); school counseling (MA); teaching and learning (MA Ed, Ed D, Ed S).

College of Health Sciences Offers public health (MPH).

Florida School of Professional Psychology Offers clinical psychology (MA, Psy D); counselor education and supervision (Ed D); industrial organizational psychology (MA); marriage and family therapy (MA); mental health counseling (MA).

ARGOSY UNIVERSITY, TWIN CITIES, Eagan, MN 55121

General Information Proprietary, coed, university.

GRADUATE UNITS

College of Business Offers accounting (DBA); customized professional concentration (MBA, DBA); finance (MBA); fraud examination (MBA); global business sustainability (DBA); healthcare administration (MBA); information systems (DBA); information systems management (MBA); international business (MBA, DBA); management (MBA, MSM, DBA); marketing (MBA, DBA); organizational leadership (Ed D); public administration (MBA); sustainable management (MBA).

College of Education Offers advanced educational administration (Ed D, Ed S); educational leadership (MA Ed, Ed D, Ed S); higher and postsecondary education (MA Ed); initial educational administration (Ed D, Ed S); instructional leadership (MA Ed, Ed D, Ed S).

College of Health Sciences Offers health services management (MS); public health (MPH).

Minnesota School of Professional Psychology Offers clinical psychology (MA, Psy D); forensic counseling (Post-Graduate Certificate); forensic psychology (MA); industrial organizational psychology (MA); marriage and family therapy (MA, DMFT).

ARIZONA SCHOOL OF ACUPUNCTURE AND ORIENTAL MEDICINE, Tucson, AZ 85712

General Information Proprietary, coed, graduate-only institution.

GRADUATE UNITS

Graduate Programs Offers acupuncture (M Ac, M Ac OM).

ARIZONA STATE UNIVERSITY AT THE TEMPE CAMPUS, Tempe, AZ 85287

General Information State-supported, coed, university. CGS member. *Graduate housing:* Room and/or apartments available to single students; on-campus housing not available to married students. *Research affiliation:* Arizona Public Service (electrical, computer and energy engineering), Banner Health (health, biomedical, and life sciences), Honeywell (mechanical and aerospace engineering), Mayo Clinic (healthcare, biomedical informatics), Raytheon Corporation (computer science and engineering), Translational Genomics Research Institute (TGEN) (biomedicine).

GRADUATE UNITS

College of Health Solutions Offers audiology (Au D); behavioral health (DBH); biomedical informatics (MS, PhD); communication disorders (MS); health solutions (MS, Au D, DBH, PhD); speech and hearing science (PhD).

School of Nutrition and Health Promotion Offers clinical exercise physiology (MS); exercise and wellness (MS); nutrition (MS); obesity prevention and management (MS); physical activity, nutrition and wellness (PhD).

College of Liberal Arts and Sciences *Program availability:* Part-time, online learning. Offers American media and popular culture (MAS); applied behavior analysis (MS); applied linguistics (PhD); behavioral neuroscience (PhD); biochemistry (MS, PhD); chemistry (MS, PhD); clinical psychology (PhD); cognitive science (PhD); creative writing (MFA); developmental psychology (PhD); English (MA, PhD); film and media studies (MAS); liberal arts and sciences (MA, MAS, MFA, MLS, MNS, MS, MTESOL, MUEP, PSM, PSM, PhD, Graduate Certificate); liberal studies (MLS); linguistics (Graduate Certificate); nanoscience (PSM, PSM); physics (MNS, PhD); quantitative psychology (PhD); science and technology policy (MS); social psychology (PhD); teaching English to speakers of other languages (MTESOL); translation studies (Graduate Certificate). Electronic applications accepted.

Hugh Downs School of Human Communication *Program availability:* Evening/weekend. Offers communication (PhD). Electronic applications accepted.

School of Earth and Space Exploration Offers astrophysics (MS, PhD); exploration systems design (PhD); geological sciences (MS, PhD). PhD in exploration systems design is offered in collaboration with the Ira A. Fulton School of Engineering. Electronic applications accepted.

School of Geographical Sciences and Urban Planning Offers geographic information systems (MAS); geographical information science (Graduate Certificate); geography (MA, PhD); transportation systems (Graduate Certificate); urban and environmental planning (MUEP); urban planning (PhD). Electronic applications accepted.

School of Historical, Philosophical and Religious Studies *Program availability:* Part-time. Offers European history (MA, PhD); medieval studies (Graduate Certificate); North American history (MA, PhD); philosophy (MA, PhD); public history (MA); religious studies (MA, PhD); Renaissance studies (Graduate Certificate); scholarly publishing (Graduate Certificate). Electronic applications accepted.

School of Human Evolution and Social Change Offers anthropology (MA, PhD); applied mathematics for the life and social sciences (PhD); environmental social science (PhD); global health (MA, PhD); immigration studies (Graduate Certificate). Electronic applications accepted.

School of International Letters and Cultures Offers Asian languages and civilizations: Chinese (MA); Asian languages and civilizations: Japanese (MA); Chinese (MA, PhD); comparative literature (MA); cultural studies (PhD); French (MA); German (MA); Japanese (MA); language and culture (MA); linguistics (MA); literature (MA, PhD); literature and culture (MA); Spanish (MA, PhD). Electronic applications accepted.

School of Life Sciences Offers animal behavior (PhD); applied ethics (biomedical and health ethics) (MA); biology (MS, PhD); environmental life sciences (PhD); evolutionary biology (PhD); history and philosophy of science (PhD); human and social dimensions of science and technology (PhD); microbiology (PhD); molecular and cellular biology (PhD); neuroscience (PhD). Electronic applications accepted.

School of Mathematical and Statistical Sciences *Program availability:* Part-time. Offers applied mathematics (PhD); mathematics (MA, PhD); mathematics education (PhD); statistics (MS, PhD, Graduate Certificate). Electronic applications accepted.

School of Politics and Global Studies *Program availability:* Part-time. Offers political science (MA, PhD). Electronic applications accepted.

School of Social and Family Dynamics Offers family and human development (MS, PhD); infant-family practice (MAS); marriage and family therapy (MAS); sociology (MA, PhD). Electronic applications accepted.

School of Social Transformation *Program availability:* Part-time. Offers African studies (Graduate Certificate); gender studies (PhD, Graduate Certificate); justice studies (MS, PhD); social and cultural pedagogy (MA); socio-economic justice (Graduate Certificate). Electronic applications accepted.

College of Nursing and Health Innovation *Program availability:* Online learning. Offers advanced nursing practice (DNP); clinical research management (MS); community and public health practice (Graduate Certificate); family mental health nurse practitioner (Graduate Certificate); family nurse practitioner (Graduate Certificate); geriatric nursing (Graduate Certificate); healthcare innovation (MHI); nurse education in academic and practice settings (Graduate Certificate); nurse educator (MS); nursing and healthcare innovation (PhD). Electronic applications accepted.

College of Public Programs *Program availability:* Part-time, evening/weekend, online learning. Electronic applications accepted.

School of Community Resources and Development *Program availability:* Part-time, evening/weekend. Offers community resources and development (MS, PhD); nonprofit leadership and management (Graduate Certificate); nonprofit studies (MNpS); sustainable tourism (MAS). Electronic applications accepted.

School of Criminology and Criminal Justice *Program availability:* Part-time, evening/weekend, online learning. Offers corrections management (Graduate Certificate); criminal justice (MA); criminology and criminal justice (MS, PhD); law enforcement administration (Graduate Certificate). Electronic applications accepted.

School of Public Affairs *Program availability:* Part-time, evening/weekend. Offers emergency management and homeland security (MA); program evaluation (MS); public administration (MPA, PhD); public policy (MPP). Electronic applications accepted.

School of Social Work *Program availability:* Part-time. Offers advanced direct practice (MSW); assessment of integrative health modalities (Graduate Certificate); gerontology (Graduate Certificate); Latino cultural competency (Graduate Certificate); planning, administration and community practice (MSW); social work (PhD); trauma and bereavement (Graduate Certificate). Electronic applications accepted.

Graduate College *Program availability:* Part-time, evening/weekend, online learning. Offers human and social dimensions of science and technology (PhD); neuroscience (PhD). Electronic applications accepted.

Herberger Institute for Design and the Arts Offers design and the arts (M Arch, MA, MFA, MLA, MM, MS, MSD, MUD, DMA, PhD). Electronic applications accepted.

The Design School Offers architecture (M Arch); building design/built environment (MS); design (MSD, PhD); design, environment and the arts (PhD); digital culture (PhD); healthcare and healing environments (PhD); history, theory, and criticism (PhD); landscape architecture (MLA); urban design (MUD). Electronic applications accepted.

School of Art Offers art education (MA); art history (MA); ceramics (MFA); design, environment and the arts (PhD); drawing (MFA); fibers (MFA); intermedia (MFA); metals (MFA); museum studies (MFA); painting (MFA); printmaking (MFA); sculpture (MFA); wood (MFA). Electronic applications accepted.

School of Arts, Media and Engineering Offers media arts and sciences (PhD). Electronic applications accepted.

School of Film, Dance and Theatre Offers dance (MFA); interdisciplinary digital media and performance (MFA); theatre (MA, MFA, PhD). Electronic applications accepted.

School of Music Offers composition (MM, DMA); conducting (DMA); ethnomusicology (MA); interdisciplinary digital media/performance (DMA); music education (MM, PhD); music history and literature (MA); music therapy (MM); performance (MM, DMA). Electronic applications accepted.

Ira A. Fulton Schools of Engineering *Program availability:* Part-time, evening/weekend, online learning. Offers aerospace engineering (MS, PhD); chemical engineering (MS, PhD); construction (MS); embedded systems (M Eng); engineering (M Eng, MA, MCS, MS, MSE, PSM, PhD, Graduate Certificate); enterprise systems innovation and management (MSE); materials science and engineering (MS, PhD); mechanical engineering (MS, PhD); modeling and simulation (M Eng); quality and reliability engineering (M Eng); software engineering (MSE); solar energy engineering and commercialization (PSM); systems engineering (M Eng). Electronic applications accepted.

The Polytechnic School *Program availability:* Part-time, evening/weekend. Offers applied psychology (MS); aviation management and human factors (MS); environmental technology management (MS); global technology and development (MS); graphic information technology (MS); management of technology (MS); manufacturing engineering technology (MS); simulation, modeling, and applied cognitive science (PhD); technology and innovation (MS, PhD). Electronic applications accepted.

School of Biological and Health Systems Engineering *Program availability:* Part-time, evening/weekend. Offers biological design (PhD); biomedical engineering (MS, PhD). Electronic applications accepted.

School of Computing, Informatics, and Decision Systems Engineering *Program availability:* Part-time, evening/weekend, online learning. Offers computer engineering (MS, PhD); computer science (MCS, MS, PhD); industrial engineering (MS, PhD); software engineering (MS). Electronic applications accepted.

School of Electrical, Computer and Energy Engineering *Program availability:* Part-time, evening/weekend, online learning. Offers electrical engineering (MS, MSE, PhD); nuclear power generation (Graduate Certificate). Electronic applications accepted.

School of Sustainable Engineering and the Built Environment *Program availability:* Part-time, evening/weekend, online learning. Offers civil, environmental and sustainable engineering (MS, MSE, PhD); construction engineering (MSE); construction management (MS, PhD). Electronic applications accepted.

Mary Lou Fulton Teachers College *Program availability:* Part-time, evening/weekend, online learning. Offers autism spectrum disorder (Graduate Certificate); curriculum and instruction (M Ed, MA); education (M Ed, MA, MC, MPE, Ed D, PhD, Graduate Certificate); educational leadership (M Ed); educational policy and evaluation (PhD); educational technology (M Ed); elementary education (M Ed); higher and postsecondary education (M Ed); instructional design and performance improvement (Graduate Certificate); leadership and innovation (Ed D); online teaching for grades K-12 (Graduate Certificate); physical education (MPE); secondary education (M Ed); special education (M Ed). Electronic applications accepted.

New College of Interdisciplinary Arts and Sciences *Program availability:* Part-time, evening/weekend. Offers applied ethics and the professions (MA); communication studies (MA); interdisciplinary studies (MA); psychology (MS); social justice and human rights (MA). Electronic applications accepted.

Sandra Day O'Connor College of Law Students: 718 full-time (300 women); includes 195 minority (17 Black or African American, non-Hispanic/Latino; 14 American Indian or Alaska Native, non-Hispanic/Latino; 27 Asian, non-Hispanic/Latino; 98 Hispanic/Latino; 3 Native Hawaiian or other Pacific Islander, non-Hispanic/Latino; 36 Two or more races, non-Hispanic/Latino), 13 international. Average age 28. 1,860 applicants, 42% accepted, 228 enrolled. *Faculty:* 71 full-time (31 women), 67 part-time/adjunct (16 women). Expenses: Contact institution. *Financial support:* In 2016–17, 432 students received support. Institutionally sponsored loans and scholarships/grants available. Financial award application deadline: 3/15; financial award applicants required to submit FAFSA. In 2016, 52 master's, 190 doctorates awarded. *Program availability:* 100% online. Offers biotechnology and genomics (LL M); law (JD); legal studies (MLS); patent practice (MLS); sports law and business (MSLB); tribal policy, law and government (LL M). *Application deadline:* For fall admission, 3/1 priority date for domestic and international students. Applications are processed on a rolling basis. *Application fee:* $65. Electronic applications accepted. *Application Contact:* Chitra Damania, Director of Operations, 480-965-1474, Fax: 480-727-7930, E-mail: law.admissions@asu.edu. *Dean/Professor,* Douglas Sylvester, 480-965-6188, Fax: 480-965-6521, E-mail: douglas.sylvester@asu.edu.

School of Letters and Sciences *Program availability:* Part-time, evening/weekend, online learning. Offers biomedical and health ethics (MA); counseling (MC); counseling psychology (PhD); ethics and emerging technologies (MA); letters and sciences (MA, MC, PhD); public administration, policy and ethics (MA); science, technology and ethics (MA). Electronic applications accepted.

School of Sustainability *Program availability:* Part-time, evening/weekend. Offers sustainability (MA, MS, PhD); sustainable technology and management (Graduate Certificate). Electronic applications accepted.

Thunderbird School of Global Management *Program availability:* Online learning. Offers global affairs and management (MA); global management (MGM).

Walter Cronkite School of Journalism and Mass Communication Offers journalism and mass communication (PhD); mass communication (MMC). Electronic applications accepted.

W. P. Carey School of Business *Program availability:* Part-time, evening/weekend, online learning. Offers business (M Acc, M Tax, MBA, MRED, MS, PhD, Graduate Certificate); business administration (PhD); economics (PhD); entrepreneurship (MBA); finance (MBA); health sector management (MBA); information management (MS); international business (MBA); leadership (MBA); marketing (MBA); organizational behavior (PhD); real estate development (MRED); strategic management (PhD); supply chain management (MBA, PhD). Electronic applications accepted.

Morrison School of Agribusiness *Program availability:* Part-time, evening/weekend. Offers agribusiness (PhD). Electronic applications accepted.

School of Accountancy *Program availability:* Part-time, evening/weekend. Offers accountancy (M Acc, M Tax); business administration (PhD). Electronic applications accepted.

ARIZONA SUMMIT LAW SCHOOL, Phoenix, AZ 85004

General Information Proprietary, coed, graduate-only institution. *Enrollment by degree level:* 386 doctoral. *Graduate faculty:* 17 full-time (13 women), 25 part-time/adjunct (7 women). *Tuition:* Full-time $43,306. *Required fees:* $2048. One-time fee: $70 part-time. Tuition and fees vary according to course load. *Graduate housing:* On-campus housing not available. *Student services:* Campus employment opportunities, career counseling, free psychological counseling, international student services, services for students with disabilities, writing training.
Website: http://www.azsummitlaw.edu/

General Application Contact: Rick Jackson, Associate Dean of Admissions, 602-682-6817, E-mail: admissions@azsummitlaw.edu.

GRADUATE UNITS

JD Program Students: 184 full-time (91 women), 202 part-time (113 women); includes 165 minority (68 Black or African American, non-Hispanic/Latino; 11 American Indian or Alaska Native, non-Hispanic/Latino; 20 Asian, non-Hispanic/Latino; 63 Hispanic/Latino; 2 Native Hawaiian or other Pacific Islander, non-Hispanic/Latino; 1 Two or more races, non-Hispanic/Latino), 5 international. Average age 33. *Faculty:* 17 full-time (13 women), 25 part-time/adjunct (7 women). Expenses: Contact institution. *Financial support:* Applicants required to submit FAFSA. In 2016, 221 doctorates awarded. *Program availability:* Part-time, evening/weekend. Offers law (JD). *Application Contact:* Rick Jackson, Associate Dean of Admissions, 602-682-6817, E-mail: admissions@azsummitlaw.edu.

ARKANSAS STATE UNIVERSITY, State University, AR 72467

General Information State-supported, coed, comprehensive institution. CGS member. *Graduate housing:* Rooms and/or apartments available on a first-come, first-served basis to single and married students. *Research affiliation:* Oak Ridge Associated Universities (scientific research and education development), Applied Biotechnologies Institute (recombinant proteins), Biostrategies, LLC (biotechnology), Infinite Enzymes (plant biotechnology), Nature West (physical, engineering, and life sciences), GeneCoMe (biotechnology).

GRADUATE UNITS

Graduate School *Program availability:* Part-time, online learning. Electronic applications accepted.

College of Agriculture and Technology *Program availability:* Part-time. Offers agricultural education (SCCT); agriculture (MSA); vocational-technical administration (SCCT). Electronic applications accepted.

College of Business *Program availability:* Part-time, evening/weekend. Offers accountancy (M Acc); business (M Acc, MBA, SCCT); business administration (MBA); business administration education (SCCT); business technology education (SCCT). Electronic applications accepted.

College of Education and Behavioral Science *Program availability:* Part-time, online learning. Offers clinical mental health counseling (Graduate Certificate); college student personnel services (MS); community college administration (SCCT); curriculum and instruction (MSE); dyslexia therapy (Graduate Certificate); early childhood education (MSE); early childhood services (MS); education and behavioral science (MAT, MRC, MS, MSE, Ed D, Ed S, Graduate Certificate, SCCT); educational leadership (MSE, Ed D, Ed S); educational theory and practice (MSE); exercise science (MS); middle level education (MAT, MSE); physical education (MSE, SCCT); psychological science (MS); psychology and counseling (Ed S); reading (MSE, Ed S); rehabilitation counseling (MRC); school counseling (MSE); special education - gifted, talented, and creative (MSE); special education - instructional specialist grades 4-12 (MSE); special education - instructional specialist grades P-4 (MSE); special education, K-12 (MSE); sports administration (MS); student affairs (Graduate Certificate). Electronic applications accepted.

College of Engineering *Program availability:* Part-time. Offers engineering (MS Eng); engineering management (MEM). Electronic applications accepted.

College of Fine Arts *Program availability:* Part-time. Offers fine arts (MM, MME, SCCT); music education (MME, SCCT); music performance (MM). Electronic applications accepted.

College of Humanities and Social Sciences *Program availability:* Part-time. Offers criminal justice (MA); English (MA); English education (MSE, SCCT); heritage studies (MA, PhD); history (MA); history education (SCCT); humanities and social sciences (MA, MPA, MSE, PhD, SCCT); political science (MA); political science education (SCCT); public administration (MPA); social science education (MSE); sociology (MA); sociology education (SCCT). Electronic applications accepted.

College of Media and Communication *Program availability:* Part-time. Offers communication studies (MA, SCCT); health communications (Graduate Certificate); mass communications (MSMC); media and communication (MA, MSMC, Graduate Certificate, SCCT). Electronic applications accepted.

College of Nursing and Health Professions *Program availability:* Part-time. Offers addiction studies (Graduate Certificate); aging studies (Graduate Certificate); communication disorders (MCD); disaster preparedness and emergency management (MS); dyslexia therapy (Graduate Certificate); health care management (Graduate Certificate); health sciences (MS); health sciences education (Graduate Certificate); healthcare emergency management (Graduate Certificate); nurse anesthesia (MSN); nursing (MSN); nursing and health professions (MCD, MS, MSN, MSW, DNP, DOT, DPT, Graduate Certificate); nursing practice (DNP); occupational therapy (DOT); physical therapy (DPT); social work (MSW). Electronic applications accepted.

College of Sciences and Mathematics *Program availability:* Part-time. Offers biological sciences (MA); biology (MS); biology education (MSE, SCCT); biotechnology (PSM); chemistry (MS); chemistry education (MSE, SCCT); computer science (MS); environmental sciences (MS, PhD); mathematics (MS); mathematics education (MSE); molecular biosciences (MS, PhD); sciences and mathematics (MA, MS, MSE, PSM, PhD, SCCT). Electronic applications accepted.

ARKANSAS TECH UNIVERSITY, Russellville, AR 72801

General Information State-supported, coed, comprehensive institution. CGS member. *Enrollment:* 11,894 graduate, professional, and undergraduate students; 206 full-time matriculated graduate/professional students (112 women), 620 part-time matriculated graduate/professional students (430 women). *Enrollment by degree level:* 790 master's, 24 doctoral, 12 other advanced degrees. *Graduate faculty:* 89 full-time (40 women), 13 part-time/adjunct (9 women). *Tuition,* state resident: full-time $4932; part-time $274 per credit hour. *Tuition,* nonresident: full-time $9864; part-time $548 per credit hour. *Required fees:* $513 per semester. Tuition and fees vary according to course load. *Graduate housing:* Room and/or apartments available on a first-come, first-served basis to single students; on-campus housing not available to married students. Typical cost: $4296 per year ($7036 including board). Housing application deadline: 8/1. *Student services:* Campus employment opportunities, campus safety program, career counseling, exercise/wellness program, free psychological counseling, international student services, low-cost health insurance, multicultural affairs office, services for students with disabilities, teacher training. *Library facilities:* Ross Pendergraft Library and Technology Center. *Collection:* Books: 313,011 (physical), 47,410 (digital/electronic); Databases: 259. Students can reserve study rooms.

Computer facilities: Computer purchase and lease plans are available. 1,124 computers available on campus for general student use. A campuswide network can be accessed from student residence rooms and from off campus. Online class registration is available.
Website: http://www.atu.edu/

General Application Contact: Dr. Mary B. Gunter, Dean of Graduate College, 479-968-0398, Fax: 479-964-0542, E-mail: gradcollege@atu.edu.

GRADUATE UNITS

College of Arts and Humanities Students: 56 full-time (42 women), 121 part-time (85 women); includes 23 minority (7 Black or African American, non-Hispanic/Latino; 1 Asian, non-Hispanic/Latino; 11 Hispanic/Latino; 4 Two or more races, non-Hispanic/Latino), 34 international. Average age 32. Expenses: Contact institution. *Financial support:* In 2016–17, research assistantships with full tuition reimbursements (averaging $4,800 per year), teaching assistantships with full tuition reimbursements (averaging $4,800 per year) were awarded; career-related internships or fieldwork, Federal Work-Study, scholarships/grants, health care benefits, and unspecified assistantships also available. Support available to part-time students. Financial award application deadline: 4/15; financial award applicants required to submit FAFSA. In 2016, 90 master's awarded. *Program availability:* Part-time. Offers applied sociology (MS); English (M Ed, MA); history (MA); liberal arts (MLA); multi-media journalism (MA); psychology (MS); teaching English as a second language (MA). *Application deadline:* For fall admission, 3/1 priority date for domestic students, 5/1 priority date for international students; for spring admission, 10/1 priority date for domestic and international students. Applications are processed on a rolling basis. *Application fee:* $25 ($75 for international students). Electronic applications accepted. *Application Contact:* Dr. Mary B. Gunter, Dean of Graduate College, 479-968-0398, Fax: 479-964-0542, E-mail: gradcollege@atu.edu. *Dean,* Dr. Jeffrey Woods, 479-968-0274, Fax: 479-964-0812, E-mail: jwoods@atu.edu.

College of Business Students: 4 full-time (all women), 22 part-time (14 women); includes 4 minority (3 Black or African American, non-Hispanic/Latino; 1 Hispanic/Latino), 2 international. Average age 33. Expenses: Contact institution. *Financial support:* Application deadline: 4/15; applicants required to submit FAFSA. In 2016, 10 master's awarded. *Program availability:* Part-time, evening/weekend, online only. Offers business (MSBA). *Application deadline:* For fall admission, 3/1 priority date for domestic students, 5/1 priority date for international students; for spring admission, 10/1 priority date for domestic and international students. Applications are processed on a rolling basis. *Application fee:* $25 ($75 for international students). Electronic applications accepted. *Application Contact:* Dr. Mary B. Gunter, Dean of Graduate College, 479-968-0398, Fax: 479-964-0542, E-mail: gradcollege@atu.edu. *Dean,* Dr. Jeff Robertson, 479-968-0498, E-mail: jrobertson@atu.edu.

College of Education Students: 72 full-time (43 women), 371 part-time (283 women); includes 108 minority (80 Black or African American, non-Hispanic/Latino; 1 American Indian or Alaska Native, non-Hispanic/Latino; 4 Asian, non-Hispanic/Latino; 13 Hispanic/Latino; 10 Two or more races, non-Hispanic/Latino), 6 international. Average age 33. Expenses: Contact institution. *Financial support:* In 2016–17, research assistantships with full tuition reimbursements (averaging $4,800 per year), teaching assistantships with full tuition reimbursements (averaging $4,800 per year) were awarded; career-related internships or fieldwork, Federal Work-Study, scholarships/grants, health care benefits, and unspecified assistantships also available. Support available to part-time students. Financial award application deadline: 4/15; financial award applicants required to submit FAFSA. In 2016, 181 master's, 1 other advanced degree awarded. *Program availability:* Part-time, evening/weekend, online learning. Offers college student personnel (MS); educational leadership (M Ed, Ed S); elementary education (M Ed); instructional improvement (M Ed); instructional technology (M Ed); school counseling and leadership (M Ed); school leadership (Ed D); strength and conditioning studies (MS); teaching (MAT); teaching, learning, and leadership (M Ed). *Application deadline:* For fall admission, 3/1 priority date for domestic students, 5/1 priority date for international students; for spring admission, 10/1 priority date for domestic and international students. Applications are processed on a rolling basis. *Application fee:* $25 ($75 for international students). Electronic applications accepted. *Dean,* Dr. Mary Gunter, 479-964-3217, E-mail: mgunter@atu.edu.

College of Engineering and Applied Sciences Students: 59 full-time (15 women), 63 part-time (21 women); includes 22 minority (8 Black or African American, non-Hispanic/Latino; 2 American Indian or Alaska Native, non-Hispanic/Latino; 4 Asian, non-Hispanic/Latino; 4 Hispanic/Latino; 4 Two or more races, non-Hispanic/Latino), 41 international. Average age 31. Expenses: Contact institution. *Financial support:* In 2016–17, research assistantships with full tuition reimbursements (averaging $4,800 per year), teaching assistantships with full tuition reimbursements (averaging $4,800 per year) were awarded; career-related internships or fieldwork, Federal Work-Study, scholarships/grants, health care benefits, and unspecified assistantships also available. Support available to part-time students. Financial award application deadline: 4/15; financial award applicants required to submit FAFSA. In 2016, 43 master's awarded. *Program availability:* Part-time, online learning. Offers emergency management (MS); engineering (M Engr); information technology (MS). *Application deadline:* For fall admission, 3/1 priority date for domestic students, 5/1 priority date for international students; for spring admission, 10/1 priority date for domestic and international students. Applications are processed on a rolling basis. *Application fee:* $25 ($75 for international students). Electronic applications accepted. *Application Contact:* Dr. Mary B. Gunter, Dean of Graduate College, 479-968-0398, Fax: 479-964-0542, E-mail: gradcollege@atu.edu. *Dean,* Dr. Douglas Barlow, 479-968-0353, E-mail: dbarlow@atu.edu.

College of Natural and Health Sciences Students: 15 full-time (8 women), 43 part-time (27 women); includes 13 minority (8 Black or African American, non-Hispanic/Latino; 1 Asian, non-Hispanic/Latino; 3 Hispanic/Latino; 1 Two or more races, non-Hispanic/Latino). Average age 37. Expenses: Contact institution. *Financial support:* In 2016–17, research assistantships with full tuition reimbursements (averaging $4,800 per year), teaching assistantships with full tuition reimbursements (averaging $4,800 per year) were awarded; career-related internships or fieldwork, Federal Work-Study, scholarships/grants, health care benefits, and unspecified assistantships also available. Support available to part-time students. Financial award application deadline: 4/15; financial award applicants required to submit FAFSA. In 2016, 16 master's awarded. *Program availability:* Part-time. Offers fisheries and wildlife biology (MS); health informatics (MS); nursing (MSN). *Application deadline:* For fall admission, 3/1 priority date for domestic students, 5/1 priority date for international students; for spring admission, 10/1 priority date for domestic and international students. Applications are processed on a rolling basis. *Application fee:* $25 ($75 for international students). Electronic applications accepted. *Application Contact:* Dr. Mary B. Gunter, Dean of Graduate College, 479-968-0398, Fax: 479-964-0542, E-mail: gradcollege@atu.edu. *Dean,* Dr. Jeff Robertson, 479-968-0498, E-mail: jrobertson@atu.edu.

ARLINGTON BAPTIST COLLEGE, Arlington, TX 76012-3425
General Information Independent-religious, coed, comprehensive institution.

GRADUATE UNITS

Program in Biblical and Theological Studies Offers Biblical and theological studies (MA). Electronic applications accepted.

Program in Education Offers curriculum and instruction (M Ed); educational leadership (M Ed).

ARMSTRONG STATE UNIVERSITY, Savannah, GA 31419-1997
General Information State-supported, coed, comprehensive institution. *Enrollment:* 7,157 graduate, professional, and undergraduate students; 310 full-time matriculated graduate/professional students (224 women), 439 part-time matriculated graduate/professional students (339 women). *Enrollment by degree level:* 624 master's, 105 doctoral, 20 other advanced degrees. *Graduate faculty:* 91 full-time (58 women), 16 part-time/adjunct (11 women). Tuition, state resident: full-time $1781; part-time $161.93 per credit hour. Tuition, nonresident: full-time $6482; part-time $589.27 per credit hour. *Required fees:* $1224 per unit. $612 per semester. Tuition and fees vary according to course load, campus/location and program. *Graduate housing:* Room and/or apartments available on a first-come, first-served basis to single students; on-campus housing not available to married students. Typical cost: $6592 per year. Room charges vary according to board plan and housing facility selected. Housing application deadline: 7/1. *Student services:* Campus employment opportunities, campus safety program, career counseling, exercise/wellness program, free psychological counseling, international student services, low-cost health insurance, multicultural affairs office, services for students with disabilities, teacher training, writing training. *Library facilities:* Lane Library plus 1 other. *Collection:* Books: 207,421 (physical), 215,400 (digital/electronic); Serial titles: 500 (physical), 2,000 (digital/electronic); Databases: 300. Weekly public service hours: 108; students can reserve study rooms.

Computer facilities: 300 computers available on campus for general student use. A campuswide network can be accessed from student residence rooms. Online class registration is available.
Website: http://www.armstrong.edu/

General Application Contact: McKenzie Peterman, Assistant Director of Graduate Admissions, 912-344-2503, Fax: 912-344-3417, E-mail: graduate@armstrong.edu.

GRADUATE UNITS

School of Graduate Studies Students: 310 full-time (224 women), 439 part-time (339 women); includes 237 minority (184 Black or African American, non-Hispanic/Latino; 14 Asian, non-Hispanic/Latino; 23 Hispanic/Latino; 16 Two or more races, non-Hispanic/Latino), 12 international. Average age 31. 728 applicants, 33% accepted, 177 enrolled. *Faculty:* 91 full-time (58 women), 16 part-time/adjunct (11 women). Expenses: Contact institution. *Financial support:* In 2016–17, 65 research assistantships with full tuition reimbursements (averaging $5,000 per year) were awarded; Federal Work-Study, scholarships/grants, and unspecified assistantships also available. Financial award application deadline: 3/15; financial award applicants required to submit FAFSA. In 2016, 219 master's, 25 doctorate, 39 other advanced degrees awarded. *Program availability:* Part-time, evening/weekend, 100% online. Offers adolescent and adult education (Certificate); adult education and community leadership (M Ed); adult-gerontological acute care nurse practitioner (Certificate); adult-gerontological clinical nurse specialist (Certificate); adult-gerontological primary care nurse practitioner (Certificate); American and European history (MA); communication sciences and disorders (MS); computer and information science (MSCIS); criminal justice (MS); curriculum and instruction (M Ed); cyber crime (Certificate); early childhood education (M Ed, MAT); family nurse practitioner (MSN); health services administration (MHSA); physical therapy (DPT); professional communication and leadership (MA, Certificate); public health (MPH); public history (MA); reading (Certificate); secondary education

(MAT); special education (M Ed, MAT); special education transition specialist (Certificate); sports health sciences (MSSM); strength and conditioning (Certificate). *Application deadline:* For fall admission, 7/1 priority date for domestic students, 5/1 priority date for international students; for spring admission, 11/15 priority date for domestic students, 9/15 priority date for international students; for summer admission, 4/15 priority date for domestic students, 9/15 priority date for international students. Applications are processed on a rolling basis. *Application fee:* $30. Electronic applications accepted. *Application Contact:* McKenzie Peterman, Assistant Director of Graduate Admissions, 912-344-2503, Fax: 912-344-3417, E-mail: graduate@armstrong.edu. *Associate Provost for Academic Affairs and Graduate Studies,* Donna Brooks, 912-344-2589, Fax: 912-344-3417, E-mail: graduate@armstrong.edu.

ART ACADEMY OF CINCINNATI, Cincinnati, OH 45202
General Information Independent, coed, comprehensive institution. *Graduate housing:* Rooms and/or apartments available on a first-come, first-served basis to single and married students. Housing application deadline: 5/1.

GRADUATE UNITS

Program in Art Education *Program availability:* Part-time. Offers art education (MAAE). Offered during summer only. Electronic applications accepted.

ARTCENTER COLLEGE OF DESIGN, Pasadena, CA 91103
General Information Independent, coed, comprehensive institution. *Graduate housing:* On-campus housing not available.

GRADUATE UNITS

Graduate Art Program Offers art (MFA). Electronic applications accepted.

Graduate Environmental Design Program Offers furniture and fixtures (MS); spatial experience (MS). Electronic applications accepted.

Graduate Film Program Offers film (MFA). Electronic applications accepted.

Graduate Graphic Design Program Offers graphic design (MFA).

Graduate Industrial Design Program Offers industrial design (MS). Electronic applications accepted.

Graduate Media Design Practices Program Offers media design practices (MFA). Electronic applications accepted.

Graduate Transportation Design Program Offers transportation systems (MS).

THE ART INSTITUTE OF CALIFORNIA–SAN FRANCISCO, A CAMPUS OF ARGOSY UNIVERSITY, San Francisco, CA 94102-4928
General Information Proprietary, coed, comprehensive institution.

GRADUATE UNITS

Program in Computer Animation Offers computer animation (MFA).

THE ART INSTITUTE OF DALLAS, A BRANCH OF MIAMI INTERNATIONAL UNIVERSITY OF ART & DESIGN, Dallas, TX 75231-5993
General Information Proprietary, coed, comprehensive institution.

GRADUATE UNITS

Program in Design and Media Management Offers design and media management (MA).

ASBURY THEOLOGICAL SEMINARY, Wilmore, KY 40390-1199
General Information Independent-religious, coed, primarily men, graduate-only institution. *Graduate housing:* Rooms and/or apartments available on a first-come, first-served basis to single and married students. Housing application deadline: 8/15.

GRADUATE UNITS

Graduate and Professional Programs *Program availability:* Part-time, online learning. Offers theology (M Div, MA, MAAS, MACE, MACL, MACM, MACP, MAMFC, MAMHC, MAPC, MASF, MAYM, Th M, D Min, PhD, Certificate). Electronic applications accepted.

ASBURY UNIVERSITY, Wilmore, KY 40390-1198
General Information Independent-religious, coed, comprehensive institution. *Graduate housing:* On-campus housing not available.

GRADUATE UNITS

School of Graduate and Professional Studies *Program availability:* Part-time. Offers biology: alternative certificate (MA Ed); chemistry: alternative certificate (MA Ed); child and family services (MSW); English (MA Ed); English as a second language (MA Ed); ESL (MA Ed); French (MA Ed); Latin: alternative certificate (MA Ed); mathematics: alternative certificate (MA Ed); reading/writing endorsement (MA Ed); social studies (MA Ed); social work (MSW); Spanish (MA Ed); special education (MA Ed); special education: alternative certificate (MA Ed); teacher as leader endorsement (MA Ed). Electronic applications accepted.

ASHLAND THEOLOGICAL SEMINARY, Ashland, OH 44805
General Information Independent-religious, coed, graduate-only institution. *Tuition:* Full-time $15,120; part-time $630 per semester hour. Tuition and fees vary according to program. *Graduate housing:* Rooms and/or apartments available on a first-come, first-served basis to single and married students. Housing application deadline: 8/30. *Student services:* Campus employment opportunities, career counseling, free psychological counseling, international student services, low-cost health insurance, services for students with disabilities, writing training. *Library facilities:* Roger Darling Memorial Library. *Research affiliation:* Tel Gezer Excavation and Publication Program (archaeological studies), Tyndale House, Cambridge England (faculty study and research).

Computer facilities: 20 computers available on campus for general student use. Online class registration is available.
Website: http://seminary.ashland.edu/

General Application Contact: Renee Johnson, Coordinator of Admissions, 419-289-5704, Fax: 419-207-6077, E-mail: rjohns13@ashland.edu.

GRADUATE UNITS

Graduate Programs Expenses: Contact institution. *Financial support:* Research assistantships, teaching assistantships, career-related internships or fieldwork, institutionally sponsored loans, scholarships/grants, and unspecified assistantships available. Support available to part-time students. Financial award application deadline: 5/15; financial award applicants required to submit FAFSA. *Program availability:* Part-time. Offers Biblical studies (MA); Christian ministries (MACM); clinical mental health counseling (MA); counseling (MAC); historical and theological studies (MA); ministry

(D Min); pastoral ministry (M Div). MAC program offered in Detroit, MI. *Application deadline:* For fall admission, 8/30 for domestic students. Applications are processed on a rolling basis. *Application fee:* $35. Electronic applications accepted. *Application Contact:* Dr. Mark Harden, President, 419-289-5160, Fax: 419-289-5969, E-mail: mharden@ashland.edu. *President,* Dr. Mark Harden, 419-289-5160, Fax: 419-289-5969, E-mail: mharden@ashland.edu.

ASHLAND UNIVERSITY, Ashland, OH 44805-3702

General Information Independent-religious, coed, comprehensive institution. *Graduate housing:* On-campus housing not available. *Student services:* Campus employment opportunities, campus safety program, career counseling, exercise/wellness program, free psychological counseling, international student services, low-cost health insurance, multicultural affairs office, services for students with disabilities, teacher training, writing training. *Library facilities:* Ashland University Library plus 2 others. *Collection:* Books: 223,607 (physical), 255,789 (digital/electronic); Serial titles: 1,070 (physical), 114,001 (digital/electronic); Databases: 200. Weekly public service hours: 102; students can reserve study rooms. *Research affiliation:* Teacher Quality Project (TQP) (education).

Computer facilities: Computer purchase and lease plans are available. 760 computers available on campus for general student use. A campuswide network can be accessed from student residence rooms and from off campus. Online class registration is available.
Website: http://www.ashland.edu/

General Application Contact: Dr. W. Gregory Gerrick, Dean, Graduate School, 419-289-5750, Fax: 419-289-5949, E-mail: ggerrick@ashland.edu.

GRADUATE UNITS

College of Arts and Sciences Expenses: Contact institution. *Financial support:* Application deadline: 4/1. Offers American history and government (MAHG); arts and sciences (MA, MAHG, MFA); corporate and strategic communication (MA); creative writing (MFA). *Application deadline:* Applications are processed on a rolling basis. *Application fee:* $30. Electronic applications accepted. *Application Contact:* Dr. W. Gregory Gerrick, Dean, Graduate School, 419-289-5750, Fax: 419-289-5949, E-mail: ggerrick@ashland.edu. *Dean,* Dr. Dawn Weber, 419-289-5107.

Dauch College of Business and Economics Expenses: Contact institution. *Financial support:* Tuition waivers (partial) and unspecified assistantships available. Financial award application deadline: 4/15; financial award applicants required to submit FAFSA. *Program availability:* Part-time, evening/weekend. Offers business and economics (MBA). *Application deadline:* For fall admission, 8/1 priority date for domestic students; for spring admission, 12/1 priority date for domestic students. Applications are processed on a rolling basis. *Application fee:* $30. Electronic applications accepted. *Application Contact:* Stephen W. Krispinsky, Executive Director of MBA Program, 419-289-5236, Fax: 419-289-5910, E-mail: skrispin@ashland.edu. *Associate Dean,* Dr. Raymond Jacobs, 419-289-5931, E-mail: rjacobs@ashland.edu.

Dwight Schar College of Education Expenses: Contact institution. *Financial support:* Teaching assistantships with partial tuition reimbursements and scholarships/grants available. Financial award application deadline: 4/15. *Program availability:* Part-time, evening/weekend. Offers building principal (M Ed); education (M Ed, Ed D); educational leadership studies (Ed D); educational technology (M Ed); intervention specialist, mild/moderate (M Ed); intervention specialist, moderate/intensive (M Ed); literacy (M Ed); talented and gifted (M Ed); teaching and learning in the 21st century (M Ed). *Application deadline:* For fall admission, 8/27 for domestic students; for spring admission, 1/14 for domestic students. Applications are processed on a rolling basis. *Application fee:* $30. *Application Contact:* Dr. Linda Billman, Associate Dean, 419-289-5369, Fax: 419-289-5331, E-mail: lbillman@ashland.edu. *Dean,* Dr. James P. Van Keuren, 419-289-5377, E-mail: jvankeu1@ashland.edu.

Dwight Schar College of Nursing and Health Sciences Expenses: Contact institution. Offers applied exercise science (MS); family nurse practitioner (DNP); nursing and health sciences (MS, DNP). *Application Contact:* Dr. Faye Grund, Dean and Administrative Officer, 419-521-6802, E-mail: fgrund@ashland.edu. *Dean and Administrative Officer,* Dr. Faye Grund, 419-521-6802, E-mail: fgrund@ashland.edu.

ASHWORTH COLLEGE, Norcross, GA 30092

General Information Proprietary, coed, comprehensive institution.

GRADUATE UNITS

Graduate Programs Offers business administration (MBA); criminal justice (MS); health care administration (MBA, MS); human resource management (MBA, MS); international business (MBA); management (MS); marketing (MBA, MS).

ASPEN UNIVERSITY, Denver, CO 80246-1930

General Information Independent, coed, comprehensive institution. *Graduate housing:* On-campus housing not available.

GRADUATE UNITS

Program in Business Administration *Program availability:* Part-time, evening/weekend, online learning. Offers business administration (MBA); finance (MBA); information management (MBA); project management (MBA, Certificate). Electronic applications accepted.

Program in Information Technology *Program availability:* Part-time, evening/weekend, online learning. Offers information technology (MS, Certificate). Electronic applications accepted.

Program in Nursing Offers forensic nursing (MSN); informatics (MSN); nursing (MSN); nursing administration and management (MSN); nursing education (MSN); public health (MSN).

Programs in Information Management *Program availability:* Part-time, evening/weekend, online learning. Offers information management (MS); information systems (Certificate). Electronic applications accepted.

ASSEMBLIES OF GOD THEOLOGICAL SEMINARY, Springfield, MO 65802

General Information Independent-religious, coed, graduate-only institution. *Graduate housing:* On-campus housing not available.

GRADUATE UNITS

Graduate and Professional Programs *Program availability:* Part-time, evening/weekend, 100% online. Offers Biblical interpretation and theology (PhD); Christian ministries (MA); divinity (M Div); intercultural studies (MA, PhD); ministry (D Min); missiology (DAIS); pastoral studies (MPL); theological studies (MA, Th M). Electronic applications accepted.

ASSUMPTION COLLEGE, Worcester, MA 01609-1296

General Information Independent-religious, coed, comprehensive institution. *Enrollment:* 2,407 graduate, professional, and undergraduate students; 162 full-time matriculated graduate/professional students (112 women), 234 part-time matriculated graduate/professional students (163 women). Enrollment by degree level: 366 master's, 30 other advanced degrees. *Graduate faculty:* 16 full-time (8 women), 51 part-time/adjunct (19 women). *Tuition:* Full-time $11,610; part-time $645 per credit. *Required fees:* $70 per term. Tuition and fees vary according to course load and program. *Graduate housing:* On-campus housing not available. *Student services:* Campus employment opportunities, campus safety program, career counseling, exercise/wellness program, international student services, low-cost health insurance, multicultural affairs office, services for students with disabilities. *Library facilities:* Emmanuel d'Alzon Library. *Collection:* Books: 140,638 (physical), 148,508 (digital/electronic); Serial titles: 268 (physical), 40,818 (digital/electronic); Databases: 75. Weekly public service hours: 102; students can reserve study rooms.

Computer facilities: Computer purchase and lease plans are available. 361 computers available on campus for general student use. A campuswide network can be accessed from student residence rooms and from off campus. Online class registration is available.
Website: http://www.assumption.edu/

General Application Contact: Karen Stoyanoff, Director of Recruitment for Graduate Enrollment, 508-767-7442, Fax: 508-799-4412, E-mail: graduate@assumption.edu.

GRADUATE UNITS

Addiction Counseling Program Expenses: Contact institution. *Program availability:* Part-time, evening/weekend. Offers addiction counseling (CGS). *Application deadline:* Applications are processed on a rolling basis. *Application fee:* $30. Electronic applications accepted. *Application Contact:* Karen Stoyanoff, Director of Recruitment for Graduate Enrollment, 508-767-7442, Fax: 508-799-4412, E-mail: graduate@assumption.edu. *Director,* Dr. Leonard A. Doerfler, 508-767-7549, Fax: 508-767-7263, E-mail: doerfler@assumption.edu.

Applied Behavior Analysis Program Students: 1 part-time. 9 applicants, 44% accepted, 1 enrolled. *Faculty:* 1 (woman) full-time. Expenses: Contact institution. *Financial support:* Tuition waivers (full and partial) and institutional discounts available. Financial award applicants required to submit FAFSA. *Program availability:* Part-time, evening/weekend. Offers applied behavior analysis (MA, CAGS). *Application deadline:* For fall admission, 7/1 for domestic and international students. *Application fee:* $30. Electronic applications accepted. *Application Contact:* Karen Stoyanoff, Director of Recruitment for Graduate Enrollment, 508-767-7442, Fax: 508-799-4412, E-mail: graduate@assumption.edu. *Director,* Dr. Karen Lionello-DeNolf, 508-767-7498, E-mail: k.lionellodenolf@assumption.edu.

Business Studies Program Students: 44 full-time (16 women), 97 part-time (47 women); includes 20 minority (8 Black or African American, non-Hispanic/Latino; 5 Asian, non-Hispanic/Latino; 6 Hispanic/Latino; 1 Two or more races, non-Hispanic/Latino), 4 international. Average age 29. 34 applicants, 59% accepted, 16 enrolled. *Faculty:* 4 full-time (1 woman), 19 part-time/adjunct (6 women). Expenses: Contact institution. *Financial support:* In 2016–17, 19 students received support. Tuition waivers (full and partial), unspecified assistantships, and institutional discounts available. Financial award applicants required to submit FAFSA. In 2016, 97 master's, 1 other advanced degree awarded. *Program availability:* Part-time, evening/weekend. Offers accounting (MBA); business studies (CAGS); finance/economics (MBA); human resources (MBA); international business (MBA); management (MBA); marketing (MBA); nonprofit leadership (MBA). *Application deadline:* For fall admission, 7/1 priority date for domestic and international students; for spring admission, 12/1 priority date for domestic and international students; for summer admission, 4/1 priority date for domestic and international students. *Application fee:* $30. Electronic applications accepted. *Application Contact:* Karen Stoyanoff, Director of Recruitment for Graduate Enrollment, 508-767-7442, Fax: 508-799-4412, E-mail: graduate@assumption.edu. *Director,* Dr. Robin Frkal, 508-767-7622, E-mail: rafrkal@assumption.edu.

Clinical Counseling Psychology Program Students: 40 full-time (31 women), 29 part-time (26 women); includes 11 minority (1 Black or African American, non-Hispanic/Latino; 1 American Indian or Alaska Native, non-Hispanic/Latino; 4 Asian, non-Hispanic/Latino; 5 Hispanic/Latino). Average age 27. 63 applicants, 51% accepted, 20 enrolled. *Faculty:* 4 full-time (2 women), 7 part-time/adjunct (2 women). Expenses: Contact institution. *Financial support:* In 2016–17, 17 students received support, including 12 fellowships with full tuition reimbursements available; tuition waivers (full and partial), unspecified assistantships, and institutional discounts also available. Financial award application deadline: 3/7; financial award applicants required to submit FAFSA. In 2016, 25 master's awarded. *Program availability:* Part-time, evening/weekend. Offers child and family interventions (MA); clinical counseling (CAGS); cognitive-behavioral therapies (MA). *Application deadline:* For fall admission, 3/7 priority date for domestic and international students; for spring admission, 10/5 for domestic and international students; for summer admission, 2/8 for domestic and international students. *Application fee:* $30. Electronic applications accepted. *Application Contact:* Karen Stoyanoff, Director of Recruitment for Graduate Enrollment, 508-767-7442, Fax: 508-799-4412, E-mail: graduate@assumption.edu. *Director,* Dr. Leonard A. Doerfler, 508-767-7549, Fax: 508-767-7263, E-mail: doerfler@assumption.edu.

Health Advocacy Program Students: 1 (woman) full-time, 13 part-time (all women). Average age 47. 16 applicants, 69% accepted, 8 enrolled. *Faculty:* 1 (woman) full-time, 2 part-time/adjunct (0 women). Expenses: Contact institution. *Financial support:* In 2016–17, 2 students received support. Tuition waivers (full and partial) and institutional discounts available. Financial award applicants required to submit FAFSA. In 2016, 2 other advanced degrees awarded. *Program availability:* Part-time, evening/weekend, online only, 100% online. Offers health advocacy (MA, Professional Certificate). *Application deadline:* For fall admission, 7/1 for domestic and international students; for spring admission, 12/1 for domestic and international students. *Application fee:* $30. Electronic applications accepted. *Application Contact:* Karen Stoyanoff, Director of Recruitment for Graduate Enrollment, 508-767-7442, Fax: 508-799-4412, E-mail: graduate@assumption.edu. *Director,* Lea Christo, 508-767-7503, Fax: 508-798-2872, E-mail: l.christo@assumption.edu.

Rehabilitation Counseling Program Students: 31 full-time (25 women), 45 part-time (33 women); includes 19 minority (11 Black or African American, non-Hispanic/Latino; 1 Asian, non-Hispanic/Latino; 6 Hispanic/Latino; 1 Two or more races, non-Hispanic/Latino). Average age 34. 25 applicants, 68% accepted, 16 enrolled. *Faculty:* 1 full-time (0 women), 14 part-time/adjunct (6 women). Expenses: Contact institution. *Financial support:* In 2016–17, 21 students received support. Scholarships/grants, tuition waivers (full and partial), unspecified assistantships, and institutional discounts available. Financial award application deadline: 4/15; financial award applicants required to submit FAFSA. In 2016, 22 master's, 1 other advanced degree awarded. *Program availability:* Part-time, evening/weekend, blended/hybrid learning. Offers rehabilitation counseling (MA, CAGS). *Application deadline:* For fall admission, 7/1 for domestic and international students; for spring admission, 12/1 for domestic and international

Assumption College

students; for summer admission, 4/15 for domestic and international students. *Application fee:* $30. Electronic applications accepted. *Application Contact:* Karen Stoyanoff, Director of Recruitment for Graduate Enrollment, 508-767-7442, Fax: 508-799-4915, E-mail: graduate@assumption.edu. *Director,* Dr. Nicholas Cioe, 508-767-7370, Fax: 508-798-2872, E-mail: nj.cioe@assumption.edu.

Resiliency in the Helping Professions Program *Expenses:* Contact institution. *Program availability:* Part-time, evening/weekend. Offers resiliency in the helping professions (CAGS, CGS). *Application deadline:* Applications are processed on a rolling basis. *Application fee:* $30. *Application Contact:* Karen Stoyanoff, Director of Recruitment for Graduate Enrollment, 508-767-7442, Fax: 508-799-4412, E-mail: graduate@assumption.edu. *Director,* Lea Christo, 508-767-7503, Fax: 508-798-2872, E-mail: l.christo@assumption.edu.

School Counseling Program Students: 43 full-time (36 women), 24 part-time (22 women); includes 7 minority (6 Hispanic/Latino; 1 Two or more races, non-Hispanic/Latino). Average age 27. 44 applicants, 66% accepted, 16 enrolled. *Faculty:* 3 full-time (1 woman), 7 part-time/adjunct (4 women). *Expenses:* Contact institution. *Financial support:* In 2016–17, 8 students received support. Tuition waivers (full and partial), unspecified assistantships, and institutional discounts available. Financial award applicants required to submit FAFSA. In 2016, 22 master's, 6 other advanced degrees awarded. *Program availability:* Part-time, evening/weekend. Offers resiliency (CAGS); school counseling (MA, CAGS). *Application deadline:* Applications are processed on a rolling basis. *Application fee:* $30. Electronic applications accepted. *Application Contact:* Karen Stoyanoff, Director of Recruitment for Graduate Enrollment, 508-767-7442, Fax: 508-799-4915, E-mail: graduate@assumption.edu. *Interim Director,* Dr. Susan Scully-Hill, 508-767-7319, Fax: 508-798-2872, E-mail: sscully@assumption.edu.

Special Education Program Students: 3 full-time (all women), 25 part-time (22 women); includes 1 minority (Hispanic/Latino). Average age 27. 17 applicants, 82% accepted, 11 enrolled. *Faculty:* 2 full-time (both women), 3 part-time/adjunct (2 women). *Expenses:* Contact institution. *Financial support:* In 2016–17, 5 students received support. Tuition waivers (full and partial), unspecified assistantships, and institutional discounts available. Financial award applicants required to submit FAFSA. In 2016, 18 master's, 12 other advanced degrees awarded. *Program availability:* Part-time, evening/weekend. Offers positive behavior support (CAGS); special education (MA). *Application deadline:* Applications are processed on a rolling basis. *Application fee:* $30. Electronic applications accepted. *Application Contact:* Karen Stoyanoff, Director of Recruitment for Graduate Enrollment, 508-767-7442, Fax: 508-799-4915, E-mail: graduate@assumption.edu. *Director,* Dr. Nanho Vander Hart, 508-767-7380, Fax: 508-767-7263, E-mail: nvanderh@assumption.edu.

ATHABASCA UNIVERSITY, Athabasca, AB T9S 3A3, Canada

General Information Province-supported, coed, comprehensive institution. *Graduate housing:* On-campus housing not available. *Research affiliation:* SAP (software), IBM (software).

GRADUATE UNITS

Centre for Distance Education *Program availability:* Part-time, online learning. Offers distance education (MDE, Ed D); distance education technology (Advanced Diploma). Electronic applications accepted.

Centre for Interdisciplinary Studies *Program availability:* Part-time, evening/weekend, online learning. Offers adult education (MA); community studies (MA); cultural studies (MA); educational studies (MA); global change (MA); heritage resource management (Postbaccalaureate Certificate); legislative drafting (Postbaccalaureate Certificate); work, organization, and leadership (MA). Electronic applications accepted.

Faculty of Business *Program availability:* Part-time, evening/weekend, online learning. Offers business administration (MBA); information technology management (MBA); innovative management (DBA); management (GDM); project management (MBA, GDM). Electronic applications accepted.

Faculty of Health Disciplines *Program availability:* Part-time, online learning. Offers advanced nursing practice (MN, Advanced Diploma); generalist (MN); health studies (MHS). Electronic applications accepted.

Faculty of Science and Technology *Program availability:* Part-time, online learning. Offers architecture (Postgraduate Diploma); information systems (M Sc). Electronic applications accepted.

Program in Counseling Offers applied psychology (Post Master's Certificate); art therapy (MC); career counseling (MC); counseling (Advanced Certificate); counseling psychology (MC); school counseling (MC).

THE ATHENAEUM OF OHIO, Cincinnati, OH 45230-5900

General Information Independent-religious, coed, graduate-only institution. *Enrollment by degree level:* 110 master's, 77 other advanced degrees. *Tuition:* Full-time $10,080; part-time $5040 per credit. *One-time fee:* $30. *Graduate housing:* On-campus housing not available. *Library facilities:* Eugene H. Maly Memorial Library.

Computer facilities: 3 computers available on campus for general student use. Website: http://www.mtsm.org/

General Application Contact: Nicholas Jobe, Registrar, 513-231-2223, Fax: 513-231-3254, E-mail: njobe@athenaeum.edu.

GRADUATE UNITS

Graduate Programs Students: 64 full-time (0 women), 57 part-time (31 women); includes 10 minority (1 Black or African American, non-Hispanic/Latino; 4 Asian, non-Hispanic/Latino; 4 Hispanic/Latino; 1 Two or more races, non-Hispanic/Latino), 3 international. *Expenses:* Contact institution. *Financial support:* Scholarships/grants available. Support available to part-time students. Financial award application deadline: 8/1. In 2016, 45 master's awarded. *Program availability:* Part-time, evening/weekend. Offers theology (M Div, MA, MA Th, MABS, Certificate). *Application deadline:* For fall admission, 4/15 priority date for domestic students; for winter admission, 11/1 priority date for domestic students. Applications are processed on a rolling basis. *Application fee:* $30. *Application Contact:* Nicholas Jobe, Registrar, 513-231-2223, Fax: 513-231-3254, E-mail: njobe@athenaeum.edu. *Dean,* Fr. David J. Endres, 513-231-2223, Fax: 513-231-3254, E-mail: dendres@athenaeum.edu.

ATLANTA'S JOHN MARSHALL LAW SCHOOL, Atlanta, GA 30309

General Information Private, coed, graduate-only institution.

GRADUATE UNITS

JD and LL M Programs *Program availability:* Part-time, evening/weekend, online learning. Offers American legal studies (LL M); employment law (LL M); law (JD). Electronic applications accepted.

ATLANTIC INSTITUTE OF ORIENTAL MEDICINE, Fort Lauderdale, FL 33301

General Information Independent, coed, graduate-only institution. *Enrollment by degree level:* 105 master's, 51 doctoral. *Graduate faculty:* 7 full-time (1 woman), 15 part-time/adjunct (6 women). *Tuition:* Full-time $17,000. *Required fees:* $250. *Student services:* Campus employment opportunities, campus safety program, career counseling, exercise/wellness program, international student services. *Collection:* Books: 3,300 (physical). Weekly public service hours: 50.

Computer facilities: 4 computers available on campus for general student use. Online class registration is available.
Website: http://www.atom.edu/

General Application Contact: Karen Gemignani, Admissions Counselor, 954-763-9840 Ext. 213, Fax: 954-763-9844, E-mail: admissions@atom.edu.

GRADUATE UNITS

Graduate Program Students: 156 full-time (114 women); includes 80 minority (12 Black or African American, non-Hispanic/Latino; 18 Asian, non-Hispanic/Latino; 50 Hispanic/Latino), 5 international. *Faculty:* 7 full-time (1 woman), 15 part-time/adjunct (6 women). *Expenses:* Contact institution. *Financial support:* Applicants required to submit FAFSA. In 2016, 47 master's, 12 doctorates awarded. *Program availability:* Evening/weekend. Offers Oriental medicine (MS, DAOM). *Application deadline:* For fall admission, 7/1 for domestic students, 5/1 for international students; for spring admission, 11/30 for domestic students, 2/28 for international students. Applications are processed on a rolling basis. *Application fee:* $20 ($30 for international students). *Application Contact:* Karen Gemignana, Admissions Counselor, 954-763-9840 Ext. 213, Fax: 954-763-9844, E-mail: admissions@atom.edu. *President,* Dr. Johanna C. Yen, 954-763-9840 Ext. 202, Fax: 954-763-9844, E-mail: president@atom.edu.

ATLANTIC SCHOOL OF THEOLOGY, Halifax, NS B3H 3B5, Canada

General Information Independent, coed, graduate-only institution. *Graduate housing:* Rooms and/or apartments available on a first-come, first-served basis to single and married students. Housing application deadline: 6/1.

GRADUATE UNITS

Graduate and Professional Programs *Program availability:* Part-time, online learning. Offers ministry (M Div); theological studies (Graduate Certificate).

ATLANTIC UNIVERSITY, Virginia Beach, VA 23451-2061

General Information Independent, coed, primarily women, graduate-only institution. *Graduate housing:* On-campus housing not available. *Library facilities:* A.R.E. Library plus 1 other.
Website: http://www.atlanticuniv.edu/

General Application Contact: Rachel Alvidrez, Associate Vice President of Enrollment Management Services, 757-631-8101, Fax: 757-631-8096, E-mail: rachel.alvidrez@atlanticuniv.edu.

GRADUATE UNITS

Program in Integrated Imagery: Regression Hypnosis *Expenses:* Contact institution. *Program availability:* Blended/hybrid learning. Offers integrated imagery: regression hypnosis (Graduate Certificate). *Application deadline:* For fall admission, 8/13 for domestic students; for spring admission, 11/13 for domestic students; for summer admission, 4/9 for domestic students. *Application fee:* $50. *Application Contact:* Rachel Alvidrez, Educational Services Manager, 757-631-8101, Fax: 757-631-8096, E-mail: info@atlanticuniv.edu.

Program in Transpersonal Psychology *Expenses:* Contact institution. *Program availability:* Part-time, evening/weekend, online learning. Offers applied spirituality (MA); consciousness (MA); creativity (MA); general studies (MA); leadership and conflict transformation (MA). *Application deadline:* For fall admission, 7/19 for domestic students; for spring admission, 11/16 for domestic students; for summer admission, 3/15 for domestic students. Applications are processed on a rolling basis. *Application fee:* $50. Electronic applications accepted. *Application Contact:* Rachel Alvidrez, Associate Vice President of Enrollment Management Services, 757-631-8101, Fax: 757-631-8096, E-mail: info@atlanticuniv.edu.

Spiritual Guidance Mentor Program *Expenses:* Contact institution. Offers spiritual guidance mentor (Certificate). *Application deadline:* For fall admission, 8/13 for domestic students; for spring admission, 11/13 for domestic students; for summer admission, 4/9 for domestic students. *Application fee:* $35. *Application Contact:* Rachel Alvidrez, Educational Services Manager, 757-631-8101, Fax: 757-631-8096, E-mail: info@atlanticuniv.edu.

ATLANTIC UNIVERSITY COLLEGE, Guaynabo, PR 00970

General Information Independent, coed, comprehensive institution.

GRADUATE UNITS

Program in Graphic Arts *Program availability:* Part-time. Offers digital graphic design (MGD).

A.T. STILL UNIVERSITY, Kirksville, MO 63501

General Information Independent, coed, graduate-only institution. *Enrollment by degree level:* 718 master's, 2,723 doctoral, 128 other advanced degrees. *Graduate faculty:* 231 full-time (107 women), 509 part-time/adjunct (244 women). *Graduate housing:* Rooms and/or apartments available on a first-come, first-served basis to single and married students. Housing application deadline: 3/1. *Student services:* Campus employment opportunities, campus safety program, career counseling, exercise/wellness program, free psychological counseling, multicultural affairs office, services for students with disabilities. *Library facilities:* A.T. Still Memorial Library plus 1 other. *Collection:* Books: 16,385 (physical), 220,642 (digital/electronic); Serial titles: 1,281 (physical), 41,028 (digital/electronic); Databases: 71. Weekly public service hours: 156. *Research affiliation:* Nordic Academy of Osteopathy (osteopathic clinical research), Truman State University (osteopathic clinical research), The University of Arizona, College of Medicine-Phoenix (osteopathic and biomedical clinical research), Pennsylvania State University (exercise pressor reflex), Banner Heart Hospital (education and readmissions), Zimmer DeNovo (orthopedic clinical trials).

Computer facilities: 45 computers available on campus for general student use. Website: http://www.atsu.edu/

General Application Contact: Donna Sparks, Associate Director for Admissions, 660-626-2237, Fax: 660-626-2969, E-mail: admissions@atsu.edu.

GRADUATE UNITS

Arizona School of Dentistry and Oral Health Students: 310 full-time (162 women), 1 part-time (0 women); includes 122 minority (8 Black or African American, non-Hispanic/Latino; 5 American Indian or Alaska Native, non-Hispanic/Latino; 79 Asian, non-Hispanic/Latino; 20 Hispanic/Latino; 10 Two or more races, non-Hispanic/Latino; 2 international. 2,654 applicants, 5% accepted, 76 enrolled. *Faculty:* 58 full-time (29 women), 132 part-time/adjunct (88 women). Expenses: Contact institution. *Financial support:* In 2016–17, 48 students received support. Federal Work-Study and scholarships/grants available. Financial award application deadline: 6/1; financial award applicants required to submit FAFSA. In 2016, 82 doctorates, 5 Certificates awarded. Offers dental medicine (DMD); orthodontics (Certificate). *Application deadline:* For fall admission, 11/15 for domestic and international students; for summer admission, 11/15 for domestic and international students. Applications are processed on a rolling basis. *Application fee:* $70. Electronic applications accepted. *Application Contact:* Donna Sparks, Associate Director, Admissions Processing, 660-626-2117, Fax: 660-626-2969, E-mail: admissions@atsu.edu. *Dean,* Dr. Jack Dillenberg, 480-219-6000, Fax: 480-219-6110, E-mail: jdillenberg@atsu.edu.

Arizona School of Health Sciences Students: 555 full-time (370 women), 411 part-time (297 women); includes 243 minority (49 Black or African American, non-Hispanic/Latino; 6 American Indian or Alaska Native, non-Hispanic/Latino; 90 Asian, non-Hispanic/Latino; 79 Hispanic/Latino; 19 Two or more races, non-Hispanic/Latino), 64 international. Average age 33. 4,529 applicants, 9% accepted, 271 enrolled. *Faculty:* 54 full-time (31 women), 188 part-time/adjunct (132 women). Expenses: Contact institution. *Financial support:* In 2016–17, 140 students received support. Federal Work-Study and scholarships/grants available. Financial award application deadline: 6/1; financial award applicants required to submit FAFSA. In 2016, 139 master's, 253 doctorates, 1 other advanced degree awarded. *Program availability:* Part-time, 100% online. Offers advanced occupational therapy (MS); advanced physician assistant studies (MS); athletic training (MS, DAT); audiology (Au D); clinical decision making in athletic training (Graduate Certificate); occupational therapy (MS, OTD); orthopedic rehabilitation (Graduate Certificate); physical therapy (DPT); physician assistant studies (MS); transitional audiology (Au D); transitional physical therapy (DPT). *Application deadline:* For fall admission, 7/7 for domestic and international students; for winter admission, 10/3 for domestic and international students; for spring admission, 1/16 for domestic and international students; for summer admission, 4/17 for domestic and international students. Applications are processed on a rolling basis. *Application fee:* $70. Electronic applications accepted. *Application Contact:* Donna Sparks, Associate Director, Admissions Processing, 660-626-2117, Fax: 660-626-2969, E-mail: admissions@atsu.edu. *Dean,* Dr. Randy Danielsen, 480-219-6000, Fax: 480-219-6110, E-mail: rdanielsen@atsu.edu.

College of Graduate Health Studies Students: 505 full-time (319 women), 461 part-time (276 women); includes 337 minority (151 Black or African American, non-Hispanic/Latino; 19 American Indian or Alaska Native, non-Hispanic/Latino; 70 Asian, non-Hispanic/Latino; 89 Hispanic/Latino; 1 Native Hawaiian or other Pacific Islander, non-Hispanic/Latino; 7 Two or more races, non-Hispanic/Latino), 29 international. Average age 37. 366 applicants, 98% accepted, 370 enrolled. *Faculty:* 29 full-time (18 women), 89 part-time/adjunct (46 women). Expenses: Contact institution. *Financial support:* Scholarships/grants available. Financial award applicants required to submit FAFSA. In 2016, 113 master's, 94 doctorates, 110 other advanced degrees awarded. *Program availability:* Part-time, online only, 100% online, blended/hybrid learning. Offers dental public health (MPH); exercise and sport psychology (Certificate); fundamentals of education (Certificate); geriatric exercise science (Certificate); global health (Certificate); health administration (MHA, DHA); health professions (Ed D); health sciences (DH Sc); kinesiology (MS); leadership and organizational behavior (Certificate); public health (MPH); sports conditioning (Certificate). *Application deadline:* For fall admission, 5/20 for domestic and international students; for winter admission, 9/12 for domestic and international students; for spring admission, 12/12 for domestic and international students; for summer admission, 3/6 for domestic and international students. Applications are processed on a rolling basis. *Application fee:* $70. Electronic applications accepted. *Application Contact:* Amie Waldemer, Associate Director, Online Admissions, 480-219-6146, E-mail: awaldemer@atsu.edu. *Dean,* Dr. Donald Altman, 660-626-2820, Fax: 660-626-2826, E-mail: daltman@atsu.edu.

Kirksville College of Osteopathic Medicine Students: 713 full-time (293 women), 16 part-time (8 women); includes 130 minority (18 Black or African American, non-Hispanic/Latino; 1 American Indian or Alaska Native, non-Hispanic/Latino; 43 Asian, non-Hispanic/Latino; 36 Hispanic/Latino; 32 Two or more races, non-Hispanic/Latino), 3 international. Average age 26. 4,806 applicants, 8% accepted, 180 enrolled. *Faculty:* 40 full-time (7 women), 32 part-time/adjunct (4 women). Expenses: Contact institution. *Financial support:* In 2016–17, 152 students received support, including 24 fellowships with full tuition reimbursements available (averaging $52,141 per year); Federal Work-Study and scholarships/grants also available. Financial award application deadline: 6/1; financial award applicants required to submit FAFSA. In 2016, 1 master's, 168 doctorates awarded. Offers biomedical sciences (MS); osteopathic medicine (DO). *Application deadline:* For fall admission, 2/1 for domestic students; for summer admission, 2/1 for domestic students. Applications are processed on a rolling basis. *Application fee:* $70. Electronic applications accepted. *Application Contact:* Donna Sparks, Associate Director, Admissions Processing, 660-626-2117, Fax: 660-626-2969, E-mail: admissions@atsu.edu. *Dean,* Dr. Margaret Wilson, 660-626-2354, Fax: 660-626-2080, E-mail: mwilson@atsu.edu.

Missouri School of Dentistry and Oral Health Students: 168 full-time (92 women); includes 44 minority (1 Black or African American, non-Hispanic/Latino; 1 American Indian or Alaska Native, non-Hispanic/Latino; 32 Asian, non-Hispanic/Latino; 10 Hispanic/Latino). Average age 27. 1,269 applicants, 8% accepted, 42 enrolled. *Faculty:* 11 full-time (4 women), 34 part-time/adjunct (8 women). Expenses: Contact institution. *Financial support:* In 2016–17, 33 students received support. Federal Work-Study and scholarships/grants available. Financial award application deadline: 6/1; financial award applicants required to submit FAFSA. Offers dental medicine (DMD). *Application deadline:* For fall admission, 12/1 for domestic students; for summer admission, 12/1 for domestic students. Applications are processed on a rolling basis. *Application fee:* $70. Electronic applications accepted. *Application Contact:* Donna Sparks, Associate Director for Admissions, 660-626-2237, Fax: 660-626-2969, E-mail: admissions@atsu.edu. *Dean,* Dr. Dwight McLeod, 660-626-2842, E-mail: dmcleod@atsu.edu.

School of Osteopathic Medicine in Arizona Students: 428 full-time (231 women), 1 part-time (0 women); includes 219 minority (8 Black or African American, non-Hispanic/Latino; 1 American Indian or Alaska Native, non-Hispanic/Latino; 149 Asian, non-Hispanic/Latino; 34 Hispanic/Latino; 1 Native Hawaiian or other Pacific Islander, non-Hispanic/Latino; 26 Two or more races, non-Hispanic/Latino). Average age 27. 5,876 applicants, 4% accepted, 108 enrolled. *Faculty:* 39 full-time (18 women), 14 part-time/adjunct (10 women). Expenses: Contact institution. *Financial support:* In 2016–17, 38 students received support, including 2 fellowships (averaging $52,992 per year); Federal Work-Study and scholarships/grants also available. Financial award application deadline: 6/1; financial award applicants required to submit FAFSA. In 2016, 104 doctorates awarded. Offers osteopathic medicine (DO). *Application deadline:* For fall admission, 3/1 for domestic students; for summer admission, 3/1 for domestic students.

Applications are processed on a rolling basis. *Application fee:* $70. Electronic applications accepted. *Application Contact:* Donna Sparks, Associate Director for Admissions, 660-626-2117, Fax: 660-626-2969, E-mail: admissions@atsu.edu. *Dean,* Dr. Jeffrey Morgan, 480-219-6000, Fax: 480-219-6110, E-mail: jeffreymorgan@atsu.edu.

AUBURN UNIVERSITY, Auburn University, AL 36849

General Information State-supported, coed, university. *Enrollment:* 28,290 graduate, professional, and undergraduate students; 3,180 full-time matriculated graduate/professional students (1,828 women), 2,340 part-time matriculated graduate/professional students (1,060 women). *Enrollment by degree level:* 2,610 master's, 2,769 doctoral, 141 other advanced degrees. *Graduate faculty:* 1,186 full-time (453 women), 98 part-time/adjunct (40 women). *Tuition,* state resident: full-time $9072; part-time $504 per credit hour. Tuition, nonresident: full-time $27,216; part-time $1512 per credit hour. *Required fees:* $812 per semester. Tuition and fees vary according to degree level and program. *Graduate housing:* Rooms and/or apartments available on a first-come, first-served basis to single and married students. Typical cost: $12,898 (including board) for married students. *Student services:* Campus employment opportunities, campus safety program, career counseling, exercise/wellness program, free psychological counseling, international student services, low-cost health insurance, multicultural affairs office, services for students with disabilities, teacher training, writing training. *Library facilities:* R. B. Draughon Library plus 3 others. *Collection:* Books: 4.5 million (physical), 998,420 (digital/electronic); Serial titles: 76,117 (physical), 81,492 (digital/electronic). Study areas open 24 hours, 5–7 days a week. *Research affiliation:* National Center of Excellence for Airliner Cabin Environmental Research (aerospace, polymer and fibers engineering), National Textile Center Consortium (polymer and fibers engineering), National Asphalt Pavement Association (asphalt technology, civil engineering), Consortium for Vehicle Electronics (mechanical and automotive engineering, electrical engineering), Tay-Sachs Gene Therapy Consortium (veterinary medicine, clinical sciences), Higher Education Consortium for Special Education (special and rehabilitative education).

Computer facilities: Computer purchase and lease plans are available. 1,722 computers available on campus for general student use. A campuswide network can be accessed from student residence rooms and from off campus. Online class registration, bursar payments, course materials are available. Website: http://www.auburn.edu/

General Application Contact: Dr. George Flowers, Dean of the Graduate School, 334-844-2125, E-mail: flowegt@auburn.edu.

GRADUATE UNITS

College of Veterinary Medicine Students: 506 full-time (406 women), 90 part-time (60 women); includes 54 minority (9 Black or African American, non-Hispanic/Latino; 2 American Indian or Alaska Native, non-Hispanic/Latino; 11 Asian, non-Hispanic/Latino; 25 Hispanic/Latino; 7 Two or more races, non-Hispanic/Latino), 24 international. Average age 26. 789 applicants, 42% accepted, 137 enrolled. *Faculty:* 94 full-time (39 women), 5 part-time/adjunct (2 women). Expenses: Contact institution. *Financial support:* Fellowships, research assistantships, teaching assistantships, and Federal Work-Study available. Support available to part-time students. Financial award application deadline: 3/15; financial award applicants required to submit FAFSA. In 2016, 11 master's, 123 doctorates awarded. *Program availability:* Part-time. Offers veterinary medicine (MS, DVM, PhD). *Application deadline:* Applications are processed on a rolling basis. *Application fee:* $50 ($60 for international students). *Application Contact:* Dr. George Flowers, Interim Dean of the Graduate School, 334-844-4700. *Acting Dean,* Dr. Calvin Johnson, 334-844-2650.

Graduate School Students: 3,180 full-time (1,828 women), 2,340 part-time (1,060 women); includes 839 minority (428 Black or African American, non-Hispanic/Latino; 24 American Indian or Alaska Native, non-Hispanic/Latino; 142 Asian, non-Hispanic/Latino; 166 Hispanic/Latino; 5 Native Hawaiian or other Pacific Islander, non-Hispanic/Latino; 74 Two or more races, non-Hispanic/Latino), 1,134 international. Average age 29. 5,966 applicants, 48% accepted, 1520 enrolled. *Faculty:* 1,186 full-time (453 women), 98 part-time/adjunct (40 women). Expenses: Contact institution. *Financial support:* Fellowships, research assistantships, teaching assistantships, career-related internships or fieldwork, and Federal Work-Study available. Support available to part-time students. Financial award applicants required to submit FAFSA. In 2016, 1,186 master's, 523 doctorates, 198 other advanced degrees awarded. *Program availability:* Part-time, evening/weekend. Offers applied economics (PhD); cell and molecular biology (PhD); real estate development (MRED); sociology and rural sociology (MA, MS). *Application fee:* $50 ($60 for international students). *Dean,* Dr. George Flowers, 334-844-4700, E-mail: gradadm@auburn.edu.

College of Agriculture Students: 127 full-time (75 women), 138 part-time (56 women); includes 17 minority (6 Black or African American, non-Hispanic/Latino; 1 American Indian or Alaska Native, non-Hispanic/Latino; 1 Asian, non-Hispanic/Latino; 7 Hispanic/Latino; 2 Two or more races, non-Hispanic/Latino), 102 international. Average age 28. 147 applicants, 55% accepted, 67 enrolled. *Faculty:* 119 full-time (35 women). Expenses: Contact institution. *Financial support:* Fellowships, research assistantships, teaching assistantships, and Federal Work-Study available. Support available to part-time students. Financial award application deadline: 3/1; financial award applicants required to submit FAFSA. In 2016, 71 master's, 21 doctorates awarded. *Program availability:* Part-time. Offers agricultural economics (M Ag); agriculture (M Ag, M Aq, MS, PhD); agronomy and soils (M Ag, MS, PhD); animal sciences (M Ag, MS, PhD); entomology (M Ag, MS); fisheries and allied aquacultures (M Aq, MS, PhD); horticulture (M Ag, MS, PhD); plant pathology (M Ag, MS, PhD); poultry science (M Ag, MS, PhD). *Application deadline:* Applications are processed on a rolling basis. *Application fee:* $50 ($60 for international students). Electronic applications accepted. *Application Contact:* Dr. George Flowers, Dean of the Graduate School, 334-844-2125. *Dean,* Paul Patterson, 334-844-3254.

College of Architecture, Design, and Construction Students: 79 full-time (36 women), 68 part-time (21 women); includes 27 minority (12 Black or African American, non-Hispanic/Latino; 4 Asian, non-Hispanic/Latino; 8 Hispanic/Latino; 1 Native Hawaiian or other Pacific Islander, non-Hispanic/Latino; 2 Two or more races, non-Hispanic/Latino), 41 international. Average age 31. 223 applicants, 71% accepted, 66 enrolled. *Faculty:* 62 full-time (14 women), 7 part-time/adjunct (1 woman). Expenses: Contact institution. *Financial support:* Fellowships and Federal Work-Study available. Support available to part-time students. Financial award application deadline: 3/15; financial award applicants required to submit FAFSA. In 2016, 73 master's awarded. *Program availability:* Part-time. Offers architecture, design, and construction (MBC, MCP, MID, MIDC, ML Arch); building science (MBC, MIDC); community planning (MCP); industrial design (MID); integrated design and construction (MIDC); landscape architecture (ML Arch). *Application deadline:* Applications are processed on a rolling basis. *Application fee:* $50 ($60 for international students). Electronic applications accepted. *Application Contact:* Dr.

George Flowers, Dean of the Graduate School, 334-844-2125. *Dean/Chair*, Dr. Vini Nathan, 334-844-4285.

College of Business Students: 197 full-time (85 women), 590 part-time (164 women); includes 124 minority (46 Black or African American, non-Hispanic/Latino; 5 American Indian or Alaska Native, non-Hispanic/Latino; 30 Asian, non-Hispanic/Latino; 31 Hispanic/Latino; 12 Two or more races, non-Hispanic/Latino; 58 international. Average age 33. 792 applicants, 57% accepted, 273 enrolled. *Faculty:* 73 full-time (19 women), 9 part-time/adjunct (5 women). Expenses: Contact institution. *Financial support:* Fellowships, research assistantships, teaching assistantships, career-related internships or fieldwork, and Federal Work-Study available. Support available to part-time students. Financial award application deadline: 3/15; financial award applicants required to submit FAFSA. In 2016, 276 master's, 4 doctorates awarded. *Program availability:* Part-time. Offers accountancy (M Acc); business (M Acc, MBA, MRED, MS, PhD); business administration (MBA); finance (MS); management (PhD). *Application deadline:* Applications are processed on a rolling basis. *Application fee:* $50 ($60 for international students). Electronic applications accepted. *Application Contact:* Dr. George Flowers, Dean of the Graduate School, 334-844-2125. *Dean*, Dr. Bill Hardgrave, 334-844-4832, E-mail: bch0014@auburn.edu.

College of Education Students: 457 full-time (321 women), 515 part-time (344 women); includes 273 minority (209 Black or African American, non-Hispanic/Latino; 4 American Indian or Alaska Native, non-Hispanic/Latino; 8 Asian, non-Hispanic/Latino; 33 Hispanic/Latino; 2 Native Hawaiian or other Pacific Islander, non-Hispanic/Latino; 17 Two or more races, non-Hispanic/Latino; 37 international. Average age 33. 726 applicants, 55% accepted, 256 enrolled. *Faculty:* 97 full-time (60 women), 12 part-time/adjunct (7 women). Expenses: Contact institution. *Financial support:* Fellowships, research assistantships, teaching assistantships, career-related internships or fieldwork, and Federal Work-Study available. Support available to part-time students. Financial award application deadline: 3/15; financial award applicants required to submit FAFSA. In 2016, 251 master's, 71 doctorates, 65 other advanced degrees awarded. *Program availability:* Part-time. Offers adult education (PhD, Ed S); curriculum supervision (M Ed, PhD); education (M Ed, MS, Ed D, Ed S, Graduate Certificate); elementary education (Ed S); exercise science (M Ed); higher education administration (PhD); library media (Ed S); school administration (M Ed, PhD); special education, rehabilitation, counseling and school psychology (M Ed, MS, PhD). *Application fee:* $50 ($60 for international students). Electronic applications accepted. *Application Contact:* Dr. George Flowers, Dean of the Graduate School, 334-844-2125. *Dean*, Dr. Betty Lou Whitford, 334-844-4446.

College of Human Sciences Students: 73 full-time (57 women), 72 part-time (46 women); includes 24 minority (10 Black or African American, non-Hispanic/Latino; 1 American Indian or Alaska Native, non-Hispanic/Latino; 3 Asian, non-Hispanic/Latino; 7 Hispanic/Latino; 3 Two or more races, non-Hispanic/Latino; 32 international. Average age 30. 141 applicants, 53% accepted, 49 enrolled. *Faculty:* 54 full-time (36 women). Expenses: Contact institution. *Financial support:* Fellowships, research assistantships, teaching assistantships, career-related internships or fieldwork, and Federal Work-Study available. Support available to part-time students. Financial award application deadline: 3/15; financial award applicants required to submit FAFSA. In 2016, 21 master's, 8 doctorates, 14 other advanced degrees awarded. *Program availability:* Part-time. Offers consumer affairs (MS, PhD); human development and family studies (MS, PhD); human sciences (MS, PhD, Graduate Certificate); nutrition and food science (MS, PhD, Graduate Certificate). *Application deadline:* Applications are processed on a rolling basis. *Application fee:* $50 ($60 for international students). Electronic applications accepted. *Application Contact:* Dr. George Flowers, Dean of the Graduate School, 334-844-2125. *Dean*, Dr. June Henton, 334-844-3790, E-mail: jhenton@humsci.auburn.edu.

College of Liberal Arts Students: 275 full-time (195 women), 138 part-time (80 women); includes 52 minority (25 Black or African American, non-Hispanic/Latino; 2 American Indian or Alaska Native, non-Hispanic/Latino; 6 Asian, non-Hispanic/Latino; 12 Hispanic/Latino; 7 Native Hawaiian or other Pacific Islander, non-Hispanic/Latino; 50 international. Average age 29. 905 applicants, 20% accepted, 128 enrolled. *Faculty:* 237 full-time (127 women), 30 part-time/adjunct (15 women). Expenses: Contact institution. *Financial support:* Fellowships, research assistantships, teaching assistantships, career-related internships or fieldwork, and Federal Work-Study available. Support available to part-time students. Financial award application deadline: 3/15; financial award applicants required to submit FAFSA. In 2016, 105 master's, 46 doctorates, 6 other advanced degrees awarded. *Program availability:* Part-time. Offers audiology (MCD, Au D); communication and journalism (MA, Graduate Certificate); economics (MS); English (MA, MTPC, PhD, Graduate Certificate); foreign languages and literatures (MA, MHS); history (MA, PhD, Graduate Certificate); liberal arts (MA, MCD, MHS, MPA, MS, MTPC, Au D, PhD, Graduate Certificate); psychology (MS, PhD); public administration (MPA, PhD, Graduate Certificate). *Application deadline:* Applications are processed on a rolling basis. *Application fee:* $50 ($60 for international students). Electronic applications accepted. *Application Contact:* Dr. George Flowers, Dean of the Graduate School, 334-844-2125. *Dean*, Dr. Joe Aistrup, 334-844-2183.

College of Sciences and Mathematics Students: 196 full-time (67 women), 180 part-time (75 women); includes 40 minority (12 Black or African American, non-Hispanic/Latino; 1 American Indian or Alaska Native, non-Hispanic/Latino; 14 Asian, non-Hispanic/Latino; 7 Hispanic/Latino; 6 Two or more races, non-Hispanic/Latino; 148 international. Average age 28. 317 applicants, 51% accepted, 86 enrolled. *Faculty:* 164 full-time (35 women), 15 part-time/adjunct (5 women). Expenses: Contact institution. *Financial support:* Fellowships, research assistantships, teaching assistantships, career-related internships or fieldwork, and Federal Work-Study available. Support available to part-time students. Financial award applicants required to submit FAFSA. In 2016, 61 master's, 25 doctorates awarded. *Program availability:* Part-time. Offers analytical chemistry (MS, PhD); applied mathematics (MAM, MS); biochemistry (MS, PhD); botany (MS); geology and geography (MS); inorganic chemistry (MS); mathematics (MS, PhD); organic chemistry (PhD); physical chemistry (MS, PhD); physics (MS, PhD); probability and statistics (M Prob S); sciences and mathematics (M Prob S, MAM, MS, PhD); statistics (MS); zoology (MS). *Application deadline:* Applications are processed on a rolling basis. *Application fee:* $50 ($60 for international students). *Application Contact:* Dr. George Flowers, Dean of the Graduate School, 334-844-2125. *Dean*, Nicholas Giordano, 334-844-5737.

Ginn College of Engineering Students: 565 full-time (141 women), 334 part-time (63 women); includes 56 minority (24 Black or African American, non-Hispanic/Latino; 2 American Indian or Alaska Native, non-Hispanic/Latino; 10 Asian, non-Hispanic/Latino; 16 Hispanic/Latino; 4 Two or more races, non-Hispanic/Latino; 557 international. Average age 27. 1,346 applicants, 46% accepted, 225 enrolled. *Faculty:* 162 full-time (15 women), 16 part-time/adjunct (2 women). Expenses: Contact institution. *Financial support:* Fellowships, research assistantships, teaching assistantships, and Federal Work-Study available. Support available to part-time

students. Financial award application deadline: 3/15; financial award applicants required to submit FAFSA. In 2016, 220 master's, 75 doctorates, 14 other advanced degrees awarded. *Program availability:* Part-time. Offers aerospace engineering (MAE, MS, PhD); biosystems engineering (MS, PhD); chemical engineering (M Ch E, MS, PhD); civil engineering (MCE, MS, PhD); computer science and software engineering (MS, MSWE, PhD); electrical and computer engineering (MEE, MS, PhD); engineering (M Ch E, M Mtl E, MAE, MCE, MEE, MISE, MME, MS, MSWE, PhD, Graduate Certificate); industrial and systems engineering (MISE, MS, PhD, Graduate Certificate); materials engineering (M Mtl E, MS, PhD); mechanical engineering (M Mtl E, MME, MS, PhD); polymer and fiber engineering (MS, PhD). *Application deadline:* Applications are processed on a rolling basis. *Application fee:* $50 ($60 for international students). Electronic applications accepted. *Application Contact:* Dr. George Flowers, Dean of the Graduate School, 334-844-2125. *Dean*, Dr. Chris Roberts, 334-844-2308.

School of Forestry and Wildlife Sciences Students: 32 full-time (12 women), 39 part-time (20 women); includes 5 minority (1 Black or African American, non-Hispanic/Latino; 1 American Indian or Alaska Native, non-Hispanic/Latino; 1 Asian, non-Hispanic/Latino; 2 Hispanic/Latino), 24 international. Average age 28. 27 applicants, 78% accepted, 17 enrolled. *Faculty:* 29 full-time (7 women), 1 (woman) part-time/adjunct. Expenses: Contact institution. *Financial support:* Fellowships, research assistantships, teaching assistantships, and Federal Work-Study available. Support available to part-time students. Financial award application deadline: 3/15; financial award applicants required to submit FAFSA. In 2016, 21 master's, 5 doctorates awarded. *Program availability:* Part-time. Offers forestry (MS); natural resource conservation (MNR); wildlife sciences (MS, PhD). *Application deadline:* Applications are processed on a rolling basis. *Application fee:* $50 ($60 for international students). Electronic applications accepted. *Application Contact:* Dr. George Flowers, Dean of the Graduate School, 334-844-2125. *Dean*, Dr. Janaki Alavalapati, 334-844-1004, Fax: 334-844-1084, E-mail: jra0024@auburn.edu.

School of Nursing Students: 2 full-time (1 woman), 124 part-time (112 women); includes 25 minority (18 Black or African American, non-Hispanic/Latino; 1 Asian, non-Hispanic/Latino; 2 Hispanic/Latino; 4 Two or more races, non-Hispanic/Latino). Average age 33. 93 applicants, 61% accepted, 46 enrolled. *Faculty:* 25 full-time (23 women). Expenses: Contact institution. In 2016, 49 master's awarded. Offers nursing educator (MSN); primary care practitioner (MSN). *Application Contact:* Dr. George Flowers, Dean of the Graduate School, 334-844-4700, E-mail: gradadm@auburn.edu. *Dean*, Dr. Gregg Newschwander, 334-844-3658, E-mail: gen0002@auburn.edu.

Harrison School of Pharmacy Students: 636 full-time (414 women), 12 part-time (8 women); includes 129 minority (47 Black or African American, non-Hispanic/Latino; 5 American Indian or Alaska Native, non-Hispanic/Latino; 51 Asian, non-Hispanic/Latino; 14 Hispanic/Latino; 2 Native Hawaiian or other Pacific Islander, non-Hispanic/Latino; 10 Two or more races, non-Hispanic/Latino; 38 international. Average age 25. 537 applicants, 56% accepted, 158 enrolled. *Faculty:* 55 full-time (32 women), 2 part-time/adjunct (both women). Expenses: Contact institution. *Financial support:* Fellowships, research assistantships, teaching assistantships, and Federal Work-Study available. Support available to part-time students. Financial award applicants required to submit FAFSA. In 2016, 4 master's, 139 doctorates awarded. *Program availability:* Part-time. Offers pharmacal sciences (MS, PhD); pharmaceutical sciences (PhD); pharmacy (MS, PhD, Pharm D); pharmacy care systems (MS, PhD). *Application deadline:* Applications are processed on a rolling basis. *Application fee:* $50 ($60 for international students). Electronic applications accepted. *Application Contact:* Dr. George Flowers, Dean of the Graduate School, 334-844-2125. *Dean*, Dr. R. Lee Evans, 334-844-8348.

AUBURN UNIVERSITY AT MONTGOMERY, Montgomery, AL 36124-4023

General Information State-supported, coed, comprehensive institution. *Enrollment:* 4,878 graduate, professional, and undergraduate students; 217 full-time matriculated graduate/professional students (131 women), 445 part-time matriculated graduate/professional students (312 women). *Enrollment by degree level:* 583 master's, 15 doctoral, 64 other advanced degrees. Graduate faculty: 91 full-time (39 women), 23 part-time/adjunct (8 women). Tuition, state resident: full-time $6462; part-time $359 per credit hour. Tuition, nonresident: full-time $14,526; part-time $807 per credit hour. *Required fees:* $554. Graduate housing: Rooms and/or apartments available on a first-come, first-served basis to single and married students. Typical cost: $4450 per year ($5650 including board) for single students. Room and board charges vary according to housing facility selected. Housing application deadline: 5/1. *Student services:* Campus employment opportunities, campus safety program, career counseling, exercise/wellness program, free psychological counseling, international student services, low-cost health insurance, multicultural affairs office, services for students with disabilities. *Library facilities:* Auburn University at Montgomery Library. *Collection:* Books: 340,819 (physical). Weekly public service hours: 86; students can reserve study rooms.

Computer facilities 600 computers available on campus for general student use. A campuswide network can be accessed from student residence rooms. Online class registration is available.
Website: http://www.aum.edu/

General Application Contact: Ashley Warren, Administrative Coordinator, Provost's Office, 334-244-3623, Fax: 334-244-3947, E-mail: awarren3@aum.edu.

GRADUATE UNITS

College of Arts and Sciences Students: 53 full-time (34 women), 53 part-time (34 women); includes 21 minority (17 Black or African American, non-Hispanic/Latino; 2 Asian, non-Hispanic/Latino; 1 Hispanic/Latino; 1 Two or more races, non-Hispanic/Latino), 20 international. 75 applicants, 80% accepted, 38 enrolled. *Faculty:* 37 full-time (10 women), 1 part-time/adjunct (0 women). Expenses: Contact institution. *Financial support:* In 2016–17, 9 teaching assistantships were awarded; career-related internships or fieldwork and scholarships/grants also available. Support available to part-time students. Financial award application deadline: 3/1; financial award applicants required to submit FAFSA. *Program availability:* Part-time, evening/weekend. Offers arts and sciences (MLA, MS, MTW); clinical psychology (MS); teaching writing (MTW). *Application deadline:* For fall admission, 7/1 for international students; for spring admission, 11/1 for international students; for summer admission, 4/15 for international students. Applications are processed on a rolling basis. *Application fee:* $25 ($0 for international students). Electronic applications accepted. *Application Contact:* Dr. Pamela Tidwell, Associate Dean, 334-244-3362, Fax: 334-244-3826, E-mail: ptidwell@aum.edu. *Dean*, Dr. Michael Burger, 334-244-3678, Fax: 334-244-3826, E-mail: mburger1@aum.edu.

Department of Mathematics and Computer Science Students: 14 full-time (3 women), 8 part-time (2 women); includes 1 minority (Asian, non-Hispanic/Latino), 19 international. Average age 27. 28 applicants, 71% accepted, 6 enrolled. *Faculty:* 6 full-time (0 women), 1 part-time/adjunct (0 women). Expenses: Contact institution. *Financial support:* In 2016–17, 1 teaching assistantship was awarded. Financial award application deadline: 3/1; financial award applicants required to submit FAFSA. In 2016, 22 master's awarded. Offers cybersystems and information security (MS). *Application deadline:* Applications are processed on a rolling basis. *Application fee:* $25 ($0 for international students). Electronic applications accepted. *Application Contact:* Dr. Luis Cueva-Parra, Associate Dean, 334-244-3321, Fax: 334-244-3826, E-mail: lcuevapa@aum.edu. *Chair,* Dr. Yi Wang, 334-244-3318, Fax: 334-244-3826, E-mail: ywang2@aum.edu.

College of Business Students: 50 full-time (22 women), 83 part-time (54 women); includes 33 minority (28 Black or African American, non-Hispanic/Latino; 3 Asian, non-Hispanic/Latino; 1 Hispanic/Latino; 1 Two or more races, non-Hispanic/Latino), 24 international. Average age 37. 122 applicants, 82% accepted, 74 enrolled. *Faculty:* 18 full-time (5 women), 1 part-time/adjunct (0 women). Expenses: Contact institution. *Financial support:* Research assistantships, career-related internships or fieldwork, and scholarships/grants available. Support available to part-time students. Financial award application deadline: 3/1; financial award applicants required to submit FAFSA. In 2016, 79 master's awarded. *Program availability:* Part-time, evening/weekend. Offers business (M Acc, MBA, MS); business and management (MBA); information systems management (MS). *Application deadline:* For fall admission, 7/1 for international students; for spring admission, 11/1 for international students; for summer admission, 4/15 for international students. Applications are processed on a rolling basis. *Application fee:* $25 ($0 for international students). Electronic applications accepted. *Application Contact:* Jennifer Taylor, Assistant Director of Graduate Programs, 334-244-3587, Fax: 334-244-3137, E-mail: jtaylor5@aum.edu. *Dean,* Dr. Rhea Ingram, 334-244-3476, Fax: 334-244-3792, E-mail: wingram4@aum.edu.

School of Accountancy Students: 5 full-time (2 women), 26 part-time (19 women); includes 6 minority (5 Black or African American, non-Hispanic/Latino; 1 Two or more races, non-Hispanic/Latino), 4 international. 28 applicants, 93% accepted, 20 enrolled. *Faculty:* 5 full-time (3 women). Expenses: Contact institution. *Financial support:* Scholarships/grants available. *Program availability:* Part-time. Offers accountancy (M Acc). *Application deadline:* Applications are processed on a rolling basis. *Application fee:* $25 ($0 for international students). Electronic applications accepted. *Application Contact:* Rhonda Seay, Graduate Advisor, 334-244-3115, E-mail: rseay@aum.edu.

College of Education Students: 80 full-time (63 women), 170 part-time (141 women); includes 72 minority (68 Black or African American, non-Hispanic/Latino; 2 Asian, non-Hispanic/Latino; 1 Hispanic/Latino; 1 Two or more races, non-Hispanic/Latino), 3 international. Average age 33. *Faculty:* 25 full-time (15 women), 11 part-time/adjunct (9 women). Expenses: Contact institution. *Financial support:* In 2016–17, 5 teaching assistantships were awarded; career-related internships or fieldwork and scholarships/grants also available. Support available to part-time students. Financial award application deadline: 3/1; financial award applicants required to submit FAFSA. *Program availability:* Part-time, evening/weekend. Offers counselor education (M Ed, Ed S); early childhood special education (M Ed); education (M Ed, Ed S); elementary education (M Ed, Ed S); exercise science (M Ed); instructional leadership (M Ed); instructional technology (Ed S); physical education (Ed S); secondary education (M Ed); special education/collaborative teacher (M Ed, Ed S); sport management (M Ed). *Application deadline:* Applications are processed on a rolling basis. Electronic applications accepted. *Application Contact:* Dr. Rhonda Morton, Associate Dean/Graduate Coordinator, 334-224-3287, Fax: 334-244-3978, E-mail: rmorton@aum.edu. *Dean,* Dr. Sheila Austin, 334-244-3425, Fax: 334-244-3102, E-mail: saustin1@aum.edu.

College of Nursing and Health Sciences Students: 23 full-time (14 women), 19 part-time (9 women); includes 10 minority (9 Black or African American, non-Hispanic/Latino; 1 Hispanic/Latino), 2 international. 28 applicants, 75% accepted, 14 enrolled. Expenses: Contact institution. Offers nurse educator (MSN); nurse practitioner (MSN). Programs offered jointly with Auburn University. *Application deadline:* For fall admission, 7/1 for domestic students; for spring admission, 10/1 for domestic students; for summer admission, 3/1 for domestic students. Applications are processed on a rolling basis. *Application fee:* $25 ($0 for international students). Electronic applications accepted. *Application Contact:* Dr. Barbara Wilder, Graduate Program Director, 334-844-6766, E-mail: wildebf@auburn.edu. *Dean,* Dr. Jean Leuner, 334-244-3658, E-mail: jleuner@aum.edu.

College of Public Policy and Justice Students: 20 full-time (10 women), 91 part-time (50 women); includes 38 minority (34 Black or African American, non-Hispanic/Latino; 2 Asian, non-Hispanic/Latino; 2 Two or more races, non-Hispanic/Latino), 5 international. Average age 32. 42 applicants, 90% accepted, 15 enrolled. *Faculty:* 14 full-time (4 women), 6 part-time/adjunct (2 women). Expenses: Contact institution. *Financial support:* In 2016–17, 6 teaching assistantships were awarded; career-related internships or fieldwork and scholarships/grants also available. Support available to part-time students. Financial award application deadline: 3/1; financial award applicants required to submit FAFSA. In 2016, 34 master's awarded. *Program availability:* Part-time, evening/weekend. Offers criminal justice (MSJPS); geographic information systems (MS); homeland security (MSJPS); homeland security and emergency management (MS); legal studies (MSJPS); organizational leadership (MSJPS); political science (MPS); public administration (MPA); public administration and public policy (PhD); public policy and justice (MPA, MPS, MS, MSJPS, PhD). *Application deadline:* Applications are processed on a rolling basis. Electronic applications accepted. *Application Contact:* Dr. Keivan Deravi, Dean, 334-244-3422, Fax: 334-244-3920, E-mail: mderavi@aum.edu. *Dean,* Dr. Keivan Deravi, 334-244-3422, Fax: 334-244-3920, E-mail: mderavi@aum.edu.

AUGSBURG COLLEGE, Minneapolis, MN 55454-1351

General Information Independent-religious, coed, comprehensive institution. *Graduate housing:* On-campus housing not available.

GRADUATE UNITS

Program in Business Administration *Program availability:* Evening/weekend. Offers business administration (MBA). Electronic applications accepted.

Program in Education *Program availability:* Part-time, evening/weekend. Offers education (MAE). Electronic applications accepted.

Program in Leadership *Program availability:* Part-time, evening/weekend. Offers leadership (MA).

Program in Physician Assistant Studies Offers physician assistant studies (MS).

Program in Social Work *Program availability:* Part-time, evening/weekend. Offers social work (MSW).

Programs in Nursing Offers nursing (MA, DNP).

AUGUSTANA UNIVERSITY, Sioux Falls, SD 57197

General Information Independent-religious, coed, comprehensive institution. *Enrollment:* 1,937 graduate, professional, and undergraduate students; 10 full-time matriculated graduate/professional students (9 women), 262 part-time matriculated graduate/professional students (214 women). *Enrollment by degree level:* 272 master's. *Graduate faculty:* 11 full-time (5 women), 13 part-time/adjunct (12 women). *Graduate housing:* Rooms and/or apartments available on a first-come, first-served basis to single and married students. Typical cost: $4750 per year ($8964 including board) for single students; $5364 per year ($6764 including board) for married students. Room and board charges vary according to board plan, campus/location and housing facility selected. Housing application deadline: 9/1. *Student services:* Campus employment opportunities, campus safety program, career counseling, child daycare facilities, exercise/wellness program, free psychological counseling, international student services, low-cost health insurance, multicultural affairs office, services for students with disabilities, teacher training, writing training. *Library facilities:* Mikkelsen Library. *Collection:* Students can reserve study rooms. *Research affiliation:* Binghamton University, State University of New York (chemistry), Sanford Underground Science and Engineering Lab (physics), JR Macdonald Laboratory (physics), NASA (computer science), Labratori Nazionalidd Gran Sasso, Italy (physics), Sanford Research (biology, biochemistry, genetic counseling).

Computer facilities: Computer purchase and lease plans are available. 250 computers available on campus for general graduate student use. A campuswide network can be accessed from student residence rooms and from off campus. Online class registration is available.
Website: http://www.augie.edu/

General Application Contact: Julia Paluch, Administrative Assistant, Graduate Education, 605-274-4043, Fax: 605-274-4450, E-mail: julia.paluch@augie.edu.

GRADUATE UNITS

MA in Education Program Expenses: Contact institution. *Financial support:* Application deadline: 3/1; applicants required to submit FAFSA. *Program availability:* Part-time, evening/weekend, online only, 100% online. Offers instructional strategies (MA); reading (MA); special populations (MA); STEM (MA); technology (MA). *Application deadline:* For fall admission, 8/1 for domestic and international students; for spring admission, 11/1 for domestic and international students; for summer admission, 4/1 for domestic and international students. Applications are processed on a rolling basis. *Application fee:* $50. Electronic applications accepted. *Application Contact:* Jody Nitz, Graduate Coordinator, 605-274-4043, Fax: 605-274-4450, E-mail: graduate@augie.edu. *Chair,* Dr. Laurie Daily, 605-274-5211, E-mail: laurie.daily@augie.edu.

Sports Administration and Leadership Program Expenses: Contact institution. *Financial support:* Unspecified assistantships available. Financial award application deadline: 3/1; financial award applicants required to submit FAFSA. *Program availability:* Part-time. Offers sports administration and leadership (MA). *Application deadline:* For fall admission, 6/1 priority date for domestic and international students. Applications are processed on a rolling basis. *Application fee:* $50. Electronic applications accepted. *Application Contact:* Jody Nitz, Graduate Education Assistant, 605-274-4043, Fax: 605-274-4450, E-mail: graduate@augie.edu. *Director,* Dr. Sherry Barkley, 605-274-4312, E-mail: sherry.barkley@augie.edu.

AUGUSTA UNIVERSITY, Augusta, GA 30912

General Information State-supported, coed, university. CGS member. *Enrollment:* 7,938 graduate, professional, and undergraduate students; 2,344 full-time matriculated graduate/professional students (1,387 women), 406 part-time matriculated graduate/professional students (298 women). *Enrollment by degree level:* 964 master's, 1,718 doctoral, 68 other advanced degrees. *Graduate faculty:* 643 full-time (338 women), 114 part-time/adjunct (57 women). *Graduate housing:* Rooms and/or apartments available on a first-come, first-served basis to single and married students. *Student services:* Campus employment opportunities, campus safety program, career counseling, child daycare facilities, exercise/wellness program, free psychological counseling, international student services, multicultural affairs office, services for students with disabilities. *Library facilities:* Main library plus 2 others. *Research affiliation:* Georgia Cancer Coalition (cancer research programs), Advanced Technology Development Center (biotechnology transfer), Medical College of Georgia Research Institute, Inc. (biomedical research), Georgia Center of Innovation for Life Sciences (research commercialization and economic development), Georgia Research Alliance (science and technology development).

Computer facilities: A campuswide network can be accessed from student residence rooms. Online class registration is available.
Website: http://www.augusta.edu/

General Application Contact: Maura Flaschner, Director of Academic Admissions, 706-721-2725, Fax: 706-721-7279, E-mail: admissions@augusta.edu.

GRADUATE UNITS

Clinical Nurse Leader Program Students: 237 full-time (192 women), 1 (woman) part-time; includes 63 minority (32 Black or African American, non-Hispanic/Latino; 7 Asian, non-Hispanic/Latino; 10 Hispanic/Latino; 14 Two or more races, non-Hispanic/Latino). Average age 26. 308 applicants, 49% accepted, 119 enrolled. Expenses: Contact institution. In 2016, 100 master's awarded. Offers clinical nurse leader (MSN). *Application deadline:* For fall admission, 2/1 for domestic students. *Application fee:* $50. Electronic applications accepted. *Application Contact:* Emily Holsey, Program Manager, 706-721-9767, Fax: 706-721-8169, E-mail: cnl@augusta.edu. *Director,* Dr. Stephanie Wright, 706-721-9767, Fax: 706-721-8169.

College of Allied Health Sciences Students: 379 full-time (289 women), 40 part-time (31 women); includes 88 minority (39 Black or African American, non-Hispanic/Latino; 1 American Indian or Alaska Native, non-Hispanic/Latino; 26 Asian, non-Hispanic/Latino; 14 Hispanic/Latino; 8 Two or more races, non-Hispanic/Latino), 3 international. Average age 27. Expenses: Contact institution. *Financial support:* Federal Work-Study available. Support available to part-time students. Financial award application deadline: 5/31; financial award applicants required to submit FAFSA. *Program availability:* Online learning. Offers allied health sciences (MHS, MPA, MPH, MS, DPT, PhD); clinical laboratory sciences (MHS); diagnostic sciences (PhD); environmental health (MPH); health care outcomes (PhD); health informatics (MPH); health management (MPH); medical illustration (MS); occupational therapy (MHS); physical therapy (DPT); physician assistant (MPA); rehabilitation science (PhD); social and behavioral sciences (MPH). *Application deadline:* For fall admission, 6/15 for domestic students, 1/15 for international students. Applications are processed on a rolling basis. *Application Contact:* Leslie Bell, Administrative Assistant, 706-721-2621, Fax: 706-721-7279, E-mail: lebell@augusta.edu. *Dean and Professor,* Dr. Andrew Balas, 706-721-2621, Fax: 706-721-7312, E-mail: andrew.balas@augusta.edu.

The Dental College of Georgia Students: 343 full-time (160 women), 4 part-time (1 woman); includes 115 minority (39 Black or African American, non-Hispanic/Latino; 46 Asian, non-Hispanic/Latino; 15 Hispanic/Latino; 15 Two or more races, non-

Hispanic/Latino), 2 international. Average age 26. Expenses: Contact institution. *Financial support:* Federal Work-Study and scholarships/grants available. Financial award application deadline: 5/1; financial award applicants required to submit FAFSA. Offers dentistry (DMD). *Application deadline:* For fall admission, 10/15 for domestic students. Electronic applications accepted. *Application Contact:* Dr. Carole M. Hanes, Associate Dean for Students, Admissions, and Alumni, 706-721-2813, Fax: 706-723-0237, E-mail: chanes@augusta.edu. *Dean,* Dr. Carol Lefebvre, 706-721-2117, Fax: 706-723-0237, E-mail: clefebvr@augusta.edu.

Doctor of Nursing Practice Program Students: 85 full-time (77 women), 78 part-time (65 women); includes 43 minority (24 Black or African American, non-Hispanic/Latino; 11 Asian, non-Hispanic/Latino; 3 Hispanic/Latino; 1 Native Hawaiian or other Pacific Islander, non-Hispanic/Latino; 4 Two or more races, non-Hispanic/Latino). Average age 33. Expenses: Contact institution. Offers adult gerontology acute care nurse practitioner (DNP); family nurse practitioner (DNP); nurse executive (DNP); nursing (DNP); nurse anesthesia (DNP); pediatric nurse practitioner (DNP); psychiatric mental health nurse practitioner (DNP). *Application deadline:* For fall admission, 3/1 for domestic and international students; for spring admission, 7/1 for domestic and international students. Applications are processed on a rolling basis. *Application fee:* $50. Electronic applications accepted. *Application Contact:* Karen Sturgill, Program Manager, 706-721-3676, Fax: 706-721-8169, E-mail: dnp@augusta.edu. *Program Director, Acute Care Tracks,* Dr. Marguerite Murphy, RN, 706-721-3676, Fax: 706-721-8169.

College of Education Students: 42 full-time (27 women), 58 part-time (34 women); includes 30 minority (23 Black or African American, non-Hispanic/Latino; 6 Hispanic/Latino; 1 Two or more races, non-Hispanic/Latino), 1 international. Average age 31. Expenses: Contact institution. *Financial support:* Career-related internships or fieldwork, Federal Work-Study, institutionally sponsored loans, and unspecified assistantships available. Support available to part-time students. Financial award application deadline: 4/15; financial award applicants required to submit FAFSA. *Program availability:* Part-time, evening/weekend. Offers counselor education (M Ed, Ed S); curriculum and instruction (Ed S); education (M Ed, MAT, Ed D, Ed S); educational innovation (Ed D); elementary education (MAT); foreign language education (MAT); instruction (M Ed); leadership (Ed S); middle grades education (MAT); music education (MAT); school administration (M Ed); secondary education (MAT); special education (MAT); teacher leadership (M Ed). *Application deadline:* For fall admission, 7/16 priority date for domestic students. Applications are processed on a rolling basis. *Application fee:* $20. *Application Contact:* Dr. Zach Kelehear, Dean, 706-737-1499, Fax: 706-667-4706, E-mail: zkelehear@augusta.edu. *Dean,* Dr. Zach Kelehear, 706-737-1499, Fax: 706-667-4706, E-mail: zkelehear@augusta.edu.

College of Science and Mathematics Expenses: Contact institution. Offers psychological sciences (MS); science and mathematics (MS). *Application Contact:* Dr. John C. Sutherland, Interim Dean, Fax: 706-721-6829, E-mail: jsutherland@augusta.edu. *Interim Dean,* Dr. John C. Sutherland, 706-729-2260, Fax: 706-721-6829, E-mail: jsutherland@augusta.edu.

Hull College of Business Expenses: Contact institution. *Financial support:* Research assistantships with partial tuition reimbursements, Federal Work-Study, and institutionally sponsored loans available. Support available to part-time students. Financial award application deadline: 4/15; financial award applicants required to submit FAFSA. *Program availability:* Part-time, evening/weekend. Offers business administration (MBA); information security management (MS). *Application deadline:* For fall admission, 7/2 for domestic and international students; for spring admission, 12/2 priority date for domestic students, 12/2 for international students; for summer admission, 4/2 for domestic and international students. Applications are processed on a rolling basis. *Application fee:* $20. *Application Contact:* Melissa Furman, Assistant Dean, 706-729-2056, Fax: 706-667-4064, E-mail: mfurman@augusta.edu. *Dean,* Dr. Richard Franza, 706-737-1418, Fax: 706-667-4064, E-mail: rfranza@augusta.edu.

Medical College of Georgia Students: 913 full-time (426 women), 3 part-time (all women); includes 370 minority (86 Black or African American, non-Hispanic/Latino; 2 American Indian or Alaska Native, non-Hispanic/Latino; 202 Asian, non-Hispanic/Latino; 70 Hispanic/Latino; 10 Two or more races, non-Hispanic/Latino). Average age 25. 2,986 applicants, 12% accepted, 230 enrolled. Expenses: Contact institution. *Financial support:* Fellowships with tuition reimbursements, career-related internships or fieldwork, Federal Work-Study, institutionally sponsored loans, and scholarships/grants available. Support available to part-time students. Financial award applicants required to submit FAFSA. In 2016, 222 doctorates awarded. Offers medicine (MD). *Application deadline:* For fall admission, 11/1 for domestic students. *Application Contact:* Esther Holland, Director of Admissions, 706-721-3186, Fax: 706-721-0959, E-mail: eholland@augusta.edu. *Dean,* Dr. David Hess, 706-721-2231, Fax: 706-721-7035, E-mail: mcgdean@augusta.edu.

Nursing PhD Program Students: 17 full-time (14 women), 4 part-time (all women); includes 7 minority (5 Black or African American, non-Hispanic/Latino; 1 Asian, non-Hispanic/Latino; 1 Two or more races, non-Hispanic/Latino). Average age 44. 12 applicants, 50% accepted, 6 enrolled. Expenses: Contact institution. *Financial support:* Research assistantships with partial tuition reimbursements available. Financial award applicants required to submit FAFSA. Offers nursing (PhD). *Application deadline:* For fall admission, 5/1 for domestic and international students; for spring admission, 10/1 for domestic and international students. *Application fee:* $50. Electronic applications accepted. *Application Contact:* Bridgett Hill, Program Manager, 706-721-9749, Fax: 706-721-7390. *Director,* Dr. Julie Zadinsky, 706-721-9749, Fax: 706-721-8169.

Program in Biochemistry and Cancer Biology Students: 25 full-time (14 women); includes 4 minority (1 Black or African American, non-Hispanic/Latino; 2 Asian, non-Hispanic/Latino; 1 Hispanic/Latino), 10 international. Average age 28. Expenses: Contact institution. *Financial support:* Research assistantships with partial tuition reimbursements, Federal Work-Study, institutionally sponsored loans, and scholarships/grants available. Support available to part-time students. Financial award application deadline: 5/31; financial award applicants required to submit FAFSA. Offers biochemistry and cancer biology (PhD). *Application deadline:* For fall admission, 1/15 for domestic and international students. *Application fee:* $50. Electronic applications accepted. *Application Contact:* Dr. Darren Browning, Director, 706-721-7658, E-mail: dbrowning@augusta.edu. *Chair,* Dr. Vinata Lokeshwar, 706-721-7652, Fax: 706-721-9947, E-mail: vlokeshwar@augusta.edu.

Program in Cellular Biology and Anatomy Students: 11 full-time (7 women); includes 3 minority (2 Black or African American, non-Hispanic/Latino; 1 Asian, non-Hispanic/Latino), 6 international. Average age 29. Expenses: Contact institution. *Financial support:* Fellowships with partial tuition reimbursements, research assistantships with partial tuition reimbursements, teaching assistantships with partial tuition reimbursements, Federal Work-Study, institutionally sponsored loans, and scholarships/grants available. Support available to part-time students. Financial award application deadline: 5/31; financial award applicants required to submit FAFSA. Offers cellular biology and anatomy (PhD). *Application deadline:* For fall admission, 1/15 for domestic and international students. Applications are processed on a rolling basis.

Application fee: $50. *Application Contact:* Dr. Mark Hamrick, Director, 706-721-1958. *Chair and Professor,* Dr. Sylvia B. Smith, 706-721-3731, Fax: 706-721-6120, E-mail: sbsmith@augusta.edu.

Program in Genomic Medicine Students: 7 full-time (2 women); includes 3 minority (all Asian, non-Hispanic/Latino), 1 international. Average age 27. *Faculty:* 1 full-time, 8 part-time/adjunct. Expenses: Contact institution. *Financial support:* Research assistantships with partial tuition reimbursements, Federal Work-Study, institutionally sponsored loans, and scholarships/grants available. Support available to part-time students. Financial award application deadline: 5/31; financial award applicants required to submit FAFSA. Offers genomic medicine (PhD). *Application deadline:* For fall admission, 1/15 for domestic and international students. *Application fee:* $50. Electronic applications accepted. *Application Contact:* Dr. Rafal Pacholczyk, Program Director, 706-721-3542. *Director, Center for Biotechnology and Genomic Medicine,* Dr. Jin-Xiong She, 706-721-3410, E-mail: jshe@augusta.edu.

Program in Molecular Medicine Students: 9 full-time (4 women); includes 1 minority (Asian, non-Hispanic/Latino), 5 international. Average age 31. Expenses: Contact institution. *Financial support:* Fellowships with partial tuition reimbursements, research assistantships with partial tuition reimbursements, teaching assistantships, Federal Work-Study, institutionally sponsored loans, and scholarships/grants available. Support available to part-time students. Financial award application deadline: 5/31; financial award applicants required to submit FAFSA. Offers molecular medicine (PhD). *Application deadline:* For fall admission, 1/15 for domestic and international students. *Application fee:* $50. Electronic applications accepted. *Application Contact:* Angie Compton, Program Administrator, 706-721-4548, E-mail: acompton@augusta.edu. *Director,* Dr. Lynnette McCluskey, 706-721-5616, Fax: 706-721-0340, E-mail: lmccluskey@augusta.edu.

Program in Neuroscience Students: 19 full-time (12 women); includes 4 minority (3 Asian, non-Hispanic/Latino; 1 Two or more races, non-Hispanic/Latino), 6 international. Average age 26. Expenses: Contact institution. *Financial support:* Research assistantships with partial tuition reimbursements and Federal Work-Study available. Support available to part-time students. Financial award application deadline: 5/31. Offers neuroscience (PhD). *Application deadline:* For fall admission, 1/15 for domestic and international students. *Application fee:* $50. Electronic applications accepted. *Application Contact:* Angie Compton, Coordinator, 706-721-0487, E-mail: acompton@augusta.edu. *Director,* Dr. Darrell Brann, 706-721-7779, Fax: 706-721-8685, E-mail: dbrann@augusta.edu.

Program in Oral Biology Students: 9 full-time (6 women), 2 part-time (both women); includes 3 minority (all Asian, non-Hispanic/Latino), 5 international. Average age 31. Expenses: Contact institution. *Financial support:* Federal Work-Study, institutionally sponsored loans, scholarships/grants, and tuition waivers available. Support available to part-time students. Financial award application deadline: 5/31; financial award applicants required to submit FAFSA. *Program availability:* Part-time. Offers oral biology (MS, PhD). *Application deadline:* For fall admission, 5/1 for domestic students, 3/1 for international students. *Application fee:* $50. Electronic applications accepted. *Application Contact:* Dr. Regina Messer, Director, 706-721-8979, Fax: 706-721-3392. *Director,* Dr. Regina Messer, 706-721-8979, Fax: 706-721-3392.

Program in Pharmacology Students: 3 full-time (2 women), 2 international. Average age 27. Expenses: Contact institution. *Financial support:* Fellowships with partial tuition reimbursements, research assistantships with partial tuition reimbursements, Federal Work-Study, institutionally sponsored loans, and scholarships/grants available. Support available to part-time students. Financial award applicants required to submit FAFSA. Offers pharmacology (PhD). *Application deadline:* For fall admission, 1/15 for domestic and international students. *Application fee:* $50. Electronic applications accepted. *Application Contact:* Dr. John A. Johnson, Director, 706-721-4173, Fax: 706-721-6059, E-mail: jjohnson@augusta.edu. *Director,* Dr. John A. Johnson, 706-721-4173, Fax: 706-721-6059, E-mail: jjohnson@augusta.edu.

Program in Physiology Students: 4 full-time (2 women); includes 2 minority (1 Black or African American, non-Hispanic/Latino; 1 Hispanic/Latino), 1 international. Average age 28. Expenses: Contact institution. *Financial support:* Fellowships with partial tuition reimbursements, research assistantships with partial tuition reimbursements, Federal Work-Study, institutionally sponsored loans, scholarships/grants, and traineeships available. Support available to part-time students. Financial award applicants required to submit FAFSA. In 2016, 1 doctorate awarded. Offers physiology (PhD). *Application deadline:* For fall admission, 1/15 for domestic and international students. *Application fee:* $50. Electronic applications accepted. *Application Contact:* Dr. Adviye Ergul, Professor/Director, 706-721-9103, E-mail: aergul@augusta.edu. *Chair and Professor,* Dr. Clinton Webb, 706-721-7742, Fax: 706-721-7299, E-mail: cwebb@augusta.edu.

Program in Vascular Biology Students: 9 full-time (5 women); includes 2 minority (1 Black or African American, non-Hispanic/Latino; 1 Hispanic/Latino), 6 international. Average age 29. Expenses: Contact institution. *Financial support:* Fellowships with partial tuition reimbursements, research assistantships with partial tuition reimbursements, Federal Work-Study, institutionally sponsored loans, scholarships/grants, and traineeships available. Support available to part-time students. In 2016, 1 doctorate awarded. Offers vascular biology (PhD). *Application fee:* $50. *Application Contact:* Dr. David J. Fulton, Director, Vascular Biology Center, 706-721-6338, Fax: 706-721-9799, E-mail: dfulton@augusta.edu. *Director, Vascular Biology Center,* Dr. David J. Fulton, 706-721-6338, Fax: 706-721-9799, E-mail: dfulton@augusta.edu.

AURORA UNIVERSITY, Aurora, IL 60506-4892

General Information Independent, coed, comprehensive institution. *Enrollment:* 5,643 graduate, professional, and undergraduate students; 678 full-time matriculated graduate/professional students (587 women), 1,075 part-time matriculated graduate/professional students (751 women). *Enrollment by degree level:* 1,510 master's, 243 doctoral. *Graduate faculty:* 51 full-time (25 women), 136 part-time/adjunct (93 women). *Tuition:* Full-time $10,800; part-time $600 per credit hour. Tuition and fees vary according to degree level, campus/location and program. *Graduate housing:* On-campus housing not available. *Student services:* Campus employment opportunities, campus safety program, career counseling, exercise/wellness program, free psychological counseling, international student services, multicultural affairs office, services for students with disabilities, teacher training, writing training. *Library facilities:* Charles B. Phillips Library plus 1 other. *Collection:* Books: 38,404 (physical), 160,012 (digital/electronic); Serial titles: 62 (physical), 46,444 (digital/electronic); Databases: 61. Weekly public service hours: 97; students can reserve study rooms.

Computer facilities: 287 computers available on campus for general student use. A campuswide network can be accessed from student residence rooms and from off campus. Online class registration, learning management system are available. Website: http://www.aurora.edu/

General Application Contact: Judson Curry, Dean of Adult and Graduate Studies, 630-947-8946, E-mail: jcurry@aurora.edu.

GRADUATE UNITS

College of Arts and Sciences Students: 24 part-time (13 women); includes 1 minority (Asian, non-Hispanic/Latino). Average age 30. 12 applicants, 100% accepted, 6 enrolled. *Faculty:* 3 full-time (1 woman), 5 part-time/adjunct (0 women). Expenses: Contact institution. *Financial support:* Federal Work-Study, scholarships/grants, and unspecified assistantships available. Support available to part-time students. Financial award application deadline: 4/1; financial award applicants required to submit FAFSA. In 2016, 11 master's awarded. *Program availability:* Part-time, evening/weekend. Offers homeland security (MS); mathematics (MS). *Application deadline:* For fall admission, 6/1 for international students; for spring admission, 10/1 for international students. Applications are processed on a rolling basis. *Application fee:* $0. Electronic applications accepted. *Application Contact:* Judson Curry, Dean of Adult and Graduate Studies, 630-947-8946, E-mail: jcurry@aurora.edu. *Vice President for Academic Affairs,* Dr. Frank Buscher, 630-844-5252, E-mail: fbuscher@aurora.edu.

Dunham School of Business and Public Policy Students: 67 full-time (42 women), 186 part-time (98 women); includes 76 minority (32 Black or African American, non-Hispanic/Latino; 2 Asian, non-Hispanic/Latino; 35 Hispanic/Latino; 7 Two or more races, non-Hispanic/Latino), 5 international. Average age 33. 123 applicants, 99% accepted, 21 enrolled. *Faculty:* 8 full-time (1 woman), 19 part-time/adjunct (9 women). Expenses: Contact institution. *Financial support:* In 2016–17, 58 students received support. Federal Work-Study, scholarships/grants, and unspecified assistantships available. Support available to part-time students. Financial award applicants required to submit FAFSA. In 2016, 99 master's awarded. *Program availability:* Part-time, evening/weekend, 100% online. Offers accountancy (MS); business (MBA); digital marketing and analytics (MS). *Application deadline:* For fall admission, 6/1 for international students; for spring admission, 10/1 for international students. Applications are processed on a rolling basis. *Application fee:* $0. Electronic applications accepted. *Application Contact:* Ed Miranda, Senior Recruiter for Adult and Graduate Programs, 630-947-8923, E-mail: emiranda@aurora.edu. *Executive Director of School of Business and Policy,* Dr. Toby Arquette, 630-844-5614, E-mail: tarquett@aurora.edu.

School of Education and Human Performance Students: 36 full-time (30 women), 559 part-time (372 women); includes 68 minority (27 Black or African American, non-Hispanic/Latino; 1 American Indian or Alaska Native, non-Hispanic/Latino; 6 Asian, non-Hispanic/Latino; 29 Hispanic/Latino; 2 Native Hawaiian or other Pacific Islander, non-Hispanic/Latino; 3 Two or more races, non-Hispanic/Latino). Average age 37. 126 applicants, 98% accepted, 72 enrolled. *Faculty:* 22 full-time (12 women), 46 part-time/adjunct (27 women). Expenses: Contact institution. *Financial support:* In 2016–17, 10 students received support. Federal Work-Study, scholarships/grants, and unspecified assistantships available. Support available to part-time students. Financial award applicants required to submit FAFSA. In 2016, 178 master's, 27 doctorates awarded. *Program availability:* Part-time, evening/weekend. Offers bilingual-ESL education (MA); educational leadership (MA); educational technology (MA); leadership in administration (Ed D); leadership in adult learning and higher education (Ed D); leadership in curriculum and instruction (Ed D); reading instruction (MA); special education (MA). *Application deadline:* For fall admission, 6/1 for international students; for spring admission, 10/1 for international students. Applications are processed on a rolling basis. *Application fee:* $0. Electronic applications accepted. *Application Contact:* Elizabeth Botica, Graduate Education Recruiter, 630-947-8918, E-mail: ebotica@aurora.edu. *Executive Director of the School of Education and Human Performance,* Dr. Jen Buckley, 630-844-1542, Fax: 630-844-6155, E-mail: jbuckley@aurora.edu.

School of Nursing and Allied Health Students: 18 full-time (all women), 62 part-time (59 women); includes 18 minority (3 Black or African American, non-Hispanic/Latino; 2 Asian, non-Hispanic/Latino; 11 Hispanic/Latino; 2 Two or more races, non-Hispanic/Latino). Average age 34. 37 applicants, 81% accepted, 25 enrolled. *Faculty:* 5 full-time (4 women), 10 part-time/adjunct (9 women). Expenses: Contact institution. *Financial support:* In 2016–17, 25 students received support. Federal Work-Study, scholarships/grants, and unspecified assistantships available. Support available to part-time students. Financial award applicants required to submit FAFSA. In 2016, 31 master's awarded. *Program availability:* Part-time, evening/weekend. Offers applied behavior analysis (MS); nursing (MSN). *Application deadline:* For fall admission, 6/1 for international students; for spring admission, 10/1 for international students. Applications are processed on a rolling basis. *Application fee:* $0. Electronic applications accepted. *Application Contact:* Judson Curry, Dean of Adult and Graduate Studies, 630-947-8946, E-mail: jcurry@aurora.edu. *Interim Executive Director for the School of Nursing and Allied Health,* Dr. Carmella Moran, 630-844-5132, E-mail: cmoran@aurora.edu.

School of Social Work Students: 557 full-time (497 women), 242 part-time (207 women); includes 250 minority (105 Black or African American, non-Hispanic/Latino; 1 American Indian or Alaska Native, non-Hispanic/Latino; 16 Asian, non-Hispanic/Latino; 111 Hispanic/Latino; 17 Two or more races, non-Hispanic/Latino), 1 international. Average age 31. 356 applicants, 98% accepted, 205 enrolled. *Faculty:* 13 full-time (7 women), 56 part-time/adjunct (48 women). Expenses: Contact institution. *Financial support:* In 2016–17, 524 students received support. Federal Work-Study, scholarships/grants, and unspecified assistantships available. Support available to part-time students. Financial award applicants required to submit FAFSA. In 2016, 349 master's, 9 doctorates awarded. *Program availability:* Part-time, evening/weekend. Offers social work (MSW, DSW). *Application deadline:* For fall admission, 6/1 for international students; for spring admission, 10/1 for international students. Applications are processed on a rolling basis. *Application fee:* $0. Electronic applications accepted. *Application Contact:* Debbie Enlow, Senior Recruiter/Advisor for Adult and Graduate Studies, 630-947-8904, E-mail: denlow@aurora.edu. *Executive Director,* Dr. Fred McKenzie, 630-947-8930, E-mail: mckenzie@aurora.edu.

AUSTIN COLLEGE, Sherman, TX 75090-4400

General Information Independent-religious, coed, comprehensive institution. *Enrollment:* 1,294 graduate, professional, and undergraduate students; 13 full-time matriculated graduate/professional students (10 women), 3 part-time matriculated graduate/professional students (2 women). *Enrollment by degree level:* 16 master's. *Graduate faculty:* 4 full-time (all women), 2 part-time/adjunct (both women). *Tuition:* Part-time $5285 per course. *Graduate housing:* Room and/or apartments available on a first-come, first-served basis to single students; on-campus housing not available to married students. Typical cost: $5690 per year ($12,082 including board). Room and board charges vary according to board plan. Housing application deadline: 5/1. *Student services:* Campus employment opportunities, campus safety program, career counseling, free psychological counseling, teacher training. *Library facilities:* Abell

Library. *Collection:* Books: 227,390 (physical). Study areas open 24 hours, 5–7 days a week; students can reserve study rooms.

Computer facilities: 160 computers available on campus for general student use. A campuswide network can be accessed from student residence rooms and from off campus. Online class registration is available.
Website: http://www.austincollege.edu/

General Application Contact: Nikki Christensen, Administrative Assistant, Academic Affairs, 903-813-2327, E-mail: nchristensen@austincollege.edu.

GRADUATE UNITS

Austin Teacher Program Students: 13 full-time (10 women), 3 part-time (2 women); includes 4 minority (1 Black or African American, non-Hispanic/Latino; 2 Hispanic/Latino; 1 Two or more races, non-Hispanic/Latino), 1 international. Average age 23. *Faculty:* 5 full-time (4 women), 1 (woman) part-time/adjunct. Expenses: Contact institution. *Financial support:* Career-related internships or fieldwork, Federal Work-Study, scholarships/grants, and unspecified assistantships available. Support available to part-time students. Financial award application deadline: 4/1; financial award applicants required to submit FAFSA. In 2016, 16 master's awarded. *Program availability:* Part-time. Offers teaching (MAT). *Application deadline:* For fall admission, 5/1 priority date for domestic students; for spring admission, 1/15 priority date for domestic students. Applications are processed on a rolling basis. *Application fee:* $35. Electronic applications accepted. *Application Contact:* Nikki Christensen, 903-813-2327, E-mail: nchristensen@austincollege.edu. *Department Chair,* Julia Shahid, 903-813-2457, E-mail: jshahid@austincollege.edu.

AUSTIN GRADUATE SCHOOL OF THEOLOGY, Austin, TX 78752

General Information Independent-religious, coed, upper-level institution. *Enrollment:* 41 graduate, professional, and undergraduate students; 9 full-time matriculated graduate/professional students (2 women), 12 part-time matriculated graduate/professional students (4 women). *Enrollment by degree level:* 21 master's. *Graduate faculty:* 4 full-time (0 women), 4 part-time/adjunct (0 women). *Tuition:* Full-time $6300; part-time $4200 per credit. *Required fees:* $350; $350 per credit. $175 per semester. *Graduate housing:* On-campus housing not available. *Student services:* Campus employment opportunities, international student services, services for students with disabilities. *Library facilities:* David Worley Library.

Computer facilities: 6 computers available on campus for general student use. A campuswide network can be accessed.
Website: http://www.austingrad.edu/

General Application Contact: Dawn Bond, Director of Admissions/Registrar, 512-476-2772 Ext. 103, Fax: 512-476-3919, E-mail: dbond@austingrad.edu.

GRADUATE UNITS

Program in Theological Studies Students: 9 full-time (2 women), 12 part-time (4 women). *Faculty:* 4 full-time (0 women), 4 part-time/adjunct (0 women). Expenses: Contact institution. *Financial support:* Federal Work-Study and scholarships/grants available. Support available to part-time students. Financial award application deadline: 7/1. *Program availability:* Part-time. Offers theological studies (MATS). *Application deadline:* For fall admission, 7/1 priority date for domestic and international students; for spring admission, 10/1 priority date for domestic and international students. Applications are processed on a rolling basis. *Application fee:* $25. Electronic applications accepted. *Application Contact:* Dawn Bond, Director of Admissions/Registrar, 512-476-2772 Ext. 103, Fax: 512-476-3919, E-mail: dbond@austingrad.edu. *Graduate Student Advisor,* Dr. Keith Stanglin, 512-476-2772, Fax: 512-476-3919, E-mail: stanglin@austingrad.edu.

AUSTIN PEAY STATE UNIVERSITY, Clarksville, TN 37044

General Information State-supported, coed, comprehensive institution. CGS member. *Enrollment:* 10,344 graduate, professional, and undergraduate students; 248 full-time matriculated graduate/professional students (163 women), 568 part-time matriculated graduate/professional students (415 women). *Enrollment by degree level:* 786 master's, 30 other advanced degrees. *Graduate faculty:* 127 full-time (63 women), 19 part-time/adjunct (all women). *Tuition,* state resident: full-time $8300; part-time $415 per credit hour. Tuition, nonresident: full-time $22,280; part-time $1114 per credit hour. *Required fees:* $1473; $73.65 per credit hour. *Graduate housing:* Rooms and/or apartments available on a first-come, first-served basis to single and married students. Typical cost: $6500 per year ($9848 including board) for single students; $6500 per year ($9848 including board) for married students. Room and board charges vary according to board plan, campus/location and housing facility selected. *Student services:* Campus employment opportunities, campus safety program, career counseling, child daycare facilities, exercise/wellness program, free psychological counseling, international student services, low-cost health insurance, multicultural affairs office, services for students with disabilities, teacher training, writing training. *Library facilities:* Felix G. Woodward Library. *Collection:* Books: 219,393 (physical), 302,794 (digital/electronic); Serial titles: 2,800 (physical), 54,016 (digital/electronic); Databases: 281. Weekly public service hours: 109.

Computer facilities: Computer purchase and lease plans are available. 1,062 computers available on campus for general student use. A campuswide network can be accessed from student residence rooms and from off campus. Online class registration is available.
Website: http://www.apsu.edu/

General Application Contact: Brad Averitt, Coordinator of Graduate Recruitment, 800-859-4723, Fax: 931-221-7641, E-mail: gradadmissions@apsu.edu.

GRADUATE UNITS

College of Graduate Studies Students: 248 full-time (163 women), 568 part-time (415 women); includes 173 minority (110 Black or African American, non-Hispanic/Latino; 8 Asian, non-Hispanic/Latino; 32 Hispanic/Latino; 23 Two or more races, non-Hispanic/Latino), 6 international. Average age 33. 505 applicants, 66% accepted, 250 enrolled. *Faculty:* 120 full-time (63 women), 23 part-time/adjunct (18 women). Expenses: Contact institution. *Financial support:* In 2016–17, 136 students received support, including 136 research assistantships with full tuition reimbursements available (averaging $5,184 per year); career-related internships or fieldwork, Federal Work-Study, institutionally sponsored loans, scholarships/grants, and unspecified assistantships also available. Support available to part-time students. Financial award applicants required to submit FAFSA. In 2016, 314 master's, 13 other advanced degrees awarded. *Program availability:* Part-time, evening/weekend, online learning. *Application deadline:* For fall admission, 8/9 priority date for domestic students. Applications are processed on a rolling basis. *Application fee:* $45 ($50 for international students). Electronic applications accepted. *Application Contact:* Brad Averitt, Coordinator of Graduate Recruitment, 931-221-6189, Fax: 931-221-7641, E-mail: gradadmissions@apsu.edu. *Interim Associate Provost of Research and Dean of the College of Graduate Studies,* Dr. Chad Brooks, 931-221-7414, Fax: 931-221-7641, E-mail: dakshinamurthyr@apsu.edu.

College of Arts and Letters Students: 34 full-time (17 women), 82 part-time (46 women); includes 26 minority (17 Black or African American, non-Hispanic/Latino; 1 Asian, non-Hispanic/Latino; 4 Hispanic/Latino; 4 Two or more races, non-Hispanic/Latino), 1 international. Average age 33. 69 applicants, 70% accepted, 38 enrolled. *Faculty:* 40 full-time (16 women), 4 part-time/adjunct (2 women). Expenses: Contact institution. *Financial support:* Research assistantships with full tuition reimbursements, teaching assistantships, career-related internships or fieldwork, Federal Work-Study, institutionally sponsored loans, scholarships/grants, and unspecified assistantships available. Support available to part-time students. Financial award application deadline: 4/1; financial award applicants required to submit FAFSA. In 2016, 47 master's awarded. *Program availability:* Part-time, online learning. Offers arts and letters (M Mu, MA); communication arts (MA); English (MA); military history (MA); music education (M Mu); music performance (M Mu). *Application deadline:* For fall admission, 8/9 priority date for domestic students. Applications are processed on a rolling basis. *Application fee:* $45 ($50 for international students). Electronic applications accepted. *Application Contact:* Brad Averitt, Coordinator of Graduate Admissions, 800-859-4723, Fax: 931-221-7641, E-mail: gradadmissions@apsu.edu. *Dean,* Dr. Dixie Webb, 931-221-6445, Fax: 931-221-1024, E-mail: webbd@apsu.edu.

College of Behavioral and Health Sciences Students: 131 full-time (94 women), 217 part-time (182 women); includes 89 minority (63 Black or African American, non-Hispanic/Latino; 2 Asian, non-Hispanic/Latino; 13 Hispanic/Latino; 11 Two or more races, non-Hispanic/Latino), 3 international. Average age 33. 241 applicants, 67% accepted, 131 enrolled. *Faculty:* 32 full-time (23 women), 13 part-time/adjunct (12 women). Expenses: Contact institution. *Financial support:* Research assistantships with full tuition reimbursements, career-related internships or fieldwork, Federal Work-Study, institutionally sponsored loans, scholarships/grants, and unspecified assistantships available. Support available to part-time students. Financial award application deadline: 4/1; financial award applicants required to submit FAFSA. In 2016, 149 master's awarded. *Program availability:* Part-time, evening/weekend, online learning. Offers behavioral and health sciences (MA, MPS, MS, MSN, MSW); family nurse practitioner (MSN); human resources leadership (MPS); industrial-organizational psychology (MS); mental health counseling (MS); nursing administration (MSN); nursing education (MSN); nursing informatics (MSN); public health education (MS); school counseling (MS); social work (MSW); sports and wellness leadership (MS); strategic leadership (MPS); training and development (MPS). *Application deadline:* For fall admission, 8/9 priority date for domestic students. Applications are processed on a rolling basis. *Application fee:* $45 ($50 for international students). Electronic applications accepted. *Application Contact:* Brad Averitt, Coordinator of Graduate Admissions, 800-859-4723, Fax: 931-221-7641, E-mail: gradadmissions@apsu.edu. *Dean,* Dr. David Denton, 931-221-7423, Fax: 931-221-6382, E-mail: dentond@apsu.edu.

College of Business Students: 3 full-time (2 women), 68 part-time (35 women); includes 11 minority (3 Black or African American, non-Hispanic/Latino; 2 Asian, non-Hispanic/Latino; 3 Hispanic/Latino; 3 Two or more races, non-Hispanic/Latino). Average age 34. 68 applicants, 49% accepted, 24 enrolled. *Faculty:* 6 full-time (3 women). Expenses: Contact institution. *Financial support:* Research assistantships with full tuition reimbursements, career-related internships or fieldwork, Federal Work-Study, institutionally sponsored loans, scholarships/grants, and unspecified assistantships available. Support available to part-time students. Financial award application deadline: 4/1; financial award applicants required to submit FAFSA. In 2016, 21 master's awarded. *Program availability:* Part-time, evening/weekend, online learning. Offers management (MS). *Application deadline:* For fall admission, 8/9 priority date for domestic students. Applications are processed on a rolling basis. *Application fee:* $45 ($50 for international students). Electronic applications accepted. *Application Contact:* Brad Averitt, Coordinator of Graduate Admissions, 800-859-4723, Fax: 931-221-7641, E-mail: gradadmissions@apsu.edu. *Interim Dean,* Charles Moses, 931-221-7674, Fax: 931-221-7355, E-mail: mosesc@apsu.edu.

College of Education Students: 66 full-time (42 women), 156 part-time (132 women); includes 44 minority (24 Black or African American, non-Hispanic/Latino; 2 Asian, non-Hispanic/Latino; 11 Hispanic/Latino; 7 Two or more races, non-Hispanic/Latino), 2 international. Average age 35. 78 applicants, 82% accepted, 47 enrolled. *Faculty:* 19 full-time (12 women), 5 part-time/adjunct (4 women). Expenses: Contact institution. *Financial support:* Research assistantships with full tuition reimbursements, career-related internships or fieldwork, Federal Work-Study, institutionally sponsored loans, scholarships/grants, and unspecified assistantships available. Support available to part-time students. Financial award application deadline: 4/1; financial award applicants required to submit FAFSA. In 2016, 87 master's, 9 other advanced degrees awarded. *Program availability:* Part-time, evening/weekend, online learning. Offers administration and supervision (Ed S); counseling and guidance (Ed S); curriculum and instruction (MA Ed); education (MA Ed, MAT, Ed S); education leadership (MA Ed); elementary education (Ed S); elementary education K-6 (MAT); reading (MA Ed); secondary education (Ed S); secondary education 7-12 (MAT); special education K-12 (MAT). *Application deadline:* For fall admission, 8/9 priority date for domestic students. Applications are processed on a rolling basis. *Application fee:* $45 ($50 for international students). Electronic applications accepted. *Application Contact:* Brad Averitt, Coordinator of Graduate Admissions, 800-859-4723, Fax: 931-221-7641, E-mail: gradadmissions@apsu.edu. *Director,* Dr. Carlette Hardin, 931-221-7696, Fax: 931-221-1292, E-mail: hardinc@apsu.edu.

College of Science and Mathematics Students: 14 full-time (8 women), 44 part-time (19 women); includes 9 minority (2 Black or African American, non-Hispanic/Latino; 1 Asian, non-Hispanic/Latino; 1 Hispanic/Latino; 5 Two or more races, non-Hispanic/Latino). Average age 33. 49 applicants, 51% accepted, 19 enrolled. *Faculty:* 23 full-time (9 women), 1 part-time/adjunct (0 women). Expenses: Contact institution. *Financial support:* Research assistantships with full tuition reimbursements, career-related internships or fieldwork, Federal Work-Study, institutionally sponsored loans, scholarships/grants, and unspecified assistantships available. Support available to part-time students. Financial award application deadline: 4/1; financial award applicants required to submit FAFSA. In 2016, 13 master's awarded. *Program availability:* Part-time, online learning. Offers clinical laboratory science (MS); data management and analysis (PSM); engineering technology (MS); predictive analytics (PSM); science and mathematics (MS, PSM). *Application deadline:* For fall admission, 8/9 priority date for domestic students. Applications are processed on a rolling basis. *Application fee:* $45 ($50 for international students). Electronic applications accepted. *Application Contact:* Brad Averitt, Graduate Coordinator, 800-859-4723, Fax: 931-221-7641, E-mail: gradadmissions@apsu.edu. *Dean,* Dr. Jaime Taylor, 931-221-7971, Fax: 931-221-7984, E-mail: taylorj@apsu.edu.

AUSTIN PRESBYTERIAN THEOLOGICAL SEMINARY, Austin, TX 78705-5797

General Information Independent-religious, coed, graduate-only institution. *Enrollment by degree level:* 118 master's, 44 doctoral. *Graduate faculty:* 20 full-time (6 women), 5 part-time/adjunct (1 woman). *Tuition:* Full-time $13,200; part-time $220 per credit. *Required fees:* $120; $120 per credit. $25 per semester. One-time fee: $175 full-time; $120 part-time. Tuition and fees vary according to degree level and program. *Graduate housing:* Rooms and/or apartments available on a first-come, first-served basis to single and married students. Typical cost: $2030 (including board) for single students; $7250 (including board) for married students. Room and board charges vary according to housing facility selected. Housing application deadline: 5/31. *Student services:* Campus employment opportunities, campus safety program, career counseling, free psychological counseling, international student services, services for students with disabilities, writing training. *Library facilities:* Stitt Library. *Collection:* Books: 136,132 (physical), 182,854 (digital/electronic); Serial titles: 1,202 (physical), 68,395 (digital/electronic); Databases: 87. Weekly public service hours: 37; students can reserve study rooms.

Computer facilities: 20 computers available on campus for general student use. A campuswide network can be accessed from student residence rooms. Website: http://www.austinseminary.edu/

General Application Contact: Dr. Jack Barden, Vice President for Admissions, 512-404-4827, Fax: 512-472-7089, E-mail: admissions@austinseminary.edu.

GRADUATE UNITS

Graduate and Professional Programs Students: 88 full-time (50 women), 74 part-time (41 women). *Faculty:* 20 full-time (6 women), 5 part-time/adjunct (1 woman). Expenses: Contact institution. *Financial support:* Fellowships, career-related internships or fieldwork, institutionally sponsored loans, and scholarships/grants available. Support available to part-time students. Financial award application deadline: 3/1; financial award applicants required to submit FAFSA. In 2016, 44 master's, 4 doctorates awarded. Offers divinity (M Div); ministry (D Min); ministry practice (MA); theological studies (MA); youth ministry (MA). M Div/MSSW offered in collaboration with The University of Texas at Austin School of Social Work. *Application deadline:* For fall admission, 5/1 for domestic students, 1/1 for international students; for summer admission, 2/2 for domestic students. Applications are processed on a rolling basis. Electronic applications accepted. *Application Contact:* Dr. Jack Barden, Vice President for Admissions, 512-404-4827, Fax: 512-472-7089, E-mail: admissions@austinseminary.edu. *Academic Dean,* Dr. David Jensen, 512-404-4821, Fax: 512-479-0738, E-mail: dean@austinseminary.edu.

AVE MARIA SCHOOL OF LAW, Naples, FL 34119

General Information Independent-religious, coed, graduate-only institution. *Enrollment by degree level:* 248 doctoral. *Graduate faculty:* 24 full-time (6 women), 9 part-time/adjunct (3 women). *Tuition:* Full-time $39,450. *Required fees:* $2256. *Graduate housing:* Rooms and/or apartments available on a first-come, first-served basis to single and married students. Typical cost: $10,350 per year ($14,562 including board) for single students; $10,350 per year ($14,562 including board) for married students. Housing application deadline: 5/1. *Student services:* Campus employment opportunities, campus safety program, career counseling, international student services, services for students with disabilities, writing training. *Library facilities:* Veterans Memorial Law Library. *Collection:* Books: 53,471 (physical), 48,624 (digital/electronic); Serial titles: 2,330 (physical), 29,769 (digital/electronic); Databases: 206. Weekly public service hours: 168; study areas open 24 hours, 5–7 days a week; students can reserve study rooms.

Computer facilities: 24 computers available on campus for general student use. A campuswide network can be accessed from student residence rooms and from off campus. Online class registration is available.
Website: http://www.avemarialaw.edu/

General Application Contact: Claire T. O'Keefe, Assistant Dean of Admissions, 239-687-5423, Fax: 239-352-2890, E-mail: info@avemarialaw.edu.

GRADUATE UNITS

Professional Program Students: 248 full-time (130 women); includes 78 minority (16 Black or African American, non-Hispanic/Latino; 5 American Indian or Alaska Native, non-Hispanic/Latino; 3 Asian, non-Hispanic/Latino; 54 Hispanic/Latino), 5 international. Average age 26. 637 applicants, 54% accepted, 88 enrolled. *Faculty:* 24 full-time (6 women), 9 part-time/adjunct (3 women). Expenses: Contact institution. *Financial support:* In 2016–17, 158 students received support. Research assistantships, career-related internships or fieldwork, Federal Work-Study, and scholarships/grants available. Financial award application deadline: 6/30; financial award applicants required to submit FAFSA. In 2016, 88 doctorates awarded. Offers law (JD). *Application deadline:* For fall admission, 7/15 priority date for domestic and international students. Applications are processed on a rolling basis. *Application fee:* $0. Electronic applications accepted. *Application Contact:* Claire T. O'Keefe, Assistant Dean of Admissions, 239-687-5423, Fax: 239-352-2890, E-mail: info@avemarialaw.edu. *President/Dean,* Kevin Cieply, 239-687-5300, E-mail: kcieply@avemarialaw.edu.

AVE MARIA UNIVERSITY, Ave Maria, FL 34142

General Information Independent-religious, coed, comprehensive institution. *Graduate housing:* Room and/or apartments available on a first-come, first-served basis to single students; on-campus housing not available to married students. Housing application deadline: 7/15.

GRADUATE UNITS
Graduate Programs

AVERETT UNIVERSITY, Danville, VA 24541-3692

General Information Independent-religious, coed, comprehensive institution. *Enrollment:* 859 graduate, professional, and undergraduate students; 142 full-time matriculated graduate/professional students (125 women), 255 part-time matriculated graduate/professional students (193 women). *Enrollment by degree level:* 397 master's. *Graduate faculty:* 9 full-time (1 woman), 36 part-time/adjunct (18 women). Tuition and fees vary according to campus/location and program. *Graduate housing:* On-campus housing not available. *Student services:* Campus employment opportunities, campus safety program, career counseling, free psychological counseling, services for students with disabilities, teacher training, writing training. *Library facilities:* Mary B. Blount Library. *Collection:* Books: 87,139 (physical), 184,225 (digital/electronic); Serial titles:

284 (physical), 34,278 (digital/electronic); Databases: 124. Weekly public service hours: 81; students can reserve study rooms.

Computer facilities: 150 computers available on campus for general student use. A campuswide network can be accessed from student residence rooms. Online class registration is available.
Website: http://www.averett.edu/

General Application Contact: Melissa Anderson, Director of Admissions, Graduate and Professional Studies, 804-729-8285, E-mail: manderson@averett.edu.

GRADUATE UNITS

Master in Education Program Students: 26 full-time (22 women), 98 part-time (73 women); includes 39 minority (34 Black or African American, non-Hispanic/Latino; 3 American Indian or Alaska Native, non-Hispanic/Latino; 2 Hispanic/Latino). Average age 36. 109 applicants, 54% accepted, 56 enrolled. *Faculty:* 1 full-time (0 women), 15 part-time/adjunct (12 women). Expenses: Contact institution. *Financial support:* Application deadline: 3/1; applicants required to submit FAFSA. In 2016, 19 master's awarded. *Program availability:* Part-time, online only, 100% online. Offers administration and supervision (M Ed); curriculum and instruction (M Ed); special education with endorsement (M Ed); special education with licensure (M Ed). Program offered on Danville Campus only. *Application deadline:* Applications are processed on a rolling basis. Electronic applications accepted. *Education Chair,* Dr. Sue Davis, 434-791-5741, Fax: 434-791-5020, E-mail: suedavis@averett.edu.

Master of Accountancy Program Students: 1 full-time (0 women), 5 part-time (3 women); includes 1 minority (Black or African American, non-Hispanic/Latino). Average age 29. 6 applicants, 100% accepted, 6 enrolled. *Faculty:* 2 full-time (1 woman). Expenses: Contact institution. *Financial support:* In 2016–17, 1 student received support. Application deadline: 3/1; applicants required to submit FAFSA. In 2016, 1 master's awarded. *Program availability:* Part-time, online only, 100% online. Offers accountancy (M Acc). *Application deadline:* Applications are processed on a rolling basis. Electronic applications accepted. *Application Contact:* Melissa Anderson, Director of Admissions, Graduate and Professional Studies, 804-729-8285, E-mail: manderson@averett.edu. *Director of the Master in Accountancy Program,* Dr. Peggy C. Wright, 434-791-7118, E-mail: pwright@averett.edu.

Master of Business Administration Program Students: 52 full-time (40 women), 215 part-time (117 women); includes 133 minority (110 Black or African American, non-Hispanic/Latino; 5 American Indian or Alaska Native, non-Hispanic/Latino; 9 Asian, non-Hispanic/Latino; 9 Hispanic/Latino), 6 international. Average age 38. 143 applicants, 78% accepted, 104 enrolled. *Faculty:* 6 full-time (0 women), 21 part-time/adjunct (6 women). Expenses: Contact institution. *Financial support:* Application deadline: 3/1; applicants required to submit FAFSA. In 2016, 99 master's awarded. *Program availability:* Part-time, evening/weekend, 100% online, blended/hybrid learning. Offers business administration (MBA); human resources management (MBA); leadership (MBA); marketing (MBA). *Application deadline:* Applications are processed on a rolling basis. Electronic applications accepted. *Application Contact:* Melissa Anderson, Director of Admissions, Graduate and Professional Studies, 804-729-8285, E-mail: manderson@averett.edu. *Chair, Business Department,* Dr. Peggy C. Wright, 434-791-7118, E-mail: pwright@averett.edu.

AVILA UNIVERSITY, Kansas City, MO 64145-1698

General Information Independent-religious, coed, comprehensive institution. *Enrollment:* 1,745 graduate, professional, and undergraduate students; 305 full-time matriculated graduate/professional students (209 women), 113 part-time matriculated graduate/professional students (87 women). *Enrollment by degree level:* 353 master's, 65 other advanced degrees. *Graduate faculty:* 21 full-time (15 women), 40 part-time/adjunct (21 women). *Tuition:* Full-time $6600; part-time $550 per credit hour. Full-time tuition and fees vary according to program. *Graduate housing:* Room and/or apartments available on a first-come, first-served basis to single students; on-campus housing not available to married students. Typical cost: $3300 per year ($6600 including board). *Student services:* Campus employment opportunities, campus safety program, career counseling, child daycare facilities, exercise/wellness program, free psychological counseling, international student services, low-cost health insurance, multicultural affairs office, services for students with disabilities, teacher training, writing training. *Library facilities:* Hooley-Bundshu Library plus 1 other. *Collection:* Books: 39,963 (physical), 309,063 (digital/electronic); Serial titles: 205 (physical), 389,497 (digital/electronic); Databases: 72. Weekly public service hours: 91; students can reserve study rooms.

Computer facilities: 141 computers available on campus for general student use. A campuswide network can be accessed from student residence rooms and from off campus. Online class registration, laptop checkout through library are available.
Website: http://www.avila.edu/

General Application Contact: Jamie McConnell, Director of Graduate and Advantage Admission, 816-501-0428, E-mail: jamie.mcconnell@avila.edu.

GRADUATE UNITS

Department of Psychology Students: 92 full-time (78 women), 22 part-time (20 women); includes 39 minority (25 Black or African American, non-Hispanic/Latino; 1 American Indian or Alaska Native, non-Hispanic/Latino; 3 Asian, non-Hispanic/Latino; 8 Hispanic/Latino; 2 Two or more races, non-Hispanic/Latino), 1 international. Average age 34. 93 applicants, 43% accepted, 30 enrolled. *Faculty:* 7 full-time (6 women), 10 part-time/adjunct (4 women). Expenses: Contact institution. *Financial support:* In 2016–17, 15 students received support, including 5 research assistantships with partial tuition reimbursements available; career-related internships or fieldwork, scholarships/grants, and unspecified assistantships also available. Support available to part-time students. Financial award applicants required to submit FAFSA. In 2016, 48 master's awarded. *Program availability:* Part-time. Offers counseling psychology (MS); psychology (MS). *Application deadline:* Applications are processed on a rolling basis. *Application fee:* $0. Electronic applications accepted. *Application Contact:* Tamika Doolin, Graduate Admissions Advisor, 816-501-3661, Fax: 816-501-2455, E-mail: gradpsych@avila.edu. *Director of Graduate Psychology Enrollment Management,* Aaron R. Coffey, 816-501-0419, Fax: 816-501-2455, E-mail: aaron.coffey@avila.edu.

School of Business Students: 58 full-time (22 women), 21 part-time (10 women); includes 20 minority (10 Black or African American, non-Hispanic/Latino; 2 Asian, non-Hispanic/Latino; 5 Hispanic/Latino; 3 Two or more races, non-Hispanic/Latino), 18 international. Average age 30. 75 applicants, 28% accepted, 14 enrolled. *Faculty:* 8 full-time (4 women), 4 part-time/adjunct (2 women). Expenses: Contact institution. *Financial support:* In 2016–17, 11 students received support. Career-related internships or fieldwork and scholarships/grants available. Support available to part-time students. Financial award applicants required to submit FAFSA. In 2016, 40 master's awarded. *Program availability:* Part-time, evening/weekend. Offers accounting (MBA); finance (MBA); health care administration (MBA); international business (MBA); management (MBA); management information systems (MBA); marketing (MBA). *Application deadline:* For fall admission, 7/30 priority date for domestic and international students;

for winter admission, 11/30 priority date for domestic and international students; for spring admission, 2/28 priority date for domestic and international students; for summer admission, 6/1 priority date for domestic and international students. Applications are processed on a rolling basis. *Application fee:* $0. Electronic applications accepted. *Application Contact:* Brandon Black, MBA Admission Advisor, 816-501-3601, Fax: 816-501-2463, E-mail: brandon.black@avila.edu. *Dean,* Dr. Richard Woodall, 816-501-3720, Fax: 816-501-2463, E-mail: richard.woodall@avila.edu.

School of Education Students: 65 full-time (50 women), 23 part-time (17 women); includes 12 minority (8 Black or African American, non-Hispanic/Latino; 2 Asian, non-Hispanic/Latino; 1 Hispanic/Latino; 1 Two or more races, non-Hispanic/Latino), 3 international. Average age 34. 135 applicants, 44% accepted, 33 enrolled. *Faculty:* 6 full-time (5 women), 11 part-time/adjunct (6 women). Expenses: Contact institution. *Financial support:* In 2016–17, 6 students received support. Unspecified assistantships available. Financial award applicants required to submit FAFSA. In 2016, 29 master's awarded. *Program availability:* Part-time, evening/weekend, online learning. Offers English language learners (Advanced Certificate); international advocacy and leadership (MA, Certificate); literacy (MA); special reading (Advanced Certificate); teaching and learning (MA); TESL (MA). *Application deadline:* Applications are processed on a rolling basis. Electronic applications accepted. *Application Contact:* Cory Roup, Graduate Education Enrollment and Academic Advisor, 816-501-2464, E-mail: cory.roup@avila.edu. *Director of Graduate Education,* Dr. Stacy Keith, 816-501-2446, Fax: 816-501-2915, E-mail: stacy.keith@avila.edu.

School of Professional Studies Students: 90 full-time (59 women), 47 part-time (40 women); includes 50 minority (38 Black or African American, non-Hispanic/Latino; 1 American Indian or Alaska Native, non-Hispanic/Latino; 3 Asian, non-Hispanic/Latino; 7 Hispanic/Latino; 1 Two or more races, non-Hispanic/Latino), 6 international. Average age 38. 95 applicants, 58% accepted, 38 enrolled. *Faculty:* 15 part-time/adjunct (9 women). Expenses: Contact institution. *Financial support:* In 2016–17, 14 students received support. Unspecified assistantships available. Support available to part-time students. Financial award applicants required to submit FAFSA. In 2016, 37 master's awarded. *Program availability:* Part-time-only, evening/weekend, 100% online, blended/hybrid learning. Offers executive leadership development (MS); fundraising (MA); instructional design and technology (MA, MS); leadership coaching (MS); organizational development (MS); project management (MA); strategic human resources (MS). *Application deadline:* Applications are processed on a rolling basis. *Application fee:* $0. Electronic applications accepted. *Application Contact:* Jessica Burson, Graduate Admission Advisor, 816-501-2482, Fax: 816-941-4650, E-mail: advantage@avila.edu. *Associate Dean/Director,* Dr. Steve Iliff, 816-501-3675, Fax: 816-941-4650, E-mail: advantage@avila.edu.

BABEL UNIVERSITY PROFESSIONAL SCHOOL OF TRANSLATION, Honolulu, HI 96815

General Information Proprietary, coed, primarily women, graduate-only institution. *Graduate housing:* On-campus housing not available.

GRADUATE UNITS

Program in Translation *Program availability:* Part-time, evening/weekend, online learning. Offers translation (MA).

BABSON COLLEGE, Babson Park, MA 02457-0310

General Information Independent, coed, comprehensive institution. *Graduate housing:* Rooms and/or apartments available on a first-come, first-served basis to single and married students. Housing application deadline: 5/1.

GRADUATE UNITS

F. W. Olin Graduate School of Business *Program availability:* Part-time, evening/weekend, online learning. Offers accounting (MSA); advanced management (Certificate); business administration (MBA); global entrepreneurship (MS); technological entrepreneurship (MS). Electronic applications accepted.

BAKER COLLEGE CENTER FOR GRADUATE STUDIES—ONLINE, Flint, MI 48507

General Information Independent, coed, graduate-only institution. *Graduate housing:* On-campus housing not available.

GRADUATE UNITS

Graduate Programs *Program availability:* Part-time, evening/weekend, online learning. Offers accounting (MBA); business administration (DBA); finance (MBA); general business (MBA); health care management (MBA); human resources management (MBA); information management (MBA); leadership studies (MBA); management information systems (MSIS); marketing (MBA). Electronic applications accepted.

BAKER UNIVERSITY, Baldwin City, KS 66006-0065

General Information Independent-religious, coed, comprehensive institution. *Enrollment:* 1,144 graduate, professional, and undergraduate students; 136 full-time matriculated graduate/professional students (77 women), 723 part-time matriculated graduate/professional students (461 women). *Enrollment by degree level:* 750 master's, 109 doctoral. *Graduate housing:* On-campus housing not available. *Student services:* Campus safety program, international student services, services for students with disabilities. *Library facilities:* Baker University Library. *Collection:* Books: 89,076 (physical), 149,796 (digital/electronic); Serial titles: 1,564 (physical); Databases: 48. Study areas open 24 hours, 5–7 days a week; students can reserve study rooms.

Computer facilities: 140 computers available on campus for general student use. A campuswide network can be accessed from student residence rooms. Online class registration is available.
Website: http://www.bakeru.edu/

General Application Contact: Kelly Belk, Vice President of Enrollment Management, 913-491-4432, E-mail: kbelk@bakeru.edu.

GRADUATE UNITS

School of Education Students: 16 full-time (10 women), 375 part-time (276 women); includes 45 minority (19 Black or African American, non-Hispanic/Latino; 7 American Indian or Alaska Native, non-Hispanic/Latino; 3 Asian, non-Hispanic/Latino; 11 Hispanic/Latino; 1 Native Hawaiian or other Pacific Islander, non-Hispanic/Latino; 4 Two or more races, non-Hispanic/Latino). Average age 36. Expenses: Contact institution. *Financial support:* Applicants required to submit FAFSA. In 2016, 187 master's, 43 doctorates awarded. *Program availability:* Part-time, evening/weekend, 100% online. Offers education (MA Ed, MSSE, MSSL, MST, Ed D). Master's-level programs also offered in Wichita, KS. *Application deadline:* Applications are processed on a rolling basis. Electronic applications accepted. *Application Contact:* Linda Reynolds, Director of Graduate Education Enrollment, 913-344-6037, E-mail: linda.reynolds@bakeru.edu. *Dean of the School of Education,* Dr. Marc Childress, 913-344-1235, E-mail: marcus.childress@bakeru.edu.

School of Professional and Graduate Studies Students: 120 full-time (67 women), 338 part-time (176 women); includes 102 minority (47 Black or African American, non-Hispanic/Latino; 11 American Indian or Alaska Native, non-Hispanic/Latino; 13 Asian, non-Hispanic/Latino; 26 Hispanic/Latino; 5 Two or more races, non-Hispanic/Latino), 2 international. Average age 35. Expenses: Contact institution. *Financial support:* Applicants required to submit FAFSA. In 2016, 258 master's awarded. *Program availability:* Part-time, evening/weekend, online learning. Offers business (MAOL, MBA, MSM, MSSM); liberal arts (MLA). *Application deadline:* Applications are processed on a rolling basis. *Application Contact:* Kelly Belk, Vice President of Enrollment Management, 913-491-4432, E-mail: kelly.belk@learn.bakeru.edu. *Dean of the School of Professional and Graduate Studies*, Dr. Jacob Bucher, 785-594-8475, E-mail: jacob.bucher@bakeru.edu.

BAKKE GRADUATE UNIVERSITY, Dallas, TX 75243-7039
General Information Independent-religious, coed, primarily men, graduate-only institution. *Graduate housing:* On-campus housing not available.

GRADUATE UNITS

Programs in Pastoral Ministry and Business *Program availability:* Part-time, online learning. Offers business administration (MBA); church and ministry multiplication (D Min); global urban leadership (MA); leadership (D Min); ministry in complex contexts (D Min); social and civic entrepreneurship (MA); theology of work (D Min); theology reflection (D Min); transformational leadership (DTL); urban youth ministry (D Min). Electronic applications accepted.

BALDWIN WALLACE UNIVERSITY, Berea, OH 44017-2088
General Information Independent-religious, coed, comprehensive institution. *Enrollment:* 3,951 graduate, professional, and undergraduate students; 436 full-time matriculated graduate/professional students (278 women), 204 part-time matriculated graduate/professional students (128 women). *Enrollment by degree level:* 640 master's. *Graduate faculty:* 39 full-time (19 women), 42 part-time/adjunct (15 women). *Graduate housing:* Room and/or apartments available to single students; on-campus housing not available to married students. *Student services:* Campus employment opportunities, campus safety program, career counseling, exercise/wellness program, free psychological counseling, international student services, low-cost health insurance, multicultural affairs office, services for students with disabilities, teacher training, writing training. *Library facilities:* Ritter Library plus 2 others. *Collection:* Books: 106,767 (physical), 408,078 (digital/electronic); Serial titles: 174 (physical), 71,231 (digital/electronic); Databases: 265. Weekly public service hours: 90; study areas open 24 hours, 5–7 days a week; students can reserve study rooms. *Research affiliation:* Cuyahoga Community College (early childhood education), Berea City Schools (co-teaching models), Head Start Programs (early childhood education).

Computer facilities: 500 computers available on campus for general student use. A campuswide network can be accessed from student residence rooms. Online class registration is available.
Website: http://www.bw.edu/

General Application Contact: Winifred W. Gerhardt, Director of Transfer, Adult and Graduate Admission, 440-826-2222, Fax: 440-826-3830, E-mail: admission@bw.edu.

GRADUATE UNITS

Graduate Programs Students: 436 full-time (278 women), 204 part-time (128 women); includes 96 minority (43 Black or African American, non-Hispanic/Latino; 15 Asian, non-Hispanic/Latino; 27 Hispanic/Latino; 11 Two or more races, non-Hispanic/Latino), 3 international. Average age 32. 841 applicants, 34% accepted, 196 enrolled. *Faculty:* 39 full-time (19 women), 42 part-time/adjunct (15 women). Expenses: Contact institution. In 2016, 246 master's awarded. *Program availability:* Part-time, evening/weekend, 100% online, blended/hybrid learning. Offers health education and disease prevention (MPH); physician assistant (MMS); population health leadership and management (MPH); speech-language pathology (MS). *Application deadline:* Applications are processed on a rolling basis. *Application fee:* $25. Electronic applications accepted. *Application Contact:* Winifred W. Gerhardt, Director of Transfer, Adult and Graduate Admission, 440-826-2222, Fax: 440-826-3830, E-mail: admission@bw.edu. *Provost, Academic Affairs*, Stephen D. Stahl, 440-826-2271, E-mail: sstahl@bw.edu.

School of Business Students: 200 full-time (84 women), 121 part-time (68 women); includes 61 minority (28 Black or African American, non-Hispanic/Latino; 11 Asian, non-Hispanic/Latino; 17 Hispanic/Latino; 5 Two or more races, non-Hispanic/Latino), 3 international. Average age 34. 131 applicants, 77% accepted, 71 enrolled. *Faculty:* 21 full-time (8 women), 23 part-time/adjunct (8 women). Expenses: Contact institution. *Financial support:* Applicants required to submit FAFSA. In 2016, 168 master's awarded. *Program availability:* Part-time, evening/weekend, blended/hybrid learning. Offers accounting (MBA); analytics (MBA); entrepreneurship (MBA); executive management (MBA); health care (MBA); human resources (MBA); international management (MBA); management (MAM, MBA); sustainability (MBA). *Application deadline:* For fall admission, 7/25 priority date for domestic students, 4/30 priority date for international students; for spring admission, 12/15 priority date for domestic students, 9/30 priority date for international students; for summer admission, 4/15 for domestic students. Applications are processed on a rolling basis. Electronic applications accepted. *Application Contact:* Laura Spencer, Graduate Application Specialist, 440-826-2191, Fax: 440-826-3868, E-mail: lspencer@bw.edu. *MBA Program Director*, Dale Kramer, 440-826-3331, Fax: 440-826-3868, E-mail: dkramer@bw.edu.

School of Education Students: 126 full-time (99 women), 82 part-time (59 women); includes 20 minority (12 Black or African American, non-Hispanic/Latino; 1 Asian, non-Hispanic/Latino; 3 Hispanic/Latino; 4 Two or more races, non-Hispanic/Latino). Average age 32. 123 applicants, 50% accepted, 49 enrolled. *Faculty:* 7 full-time (3 women), 9 part-time/adjunct (1 woman). Expenses: Contact institution. *Financial support:* Career-related internships or fieldwork available. Financial award applicants required to submit FAFSA. In 2016, 54 master's awarded. *Program availability:* Part-time, evening/weekend, 100% online, blended/hybrid learning. Offers leadership in higher education (MA Ed); literacy (MA Ed); mild/moderate educational needs (MA Ed); school leadership (MA Ed); technology leadership (MA Ed). *Application deadline:* For fall admission, 8/15 priority date for domestic students; for spring admission, 12/15 priority date for domestic students. Applications are processed on a rolling basis. *Application fee:* $25. Electronic applications accepted. *Application Contact:* Winifred W. Gerhardt, Director of Transfer, Adult and Graduate Admission, 440-826-2222, Fax: 440-826-3830, E-mail: admission@bw.edu. *Dean*, Dr. Karen Kaye, 440-826-2168, Fax: 440-826-3779, E-mail: kkaye@bw.edu.

BALL STATE UNIVERSITY, Muncie, IN 47306
General Information State-supported, coed, university. CGS member. *Graduate housing:* Rooms and/or apartments available on a first-come, first-served basis to single and married students. Housing application deadline: 6/1. *Research affiliation:* DowAgro

(biochemistry), Lilly Company (biochemistry), Cisco (networking, information management), Element (biochemistry), ConforMIS (biomechanics), Monell (chemistry).

GRADUATE UNITS

Graduate School *Program availability:* Part-time, evening/weekend, 100% online, blended/hybrid learning. Electronic applications accepted.

College of Applied Sciences and Technology Program availability: Part-time, evening/weekend, 100% online. Offers adult/gerontology nurse practitioner (Post Master's Certificate); applied sciences and technology (MA, MS, DNP, PhD, Certificate, Post Master's Certificate, Postbaccalaureate Certificate); athletic coaching education (Certificate); career and technical education (MA); evidence-based clinical practice (Postbaccalaureate Certificate); exercise science (MA, MS); family and consumer science (MS); family and consumer sciences (MA); family nurse practitioner (Post Master's Certificate); family nurse practitioner for the adult nurse practitioner or adult/gerontology nurse practitioner (Post Master's Certificate); human bioenergetics (PhD); nurse educator (Post Master's Certificate); nursing (MS); nursing education (Postbaccalaureate Certificate); nursing practice (DNP); nutrition and dietetics (MA, MS); physical education (MS); physical education and sport (MA, MS); technology education (MA); wellness management (MA, MS). Electronic applications accepted.

College of Architecture and Planning Program availability: Part-time. Offers architecture (M Arch, M Arch II); architecture and planning (M Arch, M Arch II, MLA, MS, MUD, MURP, Certificate); digital fabrication (Certificate); historic preservation (MS); landscape architecture (MLA); urban and regional planning (MURP); urban design (MUD). Electronic applications accepted.

College of Communication, Information, and Media Program availability: Part-time, 100% online, blended/hybrid learning. Offers communication studies (MA); communication, information, and media (MA, MS, Certificate); emerging media and visual reporting (Certificate); emerging media design and development (MA); information and communication sciences (MS); information and communication technologies (Certificate); journalism (MA); literary journalism (Certificate); public relations (MA); telecommunications (MA). Electronic applications accepted.

College of Fine Arts Program availability: Part-time. Offers fine arts (MFA); music (MA, MM, DA, Artist Diploma); visual arts studio (MA). Electronic applications accepted.

College of Sciences and Humanities Program availability: Part-time, 100% online, blended/hybrid learning. Offers actuarial science (MA); anthropology (MA); audiology (Au D); biology (MA, MS); chemistry (MA, MS); clinical psychology (MA); cognitive and social processes (MA); computer science (MA, MS); elementary mathematics teacher leadership (Certificate); emergency management and homeland security (Certificate); English (MA, PhD); environmental science (PhD); geographic information systems (Certificate); geography (MS); geology (MA, MS); history (MA); interpretive ethnography (Certificate); linguistics (MA); mathematics (MA, MS); mathematics education (MA); middle school mathematics education (Certificate); natural resources and environmental management (MA, MS); physics (MA, MAE, MS); physiology (MA, MS); political science (MA, MPA, Certificate); post-secondary foundational mathematics teaching (MA, Certificate); professional meteorology and climatology (Certificate); public administration (MPA, Certificate); sciences and humanities (MA, MAE, MPA, MS, Au D, PhD, Certificate); sociology (MA); speech-language pathology (MA); statistical modeling (Certificate); statistics (MA, MS); teaching English to speakers of other languages (TESOL) and linguistics (MA). Electronic applications accepted.

Miller College of Business Program availability: Part-time, evening/weekend, 100% online, blended/hybrid learning. Offers accounting (MS); business administration (MBA, Certificate, Graduate Certificate); business education (MA); business essentials (Graduate Certificate); community and economic development (Certificate); health economics, policy and administration (Certificate); information systems and operations management (MA, Certificate); information systems security management (Certificate); selling and sales management (Certificate). Electronic applications accepted.

Teachers College Program availability: Part-time, evening/weekend, 100% online, blended/hybrid learning. Offers adult and community education (MA); adult education (MA, Ed D, Certificate); adult, higher and community education (Ed D); applied behavior analysis (MA, Certificate); autism (Certificate); charter school leadership (Certificate); college and university teaching (Certificate); community college leadership (Certificate); community education (Certificate); computer education (Certificate); counseling (MA); counseling psychology (MA, PhD); curriculum and educational technology (MA); diversity studies (Certificate); early childhood administration (Certificate); education (MA, MAE, MS, Ed D, PhD, Certificate, Ed S); educational administration and supervision (MA, Ed D); educational psychology (MA, MS); educational psychology (PhD); educational studies (PhD); elementary education (MAE, Ed D, PhD); enhanced teaching practice for elementary teachers (Certificate); executive development for public service (MA); gifted and talented education (Certificate); human development and learning (Certificate); identity and leadership development for counselors (Certificate); instructional design and assessment (Certificate); literacy instruction (Certificate); middle-level education (Certificate); neuropsychology (Certificate); qualitative research in education (Certificate); quantitative psychology (MS); response to intervention (Certificate); school psychology (MA, PhD, Ed S); school psychology (Ed S); school superintendent (Ed S); secondary education (MA); social psychology (MA); social psychology and clinical mental health counseling (MA, MAE, Ed D); special education (MA, MAE, Ed D); student affairs administration in higher education (MA). Electronic applications accepted.

BANK STREET COLLEGE OF EDUCATION, New York, NY 10025
General Information Independent, coed, graduate-only institution. *Research affiliation:* Annenberg Institute (education), Stanford University (education), Educational Development Center (education), Mathematica Policy Research, Inc. (education), Center for Teaching Quality (education).

GRADUATE UNITS

Graduate School Offers advanced literacy specialization (Ed M); bilingual childhood special education (Ed M); bilingual early childhood general education (MS Ed); bilingual early childhood special and general education (MS Ed); bilingual early childhood special education (Ed M, MS Ed); bilingual elementary/childhood general education (MS Ed); bilingual elementary/childhood special and general education (MS Ed); bilingual elementary/childhood special education (MS Ed); child life (MS); early childhood and elementary/childhood education (MS Ed); early childhood education (MS Ed); early childhood leadership (MS Ed); early childhood special and general education (MS Ed); early childhood special education (Ed M, MS Ed); education (Ed M, MS, MS Ed); educational leadership (MS Ed); elementary/childhood education (MS Ed); elementary/childhood special and general education (MS Ed); elementary/childhood special education (MS Ed); elementary/childhood special education certification (Ed M); infant and family development (MS Ed); infant and family early childhood special and general education (MS Ed); infant and family/early childhood special education (Ed M); leadership for educational change (Ed M, MS Ed); leadership in community-based learning (MS Ed); leadership in mathematics education (MS Ed); leadership in museum education (MS Ed); leadership in the arts: creative writing (MS Ed); leadership in the arts: visual arts (MS Ed); museum education (MS Ed); museum education: elementary education certification (MS Ed); reading and literacy (MS Ed); teaching literacy (MS Ed); teaching literacy and childhood general education (MS Ed). Electronic applications accepted.

BAPTIST BIBLE COLLEGE, Springfield, MO 65803-3498

General Information Independent-religious, coed, comprehensive institution. *Graduate housing:* Rooms and/or apartments available on a first-come, first-served basis to single and married students.

GRADUATE UNITS

Graduate School of Theology *Program availability:* Part-time. Offers biblical counseling (MA); biblical studies (MA); church ministry (MA); intercultural studies (MA); theology (M Div). Electronic applications accepted.

THE BAPTIST COLLEGE OF FLORIDA, Graceville, FL 32440-1898

General Information Independent-religious, coed, comprehensive institution. *Graduate housing:* Rooms and/or apartments available on a first-come, first-served basis to single and married students.

GRADUATE UNITS

Graduate Programs *Program availability:* Part-time, 100% online, blended/hybrid learning. Offers Christian ministry (MA); Christian studies (MA); music and worship leadership (MA). Electronic applications accepted.

BAPTIST MISSIONARY ASSOCIATION THEOLOGICAL SEMINARY, Jacksonville, TX 75766-5407

General Information Independent-religious, coed, primarily men, comprehensive institution. *Graduate housing:* Rooms and/or apartments available on a first-come, first-served basis to single and married students. Housing application deadline: 6/1.

GRADUATE UNITS

Graduate and Professional Programs *Program availability:* Part-time. Offers theology (M Div, MAR). Electronic applications accepted.

BAPTIST THEOLOGICAL SEMINARY AT RICHMOND, Richmond, VA 23227

General Information Independent-religious, coed, graduate-only institution. *Enrollment by degree level:* 52 master's, 9 doctoral, 3 other advanced degrees. *Graduate faculty:* 5 full-time (1 woman), 11 part-time/adjunct (2 women). *Tuition:* Full-time $9900; part-time $6600 per year. *Required fees:* $620; $620 per year. *One-time fee:* $410. *Graduate housing:* Rooms and/or apartments available on a first-come, first-served basis to single and married students. Typical cost: $9120 (including board) for single students; $9120 (including board) for married students. Room and board charges vary according to housing facility selected. Housing application deadline: 2/15. *Student services:* Campus employment opportunities, campus safety program, free psychological counseling, international student services, services for students with disabilities, writing training. *Library facilities:* Morton Library. *Collection:* Students can reserve study rooms.

Computer facilities: 2 computers available on campus for general student use. A campuswide network can be accessed. Online class registration is available. Website: http://www.btsr.edu/

General Application Contact: Melissa Fallen, Director of Admissions and Recruitment, 804-204-1208, E-mail: admissions@btsr.edu.

GRADUATE UNITS

Graduate and Professional Programs Students: 42 full-time (23 women), 34 part-time (19 women); includes 11 minority (all Black or African American, non-Hispanic/Latino), 2 international. Average age 46. Faculty: 5 full-time (1 woman), 11 part-time/adjunct (2 women). Expenses: Contact institution. *Financial support:* In 2016–17, 46 students received support, including 11 teaching assistantships (averaging $3,300 per year); scholarships/grants also available. Financial award application deadline: 2/1. In 2016, 8 master's, 2 doctorates awarded. *Program availability:* Part-time, 100% online, blended/hybrid learning. Offers Biblical interpretation (M Div); Christian education formation (M Div); Christian ministry (MCM); justice and peacebuilding (M Div); ministry (D Min); religious freedom (M Div); theological studies (MTS, Graduate Certificate); theology (M Div); youth and student ministries (M Div). *Application deadline:* For fall admission, 7/1 for domestic students, 5/1 for international students; for winter admission, 12/15 for domestic students, 9/1 for international students; for spring admission, 1/15 for domestic students, 10/1 for international students. Applications are processed on a rolling basis. *Application fee:* $35. Electronic applications accepted. *Application Contact:* Melissa Fallen, Director of Admissions and Recruitment, 804-204-1208, E-mail: admissions@btsr.edu. *President,* Dr. Ronald W. Crawford, 804-204-1201, Fax: 804-355-8182, E-mail: rcrawford@btsr.edu.

BARCLAY COLLEGE, Haviland, KS 67059-0288

General Information Independent-religious, coed, comprehensive institution.

GRADUATE UNITS

Master of Arts Program *Program availability:* Online learning. Offers transformational leadership (MA). Electronic applications accepted.

BARD COLLEGE, Annandale-on-Hudson, NY 12504

General Information Independent, coed, comprehensive institution. *Enrollment:* 2,335 graduate, professional, and undergraduate students; 424 matriculated graduate/professional students. *Enrollment by degree level:* 397 master's, 15 doctoral, 22 other advanced degrees. *Graduate housing:* On-campus housing not available. *Student services:* Low-cost health insurance. *Library facilities:* Stevenson Library plus 3 others. *Collection:* Books: 346,724 (physical), 129,695 (digital/electronic); Serial titles: 1,419 (physical), 33,229 (digital/electronic); Databases: 41. Weekly public service hours: 75; students can reserve study rooms.

Computer facilities: 425 computers available on campus for general student use. A campuswide network can be accessed from student residence rooms and from off campus. Online class registration is available. Website: http://www.bard.edu/

General Application Contact: Dr. Norton Batkin, Vice President and Dean of Graduate Studies, 845-758-7895, Fax: 845-752-4901, E-mail: dgs@bard.edu.

GRADUATE UNITS

Bard Center for Environmental Policy *Program availability:* Part-time. Offers climate science and policy (MS, Professional Certificate); environmental policy (MS, Professional Certificate); sustainability (MBA). Electronic applications accepted.

Center for Curatorial Studies Expenses: Contact institution. *Financial support:* Fellowships, research assistantships, career-related internships or fieldwork, scholarships/grants, and unspecified assistantships available. Financial award application deadline: 3/15; financial award applicants required to submit FAFSA. Offers curatorial studies (MA). *Application deadline:* For fall admission, 2/1 for domestic and international students. *Application fee:* $65. Electronic applications accepted. *Application Contact:* Tom Eccles, Executive Director, 845-758-7598, Fax: 845-758-2442, E-mail: ccs@bard.edu. *Executive Director,* Tom Eccles, 845-758-7598, Fax: 845-758-2442, E-mail: ccs@bard.edu.

Conservatory of Music Expenses: Contact institution. Offers music (MM); vocal arts (MM). *Application Contact:* Kristin Roca, Graduate Program Coordinator, 845-758-7895, Fax: 845-758-7897, E-mail: kroca@bard.edu. *Director,* Robert Martin, 845-758-7419, E-mail: martin@bard.edu.

The Conductors Institute Expenses: Contact institution. Offers choral conducting (MM); orchestral conducting (MM). *Application fee:* $30. *Application Contact:* Harold Farberman, Artistic Director, 845-758-7425, E-mail: ci@bard.edu. *Artistic Director,* Harold Farberman, 845-758-7425, E-mail: ci@bard.edu.

International Center of Photography Expenses: Contact institution. Offers advanced photographic studies (MFA). *Application Contact:* Nayland Blake, Chair, 212-857-0001, E-mail: icpbard@icp.edu. *Chair,* Nayland Blake, 212-857-0001, E-mail: icpbard@icp.edu.

Levy Economics Institute Expenses: Contact institution. Offers economic theory and policy (MS). *Application deadline:* For fall admission, 11/15 priority date for domestic students. *Application Contact:* Jan Kregel, Program Director, 845-758-7776, E-mail: kregel@levy.org. *Program Director,* Jan Kregel, 845-758-7776, E-mail: kregel@levy.org.

Longy School of Music Expenses: Contact institution. *Financial support:* Teaching assistantships, scholarships/grants, and unspecified assistantships available. Financial award application deadline: 3/1; financial award applicants required to submit FAFSA. *Program availability:* Part-time. Offers chamber music (Artist Diploma); collaborative piano (MM, Artist Diploma, GPD); composition (MM); opera (MM, GPD); organ (MM, Artist Diploma, GPD); piano (MM, Artist Diploma, GPD); voice (MM, Artist Diploma, GPD). MAT offered in partnership with the Los Angeles Philharmonic at the Los Angeles campus only. *Application deadline:* For fall admission, 12/1 priority date for domestic and international students; for spring admission, 11/1 for domestic and international students. *Application fee:* $100. Electronic applications accepted. *Application Contact:* Azusa Chapman, Director of Admissions and Student Services, 617-876-0956 Ext. 1790, Fax: 617-876-9326, E-mail: admissions@longy.edu. *President,* Karen Zorn, 617-876-0956, Fax: 617-876-9326, E-mail: music@longy.edu.

Master of Arts in Teaching Program Expenses: Contact institution. *Financial support:* Fellowships, institutionally sponsored loans, and scholarships/grants available. Support available to part-time students. Financial award application deadline: 4/28; financial award applicants required to submit FAFSA. *Program availability:* Part-time. Offers secondary education (MAT). *Application deadline:* For winter admission, 1/30 priority date for domestic students; for spring admission, 4/27 for domestic students, 4/30 for international students. Applications are processed on a rolling basis. *Application fee:* $65. Electronic applications accepted. *Application Contact:* Cecilia Maple, Assistant Director for Admission and Student Affairs, 845-758-7145, E-mail: mat@bard.edu. *Director,* Derek Furr, 845-758-7136, Fax: 845-758-7149, E-mail: mat@bard.edu.

Milton Avery Graduate School of the Arts Expenses: Contact institution. *Financial support:* Fellowships and scholarships/grants available. Financial award application deadline: 3/15; financial award applicants required to submit FAFSA. Offers film/video (MFA); music/sound (MFA); painting (MFA); photography (MFA); sculpture (MFA); writing (MFA). *Application deadline:* For fall admission, 1/15 for international students. *Application fee:* $65. Electronic applications accepted. *Application Contact:* Arthur Gibbons, Director, 845-758-7481, Fax: 845-758-7507, E-mail: mfa@bard.edu. *Director,* Arthur Gibbons, 845-758-7481, Fax: 845-758-7507, E-mail: mfa@bard.edu.

BARD GRADUATE CENTER, New York, NY 10024-3602

General Information Independent, coed, primarily women, graduate-only institution. *Enrollment by degree level:* 42 master's, 36 doctoral. *Graduate faculty:* 15 full-time (7 women), 5 part-time/adjunct (4 women). *Graduate housing:* Rooms and/or apartments available on a first-come, first-served basis to single and married students. Housing application deadline: 4/1. *Student services:* Campus employment opportunities, campus safety program, career counseling, free psychological counseling, grant writing training, low-cost health insurance, writing training. *Research affiliation:* Association of Research Institutes in Art History, Metropolitan Museum of Art, Brooklyn Museum, American Museum of Natural History, Museum of Arts and Design, The Frick Collection.

Computer facilities: A campuswide network can be accessed from student residence rooms. Website: http://www.bgc.bard.edu/

General Application Contact: Elena Pinto Simon, Dean for Academic Administration, Student and Alumni Affairs, 212-501-3057, Fax: 212-501-3065, E-mail: simon@bgc.bard.edu.

GRADUATE UNITS

Graduate Studies Students: 67 full-time (55 women), 11 part-time (all women). *Faculty:* 15 full-time (7 women), 5 part-time/adjunct (4 women). Expenses: Contact institution. *Financial support:* Fellowships with tuition reimbursements, research assistantships, teaching assistantships, career-related internships or fieldwork, institutionally sponsored loans, scholarships/grants, traineeships, health care benefits, and unspecified assistantships available. Financial award application deadline: 1/6; financial award applicants required to submit FAFSA. In 2016, 23 master's, 5 doctorates awarded. *Program availability:* Part-time. Offers decorative arts, design history, and material culture (M Phil, MA, PhD). *Application deadline:* For fall admission, 1/6 for domestic and international students. *Application fee:* $70. *Application Contact:* Elena Pinto Simon, Dean for Academic Administration, Student and Alumni Affairs, 212-501-3057, Fax: 212-501-3065, E-mail: simon@bgc.bard.edu. *Founder and Director,* Susan Weber, 212-501-3000, Fax: 212-501-3079.

BARRY UNIVERSITY, Miami Shores, FL 33161-6695

General Information Independent-religious, coed, university. *Graduate housing:* On-campus housing not available. *Research affiliation:* Baxter Corporation (immunology, diagnostics), Coulter Corporation (immunology, cytology), Cordis Corporation (cardiac product development), Diamedix (immunological diagnostics), Noven Pharmaceutical, Sano Pharmaceuticals.

GRADUATE UNITS

Andreas School of Business *Program availability:* Part-time, evening/weekend. Offers accounting (MSA); business (MBA, MSA, MSM, Certificate); business administration (MBA); finance (Certificate); health services administration (Certificate); international business (Certificate); management (MSM); management information systems (Certificate); marketing (Certificate). Electronic applications accepted.

College of Arts and Sciences *Program availability:* Part-time, evening/weekend. Offers arts and sciences (MA, MFA, MS, D Min, Certificate, SSP); broadcasting (Certificate); clinical psychology (MS); communication (MA); liberal studies (MA); ministry (D Min); organizational communication (MS); pastoral ministry for Hispanics (MA); pastoral theology (MA); photography (MA, MFA); practical theology (MA); school psychology (MS, SSP). Electronic applications accepted.

College of Health Sciences *Program availability:* Part-time, evening/weekend. Offers anesthesiology (MS); biology (MS); biomedical sciences (MS); health care leadership (Certificate); health care planning and informatics (Certificate); health sciences (MS, Certificate); health services administration (MS); histotechnology (Certificate); long term care management (Certificate); medical group practice management (Certificate); occupational therapy (MS); quality improvement and outcomes management (Certificate). Electronic applications accepted.

Dwayne O. Andreas School of Law Offers law (JD).

Physician Assistant Program Offers physician assistant (MCMS). Electronic applications accepted.

School of Adult and Continuing Education *Program availability:* Part-time, evening/weekend. Offers administrative studies (MA); adult and continuing education (MA, MPA, MS, MSN, PhD, Certificate); information technology (MS); public administration (MPA). Electronic applications accepted.

Division of Nursing *Program availability:* Part-time, evening/weekend. Offers acute care nurse practitioner (MSN); family nurse practitioner (MSN); nurse practitioner (Certificate); nursing (MSN, PhD, Certificate); nursing administration (MSN, PhD, Certificate); nursing education (MSN, Certificate). Electronic applications accepted.

School of Education *Program availability:* Part-time, evening/weekend, online learning. Offers accomplished teacher (Ed S); advanced teaching and learning with technology (Certificate); counseling (MS, PhD, Ed S); culture, language and literacy (TESOL) (PhD); curriculum evaluation and research (PhD); distance education (Certificate); early childhood (Ed S); early childhood education (PhD); education (MS, Ed D, PhD, Certificate, Ed S); education for teachers of students with hearing impairments (MS); educational computing and technology (MS, Ed S); educational leadership (MS, Ed D, Certificate, Ed S); educational technology (PhD); elementary (Ed S); elementary education (MS, PhD); elementary education/ESOL (MS); ESOL (Ed S); exceptional student education (MS, Ed S); gifted (Ed S); higher education administration (PhD); higher education technology integration (Certificate); human resource development (PhD); human resource development and administration (MS); human resources: not for profit and religious organizations (Certificate); K-12 technology integration (Certificate); leadership (PhD); marital, couple and family counseling/therapy (MS, Ed S); mental health counseling (MS, Ed S); Montessori (Ed S); Montessori education (MS, Ed S); PKP/elementary (Ed S); pre-k/primary (MS); pre-k/primary/ESOL (MS); reading (MS, Ed S); reading, language and cognition (PhD); rehabilitation counseling (MS, Ed S); school counseling (MS, Ed S); technology and TESOL (MS, Ed S); TESOL (MS); TESOL international (MS). Electronic applications accepted.

School of Human Performance and Leisure Sciences *Program availability:* Part-time, evening/weekend. Offers athletic training (MS); biomechanics (MS); exercise science (MS); general movement science (MS); human performance and leisure sciences (MS); sport and exercise psychology (MS); sport management (MS). Electronic applications accepted.

School of Podiatric Medicine Offers anatomy (MS); podiatric medicine (MS, DPM); podiatric medicine and surgery (DPM). Electronic applications accepted.

School of Social Work *Program availability:* Part-time, evening/weekend. Offers social work (MSW, PhD). Electronic applications accepted.

BARTON COLLEGE, Wilson, NC 27893-7000

General Information Independent-religious, coed, comprehensive institution.

GRADUATE UNITS

Program in Elementary Education Offers elementary education (M Ed). Electronic applications accepted.

BARUCH COLLEGE OF THE CITY UNIVERSITY OF NEW YORK, New York, NY 10010-5585

General Information State and locally supported, coed, comprehensive institution. *Graduate housing:* On-campus housing not available.

GRADUATE UNITS

Austin W. Marxe School of Public and International Affairs *Program availability:* Part-time, evening/weekend. Offers educational leadership (MS Ed); general public administration (MPA); health care policy (MPA); higher education administration (MS Ed); international nongovernmental organizations (MIA); nonprofit administration (MPA); policy analysis and evaluation (MPA); public and international affairs (MIA, MPA, MS Ed, Advanced Certificate); public management (MPA); school building leadership (Advanced Certificate); school district leadership (Advanced Certificate); trade policy and global economic governance (MIA); urban development and sustainability (MPA); Western Hemisphere affairs (MIA). Electronic applications accepted.

Weissman School of Arts and Sciences Students: 164 full-time (107 women), 99 part-time (59 women); includes 67 minority (24 Black or African American, non-Hispanic/Latino; 2 American Indian or Alaska Native, non-Hispanic/Latino; 14 Asian, non-Hispanic/Latino; 23 Hispanic/Latino; 4 Two or more races, non-Hispanic/Latino), 73 international. Expenses: Contact institution. *Financial support:* Career-related internships or fieldwork, Federal Work-Study, scholarships/grants, traineeships, tuition waivers (partial), and unspecified assistantships available. Financial award applicants required to submit FAFSA. *Program availability:* Part-time, evening/weekend. Offers arts administration (MA); arts and sciences (MA, MS); corporate communication (MA); financial engineering (MS); industrial/organizational psychology (MS); mental health counseling (MA). *Application fee:* $125. Electronic applications accepted. *Application Contact:* Michael J. Lovaglio, Director of Graduate Programs, 646-312-3897, Fax: 646-312-3871, E-mail: wsas.graduate.studies@baruch.cuny.edu.

Zicklin School of Business *Program availability:* Part-time, evening/weekend. Offers accounting (MBA, MS, PhD); business (MBA, MS, PhD, Certificate); business administration (MBA); decision sciences (MBA); economics (MBA); entrepreneurship (MBA, MS); finance (MBA, MS, PhD); general business administration (MBA); health care administration (MBA); industrial and labor relations (MS); industrial and organizational psychology (MBA, MS, PhD); information systems (MBA, MS, PhD);

international business (MBA); management (PhD); marketing (MBA, MS, PhD); operations management (MBA); organizational behavior/human resources management (MBA); quantitative methods and modeling (MBA, MS); real estate (MBA, MS); statistics (MBA, MS); sustainable business (MBA); taxation (MBA, MS). JD/MBA offered jointly with Brooklyn Law School and New York Law School. Electronic applications accepted.

BASTYR UNIVERSITY, Kenmore, WA 98028-4966

General Information Independent, coed, upper-level institution. *Graduate housing:* Room and/or apartments available on a first-come, first-served basis to single students; on-campus housing not available to married students. Housing application deadline: 5/1. *Research affiliation:* University of Washington (health), Fred Hutchinson Cancer Research Center (oncology), Seattle Cancer Care Alliance (oncology), Benaroya Research Institute at Virginia Mason (health).

GRADUATE UNITS

School of Acupuncture and Oriental Medicine *Program availability:* Evening/weekend. Offers acupuncture and Oriental medicine (MS, DAOM, Certificate). Electronic applications accepted.

School of Natural Health Arts and Sciences *Program availability:* Part-time. Offers counseling psychology (MA); holistic landscape design (Certificate); midwifery (MS); nutrition (MS); nutrition and clinical health psychology (MS).

School of Naturopathic Medicine *Program availability:* Part-time. Offers naturopathic medicine (ND). Electronic applications accepted.

BAYAMÓN CENTRAL UNIVERSITY, Bayamón, PR 00960-1725

General Information Independent-religious, coed, comprehensive institution. *Graduate housing:* On-campus housing not available.

GRADUATE UNITS

Graduate Programs *Program availability:* Part-time, evening/weekend. Offers accounting (MBA); administration and supervision (MA Ed); commercial education (MA Ed); elementary education (K–3) (MA Ed); family counseling (Graduate Certificate); finance (MBA); general business (MBA); guidance and counseling (MA Ed); management (MBA); marketing (MBA); organizational psychology (MA); pre-elementary teacher (MA Ed); rehabilitation counseling (MA Ed); special education (MA Ed).

BAYLOR COLLEGE OF MEDICINE, Houston, TX 77030-3498

General Information Independent, coed, graduate-only institution. CGS member. *Graduate housing:* On-campus housing not available. *Research affiliation:* Veterans Affairs Medical Center (biomedical research), Texas Children's Hospital (pediatric biomedical research), St. Luke's Episcopal Hospital (biomedical research), National Space Biomedical Research Institute (biomedical research), Harris Health System (biomedical research), Children's Nutrition Research Center (pediatric nutrition).

GRADUATE UNITS

Graduate School of Biomedical Sciences Offers biochemistry (PhD); biochemistry and molecular biology (PhD); biomedical sciences (MS, PhD); cardiovascular sciences (PhD); cell and molecular biology (PhD); clinical scientist training (MS, PhD); developmental biology (PhD); genetics (PhD); human genetics (PhD); immunology (PhD); microbiology (PhD); molecular and cellular biology (PhD); molecular and human genetics (PhD); molecular physiology and biophysics (PhD); molecular virology and microbiology (PhD); neuroscience (PhD); pharmacology (PhD); structural and computational biology and molecular biophysics (PhD); translational biology and molecular medicine (PhD); virology (PhD). Electronic applications accepted.

Medical School Offers medicine (MD). Electronic applications accepted.

School of Allied Health Sciences Offers allied health sciences (MS, DNP); nurse anesthesia (DNP); physician assistant (MS). Electronic applications accepted.

BAYLOR UNIVERSITY, Waco, TX 76798

General Information Independent-religious, coed, university. CGS member. *Enrollment:* 16,959 graduate, professional, and undergraduate students; 2,157 full-time matriculated graduate/professional students (1,043 women), 351 part-time matriculated graduate/professional students (163 women). *Enrollment by degree level:* 1,320 master's, 1,169 doctoral, 19 other advanced degrees. *Graduate faculty:* 789. *Tuition:* Full-time $28,494; part-time $1583 per credit hour. *Required fees:* $167 per credit hour. Tuition and fees vary according to course load and program. *Graduate housing:* Rooms and/or apartments available to single and married students. *Student services:* Campus employment opportunities, campus safety program, career counseling, exercise/wellness program, free psychological counseling, international student services, low-cost health insurance, multicultural affairs office, services for students with disabilities. *Library facilities:* Moody Memorial Library plus 8 others. *Research affiliation:* Sandia National Laboratories (physics), Zyvex Corporation (physics), OXiGENE, Inc. (pharmaceuticals), Brookhaven National Laboratory (physics), Fermi National Accelerator Laboratory (physics), National Center for Supercomputing Applications (physics).

Computer facilities: Computer purchase and lease plans are available. A campuswide network can be accessed from student residence rooms and from off campus. Online class registration is available.
Website: http://www.baylor.edu/

General Application Contact: Lori McNamara, Admissions Coordinator, 254-710-3588, Fax: 254-710-3870.

GRADUATE UNITS

Diana R. Garland School of Social Work Students: 106 full-time (90 women), 18 part-time (15 women); includes 39 minority (19 Black or African American, non-Hispanic/Latino; 1 Asian, non-Hispanic/Latino; 16 Hispanic/Latino; 3 Two or more races, non-Hispanic/Latino), 3 international. Average age 27. 190 applicants, 72% accepted, 71 enrolled. *Faculty:* 11 full-time (5 women), 13 part-time/adjunct (7 women). Expenses: Contact institution. *Financial support:* In 2016–17, 138 students received support, including 12 research assistantships with tuition reimbursements available (averaging $6,800 per year); career-related internships or fieldwork, Federal Work-Study, institutionally sponsored loans, scholarships/grants, traineeships, tuition waivers (full and partial), and unspecified assistantships also available. Support available to part-time students. Financial award application deadline: 6/1; financial award applicants required to submit FAFSA. In 2016, 64 master's awarded. *Program availability:* Part-time, blended/hybrid learning. Offers social work (MSW, PhD). *Application deadline:* For spring admission, 3/15 for domestic and international students. Applications are processed on a rolling basis. *Application fee:* $45. Electronic applications accepted. *Application Contact:* Dr. Crystal Diaz-Espinoza, Director of Recruitment and Career Services, 254-710-4479, Fax: 254-710-6455, E-mail: crystal_diaz-espinoza@baylor.edu. *Associate Dean for Academic Affairs,* Dr. David Pooler, 254-710-3884, Fax: 254-710-7412, E-mail: david_pooler@baylor.edu.

George W. Truett Theological Seminary Students: 258 full-time (89 women), 79 part-time (25 women); includes 95 minority (50 Black or African American, non-Hispanic/Latino; 10 Asian, non-Hispanic/Latino; 23 Hispanic/Latino; 12 Two or more races, non-Hispanic/Latino), 20 international. Average age 30. 157 applicants, 82% accepted, 84 enrolled. *Faculty:* 20 full-time (2 women), 18 part-time/adjunct (5 women). Expenses: Contact institution. *Financial support:* In 2016–17, 328 students received support, including 33 research assistantships with partial tuition reimbursements available (averaging $3,474 per year); teaching assistantships, career-related internships or fieldwork, Federal Work-Study, institutionally sponsored loans, scholarships/grants, traineeships, health care benefits, tuition waivers, and unspecified assistantships also available. Support available to part-time students. Financial award application deadline: 8/1; financial award applicants required to submit FAFSA. In 2016, 81 master's, 7 doctorates awarded. *Program availability:* Part-time. Offers theology (M Div, MACM, MTS, D Min). *Application deadline:* For fall admission, 5/1 for domestic students, 6/10 for international students; for spring admission, 11/15 for domestic students, 10/10 for international students; for summer admission, 4/1 for domestic students, 3/10 for international students. Applications are processed on a rolling basis. *Application fee:* $35. Electronic applications accepted. *Application Contact:* Carley Joy Collier, Administrative Associate, Admissions Services, 254-710-7334, Fax: 254-710-7233, E-mail: carley_lund@baylor.edu. *Dean,* Dr. Todd D. Still, 254-710-3755, Fax: 254-710-3753, E-mail: todd_still@baylor.edu.

Graduate School Students: 1,432 full-time (680 women), 260 part-time (127 women); includes 315 minority (72 Black or African American, non-Hispanic/Latino; 3 American Indian or Alaska Native, non-Hispanic/Latino; 56 Asian, non-Hispanic/Latino; 117 Hispanic/Latino; 1 Native Hawaiian or other Pacific Islander, non-Hispanic/Latino; 66 Two or more races, non-Hispanic/Latino), 201 international. 1,692 applicants. *Faculty:* 789. Expenses: Contact institution. *Financial support:* Fellowships, research assistantships with tuition reimbursements, teaching assistantships with tuition reimbursements, career-related internships or fieldwork, Federal Work-Study, institutionally sponsored loans, scholarships/grants, health care benefits, tuition waivers (full and partial), and unspecified assistantships available. Support available to part-time students. Financial award applicants required to submit FAFSA. In 2016, 605 master's, 137 doctorates, 7 other advanced degrees awarded. *Program availability:* Part-time, evening/weekend, 100% online, blended/hybrid learning. Offers emergency medicine (D Sc PA); health care administration (MHA); health sciences (MHA, MS, D Sc, D Sc PA, DPT, DScPT); nutrition (MS); orthopedics (D Sc); physical therapy (DPT, DScPT). *Application deadline:* For fall admission, 2/15 for domestic students; for spring admission, 12/1 for domestic students; for summer admission, 5/1 for domestic students. Applications are processed on a rolling basis. *Application fee:* $50. Electronic applications accepted. *Application Contact:* Lori McNamara, Graduate Admissions Coordinator, 254-710-3588, Fax: 254-710-3870, E-mail: lori_mcnamara@baylor.edu. *Dean,* Dr. Larry Lyon, 254-710-3588, Fax: 254-710-3870, E-mail: larry_lyon@baylor.edu.

College of Arts and Sciences Students: 536 full-time (228 women), 88 part-time (40 women); includes 90 minority (11 Black or African American, non-Hispanic/Latino; 17 Asian, non-Hispanic/Latino; 32 Hispanic/Latino; 30 Two or more races, non-Hispanic/Latino), 92 international. Expenses: Contact institution. *Financial support:* Fellowships, research assistantships with partial tuition reimbursements, teaching assistantships, career-related internships or fieldwork, Federal Work-Study, institutionally sponsored loans, scholarships/grants, tuition waivers (full and partial), and laboratory assistantships, practicum stipends available. Support available to part-time students. In 2016, 101 master's, 67 doctorates awarded. *Program availability:* Part-time, evening/weekend. Offers American studies (MA); arts and sciences (IMES, MA, MES, MFA, MIJ, MPPA, MS, MSCSD, MSW, PhD, Psy D); biochemistry (MS, PhD); biology (MA, MS, PhD); chemistry (MS, PhD); clinical psychology (Psy D); communication (MA); community analytics (PhD); ecological, earth and environmental sciences (PhD); English (MA, PhD); environmental biology (MS); environmental science (MES, MS); geosciences (MS, PhD); history (MA, PhD); international journalism (MIJ); international studies (MA); journalism (MA); limnology (MS); mathematics (MS, PhD); museum studies (MA); philosophy (MA, PhD); physics (MA, MS, PhD); political science (MA, PhD); psychology (MA, PhD); public policy and administration (MPPA); religion (MA, PhD); sociology (MA); sociology of religion (PhD); Spanish (MA); statistical science (MA, PhD); theatre arts (MA, MFA). *Application deadline:* Applications are processed on a rolling basis. *Application fee:* $25. Electronic applications accepted. *Application Contact:* Suzanne Keener, Administrative Assistant, 254-710-3588, Fax: 254-710-3870. *Dean,* Dr. Larry Lyon, 254-710-3588, Fax: 254-710-3870, E-mail: larry_lyon@baylor.edu.

Hankamer School of Business Students: 292 full-time (124 women), 31 part-time (12 women); includes 80 minority (22 Black or African American, non-Hispanic/Latino; 17 Asian, non-Hispanic/Latino; 31 Hispanic/Latino; 10 Two or more races, non-Hispanic/Latino), 41 international. Expenses: Contact institution. *Financial support:* Research assistantships, teaching assistantships, career-related internships or fieldwork, Federal Work-Study, and institutionally sponsored loans available. In 2016, 250 master's, 2 doctorates awarded. *Program availability:* Part-time. Offers accounting and business law (M Acc, MT); business (M Acc, MBA, MS Eco, MSIS, MT, PhD); business administration (MBA); economics (MS Eco); entrepreneurship (PhD); information systems (MSIS, PhD); information systems management (MBA). *Application deadline:* For fall admission, 8/1 for domestic students; for spring admission, 12/1 for domestic students. Applications are processed on a rolling basis. *Application fee:* $25. *Application Contact:* Laurie Wilson, Director, Graduate Business Programs, 254-710-4163, Fax: 254-710-1066, E-mail: laurie_wilson@baylor.edu. *Associate Dean,* Dr. Gary Carini, 254-710-3718, Fax: 254-710-1092, E-mail: gary_carini@baylor.edu.

Institute of Biomedical Studies Students: 23 full-time (8 women), 1 part-time (0 women); includes 4 minority (1 Black or African American, non-Hispanic/Latino; 1 Asian, non-Hispanic/Latino; 2 Hispanic/Latino), 11 international. Average age 24. 69 applicants, 10% accepted, 5 enrolled. *Faculty:* 17 part-time/adjunct (3 women). Expenses: Contact institution. *Financial support:* In 2016–17, 22 students received support, including 11 research assistantships (averaging $20,000 per year), 11 teaching assistantships (averaging $20,000 per year); tuition waivers also available. In 2016, 1 master's, 6 doctorates awarded. Offers biomedical studies (MS, PhD). *Application deadline:* Applications are processed on a rolling basis. *Application fee:* $25. Electronic applications accepted. *Application Contact:* Rhonda Bellert, Administrative Associate, 254-710-2514, Fax: 254-710-2199, E-mail: rhonda_bellert@baylor.edu. *Graduate Program Director,* Dr. Chris Kearney, 254-710-2131, Fax: 254-710-3878, E-mail: chris_kearney@baylor.edu.

Louise Herrington School of Nursing Students: 49 full-time (45 women), 9 part-time (all women); includes 21 minority (6 Black or African American, non-Hispanic/Latino; 1 American Indian or Alaska Native, non-Hispanic/Latino; 3 Asian, non-Hispanic/Latino; 9 Hispanic/Latino; 2 Two or more races, non-Hispanic/Latino). Average age 35. 47 applicants, 70% accepted, 26 enrolled. *Faculty:* 11 full-time (all women), 3 part-time/adjunct (2 women). Expenses: Contact institution. *Financial support:* In 2016–17, 66 students received support, including 1 teaching assistantship (averaging $4,167 per year); Federal Work-Study, scholarships/grants, and unspecified assistantships also available. Support available to part-time students. Financial award application deadline: 6/30; financial award applicants required to submit FAFSA. In 2016, 10 master's, 5 doctorates awarded. *Program availability:* Part-time, online learning. Offers family nurse practitioner (MSN); neonatal nurse practitioner (MSN); nurse-midwifery (DNP). *Application deadline:* For fall admission, 2/1 for domestic students. *Application fee:* $50. Electronic applications accepted. *Application Contact:* Elaine Lark, Coordinator of Recruitment and Enrollment, 214-818-7839, Fax: 214-820-3835, E-mail: elaine_lark@baylor.edu. *Graduate Program Director,* Dr. Barbara Camune, 214-367-3754, Fax: 214-820-3375, E-mail: barbara_camune@baylor.edu.

Robbins College of Health and Human Sciences Students: 130 full-time (100 women), 16 part-time (7 women); includes 29 minority (5 Black or African American, non-Hispanic/Latino; 4 Asian, non-Hispanic/Latino; 12 Hispanic/Latino; 8 Two or more races, non-Hispanic/Latino), 8 international. Expenses: Contact institution. In 2016, 69 master's, 1 doctorate awarded. Offers communication sciences and disorders (MS); health and human sciences (MA, MPH, MS, MS Ed, PhD); health, human performance and recreation (MPH, MS, PhD); nutrition sciences (MS). *Application Contact:* Lori McNamara, Graduate Admissions Coordinator, 254-710-3588, Fax: 254-710-3870, E-mail: lori_mcnamara@baylor.edu. *Interim Dean,* Dr. Rodney G. Bowden, 254-710-6111, Fax: 254-710-3699, E-mail: rodney_bowden@baylor.edu.

School of Education Students: 133 full-time (90 women), 41 part-time (28 women); includes 38 minority (15 Black or African American, non-Hispanic/Latino; 3 Asian, non-Hispanic/Latino; 12 Hispanic/Latino; 1 Native Hawaiian or other Pacific Islander, non-Hispanic/Latino; 7 Two or more races, non-Hispanic/Latino), 5 international. 248 applicants, 35% accepted, 28 enrolled. *Faculty:* 44 full-time (20 women). Expenses: Contact institution. *Financial support:* In 2016–17, 181 students received support, including 38 research assistantships (averaging $12,050 per year), 68 teaching assistantships (averaging $12,050 per year); career-related internships or fieldwork, Federal Work-Study, institutionally sponsored loans, scholarships/grants, and tuition waivers (partial) also available. Financial award applicants required to submit FAFSA. In 2016, 60 master's, 13 doctorates, 7 other advanced degrees awarded. *Program availability:* Part-time, online learning. Offers applied behavior analysis (MS Ed); curriculum and instruction (MA, MS Ed, Ed D, PhD); education (MA, MPH, MS Ed, Ed D, PhD, Ed S); educational leadership (MS Ed, Ed S); educational psychology (MA, MS Ed, PhD); exceptionalities (PhD); gifted and talented studies (MS Ed); learning and development (PhD); measurement (PhD); quantitative methods (MA); school psychology (Ed S). *Application deadline:* Applications are processed on a rolling basis. *Application fee:* $25. Electronic applications accepted. *Application Contact:* Julie Baker, Administrative Assistant, 254-710-3050, Fax: 254-710-3870, E-mail: julie_baker@baylor.edu. *Dean,* Dr. Jon Engelhardt, 254-710-3111, Fax: 254-710-3987.

School of Engineering and Computer Science Students: 90 full-time (16 women), 9 part-time (0 women); includes 13 minority (3 Black or African American, non-Hispanic/Latino; 4 Asian, non-Hispanic/Latino; 5 Hispanic/Latino; 1 Two or more races, non-Hispanic/Latino), 39 international. *Faculty:* 31 full-time (3 women). Expenses: Contact institution. *Financial support:* In 2016–17, research assistantships with tuition reimbursements (averaging $15,000 per year), teaching assistantships with tuition reimbursements (averaging $15,000 per year) were awarded. Financial award application deadline: 3/15. In 2016, 30 master's, 2 doctorates awarded. *Program availability:* Part-time. Offers biomedical engineering (MSBME); computer science (MS, PhD); electrical and computer engineering (MS, PhD); engineering (ME); engineering and computer science (ME, MS, MSBME, PhD); mechanical engineering (MS, PhD). *Application deadline:* For fall admission, 8/1 for domestic students; for spring admission, 12/1 for domestic students. Applications are processed on a rolling basis. *Application fee:* $25. *Application Contact:* 254-710-3588, Fax: 254-710-3870. *Dean,* Dr. Dennis L. O'Neal, 254-710-3871, Fax: 254-710-3839, E-mail: dennis_oneal@baylor.edu.

School of Music Students: 15 full-time (9 women), 59 part-time (26 women); includes 11 minority (2 Black or African American, non-Hispanic/Latino; 2 Asian, non-Hispanic/Latino; 7 Hispanic/Latino), 16 international. Expenses: Contact institution. *Financial support:* In 2016–17, 43 teaching assistantships with full tuition reimbursements (averaging $5,990 per year) were awarded; Federal Work-Study and institutionally sponsored loans also available. In 2016, 24 master's awarded. Offers church music (MM, DMA); collaborative piano (MM); composition (MM); conducting (MM); music history and literature (MM); music theory (MM); performance (MM); piano pedagogy and performance (MM). *Application deadline:* For fall admission, 8/1 for domestic students; for spring admission, 12/1 for domestic students. Applications are processed on a rolling basis. *Application fee:* $25. *Application Contact:* Melinda Coates, Administrative Assistant, 254-710-2360, Fax: 254-710-3870, E-mail: melinda_coats@baylor.edu. *Graduate Program Director,* Dr. David Music, 254-710-2360, Fax: 254-710-1191, E-mail: david_music@baylor.edu.

School of Law Students: 367 full-time (190 women), 2 part-time (1 woman); includes 89 minority (14 Black or African American, non-Hispanic/Latino; 4 American Indian or Alaska Native, non-Hispanic/Latino; 18 Asian, non-Hispanic/Latino; 48 Hispanic/Latino; 2 Native Hawaiian or other Pacific Islander, non-Hispanic/Latino; 3 Two or more races, non-Hispanic/Latino), 4 international. Average age 24. 1,724 applicants, 41% accepted, 72 enrolled. *Faculty:* 28 full-time (9 women), 20 part-time/adjunct (2 women). Expenses: Contact institution. *Financial support:* In 2016–17, 259 students received support. Career-related internships or fieldwork, Federal Work-Study, and scholarships/grants available. Financial award application deadline: 2/1; financial award applicants required to submit FAFSA. In 2016, 140 doctorates awarded. Offers law (JD). *Application deadline:* For fall admission, 3/15 for domestic and international students; for spring admission, 11/15 for domestic and international students; for summer admission, 3/15 for domestic and international students. Applications are processed on a rolling basis. *Application fee:* $0. Electronic applications accepted. *Application Contact:* Jenny Branson, Assistant Dean of Admissions and Financial Aid, 254-710-1911, Fax: 254-710-2316, E-mail: jenny_branson@baylor.edu. *Dean,* Bradley J. B. Toben, 254-710-1911, Fax: 254-710-2316.

BAY PATH UNIVERSITY, Longmeadow, MA 01106-2292

General Information Independent, Undergraduate; women only; graduate: coed, comprehensive institution. *Enrollment:* 3,224 graduate, professional, and undergraduate students; 570 full-time matriculated graduate/professional students (484 women), 762 part-time matriculated graduate/professional students (664 women). *Enrollment by degree level:* 1,290 master's, 41 other advanced degrees. *Graduate faculty:* 35 full-time (28 women), 116 part-time/adjunct (89 women). Tuition and fees vary according to program. *Graduate housing:* Room and/or apartments available on a first-come, first-served basis to single students; on-campus housing not available to married students. Housing application deadline: 7/2. *Student services:* Campus employment opportunities, campus safety program, career counseling, exercise/wellness program, free psychological counseling, international student services, low-cost health insurance, multicultural affairs office, services for students with disabilities. *Library facilities:* Hatch Library. *Collection:* Books: 52,565 (physical), 408,000 (digital/electronic); Serial titles: 80 (physical), 55,000 (digital/electronic); Databases: 110. Weekly public service hours: 86; students can reserve study rooms.

Computer facilities: 235 computers available on campus for general student use. A campuswide network can be accessed from student residence rooms and from off campus. Online class registration is available.
Website: http://www.baypath.edu/

General Application Contact: Diane Ranaldi, Dean of Graduate Admissions, 413-565-1332, Fax: 413-565-1250, E-mail: dranaldi@baypath.edu.

GRADUATE UNITS

Program in Accounting Students: 1 (woman) full-time, 27 part-time (25 women); includes 12 minority (5 Black or African American, non-Hispanic/Latino; 2 Asian, non-Hispanic/Latino; 4 Hispanic/Latino; 1 Two or more races, non-Hispanic/Latino). Average age 34. 18 applicants, 83% accepted, 11 enrolled. Expenses: Contact institution. *Financial support:* In 2016–17, 2 students received support. Scholarships/grants and unspecified assistantships available. Financial award applicants required to submit FAFSA. In 2016, 3 master's awarded. *Program availability:* Part-time, online only, 100% online. Offers forensic accounting (MS); private accounting (MS); public accounting (tax and audit) (MS). *Application deadline:* Applications are processed on a rolling basis. *Application fee:* $45. Electronic applications accepted. *Application Contact:* Diane Ranaldi, Dean of Graduate Admissions, 413-565-1332, Fax: 413-565-1250, E-mail: dranaldi@baypath.edu. *Director,* Kara Stevens, 413-565-1344, E-mail: kastevens@baypath.edu.

Program in Applied Behavior Analysis Students: 115 part-time (103 women); includes 11 minority (3 Black or African American, non-Hispanic/Latino; 2 Asian, non-Hispanic/Latino; 4 Hispanic/Latino; 2 Two or more races, non-Hispanic/Latino), 1 international. Average age 30. 85 applicants, 75% accepted, 57 enrolled. Expenses: Contact institution. *Financial support:* Unspecified assistantships available. Financial award applicants required to submit FAFSA. In 2016, 18 master's awarded. *Program availability:* Part-time, online learning. Offers applied behavior analysis (MS); autism spectrum disorders (MS). *Application deadline:* Applications are processed on a rolling basis. *Application fee:* $45. Electronic applications accepted. *Application Contact:* Diane Ranaldi, Dean of Graduate Admissions, 413-565-1332, Fax: 413-565-1250, E-mail: dranaldi@baypath.edu. *Director,* Susan Ainsleigh, E-mail: sainsleigh@baypath.edu.

Program in Applied Data Science Students: 5 full-time (1 woman), 6 part-time (1 woman); includes 5 minority (3 Black or African American, non-Hispanic/Latino; 1 Asian, non-Hispanic/Latino; 1 Two or more races, non-Hispanic/Latino), 1 international. Average age 35. 10 applicants, 90% accepted, 9 enrolled. Expenses: Contact institution. *Financial support:* Applicants required to submit FAFSA. *Program availability:* Part-time, 100% online. Offers applied data science (MS). *Application deadline:* Applications are processed on a rolling basis. *Application fee:* $45. Electronic applications accepted. *Application Contact:* Diane Ranaldi, Dean of Graduate Admissions, 413-565-1332, Fax: 413-565-1250, E-mail: dranaldi@baypath.edu. *Director,* Ning Jia, E-mail: njia@baypath.edu.

Program in Applied Laboratory Science and Operations Students: 5 full-time (all women), 1 (woman) part-time; includes 2 minority (both Hispanic/Latino). Average age 27. 11 applicants, 100% accepted, 6 enrolled. Expenses: Contact institution. *Financial support:* Unspecified assistantships available. Financial award applicants required to submit FAFSA. *Program availability:* Part-time, evening/weekend. Offers applied laboratory science and operations (MS). *Application deadline:* Applications are processed on a rolling basis. *Application fee:* $45. Electronic applications accepted. *Application Contact:* Diane Ranaldi, Dean of Graduate Admissions, 413-565-1332, Fax: 413-565-1250, E-mail: dranaldi@baypath.edu. *Program Director,* Dr. Thomas Mennella, 413-565-1318, E-mail: tmennella@baypath.edu.

Program in Clinical Mental Health Counseling Students: 85 full-time (78 women), 83 part-time (76 women); includes 43 minority (19 Black or African American, non-Hispanic/Latino; 1 Asian, non-Hispanic/Latino; 17 Hispanic/Latino; 6 Two or more races, non-Hispanic/Latino), 16 international. Average age 31. 75 applicants, 72% accepted, 40 enrolled. Expenses: Contact institution. *Financial support:* Unspecified assistantships available. Financial award applicants required to submit FAFSA. In 2016, 21 master's awarded. *Program availability:* Part-time, blended/hybrid learning. Offers clinical mental health counseling (MS). Program also offered in Sturbridge and Burlington, MA. *Application deadline:* Applications are processed on a rolling basis. *Application fee:* $45. Electronic applications accepted. *Application Contact:* Diane Ranaldi, Dean of Graduate Admissions, 413-565-1332, Fax: 413-565-1250, E-mail: dranaldi@baypath.edu. *Director,* Dr. Mark Benander, 413-565-1332, E-mail: mbenander@baypath.edu.

Program in Communications and Information Management Students: 12 full-time (8 women), 23 part-time (21 women); includes 10 minority (4 Black or African American, non-Hispanic/Latino; 3 Hispanic/Latino; 1 Native Hawaiian or other Pacific Islander, non-Hispanic/Latino; 2 Two or more races, non-Hispanic/Latino), 4 international. Average age 37. 26 applicants, 92% accepted, 16 enrolled. Expenses: Contact institution. *Financial support:* Unspecified assistantships available. Financial award applicants required to submit FAFSA. In 2016, 27 master's awarded. *Program availability:* Part-time, evening/weekend, 100% online. Offers communications and information management (MS). *Application deadline:* Applications are processed on a rolling basis. *Application fee:* $45. Electronic applications accepted. *Application Contact:* Diane Ranaldi, Dean of Graduate Admissions, 413-565-1332, Fax: 413-565-1250, E-mail: dranaldi@baypath.edu. *Program Director,* Robin Saunders, 413-565-1009.

Program in Creative Nonfiction Students: 13 full-time (11 women), 37 part-time (35 women); includes 7 minority (5 Black or African American, non-Hispanic/Latino; 2 Hispanic/Latino). Average age 47. 28 applicants, 75% accepted, 18 enrolled. Expenses: Contact institution. *Financial support:* Applicants required to submit FAFSA. In 2016, 7 master's awarded. *Program availability:* Part-time, evening/weekend, online only, 100% online. Offers creative nonfiction (MFA). *Application deadline:* Applications are processed on a rolling basis. *Application fee:* $45. Electronic applications accepted. *Application Contact:* Diane Ranaldi, Dean of Graduate Admissions, 413-565-1332, Fax: 413-565-1250, E-mail: dranaldi@baypath.edu. *Director,* Leanne James Blackwell, 413-565-1232, E-mail: ljblackwell@baypath.edu.

Program in Curriculum and Instruction Students: 16 full-time (all women), 30 part-time (28 women); includes 8 minority (3 Black or African American, non-Hispanic/Latino; 2 Hispanic/Latino; 3 Two or more races, non-Hispanic/Latino). Average age 31. 27 applicants, 67% accepted, 15 enrolled. Expenses: Contact institution. *Financial support:* Unspecified assistantships available. Financial award applicants required to submit FAFSA. In 2016, 4 master's awarded. *Program availability:* Part-time, 100% online.

Offers curriculum and instruction (MS Ed). *Application deadline:* Applications are processed on a rolling basis. *Application fee:* $45. Electronic applications accepted. *Application Contact:* Diane Ranaldi, Dean of Graduate Admissions, 413-565-1332, Fax: 413-565-1250, E-mail: dranaldi@baypath.edu. *Program Director,* Andrea Hickson, E-mail: ahickson@baypath.edu.

Program in Cybersecurity Management Students: 10 full-time (6 women), 19 part-time (11 women); includes 13 minority (6 Black or African American, non-Hispanic/Latino; 6 Hispanic/Latino; 1 Two or more races, non-Hispanic/Latino). Average age 36. 19 applicants, 95% accepted, 14 enrolled. Expenses: Contact institution. *Financial support:* Unspecified assistantships available. Financial award applicants required to submit FAFSA. In 2016, 4 master's awarded. *Program availability:* Part-time, evening/weekend, online only, 100% online. Offers cybersecurity management (MS). *Application deadline:* Applications are processed on a rolling basis. *Application fee:* $45. Electronic applications accepted. *Application Contact:* Diane Ranaldi, Dean of Graduate Admissions, 413-565-1332, Fax: 413-565-1250, E-mail: dranaldi@baypath.edu. *Director,* Dr. Larry Snyder, 413-565-1294, E-mail: lsnyder@baypath.edu.

Program in Developmental Psychology Students: 4 full-time (3 women), 15 part-time (14 women); includes 8 minority (3 Black or African American, non-Hispanic/Latino; 4 Hispanic/Latino; 1 Two or more races, non-Hispanic/Latino). Average age 38. 24 applicants, 54% accepted, 8 enrolled. Expenses: Contact institution. *Financial support:* Unspecified assistantships available. Financial award applicants required to submit FAFSA. In 2016, 7 master's awarded. *Program availability:* Part-time, 100% online. Offers developmental psychology (MS). *Application deadline:* Applications are processed on a rolling basis. *Application fee:* $45. Electronic applications accepted. *Application Contact:* Diane Ranaldi, Dean of Graduate Admissions, 413-565-1332, Fax: 413-565-1250, E-mail: dranaldi@baypath.edu. *Program Director,* Dr. Mark Benander, 413-565-1332, E-mail: mbenander@baypath.edu.

Program in Education Students: 37 full-time (33 women), 124 part-time (104 women); includes 15 minority (6 Black or African American, non-Hispanic/Latino; 1 Asian, non-Hispanic/Latino; 6 Hispanic/Latino; 1 Native Hawaiian or other Pacific Islander, non-Hispanic/Latino; 1 Two or more races, non-Hispanic/Latino). Average age 33. 65 applicants, 68% accepted, 36 enrolled. Expenses: Contact institution. *Financial support:* Unspecified assistantships available. Financial award applicants required to submit FAFSA. *Program availability:* Part-time, 100% online. Offers education. *Application deadline:* Applications are processed on a rolling basis. *Application fee:* $45. Electronic applications accepted. *Application Contact:* Diane Ranaldi, Dean of Graduate Admissions, 413-565-1332, Fax: 413-565-1250, E-mail: dranaldi@baypath.edu. *Program Coordinator,* Dr. Karen DeAngelis, E-mail: kdeangelis@baypath.edu.

Program in Entrepreneurial Thinking and Innovative Practices Students: 21 full-time (19 women), 60 part-time (53 women); includes 17 minority (8 Black or African American, non-Hispanic/Latino; 8 Hispanic/Latino; 1 Two or more races, non-Hispanic/Latino), 2 international. Average age 33. 48 applicants, 92% accepted, 37 enrolled. Expenses: Contact institution. *Financial support:* Unspecified assistantships available. Financial award applicants required to submit FAFSA. In 2016, 34 master's awarded. *Program availability:* Part-time, 100% online. Offers entrepreneurial thinking and innovative practices (MBA). *Application deadline:* Applications are processed on a rolling basis. *Application fee:* $45. Electronic applications accepted. *Application Contact:* Diane Ranaldi, Dean of Graduate Admissions, 413-565-1332, Fax: 413-565-1250, E-mail: dranaldi@baypath.edu. *Program Director,* Mo Sattar, 413-565-1228, E-mail: msattar@baypath.edu.

Program in Higher Education Administration Students: 9 full-time (8 women), 50 part-time (39 women); includes 18 minority (8 Black or African American, non-Hispanic/Latino; 1 American Indian or Alaska Native, non-Hispanic/Latino; 7 Hispanic/Latino; 2 Two or more races, non-Hispanic/Latino). Average age 36. 27 applicants, 67% accepted, 14 enrolled. Expenses: Contact institution. *Financial support:* Unspecified assistantships available. Financial award applicants required to submit FAFSA. In 2016, 15 master's awarded. *Program availability:* Part-time, online only, 100% online. Offers enrollment management (MS); general administration (MS); institutional advancement (MS); online teaching and program administration (MS). *Application deadline:* Applications are processed on a rolling basis. *Application fee:* $45. Electronic applications accepted. *Application Contact:* Diane Ranaldi, Dean of Graduate Admissions, 413-565-1332, Fax: 413-565-1250, E-mail: dranaldi@baypath.edu. *Program Director,* Dr. Lauren Way, 413-565-1193, E-mail: lway@baypath.edu.

Program in Information Management Students: 1 (woman) full-time, all international. Average age 24. Expenses: Contact institution. *Financial support:* Unspecified assistantships available. Financial award applicants required to submit FAFSA. *Program availability:* Part-time, 100% online. Offers information management (MS). *Application deadline:* Applications are processed on a rolling basis. *Application fee:* $45. Electronic applications accepted. *Application Contact:* Diane Ranaldi, Dean of Graduate Admissions, 413-565-1332, Fax: 413-565-1250, E-mail: dranaldi@baypath.edu. *Director,* Robin Saunders, 413-565-1009, E-mail: rsaunders@baypath.edu.

Program in Leadership and Negotiation Students: 7 full-time (6 women), 24 part-time (19 women); includes 7 minority (5 Black or African American, non-Hispanic/Latino; 2 Hispanic/Latino). Average age 38. Expenses: Contact institution. *Financial support:* Unspecified assistantships available. Financial award applicants required to submit FAFSA. *Program availability:* Part-time, 100% online, blended/hybrid learning. Offers leadership and negotiation (MS). *Application deadline:* Applications are processed on a rolling basis. *Application fee:* $45. Electronic applications accepted. *Application Contact:* Diane Ranaldi, Dean of Graduate Admissions, 413-565-1332, Fax: 413-565-1250, E-mail: dranaldi@baypath.edu. *Director,* Dr. Joshua Weiss, E-mail: joweiss@baypath.edu.

Program in Nonprofit Management and Philanthropy Students: 7 full-time (6 women), 36 part-time (33 women); includes 12 minority (5 Black or African American, non-Hispanic/Latino; 1 Asian, non-Hispanic/Latino; 3 Hispanic/Latino; 3 Two or more races, non-Hispanic/Latino). Average age 36. 28 applicants, 79% accepted, 20 enrolled. Expenses: Contact institution. *Financial support:* Unspecified assistantships available. Financial award applicants required to submit FAFSA. In 2016, 13 master's awarded. *Program availability:* Part-time, 100% online. Offers nonprofit management and philanthropy (MS). *Application deadline:* Applications are processed on a rolling basis. *Application fee:* $45. Electronic applications accepted. *Application Contact:* Diane Ranaldi, Dean of Graduate Admissions, 413-565-1332, Fax: 413-565-1250, E-mail: dranaldi@baypath.edu. *Program Director,* Silvia de Haas-Phillips, E-mail: sdphillips@baypath.edu.

Program in Occupational Therapy Students: 275 full-time (242 women), 24 part-time (all women); includes 54 minority (19 Black or African American, non-Hispanic/Latino; 1 American Indian or Alaska Native, non-Hispanic/Latino; 9 Asian, non-Hispanic/Latino; 14 Hispanic/Latino; 11 Two or more races, non-Hispanic/Latino), 1 international. Average age 27. 371 applicants, 52% accepted, 94 enrolled. Expenses: Contact institution. *Financial support:* Unspecified assistantships available. Financial award applicants required to submit FAFSA. In 2016, 81 master's awarded. *Program* *availability:* Part-time. Offers occupational therapy (MOT). *Application deadline:* Applications are processed on a rolling basis. *Application fee:* $45. Electronic applications accepted. *Application Contact:* Diane Ranaldi, Dean of Graduate Admissions, 413-565-1332, Fax: 413-565-1250, E-mail: dranaldi@baypath.edu. *Program Director,* Dr. Beverly St. Pierre, E-mail: bstpierre@baypath.edu.

Program in Physician Assistant Studies Students: 53 full-time (30 women), 5 part-time (2 women); includes 4 minority (1 Black or African American, non-Hispanic/Latino; 1 Asian, non-Hispanic/Latino; 2 Two or more races, non-Hispanic/Latino). Average age 29. Expenses: Contact institution. *Financial support:* Unspecified assistantships available. Financial award applicants required to submit FAFSA. In 2016, 23 master's awarded. Offers physician assistant studies (MS). *Application deadline:* Applications are processed on a rolling basis. *Application fee:* $60. Electronic applications accepted. *Application Contact:* Diane Ranaldi, Dean of Graduate Admissions, 413-565-1332, Fax: 413-565-1250, E-mail: dranaldi@baypath.edu. *Director,* Theresa Riethle, 413-565-1206, E-mail: triethle@baypath.edu.

Program in Strategic Fundraising and Philanthropy Students: 1 full-time (0 women), 15 part-time (14 women); includes 2 minority (both Black or African American, non-Hispanic/Latino). Average age 35. 7 applicants, 71% accepted, 5 enrolled. Expenses: Contact institution. *Financial support:* Unspecified assistantships available. Financial award applicants required to submit FAFSA. In 2016, 4 master's awarded. *Program availability:* Part-time, 100% online. Offers higher education fundraising (MS); nonprofit fundraising (MS). *Application deadline:* Applications are processed on a rolling basis. *Application fee:* $45. Electronic applications accepted. *Application Contact:* Diane Ranaldi, Dean of Graduate Admissions, 413-565-1332, Fax: 413-565-1250, E-mail: dranaldi@baypath.edu. *Program Director,* Silvia de Haas-Phillips, E-mail: sdphillips@baypath.edu.

BECKER COLLEGE, Worcester, MA 01609
General Information Independent, coed, comprehensive institution.

GRADUATE UNITS
Program in Mental Health Counseling Offers community mental health (MA); school consultation (MA). Electronic applications accepted.

BELHAVEN UNIVERSITY, Jackson, MS 39202-1789
General Information Independent-religious, coed, comprehensive institution. *Enrollment:* 4,759 graduate, professional, and undergraduate students; 27 full-time matriculated graduate/professional students (18 women), 2,056 part-time matriculated graduate/professional students (1,554 women). *Enrollment by degree level:* 1,990 master's, 111 other advanced degrees. *Graduate faculty:* 29 full-time (14 women), 119 part-time/adjunct (60 women). *Tuition:* Full-time $9630; part-time $535 per credit hour. *Required fees:* $225; $75 per course. *Graduate housing:* On-campus housing not available. *Student services:* Career counseling, free psychological counseling. *Library facilities:* Warren A. Hood Library plus 1 other. *Collection:* Books: 45,076 (physical), 50,445 (digital/electronic); Serial titles: 160 (physical), 40,370 (digital/electronic); Databases: 46. Weekly public service hours: 104.

Computer facilities: 36 computers available on campus for general student use. A campuswide network can be accessed from student residence rooms and from off campus. Online class registration is available.
Website: http://www.belhaven.edu/

General Application Contact: Dr. Audrey Kelleher, Vice President for Adult and Graduate Marketing and Development, 407-804-1424, Fax: 407-620-5210, E-mail: akelleher@belhaven.edu.

GRADUATE UNITS
School of Business Students: 953 full-time (677 women), 392 part-time (292 women); includes 1,082 minority (1,027 Black or African American, non-Hispanic/Latino; 14 American Indian or Alaska Native, non-Hispanic/Latino; 4 Asian, non-Hispanic/Latino; 20 Hispanic/Latino; 2 Native Hawaiian or other Pacific Islander, non-Hispanic/Latino; 15 Two or more races, non-Hispanic/Latino), 11 international. Average age 35. *Faculty:* 16 full-time (3 women), 82 part-time/adjunct (32 women). Expenses: Contact institution. *Financial support:* Applicants required to submit FAFSA. In 2016, 235 master's awarded. *Program availability:* Part-time, evening/weekend, 100% online. Offers business administration (MBA); health administration (MBA, MHA); human resources (MBA, MSL); leadership (MBA); public administration (MPA); sports administration (MBA, MSA). *Application deadline:* Applications are processed on a rolling basis. *Application fee:* $25. Electronic applications accepted. *Application Contact:* Dr. Audrey Kelleher, Vice President of Adult and Graduate Marketing and Development, 407-804-1424, Fax: 407-620-5210, E-mail: akelleher@belhaven.edu. *Dean,* Dr. Ralph Mason, 601-968-8949, Fax: 601-968-8951, E-mail: cmason@belhaven.edu.

School of Education Students: 319 full-time (270 women), 403 part-time (318 women); includes 502 minority (486 Black or African American, non-Hispanic/Latino; 2 Asian, non-Hispanic/Latino; 3 Hispanic/Latino; 11 Two or more races, non-Hispanic/Latino). Average age 35. *Faculty:* 36 full-time (27 women), 9 part-time/adjunct (6 women). Expenses: Contact institution. *Financial support:* Applicants required to submit FAFSA. In 2016, 78 master's awarded. *Program availability:* Part-time, evening/weekend, 100% online, blended/hybrid learning. Offers educational technology (M Ed); elementary education (M Ed, MAT); reading literacy (M Ed); secondary education (M Ed, MAT). *Application deadline:* Applications are processed on a rolling basis. *Application fee:* $25. Electronic applications accepted. *Application Contact:* Sean Kirnan, Assistant Vice President for Adult and Graduate Enrollment and Student Services, 601-968-8727, Fax: 601-968-5953, E-mail: gradadmission@belhaven.edu. *Dean,* Dr. David Hand, 601-965-7020, E-mail: dhand@belhaven.edu.

BELLARMINE UNIVERSITY, Louisville, KY 40205
General Information Independent-religious, coed, comprehensive institution. *Enrollment:* 3,971 graduate, professional, and undergraduate students; 306 full-time matriculated graduate/professional students (197 women), 402 part-time matriculated graduate/professional students (295 women). *Enrollment by degree level:* 369 master's, 308 doctoral, 31 other advanced degrees. *Graduate faculty:* 73 full-time (45 women), 75 part-time/adjunct (51 women). Tuition and fees vary according to program. *Graduate housing:* Room and/or apartments available on a first-come, first-served basis to single students; on-campus housing not available to married students. Typical cost: $7520 per year ($11,920 including board). Room and board charges vary according to board plan and housing facility selected. *Student services:* Campus employment opportunities, campus safety program, career counseling, exercise/wellness program, free psychological counseling, international student services, multicultural affairs office, services for students with disabilities, teacher training, writing training. *Library facilities:* W. L. Lyons Brown Library. *Collection:* Books: 121,125 (physical), 233,857 (digital/electronic); Serial titles: 207 (physical), 88,144 (digital/electronic); Databases: 145. Weekly public service hours: 140; study areas open 24 hours, 5–7 days a week.

Computer facilities: 440 computers available on campus for general student use. A campuswide network can be accessed from student residence rooms and from off campus. Online class registration, mobile app are available.
Website: http://www.bellarmine.edu/

General Application Contact: Dr. Sara Pettingill, Dean of Graduate Admission, 502-272-8401, Fax: 502-272-8002, E-mail: spettingill@bellarmine.edu.

GRADUATE UNITS
Annsley Frazier Thornton School of Education Students: 39 full-time (28 women), 211 part-time (164 women); includes 46 minority (35 Black or African American, non-Hispanic/Latino; 3 Asian, non-Hispanic/Latino; 5 Hispanic/Latino; 3 Two or more races, non-Hispanic/Latino). Average age 34. *Faculty:* 15 full-time (7 women), 44 part-time/adjunct (36 women). Expenses: Contact institution. *Financial support:* Scholarships/grants available. Financial award applicants required to submit FAFSA. In 2016, 66 master's, 3 doctorates, 43 other advanced degrees awarded. *Program availability:* Part-time, evening/weekend. Offers education and district leadership (Ed D); education and social change (PhD); elementary education (MA Ed, MAT); leadership in higher education (PhD); learning and behavior disorders (MA Ed, MAT); middle grades education (MA Ed, MAT); principalship (Ed S); reading and writing (MA Ed); secondary education (MAT); teacher leadership (MA Ed). *Application deadline:* For fall admission, 8/1 priority date for domestic and international students; for spring admission, 12/1 priority date for domestic and international students; for summer admission, 4/10 priority date for domestic and international students. Applications are processed on a rolling basis. *Application fee:* $40. Electronic applications accepted. *Application Contact:* Sarah Shumway Schuble, Senior Graduate Recruiter, 502-272-8271, Fax: 502-272-8002, E-mail: sshumway@bellarmine.edu. *Dean,* Dr. Robert Cooter, 502-272-8191, Fax: 502-272-8189, E-mail: rcooter@bellarmine.edu.

Donna and Allan Lansing School of Nursing and Health Sciences Students: 210 full-time (145 women), 98 part-time (89 women); includes 17 minority (2 Black or African American, non-Hispanic/Latino; 1 American Indian or Alaska Native, non-Hispanic/Latino; 7 Asian, non-Hispanic/Latino; 1 Hispanic/Latino; 6 Two or more races, non-Hispanic/Latino), 1 international. Average age 28. *Faculty:* 28 full-time (23 women), 5 part-time/adjunct (all women). Expenses: Contact institution. *Financial support:* Career-related internships or fieldwork and scholarships/grants available. Financial award applicants required to submit FAFSA. In 2016, 43 master's, 68 doctorates awarded. *Program availability:* Part-time, evening/weekend. Offers family nurse practitioner (MSN); health science (MHS); nursing administration (MSN); nursing education (MSN); nursing practice (DNP); physical therapy (DPT). *Application deadline:* Applications are processed on a rolling basis. *Application fee:* $40. Electronic applications accepted. *Application Contact:* Julie Armstrong-Binnix, Health Science Recruiter, 800-274-4723 Ext. 8364, E-mail: julieab@bellarmine.edu. *Dean,* Dr. Mark Wiegand, 800-274-4723 Ext. 8368, E-mail: mwiegand@bellarmine.edu.

School of Communication Students: 3 full-time (all women), 25 part-time (16 women); includes 6 minority (5 Black or African American, non-Hispanic/Latino; 1 Hispanic/Latino), 3 international. Average age 29. *Faculty:* 6 full-time (3 women). Expenses: Contact institution. *Financial support:* Applicants required to submit FAFSA. In 2016, 15 master's awarded. *Program availability:* Part-time, evening/weekend. Offers communication (MA, MSDM). *Application deadline:* Applications are processed on a rolling basis. *Application fee:* $40. Electronic applications accepted. *Application Contact:* Dr. Sara Pettingill, Dean of Graduate Admission, 502-272-8401, Fax: 502-272-8002, E-mail: spettingill@bellarmine.edu. *Dean,* Dr. Lara Needham, 502-272-7965, E-mail: lneedham@bellarmine.edu.

School of Continuing and Professional Studies Students: 25 part-time (3 women); includes 4 minority (1 Black or African American, non-Hispanic/Latino; 1 Asian, non-Hispanic/Latino; 2 Hispanic/Latino). Average age 32. *Faculty:* 1 part-time/adjunct (0 women). Expenses: Contact institution. *Program availability:* Part-time, evening/weekend. Offers analytics (MSA). *Application deadline:* Applications are processed on a rolling basis. *Application fee:* $40. Electronic applications accepted. *Application Contact:* Dr. Sara Pettingill, Dean of Graduate Admission, 502-272-8401, E-mail: spettingill@bellarmine.edu. *Vice President of Enrollment Management/Dean of the School of Professional and Continuing Studies,* Dr. Sean Ryan, 502-272-8376, E-mail: sryan@bellarmine.edu.

W. Fielding Rubel School of Business Students: 54 full-time (21 women), 43 part-time (23 women); includes 14 minority (6 Black or African American, non-Hispanic/Latino; 2 Asian, non-Hispanic/Latino; 4 Hispanic/Latino; 2 Two or more races, non-Hispanic/Latino), 2 international. Average age 29. *Faculty:* 13 full-time (4 women). Expenses: Contact institution. *Financial support:* Career-related internships or fieldwork, scholarships/grants, and unspecified assistantships available. Support available to part-time students. Financial award application deadline: 7/1. In 2016, 74 master's awarded. *Program availability:* Part-time, evening/weekend. Offers business (EMBA, MBA, MST). *Application deadline:* Applications are processed on a rolling basis. *Application fee:* $40. Electronic applications accepted. *Application Contact:* Dr. Sara Pettingill, Dean of Graduate Admission, 800-274-4723 Ext. 8258, Fax: 502-272-8002, E-mail: spettingill@bellarmine.edu. *Dean,* Dr. Sharon Kerrick, 800-272-8249, Fax: 502-272-7443, E-mail: skerrick@bellarmine.edu.

BELLEVUE UNIVERSITY, Bellevue, NE 68005-3098
General Information Independent, coed, comprehensive institution. *Graduate housing:* Room and/or apartments available on a first-come, first-served basis to single students; on-campus housing not available to married students.

GRADUATE UNITS
Graduate School *Program availability:* Part-time, evening/weekend, online learning.

College of Arts and Sciences *Program availability:* Online learning. Offers clinical counseling (MS); healthcare administration (MHA); human services (MA); international security and intelligence studies (MS); managerial communication (MA).

College of Business Offers acquisition and contract management (MS); business administration (MBA); finance (MS); human capital management (PhD); management (MSM).

College of Information Technology Offers computer information systems (MS); cybersecurity (MS); management of information systems (MS); project management (MPM).

College of Professional Studies

BELLIN COLLEGE, Green Bay, WI 54305
General Information Independent, coed, primarily women, comprehensive institution. *Graduate housing:* On-campus housing not available.

GRADUATE UNITS
School of Nursing Offers family nurse practitioner (MSN); nurse educator (MSN).

BELMONT UNIVERSITY, Nashville, TN 37212

General Information Independent-religious, coed, university. *Enrollment:* 7,723 graduate, professional, and undergraduate students; 1,331 full-time matriculated graduate/professional students (849 women), 99 part-time matriculated graduate/professional students (61 women). *Enrollment by degree level:* 586 master's, 844 doctoral. *Graduate faculty:* 159 full-time (86 women), 65 part-time/adjunct (29 women). Tuition and fees vary according to program. *Graduate housing:* On-campus housing not available. *Student services:* Campus employment opportunities, campus safety program, career counseling, exercise/wellness program, free psychological counseling, international student services, low-cost health insurance, multicultural affairs office, services for students with disabilities. *Library facilities:* Lila D. Bunch Library plus 1 other. *Collection:* Books: 236,551 (physical), 78,431 (digital/electronic); Serial titles: 35,012 (physical), 800,919 (digital/electronic); Databases: 299. Weekly public service hours: 127; students can reserve study rooms.

Computer facilities: Computer purchase and lease plans are available. 500 computers available on campus for general student use. A campuswide network can be accessed from student residence rooms and from off campus. Online class registration, individual student information via course management system are available.
Website: http://www.belmont.edu/

General Application Contact: David Mee, Dean of Enrollment Services, 615-460-6785, Fax: 615-460-5434, E-mail: david.mee@belmont.edu.

GRADUATE UNITS

College of Health Sciences Students: 384 full-time (320 women), 11 part-time (all women); includes 41 minority (9 Black or African American, non-Hispanic/Latino; 17 Asian, non-Hispanic/Latino; 5 Hispanic/Latino; 10 Two or more races, non-Hispanic/Latino), 2 international. Average age 26. *Faculty:* 30 full-time (26 women), 16 part-time/adjunct (11 women). Expenses: Contact institution. *Financial support:* Teaching assistantships with full tuition reimbursements, career-related internships or fieldwork, scholarships/grants, and traineeships available. Financial award application deadline: 3/1; financial award applicants required to submit FAFSA. In 2016, 52 master's, 79 doctorates awarded. *Program availability:* Part-time, blended/hybrid learning. Offers nursing (MSN, DNP); occupational therapy (MSOT, OTD); physical therapy (DPT). *Application deadline:* Applications are processed on a rolling basis. *Application fee:* $50. Electronic applications accepted. *Application Contact:* Bill Nichols, Director of Enrollment Services, 615-460-6107, E-mail: bill.nichols@belmont.edu. *Dean,* Dr. Cathy Taylor, 615-460-6916, Fax: 615-460-6750.

College of Law Students: 261 full-time (139 women); includes 33 minority (9 Black or African American, non-Hispanic/Latino; 18 Asian, non-Hispanic/Latino; 3 Hispanic/Latino; 1 Native Hawaiian or other Pacific Islander, non-Hispanic/Latino; 3 Two or more races, non-Hispanic/Latino). Average age 26. *Faculty:* 27 full-time (10 women), 8 part-time/adjunct (3 women). Expenses: Contact institution. *Financial support:* Applicants required to submit FAFSA. Offers law (JD). *Application deadline:* For fall admission, 7/31 priority date for domestic students, 7/30 priority date for international students. Applications are processed on a rolling basis. Electronic applications accepted. *Application Contact:* Ehren Green, Director of Admissions, 615-460-8273, Fax: 615-460-5434, E-mail: ehren.green@belmont.edu. *Dean,* Alberto R. Gonzales, 615-460-8259, E-mail: alberto.gonzales@belmont.edu.

College of Pharmacy Students: 305 full-time (185 women); includes 71 minority (23 Black or African American, non-Hispanic/Latino; 37 Asian, non-Hispanic/Latino; 5 Hispanic/Latino; 6 Two or more races, non-Hispanic/Latino), 1 international. Average age 25. *Faculty:* 21 full-time (12 women), 6 part-time/adjunct (3 women). Expenses: Contact institution. *Financial support:* Applicants required to submit FAFSA. Offers pharmacy (Pharm D). *Application deadline:* For fall admission, 8/31 priority date for domestic students; for spring admission, 3/1 for domestic students. Applications are processed on a rolling basis. *Application fee:* $50. Electronic applications accepted. *Application Contact:* Dr. Elinor Gray, Dean of Enrollment Services, 615-460-6790, Fax: 615-460-6741, E-mail: elinor.gray@belmont.edu. *Dean,* Dr. Phil Johnston, 615-460-6746, Fax: 615-460-6741, E-mail: phil.johnston@belmont.edu.

Jack C. Massey Graduate School of Business Students: 154 full-time (72 women), 49 part-time (25 women); includes 30 minority (12 Black or African American, non-Hispanic/Latino; 11 Asian, non-Hispanic/Latino; 4 Hispanic/Latino; 3 Two or more races, non-Hispanic/Latino), 10 international. Average age 28. 148 applicants, 64% accepted, 77 enrolled. *Faculty:* 27 full-time (10 women), 8 part-time/adjunct (3 women). Expenses: Contact institution. *Financial support:* Scholarships/grants, tuition waivers (partial), and unspecified assistantships available. Financial award application deadline: 7/1; financial award applicants required to submit FAFSA. In 2016, 136 master's awarded. *Program availability:* Part-time, evening/weekend. Offers accounting (M Acc); business (AMBA, PMBA); healthcare (MBA). *Application deadline:* For fall admission, 7/1 for domestic and international students; for spring admission, 11/1 for domestic and international students. Applications are processed on a rolling basis. *Application fee:* $50. Electronic applications accepted. *Application Contact:* E-mail: masseyadmissions@belmont.edu. *Dean,* Dr. Patrick Raines, 615-460-6480, Fax: 615-460-6455, E-mail: pat.raines@belmont.edu.

BEMIDJI STATE UNIVERSITY, Bemidji, MN 56601-2699

General Information State-supported, coed, comprehensive institution. CGS member. *Graduate housing:* Room and/or apartments available on a first-come, first-served basis to single students; on-campus housing not available to married students. Housing application deadline: 8/1. *Research affiliation:* National Interscholastic Athletic Administrators Association, Sanford Research, Mossy Oak, Bass Pro Shops.

GRADUATE UNITS

School of Graduate Studies *Program availability:* Part-time, online learning. Offers biology (MS); education (MS); English (MA, MS); environmental studies (MS); mathematics (MS); mathematics (elementary and middle level education) (MS); special education (M Sp Ed). Electronic applications accepted.

BENEDICTINE COLLEGE, Atchison, KS 66002-1499

General Information Independent-religious, coed, comprehensive institution. *Enrollment:* 2,189 graduate, professional, and undergraduate students; 48 full-time matriculated graduate/professional students (19 women), 22 part-time matriculated graduate/professional students (11 women). *Enrollment by degree level:* 67 master's, 3 other advanced degrees. *Graduate faculty:* 10 part-time/adjunct (1 woman). *Tuition:* Part-time $800 per credit hour. *Required fees:* $750 per credit hour. Tuition and fees vary according to program. *Graduate housing:* Room and/or apartments available on a first-come, first-served basis to single students; on-campus housing not available to married students. Typical cost: $9530 (including board). Room and board charges vary according to board plan and housing facility selected. *Student services:* Campus employment opportunities, campus safety program, career counseling, exercise/wellness program, free psychological counseling, international student services, services for students with disabilities, teacher training. *Library facilities:* Benedictine College Library. *Collection:* Books: 198,277 (physical), 139,987 (digital/electronic); Serial titles: 45,794 (physical); Databases: 88. Weekly public service hours: 85.

Computer facilities: Computer purchase and lease plans are available. 100 computers available on campus for general student use. A campuswide network can be accessed from student residence rooms and from off campus. Online class registration is available.
Website: http://www.benedictine.edu/

General Application Contact: Dr. Cheryl Reding, Director, Graduate Programs in Education, 913-360-7384, E-mail: creding@benedictine.edu.

GRADUATE UNITS

Master of Arts in Education Program Expenses: Contact institution. *Financial support:* Unspecified assistantships available. Financial award applicants required to submit FAFSA. In 2016, 3 master's awarded. *Program availability:* Part-time, evening/weekend. Offers education (MA). *Application deadline:* Applications are processed on a rolling basis. *Application fee:* $50. Electronic applications accepted. *Application Contact:* Dr. Cheryl Reding, Director, Graduate Programs in Education, 913-360-7384, E-mail: creding@benedictine.edu.

Master of Arts in School Leadership Program Students: 12 full-time (7 women), 16 part-time (8 women), 1 international. Average age 33. 12 applicants, 83% accepted, 10 enrolled. *Faculty:* 3 part-time/adjunct (1 woman). Expenses: Contact institution. *Financial support:* Scholarships/grants and unspecified assistantships available. Financial award applicants required to submit FAFSA. In 2016, 8 master's awarded. *Program availability:* Part-time, evening/weekend. Offers school leadership (MA). *Application deadline:* Applications are processed on a rolling basis. *Application fee:* $50. Electronic applications accepted. *Application Contact:* Dr. Cheryl Reding, Director, Graduate Programs in Education, 913-360-7384, E-mail: creding@benedictine.edu.

Master of Business Administration Program Students: 36 full-time (12 women), 3 part-time (1 woman); includes 2 minority (1 Black or African American, non-Hispanic/Latino; 1 Hispanic/Latino), 3 international. Average age 27. 34 applicants, 85% accepted, 27 enrolled. *Faculty:* 6 part-time/adjunct (0 women). Expenses: Contact institution. *Financial support:* In 2016–17, 7 students received support. Unspecified assistantships available. Financial award application deadline: 3/15; financial award applicants required to submit FAFSA. In 2016, 12 master's awarded. *Program availability:* Part-time, evening/weekend. Offers business administration (MBA). *Application deadline:* Applications are processed on a rolling basis. *Application fee:* $50. Electronic applications accepted. *Chair, School of Business,* Michael King, 913-360-7160, E-mail: mking@benedictine.edu.

BENEDICTINE UNIVERSITY, Lisle, IL 60532

General Information Independent-religious, coed, comprehensive institution. *Enrollment:* 519 full-time matriculated graduate/professional students (359 women), 2,202 part-time matriculated graduate/professional students (1,563 women). *Enrollment by degree level:* 2,600 master's, 112 doctoral, 9 other advanced degrees. *Graduate faculty:* 34 full-time (21 women), 241 part-time/adjunct (128 women). *Tuition:* Full-time $15,600; part-time $650 per hour. *Required fees:* $300. One-time fee: $125 part-time. Tuition and fees vary according to class time, course load, campus/location and program. *Graduate housing:* On-campus housing not available. *Student services:* Campus employment opportunities, campus safety program, career counseling, free psychological counseling, international student services, services for students with disabilities. *Library facilities:* Benedictine Library.

Computer facilities: A campuswide network can be accessed from student residence rooms and from off campus. Online class registration is available.
Website: http://www.ben.edu/

General Application Contact: Kari Gibbons, Associate Vice President, Enrollment Center, 630-829-6200, Fax: 630-829-6584, E-mail: kgibbons@ben.edu.

GRADUATE UNITS

Graduate Programs Students: 478 full-time (299 women), 1,930 part-time (1,407 women); includes 590 minority (345 Black or African American, non-Hispanic/Latino; 16 American Indian or Alaska Native, non-Hispanic/Latino; 149 Asian, non-Hispanic/Latino; 75 Hispanic/Latino; 5 Native Hawaiian or other Pacific Islander, non-Hispanic/Latino), 47 international. Average age 33. 801 applicants, 87% accepted, 537 enrolled. *Faculty:* 34 full-time (21 women), 241 part-time/adjunct (128 women). Expenses: Contact institution. *Financial support:* Career-related internships or fieldwork and health care benefits available. Support available to part-time students. In 2016, 933 master's, 29 doctorates awarded. *Program availability:* Part-time, evening/weekend, online learning. Offers accountancy (MS); accounting (MS); administration of health care institutions (MPH); clinical exercise physiology (MS); clinical psychology (MS); curriculum and instruction and collaborative teaching (M Ed); dietetics (MPH); disaster management (MPH); elementary education (MA Ed); entrepreneurship and managing innovation (MBA); financial management (MBA); health administration (MBA); health education (MPH); health information systems (MPH); higher education and organizational change (Ed D); human resource management (MBA); information systems security (MBA); international business (MBA); leadership (MS); leadership and administration (M Ed); management and organizational behavior (MS, PhD); management consulting (MBA); management information systems (MS); marketing management (MBA); nursing (MSN); nutrition and wellness (MS); operations management and logistics (MBA); organization development (PhD); organizational leadership (MBA); reading and literacy (M Ed); science content and process (MS); secondary education (MA Ed); special education (MA Ed); values-driven leadership (DBA, PhD). *Application deadline:* For fall admission, 9/1 for domestic students; for winter admission, 12/1 for domestic students; for spring admission, 2/15 for domestic students. Applications are processed on a rolling basis. *Application fee:* $40. Electronic applications accepted. *Application Contact:* Kari Gibbons, Associate Vice President, Enrollment Center, 630-829-6200, Fax: 630-829-6584, E-mail: kgibbons@ben.edu. *Provost and Vice President for Academic Affairs,* Dr. Donald B. Taylor, 630-829-6240, Fax: 630-829-6369.

BENNINGTON COLLEGE, Bennington, VT 05201

General Information Independent, coed, comprehensive institution. *Graduate housing:* Room and/or apartments available on a first-come, first-served basis to single students; on-campus housing not available to married students.

GRADUATE UNITS

Graduate Programs *Program availability:* Part-time, online learning. Offers allied and health sciences (Certificate); dance (MFA); music (MFA); writing (MFA).

BENTLEY UNIVERSITY, Waltham, MA 02452-4705

General Information Independent, coed, comprehensive institution. *Enrollment:* 5,508 graduate, professional, and undergraduate students; 750 full-time matriculated graduate/professional students (466 women), 534 part-time matriculated graduate/professional students (262 women). *Enrollment by degree level:* 1,250 master's, 24 doctoral, 10 other advanced degrees. *Graduate faculty:* 71 full-time (25 women), 33 part-time/adjunct (15 women). *Tuition:* Part-time $1408 per credit. *Required fees:* $160 per credit. *Graduate housing:* Room and/or apartments available on a first-come, first-served basis to single students; on-campus housing not available to married students. Typical cost: $11,570 per year ($17,390 including board). *Student services:* Campus employment opportunities, campus safety program, career counseling, exercise/wellness program, free psychological counseling, international student services, low-cost health insurance, multicultural affairs office, services for students with disabilities. *Library facilities:* Bentley Library. *Collection:* Books: 183,873 (physical), 202,640 (digital/electronic); Serial titles: 1,650 (physical), 80,549 (digital/electronic); Databases: 87. Weekly public service hours: 110; students can reserve study rooms.

Computer facilities: Computer purchase and lease plans are available. 4,490 computers available on campus for general student use. A campuswide network can be accessed from student residence rooms and from off campus. Online class registration, learning management system, student employment, free software are available. Website: http://www.bentley.edu/

General Application Contact: Sharon Hill, Assistant Dean/Director of Graduate Admissions, 781-891-2108, Fax: 781-891-2464, E-mail: bentleygraduateadmissions@bentley.edu.

GRADUATE UNITS

Graduate School of Business Students: 750 full-time (466 women), 534 part-time (262 women); includes 145 minority (29 Black or African American, non-Hispanic/Latino; 3 American Indian or Alaska Native, non-Hispanic/Latino; 74 Asian, non-Hispanic/Latino; 29 Hispanic/Latino; 10 Two or more races, non-Hispanic/Latino; 577 international). Average age 28. 1,680 applicants, 68% accepted, 511 enrolled. *Faculty:* 71 full-time (25 women), 33 part-time/adjunct (15 women). Expenses: Contact institution. *Financial support:* In 2016–17, 277 students received support. Scholarships/grants, tuition waivers (partial), and unspecified assistantships available. Support available to part-time students. Financial award application deadline: 6/1; financial award applicants required to submit FAFSA. In 2016, 620 master's, 6 doctorates, 118 other advanced degrees awarded. *Program availability:* Part-time, evening/weekend, 100% online, blended/hybrid learning. Offers accountancy (PhD); accounting (GBC); business (MBA, MSA, MSF, MSFP, MSHFID, MSIT, MSMA, MST, PhD, Certificate, GBC, GSS); business administration (MBA); business analytics (GBC); business ethics (GBC); finance (MSF); financial planning (MSFP); fraud and forensic accounting (GBC); human factors in information design (MSHFID); information technology (MSIT); marketing analytics (MSMA); taxation (MST). *Application deadline:* Applications are processed on a rolling basis. *Application fee:* $50. Electronic applications accepted. *Application Contact:* Sharon Hill, Assistant Dean/Director of Graduate Admissions, 781-891-2108, Fax: 781-891-2464, E-mail: bentleygraduateadmissions@bentley.edu. *Acting Co-Provost, Dean of Business,* Dr. Roy A. Wiggins, III, 781-891-3166.

BERGIN UNIVERSITY OF CANINE STUDIES, Rohnert Park, CA 94928

General Information Independent, coed, comprehensive institution. *Graduate housing:* On-campus housing not available.

GRADUATE UNITS

Program in Canine Life Sciences *Program availability:* Online learning. Offers canine life sciences (MS).

BERKELEY COLLEGE–WOODLAND PARK CAMPUS, Woodland Park, NJ 07424

General Information Proprietary, coed, comprehensive institution.

GRADUATE UNITS

MBA Program Offers management (MBA).

BERKLEE COLLEGE OF MUSIC, Boston, MA 02215-3693

General Information Independent, coed, comprehensive institution. *Enrollment:* 368 full-time matriculated graduate/professional students (174 women), 41 part-time matriculated graduate/professional students (27 women). *Enrollment by degree level:* 363 master's, 46 other advanced degrees. *Graduate faculty:* 140 full-time (53 women), 82 part-time/adjunct (31 women). *Tuition:* Full-time $47,500. *Required fees:* $1215. Tuition and fees vary according to campus/location and program. *Graduate housing:* On-campus housing not available. *Student services:* Campus employment opportunities, campus safety program, career counseling, exercise/wellness program, free psychological counseling, grant writing training, international student services, low-cost health insurance, multicultural affairs office, services for students with disabilities, teacher training, writing training. *Library facilities:* The Stan Getz Media Center and Library.

Computer facilities: Computer purchase and lease plans are available. A campuswide network can be accessed from student residence rooms. Online class registration is available. Website: http://www.berklee.edu/

General Application Contact: 617-747-2221, Fax: 617-747-2047, E-mail: admissions@berklee.edu.

GRADUATE UNITS

Berklee Graduate Programs Students: 159 full-time (51 women), 30 part-time (24 women); includes 35 minority (12 Black or African American, non-Hispanic/Latino; 7 Asian, non-Hispanic/Latino; 12 Hispanic/Latino; 4 Two or more races, non-Hispanic/Latino; 78 international. Average age 26. 774 applicants, 36% accepted, 177 enrolled. *Faculty:* 53 full-time (18 women), 39 part-time/adjunct (7 women). Expenses: Contact institution. *Financial support:* In 2016–17, 161 students received support, including 120 fellowships with full and partial tuition reimbursements available (averaging $18,507 per year), 41 research assistantships (averaging $4,220 per year); career-related internships or fieldwork, scholarships/grants, and tuition waivers (full and partial) also available. Support available to part-time students. Financial award application deadline: 2/1; financial award applicants required to submit CSS PROFILE or FAFSA. In 2016, 137 master's awarded. *Program availability:* Part-time, blended/hybrid learning. Offers contemporary performance (MM); global entertainment and music business (MA); music production, technology, and innovation (MM); music therapy (MA); scoring for film, television, and video games (MM). Production: global entertainment and music business; music production, technology, and innovation; and scoring for film, television, and video games programs offered at Valencia, Spain campus. *Application deadline:* For fall admission, 2/1 for domestic and international students. *Application fee:* $150.

Electronic applications accepted. *Application Contact:* Office of Admissions, 617-747-2221, E-mail: admissions@berklee.edu. *Dean, Institutional Assessment and Graduate Studies,* Camille Colatosi, PhD, E-mail: ccolatosti@berklee.edu.

The Boston Conservatory at Berklee Students: 209 full-time (123 women), 11 part-time (3 women); includes 44 minority (7 Black or African American, non-Hispanic/Latino; 11 Asian, non-Hispanic/Latino; 15 Hispanic/Latino; 1 Native Hawaiian or other Pacific Islander, non-Hispanic/Latino; 10 Two or more races, non-Hispanic/Latino; 67 international). Average age 25. 568 applicants, 41% accepted, 86 enrolled. *Faculty:* 87 full-time (35 women), 43 part-time/adjunct (24 women). Expenses: Contact institution. *Financial support:* In 2016–17, 236 students received support. Federal Work-Study and scholarships/grants available. Financial award application deadline: 12/1; financial award applicants required to submit FAFSA. In 2016, 77 master's, 14 other advanced degrees awarded. *Program availability:* Part-time. Offers bassoon performance (MM); cello performance (MM); choral conducting (MM); clarinet performance (MM); collaborative piano (MM); composition (MM); contemporary music performance (MM); double bass performance (MM); flute performance (MM); harp performance (MM); horn performance (MM); marimba performance (MM); music and autism (Certificate); music education (MM); music education and autism (MM); music performance (ADP); musical theater (MFA); oboe performance (MM); opera performance (MM); orchestral conducting (MM); percussion performance (MM); piano performance (MM); saxophone performance (MM); trombone performance (MM); trumpet performance (MM). *Application deadline:* For fall admission, 12/15 for domestic and international students. *Application fee:* $110. Electronic applications accepted. *Application Contact:* Director of Admissions, 617-912-9153, Fax: 617-912-9217, E-mail: admissions@bostonconservatory.edu. *Dean, Institutional Assessment and Graduate Studies,* Camille Colatosi, PhD, E-mail: ccolatosti@berklee.edu.

BERRY COLLEGE, Mount Berry, GA 30149-0159

General Information Independent-religious, coed, comprehensive institution. *Enrollment:* 2,174 graduate, professional, and undergraduate students; 36 full-time matriculated graduate/professional students (28 women), 65 part-time matriculated graduate/professional students (39 women). *Enrollment by degree level:* 33 master's, 68 other advanced degrees. *Graduate faculty:* 2 full-time (0 women), 17 part-time/adjunct (10 women). *Tuition:* Full-time $10,890; part-time $605 per credit hour. *Graduate housing:* On-campus housing not available. *Student services:* Campus employment opportunities, campus safety program, career counseling, child daycare facilities, exercise/wellness program, free psychological counseling, grant writing training, international student services, multicultural affairs office, services for students with disabilities, teacher training, writing training. *Library facilities:* Memorial Library plus 1 other. *Collection:* Books: 213,724 (physical), 375,698 (digital/electronic); Serial titles: 9,234 (physical), 52,975 (digital/electronic); Databases: 266. Weekly public service hours: 106; students can reserve study rooms. *Research affiliation:* Georgia Professional Standards Commission (education), Koch Foundation (business and economics), South Rome Early Learning Center (education), Marcus Autism Center (psychology and education), South Rome Development Corporation (education), Rome-Floyd County Commission on Children and Youth (education and psychology).

Computer facilities: 200 computers available on campus for general student use. A campuswide network can be accessed from student residence rooms and from off campus. Online class registration is available. Website: http://www.berry.edu/

General Application Contact: Brett Kennedy, Assistant Vice President of Enrollment Management, 706-236-2215, Fax: 706-290-2178, E-mail: admissions@berry.edu.

GRADUATE UNITS

Graduate Programs Students: 36 full-time (28 women), 65 part-time (39 women); includes 24 minority (19 Black or African American, non-Hispanic/Latino; 5 Hispanic/Latino). Average age 38. *Faculty:* 2 full-time (0 women), 17 part-time/adjunct (10 women). Expenses: Contact institution. *Financial support:* In 2016–17, 24 students received support, including 11 research assistantships with full tuition reimbursements available (averaging $6,930 per year); scholarships/grants, tuition waivers (partial), and unspecified assistantships also available. Support available to part-time students. Financial award application deadline: 3/1; financial award applicants required to submit FAFSA. In 2016, 17 master's, 76 other advanced degrees awarded. *Program availability:* Part-time, evening/weekend. Offers curriculum and instruction (M Ed, Ed S); early childhood education (M Ed, MAT); educational leadership (Ed S); middle grades education (M Ed); middle-grades education (M Ed); middle-grades education and reading (M Ed, MAT); reading (M Ed); secondary education (MAT). *Application deadline:* For fall admission, 7/21 for domestic students; 5/1 for international students; for spring admission, 12/1 for domestic students, 2/1 for international students. Applications are processed on a rolling basis. *Application fee:* $25 ($30 for international students). Electronic applications accepted. *Application Contact:* Brett Kennedy, Assistant Vice President of Enrollment Management, 706-236-2215, Fax: 706-290-2178, E-mail: admissions@berry.edu. *Interim Provost,* Dr. Andrew R. Bressette, 706-236-2216, Fax: 706-290-2179, E-mail: provostoffice@berry.edu.

Campbell School of Business Students: 2 full-time (1 woman), 21 part-time (7 women); includes 3 minority (2 Black or African American, non-Hispanic/Latino; 1 Hispanic/Latino). Average age 31. *Faculty:* 6 part-time/adjunct (2 women). Expenses: Contact institution. *Financial support:* In 2016–17, 18 students received support, including 11 research assistantships with full tuition reimbursements available (averaging $6,930 per year); scholarships/grants, tuition waivers (partial), and unspecified assistantships also available. Support available to part-time students. Financial award application deadline: 3/1; financial award applicants required to submit FAFSA. In 2016, 11 master's awarded. *Program availability:* Part-time, evening/weekend. Offers business (MBA). *Application deadline:* For fall admission, 7/21 for domestic students; for spring admission, 12/1 for domestic students. Applications are processed on a rolling basis. *Application fee:* $25 ($30 for international students). Electronic applications accepted. *Application Contact:* Brett Kennedy, Assistant Vice President of Enrollment Management, 706-236-2215, Fax: 706-290-2178, E-mail: admissions@berry.edu. *Dean,* Dr. Joyce Heames, 706-236-2233, Fax: 706-802-6728, E-mail: jheames@berry.edu.

BETHANY COLLEGE, Bethany, WV 26032

General Information Independent-religious, coed, comprehensive institution. *Graduate housing:* Room and/or apartments available on a first-come, first-served basis to single students; on-campus housing not available to married students. *Student services:* Campus employment opportunities, career counseling, free psychological counseling, services for students with disabilities, teacher training. *Library facilities:* T. W. Phillips

Memorial Library. *Collection:* Books: 126,369 (physical), 135,500 (digital/electronic); Serial titles: 3,975 (physical); Databases: 50. Weekly public service hours: 88.

Computer facilities: 145 computers available on campus for general student use. A campuswide network can be accessed from student residence rooms and from off campus. Online class registration is available.
Website: http://www.bethanywv.edu/

General Application Contact: Mollie Cecere, Vice President for Enrollment Management, 800-922-7611, E-mail: enrollment@bethanywv.edu.

GRADUATE UNITS

Master of Arts in Teaching Program Expenses: Contact institution. *Financial support:* Unspecified assistantships available. Financial award applicants required to submit FAFSA. *Program availability:* Part-time. Offers teaching (MAT). *Application deadline:* Applications are processed on a rolling basis. *Application fee:* $0. Electronic applications accepted. *Application Contact:* Mollie Cecere, Vice President for Enrollment Management, 304-829-7611, E-mail: mcecere@bethanywv.edu. *MAT Program Director,* Dr. Edward Shephard, 304-829-7176, E-mail: eshephard@bethanywv.edu.

BETHANY GLOBAL UNIVERSITY, Bloomington, MN 55438

General Information Independent-religious, coed, comprehensive institution. *Enrollment by degree level:* 39 master's. *Graduate faculty:* 1 full-time (0 women), 5 part-time/adjunct (0 women). *Graduate housing:* On-campus housing not available. *Student services:* International student services, teacher training, writing training.
Website: http://www.bethanygu.edu/

General Application Contact: Katherin Lawlor, Admissions Coordinator, 952-918-1894, E-mail: katherin.lawlor@bethanygu.edu.

GRADUATE UNITS

Graduate Programs Students: 39 part-time (13 women). *Faculty:* 1 full-time (0 women), 5 part-time/adjunct (0 women). Expenses: Contact institution. *Program availability:* Part-time, evening/weekend, online only, 100% online. Offers intercultural ministry education (MA); intercultural ministry leadership (MA); intercultural ministry studies (MA). Electronic applications accepted. *Application Contact:* Dr. Jim Raymo, Director, 952-829-4680, E-mail: jim.raymo@bethanygu.edu. *Director,* Dr. Jim Raymo, 952-829-4680, E-mail: jim.raymo@bethanygu.edu.

BETHANY THEOLOGICAL SEMINARY, Richmond, IN 47374-4019

General Information Independent-religious, coed, graduate-only institution. *Graduate housing:* On-campus housing not available.

GRADUATE UNITS

Graduate and Professional Programs *Program availability:* Part-time, online learning. Offers biblical studies (MA Th); ministry studies (M Div); peace studies (M Div, MA Th); theological studies (MA Th, CATS); youth ministry (M Div).

BETHEL COLLEGE, Mishawaka, IN 46545-5591

General Information Independent-religious, coed, comprehensive institution. *Enrollment:* 1,639 graduate, professional, and undergraduate students; 59 full-time matriculated graduate/professional students (40 women), 192 part-time matriculated graduate/professional students (117 women). *Enrollment by degree level:* 251 master's. *Graduate faculty:* 1 (woman) full-time, 38 part-time/adjunct (16 women). *Tuition:* Full-time $6750; part-time $3375 per credit hour. *Required fees:* $75 per semester. Tuition and fees vary according to course load and program. *Graduate housing:* On-campus housing not available. *Student services:* Campus employment opportunities, campus safety program, career counseling, free psychological counseling, international student services, services for students with disabilities, writing training. *Library facilities:* Otis and Elizabeth Bowen Library. *Collection:* Books: 95,315 (physical), 159,582 (digital/electronic); Serial titles: 825 (physical), 53,615 (digital/electronic); Databases: 90. Weekly public service hours: 83.

Computer facilities: 160 computers available on campus for general student use. A campuswide network can be accessed from student residence rooms.
Website: http://www.bethelcollege.edu/

General Application Contact: Dr. Toni Steffensen Pauls, Vice President of Adult and Graduate Studies, 574-807-7550, Fax: 574-807-7551.

GRADUATE UNITS

Adult and Graduate Programs Students: 59 full-time (40 women), 192 part-time (117 women); includes 45 minority (29 Black or African American, non-Hispanic/Latino; 11 Hispanic/Latino; 5 Two or more races, non-Hispanic/Latino), 6 international. Average age 37. 148 applicants, 66% accepted, 91 enrolled. *Faculty:* 1 (woman) full-time, 38 part-time/adjunct (16 women). Expenses: Contact institution. *Financial support:* Career-related internships or fieldwork available. Financial award applicants required to submit FAFSA. In 2016, 71 master's awarded. *Program availability:* Part-time, evening/weekend, 100% online, blended/hybrid learning. Offers business administration (MBA); education (M Ed, MAT); ministries (M Min); nursing (MSN); theological studies (MATS). *Application deadline:* For fall admission, 5/1 for international students; for spring admission, 10/1 for international students. Applications are processed on a rolling basis. *Application fee:* $0. Electronic applications accepted. *Vice President for Adult and Graduate Studies,* Dr. Toni Pauls, 574-807-7400, Fax: 574-807-7551, E-mail: toni.pauls@bethelcollege.edu.

BETHEL SEMINARY, St. Paul, MN 55112-6998

General Information Independent-religious, coed, graduate-only institution. *Enrollment by degree level:* 457 master's, 52 doctoral, 7 other advanced degrees. *Graduate faculty:* 14 full-time (4 women), 37 part-time/adjunct (17 women). *Tuition:* Full-time $7425; part-time $495 per credit. *Required fees:* $31 per semester. *Graduate housing:* On-campus housing not available. *Student services:* Campus employment opportunities, campus safety program, career counseling, child daycare facilities, exercise/wellness program, free psychological counseling, international student services, multicultural affairs office, services for students with disabilities, writing training. *Library facilities:* Carl H. Lundquist Library plus 2 others. *Collection:* Books: 262,412 (physical), 150,147 (digital/electronic); Serial titles: 25,812 (physical), 30,657 (digital/electronic); Databases: 120. Weekly public service hours: 57; students can reserve study rooms.

Computer facilities: 19 computers available on campus for general student use. A campuswide network can be accessed. Online class registration is available.
Website: http://seminary.bethel.edu/

General Application Contact: Jen Niska, Director of Admissions, 651-638-6288, Fax: 651-638-6002, E-mail: seminary-admissions@bethel.edu.

GRADUATE UNITS

Graduate and Professional Programs Students: 369 full-time (165 women), 147 part-time (43 women); includes 138 minority (48 Black or African American, non-Hispanic/Latino; 45 Asian, non-Hispanic/Latino; 28 Hispanic/Latino; 2 Native Hawaiian or other Pacific Islander, non-Hispanic/Latino; 15 Two or more races, non-Hispanic/Latino), 15 international. 322 applicants, 75% accepted, 174 enrolled. *Faculty:* 14 full-time (4 women), 37 part-time/adjunct (17 women). Expenses: Contact institution. *Financial support:* In 2016–17, 404 students received support. Teaching assistantships, career-related internships or fieldwork, Federal Work-Study, and scholarships/grants available. Financial award applicants required to submit FAFSA. In 2016, 168 master's, 24 doctorates, 6 other advanced degrees awarded. *Program availability:* Part-time, evening/weekend, blended/hybrid learning. Offers Anglican studies (Certificate); children's and family ministry (MA); Christian studies (Certificate); Christian thought (MA); church planting (Certificate); Greek and Hebrew language (M Div); Greek language (M Div); Hebrew language (M Div); marriage and family therapy (MA, Certificate); mental health counseling (MA); ministry (MA, D Min); ministry practice (Certificate); theological studies (MA, Certificate); transformational leadership (MA); young life youth ministry (Certificate). *Application deadline:* For fall admission, 8/1 priority date for domestic students; for winter admission, 12/1 priority date for domestic students; for spring admission, 1/1 priority date for domestic students. Applications are processed on a rolling basis. *Application fee:* $0. Electronic applications accepted. *Application Contact:* Jen Niska, Director of Admissions, 651-638-6288, Fax: 651-638-6002, E-mail: seminary-admissions@bethel.edu. *Vice-President and Dean,* Dr. David Clark, 651-638-6659, E-mail: d-clark@bethel.edu.

BETHEL UNIVERSITY, St. Paul, MN 55112-6999

General Information Independent-religious, coed, comprehensive institution. *Enrollment:* 4,615 graduate, professional, and undergraduate students; 674 full-time matriculated graduate/professional students (466 women), 378 part-time matriculated graduate/professional students (256 women). *Enrollment by degree level:* 930 master's, 266 doctoral, 64 other advanced degrees. *Graduate faculty:* 19 full-time (15 women), 57 part-time/adjunct (37 women). *Tuition:* Full-time $12,840; part-time $535 per credit. *Graduate housing:* On-campus housing not available. *Student services:* Campus employment opportunities, campus safety program, career counseling, child daycare facilities, exercise/wellness program, international student services, low-cost health insurance, multicultural affairs office, services for students with disabilities, teacher training, writing training. *Library facilities:* Bethel University Library plus 1 other. *Collection:* Books: 141,904 (physical), 153,597 (digital/electronic); Serial titles: 890 (physical), 31,538 (digital/electronic); Databases: 93. Weekly public service hours: 96; students can reserve study rooms.

Computer facilities: Computer purchase and lease plans are available. 203 computers available on campus for general student use. A campuswide network can be accessed from student residence rooms and from off campus. Online class registration is available.
Website: http://www.bethel.edu/

General Application Contact: Director of Admissions, 651-635-8000, Fax: 651-635-8004, E-mail: gs@bethel.edu.

GRADUATE UNITS

Graduate School Students: 674 full-time (466 women), 378 part-time (256 women); includes 188 minority (94 Black or African American, non-Hispanic/Latino; 3 American Indian or Alaska Native, non-Hispanic/Latino; 43 Asian, non-Hispanic/Latino; 31 Hispanic/Latino; 1 Native Hawaiian or other Pacific Islander, non-Hispanic/Latino; 16 Two or more races, non-Hispanic/Latino), 33 international. *Faculty:* 19 full-time (15 women), 57 part-time/adjunct (37 women). Expenses: Contact institution. *Financial support:* Teaching assistantships, career-related internships or fieldwork, and scholarships/grants available. Support available to part-time students. Financial award applicants required to submit FAFSA. *Program availability:* Part-time, evening/weekend, 100% online, blended/hybrid learning. Offers business administration (MBA); classroom management (Certificate); counseling (MA); international baccalaureate teaching and learning (Certificate); K-12 education (MA); leadership (Ed D); leadership foundations (Certificate); nurse educator (MS, Certificate); nurse-midwifery (MS); physician assistant (MS); special education (MA); strategic leadership (MA); teaching (MA). *Application deadline:* Applications are processed on a rolling basis. *Application fee:* $0. Electronic applications accepted. *Application Contact:* Director of Admissions, 651-635-8000, Fax: 651-635-8004, E-mail: gs@bethel.edu. *Vice-President/Dean,* Dick Crombie, 651-635-8000, Fax: 651-635-8004, E-mail: gs@bethel.edu.

BETHEL UNIVERSITY, McKenzie, TN 38201

General Information Independent-religious, coed, comprehensive institution. *Graduate housing:* Room and/or apartments available on a first-come, first-served basis to single students; on-campus housing not available to married students. Housing application deadline: 7/31.

GRADUATE UNITS

Graduate Programs *Program availability:* Part-time, evening/weekend. Offers administration and supervision (MA Ed); business administration (MBA); conflict resolution (MA); physician assistant studies (MS).

BETHESDA UNIVERSITY, Anaheim, CA 92801

General Information Independent-religious, coed, comprehensive institution.

GRADUATE UNITS

Graduate and Professional Programs Offers biblical studies (MA); music (MA); theology (M Div).

BETH HAMEDRASH SHAAREI YOSHER INSTITUTE, Brooklyn, NY 11204

General Information Independent-religious, men only, comprehensive institution.
GRADUATE UNITS
Graduate Programs

BETH HATALMUD RABBINICAL COLLEGE, Brooklyn, NY 11214

General Information Independent-religious, men only, comprehensive institution.
GRADUATE UNITS
Graduate Programs

BETH MEDRASH GOVOHA, Lakewood, NJ 08701-2797

General Information Independent-religious, men only, comprehensive institution.
GRADUATE UNITS
Graduate Programs

BETHUNE-COOKMAN UNIVERSITY, Daytona Beach, FL 32114-3099

General Information Independent-religious, coed, comprehensive institution.

GRADUATE UNITS

School of Graduate Studies *Program availability:* Online learning. Offers transformative leadership (MS). Electronic applications accepted.

BEULAH HEIGHTS UNIVERSITY, Atlanta, GA 30316

General Information Independent-religious, coed, comprehensive institution.

GRADUATE UNITS

Graduate School Offers biblical studies (MA); leadership studies (MA). Electronic applications accepted.

BEXLEY SEABURY SEMINARY, Chicago, IL 60637

General Information Independent-religious, coed, graduate-only institution. *Enrollment by degree level:* 28 doctoral, 17 other advanced degrees. *Graduate faculty:* 2 full-time (1 woman), 10 part-time/adjunct (3 women). *Tuition:* Full-time $14,160; part-time $3540 per course. One-time fee: $150. *Graduate housing:* On-campus housing not available. *Student services:* Career counseling, low-cost health insurance. *Library facilities:* United Library.

Computer facilities: A campuswide network can be accessed.
Website: http://www.bexleyseabury.edu/

General Application Contact: Jaime Briceno, Recruiter and Digital Missioner, 773-380-7045, Fax: 773-380-6788, E-mail: jbriceno@bexleyseabury.edu.

GRADUATE UNITS

Graduate Programs Students: 45 part-time (20 women); includes 6 minority (2 Black or African American, non-Hispanic/Latino; 2 American Indian or Alaska Native, non-Hispanic/Latino; 2 Hispanic/Latino), 2 international. *Faculty:* 2 full-time (1 woman), 10 part-time/adjunct (3 women). Expenses: Contact institution. *Financial support:* Career-related internships or fieldwork, institutionally sponsored loans, and scholarships/grants available. Financial award application deadline: 5/1; financial award applicants required to submit FAFSA. *Program availability:* Part-time. Offers Anglican studies (Diploma); congregational development (D Min); preaching (D Min); theology (M Div). *Application deadline:* Applications are processed on a rolling basis. *Application fee:* $25. *Application Contact:* Jaime Briceno, Recruiter and Digital Missioner, 773-380-7045, Fax: 773-380-5788, E-mail: jbriceno@bexleyseabury.edu. *President,* Roger A. Ferlo, 773-380-6782, E-mail: rferlo@bexleyseabury.edu.

BIBLICAL THEOLOGICAL SEMINARY, Hatfield, PA 19440-2499

General Information Independent-religious, coed, graduate-only institution. *Enrollment by degree level:* 204 master's, 34 doctoral, 18 other advanced degrees. *Graduate faculty:* 9 full-time (1 woman), 21 part-time/adjunct (4 women). *Tuition:* Full-time $12,360; part-time $6180 per credit. *Required fees:* $75; $75 per credit. $50 per semester. *Graduate housing:* Rooms and/or apartments available on a first-come, first-served basis to single and married students. Typical cost: $7565 per year for single students; $15,130 per year for married students. Housing application deadline: 8/30. *Student services:* Campus employment opportunities, career counseling, international student services. *Library facilities:* BTS Library plus 1 other. *Collection:* Books: 43,390 (physical), 140,000 (digital/electronic); Serial titles: 13,572 (physical), 220 (digital/electronic); Databases: 10. Weekly public service hours: 36. *Research affiliation:* Christian Counseling and Education Foundation (psychology).

Computer facilities: 20 computers available on campus for general student use.
Website: http://www.biblical.edu/

General Application Contact: Patsy Byrd, Administrative Coordinator for Student Advancement, 215-368-5000 Ext. 106, Fax: 215-368-7002, E-mail: pbyrd@biblical.edu.

GRADUATE UNITS

Graduate and Professional Programs Students: 145 full-time (54 women), 111 part-time (44 women); includes 98 minority (57 Black or African American, non-Hispanic/Latino; 1 American Indian or Alaska Native, non-Hispanic/Latino; 35 Asian, non-Hispanic/Latino; 4 Hispanic/Latino; 1 Two or more races, non-Hispanic/Latino), 67 international. Average age 39. 165 applicants, 64% accepted, 95 enrolled. *Faculty:* 9 full-time (1 woman), 21 part-time/adjunct (4 women). Expenses: Contact institution. *Financial support:* In 2016–17, 170 students received support. Career-related internships or fieldwork, institutionally sponsored loans, and scholarships/grants available. Support available to part-time students. Financial award application deadline: 8/30; financial award applicants required to submit FAFSA. In 2016, 47 master's, 7 doctorates awarded. *Program availability:* Part-time, evening/weekend. Offers advanced missional leadership (D Min); advanced pastoral studies (Certificate); biblical counseling (Certificate); biblical studies (MA, Certificate); counseling (MA); ministry (M Div, MA); missional theology (MA). *Application deadline:* Applications are processed on a rolling basis. *Application fee:* $30. Electronic applications accepted. *Application Contact:* Rev. Michael Heath, Student Advancement Counselor, 215-368-5000 Ext. 152, Fax: 215-368-7002, E-mail: mheath@biblical.edu.

BINGHAMTON UNIVERSITY, STATE UNIVERSITY OF NEW YORK, Binghamton, NY 13902-6000

General Information State-supported, coed, university. CGS member. *Enrollment:* 17,292 graduate, professional, and undergraduate students; 2,076 full-time matriculated graduate/professional students (915 women), 1,498 part-time matriculated graduate/professional students (792 women). *Enrollment by degree level:* 2,125 master's, 1,394 doctoral, 55 other advanced degrees. *Graduate faculty:* 667 full-time (282 women), 333 part-time/adjunct (164 women). *Graduate housing:* Room and/or apartments available on a first-come, first-served basis to single students; on-campus housing not available to married students. *Student services:* Campus employment opportunities, campus safety program, career counseling, child daycare facilities, exercise/wellness program, free psychological counseling, grant writing training, international student services, low-cost health insurance, multicultural affairs office, services for students with disabilities, teacher training, writing training. *Library facilities:* Glenn G. Bartle Library plus 4 others. *Collection:* Books: 2.3 million (physical), 1.1 million (digital/electronic); Serial titles: 683 (physical), 125,064 (digital/electronic); Databases: 358. Weekly public service hours: 136; study areas open 24 hours, 5–7 days a week; students can reserve study rooms. *Research affiliation:* United Health Services Hospitals (health care, engineering), Mount Sinai Hospital (health care, engineering), Lockheed Martin Corporation (engineering, management, mathematics), Matco Company (engineering), IBM (engineering), Universal Instruments (engineering).

Computer facilities: 1,190 computers available on campus for general student use. A campuswide network can be accessed from student residence rooms and from off campus. Online class registration, course management system, personal Web space, wiki, virtual desktop are available.
Website: http://www.binghamton.edu/

General Application Contact: Dr. Susan Strehle, Vice Provost and Dean of the Graduate School, 607-777-2070, Fax: 607-777-2501, E-mail: sstrehle@binghamton.edu.

GRADUATE UNITS

Graduate School Students: 2,076 full-time (915 women), 1,498 part-time (792 women); includes 485 minority (115 Black or African American, non-Hispanic/Latino; 10 American Indian or Alaska Native, non-Hispanic/Latino; 181 Asian, non-Hispanic/Latino; 147 Hispanic/Latino; 3 Native Hawaiian or other Pacific Islander, non-Hispanic/Latino; 29 Two or more races, non-Hispanic/Latino), 1,523 international. Average age 29. 5,044 applicants, 65% accepted, 1299 enrolled. *Faculty:* 667 full-time (282 women), 333 part-time/adjunct (164 women). Expenses: Contact institution. *Financial support:* In 2016–17, 1,150 students received support, including 7 fellowships with full tuition reimbursements available (averaging $11,000 per year), 180 research assistantships with full tuition reimbursements available (averaging $15,000 per year), 543 teaching assistantships with full tuition reimbursements available (averaging $15,000 per year); career-related internships or fieldwork, Federal Work-Study, institutionally sponsored loans, scholarships/grants, traineeships, health care benefits, tuition waivers (full and partial), and unspecified assistantships also available. Support available to part-time students. Financial award applicants required to submit FAFSA. In 2016, 1,013 master's, 139 doctorates, 43 other advanced degrees awarded. *Program availability:* Part-time, evening/weekend, online learning. Offers sustainable communities (MA, MS). *Application deadline:* Applications are processed on a rolling basis. *Application fee:* $75. Electronic applications accepted. *Application Contact:* Ben Balkaya, Assistant Dean and Director, 607-777-2151, Fax: 607-777-2501, E-mail: balkaya@binghamton.edu. *Vice Provost and Dean of the Graduate School,* Dr. Susan Strehle, 607-777-2070, Fax: 607-777-2501, E-mail: sstrehle@binghamton.edu.

College of Community and Public Affairs Students: 225 full-time (159 women), 144 part-time (118 women); includes 87 minority (27 Black or African American, non-Hispanic/Latino; 14 Asian, non-Hispanic/Latino; 34 Hispanic/Latino; 1 Native Hawaiian or other Pacific Islander, non-Hispanic/Latino; 11 Two or more races, non-Hispanic/Latino), 24 international. Average age 30. 394 applicants, 75% accepted, 161 enrolled. *Faculty:* 48 full-time (34 women), 22 part-time/adjunct (18 women). Expenses: Contact institution. *Financial support:* In 2016–17, 132 students received support. Fellowships, research assistantships, career-related internships or fieldwork, Federal Work-Study, institutionally sponsored loans, scholarships/grants, health care benefits, and unspecified assistantships available. Financial award applicants required to submit FAFSA. In 2016, 99 master's awarded. *Program availability:* Part-time, evening/weekend. Offers community and public affairs (MPA, MS, MSW); public administration (MPA); social work (MSW); student affairs administration (MS). *Application deadline:* Applications are processed on a rolling basis. *Application fee:* $75. Electronic applications accepted. *Application Contact:* Ben Balkaya, Assistant Dean and Director, 607-777-2151, Fax: 607-777-2501, E-mail: balkaya@binghamton.edu. *Dean,* Dr. Laura Bronstein, 607-777-5572, Fax: 607-777-2406, E-mail: lbronst@binghamton.edu.

Decker School of Nursing Students: 90 full-time (72 women), 124 part-time (110 women); includes 35 minority (16 Black or African American, non-Hispanic/Latino; 7 Asian, non-Hispanic/Latino; 7 Hispanic/Latino; 5 Two or more races, non-Hispanic/Latino), 13 international. Average age 37. 152 applicants, 92% accepted, 84 enrolled. *Faculty:* 52 full-time (47 women), 40 part-time/adjunct (36 women). Expenses: Contact institution. *Financial support:* In 2016–17, 35 students received support, including 1 fellowship with partial tuition reimbursement available (averaging $16,500 per year), research assistantships with full tuition reimbursements available (averaging $12,500 per year), 1 teaching assistantship with full tuition reimbursement available (averaging $16,500 per year); career-related internships or fieldwork, Federal Work-Study, institutionally sponsored loans, traineeships, health care benefits, tuition waivers (full and partial), and unspecified assistantships also available. Financial award applicants required to submit FAFSA. In 2016, 39 master's, 13 doctorates, 13 other advanced degrees awarded. *Program availability:* Part-time, evening/weekend. Offers nursing (MS, DNP, PhD, Certificate). *Application fee:* $75. Electronic applications accepted. *Application Contact:* Ben Balkaya, Assistant Dean and Director, 607-777-2151, Fax: 607-777-2501, E-mail: balkaya@binghamton.edu. *Dean,* Dr. Mario R. Ortiz, 607-777-2311, E-mail: mortiz@binghamton.edu.

Graduate School of Education Students: 103 full-time (75 women), 130 part-time (101 women); includes 21 minority (7 Black or African American, non-Hispanic/Latino; 2 American Indian or Alaska Native, non-Hispanic/Latino; 3 Asian, non-Hispanic/Latino; 7 Hispanic/Latino; 2 Two or more races, non-Hispanic/Latino), 5 international. Average age 32. 139 applicants, 86% accepted, 77 enrolled. *Faculty:* 18 full-time (12 women), 24 part-time/adjunct (20 women). Expenses: Contact institution. *Financial support:* In 2016–17, 21 students received support, including 2 fellowships with full tuition reimbursements available (averaging $10,000 per year), 3 teaching assistantships with full tuition reimbursements available (averaging $15,500 per year); research assistantships, career-related internships or fieldwork, Federal Work-Study, institutionally sponsored loans, scholarships/grants, health care benefits, tuition waivers (full and partial), and unspecified assistantships also available. Financial award applicants required to submit FAFSA. In 2016, 79 master's, 4 doctorates, 9 other advanced degrees awarded. *Program availability:* Part-time, evening/weekend. Offers biology education (MAT, MS Ed); chemistry education (MAT, MS Ed); childhood education (MS Ed); earth science education (MAT, MS Ed); education (MAT, MS, MS Ed, Ed D, Certificate); educational leadership (Certificate); educational studies (MS); educational theory and practice (Ed D); English education (MAT, MS Ed); French education (MAT, MS Ed); literacy education (MS Ed); mathematical sciences education (MAT, MS Ed); physics (MAT, MS Ed); social studies (MAT, MS Ed); Spanish education (MAT, MS Ed); special education (MS Ed); TESOL education (MS Ed). *Application fee:* $75. Electronic applications accepted. *Application Contact:* Ben Balkaya, Assistant Dean and Director, 607-777-2151, Fax: 607-777-2501, E-mail: balkaya@binghamton.edu. *Dean,* Dr. Susan Strehle, 607-777-7329, E-mail: sstrehle@binghamton.edu.

Harpur College of Arts and Sciences Students: 513 full-time (243 women), 619 part-time (326 women); includes 150 minority (30 Black or African American, non-Hispanic/Latino; 8 American Indian or Alaska Native, non-Hispanic/Latino; 48 Asian, non-Hispanic/Latino; 53 Hispanic/Latino; 1 Native Hawaiian or other Pacific Islander, non-Hispanic/Latino; 10 Two or more races, non-Hispanic/Latino), 406 international. Average age 30. 1,258 applicants, 53% accepted, 271 enrolled. *Faculty:* 392 full-time (151 women), 189 part-time/adjunct (83 women). Expenses: Contact institution. *Financial support:* In 2016–17, 589 students received support, including 2 fellowships with full tuition reimbursements available (averaging $8,000 per year), 42 research assistantships with full tuition reimbursements available (averaging $16,500 per year), 429 teaching assistantships with full tuition reimbursements available (averaging $15,000 per year); career-related internships or fieldwork, Federal Work-Study, institutionally sponsored loans, scholarships/grants, health care benefits, tuition waivers (full and partial), and unspecified assistantships also available. Financial award applicants required to submit FAFSA. In 2016, 149 master's, 85 doctorates, 4 other advanced degrees awarded. *Program availability:* Part-time, evening/weekend. Offers analytical chemistry (PhD); anthropology (MA, PhD); applied statistics (MA); art history (MA, PhD); arts and sciences (MA, MM, MS, PhD, Certificate); Asian and Asian American studies (MA, Certificate); behavioral neuroscience (PhD); biological sciences (MA, MS, PhD); biomedical anthropology (MS); chemistry (MA, MS); clinical psychology (PhD); cognitive and behavioral science (PhD); comparative literature (MA, PhD); creative writing (MA); economics (MA, PhD); English (PhD); English/American literature (MA); environmental chemistry (PhD); environmental studies (MS); French (MA); geography (MA); geological sciences (MS, PhD); history (MA, PhD); inorganic chemistry (PhD); Italian (MA); mathematical sciences (MA, PhD); music (MM); organic chemistry (PhD); philosophy (MA, PhD); philosophy, interpretation and culture (MA, PhD); physical chemistry (PhD); physics, applied physics, and astronomy (MS, PhD); political science (MA, PhD); social, political, ethical and legal philosophy (MA, PhD); sociology (MA, PhD); Spanish (MA); theatre (MA); translation research and instruction (PhD, Certificate). *Application deadline:* Applications are processed on a rolling basis. *Application fee:* $75. Electronic applications accepted. *Application Contact:* Ben Balkaya, Assistant Dean and Director, 607-777-2151, Fax: 607-777-2501, E-mail: balkaya@binghamton.edu. *Dean,* Dr. Terrence Deak, 607-777-2145, E-mail: tdeak@binghamton.edu.

School of Management Students: 351 full-time (167 women), 64 part-time (45 women); includes 77 minority (3 Black or African American, non-Hispanic/Latino; 57 Asian, non-Hispanic/Latino; 16 Hispanic/Latino; 1 Two or more races, non-Hispanic/Latino), 182 international. Average age 24. 843 applicants, 56% accepted, 269 enrolled. *Faculty:* 44 full-time (11 women), 32 part-time/adjunct (4 women). Expenses: Contact institution. *Financial support:* In 2016–17, 41 students received support, including 16 teaching assistantships with full tuition reimbursements available (averaging $17,000 per year); career-related internships or fieldwork, Federal Work-Study, institutionally sponsored loans, scholarships/grants, health care benefits, tuition waivers (full and partial), and unspecified assistantships also available. Financial award applicants required to submit FAFSA. In 2016, 262 master's, 4 doctorates awarded. *Program availability:* Part-time, evening/weekend. Offers accounting (MS); business administration (MBA); corporate executive (MBA); executive business administration (MBA); health care professional executive (MBA); management (MBA, MS, PhD); professional business administration (MBA). *Application deadline:* Applications are processed on a rolling basis. *Application fee:* $75. Electronic applications accepted. *Application Contact:* Ben Balkaya, Assistant Dean and Director, 607-777-2151, Fax: 607-777-2501, E-mail: balkaya@binghamton.edu. *Dean,* Dr. Upinder Dhillon, 607-777-2314, E-mail: dhillon@binghamton.edu.

Thomas J. Watson School of Engineering and Applied Science Students: 789 full-time (195 women), 416 part-time (91 women); includes 113 minority (31 Black or African American, non-Hispanic/Latino; 51 Asian, non-Hispanic/Latino; 30 Hispanic/Latino; 1 Native Hawaiian or other Pacific Islander, non-Hispanic/Latino), 893 international. Average age 27. 2,243 applicants, 69% accepted, 431 enrolled. *Faculty:* 101 full-time (16 women), 26 part-time/adjunct (3 women). Expenses: Contact institution. *Financial support:* In 2016–17, 332 students received support, including 2 fellowships with full tuition reimbursements available (averaging $10,000 per year), 138 research assistantships with full tuition reimbursements available (averaging $16,500 per year), 94 teaching assistantships with full tuition reimbursements available (averaging $16,500 per year); career-related internships or fieldwork, Federal Work-Study, institutionally sponsored loans, scholarships/grants, health care benefits, tuition waivers (full and partial), and unspecified assistantships also available. Financial award application deadline: 2/15; financial award applicants required to submit FAFSA. In 2016, 385 master's, 32 doctorates awarded. *Program availability:* Part-time, evening/weekend, online learning. Offers biomedical engineering (MS, PhD); computer science (MS, PhD); electrical and computer engineering (M Eng, MS, PhD); engineering and applied science (M Eng, MS, PhD); executive health systems (MS); industrial and systems engineering (M Eng); materials science and engineering (MS, PhD); mechanical engineering (M Eng, MS, PhD); systems science and industrial engineering (MS, PhD). *Application deadline:* Applications are processed on a rolling basis. *Application fee:* $75. Electronic applications accepted. *Application Contact:* Ben Balkaya, Assistant Dean and Director, 607-777-2151, Fax: 607-777-2501, E-mail: balkaya@binghamton.edu. *Coordinator of Graduate Programs, The Watson School,* Ellen Tilden, 607-777-2873, E-mail: etilden@binghamton.edu.

BIOLA UNIVERSITY, La Mirada, CA 90639-0001
General Information Independent-religious, coed, university. *Graduate housing:* Rooms and/or apartments available on a first-come, first-served basis to single and married students.

GRADUATE UNITS
Cook School of Intercultural Studies *Program availability:* Part-time, 100% online. Offers anthropology (MA); applied linguistics (MA); intercultural education (PhD); intercultural studies (MA, PhD); linguistics (Certificate); linguistics and Biblical languages (MA); missiology (D Miss); missions (MA); teaching English to speakers of other languages (MA, Certificate); teaching English to speakers of other languages (online) (MA). Electronic applications accepted.

Crowell School of Business *Program availability:* Part-time, evening/weekend. Offers business (MBA, MP Acc). Electronic applications accepted.

Rosemead School of Psychology Offers clinical psychology (PhD, Psy D). Electronic applications accepted.

School of Arts and Sciences *Program availability:* Part-time, evening/weekend, online learning. Offers Christian apologetics (MA, Certificate); science and religion (MA); speech language pathology (MA). Electronic applications accepted.

School of Education *Program availability:* Part-time, evening/weekend, online learning. Offers curriculum and instruction (Certificate); early childhood (MA Ed, MAT); multiple subject (MAT); single subject (MAT); special education (MA Ed, MAT, Certificate). Electronic applications accepted.

Talbot School of Theology *Program availability:* Part-time, evening/weekend. Offers adult/family ministry (MACE); Bible exposition (MA, Th M); Biblical and theological studies (Certificate); biblical and theological studies/diversified (MA); children's ministry (MACE); Christian education (M Div); cross-cultural education ministry (MACE); educational studies (Ed D, PhD); evangelism and discipleship (M Div); general Christian education (MACE); Messianic Jewish studies (M Div, Certificate); missions and intercultural studies (M Div); New Testament (MA, Th M); Old Testament (MA); Old Testament and Semitics (Th M); pastoral and general ministry (M Div); pastoral care and counseling (M Div, MACML); philosophy (MA); preaching and pastoral ministry (MACML); spiritual formation (M Div, Certificate); spiritual formation and soul care (MA);

sports ministry (MACML); theology (MA, Th M, D Min, Certificate); youth ministry (MACE). Electronic applications accepted.

BISHOP'S UNIVERSITY, Sherbrooke, QC J1M 1Z7, Canada
General Information Province-supported, coed, comprehensive institution. *Graduate housing:* Room and/or apartments available on a first-come, first-served basis to single students; on-campus housing not available to married students. Housing application deadline: 7/1.

GRADUATE UNITS
School of Education *Program availability:* Part-time, online learning. Offers advanced studies in education (Diploma); education (M Ed, MA); teaching English as a second language (Certificate).

BLACK HILLS STATE UNIVERSITY, Spearfish, SD 57799
General Information State-supported, coed, comprehensive institution. *Graduate housing:* Room and/or apartments available on a first-come, first-served basis to single students; on-campus housing not available to married students. Housing application deadline: 4/1.

GRADUATE UNITS
Graduate Studies *Program availability:* Part-time, evening/weekend, online learning. Offers business administration (MBA); curriculum and instruction (MS); integrative genomics (MS); strategic leadership (MS). Electronic applications accepted.

BLESSING-RIEMAN COLLEGE OF NURSING & HEALTH SCIENCES, Quincy, IL 62305-7005
General Information Independent, coed, primarily women, comprehensive institution. *Enrollment:* 15 part-time matriculated graduate/professional students (13 women). *Enrollment by degree level:* 15 master's. *Graduate faculty:* 7 full-time (all women). *Tuition:* Part-time $500 per credit hour. *Required fees:* $200 per degree program. $100 per semester. *Graduate housing:* On-campus housing not available. *Student services:* Campus safety program, services for students with disabilities. *Library facilities:* Blessing Health Professions Library plus 1 other.

Computer facilities: 28 computers available on campus for general student use. A campuswide network can be accessed.
Website: http://www.brcn.edu/

General Application Contact: Heather Mutter, Admissions Counselor, 217-228-5520 Ext. 6964, Fax: 217-223-4661, E-mail: hmutter@brcn.edu.

GRADUATE UNITS
Master of Science in Nursing Program Students: 15 part-time (13 women). Average age 35. *Faculty:* 6 full-time (all women). Expenses: Contact institution. *Financial support:* Scholarships/grants available. Financial award application deadline: 4/30; financial award applicants required to submit FAFSA. In 2016, 6 master's awarded. *Program availability:* Part-time-only, evening/weekend, online only, 100% online. Offers nursing administration (MSN); nursing education (MSN). *Application deadline:* Applications are processed on a rolling basis. Electronic applications accepted. *Application Contact:* Heather Mutter, Admissions Counselor, 217-228-5520 Ext. 6964, Fax: 217-223-1781, E-mail: hmutter@brcn.edu. *Administrative Coordinator, Accreditation,* Dr. Karen Mayville, 217-228-5520 Ext. 6968, Fax: 217-223-4661, E-mail: kmayville@brcn.edu.

BLOOMFIELD COLLEGE, Bloomfield, NJ 07003-9981
General Information Independent-religious, coed, comprehensive institution.
GRADUATE UNITS
Program in Accounting Offers accounting (MS).

BLOOMSBURG UNIVERSITY OF PENNSYLVANIA, Bloomsburg, PA 17815-1301
General Information State-supported, coed, comprehensive institution. *Enrollment:* 9,658 graduate, professional, and undergraduate students; 336 full-time matriculated graduate/professional students (227 women), 320 part-time matriculated graduate/professional students (224 women). *Enrollment by degree level:* 590 master's, 48 doctoral, 18 other advanced degrees. *Graduate faculty:* 71 full-time (34 women), 22 part-time/adjunct (17 women). *Tuition, state resident:* full-time $9660; part-time $483 per credit. *Tuition, nonresident:* full-time $14,500; part-time $725 per credit. *Required fees:* $2410; $107 per credit. $75 per term. Tuition and fees vary according to course load, degree level and program. *Graduate housing:* Room and/or apartments available on a first-come, first-served basis to single students; on-campus housing not available to married students. Typical cost: $3176 per year ($5736 including board). *Student services:* Campus employment opportunities, campus safety program, career counseling, child daycare facilities, exercise/wellness program, free psychological counseling, international student services, low-cost health insurance, multicultural affairs office, services for students with disabilities, teacher training, writing training. *Library facilities:* Andruss Library. *Collection:* Books: 473,456 (physical), 229,760 (digital/electronic); Serial titles: 5,900 (physical), 451,151 (digital/electronic); Databases: 154. Weekly public service hours: 98; students can reserve study rooms. *Research affiliation:* American Chemical Society Petroleum Research Fund (chemistry), Consortium of Big Ten Universities Research and Training Reactors (physics), Melanoma Research Fund (biology), Merck & Company, Inc. (biology), Marine Science Consortium (biology).

Computer facilities: Computer purchase and lease plans are available. 1,571 computers available on campus for general student use. A campuswide network can be accessed from student residence rooms and from off campus. Online class registration is available.
Website: http://www.bloomu.edu/

General Application Contact: Jennifer Kessler, Administrative Assistant, 570-389-4015, Fax: 570-389-3054, E-mail: jkessler@bloomu.edu.

GRADUATE UNITS
School of Graduate Studies Students: 336 full-time (227 women), 320 part-time (224 women); includes 73 minority (25 Black or African American, non-Hispanic/Latino; 17 Asian, non-Hispanic/Latino; 15 Hispanic/Latino; 3 Native Hawaiian or other Pacific Islander, non-Hispanic/Latino; 13 Two or more races, non-Hispanic/Latino), 6 international. Average age 29. 950 applicants, 37% accepted, 265 enrolled. *Faculty:* 71 full-time (34 women), 22 part-time/adjunct (17 women). Expenses: Contact institution. *Financial support:* Research assistantships, Federal Work-Study, scholarships/grants, and unspecified assistantships available. Financial award application deadline: 3/15; financial award applicants required to submit FAFSA. In 2016, 260 master's, 12 doctorates, 1 other advanced degree awarded. *Program availability:* Part-time, evening/weekend. *Application deadline:* Applications are processed on a rolling basis. *Application fee:* $35 ($60 for international students). Electronic applications accepted.

Application Contact: Jennifer Kessler, Administrative Assistant, 570-389-4015, Fax: 570-389-3054, E-mail: jkessler@bloomu.edu. *Interim Assistant Vice President/Dean of Graduate Studies and Sponsored Research*, Dr. Mark Tapsak, 570-389-4015, Fax: 570-389-3054, E-mail: mtapsak@bloomu.edu.

College of Education Students: 106 full-time (67 women), 128 part-time (97 women); includes 26 minority (10 Black or African American, non-Hispanic/Latino; 5 Asian, non-Hispanic/Latino; 5 Hispanic/Latino; 1 Native Hawaiian or other Pacific Islander, non-Hispanic/Latino; 5 Two or more races, non-Hispanic/Latino), 1 international. Average age 28. 181 applicants, 66% accepted, 98 enrolled. *Faculty:* 26 full-time (13 women), 4 part-time/adjunct (all women). Expenses: Contact institution. *Financial support:* Federal Work-Study and unspecified assistantships available. In 2016, 86 master's awarded. *Program availability:* Part-time. Offers college student affairs (M Ed); curriculum and instruction (M Ed, Certificate); early childhood education (M Ed); education (M Ed, MS, Certificate); education of the deaf/hard of hearing (MS); educational leadership (M Ed); language arts (M Ed); math (M Ed); middle level education grades 4-8 (M Ed); PreK-12 curriculum and instruction (M Ed); PreK-12 school counseling (M Ed); PreK-12 school principal (M Ed); reading (M Ed); school principal (Certificate); science (M Ed); social studies (M Ed); special education (M Ed, MS, Certificate). *Application fee:* $35 ($60 for international students). Electronic applications accepted. *Application Contact:* Jennifer Kessler, Administrative Assistant, 570-389-4015, Fax: 570-389-3054, E-mail: jkessler@bloomu.edu. *College of Education Graduate Program Coordinator*, Dr. Ingrid Everett, 570-389-5120, Fax: 570-389-3030, E-mail: ieverett@bloomu.edu.

College of Science and Technology Students: 191 full-time (147 women), 154 part-time (110 women); includes 37 minority (12 Black or African American, non-Hispanic/Latino; 9 Asian, non-Hispanic/Latino; 8 Hispanic/Latino; 1 Native Hawaiian or other Pacific Islander, non-Hispanic/Latino; 7 Two or more races, non-Hispanic/Latino), 3 international. Average age 29. 652 applicants, 25% accepted, 124 enrolled. *Faculty:* 36 full-time (18 women), 17 part-time/adjunct (13 women). Expenses: Contact institution. *Financial support:* Federal Work-Study and unspecified assistantships available. Financial award applicants required to submit FAFSA. In 2016, 138 master's, 12 doctorates, 1 other advanced degree awarded. Offers adult and family nurse practitioner (MSN); audiology (Au D); biology (MS); clinical athletic training (MS); community health (MSN); corporate instructional technology (MS); eLearning developer (Certificate); exercise science (MS); intraoperative neurophysiological monitoring (Certificate); nurse anesthesia (MSN); nursing (MSN); nursing administration (MSN); science and technology (M Ed, MS, MSN, Au D, Certificate); speech pathology (MS); speech-language pathology (MS). *Application deadline:* Applications are processed on a rolling basis. *Application fee:* $35 ($60 for international students). Electronic applications accepted. *Application Contact:* Jennifer Kessler, Administrative Assistant, 570-389-4015, Fax: 570-389-3054, E-mail: jkessler@bloomu.edu. *Dean of the College of Science and Technology*, Dr. Robert Aronstam, 570-389-5333, Fax: 570-389-5063, E-mail: aronstam@bloomu.edu.

Zeigler College of Business Students: 39 full-time (13 women), 38 part-time (17 women); includes 10 minority (3 Black or African American, non-Hispanic/Latino; 3 Asian, non-Hispanic/Latino; 2 Hispanic/Latino; 1 Native Hawaiian or other Pacific Islander, non-Hispanic/Latino; 1 Two or more races, non-Hispanic/Latino), 2 international. Average age 27. 114 applicants, 60% accepted, 56 enrolled. *Faculty:* 9 full-time (3 women), 1 part-time/adjunct (0 women). Expenses: Contact institution. *Financial support:* Unspecified assistantships available. In 2016, 36 master's awarded. *Program availability:* Part-time, evening/weekend. Offers accounting (M Acc); business (M Acc, M Ed, MBA, Certificate); business administration (MBA); business education (M Ed); management (Certificate). *Application deadline:* Applications are processed on a rolling basis. *Application fee:* $35 ($60 for international students). Electronic applications accepted. *Application Contact:* Jennifer Kessler, Administrative Assistant, 570-389-4015, Fax: 570-389-3054, E-mail: jkessler@bloomu.edu. *Dean of Zeigler College of Business*, Dr. Jeffrey Krug, 570-389-4883, Fax: 570-389-3892, E-mail: jakrug@bloomu.edu.

BLUEFIELD COLLEGE, Bluefield, VA 24605-1799

General Information Independent-religious, coed, comprehensive institution. *Enrollment:* 982 graduate, professional, and undergraduate students; 10 full-time matriculated graduate/professional students (6 women), 3 part-time matriculated graduate/professional students (all women). *Enrollment by degree level:* 13 master's. *Graduate faculty:* 2 full-time (1 woman), 2 part-time/adjunct (1 woman). *Tuition:* Full-time $5520; part-time $460 per credit. *Graduate housing:* On-campus housing not available. *Student services:* Low-cost health insurance. *Library facilities:* Easley Library. *Collection:* Books: 44,352 (physical), 165,829 (digital/electronic); Serial titles: 7,976 (physical), 334 (digital/electronic); Databases: 72. Students can reserve study rooms.

Computer facilities: 110 computers available on campus for general student use. A campuswide network can be accessed from student residence rooms. Online class registration is available.
Website: http://www.bluefield.edu/

General Application Contact: Trent Argo, Vice President for Enrollment Management, 276-326-4231, Fax: 276-326-4395, E-mail: targo@bluefield.edu.

GRADUATE UNITS

School of Education Students: 10 full-time (6 women), 3 part-time (all women); includes 2 minority (1 Black or African American, non-Hispanic/Latino; 1 Two or more races, non-Hispanic/Latino). Average age 32. 13 applicants, 23% accepted, 3 enrolled. *Faculty:* 2 full-time (1 woman), 2 part-time/adjunct (1 woman). Expenses: Contact institution. *Financial support:* Applicants required to submit FAFSA. In 2016, 7 master's awarded. *Program availability:* Part-time, online only, 100% online. Offers education (MA Ed). *Application deadline:* Applications are processed on a rolling basis. *Application fee:* $0. Electronic applications accepted. *Dean*, Dr. Donna Hardy Watson, 276-326-4475, E-mail: dwatson@bluefield.edu.

BLUE MOUNTAIN COLLEGE, Blue Mountain, MS 38610

General Information Independent-religious, coed, comprehensive institution. *Graduate housing:* Room and/or apartments available on a first-come, first-served basis to single students; on-campus housing not available to married students.

GRADUATE UNITS

Program in Elementary Education *Program availability:* Part-time, evening/weekend. Offers elementary education (M Ed). Electronic applications accepted.

Program in Literacy/Reading (K-12) *Program availability:* Part-time, evening/weekend. Offers literacy/reading (K-12) (M Ed). Electronic applications accepted.

BLUFFTON UNIVERSITY, Bluffton, OH 45817

General Information Independent-religious, coed, comprehensive institution. *Enrollment:* 952 graduate, professional, and undergraduate students; 64 full-time matriculated graduate/professional students (41 women), 3 part-time matriculated graduate/professional students (all women). *Enrollment by degree level:* 67 master's. *Graduate faculty:* 14 full-time (6 women), 13 part-time/adjunct (4 women). Full-time $6420. Tuition and fees vary according to program. *Graduate housing:* Room and/or apartments available on a first-come, first-served basis to single students; on-campus housing not available to married students. Typical cost: $6460 per year. Room charges vary according to housing facility selected. *Student services:* Campus employment opportunities, career counseling, exercise/wellness program, free psychological counseling, international student services, multicultural affairs office, services for students with disabilities, writing training. *Library facilities:* Musselman Library plus 1 other. *Collection:* Books: 73,858 (physical), 282,112 (digital/electronic); Serial titles: 1,086 (physical), 44,747 (digital/electronic); Databases: 261. Weekly public service hours: 81; students can reserve study rooms.

Computer facilities: 170 computers available on campus for general student use. A campuswide network can be accessed from student residence rooms and from off campus. Online class registration is available.
Website: http://www.bluffton.edu/

General Application Contact: Rebecca Cox, 419-488-3257, Fax: 419-358-3399.

GRADUATE UNITS

Programs in Business Students: 55 full-time (34 women), 2 part-time (1 woman); includes 5 minority (1 Black or African American, non-Hispanic/Latino; 2 Asian, non-Hispanic/Latino; 2 Hispanic/Latino), 2 international. Average age 34. 31 applicants, 77% accepted, 22 enrolled. *Faculty:* 9 full-time (3 women), 12 part-time/adjunct (4 women). Expenses: Contact institution. *Financial support:* Scholarships/grants and unspecified assistantships available. Financial award application deadline: 5/1. In 2016, 44 master's awarded. *Program availability:* Evening/weekend, online learning. Offers accounting and financial management (MBA); business administration (MBA); health care management (MBA); leadership (MBA); organizational management (MA); production and operations management (MBA). *Application deadline:* For fall admission, 7/31 priority date for domestic and international students. Applications are processed on a rolling basis. *Application fee:* $25. Electronic applications accepted. *Application Contact:* Carrie Mast, Administrative Assistant, Graduate Programs in Business, 419-358-3065, E-mail: mastc@bluffton.edu. *Director of Graduate Programs in Business*, Dr. Melissa Green, 419-358-3447, E-mail: greenm@bluffton.edu.

Programs in Education Students: 9 full-time (all women), 10 part-time (9 women); includes 1 minority (Black or African American, non-Hispanic/Latino). Average age 34. 14 applicants, 50% accepted, 6 enrolled. *Faculty:* 6 full-time (3 women), 1 part-time/adjunct (0 women). Expenses: Contact institution. *Financial support:* Health care benefits available. Support available to part-time students. Financial award application deadline: 9/15; financial award applicants required to submit FAFSA. In 2016, 1 master's awarded. *Program availability:* Part-time. Offers faith-based education (MA Ed); intervention specialist (MA Ed); leadership (MA Ed); reading (MA Ed). *Application deadline:* For fall admission, 8/15 priority date for domestic students, 6/15 priority date for international students; for spring admission, 12/15 priority date for domestic students, 9/15 priority date for international students. Applications are processed on a rolling basis. *Application fee:* $25. Electronic applications accepted. *Application Contact:* Nancey Schortgen, Program Representative, 419-358-3202, Fax: 419-358-3399, E-mail: schortgenn@bluffton.edu. *Director of Graduate Programs in Education*, Dr. Gayle M. Trollinger, 419-358-3341, E-mail: trollingerg@bluffton.edu.

BOB JONES UNIVERSITY, Greenville, SC 29614

General Information Independent-religious, coed, university.

GRADUATE UNITS

Graduate Programs

BOISE STATE UNIVERSITY, Boise, ID 83725-0399

General Information State-supported, coed, university. CGS member. *Enrollment:* 23,886 graduate, professional, and undergraduate students; 903 full-time matriculated graduate/professional students (505 women), 2,088 part-time matriculated graduate/professional students (1,309 women). *Enrollment by degree level:* 1,971 master's, 209 doctoral, 107 other advanced degrees. *Graduate faculty:* 457. Tuition, state resident: full-time $6058; part-time $358 per credit hour. Tuition, nonresident: full-time $20,108; part-time $608 per credit hour. *Required fees:* $2108. Tuition and fees vary according to program. *Graduate housing:* Rooms and/or apartments available on a first-come, first-served basis to single and married students. Housing application deadline: 6/1. *Student services:* Campus employment opportunities, campus safety program, career counseling, child daycare facilities, exercise/wellness program, free psychological counseling, grant writing training, international student services, low-cost health insurance, multicultural affairs office, services for students with disabilities, teacher training, writing training. *Library facilities:* Albertsons Library plus 1 other. *Collection:* Books: 800,205 (physical), 60,977 (digital/electronic); Serial titles: 112,213 (digital/electronic); Databases: 303. Weekly public service hours: 115; study areas open 24 hours, 5–7 days a week; students can reserve study rooms. *Research affiliation:* Federal Aviation Administration (airliner cabin environment research), Lee Pesky Learning Center (elementary mathematics education), Prewitt & Associates, Inc. (C-130 drop zones), Bechtel BWXT Idaho, LLC (energy policy analysis), Argonne National Laboratory (energy policy analysis), American Chemical Society (petroleum research).

Computer facilities: 900 computers available on campus for general student use. A campuswide network can be accessed from student residence rooms and from off campus. Online class registration is available.
Website: http://www.boisestate.edu/

General Application Contact: Dean, 208-426-3647, Fax: 208-426-2789.

GRADUATE UNITS

College of Arts and Sciences Students: 233 full-time (115 women), 122 part-time (75 women); includes 37 minority (2 Black or African American, non-Hispanic/Latino; 3 American Indian or Alaska Native, non-Hispanic/Latino; 10 Asian, non-Hispanic/Latino; 18 Hispanic/Latino; 1 Native Hawaiian or other Pacific Islander, non-Hispanic/Latino; 3 Two or more races, non-Hispanic/Latino), 24 international. Average age 32. 495 applicants, 26% accepted, 93 enrolled. *Faculty:* 140. Expenses: Contact institution. *Financial support:* In 2016–17, 61 students received support, including 39 research assistantships (averaging $8,157 per year), 108 teaching assistantships (averaging $8,021 per year); scholarships/grants and unspecified assistantships also available. Financial award applicants required to submit FAFSA. In 2016, 81 master's, 1 doctorate awarded. *Program availability:* Part-time. Offers anthropology (MA); applied anthropology (MAA); applied historical research (MAHR); art education (MA); arts and sciences (M E Sci, MA, MAA, MAHR, MFA, MM, MS, PhD); biology (MA, MS); biomolecular sciences (PhD); chemistry (MS); communication (MA); creative writing (MFA); earth science (M E Sci); English (MA); geophysics (MS, PhD); geosciences (MS, PhD); history (MA); hydrology (MS); interdisciplinary studies (MA, MS); mathematics (MS); mathematics education (MS); music education (MM); performance (MM); raptor biology (MS); rhetoric and composition (MA); teaching English language (MA); technical communication (MA); visual arts (MFA). *Application deadline:* For fall admission, 5/1 for domestic and international students. *Application fee:* $65 ($95 for international students). Electronic applications accepted. *Dean,* Dr. Tony Roark, 208-426-1414, Fax: 208-426-3006.

College of Business and Economics Students: 146 full-time (52 women), 187 part-time (59 women); includes 33 minority (3 Black or African American, non-Hispanic/Latino; 1 American Indian or Alaska Native, non-Hispanic/Latino; 8 Asian, non-Hispanic/Latino; 16 Hispanic/Latino; 5 Two or more races, non-Hispanic/Latino), 12 international. Average age 33. 234 applicants, 63% accepted, 116 enrolled. *Faculty:* 22. Expenses: Contact institution. *Financial support:* In 2016–17, 29 students received support, including 2 research assistantships (averaging $7,596 per year); scholarships/grants and unspecified assistantships also available. Financial award applicants required to submit FAFSA. In 2016, 125 master's awarded. *Program availability:* Part-time, online learning. Offers accountancy (MSA); accountancy taxation (MSAT); business and economics (MBA, MSA, MSAT); executive (MBA). *Application deadline:* For fall admission, 5/1 for domestic and international students. Applications are processed on a rolling basis. *Application fee:* $65 ($95 for international students). Electronic applications accepted. *Application Contact:* Scott Lowe, Program Coordinator, 208-426-5439, E-mail: scottlowe@boisestate.edu. *Dean,* Dr. Kenneth J. Petersen, 208-426-1125, E-mail: kenpetersen@boisestate.edu.

College of Education Students: 131 full-time (106 women), 762 part-time (486 women); includes 88 minority (13 Black or African American, non-Hispanic/Latino; 4 American Indian or Alaska Native, non-Hispanic/Latino; 19 Asian, non-Hispanic/Latino; 46 Hispanic/Latino; 4 Native Hawaiian or other Pacific Islander, non-Hispanic/Latino; 2 Two or more races, non-Hispanic/Latino), 32 international. Average age 37. 399 applicants, 61% accepted, 146 enrolled. *Faculty:* 106. Expenses: Contact institution. *Financial support:* In 2016–17, 36 students received support, including 1 teaching assistantship (averaging $2,148 per year); scholarships/grants and unspecified assistantships also available. Financial award applicants required to submit FAFSA. In 2016, 234 master's, 12 doctorates awarded. *Program availability:* Part-time, 100% online, blended/hybrid learning. Offers bilingual education (M Ed); counselor education (MA, Graduate Certificate); curriculum and instruction (MA Ed, Ed D); early and special education (M Ed); education (M Ed, MA, MET, MPE, MS, MS Ed, Ed D, Ed S, Graduate Certificate); educational leadership (M Ed); educational technology (MET, MS, Ed D); English as a new language (M Ed); executive educational leadership (Ed S); literacy (MA); online teaching (Graduate Certificate); school technology coordination (Graduate Certificate); technology integration (Graduate Certificate). *Application fee:* $65 ($95 for international students). Electronic applications accepted. *Dean,* Dr. Rich Osguthorpe, 208-426-1611, E-mail: richardosguthorpe@boisestate.edu.

College of Engineering Students: 136 full-time (42 women), 231 part-time (117 women); includes 52 minority (15 Black or African American, non-Hispanic/Latino; 17 Asian, non-Hispanic/Latino; 15 Hispanic/Latino; 5 Two or more races, non-Hispanic/Latino), 78 international. Average age 34. 309 applicants, 51% accepted, 81 enrolled. *Faculty:* 78. Expenses: Contact institution. *Financial support:* In 2016–17, 50 students received support, including 63 research assistantships (averaging $9,326 per year), 7 teaching assistantships with partial tuition reimbursements available (averaging $10,656 per year); scholarships/grants and unspecified assistantships also available. Financial award applicants required to submit FAFSA. In 2016, 72 master's, 1 doctorate awarded. *Program availability:* Part-time, online learning. Offers civil engineering (M Engr, MS); computer science (MS); computer science teacher endorsement (Graduate Certificate); electrical and computer engineering (M Engr, MS, PhD); engineering (M Engr, MS, PhD, Graduate Certificate); mechanical engineering (M Engr, MS); organizational performance and workplace learning (MS); STEM education (MS); workplace e-learning and performance support (Graduate Certificate); workplace instructional design (Graduate Certificate); workplace performance improvement (Graduate Certificate). *Application fee:* $65 ($95 for international students). Electronic applications accepted. *Application Contact:* Hao Chen, Program Coordinator, 208-426-1020, E-mail: haochen@boisestate.edu. *Dean,* Dr. Amy Moll, 208-426-5719.

Micron School of Materials Science and Engineering Students: 37 full-time (13 women), 6 part-time (3 women); includes 6 minority (5 Asian, non-Hispanic/Latino; 1 Hispanic/Latino), 8 international. Average age 29. 61 applicants, 36% accepted, 7 enrolled. *Faculty:* 16. Expenses: Contact institution. *Financial support:* In 2016–17, 6 students received support, including 32 research assistantships (averaging $8,599 per year); scholarships/grants and unspecified assistantships also available. Financial award application deadline: 1/15; financial award applicants required to submit FAFSA. In 2016, 10 master's, 1 doctorate awarded. Offers materials science and engineering (M Engr, MS, PhD). *Application deadline:* For fall admission, 1/15 priority date for domestic and international students. *Application fee:* $65 ($95 for international students). Electronic applications accepted. *Application Contact:* Dr. David Estrada, Graduate Program Coordinator, 208-426-5693, E-mail: daveestrada@boisestate.edu. *Department Chair,* Dr. Janet Callahan, 208-426-5983, E-mail: janetcallahan@boisestate.edu.

College of Health Sciences Students: 221 full-time (174 women), 183 part-time (138 women); includes 42 minority (11 Black or African American, non-Hispanic/Latino; 3 Asian, non-Hispanic/Latino; 24 Hispanic/Latino; 1 Native Hawaiian or other Pacific Islander, non-Hispanic/Latino; 3 Two or more races, non-Hispanic/Latino). Average age 35. 246 applicants, 49% accepted, 85 enrolled. *Faculty:* 72. Expenses: Contact institution. *Financial support:* In 2016–17, 79 students received support, including 4 research assistantships (averaging $3,510 per year); scholarships/grants and unspecified assistantships also available. Financial award applicants required to submit FAFSA. In 2016, 151 master's, 13 other advanced degrees awarded. *Program availability:* Part-time, 100% online. Offers athletic leadership (MAL); community and environmental health (MHS); health science (MHS); health sciences (MAL, MHS, MK, MS, MSN, MSW, DNP, Graduate Certificate); health services leadership (Graduate Certificate); kinesiology (MK, MS). *Application deadline:* Applications are processed on a rolling basis. *Application fee:* $65 ($95 for international students). Electronic applications accepted. *Application Contact:* Dr. Tedd McDonald, Program Director, 208-426-2425, E-mail: tmcdonal@boisestate.edu. *Dean,* Dr. Tim Dunnagan, 208-426-4150, E-mail: timdunnagan@boisestate.edu.

School of Nursing Students: 1 (woman) full-time, 91 part-time (73 women); includes 11 minority (5 Black or African American, non-Hispanic/Latino; 2 Asian, non-Hispanic/Latino; 3 Hispanic/Latino; 1 Native Hawaiian or other Pacific Islander, non-Hispanic/Latino). Average age 43. 32 applicants, 44% accepted, 12 enrolled. Expenses: Contact institution. *Financial support:* In 2016–17, 1 student received support. Scholarships/grants and unspecified assistantships available. Financial award application deadline: 10/15; financial award applicants required to submit FAFSA. In 2016, 3 master's awarded. Offers acute care adult gerontology (Graduate Certificate); adult gerontology acute care (MSN); adult gerontology primary care (MSN); healthcare simulation (Graduate Certificate); nursing practice (DNP); primary

care adult gerontology (Graduate Certificate). *Application deadline:* For spring admission, 10/15 priority date for domestic and international students. Applications are processed on a rolling basis. *Application fee:* $65 ($95 for international students). Electronic applications accepted. *Application Contact:* Dr. Nancy Loftus, Program Coordinator, 208-426-3819, E-mail: nancyloftus@boisestate.edu. *Director,* Dr. Ann Hubbert, 208-426-3404, E-mail: annhubbert@boisestate.edu.

School of Social Work Students: 177 full-time (146 women), 23 part-time (22 women); includes 13 minority (2 Black or African American, non-Hispanic/Latino; 10 Hispanic/Latino; 1 Two or more races, non-Hispanic/Latino). Average age 34. 139 applicants, 46% accepted, 47 enrolled. *Faculty:* 33. Expenses: Contact institution. *Financial support:* In 2016–17, 37 students received support, including 2 research assistantships (averaging $4,083 per year); scholarships/grants and unspecified assistantships also available. Financial award applicants required to submit FAFSA. In 2016, 104 master's awarded. *Program availability:* Part-time, 100% online. Offers social work (MSW). *Application deadline:* For fall admission, 1/10 for domestic and international students. *Application fee:* $65 ($95 for international students). Electronic applications accepted. *Application Contact:* Dr. Cynthia Sanders, Program Coordinator, 208-426-1780, E-mail: cynthiasanders@boisestate.edu. *Director,* Dr. Randy Magen, 208-426-1789, E-mail: randymagen@boisestate.edu.

School of Public Service Students: 63 full-time (32 women), 111 part-time (68 women); includes 21 minority (1 American Indian or Alaska Native, non-Hispanic/Latino; 2 Asian, non-Hispanic/Latino; 16 Hispanic/Latino; 1 Native Hawaiian or other Pacific Islander, non-Hispanic/Latino; 1 Two or more races, non-Hispanic/Latino), 2 international. Average age 36. 114 applicants, 48% accepted, 44 enrolled. *Faculty:* 28. Expenses: Contact institution. *Financial support:* In 2016–17, 51 students received support, including 4 research assistantships (averaging $5,064 per year); scholarships/grants and unspecified assistantships also available. Financial award applicants required to submit FAFSA. In 2016, 44 master's awarded. *Program availability:* Part-time. Offers criminal justice (MA); political science (MA); public policy and administration (MPA, PhD, Graduate Certificate); public service (MA, MPA, PhD, Graduate Certificate). *Application fee:* $65 ($95 for international students). Electronic applications accepted. *Dean,* Dr. Corey Cook, 208-426-3349, E-mail: coreydcook@boisestate.edu.

BORICUA COLLEGE, New York, NY 10032-1560
General Information Independent, coed, comprehensive institution. *Enrollment:* 109 full-time matriculated graduate/professional students (92 women). *Enrollment by degree level:* 109 master's. *Graduate faculty:* 2 full-time (1 woman), 6 part-time/adjunct (4 women). *Tuition:* Full-time $13,000. *Required fees:* $100. *Student services:* Career counseling, teacher training. *Library facilities:* Boricua College Library plus 1 other.

Computer facilities: 120 computers available on campus for general student use. Website: http://www.boricuacollege.edu/

General Application Contact: Brenda Rodriguez, Director of Admissions, 347-964-8680, E-mail: brodriguez@boricuacollege.edu.

GRADUATE UNITS

Program in Human Services Expenses: Contact institution. *Financial support:* Career-related internships or fieldwork and Federal Work-Study available. Financial award applicants required to submit FAFSA. *Program availability:* Evening/weekend. Offers human services (MS). Program offered in Brooklyn and Manhattan. *Application deadline:* Applications are processed on a rolling basis. *Application fee:* $100. *Application Contact:* Miriam Pfeffer, Director of Admissions, 718-782-2200 Ext. 210, E-mail: mpfeffer@boricuacollege.edu. *Co-Chairperson,* Victor Garcia, 718-782-2200 Ext. 271.

Program in Latin American and Caribbean Studies Expenses: Contact institution. *Financial support:* Career-related internships or fieldwork and Federal Work-Study available. Financial award applicants required to submit FAFSA. *Program availability:* Evening/weekend. Offers Latin American and Caribbean studies (MA). Program offered in Brooklyn and Manhattan. *Application deadline:* Applications are processed on a rolling basis. *Application fee:* $100. *Application Contact:* Miriam Pfeffer, Director of Admissions, 718-782-2200 Ext. 210, E-mail: mpfeffer@boricuacollege.edu. *Senior Vice President,* Dr. Maria Montes, 718-782-2200 Ext. 222.

Program in TESOL Education (K-12) Expenses: Contact institution. *Financial support:* Career-related internships or fieldwork and Federal Work-Study available. Financial award applicants required to submit FAFSA. *Program availability:* Evening/weekend. Offers TESOL education (MS). *Application deadline:* Applications are processed on a rolling basis. *Application fee:* $100. *Application Contact:* Dr. Shivaji Sengupta, Vice President, 212-694-1000 Ext. 650, Fax: 212-694-1015, E-mail: ssengupta@boricuacollege.edu. *Co-Chairperson,* Dr. Joseph H. Gaines, 212-694-1000.

BOSTON ARCHITECTURAL COLLEGE, Boston, MA 02115-2795
General Information Independent, coed, comprehensive institution.

GRADUATE UNITS

Graduate Programs Offers architecture (M Arch); historic preservation (MDS); interior design (MID); landscape architecture (MLA); sustainable design (MDS). Electronic applications accepted.

BOSTON COLLEGE, Chestnut Hill, MA 02467-3800
General Information Independent-religious, coed, university. CGS member. *Enrollment:* 13,851 graduate, professional, and undergraduate students; 3,078 full-time matriculated graduate/professional students (1,828 women), 986 part-time matriculated graduate/professional students (489 women). *Graduate faculty:* 861. Tuition and fees vary according to program. *Graduate housing:* On-campus housing not available. *Student services:* Campus employment opportunities, campus safety program, career counseling, child daycare facilities, exercise/wellness program, free psychological counseling, grant writing training, international student services, low-cost health insurance, multicultural affairs office, services for students with disabilities, teacher training, writing training. *Library facilities:* O'Neill Library plus 8 others. *Collection:* Books: 3.2 million (physical), 817,757 (digital/electronic); Serial titles: 3,937 (physical), 41,900 (digital/electronic). Study areas open 24 hours, 5–7 days a week; students can reserve study rooms.

Computer facilities: Computer purchase and lease plans are available. 1,000 computers available on campus for general student use. A campuswide network can be accessed from student residence rooms and from off campus. Online class registration is available.
Website: http://www.bc.edu/

General Application Contact: Robert V. Howe, Associate Dean, 617-552-3265, Fax: 617-552-3700, E-mail: hower@bc.edu.

GRADUATE UNITS

Carroll School of Management *Program availability:* Part-time, evening/weekend. Offers accounting (MSA); business administration (MBA); finance (MSF, PhD); management (MBA, MSA, MSF, PhD); management and organization (PhD). Electronic applications accepted.

Graduate School of Arts and Sciences Students: 752 full-time (328 women), 39 part-time (9 women). 2,070 applicants, 27% accepted, 177 enrolled. *Faculty:* 473 full-time (155 women). Expenses: Contact institution. *Financial support:* In 2016–17, fellowships with tuition reimbursements (averaging $21,500 per year), research assistantships with tuition reimbursements (averaging $21,500 per year), teaching assistantships with tuition reimbursements (averaging $21,500 per year) were awarded; career-related internships or fieldwork, Federal Work-Study, scholarships/grants, health care benefits, tuition waivers (full and partial), and unspecified assistantships also available. Support available to part-time students. Financial award application deadline: 3/1; financial award applicants required to submit FAFSA. In 2016, 136 master's, 90 doctorates awarded. *Program availability:* Part-time. Offers arts and sciences (MA, MS, MST, PhD); biochemistry (PhD); biology (PhD); classics (MA); earth and environmental sciences (MS); economics (PhD); English (MA, PhD); European national studies (MA); French (MA); Greek (MA); history (MA, PhD); inorganic chemistry (PhD); Irish studies (MA, PhD); Italian (MA); Latin (MA); linguistics (MA); mathematics (PhD); medieval studies (MA); organic chemistry (PhD); philosophy (MA, PhD); philosophy and theology (PhD); physical chemistry (PhD); physics (MS, PhD); political science (MA, PhD); psychology (PhD); Russian (MA); science education (MST); Slavic studies (MA); sociology (MA, PhD); Spanish (MA); theology (PhD). *Application deadline:* For fall admission, 1/2 priority date for domestic and international students. *Application fee:* $75. Electronic applications accepted. *Application Contact:* Robert V. Howe, Associate Dean, 617-552-3265, Fax: 617-552-3700, E-mail: hower@bc.edu. *Dean,* Dr. Gregory Kalscheur, 617-552-6850, E-mail: gregory.kalscheur@bc.edu.

Law School Offers law (JD). Electronic applications accepted.

Lynch School of Education Students: 345 full-time (277 women), 422 part-time (318 women); includes 157 minority (50 Black or African American, non-Hispanic/Latino; 36 Asian, non-Hispanic/Latino; 50 Hispanic/Latino; 1 Native Hawaiian or other Pacific Islander, non-Hispanic/Latino; 20 Two or more races, non-Hispanic/Latino), 103 international. Average age 28. 1,385 applicants, 58% accepted, 322 enrolled. *Faculty:* 62 full-time (37 women). Expenses: Contact institution. *Financial support:* Fellowships with tuition reimbursements, research assistantships with tuition reimbursements, teaching assistantships with tuition reimbursements, career-related internships or fieldwork, Federal Work-Study, scholarships/grants, traineeships, health care benefits, tuition waivers (partial), and unspecified assistantships available. Support available to part-time students. Financial award applicants required to submit FAFSA. In 2016, 375 master's, 56 doctorates, 7 other advanced degrees awarded. *Program availability:* Part-time, evening/weekend. Offers applied developmental and educational psychology (MA, PhD); counseling psychology (PhD); curriculum and instruction (M Ed, PhD, CAES); education (M Ed, MA, MAT, MS, MST, Ed D, PhD, CAES); educational leadership (M Ed, Ed D, CAES); educational research, measurement, and evaluation (M Ed, MS, PhD); elementary education (M Ed, MAT); higher education (MA, PhD); international higher education (MA); mental health counseling (MA); reading and literacy (M Ed, MAT, CAES); secondary education (M Ed, MAT, MST); special needs: moderate disabilities (M Ed, CAES); special needs: severe disabilities (M Ed, CAES). *Application deadline:* For fall admission, 12/1 priority date for domestic and international students; for spring admission, 11/1 for domestic and international students. *Application fee:* $65. Electronic applications accepted. *Application Contact:* Jamie Grenon, Associate Dean for Graduate Admissions and Financial Aid, 617-552-4214, Fax: 617-552-0398, E-mail: grenonj@bc.edu. *Dean,* Dr. Stanton Wortham, 617-552-4200, Fax: 617-552-0812.

School of Social Work *Program availability:* Part-time. Offers social work (MSW, PhD). Electronic applications accepted.

School of Theology and Ministry *Program availability:* Part-time. Offers church leadership (MA); divinity (M Div); pastoral ministry (MA); religious education (MA, PhD); sacred theology (STD, STL); social justice/social ministry (MA); spiritual direction (MA); theological studies (MTS); theology (Th M, PhD); youth ministry (MA). Electronic applications accepted.

William F. Connell School of Nursing Students: 188 full-time (162 women), 70 part-time (63 women); includes 39 minority (8 Black or African American, non-Hispanic/Latino; 15 Asian, non-Hispanic/Latino; 11 Hispanic/Latino; 5 Two or more races, non-Hispanic/Latino). Average age 30. 322 applicants, 52% accepted, 75 enrolled. *Faculty:* 52 full-time (47 women), 48 part-time/adjunct (45 women). Expenses: Contact institution. *Financial support:* In 2016–17, 165 students received support, including 12 fellowships with full tuition reimbursements available (averaging $24,288 per year), 27 teaching assistantships (averaging $5,652 per year); research assistantships, scholarships/grants, health care benefits, tuition waivers (partial), and unspecified assistantships also available. Support available to part-time students. Financial award application deadline: 4/18; financial award applicants required to submit FAFSA. In 2016, 93 master's, 4 doctorates awarded. *Program availability:* Part-time. Offers adult-gerontology nursing (MS); family health nursing (MS); forensic nursing (MS); nurse anesthesia (MS); nursing (PhD); pediatric nursing (MS); psychiatric-mental health nursing (MS); women's health nursing (MS). *Application deadline:* For fall admission, 9/30 for domestic and international students; for winter admission, 1/15 for domestic and international students; for spring admission, 3/15 for domestic and international students. *Application fee:* $40. Electronic applications accepted. *Application Contact:* Sean Sendall, Assistant Dean, Graduate Enrollment and Data Analytics, 617-552-4745, Fax: 617-552-2121, E-mail: sean.sendall@bc.edu. *Dean,* Dr. Susan Gennaro, 617-552-4251, Fax: 617-552-0931, E-mail: susan.gennaro@bc.edu.

BOSTON GRADUATE SCHOOL OF PSYCHOANALYSIS, Brookline, MA 02446-4602

General Information Independent, coed, graduate-only institution. *Graduate housing:* On-campus housing not available. *Research affiliation:* Boston Institute for Psychotherapy (psychotherapy).

GRADUATE UNITS

BGSP-New Jersey Offers psychoanalysis (MA); psychoanalytic counseling (MA). Programs offered in conjunction with Academic of Clinical and Applied Psychoanalysis in Livingston, NJ.

CAGS and Certificate Programs *Program availability:* Part-time. Offers child and adolescent intervention (CAGS); psychoanalysis (Certificate); psychoanalytic psychotherapy (CAGS).

Doctoral Programs *Program availability:* Part-time. Offers psychoanalysis (Psya D); psychoanalysis, society and culture (Psya D).

Master's Programs *Program availability:* Part-time. Offers mental health counseling (MA); psychoanalysis (MA); psychoanalysis, society and culture (MA).

New York Graduate School of Psychoanalysis *Program availability:* Part-time. Offers psychoanalysis (MA).

BOSTON UNIVERSITY, Boston, MA 02215

General Information Independent, coed, university. CGS member. *Enrollment:* 32,695 graduate, professional, and undergraduate students; 9,756 full-time matriculated graduate/professional students (5,479 women), 4,866 part-time matriculated graduate/professional students (2,722 women). *Enrollment by degree level:* 9,421 master's, 5,003 doctoral, 198 other advanced degrees. *Graduate housing:* On-campus housing not available. *Student services:* Campus employment opportunities, campus safety program, career counseling, child daycare facilities, exercise/wellness program, free psychological counseling, international student services, low-cost health insurance, services for students with disabilities, writing training. *Library facilities:* Mugar Memorial Library plus 20 others. *Collection:* Books: 2.6 million (physical), 1.5 million (digital/electronic); Databases: 578. Weekly public service hours: 123; students can reserve study rooms. *Research affiliation:* NASA-Ames Research Center, Society for the Preservation of New England Antiquities, Massachusetts Historical Society, Woods Hole Oceanographic Institution-Marine Biological Laboratory.

Computer facilities: Computer purchase and lease plans are available. 250 computers available on campus for general student use. A campuswide network can be accessed from student residence rooms and from off campus. Online class registration, research and educational networks are available.
Website: http://www.bu.edu/

GRADUATE UNITS

College of Communication Students: 333 full-time (256 women), 16 part-time (12 women); includes 46 minority (7 Black or African American, non-Hispanic/Latino; 8 Asian, non-Hispanic/Latino; 24 Hispanic/Latino; 7 Two or more races, non-Hispanic/Latino), 149 international. Average age 24. 975 applicants, 61% accepted, 222 enrolled. *Faculty:* 67 full-time, 73 part-time/adjunct. Expenses: Contact institution. *Financial support:* In 2016–17, 125 students received support, including 5 research assistantships (averaging $10,000 per year), 50 teaching assistantships (averaging $8,000 per year); career-related internships or fieldwork, Federal Work-Study, institutionally sponsored loans, scholarships/grants, health care benefits, and unspecified assistantships also available. Support available to part-time students. Financial award application deadline: 5/1; financial award applicants required to submit FAFSA. In 2016, 169 master's awarded. *Program availability:* Part-time. Offers advertising (MS); communication (MA, MFA, MS, PhD); film and television (MFA, MS); journalism (MS). *Application deadline:* For fall admission, 5/1 for domestic and international students. Applications are processed on a rolling basis. *Application fee:* $95. Electronic applications accepted. *Application Contact:* Manny Dotel, Assistant Director, Graduate Affairs, 617-353-3481, E-mail: comgrad@bu.edu. *Dean,* Thomas Fiedler, 617-353-3450, Fax: 617-358-0399, E-mail: comdean@bu.edu.

Division of Emerging Media Studies Students: 46 full-time (37 women), 5 part-time (3 women); includes 7 minority (3 Black or African American, non-Hispanic/Latino; 2 Asian, non-Hispanic/Latino; 1 Hispanic/Latino; 1 Two or more races, non-Hispanic/Latino), 24 international. Average age 24. 72 applicants, 44% accepted, 15 enrolled. *Faculty:* 4 full-time (1 woman). Expenses: Contact institution. *Financial support:* Fellowships, research assistantships, teaching assistantships, career-related internships or fieldwork, Federal Work-Study, institutionally sponsored loans, scholarships/grants, health care benefits, and unspecified assistantships available. Financial award applicants required to submit FAFSA. In 2016, 18 master's awarded. *Program availability:* Part-time. Offers emerging media studies (MA, PhD). *Application deadline:* For fall admission, 5/1 for domestic and international students. Applications are processed on a rolling basis. *Application fee:* $95. Electronic applications accepted. *Application Contact:* Haley Nielsen, Administrator of Admission and Financial Aid, 617-353-3481, E-mail: comgrad@bu.edu. *Professor of Emerging Media/Chair of the Division of Emerging Media Studies,* Dr. James Katz, 617-353-7733, E-mail: katz2020@bu.edu.

College of Engineering Students: 858 full-time (266 women), 183 part-time (48 women); includes 140 minority (6 Black or African American, non-Hispanic/Latino; 85 Asian, non-Hispanic/Latino; 31 Hispanic/Latino; 2 Native Hawaiian or other Pacific Islander, non-Hispanic/Latino; 16 Two or more races, non-Hispanic/Latino), 552 international. Average age 25. 3,089 applicants, 30% accepted, 372 enrolled. *Faculty:* 112 full-time (12 women), 9 part-time/adjunct (1 woman). Expenses: Contact institution. *Financial support:* In 2016–17, 458 students received support, including 115 fellowships with full tuition reimbursements available (averaging $33,000 per year), 246 research assistantships with full tuition reimbursements available (averaging $33,000 per year), 7 teaching assistantships with full tuition reimbursements available (averaging $22,000 per year); scholarships/grants and unspecified assistantships also available. Support available to part-time students. Financial award application deadline: 1/15; financial award applicants required to submit FAFSA. In 2016, 283 master's, 62 doctorates awarded. *Program availability:* Part-time, blended/hybrid learning. Offers biomedical engineering (M Eng, MS, PhD); computer engineering (M Eng, MS, PhD); engineering (M Eng, MS, PhD); manufacturing engineering (M Eng, MS); materials science and engineering (M Eng, MS, PhD); mechanical engineering (PhD); systems engineering (M Eng, MS, PhD). *Application deadline:* For fall admission, 12/15 for domestic and international students; for spring admission, 10/1 for domestic and international students. *Application fee:* $95. Electronic applications accepted. *Application Contact:* Andrew Butler, 617-353-9760, Fax: 617-353-0259, E-mail: enggrad@bu.edu. *Dean,* Dr. Kenneth R. Lutchen, 617-353-2800, Fax: 617-358-3468, E-mail: klutch@bu.edu.

College of Fine Arts Students: 1,054 full-time (618 women), 30 part-time (16 women); includes 151 minority (40 Black or African American, non-Hispanic/Latino; 2 American Indian or Alaska Native, non-Hispanic/Latino; 37 Asian, non-Hispanic/Latino; 49 Hispanic/Latino; 1 Native Hawaiian or other Pacific Islander, non-Hispanic/Latino; 22 Two or more races, non-Hispanic/Latino), 281 international. Average age 32. 1,472 applicants, 32% accepted, 169 enrolled. Expenses: Contact institution. *Financial support:* Fellowships, teaching assistantships, Federal Work-Study, and scholarships/grants available. Support available to part-time students. Financial award application deadline: 1/1. In 2016, 267 master's, 53 doctorates, 11 other advanced degrees awarded. *Program availability:* Part-time. Offers fine arts (MA, MFA, MM, DMA, Artist Diploma, CAS, Certificate, Performance Diploma). *Application deadline:* For fall admission, 1/15 for domestic and international students. *Application fee:* $80. Electronic applications accepted. *Application Contact:* Mark Krone, Manager, Graduate Admissions and Online Marketing, 617-353-3350, E-mail: arts@bu.edu. *Dean,* Lynne Allen, 617-353-3350.

School of Music Students: 378 full-time (218 women), 6 part-time (4 women); includes 48 minority (8 Black or African American, non-Hispanic/Latino; 14 Asian, non-Hispanic/Latino; 16 Hispanic/Latino; 10 Two or more races, non-Hispanic/Latino), 190 international. Average age 28. 1,027 applicants, 35% accepted, 111 enrolled. *Faculty:* 36 full-time, 21 part-time/adjunct. Expenses: Contact institution. *Financial support:*

Fellowships, teaching assistantships, scholarships/grants, and unspecified assistantships available. Financial award application deadline: 12/1. In 2016, 131 master's, 53 doctorates, 11 Artist Diplomas awarded. *Program availability:* Part-time. Offers choral conducting (MM); collaborative piano (DMA); composition and theory (DMA); conducting (Performance Diploma); historical performance (MM, Artist Diploma); music education (MM, DMA, CAS); music theory (MM); opera performance (Certificate); performance (MM). *Application deadline:* For fall admission, 12/1 priority date for domestic and international students. *Application fee:* $95. Electronic applications accepted. *Application Contact:* Shaun Ramsay, Assistant Director, Admissions and Student Affairs, 617-353-3341, E-mail: arts@bu.edu. *Director,* Shiela Kibbe, 617-353-3341, Fax: 617-353-7455, E-mail: cfamusic@bu.edu.

School of Theatre Students: 48 full-time (28 women), 2 part-time (0 women); includes 7 minority (1 Black or African American, non-Hispanic/Latino; 1 American Indian or Alaska Native, non-Hispanic/Latino; 3 Asian, non-Hispanic/Latino; 1 Hispanic/Latino; 1 Two or more races, non-Hispanic/Latino), 3 international. Average age 27. 142 applicants, 15% accepted, 16 enrolled. *Faculty:* 16 full-time, 9 part-time/adjunct. Expenses: Contact institution. *Financial support:* In 2016–17, 16 students received support. Fellowships, teaching assistantships, scholarships/grants, unspecified assistantships, and stipends available. Financial award application deadline: 2/1. In 2016, 14 master's awarded. Offers design (MFA); lighting crafts (Certificate); management (MFA); production (MFA); scenic painting (Certificate). *Application deadline:* For fall admission, 2/1 priority date for domestic and international students. *Application fee:* $95. Electronic applications accepted. *Application Contact:* Mark Krone, Manager, Graduate Admissions and Online Marketing, 617-353-3350, E-mail: arts@bu.edu. *Director,* Jim Petosa, 617-353-3390.

School of Visual Arts Students: 197 full-time (166 women), 3 part-time (all women); includes 24 minority (2 Black or African American, non-Hispanic/Latino; 9 Asian, non-Hispanic/Latino; 8 Hispanic/Latino; 5 Two or more races, non-Hispanic/Latino), 58 international. Average age 31. 257 applicants, 27% accepted, 21 enrolled. *Faculty:* 17 full-time, 4 part-time/adjunct. Expenses: Contact institution. *Financial support:* In 2016–17, 36 students received support. Fellowships, teaching assistantships, scholarships/grants, and unspecified assistantships available. Financial award application deadline: 2/1. In 2016, 122 master's awarded. Offers art education (MA); graphic design (MFA); painting (MFA); sculpture (MFA); studio teaching (MA). *Application deadline:* For fall admission, 2/1 for domestic and international students. Applications are processed on a rolling basis. *Application fee:* $80. *Application Contact:* Jessica Caccamo, Assistant Director, 617-353-3371, E-mail: visuarts@bu.edu. *Interim Director,* Jeannette Guillemin, 617-353-3371.

College of Health and Rehabilitation Sciences: Sargent College Students: 535 full-time (456 women), 57 part-time (52 women); includes 102 minority (4 Black or African American, non-Hispanic/Latino; 54 Asian, non-Hispanic/Latino; 24 Hispanic/Latino; 20 Two or more races, non-Hispanic/Latino), 31 international. Average age 25. 1,626 applicants, 21% accepted, 126 enrolled. *Faculty:* 54 full-time (42 women), 44 part-time/adjunct (28 women). Expenses: Contact institution. *Financial support:* In 2016–17, 302 students received support, including 24 research assistantships with full tuition reimbursements available (averaging $21,500 per year), 18 teaching assistantships (averaging $2,500 per year); career-related internships or fieldwork, Federal Work-Study, institutionally sponsored loans, scholarships/grants, and health care benefits also available. Support available to part-time students. Financial award application deadline: 1/1; financial award applicants required to submit FAFSA. In 2016, 123 master's, 125 doctorates awarded. *Program availability:* Blended/hybrid learning. Offers athletic training (PhD); health and rehabilitation sciences (MS, DPT, OTD, PhD); human physiology (MS, PhD); nutrition (MS); occupational therapy (OTD); physical therapy (DPT); rehabilitation sciences (PhD); speech, language and hearing sciences (PhD); speech-language pathology (MS). *Application deadline:* For fall admission, 1/1 priority date for domestic and international students. Applications are processed on a rolling basis. *Application fee:* $80. Electronic applications accepted. *Application Contact:* Sharon Sankey, Assistant Dean, Student Services, 617-353-2713, Fax: 617-353-7500, E-mail: ssankey@bu.edu. *Dean,* Dr. Christopher Moore, 617-353-2705, Fax: 617-353-7500, E-mail: mooreca@bu.edu.

Graduate School of Arts and Sciences Students: 1,850 full-time (913 women), 176 part-time (93 women); includes 236 minority (38 Black or African American, non-Hispanic/Latino; 90 Asian, non-Hispanic/Latino; 80 Hispanic/Latino; 28 Two or more races, non-Hispanic/Latino), 818 international. Average age 28. 8,109 applicants, 26% accepted, 577 enrolled. Expenses: Contact institution. *Financial support:* In 2016–17, 1,375 students received support, including 210 fellowships with full tuition reimbursements available (averaging $21,500 per year), 400 research assistantships with full tuition reimbursements available (averaging $21,500 per year), 575 teaching assistantships with full tuition reimbursements available (averaging $21,500 per year); career-related internships or fieldwork, Federal Work-Study, scholarships/grants, traineeships, health care benefits, and unspecified assistantships also available. In 2016, 407 master's, 202 doctorates awarded. Offers African American studies (MA); American and New England studies (MA); anthropology (PhD); applied anthropology (MA); archaeology (MA, PhD); art history (MA, PhD); arts and sciences (MA, MAEP, MFA, MM, MS, PhD, Certificate); astronomy (MA, PhD); bioinformatics (MS, PhD); biology (MA, PhD); biostatistics (MA, PhD); chemistry (MA, PhD); classical studies (MA, PhD); computer science (MS, PhD); creative writing (MFA); cyber security (MS); data-centric computing (MS); earth and environment (PhD); earth sciences (MA, PhD); economics (MA, MAEP, PhD); energy and environment (MA); English (MA, PhD); ethnomusicology (PhD); French language and literature (MA, PhD); geography (MA, PhD); global development policy (MA); Hispanic language and literatures (MA, PhD); historical musicology (PhD); historical musicology and ethnomusicology (PhD); history (MA, PhD); international relations and environmental policy (MA); linguistics (MA, PhD); mathematics (MA, PhD); molecular biology, cell biology, and biochemistry (MA, PhD); museum studies (Certificate); musicology (MM); philosophy (MA, PhD); physics (MA, PhD); playwriting (MFA); political science (PhD); preservation studies (MA); psychological and brain sciences (MA, PhD); remote sensing and geospatial sciences (MA); sociology (MA, PhD); statistical practice (MS); statistics (MA, PhD). *Application deadline:* For fall admission, 1/15 priority date for domestic and international students; for spring admission, 10/15 priority date for domestic and international students. *Application fee:* $95. Electronic applications accepted. *Application Contact:* Martin Gastmann, Assistant Director of Admissions and Financial Aid, 617-353-2696, Fax: 617-358-5492, E-mail: grs@bu.edu. *Associate Dean,* Dr. Emily Barman, 617-353-2696, Fax: 617-358-5492.

Editorial Institute Students: 16 full-time (10 women), 5 part-time (3 women); includes 5 minority (4 Hispanic/Latino; 1 Two or more races, non-Hispanic/Latino), 1 international. Average age 35. 1 applicant. Expenses: Contact institution. *Financial support:* In 2016–17, 16 students received support, including fellowships with full tuition reimbursements available (averaging $21,500 per year), 5 research assistantships with full tuition reimbursements available (averaging $21,500 per year), 3 teaching assistantships with full tuition reimbursements available (averaging

$21,500 per year); Federal Work-Study, scholarships/grants, and health care benefits also available. Financial award application deadline: 1/15. Offers editorial studies (MA). *Application deadline:* For fall admission, 4/15 for domestic and international students. *Application fee:* $95. Electronic applications accepted. *Application Contact:* Ellen Wrigley, Administrative Assistant, 617-353-6631, Fax: 617-353-6917, E-mail: ellen@bu.edu. *Director,* Archie Burnett, 617-353-6631, E-mail: burnetta@bu.edu.

Frederick S. Pardee School of Global Studies Students: 83 full-time (46 women), 18 part-time (11 women); includes 15 minority (5 Black or African American, non-Hispanic/Latino; 4 Asian, non-Hispanic/Latino; 5 Hispanic/Latino; 1 Two or more races, non-Hispanic/Latino), 37 international. Average age 26. 360 applicants, 73% accepted, 35 enrolled. *Faculty:* 33 full-time (8 women), 10 part-time/adjunct (4 women). Expenses: Contact institution. *Financial support:* In 2016–17, 30 students received support. Federal Work-Study, scholarships/grants, and unspecified assistantships available. Financial award application deadline: 1/15. In 2016, 35 master's awarded. Offers global studies (MA). *Application deadline:* For fall admission, 4/15 for domestic and international students; for spring admission, 10/15 for domestic and international students. Applications are processed on a rolling basis. *Application fee:* $95. Electronic applications accepted. *Application Contact:* Michael Williams, Graduate Program Administrator, 617-353-9349, Fax: 617-353-9290, E-mail: psgsgrad@bu.edu. *Dean,* Adil Najam, 617-358-0988, Fax: 617-353-9290, E-mail: anajam@bu.edu.

Graduate Division of Religious Studies Students: 52 full-time (24 women), 6 part-time (1 woman); includes 11 minority (3 Black or African American, non-Hispanic/Latino; 4 Asian, non-Hispanic/Latino; 3 Hispanic/Latino; 1 Two or more races, non-Hispanic/Latino), 6 international. Average age 32. 78 applicants, 18% accepted, 8 enrolled. Expenses: Contact institution. *Financial support:* In 2016–17, 52 students received support, including 22 fellowships with full tuition reimbursements available (averaging $21,500 per year), 3 research assistantships with full tuition reimbursements available (averaging $21,500 per year), 9 teaching assistantships with full tuition reimbursements available (averaging $21,500 per year); career-related internships or fieldwork, Federal Work-Study, scholarships/grants, health care benefits, and unspecified assistantships also available. Financial award application deadline: 1/15. In 2016, 5 master's, 10 doctorates awarded. Offers religious studies (MA, PhD). *Application deadline:* For fall admission, 1/15 for domestic and international students. *Application fee:* $95. Electronic applications accepted. *Application Contact:* Karen Nardella, Department Administrator, 617-353-2636, Fax: 617-358-3087, E-mail: kcn@bu.edu. *Director,* Adam Seligman, 617-358-0262, Fax: 617-358-3087, E-mail: seligman@bu.edu.

Henry M. Goldman School of Dental Medicine Students: 815 full-time (429 women); includes 194 minority (12 Black or African American, non-Hispanic/Latino; 128 Asian, non-Hispanic/Latino; 40 Hispanic/Latino; 14 Two or more races, non-Hispanic/Latino), 315 international. Average age 28. 6,456 applicants, 7% accepted, 270 enrolled. *Faculty:* 139 full-time (61 women), 100 part-time/adjunct (36 women). Expenses: Contact institution. *Financial support:* In 2016–17, 98 students received support. Career-related internships or fieldwork, institutionally sponsored loans, scholarships/grants, and stipends available. Financial award application deadline: 4/15; financial award applicants required to submit FAFSA. In 2016, 19 master's, 212 doctorates, 33 other advanced degrees awarded. Offers dental medicine (MS, MSD, D Sc, D Sc D, DMD, CAGS). *Application deadline:* For fall admission, 12/1 for domestic and international students. Applications are processed on a rolling basis. *Application fee:* $75. Electronic applications accepted. *Application Contact:* Admissions Representative, 617-638-4787, Fax: 617-638-4798, E-mail: applydmd@bu.edu. *Dean,* Dr. Jeffrey W. Hutter, 617-638-4780, E-mail: jhutter@bu.edu.

Metropolitan College Students: 430 full-time (200 women), 3,179 part-time (1,492 women); includes 912 minority (304 Black or African American, non-Hispanic/Latino; 9 American Indian or Alaska Native, non-Hispanic/Latino; 282 Asian, non-Hispanic/Latino; 262 Hispanic/Latino; 4 Native Hawaiian or other Pacific Islander, non-Hispanic/Latino; 51 Two or more races, non-Hispanic/Latino), 951 international. Average age 32. 1,745 applicants, 70% accepted, 748 enrolled. *Faculty:* 36 full-time (12 women), 199 part-time/adjunct (57 women). Expenses: Contact institution. *Financial support:* In 2016–17, 948 students received support, including 60 research assistantships (averaging $8,200 per year), 8 teaching assistantships (averaging $2,500 per year); career-related internships or fieldwork, scholarships/grants, and unspecified assistantships also available. Support available to part-time students. Financial award applicants required to submit FAFSA. In 2016, 1,078 master's awarded. *Program availability:* Part-time, evening/weekend, 100% online, blended/hybrid learning. Offers actuarial science (MS); advertising (MS); applied business analytics (MS); arts administration (MS, Graduate Certificate); city planning (MCP); communications (MLA); computer information systems (MS); computer networks (Certificate); computer science (MS); criminal justice (MCJ); data analytics (Certificate); digital forensics (Certificate); economic development and tourism management (MSAS); enterprise risk management (MS); financial management (MS); fundraising management (Graduate Certificate); global marketing management (MS); health communication (MS); health informatics (Certificate); history and culture (MLA); information technology project management (Certificate); innovation and technology (MSAS); insurance management (MSM); leadership (MS); project management (MS); software development (MS); software engineering in health care systems (Certificate); supply chain management (MS); telecommunications (MS); urban affairs (MUA). *Application deadline:* Applications are processed on a rolling basis. *Application fee:* $85. Electronic applications accepted. *Application Contact:* Kristin McAullife, Director, Enrollment Services, 617-353-6000, E-mail: met@bu.edu. *Dean,* Dr. Tanya Zlateva, 617-353-3010, Fax: 617-353-6066.

Questrom School of Business Students: 744 full-time (331 women), 734 part-time (315 women); includes 257 minority (41 Black or African American, non-Hispanic/Latino; 2 American Indian or Alaska Native, non-Hispanic/Latino; 123 Asian, non-Hispanic/Latino; 72 Hispanic/Latino; 1 Native Hawaiian or other Pacific Islander, non-Hispanic/Latino; 18 Two or more races, non-Hispanic/Latino), 441 international. Average age 28. 1,098 applicants, 37% accepted, 159 enrolled. *Faculty:* 77 full-time (21 women), 41 part-time/adjunct (7 women). Expenses: Contact institution. *Financial support:* Career-related internships or fieldwork, Federal Work-Study, institutionally sponsored loans, scholarships/grants, and tuition waivers (partial) available. Support available to part-time students. Financial award applicants required to submit FAFSA. In 2016, 492 master's, 7 doctorates awarded. *Program availability:* Part-time, evening/weekend. Offers business (EMBA, MBA); management (PhD); management studies (MSMS); mathematical finance (MS, PhD). *Application deadline:* For fall admission, 3/19 for domestic and international students; for spring admission, 11/8 for domestic students. *Application fee:* $125. Electronic applications accepted. *Application Contact:* Meredith C. Siegel, Assistant Dean, Graduate Admission, 617-353-2670, Fax: 617-353-7368, E-mail: mba@bu.edu. *Professor/Dean,* Kenneth W. Freeman, 617-353-9720, Fax: 617-353-5581, E-mail: kfreeman@bu.edu.

School of Education Students: 293 full-time (222 women), 492 part-time (361 women); includes 186 minority (60 Black or African American, non-Hispanic/Latino; 46 Asian, non-Hispanic/Latino; 62 Hispanic/Latino; 1 Native Hawaiian or other Pacific Islander, non-Hispanic/Latino; 17 Two or more races, non-Hispanic/Latino), 78 international. Average age 28. 1,039 applicants, 64% accepted, 292 enrolled. Expenses: Contact institution. *Financial support:* Fellowships with full tuition reimbursements, research assistantships, teaching assistantships with partial tuition reimbursements, career-related internships or fieldwork, Federal Work-Study, and scholarships/grants available. Support available to part-time students. Financial award applicants required to submit FAFSA. In 2016, 276 master's, 19 doctorates, 13 other advanced degrees awarded. *Program availability:* Part-time, evening/weekend. Offers education (Ed M, MAT, Ed D, PhD, CAGS). *Application deadline:* For fall admission, 1/15 priority date for domestic and international students; for spring admission, 9/15 priority date for domestic and international students. Applications are processed on a rolling basis. *Application fee:* $95. Electronic applications accepted. *Application Contact:* Katharine Nelson, Director of Graduate Student Services, 617-353-4237, E-mail: sedgrad@bu.edu. *Dean,* Dr. Hardin Coleman, 617-353-3213.

School of Law Students: 903 full-time (492 women), 150 part-time (76 women); includes 227 minority (43 Black or African American, non-Hispanic/Latino; 2 American Indian or Alaska Native, non-Hispanic/Latino; 61 Asian, non-Hispanic/Latino; 94 Hispanic/Latino; 1 Native Hawaiian or other Pacific Islander, non-Hispanic/Latino; 26 Two or more races, non-Hispanic/Latino). Average age 27. 4,800 applicants, 29% accepted, 208 enrolled. *Faculty:* 45 full-time (23 women), 111 part-time/adjunct (34 women). Expenses: Contact institution. *Financial support:* In 2016–17, 616 students received support. Career-related internships or fieldwork, Federal Work-Study, institutionally sponsored loans, and scholarships/grants available. Financial award application deadline: 3/1; financial award applicants required to submit FAFSA. In 2016, 258 master's, 224 doctorates awarded. *Program availability:* 100% online, blended/hybrid learning. Offers law (LL M, JD). MD/JD offered jointly with the School of Medicine. *Application deadline:* For fall admission, 4/1 for domestic and international students. Applications are processed on a rolling basis. *Application fee:* $85. Electronic applications accepted. *Application Contact:* Alissa Leonard, Director of Admissions and Financial Aid, 617-353-3100, Fax: 617-353-0578, E-mail: bulawadm@bu.edu. *Dean,* Maureen A. O'Rourke, 617-353-3112, Fax: 617-358-4706, E-mail: lawdean@bu.edu.

School of Medicine Students: 1,777 full-time (995 women), 128 part-time (62 women); includes 589 minority (53 Black or African American, non-Hispanic/Latino; 2 American Indian or Alaska Native, non-Hispanic/Latino; 353 Asian, non-Hispanic/Latino; 131 Hispanic/Latino; 3 Native Hawaiian or other Pacific Islander, non-Hispanic/Latino; 47 Two or more races, non-Hispanic/Latino), 154 international. Average age 26. Expenses: Contact institution. *Financial support:* In 2016–17, 377 students received support. Fellowships, research assistantships, teaching assistantships, career-related internships or fieldwork, Federal Work-Study, institutionally sponsored loans, and scholarships/grants available. Support available to part-time students. Financial award application deadline: 4/15; financial award applicants required to submit FAFSA. In 2016, 314 master's, 253 doctorates awarded. *Program availability:* Part-time, evening/weekend. Offers medicine (MA, MS, MD, PhD). *Application Contact:* Dr. Robert Witzburg, Associate Dean for Admissions, 617-638-4630. *Dean,* Dr. Karen H. Antman, 617-638-5300.

Division of Graduate Medical Sciences Students: 988 full-time (576 women), 106 part-time (56 women); includes 340 minority (33 Black or African American, non-Hispanic/Latino; 2 American Indian or Alaska Native, non-Hispanic/Latino; 199 Asian, non-Hispanic/Latino; 72 Hispanic/Latino; 1 Native Hawaiian or other Pacific Islander, non-Hispanic/Latino; 33 Two or more races, non-Hispanic/Latino), 101 international. Average age 26. 2,525 applicants, 32% accepted, 386 enrolled. *Faculty:* 1,020 full-time (460 women), 517 part-time/adjunct (212 women). Expenses: Contact institution. *Financial support:* In 2016–17, fellowships (averaging $32,250 per year), research assistantships (averaging $32,250 per year), teaching assistantships (averaging $32,250 per year) were awarded; Federal Work-Study, scholarships/grants, and traineeships also available. Financial award applicants required to submit FAFSA. In 2016, 314 master's, 66 doctorates awarded. *Program availability:* Part-time. Offers anatomy and neurobiology (MA, PhD); behavioral neuroscience (PhD); biochemistry (MA, PhD); bioimaging (MS); biomedical forensic sciences (MS); biomedical sciences (PhD); cell and molecular biology (PhD); clinical investigation (MA); forensic anthropology (MS); genetic counseling (MS); genetics and genomics (PhD); healthcare emergency management (MS); immunology (PhD); medical anthropology and cross cultural practice (MA); medical sciences (MA, MS, PhD); mental health counseling and behavioral medicine (MA); microbiology (PhD); molecular medicine (PhD); neuroscience (PhD); nutrition and metabolism (MS, PhD); oral biology (PhD); oral health sciences (MS); pathology and laboratory medicine (PhD); pharmacology and experimental therapeutics (MA, PhD); physician assistant (MS); physiology and biophysics (MA, PhD). *Application deadline:* For fall admission, 1/31 for domestic and international students; for spring admission, 10/15 for domestic and international students. *Application fee:* $95. Electronic applications accepted. *Application Contact:* GMS Admissions Office, 617-638-5255, Fax: 617-638-5740, E-mail: askgms@bu.edu. *Associate Provost,* Dr. Linda Hyman, 617-638-5255, Fax: 617-638-5740.

School of Public Health Students: 677 full-time (548 women), 390 part-time (333 women); includes 298 minority (82 Black or African American, non-Hispanic/Latino; 2 American Indian or Alaska Native, non-Hispanic/Latino; 113 Asian, non-Hispanic/Latino; 73 Hispanic/Latino; 1 Native Hawaiian or other Pacific Islander, non-Hispanic/Latino; 27 Two or more races, non-Hispanic/Latino), 121 international. Average age 27. 2,594 applicants, 43% accepted, 396 enrolled. *Faculty:* 153 full-time, 271 part-time/adjunct. Expenses: Contact institution. *Financial support:* In 2016–17, 421 students received support. Fellowships, teaching assistantships, career-related internships or fieldwork, Federal Work-Study, institutionally sponsored loans, scholarships/grants, traineeships, and tuition waivers (partial) available. Support available to part-time students. Financial award application deadline: 5/31; financial award applicants required to submit FAFSA. In 2016, 480 master's, 18 doctorates awarded. *Program availability:* Part-time, evening/weekend. Offers biostatistics (MA, MPH, PhD); community health sciences (MPH, Dr PH); environmental health (MPH, MS, PhD); epidemiology (MPH, MS, PhD); global health (MPH, Dr PH); health services research (MS); public health (MA, MPH, MS, Dr PH, PhD). *Application deadline:* For fall admission, 1/1 priority date for domestic and international students; for spring admission, 10/1 priority date for domestic and international students. Applications are processed on a rolling basis. *Application fee:* $120. Electronic applications accepted. *Application Contact:* LePhan Quan, Associate Director of Admissions, 617-638-4640, Fax: 617-638-5299, E-mail: asksph@bu.edu. *Dean,* Dr. Sandro Galea, 617-638-4640, Fax: 617-638-5299, E-mail: asksph@bu.edu.

School of Social Work Students: 244 full-time (221 women), 655 part-time (587 women); includes 234 minority (78 Black or African American, non-Hispanic/Latino; 4 American Indian or Alaska Native, non-Hispanic/Latino; 24 Asian, non-Hispanic/Latino; 103 Hispanic/Latino; 3 Native Hawaiian or other Pacific Islander, non-Hispanic/Latino; 22 Two or more races, non-Hispanic/Latino), 8 international. Average age 31. 937 applicants, 64% accepted, 179 enrolled. *Faculty:* 28 full-time (18 women), 39 part-time/adjunct (28 women). Expenses: Contact institution. *Financial support:* In 2016–17, 158 students received support. Career-related internships or fieldwork, Federal Work-Study, institutionally sponsored loans, and scholarships/grants available. Support available to part-time students. Financial award application deadline: 3/1; financial award applicants required to submit FAFSA. In 2016, 241 master's, 5 doctorates awarded. *Program availability:* Part-time, evening/weekend, 100% online. Offers social work (MSW, PhD). *Application deadline:* For fall admission, 1/13 priority date for domestic students, 1/13 for international students. *Application fee:* $95. Electronic applications accepted. *Application Contact:* Julie Billings, Admissions and Financial Aid Coordinator, 617-353-3750, Fax: 617-353-5612, E-mail: busswad@bu.edu. *Dean,* Gail Steketee, 617-353-3760, Fax: 617-353-5612.

School of Theology Students: 260 full-time (131 women), 69 part-time (30 women); includes 69 minority (36 Black or African American, non-Hispanic/Latino; 10 Asian, non-Hispanic/Latino; 16 Hispanic/Latino; 7 Two or more races, non-Hispanic/Latino), 53 international. Average age 35. 234 applicants, 71% accepted, 106 enrolled. *Faculty:* 34 full-time (14 women), 7 part-time/adjunct (3 women). Expenses: Contact institution. *Financial support:* In 2016–17, 252 students received support, including 78 fellowships with full tuition reimbursements available (averaging $4,537 per year), 32 research assistantships (averaging $6,000 per year), 32 teaching assistantships with full and partial tuition reimbursements available (averaging $20,000 per year); career-related internships or fieldwork, Federal Work-Study, institutionally sponsored loans, scholarships/grants, traineeships, health care benefits, tuition waivers (full and partial), and unspecified assistantships also available. Support available to part-time students. Financial award application deadline: 7/15; financial award applicants required to submit FAFSA. In 2016, 78 master's, 9 doctorates awarded. *Program availability:* Part-time, blended/hybrid learning. Offers chaplaincy (M Div); choral conducting (MSM); church and the arts (M Div); constructive theology and ethics (PhD); ecological theology and ethics (MTS); global and community engagement (M Div); history and hermeneutics (PhD); organ (MSM); pastoral ministry (M Div); practical theology (PhD); religion and conflict transformation (MTS); religion and science (MTS); religion and the academy (M Div); spirituality studies (MTS); theology (MTS, STM); transcultural studies (MTS); transformational leadership (D Min). PhD in history and hermeneutics: mission studies offered in collaboration with Gordon-Conwell Theological Seminary. *Application deadline:* For fall admission, 1/15 priority date for domestic and international students; for spring admission, 10/15 priority date for domestic and international students. Applications are processed on a rolling basis. *Application fee:* $95. Electronic applications accepted. *Application Contact:* Rev. Anastasia Kidd, Director of Admissions and College Relations, 617-353-3036, Fax: 617-358-0140, E-mail: sthadmis@bu.edu. *Dean,* Rev. Dr. Mary Elizabeth Moore, 617-353-3050, Fax: 617-353-3061, E-mail: memoore@bu.edu.

BOWIE STATE UNIVERSITY, Bowie, MD 20715-9465

General Information State-supported, coed, comprehensive institution. CGS member. *Graduate housing:* Room and/or apartments available on a first-come, first-served basis to single students; on-campus housing not available to married students. Housing application deadline: 8/1.

GRADUATE UNITS

Graduate Programs *Program availability:* Part-time, evening/weekend. Offers administration of nursing services (MS); applied and computational mathematics (MS); business administration (MBA); computer science (MS, App Sc D); counseling psychology (MA); educational leadership (Ed D); elementary and secondary school administration (M Ed); elementary education (M Ed); English (MA); family nurse practitioner (MS); guidance and counseling (M Ed); human resource development (MA); information systems analyst (Certificate); management information systems (MS); mental health counseling (MA); nursing education (MS); organizational communication (MA, Certificate); public administration (MPA); reading education (M Ed); school administration and supervision (M Ed); secondary education (M Ed); special education (M Ed); teaching (MAT). Electronic applications accepted.

BOWLING GREEN STATE UNIVERSITY, Bowling Green, OH 43403

General Information State-supported, coed, university. CGS member. *Graduate housing:* Rooms and/or apartments available to single and married students. *Student services:* Campus employment opportunities, campus safety program, career counseling, child daycare facilities, exercise/wellness program, free psychological counseling, grant writing training, international student services, low-cost health insurance, multicultural affairs office, services for students with disabilities, teacher training, writing training. *Library facilities:* William T. Jerome Library. *Collection:* Books: 143,305 (physical), 104,852 (digital/electronic); Serial titles: 825 (physical), 11,511 (digital/electronic); Databases: 268. Weekly public service hours: 110; students can reserve study rooms. *Research affiliation:* Spectra Group, Inc. (photoscience).

Computer facilities: Computer purchase and lease plans are available. 1,500 computers available on campus for general student use. A campuswide network can be accessed from student residence rooms and from off campus. Online class registration, wireless networking, filesharing software, bursar billing information and payment, view and change personal information, order official and unofficial transcripts, check meal plan balance, apply for graduation are available. Website: http://www.bgsu.edu/

General Application Contact: Dr. Alexander Goberman, Associate Dean, Graduate College, 419-372-7710, Fax: 419-372-8569, E-mail: goberma@bgsu.edu.

GRADUATE UNITS

Graduate College Expenses: Contact institution. *Financial support:* Fellowships with full tuition reimbursements, research assistantships with full and partial tuition reimbursements, teaching assistantships with full and partial tuition reimbursements, career-related internships or fieldwork, Federal Work-Study, institutionally sponsored loans, tuition waivers (full and partial), and unspecified assistantships available. Support available to part-time students. Financial award applicants required to submit FAFSA. *Program availability:* Part-time, evening/weekend. *Application fee:* $30. Electronic applications accepted. *Application Contact:* Dr. Terry L. Lawrence, Assistant Dean for Graduate Admissions and Studies, 419-372-7713, Fax: 419-372-8569, E-mail: tlawren@bgnet.bgsu.edu. *Acting Vice Provost for Research/Dean,* Dr. Deanne Snavely, 419-372-7714, Fax: 419-372-8569, E-mail: snavely@bgsu.edu.

College of Arts and Sciences Expenses: Contact institution. *Financial support:* Fellowships, research assistantships with full and partial tuition reimbursements, teaching assistantships with full and partial tuition reimbursements, career-related internships or fieldwork, Federal Work-Study, institutionally sponsored loans, tuition waivers (full and partial), and unspecified assistantships available. Support available to part-time students. Financial award applicants required to submit FAFSA. *Program availability:* Part-time. Offers 2-D studio art (MA, MFA); 3-D studio art (MA, MFA);

Bowling Green State University

American culture studies (MA, PhD); applied philosophy (PhD); art education (MA); art history (MA); arts and sciences (MA, MAT, MFA, MPA, MS, PhD); biological sciences (MS, PhD); chemistry (MS, PhD); clinical psychology (MA, PhD); computer art (MA); computer science (MS); creative writing (MFA); demography and population studies (MA); design (MFA); developmental psychology (MA, PhD); digital arts (MFA); English (MA, PhD); experimental psychology (MA, PhD); fiction (MFA); French (MA); geology (MS); geophysics (MS); German (MA); graphics (MFA); history (MA, MAT, PhD); industrial/organizational psychology (MA, PhD); institutional theory and history (PhD); literature (MA); mathematics (MA, MAT, PhD); media and communication (MA, PhD); philosophy (MA); photochemical sciences (PhD); physics (MAT, MS); poetry (MFA); popular culture (MA); public administration (MPA); public history (MA); quantitative psychology (MA, PhD); rhetoric and writing (PhD); scientific and technical communication (MA); social psychology (MA); sociology (PhD); Spanish (MA); statistics (PhD); strategic communication (MA); theatre and film (MA, PhD). *Application fee:* $30. Electronic applications accepted. *Application Contact:* Dr. Terry L. Lawrence, Assistant Dean for Graduate Admissions and Studies, 419-372-7713, Fax: 419-372-8569, E-mail: tlawren@bgnet.bgsu.edu. *Dean,* Dr. Donald Nieman, 419-372-2340.

College of Business Expenses: Contact institution. *Financial support:* Research assistantships with full tuition reimbursements, teaching assistantships with full tuition reimbursements, career-related internships or fieldwork, Federal Work-Study, institutionally sponsored loans, and unspecified assistantships available. Financial award applicants required to submit FAFSA. *Program availability:* Part-time, evening/weekend. Offers accountancy (M Acc); applied statistics (MS); business (M Acc, MA, MBA, MOD, MS); business administration (MBA); financial economics (MA); organization development (MOD). *Application deadline:* Applications are processed on a rolling basis. *Application fee:* $30. Electronic applications accepted. *Application Contact:* Dr. Terry L. Lawrence, Assistant Dean for Graduate Admissions and Studies, 419-372-7713, Fax: 419-372-8569, E-mail: tlawren@bgnet.bgsu.edu. *Dean,* Dr. Rodney Rogers, 419-372-2747.

College of Education and Human Development Expenses: Contact institution. *Financial support:* Research assistantships with full tuition reimbursements, teaching assistantships with full tuition reimbursements, career-related internships or fieldwork, Federal Work-Study, institutionally sponsored loans, tuition waivers (full and partial), and unspecified assistantships available. Support available to part-time students. Financial award applicants required to submit FAFSA. *Program availability:* Part-time, evening/weekend. Offers assistive technology (M Ed); autism spectrum disorders (M Ed); classroom technology (M Ed); clinical mental health counseling (M Ed, MA); college student personnel (MA); cross-cultural and international education (MA); curriculum and teaching (M Ed); developmental kinesiology (M Ed); education and human development (M Ed, MA, Ed D, PhD, Ed S); educational administration and supervision (M Ed, Ed D, Ed S); educational leadership (M Ed, Ed S); general special education (M Ed); higher education administration (PhD); intervention specialist: mild/moderate disabilities (M Ed); intervention specialist: moderate/intensive disabilities (M Ed); leadership studies (Ed D); reading (M Ed, Ed S); recreation and leisure (M Ed); school counseling (M Ed); secondary transition/transition-to-work (M Ed); special education (M Ed); sport administration (M Ed); workforce education and development (M Ed). *Application deadline:* Applications are processed on a rolling basis. *Application fee:* $30. Electronic applications accepted. *Application Contact:* Dr. Terry L. Lawrence, Assistant Dean for Graduate Admissions and Studies, 419-372-7713, Fax: 419-372-8569, E-mail: tlawren@bgnet.bgsu.edu. *Interim Dean,* Dr. Rosalino Hammond.

College of Health and Human Services Expenses: Contact institution. *Financial support:* Fellowships with full tuition reimbursements, research assistantships with full tuition reimbursements, teaching assistantships with full tuition reimbursements, career-related internships or fieldwork, Federal Work-Study, institutionally sponsored loans, and unspecified assistantships available. Financial award applicants required to submit FAFSA. *Program availability:* Part-time, evening/weekend. Offers communication disorders (PhD); criminal justice (MSCJ); health and human services (MPH, MS, MSCJ, PhD); public health (MPH); speech-language pathology (MS). *Application fee:* $30. Electronic applications accepted. *Application Contact:* Dr. Terry L. Lawrence, Assistant Dean for Graduate Admissions and Studies, 419-372-7713, Fax: 419-372-8569, E-mail: tlawren@bgnet.bgsu.edu. *Dean,* Dr. Linda Petrosino, 419-372-8243.

College of Musical Arts Expenses: Contact institution. *Financial support:* Research assistantships with full tuition reimbursements, teaching assistantships with full tuition reimbursements, career-related internships or fieldwork, Federal Work-Study, and unspecified assistantships available. Financial award applicants required to submit FAFSA. *Program availability:* Part-time. Offers composition (MM); contemporary music (DMA); ethnomusicology (MM); music education (MM); music history (MM); music theory (MM); performance (MM). *Application deadline:* For fall admission, 3/1 priority date for domestic students. *Application fee:* $30. Electronic applications accepted. *Application Contact:* Dr. Robert Satterlee, Graduate Coordinator, 419-372-2360. *Dean,* Dr. Richard Kennell, 419-372-2188.

College of Technology Expenses: Contact institution. *Financial support:* Research assistantships with full tuition reimbursements, teaching assistantships with full tuition reimbursements, career-related internships or fieldwork, Federal Work-Study, institutionally sponsored loans, tuition waivers (full and partial), and unspecified assistantships available. Financial award applicants required to submit FAFSA. *Program availability:* Part-time. Offers career and technology education (M Ed); technology (M Ed). *Application fee:* $30. Electronic applications accepted. *Application Contact:* Dr. Terry L. Lawrence, Assistant Dean for Graduate Admissions and Studies, 419-372-7713, Fax: 419-372-8569, E-mail: tlawren@bgnet.bgsu.edu. *Dean,* Dr. C. Wayne Unsell, 419-372-2438.

Interdisciplinary Studies Expenses: Contact institution. *Financial support:* Fellowships with full tuition reimbursements, research assistantships with full tuition reimbursements, teaching assistantships with full tuition reimbursements, Federal Work-Study, and unspecified assistantships available. Financial award applicants required to submit FAFSA. *Program availability:* Part-time. Offers interdisciplinary studies (M Ed, MA, MS, PhD). *Application fee:* $30. Electronic applications accepted. *Application Contact:* Dr. Terry L. Lawrence, Assistant Dean for Graduate Admissions and Studies, 419-372-7713, Fax: 419-372-8569, E-mail: tlawren@bgnet.bgsu.edu. *Acting Vice Provost for Research/Dean,* Dr. Deanne Snavely, 419-372-7714, Fax: 419-372-8569, E-mail: snavely@bgsu.edu.

BRADLEY UNIVERSITY, Peoria, IL 61625-0002

General Information Independent, coed, comprehensive institution. CGS member. *Enrollment:* 5,598 graduate, professional, and undergraduate students; 386 full-time matriculated graduate/professional students (166 women), 588 part-time matriculated graduate/professional students (424 women). *Enrollment by degree level:* 669 master's, 227 doctoral, 79 other advanced degrees. *Graduate faculty:* 197 full-time (78 women), 24 part-time/adjunct (15 women). *Tuition:* Full-time $7650; part-time $850 per credit. *Required fees:* $50 per credit. One-time fee: $100 full-time. *Graduate housing:* On-campus housing not available. *Student services:* Campus employment opportunities, campus safety program, career counseling, exercise/wellness program, free psychological counseling, international student services, low-cost health insurance, multicultural affairs office, services for students with disabilities, teacher training. *Library facilities:* Cullom-Davis Library. *Collection:* Books: 446,041 (physical), 43,242 (digital/electronic); Serial titles: 280 (physical), 57,963 (digital/electronic); Databases: 54. Weekly public service hours: 108; students can reserve study rooms. *Research affiliation:* Illinois Manufacturing Extension Center, Northern Research Laboratory, Peoria School of Medicine, Caterpillar, Inc., Ford Motor Credit/Visteon.

Computer facilities: Computer purchase and lease plans are available. 103 computers available on campus for general student use. A campuswide network can be accessed from student residence rooms and from off campus. Online class registration, online directory, catalog and other resources are available.
Website: http://www.bradley.edu/

General Application Contact: Kayla Carroll, Director, Graduate International Admissions and Student Services, 309-677-2375, Fax: 309-677-3343, E-mail: bugrad@bradley.edu.

GRADUATE UNITS

The Graduate School Expenses: Contact institution. *Financial support:* Fellowships with full tuition reimbursements, research assistantships with full tuition reimbursements, career-related internships or fieldwork, institutionally sponsored loans, scholarships/grants, tuition waivers (partial), and unspecified assistantships available. Support available to part-time students. Financial award application deadline: 4/1. *Program availability:* Part-time, evening/weekend. *Application deadline:* For fall admission, 5/15 priority date for domestic and international students; for spring admission, 10/15 priority date for domestic and international students. Applications are processed on a rolling basis. *Application fee:* $40 ($50 for international students). Electronic applications accepted. *Application Contact:* Kayla Carroll, Director of International Admissions and Student Services, 309-677-2375, E-mail: klcarroll@fsmail.bradley.edu. *Dean,* Jeffrey Bakken, 309-677-2375, E-mail: jbakken@fsmail.bradley.edu.

Caterpillar College of Engineering and Technology Expenses: Contact institution. *Financial support:* Research assistantships with full and partial tuition reimbursements, teaching assistantships, institutionally sponsored loans, scholarships/grants, tuition waivers (partial), and unspecified assistantships available. Support available to part-time students. Financial award application deadline: 4/1. *Program availability:* Part-time, evening/weekend. Offers civil engineering and construction (MSCE); electrical and computer engineering (MSEE); engineering and technology (MS, MSCE, MSEE, MSME); industrial engineering (MS); manufacturing engineering (MS); mechanical engineering (MSME). *Application deadline:* For fall admission, 5/15 priority date for domestic and international students; for spring admission, 10/15 priority date for domestic and international students. Applications are processed on a rolling basis. *Application fee:* $40 ($50 for international students). Electronic applications accepted. *Application Contact:* Kayla Carroll, Director of International Admissions and Student Services, 309-677-2375, E-mail: klcarroll@fsmail.bradley.edu. *Dean,* Lex Akers, 309-677-2721, E-mail: lakers@bradley.edu.

College of Education and Health Sciences Expenses: Contact institution. *Financial support:* Research assistantships with full and partial tuition reimbursements, career-related internships or fieldwork, institutionally sponsored loans, scholarships/grants, tuition waivers (partial), and unspecified assistantships available. Support available to part-time students. Financial award application deadline: 4/1. *Program availability:* Part-time, evening/weekend. Offers counseling (MA); curriculum and instruction (MA); dietetic internship (MS); education and health sciences (MA, MS, MSN, DNP, DPT, Certificate); family nurse practitioner (MSN, DNP, Certificate); leadership (DNP); leadership in educational administration (MA); nonprofit leadership (MA); nursing administration (MSN); nursing education (MSN, Certificate); physical therapy (DPT). *Application deadline:* For fall admission, 5/15 priority date for domestic students, 5/15 for international students; for spring admission, 10/15 priority date for domestic students, 10/15 for international students. Applications are processed on a rolling basis. *Application fee:* $40 ($50 for international students). Electronic applications accepted. *Application Contact:* Kayla Carroll, Director of International Admissions and Student Services, 309-677-2375, E-mail: klcarroll@fsmail.bradley.edu. *Dean,* Dr. Joan Sattler, 309-677-3181, E-mail: jls@bradley.edu.

College of Liberal Arts and Sciences Expenses: Contact institution. *Financial support:* Research assistantships with full and partial tuition reimbursements, teaching assistantships, career-related internships or fieldwork, institutionally sponsored loans, scholarships/grants, tuition waivers (partial), and unspecified assistantships available. Support available to part-time students. Financial award application deadline: 4/1. *Program availability:* Part-time, evening/weekend. Offers biochemistry (MS); biology (MS); chemistry (MS); computer information systems (MS); computer science (MS); English (MA); liberal arts and sciences (MA, MS). *Application deadline:* For fall admission, 5/15 priority date for domestic and international students; for spring admission, 10/15 priority date for domestic and international students. Applications are processed on a rolling basis. *Application fee:* $40 ($50 for international students). Electronic applications accepted. *Application Contact:* Kayla Carroll, Director of International Admissions and Student Services, 309-677-2375, E-mail: klcarroll@fsmail.bradley.edu. *Dean,* Dr. Christopher Jones, 309-677-2380, E-mail: cmjones@bradley.edu.

Foster College of Business Expenses: Contact institution. *Financial support:* Research assistantships with full and partial tuition reimbursements, teaching assistantships with full and partial tuition reimbursements, career-related internships or fieldwork, scholarships/grants, tuition waivers (partial), and unspecified assistantships available. Support available to part-time students. Financial award application deadline: 4/1. *Program availability:* Part-time, evening/weekend. Offers accounting (MSA); business (MBA, MSA); business administration (MBA). *Application deadline:* For fall admission, 5/15 priority date for domestic and international students; for spring admission, 10/15 priority date for domestic and international students. Applications are processed on a rolling basis. *Application fee:* $40 ($50 for international students). Electronic applications accepted. *Application Contact:* Kayla Carroll, Director of International Admission and Student Services, 309-677-2375, E-mail: klcarroll@fsmail.bradley.edu. *Dean,* Dr. Darrell Radson, 309-677-2255, E-mail: radson@bradley.edu.

Slane College of Communications and Fine Arts Expenses: Contact institution. *Financial support:* Teaching assistantships with full and partial tuition reimbursements, scholarships/grants, tuition waivers (partial), and unspecified assistantships available. Support available to part-time students. Financial award application deadline: 4/1. *Program availability:* Part-time, evening/weekend. Offers ceramics (MA, MFA); communications and fine arts (MA, MFA); drawing (MA, MFA); electronic graphic design (MA, MFA); painting (MA, MFA); photography (MA, MFA); printmaking (MA, MFA); sculpture (MA, MFA). *Application deadline:* For fall admission, 4/1 priority date for domestic students, 4/11 priority date for international students; for spring admission, 11/1 priority date for domestic and international students. Applications are processed on a rolling basis. *Application fee:* $40 ($50 for international students). Electronic applications accepted. *Application Contact:* Kayla Carroll, Director of International Admission and Student Services, 309-677-2375, E-mail: klcarroll@fsmail.bradley.edu. *Dean,* Dr. Jeffrey Huberman, 309-677-2360.

BRANDEIS UNIVERSITY, Waltham, MA 02454-9110

General Information Independent, coed, university. CGS member. *Enrollment:* 5,729 graduate, professional, and undergraduate students; 1,608 full-time matriculated graduate/professional students (898 women), 513 part-time matriculated graduate/professional students (252 women). *Enrollment by degree level:* 1,404 master's, 604 doctoral, 113 other advanced degrees. *Graduate faculty:* 361 full-time (156 women), 208 part-time/adjunct (88 women). *Graduate housing:* On-campus housing not available. *Student services:* Campus employment opportunities, campus safety program, career counseling, child daycare facilities, exercise/wellness program, free psychological counseling, grant writing training, international student services, low-cost health insurance, multicultural affairs office, services for students with disabilities, teacher training, writing training. *Library facilities:* Goldfarb Library plus 1 other. *Collection:* Books: 984,446 (physical), 1.2 million (digital/electronic); Serial titles: 10,862 (physical), 35,968 (digital/electronic); Databases: 285. Students can reserve study rooms.

Computer facilities: Computer purchase and lease plans are available. 130 computers available on campus for general student use. A campuswide network can be accessed from student residence rooms and from off campus. Online class registration, educational software are available.
Website: http://www.brandeis.edu/
General Application Contact: 781-736-2000.

GRADUATE UNITS

Graduate School of Arts and Sciences Students: 805 full-time (394 women), 50 part-time (33 women); includes 117 minority (21 Black or African American, non-Hispanic/Latino; 2 American Indian or Alaska Native, non-Hispanic/Latino; 36 Asian, non-Hispanic/Latino; 47 Hispanic/Latino; 11 Two or more races, non-Hispanic/Latino), 251 international. 2,556 applicants, 36% accepted, 339 enrolled. *Faculty:* 306 full-time (132 women), 125 part-time/adjunct (62 women). Expenses: Contact institution. *Financial support:* In 2016–17, 298 fellowships with tuition reimbursements, 108 research assistantships with tuition reimbursements, 162 teaching assistantships with partial tuition reimbursements were awarded; Federal Work-Study, scholarships/grants, health care benefits, tuition waivers (full and partial), and unspecified assistantships also available. Support available to part-time students. Financial award application deadline: 4/15; financial award applicants required to submit FAFSA. In 2016, 258 master's, 61 doctorates awarded. *Program availability:* Part-time, blended/hybrid learning. Offers acting (MFA); anthropology (MA, PhD); anthropology and women's, gender, and sexuality studies (MA); anthropology/women's, gender, and sexuality studies (MA); arts and sciences (Ed M, MA, MAT, MFA, MS, PhD, CAGS, Postbaccalaureate Certificate); biochemistry and biophysics (MS, PhD); biotechnology (MS); brain, body and behavior (PhD); classical studies (MA); cognitive neuroscience (PhD); comparative humanities (MA); composition and theory (MA, MFA, PhD); computational linguistics (MA); computer science (MA, PhD); English (MA, PhD); English and women's, gender, and sexuality studies (MA); general psychology (MA); genetic counseling (MS); genetics (PhD); global studies (MA); history (MA, PhD); inorganic chemistry (MA, MS, PhD); Jewish day school (MAT); mathematics (MA, PhD, Postbaccalaureate Certificate); microbiology (PhD); molecular and cell biology (MS, PhD); molecular biology (PhD); musicology (MA, MFA, PhD); Near Eastern and Judaic studies (MA, PhD); Near Eastern and Judaic studies and women's, gender, and sexuality studies (MA); near Eastern and Judaic studies and women's, gender, and sexuality studies (MA); neurobiology (PhD); neuroscience (MS, PhD); organic chemistry (MA, MS, PhD); philosophy (MA); physical chemistry (MS, PhD); physics (MA, PhD); politics (MA, PhD); premedical studies (Postbaccalaureate Certificate); public elementary education (MAT); public policy and women's, gender, and sexuality studies (MA); quantitative biology (PhD); secondary education (MAT); social policy and sociology (PhD); social/developmental psychology (PhD); sociology (PhD); sociology and women's, gender, and sexuality studies (MA); studio art (Postbaccalaureate Certificate); sustainable international development and women's, gender, and sexuality studies (MA); teacher leadership (Ed M, CAGS); teaching of Hebrew (MAT); women's and gender studies (PhD). *Application deadline:* For fall admission, 1/15 priority date for domestic and international students; for spring admission, 11/1 for domestic and international students. Applications are processed on a rolling basis. *Application fee:* $75. Electronic applications accepted. *Application Contact:* Jaclyn Farina, Director of Admission, Graduate School of Arts and Sciences, 781-736-3410, Fax: 781-736-3412, E-mail: gradschool@brandeis.edu. *Dean,* Dr. Eric Chasalow, 781-736-3410, Fax: 781-736-3412, E-mail: gradschool@brandeis.edu.

The Heller School for Social Policy and Management *Program availability:* Part-time. Offers aging (MPP); assets and inequalities (PhD); behavioral health (MPP); child, youth, and family management (MBA); children, youth and families (MPP, PhD); coexistence and conflict (MA); general social policy (MPP); global health and development (PhD); health (MPP); health and behavioral health (PhD); health care management (MBA); international development (MA); international health policy and management (MS); poverty alleviation and development (MPP); social impact management (MBA); social policy and management (MBA); sustainable development (MBA). Electronic applications accepted.

International Business School (IBS) Students: 387 full-time (174 women), 26 part-time (11 women); includes 270 minority (21 Black or African American, non-Hispanic/Latino; 226 Asian, non-Hispanic/Latino; 23 Hispanic/Latino). Average age 26. 1,383 applicants, 26% accepted, 139 enrolled. *Faculty:* 32 full-time (13 women), 27 part-time/adjunct (4 women). Expenses: Contact institution. *Financial support:* In 2016–17, 176 students received support, including 11 fellowships (averaging $9,545 per year); research assistantships, teaching assistantships, career-related internships or fieldwork, institutionally sponsored loans, scholarships/grants, and health care benefits also available. Financial award application deadline: 1/15. In 2016, 171 master's, 3 doctorates awarded. Offers asset management (MSF); business economics (MA); corporate finance (MBA, MSF); data analytics (MBA); global trade (PhD); international business (MA, MBA, MSF, PhD); macroeconomics (PhD); marketing (MBA); real estate (MBA); risk management (MSF); transfer pricing and valuation (MSF). *Application deadline:* For fall admission, 11/1 for domestic and international students; for winter admission, 1/15 for domestic and international students; for spring admission, 3/15 for

domestic students, 3/15 priority date for international students; for summer admission, 5/1 for domestic and international students. *Application fee:* $100. Electronic applications accepted. *Application Contact:* Kelly Sugrue, Director of Admissions, 781-736-2252, Fax: 781-736-2263, E-mail: globaladmissions@brandeis.edu. *Dean,* Peter Petri, 781-736-2256.

Rabb School of Continuing Studies, Division of Graduate Professional Studies Students: 3 full-time (2 women), 352 part-time (156 women); includes 87 minority (37 Black or African American, non-Hispanic/Latino; 40 Asian, non-Hispanic/Latino; 3 Hispanic/Latino; 7 Two or more races, non-Hispanic/Latino), 1 international. Average age 38. 83 applicants, 98% accepted, 77 enrolled. *Faculty:* 45 part-time/adjunct (16 women). Expenses: Contact institution. *Financial support:* Applicants required to submit FAFSA. In 2016, 97 master's awarded. *Program availability:* Part-time-only. Offers bioinformatics (MS); digital innovation for finance technology (MS); digital marketing and design (MS); health and medical informatics (MS); information security (MS); instructional design and technology (MS); learning analytics (Graduate Certificate); project and program management (MS); software engineering (MSE); strategic analytics (MS); technology management (MS); user-centered design (MS). *Application deadline:* For fall admission, 6/21 priority date for domestic and international students; for winter admission, 9/13 priority date for domestic and international students; for spring admission, 12/20 priority date for domestic and international students; for summer admission, 3/14 priority date for domestic and international students. Applications are processed on a rolling basis. *Application fee:* $50. Electronic applications accepted. *Application Contact:* Frances Stearns, Director of Admissions and Recruitment, 781-736-8785, E-mail: fstearns@brandeis.edu. *Executive Director,* Anne M. Marando, 781-736-8782, E-mail: marando@brandeis.edu.

BRANDMAN UNIVERSITY, Irvine, CA 92618

General Information Independent, coed, comprehensive institution. *Enrollment:* 7,388 graduate, professional, and undergraduate students; 1,267 full-time matriculated graduate/professional students (903 women), 1,692 part-time matriculated graduate/professional students (1,104 women). *Enrollment by degree level:* 2,539 master's, 394 doctoral, 26 other advanced degrees. *Graduate faculty:* 44 full-time (26 women), 432 part-time/adjunct (254 women). *Tuition:* Full-time $14,880; part-time $620 per credit hour. Tuition and fees vary according to degree level and program. *Student services:* Career counseling, services for students with disabilities, writing training. *Library facilities:* Leatherby Library plus 1 other.

Computer facilities: 837 computers available on campus for general student use. A campuswide network can be accessed. Online class registration is available.
Website: http://www.brandman.edu/irvine/

General Application Contact: Office of Admission, 877-516-4501, Fax: 866-659-1143, E-mail: adminfo@brandman.edu.

GRADUATE UNITS

Marybelle and S. Paul Musco School of Nursing and Health Professions Expenses: Contact institution. Offers nursing (DNP). *Dean,* Dr. Tyke Hanisch, 949-341-9815.

School of Arts and Sciences Expenses: Contact institution. Offers psychology (MA). *Dean,* Dr. Jeremy Korr, 949-341-9831.

School of Business and Professional Studies Expenses: Contact institution. Offers accounting (MBA); business administration (MBA); e-business strategic management (MBA); entrepreneurship (MBA); finance (MBA); health administration (MBA); human resources (MBA, MS); international business (MBA); marketing (MBA); organizational leadership (MA, MBA, MPA); public administration (MPA). *Dean,* Dr. Glenn Worthington, 253-861-1024, E-mail: gworthin@brandman.edu.

School of Education Expenses: Contact institution. Offers education (MA); elementary education (MAT); organizational leadership (Ed D); school counseling (MA); secondary education (MAT); special education (MA). *Dean,* Dr. Christine G. Zeppos, 949-341-9948, E-mail: zeppos@brandman.edu.

BRANDON UNIVERSITY, Brandon, MB R7A 6A9, Canada

General Information Province-supported, coed, comprehensive institution. *Graduate housing:* Room and/or apartments available on a first-come, first-served basis to single students; on-campus housing not available to married students.

GRADUATE UNITS

Department of Rural Development Offers rural development (MRD, Diploma). Electronic applications accepted.

Faculty of Education Offers curriculum and instruction (M Ed, Diploma); educational administration (M Ed, Diploma); guidance and counseling (M Ed, Diploma); special education (M Ed, Diploma).

School of Music *Program availability:* Part-time. Offers composition (M Mus); music education (M Mus); performance and literature (M Mus). Electronic applications accepted.

BRENAU UNIVERSITY, Gainesville, GA 30501

General Information Independent, coed, primarily women, comprehensive institution. *Graduate housing:* Room and/or apartments available on a first-come, first-served basis to single students; on-campus housing not available to married students.

GRADUATE UNITS

Sydney O. Smith Graduate School *Program availability:* Part-time, evening/weekend, online learning. Electronic applications accepted.

College of Business and Mass Communication *Program availability:* Part-time, evening/weekend, online learning. Offers accounting (MBA); business administration (MBA); healthcare management (MBA); organizational leadership (MS); project management (MBA). Electronic applications accepted.

College of Education *Program availability:* Part-time, evening/weekend, online learning. Offers early childhood (Ed S); early childhood education (M Ed, MAT); middle grades (Ed S); middle grades education (M Ed, MAT); secondary education (MAT); special education (M Ed, MAT). Electronic applications accepted.

College of Fine Arts and Humanities *Program availability:* Part-time. Offers interior design (MID). Electronic applications accepted.

College of Health Sciences *Program availability:* Part-time, evening/weekend. Offers family nurse practitioner (MSN); nurse educator (MSN); nursing management (MSN); occupational therapy (MS); psychology (MS). Electronic applications accepted.

BRESCIA UNIVERSITY, Owensboro, KY 42301-3023

General Information Independent-religious, coed, comprehensive institution. *Graduate housing:* Room and/or apartments available on a first-come, first-served basis to single students; on-campus housing not available to married students.

GRADUATE UNITS

Program in Business Administration *Program availability:* Part-time, evening/weekend. Offers business administration (MBA). Electronic applications accepted.

Program in Management *Program availability:* Part-time, evening/weekend. Offers management (MSM).

Program in Social Work *Program availability:* Online learning. Offers social work (MSW). Electronic applications accepted.

Program in Teacher Leadership *Program availability:* Part-time, evening/weekend. Offers teacher leadership (MSTL). Electronic applications accepted.

BRIAR CLIFF UNIVERSITY, Sioux City, IA 51104-0100

General Information Independent-religious, coed, comprehensive institution. *Enrollment:* 1,316 graduate, professional, and undergraduate students; 87 full-time matriculated graduate/professional students (43 women), 112 part-time matriculated graduate/professional students (78 women). *Enrollment by degree level:* 145 master's, 52 doctoral, 2 other advanced degrees. *Graduate faculty:* 21 full-time (8 women), 5 part-time/adjunct (2 women). *Graduate housing:* Room and/or apartments available on a first-come, first-served basis to single students; on-campus housing not available to married students. Typical cost: $8000 (including board). Housing application deadline: 6/1. *Student services:* Campus employment opportunities, campus safety program, career counseling, exercise/wellness program, free psychological counseling, international student services, services for students with disabilities. *Library facilities:* Bishop Mueller Library.

Computer facilities: A campuswide network can be accessed from student residence rooms and from off campus.
Website: http://www.briarcliff.edu/

General Application Contact: Cheryl Olson, Director of Graduate Admissions, 712-279-1777, Fax: 712-279-1632, E-mail: cheryl.olson@briarcliff.edu.

GRADUATE UNITS

Graduate Nursing Programs Students: 59 part-time (48 women); includes 3 minority (all Black or African American, non-Hispanic/Latino). Average age 38. 64 applicants, 47% accepted, 27 enrolled. *Faculty:* 5 full-time (4 women). Expenses: Contact institution. *Financial support:* Application deadline: 8/1; applicants required to submit FAFSA. *Program availability:* Part-time, online only, 100% online, blended/hybrid learning. Offers nursing (MSN, DNP, Post-Master's Certificate). *Application deadline:* For fall admission, 8/1 for domestic students. Applications are processed on a rolling basis. *Application fee:* $25. Electronic applications accepted. *Application Contact:* Cheryl Olson, Director of Graduate Admissions, 712-279-1777, Fax: 712-279-1632, E-mail: cheryl.olson@briarcliff.edu. *Director,* Dr. Richard Peterson, 712-279-1662, Fax: 712-279-1698, E-mail: richard.petersen@briarcliff.edu.

BRIDGEWATER COLLEGE, Bridgewater, VA 22812-1599

General Information Independent-religious, coed, comprehensive institution.

GRADUATE UNITS

Program in Athletic Training Offers athletic training (MS). Electronic applications accepted.

BRIDGEWATER STATE UNIVERSITY, Bridgewater, MA 02325

General Information State-supported, coed, comprehensive institution. CGS member. *Graduate housing:* On-campus housing not available.

GRADUATE UNITS

College of Graduate Studies *Program availability:* Part-time, evening/weekend.

Bartlett College of Science and Mathematics Offers biology (MAT); computer science (MS); mathematics (MAT); physics (MAT); science and mathematics (MAT, MS).

College of Education and Allied Studies *Program availability:* Part-time, evening/weekend. Offers counseling (M Ed, CAGS); early childhood education (M Ed); education and allied studies (M Ed, MAT, MS, CAGS); educational leadership (M Ed, CAGS); elementary education (M Ed); health promotion (M Ed); instructional technology (M Ed); physical education (MS); reading (M Ed, CAGS); secondary education (MAT); special education (M Ed); speech/language pathology (MS).

College of Humanities and Social Sciences *Program availability:* Part-time, evening/weekend. Offers art (MAT); criminal justice (MS); English (MA, MAT); history (MAT); humanities and social sciences (MA, MAT, MPA, MS, MSW); physical sciences (MAT); psychology (MA); public administration (MPA); social work (MSW).

Ricciardi College of Business *Program availability:* Part-time, evening/weekend. Offers accounting and finance (MSM); business (MSM); management (MSM).

BRIERCREST SEMINARY, Caronport, SK S0H 0S0, Canada

General Information Independent-religious, coed, graduate-only institution. *Graduate housing:* Rooms and/or apartments guaranteed to single students and available on a first-come, first-served basis to married students.

GRADUATE UNITS

Graduate Programs *Program availability:* Part-time. Offers Biblical studies (M Div); leadership (MA); leadership and management (M Div); marriage and family counseling (MA); missions (MA); New Testament (MATS); Old Testament (MATS); organizational leadership (MA); pastoral counseling (M Div, MA); pastoral ministry (M Div); theological studies (M Div); theology (MATS); worship (M Div, MA); youth and family ministry (M Div, MA).

BRIGHAM YOUNG UNIVERSITY, Provo, UT 84602-1001

General Information Independent-religious, coed, university. CGS member. *Enrollment:* 34,240 graduate, professional, and undergraduate students; 2,120 full-time matriculated graduate/professional students (790 women), 1,095 part-time matriculated graduate/professional students (412 women). *Enrollment by degree level:* 2,212 master's, 957 doctoral, 46 other advanced degrees. *Graduate faculty:* 1,039 full-time (171 women), 3 part-time/adjunct (0 women). *Tuition:* Full-time $6680; part-time $393 per credit. Tuition and fees vary according to course load, program and student's religious affiliation. *Graduate housing:* Rooms and/or apartments available on a first-come, first-served basis to single and married students. Typical cost: $3450 per year ($7330 including board) for single students; $7860 per year ($12,252 including board) for married students. Room and board charges vary according to board plan, campus/location and housing facility selected. Housing application deadline: 2/1. *Student services:* Campus employment opportunities, campus safety program, career counseling, exercise/wellness program, free psychological counseling, grant writing training, international student services, low-cost health insurance, multicultural affairs office, services for students with disabilities, teacher training, writing training. *Library facilities:* Harold B. Lee Library plus 2 others.

Computer facilities: Computer purchase and lease plans are available. A campuswide network can be accessed from student residence rooms and from off campus. Online class registration is available.
Website: http://www.byu.edu/

General Application Contact: Graduate Studies, 801-422-4091, Fax: 801-422-0270, E-mail: gradstudies@byu.edu.

GRADUATE UNITS

Graduate Studies Students: 2,120 full-time (790 women), 1,095 part-time (412 women); includes 344 minority (19 Black or African American, non-Hispanic/Latino; 7 American Indian or Alaska Native, non-Hispanic/Latino; 55 Asian, non-Hispanic/Latino; 153 Hispanic/Latino; 13 Native Hawaiian or other Pacific Islander, non-Hispanic/Latino; 97 Two or more races, non-Hispanic/Latino); 317 international. Average age 30. 2,301 applicants, 60% accepted, 1121 enrolled. *Faculty:* 1,039 full-time (171 women), 3 part-time/adjunct (0 women). Expenses: Contact institution. *Financial support:* In 2016–17, 53 students received support, including 35 fellowships (averaging $12,000 per year), 13 research assistantships (averaging $30,000 per year), 5 teaching assistantships (averaging $4,000 per year); career-related internships or fieldwork, institutionally sponsored loans, scholarships/grants, health care benefits, and tuition waivers (full and partial) also available. Support available to part-time students. Financial award applicants required to submit FAFSA. In 2016, 1,041 master's, 256 doctorates, 14 other advanced degrees awarded. *Program availability:* Part-time, evening/weekend. *Application deadline:* For fall admission, 12/1 priority date for domestic and international students; for winter admission, 6/30 priority date for domestic and international students; for spring admission, 1/15 priority date for domestic and international students; for summer admission, 2/1 for domestic and international students. Applications are processed on a rolling basis. *Application fee:* $50. Electronic applications accepted. *Application Contact:* Logan Gillette, Director of Graduate Admissions and Recruitment, 801-422-7308, E-mail: logangillette@byu.edu. *Dean,* Dr. Wynn Stirling, 801-422-4465, Fax: 801-422-0089, E-mail: gradstudies@byu.edu.

College of Family, Home, and Social Sciences Students: 226 full-time (153 women); includes 43 minority (3 Black or African American, non-Hispanic/Latino; 14 Asian, non-Hispanic/Latino; 20 Hispanic/Latino; 3 Native Hawaiian or other Pacific Islander, non-Hispanic/Latino; 3 Two or more races, non-Hispanic/Latino), 6 international. Average age 26. *Faculty:* 96 full-time (20 women), 21 part-time/adjunct (12 women). Expenses: Contact institution. *Financial support:* In 2016–17, 168 students received support, including 56 fellowships with tuition reimbursements available (averaging $1,850 per year), 120 research assistantships with tuition reimbursements available (averaging $12,804 per year), 7 teaching assistantships with tuition reimbursements available (averaging $6,050 per year); career-related internships or fieldwork, institutionally sponsored loans, scholarships/grants, tuition waivers (partial), unspecified assistantships, and administrative aides, paid field practicum, AmeriCorps education awards also available. Financial award application deadline: 3/27; financial award applicants required to submit FAFSA. In 2016, 72 master's, 19 doctorates awarded. Offers anthropology (MA); applied social psychology (PhD); clinical psychology (PhD); cognitive and behavioral neuroscience (PhD); developmental psychology (PhD); family, home, and social sciences (MA, MS, MSW, PhD); marriage and family therapy (MS, PhD); marriage, family and human development (MS, PhD); social work (MSW); sociology (MS). *Application deadline:* For fall admission, 1/15 for domestic and international students. *Application fee:* $50. Electronic applications accepted. *Application Contact:* Adviser, 801-422-4541, Fax: 801-378-5238, E-mail: gradstudies@byu.edu. *Dean,* Dr. Benjamin M. Ogles, 801-422-2083, Fax: 801-422-2084, E-mail: ben_ogles@byu.edu.

College of Fine Arts and Communications Students: 87 full-time (53 women), 29 part-time (17 women); includes 19 minority (1 American Indian or Alaska Native, non-Hispanic/Latino; 10 Asian, non-Hispanic/Latino; 6 Hispanic/Latino; 2 Native Hawaiian or other Pacific Islander, non-Hispanic/Latino), 6 international. Average age 30. 82 applicants, 44% accepted, 30 enrolled. *Faculty:* 97 full-time (18 women), 58 part-time/adjunct (33 women). Expenses: Contact institution. *Financial support:* In 2016–17, 86 students received support, including 70 research assistantships with full and partial tuition reimbursements available (averaging $3,187 per year), 51 teaching assistantships with partial tuition reimbursements available (averaging $3,162 per year); career-related internships or fieldwork, institutionally sponsored loans, scholarships/grants, tuition waivers (partial), unspecified assistantships, and supplementary awards also available. Support available to part-time students. In 2016, 48 master's awarded. Offers art education (MA); composition (MM); conducting (MM); fine arts and communications (MA, MFA, MM); mass communications (MA); music education (MA, MM); performance (MM); studio arts (MFA); theatre and media arts (MA). *Application deadline:* Applications are processed on a rolling basis. *Application fee:* $50. Electronic applications accepted. *Application Contact:* Adviser, 801-422-4541, Fax: 801-378-5238, E-mail: gradstudies@byu.edu. *Dean,* Edward E. Adams, 801-422-8271, Fax: 801-422-0253, E-mail: francie_jenson@byu.edu.

College of Humanities Students: 183 full-time (119 women), 52 part-time (32 women); includes 40 minority (1 American Indian or Alaska Native, non-Hispanic/Latino; 15 Asian, non-Hispanic/Latino; 23 Hispanic/Latino; 1 Native Hawaiian or other Pacific Islander, non-Hispanic/Latino), 14 international. Average age 30. 110 applicants, 72% accepted, 66 enrolled. *Faculty:* 173 full-time (43 women), 8 part-time/adjunct (6 women). Expenses: Contact institution. *Financial support:* In 2016–17, 53 students received support, including 57 fellowships (averaging $2,324 per year), 29 research assistantships (averaging $3,648 per year), 180 teaching assistantships (averaging $2,379 per year); career-related internships or fieldwork, institutionally sponsored loans, scholarships/grants, tuition waivers (full and partial), unspecified assistantships, and student instructorships, travel money for conference presentations also available. Support available to part-time students. In 2016, 59 master's awarded. *Program availability:* Part-time. Offers comparative studies (MA); creative writing (MFA); French studies (MA); humanities (MA, MFA); linguistics (MA); literature (MA); Portuguese (MA); rhetoric/composition (MA); second language teaching (MA); Spanish (MA); teaching English as a second language (MA). *Application fee:* $50. Electronic applications accepted. *Application Contact:* Adviser, 801-422-4541, Fax: 801-378-5238, E-mail: gradstudies@byu.edu. *Dean,* Scott J. Miller, 801-422-2779, Fax: 801-422-0308, E-mail: scott_miller@byu.edu.

College of Life Sciences Students: 155 full-time (83 women), 79 part-time (34 women); includes 39 minority (1 Black or African American, non-Hispanic/Latino; 1 American Indian or Alaska Native, non-Hispanic/Latino; 16 Asian, non-Hispanic/Latino; 16 Hispanic/Latino; 5 Native Hawaiian or other Pacific Islander, non-Hispanic/Latino), 5 international. Average age 28. 167 applicants, 49% accepted, 64 enrolled. *Faculty:* 138 full-time (23 women), 17 part-time/adjunct (15 women). Expenses: Contact institution. *Financial support:* In 2016–17, 216 students received support, including 38 fellowships with tuition reimbursements available (averaging $10,700 per year), 181 research assistantships with tuition reimbursements available (averaging $12,578 per year), 136 teaching assistantships with tuition reimbursements available (averaging

$12,310 per year); career-related internships or fieldwork, institutionally sponsored loans, scholarships/grants, health care benefits, tuition waivers (full and partial), and unspecified assistantships also available. Financial award application deadline: 2/1; financial award applicants required to submit FAFSA. In 2016, 81 master's, 13 doctorates awarded. Offers athletic training (MS); biological science medicine (MS); biology (MS, PhD); environmental science (MS); exercise physiology (MS, PhD); exercise sciences (MS); food science (MS); genetics and biotechnology (MS); health promotion (MS, PhD); health science (MPH); life sciences (MPH, MS, PhD); microbiology and molecular biology (MS, PhD); neuroscience (MS, PhD); nutrition (MS); physical medicine and rehabilitation (PhD); physiology and developmental biology (MS, PhD); wildlife and wildlands conservation (MS, PhD). *Application deadline:* For fall admission, 2/1 for domestic and international students; for winter admission, 2/1 for international students. *Application fee:* $50. Electronic applications accepted. *Application Contact:* Sue Pratley, Application Contact, 801-422-3963, Fax: 801-422-0050, E-mail: sue_pratley@byu.edu. *Dean,* James P. Porter, 801-422-3963, Fax: 801-422-0050, E-mail: james_porter@byu.edu.

College of Nursing Students: 30 full-time (21 women); includes 1 minority (Hispanic/Latino). Average age 33. 57 applicants, 30% accepted, 16 enrolled. *Faculty:* 4 full-time (all women), 6 part-time/adjunct (2 women). Expenses: Contact institution. *Financial support:* In 2016–17, 30 students received support, including 1 research assistantship (averaging $12,800 per year); teaching assistantships, institutionally sponsored loans, and scholarships/grants also available. Financial award application deadline: 3/1; financial award applicants required to submit FAFSA. In 2016, 15 master's awarded. Offers family nurse practitioner (MS). *Application deadline:* For spring admission, 12/1 for domestic and international students. *Application fee:* $50. Electronic applications accepted. *Application Contact:* Cherie Top, Graduate Secretary, 801-422-4142, Fax: 801-422-0538, E-mail: cherie-top@byu.edu. *Dean,* Dr. Patricia Ravert, 801-422-1167, Fax: 801-422-0536, E-mail: patricia_ravert@byu.edu.

College of Physical and Mathematical Sciences Students: 294 full-time (62 women), 38 part-time (11 women); includes 40 minority (28 Asian, non-Hispanic/Latino; 9 Hispanic/Latino; 3 Native Hawaiian or other Pacific Islander, non-Hispanic/Latino), 51 international. Average age 27. 229 applicants, 53% accepted, 97 enrolled. *Faculty:* 159 full-time (11 women), 8 part-time/adjunct (2 women). Expenses: Contact institution. *Financial support:* In 2016–17, 316 students received support, including 14 fellowships with full tuition reimbursements available (averaging $21,660 per year), 162 research assistantships with tuition reimbursements available (averaging $16,778 per year), 140 teaching assistantships with tuition reimbursements available (averaging $16,191 per year); career-related internships or fieldwork, institutionally sponsored loans, scholarships/grants, health care benefits, tuition waivers (full and partial), and unspecified assistantships also available. Support available to part-time students. In 2016, 59 master's, 23 doctorates awarded. *Program availability:* Part-time. Offers applied statistics (MS); biochemistry (MS, PhD); chemistry (MS, PhD); computer science (MS, PhD); geological sciences (MS); mathematics (MS, PhD); mathematics education (MA); physical and mathematical sciences (MA, MS, PhD); physics (MS, PhD); physics and astronomy (PhD). *Application deadline:* Applications are processed on a rolling basis. *Application fee:* $50. Electronic applications accepted. *Application Contact:* Lynn Patten, Executive Secretary, 801-422-4022, Fax: 801-422-0550, E-mail: lynn_patten@byu.edu. *Dean,* Dr. Scott D. Sommerfeldt, 801-422-2205, Fax: 801-422-0550, E-mail: scott_sommerfeldt@byu.edu.

College of Religious Education Students: 17 full-time (2 women). Average age 32. 7 applicants, 43% accepted, 3 enrolled. *Faculty:* 42 full-time (4 women), 2 part-time/adjunct (0 women). Expenses: Contact institution. *Financial support:* In 2016–17, 6 students received support. Scholarships/grants available. In 2016, 8 master's awarded. Offers religious education (MA). *Application deadline:* For fall admission, 12/1 for domestic and international students. *Application fee:* $50. Electronic applications accepted. *Application Contact:* Dr. Terry B. Ball, Professor of Ancient Scripture, 801-422-3357, Fax: 801-422-0616, E-mail: terry_ball@byu.edu. *Dean,* Dr. Brent L. Top, 801-422-2736, Fax: 801-422-0616, E-mail: brent_top@byu.edu.

David O. McKay School of Education Students: 189 full-time (102 women), 115 part-time (81 women); includes 28 minority (1 Black or African American, non-Hispanic/Latino; 2 American Indian or Alaska Native, non-Hispanic/Latino; 7 Asian, non-Hispanic/Latino; 8 Hispanic/Latino; 8 Native Hawaiian or other Pacific Islander, non-Hispanic/Latino; 2 Two or more races, non-Hispanic/Latino), 8 international. Average age 34. 337 applicants, 42% accepted, 123 enrolled. *Faculty:* 71 full-time (24 women), 10 part-time/adjunct (3 women). Expenses: Contact institution. *Financial support:* In 2016–17, 118 students received support, including 108 research assistantships with tuition reimbursements available (averaging $6,525 per year), 30 teaching assistantships with tuition reimbursements available (averaging $4,893 per year); fellowships, career-related internships or fieldwork, institutionally sponsored loans, scholarships/grants, tuition waivers (partial), and unspecified assistantships also available. Support available to part-time students. Financial award application deadline: 3/15; financial award applicants required to submit FAFSA. In 2016, 83 master's, 29 doctorates, 14 other advanced degrees awarded. *Program availability:* Part-time, evening/weekend. Offers counseling psychology (PhD); education (M Ed, MA, MS, Ed D, PhD, Ed S); educational inquiry, measurement, and evaluation (PhD); educational leadership and foundations (Ed D); educational leadership: education policy and social foundations (M Ed); educational leadership: school leadership (M Ed); instructional psychology and technology (MS, PhD); integrative science-technology-engineering-mathematics (STEM) (MA); literacy education (MA); physical education teacher education (MA); school psychology (Ed S); special education (MS); speech language pathology (MS); teacher education (MA). *Application deadline:* For fall admission, 2/1 for domestic and international students; for winter admission, 2/1 for domestic and international students; for spring admission, 1/15 for domestic and international students; for summer admission, 3/1 for domestic and international students. *Application fee:* $50. Electronic applications accepted. *Application Contact:* Brandan Beerli, Director, Education Student Services, 801-422-9199, Fax: 801-422-0195. *Dean,* Dr. Mary Anne Prater, 801-422-1592, Fax: 801-422-0200, E-mail: prater@byu.edu.

Ira A. Fulton College of Engineering and Technology Students: 363 full-time (42 women); includes 14 minority (3 American Indian or Alaska Native, non-Hispanic/Latino; 4 Asian, non-Hispanic/Latino; 4 Hispanic/Latino; 3 Native Hawaiian or other Pacific Islander, non-Hispanic/Latino), 56 international. Average age 27. 203 applicants, 63% accepted, 98 enrolled. *Faculty:* 107 full-time (3 women), 10 part-time/adjunct (2 women). Expenses: Contact institution. *Financial support:* In 2016–17, 475 students received support, including 26 fellowships with full and partial tuition reimbursements available (averaging $22,961 per year), 631 research assistantships with full and partial tuition reimbursements available (averaging $13,681 per year), 138 teaching assistantships with full and partial tuition reimbursements available (averaging $10,574 per year); scholarships/grants and health care benefits also available. Financial award application deadline: 3/1; financial award applicants

required to submit FAFSA. In 2016, 87 master's, 18 doctorates awarded. Offers chemical engineering (MS, PhD); civil engineering (MS, PhD); construction management (MS); electrical and computer engineering (MS, PhD); engineering and technology (MS, PhD); information technology (MS); manufacturing engineering technology (MS); mechanical engineering (MS, PhD); technology and engineering education (MS). *Application deadline:* For fall admission, 1/15 for domestic and international students; for winter admission, 6/15 for domestic and international students; for spring admission, 2/5 for domestic and international students; for summer admission, 2/5 for domestic and international students. *Application fee:* $50. Electronic applications accepted. *Application Contact:* Claire A. DeWitt, Adviser, 801-422-4541, Fax: 801-422-0270, E-mail: gradstudies@byu.edu. *Dean,* Dr. Michael A. Jensen, 801-422-5736, Fax: 801-422-0218, E-mail: college@et.byu.edu.

J. Reuben Clark Law School Students: 397 full-time (146 women), 12 part-time (8 women); includes 65 minority (4 Black or African American, non-Hispanic/Latino; 5 American Indian or Alaska Native, non-Hispanic/Latino; 12 Asian, non-Hispanic/Latino; 20 Hispanic/Latino; 9 Native Hawaiian or other Pacific Islander, non-Hispanic/Latino; 15 Two or more races, non-Hispanic/Latino), 10 international. Average age 27. 436 applicants, 44% accepted, 138 enrolled. *Faculty:* 26 full-time (10 women), 35 part-time/adjunct (7 women). Expenses: Contact institution. *Financial support:* In 2016–17, 221 students received support, including 12 fellowships (averaging $36,299 per year); career-related internships or fieldwork, institutionally sponsored loans, scholarships/grants, unspecified assistantships, and student employment also available. Financial award application deadline: 6/1; financial award applicants required to submit FAFSA. In 2016, 4 master's, 143 doctorates awarded. Offers law (LL M, JD). *Application deadline:* For fall admission, 3/1 priority date for domestic students, 3/1 for international students. Applications are processed on a rolling basis. *Application fee:* $50. Electronic applications accepted. *Application Contact:* Rebeca Welch, Admissions Coordinator, 801-422-4356, Fax: 801-422-0389, E-mail: welchr@law.byu.edu. *Dean,* D. Gordon Smith, 801-422-6383, Fax: 801-422-0389, E-mail: smithg@law.byu.edu.

Marriott School of Management Students: 419 full-time (117 women), 261 part-time (71 women); includes 56 minority (6 Black or African American, non-Hispanic/Latino; 17 Asian, non-Hispanic/Latino; 24 Hispanic/Latino; 9 Native Hawaiian or other Pacific Islander, non-Hispanic/Latino), 101 international. Average age 34. 674 applicants, 57% accepted, 315 enrolled. *Faculty:* 138 full-time (18 women), 73 part-time/adjunct (24 women). Expenses: Contact institution. *Financial support:* In 2016–17, 378 students received support. Research assistantships, teaching assistantships, career-related internships or fieldwork, institutionally sponsored loans, and scholarships/grants available. Financial award applicants required to submit FAFSA. In 2016, 299 master's awarded. *Program availability:* Part-time, evening/weekend. Offers business administration (MBA); entrepreneurship (MBA); federal government (MPA); finance (MBA); global supply chain management (MBA); health care (MPA); local government management (MPA); management (EMBA, MBA, MPA); marketing (MBA); nonprofit management (MPA); public administration (MPA); strategic human resources (MBA). *Application fee:* $50. Electronic applications accepted. *Dean,* Dr. Lee Perry, 801-422-4121, Fax: 801-422-4501.

BRISTOL UNIVERSITY, Anaheim, CA 92806

General Information Proprietary, coed, comprehensive institution.

GRADUATE UNITS

Program in Business Administration Offers business administration (MBA); international business (MBA); marketing (MBA); sports management (MBA).

BRITE DIVINITY SCHOOL, Fort Worth, TX 76109

General Information Independent-religious, coed, graduate-only institution. *Enrollment by degree level:* 159 master's, 58 doctoral, 217 other advanced degrees. *Graduate faculty:* 18 full-time (6 women), 4 part-time/adjunct (1 woman). *Graduate housing:* Rooms and/or apartments available on a first-come, first-served basis to single and married students. Typical cost: $5940 per year for single students; $9900 per year for married students. Room charges vary according to housing facility selected. Housing application deadline: 4/1. *Library facilities:* Mary Couts Burnett. *Collection:* Study areas open 24 hours, 5–7 days a week; students can reserve study rooms.

Computer facilities: A campuswide network can be accessed from student residence rooms and from off campus.
Website: http://www.brite.edu/

General Application Contact: Dr. Valerie Forstman, Assistant Dean for Common Life/Director of Admissions, 817-257-7513, E-mail: v.forstman@tcu.edu.

GRADUATE UNITS

Graduate and Professional Programs *Faculty:* 18 full-time (6 women), 4 part-time/adjunct (1 woman). Expenses: Contact institution. *Financial support:* Career-related internships or fieldwork and unspecified assistantships available. Financial award application deadline: 3/1. *Program availability:* Part-time, evening/weekend. Offers Biblical interpretation (PhD); divinity (M Div); ministry (D Min); pastoral theology (PhD); theological studies (MTS, CTS); theology (Th M); theology and ministry (MA). *Application deadline:* For fall admission, 3/1 for domestic students; for spring admission, 12/1 for domestic students. Applications are processed on a rolling basis. *Application fee:* $0. *Application Contact:* Dr. Valerie Forstman, Director of Admissions, 817-257-7513, E-mail: v.forstman@tcu.edu. *President,* Dr. D. Newell Williams, 817-257-7231.

BROADVIEW UNIVERSITY–WEST JORDAN, West Jordan, UT 84088

General Information Proprietary, coed, comprehensive institution.

GRADUATE UNITS
Graduate Programs

BROCK UNIVERSITY, St. Catharines, ON L2S 3A1, Canada

General Information Province-supported, coed, university. *Graduate housing:* Room and/or apartments available on a first-come, first-served basis to single students; on-campus housing not available to married students. *Research affiliation:* Registered Nurses Association of Ontario (nursing best practices), Canadian Honey Council (agriculture, therapeutic product development), Fly Fishing Canada/Trout Unlimited Canada (fisheries management), Henry Ford Health Centre (cancer epidemiology).

GRADUATE UNITS

Faculty of Graduate Studies *Program availability:* Part-time, evening/weekend. Electronic applications accepted.

Faculty of Applied Health Sciences Offers applied health sciences (M Sc, MA, PhD). Electronic applications accepted.

Faculty of Business *Program availability:* Part-time. Offers accountancy (M Acc); business (M Acc, M Sc, MBA); business administration (MBA); management (M Sc). Electronic applications accepted.

Faculty of Education *Program availability:* Part-time, evening/weekend. Offers education (M Ed, PhD). Electronic applications accepted.

Faculty of Humanities *Program availability:* Part-time. Offers applied linguistics (MA); classics (MA); English (MA); history (MA); humanities (MA); philosophy (MA); studies in comparative literatures and arts (MA). Electronic applications accepted.

Faculty of Mathematics and Science *Program availability:* Part-time. Offers biological sciences (M Sc, PhD); biotechnology (M Sc, PhD); chemistry (M Sc, PhD); computer science (M Sc); earth sciences (M Sc); mathematics and science (M Sc); mathematics and statistics (M Sc); physics (M Sc). Electronic applications accepted.

Faculty of Social Sciences *Program availability:* Part-time. Offers applied disability studies (MA, MADS, Diploma); behavioral neuroscience (MA, PhD); business economics (MBE); Canadian politics (MA); child and youth studies (MA); comparative politics (MA); critical sociology (MA); geography (MA); international relations (MA); life span development (MA, PhD); political theory or philosophy (MA); popular culture (MA); public policy (MA); social justice and equity studies (MA); social personality (MA, PhD); social sciences (MA, MADS, MBE, PhD, Diploma). Electronic applications accepted.

BROOKLINE COLLEGE, Phoenix, AZ 85021

General Information Proprietary, coed, comprehensive institution.

GRADUATE UNITS

Nursing Programs *Program availability:* Part-time, online learning. Offers health systems administration (MSN); nursing (MSN).

BROOKLYN COLLEGE OF THE CITY UNIVERSITY OF NEW YORK, Brooklyn, NY 11210-2889

General Information State and locally supported, coed, comprehensive institution. *Graduate housing:* Room and/or apartments available on a first-come, first-served basis to single students; on-campus housing not available to married students. *Research affiliation:* Biothera Inc. (biology), Silicon Valley Community Foundation (computer and information science), Jessie Smith Noyes Foundation (sustainability), Sloan-Kettering Memorial Cancer Center (health/biology), Community Health Care Association of New York State (health and nutrition sciences), Welfare Research Inc. (education).

GRADUATE UNITS

School of Business *Program availability:* Part-time, evening/weekend. Offers accounting (MS); business administration (MS). Electronic applications accepted.

School of Education *Program availability:* Part-time, evening/weekend. Offers adolescence science education (MAT); art teacher (K-12) (MA); autism spectrum disorders (AC); bilingual education (MS Ed); biology (MA); biology teacher (7-12) (MA); birth-grade 2 (MS Ed); chemistry (MA); chemistry teacher (7-12) (MA); earth science (MA); earth science teacher (7-12) (MAT); education (MA, MAT, MS Ed, AC); English teacher (7-12) (MA); French teacher (7-12) (MA); general science (MA); liberal arts (MS Ed); mathematics (MS Ed); mathematics teacher (7-12) (MA); middle childhood mathematics education (MS Ed); music teacher (MA); physics (MA); physics teacher (7-12) (MA); play therapy (AC); school building leader (MS Ed); school counseling (MS Ed); school district leader (MS Ed); school psychologist (MS Ed); science and environmental education (MS Ed); social studies teacher (7-12) (MA); Spanish teacher (7-12) (MA); teacher of students with disabilities (MS Ed). Electronic applications accepted.

School of Humanities and Social Sciences *Program availability:* Part-time, evening/weekend. Offers audiology (Au D); creative writing (MFA); English (MA); French (MA); history (MA); humanities and social sciences (MA, MFA, MS, Au D, PhD); international affairs (MA); Judaic studies (MA); political science (MA); sociology (MA, PhD); Spanish (MA); speech (MA); speech-language pathology (MS); urban policy and administration (MA). Electronic applications accepted.

School of Natural and Behavioral Sciences *Program availability:* Part-time, evening/weekend. Offers biology (MA); chemistry (MA, MS, PhD); community health (MA); community health education (MA); computer science (MA); earth and environmental sciences (MA, PhD); exercise and sports science (MS); experimental psychology (MA); general public health (MPH); grief counseling (CAS); health care policy and administration (MPH); health informatics (MS); industrial and organizational psychology (MA); information systems (MS); mathematics (MA); mental health counseling (MA); natural and behavioral sciences (MA, MPH, MS, PhD, AC, Advanced Certificate); nutrition (MS); parallel and distributed computing (Advanced Certificate); physical education teacher (MS); physics (MA); psychology (PhD); public health (MPH); sport management (MS); thanatology (MA). Electronic applications accepted.

School of Visual, Media and Performing Arts *Program availability:* Part-time, evening/weekend. Offers acting (MFA); art history (MA); cinema arts (MFA); cinema studies (MA); design and technical theater (MFA); digital art (MFA); directing (MFA); drawing and painting (MFA); media studies (MS); performance and interactive media arts (MFA); performing arts management (MFA); photography (MFA); printmaking (MFA); sculpture (MFA); television production (MFA); theater history and criticism (MA); visual, media and performing arts (M Mus, MA, MFA, MS). Electronic applications accepted.

Conservatory of Music *Program availability:* Part-time. Offers composition (MM); music teacher (MA); musicology (MA); performance (MM). Electronic applications accepted.

BROOKLYN LAW SCHOOL, Brooklyn, NY 11201-3798

General Information Independent, coed, graduate-only institution. *Graduate housing:* Rooms and/or apartments available to single students and guaranteed to married students. Housing application deadline: 5/1.

GRADUATE UNITS

Graduate and Professional Programs *Program availability:* Part-time, evening/weekend. Offers law (LL M, JD). JD/MBA offered jointly with Bernard M. Baruch College of the City University of New York; JD/MS with Pratt Institute; JD/MUP with Hunter College of the City University of New York; and JD/MA with Brooklyn College of the City University of New York. Electronic applications accepted.

BROWN UNIVERSITY, Providence, RI 02912

General Information Independent, coed, university. CGS member. *Graduate housing:* Room and/or apartments available to single students; on-campus housing not available to married students. *Research affiliation:* Woods Hole Oceanographic Institution-Marine Biological Laboratory, Rhode Island Reactor, International Center for Numismatic Studies, Meeting Street School.

GRADUATE UNITS

Graduate School *Program availability:* Part-time. Offers acting and directing (MFA); American studies (PhD); American studies for international students (MA); ancient western Asian studies (PhD); anthropology (MA, PhD); Asian religious traditions (PhD); Brazilian studies (AM); chemistry (PhD); classics (MA, PhD); cognitive science (Sc M, PhD); comparative literature (PhD); computer music and multimedia (PhD); computer science (Sc M, PhD); economics (PhD); Egyptology (PhD); elementary education (MAT); English (MAT, PhD); English as a second language and cross-cultural studies (MA); ethnomusicology (PhD); French studies (PhD); geological sciences (PhD); German (PhD); Hispanic studies (PhD); history (MA, PhD); history of art and architecture (PhD); history of the exact sciences in antiquity (PhD); history/social studies (MAT); Italian studies (PhD); linguistics (AM, PhD); literary arts (MFA); mathematics (PhD); philosophy (PhD); physics (Sc M, PhD); playwriting (MFA); political science (PhD); Portuguese and Brazilian studies (AM, PhD); Portuguese bilingual education and cross-cultural studies (AM); psychology (PhD); public humanities (MA); religion and critical thought (PhD); religions of the ancient Mediterranean (PhD); Russian language and literature (AM); science (MAT); secondary education (MAT); Slavic linguistics (AM); Slavic studies (PhD); sociology (MA, PhD); teaching (MAT); theatre and performance studies (PhD); urban education policy (AM).

A. Alfred Taubman Center for Public Policy and American Institutions Offers public policy and American institutions (MPA, MPP).

Division of Applied Mathematics Offers applied mathematics (Sc M, PhD).

Division of Biology and Medicine *Program availability:* Part-time. Offers behavioral and social sciences intervention (M Sc); biology and medicine (AM, M Sc, MA, MPH, Sc M, MD, PhD); biomedical engineering (Sc M, PhD); biostatistics (AM, Sc M, PhD); biotechnology (PhD); ecology and evolutionary biology (PhD); epidemiology (Sc M); health services, policy and practice (PhD); medicine (MD); molecular biology, cell biology, and biochemistry (MA, PhD); molecular pharmacology and physiology (PhD); neuroscience (PhD); pathology and laboratory medicine (Sc M, PhD); public health (MPH). Electronic applications accepted.

Joukowsky Institute for Archaeology and the Ancient World Offers archaeology and the ancient world (PhD).

School of Engineering Offers biomedical engineering (Sc M, PhD); chemical and biochemical engineering (Sc M, PhD); electrical sciences and computer engineering (Sc M, PhD); fluid and thermal sciences (Sc M, PhD); materials science and engineering (Sc M, PhD); mechanics of solids and structures (Sc M, PhD).

National Institutes of Health Sponsored Programs Offers neuroscience (PhD).

BRYAN COLLEGE, Dayton, TN 37321

General Information Independent-religious, coed, comprehensive institution. *Graduate housing:* On-campus housing not available. *Library facilities:* Bryan College Library.

Computer facilities: A campuswide network can be accessed from student residence rooms and from off campus. Online class registration is available.
Website: http://www.bryan.edu/

GRADUATE UNITS

MBA Program *Expenses:* Contact institution. *Financial support:* Applicants required to submit FAFSA. Offers business administration (MBA). *Application fee:* $50. *Application Contact:* Carla Harle, MBA Coordinator, 423-775-7480, E-mail: carla.harle@bryan.edu. *MBA Director*, Dr. Adina Scruggs, 423-634-2057, E-mail: adina.scruggs@bryan.edu.

BRYAN COLLEGE OF HEALTH SCIENCES, Lincoln, NE 68506-1398

General Information Independent, coed, comprehensive institution. CGS member.

GRADUATE UNITS

School of Nurse Anesthesia Offers nurse anesthesia (MS).

BRYANT UNIVERSITY, Smithfield, RI 02917

General Information Independent, coed, comprehensive institution. *Enrollment:* 3,698 graduate, professional, and undergraduate students; 142 full-time matriculated graduate/professional students (72 women), 93 part-time matriculated graduate/professional students (40 women). *Enrollment by degree level:* 235 master's. *Graduate faculty:* 21 full-time (4 women), 7 part-time/adjunct (3 women). *Tuition:* Full-time $26,832; part-time $1118 per credit hour. Tuition and fees vary according to degree level and program. *Graduate housing:* Room and/or apartments available on a first-come, first-served basis to single students; on-campus housing not available to married students. Typical cost: $10,693 per year ($16,587 including board). Room and board charges vary according to board plan and housing facility selected. Housing application deadline: 8/1. *Student services:* Campus employment opportunities, campus safety program, career counseling, exercise/wellness program, free psychological counseling, international student services, low-cost health insurance, multicultural affairs office, services for students with disabilities, teacher training, writing training. *Library facilities:* Douglas and Judith Krupp Library plus 1 other. *Collection:* Books: 150,000 (physical), 31,110 (digital/electronic); Serial titles: 3,343 (physical), 299 (digital/electronic); Databases: 79. Weekly public service hours: 107; students can reserve study rooms.

Computer facilities: Computer purchase and lease plans are available. 526 computers available on campus for general student use. A campuswide network can be accessed from student residence rooms and from off campus. Online class registration, e-mail, online library, student Web hosts are available.
Website: http://www.bryant.edu/

General Application Contact: Terri Rogers, Admissions Assistant, 401-232-6230, E-mail: graduateprograms@bryant.edu.

GRADUATE UNITS

College of Arts and Sciences Students: 4 full-time (all women), 10 part-time (8 women); includes 2 minority (1 Black or African American, non-Hispanic/Latino; 1 Two or more races, non-Hispanic/Latino), 1 international. Average age 32. 29 applicants, 31% accepted, 6 enrolled. *Faculty:* 2 full-time (0 women), 2 part-time/adjunct (1 woman). *Expenses:* Contact institution. *Financial support:* Fellowships and research assistantships available. Financial award applicants required to submit FAFSA. In 2016, 6 master's, 2 other advanced degrees awarded. *Program availability:* Part-time, evening/weekend. Offers communication (MA, Graduate Certificate); global environmental studies (MS); health care communication (MA); organizational communication (MA); sustainability practices (Graduate Certificate). *Application deadline:* For fall admission, 8/15 for domestic and international students; for spring admission, 1/15 for domestic and international students; for summer admission, 5/15 for domestic and international students. Applications are processed on a rolling basis. *Application fee:* $80. Electronic applications accepted. *Application Contact:* Terri Rogers, Admission Assistant, Graduate School, 401-232-6230, E-mail: graduateprograms@bryant.edu. *Associate Dean, College of Arts and Sciences,* Bradford Martin, 401-232-6929, E-mail: bmartin@bryant.edu.

Graduate School of Business Students: 71 full-time (23 women), 83 part-time (32 women); includes 17 minority (5 Black or African American, non-Hispanic/Latino; 4

Asian, non-Hispanic/Latino; 5 Hispanic/Latino; 3 Two or more races, non-Hispanic/Latino), 17 international. Average age 27. 165 applicants, 57% accepted, 66 enrolled. *Faculty:* 16 full-time (3 women), 2 part-time/adjunct (0 women). Expenses: Contact institution. *Financial support:* Research assistantships, scholarships/grants, and unspecified assistantships available. Support available to part-time students. Financial award application deadline: 2/15; financial award applicants required to submit FAFSA. In 2016, 106 master's, 12 other advanced degrees awarded. *Program availability:* Part-time, evening/weekend. Offers accounting (MPAC); business administration (MBA); business analytics (Graduate Certificate); taxation (MST). *Application deadline:* For fall admission, 7/15 for domestic and international students; for spring admission, 11/15 for domestic and international students; for summer admission, 4/15 for domestic and international students. Applications are processed on a rolling basis. *Application fee:* $80. Electronic applications accepted. *Application Contact:* Terri Rogers, Admissions Assistant, 401-232-6230, Fax: 401-232-6494, E-mail: graduateprograms@bryant.edu. *Graduate Program Director*, Bjorn Carlsson, 401-232-6707, E-mail: bcarlsson@bryant.edu.

School of Health Sciences Students: 67 full-time (45 women); includes 3 minority (2 Asian, non-Hispanic/Latino; 1 Two or more races, non-Hispanic/Latino). Average age 29. 64 applicants, 100% accepted, 43 enrolled. *Faculty:* 3 full-time (1 woman), 3 part-time/adjunct (2 women). Expenses: Contact institution. *Financial support:* Fund for a Healthy Rhode Island awards available. Financial award applicants required to submit FAFSA. Offers physician assistant studies (MPAS). *Application deadline:* For winter admission, 10/1 for domestic and international students. Applications are processed on a rolling basis. *Application fee:* $80. Electronic applications accepted. *Application Contact:* Amy Paul, Program Coordinator, 401-232-6556, E-mail: pa_program@bryant.edu. *Program Director*, Jay Amrien, 401-232-6556, E-mail: jamrien@bryant.edu.

BRYAN UNIVERSITY, Springfield, MO 65804

General Information Proprietary, coed, comprehensive institution.

GRADUATE UNITS

Program in Business Administration *Program availability:* Online learning. Offers business administration (MBA).

BRYN ATHYN COLLEGE OF THE NEW CHURCH, Bryn Athyn, PA 19009-0717

General Information Independent-religious, coed, comprehensive institution. *Graduate housing:* Room and/or apartments available on a first-come, first-served basis to single students; on-campus housing not available to married students. Housing application deadline: 1/31.

GRADUATE UNITS

Academy of the New Church Theological School *Program availability:* Part-time, online learning. Offers divinity (M Div); religious studies (MA).

BRYN MAWR COLLEGE, Bryn Mawr, PA 19010-2899

General Information Independent, Undergraduate: women only; graduate: coed, university. CGS member. *Enrollment:* 1,708 graduate, professional, and undergraduate students; 276 full-time matriculated graduate/professional students (212 women), 51 part-time matriculated graduate/professional students (41 women). *Enrollment by degree level:* 150 master's, 99 doctoral, 78 other advanced degrees. *Graduate faculty:* 48 full-time (28 women), 20 part-time/adjunct (9 women). *Tuition:* Full-time $40,620; part-time $6770 per unit. Tuition and fees vary according to program. *Graduate housing:* On-campus housing not available. *Student services:* Campus employment opportunities, career counseling, exercise/wellness program, international student services, low-cost health insurance, multicultural affairs office, services for students with disabilities, teacher training. *Library facilities:* Canaday Library plus 3 others. *Collection:* Books: 731,197 (physical), 700,741 (digital/electronic); Serial titles: 9,382 (physical), 96,451 (digital/electronic); Databases: 184. Weekly public service hours: 105; study areas open 24 hours, 5–7 days a week.

Computer facilities: 125 computers available on campus for general student use. A campuswide network can be accessed from student residence rooms and from off campus. Online class registration is available. Website: http://www.brynmawr.edu/

General Application Contact: Office of Admissions, 610-526-5152, Fax: 610-526-7471, E-mail: admissions@brynmawr.edu.

GRADUATE UNITS

Graduate School of Arts and Sciences Students: 61 full-time (43 women), 19 part-time (13 women); includes 8 minority (1 Black or African American, non-Hispanic/Latino; 5 Hispanic/Latino; 1 Native Hawaiian or other Pacific Islander, non-Hispanic/Latino; 1 Two or more races, non-Hispanic/Latino), 3 international. Average age 30. 94 applicants, 27% accepted, 15 enrolled. *Faculty:* 40 full-time (23 women), 9 part-time/adjunct (3 women). Expenses: Contact institution. *Financial support:* In 2016–17, 79 students received support, including 45 fellowships with tuition reimbursements available (averaging $17,087 per year), 3 research assistantships with tuition reimbursements available (averaging $12,667 per year), 23 teaching assistantships with tuition reimbursements available (averaging $17,761 per year); career-related internships or fieldwork, Federal Work-Study, institutionally sponsored loans, health care benefits, unspecified assistantships, and tuition awards also available. Support available to part-time students. Financial award application deadline: 12/15. In 2016, 12 master's, 9 doctorates awarded. *Program availability:* Part-time. Offers arts and sciences (MA, PhD); chemistry (MA, PhD); classical and Near Eastern archaeology (MA, PhD); Greek, Latin, and classical studies (MA, PhD); history of art (MA, PhD); mathematics (MA, PhD); physics (MA, PhD). *Application deadline:* For fall admission, 12/15 for domestic and international students. *Application fee:* $50. Electronic applications accepted. *Application Contact:* Maria Dantis, Graduate Program Administrator, 610-526-5074, E-mail: gsas@brynmawr.edu. *Dean of Graduate Studies*, Sharon Burgmayer, 610-526-5106, E-mail: sburgmay@brynmawr.edu.

Graduate School of Social Work and Social Research Students: 137 full-time (118 women), 32 part-time (28 women); includes 36 minority (20 Black or African American, non-Hispanic/Latino; 6 Asian, non-Hispanic/Latino; 6 Hispanic/Latino; 4 Two or more races, non-Hispanic/Latino), 1 international. Average age 33. 164 applicants, 79% accepted, 90 enrolled. *Faculty:* 8 full-time (5 women), 11 part-time/adjunct (6 women). Expenses: Contact institution. *Financial support:* In 2016–17, 147 students received support. Fellowships, research assistantships, teaching assistantships, career-related internships or fieldwork, Federal Work-Study, institutionally sponsored loans, scholarships/grants, tuition waivers, and dissertation awards (for PhD) available. Support available to part-time students. Financial award application deadline: 4/15; financial award applicants required to submit FAFSA. In 2016, 81 master's, 3 doctorates awarded. *Program availability:* Part-time, evening/weekend. Offers social work and social research (MSS, PhD). *Application deadline:* For fall admission, 4/15 for domestic and international

students. Applications are processed on a rolling basis. *Application fee:* $50. Electronic applications accepted. *Application Contact:* Sheila Gillin, Director of Graduate Admissions, 610-520-7533, E-mail: sgillin@brynmawr.edu. *Dean*, Dr. Darlyne Bailey, 610-520-2610, Fax: 610-520-2613, E-mail: dbailey01@brynmawr.edu.

BUCKNELL UNIVERSITY, Lewisburg, PA 17837

General Information Independent, coed, comprehensive institution. CGS member. *Tuition:* Part-time $5475 per course. *Graduate housing:* On-campus housing not available. *Student services:* Campus employment opportunities, campus safety program, career counseling, free psychological counseling, international student services, low-cost health insurance, multicultural affairs office, services for students with disabilities, teacher training, writing training. *Library facilities:* Ellen Clarke Bertrand Library. *Collection:* Books: 721,500 (physical), 360,572 (digital/electronic); Serial titles: 351 (physical), 52,048 (digital/electronic); Databases: 221. Weekly public service hours: 125.

Computer facilities: 1,031 computers available on campus for general student use. A campuswide network can be accessed from student residence rooms and from off campus. Online class registration is available. Website: http://www.bucknell.edu/

General Application Contact: Robert M. Midkiff, Dean of Graduate Studies, 570-577-1547, Fax: 570-577-1826, E-mail: gradstds@bucknell.edu.

GRADUATE UNITS

Graduate Studies Expenses: Contact institution. *Financial support:* Fellowships with full and partial tuition reimbursements, research assistantships with full tuition reimbursements, scholarships/grants, tuition waivers (partial), and unspecified assistantships available. Financial award application deadline: 2/1. *Program availability:* Part-time. *Application deadline:* For fall admission, 2/1 priority date for domestic students, 1/1 priority date for international students; for spring admission, 12/1 priority date for domestic students. *Application fee:* $25. *Application Contact:* Gretchen H. Fegley, Coordinator, 570-577-3655, Fax: 570-577-3760, E-mail: gfegley@bucknell.edu. *Dean*, Robert M. Midkiff, 570-577-1304, Fax: 570-577-3760, E-mail: gradstds@bucknell.edu.

College of Arts and Sciences Expenses: Contact institution. *Financial support:* Fellowships, research assistantships, scholarships/grants, and unspecified assistantships available. Financial award application deadline: 3/1. *Program availability:* Part-time. Offers animal behavior (MS); arts and sciences (MA, MS, MS Ed); biology (MS); chemistry (MA, MS); college student personnel (MS Ed); English (MA); mathematics (MA, MS); psychology (MS). *Application deadline:* For fall admission, 6/1 priority date for domestic students, 3/1 for international students; for spring admission, 12/1 priority date for domestic students. Applications are processed on a rolling basis. *Application fee:* $25. *Application Contact:* Gretchen H. Fegley, Coordinator, 570-577-3655, Fax: 570-577-3760, E-mail: gfegley@bucknell.edu. *Dean of Graduate Studies*, Robert M. Midkiff, 570-577-1304.

College of Engineering Expenses: Contact institution. *Financial support:* Research assistantships with full tuition reimbursements and unspecified assistantships available. Financial award application deadline: 2/1. *Program availability:* Part-time. Offers chemical engineering (MS Ch E); civil and environmental engineering (MSCE, MSEV); electrical and computer engineering (MSEE); engineering (MS Ch E, MSCE, MSEE, MSEV, MSME); mechanical engineering (MSME). *Application deadline:* For fall admission, 2/1 priority date for domestic students, 1/1 priority date for international students. *Application fee:* $25. *Application Contact:* Gretchen H. Fegley, Coordinator, 570-577-3655, Fax: 570-577-3760, E-mail: gfegley@bucknell.edu. *Dean of Graduate Studies*, Robert M. Midkiff, 570-577-1304.

BUENA VISTA UNIVERSITY, Storm Lake, IA 50588

General Information Independent-religious, coed, comprehensive institution. *Graduate housing:* Room and/or apartments available on a first-come, first-served basis to single students; on-campus housing not available to married students. Housing application deadline: 5/1.

GRADUATE UNITS

School of Education *Program availability:* Part-time, evening/weekend, online learning. Offers curriculum and instruction (M Ed); school guidance and counseling (MS Ed). Program offered in summer only. Electronic applications accepted.

BUFFALO STATE COLLEGE, STATE UNIVERSITY OF NEW YORK, Buffalo, NY 14222-1095

General Information State-supported, coed, comprehensive institution. CGS member. *Graduate housing:* Room and/or apartments available on a first-come, first-served basis to single students; on-campus housing not available to married students. Housing application deadline: 8/15. *Research affiliation:* Friends of Buffalo River, Research Institute on Addictions at the University of Buffalo, Roswell Park Memorial Institute, Hauptman-Woodward Medical Research Institute, Ecology and Environment Corporation, Phillip Morris Foundation.

GRADUATE UNITS

The Graduate School *Program availability:* Part-time, evening/weekend, online learning. Offers multidisciplinary studies (MA, MS).

Faculty of Applied Science and Education *Program availability:* Part-time, evening/weekend, online learning. Offers adult education (MS, Certificate); applied science and education (MPS, MS, MS Ed, CAS, Certificate); business and marketing education (MS Ed); career and technical education (MS Ed); childhood education (grades 1-6) (MS Ed); creative studies (MS); criminal justice (MS); early childhood and childhood curriculum and instruction (MS Ed); early childhood education (birth-grade 2) (MS Ed); educational computing (MS Ed); educational leadership (CAS); elementary education (MS Ed); human resources development (Certificate); industrial technology (MS); literacy specialist (MPS, MS Ed); literacy specialist (birth-grade 6) (MS Ed); literacy specialist (grades 5-12) (MPS); special education (MS Ed); special education: adolescents (MS Ed); special education: childhood (MS Ed); special education: early childhood (MS Ed); speech-language pathology (MS Ed); student personnel administration (MS); teaching bilingual exceptional individuals (MS Ed); technology education (MS Ed).

Faculty of Arts and Humanities *Program availability:* Part-time, evening/weekend. Offers art conservation (CAS); art education (MS Ed); arts and humanities (MA, MS Ed, CAS); conservation of historic works and art works (MA); English (MA); secondary education (MS Ed).

Faculty of Natural and Social Sciences *Program availability:* Part-time, evening/weekend. Offers applied economics (MA); biology (MA); chemistry (MA); history (MA); mathematics education (MS Ed); natural and social sciences (MA, MS Ed); secondary education (MS Ed); secondary education physics (MS Ed).

BUTLER UNIVERSITY, Indianapolis, IN 46208-3485

General Information Independent, coed, comprehensive institution. *Enrollment:* 5,095 graduate, professional, and undergraduate students; 440 full-time matriculated graduate/professional students (295 women), 330 part-time matriculated graduate/professional students (162 women). *Enrollment by degree level:* 495 master's, 259 doctoral, 14 other advanced degrees. *Graduate faculty:* 141 full-time (74 women), 59 part-time/adjunct (29 women). *Tuition:* Full-time $10,080. Tuition and fees vary according to course level, degree level, program and student level. *Graduate housing:* Room and/or apartments available on a first-come, first-served basis to single students; on-campus housing not available to married students. Typical cost: $9194 per year ($15,824 including board). Room and board charges vary according to board plan and housing facility selected. Housing application deadline: 8/1. *Student services:* Campus employment opportunities, campus safety program, career counseling, exercise/wellness program, free psychological counseling, international student services, low-cost health insurance, multicultural affairs office, services for students with disabilities. *Library facilities:* Irwin Library plus 2 others. *Collection:* Books: 196,295 (physical), 293,303 (digital/electronic); Serial titles: 18,930 (physical), 44,712 (digital/electronic); Databases: 243. Weekly public service hours: 106; students can reserve study rooms.

Computer facilities: Computer purchase and lease plans are available. 490 computers available on campus for general student use. A campuswide network can be accessed from student residence rooms and from off campus. Online class registration is available.
Website: http://www.butler.edu/

General Application Contact: Diane Dubord, Graduate Student Services Specialist, 317-940-8107, Fax: 317-940-8250, E-mail: ddubord@butler.edu.

GRADUATE UNITS

College of Education Students: 9 full-time (7 women), 119 part-time (85 women); includes 14 minority (10 Black or African American, non-Hispanic/Latino; 1 Asian, non-Hispanic/Latino; 2 Hispanic/Latino; 1 Two or more races, non-Hispanic/Latino). Average age 32. 79 applicants, 76% accepted, 63 enrolled. *Faculty:* 13 full-time (10 women), 5 part-time/adjunct (4 women). Expenses: Contact institution. *Financial support:* In 2016–17, 60 students received support. Scholarships/grants and unspecified assistantships available. Financial award application deadline: 7/15; financial award applicants required to submit FAFSA. In 2016, 42 master's, 30 other advanced degrees awarded. *Program availability:* Part-time. Offers alternative special education licensure (Certificate); educational administration (MS); effective teaching and leadership (MS); international baccalaureate teaching and learning (Certificate); licensed mental health counselor (Certificate); school counseling (MS); teachers of the visually impaired (Certificate). *Application deadline:* For fall admission, 2/1 for domestic and international students; for spring admission, 11/1 for domestic and international students; for summer admission, 4/1 for domestic and international students. Applications are processed on a rolling basis. *Application fee:* $0. Electronic applications accepted. *Application Contact:* Diane Dubord, Graduate Student Services Specialist, 317-940-8100, Fax: 317-940-8250, E-mail: ddubord@butler.edu. *Dean,* Dr. Ena Shelley, 317-940-9752, Fax: 317-940-6481.

College of Liberal Arts and Sciences Students: 10 full-time (4 women), 51 part-time (30 women); includes 7 minority (4 Black or African American, non-Hispanic/Latino; 1 Hispanic/Latino; 2 Two or more races, non-Hispanic/Latino), 2 international. Average age 34. 52 applicants, 60% accepted, 15 enrolled. *Faculty:* 20 full-time (6 women), 4 part-time/adjunct (2 women). Expenses: Contact institution. *Financial support:* Scholarships/grants, tuition waivers (full and partial), and unspecified assistantships available. Financial award application deadline: 7/15; financial award applicants required to submit FAFSA. In 2016, 12 master's awarded. *Program availability:* Part-time, evening/weekend. Offers creative writing (MFA); English (MA); history (MA); liberal arts and sciences (MA, MFA). *Application deadline:* For fall admission, 2/15 for domestic and international students; for spring admission, 9/15 for domestic and international students. Applications are processed on a rolling basis. *Application fee:* $0. Electronic applications accepted. *Application Contact:* Diane Dubord, Graduate Student Services Specialist, 317-940-8107, Fax: 317-940-8250, E-mail: ddubord@butler.edu. *Dean,* Dr. Jay Howard, 317-940-9874, E-mail: jrhoward@butler.edu.

College of Pharmacy and Health Sciences Students: 374 full-time (268 women), 6 part-time (3 women); includes 28 minority (1 Black or African American, non-Hispanic/Latino; 15 Asian, non-Hispanic/Latino; 7 Hispanic/Latino; 5 Two or more races, non-Hispanic/Latino), 5 international. Average age 24. 420 applicants, 20% accepted, 92 enrolled. *Faculty:* 61 full-time (42 women). Expenses: Contact institution. *Financial support:* In 2016–17, 4 students received support. Scholarships/grants, tuition waivers (full and partial), and unspecified assistantships available. Financial award application deadline: 7/15; financial award applicants required to submit FAFSA. In 2016, 51 master's, 103 doctorates awarded. Offers pharmaceutical science (MS); pharmacy (Pharm D); physician assistant studies (MS). *Application deadline:* For fall admission, 4/1 for domestic and international students. *Application fee:* $0. Electronic applications accepted. *Application Contact:* Diane Dubord, Graduate Student Services Specialist, 317-940-8107, E-mail: ddubord@butler.edu. *Dean,* Dr. Robert Soltis, 317-940-8056, E-mail: rsoltis@butler.edu.

Jordan College of the Arts Students: 16 full-time (5 women), 21 part-time (4 women); includes 7 minority (3 Black or African American, non-Hispanic/Latino; 1 Asian, non-Hispanic/Latino; 1 Hispanic/Latino; 2 Two or more races, non-Hispanic/Latino), 1 international. Average age 26. 41 applicants, 66% accepted, 13 enrolled. *Faculty:* 29 full-time (10 women), 36 part-time/adjunct (18 women). Expenses: Contact institution. *Financial support:* Scholarships/grants, tuition waivers (full and partial), and unspecified assistantships available. Financial award application deadline: 7/15; financial award applicants required to submit FAFSA. In 2016, 16 master's awarded. *Program availability:* Part-time. Offers composition (MM); conducting (MM); music education (MM); music history (MM). *Application deadline:* For fall admission, 2/1 for domestic and international students; for spring admission, 12/15 for domestic and international students; for summer admission, 4/15 for domestic and international students. Applications are processed on a rolling basis. *Application fee:* $0. Electronic applications accepted. *Application Contact:* Diane Dubord, Graduate Student Services Specialist, 317-940-8107, E-mail: ddubord@butler.edu. *Interim Dean,* Michele Jarvis, 317-940-9231, E-mail: mjarvis@butler.edu.

Lacy School of Business Students: 31 full-time (11 women), 133 part-time (40 women); includes 10 minority (2 Black or African American, non-Hispanic/Latino; 2 Asian, non-Hispanic/Latino; 6 Hispanic/Latino), 2 international. Average age 31. 122 applicants, 68% accepted, 42 enrolled. *Faculty:* 18 full-time (6 women), 14 part-time/adjunct (5 women). Expenses: Contact institution. *Financial support:* In 2016–17, 15 students received support. Scholarships/grants, tuition waivers (full and partial), and unspecified assistantships available. Financial award application deadline: 7/15; financial award applicants required to submit FAFSA. In 2016, 89 master's awarded. *Program availability:* Part-time. Offers finance (MBA); international business (MBA);

leadership (MBA); marketing (MBA); professional accounting (MP Acc). *Application deadline:* For fall admission, 8/1 for domestic and international students; for spring admission, 12/1 for domestic and international students; for summer admission, 4/1 for domestic and international students. Applications are processed on a rolling basis. *Application fee:* $0. Electronic applications accepted. *Application Contact:* Diane Dubord, Graduate Student Service Specialist, 317-940-8107, Fax: 317-940-8250, E-mail: ddubord@butler.edu. *Dean,* Dr. Stephen Standifird.

BYZANTINE CATHOLIC SEMINARY OF SAINTS CYRIL AND METHODIUS, Pittsburgh, PA 15214

General Information Independent-religious, coed, graduate-only institution.

GRADUATE UNITS

Graduate and Professional Programs Offers theology (M Div, MAT).

CABARRUS COLLEGE OF HEALTH SCIENCES, Concord, NC 28025

General Information Independent, coed, primarily women, comprehensive institution.

GRADUATE UNITS

Program in Occupational Therapy Offers occupational therapy (MOT).

CABRINI UNIVERSITY, Radnor, PA 19087

General Information Independent-religious, coed, comprehensive institution. *Graduate housing:* On-campus housing not available.

GRADUATE UNITS

Graduate Studies *Program availability:* Part-time, evening/weekend. Offers accounting (M Acc); education (M Ed); leadership (MS). Electronic applications accepted.

CAIRN UNIVERSITY, Langhorne, PA 19047-2990

General Information Independent-religious, coed, comprehensive institution. *Enrollment:* 1,042 graduate, professional, and undergraduate students; 54 full-time matriculated graduate/professional students (24 women), 244 part-time matriculated graduate/professional students (129 women). *Enrollment by degree level:* 292 master's, 6 other advanced degrees. *Graduate faculty:* 15 full-time (4 women), 17 part-time/adjunct (8 women). *Tuition:* Full-time $11,790; part-time $655 per credit hour. Tuition and fees vary according to program. *Graduate housing:* Rooms and/or apartments available on a first-come, first-served basis to single and married students. Typical cost: $4566 per year ($9583 including board) for single students. Room and board charges vary according to housing facility selected. *Student services:* Campus employment opportunities, campus safety program, career counseling, exercise/wellness program, international student services, low-cost health insurance, services for students with disabilities, teacher training, writing training. *Library facilities:* Masland Learning Resource Center. *Collection:* Books: 104,860 (physical), 421,604 (digital/electronic); Serial titles: 945 (physical), 53,295 (digital/electronic); Databases: 177. Weekly public service hours: 86; students can reserve study rooms.

Computer facilities: Computer purchase and lease plans are available. 66 computers available on campus for general student use. A campuswide network can be accessed from student residence rooms and from off campus. Online class registration is available. Website: http://cairn.edu/

General Application Contact: Rebecca Lippert, Director, Admissions, 800-572-2472, Fax: 215-702-4241, E-mail: blippert@cairn.edu.

GRADUATE UNITS

Department of Counseling Students: 20 full-time (15 women), 58 part-time (35 women); includes 29 minority (18 Black or African American, non-Hispanic/Latino; 1 Asian, non-Hispanic/Latino; 8 Hispanic/Latino; 2 Two or more races, non-Hispanic/Latino), 3 international. Average age 37. 30 applicants, 80% accepted, 22 enrolled. *Faculty:* 3 full-time (1 woman), 4 part-time/adjunct (all women). Expenses: Contact institution. *Financial support:* Scholarships/grants available. Support available to part-time students. Financial award applicants required to submit FAFSA. In 2016, 19 master's awarded. *Program availability:* Part-time, evening/weekend. Offers counseling (MS). *Application deadline:* Applications are processed on a rolling basis. *Application fee:* $25. Electronic applications accepted. *Application Contact:* Gwen Dorsey, Enrollment Counselor, Graduate Counseling, 800-572-2472, Fax: 215-702-4248, E-mail: gdorsey@cairn.edu. *Chair,* Dr. Jeff Black, 215-702-4347, E-mail: jblack@cairn.edu.

School of Business Students: 7 full-time (5 women), 43 part-time (19 women); includes 20 minority (10 Black or African American, non-Hispanic/Latino; 1 American Indian or Alaska Native, non-Hispanic/Latino; 4 Asian, non-Hispanic/Latino; 3 Hispanic/Latino; 2 Two or more races, non-Hispanic/Latino), 4 international. Average age 36. 17 applicants, 100% accepted, 16 enrolled. *Faculty:* 3 full-time (0 women), 6 part-time/adjunct (1 woman). Expenses: Contact institution. *Financial support:* Scholarships/grants available. Support available to part-time students. Financial award applicants required to submit FAFSA. In 2016, 16 master's awarded. *Program availability:* Part-time, evening/weekend, 100% online, blended/hybrid learning. Offers accounting (MBA); business administration (MBA); international entrepreneurship (MBA); nonprofit leadership (MBA); organizational leadership (MSOL, Postbaccalaureate Certificate). *Application deadline:* Applications are processed on a rolling basis. *Application fee:* $25. Electronic applications accepted. *Application Contact:* Gwen Dorsey, Assistant Director, Graduate Admissions, 800-572-2472, Fax: 215-702-4248, E-mail: gdorsey@cairn.edu. *Dean, School of Business,* Yunn Kang, 215-702-4461, Fax: 215-702-4248, E-mail: ykang@cairn.edu.

School of Divinity Students: 24 full-time (2 women), 54 part-time (13 women); includes 29 minority (19 Black or African American, non-Hispanic/Latino; 4 Asian, non-Hispanic/Latino; 5 Hispanic/Latino; 1 Two or more races, non-Hispanic/Latino), 1 international. Average age 37. 29 applicants, 97% accepted, 26 enrolled. *Faculty:* 6 full-time (0 women), 3 part-time/adjunct (0 women). Expenses: Contact institution. *Financial support:* Scholarships/grants available. Support available to part-time students. Financial award applicants required to submit FAFSA. In 2016, 31 master's awarded. *Program availability:* Part-time, evening/weekend, 100% online, blended/hybrid learning. Offers divinity (M Div); religion (MA); theology (Th M). *Application deadline:* Applications are processed on a rolling basis. *Application fee:* $25. Electronic applications accepted. *Application Contact:* Abigail Simon, Assistant Director, Graduate Admissions, 800-572-2472, Fax: 215-702-4248, E-mail: asimon@cairn.edu. *Dean,* Dr. Jonathan L. Master, 215-702-4358, Fax: 215-702-4359, E-mail: divinity@cairn.edu.

School of Education Students: 3 full-time (2 women), 89 part-time (62 women); includes 18 minority (10 Black or African American, non-Hispanic/Latino; 6 Asian, non-Hispanic/Latino; 2 Hispanic/Latino), 21 international. Average age 38. 35 applicants, 100% accepted, 25 enrolled. *Faculty:* 2 full-time (both women), 4 part-time/adjunct (3 women). Expenses: Contact institution. *Financial support:* Scholarships/grants available. Support available to part-time students. Financial award applicants required to submit FAFSA. In 2016, 17 master's awarded. *Program availability:* Part-time, evening/weekend, 100% online, blended/hybrid learning. Offers applied behavior analysis (MS Sp Ed, Certificate); educational leadership and administration (MS El); instruction (MS Sp Ed); teacher education (MS Ed). *Application deadline:* Applications are processed on a rolling basis. *Application fee:* $25. Electronic applications accepted. *Application Contact:* Abigail Simon, Enrollment Counselor, Graduate Education, 800-572-2472, Fax: 215-702-4248, E-mail: asimon@cairn.edu. *Interim Dean,* Joseph Beeson, 215-702-4498, E-mail: teacher.ed@cairn.edu.

CALDWELL UNIVERSITY, Caldwell, NJ 07006-6195

General Information Independent-religious, coed, comprehensive institution. CGS member.

GRADUATE UNITS

Graduate Studies *Program availability:* Part-time, evening/weekend. Offers art therapy (MA); counseling (MA); director of school counseling (Post-Master's Certificate); professional counselor (Post-Master's Certificate); school counselor (Post-Master's Certificate). Electronic applications accepted.

Division of Applied Behavior Analysis *Program availability:* Part-time. Offers applied behavior analysis (MA, PhD, Post-Master's Certificate). Electronic applications accepted.

Division of Business *Program availability:* Part-time. Offers accounting (MS); business administration (MBA). Electronic applications accepted.

Division of Education *Program availability:* Part-time, evening/weekend. Offers curriculum and instruction (MA); education (Ed D, Postbaccalaureate Certificate); educational administration (MA); learning disabilities teacher-consultant (Post-Master's Certificate); literacy instruction (MA); principal (Post-Master's Certificate); reading specialist (Post-Master's Certificate); special education (MA); superintendent (Post-Master's Certificate); supervisor (Post-Master's Certificate). Electronic applications accepted.

CALIFORNIA BAPTIST UNIVERSITY, Riverside, CA 92504-3206

General Information Independent-religious, coed, comprehensive institution. *Enrollment:* 9,157 graduate, professional, and undergraduate students; 1,202 full-time matriculated graduate/professional students (869 women), 1,016 part-time matriculated graduate/professional students (714 women). *Enrollment by degree level:* 2,170 master's, 48 doctoral. *Graduate faculty:* 171 full-time (93 women), 84 part-time/adjunct (42 women). *Tuition:* Full-time $12,240; part-time $680 per unit. *Required fees:* $175 per semester. One-time fee: $45. Tuition and fees vary according to course load, degree level and program. *Graduate housing:* Room and/or apartment available on a first-come, first-served basis to single students; on-campus housing not available to married students. Typical cost: $7890 per year ($11,990 including board). Room and board charges vary according to board plan and housing facility selected. Housing application deadline: 8/1. *Student services:* Campus employment opportunities, campus safety program, career counseling, exercise/wellness program, free psychological counseling, international student services, low-cost health insurance, multicultural affairs office, services for students with disabilities, teacher training, writing training. *Library facilities:* Annie Gabriel Library. *Collection:* Books: 130,837 (physical), 190,918 (digital/electronic); Serial titles: 59,915 (physical), 21,548 (digital/electronic); Databases: 83. Weekly public service hours: 101; students can reserve study rooms.

Computer facilities: Computer purchase and lease plans are available. 279 computers available on campus for general student use. A campuswide network can be accessed from student residence rooms and from off campus. Online class registration, online course evaluations are available.
Website: http://www.calbaptist.edu/

General Application Contact: Alma Salazar, Director of Graduate Admissions, 951-552-8086, Fax: 951-552-8700, E-mail: graduateadmissions@calbaptist.edu.

GRADUATE UNITS

Doctor of Nursing Practice Program Students: 7 part-time (5 women); includes 3 minority (1 Black or African American, non-Hispanic/Latino; 1 American Indian or Alaska Native, non-Hispanic/Latino; 1 Hispanic/Latino). Average age 51. 13 applicants, 31% accepted, 4 enrolled. *Faculty:* 6 full-time (5 women). Expenses: Contact institution. *Financial support:* Federal Work-Study and scholarships/grants available. Financial award applicants required to submit CSS PROFILE or FAFSA. *Program availability:* Part-time. Offers nursing (DNP). *Application deadline:* For fall admission, 8/1 priority date for domestic students, 7/1 priority date for international students; for spring admission, 12/1 priority date for domestic students, 11/1 priority date for international students. Applications are processed on a rolling basis. *Application fee:* $45. Electronic applications accepted. *Application Contact:* Dr. Lisa Bursch, DNP Program Director, 951-343-4940, E-mail: lbursch@calbaptist.edu. *Dean, School of Nursing,* Dr. Geneva Oaks, 951-343-4702, E-mail: goaks@calbaptist.edu.

Program in Accounting Students: 13 full-time (9 women), 12 part-time (7 women); includes 15 minority (5 Black or African American, non-Hispanic/Latino; 1 Asian, non-Hispanic/Latino; 6 Hispanic/Latino; 1 Native Hawaiian or other Pacific Islander, non-Hispanic/Latino; 2 Two or more races, non-Hispanic/Latino). Average age 33. 13 applicants, 62% accepted, 4 enrolled. *Faculty:* 8 full-time (2 women). Expenses: Contact institution. *Financial support:* In 2016–17, 5 students received support. Federal Work-Study and scholarships/grants available. Financial award applicants required to submit CSS PROFILE or FAFSA. In 2016, 2 master's awarded. *Program availability:* Part-time, evening/weekend, online only, 100% online. Offers accounting (MS). *Application deadline:* For fall admission, 8/1 priority date for domestic students, 7/1 priority date for international students; for spring admission, 12/1 priority date for domestic students, 11/1 priority date for international students. Applications are processed on a rolling basis. *Application fee:* $45. Electronic applications accepted. *Application Contact:* Karin Nelson, Program Director, Accounting, 951-552-8777, E-mail: knelson@calbaptist.edu. *Vice President, Online and Professional Studies,* Dr. David Poole, 951-343-3902, E-mail: dpoole@calbaptist.edu.

Program in Applied Mathematics Students: 8 full-time (4 women), 2 part-time (1 woman); includes 5 minority (1 Black or African American, non-Hispanic/Latino; 4 Hispanic/Latino), 1 international. Average age 26. 7 applicants, 57% accepted, 2 enrolled. *Faculty:* 8 full-time (3 women). Expenses: Contact institution. *Financial support:* In 2016–17, 2 students received support. Scholarships/grants and unspecified assistantships available. Financial award applicants required to submit CSS PROFILE or FAFSA. *Program availability:* Part-time. Offers applied mathematics (MS). *Application deadline:* For fall admission, 8/1 priority date for domestic students, 7/1 priority date for international students; for spring admission, 12/1 priority date for domestic students, 11/1 priority date for international students. Applications are processed on a rolling basis. *Application fee:* $45. Electronic applications accepted. *Application Contact:* Dr. Ricardo J. Cordero-Soto, Associate Professor of Mathematics, 951-552-8632, E-mail: rcordero@calbaptist.edu. *Dean of the College of Arts and Science,* Dr. Gayne Anacker, 951-343-4682.

Program in Architecture Students: 73 full-time (28 women), 2 part-time (1 woman); includes 46 minority (8 Black or African American, non-Hispanic/Latino; 1 American Indian or Alaska Native, non-Hispanic/Latino; 4 Asian, non-Hispanic/Latino; 31 Hispanic/Latino; 1 Native Hawaiian or other Pacific Islander, non-Hispanic/Latino; 1 Two or more races, non-Hispanic/Latino), 3 international. Average age 21. *Faculty:* 8 full-time (3 women), 5 part-time/adjunct (2 women). Expenses: Contact institution. *Financial support:* Federal Work-Study and scholarships/grants available. Financial award applicants required to submit CSS PROFILE or FAFSA. Offers architecture (M Arch). *Application deadline:* For fall admission, 8/1 priority date for domestic students, 7/1 for international students; for spring admission, 12/1 priority date for domestic students, 11/1 for international students. Applications are processed on a rolling basis. *Application fee:* $45. Electronic applications accepted. *Dean, College of Architecture, Visual Arts and Design,* Mark Roberson, 951-552-8652, E-mail: maroberson@calbaptist.edu.

Program in Athletic Training Students: 37 full-time (22 women); includes 17 minority (3 Black or African American, non-Hispanic/Latino; 4 Asian, non-Hispanic/Latino; 10 Hispanic/Latino). Average age 25. *Faculty:* 4 full-time (3 women). Expenses: Contact institution. *Financial support:* In 2016–17, 3 students received support. Research assistantships, Federal Work-Study, and scholarships/grants available. Financial award applicants required to submit CSS PROFILE or FAFSA. In 2016, 20 master's awarded. *Program availability:* Part-time. Offers athletic training (MS). *Application deadline:* For fall admission, 8/1 priority date for domestic students, 7/1 for international students; for spring admission, 12/1 priority date for domestic students, 11/1 for international students. Applications are processed on a rolling basis. *Application fee:* $45. Electronic applications accepted. *Application Contact:* Dr. Nicole MacDonald, Director, Athletic Training Program, 951-343-4379, E-mail: nmacdona@calbaptist.edu. *Dean of the College of Health Science,* Dr. David Pearson, 951-343-4298, E-mail: dpearson@calbaptist.edu.

Program in Business Administration Students: 105 full-time (48 women), 122 part-time (63 women); includes 101 minority (23 Black or African American, non-Hispanic/Latino; 1 American Indian or Alaska Native, non-Hispanic/Latino; 10 Asian, non-Hispanic/Latino; 59 Hispanic/Latino; 2 Native Hawaiian or other Pacific Islander, non-Hispanic/Latino; 6 Two or more races, non-Hispanic/Latino), 54 international. Average age 29. 136 applicants, 65% accepted, 62 enrolled. *Faculty:* 14 full-time (3 women), 10 part-time/adjunct (1 woman). Expenses: Contact institution. *Financial support:* In 2016–17, 38 students received support. Federal Work-Study and scholarships/grants available. Financial award applicants required to submit CSS PROFILE or FAFSA. In 2016, 71 master's awarded. *Program availability:* Part-time, evening/weekend, 100% online, blended/hybrid learning. Offers accounting (MBA); construction management (MBA); healthcare management (MBA); management (MBA). *Application deadline:* For fall admission, 8/1 priority date for domestic students, 7/1 for international students; for spring admission, 12/1 priority date for domestic students, 11/1 for international students. Applications are processed on a rolling basis. *Application fee:* $45. Electronic applications accepted. *Application Contact:* Stephanie Fluitt, Graduate Admissions Counselor, 951-343-4696, E-mail: sfluitt@calbaptist.edu. *Interim Dean, School of Business,* Dr. Steve Strombeck, 951-343-4701, Fax: 951-343-4361, E-mail: sstrombeck@calbaptist.edu.

Program in Civil Engineering Students: 6 full-time (3 women), 2 part-time (1 woman); includes 1 minority (Hispanic/Latino), 5 international. Average age 24. 7 applicants, 71% accepted, 5 enrolled. *Faculty:* 6 full-time (1 woman), 1 part-time/adjunct (0 women). Expenses: Contact institution. *Financial support:* Federal Work-Study and scholarships/grants available. Financial award applicants required to submit CSS PROFILE or FAFSA. *Program availability:* Part-time. Offers civil engineering (MS). *Application deadline:* For fall admission, 8/1 priority date for domestic students, 7/1 priority date for international students; for spring admission, 12/1 priority date for domestic students, 11/1 priority date for international students. Applications are processed on a rolling basis. *Application fee:* $45. Electronic applications accepted. *Application Contact:* Taylor Neece, Director of Graduate Admissions, 951-343-4871, Fax: 877-228-8877, E-mail: graduateadmissions@calbaptist.edu. *Associate Dean, College of Engineering,* Dr. Helen Jung, 951-343-4510.

Program in Communication Students: 13 full-time (8 women), 7 part-time (3 women); includes 11 minority (2 Black or African American, non-Hispanic/Latino; 8 Hispanic/Latino; 1 Two or more races, non-Hispanic/Latino). Average age 29. 14 applicants, 71% accepted, 6 enrolled. *Faculty:* 5 full-time (2 women). Expenses: Contact institution. *Financial support:* In 2016–17, 2 students received support. Federal Work-Study and scholarships/grants available. Financial award applicants required to submit CSS PROFILE or FAFSA. In 2016, 9 master's awarded. *Program availability:* Part-time, evening/weekend, online only, 100% online. Offers communication (MA). *Application deadline:* For fall admission, 8/1 priority date for domestic students, 7/1 priority date for international students; for spring admission, 12/1 priority date for domestic students, 11/1 priority date for international students. Applications are processed on a rolling basis. *Application fee:* $45. Electronic applications accepted. *Application Contact:* Dr. MaryAnn Pearson, Program Director of MA in Communication, 951-343-3967, E-mail: mpearson@calbaptist.edu. *Vice President of Online and Professional Studies,* Dr. David Poole, 951-343-3901, E-mail: dpoole@calbaptist.edu.

Program in Counseling Ministry Students: 3 full-time (2 women), 9 part-time (8 women); includes 4 minority (1 Black or African American, non-Hispanic/Latino; 3 Hispanic/Latino). Average age 36. 4 applicants, 100% accepted, 2 enrolled. *Faculty:* 4 full-time (1 woman), 1 (woman) part-time/adjunct. Expenses: Contact institution. *Financial support:* In 2016–17, 2 students received support. Federal Work-Study and scholarships/grants available. Financial award applicants required to submit CSS PROFILE or FAFSA. In 2016, 4 master's awarded. *Program availability:* Part-time, evening/weekend. Offers professional ministry (MA); research in counseling ministry (MA). *Application deadline:* For fall admission, 8/1 priority date for domestic students, 7/1 for international students; for spring admission, 12/1 priority date for domestic students, 11/1 for international students. Applications are processed on a rolling basis. *Application fee:* $45. Electronic applications accepted. *Application Contact:* Dr. Nathan Lewis, Program Director of Counseling Ministry, 951-343-4348, E-mail: nlewis@calbaptist.edu. *Dean, School of Behavioral Sciences,* Dr. Jacqueline Gustafson, 951-343-4487, E-mail: jcraig@calbaptist.edu.

Program in Counseling Ministry and Counseling Psychology (Dual Master's) Students: 14 full-time (11 women), 2 part-time (1 woman); includes 12 minority (2 Black or African American, non-Hispanic/Latino; 1 Asian, non-Hispanic/Latino; 9 Hispanic/Latino). Average age 31. 11 applicants, 45% accepted, 5 enrolled. *Faculty:* 18 full-time (11 women), 10 part-time/adjunct (7 women). Expenses: Contact institution. *Financial support:* In 2016–17, 2 students received support. Federal Work-Study and scholarships/grants available. Financial award applicants required to submit CSS PROFILE or FAFSA. *Program availability:* Part-time, evening/weekend. *Application deadline:* For fall admission, 8/1 priority date for domestic students, 7/1 for international students; for spring admission, 12/1 priority date for domestic students, 11/1 for

California Baptist University

international students. Applications are processed on a rolling basis. *Application fee:* $45. Electronic applications accepted. *Application Contact:* Mischa Routon, Director of Counseling Psychology Program, 951-343-4206, Fax: 877-228-8877, E-mail: mrouton@calbaptist.edu. *Dean, School of Behavioral Sciences,* Dr. Jacqueline Gustafson, 951-343-4487, E-mail: jcraig@calbaptist.edu.

Program in Counseling Psychology Students: 258 full-time (211 women), 97 part-time (82 women); includes 238 minority (64 Black or African American, non-Hispanic/Latino; 1 American Indian or Alaska Native, non-Hispanic/Latino; 14 Asian, non-Hispanic/Latino; 146 Hispanic/Latino; 1 Native Hawaiian or other Pacific Islander, non-Hispanic/Latino; 12 Two or more races, non-Hispanic/Latino), 1 international. Average age 31. 98 applicants, 78% accepted, 64 enrolled. *Faculty:* 18 full-time (11 women), 10 part-time/adjunct (7 women). Expenses: Contact institution. *Financial support:* In 2016–17, 79 students received support. Federal Work-Study and scholarships/grants available. Financial award applicants required to submit CSS PROFILE or FAFSA. In 2016, 106 master's awarded. *Program availability:* Part-time, evening/weekend, 100% online, blended/hybrid learning. Offers counseling psychology (MS); forensic psychology (MS); professional clinical counselor (MS). *Application deadline:* For fall admission, 8/1 priority date for domestic students, 7/1 for international students; for spring admission, 12/1 priority date for domestic students, 11/1 for international students. Applications are processed on a rolling basis. *Application fee:* $45. Electronic applications accepted. *Application Contact:* Mischa Routon, Associate Dean of Graduate Programs, 951-343-4206, Fax: 951-343-4569, E-mail: mrouton@calbaptist.edu. *Dean, School of Behavioral Sciences,* Dr. Jacqueline Gustafson, 951-343-4487, E-mail: jcraig@calbaptist.edu.

Program in Disability Studies Students: 6 part-time (all women); includes 2 minority (1 Black or African American, non-Hispanic/Latino; 1 Two or more races, non-Hispanic/Latino). Average age 43. 8 applicants. *Faculty:* 5 full-time (2 women), 4 part-time/adjunct (2 women). Expenses: Contact institution. *Financial support:* In 2016–17, 1 student received support. Federal Work-Study and scholarships/grants available. Financial award applicants required to submit CSS PROFILE or FAFSA. In 2016, 8 master's awarded. *Program availability:* Part-time, evening/weekend, 100% online. Offers disability ministry (MA); disability policy (MA). *Application deadline:* For fall admission, 8/1 priority date for domestic students, 7/1 for international students; for spring admission, 12/1 priority date for domestic students, 11/1 for international students. Applications are processed on a rolling basis. *Application fee:* $45. Electronic applications accepted. *Application Contact:* Dr. Jeff McNair, Program Director, MA in Disability Studies, 951-343-4489, E-mail: jmcnair@calbaptist.edu. *Vice President, Online and Professional Studies,* Dr. David Poole, 951-343-3901, E-mail: dpoole@calbaptist.edu.

Program in Education Students: 191 full-time (148 women), 234 part-time (178 women); includes 194 minority (23 Black or African American, non-Hispanic/Latino; 5 American Indian or Alaska Native, non-Hispanic/Latino; 15 Asian, non-Hispanic/Latino; 131 Hispanic/Latino; 4 Native Hawaiian or other Pacific Islander, non-Hispanic/Latino; 16 Two or more races, non-Hispanic/Latino), 2 international. Average age 31. 277 applicants, 61% accepted, 150 enrolled. *Faculty:* 20 full-time (8 women), 11 part-time/adjunct (7 women). Expenses: Contact institution. *Financial support:* In 2016–17, 162 students received support. Federal Work-Study and scholarships/grants available. Financial award applicants required to submit CSS PROFILE or FAFSA. In 2016, 280 master's awarded. *Program availability:* Part-time, evening/weekend, 100% online, blended/hybrid learning. Offers educational leadership (MS); educational leadership for faith-based institutions (MS); educational leadership for public institutions (MS); educational technology (MS); instructional computer applications (MS); international education (MS); leadership and adult learning (MS); leadership and organizational studies (MS); online teaching and learning (MS); reading (MS); science education (MA); special education in mild/moderate disabilities (MS); special education in moderate/severe disabilities (MS); teacher leadership (MS); teaching (MS); teaching and learning (MS). *Application deadline:* For fall admission, 8/1 priority date for domestic students, 7/1 for international students; for spring admission, 12/1 priority date for domestic students, 11/1 for international students. Applications are processed on a rolling basis. *Application fee:* $45. Electronic applications accepted. *Dean, School of Education,* Dr. John Shoup, 951-343-4516, E-mail: jshoup@calbaptist.edu.

Program in English Students: 3 full-time (2 women), 26 part-time (19 women); includes 14 minority (4 Black or African American, non-Hispanic/Latino; 1 Asian, non-Hispanic/Latino; 9 Hispanic/Latino), 3 international. Average age 28. 8 applicants, 88% accepted, 6 enrolled. *Faculty:* 9 full-time (7 women), 1 (woman) part-time/adjunct. Expenses: Contact institution. *Financial support:* In 2016–17, 5 students received support. Federal Work-Study and scholarships/grants available. Financial award applicants required to submit CSS PROFILE or FAFSA. In 2016, 4 master's awarded. *Program availability:* Part-time, evening/weekend. Offers English pedagogy (MA); literature (MA); teaching English to speakers of other languages (TESOL) (MA). *Application deadline:* For fall admission, 8/1 priority date for domestic students, 7/1 for international students; for spring admission, 12/1 priority date for domestic students, 11/1 for international students. Applications are processed on a rolling basis. *Application fee:* $45. Electronic applications accepted. *Application Contact:* Dr. Laura Veltman, Director, Master of Arts Program in English, 951-343-4276, Fax: 951-343-4661, E-mail: lveltman@calbaptist.edu. *Dean, College of Arts and Sciences,* Dr. Gayne Anacker, 951-343-4682, E-mail: ganacker@calbaptist.edu.

Program in Forensic Psychology Students: 68 full-time (55 women), 9 part-time (7 women); includes 44 minority (11 Black or African American, non-Hispanic/Latino; 31 Hispanic/Latino; 2 Two or more races, non-Hispanic/Latino), 1 international. Average age 26. 48 applicants, 75% accepted, 32 enrolled. *Faculty:* 4 full-time (3 women), 1 (woman) part-time/adjunct. Expenses: Contact institution. *Financial support:* In 2016–17, 12 students received support. Federal Work-Study and scholarships/grants available. Financial award applicants required to submit CSS PROFILE or FAFSA. In 2016, 20 master's awarded. *Program availability:* Part-time, evening/weekend. Offers forensic psychology (MA). *Application deadline:* For fall admission, 8/1 priority date for domestic students, 7/1 for international students; for spring admission, 12/1 priority date for domestic students, 11/1 for international students. Applications are processed on a rolling basis. *Application fee:* $45. Electronic applications accepted. *Application Contact:* Dr. Anne-Marie Larsen, Director, Graduate Program in Forensic Psychology, 951-343-4761, E-mail: alarsen@calbaptist.edu. *Dean, School of Behavioral Sciences,* Dr. Jacqueline Gustafson, 951-343-4487, E-mail: jcraig@calbaptist.edu.

Program in Higher Education Leadership and Student Development Students: 23 part-time (16 women); includes 11 minority (4 Black or African American, non-Hispanic/Latino; 7 Hispanic/Latino), 2 international. Average age 29. 24 applicants, 67% accepted, 16 enrolled. *Faculty:* 5 full-time (2 women), 2 part-time/adjunct (1 woman). Expenses: Contact institution. *Financial support:* In 2016–17, 5 students received support. Federal Work-Study and scholarships/grants available. Financial award applicants required to submit CSS PROFILE or FAFSA. In 2016, 11 master's awarded. *Program availability:* Part-time, evening/weekend. Offers higher education leadership

and student development (MS). *Application deadline:* For fall admission, 8/1 priority date for domestic students, 7/1 for international students; for spring admission, 12/1 priority date for domestic students, 11/1 for international students. Applications are processed on a rolling basis. *Application fee:* $45. Electronic applications accepted. *Application Contact:* Dr. Shana Matamala, Associate Dean, School of Education, 951-343-4760, E-mail: smatamala@calbaptist.edu. *Dean, School of Education,* Dr. John Shoup, 951-343-4205, E-mail: jshoup@calbaptist.edu.

Program in Kinesiology Students: 77 full-time (43 women), 37 part-time (16 women); includes 48 minority (16 Black or African American, non-Hispanic/Latino; 9 Asian, non-Hispanic/Latino; 20 Hispanic/Latino; 1 Native Hawaiian or other Pacific Islander, non-Hispanic/Latino; 2 Two or more races, non-Hispanic/Latino), 26 international. Average age 28. 71 applicants, 76% accepted, 47 enrolled. *Faculty:* 10 full-time (3 women), 3 part-time/adjunct (0 women). Expenses: Contact institution. *Financial support:* In 2016–17, 11 students received support. Federal Work-Study, scholarships/grants, and unspecified assistantships available. Financial award applicants required to submit CSS PROFILE or FAFSA. In 2016, 43 master's awarded. *Program availability:* Part-time, 100% online, blended/hybrid learning. Offers exercise science (MS); physical education (MS); sport management (MS). *Application deadline:* For fall admission, 8/1 priority date for domestic students, 7/1 for international students; for spring admission, 12/1 priority date for domestic students, 11/1 for international students. Applications are processed on a rolling basis. *Application fee:* $45. Electronic applications accepted. *Application Contact:* Dr. Sean Sullivan, Chair, Department of Kinesiology, 951-343-4528, Fax: 951-343-5095, E-mail: ssullivan@calbaptist.edu. *Dean, College of Allied Health,* Dr. David Pearson, 951-343-4298, E-mail: dpearson@calbaptist.edu.

Program in Leadership and Adult Learning Expenses: Contact institution. *Financial support:* Applicants required to submit CSS PROFILE or FAFSA. *Program availability:* Part-time, evening/weekend. Offers leadership and adult learning (MA). *Application deadline:* For fall admission, 8/1 priority date for domestic students, 7/1 priority date for international students; for spring admission, 12/1 priority date for domestic students, 11/1 priority date for international students. Applications are processed on a rolling basis. *Application fee:* $45. Electronic applications accepted. *Dean, School of Education,* Dr. John Shoup, 951-343-4205, E-mail: jshoup@calbaptist.edu.

Program in Leadership and Community Development Students: 2 full-time (0 women), 1 (woman) part-time; includes 2 minority (both Hispanic/Latino). Average age 24. 3 applicants, 67% accepted, 2 enrolled. *Faculty:* 3 full-time (0 women), 1 part-time/adjunct (0 women). Expenses: Contact institution. *Financial support:* In 2016–17, 1 student received support. Applicants required to submit CSS PROFILE or FAFSA. *Program availability:* Part-time, evening/weekend. Offers leadership and community development (MA). *Application deadline:* For fall admission, 8/1 priority date for domestic students, 7/1 priority date for international students; for spring admission, 12/1 for domestic students, 11/1 priority date for international students. Applications are processed on a rolling basis. *Application fee:* $45. Electronic applications accepted. *Application Contact:* Taylor Neece, Director of Graduate Admissions, 951-343-4871, Fax: 877-228-8877, E-mail: graduateadmissions@calbaptist.edu. *Dean, School of Education,* Dr. John Shoup, 951-343-4205, E-mail: jshoup@calbaptist.edu.

Program in Leadership and Organizational Studies Students: 17 part-time (11 women); includes 9 minority (1 Black or African American, non-Hispanic/Latino; 6 Hispanic/Latino; 2 Two or more races, non-Hispanic/Latino). Average age 41. 26 applicants, 69% accepted, 15 enrolled. *Faculty:* 7 full-time (2 women), 3 part-time/adjunct (0 women). Expenses: Contact institution. *Financial support:* In 2016–17, 7 students received support. Federal Work-Study and scholarships/grants available. Financial award applicants required to submit CSS PROFILE or FAFSA. In 2016, 7 master's awarded. *Program availability:* Part-time, evening/weekend. Offers leadership and organizational studies (MA). *Application deadline:* For fall admission, 8/1 priority date for domestic students, 7/1 for international students; for spring admission, 11/1 priority date for domestic students, 11/1 for international students. Applications are processed on a rolling basis. *Application fee:* $45. Electronic applications accepted. *Application Contact:* Dr. Shana Matamala, Associate Dean, School of Education, Dr. John Shoup, 951-343-4205, E-mail: jshoup@calbaptist.edu.

Program in Mechanical Engineering Students: 4 full-time (0 women); includes 1 minority (Asian, non-Hispanic/Latino), 1 international. Average age 24. 14 applicants, 71% accepted, 10 enrolled. *Faculty:* 7 full-time (2 women). Expenses: Contact institution. *Financial support:* Federal Work-Study and scholarships/grants available. Financial award applicants required to submit CSS PROFILE or FAFSA. *Program availability:* Part-time. Offers mechanical engineering (MS). *Application deadline:* For fall admission, 8/1 priority date for domestic students, 7/1 priority date for international students; for spring admission, 12/1 priority date for domestic students, 11/1 priority date for international students. Applications are processed on a rolling basis. *Application fee:* $45. Electronic applications accepted. *Application Contact:* Felicia Tasabia, Administrative Assistant, 951-343-4972, E-mail: ftasabia@calbaptist.edu. *Assistant Dean, College of Engineering,* Dr. Ziliang Zhou, 951-343-4681, E-mail: zzhou@calbaptist.edu.

Program in Music Students: 12 full-time (6 women), 8 part-time (6 women); includes 8 minority (2 Black or African American, non-Hispanic/Latino; 3 Asian, non-Hispanic/Latino; 3 Hispanic/Latino), 8 international. Average age 26. 7 applicants, 57% accepted, 3 enrolled. *Faculty:* 14 full-time (8 women), 18 part-time/adjunct (7 women). Expenses: Contact institution. *Financial support:* In 2016–17, 8 students received support. Federal Work-Study and scholarships/grants available. Financial award applicants required to submit CSS PROFILE or FAFSA. In 2016, 7 master's awarded. *Program availability:* Part-time, evening/weekend. Offers conducting (MM); music education (MM); performance (MM). *Application deadline:* For fall admission, 8/1 priority date for domestic students, 7/1 for international students; for spring admission, 12/1 priority date for domestic students, 11/1 for international students. Applications are processed on a rolling basis. *Application fee:* $45. Electronic applications accepted. *Application Contact:* Stephanie Fluitt, Graduate Admissions Counselor, 952-343-4696, E-mail: sfluitt@calbaptist.edu. *Dean, School of Music,* Dr. Joseph Bolin, 951-343-4714, Fax: 951-343-4570, E-mail: jbolin@calbaptist.edu.

Program in Nursing Students: 92 full-time (76 women), 132 part-time (102 women); includes 124 minority (32 Black or African American, non-Hispanic/Latino; 2 American Indian or Alaska Native, non-Hispanic/Latino; 36 Asian, non-Hispanic/Latino; 51 Hispanic/Latino; 2 Native Hawaiian or other Pacific Islander, non-Hispanic/Latino; 1 Two or more races, non-Hispanic/Latino), 3 international. Average age 33. 57 applicants, 54% accepted, 28 enrolled. *Faculty:* 22 full-time (21 women), 13 part-time/adjunct (11 women). Expenses: Contact institution. *Financial support:* In 2016–17, 38 students received support. Federal Work-Study and scholarships/grants available. Financial award applicants required to submit CSS PROFILE or FAFSA. In 2016, 49 master's awarded. *Program availability:* Part-time. Offers clinical nurse specialist (MSN); family nurse practitioner (MSN); healthcare systems management (MSN); teaching-learning (MSN). *Application deadline:* For fall admission, 8/1 priority date for domestic students,

7/1 for international students; for spring admission, 12/1 priority date for domestic students, 11/1 for international students. Applications are processed on a rolling basis. *Application fee:* $45. Electronic applications accepted. *Application Contact:* Dr. Rebecca Meyer, Director, Graduate Program in Nursing, 951-343-4952, Fax: 951-343-5095, E-mail: rmeyer@calbaptist.edu. *Dean, School of Nursing,* Dr. Geneva Oaks, 951-343-4702, E-mail: goaks@calbaptist.edu.

Program in Organizational Leadership Students: 58 full-time (47 women), 31 part-time (20 women); includes 54 minority (14 Black or African American, non-Hispanic/Latino; 2 Asian, non-Hispanic/Latino; 31 Hispanic/Latino; 2 Native Hawaiian or other Pacific Islander, non-Hispanic/Latino; 5 Two or more races, non-Hispanic/Latino). Average age 38. 51 applicants, 76% accepted, 32 enrolled. *Faculty:* 9 full-time (2 women), 4 part-time/adjunct (1 woman). Expenses: Contact institution. *Financial support:* In 2016–17, 36 students received support. Federal Work-Study and scholarships/grants available. Financial award applicants required to submit CSS PROFILE or FAFSA. In 2016, 34 master's awarded. *Program availability:* Part-time, evening/weekend, 100% online. Offers organizational leadership (MA). *Application deadline:* For fall admission, 8/1 priority date for domestic students, 7/1 for international students; for spring admission, 12/1 priority date for domestic students, 11/1 for international students. Applications are processed on a rolling basis. Electronic applications accepted. *Application Contact:* Dr. Greg Bowden, Director of Master's in Organizational Leadership, 951-343-5560, E-mail: abowden@calbaptist.edu. *Vice President, Online and Professional Studies,* Dr. David Poole, 951-343-3902, E-mail: dpoole@calbaptist.edu.

Program in Physician Assistant Studies Students: 30 full-time (23 women); includes 18 minority (7 Asian, non-Hispanic/Latino; 8 Hispanic/Latino; 1 Native Hawaiian or other Pacific Islander, non-Hispanic/Latino; 2 Two or more races, non-Hispanic/Latino). Average age 26. 236 applicants, 14% accepted, 30 enrolled. *Faculty:* 6 full-time (3 women). Expenses: Contact institution. *Financial support:* In 2016–17, 2 students received support. Federal Work-Study and scholarships/grants available. Financial award applicants required to submit CSS PROFILE or FAFSA. *Program availability:* Part-time. Offers physician assistant studies (MS). *Application deadline:* For fall admission, 12/1 priority date for domestic students, 11/1 priority date for international students; for spring admission, 8/1 priority date for domestic students, 7/1 priority date for international students. Applications are processed on a rolling basis. *Application fee:* $45. Electronic applications accepted. *Application Contact:* Taylor Neece, Director of Graduate Admissions, 951-343-4871, Fax: 877-228-8877, E-mail: graduateadmissions@calbaptist.edu. *Director,* Dr. Allan M. Bedashi, 951-552-8838, E-mail: abedashi@calbaptist.edu.

Program in Public Administration Students: 47 full-time (30 women), 26 part-time (13 women); includes 44 minority (7 Black or African American, non-Hispanic/Latino; 1 American Indian or Alaska Native, non-Hispanic/Latino; 1 Asian, non-Hispanic/Latino; 31 Hispanic/Latino; 4 Two or more races, non-Hispanic/Latino). Average age 34. 59 applicants, 56% accepted, 26 enrolled. *Faculty:* 5 full-time (3 women), 3 part-time/adjunct (2 women). Expenses: Contact institution. *Financial support:* In 2016–17, 37 students received support. Federal Work-Study and scholarships/grants available. Financial award applicants required to submit CSS PROFILE or FAFSA. In 2016, 47 master's awarded. *Program availability:* Part-time, evening/weekend, 100% online, blended/hybrid learning. Offers public administration (MPA); strategic innovation (MPA). *Application deadline:* For fall admission, 8/1 priority date for domestic students, 7/1 for international students; for spring admission, 12/1 priority date for domestic students, 11/1 for international students. Applications are processed on a rolling basis. *Application fee:* $45. Electronic applications accepted. *Application Contact:* Dr. Elaine Ahumada, Director, MPA Program, 951-343-3929, Fax: 951-343-4661, E-mail: eahumada@calbaptist.edu. *Vice President, Online and Professional Studies,* Dr. David Poole, 951-343-3902, E-mail: dpoole@calbaptist.edu.

Program in Public Health Students: 48 full-time (40 women), 27 part-time (23 women); includes 58 minority (8 Black or African American, non-Hispanic/Latino; 4 Asian, non-Hispanic/Latino; 40 Hispanic/Latino; 6 Two or more races, non-Hispanic/Latino). Average age 28. 61 applicants, 75% accepted, 28 enrolled. *Faculty:* 10 full-time (6 women), 4 part-time/adjunct (3 women). Expenses: Contact institution. *Financial support:* In 2016–17, 22 students received support. Federal Work-Study and scholarships/grants available. Financial award applicants required to submit CSS PROFILE or FAFSA. *Program availability:* Part-time, evening/weekend. Offers health education and promotion (MPH); health policy and administration (MPH). *Application deadline:* For fall admission, 8/1 priority date for domestic students, 7/1 for international students; for spring admission, 12/1 priority date for domestic students, 11/1 for international students. Applications are processed on a rolling basis. *Application fee:* $45. Electronic applications accepted. *Application Contact:* Dr. Robert LaChausse, Chair, Department of Public Health Sciences, 951-552-8484, E-mail: rlachausse@calbaptist.edu. *Dean, College of Health Science,* Dr. David Pearson, 951-343-4298, E-mail: dpearson@calbaptist.edu.

Program in Public Relations Students: 8 full-time (5 women), 8 part-time (6 women); includes 11 minority (6 Black or African American, non-Hispanic/Latino; 3 Hispanic/Latino; 2 Two or more races, non-Hispanic/Latino). Average age 32. 10 applicants, 60% accepted, 5 enrolled. *Faculty:* 3 full-time (2 women), 1 (woman) part-time/adjunct. Expenses: Contact institution. *Financial support:* Applicants required to submit CSS PROFILE or FAFSA. In 2016, 11 master's awarded. *Program availability:* Part-time, evening/weekend, online learning. Offers public relations (MA). *Application deadline:* For fall admission, 8/1 priority date for domestic students, 7/1 for international students; for spring admission, 12/1 priority date for domestic students, 11/1 priority date for international students. Applications are processed on a rolling basis. *Application fee:* $45. Electronic applications accepted. *Application Contact:* Dr. MaryAnn Pearson, Program Director, MA in Public Relations, 951-343-3967, E-mail: mpearson@calbaptist.edu. *Vice President of Online and Professional Studies,* Dr. David Poole, 951-343-3902, E-mail: dpoole@calbaptist.edu.

Program in School Counseling Students: 2 full-time (1 woman), 46 part-time (41 women); includes 25 minority (4 Black or African American, non-Hispanic/Latino; 1 American Indian or Alaska Native, non-Hispanic/Latino; 19 Hispanic/Latino; 1 Two or more races, non-Hispanic/Latino). Average age 33. 45 applicants, 56% accepted, 21 enrolled. *Faculty:* 2 full-time (both women), 2 part-time/adjunct (1 woman). Expenses: Contact institution. *Financial support:* In 2016–17, 17 students received support. Federal Work-Study and scholarships/grants available. Financial award applicants required to submit CSS PROFILE or FAFSA. In 2016, 1 master's awarded. *Program availability:* Part-time, evening/weekend. Offers school counseling (MS). *Application deadline:* For fall admission, 8/1 priority date for domestic students, 7/7 priority date for international students; for spring admission, 12/1 priority date for domestic students, 11/1 priority date for international students. Applications are processed on a rolling basis. *Application fee:* $45. Electronic applications accepted. *Application Contact:* Dr. Nona Cabral, Program Coordinator, School Counseling, 951-343-4804, E-mail: ncabral@calbaptist.edu. *Dean, School of Education,* Dr. John Shoup, 951-343-4205, E-mail: jshoup@calbaptist.edu.

Program in School Psychology Students: 23 full-time (all women), 23 part-time (21 women); includes 23 minority (3 Black or African American, non-Hispanic/Latino; 3 Asian, non-Hispanic/Latino; 17 Hispanic/Latino). Average age 31. 43 applicants, 67% accepted, 26 enrolled. *Faculty:* 2 full-time (both women), 5 part-time/adjunct (3 women). Expenses: Contact institution. *Financial support:* In 2016–17, 16 students received support. Federal Work-Study and scholarships/grants available. Financial award applicants required to submit CSS PROFILE or FAFSA. In 2016, 9 master's awarded. *Program availability:* Part-time, evening/weekend. Offers school psychology (MS). *Application deadline:* For fall admission, 7/1 priority date for domestic and international students; for spring admission, 12/1 priority date for domestic students, 11/1 priority date for international students. Applications are processed on a rolling basis. *Application fee:* $45. Electronic applications accepted. *Application Contact:* Dr. Jane McGuire, Program Coordinator, School Psychology, 951-343-4707, E-mail: jmcguire@calbaptist.edu. *Dean, School of Education,* Dr. John Shoup, 951-343-4205, E-mail: jshoup@calbaptist.edu.

Program in Social Work *Faculty:* 3 full-time (2 women). Expenses: Contact institution. *Financial support:* Federal Work-Study and scholarships/grants available. *Program availability:* Part-time. Offers clinical social work (MSW); community social work practice (MSW). *Application deadline:* For fall admission, 8/1 priority date for domestic students, 7/1 for international students; for spring admission, 12/1 priority date for domestic students, 11/1 for international students. Applications are processed on a rolling basis. *Application fee:* $45. Electronic applications accepted. *Application Contact:* Taylor Neece, Director of Graduate Admissions, 951-343-4871, Fax: 877-228-8877, E-mail: graduateadmissions@calbaptist.edu. *Director, Social Work Program,* Dr. Satara Armstrong, 951-552-8442, E-mail: sarmstrong@calbaptist.edu.

Program in Software Engineering Students: 17 full-time (3 women), 2 part-time (0 women); includes 1 minority (Asian, non-Hispanic/Latino), 16 international. Average age 24. 57 applicants, 39% accepted, 11 enrolled. *Faculty:* 4 full-time (2 women). Expenses: Contact institution. *Financial support:* Federal Work-Study and scholarships/grants available. Financial award applicants required to submit CSS PROFILE or FAFSA. *Program availability:* Part-time. Offers software engineering (MS). *Application deadline:* For fall admission, 8/1 priority date for domestic students, 7/1 priority date for international students; for spring admission, 12/1 priority date for domestic students, 11/1 priority date for international students. Applications are processed on a rolling basis. *Application fee:* $45. Electronic applications accepted. *Application Contact:* Taylor Neece, Director of Graduate Admissions, 951-343-4871, Fax: 877-228-8877, E-mail: graduateadmissions@calbaptist.edu. *Chair, Computer Science and Software Engineering,* Dr. Arlene Perkins, 951-552-8630, E-mail: aperkins@calbaptist.edu.

Program in Speech Language Pathology Students: 25 full-time (22 women); includes 16 minority (2 Black or African American, non-Hispanic/Latino; 4 Asian, non-Hispanic/Latino; 9 Hispanic/Latino; 1 Two or more races, non-Hispanic/Latino). Average age 25. 92 applicants, 27% accepted, 25 enrolled. *Faculty:* 5 full-time (4 women). Expenses: Contact institution. *Financial support:* In 2016–17, 1 student received support. Federal Work-Study and scholarships/grants available. Financial award applicants required to submit CSS PROFILE or FAFSA. Offers speech language pathology (MS). *Application deadline:* For fall admission, 12/1 priority date for domestic students, 11/1 priority date for international students; for spring admission, 8/1 priority date for domestic students, 7/1 priority date for international students. Applications are processed on a rolling basis. *Application fee:* $45. Electronic applications accepted. *Application Contact:* Taylor Neece, Director of Graduate Admissions, 951-343-4871, Fax: 877-228-8877, E-mail: graduateadmissions@calbaptist.edu. *Director,* Dr. Candace Vickers, 951-552-8129, E-mail: cvickers@calbaptist.edu.

CALIFORNIA COAST UNIVERSITY, Santa Ana, CA 92701

General Information Proprietary, coed, comprehensive institution.

GRADUATE UNITS

School of Administration and Management *Program availability:* Online learning. Offers business marketing (MBA); health care management (MBA); human resource management (MBA); management (MBA, MS). Electronic applications accepted.

School of Behavioral Science *Program availability:* Online learning. Offers psychology (MS).

School of Criminal Justice Offers criminal justice (MS).

School of Education *Program availability:* Online learning. Offers administration (M Ed); curriculum and instruction (M Ed); educational administration (Ed D); educational psychology (Ed D); organizational leadership (Ed D).

CALIFORNIA COLLEGE OF THE ARTS, San Francisco, CA 94107

General Information Independent, coed, comprehensive institution. *Enrollment:* 1,983 graduate, professional, and undergraduate students; 430 full-time matriculated graduate/professional students (277 women); 25 part-time matriculated graduate/professional students (10 women). *Enrollment by degree level:* 455 master's. *Graduate faculty:* 46 full-time (24 women), 93 part-time/adjunct (44 women). *Tuition:* Full-time $47,340; part-time $1578 per credit. *Required fees:* $490; $245 per semester. Full-time tuition and fees vary according to course load and program. *Graduate housing:* Room and/or apartments available on a first-come, first-served basis to single students; on-campus housing not available to married students. Typical cost: $11,230 per year. Room charges vary according to housing facility selected. Housing application deadline: 5/15. *Student services:* Campus employment opportunities, campus safety program, career counseling, exercise/wellness program, free psychological counseling, grant writing training, international student services, low-cost health insurance, multicultural affairs office, services for students with disabilities, writing training. *Library facilities:* Meyer Library plus 1 other.

Computer facilities: Computer purchase and lease plans are available. 400 computers available on campus for general student use. A campuswide network can be accessed from student residence rooms and from off campus. Online class registration, online course evaluations, learning management system, media applications, software training, print payments are available.
Website: http://www.cca.edu/

General Application Contact: Wes Fanelli, Assistant Director of Graduate Admissions, 415-703-9533, Fax: 415-703-9539, E-mail: graduateprograms@cca.edu.

GRADUATE UNITS

Graduate Programs Students: 438 full-time (270 women), 25 part-time (16 women); includes 136 minority (30 Black or African American, non-Hispanic/Latino; 4 American Indian or Alaska Native, non-Hispanic/Latino; 57 Asian, non-Hispanic/Latino; 45 Hispanic/Latino), 72 international. Average age 31. 1,267 applicants, 51% accepted, 217 enrolled. Expenses: Contact institution. *Financial support:* In 2016–17, 345 students received support, including 119 teaching assistantships; Federal Work-Study, scholarships/grants, and unspecified assistantships also available. Financial award applicants required to submit FAFSA. In 2016, 213 master's awarded. *Program* *availability:* Part-time. Offers advanced architecture design (MAAD); architecture (M Arch); ceramics (MFA); creative non-fiction (MFA); curatorial practice (MA); design strategy (MBA); fiction (MFA); film/video/performance (MFA); glass (MFA); graphic design (MFA); industrial design (MFA); interaction design (MFA); interdisciplinary studies (MFA); jewelry/metal arts (MFA); media studies (MFA); painting/drawing (MFA); photography (MFA); poetry (MFA); printmaking (MFA); sculpture (MFA); textiles (MFA); visual and critical studies (MA); wood/furniture (MFA). *Application deadline:* For fall admission, 1/10 priority date for domestic and international students. Applications are processed on a rolling basis. *Application fee:* $70. Electronic applications accepted. *Application Contact:* Wes Fanelli, Assistant Director of Graduate Admissions, 415-703-9533, Fax: 415-703-9539, E-mail: wfanelli@cca.edu. *Director of Graduate Admissions,* Noel Dahl, 415-703-9537, Fax: 415-703-9539, E-mail: ndahl@cca.edu.

CALIFORNIA INSTITUTE OF INTEGRAL STUDIES, San Francisco, CA 94103

General Information Independent, coed, upper-level institution. CGS member. *Enrollment:* 1,495 graduate, professional, and undergraduate students; 1,083 full-time matriculated graduate/professional students (794 women), 323 part-time matriculated graduate/professional students (243 women). *Enrollment by degree level:* 721 master's, 685 doctoral. *Tuition:* Full-time $19,728; part-time $1098 per semester hour. *Required fees:* $320; $320 per semester hour. *Graduate housing:* On-campus housing not available. *Student services:* Campus employment opportunities, campus safety program, career counseling, grant writing training, international student services, low-cost health insurance, multicultural affairs office, services for students with disabilities, writing training. *Library facilities:* The Laurance S. Rockefeller Library plus 1 other. *Research affiliation:* Bay Area Reference Service.

Computer facilities: 25 computers available on campus for general student use. A campuswide network can be accessed from off campus. Online class registration is available.
Website: http://www.ciis.edu/

General Application Contact: Ellen Durst, Interim Director of Admissions, 415-575-6153, Fax: 415-575-1264, E-mail: admissions@ciis.edu.

GRADUATE UNITS

American College of Traditional Chinese Medicine Students: 167 full-time (130 women), 89 part-time (63 women); includes 107 minority (5 Black or African American, non-Hispanic/Latino; 2 American Indian or Alaska Native, non-Hispanic/Latino; 63 Asian, non-Hispanic/Latino; 17 Hispanic/Latino; 6 Native Hawaiian or other Pacific Islander, non-Hispanic/Latino; 14 Two or more races, non-Hispanic/Latino), 8 international. Average age 37. 69 applicants, 99% accepted, 55 enrolled. Expenses: Contact institution. Offers acupuncture and Chinese medicine (DACM, tDACM); acupuncture and Oriental medicine (DAOM); traditional Chinese medicine (MSTCM). *Application deadline:* For fall admission, 8/1 priority date for domestic students. *Application fee:* $65. Electronic applications accepted. *Application Contact:* Yuwen Chiu, Associate Director of Admissions, 415-828-7600, E-mail: yuwenchiu@actcm.edu. *Academic Dean,* Dr. Bingzen Zou, 415-828-7600, E-mail: bingzou@actcm.edu.

School of Consciousness and Transformation Students: 390 full-time (256 women), 121 part-time (84 women); includes 135 minority (39 Black or African American, non-Hispanic/Latino; 2 American Indian or Alaska Native, non-Hispanic/Latino; 22 Asian, non-Hispanic/Latino; 40 Hispanic/Latino; 2 Native Hawaiian or other Pacific Islander, non-Hispanic/Latino; 30 Two or more races, non-Hispanic/Latino), 51 international. Average age 38. 195 applicants, 92% accepted, 124 enrolled. Expenses: Contact institution. *Financial support:* Research assistantships, teaching assistantships, career-related internships or fieldwork, Federal Work-Study, and scholarships/grants available. Support available to part-time students. Financial award application deadline: 4/15; financial award applicants required to submit FAFSA. In 2016, 35 master's, 41 doctorates awarded. *Program availability:* Part-time, evening/weekend, 100% online, blended/hybrid learning. Offers anthropology and social change (MA, PhD); Asian philosophies and cultures (MA); creative inquiry/interdisciplinary arts (MFA); East-West psychology (MA, PhD); integral and transpersonal psychology (PhD); philosophy and religion (PhD); theater and performance making (MFA); transformative leadership (MA); transformative studies (PhD); women, gender, spirituality and social justice (MA); writing and consciousness (MFA). *Application deadline:* For fall admission, 2/1 priority date for domestic and international students; for spring admission, 10/15 priority date for domestic and international students. Applications are processed on a rolling basis. *Application fee:* $65. Electronic applications accepted. *Application Contact:* Ellen Durst, Director of Admissions, 415-575-6100, Fax: 415-575-1268, E-mail: admissions@ciis.edu.

School of Professional Psychology and Health Students: 526 full-time (408 women), 113 part-time (96 women); includes 173 minority (34 Black or African American, non-Hispanic/Latino; 5 American Indian or Alaska Native, non-Hispanic/Latino; 31 Asian, non-Hispanic/Latino; 58 Hispanic/Latino; 1 Native Hawaiian or other Pacific Islander, non-Hispanic/Latino; 44 Two or more races, non-Hispanic/Latino), 52 international. Average age 38. 319 applicants, 85% accepted, 164 enrolled. Expenses: Contact institution. *Financial support:* Research assistantships with tuition reimbursements, teaching assistantships with tuition reimbursements, career-related internships or fieldwork, Federal Work-Study, and scholarships/grants available. Support available to part-time students. Financial award application deadline: 4/15; financial award applicants required to submit FAFSA. In 2016, 157 master's, 21 doctorates awarded. *Program availability:* Part-time, evening/weekend, 100% online, blended/hybrid learning. Offers clinical psychology (Psy D); community mental health (MA); drama therapy (MA); expressive arts therapy (MA); human sexuality (PhD); integral counseling psychology (MA); integrative health studies (MA); psychological studies (MA); somatic psychology (MA). *Application deadline:* For fall admission, 2/1 priority date for domestic and international students; for spring admission, 10/15 priority date for domestic and international students. Applications are processed on a rolling basis. *Application fee:* $65. Electronic applications accepted. *Application Contact:* Ellen Durst, Director of Admissions, 415-575-6100, Fax: 415-575-1268, E-mail: admissions@ciis.edu.

CALIFORNIA INSTITUTE OF TECHNOLOGY, Pasadena, CA 91125-0001

General Information Independent, coed, university. CGS member. *Graduate housing:* Rooms and/or apartments available on a first-come, first-served basis to single students and available to married students. Housing application deadline: 5/1. *Research affiliation:* Scripps Institute of Oceanography, Stanford Linear Accelerator Center (high-energy physics), European Center for Nuclear Research (high-energy physics), National Science Foundation Center for Research in Parallel Computing, Cosmic Gravitational Waves Observatory (laser interferometer gravitational waves).

GRADUATE UNITS

Division of Biology Offers biochemistry and molecular biophysics (PhD); cell biology and biophysics (PhD); developmental biology (PhD); genetics (PhD); immunology (PhD); molecular biology (PhD); neurobiology (PhD). Electronic applications accepted.

Division of Chemistry and Chemical Engineering Students: 239 full-time (88 women); includes 69 minority (1 Black or African American, non-Hispanic/Latino; 43 Asian, non-Hispanic/Latino; 18 Hispanic/Latino; 7 Two or more races, non-Hispanic/Latino), 48 international. Average age 25. 638 applicants, 23% accepted, 43 enrolled. Faculty: 41 full-time (7 women). Expenses: Contact institution. *Financial support:* In 2016–17, 309 students received support, including fellowships (averaging $31,000 per year), research assistantships (averaging $25,900 per year), teaching assistantships (averaging $5,100 per year); Federal Work-Study, institutionally sponsored loans, scholarships/grants, traineeships, health care benefits, and unspecified assistantships also available. Financial award application deadline: 12/15. In 2016, 14 master's, 59 doctorates awarded. Offers biochemistry and molecular biophysics (MS, PhD); chemical engineering (MS, PhD); chemistry (MS, PhD). *Application deadline:* For fall admission, 12/15 for domestic and international students. *Application fee:* $100. Electronic applications accepted. *Application Contact:* Natalie Gilmore, Graduate Office, 626-395-3812, Fax: 626-577-9246, E-mail: ngilmore@its.caltech.edu. *Chair, Division of Chemistry and Chemical Engineering,* Prof. Jacqueline K. Barton, 626-395-3646, Fax: 626-395-6948, E-mail: jkbarton@caltech.edu.

Division of Engineering and Applied Science Offers aeronautics (MS, PhD, Engr); applied and computational mathematics (MS, PhD); applied mechanics (MS, PhD); applied physics (MS, PhD); bioengineering (MS, PhD); civil engineering (MS, PhD, Engr); computation and neural systems (MS, PhD); computer science (MS, PhD); control and dynamical systems (MS, PhD); electrical engineering (MS, PhD, Engr); environmental science and engineering (MS, PhD); materials science (MS, PhD); mechanical engineering (MS, PhD, Engr). Electronic applications accepted.

Division of Geological and Planetary Sciences Offers environmental science and engineering (MS, PhD); geobiology (MS, PhD); geochemistry (MS, PhD); geology (MS, PhD); geophysics (MS, PhD); planetary science (MS, PhD). Electronic applications accepted.

Division of Physics, Mathematics and Astronomy Offers astronomy (PhD); mathematics (PhD); physics (PhD).

Division of the Humanities and Social Sciences Offers humanities and social sciences (MS, PhD); social science (MS, PhD). Electronic applications accepted.

CALIFORNIA INSTITUTE OF THE ARTS, Valencia, CA 91355-2340

General Information Independent, coed, comprehensive institution. *Graduate housing:* Room and/or apartments available on a first-come, first-served basis to single students; on-campus housing not available to married students. Housing application deadline: 7/1.

GRADUATE UNITS

School of Art Offers art (MFA, Adv C); graphic design (MFA, Adv C); photography (MFA, Adv C). Electronic applications accepted.

School of Critical Studies Offers writing (MFA, Adv C).

School of Dance Offers dance (MFA, Adv C).

School of Film/Video Offers experimental animation (MFA); film directing (MFA, Adv C); film/video (Adv C). Electronic applications accepted.

School of Music *Program availability:* Part-time. Offers African music (MFA, Adv C); composition (MFA, Adv C); composition/new media (MFA, Adv C); Indonesian music (MFA, Adv C); jazz (MFA, Adv C); North Indian music (MFA, Adv C); performance (MFA, Adv C); performer/composer (MFA, Adv C); voice (MFA, Adv C); world music performance (MFA). Electronic applications accepted.

School of Theater Offers acting (MFA, Adv C); creative producing and management (MFA); design and production (MFA); design and technology (Adv C); directing (MFA); theater management (Adv C). Electronic applications accepted.

CALIFORNIA INTERCONTINENTAL UNIVERSITY, Irvine, CA 92614

General Information Proprietary, coed, comprehensive institution.

GRADUATE UNITS

Hollywood College of the Entertainment Industry Offers Hollywood and entertainment management (MBA).

School of Business Offers banking and finance (MBA); entrepreneurship and business management (DBA); global business leadership (DBA); international management and marketing (MBA); organizational management and human resource management (MBA).

School of Healthcare Offers healthcare management and leadership (MBA, DBA).

School of Information Technology Offers information systems and enterprise resource management (DBA); information systems and knowledge management (MBA); project and quality management (MBA).

CALIFORNIA INTERNATIONAL BUSINESS UNIVERSITY, San Diego, CA 92101

General Information Independent, coed, graduate-only institution.

GRADUATE UNITS

Graduate Programs Offers business (MBA, MSIM, DBA).

CALIFORNIA LUTHERAN UNIVERSITY, Thousand Oaks, CA 91360-2787

General Information Independent-religious, coed, comprehensive institution. CGS member. *Enrollment:* 4,173 graduate, professional, and undergraduate students; 1,123 full-time matriculated graduate/professional students (716 women), 306 part-time matriculated graduate/professional students (187 women). *Enrollment by degree level:* 1,197 master's, 151 doctoral, 81 other advanced degrees. *Graduate faculty:* 65 full-time (38 women), 92 part-time/adjunct (51 women). *Graduate housing:* Room and/or apartments available on a first-come, first-served basis to single students; on-campus housing not available to married students. *Student services:* Campus employment opportunities, career counseling, free psychological counseling, international student services, low-cost health insurance, multicultural affairs office, services for students with disabilities, writing training. *Library facilities:* Pearson Library. *Collection:* Books: 133,915 (physical), 194,230 (digital/electronic); Serial titles: 152 (physical); Databases: 179. Students can reserve study rooms.

Computer facilities: 334 computers available on campus for general student use. A campuswide network can be accessed from student residence rooms and from off campus. Online class registration is available.
Website: http://www.callutheran.edu/

General Application Contact: Information Contact, 805-493-3325, Fax: 805-493-3861, E-mail: clugrad@calutheran.edu.

GRADUATE UNITS

Graduate Studies Students: 1,123 full-time (716 women), 306 part-time (187 women); includes 445 minority (29 Black or African American, non-Hispanic/Latino; 7 American Indian or Alaska Native, non-Hispanic/Latino; 40 Asian, non-Hispanic/Latino; 176 Hispanic/Latino; 1 Native Hawaiian or other Pacific Islander, non-Hispanic/Latino; 192 Two or more races, non-Hispanic/Latino), 362 international. Average age 35. 1,173 applicants, 65% accepted, 415 enrolled. *Faculty:* 65 full-time (38 women), 92 part-time/adjunct (51 women). Expenses: Contact institution. *Financial support:* Scholarships/grants and unspecified assistantships available. Support available to part-time students. Financial award applicants required to submit FAFSA. In 2016, 518 master's, 20 doctorates awarded. *Program availability:* Part-time, evening/weekend. Offers clinical psychology (MS, Psy D); marital and family therapy (MS). *Application deadline:* Applications are processed on a rolling basis. *Application fee:* $50. Electronic applications accepted. *Application Contact:* 805-493-3325, Fax: 805-493-3861, E-mail: clugrad@calutheran.edu. *Provost/Vice President for Academic Affairs,* Dr. Leanne Neilson, 805-493-3145, E-mail: neilson@calutheran.edu.

Graduate School of Education Students: 518 full-time (411 women), 79 part-time (67 women); includes 252 minority (12 Black or African American, non-Hispanic/Latino; 3 American Indian or Alaska Native, non-Hispanic/Latino; 17 Asian, non-Hispanic/Latino; 108 Hispanic/Latino; 1 Native Hawaiian or other Pacific Islander, non-Hispanic/Latino; 111 Two or more races, non-Hispanic/Latino), 14 international. Average age 35. 319 applicants, 74% accepted, 192 enrolled. *Faculty:* 23 full-time (17 women), 39 part-time/adjunct (26 women). Expenses: Contact institution. In 2016, 93 master's, 13 doctorates awarded. *Program availability:* Part-time, evening/weekend. Offers counseling and guidance (MS); educational leadership (MA, Ed D); special education (MS); teacher leadership (M Ed); teaching (M Ed). *Application deadline:* For fall admission, 7/1 priority date for domestic students; for spring admission, 11/1 priority date for domestic students; for summer admission, 4/1 priority date for domestic students. Applications are processed on a rolling basis. *Application fee:* $50. Electronic applications accepted. *Application Contact:* 805-493-3325, Fax: 805-493-3861, E-mail: clugrad@calutheran.edu. *Dean,* Dr. Michael Hillis, 805-493-3421.

Pacific Lutheran Theological Seminary Students: 45 full-time (24 women), 1 (woman) part-time; includes 10 minority (1 Black or African American, non-Hispanic/Latino; 1 Hispanic/Latino; 8 Two or more races, non-Hispanic/Latino), 1 international. Average age 34. 29 applicants, 86% accepted, 19 enrolled. *Faculty:* 6 full-time (5 women), 2 part-time/adjunct (0 women). Expenses: Contact institution. *Financial support:* In 2016–17, 104 students received support. Teaching assistantships, career-related internships or fieldwork, Federal Work-Study, institutionally sponsored loans, and scholarships/grants available. Support available to part-time students. Financial award application deadline: 3/15; financial award applicants required to submit FAFSA. In 2016, 10 master's, 3 other advanced degrees awarded. *Program availability:* Part-time. Offers theology (M Div, MA, MCM, MTS, PhD, Th D, Certificate). MA, Th D, PhD offered jointly with Graduate Theological Union; PhD with University of California, Berkeley. *Application deadline:* For fall admission, 8/1 priority date for domestic students; for spring admission, 1/1 priority date for domestic students. Applications are processed on a rolling basis. *Application fee:* $25. Electronic applications accepted. *Application Contact:* 805-493-3325, Fax: 805-493-3861, E-mail: clugrad@calutheran.edu. *Dean,* Alica Vargas, 510-559-2732, E-mail: avargas@plts.edu.

School of Management Students: 427 full-time (172 women), 189 part-time (87 women); includes 120 minority (14 Black or African American, non-Hispanic/Latino; 2 American Indian or Alaska Native, non-Hispanic/Latino; 19 Asian, non-Hispanic/Latino; 37 Hispanic/Latino; 48 Two or more races, non-Hispanic/Latino), 338 international. Average age 30. 591 applicants, 64% accepted, 131 enrolled. *Faculty:* 25 full-time (10 women), 36 part-time/adjunct (12 women). Expenses: Contact institution. In 2016, 305 master's awarded. *Program availability:* Part-time, evening/weekend, 100% online, blended/hybrid learning. Offers business (IMBA); computer science (MS); econometrics (MBA); economics (MS); entrepreneurship (MBA, Certificate); finance (MBA, Certificate); financial planning (MBA, Certificate); information systems and technology (MS); information technology management (MBA, Certificate); international business (MBA, Certificate); management and organization behavior (MBA); management and organizational behavior (Certificate); marketing (MBA, Certificate); microeconomics (MBA); nonprofit and social enterprise (MBA); public policy and administration (MPPA). *Application deadline:* Applications are processed on a rolling basis. *Application fee:* $50. Electronic applications accepted. *Application Contact:* 805-493-3325, Fax: 805-493-3861, E-mail: clugrad@calutheran.edu. *Dean,* Dr. Gerhard Apfelthaler, 805-493-3360.

CALIFORNIA MIRAMAR UNIVERSITY, San Diego, CA 92108

General Information Proprietary, coed, comprehensive institution.

GRADUATE UNITS

Program in Business Administration Offers business administration (MBA).

Program in Strategic Leadership Offers strategic leadership (MS).

Program in Taxation and Trade for Executives Offers taxation and trade for executives (MT).

Program in Telecommunications Management Offers telecommunications management (MST).

CALIFORNIA POLYTECHNIC STATE UNIVERSITY, SAN LUIS OBISPO, San Luis Obispo, CA 93407

General Information State-supported, coed, comprehensive institution. CGS member. Enrollment: 21,306 graduate, professional, and undergraduate students; 471 full-time matriculated graduate/professional students (221 women), 226 part-time matriculated graduate/professional students (102 women). Enrollment by degree level: 697 master's. Graduate faculty: 155 full-time (52 women), 19 part-time/adjunct (9 women). Tuition, state resident: full-time $6738; part-time $3906 per year. Tuition, nonresident: full-time $15,666; part-time $8370 per year. Required fees: $3603; $3141 per unit. $1047 per term. Graduate housing: Room and/or apartments available on a first-come, first-served basis to single students; on-campus housing not available to married students. Typical cost: $7360 per year ($12,507 including board). Room and board charges vary according to housing facility selected. Student services: Campus employment opportunities, campus safety program, career counseling, child daycare facilities, exercise/wellness program, free psychological counseling, grant writing training, international student services, low-cost health insurance, multicultural affairs office, services for students with disabilities, teacher training, writing training. Library facilities: Robert E. Kennedy Library.

Computer facilities: A campuswide network can be accessed from student residence rooms and from off campus. Online class registration is available. Website: http://www.calpoly.edu/

General Application Contact: Dr. James Maraviglia, Associate Vice Provost for Marketing and Enrollment Development, 805-756-2311, Fax: 805-756-5400, E-mail: admissions@calpoly.edu.

GRADUATE UNITS

College of Agriculture, Food and Environmental Sciences Students: 68 full-time (42 women), 22 part-time (14 women); includes 21 minority (6 Asian, non-Hispanic/Latino; 11 Hispanic/Latino; 4 Two or more races, non-Hispanic/Latino), 5 international. Average age 26. 97 applicants, 39% accepted, 30 enrolled. *Faculty:* 24 full-time (10 women), 1 (woman) part-time/adjunct. Expenses: Contact institution. *Financial support:* Fellowships, research assistantships, teaching assistantships, career-related internships or fieldwork, institutionally sponsored loans, scholarships/grants, and health care benefits available. Financial award application deadline: 3/2; financial award applicants required to submit FAFSA. In 2016, 61 master's awarded. *Program availability:* Part-time. Offers agribusiness (MS); agricultural education and communication (MAE); agriculture (MS); agriculture, food and environmental sciences (MAE, MS); food science and nutrition (MS); forestry sciences (MS); nutrition (MS). *Application deadline:* For fall admission, 4/1 for domestic students, 11/30 for international students; for winter admission, 10/1 for domestic students; for spring admission, 1/1 for domestic students. Applications are processed on a rolling basis. *Application fee:* $55. Electronic applications accepted. *Application Contact:* Dr. Jim Prince, Associate Dean, Research and Graduate Programs, 805-756-5104, E-mail: jpprince@calpoly.edu. *Dean,* Dr. Andrew Thulin, 805-756-2161, Fax: 805-756-6577, E-mail: athulin@calpoly.edu.

College of Architecture and Environmental Design Students: 39 full-time (17 women), 5 part-time (4 women); includes 4 minority (1 Asian, non-Hispanic/Latino; 3 Hispanic/Latino), 5 international. Average age 25. 72 applicants, 47% accepted, 15 enrolled. *Faculty:* 14 full-time (5 women), 1 part-time/adjunct (0 women). Expenses: Contact institution. *Financial support:* Research assistantships, teaching assistantships, career-related internships or fieldwork, and institutionally sponsored loans available. Financial award application deadline: 3/2; financial award applicants required to submit FAFSA. In 2016, 36 master's awarded. *Program availability:* Part-time. Offers architectural engineering (MS); architecture (MS); architecture and environmental design (MCRP, MS); city and regional planning (MCRP). *Application deadline:* For fall admission, 6/1 for domestic students, 11/30 for international students; for winter admission, 11/1 for domestic students, 6/30 for international students. Applications are processed on a rolling basis. *Application fee:* $55. Electronic applications accepted. *Associate Dean,* Dr. Michael Lucas, E-mail: mlucas@calpoly.edu.

College of Engineering Students: 195 full-time (40 women), 124 part-time (25 women); includes 106 minority (3 Black or African American, non-Hispanic/Latino; 52 Asian, non-Hispanic/Latino; 34 Hispanic/Latino; 1 Native Hawaiian or other Pacific Islander, non-Hispanic/Latino; 16 Two or more races, non-Hispanic/Latino), 25 international. Average age 26. 482 applicants, 31% accepted, 109 enrolled. *Faculty:* 58 full-time (14 women), 1 part-time/adjunct (0 women). Expenses: Contact institution. *Financial support:* Fellowships, research assistantships, teaching assistantships, career-related internships or fieldwork, institutionally sponsored loans, and unspecified assistantships available. Financial award application deadline: 3/2; financial award applicants required to submit FAFSA. In 2016, 209 master's awarded. *Program availability:* Part-time. Offers aerospace engineering (MS); biomedical and general engineering (MS); civil and environmental engineering (MS); computer science (MS); electrical engineering (MS); engineering (MS); industrial engineering (MS); mechanical engineering (MS). *Application deadline:* For fall admission, 4/1 for domestic students, 3/1 for international students; for winter admission, 10/1 for domestic students; for spring admission, 1/1 for domestic students. Applications are processed on a rolling basis. *Application fee:* $55. Electronic applications accepted. *Associate Dean,* Dr. Rakesh Goel, 805-756-6402, E-mail: rgoel@calpoly.edu.

College of Liberal Arts Students: 37 full-time (29 women), 44 part-time (27 women); includes 19 minority (1 Black or African American, non-Hispanic/Latino; 1 Asian, non-Hispanic/Latino; 11 Hispanic/Latino; 1 Native Hawaiian or other Pacific Islander, non-Hispanic/Latino; 5 Two or more races, non-Hispanic/Latino). Average age 28. 100 applicants, 58% accepted, 31 enrolled. *Faculty:* 19 full-time (8 women), 1 (woman) part-time/adjunct. Expenses: Contact institution. *Financial support:* Fellowships, teaching assistantships, career-related internships or fieldwork, Federal Work-Study, institutionally sponsored loans, scholarships/grants, and tutorships, writing laboratory assistantships available. Support available to part-time students. Financial award application deadline: 3/2; financial award applicants required to submit FAFSA. In 2016, 47 master's awarded. *Program availability:* Part-time. Offers English (MA); history (MA); liberal arts (MA, MPP, MS); political science (MPP); psychology (MS). *Application deadline:* For fall admission, 4/1 for domestic students, 3/1 for international students. *Application fee:* $55. *Associate Dean,* Dr. Debra Valencia-Laver, 805-756-2706, Fax: 805-756-5748, E-mail: dlvalenc@calpoly.edu.

College of Science and Mathematics Students: 122 full-time (87 women), 54 part-time (29 women); includes 56 minority (1 Black or African American, non-Hispanic/Latino; 1 American Indian or Alaska Native, non-Hispanic/Latino; 8 Asian, non-Hispanic/Latino; 39 Hispanic/Latino; 7 Two or more races, non-Hispanic/Latino), 3 international. Average age 29. 335 applicants, 43% accepted, 117 enrolled. *Faculty:* 36 full-time (14 women), 15 part-time/adjunct (7 women). Expenses: Contact institution. *Financial support:* Fellowships, research assistantships, teaching assistantships, career-related internships or fieldwork, and Federal Work-Study available. Support available to part-time students. Financial award application deadline: 3/2; financial award applicants required to submit FAFSA. In 2016, 102 master's awarded. *Program availability:* Part-time. Offers biological sciences (MA, MS); kinesiology (MS); mathematics (MS); polymers and coating science (MS); science and mathematics (MA, MS). *Application deadline:* For fall admission, 4/1 for domestic students, 3/1 for international students. Applications are processed on a rolling basis. *Application fee:* $55. Electronic applications accepted. *Associate Dean,* Dr. Kellie G. Hall, 805-756-2226, Fax: 805-756-1670, E-mail: kghall@calpoly.edu.

School of Education Students: 82 full-time (63 women), 21 part-time (17 women); includes 30 minority (1 Black or African American, non-Hispanic/Latino; 1 American Indian or Alaska Native, non-Hispanic/Latino; 2 Asian, non-Hispanic/Latino; 22 Hispanic/Latino; 4 Two or more races, non-Hispanic/Latino), 1 international. Average age 31. 202 applicants, 49% accepted, 87 enrolled. *Faculty:* 8 full-time (6 women), 14 part-time/adjunct (6 women). Expenses: Contact institution. *Financial support:* Fellowships, research assistantships, career-related internships or fieldwork, Federal Work-Study, and institutionally sponsored loans available. Support available to part-time students. Financial award application deadline: 3/2; financial award applicants required to submit FAFSA. In 2016, 63 master's awarded. *Program availability:* Part-time, evening/weekend. Offers education (MA). *Application deadline:* For fall admission, 4/1 for domestic students, 3/1 for international students. Applications are processed on a rolling basis. *Application fee:* $55. Electronic applications accepted.

California Polytechnic State University, San Luis Obispo

Application Contact: E-mail: soe@calpoly.edu. *Director,* Dr. Kevin Taylor, 805-756-1503, E-mail: jktaylor@calpoly.edu.

Orfalea College of Business Students: 114 full-time (50 women), 20 part-time (8 women); includes 34 minority (18 Asian, non-Hispanic/Latino; 12 Hispanic/Latino; 4 Two or more races, non-Hispanic/Latino), 11 international. Average age 24. 69 applicants, 49% accepted, 25 enrolled. *Faculty:* 4 full-time (1 woman). Expenses: Contact institution. *Financial support:* Fellowships, career-related internships or fieldwork, Federal Work-Study, institutionally sponsored loans, scholarships/grants, and unspecified assistantships available. Support available to part-time students. Financial award application deadline: 3/2; financial award applicants required to submit FAFSA. In 2016, 81 master's awarded. Offers accounting (MBA); business administration (MBA); business analytics (MS); economics (MS); taxation (MS). *Application deadline:* For fall admission, 4/1 for domestic students, 3/1 for international students. Applications are processed on a rolling basis. *Application fee:* $55. Electronic applications accepted. *Application Contact:* Dr. Beena Khurana, Associate Dean, 805-756-7519, E-mail: bkhurana@calpoly.edu. *Associate Dean,* Dr. Sanjiv Jaggia, 805-756-2705, E-mail: sjaggia@calpoly.edu.

CALIFORNIA STATE POLYTECHNIC UNIVERSITY, POMONA, Pomona, CA 91768-2557

General Information State-supported, coed, comprehensive institution. *Enrollment:* 25,326 graduate, professional, and undergraduate students; 397 full-time matriculated graduate/professional students (192 women), 882 part-time matriculated graduate/professional students (404 women). *Enrollment by degree level:* 1,229 master's, 50 doctoral. *Graduate faculty:* 611 full-time (256 women), 610 part-time/adjunct (242 women). Tuition, state resident: full-time $6738. Tuition, nonresident: full-time $12,690. *Required fees:* $1555. Tuition and fees vary according to course load, degree level and program. *Graduate housing:* Room and/or apartments available on a first-come, first-served basis to single students; on-campus housing not available to married students. Typical cost: $9027 per year ($14,514 including board). Room and board charges vary according to board plan and housing facility selected. Housing application deadline: 5/1. *Student services:* Campus employment opportunities, campus safety program, career counseling, child daycare facilities, free psychological counseling, international student services, low-cost health insurance, multicultural affairs office, services for students with disabilities. *Library facilities:* University Library. *Collection:* Books: 577,476 (physical), 14,408 (digital/electronic); Serial titles: 277,642 (physical), 13,362 (digital/electronic); Databases: 143. Weekly public service hours: 92; study areas open 24 hours, 5–7 days a week; students can reserve study rooms.

Computer facilities: Computer purchase and lease plans are available. 2,117 computers available on campus for general student use. A campuswide network can be accessed from student residence rooms and from off campus. Website: http://www.cpp.edu/

General Application Contact: Andrew M. Wright, Director of Admissions, 909-869-3130, Fax: 909-869-4529, E-mail: awright@cpp.edu.

GRADUATE UNITS

Ed D Program in Educational Leadership Students: 51 part-time (37 women); includes 36 minority (8 Black or African American, non-Hispanic/Latino; 5 Asian, non-Hispanic/Latino; 21 Hispanic/Latino; 2 Two or more races, non-Hispanic/Latino), 1 international. Average age 43. 21 applicants, 100% accepted, 15 enrolled. Expenses: Contact institution. *Financial support:* Applicants required to submit FAFSA. In 2016, 14 doctorates awarded. *Program availability:* Part-time, evening/weekend. Offers educational leadership (Ed D). *Application deadline:* Applications are processed on a rolling basis. *Application fee:* $55. Electronic applications accepted. *Application Contact:* Andrew M. Wright, Director of Admissions. *Doctoral Studies Coordinator,* Michael M. Bandoni, 909-869-3060, Fax: 909-869-5416, E-mail: mmbandoni@cpp.edu.

John T. Lyle Center for Regenerative Studies Students: 9 full-time (7 women), 7 part-time (5 women); includes 9 minority (3 Asian, non-Hispanic/Latino; 5 Hispanic/Latino; 1 Two or more races, non-Hispanic/Latino), 2 international. Average age 27. 8 applicants, 100% accepted, 8 enrolled. Expenses: Contact institution. *Financial support:* Application deadline: 3/2; applicants required to submit FAFSA. In 2016, 6 master's awarded. *Program availability:* Part-time. Offers regenerative studies (MS). *Application deadline:* Applications are processed on a rolling basis. *Application fee:* $55. Electronic applications accepted. *Application Contact:* Andrew M. Wright, Director of Admissions, 909-869-3130, Fax: 909-869-4529, E-mail: awright@cpp.edu. *Interim Graduate Coordinator,* Dr. Kyle D. Brown, 909-869-5178, Fax: 909-869-5188, E-mail: kdbrown@cpp.edu.

Master of Science in Business Administration Program Students: 6 part-time (1 woman); includes 4 minority (3 Asian, non-Hispanic/Latino; 1 Hispanic/Latino), 1 international. Average age 34. 2 applicants, 100% accepted, 2 enrolled. Expenses: Contact institution. *Financial support:* Application deadline: 3/2; applicants required to submit FAFSA. In 2016, 4 master's awarded. *Program availability:* Part-time, evening/weekend. Offers information systems auditing (MS). *Application deadline:* Applications are processed on a rolling basis. *Application fee:* $55. Electronic applications accepted. *Application Contact:* Andrew M. Wright, Director of Admissions, 909-869-3130, Fax: 909-869-4529, E-mail: awright@cpp.edu. *Dean,* Dr. Erik Rolland, 909-869-2400, Fax: 909-869-6799, E-mail: erolland@cpp.edu.

Master's Programs in Education Students: 21 full-time (14 women), 95 part-time (67 women); includes 69 minority (8 Black or African American, non-Hispanic/Latino; 1 American Indian or Alaska Native, non-Hispanic/Latino; 10 Asian, non-Hispanic/Latino; 48 Hispanic/Latino; 2 Two or more races, non-Hispanic/Latino), 4 international. Average age 34. 27 applicants, 93% accepted, 14 enrolled. Expenses: Contact institution. *Financial support:* Application deadline: 3/2; applicants required to submit FAFSA. In 2016, 50 master's awarded. *Program availability:* Part-time, evening/weekend. Offers curriculum and instruction (MA). *Application deadline:* Applications are processed on a rolling basis. *Application fee:* $55. Electronic applications accepted. *Application Contact:* Andrew M Wright, Director of Admissions, 909-869-3130, Fax: 909-869-4529, E-mail: awright@cpp.edu. *Graduate Studies Coordinator,* Kelly Mitchell, 909-869-2358, Fax: 909-869-2722, E-mail: klmitchell@cpp.edu.

MBA Program Students: 7 full-time (3 women), 29 part-time (11 women); includes 18 minority (1 Black or African American, non-Hispanic/Latino; 10 Asian, non-Hispanic/Latino; 7 Hispanic/Latino), 6 international. Average age 29. 20 applicants, 95% accepted, 15 enrolled. Expenses: Contact institution. *Financial support:* Application deadline: 3/2; applicants required to submit FAFSA. In 2016, 29 master's awarded. *Program availability:* Part-time, evening/weekend. Offers business administration (MBA). *Application deadline:* Applications are processed on a rolling basis. *Application fee:* $55. Electronic applications accepted. *Application Contact:* Andrew M. Wright, Director of Admissions, 909-869-3130, Fax: 909-869-4529, E-mail: awright@cpp.edu. *Dean,* Dr. Erik Rolland, 909-869-2400, E-mail: erolland@cpp.edu.

Program in Accountancy Students: 12 full-time (6 women), 10 part-time (7 women); includes 10 minority (7 Asian, non-Hispanic/Latino; 2 Hispanic/Latino; 1 Two or more races, non-Hispanic/Latino), 7 international. Average age 29. 30 applicants, 100% accepted, 19 enrolled. Expenses: Contact institution. *Financial support:* Application deadline: 3/2; applicants required to submit FAFSA. In 2016, 8 master's awarded. *Program availability:* Part-time, evening/weekend. Offers accountancy (MS). *Application deadline:* Applications are processed on a rolling basis. *Application fee:* $55. Electronic applications accepted. *Application Contact:* Andrew M. Wright, Director of Admissions, 909-869-3130, Fax: 909-869-4529, E-mail: awright@cpp.edu. *Program Coordinator,* Dr. Meihua Koo, 909-869-4531, Fax: 909-869-4511, E-mail: mkoo@cpp.edu.

Program in Agriculture Students: 18 full-time (13 women), 27 part-time (13 women); includes 23 minority (2 Black or African American, non-Hispanic/Latino; 6 Asian, non-Hispanic/Latino; 14 Hispanic/Latino; 1 Two or more races, non-Hispanic/Latino), 2 international. Average age 29. 27 applicants, 100% accepted, 24 enrolled. Expenses: Contact institution. *Financial support:* Application deadline: 3/2; applicants required to submit FAFSA. In 2016, 12 master's awarded. *Program availability:* Part-time, evening/weekend. Offers agricultural science (MS). *Application deadline:* Applications are processed on a rolling basis. *Application fee:* $55. Electronic applications accepted. *Application Contact:* Andrew M. Wright, Director of Admissions, 909-869-3130, Fax: 909-869-4529, E-mail: awright@cpp.edu. *Director of Research and Graduate Studies,* Dr. Harmit Singh, 909-869-3023, Fax: 909-869-5078, E-mail: harmitsingh@cpp.edu.

Program in Architecture Students: 43 full-time (21 women), 2 part-time (1 woman); includes 23 minority (7 Asian, non-Hispanic/Latino; 16 Hispanic/Latino), 8 international. Average age 28. 19 applicants, 100% accepted, 18 enrolled. Expenses: Contact institution. *Financial support:* Application deadline: 3/2; applicants required to submit FAFSA. In 2016, 24 master's awarded. *Program availability:* Part-time, evening/weekend. Offers architecture (M Arch). *Application deadline:* Applications are processed on a rolling basis. *Application fee:* $55. Electronic applications accepted. *Application Contact:* Andrew M. Wright, Director of Admissions, 909-869-3130, Fax: 909-869-4529, E-mail: awright@cpp.edu. *Graduate Coordinator,* Dr. Weimin Li, 909-869-2715, Fax: 909-869-2580, E-mail: wli@cpp.edu.

Program in Biological Sciences Students: 29 full-time (17 women), 52 part-time (28 women); includes 44 minority (1 Black or African American, non-Hispanic/Latino; 15 Asian, non-Hispanic/Latino; 26 Hispanic/Latino; 2 Two or more races, non-Hispanic/Latino), 6 international. Average age 26. 21 applicants, 100% accepted, 17 enrolled. Expenses: Contact institution. *Financial support:* Application deadline: 3/2; applicants required to submit FAFSA. In 2016, 19 master's awarded. *Program availability:* Part-time, evening/weekend. Offers biological sciences (MS). *Application deadline:* Applications are processed on a rolling basis. *Application fee:* $55. Electronic applications accepted. *Application Contact:* Andrew M. Wright, Director of Admissions, 909-869-2715, Fax: 909-869-2580, E-mail: wli@cpp.edu. *Graduate Coordinator,* Dr. Robert J. Talmadge, 909-869-3025, Fax: 909-869-4078, E-mail: rjtalmadge@cpp.edu.

Program in Chemistry Students: 9 full-time (2 women), 9 part-time (2 women); includes 8 minority (7 Asian, non-Hispanic/Latino; 1 Hispanic/Latino), 3 international. Average age 27. 8 applicants, 100% accepted, 7 enrolled. Expenses: Contact institution. *Financial support:* Application deadline: 3/2; applicants required to submit FAFSA. In 2016, 9 master's awarded. *Program availability:* Part-time, evening/weekend. Offers chemistry (MS). *Application deadline:* Applications are processed on a rolling basis. *Application fee:* $55. Electronic applications accepted. *Application Contact:* Andrew M. Wright, Director of Admissions, 909-869-3130, Fax: 909-869-4529, E-mail: awright@cpp.edu. *Graduate Coordinator,* Dr. Gregory Barding, 909-869-3681, E-mail: gabarding@cpp.edu.

Program in Civil Engineering Students: 29 full-time (9 women), 86 part-time (73 women); includes 56 minority (2 Black or African American, non-Hispanic/Latino; 29 Asian, non-Hispanic/Latino; 24 Hispanic/Latino; 1 Two or more races, non-Hispanic/Latino), 14 international. Average age 27. 49 applicants, 96% accepted, 36 enrolled. Expenses: Contact institution. *Financial support:* Application deadline: 3/2; applicants required to submit FAFSA. In 2016, 32 master's awarded. *Program availability:* Part-time, evening/weekend. Offers civil engineering (MS). *Application deadline:* Applications are processed on a rolling basis. *Application fee:* $55. Electronic applications accepted. *Application Contact:* Andrew M. Wright, Director of Admissions, 909-869-3130, Fax: 909-869-4529, E-mail: awright@cpp.edu. *Graduate Coordinator,* Dr. Ronald Yeung, 909-869-2640, Fax: 909-869-4342, E-mail: mryeung@cpp.edu.

Program in Computer Science Students: 13 full-time (5 women), 67 part-time (22 women); includes 31 minority (2 Black or African American, non-Hispanic/Latino; 20 Asian, non-Hispanic/Latino; 9 Hispanic/Latino), 32 international. Average age 28. 30 applicants, 100% accepted, 24 enrolled. Expenses: Contact institution. *Financial support:* Application deadline: 3/2; applicants required to submit FAFSA. In 2016, 22 master's awarded. *Program availability:* Part-time, evening/weekend. Offers computer science (MS). *Application deadline:* Applications are processed on a rolling basis. *Application fee:* $55. Electronic applications accepted. *Application Contact:* Andrew M. Wright, Director of Admissions, 909-869-3130, Fax: 909-869-4529, E-mail: awright@cpp.edu. *Graduate Coordinator,* Dr. Gilbert S. Young, 909-869-4413, Fax: 909-869-4733, E-mail: gsyoung@cpp.edu.

Program in Economics Students: 8 full-time (3 women), 32 part-time (15 women); includes 11 minority (1 Black or African American, non-Hispanic/Latino; 1 American Indian or Alaska Native, non-Hispanic/Latino; 3 Asian, non-Hispanic/Latino; 6 Hispanic/Latino), 22 international. Average age 28. 15 applicants, 93% accepted, 11 enrolled. Expenses: Contact institution. *Financial support:* Application deadline: 3/2; applicants required to submit FAFSA. In 2016, 11 master's awarded. *Program availability:* Part-time, evening/weekend. Offers economics (MS). *Application deadline:* Applications are processed on a rolling basis. *Application fee:* $55. Electronic applications accepted. *Application Contact:* Andrew M. Wright, Director of Admissions, 909-869-3130, Fax: 909-869-4529, E-mail: awright@cpp.edu. *Graduate Coordinator,* Dr. Gregory Hunter, 909-869-4888, Fax: 909-869-6987, E-mail: gwhunter@cpp.edu.

Program in Electrical Engineering Students: 15 full-time (3 women), 56 part-time (7 women); includes 31 minority (1 American Indian or Alaska Native, non-Hispanic/Latino; 21 Asian, non-Hispanic/Latino; 9 Hispanic/Latino), 14 international. Average age 27. 27 applicants, 96% accepted, 15 enrolled. Expenses: Contact institution. *Financial support:* Application deadline: 3/2; applicants required to submit FAFSA. In 2016, 34 master's awarded. *Program availability:* Part-time, evening/weekend. Offers communication systems (MSEE). *Application deadline:* Applications are processed on a rolling basis. *Application fee:* $55. Electronic applications accepted. *Application Contact:* Andrew M. Wright, Director of Admissions, 909-869-3130, Fax: 909-869-4529, E-mail: awright@cpp.edu. *Graduate Coordinator,* Dr. Halima M. El Naga, 909-869-2515, Fax: 909-869-4687, E-mail: helnaga@cpp.edu.

Program in Engineering Students: 23 part-time (3 women); includes 5 minority (3 Asian, non-Hispanic/Latino; 2 Hispanic/Latino), 2 international. Average age 28. 11 applicants, 100% accepted, 10 enrolled. Expenses: Contact institution. *Financial support:* Application deadline: 3/2; applicants required to submit FAFSA. In 2016, 8 master's awarded. *Program availability:* Part-time, evening/weekend. Offers engineering (MSE). *Application deadline:* Applications are processed on a rolling basis. *Application fee:* $55. Electronic applications accepted. *Application Contact:* Andrew M. Wright, Director of Admissions, 909-869-3130, Fax: 909-869-4529, E-mail: awright@cpp.edu. *Department Chair/Coordinator,* Dr. Ali R. Ahmadi, 909-869-2470, Fax: 909-869-6920, E-mail: arahmadi@cpp.edu.

Program in Engineering Management Students: 3 full-time (1 woman), 39 part-time (10 women); includes 15 minority (4 Asian, non-Hispanic/Latino; 8 Hispanic/Latino; 3 Two or more races, non-Hispanic/Latino), 13 international. Average age 29. 15 applicants, 100% accepted, 12 enrolled. Expenses: Contact institution. *Financial support:* Application deadline: 3/2; applicants required to submit FAFSA. In 2016, 15 master's awarded. *Program availability:* Part-time, evening/weekend. Offers engineering management (MS). *Application deadline:* Applications are processed on a rolling basis. *Application fee:* $55. Electronic applications accepted. *Application Contact:* Andrew M. Wright, Director of Admissions, 909-869-3130, Fax: 909-869-4529, E-mail: awright@cpp.edu. *Chair/Graduate Coordinator,* Dr. Kamran Abedini, 909-869-2569, Fax: 909-869-2564, E-mail: kabedini@cpp.edu.

Program in English Students: 31 full-time (19 women), 45 part-time (32 women); includes 41 minority (3 Black or African American, non-Hispanic/Latino; 2 American Indian or Alaska Native, non-Hispanic/Latino; 10 Asian, non-Hispanic/Latino; 25 Hispanic/Latino; 1 Two or more races, non-Hispanic/Latino), 4 international. Average age 27. 31 applicants, 100% accepted, 26 enrolled. Expenses: Contact institution. *Financial support:* Application deadline: 3/2; applicants required to submit FAFSA. In 2016, 27 master's awarded. *Program availability:* Part-time, evening/weekend. Offers English (MA). *Application deadline:* Applications are processed on a rolling basis. *Application fee:* $55. Electronic applications accepted. *Application Contact:* Andrew M. Wright, Director of Admissions, 909-869-3130, Fax: 909-869-4529, E-mail: awright@cpp.edu. *Graduate Coordinator,* Dr. Lise-Hélène Smith, 909-869-3979, Fax: 909-869-4896, E-mail: lvtrouilloud@cpp.edu.

Program in Geology Students: 7 full-time (1 woman), 23 part-time (8 women); includes 13 minority (1 Black or African American, non-Hispanic/Latino; 2 Asian, non-Hispanic/Latino; 9 Hispanic/Latino; 1 Two or more races, non-Hispanic/Latino), 2 international. Average age 29. 15 applicants, 100% accepted, 13 enrolled. Expenses: Contact institution. *Financial support:* Application deadline: 3/2; applicants required to submit FAFSA. In 2016, 6 master's awarded. *Program availability:* Part-time, evening/weekend. Offers geology (MS). *Application deadline:* Applications are processed on a rolling basis. Electronic applications accepted. *Application Contact:* Andrew M. Wright, Director of Admissions, 909-869-3130, Fax: 909-869-4529, E-mail: awright@cpp.edu. *Department Chair/Graduate Coordinator,* Dr. Jonathan A. Nourse, 909-869-3460, Fax: 909-869-2920, E-mail: janourse@cpp.edu.

Program in History Students: 13 part-time (8 women); includes 8 minority (7 Hispanic/Latino; 1 Two or more races, non-Hispanic/Latino). Average age 32. 8 applicants, 100% accepted, 7 enrolled. Expenses: Contact institution. *Financial support:* Application deadline: 3/2; applicants required to submit FAFSA. In 2016, 9 master's awarded. *Program availability:* Part-time, evening/weekend. Offers history (MA). *Application deadline:* Applications are processed on a rolling basis. *Application fee:* $55. Electronic applications accepted. *Application Contact:* Andrew M. Wright, Director of Admissions, 909-869-3139, Fax: 909-869-4529, E-mail: awright@cpp.edu. *Graduate Coordinator,* Dr. Amanda H. Podany, 909-869-3875, Fax: 909-869-4724, E-mail: ahpodany@cpp.edu.

Program in Hospitality Management Students: 12 full-time (10 women), 35 part-time (22 women); includes 14 minority (3 Black or African American, non-Hispanic/Latino; 7 Asian, non-Hispanic/Latino; 2 Hispanic/Latino; 2 Two or more races, non-Hispanic/Latino), 25 international. Average age 29. 17 applicants, 88% accepted, 12 enrolled. Expenses: Contact institution. *Financial support:* Application deadline: 3/2; applicants required to submit FAFSA. In 2016, 19 master's awarded. *Program availability:* Part-time, evening/weekend. Offers hospitality management (MS). *Application deadline:* Applications are processed on a rolling basis. *Application fee:* $55. Electronic applications accepted. *Application Contact:* Andrew M. Wright, Director of Admissions, 909-869-3130, Fax: 909-869-4529, E-mail: awright@cpp.edu. *Program Director,* Dr. Neha Singh, 909-869-4565, Fax: 909-869-4805, E-mail: nsingh@cpp.edu.

Program in Interior Architecture Students: 19 full-time (all women), 39 part-time (35 women); includes 12 minority (3 Black or African American, non-Hispanic/Latino; 8 Asian, non-Hispanic/Latino; 1 Hispanic/Latino), 20 international. Average age 30. 31 applicants, 100% accepted, 27 enrolled. Expenses: Contact institution. *Financial support:* Application deadline: 3/2; applicants required to submit FAFSA. In 2016, 49 master's awarded. *Program availability:* Part-time, evening/weekend. Offers interior architecture (MIA). Program offered in partnership with UCLA Extension. *Application deadline:* Applications are processed on a rolling basis. *Application fee:* $55. Electronic applications accepted. *Application Contact:* Andrew M. Wright, Director of Admissions, 909-869-3130, Fax: 909-869-4529, E-mail: awright@cpp.edu. *Program Coordinator,* George R. Proctor, 909-869-4728, Fax: 909-869-4331, E-mail: grproctor@cpp.edu.

Program in Kinesiology Students: 7 full-time (3 women), 10 part-time (6 women); includes 10 minority (6 Asian, non-Hispanic/Latino; 3 Hispanic/Latino; 1 Two or more races, non-Hispanic/Latino). Average age 26. 6 applicants, 100% accepted, 5 enrolled. Expenses: Contact institution. *Financial support:* Application deadline: 3/2; applicants required to submit FAFSA. In 2016, 2 master's awarded. *Program availability:* Part-time, evening/weekend. Offers kinesiology (MS). *Application deadline:* Applications are processed on a rolling basis. *Application fee:* $55. Electronic applications accepted. *Application Contact:* Andrew M. Wright, Director of Admissions, 909-869-3130, Fax: 909-869-4529, E-mail: awright@cpp.edu. *Graduate Coordinator,* Dr. Ken Hansen, 909-869-4638, Fax: 909-869-4797, E-mail: kahansen@cpp.edu.

Program in Landscape Architecture Students: 17 full-time (7 women), 8 part-time (7 women); includes 7 minority (2 Asian, non-Hispanic/Latino; 4 Hispanic/Latino; 1 Two or more races, non-Hispanic/Latino), 7 international. Average age 31. 8 applicants, 100% accepted, 8 enrolled. Expenses: Contact institution. *Financial support:* Application deadline: 3/2; applicants required to submit FAFSA. In 2016, 25 master's awarded. *Program availability:* Part-time, evening/weekend. Offers landscape architecture (M Land Arch). *Application deadline:* Applications are processed on a rolling basis. *Application fee:* $55. Electronic applications accepted. *Application Contact:* Andrew M. Wright, Director of Admissions, 909-869-3130, Fax: 909-869-4529, E-mail: awright@cpp.edu. *Graduate Coordinator,* Dr. Weimin Li, 909-869-2715, Fax: 909-869-2580, E-mail: wli@cpp.edu.

Program in Mathematics Students: 10 full-time (3 women), 28 part-time (16 women); includes 23 minority (2 Black or African American, non-Hispanic/Latino; 4 Asian, non-Hispanic/Latino; 16 Hispanic/Latino; 1 Two or more races, non-Hispanic/Latino), 2 international. Average age 26. 26 applicants, 92% accepted, 18 enrolled. Expenses: Contact institution. *Financial support:* Application deadline: 3/2; applicants required to submit FAFSA. In 2016, 12 master's awarded. *Program availability:* Part-time, evening/weekend. Offers applied mathematics (MS). *Application deadline:* Applications

are processed on a rolling basis. *Application fee:* $55. Electronic applications accepted. *Application Contact:* Andrew M. Wright, Director of Admissions, 909-869-3130, Fax: 909-869-4529, E-mail: awright@cpp.edu. *Graduate Coordinator,* Dr. John Rock, 909-869-2404, Fax: 909-869-4904, E-mail: jarock@cpp.edu.

Program in Mechanical Engineering Students: 8 full-time (1 woman), 64 part-time (7 women); includes 46 minority (1 Black or African American, non-Hispanic/Latino; 24 Asian, non-Hispanic/Latino; 18 Hispanic/Latino; 3 Two or more races, non-Hispanic/Latino), 11 international. Average age 27. 22 applicants, 100% accepted, 17 enrolled. Expenses: Contact institution. *Financial support:* Application deadline: 3/2; applicants required to submit FAFSA. In 2016, 14 master's awarded. *Program availability:* Part-time, evening/weekend. Offers mechanical engineering (MS). *Application deadline:* Applications are processed on a rolling basis. *Application fee:* $55. Electronic applications accepted. *Application Contact:* Andrew M. Wright, Director of Admissions, 909-869-3130, Fax: 909-869-4529, E-mail: awright@cpp.edu. *Graduate Coordinator,* Dr. Henry Xue, 909-869-4304, Fax: 909-869-4341, E-mail: hxue@cpp.edu.

Program in Psychology Students: 31 full-time (26 women); includes 23 minority (1 Black or African American, non-Hispanic/Latino; 4 Asian, non-Hispanic/Latino; 16 Hispanic/Latino; 2 Two or more races, non-Hispanic/Latino), 1 international. Average age 24. 16 applicants, 100% accepted, 16 enrolled. Expenses: Contact institution. *Financial support:* Application deadline: 3/2; applicants required to submit FAFSA. In 2016, 15 master's awarded. *Program availability:* Part-time, evening/weekend. Offers psychology (MS). *Application deadline:* Applications are processed on a rolling basis. *Application fee:* $55. Electronic applications accepted. *Application Contact:* Andrew M. Wright, Director of Admissions, 909-869-3130, Fax: 909-869-4529, E-mail: awright@cpp.edu. *Director of Graduate Studies,* Dr. Jeffery Mio, 909-869-3899, Fax: 909-869-4930, E-mail: jsmio@cpp.edu.

Program in Public Administration Students: 3 full-time (2 women), 34 part-time (19 women); includes 29 minority (3 Black or African American, non-Hispanic/Latino; 4 Asian, non-Hispanic/Latino; 18 Hispanic/Latino; 4 Two or more races, non-Hispanic/Latino), 3 international. Average age 31. 17 applicants, 94% accepted, 13 enrolled. Expenses: Contact institution. *Financial support:* Application deadline: 3/2; applicants required to submit FAFSA. In 2016, 13 master's awarded. *Program availability:* Part-time, evening/weekend. Offers public administration (MPA). *Application deadline:* Applications are processed on a rolling basis. *Application fee:* $55. Electronic applications accepted. *Application Contact:* Andrew M. Wright, Director of Admissions, 909-869-3130, Fax: 909-869-4529, E-mail: awright@cpp.edu. *MPA Director,* Dr. Sandra M. Emerson, 909-869-3879, Fax: 909-869-6995, E-mail: smemerson@cpp.edu.

Program in Systems Engineering Students: 8 part-time (4 women); includes 4 minority (2 Asian, non-Hispanic/Latino; 1 Hispanic/Latino; 1 Two or more races, non-Hispanic/Latino), 2 international. Average age 29. 6 applicants, 83% accepted, 4 enrolled. Expenses: Contact institution. *Financial support:* Application deadline: 3/2. *Program availability:* Part-time, evening/weekend. Offers systems engineering (MS). *Application deadline:* Applications are processed on a rolling basis. *Application fee:* $55. Electronic applications accepted. *Application Contact:* Andrew M. Wright, Director of Admissions, 909-869-3130, Fax: 909-869-4529, E-mail: awright@cpp.edu. *Professor/Coordinator,* Dr. Kamran Abedini, 909-869-2569, Fax: 909-869-2564, E-mail: kabedini@cpp.edu.

Program in Urban and Regional Planning Students: 29 full-time (16 women), 11 part-time (6 women); includes 30 minority (3 Black or African American, non-Hispanic/Latino; 7 Asian, non-Hispanic/Latino; 20 Hispanic/Latino), 2 international. Average age 27. 21 applicants, 100% accepted, 19 enrolled. Expenses: Contact institution. *Financial support:* Application deadline: 3/2; applicants required to submit FAFSA. In 2016, 18 master's awarded. *Program availability:* Part-time, evening/weekend. Offers urban and regional planning (MURP). *Application deadline:* Applications are processed on a rolling basis. *Application fee:* $55. Electronic applications accepted. *Application Contact:* Andrew M. Wright, Director of Admissions, 909-869-3130, Fax: 909-869-4529, E-mail: awright@cpp.edu. *Graduate Coordinator,* Dr. Courtney Knapp, 909-869-4507, E-mail: ceknapp@cpp.edu.

CALIFORNIA STATE UNIVERSITY, BAKERSFIELD, Bakersfield, CA 93311

General Information State-supported, coed, comprehensive institution. *Enrollment:* 9,341 graduate, professional, and undergraduate students; 442 full-time matriculated graduate/professional students (334 women), 223 part-time matriculated graduate/professional students (137 women). *Enrollment by degree level:* 647 master's, 18 doctoral. *Graduate faculty:* 48 full-time (23 women), 39 part-time/adjunct (23 women). *Tuition, state resident:* full-time $2246; part-time $1302 per semester. *Graduate housing:* Room and/or apartments available on a first-come, first-served basis to single students; on-campus housing not available to married students. Typical cost: $4411 per year ($6410 including board). Room and board charges vary according to board plan. Housing application deadline: 8/1. *Student services:* Campus employment opportunities, campus safety program, career counseling, child daycare facilities, exercise/wellness program, free psychological counseling, grant writing training, international student services, multicultural affairs office, services for students with disabilities, teacher training, writing training. *Library facilities:* Walter W. Stiern Library.

Computer facilities: A campuswide network can be accessed from student residence rooms and from off campus. Online class registration is available. Website: http://www.csub.edu/

General Application Contact: Dr. Vandana Kohli, Director, Graduate Programs, 661-664-2786, E-mail: vkohli@csub.edu.

GRADUATE UNITS

Division of Graduate Studies Expenses: Contact institution. *Financial support:* Fellowships, research assistantships with partial tuition reimbursements, teaching assistantships with partial tuition reimbursements, career-related internships or fieldwork, Federal Work-Study, institutionally sponsored loans, scholarships/grants, and traineeships available. Support available to part-time students. Financial award application deadline: 1/15; financial award applicants required to submit CSS PROFILE. *Program availability:* Part-time, evening/weekend, online learning. Offers administration (MSA); interdisciplinary studies (MA). *Application deadline:* For fall admission, 8/1 priority date for domestic students; for winter admission, 11/1 priority date for domestic students; for spring admission, 3/1 priority date for domestic students. Applications are processed on a rolling basis. *Application fee:* $55. *Application Contact:* Debbie Blowers, Assistant Director, Admissions and Evaluations, 661-654-3381, Fax: 661-654-3389, E-mail: dblowers@csub.edu. *Associate Vice President for Academic Affairs,* Dr. Vernon B. Harper, Jr., 661-664-3420, Fax: 661-664-6911, E-mail: vharper@csub.edu.

School of Arts and Humanities Students: 15 full-time (7 women), 25 part-time (15 women); includes 22 minority (1 Black or African American, non-Hispanic/Latino; 3 Asian, non-Hispanic/Latino; 16 Hispanic/Latino; 2 Two or more races, non-Hispanic/Latino). Average age 36. 25 applicants, 72% accepted, 14 enrolled.

California State University, Bakersfield

Expenses: Contact institution. *Financial support:* Fellowships, career-related internships or fieldwork, institutionally sponsored loans, scholarships/grants, and traineeships available. *Program availability:* Part-time, evening/weekend. Offers arts and humanities (MA); English (MA); history (MA); Spanish (MA). *Application deadline:* Applications are processed on a rolling basis. *Application fee:* $55. *Application Contact:* Debbie Blowers, Assistant Director of Admissions, 661-664-3381, E-mail: dblowers@csub.edu. *Interim Dean,* Dr. Liora Gubkin, 661-654-2221, E-mail: lgubkin_malicdem@csub.edu.

School of Business and Public Administration Students: 95 full-time (58 women), 74 part-time (40 women); includes 90 minority (20 Black or African American, non-Hispanic/Latino; 12 Asian, non-Hispanic/Latino; 53 Hispanic/Latino; 5 Two or more races, non-Hispanic/Latino), 14 international. Average age 30. 161 applicants, 57% accepted, 77 enrolled. Expenses: Contact institution. *Financial support:* Career-related internships or fieldwork available. Offers business administration (MBA); business and public administration (MBA, MPA, MS); health care administration (MS); public administration (MPA). *Application deadline:* Applications are processed on a rolling basis. *Application fee:* $55. *Application Contact:* Debbie Blowers, Assistant Director of Admissions, 661-664-3381, E-mail: dblowers@csub.edu. *Interim Dean,* Dr. John Stark, 661-654-2323, Fax: 661-654-2438, E-mail: jstark@csub.edu.

School of Natural Sciences, Mathematics, and Engineering Students: 19 full-time (7 women), 33 part-time (13 women); includes 25 minority (2 Black or African American, non-Hispanic/Latino; 7 Asian, non-Hispanic/Latino; 15 Hispanic/Latino; 1 Two or more races, non-Hispanic/Latino). Average age 29. 16 applicants, 88% accepted, 10 enrolled. Expenses: Contact institution. Offers biology (MS); geological sciences (MS); hydrogeology (MS); natural sciences, mathematics, and engineering (MA, MS); nursing (MSN); petroleum geology (MS); science education (MS); teaching mathematics (MA). *Application fee:* $55. *Application Contact:* Debbie Blowers, Assistant Director of Admissions, 661-664-3381, E-mail: dblowers@csub.edu. *Dean,* Dr. Kathleen Madden, 661-654-3450, E-mail: kmadden2@csub.edu.

School of Social Sciences and Education Students: 239 full-time (206 women), 74 part-time (57 women); includes 222 minority (23 Black or African American, non-Hispanic/Latino; 4 American Indian or Alaska Native, non-Hispanic/Latino; 18 Asian, non-Hispanic/Latino; 161 Hispanic/Latino; 16 Two or more races, non-Hispanic/Latino), 8 international. Average age 33. 312 applicants, 64% accepted, 156 enrolled. Expenses: Contact institution. Offers anthropology (MA); counseling psychology (MS); educational administration (MA); educational leadership (Ed D); school counseling (MS); social sciences and education (MA, MS, MSW, Ed D); social work (MSW); sociology (MA); special education (MA); student affairs (MS). *Application deadline:* Applications are processed on a rolling basis. *Application fee:* $55. *Application Contact:* Debbie Blowers, Assistant Director of Admissions, 661-664-3381, E-mail: dblowers@csub.edu. *Dean,* Dr. Steve Bacon, 661-664-2210, Fax: 661-664-2016, E-mail: sbacon@csub.edu.

CALIFORNIA STATE UNIVERSITY CHANNEL ISLANDS, Camarillo, CA 93012

General Information State-supported, coed, comprehensive institution. *Graduate housing:* Room and/or apartments available on a first-come, first-served basis to single students; on-campus housing not available to married students. Housing application deadline: 6/1.

GRADUATE UNITS

Extended University and International Programs *Program availability:* Part-time, evening/weekend. Offers biotechnology and bioinformatics (MS); business administration (MBA); computer science (MS); mathematics (MS).

CALIFORNIA STATE UNIVERSITY, CHICO, Chico, CA 95929-0722

General Information State-supported, coed, comprehensive institution. CGS member. *Enrollment:* 17,557 graduate, professional, and undergraduate students; 759 full-time matriculated graduate/professional students (537 women), 327 part-time matriculated graduate/professional students (200 women). *Enrollment by degree level:* 1,086 master's. *Graduate faculty:* 13 full-time (3 women), 30 part-time/adjunct (11 women). *Graduate housing:* Room and/or apartments available on a first-come, first-served basis to single students; on-campus housing not available to married students. Typical cost: $12,824 (including board). Housing application deadline: 3/22. *Student services:* Campus employment opportunities, campus safety program, career counseling, child daycare facilities, exercise/wellness program, free psychological counseling, grant writing training, international student services, low-cost health insurance, multicultural affairs office, services for students with disabilities, teacher training, writing training. *Library facilities:* Meriam Library plus 1 other. *Collection:* Books: 923,470 (physical), 180,505 (digital/electronic); Serial titles: 660 (physical). Study areas open 24 hours, 5–7 days a week; students can reserve study rooms. *Research affiliation:* Sierra Nevada Brewery (nutrition, food sciences, agriculture), Lawrence Livermore Labs - Inspection and Surveillance Robots (engineering and computer science), U.S. Navy Office of Naval Research (engineering), California Department of Transportation Pavement Preservation and Recycling (engineering, computer science, construction management), U.S. Navy Office of Naval Research (engineering), Verizon Wireless/Samsung (business).

Computer facilities: Computer purchase and lease plans are available. 243 computers available on campus for general student use. A campuswide network can be accessed from student residence rooms and from off campus. Online class registration, student account information, calendar, transcripts are available. Website: http://www.csuchico.edu/

General Application Contact: Judy L. Morris, Admissions Counselor, 530-898-6880, Fax: 530-898-3342, E-mail: graduatestudies@csuchico.edu.

GRADUATE UNITS

Office of Graduate Studies Students: 759 full-time (537 women), 327 part-time (200 women); includes 431 minority (17 Black or African American, non-Hispanic/Latino; 6 American Indian or Alaska Native, non-Hispanic/Latino; 56 Asian, non-Hispanic/Latino; 170 Hispanic/Latino; 182 Two or more races, non-Hispanic/Latino), 95 international. Average age 29. 811 applicants, 47% accepted, 229 enrolled. *Faculty:* 131 full-time (66 women), 56 part-time/adjunct (36 women). Expenses: Contact institution. *Financial support:* Fellowships, research assistantships, teaching assistantships, career-related internships or fieldwork, Federal Work-Study, scholarships/grants, unspecified assistantships, and stipends available. Support available to part-time students. Financial award application deadline: 3/1; financial award applicants required to submit FAFSA. In 2016, 373 master's awarded. *Program availability:* Part-time, 100% online, blended/hybrid learning. *Application deadline:* For fall admission, 3/1 priority date for domestic students, 3/1 for international students; for spring admission, 9/15 priority date for domestic students, 9/15 for international students. *Application fee:* $55. Electronic applications accepted. *Application Contact:* Judy L. Morris, Graduate Admissions

Coordinator, 530-898-5416, Fax: 530-898-3342, E-mail: jlmorris@csuchico.edu. *Office of Graduate Studies,* Dr. Sharon Barrios, 530-898-6880, Fax: 530-898-3342, E-mail: sbarrios@csuchico.edu.

College of Agriculture 1 applicant. Expenses: Contact institution. *Financial support:* Fellowships and teaching assistantships available. Financial award application deadline: 3/1; financial award applicants required to submit FAFSA. In 2016, 9 master's awarded. Offers agricultural education (MS). *Application Contact:* Judy L. Morris, Graduate Admissions Coordinator, 530-898-5416, Fax: 530-898-3342, E-mail: jlmorris@csuchico.edu. *Dean,* Thomas E. Dickinson, 530-898-5844.

College of Behavioral and Social Sciences Students: 221 full-time (169 women), 64 part-time (43 women); includes 97 minority (8 Black or African American, non-Hispanic/Latino; 1 American Indian or Alaska Native, non-Hispanic/Latino; 19 Asian, non-Hispanic/Latino; 52 Hispanic/Latino; 17 Two or more races, non-Hispanic/Latino). 319 applicants, 41% accepted, 81 enrolled. *Faculty:* 112 full-time (60 women), 132 part-time/adjunct (83 women). Expenses: Contact institution. *Financial support:* Fellowships, teaching assistantships, career-related internships or fieldwork, Federal Work-Study, scholarships/grants, and unspecified assistantships available. Support available to part-time students. Financial award application deadline: 3/1; financial award applicants required to submit FAFSA. In 2016, 116 master's awarded. Offers anthropology (MA); applied/school psychology (MA); behavioral and social sciences (MA, MPA, MS, MSW); health administration (MPA); local government management (MPA); marriage and family therapy (MS); museum studies (MA); political science (MA); psychological science (MA); public administration (MPA); social science (MA); social work (MSW). *Application deadline:* For fall admission, 3/1 for domestic and international students. *Application fee:* $55. Electronic applications accepted. *Application Contact:* Judy L. Morris, Graduate Admissions Coordinator, 530-898-6880, Fax: 530-898-6889, E-mail: jlmorris@csuchico.edu. *Dean,* Dr. Eddie Vela, 530-898-6171, Fax: 530-898-5986, E-mail: bss@csuchico.edu.

College of Business Students: 33 full-time (15 women), 37 part-time (16 women); includes 29 minority (1 American Indian or Alaska Native, non-Hispanic/Latino; 18 Asian, non-Hispanic/Latino; 8 Hispanic/Latino; 2 Two or more races, non-Hispanic/Latino). 53 applicants, 75% accepted, 24 enrolled. *Faculty:* 60 full-time (21 women), 54 part-time/adjunct (19 women). Expenses: Contact institution. *Financial support:* Career-related internships or fieldwork, institutionally sponsored loans, scholarships/grants, traineeships, and unspecified assistantships available. Financial award application deadline: 3/1; financial award applicants required to submit FAFSA. In 2016, 26 master's awarded. *Program availability:* Part-time. Offers business (MBA). *Application deadline:* For fall admission, 3/1 for domestic and international students; for spring admission, 9/15 for domestic and international students. *Application fee:* $55. Electronic applications accepted. *Application Contact:* Dr. Matthew Meuter, MBA Director, 530-898-5880, Fax: 530-898-4584, E-mail: mmeuter@csuchico.edu. *Dean,* Dr. Judy Hennessey, 530-898-6272, Fax: 530-898-4584, E-mail: jehennessey@csuchico.edu.

College of Communication and Education Students: 118 full-time (93 women), 55 part-time (37 women); includes 57 minority (2 Black or African American, non-Hispanic/Latino; 8 Asian, non-Hispanic/Latino; 35 Hispanic/Latino; 1 Native Hawaiian or other Pacific Islander, non-Hispanic/Latino; 11 Two or more races, non-Hispanic/Latino). 233 applicants, 35% accepted, 63 enrolled. *Faculty:* 82 full-time (47 women), 132 part-time/adjunct (80 women). Expenses: Contact institution. *Financial support:* Fellowships, teaching assistantships, career-related internships or fieldwork, Federal Work-Study, and stipends available. Support available to part-time students. Financial award application deadline: 3/1; financial award applicants required to submit FAFSA. In 2016, 120 master's awarded. *Program availability:* Part-time. Offers communication and education (MA, MS); communication sciences and disorders (MA); communication studies (MA); curriculum and instruction (MA); kinesiology (MA); recreation, parks, and tourism (MA); teaching English learners and special education advising patterns (MA). *Application deadline:* For fall admission, 3/1 for domestic and international students; for spring admission, 9/15 for domestic and international students. *Application fee:* $55. Electronic applications accepted. *Application Contact:* Judy L. Rice, School of Graduate, International, and Interdisciplinary Studies, 530-898-5416, Fax: 530-898-3342, E-mail: jlrice@csuchico.edu. *Dean,* Dr. Angela Trethewey, 530-898-4015, Fax: 530-898-4345, E-mail: cme@csuchico.edu.

College of Engineering, Computer Science, and Construction Management Students: 28 full-time (6 women), 47 part-time (13 women); includes 56 minority (55 Asian, non-Hispanic/Latino; 1 Hispanic/Latino). 89 applicants, 74% accepted, 12 enrolled. *Faculty:* 59 full-time (12 women), 37 part-time/adjunct (4 women). Expenses: Contact institution. *Financial support:* Fellowships, research assistantships, teaching assistantships, career-related internships or fieldwork, Federal Work-Study, scholarships/grants, and traineeships available. Support available to part-time students. Financial award application deadline: 3/1; financial award applicants required to submit FAFSA. In 2016, 34 master's awarded. *Program availability:* Part-time, online learning. Offers computer engineering (MS); computer science (MS); electronic engineering (MS); electronics engineering (MS); engineering, computer science, and construction management (MS). *Application deadline:* For fall admission, 3/1 priority date for domestic students, 3/1 for international students; for spring admission, 9/15 priority date for domestic students, 9/15 for international students. *Application fee:* $55. Electronic applications accepted. *Application Contact:* Judy L. Rice, Graduate Admissions Counselor, 530-898-5416, Fax: 530-898-3342, E-mail: jlrice@csuchico.edu. *Dean,* Ricardo Jacquez, 530-898-5963, Fax: 530-898-4070, E-mail: ecc@csuchico.edu.

College of Humanities and Fine Arts Students: 33 full-time (16 women), 9 part-time (8 women); includes 10 minority (1 Asian, non-Hispanic/Latino; 5 Hispanic/Latino; 4 Two or more races, non-Hispanic/Latino). 32 applicants, 63% accepted, 17 enrolled. *Faculty:* 107 full-time (43 women), 89 part-time/adjunct (49 women). Expenses: Contact institution. *Financial support:* Teaching assistantships, career-related internships or fieldwork, Federal Work-Study, scholarships/grants, and unspecified assistantships available. Support available to part-time students. Financial award application deadline: 3/1; financial award applicants required to submit FAFSA. In 2016, 14 master's awarded. Offers art history (MA); art studio (MFA); English (MA); fine arts (MFA); history (MA); humanities and fine arts (MA, MFA). *Application deadline:* For fall admission, 3/1 priority date for domestic students, 3/1 for international students; for spring admission, 9/15 priority date for domestic students, 9/15 for international students. *Application fee:* $55. Electronic applications accepted. *Application Contact:* Judy L. Rice, Graduate Admissions Coordinator, 530-898-5416, Fax: 530-898-3342, E-mail: jlrice@csuchico.edu. *Dean,* Dr. Robert M. Knight, 530-898-5351, Fax: 530-898-5581, E-mail: hfa@csuchico.edu.

College of Natural Sciences Students: 33 full-time (20 women), 33 part-time (20 women); includes 18 minority (5 Asian, non-Hispanic/Latino; 10 Hispanic/Latino; 1 Native Hawaiian or other Pacific Islander, non-Hispanic/Latino; 2 Two or more races, non-Hispanic/Latino). 79 applicants, 52% accepted, 29 enrolled. *Faculty:* 108 full-time

(65 women), 114 part-time/adjunct (64 women). Expenses: Contact institution. *Financial support:* Fellowships, research assistantships, teaching assistantships, career-related internships or fieldwork, and Federal Work-Study available. Support available to part-time students. Financial award application deadline: 3/1; financial award applicants required to submit FAFSA. In 2016, 42 master's awarded. *Program availability:* Part-time. Offers biological sciences (MS); environmental science (MS, PSM); general nutritional science (MS); geosciences (MS); mathematics in education (MS); natural sciences (MS, MSN, PSM); nursing (MSN); nutrition education (MS). *Application deadline:* For fall admission, 3/1 priority date for domestic students, 3/1 for international students; for spring admission, 9/15 priority date for domestic students, 9/15 for international students. *Application fee:* $55. Electronic applications accepted. *Application Contact:* Judy L. Rice, Graduate Admissions Coordinator, 530-898-5416, Fax: 530-898-3342, E-mail: jlrice@csuchico.edu. *Dean,* Dr. David Hassenzahl, 530-898-6121, Fax: 530-898-4363, E-mail: ns@csuchico.edu.

CALIFORNIA STATE UNIVERSITY, DOMINGUEZ HILLS, Carson, CA 90747-0001

General Information State-supported, coed, comprehensive institution. CGS member. *Enrollment:* 14,635 graduate, professional, and undergraduate students; 766 full-time matriculated graduate/professional students (569 women), 715 part-time matriculated graduate/professional students (536 women). *Enrollment by degree level:* 1,508 master's. *Graduate faculty:* 76 full-time (49 women), 107 part-time/adjunct (78 women). *Tuition, area resident:* Full-time $6738; part-time $3906 per unit. Tuition and fees vary according to course load, program and reciprocity agreements. *Graduate housing:* Rooms and/or apartments available on a first-come, first-served basis to single and married students. Typical cost: $9012 per year for married students. Housing application deadline: 4/15. *Student services:* Campus employment opportunities, campus safety program, career counseling, child daycare facilities, exercise/wellness program, free psychological counseling, international student services, low-cost health insurance, multicultural affairs office, services for students with disabilities, writing training. *Library facilities:* Leo F. Cain Educational Resource Center. *Collection:* Books: 457,885 (physical), 300,523 (digital/electronic); Serial titles: 6,542 (physical), 75,366 (digital/electronic); Databases: 94. Weekly public service hours: 81; students can reserve study rooms. *Research affiliation:* Los Angeles Biomedical Research Institute at Harbor UCLA Medical Center (biomedical science), Hewlett Packard (catalyst initiative grants).

Computer facilities: 1,100 computers available on campus for general student use. A campuswide network can be accessed from student residence rooms and from off campus. Online class registration is available.
Website: http://www.csudh.edu/

General Application Contact: Brandy McLelland, Director of Student Records and Student Information Services, 310-243-3645, E-mail: bmclelland@csudh.edu.

GRADUATE UNITS

College of Arts and Humanities *Faculty:* 313 full-time (162 women), 517 part-time/adjunct (291 women). Expenses: Contact institution. *Financial support:* Institutionally sponsored loans available. Support available to part-time students. Financial award application deadline: 3/2; financial award applicants required to submit FAFSA. In 2016, 99 master's awarded. *Program availability:* Part-time, evening/weekend, 100% online. Offers arts and humanities (MA, Certificate); English literature (MA); negotiation, conflict resolution and peacebuilding (MA); rhetoric and composition (Certificate); teaching English as a second language (MA, Certificate). *Application deadline:* For fall admission, 6/1 for domestic students. *Application fee:* $55. *Application Contact:* Brandy McLelland, Director of Student Information Services/Registrar, 310-243-3645, E-mail: bmclelland@csudh.edu. *Dean,* Dr. Mitch Avila, 310-243-3389, E-mail: mitchavila@csudh.edu.

College of Business Administration and Public Policy Expenses: Contact institution. *Program availability:* Part-time, evening/weekend, online learning. Offers business administration (MBA); business administration and public policy (MBA, MPA); public administration (MPA). *Application deadline:* For fall admission, 4/1 for domestic and international students; for spring admission, 11/1 for domestic students, 10/1 for international students. *Application fee:* $55. *Application Contact:* Betty Vu, Assistant Dean, Graduate and Professional Programs, 310-243-3165, E-mail: bvu@csudh.edu. *Dean,* Dr. Joseph Wen, 310-243-2124, E-mail: jwen@csudh.edu.

College of Education Expenses: Contact institution. *Program availability:* Part-time, evening/weekend. Offers education (MA, MS). *Application deadline:* For fall admission, 6/1 priority date for domestic students; for spring admission, 10/1 priority date for domestic students. Applications are processed on a rolling basis. *Application fee:* $55. *Application Contact:* Brandy McLelland, Director of Student Information Services/Registrar, 310-243-3645, E-mail: bmclelland@csudh.edu. *Dean,* Dr. John Davis, 310-243-3510, Fax: 310-243-3518, E-mail: jdavis@csudh.edu.

Division of Graduate Education Expenses: Contact institution. *Program availability:* Part-time, evening/weekend. Offers college counseling (MS); counseling (MS); school counseling (MS). *Application deadline:* For fall admission, 6/1 for domestic students. *Application fee:* $55. *Application Contact:* Admissions Office, 310-243-3530. *Chair,* Anthony Normore, 310-243-3925, E-mail: anormore@csudh.edu.

Division of Teacher Education Expenses: Contact institution. *Program availability:* Part-time, evening/weekend. Offers early childhood special education (MA); special education (MA). *Application deadline:* For fall admission, 6/1 for domestic students. *Application fee:* $55. *Application Contact:* Admissions Office, 310-243-3530. *Chair,* Dr. Deandrea Nelson, 310-243-2489, E-mail: dnelson@csudh.edu.

College of Extended and International Education Expenses: Contact institution. *Program availability:* Part-time, evening/weekend, online learning. Offers extended and international education (MA, MS); humanities (MA); quality assurance (MA). *Application fee:* $55. Electronic applications accepted. *Application Contact:* Jackie McKenzie, Extended Education Registrar, 310-243-3741, E-mail: jmckenzie@csudh.edu. *Dean,* Dr. Kim McNutt, 310-243-3737, Fax: 310-516-4423, E-mail: kmncnutt@csudh.edu.

College of Health, Human Services and Nursing Expenses: Contact institution. Offers health, human services and nursing (MS, MSN, MSW); marital and family therapy (MS); nursing (MSN); occupational therapy (MS); social work (MSW). *Application fee:* $55. Electronic applications accepted. *Application Contact:* Brandy McLelland, Director of Student Information Services/Registrar, 310-243-3645, E-mail: bmclelland@csudh.edu. *Dean,* Dr. Gary Sayed, 301-243-2046, Fax: 310-217-6800, E-mail: gsayed@csudh.edu.

College of Natural and Behavioral Sciences Expenses: Contact institution. Offers biology (MS); clinical psychology (MA); computer science (MS); health psychology (MA); natural and behavioral sciences (MA, MS, Certificate); social research (MA); sociology (MA). *Application Contact:* Brandy McLelland, Director of Student Information Services/Registrar, 310-243-3645, E-mail: bmclelland@csudh.edu. *Dean,* Dr. Rodrick Hay, 310-243-2547, E-mail: rhay@csudh.edu.

CALIFORNIA STATE UNIVERSITY, EAST BAY, Hayward, CA 94542-3000

General Information State-supported, coed, comprehensive institution. *Enrollment:* 15,855 graduate, professional, and undergraduate students; 949 full-time matriculated graduate/professional students (622 women), 1,182 part-time matriculated graduate/professional students (677 women). *Enrollment by degree level:* 2,070 master's, 61 doctoral. *Graduate faculty:* 371 full-time (188 women), 504 part-time/adjunct (293 women). *Graduate housing:* On-campus housing not available. *Student services:* Campus employment opportunities, campus safety program, career counseling, exercise/wellness program, free psychological counseling, international student services, low-cost health insurance, services for students with disabilities. *Library facilities:* Hayward Campus Library. *Research affiliation:* Bayer USA Foundation (STEM), Chevron (STEM), Hearst Foundation (STEM), NASA (earth and environmental sciences), Irvine Foundation (education: teacher preparation), Carnegie Foundation (statistics for non-STEM majors).

Computer facilities: Computer purchase and lease plans are available. 700 computers available on campus for general student use. A campuswide network can be accessed from student residence rooms and from off campus. Online class registration is available.
Website: http://www.csueastbay.edu/

General Application Contact: Dr. Donna Wiley, Senior Director of Graduate Studies and Academic Programs, 510-885-2928, Fax: 510-885-4777, E-mail: donna.wiley@csueastbay.edu.

GRADUATE UNITS

Office of Graduate Studies Students: 949 full-time (622 women), 1,182 part-time (677 women); includes 973 minority (201 Black or African American, non-Hispanic/Latino; 5 American Indian or Alaska Native, non-Hispanic/Latino; 392 Asian, non-Hispanic/Latino; 285 Hispanic/Latino; 16 Native Hawaiian or other Pacific Islander, non-Hispanic/Latino; 74 Two or more races, non-Hispanic/Latino), 569 international. Average age 32. 3,725 applicants, 42% accepted, 697 enrolled. Expenses: Contact institution. *Financial support:* Fellowships, teaching assistantships, career-related internships or fieldwork, Federal Work-Study, institutionally sponsored loans, and scholarships/grants available. Support available to part-time students. Financial award application deadline: 3/2; financial award applicants required to submit FAFSA. In 2016, 1,088 master's, 16 doctorates awarded. *Program availability:* Part-time, evening/weekend, online learning. Offers interdisciplinary studies (MA, MS). *Application deadline:* For fall admission, 6/30 for domestic and international students. Applications are processed on a rolling basis. *Application fee:* $55. Electronic applications accepted. *Interim Associate Vice President,* Dr. Donna Wiley, 510-885-3716, Fax: 510-885-4777, E-mail: donna.wiley@csueastbay.edu.

College of Business and Economics Students: 189 full-time (100 women), 238 part-time (111 women); includes 183 minority (26 Black or African American, non-Hispanic/Latino; 121 Asian, non-Hispanic/Latino; 25 Hispanic/Latino; 4 Native Hawaiian or other Pacific Islander, non-Hispanic/Latino; 7 Two or more races, non-Hispanic/Latino), 159 international. Average age 32. 682 applicants, 44% accepted, 134 enrolled. Expenses: Contact institution. *Financial support:* Fellowships, career-related internships or fieldwork, Federal Work-Study, institutionally sponsored loans, and scholarships/grants available. Support available to part-time students. Financial award application deadline: 3/2; financial award applicants required to submit FAFSA. In 2016, 200 master's awarded. *Program availability:* Part-time, evening/weekend, online learning. Offers accountancy (MS); business analytics (MS); business and economics (MA, MBA); computer information systems (MBA); economics (MA); entrepreneurship (MBA); finance (MBA); global innovators (MBA); human resources and organizational behavior (MBA); human resources/personnel management (MBA); information technology management (MBA); marketing (MBA); marketing management (MBA); operations and supply chain management (MBA); small business management (MBA); strategy and international business (MBA). *Application deadline:* For fall admission, 6/30 for domestic and international students. Applications are processed on a rolling basis. *Application fee:* $55. Electronic applications accepted. *Application Contact:* Dr. Donna Wiley, Interim Associate Vice President for Academic Programs and Graduate Studies, 510-885-3716, Fax: 510-885-4777, E-mail: donna.wiley@csueastbay.edu. *Interim Dean,* Xinjian Lu, 510-885-3291, E-mail: xinjian.lu@csueastbay.edu.

College of Education and Allied Studies Students: 274 full-time (203 women), 148 part-time (108 women); includes 220 minority (44 Black or African American, non-Hispanic/Latino; 2 American Indian or Alaska Native, non-Hispanic/Latino; 59 Asian, non-Hispanic/Latino; 86 Hispanic/Latino; 5 Native Hawaiian or other Pacific Islander, non-Hispanic/Latino; 24 Two or more races, non-Hispanic/Latino), 8 international. Average age 35. 369 applicants, 58% accepted, 118 enrolled. Expenses: Contact institution. *Financial support:* Career-related internships or fieldwork, Federal Work-Study, and institutionally sponsored loans available. Support available to part-time students. Financial award application deadline: 3/2; financial award applicants required to submit FAFSA. In 2016, 189 master's, 16 doctorates awarded. *Program availability:* Part-time, evening/weekend, online learning. Offers counseling (MS); education (MS); education and allied studies (MS, Ed D); educational leadership (MS, Ed D); kinesiology (MS); marriage and family therapy (MS); mild-moderate disabilities (MS); moderate-severe disabilities (MS); recreation and tourism (MS); school counseling (MS); school psychology (MS); special education (MS). *Application deadline:* For fall admission, 6/30 for domestic and international students. *Application fee:* $55. Electronic applications accepted. *Application Contact:* Dr. Donna Wiley, Interim Associate Vice President for Academic Programs and Graduate Studies, 510-885-3716, Fax: 510-885-4777, E-mail: donna.wiley@csueastbay.edu. *Dean,* Dr. Carolyn Nelson, 510-885-3942, Fax: 510-885-2283, E-mail: carolyn.nelson@csueastbay.edu.

College of Letters, Arts, and Social Sciences Students: 290 full-time (232 women), 399 part-time (286 women); includes 429 minority (114 Black or African American, non-Hispanic/Latino; 3 American Indian or Alaska Native, non-Hispanic/Latino; 126 Asian, non-Hispanic/Latino; 143 Hispanic/Latino; 8 Native Hawaiian or other Pacific Islander, non-Hispanic/Latino; 35 Two or more races, non-Hispanic/Latino), 51 international. Average age 32. 1,211 applicants, 33% accepted, 233 enrolled. Expenses: Contact institution. *Financial support:* Fellowships, research assistantships, teaching assistantships, career-related internships or fieldwork, Federal Work-Study, institutionally sponsored loans, and scholarships/grants available. Support available to part-time students. Financial award application deadline: 3/2; financial award applicants required to submit FAFSA. In 2016, 410 master's awarded. *Program availability:* Part-time, evening/weekend, online learning. Offers anthropology (MA); children, youth, and family services (MSW); communication (MA); community mental health services (MSW); creative writing (MA); geography (MA); health care administration (MPA, MS); history (MA); letters, arts, and social sciences (MA, MPA, MS, MSW); literary studies (MA); management and change in health care (MS); multimedia (MA); music (MA); public administration (MPA); public history (MA); public management and policy analysis (MPA); speech-language pathology (MS); teaching (MA); teaching English to speakers of other languages (MA). *Application deadline:* For fall admission, 6/30 for domestic and international students. Applications are processed on a rolling basis. *Application fee:* $55. Electronic applications accepted. *Application Contact:* Dr. Donna Wiley, Interim Associate Vice President for Academic Programs and Graduate Studies, 510-885-3716, Fax: 510-885-4777, E-mail: donna.wiley@csueastbay.edu. *Dean,* Dr. Kathleen Rountree, 510-885-3161, Fax: 510-885-3164, E-mail: kathleen.rountree@csueastbay.edu.

College of Science Students: 196 full-time (87 women), 396 part-time (172 women); includes 143 minority (16 Black or African American, non-Hispanic/Latino; 86 Asian, non-Hispanic/Latino; 31 Hispanic/Latino; 2 Native Hawaiian or other Pacific Islander, non-Hispanic/Latino; 8 Two or more races, non-Hispanic/Latino), 351 international. Average age 29. 1,458 applicants, 45% accepted, 212 enrolled. Expenses: Contact institution. *Financial support:* Career-related internships or fieldwork, Federal Work-Study, and institutionally sponsored loans available. Support available to part-time students. Financial award application deadline: 3/2; financial award applicants required to submit FAFSA. In 2016, 289 master's awarded. *Program availability:* Part-time, evening/weekend. Offers actuarial science (MS); applied mathematics (MS); applied statistics (MS); biochemistry (MS); biological sciences (MS); biostatistics (MS); computational statistics (MS); computer networks (MS); computer science (MS); construction management (MS); engineering management (MS); geology (MS); marine science (MS); mathematical statistics (MS); mathematics (MS); mathematics teaching (MS); science (MS); statistics (MS). *Application deadline:* For fall admission, 6/30 for domestic and international students. *Application fee:* $55. Electronic applications accepted. *Application Contact:* Dr. Donna Wiley Interim Associate Vice President for Academic Programs and Graduate Studies, 510-885-3716, Fax: 510-885-4777, E-mail: donna.wiley@csueastbay.edu. *Dean,* Dr. Jason Singley, 510-885-3441, Fax: 510-885-2035, E-mail: jason.singley@csueastbay.edu.

CALIFORNIA STATE UNIVERSITY, FRESNO, Fresno, CA 93740-8027

General Information State-supported, coed, comprehensive institution. CGS member. *Enrollment:* 24,403 graduate, professional, and undergraduate students; 2,092 full-time matriculated graduate/professional students (1,443 women), 782 part-time matriculated graduate/professional students (475 women). *Enrollment by degree level:* 2,817 master's, 57 doctoral. *Graduate housing:* Room and/or apartments available on a first-come, first-served basis to single students; on-campus housing not available to married students. Housing application deadline: 4/1. *Student services:* Campus employment opportunities, campus safety program, career counseling, child daycare facilities, exercise/wellness program, free psychological counseling, international student services, low-cost health insurance, multicultural affairs office, services for students with disabilities. *Library facilities:* Henry Madden Library. *Research affiliation:* Coleman Foundation (administration), Starburst Foundation (engineering), Garabedian Foundation (agribusiness), California Endowment (arts and humanities).

Computer facilities: A campuswide network can be accessed from student residence rooms and from off campus. Online class registration is available.
Website: http://www.csufresno.edu/

General Application Contact: Helen M. Martinez, Administrative Analyst/Specialist, 559-278-2448, Fax: 559-278-4658, E-mail: helen_martinez@csufresno.edu.

GRADUATE UNITS

Division of Research and Graduate Studies Students: 2,092 full-time (1,443 women), 782 part-time (475 women). Expenses: Contact institution. *Financial support:* Teaching assistantships, career-related internships or fieldwork, Federal Work-Study, scholarships/grants, traineeships, tuition waivers (partial), unspecified assistantships, and research awards available. Support available to part-time students. Financial award application deadline: 3/1; financial award applicants required to submit FAFSA. In 2016, 835 master's, 64 doctorates awarded. *Program availability:* Part-time, evening/weekend. *Application deadline:* For fall admission, 5/1 for domestic and international students; for spring admission, 10/1 for domestic and international students. Applications are processed on a rolling basis. *Application fee:* $55. Electronic applications accepted. *Dean,* Dr. James Marshall, 559-278-2448, Fax: 559-278-4658.

College of Arts and Humanities Expenses: Contact institution. *Financial support:* Teaching assistantships, career-related internships or fieldwork, Federal Work-Study, scholarships/grants, and unspecified assistantships available. Support available to part-time students. Financial award application deadline: 3/1; financial award applicants required to submit FAFSA. *Program availability:* Part-time, evening/weekend. Offers art (MA); arts and humanities (MA, MFA); communication (MA); creative writing (MFA); linguistics (MA); literature (MA); music (MA); music education (MA); performance (MA); rhetoric and writing studies (MA); Spanish (MA). *Application deadline:* For fall admission, 5/1 for domestic and international students; for spring admission, 10/1 for domestic and international students. Applications are processed on a rolling basis. *Application fee:* $55. Electronic applications accepted. *Application Contact:* Cathie Salanitro, Administrative Analyst, 559-278-2448, Fax: 559-278-4658, E-mail: cathies@csufresno.edu. *Dean,* Dr. Saul Jimenez-Sandoval, 559-278-3056, Fax: 559-278-6758.

College of Health and Human Services Expenses: Contact institution. *Financial support:* Teaching assistantships, career-related internships or fieldwork, Federal Work-Study, scholarships/grants, traineeships, and unspecified assistantships available. Support available to part-time students. Financial award application deadline: 3/1; financial award applicants required to submit FAFSA. *Program availability:* Part-time, evening/weekend. Offers communicative disorders (MA); exercise science (MA); general kinesiology (MA); health and human services (MA, MPH, MS, MSW, DNP, DPT); health policy and management (MPH); health promotion (MPH); nursing (MS, DNP); physical therapy (DPT); social work education (MSW); sport administration (MA); sport psychology (MA). *Application deadline:* For fall admission, 5/1 for domestic and international students; for spring admission, 10/1 for domestic and international students. Applications are processed on a rolling basis. *Application fee:* $55. Electronic applications accepted. *Dean,* Dr. Jody Hironaka-Juteau, 559-278-4004, Fax: 559-278-4437, E-mail: jhironak@csufresno.edu.

College of Science and Mathematics Expenses: Contact institution. *Financial support:* Teaching assistantships, career-related internships or fieldwork, Federal Work-Study, scholarships/grants, and unspecified assistantships available. Support available to part-time students. Financial award application deadline: 3/1; financial award applicants required to submit FAFSA. *Program availability:* Part-time, evening/weekend. Offers applied behavior analysis (MA); biology (MS); biotechnology (MBT); chemistry (MS); computer science (MS); general/experimental psychology

(MA); geology (MS); marine science (MS); mathematics (MA); mathematics teaching (MA); physics (MS); school psychology (Ed S); science and mathematics (MA, MBT, MS, Ed S). *Application deadline:* For fall admission, 5/1 for domestic and international students; for spring admission, 10/1 for domestic and international students. Applications are processed on a rolling basis. *Application fee:* $55. Electronic applications accepted. *Application Contact:* Teresa Ramos, Administrative Analyst, 559-278-3936, Fax: 559-278-4658, E-mail: teresar@csufresno.edu. *Interim Dean,* Dr. Robert G. Dundas, 559-278-3936, Fax: 559-278-7139, E-mail: rdundas@csufresno.edu.

College of Social Sciences Expenses: Contact institution. *Financial support:* Teaching assistantships, career-related internships or fieldwork, Federal Work-Study, scholarships/grants, and unspecified assistantships available. Support available to part-time students. Financial award application deadline: 3/1; financial award applicants required to submit FAFSA. *Program availability:* Part-time, evening/weekend. Offers criminology (MS); history (MA); history teaching (MA); public administration (MPA); social sciences (MA, MPA, MS). *Application deadline:* For fall admission, 5/1 for domestic and international students; for spring admission, 10/1 for domestic and international students. Applications are processed on a rolling basis. *Application fee:* $55. Electronic applications accepted. *Application Contact:* Fabiola Alvarez, Administrative Analyst/Specialist, 559-278-2448, Fax: 559-278-4658. *Interim Dean,* Michelle DenBeste, 559-278-3013, Fax: 559-278-7664.

Craig School of Business Expenses: Contact institution. *Financial support:* Teaching assistantships, career-related internships or fieldwork, Federal Work-Study, scholarships/grants, and unspecified assistantships available. Support available to part-time students. Financial award application deadline: 3/1; financial award applicants required to submit FAFSA. *Program availability:* Part-time, blended/hybrid learning. Offers business (MBA). *Application deadline:* For fall admission, 6/1 for domestic and international students; for spring admission, 11/1 for domestic and international students. Applications are processed on a rolling basis. *Application fee:* $55. Electronic applications accepted. *Dean,* Dr. Robert Harper, 559-278-2482, Fax: 559-278-6931, E-mail: roberth@csufresno.edu.

Jordan College of Agricultural Sciences and Technology Expenses: Contact institution. *Financial support:* Teaching assistantships, career-related internships or fieldwork, Federal Work-Study, and scholarships/grants available. Support available to part-time students. Financial award application deadline: 3/1; financial award applicants required to submit FAFSA. *Program availability:* Part-time, evening/weekend. Offers agricultural sciences and technology (MS); animal science (MS); industrial technology (MS); plant science (MS); viticulture and enology (MS). *Application deadline:* For fall admission, 5/1 for domestic and international students; for spring admission, 10/1 for domestic and international students. Applications are processed on a rolling basis. *Application fee:* $55. Electronic applications accepted. *Dean,* Dr. Sandra J. Witte, 559-278-2061, Fax: 559-278-4496.

Kremen School of Education and Human Development Expenses: Contact institution. *Financial support:* Career-related internships or fieldwork, Federal Work-Study, scholarships/grants, and research awards available. Support available to part-time students. Financial award application deadline: 3/1; financial award applicants required to submit FAFSA. *Program availability:* Part-time, evening/weekend. Offers clinical rehabilitation and mental health counseling (MS); clinical rehabilitation and mental health counseling (MS); education (MA); education and human development (MA, MS, Ed D); educational leadership (MA, Ed D); marriage, family and child counseling (MS); special education (MA); student affairs and college counseling (MS). *Application deadline:* For fall admission, 5/1 for domestic and international students; for spring admission, 10/1 for domestic and international students. Applications are processed on a rolling basis. *Application fee:* $55. Electronic applications accepted. *Application Contact:* Administrative Assistant, 559-278-2448, Fax: 559-278-4658. *Dean,* Dr. Paul Beare, 559-278-0210, Fax: 559-278-0113, E-mail: pbeare@csufresno.edu.

Lyles College of Engineering Expenses: Contact institution. *Financial support:* Teaching assistantships, career-related internships or fieldwork, Federal Work-Study, scholarships/grants, and unspecified assistantships available. Support available to part-time students. Financial award application deadline: 3/1; financial award applicants required to submit FAFSA. *Program availability:* Part-time, evening/weekend. Offers civil and geomatics engineering (MS); computer engineering (MSE); electrical engineering (MSE); engineering (MS, MSE); mechanical engineering (MS). *Application deadline:* For fall admission, 5/1 for domestic and international students; for spring admission, 10/1 for domestic students, 5/1 for international students. Applications are processed on a rolling basis. *Application fee:* $55. Electronic applications accepted. *Dean,* Dr. Ram Nunna, 559-278-2500, Fax: 559-278-4475.

CALIFORNIA STATE UNIVERSITY, FULLERTON, Fullerton, CA 92834-9480

General Information State-supported, coed, comprehensive institution. CGS member. *Enrollment:* 40,235 graduate, professional, and undergraduate students; 2,613 full-time matriculated graduate/professional students (1,659 women), 3,046 part-time matriculated graduate/professional students (1,707 women). *Enrollment by degree level:* 3,984 master's, 884 doctoral, 791 other advanced degrees. *Graduate faculty:* 800 full-time (373 women), 44 part-time/adjunct (21 women). Tuition, state resident: full-time $3369; part-time $1953 per unit. Tuition, nonresident: full-time $3915; part-time $2499 per unit. Tuition and fees vary according to course load, degree level and program. *Graduate housing:* Rooms and/or apartments available on a first-come, first-served basis to single and married students. Typical cost: $13,000 (including board) for single students; $13,000 (including board) for married students. Room and board charges vary according to board plan, campus/location and housing facility selected. Housing application deadline: 6/30. *Student services:* Campus employment opportunities, campus safety program, career counseling, child daycare facilities, exercise/wellness program, free psychological counseling, international student services, low-cost health insurance, multicultural affairs office, services for students with disabilities, teacher training, writing training. *Library facilities:* Pollak Library. *Research affiliation:* U.S. Department of Interior (desert studies), County of Orange (demographic research), Department of Literacy and Reading Education, SchoolsFirst Federal Credit Uniton (creativity and critical thinking), California Office of Historic Preservation and the State Historic Resources Commission (South Central coastal information).

Computer facilities: 2,000 computers available on campus for general student use. A campuswide network can be accessed from student residence rooms and from off campus. Online class registration is available.
Website: http://www.fullerton.edu/

General Application Contact: Admissions/Applications, 657-278-2371, E-mail: admissions@fullerton.edu.

GRADUATE UNITS

Graduate Studies Students: 1,927 full-time (1,116 women), 2,703 part-time (1,364 women); includes 1,939 minority (131 Black or African American, non-Hispanic/Latino; 9 American Indian or Alaska Native, non-Hispanic/Latino; 753 Asian, non-Hispanic/Latino; 930 Hispanic/Latino; 6 Native Hawaiian or other Pacific Islander, non-Hispanic/Latino; 110 Two or more races, non-Hispanic/Latino), 1,081 international. Average age 30. Expenses: Contact institution. *Financial support:* Research assistantships, teaching assistantships, career-related internships or fieldwork, Federal Work-Study, institutionally sponsored loans, and scholarships/grants available. Support available to part-time students. Financial award application deadline: 3/1; financial award applicants required to submit FAFSA. *Program availability:* Part-time, evening/weekend, online learning. *Application deadline:* For fall admission, 3/1 for domestic and international students; for spring admission, 10/1 for domestic and international students. Applications are processed on a rolling basis. *Application fee:* $55. Electronic applications accepted. *Application Contact:* Admissions/Applications, 657-278-2371, Fax: 657-278-2356, E-mail: admissions@fullerton.edu. *Director,* Dr. Katherine Powers, 657-278-2618, E-mail: gradstudiesrecept@fullerton.edu.

College of Business and Economics Expenses: Contact institution. *Financial support:* Career-related internships or fieldwork, Federal Work-Study, institutionally sponsored loans, and scholarships/grants available. Support available to part-time students. Financial award application deadline: 3/1; financial award applicants required to submit FAFSA. *Program availability:* Part-time. Offers accounting (MBA, MS); business administration (MBA); business analytics (MBA); business and economics (MA, MBA, MS); decision science (MBA); economics (MA, MBA); entrepreneurship (MBA); finance (MBA); information systems (MBA, MS); information systems and decision sciences (MS); information systems and e-commerce (MS); information technology (MS); international business (MBA); management (MBA); marketing (MBA); organizational leadership (MBA); risk management and insurance (MBA). *Application deadline:* Applications are processed on a rolling basis. *Application fee:* $55. Electronic applications accepted. *Application Contact:* Admissions/Applications, 657-278-2371. *Interim Dean,* Dr. Morteza Rahmatian, 657-773-2592.

College of Communications Expenses: Contact institution. *Financial support:* Teaching assistantships, career-related internships or fieldwork, Federal Work-Study, institutionally sponsored loans, and scholarships/grants available. Support available to part-time students. Financial award application deadline: 3/1; financial award applicants required to submit FAFSA. *Program availability:* Part-time. Offers communication studies (MA); communications (MA, MFA); communications in tourism and entertainment (MA); communicative disorders (MA); mass communications research and theory (MA); professional communications (MA); screenwriting (MFA). *Application fee:* $55. *Application Contact:* Admissions/Applications, 657-278-2371. *Dean,* Dr. William G. Briggs, 657-278-3355.

College of Education Expenses: Contact institution. *Financial support:* Research assistantships and teaching assistantships available. Financial award application deadline: 3/1; financial award applicants required to submit FAFSA. Offers bilingual/bicultural education (MS); education (MS, Ed D); educational administration (MS); educational leadership (Ed D); educational technology (MS); elementary curriculum and instruction (MS); instructional design and technology (MS); special education (MS); teacher instruction (MS); teaching foundational mathematics (MS). *Application fee:* $55. *Application Contact:* Admissions/Applications, 657-278-2371. *Dean,* Dr. Claire Cavallaro, 657-278-4021.

College of Engineering and Computer Science Expenses: Contact institution. *Financial support:* Career-related internships or fieldwork, Federal Work-Study, institutionally sponsored loans, and scholarships/grants available. Support available to part-time students. Financial award application deadline: 3/1; financial award applicants required to submit FAFSA. *Program availability:* Part-time. Offers civil engineering (MS); computer engineering (MS); computer science (MS); electrical engineering (MS); engineering and computer science (MS); mechanical engineering (MS); software engineering (MS); systems engineering (MS). *Application fee:* $55. *Application Contact:* Admissions/Applications, 657-278-2371. *Dean,* Dr. Raman Unnikrishnan, 657-278-3362.

College of Health and Human Development Expenses: Contact institution. *Financial support:* Career-related internships or fieldwork, Federal Work-Study, institutionally sponsored loans, and scholarships/grants available. Support available to part-time students. Financial award application deadline: 3/1; financial award applicants required to submit FAFSA. *Program availability:* Part-time. Offers aging (MSW); child welfare (MSW); community mental health (MSW); counseling (MS); health and human development (MS, MSW, DNP); kinesiology (MS); leadership (MS); nurse anesthesia (MS); nurse educator (MS); nursing (DNP); school nursing (MS); women's health care (MS). *Application fee:* $55. *Application Contact:* Admissions/Applications, 657-278-2371. *Dean,* Dr. Shari McMahan, 657-278-3311.

College of Humanities and Social Sciences Expenses: Contact institution. *Financial support:* Career-related internships or fieldwork, Federal Work-Study, institutionally sponsored loans, and scholarships/grants available. Support available to part-time students. Financial award application deadline: 3/1; financial award applicants required to submit FAFSA. *Program availability:* Part-time. Offers American studies (MA); anthropology (MA); clinical psychology (MS); English (MA); environmental studies (MS); geography (MA); gerontology (MS); history (MA); humanities and social sciences (MA, MPA, MS); linguistics (MA); political science (MA); psychology (MA); public administration (MPA); sociology (MA); Spanish (MA). *Application fee:* $55. *Application Contact:* Admissions/Applications, 657-278-2371. *Dean,* Dr. Angela Della-Volpe, 657-278-3528.

College of Natural Science and Mathematics Expenses: Contact institution. *Financial support:* Research assistantships, teaching assistantships, career-related internships or fieldwork, Federal Work-Study, institutionally sponsored loans, and scholarships/grants available. Support available to part-time students. Financial award application deadline: 3/1; financial award applicants required to submit FAFSA. *Program availability:* Part-time. Offers applied mathematics (MA); biology (MS); biotechnology (MBT); chemistry (MA, MS); geological sciences (MS); mathematics education (MA); natural science and mathematics (MA, MAT, MBT, MS); physics (MS); teaching science (MAT). *Application fee:* $55. *Application Contact:* Admissions/Applications, 657-278-2371. *Acting Dean,* Dr. Robert Koch, 657-278-2638.

College of the Arts Expenses: Contact institution. *Financial support:* Teaching assistantships, career-related internships or fieldwork, Federal Work-Study, institutionally sponsored loans, and scholarships/grants available. Support available to part-time students. Financial award application deadline: 3/1; financial award applicants required to submit FAFSA. *Program availability:* Part-time. Offers arts (MA, MFA, MM); music education (MA); performance (MM); theatre arts (MFA). *Application fee:* $55. *Director,* Larry M. Timm, 657-278-3511, E-mail: ltimm@fullerton.edu.

CALIFORNIA STATE UNIVERSITY, LONG BEACH, Long Beach, CA 90840

General Information State-supported, coed, comprehensive institution. *Graduate housing:* Room and/or apartments available on a first-come, first-served basis to single students; on-campus housing not available to married students. Housing application deadline: 4/1. *Student services:* Campus employment opportunities, campus safety program, career counseling, child daycare facilities, exercise/wellness program, free psychological counseling, grant writing training, international student services, low-cost health insurance, multicultural affairs office, services for students with disabilities, teacher training, writing training. *Library facilities:* CSULB University Library. *Collection:* Books: 746,820 (physical), 764,807 (digital/electronic); Serial titles: 16,579 (physical), 69,287 (digital/electronic); Databases: 227. Weekly public service hours: 97. *Research affiliation:* Boeing (aerospace engineering and manufacturing).

Computer facilities: 2,000 computers available on campus for general student use. A campuswide network can be accessed from student residence rooms and from off campus. Online class registration is available. Website: http://www.csulb.edu/

General Application Contact: Amy Paulsen, Executive Assistant to the Provost, 562-985-4129, Fax: 562-985-1680, E-mail: amy.paulsen@csulb.edu.

GRADUATE UNITS

Graduate Studies Expenses: Contact institution. *Financial support:* Fellowships, research assistantships, teaching assistantships, career-related internships or fieldwork, Federal Work-Study, institutionally sponsored loans, scholarships/grants, traineeships, tuition waivers (partial), and unspecified assistantships available. Financial award application deadline: 3/2; financial award applicants required to submit FAFSA. *Program availability:* Part-time, evening/weekend, online learning. *Application deadline:* For fall admission, 7/1 for domestic and international students; for spring admission, 12/1 for domestic and international students. Applications are processed on a rolling basis. *Application fee:* $55. Electronic applications accepted. *Application Contact:* Rachel Brophy, Student Programs Coordinator, 562-985-4546, Fax: 562-985-7786, E-mail: rpbrophy@csulb.edu. *Director,* Dr. Cecile Lindsay, 562-985-8225, Fax: 562-985-1680, E-mail: clindsay@csulb.edu.

College of Business Administration Expenses: Contact institution. *Financial support:* Career-related internships or fieldwork and scholarships/grants available. Financial award application deadline: 3/2; financial award applicants required to submit FAFSA. *Program availability:* Part-time, evening/weekend. Offers business administration (MS). *Application deadline:* For fall admission, 3/30 for domestic students. Applications are processed on a rolling basis. *Application fee:* $55. Electronic applications accepted. *Application Contact:* Dr. H. Michael Chung, Director, Graduate Programs and Executive Education, 562-985-5565, Fax: 562-985-5742, E-mail: hmchung@csulb.edu. *Dean,* Dr. Michael E. Solt, 562-985-5307, E-mail: msolt@csulb.edu.

College of Education Expenses: Contact institution. *Financial support:* Federal Work-Study, institutionally sponsored loans, and scholarships/grants available. Financial award application deadline: 3/2. *Program availability:* Part-time, evening/weekend. Offers counseling (MS); education (MA, Ed D); educational administration (MA, Ed D); educational psychology (MA); elementary education (MA); secondary education (MA); special education (MS). *Application deadline:* For fall admission, 3/1 for domestic students. Applications are processed on a rolling basis. *Application fee:* $55. Electronic applications accepted. *Dean,* Shireen Pavri, 562-985-4513, Fax: 562-985-4951.

College of Engineering Expenses: Contact institution. *Financial support:* Research assistantships, teaching assistantships, career-related internships or fieldwork, Federal Work-Study, institutionally sponsored loans, scholarships/grants, and unspecified assistantships available. Financial award application deadline: 3/2. *Program availability:* Part-time, evening/weekend. Offers aerospace engineering (MSAE); civil engineering (MSCE); computer engineering (MSCS); computer science (MSCS); electrical engineering (MSEE); engineering (MS, MSAE, MSCE, MSCS, MSE, MSEE, MSME, PhD); engineering and industrial applied mathematics (PhD); interdisciplinary engineering (MSE); management engineering (MSE); mechanical engineering (MSME). *Application deadline:* For fall admission, 4/20 for domestic students. *Application fee:* $55. Electronic applications accepted. *Application Contact:* Dr. Sandra Cynar, Special Assistant to the Dean for Outreach, 562-985-1512, Fax: 562-985-7561, E-mail: cynar@csulb.edu. *Dean,* Dr. Forouzan Golshani, 562-985-5123, Fax: 562-985-7561, E-mail: coe-dean@csulb.edu.

College of Health and Human Services Expenses: Contact institution. *Financial support:* Fellowships, research assistantships, teaching assistantships, career-related internships or fieldwork, Federal Work-Study, institutionally sponsored loans, and scholarships/grants available. Financial award application deadline: 3/2; financial award applicants required to submit FAFSA. *Program availability:* Part-time, evening/weekend, online learning. Offers adapted physical education (MA); coaching and student athlete development (MA); criminal justice (MS); emergency services administration (MS); exercise physiology and nutrition (MS); exercise science (MS); gerontology (MS); health and human services (MA, MPA, MPH, MS, MSN, MSW, DNP, DPT, Graduate Certificate); health care administration (MS); health science (MPH); individualized studies (MA); kinesiology (MA); nursing (MSN, DNP, Graduate Certificate); pedagogical studies (MA); physical therapy (DPT); public policy and administration (MPA, Graduate Certificate); recreation administration (MS); social work (MSW); sport and exercise psychology (MS); sport management (MA); sports medicine and injury studies (MS). *Application deadline:* For fall admission, 7/1 for domestic students; for spring admission, 12/1 for domestic students. Applications are processed on a rolling basis. *Application fee:* $55. Electronic applications accepted. *Dean,* Monica Lounsbery.

College of Liberal Arts Expenses: Contact institution. *Financial support:* Research assistantships, teaching assistantships, career-related internships or fieldwork, Federal Work-Study, institutionally sponsored loans, and scholarships/grants available. Financial award application deadline: 3/2. *Program availability:* Part-time, evening/weekend. Offers Africa and the Middle East (MA); anthropology (MA); applied anthropology (MA); Asian studies (MA); communication studies (MA); creative writing (MFA); economics (MA); English (MA); French and Francophone studies (MA); general linguistics (MA); geography (MA, MS); German (MA); human factors (MS); industrial/organizational psychology (MS); language and culture (MA); liberal arts (MA, MFA, MS, Graduate Certificate); philosophy (MA); political science (MA); psychology (MA); religious studies (MA); Spanish (MA); special concentration (MA); teaching English to speakers of other languages (MA, Graduate Certificate). *Application deadline:* For fall admission, 7/1 for domestic and international students; for spring admission, 12/1 for international students. Applications are processed on a rolling basis. *Application fee:* $55. Electronic applications accepted. *Dean,* David Wallace, 562-985-5381, Fax: 562-985-2463.

College of Natural Sciences and Mathematics Expenses: Contact institution. *Financial support:* Research assistantships, teaching assistantships, Federal Work-Study, institutionally sponsored loans, scholarships/grants, traineeships, and unspecified assistantships available. Financial award application deadline: 3/2. *Program availability:* Part-time. Offers biochemistry (MS); biology (MS); chemistry (MS); geology (MS); mathematics (MS); microbiology (MS); natural sciences and mathematics (MS); physics (MS); science education (MS). *Application deadline:* For fall admission, 7/1 for domestic students. Applications are processed on a rolling basis. *Application fee:* $55. Electronic applications accepted. *Application Contact:* Dr. Henry Fung, Associate Dean for Curriculum and Instruction, 562-985-7898, Fax: 562-985-2315, E-mail: hcfung@csulb.edu. *Dean,* Dr. Laura Kingsford, 562-985-4707, Fax: 562-985-2315, E-mail: lking@csulb.edu.

College of the Arts Expenses: Contact institution. *Financial support:* Research assistantships, teaching assistantships, Federal Work-Study, institutionally sponsored loans, scholarships/grants, and traineeships available. Financial award application deadline: 3/2. *Program availability:* Part-time. Offers acting (MFA); art education (MA); arts (MA, MFA, MM); composition (MM); dance (MA, MFA); music (MA); studio art (MFA). *Application deadline:* For fall admission, 1/31 for domestic students. Applications are processed on a rolling basis. *Application fee:* $55. Electronic applications accepted. *Application Contact:* Rachel Brophy, Student Programs Coordinator, 562-985-4546, Fax: 562-985-7786, E-mail: rpbrophy@csulb.edu. *Dean,* Donald Para, 562-985-4366, Fax: 562-985-7883, E-mail: cota@csulb.edu.

CALIFORNIA STATE UNIVERSITY, LOS ANGELES, Los Angeles, CA 90032-8530

General Information State-supported, coed, comprehensive institution. CGS member. *Graduate housing:* Room and/or apartments available on a first-come, first-served basis to single students; on-campus housing not available to married students. *Research affiliation:* NASA (engineering), General Motors (engineering).

GRADUATE UNITS

Graduate Studies *Program availability:* Part-time, evening/weekend. Electronic applications accepted.

Charter College of Education *Program availability:* Part-time, evening/weekend. Offers applied and advanced studies in education (Graduate Certificate); counseling (MS); education (MA, MS, Ed D, PhD, Graduate Certificate); elementary teaching (MA); special education (MA, PhD). Electronic applications accepted.

College of Arts and Letters *Program availability:* Part-time, evening/weekend. Offers art (MA); arts and letters (MA, MFA, MM, Certificate, Graduate Certificate); communication studies (MA, MFA); English (MA, Certificate); fine arts (MFA); French (MA); music composition (MM); music education (MA); musicology (MA); performance (MM); philosophy (MA, Graduate Certificate); Spanish (MA); theater arts (MA). Electronic applications accepted.

College of Business and Economics *Program availability:* Part-time, evening/weekend. Offers accounting (MBA); business and economics (MA, MBA, MS, Postbaccalaureate Certificate); finance and banking (MBA, MS); financial economics (MA); global economics (MA); health care management (MS); international business (MBA, MS); management (MBA, MS). Electronic applications accepted.

College of Engineering, Computer Science, and Technology *Program availability:* Part-time, evening/weekend. Offers civil engineering (MS); computer science (MS); electrical engineering (MS); engineering, computer science, and technology (MA, MS); industrial and technical studies (MA); mechanical engineering (MS). Electronic applications accepted.

College of Health and Human Services *Program availability:* Part-time, evening/weekend. Offers child development (MA); criminal justice (MS); criminalistics (MS); health and human services (MA, MS, MSW, Certificate, Post Master's Certificate); nursing (MS, Post Master's Certificate); nutritional science (MS); physical education and kinesiology (MA); social work (MSW); speech and hearing (MA); speech-language pathology (MA). Electronic applications accepted.

College of Natural and Social Sciences *Program availability:* Part-time, evening/weekend. Offers analytical chemistry (MS); anthropology (MA); biology (MS); geography (MA); geological sciences (MS); history (MA); Latin American studies (MA); mathematics (MS); Mexican-American studies (MA); natural and social sciences (MA, MS); physics (MS); political science (MA); psychology (MA, MS); public administration (MS); sociology (MA).

CALIFORNIA STATE UNIVERSITY MARITIME ACADEMY, Vallejo, CA 94590

General Information State-supported, coed, comprehensive institution. *Enrollment:* 1,150 graduate, professional, and undergraduate students; 49 full-time matriculated graduate/professional students (10 women). *Enrollment by degree level:* 49 master's. *Graduate faculty:* 16 part-time/adjunct (2 women). *Graduate housing:* On-campus housing not available. *Student services:* Career counseling, services for students with disabilities.

Computer facilities: 75 computers available on campus for general student use. A campuswide network can be accessed from student residence rooms and from off campus. Online class registration is available.
Website: http://www.csum.edu/

General Application Contact: Kathy Arnold, Graduate Program Coordinator, 707-654-1271, Fax: 707-654-1158, E-mail: karnold@csum.edu.

GRADUATE UNITS

Graduate Studies Students: 49 full-time (10 women); includes 11 minority (2 Black or African American, non-Hispanic/Latino; 5 Asian, non-Hispanic/Latino; 2 Hispanic/Latino; 2 Native Hawaiian or other Pacific Islander, non-Hispanic/Latino; 1 international. Average age 32. 29 applicants, 93% accepted, 26 enrolled. *Faculty:* 16 part-time/adjunct (2 women). Expenses: Contact institution. *Financial support:* Applicants required to submit FAFSA. In 2016, 24 master's awarded. *Program availability:* Evening/weekend, online only, 100% online. Offers transportation and engineering management (MS). *Application deadline:* Applications are processed on a rolling basis. *Application fee:* $55. Electronic applications accepted. *Application Contact:* Kathy Arnold, Program Coordinator, 707-654-1271, Fax: 707-654-1158, E-mail: karnold@csum.edu. *Dean, Graduate Studies,* Dr. Jim Burns.

CALIFORNIA STATE UNIVERSITY, MONTEREY BAY, Seaside, CA 93955-8001

General Information State-supported, coed, comprehensive institution. *Graduate housing:* Rooms and/or apartments available on a first-come, first-served basis to single and married students.

GRADUATE UNITS

College of Business *Program availability:* Part-time, evening/weekend, online learning. Offers business (MBA). Electronic applications accepted.

College of Education *Program availability:* Part-time, evening/weekend. Offers education (MAE). Electronic applications accepted.

College of Health Sciences and Human Services *Program availability:* Part-time. Offers social work (MSW). Electronic applications accepted.

College of Science *Program availability:* Part-time. Offers applied marine and watershed science (MS); marine science (MS); science (MS, MSMIT). Electronic applications accepted.

School of Computing and Design Offers computing and design (MS, MSMIT). MSMIT offered in conjunction with College of Business. Electronic applications accepted.

CALIFORNIA STATE UNIVERSITY, NORTHRIDGE, Northridge, CA 91330

General Information State-supported, coed, comprehensive institution. CGS member. *Enrollment:* 39,916 graduate, professional, and undergraduate students; 1,773 full-time matriculated graduate/professional students (1,135 women), 1,536 part-time matriculated graduate/professional students (910 women). *Enrollment by degree level:* 3,175 master's, 134 doctoral. *Graduate faculty:* 762 full-time (375 women), 1,588 part-time/adjunct (781 women). *Tuition,* state resident: full-time $4152. *Graduate housing:* Room and/or apartments available to single students; on-campus housing not available to married students. *Student services:* Campus employment opportunities, campus safety program, career counseling, child daycare facilities, free psychological counseling, international student services, low-cost health insurance, multicultural affairs office, services for students with disabilities, teacher training. *Library facilities:* Oviatt Library plus 1 other. *Collection:* Students can reserve study rooms. *Research affiliation:* Haagen Company (archaeology), Northridge Hospital (biology), Warner Center Institute (child care), Jet Propulsion Laboratory (engineering), Hughes Aircraft Corporation (engineering), California Institute of Technology (science).

Computer facilities: A campuswide network can be accessed from student residence rooms and from off campus. Online class registration is available.
Website: http://www.csun.edu/

General Application Contact: Dr. Crist Khachikian, Associate Vice President, 818-677-2138.

GRADUATE UNITS

Graduate Studies Students: 1,773 full-time (1,135 women), 1,536 part-time (910 women); includes 1,467 minority (111 Black or African American, non-Hispanic/Latino; 8 American Indian or Alaska Native, non-Hispanic/Latino; 284 Asian, non-Hispanic/Latino; 944 Hispanic/Latino; 6 Native Hawaiian or other Pacific Islander, non-Hispanic/Latino; 114 Two or more races, non-Hispanic/Latino), 462 international. Average age 30. 5,460 applicants, 40% accepted, 1124 enrolled. *Faculty:* 762 full-time (375 women), 1,588 part-time/adjunct (781 women). Expenses: Contact institution. *Financial support:* Fellowships, research assistantships, teaching assistantships, career-related internships or fieldwork, Federal Work-Study, institutionally sponsored loans, scholarships/grants, tuition waivers (partial), and unspecified assistantships available. Support available to part-time students. Financial award applicants required to submit FAFSA. In 2016, 1,962 master's awarded. *Program availability:* Part-time, evening/weekend. *Application deadline:* For fall admission, 3/31 for domestic students; for spring admission, 10/31 for domestic students. Applications are processed on a rolling basis. *Application fee:* $55. *Application Contact:* 818-677-3755. *Associate Vice President,* Dr. Crist Khachikian, 818-677-2138.

College of Arts, Media, and Communication Students: 128 full-time (74 women), 91 part-time (52 women); includes 74 minority (7 Black or African American, non-Hispanic/Latino; 2 American Indian or Alaska Native, non-Hispanic/Latino; 10 Asian, non-Hispanic/Latino; 38 Hispanic/Latino; 2 Native Hawaiian or other Pacific Islander, non-Hispanic/Latino; 15 Two or more races, non-Hispanic/Latino), 42 international. Average age 31. 365 applicants, 41% accepted, 81 enrolled. *Faculty:* 102 full-time (47 women), 275 part-time/adjunct (128 women). Expenses: Contact institution. *Financial support:* Teaching assistantships, career-related internships or fieldwork, Federal Work-Study, and unspecified assistantships available. Support available to part-time students. Financial award application deadline: 3/1. *Program availability:* Part-time, evening/weekend. Offers art education (MA); art history (MA); arts, media, and communication (MA, MFA, MM); communication studies (MA); composition (MM); conducting (MM); mass communication (MA); music education (MA); performance (MM); screenwriting (MM); studio art (MA, MFA); theatre (MA); visual communications (MA, MFA). *Application deadline:* For fall admission, 11/30 for domestic students. *Application fee:* $55. *Interim Dean,* Dan Hosken, 818-677-2246, E-mail: dan.hosken@csun.edu.

College of Business and Economics Students: 49 full-time (26 women), 94 part-time (50 women); includes 59 minority (6 Black or African American, non-Hispanic/Latino; 29 Asian, non-Hispanic/Latino; 19 Hispanic/Latino; 5 Two or more races, non-Hispanic/Latino), 12 international. Average age 32. 401 applicants, 31% accepted, 59 enrolled. Expenses: Contact institution. *Financial support:* Teaching assistantships and Federal Work-Study available. Support available to part-time students. Financial award application deadline: 3/1. *Program availability:* Part-time. Offers business and economics (MBA). *Application deadline:* For fall admission, 11/30 for domestic students. *Application fee:* $55. *Application Contact:* Dr. Deborah Heisley, Director of Graduate Programs, 818-677-2467, E-mail: deborah.heisley@csun.edu. *Dean,* Dr. Kenneth Lord, 818-677-2455.

College of Engineering and Computer Science Students: 281 full-time (65 women), 273 part-time (47 women); includes 54 minority (2 Black or African American, non-Hispanic/Latino; 1 American Indian or Alaska Native, non-Hispanic/Latino; 42 Asian, non-Hispanic/Latino; 1 Native Hawaiian or other Pacific Islander, non-Hispanic/Latino; 8 Two or more races, non-Hispanic/Latino), 286 international. Average age 28. 1,195 applicants, 29% accepted, 145 enrolled. *Faculty:* 64 full-time (14 women), 108 part-time/adjunct (18 women). Expenses: Contact institution. *Financial support:* Teaching assistantships, career-related internships or fieldwork, and Federal Work-Study available. Support available to part-time students. Financial award application deadline: 3/1. *Program availability:* Part-time, evening/weekend. Offers computer science (MS); electrical engineering (MS); engineering (MS); engineering and computer science (MS); engineering automation (MS); engineering management (MS); manufacturing systems engineering (MS); materials engineering (MS); mechanical engineering (MS); software engineering (MS). *Application deadline:* For fall admission, 11/30 for domestic students. *Application fee:* $55. *Dean,* Dr. S. K. Ramesh, 818-677-4501, E-mail: s.ramesh@csun.edu.

College of Health and Human Development Students: 434 full-time (327 women), 214 part-time (164 women); includes 317 minority (27 Black or African American, non-Hispanic/Latino; 1 American Indian or Alaska Native, non-Hispanic/Latino; 83 Asian, non-Hispanic/Latino; 172 Hispanic/Latino; 4 Native Hawaiian or other Pacific Islander, non-Hispanic/Latino; 30 Two or more races, non-Hispanic/Latino; 47 international. Average age 29. 850 applicants, 34% accepted, 179 enrolled. *Faculty:* 106 full-time (72 women), 258 part-time/adjunct (162 women). Expenses: Contact institution. *Financial support:* Teaching assistantships, career-related internships or fieldwork, Federal Work-Study, and institutionally sponsored loans available. Support available to part-time students. Financial award application deadline: 3/1. *Program availability:* Part-time, evening/weekend. Offers audiology (MS); environmental and occupational health (MS); family and consumer sciences (MS); health administration (MS); health and human development (MPH, MPT, MS); hospitality and tourism (MS); industrial hygiene (MS); kinesiology (MS); physical therapy (MPT); public health (MPH); recreational sport management/campus recreation (MS); speech language pathology (MS). *Application deadline:* For fall admission, 11/30 for domestic students. *Application fee:* $55. *Application Contact:* 818-677-3755. *Dean,* Farrell J. Webb, 818-677-3001.

College of Humanities Students: 97 full-time (62 women), 121 part-time (83 women); includes 107 minority (4 Black or African American, non-Hispanic/Latino; 1 American Indian or Alaska Native, non-Hispanic/Latino; 12 Asian, non-Hispanic/Latino; 84 Hispanic/Latino; 6 Two or more races, non-Hispanic/Latino; 17 international. Average age 33. 174 applicants, 74% accepted, 68 enrolled. *Faculty:* 113 full-time (66 women), 243 part-time/adjunct (147 women). Expenses: Contact institution. *Financial support:* Teaching assistantships and Federal Work-Study available. Support available to part-time students. Financial award application deadline: 3/1. *Program availability:* Part-time, evening/weekend. Offers Chicana and Chicano studies (MA); creative writing (MA); humanities (MA); linguistics (MA); literature (MA); rhetoric and composition theory (MA); Spanish (MA). *Application deadline:* For fall admission, 11/30 for domestic students. *Application fee:* $55. *Dean,* Dr. Elizabeth Say, 818-677-3301.

College of Science and Mathematics Students: 66 full-time (31 women), 149 part-time (59 women); includes 80 minority (5 Black or African American, non-Hispanic/Latino; 1 American Indian or Alaska Native, non-Hispanic/Latino; 27 Asian, non-Hispanic/Latino; 42 Hispanic/Latino; 5 Two or more races, non-Hispanic/Latino; 17 international. Average age 28. 242 applicants, 45% accepted, 75 enrolled. *Faculty:* 114 full-time (37 women), 255 part-time/adjunct (105 women). Expenses: Contact institution. *Financial support:* Research assistantships, teaching assistantships, Federal Work-Study, institutionally sponsored loans, tuition waivers (partial), and unspecified assistantships available. Support available to part-time students. Financial award applicants required to submit FAFSA. *Program availability:* Part-time, evening/weekend. Offers applied mathematics (MS); biochemistry (MS); biology (MS); chemistry (MS); geology (MS); mathematics (MS); physics (MS); science and mathematics (MS). *Application fee:* $55. *Dean,* Dr. Jerry Stinner, 818-677-2004, E-mail: jerry.stinner@csun.edu.

College of Social and Behavioral Sciences Students: 349 full-time (258 women), 128 part-time (83 women); includes 295 minority (33 Black or African American, non-Hispanic/Latino; 1 American Indian or Alaska Native, non-Hispanic/Latino; 32 Asian, non-Hispanic/Latino; 215 Hispanic/Latino; 14 Two or more races, non-Hispanic/Latino; 15 international. Average age 30. 4,193 applicants, 16% accepted, 198 enrolled. *Faculty:* 125 full-time (67 women), 135 part-time/adjunct (66 women). Expenses: Contact institution. *Financial support:* Teaching assistantships, career-related internships or fieldwork, Federal Work-Study, and institutionally sponsored loans available. Support available to part-time students. Financial award application deadline: 3/1. *Program availability:* Part-time, evening/weekend. Offers clinical psychology (MA); general anthropology (MA); general experimental psychology (MA); geography (MA); history (MA); political science (MA); public archaeology (MA); social and behavioral sciences (MA, MSW); social work (MSW); sociology (MA). *Application deadline:* For fall admission, 11/30 for domestic students. *Application fee:* $55. *Dean,* Dr. Stella Z. Theodoulou, 818-677-3317.

Michael D. Eisner College of Education Students: 368 full-time (291 women), 465 part-time (371 women); includes 430 minority (27 Black or African American, non-Hispanic/Latino; 1 American Indian or Alaska Native, non-Hispanic/Latino; 49 Asian, non-Hispanic/Latino; 321 Hispanic/Latino; 1 Native Hawaiian or other Pacific Islander, non-Hispanic/Latino; 31 Two or more races, non-Hispanic/Latino; 26 international. Average age 33. 948 applicants, 53% accepted, 319 enrolled. *Faculty:* 65 full-time (46 women), 176 part-time/adjunct (104 women). Expenses: Contact institution. *Financial support:* Fellowships, career-related internships or fieldwork, Federal Work-Study, institutionally sponsored loans, scholarships/grants, and tuition waivers (partial) available. Support available to part-time students. Financial award application deadline: 3/1. *Program availability:* Part-time, evening/weekend. Offers counseling (MS); curriculum and instruction (MA); early childhood special education (MA); education (MA, MA Ed, MS, Ed D); education of the deaf and hard of hearing (MA); educational administration (MA); educational leadership (Ed D); educational psychology (MA Ed); educational technology (MA); educational therapy (MA); English education (MA); language and literacy (MA); mathematics education (MA); mild/moderate disabilities (MA); moderate/severe disabilities (MA); multilingual/multicultural education (MA); secondary science education (MA); teaching and learning (MA). *Application deadline:* For fall admission, 11/30 for domestic students. *Application fee:* $55. *Dean,* Dr. Michael E. Spagna, 818-677-2590.

The Tseng College of Extended Learning Students: 1 (woman) full-time, 1 (woman) part-time. Average age 40. *Faculty:* 55 part-time/adjunct (28 women). Expenses: Contact institution. Offers business administration (Graduate Certificate); health administration (MPA); health education (MPH); knowledge management (MKM); music industry administration (MA); nonprofit-sector management (Graduate Certificate); public administration (MPA); public sector management and leadership (MPA); social work (MSW); taxation (MS); tourism, hospitality and recreation management (MS). *Dean,* Joyce Feucht-Haviar, 866-873-6439.

CALIFORNIA STATE UNIVERSITY, SACRAMENTO, Sacramento, CA 95819

General Information State-supported, coed, comprehensive institution. CGS member. *Enrollment:* 30,510 graduate, professional, and undergraduate students; 1,409 full-time matriculated graduate/professional students (966 women), 1,022 part-time matriculated graduate/professional students (577 women). *Enrollment by degree level:* 2,291 master's, 140 doctoral. Tuition and fees vary according to degree level and program. *Graduate housing:* Room and/or apartments available on a first-come, first-served basis to single students; on-campus housing not available to married students. *Student services:* Campus employment opportunities, career counseling, child daycare facilities, free psychological counseling, grant writing training, international student services, low-cost health insurance, multicultural affairs office, services for students with disabilities, teacher training, writing training. *Library facilities:* California State University, Sacramento Library.

Computer facilities: Computer purchase and lease plans are available. A campuswide network can be accessed from student residence rooms and from off campus. Online class registration, online transcripts are available. Website: http://www.csus.edu/

General Application Contact: Dr. Chevelle Newsome, Dean of Graduate Admissions, 916-278-6470, Fax: 916-278-5669, E-mail: cnewsome@skymail.csus.edu.

GRADUATE UNITS

Office of Graduate Studies Expenses: Contact institution. *Financial support:* Research assistantships, teaching assistantships, career-related internships or fieldwork, and Federal Work-Study available. Support available to part-time students. Financial award application deadline: 3/1; financial award applicants required to submit FAFSA. *Program availability:* Part-time, evening/weekend. *Application deadline:* For fall admission, 3/1 for international students; for spring admission, 9/30 for international students. Applications are processed on a rolling basis. *Application fee:* $55. Electronic applications accepted. *Application Contact:* Jose Martinez, Graduate Admissions Supervisor, 916-278-7871, E-mail: martinj@skymail.csus.edu. *Dean,* Dr. Chevelle Newsome, 916-248-2738, E-mail: cnewsome@csus.edu.

College of Arts and Letters Students: 93 full-time (53 women), 141 part-time (85 women); includes 78 minority (12 Black or African American, non-Hispanic/Latino; 1 American Indian or Alaska Native, non-Hispanic/Latino; 19 Asian, non-Hispanic/Latino; 44 Hispanic/Latino; 2 Native Hawaiian or other Pacific Islander, non-Hispanic/Latino). Average age 31. Expenses: Contact institution. *Financial support:* Research assistantships, teaching assistantships, career-related internships or fieldwork, and Federal Work-Study available. Support available to part-time students. Financial award applicants required to submit FAFSA. In 2016, 87 master's awarded. *Program availability:* Part-time, evening/weekend. Offers arts and letters (MA, MM, PhD); communication studies (MA); composition (MA); creative writing (MA); history (MA); literature (MA); music (MM); public historical studies (PhD); public history (MA); studio art (MA); teaching English to speakers of other languages (MA); world languages and literatures (MA). *Application deadline:* For fall admission, 3/1 for domestic students, 2/1 for international students; for spring admission, 9/15 for domestic students, 8/15 for international students. Applications are processed on a rolling basis. *Application fee:* $55. Electronic applications accepted. *Application Contact:* Jose Martinez, Graduate Admissions Supervisor, 916-278-7871, E-mail: martinj@skymail.csus.edu. *Dean,* Dr. Sheree Meyer, 916-278-6502.

College of Business Administration Students: 138 full-time (68 women), 129 part-time (63 women); includes 211 minority (12 Black or African American, non-Hispanic/Latino; 132 American Indian or Alaska Native, non-Hispanic/Latino; 63 Asian, non-Hispanic/Latino; 4 Native Hawaiian or other Pacific Islander, non-Hispanic/Latino). Average age 34. 198 applicants, 77% accepted, 85 enrolled. Expenses: Contact institution. *Financial support:* Research assistantships, teaching assistantships, career-related internships or fieldwork, and Federal Work-Study available. Support available to part-time students. Financial award applicants required to submit FAFSA. In 2016, 168 master's awarded. *Program availability:* Part-time, evening/weekend. Offers accountancy (MS); business administration (IMBA, MBA); human resources (MBA); urban land development (MBA). *Application deadline:* For fall admission, 2/1 for domestic students, 3/1 for international students; for spring admission, 9/15 for domestic students, 9/30 for international students. Applications are processed on a rolling basis. *Application fee:* $55. Electronic applications accepted. *Application Contact:* Jose Martinez, Graduate Admissions Supervisor, 916-278-7871, E-mail: martinj@skymail.csus.edu. *Dean,* Dr. Pierre A. Balthazard, 916-278-6578, Fax: 916-278-5793, E-mail: cba@csus.edu.

College of Education Students: 429 full-time (297 women), 179 part-time (102 women); includes 368 minority (41 Black or African American, non-Hispanic/Latino; 3 American Indian or Alaska Native, non-Hispanic/Latino; 176 Asian, non-Hispanic/Latino; 142 Hispanic/Latino; 6 Native Hawaiian or other Pacific Islander, non-Hispanic/Latino). Average age 32. 540 applicants, 80% accepted, 250 enrolled. Expenses: Contact institution. *Financial support:* Research assistantships, teaching assistantships, career-related internships or fieldwork, and Federal Work-Study available. Support available to part-time students. Financial award application deadline: 3/1; financial award applicants required to submit FAFSA. In 2016, 107 master's, 7 doctorates awarded. *Program availability:* Part-time. Offers child development (MA); counseling (MS); curriculum and instruction (MA); education (MA, MS, Ed D); education leadership and policy studies (MA); educational technology (MA); gender equity (MA); language and literacy (MA); multicultural education (MA); school psychology (MA); special education (MA); workforce development advocacy (MA). *Application deadline:* Applications are processed on a rolling basis. *Application fee:* $55. Electronic applications accepted. *Application Contact:* Jose Martinez, Graduate Admissions Supervisor, 916-278-7871, E-mail: martinj@skymail.csus.edu. *Dean,* Dr. Alexander Sidorkin, 916-278-6639, E-mail: sidorkin@csus.edu.

College of Engineering and Computer Science Students: 161 full-time (54 women), 206 part-time (55 women); includes 273 minority (18 Black or African American, non-Hispanic/Latino; 1 American Indian or Alaska Native, non-Hispanic/Latino; 224 Asian, non-Hispanic/Latino; 29 Hispanic/Latino; 1 Native Hawaiian or other Pacific Islander, non-Hispanic/Latino). Average age 28. 661 applicants, 72% accepted, 139 enrolled. Expenses: Contact institution. *Financial support:* Research assistantships, teaching assistantships, career-related internships or fieldwork, and Federal Work-Study available. Support available to part-time students. Financial award application deadline: 3/1; financial award applicants required to submit FAFSA. In 2016, 95 master's awarded. *Program availability:* Part-time, evening/weekend. Offers civil engineering (MS); computer science (MS); electrical and electronic engineering (MS); engineering and computer science (MS); mechanical engineering (MS); software engineering (MS). *Application deadline:* Applications are processed on a rolling basis. *Application fee:* $55. Electronic applications accepted. *Application Contact:* Jose Martinez, Graduate Admissions Supervisor, 916-278-7871, E-mail: martinj@skymail.csus.edu. *Dean,* Dr. Lorenzo M. Smith, 916-278-6127, Fax: 916-278-5949, E-mail: lsmith@csus.edu.

College of Health and Human Services Students: 497 full-time (408 women), 214 part-time (170 women); includes 259 minority (40 Black or African American, non-Hispanic/Latino; 6 American Indian or Alaska Native, non-Hispanic/Latino; 93 Asian, non-Hispanic/Latino; 115 Hispanic/Latino; 5 Native Hawaiian or other Pacific Islander, non-Hispanic/Latino). Average age 32. 102 applicants, 47% accepted, 42 enrolled. Expenses: Contact institution. *Financial support:* Research assistantships, teaching assistantships, career-related internships or fieldwork, and Federal Work-Study available. Support available to part-time students. Financial award application deadline: 3/1; financial award applicants required to submit FAFSA. In 2016, 218 master's, 30 doctorates awarded. *Program availability:* Part-time. Offers communication sciences and disorders (MS); criminal justice (MS); family and children's services (MSW); health and human services (MS, MSW, DPT); kinesiology and health science (MS); nursing (MS); physical therapy (DPT); recreation, parks and tourism administration (MS). *Application deadline:* Applications are processed on a rolling basis. *Application fee:* $55. Electronic applications accepted. *Application Contact:* Jose Martinez, Graduate Admissions Supervisor, 916-278-7871, E-mail: martinj@skymail.csus.edu. *Dean,* Dr. Fred Baldini, 916-278-7255, Fax: 916-278-7421, E-mail: baldinif@csus.edu.

College of Natural Sciences and Mathematics Students: 30 full-time (16 women), 84 part-time (39 women); includes 35 minority (4 Black or African American, non-Hispanic/Latino; 3 American Indian or Alaska Native, non-Hispanic/Latino; 19 Asian, non-Hispanic/Latino; 9 Hispanic/Latino). Average age 31. 136 applicants, 63% accepted, 56 enrolled. Expenses: Contact institution. *Financial support:* Research assistantships, teaching assistantships, career-related internships or fieldwork, and Federal Work-Study available. Support available to part-time students. Financial award application deadline: 3/1; financial award applicants required to submit FAFSA. In 2016, 22 master's awarded. *Program availability:* Part-time. Offers biochemistry (MS); biological conservation (MS); chemistry (MS); mathematics (MA); molecular and cellular biology (MS); natural sciences and mathematics (MA, MS); stem cell (MA). *Application deadline:* Applications are processed on a rolling basis. *Application fee:* $55. Electronic applications accepted. *Application Contact:* Jose Martinez, Graduate Admissions Supervisor, 916-278-7871, E-mail: martinj@skymail.csus.edu. *Dean,* Dr. Jill Trainer, 916-278-4655, E-mail: jill.trainer@csus.edu.

College of Social Sciences and Interdisciplinary Studies Students: 50 full-time (30 women), 149 part-time (85 women); includes 70 minority (12 Black or African American, non-Hispanic/Latino; 2 American Indian or Alaska Native, non-Hispanic/Latino; 19 Asian, non-Hispanic/Latino; 34 Hispanic/Latino; 3 Native Hawaiian or other Pacific Islander, non-Hispanic/Latino). Average age 30. 213 applicants, 52% accepted, 86 enrolled. Expenses: Contact institution. *Financial support:* Teaching assistantships, career-related internships or fieldwork, and Federal Work-Study available. Support available to part-time students. Financial award application deadline: 3/1; financial award applicants required to submit FAFSA. In 2016, 39 master's awarded. *Program availability:* Part-time. Offers anthropology (MA); applied behavior analysis (MA); counseling psychology (MA); government (MA); industrial/organizational psychology (MA); public policy and administration (MPPA); social sciences and interdisciplinary studies (MA, MPPA); sociology (MA). *Application deadline:* Applications are processed on a rolling basis. *Application fee:* $55. Electronic applications accepted. *Application Contact:* Jose Martinez, Graduate Admissions Supervisor, 916-278-7871, E-mail: martinj@skymail.csus.edu. *Dean,* Dr. Orn Bodvarsson, 916-278-6504, Fax: 916-278-4678, E-mail: obbodvarsson@csus.edu.

CALIFORNIA STATE UNIVERSITY, SAN BERNARDINO, San Bernardino, CA 92407

General Information State-supported, coed, comprehensive institution. CGS member. *Enrollment:* 20,767 graduate, professional, and undergraduate students; 752 full-time matriculated graduate/professional students (521 women), 1,110 part-time matriculated graduate/professional students (658 women). *Enrollment by degree level:* 1,783 master's, 79 doctoral. *Graduate faculty:* 160 full-time (77 women), 80 part-time/adjunct (49 women). Tuition, state resident: full-time $7843; part-time $5011.20 per year. Tuition and fees vary according to course load, degree level, program and reciprocity agreements. *Graduate housing:* Room and/or apartments available on a first-come, first-served basis to single students; on-campus housing not available to married students. *Student services:* Campus employment opportunities, campus safety program, career counseling, child daycare facilities, exercise/wellness program, free psychological counseling, international student services, low-cost health insurance, multicultural affairs office, services for students with disabilities, teacher training. *Library facilities:* Pfau Library.

Computer facilities: Computer purchase and lease plans are available. A campuswide network can be accessed from student residence rooms and from off campus. Online class registration is available.
Website: http://www.csusb.edu/

General Application Contact: Dr. Francisca Beer, Dean of Graduate Studies, 909-537-5058, Fax: 909-537-5078, E-mail: fbeer@csusb.edu.

GRADUATE UNITS

Graduate Studies Students: 752 full-time (521 women), 1,110 part-time (658 women); includes 1,036 minority (143 Black or African American, non-Hispanic/Latino; 7 American Indian or Alaska Native, non-Hispanic/Latino; 93 Asian, non-Hispanic/Latino; 736 Hispanic/Latino; 3 Native Hawaiian or other Pacific Islander, non-Hispanic/Latino; 54 Two or more races, non-Hispanic/Latino), 202 international. 1,879 applicants, 49% accepted, 627 enrolled. *Faculty:* 160 full-time (77 women), 80 part-time/adjunct (49 women). Expenses: Contact institution. In 2016, 834 master's, 3 doctorates awarded. *Program availability:* Part-time, evening/weekend. Offers integrative studies (MA). *Application deadline:* For fall admission, 7/17 for domestic students. *Application fee:* $55. *Application Contact:* Olivia Rosas, Director of Admissions, 909-537-7577, Fax: 909-537-7034, E-mail: orosas@csusb.edu. *Dean,* Dr. Francisca Beer, 909-537-5058, Fax: 909-537-5078, E-mail: fbeer@csusb.edu.

College of Arts and Letters Students: 42 full-time (29 women), 101 part-time (72 women); includes 81 minority (11 Black or African American, non-Hispanic/Latino; 3 Asian, non-Hispanic/Latino; 62 Hispanic/Latino; 5 Two or more races, non-Hispanic/Latino), 10 international. 83 applicants, 64% accepted, 45 enrolled. *Faculty:* 21 full-time (15 women). Expenses: Contact institution. *Financial support:* Application deadline: 3/1. In 2016, 35 master's awarded. *Program availability:* Part-time, evening/weekend. Offers arts and letters (MA, MFA); communication studies (MA); creative writing (MFA); English composition (MA); integrated marketing communication (MA); Spanish (MA); studio art (MA). *Application deadline:* For fall admission, 7/17 priority date for domestic students. Applications are processed on a rolling basis. *Application fee:* $55. Electronic applications accepted. *Application Contact:* Dr. Francisca Beer, Dean of Graduate Studies, 909-537-5058, Fax: 909-537-5078, E-mail: fbeer@csusb.edu. *Dean,* Dr. Terry L. Ballman, 909-537-5800, Fax: 909-537-5926, E-mail: tballman@csusb.edu.

College of Business and Public Administration Students: 97 full-time (39 women), 347 part-time (168 women); includes 237 minority (41 Black or African American, non-Hispanic/Latino; 2 American Indian or Alaska Native, non-Hispanic/Latino; 40 Asian, non-Hispanic/Latino; 144 Hispanic/Latino; 1 Native Hawaiian or other Pacific Islander, non-Hispanic/Latino; 9 Two or more races, non-Hispanic/Latino), 89 international. 442 applicants, 48% accepted, 114 enrolled. *Faculty:* 25 full-time (6 women), 8 part-time/adjunct (3 women). Expenses: Contact institution. *Financial support:* Application deadline: 3/1. In 2016, 301 master's awarded. *Program availability:* Part-time, evening/weekend. Offers accountancy (MSA); accounting (MBA); business and public administration (MBA, MPA, MSA); entrepreneurship (MBA); finance (MBA); global business (MBA); information management (MBA);

information security (MBA); management (MBA); public administration (MPA); supply chain management (MBA). *Application deadline:* For fall admission, 7/17 for domestic students. Applications are processed on a rolling basis. *Application fee:* $55. *Application Contact:* Dr. Francisca Beer, Dean of Graduate Studies, 909-537-5058, Fax: 909-537-5078, E-mail: fbeer@csusb.edu. *Dean,* Dr. Lawrence C. Rose, 909-537-3703, E-mail: lrose@csusb.edu.

College of Education Students: 288 full-time (212 women), 372 part-time (249 women); includes 359 minority (55 Black or African American, non-Hispanic/Latino; 1 American Indian or Alaska Native, non-Hispanic/Latino; 23 Asian, non-Hispanic/Latino; 261 Hispanic/Latino; 19 Two or more races, non-Hispanic/Latino), 52 international. 410 applicants, 76% accepted, 232 enrolled. *Faculty:* 34 full-time (21 women), 45 part-time/adjunct (30 women). Expenses: Contact institution. In 2016, 264 master's, 3 doctorates awarded. *Program availability:* Part-time, evening/weekend. Offers counseling and guidance (MS); education (MA, MS, Ed D); educational administration (MA); educational leadership: community college (MA); educational leadership: P-12 (Ed D); rehabilitation counseling (MA). *Application deadline:* For fall admission, 7/17 for domestic students. *Application fee:* $55. *Application Contact:* Dr. Francisca Beer, Dean of Graduate Studies, 909-537-5808, E-mail: fbeer@csusb.edu. *Dean,* Dr. Jay Fiene, 909-537-5600, Fax: 909-537-7011, E-mail: jfiene@csusb.edu.

College of Natural Sciences Students: 46 full-time (28 women), 133 part-time (69 women); includes 94 minority (8 Black or African American, non-Hispanic/Latino; 1 American Indian or Alaska Native, non-Hispanic/Latino; 15 Asian, non-Hispanic/Latino; 67 Hispanic/Latino; 2 Native Hawaiian or other Pacific Islander, non-Hispanic/Latino; 1 Two or more races, non-Hispanic/Latino), 40 international. 351 applicants, 32% accepted, 68 enrolled. *Faculty:* 33 full-time (11 women), 4 part-time/adjunct (3 women). Expenses: Contact institution. *Financial support:* Fellowships, research assistantships, and teaching assistantships available. In 2016, 70 master's awarded. *Program availability:* Part-time. Offers biology (MS); computer science (MS); earth and environmental sciences (MS); health services administration (MS); mathematics (MA); natural sciences (MA, MAT, MPH, MS, MSN); nursing (MSN); public health (MPH); teaching mathematics (MAT). *Application fee:* $55. *Application Contact:* Dr. Francisca Beer, Dean of Graduate Studies, 909-537-5052, E-mail: fbeer@csusb.edu. *Dean,* Dr. Kirsten Fleming, 909-537-5300, Fax: 909-537-7005, E-mail: kfleming@csusb.edu.

College of Social and Behavioral Sciences Students: 240 full-time (187 women), 148 part-time (95 women); includes 237 minority (23 Black or African American, non-Hispanic/Latino; 3 American Indian or Alaska Native, non-Hispanic/Latino; 12 Asian, non-Hispanic/Latino; 179 Hispanic/Latino; 20 Two or more races, non-Hispanic/Latino), 11 international. 591 applicants, 38% accepted, 167 enrolled. *Faculty:* 39 full-time (20 women), 18 part-time/adjunct (12 women). Expenses: Contact institution. *Financial support:* Career-related internships or fieldwork, Federal Work-Study, institutionally sponsored loans, and unspecified assistantships available. Support available to part-time students. In 2016, 162 master's awarded. *Program availability:* Part-time, evening/weekend. Offers child development (MA); clinical psychology (MS); clinical/counseling psychology (MS); criminal justice (MA); general/experimental psychology (MA); industrial/organizational psychology (MS); national cyber security studies (MA); national security studies (MA); psychology-life span (MA); social and behavioral sciences (MA, MS, MSW); social sciences and globalization (MA); social work (MSW). *Application deadline:* For fall admission, 7/17 for domestic students. *Application fee:* $55. *Application Contact:* Dr. Francisca Beer, Dean of Graduate Studies, 909-537-5058, E-mail: fbeer@csusb.edu. *Dean,* Dr. Rafik Mohamed, 909-537-7500, Fax: 909-537-7107, E-mail: rafik.mohamed@csusb.edu.

CALIFORNIA STATE UNIVERSITY, SAN MARCOS, San Marcos, CA 92096-0001

General Information State-supported, coed, comprehensive institution. CGS member. *Enrollment:* 13,144 graduate, professional, and undergraduate students; 403 full-time matriculated graduate/professional students (277 women), 213 part-time matriculated graduate/professional students (144 women). *Enrollment by degree level:* 616 master's. *Graduate faculty:* 103 full-time (54 women), 269 part-time/adjunct (136 women). Tuition, state resident: full-time $6738. Tuition, nonresident: full-time $13,434. *Required fees:* $1906. Tuition and fees vary according to campus/location and program. *Graduate housing:* Room and/or apartments available on a first-come, first-serve basis to single students; on-campus housing not available to married students. Typical cost: $13,240 (including board). Room and board charges vary according to board plan, campus/location and housing facility selected. Housing application deadline: 10/1. *Student services:* Campus employment opportunities, campus safety program, career counseling, child daycare facilities, exercise/wellness program, free psychological counseling, international student services, low-cost health insurance, multicultural affairs office, services for students with disabilities, teacher training, writing training. *Library facilities:* Kellogg Library. *Collection:* Books: 215,402 (physical), 268,189 (digital/electronic); Serial titles: 3,130 (physical), 81,643 (digital/electronic); Databases: 100. Weekly public service hours: 100; students can reserve study rooms.

Computer facilities: A campuswide network can be accessed from student residence rooms and from off campus. Online class registration is available.
Website: http://www.csusm.edu/

General Application Contact: Dr. Wesley Schultz, Dean of Office of Graduate Studies and Research, 760-750-8045, Fax: 760-750-8045, E-mail: apply@csusm.edu.

GRADUATE UNITS

College of Business Administration *Program availability:* Evening/weekend. Offers business administration (MBA).

College of Education, Health and Human Services Offers behavioral health (MSW); children, youth and families (MSW); education, health and human services (MA, MSW, Ed D); speech-language pathology (MA).

School of Education *Program availability:* Part-time, evening/weekend. Offers educational administration (MA); educational leadership (Ed D); general education (MA); literacy education (MA); special education (MA).

School of Nursing Offers advanced practice nursing (MSN); clinical nurse leader (MSN); nursing education (MSN).

College of Humanities, Arts, Behavioral and Social Sciences *Program availability:* Part-time, evening/weekend. Offers Hispanic cultures and society (MA); Hispanic language and linguistics (MA); Hispanic literatures and literary theory (MA); history (MA); humanities, arts, behavioral and social sciences (MA); literature and writing studies (MA); psychology (MA); sociological practice (MA). Electronic applications accepted.

College of Science and Mathematics Offers biological sciences (MS); computer science (MS); mathematics (MS); science and mathematics (MS).

CALIFORNIA STATE UNIVERSITY, STANISLAUS, Turlock, CA 95382

General Information State-supported, coed, comprehensive institution. CGS member. *Required fees:* $8472. *Graduate housing:* Room and/or apartments available on a first-come, first-served basis to single students; on-campus housing not available to married students. Typical cost: $9766 (including board). Housing application deadline: 7/15. *Student services:* Campus employment opportunities, campus safety program, career counseling, child daycare facilities, exercise/wellness program, free psychological counseling, international student services, low-cost health insurance, services for students with disabilities, teacher training, writing training. *Library facilities:* Vasche Library. Collection: Books: 514,045 (physical), 8,002 (digital/electronic); Serial titles: 634 (physical), 60,803 (digital/electronic); Databases: 187. Weekly public service hours: 90; students can reserve study rooms. *Research affiliation:* California Campus Compact–Carnegie Fellowship Program (teaching development for faculty), Valley Mountain Regional Center (development disability), Friends of Turlock Library, EDAW, Inc. (environmental sustainable development), Mathematical Association of America (mathematics), Kaiser Permanente (health care).

Computer facilities: 200 computers available on campus for general student use. A campuswide network can be accessed from student residence rooms and from off campus. Online class registration is available.
Website: http://www.csustan.edu/

General Application Contact: Graduate School, 209-667-3129, Fax: 209-664-7025, E-mail: graduate_school@csustan.edu.

GRADUATE UNITS

College of Business Administration Expenses: Contact institution. *Financial support:* Fellowships and Federal Work-Study available. Financial award application deadline: 3/1; financial award applicants required to submit FAFSA. *Program availability:* Part-time, evening/weekend. Offers business administration (EMBA, MBA). *Application deadline:* For fall admission, 6/30 for domestic students; for winter admission, 11/30 for domestic students; for spring admission, 11/30 for domestic students. *Application fee:* $55. *Application Contact:* Dr. Randall Brown, Director, 209-667-3280, Fax: 209-667-3080. *Dean,* Dr. Nael Aly, 209-667-3288, Fax: 209-667-3080.

College of Education, Kinesiology and Social Work Expenses: Contact institution. *Financial support:* Fellowships, career-related internships or fieldwork, and Federal Work-Study available. Financial award application deadline: 3/1; financial award applicants required to submit FAFSA. *Program availability:* Part-time, evening/weekend. Offers community college leadership (Ed D); curriculum and instruction (MA); education, kinesiology and social work (MA, MSW, Ed D); P-12 leadership (Ed D); school administration (MA); school counseling (MA); social work (MSW). *Application deadline:* For fall admission, 6/30 for domestic students; for winter admission, 11/30 for domestic students; for spring admission, 11/30 for domestic students. *Application fee:* $55. *Application Contact:* Graduate School, 209-667-3129, Fax: 209-664-7025, E-mail: graduate_school@csustan.edu. *Dean,* Dr. Oddmund Myhre, 209-667-3652.

College of Natural Sciences Expenses: Contact institution. Offers ecological conservation (MS); genetic counseling (MS); natural sciences (MS). *Application Contact:* Graduate School, 209-667-3129, Fax: 209-664-7025, E-mail: graduate_school@csustan.edu. *Dean,* Dr. Roger McNeil, 209-667-3153.

College of Science Expenses: Contact institution. Offers behavior analysis (MA, MS); counseling psychology (MS); general psychology (MA); gerontological nursing (MS); nursing education (MS); science (MA, MS). *Application Contact:* Graduate School, 209-667-3129, Fax: 209-664-7025, E-mail: graduate_school@csustan.edu. *Dean,* Dr. David Evans, 209-667-3155, Fax: 209-667-7113.

College of the Arts, Humanities and Social Sciences Expenses: Contact institution. Offers arts, humanities and social sciences (MA, MPA, MS, Certificate); criminal justice (MA); history (MA); interdisciplinary studies (MA, MS); literature (Certificate); public administration (MPA); rhetoric and teaching writing (MA); teaching English to speakers of other languages (MA). *Application Contact:* Graduate School, 209-667-3129, Fax: 209-664-7025, E-mail: graduate_school@csustan.edu. *Dean,* Dr. James A. Tuedio, 209-667-3531.

CALIFORNIA UNIVERSITY OF MANAGEMENT AND SCIENCES, Anaheim, CA 92801

General Information Independent, coed, comprehensive institution.

GRADUATE UNITS

Graduate Programs Offers business administration (MBA, DBA); computer information systems (MS); economics (MS); international business (MS); sports management (MS).

CALIFORNIA UNIVERSITY OF PENNSYLVANIA, California, PA 15419-1394

General Information State-supported, coed, comprehensive institution. CGS member. *Enrollment:* 7,553 graduate, professional, and undergraduate students; 833 full-time matriculated graduate/professional students (536 women), 1,198 part-time matriculated graduate/professional students (746 women). *Enrollment by degree level:* 1,959 master's, 4 doctoral, 68 other advanced degrees. *Graduate faculty:* 91 full-time (54 women), 54 part-time/adjunct (20 women). Tuition, state resident: full-time $11,592; part-time $483 per credit. Tuition, nonresident: full-time $17,400; part-time $725 per credit. *Required fees:* $3916. Tuition and fees vary according to course load, degree level, campus/location and reciprocity agreements. *Graduate housing:* Room and/or apartments available on a first-come, first-served basis to single students; on-campus housing not available to married students. Typical cost: $6592 per year ($10,086 including board). Room and board charges vary according to board plan and housing facility selected. *Student services:* Campus employment opportunities, campus safety program, career counseling, exercise/wellness program, free psychological counseling, grant writing training, international student services, low-cost health insurance, multicultural affairs office, services for students with disabilities, teacher training, writing training. *Library facilities:* Manderino Library. Collection: Books: 236,664 (physical), 83,157 (digital/electronic); Databases: 107. Students can reserve study rooms. *Research affiliation:* The Center for Rural Pennsylvania (agriculture), The Technology Collaborative (robotics), International Technical Education Association (curricular development), National Collegiate Athletic Association (NCAA) (tobacco use), Gettysburg Travel Council (travel and tourism), NASA.

Computer facilities: 1,300 computers available on campus for general student use. A campuswide network can be accessed from student residence rooms and from off campus. Online class registration is available.
Website: http://www.calu.edu/

General Application Contact: Nicole Popielarcheck, Assistant Director of Graduate Admissions and Recruitment, 724-938-4029, Fax: 724-938-5712, E-mail: popielarcheck@calu.edu.

GRADUATE UNITS

School of Graduate Studies and Research *Program availability:* Part-time, evening/weekend, online learning. Electronic applications accepted.

College of Education and Human Services *Program availability:* Part-time, evening/weekend, online learning. Offers athletic training (MS); clinical mental health counseling (MS); communication disorders (MS); education and human services (M Ed, MAT, MS, MSW); elementary education (M Ed); intercollegiate athletic administration (MS); mentally and/or physically handicapped education (M Ed); performance enhancement and injury prevention (MS); reading specialist (M Ed); rehabilitation science (MS); school administration (M Ed); school counseling (M Ed); secondary education (MAT); social work (MSW); sport management (MS); sport psychology (MS); sports counseling (MS); technology education (M Ed); wellness and fitness (MS). Electronic applications accepted.

College of Liberal Arts *Program availability:* Part-time, evening/weekend. Offers applied criminology (MA); liberal arts (MA, MS); school psychology (MS). Electronic applications accepted.

Eberly College of Science and Technology *Program availability:* Part-time, evening/weekend, online learning. Offers business administration (MBA); business analytics (MBA); entrepreneurship (MBA); legal studies (MS); nursing administration and leadership (MBA); science and technology (MBA, MS). Electronic applications accepted.

CALIFORNIA WESTERN SCHOOL OF LAW, San Diego, CA 92101-3090

General Information Independent, coed, graduate-only institution. *Enrollment by degree level:* 117 master's, 640 doctoral. *Graduate faculty:* 43 full-time (18 women), 48 part-time/adjunct (20 women). Tuition: Full-time $48,800; part-time $34,200 per year. *Required fees:* $100; $100 per unit. Tuition and fees vary according to degree level. *Graduate housing:* On-campus housing not available. *Student services:* Campus employment opportunities, campus safety program, career counseling, free psychological counseling, international student services, multicultural affairs office, services for students with disabilities, writing training. *Library facilities:* California Western School of Law Library plus 1 other. Collection: Books: 207,884 (physical), 61,814 (digital/electronic); Serial titles: 4,494 (physical), 1,763 (digital/electronic); Databases: 95. Weekly public service hours: 110; students can reserve study rooms.

Computer facilities: 36 computers available on campus for general student use. A campuswide network can be accessed from off campus. Online class registration is available.
Website: https://www.cwsl.edu/

General Application Contact: 619-525-1401, E-mail: admissions@cwsl.edu.

GRADUATE UNITS

Graduate and Professional Programs Students: 568 full-time (339 women), 189 part-time (84 women); includes 267 minority (41 Black or African American, non-Hispanic/Latino; 9 American Indian or Alaska Native, non-Hispanic/Latino; 42 Asian, non-Hispanic/Latino; 123 Hispanic/Latino; 9 Native Hawaiian or other Pacific Islander, non-Hispanic/Latino; 43 Two or more races, non-Hispanic/Latino), 12 international. Average age 27. 1,408 applicants, 70% accepted, 230 enrolled. *Faculty:* 43 full-time (18 women), 48 part-time/adjunct (20 women). Expenses: Contact institution. *Financial support:* Career-related internships or fieldwork, Federal Work-Study, institutionally sponsored loans, and scholarships/grants available. Support available to part-time students. Financial award applicants required to submit FAFSA. *Program availability:* Part-time. Offers law (JD); Spanish language in trial advocacy (LL M). JD/MSW and JD/MBA offered jointly with San Diego State University. *Application deadline:* For fall admission, 4/1 for domestic students; for spring admission, 11/1 for domestic students. Applications are processed on a rolling basis. Electronic applications accepted. *Application Contact:* Traci D. Howard, Assistant Dean for Admissions, 619-525-1404, Fax: 619-615-1404, E-mail: admissions@cwsl.edu. *Dean,* Niels B. Schaumann, 619-239-0391, Fax: 619-685-2916.

CALUMET COLLEGE OF SAINT JOSEPH, Whiting, IN 46394-2195

General Information Independent-religious, coed, comprehensive institution.

GRADUATE UNITS

Program in Leadership in Teaching Offers leadership in teaching (MS Ed).

Program in Public Safety Administration Offers public safety administration (MS).

Program in Quality Assurance Offers quality assurance (MS).

CALVARY UNIVERSITY, Kansas City, MO 64147

General Information Independent-religious, coed, comprehensive institution. *Enrollment:* 271 graduate, professional, and undergraduate students; 11 full-time matriculated graduate/professional students (3 women), 29 part-time matriculated graduate/professional students (15 women). *Enrollment by degree level:* 40 master's. *Graduate faculty:* 6 full-time (2 women), 2 part-time/adjunct (1 woman). Tuition: Full-time $7200; part-time $4800 per credit. *Required fees:* $640; $520 per credit. $140 per semester. One-time fee: $100. Tuition and fees vary according to program. *Graduate housing:* Rooms and/or apartments available on a first-come, first-served basis to single and married students. Typical cost: $5175 per year ($9135 including board) for single students; $6600 per year ($10,560 including board) for married students. Room and board charges vary according to board plan and housing facility selected. *Student services:* Campus employment opportunities, services for students with disabilities, writing training. *Library facilities:* Hilda Kroeker Library. Collection: Books: 41,841 (physical), 420 (digital/electronic); Serial titles: 268 (physical); Databases: 4.

Computer facilities: 32 computers available on campus for general student use. A campuswide network can be accessed from student residence rooms. Online class registration is available.
Website: http://www.calvary.edu/

General Application Contact: Ann Rogers, Admissions Office Assistant, 800-326-3960 Ext. 1321, Fax: 816-331-4474, E-mail: admissions@calvary.edu.

GRADUATE UNITS

Graduate School and Seminary Students: 11 full-time (3 women), 29 part-time (15 women); includes 12 minority (4 Black or African American, non-Hispanic/Latino; 1 American Indian or Alaska Native, non-Hispanic/Latino; 6 Asian, non-Hispanic/Latino; 1 Native Hawaiian or other Pacific Islander, non-Hispanic/Latino). Average age 39. *Faculty:* 6 full-time (2 women), 2 part-time/adjunct (1 woman). Expenses: Contact institution. *Financial support:* In 2016–17, 8 students received support. Scholarships/grants available. Financial award application deadline: 11/5; financial award applicants required to submit FAFSA. In 2016, 19 master's awarded. *Program availability:* Part-time, evening/weekend. Offers Bible and theology (MS); Biblical counseling (MA); education (MS); organization development (MS); pastoral studies

(M Div). *Application deadline:* Applications are processed on a rolling basis. *Application fee:* $0. Electronic applications accepted. *Application Contact:* Ann Rogers, Admissions Office Assistant, 800-326-3960 Ext. 1321, Fax: 816-331-4474, E-mail: admissions@calvary.edu. *Director of Seminary,* Dr. Thomas Baurain, 816-322-0110 Ext. 1502, Fax: 816-331-4474, E-mail: thomas.baurain@calvary.edu.

CALVIN COLLEGE, Grand Rapids, MI 49546-4388

General Information Independent-religious, coed, comprehensive institution. *Enrollment:* 3,918 graduate, professional, and undergraduate students; 4 full-time matriculated graduate/professional students (3 women), 120 part-time matriculated graduate/professional students (80 women). *Enrollment by degree level:* 124 master's. *Graduate faculty:* 12 full-time (5 women). *Graduate housing:* Room and/or apartments available on a first-come, first-served basis to single students; on-campus housing not available to married students. Housing application deadline: 4/1. *Student services:* Campus employment opportunities, campus safety program, career counseling, exercise/wellness program, free psychological counseling, international student services, low-cost health insurance, multicultural affairs office, services for students with disabilities, writing training. *Library facilities:* Hekman Library. *Collection:* Books: 714,950 (physical), 346,117 (digital/electronic); Serial titles: 5,893 (physical), 34,583 (digital/electronic); Databases: 137. Weekly public service hours: 90.

Computer facilities: Computer purchase and lease plans are available. 1,025 computers available on campus for general student use. A campuswide network can be accessed from student residence rooms and from off campus. Online class registration is available.
Website: http://www.calvin.edu/

General Application Contact: Cindi Hoekstra, Graduate Program Manager, 616-516-6158, Fax: 616-526-6505, E-mail: choekstr@calvin.edu.

GRADUATE UNITS

Graduate Programs in Education Students: 4 full-time (3 women), 120 part-time (80 women); includes 13 minority (3 Black or African American, non-Hispanic/Latino; 4 Asian, non-Hispanic/Latino; 1 Hispanic/Latino; 5 Two or more races, non-Hispanic/Latino), 15 international. Average age 29. 24 applicants, 100% accepted, 24 enrolled. *Faculty:* 12 full-time (5 women). Expenses: Contact institution. *Financial support:* Federal Work-Study, scholarships/grants, and tuition waivers (full and partial) available. Financial award application deadline: 4/3; financial award applicants required to submit FAFSA. In 2016, 23 master's awarded. *Program availability:* Part-time. Offers curriculum and instruction (M Ed). *Application deadline:* For fall admission, 8/1 priority date for domestic students, 5/1 priority date for international students; for spring admission, 1/1 priority date for domestic students, 12/1 priority date for international students; for summer admission, 5/18 for domestic students. Applications are processed on a rolling basis. *Application fee:* $0. Electronic applications accepted. *Application Contact:* Cindi Hoekstra, Program Manager, 616-526-6158, Fax: 616-526-6505, E-mail: choekstr@calvin.edu. *Graduate Program Director,* Dr. David Smith, 616-526-6158, Fax: 616-526-6505, E-mail: dsmith@calvin.edu.

CALVIN THEOLOGICAL SEMINARY, Grand Rapids, MI 49546-4387

General Information Independent-religious, coed, graduate-only institution. *Graduate housing:* Rooms and/or apartments available on a first-come, first-served basis to single and married students. Housing application deadline: 4/1.

GRADUATE UNITS

Graduate and Professional Programs *Program availability:* Part-time. Offers Bible and theology (MA); divinity (M Div); educational ministry (MA); historical theology (PhD); missions and evangelism (MA); pastoral care (MA); philosophical and moral theology (PhD); systematic theology (PhD); theological studies (MTS); theology (Th M); worship (MA); youth and family ministries (MA). Electronic applications accepted.

CAMBRIDGE COLLEGE, Cambridge, MA 02138-5304

General Information Independent, coed, comprehensive institution. CGS member. *Graduate housing:* On-campus housing not available.

GRADUATE UNITS

School of Education *Program availability:* Part-time, evening/weekend, online learning. Offers autism specialist (M Ed); autism/behavior analyst (Post-Master's Certificate); behavior analyst (Post-Master's Certificate); behavioral management (M Ed); early childhood teacher (M Ed); education specialist in curriculum and instruction (CAGS); educational leadership (Ed D); elementary teacher (M Ed); English as a second language (M Ed, Certificate); general science (M Ed); health education (Post-Master's Certificate); health/family and consumer sciences (M Ed); history (M Ed); individualized (M Ed); information technology literacy (M Ed); instructional technology (M Ed); interdisciplinary studies (M Ed); library teacher (M Ed); literacy education (M Ed); mathematics (M Ed); mathematics specialist (Certificate); middle school mathematics and science (M Ed); school administration (M Ed, CAGS); school guidance counselor (M Ed); school nurse education (M Ed); school social worker/adjustment counselor (M Ed); special education administrator (CAGS); special education/moderate disabilities (M Ed); teaching skills and methodologies (M Ed). Electronic applications accepted.

School of Management *Program availability:* Part-time, evening/weekend. Offers business negotiation and conflict resolution (M Mgt); general business (M Mgt); health care informatics (M Mgt); health care management (M Mgt); leadership in human and organizational dynamics (M Mgt); non-profit and public organization management (M Mgt); small business development (M Mgt); technology management (M Mgt). Electronic applications accepted.

School of Psychology and Counseling *Program availability:* Part-time, evening/weekend. Offers addiction counseling (Certificate); alcohol and drug counseling (Certificate); counseling psychology (M Ed, CAGS); counseling psychology: forensic counseling (M Ed); marriage and family therapy (M Ed); mental health and addiction counseling (M Ed); mental health counseling (M Ed); mental health counseling for school guidance counselors (Post Master's Certificate); psychological studies (M Ed); school adjustment and mental health counseling (M Ed); school adjustment, mental health and addiction counseling (M Ed); school guidance counselor (M Ed); trauma studies (Certificate). Electronic applications accepted.

CAMERON UNIVERSITY, Lawton, OK 73505-6377

General Information State-supported, coed, comprehensive institution. *Graduate housing:* Room and/or apartments available on a first-come, first-served basis to single students; on-campus housing not available to married students. *Research affiliation:* Telos OK, LLC (simulations), Army Research Institute (human factors), Advanced Systems Technology, Inc. (informational systems), Dynamics Research Corporation (multimedia systems), Eagle Systems, Inc. (multimedia systems), Halliburton (energy systems).

GRADUATE UNITS

Office of Graduate Studies *Program availability:* Part-time, evening/weekend, online learning. Offers behavioral sciences (MS); business administration (MBA); education (M Ed); educational leadership (MS); entrepreneurial studies (MS); teaching (MAT). Electronic applications accepted.

CAMPBELLSVILLE UNIVERSITY, Campbellsville, KY 42718-2799

General Information Independent-religious, coed, comprehensive institution. *Enrollment:* 4,305 graduate, professional, and undergraduate students; 508 full-time matriculated graduate/professional students (302 women), 434 part-time matriculated graduate/professional students (196 women). *Enrollment by degree level:* 942 master's. *Graduate faculty:* 66 full-time (31 women), 45 part-time/adjunct (24 women). *Tuition:* Full-time $14,250; part-time $475 per credit hour. *Required fees:* $75 per term. Tuition and fees vary according to campus/location and program. *Graduate housing:* Rooms and/or apartments available on a first-come, first-served basis to single and married students. Typical cost: $7896 (including board) for single students; $7896 (including board) for married students. Room and board charges vary according to housing facility selected. Housing application deadline: 6/30. *Student services:* Campus employment opportunities, campus safety program, career counseling, exercise/wellness program, international student services, teacher training, writing training. *Library facilities:* Montgomery Library. *Collection:* Books: 172,863 (physical), 236,674 (digital/electronic); Serial titles: 126 (physical); Databases: 72. Weekly public service hours: 77; students can reserve study rooms.

Computer facilities: 220 computers available on campus for general student use. A campuswide network can be accessed from student residence rooms and from off campus. Online class registration is available.
Website: http://www.campbellsville.edu/

General Application Contact: Monica Bamwine, Assistant Director of Graduate Admissions, 270-789-5221, Fax: 270-789-5071, E-mail: mkbamwine@campbellsville.edu.

GRADUATE UNITS

Carver School of Social Work Students: 107 full-time (101 women), 63 part-time (55 women); includes 20 minority (15 Black or African American, non-Hispanic/Latino; 1 American Indian or Alaska Native, non-Hispanic/Latino; 2 Asian, non-Hispanic/Latino; 2 Hispanic/Latino), 3 international. Average age 33. 254 applicants, 71% accepted, 121 enrolled. *Faculty:* 11 full-time (9 women), 7 part-time/adjunct (all women). Expenses: Contact institution. *Financial support:* Applicants required to submit FAFSA. In 2016, 47 master's awarded. *Program availability:* Part-time, evening/weekend, 100% online, blended/hybrid learning. Offers social work (MA). *Application deadline:* Applications are processed on a rolling basis. *Application fee:* $25. Electronic applications accepted. *Application Contact:* Monica Bamwine, Assistant Director of Graduate Admissions, 270-789-5221, Fax: 270-789-5071, E-mail: mkbamwine@campbellsville.edu. *Program Director,* Dr. Helen K. Mudd, 270-789-5045, Fax: 270-789-5542, E-mail: hkmudd@campbellsville.edu.

College of Arts and Sciences Students: 1 full-time (0 women), 23 part-time (13 women); includes 4 minority (1 Black or African American, non-Hispanic/Latino; 1 Asian, non-Hispanic/Latino; 2 Hispanic/Latino), 5 international. Average age 25. 28 applicants, 71% accepted, 17 enrolled. *Faculty:* 6 full-time (2 women), 3 part-time/adjunct (1 woman). Expenses: Contact institution. *Financial support:* Unspecified assistantships available. Financial award application deadline: 6/1; financial award applicants required to submit FAFSA. In 2016, 4 master's awarded. *Program availability:* Part-time, evening/weekend, 100% online, blended/hybrid learning. Offers social science (MA). *Application deadline:* Applications are processed on a rolling basis. *Application fee:* $25. Electronic applications accepted. *Application Contact:* Monica Bamwine, Assistant Director of Graduate Admissions, 270-789-5221, Fax: 270-789-5071, E-mail: mkbamwine@campbellsville.edu. *Dean,* Dr. Mike Page, 270-789-5394.

School of Business and Economics Students: 35 full-time (17 women), 414 part-time (112 women); includes 35 minority (21 Black or African American, non-Hispanic/Latino; 10 Asian, non-Hispanic/Latino; 4 Hispanic/Latino), 323 international. Average age 28. 351 applicants, 79% accepted, 209 enrolled. *Faculty:* 12 full-time (2 women), 11 part-time/adjunct (6 women). Expenses: Contact institution. *Financial support:* Application deadline: 6/1; applicants required to submit FAFSA. In 2016, 47 master's awarded. *Program availability:* Part-time, evening/weekend, 100% online, blended/hybrid learning. Offers business administration (MBA). *Application deadline:* Applications are processed on a rolling basis. *Application fee:* $25. Electronic applications accepted. *Application Contact:* Monica Bamwine, Assistant Director of Graduate Admissions, 270-789-5221, Fax: 270-789-5071, E-mail: mkbamwine@campbellsville.edu. *Dean,* Dr. Patricia H. Cowherd, 270-789-5553, Fax: 270-789-5066, E-mail: phcowherd@campbellsville.edu.

School of Education Students: 36 full-time (29 women), 163 part-time (128 women); includes 16 minority (14 Black or African American, non-Hispanic/Latino; 1 Hispanic/Latino; 1 Two or more races, non-Hispanic/Latino). Average age 35. 173 applicants, 58% accepted, 87 enrolled. *Faculty:* 13 full-time (11 women), 12 part-time/adjunct (7 women). Expenses: Contact institution. *Financial support:* Applicants required to submit FAFSA. In 2016, 58 master's awarded. *Program availability:* Part-time, evening/weekend, 100% online, blended/hybrid learning. Offers special education (MASE). *Application deadline:* Applications are processed on a rolling basis. *Application fee:* $25. Electronic applications accepted. *Application Contact:* Monica Bamwine, Assistant Director of Graduate Admissions, 270-789-5221, Fax: 270-789-5071, E-mail: mkbamwine@campbellsville.edu. *Dean,* Dr. Beverly Ennis, 270-789-5344, Fax: 270-789-5206, E-mail: bcennis@campbellsville.edu.

School of Music Students: 1 (woman) full-time, 26 part-time (13 women), 14 international. Average age 30. 17 applicants, 76% accepted, 12 enrolled. *Faculty:* 13 full-time (6 women), 10 part-time/adjunct (4 women). Expenses: Contact institution. *Financial support:* Application deadline: 6/1; applicants required to submit FAFSA. In 2016, 10 master's awarded. *Program availability:* Part-time, 100% online, blended/hybrid learning. Offers church music (MM); conducting (MM); instrumental performance (MM); music (MA); music education (MM); musicology (MA); pedagogy and performance (MM); worship (MA). *Application deadline:* Applications are processed on a rolling basis. *Application fee:* $25. Electronic applications accepted. *Application Contact:* Monica Bamwine, Assistant Director of Graduate Admissions, 270-789-5221, Fax: 270-789-5071, E-mail: mkbamwine@campbellsville.edu. *Dean,* Dr. Tony Cunha, 270-789-5240, Fax: 270-789-5524, E-mail: accunha@campbellsville.edu.

School of Theology Students: 5 full-time (2 women), 83 part-time (41 women); includes 33 minority (27 Black or African American, non-Hispanic/Latino; 1 American Indian or Alaska Native, non-Hispanic/Latino; 4 Hispanic/Latino; 1 Two or more races, non-Hispanic/Latino), 1 international. Average age 43. 60 applicants, 62% accepted, 30 enrolled. *Faculty:* 12 full-time (2 women), 5 part-time/adjunct (1 woman). Expenses: Contact institution. *Financial support:* Application deadline: 6/1; applicants required to submit FAFSA. In 2016, 31 master's awarded. *Program availability:* Part-time, evening/weekend, 100% online, blended/hybrid learning. Offers marriage and family therapy (MMFT); theology (M Th). *Application deadline:* Applications are processed on a rolling basis. *Application fee:* $25. Electronic applications accepted. *Application Contact:* Monica Bamwine, Assistant Director of Graduate Admissions, 270-789-5221, Fax: 270-789-5071, E-mail: mkbamwine@campbellsville.edu. *Dean,* Dr. John E. Hurtgen, 270-789-5077, Fax: 270-789-5050, E-mail: jehurtgen@campbellsville.edu.

CAMPBELL UNIVERSITY, Buies Creek, NC 27506

General Information Independent-religious, coed, university. *Graduate housing:* Rooms and/or apartments available on a first-come, first-served basis to single and married students. Housing application deadline: 6/2.

GRADUATE UNITS

Graduate and Professional Programs *Program availability:* Part-time, evening/weekend.

College of Pharmacy and Health Sciences *Program availability:* Part-time, evening/weekend. Offers clinical research (MS); pharmaceutical sciences (MS); pharmacy (Pharm D); physician assistant (MPAP); public health (MS). Electronic applications accepted.

Divinity School Offers Christian ministry (MA); divinity (M Div); ministry (D Min).

Jerry M. Wallace School of Osteopathic Medicine Offers osteopathic medicine (DO).

Lundy-Fetterman School of Business *Program availability:* Part-time, evening/weekend. Offers business (MBA, MTWM).

Norman Adrian Wiggins School of Law Offers law (JD). JD/MPA offered in partnership with North Carolina State University. Electronic applications accepted.

School of Education *Program availability:* Part-time, evening/weekend. Offers elementary education (M Ed); interdisciplinary studies (M Ed); middle grades education (M Ed); physical education (M Ed); school administration (MSA); school counseling (M Ed); secondary education (M Ed).

CANADIAN COLLEGE OF NATUROPATHIC MEDICINE, Toronto, ON M2K 1E2, Canada

General Information Independent, coed, primarily women, graduate-only institution. *Graduate housing:* Room and/or apartments available on a first-come, first-served basis to single students; on-campus housing not available to married students. Housing application deadline: 4/30. *Research affiliation:* Ottawa Regional Cancer Centre, McMaster University, University of Oxford, Hospital for Sick Children, Mayo Clinic, Johns Hopkins University.

GRADUATE UNITS

Bachelor of Naturopathy Program Offers naturopathy (BN). Electronic applications accepted.

CANADIAN MEMORIAL CHIROPRACTIC COLLEGE, Toronto, ON M2H 3J1, Canada

General Information Independent, coed, graduate-only institution. *Graduate housing:* On-campus housing not available. *Research affiliation:* University of Waterloo, University of Calgary, University of Toronto.

GRADUATE UNITS

Certificate Programs Offers chiropractic clinical sciences (Certificate); chiropractic radiology (Certificate); chiropractic sports sciences (Certificate); clinical acupuncture (Certificate).

Professional Program Offers chiropractic (DC).

CANADIAN SOUTHERN BAPTIST SEMINARY, Cochrane, AB T4C 2G1, Canada

General Information Independent-religious, coed, graduate-only institution. *Enrollment by degree level:* 42 master's. *Graduate faculty:* 3 full-time (0 women), 8 part-time/adjunct (1 woman). *Tuition:* Full-time $6900 Canadian dollars; part-time $345 Canadian dollars per credit hour. *Required fees:* $20 Canadian dollars per credit hour. $35 Canadian dollars per semester. Tuition and fees vary according to course load. *Graduate housing:* Rooms and/or apartments available on a first-come, first-served basis to single and married students. Housing application deadline: 7/1. *Student services:* Campus employment opportunities, international student services. *Library facilities:* Keith C. Wills Library. *Collection:* Books: 40,100 (physical), 1,970 (digital/electronic). Weekly public service hours: 65.

Computer facilities: 6 computers available on campus for general student use. A campuswide network can be accessed from off campus. Online class registration is available.
Website: http://www.csbs.ca/

General Application Contact: Mike Sharkey, Admissions Counselor, 403-932-6622 Ext. 251, Fax: 403-932-7049, E-mail: admissions@csbs.ca.

GRADUATE UNITS

Graduate Programs Students: 24 full-time (9 women), 18 part-time (2 women); includes 4 minority (1 Black or African American, non-Hispanic/Latino; 3 Asian, non-Hispanic/Latino), 11 international. Average age 29. 17 applicants, 76% accepted, 11 enrolled. *Faculty:* 3 full-time (0 women), 8 part-time/adjunct (1 woman). Expenses: Contact institution. *Financial support:* Scholarships/grants available. Financial award application deadline: 7/1. In 2016, 10 master's awarded. *Program availability:* Part-time, 100% online, blended/hybrid learning. Offers Biblical studies (MBS); Christian ministry (MCMin); Christian studies (MCS); ministry (M Div). *Application deadline:* For fall admission, 7/1 priority date for domestic students, 3/1 priority date for international students; for winter admission, 11/15 priority date for domestic students. Applications are processed on a rolling basis. *Application fee:* $50 ($150 for international students). *Application Contact:* Kathleen McNaughton, Registrar, 403-932-6622 Ext. 221, E-mail: kathleen.mcnaughton@csbs.ca. *Academic Dean,* Dr. Steve Booth, 403-932-6622 Ext. 232, E-mail: steve.booth@csbs.ca.

CANISIUS COLLEGE, Buffalo, NY 14208-1098

General Information Independent-religious, coed, comprehensive institution. *Enrollment:* 3,734 graduate, professional, and undergraduate students; 484 full-time matriculated graduate/professional students (299 women), 639 part-time matriculated graduate/professional students (387 women). *Enrollment by degree level:* 1,015 master's, 108 other advanced degrees. *Graduate faculty:* 58 full-time (27 women), 77 part-time/adjunct (43 women). *Tuition:* Full-time $14,742. *Required fees:* $724. *Graduate housing:* Room and/or apartments available on a first-come, first-served basis to single students; on-campus housing not available to married students. Typical cost: $7764 per year ($13,218 including board). Room and board charges vary according to board plan, campus/location and housing facility selected. Housing application deadline: 5/1. *Student services:* Campus employment opportunities, campus safety program, career

counseling, exercise/wellness program, free psychological counseling, international student services, multicultural affairs office, services for students with disabilities, teacher training. *Library facilities:* Andrew L. Bouwhuis Library plus 1 other. *Collection:* Books: 300,786 (physical), 96,476 (digital/electronic); Serial titles: 1,140 (physical), 66,335 (digital/electronic); Databases: 110. Weekly public service hours: 110; students can reserve study rooms. *Research affiliation:* Eduventures (enrollment management).

Computer facilities: Computer purchase and lease plans are available. 700 computers available on campus for general student use. A campuswide network can be accessed from student residence rooms and from off campus. Online class registration, online accounts are available.
Website: http://www.canisius.edu/

General Application Contact: Kathleen B Davis, Interim Director of Graduate Admissions, 716-888-2210, Fax: 716-888-3290, E-mail: davisb@canisius.edu.

GRADUATE UNITS

Graduate Division Students: 484 full-time (299 women), 639 part-time (387 women); includes 146 minority (77 Black or African American, non-Hispanic/Latino; 4 American Indian or Alaska Native, non-Hispanic/Latino; 18 Asian, non-Hispanic/Latino; 34 Hispanic/Latino; 13 Two or more races, non-Hispanic/Latino), 49 international. Average age 29. 905 applicants, 70% accepted, 450 enrolled. *Faculty:* 58 full-time (27 women), 77 part-time/adjunct (43 women). Expenses: Contact institution. *Financial support:* Career-related internships or fieldwork, Federal Work-Study, scholarships/grants, tuition waivers (partial), and unspecified assistantships available. Support available to part-time students. Financial award application deadline: 4/30; financial award applicants required to submit FAFSA. In 2016, 578 master's, 39 other advanced degrees awarded. *Program availability:* Part-time, evening/weekend, 100% online, blended/hybrid learning. *Application deadline:* Applications are processed on a rolling basis. *Application fee:* $25. Electronic applications accepted. *Application Contact:* Kathleen B. Davis, Vice President for Enrollment Management, 716-888-2500, Fax: 716-888-3195, E-mail: daviskb@canisius.edu. *Vice President for Academic Affairs,* Dr. Margaret C. McCarthy, 716-888-2120, Fax: 716-888-2120, E-mail: mmccarth@canisius.edu.

College of Arts and Sciences Students: 19 full-time (17 women), 49 part-time (39 women); includes 7 minority (3 Black or African American, non-Hispanic/Latino; 1 Asian, non-Hispanic/Latino; 2 Hispanic/Latino; 1 Two or more races, non-Hispanic/Latino), 3 international. Average age 31. 102 applicants, 33% accepted, 25 enrolled. *Faculty:* 7 full-time (5 women), 3 part-time/adjunct (all women). Expenses: Contact institution. *Financial support:* Career-related internships or fieldwork, Federal Work-Study, scholarships/grants, tuition waivers (partial), and unspecified assistantships available. Financial award application deadline: 4/30; financial award applicants required to submit FAFSA. In 2016, 33 master's awarded. *Program availability:* Part-time, evening/weekend, 100% online, blended/hybrid learning. Offers anthrozoology (MS); arts and sciences (MS); communication and leadership (MS). *Application deadline:* For fall admission, 7/15 priority date for domestic students; for spring admission, 4/15 priority date for domestic students. Applications are processed on a rolling basis. *Application fee:* $25. Electronic applications accepted. *Application Contact:* Kathleen B. Davis, Vice President for Enrollment Management, 716-888-2500, Fax: 716-888-3195, E-mail: daviskb@canisius.edu. *Dean of Arts and Sciences,* Dr. Beth A. Gill, 716-888-2150, E-mail: gille@canisius.edu.

Richard J. Wehle School of Business Students: 151 full-time (65 women), 148 part-time (50 women); includes 36 minority (16 Black or African American, non-Hispanic/Latino; 1 American Indian or Alaska Native, non-Hispanic/Latino; 10 Asian, non-Hispanic/Latino; 8 Hispanic/Latino; 1 Two or more races, non-Hispanic/Latino), 30 international. Average age 27. 274 applicants, 66% accepted, 110 enrolled. *Faculty:* 23 full-time (4 women), 14 part-time/adjunct (3 women). Expenses: Contact institution. *Financial support:* Career-related internships or fieldwork, Federal Work-Study, scholarships/grants, tuition waivers (partial), and unspecified assistantships available. Support available to part-time students. Financial award application deadline: 4/30; financial award applicants required to submit FAFSA. In 2016, 150 master's awarded. *Program availability:* Part-time, evening/weekend. Offers accounting (MBA); business (MBA, MS); business administration (MBA); forensic accounting (MS); international business (MS); professional accounting (MBA). *Application deadline:* For fall admission, 7/1 priority date for domestic students; for spring admission, 11/1 priority date for domestic students. Applications are processed on a rolling basis. *Application fee:* $25. Electronic applications accepted. *Application Contact:* Kathleen B. Davis, Vice President of Enrollment Management, 716-888-2500, Fax: 716-888-3195, E-mail: daviskb@canisius.edu. *Dean,* Dr. Daniel J. Borgia, 716-888-2160, Fax: 716-888-2145, E-mail: gradbus@canisius.edu.

School of Education and Human Services Students: 314 full-time (217 women), 442 part-time (298 women); includes 103 minority (58 Black or African American, non-Hispanic/Latino; 3 American Indian or Alaska Native, non-Hispanic/Latino; 7 Asian, non-Hispanic/Latino; 24 Hispanic/Latino; 11 Two or more races, non-Hispanic/Latino), 16 international. Average age 29. 490 applicants, 86% accepted, 315 enrolled. *Faculty:* 28 full-time (18 women), 60 part-time/adjunct (37 women). Expenses: Contact institution. *Financial support:* Career-related internships or fieldwork, Federal Work-Study, scholarships/grants, tuition waivers (partial), and unspecified assistantships available. Support available to part-time students. Financial award application deadline: 4/30; financial award applicants required to submit FAFSA. In 2016, 455 master's awarded. *Program availability:* Part-time, evening/weekend, 100% online, blended/hybrid learning. Offers adolescence education (MS Ed); applied nutrition (MS, Certificate); business and marketing education (MS Ed); childhood education (MS Ed); college student personnel (MS Ed); community and school health (MS); community mental health counseling (MS); counseling and human services (MS); deaf education (MS Ed); deaf/adolescent education, grades 7-12 (MS Ed); deaf/childhood education, grades 1-6 (MS Ed); differentiated instruction (MS Ed); education administration (MS, MS Ed, MSA, Certificate); educational administration (MS Ed); educational technologies (Certificate); general education (MS Ed); gifted education extension (Certificate); health and human performance (MS); health information technology (MS Ed); physical education (MS Ed); physical education birth - 12 (MS Ed); reading (Certificate); respiratory care (MS); school agency counseling (MS); school building leadership (MS Ed, Certificate); school district leadership (Certificate); special education (MS); sport administration (MSA); teacher leader (Certificate); TESOL (MS Ed). *Application deadline:* Applications are processed on a rolling basis. *Application fee:* $25. Electronic applications accepted. *Application Contact:* Kathleen B. Davis, Vice President of Enrollment Management, 716-888-2500, Fax: 716-888-3195, E-mail: daviskb@canisius.edu. *Dean,* Dr. Jeffrey R. Lindauer, 716-888-3294, Fax: 716-888-3164, E-mail: lindauej@canisius.edu.

CAPE BRETON UNIVERSITY, Sydney, NS B1P 6L2, Canada

General Information Province-supported, coed, comprehensive institution. *Graduate housing:* Room and/or apartments available on a first-come, first-served basis to single students; on-campus housing not available to married students. Housing application deadline: 3/31. *Research affiliation:* Hyperspectral Data International (marine remote sensing), Sable Offshore Energy, Inc. (petroleum resources), Fortress Louisbourg National Historic Park (museum/heritage projects), Dynagen Industrial Mine Technology (mining industry equipment), Atlantic Geomatics (computer networking and software development), Advanced Glazing, Limited (transparent insulation).

GRADUATE UNITS

Shannon School of Business *Program availability:* Part-time. Offers business (MBA). Electronic applications accepted.

CAPELLA UNIVERSITY, Minneapolis, MN 55402

General Information Proprietary, coed, upper-level institution. CGS member.

GRADUATE UNITS

Harold Abel School of Social and Behavioral Science *Program availability:* Part-time, evening/weekend, online learning. Offers addiction psychology (PhD); applied behavior analysis (MS); child and adolescent development (MS); clinical psychology (MS, Psy D); counseling psychology (MS); educational psychology (MS, PhD); evaluation, research, and measurement (MS); general addiction counseling (MS); general advanced studies in human behavior (MS, PhD); general counselor education and supervision (PhD); general marriage and family counseling/therapy (MS); general mental health counseling (MS); general psychology (MS, PhD); general school counseling (MS); general social work (DSW); industrial/organizational psychology (MS, PhD); leadership coaching psychology (MS); school psychology (MS, Psy D); social and behavioral science (MS, PhD, Psy D); sport psychology (MS). Electronic applications accepted.

School of Business and Technology *Program availability:* Part-time, evening/weekend, online learning. Offers accounting (MBA, DBA, PhD); business analysis (MS); business and technology (MBA, MS, DBA, PhD); business intelligence (MBA, DBA); enterprise software architecture (MS); entrepreneurship (MBA); finance (MBA, DBA, PhD); general business administration (MBA); general business management (PhD); general human resource management (MS); general information systems and technology management (MS); general information technology (PhD); general leadership (MS); global operations and supply chain management (MBA, DBA); health care management (MBA); human resource management (MBA, DBA, PhD); information assurance and security (MS, PhD); information technology education (PhD); information technology management (MBA, DBA, PhD); leadership (DBA, PhD); management education (PhD); marketing (MBA, DBA, PhD); network management (MS); project management (MBA, MS, DBA, PhD); strategy and innovation (DBA, PhD). Electronic applications accepted.

School of Education *Program availability:* Part-time, evening/weekend, online learning. Offers adult education (MS); curriculum and instruction (MS, PhD); early childhood education (MS); education (MS, Ed D, PhD); educational leadership and management (Ed D); enrollment management (MS); higher education leadership and management (MS); instructional design for online learning (MS, PhD); integrative studies (MS); K-12 studies in education (MS, PhD); leadership for higher education (PhD); leadership in educational administration (MS, PhD); postsecondary and adult education (PhD); professional studies in education (PhD); reading and literacy (MS, Ed D); special education leadership (PhD); special education teaching (MS); training and performance improvement (PhD). Electronic applications accepted.

School of Public Service Leadership Offers criminal justice (MS, PhD); diabetes nursing (MSN); emergency management (MS, PhD); epidemiology (Dr PH); general health administration (DHA); general nursing (MSN); general public administration (DPA); general public health (MPH); gerontology (MS); gerontology nursing (MSN); health administration (MHA); health advocacy and leadership (Dr PH); health care administration (PhD); health care leadership (DHA); health care operations (MHA); health information management (MS); health management policy (MPH); health policy (MHA); health policy advocacy (DHA); homeland security (MS); multidisciplinary human services (MS, PhD); nonprofit management and leadership (PhD); nurse educator (MSN); nursing education (PhD); nursing leadership and administration (MSN); nursing practice (DNP); public administration (MPA); public safety leadership (MS, PhD); public service leadership (MHA, MPA, MPH, MS, DHA, DPA, Dr PH, PhD); social and community services (MS, PhD); social behavioral sciences (MPH).

CAPITAL UNIVERSITY, Columbus, OH 43209-2394

General Information Independent-religious, coed, comprehensive institution. *Graduate housing:* On-campus housing not available.

GRADUATE UNITS

Conservatory of Music *Program availability:* Part-time. Offers music education (MM). Program offered only in summer. Electronic applications accepted.

Law School *Program availability:* Part-time, evening/weekend. Offers business (LL M); business and taxation (LL M); law (LL M, MT, JD); taxation (LL M, MT). Electronic applications accepted.

School of Management Students: 165 (70 women); includes 16 minority (8 Black or African American, non-Hispanic/Latino; 6 Asian, non-Hispanic/Latino; 2 Hispanic/Latino), 6 international. Average age 32. 71 applicants, 56% accepted, 32 enrolled. *Faculty:* 17 full-time (7 women), 23 part-time/adjunct (1 woman). *Expenses:* Contact institution. *Financial support:* Unspecified assistantships available. Financial award application deadline: 8/1; financial award applicants required to submit FAFSA. In 2016, 1 master's awarded. *Program availability:* Part-time, evening/weekend. Offers leadership (MBA). *Application deadline:* For fall admission, 7/1 priority date for domestic and international students; for winter admission, 11/1 for domestic students; for spring admission, 11/1 priority date for domestic and international students; for summer admission, 4/1 priority date for domestic and international students. Applications are processed on a rolling basis. Electronic applications accepted. *Application Contact:* Carli Isgrigg, Assistant Director of Adult and Graduate Education Recruitment, 614-236-6546, Fax: 614-236-6923, E-mail: cisgrigg@capital.edu. *MBA Director,* John Gentner, 614-236-6544, Fax: 614-236-6923, E-mail: jgentner@capital.edu.

School of Nursing *Program availability:* Part-time, evening/weekend. Offers administration (MSN); legal studies (MSN); theological studies (MSN).

CAPITOL TECHNOLOGY UNIVERSITY, Laurel, MD 20708-9759

General Information Independent, coed, comprehensive institution. *Graduate housing:* On-campus housing not available.

GRADUATE UNITS

Graduate Programs *Program availability:* Part-time, evening/weekend, online learning. Offers business administration (MBA); computer science (MS); electrical engineering (MS); information and telecommunications systems management (MS); information architecture (MS); network security (MS). Electronic applications accepted.

CARDINAL STRITCH UNIVERSITY, Milwaukee, WI 53217-3985

General Information Independent-religious, coed, university. *Enrollment:* 2,464 graduate, professional, and undergraduate students; 316 full-time matriculated graduate/professional students (203 women), 614 part-time matriculated graduate/professional students (407 women). *Enrollment by degree level:* 786 master's, 144 doctoral. *Tuition:* Full-time $11,890; part-time $765 per credit hour. Tuition and fees vary according to class time, course load, degree level, program and student's religious affiliation. *Graduate housing:* Room and or apartments available on a first-come, first-served basis to single students; on-campus housing not available to married students. Typical cost: $7940 (including board). Room and board charges vary according to board plan and housing facility selected. *Student services:* Campus employment opportunities, career counseling, exercise/wellness program, free psychological counseling, international student services, multicultural affairs office, services for students with disabilities, teacher training, writing training. *Library facilities:* Cardinal Stritch University Library. *Collection:* Books: 123,152 (physical), 146,127 (digital/electronic); Serial titles: 121 (physical), 71 (digital/electronic); Databases: 74. Weekly public service hours: 90.

Computer facilities: Computer purchase and lease plans are available. 454 computers available on campus for general student use. A campuswide network can be accessed from student residence rooms and from off campus. Online class registration is available.
Website: http://www.stritch.edu/

General Application Contact: Allan D. Mitchler, Vice President for Graduate, Adult and Online Enrollment Service, 800-347-8822 Ext. 4042, E-mail: admissions@stritch.edu.

GRADUATE UNITS

College of Arts and Sciences Students: 11 full-time (8 women), 45 part-time (24 women); includes 12 minority (7 Black or African American, non-Hispanic/Latino; 1 American Indian or Alaska Native, non-Hispanic/Latino; 3 Hispanic/Latino; 1 Two or more races, non-Hispanic/Latino), 5 international. Average age 30. 92 applicants, 24% accepted, 13 enrolled. *Expenses:* Contact institution. *Financial support:* Research assistantships with partial tuition reimbursements, career-related internships or fieldwork, Federal Work-Study, scholarships/grants, and unspecified assistantships available. Financial award applicants required to submit FAFSA. In 2016, 54 master's awarded. *Program availability:* Part-time, evening/weekend. Offers arts and sciences (MA, MS); clinical psychology (MA); ministry (MA); religious studies (MA); sport management (MS). *Application deadline:* For fall admission, 7/15 priority date for domestic students; for spring admission, 12/15 priority date for domestic students. Applications are processed on a rolling basis. *Application fee:* $0. Electronic applications accepted. *Application Contact:* 800-347-8822 Ext. 4042, E-mail: admissions@stritch.edu. *Dean,* Dr. Dan J. Scholz, 414-410-4162, E-mail: djscholz@stritch.edu.

College of Business and Management Students: 226 full-time (130 women), 84 part-time (47 women); includes 117 minority (78 Black or African American, non-Hispanic/Latino; 1 American Indian or Alaska Native, non-Hispanic/Latino; 20 Asian, non-Hispanic/Latino; 14 Hispanic/Latino; 1 Native Hawaiian or other Pacific Islander, non-Hispanic/Latino; 3 Two or more races, non-Hispanic/Latino), 14 international. Average age 35. 247 applicants, 66% accepted, 120 enrolled. *Expenses:* Contact institution. *Financial support:* Career-related internships or fieldwork, Federal Work-Study, and scholarships/grants available. Financial award applicants required to submit FAFSA. In 2016, 309 master's awarded. *Program availability:* Part-time, evening/weekend, 100% online, blended/hybrid learning. Offers healthcare management (MBA). Programs also offered in Madison, WI. *Application deadline:* Applications are processed on a rolling basis. *Application fee:* $0. Electronic applications accepted. *Application Contact:* Graduate Admissions, 414-410-4042, E-mail: admissions@stritch.edu. *Dean,* Dr. Philip Anderson, 414-410-4004, E-mail: ptanderson@stritch.edu.

College of Education and Leadership Students: 106 full-time (87 women), 499 part-time (334 women); includes 147 minority (89 Black or African American, non-Hispanic/Latino; 6 American Indian or Alaska Native, non-Hispanic/Latino; 8 Asian, non-Hispanic/Latino; 33 Hispanic/Latino; 2 Native Hawaiian or other Pacific Islander, non-Hispanic/Latino; 9 Two or more races, non-Hispanic/Latino), 17 international. Average age 36. 344 applicants, 100% accepted, 137 enrolled. *Expenses:* Contact institution. *Financial support:* Fellowships, research assistantships with partial tuition reimbursements, career-related internships or fieldwork, Federal Work-Study, and scholarships/grants available. Financial award applicants required to submit FAFSA. In 2016, 155 master's, 42 doctorates awarded. *Program availability:* Part-time, evening/weekend, 100% online. Offers education and leadership (MA, MS, Ed D, PhD); educational leadership (MS); higher education student affairs leadership (MS); language and literacy (MA, PhD); leadership for the advancement of learning and service (Ed D, PhD); leadership for the advancement of learning and service in higher education (Ed D, PhD); special education (PhD); teaching (MAT); urban education (MA); urban special education (MA). *Application deadline:* For fall admission, 7/15 priority date for domestic students; for spring admission, 12/15 priority date for domestic students. Applications are processed on a rolling basis. Electronic applications accepted. *Application Contact:* Graduate Admissions, 800-347-8822 Ext. 4042, E-mail: admissions@stritch.edu. *Dean,* Dr. Freda Russell, 414-410-4735, E-mail: frrussell@stritch.edu.

Ruth S. Coleman College of Nursing and Health Sciences Students: 9 part-time (all women); includes 3 minority (1 Black or African American, non-Hispanic/Latino; 1 Asian, non-Hispanic/Latino; 1 Two or more races, non-Hispanic/Latino). Average age 33. 18 applicants, 100% accepted. *Expenses:* Contact institution. *Financial support:* Federal Work-Study and scholarships/grants available. Financial award applicants required to submit FAFSA. In 2016, 9 master's awarded. *Program availability:* Part-time, evening/weekend. Offers nursing and health sciences (MSN). *Application deadline:* For fall admission, 6/15 priority date for domestic students; for spring admission, 11/15 priority date for domestic students. Applications are processed on a rolling basis. Electronic applications accepted. *Application Contact:* Graduate Admissions, 800-347-8822 Ext. 4042, E-mail: admissions@stritch.edu. *Dean,* Dr. Kelly J. Dries, 414-410-4397, E-mail: kjdries@stritch.edu.

CAREY THEOLOGICAL COLLEGE, Vancouver, BC V6T 1J6, Canada

General Information Independent-religious, coed, graduate-only institution. *Graduate housing:* Rooms and/or apartments available on a first-come, first-served basis to single and married students. Housing application deadline: 5/31.

GRADUATE UNITS

Graduate Programs *Program availability:* Part-time. Offers theology (M Div, MASF, D Min). Electronic applications accepted.

CARIBBEAN UNIVERSITY, Bayamón, PR 00960-0493

General Information Independent, coed, comprehensive institution.

GRADUATE UNITS
Graduate School

CARLETON UNIVERSITY, Ottawa, ON K1S 5B6, Canada

General Information Province-supported, coed, university. *Graduate housing:* Room and/or apartments guaranteed to single students; on-campus housing not available to married students. Housing application deadline: 5/31.

GRADUATE UNITS

Faculty of Graduate Studies *Program availability:* Part-time, evening/weekend. Electronic applications accepted.

Faculty of Arts and Social Sciences *Program availability:* Part-time, evening/weekend. Offers anthropology (MA); applied language studies (MA); art history: art and its institutions (MA); arts and social sciences (M Sc, MA, PhD); Canadian studies (MA, PhD); cognitive science (PhD); cultural mediations (PhD); English (MA, PhD); film studies (MA); French (MA); geography (M Sc, MA, PhD); history (MA, PhD); music and culture (MA); neuroscience (M Sc); philosophy (MA); psychology (MA, PhD); sociology (MA, PhD).

Faculty of Business Offers business (MBA, PhD); business administration (MBA); management (PhD).

Faculty of Engineering and Design Offers aerospace engineering (M Eng, MA Sc, PhD); biomedical engineering (MA Sc); civil and environmental engineering (M Eng, MA Sc, PhD); design studies (M Arch); electrical engineering (M Eng, M Sc, MA Sc, PhD); engineering and design (M Arch, M Des, M Eng, M Sc, MA Sc, PhD); industrial design (M Des); information and systems science (M Sc); materials engineering (M Eng, MA Sc); mechanical engineering (M Eng, MA Sc, PhD); technology innovation management (M Eng, MA Sc).

Faculty of Public Affairs and Management *Program availability:* Part-time. Offers communication (MA, PhD); conflict resolution (Certificate); economics (MA, PhD); European and European Union studies (MA); European integration studies (Diploma); international affairs (MA, PhD); journalism (MJ); legal studies (MA); political economy (MA, PhD); political science (MA, PhD); public administration (MA, DPA); public affairs and management (MA, MJ, MSW, DPA, PhD, Certificate, Diploma); public policy (PhD); Russian, Eurasian and transition studies (MA); social work (MSW).

Faculty of Science *Program availability:* Part-time, evening/weekend. Offers biology (M Sc, PhD); chemistry (M Sc, PhD); computer science (MCS, PhD); earth sciences (M Sc, PhD); information and system science (M Sc); information and systems science (M Sc); mathematics (M Sc, PhD); physics (M Sc, PhD); science (M Sc, MCS, PhD).

CARLOS ALBIZU UNIVERSITY, San Juan, PR 00901

General Information Independent, coed, university. *Graduate housing:* On-campus housing not available.

GRADUATE UNITS

Graduate Programs *Program availability:* Part-time, evening/weekend. Offers clinical psychology (MS, PhD, Psy D); general psychology (PhD); industrial/organizational psychology (MS, PhD); speech and language pathology (MS).

CARLOS ALBIZU UNIVERSITY, MIAMI CAMPUS, Miami, FL 33172-2209

General Information Independent, coed, comprehensive institution. *Enrollment:* 475 full-time matriculated graduate/professional students (396 women), 191 part-time matriculated graduate/professional students (161 women). *Enrollment by degree level:* 371 master's, 285 doctoral, 10 other advanced degrees. *Graduate faculty:* 28 full-time (22 women), 31 part-time/adjunct (19 women). *Tuition:* Full-time $10,260; part-time $5130 per credit hour. *Required fees:* $302 per term. Tuition and fees vary according to course load, degree level and program. *Graduate housing:* On-campus housing not available. *Student services:* Campus employment opportunities, campus safety program, career counseling, exercise/wellness program, international student services, low-cost health insurance, services for students with disabilities, teacher training, writing training. *Library facilities:* Albizu Library. *Collection:* Books: 27,760 (physical), 22,900 (digital/electronic); Serial titles: 295 (physical), 17,034 (digital/electronic); Databases: 73. Weekly public service hours: 66.

Computer facilities: 268 computers available on campus for general student use. A campuswide network can be accessed from off campus. Online class registration, Campus Portal; Virtual Library; 24/7 Support; Cloud Computing; Learning Center are available.
Website: http://www.albizu.edu/

General Application Contact: Chantel Caraza-Garcia, Administrative Assistant, 305-593-1223 Ext. 3137, Fax: 305-593-1854, E-mail: ccaraza@albizu.edu.

GRADUATE UNITS

Graduate Programs Students: 475 full-time (396 women), 191 part-time (161 women); includes 560 minority (56 Black or African American, non-Hispanic/Latino; 1 American Indian or Alaska Native, non-Hispanic/Latino; 4 Asian, non-Hispanic/Latino; 494 Hispanic/Latino; 5 Two or more races, non-Hispanic/Latino), 15 international. Average age 34. 335 applicants, 46% accepted, 122 enrolled. *Faculty:* 28 full-time (22 women), 31 part-time/adjunct (19 women). Expenses: Contact institution. *Financial support:* In 2016–17, 131 students received support. Federal Work-Study, scholarships/grants, unspecified assistantships, and tuition discounts available. Financial award application deadline: 6/1; financial award applicants required to submit FAFSA. In 2016, 143 master's, 48 doctorates awarded. *Program availability:* Part-time, evening/weekend, 100% online. Offers clinical psychology (PhD, Psy D); entrepreneurship (MBA); exceptional student education (MS); human services (PhD); industrial/organizational psychology (MS); marriage and family therapy (MS); mental health counseling (MS); nonprofit management (MBA); organizational management (MBA); psychology (MS); school counseling (MS); speech and language pathology (MS); teaching English for speakers of other languages (MS). *Application deadline:* For fall admission, 4/1 priority date for domestic students, 5/1 priority date for international students; for spring admission, 11/1 priority date for domestic students, 9/1 priority date for international students. Applications are processed on a rolling basis. *Application fee:* $50. Electronic applications accepted. *Application Contact:* Sonia Feliciano, Institutional Director of Student Recruitment, 305-593-1223 Ext. 3108, Fax: 305-477-8983, E-mail: sfeliciano@albizu.edu. *Provost,* Dr. Etiony Aldarondo, 305-593-1223 Ext. 3138, Fax: 305-592-7930, E-mail: ealdarondo@albizu.edu.

CARLOW UNIVERSITY, Pittsburgh, PA 15213-3165

General Information Independent-religious, coed, primarily women, comprehensive institution. CGS member. *Enrollment:* 2,255 graduate, professional, and undergraduate students; 651 full-time matriculated graduate/professional students (571 women), 194 part-time matriculated graduate/professional students (163 women). *Enrollment by degree level:* 758 master's, 70 doctoral, 17 other advanced degrees. *Graduate faculty:* 25 full-time, 86 part-time/adjunct. *Tuition:* Full-time $11,855; part-time $801 per credit. *Required fees:* $182; $13 per credit. Tuition and fees vary according to course load, degree level and program. *Graduate housing:* Room and/or apartments available on a first-come, first-served basis to single students; on-campus housing not available to married students. Typical cost: $5514 per year ($10,784 including board). Room and board charges vary according to board plan. *Student services:* Campus employment opportunities, campus safety program, career counseling, exercise/wellness program, free psychological counseling, international student services, multicultural affairs office, services for students with disabilities, teacher training, writing training. *Library facilities:* Grace Library.

Computer facilities: A campuswide network can be accessed from student residence rooms and from off campus. Online class registration is available.
Website: http://www.carlow.edu/

General Application Contact: Wendy Phillips, Director, Graduate Admissions, 412-578-8861, Fax: 412-578-6321, E-mail: gradstudies@carlow.edu.

GRADUATE UNITS

College of Health and Wellness Students: 283 full-time (260 women), 74 part-time (67 women); includes 26 minority (9 Black or African American, non-Hispanic/Latino; 1 American Indian or Alaska Native, non-Hispanic/Latino; 6 Asian, non-Hispanic/Latino; 6 Hispanic/Latino; 4 Two or more races, non-Hispanic/Latino), 2 international. Average age 38. 134 applicants, 92% accepted, 80 enrolled. Expenses: Contact institution. *Financial support:* Application deadline: 4/1; applicants required to submit FAFSA. In 2016, 94 master's, 12 doctorates, 4 other advanced degrees awarded. *Program availability:* Part-time, evening/weekend, 100% online, blended/hybrid learning, low-residency. Offers family nurse practitioner (MSN, Certificate); health and wellness (MSN, DNP, Certificate); nursing leadership and education (MSN); nursing practice (DNP). *Application deadline:* For fall admission, 6/15 priority date for domestic and international students; for spring admission, 11/15 priority date for domestic and international students. Applications are processed on a rolling basis. Electronic applications accepted. *Application Contact:* E-mail: gradstudies@carlow.edu. *Dean,* Dr. Lynn George, Fax: 412-578-6114.

College of Leadership and Social Change Students: 288 full-time (238 women), 71 part-time (53 women); includes 100 minority (74 Black or African American, non-Hispanic/Latino; 1 American Indian or Alaska Native, non-Hispanic/Latino; 8 Asian, non-Hispanic/Latino; 9 Hispanic/Latino; 8 Two or more races, non-Hispanic/Latino), 2 international. Average age 32. 189 applicants, 89% accepted, 113 enrolled. Expenses: Contact institution. *Financial support:* Application deadline: 4/1; applicants required to submit FAFSA. In 2016, 124 master's, 12 doctorates, 1 other advanced degree awarded. *Program availability:* Part-time, evening/weekend, 100% online, blended/hybrid learning. Offers addictions (MS); adult/generalist (MS); child and family (MS); counseling psychology (Psy D); fraud and forensics (MS); healthcare management (MBA); human resource management (MBA); leadership and management (MBA); leadership and social change (MBA, MS, Psy D, Certificate); professional counseling (Certificate); project management (MBA); trauma-informed (MS). *Application deadline:* For fall admission, 6/15 priority date for domestic and international students; for spring admission, 11/15 priority date for domestic and international students. Applications are processed on a rolling basis. *Application fee:* $0. Electronic applications accepted. *Application Contact:* 412-578-6059, Fax: 412-578-6321, E-mail: gradstudies@carlow.edu. *Dean,* Dr. Allyson M. Lowe, 412-578-6663, Fax: 412-578-6357, E-mail: amlowe@carlow.edu.

College of Learning and Innovation Students: 79 full-time (72 women), 49 part-time (43 women); includes 17 minority (10 Black or African American, non-Hispanic/Latino; 1 American Indian or Alaska Native, non-Hispanic/Latino; 1 Hispanic/Latino; 5 Two or more races, non-Hispanic/Latino). Average age 34. 51 applicants, 86% accepted, 28 enrolled. Expenses: Contact institution. *Financial support:* Application deadline: 4/1; applicants required to submit FAFSA. In 2016, 26 master's, 3 other advanced degrees awarded. *Program availability:* Part-time, evening/weekend, 100% online, blended/hybrid learning, low-residency. Offers early childhood education (M Ed); educational leadership for high performance learning (MS); educational leadership for high performance learning with principal certification (MS); fiction (MFA); learning and innovation (M Ed, MFA, MS, Graduate Certificate); non-fiction (MFA); poetry (MFA); special education (M Ed). *Application deadline:* Applications are processed on a rolling basis. *Application fee:* $0. Electronic applications accepted. *Dean,* Dr. Matthew Gordley, 412-578-6262, E-mail: megordley@carlow.edu.

CARNEGIE MELLON UNIVERSITY, Pittsburgh, PA 15213-3891

General Information Independent, coed, university. CGS member. *Graduate housing:* On-campus housing not available. *Research affiliation:* National Census Data Research Center (public policy), Robotics Engineering Consortium (computer science and engineering), Software Engineering Institute (computer science and engineering), Carnegie Bosch Institute for Applied Studies in International Management (business and management), Pittsburgh Supercomputer Center.

GRADUATE UNITS

Carnegie Institute of Technology *Program availability:* Part-time, evening/weekend. Offers advanced infrastructure systems (MS, PhD); advanced infrastructure systems technology development and application (MS); air quality engineering and science (MS); bioengineering (MS, PhD); chemical engineering (M Ch E, MS, PhD); civil and environmental engineering (MS, PhD); civil and environmental engineering/engineering and public policy (PhD); civil engineering (MS, PhD); colloids, polymers and surfaces (MS); computational mechanics (MS, PhD); computational modeling and monitoring for resilient structural and material systems (MS); electrical and computer engineering (MS, PhD); energy infrastructure systems (MS); engineering and public policy (PhD); environmental engineering (MS, PhD); environmental management and science (MS, PhD); IT-based sustainable global infrastructure and construction management (MS); materials science and engineering (MS, PhD); mechanical engineering (MS, PhD); product development (MPD); sustainability and green design (MS); technology (M Ch E, MPD, MS, PhD); water quality engineering and science (MS).

Information Networking Institute Offers information networking (MS); information security (MS); information technology - information security (MS); information technology - mobility (MS); information technology - software management (MS).

Center for the Neural Basis of Cognition Offers neural basis of cognition (PhD).

College of Fine Arts *Program availability:* Part-time. Offers fine arts (M Des, M Sc, MAM, MET, MFA, MM, MPD, MS, MSA, MTID, MUD, D Des, PhD). Electronic applications accepted.

School of Architecture Offers architecture (MSA); architecture, engineering, and construction management (PhD); building performance and diagnostics (MS, PhD); computational design (MS, PhD); engineering construction management (MSA); tangible interaction design (MTID); urban design (MUD).

School of Art Offers art (MFA).

School of Design Offers design (M Des, MA, MPD, D Des, PhD); design for interaction (M Des); design for interactions (M Des); design theory (PhD); new product development (PhD); product development (MPD); typography and information design (PhD).

School of Drama Offers design (MFA); directing (MFA); dramatic writing (MFA); production technology and management (MFA); video and media design (MFA).

School of Music *Program availability:* Part-time. Offers collaborative piano (MM); composition (MM); instrumental performance (MM); music and technology (MS); music education (MM); vocal performance (MM).

Dietrich College of Humanities and Social Sciences *Program availability:* Part-time. Offers African and African-American diaspora (PhD); behavioral decision research (PhD); cognitive neuroscience (PhD); cognitive psychology (PhD); communication planning and design (M Des); culture and power (PhD); developmental psychology (PhD); editing and publishing (MAPW); humanities and social sciences (M Des, MA, MAPW, MS, PhD); labor, politics and social movements (PhD); literary and cultural studies (MA, PhD); logic, computation and methodology (MS, PhD); machine learning and statistics (PhD); mathematical finance (PhD); philosophy (MA, PhD); policy and non-profit communication (MAPW); professional writing (MAPW); public and media relations/corporate communications (MAPW); pure and applied logic (PhD); rhetoric (MA, PhD); science or healthcare communication (MAPW); second language acquisition (MA, PhD); social and decision science (PhD); social/personality/health psychology (PhD); statistics (MS, PhD); statistics and public policy (PhD); strategy, entrepreneurship, and technological change (PhD); technical writing (MAPW); technology, environment, science and health (PhD); women, gender and the family (PhD); writing for new media (MAPW); writing for print media (MAPW). Electronic applications accepted.

Heinz College *Program availability:* Part-time, evening/weekend. Offers information systems, public policy, and management (MAM, MEIM, MISM, MMM, MPM, MSBTM, MSHCPM, MSISPM, MSIT, MSPPM, PhD). Electronic applications accepted.

Heinz College Australia Offers information technology (MSIT); public policy and management (MS).

School of Information Systems and Management Offers information security policy and management (MSISPM); information systems and management (MISM, MSISPM, MSIT); information systems management (MISM); information technology (MSIT).

School of Public Policy and Management Offers arts management (MAM); biotechnology and management (MS); entertainment industry management (MEIM); health care policy and management (MSHCPM); medical management (MMM); public management (MPM); public policy and management (MMM, MPM, MS, MSHCPM, PhD).

Joint CMU-Pitt PhD Program in Computational Biology Offers computational biology (PhD).

Mellon College of Science *Program availability:* Part-time. Offers algorithms, combinatorics, and optimization (PhD); applied physics (PhD); atmospheric chemistry (PhD); biochemistry (PhD); bioinorganic chemistry (PhD); bioorganic chemistry and chemical biology (PhD); biophysical chemistry (PhD); biophysics (PhD); catalysis (PhD); cell and developmental biology (PhD); computational biology (MS, PhD); computational finance (MS); genetics (PhD); green and environmental chemistry (PhD); materials and nanoscience (PhD); mathematical finance (PhD); mathematical sciences (DA, PhD); molecular biology (PhD); molecular biophysics and structural biology (PhD); neuroscience (PhD); physics (MS, PhD); pure and applied logic (PhD); renewable energy (PhD); science (MS, DA, PhD); sensors, probes, and imaging (PhD); spectroscopy and single molecule analysis (PhD); structural biology (PhD); theoretical and computational chemistry (PhD). Electronic applications accepted.

School of Computer Science Offers algorithms, combinatorics, and optimization (PhD); computer science (MS, PhD); entertainment technology (MET); human-computer interaction (MHCI, PhD); machine learning (MS, PhD); pure and applied logic (PhD); software engineering (MSE, PhD).

Language Technologies Institute Offers language technologies (MLT, MS, PhD).

Robotics Institute Offers computer vision (MS); robotic systems development (MS); robotics (MS, PhD); robotics technology (MS).

Tepper School of Business *Program availability:* Part-time. Offers accounting (PhD); business management and software engineering (MBMSE); business technologies (PhD); civil engineering and industrial management (MS); computational finance (MSCF); economics (PhD); environmental engineering and management (MEEM); financial economics (PhD); industrial administration (MBA); marketing (PhD); mathematical finance (PhD); operations management (PhD); operations research (PhD); organizational behavior and theory (PhD); production and operations management (PhD); public policy and management (MS, MSED); software engineering and business management (MS). JD/MSIA offered jointly with University of Pittsburgh.

CAROLINA CHRISTIAN COLLEGE, Winston-Salem, NC 27102-0777
General Information Independent-religious, coed, comprehensive institution.
GRADUATE UNITS
Program in Religious Education Offers Christian education (MRE); pastoral care (MRE).

CARROLL UNIVERSITY, Waukesha, WI 53186-5593
General Information Independent-religious, coed, comprehensive institution. *Tuition:* Full-time $10,548; part-time $586 per credit. *Required fees:* $520 per semester. Tuition and fees vary according to course load, degree level and program. *Graduate housing:* On-campus housing not available. *Student services:* Campus employment opportunities, campus safety program, career counseling, exercise/wellness program, free psychological counseling, international student services, multicultural affairs office, services for students with disabilities. *Library facilities:* Todd Wehr Memorial Library.
Computer facilities: Computer purchase and lease plans are available. 400 computers available on campus for general student use. A campuswide network can be accessed from student residence rooms and from off campus. Online class registration is available.
Website: http://www.carrollu.edu/
General Application Contact: Lori Aliota, Director of Graduate Admission, 262-524-7226, E-mail: laliota@carrollu.edu.
GRADUATE UNITS
Graduate Programs in Education Students: 11 full-time (10 women), 163 part-time (125 women); includes 11 minority (3 Black or African American, non-Hispanic/Latino; 3 American Indian or Alaska Native, non-Hispanic/Latino; 2 Asian, non-Hispanic/Latino; 3 Hispanic/Latino), 1 international. Average age 34. 96 applicants, 38% accepted, 18

enrolled. *Faculty:* 7 full-time (5 women), 14 part-time/adjunct (all women). Expenses: Contact institution. *Financial support:* Available to part-time students. Application deadline: 3/15; applicants required to submit FAFSA. In 2016, 43 master's awarded. *Program availability:* Part-time, evening/weekend. Offers adult and continuing education (M Ed); educational leadership (MS); PK-12 (M Ed). *Application deadline:* For fall admission, 8/15 priority date for domestic students. Applications are processed on a rolling basis. *Application fee:* $0. Electronic applications accepted. *Application Contact:* Lori Aliota, Graduate Admission Counselor, 262-524-7226, E-mail: laliota@carrollu.edu. *Director of Graduate Studies,* Dr. Kathrine Kramer, 262-650-4917, E-mail: kkramer@carrollu.edu.

Program in Business Administration Students: 15 part-time (6 women). Average age 28. 54 applicants, 43% accepted. *Faculty:* 2 full-time (both women). Expenses: Contact institution. *Financial support:* Applicants required to submit FAFSA. *Program availability:* Part-time. Offers business administration (MBA). *Application deadline:* Applications are processed on a rolling basis. Electronic applications accepted. *Application Contact:* Kyle Jones, MBA Admission Counselor, 262-524-7225, E-mail: mbainfo@carrollu.edu. *Professor and Academic Leader,* Carol Tallarico, 262-951-3027, E-mail: ctallari@carrollu.edu.

Program in Physical Therapy Students: 78 full-time (59 women); includes 4 minority (2 Asian, non-Hispanic/Latino; 2 Hispanic/Latino). Average age 24. 150 applicants, 69% accepted, 57 enrolled. *Faculty:* 6 full-time (3 women), 5 part-time/adjunct (4 women). Expenses: Contact institution. *Financial support:* Available to part-time students. Application deadline: 3/15; applicants required to submit FAFSA. In 2016, 33 doctorates awarded. Offers physical therapy (DPT). *Application deadline:* For fall admission, 1/14 for domestic students. Applications are processed on a rolling basis. *Application fee:* $50. *Application Contact:* Lori Aliota, Associate Director of Graduate Admission, 262-524-7226, E-mail: ptinfo@carrollu.edu. *Dean, Natural and Health Sciences,* Dr. Jane F. Hopp, 262-524-7294, E-mail: jhopp@carrollu.edu.

Program in Physician Assistant Studies 167 applicants, 16% accepted, 22 enrolled. Expenses: Contact institution. *Financial support:* Applicants required to submit FAFSA. Offers physician assistant studies (MS). *Application fee:* $50. *Application Contact:* Cindy Holahan, Assistant Director of Graduate Admission, 262-524-7361, E-mail: cholahan@carrollu.edu. *Director,* Jessica M. Grusnick, 262-524-7398, E-mail: jgrusnic@carrollu.edu.

Program in Software Engineering Expenses: Contact institution. *Financial support:* Institutionally sponsored loans available. Support available to part-time students. Financial award applicants required to submit FAFSA. *Program availability:* Part-time, evening/weekend. Offers software engineering (MSE). *Application deadline:* For fall admission, 9/15 priority date for domestic students. Applications are processed on a rolling basis. *Application fee:* $0. Electronic applications accepted. *Application Contact:* Lori Aliota, Director of Graduate Admission, 262-524-7226, E-mail: laliota@carrollu.edu. *Professor/Director,* Dr. Chenglie Hu, 262-524-7170, E-mail: chu@carrollu.edu.

CARSON-NEWMAN UNIVERSITY, Jefferson City, TN 37760
General Information Independent-religious, coed, comprehensive institution. *Enrollment:* 2,659 graduate, professional, and undergraduate students; 114 full-time matriculated graduate/professional students (78 women), 658 part-time matriculated graduate/professional students (466 women). *Enrollment by degree level:* 580 master's, 149 doctoral, 43 other advanced degrees. *Graduate faculty:* 38 full-time (20 women), 14 part-time/adjunct (10 women). *Tuition:* Full-time $10,142; part-time $461 per credit hour. *Required fees:* $300; $150 per semester. One-time fee: $150. *Graduate housing:* Room and/or apartments available to single students. Housing application deadline: 7/15. *Student services:* Campus employment opportunities, career counseling, free psychological counseling, international student services, low-cost health insurance, services for students with disabilities. *Library facilities:* Stephens-Burnett Library plus 3 others. *Collection:* Study areas open 24 hours, 5–7 days a week; students can reserve study rooms.
Computer facilities: A campuswide network can be accessed from student residence rooms and from off campus. Online class registration is available.
Website: http://www.cn.edu/
General Application Contact: Nilma Stewart, Graduate Admissions and Services Adviser, 865-471-3230, Fax: 865-471-3875, E-mail: adults@cn.edu.
GRADUATE UNITS
Department of Nursing *Program availability:* Part-time. Offers family nurse practitioner (MSN); nurse educator (MSN).
Graduate Program in Education *Program availability:* Part-time, evening/weekend, 100% online, blended/hybrid learning. Offers curriculum and instruction (M Ed); educational leadership (M Ed); elementary education (MAT); school counseling (MS); secondary education (MAT); teaching English as a second language (MATESL).
Program in Applied Theology *Program availability:* Part-time, evening/weekend. Offers applied theology (MAAT).
Program in Business Administration *Program availability:* Part-time, evening/weekend, 100% online, blended/hybrid learning. Offers business administration (MBA).
Program in Counseling *Program availability:* Part-time, evening/weekend. Offers counseling (MSC).
Program in Social Entrepreneurship *Program availability:* Part-time, evening/weekend, 100% online, blended/hybrid learning. Offers social entrepreneurship (MAASJ).

CARTHAGE COLLEGE, Kenosha, WI 53140
General Information Independent-religious, coed, comprehensive institution. *Graduate housing:* On-campus housing not available.
GRADUATE UNITS
Division of Teacher Education *Program availability:* Part-time, evening/weekend. Offers classroom guidance and counseling (M Ed); creative arts (M Ed); gifted and talented children (M Ed); language arts (M Ed); modern language (M Ed); natural sciences (M Ed); reading (M Ed, Certificate); social sciences (M Ed); teacher leadership (M Ed).

CASE WESTERN RESERVE UNIVERSITY, Cleveland, OH 44106
General Information Independent, coed, university. CGS member. *Enrollment:* 11,664 graduate, professional, and undergraduate students; 5,370 full-time matriculated graduate/professional students (2,873 women), 934 part-time matriculated graduate/professional students (564 women). *Enrollment by degree level:* 3,192 master's, 3,084 doctoral, 28 other advanced degrees. *Graduate faculty:* 3,501 full-time (1,326 women). *Tuition:* Full-time $42,576; part-time $1774 per credit hour. *Required fees:* $34. Tuition and fees vary according to course load and program. *Graduate housing:* On-campus housing not available. *Student services:* Campus employment

opportunities, campus safety program, career counseling, exercise/wellness program, free psychological counseling, grant writing training, international student services, low-cost health insurance, multicultural affairs office, services for students with disabilities, teacher training, writing training. *Library facilities:* Kelvin Smith Library plus 6 others. *Collection:* Books: 3.4 million (physical); Serial titles: 191,970 (physical); Databases: 423. Students can reserve study rooms. *Research affiliation:* Bayer Materials Science (wind materials research), Cleveland Clinic Foundation (biomedical science), Johnson & Johnson Services, Inc. (human health), Cleveland Botanical Garden (plant sciences and ecology), Swagelok Company (surface analysis and materials technology), University Hospitals of Cleveland (biomedical science).

Computer facilities: Computer purchase and lease plans are available. 254 computers available on campus for general student use. A campuswide network can be accessed from student residence rooms and from off campus. Online class registration, software library, online reference databases, electronic books and journals, research computing, training are available.
Website: http://www.case.edu/

GRADUATE UNITS
Frances Payne Bolton School of Nursing Students: 265 full-time (218 women), 231 part-time (191 women); includes 90 minority (38 Black or African American, non-Hispanic/Latino; 29 Asian, non-Hispanic/Latino; 11 Hispanic/Latino; 1 Native Hawaiian or other Pacific Islander, non-Hispanic/Latino; 11 Two or more races, non-Hispanic/Latino), 30 international. Average age 37. 329 applicants, 68% accepted, 161 enrolled. *Faculty:* 31 full-time (27 women). Expenses: Contact institution. *Financial support:* In 2016–17, 254 students received support, including 16 fellowships with full tuition reimbursements available (averaging $13,673 per year), 16 research assistantships with partial tuition reimbursements available (averaging $17,568 per year), 26 teaching assistantships with partial tuition reimbursements available (averaging $17,568 per year); scholarships/grants, traineeships, and Nurse Faculty Loan Program also available. Financial award application deadline: 5/15; financial award applicants required to submit FAFSA. In 2016, 105 master's, 45 doctorates awarded. *Program availability:* Part-time. Offers acute care pediatric nurse practitioner (MSN); acute care/cardiovascular nursing (MSN); acute care/flight nurse (MSN); adult gerontology acute care nurse practitioner (MSN); adult gerontology primary care nurse practitioner (MSN); educational leadership (DNP); family nurse practitioner (MSN); family systems psychiatric mental health nursing (MSN); neonatal nurse practitioner (MSN); nurse anesthesia (MSN); nurse education (MSN); nurse midwifery (MSN); nurse practitioner (MSN); nursing (MN); palliative care (MSN); pediatric nurse practitioner (MSN); practice leadership (DNP); women's health nurse practitioner (MSN). *Application deadline:* For fall admission, 3/1 for domestic students, 6/1 for international students; for spring admission, 9/1 for domestic students, 10/1 for international students; for summer admission, 3/1 for domestic and international students. Applications are processed on a rolling basis. *Application fee:* $75. Electronic applications accepted. *Application Contact:* Jackie Tepale, Admissions Coordinator, Graduate Programs, 216-368-5253, Fax: 216-368-0124, E-mail: yyd@case.edu. *Dean/Professor*, Dr. Mary E. Kerr, 216-368-2545, Fax: 216-368-5050, E-mail: mek55@case.edu.

Jack, Joseph and Morton Mandel School of Applied Social Sciences *Program availability:* Evening/weekend, online learning. Offers nonprofit management (MNO); social welfare (PhD); social work (MSSA). Electronic applications accepted.

School of Dental Medicine Offers advanced general dentistry (Certificate); dental medicine (MSD, DMD, Certificate); dentistry (MSD, DMD, Certificate); endodontics (MSD, Certificate); oral surgery (Certificate); orthodontics (MSD, Certificate); pedodontics (MSD, Certificate); periodontics (MSD, Certificate). Electronic applications accepted.

School of Graduate Studies Students: 2,151 full-time (1,003 women), 319 part-time (156 women); includes 515 minority (134 Black or African American, non-Hispanic/Latino; 234 Asian, non-Hispanic/Latino; 99 Hispanic/Latino; 2 Native Hawaiian or other Pacific Islander, non-Hispanic/Latino; 46 Two or more races, non-Hispanic/Latino), 772 international. Average age 28. 4,979 applicants, 36% accepted, 868 enrolled. *Faculty:* 3,501 full-time (1,326 women). Expenses: Contact institution. *Financial support:* Fellowships with tuition reimbursements, research assistantships with tuition reimbursements, teaching assistantships with tuition reimbursements, career-related internships or fieldwork, Federal Work-Study, institutionally sponsored loans, scholarships/grants, traineeships, health care benefits, tuition waivers (full and partial), and unspecified assistantships available. Support available to part-time students. Financial award applicants required to submit CSS PROFILE or FAFSA. In 2016, 611 master's, 215 doctorates awarded. *Program availability:* Part-time, evening/weekend, online learning. Offers acting (MFA); anthropology (MA, PhD); applied mathematics (MS, PhD); art education (MA); art history (MA, PhD); art history and museum studies (MA); astronomy (MS, PhD); biology (MS, PhD); chemistry (MS, PhD); clinical psychology (PhD); cognitive linguistics (MA); communication sciences (MA, PhD); dance (MA, MFA); early music (MA, D Mus A); earth, environmental, and planetary sciences (MS, PhD); English (MA, PhD); experimental psychology (PhD); French (MA); historical musicology (MA, PhD); historical performance practice (DMA); history (MA, PhD); mathematics (MS, PhD); music education (MA, PhD); music history (MA); physician assistant (MS); physics (MS, PhD); political science (MA, PhD); sociology (MA, PhD); speech-language pathology (MA, PhD); theater (MA); world literature (MA). *Application deadline:* For fall admission, 3/1 for domestic students; for spring admission, 11/1 for domestic students. *Application fee:* $50. Electronic applications accepted. *Vice Provost and Dean*, Dr. Charles E. Rozek, 216-368-4390, Fax: 216-368-4250, E-mail: charles.rozek@case.edu.

Case School of Engineering Students: 632 full-time (173 women), 70 part-time (21 women); includes 75 minority (11 Black or African American, non-Hispanic/Latino; 48 Asian, non-Hispanic/Latino; 11 Hispanic/Latino; 5 Two or more races, non-Hispanic/Latino), 433 international. 1,310 applicants, 48% accepted, 447 enrolled. *Faculty:* 112 full-time (15 women). Expenses: Contact institution. *Financial support:* In 2016–17, 334 students received support, including 35 fellowships with tuition reimbursements available, 258 research assistantships with tuition reimbursements available, 32 teaching assistantships; career-related internships or fieldwork, Federal Work-Study, and institutionally sponsored loans also available. Support available to part-time students. Financial award applicants required to submit FAFSA. In 2016, 153 master's, 70 doctorates awarded. *Program availability:* Part-time, evening/weekend, 100% online, blended/hybrid learning. Offers biomedical engineering (MS, PhD); chemical and biomolecular engineering (MS, PhD); civil engineering (MS, PhD); computer engineering (MS, PhD); computing and information sciences (MS, PhD); electrical engineering (MS, PhD); engineering (ME, MEM, MS, PhD); macromolecular science and engineering (MS, PhD); management and engineering (MEM); materials science and engineering (MS, PhD); mechanical and aerospace engineering (MS, PhD); systems and control engineering (MS, PhD). *Application deadline:* Applications are processed on a rolling basis. *Application fee:* $50. Electronic applications accepted. *Application Contact:* Dr. Marc Buchner,

Associate Dean, Academics, 216-368-4096, Fax: 216-368-6939, E-mail: marc.buchner@case.edu. *Dean/Professor*, Jeffrey L. Duerk, 216-368-4436, Fax: 216-368-6939, E-mail: duerk@case.edu.

Cleveland Clinic Lerner Research Institute–Molecular Medicine PhD Program Students: 38 full-time (26 women); includes 7 minority (5 Black or African American, non-Hispanic/Latino; 2 Asian, non-Hispanic/Latino), 4 international. Average age 27. 62 applicants, 11% accepted, 7 enrolled. *Faculty:* 157 full-time (46 women). Expenses: Contact institution. *Financial support:* Fellowships with full tuition reimbursements, health care benefits, and stipends available. In 2016, 10 doctorates awarded. Offers molecular medicine (PhD). *Application deadline:* For fall admission, 1/15 priority date for domestic students, 11/1 for international students. *Application fee:* $50. Electronic applications accepted. *Director of Research Education and Training*, Dr. Christine Moravec, 216-445-9949, E-mail: moravec@ccf.org.

School of Law Students: 421 full-time (215 women), 1 (woman) part-time; includes 76 minority (37 Black or African American, non-Hispanic/Latino; 17 Asian, non-Hispanic/Latino; 19 Hispanic/Latino; 3 Two or more races, non-Hispanic/Latino), 37 international. Average age 24. 1,645 applicants, 43% accepted, 144 enrolled. *Faculty:* 40 full-time (15 women), 25 part-time/adjunct (4 women). Expenses: Contact institution. *Financial support:* In 2016–17, 345 students received support. Career-related internships or fieldwork, Federal Work-Study, institutionally sponsored loans, and scholarships/grants available. Financial award application deadline: 5/1; financial award applicants required to submit FAFSA. In 2016, 72 master's, 99 doctorates awarded. Offers financial integrity (MA); health law (SJD); intellectual property (LL M); international business law (LL M); international criminal law (LL M); law (JD, SJD); patent practice (MA); U.S. legal studies (LL M). *Application deadline:* For fall admission, 4/1 priority date for domestic and international students. Applications are processed on a rolling basis. *Application fee:* $40. Electronic applications accepted. *Application Contact:* Kelli Curtis, Associate Dean for Admissions, 216-368-3600, Fax: 216-368-0185, E-mail: lawadmissions@case.edu. *Co-Dean*, Jessica Berg, 216-368-3283.

School of Medicine Expenses: Contact institution. *Financial support:* Fellowships, research assistantships, teaching assistantships, career-related internships or fieldwork, Federal Work-Study, institutionally sponsored loans, and tuition waivers (full and partial) available. Support available to part-time students. *Program availability:* Part-time. Offers clinical research (MS, PhD); medicine (MA, MPH, MS, MD, PhD). *Application deadline:* Applications are processed on a rolling basis. *Application fee:* $50. *Application Contact:* Dr. Alison K. Hall, Director, Graduate Education, 216-368-8668, Fax: 216-368-0795, E-mail: alison.hall@case.edu. *Dean*, Dr. Pamela Davis, 216-368-2825.

Graduate Programs in Medicine Expenses: Contact institution. *Financial support:* Fellowships, research assistantships, teaching assistantships, career-related internships or fieldwork, Federal Work-Study, institutionally sponsored loans, tuition waivers (full and partial), and unspecified assistantships available. Support available to part-time students. *Program availability:* Part-time. Offers anesthesiologist assistant (MS); applied anatomy (MS); biochemistry (MS, PhD); bioethics (MA); biostatistics (MS); cancer biology (PhD); cell biology (PhD); dietetics (MS); epidemiology and biostatistics (PhD); genetic counseling (MS); genetics and genome sciences (PhD); immunology (PhD); medical physiology (MS); medicine (MA, MPH, MS, PhD); molecular and cellular basis of disease (PhD); molecular biology (PhD); molecular medicine (PhD); molecular nutrition (MS); molecular virology (PhD); neuroscience (PhD); nutrition (MS, PhD); nutritional biochemistry and metabolism (MS); pathology (MS); pharmacology (PhD); physiology and biophysics (PhD); public health (MPH); public health nutrition (MS). *Application deadline:* For fall admission, 3/1 priority date for domestic students, 2/1 priority date for international students; for spring admission, 11/1 priority date for domestic students, 10/1 priority date for international students. Applications are processed on a rolling basis. *Application fee:* $50. Electronic applications accepted. *Application Contact:* Deborah Noureddine, Coordinator, 216-368-3347, Fax: 216-368-0795, E-mail: deborah.noureddine@case.edu. *Dean*, Dr. Alison K. Hall, 216-368-8668, Fax: 216-368-0795, E-mail: alison.hall@case.edu.

Weatherhead School of Management *Program availability:* Part-time, evening/weekend. Offers accountancy (M Acc, PhD); business administration (EMBA, MBA); business analytics (MSM); designing sustainable systems (PhD); finance (MSM); healthcare (MSM); management (EMBA, M Acc, MBA, MNO, MPOD, MS, MSM, EDM, PhD, CNM); operations and supply chain management (MSM); operations research (PhD); organizational behavior (PhD); positive organization development and change (MS). Electronic applications accepted.

Mandel Center for Nonprofit Organizations Offers nonprofit management (MNO, CNM).

CASTLETON UNIVERSITY, Castleton, VT 05735
General Information State-supported, coed, comprehensive institution. *Graduate housing:* Room and/or apartments available on a first-come, first-served basis to single students; on-campus housing not available to married students. Housing application deadline: 5/19.

GRADUATE UNITS
Division of Graduate Studies *Program availability:* Part-time, evening/weekend. Offers curriculum and instruction (MA Ed); educational leadership (MA Ed, CAGS); forensic psychology (MA); language arts and reading (MA Ed, CAGS); special education (MA Ed, CAGS).

CATAWBA COLLEGE, Salisbury, NC 28144-2488
General Information Independent-religious, coed, comprehensive institution. *Enrollment:* 1,306 graduate, professional, and undergraduate students; 9 part-time matriculated graduate/professional students (all women). *Enrollment by degree level:* 9 master's. *Graduate faculty:* 4 full-time (3 women), 1 part-time/adjunct (0 women). *Tuition:* Part-time $185 per semester hour. *Required fees:* $25 per semester. *Graduate housing:* On-campus housing not available. *Student services:* Campus safety program, career counseling, exercise/wellness program, teacher training. *Library facilities:* Corriher-Linn-Black Memorial Library plus 1 other. *Collection:* Books: 151,650 (physical), 184,548 (digital/electronic); Serial titles: 95 (physical), 32,589 (digital/electronic); Databases: 102. Weekly public service hours: 83; students can reserve study rooms.

Computer facilities: 173 computers available on campus for general student use. A campuswide network can be accessed from student residence rooms and from off campus. Online class registration is available.
Website: http://www.catawba.edu/

General Application Contact: Dr. Kimberly Creamer, Director, Graduate Program, 704-637-4462, Fax: 704-637-4732, E-mail: kcreamer14@catawba.edu.

GRADUATE UNITS
Department of Teacher Education Students: 9 part-time (all women). Average age 30. 9 applicants, 100% accepted, 9 enrolled. *Faculty:* 4 full-time (3 women), 1 part-

time/adjunct (0 women). Expenses: Contact institution. *Financial support:* In 2016–17, 9 students received support. Scholarships/grants and free tuition (for Rowan-Salisbury teachers only) available. Financial award application deadline: 10/1. In 2016, 3 master's awarded. *Program availability:* Part-time-only. Offers elementary education (M Ed); STEM education (M Ed). *Application deadline:* For spring admission, 10/1 for domestic students. Applications are processed on a rolling basis. *Application fee:* $25. Electronic applications accepted. *Application Contact:* Jane V. Snider, Administrative Assistant, 704-637-4461, Fax: 704-637-4732, E-mail: jvsnider@catawba.edu. *Director, Graduate Program,* Dr. Kimberly Creamer, 704-637-4462, Fax: 704-637-4732, E-mail: kcreamer14@catawba.edu.

CATHOLIC DISTANCE UNIVERSITY, Charles Town, WV 25414

General Information Independent-religious, coed, graduate-only institution. *Graduate housing:* On-campus housing not available.

GRADUATE UNITS

Graduate Programs *Program availability:* Part-time, evening/weekend, online learning. Offers religious studies (MRS); theology (MA).

CATHOLIC THEOLOGICAL UNION, Chicago, IL 60615-5698

General Information Independent-religious, coed, graduate-only institution. *Graduate housing:* Rooms and/or apartments available on a first-come, first-served basis to single and married students. Housing application deadline: 7/1.

GRADUATE UNITS

Graduate and Professional Programs *Program availability:* Part-time, evening/weekend. Offers biblical spirituality (Certificate); cross-cultural ministries (D Min); cross-cultural missions (Certificate); divinity (M Div); liturgical studies (Certificate); liturgy (D Min); pastoral studies (MAPS, Certificate); spiritual formation (Certificate); spirituality (Certificate); theology (MA). M Div/PhD offered jointly with University of Chicago; M Div/MSW with Loyola University Chicago and University of Chicago.

THE CATHOLIC UNIVERSITY OF AMERICA, Washington, DC 20064

General Information Independent-religious, coed, university. CGS member. *Enrollment:* 6,060 graduate, professional, and undergraduate students; 1,072 full-time matriculated graduate/professional students (474 women), 1,706 part-time matriculated graduate/professional students (1,015 women). *Enrollment by degree level:* 1,469 master's, 1,268 doctoral, 41 other advanced degrees. *Graduate faculty:* 413 full-time (157 women), 323 part-time/adjunct (123 women). *Tuition:* $42,850; part-time $1710 per credit. *Required fees:* $600; $400 per credit. $200 per semester. Part-time tuition and fees vary according to course load and program. *Graduate housing:* Room and/or apartments available on a first-come, first-served basis to single students; on-campus housing not available to married students. Typical cost: $16,372 (including board). Room and board charges vary according to board plan. Housing application deadline: 5/15. *Student services:* Campus employment opportunities, campus safety program, career counseling, exercise/wellness program, free psychological counseling, international student services, low-cost health insurance, multicultural affairs office, services for students with disabilities, teacher training, writing training. *Library facilities:* Mullen Library plus 7 others. *Collection:* Books: 739,107 (physical), 216,309 (digital/electronic); Serial titles: 338,081 (physical), 87,846 (digital/electronic); Databases: 418. Weekly public service hours: 102. *Research affiliation:* EnergySolutions (waste vitrification research), National Rehabilitation Hospital (rehabilitation engineering research), Samsung (building environmental control), Space Telescope Science Institute (astronomy and space physics research), Better Way Foundation (early childhood education), Eco-Convergence Group, Inc. (concrete materials research).

Computer facilities: Computer purchase and lease plans are available. 542 computers available on campus for general student use. A campuswide network can be accessed from student residence rooms and from off campus. Online class registration is available.

Website: http://www.cua.edu/

General Application Contact: Director of Graduate Admissions, 202-319-5057, Fax: 202-319-6533, E-mail: cua-admissions@cua.edu.

GRADUATE UNITS

Benjamin T. Rome School of Music Students: 29 full-time (15 women), 71 part-time (31 women); includes 26 minority (7 Black or African American, non-Hispanic/Latino; 13 Asian, non-Hispanic/Latino; 6 Hispanic/Latino), 22 international. Average age 33. 80 applicants, 73% accepted, 24 enrolled. *Faculty:* 20 full-time (4 women), 53 part-time/adjunct (21 women). Expenses: Contact institution. *Financial support:* Fellowships, research assistantships, teaching assistantships, Federal Work-Study, scholarships/grants, tuition waivers (full and partial), and unspecified assistantships available. Financial award application deadline: 2/1; financial award applicants required to submit FAFSA. In 2016, 15 master's, 9 doctorates awarded. *Program availability:* Part-time. Offers cello (Artist Diploma); chamber music (piano) (MM, DMA); composition (MM, DMA); music (MAT); musicology (MA, PhD); orchestral conducting (MM, DMA, Artist Diploma); orchestral instruments/guitar (MM, DMA); piano (Artist Diploma); piano pedagogy (MM, DMA); piano performance (MM, DMA); sacred music (MMSM, DMA); violin (Artist Diploma); vocal accompanying (MM, DMA); vocal pedagogy (MM, DMA); vocal performance (MM, DMA); voice (Artist Diploma). MA/MSLIS offered in partnership with Department of Library and Information Science. *Application deadline:* For fall admission, 7/15 priority date for domestic students, 7/1 for international students; for spring admission, 11/15 priority date for domestic students, 11/1 for international students. Applications are processed on a rolling basis. *Application fee:* $55. Electronic applications accepted. *Application Contact:* Director of Graduate Admissions, 202-319-5057, Fax: 202-319-6533, E-mail: cua-admissions@cua.edu. *Dean,* Dr. Grayson Wagstaff, 202-319-5417, Fax: 202-319-6280, E-mail: cua-music@cua.edu.

Busch School of Business and Economics Students: 60 full-time (32 women), 26 part-time (14 women); includes 26 minority (11 Black or African American, non-Hispanic/Latino; 8 Asian, non-Hispanic/Latino; 5 Hispanic/Latino; 2 Two or more races, non-Hispanic/Latino), 22 international. Average age 29. 121 applicants, 77% accepted, 64 enrolled. *Faculty:* 30 full-time (7 women), 30 part-time/adjunct (5 women). Expenses: Contact institution. *Financial support:* Fellowships, research assistantships, teaching assistantships, Federal Work-Study, scholarships/grants, tuition waivers (full and partial), and unspecified assistantships available. Financial award application deadline: 2/1; financial award applicants required to submit FAFSA. In 2016, 48 master's awarded. *Program availability:* Part-time. Offers accounting (MS); business analysis (MSBA); integral economic development management (MA); integral economic development policy (MA); management (MS). *Application deadline:* For fall admission, 7/15 priority date for domestic students, 7/1 for international students; for spring admission, 11/15 priority date for domestic students, 11/1 for international students. Applications are processed on a rolling basis. *Application fee:* $55. Electronic applications accepted.

Application Contact: Director of Graduate Admissions, 202-319-5057, Fax: 202-319-6533, E-mail: cua-admissions@cua.edu. *Dean,* Dr. William Bowman, 202-319-5290, Fax: 202-319-4426, E-mail: otey@cua.edu.

Columbus School of Law Students: 262 full-time (141 women), 131 part-time (62 women); includes 70 minority (32 Black or African American, non-Hispanic/Latino; 2 American Indian or Alaska Native, non-Hispanic/Latino; 2 Asian, non-Hispanic/Latino; 22 Hispanic/Latino; 12 Two or more races, non-Hispanic/Latino), 3 international. Average age 26. 1,265 applicants, 51% accepted, 123 enrolled. *Faculty:* 43 full-time (21 women), 83 part-time/adjunct (19 women). Expenses: Contact institution. *Financial support:* In 2016–17, 330 students received support. Career-related internships or fieldwork, Federal Work-Study, institutionally sponsored loans, and scholarships/grants available. Support available to part-time students. Financial award application deadline: 8/15; financial award applicants required to submit FAFSA. In 2016, 138 doctorates awarded. *Program availability:* Part-time, evening/weekend. Offers law (MLS, JD). *Application deadline:* For fall admission, 3/16 priority date for domestic students, 3/16 for international students. Applications are processed on a rolling basis. *Application fee:* $65. Electronic applications accepted. *Application Contact:* Shani J. P. Butts, Assistant Dean of Admissions, 202-319-5151, Fax: 202-319-4462, E-mail: butts@law.edu. *Dean,* Daniel F. Attridge, 202-319-5139, Fax: 202-319-5473.

Metropolitan School of Professional Studies Students: 12 full-time (5 women), 85 part-time (42 women); includes 53 minority (29 Black or African American, non-Hispanic/Latino; 2 Asian, non-Hispanic/Latino; 12 Hispanic/Latino; 10 Two or more races, non-Hispanic/Latino), 2 international. Average age 37. 9 applicants, 89% accepted, 4 enrolled. *Faculty:* 35 part-time/adjunct (10 women). Expenses: Contact institution. *Financial support:* Scholarships/grants available. Financial award application deadline: 3/15; financial award applicants required to submit FAFSA. In 2016, 97 master's awarded. *Program availability:* Part-time, evening/weekend, 100% online. Offers emergency service administration (MS); health administration (MHA); social service administration (MS). *Application deadline:* For fall admission, 7/15 priority date for domestic students, 7/1 for international students; for spring admission, 11/15 priority date for domestic students, 11/1 for international students. Applications are processed on a rolling basis. *Application fee:* $55. Electronic applications accepted. *Application Contact:* Director of Graduate Admissions, 202-319-5057, Fax: 202-319-6533, E-mail: cua-admissions@cua.edu. *Dean,* Dr. Vince Kiernan, 202-319-5256, Fax: 202-319-6260, E-mail: kiernan@cua.edu.

National Catholic School of Social Service Students: 121 full-time (98 women), 408 part-time (360 women); includes 238 minority (142 Black or African American, non-Hispanic/Latino; 12 Asian, non-Hispanic/Latino; 50 Hispanic/Latino; 34 Two or more races, non-Hispanic/Latino), 7 international. Average age 35. 414 applicants, 64% accepted, 157 enrolled. *Faculty:* 16 full-time (13 women), 21 part-time/adjunct (15 women). Expenses: Contact institution. *Financial support:* Fellowships, research assistantships, teaching assistantships, Federal Work-Study, scholarships/grants, tuition waivers (full and partial), and unspecified assistantships available. Financial award application deadline: 3/15; financial award applicants required to submit FAFSA. In 2016, 84 master's, 5 doctorates awarded. *Program availability:* Part-time, 100% online. Offers clinical (MSW); combined (clinical and social change) (MSW); social change (MSW); social work (PhD). MSW/JD offered with Columbus School of Law. *Application deadline:* For fall admission, 7/15 priority date for domestic students, 7/1 for international students; for spring admission, 11/15 priority date for domestic students, 11/1 for international students. Applications are processed on a rolling basis. *Application fee:* $60. Electronic applications accepted. *Application Contact:* Director of Graduate Admissions, 202-319-5057, Fax: 202-319-6533, E-mail: cua-admissions@cua.edu. *Dean,* Dr. Will Rainford, 202-319-5454, Fax: 202-319-5093, E-mail: rainford@cua.edu.

School of Architecture and Planning Students: 69 full-time (28 women), 21 part-time (13 women); includes 35 minority (11 Black or African American, non-Hispanic/Latino; 5 Asian, non-Hispanic/Latino; 11 Hispanic/Latino; 8 Two or more races, non-Hispanic/Latino), 13 international. Average age 28. 73 applicants, 84% accepted, 24 enrolled. *Faculty:* 20 full-time (7 women), 15 part-time/adjunct (1 woman). Expenses: Contact institution. *Financial support:* Fellowships, research assistantships, teaching assistantships, Federal Work-Study, scholarships/grants, tuition waivers (full and partial), and unspecified assistantships available. Financial award application deadline: 2/1; financial award applicants required to submit FAFSA. In 2016, 42 master's awarded. *Program availability:* Part-time. Offers architecture and planning (M Arch, MS Arch St); city and regional planning (M Arch); facilities management (MS Arch); regional development (Certificate); sustainable design (M Arch, Certificate). *Application deadline:* For fall admission, 1/15 priority date for domestic students, 7/1 for international students; for spring admission, 10/15 priority date for domestic students, 11/1 for international students. Applications are processed on a rolling basis. *Application fee:* $55. Electronic applications accepted. *Application Contact:* Director of Graduate Admissions, 202-319-5057, Fax: 202-319-6533, E-mail: cua-admissions@cua.edu. *Dean,* Randall Ott, 202-319-5784, Fax: 202-319-2023, E-mail: ott@cua.edu.

School of Arts and Sciences Students: 184 full-time (91 women), 326 part-time (189 women); includes 92 minority (30 Black or African American, non-Hispanic/Latino; 14 Asian, non-Hispanic/Latino; 22 Hispanic/Latino; 26 Two or more races, non-Hispanic/Latino), 93 international. Average age 31. 551 applicants, 52% accepted, 130 enrolled. *Faculty:* 162 full-time (73 women), 62 part-time/adjunct (29 women). Expenses: Contact institution. *Financial support:* Fellowships, research assistantships, teaching assistantships, Federal Work-Study, scholarships/grants, tuition waivers (full and partial), and unspecified assistantships available. Financial award application deadline: 2/1; financial award applicants required to submit FAFSA. In 2016, 142 master's, 41 doctorates awarded. *Program availability:* Part-time. Offers acting (MFA); American government (MA); ancient Near East (Biblical Hebrew/Aramaic) (MA, PhD); anthropology (MA); applied experimental psychology (PhD); Arabic (PhD); arts and sciences (MA, MFA, MS, MSBA, MSLS, PhD, Certificate); biotechnology (MS); Byzantine and Orthodox studies (MA); Catholic school leadership (MA); cell and microbial biology (MS, PhD); Christian Near East (Biblical Hebrew/Aramaic) (MA); clinical laboratory science (MS, PhD); clinical psychology (PhD); Congressional and Presidential studies (MA); Coptic (MA, PhD); creative teaching through drama (Certificate); crime and justice studies (MA); directing (MFA); early Christian studies (MA, PhD); education (Certificate); English (MA, PhD); general psychology (MA); global and comparative sociology (MA); Greek (MA, Certificate); Greek and Latin (MA, PhD, Certificate); Hispanic studies (MA, PhD); history (MA, PhD); human development psychology (PhD); human factors (MA); international affairs (MA); international political economics (MA); Latin (MA, Certificate); library and information science (MSLS, Certificate); Medieval and Byzantine studies (PhD, Certificate); nuclear environmental protection (MS); physics (MS, PhD); playwriting (MFA); political theory (MA, PhD); public policy (MA); religion and society in the late medieval and early modern world (MA); rhetoric (Certificate); secondary education (MA); special education (MA); Syriac (MA, PhD); the Islamic world (MA); the Medieval West (MA); theatre education (MA); theatre history and criticism (MA); world politics (MA, PhD). *Application deadline:* For fall admission, 2/1 priority date for domestic students, 7/1 for international students; for spring admission, 11/15 priority date for domestic students, 11/1 for international students. Applications are processed on a rolling basis. *Application fee:* $55. Electronic applications accepted. *Application Contact:* Director of Graduate Admissions, 202-319-5057, Fax: 202-319-6533, E-mail: cua-admissions@cua.edu. *Dean,* Dr. Aaron Dominguez, 202-319-5115, Fax: 202-319-4463, E-mail: artsandsciences@cua.edu.

School of Canon Law Students: 25 full-time (2 women), 49 part-time (7 women); includes 9 minority (1 Black or African American, non-Hispanic/Latino; 2 Asian, non-Hispanic/Latino; 5 Hispanic/Latino; 1 Two or more races, non-Hispanic/Latino), 11 international. Average age 38. 26 applicants, 88% accepted, 21 enrolled. *Faculty:* 8 full-time (1 woman), 2 part-time/adjunct (0 women). Expenses: Contact institution. *Financial support:* Fellowships, research assistantships, teaching assistantships, Federal Work-Study, scholarships/grants, tuition waivers (full and partial), and unspecified assistantships available. Financial award application deadline: 2/1; financial award applicants required to submit FAFSA. In 2016, 25 master's, 2 doctorates awarded. *Program availability:* Part-time. Offers Canon law (JCD, JCL); church administration (MCA). JD/JCL offered jointly with Columbus School of Law. *Application deadline:* For fall admission, 7/15 priority date for domestic students, 7/1 for international students; for spring admission, 11/15 priority date for domestic students, 11/1 for international students. Applications are processed on a rolling basis. *Application fee:* $55. Electronic applications accepted. *Application Contact:* Director of Graduate Admissions, 202-319-5057, Fax: 202-319-6533, E-mail: cua.edu. *Dean,* Msgr. Ronny Jenkins, 202-319-5492, Fax: 202-319-4187, E-mail: cua-canonlaw@cua.edu.

School of Engineering Students: 70 full-time (18 women), 104 part-time (28 women); includes 32 minority (13 Black or African American, non-Hispanic/Latino; 4 Asian, non-Hispanic/Latino; 2 Hispanic/Latino; 13 Two or more races, non-Hispanic/Latino), 104 international. Average age 32. 166 applicants, 68% accepted, 48 enrolled. *Faculty:* 33 full-time (3 women), 26 part-time/adjunct (2 women). Expenses: Contact institution. *Financial support:* Fellowships, research assistantships, teaching assistantships, Federal Work-Study, scholarships/grants, tuition waivers (full and partial), and unspecified assistantships available. Financial award application deadline: 2/1; financial award applicants required to submit FAFSA. In 2016, 72 master's, 13 doctorates awarded. *Program availability:* Part-time. Offers biomedical engineering (MBE, PhD); civil engineering (MS, PhD); computer science (MSCS, PhD); electrical engineering (MEE, PhD); energy and environment (MME); engineering (MBE, MCE, MEE, MME, MS, MSCS, MSE, PhD, Certificate); engineering management (MSE, Certificate); general (MME); materials science and engineering (MS); mechanical engineering (MSE, PhD); program management (Certificate); systems engineering and management of information technology (Certificate); transportation and infrastructure systems (Certificate). *Application deadline:* For fall admission, 7/15 priority date for domestic students, 7/1 for international students; for spring admission, 11/15 priority date for domestic students, 11/1 for international students. Applications are processed on a rolling basis. *Application fee:* $55. Electronic applications accepted. *Application Contact:* Director of Graduate Admissions, 202-319-5057, Fax: 202-319-6533, E-mail: cua-admissions@cua.edu. *Dean,* Dr. Charles C. Nguyen, 202-319-5160, Fax: 202-319-4499, E-mail: nguyen@cua.edu.

School of Nursing Students: 23 full-time (21 women), 215 part-time (198 women); includes 81 minority (57 Black or African American, non-Hispanic/Latino; 8 Asian, non-Hispanic/Latino; 6 Hispanic/Latino; 10 Two or more races, non-Hispanic/Latino), 12 international. Average age 40. 129 applicants, 69% accepted, 56 enrolled. *Faculty:* 21 full-time (all women), 38 part-time/adjunct (31 women). Expenses: Contact institution. *Financial support:* Fellowships, research assistantships, teaching assistantships, Federal Work-Study, scholarships/grants, tuition waivers (full and partial), and unspecified assistantships available. Financial award application deadline: 2/1; financial award applicants required to submit FAFSA. In 2016, 24 master's, 9 doctorates awarded. *Program availability:* Part-time, 100% online. Offers nursing (MSN, DNP, PhD, Certificate). *Application deadline:* For fall admission, 7/15 priority date for domestic students, 7/1 for international students; for spring admission, 11/15 priority date for domestic students, 11/1 for international students. Applications are processed on a rolling basis. *Application fee:* $55. Electronic applications accepted. *Application Contact:* Director of Graduate Admissions, 202-319-5057, Fax: 202-319-6533, E-mail: cua-admissions@cua.edu. *Dean,* Dr. Patricia McMullen, 202-319-5403, Fax: 202-319-6485, E-mail: mcmullep@cua.edu.

School of Philosophy Students: 57 full-time (8 women), 70 part-time (12 women); includes 10 minority (3 Asian, non-Hispanic/Latino; 6 Hispanic/Latino; 1 Two or more races, non-Hispanic/Latino), 8 international. Average age 32. 75 applicants, 53% accepted, 25 enrolled. *Faculty:* 22 full-time (5 women), 4 part-time/adjunct (0 women). Expenses: Contact institution. *Financial support:* Fellowships, research assistantships, teaching assistantships, Federal Work-Study, scholarships/grants, tuition waivers (full and partial), and unspecified assistantships available. Financial award application deadline: 2/1; financial award applicants required to submit FAFSA. In 2016, 11 master's, 4 doctorates awarded. *Program availability:* Part-time. Offers philosophy (MA, PhD, Ph L). MA/JD offered in combination with Columbus School of Law. *Application deadline:* For fall admission, 7/15 priority date for domestic students, 7/1 for international students; for spring admission, 11/15 priority date for domestic students, 11/1 for international students. Applications are processed on a rolling basis. *Application fee:* $55. Electronic applications accepted. *Application Contact:* Director of Graduate Admissions, 202-319-5057, Fax: 202-319-6533, E-mail: cua-admissions@cua.edu. *Dean,* Dr. John McCarthy, 202-319-6649, Fax: 202-319-4731, E-mail: mccartjc@cua.edu.

School of Theology and Religious Studies Students: 156 full-time (11 women), 193 part-time (51 women); includes 61 minority (9 Black or African American, non-Hispanic/Latino; 1 American Indian or Alaska Native, non-Hispanic/Latino; 13 Asian, non-Hispanic/Latino; 24 Hispanic/Latino; 14 Two or more races, non-Hispanic/Latino), 51 international. Average age 36. 168 applicants, 65% accepted, 58 enrolled. *Faculty:* 40 full-time (2 women), 8 part-time/adjunct (2 women). Expenses: Contact institution. *Financial support:* Fellowships, research assistantships, teaching assistantships, Federal Work-Study, scholarships/grants, tuition waivers (full and partial), and unspecified assistantships available. Financial award application deadline: 2/1; financial award applicants required to submit FAFSA. In 2016, 96 master's, 20 doctorates awarded. *Program availability:* Part-time. Offers theology and religious studies (M Cat, M Div, MA, D Min, PhD, STD, Certificate, STB, STL). MSLA/MA offered in conjunction with Department of Library and Information Science. *Application deadline:* For fall admission, 7/15 priority date for domestic students, 7/1 for international students; for spring admission, 11/15 priority date for domestic students, 11/1 for international students. Applications are processed on a rolling basis. *Application fee:* $55. Electronic applications accepted. *Application Contact:* Director of Graduate Admissions, 202-319-5057, Fax: 202-319-6533, E-mail: cua-admissions@cua.edu. *Dean,* Very Rev. Mark Morozowich, 202-319-5684, Fax: 202-319-4967, E-mail: morozowich@cua.edu.

CEDAR CREST COLLEGE, Allentown, PA 18104-6196

General Information Independent-religious, coed, primarily women, comprehensive institution. *Enrollment:* 1,669 graduate, professional, and undergraduate students; 50 full-time matriculated graduate/professional students (43 women), 153 part-time matriculated graduate/professional students (140 women). *Enrollment by degree level:* 172 master's, 31 other advanced degrees. *Graduate faculty:* 20 full-time (15 women), 20 part-time/adjunct (11 women). *Tuition:* Full-time $6489; part-time $721 per credit. *Required fees:* $50 per credit. *Graduate housing:* On-campus housing not available. *Student services:* Campus employment opportunities, campus safety program, career counseling, exercise/wellness program, free psychological counseling, international student services, multicultural affairs office, services for students with disabilities, teacher training. *Library facilities:* Frank M. Cressman Library.

Computer facilities: Computer purchase and lease plans are available. 285 computers available on campus for general student use. A campuswide network can be accessed from student residence rooms and from off campus. Online class registration is available.

Website: http://www.cedarcrest.edu/

General Application Contact: Mary Ellen Hickes, Director of School of Adult and Graduate Education, 610-437-4471, E-mail: sage@cedarcrest.edu.

GRADUATE UNITS

Department of Education Students: 11 full-time (9 women), 68 part-time (63 women); includes 10 minority (3 Black or African American, non-Hispanic/Latino; 2 American Indian or Alaska Native, non-Hispanic/Latino; 1 Asian, non-Hispanic/Latino; 4 Hispanic/Latino). Average age 34. *Faculty:* 4 full-time (all women), 5 part-time/adjunct (4 women). Expenses: Contact institution. *Financial support:* In 2016–17, 60 students received support. Available to part-time students. Applicants required to submit FAFSA. In 2016, 18 master's awarded. *Program availability:* Part-time, evening/weekend. Offers education (M Ed). *Application deadline:* For fall admission, 8/7 priority date for domestic and international students; for winter admission, 11/7 priority date for domestic and international students; for spring admission, 1/8 priority date for domestic and international students. Applications are processed on a rolling basis. Electronic applications accepted. *Application Contact:* Mary Ellen Hickes, Director of School of Adult and Graduate Education, 610-606-4666, E-mail: sage@cedarcrest.edu. *Graduate Program Director,* Dr. Jill Purdy, 610-606-4666 Ext. 3419, E-mail: jepurdy@cedarcrest.edu.

Dietetic Internship Certificate Program Students: 26 part-time (24 women). Average age 26. *Faculty:* 2 full-time (both women), 3 part-time/adjunct (2 women). Expenses: Contact institution. In 2016, 26 Graduate Certificates awarded. *Program availability:* Part-time, evening/weekend, blended/hybrid learning. Offers dietetic internship (Graduate Certificate). *Application deadline:* Applications are processed on a rolling basis. Electronic applications accepted. *Application Contact:* Mary Ellen Hickes, Director of School of Adult and Graduate Education, 610-437-4471, E-mail: sage@cedarcrest.edu. *Director,* Marilou Wieder, 610-606-4666 Ext. 3445, E-mail: mwieder@cedarcrest.edu.

Program in Art Therapy Students: 16 full-time (all women), 7 part-time (all women); includes 2 minority (1 Asian, non-Hispanic/Latino; 1 Hispanic/Latino). Average age 31. *Faculty:* 2 full-time (both women), 4 part-time/adjunct (all women). Expenses: Contact institution. In 2016, 7 master's awarded. *Program availability:* Part-time, evening/weekend, blended/hybrid learning. Offers art therapy (MA). *Application deadline:* Applications are processed on a rolling basis. Electronic applications accepted. *Application Contact:* Mary Ellen Hickes, Director of School of Adult and Graduate Education, 610-437-4471, E-mail: sage@cedarcrest.edu. *Director,* Rebecca Arnold, 610-437-4471 Ext. 3594, E-mail: rarnold@cedarcrest.edu.

Program in Business Administration Students: 27 full-time (18 women), 18 part-time (13 women); includes 15 minority (8 Black or African American, non-Hispanic/Latino; 7 Hispanic/Latino). Average age 41. *Faculty:* 1 full-time (0 women), 9 part-time/adjunct (5 women). Expenses: Contact institution. *Program availability:* Part-time, evening/weekend. Offers business administration (MBA). *Application deadline:* Applications are processed on a rolling basis. Electronic applications accepted. *Application Contact:* Mary Ellen Hickes, Director of School of Adult and Graduate Education, 610-437-4471, E-mail: sage@cedarcrest.edu. *Chair,* Ibolya Balog, 610-437-4471 Ext. 4453, E-mail: ibalog@cedarcrest.edu.

Program in Creative Writing Students: 14 part-time (11 women). Average age 38. *Faculty:* 5 part-time/adjunct (2 women). Expenses: Contact institution. In 2016, 10 master's awarded. *Program availability:* Part-time, evening/weekend, blended/hybrid learning. Offers creative writing (MFA). *Application deadline:* Applications are processed on a rolling basis. Electronic applications accepted. *Application Contact:* Mary Ellen Hickes, Director of School of Adult and Graduate Education, 610-437-4471, E-mail: sage@cedarcrest.edu. *Director of Writing Program,* Allison Wellford, 610-606-4666 Ext. 3474, E-mail: acwellfo@cedarcrest.edu.

Program in Forensic Science Students: 16 full-time (12 women), 9 part-time (8 women); includes 3 minority (1 Black or African American, non-Hispanic/Latino; 1 American Indian or Alaska Native, non-Hispanic/Latino; 1 Asian, non-Hispanic/Latino). Average age 25. *Faculty:* 4 full-time (2 women), 2 part-time/adjunct (1 woman). Expenses: Contact institution. *Financial support:* In 2016–17, 4 students received support. Unspecified assistantships available. In 2016, 2 master's awarded. Offers forensic science (MS). *Application deadline:* For fall admission, 1/2 priority date for domestic students. Applications are processed on a rolling basis. Electronic applications accepted. *Application Contact:* Mary Ellen Hickes, Director of School of Adult and Graduate Education, 610-606-4666, E-mail: sage@cedarcrest.edu. *Director and Associate Professor,* Dr. Lawrence A. Quarino, 610-606-4666 Ext. 3507, Fax: 610-740-3787, E-mail: laquarin@cedarcrest.edu.

Program in Nursing Students: 11 part-time (9 women). Average age 35. *Faculty:* 3 full-time (all women), 1 part-time/adjunct (0 women). Expenses: Contact institution. In 2016, 10 master's awarded. *Program availability:* Part-time. Offers nursing administration (MS); nursing education (MS). *Application deadline:* Applications are processed on a rolling basis. Electronic applications accepted. *Application Contact:* Mary Ellen Hickes, Director of School of Adult and Graduate Education, 610-606-4666, E-mail: sage@cedarcrest.edu. *Director,* Dr. Wendy Robb, 610-606-4666, E-mail: wjrobb@cedarcrest.edu.

CEDARS-SINAI MEDICAL CENTER, Los Angeles, CA 90048

General Information Independent, coed, graduate-only institution. *Enrollment by degree level:* 2 master's, 40 doctoral. *Graduate faculty:* 60 full-time (15 women). *Graduate housing:* On-campus housing not available. *Student services:* Exercise/wellness program, free psychological counseling, grant writing training, low-cost health insurance. *Library facilities:* Cedars-Sinai Medical Library.

Computer facilities: 15 computers available on campus for general student use.
Website: http://www.cedars-sinai.edu/Education/

Cedars-Sinai Medical Center

General Application Contact: Emma Yates Casler, Program Coordinator, 310-423-8294, E-mail: yatese@cshs.org.

GRADUATE UNITS

Graduate Program in Biomedical Sciences and Translational Medicine Students: 40 full-time (26 women); includes 12 minority (2 Black or African American, non-Hispanic/Latino; 4 Asian, non-Hispanic/Latino; 4 Hispanic/Latino; 2 Native Hawaiian or other Pacific Islander, non-Hispanic/Latino). Average age 29. 55 applicants, 15% accepted, 8 enrolled. *Faculty:* 60 full-time (15 women). Expenses: Contact institution. *Financial support:* Health care benefits and annual stipends ($36,000) available. Offers biomedical sciences and translational medicine (PhD). *Application deadline:* For fall admission, 1/31 for domestic students. *Application fee:* $35. Electronic applications accepted. *Application Contact:* Emma Yates Casler, Program Coordinator, 310-423-8294, E-mail: yatese@cshs.org.

CEDARVILLE UNIVERSITY, Cedarville, OH 45314

General Information Independent-religious, coed, comprehensive institution. *Graduate faculty:* 46 full-time (17 women), 19 part-time/adjunct (8 women). *Tuition, area resident:* Full-time $12,594; part-time $566 per credit. One-time fee: $100 full-time. Tuition and fees vary according to degree level and program. *Graduate housing:* On-campus housing not available. *Student services:* Campus employment opportunities, campus safety program, career counseling, exercise/wellness program, free psychological counseling, international student services, low-cost health insurance, services for students with disabilities, writing training. *Library facilities:* Centennial Library. *Collection:* Books: 183,128 (physical), 117,396 (digital/electronic); Serial titles: 763 (physical), 25,339 (digital/electronic); Databases: 199. Weekly public service hours: 91; students can reserve study rooms.

Computer facilities: 1,500 computers available on campus for general student use. A campuswide network can be accessed from student residence rooms and from off campus. Online class registration, over 70 software packages are available.
Website: http://www.cedarville.edu/

General Application Contact: Jim Amstutz, Director of Graduate Admissions, 937-766-8000, Fax: 937-766-7575, E-mail: gradadmissions@cedarville.edu.

GRADUATE UNITS

Graduate Programs Expenses: Contact institution. *Financial support:* Scholarships/grants and unspecified assistantships available. Support available to part-time students. Financial award applicants required to submit FAFSA. *Program availability:* Part-time, evening/weekend, online learning. Offers business administration (MBA); family nurse practitioner (MSN); global ministry (M Div); global public health nursing (MSN); healthcare administration (MBA); ministry (M Min); nurse educator (MSN); operations management (MBA); pharmacy (Pharm D). *Application deadline:* For fall admission, 5/1 priority date for domestic and international students; for spring admission, 11/1 priority date for domestic and international students. Applications are processed on a rolling basis. *Application fee:* $0. Electronic applications accepted. *Application Contact:* Jim Amstutz, Director of Graduate Admissions, 937-766-7878, Fax: 937-766-7575, E-mail: amstutzj@cedarville.edu. *Dean of Graduate Studies,* 937-766-7700.

CENTENARY COLLEGE OF LOUISIANA, Shreveport, LA 71104

General Information Independent-religious, coed, comprehensive institution. *Enrollment:* 540 graduate, professional, and undergraduate students. *Enrollment by degree level:* 77 master's. *Graduate faculty:* 5 full-time (1 woman), 6 part-time/adjunct (all women). *Graduate housing:* Room and/or apartments available on a first-come, first-served basis to single students; on-campus housing not available to married students. *Student services:* Career counseling, exercise/wellness program, free psychological counseling, multicultural affairs office. *Library facilities:* Magale Library plus 1 other. *Collection:* Books: 151,971 (physical), 155,940 (digital/electronic); Serial titles: 9,794 (physical), 255,780 (digital/electronic); Databases: 323. Weekly public service hours: 82; students can reserve study rooms.

Computer facilities: A campuswide network can be accessed from student residence rooms and from off campus. Online class registration is available.
Website: http://www.centenary.edu/

General Application Contact: Dr. Jenifer K. Ward, Provost and Dean of the College, 318-869-5104, Fax: 318-869-5026, E-mail: provost@centenary.edu.

GRADUATE UNITS

Graduate Programs Students: 1 (woman) full-time, 57 part-time (36 women). *Faculty:* 5 full-time (1 woman), 5 part-time/adjunct (all women). Expenses: Contact institution. *Financial support:* Career-related internships or fieldwork and Federal Work-Study available. Support available to part-time students. Financial award applicants required to submit FAFSA. In 2016, 31 master's awarded. *Program availability:* Part-time, evening/weekend. Offers elementary education (MAT); secondary education (MAT). *Provost and Dean of the College,* Dr. Jenifer Ward, 318-869-5104, Fax: 318-869-5026, E-mail: jward@centenary.edu.

Frost School of Business Students: 10 part-time (6 women). *Faculty:* 3 full-time, 2 part-time/adjunct (both women). Expenses: Contact institution. In 2016, 13 master's awarded. *Program availability:* Part-time, evening/weekend. Offers business (MBA). *Application deadline:* For fall admission, 8/1 for domestic students; for winter admission, 10/1 for domestic students; for spring admission, 3/1 for domestic students; for summer admission, 5/1 for domestic students. Applications are processed on a rolling basis. *Application fee:* $20. *Application Contact:* Patricia F. Gallion, MBA Coordinator, 318-869-5141, Fax: 318-869-5139, E-mail: pgallion@centenary.edu. *Dean,* Dr. Harold Christensen, 318-869-5141, Fax: 318-869-5139, E-mail: hchriste@centenary.edu.

CENTENARY UNIVERSITY, Hackettstown, NJ 07840-2100

General Information Independent-religious, coed, comprehensive institution. *Graduate housing:* Room and/or apartments available on a first-come, first-served basis to single students; on-campus housing not available to married students. Housing application deadline: 6/1.

GRADUATE UNITS

Program in Business Administration *Program availability:* Part-time, evening/weekend, online learning. Offers business administration (MBA).

Program in Counseling Psychology *Program availability:* Part-time, evening/weekend, online learning. Offers counseling (MA); counseling psychology (MA).

Program in Education *Program availability:* Part-time, evening/weekend, online learning. Offers education practice (M Ed); educational leadership (MA, Ed D); instructional leadership (MA); reading (M Ed); special education (MA).

Program in Professional Accounting *Program availability:* Part-time, evening/weekend, online learning. Offers professional accounting (MS).

CENTRAL BAPTIST THEOLOGICAL SEMINARY, Shawnee, KS 66226

General Information Independent-religious, coed, graduate-only institution. *Graduate housing:* On-campus housing not available.

GRADUATE UNITS

Graduate and Professional Programs *Program availability:* Part-time. Offers missional church studies (MA); theological studies (MA); theology (M Div, Diploma). Electronic applications accepted.

CENTRAL CONNECTICUT STATE UNIVERSITY, New Britain, CT 06050-4010

General Information State-supported, coed, comprehensive institution. *Enrollment:* 11,784 graduate, professional, and undergraduate students; 571 full-time matriculated graduate/professional students (369 women), 1,505 part-time matriculated graduate/professional students (964 women). *Enrollment by degree level:* 1,591 master's, 49 doctoral, 436 other advanced degrees. *Graduate faculty:* 182 full-time (73 women), 61 part-time/adjunct (41 women). *Tuition, area resident:* Full-time $6497; part-time $606 per credit. Tuition, state resident: full-time $9748; part-time $622 per credit. Tuition, nonresident: full-time $18,102; part-time $622 per credit. *Required fees:* $4459; $246 per credit. *Graduate housing:* Room and/or apartments available on a first-come, first-served basis to single students; on-campus housing not available to married students. Typical cost: $6636 per year ($11,462 including board). Room and board charges vary according to board plan, campus/location and housing facility selected. Housing application deadline: 5/1. *Student services:* Campus employment opportunities, campus safety program, career counseling, child daycare facilities, exercise/wellness program, free psychological counseling, international student services, low-cost health insurance, multicultural affairs office, services for students with disabilities, teacher training, writing training. *Library facilities:* Elihu Burritt Library plus 1 other. *Collection:* Books: 572,464 (physical), 160,771 (digital/electronic); Serial titles: 3,957 (physical), 57,143 (digital/electronic); Databases: 105. Weekly public service hours: 84.

Computer facilities: 750 computers available on campus for general student use. A campuswide network can be accessed from student residence rooms and from off campus. Online class registration is available.
Website: http://www.ccsu.edu/

General Application Contact: Patricia Gardner, Associate Director of Graduate Studies, 860-832-2350, Fax: 860-832-2362.

GRADUATE UNITS

School of Graduate Studies Students: 571 full-time (369 women), 1,505 part-time (964 women); includes 435 minority (164 Black or African American, non-Hispanic/Latino; 74 Asian, non-Hispanic/Latino; 150 Hispanic/Latino; 2 Native Hawaiian or other Pacific Islander, non-Hispanic/Latino; 45 Two or more races, non-Hispanic/Latino), 71 international. Average age 32. 1,064 applicants, 71% accepted, 506 enrolled. *Faculty:* 182 full-time (73 women), 61 part-time/adjunct (41 women). Expenses: Contact institution. *Financial support:* In 2016–17, 175 students received support. Career-related internships or fieldwork, Federal Work-Study, scholarships/grants, and unspecified assistantships available. Support available to part-time students. Financial award application deadline: 3/1; financial award applicants required to submit FAFSA. In 2016, 539 master's, 5 doctorates, 145 other advanced degrees awarded. *Program availability:* Part-time, evening/weekend, 100% online. *Application deadline:* For fall admission, 6/1 for domestic students, 5/1 for international students; for spring admission, 11/1 for domestic and international students. Applications are processed on a rolling basis. *Application fee:* $50. Electronic applications accepted. *Associate Director of Graduate Studies,* Patricia Gardner, 860-832-2350, Fax: 860-832-2362.

College of Liberal Arts and Social Sciences Students: 132 full-time (88 women), 223 part-time (147 women); includes 78 minority (25 Black or African American, non-Hispanic/Latino; 12 Asian, non-Hispanic/Latino; 32 Hispanic/Latino; 9 Two or more races, non-Hispanic/Latino), 11 international. Average age 31. 232 applicants, 68% accepted, 111 enrolled. *Faculty:* 67 full-time (32 women), 3 part-time/adjunct (2 women). Expenses: Contact institution. *Financial support:* In 2016–17, 47 students received support. Career-related internships or fieldwork, Federal Work-Study, scholarships/grants, and unspecified assistantships available. Support available to part-time students. Financial award application deadline: 3/1; financial award applicants required to submit FAFSA. In 2016, 78 master's, 13 other advanced degrees awarded. *Program availability:* Part-time, evening/weekend. Offers art education (MS, Certificate); communication (MS, Certificate); criminal justice (MS); English (MA, MAT, MS, Certificate); geography (MS); history (MA, Certificate); information design (MA); international studies (MS); liberal arts and social sciences (MA, MAT, MS, Certificate); modern language (MA, Certificate); music education (MS, Certificate); psychological science (MA); Spanish (MS, Certificate). *Application deadline:* For fall admission, 6/1 for domestic students, 5/1 for international students; for spring admission, 11/1 for domestic and international students. Applications are processed on a rolling basis. *Application fee:* $50. Electronic applications accepted. *Application Contact:* Patricia Gardner, Associate Director of Graduate Studies, 860-832-2350, Fax: 860-832-2362. *Interim Dean,* Dr. Brian Sommers, 860-832-2604, E-mail: sommersb@ccsu.edu.

School of Business Students: 21 full-time (12 women), 194 part-time (83 women); includes 65 minority (25 Black or African American, non-Hispanic/Latino; 17 Asian, non-Hispanic/Latino; 19 Hispanic/Latino; 4 Two or more races, non-Hispanic/Latino), 1 international. Average age 30. 158 applicants, 72% accepted, 76 enrolled. *Faculty:* 16 full-time (4 women), 1 part-time/adjunct (0 women). Expenses: Contact institution. *Financial support:* In 2016–17, 14 students received support. Career-related internships or fieldwork, Federal Work-Study, scholarships/grants, and unspecified assistantships available. Support available to part-time students. Financial award application deadline: 3/1; financial award applicants required to submit FAFSA. In 2016, 23 master's awarded. *Program availability:* Part-time, evening/weekend. Offers accounting (MSA); business (MBA, MSA); business administration (MBA). *Application deadline:* For fall admission, 6/1 for domestic students, 5/1 for international students; for spring admission, 11/1 for domestic and international students. Applications are processed on a rolling basis. *Application fee:* $50. Electronic applications accepted. *Application Contact:* Patricia Gardner, Associate Director of Graduate Admissions, 860-832-2350, Fax: 860-832-2362. *Dean,* Dr. Ken Colwell, 860-832-3209, E-mail: colwell@ccsu.edu.

School of Education and Professional Studies Students: 229 full-time (172 women), 789 part-time (608 women); includes 183 minority (75 Black or African American, non-Hispanic/Latino; 12 Asian, non-Hispanic/Latino; 76 Hispanic/Latino; 1 Native Hawaiian or other Pacific Islander, non-Hispanic/Latino; 19 Two or more races, non-Hispanic/Latino), 2 international. Average age 33. 403 applicants, 73% accepted, 212 enrolled. *Faculty:* 45 full-time (21 women), 52 part-time/adjunct (38 women). Expenses: Contact institution. *Financial support:* In 2016–17, 67 students received support. Career-related internships or fieldwork, Federal Work-Study, scholarships/grants, and unspecified assistantships available. Support available to part-time students. Financial award application deadline: 3/1; financial award applicants required to submit FAFSA. In 2016, 289 master's, 5 doctorates, 124 other advanced degrees awarded. *Program availability:* Part-time, evening/weekend. Offers education and professional studies (MAT, MS, Ed D, AC, Certificate, Sixth Year Certificate); educational leadership, policy and instructional technology (MS, Ed D, AC, Sixth Year Certificate); literacy, elementary, and early childhood education (MS, AC, Sixth Year Certificate); marriage and family therapy (MS); physical education (MS); professional counseling (MS, AC, Certificate); school counseling (MS); special education and interventions (MS, Certificate); student development in higher education (MS). *Application deadline:* For fall admission, 6/1 for domestic students, 5/1 for international students; for spring admission, 11/1 for domestic and international students. Applications are processed on a rolling basis. *Application fee:* $50. Electronic applications accepted. *Application Contact:* Patricia Gardner, Associate Director of Graduate Studies, 860-832-2350, Fax: 860-832-2362. *Dean,* Dr. Michael Alfano, 860-832-2101, E-mail: malfano@ccsu.edu.

School of Engineering, Science and Technology Students: 189 full-time (97 women), 299 part-time (126 women); includes 109 minority (39 Black or African American, non-Hispanic/Latino; 33 Asian, non-Hispanic/Latino; 23 Hispanic/Latino; 1 Native Hawaiian or other Pacific Islander, non-Hispanic/Latino; 13 Two or more races, non-Hispanic/Latino), 57 international. Average age 32. 271 applicants, 70% accepted, 107 enrolled. *Faculty:* 54 full-time (16 women), 5 part-time/adjunct (1 woman). Expenses: Contact institution. *Financial support:* In 2016–17, 47 students received support. Career-related internships or fieldwork, Federal Work-Study, scholarships/grants, and unspecified assistantships available. Support available to part-time students. Financial award application deadline: 3/1; financial award applicants required to submit FAFSA. In 2016, 149 master's, 8 other advanced degrees awarded. *Program availability:* Part-time, evening/weekend, 100% online. Offers biological sciences (MA); biomolecular sciences (MS, Certificate); computer information technology (MS); construction management (MS, Certificate); data mining (MS, Certificate); engineering (MS); engineering, science and technology (MA, MS, Certificate, Sixth Year Certificate); environmental and occupational safety (Certificate); lean manufacturing and Six Sigma (Certificate); mathematics (MA, MS); mathematics education leadership (Sixth Year Certificate); mathematics for secondary education (Certificate); STEM education (MS); supply chain and logistics (Certificate); technology management (MS). *Application deadline:* For fall admission, 6/1 for domestic students, 5/1 for international students; for spring admission, 11/1 for domestic and international students. Applications are processed on a rolling basis. *Application fee:* $50. Electronic applications accepted. *Application Contact:* Patricia Gardner, Associate Director of Graduate Studies, 860-832-2350, Fax: 860-832-2362. *Dean,* Dr. Faris Malhas, 860-832-1800, E-mail: fmalhas@ccsu.edu.

CENTRAL EUROPEAN UNIVERSITY, H-1051 Budapest, Hungary

General Information Independent, coed, graduate-only institution. CGS member. *Enrollment by degree level:* 868 master's, 433 doctoral. *Graduate faculty:* 190 full-time (63 women), 112 part-time/adjunct (36 women). *Tuition:* Full-time 13,500 euros. Tuition and fees vary according to degree level, program and student level. *Graduate housing:* Room and/or apartments guaranteed to single students; on-campus housing not available to married students. Housing application deadline: 2/4. *Student services:* Campus employment opportunities, campus safety program, career counseling, exercise/wellness program, free psychological counseling, grant writing training, international student services, low-cost health insurance, multicultural affairs office, services for students with disabilities, teacher training, writing training. *Library facilities:* CEU Library plus 1 other. *Collection:* Books: 184,083 (physical), 164,176 (digital/electronic); Serial titles: 208 (physical), 44,700 (digital/electronic); Databases: 95. Weekly public service hours: 89; students can reserve study rooms. *Research affiliation:* Institute of Human Sciences Vienna (social sciences), Open Society Institute (social sciences), Alfréd Rényi Institute of Mathematics.

Computer facilities: 290 computers available on campus for general student use. A campuswide network can be accessed from student residence rooms and from off campus. Online class registration is available.
Website: http://www.ceu.hu/

General Application Contact: Zsuzsanna Jaszberenyi, Admissions Officer, 361-327-3009, Fax: 361-327-3211, E-mail: admissions@ceu.edu.

GRADUATE UNITS

Center for Network Science Students: 10 full-time (4 women). Average age 33. 33 applicants, 27% accepted, 7 enrolled. *Faculty:* 2 full-time (1 woman), 1 part-time/adjunct (0 women). Expenses: Contact institution. *Financial support:* In 2016–17, 10 students received support. Fellowships, research assistantships, teaching assistantships, scholarships/grants, health care benefits, and tuition waivers (full) available. Financial award applicants required to submit FAFSA. Offers network science (PhD). *Application deadline:* For fall admission, 2/4 for domestic and international students. *Application fee:* $30. Electronic applications accepted. *Application Contact:* Janos Kertesz, Program Director, 36-1-327-3000 Ext. 2655, E-mail: cns@ceu.edu. *Director,* Balazs Vedres, 36-1-327-3000.

CEU Business School Students: 73 full-time (29 women), 108 part-time (28 women). Average age 33. 218 applicants, 57% accepted, 69 enrolled. *Faculty:* 16 full-time (4 women), 15 part-time/adjunct (5 women). Expenses: Contact institution. *Financial support:* Scholarships/grants, health care benefits, and tuition waivers (full and partial) available. In 2016, 108 master's awarded. *Program availability:* Part-time. Offers business administration (PhD); business analytics (M Sc); executive business administration (EMBA); finance (M Sc); general management (MBA); information technology management (M Sc); international executive (MBA). *Application deadline:* For fall admission, 2/4 for domestic and international students. *Application fee:* $30. Electronic applications accepted. *Application Contact:* Agnes Schram, Admissions Coordinator, 361-887-5111, E-mail: schrama@business.ceu.edu. *Dean/Managing Director,* Dr. Mel Horwitch, 36 1 887-5050, E-mail: mhorwitch@ceubusiness.com.

Department of Cognitive Science Students: 29 full-time (16 women). Average age 27. 69 applicants, 14% accepted, 5 enrolled. *Faculty:* 26 full-time (12 women), 1 part-time/adjunct (0 women). Expenses: Contact institution. *Financial support:* In 2016–17, 6 students received support. Fellowships, career-related internships or fieldwork, scholarships/grants, and health care benefits available. Offers cognitive science (PhD). *Application deadline:* For fall admission, 2/4 priority date for domestic and international students. *Application fee:* $30. Electronic applications accepted. *Application Contact:* Zsuzsanna Jaszberenyi, Admissions Officer, 361-324-3009, Fax: 367-327-3211, E-mail: admissions@ceu.edu. *Head of Department,* Dr. Natalie Sebanz, 36 1 887-5137, E-mail: sebanzn@ceu.edu.

Department of Economics Students: 122 full-time (44 women). Average age 26. 300 applicants, 24% accepted, 51 enrolled. *Faculty:* 14 full-time (1 woman), 9 part-

time/adjunct (1 woman). Expenses: Contact institution. *Financial support:* Fellowships, teaching assistantships, career-related internships or fieldwork, institutionally sponsored loans, scholarships/grants, health care benefits, and tuition waivers (full and partial) available. In 2016, 34 master's, 5 doctorates awarded. Offers business analytics (M Sc); economic policy in global markets (MA); economics (MA, PhD); global economic relations (MA). *Application deadline:* For fall admission, 2/4 for domestic and international students. *Application fee:* $30. Electronic applications accepted. *Application Contact:* Zsuzsanna Jaszberenyi, Admissions Officer, 361-324-3009, Fax: 367-327-3211, E-mail: admissions@ceu.edu. *Head of Department,* Miklos Koren, 36 1 327-3000 Ext. 2212, E-mail: econdept@ceu.edu.

Department of Environmental Sciences and Policy Students: 86 full-time (52 women), 5 part-time (3 women). Average age 29. 533 applicants, 19% accepted, 46 enrolled. *Faculty:* 11 full-time (3 women), 3 part-time/adjunct (0 women). Expenses: Contact institution. *Financial support:* Fellowships, teaching assistantships, career-related internships or fieldwork, institutionally sponsored loans, scholarships/grants, health care benefits, and tuition waivers (full and partial) available. Financial award application deadline: 2/4. In 2016, 42 master's, 8 doctorates awarded. *Program availability:* Part-time. Offers environmental sciences and policy (MS, PhD). *Application deadline:* For fall admission, 2/4 for domestic and international students. *Application fee:* $30. Electronic applications accepted. *Application Contact:* Zsuzsanna Jaszberenyi, Head of Admissions Services, 361-327-3009, E-mail: admissions@ceu.edu. *Head of Department,* Dr. Ruben Mnatsakanian, 36 1 327-3021, Fax: 36-1-327-3031, E-mail: envsci@ceu.edu.

Department of Gender Studies Students: 85 full-time (74 women). Average age 29. 436 applicants, 11% accepted, 38 enrolled. *Faculty:* 10 full-time (9 women), 1 (woman) part-time/adjunct. Expenses: Contact institution. *Financial support:* Fellowships, career-related internships or fieldwork, scholarships/grants, health care benefits, and tuition waivers (full and partial) available. Financial award application deadline: 2/4. In 2016, 38 master's, 4 doctorates awarded. Offers gender studies (MA, PhD). *Application deadline:* For fall admission, 2/4 for domestic and international students. *Application fee:* $30. Electronic applications accepted. *Application Contact:* Zsuzsanna Jaszberenyi, Admissions Officer, 361-324-3009, Fax: 367-327-3211, E-mail: admissions@ceu.edu. *Head of Department,* Elissa Helms, 36 1 327-3034, Fax: 36-1-327-3296, E-mail: gender@ceu.edu.

Department of History Students: 94 full-time (35 women). Average age 28. 191 applicants, 35% accepted, 51 enrolled. *Faculty:* 14 full-time (3 women), 8 part-time/adjunct (2 women). Expenses: Contact institution. *Financial support:* Fellowships, career-related internships or fieldwork, institutionally sponsored loans, scholarships/grants, and tuition waivers (full and partial) available. In 2016, 30 master's, 4 doctorates awarded. Offers history (MA, PhD). *Application deadline:* For fall admission, 2/4 for domestic and international students. *Application fee:* $30. Electronic applications accepted. *Application Contact:* Agnes Bendik, Coordinator, 361-327-3000 Ext. 2591, Fax: 361-235-6145, E-mail: history@ceu.edu. *Head,* Dr. Matthias Riedl, 36 1 327-3022, Fax: 361-327-3191, E-mail: history@ceu.edu.

Department of International Relations Students: 76 full-time (40 women), 2 part-time (1 woman). Average age 28. 650 applicants, 15% accepted, 60 enrolled. *Faculty:* 11 full-time (3 women), 4 part-time/adjunct (1 woman). Expenses: Contact institution. *Financial support:* In 2016–17, 71 students received support. Fellowships, career-related internships or fieldwork, scholarships/grants, health care benefits, and tuition waivers (full and partial) available. In 2016, 40 master's, 4 doctorates awarded. Offers global economic relations (MA); international relations (MA, PhD). *Application deadline:* For fall admission, 2/4 for domestic and international students. *Application fee:* $30. Electronic applications accepted. *Application Contact:* Zsuzsanna Jaszberenyi, Admissions Officer, 361-324-3009, Fax: 367-327-3211, E-mail: admissions@ceu.edu. *Head of Department,* Matteo Fumagalli, 36 1 327-3243 Ext. 2219, E-mail: fumagallim@ceu.edu.

Department of Legal Studies Students: 89 full-time (43 women). Average age 27. 420 applicants, 27% accepted, 66 enrolled. *Faculty:* 10 full-time (5 women), 15 part-time/adjunct (3 women). Expenses: Contact institution. *Financial support:* Fellowships, career-related internships or fieldwork, institutionally sponsored loans, scholarships/grants, and tuition waivers (full and partial) available. Financial award application deadline: 2/4. In 2016, 52 master's, 4 doctorates awarded. Offers comparative Constitutional law (LL M); human rights (LL M, MA); international business law (LL M); juridical sciences (SJD); law and economics (LL M, MA). *Application deadline:* For fall admission, 2/4 for domestic and international students. *Application fee:* $30. Electronic applications accepted. *Application Contact:* Zsuzsanna Jaszberenyi, Department Coordinator, 361-327-3272, Fax: 361-327-3198, E-mail: admissions@ceu.edu. *Head of Department,* Dr. Karoly Bard, 36 1 327-3294, Fax: 361-327-3198, E-mail: legalst@ceu.edu.

Department of Mathematics and its Applications Students: 41 full-time (8 women). Average age 26. 81 applicants, 16% accepted, 11 enrolled. *Faculty:* 2 full-time (0 women), 11 part-time/adjunct (1 woman). Expenses: Contact institution. *Financial support:* Fellowships, career-related internships or fieldwork, scholarships/grants, health care benefits, and tuition waivers (full and partial) available. Financial award application deadline: 2/4. In 2016, 3 master's, 8 doctorates awarded. Offers applied mathematics (MS); mathematics and its applications (PhD). *Application deadline:* For fall admission, 2/4 for domestic and international students. *Application fee:* $30. Electronic applications accepted. *Application Contact:* Zsuzsanna Jaszberenyi, Admissions Officer, 361-324-3009, Fax: 367-327-3211, E-mail: admissions@ceu.edu. *Head,* Dr. Karoly Boroczky, 36 1 327-3053, E-mail: mathematics@ceu.edu.

Department of Medieval Studies Students: 101 full-time (60 women). Average age 27. 139 applicants, 32% accepted, 41 enrolled. *Faculty:* 12 full-time (3 women), 9 part-time/adjunct (5 women). Expenses: Contact institution. *Financial support:* In 2016–17, 74 students received support. Fellowships, scholarships/grants, health care benefits, and tuition waivers (full and partial) available. In 2016, 21 master's, 4 doctorates awarded. Offers comparative history: interdisciplinary Medieval studies (MA); cultural heritage studies (MA); Medieval studies (MA, PhD). *Application deadline:* For fall admission, 2/4 for domestic and international students. *Application fee:* $30. Electronic applications accepted. *Application Contact:* Zsuzsanna Jaszberenyi, Admissions Officer, 361-324-3009, Fax: 367-327-3211, E-mail: admissions@ceu.edu. *Head,* Dr. Katalin Szende, 36 1 327-3046, E-mail: ziemannd@ceu.edu.

Department of Philosophy Students: 47 full-time (14 women). Average age 28. 153 applicants, 18% accepted, 16 enrolled. *Faculty:* 8 full-time (2 women), 3 part-time/adjunct (1 woman). Expenses: Contact institution. *Financial support:* In 2016–17, 45 students received support. Fellowships, teaching assistantships, scholarships/grants, health care benefits, and tuition waivers (full and partial) available. In 2016, 14 master's, 6 doctorates awarded. Offers philosophy (MA, PhD). *Application deadline:* For fall admission, 2/4 for domestic and international students. *Application fee:* $30. Electronic applications accepted. *Application Contact:* Zsuzsanna Jaszberenyi, Admissions Officer, 361-324-3009, Fax: 367-327-3211, E-mail: admissions@ceu.edu. *Head of Department,* Dr. Hanoch Ben-Yami, 36 1 327-3806, Fax: 361-327-3072, E-mail: philosophy@ceu.edu.

Department of Political Science Students: 108 full-time (42 women). Average age 27. 340 applicants, 26% accepted, 54 enrolled. *Faculty:* 16 full-time (5 women), 6 part-time/adjunct (2 women). Expenses: Contact institution. *Financial support:* Fellowships, teaching assistantships, career-related internships or fieldwork, scholarships/grants, health care benefits, and tuition waivers (full and partial) available. In 2016, 47 master's, 10 doctorates awarded. Offers political science (MA, PhD). *Application deadline:* For fall admission, 2/4 for domestic and international students. *Application fee:* $30. Electronic applications accepted. *Application Contact:* Zsuzsanna Jaszbrenyi, Admissions Officer, 361-324-3009, Fax: 367-327-3211, E-mail: admissions@ceu.edu. *Head of Department,* Dr. Carsten Q. Schneider, 36 1 235-6164, E-mail: polsci@ceu.edu.

Department of Sociology and Social Anthropology Students: 77 full-time (47 women). Average age 28. 339 applicants, 14% accepted, 39 enrolled. *Faculty:* 11 full-time (4 women), 4 part-time/adjunct (1 woman). Expenses: Contact institution. *Financial support:* Fellowships, career-related internships or fieldwork, scholarships/grants, health care benefits, and tuition waivers (full and partial) available. In 2016, 27 master's, 8 doctorates awarded. Offers sociology and social anthropology (MA, PhD). *Application deadline:* For fall admission, 2/4 for domestic and international students. *Application fee:* $30. Electronic applications accepted. *Application Contact:* Zsuzsanna Jaszbrenyi, Admissions Officer, 361-324-3009, Fax: 367-327-3211, E-mail: admissions@ceu.edu. *Head of Department,* Dr. Andreas Dafinger, 36 1 327-3000 Ext. 2131, E-mail: sociology@ceu.edu.

Nationalism Studies Program Students: 32 full-time (22 women). Average age 26. 116 applicants, 28% accepted, 24 enrolled. *Faculty:* 5 full-time (1 woman), 5 part-time/adjunct (3 women). Expenses: Contact institution. *Financial support:* In 2016–17, 32 students received support. Fellowships, scholarships/grants, health care benefits, and tuition waivers (full and partial) available. In 2016, 22 master's awarded. Offers nationalism studies (MA). *Application deadline:* For fall admission, 2/4 for domestic and international students. *Application fee:* $30. Electronic applications accepted. *Application Contact:* Zsuzsanna Jaszbrenyi, Admissions Officer, 361-324-3009, Fax: 367-327-3211, E-mail: admissions@ceu.edu. *Program Director,* Dr. Michael Laurence Miller, 36 1 327-3081, E-mail: nationalism@ceu.edu.

School of Public Policy Students: 141 full-time (90 women). Average age 29. 931 applicants, 30% accepted, 75 enrolled. *Faculty:* 22 full-time (7 women), 17 part-time/adjunct (10 women). Expenses: Contact institution. *Financial support:* Fellowships, career-related internships or fieldwork, scholarships/grants, health care benefits, and tuition waivers (full and partial) available. In 2016, 68 master's, 7 doctorates awarded. Offers public administration (MPA); public policy (MA, PhD). *Application deadline:* For fall admission, 2/4 for domestic and international students. *Application fee:* $30. Electronic applications accepted. *Application Contact:* Zsuzsanna Jaszbrenyi, Admissions Officer, 361-324-3009, Fax: 367-327-3211, E-mail: admissions@ceu.edu. *Head,* Dr. Julia Buxton, 36 1 327-3110, E-mail: spp@ceu.edu.

CENTRAL METHODIST UNIVERSITY, Fayette, MO 65248-1198

General Information Independent-religious, coed, comprehensive institution. *Graduate housing:* Rooms and/or apartments available on a first-come, first-served basis to single and married students.

GRADUATE UNITS

College of Graduate and Extended Studies *Program availability:* Part-time, evening/weekend, online learning. Offers clinical counseling (MS); clinical nurse leader (MSN); education (M Ed); music education (MME); nurse educator (MSN). Electronic applications accepted.

CENTRAL MICHIGAN UNIVERSITY, Mount Pleasant, MI 48859

General Information State-supported, coed, university. CGS member. *Graduate housing:* Rooms and/or apartments available on a first-come, first-served basis to single and married students. *Research affiliation:* IBM (information technology), Dendritic Nanotechnologies, Inc. (chemistry, physics), Dow Corning Corporation (silicon-based technology), Dow Chemical Company (chemicals and plastics), SAS Business Analytics (business analysis), SAP (information technology).

GRADUATE UNITS

Central Michigan University Global Campus Students: 544 full-time (313 women), 3,485 part-time (2,215 women); includes 1,720 minority (1,263 Black or African American, non-Hispanic/Latino; 41 American Indian or Alaska Native, non-Hispanic/Latino; 100 Asian, non-Hispanic/Latino; 68 Hispanic/Latino; 7 Native Hawaiian or other Pacific Islander, non-Hispanic/Latino; 241 Two or more races, non-Hispanic/Latino). Average age 38. 2,006 applicants, 81% accepted, 1084 enrolled. *Faculty:* 168 full-time, 340 part-time/adjunct. Expenses: Contact institution. *Financial support:* Scholarships/grants and tuition waivers (partial) available. Support available to part-time students. Financial award applicants required to submit FAFSA. In 2016, 1,219 master's, 30 doctorates, 118 other advanced degrees awarded. *Program availability:* Part-time, evening/weekend, online learning. Offers acquisitions administration (MSA, Certificate); college teaching (Graduate Certificate); community college (MA); curriculum and instruction (MA); cybersecurity (Certificate); educational technology (MA, DET); engineering management administration (MSA, Certificate); enterprise resource planning (MBA, Certificate); general administration (MSA, Certificate); general public administration (MSA, Certificate); health administration (DHA); health services administration (MSA, Certificate); human resource management (MBA); human resources administration (MSA, Certificate); information resource management (MSA); information resource management administration (Certificate); international administration (MSA, Certificate); international health (Certificate); K-12 leadership (Ed D); leadership (MSA, Certificate); logistics management (MBA, Certificate); marketing (MBA); nutrition and dietetics (MS); philanthropy and fundraising administration (MSA, Certificate); professional counseling (MA); public administration (MSA, Certificate); public management (MPA); reading and literacy K-12 (MA); recreation and park administration (MSA); research administration (MSA, Certificate); school counseling (MA); school principalship (MA); state and local government (MPA); training and development (MA); value-driven organization (MBA). *Application deadline:* Applications are processed on a rolling basis. *Application fee:* $50. Electronic applications accepted. *Application Contact:* Global Campus Call Center, 877-268-4636, Fax: 989-774-2461, E-mail: cmuglobal@cmich.edu. *Vice President and Executive Director,* Dr. Peter Ross, 989-774-4456, Fax: 989-774-3232, E-mail: ross1pg@cmich.edu.

College of Graduate Studies *Program availability:* Part-time, evening/weekend, online learning. Offers acquisitions administration (MSA, Graduate Certificate); general administration (MSA, Graduate Certificate); health services administration (MSA, Graduate Certificate); human resource administration (Graduate Certificate); human resources administration (MSA); information resource management (MSA, Graduate Certificate); international administration (MSA, Graduate Certificate); leadership (MSA, Graduate Certificate); public administration (MSA, Graduate Certificate); research administration (Graduate Certificate); sport administration (MSA). Electronic applications accepted.

College of Business Administration *Program availability:* Part-time, evening/weekend. Offers accounting (MBA); business administration (MA, MBA, MS, Graduate Certificate); business computing (Graduate Certificate); business economics (MBA); consulting (MBA); economics (MA); finance (MBA); general business (MBA); human resource management (MBA); information systems (MBA, MS); international business (MBA); logistics management (MBA); marketing (MBA); value-driven organization (MBA). Electronic applications accepted.

College of Communication and Fine Arts *Program availability:* Part-time. Offers communication (MA); communication and fine arts (MA, MM); composition (MM); conducting (MM); electronic media management (MA); electronic media production (MA); electronic media studies (MA); film theory and criticism (MA); music education (MM); performance (MM). Electronic applications accepted.

College of Education and Human Services *Program availability:* Part-time, evening/weekend. Offers apparel product development and merchandising technology (MS); autism (Graduate Certificate); counseling (MA); education and human services (MA, MS, Ed D, Ed S, Graduate Certificate); educational leadership (Ed D); educational technology (MA, Graduate Certificate); elementary education (MA); general educational administration (Ed S); gerontology (Graduate Certificate); human development and family studies (MA); nutrition and dietetics (MS); reading and literacy K-12 (MA); school principalship (MA); secondary education (MA); special education (MA, Graduate Certificate); student affairs administration (MA); teacher leadership (MA). Electronic applications accepted.

College of Humanities and Social and Behavioral Sciences *Program availability:* Part-time, evening/weekend. Offers American politics (MA); applied experimental psychology (PhD); clinical psychology (PhD); English composition and communication (MA); English language and literature (MA); European history (Graduate Certificate); experimental psychology (MS, PhD); history (MA); humanities (MA); humanities and social and behavioral sciences (MA, MPA, MS, PhD, Graduate Certificate, S Psy S); industrial and organizational psychology (MA, PhD); modern history (Graduate Certificate); neuroscience (MS, PhD); occupational health psychology (PhD); political science (MA); professional development in public administration (Graduate Certificate); public administration (MPA, Graduate Certificate); public management (MPA); school psychology (PhD, S Psy S); Spanish (MA); state and local government (MPA); TESOL: teaching English to speakers of other languages (MA); United States history (Graduate Certificate). Electronic applications accepted.

College of Science and Technology *Program availability:* Part-time, evening/weekend. Offers biology (MS); chemistry (MS); computer science (MS); conservation biology (MS); geographic information sciences (MS); industrial management and technology (MA); mathematics (MA, PhD); physics (MS); science and technology (MA, MAT, MS, PhD, Graduate Certificate); science of advanced materials (PhD); teaching chemistry (MA). Electronic applications accepted.

The Herbert H. and Grace A. Dow College of Health Professions *Program availability:* Part-time. Offers audiology (Au D); exercise science (MA); health administration (DHA); health professions (MA, MS, Au D, DHA, DPT, Graduate Certificate); physical therapy (DPT); physician assistant (MS); speech-language pathology (MA); sport administration (MA). Electronic applications accepted.

CENTRAL PENN COLLEGE, Summerdale, PA 17093-0309

General Information Proprietary, coed, comprehensive institution.

GRADUATE UNITS

Graduate Programs *Program availability:* Evening/weekend. Offers information systems management (MPS); organizational development (MPS). Programs offered in Harrisburg, PA.

CENTRAL WASHINGTON UNIVERSITY, Ellensburg, WA 98926

General Information State-supported, coed, comprehensive institution. CGS member. *Graduate housing:* Rooms and/or apartments available on a first-come, first-served basis to single and married students. *Research affiliation:* East-West Center (Pacific area studies), Associated Western Universities (science and engineering), Jet Propulsion Laboratory (engineering).

GRADUATE UNITS

Graduate Studies and Research *Program availability:* Part-time, evening/weekend. Offers individual studies (M Ed, MA, MS). Electronic applications accepted.

College of Arts and Humanities *Program availability:* Part-time. Offers art (MA, MFA); arts and humanities (MA, MFA, MM); English (MA); history (MA); music (MM); teaching English as a second language (MA); theatre production (MA); theatre studies (MA). Electronic applications accepted.

College of Business *Program availability:* Part-time. Offers accounting (MPA); business (MPA). Electronic applications accepted.

College of Education and Professional Studies *Program availability:* Part-time. Offers athletic administration (MS); career and technical education (MS); education and professional studies (M Ed, MS); engineering technology (MS); exercise science (MS); family and consumer sciences education (MS); family studies (MS); health and physical education (MS); higher education (M Ed); master teacher (M Ed); nutrition (MS); reading education (M Ed); school administration (M Ed); school instructional leadership (M Ed); special education (M Ed). Electronic applications accepted.

College of the Sciences *Program availability:* Part-time, evening/weekend. Offers biological sciences (MS); chemistry (MS); experimental psychology (MS); geological sciences (MS); mathematics (MAT); mental health counseling (MS); resource management (MS); school counseling (M Ed); school psychology (M Ed); sciences (M Ed, MAT, MS). Electronic applications accepted.

CENTRAL YESHIVA TOMCHEI TMIMIM-LUBAVITCH, Brooklyn, NY 11230

General Information Independent-religious, men only, comprehensive institution.

GRADUATE UNITS

Graduate Programs Offers Jewish/Judaic studies (MA); Talmudic studies (MA).

CENTRO DE ESTUDIOS AVANZADOS DE PUERTO RICO Y EL CARIBE, Old San Juan, PR 00902-3970

General Information Independent, coed, graduate-only institution. *Graduate housing:* On-campus housing not available. *Research affiliation:* Museo de las Americas, Museo Hombre Dominicano, Archivo General, Museo Universidad del Turabo.

GRADUATE UNITS

Graduate Program in Puerto Rican and Caribbean Studies *Program availability:* Part-time, evening/weekend. Offers Puerto Rican and Caribbean history (MA, PhD); Puerto Rican and Caribbean literature (MA, PhD); Puerto Rican studies (MA).

CHADRON STATE COLLEGE, Chadron, NE 69337

General Information State-supported, coed, comprehensive institution. *Graduate housing:* Rooms and/or apartments available on a first-come, first-served basis to single and married students. Housing application deadline: 6/1.

GRADUATE UNITS

School of Professional and Graduate Studies *Program availability:* Part-time, evening/weekend, online learning. Offers business (MA Ed); business and economics (MBA); community counseling (MA Ed); educational administration (MS Ed, Sp Ed); elementary education (MS Ed); history (MA Ed); language and literature (MA Ed); secondary administration (MS Ed); secondary education (MS Ed). Electronic applications accepted.

CHAMINADE UNIVERSITY OF HONOLULU, Honolulu, HI 96816-1578

General Information Independent-religious, coed, comprehensive institution. *Enrollment:* 1,769 graduate, professional, and undergraduate students; 406 full-time matriculated graduate/professional students (280 women), 191 part-time matriculated graduate/professional students (138 women). *Enrollment by degree level:* 597 master's. *Graduate faculty:* 30 full-time (10 women), 35 part-time/adjunct (16 women). *Tuition:* Full-time $18,600; part-time $775 per credit hour. Tuition and fees vary according to campus/location and program. *Graduate housing:* On-campus housing not available. *Student services:* Campus safety program, career counseling, free psychological counseling, international student services, services for students with disabilities, teacher training, writing training. *Library facilities:* Sullivan Library. *Collection:* Books: 51,328 (physical), 133,447 (digital/electronic); Serial titles: 11,276 (physical), 144,925 (digital/electronic); Databases: 82.

Computer facilities: 200 computers available on campus for general student use. A campuswide network can be accessed from student residence rooms and from off campus. Online class registration is available.
Website: http://www.chaminade.edu/

General Application Contact: 808-735-4755, E-mail: gradserv@chaminade.edu.

GRADUATE UNITS

Office of Professional and Continuing Education Students: 406 full-time (280 women), 191 part-time (138 women); includes 393 minority (32 Black or African American, non-Hispanic/Latino; 7 American Indian or Alaska Native, non-Hispanic/Latino; 173 Asian, non-Hispanic/Latino; 33 Hispanic/Latino; 138 Native Hawaiian or other Pacific Islander, non-Hispanic/Latino; 10 Two or more races, non-Hispanic/Latino), 3 international. Average age 33. 175 applicants, 97% accepted, 119 enrolled. *Faculty:* 30 full-time (10 women), 35 part-time/adjunct (16 women). Expenses: Contact institution. *Financial support:* Applicants required to submit FAFSA. In 2016, 231 master's awarded. *Program availability:* Part-time, evening/weekend, 100% online, blended/hybrid learning. Offers accounting (MBA); business (MBA); child development (M Ed); correctional (MSCJA); criminal justice (MSCJA); diaconate education (MPT); early childhood education (MAT); educational leadership (M Ed); elementary education (MAT); instructional leadership (M Ed); island business (MBA); law enforcement (MSCJA); marriage and family counseling (MSCP); mental health counseling (MSCP); Montessori (M Ed); not-for-profit (MBA); pastoral counseling and spiritual direction (MPT); pastoral theology (MPT); school counseling (MSCP); secondary education (MAT); special education (MAT). *Application deadline:* Applications are processed on a rolling basis. *Application fee:* $40. Electronic applications accepted. *Application Contact:* 808-739-4664, E-mail: gradserv@chaminade.edu. *Director,* Michelle Cohen, 808-735-4755, E-mail: gradserv@chaminade.edu.

CHAMPLAIN COLLEGE, Burlington, VT 05402-0670

General Information Independent, coed, comprehensive institution. *Graduate housing:* Rooms and/or apartments available on a first-come, first-served basis to single and married students.

GRADUATE UNITS

Graduate Studies *Program availability:* Part-time, online learning. Offers business (MBA); digital forensic science (MS); early childhood education (M Ed); emergent media (MFA, MS); executive leadership (MS); health care administration (MS); information security operations (MS); law (MS); mediation and applied conflict studies (MS). MS in emergent media program held in Shanghai. Electronic applications accepted.

CHAPMAN UNIVERSITY, Orange, CA 92866

General Information Independent-religious, coed, comprehensive institution. CGS member. *Enrollment:* 8,542 graduate, professional, and undergraduate students; 1,635 full-time matriculated graduate/professional students (952 women), 493 part-time matriculated graduate/professional students (307 women). *Enrollment by degree level:* 1,146 master's, 965 doctoral, 17 other advanced degrees. *Graduate faculty:* 313 full-time (129 women), 228 part-time/adjunct (107 women). Tuition and fees vary according to course load and program. *Graduate housing:* Rooms and/or apartments available on a first-come, first-served basis to single and married students. Housing application deadline: 6/1. *Student services:* Campus employment opportunities, campus safety program, career counseling, exercise/wellness program, free psychological counseling, grant writing training, international student services, low-cost health insurance, multicultural affairs office, services for students with disabilities, teacher training, writing training. *Library facilities:* Leatherby Libraries plus 1 other. *Collection:* Books: 334,330 (physical), 16,370 (digital/electronic); Serial titles: 326 (physical), 67,937 (digital/electronic); Databases: 274. Weekly public service hours: 127; students can reserve study rooms. *Research affiliation:* National Science Foundation (science, engineering), National Endowment for the Arts (NEA) (art), U.S. Department of Education (DOE) (education), U.S. Geological Survey (USGS) (earth sciences), U.S. Department of Agriculture (USDA) (agriculture, food, nutrition).

Computer facilities: Computer purchase and lease plans are available. A campuswide network can be accessed from student residence rooms and from off campus. Online class registration is available.
Website: http://www.chapman.edu/

General Application Contact: Eva Yen, Director of Graduate Admissions, 888-CU-APPLY, Fax: 714-997-6713, E-mail: eyen@chapman.edu.

GRADUATE UNITS

College of Educational Studies Students: 186 full-time (148 women), 186 part-time (134 women); includes 144 minority (9 Black or African American, non-Hispanic/Latino; 39 Asian, non-Hispanic/Latino; 78 Hispanic/Latino; 2 Native Hawaiian or other Pacific Islander, non-Hispanic/Latino; 16 Two or more races, non-Hispanic/Latino), 8 international. Average age 29. 143 applicants, 63% accepted, 64 enrolled. *Faculty:* 29 full-time (14 women), 36 part-time/adjunct (28 women). Expenses: Contact institution. *Financial support:* Fellowships and scholarships/grants available. Financial award

application deadline: 3/2; financial award applicants required to submit FAFSA. In 2016, 111 master's, 24 doctorates awarded. *Program availability:* Part-time, evening/weekend. Offers counseling (MA); education (PhD); educational psychology (MA); leadership development (MA); multiple subjects (Credential); pupil personnel services (Credential); school psychology (Ed S); single subject (Credential); special education (MA, Credential); teaching (MA). *Application deadline:* Applications are processed on a rolling basis. *Application fee:* $60. Electronic applications accepted. *Application Contact:* Sara Simon, Graduate Admission Counselor, 714-997-6770, E-mail: simon@chapman.edu. *Dean,* Dr. Margaret Grogan, 714-516-5968, E-mail: grogan@chapman.edu.

Crean College of Health and Behavioral Sciences Students: 292 full-time (196 women), 99 part-time (72 women); includes 166 minority (6 Black or African American, non-Hispanic/Latino; 1 American Indian or Alaska Native, non-Hispanic/Latino; 80 Asian, non-Hispanic/Latino; 64 Hispanic/Latino; 15 Two or more races, non-Hispanic/Latino), 5 international. Average age 27. 1,897 applicants, 12% accepted, 115 enrolled. *Faculty:* 31 full-time (23 women), 17 part-time/adjunct (14 women). Expenses: Contact institution. In 2016, 55 master's, 60 doctorates awarded. Offers athletic training (MS); communication sciences and disorders (MS); health and behavioral sciences (MA, MMS, MS, DPT, TDPT); marriage and family therapy (MA); physical therapy (DPT, TDPT); physician assistant studies (MMS). *Application fee:* $60. Electronic applications accepted. *Application Contact:* Monica Chen, Graduate Admission Counselor, 714-289-3590, Fax: 714-997-6713, E-mail: mchen@chapman.edu. *Dean,* Dr. Janeen Hill, 714-628-7223, E-mail: jhill@chapman.edu.

Dodge College of Film and Media Arts Students: 241 full-time (115 women), 6 part-time (1 woman); includes 45 minority (3 Black or African American, non-Hispanic/Latino; 8 Asian, non-Hispanic/Latino; 19 Hispanic/Latino; 5 Two or more races, non-Hispanic/Latino), 99 international. Average age 26. 467 applicants, 50% accepted, 113 enrolled. *Faculty:* 44 full-time (11 women), 69 part-time/adjunct (26 women). Expenses: Contact institution. *Financial support:* Fellowships, Federal Work-Study, and scholarships/grants available. Financial award applicants required to submit FAFSA. In 2016, 79 master's awarded. Offers documentary filmmaking (MFA); film and television producing (MFA); film production (MFA); film studies (MA); production design (MFA); screenwriting (MFA). *Application deadline:* For fall admission, 12/1 for domestic students. *Application fee:* $60. Electronic applications accepted. *Application Contact:* Lauren Kacura, Assistant Director of Admissions, 714-744-7856, E-mail: kacura@chapman.edu. *Dean,* Robert Bassett, 714-997-6715, E-mail: bassett@chapman.edu.

Fowler School of Law Students: 471 full-time (252 women), 38 part-time (19 women); includes 208 minority (8 Black or African American, non-Hispanic/Latino; 3 American Indian or Alaska Native, non-Hispanic/Latino; 76 Asian, non-Hispanic/Latino; 92 Hispanic/Latino; 29 Two or more races, non-Hispanic/Latino), 13 international. Average age 26. 1,499 applicants, 50% accepted, 190 enrolled. *Faculty:* 44 full-time (18 women), 22 part-time/adjunct (6 women). Expenses: Contact institution. *Financial support:* Fellowships, Federal Work-Study, and scholarships/grants available. Financial award applicants required to submit FAFSA. In 2016, 21 master's, 159 doctorates awarded. *Program availability:* Part-time. Offers advocacy and dispute resolution (JD); business law (LL M, JD); criminal law (JD); entertainment and media law (LL M); entertainment law (JD); environmental, land use, and real estate law (JD); international and comparative law (LL M); international law (JD); law (JD); prosecutorial science (LL M); tax law (JD); taxation (LL M); trial advocacy (LL M). *Application deadline:* For fall admission, 4/15 priority date for domestic students. Applications are processed on a rolling basis. Electronic applications accepted. *Application Contact:* Grace Alcantara, Assistant Dean of Admissions and Diversity Initiatives, 714-628-2500, E-mail: lawadmission@chapman.edu. *Dean,* Matthew J. Parlow, 714-628-2678, E-mail: parlow@chapman.edu.

The George L. Argyros School of Business and Economics Students: 179 full-time (83 women), 94 part-time (44 women); includes 77 minority (4 Black or African American, non-Hispanic/Latino; 2 American Indian or Alaska Native, non-Hispanic/Latino; 30 Asian, non-Hispanic/Latino; 30 Hispanic/Latino; 3 Native Hawaiian or other Pacific Islander, non-Hispanic/Latino; 8 Two or more races, non-Hispanic/Latino), 96 international. Average age 28. 250 applicants, 75% accepted, 94 enrolled. *Faculty:* 54 full-time (10 women), 35 part-time/adjunct (7 women). Expenses: Contact institution. *Financial support:* Fellowships, Federal Work-Study, and scholarships/grants available. Financial award applicants required to submit FAFSA. In 2016, 114 master's awarded. *Program availability:* Part-time, evening/weekend. Offers accounting (MS); business administration (Exec MBA, MBA); economic systems design (MS). *Application fee:* $60. Electronic applications accepted. *Application Contact:* Debra Gonda, Associate Dean, 714-997-6894, E-mail: gonda@chapman.edu. *Dean,* Reginald Gilyard, 714-997-6684.

Schmid College of Science and Technology Students: 44 full-time (27 women), 58 part-time (24 women); includes 35 minority (2 Black or African American, non-Hispanic/Latino; 18 Asian, non-Hispanic/Latino; 11 Hispanic/Latino; 4 Two or more races, non-Hispanic/Latino), 19 international. Average age 28. 104 applicants, 61% accepted, 43 enrolled. *Faculty:* 18 full-time (5 women), 8 part-time/adjunct (5 women). Expenses: Contact institution. In 2016, 21 master's awarded. *Program availability:* Part-time, evening/weekend. Offers computational and data sciences (MS, PhD); food science (MS); science and technology (MS, PhD). *Application fee:* $60. Electronic applications accepted. *Dean,* Dr. Andrew Lyon, 714-997-6730, E-mail: lyon@chapman.edu.

School of Pharmacy Students: 195 full-time (117 women), 2 part-time (both women); includes 122 minority (7 Black or African American, non-Hispanic/Latino; 1 American Indian or Alaska Native, non-Hispanic/Latino; 94 Asian, non-Hispanic/Latino; 15 Hispanic/Latino; 1 Native Hawaiian or other Pacific Islander, non-Hispanic/Latino; 4 Two or more races, non-Hispanic/Latino), 20 international. Average age 28. 725 applicants, 26% accepted, 107 enrolled. *Faculty:* 32 full-time (15 women), 5 part-time/adjunct (2 women). Expenses: Contact institution. *Financial support:* Fellowships, research assistantships, Federal Work-Study, and scholarships/grants available. Offers pharmaceutical sciences (MS, PhD); pharmacy (Pharm D). *Application deadline:* Applications are processed on a rolling basis. Electronic applications accepted. *Application Contact:* Dr. Lawrence Brown, Associate Dean of Student and Academic Affairs, 714-516-5600, E-mail: pharmacyadmissions@chapman.edu. *Dean,* Ronald P. Jordan, 714-516-5486, E-mail: rpjordan@chapman.edu.

Wilkinson College of Arts, Humanities, and Social Sciences Students: 50 full-time (31 women), 28 part-time (19 women); includes 25 minority (1 Black or African American, non-Hispanic/Latino; 5 Asian, non-Hispanic/Latino; 16 Hispanic/Latino; 3 Two or more races, non-Hispanic/Latino), 3 international. Average age 29. 110 applicants, 87% accepted, 32 enrolled. *Faculty:* 22 full-time (13 women), 24 part-time/adjunct (16 women). Expenses: Contact institution. In 2016, 39 master's awarded. *Program availability:* Part-time, evening/weekend. Offers arts, humanities, and social sciences (MA, MFA, MS); creative writing (MFA); English (MA); health and strategic

Charles R. Drew University of Medicine and Science

communication (MS); international studies (MA); war and society (MA). *Application fee:* $60. Electronic applications accepted. *Dean,* Dr. Patrick Fuery, 714-516-4580, E-mail: fuery@chapman.edu.

CHARLES R. DREW UNIVERSITY OF MEDICINE AND SCIENCE, Los Angeles, CA 90059

General Information Independent, coed, comprehensive institution. *Graduate housing:* On-campus housing not available.

GRADUATE UNITS

College of Science and Health

Professional Program in Medicine Offers medicine (MD).

CHARLESTON SCHOOL OF LAW, Charleston, SC 29403

General Information Proprietary, coed, graduate-only institution. *Enrollment by degree level:* 417 doctoral, 1 other advanced degree. *Graduate faculty:* 25 full-time (13 women), 45 part-time/adjunct (18 women). *Tuition:* Full-time $40,596; part-time $16,309 per semester. *Required fees:* $120; $60 per semester. *Graduate housing:* On-campus housing not available. *Student services:* Campus employment opportunities, campus safety program, career counseling, free psychological counseling, services for students with disabilities, writing training. *Library facilities:* Sol Blatt Jr. Law Library. *Collection:* Books: 6,476 (physical), 303,861 (digital/electronic). Weekly public service hours: 105; students can reserve study rooms.

Computer facilities: A campuswide network can be accessed. Online class registration is available.
Website: http://www.charlestonlaw.edu/

General Application Contact: Jacqueline B. Bell, Assistant Dean of Admission, 843-377-2143, Fax: 843-329-4091, E-mail: info@charlestonlaw.edu.

GRADUATE UNITS

Graduate and Professional Programs Students: 363 full-time (189 women), 53 part-time (34 women). *Faculty:* 25 full-time (13 women), 45 part-time/adjunct (18 women). Expenses: Contact institution. *Financial support:* Scholarships/grants available. Offers admiralty and maritime law (LL M); law (JD). *Application deadline:* For fall admission, 6/1 for domestic students; for spring admission, 11/1 for domestic students. Applications are processed on a rolling basis. Electronic applications accepted. *Application Contact:* Jacqueline B. Bell, Assistant Dean of Admission, 843-377-2143, Fax: 843-329-4091, E-mail: info@charlestonlaw.edu.

CHARLESTON SOUTHERN UNIVERSITY, Charleston, SC 29423-8087

General Information Independent-religious, coed, comprehensive institution. *Enrollment:* 3,616 graduate, professional, and undergraduate students; 41 full-time matriculated graduate/professional students (31 women), 371 part-time matriculated graduate/professional students (220 women). *Enrollment by degree level:* 412 master's. *Graduate faculty:* 12 full-time (1 woman), 4 part-time/adjunct (0 women). *Tuition:* Full-time $6000. Tuition and fees vary according to program. *Graduate housing:* On-campus housing not available. *Student services:* Campus employment opportunities, campus safety program, career counseling, free psychological counseling, international student services, services for students with disabilities, writing training. *Library facilities:* L. Mendel Rivers Library plus 1 other. *Collection:* Books: 117,095 (physical), 303,641 (digital/electronic); Serial titles: 4,761 (physical), 53,688 (digital/electronic); Databases: 177. Weekly public service hours: 83; students can reserve study rooms. *Research affiliation:* Waccamaw Regional Planning and Development Council (economic forecasting), Metro Charleston Chamber of Commerce (economic forecasting), Santee Lynches Council of Governments (economic forecasting).

Computer facilities: 250 computers available on campus for general student use. A campuswide network can be accessed from student residence rooms and from off campus. Online class registration, online course work are available.
Website: http://www.charlestonsouthern.edu/

General Application Contact: Janie Cogdill, Graduate Enrollment Counselor, 843-863-7050, Fax: 843-863-7070, E-mail: jcogdill@csuniv.edu.

GRADUATE UNITS

Department of Criminal Justice Expenses: Contact institution. *Financial support:* Research assistantships with full tuition reimbursements available. Financial award application deadline: 4/15; financial award applicants required to submit FAFSA. *Program availability:* Part-time, evening/weekend. Offers criminal justice (MSCJ). *Application deadline:* Applications are processed on a rolling basis. *Application fee:* $40. *Application Contact:* Gary Metts, Interim Chair, 843-863-7330, Fax: 843-863-7198, E-mail: gmetts@csuniv.edu. *Interim Chair,* Gary Metts, 843-863-7330, Fax: 843-863-7198, E-mail: gmetts@csuniv.edu.

School of Business Expenses: Contact institution. *Financial support:* Research assistantships with full tuition reimbursements available. Financial award application deadline: 4/15; financial award applicants required to submit FAFSA. *Program availability:* Part-time, evening/weekend. Offers accounting (MBA); finance (MBA); general management (MBA); human resource management (MS); leadership (MBA); management information systems (MBA); organizational leadership (MA). *Application deadline:* Applications are processed on a rolling basis. *Application fee:* $40. *Application Contact:* Dr. Darin L. Gerdes, Director of the MBA Program, 843-863-7814, Fax: 843-863-7922, E-mail: dgerdes@csuniv.edu. *Interim Dean,* Dr. David Palmer, 843-863-7025, Fax: 843-863-7922, E-mail: dpalmer@csuniv.edu.

School of Education Expenses: Contact institution. *Financial support:* Research assistantships with full tuition reimbursements, career-related internships or fieldwork, and Federal Work-Study available. Financial award application deadline: 4/15; financial award applicants required to submit FAFSA. *Program availability:* Part-time, evening/weekend. Offers elementary administration and supervision (M Ed); elementary education (M Ed); secondary administration and supervision (M Ed). *Application deadline:* Applications are processed on a rolling basis. *Application fee:* $40. *Application Contact:* Dr. Melanie G. Reynolds-Murphy, Interim Dean, 843-863-7765, Fax: 843-863-7784, E-mail: mmurphy@csuniv.edu. *Interim Dean,* Dr. Melanie G. Reynolds-Murphy, 843-863-7765, Fax: 843-863-7784, E-mail: mmurphy@csuniv.edu.

CHARLOTTE CHRISTIAN COLLEGE AND THEOLOGICAL SEMINARY, Charlotte, NC 28205

General Information Independent-religious, coed, comprehensive institution.

GRADUATE UNITS

Graduate Program *Program availability:* Part-time, evening/weekend. Offers urban Christian ministry (MA). Electronic applications accepted.

CHATHAM UNIVERSITY, Pittsburgh, PA 15232-2826

General Information Independent, coed, primarily women, university. CGS member. *Enrollment:* 2,110 graduate, professional, and undergraduate students; 780 full-time matriculated graduate/professional students (607 women), 317 part-time matriculated graduate/professional students (265 women). *Enrollment by degree level:* 737 master's, 360 doctoral. *Graduate faculty:* 68 full-time (48 women), 107 part-time/adjunct (84 women). *Tuition:* Full-time $16,254; part-time $903 per credit hour. *Required fees:* $468; $26 per credit hour. *Graduate housing:* Rooms and/or apartments available on a first-come, first-served basis to single and married students. Typical cost: $5634 per year ($11,042 including board) for single students; $6634 per year ($12,042 including board) for married students. Housing application deadline: 3/26. *Student services:* Campus employment opportunities, campus safety program, career counseling, exercise/wellness program, free psychological counseling, international student services, low-cost health insurance, services for students with disabilities, teacher training, writing training. *Library facilities:* Jennie King Mellon Library. *Collection:* Books: 88,368 (physical), 1,200 (digital/electronic); Serial titles: 92 (physical), 32,874 (digital/electronic); Databases: 65. Weekly public service hours: 99; study areas open 24 hours, 5–7 days a week; students can reserve study rooms.

Computer facilities: Computer purchase and lease plans are available. 180 computers available on campus for general student use. A campuswide network can be accessed from student residence rooms and from off campus. Online class registration is available.
Website: http://www.chatham.edu/

General Application Contact: Katie Noel, Assistant Director of Graduate Admission, 412-365-1695, Fax: 412-365-1609, E-mail: knoel@chatham.edu.

GRADUATE UNITS

Nursing Programs *Program availability:* Online learning. Offers education/leadership (MSN); nursing (DNP). Electronic applications accepted.

Program in Accounting *Program availability:* Part-time, evening/weekend. Offers accounting (M Acc, MAC). Electronic applications accepted.

Program in Biology *Program availability:* Part-time. Offers environmental biology (MS); human biology (MS). Electronic applications accepted.

Program in Business Administration *Program availability:* Part-time, evening/weekend. Offers business administration (MBA); healthcare management (MBA); sustainability (MBA); women's leadership (MBA). Electronic applications accepted.

Program in Communication *Program availability:* Online learning. Offers environmental communication (M Comm); health communication (M Comm); strategic communication (M Comm).

Program in Counseling Psychology *Program availability:* Part-time, evening/weekend. Offers child, adolescent and family (MSCP); counseling psychology (Psy D); health and holistic (MSCP); infant mental health (MSCP); organization and supervision (MSCP); sport and exercise (MSCP). Electronic applications accepted.

Program in Education Offers early childhood education (MAT); elementary education (MAT); environmental education (K-12) (MAT); secondary art (MAT); secondary biology education (MAT); secondary chemistry education (MAT); secondary English education (MAT); secondary math education (MAT); secondary physics education (MAT); secondary social studies education (MAT); special education (MAT). Electronic applications accepted.

Program in Film and Digital Technology *Program availability:* Part-time, evening/weekend. Offers film and digital technology (MFA). Electronic applications accepted.

Program in Healthcare Informatics *Program availability:* Online learning. Offers healthcare informatics (MHI).

Program in Interior Architecture *Program availability:* Part-time, evening/weekend, online learning. Offers interior architecture (MIA). Electronic applications accepted.

Program in Landscape Architecture *Program availability:* Part-time, evening/weekend. Offers landscape architecture (ML Arch); landscape design and development (MA). Electronic applications accepted.

Program in Occupational Therapy Offers occupational therapy (MOT, OTD). Electronic applications accepted.

Program in Physical Therapy Offers physical therapy (DPT, TDPT). Electronic applications accepted.

Program in Physician Assistant Studies Offers physician assistant studies (MPAS). Electronic applications accepted.

Program in Writing *Program availability:* Part-time, evening/weekend, online learning. Offers children's writing (MFA); fiction (MFA); non-fiction (MFA); poetry (MFA); professional writing (MPW); screenwriting (MFA). Electronic applications accepted.

CHESTNUT HILL COLLEGE, Philadelphia, PA 19118-2693

General Information Independent-religious, coed, comprehensive institution. *Graduate housing:* On-campus housing not available.

GRADUATE UNITS

School of Graduate Studies *Program availability:* Part-time, evening/weekend. Offers administration of human services (MS, CAS); early education (M Ed); educational leadership (M Ed); elementary/middle education (M Ed); instructional technology (MS, CAS); reading (M Ed); reading specialist (M Ed); secondary education (M Ed); special education (M Ed). Electronic applications accepted.

Division of Psychology *Program availability:* Part-time, evening/weekend. Offers clinical and counseling psychology (MS, CAS); clinical psychology (Psy D).

CHEYNEY UNIVERSITY OF PENNSYLVANIA, Cheyney, PA 19319

General Information State-supported, coed, comprehensive institution. *Graduate housing:* On-campus housing not available.

GRADUATE UNITS

Graduate Programs *Program availability:* Part-time, evening/weekend. Offers educational leadership (M Ed, Certificate); elementary education (M Ed); principal certification (Certificate); public administration (MPA); special education (M Ed); urban education (M Ed). Electronic applications accepted.

THE CHICAGO SCHOOL OF PROFESSIONAL PSYCHOLOGY, Chicago, IL 60610

General Information Independent, coed, primarily women, graduate-only institution. CGS member. *Graduate housing:* On-campus housing not available.

GRADUATE UNITS

Program in Applied Behavior Analysis Offers applied behavior analysis (MS, PhD).

Program in Business Psychology Offers business psychology (PhD); industrial and organizational business psychology (Psy D); industrial and organizational psychology (MA); organizational leadership (MA, PhD).

Program in Clinical Forensic Psychology Offers clinical forensic psychology (Psy D).

Program in Clinical Mental Health Counseling *Program availability:* Part-time. Offers clinical mental health counseling (MA).

Program in Clinical Psychology Offers clinical psychology (Psy D). Electronic applications accepted.

Program in Forensic Psychology Offers forensic psychology (MA).

Program in Industrial and Organizational Psychology *Program availability:* Part-time, evening/weekend. Offers business psychology (Psy D); industrial and organizational psychology (MA).

Program in School Psychology *Program availability:* Part-time. Offers school psychology (Ed D, Ed S).

THE CHICAGO SCHOOL OF PROFESSIONAL PSYCHOLOGY AT DOWNTOWN LOS ANGELES, Los Angeles, CA 90017

General Information Independent, coed, graduate-only institution.

GRADUATE UNITS

Program in Applied Behavior Analysis Offers applied behavior analysis (Psy D).

Program in Clinical Forensic Psychology Offers clinical forensic psychology (Psy D).

Program in Clinical Psychology Offers applied behavior analysis (MA); clinical psychology (Psy D); marital and family therapy (MA).

Program in Industrial and Organizational Psychology Offers industrial and organizational psychology (MA).

THE CHICAGO SCHOOL OF PROFESSIONAL PSYCHOLOGY AT IRVINE, Irvine, CA 92612

General Information Independent, coed, graduate-only institution.

GRADUATE UNITS

Program in Clinical Forensic Psychology Offers clinical forensic psychology (Psy D).

Program in Marital and Family Therapy Offers clinical psychology (MA); management practice (Psy D); psychodynamic psychotherapy (Psy D).

Program in Psychology Offers generalist (Psy D); psychodynamic psychotherapy (Psy D).

THE CHICAGO SCHOOL OF PROFESSIONAL PSYCHOLOGY: ONLINE, Chicago, IL 60654

General Information Independent, coed, graduate-only institution. *Graduate housing:* On-campus housing not available.

GRADUATE UNITS

PhD Program in Organizational Leadership Offers organizational leadership (PhD).

Program in Applied Industrial and Organizational Psychology Offers applied industrial and organizational psychology (MA, Certificate).

Program in Forensic Psychology Offers forensic psychology (MA, Certificate).

Program in International Psychology Offers international psychology (PhD).

Program in Psychology Offers child and adolescent psychology (MA); generalist (MA); gerontology (MA); international psychology (MA); organizational leadership (MA); sport and exercise psychology (MA).

CHICAGO STATE UNIVERSITY, Chicago, IL 60628

General Information State-supported, coed, comprehensive institution. *Graduate housing:* Room and/or apartments available on a first-come, first-served basis to single students; on-campus housing not available to married students.

GRADUATE UNITS

College of Pharmacy Offers pharmacy (Pharm D).

School of Graduate and Professional Studies *Program availability:* Part-time, evening/weekend. Electronic applications accepted.

College of Arts and Sciences *Program availability:* Part-time, evening/weekend. Offers arts and sciences (MA, MFA, MS, MSW); biological sciences (MS); computer science (MS); counseling (MA); creative writing (MFA); criminal justice (MS); English (MA); geographic information systems (MA); geography (MA); history (MA); mathematics (MS); social work (MSW).

College of Education *Program availability:* Part-time. Offers bilingual education (M Ed); curriculum and instruction (MS Ed); early childhood education (MAT, MS Ed); education (M Ed, MA, MAT, MS Ed, Ed D); educational leadership (MA, Ed D); elementary education (MAT); general administration (MA); higher education administration (MA); instructional foundations (MS Ed); library information and media studies (MS Ed); middle school education (MAT); physical education (MS Ed); reading (MS Ed); secondary education (MAT); special education (M Ed); teaching of reading (MS Ed); technology and education (MS Ed).

College of Health Sciences Offers health sciences (MOT, MPH, MSN); nursing (MSN); occupational therapy (MOT); public health (MPH).

CHICAGO THEOLOGICAL SEMINARY, Chicago, IL 60637-1507

General Information Independent-religious, coed, graduate-only institution. *Graduate housing:* On-campus housing not available.

GRADUATE UNITS

Graduate and Professional Programs *Program availability:* Part-time. Offers Bible, culture and hermeneutics (PhD); preaching (D Min); religion and health (D Min); religious studies (MA); spirituality and spiritual direction (D Min); theology (M Div); theology, ethics and the human sciences (PhD).

CHOWAN UNIVERSITY, Murfreesboro, NC 27855

General Information Independent-religious, coed, comprehensive institution. *Graduate housing:* Room and/or apartments available to single students; on-campus housing not available to married students.

GRADUATE UNITS

School of Graduate Studies Offers education (M Ed). Electronic applications accepted.

CHRISTENDOM COLLEGE, Front Royal, VA 22630-5103

General Information Independent-religious, coed, comprehensive institution. *Enrollment:* 583 graduate, professional, and undergraduate students; 5 full-time matriculated graduate/professional students (2 women), 126 part-time matriculated graduate/professional students (53 women). *Enrollment by degree level:* 131 master's. *Graduate faculty:* 2 full-time (0 women), 9 part-time/adjunct (3 women). *Tuition:* Part-time

$380 per credit. *Graduate housing:* On-campus housing not available. *Student services:* Campus employment opportunities, campus safety program. *Library facilities:* St. John the Evangelist Library. *Collection:* Books: 100,000 (physical), 1,000 (digital/electronic); Serial titles: 250 (physical), 1,000 (digital/electronic); Databases: 45. Weekly public service hours: 97.

Computer facilities: 60 computers available on campus for general student use. A campuswide network can be accessed.
Website: http://www.christendom.edu/

General Application Contact: Virginia Norris, Director of Admissions, 703-658-4304, E-mail: graduate.school@christendom.edu.

GRADUATE UNITS

Graduate School Students: 5 full-time (2 women), 126 part-time (53 women). Average age 30. 10 applicants, 100% accepted, 8 enrolled. *Faculty:* 2 full-time (0 women), 9 part-time/adjunct (3 women). Expenses: Contact institution. In 2016, 25 master's awarded. *Program availability:* Part-time, evening/weekend, 100% online, blended/hybrid learning. Offers theological studies (MA). *Application deadline:* For fall admission, 6/1 priority date for domestic students; for spring admission, 11/1 priority date for domestic students. Applications are processed on a rolling basis. *Application fee:* $100. Electronic applications accepted. *Application Contact:* Virginia Norris, Director of Admissions, 703-658-4304, E-mail: graduate.school@christendom.edu. *Dean,* Dr. Robert J. Matava, 703-658-4304.

CHRISTIAN BROTHERS UNIVERSITY, Memphis, TN 38104-5581

General Information Independent-religious, coed, comprehensive institution. *Graduate housing:* On-campus housing not available.

GRADUATE UNITS

School of Arts *Program availability:* Part-time, evening/weekend. Offers Catholic studies (MACS); educational leadership (MSEL); teacher-leadership (M Ed); teaching (MAT).

School of Business *Program availability:* Part-time, evening/weekend. Offers accountancy (M Acc); business (MBA); international business (MIB); project management (Certificate).

School of Engineering *Program availability:* Part-time, evening/weekend, online learning. Offers engineering (MEM, MSEM).

School of Sciences Offers physician assistant studies (MS).

CHRISTIAN THEOLOGICAL SEMINARY, Indianapolis, IN 46208-3301

General Information Independent-religious, coed, graduate-only institution. *Graduate housing:* Rooms and/or apartments available on a first-come, first-served basis to single and married students.

GRADUATE UNITS

Graduate and Professional Programs *Program availability:* Part-time. Offers educational and arts ministries (MA); marriage and family therapy (MA); pastoral care and counseling (D Min); psychotherapy and faith (MA); theological studies (MTS); theology (M Div). Electronic applications accepted.

CHRISTIE'S EDUCATION, New York, NY 10020

General Information Proprietary, coed, primarily women, graduate-only institution. *Enrollment by degree level:* 63 master's, 6 other advanced degrees. *Graduate faculty:* 6 full-time (4 women). *Graduate housing:* On-campus housing not available. *Student services:* Campus employment opportunities, career counseling, international student services, services for students with disabilities, writing training. *Library facilities:* Christie's Education Library. *Collection:* Books: 6,000 (physical); Databases: 20.

Computer facilities: 11 computers available on campus for general student use. Website: http://www.christies.edu/

General Application Contact: Hilary Smith, Recruitment and Admissions Officer, 212-355-1501 Ext. 3309, Fax: 212-355-7370, E-mail: hsmith@christies.edu.

GRADUATE UNITS

Certificate Program in Art Business Expenses: Contact institution. Offers art business (Certificate). *Application deadline:* Applications are processed on a rolling basis. Electronic applications accepted. *Application Contact:* Catherine Warden, Academic Coordinator, 212-355-1501, Fax: 212-355-7370, E-mail: shortcoursesus@christies.edu. *Director of Continuing Education,* Dr. Marisa Kayyem, 212-355-1501, Fax: 212-355-7370, E-mail: mkayyem@christies.edu.

Certificate Program in Modern and Contemporary Art in New York Students: 6 (4 women). *Faculty:* 5 full-time (4 women). Expenses: Contact institution. *Program availability:* Part-time. Offers modern and contemporary art (Certificate). *Application deadline:* Applications are processed on a rolling basis. *Application fee:* $95. *Application Contact:* Hilary Smith, Recruitment and Admissions Officer, 212-355-1501 Ext. 3309, Fax: 212-355-7370, E-mail: hsmith@christies.edu. *Program Director,* Dr. Julie Reiss, 212-355-1501 Ext. 3307, E-mail: jreiss@christies.edu.

MA Program in Art, Law and Business Students: 13 full-time (12 women). *Faculty:* 3 full-time (2 women). Expenses: Contact institution. *Financial support:* In 2016–17, 1 student received support. Scholarships/grants and unspecified assistantships available. Financial award applicants required to submit FAFSA. *Program availability:* Part-time. Offers art, law and business (MA). *Application deadline:* For fall admission, 1/15 priority date for domestic and international students. Applications are processed on a rolling basis. *Application fee:* $95. *Application Contact:* Hilary Smith, Recruitment and Admissions Officer, 212-355-1501 Ext. 3309, Fax: 212-355-7370, E-mail: hsmith@christies.edu. *Program Director,* Noah Kupferman, 212-355-1501 Ext. 7101, E-mail: nkupferman@christies.edu.

MA Program in Modern and Contemporary Art and the Market Students: 47 full-time (43 women), 4 part-time (all women). *Faculty:* 5 full-time (4 women). Expenses: Contact institution. *Financial support:* In 2016–17, 3 students received support. Scholarships/grants and unspecified assistantships available. Financial award applicants required to submit FAFSA. In 2016, 21 master's awarded. *Program availability:* Part-time. Offers modern and contemporary art and the market (MA). *Application deadline:* For fall admission, 1/15 priority date for domestic and international students. Applications are processed on a rolling basis. *Application fee:* $95. *Application Contact:* Hilary Smith, Recruitment and Admissions Officer, 212-355-1501 Ext. 3309, Fax: 212-355-7370, E-mail: hsmith@christies.edu. *Program Director,* Dr. Julie Reiss, 212-355-1501 Ext. 3307, Fax: 212-355-7370, E-mail: jreiss@christies.edu.

CHRISTOPHER NEWPORT UNIVERSITY, Newport News, VA 23606-3072

General Information State-supported, coed, comprehensive institution. *Enrollment:* 5,042 graduate, professional, and undergraduate students; 81 full-time matriculated graduate/professional students (60 women), 25 part-time matriculated graduate/professional students (10 women). *Enrollment by degree level:* 106 master's. *Graduate faculty:* 31 full-time (13 women), 14 part-time/adjunct (11 women). Tuition, state resident: full-time $6660; part-time $370 per credit hour. Tuition, nonresident: full-time $15,138; part-time $841 per credit hour. *Required fees:* $3906; $217 per credit hour. Tuition and fees vary according to course load. *Graduate housing:* On-campus housing not available. *Student services:* Campus employment opportunities, campus safety program, career counseling, exercise/wellness program, free psychological counseling, grant writing training, multicultural affairs office, services for students with disabilities, writing training. *Library facilities:* Paul and Rosemary Trible Library. *Collection:* Books: 226,712 (physical), 567,490 (digital/electronic); Serial titles: 760 (physical), 64,477 (digital/electronic); Databases: 282. Weekly public service hours: 101; study areas open 24 hours, 5–7 days a week; students can reserve study rooms. *Research affiliation:* Thomas Jefferson National Accelerator Facility (instrument and nuclear physics), Langley Research Center, Center for Distance Learning (flow visualization), National Science Foundation (science), Langley Research Center, Center for Distance Learning (flow visualization), National Science Foundation (science).

Computer facilities: 540 computers available on campus for general student use. A campuswide network can be accessed from student residence rooms and from off campus. Online class registration is available.
Website: http://www.cnu.edu/

General Application Contact: Lyn Sawyer, Associate Director, Graduate Admissions, 757-594-7544, Fax: 757-594-7649, E-mail: gradstdy@cnu.edu.

GRADUATE UNITS

Graduate Studies Students: 81 full-time (60 women), 25 part-time (10 women); includes 14 minority (2 Black or African American, non-Hispanic/Latino; 5 Hispanic/Latino; 7 Two or more races, non-Hispanic/Latino), 2 international. Average age 24. 98 applicants, 84% accepted, 70 enrolled. *Faculty:* 31 full-time (13 women), 14 part-time/adjunct (11 women). Expenses: Contact institution. *Financial support:* In 2016–17, 13 students received support, including 9 research assistantships with full tuition reimbursements available (averaging $2,000 per year), 4 teaching assistantships (averaging $1,000 per year); scholarships/grants and unspecified assistantships also available. Financial award application deadline: 3/1; financial award applicants required to submit FAFSA. In 2016, 83 master's awarded. *Program availability:* Part-time. Offers applied physics and computer science (MS); environmental science (MS); teacher preparation (MAT). *Application deadline:* For fall admission, 7/15 for domestic students, 3/1 for international students; for spring admission, 10/15 for domestic students, 10/1 for international students; for summer admission, 12/1 for domestic and international students. Applications are processed on a rolling basis. *Application fee:* $65. Electronic applications accepted. *Application Contact:* Lyn Sawyer, Associate Director, Graduate Admissions and Records, 757-594-7544, Fax: 757-594-7649, E-mail: gradstdy@cnu.edu. *Vice Provost for Research, Graduate Studies, and Assessment,* Dr. Geoffrey C. Klein, 757-594-7477, E-mail: geoffrey.klein@cnu.edu.

CHRIST THE KING SEMINARY, East Aurora, NY 14052

General Information Independent-religious, coed, graduate-only institution. *Graduate housing:* On-campus housing not available.

GRADUATE UNITS

Graduate and Professional Programs *Program availability:* Part-time, evening/weekend. Offers divinity (M Div); pastoral ministry (MA); theology (MA).

CHURCH DIVINITY SCHOOL OF THE PACIFIC, Berkeley, CA 94709-1217

General Information Independent-religious, coed, graduate-only institution. *Graduate housing:* Rooms and/or apartments available on a first-come, first-served basis to single and married students. Housing application deadline: 5/1.

GRADUATE UNITS

Graduate and Professional Programs *Program availability:* Part-time. Offers theology (M Div, MA, MTS, D Min, Certificate). MA program offered jointly with Graduate Theological Union. Electronic applications accepted.

CINCINNATI CHRISTIAN UNIVERSITY, Cincinnati, OH 45204-3200

General Information Independent-religious, coed, comprehensive institution. *Graduate housing:* On-campus housing not available.

GRADUATE UNITS

Graduate School *Program availability:* Part-time. Offers biblical studies (MA); church history (MA); counseling (MAC); divinity (M Div); ministry (M Min); practical ministries (MA); theological studies (MA). Electronic applications accepted.

THE CITADEL, THE MILITARY COLLEGE OF SOUTH CAROLINA, Charleston, SC 29409

General Information State-supported, coed, primarily men, comprehensive institution. *Enrollment:* 3,602 graduate, professional, and undergraduate students; 173 full-time matriculated graduate/professional students (106 women), 634 part-time matriculated graduate/professional students (378 women). *Enrollment by degree level:* 686 master's, 121 other advanced degrees. *Graduate faculty:* 24 full-time (8 women), 23 part-time/adjunct (9 women). Tuition, state resident: full-time $5121; part-time $569 per credit hour. Tuition, nonresident: full-time $8613; part-time $957 per credit hour. *Required fees:* $90 per term. *Graduate housing:* On-campus housing not available. *Student services:* Campus employment opportunities, career counseling, exercise/wellness program, free psychological counseling, international student services, low-cost health insurance, multicultural affairs office, services for students with disabilities, teacher training, writing training. *Library facilities:* Daniel Library. *Collection:* Books: 201,000 (physical), 190,000 (digital/electronic). Students can reserve study rooms.

Computer facilities: 350 computers available on campus for general student use. A campuswide network can be accessed from student residence rooms and from off campus. Online class registration is available.
Website: http://www.citadel.edu/

General Application Contact: Dr. Tara Hornor, Associate Provost for Planning, Assessment and Evaluation/Dean of Enrollment Management, 843-953-5089, E-mail: cgc@citadel.edu.

GRADUATE UNITS

Citadel Graduate College Students: 173 full-time (106 women), 634 part-time (378 women); includes 167 minority (113 Black or African American, non-Hispanic/Latino; 2 American Indian or Alaska Native, non-Hispanic/Latino; 8 Asian, non-Hispanic/Latino; 27 Hispanic/Latino; 3 Native Hawaiian or other Pacific Islander, non-Hispanic/Latino; 14 Two or more races, non-Hispanic/Latino), 8 international. Average age 32. 437 applicants, 95% accepted, 268 enrolled. *Faculty:* 24 full-time (8 women), 23 part-

time/adjunct (9 women). Expenses: Contact institution. *Financial support:* Fellowships and unspecified assistantships available. Support available to part-time students. Financial award application deadline: 7/1; financial award applicants required to submit FAFSA. In 2016, 292 master's, 11 other advanced degrees awarded. *Program availability:* Part-time, evening/weekend, 100% online, blended/hybrid learning. Offers leadership studies (MS, Graduate Certificate). *Application deadline:* Applications are processed on a rolling basis. *Application fee:* $40. Electronic applications accepted. *Application Contact:* Dr. Tara Hornor, Associate Provost for Planning, Assessment and Evaluation/Dean of Enrollment Management, 843-953-5089, E-mail: cgc@citadel.edu. *Provost and Dean of the College,* Dr. Connie Ledoux Book, 843-953-5007, E-mail: cbook1@citadel.edu.

School of Engineering Students: 5 full-time (2 women), 98 part-time (38 women); includes 23 minority (11 Black or African American, non-Hispanic/Latino; 1 American Indian or Alaska Native, non-Hispanic/Latino; 3 Asian, non-Hispanic/Latino; 6 Hispanic/Latino; 1 Native Hawaiian or other Pacific Islander, non-Hispanic/Latino; 1 Two or more races, non-Hispanic/Latino), 1 international. 76 applicants, 96% accepted, 43 enrolled. *Faculty:* 3 full-time (0 women), 6 part-time/adjunct (0 women). Expenses: Contact institution. *Financial support:* Fellowships and unspecified assistantships available. Support available to part-time students. Financial award application deadline: 7/1; financial award applicants required to submit FAFSA. In 2016, 35 master's, 45 other advanced degrees awarded. *Program availability:* Part-time, evening/weekend. Offers aeronautical engineering (Graduate Certificate); built environment and public health (Graduate Certificate); civil engineering (MS); composites engineering (Graduate Certificate); computer engineering (Graduate Certificate); electrical engineering (MS); engineering (MS, Graduate Certificate); geotechnical engineering (Graduate Certificate); manufacturing engineering (Graduate Certificate); mechanical engineering (MS); mechatronics engineering (Graduate Certificate); power and energy (Graduate Certificate); project management (MS); structural engineering (Graduate Certificate); systems engineering management (Graduate Certificate); technical program management (Graduate Certificate); technical project management (Graduate Certificate); transportation engineering (Graduate Certificate). *Application deadline:* Applications are processed on a rolling basis. *Application fee:* $40. Electronic applications accepted. *Application Contact:* Dr. Tara Hornor, Associate Provost for Planning, Assessment and Evaluation/Dean of Enrollment Management, 843-953-5089, E-mail: cgc@citadel.edu. *Dean,* Dr. Ronald W. Welch, 843-953-6588, E-mail: ronald.welch@citadel.edu.

School of Humanities and Social Sciences Students: 74 full-time (49 women), 88 part-time (67 women); includes 27 minority (16 Black or African American, non-Hispanic/Latino; 6 Hispanic/Latino; 1 Native Hawaiian or other Pacific Islander, non-Hispanic/Latino; 4 Two or more races, non-Hispanic/Latino). 42 applicants, 88% accepted, 12 enrolled. *Faculty:* 14 full-time (3 women), 4 part-time/adjunct (3 women). Expenses: Contact institution. *Financial support:* Fellowships and unspecified assistantships available. Support available to part-time students. Financial award application deadline: 7/1; financial award applicants required to submit FAFSA. In 2016, 32 master's, 20 other advanced degrees awarded. *Program availability:* Part-time, evening/weekend, 100% online, blended/hybrid learning. Offers English (MA); Hispanic studies (Graduate Certificate); history (MA); history and teaching content (Graduate Certificate); homeland security (Graduate Certificate); humanities and social sciences (MA, Ed S, Graduate Certificate); intelligence analysis (Graduate Certificate); intelligence and security studies (MA); international politics and military affairs (MA); psychology (MA); school psychology (Ed S); social science (MA). *Application deadline:* Applications are processed on a rolling basis. *Application fee:* $40. Electronic applications accepted. *Application Contact:* Dr. Tara Hornor, Associate Provost for Planning, Assessment and Evaluation/Dean of Enrollment Management, 843-953-5089, E-mail: cgc@citadel.edu. *Dean,* Dr. Winfred B. Moore, Jr., 843-953-7477, E-mail: moorew@citadel.edu.

School of Science and Mathematics Students: 16 full-time (8 women), 32 part-time (15 women); includes 10 minority (8 Black or African American, non-Hispanic/Latino; 1 Hispanic/Latino; 1 Native Hawaiian or other Pacific Islander, non-Hispanic/Latino), 1 international. 31 applicants, 90% accepted, 11 enrolled. *Faculty:* 8 full-time (3 women), 1 (woman) part-time/adjunct. Expenses: Contact institution. *Financial support:* Fellowships and unspecified assistantships available. Support available to part-time students. Financial award application deadline: 7/1; financial award applicants required to submit FAFSA. In 2016, 33 master's, 3 other advanced degrees awarded. *Program availability:* Part-time, evening/weekend. Offers biology (MA); computer and information sciences (MS); environmental studies (Graduate Certificate); health, exercise, and sport science (MS); science and mathematics (MA, MA Ed, MAT, MS, Graduate Certificate); sport management (MA, Graduate Certificate). *Application deadline:* Applications are processed on a rolling basis. *Application fee:* $40. Electronic applications accepted. *Application Contact:* Dr. Tara Hornor, Associate Provost for Planning, Assessment and Evaluation/Dean of Enrollment Management, 843-953-5089, E-mail: cgc@citadel.edu. *Interim Dean,* Dr. John E. Weinstein, 843-953-5300, E-mail: weinsteinj@citadel.edu.

Tommy and Victoria Baker School of Business Students: 27 full-time (10 women), 137 part-time (51 women); includes 17 minority (7 Black or African American, non-Hispanic/Latino; 1 American Indian or Alaska Native, non-Hispanic/Latino; 2 Asian, non-Hispanic/Latino; 4 Hispanic/Latino; 3 Two or more races, non-Hispanic/Latino), 3 international. 100 applicants, 94% accepted, 56 enrolled. *Faculty:* 3 full-time (0 women), 1 part-time/adjunct (0 women). Expenses: Contact institution. *Financial support:* Fellowships and unspecified assistantships available. Support available to part-time students. Financial award application deadline: 7/1; financial award applicants required to submit FAFSA. In 2016, 91 master's awarded. *Program availability:* Part-time, evening/weekend, 100% online, blended/hybrid learning. Offers business (MBA). *Application deadline:* Applications are processed on a rolling basis. *Application fee:* $40. Electronic applications accepted. *Application Contact:* Morgan LaForge, MBA Academic Advisor, 843-953-5257, E-mail: mlaforge@citadel.edu. *MBA Program Director,* Dr. William Sharbrough, 843-953-5056, E-mail: sharbroughw@citadel.edu.

Zucker Family School of Education Students: 70 full-time (58 women), 249 part-time (200 women); includes 87 minority (70 Black or African American, non-Hispanic/Latino; 1 Asian, non-Hispanic/Latino; 9 Hispanic/Latino; 7 Two or more races, non-Hispanic/Latino), 2 international. 146 applicants, 98% accepted, 105 enrolled. *Faculty:* 9 full-time (4 women), 9 part-time/adjunct (5 women). Expenses: Contact institution. *Financial support:* Fellowships and unspecified assistantships available. Support available to part-time students. Financial award application deadline: 7/1; financial award applicants required to submit FAFSA. In 2016, 85 master's, 7 other advanced degrees awarded. *Program availability:* Part-time, evening/weekend, 100% online, blended/hybrid learning. Offers elementary/secondary school administration and supervision (M Ed);

elementary/secondary school counseling (M Ed); interdisciplinary STEM education (M Ed); literacy education (M Ed, Graduate Certificate); middle grades (MAT); physical education (grades K-12) (MAT); school superintendency (Ed S); secondary education (MAT); student affairs (Graduate Certificate); student affairs and college counseling (M Ed). *Application deadline:* Applications are processed on a rolling basis. *Application fee:* $40. Electronic applications accepted. *Application Contact:* Dr. Tammy J. Graham, Associate Professor, 843-953-6854, E-mail: tammy.graham@citadel.edu. *Dean,* Dr. Larry G. Daniel, 843-953-5097, E-mail: ldaniel@citadel.edu.

CITY COLLEGE OF THE CITY UNIVERSITY OF NEW YORK, New York, NY 10031-9198

General Information State and locally supported, coed, comprehensive institution. CGS member. *Enrollment:* 16,161 graduate, professional, and undergraduate students; 625 full-time matriculated graduate/professional students (200 women), 2,464 part-time matriculated graduate/professional students (1,460 women). *Enrollment by degree level:* 2,562 master's, 83 doctoral, 4 other advanced degrees. *Graduate faculty:* 519 full-time (199 women), 610 part-time/adjunct (291 women). Tuition and fees vary according to course load, degree level and program. *Graduate housing:* Room and/or apartments available on a first-come, first-served basis to single students; on-campus housing not available to married students. *Student services:* Campus employment opportunities, campus safety program, career counseling, child daycare facilities, exercise/wellness program, free psychological counseling, international student services, multicultural affairs office, services for students with disabilities, teacher training, writing training. *Library facilities:* Morris Raphael Cohen Library plus 8 others. *Research affiliation:* New York Center for Biological Structures, Lucent Laboratories (engineering), Hospital for Joint Diseases (biomedical engineering), Museum of Natural History.

Computer facilities: Computer purchase and lease plans are available. 3,000 computers available on campus for general student use. A campuswide network can be accessed from off campus. Online class registration is available.
Website: http://www.ccny.cuny.edu/

General Application Contact: Pauline Pabon, Assistant Director of Graduate Admissions, 212-650-6977, Fax: 212-650-6417, E-mail: graduateadmissions@ccny.cuny.edu.

GRADUATE UNITS

Graduate School *Program availability:* Part-time, evening/weekend. Offers sustainability in the urban environment (MS).

The Bernard and Anne Spitzer School of Architecture *Program availability:* Part-time. Offers architecture (M Arch); landscape architecture (MLA); urban design (MUP).

Colin Powell School for Civic and Global Leadership *Program availability:* Part-time. Offers clinical psychology (PhD); economics (MA); economics and business (MA); general psychology (MA); international relations (MA); mental health counseling (MA); psychology (MA, PhD); public service management (MPA); sociology (MA). Electronic applications accepted.

Division of Humanities and the Arts *Program availability:* Part-time. Offers advertising design (MFA); art history (MA); art history and museum studies (MA); art museum education (MA); branding and integrated communications (MPS); ceramic design (MFA); creative writing (MFA); digital and interdisciplinary art practice (MFA); film (MFA); fine arts (MFA); history (MA); humanities and the arts (MA, MFA, MPS); language and literacy (MA); literature (MA); museum studies (MA); painting (MFA); printmaking (MFA); sculpture (MFA); Spanish (MA); wood and metal design (MFA). Electronic applications accepted.

Division of Science *Program availability:* Part-time. Offers biochemistry (MS, PhD); biology (MS, PhD); chemistry (MS, PhD); geology (MS); mathematics (MS); physics (MS, PhD); science (MS, PhD). Electronic applications accepted.

Grove School of Engineering *Program availability:* Part-time. Offers biomedical engineering (MS, PhD); chemical engineering (ME, PhD); civil engineering (ME, MS, PhD); computer science (MS, PhD); electrical engineering (ME, MS, PhD); engineering (ME, MIS, MS, PhD); information systems (MIS); mechanical engineering (ME, MS, PhD).

School of Education *Program availability:* Part-time, evening/weekend. Offers adolescent mathematics education (MA, AC); bilingual education (MS); childhood education (MS); early childhood education (MS); education (MA, MS, MS Ed, AC); educational leadership (MS, AC); educational theatre (MS); English education (MA); literacy (MS); middle school mathematics education (MS); science education (MS); social studies education (AC); teacher of students with disabilities in adolescent education (MS Ed); teacher of students with disabilities in childhood education (MS Ed); TESOL (MS).

CITY UNIVERSITY OF NEW YORK SCHOOL OF LAW, Long Island City, NY 11101-4356

General Information State and locally supported, coed, graduate-only institution. *Enrollment by degree level:* 424 doctoral. *Graduate faculty:* 47 full-time (30 women), 3 part-time/adjunct (all women). Tuition, state resident: full-time $14,663; part-time $10,028 per year. Tuition, nonresident: full-time $23,983; part-time $16,448 per year. *Required fees:* $563; $173.95 per term. *Graduate housing:* On-campus housing not available. *Student services:* Campus employment opportunities, campus safety program, career counseling, exercise/wellness program, free psychological counseling, services for students with disabilities, writing training. *Library facilities:* CUNY School of Law Library. *Collection:* Books: 59,596 (physical), 478,975 (digital/electronic); Serial titles: 1,642 (physical), 95,611 (digital/electronic); Databases: 376. Weekly public service hours: 61; study areas open 24 hours, 5–7 days a week; students can reserve study rooms.

Computer facilities: 105 computers available on campus for general student use. A campuswide network can be accessed from off campus. Online class registration is available.
Website: http://www.law.cuny.edu/

General Application Contact: Degna P. Levister, Assistant Dean of Admissions and Enrollment Management, 718-340-4210, Fax: 718-340-4435, E-mail: admissions@law.cuny.edu.

GRADUATE UNITS

Professional Program Students: 336 full-time (217 women), 88 part-time (50 women); includes 205 minority (55 Black or African American, non-Hispanic/Latino; 3 American Indian or Alaska Native, non-Hispanic/Latino; 50 Asian, non-Hispanic/Latino; 81 Hispanic/Latino; 16 Two or more races, non-Hispanic/Latino), 14 international. Average age 29. 1,427 applicants, 46% accepted, 193 enrolled. *Faculty:* 47 full-time (30 women), 3 part-time/adjunct (all women). Expenses: Contact institution. *Financial support:* In 2016–17, 171 students received support, including 37 fellowships (averaging $13,849 per year), 18 research assistantships (averaging $839 per year); Federal Work-Study,

scholarships/grants, tuition waivers (full and partial), and unspecified assistantships also available. Support available to part-time students. Financial award application deadline: 5/1; financial award applicants required to submit FAFSA. In 2016, 104 doctorates awarded. *Program availability:* Part-time, evening/weekend. Offers law (JD). *Application deadline:* For fall admission, 6/15 priority date for domestic students. Applications are processed on a rolling basis. *Application fee:* $60. Electronic applications accepted. *Application Contact:* Degna P. Levister, Assistant Dean of Admissions and Enrollment Management, 718-340-4210, Fax: 718-340-4435, E-mail: admissions@law.cuny.edu. *Dean/Professor of Law,* Mary Lu Bilek, 718-340-4201, Fax: 718-340-4482.

CITY UNIVERSITY OF SEATTLE, Seattle, WA 98121

General Information Independent, coed, comprehensive institution. *Graduate housing:* Room and/or apartments available on a first-come, first-served basis to single students; on-campus housing not available to married students.

GRADUATE UNITS

Graduate Division *Program availability:* Part-time, evening/weekend, online learning. Electronic applications accepted.

Albright School of Education *Program availability:* Part-time, evening/weekend, online learning. Offers administrator certification (Certificate); curriculum and instruction (M Ed); elementary education (MIT); guidance and counseling (M Ed); leadership (M Ed); reading and literacy (M Ed); school counseling (M Ed); special education (MIT); superintendent certification (Certificate). Electronic applications accepted.

Division of Arts and Sciences *Program availability:* Part-time, evening/weekend, online learning. Offers counseling psychology (MA). Electronic applications accepted.

Division of Doctoral Studies *Program availability:* Online learning. Offers leadership (Ed D).

School of Management *Program availability:* Part-time, evening/weekend, online learning. Offers accounting (Certificate); change leadership (MBA, Certificate); computer systems (MS); finance (Certificate); financial management (MBA); general management (MBA); general management-Europe (MBA); global marketing (MBA); human resources management (Certificate); individualized study (MBA); information security (MS); information systems (MBA); leadership (MA); marketing (MBA, Certificate); project management (MBA, MS, Certificate); sustainable business (Certificate); technology management (MBA, Certificate). Electronic applications accepted.

CITY VISION UNIVERSITY, Kansas City, MO 64109-1845

General Information Independent-religious, coed, comprehensive institution.

GRADUATE UNITS

Program in Technology and Ministry *Program availability:* Online learning. Offers technology and ministry (MS).

CLAFLIN UNIVERSITY, Orangeburg, SC 29115

General Information Independent-religious, coed, comprehensive institution. *Graduate housing:* Room and/or apartments available on a first-come, first-served basis to single students; on-campus housing not available to married students. Housing application deadline: 4/15.

GRADUATE UNITS

Graduate Programs *Program availability:* Part-time. Offers biotechnology (MS); business administration (MBA).

CLAREMONT GRADUATE UNIVERSITY, Claremont, CA 91711-6160

General Information Independent, coed, graduate-only institution. CGS member. *Enrollment by degree level:* 741 master's, 1,236 doctoral, 61 other advanced degrees. *Graduate faculty:* 117 full-time (51 women), 17 part-time/adjunct (0 women). *Tuition:* Full-time $44,328; part-time $1847 per unit. *Required fees:* $600; $300 per semester. Tuition and fees vary according to course load and program. *Graduate housing:* Rooms and/or apartments available on a first-come, first-served basis to single and married students. Typical cost: $8412 per year for single students; $17,880 per year for married students. Room charges vary according to housing facility selected. Housing application deadline: 5/15. *Student services:* Campus employment opportunities, campus safety program, career counseling, exercise/wellness program, free psychological counseling, grant writing training, international student services, low-cost health insurance, multicultural affairs office, services for students with disabilities, teacher training, writing training. *Library facilities:* Honnold/Mudd Library plus 3 others. *Collection:* Students can reserve study rooms. *Research affiliation:* Claremont School of Theology (religion), Rancho Santa Ana Botanic Garden (botany, native plants).

Computer facilities: 136 computers available on campus for general student use. A campuswide network can be accessed from student residence rooms. Online class registration is available.
Website: http://www.cgu.edu/

General Application Contact: Loren Bryant, Admissions Coordinator, 909-607-7811, Fax: 909-607-7285, E-mail: admissions@cgu.edu.

GRADUATE UNITS

Graduate Programs Students: 1,355 full-time (757 women), 683 part-time (378 women); includes 678 minority (118 Black or African American, non-Hispanic/Latino; 10 American Indian or Alaska Native, non-Hispanic/Latino; 194 Asian, non-Hispanic/Latino; 275 Hispanic/Latino; 11 Native Hawaiian or other Pacific Islander, non-Hispanic/Latino; 70 Two or more races, non-Hispanic/Latino), 452 international. Average age 34. *Faculty:* 117 full-time (51 women), 17 part-time/adjunct (0 women). Expenses: Contact institution. *Financial support:* Fellowships, research assistantships, teaching assistantships, career-related internships or fieldwork, Federal Work-Study, institutionally sponsored loans, scholarships/grants, tuition waivers (full and partial), and unspecified assistantships available. Support available to part-time students. Financial award application deadline: 2/15; financial award applicants required to submit FAFSA. In 2016, 416 master's, 165 doctorates, 41 other advanced degrees awarded. *Program availability:* Part-time, evening/weekend. Offers arts management (MA); botany (MS, PhD); financial engineering (MSFE). *Application deadline:* For fall admission, 2/1 priority date for domestic and international students; for spring admission, 11/1 priority date for domestic and international students. Applications are processed on a rolling basis. *Application fee:* $80. Electronic applications accepted. *Application Contact:* Loren Bryant, Admissions Coordinator, 909-607-7811, Fax: 909-607-7285, E-mail: admissions@cgu.edu. *Interim President,* Jacob Adams, 909-621-8025, Fax: 909-607-9103, E-mail: jacob.adams@cgu.edu.

Center for Information Systems and Technology Students: 60 full-time (18 women), 81 part-time (27 women); includes 34 minority (7 Black or African American, non-Hispanic/Latino; 18 Asian, non-Hispanic/Latino; 7 Hispanic/Latino; 1 Native Hawaiian or other Pacific Islander, non-Hispanic/Latino; 1 Two or more races, non-

Hispanic/Latino), 80 international. Average age 35. *Faculty:* 8 full-time (1 woman), 1 part-time/adjunct (0 women). Expenses: Contact institution. *Financial support:* Fellowships, research assistantships, teaching assistantships, Federal Work-Study, institutionally sponsored loans, and scholarships/grants available. Support available to part-time students. Financial award application deadline: 2/15; financial award applicants required to submit FAFSA. In 2016, 21 master's, 10 doctorates awarded. *Program availability:* Part-time. Offers cybersecurity and networking (MS); data science and analytics (MS); electronic commerce (PhD); geographic information systems (MS); health informatics (MS); information systems (Certificate); IT strategy and innovation (MS); knowledge management (PhD); systems development (PhD); telecommunications and networking (PhD). *Application deadline:* For fall admission, 2/1 priority date for domestic and international students. Applications are processed on a rolling basis. *Application fee:* $80. Electronic applications accepted. *Application Contact:* Jake Campbell, Senior Assistant Director of Admissions, 909-607-3024, E-mail: jake.campbell@cgu.edu. *Acting Director,* Lorne Olfman, 909-607-3035, E-mail: lorne.olfman@cgu.edu.

Institute of Mathematical Sciences Students: 45 full-time (15 women), 40 part-time (17 women); includes 22 minority (3 Black or African American, non-Hispanic/Latino; 9 Asian, non-Hispanic/Latino; 9 Hispanic/Latino; 1 Two or more races, non-Hispanic/Latino; 34 international. Average age 32. *Faculty:* 5 full-time (1 woman), 3 part-time/adjunct (0 women). Expenses: Contact institution. *Financial support:* Fellowships, research assistantships, Federal Work-Study, institutionally sponsored loans, scholarships/grants, and tuition waivers (full and partial) available. Support available to part-time students. Financial award application deadline: 2/15; financial award applicants required to submit FAFSA. In 2016, 11 master's, 16 doctorates awarded. *Program availability:* Part-time. Offers computational and systems biology (PhD); computational mathematics and numerical analysis (MA, MS); computational science (PhD); engineering and industrial applied mathematics (PhD); mathematics (PhD); operations research and statistics (MA, MS); physical applied mathematics (MA, MS); pure mathematics (MA, MS); scientific computing (MA, MS); systems and control theory (MA, MS). PhD programs offered jointly with San Diego State University and California State University, Long Beach. *Application deadline:* For fall admission, 2/1 priority date for domestic and international students. Applications are processed on a rolling basis. *Application fee:* $80. Electronic applications accepted. *Application Contact:* Jake Campbell, Assistant Director of Admissions, 909-607-3024, E-mail: jake.campbell@cgu.edu. *Director,* John Angus, 909-607-3376, E-mail: john.angus@cgu.edu.

Peter F. Drucker and Masatoshi Ito Graduate School of Management Students: 137 full-time (84 women), 73 part-time (34 women); includes 57 minority (10 Black or African American, non-Hispanic/Latino; 22 Asian, non-Hispanic/Latino; 19 Hispanic/Latino; 3 Native Hawaiian or other Pacific Islander, non-Hispanic/Latino; 3 Two or more races, non-Hispanic/Latino), 75 international. Average age 32. *Faculty:* 15 full-time (5 women), 1 part-time/adjunct (0 women). Expenses: Contact institution. *Financial support:* Fellowships, research assistantships, teaching assistantships, Federal Work-Study, institutionally sponsored loans, and scholarships/grants available. Support available to part-time students. Financial award application deadline: 2/15; financial award applicants required to submit FAFSA. In 2016, 102 master's, 2 doctorates, 26 other advanced degrees awarded. *Program availability:* Part-time. Offers advanced management (MS); art business (MA); executive management (EMBA); leadership (Certificate); management (EMBA, MA, MBA, MS, PhD, Certificate); strategy (Certificate). *Application deadline:* For fall admission, 2/1 priority date for domestic and international students. Applications are processed on a rolling basis. *Application fee:* $80. Electronic applications accepted. *Application Contact:* Alice Liu, Assistant Director of Admissions, 909-607-7583, E-mail: alice.liu@cgu.edu. *Dean,* Jenny Darroch, 909-607-2471, E-mail: jenny.darroch@cgu.edu.

School of Arts and Humanities Students: 372 full-time (202 women), 97 part-time (57 women); includes 138 minority (23 Black or African American, non-Hispanic/Latino; 4 American Indian or Alaska Native, non-Hispanic/Latino; 44 Asian, non-Hispanic/Latino; 47 Hispanic/Latino; 2 Native Hawaiian or other Pacific Islander, non-Hispanic/Latino; 18 Two or more races, non-Hispanic/Latino), 54 international. Average age 37. *Faculty:* 28 full-time (14 women), 5 part-time/adjunct (0 women). Expenses: Contact institution. *Financial support:* Fellowships, research assistantships, teaching assistantships, Federal Work-Study, institutionally sponsored loans, and scholarships/grants available. Support available to part-time students. Financial award application deadline: 2/15; financial award applicants required to submit FAFSA. In 2016, 65 master's, 42 doctorates, 3 other advanced degrees awarded. *Program availability:* Part-time. Offers Africana history (Certificate); Africana studies (Certificate); American studies (MA, PhD); American studies and U.S. history (MA, PhD); applied women's studies (MA); archival studies (MA); arts and humanities (M Phil, MA, MFA, DCM, DMA, PhD, Certificate); church music (MA, DCM); composition (MA, DMA); critical theory (MA, PhD); cultural studies (MA, PhD); digital media (MFA); drawing (MFA); early modern studies (MA, PhD); English (M Phil, MA, PhD); European studies (MA, PhD); Hebrew Bible (MA, PhD); historical performance practices (MA, DMA); history of Christianity and religions of North America (MA, PhD); installation (MFA); literary theory (MA, PhD); literature (MA, PhD); literature and creative writing (MA); literature and film (MA); media studies (MA, PhD); museum studies (MA); musicology (MA, PhD); New Testament (MA, PhD); oral history (MA, PhD); painting (MFA); performance (MA, MFA, DMA); philosophy (MA, PhD); philosophy of religion and theology (MA, PhD); photography (MFA); sculpture (MFA); studio (MFA); theology, ethics and culture (MA); women's studies in religion (MA, PhD). *Application deadline:* For fall admission, 2/1 priority date for domestic and international students. Applications are processed on a rolling basis. *Application fee:* $80. Electronic applications accepted. *Application Contact:* Amy Sandefur, Assistant Director of Admissions, 909-607-9101, E-mail: amy.sandefur@cgu.edu. *Dean,* Patrick Mason, 909-607-8362, E-mail: patrick.mason@cgu.edu.

School of Community and Global Health Students: 64 full-time (43 women), 33 part-time (21 women); includes 47 minority (7 Black or African American, non-Hispanic/Latino; 18 Asian, non-Hispanic/Latino; 16 Hispanic/Latino; 1 Native Hawaiian or other Pacific Islander, non-Hispanic/Latino; 5 Two or more races, non-Hispanic/Latino), 16 international. Average age 30. *Faculty:* 9 full-time (4 women). Expenses: Contact institution. *Financial support:* Fellowships, research assistantships, teaching assistantships, Federal Work-Study, institutionally sponsored loans, and scholarships/grants available. Support available to part-time students. Financial award application deadline: 2/15; financial award applicants required to submit FAFSA. In 2016, 27 master's, 2 doctorates awarded. Offers health promotion science (PhD); public health (MPH). *Application deadline:* For fall admission, 2/1 priority date for domestic and international students; for spring admission, 11/1 priority date for domestic and international students. Applications are processed on a rolling basis. *Application fee:* $80. Electronic applications accepted. *Application Contact:*

Paige Piontkowsky, Senior Assistant Director of Admissions, 909-607-3240, E-mail: paige.piontkowsky@cgu.edu. *Dean,* Stewart Donaldson, 909-607-8235, E-mail: stewart.donaldson@cgu.edu.

School of Educational Studies Students: 195 full-time (143 women), 196 part-time (137 women); includes 217 minority (43 Black or African American, non-Hispanic/Latino; 4 American Indian or Alaska Native, non-Hispanic/Latino; 32 Asian, non-Hispanic/Latino; 117 Hispanic/Latino; 2 Native Hawaiian or other Pacific Islander, non-Hispanic/Latino; 19 Two or more races, non-Hispanic/Latino), 14 international. Average age 38. *Faculty:* 14 full-time (9 women), 1 part-time/adjunct (0 women). Expenses: Contact institution. *Financial support:* Fellowships, research assistantships, Federal Work-Study, institutionally sponsored loans, and scholarships/grants available. Support available to part-time students. Financial award application deadline: 2/15; financial award applicants required to submit FAFSA. In 2016, 48 master's, 39 doctorates, 7 other advanced degrees awarded. *Program availability:* Part-time. Offers Africana education (Certificate); education and policy (MA, PhD); higher education/student affairs (MA, PhD); human development (MA, PhD); public school administration (MA, PhD); quantitative evaluation (MA, PhD); special education (MA, PhD); teacher education (MA); teaching and learning (MA, PhD); urban leadership (PhD). PhD program offered jointly with San Diego State University. *Application deadline:* For fall admission, 3/1 priority date for domestic and international students. Applications are processed on a rolling basis. *Application fee:* $80. Electronic applications accepted. *Application Contact:* Rachel Camacho, Senior Assistant Director of Admission, 909-607-9418, E-mail: camacho@cgu.edu. *Dean,* Allen Omoto, 909-607-3786, E-mail: allen.omoto@cgu.edu.

School of Social Science, Policy and Evaluation Students: 452 full-time (234 women), 139 part-time (69 women); includes 160 minority (27 Black or African American, non-Hispanic/Latino; 2 American Indian or Alaska Native, non-Hispanic/Latino; 52 Asian, non-Hispanic/Latino; 54 Hispanic/Latino; 2 Native Hawaiian or other Pacific Islander, non-Hispanic/Latino; 23 Two or more races, non-Hispanic/Latino), 139 international. Average age 32. *Faculty:* 31 full-time (14 women), 6 part-time/adjunct (0 women). Expenses: Contact institution. In 2016, 109 master's, 53 doctorates, 5 other advanced degrees awarded. Offers advanced study in evaluation (Certificate); American politics (MA, PhD); behavioral economics and neuroeconomics (PhD); business and financial economics (MA, PhD); cognitive psychology (MA, PhD); comparative politics (PhD); developmental psychology (MA, PhD); economic development (Certificate); evaluation and applied research methods (MA, PhD); health behavior research and evaluation (MA, PhD); human resource development and evaluation (MA); human resource management (MS); industrial/organizational psychology (MA, PhD); international economic and development policy (PhD); international economics policy and development (MA); international money and finance (PhD); international political economy (MA); international studies (MA); organizational behavior (MA, PhD); organizational psychology (MA, PhD); political economy and public economics (PhD); political economy and public policy (MA); political philosophy (PhD); political science (PhD); politics, economics and business (MA); politics, economics, and business (MA); public policy (MA, PhD); public policy and evaluation (MA); social psychology (MA, PhD); social science, policy and evaluation (MA, MS, PhD, Certificate); world politics (PhD). *Application fee:* $80. *Application Contact:* Paige Piontkowsky, Senior Assistant Director of Admissions, 909-607-3240, E-mail: paige.piontkowsky@cgu.edu. *Dean,* Stewart Donaldson.

CLAREMONT LINCOLN UNIVERSITY, Claremont, CA 91711

General Information Independent, coed, graduate-only institution.

GRADUATE UNITS

Graduate Programs Offers ethical leadership (MA); interfaith action (MA); social impact (MA).

CLAREMONT MCKENNA COLLEGE, Claremont, CA 91711

General Information Independent, coed, comprehensive institution. *Graduate housing:* On-campus housing not available.

GRADUATE UNITS

Robert Day School of Economics and Finance Offers finance (MA). Electronic applications accepted.

CLAREMONT SCHOOL OF THEOLOGY, Claremont, CA 91711-3199

General Information Independent-religious, coed, graduate-only institution. *Enrollment by degree level:* 168 master's, 168 doctoral, 25 other advanced degrees. *Graduate faculty:* 18 full-time (6 women), 45 part-time/adjunct (20 women). *Tuition:* Full-time $21,120. Tuition and fees vary according to course level, course load and degree level. *Graduate housing:* Rooms and/or apartments available on a first-come, first-served basis to single students and guaranteed to married students. Typical cost: $14,400 (including board) for single students. Room and board charges vary according to housing facility selected. Housing application deadline: 5/1. *Student services:* Campus employment opportunities, career counseling, international student services, low-cost health insurance, services for students with disabilities, writing training. *Library facilities:* Claremont School of Theology Library plus 1 other. *Collection:* Weekly public service hours: 80; students can reserve study rooms. *Research affiliation:* Moore Multicultural Resource and Research Center, Institute for Antiquity and Christianity, Center for Process Studies, National United Methodist Native American Center, Center for Pacific and Asian-American Ministries, Ancient Biblical Manuscript Center.

Computer facilities: 20 computers available on campus for general student use. A campuswide network can be accessed from student residence rooms. Online class registration is available.
Website: http://www.cst.edu/

General Application Contact: Murad Dibbini, Director of Admissions, 626-447-6321, Fax: 909-447-6389, E-mail: admission@cst.edu.

GRADUATE UNITS

Graduate and Professional Programs Expenses: Contact institution. *Financial support:* Research assistantships, teaching assistantships, career-related internships or fieldwork, Federal Work-Study, institutionally sponsored loans, scholarships/grants, and tuition waivers (full and partial) available. Support available to part-time students. Financial award application deadline: 4/1; financial award applicants required to submit FAFSA. *Program availability:* Part-time. Offers interfaith chaplaincy (M Div); Islamic chaplaincy (M Div); ministerial leadership (M Div); practical theology (PhD); practical theology of conflict, healing and transformation in Korean contexts (D Min); religion (MA, PhD); spiritual renewal, contemplative practice, and strategic leadership (D Min). *Application deadline:* For fall admission, 5/1 for domestic students, 4/1 for international students; for winter admission, 11/1 for domestic and international students; for spring admission, 11/1 priority date for domestic students, 11/1 for international students. Applications are processed on a rolling basis. *Application fee:* $50. Electronic applications accepted. *Application Contact:* Director of Admissions, 866-274-6500, E-mail: admission@cst.edu. *Vice President for Academic Affairs/Dean,* Sheryl A. Kujawa-Holbrook, 909-447-2520, Fax: 909-447-6274, E-mail: skujawaholbrook@cst.edu.

CLARION UNIVERSITY OF PENNSYLVANIA, Clarion, PA 16214

General Information State-supported, coed, comprehensive institution. *Enrollment:* 5,224 graduate, professional, and undergraduate students; 230 full-time matriculated graduate/professional students (196 women), 664 part-time matriculated graduate/professional students (506 women). *Enrollment by degree level:* 857 master's, 9 doctoral, 28 other advanced degrees. *Graduate faculty:* 64 full-time (34 women), 20 part-time/adjunct (17 women). Tuition, state resident: full-time $4347; part-time $483 per credit hour. Tuition, nonresident: full-time $4698; part-time $522 per credit hour. *Required fees:* $149.35 per credit hour. Tuition and fees vary according to class time, course level, course load, degree level, campus/location and program. *Graduate housing:* Room and/or apartments available on a first-come, first-served basis to single students; on-campus housing not available to married students. Typical cost: $7100 per year ($10,576 including board). Room and board charges vary according to board plan, campus/location and housing facility selected. Housing application deadline: 6/28. *Student services:* Campus employment opportunities, campus safety program, career counseling, exercise/wellness program, free psychological counseling, international student services, low-cost health insurance, multicultural affairs office, services for students with disabilities, teacher training, writing training. *Library facilities:* Carlson Library plus 1 other. *Collection:* Books: 447,828 (physical), 184,427 (digital/electronic); Serial titles: 190 (physical), 39,855 (digital/electronic); Databases: 101. Weekly public service hours: 93; students can reserve study rooms.

Computer facilities: 950 computers available on campus for general student use. A campuswide network can be accessed from student residence rooms and from off campus. Online class registration, Online Learning Management System, web-based personal disk space, other online student services (financial aid, billing etc.) are available.

Website: http://www.clarion.edu/

General Application Contact: Dana Bearer, Associate Director, Transfer, Adult, and Graduate Admissions Office, 814-393-2337, Fax: 814-393-2722, E-mail: gradstudies@clarion.edu.

GRADUATE UNITS

Office of Transfer, Adult and Graduate Admissions Students: 230 full-time (196 women), 664 part-time (506 women); includes 76 minority (34 Black or African American, non-Hispanic/Latino; 11 Asian, non-Hispanic/Latino; 14 Hispanic/Latino; 1 Native Hawaiian or other Pacific Islander, non-Hispanic/Latino; 16 Two or more races, non-Hispanic/Latino), 6 international. Average age 32. 714 applicants, 70% accepted, 301 enrolled. *Faculty:* 64 full-time (34 women), 20 part-time/adjunct (17 women). Expenses: Contact institution. *Financial support:* Career-related internships or fieldwork, Federal Work-Study, scholarships/grants, and unspecified assistantships available. Support available to part-time students. Financial award application deadline: 5/1; financial award applicants required to submit FAFSA. In 2016, 292 master's awarded. *Program availability:* Part-time, evening/weekend, 100% online, blended/hybrid learning. Offers accounting (MS); applied data analytics (MS); clinical mental health counseling (MS); curriculum and instruction (M Ed); early childhood (M Ed); family nurse practitioner (MSN, Post-Master's Certificate); finance (MBA); health care administration (MBA); innovation and entrepreneurship (MBA); library science (MSLS, CAS); mass media arts and journalism (MS); math education (M Ed); nurse educator (MSN, Post-Master's Certificate); public relations (Certificate); reading (M Ed); science education (M Ed); special education (M Ed, MS); speech language pathology (MS); technology (M Ed). *Application deadline:* For fall admission, 7/15 priority date for domestic students, 7/15 for international students; for winter admission, 12/1 for domestic students; for spring admission, 12/1 for domestic students, 11/15 for international students; for summer admission, 4/1 for domestic students. Applications are processed on a rolling basis. *Application fee:* $40. Electronic applications accepted. *Application Contact:* Dana Bearer, Associate Director for Transfer, Adult and Graduate Admissions, 814-393-2337, Fax: 814-393-2722, E-mail: gradstudies@clarion.edu. *Interim Dean of Enrollment Management,* Merrilyn Dunlap, 814-393-2306, Fax: 814-393-2722, E-mail: gradstudies@clarion.edu.

CLARK ATLANTA UNIVERSITY, Atlanta, GA 30314

General Information Independent-religious, coed, university. CGS member. *Enrollment:* 3,884 graduate, professional, and undergraduate students; 559 full-time matriculated graduate/professional students (382 women), 232 part-time matriculated graduate/professional students (147 women). *Enrollment by degree level:* 570 master's, 218 doctoral, 3 other advanced degrees. *Graduate faculty:* 100 full-time (41 women), 23 part-time/adjunct (11 women). *Tuition:* Full-time $15,498; part-time $861 per credit hour. *Required fees:* $1326; $1326 per credit hour. Tuition and fees vary according to course load. *Graduate housing:* Room and/or apartments available on a first-come, first-served basis to single students; on-campus housing not available to married students. Housing application deadline: 6/1. *Student services:* Campus employment opportunities, campus safety program, career counseling, free psychological counseling, international student services, low-cost health insurance, services for students with disabilities. *Library facilities:* Robert W. Woodruff Library.

Computer facilities: 741 computers available on campus for general student use. A campuswide network can be accessed from student residence rooms. Online class registration is available.

Website: http://www.cau.edu/

General Application Contact: Graduate Program Admissions, 404-880-8483, E-mail: graduateadmissions@cau.edu.

GRADUATE UNITS

School of Arts and Sciences Students: 174 full-time (91 women), 146 part-time (89 women); includes 185 minority (175 Black or African American, non-Hispanic/Latino; 8 Asian, non-Hispanic/Latino; 2 Hispanic/Latino), 85 international. Average age 32. 198 applicants, 70% accepted, 78 enrolled. *Faculty:* 59 full-time (20 women), 5 part-time/adjunct (0 women). Expenses: Contact institution. *Financial support:* Fellowships, research assistantships, teaching assistantships, career-related internships or fieldwork, Federal Work-Study, institutionally sponsored loans, scholarships/grants, and unspecified assistantships available. Support available to part-time students. Financial award application deadline: 4/30; financial award applicants required to submit FAFSA. In 2016, 64 master's, 11 doctorates awarded. *Program availability:* Part-time. Offers African-American studies (MA, DAH); Africana women's studies (MA, DAH); arts and sciences (MA, MPA, MS, DAH, PhD); biology (MS, PhD); chemistry (MS, PhD);

computer and information science (MS); criminal justice (MA); English (MA, DAH); history (MA, DAH); mathematical sciences (MS); physics (MS); political science (MA, PhD); public administration (MPA); Romance languages (MA, DAH); sociology (MA). *Application deadline:* For fall admission, 4/1 for domestic and international students; for spring admission, 11/1 for domestic and international students. Applications are processed on a rolling basis. *Application fee:* $40 ($55 for international students). *Application Contact:* Graduate Program Admissions, 404-880-8483, E-mail: graduateadmissions@cau.edu. *Dean,* Dr. Danille K. Taylor, 404-880-6774, E-mail: dtaylor3@cau.edu.

School of Business Administration Students: 62 full-time (41 women), 9 part-time (5 women); includes 44 minority (all Black or African American, non-Hispanic/Latino), 14 international. Average age 32. 88 applicants, 56% accepted, 26 enrolled. *Faculty:* 16 full-time (6 women), 3 part-time/adjunct (1 woman). Expenses: Contact institution. *Financial support:* Career-related internships or fieldwork, scholarships/grants, and unspecified assistantships available. Support available to part-time students. Financial award application deadline: 4/30; financial award applicants required to submit FAFSA. In 2016, 34 master's awarded. *Program availability:* Part-time. Offers accounting (MA); business administration (MA, MBA); economics (MA). *Application deadline:* For fall admission, 4/1 for domestic and international students; for spring admission, 11/1 for domestic and international students. Applications are processed on a rolling basis. *Application fee:* $40 ($55 for international students). Electronic applications accepted. *Application Contact:* Graduate Program Admissions, 404-880-8483, E-mail: graduateadmissions@cau.edu. *Interim Dean,* Dr. Edward L. Davis, 404-880-8475, E-mail: edavis@cau.edu.

School of Education Students: 85 full-time (49 women), 49 part-time (29 women); includes 101 minority (99 Black or African American, non-Hispanic/Latino; 1 Asian, non-Hispanic/Latino; 1 Hispanic/Latino), 16 international. Average age 33. 63 applicants, 86% accepted, 25 enrolled. *Faculty:* 10 full-time (6 women), 11 part-time/adjunct (8 women). Expenses: Contact institution. *Financial support:* Career-related internships or fieldwork, Federal Work-Study, scholarships/grants, and unspecified assistantships available. Support available to part-time students. Financial award application deadline: 4/30; financial award applicants required to submit FAFSA. In 2016, 36 master's, 12 doctorates, 2 other advanced degrees awarded. *Program availability:* Part-time, evening/weekend. Offers counseling and psychological studies (MA); education (MA, MAT, Ed D, Ed S); educational leadership (MA, Ed D, Ed S); special education general curriculum (MA); teaching math and science (MAT). *Application deadline:* For fall admission, 4/1 for domestic and international students; for spring admission, 11/1 for domestic and international students. Applications are processed on a rolling basis. *Application fee:* $40 ($55 for international students). Electronic applications accepted. *Application Contact:* Graduate Program Admissions, 404-880-8483, E-mail: graduateadmissions@cau.edu. *Dean,* Dr. Moses C. Norman, 404-880-8495, E-mail: mnorman@cau.edu.

School of Social Work Students: 238 full-time (201 women), 28 part-time (24 women); includes 209 minority (208 Black or African American, non-Hispanic/Latino; 1 Hispanic/Latino), 12 international. Average age 31. 184 applicants, 74% accepted, 93 enrolled. *Faculty:* 15 full-time (9 women), 4 part-time/adjunct (2 women). Expenses: Contact institution. *Financial support:* Career-related internships or fieldwork, Federal Work-Study, scholarships/grants, and unspecified assistantships available. Support available to part-time students. Financial award application deadline: 4/30; financial award applicants required to submit FAFSA. In 2016, 148 master's, 5 doctorates awarded. *Program availability:* Part-time. Offers social work (MSW, PhD). *Application deadline:* For fall admission, 4/1 for domestic and international students; for spring admission, 11/1 for domestic and international students. Applications are processed on a rolling basis. *Application fee:* $40 ($55 for international students). Electronic applications accepted. *Application Contact:* Graduate Program Admissions, 404-880-8483, E-mail: graduateadmissions@cau.edu. *Dean,* Dr. Jenny Jones, 404-880-8549, E-mail: jjones@cau.edu.

CLARKE UNIVERSITY, Dubuque, IA 52001-3198

General Information Independent-religious, coed, comprehensive institution. *Enrollment:* 1,043 graduate, professional, and undergraduate students; 175 full-time matriculated graduate/professional students (142 women), 54 part-time matriculated graduate/professional students (44 women). *Enrollment by degree level:* 77 master's, 152 doctoral. *Graduate faculty:* 35 full-time (28 women), 9 part-time/adjunct (6 women). *Tuition:* Part-time $535 per credit hour. *Required fees:* $35 per credit hour. Tuition and fees vary according to degree level and program. *Graduate housing:* On-campus housing not available. *Student services:* Career counseling, exercise/wellness program, free psychological counseling, low-cost health insurance, multicultural affairs office, services for students with disabilities, writing training. *Library facilities:* Nicholas J. Schrupp Library. *Collection:* Books: 78,500 (physical), 136,800 (digital/electronic); Serial titles: 150 (physical), 53,000 (digital/electronic); Databases: 60. Weekly public service hours: 90.

Computer facilities: 237 computers available on campus for general student use. A campuswide network can be accessed from student residence rooms and from off campus. Online class registration is available.

Website: http://www.clarke.edu/

General Application Contact: Kimberly Roush, Director of Admission, Graduate and Adult Programs, 563-588-6635, Fax: 563-552-7994, E-mail: graduate@clarke.edu.

GRADUATE UNITS

Department of Nursing and Health Students: 62 full-time (61 women), 12 part-time (all women); includes 2 minority (1 Black or African American, non-Hispanic/Latino; 1 Asian, non-Hispanic/Latino). Average age 34. 53 applicants, 55% accepted, 27 enrolled. *Faculty:* 8 full-time (all women), 2 part-time/adjunct (both women). Expenses: Contact institution. *Financial support:* Applicants required to submit FAFSA. In 2016, 20 doctorates awarded. *Program availability:* Part-time. Offers family nurse practitioner (DNP). *Application deadline:* For fall admission, 2/1 priority date for domestic students. *Application fee:* $35. Electronic applications accepted. *Application Contact:* Kimberly Roush, Director of Admission, Graduate and Adult Programs, 563-588-6539, Fax: 563-552-7994, E-mail: graduate@clarke.edu. *Chair,* Dr. Jan Lee, 563-588-6339.

Department of Social Work Students: 16 full-time (13 women), 3 part-time (all women); includes 4 minority (1 Black or African American, non-Hispanic/Latino; 2 Hispanic/Latino; 1 Two or more races, non-Hispanic/Latino). Average age 29. 16 applicants, 94% accepted, 15 enrolled. *Faculty:* 7 full-time (all women). Expenses: Contact institution. *Financial support:* Applicants required to submit FAFSA. In 2016, 5 master's awarded. *Program availability:* Part-time, evening/weekend. Offers social work (MSW). *Application deadline:* For fall admission, 2/1 priority date for domestic students. *Application fee:* $35. Electronic applications accepted. *Application Contact:* Kimberly Roush, Director of Admission, Graduate and Adult Programs, 563-588-6539, Fax: 563-552-7994, E-mail: graduate@clarke.edu. *Chair,* Regina Boarman, 888-825-2753 Ext. 6583, E-mail: regina.boarman@clarke.edu.

Graduate Business Programs Students: 13 full-time (9 women), 26 part-time (16 women); includes 5 minority (2 Black or African American, non-Hispanic/Latino; 1 Asian, non-Hispanic/Latino; 2 Hispanic/Latino), 1 international. Average age 33. 37 applicants, 54% accepted, 12 enrolled. *Faculty:* 6 full-time (3 women). Expenses: Contact institution. *Financial support:* Applicants required to submit FAFSA. In 2016, 19 master's awarded. *Program availability:* Part-time, evening/weekend, blended/hybrid learning. Offers business (MBA, MOL). *Application deadline:* Applications are processed on a rolling basis. *Application fee:* $35. Electronic applications accepted. *Application Contact:* Kimberly Roush, Director of Admission, Graduate and Adult Programs, 563-588-6539, Fax: 563-552-7994, E-mail: graduate@clarke.edu. *Director of Graduate Business Studies,* B'Ann Dittmar, 563-588-6419, E-mail: bann.dittmar@clarke.edu.

Physical Therapy Program Students: 78 full-time (53 women); includes 2 minority (1 Hispanic/Latino; 1 Two or more races, non-Hispanic/Latino). Average age 24. 166 applicants, 33% accepted, 38 enrolled. *Faculty:* 8 full-time (4 women), 6 part-time/adjunct (2 women). Expenses: Contact institution. *Financial support:* Applicants required to submit FAFSA. In 2016, 22 doctorates awarded. Offers physical therapy (DPT). *Application deadline:* For fall admission, 11/2 for domestic students. *Application fee:* $0. Electronic applications accepted. *Application Contact:* Kimberly Roush, Director of Admission, Graduate and Adult Programs, 563-588-6539, Fax: 563-552-7994, E-mail: graduate@clarke.edu. *Chair,* Dr. Bill O'Dell, 563-588-6618, E-mail: bill.odell@clarke.edu.

Program in Education Students: 6 full-time (all women), 13 part-time (all women); includes 2 minority (1 Hispanic/Latino; 1 Two or more races, non-Hispanic/Latino). Average age 26. 17 applicants, 82% accepted, 10 enrolled. *Faculty:* 6 full-time (all women), 1 (woman) part-time/adjunct. Expenses: Contact institution. *Financial support:* Applicants required to submit FAFSA. In 2016, 16 master's awarded. *Program availability:* Part-time, 100% online, blended/hybrid learning. Offers instructional leadership (MAE). *Application deadline:* Applications are processed on a rolling basis. *Application fee:* $35. Electronic applications accepted. *Application Contact:* Kimberly Roush, Director of Admission, Graduate and Adult Programs, 563-588-6539, Fax: 563-552-7994, E-mail: graduate@clarke.edu. *Director of Graduate Education,* Dr. Paula Schmidt, 563-588-6573, E-mail: paula.schmidt@clarke.edu.

CLARKSON COLLEGE, Omaha, NE 68131-2739

General Information Independent, coed, primarily women, comprehensive institution. *Graduate housing:* Room and/or apartments available on a first-come, first-served basis to single students; on-campus housing not available to married students. Housing application deadline: 6/30.

GRADUATE UNITS

Master of Science in Nursing Program *Program availability:* Part-time, evening/weekend, online learning. Offers adult nurse practitioner (MSN, Post-Master's Certificate); family nurse practitioner (MSN, Post-Master's Certificate); nursing education (MSN, Post-Master's Certificate); nursing health care leadership (MSN, Post-Master's Certificate). Electronic applications accepted.

Program in Health Care Administration *Program availability:* Part-time, evening/weekend, online learning. Offers health care administration (MHCA). Electronic applications accepted.

CLARKSON UNIVERSITY, Potsdam, NY 13699

General Information Independent, coed, university. *Enrollment:* 4,384 graduate, professional, and undergraduate students; 679 full-time matriculated graduate/professional students (288 women), 392 part-time matriculated graduate/professional students (127 women). *Enrollment by degree level:* 805 master's, 256 doctoral, 10 other advanced degrees. *Graduate faculty:* 248 full-time (71 women), 120 part-time/adjunct (45 women). *Tuition:* Full-time $23,400; part-time $1300 per credit hour. Tuition and fees vary according to campus/location and program. *Graduate housing:* On-campus housing not available. *Student services:* Campus employment opportunities, campus safety program, career counseling, free psychological counseling, international student services, low-cost health insurance, multicultural affairs office, services for students with disabilities, teacher training. *Library facilities:* Harriet Call Burnap Memorial Library plus 1 other. *Collection:* Books: 111,436 (physical), 188,698 (digital/electronic); Serial titles: 1,975 (physical), 54,563 (digital/electronic); Databases: 76. Weekly public service hours: 97; students can reserve study rooms. *Research affiliation:* Trudeau Institute (biomedical sciences).

Computer facilities: 350 computers available on campus for general student use. A campuswide network can be accessed from student residence rooms and from off campus. Online class registration is available.
Website: http://www.clarkson.edu/

General Application Contact: Dan Capogna, Graduate Admissions Contact, 518-631-9910, E-mail: graduate@clarkson.edu.

GRADUATE UNITS

Department of Bioethics Students: 13 full-time (10 women), 21 part-time (19 women); includes 6 minority (1 Black or African American, non-Hispanic/Latino; 2 Asian, non-Hispanic/Latino; 2 Hispanic/Latino; 1 Two or more races, non-Hispanic/Latino), 4 international. 27 applicants, 59% accepted, 14 enrolled. *Faculty:* 1 full-time (0 women), 8 part-time/adjunct (7 women). Expenses: Contact institution. *Financial support:* Scholarships/grants available. In 2016, 14 master's, 3 other advanced degrees awarded. *Program availability:* Part-time, evening/weekend, 100% online, blended/hybrid learning. Offers bioethics (MS, AC). Offered jointly with Icahn School of Medicine at Mount Sinai. *Application deadline:* Applications are processed on a rolling basis. *Application fee:* $50. Electronic applications accepted. *Application Contact:* Ann Nolte, Assistant Chair of Bioethics, 518-631-9860, E-mail: anolte@clarkson.edu. *Chair of Bioethics,* Dr. Sean Philpott, 518-631-9860, E-mail: sphilpott@clarkson.edu.

Division of Health Sciences Students: 154 full-time (105 women); includes 27 minority (4 Black or African American, non-Hispanic/Latino; 14 Asian, non-Hispanic/Latino; 6 Hispanic/Latino; 3 Two or more races, non-Hispanic/Latino), 4 international. *Faculty:* 20 full-time (12 women), 16 part-time/adjunct (11 women). Expenses: Contact institution. Offers health sciences (MS, DPT); occupational therapy (MS); physical therapy (DPT); physician assistant studies (MS). *Application Contact:* Melissa Roberts, Graduate Admissions Coordinator, 315-268-2161, E-mail: mroberts@clarkson.edu. *Chair of Physical Therapy / Associate Dean of Health Sciences,* Dr. George Fulk, 315-268-3786, E-mail: gfulk@clarkson.edu.

Institute for a Sustainable Environment Students: 21 full-time (7 women), 12 international. *Faculty:* 4 full-time (2 women), 6 part-time/adjunct (2 women). Expenses: Contact institution. Offers environmental politics and governance (MS); environmental science and engineering (MS, PhD); sustainable environment (MS). *Application Contact:* Dan Capogna, Graduate Admissions Contact, 518-631-9910, E-mail: graduate@clarkson.edu. *Interim Director of the Institute for a Sustainable*

Environment/Associate Director of Sustainability, Dr. Susan Powers, 315-268-6542, E-mail: spowers@clarkson.edu.

Program in Data Analytics Students: 12 full-time (2 women), 2 part-time (1 woman); includes 1 minority (Black or African American, non-Hispanic/Latino), 9 international. 36 applicants, 92% accepted, 19 enrolled. *Faculty:* 8 full-time (0 women). Expenses: Contact institution. *Financial support:* Scholarships/grants and unspecified assistantships available. In 2016, 11 master's awarded. *Program availability:* Part-time, evening/weekend, 100% online. Offers data analytics (MS). *Application deadline:* Applications are processed on a rolling basis. *Application fee:* $50. Electronic applications accepted. *Application Contact:* Dan Capogna, Graduate Admissions Contact, 518-631-9910, E-mail: graduate@clarkson.edu. *Director of Business Analytics,* Dr. Boris Jukic, 315-268-3884, E-mail: bjukic@clarkson.edu.

Program in Education Students: 38 full-time (23 women), 2 part-time (0 women); includes 6 minority (3 Asian, non-Hispanic/Latino; 2 Hispanic/Latino; 1 Two or more races, non-Hispanic/Latino), 7 international. 39 applicants, 79% accepted, 26 enrolled. *Faculty:* 8 full-time (all women), 31 part-time/adjunct (17 women). Expenses: Contact institution. *Financial support:* Scholarships/grants available. In 2016, 15 master's awarded. Offers adolescence education 7-12 (MAT); technology education K-12 (MAT). *Application deadline:* Applications are processed on a rolling basis. *Application fee:* $50. Electronic applications accepted. *Application Contact:* Dan Capogna, Graduate Admissions Contact, 518-631-9910, E-mail: graduate@clarkson.edu. *Chair of Education,* Dr. Catherine Snyder, 518-631-9870, E-mail: csnyder@clarkson.edu.

Program in Engineering Management Students: 2 full-time (0 women), 142 part-time (34 women); includes 25 minority (4 Black or African American, non-Hispanic/Latino; 11 Asian, non-Hispanic/Latino; 9 Hispanic/Latino; 1 Two or more races, non-Hispanic/Latino), 7 international. 90 applicants, 74% accepted, 67 enrolled. *Faculty:* 2 full-time (0 women), 11 part-time/adjunct (1 woman). Expenses: Contact institution. *Financial support:* Scholarships/grants available. In 2016, 65 master's awarded. *Program availability:* Part-time-only, evening/weekend, blended/hybrid learning. Offers engineering management (MS). *Application deadline:* Applications are processed on a rolling basis. *Application fee:* $50. Electronic applications accepted. *Application Contact:* Dan Capogna, Graduate Admissions Contact, 518-631-9910, E-mail: graduate@clarkson.edu. *Associate Vice President of Graduate Business Development,* Mike Walsh, 518-631-9846, E-mail: mwalsh@clarkson.edu.

School of Arts and Sciences Students: 142 full-time (59 women), 24 part-time (19 women); includes 20 minority (2 Black or African American, non-Hispanic/Latino; 9 Asian, non-Hispanic/Latino; 5 Hispanic/Latino; 4 Two or more races, non-Hispanic/Latino), 55 international. *Faculty:* 93 full-time (31 women), 32 part-time/adjunct (16 women). Expenses: Contact institution. Offers arts and sciences (MS, DPT, PhD); basic science (MS); chemistry (MS, PhD); computer science (MS, PhD); information technology (MS); interdisciplinary bioscience and biotechnology (PhD); mathematics (MS, PhD); physics (MS, PhD). *Application Contact:* Dan Capogna, Graduate Admissions Contact, 518-631-9910, E-mail: graduate@clarkson.edu. *Senior Vice President and Provost/Interim Dean of Arts and Sciences,* Dr. Charles Thorpe, 315-268-6544, E-mail: cthorpe@clarkson.edu.

School of Business Students: 176 full-time (78 women), 113 part-time (52 women); includes 64 minority (12 Black or African American, non-Hispanic/Latino; 1 American Indian or Alaska Native, non-Hispanic/Latino; 38 Asian, non-Hispanic/Latino; 6 Hispanic/Latino; 1 Native Hawaiian or other Pacific Islander, non-Hispanic/Latino; 6 Two or more races, non-Hispanic/Latino), 23 international. *Faculty:* 46 full-time (11 women), 22 part-time/adjunct (6 women). Expenses: Contact institution. Offers business (MBA, MS, Advanced Certificate); business administration (MBA); business fundamentals (Advanced Certificate); clinical leadership in healthcare management (MS); global supply chain management (Advanced Certificate); healthcare data analytics (MS); healthcare management (MBA, Advanced Certificate); human resource management (Advanced Certificate); management and leadership (Advanced Certificate). *Application Contact:* Erin Wheeler, 518-631-9910, E-mail: ewheeler@clarkson.edu. *Dean of Business,* Dr. Dayle Smith, 315-268-2300, E-mail: dsmith@clarkson.edu.

Wallace H. Coulter School of Engineering Students: 172 full-time (37 women), 111 part-time (21 women); includes 27 minority (5 Black or African American, non-Hispanic/Latino; 11 Asian, non-Hispanic/Latino; 10 Hispanic/Latino; 1 Two or more races, non-Hispanic/Latino), 97 international. *Faculty:* 75 full-time (13 women), 31 part-time/adjunct (5 women). Expenses: Contact institution. Offers business of energy (Advanced Certificate); chemical engineering (ME, MS, PhD); civil and environmental engineering (ME, MS, PhD); electrical and computer engineering (PhD); electrical engineering (ME, MS); energy systems (MS); engineering (ME, MS, PhD, Advanced Certificate); engineering and management systems (MS); interdisciplinary engineering science (MS, PhD); materials science and engineering (PhD); mechanical engineering (ME, MS, PhD). *Application Contact:* Dan Capogna, Graduate Admissions Contact, 518-631-9910, E-mail: graduate@clarkson.edu. *Dean of Engineering,* Dr. William Jemison, 315-268-6446, E-mail: wjemison@clarkson.edu.

CLARKS SUMMIT UNIVERSITY, South Abington Township, PA 18411

General Information Independent-religious, coed, comprehensive institution. *Graduate housing:* Room and/or apartments available on a first-come, first-served basis to single students; on-campus housing not available to married students.

GRADUATE UNITS

Baptist Bible Seminary *Program availability:* Part-time, evening/weekend, online learning. Offers Biblical apologetics (MA); church education (M Div, M Min); church planting (M Div, M Min); global ministry (M Div, M Min); leadership in communication (D Min); leadership in counseling and spiritual development (D Min); leadership in global ministry (D Min); leadership in pastoral ministry (D Min); leadership in theological studies (D Min); military chaplaincy (M Div); ministry (PhD); organizational leadership (M Min); outreach pastor (M Div, M Min); pastoral counseling (M Div, M Min); pastoral leadership (M Div, M Min); theology (Th M); worship ministries leadership (M Div, M Min); youth pastor (M Div, M Min). Electronic applications accepted.

Graduate Studies *Program availability:* Part-time, evening/weekend, online learning. Offers Bible (MA); counseling (MA, MS); curriculum and instruction (M Ed); educational administration (M Ed); intercultural studies (MA); literature (MA); missions (MA); organizational leadership (MA); reading specialist (M Ed); secondary English/communications (M Ed); social entrepreneurship (MA); worldview studies (MA). MA in missions program available only for Association of Baptists for World Evangelism missionary personnel.

CLARK UNIVERSITY, Worcester, MA 01610-1477

General Information Independent, coed, university. CGS member. *Enrollment:* 3,298 graduate, professional, and undergraduate students; 760 full-time matriculated graduate/professional students (437 women), 218 part-time matriculated graduate/professional students (116 women). *Enrollment by degree level:* 769 master's,

207 doctoral, 2 other advanced degrees. *Graduate faculty:* 205 full-time (92 women), 146 part-time/adjunct (60 women). *Tuition:* Full-time $44,050. *Required fees:* $80. Tuition and fees vary according to course load and program. *Graduate housing:* Rooms and/or apartments available on a first-come, first-served basis to single and married students. Typical cost: $7750 per year ($9530 including board) for single students. Room and board charges vary according to board plan and housing facility selected. *Student services:* Campus employment opportunities, campus safety program, career counseling, exercise/wellness program, free psychological counseling, grant writing training, international student services, low-cost health insurance, multicultural affairs office, services for students with disabilities, teacher training, writing training. *Library facilities:* Robert Hutchings Goddard Library plus 8 others. *Collection:* Students can reserve study rooms. *Research affiliation:* Worcester Area Computation Center, Worcester Foundation for Experimental Biology, Massachusetts Biotechnology Research Institute.

Computer facilities: A campuswide network can be accessed from student residence rooms and from off campus. Online class registration, online course support are available.
Website: http://www.clarku.edu/

General Application Contact: Ethan Bernstein, Director of Graduate Admissions, 508-793-7676, Fax: 508-793-8834, E-mail: graduateadmissions@clarku.edu.

GRADUATE UNITS

Graduate School Students: 760 full-time (437 women), 218 part-time (116 women); includes 94 minority (29 Black or African American, non-Hispanic/Latino; 1 American Indian or Alaska Native, non-Hispanic/Latino; 27 Asian, non-Hispanic/Latino; 28 Hispanic/Latino; 9 Two or more races, non-Hispanic/Latino), 476 international. Average age 28. 2,048 applicants, 72% accepted, 388 enrolled. *Faculty:* 206 full-time (90 women), 148 part-time/adjunct (64 women). Expenses: Contact institution. *Financial support:* In 2016–17, 10 fellowships with tuition reimbursements (averaging $17,000 per year), 39 research assistantships with tuition reimbursements (averaging $17,000 per year), 84 teaching assistantships with tuition reimbursements (averaging $17,000 per year) were awarded; career-related internships or fieldwork, Federal Work-Study, institutionally sponsored loans, scholarships/grants, and tuition waivers (full and partial) also available. Support available to part-time students. In 2016, 491 master's, 38 doctorates awarded. *Program availability:* Part-time, evening/weekend. Offers biology (PhD); community and global health (MHS); community development and planning (MA); economics (PhD); English (MA); environmental science and policy (MS); genocide studies (PhD); geographic information science for development and environment (MS); history of the Atlantic world (PhD); history of the Holocaust (PhD); history of the United States (PhD); Holocaust history and genocide studies (PhD); international development and social change (MA); physics (PhD); United States and Atlantic history (PhD). *Application deadline:* Applications are processed on a rolling basis. *Application fee:* $75. Electronic applications accepted. *Application Contact:* Ethan Bernstein, Director of Graduate Admission, 508-793-7373, E-mail: gradadmissions@clarku.edu. *Associate Provost and Dean of Graduate Studies,* Dr. William Fisher, 508-793-7676.

Adam Institute for Urban Teaching and School Practice Students: 24 full-time (18 women), 6 part-time (4 women); includes 8 minority (1 Black or African American, non-Hispanic/Latino; 3 Asian, non-Hispanic/Latino; 3 Hispanic/Latino; 1 Two or more races, non-Hispanic/Latino). Average age 26. 48 applicants, 69% accepted, 29 enrolled. *Faculty:* 9 full-time (6 women), 5 part-time/adjunct (3 women). Expenses: Contact institution. *Financial support:* Fellowships with tuition reimbursements, research assistantships with tuition reimbursements, teaching assistantships with tuition reimbursements, institutionally sponsored loans, and tuition waivers (partial) available. Financial award application deadline: 5/1. In 2016, 29 master's awarded. Offers urban teaching and school practice (MAT). *Application deadline:* For fall admission, 1/15 priority date for domestic students. Applications are processed on a rolling basis. *Application fee:* $75. *Application Contact:* Andrea Allen, Program Administrator, 508-793-7685, E-mail: aallen@clarku.edu. *Director,* Dr. Thomas Del Prete, 508-793-7197.

Graduate School of Management Students: 307 full-time (169 women), 120 part-time (58 women); includes 27 minority (9 Black or African American, non-Hispanic/Latino; 7 Asian, non-Hispanic/Latino; 10 Hispanic/Latino; 1 Native Hawaiian or other Pacific Islander, non-Hispanic/Latino), 259 international. Average age 28. 1,183 applicants, 79% accepted, 183 enrolled. *Faculty:* 27 full-time (12 women), 19 part-time/adjunct (6 women). Expenses: Contact institution. *Financial support:* In 2016–17, research assistantships with partial tuition reimbursements (averaging $4,800 per year), teaching assistantships with partial tuition reimbursements (averaging $4,800 per year) were awarded; fellowships, career-related internships or fieldwork, Federal Work-Study, institutionally sponsored loans, and tuition waivers (partial) also available. Support available to part-time students. Financial award application deadline: 5/31. In 2016, 214 master's awarded. *Program availability:* Part-time, evening/weekend. Offers accounting (MSA); business analytics (MSBA); finance (MBA); information management and business analytics (MBA); management (MBA); marketing (MBA); social change (MBA); sustainability (MBA). *Application deadline:* For fall admission, 6/1 priority date for domestic students; for spring admission, 12/1 priority date for domestic students. Applications are processed on a rolling basis. *Application fee:* $75. Electronic applications accepted. *Application Contact:* Jerry Czub, Director of Graduate Enrollment Management, 508-793-7559, E-mail: graduateadmissions@clarku.edu. *Dean,* Dr. Catherine Usoff, 508-793-7670, Fax: 508-793-8822, E-mail: cusoff@clarku.edu.

Gustav H. Carlson School of Chemistry Students: 17 full-time (6 women), 2 part-time (1 woman); includes 4 minority (2 Asian, non-Hispanic/Latino; 2 Hispanic/Latino), 9 international. Average age 27. 52 applicants, 23% accepted, 5 enrolled. *Faculty:* 10 full-time (1 woman), 1 (woman) part-time/adjunct. Expenses: Contact institution. *Financial support:* In 2016–17, fellowships with tuition reimbursements (averaging $21,875 per year), 11 teaching assistantships with full tuition reimbursements (averaging $21,875 per year) were awarded; research assistantships with full tuition reimbursements and tuition waivers (full) also available. Offers biochemistry (PhD); chemistry (PhD). *Application deadline:* For fall admission, 1/15 priority date for domestic students. Applications are processed on a rolling basis. *Application fee:* $75. *Application Contact:* Rene Baril, Managerial Secretary, 508-793-7130, Fax: 528-793-7117, E-mail: mbaril@clarku.edu. *Chair,* Dr. Shuanghong Huo, 508-793-7533.

Hiatt School of Psychology Students: 35 full-time (31 women), 3 part-time (1 woman); includes 8 minority (1 Black or African American, non-Hispanic/Latino; 1 American Indian or Alaska Native, non-Hispanic/Latino; 2 Asian, non-Hispanic/Latino; 4 Hispanic/Latino), 5 international. Average age 29. 243 applicants, 9% accepted, 10 enrolled. *Faculty:* 16 full-time (11 women), 2 part-time/adjunct (both women). Expenses: Contact institution. *Financial support:* In 2016–17, 8 fellowships with full tuition reimbursements (averaging $17,325 per year), 6 research assistantships with full tuition reimbursements (averaging $17,325 per year), 16 teaching assistantships

with full tuition reimbursements (averaging $17,325 per year) were awarded; career-related internships or fieldwork and tuition waivers (full and partial) also available. In 2016, 9 doctorates awarded. Offers clinical psychology (PhD); developmental psychology (PhD); social psychology (PhD). *Application deadline:* For fall admission, 12/15 priority date for domestic and international students. Applications are processed on a rolling basis. *Application fee:* $75. *Application Contact:* Kelly Boulay, Department Administrator, 508-793-7274, Fax: 508-793-7265, E-mail: psychology@clarku.edu. *Chair,* Dr. James Cordova, 508-793-7268.

School of Geography Students: 56 full-time (27 women), 1 (woman) part-time; includes 7 minority (2 Black or African American, non-Hispanic/Latino; 2 Asian, non-Hispanic/Latino; 3 Hispanic/Latino), 23 international. Average age 31. 103 applicants, 28% accepted, 20 enrolled. *Faculty:* 17 full-time (6 women). Expenses: Contact institution. *Financial support:* In 2016–17, 3 fellowships with full tuition reimbursements (averaging $17,325 per year), 12 research assistantships with full tuition reimbursements (averaging $17,325 per year), 16 teaching assistantships with full tuition reimbursements (averaging $17,325 per year) were awarded; career-related internships or fieldwork and tuition waivers (full) also available. In 2016, 7 doctorates awarded. Offers geography (PhD). *Application deadline:* For fall admission, 12/31 priority date for domestic and international students. Applications are processed on a rolling basis. *Application fee:* $75. *Application Contact:* Brenda Nikas-Hayes, Admission Coordinator, 508-793-7336, Fax: 508-793-8881, E-mail: geography@clarku.edu. *Director,* Dr. Anthony Bebbington, 508-793-7370.

School of Professional Studies Students: 93 full-time (64 women), 65 part-time (38 women); includes 15 minority (8 Black or African American, non-Hispanic/Latino; 4 Hispanic/Latino; 3 Two or more races, non-Hispanic/Latino), 94 international. Average age 29. 245 applicants, 80% accepted, 82 enrolled. *Faculty:* 36 part-time/adjunct (14 women). Expenses: Contact institution. *Financial support:* Career-related internships or fieldwork available. Support available to part-time students. In 2016, 88 master's awarded. *Program availability:* Part-time, evening/weekend. Offers information technology (MSIT); professional communication (MSPC); public administration (MPA, Certificate). *Application deadline:* Applications are processed on a rolling basis. *Application fee:* $75. Electronic applications accepted. *Application Contact:* Ethan Bernstein, Director of Graduate Admissions, 508-793-7373, E-mail: gradadmissions@clarku.edu. *Associate Dean,* Dr. John Chetro-Szivos, 508-793-7217.

CLAYTON STATE UNIVERSITY, Morrow, GA 30260-0285

General Information State-supported, coed, comprehensive institution. *Enrollment:* 6,996 graduate, professional, and undergraduate students; 175 full-time matriculated graduate/professional students (103 women), 266 part-time matriculated graduate/professional students (195 women). *Enrollment by degree level:* 441 master's. *Graduate faculty:* 76 full-time (34 women), 8 part-time/adjunct (5 women). *Tuition,* state resident: full-time $3528; part-time $196 per credit hour. *Tuition,* nonresident: full-time $13,176; part-time $732 per credit hour. *Required fees:* $1454; $1454 per credit hour. $727 per semester. Tuition and fees vary according to campus/location and program. *Graduate housing:* On-campus housing not available. *Student services:* Campus employment opportunities, career counseling, exercise/wellness program, free psychological counseling, international student services, low-cost health insurance, multicultural affairs office, services for students with disabilities. *Library facilities:* Clayton State University Library.

Computer facilities: 3,500 computers available on campus for general student use. A campuswide network can be accessed from student residence rooms and from off campus. Online class registration is available.
Website: http://www.clayton.edu/

General Application Contact: Elizabeth Taylor, Assistant to the Dean of Graduate Studies, 678-466-4113, Fax: 678-466-4119, E-mail: elizabethtaylor@clayton.edu.

GRADUATE UNITS

School of Graduate Studies Electronic applications accepted.

College of Arts and Sciences Offers administration of justice (MS); applied developmental psychology (MS); arts and sciences (MA, MAT, MS); biology (MAT); clinical/counseling psychology (MS); criminology, law, and society (MS); English (MAT); history (MAT); liberal studies (MA); mathematics (MAT).

College of Business Offers accounting (MBA); business (MBA); human resource leadership (MBA); international business (MBA); sports and entertainment management (MBA); supply chain management (MBA).

College of Health Offers family nurse practitioner (MSN); health (MHA, MSN).

College of Information and Mathematical Sciences Offers archival studies (MAS); information and mathematical sciences (MAS).

CLEARY UNIVERSITY, Howell, MI 48843

General Information Independent, coed, comprehensive institution. *Enrollment:* 92 full-time matriculated graduate/professional students (47 women), 25 part-time matriculated graduate/professional students (14 women). *Enrollment by degree level:* 117 master's. *Graduate faculty:* 13 part-time/adjunct (6 women). *Tuition:* Full-time $16,560; part-time $920 per credit hour. *Required fees:* $100 per semester. *Graduate housing:* On-campus housing not available. *Student services:* Campus employment opportunities, career counseling, free psychological counseling, international student services, services for students with disabilities, writing training. *Library facilities:* Cleary Online Library.

Computer facilities: 26 computers available on campus for general student use. A campuswide network can be accessed from student residence rooms and from off campus.
Website: http://www.cleary.edu/

General Application Contact: Cassandra Tarnowski, Director of Admissions, 800-686-1883, Fax: 517-338-3336, E-mail: ctarnowski@cleary.edu.

GRADUATE UNITS

Online Program in Business Administration Students: 92 full-time (47 women), 25 part-time (14 women). *Faculty:* 13 part-time/adjunct (6 women). Expenses: Contact institution. *Financial support:* Fellowships, Federal Work-Study, and scholarships/grants available. Support available to part-time students. Financial award application deadline: 8/15; financial award applicants required to submit FAFSA. *Program availability:* Part-time, evening/weekend, online learning. Offers analytics, technology, and innovation (MBA, Graduate Certificate); financial planning (Graduate Certificate); global leadership (MBA, Graduate Certificate); health care leadership (MBA, Graduate Certificate). *Application deadline:* For fall admission, 8/15 for domestic students, 7/15 for international students; for spring admission, 4/2 for domestic students, 1/2 for international students. Applications are processed on a rolling basis. *Application fee:* $50. Electronic applications accepted. *Application Contact:* Cassandra Tarnowski,

Director of Admissions, 800-686-1883, Fax: 517-338-3336, E-mail: ctarnowski@cleary.edu. *Provost and Chief Academic Officer*, Dr. Lance B. Lewis, 800-686-1883, E-mail: llewis@cleary.edu.

CLEMSON UNIVERSITY, Clemson, SC 29634

General Information State-supported, coed, university. CGS member. *Enrollment:* 23,406 graduate, professional, and undergraduate students; 2,925 full-time matriculated graduate/professional students (1,263 women), 2,086 part-time matriculated graduate/professional students (1,158 women). *Enrollment by degree level:* 2,882 master's, 1,484 doctoral, 600 other advanced degrees. *Graduate faculty:* 1,243 full-time (456 women), 96 part-time/adjunct (34 women). Tuition, state resident: full-time $8826; part-time $612 per credit hour. Tuition, nonresident: full-time $18,424; part-time $1223 per credit hour. *Required fees:* $856; $10 per credit hour. $310 per semester. Tuition and fees vary according to course load and program. *Graduate housing:* On-campus housing not available. *Student services:* Campus employment opportunities, campus safety program, career counseling, exercise/wellness program, free psychological counseling, grant writing training, international student services, low-cost health insurance, multicultural affairs office, services for students with disabilities, teacher training, writing training. *Library facilities:* Robert Muldrow Cooper Library plus 1 other. *Research affiliation:* Savannah National Research Lab (energy), Fluor Corporation (supply chain logistics), Greenville Hospital System (biological sciences), South Carolina Universities Research and Education Foundation (energy), Oak Ridge National Laboratory (materials science, physics), BMW (automotive, electrical and mechanical engineering).

Computer facilities: Computer purchase and lease plans are available. 1,250 computers available on campus for general student use. A campuswide network can be accessed from student residence rooms and from off campus. Online class registration is available.
Website: http://www.clemson.edu/

General Application Contact: Laura Kinard, Admissions Coordinator, 864-656-5336, E-mail: lkinard@clemson.edu.

GRADUATE UNITS

Graduate School Students: 2,925 full-time (1,263 women), 2,086 part-time (1,158 women); includes 499 minority (239 Black or African American, non-Hispanic/Latino; 3 American Indian or Alaska Native, non-Hispanic/Latino; 77 Asian, non-Hispanic/Latino; 110 Hispanic/Latino; 4 Native Hawaiian or other Pacific Islander, non-Hispanic/Latino; 66 Two or more races, non-Hispanic/Latino), 1,381 international. Average age 30. 6,655 applicants, 34% accepted, 1429 enrolled. *Faculty:* 1,243 full-time (456 women), 96 part-time/adjunct (34 women). Expenses: Contact institution. *Financial support:* In 2016–17, 2,193 students received support, including 254 fellowships with partial tuition reimbursements available (averaging $6,466 per year), 713 research assistantships with partial tuition reimbursements available (averaging $18,437 per year), 852 teaching assistantships with partial tuition reimbursements available (averaging $17,582 per year); career-related internships or fieldwork and unspecified assistantships also available. In 2016, 1,364 master's, 230 doctorates, 136 other advanced degrees awarded. *Program availability:* Part-time, evening/weekend, 100% online, blended/hybrid learning. *Application deadline:* For fall admission, 4/15 for international students; for spring admission, 10/15 for international students. Applications are processed on a rolling basis. *Application fee:* $80 ($90 for international students). Electronic applications accepted. *Application Contact:* Kathleen Costello, Director of Graduate Admissions and Recruitment, 864-656-2561, E-mail: kcostel@clemson.edu. *Associate Provost and Dean of the Graduate School*, Dr. Jason Osborne, 864-656-4172, Fax: 864-656-5344, E-mail: jwo@clemson.edu.

College of Agriculture, Forestry and Life Sciences Students: 203 full-time (102 women), 55 part-time (25 women); includes 19 minority (4 Black or African American, non-Hispanic/Latino; 1 Asian, non-Hispanic/Latino; 7 Hispanic/Latino; 7 Two or more races, non-Hispanic/Latino), 52 international. Average age 29. 147 applicants, 39% accepted, 47 enrolled. *Faculty:* 122 full-time (35 women), 3 part-time/adjunct (2 women). Expenses: Contact institution. *Financial support:* In 2016–17, 229 students received support, including 15 fellowships with partial tuition reimbursements available (averaging $6,733 per year), 134 research assistantships with partial tuition reimbursements available (averaging $16,750 per year), 71 teaching assistantships with partial tuition reimbursements available (averaging $15,425 per year); career-related internships or fieldwork and unspecified assistantships also available. In 2016, 41 master's, 22 doctorates awarded. *Program availability:* 100% online, blended/hybrid learning. Offers agricultural education (M Ag Ed); agriculture, forestry and life sciences (M Ag Ed, MFR, MS, PhD); animal and veterinary sciences (MS, PhD); applied economics (PhD); applied economics and statistics (MS); entomology (MS, PhD); food technology (PhD); food, nutrition and culinary sciences (MS); food, nutrition and packaging sciences (MS, PhD); forest resources (MFR, MS, PhD); packaging science (MS); plant and environmental sciences (MS, PhD); wildlife and fisheries biology (MS, PhD). *Application deadline:* Applications are processed on a rolling basis. *Application fee:* $80 ($90 for international students). Electronic applications accepted. *Application Contact:* Dr. Joseph Culin, Associate Dean for Research and Graduate Studies, 864-656-2810, E-mail: jculin@clemson.edu. *Dean*, Dr. George Askew, 864-656-3013, Fax: 864-656-1286, E-mail: caflsdean-l@clemson.edu.

College of Architecture, Arts, and Humanities Students: 336 full-time (179 women), 41 part-time (21 women); includes 31 minority (12 Black or African American, non-Hispanic/Latino; 4 Asian, non-Hispanic/Latino; 12 Hispanic/Latino; 3 Two or more races, non-Hispanic/Latino), 97 international. Average age 28. 644 applicants, 44% accepted, 143 enrolled. *Faculty:* 251 full-time (105 women), 23 part-time/adjunct (11 women). Expenses: Contact institution. *Financial support:* In 2016–17, 310 students received support, including 89 fellowships with partial tuition reimbursements available (averaging $2,091 per year), 47 research assistantships with partial tuition reimbursements available (averaging $6,777 per year), 69 teaching assistantships with partial tuition reimbursements available (averaging $16,436 per year); career-related internships or fieldwork and unspecified assistantships also available. In 2016, 131 master's, 6 doctorates, 13 other advanced degrees awarded. *Program availability:* Part-time, 100% online. Offers architecture (M Arch, MS, Certificate); architecture, arts, and humanities (M Arch, MA, MCRP, MCSM, MFA, MLA, MRED, MS, PhD, Certificate); city and regional planning (MCRP); construction science and management (MCSM, Certificate); English (MA); historic preservation (MS, Certificate); history (MA); landscape architecture (MLA); planning, design and the built environment (PhD); professional communication (MA); real estate development (MRED); rhetorics, communication, and information design (PhD); visual arts (MFA). *Application deadline:* For fall admission, 4/15 for international students; for spring admission, 9/15 for international students. Applications are processed on a rolling basis. *Application fee:* $80 ($90 for international students). Electronic applications

accepted. *Application Contact:* Dr. James London, Associate Dean for Research and Graduate Studies, 864-656-3927, E-mail: london1@clemson.edu. *Dean*, Dr. Richard Goodstein, 864-656-3084, Fax: 864-656-0204, E-mail: regst@clemson.edu.

College of Behavioral, Social and Health Sciences Students: 222 full-time (158 women), 306 part-time (219 women); includes 80 minority (48 Black or African American, non-Hispanic/Latino; 6 Asian, non-Hispanic/Latino; 16 Hispanic/Latino; 10 Two or more races, non-Hispanic/Latino), 45 international. Average age 33. 485 applicants, 32% accepted, 132 enrolled. *Faculty:* 180 full-time (99 women), 10 part-time/adjunct (4 women). Expenses: Contact institution. *Financial support:* In 2016–17, 206 students received support, including 5 fellowships with partial tuition reimbursements available (averaging $3,700 per year), 28 research assistantships with partial tuition reimbursements available (averaging $17,624 per year), 155 teaching assistantships with partial tuition reimbursements available (averaging $10,470 per year); unspecified assistantships also available. In 2016, 90 master's, 20 doctorates, 43 other advanced degrees awarded. *Program availability:* Part-time, evening/weekend, 100% online, blended/hybrid learning. Offers applied health research and evaluation (MS, PhD); applied psychology (MS); applied sociology (MS); behavioral, social and health sciences (MA, MPA, MS, PhD, Certificate); clinical and translational research (Certificate); communication, technology and society (MA); global health (Certificate); healthcare genetics (PhD); human factors psychology (PhD); industrial-organizational psychology (PhD); international parks and tourism (Certificate); nursing (MS); parks, recreation and tourism management (MS, PhD); policy studies (PhD, Certificate); public administration (MPA, Certificate); recreational therapy (MS); youth development leadership (MS, Certificate); youth leadership development (Certificate); youth, family and community studies (PhD, Certificate). *Application deadline:* Applications are processed on a rolling basis. *Application fee:* $80 ($90 for international students). Electronic applications accepted. *Application Contact:* Dr. Eric Muth, Associate Dean for Research and Graduate Programs, 864-656-6741, Fax: 864-656-7641, E-mail: muth@clemson.edu. *Interim Dean*, Dr. Brett Wright, 864-656-7640, Fax: 864-656-7641, E-mail: wright@clemson.edu.

College of Business Students: 358 full-time (138 women), 348 part-time (114 women); includes 105 minority (55 Black or African American, non-Hispanic/Latino; 17 Asian, non-Hispanic/Latino; 21 Hispanic/Latino; 1 Native Hawaiian or other Pacific Islander, non-Hispanic/Latino; 11 Two or more races, non-Hispanic/Latino), 109 international. Average age 29. 743 applicants, 46% accepted, 233 enrolled. *Faculty:* 131 full-time (41 women), 25 part-time/adjunct (5 women). Expenses: Contact institution. *Financial support:* In 2016–17, 152 students received support, including 33 fellowships with partial tuition reimbursements available (averaging $6,876 per year), 5 research assistantships with partial tuition reimbursements available (averaging $18,557 per year), 53 teaching assistantships with partial tuition reimbursements available (averaging $20,528 per year); career-related internships or fieldwork and unspecified assistantships also available. In 2016, 284 master's, 14 doctorates awarded. *Program availability:* Part-time, evening/weekend. Offers accounting (MP Acc); business (MA, MBA, MP Acc, MS, PhD); business administration (MBA, PhD); business analytics (MBA); economics (MA, PhD); entrepreneurship and innovation (MBA); graphic communications (MS); management (MS); marketing (MS). *Application deadline:* Applications are processed on a rolling basis. *Application fee:* $80 ($90 for international students). Electronic applications accepted. *Application Contact:* Dr. Gregory Pickett, Senior Associate Dean, 864-656-3975, E-mail: pgregor@clemson.edu. *Interim Dean*, Dr. Robert McCormick, 864-656-3178, E-mail: sixmile@clemson.edu.

College of Education Students: 120 full-time (84 women), 309 part-time (206 women); includes 96 minority (68 Black or African American, non-Hispanic/Latino; 1 American Indian or Alaska Native, non-Hispanic/Latino; 3 Asian, non-Hispanic/Latino; 19 Hispanic/Latino; 5 Two or more races, non-Hispanic/Latino), 11 international. Average age 34. 417 applicants, 50% accepted, 133 enrolled. *Faculty:* 75 full-time (54 women), 1 part-time/adjunct (0 women). Expenses: Contact institution. *Financial support:* In 2016–17, 75 students received support, including 22 fellowships with partial tuition reimbursements available (averaging $6,316 per year), 28 research assistantships with partial tuition reimbursements available (averaging $15,399 per year), 5 teaching assistantships with partial tuition reimbursements available (averaging $30,000 per year); unspecified assistantships also available. In 2016, 239 master's, 21 doctorates, 59 other advanced degrees awarded. *Program availability:* Part-time, evening/weekend, 100% online. Offers administration and supervision (M Ed, Ed S); administration and supervision (K-12) (M Ed, Ed S); athletic leadership (MS, Certificate); counselor education (M Ed, Ed S); curriculum and instruction (PhD); education and organizational leadership (MS); educational leadership (PhD); human resource development (MHRD); learning sciences (PhD); literacy (M Ed); literacy, language and culture (PhD); middle level education (MAT); middle-level education (MAT); science, technology, engineering, arts and mathematics education (Certificate); secondary math and science (MAT); special education (M Ed, MAT, PhD); STEAM education (Certificate); student affairs (M Ed); teaching and learning (M Ed). *Application deadline:* Applications are processed on a rolling basis. *Application fee:* $80 ($90 for international students). Electronic applications accepted. *Application Contact:* Dr. David Fleming, Graduate Programs Coordinator, 864-656-1881, Fax: 864-656-0311, E-mail: dflemin@clemson.edu. *Dean*, Dr. George Petersen, 864-656-4444, Fax: 864-656-0311, E-mail: soedean@clemson.edu.

College of Engineering, Computing and Applied Sciences Students: 1,165 full-time (323 women), 250 part-time (52 women); includes 91 minority (26 Black or African American, non-Hispanic/Latino; 25 Asian, non-Hispanic/Latino; 21 Hispanic/Latino; 2 Native Hawaiian or other Pacific Islander, non-Hispanic/Latino; 17 Two or more races, non-Hispanic/Latino), 853 international. Average age 27. 3,474 applicants, 23% accepted, 410 enrolled. *Faculty:* 273 full-time (55 women), 15 part-time/adjunct (4 women). Expenses: Contact institution. *Financial support:* In 2016–17, 908 students received support, including 81 fellowships with partial tuition reimbursements available (averaging $10,920 per year), 428 research assistantships with partial tuition reimbursements available (averaging $19,916 per year), 227 teaching assistantships with partial tuition reimbursements available (averaging $18,618 per year); career-related internships or fieldwork and unspecified assistantships also available. In 2016, 460 master's, 101 doctorates, 10 other advanced degrees awarded. *Program availability:* Part-time, 100% online. Offers automotive engineering (MS, PhD); bioengineering (MS, PhD); biomedical engineering (M Engr); biosystems engineering (MS, PhD); chemical engineering (MS, PhD); civil engineering (MS, PhD); computer engineering (MS, PhD); computer science (MS, PhD); computing (MFA, MS, PhD); digital production arts (MFA); electrical engineering (M Engr, MS, PhD); engineering and science education (PhD, Certificate); engineering, computing and applied sciences (M Engr, MFA, MS, PhD, Certificate); environmental engineering and science (MS, PhD); environmental health physics (MS); human-centered computing (PhD); hydrogeology (MS); industrial engineering (M Engr, MS, PhD); materials science and engineering (MS, PhD); mechanical engineering (MS, PhD); medical device recycling and reprocessing (Certificate). *Application deadline:* Applications are processed on a rolling basis. *Application fee:* $80 ($90 for international students). Electronic applications accepted. *Application Contact:* Dr. Douglas Hirt, Associate Dean for Research and Graduate Studies, 864-656-3201, E-mail: hirtd@clemson.edu. *Dean,* Dr. Anand Gramopadhye, 864-656-3200, E-mail: agrampo@clemson.edu.

College of Science Students: 333 full-time (143 women), 264 part-time (184 women); includes 50 minority (17 Black or African American, non-Hispanic/Latino; 2 American Indian or Alaska Native, non-Hispanic/Latino; 10 Asian, non-Hispanic/Latino; 10 Hispanic/Latino; 1 Native Hawaiian or other Pacific Islander, non-Hispanic/Latino; 10 Two or more races, non-Hispanic/Latino), 181 international. Average age 31. 502 applicants, 34% accepted, 114 enrolled. *Faculty:* 211 full-time (67 women), 17 part-time/adjunct (7 women). Expenses: Contact institution. *Financial support:* In 2016–17, 345 students received support, including 9 fellowships with partial tuition reimbursements available (averaging $9,583 per year), 63 research assistantships with partial tuition reimbursements available (averaging $21,421 per year), 246 teaching assistantships with partial tuition reimbursements available (averaging $21,746 per year); career-related internships or fieldwork and health care benefits also available. In 2016, 119 master's, 49 doctorates awarded. *Program availability:* Part-time, 100% online. Offers biochemistry and molecular biology (PhD); biological sciences for science educators (MBS); chemistry (MS, PhD); environmental toxicology (MS, PhD); genetics (PhD); mathematical sciences (MS, PhD); microbiology (MS, PhD); physics (MS, PhD); science (MBS, MS, PhD). *Application deadline:* Applications are processed on a rolling basis. *Application fee:* $80 ($90 for international students). Electronic applications accepted. *Application Contact:* Dr. Brian Dominy, Interim Associate Dean for Academic Affairs, 864-656-7702, E-mail: dominy@clemson.edu. *Interim Dean,* Dr. Mark Leising, 864-656-7137, E-mail: lmark@clemson.edu.

CLEVELAND INSTITUTE OF MUSIC, Cleveland, OH 44106-1776

General Information Independent, coed, comprehensive institution. *Graduate housing:* Room and/or apartments available on a first-come, first-served basis to single students; on-campus housing not available to married students. Housing application deadline: 5/30.

GRADUATE UNITS

Graduate Programs Offers performance (MM, DMA, AD, CPS). DMA and MM programs offered jointly with Case Western Reserve University. Electronic applications accepted.

CLEVELAND STATE UNIVERSITY, Cleveland, OH 44115

General Information State-supported, coed, university. CGS member. *Enrollment:* 16,949 graduate, professional, and undergraduate students; 1,844 full-time matriculated graduate/professional students (1,044 women), 1,946 part-time matriculated graduate/professional students (1,171 women). *Enrollment by degree level:* 3,186 master's, 414 doctoral, 190 other advanced degrees. *Graduate faculty:* 273 full-time (125 women), 316 part-time/adjunct (162 women). Tuition, state resident: full-time $9565. Tuition, nonresident: full-time $17,980. Tuition and fees vary according to program. *Graduate housing:* Room and/or apartments available on a first-come, first-served basis to single students; on-campus housing not available to married students. Housing application deadline: 7/15. *Student services:* Campus employment opportunities, campus safety program, career counseling, exercise/wellness program, international student services, low-cost health insurance, multicultural affairs office, services for students with disabilities, teacher training, writing training. *Library facilities:* Michael Schwartz Library plus 1 other. *Collection:* Books: 524,556 (physical), 228,146 (digital/electronic); Serial titles: 6,155 (physical), 194 (digital/electronic); Databases: 733. Students can reserve study rooms. *Research affiliation:* Cleveland Clinic Foundation, Metro Health System.

Computer facilities: Computer purchase and lease plans are available. 736 computers available on campus for general student use. A campuswide network can be accessed from student residence rooms and from off campus. Online class registration, each general purpose computer lab has a scanner and printer, students are allowed free black and white printing up to 2,000 pages per semester are available. Website: http://www.csuohio.edu/

General Application Contact: Dianne C. Oloff, Graduate Student Services Specialist, 216-687-5230, Fax: 216-875-9933, E-mail: d.oloff@csuohio.edu.

GRADUATE UNITS

Cleveland-Marshall College of Law Students: 240 full-time (113 women), 140 part-time (83 women); includes 75 minority (40 Black or African American, non-Hispanic/Latino; 10 Asian, non-Hispanic/Latino; 17 Hispanic/Latino; 8 Two or more races, non-Hispanic/Latino), 4 international. Average age 28. 711 applicants, 44% accepted, 118 enrolled. *Faculty:* 34 full-time (17 women), 61 part-time/adjunct (16 women). Expenses: Contact institution. *Financial support:* In 2016–17, 198 students received support, including 17 fellowships (averaging $2,500 per year), 34 research assistantships, 7 teaching assistantships with partial tuition reimbursements available (averaging $6,700 per year); career-related internships or fieldwork, Federal Work-Study, scholarships/grants, and unspecified assistantships also available. Support available to part-time students. Financial award application deadline: 5/1; financial award applicants required to submit FAFSA. In 2016, 10 master's, 115 doctorates, 2 Certificates awarded. *Program availability:* Part-time, evening/weekend. Offers law (LL M, MLS, JD, Certificate). *Application deadline:* For fall admission, 5/1 for domestic and international students. Applications are processed on a rolling basis. *Application fee:* $0. Electronic applications accepted. *Application Contact:* Christopher Lucak, Assistant Dean for Admission and Financial Aid, 216-687-2304, Fax: 216-687-6881, E-mail: law.admissions@csuohio.edu. *Dean,* Craig M. Boise, 216-687-2300, Fax: 216-687-6881, E-mail: c.boise@csuohio.edu.

College of Graduate Studies Students: 1,844 full-time (1,044 women), 1,946 part-time (1,171 women); includes 792 minority (518 Black or African American, non-Hispanic/Latino; 4 American Indian or Alaska Native, non-Hispanic/Latino; 91 Asian, non-Hispanic/Latino; 118 Hispanic/Latino; 2 Native Hawaiian or other Pacific Islander, non-Hispanic/Latino; 59 Two or more races, non-Hispanic/Latino), 812 international. Average age 31. 4,931 applicants, 46% accepted, 966 enrolled. *Faculty:* 383 full-time (145 women), 151 part-time/adjunct (55 women). Expenses: Contact institution. *Financial support:* In 2016–17, 306 research assistantships with tuition reimbursements (averaging $3,480 per year), 123 teaching assistantships with tuition reimbursements (averaging $3,480 per year) were awarded; career-related internships or fieldwork, scholarships/grants, tuition waivers (full and partial), and unspecified assistantships also available. Financial award applicants required to submit FAFSA. In 2016, 1,426 master's, 202 doctorates, 8 other advanced degrees awarded. *Program availability:* Part-time, evening/weekend, 100% online, blended/hybrid learning. *Application deadline:* For fall admission, 7/1 priority date for domestic students, 5/15 priority date for international

students; for spring admission, 11/15 priority date for domestic students, 11/1 priority date for international students; for summer admission, 4/1 for domestic students, 3/15 for international students. Applications are processed on a rolling basis. *Application fee:* $30. Electronic applications accepted. *Application Contact:* Dianne C. Oloff, Graduate Student Services Specialist, 216-523-7572, Fax: 216-875-9933, E-mail: d.oloff@csuohio.edu. *Dean, College of Graduate Studies,* Dr. Jianping Zhu, 216-687-3595, Fax: 216-875-9933, E-mail: j.zhu94@csuohio.edu.

College of Education and Human Services Students: 253 full-time (188 women), 751 part-time (576 women); includes 320 minority (249 Black or African American, non-Hispanic/Latino; 2 American Indian or Alaska Native, non-Hispanic/Latino; 8 Asian, non-Hispanic/Latino; 41 Hispanic/Latino; 1 Native Hawaiian or other Pacific Islander, non-Hispanic/Latino; 19 Two or more races, non-Hispanic/Latino), 65 international. Average age 34. 487 applicants, 58% accepted, 178 enrolled. *Faculty:* 86 full-time (60 women), 106 part-time/adjunct (81 women). Expenses: Contact institution. *Financial support:* In 2016–17, 64 students received support, including 38 research assistantships with full tuition reimbursements available (averaging $6,960 per year), 2 teaching assistantships with full tuition reimbursements available (averaging $7,800 per year); career-related internships or fieldwork, Federal Work-Study, scholarships/grants, tuition waivers (partial), and unspecified assistantships also available. Support available to part-time students. Financial award application deadline: 8/1; financial award applicants required to submit FAFSA. In 2016, 314 master's, 20 doctorates awarded. *Program availability:* Part-time, evening/weekend, 100% online, blended/hybrid learning. Offers adult learning and development (M Ed); adult, continuing, and higher education (PhD); art education (M Ed); counseling psychology (PhD); counselor education (PhD); early childhood education (M Ed); early childhood mental health counseling (Certificate); education and human services (M Ed, MPH, PhD, Certificate, Ed S); educational administration and supervision (M Ed); foreign language education (M Ed); learning and development (PhD); middle childhood mathematics and science education (M Ed); nursing education (PhD); physical education pedagogy (M Ed); policy studies (PhD); public health (MPH); school administration (PhD); special education (M Ed); teaching English to speakers of other languages (M Ed); urban education (PhD). *Application deadline:* For fall admission, 7/1 priority date for domestic students, 5/15 for international students; for spring admission, 11/15 priority date for domestic students, 11/1 for international students; for summer admission, 4/1 for domestic students, 3/15 for international students. Applications are processed on a rolling basis. *Application fee:* $30. Electronic applications accepted. *Application Contact:* Patricia Sokolowski, Office Coordinator/Assistant to the Dean, 216-523-7143, Fax: 216-687-5415, E-mail: p.sokolowski@csuohio.edu. *Dean,* Dr. Sajit Zachariah, 216-523-7143, Fax: 216-687-5415, E-mail: sajit.zachariah@csuohio.edu.

College of Liberal Arts and Social Sciences Students: 240 full-time (170 women), 141 part-time (89 women); includes 134 minority (98 Black or African American, non-Hispanic/Latino; 5 Asian, non-Hispanic/Latino; 15 Hispanic/Latino; 16 Two or more races, non-Hispanic/Latino), 19 international. Average age 33. 499 applicants, 46% accepted, 123 enrolled. *Faculty:* 156 full-time (64 women), 184 part-time/adjunct (79 women). Expenses: Contact institution. *Financial support:* In 2016–17, 99 research assistantships with tuition reimbursements (averaging $4,172 per year), 67 teaching assistantships with tuition reimbursements (averaging $4,657 per year) were awarded; fellowships, career-related internships or fieldwork, Federal Work-Study, institutionally sponsored loans, tuition waivers (full and partial), and unspecified assistantships also available. Support available to part-time students. Financial award applicants required to submit FAFSA. In 2016, 177 master's awarded. *Program availability:* Part-time, evening/weekend. Offers applied communication theory and methodology (MA); art history (MA); bioethics (MA, Certificate); composition (MM); creative writing (MFA); economics (MA); global interactions (MA); liberal arts and social sciences (M Ed, MA, MFA, MM, MSW, Certificate); museum studies (MA); music education (MM); philosophy (MA); social work (MSW); Spanish (MA). *Application deadline:* For fall admission, 7/1 priority date for domestic students, 5/15 for international students; for spring admission, 11/15 priority date for domestic students, 11/1 for international students; for summer admission, 4/1 for domestic students, 3/15 for international students. Applications are processed on a rolling basis. *Application fee:* $30. Electronic applications accepted. *Application Contact:* Deborah L. Brown, Interim Assistant Director, Graduate Admissions, 216-523-7572, Fax: 216-687-5400, E-mail: d.l.brown@csuohio.edu. *Dean,* Dr. Gregory M. Sadlek, 216-687-3660.

College of Sciences and Health Professions Students: 579 full-time (413 women), 181 part-time (134 women); includes 102 minority (46 Black or African American, non-Hispanic/Latino; 1 American Indian or Alaska Native, non-Hispanic/Latino; 19 Asian, non-Hispanic/Latino; 27 Hispanic/Latino; 9 Two or more races, non-Hispanic/Latino), 98 international. Average age 28. 912 applicants, 34% accepted, 204 enrolled. *Faculty:* 107 full-time (35 women), 76 part-time/adjunct (43 women). Expenses: Contact institution. *Financial support:* In 2016–17, 174 students received support, including 47 research assistantships with full tuition reimbursements available (averaging $17,000 per year), 127 teaching assistantships with tuition reimbursements available (averaging $10,700 per year); unspecified assistantships also available. Financial award applicants required to submit FAFSA. In 2016, 223 master's, 52 doctorates, 6 other advanced degrees awarded. *Program availability:* Part-time, evening/weekend, online learning. Offers applied statistics (MS); biological, geological, and environmental sciences (MS, PhD); clinical chemistry (PhD); health sciences (MS); mathematics (MS); occupational therapy (MOT); organic chemistry (MS); physical chemistry (MS); physical therapy (DPT); physician assistant science (MS); physics (MS); psychology (MA, PhD, Psy S); sciences and health professions (MA, MOT, MS, DPT, PhD, Psy S); speech pathology and audiology (MA). *Application deadline:* For fall admission, 7/1 priority date for domestic students, 5/15 priority date for international students; for spring admission, 11/15 priority date for domestic students, 11/1 priority date for international students; for summer admission, 4/1 for domestic students, 3/15 for international students. Applications are processed on a rolling basis. *Application fee:* $30. Electronic applications accepted. *Application Contact:* Dianne C. Oloff, Graduate Student Services Specialist, 216-687-5230, Fax: 216-875-9933, E-mail: d.oloff@csuohio.edu. *Dean of the College of Graduate Studies,* Dr. Jianping Zhu, 216-687-3595, Fax: 216-875-9933, E-mail: j.zhu94@csuohio.edu.

Fenn College of Engineering Students: 389 full-time (75 women), 258 part-time (53 women); includes 37 minority (13 Black or African American, non-Hispanic/Latino; 18 Asian, non-Hispanic/Latino; 5 Hispanic/Latino; 1 Two or more races, non-Hispanic/Latino), 453 international. Average age 26. 1,037 applicants, 48% accepted, 143 enrolled. *Faculty:* 54 full-time (5 women), 12 part-time/adjunct (0 women). Expenses: Contact institution. *Financial support:* In 2016–17, 93 students received support, including 1 fellowship with full tuition reimbursement available, 120 research assistantships with tuition reimbursements available (averaging $8,694 per year), 20

Cleveland State University

teaching assistantships with tuition reimbursements available (averaging $8,082 per year); career-related internships or fieldwork, institutionally sponsored loans, scholarships/grants, tuition waivers (full and partial), and unspecified assistantships also available. Support available to part-time students. Financial award application deadline: 3/30; financial award applicants required to submit FAFSA. In 2016, 250 master's, 9 doctorates awarded. *Program availability:* Part-time, evening/weekend. Offers applied biomedical engineering (D Eng); chemical and biomedical engineering (MS, D Eng); civil and environmental engineering (MS, D Eng); electrical engineering (MS, D Eng); engineering (MS, D Eng); industrial and manufacturing engineering (MS, D Eng); mechanical engineering (MS, D Eng); software engineering (MS). *Application deadline:* For fall admission, 7/15 for domestic students, 5/15 for international students; for spring admission, 12/5 for domestic students, 11/1 for international students. Applications are processed on a rolling basis. *Application fee:* $30. Electronic applications accepted. *Application Contact:* Deborah L. Brown, Interim Assistant Director, Graduate Admissions, 216-523-7572, Fax: 216-687-9214, E-mail: d.l.brown@csuohio.edu. *Associate Dean,* Dr. Paul P. Lin, 216-687-2556, Fax: 216-687-9280, E-mail: p.lin@csuohio.edu.

Maxine Goodman Levin College of Urban Affairs Students: 49 full-time (28 women), 113 part-time (64 women); includes 34 minority (24 Black or African American, non-Hispanic/Latino; 2 Asian, non-Hispanic/Latino; 4 Hispanic/Latino; 4 Two or more races, non-Hispanic/Latino), 14 international. Average age 33. 195 applicants, 47% accepted, 38 enrolled. *Faculty:* 22 full-time (9 women), 8 part-time/adjunct (4 women). Expenses: Contact institution. *Financial support:* In 2016–17, 60 students received support, including 40 research assistantships with full tuition reimbursements available (averaging $8,000 per year), 15 teaching assistantships with tuition reimbursements available (averaging $7,000 per year); career-related internships or fieldwork, Federal Work-Study, institutionally sponsored loans, scholarships/grants, and unspecified assistantships also available. Support available to part-time students. Financial award application deadline: 3/1; financial award applicants required to submit FAFSA. In 2016, 66 master's, 4 doctorates awarded. *Program availability:* Part-time, evening/weekend. Offers communication (PhD); economic development (MPA); environmental nonprofit management (MAES); environmental planning (MAES); environmental sustainability (MUPDD); housing and neighborhood development (MUPDD); local and urban management (Certificate); non-profit management (MPA); nonprofit administration and leadership (MNAL); nonprofit management (Certificate); policy and administration (MAES); public administration (PhD); public management (MPA); sustainable economic development (MAES); urban affairs (MAES, MNAL, MPA, MS, MUPDD, PhD, Certificate); urban economic development (Certificate); urban policy and development (PhD); urban studies (MS, Certificate). *Application deadline:* For fall admission, 7/1 priority date for domestic students, 5/15 for international students; for spring admission, 11/15 for domestic students, 11/1 for international students; for summer admission, 4/1 for domestic students, 3/15 for international students. Applications are processed on a rolling basis. *Application fee:* $30. Electronic applications accepted. *Application Contact:* Graduate Program Coordinator, 216-523-7522, Fax: 216-687-5398, E-mail: urbanprograms@csuohio.edu. *Dean,* Dr. Roland V. Anglin, 216-687-2135, E-mail: r.anglin@csuohio.edu.

Monte Ahuja College of Business Students: 322 full-time (159 women), 462 part-time (217 women); includes 148 minority (75 Black or African American, non-Hispanic/Latino; 1 American Indian or Alaska Native, non-Hispanic/Latino; 38 Asian, non-Hispanic/Latino; 23 Hispanic/Latino; 1 Native Hawaiian or other Pacific Islander, non-Hispanic/Latino; 10 Two or more races, non-Hispanic/Latino), 163 international. Average age 30. 1,052 applicants, 46% accepted, 258 enrolled. *Faculty:* 48 full-time (16 women), 33 part-time/adjunct (12 women). Expenses: Contact institution. *Financial support:* In 2016–17, 110 students received support, including 45 research assistantships with full tuition reimbursements available (averaging $6,960 per year), 1 teaching assistantship with full tuition reimbursement available (averaging $7,800 per year); career-related internships or fieldwork, scholarships/grants, tuition waivers (full), and unspecified assistantships also available. Financial award application deadline: 5/15; financial award applicants required to submit FAFSA. In 2016, 428 master's, 5 doctorates awarded. *Program availability:* Part-time, evening/weekend. Offers business (AMBA, EMBA, M Acc, MBA, MLRHR, DBA); business administration (AMBA, EMBA, MBA, DBA); financial accounting/audit (M Acc); health care administration (MBA); information systems (DBA); labor relations and human resources (MLRHR); marketing (DBA). *Application deadline:* For fall admission, 7/1 priority date for domestic students, 5/15 for international students; for spring admission, 11/15 priority date for domestic students, 11/1 for international students; for summer admission, 4/1 for domestic students, 3/15 for international students. Applications are processed on a rolling basis. *Application fee:* $30. Electronic applications accepted. *Application Contact:* Kenneth Dippong, Director, Student Services, 216-523-7545, Fax: 216-687-9354, E-mail: k.dippong@csuohio.edu. *Dean,* Dr. Robert F. Scherer, 216-687-3786, Fax: 216-687-9354, E-mail: r.scherer@csuohio.edu.

School of Nursing Students: 12 full-time (11 women), 40 part-time (38 women); includes 17 minority (13 Black or African American, non-Hispanic/Latino; 1 Asian, non-Hispanic/Latino; 3 Hispanic/Latino). Average age 36. 60 applicants, 62% accepted, 26 enrolled. *Faculty:* 7 full-time (all women). Expenses: Contact institution. *Financial support:* Tuition waivers (full) and unspecified assistantships available. Financial award application deadline: 5/1; financial award applicants required to submit FAFSA. In 2016, 14 master's awarded. *Program availability:* Part-time, 100% online. Offers nursing (MSN, PhD). *Application deadline:* For fall admission, 3/1 priority date for domestic and international students. *Application fee:* $55. Electronic applications accepted. *Application Contact:* Maureen Mitchell, Assistant Professor and Graduate Program Director, 216-523-7128, Fax: 216-687-3556, E-mail: m.m.mitchell1@csuohio.edu. *Dean,* Dr. Vida Lock, 216-523-7237, Fax: 216-687-3556, E-mail: v.lock@csuohio.edu.

CLEVELAND UNIVERSITY–KANSAS CITY, Overland Park, KS 66210

General Information Independent, coed, comprehensive institution. *Graduate housing:* On-campus housing not available.

GRADUATE UNITS

Professional Program *Program availability:* Part-time. Offers chiropractic (DC). Electronic applications accepted.

Program in Health Promotion *Program availability:* Part-time. Offers health promotion (MSHP). Electronic applications accepted.

COASTAL CAROLINA UNIVERSITY, Conway, SC 29528-6054

General Information State-supported, coed, comprehensive institution. *Enrollment:* 10,479 graduate, professional, and undergraduate students; 205 full-time matriculated

graduate/professional students (105 women), 413 part-time matriculated graduate/professional students (312 women). Enrollment by degree level: 561 master's, 9 doctoral, 48 other advanced degrees. *Graduate faculty:* 69 full-time (27 women), 17 part-time/adjunct (8 women). Tuition, state resident: full-time $9990; part-time $555 per credit hour. Tuition, nonresident: full-time $18,108; part-time $1006 per credit hour. *Required fees:* $90; $5 per credit hour. *Graduate housing:* Room and/or apartments available on a first-come, first-served basis to single students; on-campus housing not available to married students. Typical cost: $5440 per year ($8890 including board). Room and board charges vary according to board plan and housing facility selected. Housing application deadline: 5/1. *Student services:* Campus employment opportunities, campus safety program, career counseling, exercise/wellness program, free psychological counseling, grant writing training, international student services, low-cost health insurance, multicultural affairs office, services for students with disabilities, teacher training, writing training. *Library facilities:* Kimbel Library. *Collection:* Books: 138,355 (physical), 375,066 (digital/electronic); Serial titles: 588 (physical), 45,000 (digital/electronic); Databases: 175. Weekly public service hours: 168; study areas open 24 hours, 5–7 days a week.

Computer facilities: Computer purchase and lease plans are available. 1,322 computers available on campus for general student use. A campuswide network can be accessed from student residence rooms and from off campus. Online class registration is available.

Website: http://www.coastal.edu/

General Application Contact: Dr. James O. Luken, Associate Provost/Interim Vice Dean of the School of the Coastal Environment, 843-349-2235, Fax: 843-349-6444, E-mail: joluken@coastal.edu.

GRADUATE UNITS

College of Science Students: 41 full-time (14 women), 29 part-time (15 women); includes 7 minority (4 Black or African American, non-Hispanic/Latino; 1 American Indian or Alaska Native, non-Hispanic/Latino; 1 Hispanic/Latino; 1 Two or more races, non-Hispanic/Latino), 6 international. Average age 27. 72 applicants, 57% accepted, 35 enrolled. *Faculty:* 23 full-time (5 women), 1 part-time/adjunct (0 women). Expenses: Contact institution. *Financial support:* Fellowships, research assistantships, and unspecified assistantships available. Support available to part-time students. Financial award application deadline: 3/1; financial award applicants required to submit FAFSA. In 2016, 13 master's awarded. *Program availability:* Part-time, evening/weekend. Offers applied computing and information systems (Certificate); coastal marine and wetland studies (MS); information systems technology (MS); marine science (PhD); sports management (MS). *Application deadline:* For fall admission, 1/15 priority date for domestic and international students; for spring admission, 11/1 priority date for domestic and international students. Applications are processed on a rolling basis. *Application fee:* $45. Electronic applications accepted. *Application Contact:* Dr. James O. Luken, Associate Provost/Vice-Dean of the Coastal Environment, 843-349-2235, Fax: 843-349-6444, E-mail: joluken@coastal.edu. *Dean,* Dr. Michael H. Roberts, 843-349-2282, Fax: 843-349-2545, E-mail: mroberts@coastal.edu.

E. Craig Wall, Sr. College of Business Administration Students: 67 full-time (28 women), 30 part-time (15 women); includes 25 minority (16 Black or African American, non-Hispanic/Latino; 2 Asian, non-Hispanic/Latino; 3 Hispanic/Latino; 1 Native Hawaiian or other Pacific Islander, non-Hispanic/Latino; 3 Two or more races, non-Hispanic/Latino), 11 international. Average age 27. 88 applicants, 78% accepted, 56 enrolled. *Faculty:* 14 full-time (7 women), 3 part-time/adjunct (0 women). Expenses: Contact institution. *Financial support:* Fellowships, research assistantships, and unspecified assistantships available. Support available to part-time students. Financial award application deadline: 3/1; financial award applicants required to submit FAFSA. In 2016, 70 master's, 1 other advanced degree awarded. *Program availability:* Part-time, evening/weekend. Offers accounting (M Acc); business administration (MBA); business foundations (Certificate); fraud examination (Certificate). *Application deadline:* For fall admission, 6/15 priority date for domestic and international students; for spring admission, 11/15 priority date for domestic and international students; for summer admission, 4/15 priority date for domestic and international students. Applications are processed on a rolling basis. *Application fee:* $45. Electronic applications accepted. *Application Contact:* Dr. James O. Luken, Associate Provost/Interim Vice-Dean of the Coastal Environment, 843-349-2235, Fax: 843-349-6444, E-mail: joluken@coastal.edu. *Associate Professor/Director of Graduate Programs and Executive Education,* Dr. Arlise P. McKinney, 843-349-2390, Fax: 843-349-2455, E-mail: amckinney@coastal.edu.

Spadoni College of Education Students: 74 full-time (48 women), 340 part-time (271 women); includes 78 minority (70 Black or African American, non-Hispanic/Latino; 1 American Indian or Alaska Native, non-Hispanic/Latino; 2 Asian, non-Hispanic/Latino; 4 Hispanic/Latino; 1 Two or more races, non-Hispanic/Latino), 2 international. Average age 33. 298 applicants, 93% accepted, 213 enrolled. *Faculty:* 16 full-time (8 women), 12 part-time/adjunct (7 women). Expenses: Contact institution. *Financial support:* Fellowships, research assistantships, and unspecified assistantships available. Support available to part-time students. Financial award application deadline: 3/1; financial award applicants required to submit FAFSA. In 2016, 167 master's, 8 other advanced degrees awarded. *Program availability:* Part-time, evening/weekend. Offers education (MAT); educational leadership (M Ed, Ed S); English for speakers of other languages (Certificate); instructional technology (M Ed, Ed S); learning and teaching (M Ed); online teaching and training (Certificate); special education (M Ed). *Application deadline:* For fall admission, 7/1 priority date for domestic and international students; for spring admission, 11/1 priority date for domestic and international students; for summer admission, 3/1 priority date for domestic and international students. Applications are processed on a rolling basis. *Application fee:* $45. Electronic applications accepted. *Application Contact:* Dr. James O. Luken, Associate Provost/Vice-Dean of the Coastal Environment, 843-349-2235, Fax: 843-349-6444, E-mail: joluken@coastal.edu. *Dean,* Dr. Edward Jadallah, 843-349-2773, Fax: 843-349-2106, E-mail: ejadalla@coastal.edu.

Thomas W. and Robin W. Edwards College of Humanities and Fine Arts Students: 23 full-time (15 women), 14 part-time (11 women); includes 7 minority (4 Black or African American, non-Hispanic/Latino; 1 American Indian or Alaska Native, non-Hispanic/Latino; 2 Hispanic/Latino). Average age 34. 24 applicants, 83% accepted, 13 enrolled. *Faculty:* 16 full-time (7 women), 1 (woman) part-time/adjunct. Expenses: Contact institution. *Financial support:* Fellowships, research assistantships, and unspecified assistantships available. Support available to part-time students. Financial award application deadline: 3/1; financial award applicants required to submit FAFSA. In 2016, 13 master's awarded. *Program availability:* Part-time, evening/weekend. Offers liberal studies (MA); writing (MA). *Application deadline:* For fall admission, 5/15 priority date for domestic and international students; for spring admission, 11/15 priority date for domestic and international students. Applications are processed on a rolling basis. *Application fee:* $45. Electronic applications accepted. *Application Contact:* Dr. James O. Luken, Associate Provost/Vice-Dean of the Coastal Environment, 843-349-2235, Fax: 843-349-6444, E-mail: joluken@coastal.edu. *Associate Professor/Coordinator of Graduate Study,* Joseph R. Oestreich, 843-349-2433, E-mail: joeo@coastal.edu.

COGSWELL POLYTECHNICAL COLLEGE, San Jose, CA 95134

General Information Proprietary, coed, comprehensive institution.

GRADUATE UNITS

Program in Entrepreneurship and Innovation Offers entrepreneurship and innovation (MA).

COKER COLLEGE, Hartsville, SC 29550

General Information Independent, coed, comprehensive institution.

GRADUATE UNITS

Graduate Programs *Program availability:* Part-time, 100% online. Offers athletic administration (MS); literacy studies (M Ed). Electronic applications accepted.

THE COLBURN SCHOOL CONSERVATORY OF MUSIC, Los Angeles, CA 90012

General Information Independent, coed, comprehensive institution.

GRADUATE UNITS

Graduate Programs Offers music (AD); performance (MM).

COLD SPRING HARBOR LABORATORY, Cold Spring Harbor, NY 11724

General Information Independent, coed, graduate-only institution. *Enrollment by degree level:* 44 doctoral. *Graduate faculty:* 51 full-time (10 women). *Graduate housing:* Rooms and/or apartments guaranteed to single students and available on a first-come, first-served basis to married students. Housing application deadline: 8/1. *Student services:* Campus safety program, career counseling, child daycare facilities, exercise/wellness program, free psychological counseling, grant writing training, international student services, low-cost health insurance, services for students with disabilities, teacher training, writing training. *Library facilities:* Cold Spring Harbor Laboratory Library. *Collection:* Study areas open 24 hours, 5–7 days a week; students can reserve study rooms.

Computer facilities: A campuswide network can be accessed from student residence rooms and from off campus.
Website: http://www.cshl.edu/gradschool/

General Application Contact: Kimberly Creteur, Admissions and Recruitment Manager, 516-367-6890, Fax: 516-367-6919, E-mail: gradschool@cshl.edu.

GRADUATE UNITS

Watson School of Biological Sciences Students: 44 full-time (24 women); includes 8 minority (2 Black or African American, non-Hispanic/Latino; 2 Asian, non-Hispanic/Latino; 3 Hispanic/Latino; 1 Two or more races, non-Hispanic/Latino), 24 international. Average age 27. 300 applicants, 10% accepted, 11 enrolled. *Faculty:* 51 full-time (10 women). Expenses: Contact institution. *Financial support:* In 2016–17, 44 students received support, including 44 fellowships with full tuition reimbursements available (averaging $33,000 per year); scholarships/grants, health care benefits, and tuition waivers (full) also available. Financial award application deadline: 12/1. In 2016, 8 doctorates awarded. Offers biological sciences (PhD). *Application deadline:* For fall admission, 12/1 for domestic and international students. *Application fee:* $60. Electronic applications accepted. *Application Contact:* Admissions and Recruitment Manager, 516-367-6890, E-mail: gradschool@cshl.edu. *Dean,* Dr. Alexander Gann, 516-367-6890, E-mail: ganna@cshl.edu.

COLEMAN UNIVERSITY, San Diego, CA 92123

General Information Independent, coed, comprehensive institution. *Graduate housing:* On-campus housing not available.

GRADUATE UNITS

Program in Business and Technology Management *Program availability:* Evening/weekend, online learning. Offers business and technology management (MS).

Program in Information Technology *Program availability:* Evening/weekend. Offers information technology (MSIT).

COLGATE ROCHESTER CROZER DIVINITY SCHOOL, Rochester, NY 14620-2530

General Information Independent-religious, coed, graduate-only institution. *Enrollment by degree level:* 57 master's, 51 doctoral, 6 other advanced degrees. *Graduate faculty:* 6 full-time (3 women), 8 part-time/adjunct (3 women). *Tuition:* Full-time $14,360; part-time $1795 per course. *Required fees:* $330; $35 per course. $70 per semester. One-time fee: $225. Tuition and fees vary according to course load. *Graduate housing:* Rooms and/or apartments available on a first-come, first-served basis to single and married students. Typical cost: $6525 per year for single students; $6525 per year for married students. Room charges vary according to housing facility selected. Housing application deadline: 7/1. *Student services:* Campus employment opportunities, campus safety program, services for students with disabilities. *Library facilities:* Ambrose Swasey Library plus 1 other. *Collection:* Books: 19,227 (physical); Serial titles: 57 (physical). Weekly public service hours: 41.

Computer facilities: 8 computers available on campus for general student use. A campuswide network can be accessed from student residence rooms.
Website: http://www.crcds.edu/

General Application Contact: Rev. Melissa M. Morral, Vice President for Enrollment Services, 585-340-9500, Fax: 585-340-9644, E-mail: mmorral@crcds.edu.

GRADUATE UNITS

Graduate and Professional Programs Students: 85 full-time, 29 part-time; includes 66 minority (56 Black or African American, non-Hispanic/Latino; 6 Asian, non-Hispanic/Latino; 4 Hispanic/Latino). Average age 43. 33 applicants, 91% accepted, 27 enrolled. *Faculty:* 6 full-time (3 women), 8 part-time/adjunct (3 women). Expenses: Contact institution. *Financial support:* In 2016–17, 43 students received support. Scholarships/grants available. Financial award application deadline: 9/1; financial award applicants required to submit FAFSA. In 2016, 12 master's, 3 doctorates awarded. *Program availability:* Part-time, evening/weekend. Offers divinity (M Div, MA, Certificate); peace building and interfaith dialogue (D Min); prophetic preaching (D Min); transformative leadership (D Min). *Application deadline:* For fall admission, 7/1 priority date for domestic students, 3/1 for international students; for spring admission, 12/1 priority date for domestic students, 9/1 for international students. Applications are processed on a rolling basis. *Application fee:* $35. Electronic applications accepted. *Application Contact:* Rev. Melissa M. Morral, Vice President for Enrollment Services, 585-340-9633, Fax: 585-340-9644, E-mail: mmorral@crcds.edu. *President,* Marvin A. McMickle, PhD, 585-271-1320 Ext. 680, Fax: 585-271-8013.

COLGATE UNIVERSITY, Hamilton, NY 13346-1386

General Information Independent, coed, comprehensive institution. *Graduate housing:* On-campus housing not available.

GRADUATE UNITS

Master of Arts in Teaching Program Offers teaching (MAT).

THE COLLEGE AT BROCKPORT, STATE UNIVERSITY OF NEW YORK, Brockport, NY 14420-2997

General Information State-supported, coed, comprehensive institution. CGS member. *Enrollment:* 8,243 graduate, professional, and undergraduate students; 354 full-time matriculated graduate/professional students (223 women), 659 part-time matriculated graduate/professional students (452 women). *Graduate faculty:* 121 full-time (62 women), 39 part-time/adjunct (23 women). Tuition, state resident: full-time $10,870; part-time $453 per credit hour. *Required fees:* $994. *Graduate housing:* On-campus housing not available. *Student services:* Campus employment opportunities, campus safety program, career counseling, child daycare facilities, exercise/wellness program, free psychological counseling, grant writing training, international student services, low-cost health insurance, multicultural affairs office, services for students with disabilities, teacher training, writing training. *Library facilities:* Drake Memorial Library. *Collection:* Books: 500,461 (physical), 185,000 (digital/electronic); Serial titles: 4,747 (physical), 113,396 (digital/electronic); Databases: 270. Weekly public service hours: 93; students can reserve study rooms.

Computer facilities: 1,000 computers available on campus for general student use. A campuswide network can be accessed from student residence rooms and from off campus. Online class registration is available.
Website: http://www.brockport.edu/

General Application Contact: Danielle A. Welch, Graduate Admissions Counselor, 585-395-2525, Fax: 585-395-2515, E-mail: dwelch@brockport.edu.

GRADUATE UNITS

General Education Division Students: 3 full-time (1 woman), 18 part-time (11 women); includes 7 minority (3 Black or African American, non-Hispanic/Latino; 2 Asian, non-Hispanic/Latino; 1 Hispanic/Latino; 1 Two or more races, non-Hispanic/Latino). 13 applicants, 85% accepted, 10 enrolled. Expenses: Contact institution. *Financial support:* Federal Work-Study, scholarships/grants, and unspecified assistantships available. Support available to part-time students. Financial award application deadline: 3/15; financial award applicants required to submit FAFSA. In 2016, 11 master's awarded. *Program availability:* Part-time, 100% online. Offers liberal studies (MA). *Application deadline:* For fall admission, 6/15 priority date for domestic and international students; for spring admission, 10/15 priority date for domestic and international students; for summer admission, 3/15 priority date for domestic and international students. *Application fee:* $50. Electronic applications accepted. *Application Contact:* Danielle A. Welch, Graduate Admissions Counselor, 585-395-5465, Fax: 585-395-2515. *Vice Provost,* Dr. P. Michael Fox, 585-395-2524, Fax: 585-395-2401, E-mail: mmallory@brockport.edu.

School of Arts and Sciences Students: 32 full-time (17 women), 30 part-time (12 women); includes 5 minority (1 Black or African American, non-Hispanic/Latino; 1 Asian, non-Hispanic/Latino; 3 Two or more races, non-Hispanic/Latino). 71 applicants, 44% accepted, 21 enrolled. *Faculty:* 27 full-time (11 women), 2 part-time/adjunct (both women). Expenses: Contact institution. In 2016, 30 master's awarded. Offers arts and sciences (MA, MFA, MS, PSM, AGC); biology (MS, PSM); communication (MA); creative writing (AGC); dance (MA, MFA); English (MA); environmental science and biology (MS); history (MA); mathematics (MA); psychology (MA); visual studies (MFA). *Application Contact:* Danielle A. Welch, Graduate Admissions Counselor, 585-395-2525, Fax: 585-395-2515. *Dean,* Dr. Jose A. Maliekal, 585-395-2394, Fax: 585-395-2172, E-mail: kkifer@brockport.edu.

School of Business and Management Students: 13 full-time (5 women), 8 part-time (5 women); includes 4 minority (3 Black or African American, non-Hispanic/Latino; 1 Asian, non-Hispanic/Latino). 29 applicants, 79% accepted, 19 enrolled. *Faculty:* 5 full-time (1 woman), 1 part-time/adjunct (0 women). Expenses: Contact institution. *Financial support:* Career-related internships or fieldwork, Federal Work-Study, scholarships/grants, and unspecified assistantships available. Financial award application deadline: 3/15; financial award applicants required to submit FAFSA. In 2016, 17 master's awarded. *Program availability:* Part-time. Offers arts administration (AGC); forensic accounting (MS); nonprofit management (AGC); public administration (MPA, AGC). *Application deadline:* For fall admission, 7/1 priority date for domestic and international students; for spring admission, 12/1 priority date for domestic and international students. *Application fee:* $50. Electronic applications accepted. *Application Contact:* Dr. Donald A. Kent, Graduate Director, 585-395-5521, Fax: 585-395-2515, E-mail: dkent@brockport.edu. *Department Chair,* Dr. James Cordeiro, 585-395-5793, Fax: 585-395-2542.

School of Education, Health, and Human Services Students: 194 full-time (142 women), 575 part-time (430 women); includes 114 minority (55 Black or African American, non-Hispanic/Latino; 4 American Indian or Alaska Native, non-Hispanic/Latino; 12 Asian, non-Hispanic/Latino; 22 Hispanic/Latino; 1 Native Hawaiian or other Pacific Islander, non-Hispanic/Latino; 20 Two or more races, non-Hispanic/Latino), 4 international. 523 applicants, 72% accepted, 275 enrolled. *Faculty:* 33 full-time (20 women), 35 part-time/adjunct (23 women). Expenses: Contact institution. *Financial support:* In 2016–17, 3 teaching assistantships with full tuition reimbursements (averaging $3,000 per year) were awarded; institutionally sponsored loans, scholarships/grants, and unspecified assistantships also available. Financial award applicants required to submit FAFSA. In 2016, 231 master's, 82 other advanced degrees awarded. *Program availability:* 100% online. Offers adapted physical education (AGC); adolescence biology education (MS Ed); adolescence chemistry education (MS Ed); adolescence earth science education (MS Ed); adolescence education (MS Ed); adolescence English education (MS Ed); adolescence mathematics education (MS Ed); adolescence physics education (MS Ed); adolescence social studies education (MS Ed); bilingual education (MS Ed, AGC); biology (MS Ed, AGC); chemistry (MS Ed, AGC); childhood curriculum specialist (MS Ed); college counseling (MS Ed, CAS); education, health, and human services (MPA, MS, MS Ed, MSW, AGC, Advanced Certificate, CAS, Graduate Certificate); English (MS Ed, Advanced Certificate); family and community practice (MSW); gerontology (AGC); health education (MS Ed); inclusive generalist education (MS Ed, AGC, Advanced Certificate); interdisciplinary health practice (MSW); literacy education B-12 (MS Ed); mathematics (MS Ed, Advanced Certificate); mental health counseling (MS, CAS); physical education (MS Ed); school building leader (CAS); school building leader/school district leader (CAS); school counseling (MS Ed, CAS); school counselor supervision (CAS); school district business leader (CAS); school district leader (CAS); science (MS Ed, Advanced Certificate); social studies (MS Ed, Advanced Certificate); teacher leadership (Graduate Certificate).

Application Contact: Danielle A. Welch, Graduate Admissions Counselor, 585-395-2525, Fax: 585-395-2515. *Dean,* Dr. Thomas Hernandez, 585-395-2510, Fax: 585-395-2172, E-mail: thernandez@brockport.edu.

COLLÈGE DOMINICAIN DE PHILOSOPHIE ET DE THÉOLOGIE, Ottawa, ON K1R 7G3, Canada

General Information Independent-religious, coed, university. *Graduate housing:* Room and/or apartments available on a first-come, first-served basis to single students; on-campus housing not available to married students.

GRADUATE UNITS

Graduate Programs *Program availability:* Part-time, evening/weekend.

Faculty of Philosophy Offers philosophy (MA Ph, PhD).

Faculty of Theology Program availability: Part-time, evening/weekend. Offers theology (M Th, MA Th, PhD, Th D, L Th).

COLLEGE FOR CREATIVE STUDIES, Detroit, MI 48202-4034

General Information Independent, coed, comprehensive institution.

GRADUATE UNITS

Graduate Programs

COLLEGE FOR FINANCIAL PLANNING, Centennial, CO 80112

General Information Proprietary, coed, primarily men, graduate-only institution. *Enrollment by degree level:* 230 master's, 2,894 other advanced degrees. *Graduate faculty:* 9 full-time (2 women), 24 part-time/adjunct (4 women). *Tuition:* Full-time $6750; part-time $450 per credit hour. *Graduate housing:* On-campus housing not available. *Student services:* Services for students with disabilities. *Library facilities:* Apollo University Library. *Collection:* Books: 190,000 (digital/electronic); Databases: 7.

Computer facilities: A campuswide network can be accessed. Online class registration is available.

Website: http://www.cffp.edu/

General Application Contact: Alicia Christensen, Director of Enrollment, 303-220-4835, Fax: 303-220-1810, E-mail: alicia.mead@cffp.edu.

GRADUATE UNITS

Graduate Programs Students: 4,318 full-time. *Faculty:* 9 full-time (2 women), 32 part-time/adjunct (6 women). Expenses: Contact institution. *Program availability:* Part-time, evening/weekend, online only, 100% online. Offers finance (MSF); personal financial planning (MS). *Application deadline:* Applications are processed on a rolling basis. Electronic applications accepted. *Application Contact:* Alicia Christensen, Director of Enrollment, 303-220-4835, Fax: 303-220-1810, E-mail: alicia.mead@cffp.edu. *President,* John Sears, 303-220-4918, E-mail: john.sears@cffp.edu.

COLLEGE OF CHARLESTON, Charleston, SC 29424-0001

General Information State-supported, coed, comprehensive institution. CGS member. *Graduate housing:* On-campus housing not available. *Student services:* Campus employment opportunities, campus safety program, career counseling, child daycare facilities, exercise/wellness program, free psychological counseling, grant writing training, international student services, low-cost health insurance, multicultural affairs office, services for students with disabilities, teacher training, writing training. *Library facilities:* Marlene and Nathan Addlestone Library plus 3 others. *Collection:* Books: 700,910 (physical), 573,884 (digital/electronic); Serial titles: 2,721 (physical), 84,039 (digital/electronic); Databases: 328. Weekly public service hours: 121; students can reserve study rooms. *Research affiliation:* Oak Ridge Associated Universities (science), South Carolina Department of Natural Resources, Marine Resources Division (marine biology, environmental studies), National Institute of Standards and Technology (NIST) (marine biology, environmental studies), National Oceanic and Atmospheric Administration (NOAA) (marine biology, environmental studies), U.S. Department of Agriculture (USDA) (environmental studies), South Carolina Aquarium (marine biology, environmental studies).

Computer facilities: Computer purchase and lease plans are available. 1,024 computers available on campus for general student use. A campuswide network can be accessed. Online class registration is available.

Website: http://www.cofc.edu/

General Application Contact: Susan Hallatt, Assistant Director of Graduate Admissions, 843-953-5614, Fax: 843-953-1434, E-mail: hallatts@cofc.edu.

GRADUATE UNITS

Graduate School Expenses: Contact institution. *Financial support:* Fellowships, research assistantships, teaching assistantships, career-related internships or fieldwork, Federal Work-Study, institutionally sponsored loans, scholarships/grants, tuition waivers (partial), and unspecified assistantships available. Support available to part-time students. Financial award application deadline: 5/1; financial award applicants required to submit FAFSA. *Program availability:* Part-time, evening/weekend. *Application deadline:* For fall admission, 4/1 priority date for domestic students, 4/1 for international students; for spring admission, 10/1 priority date for domestic students, 8/1 for international students. *Application fee:* $45. Electronic applications accepted. *Application Contact:* Susan Hallatt, Director of Admissions, 843-953-5614, Fax: 843-953-1434, E-mail: hallatts@cofc.edu. *Dean,* Dr. Amy Thompson McCandless, 843-953-5730, Fax: 843-953-1434, E-mail: mccandlessa@cofc.edu.

School of Business Expenses: Contact institution. *Financial support:* Research assistantships, scholarships/grants, and unspecified assistantships available. Support available to part-time students. Financial award applicants required to submit FAFSA. Offers accountancy (MS); business (MBA, MS); business administration (MBA). *Application deadline:* For fall admission, 7/1 for domestic students. Applications are processed on a rolling basis. *Application fee:* $45. Electronic applications accepted. *Application Contact:* Susan Hallatt, Director of Graduate Admissions, 843-953-5614, Fax: 843-953-1434, E-mail: hallatts@cofc.edu. *Dean,* Dr. Alan Shao, 843-953-6651, Fax: 843-953-5697, E-mail: shaoa@cofc.edu.

School of Education, Health, and Human Performance Expenses: Contact institution. *Financial support:* Research assistantships, teaching assistantships, career-related internships or fieldwork, Federal Work-Study, scholarships/grants, and unspecified assistantships available. Support available to part-time students. Financial award application deadline: 4/1; financial award applicants required to submit FAFSA. *Program availability:* Part-time, evening/weekend. Offers early childhood education (MAT); education, health, and human performance (M Ed, MAT, Certificate); elementary education (MAT); English to speakers of other languages (Certificate); languages (M Ed); performing arts education (MAT); science and mathematics for teachers (M Ed); special education (MAT); teaching, learning and advocacy (M Ed). *Application deadline:* For fall admission, 4/1 for domestic students; for spring admission, 11/1 for domestic students. Applications are processed on a rolling basis.

Application fee: $45. Electronic applications accepted. *Application Contact:* Susan Hallatt, Director of Graduate Admissions, 843-953-5614, Fax: 843-953-1434, E-mail: hallatts@cofc.edu. *Dean,* Dr. Frances Welch, 843-953-5613, Fax: 843-953-5407, E-mail: welchf@cofc.edu.

School of Humanities and Social Sciences Expenses: Contact institution. *Financial support:* Fellowships, research assistantships, teaching assistantships, career-related internships or fieldwork, Federal Work-Study, scholarships/grants, and unspecified assistantships available. Support available to part-time students. Financial award application deadline: 4/1; financial award applicants required to submit FAFSA. *Program availability:* Part-time, evening/weekend. Offers creative writing (MFA); English (MA); history (MA); humanities and social sciences (MA, MFA, MPA, Certificate); public administration (MPA); urban and regional planning (Certificate). *Application fee:* $45. Electronic applications accepted. *Application Contact:* Susan Hallatt, Director of Graduate Admissions, 843-953-5614, Fax: 843-953-1434, E-mail: hallatts@cofc.edu. *Dean,* Dr. Cynthia Lowenthal, 843-953-0760, Fax: 843-953-0758.

School of Sciences and Mathematics Expenses: Contact institution. *Financial support:* Fellowships, research assistantships, teaching assistantships, career-related internships or fieldwork, Federal Work-Study, institutionally sponsored loans, scholarships/grants, and unspecified assistantships available. Support available to part-time students. Financial award application deadline: 4/1; financial award applicants required to submit FAFSA. *Program availability:* Part-time, evening/weekend. Offers computer and information sciences (MS); environmental studies (MS); marine biology (MS); mathematics (MS); sciences and mathematics (MS). *Application deadline:* Applications are processed on a rolling basis. *Application fee:* $45. Electronic applications accepted. *Application Contact:* John Peters, Dean, 843-953-1422. *Dean,* John Peters, 843-953-1422.

School of the Arts Expenses: Contact institution. *Financial support:* Scholarships/grants and unspecified assistantships available. Financial award application deadline: 4/1; financial award applicants required to submit FAFSA. Offers arts (MS, Certificate); arts management (Certificate); historic preservation (MS). *Application fee:* $45. *Application Contact:* Susan Hallatt, Director of Graduate Admissions, 843-953-5614, Fax: 843-953-1434, E-mail: hallatts@cofc.edu. *Dean,* Dr. Valerie B. Morris, 843-953-8222, Fax: 843-953-4988, E-mail: morrisv@cofc.edu.

COLLEGE OF EMMANUEL AND ST. CHAD, Saskatoon, SK S7N 0W6, Canada

General Information Independent-religious, coed, graduate-only institution. *Tuition:* Part-time $975 per course. Part-time tuition and fees vary according to degree level and program. *Graduate housing:* Room and/or apartments available to single students; on-campus housing not available to married students. Housing application deadline: 6/15. *Student services:* Campus employment opportunities, campus safety program, career counseling, free psychological counseling, international student services, writing training. Website: http://www.usask.ca/stu/emmanuel/

General Application Contact: Lisa McInnis, Registrar, 306-975-1550, Fax: 306-934-2683, E-mail: esc.registrar@usask.ca.

GRADUATE UNITS

Bachelor of Theology Program Expenses: Contact institution. *Financial support:* Career-related internships or fieldwork and bursaries available. Support available to part-time students. Financial award application deadline: 9/30. *Program availability:* Part-time, online learning. Offers theology (B Th). *Application deadline:* For fall admission, 5/31 priority date for domestic students. Applications are processed on a rolling basis. *Application fee:* $75. *Application Contact:* Lisa McInnis, Registrar, 306-975-1550, Fax: 306-934-2683, E-mail: esc.registrar@usask.ca. *Principal,* Rev. Dr. Iain Luke, 306-975-1555, Fax: 306-934-2683, E-mail: iain.luke@usask.ca.

Graduate Programs Expenses: Contact institution. *Financial support:* Career-related internships or fieldwork and bursaries available. Support available to part-time students. Financial award application deadline: 9/30. *Program availability:* Part-time. Offers theology (M Div, MTS, STM, D Min, L Th). STM and D Min programs offered jointly with Lutheran Theological Seminary and St. Andrew's College. *Application deadline:* For fall admission, 5/31 priority date for domestic students. Applications are processed on a rolling basis. *Application fee:* $75. *Application Contact:* Lisa McInnis, Registrar, 306-975-1550, Fax: 306-934-2683. *Principal,* Rev. Dr. Iain Luke, 306-975-1555, Fax: 306-934-2683, E-mail: iain.luke@usask.ca.

THE COLLEGE OF IDAHO, Caldwell, ID 83605

General Information Independent, coed, comprehensive institution. *Graduate housing:* Room and/or apartments available on a first-come, first-served basis to single students; on-campus housing not available to married students. Housing application deadline: 5/1.

GRADUATE UNITS

Department of Education Offers curriculum and instruction (M Ed); teaching (MAT).

COLLEGE OF MOUNT SAINT VINCENT, Riverdale, NY 10471-1093

General Information Independent, coed, comprehensive institution. *Graduate housing:* On-campus housing not available.

GRADUATE UNITS

School of Professional and Graduate Studies Offers family nurse practitioner (MSN, PMC); instructional technology and global perspectives (Certificate); middle level education (Certificate); multicultural studies (Certificate); nurse educator (PMC); nursing administration (MSN); nursing education (MSN); teaching English to speakers of other languages (MS Ed); urban and multicultural education (MS Ed).

THE COLLEGE OF NEW JERSEY, Ewing, NJ 08628

General Information State-supported, coed, comprehensive institution. CGS member. *Enrollment:* 7,396 graduate, professional, and undergraduate students; 413 full-time matriculated graduate/professional students (311 women), 867 part-time matriculated graduate/professional students (720 women). *Enrollment by degree level:* 724 master's, 274 other advanced degrees. *Student services:* Campus employment opportunities, campus safety program, career counseling, exercise/wellness program, free psychological counseling, international student services, low-cost health insurance, services for students with disabilities, teacher training. *Library facilities:* The College of New Jersey Library. *Collection:* Books: 694,461 (physical), 6,455 (digital/electronic); Serial titles: 44,898 (physical), 8,859 (digital/electronic); Databases: 114. Weekly public service hours: 98; students can reserve study rooms.

Computer facilities: Computer purchase and lease plans are available. 631 computers available on campus for general student use. A campuswide network can be accessed from student residence rooms and from off campus. Online class registration is available.

Website: http://www.tcnj.edu/

General Application Contact: Susan L. Hydro, Director of Graduate and Intersession Programs, 609-771-2300, Fax: 609-637-5105, E-mail: graduate@tcnj.edu.

GRADUATE UNITS

Office of Graduate and Advancing Education Students: 413 full-time (311 women), 867 part-time (720 women); includes 207 minority (64 Black or African American, non-Hispanic/Latino; 3 American Indian or Alaska Native, non-Hispanic/Latino; 63 Asian, non-Hispanic/Latino; 71 Hispanic/Latino; 2 Native Hawaiian or other Pacific Islander, non-Hispanic/Latino; 4 Two or more races, non-Hispanic/Latino). 694 applicants, 79% accepted, 499 enrolled. Expenses: Contact institution. *Financial support:* Tuition waivers (partial) and unspecified assistantships available. Financial award application deadline: 5/1; financial award applicants required to submit FAFSA. In 2016, 375 master's, 129 other advanced degrees awarded. *Program availability:* Part-time, evening/weekend. Offers overseas education (M Ed, Certificate). *Application deadline:* For fall admission, 2/1 priority date for domestic students; for spring admission, 10/1 priority date for domestic students. *Application fee:* $75. Electronic applications accepted. *Application Contact:* Susan L. Hydro, Director of Graduate and Intersession Programs, 609-771-2300, Fax: 609-637-5105, E-mail: graduate@tcnj.edu. *Director of Graduate and Intersession Programs,* Susan L. Hydro, 609-771-2300, Fax: 609-637-5105, E-mail: graduate@tcnj.edu.

School of Education *Program availability:* Part-time, evening/weekend. Offers community counseling: human services (MA); community counseling: substance abuse and addiction (MA, Certificate); developmental reading (M Ed); early childhood education (M Ed, MAT); education (M Ed, MA, MAT, Certificate, Ed S); educational leadership (M Ed, Certificate); elementary education (M Ed, MAT); elementary teaching (MAT); English as a second language (M Ed); marriage and family therapy (Ed S); reading certification (Certificate); school counseling (MA); school personnel: preschool-grade 3 (M Ed); secondary education (MAT); special education (M Ed, MAT); special education with learning disabilities (Certificate); teaching English as a second language (M Ed, Certificate). Electronic applications accepted.

School of Humanities and Social Sciences *Program availability:* Part-time. Offers English (MA); gender studies (Certificate); humanities and social sciences (MA, Certificate). Electronic applications accepted.

School of Nursing, Health and Exercise Science *Program availability:* Part-time. Offers health (MAT); health education (M Ed, MAT); nursing (MSN, Certificate); nursing, health and exercise science (M Ed, MAT, MSN, Certificate); physical education (M Ed, MAT). Electronic applications accepted.

See Display below and Close-Up on page 873.

THE COLLEGE OF NEW ROCHELLE, New Rochelle, NY 10805-2308

General Information Independent, coed, primarily women, comprehensive institution. *Graduate housing:* Room and/or apartments available on a first-come, first-served basis to single students; on-campus housing not available to married students. Housing application deadline: 8/1.

GRADUATE UNITS

Graduate School *Program availability:* Part-time, evening/weekend. Offers acute care nurse practitioner (MS, Certificate); clinical specialist in holistic nursing (MS, Certificate); family nurse practitioner (MS, Certificate); nursing and health care management (MS); nursing education (Certificate). Electronic applications accepted.

Division of Art and Communication Studies *Program availability:* Part-time, evening/weekend. Offers art therapy (MS); art therapy/counseling (MS); communication studies (MS, Certificate).

Division of Education *Program availability:* Part-time, evening/weekend. Offers art education (MS); bilingual education (Certificate); childhood education (MS Ed); childhood education/early childhood education (MS Ed); early childhood education (MS Ed); educational leadership (MS, Advanced Certificate, Advanced Diploma); gifted education (Certificate); literacy education (MS Ed); multilingual/multicultural education (MS Ed, Certificate); school building leader (MS, Advanced Certificate); school district leader (MS, Advanced Diploma); special education (MS Ed); teaching English to speakers of other languages (MS Ed, Certificate). Electronic applications accepted.

Division of Human Services *Program availability:* Part-time, evening/weekend. Offers career development (MS, Advanced Certificate); guidance and counseling (MS, Advanced Certificate); long term care administration (MPA); marriage and family therapy (MMFT); mental health counseling (MS, Certificate); public administration (MPA); school psychology (MS); thanatology (Certificate). Electronic applications accepted.

COLLEGE OF SAINT ELIZABETH, Morristown, NJ 07960-6989

General Information Independent-religious, coed, primarily women, comprehensive institution. *Graduate housing:* Room and/or apartments available on a first-come, first-served basis to single students; on-campus housing not available to married students. Housing application deadline: 7/1. *Research affiliation:* National Figure Skating Association (sports nutrition), National Institute of Mental Health (NIMH) (mental health service), Cornell University/The University of Texas at Houston (food biotechnology) (attitude research)).

GRADUATE UNITS

Department of Business Administration and Management *Program availability:* Part-time. Offers human resource management (MS); organizational change (MS). Electronic applications accepted.

Department of Educational Leadership *Program availability:* Part-time. Offers assistive technology (Certificate); education (MA); educational leadership (MA, Ed D). Electronic applications accepted.

Department of Foods and Nutrition *Program availability:* Part-time, blended/hybrid learning. Offers dietetic internship (Certificate); dietetics verification (Certificate); nutrition (MS); sports nutrition and wellness (Certificate). Electronic applications accepted.

Department of Nursing *Program availability:* Part-time. Offers nursing (MSN). Electronic applications accepted.

Department of Psychology *Program availability:* Part-time. Offers counseling psychology (MA); forensic psychology (MA); mental health counseling (Certificate); psychology (Psy D); student affairs in higher education (Certificate). Electronic applications accepted.

Department of Theology and Philosophy *Program availability:* Part-time. Offers theology (MA). Electronic applications accepted.

Health Administration Program *Program availability:* Part-time. Offers health administration (MS). Electronic applications accepted.

Program in Justice Administration and Public Service *Program availability:* Part-time. Offers justice administration and public service (MA). Electronic applications accepted.

COLLEGE OF ST. JOSEPH, Rutland, VT 05701-3899

General Information Independent-religious, coed, comprehensive institution. *Tuition:* Full-time $13,800; part-time $560 per credit. *Required fees:* $75 per semester. Full-time tuition and fees vary according to course load. *Graduate housing:* Room and/or apartments guaranteed to single students; on-campus housing not available to married students. Typical cost: $6500 per year ($11,900 including board). Housing application deadline: 7/1. *Student services:* Campus employment opportunities, campus safety program, career counseling, free psychological counseling, low-cost health insurance, services for students with disabilities, teacher training, writing training. *Library facilities:* Giorgetti Library.

Computer facilities: 33 computers available on campus for general student use. A campuswide network can be accessed. Online statements/ability to pay tuition online available.

Website: http://www.csj.edu/

General Application Contact: Ken Labate, Vice President of Student Recruitment and Admissions, 802-776-5268, Fax: 802-776-5258, E-mail: ken.labate@csj.edu.

GRADUATE UNITS

Graduate Programs Expenses: Contact institution. *Financial support:* Career-related internships or fieldwork, tuition waivers (partial), and unspecified assistantships available. Financial award application deadline: 3/1; financial award applicants required to submit FAFSA. *Program availability:* Part-time, evening/weekend. *Application deadline:* Applications are processed on a rolling basis. *Application fee:* $35. Electronic applications accepted. *Application Contact:* Joel Wincowski, Interim Dean of Admissions, 802-773-5900 Ext. 3227, Fax: 802-776-5310, E-mail: joel.wincowski@csj.edu. *Academic Dean,* Dr. Nancy Kline, 802-773-5900 Ext. 3213, Fax: 802-776-5258, E-mail: nkline@csj.edu.

Division of Business Expenses: Contact institution. *Financial support:* Teaching assistantships with full tuition reimbursements, Federal Work-Study, and unspecified assistantships available. Support available to part-time students. Financial award application deadline: 3/1. *Program availability:* Part-time, evening/weekend. Offers business administration (MBA). *Application deadline:* Applications are processed on a rolling basis. *Application fee:* $35. Electronic applications accepted. *Application Contact:* Alan Young, Dean of Admissions, 802-773-5900 Ext. 3227, Fax: 802-776-5310, E-mail: alanyoung@csj.edu. *Chair,* Robert Foley, 802-773-5900 Ext. 3248, Fax: 802-776-5258, E-mail: rfoley@csj.edu.

Division of Education Expenses: Contact institution. *Financial support:* Career-related internships or fieldwork, Federal Work-Study, and unspecified assistantships available. Support available to part-time students. Financial award application deadline: 3/1. *Program availability:* Part-time, evening/weekend. Offers elementary education (M Ed); English (M Ed); general education (M Ed); reading (M Ed); secondary education (M Ed); social studies (M Ed); special education (M Ed). *Application deadline:* Applications are processed on a rolling basis. *Application fee:* $35. Electronic applications accepted. *Application Contact:* Alan Young, Dean of Admissions, 802-773-5900 Ext. 3227, Fax: 802-776-5310, E-mail: alanyoung@csj.edu. *Chair,* Dr. Maria Bove, 802-773-5900 Ext. 3243, Fax: 802-776-5258, E-mail: mbove@csj.edu.

Division of Psychology and Human Services Expenses: Contact institution. *Financial support:* Teaching assistantships with tuition reimbursements, career-related internships or fieldwork, Federal Work-Study, and unspecified assistantships available. Support available to part-time students. Financial award application deadline: 3/1. *Program availability:* Part-time, evening/weekend. Offers alcohol and substance abuse counseling (MS); clinical mental health counseling (MS); clinical psychology (MS); community counseling (MS); school guidance counseling (MS). *Application deadline:* Applications are processed on a rolling basis. *Application fee:* $35. Electronic applications accepted. *Application Contact:* Alan Young, Dean of Admissions, 802-773-5900 Ext. 3227, Fax: 802-776-5310, E-mail: alanyoung@csj.edu. *Chair,* Dr. Craig Knapp, 802-773-5900 Ext. 3219, Fax: 802-776-5258, E-mail: cknapp@csj.edu.

COLLEGE OF SAINT MARY, Omaha, NE 68106

General Information Independent-religious, women only, comprehensive institution.

GRADUATE UNITS

Program in Education *Program availability:* Part-time. Offers assessment leadership (MSE); English as a second language (MSE).

Program in Health Professions Education *Program availability:* Part-time. Offers health professions education (Ed D).

Program in Nursing *Program availability:* Part-time. Offers nursing (MSN).

Program in Occupational Therapy Offers occupational therapy (MOT).

Program in Organizational Leadership *Program availability:* Part-time, evening/weekend. Offers organizational leadership (MOL). Electronic applications accepted.

Program in Teaching *Program availability:* Evening/weekend. Offers teaching (MAT).

THE COLLEGE OF SAINT ROSE, Albany, NY 12203-1419

General Information Independent, coed, comprehensive institution. CGS member. *Enrollment:* 4,211 graduate, professional, and undergraduate students; 569 full-time matriculated graduate/professional students (406 women), 1,025 part-time matriculated graduate/professional students (780 women). *Enrollment by degree level:* 755 master's, 839 other advanced degrees. *Graduate faculty:* 79 full-time (39 women), 71 part-time/adjunct (39 women). *Tuition:* Full-time $14,382; part-time $799 per credit. *Required fees:* $814; $32 per credit. $88 per semester. Tuition and fees vary according to course load. *Graduate housing:* Room and/or apartments available on a first-come, first-served basis to single students; on-campus housing not available to married students. Typical cost: $7994 per year ($14,136 including board). Room and board charges vary according to board plan. Housing application deadline: 3/15. *Student services:* Campus employment opportunities, campus safety program, career counseling, child daycare facilities, exercise/wellness program, free psychological counseling, international student services, multicultural affairs office, services for students with disabilities, teacher training, writing training. *Library facilities:* Neil Hellman Library plus 2 others. *Collection:* Books: 241,000 (physical), 116,500 (digital/electronic); Serial titles: 1,200 (physical), 10 (digital/electronic); Databases: 104. Students can reserve study rooms.

Computer facilities: 755 computers available on campus for general student use. A campuswide network can be accessed from student residence rooms and from off campus. Online class registration is available.

Website: http://www.strose.edu/

General Application Contact: Cris Murray, Assistant Vice President for Graduate Recruitment and Enrollment, 518-485-3390, Fax: 518-458-5479, E-mail: grad@strose.edu.

GRADUATE UNITS

Graduate Studies Students: 569 full-time (406 women), 1,025 part-time (780 women); includes 417 minority (205 Black or African American, non-Hispanic/Latino; 4 American Indian or Alaska Native, non-Hispanic/Latino; 40 Asian, non-Hispanic/Latino; 148 Hispanic/Latino; 1 Native Hawaiian or other Pacific Islander, non-Hispanic/Latino; 19 Two or more races, non-Hispanic/Latino), 138 international. Average age 32. 1,372 applicants, 67% accepted, 534 enrolled. *Faculty:* 79 full-time (39 women), 71 part-time/adjunct (39 women). Expenses: Contact institution. *Financial support:* Career-related internships or fieldwork, scholarships/grants, tuition waivers (partial), and unspecified assistantships available. Support available to part-time students. Financial award application deadline: 4/15. In 2016, 458 master's, 631 other advanced degrees awarded. *Program availability:* Part-time, evening/weekend, 100% online. *Application deadline:* For fall admission, 4/1 priority date for domestic and international students; for spring admission, 10/15 priority date for domestic and international students; for summer admission, 3/15 priority date for domestic and international students. Applications are processed on a rolling basis. *Application fee:* $40. Electronic applications accepted. *Application Contact:* Cris Murray, Assistant Vice President for Recruitment and Enrollment, 518-485-3390, Fax: 518-458-5479, E-mail: grad@strose.edu.

Huether School of Business Students: 70 full-time (37 women), 67 part-time (29 women); includes 24 minority (17 Black or African American, non-Hispanic/Latino; 1 Asian, non-Hispanic/Latino; 5 Hispanic/Latino; 1 Two or more races, non-Hispanic/Latino), 20 international. Average age 28. 117 applicants, 76% accepted, 33 enrolled. *Faculty:* 11 full-time (5 women), 6 part-time/adjunct (2 women). Expenses: Contact institution. *Financial support:* Career-related internships or fieldwork, scholarships/grants, tuition waivers (partial), and unspecified assistantships available. Support available to part-time students. Financial award application deadline: 4/15. In 2016, 67 master's, 15 other advanced degrees awarded. *Program availability:* Part-time, evening/weekend. Offers accounting (MS); business administration (MBA); financial planning (Advanced Certificate); organizational leadership and change management (Advanced Certificate). *Application deadline:* For fall admission, 4/1 priority date for domestic and international students; for spring admission, 10/15 priority date for domestic and international students; for summer admission, 3/15 priority date for domestic and international students. Applications are processed on a rolling basis. *Application fee:* $40. Electronic applications accepted. *Application Contact:* Cris Murray, Assistant Vice President for Graduate Recruitment and Enrollment, 518-485-3390, Fax: 518-458-5479, E-mail: grad@strose.edu. *Interim Dean,* Gretchen Guenther-Collins, 518-454-2122, E-mail: guentheg@strose.edu.

School of Mathematics and Sciences Students: 89 full-time (28 women), 16 part-time (6 women); includes 4 minority (2 Black or African American, non-Hispanic/Latino; 1 Asian, non-Hispanic/Latino; 1 Two or more races, non-Hispanic/Latino), 97 international. Average age 25. 220 applicants, 83% accepted, 13 enrolled. *Faculty:* 10 full-time (4 women), 3 part-time/adjunct (0 women). Expenses: Contact institution. *Financial support:* Career-related internships or fieldwork, scholarships/grants, tuition waivers (partial), and unspecified assistantships available. Support available to part-time students. Financial award application deadline: 4/15. In 2016, 18 master's, 3 other advanced degrees awarded. *Program availability:* Part-time, evening/weekend, 100% online. Offers computer information systems (MS, Advanced Certificate); mathematics and sciences (MS, MSSW, Advanced Certificate); social work (MSSW). *Application deadline:* For fall admission, 4/1 priority date for domestic and international students; for spring admission, 10/15 priority date for domestic and international students; for summer admission, 3/15 priority date for domestic and international students. Applications are processed on a rolling basis. *Application fee:* $40. Electronic applications accepted. *Application Contact:* Cris Murray, Assistant Vice President for Graduate Recruitment and Enrollment, 518-485-3390, Fax: 518-458-5479, E-mail: grad@strose.edu. *Dean,* Dr. Richard J. Thompson, Jr., 518-337-4853, E-mail: thompsor@strose.edu.

Thelma P. Lally School of Education Students: 398 full-time (337 women), 923 part-time (731 women); includes 385 minority (186 Black or African American, non-Hispanic/Latino; 4 American Indian or Alaska Native, non-Hispanic/Latino; 37 Asian, non-Hispanic/Latino; 142 Hispanic/Latino; 1 Native Hawaiian or other Pacific Islander, non-Hispanic/Latino; 15 Two or more races, non-Hispanic/Latino), 21 international. Average age 33. 1,023 applicants, 62% accepted, 487 enrolled. *Faculty:* 42 full-time (24 women), 60 part-time/adjunct (36 women). Expenses: Contact institution. *Financial support:* Career-related internships or fieldwork, scholarships/grants, tuition waivers (partial), and unspecified assistantships available. Support available to part-time students. Financial award application deadline: 4/15. In 2016, 347 master's, 610 other advanced degrees awarded. *Program availability:* Part-time, evening/weekend, 100% online. Offers adolescence education (MS Ed, Advanced Certificate); adolescence education and special education (MS Ed); adolescence education/special education (Advanced Certificate); childhood education (MS Ed); childhood education and special education (MS Ed); childhood special education (MS Ed); clinical mental health counseling (Certificate); college student services administration (MS Ed); communication sciences and disorders (MS Ed); curriculum and instruction (MS Ed); early childhood education (MS Ed); early childhood special education (MS Ed); education (MS, MS Ed, Advanced Certificate, Certificate); educational leadership (MS Ed); educational psychology (MS Ed, Certificate); higher education leadership and administration (MS Ed, Advanced Certificate); literacy: birth-grade 6 (MS Ed, Advanced Certificate); literacy: grades 5-12 (MS Ed, Advanced Certificate); school building leader (Certificate); school counseling (MS Ed, Certificate); school district business leader (Certificate); school district leader (Certificate); school psychology (MS Ed); special education (Certificate); special education professional (MS Ed). *Application deadline:* For fall admission, 4/1 priority date for domestic and international students; for spring admission, 10/15 priority date for domestic and international students; for summer admission, 3/15 priority date for domestic and international students. Applications are processed on a rolling basis. *Application fee:* $40. Electronic applications accepted. *Application Contact:* Cris Murray, Assistant Vice President for Graduate Recruitment and Enrollment, 518-454-5136, Fax: 518-458-5479, E-mail: grad@strose.edu. *Dean,* Dr. Margaret McLane, 518-454-2147.

THE COLLEGE OF ST. SCHOLASTICA, Duluth, MN 55811-4199

General Information Independent-religious, coed, comprehensive institution. *Graduate housing:* On-campus housing not available.

GRADUATE UNITS

Graduate Studies *Program availability:* Part-time, evening/weekend, online learning. Offers athletic training (MS); computer information systems (MA, Certificate); education (M Ed, MS, Certificate); exercise physiology (MA); health information management (MA,

Certificate); management (MA, Certificate); nursing (MA, PMC); occupational therapy (MA); physical therapy (DPT); social work (MSW). Electronic applications accepted.

COLLEGE OF STATEN ISLAND OF THE CITY UNIVERSITY OF NEW YORK, Staten Island, NY 10314-6600

General Information State and locally supported, coed, comprehensive institution. *Enrollment:* 13,775 graduate, professional, and undergraduate students; 200 full-time matriculated graduate/professional students (134 women), 686 part-time matriculated graduate/professional students (505 women). *Enrollment by degree level:* 769 master's, 59 doctoral, 58 other advanced degrees. *Graduate faculty:* 84 full-time (48 women), 90 part-time/adjunct (53 women). Tuition, state resident: full-time $10,130; part-time $425 per credit. Tuition, nonresident: full-time $18,720; part-time $780 per credit. *Required fees:* $181.10 per semester. Tuition and fees vary according to program. *Graduate housing:* Room and/or apartments available on a first-come, first-served basis to single students; on-campus housing not available to married students. Typical cost: $13,627 per year ($17,227 including board). Room and board charges vary according to housing facility selected. *Student services:* Career counseling, child daycare facilities, international student services. *Library facilities:* College of Staten Island Library. *Collection:* Books: 261,252 (physical), 457,488 (digital/electronic); Serial titles: 65,800 (physical); Databases: 167. Weekly public service hours: 112; students can reserve study rooms. *Research affiliation:* Alfred P. Sloan Foundation, Craig H. Neilson Foundation, Northfield Bank Foundation, Simons Foundation, Eurasia Foundation, Massachusetts Clean Energy Technology Center (field survey for off shore wind).

Computer facilities: A campuswide network can be accessed from off campus. Online class registration is available.
Website: http://www.csi.cuny.edu/

General Application Contact: Sasha Spence, Associate Director for Graduate Recruitment and Admissions, 718-982-2019, Fax: 718-982-2500, E-mail: sasha.spence@csi.cuny.edu.

GRADUATE UNITS

Graduate Programs Average age 30. Expenses: Contact institution. In 2016, 277 master's, 43 other advanced degrees awarded. *Application Contact:* Sasha Spence, Associate Director for Graduate Admissions, 718-982-2019, Fax: 718-982-2500, E-mail: sasha.spence@csi.cuny.edu. *Provost/Senior Vice President for Academic Affairs,* Dr. Gary Reichard, 718-982-2440, Fax: 718-982-2442, E-mail: provost@csi.cuny.edu.

Division of Humanities and Social Sciences Students: 97 full-time, 115 part-time. Average age 31. *Faculty:* 23 full-time, 18 part-time/adjunct. Expenses: Contact institution. In 2016, 72 master's, 3 other advanced degrees awarded. Offers autism spectrum disorders (Advanced Certificate); cinema and media studies (MA); English (MA); history (MA); history of Africa and the Middle East (MA); history of Asia (MA); history of Europe (MA); history of Latin America and the Caribbean (MA); history of the United States (MA); liberal studies (MA); mental health counseling (MA). *Application Contact:* Sasha Spence, Associate Director for Graduate Admissions, 718-982-2019, Fax: 718-982-2500, E-mail: sasha.spence@csi.cuny.edu. *Dean of Humanities and Social Sciences,* Dr. Nan Sussman, 718-982-2315, Fax: 718-982-2316, E-mail: nan.sussman@csi.cuny.edu.

Division of Science and Technology Students: 11 full-time, 96 part-time. Average age 28. 152 applicants, 47% accepted, 43 enrolled. *Faculty:* 19 full-time, 5 part-time/adjunct. Expenses: Contact institution. In 2016, 39 master's awarded. Offers biology (MS); computer science (MS); environmental science (MS); neuroscience and developmental disabilities (MS). *Application Contact:* Sasha Spence, Associate Director for Graduate Admissions, 718-982-2019, Fax: 718-982-2500, E-mail: sasha.spence@csi.cuny.edu.

School of Business Students: 5 full-time, 53 part-time. Average age 31. 79 applicants, 39% accepted, 26 enrolled. *Faculty:* 7 full-time, 2 part-time/adjunct. Expenses: Contact institution. In 2016, 22 master's awarded. Offers accounting (MS); business (MS, Advanced Certificate); business analytics of large-scale data (Advanced Certificate); business management (MS). *Application Contact:* Sasha Spence, Associate Director for Graduate Admissions, 718-982-2019, Fax: 718-982-2500, E-mail: sasha.spence@csi.cuny.edu. *Dean of School of Business,* Dr. Susan L. Holak, 718-982-2920, Fax: 718-982-3183, E-mail: susan.holak@csi.cuny.edu.

School of Education Students: 32 full-time, 414 part-time. Average age 30. *Faculty:* 25 full-time, 40 part-time/adjunct. Expenses: Contact institution. In 2016, 117 master's, 26 Advanced Certificates awarded. Offers biology (MS Ed); education (MS Ed, Advanced Certificate, Post-Master's Certificate); English (MS Ed); learning and development (MS Ed); literacy education (MS Ed); mathematics (MS Ed); mathematics education (MS Ed); music education (MS Ed); school administrator and supervisor (Post-Master's Certificate); school building leader (Post-Master's Certificate); school district leader (Post-Master's Certificate); science education (MS Ed); social foundations of education (MS Ed); social studies (MS Ed); social studies education (MS Ed); special education (MS Ed); teaching of English to speakers of other languages (MS Ed, Advanced Certificate). *Application Contact:* Sasha Spence, Associate Director for Graduate Admissions, 718-982-2019, Fax: 718-982-2500, E-mail: sasha.spence@csi.cuny.edu.

School of Health Sciences Students: 60 full-time, 61 part-time. Average age 31. 354 applicants, 17% accepted, 53 enrolled. *Faculty:* 10 full-time, 25 part-time/adjunct. Expenses: Contact institution. In 2016, 27 master's, 14 other advanced degrees awarded. Offers clinical nurse specialist (MS, Advanced Certificate); cultural competence (Advanced Certificate); health sciences (MS, MSW, DNP, DPT, Advanced Certificate); nurse practitioner (MS, Advanced Certificate); nursing practice (DNP); physical therapy (DPT); social work (MSW). *Application Contact:* Sasha Spence, Associate Director for Graduate Admissions, 718-982-2019, Fax: 718-982-2500, E-mail: sasha.spence@csi.cuny.edu.

See Display on next page and Close-Up on page 875.

COLLEGE OF THE ATLANTIC, Bar Harbor, ME 04609-1198

General Information Independent, coed, comprehensive institution. *Graduate housing:* Room and/or apartments available to single students; on-campus housing not available to married students. Housing application deadline: 6/1. *Research affiliation:* Acadia National Park, National Park Service (research management, environmental education), Mount Desert Island Biological Laboratory, Jackson Laboratory (genetics), Society for Human Ecology (ecological decision making in society).

GRADUATE UNITS

Program in Human Ecology Offers human ecology (M Phil).

THE COLLEGE OF WILLIAM AND MARY, Williamsburg, VA 23187-8795

General Information State-supported, coed, university. CGS member. *Enrollment:* 8,617 graduate, professional, and undergraduate students; 1,772 full-time matriculated graduate/professional students (868 women), 464 part-time matriculated graduate/professional students (210 women). *Enrollment by degree level:* 1,175 master's, 1,051 doctoral, 6 other advanced degrees. *Graduate faculty:* 698 full-time (283 women), 188 part-time/adjunct (78 women). Tuition, state resident: full-time $9000; part-time $500 per credit hour. Tuition, nonresident: full-time $24,686; part-time $1200 per credit hour. *Required fees:* $5258. One-time fee: $400 full-time. *Graduate housing:* Room and/or apartments available on a first-come, first-served basis to single students; on-campus housing not available to married students. Typical cost: $7680 per year ($9552 including board). Housing application deadline: 2/14. *Student services:* Campus employment opportunities, campus safety program, career counseling, child daycare facilities, exercise/wellness program, free psychological counseling, grant writing training, international student services, low-cost health insurance, multicultural affairs office, services for students with disabilities, teacher training, writing training. *Library facilities:* Earl Gregg Swem Library plus 7 others. *Collection:* Books: 1.3 million (physical), 1.6 million (digital/electronic); Serial titles: 37,434 (physical), 143,090 (digital/electronic); Databases: 505. Weekly public service hours: 107; study areas open 24 hours, 5–7 days a week; students can reserve study rooms. *Research affiliation:* Colonial Williamsburg (archaeology, history), Thomas Jefferson National Accelerator Facility (nuclear physics), Court Records Solutions (law and technology), AidData (global aid flows and development finance), James City County Business and Technology Incubator (economic development), Center for Excellence in Aging and Geriatric Health (public policy, kinesiology).

Computer facilities: Computer purchase and lease plans are available. 400 computers available on campus for general student use. A campuswide network can be accessed from student residence rooms. Online class registration is available.
Website: http://www.wm.edu/

General Application Contact: Evan Davies, Director of Institutional Research, 757-221-2147, Fax: 757-221-2080, E-mail: esdav2@wm.edu.

GRADUATE UNITS

Faculty of Arts and Sciences Students: 364 full-time (140 women), 12 part-time (6 women); includes 47 minority (10 Black or African American, non-Hispanic/Latino; 1 American Indian or Alaska Native, non-Hispanic/Latino; 10 Asian, non-Hispanic/Latino; 15 Hispanic/Latino; 11 Two or more races, non-Hispanic/Latino), 117 international. Average age 26. 703 applicants, 31% accepted, 111 enrolled. *Faculty:* 481 full-time (195 women), 102 part-time/adjunct (43 women). Expenses: Contact institution. *Financial support:* Fellowships, research assistantships, teaching assistantships, career-related internships or fieldwork, Federal Work-Study, institutionally sponsored loans, and unspecified assistantships available. Financial award applicants required to submit FAFSA. In 2016, 83 master's, 33 doctorates awarded. *Program availability:* Part-time. Offers accelerator science (PhD); American studies (MA, PhD); anthropology (MA, PhD); applied mathematics (PhD); applied mechanics (PhD); applied robotics (PhD); applied science (MS); arts and sciences (MA, MPP, MS, PhD); atmospheric and environmental science (PhD); biology (MS); chemistry (MA, MS); computational neuroscience (PhD); computational operations research (MS); computer science (MS, PhD); history (MA, PhD); interface, thin film and surface science (PhD); lasers and optics (PhD); magnetic resonance (PhD); materials science and engineering (PhD); mathematical and computational biology (PhD); medical imaging (PhD); nanotechnology (PhD); neuroscience (PhD); non-destructive evaluation (PhD); physics (MS, PhD); polymer chemistry (PhD); psychological sciences (PhD); public policy (MPP); remote sensing (PhD). *Application fee:* $45. Electronic applications accepted. *Application Contact:* Wanda Carter, Graduate Registrar, 757-221-2467, Fax: 757-221-4874, E-mail: wdcart@wm.edu. *Dean of Graduate Studies and Research,* Dr. Virginia Torczon, 757-221-2468, E-mail: vjtorc@wm.edu.

Raymond A. Mason School of Business Students: 279 full-time (88 women), 300 part-time (101 women); includes 131 minority (59 Black or African American, non-Hispanic/Latino; 2 American Indian or Alaska Native, non-Hispanic/Latino; 24 Asian, non-Hispanic/Latino; 33 Hispanic/Latino; 2 Native Hawaiian or other Pacific Islander, non-Hispanic/Latino; 11 Two or more races, non-Hispanic/Latino), 76 international. Average age 33. 791 applicants, 58% accepted, 275 enrolled. *Faculty:* 62 full-time (20 women), 10 part-time/adjunct (2 women). Expenses: Contact institution. *Financial support:* In 2016–17, 141 students received support. Scholarships/grants and unspecified assistantships available. Financial award applicants required to submit FAFSA. In 2016, 193 master's awarded. *Program availability:* Part-time, evening/weekend, online learning. Offers accounting (M Acc); business (EMBA, M Acc, MBA, MS). *Application deadline:* For fall admission, 11/16 for domestic and international students; for winter admission, 1/18 for domestic and international students; for spring admission, 5/16 for domestic and international students; for summer admission, 7/15 for domestic students. *Application fee:* $100. Electronic applications accepted. *Application Contact:* Amanda K. Barth, Director, Full-time MBA Admissions, 757-221-2944, Fax: 757-221-2958, E-mail: amanda.barth@mason.wm.edu. *Dean,* Dr. Lawrence Pulley, 757-221-2891, Fax: 757-221-2937, E-mail: larry.pulley@mason.wm.edu.

School of Education Students: 201 full-time (147 women), 167 part-time (118 women); includes 80 minority (43 Black or African American, non-Hispanic/Latino; 1 American Indian or Alaska Native, non-Hispanic/Latino; 7 Asian, non-Hispanic/Latino; 19 Hispanic/Latino; 10 Two or more races, non-Hispanic/Latino), 9 international. Average age 33. 432 applicants, 65% accepted, 167 enrolled. *Faculty:* 54 full-time (31 women), 84 part-time/adjunct (57 women). Expenses: Contact institution. *Financial support:* In 2016–17, 140 students received support, including 1 fellowship with full tuition reimbursement available (averaging $20,000 per year), 96 research assistantships (averaging $17,926 per year); career-related internships or fieldwork, scholarships/grants, and unspecified assistantships also available. Financial award application deadline: 1/15; financial award applicants required to submit FAFSA. In 2016, 127 master's, 30 doctorates, 12 other advanced degrees awarded. *Program availability:* Part-time, evening/weekend. Offers addictions counseling (M Ed); community counseling (M Ed); counselor education (PhD); curriculum and educational technology (PhD); curriculum leadership (Ed D, PhD); education (M Ed, MA Ed, Ed D, PhD, Ed S); educational leadership (M Ed); educational policy, planning, and leadership (Ed D, PhD); elementary education (MA Ed); family counseling (M Ed); gifted education (MA Ed); literacy leadership (MA Ed); math specialist (MA Ed); school counseling (M Ed); school psychology (M Ed, Ed S); secondary education (MA Ed); special education (MA Ed). *Application deadline:* For fall admission, 1/15 for domestic and international students; for spring admission, 10/1 for domestic and international students. *Application fee:* $50. Electronic applications accepted. *Application Contact:* Dorothy Smith Osborne, Assistant Dean for Academic Programs and Student Services,

GRADUATE STUDIES

MASTER OF ARTS AND SCIENCES
Accounting (MS)
Biology (MS)
Business Management (MS)
Cinema and Media Studies (MA) Clinical
Mental Health Counseling (MA) Computer
Science (MS)
Education (MSEd)

- Childhood Education
- Adolescence Education
  (Biology, English, Mathematics, or Social Studies)
- Special Education – Childhood
- Special Education – Adolescence Generalist
- Teaching of English to Speakers of Other Languages

Electrical Egineering (ME)
English (MA)
Environmental Science (MS)
History (MA)
Liberal Studies (MA)
Neuroscience and Developmental Disabilities (MS)
Nursing (MS)

- Adult-Gerontological Health Nursing

Social Work (MSW)

POST-MASTER'S
Education

- School District Leader
- School Building Leader and School District Leader
  (Dual Certificate)

Nursing

- Adult-Gerontological Health Nursing

ADVANCED CERTIFICATES
Autism Spectrum Disorders
Bilingual Education
Business Analytics of Large-Scale Data
Cultural Competence
Teaching of English to Speakers of Other Languages

DOCTORAL PROGRAMS
Adult-Gerontological Health Nursing (DNP)
Clinical Doctorate in Physical Therapy (DPT)

The College of Staten Island offers additional Doctoral programs jointly with The Graduate Center, CUNY:
Biochemistry (PhD)
Biology (Specialty in Neuroscience, PhD)
Computer Science (PhD)
Nursing (PhD)
Physics (PhD)
Polymer Chemistry (PhD)

www.csi.cuny.edu/graduatestudies
718.982.2019 • masterit@csi.cuny.edu
2800 Victory Boulevard • Staten Island, NY 10314

THE CITY UNIVERSITY OF NEW YORK
College of Staten Island
CU NY

757-221-2317, E-mail: dsosbo@wm.edu. *Dean*, Dr. Spencer G. Niles, 757-221-2317, E-mail: sgniles@wm.edu.

Virginia Institute of Marine Science Students: 80 full-time (47 women), 3 part-time (2 women); includes 7 minority (1 Black or African American, non-Hispanic/Latino; 2 Asian, non-Hispanic/Latino; 2 Hispanic/Latino; 2 Two or more races, non-Hispanic/Latino), 19 international. Average age 27. 105 applicants, 28% accepted, 21 enrolled. *Faculty:* 63 full-time (20 women). Expenses: Contact institution. *Financial support:* In 2016–17, 56 students received support, including fellowships with full tuition reimbursements available (averaging $25,000 per year), research assistantships with full tuition reimbursements available (averaging $20,452 per year), teaching assistantships with full tuition reimbursements available (averaging $20,452 per year); career-related internships or fieldwork, scholarships/grants, health care benefits, and unspecified assistantships also available. Financial award application deadline: 1/5. In 2016, 11 master's, 6 doctorates awarded. Offers marine science (MS, PhD). *Application deadline:* For fall admission, 1/5 for domestic and international students. *Application fee:* $53. Electronic applications accepted. *Application Contact:* Dr. Linda C. Schaffner, Associate Dean of Academic Studies, 804-684-7105, Fax: 804-684-7881, E-mail: admissions@vims.edu. *Dean/Director,* Dr. John T. Wells, 804-684-7102, Fax: 804-684-7009, E-mail: wells@vims.edu.

William and Mary Law School Students: 654 full-time (351 women), 15 part-time (10 women); includes 76 minority (24 Black or African American, non-Hispanic/Latino; 11 Asian, non-Hispanic/Latino; 27 Hispanic/Latino; 14 Two or more races, non-Hispanic/Latino), 49 international. Average age 25. 4,833 applicants, 38% accepted, 238 enrolled. *Faculty:* 44 full-time (19 women), 41 part-time/adjunct (10 women). Expenses: Contact institution. *Financial support:* In 2016–17, 604 students received support, including 242 fellowships (averaging $4,000 per year), 62 research assistantships (averaging $2,419 per year), 35 teaching assistantships (averaging $5,391 per year); career-related internships or fieldwork, Federal Work-Study, and scholarships/grants also available. Financial award application deadline: 2/15; financial award applicants required to submit FAFSA. In 2016, 33 master's, 178 doctorates awarded. Offers law (LL M, JD). *Application deadline:* For fall admission, 3/1 priority date for domestic and international students. *Application fee:* $50. Electronic applications accepted. *Application Contact:* Faye F. Shealy, Associate Dean for Admission, 757-221-3785, Fax: 757-221-3261, E-mail: ffshea@wm.edu. *Dean/Professor,* Davison M. Douglas, 757-221-3790, Fax: 757-221-3261, E-mail: dmdoug@wm.edu.

COLORADO CHRISTIAN UNIVERSITY, Lakewood, CO 80226

General Information Independent-religious, coed, comprehensive institution. *Graduate housing:* On-campus housing not available.

GRADUATE UNITS

Program in Business Administration *Program availability:* Part-time, evening/weekend, online learning. Offers corporate training (MBA); information security (MA); leadership (MBA); project management (MBA). Electronic applications accepted.

Program in Counseling *Program availability:* Part-time, evening/weekend. Offers counseling (MAC). Electronic applications accepted.

Program in Curriculum and Instruction *Program availability:* Part-time, evening/weekend. Offers corporate education (MACI); early childhood educator (MACI); elementary educator (MACI); instructional technology (MACI); master educator (MACI); online course developer (MACI); online teaching and learning (MACI); special education generalist (MACI). Electronic applications accepted.

THE COLORADO COLLEGE, Colorado Springs, CO 80903-3294

General Information Independent, coed, comprehensive institution. *Graduate housing:* On-campus housing not available.

GRADUATE UNITS

Education Department Offers art teaching (K-12) (MAT); arts and humanities (MAT); elementary education (MAT); elementary school teaching (MAT); English teaching (MAT); foreign language teaching (MAT); integrated natural sciences (MAT); liberal arts (MAT); mathematics teaching (MAT); music teaching (MAT); science teaching (MAT); secondary education (MAT); social studies teaching (MAT); Southwest studies (MAT); teaching (MAT). Electronic applications accepted.

COLORADO MESA UNIVERSITY, Grand Junction, CO 81501-3122

General Information State-supported, coed, comprehensive institution. *Enrollment:* 9,735 graduate, professional, and undergraduate students; 27 full-time matriculated graduate/professional students (14 women), 113 part-time matriculated graduate/professional students (92 women). *Enrollment by degree level:* 87 master's, 30 doctoral, 23 other advanced degrees. *Graduate faculty:* 18 full-time (8 women), 12 part-time/adjunct (5 women). Tuition, state resident: full-time $3582; part-time $398 per credit hour. Tuition, nonresident: full-time $10,080; part-time $1120 per credit hour. *Required fees:* $27.43 per credit hour. Tuition and fees vary according to course load and program. *Graduate housing:* Room and/or apartments available on a first-come, first-served basis to single students; on-campus housing not available to married students. Typical cost: $5850 per year ($10,560 including board). Room and board charges vary according to board plan and housing facility selected. Housing application deadline: 8/1. *Student services:* Campus safety program, child daycare facilities, exercise/wellness program, free psychological counseling, international student services, low-cost health insurance, multicultural affairs office, services for students with disabilities, teacher training. *Library facilities:* John U. Tomlinson Library. *Collection:* Books: 354,788 (physical), 43,611 (digital/electronic). Study areas open 24 hours, 5–7 days a week; students can reserve study rooms.

Computer facilities: 525 computers available on campus for general student use. A campuswide network can be accessed from student residence rooms and from off campus. Online class registration is available. Website: http://www.coloradomesa.edu/

General Application Contact: Office of Graduate Studies, 970-248-1020.

GRADUATE UNITS

Center for Teacher Education Students: 18 full-time (13 women), 35 part-time (28 women); includes 4 minority (1 American Indian or Alaska Native, non-Hispanic/Latino; 3 Hispanic/Latino), 1 international. Average age 34. 28 applicants, 25% accepted, 6 enrolled. *Faculty:* 6 full-time (5 women), 12 part-time/adjunct (6 women). Expenses: Contact institution. *Financial support:* In 2016–17, 2 students received support. Scholarships/grants available. Financial award applicants required to submit FAFSA. In 2016, 26 master's, 36 other advanced degrees awarded. *Program availability:* Part-time. Offers educational leadership (MAEd); English for speakers of other languages (MAEd); exceptional learner/special education (MAEd); teacher education (Graduate Certificate); teacher leader (MAEd). *Application deadline:* For fall admission, 6/1 priority date for domestic and international students; for spring admission, 11/1 priority date for domestic and international students; for summer admission, 3/1 priority date for domestic and international students. Applications are processed on a rolling basis. *Application fee:*

$50. Electronic applications accepted. *Application Contact:* Mary Kienietz, Administrative Assistant, 970-248-1786, E-mail: mkieniet@coloradomesa.edu. *Department Head,* Dr. Blake Bickham, 970-248-1729, E-mail: bbickham@coloradomesa.edu.

Department of Business Students: 8 full-time (0 women), 18 part-time (11 women); includes 5 minority (4 Hispanic/Latino; 1 Native Hawaiian or other Pacific Islander, non-Hispanic/Latino), 3 international. Average age 27. 30 applicants, 43% accepted, 9 enrolled. *Faculty:* 12 full-time (1 woman), 1 part-time/adjunct (0 women). Expenses: Contact institution. *Financial support:* In 2016–17, 4 students received support. Scholarships/grants available. Financial award applicants required to submit FAFSA. In 2016, 10 master's awarded. *Program availability:* Part-time, evening/weekend. Offers business (MBA). *Application deadline:* For fall admission, 4/1 priority date for domestic and international students; for spring admission, 10/1 priority date for domestic and international students. Applications are processed on a rolling basis. *Application fee:* $50. Electronic applications accepted. *Application Contact:* Jane Sandoval, MBA Coordinator, 970-248-1778, Fax: 970-248-1730, E-mail: jsandova@coloradomesa.edu. *Department Head,* Dr. Steven Norman, 970-248-1944, Fax: 970-248-1730, E-mail: snorman@coloradomesa.edu.

Department of Health Sciences Students: 3 full-time (all women), 39 part-time (35 women); includes 6 minority (1 American Indian or Alaska Native, non-Hispanic/Latino; 3 Asian, non-Hispanic/Latino; 1 Hispanic/Latino; 1 Two or more races, non-Hispanic/Latino), 1 international. Average age 38. 35 applicants, 34% accepted, 6 enrolled. *Faculty:* 6 full-time (all women), 2 part-time/adjunct (0 women). Expenses: Contact institution. *Financial support:* In 2016–17, 1 student received support. Scholarships/grants available. Financial award applicants required to submit FAFSA. In 2016, 3 master's, 6 doctorates, 1 other advanced degree awarded. *Program availability:* Part-time, evening/weekend, 100% online, blended/hybrid learning. Offers advanced nursing practice (MSN); family nurse practitioner (DNP); health information technology systems (Graduate Certificate); nursing education (MSN). *Application deadline:* For fall admission, 4/1 for domestic and international students; for spring admission, 11/1 for domestic and international students. Applications are processed on a rolling basis. *Application fee:* $50. Electronic applications accepted. *Application Contact:* Renae Phillips, Professional Staff Assistant, 970-248-1235, E-mail: rdphilli@coloradomesa.edu. *Director,* Dr. Debra Bailey, 970-248-1772, E-mail: dbailey@coloradomesa.edu.

COLORADO SCHOOL OF MINES, Golden, CO 80401-1887

General Information State-supported, coed, university. CGS member. *Enrollment:* 5,876 graduate, professional, and undergraduate students; 1,077 full-time matriculated graduate/professional students (318 women), 150 part-time matriculated graduate/professional students (34 women). *Enrollment by degree level:* 684 master's, 543 doctoral. *Graduate faculty:* 404 full-time (121 women), 194 part-time/adjunct (54 women). Tuition, state resident: full-time $15,690. Tuition, nonresident: full-time $34,020. *Required fees:* $2152. Tuition and fees vary according to course load. *Graduate housing:* Rooms and/or apartments available on a first-come, first-served basis to single and married students. Typical cost: $8712 per year for single students; $8712 per year for married students. Room charges vary according to campus/location and housing facility selected. Housing application deadline: 6/1. *Student services:* Campus employment opportunities, campus safety program, career counseling, exercise/wellness program, free psychological counseling, international student services, low-cost health insurance, multicultural affairs office, services for students with disabilities, teacher training, writing training. *Library facilities:* Arthur Lakes Library. *Collection:* Books: 503,801 (physical), 134,211 (digital/electronic); Serial titles: 578 (physical), 104,424 (digital/electronic); Databases: 128. Weekly public service hours: 107; students can reserve study rooms.

Computer facilities: Computer purchase and lease plans are available. 1,000 computers available on campus for general student use. A campuswide network can be accessed from student residence rooms and from off campus. Online class registration is available. Website: http://www.mines.edu/

General Application Contact: Angel Dotson, Graduate Admissions Coordinator, 303-273-3348, E-mail: grad-app@mines.edu.

GRADUATE UNITS

Office of Graduate Studies Students: 1,162 full-time (338 women), 159 part-time (44 women); includes 150 minority (10 Black or African American, non-Hispanic/Latino; 3 American Indian or Alaska Native, non-Hispanic/Latino; 33 Asian, non-Hispanic/Latino; 76 Hispanic/Latino; 1 Native Hawaiian or other Pacific Islander, non-Hispanic/Latino; 27 Two or more races, non-Hispanic/Latino), 409 international. Average age 28. 2,204 applicants, 44% accepted, 394 enrolled. *Faculty:* 408 full-time (119 women), 192 part-time/adjunct (68 women). Expenses: Contact institution. *Financial support:* In 2016–17, 63 fellowships with full tuition reimbursements, 486 research assistantships with full tuition reimbursements, 154 teaching assistantships with full tuition reimbursements were awarded; career-related internships or fieldwork, Federal Work-Study, institutionally sponsored loans, scholarships/grants, health care benefits, and unspecified assistantships also available. Financial award application deadline: 12/15; financial award applicants required to submit FAFSA. In 2016, 388 master's, 115 doctorates awarded. *Program availability:* Part-time. Offers applied physics (MS, PhD); chemical and biological engineering (MS, PhD); chemistry (MS, PhD); civil and environmental engineering (MS, PhD); computer science (MS, PhD); electrical engineering (MS, PhD); engineering and technology management (MS); environmental engineering science (MS, PhD); geochemistry (MS, PMS, PhD); geological engineering (ME, MS, PhD); geology (MS, PhD); geophysical engineering (ME, MS, PhD); geophysics (MS, PhD); hydrology (MS, PhD); international political economy (Graduate Certificate); materials science (MS, PhD); mechanical engineering (MS, PhD); metallurgical and materials engineering (ME, MS, PhD); mineral economics (PhD); mineral exploration and mining geosciences (PMS); mining and earth systems engineering (MS); mining engineering (PhD); nuclear engineering (ME, MS, PhD); operations research and engineering (PhD); petroleum engineering (ME, MS, PhD); petroleum reservoir systems (PMS); science and technology policy (Graduate Certificate); underground construction and tunneling (MS, PhD). *Application deadline:* For fall admission, 12/15 priority date for domestic and international students; for spring admission, 9/1 priority date for domestic and international students. *Application fee:* $50 ($70 for international students). Electronic applications accepted. *Application Contact:* Angel Dotson, Graduate Admissions Coordinator, 303-273-3348, Fax: 303-273-3247, E-mail: grad-app@mines.edu. *Dean of Graduate Studies,* Dr. Tina Voelker, 303-273-3152, E-mail: bvoelker@mines.edu.

See Display below and Close-Up on page 877.

COLORADO SCHOOL OF TRADITIONAL CHINESE MEDICINE, Denver, CO 80206-2127

General Information Independent, coed, graduate-only institution. *Enrollment by degree level:* 100 master's. *Graduate faculty:* 52 part-time/adjunct (20 women). *Tuition:* Full-time $17,000; part-time $9000 per year. *Required fees:* $450; $1020 per unit. $340 per trimester. Part-time tuition and fees vary according to course load and program.

COLORADO SCHOOL OF MINES
GRADUATE SCHOOL

Colorado School of Traditional Chinese Medicine

Graduate housing: On-campus housing not available. *Student services:* Campus employment opportunities, exercise/wellness program. *Library facilities:* CSTCM Library. *Collection:* Books: 8,000 (physical), 200 (digital/electronic).

Computer facilities: 4 computers available on campus for general student use. X available. Website: http://www.cstcm.edu/

General Application Contact: Chris Duxbury-Edwards, Recruiting Director, 303-329-6355 Ext. 21, Fax: 303-388-8165, E-mail: recruiting@cstcm.edu.

GRADUATE UNITS

Graduate Programs Students: 100 full-time (75 women). Average age 33. 43 applicants, 58% accepted, 19 enrolled. *Faculty:* 52 part-time/adjunct (20 women). Expenses: Contact institution. *Financial support:* Scholarships/grants available. Financial award applicants required to submit FAFSA. In 2016, 1 master's awarded. *Program availability:* Part-time. Offers acupuncture (MS); traditional Chinese medicine (MS). *Application deadline:* For fall admission, 8/19 for domestic and international students; for winter admission, 12/23 for domestic and international students; for summer admission, 4/22 for domestic and international students. Applications are processed on a rolling basis. *Application fee:* $50. *Application Contact:* Chris Duxbury-Edwards, Recruiting Director, 303-329-6355 Ext. 21, Fax: 303-388-8165, E-mail: recruiting@cstcm.edu. *Administrative Director,* Vladimir Dibrigida, 303-329-6355 Ext. 11, Fax: 303-388-8165, E-mail: director@cstcm.edu.

COLORADO STATE UNIVERSITY, Fort Collins, CO 80523

General Information State-supported, coed, university. CGS member. *Enrollment:* 33,058 graduate, professional, and undergraduate students; 2,795 full-time matriculated graduate/professional students (1,696 women), 4,020 part-time matriculated graduate/professional students (1,842 women). *Enrollment by degree level:* 4,501 master's, 2,266 doctoral, 48 other advanced degrees. *Graduate faculty:* 1,057 full-time (425 women), 249 part-time/adjunct (124 women). Tuition, state resident: full-time $9628. Tuition, nonresident: full-time $23,603. *Required fees:* $2253; $528.14 per credit hour. $264.07 per semester. Tuition and fees vary according to course load and program. *Graduate housing:* Rooms and/or apartments available on a first-come, first-served basis to single and married students. Typical cost: $5416 per year ($11,110 including board) for single students. Room and board charges vary according to board plan and housing facility selected. *Student services:* Campus employment opportunities, campus safety program, career counseling, child daycare facilities, exercise/wellness program, free psychological counseling, grant writing training, international student services, low-cost health insurance, multicultural affairs office, services for students with disabilities, teacher training, writing training. *Library facilities:* William E. Morgan Library plus 2 others. *Collection:* Books: 1.2 million (physical), 534,252 (digital/electronic); Serial titles: 53,973 (physical), 84,523 (digital/electronic); Databases: 343. Weekly public service hours: 108; study areas open 24 hours, 5–7 days a week; students can reserve study rooms. *Research affiliation:* U.S. Department of Commerce/National Oceanic and Atmospheric Administration (NOAA) Joint Institutes (meteorological satellite imagery), Natural Resources Research Center/Agencies of U.S. Departments of Agriculture (USDA) and Interior (infectious disease), National Center for Genetic Resources Preservation (genetic resources of crops), National Wildlife Research Center (interactions of wild animals and society), National Centers for Atmospheric Research (climate, meteorology), Solix (algae-produced biofuels).

Computer facilities: Computer purchase and lease plans are available. 1,700 computers available on campus for general student use. A campuswide network can be accessed from student residence rooms and from off campus. Online class registration, personalized portal services including transcripts and financials (billing, financial aid) are available. Website: http://www.colostate.edu/

General Application Contact: Sandra Dailey, Academic Progress and Special Admissions Coordinator, Graduate School, 970-491-6817, Fax: 970-491-2194, E-mail: gradschool@colostate.edu.

GRADUATE UNITS

College of Agricultural Sciences Students: 116 full-time (67 women), 223 part-time (131 women); includes 28 minority (2 Black or African American, non-Hispanic/Latino; 1 American Indian or Alaska Native, non-Hispanic/Latino; 15 Hispanic/Latino; 10 Two or more races, non-Hispanic/Latino), 63 international. Average age 32. 189 applicants, 61% accepted, 63 enrolled. *Faculty:* 92 full-time (26 women), 10 part-time/adjunct (6 women). Expenses: Contact institution. *Financial support:* In 2016–17, 14 fellowships with full tuition reimbursements (averaging $42,047 per year), 98 research assistantships with tuition reimbursements (averaging $18,965 per year), 36 teaching assistantships (averaging $16,089 per year) were awarded; Federal Work-Study, scholarships/grants, tuition waivers, and unspecified assistantships also available. Financial award application deadline: 1/15; financial award applicants required to submit FAFSA. In 2016, 79 master's, 20 doctorates awarded. *Program availability:* Part-time, evening/weekend, 100% online, blended/hybrid learning. Offers agricultural and resource economics (MS, PhD); agricultural sciences (M Agr, MAEE, MLA, MS, PhD); animal sciences (MS, PhD); entomology (MS, PhD); horticulture and landscape architecture (MLA, MS, PhD); pest management (MS); plant pathology (MS, PhD); soil and crop sciences (MS, PhD); weed science (MS, PhD). *Application fee:* $60 ($70 for international students). Electronic applications accepted. *Application Contact:* Pam Schell, Administrative Assistant, 970-491-2410, Fax: 970-491-4895, E-mail: pam.schell@colostate.edu. *Dean,* Dr. Ajay Menon, 970-491-6274, Fax: 970-491-4895, E-mail: ajay.menon@colostate.edu.

College of Business Students: 241 full-time (104 women), 931 part-time (301 women); includes 210 minority (31 Black or African American, non-Hispanic/Latino; 6 American Indian or Alaska Native, non-Hispanic/Latino; 65 Asian, non-Hispanic/Latino; 79 Hispanic/Latino; 3 Native Hawaiian or other Pacific Islander, non-Hispanic/Latino; 26 Two or more races, non-Hispanic/Latino), 137 international. Average age 35. 661 applicants, 79% accepted, 378 enrolled. *Faculty:* 39 full-time (7 women), 13 part-time/adjunct (4 women). Expenses: Contact institution. *Financial support:* Career-related internships or fieldwork, scholarships/grants, and unspecified assistantships available. Financial award application deadline: 2/15; financial award applicants required to submit FAFSA. In 2016, 540 master's awarded. *Program availability:* Part-time, evening/weekend, 100% online, blended/hybrid learning. Offers accounting (M Acc); business (M Acc, M Fin, MBA, MCIS); business administration (MBA); computer information systems (MCIS); finance (M Fin); global social and sustainable enterprise (MBA); taxation (M Acc). *Application fee:* $60 ($70 for international students). Electronic applications accepted. *Application Contact:* Graduate Programs Admissions Contact, 970-491-4622, E-mail: cobgradinfo@colostate.edu. *Dean,* Dr. Beth Walker, 970-491-6471, E-mail: beth.walker@colostate.edu.

College of Health and Human Sciences Students: 416 full-time (323 women), 715 part-time (491 women); includes 209 minority (35 Black or African American, non-Hispanic/Latino; 3 American Indian or Alaska Native, non-Hispanic/Latino; 27 Asian, non-Hispanic/Latino; 114 Two or more races, non-Hispanic/Latino; 30 Two or more races, non-Hispanic/Latino),

52 international. Average age 34. 1,346 applicants, 30% accepted, 298 enrolled. *Faculty:* 104 full-time (73 women), 43 part-time/adjunct (26 women). Expenses: Contact institution. *Financial support:* In 2016–17, 3 fellowships with full tuition reimbursements (averaging $45,989 per year), 58 research assistantships with tuition reimbursements (averaging $14,525 per year), 59 teaching assistantships with tuition reimbursements (averaging $12,197 per year) were awarded; Federal Work-Study, scholarships/grants, and unspecified assistantships also available. Financial award application deadline: 1/15; financial award applicants required to submit FAFSA. In 2016, 338 master's, 41 doctorates awarded. *Program availability:* Part-time, evening/weekend, 100% online, blended/hybrid learning. Offers apparel and merchandising (MS); applied developmental science (PhD); construction management (MS); dietetics (MS); exercise science and nutrition (MS); family and developmental studies (MS); food science and human nutrition (PhD); food science and nutrition (MS); health and exercise science (MS); health and human sciences (M Ed, MOT, MS, MSW, PhD); human bioenergetics (PhD); interior design (MS); marriage and family therapy (MS); nutrition and exercise science (MS); occupational therapy (MOT, MS, PhD). *Application fee:* $60 ($70 for international students). Electronic applications accepted. *Application Contact:* Patricia Davies, Associate Dean for Research and Graduate Programs, 970-491-7294, Fax: 970-491-7859, E-mail: patricia.davies@colostate.edu. *Dean,* Dr. Jeff McCubbin, 970-491-6331, Fax: 970-491-7859, E-mail: jeff.mccubbin@colostate.edu.

School of Education Students: 80 full-time (56 women), 541 part-time (353 women); includes 142 minority (26 Black or African American, non-Hispanic/Latino; 2 American Indian or Alaska Native, non-Hispanic/Latino; 22 Asian, non-Hispanic/Latino; 71 Hispanic/Latino; 21 Two or more races, non-Hispanic/Latino), 18 international. Average age 37. 483 applicants, 31% accepted, 137 enrolled. *Faculty:* 29 full-time (21 women), 23 part-time/adjunct (11 women). Expenses: Contact institution. *Financial support:* In 2016–17, 3 students received support, including 7 research assistantships with full tuition reimbursements available (averaging $11,749 per year), 5 teaching assistantships with full tuition reimbursements available (averaging $15,886 per year); fellowships with full tuition reimbursements available, scholarships/grants, and unspecified assistantships also available. Financial award application deadline: 3/1; financial award applicants required to submit FAFSA. In 2016, 183 master's, 33 doctorates awarded. *Program availability:* Part-time, online only, 100% online, blended/hybrid learning, face-to-face off-campus courses. Offers adult education and training (M Ed); counseling and career development (M Ed); education sciences (PhD); higher education leadership (PhD); organization learning, performance, and change (PhD); organizational learning, performance, and change (M Ed); student affairs in higher education (MS); teaching and learning (M Ed). *Application deadline:* Applications are processed on a rolling basis. *Application fee:* $60 ($70 for international students). Electronic applications accepted. *Application Contact:* Kelli Clark, Graduate Programs Coordinator, 970-491-2093, Fax: 970-491-1317, E-mail: kelli.clark@colostate.edu. *Co-Director,* Dr. Louise Jennings, 970-491-6317, Fax: 970-491-1317, E-mail: louise.jennings@colostate.edu.

School of Social Work Students: 77 full-time (64 women), 75 part-time (64 women); includes 32 minority (8 Black or African American, non-Hispanic/Latino; 1 American Indian or Alaska Native, non-Hispanic/Latino; 21 Hispanic/Latino; 2 Two or more races, non-Hispanic/Latino), 4 international. Average age 32. 64 applicants, 98% accepted, 31 enrolled. *Faculty:* 6 full-time (5 women), 12 part-time/adjunct (10 women). Expenses: Contact institution. *Financial support:* In 2016–17, 7 students received support, including 2 research assistantships with partial tuition reimbursements available (averaging $20,976 per year), 1 teaching assistantship with partial tuition reimbursement available (averaging $6,966 per year); fellowships with partial tuition reimbursements available, scholarships/grants, and unspecified assistantships also available. Financial award application deadline: 3/1; financial award applicants required to submit FAFSA. In 2016, 54 master's, 8 doctorates awarded. *Program availability:* Part-time, evening/weekend, 100% online, blended/hybrid learning. Offers social work (MSW, PhD). *Application deadline:* For fall admission, 12/31 for domestic and international students; for spring admission, 5/31 for domestic and international students; for summer admission, 12/31 for domestic and international students. *Application fee:* $60 ($70 for international students). Electronic applications accepted. *Application Contact:* Timothy Frank, Graduate Program Coordinator, 970-491-2536, Fax: 970-491-7280, E-mail: timothy.frank@colostate.edu. *Director,* Dr. Audrey Shillington, 970-491-2378, Fax: 970-491-7280, E-mail: audrey.shillington@colostate.edu.

College of Liberal Arts Students: 338 full-time (212 women), 350 part-time (235 women); includes 83 minority (11 Black or African American, non-Hispanic/Latino; 5 American Indian or Alaska Native, non-Hispanic/Latino; 14 Asian, non-Hispanic/Latino; 39 Hispanic/Latino; 14 Two or more races, non-Hispanic/Latino), 79 international. Average age 30. 669 applicants, 57% accepted, 211 enrolled. *Faculty:* 163 full-time (79 women), 48 part-time/adjunct (37 women). Expenses: Contact institution. *Financial support:* In 2016–17, 5 research assistantships with tuition reimbursements (averaging $17,455 per year), 253 teaching assistantships with tuition reimbursements (averaging $14,063 per year) were awarded; career-related internships or fieldwork, Federal Work-Study, scholarships/grants, and unspecified assistantships also available. Support available to part-time students. Financial award application deadline: 1/15; financial award applicants required to submit FAFSA. In 2016, 191 master's, 7 doctorates awarded. *Program availability:* Part-time. Offers anthropology of health and well-being (MA); communication (PhD); communication studies (MA); communications and media management (MCMM); creative nonfiction (MA); creative writing (MFA); economics (MA, PhD); environmental politics and policy (PhD); ethnic studies (MA); French (MA); German (MA); humans and the environment (MA); international development (MA); liberal arts (MA, MALCM, MCMM, MFA, MM, MS, PhD); literature (MA); philosophy (MA); political science (MA); professional methods and techniques (MA); public communication and technology (MS, PhD); public history (MA); rhetoric and composition (MA); sociology (MA); Spanish (MA); studio art (MFA); TESL/TEFL (MA). *Application fee:* $60 ($70 for international students). Electronic applications accepted. *Application Contact:* Dr. Bruce Ronda, Associate Dean for Faculty and Graduate Studies, 970-491-5421, Fax: 970-491-0528, E-mail: bruce.ronda@colostate.edu. *Dean,* Dr. Ben Withers, 970-491-5421, Fax: 970-491-0528, E-mail: ben.withers@colostate.edu.

LEAP Institute for the Arts Students: 7 part-time (6 women); includes 1 minority (Black or African American, non-Hispanic/Latino). Average age 31. 4 applicants, 100% accepted, 3 enrolled. Expenses: Contact institution. *Financial support:* In 2016–17, 3 students received support. Fellowships, research assistantships, teaching assistantships, career-related internships or fieldwork, scholarships/grants, and tuition waivers available. Financial award application deadline: 3/1; financial award applicants required to submit FAFSA. *Program availability:* Part-time, evening/weekend, 100% online. Offers leadership, entrepreneurship, arts advocacy and the public (MALCM). *Application deadline:* For fall admission, 4/15 for domestic and international students; for spring admission, 9/15 for domestic and international students; for summer admission, 2/15 for domestic and international students.

Applications are processed on a rolling basis. *Application fee:* $60 ($70 for international students). Electronic applications accepted. *Application Contact:* Dulcie Willis, Coordinator, 970-491-3746, E-mail: dulcie.willis@colostate.edu. *Director,* Dr. Constance DeVereaux, 970-491-3902, E-mail: constance.devereaux@colostate.edu.

School of Music, Theatre and Dance Students: 54 full-time (31 women), 100 part-time (77 women); includes 16 minority (2 Black or African American, non-Hispanic/Latino; 4 Asian, non-Hispanic/Latino; 8 Hispanic/Latino; 2 Two or more races, non-Hispanic/Latino), 13 international. Average age 30. 77 applicants, 79% accepted, 43 enrolled. *Faculty:* 25 full-time (7 women), 9 part-time/adjunct (5 women). Expenses: Contact institution. *Financial support:* In 2016–17, 25 students received support, including 24 teaching assistantships with full and partial tuition reimbursements available (averaging $8,998 per year); research assistantships, scholarships/grants, traineeships, and unspecified assistantships also available. Financial award application deadline: 2/15; financial award applicants required to submit FAFSA. In 2016, 69 master's awarded. *Program availability:* Part-time. Offers choral conducting (MM); collaborative piano (MM); instrumental conducting (MM); music education (MM); music performance (MM); music therapy (MM). *Application deadline:* For fall admission, 2/15 for domestic and international students. Applications are processed on a rolling basis. *Application fee:* $60 ($70 for international students). Electronic applications accepted. *Application Contact:* Dr. G. Murray Oliver, Graduate Program Coordinator, 970-491-5193, Fax: 970-491-7541, E-mail: murray.oliver@colostate.edu. *Director,* Dr. Daniel Goble, 970-491-5529, E-mail: dan.goble@colostate.edu.

College of Natural Sciences Students: 319 full-time (134 women), 539 part-time (211 women); includes 105 minority (6 Black or African American, non-Hispanic/Latino; 1 American Indian or Alaska Native, non-Hispanic/Latino; 32 Asian, non-Hispanic/Latino; 44 Hispanic/Latino; 22 Two or more races, non-Hispanic/Latino), 149 international. Average age 29. 508 applicants, 65% accepted, 241 enrolled. *Faculty:* 194 full-time (74 women), 25 part-time/adjunct (10 women). Expenses: Contact institution. *Financial support:* In 2016–17, 49 fellowships (averaging $44,497 per year), 186 research assistantships with full and partial tuition reimbursements (averaging $22,020 per year), 362 teaching assistantships with full and partial tuition reimbursements (averaging $19,006 per year) were awarded; scholarships/grants also available. Financial award application deadline: 2/15; financial award applicants required to submit FAFSA. In 2016, 146 master's, 63 doctorates awarded. *Program availability:* Part-time, 100% online. Offers biochemistry and molecular biology (MS, PhD); botany (MS, PhD); chemistry (MS, PhD); computer science (MCS, MS, PhD); mathematics (MS, PhD); natural sciences (MAIOP, MAS, MCS, MS, PhD); physics (MS, PhD); psychology (PhD); statistics (MAS, MS, PhD); zoology (MS, PhD). *Application fee:* $60 ($70 for international students). Electronic applications accepted. *Application Contact:* Dr. Simon Tavener, Associate Dean for Academics, 970-491-1300, Fax: 970-491-6639, E-mail: cns@colostate.edu. *Dean,* Dr. Janice Nerger, 970-491-1300, Fax: 970-491-6639, E-mail: janice.nerger@colostate.edu.

College of Veterinary Medicine and Biomedical Sciences Students: 847 full-time (650 women), 179 part-time (118 women); includes 189 minority (8 Black or African American, non-Hispanic/Latino; 4 American Indian or Alaska Native, non-Hispanic/Latino; 53 Asian, non-Hispanic/Latino; 84 Hispanic/Latino; 40 Two or more races, non-Hispanic/Latino), 58 international. Average age 28. 1,552 applicants, 29% accepted, 351 enrolled. *Faculty:* 230 full-time (111 women), 35 part-time/adjunct (20 women). Expenses: Contact institution. *Financial support:* In 2016–17, 94 research assistantships with tuition reimbursements (averaging $21,923 per year), 15 teaching assistantships with tuition reimbursements (averaging $18,206 per year) were awarded; fellowships with full tuition reimbursements, scholarships/grants, traineeships, and unspecified assistantships also available. Financial award application deadline: 2/15; financial award applicants required to submit FAFSA. In 2016, 152 master's, 20 doctorates awarded. Offers biomedical sciences (PhD); clinical sciences (MS, PhD); environmental health (MS, PhD); microbiology, immunology and pathology (MS, PhD); pathology (PhD); radiological health sciences (MS, PhD); reproductive technology (MS); toxicology (MS, PhD); veterinary medicine (DVM); veterinary medicine and biomedical sciences (MS, DVM, PhD). *Application fee:* $60 ($70 for international students). Electronic applications accepted. *Application Contact:* Graduate Program Coordinator. *Dean,* Dr. Mark Stetter, 970-491-7051, E-mail: mark.stetter@colostate.edu.

Interdisciplinary College Students: 69 full-time (49 women), 137 part-time (73 women); includes 23 minority (3 Black or African American, non-Hispanic/Latino; 7 Asian, non-Hispanic/Latino; 8 Hispanic/Latino; 5 Two or more races, non-Hispanic/Latino), 36 international. Average age 31. 186 applicants, 22% accepted, 31 enrolled. Expenses: Contact institution. In 2016, 28 master's, 32 doctorates awarded. Offers cancer biology (PhD); cell and molecular biology (MS); ecological risk assessment and management (MS, PhD); human-environment interactions (MS, PhD); molecular, cellular and integrative neurosciences (PhD). *Application fee:* $60 ($70 for international students). Electronic applications accepted. *Application Contact:* Sandra Dailey, Graduate School Academic Progress and Special Admissions Coordinator, 970-491-6817, Fax: 970-491-2194, E-mail: gradschool@colostate.edu.

Walter Scott, Jr. College of Engineering Students: 333 full-time (88 women), 662 part-time (148 women); includes 94 minority (11 Black or African American, non-Hispanic/Latino; 1 American Indian or Alaska Native, non-Hispanic/Latino; 35 Asian, non-Hispanic/Latino; 33 Hispanic/Latino; 14 Two or more races, non-Hispanic/Latino), 388 international. Average age 30. 875 applicants, 66% accepted, 255 enrolled. *Faculty:* 170 full-time (37 women), 45 part-time/adjunct (11 women). Expenses: Contact institution. *Financial support:* In 2016–17, 30 fellowships with full tuition reimbursements (averaging $45,899 per year), 234 research assistantships with tuition reimbursements (averaging $24,506 per year), 65 teaching assistantships with tuition reimbursements (averaging $16,723 per year) were awarded; scholarships/grants, traineeships, health care benefits, and unspecified assistantships also available. Financial award application deadline: 1/15; financial award applicants required to submit FAFSA. In 2016, 203 master's, 50 doctorates awarded. *Program availability:* Part-time, evening/weekend, 100% online, blended/hybrid learning. Offers atmospheric science (MS, PhD); chemical engineering (ME, MS, PhD); civil and environmental engineering (MS, PhD); civil engineering (ME); computer engineering (ME, MS, PhD); electrical engineering (ME, MS, PhD); engineering (ME, MS, PhD); industrial engineering (PhD); mechanical engineering (ME, MS, PhD); systems engineering (ME, MS, PhD). *Application fee:* $60 ($70 for international students). Electronic applications accepted. *Application Contact:* Dr. Anthony Marchese, Associate Dean of Academic and Student Affairs, 970-491-6226, Fax: 970-491-3429, E-mail: anthony.marchese@colostate.edu. *Dean,* Dr. David McLean, 970-491-3366, E-mail: david.mclean@colostate.edu.

School of Biomedical Engineering Students: 15 full-time (6 women), 20 part-time (11 women); includes 4 minority (2 Asian, non-Hispanic/Latino; 2 Hispanic/Latino), 6 international. Average age 27. 52 applicants, 17% accepted, 7 enrolled. *Faculty:* 1 (woman) part-time/adjunct. Expenses: Contact institution. *Financial support:* In 2016–17, 18 students received support, including 17 research assistantships with full tuition reimbursements available (averaging $23,940 per year), 2 teaching assistantships

with full tuition reimbursements available (averaging $18,000 per year); unspecified assistantships also available. Financial award application deadline: 1/15; financial award applicants required to submit FAFSA. In 2016, 2 master's, 3 doctorates awarded. *Program availability:* Part-time, evening/weekend, 100% online. Offers bioengineering (MS, PhD); biomedical engineering (ME). *Application deadline:* For fall admission, 1/15 priority date for domestic and international students; for spring admission, 9/1 priority date for domestic and international students. *Application fee:* $60 ($70 for international students). Electronic applications accepted. *Application Contact:* Sara Mattern, Graduate Academic Adviser, 970-491-7157, Fax: 970-491-5569, E-mail: sara.mattern@colostate.edu. *Director and Professor,* Dr. Stu Tobet, 970-491-7157, Fax: 970-491-5569, E-mail: stuart.tobet@colostate.edu.

Warner College of Natural Resources Students: 116 full-time (69 women), 284 part-time (134 women); includes 50 minority (7 Black or African American, non-Hispanic/Latino; 3 American Indian or Alaska Native, non-Hispanic/Latino; 2 Asian, non-Hispanic/Latino; 28 Hispanic/Latino; 10 Two or more races, non-Hispanic/Latino), 37 international. Average age 30. 307 applicants, 61% accepted, 155 enrolled. *Faculty:* 65 full-time (18 women), 30 part-time/adjunct (10 women). Expenses: Contact institution. *Financial support:* In 2016–17, 50 fellowships with full and partial tuition reimbursements (averaging $47,291 per year), 81 research assistantships with full and partial tuition reimbursements (averaging $24,042 per year), 41 teaching assistantships with full and partial tuition reimbursements (averaging $13,982 per year) were awarded; career-related internships or fieldwork, Federal Work-Study, scholarships/grants, and unspecified assistantships also available. Financial award application deadline: 2/15; financial award applicants required to submit FAFSA. In 2016, 97 master's, 16 doctorates awarded. *Program availability:* Part-time, evening/weekend, 100% online, blended/hybrid learning. Offers conservation leadership (MS); earth sciences (PhD); ecological restoration (MNRS); fish, wildlife, and conservation biology (MFWCB, MS, PhD); forest sciences (MNRS, MS, PhD); greenhouse gas management and accounting (MGMA); human dimensions of natural resources (MS, PhD); natural resources (MFWCB, MGMA, MNRS, MS, MTM, PhD); rangeland ecosystem science (MS, PhD); rangeland ecosystems (MNRS); sustainable military lands management (MNRS); tourism management (MTM); watershed science (MS). *Application fee:* $60 ($70 for international students). Electronic applications accepted. *Application Contact:* Dr. Rich Conant, Associate Dean for Academic Affairs, 970-491-1919, Fax: 970-491-0279, E-mail: conant@nrel.colostate.edu. *Dean and Professor,* John P. Hayes, 970-491-6675, Fax: 970-491-0279, E-mail: wcnr_deans_office@mail.colostate.edu.

COLORADO STATE UNIVERSITY–GLOBAL CAMPUS, Greenwood Village, CO 80111
General Information State-supported, coed, comprehensive institution.
GRADUATE UNITS
Graduate Programs *Program availability:* Online learning.

COLORADO STATE UNIVERSITY–PUEBLO, Pueblo, CO 81001-4901
General Information State-supported, coed, comprehensive institution. *Graduate housing:* Room and/or apartments available on a first-come, first-served basis to single students; on-campus housing not available to married students. Housing application deadline: 8/1.
GRADUATE UNITS
College of Education, Engineering and Professional Studies *Program availability:* Part-time, evening/weekend. Offers art education (M Ed); education, engineering and professional studies (M Ed, MS); foreign language education (M Ed); health and physical education (M Ed); industrial and systems engineering (MS); instructional technology (M Ed); linguistically diverse education (M Ed); music education (M Ed); nursing (MS); special education (M Ed). Electronic applications accepted.
College of Science and Mathematics *Program availability:* Part-time, evening/weekend. Offers applied natural science (MS).
Malik and Seeme Hasan School of Business *Program availability:* Part-time, evening/weekend. Offers business (MBA).

COLORADO TECHNICAL UNIVERSITY AURORA, Aurora, CO 80014
General Information Proprietary, coed, comprehensive institution. *Graduate housing:* On-campus housing not available.
GRADUATE UNITS
Program in Computer Engineering Offers computer engineering (MS).
Program in Computer Science *Program availability:* Part-time, evening/weekend. Offers computer systems security (MSCS); database systems (MSCS); software engineering (MSCS).
Program in Electrical Engineering Offers electrical engineering (MS).
Program in Information Science Offers information systems security (MSM).
Program in Systems Engineering Offers systems engineering (MS).
Programs in Business Administration and Management *Program availability:* Part-time, evening/weekend. Offers accounting (MBA); business administration (MBA); business administration and management (EMBA); finance (MBA); human resource management (MBA); marketing (MBA); mediation and dispute resolution (MBA); operations management (MBA); project management (MBA); technology management (MBA).

COLORADO TECHNICAL UNIVERSITY COLORADO SPRINGS, Colorado Springs, CO 80907
General Information Proprietary, coed, university. *Graduate housing:* On-campus housing not available.
GRADUATE UNITS
Graduate Studies *Program availability:* Part-time, evening/weekend. Offers accounting (MBA, MSA); business administration (MBA); computer engineering (MSCE); computer science (DCS); computer systems security (MSCS); criminal justice (MSM); database systems (MSCS); electrical engineering (MSEE); finance (MBA); human resources management (MBA); information systems security (MSM); logistics/supply chain management (MBA); management (DM); marketing (MBA); mediation and dispute resolution (MBA); operations management (MBA); project management (MBA); software engineering (MSCS); systems engineering (MS); technology management (MBA).

COLUMBIA COLLEGE, Columbia, MO 65216-0002
General Information Independent-religious, coed, comprehensive institution. *Enrollment:* 1,093 graduate, professional, and undergraduate students; 101 full-time matriculated graduate/professional students (67 women), 724 part-time matriculated

graduate/professional students (433 women). *Enrollment by degree level:* 825 master's. *Graduate faculty:* 22 full-time (7 women), 70 part-time/adjunct (38 women). *Tuition:* Full-time $10,500; part-time $350 per credit hour. *Graduate housing:* On-campus housing not available. *Student services:* Campus employment opportunities, campus safety program, career counseling, exercise/wellness program, free psychological counseling, international student services, low-cost health insurance, services for students with disabilities, teacher training, writing training. *Library facilities:* J. W. and Lois Stafford Library. *Collection:* Books: 61,486 (physical), 128,017 (digital/electronic); Serial titles: 133 (physical), 107,640 (digital/electronic); Databases: 60. Weekly public service hours: 94; students can reserve study rooms.

Computer facilities: Computer purchase and lease plans are available. 134 computers available on campus for general student use. A campuswide network can be accessed from student residence rooms and from off campus. Online class registration is available.
Website: http://www.ccis.edu/

General Application Contact: Stephanie Johnson, Director of Admissions, 573-875-7352, Fax: 573-875-7506, E-mail: sjohnson@ccis.edu.

GRADUATE UNITS

Master of Arts in Teaching Program Students: 14 full-time (11 women), 86 part-time (66 women); includes 20 minority (7 Black or African American, non-Hispanic/Latino; 1 American Indian or Alaska Native, non-Hispanic/Latino; 2 Asian, non-Hispanic/Latino; 7 Hispanic/Latino; 3 Two or more races, non-Hispanic/Latino), 2 international. Average age 35. 58 applicants, 86% accepted, 40 enrolled. *Faculty:* 6 full-time (4 women), 18 part-time/adjunct (14 women). Expenses: Contact institution. *Financial support:* In 2016–17, 1 student received support. Career-related internships or fieldwork, Federal Work-Study, and scholarships/grants available. Financial award application deadline: 3/15; financial award applicants required to submit FAFSA. In 2016, 45 master's awarded. *Program availability:* Part-time, evening/weekend, 100% online, blended/hybrid learning. Offers teaching (MAT). *Application deadline:* For fall admission, 8/9 priority date for domestic and international students; for spring admission, 12/27 priority date for domestic and international students. Applications are processed on a rolling basis. *Application fee:* $55. Electronic applications accepted. *Application Contact:* Stephanie Johnson, Director of Admissions, 573-875-7352, Fax: 573-875-7506, E-mail: sjohnson@ccis.edu. *Graduate Program Coordinator,* Dr. Kristi Clevenger, 573-875-7590, Fax: 573-876-4493, E-mail: kclevenger@ccis.edu.

Master of Business Administration Program Students: 76 full-time (51 women), 415 part-time (240 women); includes 109 minority (60 Black or African American, non-Hispanic/Latino; 3 American Indian or Alaska Native, non-Hispanic/Latino; 7 Asian, non-Hispanic/Latino; 25 Hispanic/Latino; 2 Native Hawaiian or other Pacific Islander, non-Hispanic/Latino; 12 Two or more races, non-Hispanic/Latino), 26 international. Average age 36. 121 applicants, 90% accepted, 63 enrolled. *Faculty:* 5 full-time (2 women), 39 part-time/adjunct (15 women). Expenses: Contact institution. *Financial support:* Federal Work-Study and scholarships/grants available. Financial award application deadline: 3/1; financial award applicants required to submit FAFSA. In 2016, 194 master's awarded. *Program availability:* Part-time, evening/weekend, 100% online, blended/hybrid learning. Offers accounting (MBA); human resources (MBA). *Application deadline:* For fall admission, 8/9 priority date for domestic and international students; for spring admission, 12/27 priority date for domestic and international students. Applications are processed on a rolling basis. *Application fee:* $55. Electronic applications accepted. *Application Contact:* Stephanie Johnson, Director of Admissions, 573-875-7352, Fax: 573-875-7506, E-mail: sjohnson@ccis.edu. *Dean, School of Business Administration,* Dr. Shanda Traiser, 573-875-7561, Fax: 573-876-4493, E-mail: strasier@ccis.edu.

Master of Education in Educational Leadership Program Students: 4 full-time (3 women), 39 part-time (12 women); includes 3 minority (2 Black or African American, non-Hispanic/Latino; 1 Asian, non-Hispanic/Latino). Average age 39. 8 applicants, 100% accepted, 6 enrolled. *Faculty:* 1 (woman) full-time, 4 part-time/adjunct (all women). Expenses: Contact institution. *Financial support:* Federal Work-Study and scholarships/grants available. Financial award application deadline: 3/1; financial award applicants required to submit FAFSA. In 2016, 4 master's awarded. *Program availability:* Part-time, evening/weekend, 100% online, blended/hybrid learning. Offers educational leadership (M Ed). *Application deadline:* For fall admission, 8/9 priority date for domestic and international students; for spring admission, 12/27 priority date for domestic and international students. Applications are processed on a rolling basis. *Application fee:* $55. Electronic applications accepted. *Application Contact:* Stephanie Johnson, Director of Admissions, 573-875-7352, Fax: 573-875-7506, E-mail: sjohnson@ccis.edu. *M Ed Coordinator,* Teresa VanDover, 573-875-7794, E-mail: tmvandover@ccis.edu.

Master of Science in Criminal Justice Program Students: 7 full-time (3 women), 126 part-time (71 women); includes 43 minority (28 Black or African American, non-Hispanic/Latino; 1 American Indian or Alaska Native, non-Hispanic/Latino; 11 Hispanic/Latino; 1 Native Hawaiian or other Pacific Islander, non-Hispanic/Latino; 2 Two or more races, non-Hispanic/Latino), 1 international. Average age 39. 33 applicants, 97% accepted, 28 enrolled. *Faculty:* 3 full-time (0 women), 14 part-time/adjunct (8 women). Expenses: Contact institution. *Financial support:* Federal Work-Study and scholarships/grants available. Financial award application deadline: 3/1; financial award applicants required to submit FAFSA. In 2016, 59 master's awarded. *Program availability:* Part-time, evening/weekend, 100% online, blended/hybrid learning. Offers criminal justice (MSCJ). *Application deadline:* For fall admission, 8/9 priority date for domestic and international students; for spring admission, 12/27 priority date for domestic and international students. Applications are processed on a rolling basis. *Application fee:* $55. Electronic applications accepted. *Application Contact:* Stephanie Johnson, Director of Admissions, 573-875-7352, Fax: 573-875-7506, E-mail: sjohnson@ccis.edu. *Graduate Program Coordinator,* Dr. Mike Lyman, 573-875-7472, E-mail: mlyman@ccis.edu.

COLUMBIA COLLEGE, Columbia, SC 29203-5998

General Information Independent-religious, coed, primarily women, comprehensive institution. *Graduate housing:* On-campus housing not available.

GRADUATE UNITS

Graduate Programs *Program availability:* Part-time, evening/weekend. Offers organizational change and leadership (MA). Electronic applications accepted.

Education Division *Program availability:* Part-time, evening/weekend, online learning. Offers divergent learning (M Ed); higher education administration (M Ed). Electronic applications accepted.

COLUMBIA COLLEGE CHICAGO, Chicago, IL 60605-1996

General Information Independent, coed, comprehensive institution. CGS member. *Graduate housing:* Room and/or apartments available on a first-come, first-served basis to single students; on-campus housing not available to married students. Housing application deadline: 5/1.

GRADUATE UNITS

Graduate School *Program availability:* Part-time, evening/weekend, online learning. Offers arts, entertainment and media management (MA); cinema directing (MFA); creative producing (MFA); dance/movement therapy and counseling (MA, Certificate); drama therapy and counseling (MA); fiction (MFA); interdisciplinary arts (MA); interdisciplinary arts and media (MFA); interdisciplinary book and paper arts (MFA); journalism (MA); Laban movement analysis (Certificate); movement pattern analysis (Certificate); music composition for the screen (MFA); nonfiction (MFA); photography (MFA); poetry (MFA). Electronic applications accepted.

COLUMBIA COLLEGE OF NURSING, Glendale, WI 53212

General Information Independent, coed, primarily women, upper-level institution.
GRADUATE UNITS
Graduate Program Offers nursing (MSN).

COLUMBIA INTERNATIONAL UNIVERSITY, Columbia, SC 29230-3122

General Information Independent-religious, coed, university. *Graduate housing:* Rooms and/or apartments available on a first-come, first-served basis to single and married students. Housing application deadline: 8/1.

GRADUATE UNITS

Columbia Graduate School *Program availability:* Part-time, evening/weekend, online learning. Offers Bible teaching (MABT); counseling (MACN); early childhood and elementary education (MAT); educational administration (M Ed); educational leadership (PhD); instruction and learning (M Ed); teaching English as a foreign language (Certificate); teaching English as a foreign language and intercultural studies (MATF). Electronic applications accepted.

Seminary and School of Ministry *Program availability:* Part-time, evening/weekend. Offers academic ministries (M Div); Bible and theology (Certificate); bible exposition (M Div, MABE); Biblical ministry (Certificate); chaplaincy (M Div); intercultural studies (MAIS); leadership (D Min); member care (D Min); missions (D Min); preaching (D Min); theological studies (MA). Electronic applications accepted.

COLUMBIA SOUTHERN UNIVERSITY, Orange Beach, AL 36561

General Information Proprietary, coed, comprehensive institution. *Graduate housing:* On-campus housing not available.

GRADUATE UNITS

College of Safety and Emergency Services *Program availability:* Part-time, evening/weekend, online learning. Offers criminal justice administration (MS); emergency services management (MS); occupational safety and health (MS). Electronic applications accepted.

DBA Program *Program availability:* Part-time, evening/weekend, online learning. Offers business administration (DBA). Electronic applications accepted.

MBA Program *Program availability:* Part-time, evening/weekend, online learning. Offers finance (MBA); health care management (MBA); human resource management (MBA); marketing (MBA); project management (MBA); public administration (MBA). Electronic applications accepted.

Program in Organizational Leadership Offers organizational leadership (MS).

COLUMBIA THEOLOGICAL SEMINARY, Decatur, GA 30031-0520

General Information Independent-religious, coed, graduate-only institution. *Graduate housing:* Rooms and/or apartments available on a first-come, first-served basis to single students and available to married students. Housing application deadline: 4/30.

GRADUATE UNITS

Graduate and Professional Programs Offers theology (M Div, MATS, Th M, D Min, Th D). Th D program offered jointly with Emory University; D Min with Interdenominational Theological Center.

COLUMBIA UNIVERSITY, New York, NY 10027

General Information Independent, coed, university. CGS member. *Graduate housing:* Rooms and/or apartments available on a first-come, first-served basis to single and married students. Housing application deadline: 7/10. *Research affiliation:* Long Island Biological Laboratory, Brookhaven National Laboratory, New York Botanical Gardens, American Museum of Natural History, Marine Biological Laboratory, Goddard Space Flight Center.

GRADUATE UNITS

College of Dental Medicine Offers advanced education in general dentistry (Certificate); biomedical informatics (MA, PhD); dental and oral surgery (DDS); dental medicine (MA, MS, DDS, PhD, Certificate); endodontics (Certificate); orthodontics (MS, Certificate); periodontics (MS, Certificate); prosthodontics (MS, Certificate); science education (MA).

College of Physicians and Surgeons *Program availability:* Part-time. Offers anatomy (M Phil, MA, PhD); anatomy and cell biology (PhD); biochemistry and molecular biophysics (M Phil, PhD); biomedical informatics (M Phil, MA, PhD); biomedical sciences (M Phil, MA, PhD); biophysics (PhD); cellular, molecular, structural and genetic studies (PhD); genetics (M Phil, MA, PhD); medicine (M Phil, MA, MS, DN Sc, DPT, Ed D, MD, OTD, PhD, Adv C); movement science (Ed D); neurobiology and behavior (PhD); occupational therapy (MS); occupational therapy and cognition (OTD); pathobiology (M Phil, MA, PhD); pharmacology (M Phil, MA, PhD); pharmacology-toxicology (M Phil, MA, PhD); physical therapy (DPT); physiology and cellular biophysics (M Phil, MA, PhD).

Institute of Human Nutrition Students: 73 full-time (37 women), 2 part-time (1 woman); includes 27 minority (all Asian, non-Hispanic/Latino). Average age 23. 200 applicants, 63% accepted, 75 enrolled. *Faculty:* 46 full-time (22 women). Expenses: Contact institution. *Financial support:* In 2016–17, 65 students received support, including 12 fellowships (averaging $28,164 per year), 17 research assistantships (averaging $28,164 per year); Federal Work-Study, institutionally sponsored loans, and traineeships also available. Support available to part-time students. Financial award application deadline: 1/4; financial award applicants required to submit FAFSA. In 2016, 85 master's, 3 doctorates awarded. *Program availability:* Part-time. Offers nutrition (MS, PhD). *Application deadline:* For spring admission, 8/1 priority date for domestic and international students. Applications are processed on a rolling basis. *Application fee:* $95. Electronic applications accepted. *Application Contact:* Dr. Sharon R. Akabas, Director, MS Program in Human Nutrition, 212-305-4808, Fax: 212-305-3079, E-mail: sa109@cumc.columbia.edu. *Director,* Dr. Richard J. Deckelbaum, 212-305-4808, Fax: 212-305-3079, E-mail: nutrition@cumc.columbia.edu.

Columbia University Mailman School of Public Health Students: 1,000 full-time (773 women), 393 part-time (283 women); includes 499 minority (101 Black or African American, non-Hispanic/Latino; 6 American Indian or Alaska Native, non-

Hispanic/Latino; 263 Asian, non-Hispanic/Latino; 97 Hispanic/Latino; 32 Two or more races, non-Hispanic/Latino; 246 international. Average age 28. 3,008 applicants, 54% accepted, 664 enrolled. Expenses: Contact institution. *Financial support:* In 2016–17, 619 students received support. Fellowships, research assistantships, teaching assistantships, career-related internships or fieldwork, Federal Work-Study, and traineeships available. Support available to part-time students. Financial award application deadline: 2/1; financial award applicants required to submit FAFSA. In 2016, 647 master's, 24 doctorates awarded. *Program availability:* Part-time, evening/weekend. Offers biostatistics (MPH, MS, Dr PH, PhD); environmental health sciences (MPH, Dr PH, PhD); epidemiology (MPH, MS, Dr PH, PhD); health policy and management (Exec MHA, Exec MPH, MHA, MPH); population and family health (MPH, Dr PH); public health (Exec MHA, Exec MPH, MHA, MPH, MS, Dr PH, PhD); radiological sciences (MS); sociomedical sciences (MPH, MS, Dr PH, PhD); toxicology (MS). PhD offered in cooperation with the Graduate School of Arts and Sciences. *Application deadline:* For fall admission, 12/1 priority date for domestic and international students. *Application fee:* $120. Electronic applications accepted. *Application Contact:* Dr. Joseph Korevec, Senior Director of Admissions and Financial Aid, 212-305-8698, Fax: 212-342-1861, E-mail: ph-admit@columbia.edu. *Dean/Professor,* Dr. Linda P. Fried, 212-305-9300, Fax: 212-305-9342, E-mail: lpfried@columbia.edu.

Fu Foundation School of Engineering and Applied Science Students: 1,968 full-time (622 women), 1,137 part-time (381 women); includes 260 minority (15 Black or African American, non-Hispanic/Latino; 176 Asian, non-Hispanic/Latino; 9 Hispanic/Latino; 1 Native Hawaiian or other Pacific Islander, non-Hispanic/Latino; 59 Two or more races, non-Hispanic/Latino), 2,453 international. Average age 25. 10,741 applicants, 28% accepted, 1373 enrolled. *Faculty:* 249 full-time (35 women), 132 part-time/adjunct (8 women). Expenses: Contact institution. *Financial support:* In 2016–17, 1,012 students received support, including 290 fellowships with full tuition reimbursements available (averaging $5,334 per year), 647 research assistantships with full tuition reimbursements available (averaging $27,270 per year), 215 teaching assistantships with full tuition reimbursements available (averaging $27,270 per year); career-related internships or fieldwork, Federal Work-Study, institutionally sponsored loans, scholarships/grants, traineeships, health care benefits, tuition waivers (full), unspecified assistantships, and Awards also available. Support available to part-time students. Financial award application deadline: 12/15; financial award applicants required to submit FAFSA. In 2016, 1,294 master's, 111 doctorates awarded. *Program availability:* Part-time, 100% online. Offers applied mathematics (MS, Eng Sc D, PhD); applied physics (MS, Eng Sc D, PhD); biomedical engineering (MS, Eng Sc D, PhD); chemical engineering (MS, PhD); civil engineering (MS, Eng Sc D, PhD); computer engineering (MS); computer science (MS, Eng Sc D, PhD); construction engineering and management (MS); earth and environmental engineering (Eng Sc D, PhD); earth resources engineering (MS); electrical engineering (MS, PhD); engineering and applied science (MS, Eng Sc D, PhD); engineering mechanics (MS, Eng Sc D, PhD); financial engineering (MS); industrial engineering (MS); industrial engineering and operations research (PhD); management science and engineering (MS); materials science and engineering (MS, Eng Sc D, PhD); mechanical engineering (MS, Eng Sc D, PhD); medical physics (MS); operations research (MS). *Application deadline:* For fall admission, 12/15 priority date for domestic and international students; for spring admission, 10/1 priority date for domestic and international students. Applications are processed on a rolling basis. *Application fee:* $85. Electronic applications accepted. *Application Contact:* Jocelyn Morales, Associate Director, 212-854-6901, Fax: 212-854-5900, E-mail: seasgradmit@columbia.edu. *Dean,* Dr. Mary C. Boyce, 212-854-1123, Fax: 212-864-0104, E-mail: seasdean@columbia.edu.

Data Science Institute Expenses: Contact institution. *Financial support:* Applicants required to submit FAFSA. *Program availability:* Part-time. Offers data science (MS). *Application deadline:* For fall admission, 2/15 for domestic students. *Application fee:* $85. *Application Contact:* Dr. Kathleen R. McKeown, Director, 212-854-5660, Fax: 212-864-0104, E-mail: kathy@cs.columbia.edu. *Director,* Dr. Kathleen R. McKeown, 212-854-5660, Fax: 212-864-0104, E-mail: kathy@cs.columbia.edu.

Graduate School of Architecture, Planning, and Preservation Offers advanced architectural design (MS); architecture (M Arch, PhD); architecture, planning, and preservation (M Arch, MS, PhD, Certificate); historic preservation (MS, Certificate); real estate development (MS); urban planning (MS, PhD). PhD offered through the Graduate School of Arts and Sciences.

Graduate School of Arts and Sciences *Program availability:* Part-time. Offers African-American studies (MA); American studies (MA); anthropology (MA, PhD); art history and archaeology (MA, PhD); astronomy (PhD); biological sciences (PhD); biotechnology (MA); chemical physics (PhD); chemistry (PhD); classical studies (MA, PhD); classics (MA, PhD); climate and society (MA); conservation biology (MA); earth and environmental sciences (PhD); East Asia: regional studies (MA); East Asian languages and cultures (MA, PhD); ecology, evolution and environmental biology (MA); ecology, evolution, and environmental biology (PhD); economics (MA, PhD); English and comparative literature (MA, PhD); French and Romance philology (MA, PhD); Germanic languages (MA, PhD); global French studies (MA); global thought (MA); Hispanic cultural studies (MA); history (PhD); history and literature (MA); human rights studies (MA); Islamic studies (MA); Italian (MA, PhD); Japanese pedagogy (MA); Jewish studies (MA); Latin America and the Caribbean: regional studies (MA); Latin American and Iberian cultures (PhD); mathematics (MA, PhD); medieval and Renaissance studies (MA); Middle Eastern, South Asian, and African studies (MA, PhD); modern art: critical and curatorial studies (MA); modern European studies (MA); museum anthropology (MA); music (DMA, PhD); oral history (MA); philosophical foundations of physics (MA); philosophy (MA, PhD); physics (PhD); political science (MA, PhD); psychology (PhD); quantitative methods in the social sciences (MA); religion (MA, PhD); Russia, Eurasia and East Europe: regional studies (MA); Russian translation (MA); Slavic cultures (MA); Slavic languages (MA, PhD); sociology (MA, PhD); South Asian studies (MA); statistics (MA, PhD); theatre (PhD). Dual-degree programs require admission to both Graduate School of Arts and Sciences and another Columbia school. Electronic applications accepted.

Graduate School of Business Offers accounting (MBA); business (EMBA, MBA, PhD); business administration (EMBA, MBA); decision, risk, and operations (MBA); entrepreneurship (MBA); finance and economics (MBA); global business administration (EMBA); healthcare and pharmaceutical management (MBA); human resource management (MBA); international business (MBA); leadership and ethics (MBA); management (MBA); marketing (MBA); media (MBA); private equity (MBA); real estate (MBA); social enterprise (MBA); value investing (MBA). Electronic applications accepted.

Graduate School of Journalism *Program availability:* Part-time. Offers journalism (MA, MS, PhD).

School of Continuing Education *Program availability:* Part-time, evening/weekend. Offers actuarial science (MS); bioethics (MS); communications practice (MS); construction administration (MS); fundraising management (MS); information and

archive management (MS); landscape design (MS); narrative medicine (MS); negotiation and conflict resolution (MS); sports management (MS); strategic communications (MS); sustainability management (MS); technology management (Exec MS). Electronic applications accepted.

School of International and Public Affairs Students: 3,163 full-time (1,781 women). Average age 27. 2,700 applicants, 56% accepted, 628 enrolled. *Faculty:* 70 full-time (18 women), 203 part-time/adjunct (80 women). Expenses: Contact institution. *Financial support:* Fellowships, research assistantships, teaching assistantships, career-related internships or fieldwork, Federal Work-Study, institutionally sponsored loans, and scholarships/grants available. Financial award application deadline: 1/5; financial award applicants required to submit FAFSA. In 2016, 700 master's awarded. *Program availability:* Part-time, evening/weekend. Offers development practice (MPA); environmental science and policy (MPA); international affairs (MIA); international and public affairs (MA, MIA, MPA, Certificate); public policy and administration (MPA). *Application deadline:* For fall admission, 1/5 for domestic and international students; for spring admission, 10/15 for domestic and international students. *Application fee:* $95. Electronic applications accepted. *Application Contact:* Grace Han, Executive Director of Admissions and Financial Aid, 212-854-6216, Fax: 212-854-3010, E-mail: sipa_admission@columbia.edu. *Dean,* Merit Janow, 212-854-4604, Fax: 212-864-4847, E-mail: njc2138@sipa.columbia.edu.

School of Law Offers law (LL M, JD, JSD). Electronic applications accepted.

School of Nursing Students: 256 full-time (222 women); includes 115 minority (23 Black or African American, non-Hispanic/Latino; 2 American Indian or Alaska Native, non-Hispanic/Latino; 61 Asian, non-Hispanic/Latino; 27 Hispanic/Latino; 2 Native Hawaiian or other Pacific Islander, non-Hispanic/Latino), 5 international. Average age 32. 1,683 applicants, 31% accepted, 256 enrolled. *Faculty:* 60 full-time (54 women), 33 part-time/adjunct (24 women). Expenses: Contact institution. *Financial support:* In 2016–17, 245 students received support. Research assistantships, teaching assistantships, Federal Work-Study, institutionally sponsored loans, and scholarships/grants available. Support available to part-time students. Financial award application deadline: 2/1; financial award applicants required to submit FAFSA. In 2016, 164 master's, 17 doctorates, 8 other advanced degrees awarded. Offers adult-gerontology acute care nurse practitioner (MS, Adv C); adult-gerontology primary care nurse practitioner (MS, Adv C); family nurse practitioner (MS, Adv C); nurse anesthesia (MS, Adv C); nurse midwifery (MS); nursing (MS, DNP, PhD, Adv C); pediatric nurse practitioner (MS, Adv C); psychiatric mental health nursing (MS, Adv C). *Application deadline:* For fall admission, 4/15 for domestic and international students; for spring admission, 1/15 for domestic and international students; for summer admission, 10/15 for domestic and international students. *Application fee:* $65. Electronic applications accepted. *Application Contact:* Jose Villa, Director of Admissions, 212-305-5756, E-mail: nursing@columbia.edu. *Dean,* Dr. Bobbie Berkowitz, 212-305-3582.

School of Social Work *Program availability:* 100% online. Offers social work (MSSW, PhD). MS/MS Ed offered jointly with Bank Street College of Education; MS/M Div with Union Theological Seminary in New York; MS/MA with The Jewish Theological Seminary; MS/MS dual degree with the Graduate School of Architecture, Planning, and Preservation. Electronic applications accepted.

School of the Arts Offers acting (MFA); arts (MA, MFA); creative producing (MFA); directing (MFA); dramaturgy (MFA); fiction (MFA); film studies (MA); new genres (MFA); nonfiction (MFA); painting (MFA); photography (MFA); playwriting (MFA); poetry (MFA); printmaking (MFA); screenwriting (MFA); sculpture (MFA); stage management (MFA); theater management and producing (MFA). Electronic applications accepted.

South Asia Institute Offers South Asia studies (MA, Certificate). Students must be enrolled in a separate graduate degree program at Columbia University. Electronic applications accepted.

COLUMBUS COLLEGE OF ART & DESIGN, Columbus, OH 43215-1758

General Information Independent, coed, comprehensive institution. *Enrollment:* 1,095 graduate, professional, and undergraduate students; 33 full-time matriculated graduate/professional students (21 women). *Enrollment by degree level:* 33 master's. *Graduate faculty:* 64 full-time (28 women), 111 part-time/adjunct (52 women). *Tuition:* Full-time $32,400. *Required fees:* $1080. *Graduate housing:* Rooms and/or apartments available on a first-come, first-served basis to single and married students. Typical cost: $7790 per year ($9830 including board) for single students; $7790 per year ($9830 including board) for married students. Room and board charges vary according to campus/location. Housing application deadline: 5/6. *Student services:* Campus employment opportunities, campus safety program, career counseling, exercise/wellness program, free psychological counseling, grant writing training, international student services, services for students with disabilities, teacher training, writing training. *Library facilities:* Packard Library. *Collection:* Books: 40,836 (physical), 28,701 (digital/electronic); Serial titles: 434 (physical), 253,828 (digital/electronic).

Computer facilities: 485 computers available on campus for general student use. A campuswide network can be accessed. Online class registration is available. Website: http://www.ccad.edu/

General Application Contact: John Cairns, Graduate Admissions Counselor, 614-222-3249, E-mail: jcairns.1@ccad.edu.

GRADUATE UNITS

Graduate Programs Students: 33 full-time (21 women). *Faculty:* 64 full-time (28 women), 111 part-time/adjunct (52 women). Expenses: Contact institution. *Financial support:* Scholarships/grants available. Financial award applicants required to submit FAFSA. Offers integrative design (M Des); visual arts (MFA). *Application deadline:* For fall admission, 2/15 priority date for domestic students. Applications are processed on a rolling basis. *Application fee:* $65. Electronic applications accepted. *Application Contact:* John Cairns, Graduate Admissions Counselor, 614-222-3249, E-mail: jcairns.1@ccad.edu.

COLUMBUS STATE UNIVERSITY, Columbus, GA 31907-5645

General Information State-supported, coed, comprehensive institution. CGS member. *Enrollment:* 8,407 graduate, professional, and undergraduate students; 599 full-time matriculated graduate/professional students (353 women), 1,012 part-time matriculated graduate/professional students (613 women). *Enrollment by degree level:* 1,123 master's, 154 doctoral, 334 other advanced degrees. *Graduate faculty:* 116 full-time (44 women), 59 part-time/adjunct (33 women). Tuition, state resident: full-time $4804; part-time $2412 per semester. Tuition, nonresident: full-time $19,218; part-time $9612 per semester. *Required fees:* $1850. Tuition and fees vary according to program. *Graduate housing:* Rooms and/or apartments available on a first-come, first-served basis to single and married students. Housing application deadline: 6/30. *Student services:* Campus employment opportunities, campus safety program, career counseling, exercise/wellness program, free psychological counseling, international student services, low-cost health insurance, multicultural affairs office, services for students with disabilities, teacher training, writing training. *Library facilities:* Simon Schwob Memorial Library plus 1 other. *Collection:* Books: 383,649 (physical).

Computer facilities: A campuswide network can be accessed from student residence rooms and from off campus. Online class registration is available.
Website: http://www.columbusstate.edu/

General Application Contact: Kristin Williams, Director of International and Graduate Admissions, 706-507-8848, Fax: 706-568-5091, E-mail: williams_kristin@columbusstate.edu.

GRADUATE UNITS

Graduate Studies Students: 599 full-time (353 women), 1,012 part-time (613 women); includes 697 minority (577 Black or African American, non-Hispanic/Latino; 7 American Indian or Alaska Native, non-Hispanic/Latino; 31 Asian, non-Hispanic/Latino; 50 Hispanic/Latino; 2 Native Hawaiian or other Pacific Islander, non-Hispanic/Latino; 30 Two or more races, non-Hispanic/Latino), 68 international. Average age 36. 1,254 applicants, 52% accepted, 452 enrolled. *Faculty:* 116 full-time (44 women), 59 part-time/adjunct (33 women). Expenses: Contact institution. *Financial support:* In 2016–17, 185 students received support, including 102 research assistantships with partial tuition reimbursements available (averaging $3,000 per year); career-related internships or fieldwork, Federal Work-Study, institutionally sponsored loans, scholarships/grants, tuition waivers (partial), and unspecified assistantships also available. Support available to part-time students. Financial award application deadline: 5/1; financial award applicants required to submit FAFSA. In 2016, 425 master's, 7 doctorates, 146 other advanced degrees awarded. *Program availability:* Part-time, evening/weekend, 100% online, blended/hybrid learning. *Application deadline:* For fall admission, 6/30 for domestic and international students; for spring admission, 11/1 for domestic and international students; for summer admission, 5/1 for domestic and international students. Applications are processed on a rolling basis. *Application fee:* $50. Electronic applications accepted. *Application Contact:* Kristin Williams, Director of International and Graduate Admissions, 706-507-8848, Fax: 706-568-5091, E-mail: williams_kristin@columbusstate.edu. *Assistant Vice President for Academic Affairs,* Dr. Ellen Roberts, 706-507-8573, Fax: 706-569-3168, E-mail: roberts_ellen@columbusstate.edu.

College of Education and Health Professions Students: 365 full-time (260 women), 597 part-time (476 women); includes 483 minority (428 Black or African American, non-Hispanic/Latino; 2 American Indian or Alaska Native, non-Hispanic/Latino; 12 Asian, non-Hispanic/Latino; 23 Hispanic/Latino; 18 Two or more races, non-Hispanic/Latino), 6 international. Average age 37. 748 applicants, 53% accepted, 283 enrolled. *Faculty:* 43 full-time (24 women), 45 part-time/adjunct (31 women). Expenses: Contact institution. *Financial support:* In 2016–17, 113 students received support, including 25 research assistantships with partial tuition reimbursements available (averaging $3,000 per year); career-related internships or fieldwork, Federal Work-Study, institutionally sponsored loans, scholarships/grants, tuition waivers (partial), and unspecified assistantships also available. Support available to part-time students. Financial award application deadline: 5/1; financial award applicants required to submit FAFSA. In 2016, 162 master's, 7 doctorates, 139 other advanced degrees awarded. *Program availability:* Part-time, evening/weekend, 100% online, blended/hybrid learning. Offers clinical mental health counseling (MS); curriculum and instruction in accomplished teaching (M Ed); curriculum and leadership (Ed D); early childhood education (M Ed, MAT, Ed S); education and health professions (M Ed, MAT, MS, MSN, Ed D, Ed S); educational leadership (M Ed, Ed S); exercise science (MS); family nurse practitioner (MSN); health and physical education (M Ed, MAT); middle grades education (M Ed, MAT, Ed S); nursing (MSN); school counseling (M Ed, Ed S); secondary education (M Ed, MAT, Ed S); special education (M Ed, MAT, Ed S); teacher leadership (M Ed). *Application deadline:* For fall admission, 6/30 for domestic students, 5/1 for international students; for spring admission, 11/1 for domestic and international students; for summer admission, 3/1 for domestic and international students. Applications are processed on a rolling basis. *Application fee:* $50. Electronic applications accepted. *Application Contact:* Kristin Williams, Director of International and Graduate Recruitment, 706-507-8848, Fax: 706-568-5091, E-mail: williams_kristin@columbusstate.edu. *Dean,* Dr. Deirdre Greer, 706-507-8505, Fax: 706-569-3134, E-mail: greer_deirdre@columbusstate.edu.

College of Letters and Sciences Students: 93 full-time (50 women), 259 part-time (76 women); includes 132 minority (107 Black or African American, non-Hispanic/Latino; 4 American Indian or Alaska Native, non-Hispanic/Latino; 6 Asian, non-Hispanic/Latino; 9 Hispanic/Latino; 1 Native Hawaiian or other Pacific Islander, non-Hispanic/Latino; 5 Two or more races, non-Hispanic/Latino), 2 international. Average age 39. 148 applicants, 58% accepted, 72 enrolled. *Faculty:* 14 full-time (2 women), 10 part-time/adjunct (0 women). Expenses: Contact institution. *Financial support:* In 2016–17, 9 students received support, including 27 research assistantships with tuition reimbursements available (averaging $3,000 per year); career-related internships or fieldwork, Federal Work-Study, institutionally sponsored loans, scholarships/grants, tuition waivers (partial), and unspecified assistantships also available. Support available to part-time students. Financial award application deadline: 5/1; financial award applicants required to submit FAFSA. In 2016, 146 master's awarded. *Program availability:* Part-time, evening/weekend, 100% online, blended/hybrid learning. Offers history (MA); letters and sciences (MA, MPA, MPSA, MS, Certificate); natural sciences (MS); public administration (MPA); public safety administration (MPSA); teaching English to speakers of other languages (Certificate). *Application deadline:* For fall admission, 6/30 for domestic students, 5/1 for international students; for spring admission, 11/1 for domestic students, 10/1 for international students; for summer admission, 3/1 for domestic and international students. Applications are processed on a rolling basis. *Application fee:* $50. Electronic applications accepted. *Application Contact:* Kristin Williams, Director of International and Graduate Recruitment, 706-507-8848, Fax: 706-568-5091, E-mail: williams_kristin@columbusstate.edu. *Dean,* Dr. Dennis Rome, 706-568-2056, E-mail: rome_dennis@columbusstate.edu.

College of the Arts Students: 48 full-time (22 women), 24 part-time (14 women); includes 12 minority (6 Black or African American, non-Hispanic/Latino; 1 Asian, non-Hispanic/Latino; 4 Hispanic/Latino; 1 Native Hawaiian or other Pacific Islander, non-Hispanic/Latino), 26 international. Average age 27. 71 applicants, 52% accepted, 31 enrolled. *Faculty:* 27 full-time (10 women), 2 part-time/adjunct (both women). Expenses: Contact institution. *Financial support:* In 2016–17, 44 students received support, including 34 research assistantships with partial tuition reimbursements available (averaging $3,000 per year); career-related internships or fieldwork, Federal Work-Study, institutionally sponsored loans, scholarships/grants, tuition waivers (partial), and unspecified assistantships also available. Support available to part-time students. Financial award application deadline: 5/1; financial award applicants required to submit FAFSA. In 2016, 11 master's, 7 other advanced degrees awarded. *Program availability:* Part-time, evening/weekend. Offers art education (M Ed, MAT); arts (M Ed, MAT, MM, Artist Diploma); music (Artist Diploma); music education (MM);

music performance (MM); theatre education (M Ed, MAT). *Application deadline:* For fall admission, 6/30 for domestic students, 5/1 for international students; for spring admission, 11/1 for domestic and international students; for summer admission, 3/1 for domestic and international students. Applications are processed on a rolling basis. *Application fee:* $50. Electronic applications accepted. *Application Contact:* Kristin Williams, Director of International and Graduate Recruitment, 706-507-8848, Fax: 706-568-5091, E-mail: williams_kristin@columbusstate.edu. *Dean,* Dr. Richard Baxter, 706-507-8043, E-mail: baxter_richard@columbusstate.edu.

Turner College of Business Students: 93 full-time (21 women), 132 part-time (47 women); includes 69 minority (36 Black or African American, non-Hispanic/Latino; 1 American Indian or Alaska Native, non-Hispanic/Latino; 11 Asian, non-Hispanic/Latino; 14 Hispanic/Latino; 7 Two or more races, non-Hispanic/Latino), 35 international. Average age 31. 279 applicants, 44% accepted, 64 enrolled. *Faculty:* 10 full-time (3 women). Expenses: Contact institution. *Financial support:* In 2016–17, 18 students received support, including 16 research assistantships (averaging $3,000 per year); Federal Work-Study also available. Financial award application deadline: 5/1; financial award applicants required to submit FAFSA. In 2016, 106 master's awarded. *Program availability:* Part-time, evening/weekend, 100% online, blended/hybrid learning. Offers applied computer science (MS); business administration (MBA); human resource management (Certificate); information systems security (Certificate); modeling and simulation (Certificate); organizational leadership (MS); servant leadership (Certificate). *Application deadline:* For fall admission, 6/30 for domestic students, 5/1 for international students; for spring admission, 11/1 for domestic and international students; for summer admission, 3/1 for domestic and international students. Applications are processed on a rolling basis. *Application fee:* $50. Electronic applications accepted. *Application Contact:* Kristin Williams, Director of International and Graduate Recruitment, 706-507-8848, Fax: 706-568-5091, E-mail: thornton_katie@colstate.edu. *Dean,* Dr. Linda U. Hadley, 706-507-8153, Fax: 706-568-2184, E-mail: hadley_linda@columbusstate.edu.

CONCORDIA COLLEGE, Moorhead, MN 56562

General Information Independent-religious, coed, comprehensive institution.

GRADUATE UNITS

Program in Education Offers world language instruction (M Ed).

CONCORDIA COLLEGE–NEW YORK, Bronxville, NY 10708-1998

General Information Independent-religious, coed, comprehensive institution.

GRADUATE UNITS

Program in Business Leadership Offers business leadership (MS).

Program in Childhood Special Education Offers childhood special education (MS Ed).

CONCORDIA LUTHERAN SEMINARY, Edmonton, AB T5B 4E3, Canada

General Information Independent-religious, coed, primarily men, graduate-only institution. *Graduate housing:* On-campus housing not available.

GRADUATE UNITS

Graduate and Professional Programs *Program availability:* Part-time. Offers theology (M Div, Graduate Certificate).

CONCORDIA SEMINARY, St. Louis, MO 63105-3199

General Information Independent-religious, coed, primarily men, graduate-only institution. *Graduate housing:* Rooms and/or apartments guaranteed to single students and available to married students. Housing application deadline: 3/4. *Research affiliation:* Center for Reformation Research, Concordia Historical Institute.

GRADUATE UNITS

Graduate Programs Offers theology (M Div, MA, STM, D Min, PhD, Certificate).

CONCORDIA THEOLOGICAL SEMINARY, Fort Wayne, IN 46825-4996

General Information Independent-religious, coed, primarily men, graduate-only institution. *Graduate housing:* Room and/or apartments available to single students; on-campus housing not available to married students.

GRADUATE UNITS

Graduate and Professional Programs *Program availability:* Part-time. Offers theology (M Div, MA, STM, D Min, PhD).

CONCORDIA UNIVERSITY, Montréal, QC H3G 1M8, Canada

General Information Province-supported, coed, university. CGS member. *Graduate housing:* Room and/or apartments available on a first-come, first-served basis to single students; on-campus housing not available to married students. *Research affiliation:* Canadian Rural Revitalization Foundation (sociology), Blue Metropolis Literary Series (English), Canadian Journalism Project (journalism), Centre de Recherche en Plasturgie et Composites (CREPEC) (mechanical and industrial engineering), Centre de Recherche Informatique de Montreal (CRIM) (computer science), Center d'experise et de services en application Multimedia (multimedia).

GRADUATE UNITS

School of Graduate Studies *Program availability:* Part-time, evening/weekend. Offers individualized research (M Sc, MA, PhD).

Faculty of Arts and Science Offers adult education (Certificate, Diploma); Anglais-Franlfcais en langue et techniques de localization (Certificate); applied linguistics (MA, Certificate); arts and science (M Env, M Sc, MA, MTM, PhD, Certificate, Diploma, Graduate Diploma); biology (M Sc, PhD); biotechnology and genomics (Diploma); chemistry (M Sc, PhD); child studies (MA); communication (PhD); communication studies (Diploma); community economic development (Diploma); creative writing (MA); economics (MA, PhD, Diploma); educational studies (MA); educational technology (MA); English literature (MA, PhD); environmental assessment (M Env, Diploma); exercise science (M Sc); geography, urban and environmental studies (M Sc, PhD); history (MA, PhD); human systems intervention (MA); humanities (PhD); instructional technology (Diploma); journalism (Graduate Diploma); journalism studies (MA); Judaic studies (MA); littératures Francophones et résonances médiatiques (MA); mathematics (PhD); mathematics and statistics (M Sc, MA); media studies (MA); philosophy (MA); physics (M Sc, PhD); political science (PhD); psychology (MA, PhD, Certificate); public policy and public administration (MA); religion (MA, PhD); social and cultural analysis (PhD); social and cultural anthropology (MA); sociology (MA); teaching English as a second language (Certificate); teaching of mathematics (MTM); theological studies (MA); translation (Diploma); translation studies (MA); visual journalism (Diploma); youth work (Graduate Diploma).

Faculty of Engineering and Computer Science Offers 3D graphics and game development (Certificate); aerospace engineering (M Eng); building engineering (M Eng, MA Sc, PhD, Certificate); civil engineering (M Eng, MA Sc, PhD); computer science (M App Comp Sc, M Comp Sc, PhD, Diploma); electrical and computer engineering (M Eng, MA Sc, PhD); engineering and computer science (M App Comp Sc, M Comp Sc, M Eng, MA Sc, PhD, Certificate, Diploma); environmental engineering (Certificate); industrial engineering (M Eng, MA Sc, PhD); information and systems engineering (PhD); information systems security (M Eng, MA Sc); mechanical engineering (M Eng, MA Sc, PhD, Certificate); quality systems engineering (M Eng, MA Sc); service engineering and network management (Certificate); software engineering (M Eng, MA Sc).

Faculty of Fine Arts *Program availability:* Part-time. Offers advanced music performance studies (Diploma); art education (MA, PhD); art history (MA, PhD); art therapy (MA); design (M Des); digital technologies in design art practice (Certificate); drama therapy (MA); film and moving image studies (PhD); film production (MFA); film studies (MA); fine arts (M Des, MA, MFA, PhD, Certificate, Diploma); music therapy (MA); studio arts (MFA).

John Molson School of Business *Program availability:* Part-time, evening/weekend. Offers administration (M Sc); business administration (MBA, PhD, Certificate, Diploma); executive business administration (EMBA); supply chain management (MSCM). PhD program offered jointly with HEC Montreal, McGill University, and Université du Québec à Montréal. Electronic applications accepted.

CONCORDIA UNIVERSITY, Portland, OR 97211-6099

General Information Independent-religious, coed, comprehensive institution. *Graduate housing:* Room and/or apartments available on a first-come, first-served basis to single students; on-campus housing not available to married students. Housing application deadline: 8/1.

GRADUATE UNITS

College of Education *Program availability:* Part-time, online learning. Offers career and technical education (M Ed); curriculum and instruction (M Ed); early childhood (MAT); education leadership (Ed D); educational administration (M Ed); elementary education (MAT); secondary education (MAT); special education (M Ed); teacher leadership (Ed D). Electronic applications accepted.

School of Management *Program availability:* Evening/weekend. Offers management (MBA).

CONCORDIA UNIVERSITY ANN ARBOR, Ann Arbor, MI 48105-2797

General Information Independent-religious, coed, comprehensive institution. *Graduate housing:* On-campus housing not available.

GRADUATE UNITS

Graduate Programs *Program availability:* Part-time, evening/weekend. Offers curriculum and instruction (MS); educational leadership (MS); organizational leadership and administration (MS). Electronic applications accepted.

CONCORDIA UNIVERSITY CHICAGO, River Forest, IL 60305-1499

General Information Independent-religious, coed, comprehensive institution. CGS member. *Graduate housing:* Rooms and/or apartments available on a first-come, first-served basis to single and married students.

GRADUATE UNITS

College of Education Offers Christian education (MA); curriculum and instruction (MA); early childhood education (MA, Ed D); elementary education (MAT); reading education (MA); school leadership (MA, Ed D, CAS); secondary education (MAT).

College of Graduate and Innovative Programs Offers business administration (MBA); church music (MCM); community counseling (MA); educational technology (MA); gerontology (MA); human services (MA); liberal studies (MA); music (MA); psychology (MA); religion (MA); school counseling (MA, CAS).

CONCORDIA UNIVERSITY IRVINE, Irvine, CA 92612-3299

General Information Independent-religious, coed, comprehensive institution. *Graduate housing:* Room and/or apartments available on a first-come, first-served basis to single students; on-campus housing not available to married students. Housing application deadline: 6/1.

GRADUATE UNITS

School of Arts and Sciences *Program availability:* Part-time, evening/weekend, online learning. Offers coaching and athletic administration (MA). Electronic applications accepted.

School of Business *Program availability:* Part-time, evening/weekend. Offers business administration (MBA). Electronic applications accepted.

School of Education *Program availability:* Part-time, evening/weekend, online learning. Offers curriculum and instruction (MA); education and preliminary teaching credential (M Ed); educational administration and preliminary administrative services credential (MA); educational technology (MA); school counseling with pupil personnel services credential (MA). Electronic applications accepted.

School of Professional Studies

School of Theology *Program availability:* Part-time, evening/weekend. Offers Christian leadership (MA); research in theology (MA); theology and culture (MA). Electronic applications accepted.

CONCORDIA UNIVERSITY, NEBRASKA, Seward, NE 68434-1556

General Information Independent-religious, coed, comprehensive institution. *Graduate housing:* Rooms and/or apartments available on a first-come, first-served basis to single and married students.

GRADUATE UNITS

Graduate Programs in Education *Program availability:* Part-time, evening/weekend. Offers early childhood education (M Ed); education (M Ed, MPE, MS); elementary and secondary education (M Ed); elementary education (M Ed); family life ministry (MS); parish education (MPE); reading education (M Ed); secondary education (M Ed). Electronic applications accepted.

Program in Computer Science *Program availability:* Online learning. Offers cyber operations (MS).

CONCORDIA UNIVERSITY OF EDMONTON, Edmonton, AB T5B 4E4, Canada

General Information Independent-religious, coed, comprehensive institution.

GRADUATE UNITS

Program in Biblical and Christian Studies Offers Biblical and Christian studies (MA).

Program in Information Systems Security Management Offers information systems security management (MA).

CONCORDIA UNIVERSITY, ST. PAUL, St. Paul, MN 55104-5494

General Information Independent-religious, coed, comprehensive institution. CGS member. *Enrollment:* 4,535 graduate, professional, and undergraduate students; 1,794 full-time matriculated graduate/professional students (1,228 women), 82 part-time matriculated graduate/professional students (26 women). *Enrollment by degree level:* 1,666 master's, 123 doctoral, 87 other advanced degrees. *Graduate faculty:* 27 full-time (11 women), 149 part-time/adjunct (75 women). *Tuition:* Full-time $4536; part-time $378 per credit. Tuition and fees vary according to degree level and program. *Graduate housing:* Rooms and/or apartments available on a first-come, first-served basis to single and married students. Typical cost: $10,750 (including board) for single students; $6500 per year for married students. Room and board charges vary according to housing facility selected. Housing application deadline: 6/1. *Student services:* Campus employment opportunities, campus safety program, career counseling, child daycare facilities, exercise/wellness program, free psychological counseling, international student services, multicultural affairs office, services for students with disabilities, teacher training, writing training. *Library facilities:* Library Technology Center. *Collection:* Books: 113,983 (physical), 170,320 (digital/electronic); Serial titles: 726 (physical), 119,903 (digital/electronic); Databases: 60. Weekly public service hours: 74; students can reserve study rooms.

Computer facilities: 10 computers available on campus for general student use. A campuswide network can be accessed from student residence rooms and from off campus. Online class registration is available. Website: http://www.csp.edu/

General Application Contact: Kimberly Craig, Associate Vice President, Cohort Enrollment Management, 651-603-6223, Fax: 651-603-6320, E-mail: craig@csp.edu.

GRADUATE UNITS

College of Business Students: 462 full-time (288 women), 25 part-time (16 women); includes 123 minority (59 Black or African American, non-Hispanic/Latino; 1 American Indian or Alaska Native, non-Hispanic/Latino; 36 Asian, non-Hispanic/Latino; 10 Hispanic/Latino; 1 Native Hawaiian or other Pacific Islander, non-Hispanic/Latino; 16 Two or more races, non-Hispanic/Latino), 28 international. Average age 34. 269 applicants, 73% accepted, 137 enrolled. *Faculty:* 12 full-time (4 women), 36 part-time/adjunct (15 women). Expenses: Contact institution. *Financial support:* In 2016–17, 259 students received support. Scholarships/grants and unspecified assistantships available. Financial award applicants required to submit FAFSA. In 2016, 192 master's awarded. *Program availability:* Part-time, evening/weekend, 100% online, blended/hybrid learning. Offers business administration (MBA); business and organizational leadership (MBA); health care management (MBA); human resource management (MA); leadership and management (MA); strategic communication management (MA). *Application deadline:* For fall admission, 8/1 for domestic and international students; for spring admission, 12/1 for domestic and international students; for summer admission, 5/1 for domestic and international students. Applications are processed on a rolling basis. *Application fee:* $50. Electronic applications accepted. *Application Contact:* Kimberly Craig, Associate Vice President, Cohort Enrollment Management, 651-603-6223, Fax: 651-603-6320, E-mail: craig@csp.edu. *Dean,* Dr. Kevin Hall, 651-603-6165, Fax: 651-641-8807, E-mail: khall@csp.edu.

College of Education Students: 994 full-time (745 women), 40 part-time (34 women); includes 118 minority (40 Black or African American, non-Hispanic/Latino; 7 American Indian or Alaska Native, non-Hispanic/Latino; 33 Asian, non-Hispanic/Latino; 20 Hispanic/Latino; 18 Two or more races, non-Hispanic/Latino), 15 international. Average age 34. 549 applicants, 82% accepted, 372 enrolled. *Faculty:* 9 full-time (5 women), 88 part-time/adjunct (52 women). Expenses: Contact institution. *Financial support:* In 2016–17, 112 students received support. Scholarships/grants and unspecified assistantships available. Financial award applicants required to submit FAFSA. In 2016, 399 master's, 108 other advanced degrees awarded. *Program availability:* Part-time, evening/weekend, 100% online, blended/hybrid learning. Offers classroom instruction (MA Ed); differentiated instruction (MA Ed); education (Ed D); educational leadership (MA Ed); educational technology (MA Ed); K-12 principal licensure (Ed S); special education (MA Ed, Certificate); superintendent (Ed S); teaching (MAT). *Application deadline:* For fall admission, 8/1 for domestic and international students; for spring admission, 12/1 for domestic and international students; for summer admission, 5/1 for domestic and international students. Applications are processed on a rolling basis. *Application fee:* $50. Electronic applications accepted. *Application Contact:* Kimberly Craig, Associate Vice President, Cohort Enrollment Management, 651-603-6223, Fax: 651-603-6320, E-mail: craig@csp.edu. *Dean,* Lonn Maly, 651-641-8203, E-mail: maly@csp.edu.

College of Health and Science Students: 337 full-time (194 women), 18 part-time (7 women); includes 65 minority (35 Black or African American, non-Hispanic/Latino; 7 Asian, non-Hispanic/Latino; 8 Hispanic/Latino; 4 Native Hawaiian or other Pacific Islander, non-Hispanic/Latino; 11 Two or more races, non-Hispanic/Latino), 3 international. Average age 30. 388 applicants, 40% accepted, 117 enrolled. *Faculty:* 7 full-time (2 women), 27 part-time/adjunct (9 women). Expenses: Contact institution. *Financial support:* In 2016–17, 114 students received support. Scholarships/grants and unspecified assistantships available. Financial award applicants required to submit FAFSA. In 2016, 92 master's awarded. *Program availability:* Part-time, evening/weekend, 100% online, blended/hybrid learning. Offers criminal justice leadership (MA); exercise science (MS); family science (MA); human services (MA); orthotics and prosthetics (MS); physical therapy (DPT); sports management (MA). *Application deadline:* For fall admission, 4/1 for domestic students. Applications are processed on a rolling basis. *Application fee:* $50. Electronic applications accepted. *Application Contact:* Kimberly Craig, Associate Vice President, Cohort Enrollment Management, 651-603-6223, Fax: 651-603-6320, E-mail: craig@csp.edu. *Interim Dean,* Dr. Katie Fischer, 651-641-8735, E-mail: fischer@csp.edu.

CONCORDIA UNIVERSITY TEXAS, Austin, TX 78726

General Information Independent-religious, coed, comprehensive institution.

GRADUATE UNITS

College of Education *Program availability:* Part-time, evening/weekend. Offers education (M Ed).

CONCORDIA UNIVERSITY WISCONSIN, Mequon, WI 53097-2402

General Information Independent-religious, coed, comprehensive institution. *Graduate housing:* Room and/or apartments available to single students; on-campus housing not available to married students. Housing application deadline: 8/1. *Student services:* Campus employment opportunities, campus safety program, career counseling, exercise/wellness program, free psychological counseling, international student services, low-cost health insurance, services for students with disabilities, writing training. *Library facilities:* Rinker Memorial Library.

Computer facilities: A campuswide network can be accessed from student residence rooms and from off campus.
Website: http://www.cuw.edu/

General Application Contact: Kenneth K. Gaschk, Senior Vice President of Enrollment Services, 262-243-4500.

GRADUATE UNITS

Graduate Programs Expenses: Contact institution. *Financial support:* Career-related internships or fieldwork and tuition waivers (partial) available. Financial award application deadline: 8/1. *Program availability:* Part-time, evening/weekend, online learning. Offers art education (MS Ed); early childhood (MS Ed); educational administration (MS Ed); environmental education (MS Ed); family studies (MS Ed); literacy (MS Ed); school counseling (MS Ed); special education (MS Ed). *Application deadline:* For fall admission, 8/1 priority date for domestic students; for winter admission, 12/1 priority date for domestic students; for spring admission, 1/1 priority date for domestic students. Applications are processed on a rolling basis. *Application fee:* $35. Electronic applications accepted. *Application Contact:* Mary Eberhardt, Graduate Admissions, 262-243-4551, Fax: 262-243-4428, E-mail: mary.eberhardt@cuw.edu. *Dean of Graduate Studies,* Dr. Marsha K. Konz, 262-243-4253, Fax: 262-243-4428, E-mail: marsha.konz@cuw.edu.

School of Arts and Sciences Expenses: Contact institution. Offers arts and sciences (MCM); church music (MCM). *Application fee:* $35 ($125 for international students). *Application Contact:* Bill V. Mueller, Graduate Admissions Counselor, 262-243-4551, Fax: 262-243-4428, E-mail: williamvmueller@cuw.edu. *Dean of Graduate Studies,* Dr. Marsha K. Konz, 262-243-4253, Fax: 262-243-4428, E-mail: marsha.konz@cuw.edu.

School of Business Administration Expenses: Contact institution. Offers business administration (MBA, MS); finance (MBA); health care administration (MBA); human resource management (MBA); international business (MBA); international business-bilingual English/Chinese (MBA); management (MBA); management information systems (MBA); managerial communications (MBA); marketing (MBA); organizational leadership administration (MS); public administration (MBA); risk management (MBA). *Application Contact:* Mary Eberhardt, Graduate Admissions, 262-243-4551, Fax: 262-243-4428, E-mail: mary.eberhardt@cuw.edu. *Dean of Graduate Studies,* Dr. Marsha K. Konz, 262-243-4253, Fax: 262-243-4428, E-mail: marsha.konz@cuw.edu.

School of Health Professions Expenses: Contact institution. Offers health professions (MOT, MSRS, DPT); occupational therapy (MOT); physical therapy (DPT); rehabilitation science (MSRS). *Application Contact:* Bill V. Mueller, Graduate Admissions Counselor, 262-243-4551, Fax: 262-243-4428, E-mail: williamvmueller@cuw.edu. *Dean of Graduate Studies,* Dr. Marsha K. Konz, 262-243-4253, Fax: 262-243-4428, E-mail: marsha.konz@cuw.edu.

School of Nursing Expenses: Contact institution. *Financial support:* Application deadline: 8/1. *Program availability:* Online learning. Offers family nurse practitioner (MSN). *Application deadline:* For fall admission, 8/1 priority date for domestic students. Applications are processed on a rolling basis. *Application fee:* $35. *Application Contact:* Mary Eberhardt, Graduate Admissions, 262-243-4551, Fax: 262-243-4428, E-mail: mary.eberhardt@cuw.edu. *Director,* Dr. Ruth Gresley, 262-243-4452, E-mail: ruth.gresley@cuw.edu.

School of Pharmacy Expenses: Contact institution. Offers pharmaceutical/chemical product development (MPD); pharmacy (Pharm D). *Application Contact:* Dr. Dean L. Arneson, Dean, 262-243-2753, E-mail: dean.arneson@cuw.edu. *Dean,* Dr. Dean L. Arneson, 262-243-2753, E-mail: dean.arneson@cuw.edu.

CONCORD LAW SCHOOL, Los Angeles, CA 90024
General Information Proprietary, coed, graduate-only institution.

GRADUATE UNITS

Program in Law *Program availability:* Part-time, evening/weekend, online learning. Offers law (EJD, JD). Electronic applications accepted.

CONCORD UNIVERSITY, Athens, WV 24712-1000
General Information State-supported, coed, comprehensive institution. *Enrollment:* 2,451 graduate, professional, and undergraduate students; 129 full-time matriculated graduate/professional students (105 women), 220 part-time matriculated graduate/professional students (169 women). *Enrollment by degree level:* 302 master's, 47 other advanced degrees. *Graduate faculty:* 16 full-time (10 women), 7 part-time/adjunct (4 women). Tuition, state resident: full-time $3800; part-time $2539 per semester. Tuition, nonresident: full-time $6627; part-time $4416 per semester. Tuition and fees vary according to course load. *Graduate housing:* Room and/or apartments available on a first-come, first-served basis to single students; on-campus housing not available to married students. Typical cost: $4308 per year ($8601 including board). Room and board charges vary according to board plan. *Student services:* Campus employment opportunities, career counseling, child daycare facilities, free psychological counseling, international student services, multicultural affairs office, services for students with disabilities. *Library facilities:* J. Frank Marsh Library. *Collection:* Books: 156,138 (physical), 3,029 (digital/electronic); Serial titles: 86 (physical), 110 (digital/electronic); Databases: 21. Weekly public service hours: 77; study areas open 24 hours, 5–7 days a week; students can reserve study rooms.

Computer facilities: 350 computers available on campus for general student use. A campuswide network can be accessed from student residence rooms and from off campus. Online class registration is available.
Website: http://www.concord.edu/

General Application Contact: Debra Moore, Special Events Assistant, 304-384-5113, E-mail: dlm@concord.edu.

GRADUATE UNITS

Graduate Studies Students: 129 full-time (105 women), 220 part-time (169 women); includes 28 minority (26 Black or African American; 1 American Indian or Alaska Native, non-Hispanic/Latino; 1 Hispanic/Latino), 2 international. *Faculty:* 16 full-time (10 women), 7 part-time/adjunct (4 women). Expenses: Contact institution. *Financial support:* Tuition waivers and unspecified assistantships available. Financial award applicants required to submit FAFSA. *Program availability:* Part-time, evening/weekend, online learning. Offers educational leadership and supervision (M Ed); health promotion (MA); reading specialist (M Ed); social work (MSW); special education (M Ed); teaching (MAT). *Application deadline:* Applications are processed on a rolling basis. *Application fee:* $30. Electronic applications accepted. *Application Contact:* Debra Moore, Special Events Assistant, 304-384-5113, E-mail: dlm@concord.edu. *Director,* Dr. Cheryl Barnes, 304-384-6306, E-mail: cbarnes@concord.edu.

CONSERVATORIO DE MUSICA DE PUERTO RICO, San Juan, PR 00907
General Information Commonwealth-supported, coed, comprehensive institution.

GRADUATE UNITS

Program in Musical Performance Offers guitar (Diploma); orchestral instruments (Diploma); piano (Diploma); vocal performance (Diploma).
Program in Music Education Offers music education (MM Ed).

CONVERSE COLLEGE, Spartanburg, SC 29302
General Information Independent, Undergraduate: women only; graduate: coed, comprehensive institution. *Enrollment:* 1,319 graduate, professional, and undergraduate students; 108 full-time matriculated graduate/professional students (85 women), 341 part-time matriculated graduate/professional students (288 women). *Enrollment by degree level:* 416 master's, 33 other advanced degrees. *Tuition:* Full-time $3600; part-time $400 per credit hour. *Required fees:* $70 per term. *Graduate housing:* Room and/or apartments available to single students; on-campus housing not available to married students. *Student services:* Campus employment opportunities, campus safety program, career counseling, international student services, teacher training. *Library facilities:* Mickel Library. *Collection:* Books: 165,873 (physical), 252,047 (digital/electronic); Databases: 30.

Computer facilities: 140 computers available on campus for general student use. A campuswide network can be accessed from student residence rooms and from off campus. Online class registration is available.
Website: http://www.converse.edu/

General Application Contact: Graduate Admissions, 864-596-9404, E-mail: graduate@converse.edu.

GRADUATE UNITS

School of Education and Graduate Studies Expenses: Contact institution. *Financial support:* Research assistantships, career-related internships or fieldwork, and scholarships/grants available. Support available to part-time students. Financial award applicants required to submit FAFSA. *Program availability:* Part-time, evening/weekend. Offers administration and leadership (Ed S); administration and supervision (M Ed, Ed S); art education (M Ed, MAT); biology (MAT); chemistry (MAT); creative writing (MFA); education (M Ed, M Mus, MAT, MFA, MLA, MMFT, Ed S); elementary education (M Ed, MAT); English (M Ed, MAT, MLA); gifted education (M Ed); history (MLA); intellectual disabilities (MAT); language arts/English (MAT); learning disabilities (MAT); literacy (Ed S); marriage and family therapy (MMFT); mathematics (M Ed, MAT); middle level education (M Ed); natural sciences (M Ed); political science (MLA); science (MAT); social sciences (M Ed, MAT); social studies (MAT); special education (M Ed). *Application deadline:* For fall admission, 8/1 for domestic and international students; for winter admission, 11/15 for domestic and international students; for spring admission, 1/15 for domestic and international students. Applications are processed on a rolling basis. *Application fee:* $40. Electronic applications accepted. *Application Contact:* 864-596-9404, E-mail: graduate@converse.edu.

Petrie School of Music Expenses: Contact institution. *Financial support:* Career-related internships or fieldwork, Federal Work-Study, institutionally sponsored loans, and unspecified assistantships available. Support available to part-time students. Financial award application deadline: 4/15. *Program availability:* Part-time, evening/weekend. Offers music education (M Mus); performance (M Mus). *Application deadline:* For spring admission, 3/1 priority date for domestic and international students. Applications are processed on a rolling basis. *Application fee:* $40. Electronic applications accepted. *Application Contact:* 864-596-9404, E-mail: graduate@converse.edu. *Director,* Patricia S. Foy, 864-596-9172, E-mail: patti.foy@converse.edu.

THE CONWAY SCHOOL, Conway, MA 01341-0179
General Information Independent, coed, graduate-only institution. *Graduate housing:* On-campus housing not available.

GRADUATE UNITS

Program in Ecological Design Offers ecological design (MS).

COOPER UNION FOR THE ADVANCEMENT OF SCIENCE AND ART, New York, NY 10003-7120
General Information Independent, coed, comprehensive institution. *Enrollment:* 964 graduate, professional, and undergraduate students; 49 full-time matriculated graduate/professional students (14 women), 39 part-time matriculated graduate/professional students (8 women). *Enrollment by degree level:* 88 master's. *Graduate faculty:* 29 full-time (3 women), 19 part-time/adjunct (6 women). *Tuition:* Full-time $16,055; part-time $1235 per credit. *Required fees:* $925 per semester. One-time fee: $250. Tuition and fees vary according to course load. *Graduate housing:* On-campus housing not available. *Student services:* Campus employment opportunities, campus safety program, career counseling, international student services, low-cost health insurance, services for students with disabilities, writing training. *Library facilities:* Cooper Union Library. *Collection:* Books: 97,656 (physical), 15,649 (digital/electronic); Serial titles: 73 (physical), 41,326 (digital/electronic); Databases: 51. Weekly public service hours: 69. *Research affiliation:* National Science Foundation, Albert Einstein College of Medicine (child obesity and sleep apnea), National Institutes of Health, edX (STEM education), New York State Energy Research and Development Authority (energy efficiency and power regeneration), Maxentric (wireless communications).

Computer facilities: Computer purchase and lease plans are available. 100 computers available on campus for general student use. A campuswide network can be accessed from student residence rooms and from off campus. Online class registration is available.
Website: http://www.cooper.edu/

General Application Contact: Chabeli Lajara, Administrative Assistant, 212-353-4120, E-mail: admissions@cooper.edu.

GRADUATE UNITS

Albert Nerken School of Engineering Students: 36 full-time (5 women), 39 part-time (8 women); includes 34 minority (3 Black or African American, non-Hispanic/Latino; 16 Asian, non-Hispanic/Latino; 5 Hispanic/Latino; 10 Two or more races, non-Hispanic/Latino), 3 international. Average age 24. 59 applicants, 75% accepted, 34 enrolled. *Faculty:* 27 full-time (1 woman), 15 part-time/adjunct (2 women). Expenses: Contact institution. *Financial support:* In 2016–17, 70 students received support, including 4 fellowships with tuition reimbursements available (averaging $11,000 per year); career-related internships or fieldwork, tuition waivers (full and partial), and tuition scholarships offered to exceptional students also available. Support available to part-time students. Financial award application deadline: 5/1; financial award applicants required to submit FAFSA. In 2016, 25 master's awarded. *Program availability:* Part-time. Offers chemical engineering (ME); civil engineering (ME); electrical engineering (ME); mechanical engineering (ME). *Application deadline:* For fall admission, 3/31 for domestic and international students. *Application fee:* $75. Electronic applications accepted. *Application Contact:* Chabeli Lajara, Administrative Assistant, 212-353-4120, E-mail: admissions@cooper.edu. *Acting Dean of Albert Nerken School of Engineering,* Richard Stock, 212-353-4285, E-mail: stock@cooper.edu.

Irwin S. Chanin School of Architecture Students: 13 full-time (9 women), 10 international. Average age 26. 66 applicants, 29% accepted, 14 enrolled. *Faculty:* 14 full-time (3 women), 19 part-time/adjunct (6 women). Expenses: Contact institution. *Financial support:* In 2016–17, 14 students received support. Tuition waivers (partial) and tuition scholarships offered to exceptional students available. Financial award application deadline: 5/1; financial award applicants required to submit FAFSA. In 2016, 6 master's awarded. Offers architecture (M Arch II). *Application deadline:* For fall admission, 1/31 for domestic and international students. *Application fee:* $75. Electronic applications accepted. *Application Contact:* Chabeli Lajara, Administrative Assistant, 212-353-4120, E-mail: admissions@cooper.edu. *Dean,* Nader Tehrani, 212-353-4220, E-mail: ntehrani@cooper.edu.

COPPIN STATE UNIVERSITY, Baltimore, MD 21216-3698

General Information State-supported, coed, comprehensive institution. CGS member. *Graduate housing:* On-campus housing not available.

GRADUATE UNITS

Division of Graduate Studies *Program availability:* Part-time, evening/weekend, online learning.

Division of Arts and Sciences *Program availability:* Part-time, evening/weekend. Offers alcohol and substance abuse counseling (MS); arts and sciences (M Ed, MA, MS); criminal justice (MS); human services administration (MS); rehabilitation counseling (M Ed).

Division of Education *Program availability:* Part-time, evening/weekend, online learning. Offers adult and general education (MS); curriculum and instruction (M Ed); education (M Ed, MAT, MS); reading education (MS); special education (M Ed); teacher education (MAT); teaching (MAT).

Helene Fuld School of Nursing *Program availability:* Part-time, evening/weekend. Offers family nurse practitioner (PMC); nursing (MSN).

CORBAN UNIVERSITY, Salem, OR 97301-9392

General Information Independent-religious, coed, comprehensive institution.

GRADUATE UNITS

Graduate School Offers counseling (MA); education (MS Ed); management (MBA); non-profit management (MBA).

School of Ministry *Program availability:* Part-time, evening/weekend. Offers Biblical languages (M Div); Biblical leadership (Certificate); Christian leadership (MA); Church ministry (M Div); ministry (D Min).

CORNELL UNIVERSITY, Ithaca, NY 14853

General Information Independent, coed, university. CGS member. *Graduate housing:* Rooms and/or apartments available on a first-come, first-served basis to single and married students. Housing application deadline: 7/1. *Research affiliation:* Brookhaven National Laboratory (physics, biology, medicine, chemistry, energy, engineering, environmental science), Fermi National Accelerator Laboratory, Boyce Thompson Institute for Plant Research (plant research).

GRADUATE UNITS

College of Veterinary Medicine Students: 396 full-time (311 women); includes 79 minority (3 Black or African American, non-Hispanic/Latino; 26 Asian, non-Hispanic/Latino; 17 Hispanic/Latino; 33 Two or more races, non-Hispanic/Latino), 6 international. Average age 26. 1,025 applicants, 15% accepted, 101 enrolled. *Faculty:* 194 full-time (89 women). Expenses: Contact institution. *Financial support:* In 2016–17, 270 students received support. Federal Work-Study, institutionally sponsored loans, and scholarships/grants available. Financial award application deadline: 2/15; financial award applicants required to submit CSS PROFILE or FAFSA. In 2016, 98 doctorates awarded. Offers veterinary medicine (DVM). *Application deadline:* For fall admission, 9/15 for domestic and international students. Electronic applications accepted. *Application Contact:* Jennifer A. Mailey, Director of Admissions, 607-253-3700, Fax: 607-253-3709, E-mail: jam333@cornell.edu. *Dean,* Dr. Lorin Warnick, 607-253-3771, Fax: 607-253-3701.

Cornell Law School Offers law (LL M, JD, JSD). JD/MLLP offered jointly with Humboldt University, Berlin; JD/DESS offered jointly with Institut d'etudes Politiques de Paris ("Sciences Po") and Paris I. Electronic applications accepted.

Graduate School Students: 5,482 full-time (2,507 women); includes 861 minority (102 Black or African American, non-Hispanic/Latino; 10 American Indian or Alaska Native, non-Hispanic/Latino; 373 Asian, non-Hispanic/Latino; 263 Hispanic/Latino; 3 Native Hawaiian or other Pacific Islander, non-Hispanic/Latino; 110 Two or more races, non-Hispanic/Latino), 2,630 international. Average age 27. 20,805 applicants, 23% accepted, 2101 enrolled. *Faculty:* 1,961 full-time (561 women). Expenses: Contact institution. *Financial support:* In 2016–17, 2,921 students received support, including 729 fellowships with full tuition reimbursements available, 984 research assistantships with full tuition reimbursements available, 1,208 teaching assistantships with full tuition reimbursements available; career-related internships or fieldwork, institutionally sponsored loans, scholarships/grants, traineeships, health care benefits, tuition waivers (full and partial), and unspecified assistantships also available. Financial award applicants required to submit FAFSA. In 2016, 1,844 master's, 497 doctorates awarded. Offers 19th century art (PhD); acarology (MS, PhD); adult and extension education (MPS, MS, PhD); advanced composites and structures (M Eng); advanced materials processing (M Eng, MS, PhD); aerospace engineering (M Eng, MS, PhD); African history (MA, PhD); African studies (MPS); African, African American and African diaspora (PhD); African-American literature (PhD); African-American studies (MPS); Africana studies (PhD); agricultural finance (MS, PhD); agriculture and life sciences (M Eng, MFS, MLA, MPS, MS, PhD); agronomy (MS, PhD); algorithms (M Eng, PhD); American art (PhD); American history (MA, PhD); American literature after 1865 (PhD); American literature to 1865 (PhD); American politics (PhD); American studies (PhD); analytical chemistry (PhD); ancient art and archaeology (PhD); ancient Greek history (PhD); ancient history (MA, PhD); ancient Near Eastern studies (PhD); ancient philosophy (PhD); ancient Roman history (PhD); animal cytology (PhD); animal genetics (MPS, MS, PhD); animal genomics (MPS, MS, PhD); animal nutrition (MPS, MS, PhD); animal science (MS, MS); apiculture (MS, PhD); apparel design (MA, MPS); applied econometrics and qualitative analysis (MS, PhD); applied economics (PhD); applied entomology (MS, PhD); applied linguistics (MA, PhD); applied logic and automated reasoning (M Eng, MS, PhD); applied mathematics (PhD); applied mathematics and computational methods (M Eng, MS, PhD); applied physics (PhD); applied probability

and statistics (PhD); applied research in human-environment relations (MS); applied statistics (MPS); aquatic entomology (MS, PhD); Arabic and Islamic studies (MA, PhD); archaeological anthropology (PhD); architectural design (M Arch); architectural science (MS); architecture, art and planning (M Arch, MA, MFA, MPS, MRP, MS, PhD); artificial intelligence (M Eng, PhD); arts and sciences (MA, MFA, MPA, MPS, MS, DMA, PhD); Asian American art (PhD); Asian religions (MA, PhD); astronomy (PhD); astrophysics (PhD); atmospheric science (MS, PhD); Baroque art (PhD); basic analytical economics (PhD); behavioral biology (PhD); behavioral physiology (MS, PhD); biblical studies (MA, PhD); bio-organic chemistry (PhD); biochemical engineering (M Eng, MS, PhD); biochemistry (PhD); bioenergy and integrated energy systems (M Eng, MPS, MS, PhD); biological anthropology (PhD); biological control (MS, PhD); biological engineering (M Eng, MPS, MS, PhD); biomechanical engineering (M Eng, MS, PhD); biomedical engineering (M Eng, MS, PhD); biometry (MS, PhD); biophysical chemistry (PhD); biophysics (PhD); bioprocess engineering (M Eng, MPS, MS, PhD); biopsychology (PhD); breeding of horticultural crops (MPS); cardiovascular and respiratory physiology (MS, PhD); cell biology (PhD); cellular and molecular medicine (PhD); cellular and molecular toxicology (MS, PhD); cellular immunology (MS, PhD); chemical biology (PhD); chemical physics (PhD); chemical reaction engineering (M Eng, MS, PhD); Chinese philosophy (PhD); city and regional planning (MRP, PhD); classical and statistical thermodynamics (M Eng, MS, PhD); classical archaeology (PhD); classical Chinese literature (PhD); classical Japanese literature (PhD); classical literature and philology (PhD); classical myth (PhD); classical rhetoric (PhD); cognition (PhD); collective bargaining, labor law and labor history (MILR, MPS, MS, PhD); colonial and postcolonial literatures (PhD); combustion (M Eng, MS, PhD); communication (MS, PhD); community nutrition (MPS, PhD); comparative and functional anatomy (PhD); comparative biomedical sciences (MS, PhD); comparative literature (PhD); comparative modernities (PhD); comparative politics (PhD); composition (DMA); computational behavioral biology (PhD); computational biology (PhD); computational cell biology (PhD); computational ecology (PhD); computational genetics (PhD); computational macromolecular biology (PhD); computational organismal biology (PhD); computer engineering (M Eng, PhD); computer graphics (M Eng, MS, PhD); computer science (M Eng, PhD); computer vision (M Eng, PhD); concurrency and distributed computing (M Eng, PhD); conservation biology (MS, PhD); consumer policy (PhD); cytology (MS, PhD); dairy science (MPS, MS, PhD); decision theory (MS, PhD); development policy (MPS); developmental and reproductive biology (MS, PhD); developmental biology (PhD); developmental psychology (MA, PhD); digital art (PhD); drama and the theatre (PhD); dramatic literature (PhD); dynamics and space mechanics (MS, PhD); early modern European history (MA, PhD); East Asian art (PhD); East Asian linguistics (MA, PhD); East Asian literature and culture (PhD); East Asian studies (MA); ecohydrology (M Eng, MPS, MS, PhD); ecology (PhD); econometrics and economic statistics (PhD); economic and social statistics (MILR, MS, PhD); economic development and planning (PhD); economic geology (M Eng, MS, PhD); economic theory (PhD); economics of development (MS, PhD); economy and society (MA, PhD); ecosystem biology and biogeochemistry (MPS, MS, PhD); ecotoxicology and environmental chemistry (MS, PhD); electrical engineering (M Eng, PhD); electrical systems (M Eng, MS, PhD); electrophysics (M Eng, PhD); endocrinology (MS, PhD); energy and power systems (M Eng, MS, PhD); engineering (M Eng, MPS, MS, PhD); engineering geology (M Eng, MS, PhD); engineering management (M Eng, MS, PhD); engineering physics (M Eng); engineering statistics (MS, PhD); English history (MA, PhD); English linguistics (MA, PhD); English poetry (PhD); English Renaissance to 1660 (PhD); enology (MS, PhD); environmental and comparative physiology (MS, PhD); environmental archaeology (MA); environmental economics (MS, PhD); environmental engineering (M Eng, MPS, MS, PhD); environmental fluid mechanics and hydrology (M Eng, MS, PhD); environmental geophysics (M Eng, MS, PhD); environmental information science (MS, PhD); environmental management (MPS); environmental planning and design (MRP, PhD); environmental studies (MA, MS, PhD); environmental systems engineering (M Eng, MS, PhD); evolutionary biology (PhD); experimental design (MS, PhD); experimental physics (MS, PhD); facilities planning and management (MS); family and social welfare policy (PhD); farm management and production economics (MS, PhD); fiber science (MS, PhD); field crop science (MS, PhD); fishery and aquatic science (MPS, MS, PhD); fluid dynamics, rheology and biorheology (M Eng, MS, PhD); fluid mechanics (M Eng, MS, PhD); food chemistry (MPS, MS, PhD); food engineering (M Eng, MPS, MS, PhD); food microbiology (MPS, MS, PhD); food processing waste technology (MPS, MS, PhD); food science (MFS, MPS, MS, PhD); forest science (MPS, MS, PhD); French history (MA, PhD); French linguistics (PhD); French literature (PhD); fungal and oomycete biology (MPS, MS, PhD); gastrointestinal and metabolic physiology (MS, PhD); gender and life course (MA, PhD); general geology (M Eng, MS, PhD); general linguistics (MA, PhD); general space sciences (PhD); genetics (PhD); genomics (PhD); geobiology (M Eng, MS, PhD); geochemistry and isotope geology (M Eng, MS, PhD); geohydrology (M Eng, MS, PhD); geomorphology (M Eng, MS, PhD); geophysics (M Eng, MS, PhD); geotechnical engineering (M Eng, MS, PhD); geotectonics (M Eng, MS, PhD); German area studies (MA, PhD); German history (MA, PhD); German intellectual history (MA, PhD); Germanic linguistics (PhD); Germanic literature (MA, PhD); Greek and Latin language and linguistics (PhD); health administration (MHA); health management and policy (PhD); heat and mass transfer (M Eng, MS, PhD); heat transfer (M Eng, MS, PhD); Hebrew and Judaic studies (MA, PhD); Hispanic literature (PhD); histology (MS, PhD); historic preservation planning (MA); historical archaeology (MA); history and philosophy of science and technology (MA, PhD); history of architecture (MA, PhD); history of photography (PhD); history of science (MA, PhD); history of urban development (MA, PhD); horticultural crop management systems (MPS); housing and design (MS); human computer interaction (PhD); human development and family studies (MA, PhD); human dimensions of natural resources management (MPS, MS, PhD); human ecology (MA, MHA, MPA, MPS, MS, PhD); human experimental psychology (PhD); human factors and ergonomics (MS); human nutrition (MPS, PhD); human resource studies (MILR, MPS, MS, PhD); human-computer interaction (MS, PhD); human-environment relations (MS); human-plant interactions (MPS, PhD); immunochemistry (MS, PhD); immunogenetics (MS, PhD); immunopathology (MS, PhD); Indo-European linguistics (MA, PhD); industrial and labor relations problems (MILR, MPS, MS, PhD); industrial biotechnology (M Eng, MPS, MS, PhD); industrial organization and control (PhD); infection and immunity (MS, PhD); infectious diseases (MS, PhD); information organization and retrieval (M Eng, PhD); information science (PhD); information systems (PhD); infrared astronomy (PhD); inorganic chemistry (PhD); insect behavior (MS, PhD); insect biochemistry (MS, PhD); insect ecology (MS, PhD); insect genetics (MS, PhD); insect morphology (MS, PhD); insect pathology (MS, PhD); insect physiology (MS, PhD); insect systematics (MS, PhD); insect toxicology and insecticide chemistry (MS, PhD); integrated pest management (MS, PhD); interior design (MA, MPS); international agriculture and development (MPS); international and comparative labor (MILR, MPS, MS, PhD); international development (MPS); international development planning (MRP, PhD); international economics (PhD); international food science (MPS, MS, PhD);

international nutrition (MPS, PhD); international planning (MPS); international population (MPS); international relations (PhD); international spatial problems (MA, MS, PhD); Islamic art (PhD); Italian linguistics (PhD); Italian literature (PhD); kinetics and catalysis (M Eng, MS, PhD); Korean history (PhD); Korean literature (PhD); labor economics (MILR, MPS, MS, PhD); landscape architecture (MLA, MPS); language and communication (MS, PhD); Latin American archaeology (MA); Latin American art (PhD); Latin American history (MA, PhD); learning, teaching, and social policy (MPS, MS, PhD); lesbian, bisexual, and gay literary studies (PhD); literary criticism and theory (PhD); location theory (MA, MS, PhD); manufacturing systems engineering (PhD); marine geology (MS, PhD); marketing and food distribution (MS, PhD); materials and manufacturing engineering (M Eng, MS, PhD); materials chemistry (PhD); materials engineering (M Eng, PhD); materials science (M Eng, PhD); mathematical programming (PhD); mathematical statistics (MS, PhD); mathematics (PhD); mathematics 7-12 (MS); mechanical systems and design (M Eng, PhD); mechanics of materials (MS, PhD); media communication and society (MS, PhD); medical and veterinary entomology (MS, PhD); medieval and Renaissance Latin literature (PhD); medieval archaeology (MA, PhD); medieval art (PhD); medieval Chinese history (MA, PhD); medieval history (MA, PhD); medieval literature (PhD); medieval music (PhD); medieval philology and linguistics (PhD); medieval philosophy (PhD); Mediterranean and Near Eastern archaeology (MA); membrane and epithelial physiology (MS, PhD); methodology (MA, PhD); microbiology (PhD); mineralogy (M Eng, MS, PhD); modern art (PhD); modern Chinese history (MA, PhD); modern Chinese literature (PhD); modern European history (MA, PhD); modern Japanese history (PhD); modern Japanese literature (PhD); modern Middle Eastern history (PhD); molecular and cellular physiology (MS, PhD); molecular biochemistry (MPS, PhD); molecular biology (PhD); monetary and macro economics (PhD); multiphase flows (M Eng, MS, PhD); multiregional economic analysis (MA, MS, PhD); musicology (PhD); nanobiotechnology (M Eng, MPS, MS, PhD); neural and sensory physiology (MS, PhD); neurobiology (PhD); nutritional and food toxicology (MS, PhD); Old and Middle English (PhD); old Norse (PhD); operating systems (M Eng, PhD); operations research and industrial engineering (M Eng); organic chemistry (PhD); organizational behavior (MILR, MPS, MS, PhD); organizational communication (MS, PhD); organizations (MA, PhD); organometallic chemistry (PhD); paleobotany (MS, PhD); paleontology (M Eng, MS, PhD); parallel computing (M Eng, PhD); peace science (MA, MS, PhD); performance practice (DMA); personality and social psychology (PhD); petroleum geology (M Eng, MS, PhD); petrology (M Eng, MS, PhD); pharmacology (MS, PhD); philosophy (PhD); phonetics (MA, PhD); phonological theory (MA, PhD); physical chemistry (PhD); physics (MS, PhD); physiological genomics (MS, PhD); physiology and ecology of horticultural crops (MPS, MS, PhD); physiology of reproduction (MPS, MS, PhD); planetary geology (M Eng, MS, PhD); planetary studies (PhD); planning methods (MA, MS, PhD); planning theory and systems analysis (MRP, PhD); plant biochemistry (MPS, MS, PhD); plant breeding (MPS, MS, PhD); plant cell biology (MS, PhD); plant ecology (MS, PhD); plant genetics (MPS, MS, PhD); plant microbe pathology (MPS, MS, PhD); plant molecular biology (MS, PhD); plant morphology, anatomy and biomechanics (MS, PhD); plant pathology (MPS, MS, PhD); plant physiology (MS, PhD); plant protection (MPS); policy analysis (MA, PhD); policy and institutional analysis (MS, PhD); political methodology (PhD); political sociology/social movements (MA, PhD); political thought (PhD); polymer chemistry (PhD); polymer science (MS, PhD); polymers (M Eng, MS, PhD); population and development (MS, PhD); population medicine and epidemiology (MS, PhD); Precambrian geology (M Eng, MS, PhD); premodern Islamic history (MA, PhD); premodern Japanese history (MA, PhD); probability (MS, PhD); program development and evaluation (MPS, MS, PhD); programming environments (M Eng, PhD); programming languages and methodology (M Eng, PhD); prose fiction (PhD); public affairs (MPA); public finance (PhD); public policy (PhD); public policy analysis (MA, PhD); quantitative ecology (MS, PhD); Quaternary geology (M Eng, MS, PhD); racial and ethnic relations (MA, PhD); radio astronomy (PhD); radiophysics (PhD); real estate (MPS); regional economics and development planning (MRP, PhD); regional science (MRP, PhD); remote sensing (M Eng, MS, PhD); Renaissance art (PhD); Renaissance history (MA, PhD); reproductive physiology (MS, PhD); resource economics (PhD); Restoration and the eighteenth-century (PhD); risk assessment, management and public policy (MS, PhD); robotics (M Eng, PhD); rock mechanics (M Eng, MS, PhD); Romance linguistics (MA, PhD); rural and environmental sociology (MS, PhD); Russian history (MA, PhD); sampling (MS, PhD); science and technology policy (MPS); science, environment and health communication (MS, PhD); scientific computing (M Eng, PhD); second language acquisition (MA, PhD); sedimentology (M Eng, MS, PhD); seismology (M Eng, MS, PhD); semantics (MA, PhD); sensory evaluation (MPS, MS, PhD); Slavic linguistics (MA, PhD); social and health systems planning (MRP, PhD); social aspects of information (PhD); social networks (MA, PhD); social psychology (MA, PhD); social psychology of communication (MS, PhD); social stratification (MA, PhD); social studies of science and technology (MA, PhD); sociocultural anthropology (PhD); sociolinguistics (MA, PhD); soil science (MS, PhD); solid mechanics (PhD); South Asian history (PhD); South Asian linguistics (MA, PhD); South Asian literature and culture (PhD); South Asian studies (MA); Southeast Asian art (PhD); Southeast Asian history (MA, PhD); Southeast Asian linguistics (PhD); Southeast Asian literature and culture (PhD); Southeast Asian studies (MA); Spanish linguistics (PhD); state, economy, and society (MS, PhD); statistical computing (MS, PhD); stochastic processes (MS, PhD); Stone Age archaeology (MA); stratigraphy (M Eng, MS, PhD); structural and functional biology (MS, PhD); structural engineering (M Eng, MS, PhD); structural geology (M Eng, MS, PhD); structural mechanics (M Eng, MS); surface science (M Eng, MS, PhD); sustainable systems (M Eng, MPS, MS, PhD); syntactic theory (MA, PhD); synthetic biology (MS); syntheticbiology (M Eng, MPS, PhD); systematic botany (MS, PhD); systems engineering (M Eng, PhD); textile science (MS, PhD); the nineteenth century (PhD); the twentieth century (PhD); theatre history (PhD); theatre theory and aesthetics (PhD); theoretical astrophysics (PhD); theoretical chemistry (PhD); theoretical physics (MS, PhD); theory and criticism (PhD); theory and criticism of architecture (M Arch); theory of computation (M Eng, PhD); theory of music (MA); transportation engineering (MS, PhD); transportation systems engineering (M Eng); urban and regional economics (MA, MS, PhD); urban and regional theory (MRP, PhD); urban design (M Arch); urban planning history (MRP, PhD); visual studies (PhD); water resource systems (M Eng, MS, PhD); wildlife conservation (PhD); wildlife science (MPS, MS, PhD); women's literature (PhD). *Application deadline:* For fall admission, 1/15 for domestic and international students; for spring admission, 11/1 for domestic and international students. *Application fee:* $105. Electronic applications accepted. *Application Contact:* Graduate School Application Requests, 607-255-5816, E-mail: gradadmissions@cornell.edu. *Dean,* Dr. Barbara Knuth, 607-255-5417.

Field of Hotel Administration Offers hospitality management (MMH); hotel administration (MS, PhD). Electronic applications accepted.

Graduate Field in the Law School Offers law (JSD). Electronic applications accepted.

Graduate Field of Management Offers accounting (PhD); finance (PhD); marketing (PhD); organizational behavior (PhD); production and operations management (PhD). Electronic applications accepted.

Samuel Curtis Johnson Graduate School of Management Students: 580 full-time (174 women); includes 139 minority (18 Black or African American, non-Hispanic/Latino; 2 American Indian or Alaska Native, non-Hispanic/Latino; 77 Asian, non-Hispanic/Latino; 26 Hispanic/Latino; 16 Two or more races, non-Hispanic/Latino), 191 international. Average age 28. 1,960 applicants, 27% accepted, 279 enrolled. *Faculty:* 62 full-time (17 women), 65 part-time/adjunct (8 women). Expenses: Contact institution. *Financial support:* Fellowships, research assistantships, career-related internships or fieldwork, Federal Work-Study, institutionally sponsored loans, and tuition waivers (full and partial) available. Financial award applicants required to submit FAFSA. Offers business administration (Exec MBA); management (MBA); management - accounting (MPS). *Application deadline:* For fall admission, 10/5 for domestic and international students; for winter admission, 11/15 for domestic and international students; for spring admission, 1/10 for domestic and international students; for summer admission, 3/15 for domestic and international students. *Application fee:* $200. Electronic applications accepted. *Application Contact:* Admissions Office, 800-847-2082, Fax: 607-255-0065, E-mail: mba@johnson.cornell.edu. *Dean,* Dr. Mark Nelson, 607-255-6418, E-mail: dean@johnson.cornell.edu.

CORNERSTONE UNIVERSITY, Grand Rapids, MI 49525-5897
General Information Independent-religious, coed, comprehensive institution. *Graduate housing:* Rooms and/or apartments available on a first-come, first-served basis to single and married students.
GRADUATE UNITS
Graduate Programs *Program availability:* Part-time, online learning. Offers business administration (MBA); education (MA Ed); management (MSM); teaching English to speakers of other languages (MA, Graduate Certificate). Programs also offered at Holland, Kalamazoo, and Troy, MI campuses. Electronic applications accepted.

COVENANT COLLEGE, Lookout Mountain, GA 30750
General Information Independent-religious, coed, comprehensive institution. *Graduate housing:* Room and/or apartments available on a first-come, first-served basis to single students; on-campus housing not available to married students. Housing application deadline: 5/1.
GRADUATE UNITS
Program in Education *Program availability:* Part-time. Offers education (M Ed, MAT).

COVENANT THEOLOGICAL SEMINARY, St. Louis, MO 63141-8697
General Information Independent-religious, coed, graduate-only institution. *Graduate housing:* Rooms and/or apartments available on a first-come, first-served basis to single and married students.
GRADUATE UNITS
Graduate and Professional Programs *Program availability:* Part-time, evening/weekend, online learning. Offers theology (M Div, MA, MAC, MAEM, Th M, D Min, Certificate). Electronic applications accepted.

COX COLLEGE, Springfield, MO 65802
General Information Independent, coed, primarily women, comprehensive institution.
GRADUATE UNITS
Programs in Nursing Offers clinical nurse leader (MSN); family nurse practitioner (MSN); nurse educator (MSN). Electronic applications accepted.

CRANBROOK ACADEMY OF ART, Bloomfield Hills, MI 48303-0801
General Information Independent, coed, graduate-only institution. *Enrollment by degree level:* 140 master's. *Graduate faculty:* 10 full-time (4 women). *Tuition:* Full-time $37,375. *Required fees:* $1460. *Graduate housing:* Room and/or apartments available on a first-come, first-served basis to single students; on-campus housing not available to married students. Typical cost: $3270 per year. Housing application deadline: 4/1. *Student services:* Campus employment opportunities. *Library facilities:* Cranbrook Academy of Art Library. *Collection:* Books: 39,349 (physical); Serial titles: 4,343 (physical); Databases: 40.

Computer facilities: 20 computers available on campus for general student use. A campuswide network can be accessed from student residence rooms. Website: http://www.cranbrookart.edu/

General Application Contact: Leslie Tobakos, Registrar/Financial Aid and Admissions Manager, 248-645-3360, Fax: 248-645-3591, E-mail: ltobakos@cranbrook.edu.
GRADUATE UNITS
Program in Architecture Expenses: Contact institution. *Financial support:* Federal Work-Study and scholarships/grants available. Financial award application deadline: 2/15; financial award applicants required to submit FAFSA. Offers architecture (M Arch). *Application deadline:* For fall admission, 2/1 priority date for domestic and international students. *Application fee:* $85. Electronic applications accepted. *Application Contact:* Leslie Tobakos, Registrar/Financial Aid and Admissions Manager, 248-645-3360, Fax: 248-645-3591, E-mail: ltobakos@cranbrook.edu. *Interim Head,* Ceren Bingol, 248-645-3462, Fax: 248-645-3591, E-mail: cbingol@cranbrook.edu.

Program in Fine Arts Expenses: Contact institution. *Financial support:* Federal Work-Study and scholarships/grants available. Financial award application deadline: 2/15; financial award applicants required to submit FAFSA. Offers 2d design (MFA); 3d design (MFA); ceramics (MFA); fiber (MFA); metalsmithing (MFA); painting (MFA); photography (MFA); print media (MFA); sculpture (MFA). *Application deadline:* For fall admission, 2/1 priority date for domestic and international students. *Application fee:* $85. Electronic applications accepted. *Application Contact:* Leslie Tobakos, Registrar/Financial Aid and Admissions Manager, 248-645-3360, Fax: 248-645-3591, E-mail: ltobakos@cranbrook.edu. *Director,* Christopher Scoates, 248-645-3301, Fax: 248-645-3591.

CRANDALL UNIVERSITY, Moncton, NB E1C 9L7, Canada
General Information Independent-religious, coed, comprehensive institution.
GRADUATE UNITS
Graduate Programs

CREIGHTON UNIVERSITY, Omaha, NE 68178-0001
General Information Independent-religious, coed, university. CGS member. *Enrollment:* 8,393 graduate, professional, and undergraduate students; 2,796 full-time matriculated graduate/professional students (1,630 women), 1,394 part-time matriculated graduate/professional students (893 women). *Enrollment by degree level:* 1,004 master's, 3,094 doctoral, 92 other advanced degrees. *Graduate faculty:* 323 full-time (120 women). *Tuition:* Full-time $14,400; part-time $800 per credit hour. *Required fees:* $158 per semester. Tuition and fees vary according to course load, campus/location, program, reciprocity agreements and student's religious affiliation. *Graduate housing:* Rooms and/or apartments available on a first-come, first-served basis to single and

married students. Typical cost: $10,620 per year for single students; $10,620 per year for married students. Room charges vary according to board plan, campus/location and housing facility selected. Housing application deadline: 5/1. *Student services:* Campus employment opportunities, campus safety program, career counseling, child daycare facilities, exercise/wellness program, free psychological counseling, grant writing training, international student services, low-cost health insurance, multicultural affairs office, services for students with disabilities, teacher training, writing training. *Library facilities:* Reinert Alumni Memorial Library plus 2 others. *Collection:* Study areas open 24 hours, 5–7 days a week. *Research affiliation:* U.S. Department of Education (DOE) (student support services), National Institutes of Health (asthma), U.S. Department of Commerce (atmospheric science), National Science Foundation (business and education).

Computer facilities: Computer purchase and lease plans are available. 404 computers available on campus for general student use. A campuswide network can be accessed from student residence rooms and from off campus. Online class registration, financial aid information are available.
Website: http://www.creighton.edu/

General Application Contact: Lindsay Johnson, Director of Graduate and Adult Recruitment, 402-280-2703, Fax: 402-280-2423, E-mail: gradschool@creighton.edu.

GRADUATE UNITS

College of Nursing Students: 124 full-time (111 women), 242 part-time (229 women); includes 39 minority (8 Black or African American, non-Hispanic/Latino; 3 American Indian or Alaska Native, non-Hispanic/Latino; 13 Asian, non-Hispanic/Latino; 10 Hispanic/Latino; 5 Two or more races, non-Hispanic/Latino), 1 international. Average age 32. 220 applicants, 75% accepted, 140 enrolled. *Faculty:* 21 full-time (all women), 35 part-time/adjunct (30 women). Expenses: Contact institution. *Financial support:* In 2016–17, 8 students received support. Scholarships/grants available. Financial award applicants required to submit FAFSA. In 2016, 59 master's, 37 doctorates awarded. *Program availability:* Part-time, blended/hybrid learning. Offers adult gerontology acute care nurse practitioner (DNP, Post-Master's Certificate); adult gerontology nurse practitioner (DNP); clinical nurse leader (MSN, Post-Graduate Certificate); clinical systems administration (MSN, DNP); family nurse practitioner (DNP, Post-Master's Certificate); neonatal nurse practitioner (DNP, Post-Master's Certificate); nursing (Post-Graduate Certificate); pediatric acute care nurse practitioner (DNP, Post-Master's Certificate); psychiatric mental health nurse practitioner (DNP). *Application deadline:* For fall admission, 6/15 priority date for domestic and international students; for spring admission, 11/15 priority date for domestic and international students; for summer admission, 4/15 for domestic and international students. Applications are processed on a rolling basis. *Application fee:* $50. Electronic applications accepted. *Application Contact:* Shannon Cox, Enrollment Specialist, 402-280-2067, Fax: 402-280-2045, E-mail: shannoncox@creighton.edu. *Dean,* Dr. Catherine Todero, 402-280-2004, Fax: 402-280-2045.

Graduate School Students: 423 full-time (264 women), 1,312 part-time (827 women); includes 304 minority (106 Black or African American, non-Hispanic/Latino; 10 American Indian or Alaska Native, non-Hispanic/Latino; 56 Asian, non-Hispanic/Latino; 98 Hispanic/Latino; 2 Native Hawaiian or other Pacific Islander, non-Hispanic/Latino; 32 Two or more races, non-Hispanic/Latino), 70 international. Average age 35. 691 applicants, 60% accepted, 241 enrolled. *Faculty:* 323 full-time (119 women). Expenses: Contact institution. *Financial support:* In 2016–17, fellowships with tuition reimbursements (averaging $23,000 per year), research assistantships with tuition reimbursements (averaging $15,700 per year), teaching assistantships with tuition reimbursements (averaging $15,700 per year) were awarded; career-related internships or fieldwork, institutionally sponsored loans, scholarships/grants, tuition waivers (partial), and unspecified assistantships also available. Support available to part-time students. Financial award application deadline: 3/1; financial award applicants required to submit FAFSA. In 2016, 471 master's, 65 doctorates awarded. *Program availability:* Part-time, evening/weekend, 100% online, blended/hybrid learning. Offers emergency medical services (MS); health and wellness coaching (MS); leadership (Ed D); organizational leadership (MS). *Application deadline:* For fall admission, 3/1 priority date for domestic and international students; for winter admission, 10/1 for domestic students, 7/1 for international students; for spring admission, 4/1 for domestic students, 10/1 for international students. Applications are processed on a rolling basis. *Application fee:* $50. Electronic applications accepted. *Application Contact:* Lindsay Johnson, Director of Graduate and Adult Recruitment, 402-280-2703, Fax: 402-280-2423, E-mail: gradschool@creighton.edu. *Dean,* Dr. Gail M. Jensen, 402-280-2424, Fax: 402-280-2423, E-mail: gjensen@creighton.edu.

College of Arts and Sciences Students: 51 full-time (32 women), 198 part-time (139 women); includes 16 minority (4 Black or African American, non-Hispanic/Latino; 4 American Indian or Alaska Native, non-Hispanic/Latino; 1 Asian, non-Hispanic/Latino; 6 Hispanic/Latino; 1 Two or more races, non-Hispanic/Latino), 13 international. Average age 34. 72 applicants, 65% accepted, 12 enrolled. *Faculty:* 119 full-time (37 women). Expenses: Contact institution. *Financial support:* In 2016–17, teaching assistantships with full tuition reimbursements (averaging $11,465 per year) were awarded; fellowships, scholarships/grants, and tuition waivers (partial) also available. Financial award applicants required to submit FAFSA. In 2016, 93 master's awarded. *Program availability:* Part-time, evening/weekend, 100% online, blended/hybrid learning. Offers arts and sciences (M Ed, MA, MFA, MS); creative writing (MA, MFA); East-West studies (MA); educational leadership (MS); elementary school guidance (MS); elementary teaching (M Ed); international relations (MA); medical anthropology (MA); physics (MS); school counseling and preventive mental health (MS); secondary school guidance (MS); secondary teaching (M Ed); teaching (M Ed); theology (MA). *Application deadline:* For fall admission, 3/1 for domestic and international students; for winter admission, 10/1 for domestic students, 7/1 for international students; for spring admission, 4/1 for domestic students, 10/1 for international students. Applications are processed on a rolling basis. *Application fee:* $50. Electronic applications accepted. *Application Contact:* Lindsay Johnson, Director of Graduate and Adult Recruitment, 402-280-2703, Fax: 402-280-2423, E-mail: gradschool@creighton.edu. *Dean,* Dr. Bridget M. Keegan, 402-280-4015, E-mail: bridgetkeegan@creighton.edu.

Heider College of Business Students: 41 full-time (13 women), 262 part-time (79 women); includes 24 minority (16 Black or African American, non-Hispanic/Latino; 3 Asian, non-Hispanic/Latino; 1 Hispanic/Latino; 2 Native Hawaiian or other Pacific Islander, non-Hispanic/Latino; 2 Two or more races, non-Hispanic/Latino), 21 international. Average age 32. 189 applicants, 73% accepted, 74 enrolled. *Faculty:* 33 full-time (10 women), 22 part-time/adjunct (3 women). Expenses: Contact institution. *Financial support:* In 2016–17, 10 fellowships with partial tuition reimbursements (averaging $8,448 per year) were awarded; career-related internships or fieldwork, tuition waivers (partial), and unspecified assistantships also available. Financial award application deadline: 3/1. In 2016, 172 master's awarded. *Program availability:* Part-

time, evening/weekend, 100% online, blended/hybrid learning. Offers accounting (MAC); business administration (MBA); business intelligence and analytics (MS); finance (M Fin). *Application deadline:* For fall admission, 7/1 priority date for domestic students, 3/1 for international students; for winter admission, 10/1 priority date for domestic students, 7/1 for international students; for spring admission, 4/1 priority date for domestic students, 10/1 for international students; for summer admission, 5/1 for domestic and international students. Applications are processed on a rolling basis. *Application fee:* $50. Electronic applications accepted. *Application Contact:* Chris Karasek, Assistant Dean, 402-280-2829, Fax: 402-280-2172, E-mail: chriskarasek@creighton.edu. *Associate Dean for Graduate Programs,* Dr. Deborah Wells, 402-280-2841, E-mail: deborahwells@creighton.edu.

School of Dentistry Offers dentistry (DDS).

School of Law Students: 299 full-time (130 women), 8 part-time (1 woman); includes 65 minority (8 Black or African American, non-Hispanic/Latino; 1 American Indian or Alaska Native, non-Hispanic/Latino; 11 Asian, non-Hispanic/Latino; 32 Hispanic/Latino; 13 Two or more races, non-Hispanic/Latino), 2 international. Average age 25. 923 applicants, 74% accepted, 107 enrolled. *Faculty:* 29 full-time (10 women), 16 part-time/adjunct (4 women). Expenses: Contact institution. *Financial support:* In 2016–17, 216 students received support. Career-related internships or fieldwork, institutionally sponsored loans, and scholarships/grants available. Support available to part-time students. Financial award application deadline: 7/1; financial award applicants required to submit FAFSA. In 2016, 129 doctorates awarded. *Program availability:* Part-time. Offers law (MS, JD, Certificate); negotiation and conflict resolution (MS, Certificate). *Application deadline:* For fall admission, 5/1 priority date for domestic and international students; for summer admission, 4/1 priority date for domestic and international students. Applications are processed on a rolling basis. Electronic applications accepted. *Application Contact:* Andrea D. Bashara, Assistant Dean, 402-280-2586, Fax: 402-280-3161, E-mail: bashara@creighton.edu. *Dean and Professor of Law,* Paul E. McGreal, 402-280-2874, Fax: 402-280-3161.

School of Medicine Offers biomedical sciences (MS, PhD); clinical anatomy (MS); medical microbiology and immunology (MS, PhD); medicine (MS, MD, PhD); pharmaceutical sciences (MS); pharmacology (MS, PhD). Electronic applications accepted.

School of Pharmacy and Health Professions *Program availability:* Online learning. Offers occupational therapy (OTD); pharmaceutical sciences (MS); pharmacy (Pharm D); pharmacy and health professions (MS, DPT, OTD, Pharm D); physical therapy (DPT). Electronic applications accepted.

CRISWELL COLLEGE, Dallas, TX 75246-1537
General Information Independent-religious, coed, comprehensive institution. *Graduate housing:* On-campus housing not available.

GRADUATE UNITS

Graduate School of the Bible *Program availability:* Part-time. Offers biblical studies (M Div); Christian leadership (MA); counseling (MA); Jewish studies (MA); ministry (MA); theological and biblical studies (MA). Electronic applications accepted.

CROWN COLLEGE, St. Bonifacius, MN 55375-9001
General Information Independent-religious, coed, comprehensive institution. *Graduate housing:* Room and/or apartments available on a first-come, first-served basis to married students; on-campus housing not available to single students. Housing application deadline: 7/1.

GRADUATE UNITS

Adult and Graduate Studies *Program availability:* Part-time, evening/weekend, online learning. Offers Christian studies (MA); instructional leadership (MA); international leadership (MA); ministry leadership (MA); organizational leadership (MA). Electronic applications accepted.

CULVER-STOCKTON COLLEGE, Canton, MO 63435-1299
General Information Independent-religious, coed, comprehensive institution.

GRADUATE UNITS
MBA Program Offers accounting and finance (MBA).

CUMBERLAND UNIVERSITY, Lebanon, TN 37087
General Information Independent, coed, comprehensive institution. *Graduate housing:* Room and/or apartments available on a first-come, first-served basis to single students; on-campus housing not available to married students.

GRADUATE UNITS

Program in Business Administration *Program availability:* Part-time, evening/weekend. Offers business administration (MBA).

Program in Education *Program availability:* Part-time, evening/weekend, online learning. Offers education (MAE).

Program in Public Service Administration *Program availability:* Part-time, evening/weekend. Offers public service administration (MS).

CUNY GRADUATE SCHOOL OF JOURNALISM, New York, NY 10018
General Information City-supported, coed, graduate-only institution. *Graduate faculty:* 9 full-time (3 women), 68 part-time/adjunct (29 women). *International tuition:* $37,780 full-time. Tuition, state resident: full-time $17,510. Tuition, nonresident: full-time $30,780. *Student services:* Campus employment opportunities, career counseling, free psychological counseling, international student services, low-cost health insurance, services for students with disabilities, writing training. *Library facilities:* Research Center.

Computer facilities: 80 computers available on campus for general student use. Online class registration is available.
Website: http://www.journalism.cuny.edu

General Application Contact: Colleen Leigh, Director of Admissions, 646-758-7852, Fax: 646-758-7709, E-mail: colleen.leigh@journalism.cuny.edu.

GRADUATE UNITS

Graduate Program Students: 120 full-time (78 women). *Faculty:* 9 full-time (3 women), 68 part-time/adjunct (29 women). Expenses: Contact institution. *Financial support:* Career-related internships or fieldwork, Federal Work-Study, institutionally sponsored loans, and scholarships/grants available. Financial award application deadline: 3/1; financial award applicants required to submit FAFSA. Offers entrepreneurial journalism (MA); journalism (MA); social journalism (MA). *Application deadline:* For fall admission, 1/9 for domestic and international students. *Application fee:* $125. Electronic applications accepted. *Application Contact:* Colleen Leigh, Director of Admissions, 646-758-7852, Fax: 646-758-7709, E-mail: colleen.leigh@journalism.cuny.edu.

CURRY COLLEGE, Milton, MA 02186-9984
General Information Independent, coed, comprehensive institution. *Graduate housing:* On-campus housing not available. *Research affiliation:* Literacy Centers/GED Programs.
GRADUATE UNITS
Graduate Studies *Program availability:* Part-time, evening/weekend. Offers business administration (MBA); criminal justice (MA); elementary education (M Ed); finance (Certificate); foundations (non-license) (M Ed); nursing (MSN); reading (M Ed, Certificate); special education (M Ed).

CURTIS INSTITUTE OF MUSIC, Philadelphia, PA 19103-6107
General Information Independent, coed, comprehensive institution. *Graduate housing:* On-campus housing not available.
GRADUATE UNITS
Graduate Studies Offers opera (MM).

DAEMEN COLLEGE, Amherst, NY 14226-3592
General Information Independent, coed, comprehensive institution. *Graduate housing:* Room and/or apartments available on a first-come, first-served basis to single students; on-campus housing not available to married students. Housing application deadline: 7/15.
GRADUATE UNITS
Department of Accounting/Information Systems *Program availability:* Part-time, evening/weekend. Offers global business (MS). Electronic applications accepted.
Department of Nursing *Program availability:* Part-time. Offers adult nurse practitioner (MS, Post Master's Certificate); nurse executive leadership (Post Master's Certificate); nursing education (MS, Post Master's Certificate); nursing executive leadership (MS); nursing practice (DNP); palliative care nursing (Post Master's Certificate). Electronic applications accepted.
Department of Physical Therapy *Program availability:* Part-time. Offers orthopedic manual physical therapy (Advanced Certificate); physical therapy-direct entry (DPT); transitional (DPT). Electronic applications accepted.
Department of Visual and Performing Arts Offers arts administration (MS).
Education Department *Program availability:* Part-time. Offers adolescence education (MS); childhood education (MS); childhood special education (MS); childhood special-alternative certification (MS); early childhood special-alternative certification (MS). Electronic applications accepted.
Physician Assistant Department Offers physician assistant (MS). Electronic applications accepted.
Program in Executive Leadership and Change *Program availability:* Part-time, evening/weekend. Offers business (MS); health professions (MS); not-for-profit organizations (MS). Electronic applications accepted.
Program in Public Health *Program availability:* Part-time, online learning. Offers community health education (MPH); epidemiology (MPH); generalist (MPH).
Program in Social Work Offers social work (MSW).

DAKOTA STATE UNIVERSITY, Madison, SD 57042-1799
General Information State-supported, coed, comprehensive institution. CGS member. *Enrollment:* 3,190 graduate, professional, and undergraduate students; 70 full-time matriculated graduate/professional students (11 women), 231 part-time matriculated graduate/professional students (66 women). *Enrollment by degree level:* 200 master's, 91 doctoral, 10 other advanced degrees. *Graduate faculty:* 18 full-time (7 women), 5 part-time/adjunct (1 woman). Tuition, state resident: full-time $7310. Tuition, nonresident: full-time $13,824. *Required fees:* $930. Tuition and fees vary according to program and reciprocity agreements. *Graduate housing:* Room and/or apartments available on a first-come, first-served basis to single students; on-campus housing not available to married students. Typical cost: $3281 per year ($6060 including board). Room and board charges vary according to board plan. *Student services:* Campus employment opportunities, campus safety program, career counseling, exercise/wellness program, free psychological counseling, grant writing training, international student services, low-cost health insurance, multicultural affairs office, services for students with disabilities, teacher training, writing training. *Library facilities:* Karl E. Mundt Library & Learning Commons plus 1 other. *Collection:* Books: 67,151 (physical), 162,866 (digital/electronic); Serial titles: 243 (physical), 104,900 (digital/electronic); Databases: 121. Weekly public service hours: 85. *Research affiliation:* SBS–Secure Banking Solutions, LLC (information security), Secure Healthcare Solutions (information security), Chenega Logistics (information security).

Computer facilities: Computer purchase and lease plans are available. 165 computers available on campus for general student use. A campuswide network can be accessed from student residence rooms and from off campus. Online class registration is available.
Website: http://www.dsu.edu/
General Application Contact: Erin Blankespoor, Senior Secretary, Office of Graduate Studies and Research, 605-256-5799, E-mail: erin.blankespoor@dsu.edu.
GRADUATE UNITS
College of Business and Information Systems Expenses: Contact institution. *Financial support:* Fellowships with partial tuition reimbursements, research assistantships with partial tuition reimbursements, teaching assistantships with partial tuition reimbursements, career-related internships or fieldwork, Federal Work-Study, scholarships/grants, and unspecified assistantships available. Support available to part-time students. Financial award applicants required to submit FAFSA. *Program availability:* Part-time, evening/weekend, 100% online, blended/hybrid learning. Offers analytics (MSA); applied computer science (MSACS); banking security (Graduate Certificate); business analytics (Graduate Certificate); cyber security (D Sc); ethical hacking (Graduate Certificate); general management (MBA); health informatics (MSHI); information assurance and computer security (MSIA); information systems (MSIS, D Sc IS); information technology (Graduate Certificate). *Application deadline:* For fall admission, 6/15 for domestic students, 4/15 for international students; for spring admission, 11/15 for domestic students, 9/15 priority date for international students; for summer admission, 4/15 for domestic and international students. Applications are processed on a rolling basis. *Application fee:* $35. *Application Contact:* Erin Blankespoor, Senior Secretary, Office of Graduate Studies and Research, 605-256-5799, E-mail: erin.blankespoor@dsu.edu. *Dean for Graduate Studies and Research,* Mark Hawkes, 605-256-5274, E-mail: mark.hawkes@dsu.edu.
College of Education Expenses: Contact institution. *Financial support:* Fellowships with partial tuition reimbursements, career-related internships or fieldwork, Federal Work-Study, scholarships/grants, unspecified assistantships, and administrative assistantships available. Support available to part-time students. Financial award applicants required to submit FAFSA. *Program availability:* Part-time-only,

evening/weekend, online only, 100% online. Offers educational technology (MSET). *Application deadline:* For fall admission, 6/15 for domestic students; for spring admission, 11/15 for domestic students; for summer admission, 4/15 for domestic students. Applications are processed on a rolling basis. *Application fee:* $35. *Application Contact:* Mark Hawkes, Dean of Graduate Studies and Research/Academic Coordinator, 605-256-5274, Fax: 605-256-5093, E-mail: mark.hawkes@dsu.edu. *Dean,* Dr. Crystal Pauli, 605-256-5799.

DAKOTA WESLEYAN UNIVERSITY, Mitchell, SD 57301-4398
General Information Independent-religious, coed, comprehensive institution.
GRADUATE UNITS
Program in Education *Program availability:* Part-time, evening/weekend. Offers curriculum and instruction (MA Ed); educational policy and administration (MA Ed); preK-12 principal certification (MA Ed); secondary certification (MA Ed). Electronic applications accepted.

DALHOUSIE UNIVERSITY, Halifax, NS B3H 4R2, Canada
General Information Province-supported, coed, university. *Graduate housing:* Rooms and/or apartments available on a first-come, first-served basis to single and married students. Housing application deadline: 8/1.
GRADUATE UNITS
Faculty of Agriculture *Program availability:* Part-time. Offers agriculture (M Sc).
Faculty of Architecture and Planning Offers architecture and planning (M Arch, M Eng, M Plan, MEDS, MPS). Electronic applications accepted.
School of Planning Offers planning (M Eng, M Plan, MPS). Electronic applications accepted.
Faculty of Arts and Social Science *Program availability:* Part-time. Offers arts and social science (MA, PhD); classics (MA, PhD); English (MA, PhD); French (MA, PhD); German (MA); history (MA, PhD); international development studies (MA); musicology (MA); philosophy (MA, PhD); political science (MA, PhD); social anthropology (MA, PhD); sociology (MA, PhD). Electronic applications accepted.
Faculty of Computer Science Offers computational biology and bioinformatics (M Sc); computer science (M Sc, MC Sc, PhD); electronic commerce (MEC); health informatics (MHI). Electronic applications accepted.
Faculty of Dentistry Offers dentistryoral and maxillofacial surgery.
Faculty of Engineering Offers biological engineering (M Eng, MA Sc, PhD); biomedical engineering (MA Sc, PhD); chemical engineering (M Eng, MA Sc, PhD); civil and resource engineering (M Eng, MA Sc, PhD); electrical and computer engineering (M Eng, MA Sc, PhD); engineering (M Eng, MA Sc, PhD); engineering mathematics (M Sc, PhD); environmental engineering (M Eng, MA Sc, PhD); food science and technology (M Sc, PhD); industrial engineering (M Eng, MA Sc, PhD); internetworking (M Eng); materials engineering (M Eng, MA Sc, PhD); mechanical engineering (M Eng, MA Sc, PhD); mineral resource engineering (M Eng, MA Sc, PhD).
Faculty of Graduate Studies *Program availability:* Part-time, online learning. Offers anatomy and neurobiology (M Sc, PhD); interdisciplinary studies (PhD); medicine (M Sc, PhD); neuroscience (M Sc, PhD); pathology (M Sc, PhD); pharmacology (M Sc, PhD). Electronic applications accepted.
Dalhousie Law School *Program availability:* Part-time. Offers law (LL M, JSD). Electronic applications accepted.
Faculty of Health Professions *Program availability:* Part-time, online learning. Offers health professions (M Sc, MA, MAHSR, MHA, MN, MPH, MSW, PhD).
School of Health Administration *Program availability:* Part-time, online learning. Offers health administration (MAHSR, MHA, MPH, PhD). Electronic applications accepted.
School of Health and Human Performance *Program availability:* Part-time. Offers health and human performance (M Sc, MA); health promotion (MA); kinesiology (M Sc); leisure studies (MA). Electronic applications accepted.
School of Human Communication Disorders Offers audiology (M Sc); speech-language pathology (M Sc). Electronic applications accepted.
School of Nursing *Program availability:* Part-time, online learning. Offers nursing (MN, PhD). Electronic applications accepted.
School of Occupational Therapy *Program availability:* Part-time, evening/weekend, online learning. Offers occupational therapy (entry to profession) (M Sc); occupational therapy (post-professional) (M Sc). Electronic applications accepted.
School of Physiotherapy Offers physiotherapy (entry to profession) (M Sc); physiotherapy (rehabilitation research) (M Sc). Electronic applications accepted.
School of Social Work *Program availability:* Part-time, online learning. Offers social work (MSW). Electronic applications accepted.
Faculty of Management *Program availability:* Part-time. Offers management (MBA, MEC, MES, MIM, MLIS, MMM, MPA, MREM, GDPA); marine affairs (MMM). Electronic applications accepted.
Centre for Advanced Management Education *Program availability:* Part-time, online learning. Offers financial services (MBA); information management (MIM); management (MPA); natural resources (MBA). Electronic applications accepted.
Rowe School of Business *Program availability:* Part-time. Offers business administration (MBA); financial services (MBA). Electronic applications accepted.
School for Resource and Environmental Studies *Program availability:* Part-time. Offers resource and environmental studies (MES, MREM). Electronic applications accepted.
School of Information Management *Program availability:* Part-time. Offers information management (MIM, MLIS). Electronic applications accepted.
School of Public Administration *Program availability:* Part-time. Offers management (MPA); public administration (MPA, GDPA). Electronic applications accepted.
Faculty of Medicine Offers biochemistry and molecular biology (M Sc, PhD); community health and epidemiology (M Sc); medicine (M Sc, MD, PhD); microbiology and immunology (M Sc, PhD); physiology and biophysics (M Sc, PhD). Electronic applications accepted.
Faculty of Science Offers biology (M Sc, PhD); chemistry (M Sc, PhD); clinical psychology (PhD); earth sciences (M Sc, PhD); economics (MA, MDE, PhD); mathematics (M Sc, PhD); oceanography (M Sc, PhD); physics and atmospheric science (M Sc, PhD); psychology (M Sc, PhD); psychology/neuroscience (M Sc, PhD); science (M Sc, MA, MDE, PhD); statistics (M Sc, PhD). Electronic applications accepted.

DALLAS BAPTIST UNIVERSITY, Dallas, TX 75211-9299
General Information Independent-religious, coed, comprehensive institution. *Enrollment:* 5,156 graduate, professional, and undergraduate students; 716 full-time matriculated graduate/professional students (430 women), 1,217 part-time matriculated

graduate/professional students (762 women). *Enrollment by degree level:* 1,651 master's, 282 doctoral. *Graduate faculty:* 73 full-time (27 women), 216 part-time/adjunct (86 women). *Tuition:* Full-time $15,408; part-time $856 per credit hour. *Required fees:* $400 per semester. Tuition and fees vary according to course load and degree level. *Graduate housing:* Room and/or apartments available on a first-come, first-served basis to single students; on-campus housing not available to married students. Typical cost: $3685 per year ($7533 including board). Room and board charges vary according to board plan and housing facility selected. Housing application deadline: 6/1. *Student services:* Campus employment opportunities, campus safety program, career counseling, free psychological counseling, international student services, low-cost health insurance, services for students with disabilities, writing training. *Library facilities:* Vance Memorial Library plus 3 others. *Collection:* Books: 233,126 (physical), 95,122 (digital/electronic); Serial titles: 597 (physical), 35,689 (digital/electronic); Databases: 189. Weekly public service hours: 108.

Computer facilities: 199 computers available on campus for general student use. A campuswide network can be accessed from student residence rooms and from off campus. Online class registration is available.
Website: http://www.dbu.edu/

General Application Contact: Bobby Soto, Director of Admissions, 214-333-5242, Fax: 214-333-5579, E-mail: graduate@dbu.edu.

GRADUATE UNITS

College of Business Expenses: Contact institution. *Program availability:* Part-time, evening/weekend, 100% online, blended/hybrid learning. Offers accounting (MBA); business (MA, MBA, MS); business communication (MBA); conflict resolution management (MA, MBA); entrepreneurship (MBA); finance (MBA); general management (MA, MS); health care management (MA, MBA); human resource management (MA); international business (MBA); leading the non-profit organization (MBA); management (MBA); management information systems (MBA); marketing (MBA); organizational communication (MA); performance management (MA); professional sales and management optimization (MA); project management (MBA); technology and engineering management (MBA). *Application deadline:* Applications are processed on a rolling basis. *Application fee:* $25. Electronic applications accepted. *Application Contact:* Bobby Soto, Director of Admissions, 214-333-5242, E-mail: graduate@dbu.edu. *Dean,* Dr. Dale Sims, 214-333-5244, E-mail: graduate@dbu.edu.

College of Fine Arts Expenses: Contact institution. *Program availability:* Part-time, evening/weekend. Offers communication (MA). *Application deadline:* Applications are processed on a rolling basis. *Application fee:* $25. Electronic applications accepted. *Application Contact:* Dr. Joanne Morgan, Program Director, 214-333-6854, E-mail: joannem@dbu.edu. *Dean,* Ronald E. Bowles, 214-333-5316, E-mail: ronb@dbu.edu.

College of Humanities and Social Sciences Expenses: Contact institution. Offers counseling (MA); humanities (MA); humanities and social sciences (MA). *Application Contact:* Bobby Soto, Director of Admissions, 214-333-5242, Fax: 214-333-5579, E-mail: graduate@dbu.edu. *Dean,* Rob Sullivan, JD, 214-333-5238.

Dorothy M. Bush College of Education Expenses: Contact institution. *Program availability:* Part-time, evening/weekend, 100% online, blended/hybrid learning. Offers bilingual education (M Ed); charter school administration (M Ed); Christian school administration (M Ed); diagnostician (M Ed); distance learning (M Ed, MAT); dual language (M Ed); early childhood through grade 6 certification (MAT); early childhood-12 (MAT); education (M Ed, MA, MAT, MS, Ed D, Advanced Certificate); educational leadership K-12 (Ed D); elementary (MAT); English as a second language (M Ed, MAT); English as a second language/multilingual (M Ed); instructional technology (M Ed); kinesiology (M Ed); master reading teacher (M Ed); Montessori (MAT); multisensory (MAT); principal certification (M Ed); professional life coaching (M Ed); reading specialist (M Ed); school counseling (M Ed, Advanced Certificate); secondary (MAT); special education (M Ed); sport management (MA); supervision (M Ed). *Application deadline:* Applications are processed on a rolling basis. *Application fee:* $25. Electronic applications accepted. *Application Contact:* Bobby Soto, Director of Admissions, 214-333-5242, E-mail: graduate@dbu.edu. *Dean,* Dr. Neil Dugger, 214-333-5413, E-mail: graduate@dbu.edu.

Gary Cook School of Leadership Expenses: Contact institution. *Program availability:* Part-time, evening/weekend, 100% online, blended/hybrid learning. Offers administration (M Ed); East Asian studies (MA); educational leadership (Ed D); European studies (MA); general international studies (MA); global business (MA); instructional (M Ed); international immersion (MA); international ministry (MA); international relations (MA); leadership (M Ed, MA, Ed D, PhD); leadership studies (PhD). *Application deadline:* Applications are processed on a rolling basis. *Application fee:* $25. Electronic applications accepted. *Application Contact:* Bobby Soto, Director of Admissions, 214-333-5242, E-mail: graduate@dbu.edu. *Dean,* Dr. Jack Goodyear, 214-333-5595, E-mail: jackg@dbu.edu.

Graduate School of Ministry Expenses: Contact institution. *Program availability:* Part-time, evening/weekend, 100% online, blended/hybrid learning. Offers chaplaincy (MA); Christian counseling (MA); Christian heritage (MA); Christian ministry (MA); Christian ministry and education (MA); Christian scriptures (MA); church planting (MA); counseling ministry (MA); discipleship for the family (MA); discipleship through communications (MA); East Asian Studies (MA); English as a second language (MA); family ministry (MA); general (MA); general ministry (MA); general studies (MA); global communication (MA); global studies (MA); heritage and missions (MA); international business (MA); leadership (MA); leading the nonprofit organization (MA); local church discipleship (MA); ministry (MA); ministry leadership (MA); missions (MA); professional life coaching (MA); small group ministry (MA); special needs children ministry (MA); special needs family ministry (MA); student ministry (MA); urban ministry (MA); worship leadership (MA); worship ministry (MA); worship theology (MA). *Application deadline:* Applications are processed on a rolling basis. *Application fee:* $25. Electronic applications accepted. *Application Contact:* Bobby Soto, Director of Admissions, 214-333-5242, E-mail: graduate@dbu.edu. *Dean,* Dr. Robert R. Brooks, 214-333-5494, E-mail: bobb@dbu.edu.

Liberal Arts Program Expenses: Contact institution. *Program availability:* Part-time, evening/weekend, 100% online, blended/hybrid learning. Offers art (MLA); Christian studies (MLA); commercial art (MLA); East Asian studies (MLA); English (MLA); English as a second language (MLA); fine arts (MLA); history (MLA); missions (MLA); political science (MLA). *Application fee:* $25. Electronic applications accepted. *Application Contact:* Bobby Soto, Director of Admissions, 214-333-5242, E-mail: graduate@dbu.edu. *Director,* Jared Ingram, 214-333-5584, E-mail: jaredi@dbu.edu.

Professional Development Program Expenses: Contact institution. *Program availability:* Part-time, evening/weekend, 100% online, blended/hybrid learning. Offers accounting (MA); church leadership (MA); communication (MA); counseling (MA); criminal justice (MA); English as a second language (MA); finance (MA); higher education (MA); leadership studies (MA); management (MA); management information

systems (MA); marketing (MA); missions (MA); professional life coaching (MA); training and development (MA). *Application deadline:* Applications are processed on a rolling basis. *Application fee:* $25. Electronic applications accepted. *Application Contact:* Bobby Soto, Director of Admissions, 214-333-5242, E-mail: graduate@dbu.edu. *Director,* Jared Ingram, 214-333-5584, E-mail: jaredi@dbu.edu.

DALLAS THEOLOGICAL SEMINARY, Dallas, TX 75204-6499

General Information Independent, coed, graduate-only institution. *Graduate housing:* Rooms and/or apartments available on a first-come, first-served basis to single and married students.

GRADUATE UNITS

Graduate Programs *Program availability:* Part-time, online learning. Offers adult education (Th M); apologetics (Th M); Bible backgrounds (Th M); Bible translation (Th M); Biblical and theological studies (Certificate); biblical counseling (MA); biblical exegesis and linguistics (MA); biblical exposition (PhD); biblical studies (MA); Biblical theology (Th M); children's education (Th M); Christian education (MA, D Min); Christian leadership (MA); cross-cultural ministries (MA); educational administration (Th M); educational leadership (Th M); evangelism and discipleship (Th M); exposition of Biblical books (Th M); family life education (Th M); general studies (Th M); Hebrew and cognate studies (Th M); hermeneutics (Th M); historical theology (Th M); homiletics (Th M); intercultural ministries (Th M); Jesus studies (Th M); leadership studies (Th M); media and communication (MA); media arts (Th M); ministry (D Min); ministry with women (Th M); New Testament studies (Th M, PhD); Old Testament studies (Th M, PhD); parachurch ministries (Th M); pastoral care and counseling (Th M); pastoral theology and practice (Th M); philosophy (Th M); sacred theology (STM); spiritual formation (Th M); systematic theology (Th M); teaching in Christian institutions (Th M); theological studies (PhD); urban ministries (Th M); worship studies (Th M); youth education (Th M). Electronic applications accepted.

DARTMOUTH COLLEGE, Hanover, NH 03755

★ **General Information** Independent, coed, university. CGS member. *Enrollment:* 6,381 graduate, professional, and undergraduate students; 1,945 full-time matriculated graduate/professional students (916 women), 73 part-time matriculated graduate/professional students (44 women). *Enrollment by degree level:* 1,025 master's, 955 doctoral, 119 other advanced degrees. *Graduate faculty:* 453 full-time (139 women), 112 part-time/adjunct (44 women). *Graduate housing:* Rooms and/or apartments available on a first-come, first-served basis to single and married students. Typical cost: $5850 per year ($8886 including board) for single students. Room and board charges vary according to campus/location and housing facility selected. Housing application deadline: 5/15. *Student services:* Campus safety program, career counseling, free psychological counseling, international student services, low-cost health insurance, services for students with disabilities, teacher training, writing training. *Library facilities:* Baker-Berry Library plus 9 others. *Collection:* Books: 2.6 million (physical); Serial titles: 72,726 (physical). Study areas open 24 hours, 5–7 days a week; students can reserve study rooms.

Computer facilities: Computer purchase and lease plans are available. 200 computers available on campus for general student use. A campuswide network can be accessed from student residence rooms and from off campus. Online class registration is available.
Website: http://www.dartmouth.edu/

General Application Contact: Jane Seibel, Assistant Dean of Recruiting and Diversity, School of Graduate and Advanced Studies, 603-646-6578, Fax: 603-646-3488, E-mail: jane.b.seibel@dartmouth.edu.

GRADUATE UNITS

The Dartmouth Institute Students: 81 full-time (58 women), 32 part-time (20 women); includes 19 minority (1 Black or African American, non-Hispanic/Latino; 1 American Indian or Alaska Native, non-Hispanic/Latino; 13 Asian, non-Hispanic/Latino; 4 Hispanic/Latino; 8 international. Average age 31. 301 applicants, 55% accepted, 93 enrolled. *Faculty:* 48 full-time (23 women), 104 part-time/adjunct (43 women). Expenses: Contact institution. *Financial support:* In 2016–17, fellowships with full tuition reimbursements (averaging $28,200 per year) were awarded; scholarships/grants also available. In 2016, 51 master's awarded. *Program availability:* Part-time. Offers evaluative clinical sciences (MS, PhD); public health (MPH). *Application deadline:* For fall admission, 1/15 for domestic students. *Application fee:* $75. *Application Contact:* Marc Aquila, Senior Director of Recruitment and Admissions, 603-650-1539. *Director,* Dr. Elliot S. Fisher, 603-653-0802.

Geisel School of Medicine Students: 363 full-time (212 women), 3 part-time (1 woman); includes 166 minority (26 Black or African American, non-Hispanic/Latino; 2 American Indian or Alaska Native, non-Hispanic/Latino; 70 Asian, non-Hispanic/Latino; 51 Hispanic/Latino; 1 Native Hawaiian or other Pacific Islander, non-Hispanic/Latino; 16 Two or more races, non-Hispanic/Latino), 34 international. Average age 26. 6,635 applicants, 4% accepted, 92 enrolled. *Faculty:* 154 full-time (52 women), 41 part-time/adjunct (20 women). Expenses: Contact institution. *Financial support:* Institutionally sponsored loans and scholarships/grants available. In 2016, 85 doctorates awarded. Offers medicine (MD). *Application deadline:* For fall admission, 11/1 for domestic students. *Application fee:* $130. Electronic applications accepted. *Application Contact:* Rand S. Swenson, Chair, Geisel Admissions Committee, 603-650-1505, Fax: 603-650-1560, E-mail: geisel.admissions@dartmouth.edu. *Senior Associate Dean for Faculty Affairs,* Dr. Leslie Henderson, 603-650-1574, E-mail: leslie.p.henderson@dartmouth.edu.

Graduate Program in Molecular and Cellular Biology Students: 80 full-time (39 women); includes 17 minority (8 Asian, non-Hispanic/Latino; 9 Hispanic/Latino), 27 international. Average age 27. 180 applicants, 37% accepted, 24 enrolled. *Faculty:* 72 full-time (18 women), 3 part-time/adjunct (1 woman). Expenses: Contact institution. *Financial support:* Fellowships and health care benefits available. In 2016, 6 doctorates awarded. Offers biochemistry (PhD); biological sciences (PhD); genetics (PhD); immunology (PhD); microbiology and molecular pathogenesis (PhD); molecular and cellular biology (PhD). *Application deadline:* For fall admission, 12/1 for domestic students. Applications are processed on a rolling basis. *Application fee:* $75. Electronic applications accepted. *Application Contact:* Janet Cheney, Program Coordinator, 603-650-1612, E-mail: mcb@dartmouth.edu. *Vice Chair,* Dr. Patrick J. Dolph, 603-650-1092, E-mail: mcb@dartmouth.edu.

Program in Experimental and Molecular Medicine Students: 51 full-time (34 women); includes 6 minority (4 Asian, non-Hispanic/Latino; 2 Hispanic/Latino), 7 international. Average age 25. 81 applicants, 17% accepted, 8 enrolled. *Faculty:* 34 full-time (7 women), 20 part-time/adjunct (8 women). Expenses: Contact institution. *Financial support:* Fellowships and health care benefits available. Offers experimental and molecular medicine. *Application deadline:* For fall admission, 1/1 for domestic and international students. *Application fee:* $75. Electronic applications accepted.

Application Contact: Gail Egner, Program Administrator, 603-650-4933, Fax: 603-650-4932, E-mail: gail.p.egner@dartmouth.edu. *Director,* Dr. Michael Spinella, 603-650-1126, Fax: 603-650-4932.

School of Graduate and Advanced Studies Students: 574 full-time (271 women), 33 part-time (21 women); includes 86 minority (10 Black or African American, non-Hispanic/Latino; 5 American Indian or Alaska Native, non-Hispanic/Latino; 38 Asian, non-Hispanic/Latino; 21 Hispanic/Latino; 12 Two or more races, non-Hispanic/Latino), 204 international. Average age 30. *Faculty:* 167 full-time (53 women), 52 part-time/adjunct (22 women). Expenses: Contact institution. *Financial support:* In 2016–17, fellowships with full tuition reimbursements (averaging $23,832 per year), research assistantships with full tuition reimbursements (averaging $23,832 per year), teaching assistantships with full tuition reimbursements (averaging $23,832 per year) were awarded; career-related internships or fieldwork, institutionally sponsored loans, scholarships/grants, traineeships, tuition waivers (full and partial), and unspecified assistantships also available. Support available to part-time students. Financial award application deadline: 4/1; financial award applicants required to submit CSS PROFILE or FAFSA. In 2016, 131 master's, 48 doctorates awarded. Offers biophysical chemistry (MS); chemistry (PhD); cognitive neuroscience (PhD); comparative literature (MA); computer science (MS, PhD); digital music (MA); earth sciences (MS, PhD); ecology and evolutionary biology (PhD); liberal studies (MALS); mathematics (AM, PhD); physics and astronomy (PhD); psychology (PhD). *Application deadline:* For fall admission, 1/15 for domestic students. Electronic applications accepted. *Application Contact:* Gary Hutchins, Assistant Dean, School of Graduate and Advanced Studies, 603-646-2107, Fax: 603-646-3488, E-mail: g.hutchins@dartmouth.edu. *Dean of Graduate Studies,* Dr. Jon Kull, 603-646-1552, E-mail: f.jon.kull@dartmouth.edu.

Institute for Quantitative Biomedical Sciences Students: 22 full-time (13 women); includes 5 minority (1 Black or African American, non-Hispanic/Latino; 3 Asian, non-Hispanic/Latino; 1 Hispanic/Latino), 6 international. Average age 28. 29 applicants, 45% accepted, 8 enrolled. Expenses: Contact institution. *Financial support:* In 2016–17, fellowships with full tuition reimbursements (averaging $28,200 per year) were awarded. In 2016, 2 doctorates awarded. Offers quantitative biomedical sciences (PhD). Program offered in collaboration with the Department of Genetics and the Department of Community and Family Medicine. *Application deadline:* For fall admission, 3/1 for domestic students. *Application fee:* $75. Electronic applications accepted. *Application Contact:* Gary Hutchins, Assistant Dean, School of Arts and Sciences, 603-646-2107, Fax: 603-646-3488, E-mail: g.hutchins@dartmouth.edu. *Director,* Dr. Micheal Whitfield.

Thayer School of Engineering Students: 213 full-time (61 women); includes 22 minority (3 Black or African American, non-Hispanic/Latino; 14 Asian, non-Hispanic/Latino; 3 Hispanic/Latino; 2 Two or more races, non-Hispanic/Latino), 123 international. Average age 24. 765 applicants, 21% accepted, 87 enrolled. *Faculty:* 53 full-time (11 women), 9 part-time/adjunct (0 women). Expenses: Contact institution. *Financial support:* In 2016–17, 195 students received support, including 30 fellowships with full tuition reimbursements available (averaging $26,520 per year), 77 research assistantships with full tuition reimbursements available (averaging $26,520 per year), 21 teaching assistantships with partial tuition reimbursements available (averaging $7,800 per year); career-related internships or fieldwork, institutionally sponsored loans, scholarships/grants, and tuition waivers (full and partial) also available. Financial award application deadline: 2/15; financial award applicants required to submit CSS PROFILE. In 2016, 46 master's, 14 doctorates awarded. Offers biomedical engineering (M Eng, MS, PhD); biotechnology and biochemical engineering (MS, PhD); computer engineering (MS, PhD); engineering (M Eng, MEM, MS, PhD); engineering management (MEM); environmental engineering (MS, PhD); innovation (PhD); materials sciences and engineering (MS, PhD); mechanical engineering (MS, PhD). *Application deadline:* For fall admission, 1/1 priority date for domestic and international students. Applications are processed on a rolling basis. *Application fee:* $45. Electronic applications accepted. *Application Contact:* Candace S. Potter, Graduate Admissions and Financial Aid Administrator, 603-646-3844, Fax: 603-646-1620, E-mail: candace.s.potter@dartmouth.edu. *Dean,* Dr. Joseph J. Helbie, 603-646-2238, Fax: 603-646-2580, E-mail: joseph.j.helbie@dartmouth.edu.

Tuck School of Business at Dartmouth Students: 567 full-time (240 women); includes 111 minority (26 Black or African American, non-Hispanic/Latino; 5 American Indian or Alaska Native, non-Hispanic/Latino; 53 Asian, non-Hispanic/Latino; 22 Hispanic/Latino; 1 Native Hawaiian or other Pacific Islander, non-Hispanic/Latino; 4 Two or more races, non-Hispanic/Latino), 170 international. Average age 28. 2,623 applicants, 22% accepted, 285 enrolled. *Faculty:* 54 full-time (11 women). Expenses: Contact institution. *Financial support:* Institutionally sponsored loans and scholarships/grants available. Financial award application deadline: 4/1; financial award applicants required to submit FAFSA. In 2016, 275 master's awarded. Offers business (MBA). MD/MBA offered with the Geisel School of Medicine; MPH/MBA with The Dartmouth Institute for Health Policy and Clinical Practice. *Application deadline:* For fall admission, 10/1 for domestic and international students; for winter admission, 11/1 for domestic and international students; for spring admission, 1/1 for domestic and international students; for summer admission, 4/1 for domestic and international students. *Application fee:* $250. Electronic applications accepted. *Application Contact:* Amy Mitson, Interim Co-Director, Admissions, 603-646-3162, Fax: 603-646-1441, E-mail: tuck.admissions@tuck.dartmouth.edu. *Dean,* Matthew J. Slaughter, 603-646-2460, E-mail: tuck.public.relations@tuck.dartmouth.edu.

See Close-Up on page 879.

DAVENPORT UNIVERSITY, Grand Rapids, MI 49512

General Information Independent, coed, comprehensive institution. *Graduate housing:* Room and/or apartments available on a first-come, first-served basis to single students; on-campus housing not available to married students. *Research affiliation:* Human Synergistic Center for Applied Research, Inc. (leadership, organizational culture, strategy).

GRADUATE UNITS

Sneden Graduate School *Program availability:* Evening/weekend. Offers accounting (MBA); business administration (EMBA); finance (MBA); health care management (MBA); human resources (MBA); information assurance (MS); public health (MPH); strategic management (MBA). Electronic applications accepted.

DEFIANCE COLLEGE, Defiance, OH 43512-1610

General Information Independent-religious, coed, comprehensive institution. *Tuition:* Part-time $524 per credit hour. *Required fees:* $188 per semester. *Graduate housing:* On-campus housing not available. *Student services:* Career counseling, exercise/wellness program, low-cost health insurance, multicultural affairs office, services for students with disabilities, teacher training. *Library facilities:* Pilgrim Library plus 1 other. *Collection:* Books: 64,765 (physical), 248,869 (digital/electronic); Serial

titles: 308 (physical), 65,636 (digital/electronic); Databases: 146. Weekly public service hours: 83; students can reserve study rooms.

Computer facilities: Computer purchase and lease plans are available. 200 computers available on campus for general student use. A campuswide network can be accessed from student residence rooms and from off campus. Online class registration is available.

Website: http://www.defiance.edu/

General Application Contact: Sally Bissell, Director of Career Development, 419-783-2366, Fax: 419-784-0426, E-mail: sbissell@defiance.edu.

GRADUATE UNITS

Program in Business Administration Expenses: Contact institution. *Program availability:* Part-time, evening/weekend. Offers leadership (MBA). *Application deadline:* For fall admission, 8/1 for domestic and international students. Applications are processed on a rolling basis. *Application fee:* $25. Electronic applications accepted. *Assistant Professor,* Dr. Arif Sultan, 419-783-2431, Fax: 419-784-0426, E-mail: asultan@defiance.edu.

Program in Education Expenses: Contact institution. *Program availability:* Part-time. Offers education (MAE); sport coaching (MAE). *Application deadline:* For fall admission, 8/1 for domestic students. Applications are processed on a rolling basis. *Application fee:* $25. *Application Contact:* Teresa Watkins, Administrative Assistant, 419-783-2323, Fax: 419-784-0426, E-mail: twatkins@defiance.edu. *Professor,* Dr. Jo Ann Burkhardt, 419-783-2315, Fax: 419-784-0426, E-mail: jburkhardt@defiance.edu.

DELAWARE STATE UNIVERSITY, Dover, DE 19901-2277

General Information State-supported, coed, university. *Graduate housing:* Room and/or apartments available on a first-come, first-served basis to single students; on-campus housing not available to married students.

GRADUATE UNITS

Graduate Programs *Program availability:* Part-time, evening/weekend. Offers applied chemistry (MS, PhD); applied mathematics (MS); applied mathematics and theoretical physics (PhD); applied optics (MS); biological sciences (MA, MS, PhD); biology education (MS); chemistry (MS); French (MA); historic preservation (MA); mathematics (MS); mathematics education (MS); molecular and cellular neuroscience (MS); natural resources (MS); neuroscience (PhD); optics (PhD); physics (MS); physics teaching (MS); plant science (MS); Spanish (MA).

College of Business *Program availability:* Part-time, evening/weekend. Offers business administration (MBA). Electronic applications accepted.

College of Education, Health and Public Policy *Program availability:* Part-time, evening/weekend. Offers adult literacy and basic education (MA); art education (MA); curriculum and instruction (MA); education, health and public policy (MA, MS, MSW, Ed D); educational leadership (MA, Ed D); nursing (MS); science education (MA); social work (MSW); special education (MA); sport administration (MS); teaching (MA). Electronic applications accepted.

DELAWARE VALLEY UNIVERSITY, Doylestown, PA 18901-2697

General Information Independent, coed, comprehensive institution. *Graduate housing:* On-campus housing not available.

GRADUATE UNITS

MBA Program *Program availability:* Part-time, evening/weekend, online learning. Offers accounting (MBA); entrepreneurship (MBA); finance (MBA); food and agribusiness (MBA); general business (MBA); global executive leadership (MBA); human resource management (MBA); supply chain management (MBA). Electronic applications accepted.

Program in Counseling Psychology Offers child and adolescent therapy (MA); social justice community counseling (MA).

Program in Educational Leadership *Program availability:* Part-time, evening/weekend. Offers instruction, curriculum and technology (MS); school administration and leadership (MS).

DELL'ARTE INTERNATIONAL SCHOOL OF PHYSICAL THEATRE, Blue Lake, CA 95525

General Information Independent, coed, graduate-only institution. *Graduate housing:* Rooms and/or apartments available on a first-come, first-served basis to single and married students.

GRADUATE UNITS

MFA Program Offers ensemble based physical theatre (MFA). Electronic applications accepted.

DELTA STATE UNIVERSITY, Cleveland, MS 38733-0001

General Information State-supported, coed, comprehensive institution. *Graduate housing:* Rooms and/or apartments available on a first-come, first-served basis to single and married students. Housing application deadline: 6/1.

GRADUATE UNITS

Graduate Programs *Program availability:* Part-time, evening/weekend, online learning. Electronic applications accepted.

College of Arts and Sciences *Program availability:* Part-time. Offers arts and sciences (M Ed, MALS, MSCD, MSCJ, MSJC, MSNS); community development (MS); evolving human voices (MALS); gender and diversity studies (MALS); globalization studies (MALS); Mississippi Delta studies (MALS); natural sciences (MSNS); philosophy (MALS); religious studies (MALS); secondary education (M Ed); social justice and criminology (MSJC); social science secondary education (M Ed).

College of Business *Program availability:* Part-time, evening/weekend, online learning. Offers accountancy (MPA); business (MBA, MCA, MPA); business administration (MBA); commercial aviation (MCA).

College of Education *Program availability:* Part-time, evening/weekend. Offers counseling (M Ed); counselor education (Ed D); education (M Ed, MAT, MS, Ed D, Ed S); educational administration and supervision (M Ed, Ed S); elementary education (M Ed, MAT, Ed D, Ed S); health, physical education, and recreation (M Ed); higher education (Ed D); professional studies (Ed D); secondary education (MAT); special education (M Ed); sport and human performance (MS).

Robert E. Smith School of Nursing *Program availability:* Part-time. Offers family nurse practitioner (MSN); nurse administrator (MSN); nurse educator (MSN). Electronic applications accepted.

DENVER SEMINARY, Littleton, CO 80120

General Information Independent-religious, coed, graduate-only institution. *Graduate housing:* Rooms and/or apartments available on a first-come, first-served basis to single and married students. Housing application deadline: 6/1.

GRADUATE UNITS

Graduate and Professional Programs *Program availability:* Part-time, evening/weekend, online learning. Offers apologetics (Certificate); biblical studies (MA); Christian formation and soul care (MA, Certificate); Christian studies (MA, Certificate); church and parachurch leadership (D Min); counseling licensure (MA); counseling ministry (MA); intercultural ministry (Certificate); leadership (MA, Certificate); marriage and family counseling (D Min); pastoral ministry (D Min); philosophy of religion (MA); spiritual guidance (Certificate); theology (M Div, Certificate); worship (Certificate); youth and family ministry (MA). Electronic applications accepted.

DEPAUL UNIVERSITY, Chicago, IL 60604-2287

General Information Independent-religious, coed, university. CGS member. *Graduate housing:* Room and/or apartments available on a first-come, first-served basis to single students; on-campus housing not available to married students. *Research affiliation:* Civic Federation (public services), Metro Chicago Information Center (public services), International Institute of Higher Studies in the Criminal Sciences (law).

GRADUATE UNITS

College of Communication *Program availability:* Part-time, evening/weekend. Offers digital communication and media arts (MA); health communication (MA); journalism (MA); media and cinema studies (MA); organizational and multicultural communication (MA); public relations and advertising (MA); relational communication (MA). Electronic applications accepted.

College of Computing and Digital Media *Program availability:* Part-time, evening/weekend, online learning. Offers animation (MA, MFA); business information technology (MS); cinema (MFA); cinema production (MS); computational finance (MS); computer and information sciences (PhD); computer game development (MS); computer information and network security (MS); computer science (MS); e-commerce technology (MS); health informatics (MS); human-computer interaction (MS); information systems (MS); information technology project management (MS); network engineering and management (MS); predictive analytics (MS); screenwriting (MFA); software engineering (MS). Electronic applications accepted.

College of Education *Program availability:* Part-time, evening/weekend, online learning. Offers bilingual bicultural education (M Ed, MA); counseling (M Ed, MA); curriculum studies (M Ed, MA, Ed D); early childhood education (M Ed, MA, Ed D); educating adults (MA); educational leadership (M Ed, MA, Ed D); elementary education (MA); mathematics education (MA); mathematics for teaching (MS); middle school mathematics education (MS); reading specialist (M Ed, MA); secondary education (M Ed); social and cultural foundations in education (MA); special education (M Ed, MA); world languages education (M Ed, MA). Electronic applications accepted.

College of Law *Program availability:* Part-time, evening/weekend. Offers health law (LL M); intellectual property law (LL M); international law (LL M); law (JD); taxation (LL M). Electronic applications accepted.

College of Liberal Arts and Social Sciences *Program availability:* Part-time, evening/weekend, online learning. Offers Arabic (MA); Chinese (MA); English (MA); French (MA); German (MA); history (MA); interdisciplinary studies (MA, MS); international public service (MS); international studies (MA); Italian (MA); Japanese (MA); leadership and policy studies (MS); liberal studies (MA); new media studies (MA); nonprofit management (MNM); public administration (MPA); public health (MPH); public service management (MS); social work (MSW); sociology (MA); Spanish (MA); sustainable urban development (MA); women and gender studies (MA); writing and publishing (MA); writing, rhetoric, and discourse (MA). Electronic applications accepted.

College of Science and Health Offers applied mathematics (MS); applied statistics (MS); biological sciences (MA, MS); chemistry (MS); mathematics education (MA); mathematics for teaching (MS); nursing (MS); nursing practice (DNP); physics (MS); psychology (MS); pure mathematics (MS); science education (MS). Electronic applications accepted.

Kellstadt Graduate School of Business *Program availability:* Part-time, evening/weekend, online learning. Offers accountancy (M Acc, MS, MSA); applied economics (MBA); banking (MBA); behavioral finance (MBA); brand and product management (MBA); business development (MBA); business information technology (MS); business strategy and decision-making (MBA); computational finance (MS); consumer insights (MBA); corporate finance (MBA); economic policy analysis (MS); entrepreneurship (MBA, MS); finance (MBA, MS); financial analysis (MBA); general business (MBA); health sector management (MBA); hospitality leadership (MBA); hospitality leadership and operational performance (MS); human resource management (MBA); human resources (MS); investment management (MBA); leadership and change management (MBA); management accounting (MBA); marketing (MBA, MS); marketing analysis (MS); marketing strategy and planning (MBA); operations management (MBA); organizational diversity (MBA); real estate (MS); real estate finance and investment (MBA); revenue management (MBA); sports management (MBA); strategic global marketing (MBA); strategy, execution and valuation (MBA); sustainable management (MBA, MS); taxation (MBA); wealth management (MS). Electronic applications accepted.

School for New Learning *Program availability:* Part-time, evening/weekend. Offers applied professional studies (MA); applied technology (MS); educating adults (MA). Electronic applications accepted.

School of Music *Program availability:* Part-time, evening/weekend. Offers composition (MM); jazz studies (MM); music education (MM); music performance (MM); performance (Certificate). Electronic applications accepted.

The Theatre School Offers acting (MFA); arts leadership (MFA); directing (MFA). Electronic applications accepted.

DEREE - THE AMERICAN COLLEGE OF GREECE, GR-153-42 Aghia Paraskevi, Athens, Greece

General Information Independent, coed, comprehensive institution.

GRADUATE UNITS
Graduate Programs

DESALES UNIVERSITY, Center Valley, PA 18034-9568

General Information Independent-religious, coed, comprehensive institution. *Enrollment:* 3,309 graduate, professional, and undergraduate students; 410 full-time matriculated graduate/professional students (281 women), 511 part-time matriculated graduate/professional students (300 women). *Enrollment by degree level:* 816 master's, 95 doctoral, 10 other advanced degrees. *Graduate faculty:* 33 full-time (19 women), 57 part-time/adjunct (23 women). *Tuition:* Part-time $815 per credit hour. Tuition and fees vary according to degree level and program. *Graduate housing:* Room and/or apartments available on a first-come, first-served basis to single students; on-campus housing not available to married students. Typical cost: $7800 per year. Housing application deadline: 3/15. *Student services:* Campus safety program, career counseling, free psychological counseling, international student services, low-cost health insurance, multicultural affairs office, services for students with disabilities, teacher training. *Library facilities:* Trexler Library. *Collection:* Books: 167,111 (physical), 134,000 (digital/electronic); Serial titles: 207 (physical), 12,125 (digital/electronic); Databases: 88. Weekly public service hours: 102; students can reserve study rooms.

Computer facilities: 245 computers available on campus for general student use. A campuswide network can be accessed from student residence rooms and from off campus. Online class registration is available.
Website: http://www.desales.edu/

General Application Contact: Julia Ferraro, Director of Graduate Admissions, 610-282-1100 Ext. 1768, E-mail: gradadmissions@desales.edu.

GRADUATE UNITS

Division of Business Students: 73 full-time (38 women), 323 part-time (163 women); includes 59 minority (16 Black or African American, non-Hispanic/Latino; 23 Asian, non-Hispanic/Latino; 16 Hispanic/Latino; 4 Two or more races, non-Hispanic/Latino). Average age 37. 157 applicants, 87% accepted, 128 enrolled. *Faculty:* 12 full-time (4 women), 29 part-time/adjunct (5 women). Expenses: Contact institution. *Financial support:* Applicants required to submit FAFSA. In 2016, 115 master's awarded. *Program availability:* Part-time, evening/weekend, 100% online, blended/hybrid learning. Offers accounting (MBA); computer information systems (MBA); finance (MBA); health care systems management (MBA); human resources management (MBA); management (MBA); marketing (MBA); project management (MBA); self-design (MBA); supply chain management (MBA). *Application deadline:* Applications are processed on a rolling basis. *Application fee:* $50. Electronic applications accepted. *Application Contact:* Julia Ferraro, Director of Graduate Admissions, 610-282-1100 Ext. 1768, E-mail: gradadmissions@desales.edu. *Director, MBA Program,* Dr. David M. Gilfoil, 610-282-1100 Ext. 1828, Fax: 610-282-2869, E-mail: david.gilfoil@desales.edu.

Division of Healthcare Students: 274 full-time (206 women), 78 part-time (68 women); includes 40 minority (9 Black or African American, non-Hispanic/Latino; 14 Asian, non-Hispanic/Latino; 11 Hispanic/Latino; 6 Two or more races, non-Hispanic/Latino). Average age 34. 2,430 applicants, 6% accepted, 129 enrolled. *Faculty:* 22 full-time (14 women), 37 part-time/adjunct (29 women). Expenses: Contact institution. *Financial support:* Applicants required to submit FAFSA. In 2016, 76 master's, 6 doctorates awarded. *Program availability:* Part-time. Offers adult-gerontology acute care (Post Master's Certificate); adult-gerontology acute care nurse practitioner (MSN); adult-gerontology acute certified nurse practitioner (Post Master's Certificate); adult-gerontology clinical nurse specialist (MSN, Post Master's Certificate); clinical leadership (DNP); family nurse practitioner (MSN, Post Master's Certificate); general nursing practice (DNP); nurse anesthetist (MSN); nurse educator (Post Master's Certificate, Postbaccalaureate Certificate); nurse midwife (MSN); nurse practitioner (MSN); psychiatric-mental health nurse practitioner (MSN, Post Master's Certificate). *Application deadline:* Applications are processed on a rolling basis. *Application fee:* $50. Electronic applications accepted. *Application Contact:* Julia Ferraro, Director of Graduate Admissions, 610-282-1100 Ext. 1768, E-mail: gradadmissions@desales.edu. *Dean of Graduate Education,* Fr. Dr. Peter Leonard, OSFS, 610-282-1100 Ext. 1289, E-mail: peter.leonard@desales.edu.

Division of Liberal Arts and Social Sciences Students: 55 full-time (36 women), 100 part-time (64 women); includes 25 minority (5 Black or African American, non-Hispanic/Latino; 14 Hispanic/Latino; 6 Two or more races, non-Hispanic/Latino). Average age 33. 145 applicants, 80% accepted, 103 enrolled. *Faculty:* 5 full-time (3 women), 20 part-time/adjunct (13 women). Expenses: Contact institution. *Financial support:* Applicants required to submit FAFSA. In 2016, 36 master's awarded. *Program availability:* Part-time, 100% online, blended/hybrid learning. Offers criminal justice (MCJ); digital forensics (MCJ, Postbaccalaureate Certificate); education (M Ed); investigative forensics (MCJ, Postbaccalaureate Certificate). *Application deadline:* Applications are processed on a rolling basis. *Application fee:* $50. Electronic applications accepted. *Application Contact:* Julia Ferraro, Director of Graduate Admissions, 610-282-1100 Ext. 1768, E-mail: gradadmissions@desales.edu. *Division Head of Liberal Arts and Social Studies,* Dr. Brain Kane, 610-282-1100 Ext. 1274, E-mail: brian.kane@desales.edu.

Division of Science and Mathematics Students: 8 full-time (1 woman), 12 part-time (6 women); includes 1 minority (Asian, non-Hispanic/Latino). Average age 34. 20 applicants, 30% accepted, 6 enrolled. *Faculty:* 1 (woman) full-time, 3 part-time/adjunct (0 women). Expenses: Contact institution. *Financial support:* Applicants required to submit FAFSA. In 2016, 7 master's awarded. *Program availability:* Part-time, evening/weekend, 100% online, blended/hybrid learning. Offers cyber security (Postbaccalaureate Certificate); data analytics (Postbaccalaureate Certificate); information systems (MS). *Application deadline:* Applications are processed on a rolling basis. *Application fee:* $50. Electronic applications accepted. *Application Contact:* Julia Ferraro, Director of Graduate Admissions, 610-282-1100 Ext. 1768, E-mail: gradadmissions@desales.edu. *MSIS Director/Assistant Professor of Computer Science,* Dr. Patricia Riola, 610-282-1100 Ext. 1647, E-mail: patricia.riola@desales.edu.

DES MOINES UNIVERSITY, Des Moines, IA 50312-4104

General Information Independent, coed, graduate-only institution. *Graduate housing:* On-campus housing not available.

GRADUATE UNITS

College of Health Sciences *Program availability:* Part-time, evening/weekend. Offers health sciences (MHA, MPH, MS, DPT); healthcare administration (MHA); physical therapy (DPT); physician assistant (MS); public health (MPH). Electronic applications accepted.

College of Osteopathic Medicine Offers anatomy (MS); biomedical sciences (MS); osteopathic medicine (DO). Electronic applications accepted.

College of Podiatric Medicine and Surgery Offers podiatric medicine and surgery (DPM). Electronic applications accepted.

DEVRY COLLEGE OF NEW YORK–MIDTOWN MANHATTAN CAMPUS, New York, NY 10016

General Information Proprietary, coed, comprehensive institution.

GRADUATE UNITS

Keller Graduate School of Management Offers management (M Acc, MAFM, MBA, MHRM, MISM, MNCM, MPA, MPM).

DEVRY UNIVERSITY–ALPHARETTA CAMPUS, Alpharetta, GA 30009

General Information Proprietary, coed, comprehensive institution.

GRADUATE UNITS

Keller Graduate School of Management Offers management (MAFM, MBA, MHRM, MISM, MNCM, MPA, MPM).

DEVRY UNIVERSITY–ARLINGTON CAMPUS, Arlington, VA 22202

General Information Proprietary, coed, comprehensive institution. *Enrollment:* 486 graduate, professional, and undergraduate students; 26 full-time matriculated graduate/professional students (9 women), 208 part-time matriculated graduate/professional students (94 women). *Enrollment by degree level:* 234 master's. *Library facilities:* Learning Resource Center.

Computer facilities: Online class registration is available.
Website: http://www.devry.edu/

GRADUATE UNITS

Keller Graduate School of Management Students: 26 full-time (9 women), 208 part-time (94 women). Expenses: Contact institution. In 2016, 123 master's awarded. Offers management (M Acc, MAFM, MBA, MHRM, MISM, MPM). *Application Contact:* Student Application Contact, 703-414-4000.

DEVRY UNIVERSITY–CHARLOTTE CAMPUS, Charlotte, NC 28273

General Information Proprietary, coed, comprehensive institution.

GRADUATE UNITS

Keller Graduate School of Management Offers management (MAFM, MBA, MHRM, MISM, MNCM, MPA, MPM).

DEVRY UNIVERSITY–CHESAPEAKE CAMPUS, Chesapeake, VA 23320

General Information Proprietary, coed, comprehensive institution.

GRADUATE UNITS

Keller Graduate School of Management Offers management (MAFM, MBA, MHRM, MISM, MNCM, MPA, MPM).

DEVRY UNIVERSITY–CHICAGO CAMPUS, Chicago, IL 60618

General Information Proprietary, coed, comprehensive institution. *Enrollment:* 939 graduate, professional, and undergraduate students; 37 full-time matriculated graduate/professional students (18 women), 117 part-time matriculated graduate/professional students (50 women). *Enrollment by degree level:* 154 master's. *Library facilities:* Learning Resource Center.
Website: http://www.devry.edu/

GRADUATE UNITS

Keller Graduate School of Management Students: 37 full-time (18 women), 117 part-time (50 women). Expenses: Contact institution. In 2016, 58 master's awarded. Offers management (M Acc, MAFM, MBA, MHRM, MISM, MPM). *Application Contact:* Student Application Contact, 773-929-8500.

DEVRY UNIVERSITY–CHICAGO LOOP CAMPUS, Chicago, IL 60606

General Information Proprietary, coed, comprehensive institution.

GRADUATE UNITS

Keller Graduate School of Management Offers management (MAFM, MBA, MHRM, MISM, MNCM, MPM).

DEVRY UNIVERSITY–CINCINNATI CAMPUS, Cincinnati, OH 45249

General Information Proprietary, coed, comprehensive institution.

GRADUATE UNITS

Keller Graduate School of Management Offers management (MAFM, MBA, MHRM, MISM, MNCM, MPA, MPM).

DEVRY UNIVERSITY–COLUMBUS CAMPUS, Columbus, OH 43209

General Information Proprietary, coed, comprehensive institution. *Enrollment:* 1,140 graduate, professional, and undergraduate students; 26 full-time matriculated graduate/professional students (16 women), 153 part-time matriculated graduate/professional students (81 women). *Enrollment by degree level:* 179 master's.
Website: http://www.devry.edu/

GRADUATE UNITS

Keller Graduate School of Management Students: 26 full-time (16 women), 153 part-time (81 women). Expenses: Contact institution. In 2016, 24 master's awarded. Offers management (MAFM, MBA, MHRM, MISM, MPM). *Application Contact:* Student Application Contact, 614-253-7291.

DEVRY UNIVERSITY–DECATUR CAMPUS, Decatur, GA 30030

General Information Proprietary, coed, comprehensive institution. *Enrollment:* 1,087 graduate, professional, and undergraduate students; 29 full-time matriculated graduate/professional students (15 women), 154 part-time matriculated graduate/professional students (94 women). *Enrollment by degree level:* 183 master's. *Library facilities:* Learning Resource Center.
Website: http://www.devry.edu/

GRADUATE UNITS

Keller Graduate School of Management Students: 29 full-time (15 women), 154 part-time (94 women). Expenses: Contact institution. In 2016, 68 master's awarded. Offers management (MAFM, MBA, MHRM, MISM, MNCM, MPA, MPM, MSA). *Application Contact:* Student Application Contact, 404-270-2700.

DEVRY UNIVERSITY–FOLSOM CAMPUS, Folsom, CA 95630

General Information Proprietary, coed, comprehensive institution.

GRADUATE UNITS

Graduate Programs

DEVRY UNIVERSITY–FREMONT CAMPUS, Fremont, CA 94555

General Information Proprietary, coed, comprehensive institution.

GRADUATE UNITS

Keller Graduate School of Management Offers management (MAFM, MBA, MHRM, MISM, MNCM, MPA, MPM).

DEVRY UNIVERSITY–FT. WASHINGTON CAMPUS, Fort Washington, PA 19034

General Information Proprietary, coed, comprehensive institution.

GRADUATE UNITS

Keller Graduate School of Management Offers management (MAFM, MBA, MHRM, MISM, MNCM, MPA, MPM).

DEVRY UNIVERSITY–HENDERSON CAMPUS, Henderson, NV 89074

General Information Proprietary, coed, comprehensive institution.

GRADUATE UNITS

Keller Graduate School of Management Offers management (MAFM, MBA, MHRM, MISM, MNCM, MPA, MPM).

DEVRY UNIVERSITY–IRVING CAMPUS, Irving, TX 75063

General Information Proprietary, coed, comprehensive institution. *Enrollment:* 566 graduate, professional, and undergraduate students; 29 full-time matriculated graduate/professional students (14 women), 132 part-time matriculated graduate/professional students (63 women). *Enrollment by degree level:* 161 master's. *Library facilities:* Learning Resource Center.
Website: http://www.devry.edu/

GRADUATE UNITS

Keller Graduate School of Management Students: 29 full-time (14 women), 132 part-time (63 women). Expenses: Contact institution. In 2016, 102 master's awarded. Offers management (M Acc, MAFM, MBA, MHRM, MISM, MPM). *Application Contact:* Student Application Contact, 972-929-6777.

DEVRY UNIVERSITY–JACKSONVILLE CAMPUS, Jacksonville, FL 32256

General Information Proprietary, coed, comprehensive institution.

GRADUATE UNITS

Keller Graduate School of Management Offers management (MAFM, MBA, MHRM, MISM, MNCM, MPA, MPM).

DEVRY UNIVERSITY–LONG BEACH CAMPUS, Long Beach, CA 90806

General Information Proprietary, coed, comprehensive institution.

GRADUATE UNITS

Keller Graduate School of Management Offers management (MAFM, MBA, MHRM, MISM, MNCM, MPA, MPM).

DEVRY UNIVERSITY–MIRAMAR CAMPUS, Miramar, FL 33027

General Information Proprietary, coed, comprehensive institution. *Enrollment:* 406 graduate, professional, and undergraduate students; 42 full-time matriculated graduate/professional students (19 women), 118 part-time matriculated graduate/professional students (57 women). *Enrollment by degree level:* 160 master's.
Website: http://www.devry.edu/

GRADUATE UNITS

Keller Graduate School of Management Students: 42 full-time (19 women), 118 part-time (57 women). Expenses: Contact institution. In 2016, 76 master's awarded. Offers management (MAFM, MBA, MHRM, MISM, MPM, MSA). *Application Contact:* Student Application Contact, 954-499-9775.

DEVRY UNIVERSITY–MORRISVILLE CAMPUS, Morrisville, NC 27560

General Information Proprietary, coed, comprehensive institution.

GRADUATE UNITS

Keller Graduate School of Management Offers management (MBA, MHRM, MISM, MNCM, MPA, MPM).

DEVRY UNIVERSITY–NASHVILLE CAMPUS, Nashville, TN 37211

General Information Proprietary, coed, comprehensive institution.

GRADUATE UNITS

Keller Graduate School of Management Offers management (MAFM, MBA, MHRM, MISM, MNCM, MPA, MPM).

DEVRY UNIVERSITY–NORTH BRUNSWICK CAMPUS, North Brunswick, NJ 08902

General Information Proprietary, coed, comprehensive institution. *Enrollment:* 681 graduate, professional, and undergraduate students; 22 full-time matriculated graduate/professional students (8 women), 75 part-time matriculated graduate/professional students (32 women). *Enrollment by degree level:* 97 master's. *Library facilities:* Learning Resource Center.

Computer facilities: Online class registration is available.
Website: http://www.devry.edu/

GRADUATE UNITS

Keller Graduate School of Management Students: 22 full-time (8 women), 75 part-time (32 women). Expenses: Contact institution. In 2016, 48 master's awarded. Offers management (MBA).

DEVRY UNIVERSITY ONLINE, Addison, IL 60101

General Information Proprietary, coed, comprehensive institution. *Enrollment:* 15,551 graduate, professional, and undergraduate students; 451 full-time matriculated graduate/professional students (271 women), 3,007 part-time matriculated graduate/professional students (1,854 women). *Enrollment by degree level:* 3,458 master's.
Website: http://www.devry.edu/

GRADUATE UNITS

Keller Graduate School of Management Students: 451 full-time (271 women), 3,007 part-time (1,854 women). Expenses: Contact institution. In 2016, 1,519 master's awarded. *Application Contact:* Student Application Contact, 877-496-9050.

DEVRY UNIVERSITY–ORLANDO CAMPUS, Orlando, FL 32819

General Information Proprietary, coed, comprehensive institution. *Enrollment:* 764 graduate, professional, and undergraduate students; 42 full-time matriculated graduate/professional students (19 women), 187 part-time matriculated graduate/professional students (93 women). *Enrollment by degree level:* 229 master's. *Library facilities:* Learning Resource Center.

Computer facilities: Online class registration is available.
Website: http://www.devry.edu/

GRADUATE UNITS

Keller Graduate School of Management Students: 42 full-time (19 women), 187 part-time (93 women). Expenses: Contact institution. In 2016, 123 master's awarded. Offers management (MAFM, MBA, MHRM, MISM, MPA, MPM, MSA). *Application Contact:* Student Application Contact, 407-345-2800.

DEVRY UNIVERSITY–PHOENIX CAMPUS, Phoenix, AZ 85021

General Information Proprietary, coed, comprehensive institution. *Enrollment:* 616 graduate, professional, and undergraduate students; 14 full-time matriculated graduate/professional students (3 women), 86 part-time matriculated graduate/professional students (38 women). *Enrollment by degree level:* 100 master's. *Library facilities:* Learning Resource Center.

Computer facilities: Online class registration is available.
Website: http://www.devry.edu/

General Application Contact: Student Application Contact, 602-749-7301.

GRADUATE UNITS

Keller Graduate School of Management Students: 14 full-time (3 women), 86 part-time (38 women). Expenses: Contact institution. In 2016, 31 master's awarded. Offers management (MAFM, MBA, MISM, MPM, MSA). *Application Contact:* Student Application Contact, 602-749-7301.

DEVRY UNIVERSITY–POMONA CAMPUS, Pomona, CA 91768

General Information Proprietary, coed, comprehensive institution. *Enrollment:* 964 graduate, professional, and undergraduate students; 37 full-time matriculated graduate/professional students (14 women), 143 part-time matriculated graduate/professional students (66 women). *Enrollment by degree level:* 180 master's.

Computer facilities: Online class registration is available.
Website: http://www.devry.edu/

GRADUATE UNITS

Keller Graduate School of Management Students: 37 full-time (14 women), 143 part-time (66 women). Expenses: Contact institution. In 2016, 96 master's awarded. Offers management (MAFM, MBA, MHRM, MISM, MPM, MSA). *Application Contact:* Student Application Contact, 909-622-8866.

DEVRY UNIVERSITY–SAN DIEGO CAMPUS, San Diego, CA 92108

General Information Proprietary, coed, comprehensive institution.

GRADUATE UNITS

Keller Graduate School of Management Offers management (MAFM, MBA, MHRM, MISM, MNCM, MPA, MPM, Graduate Certificate).

DEVRY UNIVERSITY–SEVEN HILLS CAMPUS, Seven Hills, OH 44131

General Information Proprietary, coed, comprehensive institution.

GRADUATE UNITS

Keller Graduate School of Management Offers management (MAFM, MBA, MHRM, MISM, MNCM, MPA, MPM, Graduate Certificate).

DEVRY UNIVERSITY–TINLEY PARK CAMPUS, Tinley Park, IL 60477

General Information Proprietary, coed, comprehensive institution.

GRADUATE UNITS

Keller Graduate School of Management Offers management (MAFM, MBA, MHRM, MISM, MNCM, MPA, MPM).

DIGIPEN INSTITUTE OF TECHNOLOGY, Redmond, WA 98052

General Information Proprietary, coed, comprehensive institution. *Enrollment:* 1,054 graduate, professional, and undergraduate students; 51 full-time matriculated graduate/professional students (8 women), 27 part-time matriculated graduate/professional students (5 women). *Enrollment by degree level:* 78 master's. *Graduate faculty:* 28 full-time (7 women), 14 part-time/adjunct (1 woman). *Tuition:* Full-time $17,820; part-time $990 per credit. *Required fees:* $100 per semester. Tuition and fees vary according to program. *Graduate housing:* Room and/or apartments available on a first-come, first-served basis to single students; on-campus housing not available to married students. Typical cost: $10,754 (including board). Housing application deadline: 6/1. *Student services:* Campus employment opportunities, career counseling, free psychological counseling, international student services, multicultural affairs office, services for students with disabilities. *Library facilities:* DigiPen Library. *Collection:* Books: 5,024 (physical), 138,729 (digital/electronic); Serial titles: 29 (physical); Databases: 10. Weekly public service hours: 81. *Research affiliation:* NorthWest Research Associates (NWRA) (atmospheric modeling), Andretti Autosport (software development), Boeing (simulations), Lotus Formula 1 (software development).

Computer facilities: 794 computers available on campus for general student use. A campuswide network can be accessed from student residence rooms and from off campus. Online class registration is available.
Website: http://www.digipen.edu/

General Application Contact: Danial Powers, Director of Admissions, 425-629-5071, Fax: 425-558-0378, E-mail: dpowers@digipen.edu.

GRADUATE UNITS

Graduate Programs Students: 51 full-time (8 women), 27 part-time (5 women); includes 8 minority (3 Asian, non-Hispanic/Latino; 4 Hispanic/Latino; 1 Two or more races, non-Hispanic/Latino), 41 international. Average age 28. 107 applicants, 47% accepted, 21 enrolled. *Faculty:* 28 full-time (7 women), 14 part-time/adjunct (1 woman). Expenses: Contact institution. *Financial support:* In 2016–17, 4 students received support, including 1 fellowship (averaging $9,500 per year); career-related internships or fieldwork and scholarships/grants also available. Financial award application deadline: 5/1; financial award applicants required to submit FAFSA. In 2016, 23 master's awarded. *Program availability:* Part-time. Offers computer science (MS); digital art and animation (MFA). *Application deadline:* For fall admission, 2/1 priority date for domestic and international students; for spring admission, 7/1 for domestic and international students. Applications are processed on a rolling basis. *Application fee:* $35. Electronic applications accepted. *Application Contact:* Danial Powers, Director of Admissions, 425-629-5071, Fax: 425-558-0378, E-mail: dpowers@digipen.edu. *Senior Vice President,* Angela Kugler, 425-895-4438, Fax: 425-558-0378, E-mail: akugler@digipen.edu.

DIGITAL MEDIA ARTS COLLEGE, Boca Raton, FL 33487

General Information Proprietary, coed, comprehensive institution.

GRADUATE UNITS

Graduate Programs Offers graphic design (MFA); special FX animation (MFA).

DOANE UNIVERSITY, Crete, NE 68333-2430

General Information Independent-religious, coed, comprehensive institution. *Enrollment:* 1,047 graduate, professional, and undergraduate students; 404 full-time matriculated graduate/professional students (286 women), 568 part-time matriculated graduate/professional students (440 women). *Enrollment by degree level:* 864 master's, 63 doctoral, 45 other advanced degrees. *Graduate faculty:* 10 full-time (7 women), 138 part-time/adjunct (88 women). *Graduate housing:* On-campus housing not available. *Student services:* Career counseling, teacher training. *Library facilities:* Perkins Library plus 1 other. *Collection:* Study areas open 24 hours, 5–7 days a week; students can reserve study rooms.

Computer facilities: Computer purchase and lease plans are available. 250 computers available on campus for general student use. A campuswide network can be accessed from student residence rooms and from off campus. Online class registration is available.
Website: http://www.doane.edu/

General Application Contact: Wilma Daddario, Assistant Dean, 402-466-4774, Fax: 404-466-4228, E-mail: wilma.daddario@doane.edu.

GRADUATE UNITS

Program in Counseling Students: 71 full-time (55 women), 24 part-time (19 women); includes 11 minority (2 Black or African American, non-Hispanic/Latino; 1 American Indian or Alaska Native, non-Hispanic/Latino; 7 Hispanic/Latino; 1 Two or more races, non-Hispanic/Latino). Average age 33. *Faculty:* 2 full-time (1 woman), 15 part-time/adjunct (11 women). Expenses: Contact institution. *Financial support:* Unspecified assistantships available. Financial award application deadline: 6/1; financial award applicants required to submit FAFSA. In 2016, 45 master's awarded. *Program availability:* Evening/weekend. Offers counseling (MAC). *Application deadline:* Applications are processed on a rolling basis. *Application fee:* $25. Electronic applications accepted. *Application Contact:* Jean Kilnoski, Assistant Dean, 402-466-4774, Fax: 404-466-4228, E-mail: jean.kilnoski@doane.edu. *Associate Dean/Director of the Counseling Program,* 402-466-4774, Fax: 402-466-4228.

Program in Education Students: 224 full-time (167 women), 488 part-time (388 women); includes 22 minority (9 Black or African American, non-Hispanic/Latino; 2 American Indian or Alaska Native, non-Hispanic/Latino; 1 Asian, non-Hispanic/Latino; 7 Hispanic/Latino; 1 Native Hawaiian or other Pacific Islander, non-Hispanic/Latino; 2 Two or more races, non-Hispanic/Latino), 1 international. Average age 34. *Faculty:* 10 full-time (7 women), 66 part-time/adjunct (50 women). Expenses: Contact institution. *Financial support:* Applicants required to submit FAFSA. In 2016, 257 master's awarded. *Program availability:* Part-time, evening/weekend. Offers curriculum and instruction (M Ed); educational leadership (M Ed). *Application deadline:* Applications are processed on a rolling basis. Electronic applications accepted. *Application Contact:* Wilma Daddario, Assistant Dean, 402-464-1223, Fax: 402-466-4228, E-mail: wdaddario@doane.edu. *Dean,* Dr. Lyn C. Forester, 402-826-8604, Fax: 402-826-8278.

Program in Management Students: 109 full-time (64 women), 56 part-time (33 women); includes 27 minority (8 Black or African American, non-Hispanic/Latino; 2 American Indian or Alaska Native, non-Hispanic/Latino; 3 Asian, non-Hispanic/Latino; 13 Hispanic/Latino; 1 Two or more races, non-Hispanic/Latino), 2 international. Average age 36. *Faculty:* 3 full-time (2 women), 21 part-time/adjunct (9 women). Expenses: Contact institution. *Financial support:* Application deadline: 6/1; applicants required to submit FAFSA. In 2016, 69 master's awarded. *Program availability:* Part-time, evening/weekend. Offers management (MA). *Application deadline:* Applications are processed on a rolling basis. *Application fee:* $25. Electronic applications accepted. *Application Contact:* Kerry Fina, Advisor for Master of Arts in Management, 402-466-4774, Fax: 404-466-4228, E-mail: kerry.fina@doane.edu. *Acting Dean,* Larry Hughes, 880-333-6263, E-mail: larry.hughes@doane.edu.

DOMINICAN COLLEGE, Orangeburg, NY 10962-1210

General Information Independent, coed, comprehensive institution. *Enrollment:* 2,012 graduate, professional, and undergraduate students; 202 full-time matriculated graduate/professional students (153 women), 332 part-time matriculated graduate/professional students (221 women). *Enrollment by degree level:* 280 master's, 254 doctoral. *Graduate faculty:* 38 full-time (26 women), 83 part-time/adjunct (65 women). *Tuition:* Part-time $900 per credit. One-time fee: $200 full-time. *Graduate housing:* Room and/or apartments available on a first-come, first-served basis to single students; on-campus housing not available to married students. Typical cost: $12,420 (including board). Housing application deadline: 5/1. *Student services:* Campus employment opportunities, campus safety program, career counseling, free psychological counseling, services for students with disabilities, teacher training, writing training. *Library facilities:* Sullivan Library plus 1 other. *Collection:* Books: 81,325 (physical), 118,178 (digital/electronic); Serial titles: 612 (physical), 74,172 (digital/electronic); Databases: 82. Weekly public service hours: 89; students can reserve study rooms.

Computer facilities: 150 computers available on campus for general student use. A campuswide network can be accessed from student residence rooms and from off campus. Online class registration, Web portal, learning management system are available.
Website: http://www.dc.edu/

General Application Contact: Christina Lifshey, Assistant Director of Graduate Admissions, 845-848-7908, Fax: 845-365-3150, E-mail: graduate.admissions@dc.edu.

GRADUATE UNITS

Division of Allied Health Students: 165 full-time (124 women), 182 part-time (105 women); includes 103 minority (6 Black or African American, non-Hispanic/Latino; 1 American Indian or Alaska Native, non-Hispanic/Latino; 77 Asian, non-Hispanic/Latino; 15 Hispanic/Latino; 2 Native Hawaiian or other Pacific Islander, non-Hispanic/Latino; 2 Two or more races, non-Hispanic/Latino), 47 international. Average age 37. *Faculty:* 12 full-time (7 women), 28 part-time/adjunct (22 women). Expenses: Contact institution. *Financial support:* Applicants required to submit FAFSA. In 2016, 29 master's, 131 doctorates awarded. *Program availability:* Part-time, evening/weekend, online learning. Offers allied health (MS, DPT); occupational therapy (MS); physical therapy (MS, DPT). *Application deadline:* Applications are processed on a rolling basis. *Application fee:* $50. Electronic applications accepted. *Application Contact:* Christina Lifshey, Assistant Director of Graduate Admissions, 845-848-7900, Fax: 845-365-3150, E-mail: admissions@dc.edu. *Coordinator of Academic Study and Fieldwork,* Margaret Boyd, 845-848-6033, Fax: 845-398-4893, E-mail: margaret.boyd@dc.edu.

Division of Nursing Students: 24 full-time (20 women), 75 part-time (64 women); includes 41 minority (14 Black or African American, non-Hispanic/Latino; 13 Asian, non-Hispanic/Latino; 12 Hispanic/Latino; 1 Native Hawaiian or other Pacific Islander, non-

Hispanic/Latino; 1 Two or more races, non-Hispanic/Latino), 1 international. *Faculty:* 16 full-time (all women), 45 part-time/adjunct (38 women). Expenses: Contact institution. *Financial support:* Application deadline: 2/1; applicants required to submit FAFSA. In 2016, 20 master's awarded. *Program availability:* Part-time, evening/weekend. Offers nursing (MSN, DNP). *Application deadline:* Applications are processed on a rolling basis. *Application fee:* $50. Electronic applications accepted. *Application Contact:* Christina Lifshey, Assistant Director of Graduate Admissions, 845-848-7908, Fax: 845-365-3150, E-mail: admissions@dc.edu. *Director,* Dr. Nancy DiDona, 845-848-6051, Fax: 845-398-4891, E-mail: nancy.didona@dc.edu.

Division of Teacher Education Students: 3 full-time (all women), 53 part-time (41 women); includes 13 minority (3 Black or African American, non-Hispanic/Latino, 10 Hispanic/Latino). *Faculty:* 6 full-time (4 women), 4 part-time/adjunct (all women). Expenses: Contact institution. *Application deadline:* 2/1; applicants required to submit FAFSA. In 2016, 28 master's awarded. *Program availability:* Part-time, evening/weekend, online learning. Offers education/teaching of individuals with multiple disabilities (MS Ed). *Application deadline:* Applications are processed on a rolling basis. *Application Contact:* Christina Lifshey, Assistant Director of Graduate Admissions, 845-848-7908 Ext. 15, Fax: 845-365-3150, E-mail: admissions@dc.edu. *Director,* Dr. Mike Kelly, 845-848-4090, Fax: 845-359-7802, E-mail: mike.kelly@dc.edu.

MBA Program Students: 10 full-time (6 women), 22 part-time (11 women); includes 16 minority (9 Black or African American, non-Hispanic/Latino; 3 Asian, non-Hispanic/Latino; 3 Hispanic/Latino; 1 Two or more races, non-Hispanic/Latino), 1 international. *Faculty:* 9 full-time (2 women), 7 part-time/adjunct (1 woman). Expenses: Contact institution. *Application deadline:* 2/1; applicants required to submit FAFSA. In 2016, 16 master's awarded. *Program availability:* Part-time, evening/weekend. Offers accounting (MBA); healthcare management (MBA); management (MBA). *Application deadline:* Applications are processed on a rolling basis. *Application fee:* $50. Electronic applications accepted. *Application Contact:* Christina Lifshey, Assistant Director of Graduate Admissions, 845-848-7908, Fax: 845-365-3150, E-mail: admissions@dc.edu. *MBA Director,* Ken Mias, 845-848-4102, E-mail: ken.mias@dc.edu.

DOMINICAN HOUSE OF STUDIES, PONTIFICAL FACULTY OF THE IMMACULATE CONCEPTION, Washington, DC 20017-1585

General Information Independent-religious, coed, primarily men, graduate-only institution. *Enrollment by degree level:* 84 master's. *Graduate faculty:* 18 full-time (1 woman), 6 part-time/adjunct (3 women). *Tuition:* Full-time $16,080; part-time $2010 per credit hour. *Required fees:* $280; $280 per credit hour. $140 per semester. One-time fee: $350. *Graduate housing:* On-campus housing not available. *Student services:* Campus employment opportunities, career counseling, international student services. *Library facilities:* Dominican Theological Library. *Collection:* Books: 62,700 (physical); Serial titles: 219 (physical), 18 (digital/electronic); Databases: 6. Weekly public service hours: 61; students can reserve study rooms. *Research affiliation:* Washington Theological Consortium (theology, ecumenism), The Thomist (theology).

Computer facilities: 8 computers available on campus for general student use. A campuswide network can be accessed from off campus.
Website: http://www.dhs.edu/

General Application Contact: Rev. Albert Trudel, Registrar, 202-495-3836, Fax: 202-495-3873, E-mail: registrar@dhs.edu.

GRADUATE UNITS

Graduate and Professional Programs in Theology Students: 75 full-time (7 women), 9 part-time (3 women); includes 5 minority (2 Asian, non-Hispanic/Latino; 3 Hispanic/Latino, 13 international. Average age 33. *Faculty:* 18 full-time (1 woman), 6 part-time/adjunct (3 women). Expenses: Contact institution. *Financial support:* Career-related internships or fieldwork and Federal Work-Study available. Support available to part-time students. Financial award application deadline: 6/30; financial award applicants required to submit FAFSA. *Program availability:* Part-time. Offers moral theology (STL); sacred scripture (STL); systematic theology (STL); theology (M Div, MA, STB); Thomistic studies (MA, STD, STL). *Application deadline:* For fall admission, 7/1 for domestic and international students; for spring admission, 12/1 for domestic and international students. Applications are processed on a rolling basis. *Application fee:* $50. *Application Contact:* Rev. Albert Trudel, Registrar, 202-495-3836, Fax: 202-495-3873, E-mail: registrar@dhs.edu. *Vice-President/Academic Dean,* Rev. Thomas Petri, OP, 202-495-3832, Fax: 202-495-3873, E-mail: dean@dhs.edu.

DOMINICAN SCHOOL OF PHILOSOPHY AND THEOLOGY, Berkeley, CA 94708

General Information Independent-religious, coed, graduate-only institution. *Graduate housing:* Rooms and/or apartments available on a first-come, first-served basis to single and married students. Housing application deadline: 5/1.

GRADUATE UNITS

Graduate Programs *Program availability:* Part-time. Offers philosophy (MA); theology (M Div, MA, MTS, Certificate). Electronic applications accepted.

DOMINICAN UNIVERSITY, River Forest, IL 60305-1099

General Information Independent-religious, coed, comprehensive institution. *Enrollment:* 3,522 graduate, professional, and undergraduate students; 375 full-time matriculated graduate/professional students (313 women), 841 part-time matriculated graduate/professional students (637 women). *Enrollment by degree level:* 1,198 master's, 15 doctoral, 3 other advanced degrees. *Graduate faculty:* 59 full-time (34 women), 88 part-time/adjunct (70 women). *Tuition:* Full-time $17,850; part-time $850 per credit hour. *Required fees:* $540; $18 per course. Tuition and fees vary according to course load, degree level and program. *Graduate housing:* Room and/or apartments available on a first-come, first-served basis to single students; on-campus housing not available to married students. Typical cost: $6148 per year ($9652 including board). Room and board charges vary according to housing facility selected. Housing application deadline: 7/1. *Student services:* Campus employment opportunities, campus safety program, career counseling, child daycare facilities, exercise/wellness program, free psychological counseling, international student services, low-cost health insurance, multicultural affairs office, services for students with disabilities, teacher training, writing training. *Library facilities:* Rebecca Crown Library. *Collection:* Books: 247,967 (physical), 9,389 (digital/electronic); Serial titles: 280 (physical), 53,047 (digital/electronic); Databases: 114. Weekly public service hours: 100; students can reserve study rooms.

Computer facilities: Computer purchase and lease plans are available. 550 computers available on campus for general student use. A campuswide network can be accessed from student residence rooms and from off campus. Online class registration is available.
Website: http://www.dom.edu/

General Application Contact: Cathering Galarza-Espino, Coordinator of Graduate Marketing and Recruitment, 708-524-6983, E-mail: cgalarza@dom.edu.

GRADUATE UNITS

Brennan School of Business Students: 91 full-time (71 women), 72 part-time (36 women); includes 25 minority (7 Black or African American, non-Hispanic/Latino; 1 American Indian or Alaska Native, non-Hispanic/Latino; 9 Asian, non-Hispanic/Latino; 7 Hispanic/Latino; 1 Native Hawaiian or other Pacific Islander, non-Hispanic/Latino), 24 international. Average age 29. 84 applicants, 93% accepted, 47 enrolled. *Faculty:* 22 full-time (9 women), 13 part-time/adjunct (5 women). Expenses: Contact institution. *Financial support:* Research assistantships, career-related internships or fieldwork, scholarships/grants, tuition waivers (partial), and unspecified assistantships available. Financial award application deadline: 3/1; financial award applicants required to submit FAFSA. In 2016, 85 master's awarded. *Program availability:* Part-time, evening/weekend, 100% online, blended/hybrid learning. Offers business (MBA, MSA). JD/MBA offered jointly with John Marshall Law School. *Application deadline:* Applications are processed on a rolling basis. *Application fee:* $25. Electronic applications accepted. *Application Contact:* Dr. Kathleen Odell, Associate Dean, Brennan School of Business, 708-524-6507, Fax: 708-524-6939, E-mail: mquilty@dom.edu. *Dean,* Dr. Roberto Curci, 708-524-6321, Fax: 708-524-6939, E-mail: rcurci@dom.edu.

School of Education Students: 13 full-time (all women), 500 part-time (385 women); includes 88 minority (40 Black or African American, non-Hispanic/Latino; 3 American Indian or Alaska Native, non-Hispanic/Latino; 18 Asian, non-Hispanic/Latino; 11 Hispanic/Latino; 2 Native Hawaiian or other Pacific Islander, non-Hispanic/Latino; 14 Two or more races, non-Hispanic/Latino), 1 international. Average age 32. 162 applicants, 96% accepted, 104 enrolled. *Faculty:* 12 full-time (8 women), 64 part-time/adjunct (57 women). Expenses: Contact institution. *Financial support:* Career-related internships or fieldwork, scholarships/grants, tuition waivers (partial), and unspecified assistantships available. Support available to part-time students. Financial award application deadline: 8/15; financial award applicants required to submit FAFSA. In 2016, 200 master's awarded. *Program availability:* Part-time, evening/weekend, 100% online, blended/hybrid learning. Offers early childhood education (MS); education (MAT); elementary education (MA Ed); English as a second language (MA Ed); reading (MA Ed); special education (MS). *Application deadline:* Applications are processed on a rolling basis. *Application fee:* $25. *Application Contact:* Keven Hansen, Coordinator of Recruitment and Admissions, 708-524-6921, Fax: 708-524-6665, E-mail: educate@dom.edu. *Interim Executive Director, School of Education,* Dr. Colleen Reardon, 708-524-6643, Fax: 708-524-6665, E-mail: creardon@dom.edu.

School of Information Studies Students: 79 full-time (66 women), 170 part-time (133 women); includes 46 minority (21 Black or African American, non-Hispanic/Latino; 2 Asian, non-Hispanic/Latino; 20 Hispanic/Latino; 1 Native Hawaiian or other Pacific Islander, non-Hispanic/Latino; 2 Two or more races, non-Hispanic/Latino), 3 international. Average age 33. 121 applicants, 82% accepted, 74 enrolled. *Faculty:* 11 full-time (7 women), 8 part-time/adjunct (6 women). Expenses: Contact institution. *Financial support:* Fellowships, research assistantships, career-related internships or fieldwork, scholarships/grants, and unspecified assistantships available. Support available to part-time students. Financial award application deadline: 4/15; financial award applicants required to submit FAFSA. In 2016, 113 master's, 3 doctorates awarded. *Program availability:* Part-time, evening/weekend, 100% online, blended/hybrid learning. Offers information management (MSIM); knowledge management (Certificate); library and information science (MLIS, MPS, PhD); special studies (CSS). MLIS/M Div offered jointly with McCormick Theological Seminary, MLIS/MA with Loyola University Chicago, MLIS/MM with Northwestern University. *Application deadline:* For fall admission, 6/1 priority date for domestic students; for winter admission, 3/1 priority date for domestic students; for spring admission, 10/1 priority date for domestic students. Applications are processed on a rolling basis. *Application fee:* $25. *Application Contact:* Catherine Galarza-Espino, Coordinator of Graduate Marketing and Recruiting, 708-524-6983, E-mail: cgalarza@dom.edu. *Dean and Professor,* Dr. Kate Marek, 708-524-6648, Fax: 708-524-6657, E-mail: kmarek@dom.edu.

School of Professional and Continuing Studies Students: 30 full-time (24 women), 15 part-time (11 women); includes 17 minority (11 Black or African American, non-Hispanic/Latino; 5 Hispanic/Latino; 1 Two or more races, non-Hispanic/Latino). Average age 39. 16 applicants, 94% accepted, 15 enrolled. *Faculty:* 3 part-time/adjunct (2 women). Expenses: Contact institution. *Financial support:* Research assistantships, career-related internships or fieldwork, scholarships/grants, and unspecified assistantships available. Financial award applicants required to submit FAFSA. In 2016, 17 master's awarded. *Program availability:* Part-time, evening/weekend, 100% online, blended/hybrid learning. Offers conflict resolution (MA). *Application deadline:* Applications are processed on a rolling basis. *Application fee:* $25. Electronic applications accepted. *Application Contact:* Monica Halloran, Associate Director of Academic Advising, 708-714-9007, Fax: 708-714-9126, E-mail: mhallora@dom.edu. *Assistant Provost for Continuing Studies and Special Initiatives,* Dr. Matthew Hlinak, 708-714-9056, E-mail: mhlinak@dom.edu.

School of Social Work Students: 162 full-time (139 women), 84 part-time (72 women); includes 94 minority (50 Black or African American, non-Hispanic/Latino; 5 Asian, non-Hispanic/Latino; 37 Hispanic/Latino; 1 Native Hawaiian or other Pacific Islander, non-Hispanic/Latino; 1 Two or more races, non-Hispanic/Latino), 5 international. Average age 32. 130 applicants, 89% accepted, 77 enrolled. *Faculty:* 9 full-time (6 women), 18 part-time/adjunct (16 women). Expenses: Contact institution. *Financial support:* Research assistantships with partial tuition reimbursements, Federal Work-Study, scholarships/grants, and unspecified assistantships available. Financial award applicants required to submit FAFSA. In 2016, 87 master's awarded. *Program availability:* Part-time. Offers social work (MSW). *Application deadline:* For fall admission, 7/1 for domestic and international students; for spring admission, 11/1 for domestic and international students. Applications are processed on a rolling basis. *Application fee:* $25. Electronic applications accepted. *Application Contact:* Catherine Galarza-Espino, Coordinator of Graduate Marketing and Recruiting, 708-524-6983, E-mail: cgalarza@dom.edu. *Dean,* Dr. Charles Stoops, 708-366-3316, E-mail: cstoops@dom.edu.

DOMINICAN UNIVERSITY OF CALIFORNIA, San Rafael, CA 94901-2298

General Information Independent-religious, coed, comprehensive institution. *Enrollment:* 1,843 graduate, professional, and undergraduate students; 238 full-time matriculated graduate/professional students (181 women), 200 part-time matriculated graduate/professional students (143 women). *Enrollment by degree level:* 438 master's. *Graduate faculty:* 52 full-time (34 women), 63 part-time/adjunct (43 women). *Tuition:* Full-time $11,400; part-time $950 per credit. *Required fees:* $300 per credit. Tuition and fees vary according to course load and program. *Graduate housing:* On-campus housing not available. *Student services:* Campus employment opportunities, career counseling, free psychological counseling, international student services, low-cost health insurance, services for students with disabilities. *Library facilities:* Archbishop Alemany Library. *Collection:* Books: 110,523 (physical); Databases: 84.

Computer facilities: 195 computers available on campus for general student use. A campuswide network can be accessed from student residence rooms. Online class registration, office software are available.
Website: http://www.dominican.edu/

General Application Contact: 415-485-3204, Fax: 415-485-3214, E-mail: graduateprograms@dominican.edu.

GRADUATE UNITS

Barowsky School of Business *Program availability:* Part-time, evening/weekend. Offers global business (MBA); strategic leadership (MBA); sustainable enterprise (MBA). Electronic applications accepted.

School of Arts, Humanities and Social Sciences *Program availability:* Part-time, evening/weekend. Offers applied music (MA); art history (MA); arts, humanities and social sciences (MA); creative writing (MA); gender studies (MA); history (MA); literature (MA); philosophy (MA); political theory (MA); religion (MA). Electronic applications accepted.

School of Education and Counseling Psychology *Program availability:* Part-time, evening/weekend. Offers education and counseling psychology (MFT, MS); general (MS); marriage and family therapy (MS); multiple subject (MS); single subject (MS). Electronic applications accepted.

School of Health and Natural Sciences Offers biological sciences (MS); clinical laboratory sciences (MS); health and natural sciences (MS); occupational therapy (MS). Electronic applications accepted.

DONGGUK UNIVERSITY LOS ANGELES, Los Angeles, CA 90020

General Information Independent, coed, graduate-only institution. *Graduate housing:* On-campus housing not available.

GRADUATE UNITS

Program in Oriental Medicine *Program availability:* Part-time, evening/weekend. Offers Oriental medicine (MS).

DORDT COLLEGE, Sioux Center, IA 51250-1697

General Information Independent-religious, coed, comprehensive institution. *Graduate housing:* Rooms and/or apartments available to single and married students.

GRADUATE UNITS

Program in Education *Program availability:* Part-time, online learning. Offers education (M Ed). Electronic applications accepted.

DRAGON RISES COLLEGE OF ORIENTAL MEDICINE, Gainesville, FL 32601

General Information Proprietary, coed, graduate-only institution.

GRADUATE UNITS

Graduate Program Offers Oriental medicine (MAOM).

DRAKE UNIVERSITY, Des Moines, IA 50311-4516

General Information Independent, coed, university. *Enrollment:* 5,001 graduate, professional, and undergraduate students; 862 full-time matriculated graduate/professional students (540 women), 827 part-time matriculated graduate/professional students (571 women). *Enrollment by degree level:* 726 master's, 893 doctoral, 32 other advanced degrees. *Graduate faculty:* 107 full-time (60 women), 70 part-time/adjunct (43 women). *Tuition:* Full-time $38,244; part-time $555 per credit hour. *Required fees:* $146; $73 per semester. Tuition and fees vary according to course load, program and student level. *Graduate housing:* Room and/or apartments available on a first-come, first-served basis to single students; on-campus housing not available to married students. Typical cost: $5300 per year ($9850 including board). Room and board charges vary according to board plan, campus/location and housing facility selected. Housing application deadline: 8/1. *Student services:* Campus employment opportunities, campus safety program, career counseling, exercise/wellness program, free psychological counseling, international student services, low-cost health insurance, services for students with disabilities, teacher training, writing training. *Library facilities:* Cowles Library plus 1 other. *Collection:* Study areas open 24 hours, 5–7 days a week; students can reserve study rooms. *Research affiliation:* NASA through Iowa State University of Science and Technology (arts and sciences), Albertson's Inc. (pharmacy), U.S. Department of Agriculture (USDA) (agriculture), U.S. Department of Education (DOE) (education), Iowa Department of Education (education), National Science Foundation (biology, physics).

Computer facilities: A campuswide network can be accessed from student residence rooms and from off campus. Online class registration is available.
Website: http://www.drake.edu/

General Application Contact: Jennifer Reitano, Director, Graduate Student Programs, 515-271-2188, Fax: 515-271-2831, E-mail: jennifer.reitano@drake.edu.

GRADUATE UNITS

College of Business and Public Administration Students: 29 full-time (15 women), 199 part-time (103 women); includes 20 minority (6 Black or African American, non-Hispanic/Latino; 3 Asian, non-Hispanic/Latino; 8 Hispanic/Latino; 3 Two or more races, non-Hispanic/Latino), 12 international. Average age 32. 131 applicants, 76% accepted, 75 enrolled. *Faculty:* 15 full-time (5 women). Expenses: Contact institution. *Financial support:* Fellowships with tuition reimbursements, teaching assistantships, career-related internships or fieldwork, and institutionally sponsored loans available. Support available to part-time students. Financial award application deadline: 3/1; financial award applicants required to submit FAFSA. In 2016, 166 master's awarded. *Program availability:* Part-time, evening/weekend. Offers business and public administration (M Acc, MBA, MFM, MPA). *Application deadline:* For fall admission, 8/15 priority date for domestic students; for winter admission, 12/20 priority date for domestic students; for spring admission, 12/1 priority date for domestic students. Applications are processed on a rolling basis. *Application fee:* $25. Electronic applications accepted. *Application Contact:* Danette Kenne, Assistant Dean, 515-271-2188, Fax: 515-271-4518, E-mail: cbpa.gradprograms@drake.edu. *Dean,* Dr. Terri Vaughan, 515-271-2871, Fax: 515-271-4518, E-mail: terri.vaughan@drake.edu.

College of Pharmacy and Health Sciences Students: 447 full-time (307 women), 4 part-time (2 women); includes 61 minority (2 Black or African American, non-Hispanic/Latino; 1 American Indian or Alaska Native, non-Hispanic/Latino; 46 Asian, non-Hispanic/Latino; 5 Hispanic/Latino; 7 Two or more races, non-Hispanic/Latino), 2 international. Average age 22. 54 applicants, 31% accepted, 17 enrolled. *Faculty:* 36 full-time (18 women). Expenses: Contact institution. *Financial support:* In 2016–17, 10 teaching assistantships (averaging $3,200 per year) were awarded; career-related

internships or fieldwork, Federal Work-Study, institutionally sponsored loans, and scholarships/grants also available. Support available to part-time students. Financial award application deadline: 3/1; financial award applicants required to submit FAFSA. In 2016, 107 doctorates awarded. Offers pharmacy (Pharm D). *Application deadline:* For fall admission, 2/1 priority date for domestic students. *Application fee:* $135. Electronic applications accepted. *Dean,* Dr. Renae Chesnut, 515-271-3018, Fax: 515-271-4171, E-mail: renae.chesnut@drake.edu.

Law School Students: 306 full-time (153 women), 23 part-time (16 women); includes 49 minority (17 Black or African American, non-Hispanic/Latino; 1 American Indian or Alaska Native, non-Hispanic/Latino; 5 Asian, non-Hispanic/Latino; 16 Hispanic/Latino; 10 Two or more races, non-Hispanic/Latino), 7 international. Average age 27. 521 applicants, 44% accepted, 117 enrolled. *Faculty:* 28 full-time (10 women), 18 part-time/adjunct (5 women). Expenses: Contact institution. *Financial support:* In 2016–17, 20 research assistantships (averaging $757 per year), 6 teaching assistantships (averaging $2,142 per year) were awarded; career-related internships or fieldwork, Federal Work-Study, institutionally sponsored loans, scholarships/grants, and tuition waivers (full and partial) also available. Support available to part-time students. Financial award application deadline: 3/1; financial award applicants required to submit FAFSA. In 2016, 1 master's, 106 doctorates awarded. *Program availability:* Part-time. Offers law (LL M, MJ, JD). *Application deadline:* For fall admission, 4/1 priority date for domestic and international students. Applications are processed on a rolling basis. *Application fee:* $40. Electronic applications accepted. *Application Contact:* Kara Blanchard, Director of Admission, 515-271-2953, Fax: 515-271-2530, E-mail: kara.blanchard@drake.edu. *Dean,* Jerry Anderson, 515-271-2658, Fax: 515-271-4118, E-mail: jerry.anderson@drake.edu.

School of Education Students: 80 full-time (65 women), 582 part-time (436 women); includes 42 minority (19 Black or African American, non-Hispanic/Latino; 1 American Indian or Alaska Native, non-Hispanic/Latino; 4 Asian, non-Hispanic/Latino; 10 Hispanic/Latino; 8 Two or more races, non-Hispanic/Latino), 2 international. Average age 33. 328 applicants, 87% accepted, 219 enrolled. *Faculty:* 24 full-time (11 women), 48 part-time/adjunct (37 women). Expenses: Contact institution. *Financial support:* In 2016–17, 14 research assistantships were awarded; career-related internships or fieldwork and unspecified assistantships also available. Support available to part-time students. In 2016, 190 master's, 4 doctorates, 8 other advanced degrees awarded. *Program availability:* Part-time, evening/weekend. Offers education (MAT, MS, MSE, MST, Ed D, PhD, Ed S). *Application deadline:* For fall admission, 7/1 priority date for domestic students, 6/1 priority date for international students; for spring admission, 11/1 priority date for domestic students, 10/1 priority date for international students. Applications are processed on a rolling basis. *Application fee:* $25. Electronic applications accepted. *Dean,* Dr. Janet McMahill, 515-271-3829, E-mail: janet.mcmahill@drake.edu.

School of Journalism and Mass Communication Students: 19 part-time (14 women); includes 2 minority (1 Black or African American, non-Hispanic/Latino; 1 Hispanic/Latino). Average age 33. 5 applicants, 100% accepted, 5 enrolled. *Faculty:* 4 full-time (3 women). Expenses: Contact institution. In 2016, 8 master's awarded. *Program availability:* Part-time, evening/weekend. Offers journalism and mass communication (MCL). *Dean,* Dr. Kathleen Richardson, 515-271-2295, Fax: 515-271-4518, E-mail: kathleen.richardson@drake.edu.

DREW UNIVERSITY, Madison, NJ 07940-1493

General Information Independent-religious, coed, university. CGS member. *Enrollment:* 2,129 graduate, professional, and undergraduate students; 273 full-time matriculated graduate/professional students (145 women), 339 part-time matriculated graduate/professional students (185 women). *Enrollment by degree level:* 275 master's, 320 doctoral. *Graduate faculty:* 25 full-time (11 women), 50 part-time/adjunct (24 women). Tuition and fees vary according to program. *Graduate housing:* Rooms and/or apartments available on a first-come, first-served basis to single and married students. Housing application deadline: 7/1. *Student services:* Campus employment opportunities, campus safety program, career counseling, child daycare facilities, exercise/wellness program, free psychological counseling, international student services, low-cost health insurance, multicultural affairs office, services for students with disabilities, teacher training, writing training. *Library facilities:* Rose Memorial Library plus 1 other. *Collection:* Books: 610,346 (physical), 133,970 (digital/electronic); Databases: 370. Weekly public service hours: 83. *Research affiliation:* Center for Research Libraries (humanities), Dana Rise Institute (science), St. Barnabas Medical Center (medical humanities), Overlook Hospital (medical humanities), Methodist Archives (religion).

Computer facilities: Computer purchase and lease plans are available. A campuswide network can be accessed from student residence rooms and from off campus. Online class registration is available.
Website: http://www.drew.edu/

General Application Contact: John Witherington, Executive Director of Graduate Admissions, 973-408-3111, E-mail: gradm@drew.edu.

GRADUATE UNITS

Caspersen School of Graduate Studies Students: 62 full-time (41 women), 199 part-time (130 women); includes 38 minority (17 Black or African American, non-Hispanic/Latino; 3 Asian, non-Hispanic/Latino; 17 Hispanic/Latino; 1 Two or more races, non-Hispanic/Latino), 3 international. Average age 39. 93 applicants, 81% accepted, 46 enrolled. *Faculty:* 4 full-time (2 women), 31 part-time/adjunct (16 women). Expenses: Contact institution. *Financial support:* Fellowships, research assistantships, teaching assistantships, career-related internships or fieldwork, Federal Work-Study, scholarships/grants, and unspecified assistantships available. Support available to part-time students. Financial award applicants required to submit FAFSA. In 2016, 39 master's, 27 doctorates, 26 other advanced degrees awarded. *Program availability:* Part-time, evening/weekend. Offers conflict resolution and leadership (Certificate); history and culture (MA, PhD); K-12 education (MAT); liberal studies (M Litt, D Litt); medical humanities (MMH, DMH, CMH); poetry (MFA). *Application deadline:* For fall admission, 8/1 for domestic students, 6/1 for international students; for spring admission, 12/1 for domestic students, 10/1 for international students. Applications are processed on a rolling basis. *Application fee:* $35. Electronic applications accepted. *Application Contact:* Leanne Horinko, Director of Caspersen Admissions, 973-408-3280, E-mail: gradm@drew.edu.

Theological School Students: 208 full-time (100 women), 147 part-time (62 women); includes 134 minority (94 Black or African American, non-Hispanic/Latino; 2 American Indian or Alaska Native, non-Hispanic/Latino; 17 Asian, non-Hispanic/Latino; 16 Hispanic/Latino; 5 Two or more races, non-Hispanic/Latino), 87 international. Average age 40. 201 applicants, 78% accepted, 94 enrolled. *Faculty:* 21 full-time (9 women), 20 part-time/adjunct (9 women). Expenses: Contact institution. *Financial support:* Fellowships, career-related internships or fieldwork, Federal Work-Study, institutionally sponsored loans, and scholarships/grants available. Support available to part-time students. Financial award application deadline: 2/15; financial award applicants required

Drexel University

to submit FAFSA. In 2016, 58 master's, 33 doctorates awarded. *Program availability:* Part-time, online learning. Offers theology (M Div, MA, MA Min, STM, D Min, PhD, Certificate). *Application deadline:* For fall admission, 8/1 for domestic students, 8/1 for international students; for spring admission, 12/1 for domestic students, 10/1 for international students. Applications are processed on a rolling basis. *Application fee:* $35. Electronic applications accepted. *Application Contact:* Rev. Dr. Kevin D. Miller, Director of Theological Admissions, 973-408-3111, E-mail: kmiller@drew.edu. *Dean of the Theological School,* Dr. Javier Viera, 973-408-3418, E-mail: jviera@drew.edu.

DREXEL UNIVERSITY, Philadelphia, PA 19104-2875

General Information Independent, coed, university. CGS member. *Enrollment:* 24,232 graduate, professional, and undergraduate students; 4,489 full-time matriculated graduate/professional students (2,498 women), 4,244 part-time matriculated graduate/professional students (2,965 women). *Enrollment by degree level:* 5,389 master's, 3,031 doctoral, 313 other advanced degrees. *Graduate faculty:* 1,536 full-time (707 women), 1,017 part-time/adjunct (562 women). *Tuition:* Full-time $32,184; part-time $1192 per credit hour. *Required fees:* $280. Tuition and fees vary according to campus/location and program. *Graduate housing:* Room and/or apartments available on a first-come, first-served basis to single students; on-campus housing not available to married students. Typical cost: $4275 per year. Room charges vary according to campus/location and housing facility selected. Housing application deadline: 1/9. *Student services:* Campus safety program, career counseling, child daycare facilities, exercise/wellness program, free psychological counseling, grant writing training, international student services, low-cost health insurance, multicultural affairs office, services for students with disabilities, teacher training, writing training. *Library facilities:* W. W. Hagerty Library plus 3 others. *Collection:* Books: 286,613 (physical), 215,379 (digital/electronic); Serial titles: 126 (physical), 51,775 (digital/electronic); Databases: 465. Weekly public service hours: 87; study areas open 24 hours, 5–7 days a week; students can reserve study rooms.

Computer facilities: Computer purchase and lease plans are available. A campuswide network can be accessed from student residence rooms and from off campus. Online class registration is available.

Website: http://www.drexel.edu/

General Application Contact: Director of Graduate Admissions, 215-895-6700, Fax: 215-895-5939, E-mail: enroll@drexel.edu.

GRADUATE UNITS

College of Arts and Sciences Students: 287 full-time (163 women), 101 part-time (62 women); includes 62 minority (20 Black or African American, non-Hispanic/Latino; 1 American Indian or Alaska Native, non-Hispanic/Latino; 16 Asian, non-Hispanic/Latino; 12 Hispanic/Latino; 1 Native Hawaiian or other Pacific Islander, non-Hispanic/Latino; 12 Two or more races, non-Hispanic/Latino), 47 international. Average age 28. *Faculty:* 304 full-time (132 women), 165 part-time/adjunct (79 women). Expenses: Contact institution. *Financial support:* Research assistantships, teaching assistantships, career-related internships or fieldwork, Federal Work-Study, institutionally sponsored loans, tuition waivers (full and partial), and unspecified assistantships available. Support available to part-time students. Financial award application deadline: 2/1. In 2016, 96 master's, 39 doctorates awarded. *Program availability:* Part-time, evening/weekend. Offers arts and sciences (MA, MS, PhD); biological sciences (MS, PhD); chemistry (MS, PhD); clinical psychology (PhD); communication (MS); environmental policy (MS); environmental science (MS, PhD); forensic psychology (PhD); health psychology (PhD); law-psychology mathematics (PhD); neuropsychology (PhD); physics (MS, PhD); psychology (MS); public communication (MS); science communication (MS); science, technology and society (MS); technical communication (MS). *Application deadline:* Applications are processed on a rolling basis. *Application fee:* $50. Electronic applications accepted. *Application Contact:* Director of Graduate Admissions, 215-895-6700, Fax: 215-895-5939, E-mail: enroll@drexel.edu. *Dean,* Dr. Donna Murasko, 215-895-2620.

College of Computing and Informatics Students: 172 full-time (76 women), 344 part-time (190 women); includes 88 minority (30 Black or African American, non-Hispanic/Latino; 20 Asian, non-Hispanic/Latino; 29 Hispanic/Latino; 9 Two or more races, non-Hispanic/Latino), 105 international. Average age 33. 871 applicants, 35% accepted, 137 enrolled. *Faculty:* 64 full-time (23 women), 9 part-time/adjunct (3 women). Expenses: Contact institution. *Financial support:* In 2016–17, 97 students received support, including 1 fellowship with full tuition reimbursement available (averaging $35,000 per year), 34 research assistantships with full tuition reimbursements available (averaging $27,290 per year), 20 teaching assistantships with full tuition reimbursements available (averaging $26,750 per year); career-related internships or fieldwork, institutionally sponsored loans, scholarships/grants, health care benefits, and tuition waivers (partial) also available. Support available to part-time students. Financial award application deadline: 3/1; financial award applicants required to submit FAFSA. In 2016, 270 master's, 11 doctorates, 28 other advanced degrees awarded. *Program availability:* Part-time, evening/weekend, 100% online. Offers computer science (MS, PhD, Postbaccalaureate Certificate); computing and informatics (MS, PhD, Post-Master's Certificate, Postbaccalaureate Certificate); health informatics (MS); information science (PhD, Post-Master's Certificate, Postbaccalaureate Certificate); information systems (MS); library and information science (MS); software engineering (MS). *Application deadline:* For fall admission, 8/15 for domestic students, 7/15 for international students; for spring admission, 3/1 for domestic students, 2/1 for international students. Applications are processed on a rolling basis. *Application fee:* $65. Electronic applications accepted. *Application Contact:* Matthew Lechtenberg, Director, Recruitment, 215-895-2474, Fax: 215-895-2303, E-mail: cciinfo@drexel.edu. *Dean/Professor,* Dr. Yi Deng, 215-895-2475, Fax: 215-895-2494, E-mail: yd362@drexel.edu.

College of Engineering Students: 436 full-time (111 women), 334 part-time (73 women); includes 128 minority (46 Black or African American, non-Hispanic/Latino; 3 American Indian or Alaska Native, non-Hispanic/Latino; 40 Asian, non-Hispanic/Latino; 25 Hispanic/Latino; 14 Two or more races, non-Hispanic/Latino), 284 international. Average age 29. *Faculty:* 151 full-time (29 women), 49 part-time/adjunct (5 women). Expenses: Contact institution. *Financial support:* Research assistantships, teaching assistantships, career-related internships or fieldwork, Federal Work-Study, institutionally sponsored loans, tuition waivers (full and partial), and unspecified assistantships available. Support available to part-time students. Financial award application deadline: 2/1. In 2016, 329 master's, 54 doctorates, 12 other advanced degrees awarded. *Program availability:* Part-time, evening/weekend. Offers architectural/building systems engineering (MS, PhD); biomedical engineering (MS); chemical engineering (MS, PhD); civil engineering (PhD); computer engineering (MS); electrical and computer engineering (PhD); electrical engineering (MSEE); engineering (MS, MSEE, MSSE, PhD, Certificate); engineering management (MS, Certificate); environmental engineering (MS, PhD); geotechnical, geoenvironmental and geosynthetics engineering (MS, PhD); hydraulics, hydrology and water resources

engineering (MS, PhD); materials engineering (MS, PhD); mechanical engineering (MS, PhD); software engineering (MSSE); structures (MS); telecommunications engineering (MSEE). *Application deadline:* For fall admission, 8/21 for domestic students. Applications are processed on a rolling basis. *Application fee:* $50. Electronic applications accepted. *Application Contact:* Director of Graduate Admissions, 215-895-6700, Fax: 215-895-5939, E-mail: enroll@drexel.edu. *Interim Dean,* Dr. Giuseppe Palmese, 215-895-2210.

College of Medicine Students: 1,059 full-time (527 women); includes 483 minority (61 Black or African American, non-Hispanic/Latino; 3 American Indian or Alaska Native, non-Hispanic/Latino; 330 Asian, non-Hispanic/Latino; 50 Hispanic/Latino; 3 Native Hawaiian or other Pacific Islander, non-Hispanic/Latino; 36 Two or more races, non-Hispanic/Latino). Average age 25. *Faculty:* 365 full-time (172 women), 111 part-time/adjunct (57 women). Expenses: Contact institution. *Financial support:* Fellowships, research assistantships, teaching assistantships, career-related internships or fieldwork, Federal Work-Study, institutionally sponsored loans, and tuition waivers (full and partial) available. Support available to part-time students. Financial award application deadline: 5/1; financial award applicants required to submit FAFSA. In 2016, 3 master's, 263 other advanced degrees awarded. *Program availability:* Part-time. Offers medicine (MLAS, MMS, MS, MD, PhD, Certificate). *Application deadline:* Applications are processed on a rolling basis. Electronic applications accepted. *Application Contact:* Director of Graduate Admissions, 215-895-6700, Fax: 215-895-5939, E-mail: enroll@drexel.edu. *Dean,* Dr. Warren E. Ross, 215-762-8900, E-mail: warren.ross@drexel.edu.

Biomedical Graduate Programs Students: 151 full-time (72 women), 25 part-time (10 women); includes 32 minority (8 Black or African American, non-Hispanic/Latino; 19 Asian, non-Hispanic/Latino; 4 Hispanic/Latino; 1 Two or more races, non-Hispanic/Latino), 58 international. Average age 26. *Faculty:* 28 full-time (8 women), 4 part-time/adjunct (1 woman). Expenses: Contact institution. *Financial support:* Fellowships, research assistantships, teaching assistantships, career-related internships or fieldwork, Federal Work-Study, institutionally sponsored loans, scholarships/grants, and tuition waivers (full and partial) available. Support available to part-time students. Financial award application deadline: 5/1; financial award applicants required to submit FAFSA. In 2016, 93 master's, 14 doctorates awarded. *Program availability:* Part-time. Offers biochemistry (MS, PhD); biomedical sciences (MLAS, MMS, MS, PhD, Certificate); drug discovery and development (MS); laboratory animal science (MLAS); medical science (MMS, Certificate); microbiology and immunology (MS, PhD); molecular and cell biology and genetics (MS, PhD); molecular medicine (MS); molecular pathobiology (MS, PhD); neuroscience (MS, PhD); pharmacology and physiology (MS, PhD). *Application deadline:* For fall admission, 4/1 for domestic students. Applications are processed on a rolling basis. *Application fee:* $50. Electronic applications accepted. *Application Contact:* Director of Graduate Admissions, 215-895-6700, Fax: 215-895-5939, E-mail: enroll@drexel.edu. *Vice Dean, Biomedical Graduate and Postgraduate Studies,* Dr. Barry D. Waterhouse, 215-991-8570, E-mail: biomed.mcphu@drexel.edu.

College of Nursing and Health Professions Students: 513 full-time (398 women), 1,585 part-time (1,405 women); includes 459 minority (195 Black or African American, non-Hispanic/Latino; 3 American Indian or Alaska Native, non-Hispanic/Latino; 116 Asian, non-Hispanic/Latino; 101 Hispanic/Latino; 44 Two or more races, non-Hispanic/Latino), 52 international. Average age 34. *Faculty:* 191 full-time (152 women), 255 part-time/adjunct (210 women). Expenses: Contact institution. *Financial support:* Fellowships, research assistantships, teaching assistantships, career-related internships or fieldwork, Federal Work-Study, institutionally sponsored loans, and tuition waivers (partial) available. Support available to part-time students. Financial award application deadline: 5/1; financial award applicants required to submit FAFSA. In 2016, 529 master's, 93 doctorates, 47 other advanced degrees awarded. *Program availability:* Part-time, evening/weekend. Offers art therapy (MA, PMC); clinical biomechanics and orthopedics (PhD); couple and family therapy (MFT, PhD); creative arts therapies (PhD); dance/movement therapy (MA, PMC); emergency and public safety services (MS); hand and upper quarter rehabilitation (Certificate); hand therapy (MHS, PPDPT); music therapy (MA, PMC); nurse anesthesia (MSN); nursing and health professions (MA, MFT, MHS, MS, MSN, DPT, Dr NP, PPDPT, PhD, Certificate, PMC); nursing studies (Dr NP); orthopedics (MHS, PPDPT); pediatric rehabilitation (Certificate); pediatrics (MHS, PPDPT, PhD); physical therapy (DPT); physician assistant (MHS). *Application deadline:* Applications are processed on a rolling basis. *Application fee:* $50. Electronic applications accepted. *Application Contact:* Director of Graduate Admissions, 215-895-6700, Fax: 215-895-5939, E-mail: enroll@drexel.edu. *Dean,* Dr. Gloria Donnelly, 215-762-1336.

Division of Graduate Nursing Students: 44 part-time (41 women); includes 16 minority (13 Black or African American, non-Hispanic/Latino; 1 Hispanic/Latino; 2 Two or more races, non-Hispanic/Latino), 1 international. Average age 41. *Faculty:* 17 full-time (all women), 36 part-time/adjunct (34 women). Expenses: Contact institution. In 2016, 20 master's awarded. Offers adult acute care (MSN); adult psychiatric/mental health (MSN); advanced practice nursing (MSN); clinical trials research (MSN); family nurse practitioner (MSN); leadership in health systems management (MSN); nursing education (MSN); pediatric primary care (MSN); women's health (MSN). *Application deadline:* For fall admission, 9/1 for domestic students. Applications are processed on a rolling basis. *Application fee:* $50. Electronic applications accepted. *Application Contact:* Director of Graduate Admissions, 215-895-6700, Fax: 215-895-5939, E-mail: enroll@drexel.edu. *Director,* Elizabeth M. Blunt, 215-762-1644, E-mail: emb1@drexel.edu.

Dornsife School of Public Health Students: 263 full-time (199 women), 80 part-time (67 women); includes 121 minority (53 Black or African American, non-Hispanic/Latino; 39 Asian, non-Hispanic/Latino; 21 Hispanic/Latino; 1 Native Hawaiian or other Pacific Islander, non-Hispanic/Latino; 7 Two or more races, non-Hispanic/Latino), 62 international. Average age 28. *Faculty:* 58 full-time (33 women), 12 part-time/adjunct (11 women). Expenses: Contact institution. In 2016, 163 master's, 4 doctorates, 13 other advanced degrees awarded. Offers biostatistics (MS); epidemiology (PhD); epidemiology and biostatistics (Certificate); public health (MPH, MS, PhD, Certificate). *Application deadline:* Applications are processed on a rolling basis. *Application fee:* $35. Electronic applications accepted. *Application Contact:* Director of Graduate Admissions, 215-895-6700, Fax: 215-895-5939, E-mail: enroll@drexel.edu. *Dean,* Dr. Marla Gold, 215-762-6957.

Goodwin College of Professional Studies Students: 113 full-time, 2,262 part-time; includes 628 minority (352 Black or African American, non-Hispanic/Latino; 100 Asian, non-Hispanic/Latino; 156 Hispanic/Latino; 20 Native Hawaiian or other Pacific Islander, non-Hispanic/Latino). *Faculty:* 74 full-time (35 women). Expenses: Contact institution. In 2016, 588 master's, 23 doctorates awarded. *Application Contact:* Director of Graduate Admissions, 215-895-6700, Fax: 215-895-5939, E-mail: enroll@drexel.edu. *Dean,* Dr. William F. Lynch, 215-895-2167, E-mail: bill.lynch@drexel.edu.

School of Education *Program availability:* Part-time, evening/weekend, online learning. Offers applied behavior analysis (MS); creativity and innovation (MS); education improvement and transformation (MS); educational administration (MS); educational leadership and management (Ed D); educational leadership development and learning technologies (PhD); global and international education (MS); higher education (MS); human resources development (MS); learning technologies (MS); mathematics, learning and teaching (MS); special education (MS); teaching, learning and curriculum (MS). Electronic applications accepted.

School of Technology and Professional Studies Students: 13 full-time, 462 part-time; includes 133 minority (86 Black or African American, non-Hispanic/Latino; 24 Asian, non-Hispanic/Latino; 23 Hispanic/Latino). *Faculty:* 37 full-time (14 women). Expenses: Contact institution. *Financial support:* Applicants required to submit FAFSA. In 2016, 88 master's awarded. *Program availability:* Part-time, evening/weekend. Offers construction management (MS); creativity and innovation (MS); engineering technology (MS); food science (MS); hospitality management (MS); professional studies: creativity studies (MS); professional studies: e-learning leadership (MS); professional studies: homeland security management (MS); project management (MS); property management (MS); sport management (MS). *Application deadline:* For fall admission, 9/1 for domestic students; for winter admission, 12/1 for domestic students; for spring admission, 3/1 for domestic students. Applications are processed on a rolling basis. *Application fee:* $75. Electronic applications accepted. *Application Contact:* Matthew Gray, Manager, Recruitment and Enrollment, 215-895-6255, Fax: 215-895-2153, E-mail: mdg67@drexel.edu. *Dean,* Dr. William F. Lynch, 215-895-2159, E-mail: goodwin@drexel.edu.

LeBow College of Business Students: 406 full-time (200 women), 425 part-time (187 women); includes 119 minority (32 Black or African American, non-Hispanic/Latino; 1 American Indian or Alaska Native, non-Hispanic/Latino; 55 Asian, non-Hispanic/Latino; 20 Hispanic/Latino; 11 Two or more races, non-Hispanic/Latino), 326 international. Average age 30. *Faculty:* 132 full-time (41 women), 48 part-time/adjunct (18 women). Expenses: Contact institution. *Financial support:* Research assistantships, teaching assistantships, career-related internships or fieldwork, tuition waivers (full), and unspecified assistantships available. Financial award application deadline: 2/1. In 2016, 322 master's, 8 doctorates, 3 other advanced degrees awarded. *Program availability:* Part-time, evening/weekend. Offers accounting (MS); business (MBA, MS, PhD, APC); business administration (MBA, PhD, APC); finance (MS). *Application deadline:* For fall admission, 8/21 for domestic students. Applications are processed on a rolling basis. *Application fee:* $50. Electronic applications accepted. *Application Contact:* Director of Graduate Admissions, 215-895-6700, Fax: 215-895-5939, E-mail: enroll@drexel.edu. *Associate Dean,* Dr. George Betsekos, 215-895-1030.

School of Biomedical Engineering, Science and Health Systems Students: 151 full-time (72 women), 25 part-time (10 women); includes 32 minority (8 Black or African American, non-Hispanic/Latino; 19 Asian, non-Hispanic/Latino; 4 Hispanic/Latino; 1 Two or more races, non-Hispanic/Latino), 58 international. Average age 26. *Faculty:* 28 full-time (8 women), 4 part-time/adjunct (1 woman). Expenses: Contact institution. *Financial support:* Research assistantships, teaching assistantships, career-related internships or fieldwork, Federal Work-Study, institutionally sponsored loans, tuition waivers (full and partial), and unspecified assistantships available. Financial award application deadline: 2/1. In 2016, 93 master's, 14 doctorates awarded. Offers biomedical engineering (MS, PhD); biomedical science (MS, PhD); biostatistics (MS); clinical/rehabilitation engineering (MS). *Application deadline:* For fall admission, 8/21 for domestic students. Applications are processed on a rolling basis. *Application fee:* $50. Electronic applications accepted. *Application Contact:* Director of Graduate Admissions, 215-895-6700, Fax: 215-895-5939, E-mail: enroll@drexel.edu. *Director,* Dr. Banu Onaral, 215-895-2215.

Westphal College of Media Arts and Design Students: 126 full-time (98 women), 115 part-time (82 women); includes 61 minority (37 Black or African American, non-Hispanic/Latino; 5 Asian, non-Hispanic/Latino; 15 Hispanic/Latino; 4 Two or more races, non-Hispanic/Latino), 56 international. Average age 29. *Faculty:* 127 full-time (51 women), 14 part-time/adjunct (87 women). Expenses: Contact institution. *Financial support:* Research assistantships, teaching assistantships, career-related internships or fieldwork, and unspecified assistantships available. Support available to part-time students. Financial award application deadline: 2/1. In 2016, 84 master's awarded. *Program availability:* Part-time, evening/weekend. Offers arts administration (MS); design research (MS); digital media (MS); fashion design (MS); interior architecture and design (MS); museum leadership (MS); television management (MS). *Application deadline:* For fall admission, 8/21 for domestic students; for spring admission, 3/5 for domestic students. Applications are processed on a rolling basis. *Application fee:* $50. Electronic applications accepted. E-mail: enroll@drexel.edu. *College Recruitment Office,* 215-895-1675, Fax: 215-895-5838.

DRURY UNIVERSITY, Springfield, MO 65802

General Information Independent, coed, comprehensive institution. *Enrollment:* 1,611 graduate, professional, and undergraduate students; 237 full-time matriculated graduate/professional students (165 women). *Enrollment by degree level:* 237 master's. *Graduate faculty:* 14 full-time (7 women), 9 part-time/adjunct (6 women). One-time fee: $100 part-time. Tuition and fees vary according to program. *Graduate housing:* On-campus housing not available. *Student services:* Campus employment opportunities, campus safety program, career counseling, exercise/wellness program, grant writing training, international student services, multicultural affairs office, services for students with disabilities, teacher training, writing training. *Library facilities:* F. W. Olin Library plus 1 other. *Collection:* Books: 149,706 (physical), 185,811 (digital/electronic); Serial titles: 751 (physical), 38 (digital/electronic); Databases: 44. Weekly public service hours: 92; students can reserve study rooms. *Research affiliation:* Yale University (child development).

Computer facilities: 385 computers available on campus for general student use. A campuswide network can be accessed from student residence rooms and from off campus. Online class registration, digital imaging lab, online bill payment/student information are available. Website: http://www.drury.edu/

General Application Contact: Regina Waters, Dean, Graduate Programs, 417-873-7251, E-mail: grad@drury.edu.

GRADUATE UNITS

Cybersecurity Leadership Certificate Program *Faculty:* 3 full-time (1 woman), 2 part-time/adjunct (0 women). Expenses: Contact institution. *Financial support:* Career-related internships or fieldwork, scholarships/grants, and unspecified assistantships available. Financial award application deadline: 6/30; financial award applicants required to submit FAFSA. *Program availability:* Part-time, evening/weekend. Offers cybersecurity leadership (Certificate). *Application deadline:* For fall admission, 8/4 for domestic and international students; for spring admission, 1/5 for domestic and international students; for summer admission, 5/26 for domestic and international students. Applications are

processed on a rolling basis. *Application fee:* $25 ($50 for international students). Electronic applications accepted. *Director, Cybersecurity Leadership Certificate,* Angie Adamick, 417-873-7612, E-mail: aadamick@drury.edu.

Master in Education Program Students: 146 full-time (111 women); includes 6 minority (1 Asian, non-Hispanic/Latino; 3 Hispanic/Latino; 2 Two or more races, non-Hispanic/Latino), 1 international. Average age 34. 42 applicants, 74% accepted. Expenses: Contact institution. *Financial support:* In 2016–17, 20 students received support. Career-related internships or fieldwork, scholarships/grants, tuition waivers (partial), and unspecified assistantships available. Financial award application deadline: 6/30; financial award applicants required to submit FAFSA. In 2016, 74 master's awarded. *Program availability:* Part-time, evening/weekend, 100% online, blended/hybrid learning. Offers curriculum and instruction (M Ed); gifted education (M Ed); instructional leadership (M Ed); instructional technology (M Ed); integrated learning (M Ed); online teaching (M Ed); special education (M Ed); special reading (M Ed). *Application deadline:* For fall admission, 8/4 priority date for domestic and international students; for spring admission, 1/5 priority date for domestic and international students; for summer admission, 5/26 priority date for domestic and international students. Applications are processed on a rolling basis. *Application fee:* $25 ($50 for international students). Electronic applications accepted. *Director, Master in Education,* Dr. Asikaa Cosgrove, 417-873-7806, E-mail: acosgrov@drury.edu.

Master of Arts in Communication Program Students: 39 full-time (32 women); includes 4 minority (1 Black or African American, non-Hispanic/Latino; 2 Hispanic/Latino; 1 Two or more races, non-Hispanic/Latino), 2 international. Average age 27. 8 applicants, 88% accepted, 7 enrolled. *Faculty:* 3 full-time (1 woman), 2 part-time/adjunct (0 women). Expenses: Contact institution. *Financial support:* Career-related internships or fieldwork, scholarships/grants, and unspecified assistantships available. Financial award application deadline: 6/30; financial award applicants required to submit FAFSA. In 2016, 8 master's awarded. *Program availability:* Part-time, evening/weekend. Offers integrated marketing communications (MA); organizational leadership and change (MA). *Application deadline:* For fall admission, 8/4 priority date for domestic and international students; for spring admission, 1/5 priority date for domestic and international students; for summer admission, 5/26 priority date for domestic and international students. Applications are processed on a rolling basis. *Application fee:* $25 ($50 for international students). Electronic applications accepted. *Director, Master of Arts in Communication,* Charles Taylor, 417-873-7391, E-mail: ctaylor@drury.edu.

Master of Business Administration Program Students: 38 full-time (13 women); includes 17 minority (1 Black or African American, non-Hispanic/Latino; 2 Asian, non-Hispanic/Latino; 7 Hispanic/Latino; 7 Two or more races, non-Hispanic/Latino), 10 international. Average age 25. 38 applicants, 61% accepted, 21 enrolled. *Faculty:* 3 full-time (1 woman), 2 part-time/adjunct (0 women). Expenses: Contact institution. *Financial support:* In 2016–17, 4 students received support. Career-related internships or fieldwork, scholarships/grants, and unspecified assistantships available. Financial award application deadline: 6/30; financial award applicants required to submit FAFSA. In 2016, 26 degrees awarded. *Program availability:* Part-time, evening/weekend. Offers business administration (MBA). *Application deadline:* For fall admission, 8/4 priority date for domestic and international students; for spring admission, 1/6 priority date for domestic and international students; for summer admission, 5/26 priority date for domestic and international students. Applications are processed on a rolling basis. *Application fee:* $25 ($50 for international students). Electronic applications accepted. *Director, MBA Program,* Angie Adamick, 417-873-7612, E-mail: aadamick@drury.edu.

Master of Nonprofit and Civic Leadership Program Students: 39 full-time (32 women); includes 4 minority (1 Black or African American, non-Hispanic/Latino; 2 Hispanic/Latino; 1 Two or more races, non-Hispanic/Latino), 2 international. Average age 27. 8 applicants, 88% accepted, 7 enrolled. *Faculty:* 3 full-time (1 woman), 2 part-time/adjunct (0 women). Expenses: Contact institution. *Financial support:* Career-related internships or fieldwork, scholarships/grants, and unspecified assistantships available. Financial award application deadline: 6/30; financial award applicants required to submit FAFSA. *Program availability:* Part-time, evening/weekend. Offers nonprofit and civic leadership (MNCL). *Application deadline:* For fall admission, 8/4 for domestic and international students; for spring admission, 1/6 for domestic and international students; for summer admission, 5/24 for domestic and international students. Applications are processed on a rolling basis. *Application fee:* $25 ($50 for international students). Electronic applications accepted. *Director,* Dr. Charles Taylor, 417-873-7391, E-mail: ctaylor@drury.edu.

DUKE UNIVERSITY, Durham, NC 27708-0586

General Information Independent-religious, coed, university. CGS member. *Graduate housing:* Rooms and/or apartments available on a first-come, first-served basis to single and married students. Housing application deadline: 5/8. *Research affiliation:* Highlands Biological Station, U.S. Forest Sciences Laboratory, Organization for Tropical Studies.

GRADUATE UNITS

Divinity School *Program availability:* Part-time, online learning. Offers theology (M Div, MACP, MACS, MTS, Th M, D Min, Th D). Electronic applications accepted.

The Fuqua School of Business Students: 1,592 full-time (552 women); includes 361 minority (69 Black or African American, non-Hispanic/Latino; 6 American Indian or Alaska Native, non-Hispanic/Latino; 198 Asian, non-Hispanic/Latino; 80 Hispanic/Latino; 1 Native Hawaiian or other Pacific Islander, non-Hispanic/Latino; 7 Two or more races, non-Hispanic/Latino), 554 international. *Faculty:* 88 full-time (19 women), 50 part-time/adjunct (9 women). Expenses: Contact institution. *Financial support:* In 2016–17, 625 students received support. In 2016, 813 master's, 15 doctorates awarded. Offers academic excellence in finance (Certificate); accounting (PhD); business (EMBA, GEMBA, MBA, MMS, MQM, WEMBA, PhD, Certificate); business administration (MBA); decision sciences (MBA, PhD); energy and environment (MBA); energy finance (MBA); entrepreneurship and innovation (MBA); finance (MBA, MQM, PhD); financial analysis (MBA); forensics (MQM); foundations of business (MMS); health sector management (Certificate); leadership and ethics (MBA); management (MBA); management and organizations (PhD); management studies (MMS); marketing (MBA, MQM, PhD); operations management (MBA, PhD); social entrepreneurship (MBA); strategy (MBA, MQM, PhD). Electronic applications accepted. *Application Contact:* Sharon Thompson, Assistant Dean, Office of Admissions, 919-660-7705, Fax: 919-681-8026, E-mail: admissions-info@fuqua.duke.edu. *Dean,* William Boulding, 919-660-7822, Fax: 919-684-8742, E-mail: bb1@duke.edu.

Division of Earth and Ocean Sciences *Program availability:* Part-time. Offers earth and ocean sciences (MS, PhD). Electronic applications accepted.

Duke Global Health Institute Offers global health (MS).

Pratt School of Engineering *Program availability:* Part-time, online learning. Offers biomedical engineering (MS, PhD); civil and environmental engineering (MS, PhD); civil engineering (M Eng); electrical and computer engineering (M Eng); engineering (M Eng, MEM, MS, PhD); engineering management (MEM); environmental engineering (M Eng, MS, PhD); materials science (MS, PhD); materials science and engineering (M Eng); mechanical engineering (M Eng, MS, PhD); photonics and optical sciences (M Eng).

Nicholas School of the Environment Students: 135 full-time (94 women); includes 31 minority (1 American Indian or Alaska Native, non-Hispanic/Latino; 30 Asian, non-Hispanic/Latino), 32 international. Average age 25. *Faculty:* 50. Expenses: Contact institution. *Financial support:* In 2016–17, research assistantships (averaging $3,000 per year) were awarded; career-related internships or fieldwork, Federal Work-Study, institutionally sponsored loans, and scholarships/grants also available. Financial award application deadline: 12/15; financial award applicants required to submit FAFSA. In 2016, 130 master's, 25 doctorates awarded. *Program availability:* Online learning. Offers environment (PhD); environmental management (MEM); forestry (MF). Application deadline for PhD program is December 8. *Application deadline:* For fall admission, 12/15 priority date for domestic and international students. *Application fee:* $85. Electronic applications accepted. *Application Contact:* Sue Smith, Assistant Director of Admissions, 919-613-8070, E-mail: admissions@nicholas.duke.edu. *Assistant Director of Admissions,* Sue Smith, 919-613-8070, E-mail: admissions@nicholas.duke.edu.

Sanford School of Public Policy Expenses: Contact institution. *Financial support:* Career-related internships or fieldwork and Federal Work-Study available. Financial award application deadline: 12/31. Offers international development policy (MIDP); public policy (MIDP, MPP). *Application deadline:* For fall admission, 12/8 for domestic and international students. Electronic applications accepted. *Application Contact:* Jessica Pan, Director of Admissions, 919-613-9244, E-mail: jessica.pan@duke.edu.

School of Law Students: 676 full-time; includes 160 minority (46 Black or African American, non-Hispanic/Latino; 2 American Indian or Alaska Native, non-Hispanic/Latino; 69 Asian, non-Hispanic/Latino; 39 Hispanic/Latino; 1 Native Hawaiian or other Pacific Islander, non-Hispanic/Latino; 3 Two or more races, non-Hispanic/Latino), 44 international. Average age 24. 4,819 applicants, 23% accepted, 225 enrolled. *Faculty:* 83 full-time (39 women), 35 part-time/adjunct (11 women). Expenses: Contact institution. *Financial support:* In 2016–17, 560 students received support. Institutionally sponsored loans, scholarships/grants, and unspecified assistantships available. Financial award application deadline: 3/15; financial award applicants required to submit FAFSA. In 2016, 131 master's, 222 doctorates awarded. Offers law (LL M, MJS, JD, SJD). LL M and SJD offered only to international students; MJS offered only to sitting judges. *Application deadline:* For fall admission, 2/15 for domestic and international students. Applications are processed on a rolling basis. *Application fee:* $70. Electronic applications accepted. *Application Contact:* William J. Hoye, Associate Dean for Admissions and Student Affairs, 919-613-7020, Fax: 919-613-7257, E-mail: hoye@law.duke.edu. *Dean/Professor of Law,* David F. Levi, 919-613-7001, Fax: 919-613-7158.

School of Medicine Students: 1,028 full-time (600 women), 157 part-time (83 women); includes 426 minority (86 Black or African American, non-Hispanic/Latino; 27 American Indian or Alaska Native, non-Hispanic/Latino; 271 Asian, non-Hispanic/Latino; 42 Hispanic/Latino), 57 international. 10,710 applicants, 6% accepted, 455 enrolled. *Faculty:* 1,561 full-time (545 women), 80 part-time/adjunct (37 women). Expenses: Contact institution. *Financial support:* In 2016–17, 438 students received support. Institutionally sponsored loans and scholarships/grants available. Financial award application deadline: 5/1; financial award applicants required to submit FAFSA. In 2016, 161 master's, 204 doctorates awarded. *Program availability:* Part-time, evening/weekend. Offers biomedical sciences (MS); biostatistics (MS); clinical informatics (MS); clinical leadership (MHS); clinical research (MHS); medicine (MHS, MS, DPT, MD); pathologists' assistant (MHS); physician assistant (MHS). *Application Contact:* Andrea Lanahan, Director of Admissions, 919-684-2985, Fax: 919-684-8893, E-mail: medadm@mc.duke.edu. *Vice Dean, Medical Education,* Dr. Edward G. Buckley, 919-668-3381, Fax: 919-660-7040, E-mail: buckl002@mc.duke.edu.

Physical Therapy Division Students: 224 full-time (149 women); includes 38 minority (10 Black or African American, non-Hispanic/Latino; 10 American Indian or Alaska Native, non-Hispanic/Latino; 6 Asian, non-Hispanic/Latino; 12 Hispanic/Latino), 2 international. 872 applicants, 9% accepted, 75 enrolled. *Faculty:* 18 full-time (8 women). Expenses: Contact institution. *Financial support:* In 2016–17, 11 students received support. Application deadline: 5/1; applicants required to submit FAFSA. In 2016, 64 doctorates awarded. Offers physical therapy (DPT). *Application deadline:* For fall admission, 11/1 priority date for domestic and international students. Applications are processed on a rolling basis. *Application fee:* $50. Electronic applications accepted. *Application Contact:* Mya Shackleford, Admissions Coordinator, 919-668-5206, Fax: 919-684-1846, E-mail: mya.shackleford@duke.edu. *Program Director,* Dr. Chad Cook, 919-684-8905, Fax: 919-684-1846, E-mail: chad.cook@duke.edu.

School of Nursing Students: 161 full-time (138 women), 598 part-time (532 women); includes 161 minority (58 Black or African American, non-Hispanic/Latino; 4 American Indian or Alaska Native, non-Hispanic/Latino; 43 Asian, non-Hispanic/Latino; 30 Hispanic/Latino; 26 Two or more races, non-Hispanic/Latino), 9 international. Average age 34. 648 applicants, 48% accepted, 231 enrolled. *Faculty:* 73 full-time (62 women). Expenses: Contact institution. *Financial support:* Institutionally sponsored loans, scholarships/grants, and traineeships available. Support available to part-time students. Financial award applicants required to submit FAFSA. In 2016, 216 master's, 56 doctorates, 19 other advanced degrees awarded. *Program availability:* Part-time, evening/weekend, online learning. Offers acute care pediatric nurse practitioner (MSN, Post-Graduate Certificate); adult-gerontology nurse practitioner (MSN, Post-Graduate Certificate); family nurse practitioner (MSN, Post-Graduate Certificate); neonatal nurse practitioner (MSN); nurse anesthesia (DNP); nurse practitioner (DNP); nursing (MSN, DNP, PhD, Post-Graduate Certificate); nursing and health care leadership (MSN); nursing education (MSN); nursing informatics (MSN); pediatric nurse practitioner (MSN); women's health nurse practitioner (MSN). *Application deadline:* For fall admission, 12/1 for domestic and international students; for spring admission, 5/1 for domestic and international students. *Application fee:* $50. Electronic applications accepted. *Application Contact:* Dr. Ernie Rushing, Director of Admissions and Recruitment, 919-668-6274, Fax: 919-668-4693, E-mail: ernie.rushing@dm.duke.edu. *Dean/Vice Chancellor for Nursing Affairs/Associate Vice President for Academic Affairs for Nursing,* Dr. Marion E. Broome, 919-684-9446, Fax: 919-684-9414, E-mail: marion.broome@duke.edu.

DUNLAP-STONE UNIVERSITY, Phoenix, AZ 85024

General Information Proprietary, coed, comprehensive institution.

GRADUATE UNITS

Graduate Law Center Offers regulatory trade compliance (M Sc); U.S. regulatory trade law (LL M).

DUQUESNE UNIVERSITY, Pittsburgh, PA 15282-0001

General Information Independent-religious, coed, university. CGS member. *Enrollment:* 9,340 graduate, professional, and undergraduate students; 2,768 full-time matriculated graduate/professional students (1,743 women), 516 part-time matriculated graduate/professional students (299 women). *Enrollment by degree level:* 1,341 master's, 1,882 doctoral, 61 other advanced degrees. *Graduate faculty:* 448 full-time (203 women), 325 part-time/adjunct (152 women). *Tuition:* Full-time $22,212; part-time $1234 per credit. Tuition and fees vary according to program. *Graduate housing:* Rooms and/or apartments available on a first-come, first-served basis to single and married students. Typical cost: $6658 per year ($12,114 including board) for single students. Room and board charges vary according to board plan and housing facility selected. Housing application deadline: 5/1. *Student services:* Campus employment opportunities, campus safety program, career counseling, child daycare facilities, exercise/wellness program, free psychological counseling, international student services, low-cost health insurance, multicultural affairs office, services for students with disabilities, teacher training, writing training. *Library facilities:* Gumberg Library plus 1 other. *Collection:* Books: 647,175 (physical), 306,412 (digital/electronic); Serial titles: 203 (physical), 117,733 (digital/electronic); Databases: 205. Weekly public service hours: 111; students can reserve study rooms.

Computer facilities: Computer purchase and lease plans are available. 1,000 computers available on campus for general student use. A campuswide network can be accessed from student residence rooms and from off campus. Online class registration is available.

Website: http://www.duq.edu/

General Application Contact: Todd Eicker, Director of Graduate Admission, 412-396-6219, E-mail: eickert@duq.edu.

GRADUATE UNITS

Bayer School of Natural and Environmental Sciences Students: 118 full-time (67 women), 28 part-time (16 women); includes 13 minority (1 Black or African American, non-Hispanic/Latino; 5 Asian, non-Hispanic/Latino; 3 Hispanic/Latino; 4 Two or more races, non-Hispanic/Latino), 22 international. Average age 26. 104 applicants, 69% accepted, 35 enrolled. *Faculty:* 39 full-time (12 women), 29 part-time/adjunct (11 women). Expenses: Contact institution. *Financial support:* In 2016–17, 119 students received support, including 3 fellowships with full tuition reimbursements available, 18 research assistantships with full tuition reimbursements available, 54 teaching assistantships with full tuition reimbursements available; career-related internships or fieldwork, scholarships/grants, tuition waivers (partial), and unspecified assistantships also available. Financial award application deadline: 5/31. In 2016, 35 master's, 10 doctorates awarded. *Program availability:* Part-time. Offers biological sciences (PhD); biotechnology (MS); chemistry (PhD); environmental science and management (MS, Certificate); forensic science and law (MS); natural and environmental sciences (MS, PhD, Certificate). *Application deadline:* For fall admission, 2/15 priority date for domestic students, 2/15 for international students; for spring admission, 10/1 priority date for domestic students, 10/1 for international students. Applications are processed on a rolling basis. *Application fee:* $0. Electronic applications accepted. *Application Contact:* Heather Costello, Senior Graduate Academic Advisor, 412-396-6339, Fax: 412-396-4881, E-mail: costelloh@duq.edu. *Dean,* Dr. Philip Reeder, 412-396-4877, Fax: 412-396-4881, E-mail: reederp@duq.edu.

Graduate School of Liberal Arts Students: 464 full-time (240 women), 109 part-time (58 women); includes 82 minority (48 Black or African American, non-Hispanic/Latino; 8 Asian, non-Hispanic/Latino; 15 Hispanic/Latino; 11 Two or more races, non-Hispanic/Latino), 97 international. Average age 33. 432 applicants, 63% accepted, 132 enrolled. *Faculty:* 134 full-time (49 women), 37 part-time/adjunct (18 women). Expenses: Contact institution. *Financial support:* In 2016–17, research assistantships with full tuition reimbursements (averaging $11,000 per year), teaching assistantships with full tuition reimbursements (averaging $17,500 per year) were awarded; career-related internships or fieldwork, Federal Work-Study, institutionally sponsored loans, scholarships/grants, and tuition waivers (full and partial) also available. Support available to part-time students. Financial award application deadline: 5/1. In 2016, 240 master's, 40 doctorates, 2 other advanced degrees awarded. *Program availability:* Part-time, evening/weekend, 100% online, blended/hybrid learning. Offers clinical psychology (PhD); communication (MA); computational mathematics (MS); English (MA, PhD); historical studies (MA); leadership (MS); liberal arts (MA, MS, DHCE, PhD, Certificate); media (MS, Certificate); pastoral ministry (MA); philosophy (MA, PhD); public history (MA); religious education (MA); rhetoric (PhD); systematic theology (PhD); theology (MA). *Application deadline:* For fall admission, 8/1 for domestic students, 5/1 for international students; for spring admission, 11/1 for domestic students, 9/1 for international students. Applications are processed on a rolling basis. *Application fee:* $0. Electronic applications accepted. *Application Contact:* Linda Rendulic, Assistant to the Dean, 412-396-6400, Fax: 412-396-5265, E-mail: rendulic@duq.edu. *Dean,* Dr. James Swindal, 412-396-6400.

Center for Healthcare Ethics Students: 52 full-time (27 women); includes 9 minority (5 Black or African American, non-Hispanic/Latino; 4 Asian, non-Hispanic/Latino), 21 international. Average age 38. 26 applicants, 100% accepted, 18 enrolled. *Faculty:* 3 full-time (0 women). Expenses: Contact institution. *Financial support:* In 2016–17, 7 students received support, including 5 teaching assistantships with full and partial tuition reimbursements available (averaging $18,000 per year); Federal Work-Study and tuition waivers (full and partial) also available. Support available to part-time students. Financial award application deadline: 5/1. In 2016, 3 master's, 8 doctorates awarded. *Program availability:* Part-time, 100% online. Offers healthcare ethics (MA, DHCE, PhD, Certificate). *Application deadline:* For fall admission, 8/1 for domestic students, 5/1 for international students. *Application fee:* $0. Electronic applications accepted. *Application Contact:* Linda Rendulic, Assistant to the Dean, 412-396-6400, Fax: 412-396-5265, E-mail: rendulic@duq.edu. *Director,* Dr. Henk Ten Have, 412-396-1585, E-mail: tenhaveh@duq.edu.

John G. Rangos, Sr. School of Health Sciences Students: 232 full-time (180 women), 11 part-time (7 women); includes 18 minority (2 Black or African American, non-Hispanic/Latino; 6 Asian, non-Hispanic/Latino; 6 Hispanic/Latino; 4 Two or more races, non-Hispanic/Latino), 25 international. Average age 23. 427 applicants, 12% accepted, 34 enrolled. *Faculty:* 45 full-time (32 women), 33 part-time/adjunct (17 women). Expenses: Contact institution. *Financial support:* Federal Work-Study available. Financial award applicants required to submit FAFSA. In 2016, 98 master's, 35 doctorates awarded. *Program availability:* Minimal on-campus study. Offers health management systems (MHMS); occupational therapy (MS, OTD); physical therapy (DPT); physician assistant studies (MPAS); rehabilitation science (MS, PhD); speech-language pathology (MS). *Application deadline:* For fall admission, 2/1 for domestic and international students; for spring admission, 7/1 for domestic and international students. Applications are processed on a rolling basis. *Application fee:* $0. Electronic applications accepted. *Application Contact:* Christopher R. Hilf, Director of Enrollment

Management, 412-396-5653, Fax: 412-396-5554, E-mail: hilfc@duq.edu. *Interim Dean*, Dr. Paula Sammarone-Turocy, 412-396-5303, Fax: 412-396-5554, E-mail: turocyp@duq.edu.

Mary Pappert School of Music Students: 69 full-time (27 women), 16 part-time (6 women); includes 7 minority (3 Black or African American, non-Hispanic/Latino; 1 Asian, non-Hispanic/Latino; 1 Hispanic/Latino; 2 Two or more races, non-Hispanic/Latino), 24 international. Average age 26. 94 applicants, 93% accepted, 29 enrolled. *Faculty:* 26 full-time (9 women), 77 part-time/adjunct (22 women). Expenses: Contact institution. *Financial support:* In 2016–17, 76 students received support. Scholarships/grants and unspecified assistantships available. Financial award application deadline: 4/1. In 2016, 19 master's, 9 ADs awarded. *Program availability:* Part-time. Offers music education (MM). *Application deadline:* For fall admission, 7/1 for domestic and international students; for spring admission, 12/1 for domestic and international students; for summer admission, 6/1 for domestic students, 5/1 for international students. Applications are processed on a rolling basis. *Application fee:* $50. Electronic applications accepted. *Application Contact:* Katherine Shields, Director of Music Admissions, 412-396-5983, Fax: 412-396-5719, E-mail: shieldsk1@duq.edu. *Dean/Professor,* Dr. Seth Beckman, 412-396-6082, Fax: 412-396-1524, E-mail: beckmans@duq.edu.

Mylan School of Pharmacy Students: 751 full-time (472 women), 43 part-time (26 women); includes 74 minority (18 Black or African American, non-Hispanic/Latino; 30 Asian, non-Hispanic/Latino; 16 Hispanic/Latino; 10 Two or more races, non-Hispanic/Latino), 59 international. Average age 23. 423 applicants, 52% accepted, 197 enrolled. *Faculty:* 49 full-time (21 women), 3 part-time/adjunct (0 women). Expenses: Contact institution. *Financial support:* In 2016–17, 927 students received support, including 14 research assistantships with full tuition reimbursements available, 43 teaching assistantships with full tuition reimbursements available; Federal Work-Study also available. In 2016, 1 master's, 202 doctorates awarded. *Program availability:* Evening/weekend. Offers pharmacy (MS, PhD, Pharm D). *Application deadline:* For fall admission, 2/1 for domestic and international students; for spring admission, 12/1 for domestic and international students. Applications are processed on a rolling basis. *Application fee:* $50. Electronic applications accepted. *Dean,* Dr. J. Douglas Bricker, 412-396-6377, Fax: 412-396-5130.

Graduate School of Pharmaceutical Sciences Students: 68 full-time (32 women), 1 part-time (0 women); includes 3 minority (2 Asian, non-Hispanic/Latino; 1 Hispanic/Latino), 51 international. Average age 27. 91 applicants, 27% accepted, 17 enrolled. *Faculty:* 22 full-time (7 women). Expenses: Contact institution. *Financial support:* In 2016–17, 57 students received support, including 13 research assistantships with full tuition reimbursements available, 44 teaching assistantships with full tuition reimbursements available; unspecified assistantships also available. In 2016, 1 master's, 6 doctorates awarded. Offers medicinal chemistry (MS, PhD); pharmaceutics (MS, PhD); pharmacology (MS, PhD); pharmacy administration (MS). *Application deadline:* For fall admission, 12/1 priority date for domestic and international students; for spring admission, 10/1 priority date for domestic and international students. Applications are processed on a rolling basis. Electronic applications accepted. *Application Contact:* Information Contact, 412-396-1172, E-mail: gsps-adm@duq.edu. *Associate Dean for Research and Graduate Programs,* Dr. James K. Drennen, III, 412-396-5520.

School of Pharmacy Students: 683 full-time (440 women), 42 part-time (26 women); includes 71 minority (18 Black or African American, non-Hispanic/Latino; 28 Asian, non-Hispanic/Latino; 15 Hispanic/Latino; 10 Two or more races, non-Hispanic/Latino), 8 international. Average age 22. 332 applicants, 59% accepted, 180 enrolled. *Faculty:* 49 full-time (21 women), 3 part-time/adjunct (0 women). Expenses: Contact institution. *Financial support:* In 2016–17, 622 students received support. Federal Work-Study and scholarships/grants available. Financial award application deadline: 5/1; financial award applicants required to submit FAFSA. In 2016, 196 doctorates awarded. *Program availability:* Evening/weekend. Offers pharmacy (Pharm D). *Application deadline:* For fall admission, 12/1 priority date for domestic and international students. Applications are processed on a rolling basis. *Application fee:* $100. Electronic applications accepted. *Assistant Dean for Student Services,* Dr. Janet K. Astle, 412-396-6393, E-mail: astle@duq.edu.

Palumbo-Donahue School of Business Students: 92 full-time (43 women), 176 part-time (71 women); includes 20 minority (9 Black or African American, non-Hispanic/Latino; 8 Asian, non-Hispanic/Latino; 2 Hispanic/Latino; 1 Two or more races, non-Hispanic/Latino), 35 international. Average age 28. 272 applicants, 86% accepted, 137 enrolled. *Faculty:* 59 full-time (23 women), 25 part-time/adjunct (6 women). Expenses: Contact institution. *Financial support:* In 2016–17, 211 students received support, including 12 fellowships with partial tuition reimbursements available (averaging $14,200 per year), 20 research assistantships with partial tuition reimbursements available (averaging $22,212 per year); career-related internships or fieldwork, scholarships/grants, and unspecified assistantships also available. Support available to part-time students. Financial award application deadline: 7/1; financial award applicants required to submit FAFSA. In 2016, 137 master's awarded. *Program availability:* Part-time, evening/weekend, 100% online, minimal on-campus study. Offers accounting (M Acc); finance (MBA); information systems management (MSISM); management (MBA, MS); marketing (MBA); sports business (MS); sustainability (MBA). *Application deadline:* For fall admission, 7/1 priority date for domestic and international students; for spring admission, 12/1 for domestic and international students; for summer admission, 4/1 for domestic and international students. Applications are processed on a rolling basis. *Application fee:* $0. Electronic applications accepted. *Application Contact:* Jeff Jewett, Director of Admissions and Enrollment Management, 412-396-6244, Fax: 412-396-1726, E-mail: decrostam@duq.edu. *Associate Dean of Graduate Programs and Executive Education,* Dr. Karen Donovan, 412-396-6276, Fax: 412-396-1726, E-mail: donovan6@duq.edu.

Post-Baccalaureate Pre-Medical and Health Professions Program Students: 9 full-time (6 women), 1 part-time (0 women); includes 1 minority (Black or African American, non-Hispanic/Latino). Average age 23. 48 applicants, 27% accepted, 7 enrolled. *Faculty:* 1 (woman) full-time. Expenses: Contact institution. *Financial support:* Applicants required to submit FAFSA. In 2016, 4 Postbaccalaureate Certificates awarded. Offers pre-medical studies and health professions (Postbaccalaureate Certificate). *Application deadline:* For fall admission, 6/1 for domestic students. Applications are processed on a rolling basis. *Application fee:* $0. Electronic applications accepted. *Application Contact:* Todd Eicker, Director of Graduate Admission, 412-396-6219, E-mail: eickert@duq.edu. *Director,* Dr. Paula Sammarone-Turocy, 412-396-6335, Fax: 412-396-5587, E-mail: turocyp@duq.edu.

School of Education Students: 482 full-time (355 women), 46 part-time (35 women); includes 79 minority (47 Black or African American, non-Hispanic/Latino; 8 Asian, non-Hispanic/Latino; 15 Two or more races, non-Hispanic/Latino), 51 international. Average age 31. 453 applicants, 79% accepted, 174 enrolled. *Faculty:* 52 full-time (31 women), 83 part-time/adjunct (63 women). Expenses: Contact institution. *Financial support:* Research assistantships, teaching assistantships with tuition reimbursements, career-related internships or fieldwork, Federal Work-Study, institutionally sponsored loans, and tuition waivers available. Support available to part-time students. In 2016, 175 master's, 40 doctorates, 2 other advanced degrees awarded. *Program availability:* Part-time, evening/weekend, 100% online, blended/hybrid learning. Offers biology (MS Ed); chemistry (MS Ed); child psychology (MS Ed); clinical mental health counseling (MS Ed, Post-Master's Certificate); cognitive, behavior, physical/health disabilities (MS Ed); community and special education support (MS Ed); counselor education (MS Ed, Ed D, Post-Master's Certificate); counselor education and supervision (Ed D); counselor licensure (Post-Master's Certificate); curriculum and instruction (Post-Master's Certificate); early level (PreK-4) education (MS Ed); education (MS Ed, Ed D, PhD, Psy D, CAGS, Post-Master's Certificate); educational leadership (Ed D); educational studies (MS Ed); English (MS Ed); English as a second language (MS Ed); instructional technology (MS Ed, Ed D, Post-Master's Certificate); K-12 education (MS Ed); marriage and family counseling (MS Ed); mathematics (MS Ed); middle level (4-8) education (MS Ed); physics (MS Ed); program evaluation (MS Ed); reading and language arts (MS Ed); school administration and supervision (MS Ed, Post-Master's Certificate); school administration K-12 (MS Ed, Post-Master's Certificate); school counseling (MS Ed); school psychology (MS Ed, PhD, Psy D); school supervision (MS Ed); secondary education (MS Ed); social studies (MS Ed); special education (MS Ed, PhD); special education 7-12 (MS Ed); special education PreK-8 (MS Ed). *Application deadline:* For fall admission, 3/1 for domestic students; for spring admission, 9/1 for domestic students. Applications are processed on a rolling basis. *Application fee:* $0. Electronic applications accepted. *Application Contact:* Michael Dolinger, Director of Student and Academic Services, 412-396-6647, Fax: 412-396-5585, E-mail: dolingerm@duq.edu. *Dean,* Dr. Cindy Walker, 412-396-6102, Fax: 412-396-5585.

School of Law Students: 392 full-time (211 women); includes 30 minority (6 Black or African American, non-Hispanic/Latino; 1 American Indian or Alaska Native, non-Hispanic/Latino; 5 Asian, non-Hispanic/Latino; 8 Hispanic/Latino; 10 Two or more races, non-Hispanic/Latino), 5 international. Average age 26. 825 applicants, 61% accepted, 127 enrolled. *Faculty:* 28 full-time (13 women), 32 part-time/adjunct (9 women). Expenses: Contact institution. *Financial support:* Research assistantships with partial tuition reimbursements, teaching assistantships with partial tuition reimbursements, career-related internships or fieldwork, scholarships/grants, and tuition waivers (partial) available. Support available to part-time students. Financial award application deadline: 5/31; financial award applicants required to submit FAFSA. In 2016, 1 master's, 124 doctorates awarded. *Program availability:* Part-time, evening/weekend. Offers American law for foreign lawyers (LL M); law (JD). JD/M Div offered jointly with Pittsburgh Theological Seminary. *Application deadline:* For fall admission, 3/1 priority date for domestic and international students. Applications are processed on a rolling basis. *Application fee:* $0. Electronic applications accepted. *Application Contact:* Office of Admissions, 412-396-6296, Fax: 412-396-6659, E-mail: lawadmissions@duq.edu. *Interim Dean,* Nancy Perkins, 412-396-6285, Fax: 412-396-6283, E-mail: perkins@duq.edu.

School of Nursing Students: 159 full-time (142 women), 86 part-time (80 women); includes 42 minority (14 Black or African American, non-Hispanic/Latino; 3 American Indian or Alaska Native, non-Hispanic/Latino; 6 Asian, non-Hispanic/Latino; 14 Hispanic/Latino; 5 Two or more races, non-Hispanic/Latino), 3 international. Average age 39. 168 applicants, 77% accepted, 73 enrolled. *Faculty:* 15 full-time (12 women), 6 part-time/adjunct (all women). Expenses: Contact institution. *Financial support:* In 2016–17, 60 students received support, including 5 research assistantships with partial tuition reimbursements available (averaging $2,200 per year), 8 teaching assistantships with partial tuition reimbursements available (averaging $1,100 per year); institutionally sponsored loans, scholarships/grants, traineeships, tuition waivers (partial), and unspecified assistantships also available. Support available to part-time students. Financial award application deadline: 7/1; financial award applicants required to submit FAFSA. In 2016, 38 master's, 8 doctorates, 6 other advanced degrees awarded. *Program availability:* Part-time, evening/weekend, online only, minimal on-campus study. Offers family (individual across the life span) nurse practitioner (MSN, Post-Master's Certificate); forensic nursing (MSN, Post-Master's Certificate); nursing (MSN, DNP, PhD, Post-Master's Certificate); nursing education (MSN); nursing education and faculty role (Post-Master's Certificate); nursing practice (DNP). *Application deadline:* For fall admission, 7/10 for domestic and international students; for spring admission, 11/29 for domestic and international students; for summer admission, 4/2 for domestic and international students. Applications are processed on a rolling basis. *Application fee:* $0. Electronic applications accepted. *Application Contact:* Devon George, Nurse Recruiter, 412-396-1009, Fax: 412-396-6346, E-mail: nursing@duq.edu. *Dean/Professor,* Dr. Mary Ellen Glasgow, 412-396-6554, Fax: 412-396-5974, E-mail: glasgowm@duq.edu.

D'YOUVILLE COLLEGE, Buffalo, NY 14201-1084

General Information Independent, coed, comprehensive institution. *Graduate housing:* Room and/or apartments available on a first-come, first-served basis to single students. Housing application deadline: 8/1.

GRADUATE UNITS

Department of Business *Program availability:* Part-time, evening/weekend. Offers business administration (MBA); international business (MS). Electronic applications accepted.

Department of Chiropractic Offers chiropractic (DC). Electronic applications accepted.

Department of Dietetics Offers dietetics (MS). Five-year program begins at freshman entry. Electronic applications accepted.

Department of Education *Program availability:* Part-time, evening/weekend. Offers educational leadership (Ed D); elementary education (MS Ed); secondary education (MS Ed); special education (MS Ed). Electronic applications accepted.

Department of Health Services Administration *Program availability:* Part-time, evening/weekend. Offers clinical research associate (Certificate); health administration (Ed D); health services administration (MS, Certificate); long term care administration (Certificate). Electronic applications accepted.

Department of Physical Therapy *Program availability:* Part-time, online learning. Offers advanced orthopedic physical therapy (Certificate); manual physical therapy (Certificate); physical therapy (DPT). Electronic applications accepted.

Occupational Therapy Department Offers occupational therapy (MS). Electronic applications accepted.

Physician Assistant Department Offers physician assistant (MS). Electronic applications accepted.

School of Nursing *Program availability:* Part-time. Offers advanced practice nursing (DNP); family nurse practitioner (MSN, Certificate); nursing and health-related professions education (Certificate). Electronic applications accepted.

School of Pharmacy Offers pharmacy (Pharm D). Electronic applications accepted.

EARLHAM COLLEGE, Richmond, IN 47374-4095

General Information Independent-religious, coed, comprehensive institution. *Graduate housing:* On-campus housing not available.

GRADUATE UNITS

Graduate Programs Offers education (M Ed, MAT).

EARLHAM SCHOOL OF RELIGION, Richmond, IN 47374-5360

General Information Independent-religious, coed, graduate-only institution. *Enrollment by degree level:* 52 master's, 4 other advanced degrees. *Graduate faculty:* 8 full-time (2 women), 2 part-time/adjunct (1 woman). *Tuition:* Full-time $14,823; part-time $1647 per course. *Required fees:* $200 per semester. *Graduate housing:* On-campus housing not available. *Student services:* Campus employment opportunities, campus safety program, career counseling, exercise/wellness program, international student services, teacher training, writing training. *Library facilities:* Lilly Library plus 2 others. *Collection:* Books: 351,561 (physical); Serial titles: 292 (physical). Weekly public service hours: 112; students can reserve study rooms.

Computer facilities: 125 computers available on campus for general student use. Online class registration is available.
Website: http://www.esr.earlham.edu/

General Application Contact: Matthew Hisrich, Director of Recruitment and Admissions, 765-983-1523, Fax: 765-983-1688, E-mail: hisrima@earlham.edu.

GRADUATE UNITS

Graduate Programs Students: 38 full-time (17 women), 18 part-time (14 women). *Faculty:* 8 full-time (2 women), 2 part-time/adjunct (1 woman). *Expenses:* Contact institution. *Financial support:* Scholarships/grants and tuition waivers (full and partial) available. Financial award application deadline: 4/15; financial award applicants required to submit FAFSA. *Program availability:* Part-time, online learning. Offers religion (MA); theology (M Div, M Min). *Application deadline:* For fall admission, 7/15 priority date for domestic students; for winter admission, 12/15 priority date for domestic students. Applications are processed on a rolling basis. *Application fee:* $35. Electronic applications accepted. *Application Contact:* Matthew Hisrich, Director of Recruitment and Admissions, 765-983-1523, Fax: 765-983-1688, E-mail: hisrima@earlham.edu. *Dean,* Jay W. Marshall, 800-432-1377, Fax: 765-983-1688, E-mail: marshja@earlham.edu.

EAST CAROLINA UNIVERSITY, Greenville, NC 27858-4353

General Information State-supported, coed, university. CGS member. *Enrollment:* 28,962 graduate, professional, and undergraduate students; 2,203 full-time matriculated graduate/professional students (1,442 women), 3,330 part-time matriculated graduate/professional students (2,225 women). *Enrollment by degree level:* 4,076 master's, 1,401 doctoral, 56 other advanced degrees. *Graduate faculty:* 975 full-time (427 women), 64 part-time/adjunct (39 women). *Graduate housing:* Room and/or apartments available on a first-come, first-served basis to single students; on-campus housing not available to married students. Housing application deadline: 5/1. *Student services:* Campus employment opportunities, campus safety program, career counseling, exercise/wellness program, free psychological counseling, grant writing training, international student services, low-cost health insurance, multicultural affairs office, services for students with disabilities, teacher training, writing training. *Library facilities:* Joyner Library plus 1 other. *Collection:* Books: 1.3 million (physical), 1.6 million (digital/electronic); Serial titles: 8,391 (physical), 89,781 (digital/electronic); Databases: 428. Weekly public service hours: 142; study areas open 24 hours, 5–7 days a week; students can reserve study rooms.

Computer facilities: Computer purchase and lease plans are available. 2,375 computers available on campus for general student use. A campuswide network can be accessed from student residence rooms and from off campus. Online class registration is available.
Website: http://www.ecu.edu/

General Application Contact: Dr. Heidi Puckett, Director of Admissions, 252-328-5400, Fax: 252-328-6071, E-mail: gradschool@ecu.edu.

GRADUATE UNITS

Brody School of Medicine Students: 180 full-time (112 women), 22 part-time (15 women); includes 62 minority (23 Black or African American, non-Hispanic/Latino; 3 American Indian or Alaska Native, non-Hispanic/Latino; 19 Asian, non-Hispanic/Latino; 10 Hispanic/Latino; 7 Two or more races, non-Hispanic/Latino), 14 international. Average age 27. 166 applicants, 62% accepted, 67 enrolled. Expenses: Contact institution. *Financial support:* Fellowships with partial tuition reimbursements and institutionally sponsored loans available. Financial award application deadline: 6/1. In 2016, 40 master's, 92 doctorates awarded. Offers anatomy and cell biology (PhD); biochemistry and molecular biology (PhD); biomedical science (MS); medicine (MPH, MS, MD, PhD); microbiology and immunology (MS, MD, PhD); pharmacology and toxicology (PhD); physiology (PhD); public health (MPH). *Application fee:* $50. *Application Contact:* Contact Center, 252-744-1020.

Graduate School Students: 1,738 full-time (1,208 women), 2,628 part-time (1,861 women); includes 900 minority (580 Black or African American, non-Hispanic/Latino; 31 American Indian or Alaska Native, non-Hispanic/Latino; 88 Asian, non-Hispanic/Latino; 144 Hispanic/Latino; 1 Native Hawaiian or other Pacific Islander, non-Hispanic/Latino; 56 Two or more races, non-Hispanic/Latino), 95 international. Average age 32. 3,250 applicants, 65% accepted, 1601 enrolled. Expenses: Contact institution. *Financial support:* Fellowships with partial tuition reimbursements, research assistantships with partial tuition reimbursements, teaching assistantships with partial tuition reimbursements, career-related internships or fieldwork, Federal Work-Study, scholarships/grants, traineeships, and unspecified assistantships available. Support available to part-time students. Financial award application deadline: 6/1; financial award applicants required to submit FAFSA. *Program availability:* Part-time, evening/weekend, online learning. *Application deadline:* Applications are processed on a rolling basis. *Application fee:* $60. *Dean,* Dr. Paul Gemperline, 252-328-6073, E-mail: gemperlinep@ecu.edu.

College of Allied Health Sciences Students: 499 full-time (418 women), 207 part-time (172 women); includes 126 minority (86 Black or African American, non-Hispanic/Latino; 1 American Indian or Alaska Native, non-Hispanic/Latino; 16 Asian, non-Hispanic/Latino; 17 Hispanic/Latino; 6 Two or more races, non-Hispanic/Latino), 4 international. Average age 29. 917 applicants, 38% accepted, 266 enrolled. Expenses: Contact institution. *Financial support:* Research assistantships with partial tuition reimbursements, teaching assistantships with partial tuition reimbursements, career-related internships or fieldwork, Federal Work-Study, and scholarships/grants available. Support available to part-time students. Financial award application deadline: 6/1; financial award applicants required to submit FAFSA. In 2016, 130 master's, 32 doctorates awarded. *Program availability:* Part-time, evening/weekend, online learning. Offers allied health sciences (MS, MSOT, DPT, PhD, Certificate); communication sciences and disorders (MS, PhD); health informatics and information management (MS); military and trauma counseling (Certificate); nutrition science (MS); occupational therapy (MSOT); physical therapy (DPT); physician assistant studies (MS); rehabilitation and career counseling (MS); rehabilitation counseling (Certificate); rehabilitation counseling and administration (PhD); substance abuse and clinical counseling (MS); substance abuse counseling (Certificate); vocational evaluation (Certificate). *Application fee:* $70. *Application Contact:* Dean of Graduate School, 252-328-6012, Fax: 252-328-6071, E-mail: gradschool@ecu.edu. *Interim Dean,* Dr. Greg Hassler, 252-744-6010, E-mail: hasslerg@ecu.edu.

College of Business Students: 300 full-time (120 women), 719 part-time (354 women); includes 228 minority (139 Black or African American, non-Hispanic/Latino; 8 American Indian or Alaska Native, non-Hispanic/Latino; 29 Asian, non-Hispanic/Latino; 40 Hispanic/Latino; 12 Two or more races, non-Hispanic/Latino), 17 international. Average age 32. 527 applicants, 88% accepted, 341 enrolled. Expenses: Contact institution. *Financial support:* Research assistantships with partial tuition reimbursements, teaching assistantships with partial tuition reimbursements, and Federal Work-Study available. Support available to part-time students. Financial award application deadline: 6/1. In 2016 341 master's awarded. *Program availability:* Part-time, evening/weekend. Offers accounting (MSA); business (MBA, MSA); hospitality management (MBA); management (MBA). *Application deadline:* For fall admission, 6/1 priority date for domestic students. Applications are processed on a rolling basis. *Application fee:* $75. Electronic applications accepted. *Interim Director of Graduate Programs,* Paul Russell, 252-328-6970, E-mail: gradbus@ecu.edu.

College of Education Students: 155 full-time (126 women), 1,088 part-time (880 women); includes 259 minority (178 Black or African American, non-Hispanic/Latino; 18 American Indian or Alaska Native, non-Hispanic/Latino; 10 Asian, non-Hispanic/Latino; 39 Hispanic/Latino; 14 Two or more races, non-Hispanic/Latino), 8 international. Average age 37. 656 applicants, 95% accepted, 512 enrolled. Expenses: Contact institution. *Financial support:* Research assistantships with partial tuition reimbursements, teaching assistantships with partial tuition reimbursements, and Federal Work-Study available. Support available to part-time students. Financial award application deadline: 6/1. In 2016, 206 master's, 13 doctorates, 4 other advanced degrees awarded. *Program availability:* Part-time, evening/weekend, online learning. Offers adult education (MA Ed); assistive technology (Certificate); autism (Certificate); behavior specialist (Certificate); business and marketing education (MA); career and technical education (MA Ed); counselor education (MS); deaf-blindness (Certificate); education (MA, MA Ed, MAT, MLS, MS, MSA, Ed D, Certificate, Ed S); educational administration and supervision (Ed S); educational leadership (Ed D); elementary education (MA Ed, MAT); elementary mathematics (Certificate); English education (MAT); family and consumer science (MAT); health education (MAT); Hispanic studies (MAT); history education (MA Ed, MAT); instructional technology (MA Ed, MS); library science (MLS); mathematics education (MA Ed); middle grades education (MA Ed, MAT); music education (MAT); reading education (MA Ed); school administration (MSA); science education (MA Ed, MAT); special education (MA Ed, MAT); vocational education (MAT, MS). *Application deadline:* For fall admission, 6/1 priority date for domestic students. Applications are processed on a rolling basis. *Application fee:* $50. *Application Contact:* Dean of Graduate School, 252-328-6012, Fax: 252-328-6071, E-mail: gradschool@ecu.edu. *Dean,* Dr. Linda Ann Patriarca, 252-328-1000, Fax: 252-328-4219, E-mail: patriarcal@ecu.edu.

College of Engineering and Technology Students: 74 full-time (15 women), 280 part-time (73 women); includes 89 minority (52 Black or African American, non-Hispanic/Latino; 3 American Indian or Alaska Native, non-Hispanic/Latino; 13 Asian, non-Hispanic/Latino; 16 Hispanic/Latino; 5 Two or more races, non-Hispanic/Latino), 31 international. Average age 35. 186 applicants, 86% accepted, 109 enrolled. Expenses: Contact institution. *Financial support:* Fellowships, research assistantships, teaching assistantships, and Federal Work-Study available. Support available to part-time students. Financial award application deadline: 6/1. In 2016, 50 master's awarded. *Program availability:* Part-time. Offers biomedical engineering (MS); computer network professional (Certificate); computer science (MS); construction management (MCM); engineering and technology (MCM, MS, PhD, Certificate); information assurance (Certificate); Lean Six Sigma Black Belt (Certificate); network technology (MS); occupational safety (MS); software engineering (MS); technology management (PhD); technology systems (MS); Website developer (Certificate). *Application deadline:* For fall admission, 6/1 priority date for domestic students. Applications are processed on a rolling basis. *Application fee:* $50. *Application Contact:* Dean of Graduate School, 252-328-6012, Fax: 252-328-6071, E-mail: gradschool@ecu.edu. *Dean,* Dr. David White, 252-328-9604.

College of Fine Arts and Communication Students: 67 full-time (40 women), 69 part-time (47 women); includes 23 minority (12 Black or African American, non-Hispanic/Latino; 4 Asian, non-Hispanic/Latino; 3 Hispanic/Latino; 4 Two or more races, non-Hispanic/Latino), 1 international. Average age 30. 102 applicants, 85% accepted, 63 enrolled. Expenses: Contact institution. In 2016, 41 master's awarded. Offers advanced performance studies (Certificate); art education (MA Ed); ceramics (MFA); fine arts and communication (MA, MA Ed, MFA, MM, Certificate); graphic design (MFA); health communication (MA); illustration (MFA); metal design (MFA); music education (MM); music therapy (MM); painting and drawing (MFA); performance (MM); photography (MFA); printmaking (MFA); sculpture (MFA); Suzuki pedagogy (Certificate); textile design (MFA); theory and composition (MM); wood design (MFA). *Application fee:* $50. *Application Contact:* 252-328-6012, Fax: 252-328-6071, E-mail: gradschool@ecu.edu. *Dean,* J. Christopher Buddo, 252-328-1283, E-mail: buddoj@ecu.edu.

College of Health and Human Performance Students: 307 full-time (224 women), 154 part-time (110 women); includes 129 minority (90 Black or African American, non-Hispanic/Latino; 2 American Indian or Alaska Native, non-Hispanic/Latino; 8 Asian, non-Hispanic/Latino; 18 Hispanic/Latino; 1 Native Hawaiian or other Pacific Islander, non-Hispanic/Latino; 10 Two or more races, non-Hispanic/Latino), 10 international. Average age 29. 392 applicants, 63% accepted, 178 enrolled. Expenses: Contact institution. *Financial support:* Research assistantships, teaching assistantships, and Federal Work-Study available. Support available to part-time students. Financial award application deadline: 6/1. In 2016, 154 master's, 6 doctorates awarded. *Program availability:* Part-time, evening/weekend. Offers adapted physical education (MS); aquatic therapy (Certificate); bioenergetics and exercise science (PhD); biofeedback (Certificate); biomechanics (MS); birth through kindergarten education (MA Ed); child development and family relations (MS); environmental health (MS); exercise physiology (MS); gerontology (Certificate); health and human performance (MA, MA Ed, MAT, MS, MSW, PhD, Certificate); health education (MA Ed); health education and promotion (MS); marriage and family therapy (MS); medical family therapy (PhD); physical activity promotion (MS); physical education (MA Ed, MAT); physical education pedagogy (MS); recreation and park administration (MS); social work (MSW); sport and exercise psychology (MS); sport management (MS, Certificate); substance abuse (Certificate). *Application deadline:* For fall admission, 6/1 priority date for domestic students. Applications are processed on a rolling basis. *Application fee:* $50. *Dean,* Dr. Glen Gilbert, 252-328-0038, E-mail: gilbertg@ecu.edu.

College of Nursing Students: 157 full-time (141 women), 395 part-time (368 women); includes 105 minority (70 Black or African American, non-Hispanic/Latino; 6 American Indian or Alaska Native, non-Hispanic/Latino; 10 Asian, non-Hispanic/Latino; 9 Hispanic/Latino; 10 Two or more races, non-Hispanic/Latino). Average age 38. 225 applicants, 91% accepted, 161 enrolled. Expenses: Contact institution. *Financial support:* Research assistantships with partial tuition reimbursements, teaching assistantships with partial tuition reimbursements, and Federal Work-Study available. Support available to part-time students. Financial award application deadline: 6/1. In 2016, 89 master's, 11 doctorates, 12 other advanced degrees awarded. *Program availability:* Part-time. Offers nursing (MSN, DNP, PhD, PMC). *Application deadline:* For fall admission, 6/1 priority date for domestic students. Applications are processed on a rolling basis. *Application fee:* $70. *Application Contact:* Dean of Graduate School, 252-328-6012, Fax: 252-328-6071, E-mail: gradschool@ecu.edu. *Dean,* Dr. Sylvia Brown, 252-744-6372, E-mail: brownsy@ecu.edu.

Thomas Harriot College of Arts and Sciences Students: 447 full-time (236 women), 381 part-time (197 women); includes 160 minority (85 Black or African American, non-Hispanic/Latino; 1 American Indian or Alaska Native, non-Hispanic/Latino; 18 Asian, non-Hispanic/Latino; 39 Hispanic/Latino; 17 Two or more races, non-Hispanic/Latino), 18 international. Average age 30. 706 applicants, 58% accepted, 284 enrolled. Expenses: Contact institution. *Financial support:* Fellowships with partial tuition reimbursements, research assistantships with partial tuition reimbursements, teaching assistantships with partial tuition reimbursements, career-related internships or fieldwork, Federal Work-Study, scholarships/grants, traineeships, and unspecified assistantships available. Support available to part-time students. Financial award application deadline: 6/1. In 2016, 153 master's, 2 doctorates, 1 other advanced degree awarded. *Program availability:* Part-time, evening/weekend. Offers American history (MA); anthropology (MA); applied and resource economics (MS); applied physics (MS); arts and sciences (MA, MA Ed, MPA, MS, PhD, Certificate); Atlantic world (MA); biology (MS); biomedical physics (PhD); chemistry (MS); community health administration (Certificate); creative writing (MA); criminal justice (MA); criminal justice education (Certificate); economic development (Certificate); English studies (MA); European history (MA); geographic information science and technology (Certificate); geography (MA); geology (MS); health physics (MS); health psychology (PhD); history education (MA Ed); hydrogeology and environmental geology (Certificate); industrial and organizational psychology (MA); international studies (MA); linguistics (MA); literature (MA); maritime studies (MA); mathematics (MA); mathematics in the community college (MA); medical physics (MS); military history (MA); molecular biology and biotechnology (MS); multicultural and transnational literatures (MA, Certificate); public administration (MPA); public history (MA); public management and leadership (Certificate); rhetoric and composition (MA); rhetoric, writing, and professional communication (PhD); security studies (Certificate); sociology (MA); statistics (MA, Certificate); teaching English in the two-year college (Certificate); teaching English to speakers of other languages (MA, Certificate); technical and professional communication (MA). *Application deadline:* Applications are processed on a rolling basis. *Application fee:* $50. *Application Contact:* Dean of Graduate School, 252-328-6012, Fax: 252-328-6071, E-mail: gradschool@ecu.edu. *Dean,* Dr. William M. Downs, 252-328-6249, E-mail: downsw14@ecu.edu.

School of Dental Medicine Expenses: Contact institution. Offers dental medicine (DMD). *Application Contact:* Student Admissions, E-mail: sodmadmissions@ecu.edu. *Dean,* Dr. Greg Chadwick, 252-737-7703.

EAST CENTRAL UNIVERSITY, Ada, OK 74820

General Information State-supported, coed, comprehensive institution. *Graduate housing:* Rooms and/or apartments available on a first-come, first-served basis to single and married students.

GRADUATE UNITS

School of Graduate Studies *Program availability:* Part-time, evening/weekend. Offers administration (MSHR); counseling (MSHR); criminal justice (MSHR); education (M Ed); human services (MSHR); psychology (MSPS); rehabilitation counseling (MSHR). Electronic applications accepted.

EASTERN CONNECTICUT STATE UNIVERSITY, Willimantic, CT 06226-2295

General Information State-supported, coed, comprehensive institution. *Enrollment:* 69 full-time matriculated graduate/professional students (45 women), 127 part-time matriculated graduate/professional students (84 women). *Enrollment by degree level:* 196 master's. *Graduate faculty:* 20 full-time (11 women), 24 part-time/adjunct (17 women). *Tuition, area resident:* Full-time $11,781; part-time $560 per credit. Tuition, state resident: full-time $15,031; part-time $568 per credit. Tuition, nonresident: full-time $24,581; part-time $568 per credit. *Required fees:* $40 per semester. Full-time tuition and fees vary according to course level, course load and reciprocity agreements. *Graduate housing:* Room and/or apartments available on a first-come, first-served basis to single students; on-campus housing not available to married students. Typical cost: $4532 per year. Housing application deadline: 4/3. *Student services:* Campus employment opportunities, campus safety program, career counseling, child daycare facilities, exercise/wellness program, free psychological counseling, grant writing training, international student services, multicultural affairs office, services for students with disabilities, teacher training, writing training. *Library facilities:* J. Eugene Smith Library. *Research affiliation:* U.S. Department of Education (DOE) (early childhood education, mathematics and science education).

Computer facilities: Computer purchase and lease plans are available. 2,500 computers available on campus for general student use. A campuswide network can be accessed from student residence rooms and from off campus. Online class registration is available.
Website: http://www.easternct.edu/

General Application Contact: Paula Goyette, Graduate Division, School of Education and Professional Studies, 860-465-5292, Fax: 860-465-4538, E-mail: graduateadmissions@easternct.edu.

GRADUATE UNITS

School of Education and Professional Studies/Graduate Division Students: 69 full-time (45 women), 127 part-time (84 women); includes 38 minority (10 Black or African American, non-Hispanic/Latino; 1 American Indian or Alaska Native, non-Hispanic/Latino; 14 Asian, non-Hispanic/Latino; 11 Hispanic/Latino; 1 Native Hawaiian

or other Pacific Islander, non-Hispanic/Latino; 1 Two or more races, non-Hispanic/Latino), 6 international. Average age 34. 105 applicants, 69% accepted, 55 enrolled. *Faculty:* 20 full-time (11 women), 24 part-time/adjunct (17 women). Expenses: Contact institution. *Financial support:* Research assistantships, teaching assistantships, career-related internships or fieldwork, scholarships/grants, and unspecified assistantships available. Financial award application deadline: 3/1; financial award applicants required to submit FAFSA. In 2016, 64 master's awarded. *Program availability:* Part-time, evening/weekend. Offers accounting (MS); early childhood education (MS); education and professional studies (MS); educational technology (MS); elementary education (MS); organizational management (MS); reading and language arts (MS); secondary education (MS). *Application deadline:* For fall admission, 7/6 priority date for domestic and international students; for spring admission, 11/3 priority date for domestic and international students; for summer admission, 4/5 priority date for domestic and international students. Applications are processed on a rolling basis. *Application fee:* $50. Electronic applications accepted. *Application Contact:* Paula Goyette, Secretary II, 860-465-5292, Fax: 860-465-4538, E-mail: graduateadmissions@easternct.edu. *Dean,* Dr. Jacob Easley, II, 860-465-5293, Fax: 860-465-4538, E-mail: easleyj@easternct.edu.

EASTERN KENTUCKY UNIVERSITY, Richmond, KY 40475-3102

General Information State-supported, coed, comprehensive institution. CGS member. *Graduate housing:* Rooms and/or apartments guaranteed to single students and available to married students.

GRADUATE UNITS

The Graduate School *Program availability:* Part-time, evening/weekend, online learning. Electronic applications accepted.

College of Arts and Sciences *Program availability:* Part-time, evening/weekend. Offers arts and sciences (MA, MFA, MM, MPA, MS, PhD, Psy S); biological sciences (MS); chemistry (MS); choral conducting (MM); clinical psychology (MS); community development (MPA); community health administration (MPA); creative writing (MFA); ecology (MS); English (MA); general public administration (MPA); geology (MS, PhD); history (MA); industrial/organizational psychology (MS); mathematical sciences (MS); performance (MM); political science (MA); school psychology (Psy S); theory/composition (MM).

College of Business and Technology *Program availability:* Part-time. Offers business administration (MBA); business and technology (MBA, MS); industrial education (MS); industrial technology (MS); occupational training and development (MS); technical administration (MS); technology education (MS).

College of Education *Program availability:* Part-time, online learning. Offers communication disorders (MA Ed); education (MA, MA Ed, MAT); elementary education (MA Ed); human services (MA); instructional leadership (MA Ed); library science (MA Ed); mental health counseling (MA); music education (MA Ed); school counseling (MA Ed); secondary and higher education (MA Ed); secondary education (MA Ed); teaching (MAT).

College of Health Sciences *Program availability:* Part-time. Offers community health education (MPH); environmental health science (MPH); exercise and sport science (MS); exercise and wellness (MS); family and consumer sciences (M Ed); health sciences (MPH, MS, MSN); industrial hygiene (MPH); occupational therapy (MS); public health nutrition (MPH); recreation and park administration (MS); rural community health care (MSN); rural health family nurse practitioner (MSN); sports administration (MS).

College of Justice and Safety *Program availability:* Part-time. Offers correctional and juvenile justice studies (MS); criminal justice (MS); criminal justice education (MS); justice and safety (MS); loss prevention and safety (MS); police studies (MS).

EASTERN MENNONITE UNIVERSITY, Harrisonburg, VA 22802-2462

General Information Independent-religious, coed, comprehensive institution. *Graduate housing:* Rooms and/or apartments available on a first-come, first-served basis to single and married students. Housing application deadline: 4/15.

GRADUATE UNITS

Eastern Mennonite Seminary *Program availability:* Part-time. Offers church leadership (MA); divinity (M Div); ministry studies (Certificate); religion (MA); theological studies (Certificate).

Master of Arts in Counseling Program *Program availability:* Part-time. Offers counseling (MA). Electronic applications accepted.

Program in Biomedicine Offers biomedicine (MA). Electronic applications accepted.

Program in Business Administration *Program availability:* Part-time, evening/weekend. Offers general management (MBA); health services administration (MBA); non-profit leadership (MBA). Electronic applications accepted.

Program in Conflict Transformation *Program availability:* Part-time. Offers conflict transformation (MA, Graduate Certificate). Electronic applications accepted.

Program in Education *Program availability:* Part-time. Offers education (MA). Electronic applications accepted.

Program in Nursing *Program availability:* Part-time, online learning. Offers leadership and management (MSN); leadership and school nursing (MSN).

Program in Organizational Leadership Offers organizational leadership (MA).

EASTERN MICHIGAN UNIVERSITY, Ypsilanti, MI 48197

General Information State-supported, coed, comprehensive institution. CGS member. *Enrollment:* 21,135 graduate, professional, and undergraduate students; 988 full-time matriculated graduate/professional students (666 women), 2,529 part-time matriculated graduate/professional students (1,616 women). *Enrollment by degree level:* 2,929 master's, 240 doctoral, 336 other advanced degrees. *Graduate faculty:* 664 full-time (330 women). *Graduate housing:* Rooms and/or apartments available on a first-come, first-served basis to single and married students. *Student services:* Campus employment opportunities, campus safety program, career counseling, child daycare facilities, exercise/wellness program, free psychological counseling, grant writing training, international student services, low-cost health insurance, multicultural affairs office, services for students with disabilities, teacher training, writing training. *Library facilities:* Bruce T. Halle Library. *Research affiliation:* 3M Corporation (coatings research), Toyota Motor Company (coatings research), Beckers-Fusion (coatings research), Dima-Shield (coatings research), Signal Medical Corporation (textiles research), TRACO (coatings research).

Computer facilities: 1,600 computers available on campus for general student use. A campuswide network can be accessed from student residence rooms. Online class registration is available.
Website: http://www.emich.edu/

Eastern Michigan University

General Application Contact: Graduate Admissions, 734-487-2400, Fax: 734-487-6559, E-mail: graduate.admissions@emich.edu.

GRADUATE UNITS

Graduate School Students: 988 full-time (666 women), 2,529 part-time (1,616 women); includes 778 minority (461 Black or African American, non-Hispanic/Latino; 17 American Indian or Alaska Native, non-Hispanic/Latino; 100 Asian, non-Hispanic/Latino; 122 Hispanic/Latino; 1 Native Hawaiian or other Pacific Islander, non-Hispanic/Latino; 77 Two or more races, non-Hispanic/Latino), 317 international. Average age 32. 3,058 applicants, 57% accepted, 934 enrolled. *Faculty:* 664 full-time (330 women). Expenses: Contact institution. *Financial support:* Fellowships, research assistantships with full tuition reimbursements, teaching assistantships with full tuition reimbursements, career-related internships or fieldwork, Federal Work-Study, institutionally sponsored loans, scholarships/grants, tuition waivers (partial), and unspecified assistantships available. Support available to part-time students. Financial award applicants required to submit FAFSA. In 2016, 1,200 master's, 49 doctorates, 148 other advanced degrees awarded. *Program availability:* Part-time, evening/weekend, online learning. *Application deadline:* For fall admission, 5/15 priority date for domestic students, 2/15 priority date for international students; for winter admission, 10/15 priority date for domestic students, 9/1 priority date for international students; for summer admission, 3/15 priority date for domestic students, 3/1 priority date for international students. Applications are processed on a rolling basis. *Application fee:* $45. Electronic applications accepted. *Application Contact:* Graduate Admissions, 734-487-2400, Fax: 734-487-6559, E-mail: graduate.admissions@emich.edu. *Interim Dean, Graduate School,* Dr. Wade Tornquist, 734-487-0042, Fax: 734-487-0050, E-mail: wade.tornquist@emich.edu.

Academic and Student Affairs Division Students: 2 full-time (both women), 50 part-time (33 women); includes 8 minority (3 Black or African American, non-Hispanic/Latino; 4 Asian, non-Hispanic/Latino; 1 Two or more races, non-Hispanic/Latino), 1 international. 84 applicants, 83% accepted, 31 enrolled. Expenses: Contact institution. Offers individualized studies (MA, MS); integrated marketing communications (MS). *Application fee:* $45. *Application Contact:* Graduate Admissions, 734-487-2400, Fax: 734-487-6559, E-mail: graduate.admissions@emich.edu. *Interim Dean,* Dr. Wade Tornquist, 734-487-0042, Fax: 734-487-0050, E-mail: wade.tornquist@emich.edu.

College of Arts and Sciences Students: 274 full-time (173 women), 548 part-time (318 women); includes 167 minority (81 Black or African American, non-Hispanic/Latino; 4 American Indian or Alaska Native, non-Hispanic/Latino; 25 Asian, non-Hispanic/Latino; 32 Hispanic/Latino; 25 Two or more races, non-Hispanic/Latino), 95 international. Average age 31. 972 applicants, 53% accepted, 266 enrolled. *Faculty:* 342 full-time (148 women). Expenses: Contact institution. *Financial support:* Fellowships, research assistantships with full tuition reimbursements, teaching assistantships with full tuition reimbursements, career-related internships or fieldwork, Federal Work-Study, institutionally sponsored loans, and tuition waivers (partial) available. Support available to part-time students. Financial award applicants required to submit FAFSA. In 2016, 280 master's, 10 doctorates, 21 other advanced degrees awarded. *Program availability:* Part-time, evening/weekend. Offers Africology and African-American studies (Graduate Certificate); applied drama/theatre for the young (MFA); arts administration (MA); arts and sciences (MA, MFA, MLS, MM, MPA, MS, PhD, Graduate Certificate); cell and molecular biology (MS); chemistry (MS); children's literature (MA); clinical behavioral psychology (MS); clinical psychology (PhD); communication (MA); community college biology teaching (MS); composition (MM); computer science (MS, Graduate Certificate); creative writing (MA); criminology and criminal justice (MA); cultural museum studies (Graduate Certificate); ecology and organismal biology (MS); economics (MA, Graduate Certificate); English linguistics (MA); English studies for teachers (MA); general biology (MS); general clinical psychology (MS); general experimental psychology (MS); general public management (Graduate Certificate); general science (MS); geographic information systems (MS, Graduate Certificate); geographic information systems for educators (Graduate Certificate); geographic information systems for professionals (Graduate Certificate); heritage interpretation and museum practice (MS); historic preservation (MS, Graduate Certificate); history (MA); interpretation/performance studies (MA); language and international trade (MA); literature (MA); local government management (Graduate Certificate); management of public healthcare services (Graduate Certificate); mathematics (MA); music education (MM); nonprofit management (Graduate Certificate); performance (MM); philosophy (MA); physics (MS); piano pedagogy (MM); preservation planning and administration (MS); public administration (MPA, Graduate Certificate); public budget management (Graduate Certificate); public land planning and development management (Graduate Certificate); public personnel management (Graduate Certificate); public policy analysis (Graduate Certificate); recording, documentation and digital cultural heritage (MS); schools, society and violence (MA); social science (MA); sociology (MA); sociology - applied research specialty (MA); studio art (MA, MFA); teaching English to speakers of other languages (MA, Graduate Certificate); technical communication (Graduate Certificate); theatre arts (MA); transportation planning and modeling (Graduate Certificate); urban and regional planning (MS, Graduate Certificate); visual art education (MA); water resources (MS); women's and gender studies (MA, Graduate Certificate); world languages (MA, Graduate Certificate); written communication (MA, Graduate Certificate). *Application deadline:* Applications are processed on a rolling basis. *Application fee:* $45. *Interim Dean,* Dr. Kathleen Stacey, 734-487-4344, Fax: 734-485-9592, E-mail: kstacey@emich.edu.

College of Business Students: 167 full-time (92 women), 501 part-time (312 women); includes 197 minority (113 Black or African American, non-Hispanic/Latino; 6 American Indian or Alaska Native, non-Hispanic/Latino; 29 Asian, non-Hispanic/Latino; 28 Hispanic/Latino; 21 Two or more races, non-Hispanic/Latino), 73 international. Average age 31. 497 applicants, 67% accepted, 192 enrolled. *Faculty:* 77 full-time (30 women). Expenses: Contact institution. *Financial support:* Fellowships, research assistantships with full tuition reimbursements, teaching assistantships with full tuition reimbursements, career-related internships or fieldwork, Federal Work-Study, institutionally sponsored loans, traineeships, tuition waivers (partial), and unspecified assistantships available. Support available to part-time students. Financial award applicants required to submit FAFSA. In 2016, 260 master's, 63 other advanced degrees awarded. *Program availability:* Part-time, evening/weekend, online learning. Offers accounting (MS); accounting information systems (MS); business (MBA, MS, MSHROD, Graduate Certificate, Postbaccalaureate Certificate); business administration (MBA, Graduate Certificate); computer information systems (Graduate Certificate); e-business (MBA, Graduate Certificate); enterprise business intelligence (MBA); entrepreneurship (MBA, Graduate Certificate, Postbaccalaureate Certificate); finance (MBA, Graduate Certificate); human resources (MBA); human resources management (Graduate Certificate); human resources management and organizational development (MSHROD); information systems (MBA); integrated marketing communications (MS, Postbaccalaureate Certificate); internal auditing (MBA); international business (MBA, Graduate Certificate); marketing management (MBA, Graduate Certificate); nonprofit management (MBA); organizational development (Graduate Certificate); supply chain management (MBA, Graduate Certificate). *Application deadline:* Applications are processed on a rolling basis. *Application fee:* $45. *Application Contact:* K. Michelle Henry, Director, Graduate Business Programs, 734-487-4444, Fax: 734-483-1316, E-mail: cob.graduate@emich.edu. *Interim Dean,* Dr. Anne Balazs, 734-487-4140, Fax: 734-487-7099, E-mail: cob_dean@emich.edu.

College of Education Students: 179 full-time (159 women), 722 part-time (553 women); includes 193 minority (131 Black or African American, non-Hispanic/Latino; 4 American Indian or Alaska Native, non-Hispanic/Latino; 14 Asian, non-Hispanic/Latino; 27 Hispanic/Latino; 17 Two or more races, non-Hispanic/Latino), 20 international. Average age 34. 682 applicants, 57% accepted, 182 enrolled. *Faculty:* 72 full-time (49 women). Expenses: Contact institution. *Financial support:* Fellowships, research assistantships with full tuition reimbursements, teaching assistantships with full tuition reimbursements, career-related internships or fieldwork, Federal Work-Study, institutionally sponsored loans, scholarships/grants, tuition waivers (partial), and unspecified assistantships available. Support available to part-time students. Financial award applicants required to submit FAFSA. In 2016, 268 master's, 29 doctorates, 48 other advanced degrees awarded. *Program availability:* Part-time, evening/weekend, online learning. Offers administration and supervision (SPA); advanced teaching and learning (MA); autism spectrum disorders (MA); clinical mental health counseling (MA); cognitive impairment (M Ed); college counseling (MA); community college leadership (Graduate Certificate); counseling (MA, Graduate Certificate, Post Master's Certificate); curriculum and instruction (MA, Certificate, Graduate Certificate); curriculum development (SPA); early childhood education (MA); early literacy instruction (Graduate Certificate); education (M Ed, MA, Ed D, PhD, Graduate Certificate, Post Master's Certificate, SPA); educational assessment (Graduate Certificate); educational leadership (MA, Ed D, Graduate Certificate, Post Master's Certificate, SPA); educational media and technology (MA, Graduate Certificate); educational psychology (MA); educational psychology and assessment (MA, Graduate Certificate); educational studies (PhD); emotional impairment (M Ed); helping interventions in a multicultural society (Graduate Certificate); higher education/general administration (MA); higher education/student affairs (MA); instructional leadership (MA); K-12 administration (MA); K-12 basic administration (Post Master's Certificate); K-12 education (MA); learning disabilities (MA); learning, motivation and creativity (Graduate Certificate); literacy coaching (Graduate Certificate); middle school education (MA); online teaching (Certificate); physical/other health impairment (M Ed); reading (MA); school counseling (MA); school counselor licensure (Post Master's Certificate); secondary literacy instruction (Graduate Certificate); secondary school education (MA); social foundations (MA); special education (MA, SPA); speech-language pathology (MA); urban and diversity education (MA); urban/diversity education (MA); visual impairment (M Ed). *Application deadline:* Applications are processed on a rolling basis. *Application fee:* $45. *Dean,* Dr. Michael Sayler, 734-487-1414, Fax: 734-484-6471, E-mail: msayler@emich.edu.

College of Health and Human Services Students: 261 full-time (199 women), 416 part-time (312 women); includes 147 minority (95 Black or African American, non-Hispanic/Latino; 1 American Indian or Alaska Native, non-Hispanic/Latino; 17 Asian, non-Hispanic/Latino; 27 Hispanic/Latino; 1 Native Hawaiian or other Pacific Islander, non-Hispanic/Latino; 6 Two or more races, non-Hispanic/Latino), 24 international. Average age 32. 547 applicants, 51% accepted, 178 enrolled. *Faculty:* 113 full-time (85 women). Expenses: Contact institution. *Financial support:* Fellowships, research assistantships with full tuition reimbursements, teaching assistantships with full tuition reimbursements, career-related internships or fieldwork, Federal Work-Study, institutionally sponsored loans, scholarships/grants, tuition waivers (partial), and unspecified assistantships available. Support available to part-time students. Financial award applicants required to submit FAFSA. In 2016, 264 master's, 15 other advanced degrees awarded. *Program availability:* Part-time, evening/weekend, online learning. Offers adapted physical education (MS); clinical research administration (MS, Graduate Certificate); dementia (Graduate Certificate); dietetics (MS); exercise physiology (MS); gerontology (Graduate Certificate); health administration (MHA, MS, Graduate Certificate); health and human services (MHA, MOT, MS, MSN, MSW, Graduate Certificate); health education (MS, Graduate Certificate); health promotion and human performance (MS, Graduate Certificate); health sciences (MHA, MOT, MS, Graduate Certificate); human nutrition (MS); non-profit management (Graduate Certificate); nursing (MSN); occupational therapy (MOT, MS); orthotics (Graduate Certificate); orthotics/prosthetics (MS); physical education pedagogy (MA); physician assistant studies (MS); prosthetics (Graduate Certificate); social work (MSW); sports management (MS); sports medicine-biomechanics (MS); sports medicine-corporate adult fitness (MS); sports medicine-exercise physiology (MS); teaching in health care systems (MSN, Graduate Certificate). *Application deadline:* For fall admission, 5/15 priority date for domestic students, 2/15 priority date for international students; for winter admission, 10/15 priority date for domestic students, 9/1 priority date for international students; for summer admission, 3/15 priority date for domestic students, 3/1 priority date for international students. Applications are processed on a rolling basis. *Application fee:* $45. *Dean,* Dr. Murali Nair, 734-487-0077, Fax: 734-487-8536, E-mail: mnair@emich.edu.

College of Technology Students: 105 full-time (41 women), 292 part-time (88 women); includes 66 minority (38 Black or African American, non-Hispanic/Latino; 2 American Indian or Alaska Native, non-Hispanic/Latino; 11 Asian, non-Hispanic/Latino; 8 Hispanic/Latino; 7 Two or more races, non-Hispanic/Latino), 104 international. Average age 35. 276 applicants, 58% accepted, 85 enrolled. *Faculty:* 56 full-time (17 women). Expenses: Contact institution. *Financial support:* Fellowships, research assistantships with full tuition reimbursements, teaching assistantships with full tuition reimbursements, career-related internships or fieldwork, Federal Work-Study, institutionally sponsored loans, scholarships/grants, tuition waivers (partial), and unspecified assistantships available. Support available to part-time students. Financial award applicants required to submit FAFSA. In 2016, 128 master's, 10 doctorates, 1 other advanced degree awarded. *Program availability:* Part-time, evening/weekend, online learning. Offers apparel textiles and merchandising (MS); CAD/CAM (MS); computer-aided technology (MS); construction (Certificate); construction management (MS, Certificate); engineering management (MS); engineering technology (MS, Graduate Certificate, Postbaccalaureate Certificate); hotel and restaurant management (MS, Graduate Certificate); information assurance (Graduate Certificate); information security and applied computing (Graduate Certificate); interior design (MS); polymers and coatings technology (MS, Postbaccalaureate Certificate); project leadership (Certificate); quality management (MS, Graduate Certificate); sustainable construction (Certificate); technology (MLS, MS, PhD, Graduate Certificate); technology studies (MS). *Application deadline:* For fall admission, 5/15 priority date for domestic students, 2/15 priority date for international students; for winter admission, 10/15 priority date for domestic students, 9/1 priority date for international students; for summer admission, 3/15 priority date for domestic students, 3/1 priority date for international students. Applications are processed on a rolling basis. *Application fee:* $45. *Dean,* Dr. Mohamad Qatu, 734-487-0354, Fax: 734-487-0843, E-mail: mqatu@emich.edu.

EASTERN NAZARENE COLLEGE, Quincy, MA 02170

General Information Independent-religious, coed, comprehensive institution. *Graduate housing:* Rooms and/or apartments available to single students and available on a first-come, first-served basis to married students.

GRADUATE UNITS

Adult and Graduate Studies *Program availability:* Part-time, evening/weekend. Offers management (MSM); marriage and family therapy (MS).

Division of Teacher Education *Program availability:* Part-time, evening/weekend. Offers administration (M Ed); early childhood education (M Ed, Certificate); elementary education (M Ed, Certificate); English as a second language (Certificate); instructional enrichment and development (Certificate); middle school education (M Ed, Certificate); moderate special needs education (Certificate); principal (Certificate); program development and supervision (Certificate); secondary education (M Ed, Certificate); special education administrator (Certificate); special needs (M Ed); supervisor (Certificate); teacher of reading (M Ed, Certificate). M Ed also available through weekend program for administration, special needs, and teacher of reading only.

EASTERN NEW MEXICO UNIVERSITY, Portales, NM 88130

General Information State-supported, coed, comprehensive institution. *Graduate housing:* Rooms and/or apartments available on a first-come, first-served basis to single and married students. Housing application deadline: 8/1. *Research affiliation:* National Institutes of Health.

GRADUATE UNITS

Graduate School *Program availability:* Part-time, evening/weekend, online learning. Electronic applications accepted.

College of Business *Program availability:* Part-time, evening/weekend, online learning. Offers business (MBA). Electronic applications accepted.

College of Education and Technology *Program availability:* Part-time, online learning. Offers bilingual education (M Ed); counseling (MA); early childhood special education (M Sp Ed); education (M Ed); education and technology (M Ed, M Sp Ed, MA, MS); educational technology (M Ed); elementary education (M Ed); English as a second language (M Ed); general (M Sp Ed); pedagogy and learning (M Ed); physical education (MS); professional technical education (M Ed); reading/literacy (M Ed); school counseling (M Ed); special education (M Sp Ed). Electronic applications accepted.

College of Fine Arts *Program availability:* Part-time, online learning. Offers communicative arts and sciences (MA). Electronic applications accepted.

College of Liberal Arts and Sciences *Program availability:* Part-time, evening/weekend, online learning. Offers anthropology (MA); applied ecology (MS); botany (MS); cell, molecular biology and biotechnology (MS); chemistry (MS); English (MA); liberal arts and sciences (MA, MS, MSN); microbiology (MS); nursing (MSN); speech pathology and audiology (MS); zoology (MS). Electronic applications accepted.

EASTERN OREGON UNIVERSITY, La Grande, OR 97850-2899

General Information State-supported, coed, comprehensive institution. *Enrollment:* 3,176 graduate, professional, and undergraduate students; 102 full-time matriculated graduate/professional students (64 women), 129 part-time matriculated graduate/professional students (94 women). *Enrollment by degree level:* 549 master's. *Graduate faculty:* 25 full-time (12 women), 15 part-time/adjunct (7 women). Tuition, state resident: full-time $11,808; part-time $328 per credit. Tuition, nonresident: full-time $14,886; part-time $413.50 per credit. *Required fees:* $312 per quarter. One-time fee: $120. Tuition and fees vary according to course load, campus/location and program. *Graduate housing:* Rooms and/or apartments available on a first-come, first-served basis to single and married students. Typical cost: $6375 per year ($9930 including board) for single students; $5375 per year for married students. Room and board charges vary according to board plan and housing facility selected. *Student services:* Campus employment opportunities, campus safety program, career counseling, free psychological counseling, international student services, low-cost health insurance, multicultural affairs office, services for students with disabilities, writing training. *Library facilities:* Pierce Library. *Collection:* Students can reserve study rooms.

Computer facilities: Computer purchase and lease plans are available. A campuswide network can be accessed from student residence rooms and from off campus. Online class registration is available.
Website: http://www.eou.edu/

General Application Contact: Dr. Danny Ray Mielke, Coordinator of Graduate Studies, 541-962-3399, Fax: 541-962-3701, E-mail: danny.mielke@eou.edu.

GRADUATE UNITS

Master of Arts in Teaching Program Students: 43 full-time (31 women), 1 (woman) part-time; includes 6 minority (1 Black or African American, non-Hispanic/Latino; 1 American Indian or Alaska Native, non-Hispanic/Latino; 2 Asian, non-Hispanic/Latino; 4 Hispanic/Latino). Average age 31. *Faculty:* 6 full-time (6 women), 5 part-time/adjunct (2 women). Expenses: Contact institution. *Financial support:* In 2016–17, 13 students received support. Federal Work-Study, scholarships/grants, and tuition waivers (full and partial) available. Support available to part-time students. In 2016, 40 master's awarded. *Program availability:* Online learning. Offers elementary education (MAT); secondary education (MAT). *Application deadline:* For fall admission, 1/1 priority date for domestic students. Applications are processed on a rolling basis. *Application fee:* $50. Electronic applications accepted. *Application Contact:* Janet Frye, Administrative Support, MAT/MS Graduate Admission, 541-962-3772, Fax: 541-962-3701, E-mail: jfrye@eou.edu. *Dean of College of Business and Education,* Dr. Danny Ray Mielke, 541-962-3399, Fax: 541-962-3701, E-mail: dmeilke@eou.edu.

Master of Science Program Students: 9 full-time (8 women), 56 part-time (48 women); includes 6 minority (2 Asian, non-Hispanic/Latino; 3 Hispanic/Latino; 1 Two or more races, non-Hispanic/Latino), 1 international. Average age 37. *Faculty:* 11 full-time (8 women), 6 part-time/adjunct (4 women). Expenses: Contact institution. *Financial support:* In 2016–17, 8 students received support. Federal Work-Study, scholarships/grants, and tuition waivers (full and partial) available. Support available to part-time students. In 2016, 21 master's awarded. *Program availability:* Part-time, online only, 100% online. Offers education (MS). *Application deadline:* Applications are processed on a rolling basis. Electronic applications accepted. *Application Contact:* College of Business and Education, 541-962-3772, Fax: 541-962 3701, E-mail: ed@

eou.edu. *Coordinator,* Dr. Danny Ray Mielke, 541-962-3349, Fax: 541-962-3701, E-mail: danny.mielke@eou.edu.

MFA in Creative Writing Program Students: 10 full-time (6 women), 3 part-time (2 women); includes 2 minority (1 Black or African American, non-Hispanic/Latino; 1 American Indian or Alaska Native, non-Hispanic/Latino). Average age 49. *Faculty:* 2 full-time (1 woman), 4 part-time/adjunct (2 women). Expenses: Contact institution. *Financial support:* In 2016–17, 3 students received support. Federal Work-Study, scholarships/grants, and tuition waivers (full and partial) available. Support available to part-time students. Offers creative writing (MFA). *Application deadline:* Applications are processed on a rolling basis. *Application fee:* $50 ($90 for international students). *Application Contact:* Kerry Bullard, Administrative Program Assistant, 541-962 3555, Fax: 541-962-3701, E-mail: kbullard@eou.edu. *Interim Dean, College of Arts and Sciences,* Dr. Regina Braker, 541-962 3555, Fax: 541-962 3701, E-mail: rbraker@eou.edu.

Program in Business Administration Students: 34 full-time (16 women), 57 part-time (32 women); includes 17 minority (1 Black or African American, non-Hispanic/Latino; 3 American Indian or Alaska Native, non-Hispanic/Latino; 3 Asian, non-Hispanic/Latino; 10 Hispanic/Latino), 1 international. Average age 32. *Faculty:* 10 full-time (1 woman), 2 part-time/adjunct (0 women). Expenses: Contact institution. *Financial support:* Federal Work-Study, scholarships/grants, and tuition waivers (full and partial) available. Support available to part-time students. Financial award applicants required to submit FAFSA. In 2016, 35 master's awarded. *Program availability:* Part-time, 100% online. Offers business administration (MBA). *Application deadline:* For fall admission, 4/15 priority date for domestic students, 2/1 for international students. Applications are processed on a rolling basis. *Application fee:* $50. Electronic applications accepted. *Application Contact:* Kristin Johnson, MAT Advisor/Recruiter, 541-962-3529, Fax: 541-962-3701, E-mail: kristin.johnson@eou.edu. *Program Coordinator,* Les Mueller, 541-962-3225, E-mail: lmueller@eou.edu.

EASTERN UNIVERSITY, St. Davids, PA 19087-3696

General Information Independent-religious, coed, comprehensive institution. *Enrollment:* 3,420 graduate, professional, and undergraduate students; 473 full-time matriculated graduate/professional students (319 women), 610 part-time matriculated graduate/professional students (410 women). *Enrollment by degree level:* 911 master's, 172 doctoral. Tuition and fees vary according to course load, degree level, campus/location and program. *Graduate housing:* Room and/or apartments available on a first-come, first-served basis to single students; on-campus housing not available to married students. *Student services:* Campus employment opportunities, campus safety program, career counseling, international student services, low-cost health insurance, services for students with disabilities. *Library facilities:* Warner Memorial Library plus 4 others. *Collection:* Books: 183,941 (physical), 600,000 (digital/electronic); Serial titles: 100 (physical), 30,000 (digital/electronic); Databases: 130. Weekly public service hours: 83; students can reserve study rooms.

Computer facilities: 98 computers available on campus for general student use. A campuswide network can be accessed from student residence rooms and from off campus. Online class registration is available.
Website: http://www.eastern.edu/

General Application Contact: Michael Dziedziak, Executive Director of Enrollment, 800-452-0996, E-mail: gpsadmissions@eastern.edu.

GRADUATE UNITS

Department of Counseling Psychology Students: 104 full-time (92 women), 88 part-time (75 women); includes 83 minority (61 Black or African American, non-Hispanic/Latino; 1 American Indian or Alaska Native, non-Hispanic/Latino; 4 Asian, non-Hispanic/Latino; 13 Hispanic/Latino; 4 Two or more races, non-Hispanic/Latino), 3 international. Average age 29. Expenses: Contact institution. *Financial support:* Application deadline: 3/15. In 2016, 46 master's awarded. *Program availability:* Part-time. Offers applied behavior analysis (MA, Certificate); counseling (MA); professional counseling (Certificate); school counseling (MA, Certificate); school psychology (MS, Certificate). *Application deadline:* Applications are processed on a rolling basis. *Application fee:* $35. Electronic applications accepted. *Executive Director of Enrollment,* Michael Dziedziak, 800-452-0996, E-mail: gpsadmissions@eastern.edu.

Department of Nursing Students: 1 (woman) full-time, 23 part-time (all women); includes 3 minority (1 Black or African American, non-Hispanic/Latino; 1 Asian, non-Hispanic/Latino; 1 Hispanic/Latino). Average age 45. Expenses: Contact institution. In 2016, 7 master's awarded. Offers school health services (M Ed). *Application deadline:* Applications are processed on a rolling basis. *Application fee:* $35. Electronic applications accepted. *Executive Director of Enrollment,* Michael Dziedzak, 800-452-0996, E-mail: gpsadmissions@eastern.edu.

Department of Urban Studies Students: 8 full-time (all women), 32 part-time (27 women); includes 21 minority (16 Black or African American, non-Hispanic/Latino; 1 Asian, non-Hispanic/Latino; 3 Hispanic/Latino; 1 Two or more races, non-Hispanic/Latino), 2 international. Average age 33. Expenses: Contact institution. *Financial support:* Applicants required to submit FAFSA. In 2016, 12 master's awarded. *Program availability:* Part-time, evening/weekend, online learning. Offers urban studies (MA). *Application deadline:* Applications are processed on a rolling basis. *Application fee:* $35. Electronic applications accepted. *Executive Director of Enrollment,* Michael Dziedziak, 800-452-0996, E-mail: gpsadmissions@eastern.edu.

Graduate Programs in Business Students: 31 full-time (25 women), 167 part-time (110 women); includes 102 minority (73 Black or African American, non-Hispanic/Latino; 12 Asian, non-Hispanic/Latino; 14 Hispanic/Latino; 3 Two or more races, non-Hispanic/Latino), 15 international. Average age 33. Expenses: Contact institution. *Financial support:* Applicants required to submit FAFSA. In 2016, 105 master's awarded. *Program availability:* Part-time, evening/weekend, online learning. Offers health administration (MBA); health services management (MS); management (MBA). *Application deadline:* Applications are processed on a rolling basis. *Application fee:* $35. Electronic applications accepted. *Executive Director of Enrollment,* Michael Dziedziak, 800-452-0996, E-mail: gpsadmissions@eastern.edu.

Loeb School of Education Students: 41 full-time (32 women), 89 part-time (68 women); includes 54 minority (38 Black or African American, non-Hispanic/Latino; 3 Asian, non-Hispanic/Latino; 11 Hispanic/Latino; 2 Two or more races, non-Hispanic/Latino), 2 international. Average age 37. Expenses: Contact institution. In 2016, 64 master's awarded. *Program availability:* Part-time, evening/weekend, online learning. Offers ESL program specialist (K-12) (Certificate); general supervisor (PreK-12) (Certificate); health and physical education (K-12) (Certificate); middle level (4-8) (Certificate); multicultural education (M Ed); organizational leadership with education (PhD); Pre K-4 (Certificate); Pre K-4 with special education (Certificate); reading (M Ed); reading specialist (K-12) (Certificate); reading supervisor (K-12) (Certificate); school health supervisor (Certificate); school nurse (K-12) (Certificate); secondary biology education (7-12) (Certificate); secondary chemistry education (7-12) (Certificate);

secondary communication education (7-12) (Certificate); secondary education (7-12) (Certificate); secondary English education (7-12) (Certificate); secondary math education (7-12) (Certificate); secondary social studies education (7-12) (Certificate); special education (M Ed); special education (7-12) (Certificate); special education (Pre K-8) (Certificate); special education supervisor (N-12) (Certificate); TESOL (M Ed); world language (Certificate). *Application deadline:* Applications are processed on a rolling basis. *Application fee:* $35. Electronic applications accepted. *Executive Director of Enrollment,* Michael Dziedziak, 800-452-0996, E-mail: gpsadmissions@eastern.edu.

Palmer Theological Seminary Students: 93 full-time (43 women), 135 part-time (66 women); includes 120 minority (105 Black or African American, non-Hispanic/Latino; 2 Asian, non-Hispanic/Latino; 12 Hispanic/Latino; 1 Two or more races, non-Hispanic/Latino), 4 international. Average age 47. Expenses: Contact institution. In 2016, 42 master's, 9 doctorates awarded. *Program availability:* Part-time, online learning. Offers Biblical studies and theology (MTS); Christian counseling (MTS); Christian faith and public policy (MTS); divinity (M Div); general studies (MTS); leadership of missional church renewal (D Min); theological studies (MTS). *Application deadline:* Applications are processed on a rolling basis. *Application fee:* $30. Electronic applications accepted. *Executive Director of Enrollment,* Michael Dziedziak, 800-452-0996, E-mail: semadmis@eastern.edu.

Program in Marriage and Family Therapy Studies Students: 60 full-time (43 women); includes 41 minority (37 Black or African American, non-Hispanic/Latino; 1 Asian, non-Hispanic/Latino; 2 Hispanic/Latino; 1 Two or more races, non-Hispanic/Latino), 1 international. Average age 43. Expenses: Contact institution. In 2016, 8 doctorates awarded. *Program availability:* Evening/weekend, online learning. Offers marriage and family studies (DA); marriage and family therapy (PhD). *Application deadline:* Applications are processed on a rolling basis. *Application fee:* $75. Electronic applications accepted. *Executive Director of Enrollment,* Michael Dziedziak, 800-452-0996, E-mail: gpsadmissions@eastern.edu.

Program in Organizational Leadership Students: 74 full-time (42 women); includes 22 minority (17 Black or African American, non-Hispanic/Latino; 3 Asian, non-Hispanic/Latino; 1 Hispanic/Latino; 1 Two or more races, non-Hispanic/Latino), 4 international. Average age 46. Expenses: Contact institution. In 2016, 8 doctorates awarded. Offers organizational leadership (PhD). *Application deadline:* Applications are processed on a rolling basis. Electronic applications accepted. *Executive Director of Enrollment,* Michael Dziedziak, 800-452-0996, E-mail: gpsadmissions@eastern.edu.

Program in Theological and Cultural Anthropology Students: 2 full-time (1 woman), 9 part-time (7 women); includes 3 minority (1 Black or African American, non-Hispanic/Latino; 2 Hispanic/Latino). Average age 32. Expenses: Contact institution. In 2016, 3 master's awarded. Offers theological and cultural anthropology (MA). *Application deadline:* Applications are processed on a rolling basis. *Application fee:* $35. Electronic applications accepted. *Executive Director of Enrollment,* Michael Dziedziak, 800-452-0996, E-mail: gpsadmissions@eastern.edu.

School of Leadership and Development Students: 59 full-time (32 women), 67 part-time (35 women); includes 40 minority (32 Black or African American, non-Hispanic/Latino; 1 Asian, non-Hispanic/Latino; 2 Two or more races, non-Hispanic/Latino), 22 international. Average age 33. Expenses: Contact institution. In 2016, 44 master's awarded. *Program availability:* Part-time, evening/weekend, online learning. Offers economic development (MBA); international development (MA); nonprofit management (MS); organizational leadership (MA). *Application deadline:* Applications are processed on a rolling basis. *Application fee:* $35. Electronic applications accepted. *Executive Director of Enrollment,* Michael Dziedziak, 800-452-0996, E-mail: gpsadmissions@eastern.edu.

EASTERN VIRGINIA MEDICAL SCHOOL, Norfolk, VA 23501-1980

General Information Independent, coed, graduate-only institution. *Graduate housing:* On-campus housing not available.

GRADUATE UNITS

Biotechnology Program Offers biotechnology (MS). Electronic applications accepted.

Doctoral Program in Biomedical Sciences Offers biomedical sciences (PhD). Electronic applications accepted.

Graduate Art Therapy and Counseling Program Offers art therapy and counseling (MS). Electronic applications accepted.

Master of Physician Assistant Program Offers physician assistant (MPA). Electronic applications accepted.

Master of Public Health Program *Program availability:* Evening/weekend. Offers public health (MPH). Program offered jointly with Old Dominion University. Electronic applications accepted.

Master of Surgical Assisting Program Offers surgical assisting (MSA). Electronic applications accepted.

Master's Program in Biomedical Sciences Research Offers biomedical sciences research (MS). Electronic applications accepted.

Master's Program in Clinical Embryology and Andrology *Program availability:* Online learning. Offers clinical embryology and andrology (MS). Electronic applications accepted.

Medical Master's Program in Biomedical Sciences Offers biomedical sciences (MS). Electronic applications accepted.

Ophthalmic Technology Program Offers ophthalmic technology (Certificate). Electronic applications accepted.

Professional Program in Medicine Offers medicine (MD). Electronic applications accepted.

The Virginia Consortium Program in Clinical Psychology Offers clinical psychology (Psy D). Program offered jointly with The College of William and Mary, Norfolk State University, and Old Dominion University.

EASTERN WASHINGTON UNIVERSITY, Cheney, WA 99004-2431

General Information State-supported, coed, comprehensive institution. CGS member. *Enrollment:* 12,279 graduate, professional, and undergraduate students; 753 full-time matriculated graduate/professional students (504 women), 301 part-time matriculated graduate/professional students (233 women). *Enrollment by degree level:* 906 master's, 114 doctoral, 34 other advanced degrees. *Graduate faculty:* 505. Tuition, state resident: full-time $11,000; part-time $5500 per credit. Tuition, nonresident: full-time $24,000; part-time $12,000 per credit. *Required fees:* $1300. One-time fee: $50 full-time. Part-time tuition and fees vary according to course load, campus/location and program. *Graduate housing:* Rooms and/or apartments available on a first-come, first-served basis to single and married students. Typical cost: $7200 per year for single students; $7200 per year for married students. Room charges vary according to campus/location and housing facility selected. Housing application deadline: 5/1. *Student services:* Campus employment opportunities, campus safety program, career counseling, child daycare facilities, exercise/wellness program, free psychological counseling, grant

writing training, international student services, low-cost health insurance, multicultural affairs office, services for students with disabilities, teacher training, writing training. *Library facilities:* John F. Kennedy Library. *Collection:* Students can reserve study rooms.

Computer facilities: Computer purchase and lease plans are available. A campuswide network can be accessed from student residence rooms and from off campus. Online class registration, network disk storage; discounted software; laptops, still and video cameras, projectors for checkout; print credit; black white laser, color laser, and color photo options, large format print service are available. Website: http://www.ewu.edu/

General Application Contact: Roberta Brooke, Director of Graduate Programs, 509-359-6297, Fax: 509-359-6044, E-mail: gradprograms@ewu.edu.

GRADUATE UNITS

Graduate Studies Students: 753 full-time (504 women), 301 part-time (233 women); includes 212 minority (37 Black or African American, non-Hispanic/Latino; 34 American Indian or Alaska Native, non-Hispanic/Latino; 59 Asian, non-Hispanic/Latino; 79 Hispanic/Latino; 3 Native Hawaiian or other Pacific Islander, non-Hispanic/Latino), 15 international. Average age 33. 1,587 applicants, 25% accepted, 359 enrolled. *Faculty:* 576. Expenses: Contact institution. *Financial support:* In 2016–17, 183 teaching assistantships with partial tuition reimbursements (averaging $7,000 per year) were awarded; career-related internships or fieldwork, Federal Work-Study, institutionally sponsored loans, scholarships/grants, health care benefits, tuition waivers (full and partial), and unspecified assistantships also available. Support available to part-time students. Financial award application deadline: 2/1. In 2016, 1,604 master's, 38 doctorates, 44 other advanced degrees awarded. *Program availability:* Part-time, evening/weekend. Offers interdisciplinary studies (MA, MS). *Application deadline:* For fall admission, 3/1 priority date for domestic students. *Application fee:* $50. Electronic applications accepted. *Application Contact:* E-mail: gradprograms@ewu.edu. *Executive Director of Graduate Department,* Roberta Brooke, 509-359-6566, E-mail: rbrooke@ewu.edu.

College of Arts, Letters and Education Students: 122 full-time (75 women), 39 part-time (29 women); includes 23 minority (2 Black or African American, non-Hispanic/Latino; 3 American Indian or Alaska Native, non-Hispanic/Latino; 9 Asian, non-Hispanic/Latino; 9 Hispanic/Latino), 8 international. Average age 33. 153 applicants, 60% accepted, 61 enrolled. *Faculty:* 116. Expenses: Contact institution. *Financial support:* In 2016–17, 65 teaching assistantships with partial tuition reimbursements (averaging $10,000 per year) were awarded; career-related internships or fieldwork, Federal Work-Study, institutionally sponsored loans, scholarships/grants, health care benefits, tuition waivers (partial), and unspecified assistantships also available. Support available to part-time students. Financial award application deadline: 2/1; financial award applicants required to submit FAFSA. In 2016, 98 master's awarded. *Program availability:* Part-time. Offers adult education (M Ed); arts, letters and education (M Ed, MA, MFA, MS); composition (MA); creative writing (MFA); curriculum development (M Ed); early childhood education (M Ed); education (M Ed); educational foundations (M Ed); elementary teaching (M Ed); exercise science (MS); general (MA); instrumental/vocal performance (MA); jazz pedagogy (MA); literacy (M Ed); literature (MA); music education (MA); rhetoric, composition, and technical communication (MA); secondary teaching (M Ed); sports and recreation administration (MS); teaching English as a second language (MA); teaching K-8 (M Ed). *Application deadline:* Applications are processed on a rolling basis. *Application fee:* $75. Electronic applications accepted. *Application Contact:* Kathy White, Advisor/Recruiter for Graduate Studies, 509-359-2491, Fax: 509-359-6044, E-mail: gradprograms@ewu.edu. *Dean,* Dr. Roy Sonnema, 509-359-2227, E-mail: rsonnema1@ewu.edu.

College of Business and Public Administration Students: 60 full-time (36 women), 56 part-time (38 women); includes 34 minority (8 Black or African American, non-Hispanic/Latino; 7 American Indian or Alaska Native, non-Hispanic/Latino; 9 Asian, non-Hispanic/Latino; 10 Hispanic/Latino), 3 international. Average age 36. 123 applicants, 52% accepted, 47 enrolled. *Faculty:* 39 full-time (15 women), 6 part-time/adjunct (2 women). Expenses: Contact institution. *Financial support:* In 2016–17, 9 students received support, including 9 teaching assistantships with partial tuition reimbursements available (averaging $10,000 per year); career-related internships or fieldwork, Federal Work-Study, institutionally sponsored loans, scholarships/grants, health care benefits, tuition waivers (partial), and unspecified assistantships also available. Support available to part-time students. Financial award application deadline: 2/1. In 2016, 61 master's awarded. *Program availability:* Part-time, evening/weekend. Offers business administration (MBA); business and public administration (MBA, MPA, MURP); public administration (MPA); urban and regional planning (MURP). *Application deadline:* For fall admission, 4/1 priority date for domestic students; for spring admission, 1/15 for domestic students. Applications are processed on a rolling basis. *Application fee:* $75. Electronic applications accepted. *Application Contact:* Dr. Jill Ericson, Director of Graduate Programs, College of Business and Administration, 509-828-1248, Fax: 509-828-1275, E-mail: jericson1@ewu.edu. *Interim Dean, College of Business and Public Administration,* Dr. Danny Arnold, 509-828-1224, Fax: 509-828-1274, E-mail: darnold10@ewu.edu.

College of Health Science and Public Health Students: 33 full-time (9 women), 5 part-time (1 woman); includes 7 minority (1 Black or African American, non-Hispanic/Latino; 2 American Indian or Alaska Native, non-Hispanic/Latino; 1 Asian, non-Hispanic/Latino; 2 Hispanic/Latino; 1 Native Hawaiian or other Pacific Islander, non-Hispanic/Latino), 1 international. Average age 30. 77 applicants, 31% accepted, 16 enrolled. *Faculty:* 66 full-time (20 women). Expenses: Contact institution. *Financial support:* In 2016–17, 30 teaching assistantships with partial tuition reimbursements (averaging $10,000 per year) were awarded; career-related internships or fieldwork, Federal Work-Study, institutionally sponsored loans, scholarships/grants, health care benefits, tuition waivers (partial), and unspecified assistantships also available. Support available to part-time students. Financial award application deadline: 2/1; financial award applicants required to submit FAFSA. In 2016, 18 master's awarded. *Program availability:* Part-time. Offers communication disorders (MS); dental hygiene (MS); health science and public health (MA, MOT, MPH, MS, DPT); occupational therapy (MOT); physical therapy (DPT); public health (MPH). *Application deadline:* Applications are processed on a rolling basis. *Application fee:* $75. Electronic applications accepted. *Application Contact:* Kathy White, Advisor/Recruiter for Graduate Studies, 509-359-2491, Fax: 509-359-6044, E-mail: gradprograms@ewu.edu. *Dean,* Dr. David Bowman, 509-359-6244, E-mail: dbowman@ewu.edu.

College of Science, Technology, Engineering and Mathematics Students: 32 full-time (8 women), 6 part-time (2 women); includes 3 minority (1 Black or African American, non-Hispanic/Latino; 1 American Indian or Alaska Native, non-Hispanic/Latino; 1 Native Hawaiian or other Pacific Islander, non-Hispanic/Latino), 2 international. Average age 30. 53 applicants, 45% accepted, 19 enrolled. Expenses: Contact institution. *Financial support:* Application deadline: 2/15; applicants required to submit FAFSA. In 2016, 18 master's awarded. *Program availability:* Part-time. Offers biology (MS); computer science (MS); science, technology, engineering and mathematics (MS). *Application fee:* $75. Electronic applications accepted. *Application Contact:* Kathy White, Advisor/Recruiter for Graduate Studies, 509-359-2491, Fax: 509-359-6044, E-mail: gradprograms@ewu.edu. *Dean*, Dr. David Bowman, 509-359-6244, Fax: 509-359-6950, E-mail: dbowman@ewu.edu.

College of Social Sciences Students: 268 full-time (195 women), 149 part-time (117 women); includes 102 minority (19 Black or African American, non-Hispanic/Latino; 17 American Indian or Alaska Native, non-Hispanic/Latino; 28 Asian, non-Hispanic/Latino; 36 Hispanic/Latino; 2 Native Hawaiian or other Pacific Islander, non-Hispanic/Latino), 5 international. Average age 35. 365 applicants, 46% accepted, 117 enrolled. *Faculty:* 100 full-time (0 women), 51 part-time/adjunct (0 women). Expenses: Contact institution. *Financial support:* In 2016–17, 34 teaching assistantships with partial tuition reimbursements (averaging $10,000 per year) were awarded; research assistantships, career-related internships or fieldwork, Federal Work-Study, institutionally sponsored loans, scholarships/grants, health care benefits, tuition waivers (partial), and unspecified assistantships also available. Support available to part-time students. Financial award application deadline: 2/1; financial award applicants required to submit FAFSA. In 2016, 123 master's, 33 other advanced degrees awarded. *Program availability:* Part-time, evening/weekend. Offers applied psychology (MS); clinical psychology (MS); communication studies (MSC); experimental psychology (MS); history (MA); mental health counseling (MS); school counseling (MS); school psychology (Ed S); social sciences (MA, MS, MSC, MSW, Ed S); social work (MSW). *Application deadline:* Applications are processed on a rolling basis. *Application fee:* $75. Electronic applications accepted. *Application Contact:* Kathy White, Advisor/Recruiter for Graduate Studies, 509-359-6297, Fax: 509-359-6044, E-mail: gradprograms@ewu.edu. *Associate Dean*, Robert Saunders, 509-359-7904, E-mail: rsauders@ewu.edu.

EAST STROUDSBURG UNIVERSITY OF PENNSYLVANIA, East Stroudsburg, PA 18301-2999

General Information State-supported, coed, comprehensive institution. CGS member. *Enrollment:* 6,830 graduate, professional, and undergraduate students; 292 full-time matriculated graduate/professional students (176 women), 309 part-time matriculated graduate/professional students (55 women). *Enrollment by degree level:* 516 master's, 63 doctoral, 22 other advanced degrees. *Graduate faculty:* 83 full-time (40 women), 12 part-time/adjunct (7 women). Tuition, state resident: full-time $8694; part-time $5796 per year. Tuition, nonresident: full-time $13,050; part-time $8700 per year. *Required fees:* $2550; $1690 per unit. $845 per semester. Tuition and fees vary according to course load, campus/location and program. *Graduate housing:* Room and/or apartments available on a first-come, first-served basis to single students; on-campus housing not available to married students. Typical cost: $8510 per year ($11,110 including board). Room and board charges vary according to board plan and housing facility selected. Housing application deadline: 6/1. *Student services:* Campus employment opportunities, campus safety program, career counseling, child daycare facilities, exercise/wellness program, free psychological counseling, international student services, low-cost health insurance, multicultural affairs office, services for students with disabilities. *Library facilities:* Kemp Library. *Collection:* Books: 591,746 (physical), 215,088 (digital/electronic); Serial titles: 110,974 (physical); Databases: 82. Weekly public service hours: 99.

Computer facilities: 500 computers available on campus for general student use. A campuswide network can be accessed from student residence rooms and from off campus. Online class registration, online classes are available.
Website: http://www.esu.edu/

General Application Contact: Kevin Quintero, Coordinator of Graduate Admissions, 570-422-3536, Fax: 570-422-3711, E-mail: kquintero@esu.edu.

GRADUATE UNITS

Graduate and Extended Studies Students: 292 full-time (176 women), 309 part-time (204 women); includes 85 minority (38 Black or African American, non-Hispanic/Latino; 33 Hispanic/Latino; 1 Native Hawaiian or other Pacific Islander, non-Hispanic/Latino; 13 Two or more races, non-Hispanic/Latino), 26 international. Average age 30. 742 applicants, 47% accepted, 206 enrolled. *Faculty:* 83 full-time (40 women), 12 part-time/adjunct (7 women). Expenses: Contact institution. *Financial support:* Research assistantships with tuition reimbursements, teaching assistantships, career-related internships or fieldwork, Federal Work-Study, and unspecified assistantships available. Support available to part-time students. Financial award application deadline: 6/30; financial award applicants required to submit FAFSA. In 2016, 262 master's awarded. *Program availability:* Part-time, evening/weekend, 100% online, blended/hybrid learning. *Application deadline:* For fall admission, 7/31 priority date for domestic students, 6/30 priority date for international students; for spring admission, 11/30 for domestic students, 10/31 for international students. Applications are processed on a rolling basis. *Application fee:* $50. Electronic applications accepted. *Application Contact:* Kevin Quintero, Associate Director, Graduate and Extended Studies, 570-422-3890, Fax: 570-422-3711, E-mail: kquintero@esu.edu. *Director, Graduate and Extended Studies*, Dr. William Bajor, 570-422-3536, Fax: 570-422-3711, E-mail: wbajor@esu.edu.

College of Arts and Sciences Students: 47 full-time (15 women), 50 part-time (15 women); includes 10 minority (7 Black or African American, non-Hispanic/Latino; 3 Hispanic/Latino), 18 international. Average age 27. 100 applicants, 65% accepted, 35 enrolled. *Faculty:* 34 full-time (11 women), 2 part-time/adjunct (1 woman). Expenses: Contact institution. *Financial support:* Research assistantships with tuition reimbursements, career-related internships or fieldwork, Federal Work-Study, and unspecified assistantships available. Support available to part-time students. Financial award application deadline: 3/1; financial award applicants required to submit FAFSA. *Program availability:* Part-time, evening/weekend. Offers arts and sciences (M Ed, MA, MS); biology (MS); computer science (MS); history and geography (M Ed, MA, MS); management and leadership in public administration (MS); political science (MA). *Application deadline:* For fall admission, 7/31 for domestic students, 6/30 priority date for international students; for spring admission, 11/30 for domestic students, 10/31 for international students. Applications are processed on a rolling basis. *Application fee:* $50. Electronic applications accepted. *Application Contact:* Kevin Quintero, Associate Director, Graduate and Extended Studies, 570-422-3890, Fax: 570-422-3711, E-mail: kquintero@esu.edu. *Dean of Arts and Sciences*, Dr. Peter Hawkes, 570-422-3494, E-mail: phawkes@esu.edu.

College of Business and Management Students: 34 full-time (13 women), 28 part-time (14 women); includes 12 minority (7 Black or African American, non-Hispanic/Latino; 2 Hispanic/Latino; 3 Two or more races, non-Hispanic/Latino), 3 international. Expenses: Contact institution. *Financial support:* Research assistantships, career-related internships or fieldwork, Federal Work-Study, and unspecified assistantships available. Support available to part-time students. Financial award application deadline: 3/1; financial award applicants required to

submit FAFSA. *Program availability:* Part-time, evening/weekend, online learning. Offers business and management (MS); sport management (MS). *Application deadline:* For fall admission, 7/31 for domestic students, 6/30 priority date for international students; for spring admission, 11/30 for domestic students, 10/31 for international students. Applications are processed on a rolling basis. *Application fee:* $50. Electronic applications accepted. *Application Contact:* Kevin Quintero, Associate Director, Graduate and Extended Studies, 570-422-3890, Fax: 570-422-2711, E-mail: kquintero@esu.edu. *Dean*, Tribhuvan Puri, 570-422-3589, Fax: 570-422-3506, E-mail: tpuri@esu.edu.

College of Education Students: 27 full-time (16 women), 205 part-time (155 women); includes 25 minority (9 Black or African American, non-Hispanic/Latino; 13 Hispanic/Latino; 3 Two or more races, non-Hispanic/Latino), 1 international. Expenses: Contact institution. *Financial support:* Research assistantships with tuition reimbursements, career-related internships or fieldwork, Federal Work-Study, and unspecified assistantships available. Support available to part-time students. Financial award application deadline: 3/1; financial award applicants required to submit FAFSA. *Program availability:* Part-time, evening/weekend, online learning. Offers digital media technologies (M Ed); early childhood and elementary education (M Ed); education (M Ed, Ed D); professional and secondary education (Ed D); reading (M Ed); secondary education (M Ed); special education (M Ed). *Application deadline:* For fall admission, 7/31 priority date for domestic students, 6/30 priority date for international students; for spring admission, 11/30 for domestic students, 10/31 for international students. Applications are processed on a rolling basis. *Application fee:* $50. Electronic applications accepted. *Application Contact:* Kevin Quintero, Associate Director, Graduate and Extended Studies, 570-422-3890, Fax: 570-422-3711, E-mail: kquintero@esu.edu. *Dean*, Dr. Terry Barry, 570-422-3377, Fax: 570-422-3506, E-mail: tbarry1@esu.edu.

College of Health Sciences Students: 184 full-time (132 women), 26 part-time (20 women); includes 38 minority (15 Black or African American, non-Hispanic/Latino; 15 Hispanic/Latino; 1 Native Hawaiian or other Pacific Islander, non-Hispanic/Latino; 7 Two or more races, non-Hispanic/Latino), 4 international. Expenses: Contact institution. *Financial support:* Research assistantships with tuition reimbursements, career-related internships or fieldwork, Federal Work-Study, and institutionally sponsored loans available. Financial award application deadline: 3/1; financial award applicants required to submit FAFSA. *Program availability:* Part-time, evening/weekend, online learning. Offers athletic training (MS); communication sciences and disorders (MS); exercise science (MS); health sciences (MPH, MS); health studies (MPH, MS). *Application deadline:* For fall admission, 7/31 priority date for domestic students, 6/30 priority date for international students; for spring admission, 11/30 for domestic students, 10/31 for international students. Applications are processed on a rolling basis. *Application fee:* $50. Electronic applications accepted. *Application Contact:* Kevin Quintero, Associate Director, Graduate and Extended Studies, 570-422-3890, Fax: 570-422-2711, E-mail: kquintero@esu.edu. *Interim Dean*, Dr. William Bajor, 570-422-3425, Fax: 570-422-3347, E-mail: wbajor@esu.edu.

EAST TEXAS BAPTIST UNIVERSITY, Marshall, TX 75670-1498

General Information Independent-religious, coed, comprehensive institution. *Enrollment:* 1,461 graduate, professional, and undergraduate students; 48 full-time matriculated graduate/professional students (30 women), 74 part-time matriculated graduate/professional students (38 women). *Enrollment by degree level:* 122 master's. *Graduate faculty:* 14 full-time (6 women), 6 part-time/adjunct (3 women). *Graduate housing:* Rooms and/or apartments available on a first-come, first-served basis to single and married students. Typical cost: $4784 per year ($7947 including board) for single students; $5744 per year for married students. Room and board charges vary according to board plan and housing facility selected. *Student services:* Campus employment opportunities, campus safety program, career counseling, free psychological counseling, international student services, services for students with disabilities, teacher training, writing training. *Library facilities:* Mamye Jarrett Library. *Collection:* Books: 94,074 (physical), 3.5 million (digital/electronic); Serial titles: 21 (physical), 24,044 (digital/electronic); Databases: 228. Weekly public service hours: 89.

Computer facilities: 200 computers available on campus for general student use. A campuswide network can be accessed from student residence rooms. Online class registration is available.
Website: http://www.etbu.edu/

General Application Contact: Den Murley, Director of Graduate Admissions, 903-923-2079, Fax: 903-934-8115, E-mail: dmurley@etbu.edu.

GRADUATE UNITS

Master of Arts in Counseling Program Students: 25 full-time (20 women), 19 part-time (12 women); includes 29 minority (27 Black or African American, non-Hispanic/Latino; 2 Hispanic/Latino). Average age 32. 30 applicants, 60% accepted, 17 enrolled. *Faculty:* 4 full-time (3 women), 1 part-time/adjunct (0 women). Expenses: Contact institution. *Financial support:* In 2016–17, 6 students received support. Federal Work-Study, unspecified assistantships, and staff grants available. Financial award applicants required to submit FAFSA. In 2016, 6 master's awarded. *Program availability:* Part-time, evening/weekend. Offers counseling (MA). *Application deadline:* For fall admission, 8/17 for domestic students; for spring admission, 1/10 for domestic students; for summer admission, 5/2 for domestic students. Applications are processed on a rolling basis. *Application fee:* $50. Electronic applications accepted. *Application Contact:* Den Murley, Director of Graduate Admissions, 903-923-2079, Fax: 903-934-8115, E-mail: dmurley@etbu.edu. *Director*, Dr. David Deel, 903-923-2252, E-mail: macounsel@etbu.edu.

Master of Business Administration Program Students: 18 full-time (8 women), 16 part-time (7 women); includes 10 minority (7 Black or African American, non-Hispanic/Latino; 2 Hispanic/Latino; 1 Native Hawaiian or other Pacific Islander, non-Hispanic/Latino), 1 international. Average age 27. 19 applicants, 84% accepted, 13 enrolled. *Faculty:* 2 full-time (1 woman), 1 part-time/adjunct (0 women). Expenses: Contact institution. *Financial support:* In 2016–17, 18 students received support. Federal Work-Study, scholarships/grants, unspecified assistantships, and staff grants available. Financial award applicants required to submit FAFSA. In 2016, 8 master's awarded. *Program availability:* Part-time, evening/weekend, 100% online. Offers entrepreneurial leadership (MBA). *Application deadline:* For fall admission, 8/17 for domestic students; for spring admission, 1/10 for domestic students; for summer admission, 5/2 for domestic students. Applications are processed on a rolling basis. *Application fee:* $50. Electronic applications accepted. *Director of Graduate Admissions*, Den Murley, 903-923-2079, Fax: 903-934-8115, E-mail: dmurley@etbu.edu.

Master of Education Program Students: 33 part-time (19 women); includes 14 minority (10 Black or African American, non-Hispanic/Latino; 4 Hispanic/Latino), 1 international. Average age 29. 53 applicants, 51% accepted, 25 enrolled. *Faculty:* 3 full-time (1 woman), 3 part-time/adjunct (all women). Expenses: Contact institution. *Financial support:* In 2016–17, 14 students received support. Federal Work-Study, unspecified assistantships, and staff grants available. Financial award applicants required to submit FAFSA. In 2016, 20 master's awarded. *Program availability:* Part-time, evening/weekend. Offers college and university leadership (M Ed); curriculum and instruction (M Ed); principal certification (M Ed); sports and exercise leadership (M Ed); teacher certification (M Ed). *Application deadline:* For fall admission, 8/17 for domestic students; for spring admission, 1/10 for domestic students; for summer admission, 5/2 for domestic students. Applications are processed on a rolling basis. *Application fee:* $50. Electronic applications accepted. *Application Contact:* Den Murley, Director of Graduate Admissions, 903-923-2079, Fax: 903-934-8115, E-mail: dmurley@etbu.edu. *Director,* Dr. PJ Winters, 903-923-2276, Fax: 903-935-4318, E-mail: med@etbu.edu.

Master of Science in Kinesiology Program Students: 3 part-time (0 women); includes 1 minority (Black or African American, non-Hispanic/Latino). Average age 29. 2 applicants, 100% accepted, 2 enrolled. *Faculty:* 2 full-time (0 women). Expenses: Contact institution. *Financial support:* In 2016–17, 3 students received support. Federal Work-Study, scholarships/grants, unspecified assistantships, and staff grants available. Financial award applicants required to submit FAFSA. *Program availability:* Part-time, evening/weekend. Offers kinesiology (MS). *Application deadline:* For fall admission, 8/17 for domestic students; for spring admission, 1/10 for domestic students; for summer admission, 5/2 for domestic students. Applications are processed on a rolling basis. *Application fee:* $50. Electronic applications accepted. *Application Contact:* Den Murley, Director of Graduate Admissions, 903-923-2079, Fax: 903-934-8115, E-mail: dmurley@etbu.edu. *Dean, Frank S. Groner School of Professional Studies,* Dr. Joseph D. Brown, 903-923-2270, Fax: 903-935-4318, E-mail: jbrown@etbu.edu.

School of Christian Studies Students: 5 full-time (2 women), 3 part-time (0 women); includes 1 minority (Black or African American, non-Hispanic/Latino). Average age 24. 8 applicants, 50% accepted, 4 enrolled. *Faculty:* 3 full-time (1 woman), 1 part-time/adjunct (0 women). Expenses: Contact institution. *Financial support:* In 2016–17, 4 students received support. Federal Work-Study, scholarships/grants, unspecified assistantships, and staff grants available. Financial award applicants required to submit FAFSA. In 2016, 4 master's awarded. *Program availability:* Part-time, evening/weekend. Offers Christian ministry (MACM); religion (MA). *Application deadline:* For fall admission, 8/17 for domestic students; for spring admission, 1/10 for domestic students; for summer admission, 5/2 for domestic students. Applications are processed on a rolling basis. *Application fee:* $50. Electronic applications accepted. *Application Contact:* Den Murley, Director of Graduate Admissions, 903-923-2079, Fax: 903-934-8115, E-mail: dmurley@etbu.edu. *Director,* Dr. Warren Johnson, 903-923-2182, Fax: 903-923-2077, E-mail: christianstudiesma@etbu.edu.

EAST WEST COLLEGE OF NATURAL MEDICINE, Sarasota, FL 34234

General Information Proprietary, coed, graduate-only institution.

GRADUATE UNITS

Graduate Programs Offers Oriental medicine (MSOM).

EC-COUNCIL UNIVERSITY, Albuquerque, NM 87109

General Information Proprietary, coed, upper-level institution.

GRADUATE UNITS

Program in Security Science *Program availability:* Online learning. Offers security science (MSS).

ECOLE HÔTELIÈRE DE LAUSANNE, CH-1000 Lausanne 25, Switzerland

General Information Independent, coed, comprehensive institution.

GRADUATE UNITS

Program in Hospitality Administration Offers hospitality administration (MHA).

ÉCOLE POLYTECHNIQUE DE MONTRÉAL, Montréal, QC H3C 3A7, Canada

General Information Province-supported, coed, university. *Graduate housing:* Room and/or apartments available on a first-come, first-served basis to single students; on-campus housing not available to married students. Housing application deadline: 2/1. *Research affiliation:* Hydro-Quebec (energy), Bell Canada (telecommunications), Bombardier, Inc. (aircraft and aviation), IBM (computer research), Pratt and Whitney (aircraft and aviation), Ubisoft (video games).

GRADUATE UNITS

Graduate Programs *Program availability:* Part-time, evening/weekend. Offers aerothermics (M Eng, M Sc A, PhD); applied mechanics (M Eng, M Sc A, PhD); automation (M Eng, M Sc A, PhD); chemical engineering (M Eng, M Sc A, PhD, DESS); civil, geological and mining engineering (DESS); computer science (M Eng, M Sc A, PhD); electrical engineering (DESS); electrotechnics (M Eng, M Sc A, PhD); environmental engineering (M Eng, M Sc A, DESS); ergonomy (M Eng, M Sc A, DESS); geotechnical engineering (M Eng, M Sc A, PhD); hydraulics engineering (M Eng, M Sc A, PhD); mathematical method in CA engineering (M Eng, M Sc A, PhD); microelectronics (M Eng, M Sc A, PhD); microwave technology (M Eng, M Sc A, PhD); operational research (M Eng, M Sc A, PhD); optical engineering (M Eng, M Sc A, PhD); production (M Eng, M Sc A); solid-state physics and energy (M Eng, M Sc A, PhD); structural engineering (M Eng, M Sc A, PhD); technology management (M Eng, M Sc A); tool design (M Eng, M Sc A, PhD); transportation engineering (M Eng, M Sc A, PhD). Electronic applications accepted.

Institute of Biomedical Engineering *Program availability:* Part-time. Offers biomedical engineering (M Sc A, PhD, DESS). M Sc A and PhD programs offered jointly with Université de Montréal.

Institute of Nuclear Engineering Offers nuclear engineering (M Eng, PhD, DESS); nuclear engineering, socio-economics of energy (M Sc A).

ECUMENICAL THEOLOGICAL SEMINARY, Detroit, MI 48201

General Information Independent-religious, coed, graduate-only institution. *Graduate housing:* On-campus housing not available.

GRADUATE UNITS

Professional Program Offers theology (M Div).

Program in Ministry Offers ministry (D Min).

EDEN THEOLOGICAL SEMINARY, St. Louis, MO 63119-3192

General Information Independent-religious, coed, graduate-only institution. *Graduate housing:* Rooms and/or apartments available on a first-come, first-served basis to single and married students. Housing application deadline: 7/30.

GRADUATE UNITS

Graduate and Professional Programs Offers theology (M Div, MAPS, MTS, D Min). Electronic applications accepted.

EDGEWOOD COLLEGE, Madison, WI 53711-1997

General Information Independent-religious, coed, comprehensive institution. *Enrollment:* 2,552 graduate, professional, and undergraduate students; 208 full-time matriculated graduate/professional students (143 women), 428 part-time matriculated graduate/professional students (297 women). *Enrollment by degree level:* 467 master's, 169 doctoral. *Tuition:* Part-time $898 per credit. Tuition and fees vary according to course load. *Graduate housing:* On-campus housing not available. *Student services:* Campus employment opportunities, career counseling, free psychological counseling, international student services, low-cost health insurance, multicultural affairs office, services for students with disabilities, writing training. *Library facilities:* Oscar Rennebohm Library. *Collection:* Books: 102,707 (physical), 135,379 (digital/electronic); Serial titles: 80 (physical), 31,600 (digital/electronic); Databases: 81. Weekly public service hours: 98.

Computer facilities: Computer purchase and lease plans are available. 180 computers available on campus for general student use. A campuswide network can be accessed from student residence rooms and from off campus. Online class registration is available.

Website: http://www.edgewood.edu/

General Application Contact: Joann Eastman, Admissions Counselor, 608-663-3250, Fax: 608-663-2214, E-mail: gps@edgewood.edu.

GRADUATE UNITS

Henry Predolin School of Nursing Expenses: Contact institution. In 2016, 25 master's, 5 doctorates awarded. Offers nursing (MSN, DNP). *Application deadline:* For fall admission, 8/15 priority date for domestic students, 5/1 for international students; for spring admission, 1/8 priority date for domestic students, 11/1 for international students. Applications are processed on a rolling basis. *Application fee:* $30. Electronic applications accepted. *Application Contact:* Tracy Kantor, Enrollment and Applications Manager, 608-663-3297, Fax: 608-663-3496, E-mail: gps@edgewood.edu. *Dean,* Dr. Margaret Noreuil, 608-663-2820, Fax: 608-663-3391, E-mail: mnoreuil@edgewood.edu.

Program in Business Students: 38 full-time (22 women), 109 part-time (61 women); includes 13 minority (2 Black or African American, non-Hispanic/Latino; 4 Asian, non-Hispanic/Latino; 3 Hispanic/Latino; 1 Native Hawaiian or other Pacific Islander, non-Hispanic/Latino; 3 Two or more races, non-Hispanic/Latino), 13 international. Average age 33. Expenses: Contact institution. *Financial support:* Career-related internships or fieldwork and scholarships/grants available. In 2016, 50 master's awarded. *Program availability:* Part-time, evening/weekend. Offers accountancy (MS); sustainability leadership (MBA). *Application deadline:* For fall admission, 8/15 for domestic students, 5/1 for international students; for spring admission, 1/8 for domestic students, 11/1 for international students. Applications are processed on a rolling basis. *Application fee:* $30. Electronic applications accepted. *Application Contact:* Joann Eastman, Admissions Counselor, 608-663-3250, Fax: 608-663-2214, E-mail: gps@edgewood.edu. *Dean,* Dr. Stevie Watson, 608-663-2224, Fax: 608-663-3291, E-mail: swatson@edgewood.edu.

Program in Education Students: 137 full-time (91 women), 215 part-time (150 women); includes 51 minority (23 Black or African American, non-Hispanic/Latino; 3 American Indian or Alaska Native, non-Hispanic/Latino; 5 Asian, non-Hispanic/Latino; 17 Hispanic/Latino; 3 Two or more races, non-Hispanic/Latino), 18 international. Average age 37. *Faculty:* 13 full-time (9 women), 15 part-time/adjunct (10 women). Expenses: Contact institution. *Financial support:* Applicants required to submit FAFSA. In 2016, 74 master's, 18 doctorates awarded. *Program availability:* Part-time, evening/weekend. Offers adult learning (MA Ed); director of special education and pupil services (Certificate); education (MA Ed); teaching and learning (MA Ed). *Application deadline:* For fall admission, 8/15 for domestic students, 5/1 for international students; for spring admission, 1/8 for domestic students, 11/1 for international students. Applications are processed on a rolling basis. *Application fee:* $30. Electronic applications accepted. *Application Contact:* Joann Eastman, Admissions Counselor, 608-663-3250, Fax: 608-663-2214, E-mail: gps@edgewood.edu. *Dean,* Dr. Timothy D. Slekar, E-mail: tslekar@edgewood.edu.

Program in Marriage and Family Therapy Students: 23 full-time (20 women), 24 part-time (21 women); includes 5 minority (4 Black or African American, non-Hispanic/Latino; 1 Hispanic/Latino), 2 international. Average age 32. 34 applicants, 44% accepted, 12 enrolled. *Faculty:* 2 full-time (both women), 8 part-time/adjunct (5 women). Expenses: Contact institution. In 2016, 32 master's awarded. *Program availability:* Part-time, evening/weekend. Offers marriage and family therapy (MS). *Application deadline:* For fall admission, 2/1 for domestic students; for spring admission, 10/1 for domestic students. *Application fee:* $30. Electronic applications accepted. *Application Contact:* Jenna Alsteen, Admissions Counselor, 608-663-3250, Fax: 608-663-2214, E-mail: gps@edgewood.edu. *Associate Dean,* Dr. William Hutter, 608-663-3211, Fax: 608-663-3291, E-mail: whutter@edgewood.edu.

Program in Sustainability Leadership Students: 12 part-time (6 women); includes 2 minority (1 Black or African American, non-Hispanic/Latino; 1 Two or more races, non-Hispanic/Latino), 1 international. Average age 40. 15 applicants, 100% accepted, 14 enrolled. *Faculty:* 1 full-time (0 women), 2 part-time/adjunct (1 woman). Expenses: Contact institution. *Financial support:* In 2016–17, 14 students received support. Scholarships/grants available. Support available to part-time students. Financial award application deadline: 5/1; financial award applicants required to submit FAFSA. In 2016, 3 master's awarded. *Program availability:* Part-time, evening/weekend. Offers sustainability leadership (MA). *Application deadline:* For fall admission, 7/1 for domestic students. *Application fee:* $30. *Director,* Dr. Stephan Gilchrist, 608-663-6991, E-mail: sgilchrist@edgewood.edu.

EDINBORO UNIVERSITY OF PENNSYLVANIA, Edinboro, PA 16444

General Information State-supported, coed, comprehensive institution. *Graduate housing:* Room and/or apartments available on a first-come, first-served basis to single students; on-campus housing not available to married students. Housing application deadline: 4/3. *Research affiliation:* Arts Erie (art), State Higher Education Executive Officers Association (education and learning), Preventative Aftercare, Inc. (social work), CampusEAI (computing), Northwest Institute of Research (training and education), College Board (disability education).

GRADUATE UNITS

Department of Art *Program availability:* Evening/weekend. Offers art education (MA); fine arts (MFA); studio art (MA). Electronic applications accepted.

Department of Communication Studies *Program availability:* Part-time, evening/weekend. Offers communication studies (MA). Electronic applications accepted.

Department of Counseling, School Psychology and Special Education *Program availability:* Part-time, evening/weekend. Offers counseling (MA); educational psychology (M Ed); school psychology (Ed S); special education (M Ed). Electronic applications accepted.

Department of Early Childhood and Reading *Program availability:* Part-time, evening/weekend. Offers arts infusion (Graduate Certificate); early childhood education (M Ed); reading (M Ed); reading specialist (Graduate Certificate). Electronic applications accepted.

Department of History, Politics, Languages and Cultures *Program availability:* Part-time, evening/weekend. Offers social sciences (MA). Electronic applications accepted.

Department of Middle and Secondary Education and Educational Leadership *Program availability:* Part-time, evening/weekend. Offers educational leadership (M Ed); middle and secondary instruction (M Ed). Electronic applications accepted.

Department of Nursing *Program availability:* Part-time, evening/weekend. Offers advanced practice nursing (DNP); family nurse practitioner (MSN); nurse educator (MSN). Electronic applications accepted.

Department of Social Work *Program availability:* Evening/weekend. Offers social work (MSW). Electronic applications accepted.

Department of Speech, Language and Hearing *Program availability:* Part-time, evening/weekend. Offers speech language pathology (MA). Electronic applications accepted.

EDP UNIVERSITY OF PUERTO RICO–SAN SEBASTIAN, San Sebastian, PR 00685
General Information Independent, coed, comprehensive institution.

GRADUATE UNITS
Graduate School

EDWARD VIA COLLEGE OF OSTEOPATHIC MEDICINE–CAROLINAS CAMPUS, Spartanburg, SC 29303
General Information Independent, coed, graduate-only institution.

GRADUATE UNITS
Graduate Program Offers osteopathic medicine (DO).

EDWARD VIA COLLEGE OF OSTEOPATHIC MEDICINE–VIRGINIA CAMPUS, Blacksburg, VA 24060
General Information Independent, coed, graduate-only institution. *Research affiliation:* Virginia Polytechnic Institute and State University (biomedical research).

GRADUATE UNITS
Graduate Program Offers osteopathic medicine (DO).

ELIZABETH CITY STATE UNIVERSITY, Elizabeth City, NC 27909-7806
General Information State-supported, coed, comprehensive institution. CGS member. *Graduate housing:* Room and/or apartments available on a first-come, first-served basis to single students; on-campus housing not available to married students. Housing application deadline: 5/31.

GRADUATE UNITS
School of Education and Psychology *Program availability:* Part-time, evening/weekend. Offers education and psychology (M Ed, MSA); elementary education (M Ed); school administration (MSA). Electronic applications accepted.

School of Mathematics, Science and Technology *Program availability:* Part-time, evening/weekend. Offers applied mathematics (MS); biological sciences (MS); biology education (MS); community college teaching (MS); mathematics education (MS); mathematics, science and technology (MS); remote sensing (MS). Electronic applications accepted.

ELIZABETHTOWN COLLEGE, Elizabethtown, PA 17022-2298
General Information Independent-religious, coed, comprehensive institution.

GRADUATE UNITS
Department of Occupational Therapy Offers occupational therapy (MS).

ELMEZZI GRADUATE SCHOOL OF MOLECULAR MEDICINE, Manhasset, NY 11030
General Information Independent, coed, graduate-only institution. *Graduate housing:* On-campus housing not available. *Research affiliation:* Feinstein Institute for Medical Research (biomedical research), North Shore Long Island Jewish Health System (medicine).

GRADUATE UNITS
Graduate Program Offers molecular medicine (PhD).

ELMHURST COLLEGE, Elmhurst, IL 60126-3296
General Information Independent-religious, coed, comprehensive institution. *Enrollment:* 124 full-time matriculated graduate/professional students (110 women), 423 part-time matriculated graduate/professional students (247 women). *Enrollment by degree level:* 547 master's. *Graduate faculty:* 38 full-time (27 women), 34 part-time/adjunct (14 women). *Tuition:* Part-time $775 per semester hour. *Required fees:* $125 per term. Tuition and fees vary according to program. *Graduate housing:* On-campus housing not available. *Student services:* Campus employment opportunities, campus safety program, career counseling, exercise/wellness program, free psychological counseling, international student services, low-cost health insurance, multicultural affairs office, services for students with disabilities, teacher training, writing training. *Library facilities:* Buehler Library.

Computer facilities: 800 computers available on campus for general student use. A campuswide network can be accessed from student residence rooms and from off campus. Online class registration is available.
Website: http://www.elmhurst.edu/

General Application Contact: Timothy J. Panfil, Director of Enrollment Management, School for Professional Studies, 630-617-3300 Ext. 3256, Fax: 630-617-6471, E-mail: panfilt@elmhurst.edu.

GRADUATE UNITS
Graduate Programs Students: 124 full-time (110 women), 423 part-time (247 women); includes 116 minority (33 Black or African American, non-Hispanic/Latino; 2 American Indian or Alaska Native, non-Hispanic/Latino; 27 Asian, non-Hispanic/Latino; 48 Hispanic/Latino; 6 Two or more races, non-Hispanic/Latino), 15 international. Average age 30. 1,145 applicants, 34% accepted, 275 enrolled. *Faculty:* 38 full-time (27 women), 34 part-time/adjunct (14 women). Expenses: Contact institution. *Financial support:* In 2016–17, 275 students received support. Fellowships and scholarships/grants available.

Support available to part-time students. Financial award application deadline: 3/1; financial award applicants required to submit FAFSA. In 2016, 143 master's awarded. *Program availability:* Part-time, evening/weekend, 100% online. Offers business administration (MBA); communication sciences and disorders (MS); computer information systems (MS); data science (MS); early childhood special education (M Ed); geographic information systems (MS); health care management and administration (MHCA); industrial/organizational psychology (MA); nursing (MS, MSN); occupational therapy (MOT); project management (MPM); public health (MPH); special education (MS Ed); supply chain management (MS); teacher leadership (M Ed). *Application deadline:* For fall admission, 7/1 priority date for domestic and international students; for spring admission, 12/1 priority date for domestic students; for summer admission, 4/1 priority date for domestic students. Applications are processed on a rolling basis. *Application fee:* $0. Electronic applications accepted. *Application Contact:* Timothy J. Panfil, Director of Enrollment Management, School for Professional Studies, 630-617-3300 Ext. 3256, Fax: 630-617-6471, E-mail: panfilt@elmhurst.edu. *Dean of the School for Professional Studies*, Dr. Timothy Ricordati, 630-617-3089, E-mail: timothy.ricordati@elmhurst.edu.

ELMS COLLEGE, Chicopee, MA 01013-2839
General Information Independent-religious, coed, comprehensive institution. *Enrollment:* 1,604 graduate, professional, and undergraduate students; 96 full-time matriculated graduate/professional students (81 women), 305 part-time matriculated graduate/professional students (246 women). *Enrollment by degree level:* 251 master's, 80 doctoral, 70 other advanced degrees. *Graduate faculty:* 26 full-time (17 women), 25 part-time/adjunct (15 women). *Tuition:* Full-time $13,392. *Required fees:* $200. *Graduate housing:* On-campus housing not available. *Student services:* Career counseling, low-cost health insurance. *Library facilities:* Alumnae Library.

Computer facilities: A campuswide network can be accessed from student residence rooms and from off campus.
Website: http://www.elms.edu/

General Application Contact: Dr. Elizabeth Teahan Hukowicz, Dean, School of Graduate and Professional Studies, 413-265-2360 Ext. 238, Fax: 413-265-2459, E-mail: hukowicze@elms.edu.

GRADUATE UNITS
Division of Business Students: 51 part-time (32 women); includes 10 minority (4 Black or African American, non-Hispanic/Latino; 1 Asian, non-Hispanic/Latino; 5 Hispanic/Latino). Average age 34. 26 applicants, 100% accepted, 22 enrolled. *Faculty:* 4 full-time (all women), 6 part-time/adjunct (3 women). Expenses: Contact institution. In 2016, 24 master's awarded. *Program availability:* Part-time, evening/weekend. Offers accounting (MBA); financial planning (MBA); healthcare leadership (MBA); management (MBA). *Application deadline:* Applications are processed on a rolling basis. *Application fee:* $30. *Application Contact:* Dr. Elizabeth Teahan Hukowicz, Dean, School of Graduate and Professional Studies, 413-265-2360 Ext. 238, Fax: 413-265-2459, E-mail: hukowicze@elms.edu. *Chair, Division of Business*, Dr. David Kimball, 413-265-2300, E-mail: kimballd@elms.edu.

Division of Communication Sciences and Disorders Students: 5 full-time (all women), 22 part-time (19 women); includes 3 minority (1 Black or African American, non-Hispanic/Latino; 2 Hispanic/Latino). Average age 34. 13 applicants, 85% accepted, 6 enrolled. *Faculty:* 1 (woman) full-time, 2 part-time/adjunct (both women). Expenses: Contact institution. *Financial support:* Applicants required to submit FAFSA. In 2016, 8 master's, 4 other advanced degrees awarded. *Program availability:* Part-time. Offers autism spectrum disorders (MS, CAGS); communication sciences and disorders (CAGS). *Application deadline:* For fall admission, 7/1 priority date for domestic students; for spring admission, 11/1 priority date for domestic students. Applications are processed on a rolling basis. *Application fee:* $30. *Application Contact:* Dr. Elizabeth Teahan Hukowicz, Dean, School of Graduate and Professional Studies, 413-265-2360, Fax: 413-265-2459, E-mail: hukowicze@elms.edu. *Chair, Division of Communication Sciences and Disorders*, Dr. Kathryn James, 413-265-2253, E-mail: jamesk@elms.edu.

Division of Education Students: 6 full-time (all women), 136 part-time (111 women); includes 6 minority (1 Asian, non-Hispanic/Latino; 5 Hispanic/Latino). Average age 33. 27 applicants, 89% accepted, 20 enrolled. *Faculty:* 5 full-time (all women), 7 part-time/adjunct (6 women). Expenses: Contact institution. *Financial support:* In 2016–17, 2 teaching assistantships with partial tuition reimbursements were awarded; tuition waivers (partial) also available. Support available to part-time students. Financial award applicants required to submit FAFSA. In 2016, 47 master's, 3 other advanced degrees awarded. *Program availability:* Part-time, evening/weekend. Offers early childhood education (MAT); education (M Ed, CAGS); elementary education (MAT); English as a second language (MAT); reading (MAT); secondary education (MAT); special education (MAT). *Application deadline:* For fall admission, 7/1 priority date for domestic students; for spring admission, 11/1 priority date for domestic students. Applications are processed on a rolling basis. *Application fee:* $30. *Application Contact:* Dr. Elizabeth Teahan Hukowicz, Dean, School of Graduate and Professional Studies, 413-265-2360, Fax: 413-265-2459, E-mail: hukowicze@elms.edu. *Chair, Division of Education*, Dr. Mary Janeczek, 413-594-2761, Fax: 413-592-4871, E-mail: janeczeke@elms.edu.

Religious Studies Department Students: 3 part-time (2 women). Average age 59. *Faculty:* 3 full-time (0 women), 3 part-time/adjunct (1 woman). Expenses: Contact institution. *Financial support:* Tuition waivers (partial) available. Financial award applicants required to submit FAFSA. In 2016, 3 master's awarded. *Program availability:* Part-time, evening/weekend. Offers religious studies (MAAT). *Application deadline:* For fall admission, 7/1 priority date for domestic students; for spring admission, 11/1 priority date for domestic students. Applications are processed on a rolling basis. *Application fee:* $30. *Application Contact:* Dr. Elizabeth Teahan Hukowicz, Dean, School of Graduate and Professional Studies, 413-265-2360, Fax: 413-265-2459, E-mail: hukowicze@elms.edu. *Director of Religious Studies*, Dr. Martin Pion, 413-265-3581, Fax: 413-594-3951, E-mail: pionm@elms.edu.

School of Nursing Students: 36 full-time (34 women), 85 part-time (76 women); includes 10 minority (1 Black or African American, non-Hispanic/Latino; 1 American Indian or Alaska Native, non-Hispanic/Latino; 8 Hispanic/Latino). Average age 40. 42 applicants, 93% accepted, 28 enrolled. *Faculty:* 6 full-time (5 women), 6 part-time/adjunct (3 women). Expenses: Contact institution. *Financial support:* Applicants required to submit FAFSA. In 2016, 10 master's awarded. *Program availability:* Part-time, evening/weekend. Offers nursing and health services management (MSN); nursing education (MSN). *Application deadline:* For fall admission, 7/1 priority date for domestic students; for spring admission, 11/1 priority date for domestic students. Applications are processed on a rolling basis. *Application fee:* $30. *Application Contact:* Dr. Cynthia L. Dakin, Director of Graduate Nursing Studies, 413-265-2455, Fax: 413-265-2335, E-mail: dakinc@elms.edu. *Dean, School of Nursing*, Dr. Kathleen Scoble, 413-265-2204, E-mail: scoblek@elms.edu.

ELON UNIVERSITY, Elon, NC 27244-2010

General Information Independent-religious, coed, comprehensive institution. *Enrollment:* 6,739 graduate, professional, and undergraduate students; 643 full-time matriculated graduate/professional students (402 women), 88 part-time matriculated graduate/professional students (42 women). *Enrollment by degree level:* 255 master's, 476 doctoral. *Graduate faculty:* 116 full-time (63 women), 89 part-time/adjunct (41 women). *Graduate housing:* On-campus housing not available. *Student services:* Campus employment opportunities, campus safety program, career counseling, exercise/wellness program, free psychological counseling, international student services, low-cost health insurance, multicultural affairs office, services for students with disabilities, teacher training, writing training. *Library facilities:* Carol Grotnes Belk. *Collection:* Books: 388,971 (physical), 420,335 (digital/electronic); Serial titles: 269 (physical), 60,830 (digital/electronic); Databases: 179. Weekly public service hours: 143; study areas open 24 hours, 5–7 days a week; students can reserve study rooms.

Computer facilities: Computer purchase and lease plans are available. 1,200 computers available on campus for general student use. A campuswide network can be accessed from student residence rooms and from off campus. Online class registration is available.
Website: http://www.elon.edu/

General Application Contact: Art Fadde, Director of Graduate Admissions, 800-334-8448 Ext. 3, Fax: 336-278-7699, E-mail: afadde@elon.edu.

GRADUATE UNITS

Program in Business Administration Students: 65 full-time (27 women), 71 part-time (25 women); includes 28 minority (14 Black or African American, non-Hispanic/Latino; 1 American Indian or Alaska Native, non-Hispanic/Latino; 11 Asian, non-Hispanic/Latino; 1 Hispanic/Latino; 1 Two or more races, non-Hispanic/Latino). Average age 33. 128 applicants, 73% accepted, 80 enrolled. *Faculty:* 39 full-time (22 women), 10 part-time/adjunct (4 women). Expenses: Contact institution. *Financial support:* Federal Work-Study and scholarships/grants available. Support available to part-time students. Financial award application deadline: 3/15; financial award applicants required to submit FAFSA. In 2016, 49 master's awarded. *Program availability:* Part-time, evening/weekend. Offers business administration (MBA, MSM). *Application deadline:* For fall admission, 8/15 priority date for domestic students; for spring admission, 2/15 priority date for domestic students. Applications are processed on a rolling basis. *Application fee:* $50. Electronic applications accepted. *Application Contact:* Art Fadde, Director of Graduate Admissions, 800-334-8448 Ext. 3, Fax: 336-278-7699, E-mail: afadde@elon.edu. *Director,* Dr. William Burpitt, 336-278-5949, Fax: 336-278-5952, E-mail: wburpitt@elon.edu.

Program in Education Students: 17 part-time (all women); includes 7 minority (3 Black or African American, non-Hispanic/Latino; 1 American Indian or Alaska Native, non-Hispanic/Latino; 2 Hispanic/Latino; 1 Two or more races, non-Hispanic/Latino). Average age 33. 24 applicants, 50% accepted, 8 enrolled. *Faculty:* 9 full-time (7 women), 2 part-time/adjunct (both women). Expenses: Contact institution. *Financial support:* Federal Work-Study and scholarships/grants available. Support available to part-time students. Financial award application deadline: 6/1; financial award applicants required to submit FAFSA. In 2016, 24 master's awarded. *Program availability:* Part-time. Offers elementary education (M Ed); gifted education (M Ed); special education (M Ed). *Application deadline:* For fall admission, 5/1 for domestic students. Applications are processed on a rolling basis. *Application fee:* $50. Electronic applications accepted. *Application Contact:* Art Fadde, Director of Graduate Admissions, 800-334-8448 Ext. 3, Fax: 336-278-7699, E-mail: afadde@elon.edu. *Dean of the School of Education/Professor,* Dr. Ann Bullock, 336-278-5900, E-mail: abullock9@elon.edu.

Program in Interactive Media Students: 26 full-time (20 women); includes 7 minority (3 Black or African American, non-Hispanic/Latino; 1 American Indian or Alaska Native, non-Hispanic/Latino; 2 Hispanic/Latino; 1 Two or more races, non-Hispanic/Latino). Average age 33. 48 applicants, 81% accepted, 27 enrolled. *Faculty:* 12 full-time (3 women). Expenses: Contact institution. *Financial support:* Federal Work-Study and scholarships/grants available. Support available to part-time students. Financial award application deadline: 3/15; financial award applicants required to submit FAFSA. In 2016, 36 master's awarded. Offers interactive media (MA). *Application deadline:* For fall admission, 5/1 priority date for domestic students. Applications are processed on a rolling basis. *Application fee:* $50. Electronic applications accepted. *Application Contact:* Art Fadde, Director of Graduate Admissions, 800-334-8448 Ext. 3, Fax: 336-278-7699, E-mail: afadde@elon.edu. *Dean of the School of Communications,* Dr. Paul Parsons, 336-278-5724, E-mail: pparsons@elon.edu.

Program in Law Students: 335 full-time (195 women); includes 75 minority (53 Black or African American, non-Hispanic/Latino; 4 American Indian or Alaska Native, non-Hispanic/Latino; 2 Asian, non-Hispanic/Latino; 16 Hispanic/Latino), 1 international. Average age 26. 744 applicants, 45% accepted, 128 enrolled. *Faculty:* 34 full-time (15 women), 55 part-time/adjunct (20 women). Expenses: Contact institution. *Financial support:* Scholarships/grants available. Financial award applicants required to submit FAFSA. In 2016, 89 doctorates awarded. Offers law (JD). *Application deadline:* For fall admission, 7/30 for domestic students; for spring admission, 4/1 priority date for domestic students. Applications are processed on a rolling basis. *Application fee:* $50. Electronic applications accepted. *Application Contact:* Alan Woodlief, Associate Dean of School of Law/Director of Law School Admissions, 336-279-9203, E-mail: awoodlief@elon.edu. *Dean,* Dr. Luke Bierman, 336-279-9201, E-mail: lbierman@elon.edu.

Program in Physical Therapy Students: 141 full-time (97 women); includes 10 minority (2 Black or African American, non-Hispanic/Latino; 2 Asian, non-Hispanic/Latino; 1 Hispanic/Latino; 5 Two or more races, non-Hispanic/Latino), 1 international. Average age 26. 845 applicants, 11% accepted, 50 enrolled. *Faculty:* 14 full-time (9 women), 16 part-time/adjunct (11 women). Expenses: Contact institution. *Financial support:* Federal Work-Study and scholarships/grants available. Financial award application deadline: 10/1; financial award applicants required to submit FAFSA. In 2016, 52 doctorates awarded. Offers physical therapy (DPT). *Application deadline:* For fall admission, 11/1 for domestic students. Applications are processed on a rolling basis. *Application fee:* $50. Electronic applications accepted. *Application Contact:* Art Fadde, Director of Graduate Admissions, 800-334-8448 Ext. 3, Fax: 336-278-7699, E-mail: afadde@elon.edu. *Chair,* Dr. Becky Neiduski, 336-278-6347, E-mail: bneiduski@elon.edu.

Program in Physician Assistant Studies Students: 76 full-time (63 women); includes 5 minority (4 Asian, non-Hispanic/Latino; 1 Two or more races, non-Hispanic/Latino). Average age 26. 1,435 applicants, 5% accepted, 38 enrolled. *Faculty:* 8 full-time (7 women), 6 part-time/adjunct (4 women). Expenses: Contact institution. *Financial support:* Federal Work-Study and scholarships/grants available. Financial award application deadline: 10/1; financial award applicants required to submit FAFSA. In 2016, 37 master's awarded. Offers physician assistant studies (MS). *Application deadline:* For spring admission, 11/1 for domestic students. Applications are processed on a rolling basis. *Application fee:* $50. Electronic applications accepted. *Application Contact:* Art Fadde, Director of Graduate Admissions, 800-334-8448 Ext. 3, Fax: 336-278-7699, E-mail: afadde@elon.edu. *Department Chair/Program Director of the School of Physician Assistant Studies,* Dr. Becky Neiduski, 336-278-6850, E-mail: bneiduski@elon.edu.

EMBRY-RIDDLE AERONAUTICAL UNIVERSITY–DAYTONA, Daytona Beach, FL 32114-3900

General Information Independent, coed, university. *Enrollment:* 6,011 graduate, professional, and undergraduate students; 467 full-time matriculated graduate/professional students (131 women), 97 part-time matriculated graduate/professional students (28 women). *Enrollment by degree level:* 465 master's, 99 doctoral. *Graduate faculty:* 100 full-time (15 women), 4 part-time/adjunct (0 women). *Tuition:* Full-time $16,296; part-time $1358 per credit hour. *Required fees:* $1294; $647 per semester. One-time fee: $100 full-time. Tuition and fees vary according to course load, degree level and program. *Graduate housing:* On-campus housing not available. *Student services:* Campus employment opportunities, campus safety program, career counseling, exercise/wellness program, free psychological counseling, international student services, low-cost health insurance, multicultural affairs office, services for students with disabilities. *Library facilities:* Jack R. Hunt Memorial Library. *Collection:* Books: 54,106 (physical), 76,328 (digital/electronic); Serial titles: 1,521 (physical), 48,948 (digital/electronic); Databases: 106. Students can reserve study rooms. *Research affiliation:* Marinvent Corporation (aerospace and defense research, rapid prototyping and demonstration of novel technologies), Lockheed Martin Corporation (research, design, development, manufacturing, integration, and the sustaining of advanced technology systems, products and services), Honeywell Aerospace (aviation products and services), Boeing, Mosaic ATM (air transportation and unmanned aircraft systems industries).

Computer facilities: 1,049 computers available on campus for general student use. A campuswide network can be accessed from student residence rooms and from off campus. Online class registration is available.
Website: http://www.daytonabeach.erau.edu/

General Application Contact: Graduate Admissions, 800-388-3728, Fax: 386-226-7070, E-mail: graduate.admissions@erau.edu.

GRADUATE UNITS

Department of Aerospace Engineering Students: 109 full-time (19 women), 29 part-time (6 women); includes 9 minority (1 Black or African American, non-Hispanic/Latino; 1 American Indian or Alaska Native, non-Hispanic/Latino; 3 Asian, non-Hispanic/Latino; 2 Hispanic/Latino; 2 Two or more races, non-Hispanic/Latino), 102 international. Average age 25. 201 applicants, 26% accepted, 32 enrolled. *Faculty:* 27 full-time (3 women). Expenses: Contact institution. *Financial support:* Research assistantships, career-related internships or fieldwork, scholarships/grants, unspecified assistantships, and on-campus employment available. Financial award application deadline: 3/15; financial award applicants required to submit FAFSA. In 2016, 61 master's awarded. *Program availability:* Part-time. Offers aerodynamics and propulsion (MS, PhD); dynamics and control (MS, PhD); structures and materials (MS, PhD). *Application deadline:* For fall admission, 1/15 priority date for domestic students; for spring admission, 9/15 priority date for domestic students; for summer admission, 4/1 priority date for domestic students. Applications are processed on a rolling basis. *Application fee:* $50. Electronic applications accepted. *Application Contact:* Graduate Admissions, 386-226-6176, E-mail: graduate.admissions@erau.edu. *Professor/Chair, Aerospace Engineering,* Dr. Anastasios Lyrintzis, 386-226-7007, Fax: 386-226-6747, E-mail: lyrintzi@erau.edu.

Department of Civil Engineering Students: 5 full-time (1 woman); includes 3 minority (2 Asian, non-Hispanic/Latino; 1 Two or more races, non-Hispanic/Latino), 2 international. Average age 26. 9 applicants, 67% accepted, 5 enrolled. *Faculty:* 3 full-time (1 woman). Expenses: Contact institution. *Financial support:* Research assistantships, career-related internships or fieldwork, scholarships/grants, unspecified assistantships, and on-campus employment available. Financial award application deadline: 3/15; financial award applicants required to submit FAFSA. *Program availability:* Part-time. Offers civil engineering (MS). *Application deadline:* For fall admission, 3/1 priority date for domestic students; for spring admission, 11/1 priority date for domestic students; for summer admission, 4/1 priority date for domestic students. Applications are processed on a rolling basis. *Application fee:* $50. Electronic applications accepted. *Application Contact:* Graduate Admissions, 800-388-3728, Fax: 386-226-7070, E-mail: graduate.admissions@erau.edu. *Professor and Chair, Department of Civil Engineering,* Dr. Ashok Gurjar, 386-226-6757, E-mail: gurjara@erau.edu.

Department of Doctoral and Graduate Studies Students: 78 full-time (21 women), 46 part-time (16 women); includes 21 minority (5 Black or African American, non-Hispanic/Latino; 8 Asian, non-Hispanic/Latino; 3 Hispanic/Latino; 5 Two or more races, non-Hispanic/Latino). Average age 36. 95 applicants, 51% accepted, 26 enrolled. *Faculty:* 17 full-time (2 women), 3 part-time/adjunct (0 women). Expenses: Contact institution. *Financial support:* Research assistantships, career-related internships or fieldwork, scholarships/grants, unspecified assistantships, and on-campus employment available. Financial award application deadline: 3/15; financial award applicants required to submit FAFSA. In 2016, 21 master's, 3 doctorates awarded. *Program availability:* Part-time, primarily online, including three 6-day residencies at designated campuses. Offers aeronautics (MSA); aviation (PhD). Application fee for PhD is $100. *Application deadline:* For fall admission, 3/1 for domestic students; for spring admission, 11/1 for domestic students; for summer admission, 4/1 for domestic students. Applications are processed on a rolling basis. *Application fee:* $50. Electronic applications accepted. *Application Contact:* Graduate Admissions, 386-226-6176, E-mail: graduate.admissions@erau.edu. *Professor of Graduate Studies/Program Coordinator,* Dr. Donald Metscher, 386-226-6100, E-mail: donald.metscher@erau.edu.

Department of Electrical, Computer, Software and Systems Engineering Students: 63 full-time (17 women), 8 part-time (3 women); includes 6 minority (1 Black or African American, non-Hispanic/Latino; 1 Asian, non-Hispanic/Latino; 1 Hispanic/Latino; 3 Two or more races, non-Hispanic/Latino), 41 international. Average age 25. 93 applicants, 45% accepted, 21 enrolled. *Faculty:* 13 full-time (1 woman), 1 part-time/adjunct (0 women). Expenses: Contact institution. *Financial support:* Research assistantships, teaching assistantships, career-related internships or fieldwork, scholarships/grants, unspecified assistantships, and on-campus employment available. Financial award application deadline: 3/15; financial award applicants required to submit FAFSA. In 2016, 30 master's awarded. *Program availability:* Part-time. Offers computer engineering (MS); cybersecurity engineering (MS); electrical engineering (MSECE); electrical engineering and computer science (PhD); software engineering (MSSE); systems engineering (MS). *Application deadline:* For fall admission, 3/1 priority date for domestic students; for spring admission, 11/1 priority date for domestic students; for summer admission, 4/1 priority date for domestic students. Applications are processed on a rolling basis. *Application fee:* $50. Electronic applications accepted. *Application Contact:* Graduate Admissions, 386-226-6176, Fax: 386-226-7070, E-mail:

graduate.admissions@erau.edu. *Professor of Electrical and Computer Engineering/Chair, Department of Electrical, Computer, Software and Systems Engineering,* Timothy Wilson, PhD, 386-226-6100, E-mail: timothy.wilson@erau.edu.

Department of Human Factors Students: 42 full-time (19 women), 1 (woman) part-time; includes 9 minority (2 Black or African American, non-Hispanic/Latino; 1 American Indian or Alaska Native, non-Hispanic/Latino; 6 Two or more races, non-Hispanic/Latino), 5 international. Average age 26. 57 applicants, 32% accepted, 16 enrolled. *Faculty:* 7 full-time (2 women). Expenses: Contact institution. *Financial support:* Research assistantships, teaching assistantships, career-related internships or fieldwork, scholarships/grants, unspecified assistantships, and on-campus employment available. Financial award application deadline: 3/15; financial award applicants required to submit FAFSA. In 2016, 6 master's awarded. *Program availability:* Part-time. Offers human factors (PhD). *Application deadline:* For fall admission, 3/1 priority date for domestic students; for spring admission, 11/1 priority date for domestic students; for summer admission, 4/1 priority date for domestic students. Applications are processed on a rolling basis. *Application fee:* $50. Electronic applications accepted. *Application Contact:* Graduate Admissions, 800-862-2416, E-mail: graduate.admissions@erau.edu. *Professor/Department Chair,* Scott Shappell, PhD, E-mail: scott.shappell@erau.edu.

Department of Management, Marketing and Operations Students: 93 full-time (37 women), 15 part-time (8 women); includes 12 minority (3 Black or African American, non-Hispanic/Latino; 3 Asian, non-Hispanic/Latino; 1 Hispanic/Latino; 5 Two or more races, non-Hispanic/Latino), 71 international. Average age 26. 130 applicants, 39% accepted, 40 enrolled. *Faculty:* 13 full-time (2 women). Expenses: Contact institution. *Financial support:* Research assistantships, teaching assistantships, career-related internships or fieldwork, scholarships/grants, unspecified assistantships, and on-campus employment available. Financial award application deadline: 3/15; financial award applicants required to submit FAFSA. In 2016, 44 degrees awarded. *Program availability:* Part-time. Offers airline management (MBA); airport management (MBA); aviation finance (MSAF); aviation human resources (MBA); aviation management (MBA-AM); aviation system management (MBA); finance (MBA). *Application deadline:* For fall admission, 3/1 priority date for domestic students; for spring admission, 11/1 priority date for domestic students; for summer admission, 4/1 priority date for domestic students. Applications are processed on a rolling basis. *Application fee:* $50. Electronic applications accepted. *Application Contact:* Graduate Admissions, 386-226-6176, E-mail: graduate.admissions@erau.edu. *Dean, College of Business/Professor of Management,* Michael J. Williams, PhD, 386-226-6293, E-mail: michael.williams@erau.edu.

Department of Mechanical Engineering Students: 47 full-time (6 women), 14 part-time (4 women); includes 11 minority (3 Black or African American, non-Hispanic/Latino; 1 Asian, non-Hispanic/Latino; 1 Hispanic/Latino; 6 Two or more races, non-Hispanic/Latino), 26 international. Average age 26. 53 applicants, 43% accepted, 14 enrolled. *Faculty:* 10 full-time (4 women). Expenses: Contact institution. *Financial support:* Research assistantships, teaching assistantships, career-related internships or fieldwork, scholarships/grants, unspecified assistantships, and on-campus employment available. Financial award application deadline: 3/15; financial award applicants required to submit FAFSA. In 2016, 19 master's awarded. *Program availability:* Part-time. Offers high performance vehicles (MSME); mechanical engineering (PhD); mechanical systems (MSME). *Application deadline:* For fall admission, 3/1 priority date for domestic students; for spring admission, 11/1 priority date for domestic students; for summer admission, 4/1 priority date for domestic students. Applications are processed on a rolling basis. *Application fee:* $50. Electronic applications accepted. *Application Contact:* Graduate Admissions, 386-226-6176, Fax: 386-226-7070, E-mail: graduate.admissions@erau.edu. *Professor and Department Chair,* Charles Reinholtz, PhD, 386-323-8848, E-mail: charles.reinholtz@erau.edu.

Department of Physical Sciences Students: 36 full-time (11 women), 2 part-time (both women); includes 5 minority (1 Black or African American, non-Hispanic/Latino; 2 Hispanic/Latino; 2 Two or more races, non-Hispanic/Latino), 12 international. Average age 26. 32 applicants, 50% accepted, 9 enrolled. *Faculty:* 11 full-time (1 woman). Expenses: Contact institution. *Financial support:* Research assistantships, teaching assistantships, career-related internships or fieldwork, scholarships/grants, traineeships, unspecified assistantships, and on-campus employment available. Financial award application deadline: 3/15; financial award applicants required to submit FAFSA. In 2016, 7 master's awarded. *Program availability:* Part-time. Offers engineering physics (MS, PhD). *Application deadline:* For fall admission, 3/1 priority date for domestic students; for spring admission, 11/1 priority date for domestic students; for summer admission, 4/1 priority date for domestic students. Applications are processed on a rolling basis. *Application fee:* $50. Electronic applications accepted. *Application Contact:* Graduate Admissions, 386-226-6176, E-mail: graduate.admissions@erau.edu. *Professor of Engineering Physics/Chair, Department of Physical Sciences,* Terry Oswalt, PhD, 386-226-6100, E-mail: terry.oswalt@erau.edu.

Program in Unmanned and Autonomous Systems Engineering Students: 8 full-time (2 women), 4 international. Average age 25. 13 applicants, 38% accepted, 1 enrolled. *Faculty:* 2 full-time (0 women). Expenses: Contact institution. *Financial support:* Research assistantships, career-related internships or fieldwork, scholarships/grants, and unspecified assistantships available. Financial award application deadline: 3/15; financial award applicants required to submit FAFSA. In 2016, 2 master's awarded. *Program availability:* Part-time. Offers systems engineering (MSUASE); technical (MSUASE); unmanned aircraft systems (MSUASE). *Application deadline:* For fall admission, 3/1 priority date for domestic students; for spring admission, 11/1 priority date for domestic students. Applications are processed on a rolling basis. *Application fee:* $50. Electronic applications accepted. *Application Contact:* Graduate Admissions, 386-226-6176, E-mail: graduate.admissions@erau.edu. *Master's Program Coordinator,* Richard Stansbury, PhD, 800-862-2416, E-mail: Richard.Stansbury@erau.edu.

EMBRY-RIDDLE AERONAUTICAL UNIVERSITY–PRESCOTT, Prescott, AZ 86301-3720

General Information Independent, coed, comprehensive institution. *Enrollment:* 2,439 graduate, professional, and undergraduate students; 57 full-time matriculated graduate/professional students (14 women), 5 part-time matriculated graduate/professional students (2 women). *Enrollment by degree level:* 62 master's. *Graduate faculty:* 11 full-time (0 women), 2 part-time/adjunct (0 women). *Tuition:* Full-time $16,296; part-time $1358 per credit hour. *Required fees:* $1234; $617 per semester. One-time fee: $100 full-time. Tuition and fees vary according to course load. *Graduate housing:* On-campus housing not available. *Student services:* Campus employment opportunities, campus safety program, career counseling, exercise/wellness program, free psychological counseling, international student services, low-cost health insurance, multicultural affairs office, services for students with disabilities. *Library facilities:* Christine & Steven F. Udvar-Hazy Library & Learning Center. *Collection:* Books: 30,076 (physical), 179,675 (digital/electronic); Serial titles:

149 (physical), 51,589 (digital/electronic); Databases: 101. Students can reserve study rooms. *Research affiliation:* Boeing/Intelligent Light/Pointwise (CFD analysis on aerospace vehicles and energy systems), University of Alaska, Anchorage (development of field deployed multi-spectral computer vision systems), NASA (optimization ideas for aircraft design), Federal Aviation Administration (human factors, air traffic control interoperability, air traffic management, low-altitude operations, wake separation and noise reduction), NATO Modelling & Simulation Centre of Excellence (operational requirements, training and interoperability), Flight Research Inc. (production of world-class training and curriculum programs for aircraft loss-of-control situations).

Computer facilities: Computer purchase and lease plans are available. 730 computers available on campus for general student use. A campuswide network can be accessed from student residence rooms and from off campus. Online class registration is available.
Website: http://www.embryriddle.edu/

General Application Contact: Graduate Admissions, 928-777-6600, E-mail: prescott@erau.edu.

GRADUATE UNITS

Program in Safety Science Students: 27 full-time (7 women); includes 3 minority (1 Black or African American, non-Hispanic/Latino; 2 Two or more races, non-Hispanic/Latino), 9 international. Average age 32. 29 applicants, 69% accepted, 9 enrolled. *Faculty:* 4 full-time (0 women), 1 part-time/adjunct (0 women). Expenses: Contact institution. *Financial support:* Research assistantships, career-related internships or fieldwork, scholarships/grants, and unspecified assistantships available. Financial award application deadline: 3/15; financial award applicants required to submit FAFSA. In 2016, 20 master's awarded. *Program availability:* Part-time. Offers safety (MSSS). *Application deadline:* For fall admission, 1/15 priority date for domestic students; for spring admission, 11/1 priority date for domestic students; for summer admission, 4/1 priority date for domestic students. Applications are processed on a rolling basis. *Application fee:* $50. Electronic applications accepted. *Application Contact:* Graduate Admissions, 928-777-6600, E-mail: prescott@erau.edu. *Dean, College of Arts and Sciences,* Archie Dickey, PhD, E-mail: archie.dickey@erau.edu.

Security and Intelligence Studies Program Students: 30 full-time (7 women), 5 part-time (2 women); includes 8 minority (2 Black or African American, non-Hispanic/Latino; 2 Asian, non-Hispanic/Latino; 3 Hispanic/Latino; 1 Two or more races, non-Hispanic/Latino), 3 international. Average age 27. 50 applicants, 70% accepted, 14 enrolled. *Faculty:* 7 full-time (0 women), 1 part-time/adjunct (0 women). Expenses: Contact institution. *Financial support:* Research assistantships, career-related internships or fieldwork, scholarships/grants, and unspecified assistantships available. Financial award application deadline: 3/15; financial award applicants required to submit FAFSA. In 2016, 3 master's awarded. *Program availability:* Part-time. Offers security and intelligence studies (MSSIS). *Application deadline:* For fall admission, 1/15 priority date for domestic students; for spring admission, 11/1 priority date for domestic students; for summer admission, 4/1 priority date for domestic students. Applications are processed on a rolling basis. *Application fee:* $50. Electronic applications accepted. *Application Contact:* Graduate Admissions, 928-777-6600, E-mail: prescott@erau.edu. *Dean and Professor, College of Security and Intelligence,* Philip Jones, PhD, 928-777-6992, E-mail: philip.e.jones@erau.edu.

EMBRY-RIDDLE AERONAUTICAL UNIVERSITY–WORLDWIDE, Daytona Beach, FL 32114-3900

General Information Independent, coed, comprehensive institution. *Enrollment:* 15,457 graduate, professional, and undergraduate students; 2,145 full-time matriculated graduate/professional students (511 women), 2,114 part-time matriculated graduate/professional students (421 women). *Enrollment by degree level:* 4,256 master's, 3 other advanced degrees. *Graduate faculty:* 69 full-time (24 women), 305 part-time/adjunct (63 women). *Tuition:* Full-time $7440; part-time $620 per credit hour. Tuition and fees vary according to degree level and program. *Student services:* Career counseling, free psychological counseling, international student services, services for students with disabilities. *Library facilities:* Jack R. Hunt Memorial Library located in Daytona Beach. *Collection:* Books: 54,106 (physical), 76,328 (digital/electronic); Serial titles: 1,521 (physical), 48,948 (digital/electronic); Databases: 106. *Research affiliation:* The Society for Protective Coatings and Honda Aircraft (creation of standards for training and certification program for higher paint quality).

Computer facilities: Online class registration, ERAU Worldwide does not have a physical campus; courses are offered online and at military bases worldwide are available.
Website: http://www.worldwide.erau.edu/

General Application Contact: Worldwide Campus, 800-522-6787, E-mail: worldwide@erau.edu.

GRADUATE UNITS

Department of Aeronautics, Graduate Studies Students: 865 full-time (156 women), 998 part-time (163 women); includes 434 minority (179 Black or African American, non-Hispanic/Latino; 7 American Indian or Alaska Native, non-Hispanic/Latino; 65 Asian, non-Hispanic/Latino; 71 Hispanic/Latino; 4 Native Hawaiian or other Pacific Islander, non-Hispanic/Latino; 108 Two or more races, non-Hispanic/Latino), 128 international. Average age 37. *Faculty:* 34 full-time (9 women), 146 part-time/adjunct (20 women). Expenses: Contact institution. *Financial support:* Career-related internships or fieldwork and scholarships/grants available. Financial award applicants required to submit FAFSA. In 2016, 572 master's awarded. *Program availability:* Part-time, evening/weekend, 100% online, blended/hybrid learning, EagleVision Classroom (between classrooms), EagleVision Home (faculty and students at home), and a blend of Classroom or Home. Offers aeronautics (MSA); aeronautics and design (MS); aviation maintenance (MAM); aviation/aerospace management (MS); education (MS); human factors (MS, MSHFS); occupational safety management (MS); operations (MS); safety/emergency response (MS); small unmanned aircraft system (SUAS) operation (MS); space systems (MS); unmanned aerospace systems (MS). *Application deadline:* Applications are processed on a rolling basis. *Application fee:* $50. Electronic applications accepted. *Application Contact:* Worldwide Campus, 800-522-6787, E-mail: worldwide@erau.edu. *Department Chair,* Ian R. McAndrew, PhD, E-mail: ian.mcandrew@erau.edu.

Department of Business Administration Students: 368 full-time (81 women), 315 part-time (57 women); includes 173 minority (57 Black or African American, non-Hispanic/Latino; 4 American Indian or Alaska Native, non-Hispanic/Latino; 36 Asian, non-Hispanic/Latino; 35 Hispanic/Latino; 4 Native Hawaiian or other Pacific Islander, non-Hispanic/Latino; 37 Two or more races, non-Hispanic/Latino), 61 international. Average age 35. *Faculty:* 16 full-time (4 women), 64 part-time/adjunct (18 women). Expenses: Contact institution. *Financial support:* Career-related internships or fieldwork and scholarships/grants available. Financial award applicants required to submit FAFSA. In 2016, 204 master's awarded. *Program availability:* Part-time, evening/weekend, 100% online, blended/hybrid learning, EagleVision Classroom (between classrooms),

EagleVision Home (faculty and students at home), and a blend of Classroom or Home. Offers aviation (MBAA). *Application deadline:* Applications are processed on a rolling basis. *Application fee:* $50. Electronic applications accepted. *Application Contact:* Worldwide Campus, 800-522-6787, E-mail: worldwide@erau.edu. *Department Chair,* Ronald Mau, PhD, E-mail: ronald.mau@erau.edu.

Department of Decision Sciences Students: 572 full-time (162 women), 419 part-time (91 women); includes 307 minority (150 Black or African American, non-Hispanic/Latino; 6 American Indian or Alaska Native, non-Hispanic/Latino; 35 Asian, non-Hispanic/Latino; 51 Hispanic/Latino; 3 Native Hawaiian or other Pacific Islander, non-Hispanic/Latino; 62 Two or more races, non-Hispanic/Latino), 12 international. Average age 36. *Faculty:* 12 full-time (4 women), 40 part-time/adjunct (11 women). *Expenses:* Contact institution. *Financial support:* Career-related internships or fieldwork and scholarships/grants available. Financial award applicants required to submit FAFSA. In 2016, 217 master's awarded. *Program availability:* Part-time, evening/weekend, 100% online, blended/hybrid learning, EagleVision is a virtual classroom that combines Web video conferencing and a learning management system. EagleVision Classroom (between classrooms), EagleVision Home (faculty and students at home), and a blend of Classroom or Home. Offers aviation and aerospace management (MSEM, MSPM); financial management (MSEM, MSPM); general management (MSPM); global management (MSPM); human resources management (MSPM); information systems (MSPM); leadership (MSEM, MSPM); logistics and supply chain management (MSEM, MSLSCM, MSPM); management (MSEM, MSPM); project management (MSEM); systems engineering (MSEM, MSPM); technical management (MSPM). *Application deadline:* Applications are processed on a rolling basis. *Application fee:* $50. Electronic applications accepted. *Application Contact:* Worldwide Campus, 800-522-6787, E-mail: worldwide@erau.edu. *Department Chair,* Aman Gupta, PhD, E-mail: Aman.Gupta@erau.edu.

Department of Engineering Sciences Students: 29 full-time (8 women), 33 part-time (7 women); includes 12 minority (4 Black or African American, non-Hispanic/Latino; 3 Asian, non-Hispanic/Latino; 1 Hispanic/Latino; 4 Two or more races, non-Hispanic/Latino), 1 international. Average age 32. *Faculty:* 3 full-time (1 woman), 6 part-time/adjunct (0 women). *Expenses:* Contact institution. *Financial support:* Career-related internships or fieldwork and scholarships/grants available. Financial award applicants required to submit FAFSA. In 2016, 24 master's awarded. *Program availability:* Part-time, evening/weekend, 100% online, blended/hybrid learning. Offers aerospace engineering (MS); systems engineering (M Sys E). *Application deadline:* Applications are processed on a rolling basis. *Application fee:* $50. Electronic applications accepted. *Application Contact:* Worldwide Campus, 800-522-6787, E-mail: worldwide@erau.edu. *Department Chair,* Brian Sanders, PhD, E-mail: brian.sanders1@erau.edu.

Department of Management Students: 148 full-time (48 women), 192 part-time (52 women); includes 91 minority (46 Black or African American, non-Hispanic/Latino; 1 American Indian or Alaska Native, non-Hispanic/Latino; 11 Asian, non-Hispanic/Latino; 16 Hispanic/Latino; 17 Two or more races, non-Hispanic/Latino), 7 international. Average age 39. *Faculty:* 2 full-time (0 women), 17 part-time/adjunct (3 women). *Expenses:* Contact institution. *Financial support:* Career-related internships or fieldwork and scholarships/grants available. Financial award applicants required to submit FAFSA. In 2016, 104 master's awarded. *Program availability:* Part-time, evening/weekend, 100% online, blended/hybrid learning, EagleVision is a virtual classroom that combines Web video conferencing and a learning management system. EagleVision Classroom (between classrooms), EagleVision Home (faculty and students at home), and a blend of Classroom or Home. Offers global management (MS); human resources management (MS); leadership (MS); operations management (MS); project management (MS). *Application deadline:* Applications are processed on a rolling basis. *Application fee:* $50. Electronic applications accepted. *Application Contact:* Worldwide Campus, 800-522-6787, E-mail: worldwide@erau.edu. *Department Chair,* Thomas Henkel, PhD, E-mail: Thomas.Henkel@erau.edu.

Department of Organizational Leadership Students: 90 full-time (34 women), 68 part-time (27 women); includes 36 minority (18 Black or African American, non-Hispanic/Latino; 2 Asian, non-Hispanic/Latino; 5 Hispanic/Latino; 1 Native Hawaiian or other Pacific Islander, non-Hispanic/Latino; 10 Two or more races, non-Hispanic/Latino), 1 international. Average age 39. *Faculty:* 5 full-time (2 women), 17 part-time/adjunct (5 women). *Expenses:* Contact institution. *Financial support:* In 2016–17, 74 students received support. Career-related internships or fieldwork and scholarships/grants available. Financial award applicants required to submit FAFSA. In 2016, 47 master's awarded. *Program availability:* Part-time, evening/weekend, 100% online, blended/hybrid learning, EagleVision is a virtual classroom that combines Web video conferencing and a learning management system. EagleVision Classroom (between classrooms), EagleVision Home (faculty and students at home), and a blend of Classroom or Home. Offers leadership (MS). *Application deadline:* Applications are processed on a rolling basis. *Application fee:* $50. Electronic applications accepted. *Application Contact:* Worldwide Campus, 800-522-6787, E-mail: worldwide@erau.edu. *Department Chair,* Matt P Earnhardt, PhD, E-mail: Matthew.Earnhardt@erau.edu.

Department of Security and Emergency Services Students: 2 full-time (both women), 5 part-time (2 women); includes 27 minority (10 Black or African American, non-Hispanic/Latino; 3 Asian, non-Hispanic/Latino; 2 Hispanic/Latino; 12 Two or more races, non-Hispanic/Latino), 1 international. Average age 37. *Faculty:* 4 full-time (3 women), 5 part-time/adjunct (1 woman). *Expenses:* Contact institution. *Financial support:* Career-related internships or fieldwork and scholarships/grants available. Financial award applicants required to submit FAFSA. *Program availability:* Part-time, evening/weekend, 100% online, blended/hybrid learning, EagleVision Classroom (between classrooms), EagleVision Home (faculty and students at home), and a blend of Classroom or Home. Offers cybersecurity management and policy (MSCMP); human security and resilience (MSHSR). *Application deadline:* Applications are processed on a rolling basis. *Application fee:* $50. Electronic applications accepted. *Application Contact:* Worldwide Campus, 800-522-6787, E-mail: worldwide@erau.edu. *Department Chair,* Ronald Wakeham, E-mail: ronald.wakeham@erau.edu.

Department of Technology Management Students: 33 full-time (7 women), 44 part-time (12 women); includes 27 minority (12 Black or African American, non-Hispanic/Latino; 4 Asian, non-Hispanic/Latino; 5 Hispanic/Latino; 1 Native Hawaiian or other Pacific Islander, non-Hispanic/Latino; 5 Two or more races, non-Hispanic/Latino). Average age 36. *Faculty:* 6 full-time (3 women), 55 part-time/adjunct (15 women). *Expenses:* Contact institution. *Financial support:* Career-related internships or fieldwork and scholarships/grants available. Financial award applicants required to submit FAFSA. *Program availability:* Part-time, evening/weekend, 100% online, blended/hybrid learning, EagleVision is a virtual classroom that combines Web video conferencing and a learning management system. EagleVision Classroom (between classrooms), EagleVision Home (faculty and students at home), and a blend of Classroom or Home. Offers information security and assurance (MS); management information systems (MS). *Application deadline:* Applications are processed on a rolling basis. *Application fee:* $50. Electronic

applications accepted. *Department Chair,* Aaron Glassman, D.Mgt., E-mail: Aaron.Glassman@erau.edu.

EMERSON COLLEGE, Boston, MA 02116-4624

General Information Independent, coed, comprehensive institution. *Enrollment:* 4,431 graduate, professional, and undergraduate students; 584 full-time matriculated graduate/professional students (449 women), 64 part-time matriculated graduate/professional students (46 women). *Enrollment by degree level:* 648 master's. *Graduate faculty:* 382 full-time (253 women), 74 part-time/adjunct (41 women). *Graduate housing:* On-campus housing not available. *Student services:* Campus employment opportunities, campus safety program, career counseling, exercise/wellness program, free psychological counseling, grant writing training, international student services, low-cost health insurance, multicultural affairs office, services for students with disabilities, writing training. *Library facilities:* Iwasaki Library plus 1 other. *Collection:* Books: 336,669 (physical), 2,484 (digital/electronic); Serial titles: 67,760 (digital/electronic); Databases: 125. Weekly public service hours: 93; students can reserve study rooms.

Computer facilities: Computer purchase and lease plans are available. 480 computers available on campus for general student use. A campuswide network can be accessed from student residence rooms and from off campus. Online class registration is available.
Website: http://www.emerson.edu/
General Application Contact: Office of Graduate Admission, 617-824-8610, Fax: 617-824-8614, E-mail: gradapp@emerson.edu.

GRADUATE UNITS

Graduate Studies Students: 584 full-time (449 women), 64 part-time (46 women); includes 111 minority (28 Black or African American, non-Hispanic/Latino; 20 Asian, non-Hispanic/Latino; 45 Hispanic/Latino; 1 Native Hawaiian or other Pacific Islander, non-Hispanic/Latino; 17 Two or more races, non-Hispanic/Latino), 142 international. Average age 27. 1,348 applicants, 56% accepted, 284 enrolled. *Faculty:* 382 full-time (253 women), 74 part-time/adjunct (41 women). *Expenses:* Contact institution. *Financial support:* In 2016–17, 278 students received support, including 278 fellowships with partial tuition reimbursements available (averaging $8,649 per year); research assistantships with partial tuition reimbursements available, Federal Work-Study, scholarships/grants, and unspecified assistantships also available. Financial award application deadline: 3/1; financial award applicants required to submit FAFSA. In 2016, 312 master's awarded. *Program availability:* Part-time, evening/weekend. *Application deadline:* Applications are processed on a rolling basis. *Application fee:* $60 ($75 for international students). Electronic applications accepted. *Application Contact:* Leanda Ferland, Director of Graduate Admission, 617-824-8610, Fax: 617-824-8614, E-mail: gradapp@emerson.edu.

School of Communication Students: 262 full-time (223 women), 17 part-time (16 women); includes 42 minority (12 Black or African American, non-Hispanic/Latino; 12 Asian, non-Hispanic/Latino; 14 Hispanic/Latino; 4 Two or more races, non-Hispanic/Latino), 91 international. Average age 26. 809 applicants, 46% accepted, 133 enrolled. *Faculty:* 60 full-time (27 women), 27 part-time/adjunct (11 women). *Expenses:* Contact institution. *Financial support:* In 2016–17, 120 students received support, including 120 fellowships (averaging $6,936 per year); Federal Work-Study, scholarships/grants, and unspecified assistantships also available. Financial award application deadline: 3/1; financial award applicants required to submit FAFSA. In 2016, 172 master's awarded. Offers civic media: art and practice (MA); communication (MA, MS); communication disorders (MS); communication management (MA); global marketing communication and advertising (MA); integrated marketing communication (MA); journalism (MA). *Application deadline:* Applications are processed on a rolling basis. *Application fee:* $60 ($75 for international students). Electronic applications accepted. *Application Contact:* Leanda Ferland, Director of Graduate Admission, 617-824-8610, Fax: 617-824-8614, E-mail: gradapp@emerson.edu. *Interim Dean/Professor,* Phillip Glenn, 617-824-8739, E-mail: phillip_glenn@emerson.edu.

School of the Arts Students: 322 full-time (226 women), 47 part-time (30 women); includes 69 minority (16 Black or African American, non-Hispanic/Latino; 8 Asian, non-Hispanic/Latino; 31 Hispanic/Latino; 1 Native Hawaiian or other Pacific Islander, non-Hispanic/Latino; 13 Two or more races, non-Hispanic/Latino), 51 international. Average age 28. 539 applicants, 72% accepted, 151 enrolled. *Faculty:* 322 full-time (226 women), 47 part-time/adjunct (30 women). *Expenses:* Contact institution. *Financial support:* In 2016–17, 158 students received support, including 158 fellowships (averaging $10,362 per year); research assistantships, Federal Work-Study, scholarships/grants, and unspecified assistantships also available. Financial award application deadline: 3/1; financial award applicants required to submit FAFSA. In 2016, 140 master's awarded. *Program availability:* Part-time. Offers arts (MA, MFA); creative writing (MFA); media art (MFA); popular fiction writing and publishing (MFA); publishing and writing (MA); theatre education (MA); visual and media arts (MFA); writing for film and television (MFA). *Application deadline:* Applications are processed on a rolling basis. *Application fee:* $60 ($75 for international students). Electronic applications accepted. *Application Contact:* Leanda Ferland, Director of Graduate Admission, 617-824-8610, Fax: 617-824-8614, E-mail: gradapp@emerson.edu.

EMILY CARR UNIVERSITY OF ART + DESIGN, Vancouver, BC V6H 3R9, Canada

General Information Province-supported, coed, comprehensive institution. *Graduate housing:* On-campus housing not available. *Research affiliation:* Children's Hospital, Vancouver BC (health care research), Aldrich Pears and Associates (experience design), Kodak Communications Group (interaction design), Donat Group (e-learning), Paperny Films (television and film production), Fuel Cell Research Centre, National Research Council (clean technology).

GRADUATE UNITS

Program in Applied Arts Offers design (M Des); media arts (MAA); visual arts (MAA). Electronic applications accepted.
Program in Digital Media Offers digital media (MDM). Electronic applications accepted.

EMMANUEL COLLEGE, Boston, MA 02115

General Information Independent-religious, coed, comprehensive institution. *Enrollment:* 2,190 graduate, professional, and undergraduate students; 13 full-time matriculated graduate/professional students (7 women), 136 part-time matriculated graduate/professional students (110 women). *Enrollment by degree level:* 142 master's, 7 other advanced degrees. *Graduate faculty:* 6 full-time (all women), 24 part-time/adjunct (12 women). *Graduate housing:* On-campus housing not available. *Student services:* Campus safety program, career counseling, exercise/wellness program, multicultural affairs office, services for students with disabilities, writing training. *Library facilities:* Cardinal Cushing Library. *Collection:* Books: 93,952 (physical), 216,096 (digital/electronic); Serial titles: 228 (physical), 5,592 (digital/electronic); Databases: 68. Weekly public service hours: 106; students can reserve study rooms.

Computer facilities: 284 computers available on campus for general student use. A campuswide network can be accessed from student residence rooms. Online class registration is available.
Website: http://www.emmanuel.edu/

General Application Contact: Helen Muterperl, Associate Director of Admissions, Graduate and Professional Programs, 617-735-9700, Fax: 617-507-0434, E-mail: gpp@emmanuel.edu.

GRADUATE UNITS

Graduate and Professional Programs Students: 13 full-time (7 women), 136 part-time (110 women); includes 44 minority (23 Black or African American, non-Hispanic/Latino; 7 Asian, non-Hispanic/Latino; 13 Hispanic/Latino; 1 Two or more races, non-Hispanic/Latino). Average age 35. 110 applicants, 37% accepted, 27 enrolled. *Faculty:* 6 full-time (all women), 24 part-time/adjunct (12 women). Expenses: Contact institution. *Financial support:* Application deadline: 2/15; applicants required to submit FAFSA. In 2016, 93 master's, 27 other advanced degrees awarded. *Program availability:* Part-time, evening/weekend, blended/hybrid learning. Offers education (M Ed); human resource management (MS, Graduate Certificate); management (MSM, MSN, Graduate Certificate); management and leadership (Graduate Certificate); research administration (MSM, Graduate Certificate). *Application deadline:* Applications are processed on a rolling basis. Electronic applications accepted. *Application Contact:* Helen Muterperl, Associate Director of Admissions, Graduate and Professional Programs, 617-735-9700, Fax: 617-507-0434, E-mail: gpp@emmanuel.edu. *Executive Director, Graduate and Professional Programs,* Petia Whitmore, 617-732-1740, E-mail: gpp@emmanuel.edu.

EMORY & HENRY COLLEGE, Emory, VA 24327-0947

General Information Independent-religious, coed, comprehensive institution. *Graduate housing:* Room and/or apartments available on a first-come, first-served basis to single students; on-campus housing not available to married students.

GRADUATE UNITS

Graduate Programs *Program availability:* Part-time, evening/weekend. Offers American history (MA Ed); organizational leadership (MCOL); professional studies (M Ed); reading specialist (MA Ed).

EMORY UNIVERSITY, Atlanta, GA 30322-1100

General Information Independent-religious, coed, university. CGS member. *Graduate housing:* Rooms and/or apartments available on a first-come, first-served basis to single and married students. *Research affiliation:* Bill and Melinda Gates Foundation, Children's Pediatric Research Trust, International AIDS Vaccine Initiative, Garden City Group, Georgia Cancer Coalition, The Wistar Institute.

GRADUATE UNITS

Candler School of Theology *Program availability:* Part-time. Offers formation and witness (M Div); history, scripture and tradition (MTS); leadership in church and community (M Div); modern religious thought and experience (MTS); pastoral counseling (Th D); religion and race (M Div); religion, health and science (M Div); scripture and interpretation (M Div); society and personality (M Div); theology (Th M); theology and ethics (M Div); theology and the arts (M Div); traditions of the church (M Div); women and religion (M Div). Electronic applications accepted.

Goizueta Business School Students: 540 full-time (157 women), 265 part-time (80 women); includes 221 minority (73 Black or African American, non-Hispanic/Latino; 3 American Indian or Alaska Native, non-Hispanic/Latino; 91 Asian, non-Hispanic/Latino; 45 Hispanic/Latino; 2 Native Hawaiian or other Pacific Islander, non-Hispanic/Latino; 7 Two or more races, non-Hispanic/Latino), 189 international. Average age 32. 1,945 applicants, 37% accepted, 354 enrolled. *Faculty:* 73 full-time (17 women), 18 part-time/adjunct (5 women). Expenses: Contact institution. *Financial support:* Fellowships with full tuition reimbursements, research assistantships, teaching assistantships, career-related internships or fieldwork, Federal Work-Study, institutionally sponsored loans, and scholarships/grants available. Support available to part-time students. Financial award application deadline: 4/1; financial award applicants required to submit FAFSA. *Program availability:* Part-time, evening/weekend. Offers accounting (MBA, PhD); alternative investments (MBA); business (MBA, PhD); business administration (MBA); business process consulting (MBA); business technology management (MBA); capital markets (MBA); corporate finance (MBA); customer relationship management (MBA); decision analytics (MBA); entrepreneurship (MBA); finance (MBA, PhD); global management (MBA); information systems and operations management (PhD); investment banking (MBA); management consulting (MBA); marketing (MBA, PhD); marketing analytics (MBA); marketing consulting (MBA); operations management (MBA); organization and management (MBA, PhD); product and brand management (MBA); real estate (MBA); social enterprise (MBA); strategy consulting (MBA). *Application deadline:* For fall admission, 10/5 for domestic and international students; for winter admission, 11/30 for domestic and international students; for spring admission, 1/18 for domestic and international students. Applications are processed on a rolling basis. Electronic applications accepted. *Dean,* Erika H. James, 404-727-6377, Fax: 404-727-0868.

Laney Graduate School Offers anthropology (PhD); art history (PhD); biophysics (PhD); chemistry (PhD); choral conducting (MM, MSM); clinical psychology (PhD); clinical research (MS); cognition and development (PhD); comparative literature (PhD, Certificate); computer science (MS); computer science and informatics (PhD); development practice (MDP); economics (PhD); English (PhD, Graduate Certificate); experimental condensed matter physics (PhD); film studies (MA); French (PhD); French and educational studies (PhD); history (PhD); mathematics (MS, PhD); neuroscience and animal behavior (PhD); nursing (PhD); organ performance (MM, MSM); philosophy (PhD); political science (PhD); psychoanalytic studies (PhD); sociology (PhD); Spanish (PhD); theoretical and computational statistical physics (PhD); women's studies (Certificate); women's, gender, and sexuality studies (PhD). Electronic applications accepted.

Division of Biological and Biomedical Sciences Offers biochemistry, cell and developmental biology (PhD); biological and biomedical sciences (PhD); cancer biology (PhD); genetics and molecular biology (PhD); immunology and molecular pathogenesis (PhD); microbiology and molecular genetics (PhD); molecular and systems pharmacology (PhD); neuroscience (PhD); nutrition and health sciences (PhD); population biology, ecology and evolution (PhD). Electronic applications accepted.

Division of Educational Studies Offers educational studies (MA, PhD); middle grades teaching (MAT); secondary teaching (MAT). Electronic applications accepted.

Division of Religion Offers religion (PhD). Electronic applications accepted.

Emory Center for Ethics Offers bioethics (MA). Electronic applications accepted.

Graduate Institute of the Liberal Arts Offers liberal arts (PhD). Electronic applications accepted.

Nell Hodgson Woodruff School of Nursing *Program availability:* Part-time. Offers adult nurse practitioner (MSN); emergency nurse practitioner (MSN); family nurse practitioner (MSN); family nurse-midwife (MSN); health systems leadership (MSN); nurse-midwifery (MSN); pediatric nurse practitioner acute and primary care (MSN); women's health care (Title X) (MSN); women's health nurse practitioner (MSN). Electronic applications accepted.

Rollins School of Public Health *Program availability:* Part-time, evening/weekend, online learning. Offers applied epidemiology (MPH); applied public health informatics (MPH); behavioral sciences and health education (MPH, PhD); bioinformatics (PhD); biostatistics (MPH, MSPH); environmental health (MPH); environmental health and epidemiology (MSPH); environmental health sciences (PhD); epidemiology (MPH, MSPH, PhD); global environmental health (MPH); global health (MPH); health policy (MPH); health policy research (MSPH); health services management (MPH); health services research and health policy (PhD); prevention science (MPH); public health (MPH, MSPH, PhD); public health informatics (MSPH); public nutrition (MSPH). Electronic applications accepted.

School of Law Offers law (LL M, JD, Certificate). Electronic applications accepted.

School of Medicine Offers anesthesiology assistant (MM Sc); genetic counseling (MM Sc); medicine (MM Sc, DPT, MD); physical therapy (DPT); physician assistant (MM Sc). Electronic applications accepted.

EMPEROR'S COLLEGE OF TRADITIONAL ORIENTAL MEDICINE, Santa Monica, CA 90403

General Information Private, coed, graduate-only institution. *Graduate housing:* On-campus housing not available. *Research affiliation:* Lotus Herbs (herbs), LA Free Clinic (herbs), UCLA Ashe Center (student health).

GRADUATE UNITS

Graduate Programs *Program availability:* Part-time, evening/weekend. Offers oriental medicine (MTOM, DAOM).

EMPIRE COLLEGE, Santa Rosa, CA 95403

General Information Proprietary, coed.

GRADUATE UNITS

School of Law Offers law (MLS, JD).

EMPORIA STATE UNIVERSITY, Emporia, KS 66801-5415

General Information State-supported, coed, comprehensive institution. CGS member. *Enrollment:* 5,887 graduate, professional, and undergraduate students; 447 full-time matriculated graduate/professional students (286 women), 1,444 part-time matriculated graduate/professional students (1,003 women). *Enrollment by degree level:* 1,869 master's, 22 doctoral. *Graduate faculty:* 208 full-time (90 women), 16 part-time/adjunct (11 women). Tuition, state resident: full-time $5922; part-time $246.75 per credit hour. Tuition, nonresident: full-time $18,414; part-time $767.25 per credit hour. *Required fees:* $1884; $78.50 per credit hour. *Graduate housing:* Room and/or apartments available on a first-come, first-served basis to single students; on-campus housing not available to married students. *Typical cost:* $4836 per year ($8391 including board). Room and board charges vary according to board plan and housing facility selected. Housing application deadline: 8/1. *Student services:* Campus employment opportunities, campus safety program, career counseling, child daycare facilities, exercise/wellness program, free psychological counseling, grant writing training, international student services, low-cost health insurance, multicultural affairs office, services for students with disabilities, teacher training, writing training. *Library facilities:* William Allen White Library plus 1 other. *Collection:* Books: 389,595 (physical), 153,016 (digital/electronic); Serial titles: 35,153 (physical), 278 (digital/electronic); Databases: 97. Weekly public service hours: 79; study areas open 24 hours a week; 5–7 days a week; students can reserve study rooms.

Computer facilities: 410 computers available on campus for general student use. A campuswide network can be accessed from student residence rooms and from off campus. Online class registration is available.
Website: http://www.emporia.edu/

General Application Contact: April Huddleston, Recruitment and Development Specialist, 800-950-GRAD, Fax: 620-341-5909, E-mail: ahuddles@emporia.edu.

GRADUATE UNITS

Department of Biological Sciences Students: 21 full-time (11 women), 16 part-time (8 women); includes 2 minority (1 Hispanic/Latino; 1 Two or more races, non-Hispanic/Latino), 24 international. 33 applicants, 91% accepted, 11 enrolled. *Faculty:* 14 full-time (3 women), 1 part-time/adjunct (0 women). Expenses: Contact institution. *Financial support:* In 2016–17, 5 research assistantships with full tuition reimbursements (averaging $7,344 per year), 10 teaching assistantships with full tuition reimbursements (averaging $7,844 per year) were awarded; career-related internships or fieldwork, Federal Work-Study, institutionally sponsored loans, health care benefits, and unspecified assistantships also available. Financial award application deadline: 3/15; financial award applicants required to submit FAFSA. In 2016, 9 master's awarded. *Program availability:* Part-time. Offers botany (MS); environmental biology (MS); forensic science (MS); general biology (MS); microbial and molecular biology (MS); zoology (MS). *Application deadline:* For fall admission, 8/15 priority date for domestic students. Applications are processed on a rolling basis. *Application fee:* $30 ($75 for international students). Electronic applications accepted. *Chair,* Dr. Yixin Eric Yang, 620-341-5311, Fax: 620-341-5608, E-mail: yyang@emporia.edu.

Department of Health, Physical Education and Recreation Students: 25 full-time (9 women), 168 part-time (69 women); includes 11 minority (6 Black or African American, non-Hispanic/Latino; 1 Asian, non-Hispanic/Latino; 3 Hispanic/Latino; 1 Two or more races, non-Hispanic/Latino). 54 applicants, 33 enrolled. *Faculty:* 17 full-time (10 women), 2 part-time/adjunct (both women). Expenses: Contact institution. *Financial support:* In 2016–17, 3 research assistantships with full tuition reimbursements (averaging $7,353 per year), 10 teaching assistantships with full tuition reimbursements (averaging $7,353 per year) were awarded; career-related internships or fieldwork, Federal Work-Study, institutionally sponsored loans, health care benefits, and unspecified assistantships also available. Financial award application deadline: 3/15; financial award applicants required to submit FAFSA. In 2016, 110 master's awarded. *Program availability:* Part-time, 100% online. Offers health, physical education and recreation (MS). *Application deadline:* For fall admission, 8/15 priority date for domestic students. Applications are processed on a rolling basis. *Application fee:* $30 ($75 for international students). Electronic applications accepted. *Application Contact:* Mary Sewell, Admissions Coordinator, 800-950-GRAD, Fax: 620-341-5909, E-mail: msewell@emporia.edu. *Chair,* Dr. Shawna Shane, 620-341-5848, E-mail: sshane@emporia.edu.

Department of Instructional Design and Technology Students: 34 full-time (16 women), 53 part-time (41 women); includes 9 minority (5 Black or African American, non-Hispanic/Latino; 2 Asian, non-Hispanic/Latino; 1 Hispanic/Latino; 1 Two or more races, non-Hispanic/Latino; 29 international. 40 applicants, 98% accepted, 17 enrolled. *Faculty:* 7 full-time (3 women). Expenses: Contact institution. *Financial support:* In 2016–17, 11 teaching assistantships with full tuition reimbursements (averaging $7,344 per year) were awarded; Federal Work-Study, institutionally sponsored loans, health care benefits, and unspecified assistantships also available. Financial award application deadline: 3/15; financial award applicants required to submit FAFSA. In 2016, 42 master's awarded. *Program availability:* Part-time, online only, 100% online. Offers instructional design and technology (MS). *Application deadline:* For fall admission, 8/15 priority date for domestic students. Applications are processed on a rolling basis. *Application fee:* $30 ($75 for international students). Electronic applications accepted. *Application Contact:* Mary Sewell, Admissions Coordinator, 800-950-GRAD, Fax: 620-341-5909, E-mail: msewell@emporia.edu. *Chair,* Dr. Zeni Colorado, 620-341-5477, E-mail: jcolorad@emporia.edu.

Department of Mathematics and Economics Students: 15 full-time (6 women), 112 part-time (56 women); includes 11 minority (2 Black or African American, non-Hispanic/Latino; 1 Asian, non-Hispanic/Latino; 5 Hispanic/Latino; 1 Native Hawaiian or other Pacific Islander, non-Hispanic/Latino; 2 Two or more races, non-Hispanic/Latino), 12 international. 62 applicants, 24% accepted, 18 enrolled. *Faculty:* 15 full-time (4 women). Expenses: Contact institution. *Financial support:* In 2016–17, 4 teaching assistantships with full tuition reimbursements (averaging $7,844 per year) were awarded; research assistantships, career-related internships or fieldwork, Federal Work-Study, institutionally sponsored loans, health care benefits, and unspecified assistantships also available. Financial award application deadline: 3/15; financial award applicants required to submit FAFSA. In 2016, 16 master's awarded. *Program availability:* Part-time, evening/weekend, online only, 100% online. Offers mathematics (MS). *Application deadline:* For fall admission, 8/15 priority date for domestic students. Applications are processed on a rolling basis. *Application fee:* $30 ($75 for international students). Electronic applications accepted. *Application Contact:* Mary Sewell, Admissions Coordinator, 800-950-GRAD, Fax: 620-341-5909, E-mail: msewell@emporia.edu. *Chair,* Dr. Brian Hollenbeck, 620-341-5281, Fax: 620-341-6055, E-mail: bhollenb@emporia.edu.

Department of Music Students: 9 full-time (5 women), 3 part-time (1 woman); includes 1 minority (Black or African American, non-Hispanic/Latino), 6 international. 11 applicants, 100% accepted, 7 enrolled. *Faculty:* 12 full-time (3 women), 4 part-time/adjunct (all women). Expenses: Contact institution. *Financial support:* In 2016–17, 5 teaching assistantships with full tuition reimbursements (averaging $7,344 per year) were awarded; Federal Work-Study, institutionally sponsored loans, health care benefits, and unspecified assistantships also available. Financial award application deadline: 3/15; financial award applicants required to submit FAFSA. In 2016, 6 master's awarded. *Program availability:* Part-time. Offers music (MM). *Application deadline:* For fall admission, 8/15 priority date for domestic students. Applications are processed on a rolling basis. *Application fee:* $30 ($75 for international students). Electronic applications accepted. *Application Contact:* Dr. Andrew Houchins, Graduate Coordinator, 620-341-6089, E-mail: ahouchin@emporia.edu. *Chair,* Dr. Allan D. Comstock, 620-341-5431, E-mail: acomstoc@emporia.edu.

Department of Physical Sciences Students: 37 full-time (21 women), 19 part-time (11 women); includes 9 minority (1 Black or African American, non-Hispanic/Latino; 1 Hispanic/Latino; 7 Two or more races, non-Hispanic/Latino), 20 international. 41 applicants, 93% accepted, 17 enrolled. *Faculty:* 15 full-time (5 women), 1 part-time/adjunct (0 women). Expenses: Contact institution. *Financial support:* In 2016–17, 1 research assistantship with full tuition reimbursement (averaging $7,344 per year), 5 teaching assistantships with full tuition reimbursements (averaging $7,844 per year) were awarded; Federal Work-Study, institutionally sponsored loans, health care benefits, and unspecified assistantships also available. Financial award application deadline: 3/15; financial award applicants required to submit FAFSA. In 2016, 12 master's, 2 other advanced degrees awarded. *Program availability:* Part-time, online learning. Offers forensic science (MS); geospatial analysis (Postbaccalaureate Certificate); physical science (MS). *Application deadline:* For fall admission, 8/15 priority date for domestic students. Applications are processed on a rolling basis. *Application fee:* $30 ($75 for international students). Electronic applications accepted. *Application Contact:* Mary Sewell, Admissions Coordinator, 800-950-GRAD, Fax: 620-341-5909, E-mail: msewell@emporia.edu. *Chair,* Dr. Kim Simons, 620-341-5330, Fax: 620-341-6055, E-mail: ksimons@emporia.edu.

Program in Accountancy Students: 17 full-time (12 women), 22 part-time (13 women); includes 3 minority (1 American Indian or Alaska Native, non-Hispanic/Latino; 2 Hispanic/Latino), 11 international. 20 applicants, 95% accepted, 6 enrolled. *Faculty:* 30 full-time (5 women). Expenses: Contact institution. *Financial support:* In 2016–17, 3 research assistantships with full tuition reimbursements (averaging $7,353 per year), 3 teaching assistantships with full tuition reimbursements (averaging $7,335 per year) were awarded; unspecified assistantships also available. Financial award applicants required to submit FAFSA. In 2016, 11 master's awarded. *Program availability:* Part-time, 100% online, blended/hybrid learning. Offers accountancy (M Acc). *Application deadline:* Applications are processed on a rolling basis. *Application fee:* $40. Electronic applications accepted. *Application Contact:* April Huddleston, Recruitment and Development Specialist, 800-950-GRAD, Fax: 620-341-5909, E-mail: ahuddles@emporia.edu. *Chair of the Faculty,* Dr. Shawn Keough, 620-341-5408, E-mail: skeough@emporia.edu.

Program in Art Therapy Students: 30 full-time (27 women), 4 part-time (all women); includes 4 minority (1 American Indian or Alaska Native, non-Hispanic/Latino; 2 Hispanic/Latino; 1 Two or more races, non-Hispanic/Latino). 36 applicants, 83% accepted, 13 enrolled. *Faculty:* 11 full-time (7 women), 1 (woman) part-time/adjunct. Expenses: Contact institution. *Financial support:* In 2016–17, 7 research assistantships with full tuition reimbursements (averaging $7,353 per year), 4 teaching assistantships with full tuition reimbursements (averaging $7,335 per year) were awarded; career-related internships or fieldwork, Federal Work-Study, institutionally sponsored loans, health care benefits, and unspecified assistantships also available. Financial award application deadline: 3/15; financial award applicants required to submit FAFSA. In 2016, 12 master's awarded. *Program availability:* Part-time. Offers art therapy (MS). *Application deadline:* For fall admission, 6/1 for domestic students; for spring admission, 10/1 for domestic students. Applications are processed on a rolling basis. *Application fee:* $30 ($75 for international students). Electronic applications accepted. *Application Contact:* Mary Sewell, Admissions Coordinator, 800-950-GRAD, Fax: 620-341-5909, E-mail: msewell@emporia.edu. *Interim Chair,* Dr. Katrina Miller, 620-341-5231, E-mail: kmille12@emporia.edu.

Program in Business Administration Students: 51 full-time (19 women), 48 part-time (27 women); includes 6 minority (1 Black or African American, non-Hispanic/Latino; 1 Asian, non-Hispanic/Latino; 2 Hispanic/Latino; 2 Two or more races, non-Hispanic/Latino), 36 international. 64 applicants, 92% accepted, 14 enrolled. *Faculty:* 30 full-time (5 women). Expenses: Contact institution. *Financial support:* In 2016–17, 8 research assistantships with full tuition reimbursements (averaging $7,344 per year), 10 teaching assistantships with full tuition reimbursements (averaging $7,344 per year) were awarded; career-related internships or fieldwork, health care benefits, and unspecified assistantships also available. Financial award applicants required to submit FAFSA. In 2016, 30 master's awarded. *Program availability:* Part-time, evening/weekend, blended/hybrid learning. Offers business administration (MBA). *Application deadline:* For fall admission, 8/15 for domestic students. Applications are processed on a rolling basis. *Application fee:* $30 ($75 for international students). Electronic applications accepted. *Application Contact:* Mary Sewell, Admissions Coordinator, 800-950-GRAD, Fax: 620-341-5909, E-mail: msewell@emporia.edu. *Coordinator, Graduate and Career Services,* James Willingham, 620-341-5456, E-mail: jwilling@emporia.edu.

Program in Business Education Students: 1 full-time (0 women), 10 part-time (8 women); includes 1 minority (Asian, non-Hispanic/Latino). 9 applicants, 100% accepted, 3 enrolled. *Faculty:* 30 full-time (5 women). Expenses: Contact institution. *Financial support:* Career-related internships or fieldwork, institutionally sponsored loans, health care benefits, and unspecified assistantships available. Financial award application deadline: 3/15; financial award applicants required to submit FAFSA. In 2016, 9 master's awarded. *Program availability:* Part-time, evening/weekend, online learning. Offers business education (MS). *Application deadline:* For fall admission, 8/15 priority date for domestic students. Applications are processed on a rolling basis. *Application fee:* $30 ($75 for international students). Electronic applications accepted. *Coordinator, Graduate and Career Services,* James Willingham, 620-341-5456, E-mail: jwilling@emporia.edu.

Program in Clinical Counseling Students: 27 full-time (20 women), 10 part-time (all women); includes 7 minority (5 Black or African American, non-Hispanic/Latino; 2 Asian, non-Hispanic/Latino), 1 international. 38 applicants, 95% accepted, 10 enrolled. *Faculty:* 11 full-time (7 women), 1 (woman) part-time/adjunct. Expenses: Contact institution. *Financial support:* In 2016–17, 9 research assistantships with full tuition reimbursements (averaging $7,344 per year) were awarded; Federal Work-Study, institutionally sponsored loans, health care benefits, and unspecified assistantships also available. Financial award application deadline: 3/15; financial award applicants required to submit FAFSA. In 2016, 16 master's awarded. *Program availability:* Part-time. Offers clinical counseling (MS). *Application deadline:* For fall admission, 8/15 for domestic students. Applications are processed on a rolling basis. *Application fee:* $30 ($75 for international students). Electronic applications accepted. *Application Contact:* Mary Sewell, Admissions Coordinator, 800-950-GRAD, Fax: 620-341-5909, E-mail: msewell@emporia.edu. *Interim Chair,* Dr. Katrina Miller, 620-341-5791, E-mail: kmille12@emporia.edu.

Program in Clinical Psychology Students: 24 full-time (19 women), 5 part-time (4 women); includes 2 minority (both Hispanic/Latino), 2 international. 37 applicants, 89% accepted, 7 enrolled. *Faculty:* 8 full-time (4 women). Expenses: Contact institution. *Financial support:* In 2016–17, 3 research assistantships with full tuition reimbursements, 7 teaching assistantships with full tuition reimbursements were awarded; career-related internships or fieldwork, Federal Work-Study, institutionally sponsored loans, health care benefits, and unspecified assistantships also available. Support available to part-time students. Financial award application deadline: 3/15; financial award applicants required to submit FAFSA. In 2016, 7 master's awarded. *Program availability:* Part-time. Offers clinical psychology (MS). *Application deadline:* For fall admission, 8/15 for domestic students. Applications are processed on a rolling basis. *Application fee:* $30 ($75 for international students). Electronic applications accepted. *Application Contact:* Mary Sewell, Admissions Coordinator, 800-950-GRAD, Fax: 620-341-5909, E-mail: msewell@emporia.edu. *Chair,* Dr. Jim Persinger, 620-341-5317, E-mail: jpersing@emporia.edu.

Program in Curriculum and Instruction Students: 7 full-time (all women), 134 part-time (123 women); includes 6 minority (1 Black or African American, non-Hispanic/Latino; 1 American Indian or Alaska Native, non-Hispanic/Latino; 3 Hispanic/Latino; 1 Two or more races, non-Hispanic/Latino). 35 applicants, 100% accepted, 32 enrolled. *Faculty:* 10 full-time (3 women). Expenses: Contact institution. *Financial support:* Career-related internships or fieldwork, Federal Work-Study, institutionally sponsored loans, health care benefits, and unspecified assistantships available. Financial award application deadline: 3/15; financial award applicants required to submit FAFSA. In 2016, 57 master's awarded. *Program availability:* Part-time, online only, 100% online. Offers curriculum leadership (MS); effective practitioner (MS); national board certification (MS). *Application deadline:* For fall admission, 8/15 priority date for domestic students. Applications are processed on a rolling basis. *Application fee:* $30 ($75 for international students). Electronic applications accepted. *Application Contact:* Mary Sewell, Admissions Coordinator, 800-950-GRAD, Fax: 620-341-5909, E-mail: msewell@emporia.edu. *Chair,* Dr. Daniel Stiffler, 620-341-5776, E-mail: dstiffle@emporia.edu.

Program in Early Childhood Education Students: 2 full-time (both women), 52 part-time (50 women); includes 5 minority (all Hispanic/Latino). 13 applicants, 100% accepted, 9 enrolled. *Faculty:* 29 full-time (21 women), 3 part-time/adjunct (2 women). Expenses: Contact institution. *Financial support:* Federal Work-Study, institutionally sponsored loans, health care benefits, and unspecified assistantships available. Financial award application deadline: 3/15; financial award applicants required to submit FAFSA. In 2016, 14 master's awarded. *Program availability:* Part-time, online learning. Offers early childhood education (MS). *Application deadline:* For fall admission, 8/15 priority date for domestic students. Applications are processed on a rolling basis. *Application fee:* $30 ($75 for international students). Electronic applications accepted. *Application Contact:* Mary Sewell, Admissions Coordinator, 800-950-GRAD, Fax: 620-341-5909, E-mail: msewell@emporia.edu. *Chair,* Dr. Matt Siemears, 620-341-6057, E-mail: mseimear@emporia.edu.

Program in Educational Administration Students: 5 full-time (4 women), 1 part-time (45 women); includes 7 minority (4 Black or African American, non-Hispanic/Latino; 1 Asian, non-Hispanic/Latino; 1 Hispanic/Latino; 1 Two or more races, non-Hispanic/Latino). 28 applicants, 100% accepted, 11 enrolled. *Faculty:* 18 full-time (3 women). Expenses: Contact institution. *Financial support:* Career-related internships or fieldwork, Federal Work-Study, institutionally sponsored loans, health care benefits, and unspecified assistantships available. Financial award application deadline: 3/15; financial award applicants required to submit FAFSA. In 2016, 61 master's awarded. *Program availability:* Part-time. Offers elementary administration (MS); elementary/secondary administration (MS); secondary administration (MS). *Application deadline:* For fall admission, 8/15 priority date for domestic students. Applications are processed on a rolling basis. *Application fee:* $30 ($75 for international students). Electronic applications accepted. *Application Contact:* Mary Sewell, Admissions Coordinator, 800-950-GRAD, Fax: 620-341-5909, E-mail: msewell@emporia.edu. *Chair,* Dr. Daniel Stiffler, 620-341-5776, E-mail: dstiffle@emporia.edu.

Program in English Students: 19 full-time (10 women), 18 part-time (11 women), 8 international. 20 applicants, 100% accepted, 6 enrolled. *Faculty:* 18 full-time (10 women), 4 part-time/adjunct (3 women). Expenses: Contact institution. *Financial* *support:* In 2016–17, 1 research assistantship with full tuition reimbursement (averaging $7,353 per year), 10 teaching assistantships with full tuition reimbursements (averaging $8,244 per year) were awarded; Federal Work-Study, health care benefits, and unspecified assistantships also available. Financial award application deadline: 2/15; financial award applicants required to submit FAFSA. In 2016, 7 master's awarded. *Program availability:* Part-time. Offers English (MA). *Application deadline:* For fall admission, 8/15 for domestic students. *Application fee:* $30 ($75 for international students). *Application Contact:* Mary Sewell, Admissions Coordinator, 800-950-GRAD, Fax: 620-341-5909, E-mail: msewell@emporia.edu. *Chair,* Dr. Kevin Rabas, 620-341-5216, E-mail: krabas@emporia.edu.

Program in Forensic Science Students: 28 full-time (18 women); includes 3 minority (1 Black or African American, non-Hispanic/Latino; 1 Hispanic/Latino; 1 Two or more races, non-Hispanic/Latino), 7 international. 19 applicants, 95% accepted, 9 enrolled. *Faculty:* 15 full-time (5 women), 1 part-time/adjunct (0 women). Expenses: Contact institution. *Financial support:* In 2016–17, 4 research assistantships (averaging $7,353 per year), 6 teaching assistantships with full tuition reimbursements (averaging $7,335 per year) were awarded; unspecified assistantships also available. Financial award applicants required to submit FAFSA. *Program availability:* Part-time. Offers forensic science (MS). *Application deadline:* For fall admission, 4/15 for domestic students. Applications are processed on a rolling basis. *Application fee:* $40. Electronic applications accepted. *Application Contact:* April Huddleston, Recruitment and Development Specialist, 800-950-GRAD, Fax: 620-341-5909, E-mail: ahuddles@emporia.edu. *Interim Director,* Dr. Melissa M. Bailey, 620-341-5619, E-mail: mbailey4@emporia.edu.

Program in History Students: 8 full-time (2 women), 17 part-time (9 women); includes 3 minority (1 Black or African American, non-Hispanic/Latino; 2 Two or more races, non-Hispanic/Latino). 10 applicants, 90% accepted, 5 enrolled. *Faculty:* 13 full-time (6 women), 1 part-time/adjunct (0 women). Expenses: Contact institution. *Financial support:* In 2016–17, 1 research assistantship with full tuition reimbursement (averaging $7,344 per year), 6 teaching assistantships with full tuition reimbursements (averaging $7,344 per year) were awarded; Federal Work-Study, institutionally sponsored loans, health care benefits, and unspecified assistantships also available. Financial award application deadline: 3/15; financial award applicants required to submit FAFSA. In 2016, 4 master's awarded. *Program availability:* Part-time. Offers American history (MA); world history (MA). *Application deadline:* For fall admission, 8/15 priority date for domestic students. Applications are processed on a rolling basis. *Application fee:* $30 ($75 for international students). Electronic applications accepted. *Chair,* Dr. Michael Smith, 620-341-5566, E-mail: msmith3@emporia.edu.

Program in Informatics Students: 6 part-time (5 women); includes 2 minority (both Black or African American, non-Hispanic/Latino). 5 applicants, 100% accepted. *Faculty:* 9 full-time (6 women). Expenses: Contact institution. *Program availability:* Part-time, 100% online. Offers nursing (MS). *Application deadline:* Applications are processed on a rolling basis. *Application fee:* $40. Electronic applications accepted. *Application Contact:* April Huddleston, Recruitment and Development Specialist, 800-950-GRAD, Fax: 620-341-5909, E-mail: ahuddles@emporia.edu. *Interim Dean,* Dr. Mirah Dow, 620-341-5203, E-mail: mdow@emporia.edu.

Program in Instructional Specialist Students: 7 full-time (all women), 65 part-time (58 women). 23 applicants, 100% accepted, 16 enrolled. *Faculty:* 29 full-time (21 women), 3 part-time/adjunct (2 women). Expenses: Contact institution. *Financial support:* Federal Work-Study, institutionally sponsored loans, health care benefits, and unspecified assistantships available. Financial award application deadline: 3/15; financial award applicants required to submit FAFSA. In 2016, 27 master's awarded. *Program availability:* Part-time. Offers elementary subject matter (MS); reading (MS). *Application deadline:* For fall admission, 8/15 priority date for domestic students. Applications are processed on a rolling basis. *Application fee:* $30 ($75 for international students). Electronic applications accepted. *Application Contact:* Mary Sewell, Admissions Coordinator, 800-950-GRAD, Fax: 620-341-5909, E-mail: msewell@emporia.edu. *Chair,* Dr. Matt Siemears, 620-341-6057, E-mail: msiemear@emporia.edu.

Program in Psychology Students: 10 full-time (7 women), 9 part-time (6 women); includes 2 minority (both Black or African American, non-Hispanic/Latino), 2 international. 16 applicants, 94% accepted, 4 enrolled. *Faculty:* 8 full-time (4 women). Expenses: Contact institution. *Financial support:* In 2016–17, 8 research assistantships with full tuition reimbursements (averaging $7,353 per year), 4 teaching assistantships with full tuition reimbursements (averaging $7,344 per year) were awarded; career-related internships or fieldwork, Federal Work-Study, institutionally sponsored loans, health care benefits, and unspecified assistantships also available. Financial award application deadline: 3/15; financial award applicants required to submit FAFSA. In 2016, 8 master's awarded. *Program availability:* Part-time. Offers general psychology (MS); industrial/organizational psychology (MS). *Application deadline:* For fall admission, 6/1 priority date for domestic students; for spring admission, 10/1 for domestic students. Applications are processed on a rolling basis. *Application fee:* $30 ($75 for international students). Electronic applications accepted. *Application Contact:* Mary Sewell, Admissions Coordinator, 800-950-GRAD, Fax: 620-341-5909, E-mail: msewell@emporia.edu. *Chair,* Dr. Jim Persinger, 620-341-5317, E-mail: jpersing@emporia.edu.

Program in Rehabilitation Counseling Students: 17 full-time (all women), 7 part-time (5 women); includes 3 minority (1 Black or African American, non-Hispanic/Latino; 1 American Indian or Alaska Native, non-Hispanic/Latino; 1 Asian, non-Hispanic/Latino). 3 applicants, 100% accepted, 1 enrolled. *Faculty:* 11 full-time (7 women). Expenses: Contact institution. *Financial support:* Career-related internships or fieldwork, Federal Work-Study, institutionally sponsored loans, health care benefits, and unspecified assistantships available. Financial award application deadline: 3/15; financial award applicants required to submit FAFSA. In 2016, 3 master's awarded. *Program availability:* Part-time. Offers rehabilitation counseling (MS). *Application deadline:* For fall admission, 8/15 priority date for domestic students. Applications are processed on a rolling basis. *Application fee:* $30 ($75 for international students). Electronic applications accepted. *Application Contact:* Mary Sewell, Admissions Coordinator, 800-950-GRAD, Fax: 620-341-5909, E-mail: msewell@emporia.edu. *Chair/Graduate Co-Coordinator,* Dr. Katrina Miller, 620-341-5791, E-mail: kmille12@emporia.edu.

Program in School Counseling Students: 24 full-time (21 women), 77 part-time (68 women); includes 7 minority (1 Black or African American, non-Hispanic/Latino; 1 Asian, non-Hispanic/Latino; 4 Hispanic/Latino; 1 Two or more races, non-Hispanic/Latino), 1 international. 25 applicants, 100% accepted, 8 enrolled. *Faculty:* 11 full-time (7 women), 1 (woman) part-time/adjunct. Expenses: Contact institution. *Financial support:* In 2016–17, 4 research assistantships with full tuition reimbursements (averaging $7,353 per year), 1 teaching assistantship with full tuition reimbursement (averaging $7,335 per year) were awarded; career-related internships or fieldwork, Federal Work-Study, institutionally sponsored loans, health care benefits, and unspecified assistantships also available. Financial award application deadline: 3/15; financial award applicants required to submit FAFSA. In 2016, 28 master's awarded. *Program availability:* Part-time. Offers school counseling (MS). *Application deadline:* For fall admission, 8/15 priority date for

domestic students. Applications are processed on a rolling basis. *Application fee:* $30 ($75 for international students). Electronic applications accepted. *Application Contact:* Mary Sewell, Admissions Coordinator, 800-950-GRAD, Fax: 620-341-5909, E-mail: msewell@emporia.edu. *Chair,* Dr. Katrina Miller, 620-341-5791, E-mail: kmille12@emporia.edu.

Program in School Psychology Students: 22 full-time (18 women), 5 part-time (all women); includes 2 minority (1 Black or African American, non-Hispanic/Latino; 1 Two or more races, non-Hispanic/Latino), 1 international. 17 applicants, 100% accepted, 6 enrolled. *Faculty:* 8 full-time (4 women). Expenses: Contact institution. *Financial support:* In 2016–17, 4 teaching assistantships with full tuition reimbursements (averaging $7,335 per year) were awarded; career-related internships or fieldwork, Federal Work-Study, institutionally sponsored loans, health care benefits, and unspecified assistantships also available. Financial award application deadline: 3/15; financial award applicants required to submit FAFSA. In 2016, 5 master's, 4 other advanced degrees awarded. *Program availability:* Part-time. Offers school psychology (MS, Ed S). *Application deadline:* For fall admission, 8/15 priority date for domestic students. Applications are processed on a rolling basis. *Application fee:* $30 ($75 for international students). Electronic applications accepted. *Application Contact:* Mary Sewell, Admissions Coordinator, 800-950-GRAD, Fax: 620-341-5909, E-mail: msewell@emporia.edu. *Chair,* Dr. Jim Persinger, 620-341-5317, E-mail: jpersing@emporia.edu.

Program in Special Education Students: 5 full-time (all women), 158 part-time (119 women); includes 6 minority (1 Asian, non-Hispanic/Latino; 4 Hispanic/Latino; 1 Two or more races, non-Hispanic/Latino). 35 applicants, 100% accepted, 23 enrolled. *Faculty:* 29 full-time (21 women), 3 part-time/adjunct (2 women). Expenses: Contact institution. *Financial support:* In 2016–17, 1 teaching assistantship with full tuition reimbursement (averaging $7,335 per year) was awarded; Federal Work-Study, institutionally sponsored loans, health care benefits, and unspecified assistantships also available. Financial award application deadline: 3/15; financial award applicants required to submit FAFSA. In 2016, 40 master's awarded. *Program availability:* Part-time. Offers behavior disorders (MS); gifted, talented, and creative (MS); interrelated special education (MS). *Application deadline:* For fall admission, 8/15 priority date for domestic students. Applications are processed on a rolling basis. *Application fee:* $30 ($75 for international students). Electronic applications accepted. *Application Contact:* Mary Sewell, Admissions Coordinator, 800-950-GRAD, Fax: 620-341-5909, E-mail: msewell@emporia.edu. *Chair,* Dr. Matt Siemears, 620-341-6057, E-mail: msiemear@emporia.edu.

Program in Teaching Students: 9 full-time (7 women), 16 part-time (8 women); includes 4 minority (1 Black or African American, non-Hispanic/Latino; 3 Hispanic/Latino). 15 applicants, 100% accepted, 4 enrolled. *Faculty:* 10 full-time (3 women). Expenses: Contact institution. In 2016, 16 master's awarded. *Program availability:* Part-time, online learning. Offers teaching (M Ed). *Application fee:* $40. *Application Contact:* Mary Sewell, Admissions Coordinator, 800-950-GRAD, Fax: 620-341-5909, E-mail: msewell@emporia.edu. *Chair,* Dr. Daniel Stiffler, 620-341-5776, E-mail: dstiffle@emporia.edu.

Program in Teaching English to Speakers of Other Languages Students: 4 full-time (3 women), 16 part-time (13 women); includes 2 minority (1 Black or African American, non-Hispanic/Latino; 1 Hispanic/Latino), 2 international. 10 applicants, 100% accepted, 4 enrolled. *Faculty:* 7 full-time (3 women). Expenses: Contact institution. *Financial support:* In 2016–17, 1 research assistantship with full tuition reimbursement (averaging $7,353 per year) was awarded; Federal Work-Study, institutionally sponsored loans, health care benefits, and unspecified assistantships also available. Financial award application deadline: 2/15. In 2016, 16 master's awarded. *Program availability:* Part-time. Offers teaching English to speakers of other languages (MA). *Application deadline:* For fall admission, 8/15 priority date for domestic students. Applications are processed on a rolling basis. *Application fee:* $30 ($75 for international students). Electronic applications accepted. *Application Contact:* Mary Sewell, Admissions Coordinator, 800-950-GRAD, Fax: 620-341-5909, E-mail: msewell@emporia.edu. *Professor,* Dr. Abdelilah Salim Sehlaoui, 620-341-5237, E-mail: asehlaou@emporia.edu.

School of Library and Information Management Students: 24 full-time (18 women), 281 part-time (218 women); includes 23 minority (3 Black or African American, non-Hispanic/Latino; 1 American Indian or Alaska Native, non-Hispanic/Latino; 1 Asian, non-Hispanic/Latino; 14 Hispanic/Latino; 1 Native Hawaiian or other Pacific Islander, non-Hispanic/Latino; 3 Two or more races, non-Hispanic/Latino), 5 international. 118 applicants, 97% accepted, 71 enrolled. *Faculty:* 9 full-time (6 women). Expenses: Contact institution. *Financial support:* In 2016–17, 10 research assistantships with full tuition reimbursements (averaging $7,500 per year), 5 teaching assistantships (averaging $7,500 per year) were awarded; Federal Work-Study, institutionally sponsored loans, and unspecified assistantships also available. Financial award application deadline: 3/15; financial award applicants required to submit FAFSA. In 2016, 140 master's, 1 doctorate, 8 other advanced degrees awarded. *Program availability:* Part-time, evening/weekend, online learning. Offers archives studies (Certificate); library and information management (MLS, PhD). *Application deadline:* For fall admission, 8/15 priority date for domestic students. Applications are processed on a rolling basis. *Application fee:* $30 ($75 for international students). Electronic applications accepted. *Application Contact:* Candace Boardman, Director, Kansas MLS Program, 620-341-6159, E-mail: cboardma@emporia.edu. *Dean,* Dr. Wooseob Jeong, 620-341-5203, Fax: 620-341-5203, E-mail: wjeong1@emporia.edu.

ENDICOTT COLLEGE, Beverly, MA 01915-2096

General Information Independent, coed, comprehensive institution. *Enrollment:* 5,018 graduate, professional, and undergraduate students; 504 full-time matriculated graduate/professional students (311 women), 490 part-time matriculated graduate/professional students (362 women). *Enrollment by degree level:* 923 master's, 71 doctoral. *Graduate faculty:* 31 full-time (19 women), 115 part-time/adjunct (57 women). Tuition and fees vary according to program. *Graduate housing:* Room and/or apartments available on a first-come, first-served basis to single students; on-campus housing not available to married students. Typical cost: $10,272 per year ($14,900 including board). Housing application deadline: 5/1. *Student services:* Campus employment opportunities, campus safety program, career counseling, free psychological counseling, international student services, low-cost health insurance, multicultural affairs office, services for students with disabilities, teacher training, writing training. *Library facilities:* Diane M. Halle Library. *Collection:* Books: 103,315 (physical), 157,531 (digital/electronic); Serial titles: 64 (physical), 86,483 (digital/electronic); Databases: 173. Weekly public service hours: 97; students can reserve study rooms. *Research affiliation:* Peabody Essex Museum (history), North Shore Consortium (special needs).

Computer facilities: Computer purchase and lease plans are available. 285 computers available on campus for general student use. A campuswide network can be accessed from student residence rooms and from off campus. Online class registration is available.
Website: http://www.endicott.edu/

General Application Contact: Dr. Mary Huegel, Vice President and Dean of the School of Graduate and Professional Studies, 978-232-2084, Fax: 978-232-3000, E-mail: mhuegel@endicott.edu.

GRADUATE UNITS

Van Loan School of Graduate and Professional Studies Students: 504 full-time (311 women), 490 part-time (362 women); includes 100 minority (26 Black or African American, non-Hispanic/Latino; 21 Asian, non-Hispanic/Latino; 42 Hispanic/Latino; 11 Two or more races, non-Hispanic/Latino), 15 international. Average age 31. 323 applicants, 99% accepted, 281 enrolled. *Faculty:* 31 full-time (19 women), 115 part-time/adjunct (57 women). Expenses: Contact institution. *Financial support:* Fellowships, research assistantships, teaching assistantships, career-related internships or fieldwork, Federal Work-Study, tuition waivers (partial), and unspecified assistantships available. Financial award applicants required to submit FAFSA. In 2016, 474 master's, 2 doctorates awarded. *Program availability:* Part-time, evening/weekend, 100% online, blended/hybrid learning. Offers administrative leadership (M Ed); athletic administration (M Ed); autism and applied behavior analysis (M Ed, PhD); business administration (MBA); early childhood and elementary education (M Ed); educational leadership (Ed D); homeland security (MS); information technology (MSIT); integrative education (M Ed); interior architecture (MA, MFA); nursing (MSN, PhD); organizational management (M Ed); reading and literacy (M Ed); secondary education (M Ed); special needs and applied behavior analysis (M Ed). *Application deadline:* Applications are processed on a rolling basis. *Application fee:* $50. Electronic applications accepted. *Application Contact:* Ian Menchini, Director, Graduate Enrollment and Advising, 978-232-5292. *Dean,* Dr. Mary Huegel, 978-232-2084, Fax: 978-232-3000, E-mail: mhuegel@endicott.edu.

EPISCOPAL DIVINITY SCHOOL, Cambridge, MA 02138-3494

General Information Independent-religious, coed, graduate-only institution. *Graduate housing:* Rooms and/or apartments available on a first-come, first-served basis to single and married students. Housing application deadline: 7/31. *Research affiliation:* Boston Theological Institute.

GRADUATE UNITS

Graduate and Professional Programs *Program availability:* Part-time.

ERIKSON INSTITUTE, Chicago, IL 60654

General Information Independent, coed, primarily women, graduate-only institution.

GRADUATE UNITS

Academic Programs *Program availability:* Part-time, evening/weekend. Offers administration (Certificate); bilingual/ESL (Certificate); child development (MS); early childhood education (MS); infant mental health (Certificate); infant studies (Certificate). MS/MSW offered jointly with Loyola University Chicago.

ERSKINE THEOLOGICAL SEMINARY, Due West, SC 29639-0668

General Information Independent-religious, coed, graduate-only institution. *Graduate housing:* Room and/or apartments available on a first-come, first-served basis to single students; on-campus housing not available to married students. Housing application deadline: 6/1.

GRADUATE UNITS

Graduate and Professional Programs *Program availability:* Part-time, evening/weekend. Offers theology (M Div, MAPM, MATS, Th M, D Min). Electronic applications accepted.

EVANGELICAL SEMINARY, Myerstown, PA 17067-1212

General Information Independent-religious, coed, graduate-only institution. *Graduate housing:* Rooms and/or apartments available on a first-come, first-served basis to single and married students. Housing application deadline: 6/1.

GRADUATE UNITS

Graduate and Professional Programs *Program availability:* Part-time, online learning. Offers Biblical studies (MAR); congregational ministry (M Div); global and contextual studies (M Div, MAR); historical and theological studies (MAR); interdisciplinary studies (MAR); marriage and family counseling (M Div); marriage and family therapy (MA); New Testament (MAR); Old Testament (MAR); spiritual formation (MAR); teaching ministry (M Div); youth ministry (M Div).

EVANGELICAL SEMINARY OF PUERTO RICO, San Juan, PR 00925-2207

General Information Independent-religious, coed, graduate-only institution. *Graduate housing:* Rooms and/or apartments available on a first-come, first-served basis to single and married students. Housing application deadline: 12/15.

GRADUATE UNITS

Graduate and Professional Programs *Program availability:* Part-time. Offers theology (M Div, MAR, D Min).

EVANGEL UNIVERSITY, Springfield, MO 65802

General Information Independent-religious, coed, comprehensive institution. *Enrollment:* 1,464 graduate, professional, and undergraduate students; 116 full-time matriculated graduate/professional students (84 women), 72 part-time matriculated graduate/professional students (58 women). *Enrollment by degree level:* 157 master's, 31 doctoral. *Graduate faculty:* 16 full-time (8 women), 19 part-time/adjunct (12 women). *Tuition:* Part-time $400 per credit hour. *Required fees:* $148 per trimester. One-time fee: $25. Tuition and fees vary according to course load, degree level and program. *Graduate housing:* Rooms and/or apartments available on a first-come, first-served basis to single and married students. Housing application deadline: 5/1. *Student services:* Campus employment opportunities, campus safety program, career counseling, exercise/wellness program, free psychological counseling, international student services, multicultural affairs office, services for students with disabilities, teacher training, writing training. *Library facilities:* Claude Kendrick Library.

Computer facilities: A campuswide network can be accessed from student residence rooms. Online class registration, online payment are available. Website: http://www.evangel.edu/

General Application Contact: Karen Benitez, Admissions Representative, Graduate Studies, 417-865-2815 Ext. 7416, Fax: 417-575-5484, E-mail: benitezk@evangel.edu.

GRADUATE UNITS

Department of Behavioral Sciences Students: 35 full-time (26 women), 10 part-time (7 women); includes 5 minority (2 Black or African American, non-Hispanic/Latino; 2 Hispanic/Latino; 1 Two or more races, non-Hispanic/Latino). Average age 33. 27 applicants, 85% accepted, 20 enrolled. *Faculty:* 6 full-time (5 women), 5 part-time/adjunct (all women). Expenses: Contact institution. *Financial support:* In 2016–17,

6 students received support. Unspecified assistantships available. Financial award application deadline: 4/1; financial award applicants required to submit FAFSA. In 2016, 34 master's awarded. *Program availability:* Part-time. Offers clinical mental health counseling (MS). *Application deadline:* For fall admission, 7/15 priority date for domestic students, 8/1 for international students; for spring admission, 11/15 priority date for domestic students, 12/1 for international students. Applications are processed on a rolling basis. *Application fee:* $25. Electronic applications accepted. *Application Contact:* Matt Petry, Admissions Representative, Graduate Studies, 417-865-2815 Ext. 7416, Fax: 417-575-5484, E-mail: benitezk@evangel.edu. *Program Coordinator,* Christine Arnzen, 417-865-2815 Ext. 8618, E-mail: arnzenc@evangel.edu.

Department of Education Students: 2 full-time (1 woman), 33 part-time (29 women); includes 1 minority (Asian, non-Hispanic/Latino). Average age 30. 10 applicants, 90% accepted, 9 enrolled. *Faculty:* 3 full-time (2 women), 4 part-time/adjunct (2 women). Expenses: Contact institution. *Financial support:* In 2016–17, 11 students received support. Scholarships/grants and unspecified assistantships available. Financial award application deadline: 4/1; financial award applicants required to submit FAFSA. In 2016, 28 master's awarded. *Program availability:* Part-time, evening/weekend, 100% online, blended/hybrid learning. Offers curriculum and instruction (M Ed); educational leadership (M Ed); literacy (M Ed); secondary teaching (M Ed). *Application deadline:* For fall admission, 7/15 priority date for domestic students, 8/1 for international students; for spring admission, 11/15 priority date for domestic students, 12/1 for international students. Applications are processed on a rolling basis. *Application fee:* $25. Electronic applications accepted. *Application Contact:* Karen Benitez, Admissions Representative, Graduate Studies, 417-865-2815 Ext. 7416, Fax: 417-575-5484, E-mail: benitezk@evangel.edu. *Program Coordinator,* Dr. Susan Langston, 417-865-2815 Ext. 8552, E-mail: langstons@evangel.edu.

Doctor of Educational Leadership in Curriculum and Instruction Program Students: 26 full-time (21 women), 6 part-time (2 women); includes 2 minority (1 American Indian or Alaska Native, non-Hispanic/Latino; 1 Two or more races, non-Hispanic/Latino). Average age 41. 3 applicants, 100% accepted, 3 enrolled. *Faculty:* 4 full-time (1 woman), 2 part-time/adjunct (1 woman). Expenses: Contact institution. *Financial support:* In 2016–17, 8 students received support. Scholarships/grants available. Support available to part-time students. Financial award application deadline: 4/1; financial award applicants required to submit FAFSA. *Program availability:* Part-time, evening/weekend. Offers educational leadership in curriculum and instruction (Ed D). *Application deadline:* For fall admission, 7/15 priority date for domestic students, 8/1 for international students; for spring admission, 11/15 priority date for domestic students, 12/1 for international students. Applications are processed on a rolling basis. *Application fee:* $25. Electronic applications accepted. *Application Contact:* Karen Benitez, Admissions Representative, Graduate Studies, 417-865-2811 Ext. 7416, Fax: 417-575-5484, E-mail: benitezk@evangel.edu. *Program Coordinator,* Dr. Susan Langston, 417-865-2815 Ext. 8552, E-mail: langstons@evangel.edu.

Organizational Leadership Program Students: 32 full-time (17 women), 2 part-time (1 woman); includes 3 minority (1 Black or African American, non-Hispanic/Latino; 1 American Indian or Alaska Native, non-Hispanic/Latino; 1 Asian, non-Hispanic/Latino). Average age 38. 5 applicants, 100% accepted, 5 enrolled. *Faculty:* 3 full-time (0 women), 5 part-time/adjunct (2 women). Expenses: Contact institution. *Financial support:* In 2016–17, 17 students received support. Scholarships/grants available. Financial award application deadline: 4/1; financial award applicants required to submit FAFSA. In 2016, 24 master's awarded. *Program availability:* Part-time, evening/weekend, 100% online, blended/hybrid learning. Offers organizational leadership (MOL). *Application deadline:* For fall admission, 7/15 priority date for domestic students, 8/1 for international students; for spring admission, 11/15 priority date for domestic students, 12/1 for international students. Applications are processed on a rolling basis. *Application fee:* $25. Electronic applications accepted. *Application Contact:* Karen Benitez, Admissions Representative, Graduate Studies, 417-865-2815 Ext. 7416, Fax: 417-575-5484, E-mail: benitezk@evangel.edu. *Program Coordinator,* Dr. Duane Praschan, 417-865-2815 Ext. 8118, Fax: 417-575-5484, E-mail: praschand@evangel.edu.

School Counseling Program Students: 25 full-time (22 women), 20 part-time (15 women); includes 2 minority (both Black or African American, non-Hispanic/Latino). Average age 31. 12 applicants, 100% accepted, 12 enrolled. *Faculty:* 4 full-time (3 women), 4 part-time/adjunct (all women). Expenses: Contact institution. *Financial support:* In 2016–17, 2 students received support. Unspecified assistantships available. Financial award application deadline: 4/1; financial award applicants required to submit FAFSA. In 2016, 20 master's awarded. *Program availability:* Part-time, evening/weekend. Offers school counseling (MS). *Application deadline:* For fall admission, 7/15 priority date for domestic students, 7/1 for international students; for spring admission, 11/15 priority date for domestic students, 12/1 for international students. Applications are processed on a rolling basis. *Application fee:* $25. Electronic applications accepted. *Application Contact:* Karen Benitez, Admissions Representative, Graduate Studies, 417-865-2815 Ext. 7416, Fax: 417-575-5484, E-mail: benitezk@evangel.edu. *Program Coordinator,* Christine Arnzen, 417-865-2815 Ext. 8678, Fax: 417-575-5484, E-mail: arnzenc@evangel.edu.

EVEREST UNIVERSITY, Tampa, FL 33614

General Information Independent, coed, comprehensive institution. *Graduate housing:* On-campus housing not available.

GRADUATE UNITS

Department of Business Administration *Program availability:* Part-time, evening/weekend. Offers accounting (MBA); human resources (MBA); international business (MBA).

EVERGLADES UNIVERSITY, Boca Raton, FL 33431

General Information Independent, coed, comprehensive institution. *Enrollment:* 136 full-time matriculated graduate/professional students (92 women), 91 part-time matriculated graduate/professional students (30 women). *Enrollment by degree level:* 227 master's. *Tuition:* Full-time $16,800. *Required fees:* $1600. One-time fee: $195 part-time. *Graduate housing:* On-campus housing not available. *Student services:* Campus employment opportunities, campus safety program, career counseling, services for students with disabilities, writing training. *Library facilities:* Everglades University Library. *Collection:* Books: 19,974 (physical), 122,000 (digital/electronic); Serial titles: 48 (physical), 5,180 (digital/electronic); Databases: 55. Weekly public service hours: 6.

Computer facilities: 19 computers available on campus for general student use. Website: http://www.evergladesuniversity.edu/

GRADUATE UNITS

Graduate Programs *Program availability:* Part-time, evening/weekend, 100% online. Offers accounting for managers (MBA); aviation management (MBA); aviation operations management (MSA); aviation security (MSA); business administration

(MSA); complementary and alternative medicine (MPH); entrepreneurship (MS); human resource management (MBA); project management (MBA). Electronic applications accepted.

THE EVERGREEN STATE COLLEGE, Olympia, WA 98505

General Information State-supported, coed, comprehensive institution. *Enrollment:* 4,089 graduate, professional, and undergraduate students; 182 full-time matriculated graduate/professional students (117 women), 113 part-time matriculated graduate/professional students (84 women). *Enrollment by degree level:* 295 master's. *Graduate faculty:* 14 full-time (9 women), 17 part-time/adjunct (7 women). Tuition, state resident: full-time $9579; part-time $319 per credit. Tuition, nonresident: full-time $22,137; part-time $738 per credit. *Required fees:* $624; $9 per credit. Tuition and fees vary according to course load. *Graduate housing:* Rooms and/or apartments available on a first-come, first-served basis to single and married students. Typical cost: $6195 per year ($9360 including board) for single students; $6195 per year ($9360 including board) for married students. Housing application deadline: 6/15. *Student services:* Campus employment opportunities, campus safety program, career counseling, child daycare facilities, exercise/wellness program, free psychological counseling, grant writing training, international student services, multicultural affairs office, services for students with disabilities, teacher training, writing training. *Library facilities:* Daniel J. Evans Library. *Collection:* Books: 322,238 (physical), 158,542 (digital/electronic); Serial titles: 79 (physical), 54,617 (digital/electronic); Databases: 54. Weekly public service hours: 83; students can reserve study rooms. *Research affiliation:* Washington State Institute for Public Policy (public policy).

Computer facilities: 556 computers available on campus for general student use. A campuswide network can be accessed from student residence rooms and from off campus. Online class registration, online payment, student accounts history, financial aid records, academic history, housing application, evaluations are available.
Website: http://www.evergreen.edu/

General Application Contact: Admissions, 360-867-6170, E-mail: admissions@evergreen.edu.

GRADUATE UNITS

Graduate Programs Students: 182 full-time (117 women), 113 part-time (84 women); includes 78 minority (8 Black or African American, non-Hispanic/Latino; 25 American Indian or Alaska Native, non-Hispanic/Latino; 2 Asian, non-Hispanic/Latino; 21 Hispanic/Latino; 2 Native Hawaiian or other Pacific Islander, non-Hispanic/Latino; 20 Two or more races, non-Hispanic/Latino), 2 international. Average age 32. 309 applicants, 73% accepted, 157 enrolled. *Faculty:* 14 full-time (9 women), 17 part-time/adjunct (7 women). Expenses: Contact institution. *Financial support:* In 2016–17, 207 students received support, including 42 fellowships with partial tuition reimbursements available (averaging $1,918 per year); career-related internships or fieldwork, Federal Work-Study, institutionally sponsored loans, scholarships/grants, health care benefits, and tuition waivers (partial) also available. Support available to part-time students. Financial award application deadline: 2/1; financial award applicants required to submit FAFSA. In 2016, 141 master's awarded. *Program availability:* Part-time, evening/weekend. Offers environmental studies (MES); public administration (MPA); teaching (MIT). *Application deadline:* For fall admission, 2/1 priority date for domestic and international students. Applications are processed on a rolling basis. *Application fee:* $50. Electronic applications accepted. *Application Contact:* Amanda Mobbs, Graduate Admission Coordinator, 360-867-6856, E-mail: graduateadmissions@evergreen.edu. *Interim Vice President and Provost,* Dr. Kenneth Tabbutt, 360-867-6400, Fax: 360-867-6745, E-mail: tabbuttk@evergreen.edu.

EXCELSIOR COLLEGE, Albany, NY 12203-5159

General Information Independent, coed, comprehensive institution. *Enrollment:* 38,309 graduate, professional, and undergraduate students; 3,148 part-time matriculated graduate/professional students (1,444 women). *Enrollment by degree level:* 3,105 master's, 43 other advanced degrees. *Graduate faculty:* 72 part-time/adjunct (42 women). *Tuition:* Part-time $645 per credit. *Required fees:* $265 per credit. *Student services:* Career counseling, services for students with disabilities, writing training. *Library facilities:* Excelsior College Library.

Computer facilities: A campuswide network can be accessed from off campus. Online class registration is available.
Website: http://www.excelsior.edu/

General Application Contact: Admissions Counselor, 518-464-8500, Fax: 518-464-8777, E-mail: admissions@excelsior.edu.

GRADUATE UNITS

School of Business and Technology Students: 1,801 part-time (487 women); includes 775 minority (424 Black or African American, non-Hispanic/Latino; 5 American Indian or Alaska Native, non-Hispanic/Latino; 58 Asian, non-Hispanic/Latino; 209 Hispanic/Latino; 15 Native Hawaiian or other Pacific Islander, non-Hispanic/Latino; 64 Two or more races, non-Hispanic/Latino), 11 international. Average age 39. *Faculty:* 25 part-time/adjunct (9 women). Expenses: Contact institution. *Financial support:* Scholarships/grants available. In 2016, 288 master's awarded. *Program availability:* Part-time, evening/weekend, online learning. Offers business administration (MBA); cybersecurity management (MBA, Graduate Certificate); general business management (MS); health care management (MBA); human performance technology (MBA); human resource management (MS); human resources management (MBA); leadership (MBA, MS); mediation and arbitration (MBA, MS); social media management (MBA); technology management (MBA). *Application deadline:* Applications are processed on a rolling basis. *Application fee:* $50. Electronic applications accepted. *Application Contact:* Admissions, 888-647-2388 Ext. 133, Fax: 518-464-8777, E-mail: admissions@excelsior.edu. *Dean,* Dr. Lifang Shih, 888-647-2388.

School of Health Sciences Students: 307 part-time (240 women); includes 176 minority (101 Black or African American, non-Hispanic/Latino; 2 American Indian or Alaska Native, non-Hispanic/Latino; 17 Asian, non-Hispanic/Latino; 39 Hispanic/Latino; 3 Native Hawaiian or other Pacific Islander, non-Hispanic/Latino; 14 Two or more races, non-Hispanic/Latino), 1 international. Average age 39. *Faculty:* 5 part-time/adjunct (4 women). Expenses: Contact institution. *Financial support:* Scholarships/grants available. In 2016, 21 master's awarded. *Program availability:* Part-time, evening/weekend, online learning. Offers health administration (MS); health care informatics (Certificate); health professions education (MSHS); healthcare informatics (MS); organizational development (MS); public health (MSHS). *Application deadline:* Applications are processed on a rolling basis. *Application fee:* $50. Electronic applications accepted. *Application Contact:* Admissions Counselor, 518-464-8500, Fax: 518-464-8777, E-mail: admissions@excelsior.edu. *Dean,* Dr. Laurie Carbo-Porter, 518-464-8500, Fax: 518-464-8777.

School of Liberal Arts Students: 82 part-time (32 women); includes 40 minority (26 Black or African American, non-Hispanic/Latino; 2 American Indian or Alaska Native,

non-Hispanic/Latino; 1 Asian, non-Hispanic/Latino; 7 Hispanic/Latino; 4 Two or more races, non-Hispanic/Latino), 1 international. Average age 46. *Faculty:* 27 part-time/adjunct (18 women). Expenses: Contact institution. *Financial support:* Scholarships/grants available. In 2016, 49 master's awarded. *Program availability:* Part-time, evening/weekend, online learning. Offers liberal studies (MA). *Application deadline:* Applications are processed on a rolling basis. *Application fee:* $50. Electronic applications accepted. *Application Contact:* Admissions Counselor, 518-464-8500, Fax: 518-464-8777, E-mail: admissions@excelsior.edu. *Dean,* Dr. George Timmons, 518-464-8500, Fax: 518-464-8777, E-mail: mlsadmin@excelsior.edu.

School of Nursing Students: 777 part-time (638 women); includes 248 minority (135 Black or African American, non-Hispanic/Latino; 5 American Indian or Alaska Native, non-Hispanic/Latino; 34 Asian, non-Hispanic/Latino; 62 Hispanic/Latino; 5 Native Hawaiian or other Pacific Islander, non-Hispanic/Latino; 7 Two or more races, non-Hispanic/Latino), 2 international. Average age 44. *Faculty:* 16 part-time/adjunct (12 women). Expenses: Contact institution. *Financial support:* Scholarships/grants available. In 2016, 196 master's awarded. *Program availability:* Part-time, evening/weekend, online learning. Offers nursing (MS); nursing education (MS); nursing informatics (MS); nursing leadership and administration of health care systems (MS). *Application deadline:* Applications are processed on a rolling basis. *Application fee:* $50. Electronic applications accepted. *Application Contact:* Admissions Counselor, 888-647-2388, Fax: 518-464-8777, E-mail: gradadmissions@excelsior.edu. *Associate Dean, Graduate Program in Nursing,* Dr. Barbara Pieper, 518-464-8500, Fax: 518-464-8777, E-mail: msn@excelsior.edu.

School of Public Service Students: 181 part-time (47 women); includes 78 minority (41 Black or African American, non-Hispanic/Latino; 2 American Indian or Alaska Native, non-Hispanic/Latino; 2 Asian, non-Hispanic/Latino; 25 Hispanic/Latino; 2 Native Hawaiian or other Pacific Islander, non-Hispanic/Latino; 6 Two or more races, non-Hispanic/Latino). Average age 41. *Faculty:* 1 (woman) part-time/adjunct. Expenses: Contact institution. *Financial support:* Scholarships/grants available. In 2016, 30 master's awarded. *Program availability:* Part-time, evening/weekend, online learning. Offers criminal justice (MSCI); homeland security and emergency management (MSCJ); justice administration (MSCI); mediation and arbitration (MPA); public administration (MPA). *Application deadline:* Applications are processed on a rolling basis. *Application fee:* $50. Electronic applications accepted. *Application Contact:* Admissions Counselor, 888-647-2388, Fax: 518-464-8777, E-mail: gradadmissions@excelsior.edu. *Dean, School of Public Service,* Dr. Robert Waters, 518-464-8500, Fax: 518-464-8777.

FAIRFIELD UNIVERSITY, Fairfield, CT 06824

General Information Independent-religious, coed, comprehensive institution. *Enrollment:* 5,137 graduate, professional, and undergraduate students; 467 full-time matriculated graduate/professional students (280 women), 638 part-time matriculated graduate/professional students (475 women). *Enrollment by degree level:* 910 master's, 125 doctoral, 70 other advanced degrees. *Graduate faculty:* 71 full-time (39 women), 76 part-time/adjunct (39 women). *Tuition:* Part-time $750 per credit hour. *Required fees:* $35 per credit hour. Tuition and fees vary according to degree level and program. *Graduate housing:* Room and/or apartments available on a first-come, first-served basis to single students; on-campus housing not available to married students. Typical cost: $11,970 per year ($14,280 including board). Room and board charges vary according to housing facility selected. *Student services:* Campus employment opportunities, campus safety program, career counseling, child daycare facilities, exercise/wellness program, free psychological counseling, international student services, low-cost health insurance, multicultural affairs office, services for students with disabilities, teacher training, writing training. *Library facilities:* DiMenna-Nyselius Library. *Collection:* Books: 376,704 (physical), 898,580 (digital/electronic); Serial titles: 152 (physical), 36,383 (digital/electronic); Databases: 148. Weekly public service hours: 105; study areas open 24 hours, 5–7 days a week; students can reserve study rooms.

Computer facilities: Computer purchase and lease plans are available. 68 computers available on campus for general student use. A campuswide network can be accessed from student residence rooms and from off campus. Online class registration is available.
Website: http://www.fairfield.edu/

General Application Contact: Marianne Gumpper, Director of Graduate Admission, 203-254-4184, Fax: 203-254-4073, E-mail: gradadmis@fairfield.edu.

GRADUATE UNITS

College of Arts and Sciences Students: 60 full-time (40 women), 51 part-time (28 women); includes 24 minority (9 Black or African American, non-Hispanic/Latino; 1 Asian, non-Hispanic/Latino; 11 Hispanic/Latino; 3 Two or more races, non-Hispanic/Latino), 8 international. Average age 34. 84 applicants, 74% accepted, 38 enrolled. *Faculty:* 17 full-time (9 women), 12 part-time/adjunct (6 women). Expenses: Contact institution. *Financial support:* In 2016–17, 17 students received support. Scholarships/grants and unspecified assistantships available. Financial award applicants required to submit FAFSA. In 2016, 68 master's awarded. *Program availability:* Part-time, evening/weekend, online learning. Offers American studies (MA); communication (MA); creative writing (MFA); mathematics (MS); public administration (MPA). *Application deadline:* For fall admission, 5/15 for international students; for spring admission, 10/15 for international students. Applications are processed on a rolling basis. *Application fee:* $60. Electronic applications accepted. *Application Contact:* Marianne Gumpper, Director of Graduate Admission, 203-254-4184, Fax: 203-254-4073, E-mail: gradadmis@fairfield.edu. *Dean,* Dr. Yohuru Williams, 203-254-4000 Ext. 2221, Fax: 203-254-4119, E-mail: ywilliams@fairfield.edu.

Dolan School of Business Students: 106 full-time (41 women), 57 part-time (26 women); includes 18 minority (4 Black or African American, non-Hispanic/Latino; 1 American Indian or Alaska Native, non-Hispanic/Latino; 4 Asian, non-Hispanic/Latino; 7 Hispanic/Latino; 2 Two or more races, non-Hispanic/Latino), 39 international. Average age 26. 136 applicants, 63% accepted, 35 enrolled. *Faculty:* 20 full-time (6 women), 4 part-time/adjunct (1 woman). Expenses: Contact institution. *Financial support:* In 2016–17, 33 students received support. Scholarships/grants and unspecified assistantships available. Financial award applicants required to submit FAFSA. In 2016, 90 master's awarded. *Program availability:* Part-time, evening/weekend. Offers accounting (MBA, MS, CAS); business analytics (MS); entrepreneurship (MBA); finance (MBA, MS, CAS); general management (MBA, CAS); global management (MBA); human resource management (MBA, CAS); information systems and business analytics (MBA); marketing (MBA, CAS); taxation (MBA, CAS). *Application deadline:* For fall admission, 5/15 for international students; for spring admission, 10/15 for international students. Applications are processed on a rolling basis. *Application fee:* $60. Electronic applications accepted. *Application Contact:* Marianne Gumpper, Director of Graduate and Continuing Studies Admission, 203-254-4184, Fax: 203-254-4073, E-mail: gradadmis@fairfield.edu. *Dean,* Dr. Donald Gibson, 203-254-4070, Fax: 203-254-4105, E-mail: dgibson@fairfield.edu.

Graduate School of Education and Allied Professions Students: 153 full-time (132 women), 302 part-time (252 women); includes 97 minority (24 Black or African American, non-Hispanic/Latino; 12 Asian, non-Hispanic/Latino; 55 Hispanic/Latino; 6 Two or more races, non-Hispanic/Latino; 6 international. Average age 32. 283 applicants, 61% accepted, 97 enrolled. *Faculty:* 19 full-time (15 women), 38 part-time/adjunct (26 women). Expenses: Contact institution. *Financial support:* In 2016–17, 42 students received support. Career-related internships or fieldwork and unspecified assistantships available. Support available to part-time students. Financial award applicants required to submit FAFSA. In 2016, 130 master's awarded. *Program availability:* Part-time, evening/weekend. Offers applied behavior analysis (ATC); applied psychology (MA); clinical mental health counseling (MA, CAS); educational technology (MA); elementary education (MA, CAS); family studies (MA); integration of spirituality and religion in counseling (ATC); marriage and family therapy (MA); reading and language development (Sixth Year Certificate); school counseling (MA, CAS); school psychology (MA, CAS); school-based marriage and family therapy (ATC); secondary education (MA); special education (MA, CAS); substance abuse counseling (ATC); teaching (Certificate); teaching and foundations (MA, CAS); TESOL, world languages, and bilingual education (MA, CAS). *Application deadline:* For fall admission, 2/15 for international students; for spring admission, 10/1 for international students. *Application fee:* $60. Electronic applications accepted. *Application Contact:* Marianne Gumpper, Director of Graduate Admission, 203-254-4184, Fax: 203-254-4073, E-mail: gradadmis@fairfield.edu. *Dean:* Dr. Robert D. Hannafin, 203-254-4250, Fax: 203-254-4241, E-mail: rhannafin@fairfield.edu.

Marion Peckham Egan School of Nursing and Health Studies Students: 44 full-time (36 women), 172 part-time (154 women); includes 45 minority (17 Black or African American, non-Hispanic/Latino; 1 American Indian or Alaska Native, non-Hispanic/Latino; 10 Asian, non-Hispanic/Latino; 14 Hispanic/Latino; 3 Two or more races, non-Hispanic/Latino; 2 international. Average age 36. 107 applicants, 34% accepted, 21 enrolled. *Faculty:* 8 full-time (all women), 7 part-time/adjunct (4 women). Expenses: Contact institution. *Financial support:* In 2016–17, 47 students received support. Scholarships/grants and unspecified assistantships available. Financial award applicants required to submit FAFSA. In 2016, 20 master's, 28 doctorates awarded. *Program availability:* Part-time, evening/weekend. Offers advanced practice (DNP); family nurse practitioner (MSN, DNP); nurse anesthesia (DNP); nursing leadership (MSN); psychiatric nurse practitioner (MSN, DNP). *Application deadline:* For fall admission, 5/15 for international students; for spring admission, 10/15 for international students. Applications are processed on a rolling basis. *Application fee:* $60. Electronic applications accepted. *Application Contact:* Marianne Gumpper, Director of Graduate and Continuing Studies Admission, 203-254-4184, Fax: 203-254-4073, E-mail: gradadmis@fairfield.edu. *Dean:* Dr. Meredith Wallace Kazer, 203-254-4000 Ext. 2701, Fax: 203-254-4126, E-mail: mkazer@fairfield.edu.

School of Engineering Students: 104 full-time (31 women), 56 part-time (15 women); includes 17 minority (8 Black or African American, non-Hispanic/Latino; 5 Asian, non-Hispanic/Latino; 4 Hispanic/Latino), 108 international. Average age 28. 193 applicants, 63% accepted, 20 enrolled. *Faculty:* 7 full-time (1 woman), 15 part-time/adjunct (2 women). Expenses: Contact institution. *Financial support:* In 2016–17, 27 students received support. Scholarships/grants and unspecified assistantships available. Financial award applicants required to submit FAFSA. In 2016, 173 master's awarded. *Program availability:* Part-time, evening/weekend. Offers database management (CAS); electrical and computer engineering (MS); information security (CAS); management of technology (MS); mechanical engineering (MS); network technology (CAS); software engineering (MS); Web application development (CAS). *Application deadline:* For fall admission, 5/15 for international students; for spring admission, 10/15 for international students. Applications are processed on a rolling basis. *Application fee:* $60. Electronic applications accepted. *Application Contact:* Marianne Gumpper, Director of Graduate and Continuing Studies Admission, 203-254-4184, Fax: 203-254-4073, E-mail: gradadmis@fairfield.edu. *Dean:* Dr. Bruce Berdanier, 203-254-4147, Fax: 203-254-4013, E-mail: bberdanier@fairfield.edu.

FAIRLEIGH DICKINSON UNIVERSITY, COLLEGE AT FLORHAM, Madison, NJ 07940-1099

General Information Independent, coed, comprehensive institution. *Graduate housing:* Room and/or apartments available on a first-come, first-served basis to single students; on-campus housing not available to married students.

GRADUATE UNITS

Anthony J. Petrocelli College of Continuing Studies Offers continuing studies (MAS, MPA, MS, MSA); sports administration (MSA).

International School of Hospitality and Tourism Management Offers hospitality management studies (MS).

Public Administration Institute Offers public administration (MPA).

School of Administrative Science Offers administrative science (MAS).

Maxwell Becton College of Arts and Sciences Offers arts and sciences (MA, MFA, MS, Certificate); biology (MS); chemistry (MS); clinical mental health counseling (MA); computer science (MS); corporate and organizational communication (MA); counseling (MA); creative nonfiction (MFA); creative writing (MFA); creative writing and literature for educators (MA); fiction (MFA); industrial/organizational psychology (MA); literary translation (MFA); organizational behavior (MA, Certificate); organizational leadership (Certificate); poetry (MFA); writing for young adults (MFA).

School of Pharmacy Offers pharmacy (Pharm D).

Silberman College of Business *Program availability:* Part-time, evening/weekend. Offers accounting (MS); business (EMBA, MBA, MS, Certificate); business administration (MBA); entrepreneurial studies (MBA, Certificate); evolving technology (Certificate); finance (MBA, Certificate); health care and life sciences (EMBA); international business (MBA, Certificate); international taxation (Certificate); management (EMBA, MBA, Certificate); managing sustainability (Certificate); marketing (MBA, Certificate); pharmaceutical studies (MBA, Certificate); supply chain management (MS); taxation (MS, Certificate).

Center for Human Resource Management Studies Offers human resource management (MBA); human resource management studies (MBA).

University College: Arts, Sciences, and Professional Studies Offers arts, sciences, and professional studies (MA, MAT, MSN, Certificate).

The Henry P. Becton School of Nursing and Allied Health *Program availability:* Part-time, evening/weekend. Offers adult gerontology primary care nurse practitioner (MSN); family psychiatric/mental health nurse practitioner (MSN).

Peter Sammartino School of Education Offers education for certified teachers (MA, Certificate); educational leadership (MA); instructional technology (Certificate); literacy/reading (Certificate); PreK - 3 certification (MA, MAT); teaching (MAT).

FAIRLEIGH DICKINSON UNIVERSITY, METROPOLITAN CAMPUS, Teaneck, NJ 07666-1914

General Information Independent, coed, comprehensive institution. *Graduate housing:* Room and/or apartments available on a first-come, first-served basis to single students; on-campus housing not available to married students.

GRADUATE UNITS

Anthony J. Petrocelli College of Continuing Studies Offers continuing studies (MAS, MPA, MS, MSA, MSHS, Certificate); sports administration (MSA).

International School of Hospitality and Tourism Management Offers hospitality management (MS).

Public Administration Institute Offers public administration (MPA, Certificate); public non-profit management (Certificate).

School of Administrative Science Offers administrative science (MAS, MSHS, Certificate); homeland security (MSHS).

Silberman College of Business Offers accounting (MBA, MS, Certificate); business (EMBA, MBA, MS, Certificate); business administration (MBA); chemical studies (Certificate); entrepreneurial studies (MBA, Certificate); executive management (EMBA); finance (MBA, Certificate); healthcare and life sciences (EMBA); international business (MBA); management (MBA, Certificate); management information systems (Certificate); marketing (MBA, Certificate); pharmaceutical studies (MBA, Certificate); taxation (MS).

Center for Human Resources Management Studies Offers human resource management (MBA, Certificate).

University College: Arts, Sciences, and Professional Studies Offers arts, sciences, and professional studies (MA, MAT, MS, MSEE, MSN, DNP, PhD, Psy D, Certificate); English and literature (MA); systems science (MS).

Henry P. Becton School of Nursing and Allied Health Offers medical technology (MS); nursing (MSN, Certificate); nursing practice (DNP).

Peter Sammartino School of Education *Program availability:* Part-time. Offers dyslexia specialist (Certificate); education for certified teachers (MA); educational leadership (MA); instructional technology (Certificate); learning disabilities (MA); literacy/reading (Certificate); multilingual education (MA); PreK - 3 certification (MA, MAT); teacher of the handicapped (Certificate); teaching (MAT).

School of Art and Media Studies Offers art and media studies (MA); media and communications (MA).

School of Computer Sciences and Engineering Offers computer engineering (MS); computer science (MS); e-commerce (MS); electrical engineering (MSEE); management information systems (MS); mathematical foundation (MS).

School of Criminal Justice and Legal Studies Offers criminal justice (MA).

School of History, Political and International Studies Offers history (MA); international studies (MA); political science (MA).

School of Natural Sciences Offers biology (MS); chemistry (MS); cosmetic science (MS); science (MA).

School of Psychology Offers clinical psychology (MA, PhD); clinical psychopharmacology (MA); forensic psychology (MA); general-theoretical psychology (MA, Certificate); school psychology (MA, Psy D).

FAIRMONT STATE UNIVERSITY, Fairmont, WV 26554

General Information State-supported, coed, comprehensive institution. CGS member. *Enrollment:* 113 full-time matriculated graduate/professional students (88 women), 132 part-time matriculated graduate/professional students (98 women). *Enrollment by degree level:* 245 master's. *Graduate faculty:* 33 full-time (16 women), 7 part-time/adjunct (3 women). Tuition, state resident: full-time $7504; part-time $405 per credit hour. Tuition, nonresident: full-time $16,060; part-time $880 per credit hour. Part-time tuition and fees vary according to course load. *Graduate housing:* Room and/or apartments available on a first-come, first-served basis to single students; on-campus housing not available to married students. Typical cost: $5096 per year ($9100 including board). Room and board charges vary according to board plan and housing facility selected. *Student services:* Campus employment opportunities, campus safety program, career counseling, free psychological counseling, international student services, multicultural affairs office, services for students with disabilities, writing training. *Library facilities:* Musick Library. *Collection:* Study areas open 24 hours, 5–7 days a week.

Computer facilities: Computer purchase and lease plans are available. 1,350 computers available on campus for general student use. A campuswide network can be accessed from student residence rooms and from off campus. Online class registration is available.
Website: http://www.fairmontstate.edu/

General Application Contact: Jack Kirby, Director of Graduate Studies, 304-367-4101, E-mail: jack.kirby@fairmontstate.edu.

GRADUATE UNITS

Program in Business Administration Students: 16 full-time (9 women), 17 part-time (10 women); includes 5 minority (1 American Indian or Alaska Native, non-Hispanic/Latino; 2 Asian, non-Hispanic/Latino; 1 Hispanic/Latino; 1 Two or more races, non-Hispanic/Latino). Average age 30. 34 applicants, 79% accepted, 13 enrolled. *Faculty:* 7 full-time (3 women), 1 part-time/adjunct (0 women). Expenses: Contact institution. *Financial support:* In 2016–17, 11 students received support. Research assistantships, teaching assistantships, scholarships/grants, tuition waivers (full and partial), and unspecified assistantships available. Financial award applicants required to submit FAFSA. In 2016, 9 master's awarded. *Program availability:* Part-time, evening/weekend. Offers business administration (MBA). *Application deadline:* For fall admission, 5/1 for domestic and international students. Applications are processed on a rolling basis. *Application fee:* $40. Electronic applications accepted. *Application Contact:* Jack Kirby, Director of Graduate Studies, 304-367-4101, E-mail: jack.kirby@fairmontstate.edu. *Director,* Dr. Sunil Surendran, 304-367-4404, Fax: 304-367-4613, E-mail: sunil.surendran@fairmontstate.edu.

Program in Criminal Justice Students: 29 full-time (24 women), 13 part-time (6 women); includes 14 minority (7 Black or African American, non-Hispanic/Latino; 1 Asian, non-Hispanic/Latino; 1 Hispanic/Latino; 1 Native Hawaiian or other Pacific Islander, non-Hispanic/Latino; 4 Two or more races, non-Hispanic/Latino). Average age 30. 28 applicants, 61% accepted, 16 enrolled. *Faculty:* 5 full-time (2 women). Expenses: Contact institution. *Financial support:* In 2016–17, 4 students received support. Research assistantships, teaching assistantships, scholarships/grants, and unspecified assistantships available. Financial award applicants required to submit FAFSA. In 2016, 12 master's awarded. *Program availability:* Part-time, evening/weekend, 100% online. Offers criminal justice (MS). *Application deadline:* For fall admission, 5/1 for domestic and international students. Applications are processed on a rolling basis. *Application fee:* $40. Electronic applications accepted. *Application Contact:* Jack Kirby, Director of

Graduate Studies, 304-367-4101, E-mail: jack.kirby@fairmontstate.edu. *Director, Graduate Program in Criminal Justice*, Dr. Jennifer Myers, 304-367-4936, Fax: 304-367-4785, E-mail: jennifer.myers@fairmontstate.edu.

Programs in Education Students: 62 full-time (52 women), 102 part-time (82 women); includes 6 minority (2 Black or African American, non-Hispanic/Latino; 1 American Indian or Alaska Native, non-Hispanic/Latino; 1 Hispanic/Latino; 2 Two or more races, non-Hispanic/Latino). Average age 33. 68 applicants, 84% accepted, 47 enrolled. *Faculty:* 18 full-time (11 women), 5 part-time/adjunct (3 women). Expenses: Contact institution. *Financial support:* In 2016–17, 20 students received support. Research assistantships, teaching assistantships, scholarships/grants, and unspecified assistantships available. Financial award applicants required to submit FAFSA. In 2016, 44 degrees awarded. *Program availability:* Part-time, evening/weekend, 100% online. Offers digital media, new literacies and learning (M Ed); education (MAT); exercise science, fitness and wellness (M Ed); professional studies (M Ed); reading (M Ed); special education (M Ed). *Application deadline:* For fall admission, 5/1 for domestic and international students. Applications are processed on a rolling basis. *Application fee:* $40. Electronic applications accepted. *Application Contact:* Jack Kirby, Director of Graduate Studies, 304-367-4101, E-mail: jack.kirby@fairmontstate.edu. *Interim Dean, School of Education,* Dr. Carolyn Crislip-Tacy, 304-367-4143, Fax: 304-367-4599, E-mail: carolyn.crislip-tacy@fairmontstate.edu.

FAITH BAPTIST BIBLE COLLEGE AND THEOLOGICAL SEMINARY, Ankeny, IA 50023

General Information Independent-religious, coed, comprehensive institution. *Enrollment:* 274 graduate, professional, and undergraduate students; 18 full-time matriculated graduate/professional students (2 women), 30 part-time matriculated graduate/professional students (5 women). *Enrollment by degree level:* 48 master's. *Graduate faculty:* 3 full-time (0 women), 4 part-time/adjunct (0 women). *Graduate housing:* Rooms and/or apartments available on a first-come, first-served basis to single and married students. Housing application deadline: 8/1. *Student services:* Campus employment opportunities, career counseling, free psychological counseling, international student services, low-cost health insurance. *Library facilities:* John L. Patten Library.

Computer facilities: 45 computers available on campus for general student use. A campuswide network can be accessed from student residence rooms and from off campus. Online class registration is available.
Website: http://www.faith.edu/

General Application Contact: Jonathan Balasa, Seminary Admissions Representative, 888-FAITH4U, Fax: 515-964-1638, E-mail: seminaryrep@faith.edu.

GRADUATE UNITS

Graduate Program Students: 18 full-time (2 women), 30 part-time (5 women); includes 5 minority (1 Black or African American, non-Hispanic/Latino; 2 Asian, non-Hispanic/Latino; 1 Hispanic/Latino; 1 Two or more races, non-Hispanic/Latino). Average age 33. *Faculty:* 3 full-time (0 women), 4 part-time/adjunct (0 women). *Expenses:* Contact institution. *Financial support:* Career-related internships or fieldwork and scholarships/grants available. Support available to part-time students. Financial award application deadline: 3/1; financial award applicants required to submit FAFSA. In 2016, 13 master's awarded. *Program availability:* Part-time. Offers Biblical studies (MA); pastoral studies (M Div); pastoral training (MA); religion (MA); theological studies (MA). *Application deadline:* For fall admission, 8/1 priority date for domestic students; 8/1 for international students; for spring admission, 12/15 for domestic and international students. Applications are processed on a rolling basis. *Application fee:* $25. Electronic applications accepted. *Application Contact:* Jonathan Balasa, Seminary Admissions Representative, 888-FAITH4U, Fax: 515-964-1638, E-mail: seminaryrep@faith.edu. *President,* Rev. Jim Tillotson, 515-964-0601, E-mail: tillotsonj@faith.edu.

FAITH EVANGELICAL COLLEGE & SEMINARY, Tacoma, WA 98407

General Information Independent-religious, coed, graduate-only institution.

GRADUATE UNITS

Graduate and Professional Programs *Program availability:* Part-time, evening/weekend, online learning. Offers theology (M Div, MACM, MTS, D Min).

FAITH THEOLOGICAL SEMINARY, Baltimore, MD 21212

General Information Independent-religious, coed, comprehensive institution.

GRADUATE UNITS

Graduate Programs Offers theology (M Div, D Min, Th D).

FASHION INSTITUTE OF TECHNOLOGY, New York, NY 10001-5992

General Information State and locally supported, coed, primarily women, comprehensive institution. *Enrollment:* 9,272 graduate, professional, and undergraduate students; 120 full-time matriculated graduate/professional students (100 women), 56 part-time matriculated graduate/professional students (48 women). *Enrollment by degree level:* 176 master's. *Graduate faculty:* 9 full-time (4 women), 45 part-time/adjunct (17 women). Tuition, state resident: full-time $10,870; part-time $453 per credit. Tuition, nonresident: full-time $22,210; part-time $925 per credit. *Required fees:* $745. *Graduate housing:* Room and/or apartments available on a first-come, first-served basis to single students; on-campus housing not available to married students. Typical cost: $13,280 per year ($17,756 including board). Room and board charges vary according to board plan and housing facility selected. *Student services:* Career counseling, exercise/wellness program, free psychological counseling, international student services, low-cost health insurance, services for students with disabilities. *Library facilities:* Gladys Marcus Library. *Research affiliation:* Exhibition Designers and Producers Association (exhibition design), Society for Environmental Graphic Design (exhibition design), Lolita S. A. (global fashion management), IDEO (design and management innovation), Grove Dictionary of Art, Oxford University Press (costume history).

Computer facilities: A campuswide network can be accessed from student residence rooms.
Website: http://www.fitnyc.edu/

General Application Contact: E-mail: gradinfo@fitnyc.edu.

GRADUATE UNITS

School of Graduate Studies Expenses: Contact institution. *Financial support:* Federal Work-Study and scholarships/grants available. Financial award applicants required to submit FAFSA. *Program availability:* Part-time, evening/weekend. Offers art market studies (MA); cosmetics and fragrance marketing and management (MPS); exhibition and experience design (MA); fashion and textile studies: history, theory, museum

practice (MA); fashion design (MFA); global fashion management (MPS); illustration (MFA). *Application deadline:* For fall admission, 2/15 priority date for domestic and international students. Applications are processed on a rolling basis. *Application fee:* $50. Electronic applications accepted. *Application Contact:* Carole deSantis, Administrative Secretary, Graduate Admissions, 212-217-4314, Fax: 212-217-5156, E-mail: carole_desantis@fitnyc.edu. *Dean,* Dr. Mary Davis, 212-217-4300.

FAULKNER UNIVERSITY, Montgomery, AL 36109-3398

General Information Independent-religious, coed, university. *Graduate housing:* On-campus housing not available.

GRADUATE UNITS

Alabama Christian College of Arts and Sciences Offers arts and sciences (M Ed, MJA, MLA, MS); counseling (MS); criminal justice (MJA); liberal arts (MLA).

College of Biblical Studies Offers ministry (MABS); missions (MABS); New Testament (MABS); Old Testament (MABS); youth and family ministry (MABS).

College of Education Offers education (M Ed).

Great Books Honors College Offers Western civilization (M Litt).

Harris College of Business and Executive Education Offers management (MSM).

Thomas Goode Jones School of Law Offers law (JD). Electronic applications accepted.

FAYETTEVILLE STATE UNIVERSITY, Fayetteville, NC 28301-4298

General Information State-supported, coed, comprehensive institution. *Enrollment:* 6,223 graduate, professional, and undergraduate students; 373 full-time matriculated graduate/professional students (248 women), 307 part-time matriculated graduate/professional students (201 women). *Enrollment by degree level:* 603 master's, 77 doctoral. *Graduate faculty:* 131 full-time (59 women), 20 part-time/adjunct (9 women). *Graduate housing:* On-campus housing not available. *Student services:* Campus employment opportunities, career counseling, child daycare facilities, free psychological counseling, low-cost health insurance. *Library facilities:* Charles W. Chestnut Library. *Collection:* Books: 214,552 (physical), 180,637 (digital/electronic); Serial titles: 298 (physical), 31,619 (digital/electronic); Databases: 382. Weekly public service hours: 97; students can reserve study rooms. *Research affiliation:* Research Triangle Park.

Computer facilities: Computer purchase and lease plans are available. 600 computers available on campus for general student use. A campuswide network can be accessed from student residence rooms and from off campus. Online class registration is available.
Website: http://www.uncfsu.edu/

General Application Contact: Dr. Samuel Adu-Mireku, Associate Dean, 910-672-1042, Fax: 910-672-1083, E-mail: sadu-mireku@uncfsu.edu.

GRADUATE UNITS

Graduate School Students: 373 full-time (248 women), 307 part-time (201 women); includes 414 minority (330 Black or African American, non-Hispanic/Latino; 10 American Indian or Alaska Native, non-Hispanic/Latino; 26 Asian, non-Hispanic/Latino; 38 Hispanic/Latino; 2 Native Hawaiian or other Pacific Islander, non-Hispanic/Latino; 8 Two or more races, non-Hispanic/Latino), 6 international. Average age 35. 220 applicants, 93% accepted, 153 enrolled. *Faculty:* 131 full-time (59 women), 20 part-time/adjunct (9 women). Expenses: Contact institution. *Financial support:* In 2016–17, 19 research assistantships (averaging $4,000 per year) were awarded; institutionally sponsored loans and unspecified assistantships also available. Support available to part-time students. Financial award application deadline: 3/1; financial award applicants required to submit FAFSA. In 2016, 159 master's, 6 doctorates awarded. *Program availability:* Part-time, evening/weekend. Offers biological sciences (MS); business administration (MBA); criminal justice (MA); mathematics and computer science (MS); middle grades (MA Ed); psychology (MA); school administration (MSA); social work (MSW); sociology (MA Ed); special education (MA Ed). *Application deadline:* For fall admission, 4/1 for domestic students, 3/1 for international students; for spring admission, 10/15 for domestic students. Applications are processed on a rolling basis. *Application fee:* $40. Electronic applications accepted. *Application Contact:* 910-672-1374, Fax: 910-672-1470. *Office of Admissions,* 910-672-1374, Fax: 910-672-1470.

FELICIAN UNIVERSITY, Lodi, NJ 07644-2117

General Information Independent-religious, coed, comprehensive institution. *Enrollment:* 2,014 graduate, professional, and undergraduate students; 48 full-time matriculated graduate/professional students (31 women), 318 part-time matriculated graduate/professional students (257 women). *Enrollment by degree level:* 332 master's, 23 doctoral, 11 other advanced degrees. *Graduate faculty:* 29 full-time (17 women), 14 part-time/adjunct (5 women). *Tuition:* Full-time $18,000; part-time $1000 per credit. Tuition and fees vary according to course load and program. *Graduate housing:* Room and/or apartments available on a first-come, first-served basis to single students; on-campus housing not available to married students. Typical cost: $12,380 (including board). Housing application deadline: 5/1. *Student services:* Campus employment opportunities, campus safety program, career counseling, child daycare facilities, free psychological counseling, international student services, low-cost health insurance, services for students with disabilities, teacher training, writing training. *Library facilities:* Felician University Library plus 1 other. *Collection:* Books: 70,383 (physical), 193,005 (digital/electronic); Serial titles: 186 (physical), 33,942 (digital/electronic); Databases: 45. Weekly public service hours: 133; students can reserve study rooms.

Computer facilities: 170 computers available on campus for general student use. A campuswide network can be accessed from student residence rooms and from off campus. Online class registration is available.
Website: http://www.felician.edu/

General Application Contact: Michael Szarek, Assistant Vice-President, Graduate Admissions, 201-559-1450, E-mail: szarekm@felician.edu.

GRADUATE UNITS

Doctor of Nursing Practice Program Students: 13 part-time (12 women); includes 7 minority (4 Black or African American, non-Hispanic/Latino; 1 Asian, non-Hispanic/Latino; 2 Hispanic/Latino). Average age 53. 7 applicants, 71% accepted, 4 enrolled. *Faculty:* 4 full-time (3 women), 1 (woman) part-time/adjunct. Expenses: Contact institution. *Financial support:* Federal Work-Study and scholarships/grants available. Financial award applicants required to submit FAFSA. In 2016, 3 doctorates awarded. *Program availability:* Evening/weekend, online only, 100% online, blended/hybrid learning. Offers advanced practice (DNP); executive leadership (DNP). *Application deadline:* Applications are processed on a rolling basis. *Application fee:* $40. Electronic applications accepted. *Application Contact:* Michael Szarek, Assistant Vice-President of Graduate Admissions, 201-559-1450, E-mail: szarekm@felician.edu. *Associate Dean of Graduate Nursing,* Dr. Ann Tritak, 201-559-6151, E-mail: tritaka@felician.edu.

Felician University

Master of Science in Nursing Program Students: 1 (woman) full-time, 113 part-time (107 women); includes 53 minority (18 Black or African American, non-Hispanic/Latino; 1 American Indian or Alaska Native, non-Hispanic/Latino; 13 Asian, non-Hispanic/Latino; 18 Hispanic/Latino; 3 Native Hawaiian or other Pacific Islander, non-Hispanic/Latino). Average age 40. 88 applicants, 76% accepted, 32 enrolled. *Faculty:* 10 full-time (9 women), 1 (woman) part-time/adjunct. Expenses: Contact institution. *Financial support:* Federal Work-Study, scholarships/grants, and traineeships available. Financial award application deadline: 9/15; financial award applicants required to submit FAFSA. In 2016, 17 master's, 1 other advanced degree awarded. *Program availability:* Evening/weekend, online only, 100% online, blended/hybrid learning. Offers adult-gerontology nurse practitioner (MSN, PMC); executive leadership (MSN, PMC); family nurse practitioner (MSN, PMC); nursing education (MSN, PMC). *Application deadline:* Applications are processed on a rolling basis. *Application fee:* $40. Electronic applications accepted. *Application Contact:* Michael Szarek, Assistant Vice-President, Graduate Admissions, 201-559-1450, E-mail: szarekm@felician.edu. *Associate Dean, Department of Graduate Nursing,* Dr. Ann Tritak, 201-559-6151, E-mail: tritaka@felician.edu.

Program in Business Students: 4 full-time (2 women), 85 part-time (46 women); includes 48 minority (24 Black or African American, non-Hispanic/Latino; 10 Asian, non-Hispanic/Latino; 13 Hispanic/Latino; 1 Two or more races, non-Hispanic/Latino), 4 international. Average age 35. 71 applicants, 86% accepted, 40 enrolled. *Faculty:* 7 full-time (0 women), 9 part-time/adjunct (2 women). Expenses: Contact institution. *Financial support:* Federal Work-Study and scholarships/grants available. Financial award applicants required to submit FAFSA. In 2016, 22 master's awarded. *Program availability:* Part-time-only, evening/weekend. Offers business administration (DBA); innovation and entrepreneurship (MBA). *Application deadline:* Applications are processed on a rolling basis. *Application fee:* $40. Electronic applications accepted. *Application Contact:* Michael Szarek, Assistant Vice-President, Graduate Admissions, 201-559-1450, E-mail: szarekm@felician.edu. *Associate Dean/Associate Professor, School of Business,* Dr. David M. Turi, 201-559-3327, E-mail: turid@felician.edu.

Program in Counseling Psychology Students: 28 full-time (21 women), 23 part-time (18 women); includes 35 minority (12 Black or African American, non-Hispanic/Latino; 3 Asian, non-Hispanic/Latino; 18 Hispanic/Latino; 1 Native Hawaiian or other Pacific Islander, non-Hispanic/Latino; 1 Two or more races, non-Hispanic/Latino), 1 international. Average age 31. 28 applicants, 71% accepted, 12 enrolled. *Faculty:* 4 full-time (1 woman), 8 part-time/adjunct (7 women). Expenses: Contact institution. *Financial support:* Federal Work-Study and scholarships/grants available. Financial award applicants required to submit FAFSA. In 2016, 12 master's awarded. *Program availability:* Part-time, evening/weekend. Offers counseling psychology (MA). *Application deadline:* Applications are processed on a rolling basis. *Application fee:* $40. Electronic applications accepted. *Application Contact:* Michael Szarek, Assistant Vice-President, Graduate Admissions, 201-559-1450, E-mail: szarekm@felician.edu. *Director of the Master's in Counseling Program,* Dr. Daniel Mahoney, 201-559-6161, E-mail: mahoneyd@felician.edu.

Program in Education Students: 4 full-time (3 women), 65 part-time (60 women); includes 19 minority (9 Black or African American, non-Hispanic/Latino; 2 Asian, non-Hispanic/Latino; 8 Hispanic/Latino), 1 international. Average age 36. 36 applicants, 78% accepted, 16 enrolled. *Faculty:* 2 full-time (1 woman), 7 part-time/adjunct (2 women). Expenses: Contact institution. *Financial support:* Federal Work-Study and scholarships/grants available. Financial award applicants required to submit FAFSA. In 2016, 18 master's, 11 other advanced degrees awarded. *Program availability:* Part-time, evening/weekend. Offers education (MA); educational leadership (principal/supervision) (MA); educational supervision (PMC); principal (PMC). *Application deadline:* Applications are processed on a rolling basis. *Application fee:* $40. Electronic applications accepted. *Application Contact:* Michael Szarek, Assistant Vice-President, Graduate Admissions, 201-559-1450, E-mail: szarekm@felician.edu. *Dean and Professor, School of Education,* Dr. Rose Rudnitski, 201-559-3551, E-mail: rudnitskir@felician.edu.

Program in Health Care Administration Students: 1 full-time (0 women), 33 part-time (22 women); includes 19 minority (8 Black or African American, non-Hispanic/Latino; 4 Asian, non-Hispanic/Latino; 6 Hispanic/Latino; 1 Two or more races, non-Hispanic/Latino), 1 international. Average age 33. 31 applicants, 77% accepted, 13 enrolled. *Faculty:* 1 full-time (0 women), 6 part-time/adjunct (2 women). Expenses: Contact institution. *Financial support:* Federal Work-Study and scholarships/grants available. Financial award applicants required to submit FAFSA. In 2016, 7 master's awarded. *Program availability:* Part-time, evening/weekend. Offers health care administration (MSHA). *Application deadline:* Applications are processed on a rolling basis. *Application fee:* $40. Electronic applications accepted. *Application Contact:* Michael Szarek, Assistant Vice-President, Graduate Admissions, 201-559-1450, E-mail: szarekm@felician.edu. *Associate Dean/Associate Professor, School of Business,* Dr. David M. Turi, 201-559-3327, E-mail: turid@felician.edu.

Program in Religious Education Students: 1 (woman) full-time, 16 part-time (11 women); includes 6 minority (1 Black or African American, non-Hispanic/Latino; 3 Asian, non-Hispanic/Latino; 2 Hispanic/Latino). Average age 45. 10 applicants, 70% accepted, 4 enrolled. *Faculty:* 1 (woman) full-time, 5 part-time/adjunct (2 women). Expenses: Contact institution. *Financial support:* Federal Work-Study, scholarships/grants, and tuition waivers (partial) available. Financial award applicants required to submit FAFSA. In 2016, 8 master's awarded. *Program availability:* Part-time, evening/weekend, online only, 100% online. Offers religious education (MA, Certificate). *Application deadline:* Applications are processed on a rolling basis. *Application fee:* $40. Electronic applications accepted. *Application Contact:* Michael Szarek, Director, Graduate Admissions, 201-559-1451, E-mail: szarekm@felician.edu. *Director,* Dr. Dolores M. Henchy, 201-559-6053, Fax: 973-472-8936, E-mail: henchyd@felician.edu.

FERRIS STATE UNIVERSITY, Big Rapids, MI 49307

General Information State-supported, coed, comprehensive institution. CGS member. *Enrollment:* 14,187 graduate, professional, and undergraduate students; 890 full-time matriculated graduate/professional students (516 women), 318 part-time matriculated graduate/professional students (189 women). *Enrollment by degree level:* 381 master's, 729 doctoral, 98 other advanced degrees. *Graduate faculty:* 109 full-time (63 women), 207 part-time/adjunct (92 women). Tuition and fees vary according to degree level and program. *Graduate housing:* Rooms and/or apartments available on a first-come, first-served basis to single and married students. Typical cost: $9652 (including board) for single students. *Student services:* Campus employment opportunities, campus safety program, career counseling, child daycare facilities, exercise/wellness program, free psychological counseling, international student services, low-cost health insurance, multicultural affairs office, services for students with disabilities, teacher training. *Library facilities:* Ferris Library for Information, Technology and Education. *Collection:* 233,023 (physical), 221,325 (digital/electronic); Serial titles: 2,107 (physical), 80,766 (digital/electronic); Databases: 197. Weekly public service hours: 96; study areas open

24 hours, 5–7 days a week. *Research affiliation:* Allergan-Hydron (optometry), Bausch & Lomb (optometry), Ciba Vision (optometry), American Education Research Association (education), Vistakon-Johnson & Johnson (optometry).

Computer facilities: 1,940 computers available on campus for general student use. A campuswide network can be accessed from student residence rooms and from off campus. Online class registration is available. Website: http://www.ferris.edu/

General Application Contact: Dr. Kristen Salomonson, Dean, Enrollment Services/Director, Admissions and Records, 231-591-2100, Fax: 231-591-3944, E-mail: admissions@ferris.edu.

GRADUATE UNITS

College of Business Students: 25 full-time (11 women), 113 part-time (47 women); includes 12 minority (2 Black or African American, non-Hispanic/Latino; 1 American Indian or Alaska Native, non-Hispanic/Latino; 3 Asian, non-Hispanic/Latino; 3 Hispanic/Latino; 3 Two or more races, non-Hispanic/Latino), 50 international. Average age 31. 128 applicants, 59% accepted, 39 enrolled. *Faculty:* 18 full-time (7 women), 6 part-time/adjunct (3 women). Expenses: Contact institution. *Financial support:* Career-related internships or fieldwork, Federal Work-Study, scholarships/grants, and unspecified assistantships available. Support available to part-time students. Financial award application deadline: 3/15; financial award applicants required to submit FAFSA. In 2016, 94 master's awarded. *Program availability:* Part-time, evening/weekend, 100% online, blended/hybrid learning. Offers business intelligence (MBA); design and innovation management (MBA); incident response (MBA); information security and intelligence (MS); lean systems and leadership (MBA); performance metrics (MBA); project management (MBA); supply chain management and lean logistics (MBA). *Application deadline:* For fall admission, 7/1 priority date for domestic students, 6/15 for international students; for winter admission, 11/1 priority date for domestic students, 10/15 for international students; for spring admission, 3/1 priority date for domestic students, 2/15 for international students. Applications are processed on a rolling basis. *Application fee:* $0 ($30 for international students). Electronic applications accepted. *Application Contact:* Dr. Greg Gogolin, Professor, 231-591-3159, Fax: 231-591-3521, E-mail: greggogolin@ferris.edu. *College of Business Dean,* Dr. David Nicol, 231-591-2168, Fax: 231-591-3521, E-mail: davidnicol@ferris.edu.

College of Education and Human Services Students: 11 full-time (6 women), 87 part-time (45 women); includes 19 minority (8 Black or African American, non-Hispanic/Latino; 1 American Indian or Alaska Native, non-Hispanic/Latino; 4 Hispanic/Latino; 6 Two or more races, non-Hispanic/Latino), 9 international. Average age 36. 40 applicants, 78% accepted, 21 enrolled. *Faculty:* 15 full-time (6 women), 9 part-time/adjunct (6 women). Expenses: Contact institution. *Financial support:* In 2016–17, 1 research assistantship (averaging $4,850 per year) was awarded; career-related internships or fieldwork, Federal Work-Study, scholarships/grants, and unspecified assistantships also available. Support available to part-time students. Financial award applicants required to submit FAFSA. In 2016, 53 master's awarded. *Program availability:* Part-time, evening/weekend, blended/hybrid learning. Offers education and human services (M Ed, MS, MSCJ, MSCTE). *Application deadline:* For fall admission, 7/1 priority date for domestic and international students; for winter admission, 12/15 priority date for domestic and international students; for spring admission, 11/1 priority date for domestic and international students; for summer admission, 3/1 priority date for domestic and international students. Applications are processed on a rolling basis. *Application fee:* $30. Electronic applications accepted. *Application Contact:* Dr. Kristen Salomonson, Dean, Enrollment Services/Director, Admissions and Records, 231-591-2100, Fax: 231-591-3944, E-mail: admissions@ferris.edu. *Dean,* Arrick L. Jackson, 231-591-2702, Fax: 231-592-3792, E-mail: arrickjackson@ferris.edu.

School of Criminal Justice Students: 8 full-time (5 women), 25 part-time (11 women); includes 11 minority (5 Black or African American, non-Hispanic/Latino; 1 American Indian or Alaska Native, non-Hispanic/Latino; 3 Hispanic/Latino; 2 Two or more races, non-Hispanic/Latino). Average age 35. 16 applicants, 88% accepted, 11 enrolled. *Faculty:* 8 full-time (2 women). Expenses: Contact institution. *Financial support:* In 2016–17, 1 research assistantship (averaging $4,850 per year) was awarded; Federal Work-Study and unspecified assistantships also available. Support available to part-time students. Financial award applicants required to submit FAFSA. In 2016, 17 master's awarded. *Program availability:* Part-time, evening/weekend. Offers criminal justice administration (MSCJ). *Application deadline:* For fall admission, 8/15 for domestic students; for winter admission, 12/15 for domestic students; for spring admission, 3/15 for domestic students. Applications are processed on a rolling basis. *Application fee:* $0. Electronic applications accepted. *Application Contact:* Sara P. Rasmussen, Secretary, 231-591-3652, Fax: 231-591-3792, E-mail: sararasmussen@ferris.edu. *Professor/Graduate Program Coordinator,* Dr. Nancy L. Hogan, 231-591-2664, Fax: 231-591-3792, E-mail: hogann@ferris.edu.

School of Education Students: 3 full-time (1 woman), 62 part-time (34 women); includes 8 minority (3 Black or African American, non-Hispanic/Latino; 1 Hispanic/Latino; 4 Two or more races, non-Hispanic/Latino), 9 international. Average age 37. 24 applicants, 71% accepted, 10 enrolled. *Faculty:* 7 full-time (4 women), 9 part-time/adjunct (6 women). Expenses: Contact institution. *Financial support:* Career-related internships or fieldwork and scholarships/grants available. Support available to part-time students. Financial award applicants required to submit FAFSA. In 2016, 36 master's awarded. *Program availability:* Part-time, evening/weekend, blended/hybrid learning. Offers curriculum and instruction (M Ed); educational leadership (MS); instructor (MSCTE); post-secondary administration (MSCTE); training and development (MSCTE). *Application deadline:* For fall admission, 7/1 priority date for domestic and international students; for spring admission, 11/1 priority date for domestic and international students; for summer admission, 3/1 priority date for domestic and international students. Applications are processed on a rolling basis. *Application fee:* $30. Electronic applications accepted. *Application Contact:* Liza Ing, Graduate Program Coordinator, 231-591-5362, Fax: 231-591-2043, E-mail: lizaing@ferris.edu. *Dean,* Arrick L. Jackson, 231-591-2702, Fax: 231-591-2043, E-mail: arrickjackson@ferris.edu.

College of Health Professions Students: 4 full-time (all women), 93 part-time (84 women); includes 11 minority (3 Black or African American, non-Hispanic/Latino; 3 American Indian or Alaska Native, non-Hispanic/Latino; 2 Asian, non-Hispanic/Latino; 1 Hispanic/Latino; 1 Native Hawaiian or other Pacific Islander, non-Hispanic/Latino; 1 Two or more races, non-Hispanic/Latino). Average age 40. 31 applicants, 74% accepted, 18 enrolled. *Faculty:* 7 full-time (all women), 2 part-time/adjunct (both women). Expenses: Contact institution. *Financial support:* In 2016–17, 3 students received support. Career-related internships or fieldwork and scholarships/grants available. Financial award application deadline: 4/15; financial award applicants required to submit FAFSA. In 2016, 27 master's awarded. *Program availability:* Part-time, evening/weekend, 100% online. Offers health professions (MSN). *Application deadline:* For fall admission, 4/15 priority date for domestic students; for spring admission, 10/15 for domestic students.

Applications are processed on a rolling basis. *Application fee:* $0. Electronic applications accepted. *Application Contact:* Sharon Colley, MSN Program Coordinator, 231-591-2267, Fax: 231-591-2328, E-mail: cooleys@ferris.edu. *Chair, School of Nursing,* Dr. Susan Owens, 231-591-2267, Fax: 231-591-3788, E-mail: owenss3@ferris.edu.

School of Nursing Students: 4 full-time (all women), 93 part-time (84 women); includes 11 minority (3 Black or African American, non-Hispanic/Latino; 3 American Indian or Alaska Native, non-Hispanic/Latino; 2 Asian, non-Hispanic/Latino; 1 Hispanic/Latino; 1 Native Hawaiian or other Pacific Islander, non-Hispanic/Latino; 1 Two or more races, non-Hispanic/Latino). Average age 40. 31 applicants, 74% accepted, 18 enrolled. *Faculty:* 7 full-time (all women), 2 part-time/adjunct (both women). Expenses: Contact institution. *Financial support:* In 2016–17, 3 students received support. Career-related internships or fieldwork and scholarships/grants available. Financial award application deadline: 4/15; financial award applicants required to submit FAFSA. In 2016, 27 master's awarded. *Program availability:* Part-time, evening/weekend, online only, 100% online. Offers nursing (MSN); nursing administration (MSN); nursing education (MSN); nursing informatics (MSN). *Application deadline:* For fall admission, 4/15 priority date for domestic students; for spring admission, 10/15 for domestic students. *Application fee:* $0. Electronic applications accepted. *Application Contact:* Sharon Colley, MSN Program Coordinator, 231-591-2288, Fax: 231-591-2325, E-mail: colleys@ferris.edu. *Chair, School of Nursing,* Dr. Susan Owens, 231-591-2267, Fax: 231-591-2325, E-mail: owenss3@ferris.edu.

College of Pharmacy Students: 568 full-time (310 women), 13 part-time (6 women); includes 37 minority (6 Black or African American, non-Hispanic/Latino; 1 American Indian or Alaska Native, non-Hispanic/Latino; 8 Asian, non-Hispanic/Latino; 16 Hispanic/Latino; 6 Two or more races, non-Hispanic/Latino), 19 international. Average age 24. 446 applicants, 37% accepted, 140 enrolled. *Faculty:* 35 full-time (24 women), 4 part-time/adjunct (2 women). Expenses: Contact institution. *Financial support:* Career-related internships or fieldwork, Federal Work-Study, institutionally sponsored loans, and scholarships/grants available. Financial award applicants required to submit FAFSA. In 2016, 147 doctorates awarded. Offers pharmacy (Pharm D). *Application deadline:* For fall admission, 2/2 for domestic and international students. *Application fee:* $0. *Application Contact:* Tara M. Lee, Director of Admissions, 231-591-2249, Fax: 231-591-3829, E-mail: leet@ferris.edu. *Dean,* Dr. Stephen Durst, 231-591-2254, Fax: 231-591-3829, E-mail: dursts@ferris.edu.

Extended and International Operations Students: 94 full-time (70 women), 4 part-time (1 woman); includes 21 minority (16 Black or African American, non-Hispanic/Latino; 5 Hispanic/Latino). Average age 46. 28 applicants, 75% accepted, 19 enrolled. *Faculty:* 23 part-time/adjunct (14 women). Expenses: Contact institution. *Financial support:* In 2016–17, 4 teaching assistantships (averaging $1,000 per year) were awarded. Financial award application deadline: 5/1; financial award applicants required to submit FAFSA. In 2016, 11 doctorates awarded. *Program availability:* Evening/weekend, blended/hybrid learning. Offers community college leadership (Ed D). *Application deadline:* For fall admission, 12/15 for domestic and international students; for winter admission, 1/27 for domestic and international students; for spring admission, 4/15 for domestic students, 4/18 for international students. Applications are processed on a rolling basis. *Application fee:* $0. Electronic applications accepted. *Application Contact:* Megan Biller, Coordinator, 231-591-2710, Fax: 231-591-3539, E-mail: meganbiller@ferris.edu. *Director,* Dr. Roberta Teahen, 231-591-3805, E-mail: robertateahen@ferris.edu.

Kendall College of Art and Design Students: 40 full-time (33 women), 5 part-time (3 women); includes 9 minority (3 Black or African American, non-Hispanic/Latino; 3 Asian, non-Hispanic/Latino; 3 Hispanic/Latino), 6 international. Average age 30. 43 applicants, 53% accepted, 16 enrolled. *Faculty:* 15 full-time (10 women), 9 part-time/adjunct (2 women). Expenses: Contact institution. *Financial support:* In 2016–17, 32 students received support, including 8 fellowships (averaging $16,781 per year); scholarships/grants and unspecified assistantships also available. Financial award application deadline: 2/1; financial award applicants required to submit FAFSA. In 2016, 16 master's awarded. *Program availability:* Part-time. Offers architecture (M Arch); art education (MAE); design (MA); drawing (MFA); painting (MFA); photography (MFA); printmaking (MFA); visual and critical studies (MA). *Application deadline:* For fall admission, 2/1 priority date for domestic and international students; for spring admission, 11/1 priority date for domestic and international students. Applications are processed on a rolling basis. *Application fee:* $0. Electronic applications accepted. *Application Contact:* Thomas Post, Graduate Recruitment Specialist, 616-451-2787, Fax: 616-831-9689, E-mail: thomaspost@ferris.edu. *President,* Leslie Bellavance, 616-451-2787.

Michigan College of Optometry Students: 148 full-time (82 women); includes 10 minority (1 Black or African American, non-Hispanic/Latino; 2 Asian, non-Hispanic/Latino; 5 Hispanic/Latino; 2 Two or more races, non-Hispanic/Latino), 2 international. Average age 23. 224 applicants, 29% accepted, 39 enrolled. *Faculty:* 19 full-time (9 women), 154 part-time/adjunct (63 women). Expenses: Contact institution. *Financial support:* In 2016–17, 40 students received support. Career-related internships or fieldwork, Federal Work-Study, and scholarships/grants available. Financial award application deadline: 3/30; financial award applicants required to submit FAFSA. In 2016, 35 doctorates awarded. Offers optometry (OD). *Application deadline:* For fall admission, 2/1 for domestic and international students. Applications are processed on a rolling basis. *Application fee:* $450. Electronic applications accepted. *Application Contact:* Amy Parks, Health College Administrative Specialist, 231-591-3703, Fax: 231-591-2394, E-mail: amyparks@ferris.edu. *Dean,* Dr. David Damari, 231-591-3706, Fax: 231-591-2394, E-mail: damarid@ferris.edu.

FIELDING GRADUATE UNIVERSITY, Santa Barbara, CA 93105-3814

General Information Independent, coed, graduate-only institution. CGS member. *Enrollment by degree level:* 87 master's, 804 doctoral, 154 other advanced degrees. *Graduate faculty:* 54 full-time (35 women), 133 part-time/adjunct (81 women). *Tuition:* Full-time $27,180; part-time $720 per credit. Tuition and fees vary according to course load, degree level and program. *Graduate housing:* On-campus housing not available. *Student services:* Grant writing training, international student services, services for students with disabilities, writing training. *Library facilities:* Fielding Graduate University Library Services. *Collection:* Books: 203,776 (digital/electronic); Serial titles: 50,341 (digital/electronic); Databases: 94.

Computer facilities: Online class registration is available. *Website:* http://www.fielding.edu/

General Application Contact: Admission Office, 800-340-1099, Fax: 805-987-9793, E-mail: admission@fielding.edu.

GRADUATE UNITS

Graduate Programs Students: 871 full-time (665 women), 174 part-time (133 women); includes 383 minority (169 Black or African American, non-Hispanic/Latino; 12 American Indian or Alaska Native, non-Hispanic/Latino; 45 Asian, non-Hispanic/Latino; 109 Hispanic/Latino; 2 Native Hawaiian or other Pacific Islander, non-Hispanic/Latino; 46 Two or more races, non-Hispanic/Latino), 11 international. Average age 45. 439 applicants, 61% accepted, 188 enrolled. *Faculty:* 54 full-time (35 women), 133 part-time/adjunct (81 women). Expenses: Contact institution. *Financial support:* In 2016–17, 215 students received support, including 5 research assistantships (averaging $1,367 per year), 18 teaching assistantships (averaging $1,889 per year); scholarships/grants also available. Support available to part-time students. Financial award applicants required to submit FAFSA. In 2016, 44 master's, 113 doctorates, 118 other advanced degrees awarded. *Program availability:* Part-time, 100% online, blended/hybrid learning. *Application deadline:* For fall admission, 7/15 for domestic and international students; for spring admission, 11/1 for domestic and international students; for summer admission, 3/1 for domestic and international students. *Application fee:* $75. Electronic applications accepted. *Application Contact:* Enrollment Coordinator, 800-340-1099 Ext. 4098, Fax: 805-687-9793, E-mail: admission@fielding.edu. *President,* Dr. Katrina Rogers, 805-898-2924, Fax: 805-687-9793, E-mail: krogers@fielding.edu.

School of Leadership Studies Students: 386 full-time (293 women), 92 part-time (74 women); includes 181 minority (82 Black or African American, non-Hispanic/Latino; 10 American Indian or Alaska Native, non-Hispanic/Latino; 26 Asian, non-Hispanic/Latino; 41 Hispanic/Latino; 2 Native Hawaiian or other Pacific Islander, non-Hispanic/Latino; 20 Two or more races, non-Hispanic/Latino), 6 international. Average age 49. 119 applicants, 94% accepted, 82 enrolled. *Faculty:* 22 full-time (13 women), 89 part-time/adjunct (60 women). Expenses: Contact institution. *Financial support:* In 2016–17, 20 students received support, including 2 research assistantships (averaging $1,350 per year); scholarships/grants and tuition waivers (partial) also available. Support available to part-time students. Financial award applicants required to submit FAFSA. In 2016, 35 master's, 67 doctorates, 50 other advanced degrees awarded. *Program availability:* Part-time, 100% online, blended/hybrid learning. Offers comprehensive evidence based coaching (Certificate, Graduate Certificate); digital teaching and learning (MA); education (MA, Ed D, Certificate); educational administration (Certificate, Graduate Certificate); evidence based coaching (Certificate); evidence based coaching for organization leadership (Graduate Certificate); evidence based coaching for organizational leadership (Certificate); human and organizational development (MA, PhD, Certificate); human development (PhD); infant and early childhood development (PhD, Certificate); leadership for change (Ed D); nonprofit leadership (Certificate, Graduate Certificate); organization consulting (Graduate Certificate); organizational consulting (Certificate); organizational development and change (PhD); organizational development and leadership (MA, Certificate, Graduate Certificate); reflective practice/supervision (Certificate). *Application deadline:* For fall admission, 7/1 for domestic and international students; for spring admission, 9/1 for domestic and international students; for summer admission, 3/1 for domestic and international students. *Application fee:* $75. Electronic applications accepted. *Application Contact:* Enrollment Coordinator, 800-340-1099 Ext. 4098, Fax: 805-687-9793, E-mail: hodadmission@fielding.edu. *Provost and Senior Vice President,* Dr. Gerald Porter, 805-898-2940, Fax: 805-687-9793, E-mail: gporter@fielding.edu.

School of Psychology Students: 485 full-time (372 women), 82 part-time (59 women); includes 202 minority (87 Black or African American, non-Hispanic/Latino; 2 American Indian or Alaska Native, non-Hispanic/Latino; 19 Asian, non-Hispanic/Latino; 68 Hispanic/Latino; 26 Two or more races, non-Hispanic/Latino), 5 international. Average age 41. 320 applicants, 49% accepted, 106 enrolled. *Faculty:* 32 full-time (22 women), 44 part-time/adjunct (21 women). Expenses: Contact institution. *Financial support:* In 2016–17, 32 students received support, including 2 research assistantships (averaging $884 per year), 18 teaching assistantships (averaging $1,889 per year); scholarships/grants and health care benefits also available. Support available to part-time students. Financial award applicants required to submit FAFSA. In 2016, 9 master's, 46 doctorates, 68 other advanced degrees awarded. *Program availability:* Part-time, 100% online, blended/hybrid learning. Offers clinical psychology (PhD, Post-Doctoral Certificate, Postbaccalaureate Certificate); forensic psychology (PhD); health psychology (PhD); media psychology (MA, PhD, Certificate); neuropsychology (PhD, Post-Doctoral Certificate); parent-infant mental health (PhD); respecialization in clinical psychology (Post-Doctoral Certificate); violence prevention and control (PhD). *Application deadline:* For fall admission, 1/24 for domestic and international students; for spring admission, 11/1 for domestic and international students; for summer admission, 3/1 for domestic and international students. *Application fee:* $75. Electronic applications accepted. *Application Contact:* Enrollment Coordinator, 800-340-1099 Ext. 4098, Fax: 805-687-9793, E-mail: psyadmission@fielding.edu. *Provost and Senior Vice President,* Dr. Gerald Porter, 805-898-2940, E-mail: gporter@fielding.edu.

FISHER COLLEGE, Boston, MA 02116-1500

General Information Independent, coed, comprehensive institution. *Enrollment:* 2,030 graduate, professional, and undergraduate students; 16 full-time matriculated graduate/professional students (6 women), 18 part-time matriculated graduate/professional students (11 women). *Enrollment by degree level:* 34 master's. *Graduate faculty:* 3 full-time (1 woman), 10 part-time/adjunct (4 women). *Tuition:* Full-time $29,840; part-time $577 per contact hour. Full-time tuition and fees vary according to class time and program. *Graduate housing:* Room and/or apartments available on a first-come, first-served basis to single students; on-campus housing not available to married students. Typical cost: $13,300 per year ($15,800 including board). Housing application deadline: 8/1. *Student services:* Campus employment opportunities, campus safety program, career counseling, free psychological counseling, international student services, low-cost health insurance, multicultural affairs office, services for students with disabilities, writing training. *Library facilities:* Fisher College Library. *Collection:* Books: 22,541 (physical), 8,035 (digital/electronic); Serial titles: 40 (physical); Databases: 81. Weekly public service hours: 68; study areas open 24 hours, 5–7 days a week; students can reserve study rooms.

Computer facilities: 208 computers available on campus for general student use. A campuswide network can be accessed from student residence rooms and from off campus. Online class registration is available. *Website:* http://www.fisher.edu/

General Application Contact: Dr. Neil Trotta, Dean, 617-236-8867, Fax: 617-236-5462, E-mail: ntrotta@fisher.edu.

GRADUATE UNITS

Master of Business Administration Program Students: 16 full-time (6 women), 18 part-time (11 women); includes 11 minority (1 Black or African American, non-Hispanic/Latino; 1 American Indian or Alaska Native, non-Hispanic/Latino; 1 Asian, non-

Hispanic/Latino; 8 Hispanic/Latino), 5 international. Average age 33. 174 applicants, 17% accepted, 18 enrolled. *Faculty:* 3 full-time (1 woman), 10 part-time/adjunct (4 women). Expenses: Contact institution. *Financial support:* In 2016–17, 5 students received support. Scholarships/grants and unspecified assistantships available. Financial award applicants required to submit FAFSA. In 2016, 6 master's awarded. *Program availability:* Part-time, evening/weekend, online only, 100% online. Offers strategic leadership (MBA). *Application deadline:* For fall admission, 8/1 for domestic and international students; for winter admission, 11/1 for domestic and international students. Applications are processed on a rolling basis. Electronic applications accepted. *Dean,* Neil Trotta, 617-236-8867, Fax: 617-236-5462, E-mail: ntrotta@fisher.edu.

FISK UNIVERSITY, Nashville, TN 37208-3051
General Information Independent-religious, coed, comprehensive institution. *Graduate housing:* Rooms and/or apartments available on a first-come, first-served basis to single and married students. Housing application deadline: 4/6. *Research affiliation:* Oak Ridge Associated Universities (physics).

GRADUATE UNITS
Division of Graduate Studies *Program availability:* Part-time. Offers biology (MA); chemistry (MA); clinical psychology (MA); physics (MA); psychology (MA). Electronic applications accepted.

FITCHBURG STATE UNIVERSITY, Fitchburg, MA 01420-2697
General Information State-supported, coed, comprehensive institution. *Enrollment:* 6,763 graduate, professional, and undergraduate students; 179 full-time matriculated graduate/professional students (127 women), 805 part-time matriculated graduate/professional students (609 women). *Enrollment by degree level:* 820 master's, 57 other advanced degrees. *Graduate faculty:* 44 full-time (25 women), 202 part-time/adjunct (146 women). Tuition, state resident: full-time $2871; part-time $1914 per year. Tuition, nonresident: full-time $2871; part-time $1914 per year. *Required fees:* $3828. Tuition and fees vary according to program. *Graduate housing:* On-campus housing not available. *Student services:* Campus employment opportunities, campus safety program, career counseling, exercise/wellness program, free psychological counseling, international student services, low-cost health insurance, multicultural affairs office, services for students with disabilities, teacher training, writing training. *Library facilities:* Amelia V. Galucci-Cirio Library. *Collection:* Books: 222,517 (physical); Databases: 150. Weekly public service hours: 77.

Computer facilities: 500 computers available on campus for general student use. A campuswide network can be accessed from student residence rooms and from off campus. Online class registration is available.
Website: http://www.fitchburgstate.edu/

General Application Contact: Sean Ganas, Director of Admissions, 978-665-3144, Fax: 978-665-4540, E-mail: admissions@fitchburgstate.edu.

GRADUATE UNITS
Division of Graduate and Continuing Education *Program availability:* Part-time, evening/weekend, online learning. Offers accounting (MBA); applied communications (CAGS); arts education (M Ed); biology and teaching biology (secondary level) (MA, MAT, Certificate); computer science (MS); counseling/psychology (CAGS); curriculum and teaching (M Ed); early childhood education (M Ed); educational leadership and management (M Ed, CAGS); educational technology (Certificate); elementary education (M Ed); elementary school guidance counseling (MS); English and teaching English (secondary level) (MA, MAT, Certificate); fine arts director (Certificate); forensic nursing (MS, Certificate); guided studies (M Ed); history and teaching history (secondary level) (MA, MAT, Certificate); human resource management (MBA); individualized track (CAGS); management (MBA); mental health counseling (MS); middle school education (M Ed); occupational education (M Ed); reading specialist (M Ed, CAGS); school principal (M Ed, CAGS); science education (M Ed); secondary school guidance counseling (MS); supervisor/director (M Ed, CAGS); teaching students with moderate disabilities (M Ed); teaching students with severe disabilities (M Ed); technology education (M Ed); technology leader (M Ed, CAGS). Electronic applications accepted.

FIVE BRANCHES UNIVERSITY, Santa Cruz, CA 95062
General Information Independent, coed, graduate-only institution. *Graduate housing:* On-campus housing not available. *Research affiliation:* Highland Hospital (healthcare).

GRADUATE UNITS
Graduate School of Traditional Chinese Medicine Offers acupuncture (M Ac); acupuncture and Oriental medicine (DAOM); traditional Chinese medicine (MTCM, PhD). Electronic applications accepted.

FIVE TOWNS COLLEGE, Dix Hills, NY 11746-6055
General Information Independent, coed, comprehensive institution. *Enrollment:* 21 full-time matriculated graduate/professional students (7 women), 6 part-time matriculated graduate/professional students (2 women). *Enrollment by degree level:* 10 master's, 14 doctoral, 3 other advanced degrees. *Graduate faculty:* 12 full-time (3 women), 6 part-time/adjunct (0 women). *Tuition:* Full-time $15,000; part-time $625 per credit. *Required fees:* $600; $150 per semester. Tuition and fees vary according to degree level. *Graduate housing:* Room and/or apartments available on a first-come, first-served basis to single students; on-campus housing not available to married students. Typical cost: $8800 per year ($13,800 including board). *Student services:* Campus employment opportunities, campus safety program, career counseling, international student services, low-cost health insurance, services for students with disabilities, teacher training, writing training. *Library facilities:* Five Towns College Library plus 1 other.

Computer facilities: 110 computers available on campus for general student use. A campuswide network can be accessed from student residence rooms.
Website: http://www.ftc.edu/

General Application Contact: Ronnie MacDonald, Director of Admissions, 631-656-2110, Fax: 631-656-2172, E-mail: admissions@ftc.edu.

GRADUATE UNITS
Graduate Programs Students: 18 full-time (7 women), 6 part-time (2 women); includes 9 minority (3 Black or African American, non-Hispanic/Latino; 4 Asian, non-Hispanic/Latino; 1 Hispanic/Latino; 1 Two or more races, non-Hispanic/Latino), 1 international. Average age 35. 63 applicants, 11% accepted, 7 enrolled. *Faculty:* 12 full-time (3 women), 6 part-time/adjunct (0 women). Expenses: Contact institution. *Financial support:* Fellowships with tuition reimbursements, teaching assistantships with tuition reimbursements, and tuition waivers (partial) available. Financial award applicants required to submit FAFSA. In 2016, 4 master's, 2 doctorates awarded. *Program availability:* Part-time. Offers childhood education (MS Ed); composition and arranging (DMA); jazz/commercial music (MM); music education (MM, DMA); music history and literature (DMA); music performance (DMA). *Application deadline:* For fall admission, 9/1

for domestic and international students; for spring admission, 1/25 for domestic and international students. Applications are processed on a rolling basis. *Application fee:* $50. Electronic applications accepted. *Application Contact:* Ronnie MacDonald, Director of Admissions, 631-656-2110, Fax: 631-656-2172, E-mail: admissions@ftc.edu.

FLORIDA AGRICULTURAL AND MECHANICAL UNIVERSITY, Tallahassee, FL 32307-3200
General Information State-supported, coed, university. CGS member. *Graduate housing:* Rooms and/or apartments available on a first-come, first-served basis to single and married students. Housing application deadline: 6/1. *Research affiliation:* Boeing (aerospace science), Minority Health Professions Foundation (health science), Pfizer, Inc.

GRADUATE UNITS
College of Law *Program availability:* Part-time, evening/weekend. Offers law (JD).
Division of Graduate Studies, Research, and Continuing Education *Program availability:* Part-time, evening/weekend.
College of Education *Program availability:* Part-time, evening/weekend. Offers administration and supervision (M Ed, MS, PhD); adult education (M Ed, MS); biology (M Ed); business education (MBE); chemistry (MS Ed); education (M Ed, MBE, MS, MS Ed, PhD); educational leadership (PhD); elementary education (M Ed, MS); English (MS Ed); guidance and counseling (M Ed, MS); history (MS Ed); industrial education (MS Ed); math (MS Ed); physics (MS Ed); sport management (MS); technology education (M Ed).
College of Pharmacy and Pharmaceutical Sciences Offers environmental toxicology (PhD); health outcomes research and pharmacoeconomics (PhD); medicinal chemistry (MS, PhD); pharmaceutics (MS, PhD); pharmacology/toxicology (MS, PhD); pharmacy administration (MS); pharmacy and pharmaceutical sciences (MPH, MS, DPH, DM, Pharm D); public health (MPH, DPH).
College of Science and Technology Offers chemistry (MS); physics (MS, PhD); science and technology (MS, PhD); software engineering (MS).
College of Social Sciences, Arts and Humanities *Program availability:* Part-time. Offers community psychology (MS); criminal justice (MASS); history (MASS); history and political science (MASS, MSW); political science (MASS); public administration (MASS); social sciences, arts and humanities (MASS, MS, MSW); social work (MSW).
FAMU-FSU College of Engineering Offers biomedical engineering (MS, PhD); chemical engineering (MS, PhD); civil engineering (M Eng, MS, PhD); electrical engineering (MS, PhD); engineering (M Eng, MS, PhD); industrial engineering (MS, PhD); mechanical engineering (MS, PhD). College administered jointly by Florida State University.
School of Allied Health Sciences Offers health administration (MS); occupational therapy (MOT); physical therapy (DPT).
School of Architecture *Program availability:* Part-time. Offers architectural studies (MS Arch); architecture (professional) (M Arch); landscape architecture (MLA).
School of Business and Industry Offers accounting (MBA); finance (MBA); management information systems (MBA); marketing (MBA).
School of Journalism and Graphic Communication Offers journalism (MS).
School of Nursing Offers nursing (MSN, PhD).
School of the Environment Offers the environment (MS, PhD).

FLORIDA ATLANTIC UNIVERSITY, Boca Raton, FL 33431-0991
General Information State-supported, coed, university. CGS member. *Enrollment:* 30,538 graduate, professional, and undergraduate students; 2,116 full-time matriculated graduate/professional students (1,152 women), 2,736 part-time matriculated graduate/professional students (1,741 women). *Enrollment by degree level:* 3,687 master's, 1,127 doctoral, 38 other advanced degrees. *Graduate faculty:* 791 full-time (342 women), 541 part-time/adjunct (275 women). Tuition, state resident: full-time $7392; part-time $369.82 per credit hour. Tuition, nonresident: full-time $19,432; part-time $1024.81 per credit hour. *Graduate housing:* Room and/or apartments available on a first-come, first-served basis to single students; on-campus housing not available to married students. Typical cost: $11,906 (including board). Room and board charges vary according to campus/location and housing facility selected. *Student services:* Campus employment opportunities, campus safety program, career counseling, exercise/wellness program, free psychological counseling, international student services, low-cost health insurance, multicultural affairs office, services for students with disabilities, teacher training. *Library facilities:* S. E. Wimberly Library plus 2 others. *Collection:* Books: 1.4 million (physical), 1.3 million (digital/electronic); Serial titles: 649 (physical), 106,566 (digital/electronic); Databases: 492. Study areas open 24 hours, 5–7 days a week. *Research affiliation:* Max Planck Florida Institute for Neuroscience (neuroscience), The Vaccine and Gene Institute of Florida (biomedical sciences), Torrey Pines Institute for Molecular Studies (medical research), The Scripps Research Institute (biomedical sciences).

Computer facilities: 1,350 computers available on campus for general student use. A campuswide network can be accessed from student residence rooms and from off campus. Online class registration is available.
Website: http://www.fau.edu/

General Application Contact: Jordan Parks, Coordinator, Admissions and Registration, 561-297-1213, Fax: 561-297-1212, E-mail: jparks3@fau.edu.

GRADUATE UNITS
Charles E. Schmidt College of Medicine Students: 288 full-time (135 women), 12 part-time (10 women); includes 115 minority (30 Black or African American, non-Hispanic/Latino; 38 Asian, non-Hispanic/Latino; 40 Hispanic/Latino; 7 Two or more races, non-Hispanic/Latino). Average age 25. 45 applicants, 40% accepted, 17 enrolled. Expenses: Contact institution. *Financial support:* Fellowships and research assistantships available. Financial award applicants required to submit FAFSA. In 2016, 16 master's awarded. *Program availability:* Part-time. Offers biomedical science (MS). *Application deadline:* For fall admission, 5/1 for domestic students, 3/15 for international students; for spring admission, 10/1 for domestic and international students. *Application fee:* $30. Electronic applications accepted. *Senior Director of Administration,* Deborah Roski, 561-297-2142, E-mail: dsalerno@health.fau.edu.
Charles E. Schmidt College of Science Students: 227 full-time (95 women), 172 part-time (79 women); includes 108 minority (16 Black or African American, non-Hispanic/Latino; 19 Asian, non-Hispanic/Latino; 60 Hispanic/Latino; 13 Two or more races, non-Hispanic/Latino), 75 international. Average age 29. 412 applicants, 37% accepted, 140 enrolled. *Faculty:* 139 full-time (39 women), 6 part-time/adjunct (1 woman). Expenses: Contact institution. *Financial support:* Fellowships with partial tuition reimbursements, research assistantships with partial tuition reimbursements, teaching assistantships with partial tuition reimbursements, career-related internships or

fieldwork, Federal Work-Study, institutionally sponsored loans, scholarships/grants, tuition waivers (partial), and unspecified assistantships available. Financial award applicants required to submit FAFSA. In 2016, 112 master's, 46 doctorates awarded. *Program availability:* Part-time. Offers applied mathematics and statistics (MS); biology (MS, MST); chemistry (MS, MST, PhD); geology (MS); geosciences (PhD); mathematics (MST, PhD); physics (MS, MST, PhD); psychology (MA); science (MA, MS, MSMP, MST, PhD). *Application deadline:* For fall admission, 6/1 for domestic students, 2/15 for international students; for spring admission, 11/1 for domestic students, 8/15 for international students. Applications are processed on a rolling basis. *Application fee:* $30. Electronic applications accepted. *Dean,* Ata Sarejedini, 561-297-3301, E-mail: ata@fau.edu.

Center for Complex Systems and Brain Sciences Students: 8 full-time (2 women), 6 part-time (2 women); includes 4 minority (1 Black or African American, non-Hispanic/Latino; 1 Asian, non-Hispanic/Latino; 1 Hispanic/Latino; 1 Two or more races, non-Hispanic/Latino), 3 international. Average age 31. 15 applicants, 40% accepted, 6 enrolled. Expenses: Contact institution. *Financial support:* Fellowships with full tuition reimbursements, research assistantships with partial tuition reimbursements, teaching assistantships with partial tuition reimbursements, Federal Work-Study, and traineeships available. In 2016, 4 degrees awarded. Offers complex systems and brain sciences (PhD). *Application deadline:* For fall admission, 1/15 priority date for domestic and international students. *Application fee:* $30.

Christine E. Lynn College of Nursing Students: 39 full-time (35 women), 497 part-time (459 women); includes 285 minority (146 Black or African American, non-Hispanic/Latino; 34 Asian, non-Hispanic/Latino; 92 Hispanic/Latino; 2 Native Hawaiian or other Pacific Islander, non-Hispanic/Latino; 11 Two or more races, non-Hispanic/Latino), 6 international. Average age 38. 480 applicants, 39% accepted, 169 enrolled. *Faculty:* 39 full-time (38 women), 8 part-time/adjunct (7 women). Expenses: Contact institution. *Financial support:* Research assistantships with partial tuition reimbursements, teaching assistantships with partial tuition reimbursements, career-related internships or fieldwork, Federal Work-Study, institutionally sponsored loans, scholarships/grants, and traineeships available. Support available to part-time students. In 2016, 131 master's, 22 doctorates awarded. *Program availability:* Part-time. Offers administrative and financial leadership in nursing and health care (Post Master's Certificate); nursing (PhD); nursing practice (DNP). *Application deadline:* For fall admission, 6/1 for domestic students, 2/15 for international students; for spring admission, 10/1 for domestic students, 7/15 for international students. Applications are processed on a rolling basis. *Application fee:* $30. *Dean,* Marlaine Smith, 561-297-3206, E-mail: msmit230@health.fau.edu.

College for Design and Social Inquiry Students: 250 full-time (189 women), 278 part-time (196 women); includes 257 minority (140 Black or African American, non-Hispanic/Latino; 1 American Indian or Alaska Native, non-Hispanic/Latino; 11 Asian, non-Hispanic/Latino; 90 Hispanic/Latino; 15 Two or more races, non-Hispanic/Latino), 15 international. Average age 32. 552 applicants, 52% accepted, 221 enrolled. *Faculty:* 45 full-time (14 women), 1 (woman) part-time/adjunct. Expenses: Contact institution. *Financial support:* Fellowships with partial tuition reimbursements, research assistantships with partial tuition reimbursements, teaching assistantships with partial tuition reimbursements, career-related internships or fieldwork, Federal Work-Study, and institutionally sponsored loans available. Support available to part-time students. Financial award application deadline: 4/1. In 2016, 204 master's, 6 doctorates awarded. *Program availability:* Part-time, evening/weekend. Offers design and social inquiry (MNM, MPA, MS, MSW, MURP, DSW, PhD). *Application deadline:* For fall admission, 5/1 for domestic students, 2/15 for international students; for spring admission, 11/1 for domestic students, 7/15 for international students. Applications are processed on a rolling basis. *Application fee:* $30. *Interim Dean,* Dr. Wesley Hawkins, 561-297-4168, E-mail: whawkins@fau.edu.

School of Criminology and Criminal Justice Students: 31 full-time (21 women), 38 part-time (26 women); includes 47 minority (27 Black or African American, non-Hispanic/Latino; 3 Asian, non-Hispanic/Latino; 14 Hispanic/Latino; 3 Two or more races, non-Hispanic/Latino). Average age 29. 55 applicants, 55% accepted, 23 enrolled. *Faculty:* 9 full-time (2 women). Expenses: Contact institution. *Financial support:* Research assistantships with partial tuition reimbursements, institutionally sponsored loans, scholarships/grants, and unspecified assistantships available. Financial award application deadline: 4/1. In 2016, 19 master's awarded. *Program availability:* Part-time, evening/weekend, online learning. Offers criminology and criminal justice (MS). *Application deadline:* For fall admission, 5/1 priority date for domestic students, 2/15 for international students; for spring admission, 11/1 priority date for domestic students, 7/15 for international students. Applications are processed on a rolling basis. *Application fee:* $30. Electronic applications accepted.

School of Public Administration Students: 44 full-time (25 women), 110 part-time (60 women); includes 74 minority (43 Black or African American, non-Hispanic/Latino; 3 Asian, non-Hispanic/Latino; 24 Hispanic/Latino; 4 Two or more races, non-Hispanic/Latino), 10 international. Average age 34. 109 applicants, 52% accepted, 32 enrolled. *Faculty:* 10 full-time (2 women). Expenses: Contact institution. *Financial support:* Fellowships with full tuition reimbursements, research assistantships with partial tuition reimbursements, teaching assistantships with partial tuition reimbursements, career-related internships or fieldwork, Federal Work-Study, institutionally sponsored loans, and tuition waivers (partial) available. Support available to part-time students. Financial award application deadline: 4/1. In 2016, 65 master's, 6 doctorates awarded. *Program availability:* Part-time, evening/weekend. Offers public administration (MPA, PhD). *Application deadline:* For fall admission, 5/1 priority date for domestic students, 2/15 for international students; for spring admission, 11/1 for domestic students, 7/15 for international students. Applications are processed on a rolling basis. *Application fee:* $30.

School of Social Work Students: 147 full-time (129 women), 118 part-time (106 women); includes 121 minority (62 Black or African American, non-Hispanic/Latino; 1 American Indian or Alaska Native, non-Hispanic/Latino; 5 Asian, non-Hispanic/Latino; 45 Hispanic/Latino; 8 Two or more races, non-Hispanic/Latino), 2 international. Average age 33. 361 applicants, 52% accepted, 158 enrolled. *Faculty:* 13 full-time (8 women), 1 (woman) part-time/adjunct. Expenses: Contact institution. *Financial support:* Fellowships with tuition reimbursements, research assistantships with tuition reimbursements, career-related internships or fieldwork, Federal Work-Study, institutionally sponsored loans, and tuition waivers (partial) available. Financial award application deadline: 4/1. In 2016, 109 master's awarded. *Program availability:* Part-time, evening/weekend. Offers social work (MSW, DSW). *Application deadline:* For fall admission, 5/1 priority date for domestic students, 2/15 for international students. Applications are processed on a rolling basis. *Application fee:* $30.

School of Urban and Regional Planning Students: 28 full-time (14 women), 12 part-time (4 women); includes 16 minority (8 Black or African American, non-Hispanic/Latino; 7 Hispanic/Latino; 1 Two or more races, non-Hispanic/Latino), 3

international. Average age 29. 27 applicants, 48% accepted, 8 enrolled. *Faculty:* 4 full-time (1 woman). Expenses: Contact institution. *Financial support:* Fellowships with full tuition reimbursements, research assistantships, career-related internships or fieldwork, Federal Work-Study, institutionally sponsored loans, and tuition waivers (partial) available. Financial award application deadline: 4/1. In 2016, 11 master's awarded. *Program availability:* Part-time, evening/weekend. Offers urban and regional planning (MURP). *Application deadline:* For fall admission, 5/1 priority date for domestic students, 2/15 for international students; for spring admission, 11/1 priority date for domestic students, 7/15 for international students. Applications are processed on a rolling basis. *Application fee:* $30.

College of Business Students: 582 full-time (287 women), 943 part-time (499 women); includes 705 minority (254 Black or African American, non-Hispanic/Latino; 2 American Indian or Alaska Native, non-Hispanic/Latino; 72 Asian, non-Hispanic/Latino; 328 Hispanic/Latino; 2 Native Hawaiian or other Pacific Islander, non-Hispanic/Latino; 47 Two or more races, non-Hispanic/Latino), 81 international. Average age 32. 1,258 applicants, 59% accepted, 568 enrolled. *Faculty:* 112 full-time (38 women), 7 part-time/adjunct (5 women). Expenses: Contact institution. *Financial support:* Fellowships with partial tuition reimbursements, research assistantships with partial tuition reimbursements, teaching assistantships with full tuition reimbursements, career-related internships or fieldwork, Federal Work-Study, institutionally sponsored loans, tuition waivers (full and partial), and unspecified assistantships available. Support available to part-time students. Financial award application deadline: 3/1. *Program availability:* Part-time, evening/weekend, online learning. Offers business (M Tax, MAC, MBA, MHA, MS, PhD); business administration (MBA); economics (MS); finance (MS); information technology management (MS); marketing (MS); music business administration (MS). *Application deadline:* For fall admission, 5/1 priority date for domestic students, 2/15 priority date for international students; for spring admission, 4/1 priority date for domestic students, 1/15 priority date for international students. Applications are processed on a rolling basis. *Application fee:* $30. *Dean,* Daniel Gropper, 561-297-3635, E-mail: dgropper@fau.edu.

School of Accounting Students: 142 full-time (54 women), 457 part-time (264 women); includes 287 minority (79 Black or African American, non-Hispanic/Latino; 32 Asian, non-Hispanic/Latino; 150 Hispanic/Latino; 2 Native Hawaiian or other Pacific Islander, non-Hispanic/Latino; 24 Two or more races, non-Hispanic/Latino), 21 international. Average age 32. 500 applicants, 61% accepted, 238 enrolled. *Faculty:* 17 full-time (7 women), 4 part-time/adjunct (2 women). Expenses: Contact institution. *Financial support:* Fellowships, research assistantships with partial tuition reimbursements, teaching assistantships, career-related internships or fieldwork, Federal Work-Study, institutionally sponsored loans, scholarships/grants, and tuition waivers (partial) available. Support available to part-time students. Financial award application deadline: 3/1. In 2016, 158 master's awarded. *Program availability:* Part-time, evening/weekend, online learning. Offers accounting (MAC). *Application deadline:* For fall admission, 7/1 priority date for domestic students, 2/15 priority date for international students; for spring admission, 11/1 priority date for domestic students, 7/15 priority date for international students. Applications are processed on a rolling basis. *Application fee:* $30.

College of Education Students: 316 full-time (234 women), 501 part-time (372 women); includes 319 minority (170 Black or African American, non-Hispanic/Latino; 17 Asian, non-Hispanic/Latino; 110 Hispanic/Latino; 1 Native Hawaiian or other Pacific Islander, non-Hispanic/Latino; 21 Two or more races, non-Hispanic/Latino), 19 international. Average age 33. 974 applicants, 34% accepted, 237 enrolled. *Faculty:* 85 full-time (49 women), 28 part-time/adjunct (15 women). Expenses: Contact institution. *Financial support:* Fellowships with partial tuition reimbursements, research assistantships with partial tuition reimbursements, teaching assistantships with partial tuition reimbursements, career-related internships or fieldwork, Federal Work-Study, and unspecified assistantships available. In 2016, 207 master's, 42 doctorates, 13 other advanced degrees awarded. *Program availability:* Part-time, evening/weekend. Offers adult and community education (M Ed, PhD, Ed S); counselor education (MS, PhD); curriculum and instruction (M Ed, PhD, Ed S); early childhood education (M Ed); education (M Ed, MA, MS, Ed D, PhD, Ed S); educational leadership (M Ed, PhD, Ed S); elementary education (M Ed); environmental education (M Ed); exceptional student education (M Ed, Ed D); exercise science and health promotion (MS); higher education (M Ed, PhD); K-12 school leadership (M Ed, PhD, Ed S); multicultural education (M Ed); reading education (M Ed); social foundations of education (M Ed); speech-language pathology (MS); TESOL and bilingual education (MA). *Application deadline:* For fall admission, 5/1 for domestic students. Applications are processed on a rolling basis. *Application fee:* $30. Electronic applications accepted.

College of Engineering and Computer Science Students: 182 full-time (46 women), 200 part-time (39 women); includes 110 minority (20 Black or African American, non-Hispanic/Latino; 17 Asian, non-Hispanic/Latino; 65 Hispanic/Latino; 8 Two or more races, non-Hispanic/Latino), 135 international. Average age 31. 355 applicants, 56% accepted, 148 enrolled. *Faculty:* 74 full-time (8 women), 4 part-time/adjunct (0 women). Expenses: Contact institution. *Financial support:* Fellowships, research assistantships with partial tuition reimbursements, teaching assistantships with partial tuition reimbursements, career-related internships or fieldwork, Federal Work-Study, and unspecified assistantships available. Support available to part-time students. Financial award applicants required to submit FAFSA. In 2016, 79 master's, 12 doctorates awarded. *Program availability:* Part-time, evening/weekend, online learning. Offers bioengineering (MS); civil engineering (MS); computer engineering (MS, PhD); computer science (MS, PhD); electrical engineering (MS, PhD); engineering and computer science (MS, PhD); environmental engineering (MS); mechanical engineering (MS, PhD). *Application deadline:* For fall admission, 7/1 for domestic students, 2/15 for international students; for spring admission, 11/1 for domestic students, 7/15 for international students. Applications are processed on a rolling basis. *Application fee:* $30.

Dorothy F. Schmidt College of Arts and Letters Students: 232 full-time (131 women), 133 part-time (87 women); includes 117 minority (35 Black or African American, non-Hispanic/Latino; 8 Asian, non-Hispanic/Latino; 65 Hispanic/Latino; 9 Two or more races, non-Hispanic/Latino), 28 international. Average age 33. 307 applicants, 56% accepted, 123 enrolled. *Faculty:* 170 full-time (76 women), 14 part-time/adjunct (7 women). Expenses: Contact institution. *Financial support:* Fellowships with partial tuition reimbursements, research assistantships, teaching assistantships, career-related internships or fieldwork, Federal Work-Study, institutionally sponsored loans, and tuition waivers (partial) available. Support available to part-time students. In 2016, 104 master's, 7 doctorates awarded. *Program availability:* Part-time. Offers acting (MFA); American literature (MA); anthropology (MA, MAT); arts and letters (MA, MAT, MFA, MM, PhD, Certificate); comparative literature (MA); comparative studies (MA, PhD); design and technology (MFA); French (MA); history (MA); linguistics (MA); music (MM); political science (MA); sociology (MA); Spanish (MA); visual art (MFA). *Application deadline:* For fall admission, 6/1 priority date for domestic students. Applications are processed on a rolling basis. *Application fee:* $30. Electronic applications accepted. *Dean,* Heather Coltman, 561-297-3803, E-mail: coltman@fau.edu.

Center for Women, Gender and Sexuality Studies Students: 6 full-time (5 women), 5 part-time (all women); includes 5 minority (3 Hispanic/Latino; 2 Two or more races, non-Hispanic/Latino). Average age 27. 5 applicants, 60% accepted, 2 enrolled. Expenses: Contact institution. *Financial support:* Fellowships with tuition reimbursements, teaching assistantships with tuition reimbursements, career-related internships or fieldwork, Federal Work-Study, institutionally sponsored loans, scholarships/grants, and unspecified assistantships available. Support available to part-time students. Financial award applicants required to submit FAFSA. In 2016, 4 master's awarded. *Program availability:* Part-time. Offers women, gender and sexuality studies (MA). *Application deadline:* For fall admission, 7/1 for domestic students, 2/15 for international students; for spring admission, 11/1 for domestic students, 7/15 for international students. Applications are processed on a rolling basis. *Application fee:* $30. Electronic applications accepted. *Senior Secretary,* Regina Gloncalves, 561-297-3865, E-mail: rgoncal@fau.edu.

School of Communication and Multimedia Studies Students: 21 full-time (15 women), 17 part-time (9 women); includes 16 minority (6 Black or African American, non-Hispanic/Latino; 1 Asian, non-Hispanic/Latino; 9 Hispanic/Latino), 3 international. Average age 33. 39 applicants, 72% accepted, 14 enrolled. *Faculty:* 25 full-time (8 women). Expenses: Contact institution. *Financial support:* Teaching assistantships with partial tuition reimbursements, Federal Work-Study, institutionally sponsored loans, scholarships/grants, and unspecified assistantships available. Support available to part-time students. Financial award application deadline: 3/1; financial award applicants required to submit FAFSA. In 2016, 8 master's awarded. *Program availability:* Part-time. Offers communication studies (MA); film and video (Certificate); media, technology and entertainment (MFA). *Application deadline:* For fall admission, 7/1 priority date for domestic students, 4/1 for international students; for spring admission, 11/1 for domestic students, 10/1 for international students. Applications are processed on a rolling basis. *Application fee:* $30. Electronic applications accepted. *Application Contact:* Dr. Eric M. Freedman, Graduate Coordinator, 561-297-2534, Fax: 561-297-2615, E-mail: efreedma@fau.edu. *Director,* Dr. David Williams, 561-297-0045, Fax: 561-297-2615, E-mail: dcwill@fau.edu.

FLORIDA COASTAL SCHOOL OF LAW, Jacksonville, FL 32256

General Information Proprietary, coed, graduate-only institution.

GRADUATE UNITS

Professional Program *Program availability:* Part-time. Offers law (JD). Electronic applications accepted.

FLORIDA COLLEGE OF INTEGRATIVE MEDICINE, Orlando, FL 32809

General Information Proprietary, coed, graduate-only institution. *Graduate housing:* On-campus housing not available.

GRADUATE UNITS

Graduate Program *Program availability:* Evening/weekend. Offers Oriental medicine (MSOM). Electronic applications accepted.

FLORIDA GULF COAST UNIVERSITY, Fort Myers, FL 33965-6565

General Information State-supported, coed, comprehensive institution. CGS member. *Enrollment:* 14,840 graduate, professional, and undergraduate students; 430 full-time matriculated graduate/professional students (282 women), 699 part-time matriculated graduate/professional students (475 women). *Enrollment by degree level:* 798 master's, 72 doctoral. *Graduate faculty:* 463 full-time (212 women), 371 part-time/adjunct (167 women). *Tuition,* state resident: full-time $6721. *Tuition,* nonresident: full-time $28,170. *Required fees:* $1987. Tuition and fees vary according to course load and degree level. *Graduate housing:* Room and/or apartments available on a first-come, first-served basis to single students; on-campus housing not available to married students. Typical cost: $4820 per year. Room charges vary according to board plan. Housing application deadline: 4/1. *Student services:* Campus employment opportunities, campus safety program, career counseling, child daycare facilities, exercise/wellness program, free psychological counseling, international student services, low-cost health insurance, multicultural affairs office, services for students with disabilities, teacher training. *Library facilities:* Library Services plus 1 other. *Collection:* Books: 242,131 (physical), 73,000 (digital/electronic); Serial titles: 128,865 (digital/electronic); Databases: 389. Students can reserve study rooms. *Research affiliation:* U.S. Department of Commerce (biological sciences), Florida Department of Environmental Protection (biological sciences), Louisiana Universities Marine Consortium (LUMCON) (environmental science), South Florida Water Management District (biological sciences), Dauphin Island Sea Lab (environmental science), City of Bonita Springs (public affairs).

Computer facilities: Computer purchase and lease plans are available. 1,029 computers available on campus for general student use. A campuswide network can be accessed from student residence rooms and from off campus. Online class registration, online admissions and advising are available.
Website: http://www.fgcu.edu/

General Application Contact: Francisco Marquez, Graduate Studies Admissions, 239-590-7908, E-mail: graduate@fgcu.edu.

GRADUATE UNITS

College of Arts and Sciences Students: 89 full-time (66 women), 149 part-time (93 women); includes 47 minority (12 Black or African American, non-Hispanic/Latino; 2 Asian, non-Hispanic/Latino; 28 Hispanic/Latino; 5 Two or more races, non-Hispanic/Latino), 4 international. Average age 29. 107 applicants, 77% accepted, 68 enrolled. *Faculty:* 238 full-time (97 women), 158 part-time/adjunct (62 women). Expenses: Contact institution. *Financial support:* In 2016–17, 36 students received support. Federal Work-Study, scholarships/grants, and unspecified assistantships available. Financial award application deadline: 3/1; financial award applicants required to submit FAFSA. In 2016, 59 master's awarded. *Program availability:* Part-time, blended/hybrid learning. Offers arts and sciences (MA, MPA, MS); criminal forensic studies (MS); criminal justice studies (MS); English (MA); environmental policy (MPA); environmental science (MS); history (MA); management (MPA). *Application deadline:* For fall admission, 2/15 priority date for domestic students; for spring admission, 10/1 for domestic students. Applications are processed on a rolling basis. *Application fee:* $30. Electronic applications accepted. *Application Contact:* Patricia Rice, Executive Secretary, 239-590-7196, Fax: 239-590-7200, E-mail: price@fgcu.edu. *Dean,* Dr. Robert Gregerson, 239-590-7156, Fax: 239-590-7200, E-mail: rgregerson@fgcu.edu.

College of Education Students: 11 full-time (2 women), 114 part-time (94 women); includes 49 minority (19 Black or African American, non-Hispanic/Latino; 4 Asian, non-Hispanic/Latino; 24 Hispanic/Latino; 2 Two or more races, non-Hispanic/Latino), 2

international. Average age 33. 109 applicants, 81% accepted, 65 enrolled. *Faculty:* 26 full-time (18 women), 44 part-time/adjunct (32 women). Expenses: Contact institution. *Financial support:* In 2016–17, 9 students received support. Application deadline: 3/1; applicants required to submit FAFSA. In 2016, 52 master's awarded. *Program availability:* Part-time, evening/weekend, online learning. Offers behavior disorders (M Ed); education (M Ed, MA); educational leadership (M Ed, MA); elementary education (M Ed); English education (M Ed); gifted education (M Ed); mathematics education (M Ed); mental retardation (M Ed); middle school education (M Ed); science education (M Ed); social science education (M Ed); specific learning disabilities (M Ed); varying exceptionalities (M Ed). *Application deadline:* For fall admission, 7/1 priority date for domestic students; for spring admission, 10/15 for domestic students. Applications are processed on a rolling basis. *Application fee:* $30. Electronic applications accepted. *Application Contact:* Shannon Acosta, Graduate Studies Admissions, 239-590-7027, Fax: 239-590-7843, E-mail: sacosta@fgcu.edu. *Dean,* Dr. Eunny Hyun, 239-590-7791, Fax: 239-590-7801, E-mail: ehyun@fgcu.edu.

College of Health Professions and Social Work Students: 155 full-time (118 women), 135 part-time (105 women); includes 104 minority (29 Black or African American, non-Hispanic/Latino; 17 Asian, non-Hispanic/Latino; 51 Hispanic/Latino; 7 Two or more races, non-Hispanic/Latino), 3 international. Average age 28. 444 applicants, 45% accepted, 153 enrolled. *Faculty:* 66 full-time (45 women), 42 part-time/adjunct (21 women). Expenses: Contact institution. *Financial support:* In 2016–17, 62 students received support. Career-related internships or fieldwork, Federal Work-Study, and institutionally sponsored loans available. Financial award application deadline: 3/1; financial award applicants required to submit FAFSA. In 2016, 97 master's, 22 doctorates awarded. *Program availability:* Part-time, evening/weekend, online learning. Offers health professions and social work (M Ed, MA, MS, MSN, MSW, DNP, DPT); health science (MS); nurse anesthesia (MSN); occupational therapy (MS); physical therapy (DPT); social work (MSW). *Application deadline:* For fall admission, 2/15 for domestic students; for spring admission, 11/1 for domestic students. Applications are processed on a rolling basis. *Application fee:* $30. Electronic applications accepted. *Application Contact:* Lynn O'Hare, Administrative Assistant, 239-590-7451, Fax: 239-590-7474, E-mail: lohare@fgcu.edu. *Dean,* Dr. Mitchell Cordova, 239-590-7451, Fax: 239-590-7474.

Lutgert College of Business Students: 35 full-time (15 women), 105 part-time (45 women); includes 26 minority (5 Black or African American, non-Hispanic/Latino; 3 Asian, non-Hispanic/Latino; 14 Hispanic/Latino; 4 Two or more races, non-Hispanic/Latino), 5 international. Average age 27. 116 applicants, 53% accepted, 45 enrolled. *Faculty:* 58 full-time (23 women), 39 part-time/adjunct (16 women). Expenses: Contact institution. *Financial support:* In 2016–17, 14 students received support. Application deadline: 3/1; applicants required to submit FAFSA. In 2016, 57 master's awarded. *Program availability:* Part-time, evening/weekend. Offers accounting and taxation (MS); business (MBA, MS); business administration (MBA). *Application deadline:* For fall admission, 5/1 priority date for domestic students; for spring admission, 9/15 priority date for domestic students. Applications are processed on a rolling basis. *Application fee:* $30. Electronic applications accepted. *Application Contact:* Judy Wynekoop, Associate Dean and Professor of Computer Information Systems, 239-590-7387, Fax: 239-590-7330, E-mail: jwynekoo@fgcu.edu. *Dean, Lutgert College of Business,* Robert Beatty, 239-590-7300, Fax: 239-590-7330, E-mail: rbeatty@fgcu.edu.

FLORIDA INSTITUTE OF TECHNOLOGY, Melbourne, FL 32901-6975

General Information Independent, coed, university. *Enrollment:* 6,451 graduate, professional, and undergraduate students; 1,366 full-time matriculated graduate/professional students (630 women), 1,449 part-time matriculated graduate/professional students (475 women). *Enrollment by degree level:* 2,202 master's, 613 doctoral. *Graduate faculty:* 201 full-time (37 women), 146 part-time/adjunct (33 women). *Tuition:* full-time $22,338; part-time $1241 per credit hour. *Required fees:* $250. Tuition and fees vary according to degree level, campus/location and program. *Graduate housing:* Room and/or apartments available on a first-come, first-served basis to single students; on-campus housing not available to married students. Typical cost: $13,610 (including board). Room and board charges vary according to board plan and housing facility selected. Housing application deadline: 6/1. *Student services:* Campus employment opportunities, campus safety program, career counseling, exercise/wellness program, free psychological counseling, international student services, low-cost health insurance, multicultural affairs office, services for students with disabilities, writing training. *Library facilities:* Evans Library. *Collection:* Books: 131,973 (physical), 164,272 (digital/electronic); Serial titles: 1,548 (physical), 44,772 (digital/electronic); Databases: 172. Weekly public service hours: 96; students can reserve study rooms. *Research affiliation:* Boeing (digital signal processing aeronautics), Siemens (mechanical and aerospace engineering), General Electric-Harris (software testing), IBM (software technology, information assurance), Microsoft Corporation (simulation software development), Lockheed Martin Corporation (biological sciences).

Computer facilities: 254 computers available on campus for general student use. A campuswide network can be accessed from student residence rooms and from off campus. Online class registration is available.
Website: http://www.fit.edu/

General Application Contact: Cheryl A. Brown, Associate Director of Graduate Admissions, 321-674-7581, Fax: 321-723-9468, E-mail: cbrown@fit.edu.

GRADUATE UNITS

College of Aeronautics Students: 54 full-time (16 women), 67 part-time (13 women); includes 16 minority (6 Black or African American, non-Hispanic/Latino; 1 American Indian or Alaska Native, non-Hispanic/Latino; 2 Asian, non-Hispanic/Latino; 7 Hispanic/Latino), 46 international. Average age 33. 144 applicants, 47% accepted, 42 enrolled. *Faculty:* 10 full-time (4 women), 1 part-time/adjunct (0 women). Expenses: Contact institution. *Financial support:* In 2016–17, 1 research assistantship with partial tuition reimbursement, 2 teaching assistantships with partial tuition reimbursements were awarded; career-related internships or fieldwork, institutionally sponsored loans, tuition waivers (partial), and tuition remissions also available. Support available to part-time students. Financial award application deadline: 3/1; financial award applicants required to submit FAFSA. In 2016, 51 master's, 4 doctorates awarded. *Program availability:* Part-time, evening/weekend, 100% online. Offers airport development and management (MSA); applied aviation safety (MSA); aviation human factors (MS); aviation safety (MSA); aviation sciences (PhD); human factors in aeronautics (MS). *Application deadline:* For fall admission, 4/1 for international students; for spring admission, 9/30 for international students. Applications are processed on a rolling basis. Electronic applications accepted. *Application Contact:* Cheryl A. Brown, Associate Director of Graduate Admissions, 321-674-7581, Fax: 321-723-9468, E-mail: cbrown@fit.edu. *Dean,* Dr. Korhan Oyman, 321-674-8971, Fax: 321-674-7368, E-mail: koyman@fit.edu.

College of Engineering Students: 574 full-time (147 women), 313 part-time (58 women); includes 83 minority (20 Black or African American, non-Hispanic/Latino; 21 Asian, non-Hispanic/Latino; 36 Hispanic/Latino; 6 Two or more races, non-Hispanic/Latino), 571 international. Average age 28. 2,952 applicants, 42% accepted, 252 enrolled. *Faculty:* 94 full-time (6 women), 19 part-time/adjunct (1 woman). Expenses: Contact institution. *Financial support:* In 2016–17, 74 research assistantships with partial tuition reimbursements, 65 teaching assistantships with partial tuition reimbursements were awarded; career-related internships or fieldwork, institutionally sponsored loans, unspecified assistantships, and tuition remissions also available. Support available to part-time students. Financial award application deadline: 3/1; financial award applicants required to submit FAFSA. In 2016, 412 master's, 25 doctorates awarded. *Program availability:* Part-time. Offers aerospace engineering (MS, PhD); biological oceanography (MS); biomedical engineering (MS, PhD); chemical engineering (MS, PhD); chemical oceanography (MS); civil engineering (MS, PhD); coastal management (MS); computer engineering (MS, PhD); computer information systems (MS); computer science (MS, PhD); earth remote sensing (MS); electrical engineering (MS, PhD); engineering (MS, PhD); engineering management (MS); environmental resource management (MS); environmental science (MS, PhD); flight test engineering (MS); geological oceanography (MS); information assurance and cybersecurity (MS); mechanical engineering (MS, PhD); meteorology (MS); ocean engineering (MS, PhD); oceanography (PhD); physical oceanography (MS); software engineering (MS); systems engineering (MS, PhD). *Application deadline:* For fall admission, 4/1 for international students; for spring admission, 9/30 for international students. Applications are processed on a rolling basis. Electronic applications accepted. *Application Contact:* Cheryl A. Brown, Associate Director of Graduate Admissions, 321-674-7581, Fax: 321-723-9468, E-mail: cbrown@fit.edu. *Dean,* Dr. Martin Glicksman, 321-674-8020, Fax: 321-674-7270, E-mail: coe@fit.edu.

College of Psychology and Liberal Arts Students: 350 full-time (278 women), 35 part-time (29 women); includes 91 minority (14 Black or African American, non-Hispanic/Latino; 1 American Indian or Alaska Native, non-Hispanic/Latino; 15 Asian, non-Hispanic/Latino; 44 Hispanic/Latino; 17 Two or more races, non-Hispanic/Latino), 30 international. Average age 29. 735 applicants, 36% accepted, 138 enrolled. *Faculty:* 34 full-time (17 women), 9 part-time/adjunct (4 women). Expenses: Contact institution. *Financial support:* In 2016–17, 68 research assistantships with partial tuition reimbursements, 31 teaching assistantships with partial tuition reimbursements (averaging $8,002 per year) were awarded; fellowships, career-related internships or fieldwork, institutionally sponsored loans, tuition waivers (partial), unspecified assistantships, and tuition remissions also available. Support available to part-time students. Financial award application deadline: 3/1; financial award applicants required to submit FAFSA. In 2016, 144 master's, 28 doctorates awarded. *Program availability:* Part-time, evening/weekend, 100% online. Offers applied behavior analysis (MS); applied behavior analysis and organizational behavior management (MS); behavior analysis (PhD); clinical psychology (Psy D); global strategic communication (MS); industrial/organizational psychology (MS, PhD); organizational behavior management (MS); professional behavior analysis (MA); psychology and liberal arts (MA, MS, PhD, Psy D). *Application deadline:* For fall admission, 4/1 for international students; for spring admission, 9/30 for international students. Applications are processed on a rolling basis. Electronic applications accepted. *Application Contact:* Cheryl A. Brown, Associate Director of Graduate Admissions, 321-674-7581, Fax: 321-723-9468, E-mail: cbrown@fit.edu. *Dean,* Dr. Mary Beth Kenkel, 321-674-8142, Fax: 321-674-7105, E-mail: mkenkel@fit.edu.

College of Science Students: 216 full-time (113 women), 99 part-time (32 women); includes 36 minority (12 Black or African American, non-Hispanic/Latino; 6 Asian, non-Hispanic/Latino; 16 Hispanic/Latino; 2 Two or more races, non-Hispanic/Latino), 146 international. Average age 30. 715 applicants, 41% accepted, 85 enrolled. *Faculty:* 45 full-time (6 women), 4 part-time/adjunct (0 women). Expenses: Contact institution. *Financial support:* In 2016–17, 23 research assistantships with partial tuition reimbursements, 74 teaching assistantships with partial tuition reimbursements were awarded; career-related internships or fieldwork, institutionally sponsored loans, tuition waivers (partial), unspecified assistantships, and tuition remissions also available. Support available to part-time students. Financial award application deadline: 3/1; financial award applicants required to submit FAFSA. In 2016, 75 master's, 13 doctorates awarded. *Program availability:* Part-time, evening/weekend. Offers applied mathematics (MS, PhD); biochemistry (MS); biological science (PhD); biotechnology (MS); cell and molecular biology (MS); chemistry (MS, PhD); computer education (MS); conservation technology (MS); ecology (MS); educational technology (MS); elementary science education (M Ed); environmental education (MS); interdisciplinary science (MS); marine biology (MS); mathematics education (MS, PhD, Ed S); operations research (MS); physics (MS, PhD); science (M Ed, MAT, MS, PhD, Ed S); science education (MS, PhD, Ed S); science education: informal science education (MS); space sciences (MS, PhD); teaching (MAT). *Application deadline:* For fall admission, 3/1 for domestic students, 4/1 for international students; for spring admission, 9/1 for domestic students, 9/30 for international students. Applications are processed on a rolling basis. Electronic applications accepted. *Application Contact:* Cheryl A. Brown, Associate Director of Graduate Admissions, 321-674-7581, Fax: 321-723-9468, E-mail: cbrown@fit.edu. *Dean,* Dr. Hamid K. Rassoul, 321-674-7273, Fax: 321-674-8864, E-mail: rassoul@fit.edu.

Extended Studies Division Students: 131 full-time (58 women), 997 part-time (348 women); includes 389 minority (231 Black or African American, non-Hispanic/Latino; 9 American Indian or Alaska Native, non-Hispanic/Latino; 26 Asian, non-Hispanic/Latino; 99 Hispanic/Latino; 3 Native Hawaiian or other Pacific Islander, non-Hispanic/Latino; 21 Two or more races, non-Hispanic/Latino), 53 international. Average age 36. 962 applicants, 48% accepted, 323 enrolled. *Faculty:* 10 full-time (3 women), 122 part-time/adjunct (29 women). Expenses: Contact institution. *Financial support:* Application deadline: 3/1; applicants required to submit FAFSA. In 2016, 403 master's awarded. *Program availability:* Part-time, evening/weekend, online learning. Offers acquisition and contract management (MS); aerospace engineering (MS); business administration (MBA, DBA); computer information systems (MS); computer science (MS); electrical engineering (MS); engineering management (MS); human resources management (MS); logistics management (MS); management (MS); material acquisition management (MS); mechanical engineering (MS); operations research (MS); project management (MS); public administration (MPA); quality management (MS); software engineering (MS); space systems (MS); space systems management (MS); supply chain management (MS); systems management (MS); technology management (MS). *Application deadline:* For fall admission, 4/1 for international students; for spring admission, 9/30 for international students. Applications are processed on a rolling basis. Electronic applications accepted. *Application Contact:* Carolyn Farrior, Director of Graduate Admissions, Online Learning and Off-Campus Programs, 321-674-7118, Fax: 321-674-8216, E-mail: cfarrior@fit.edu. *Dean,* Dr. Theodore R. Richardson, III, 321-674-8123, Fax: 321-674-7597, E-mail: trichardson@fit.edu.

Nathan M. Bisk College of Business Students: 72 full-time (29 women), 208 part-time (85 women); includes 91 minority (38 Black or African American, non-Hispanic/Latino; 1 American Indian or Alaska Native, non-Hispanic/Latino; 9 Asian, non-Hispanic/Latino; 36 Hispanic/Latino; 1 Native Hawaiian or other Pacific Islander, non-Hispanic/Latino; 6 Two or more races, non-Hispanic/Latino), 24 international. Average age 33. 206 applicants, 40% accepted, 18 enrolled. *Faculty:* 7 full-time (1 woman). Expenses: Contact institution. *Financial support:* Research assistantships with partial tuition reimbursements, career-related internships or fieldwork, institutionally sponsored loans, and unspecified assistantships available. Support available to part-time students. Financial award application deadline: 3/1; financial award applicants required to submit FAFSA. In 2016, 192 master's awarded. *Program availability:* Part-time, online learning. Offers business (MBA, MS); business administration (MBA); healthcare management (MBA); innovation and entrepreneurship (MS). *Application deadline:* For fall admission, 4/1 for international students; for spring admission, 9/30 for international students. Applications are processed on a rolling basis. Electronic applications accepted. *Application Contact:* Cheryl A. Brown, Associate Director of Graduate Admissions, 321-674-7581, Fax: 321-723-9468, E-mail: cbrown@fit.edu. *Dean,* Dr. Theodore R. Richardson, III, 321-674-8123, Fax: 321-674-7597, E-mail: trichardson@fit.edu.

School of Human-Centered Design, Innovation and Art Students: 9 full-time (2 women), 4 part-time (1 woman); includes 3 minority (1 Black or African American, non-Hispanic/Latino; 1 Asian, non-Hispanic/Latino; 1 Two or more races, non-Hispanic/Latino), 6 international. Average age 35. 21 applicants, 57% accepted, 4 enrolled. *Faculty:* 3 full-time (0 women). Expenses: Contact institution. *Financial support:* In 2016–17, 5 research assistantships with partial tuition reimbursements were awarded; career-related internships or fieldwork, institutionally sponsored loans, tuition waivers (partial), unspecified assistantships, and tuition remissions also available. Financial award application deadline: 3/1; financial award applicants required to submit FAFSA. In 2016, 4 master's, 1 doctorate awarded. *Program availability:* Part-time, evening/weekend. Offers human-centered design (MS, PhD). *Application deadline:* For fall admission, 4/1 for international students; for spring admission, 9/30 for international students. Applications are processed on a rolling basis. Electronic applications accepted. *Application Contact:* Cheryl A. Brown, Associate Director of Graduate Admissions, 321-674-7581, Fax: 321-723-9468, E-mail: cbrown@fit.edu. *Director,* Dr. Guy Boy, 321-674-7631, Fax: 321-984-8461, E-mail: gboy@fit.edu.

FLORIDA INTERNATIONAL UNIVERSITY, Miami, FL 33199

General Information State-supported, coed, university. CGS member. *Enrollment:* 55,111 graduate, professional, and undergraduate students; 6,342 full-time matriculated graduate/professional students (3,675 women), 2,427 part-time matriculated graduate/professional students (1,421 women). *Enrollment by degree level:* 6,186 master's, 2,584 doctoral. *Graduate faculty:* 1,167 full-time (493 women), 1,026 part-time/adjunct (487 women). Tuition, state resident: full-time $8912; part-time $446 per credit hour. Tuition, nonresident: full-time $21,393; part-time $992 per credit hour. *Required fees:* $2185; $195 per semester. Tuition and fees vary according to program. *Graduate housing:* Rooms and/or apartments available on a first-come, first-served basis to single and married students. *Student services:* Campus employment opportunities, campus safety program, career counseling, child daycare facilities, exercise/wellness program, free psychological counseling, international student services, low-cost health insurance, multicultural affairs office, services for students with disabilities, writing training. *Library facilities:* Steven and Dorothea Green Library plus 4 others. *Collection:* Books: 1.5 million (physical), 287,899 (digital/electronic); Serial titles: 59,593 (physical), 106,720 (digital/electronic); Databases: 790. Weekly public service hours: 112; students can reserve study rooms. *Research affiliation:* National Institute of Justice (chemistry), National Science Foundation (biological sciences), Howard Hughes Medical Institute (physics), National Institute of Child Health and Human Development (social work), Boeing (mechanical engineering), American Heart Association (biomedical engineering).

Computer facilities: A campuswide network can be accessed from student residence rooms and from off campus. Online class registration, online financial and cashier's information; financial, campus maps information available on cell phones are available. Website: http://www.fiu.edu.

General Application Contact: Nanett Rojas, Assistant Director of Graduate Admissions, 305-348-7442, Fax: 305-348-7441, E-mail: gradadm@fiu.edu.

GRADUATE UNITS

Chaplin School of Hospitality and Tourism Management Students: 170 full-time (106 women), 99 part-time (76 women); includes 92 minority (23 Black or African American, non-Hispanic/Latino; 5 Asian, non-Hispanic/Latino; 59 Hispanic/Latino; 1 Native Hawaiian or other Pacific Islander, non-Hispanic/Latino; 4 Two or more races, non-Hispanic/Latino), 148 international. Average age 27. 193 applicants, 72% accepted, 85 enrolled. *Faculty:* 20 full-time (6 women), 42 part-time/adjunct (13 women). Expenses: Contact institution. *Financial support:* Institutionally sponsored loans and scholarships/grants available. Financial award application deadline: 3/1; financial award applicants required to submit FAFSA. In 2016, 161 master's awarded. *Program availability:* Part-time, evening/weekend, online learning. Offers hospitality and tourism management (MS). *Application deadline:* For fall admission, 6/1 for domestic students, 4/1 for international students; for spring admission, 10/1 for domestic students, 9/1 for international students. Applications are processed on a rolling basis. *Application fee:* $30. Electronic applications accepted. *Application Contact:* Nanett Rojas, Manager, Admissions Operations, 305-348-7464, Fax: 305-348-7441, E-mail: gradadm@fiu.edu. *Dean,* Dr. Mike Hampton, 305-919-4018, E-mail: mhampton@fiu.edu.

Chapman Graduate School of Business Students: 1,531 full-time (813 women), 622 part-time (305 women); includes 1,518 minority (269 Black or African American, non-Hispanic/Latino; 56 Asian, non-Hispanic/Latino; 1,153 Hispanic/Latino; 3 Native Hawaiian or other Pacific Islander, non-Hispanic/Latino; 37 Two or more races, non-Hispanic/Latino), 324 international. Average age 31. 2,689 applicants, 46% accepted, 855 enrolled. *Faculty:* 132 full-time (44 women), 93 part-time/adjunct (27 women). Expenses: Contact institution. *Financial support:* Institutionally sponsored loans and scholarships/grants available. Financial award application deadline: 3/1; financial award applicants required to submit FAFSA. In 2016, 1,231 master's, 4 doctorates awarded. *Program availability:* Part-time, evening/weekend. Offers business (EMBA, IMBA, M Acc, MBA, MIB, MS, MSF, MSHRM, MST, PhD); decision sciences and information systems (PhD); finance (MSF); health information management systems (MS); human resources management (MSHRM); international business (MIB); management and international business (EMBA, IMBA, MBA, PhD); marketing (MSF); systems management (MS). *Application deadline:* For fall admission, 6/1 for domestic students, 4/1 for international students; for spring admission, 10/1 for domestic students, 9/1 for international students. Applications are processed on a rolling basis. *Application fee:* $30. Electronic applications accepted. *Application Contact:* Nanett Rojas, Manager, Admissions Operations, 305-348-7464, Fax: 305-348-7441, E-mail: gradadm@fiu.edu. *Dean,* Dr. Joanne Li, 305-348-2751, Fax: 305-919-5478, E-mail: gradadm@fiu.edu.

Florida International University

Hollo School of Real Estate Students: 88 full-time (29 women), 11 part-time (5 women); includes 63 minority (16 Black or African American, non-Hispanic/Latino; 1 Asian, non-Hispanic/Latino; 43 Hispanic/Latino; 3 Two or more races, non-Hispanic/Latino), 11 international. Average age 35. 140 applicants, 56% accepted, 51 enrolled. *Faculty:* 5 full-time (1 woman), 5 part-time/adjunct (2 women). *Expenses:* Contact institution. *Financial support:* Institutionally sponsored loans and scholarships/grants available. Financial award application deadline: 3/1; financial award applicants required to submit FAFSA. In 2016, 80 master's awarded. *Program availability:* Part-time, evening/weekend. Offers international real estate (MS). *Application deadline:* For fall admission, 4/1 for domestic and international students. *Application fee:* $30. Electronic applications accepted. *Application Contact:* Isabel Lopez, Associate Director for Academic Support Services, 305-348-4198, E-mail: isabel.lopez@fiu.edu. *Director,* Eli Beracha, 305-779-7898, E-mail: eli.beracha@fiu.edu.

School of Accounting Students: 98 full-time (53 women), 19 part-time (7 women); includes 105 minority (4 Black or African American, non-Hispanic/Latino; 9 Asian, non-Hispanic/Latino; 88 Hispanic/Latino; 1 Native Hawaiian or other Pacific Islander, non-Hispanic/Latino; 3 Two or more races, non-Hispanic/Latino), 2 international. Average age 27. 242 applicants, 50% accepted, 90 enrolled. *Faculty:* 26 full-time (9 women), 10 part-time/adjunct (1 woman). *Expenses:* Contact institution. *Financial support:* Institutionally sponsored loans and scholarships/grants available. Financial award application deadline: 3/1; financial award applicants required to submit FAFSA. In 2016, 153 master's awarded. *Program availability:* Part-time, evening/weekend. Offers accounting (M Acc). *Application deadline:* For fall admission, 6/1 for domestic students, 4/1 for international students; for spring admission, 10/1 for domestic students, 9/1 for international students. Applications are processed on a rolling basis. *Application fee:* $30. Electronic applications accepted. *Application Contact:* Cynthia Teijeiro, Program Manager, 305-348-7564, E-mail: cteijeir@fiu.edu. *Director,* Ruth Ann McEwen, 305-348-2581, E-mail: rmcewen@fiu.edu.

College of Arts, Sciences, and Education Students: 993 full-time (661 women), 660 part-time (496 women); includes 1,067 minority (233 Black or African American, non-Hispanic/Latino; 24 Asian, non-Hispanic/Latino; 785 Hispanic/Latino; 25 Two or more races, non-Hispanic/Latino), 182 international. Average age 31. 1,510 applicants, 41% accepted, 408 enrolled. *Faculty:* 382 full-time (165 women), 320 part-time/adjunct (181 women). *Expenses:* Contact institution. *Financial support:* Career-related internships or fieldwork, Federal Work-Study, institutionally sponsored loans, and scholarships/grants available. Financial award application deadline: 3/1; financial award applicants required to submit FAFSA. In 2016, 515 master's, 65 doctorates awarded. *Program availability:* Part-time, evening/weekend. Offers adult education and human resource development (MS, Ed D); art education (MA, MS); arts, sciences, and education (MA, MFA, MS, PSM, Ed D, PhD, Certificate, Ed S); behavioral analysis (MS); biological sciences (MS, PhD); chemistry (MS, PhD); clinical science (PhD); cognitive neuroscience (PhD); counseling (MS); counseling psychology (MS); counselor education (MS); creative writing (MFA); curriculum and instruction (MS, Ed D, PhD, Ed S); developmental science (MS, PhD); early childhood education (MS); earth science (PhD); educational administration and supervision (Ed D); educational leadership (MS, Certificate, Ed S); English (MA); environmental studies (MS); exceptional student education (Ed D); foreign language education (MS); forensic science (MS, PSM, PhD); geosciences (MS, PhD); higher education (Ed D); higher education administration (MS); international and comparative education (MS); international/intercultural education (MS); language, literacy and culture (PhD); legal psychology (MS, PhD); liberal studies (MA); linguistics (MA); mathematical sciences (MS); mathematics, science, and learning technologies (PhD); natural resources management and policy (PSM); organizational psychology (MS, PhD); physical education (MS); physics (MS, PhD); reading education (MS); recreation and sport management (MS); school psychology (Ed S); statistics (MS); urban education (MS). *Application deadline:* For fall admission, 6/1 for domestic students, 4/1 for international students; for spring admission, 10/1 for domestic students, 9/1 for international students. Applications are processed on a rolling basis. *Application fee:* $30. Electronic applications accepted. *Application Contact:* Nanett Rojas, Assistant Director, Graduate Admissions, 305-348-7464, Fax: 305-348-7441, E-mail: gradadm@fiu.edu. *Dean,* Dr. Michael Heithaus, 305-348-2866, Fax: 305-348-4172, E-mail: casdean@fiu.edu.

College of Communication, Architecture and The Arts Students: 349 full-time (221 women), 82 part-time (48 women); includes 299 minority (44 Black or African American, non-Hispanic/Latino; 6 Asian, non-Hispanic/Latino; 241 Hispanic/Latino; 8 Two or more races, non-Hispanic/Latino), 52 international. Average age 29. 360 applicants, 53% accepted, 115 enrolled. *Faculty:* 93 full-time (38 women), 123 part-time/adjunct (59 women). *Expenses:* Contact institution. *Financial support:* Institutionally sponsored loans and scholarships/grants available. Financial award application deadline: 3/1; financial award applicants required to submit FAFSA. In 2016, 215 master's awarded. *Program availability:* Part-time, evening/weekend. Offers architecture (M Arch, MA); communication, architecture and the arts (M Arch, MA, MFA, MIA, MLA, MM, MS, Certificate, Graduate Certificate); interior architecture (MA, MIA, Certificate); landscape architecture (MLA); museum studies (Graduate Certificate); studio art (MFA). *Application deadline:* For fall admission, 6/1 for domestic students, 4/1 for international students; for spring admission, 10/1 for domestic students, 9/1 for international students. Applications are processed on a rolling basis. *Application fee:* $30. Electronic applications accepted. *Application Contact:* Nanett Rojas, Manager, Admissions Operations, 305-348-7464, Fax: 305-348-7441, E-mail: gradadm@fiu.edu. *Dean,* Dr. Brian Schriner, 305-348-3176, Fax: 305-348-6716, E-mail: schriner@fiu.edu.

School of Communication and Journalism Students: 94 full-time (72 women), 51 part-time (33 women); includes 110 minority (25 Black or African American, non-Hispanic/Latino; 81 Hispanic/Latino; 4 Two or more races, non-Hispanic/Latino), 19 international. Average age 29. 127 applicants, 62% accepted, 59 enrolled. *Faculty:* 12 full-time (6 women), 8 part-time/adjunct (4 women). *Expenses:* Contact institution. *Financial support:* Institutionally sponsored loans and scholarships/grants available. Financial award application deadline: 3/1; financial award applicants required to submit FAFSA. In 2016, 53 master's awarded. *Program availability:* Part-time, evening/weekend. Offers mass communication (MS). *Application deadline:* For fall admission, 6/1 for domestic students, 4/1 for international students; for spring admission, 10/1 for domestic students, 9/1 for international students. Applications are processed on a rolling basis. *Application fee:* $30. Electronic applications accepted. *Application Contact:* Nanett Rojas, Assistant Director, Graduate Admissions, 305-348-7442, Fax: 305-348-7441, E-mail: gradadm@fiu.edu. *Chair,* Dr. Maria Elena Villar, 305-919-5795, Fax: 305-919-5215, E-mail: mariaelena.villar@fiu.edu.

School of Music Students: 31 full-time (13 women), 18 part-time (8 women); includes 34 minority (7 Black or African American, non-Hispanic/Latino; 1 Asian, non-Hispanic/Latino; 24 Hispanic/Latino; 2 Two or more races, non-Hispanic/Latino), 3 international. Average age 29. 48 applicants, 56% accepted, 16 enrolled. *Faculty:* 21 full-time (3 women), 25 part-time/adjunct (5 women). *Expenses:* Contact institution.

Financial support: Institutionally sponsored loans and scholarships/grants available. Financial award application deadline: 3/1; financial award applicants required to submit FAFSA. In 2016, 18 master's awarded. *Program availability:* Part-time, evening/weekend. Offers music (MM); music education (MS). *Application deadline:* For fall admission, 6/1 for domestic students, 4/1 for international students; for spring admission, 10/1 for domestic students, 9/1 for international students. Applications are processed on a rolling basis. *Application fee:* $30. Electronic applications accepted. *Application Contact:* Joel Galand, Graduate Program Director, 305-348-7078, E-mail: galandj@fiu.edu. *Interim Chair,* Robert Dundas, 305-348-3587, Fax: 305-348-4073, E-mail: robert.dundas@fiu.edu.

College of Engineering and Computing Students: 560 full-time (155 women), 324 part-time (69 women); includes 369 minority (57 Black or African American, non-Hispanic/Latino; 2 American Indian or Alaska Native, non-Hispanic/Latino; 22 Asian, non-Hispanic/Latino; 280 Hispanic/Latino; 8 Two or more races, non-Hispanic/Latino), 430 international. Average age 29. 1,247 applicants, 47% accepted, 226 enrolled. *Faculty:* 129 full-time (24 women), 61 part-time/adjunct (7 women). *Expenses:* Contact institution. *Financial support:* Career-related internships or fieldwork, Federal Work-Study, institutionally sponsored loans, scholarships/grants, and unspecified assistantships available. Financial award application deadline: 3/1; financial award applicants required to submit FAFSA. In 2016, 322 master's, 45 doctorates awarded. *Program availability:* Part-time, evening/weekend, online learning. Offers biomedical engineering (MS, PhD); civil engineering (MS, PhD); computer engineering (MS); electrical engineering (MS, PhD); engineering and computing (MS, PMS, PhD); engineering management (MS); environmental engineering (MS); materials science and engineering (MS, PhD); mechanical engineering (MS, PhD). *Application deadline:* For fall admission, 6/1 for domestic students, 4/1 for international students; for spring admission, 10/1 for domestic students, 9/1 for international students. Applications are processed on a rolling basis. *Application fee:* $30. Electronic applications accepted. *Application Contact:* Sara-Michelle Lemus, Engineering Admissions Officer, 305-348-1890, E-mail: grad_eng@fiu.edu. *Dean,* Dr. John Volakis, 305-348-0273, Fax: 305-348-0127, E-mail: grad_eng@fiu.edu.

School of Computing and Information Sciences Students: 145 full-time (39 women), 109 part-time (16 women); includes 124 minority (14 Black or African American, non-Hispanic/Latino; 1 American Indian or Alaska Native, non-Hispanic/Latino; 10 Asian, non-Hispanic/Latino; 97 Hispanic/Latino; 2 Two or more races, non-Hispanic/Latino), 115 international. Average age 29. 407 applicants, 54% accepted, 78 enrolled. *Faculty:* 46 full-time (11 women), 28 part-time/adjunct (5 women). *Expenses:* Contact institution. *Financial support:* Research assistantships, teaching assistantships, institutionally sponsored loans, scholarships/grants, and unspecified assistantships available. Financial award application deadline: 3/1; financial award applicants required to submit FAFSA. In 2016, 90 master's, 8 doctorates awarded. *Program availability:* Part-time, evening/weekend. Offers computer science (MS, PhD); cybersecurity (MS); data science (MS); information technology (MS); telecommunications and networking (MS). *Application deadline:* For fall admission, 6/1 for domestic students, 4/1 for international students; for spring admission, 10/1 for domestic students, 9/1 for international students. Applications are processed on a rolling basis. *Application fee:* $30. Electronic applications accepted. *Application Contact:* Sara-Michelle Lemus, Engineering Admissions Officer, 305-348-1890, E-mail: grad_eng@fiu.edu. *Director,* Dr. S. S. Iyengar, 305-348-3947, E-mail: iyengar@cis.fiu.edu.

School of Construction Students: 35 full-time (15 women), 44 part-time (12 women); includes 39 minority (6 Black or African American, non-Hispanic/Latino; 1 Asian, non-Hispanic/Latino; 31 Hispanic/Latino; 1 Two or more races, non-Hispanic/Latino), 24 international. Average age 31. 118 applicants, 43% accepted, 20 enrolled. *Faculty:* 9 full-time (1 woman), 7 part-time/adjunct (0 women). *Expenses:* Contact institution. *Financial support:* In 2016–17, 5 students received support. Institutionally sponsored loans, scholarships/grants, and unspecified assistantships available. Financial award application deadline: 3/1; financial award applicants required to submit FAFSA. In 2016, 35 master's awarded. *Program availability:* Part-time, evening/weekend. Offers construction management (MS, PMS). *Application deadline:* For fall admission, 6/1 for domestic students, 4/1 for international students; for spring admission, 10/1 for domestic students, 9/1 for international students. Applications are processed on a rolling basis. *Application fee:* $30. Electronic applications accepted. *Application Contact:* Sara-Michelle Lemus, Engineering Admissions Officer, 305-348-1890, Fax: 305-348-7441, E-mail: grad_eng@fiu.edu. *Director,* Dr. Irtishad Ahmad, 305-348-3172, Fax: 305-348-6255, E-mail: ahmadi@fiu.edu.

College of Law Students: 494 full-time (262 women), 22 part-time (14 women); includes 319 minority (24 Black or African American, non-Hispanic/Latino; 1 American Indian or Alaska Native, non-Hispanic/Latino; 11 Asian, non-Hispanic/Latino; 278 Hispanic/Latino; 5 Two or more races, non-Hispanic/Latino), 18 international. Average age 27. 2,019 applicants, 30% accepted, 204 enrolled. *Faculty:* 30 full-time (14 women), 42 part-time/adjunct (11 women). *Expenses:* Contact institution. *Financial support:* Application deadline: 3/1; applicants required to submit FAFSA. In 2016, 20 master's, 157 doctorates awarded. *Program availability:* Part-time, evening/weekend. Offers American law for foreign lawyers (LL M); law (JD). *Application deadline:* For fall admission, 5/1 for domestic and international students. Applications are processed on a rolling basis. *Application fee:* $20. Electronic applications accepted. *Application Contact:* Chris Carbot, Assistant Dean for Administration, 305-348-1118, Fax: 305-348-1159, E-mail: christopher.carbot1@fiu.edu. *Assistant Dean for Administration,* Chris Carbot, 305-348-1118, Fax: 305-348-1159, E-mail: christopher.carbot1@fiu.edu.

Herbert Wertheim College of Medicine Students: 598 full-time (318 women); includes 379 minority (38 Black or African American, non-Hispanic/Latino; 110 Asian, non-Hispanic/Latino; 211 Hispanic/Latino; 20 Two or more races, non-Hispanic/Latino), 11 international. Average age 26. 3,990 applicants, 9% accepted, 174 enrolled. *Faculty:* 83 full-time (42 women), 76 part-time/adjunct (26 women). *Expenses:* Contact institution. *Financial support:* Institutionally sponsored loans and scholarships/grants available. Financial award application deadline: 3/1; financial award applicants required to submit FAFSA. In 2016, 108 doctorates awarded. Offers biomedical sciences (PhD); medicine (MD); physician assistant studies (MPAS). *Application deadline:* For fall admission, 12/15 for domestic students. *Application fee:* $160. Electronic applications accepted. *Application Contact:* Andria Lynn Williams, Director of Admissions, 305-348-0655, Fax: 305-348-0650, E-mail: williia@fiu.edu. *Dean,* Dr. John Rock, 305-348-0570, E-mail: med.admissions@fiu.edu.

Nicole Wertheim College of Nursing and Health Sciences Students: 789 full-time (590 women), 113 part-time (85 women); includes 692 minority (141 Black or African American, non-Hispanic/Latino; 58 Asian, non-Hispanic/Latino; 478 Hispanic/Latino; 1 Native Hawaiian or other Pacific Islander, non-Hispanic/Latino; 14 Two or more races, non-Hispanic/Latino), 15 international. Average age 29. 1,716 applicants, 25% accepted, 379 enrolled. *Faculty:* 65 full-time (47 women), 131 part-time/adjunct (94 women). *Expenses:* Contact institution. *Financial support:* Career-related internships or fieldwork, Federal Work-Study, institutionally sponsored loans, and scholarships/grants available. Financial award application deadline: 3/1; financial award applicants required to submit FAFSA. In 2016, 298 master's, 70 doctorates awarded. *Program availability:* Part-time, evening/weekend. Offers adult health nursing (MSN); athletic training (MS); family health (MSN); health services administration (MHSA); nurse anesthetist (MSN); nursing and health sciences (MHSA, MS, MSN, MSOT, DNP, DPT, PhD); nursing practice (DNP); nursing science research (PhD); occupational therapy (MSOT); pediatric nurse (MSN); physical therapy (DPT); psychiatric/mental health nursing (MSN); registered nurse (MSN); speech-language pathology (MS). *Application fee:* $30. Electronic applications accepted. *Application Contact:* Nanett Rojas, Manager, Admissions Operations, 305-348-7464, Fax: 305-348-7441, E-mail: gradadm@fiu.edu. *Dean,* Dr. Ora Strickland, 305-348-0407, E-mail: olstrick@fiu.edu.

Robert Stempel College of Public Health and Social Work Students: 355 full-time (281 women), 181 part-time (145 women); includes 405 minority (120 Black or African American, non-Hispanic/Latino; 20 Asian, non-Hispanic/Latino; 253 Hispanic/Latino; 12 Two or more races, non-Hispanic/Latino), 48 international. Average age 30. 468 applicants, 54% accepted, 151 enrolled. *Faculty:* 62 full-time (40 women), 23 part-time/adjunct (17 women). Expenses: Contact institution. *Financial support:* Institutionally sponsored loans, scholarships/grants, and unspecified assistantships available. Financial award application deadline: 3/1; financial award applicants required to submit FAFSA. In 2016, 164 master's, 12 doctorates awarded. *Program availability:* Part-time, evening/weekend, online learning. Offers biostatistics (MPH); dietetics and nutrition (MS, PhD); environmental and occupational health (MPH, PhD); epidemiology (MPH, PhD); health policy and management (MPH); health promotion and disease prevention (MPH, PhD); public health and social work (MPH, MS, MSW, PhD). *Application deadline:* For fall admission, 6/1 for domestic students, 4/1 for international students; for spring admission, 10/1 for domestic students, 9/1 for international students. Applications are processed on a rolling basis. *Application fee:* $30. Electronic applications accepted. *Application Contact:* Nanett Rojas, Manager, Admissions Operations, 305-348-7464, Fax: 305-348-7441, E-mail: gradadm@fiu.edu. *Dean,* Dr. Tomas Guilarte, 305-348-1158, Fax: 305-348-1691, E-mail: tomas.guilarte@fiu.edu.

School of Social Work Students: 165 full-time (141 women), 75 part-time (59 women); includes 210 minority (66 Black or African American, non-Hispanic/Latino; 137 Hispanic/Latino; 7 Two or more races, non-Hispanic/Latino), 5 international. Average age 31. 149 applicants, 52% accepted, 58 enrolled. *Faculty:* 20 full-time (13 women), 13 part-time/adjunct (8 women). Expenses: Contact institution. *Financial support:* Institutionally sponsored loans and scholarships/grants available. Financial award application deadline: 3/1; financial award applicants required to submit FAFSA. In 2016, 86 master's, 2 doctorates awarded. *Program availability:* Part-time, evening/weekend. Offers social welfare (PhD); social work (MSW). *Application deadline:* For fall admission, 6/1 for domestic students, 4/1 for international students; for spring admission, 10/1 for domestic students, 9/1 for international students. Applications are processed on a rolling basis. *Application fee:* $30. Electronic applications accepted. *Application Contact:* Gladys Ramos, Program Assistant, 305-348-5887, E-mail: gladys.ramos@fiu.edu. *Director,* Dr. Mary Helen Hayden, 305-348-1208, E-mail: haydenm@fiu.edu.

Steven J. Green School of International and Public Affairs Students: 503 full-time (268 women), 325 part-time (184 women); includes 533 minority (116 Black or African American, non-Hispanic/Latino; 1 American Indian or Alaska Native, non-Hispanic/Latino; 18 Asian, non-Hispanic/Latino; 382 Hispanic/Latino; 16 Two or more races, non-Hispanic/Latino), 124 international. Average age 32. 733 applicants, 57% accepted, 285 enrolled. *Faculty:* 171 full-time (71 women), 157 part-time/adjunct (65 women). Expenses: Contact institution. *Financial support:* Career-related internships or fieldwork, Federal Work-Study, institutionally sponsored loans, and scholarships/grants available. Financial award application deadline: 3/1; financial award applicants required to submit FAFSA. In 2016, 197 master's, 23 doctorates awarded. *Program availability:* Part-time, evening/weekend. Offers African and African diaspora studies (MA); Asian studies (MA); Atlantic history (PhD); criminal justice (MS); disaster management (MA); economics (MA, PhD); global and sociocultural studies (MA, PhD); history (MA); international and public affairs (MA, MPA, MS, PhD); international crime and justice (PhD); international relations (MA, PhD); Latin American and Caribbean studies (MA); political science (MA, PhD); public administration (MPA); public affairs (PhD); religious studies (MA); Spanish (MA, PhD). *Application deadline:* For fall admission, 6/1 for domestic students, 4/1 for international students; for winter admission, 10/1 for domestic students, 9/1 for international students. Applications are processed on a rolling basis. *Application fee:* $30. Electronic applications accepted. *Application Contact:* Nanett Rojas, Assistant Director of Graduate Admissions, 305-348-7442, Fax: 305-348-7441, E-mail: gradadm@fiu.edu. *Dean,* Dr. John F. Stack, Jr., 305-348-7266, Fax: 305-348-1013, E-mail: john.stack@fiu.edu.

FLORIDA MEMORIAL UNIVERSITY, Miami-Dade, FL 33054

General Information Independent-religious, coed, comprehensive institution.

GRADUATE UNITS

School of Business *Program availability:* Part-time. Offers business (MBA).

School of Education Offers elementary education (MS); exceptional student education (MS); reading (MS).

FLORIDA NATIONAL UNIVERSITY, Hialeah, FL 33012

General Information Proprietary, coed, comprehensive institution. *Enrollment:* 3,251 graduate, professional, and undergraduate students; 55 full-time matriculated graduate/professional students (28 women), 5 part-time matriculated graduate/professional students (4 women). *Enrollment by degree level:* 60 master's. *Graduate faculty:* 8 full-time (3 women), 4 part-time/adjunct (1 woman). *Tuition:* Full-time $15,600. *Required fees:* $650. *Student services:* Campus employment opportunities, campus safety program, career counseling, child daycare facilities, international student services. *Library facilities:* Hialeah Campus Library plus 1 other. *Collection:* Books: 23,301 (physical), 144,218 (digital/electronic); Serial titles: 56 (physical), 196,357 (digital/electronic); Databases: 32. Weekly public service hours: 69; students can reserve study rooms.

Computer facilities: 300 computers available on campus for general student use. A campuswide network can be accessed from off campus. Online class registration is available.
Website: http://www.fnu.edu/

General Application Contact: Virginia Rabelo, Admissions Supervisor, 305-821-3333 Ext. 1016, Fax: 305-362-0595, E-mail: vrabelo@fnu.edu.

GRADUATE UNITS

Program in Business Administration Expenses: Contact institution. *Financial support:* Federal Work-Study, institutionally sponsored loans, scholarships/grants, and tuition waivers available. Financial award applicants required to submit FAFSA. *Program availability:* Part-time, blended/hybrid learning. Offers finance (MBA); general management (MBA); health services administration (MBA); marketing (MBA); public management and leadership (MBA). *Application deadline:* Applications are processed on a rolling basis. Electronic applications accepted. *Application Contact:* Olga Rodriguez, Assistant Campus Dean, 305-821-3333 Ext. 1044, Fax: 305-362-0595, E-mail: orodriguez@fnu.edu. *Business Department Head,* Dr. Ernesto Gonzalez, 305-821-3333 Ext. 1070, Fax: 305-362-0595, E-mail: egonzalez@fnu.edu.

Program in Health Services Administration Expenses: Contact institution. *Financial support:* Scholarships/grants available. Financial award applicants required to submit FAFSA. *Program availability:* Part-time, evening/weekend, 100% online, blended/hybrid learning. Offers health services administration (MHSA). *Application deadline:* Applications are processed on a rolling basis. Electronic applications accepted. *Application Contact:* Virginia Rabelo, Admissions Supervisor, 305-821-3333 Ext. 1016, Fax: 305-362-0595, E-mail: vrabelo@fnu.edu. *Allied Health Division Head,* Dr. Loreto Almonte, 305-821-3333 Ext. 1074, Fax: 305-362-0595, E-mail: lalmonte@fnu.edu.

Program in Nursing Expenses: Contact institution. Offers family nurse practitioner (MSN); nurse educator (MSN); nurse leadership and management (MSN). *Application Contact:* Olga Rodriguez, Assistant Campus Dean, 305-821-3333 Ext. 1044, Fax: 305-362-0595, E-mail: orodriguez@fnu.edu.

FLORIDA SOUTHERN COLLEGE, Lakeland, FL 33801-5698

General Information Independent-religious, coed, comprehensive institution. *Enrollment:* 2,765 graduate, professional, and undergraduate students; 312 full-time matriculated graduate/professional students (240 women), 67 part-time matriculated graduate/professional students (50 women). *Enrollment by degree level:* 313 master's, 66 doctoral. *Graduate faculty:* 22 full-time (10 women), 10 part-time/adjunct (6 women). *Tuition:* Full-time $17,475; part-time $750 per credit hour. *Required fees:* $50 per semester. *Graduate housing:* On-campus housing not available. *Student services:* Campus employment opportunities, campus safety program, career counseling, exercise/wellness program, free psychological counseling, international student services, multicultural affairs office, services for students with disabilities, teacher training. *Library facilities:* Roux Library plus 1 other. *Collection:* Books: 160,667 (physical), 167,731 (digital/electronic); Serial titles: 22 (physical), 97,772 (digital/electronic); Databases: 118. Weekly public service hours: 104; students can reserve study rooms.

Computer facilities: Computer purchase and lease plans are available. 490 computers available on campus for general student use. A campuswide network can be accessed from student residence rooms. Online class registration, campus portal are available.
Website: http://www.flsouthern.edu/

General Application Contact: Kristen Placek, Director, Office of Adult and Graduate Education, 863-680-4205, Fax: 863-680-3872, E-mail: kplacek@flsouthern.edu.

GRADUATE UNITS

Program in Accounting Students: 27 full-time (15 women), 2 part-time (0 women); includes 7 minority (2 Black or African American, non-Hispanic/Latino; 5 Hispanic/Latino), 2 international. Average age 28. 27 applicants, 70% accepted, 17 enrolled. *Faculty:* 4 full-time (2 women). Expenses: Contact institution. *Financial support:* Federal Work-Study and unspecified assistantships available. Financial award applicants required to submit FAFSA. In 2016, 8 master's awarded. *Program availability:* Part-time, evening/weekend, blended/hybrid learning. Offers accounting (M Acc). *Application deadline:* For fall admission, 6/1 for domestic and international students; for spring admission, 10/1 for domestic and international students. Applications are processed on a rolling basis. *Application fee:* $30. Electronic applications accepted. *Application Contact:* Jared Welling, Director, Office of Adult and Graduate Education, 863-680-4914, Fax: 863-680-3872, E-mail: jwelling@flsouthern.edu. *Director,* Dr. Lynn Clements, 863-680-5022, E-mail: lclements@flsouthern.edu.

Program in Business Administration Students: 71 full-time (36 women), 6 part-time (4 women); includes 18 minority (4 Black or African American, non-Hispanic/Latino; 3 Asian, non-Hispanic/Latino; 10 Hispanic/Latino; 1 Two or more races, non-Hispanic/Latino), 8 international. Average age 29. 124 applicants, 49% accepted, 52 enrolled. *Faculty:* 4 full-time (1 woman), 1 part-time/adjunct (0 women). Expenses: Contact institution. *Financial support:* Scholarships/grants and unspecified assistantships available. Support available to part-time students. Financial award application deadline: 3/1; financial award applicants required to submit FAFSA. In 2016, 37 master's awarded. *Program availability:* Part-time, evening/weekend. Offers business administration (MBA). *Application deadline:* For fall admission, 6/1 for domestic and international students; for spring admission, 10/1 for domestic and international students. Applications are processed on a rolling basis. *Application fee:* $30. Electronic applications accepted. *Application Contact:* Kamalie Morales, Senior Assistant Director of Adult and Graduate Education, 863-680-4205, Fax: 863-680-3872, E-mail: kmorales@flsouthern.edu. *Program Coordinator,* Dr. Charles DuVal, 863-680-4280, Fax: 863-680-4355, E-mail: cduval@flsouthern.edu.

Program in Nursing Students: 50 full-time (41 women), 31 part-time (19 women); includes 19 minority (9 Black or African American, non-Hispanic/Latino; 1 American Indian or Alaska Native, non-Hispanic/Latino; 7 Hispanic/Latino; 1 Native Hawaiian or other Pacific Islander, non-Hispanic/Latino; 1 Two or more races, non-Hispanic/Latino), 2 international. Average age 40. 137 applicants, 66% accepted, 74 enrolled. *Faculty:* 5 full-time (4 women), 1 (woman) part-time/adjunct. Expenses: Contact institution. *Financial support:* In 2016–17, 1 student received support. Scholarships/grants and traineeships available. Support available to part-time students. Financial award applicants required to submit FAFSA. In 2016, 41 master's awarded. *Program availability:* Part-time, evening/weekend. Offers adult gerontology clinical nurse specialist (MSN); adult gerontology primary care nurse practitioner (MSN); family nurse practitioner (MSN); nurse educator (MSN); nursing administration (MSN). *Application deadline:* For fall admission, 6/1 for domestic and international students; for spring admission, 10/1 for domestic and international students. Applications are processed on a rolling basis. *Application fee:* $30. Electronic applications accepted. *Application Contact:* Kathy Connelly, Evening Program Assistant Director, 863-680-4205, Fax: 863-680-3872, E-mail: kconnelly@flsouthern.edu. *Dean,* Dr. Linda Comer, 863-680-4310, Fax: 863-680-3872, E-mail: lcomer@flsouthern.edu.

Programs in Teaching Students: 49 full-time (40 women), 31 part-time (19 women); includes 19 minority (9 Black or African American, non-Hispanic/Latino; 1 American Indian or Alaska Native, non-Hispanic/Latino; 7 Hispanic/Latino; 1 Native Hawaiian or other Pacific Islander, non-Hispanic/Latino; 1 Two or more races, non-Hispanic/Latino), 2 international. Average age 40. 133 applicants, 54% accepted, 50 enrolled. *Faculty:* 7 full-time (3 women), 8 part-time/adjunct (5 women). Expenses: Contact institution. *Financial support:* In 2016–17, 3 students received support. Scholarships/grants available. Support available to part-time students. Financial award applicants required to submit FAFSA. In 2016, 1 master's awarded. *Program availability:* Part-time, evening/weekend. Offers collaborative teaching and learning (M Ed); educational leadership (M Ed, Ed D);

teaching (MAT). *Application deadline:* For fall admission, 8/1 for domestic and international students; for winter admission, 4/1 for domestic and international students; for spring admission, 12/1 for domestic and international students. Applications are processed on a rolling basis. *Application fee:* $30. Electronic applications accepted. *Application Contact:* Kathy Connelly, Evening Program Assistant Director, 863-680-4205, Fax: 863-680-3872, E-mail: kconnelly@flsouthern.edu. *Dean,* Dr. Tracey Tedder, 863-680-4177, Fax: 863-680-4102, E-mail: ttedder@flsouthern.edu.

FLORIDA STATE UNIVERSITY, Tallahassee, FL 32306

General Information State-supported, coed, university. CGS member. *Enrollment:* 41,368 graduate, professional, and undergraduate students; 5,894 full-time matriculated graduate/professional students (3,108 women), 2,035 part-time matriculated graduate/professional students (1,289 women). *Enrollment by degree level:* 4,003 master's, 3,797 doctoral, 129 other advanced degrees. *Graduate faculty:* 1,906 full-time (789 women), 62 part-time/adjunct (25 women). Tuition, state resident: full-time $7263; part-time $403.51 per credit hour. Tuition, nonresident: full-time $18,087; part-time $1004.85 per credit hour. *Required fees:* $1365; $75.81 per credit hour. $20 per semester. Tuition and fees vary according to campus/location. *Graduate housing:* Room and/or apartments available on a first-come, first-served basis to single students; on-campus housing not available to married students. Typical cost: $2610 per year ($4609 including board). Room and board charges vary according to housing facility selected. Housing application deadline: 5/1. *Student services:* Campus employment opportunities, campus safety program, career counseling, child daycare facilities, exercise/wellness program, free psychological counseling, grant writing training, international student services, low-cost health insurance, multicultural affairs office, services for students with disabilities, teacher training, writing training. *Library facilities:* Robert Manning Strozier Library plus 8 others. *Collection:* Books: 3.4 million (physical), 1.6 million (digital/electronic); Serial titles: 60,740 (physical), 2.7 million (digital/electronic); Databases: 1,144. Weekly public service hours: 134; study areas open 24 hours, 5–7 days a week; students can reserve study rooms. *Research affiliation:* University Corporation for Atmospheric Research (atmospheric research), Oak Ridge National Laboratory (materials science), Southeastern Universities Research Association (energy), University Research Association (energy), Bruker, Inc. (nuclear magnetic resonance), Oak Ridge Associated Universities (education, environmental assessment).

Computer facilities: 1,100 computers available on campus for general student use. A campuswide network can be accessed from student residence rooms and from off campus. Online class registration, course home pages, course search, online fee payment are available.
Website: http://www.fsu.edu/

General Application Contact: Jermaine Williams, Associate Director for Graduate Admissions, 850-644-7145, Fax: 850-644-0197, E-mail: jawilliams@fsu.edu.

GRADUATE UNITS

College of Law Students: 550 full-time (255 women), 52 part-time (24 women); includes 174 minority (42 Black or African American, non-Hispanic/Latino; 1 American Indian or Alaska Native, non-Hispanic/Latino; 15 Asian, non-Hispanic/Latino; 91 Hispanic/Latino; 25 Two or more races, non-Hispanic/Latino), 18 international. Average age 25. 1,929 applicants, 35% accepted, 174 enrolled. *Faculty:* 57 full-time (29 women), 30 part-time/adjunct (7 women). Expenses: Contact institution. *Financial support:* In 2016–17, 406 students received support, including 4 fellowships with full tuition reimbursements available (averaging $20,683 per year), 39 research assistantships (averaging $1,557 per year), 13 teaching assistantships (averaging $1,451 per year); career-related internships or fieldwork, scholarships/grants, and unspecified assistantships also available. Financial award application deadline: 3/1; financial award applicants required to submit FAFSA. In 2016, 11 master's, 195 doctorates awarded. *Program availability:* 100% online. Offers American law for foreign lawyers (LL M); business law (LL M); environmental law and policy (LL M); law (JM, JD). *Application deadline:* For fall admission, 7/15 for domestic students, 5/15 for international students. Applications are processed on a rolling basis. Electronic applications accepted. *Application Contact:* Jennifer L. Kessinger, Director of Admissions and Records, 850-644-3787, Fax: 850-644-7284, E-mail: jkessing@law.fsu.edu. *Dean,* Erin O'Hara O'Connor, 850-644-3400, Fax: 850-644-5487, E-mail: eoconnor@law.fsu.edu.

College of Medicine Students: 485 full-time (246 women); includes 192 minority (61 Black or African American, non-Hispanic/Latino; 53 Asian, non-Hispanic/Latino; 73 Hispanic/Latino; 5 Two or more races, non-Hispanic/Latino). Average age 26. 6,503 applicants, 3% accepted, 120 enrolled. *Faculty:* 165 full-time (83 women), 56 part-time/adjunct (19 women). Expenses: Contact institution. *Financial support:* In 2016–17, 178 students received support. Scholarships/grants and tuition waivers (partial) available. Financial award application deadline: 6/30; financial award applicants required to submit FAFSA. In 2016, 119 doctorates awarded. Offers biomedical sciences (PhD); medicine (MD, PhD); neuroscience (PhD). *Application deadline:* Applications are processed on a rolling basis. Electronic applications accepted. *Application Contact:* Dana Urrutia, Admissions Coordinator, 850-644-1857, Fax: 850-645-2846, E-mail: medadmissions@med.fsu.edu. *Dean,* Dr. John Patrick Fogarty, MD, 850-644-1346, Fax: 850-645-1420, E-mail: john.fogarty@med.fsu.edu.

The Graduate School Students: 5,894 full-time (3,108 women), 2,035 part-time (1,289 women); includes 1,878 minority (681 Black or African American, non-Hispanic/Latino; 14 American Indian or Alaska Native, non-Hispanic/Latino; 228 Asian, non-Hispanic/Latino; 772 Hispanic/Latino; 7 Native Hawaiian or other Pacific Islander, non-Hispanic/Latino; 176 Two or more races, non-Hispanic/Latino), 1,387 international. Average age 30. 8,072 applicants, 45% accepted, 1989 enrolled. *Faculty:* 1,906 full-time (789 women), 62 part-time/adjunct (25 women). Expenses: Contact institution. *Financial support:* In 2016–17, 39 fellowships with full tuition reimbursements (averaging $8,949 per year), 1,892 research assistantships with full tuition reimbursements, 3,605 teaching assistantships with full tuition reimbursements were awarded; career-related internships or fieldwork, Federal Work-Study, institutionally sponsored loans, scholarships/grants, traineeships, health care benefits, tuition waivers (full and partial), and unspecified assistantships also available. Support available to part-time students. Financial award applicants required to submit FAFSA. In 2016, 2,064 master's, 406 doctorates, 53 other advanced degrees awarded. *Program availability:* Part-time, evening/weekend, 100% online, blended/hybrid learning. Offers materials science and engineering (MS, PhD). *Application deadline:* For fall admission, 7/1 for domestic and international students; for spring admission, 11/1 for domestic and international students. Electronic applications accepted. *Application fee:* $35. *Application Contact:* Jermaine Williams, Associate Director for Graduate Admissions, 850-644-7145, Fax: 850-644-0197, E-mail: jawilliams@fsu.edu. *Dean,* Dr. Nancy Marcus, 850-644-3501, Fax: 850-644-2969, E-mail: nmarcus@fsu.edu.

College of Arts and Sciences Students: 1,591 full-time, 179 part-time; includes 227 minority (50 Black or African American, non-Hispanic/Latino; 2 American Indian or Alaska Native, non-Hispanic/Latino; 48 Asian, non-Hispanic/Latino; 98 Hispanic/Latino; 1 Native Hawaiian or other Pacific Islander, non-Hispanic/Latino; 28

Two or more races, non-Hispanic/Latino), 571 international. Average age 29. *Faculty:* 587 full-time, 5 part-time/adjunct. Expenses: Contact institution. *Financial support:* Fellowships, research assistantships, teaching assistantships, career-related internships or fieldwork, institutionally sponsored loans, scholarships/grants, traineeships, and unspecified assistantships available. Support available to part-time students. Financial award applicants required to submit FAFSA. In 2016, 293 master's, 177 doctorates awarded. *Program availability:* Part-time. Offers analytical chemistry (MS, PhD); ancient history (MA); applied and computational mathematics (MS, PhD); applied behavior analysis (MS); applied statistics (MS); aquatic environmental science (MS, PSM); arts and sciences (MA, MFA, MS, MST, PSM, PhD); biochemistry (MS, PhD); biomathematics (MS, PhD); biostatistics (MS, PhD); cell and molecular biology (MS, PhD); classical archaeology (MA); classical civilization (MA); classics (PhD); clinical psychology (PhD); cognitive psychology (PhD); community college science teaching (MST); computational science (MS, PhD); computer criminology (MS); computer network and system administration (MS); computer science (MS, PhD); creative writing (MFA); cyber security (MS); developmental psychology (PhD); ecology and evolutionary biology (MS, PhD); English (PhD); financial mathematics (MS, PhD); French (MA, PhD); geological sciences (MS, PhD); geophysical fluid dynamics (PhD); German (MA); Greek (MA); Greek and Latin (MA); history (MA, MS, PhD); history and philosophy of science (MA); humanities (PhD); inorganic chemistry (MS, PhD); Italian (MA); Italian studies (MA); Latin (MA); literature (MA); materials chemistry (PhD); mathematical statistics (MS, PhD); meteorology (MS, PhD); molecular biophysics (PhD); neuroscience (PhD); oceanography (MS, PSM, PhD); organic chemistry (MS, PhD); philosophy (MA, PhD); physical chemistry (MS, PhD); physics (MS, PhD); psychobiology (MS); public history (MA); pure mathematics (MS, PhD); religion (MA, PhD); rhetoric and composition (MA); science teaching (MST); Slavic languages and literatures (MA); Slavic languages/Russian (MA); social psychology (PhD); Spanish (MA, PhD); statistical data science (MS). *Application deadline:* Applications are processed on a rolling basis. *Application fee:* $30. Electronic applications accepted. *Application Contact:* Ginger Martin, Graduate Academic Coordinator, 850-644-1081, Fax: 850-644-9656, E-mail: vmartin@fsu.edu. *Dean,* Dr. Sam Huckaba, 850-644-1081.

College of Business Students: 272 full-time (127 women), 351 part-time (133 women); includes 141 minority (45 Black or African American, non-Hispanic/Latino; 2 American Indian or Alaska Native, non-Hispanic/Latino; 20 Asian, non-Hispanic/Latino; 59 Hispanic/Latino; 2 Native Hawaiian or other Pacific Islander, non-Hispanic/Latino; 13 Two or more races, non-Hispanic/Latino), 71 international. Average age 30. 688 applicants, 60% accepted, 273 enrolled. *Faculty:* 101 full-time (27 women), 4 part-time/adjunct (2 women). Expenses: Contact institution. *Financial support:* In 2016–17, 149 students received support, including 9 fellowships (averaging $1,500 per year), 65 research assistantships with full tuition reimbursements available (averaging $20,000 per year, 75 teaching assistantships with full tuition reimbursements available (averaging $20,000 per year); career-related internships or fieldwork, scholarships/grants, health care benefits, tuition waivers (full and partial), and unspecified assistantships also available. Support available to part-time students. Financial award application deadline: 1/1; financial award applicants required to submit FAFSA. In 2016, 231 master's, 12 doctorates awarded. *Program availability:* Part-time, 100% online. Offers accounting (M Acc); business administration (MBA, PhD); finance (MS); management information systems (MS); risk management and insurance (MS). *Application deadline:* For fall admission, 6/1 for domestic and international students; for spring admission, 10/1 for domestic and international students; for summer admission, 3/1 for domestic and international students. Applications are processed on a rolling basis. *Application fee:* $30. Electronic applications accepted. *Application Contact:* Jennifer Clark, Director, 850-644-6458, E-mail: gradprograms@business.fsu.edu. *Dean,* Dr. Michael Hartline, 850-644-4405, Fax: 850-644-0915, E-mail: mhartline@business.fsu.edu.

College of Communication and Information Students: 216 full-time (172 women), 386 part-time (294 women); includes 204 minority (60 Black or African American, non-Hispanic/Latino; 50 Asian, non-Hispanic/Latino; 83 Hispanic/Latino; 11 Two or more races, non-Hispanic/Latino), 10 international. Average age 31. 733 applicants, 42% accepted, 209 enrolled. *Faculty:* 71 full-time (42 women), 17 part-time/adjunct (12 women). Expenses: Contact institution. *Financial support:* In 2016–17, 359 students received support, including 29 fellowships with full tuition reimbursements available (averaging $3,069 per year), 56 research assistantships with full tuition reimbursements available (averaging $20,371 per year), 77 teaching assistantships with full tuition reimbursements available (averaging $19,275 per year); career-related internships or fieldwork, Federal Work-Study, institutionally sponsored loans, scholarships/grants, health care benefits, tuition waivers (full and partial), and unspecified assistantships also available. Support available to part-time students. Financial award application deadline: 1/1; financial award applicants required to submit FAFSA. In 2016, 271 master's, 18 doctorates, 5 other advanced degrees awarded. *Program availability:* Part-time, evening/weekend, 100% online. Offers communication and information (MA, MS, PhD, Specialist); communication science and disorders (MS, PhD); communication theory and research (PhD); information (MA, MS, PhD, Specialist); information studies (MA, MS, PhD, Specialist); information technology (MS); integrated marketing communication (MA, MS); media and communication studies (MA, MS); public interest media and communication (MA, MS). *Application deadline:* For fall admission, 7/1 for domestic students, 5/1 for international students; for spring admission, 11/1 for domestic and international students. Applications are processed on a rolling basis. *Application fee:* $30. Electronic applications accepted. *Application Contact:* Betsy Crawford, Development and Recruiting Coordinator, Fax: 850-644-0611, E-mail: betsy.crawford@cci.fsu.edu. *Dean,* Dr. Lawrence C. Dennis, 850-644-9698, Fax: 850-644-0611, E-mail: larry.dennis@cci.fsu.edu.

College of Criminology and Criminal Justice Students: 127 full-time (84 women), 113 part-time (49 women); includes 76 minority (40 Black or African American, non-Hispanic/Latino; 1 American Indian or Alaska Native, non-Hispanic/Latino; 4 Asian, non-Hispanic/Latino; 31 Hispanic/Latino). 151 applicants, 76% accepted, 45 enrolled. *Faculty:* 19 full-time (7 women). Expenses: Contact institution. *Financial support:* In 2016–17, 50 students received support, including 3 fellowships with full tuition reimbursements available (averaging $15,000 per year), 23 research assistantships with full tuition reimbursements available (averaging $15,000 per year), 17 teaching assistantships with full tuition reimbursements available (averaging $15,000 per year); career-related internships or fieldwork, institutionally sponsored loans, scholarships/grants, health care benefits, tuition waivers (full), and unspecified assistantships also available. Financial award application deadline: 1/15; financial award applicants required to submit FAFSA. In 2016, 56 master's, 7 doctorates awarded. *Program availability:* Part-time, 100% online. Offers criminology and criminal justice (MA, MSC, PhD). *Application deadline:* For fall admission, 7/1 for domestic and international students; for spring admission, 11/1 for domestic and international students. Applications are processed on a rolling basis. *Application fee:* $30.

Electronic applications accepted. *Application Contact:* Margarita Frankeberger, Program Director, 850-644-7373, Fax: 850-644-9614, E-mail: mfrankeberger@fsu.edu. *Dean,* Dr. Thomas G. Blomberg, 850-644-7365, Fax: 850-644-9614.

College of Education Students: 611 full-time (394 women), 425 part-time (294 women); includes 252 minority (117 Black or African American, non-Hispanic/Latino; 4 American Indian or Alaska Native, non-Hispanic/Latino; 6 Asian, non-Hispanic/Latino; 95 Hispanic/Latino; 30 Two or more races, non-Hispanic/Latino; 209 international. Average age 32. 1,042 applicants, 52% accepted, 295 enrolled. *Faculty:* 99 full-time (67 women), 54 part-time/adjunct (35 women). Expenses: Contact institution. *Financial support:* In 2016–17, 313 students received support, including 22 fellowships with tuition reimbursements available, 254 research assistantships with tuition reimbursements available, 278 teaching assistantships with tuition reimbursements available; scholarships/grants, tuition waivers (full and partial), and unspecified assistantships also available. Financial award application deadline: 1/15; financial award applicants required to submit FAFSA. In 2016, 312 master's, 66 doctorates, 52 other advanced degrees awarded. *Program availability:* Part-time, evening/weekend, blended/hybrid learning, asynchronous, minimal on-campus study. Offers coaching (Certificate); counseling and human systemscounseling psychology and school psychology (PhD); curriculum and instruction (MS, PhD, Ed S); education (MS, Ed D, PhD, Certificate, Ed S); education policy and evaluation (MS, Ed D, PhD); educational leadership/administration (MS, Ed D, PhD, Certificate, Ed S); higher education (MS, Ed D, PhD); human performance technology (Certificate); instructional systems and learning technologies (MS, PhD); learning and cognition (MS, PhD); measurement and statistics (MS, PhD, Certificate); online instructional development (Certificate); program evaluation (Certificate); social, historical and philosophical foundations of education (MS); sociocultural and international development education studies (MS, Ed D, PhD); sport management (MS, PhD); sport psychology (MS, PhD). *Application fee:* $30. Electronic applications accepted. *Application Contact:* Jennie H. Kroeger, Assistant Director, Office of Communication and Recruitment, 850-644-6885, Fax: 850-644-2725, E-mail: jennie.kroeger@fsu.edu. *Dean,* Marcy P. Driscoll, 850-644-6885, Fax: 850-644-2725, E-mail: mdriscoll@fsu.edu.

College of Fine Arts Students: 261 full-time (198 women), 36 part-time (30 women); includes 76 minority (23 Black or African American, non-Hispanic/Latino; 1 American Indian or Alaska Native, non-Hispanic/Latino; 18 Asian, non-Hispanic/Latino; 30 Hispanic/Latino; 4 Two or more races, non-Hispanic/Latino), 15 international. Average age 25. 375 applicants, 89% accepted, 305 enrolled. *Faculty:* 67 full-time (40 women), 17 part-time/adjunct (12 women). Expenses: Contact institution. *Financial support:* In 2016–17, 257 students received support, including 5 fellowships with partial tuition reimbursements available (averaging $18,000 per year), 90 research assistantships with partial tuition reimbursements available (averaging $4,957 per year), 78 teaching assistantships with partial tuition reimbursements available (averaging $8,001 per year); career-related internships or fieldwork, Federal Work-Study, institutionally sponsored loans, scholarships/grants, and unspecified assistantships also available. Support available to part-time students. Financial award application deadline: 4/15; financial award applicants required to submit FAFSA. In 2016, 76 master's, 4 doctorates awarded. *Program availability:* Part-time. Offers acting (MFA); American dance studies (MA); art (MFA); art education (MA, MS, Ed D, PhD); art history (MA, PhD); costume design (MFA); dance (MFA); directing (MFA); fine arts (MA, MFA, MS, Ed D, PhD, Graduate Certificate); interior architecture and design (MA, MS); museum and cultural heritage studies (MA); studio and related studies (MA); technical production (MFA); theatre (MA, MFA); theatre management (MFA). *Application deadline:* For fall admission, 7/1 priority date for domestic students; for spring admission, 11/1 priority date for domestic students. Applications are processed on a rolling basis. *Application fee:* $30. Electronic applications accepted. *Application Contact:* Jermaine Williams, Assistant Director for Graduate Admissions, 850-644-7145, Fax: 850-644-0197, E-mail: jawilliams@fsu.edu. *Dean,* Peter Weisher, 850-664-5244, Fax: 850-644-2604, E-mail: pweishar@fsu.edu.

College of Human Sciences Students: 119 full-time (74 women), 16 part-time (12 women); includes 34 minority (12 Black or African American, non-Hispanic/Latino; 2 Asian, non-Hispanic/Latino; 10 Hispanic/Latino; 1 Native Hawaiian or other Pacific Islander, non-Hispanic/Latino; 9 Two or more races, non-Hispanic/Latino), 17 international. 171 applicants, 47% accepted, 50 enrolled. *Faculty:* 40 full-time (22 women). Expenses: Contact institution. *Financial support:* In 2016–17, 88 students received support, including 34 research assistantships with full tuition reimbursements available (averaging $7,796 per year), 78 teaching assistantships with full tuition reimbursements available (averaging $8,976 per year); career-related internships or fieldwork, Federal Work-Study, scholarships/grants, and unspecified assistantships also available. Financial award application deadline: 1/15; financial award applicants required to submit FAFSA. In 2016, 38 master's, 6 doctorates awarded. *Program availability:* Part-time. Offers exercise physiology (MS, PhD); family and child sciences (MS); family relations (PhD); human sciences (MS, PhD); marriage and family therapy (PhD); nutrition and food science (MS, PhD); retail, merchandising and product development (MS); sports nutrition (MS); sports sciences (MS). *Application deadline:* For fall admission, 4/1 for domestic and international students; for spring admission, 10/1 for domestic and international students. Applications are processed on a rolling basis. *Application fee:* $30. Electronic applications accepted. *Application Contact:* Tara L. Hartman, Academic Program Specialist, 850-644-7221, Fax: 850-644-0700, E-mail: thartman@fsu.edu. *Dean,* Dr. Michael D. Delp, 850-644-1281, Fax: 850-644-0700, E-mail: mdelp@fsu.edu.

College of Motion Picture Arts Students: 59 full-time (25 women); includes 29 minority (9 Black or African American, non-Hispanic/Latino; 13 Asian, non-Hispanic/Latino; 4 Hispanic/Latino; 3 Two or more races, non-Hispanic/Latino). Average age 25. 187 applicants, 16% accepted, 30 enrolled. *Faculty:* 24 full-time (7 women), 3 part-time/adjunct (1 woman). Expenses: Contact institution. *Financial support:* In 2016–17, 20 students received support, including 20 teaching assistantships with partial tuition reimbursements available (averaging $5,500 per year); institutionally sponsored loans and unspecified assistantships also available. Financial award application deadline: 12/1; financial award applicants required to submit FAFSA. In 2016, 30 master's awarded. Offers film production (MFA); screenwriting (MFA). *Application deadline:* For fall admission, 12/1 for domestic and international students. Electronic applications accepted. *Application Contact:* Gloria McElroy, Staff Director of Admissions and Recruitment, 850-644-2626, Fax: 850-644-2626, E-mail: gmcelroy@fsu.edu. *Interim Dean,* Reb Braddock, 850-644-0453, Fax: 850-644-2626.

College of Music Students: 324 full-time (156 women); includes 87 minority (26 Black or African American, non-Hispanic/Latino; 1 American Indian or Alaska Native, non-Hispanic/Latino; 32 Asian, non-Hispanic/Latino; 26 Hispanic/Latino; 2 Native Hawaiian or other Pacific Islander, non-Hispanic/Latino). Average age 26. 737 applicants, 42% accepted, 138 enrolled. *Faculty:* 79 full-time, 2 part-time/adjunct. Expenses: Contact institution. *Financial support:* In 2016–17, 222 students received

support, including 2 fellowships with full tuition reimbursements available (averaging $15,000 per year), 14 research assistantships with full and partial tuition reimbursements available (averaging $5,900 per year), 201 teaching assistantships with full and partial tuition reimbursements available (averaging $5,900 per year); career-related internships or fieldwork, scholarships/grants, tuition waivers (full and partial), and unspecified assistantships also available. Support available to part-time students. Financial award application deadline: 2/28; financial award applicants required to submit FAFSA. In 2016, 120 master's, 36 doctorates awarded. *Program availability:* Part-time. Offers accompanying (MM); arts administration (MA); choral conducting (MM); composition (MM, DM); ethnomusicology (MM); general music (MA); instrumental accompanying (MM); instrumental conducting (MM); jazz studies (MM); music theory (MM, PhD); music therapy (MM); musicology (MM, PhD); opera (MM); performance (MM, DM); piano pedagogy (MM); piano technology (MM); vocal accompanying (MM). *Application deadline:* For fall admission, 7/1 for domestic and international students; for spring admission, 11/1 for domestic and international students; for summer admission, 3/1 for domestic students. Applications are processed on a rolling basis. *Application fee:* $30. Electronic applications accepted. *Application Contact:* Kris Watson, Director of Admissions, 850-645-2126, Fax: 850-644-2033, E-mail: krwatson@fsu.edu. *Dean,* Dr. Patricia Flowers, 850-644-4361, Fax: 850-644-2033, E-mail: pjflowers@fsu.edu.

College of Nursing Students: 71 full-time (68 women), 29 part-time (27 women); includes 26 minority (13 Black or African American, non-Hispanic/Latino; 9 Asian, non-Hispanic/Latino; 4 Two or more races, non-Hispanic/Latino). Average age 38. 97 applicants, 46% accepted, 36 enrolled. *Faculty:* 20 full-time (19 women), 3 part-time/adjunct (all women). Expenses: Contact institution. *Financial support:* In 2016–17, 75 students received support, including fellowships with partial tuition reimbursements available (averaging $6,300 per year), research assistantships with partial tuition reimbursements available (averaging $3,000 per year), 3 teaching assistantships with partial tuition reimbursements available (averaging $3,000 per year); career-related internships or fieldwork, Federal Work-Study, institutionally sponsored loans, scholarships/grants, traineeships, and tuition waivers (partial) also available. Financial award application deadline: 4/15; financial award applicants required to submit FAFSA. In 2016, 9 master's, 20 doctorates awarded. *Program availability:* Part-time, online learning. Offers family nurse practitioner (DNP); nurse educator (MSN); nurse leader (MSN, Certificate); psychiatric mental health (Certificate). *Application deadline:* For fall admission, 4/15 for domestic and international students. *Application fee:* $30. Electronic applications accepted. *Application Contact:* Carlos Urrutia, Assistant Director for Student Services, 850-644-5638, Fax: 850-645-7249, E-mail: currutia@fsu.edu. *Dean,* Dr. Judith McFetridge-Durdle, 850-644-6846, Fax: 850-644-7660, E-mail: jdurdle@nursing.fsu.edu.

College of Social Sciences and Public Policy Students: 443 full-time (216 women), 183 part-time (95 women); includes 145 minority (66 Black or African American, non-Hispanic/Latino; 29 Asian, non-Hispanic/Latino; 32 Hispanic/Latino; 18 Two or more races, non-Hispanic/Latino), 100 international. Average age 26. 743 applicants, 64% accepted, 225 enrolled. *Faculty:* 134 full-time (47 women), 44 part-time/adjunct (7 women). Expenses: Contact institution. *Financial support:* In 2016–17, 273 students received support, including 33 fellowships with full tuition reimbursements available (averaging $21,828 per year), 85 research assistantships with full tuition reimbursements available (averaging $13,487 per year), 126 teaching assistantships with full tuition reimbursements available (averaging $18,710 per year); career-related internships or fieldwork, Federal Work-Study, institutionally sponsored loans, scholarships/grants, health care benefits, tuition waivers (full and partial), and unspecified assistantships also available. Support available to part-time students. Financial award application deadline: 1/15; financial award applicants required to submit FAFSA. In 2016, 294 master's, 31 doctorates awarded. *Program availability:* Part-time, evening/weekend. Offers applied American politics and policy (MA, MS); applied economics (MS); applied social research (MS); Asian studies (MA, MS); demography (MS); economics (PhD); geographic information science (MS); geography (MA, MS, PhD); international affairs (MA, MS); planning (MSP); political science (PhD); public administration (MPA, PhD); public administration and policy (Certificate); public health (MPH); Russian and east European studies (MA, MS); social sciences and public policy (MA, MPA, MPH, MS, MSP, PhD, Certificate); sociology (MA, MS, PhD); sociology of health and aging (MS); urban and regional planning (PhD). *Application deadline:* For fall admission, 7/1 priority date for domestic and international students; for spring admission, 11/1 priority date for domestic and international students; for summer admission, 3/1 priority date for domestic and international students. Applications are processed on a rolling basis. *Application fee:* $30. Electronic applications accepted. *Application Contact:* Jermaine Williams, Assistant Director for Graduate Admissions, 850-644-7145, Fax: 850-644-0197, E-mail: jawilliams@fsu.edu. *Interim Dean,* Dr. Timothy Chapin, 850-644-5488, Fax: 850-645-4923, E-mail: tchapin@fsu.edu.

College of Social Work Students: 254 full-time (229 women), 187 part-time (165 women); includes 161 minority (92 Black or African American, non-Hispanic/Latino; 10 Asian, non-Hispanic/Latino; 46 Hispanic/Latino; 1 Native Hawaiian or other Pacific Islander, non-Hispanic/Latino; 12 Two or more races, non-Hispanic/Latino). Average age 30. 293 applicants, 74% accepted, 167 enrolled. *Faculty:* 31 full-time (20 women), 16 part-time/adjunct (11 women). Expenses: Contact institution. *Financial support:* In 2016–17, 132 students received support, including 1 fellowship with full tuition reimbursement available (averaging $22,000 per year), 25 research assistantships with full tuition reimbursements available (averaging $4,000 per year), 7 teaching assistantships with full tuition reimbursements available (averaging $16,000 per year); career-related internships or fieldwork, scholarships/grants, health care benefits, tuition waivers (partial), and unspecified assistantships also available. Financial award application deadline: 5/1; financial award applicants required to submit FAFSA. In 2016, 220 master's, 3 doctorates awarded. *Program availability:* Part-time, evening/weekend, 100% online coursework in specified areas with mandatory in-person internships. Offers clinical social work (MSW); social leadership (MSW); social work (PhD). *Application deadline:* For fall admission, 6/1 for domestic and international students; for spring admission, 10/1 for domestic and international students; for summer admission, 3/1 for domestic and international students. Applications are processed on a rolling basis. *Application fee:* $30. Electronic applications accepted. *Application Contact:* Dana DeBoer, Coordinator of MSW Admissions, 800-378-9550, Fax: 850-644-9591, E-mail: ddeboer2@admin.fsu.edu. *Dean,* Dr. James Clark, 850-644-4752, Fax: 850-644-9750, E-mail: jclark5@fsu.edu.

FAMU-FSU College of Engineering Students: 329 full-time (66 women); includes 57 minority (32 Black or African American, non-Hispanic/Latino; 1 American Indian or Alaska Native, non-Hispanic/Latino; 7 Asian, non-Hispanic/Latino; 12 Hispanic/Latino; 5 Two or more races, non-Hispanic/Latino), 187 international. Average age 25. 484 applicants, 46% accepted, 89 enrolled. *Faculty:* 97 full-time (12 women), 10 part-time/adjunct (3 women). Expenses: Contact institution. *Financial support:* In 2016–17,

202 students received support, including 20 fellowships with full tuition reimbursements available, 123 research assistantships with full tuition reimbursements available, 79 teaching assistantships with full tuition reimbursements available; career-related internships or fieldwork, scholarships/grants, tuition waivers (full), and unspecified assistantships also available. Financial award application deadline: 1/15; financial award applicants required to submit FAFSA. In 2016, 103 master's, 23 doctorates awarded. *Program availability:* Part-time. Offers biomedical engineering (MS, PhD); chemical engineering (MS, PhD); civil and environmental engineering (M Eng, MS, PhD); electrical engineering (MS, PhD); engineering (M Eng, MS, PhD); industrial engineering (MS, PhD); mechanical engineering (MS, PhD); sustainable energy (MS). *Application deadline:* For fall admission, 3/1 for domestic and international students; for spring admission, 11/1 for domestic and international students. Applications are processed on a rolling basis. *Application fee:* $30. Electronic applications accepted. *Application Contact:* Frederika Manciagli, Director, Student Services, 850-410-6361, E-mail: manciagl@eng.famu.fsu.edu. *Dean/Professor,* Dr. John Murray Gibson, 850-410-6161, Fax: 850-410-6546, E-mail: dean@eng.fsu.edu.

FONTBONNE UNIVERSITY, St. Louis, MO 63105-3098

General Information Independent-religious, coed, comprehensive institution. *Enrollment:* 456 full-time matriculated graduate/professional students (313 women), 102 part-time matriculated graduate/professional students (77 women). *Enrollment by degree level:* 558 master's. *Graduate faculty:* 32 full-time (24 women), 43 part-time/adjunct (26 women). *Tuition:* Full-time $8436; part-time $703 per credit hour. *Required fees:* $18 per credit hour. Tuition and fees vary according to course load. *Graduate housing:* Room and/or apartments available on a first-come, first-served basis to single students; on-campus housing not available to married students. Typical cost: $5141 per year ($9364 including board). Room and board charges vary according to board plan and housing facility selected. Housing application deadline: 5/1. *Student services:* Career counseling, exercise/wellness program, free psychological counseling, international student services, multicultural affairs office, services for students with disabilities. *Library facilities:* The Jack C. Taylor Library at Fontbonne University plus 1 other. *Collection:* Books: 87,793 (physical), 210,611 (digital/electronic); Databases: 38.

Computer facilities: 215 computers available on campus for general student use. A campuswide network can be accessed from student residence rooms and from off campus. Online class registration is available.
Website: http://www.fontbonne.edu/

General Application Contact: Joseph Havis, Vice President for Enrollment Management, 314-863-2220, E-mail: admissions@fontbonne.edu.

GRADUATE UNITS

Graduate Programs Students: 456 full-time (313 women), 102 part-time (77 women); includes 138 minority (118 Black or African American, non-Hispanic/Latino; 1 American Indian or Alaska Native, non-Hispanic/Latino; 7 Asian, non-Hispanic/Latino; 9 Hispanic/Latino; 3 Two or more races, non-Hispanic/Latino), 37 international. *Faculty:* 32 full-time (24 women), 43 part-time/adjunct (26 women). *Expenses:* Contact institution. *Financial support:* Teaching assistantships with partial tuition reimbursements and scholarships/grants available. Support available to part-time students. Financial award application deadline: 4/1; financial award applicants required to submit FAFSA. *Program availability:* Part-time, evening/weekend, online learning. Offers accounting (MBA, MS); art (MA); art (K-12) (MAT); business (MBA); computer science (MS); deaf education (MA); early intervention in deaf education (MA); education (MA); elementary education (MAT); family and consumer sciences (MA); fine arts (MFA); instructional design and technology (MS); management and leadership (MM); middle school education (MAT); secondary education (MAT); special education (MAT); speech-language pathology (MS); supply chain management (MS); theatre (MA). *Application deadline:* For fall admission, 8/1 for international students; for spring admission, 12/1 for international students. Applications are processed on a rolling basis. *Application fee:* $25 ($30 for international students). Electronic applications accepted. *Application Contact:* Lauryn Filip, Coordinator, Graduate Admission and Professional Studies, 314-889-4650, E-mail: admissions@fontbonne.edu. *Vice President for Academic Affairs,* Dr. Carey Adams, 314-719-3609, E-mail: cadams@fontbonne.edu.

FORDHAM UNIVERSITY, New York, NY 10458

General Information Independent-religious, coed, university. CGS member. *Enrollment:* 15,582 graduate, professional, and undergraduate students; 4,220 full-time matriculated graduate/professional students (2,544 women), 2,284 part-time matriculated graduate/professional students (1,403 women). *Enrollment by degree level:* 4,131 master's, 2,267 doctoral, 106 other advanced degrees. *Graduate faculty:* 617 full-time (257 women), 922 part-time/adjunct (447 women). *Graduate housing:* Room and/or apartments available on a first-come, first-served basis to single students; on-campus housing not available to married students. Housing application deadline: 4/10. *Student services:* Campus employment opportunities, campus safety program, career counseling, free psychological counseling, international student services, low-cost health insurance, services for students with disabilities, teacher training, writing training. *Library facilities:* Walsh Library plus 3 others. *Collection:* Books: 2.2 million (physical), 550,000 (digital/electronic); Serial titles: 6,400 (physical), 76,500 (digital/electronic); Databases: 260. Weekly public service hours: 103; study areas open 24 hours, 5–7 days a week. *Research affiliation:* Equator Initiative/United Nations Development Programme, Folger Shakespeare Library, New York Botanical Gardens, New York Ocean Science Library, Wildlife Conservation Society, Memorial Sloan-Kettering Cancer Center.

Computer facilities: Computer purchase and lease plans are available. 1,400 computers available on campus for general student use. A campuswide network can be accessed from student residence rooms and from off campus. Online class registration is available.
Website: http://www.fordham.edu/

General Application Contact: Office of Admission, 718-817-1000.

GRADUATE UNITS

Gabelli School of Business Students: 1,117 full-time (668 women), 553 part-time (282 women); includes 207 minority (44 Black or African American, non-Hispanic/Latino; 92 Asian, non-Hispanic/Latino; 69 Hispanic/Latino; 2 Native Hawaiian or other Pacific Islander, non-Hispanic/Latino), 1,088 international. Average age 27. 4,745 applicants, 46% accepted, 752 enrolled. *Faculty:* 132 full-time (44 women), 51 part-time/adjunct (7 women). *Expenses:* Contact institution. *Financial support:* In 2016–17, 78 students received support. Career-related internships or fieldwork, institutionally sponsored loans, scholarships/grants, and unspecified assistantships available. Support available to part-time students. Financial award application deadline: 6/30; financial award applicants required to submit FAFSA. In 2016, 996 master's awarded. *Program availability:* Part-time, evening/weekend. Offers accounting (MBA, MS); applied statistics and decision-making (MS); business administration (EMBA); business analytics (MS);

communications and media management (MBA); electronic business (MBA); entrepreneurship (MBA); finance (MBA); global finance (MS); global sustainability (MBA); healthcare management (MBA); information systems (MBA, MS); investor relations (MS); management (MBA, MS); marketing (MBA); marketing intelligence (MS); media management (MBA); nonprofit leadership (MBA); quantitative finance (MS); taxation (MS). *Application deadline:* For fall admission, 11/15 priority date for domestic and international students; for winter admission, 1/15 priority date for domestic students, 1/1 priority date for international students; for spring admission, 3/1 for domestic and international students; for summer admission, 6/1 for domestic students. *Application fee:* $130. Electronic applications accepted. *Application Contact:* Lawrence Murray, Senior Assistant Dean of Graduate Admissions and Advising, 212-636-6200, Fax: 212-636-7076, E-mail: admissionsgb@fordham.edu. *Dean,* Dr. Donna Rapaccioli, 212-636-6165, Fax: 212-307-1779, E-mail: rapaccioli@fordham.edu.

Graduate School of Arts and Sciences Students: 475 full-time (232 women), 206 part-time (104 women); includes 119 minority (19 Black or African American, non-Hispanic/Latino; 2 American Indian or Alaska Native, non-Hispanic/Latino; 71 Asian, non-Hispanic/Latino; 27 Hispanic/Latino), 138 international. Average age 31. 1,883 applicants, 31% accepted, 210 enrolled. *Faculty:* 249 full-time (81 women). *Expenses:* Contact institution. *Financial support:* In 2016–17, 29 fellowships with tuition reimbursements (averaging $22,844 per year), 106 research assistantships with tuition reimbursements (averaging $16,516 per year), 280 teaching assistantships with tuition reimbursements (averaging $19,927 per year) were awarded; career-related internships or fieldwork, Federal Work-Study, institutionally sponsored loans, scholarships/grants, health care benefits, tuition waivers (full and partial), and unspecified assistantships also available. Support available to part-time students. Financial award application deadline: 1/4; financial award applicants required to submit FAFSA. In 2016, 145 master's, 56 doctorates, 87 other advanced degrees awarded. *Program availability:* Part-time, evening/weekend. Offers applied developmental psychology (PhD); applied psychological methods (MA); arts and sciences (MA, MFA, MS, PhD, Advanced Certificate, Certificate, Graduate Certificate); biological sciences (MS, PhD); classical languages and literatures (MA, PhD); clinical psychology (PhD); computer science (MS); conservation biology (Graduate Certificate); cyber security (MS); data analytics (MS); economics (MA, PhD); elections and campaign management (MA); English language and literature (MA, PhD); history (MA, PhD); international humanitarian action (MA); international political economy and development (MA, Certificate); philosophy (MA, PhD); playwriting (MFA); psychometrics (PhD); theology (MA, PhD); urban studies (MA). *Application deadline:* For fall admission, 1/4 priority date for domestic and international students; for spring admission, 10/31 for domestic and international students. Applications are processed on a rolling basis. *Application fee:* $70. Electronic applications accepted. *Application Contact:* Bernadette Valentino-Morrison, Director of Graduate Admissions, 718-817-4419, Fax: 718-817-3566, E-mail: valentinomor@fordham.edu. *Dean,* Dr. Eva Badowska, 718-817-4400, Fax: 718-817-4474, E-mail: badowska@fordham.edu.

Program in Ethics and Society Students: 8 full-time (7 women), 5 part-time (3 women); includes 3 minority (2 Black or African American, non-Hispanic/Latino; 1 Asian, non-Hispanic/Latino), 1 international. Average age 34. 39 applicants, 28% accepted, 7 enrolled. *Expenses:* Contact institution. *Financial support:* In 2016–17, 1 student received support. Teaching assistantships, Federal Work-Study, institutionally sponsored loans, scholarships/grants, tuition waivers (partial), and unspecified assistantships available. Financial award application deadline: 1/4. In 2016, 6 master's awarded. *Program availability:* Part-time. Offers ethics and society (MA); health care ethics (Certificate). *Application deadline:* For fall admission, 1/4 priority date for domestic students; for spring admission, 10/31 for domestic students. Applications are processed on a rolling basis. *Application fee:* $70. Electronic applications accepted. *Application Contact:* Bernadette Valentino-Morrison, Director of Graduate Admissions, 718-817-4419, Fax: 718-817-3566, E-mail: valentinomor@fordham.edu. *Director of Academic Programs, Fordham University Center for Ethics Education,* Dr. Bryan Pilkington, 718-817-3775, Fax: 212-759-2009, E-mail: afried@fordham.edu.

Program in Medieval Studies Students: 8 full-time (7 women), 5 part-time (3 women); includes 3 minority (2 Black or African American, non-Hispanic/Latino; 1 Asian, non-Hispanic/Latino), 1 international. Average age 27. 36 applicants, 53% accepted, 7 enrolled. *Expenses:* Contact institution. *Financial support:* In 2016–17, 4 students received support. Institutionally sponsored loans, tuition waivers (full and partial), and unspecified assistantships available. Financial award application deadline: 1/4; financial award applicants required to submit FAFSA. In 2016, 6 master's, 2 other advanced degrees awarded. *Program availability:* Part-time, evening/weekend. Offers medieval studies (MA, Certificate). *Application deadline:* For fall admission, 1/4 priority date for domestic students; for spring admission, 11/1 for domestic students. Applications are processed on a rolling basis. *Application fee:* $70. Electronic applications accepted. *Application Contact:* Bernadette Valentino-Morrison, Director of Graduate Admissions, 718-817-4419, Fax: 718-817-3566, E-mail: valentinomor@fordham.edu. *Director,* Dr. Susanne Hafner, 718-817-4655, E-mail: hafner@fordham.edu.

Graduate School of Education *Program availability:* Part-time, evening/weekend. Offers education (MSE, MST, Ed D, PhD, Adv C). Electronic applications accepted.

Division of Curriculum and Teaching *Program availability:* Part-time, evening/weekend. Offers curriculum and teaching (MSE); early childhood education (MSE); elementary education (MST); special education (MSE, Adv C); teaching English as a second language (MSE). Electronic applications accepted.

Division of Educational Leadership, Administration and Policy *Program availability:* Part-time, evening/weekend. Offers administration and supervision (MSE, Adv C); administration and supervision for church leaders (PhD); educational administration and supervision (Ed D, PhD). Electronic applications accepted.

Division of Psychological and Educational Services *Program availability:* Part-time, evening/weekend. Offers counseling and personnel services (MSE); counseling psychology (PhD); school psychology (PhD). Electronic applications accepted.

Graduate School of Religion and Religious Education *Program availability:* Part-time. Offers pastoral counseling and spiritual care (MA); pastoral ministry/spirituality/pastoral counseling (D Min); religion and religious education (MA); religious education (MS, PhD, PD); spiritual direction (Certificate). Electronic applications accepted.

Graduate School of Social Service Students: 884 full-time (787 women), 366 part-time (327 women); includes 355 minority (198 Black or African American, non-Hispanic/Latino; 1 American Indian or Alaska Native, non-Hispanic/Latino; 19 Asian, non-Hispanic/Latino; 137 Hispanic/Latino). Average age 32. *Faculty:* 48 full-time (36 women), 78 part-time/adjunct (61 women). *Expenses:* Contact institution. *Financial support:* In 2016–17, 838 students received support, including 39 research assistantships with partial tuition reimbursements available (averaging $1,980 per year); fellowships with partial tuition reimbursements available, career-related internships or fieldwork, Federal Work-Study, scholarships/grants, tuition waivers (partial), and unspecified assistantships also available. Support available to part-time students. Financial award application deadline: 2/1. In 2016, 539 master's, 4 doctorates awarded. *Program availability:* Part-time, evening/weekend, 100% online, blended/hybrid learning. Offers nonprofit leadership (MS); social work (MSW, PhD). MS jointly sponsored with Graduate School of Business and conducted through the Fordham Center for Nonprofit Leaders. *Application deadline:* For fall admission, 2/1 priority date for domestic students; for spring admission, 11/1 priority date for domestic students. Applications are processed on a rolling basis. *Application fee:* $60. Electronic applications accepted. *Application Contact:* Melba Remice, Assistant Dean of Admissions, 212-636-6600, Fax: 212-636-6613, E-mail: gssadmission@fordham.edu. *Dean,* Dr. Debra McPhee, 212-636-6616.

School of Law *Program availability:* Part-time, evening/weekend. Offers banking, corporate and finance law (LL M); corporate compliance (MSL); fashion law (MSL); intellectual property and information law (LL M); international business and trade law (LL M); law (JD). Electronic applications accepted.

FORT HAYS STATE UNIVERSITY, Hays, KS 67601-4099

General Information State-supported, coed, comprehensive institution. CGS member. *Graduate housing:* Rooms and/or apartments available to single and married students. Housing application deadline: 8/1.

GRADUATE UNITS

Graduate School *Program availability:* Part-time. Electronic applications accepted.

College of Arts and Sciences *Program availability:* Part-time. Offers arts and sciences (MA, MFA, MLS, MS, Ed S); communication (MS); English (MA); history (MA); liberal studies (MLS); psychology (MS); school psychology (Ed S); studio art (MFA). Electronic applications accepted.

College of Business and Entrepreneurship *Program availability:* Part-time. Offers business and entrepreneurship (MBA); management (MBA). Electronic applications accepted.

College of Education *Program availability:* Part-time. Offers counseling (MS); education (MS, MSE, Ed S); educational administration (MS, Ed S); instructional technology (MS); special education (MS). Electronic applications accepted.

College of Health and Life Sciences *Program availability:* Part-time. Offers health and human performance (MS); health and life sciences (MS, MSN); nursing (MSN); speech-language pathology (MS). Electronic applications accepted.

College of Science, Technology and Mathematics Offers biology (MS); geography (MS); geology (MS); geosciences (MS); science, technology and mathematics (MS).

FORT LEWIS COLLEGE, Durango, CO 81301-3999

General Information State-supported, coed, comprehensive institution.

GRADUATE UNITS

Program in Teacher Leadership Offers teacher leadership (MA, Certificate).

FORT VALLEY STATE UNIVERSITY, Fort Valley, GA 31030

General Information State-supported, coed, comprehensive institution. *Graduate housing:* Room and/or apartments available on a first-come, first-served basis to single students; on-campus housing not available to married students. Housing application deadline: 7/1.

GRADUATE UNITS

College of Graduate Studies and Extended Education *Program availability:* Part-time. Offers animal science (MS); environmental health (MPH); guidance and counseling (Ed S); mental health counseling (MS); rehabilitation counseling (MS).

FRAMINGHAM STATE UNIVERSITY, Framingham, MA 01701-9101

General Information State-supported, coed, comprehensive institution. CGS member. *Graduate housing:* On-campus housing not available.

GRADUATE UNITS

Continuing Education *Program availability:* Part-time, evening/weekend, online learning. Offers art (M Ed); business administration (MBA); counseling psychology (MA); curriculum and instructional technology (M Ed); dietetics (MS); early childhood education (M Ed); educational leadership (MA); elementary education (M Ed); English (M Ed); food science and nutrition science (MS); health care administration (MA); history (M Ed); human nutrition: education and media technologies (MS); human resource management (MA); literacy and language (M Ed); mathematics (M Ed); nursing education (MSN); nursing leadership (MSN); public administration (MA); Spanish (M Ed); special education (M Ed); teaching of English as a second language (M Ed).

FRANCISCAN SCHOOL OF THEOLOGY, Oceanside, CA 92057

General Information Independent-religious, coed, graduate-only institution. *Graduate housing:* Rooms and/or apartments available on a first-come, first-served basis to single and married students. Housing application deadline: 5/15.

GRADUATE UNITS

Graduate and Professional Programs *Program availability:* Part-time. Offers theology (M Div, MA, MAMC, MTS).

FRANCISCAN UNIVERSITY OF STEUBENVILLE, Steubenville, OH 43952-1763

General Information Independent-religious, coed, comprehensive institution. *Graduate housing:* On-campus housing not available.

GRADUATE UNITS

Graduate Programs *Program availability:* Part-time, evening/weekend, online learning. Offers administration (MS Ed); business (MBA); clinical mental health counseling (MA); nursing (MSN); philosophy (MA); teaching (MS Ed); theology and Christian ministry (MA). Electronic applications accepted.

FRANCIS MARION UNIVERSITY, Florence, SC 29502-0547

General Information State-supported, coed, comprehensive institution. *Enrollment:* 3,874 graduate, professional, and undergraduate students; 81 full-time matriculated graduate/professional students (67 women), 234 part-time matriculated graduate/professional students (181 women). *Enrollment by degree level:* 270 master's, 8 other advanced degrees. *Graduate faculty:* 29 full-time (26 women), 5 part-time/adjunct (2 women). Tuition, state resident: full-time $10,100; part-time $505 per credit hour. Tuition, nonresident: full-time $20,196; part-time $1009.80 per credit hour. *Required fees:* $14.80 per credit hour. $73 per semester. Tuition and fees vary according to course load and program. *Graduate housing:* Room and/or apartments available on a first-come, first-served basis to single students; on-campus housing not available to married students. Typical cost: $4360 per year ($7716 including board). Room and board charges vary according to board plan and housing facility selected. Housing

application deadline: 5/1. *Student services:* Campus employment opportunities, campus safety program, career counseling, child daycare facilities, free psychological counseling, international student services, low-cost health insurance, multicultural affairs office, services for students with disabilities, teacher training, writing training. *Library facilities:* James A. Rogers Library plus 1 other. *Collection:* Books: 343,000 (digital/electronic).

Computer facilities: 634 computers available on campus for general student use. A campuswide network can be accessed from student residence rooms. Online class registration, learning management system are available. Website: http://www.fmarion.edu/

General Application Contact: Jennifer Taylor, Administrative Manager, Provost's Office, 843-661-1286, Fax: 843-661-4688, E-mail: jtaylor@fmarion.edu.

GRADUATE UNITS

Graduate Programs *Program availability:* Part-time, evening/weekend. Offers applied psychology (MS); family nurse practitioner (MSN); family nurse practitioner with nurse educator certificate (MSN); nurse educator (MSN); physician assistant (MPAS); school psychology (SSP). Electronic applications accepted.

School of Business *Program availability:* Part-time, evening/weekend. Offers business (MBA); health executive management (MBA).

School of Education *Program availability:* Part-time. Offers learning disabilities (M Ed, MAT).

FRANKLIN COLLEGE, Franklin, IN 46131

General Information Independent-religious, coed, comprehensive institution.

GRADUATE UNITS

Program in Athletic Training Offers athletic training (MSAT).

FRANKLIN PIERCE UNIVERSITY, Rindge, NH 03461-0060

General Information Independent, coed, university. *Enrollment:* 2,377 graduate, professional, and undergraduate students; 380 full-time matriculated graduate/professional students (226 women), 245 part-time matriculated graduate/professional students (158 women). *Enrollment by degree level:* 365 master's, 259 doctoral, 1 other advanced degree. *Graduate faculty:* 22 full-time (16 women), 163 part-time/adjunct (106 women). *Tuition:* Full-time $15,960; part-time $665 per credit hour. Tuition and fees vary according to program. *Graduate housing:* On-campus housing not available. *Student services:* Campus employment opportunities, career counseling, exercise/wellness program, international student services, low-cost health insurance, services for students with disabilities. *Library facilities:* Frank S. DiPietro Library plus 1 other. *Collection:* Books: 115,797 (physical), 191,482 (digital/electronic); Serial titles: 112 (physical), 65,000 (digital/electronic); Databases: 64. Weekly public service hours: 95.

Computer facilities: Computer purchase and lease plans are available. 100 computers available on campus for general student use. A campuswide network can be accessed from student residence rooms and from off campus. Online class registration is available. Website: http://www.franklinpierce.edu/

General Application Contact: Linda Quimby, Assistant Vice President of Enrollment, 800-437-0048, Fax: 603-626-4815, E-mail: cgps@franklinpierce.edu.

GRADUATE UNITS

Graduate and Professional Studies Students: 380 full-time (226 women), 245 part-time (158 women); includes 52 minority (13 Black or African American, non-Hispanic/Latino; 2 American Indian or Alaska Native, non-Hispanic/Latino; 14 Asian, non-Hispanic/Latino; 22 Hispanic/Latino; 1 Native Hawaiian or other Pacific Islander, non-Hispanic/Latino), 13 international. Average age 29. 1,995 applicants, 28% accepted, 267 enrolled. *Faculty:* 47 full-time (36 women), 165 part-time/adjunct (108 women). *Expenses:* Contact institution. *Financial support:* Teaching assistantships with tuition reimbursements, career-related internships or fieldwork, and unspecified assistantships available. Support available to part-time students. Financial award applicants required to submit FAFSA. In 2016, 120 master's, 86 doctorates awarded. *Program availability:* Part-time, 100% online, blended/hybrid learning. Offers curriculum and instruction (M Ed); elementary education (MS Ed); emerging network technologies (Graduate Certificate); energy and sustainability studies (MBA, Graduate Certificate); health administration (MBA, Graduate Certificate); human resource management (MBA, Graduate Certificate); information technology (MBA); leadership (MBA); nursing education (MS); nursing leadership (MS); physical therapy (DPT); physician assistant studies (MPAS); special education (M Ed); sports management (MBA). *Application deadline:* Applications are processed on a rolling basis. *Application fee:* $0. Electronic applications accepted. *Application Contact:* Graduate Studies, 800-325-1090, Fax: 603-626-4815, E-mail: cgps@franklinpierce.edu. *Dean,* Dr. Maria Altobello, 603-647-3509, Fax: 603-229-4580, E-mail: altobellom@franklinpierce.edu.

FRANKLIN UNIVERSITY, Columbus, OH 43215-5399

General Information Independent, coed, comprehensive institution. *Graduate housing:* On-campus housing not available.

GRADUATE UNITS

Accounting Program *Program availability:* Online learning. Offers accounting (MSA).

Computer Science Program *Program availability:* Part-time, evening/weekend. Offers computer science (MS). Electronic applications accepted.

Instructional Design and Performance Technology Program Offers instructional design and performance technology (MS).

Marketing and Communication Program *Program availability:* Part-time, evening/weekend. Offers marketing and communication (MS). Electronic applications accepted.

MBA Program *Program availability:* Part-time, evening/weekend, online learning. Offers business administration (MBA). Electronic applications accepted.

FRANKLIN UNIVERSITY SWITZERLAND, CH-6924 Sorengo, Switzerland

General Information Independent, coed, comprehensive institution.

GRADUATE UNITS

The Taylor Institute for Global Enterprise Management Offers international management (MS).

FREDERICK S. PARDEE RAND GRADUATE SCHOOL, Santa Monica, CA 90407-2138

General Information Independent, coed, graduate-only institution. *Enrollment by degree level:* 107 doctoral. *Graduate faculty:* 263 part-time/adjunct (101 women). *Tuition:* Full-time $26,500. *Graduate housing:* On-campus housing not available. *Student* *services:* Campus employment opportunities, career counseling, exercise/wellness program, free psychological counseling, grant writing training, international student services, low-cost health insurance, writing training. *Library facilities:* RAND Corporation Library plus 1 other. *Collection:* Books: 17,327 (physical), 46,457 (digital/electronic); Serial titles: 1,271 (physical), 55,438 (digital/electronic); Databases: 61. Weekly public service hours: 65; study areas open 24 hours, 5–7 days a week; students can reserve study rooms. *Research affiliation:* RAND Corporation (not-for-profit research).

Computer facilities: 107 computers available on campus for general student use. Online class registration is available.
Website: http://www.prgs.edu/

General Application Contact: Stefanie Howard, Director of Admissions, 310-393-0411 Ext. 8224, Fax: 310-451-6978, E-mail: sstern@rand.org.

GRADUATE UNITS
Program in Policy Analysis Students: 107 full-time (51 women); includes 20 minority (3 Black or African American, non-Hispanic/Latino; 9 Asian, non-Hispanic/Latino; 8 Hispanic/Latino), 38 international. Average age 31. 136 applicants, 29% accepted, 22 enrolled. *Faculty:* 229 part-time/adjunct (80 women). Expenses: Contact institution. *Financial support:* In 2016–17, 107 students received support, including 107 fellowships (averaging $46,000 per year), 30 teaching assistantships (averaging $2,000 per year); scholarships/grants and health care benefits also available. Financial award application deadline: 7/1. In 2016, 19 doctorates awarded. Offers policy analysis (PhD). *Application deadline:* For fall admission, 1/10 for domestic and international students. *Application fee:* $50. Electronic applications accepted. *Application Contact:* Mary Parker, Registrar/Admissions Manager, 310-393-0411 Ext. 7690, Fax: 310-451-6978, E-mail: mfparker@prgs.edu. *Dean,* Dr. Susan L. Marquis, 310-393-0411 Ext. 7075, Fax: 310-451-6978.

FREED-HARDEMAN UNIVERSITY, Henderson, TN 38340-2399
General Information Independent-religious, coed, comprehensive institution. *Graduate housing:* Room and/or apartments available on a first-come, first-served basis to single students; on-campus housing not available to married students. Housing application deadline: 8/22.

GRADUATE UNITS
Program in Business Administration *Program availability:* Part-time, evening/weekend, online learning. Offers accounting (MBA); corporate responsibility (MBA); leadership (MBA).
Program in Counseling *Program availability:* Part-time, evening/weekend. Offers counseling (MS).
Program in Education *Program availability:* Part-time, evening/weekend. Offers curriculum and instruction (M Ed); school counseling (M Ed); school leadership (Ed S).
School of Biblical Studies *Program availability:* Part-time. Offers biblical studies (M Div, M Min, MA); divinity (M Div); ministry (M Min); New Testament (MA).

FRESNO PACIFIC UNIVERSITY, Fresno, CA 93702-4709
General Information Independent-religious, coed, comprehensive institution. *Graduate housing:* Rooms and/or apartments available on a first-come, first-served basis to single and married students. Housing application deadline: 4/20.

GRADUATE UNITS
Biblical Seminary *Program availability:* Part-time, online learning. Offers Christian ministry (MA); community leadership and transformation (MA); divinity (M Div); marriage and family therapy (MA); New Testament (MA); Old Testament (MA); theology (MA); urban mission (MA).
Graduate Programs *Program availability:* Part-time, evening/weekend. Offers business administration (MBA); church conflict and peacemaking (Certificate); family nurse practitioner (MSN); individualized study (MA); kinesiology (MA); leadership and organizational studies (MA); mediation (Certificate); peacemaking and conflict studies (MA); restorative justice (Certificate). Electronic applications accepted.
School of Education *Program availability:* Part-time, evening/weekend. Offers administrative services (MA); board certified associate behavior analyst (Certificate); curriculum and teaching (MA); education (MA, MA Ed, Certificate); educational technology (MA); reading (Certificate); reading/English as a second language (MA Ed); reading/language arts (MA Ed); school counseling (MA); school library and information technology (MA Ed); school psychology (MA); special education (MA); STEM education (MA Ed). Electronic applications accepted.

FRIENDS UNIVERSITY, Wichita, KS 67213
General Information Independent-religious, coed, comprehensive institution.

GRADUATE UNITS
Graduate School *Program availability:* Part-time, evening/weekend, online learning. Offers family therapy (MSFT); global business administration (MBA); health care leadership (MHCL); management information systems (MMIS); professional business administration (MBA). Electronic applications accepted.

FRONTIER NURSING UNIVERSITY, Hyden, KY 41749
General Information Independent, coed, primarily women, graduate-only institution.

GRADUATE UNITS
Graduate Programs Offers family nurse practitioner (MSN, DNP, Post Master's Certificate); nurse-midwifery (MSN, DNP, Post Master's Certificate); women's health care nurse practitioner (MSN, DNP, Post Master's Certificate).

FROSTBURG STATE UNIVERSITY, Frostburg, MD 21532-1099
General Information State-supported, coed, comprehensive institution. *Graduate housing:* Room and/or apartments available to single students; on-campus housing not available to married students. Housing application deadline: 6/1.

GRADUATE UNITS
Graduate School *Program availability:* Part-time, evening/weekend. Electronic applications accepted.
College of Business *Program availability:* Part-time, evening/weekend. Offers business (MBA); business administration (MBA). Electronic applications accepted.
College of Education *Program availability:* Part-time, evening/weekend. Offers curriculum and instruction (M Ed); education (M Ed, MAT, MS); educational administration and supervision (M Ed); educational technology (M Ed); elementary (M Ed); elementary education (M Ed); elementary teaching (MAT); interdisciplinary education (M Ed); parks and recreational management (MS); reading (M Ed); school counseling (M Ed); secondary (M Ed); secondary education (M Ed); secondary teaching (MAT); special education (M Ed). Electronic applications accepted.
College of Liberal Arts and Sciences *Program availability:* Part-time, evening/weekend. Offers applied computer science (MS); applied ecology and

conservation biology (MS); counseling psychology (MS); fisheries and wildlife management (MS); liberal arts and sciences (MS, MSN); nursing administration (MSN); nursing education (MSN). Electronic applications accepted.

FULLER THEOLOGICAL SEMINARY, Pasadena, CA 91182
General Information Independent-religious, coed, graduate-only institution. *Graduate housing:* Rooms and/or apartments available on a first-come, first-served basis to single and married students.

GRADUATE UNITS
Graduate Programs Offers Christian leadership (MACL); clinical psychology (PhD, Psy D); family studies (MA); global leadership (MA); global ministries (D Min); global ministries (Korean language) (D Min); intercultural studies (MA, Th M, PhD); intercultural studies (Korean language) (MA); marital and family therapy (MS); marriage and family enrichment (Certificate); ministry (M Div, D Min); missiology (D Miss); missiology (Korean language) (Th M); theology (MA, Th M, PhD); theology and ministry (MA).

FULL SAIL UNIVERSITY, Winter Park, FL 32792-7437
General Information Proprietary, coed, primarily men, comprehensive institution. *Graduate housing:* On-campus housing not available.

GRADUATE UNITS
Creative Writing Master of Fine Arts Program - Online *Program availability:* Online learning. Offers creative writing (MFA).
Education Media Design and Technology Master of Science Program - Online *Program availability:* Online learning. Offers education media design and technology (MS).
Entertainment Business Master of Science Program - Campus Expenses: Contact institution. Offers entertainment business (MS).
Entertainment Business Master of Science Program - Online *Program availability:* Online learning. Offers entertainment business (MS).
Game Design Master of Science Program - Campus Offers game design (MS).
Internet Marketing Master of Science Program - Online *Program availability:* Online learning. Offers Internet marketing (MS).
Media Design Master of Fine Arts Program - Online *Program availability:* Online learning. Offers media design (MFA).
New Media Journalism Master of Arts Program - Online Offers new media journalism (MA).

FURMAN UNIVERSITY, Greenville, SC 29613
General Information Independent, coed, comprehensive institution. CGS member. *Graduate housing:* On-campus housing not available.

GRADUATE UNITS
Graduate Division *Program availability:* Part-time, online learning. Offers chemistry (MS); curriculum and instruction (MA); early childhood education (MA); educational leadership (Ed S); English as a second language (MA); literacy (MA); school leadership (MA); special education (MA).

FUTURE GENERATIONS GRADUATE SCHOOL, Franklin, WV 26807
General Information Independent, coed, graduate-only institution. *Graduate housing:* On-campus housing not available.

GRADUATE UNITS
Program in Applied Community Change *Program availability:* Blended/hybrid learning. Offers conservation (MA). Electronic applications accepted.

GALLAUDET UNIVERSITY, Washington, DC 20002-3625
General Information Independent, coed, university. CGS member. *Enrollment:* 1,566 graduate, professional, and undergraduate students; 297 full-time matriculated graduate/professional students (231 women), 129 part-time matriculated graduate/professional students (97 women). *Enrollment by degree level:* 247 master's, 154 doctoral, 25 other advanced degrees. *Tuition:* Full-time $17,100; part-time $950 per credit hour. *Required fees:* $3725; $276 per semester. *Graduate housing:* Rooms and/or apartments available on a first-come, first-served basis to single and married students. Typical cost: $7364 per year ($13,204 including board) for single students; $8322 per year ($14,162 including board) for married students. Room and board charges vary according to housing facility selected. Housing application deadline: 4/1. *Student services:* Campus employment opportunities, campus safety program, career counseling, exercise/wellness program, free psychological counseling, grant writing training, international student services, low-cost health insurance, multicultural affairs office, services for students with disabilities, teacher training, writing training. *Library facilities:* Merrill Learning Center. *Collection:* Books: 121,359 (physical), 547,506 (digital/electronic); Serial titles: 4,142 (physical), 71,930 (digital/electronic); Databases: 79. Weekly public service hours: 90; students can reserve study rooms. *Research affiliation:* National Science Foundation/Howard University (linguistics, visual language and visual learning, integrated quantum materials), Maryland Sea Grant/University of Maryland/National Oceanic and Atmospheric Administration (NOAA) (advanced recruitment and retention in geosciences), U.S. Department of Education/Vcom3D Inc. (signing math dictionaries with mouth morphemes; accessibility and usability technologies for deaf and hard of hearing), Spencer Foundation (deaf legal discourse), University of Wisconsin-Madison/U.S. Department of Education (DOE) (telecommunications access), University of California Los Angeles/National Institutes of Health (cancer genetics).

Computer facilities: 400 computers available on campus for general student use. A campuswide network can be accessed from student residence rooms and from off campus. Online class registration is available.
Website: http://www.gallaudet.edu/

General Application Contact: Wednesday Luria, Coordinator of Prospective Graduate Student Services, 202-651-5400, Fax: 202-651-5295, E-mail: graduate.school@gallaudet.edu.

GRADUATE UNITS
The Graduate School Students: 297 full-time (231 women), 129 part-time (97 women); includes 105 minority (35 Black or African American, non-Hispanic/Latino; 20 Asian, non-Hispanic/Latino; 39 Hispanic/Latino; 11 Two or more races, non-Hispanic/Latino), 22 international. Average age 30. 471 applicants, 52% accepted, 147 enrolled. Expenses: Contact institution. *Financial support:* Fellowships, research assistantships, teaching assistantships, career-related internships or fieldwork, Federal Work-Study, scholarships/grants, tuition waivers (partial), and unspecified assistantships available. Support available to part-time students. Financial award application deadline: 7/1; financial award applicants required to submit FAFSA. In 2016, 138 master's, 25

doctorates, 14 other advanced degrees awarded. *Program availability:* Part-time. Offers American Sign Language/English bilingual early childhood deaf education: birth to 5 (Certificate); audiology (Au D); clinical psychology (PhD); deaf and hard of hearing infants, toddlers, and their families (Certificate); deaf education (MA, Ed S); deaf history (Certificate); deaf studies (Certificate); educating deaf students with disabilities (Certificate); education: teacher preparation (MA); educational neuroscience (PhD); hearing, speech and language sciences (MS, PhD); international development (MA); interpretation (MA, PhD); linguistics (MA, PhD); mental health counseling (MA); peer mentoring (Certificate); public administration (MPA); school counseling (MA); school psychology (Psy S); sign language teaching (MA); social work (MSW); speech-language pathology (MS). *Application deadline:* For fall admission, 2/15 for domestic students. Applications are processed on a rolling basis. *Application fee:* $75. Electronic applications accepted. *Application Contact:* Wednesday Luria, Coordinator of Prospective Graduate Student Services, 202-651-5400, Fax: 202-651-5295, E-mail: graduate.school@gallaudet.edu. *Dean, Graduate School and Continuing Studies,* Dr. Gaurav Mathur, 202-250-2380, Fax: 202-651-5027, E-mail: gaurav.mathur@gallaudet.edu.

GANNON UNIVERSITY, Erie, PA 16541-0001

General Information Independent-religious, coed, university. *Enrollment:* 4,343 graduate, professional, and undergraduate students; 741 full-time matriculated graduate/professional students (346 women), 475 part-time matriculated graduate/professional students (267 women). *Enrollment by degree level:* 922 master's, 266 doctoral, 28 other advanced degrees. *Graduate faculty:* 97 full-time (42 women), 41 part-time/adjunct (20 women). *Tuition:* Full-time $17,370. *Required fees:* $550. Tuition and fees vary according to course load and program. *Graduate housing:* Rooms and/or apartments available on a first-come, first-served basis to single and married students. *Student services:* Campus employment opportunities, campus safety program, career counseling, exercise/wellness program, free psychological counseling, international student services, low-cost health insurance, multicultural affairs office, services for students with disabilities, teacher training, writing training. *Library facilities:* Nash Library. *Collection:* Books: 213,041 (physical), 252,244 (digital/electronic); Serial titles: 37 (physical), 52,805 (digital/electronic); Databases: 45. Weekly public service hours: 97; students can reserve study rooms. *Research affiliation:* GE Global Research (nanotechnology), LifeLink Technologies (postural stability of flooring), Erie Insurance, Precision Rehabilitation Manufacturing (software development), AirBorn (PPS software enhancer), AirBorn (PPS software enhancer).

Computer facilities: 386 computers available on campus for general student use. A campuswide network can be accessed from student residence rooms and from off campus. Online class registration is available.

Website: http://www.gannon.edu/

General Application Contact: Bridget Philip, Director, Graduate Admissions, 814-871-7412, E-mail: graduate@gannon.edu.

GRADUATE UNITS

School of Graduate Studies Students: 741 full-time (346 women), 475 part-time (267 women); includes 59 minority (23 Black or African American, non-Hispanic/Latino; 2 American Indian or Alaska Native, non-Hispanic/Latino; 16 Asian, non-Hispanic/Latino; 11 Hispanic/Latino; 1 Native Hawaiian or other Pacific Islander, non-Hispanic/Latino; 6 Two or more races, non-Hispanic/Latino), 425 international. Average age 28. 1,820 applicants, 60% accepted, 268 enrolled. *Faculty:* 97 full-time (42 women), 41 part-time/adjunct (20 women). Expenses: Contact institution. *Financial support:* In 2016–17, 6 teaching assistantships (averaging $6,797 per year) were awarded; Federal Work-Study, scholarships/grants, and unspecified assistantships also available. Financial award application deadline: 7/1; financial award applicants required to submit FAFSA. In 2016, 533 master's, 53 doctorates, 24 other advanced degrees awarded. *Program availability:* Part-time, evening/weekend, 100% online, blended/hybrid learning. *Application deadline:* Applications are processed on a rolling basis. *Application fee:* $25. Electronic applications accepted. *Application Contact:* Bridget Philip, Director of Graduate Admissions, 814-871-7412, E-mail: graduate@gannon.edu.

College of Engineering and Business Students: 380 full-time (85 women), 177 part-time (55 women); includes 13 minority (6 Black or African American, non-Hispanic/Latino; 4 Asian, non-Hispanic/Latino; 1 Hispanic/Latino; 1 Native Hawaiian or other Pacific Islander, non-Hispanic/Latino; 1 Two or more races, non-Hispanic/Latino), 413 international. Average age 27. 1,310 applicants, 60% accepted, 83 enrolled. *Faculty:* 43 full-time (5 women), 20 part-time/adjunct (6 women). Expenses: Contact institution. *Financial support:* In 2016–17, 10 fellowships (averaging $4,338 per year) were awarded; Federal Work-Study and unspecified assistantships also available. Financial award application deadline: 7/1; financial award applicants required to submit FAFSA. In 2016, 307 master's awarded. *Program availability:* Part-time, evening/weekend, 100% online, blended/hybrid learning. Offers business administration (MBA, MPA); computer and information science (MSCIS); electrical and computer engineering (MSEE, MSES); engineering and business (MBA, MPA, MS, MSCIS, MSEE, MSEH, MSEM, MSES, MSME, Certificate); engineering management (MSEM); environmental health (MSEH); environmental health and engineering (MS); environmental science and engineering (MS, MSEH); finance (MBA); human resources management (MBA); information analytics (MSCIS, MSCIS); marketing (MBA); mechanical engineering (MSME); public administration (MPA); software engineering (MSCIS). *Application deadline:* Applications are processed on a rolling basis. *Application fee:* $25. Electronic applications accepted. *Application Contact:* Bridget Philip, Director of Graduate Admissions, 814-871-7412, E-mail: graduate@gannon.edu. *Dean,* Dr. William L. Scheller, II, 814-871-7582, E-mail: scheller002@gannon.edu.

College of Humanities, Education, and Social Sciences Students: 45 full-time (36 women), 229 part-time (168 women); includes 10 minority (4 Black or African American, non-Hispanic/Latino; 1 American Indian or Alaska Native, non-Hispanic/Latino; 2 Asian, non-Hispanic/Latino; 3 Hispanic/Latino), 8 international. Average age 34. 238 applicants, 73% accepted, 127 enrolled. *Faculty:* 23 full-time (13 women), 16 part-time/adjunct (10 women). Expenses: Contact institution. *Financial support:* In 2016–17, 5 teaching assistantships (averaging $7,446 per year) were awarded; Federal Work-Study and unspecified assistantships also available. Financial award application deadline: 7/1; financial award applicants required to submit FAFSA. In 2016, 87 master's, 2 doctorates, 24 other advanced degrees awarded. *Program availability:* Part-time, evening/weekend, 100% online, blended/hybrid learning. Offers clinical mental health counseling (MS); criminalistics (MSC); curriculum and instruction (M Ed); curriculum supervisor (Certificate); English (MA); English as a second language (Certificate); health communication (MA); humanities, education, and social sciences (M Ed, MA, MS, MSC, PhD, Certificate); organizational learning and leadership (PhD); pastoral studies (MA, Certificate); principal certification (Certificate); reading (M Ed); reading specialist (Certificate); superintendent letter of eligibility (Certificate); theological studies (Certificate). *Application deadline:*

Applications are processed on a rolling basis. *Application fee:* $25. Electronic applications accepted. *Application Contact:* Bridget Philip, Director of Graduate Admissions, 814-871-7412, E-mail: graduate@gannon.edu. *Dean,* Dr. Linda Fleming, 814-871-7549, E-mail: fleming006@gannon.edu.

Morosky College of Health Professions and Sciences Students: 316 full-time (225 women), 69 part-time (44 women); includes 36 minority (13 Black or African American, non-Hispanic/Latino; 1 American Indian or Alaska Native, non-Hispanic/Latino; 10 Asian, non-Hispanic/Latino; 7 Hispanic/Latino; 5 Two or more races, non-Hispanic/Latino), 4 international. Average age 25. 272 applicants, 53% accepted, 58 enrolled. *Faculty:* 29 full-time (24 women), 5 part-time/adjunct (4 women). Expenses: Contact institution. *Financial support:* Federal Work-Study, scholarships/grants, and unspecified assistantships available. Financial award application deadline: 7/1; financial award applicants required to submit FAFSA. In 2016, 139 master's, 51 doctorates, 1 other advanced degree awarded. *Program availability:* Part-time, evening/weekend, 100% online. Offers athletic training (MAT); family nurse practitioner (MSN, Certificate); health professions and sciences (MAT, MPAS, MS, MSN, DNP, DPT, OTD, Certificate); human performance (MS); nurse anesthesia (MSN, Certificate); nursing administration (MSN); nursing practice (DNP); occupational therapy (MS, OTD); physical therapy (DPT); physician assistant science (MPAS); sport and exercise science (MS). *Application deadline:* Applications are processed on a rolling basis. *Application fee:* $25. Electronic applications accepted. *Application Contact:* Bridget Philip, Director of Graduate Admissions, 814-871-7412, E-mail: graduate@gannon.edu. *Dean,* Dr. Sarah Ewing, 814-871-7752, E-mail: ewing003@gannon.edu.

GARDNER-WEBB UNIVERSITY, Boiling Springs, NC 28017

General Information Independent-religious, coed, university. *Enrollment:* 3,884 graduate, professional, and undergraduate students; 222 full-time matriculated graduate/professional students (132 women), 1,331 part-time matriculated graduate/professional students (969 women). *Enrollment by degree level:* 1,100 master's, 423 doctoral, 30 other advanced degrees. *Graduate faculty:* 64 full-time (34 women), 70 part-time/adjunct (31 women). *Graduate housing:* Room and/or apartments available on a first-come, first-served basis to single students; on-campus housing not available to married students. *Student services:* Campus employment opportunities, campus safety program, career counseling, exercise/wellness program, free psychological counseling, international student services, low-cost health insurance, services for students with disabilities, teacher training, writing training. *Library facilities:* Dover Memorial Library plus 1 other.

Computer facilities: Computer purchase and lease plans are available. 121 computers available on campus for general student use. A campuswide network can be accessed from student residence rooms and from off campus. Online class registration is available.

Website: http://www.gardner-webb.edu/

General Application Contact: Brandon Beach, Office of Graduate Admissions, 877-498-4723, Fax: 704-406-3895, E-mail: gradinfo@gardner-webb.edu.

GRADUATE UNITS

Graduate School Students: 2 full-time (both women), 35 part-time (18 women); includes 5 minority (3 Black or African American, non-Hispanic/Latino; 1 Asian, non-Hispanic/Latino; 1 Hispanic/Latino). Average age 27. 73 applicants, 41% accepted, 19 enrolled. *Faculty:* 9 full-time (5 women). Expenses: Contact institution. *Financial support:* Fellowships, Federal Work-Study, institutionally sponsored loans, and unspecified assistantships available. Support available to part-time students. In 2016, 11 master's awarded. *Program availability:* Part-time, evening/weekend. Offers English (MA); English education (MA); physician assistant studies (MPAS); sport science and pedagogy (MA). *Application deadline:* Applications are processed on a rolling basis. *Application fee:* $0. Electronic applications accepted. *Application Contact:* Lamont Reeves, Office of Graduate Admissions, 877-498-4723, Fax: 704-406-3895, E-mail: gradinfo@gardner-webb.edu. *Dean,* Dr. Franki Burch, 704-406-4723, E-mail: gradschool@gardner-webb.edu.

Graduate School of Business Students: 31 full-time (15 women), 250 part-time (134 women); includes 71 minority (54 Black or African American, non-Hispanic/Latino; 4 Asian, non-Hispanic/Latino; 13 Hispanic/Latino). Average age 31. 202 applicants, 65% accepted, 97 enrolled. *Faculty:* 13 full-time (3 women), 6 part-time/adjunct (2 women). Expenses: Contact institution. *Financial support:* In 2016–17, 23 students received support. Unspecified assistantships available. Support available to part-time students. Financial award applicants required to submit FAFSA. In 2016, 81 master's awarded. *Program availability:* Part-time, evening/weekend, online learning. Offers business (IMBA, M Acc, MBA). *Application deadline:* For spring admission, 1/15 for domestic students. Applications are processed on a rolling basis. Electronic applications accepted. *Application Contact:* Mischia Taylor, Director of Admissions, 877-498-4723, Fax: 704-406-3895, E-mail: mataylor@gardner-webb.edu. *Dean,* Dr. Van Graham, 704-406-4622, E-mail: vgraham@gardner-webb.edu.

School of Education Students: 10 full-time (7 women), 690 part-time (527 women); includes 286 minority (262 Black or African American, non-Hispanic/Latino; 5 American Indian or Alaska Native, non-Hispanic/Latino; 6 Asian, non-Hispanic/Latino; 11 Hispanic/Latino; 2 Two or more races, non-Hispanic/Latino), 1 international. Average age 37. 428 applicants, 52% accepted, 180 enrolled. *Faculty:* 16 full-time (6 women), 35 part-time/adjunct (20 women). Expenses: Contact institution. *Financial support:* Unspecified assistantships available. In 2016, 163 master's, 51 doctorates awarded. *Program availability:* Part-time, evening/weekend. Offers curriculum and instruction (Ed D); educational leadership (Ed D); executive leadership studies (MA, Ed S); organizational leadership (Ed D); school administration (MA). *Application deadline:* For fall admission, 8/1 priority date for domestic students. Applications are processed on a rolling basis. Electronic applications accepted. *Application Contact:* Office of Graduate Admissions, 877-498-4723, Fax: 704-406-3895, E-mail: gradinfo@gardner-webb.edu. *Dean,* Dr. Alan D. Eury, 704-406-4402, Fax: 704-406-3921, E-mail: dsimmons@gardner-webb.edu.

School of Nursing Students: 2 full-time (1 woman), 220 part-time (206 women); includes 36 minority (28 Black or African American, non-Hispanic/Latino; 2 American Indian or Alaska Native, non-Hispanic/Latino; 4 Asian, non-Hispanic/Latino; 2 Hispanic/Latino), 1 international. Average age 39. 207 applicants, 48% accepted, 85 enrolled. *Faculty:* 15 full-time (13 women), 5 part-time/adjunct (all women). Expenses: Contact institution. In 2016, 61 master's, 16 doctorates awarded. *Program availability:* Part-time, online learning. Offers family nurse practitioner (MSN, DNP). *Application Contact:* Office of Graduate Admissions, 877-498-4723, Fax: 704-406-3895, E-mail: gradinfo@gardner-webb.edu. *Dean,* Dr. Sharon Starr, 704-406-4358, Fax: 704-406-4329, E-mail: gradschool@gardner-webb.edu.

School of Psychology Students: 11 full-time (all women), 60 part-time (57 women); includes 16 minority (13 Black or African American, non-Hispanic/Latino; 3

Hispanic/Latino). Average age 29. 116 applicants, 31% accepted, 36 enrolled. *Faculty:* 5 full-time (4 women), 4 part-time/adjunct (2 women). Expenses: Contact institution. *Financial support:* Unspecified assistantships available. In 2016, 401 master's awarded. *Program availability:* Part-time, evening/weekend. Offers mental health counseling (MA); school counseling (MA). *Application deadline:* For fall admission, 7/1 priority date for domestic students. Applications are processed on a rolling basis. Electronic applications accepted. *Application Contact:* Office of Graduate Admissions, 877-498-4723, Fax: 704-406-3895, E-mail: gradinfo@gardner-webb.edu. *Chair,* Dr. David Carscaddon, 704-406-4437, Fax: 704-406-4329, E-mail: dcarscaddon@gardner-webb.edu.

School of Divinity Students: 115 full-time (59 women), 68 part-time (27 women); includes 86 minority (80 Black or African American, non-Hispanic/Latino; 5 Asian, non-Hispanic/Latino; 1 Hispanic/Latino). Average age 40. 86 applicants, 44% accepted, 16 enrolled. *Faculty:* 12 full-time (2 women), 3 part-time/adjunct (1 woman). Expenses: Contact institution. *Financial support:* Fellowships, institutionally sponsored loans, and unspecified assistantships available. Support available to part-time students. Financial award application deadline: 5/15. In 2016, 40 master's, 3 doctorates awarded. *Program availability:* Part-time. Offers biblical studies (M Div); Christian education and formation (M Div); intercultural studies (M Div); ministry (D Min); missiology (M Div); pastoral care and counseling (M Div); pastoral care and counseling/member care for missionaries (D Min); pastoral studies (M Div). *Application deadline:* Applications are processed on a rolling basis. Electronic applications accepted. *Application Contact:* Kheresa Harmon, Director of Admissions, 704-406-3205, Fax: 704-406-3895, E-mail: kharmon@gardner-webb.edu. *Dean,* Dr. Robert W. Canoy, Sr., 704-406-4400, Fax: 704-406-3935, E-mail: rcanoy@gardner-webb.edu.

GARRETT-EVANGELICAL THEOLOGICAL SEMINARY, Evanston, IL 60201-3298

General Information Independent-religious, coed, graduate-only institution. *Graduate housing:* Rooms and/or apartments guaranteed to single students and available to married students. Housing application deadline: 4/1.

GRADUATE UNITS

Graduate and Professional Programs *Program availability:* Part-time. Offers Bible and culture (PhD); Christian education (MA); Christian education and congregational studies (PhD); contemporary theology and culture (PhD); divinity (M Div); ethics, church, and society (MA); liturgical studies (PhD); ministry (D Min); music ministry (MA); pastoral care and counseling (MA); pastoral theology, personality, and culture (PhD); spiritual formation and evangelism (MA); theological studies (MTS). M Div/MSW offered jointly with Loyola University Chicago. Electronic applications accepted.

GATEWAY SEMINARY, Ontario, CA 91761-8642

General Information Independent-religious, coed, graduate-only institution. *Graduate housing:* Rooms and/or apartments available on a first-come, first-served basis to single and married students. Housing application deadline: 6/15.

GRADUATE UNITS

Graduate and Professional Programs *Program availability:* Part-time, evening/weekend. Offers divinity (M Div); early childhood education (Certificate); education leadership (MAEL, Diploma); ministry (D Min); theological studies (MTS); theology (Th M); youth ministry (Certificate). Electronic applications accepted.

GEISINGER COMMONWEALTH SCHOOL OF MEDICINE, Scranton, PA 18509

General Information Independent, coed, graduate-only institution.

GRADUATE UNITS

Graduate Programs in Medicine *Program availability:* Part-time, evening/weekend. Offers biomedical sciences (MBS). Electronic applications accepted.
Professional Program in Medicine Offers medicine (MD).

GENERAL THEOLOGICAL SEMINARY, New York, NY 10011-4977

General Information Independent-religious, coed, graduate-only institution. *Graduate housing:* Rooms and/or apartments available to single and married students. Housing application deadline: 6/1.

GRADUATE UNITS

Graduate and Professional Programs *Program availability:* Part-time, evening/weekend. Offers Anglican studies (STM, Th D, Certificate); ascetical theology (Certificate); biblical studies (Certificate); congregational development (Certificate); divinity (M Div); historical and theological studies (Certificate); spiritual direction (MASD, STM, Certificate); theology (MA).

GENEVA COLLEGE, Beaver Falls, PA 15010-3599

General Information Independent-religious, coed, comprehensive institution. *Enrollment:* 1,662 graduate, professional, and undergraduate students; 154 full-time matriculated graduate/professional students (108 women), 51 part-time matriculated graduate/professional students (31 women). *Enrollment by degree level:* 205 master's. *Graduate faculty:* 15 full-time (11 women), 17 part-time/adjunct (8 women). *Tuition:* Full-time $12,038. *Graduate housing:* On-campus housing not available. *Student services:* Campus employment opportunities, campus safety program, career counseling, free psychological counseling, international student services, low-cost health insurance, multicultural affairs office, services for students with disabilities, teacher training. *Library facilities:* McCartney Library plus 3 others. *Collection:* Books: 138,989 (physical), 15,997 (digital/electronic); Serial titles: 438 (physical), 20 (digital/electronic); Databases: 44. Weekly public service hours: 84. *Research affiliation:* INOVA Fairfax Hospital (cardiovascular science).

Computer facilities: 150 computers available on campus for general student use. A campuswide network can be accessed from student residence rooms and from off campus. Online class registration is available. Website: http://www.geneva.edu/

General Application Contact: Information Contact, 724-846-5100.

GRADUATE UNITS

Master of Arts in Counseling Program Students: 35 full-time (28 women), 32 part-time (23 women); includes 11 minority (9 Black or African American, non-Hispanic/Latino; 2 Hispanic/Latino). Average age 34. 42 applicants, 71% accepted, 21 enrolled. *Faculty:* 6 full-time (3 women), 3 part-time/adjunct (2 women). Expenses: Contact institution. *Financial support:* In 2016–17, 3 students received support. Research assistantships, teaching assistantships, career-related internships or fieldwork, and unspecified assistantships available. Financial award application deadline: 8/1; financial award applicants required to submit FAFSA. In 2016, 24 master's awarded. *Program availability:* Part-time, evening/weekend. Offers clinical mental health counseling (MA); marriage and family counseling (MA); school counseling (MA). *Application deadline:* For

fall admission, 9/1 for domestic students; for spring admission, 1/10 for domestic students. Applications are processed on a rolling basis. Electronic applications accepted. *Application Contact:* Marina Frazier, Graduate Program Manager, 724-847-6697, E-mail: counseling@geneva.edu. *Program Director,* Dr. Shannan Shiderly, 724-847-6649, Fax: 724-847-6101, E-mail: slshider@geneva.edu.

Master of Arts in Higher Education Program Students: 49 full-time (30 women), 7 part-time (2 women); includes 6 minority (3 Black or African American, non-Hispanic/Latino; 1 Hispanic/Latino; 2 Two or more races, non-Hispanic/Latino), 1 international. Average age 26. 47 applicants, 74% accepted, 23 enrolled. *Faculty:* 2 full-time (0 women), 11 part-time/adjunct (4 women). Expenses: Contact institution. *Financial support:* In 2016–17, 37 students received support. Unspecified assistantships available. Financial award application deadline: 8/1; financial award applicants required to submit FAFSA. In 2016, 23 master's awarded. *Program availability:* Part-time, evening/weekend, blended/hybrid learning. Offers campus ministry (MA); college teaching (MA); educational leadership (MA); student affairs administration (MA). *Application deadline:* For fall admission, 9/1 priority date for domestic students; for winter admission, 1/2 priority date for domestic students; for spring admission, 3/11 priority date for domestic students. Applications are processed on a rolling basis. Electronic applications accepted. *Application Contact:* Jerryn S. Carson, Program Coordinator, 724-847-6510, Fax: 724-847-6696, E-mail: hed@geneva.edu. *Program Director,* Dr. Keith Martel, 724-847-6884, Fax: 724-847-6107, E-mail: hed@geneva.edu.

Program in Business Administration Students: 22 full-time (6 women), 29 part-time (10 women); includes 4 minority (1 Black or African American, non-Hispanic/Latino; 1 American Indian or Alaska Native, non-Hispanic/Latino; 2 Asian, non-Hispanic/Latino), 1 international. Average age 35. Expenses: Contact institution. *Financial support:* In 2016–17, 1 student received support. Scholarships/grants available. Financial award application deadline: 8/1; financial award applicants required to submit FAFSA. In 2016, 15 master's awarded. *Program availability:* Part-time, evening/weekend. Offers business administration (MBA); finance (MBA); marketing (MBA); operations (MBA). *Application deadline:* For fall admission, 3/1 priority date for domestic students; for spring admission, 11/1 priority date for domestic students. Applications are processed on a rolling basis. Electronic applications accepted. *Application Contact:* Marina Frazier, Director of Graduate Enrollment, 724-847-6697, E-mail: mba@geneva.edu. *Director of the MBA Program,* Dr. Gary Vander Plaats, 724-847-6619, E-mail: gpvander@geneva.edu.

Program in Leadership Studies Students: 56 full-time (45 women), 9 part-time (6 women); includes 15 minority (12 Black or African American, non-Hispanic/Latino; 1 Asian, non-Hispanic/Latino; 2 Hispanic/Latino). Average age 45. 13 applicants, 77% accepted, 7 enrolled. *Faculty:* 1 (woman) full-time, 10 part-time/adjunct (3 women). Expenses: Contact institution. *Financial support:* In 2016–17, 50 students received support. Scholarships/grants available. Financial award application deadline: 8/1; financial award applicants required to submit FAFSA. In 2016, 38 master's awarded. *Program availability:* Online only, 100% online. Offers business management (MS); ministry leadership (MS); non-profit leadership (MS); organizational management (MS); project management (MS). *Application deadline:* For fall admission, 9/21 for domestic students; for spring admission, 2/23 for domestic students; for summer admission, 7/22 for domestic students. Applications are processed on a rolling basis. Electronic applications accepted. *Application Contact:* Lynsey Auell, Graduate Enrollment Representative, 800-576-3111, Fax: 724-847-6839, E-mail: msol@geneva.edu. *Dean of Graduate, Adult and Online Programs,* John D. Gallo, 800-576-3111, Fax: 724-847-6839, E-mail: msol@geneva.edu.

GEORGE FOX UNIVERSITY, Newberg, OR 97132-2697

General Information Independent-religious, coed, university. *Graduate housing:* On-campus housing not available.

GRADUATE UNITS

College of Business *Program availability:* Part-time, evening/weekend, online learning. Offers accounting (DBA); finance (MBA); management (DBA); management and leadership (MBA); marketing (DBA); organizational strategy (MBA); strategic human resource management (MBA). MBA offered in Newberg, OR and in Portland, OR. Electronic applications accepted.

College of Education Offers administrative leadership (Ed S); clinical mental health counseling (MA); continuing administrator license (Certificate); education (M Ed, MA, MAT, Ed D, Certificate, Ed S); educational leadership (M Ed); educational technology (M Ed); English for speakers of other languages (M Ed); ESOL (Certificate); initial administrator license (Certificate); marriage, couple and family counseling (MA, Certificate); reading (M Ed, Certificate); school counseling (MA, Certificate); school psychology (Ed S); special education (M Ed); teaching (MAT).

Portland Seminary *Program availability:* Part-time, evening/weekend, online learning. Offers Biblical studies (M Div, MA); chaplaincy (M Div); Christian history and theology (M Div, MA); creation care (M Div, MA); intercultural studies (M Div, MA); leadership (M Div, MA); leadership and global perspectives (D Min); leadership and spiritual formation (D Min); semiotics and future studies (D Min); spiritual direction (MA, Certificate); spiritual direction supervision (M Div, MA, Certificate); spiritual formation and discipleship (M Div, MA, Certificate). Electronic applications accepted.

Program in Clinical Psychology Offers clinical psychology (Psy D). Electronic applications accepted.

Program in Physical Therapy Offers physical therapy (DPT). Electronic applications accepted.

School of Social Work Offers social work (MSW).

GEORGE MASON UNIVERSITY, Fairfax, VA 22030

General Information State-supported, coed, university. CGS member. *Enrollment:* 4,185 full-time matriculated graduate/professional students (2,250 women), 5,882 part-time matriculated graduate/professional students (3,560 women). *Enrollment by degree level:* 6,878 master's, 2,724 doctoral, 465 other advanced degrees. *Graduate faculty:* 1,421 full-time (592 women), 1,199 part-time/adjunct (538 women). Tuition, state resident: full-time $10,628; part-time $443 per credit. Tuition, nonresident: full-time $29,306; part-time $1221 per credit. *Required fees:* $3096; $129 per credit. Tuition and fees vary according to program. *Graduate housing:* Room and/or apartments available on a first-come, first-served basis to single students; on-campus housing not available to married students. Typical cost: $11,180 per year. Room charges vary according to housing facility selected. Housing application deadline: 5/1. *Student services:* Campus employment opportunities, campus safety program, career counseling, child daycare facilities, exercise/wellness program, free psychological counseling, grant writing training, international student services, low-cost health insurance, multicultural affairs office, services for students with disabilities, teacher training, writing training. *Library facilities:* Fenwick Library plus 3 others. *Collection:* Books: 1.3 million (physical), 1.5 million (digital/electronic); Serial titles: 1,244 (physical), 102,222 (digital/electronic); Databases: 793. Weekly public service hours: 87; study areas open 24 hours, 5–7 days a week; students can reserve study rooms. *Research affiliation:* Science Applications

International Corporation (science and technology), Lockheed Martin Corporation (science and technology), Inova Health System (health care and medical research), L3 Communications (high-tech communication technology), Alion Science and Technology Corporation (science and technology research), Northrop Grumman Corporation (high-tech communication technology).

Computer facilities: Computer purchase and lease plans are available. 622 computers available on campus for general student use. A campuswide network can be accessed from student residence rooms and from off campus. Online class registration is available.
Website: http://www.gmu.edu/

General Application Contact: Graduate Admissions Office, 703-993-9700, Fax: 703-993-2392, E-mail: masongrad@gmu.edu.

GRADUATE UNITS

Antonin Scalia Law School Students: 382 full-time (172 women), 159 part-time (83 women). 2,587 applicants, 24% accepted, 179 enrolled. *Faculty:* 41 full-time (9 women), 84 part-time/adjunct (20 women). Expenses: Contact institution. *Financial support:* Fellowships, research assistantships, career-related internships or fieldwork, scholarships/grants, and tuition waivers (full and partial) available. Support available to part-time students. *Program availability:* Part-time, evening/weekend. Offers global antitrust law and economics (LL M); intellectual property (LL M); law (JD); law and economics (LL M); U.S. law (LL M). *Application deadline:* For fall admission, 4/1 for domestic and international students. Applications are processed on a rolling basis. *Application fee:* $0. Electronic applications accepted. *Application Contact:* Alison H. Price, Associate Dean for Admissions and Enrollment Management, 703-993-8010, Fax: 703-993-8088, E-mail: lawadmit@gmu.edu. *Dean,* Henry N. Butler, 703-993-8644, Fax: 703-993-8088.

College of Education and Human Development Students: 455 full-time (369 women), 2,127 part-time (1,746 women); includes 719 minority (282 Black or African American, non-Hispanic/Latino; 9 American Indian or Alaska Native, non-Hispanic/Latino; 168 Asian, non-Hispanic/Latino; 204 Hispanic/Latino; 4 Native Hawaiian or other Pacific Islander, non-Hispanic/Latino; 52 Two or more races, non-Hispanic/Latino), 62 international. Average age 34. 1,231 applicants, 88% accepted, 762 enrolled. *Faculty:* 167 full-time (118 women), 193 part-time/adjunct (132 women). Expenses: Contact institution. *Financial support:* In 2016–17, 104 students received support, including 13 fellowships (averaging $8,748 per year), 77 research assistantships with tuition reimbursements available (averaging $13,507 per year), 36 teaching assistantships with tuition reimbursements available (averaging $7,243 per year); career-related internships or fieldwork, Federal Work-Study, scholarships/grants, unspecified assistantships, and health care benefits (for full-time research or teaching assistantship recipients) also available. Support available to part-time students. Financial award application deadline: 3/1; financial award applicants required to submit FAFSA. In 2016, 692 master's, 45 doctorates, 198 other advanced degrees awarded. *Program availability:* Part-time, evening/weekend, online learning. Offers advanced international baccalaureate (M Ed); assistive technology (M Ed); community agency counseling (M Ed); designing digital learning in schools (M Ed); early childhood education (M Ed); early childhood education for diverse learners (M Ed); education and human development M Ed, MS, PhD, Certificate); education leadership (M Ed, Certificate); educational psychology (MS, Certificate); elementary education (M Ed); English as a second language (M Ed); exercise, fitness, and health promotion (MS); gifted child education (M Ed); higher education (PhD); history (M Ed); literacy (M Ed); literacy leadership for diverse schools (M Ed); physical education (M Ed); recreation, health and tourism (Certificate); school counseling PK-12 (M Ed); science K-12 (M Ed); secondary education (M Ed); special education (M Ed); teacher leadership (M Ed); teaching culturally, linguistically diverse and exceptional learners (M Ed); transformative teaching (M Ed). *Application fee:* $75 ($80 for international students). Electronic applications accepted. *Application Contact:* Nicole Mariam, Graduate Admissions Coordinator, 703-993-3832, Fax: 703-993-2020, E-mail: nwhite5@gmu.edu. *Dean,* Mark Ginsberg, 703-993-2004, Fax: 703-993-2001, E-mail: mginsber@gmu.edu.

College of Health and Human Services Students: 377 full-time (312 women), 385 part-time (328 women); includes 316 minority (131 Black or African American, non-Hispanic/Latino; 1 American Indian or Alaska Native, non-Hispanic/Latino; 94 Asian, non-Hispanic/Latino; 71 Hispanic/Latino; 3 Native Hawaiian or other Pacific Islander, non-Hispanic/Latino; 16 Two or more races, non-Hispanic/Latino), 72 international. Average age 33. 763 applicants, 82% accepted, 287 enrolled. *Faculty:* 97 full-time (71 women), 126 part-time/adjunct (95 women). Expenses: Contact institution. *Financial support:* In 2016–17, 70 students received support, including 64 research assistantships with tuition reimbursements available (averaging $15,817 per year), 9 teaching assistantships with tuition reimbursements available (averaging $9,077 per year); career-related internships or fieldwork, Federal Work-Study, scholarships/grants, unspecified assistantships, and health care benefits (for full-time research or teaching assistantship recipients) also available. Support available to part-time students. Financial award application deadline: 3/1; financial award applicants required to submit FAFSA. In 2016, 248 master's, 32 doctorates, 20 other advanced degrees awarded. *Program availability:* Part-time, evening/weekend, online learning. Offers global and community health (Certificate); global health (MS); health administration and policy (PhD, Certificate); health and human services (MHA, MPH, MS, MSN, MSW, DNP, PhD, Certificate); health and medical policy (MS); health systems management (MHA); nutrition (MS); public health (MPH); rehabilitation science (PhD, Certificate); social work (MSW). *Application fee:* $75 ($80 for international students). Electronic applications accepted. *Application Contact:* Kelly Benedicto, Administrative Office Specialist, Graduate Admissions, 703-993-8246, Fax: 703-993-3606, E-mail: kbenedi@gmu.edu. *Dean,* Dr. Thomas Prohaska, 703-993-1918, Fax: 703-993-1943, E-mail: tprohask@gmu.edu.

School of Nursing Students: 59 full-time (47 women), 165 part-time (148 women); includes 93 minority (46 Black or African American, non-Hispanic/Latino; 1 American Indian or Alaska Native, non-Hispanic/Latino; 30 Asian, non-Hispanic/Latino; 12 Hispanic/Latino; 1 Native Hawaiian or other Pacific Islander, non-Hispanic/Latino; 3 Two or more races, non-Hispanic/Latino), 9 international. Average age 38. 128 applicants, 87% accepted, 71 enrolled. *Faculty:* 30 full-time (29 women), 43 part-time/adjunct (41 women). Expenses: Contact institution. *Financial support:* In 2016–17, 8 students received support, including 8 research assistantships with tuition reimbursements available (averaging $15,448 per year), 2 teaching assistantships (averaging $9,394 per year); career-related internships or fieldwork, Federal Work-Study, scholarships/grants, unspecified assistantships, and health care benefits (for full-time research or teaching assistantship recipients) also available. Financial award application deadline: 3/1; financial award applicants required to submit FAFSA. In 2016, 33 master's, 31 doctorates, 4 other advanced degrees awarded. Offers nursing (MSN, DNP, PhD, Certificate). *Application deadline:* For fall admission, 2/1 for domestic and international students. Electronic applications accepted. *Application Contact:* Susan Eckis, Office

Manager, 703-993-1938, Fax: 703-993-1949, E-mail: seckis@gmu.edu. *Director,* Carol Urban, 703-993-2991, Fax: 703-993-1949, E-mail: curban@gmu.edu.

College of Humanities and Social Sciences Students: 696 full-time (410 women), 705 part-time (409 women); includes 270 minority (77 Black or African American, non-Hispanic/Latino; 4 American Indian or Alaska Native, non-Hispanic/Latino; 50 Asian, non-Hispanic/Latino; 100 Hispanic/Latino; 3 Native Hawaiian or other Pacific Islander, non-Hispanic/Latino; 36 Two or more races, non-Hispanic/Latino), 92 international. Average age 32. 1,642 applicants, 47% accepted, 337 enrolled. *Faculty:* 376 full-time (178 women), 249 part-time/adjunct (132 women). Expenses: Contact institution. *Financial support:* In 2016–17, 456 students received support, including 51 fellowships (averaging $6,970 per year), 185 research assistantships with tuition reimbursements available (averaging $16,245 per year), 282 teaching assistantships with tuition reimbursements available (averaging $13,745 per year); career-related internships or fieldwork, Federal Work-Study, scholarships/grants, unspecified assistantships, and health care benefits (for full-time research or teaching assistantship recipients) also available. Support available to part-time students. Financial award application deadline: 3/1; financial award applicants required to submit FAFSA. In 2016, 378 master's, 80 doctorates, 29 other advanced degrees awarded. *Program availability:* Part-time, evening/weekend. Offers anthropology (MA); applied developmental psychology (Certificate); art history (MA); cognitive and behavioral neuroscience (MA); communication (MA, PhD, Certificate); community college education (DA); community college teaching (MAIS); computational social science (MAIS); creative writing (MFA); criminology, law and society (MA, PhD); cultural studies (PhD); digital public humanities (Certificate); economics (MA, PhD); energy and sustainability (MAIS); English (MA, Certificate); ethics and public affairs (MA); folklore studies (MAIS); foreign languages (MA); global affairs (MA); higher education (Certificate); history (MA, PhD); humanities and social sciences (MA, MAIS, MFA, DA, PhD, Certificate); individualized studies (MAIS); industrial/organizational psychology (PhD); linguistics (PhD); Middle East and Islamic studies (MA, Certificate); neuroethics (MAIS); religion, culture, and values (MAIS); social entrepreneurship (MAIS); social justice and human rights (MAIS); sociology (PhD); war and the military in society (MAIS); women and gender studies (MAIS). *Application deadline:* For fall admission, 2/1 for domestic and international students. *Application fee:* $75 ($80 for international students). Electronic applications accepted. *Application Contact:* Stephanie Hinnenkamp, Graduate Admissions Coordinator, 703-993-2409, E-mail: shinnenk@gmu.edu. *Dean,* Deborah A. Boehm-Davis, 703-993-8715, Fax: 703-993-8714, E-mail: dbdavis@gmu.edu.

College of Science Students: 516 full-time (274 women), 472 part-time (205 women); includes 285 minority (93 Black or African American, non-Hispanic/Latino; 106 Asian, non-Hispanic/Latino; 61 Hispanic/Latino; 3 Native Hawaiian or other Pacific Islander, non-Hispanic/Latino; 22 Two or more races, non-Hispanic/Latino), 142 international. Average age 32. 832 applicants, 74% accepted, 325 enrolled. *Faculty:* 305 full-time (103 women), 86 part-time/adjunct (28 women). Expenses: Contact institution. *Financial support:* In 2016–17, 261 students received support, including 25 fellowships (averaging $9,489 per year), 115 research assistantships with tuition reimbursements available (averaging $18,554 per year), 144 teaching assistantships with tuition reimbursements available (averaging $15,747 per year); career-related internships or fieldwork, Federal Work-Study, scholarships/grants, and health care benefits (for full-time research or teaching assistantship recipients) also available. Support available to part-time students. Financial award application deadline: 3/1; financial award applicants required to submit FAFSA. In 2016, 171 master's, 89 doctorates, 91 other advanced degrees awarded. *Program availability:* Part-time, evening/weekend. Offers applied and engineering physics (MS); aquatic ecology (MS); chemistry (MS); chemistry and biochemistry (PhD); climate dynamics (PhD); computational science and informatics (PhD); earth system science (MS); earth systems and geoinformation sciences (PhD); forensic science (MS); geography and geoinformation science (Certificate); mathematical sciences (MS, PhD); neuroscience (PhD); science (MS, PhD, Certificate). *Application fee:* $75 ($80 for international students). Electronic applications accepted. *Application Contact:* Melissa C. Hayes, Graduate Programs Director, 703-993-3430, Fax: 703-993-9033, E-mail: mhayes5@gmu.edu. *Dean,* Peggy Agouris, 703-993-1362, Fax: 703-993-9614, E-mail: pagouris@gmu.edu.

School of Systems Biology Students: 102 full-time (53 women), 81 part-time (46 women); includes 52 minority (4 Black or African American, non-Hispanic/Latino; 29 Asian, non-Hispanic/Latino; 11 Hispanic/Latino; 1 Native Hawaiian or other Pacific Islander, non-Hispanic/Latino; 7 Two or more races, non-Hispanic/Latino), 41 international. Average age 31. 133 applicants, 78% accepted, 68 enrolled. *Faculty:* 10 full-time (3 women), 2 part-time/adjunct (0 women). Expenses: Contact institution. *Financial support:* In 2016–17, 53 students received support, including 11 fellowships (averaging $6,688 per year), 14 research assistantships with tuition reimbursements available (averaging $15,875 per year), 40 teaching assistantships with tuition reimbursements available (averaging $15,740 per year); career-related internships or fieldwork, Federal Work-Study, scholarships/grants, unspecified assistantships, and health care benefits (for full-time research or teaching assistantship recipients) also available. Support available to part-time students. Financial award application deadline: 3/1; financial award applicants required to submit FAFSA. In 2016, 27 master's, 15 doctorates, 1 other advanced degree awarded. Offers bioinformatics and computational biology (MS, PhD, Certificate); bioinformatics management (MS); biology (MS); biosciences (PhD); personalized medicine (Certificate). *Application fee:* $75 ($80 for international students). Electronic applications accepted. *Application Contact:* Diane St. Germain, Graduate Student Services Coordinator, 703-993-4263, Fax: 703-993-8976, E-mail: dstgerma@gmu.edu. *Director,* Dr. Iosif Vaisman, 703-993-8431, Fax: 703-993-8976, E-mail: ivaisman@gmu.edu.

College of Visual and Performing Arts Students: 81 full-time (56 women), 135 part-time (91 women); includes 57 minority (14 Black or African American, non-Hispanic/Latino; 21 Asian, non-Hispanic/Latino; 14 Hispanic/Latino; 2 Native Hawaiian or other Pacific Islander, non-Hispanic/Latino; 6 Two or more races, non-Hispanic/Latino), 30 international. Average age 31. 142 applicants, 62% accepted, 44 enrolled. *Faculty:* 73 full-time (30 women), 144 part-time/adjunct (69 women). Expenses: Contact institution. *Financial support:* In 2016–17, 22 students received support, including 2 research assistantships with tuition reimbursements available (averaging $16,753 per year), 20 teaching assistantships with tuition reimbursements available (averaging $5,907 per year); career-related internships or fieldwork, Federal Work-Study, scholarships/grants, unspecified assistantships, and health care benefits (for full-time research or teaching assistantship recipients) also available. Support available to part-time students. Financial award application deadline: 3/1; financial award applicants required to submit FAFSA. In 2016, 83 master's, 5 doctorates, 5 other advanced degrees awarded. *Program availability:* Part-time, evening/weekend. Offers art education (MAT); arts management (MA, Certificate); drawing (MFA); graphic design (MA); new media (MFA); painting (MFA); photography (MFA); printmaking (MFA); sculpture (MFA); visual and performing arts (MA, MAT, MFA, MM, DMA, PhD, Certificate). *Application fee:* $75 ($80 for international students). Electronic applications accepted. *Application Contact:*

Stevie Otto, Assistant Director, Graduate Admissions and Recruitment, 703-993-5576, Fax: 703-993-9037, E-mail: sotto2@gmu.edu. *Dean*, Rick Davis, 703-993-8624, Fax: 703-993-8883, E-mail: rdavi4@gmu.edu.

School of Music Students: 28 full-time (14 women), 50 part-time (25 women); includes 21 minority (4 Black or African American, non-Hispanic/Latino; 11 Asian, non-Hispanic/Latino; 5 Hispanic/Latino; 1 Native Hawaiian or other Pacific Islander, non-Hispanic/Latino), 3 international. Average age 34. 49 applicants, 71% accepted, 16 enrolled. *Faculty:* 20 full-time (8 women), 65 part-time/adjunct (25 women). Expenses: Contact institution. *Financial support:* In 2016–17, 19 students received support, including 2 research assistantships with tuition reimbursements available (averaging $16,753 per year), 17 teaching assistantships with tuition reimbursements available (averaging $5,573 per year); career-related internships or fieldwork, Federal Work-Study, scholarships/grants, unspecified assistantships, and health care benefits (for full-time research or teaching assistantship recipients) also available. Support available to part-time students. Financial award application deadline: 3/1; financial award applicants required to submit FAFSA. In 2016, 28 master's, 5 doctorates, 1 other advanced degree awarded. Offers composition (MM, DMA); conducting (MM, DMA); instrumental performance artist (Certificate); jazz studies (MM); music (MM); music education (MM, PhD); musical arts (DMA); pedagogy (MM); performance (MM, DMA). *Application fee:* $75 ($80 for international students). Electronic applications accepted. *Application Contact:* Dr. Lisa A. Billingham, Director of Graduate Studies, 703-993-3778, Fax: 703-993-1394, E-mail: lbillin1@gmu.edu. *Managing Director*, Dr. Linda Apple Monson, 703-993-3580, Fax: 703-993-1394, E-mail: lmonson@gmu.edu.

Schar School of Policy and Government Students: 332 full-time (165 women), 667 part-time (343 women); includes 380 minority (113 Black or African American, non-Hispanic/Latino; 65 Asian, non-Hispanic/Latino; 97 Hispanic/Latino; 2 Native Hawaiian or other Pacific Islander, non-Hispanic/Latino; 31 Two or more races, non-Hispanic/Latino), 65 international. Average age 32. 642 applicants, 78% accepted, 251 enrolled. *Faculty:* 105 full-time (38 women), 55 part-time/adjunct (17 women). Expenses: Contact institution. *Financial support:* In 2016–17, 58 students received support, including 4 fellowships (averaging $6,052 per year), 40 research assistantships with tuition reimbursements available (averaging $18,193 per year), 16 teaching assistantships (averaging $15,876 per year); career-related internships or fieldwork, Federal Work-Study, scholarships/grants, unspecified assistantships, and health care benefits (for full-time research or teaching assistantship recipients) also available. Support available to part-time students. Financial award application deadline: 3/1; financial award applicants required to submit FAFSA. In 2016, 407 master's, 25 doctorates, 26 other advanced degrees awarded. *Program availability:* Part-time, evening/weekend. Offers biodefense (MS, PhD, Certificate); international commerce and policy (MA); organization development and knowledge management (MS); peace operations (MS); policy and government (MA, MPA, MPP, MS, PhD, Certificate); political science (MA, PhD); public administration (MPA); public policy (MPP, PhD); transportation policy, operations and logistics (MA, Certificate). *Application fee:* $75 ($80 for international students). Electronic applications accepted. *Application Contact:* Travis Major, Director of Graduate Admissions, 703-993-3183, Fax: 703-993-4876, E-mail: tmajor@gmu.edu. *Dean*, Mark Rozell, 703-993-8171, Fax: 703-993-8215, E-mail: mrozell@gmu.edu.

School for Conflict Analysis and Resolution Students: 116 full-time (63 women), 159 part-time (86 women); includes 92 minority (48 Black or African American, non-Hispanic/Latino; 14 Asian, non-Hispanic/Latino; 23 Hispanic/Latino; 1 Native Hawaiian or other Pacific Islander, non-Hispanic/Latino; 6 Two or more races, non-Hispanic/Latino), 34 international. Average age 35. 224 applicants, 76% accepted, 82 enrolled. *Faculty:* 18 full-time (9 women), 21 part-time/adjunct (12 women). Expenses: Contact institution. *Financial support:* In 2016–17, 38 students received support, including 4 fellowships (averaging $10,814 per year), 24 research assistantships with tuition reimbursements available (averaging $15,919 per year), 11 teaching assistantships with tuition reimbursements available (averaging $10,483 per year); career-related internships or fieldwork, Federal Work-Study, scholarships/grants, unspecified assistantships, and health care benefits (for full-time research or teaching assistantship recipients) also available. Support available to part-time students. Financial award application deadline: 3/1; financial award applicants required to submit FAFSA. In 2016, 75 master's, 8 doctorates, 5 other advanced degrees awarded. *Program availability:* Part-time, evening/weekend. Offers conflict analysis and resolution (MS, PhD, Certificate). *Application fee:* $75 ($80 for international students). Electronic applications accepted. *Application Contact:* Monique Barner, Assistant Director for Graduate Admissions, 703-993-1300, Fax: 703-993-1302, E-mail: mwilli43@gmu.edu. *Dean*, Kevin Avruch, 703-993-3607, Fax: 703-993-1302, E-mail: kavruch@gmu.edu.

School of Business Students: 421 full-time (180 women), 130 part-time (54 women); includes 207 minority (71 Black or African American, non-Hispanic/Latino; 73 Asian, non-Hispanic/Latino; 51 Hispanic/Latino; 3 Native Hawaiian or other Pacific Islander, non-Hispanic/Latino; 9 Two or more races, non-Hispanic/Latino), 60 international. Average age 33. 503 applicants, 80% accepted, 244 enrolled. *Faculty:* 100 full-time (33 women), 65 part-time/adjunct (23 women). Expenses: Contact institution. *Financial support:* In 2016–17, 17 students received support, including 5 research assistantships with tuition reimbursements available (averaging $7,584 per year), 12 teaching assistantships with tuition reimbursements available (averaging $8,327 per year); career-related internships or fieldwork, Federal Work-Study, scholarships/grants, unspecified assistantships, and health care benefits (for full-time research or teaching assistantship recipients) also available. Support available to part-time students. Financial award application deadline: 3/1; financial award applicants required to submit FAFSA. In 2016, 263 master's, 13 other advanced degrees awarded. *Program availability:* Part-time, evening/weekend, online learning. Offers accounting (MS, Certificate); business (EMBA, MBA, MS, Certificate); business administration (MBA); management of secure information systems (MS); technology management (MS). *Application fee:* $75 ($80 for international students). Electronic applications accepted. *Application Contact:* Paige Wolf, Senior Assistant Dean of Graduate Programs, 703-993-1758, Fax: 703-993-1870, E-mail: pwolf1@gmu.edu. *Interim Dean*, Anne Magro, 703-993-1765, Fax: 703-993-2472, E-mail: amagro@gmu.edu.

Volgenau School of Engineering Students: 814 full-time (252 women), 943 part-time (233 women); includes 417 minority (85 Black or African American, non-Hispanic/Latino; 224 Asian, non-Hispanic/Latino; 75 Hispanic/Latino; 4 Native Hawaiian or other Pacific Islander, non-Hispanic/Latino; 29 Two or more races, non-Hispanic/Latino), 701 international. Average age 30. 1,661 applicants, 74% accepted, 520 enrolled. *Faculty:* 196 full-time (50 women), 175 part-time/adjunct (20 women). Expenses: Contact institution. *Financial support:* In 2016–17, 285 students received support, including 8 fellowships (averaging $9,779 per year), 107 research assistantships with tuition reimbursements available (averaging $18,402 per year), 177 teaching assistantships with tuition reimbursements available (averaging $14,732 per year); career-related internships or fieldwork, Federal Work-Study, scholarships/grants, unspecified assistantships, and health care benefits (for full-time research or teaching assistantship

recipients) also available. Support available to part-time students. Financial award application deadline: 3/1; financial award applicants required to submit FAFSA. In 2016, 484 master's, 38 doctorates, 106 other advanced degrees awarded. *Program availability:* Part-time, evening/weekend, online learning. Offers applied information technology (MS); bioengineering (PhD); biostatistics (MS); computer engineering (MS); computer science (MS, PhD, Certificate); construction project management (MS); data analytics engineering (MS); electrical and computer engineering (PhD, Certificate); engineering (M Eng, MS, PhD, Certificate); geotechnical, construction, and structural engineering (M Eng); information sciences and technology (Certificate); information technology (PhD); operations research (MS); statistical science (MS, PhD); statistics (Certificate); systems engineering and operations research (PhD, Certificate); transportation engineering (PhD). *Application fee:* $75 ($80 for international students). Electronic applications accepted. *Application Contact:* Suddaf Ismail, Director, Graduate Admissions and Recruitment, 703-993-9115, Fax: 703-993-1242, E-mail: sismail@gmu.edu. *Dean*, Kenneth S. Ball, 703-993-1498, Fax: 703-993-1734, E-mail: vsdean@gmu.edu.

GEORGETOWN COLLEGE, Georgetown, KY 40324-1696

General Information Independent-religious, coed, comprehensive institution. *Graduate housing:* On-campus housing not available.

GRADUATE UNITS

Department of Education *Program availability:* Part-time. Offers reading and writing (MA Ed); special education (MA Ed); teaching (MA Ed).

GEORGETOWN UNIVERSITY, Washington, DC 20057

General Information Independent-religious, coed, university. CGS member. *Graduate housing:* On-campus housing not available.

GRADUATE UNITS

GeorgeSquared Special Master's Program Offers biomedical sciences (MS). Program offered jointly with George Mason University.

Graduate School of Arts and Sciences Offers American government (MA); analytical chemistry (PhD); arts and sciences (EMBA, EML, EMPL, GEMBA, MA, MAE, MALS, MAT, MBA, MDSPP, MIPM, MPM, MPP, MPS, MS, DLS, DNP, PhD, Certificate); biochemistry (PhD); biochemistry and molecular and cellular biology (MS, PhD); bioethics (MA); biohazardous threat agents and emerging infectious diseases (MS); biology (PhD); biomedical science policy and advocacy (MS); biostatistics (MS, Certificate); British and American literature (MA); communication, culture, and technology (MA); computational chemistry (PhD); computer science (MS, PhD); conflict resolution (MA); democracy and governance (MA); development, management and policy (MA); econometrics (PhD); economic development (PhD); economic theory (PhD); epidemiology (Certificate); general microbiology and immunology (MS); German (MA, PhD); global history (MA); global infectious diseases (PhD); global, international and comparative history (MA); government (PhD); health physics (MS); history (MA, PhD); industrial organization (PhD); inorganic chemistry (PhD); international macro and finance (PhD); international trade (PhD); labor economics (PhD); language and communication (MA); linguistics (MS, PhD); macroeconomics (PhD); materials chemistry (PhD); mathematics and statistics (MS); microbiology and immunology (PhD); neuroscience (PhD); nuclear nonproliferation (MS); organic chemistry (PhD); pharmacology (MS, PhD); philosophy (MS); physiology (MS); psychology (PhD); public economics and political economy (PhD); Spanish (MS, PhD); theology (PhD); theoretical chemistry (PhD).

McCourt School of Public Policy *Program availability:* Part-time. Offers data science for public policy (MDSPP); international development policy (MIDP); policy leadership (EMPL); policy management (MPM); public policy (MPP). Electronic applications accepted.

McDonough School of Business Offers business administration (EMBA, GEMBA, MBA); finance (MS); leadership (EML).

School of Continuing Studies Offers American studies (MALS); Catholic studies (MALS); classical civilizations (MALS); emergency and disaster management (MPS); ethics and the professions (MALS); global strategic communications (MPS); hospitality management (MPS); human resources management (MPS); humanities (MALS); individualized study (MALS); integrated marketing communications (MPS); international affairs (MALS); Islam and Muslim-Christian relations (MALS); journalism (MPS); liberal studies (DLS); literature and society (MALS); medieval and early modern European studies (MALS); public relations and corporate communications (MPS); real estate (MPS); religious studies (MALS); social and public policy (MALS); sports industry management (MPS); systems engineering management (MPS); technology management (MPS); the theory and practice of American democracy (MALS); urban and regional planning (MPS); visual culture (MALS). MPS in systems engineering management offered jointly with Stevens Institute of Technology.

School of Nursing and Health Studies Offers acute care nurse practitioner (MS); clinical nurse specialist (MS); family nurse practitioner (MS); nurse anesthesia (MS); nurse-midwifery (MS); nursing (DNP); nursing education (MS).

Walsh School of Foreign Service Offers Asian studies (MA); contemporary Arab studies (MA, Certificate); Eurasian, Russian and East European studies (MA); foreign service (MA, MS, Certificate); German and European studies (MA); global business and finance (MS); global human development (MS); global politics and security (MS); international development (MS); Latin American studies (MA); security studies (MA); self design (MS).

Law Center *Program availability:* Part-time, evening/weekend. Offers environmental law (LL M); global health law (LL M); global health law and international institutions (LL M); individualized study (LL M); international business and economic law (LL M); law (JD, SJD); national security law (LL M); securities and financial regulation (LL M); taxation (LL M).

National Institutes of Health Sponsored Programs Offers biomedical sciences (MS, PhD).

School of Medicine Offers medicine (MD).

THE GEORGE WASHINGTON UNIVERSITY, Washington, DC 20052

General Information Independent, coed, university. CGS member. *Enrollment:* 27,159 graduate, professional, and undergraduate students; 7,816 full-time matriculated graduate/professional students (4,474 women), 7,649 part-time matriculated graduate/professional students (4,739 women). *Enrollment by degree level:* 10,448 master's, 4,566 doctoral, 451 other advanced degrees. *Graduate faculty:* 2,598 full-time (1,284 women). *Graduate housing:* Room and/or apartments available on a first-come, first-served basis to single students; on-campus housing not available to married students. *Student services:* Campus employment opportunities, campus safety program, career counseling, exercise/wellness program, free psychological counseling, international student services, low-cost health insurance, multicultural affairs office, services for students with disabilities, teacher training, writing training. *Library facilities:* Gelman Library. *Research affiliation:* Goddard Space Flight Center (radar modeling analysis, space systems technologies), Library of Congress, Smithsonian Institution, National Institutes of Health (biostatistics), NASA-Langley Research Center (aeroacoustics, aeronautics, astronautics), Children's Hospital National Medical Center.

Computer facilities: A campuswide network can be accessed from student residence rooms and from off campus.
Website: http://www.gwu.edu/
General Application Contact: Kristin Williams, Associate Provost for Graduate and Special Enrollment Management, 202-994-0467, Fax: 202-994-0371, E-mail: ksw@gwu.edu.

GRADUATE UNITS

College of Professional Studies Students: 238 full-time (89 women), 732 part-time (438 women); includes 311 minority (137 Black or African American, non-Hispanic/Latino; 4 American Indian or Alaska Native, non-Hispanic/Latino; 36 Asian, non-Hispanic/Latino; 92 Hispanic/Latino; 2 Native Hawaiian or other Pacific Islander, non-Hispanic/Latino; 40 Two or more races, non-Hispanic/Latino), 87 international. Average age 35. 833 applicants, 84% accepted, 402 enrolled. *Faculty:* 23 full-time (6 women), 91 part-time/adjunct (25 women). Expenses: Contact institution. In 2016, 447 master's, 85 other advanced degrees awarded. Offers healthcare corporate compliance (Graduate Certificate); law firm management (MPS, Graduate Certificate); paralegal studies (MPS, Graduate Certificate); publishing (MPS). *Application Contact:* Kristin Williams, Associate Provost, Graduate Enrollment, 202-994-0467, Fax: 202-994-0371, E-mail: ksw@gwu.edu. *Dean,* Dr. Ali Eskandarian, 202-994-8192, E-mail: ea1102@gwu.edu.

Graduate School of Political Management Students: 51 full-time (20 women), 212 part-time (81 women); includes 82 minority (26 Black or African American, non-Hispanic/Latino; 3 American Indian or Alaska Native, non-Hispanic/Latino; 7 Asian, non-Hispanic/Latino; 37 Hispanic/Latino; 9 Two or more races, non-Hispanic/Latino), 57 international. Average age 32. 183 applicants, 91% accepted, 98 enrolled. Expenses: Contact institution. *Financial support:* In 2016–17, 18 students received support. Fellowships with tuition reimbursements available, scholarships/grants, and tuition waivers available. Financial award application deadline: 2/1. In 2016, 96 master's, 3 other advanced degrees awarded. Offers community advocacy (Graduate Certificate); legislative affairs (MPS); PACs and political management (Graduate Certificate); political management (MPS). *Application deadline:* For fall admission, 6/15 priority date for domestic students, 4/1 priority date for international students; for spring admission, 11/15 priority date for domestic students, 10/1 priority date for international students. Applications are processed on a rolling basis. *Application fee:* $75. Electronic applications accepted. *Application Contact:* Information Contact, 202-994-6000, Fax: 202-994-6000. *Director,* Mark Kennedy, 202-994-6000, Fax: 202-994-6006, E-mail: gspmmail@gwu.edu.

Columbian College of Arts and Sciences Students: 1,641 full-time (1,060 women), 977 part-time (592 women); includes 522 minority (161 Black or African American, non-Hispanic/Latino; 6 American Indian or Alaska Native, non-Hispanic/Latino; 145 Asian, non-Hispanic/Latino; 150 Hispanic/Latino; 2 Native Hawaiian or other Pacific Islander, non-Hispanic/Latino; 58 Two or more races, non-Hispanic/Latino), 729 international. Average age 28. 6,473 applicants, 48% accepted, 998 enrolled. *Faculty:* 542 full-time (241 women). Expenses: Contact institution. *Financial support:* Fellowships with tuition reimbursements, research assistantships, teaching assistantships with tuition reimbursements, career-related internships or fieldwork, Federal Work-Study, scholarships/grants, tuition waivers, and unspecified assistantships available. Support available to part-time students. Financial award application deadline: 2/1. In 2016, 822 master's, 109 doctorates, 119 other advanced degrees awarded. *Program availability:* Part-time, evening/weekend. Offers American studies (PhD); analytical chemistry (MS, PhD); anthropology (MA, PhD); applied mathematics (MS); applied social psychology (PhD); art and the book (MA); art education (MA, MAT); art history (MA); art therapy (MA, Graduate Certificate); arts and sciences (MA, MAT, MFA, MFS, MPA, MPP, MS, PhD, Psy D, Certificate, Graduate Certificate); biological sciences (MS, PhD); biostatistics (MS, PhD); ceramics (MFA); classical acting (MFA); clinical psychology (PhD); cognitive neuroscience (PhD); crime scene investigation (MFS); criminology (MA); dance (MFA); drawing/painting (MFA); economics (MA, PhD); English (MA, PhD); environmental and resource policy (MA); exhibit design (Graduate Certificate); exhibition design (MA); financial mathematics (Graduate Certificate); folk life (MA); forensic chemistry (MFS); forensic molecular biology (MFS); forensic toxicology (MFS); geography (MA, Graduate Certificate); high-technology crime investigation (MS); historic preservation (MA); history (MA, PhD); human resources management (MA); inorganic chemistry (MS, PhD); interior design (MA, MFA); international development (MA); Islam (MA); legal institutions and theory (MA); material culture (MA); materials science (MS, PhD); mathematics (MA, PhD, Graduate Certificate); medical anthropology (MA); museum collections management and care (Graduate Certificate); museum studies (MA); museum training (MFA); new media (MFA); new media photojournalism (MA); non-profit management (Graduate Certificate); organic chemistry (MS, PhD); organizational management (Graduate Certificate); philosophy and social policy (MA); photography (MFA); physical chemistry (MS, PhD); physics (MA, PhD); political science (MA); production design (MFA); professional psychology (MA, Psy D, Graduate Certificate); sculpture (MFA); security management (MFS); sociology (MA); speech-language pathology (MA); statistics (MS, PhD); survey design and data analysis (Graduate Certificate); women's studies (MA, Certificate). *Application deadline:* For fall admission, 1/15 priority date for domestic and international students; for spring admission, 10/1 priority date for domestic and international students. Applications are processed on a rolling basis. *Application fee:* $75. Electronic applications accepted. *Application Contact:* Linda Wilkerson, Executive Assistant, 202-994-6210, Fax: 202-994-6213, E-mail: askccas@gwu.edu. *Dean,* Ben Vinson, III, 202-994-6130, E-mail: bvinson3@gwu.edu.

Institute for Biomedical Sciences Expenses: Contact institution. *Financial support:* In 2016–17, 24 students received support. Fellowships with full tuition reimbursements available, Federal Work-Study, institutionally sponsored loans, and tuition waivers available. *Program availability:* Part-time, evening/weekend. Offers biochemistry and systems biology (PhD); microbiology and immunology (PhD); molecular and cellular oncology (PhD); molecular medicine (PhD); neurosciences (PhD); pharmacology and physiology (PhD). *Application deadline:* For fall admission, 12/15 priority date for domestic and international students. Applications are processed on a rolling basis. *Application fee:* $60. Electronic applications accepted. *Application Contact:* 202-994-2179, Fax: 202-994-0967, E-mail: gwibs@gwu.edu. *Director,* Dr. Linda L. Werling, 202-994-2918, Fax: 202-994-0967, E-mail: lwerling@gwu.edu.

School of Media and Public Affairs Students: 31 full-time (20 women), 19 part-time (15 women); includes 10 minority (7 Black or African American, non-Hispanic/Latino; 1 Asian, non-Hispanic/Latino; 1 Hispanic/Latino; 1 Native Hawaiian or other Pacific

Islander, non-Hispanic/Latino), 9 international. Average age 27. 86 applicants, 59% accepted, 24 enrolled. *Faculty:* 22 full-time (10 women). Expenses: Contact institution. *Financial support:* In 2016–17, fellowships with tuition reimbursements (averaging $10,000 per year), teaching assistantships with tuition reimbursements (averaging $5,000 per year) were awarded. Financial award application deadline: 1/15. In 2016, 22 master's, 13 other advanced degrees awarded. Offers media and public affairs (MA, Graduate Certificate). *Application deadline:* For fall admission, 4/1 priority date for domestic students, 1/15 priority date for international students; for spring admission, 10/1 priority date for domestic students, 9/1 priority date for international students. Applications are processed on a rolling basis. *Application fee:* $75. Electronic applications accepted. *Application Contact:* Information Contact, 202-994-6227, Fax: 202-994-5806, E-mail: smpa@gwu.edu. *Director,* Frank Sesno, 202-994-9553, E-mail: sesno@gwu.edu.

Trachtenberg School of Public Policy and Public Administration Students: 148 full-time (96 women), 119 part-time (73 women); includes 72 minority (25 Black or African American, non-Hispanic/Latino; 2 American Indian or Alaska Native, non-Hispanic/Latino; 21 Asian, non-Hispanic/Latino; 16 Hispanic/Latino; 1 Native Hawaiian or other Pacific Islander, non-Hispanic/Latino; 7 Two or more races, non-Hispanic/Latino), 24 international. Average age 27. 548 applicants, 80% accepted, 98 enrolled. *Faculty:* 20 full-time (11 women), 12 part-time/adjunct (5 women). Expenses: Contact institution. *Financial support:* In 2016–17, 57 students received support. Fellowships, research assistantships, teaching assistantships, Federal Work-Study, scholarships/grants, health care benefits, and unspecified assistantships available. Financial award application deadline: 1/5; financial award applicants required to submit FAFSA. In 2016, 122 master's, 13 doctorates awarded. *Program availability:* Part-time, evening/weekend, online learning. Offers public administration (MPA); public policy (MPP); public policy and administration (PhD). *Application deadline:* For fall admission, 1/5 priority date for domestic and international students; for spring admission, 10/1 priority date for domestic students, 10/1 for international students. *Application fee:* $75. Electronic applications accepted. *Application Contact:* Denee' Bottoms, Assistant Director of Graduate Studies, 202-994-6662, Fax: 202-994-6792, E-mail: dbottoms@gwu.edu. *Director,* Dr. Kathryn E. Newcomer, 202-994-3959, Fax: 202-994-6792, E-mail: newcomer@gwu.edu.

Elliott School of International Affairs Students: 555 full-time (328 women), 282 part-time (174 women); includes 249 minority (62 Black or African American, non-Hispanic/Latino; 70 Asian, non-Hispanic/Latino; 86 Hispanic/Latino; 31 Two or more races, non-Hispanic/Latino), 120 international. Average age 27. 1,546 applicants, 81% accepted, 350 enrolled. *Faculty:* 79 full-time (25 women). Expenses: Contact institution. *Financial support:* In 2016–17, 155 students received support. Fellowships with partial tuition reimbursements available and Federal Work-Study available. Financial award application deadline: 1/15; financial award applicants required to submit FAFSA. In 2016, 341 master's, 1 other advanced degree awarded. *Program availability:* Part-time. Offers Asian studies (MA); European and Eurasian studies (MA); global communication (MA); global gender policy (Graduate Certificate); international affairs (MA, MIPP, MIS, Graduate Certificate); international development studies (MA); international policy and practice (MIPP); international science and technology policy (MA, Graduate Certificate); international studies (MIS); international trade and investment policy (MA); Latin American and hemispheric studies (MA); Middle East studies (MA); security policy studies (MA). *Application deadline:* For fall admission, 1/15 priority date for domestic students, 1/15 for international students; for spring admission, 10/1 for domestic and international students. *Application fee:* $75. Electronic applications accepted. *Application Contact:* Nicole A. Campbell, Director of Graduate Admissions, 202-994-7050, Fax: 202-994-9537, E-mail: esiagrad@gwu.edu. *Dean,* Rueben E. Brigety, 202-994-6240, Fax: 202-994-0335, E-mail: esiadean@gwu.edu.

Graduate School of Education and Human Development Students: 418 full-time (332 women), 1,082 part-time (828 women); includes 564 minority (326 Black or African American, non-Hispanic/Latino; 6 American Indian or Alaska Native, non-Hispanic/Latino; 79 Asian, non-Hispanic/Latino; 108 Hispanic/Latino; 2 Native Hawaiian or other Pacific Islander, non-Hispanic/Latino; 43 Two or more races, non-Hispanic/Latino), 103 international. Average age 36. 1,654 applicants, 71% accepted, 669 enrolled. *Faculty:* 83 full-time (50 women). Expenses: Contact institution. *Financial support:* In 2016–17, 279 students received support. Fellowships with tuition reimbursements available, research assistantships with tuition reimbursements available, teaching assistantships with tuition reimbursements available, career-related internships or fieldwork, Federal Work-Study, and tuition waivers (full and partial) available. Support available to part-time students. Financial award application deadline: 1/15. In 2016, 376 master's, 69 doctorates, 115 other advanced degrees awarded. *Program availability:* Part-time, evening/weekend, online learning. Offers adolescents with emotional and behavioral disabilities (MA Ed/HD); adolescents with learning disabilities (MA Ed/HD); Arabic (M Ed); art education (MA); autism spectrum disorder (MA Ed/HD); bilingual special education (MA Ed, Certificate); brain injury special education (MA Ed/HD); brain injury specialist (MA Ed/HD); clinical mental health counseling (MA); college teaching and academic leadership (MA Ed/HD, Ed S); counseling (PhD, Ed S); counseling culturally and linguistically diverse persons (MA Ed/HD, Certificate); curriculum and instruction (MA Ed, Ed D, Ed S, Graduate Certificate); design and assessment of adult learning (Graduate Certificate); e-learning (Graduate Certificate); early childhood special education (MA Ed/HD); education and human development (M Ed, MA, MA Ed, MA Ed/HD, MAT, Ed D, PhD, Certificate, Ed S, Graduate Certificate, Teaching Certificate); education policy (Ed D); education policy studies (MA Ed); educational administration (Ed D); educational administration and policy studies (Ed D); educational leadership and administration (MA Ed, Certificate, Ed S); educational technology leadership (MA Ed); elementary education (MA Ed/HD); forensic rehabilitation counseling (Graduate Certificate); general administration (MA Ed/HD, Ed S); higher education administration (MA Ed/HD, Ed D, Ed S); higher education finance (MA Ed/HD, Ed S); human and organizational learning (Ed D, Ed S); human resource development (MA); infant special education (MA Ed/HD); instructional design (Graduate Certificate); integrating technology into education (Graduate Certificate); interdisciplinary transition services (MA Ed/HD); international education (MA Ed); Italian (M Ed); job development and placement (Graduate Certificate); leadership development (Graduate Certificate); leadership in educational technology (Graduate Certificate); math (M Ed); multimedia development (Graduate Certificate); museum education (MAT); organizational learning and change (Graduate Certificate); physics (M Ed); policy (MA Ed/HD, Ed S); rehabilitation counseling (MA Ed/HD); Russian (M Ed); school counseling (MA Ed, Graduate Certificate); secondary education (M Ed); secondary special education and transition services (MA Ed/HD); special education (Ed D, Ed S); special education and transition services (Certificate); special education for children with emotional and behavioral disabilities (MA Ed/HD); special education for culturally and linguistically diverse persons (MA Ed/HD, Certificate); student affairs administration (MA Ed/HD, Ed S); substance abuse and psychiatric disabilities (MA Ed/HD); training and educational technology (Graduate Certificate); transition special education (Teaching Certificate); traumatic brain injury (MA Ed/HD).

Application deadline: For fall admission, 1/15 priority date for domestic students; for spring admission, 10/1 for domestic students. Applications are processed on a rolling basis. *Application fee:* $75. Electronic applications accepted. *Application Contact:* Sarah Lang, Director of Graduate Admissions, 202-994-1447, Fax: 202-994-7207, E-mail: slang@gwu.edu. *Dean,* Michael Feuer, 202-994-6161, Fax: 202-994-7207, E-mail: mjfeuer@gwu.edu.

Law School Students: 1,622 full-time (867 women), 315 part-time (150 women); includes 482 minority (164 Black or African American, non-Hispanic/Latino; 15 American Indian or Alaska Native, non-Hispanic/Latino; 234 Asian, non-Hispanic/Latino; 55 Hispanic/Latino; 4 Native Hawaiian or other Pacific Islander, non-Hispanic/Latino; 10 Two or more races, non-Hispanic/Latino) 222 international. Average age 27. 223 applicants, 100% accepted, 133 enrolled. *Faculty:* 84 full-time (33 women). Expenses: Contact institution. *Financial support:* Research assistantships, career-related internships or fieldwork, Federal Work-Study, institutionally sponsored loans, scholarships/grants, and tuition waivers (full and partial) available. Support available to part-time students. Financial award application deadline: 3/1; financial award applicants required to submit CSS PROFILE or FAFSA. In 2016, 166 master's, 1 doctorate awarded. *Program availability:* Part-time, evening/weekend. Offers law (SJD); national security and U.S. foreign relations (LL M). *Application deadline:* For fall admission, 3/1 for domestic students. Applications are processed on a rolling basis. *Application fee:* $75. *Application Contact:* Sophia Sim, Assistant Dean of Admissions and Financial Aid, 202-994-7235, Fax: 202-739-0624, E-mail: ssim@law.gwu.edu. *Dean,* Blake D. Morant, E-mail: bmorant@law.gwu.edu.

Milken Institute School of Public Health Students: 497 full-time (387 women), 1,400 part-time (1,063 women); includes 831 minority (349 Black or African American, non-Hispanic/Latino; 8 American Indian or Alaska Native, non-Hispanic/Latino; 276 Asian, non-Hispanic/Latino; 134 Hispanic/Latino; 6 Native Hawaiian or other Pacific Islander, non-Hispanic/Latino; 58 Two or more races, non-Hispanic/Latino), 44 international. Average age 31. 3,260 applicants, 63% accepted, 703 enrolled. *Faculty:* 130 full-time (82 women). Expenses: Contact institution. *Financial support:* In 2016–17, 71 students received support. Career-related internships or fieldwork, Federal Work-Study, institutionally sponsored loans, scholarships/grants, and tuition waivers (partial) available. Support available to part-time students. Financial award application deadline: 2/15. In 2016, 476 master's, 16 doctorates, 9 other advanced degrees awarded. *Program availability:* Part-time, evening/weekend. Offers biostatistics (MPH); environmental and occupational health (Dr PH); epidemiology (MPH); exercise and nutrition sciences (MS); global health (Dr PH); global health communication (MPH); health policy and management (EMHA, MHA, MPH, MS, Graduate Certificate); microbiology and emerging infectious diseases (MSPH); prevention and community health (MPH, Dr PH); public health (EMHA, MHA, MPH, MS, MSPH, Dr PH, Graduate Certificate). *Application deadline:* For fall admission, 2/15 priority date for domestic students, 2/15 for international students. Applications are processed on a rolling basis. *Application Contact:* Director of Admissions, 202-994-2160, Fax: 202-994-1860, E-mail: sphhsinfo@gwumc.edu. *Dean,* Dr. Lynn Goldman, 202-994-5179, E-mail: goldmanl@gwu.edu.

School of Business Students: 1,022 full-time (540 women), 816 part-time (370 women); includes 522 minority (206 Black or African American, non-Hispanic/Latino; 1 American Indian or Alaska Native, non-Hispanic/Latino; 166 Asian, non-Hispanic/Latino; 103 Hispanic/Latino; 2 Native Hawaiian or other Pacific Islander, non-Hispanic/Latino; 44 Two or more races, non-Hispanic/Latino), 701 international. Average age 32. 3,672 applicants, 47% accepted, 597 enrolled. *Faculty:* 121 full-time (38 women). Expenses: Contact institution. *Financial support:* In 2016–17, 194 students received support. Fellowships with tuition reimbursements available, teaching assistantships with tuition reimbursements available, career-related internships or fieldwork, Federal Work-Study, institutionally sponsored loans, and tuition waivers (partial) available. Financial award application deadline: 4/1. In 2016, 767 master's, 14 doctorates, 18 other advanced degrees awarded. *Program availability:* Part-time, evening/weekend, online learning. Offers accountancy (M Accy); business (M Accy, MBA, MS, MSF, MSIST, MTA, PMBA, PhD, Certificate, Professional Certificate); business administration (MBA); business analytics (MS, Certificate); destination management (Professional Certificate); event and meeting management (MTA); event management (Professional Certificate); finance (MSF, PhD); finance and investments (MBA); government contracts (MS); hospitality management (MTA); individualized studies (MTA); information and decision systems (PhD); information systems (MSIST); information systems development (MSIST); information systems management (MBA); information systems project management (MSIST); international business (PhD); management information systems (MSIST); management of science, technology, and innovation (MBA, PhD); marketing (MBA, PhD); project management (MS); sport management (MTA); strategic management and public policy (MBA, PhD); sustainable tourism destination management (MTA); tourism and hospitality management (MBA); walkable urban real estate development (Professional Certificate). PMBA also offered in Alexandria and Ashburn, VA. *Application deadline:* For fall admission, 4/1 priority date for domestic students; for spring admission, 10/1 for domestic students. Applications are processed on a rolling basis. *Application fee:* $75. Electronic applications accepted. *Application Contact:* Christopher Storer, Executive Director, Graduate Admissions, 202-994-1212, E-mail: gwmba@gwu.edu. *Dean,* Dr. Linda Livingstone.

School of Engineering and Applied Science Students: 758 full-time (191 women), 1,081 part-time (321 women); includes 409 minority (202 Black or African American, non-Hispanic/Latino; 2 American Indian or Alaska Native, non-Hispanic/Latino; 132 Asian, non-Hispanic/Latino; 53 Hispanic/Latino; 5 Native Hawaiian or other Pacific Islander, non-Hispanic/Latino; 15 Two or more races, non-Hispanic/Latino), 812 international. Average age 32. 2,657 applicants, 74% accepted, 613 enrolled. *Faculty:* 91 full-time (18 women). Expenses: Contact institution. *Financial support:* In 2016–17, 216 students received support. Fellowships with tuition reimbursements available, research assistantships with tuition reimbursements available, teaching assistantships with tuition reimbursements available, career-related internships or fieldwork, Federal Work-Study, institutionally sponsored loans, and tuition waivers (full and partial) available. Financial award application deadline: 3/1; financial award applicants required to submit FAFSA. In 2016, 449 master's, 69 doctorates, 31 other advanced degrees awarded. *Program availability:* Part-time, evening/weekend. Offers biomedical engineering (MS, PhD); civil and environmental engineering (MS, PhD, App Sc, Engr, Graduate Certificate); computer science (MS, D Sc); cybersecurity (MS); electrical engineering (MS, PhD); engineering and applied science (MS, D Sc, PhD, App Sc, Engr, Graduate Certificate); mechanical and aerospace engineering (MS, PhD, App Sc, Engr, Graduate Certificate); regulatory biomedical engineering (MS); system engineering (PhD); telecommunication and computers (MS). *Application deadline:* For fall admission, 3/1 for domestic students; for spring admission, 10/1 for domestic students. Applications are processed on a rolling basis. *Application fee:* $75. *Application Contact:* Adina Lav,

Marketing, Recruiting and Admissions, 202-994-5827, Fax: 202-994-0909, E-mail: engineering@gwu.edu. *Dean,* David S. Dolling, 202-994-6080, E-mail: dolling@gwu.edu.

School of Medicine and Health Sciences Students: 1,012 full-time (633 women), 448 part-time (336 women); includes 558 minority (150 Black or African American, non-Hispanic/Latino; 5 American Indian or Alaska Native, non-Hispanic/Latino; 249 Asian, non-Hispanic/Latino; 125 Hispanic/Latino; 6 Native Hawaiian or other Pacific Islander, non-Hispanic/Latino; 23 Two or more races, non-Hispanic/Latino), 40 international. Average age 30. 2,315 applicants, 21% accepted, 299 enrolled. *Faculty:* 1,387 full-time (745 women). Expenses: Contact institution. *Financial support:* Career-related internships or fieldwork, Federal Work-Study, and institutionally sponsored loans available. In 2016, 185 master's, 40 doctorates, 181 other advanced degrees awarded. Offers clinical practice management (MSHS); clinical research administration (MSHS); emergency services management (MSHS); end-of-life care (MSHS); immunohematology (MSHS); immunohematology and biotechnology (MSHS); medicine (MD); medicine and health sciences (MSHS, DPT, MD, OTD, Graduate Certificate); physical therapy (DPT); physician assistant (MSHS). *Application deadline:* Applications are processed on a rolling basis. *Application fee:* $75. *Application Contact:* Admissions, 202-994-3748, Fax: 202-994-1753, E-mail: medadmit@gwu.edu. *Dean,* Dr. Jeffrey Akman, 202-994-3727, E-mail: akman@gwu.edu.

School of Nursing Students: 53 full-time (47 women), 515 part-time (467 women); includes 177 minority (80 Black or African American, non-Hispanic/Latino; 4 American Indian or Alaska Native, non-Hispanic/Latino; 64 Asian, non-Hispanic/Latino; 23 Hispanic/Latino; 6 Two or more races, non-Hispanic/Latino). Average age 35. 437 applicants, 68% accepted, 174 enrolled. *Faculty:* 43 full-time (42 women). Expenses: Contact institution. In 2016, 135 master's, 35 doctorates awarded. Offers adult nurse practitioner (MSN, DNP, Post-Master's Certificate); clinical research administration (MSN); family nurse practitioner (MSN, Post-Master's Certificate); health care quality (MSN, Post-Master's Certificate); nursing leadership and management (MSN); nursing practice (DNP); palliative care nurse practitioner (Post-Master's Certificate). *Application Contact:* Kristin Williams, Associate Provost for Graduate Enrollment Management, 202-994-0467, Fax: 202-994-0371, E-mail: ksw@gwu.edu. *Dean,* Pamela R. Jeffries, 202-994-3725, E-mail: pjeffries@gwu.edu.

GEORGIA CAMPUS–PHILADELPHIA COLLEGE OF OSTEOPATHIC MEDICINE, Suwanee, GA 30024

General Information Independent, coed, graduate-only institution. *Enrollment by degree level:* 167 master's, 916 doctoral. *Graduate faculty:* 29 full-time (12 women), 174 part-time/adjunct (99 women). Tuition and fees vary according to degree level and program. *Graduate housing:* On-campus housing not available. *Student services:* Campus employment opportunities, campus safety program, career counseling, exercise/wellness program, free psychological counseling, multicultural affairs office, services for students with disabilities. *Collection:* Study areas open 24 hours, 5–7 days a week.

Website: http://www.pcom.edu/General_Information/georgia/georgia.html

General Application Contact: Craig Brown, Director of Admissions, 678-225-7500, E-mail: craigbro@pcom.edu.

GRADUATE UNITS

Doctor of Osteopathic Medicine Program Students: 534 full-time (275 women); includes 292 minority (62 Black or African American, non-Hispanic/Latino; 43 Asian, non-Hispanic/Latino; 21 Hispanic/Latino; 166 Two or more races, non-Hispanic/Latino), 6 international. 4,920 applicants, 5% accepted, 135 enrolled. Expenses: Contact institution. *Financial support:* Federal Work-Study and scholarships/grants available. Financial award application deadline: 3/15; financial award applicants required to submit FAFSA. Offers osteopathic medicine (DO). *Application deadline:* For fall admission, 3/1 for domestic and international students. Applications are processed on a rolling basis. *Application fee:* $75. Electronic applications accepted. *Application Contact:* Craig Brown, Director of Admissions, 678-225-7500, E-mail: craigbro@pcom.edu. *Dean and Chief Academic Officer,* Dr. H. William Craver, 678-225-7504, E-mail: williamcr@pcom.edu.

School of Pharmacy Students: 382 full-time (212 women); includes 254 minority (91 Black or African American, non-Hispanic/Latino; 15 Asian, non-Hispanic/Latino; 1 Hispanic/Latino; 147 Two or more races, non-Hispanic/Latino), 8 international. Average age 27. 799 applicants, 27% accepted, 88 enrolled. *Faculty:* 29 full-time (12 women), 174 part-time/adjunct (99 women). Expenses: Contact institution. *Financial support:* Federal Work-Study, institutionally sponsored loans, and scholarships/grants available. Financial award application deadline: 3/15; financial award applicants required to submit FAFSA. Offers pharmacy (Pharm D). *Application deadline:* For fall admission, 3/1 for domestic students. Applications are processed on a rolling basis. Electronic applications accepted. *Application Contact:* Marsha Williams, Associate Director of Admissions, 215-871-6700, E-mail: marshawi@pcom.edu. *Dean,* Dr. Mark Okamoto, 678-407-7330, Fax: 678-407-7339.

GEORGIA CHRISTIAN UNIVERSITY, Atlanta, GA 30360

General Information Independent-religious, coed, comprehensive institution.

GRADUATE UNITS

School of Business Offers business (MBA).

School of Divinity Offers Christian education (MA); divinity (M Div); ministry (D Min); mission studies and world Christianity (MA); theological studies (MA).

School of Music Offers music (MA).

GEORGIA COLLEGE & STATE UNIVERSITY, Milledgeville, GA 31061

General Information State-supported, coed, comprehensive institution. *Enrollment:* 6,915 graduate, professional, and undergraduate students; 289 full-time matriculated graduate/professional students (201 women), 557 part-time matriculated graduate/professional students (363 women). *Enrollment by degree level:* 680 master's, 24 doctoral, 142 other advanced degrees. *Graduate faculty:* 336 full-time (185 women). Tuition, state resident: full-time $5184; part-time $288 per credit hour. Tuition, nonresident: full-time $18,486; part-time $1027 per credit hour. Tuition and fees vary according to course load, degree level and program. *Graduate housing:* Room and/or apartments available on a first-come, first-served basis to single students; on-campus housing not available to married students. Typical cost: $6400 per year ($11,946 including board). Room and board charges vary according to board plan, campus/location and housing facility selected. Housing application deadline: 5/1. *Student services:* Campus employment opportunities, campus safety program, career counseling, free psychological counseling, grant writing training, international student services, low-cost health insurance, multicultural affairs office, services for students with disabilities, teacher training, writing training. *Library facilities:* Ina Dillard Russell Library plus 1 other. *Collection:* Books: 184,103 (physical), 597,074 (digital/electronic); Serial titles: 5,556 (physical), 162,750 (digital/electronic); Databases: 376. Weekly public service hours: 102; students can reserve study rooms.

Computer facilities: 900 computers available on campus for general student use. A campuswide network can be accessed from student residence rooms and from off campus. Online class registration is available.
Website: http://www.gcsu.edu/

General Application Contact: Kate Marshall, Graduate Admissions Coordinator, 478-445-1184, Fax: 478-445-1336, E-mail: grad-admit@gcsu.edu.

GRADUATE UNITS

Graduate School Students: 289 full-time (201 women), 557 part-time (363 women); includes 276 minority (209 Black or African American, non-Hispanic/Latino; 21 Asian, non-Hispanic/Latino; 28 Hispanic/Latino; 1 Native Hawaiian or other Pacific Islander, non-Hispanic/Latino; 17 Two or more races, non-Hispanic/Latino, 10 international. Average age 34. 362 applicants, 90% accepted, 242 enrolled. Expenses: Contact institution. *Financial support:* Scholarships/grants and unspecified assistantships available. Financial award application deadline: 3/1; financial award applicants required to submit FAFSA. In 2016, 348 master's, 9 doctorates, 78 other advanced degrees awarded. *Program availability:* Part-time, evening/weekend, 100% online. *Application deadline:* For fall admission, 7/1 priority date for domestic students, 4/1 priority date for international students; for spring admission, 11/1 priority date for domestic students, 9/1 priority date for international students; for summer admission, 4/1 priority date for domestic students. Applications are processed on a rolling basis. *Application fee:* $40. Electronic applications accepted. *Application Contact:* Kate Marshall, Graduate Admissions Coordinator, 478-445-1184, Fax: 478-445-1336, E-mail: grad-admit@gcsu.edu. *Associate Provost/Dean of Graduate Studies,* Dr. Costas Spirou, 478-445-4715, Fax: 478-445-5151, E-mail: costas.spirou@gcsu.edu.

College of Arts and Sciences Students: 66 full-time (53 women), 91 part-time (58 women); includes 45 minority (30 Black or African American, non-Hispanic/Latino; 4 Asian, non-Hispanic/Latino; 5 Hispanic/Latino; 6 Two or more races, non-Hispanic/Latino, 3 international. Average age 30. 104 applicants, 77% accepted, 57 enrolled. *Faculty:* 195 full-time (95 women). Expenses: Contact institution. *Financial support:* Unspecified assistantships available. Support available to part-time students. Financial award application deadline: 3/1; financial award applicants required to submit FAFSA. In 2016, 48 master's awarded. *Program availability:* Part-time, evening/weekend, 100% online. Offers arts and sciences (MA, MFA, MM Ed, MPA, MS, MSCJ); biology (MS); creative writing (MFA); criminal justice (MSCJ); English (MA); history, geography, and philosophy (MA); music (MM Ed); public administration (MPA). *Application deadline:* For fall admission, 7/1 priority date for domestic students, 4/1 priority date for international students; for spring admission, 11/1 priority date for domestic students, 9/1 priority date for international students; for summer admission, 4/1 priority date for domestic students. Applications are processed on a rolling basis. *Application fee:* $40. Electronic applications accepted. *Application Contact:* Kate Marshall, Graduate Admissions Coordinator, 478-445-1184, Fax: 478-445-1336, E-mail: grad-admit@gcsu.edu. *Dean,* Kenneth Proctor, 478-445-4441, E-mail: ken.proctor@gcsu.edu.

College of Health Sciences Students: 62 full-time (39 women), 139 part-time (127 women); includes 54 minority (42 Black or African American, non-Hispanic/Latino; 4 Asian, non-Hispanic/Latino; 8 Hispanic/Latino), 2 international. Average age 34. 45 applicants, 100% accepted, 36 enrolled. Expenses: Contact institution. *Financial support:* In 2016–17, 35 students received support. Unspecified assistantships available. Support available to part-time students. Financial award application deadline: 3/1; financial award applicants required to submit FAFSA. In 2016, 72 master's, 8 doctorates awarded. *Program availability:* Part-time, evening/weekend. Offers art therapy (MA); health and human performance (MS); health sciences (M Ed, MA, MAT, MMT, MS, MSN, DNP); kinesiology/health education (MAT); music therapy (MMT); nursing (MSN); nursing practice (DNP). *Application deadline:* For fall admission, 7/1 priority date for domestic students, 4/1 priority date for international students; for spring admission, 11/1 priority date for domestic students, 9/1 priority date for international students; for summer admission, 4/1 priority date for domestic students. Applications are processed on a rolling basis. *Application fee:* $40. Electronic applications accepted. *Application Contact:* Kate Marshall, Graduate Admissions Coordinator, 478-445-1184, Fax: 478-445-1336, E-mail: grad-admit@gcsu.edu. *Dean,* Dr. Sandra Gangstead, 478-445-4092, E-mail: sandra.gangstead@gcsu.edu.

The John H. Lounsbury College of Education Students: 140 full-time (98 women), 144 part-time (111 women); includes 115 minority (101 Black or African American, non-Hispanic/Latino; 2 Asian, non-Hispanic/Latino; 5 Hispanic/Latino; 7 Two or more races, non-Hispanic/Latino). Average age 35. 87 applicants, 100% accepted, 66 enrolled. Expenses: Contact institution. *Financial support:* In 2016–17, 9 students received support. Unspecified assistantships available. Support available to part-time students. Financial award application deadline: 3/1; financial award applicants required to submit FAFSA. In 2016, 108 master's, 82 other advanced degrees awarded. *Program availability:* Part-time, 100% online, blended/hybrid learning. Offers early childhood education (M Ed); education (M Ed, MAT, Ed S); educational leadership (Ed S); library media (M Ed); reading, literacy, and language (M Ed); secondary education (MAT); special education (M Ed, MAT, Ed S). *Application deadline:* For fall admission, 7/1 priority date for domestic students; for spring admission, 11/1 priority date for domestic students; for summer admission, 4/1 priority date for domestic students. Applications are processed on a rolling basis. *Application fee:* $40. Electronic applications accepted. *Application Contact:* Shanda Brand, Graduate Admissions Advisor, 478-445-1383, Fax: 478-445-6582, E-mail: shanda.brand@gcsu.edu. *Dean, College of Education,* Dr. Joseph Peters, 478-445-2518, Fax: 478-445-6582, E-mail: joseph.peters@gcsu.edu.

The J. Whitney Bunting School of Business Students: 21 full-time (11 women), 183 part-time (67 women); includes 62 minority (36 Black or African American, non-Hispanic/Latino; 11 Asian, non-Hispanic/Latino; 10 Hispanic/Latino; 1 Native Hawaiian or other Pacific Islander, non-Hispanic/Latino; 4 Two or more races, non-Hispanic/Latino), 5 international. Average age 34. 117 applicants, 91% accepted, 80 enrolled. Expenses: Contact institution. *Financial support:* In 2016–17, 19 students received support. Unspecified assistantships available. Financial award application deadline: 3/1; financial award applicants required to submit FAFSA. In 2016, 130 master's awarded. *Program availability:* Part-time, evening/weekend, 100% online, blended/hybrid learning. Offers accounting (M Acc); business (M Acc, MBA, MLSCM, MMIS); business administration (MBA); logistics (MLSCM); management information systems (MMIS). *Application deadline:* For fall admission, 7/1 priority date for domestic students, 4/1 priority date for international students; for spring admission, 11/1 priority date for domestic students, 8/1 priority date for international students; for summer admission, 4/1 priority date for domestic students. Applications are

processed on a rolling basis. *Application fee:* $40. Electronic applications accepted. *Application Contact:* Lynn Hanson, Director of Graduate Programs, 478-445-5115, E-mail: lynn.hanson@gcsu.edu. *Dean, School of Business,* Dr. Dale Young, 478-445-5497, E-mail: dael.young@gcsu.edu.

GEORGIA INSTITUTE OF TECHNOLOGY, Atlanta, GA 30332-0001

General Information State-supported, coed, university. CGS member. *Enrollment:* 26,839 graduate, professional, and undergraduate students; 6,237 full-time matriculated graduate/professional students (1,799 women), 5,046 part-time matriculated graduate/professional students (798 women). *Enrollment by degree level:* 7,868 master's, 3,415 doctoral. *Graduate faculty:* 1,054 full-time (266 women), 99 part-time/adjunct (36 women). *Graduate housing:* Rooms and/or apartments available on a first-come, first-served basis to single and married students. Housing application deadline: 6/1. *Student services:* Campus employment opportunities, campus safety program, career counseling, child daycare facilities, exercise/wellness program, free psychological counseling, grant writing training, international student services, low-cost health insurance, multicultural affairs office, services for students with disabilities, teacher training, writing training. *Library facilities:* Georgia Institute of Technology Library plus 1 other. *Collection:* Books: 931,886 (physical), 632,320 (digital/electronic); Serial titles: 361 (physical), 27,533 (digital/electronic); Databases: 314. Weekly public service hours: 168; study areas open 24 hours, 5–7 days a week; students can reserve study rooms. *Research affiliation:* Oak Ridge National Laboratory (energy, health, environment), Children's Healthcare of Atlanta (pediatric biomedical and device research), Georgia State University (brain imaging), Southeastern Universities Research Association (high-energy physics), Emory University Medical School (biomedical engineering), Zoo Atlanta (environmental design, environmental psychology).

Computer facilities: 2,500 computers available on campus for general student use. A campuswide network can be accessed from student residence rooms and from off campus. Online class registration, constant access to a virtual lab environment from a personal device or GT account are available.
Website: http://www.gatech.edu/

General Application Contact: David Bamburowski, Director of Graduate Studies, 404-894-1610, E-mail: gradinfo@mail.gatech.edu.

GRADUATE UNITS

Graduate Studies *Program availability:* Part-time, evening/weekend, online learning. Offers algorithms, combinatorics, and optimization (PhD); analytics (MS); bioengineering (MS, PhD); bioinformatics (MS, PhD); computational science and engineering (MS, PhD); human computer interaction (MS); paper science and engineering (MS, PhD); quantitative and computational finance (MS); statistics (MS). Electronic applications accepted.

College of Architecture Offers architecture (M Arch, MCRP, MS, PhD); building construction (PhD); city and regional planning (PhD); economic development (MCRP); environmental planning and management (MCRP); geographic information systems (MCRP); industrial design (MID); integrated facility and property management (MS); integrated project delivery systems (MS); land and community development (MCRP); land use planning (MCRP); music technology (MS, PhD); program management (MS); residential construction development (MS); transportation (MCRP); urban design (MCRP). Electronic applications accepted.

College of Computing *Program availability:* Part-time, online learning. Offers computer science (MS, PhD); computing (MS, PhD); human-centered computing (MS, PhD); information security (MS); robotics (PhD). Electronic applications accepted.

College of Engineering *Program availability:* Part-time, online learning. Offers aerospace engineering (MS, PhD); applied systems engineering (PMS); biomedical engineering (PhD); chemical engineering (MS, PhD); civil engineering (MS, PhD); electrical and computer engineering (MS, PhD); engineering (MS, MSMP, MSNE, PhD); engineering science and mechanics (MS, PhD); environmental engineering (MS); health systems (MS); industrial and systems engineering (MS, PhD); industrial engineering (MS, PhD); international logistics (MS); materials science and engineering (MS, PhD); mechanical engineering (MS, MSME, MSMP, MSNE, PhD); medical physics (MS, MSMP); nuclear and radiological engineering (PhD); nuclear and radiological engineering and medical physics (MS, MSMP, MSNE, PhD); nuclear engineering (MSNE); operations research (MS, PhD). Electronic applications accepted.

College of Sciences *Program availability:* Part-time. Offers applied physiology (PhD); biology (MS, PhD); chemistry and biochemistry (MS, PhD); earth and atmospheric sciences (MS, PhD); mathematics (MS, PhD); physics (MS, PhD); prosthetics and orthotics (MS); psychology (MS, PhD); sciences (MS, PhD). Electronic applications accepted.

Ivan Allen College of Liberal Arts *Program availability:* Part-time. Offers digital media (MS, PhD); economics (MS, PhD); history and sociology of technology and science (MS, PhD); international affairs (MS); liberal arts (MS, PhD); public policy (MS, PhD). Electronic applications accepted.

Scheller College of Business *Program availability:* Part-time, evening/weekend. Offers business (MBA, MS, PhD); business administration (MBA); global business (MBA); management (MS, PhD); management of technology (MBA). Electronic applications accepted.

GEORGIAN COURT UNIVERSITY, Lakewood, NJ 08701-2697

General Information Independent-religious, coed, comprehensive institution. *Enrollment:* 2,302 graduate, professional, and undergraduate students; 185 full-time matriculated graduate/professional students (152 women), 523 part-time matriculated graduate/professional students (417 women). *Enrollment by degree level:* 521 master's, 187 other advanced degrees. *Graduate faculty:* 40 full-time (22 women), 48 part-time/adjunct (25 women). *Tuition:* Full-time $15,079; part-time $839 per credit. *Required fees:* $968; $496 per credit. Tuition and fees vary according to campus/location and program. *Graduate housing:* On-campus housing not available. *Student services:* Campus employment opportunities, campus safety program, career counseling, exercise/wellness program, free psychological counseling, low-cost health insurance, services for students with disabilities, teacher training. *Library facilities:* The Sister Mary Joseph Cunningham Library. *Collection:* Books: 129,114 (physical), 85,957 (digital/electronic); Serial titles: 2,709 (physical), 31,176 (digital/electronic); Databases: 119. Weekly public service hours: 85; students can reserve study rooms.

Computer facilities: 221 computers available on campus for general student use. A campuswide network can be accessed from student residence rooms and from off campus. Online class registration is available.
Website: http://www.georgian.edu/

General Application Contact: Patrick Givens, Director of Graduate and Professional Studies Admissions, 732-987-2736, Fax: 732-987-2000, E-mail: gps@georgian.edu.

Georgian Court University

GRADUATE UNITS

School of Arts and Sciences Students: 90 full-time (75 women), 107 part-time (79 women); includes 34 minority (9 Black or African American, non-Hispanic/Latino; 20 Hispanic/Latino; 5 Two or more races, non-Hispanic/Latino), 1 international. Average age 34. 187 applicants, 49% accepted, 60 enrolled. *Faculty:* 19 full-time (11 women), 6 part-time/adjunct (3 women). Expenses: Contact institution. *Financial support:* Scholarships/grants, health care benefits, and unspecified assistantships available. Financial award application deadline: 4/15; financial award applicants required to submit FAFSA. In 2016, 66 master's, 17 other advanced degrees awarded. *Program availability:* Part-time, evening/weekend. Offers applied behavior analysis (MA); clinical mental health counseling (MA); holistic health studies (MA, Certificate); homeland security (MS, Certificate); mercy spirituality (Certificate); parish business management (Certificate); professional counselor (Certificate); school psychology (MA, Certificate); theology (MA, Certificate). *Application deadline:* For fall admission, 8/15 for domestic students, 5/1 for international students; for spring admission, 1/15 for domestic students, 10/1 for international students. Applications are processed on a rolling basis. *Application fee:* $40. Electronic applications accepted. *Application Contact:* Patrick Givens, Director of Graduate and Professional Studies Admissions, 732-987-2736, Fax: 732-987-2000, E-mail: gps@georgian.edu. *Dean,* Dr. Mary Chinery, 732-987-2493, Fax: 732-987-2007, E-mail: mchinery@georgian.edu.

School of Business and Digital Media Students: 29 full-time (22 women), 40 part-time (26 women); includes 22 minority (7 Black or African American, non-Hispanic/Latino; 2 Asian, non-Hispanic/Latino; 9 Hispanic/Latino; 4 Two or more races, non-Hispanic/Latino). Average age 31. 55 applicants, 49% accepted, 13 enrolled. *Faculty:* 7 full-time (3 women), 11 part-time/adjunct (4 women). Expenses: Contact institution. *Financial support:* Scholarships/grants, health care benefits, and unspecified assistantships available. Financial award application deadline: 4/15; financial award applicants required to submit FAFSA. In 2016, 34 master's, 3 other advanced degrees awarded. *Program availability:* Part-time, evening/weekend. Offers business (MBA); business essentials (Certificate); nonprofit management (Certificate). *Application deadline:* For fall admission, 8/15 priority date for domestic students, 5/1 for international students; for spring admission, 1/15 priority date for domestic students, 10/1 for international students. Applications are processed on a rolling basis. *Application fee:* $40. Electronic applications accepted. *Application Contact:* Patrick Givens, Director of Graduate and Professional Studies Admissions, 732-987-2736, Fax: 732-987-2000, E-mail: gps@georgian.edu. *Dean,* Dr. Janice Warner, 732-987-2662, Fax: 732-987-2024, E-mail: jwarner@georgian.edu.

School of Education Students: 66 full-time (55 women), 376 part-time (312 women); includes 92 minority (44 Black or African American, non-Hispanic/Latino; 1 American Indian or Alaska Native, non-Hispanic/Latino; 8 Asian, non-Hispanic/Latino; 34 Hispanic/Latino; 5 Two or more races, non-Hispanic/Latino). Average age 34. 409 applicants, 62% accepted, 174 enrolled. *Faculty:* 14 full-time (8 women), 31 part-time/adjunct (18 women). Expenses: Contact institution. *Financial support:* Scholarships/grants, health care benefits, and unspecified assistantships available. Financial award application deadline: 4/15; financial award applicants required to submit FAFSA. In 2016, 95 master's, 1 other advanced degree awarded. *Program availability:* Part-time, evening/weekend. Offers administration and leadership (MA); autism spectrum disorders (Certificate; education (MA); instructional technology (Certificate). *Application deadline:* For fall admission, 8/15 priority date for domestic students, 5/1 for international students; for spring admission, 1/15 priority date for domestic students, 10/1 for international students. Applications are processed on a rolling basis. *Application fee:* $40. Electronic applications accepted. *Application Contact:* Patrick Givens, Director of Graduate and Professional Studies Admissions, 732-987-2736, Fax: 732-987-2000, E-mail: gps@georgian.edu. *Dean,* Dr. Lynn DeCapua, 732-987-2729, E-mail: ldecapua@georgian.edu.

GEORGIA SOUTHERN UNIVERSITY, Statesboro, GA 30458

General Information State-supported, coed, university. CGS member. *Enrollment:* 20,673 graduate, professional, and undergraduate students; 1,132 full-time matriculated graduate/professional students (717 women), 1,470 part-time matriculated graduate/professional students (1,024 women). *Enrollment by degree level:* 1,842 master's, 523 doctoral, 237 other advanced degrees. *Graduate faculty:* 610 full-time (256 women), 36 part-time/adjunct (17 women). Tuition, state resident: full-time $7236; part-time $277 per semester hour. Tuition, nonresident: full-time $27,118; part-time $1105 per semester hour. *Required fees:* $2092. *Graduate housing:* Room and/or apartments available on a first-come, first-served basis to single students; on-campus housing not available to married students. Typical cost: $6050 per year ($9800 including board). Room and board charges vary according to board plan and housing facility selected. Housing application deadline: 5/1. *Student services:* Campus employment opportunities, campus safety program, exercise/wellness program, free psychological counseling, grant writing training, international student services, low-cost health insurance, multicultural affairs office, services for students with disabilities, teacher training, writing training. *Library facilities:* Henderson Library. *Collection:* Books: 657,965 (physical), 30,602 (digital/electronic); Serial titles: 435 (physical), 84,081 (digital/electronic); Databases: 369. Weekly public service hours: 143; study areas open 24 hours, 5–7 days a week; students can reserve study rooms. *Research affiliation:* Oak Ridge National Laboratory (physical sciences), Mount Desert Island Biological Laboratory (marine biology), Space Telescope Science Institute (astronomy, physics), St. Catherine's Island Foundation (marine science, life sciences), Skidaway Institute of Oceanography (marine sciences).

Computer facilities: Computer purchase and lease plans are available. 3,743 computers available on campus for general student use. A campuswide network can be accessed from student residence rooms and from off campus. Online class registration, online degree audit, online career services, and online healthcare are available. Website: http://www.georgiasouthern.edu/

General Application Contact: Naronda Wright, Office of Graduate Admissions, 912-478-5384, Fax: 912-478-0740, E-mail: gradadmissions@georgiasouthern.edu.

GRADUATE UNITS

Jack N. Averitt College of Graduate Studies Students: 1,132 full-time (717 women), 1,470 part-time (1,024 women); includes 809 minority (626 Black or African American, non-Hispanic/Latino; 1 American Indian or Alaska Native, non-Hispanic/Latino; 41 Asian, non-Hispanic/Latino; 98 Hispanic/Latino; 43 Two or more races, non-Hispanic/Latino; 148 international. Average age 31. 1,665 applicants, 75% accepted, 757 enrolled. *Faculty:* 610 full-time (256 women), 36 part-time/adjunct (17 women). Expenses: Contact institution. *Financial support:* In 2016–17, 670 students received support, including 192 research assistantships with partial tuition reimbursements available (averaging $7,750 per year), teaching assistantships with partial tuition reimbursements available (averaging $7,750 per year); career-related internships or fieldwork, Federal Work-Study, scholarships/grants, traineeships, tuition waivers (partial), unspecified assistantships, and doctoral stipends also available. Support

available to part-time students. Financial award application deadline: 4/15; financial award applicants required to submit FAFSA. In 2016, 801 master's, 50 doctorates, 85 other advanced degrees awarded. *Program availability:* Part-time, evening/weekend, 100% online, blended/hybrid learning. *Application deadline:* For fall admission, 4/1 priority date for domestic and international students; for spring admission, 10/1 priority date for domestic students, 10/1 for international students. Applications are processed on a rolling basis. *Application fee:* $50. Electronic applications accepted. *Application Contact:* Naronda C. Wright, Graduate Admissions Specialist, 912-478-5384, Fax: 912-478-0740, E-mail: gradadmissions@georgiasouthern.edu. *Interim Director, College of Graduate Studies,* Dr. Ashley Walker Colquitt, 912-478-0851, Fax: 912-478-8642, E-mail: awalker@georgiasouthern.edu.

Allen E. Paulson College of Engineering and Information Technology Students: 81 full-time (15 women), 61 part-time (12 women); includes 46 minority (34 Black or African American, non-Hispanic/Latino; 5 Asian, non-Hispanic/Latino; 6 Hispanic/Latino; 1 Two or more races, non-Hispanic/Latino), 42 international. Average age 29. 146 applicants, 77% accepted, 51 enrolled. *Faculty:* 54 full-time (5 women), 1 part-time/adjunct (0 women). Expenses: Contact institution. *Financial support:* In 2016–17, 8 students received support, including 3 research assistantships with full tuition reimbursements available (averaging $7,750 per year), 4 teaching assistantships with full tuition reimbursements available (averaging $7,750 per year); Federal Work-Study, scholarships/grants, tuition waivers (full), and unspecified assistantships also available. Financial award applicants required to submit FAFSA. In 2016, 30 master's awarded. *Program availability:* Part-time, online learning. Offers civil engineering and construction management (MSAE); computer science (MS); electrical and electronic systems (MSAE); engineering and information technology (MS, MSAE, Graduate Certificate); engineering and manufacturing management (Graduate Certificate); engineering/energy science (MSAE); engineering/engineering management (MSAE); engineering/mechatronics (MSAE); information technology (MSAE); occupational safety and environmental compliance (Graduate Certificate); occupational safety and environmental science (Graduate Certificate). *Application fee:* $50. *Dean,* Dr. Mohammad S. Davoud, 912-478-8046, E-mail: mdavoud@georgiasouthern.edu.

College of Business Administration Students: 113 full-time (57 women), 232 part-time (98 women); includes 90 minority (64 Black or African American, non-Hispanic/Latino; 8 Asian, non-Hispanic/Latino; 14 Hispanic/Latino; 4 Two or more races, non-Hispanic/Latino), 25 international. Average age 31. 261 applicants, 77% accepted, 139 enrolled. *Faculty:* 72 full-time (18 women), 1 part-time/adjunct (0 women). Expenses: Contact institution. *Financial support:* In 2016–17, 51 students received support. Research assistantships with partial tuition reimbursements available, teaching assistantships with partial tuition reimbursements available, career-related internships or fieldwork, Federal Work-Study, scholarships/grants, tuition waivers (partial), and unspecified assistantships available. Support available to part-time students. Financial award application deadline: 4/15; financial award applicants required to submit FAFSA. In 2016, 147 master's, 2 doctorates, 8 other advanced degrees awarded. *Program availability:* Part-time, evening/weekend, blended/hybrid learning. Offers applied economics (MS); business administration (M Acc, MBA, MS, PhD, Graduate Certificate); enterprise resources planning (Graduate Certificate); forensic accounting (M Acc); information systems (Graduate Certificate); logistics/supply chain management (PhD); taxation (M Acc). *Application deadline:* For fall admission, 3/1 priority date for domestic and international students; for spring admission, 10/1 priority date for domestic students, 10/1 for international students. Applications are processed on a rolling basis. *Application fee:* $50. Electronic applications accepted. *Dean,* Dr. Allen Amason, 912-478-2622, Fax: 912-478-0292, E-mail: aamason@georgiasouthern.edu.

College of Education Students: 322 full-time (271 women), 900 part-time (713 women); includes 374 minority (314 Black or African American, non-Hispanic/Latino; 1 American Indian or Alaska Native, non-Hispanic/Latino; 4 Asian, non-Hispanic/Latino; 36 Hispanic/Latino; 19 Two or more races, non-Hispanic/Latino), 7 international. Average age 33. 385 applicants, 88% accepted, 216 enrolled. *Faculty:* 80 full-time (55 women), 21 part-time/adjunct (11 women). Expenses: Contact institution. *Financial support:* In 2016–17, 103 students received support, including 1 teaching assistantship with full tuition reimbursement available (averaging $7,750 per year); research assistantships with partial tuition reimbursements available, career-related internships or fieldwork, Federal Work-Study, scholarships/grants, tuition waivers (full), unspecified assistantships, and doctoral stipends also available. Support available to part-time students. Financial award application deadline: 4/15; financial award applicants required to submit FAFSA. In 2016, 334 master's, 30 doctorates, 55 other advanced degrees awarded. *Program availability:* Part-time, evening/weekend, blended/hybrid learning. Offers counselor education (M Ed, Ed S); curriculum and instruction - accomplished teaching (M Ed); curriculum studies (Ed D); early childhood education (M Ed, MAT, Ed S); education (M Ed, MAT, Ed D, Ed S); educational leadership (M Ed, Ed D); English education (MAT); evaluation, assessment, research, and learning (M Ed); higher education (M Ed); higher education administration (M Ed); higher education leadership (Ed D); instructional technology (M Ed, Ed S); middle grades education (Ed S); P-12 leadership (M Ed, Ed D, Ed S); reading education (M Ed, Ed S); school library media (M Ed, Ed S); school psychology (M Ed, Ed S); secondary education (M Ed, MAT, Ed S); Spanish P-12 education (MAT); special education (Ed S). *Application deadline:* For fall admission, 3/1 priority date for domestic and international students; for spring admission, 10/1 priority date for domestic students, 10/1 for international students. Applications are processed on a rolling basis. *Application fee:* $50. Electronic applications accepted. *Dean,* Dr. Thomas Koballa, 912-478-5648, Fax: 912-478-5093, E-mail: tkoballa@georgiasouthern.edu.

College of Health and Human Sciences Students: 129 full-time (89 women), 120 part-time (84 women); includes 65 minority (44 Black or African American, non-Hispanic/Latino; 5 Asian, non-Hispanic/Latino; 13 Hispanic/Latino; 3 Two or more races, non-Hispanic/Latino), 5 international. Average age 31. 263 applicants, 57% accepted, 98 enrolled. *Faculty:* 72 full-time (47 women), 2 part-time/adjunct (both women). Expenses: Contact institution. *Financial support:* In 2016–17, 73 students received support, including 24 fellowships with full tuition reimbursements available (averaging $7,750 per year), 9 research assistantships with full tuition reimbursements available (averaging $7,750 per year), 33 teaching assistantships with full tuition reimbursements available (averaging $7,750 per year); career-related internships or fieldwork, Federal Work-Study, scholarships/grants, traineeships, tuition waivers (full), and unspecified assistantships also available. Support available to part-time students. Financial award application deadline: 4/15; financial award applicants required to submit FAFSA. In 2016, 99 master's, 16 doctorates, 3 other advanced degrees awarded. *Program availability:* Part-time, evening/weekend, blended/hybrid learning. Offers dietetics (Certificate); family nurse practitioner (MSN); health and human sciences (MS, MSN, DNP, Certificate); kinesiology (MS); nurse educator

(Certificate); nurse practitioner (MSN); nursing science (DNP); psychiatric mental health nurse practitioner (MSN); sport management (MS). *Application deadline:* For fall admission, 3/1 priority date for domestic students, 3/1 for international students; for spring admission, 10/1 priority date for domestic students, 10/1 for international students. Applications are processed on a rolling basis. *Application fee:* $50. Electronic applications accepted. *Dean,* Dr. Barry Joyner, 912-478-5322, Fax: 912-478-5349, E-mail: joyner@georgiasouthern.edu.

College of Liberal Arts and Social Sciences Students: 203 full-time (126 women), 82 part-time (59 women); includes 79 minority (46 Black or African American, non-Hispanic/Latino; 3 Asian, non-Hispanic/Latino; 18 Hispanic/Latino; 12 Two or more races, non-Hispanic/Latino), 11 international. Average age 28. 274 applicants, 63% accepted, 105 enrolled. *Faculty:* 180 full-time (81 women), 7 part-time/adjunct (2 women). Expenses: Contact institution. *Financial support:* In 2016–17, 76 students received support, including 72 fellowships with full tuition reimbursements available (averaging $7,750 per year), 10 research assistantships with full tuition reimbursements available (averaging $7,750 per year), 26 teaching assistantships with full tuition reimbursements available (averaging $7,750 per year); career-related internships or fieldwork, Federal Work-Study, scholarships/grants, tuition waivers (full), and unspecified assistantships also available. Support available to part-time students. Financial award application deadline: 4/15; financial award applicants required to submit FAFSA. In 2016, 86 master's, 3 doctorates, 6 other advanced degrees awarded. *Program availability:* Part-time. Offers clinical psychology (Psy D); composition (MM); conducting (MM); English (MA); fine arts (MFA); history (MA); liberal arts and social sciences (MA, MFA, MM, MPA, MS, Psy D, Graduate Certificate); music education (MM); music technology (MM); performance (MM); psychology (MS); public administration (MPA); public and nonprofit management (Graduate Certificate); public history (Graduate Certificate); social science (MA); Spanish (MA). *Application deadline:* For fall admission, 3/1 priority date for domestic and international students; for spring admission, 10/1 priority date for domestic students, 10/1 for international students. Applications are processed on a rolling basis. *Application fee:* $50. Electronic applications accepted. *Dean,* Dr. Curtis Ricker, 912-478-2527, Fax: 912-478-5346, E-mail: cricker@georgiasouthern.edu.

College of Science and Mathematics Students: 88 full-time (34 women), 17 part-time (8 women); includes 23 minority (13 Black or African American, non-Hispanic/Latino; 7 Asian, non-Hispanic/Latino; 3 Hispanic/Latino), 14 international. Average age 26. 63 applicants, 71% accepted, 34 enrolled. *Faculty:* 110 full-time (32 women), 3 part-time/adjunct (1 woman). Expenses: Contact institution. *Financial support:* In 2016–17, 49 students received support, including 4 fellowships with full tuition reimbursements available (averaging $7,750 per year), 22 research assistantships with full tuition reimbursements available (averaging $7,750 per year), 79 teaching assistantships with full tuition reimbursements available (averaging $7,750 per year); career-related internships or fieldwork, Federal Work-Study, scholarships/grants, tuition waivers (full), and unspecified assistantships also available. Support available to part-time students. Financial award application deadline: 4/15; financial award applicants required to submit FAFSA. In 2016, 48 master's awarded. *Program availability:* Part-time. Offers applied physical science (MS); biology (MS); mathematics (MS); science and mathematics (MS, Certificate). *Application deadline:* For fall admission, 3/1 priority date for domestic and international students; for spring admission, 10/1 priority date for domestic students, 10/1 for international students. Applications are processed on a rolling basis. *Application fee:* $50. Electronic applications accepted. *Application Contact:* Samuel T. Aldridge, Director, Graduate Admissions, 912-478-5384, Fax: 912-478-0740, E-mail: gradadmissions@georgiasouthern.edu. *Dean,* Dr. Martha Abell, 912-478-5132, Fax: 912-478-0836, E-mail: martha@georgiasouthern.edu.

Jiann-Ping Hsu College of Public Health Students: 196 full-time (125 women), 58 part-time (50 women); includes 132 minority (111 Black or African American, non-Hispanic/Latino; 9 Asian, non-Hispanic/Latino; 8 Hispanic/Latino; 4 Two or more races, non-Hispanic/Latino), 44 international. Average age 30. 273 applicants, 84% accepted, 114 enrolled. *Faculty:* 36 full-time (16 women), 1 (woman) part-time/adjunct. Expenses: Contact institution. *Financial support:* In 2016–17, 65 students received support, including 53 fellowships with full tuition reimbursements available (averaging $7,750 per year), 3 research assistantships with full tuition reimbursements available (averaging $7,750 per year), 1 teaching assistantship with full tuition reimbursement available (averaging $7,750 per year); career-related internships or fieldwork, Federal Work-Study, scholarships/grants, tuition waivers (full), and unspecified assistantships also available. Support available to part-time students. Financial award application deadline: 4/15; financial award applicants required to submit FAFSA. In 2016, 57 master's, 12 doctorates awarded. *Program availability:* Part-time. Offers biostatistics (MPH, Dr PH); community health behavior and education (Dr PH); community health education (MPH); environmental health sciences (MPH); epidemiology (MPH); health policy and management (MPH, Dr PH); healthcare administration (MHA); public health (MHA, MPH, Dr PH). *Application deadline:* For fall admission, 6/1 priority date for domestic and international students; for spring admission, 10/1 priority date for domestic students, 10/1 for international students. Applications are processed on a rolling basis. *Application fee:* $50. Electronic applications accepted. *Dean,* Dr. Greg Evans, 912-478-2676, Fax: 912-478-5605, E-mail: rgevans@georgiasouthern.edu.

GEORGIA SOUTHWESTERN STATE UNIVERSITY, Americus, GA 31709-4693

General Information State-supported, coed, comprehensive institution. *Enrollment:* 2,954 graduate, professional, and undergraduate students; 232 full-time matriculated graduate/professional students (214 women), 158 part-time matriculated graduate/professional students (116 women). *Enrollment by degree level:* 279 master's, 111 other advanced degrees. *Graduate faculty:* 41 full-time (22 women), 11 part-time/adjunct (9 women). Tuition, state resident: full-time $3330; part-time $185 per credit hour. Tuition, nonresident: full-time $13,248; part-time $736 per credit hour. *Required fees:* $1340. Tuition and fees vary according to course load, campus/location and program. *Graduate housing:* Room and/or apartments available on a first-come, first-served basis to single students; on-campus housing not available to married students. Typical cost: $5130 per year ($8952 including board). Room and board charges vary according to board plan and housing facility selected. *Student services:* Campus employment opportunities, campus safety program, career counseling, exercise/wellness program, international student services, low-cost health insurance, services for students with disabilities. *Library facilities:* James Earl Carter Library. *Collection:* Books: 207,635 (physical), 68,397 (digital/electronic); Serial titles: 76

(physical), 81 (digital/electronic); Databases: 277. Weekly public service hours: 72; students can reserve study rooms.

Computer facilities: 260 computers available on campus for general student use. A campuswide network can be accessed from student residence rooms and from off campus. Online class registration is available.
Website: http://www.gsw.edu/

General Application Contact: Whitney Ford, Admissions Specialist, Office of Graduate Admissions, 800-338-0082, Fax: 229-931-2983, E-mail: graduateadmissions@gsw.edu.

GRADUATE UNITS

School of Business Administration Students: 4 full-time (3 women), 52 part-time (32 women); includes 11 minority (10 Black or African American, non-Hispanic/Latino; 1 Hispanic/Latino). Average age 33. 31 applicants, 71% accepted, 20 enrolled. *Faculty:* 12 full-time (5 women), 2 part-time/adjunct (both women). Expenses: Contact institution. *Financial support:* Application deadline: 6/1; applicants required to submit FAFSA. In 2016, 11 master's awarded. *Program availability:* Part-time, online only, 100% online. Offers business administration (MBA). *Application deadline:* For fall admission, 6/30 for domestic students; for spring admission, 11/30 for domestic students; for summer admission, 4/30 for domestic students. Applications are processed on a rolling basis. *Application fee:* $25. Electronic applications accepted. *Application Contact:* Whitney Ford, Admissions Specialist, Office of Graduate Admissions, 800-338-0082, Fax: 229-931-2983, E-mail: graduateadmissions@gsw.edu. *Dean,* Dr. Liz Wilson, 229-931-2090.

School of Computing and Mathematics Students: 7 full-time (0 women), 11 part-time (3 women); includes 5 minority (2 Black or African American, non-Hispanic/Latino; 3 Asian, non-Hispanic/Latino), 8 international. Average age 34. 23 applicants, 57% accepted, 7 enrolled. *Faculty:* 3 full-time (0 women), 1 part-time/adjunct (0 women). Expenses: Contact institution. *Financial support:* Application deadline: 6/1; applicants required to submit FAFSA. In 2016, 5 master's, 1 other advanced degree awarded. *Program availability:* Part-time, 100% online, blended/hybrid learning. Offers computer information systems (Graduate Certificate); computer science (MS). *Application deadline:* For fall admission, 5/31 for domestic students; for spring admission, 10/15 for domestic students; for summer admission, 3/15 for domestic students. Applications are processed on a rolling basis. *Application fee:* $25. Electronic applications accepted. *Application Contact:* Whitney Ford, Admissions Specialist, Office of Graduate Admission, 800-338-0082, Fax: 229-931-2983. *Dean,* Dr. Boris V. Peltsverger, 229-931-2100.

School of Education Students: 209 full-time (199 women), 6 part-time (all women); includes 52 minority (45 Black or African American, non-Hispanic/Latino; 6 Hispanic/Latino; 1 Two or more races, non-Hispanic/Latino). Average age 33. *Faculty:* 13 full-time (8 women), 7 part-time/adjunct (6 women). Expenses: Contact institution. *Financial support:* Application deadline: 6/1; applicants required to submit FAFSA. In 2016, 57 master's awarded. Offers early childhood education (M Ed, Ed S); middle grades education (Ed S); middle grades language arts (M Ed); middle grades mathematics (M Ed); special education (M Ed). *Application deadline:* For summer admission, 4/15 for domestic students. *Application fee:* $25. Electronic applications accepted. *Application Contact:* Whitney Ford, Admissions Specialist, Office of Graduate Admissions, 800-338-0082, Fax: 229-931-2983. *Dean,* Dr. Rachel Abbott, 229-931-2145.

School of Nursing Students: 12 full-time (all women), 82 part-time (72 women); includes 32 minority (29 Black or African American, non-Hispanic/Latino; 1 Asian, non-Hispanic/Latino; 1 Hispanic/Latino; 1 Two or more races, non-Hispanic/Latino). Average age 34. 126 applicants, 59% accepted, 44 enrolled. *Faculty:* 10 full-time, 3 part-time/adjunct. Expenses: Contact institution. *Financial support:* Application deadline: 6/1; applicants required to submit FAFSA. In 2016, 6 master's awarded. *Program availability:* Part-time, online only, all theory courses are offered online. Offers family nurse practitioner (MSN); health informatics (Postbaccalaureate Certificate); nurse educator (Post Master's Certificate); nursing educator (MSN); nursing informatics (MSN); nursing leadership/management (MSN). MSN program offered by the Georgia Intercollegiate Consortium for Graduate Nursing Education, a partnership with Columbus State University. *Application deadline:* For fall admission, 2/15 for domestic students; for spring admission, 10/15 for domestic students; for summer admission, 2/15 for domestic students. *Application fee:* $25. Electronic applications accepted. *Application Contact:* Whitney Ford, Admissions Specialist, Office of Graduate Admissions, 800-338-0082, Fax: 229-931-2983, E-mail: graduateadmissions@gsw.edu. *Dean,* Dr. Sandra Daniel, 229-931-2275, E-mail: sandra.daniel@gsw.edu.

GEORGIA STATE UNIVERSITY, Atlanta, GA 30302-3083

General Information State-supported, coed, university. CGS member. *Enrollment:* 32,464 graduate, professional, and undergraduate students; 5,187 full-time matriculated graduate/professional students (3,014 women), 1,597 part-time matriculated graduate/professional students (1,036 women). *Enrollment by degree level:* 4,184 master's, 2,517 doctoral, 83 other advanced degrees. *Graduate faculty:* 760 full-time (309 women). Tuition, state resident: full-time $6876; part-time $382 per credit hour. Tuition, nonresident: full-time $22,347; part-time $1243 per credit hour. *Required fees:* $2128; $1064 per term. Part-time tuition and fees vary according to course load and program. *Graduate housing:* Rooms and/or apartments available on a first-come, first-served basis to single and married students. Typical cost: $10,252 per year ($14,084 including board) for single students. Room and board charges vary according to board plan and housing facility selected. *Student services:* Campus safety program, career counseling, child daycare facilities, exercise/wellness program, international student services, services for students with disabilities. *Library facilities:* University Library plus 1 other. *Collection:* Books: 1.7 million (physical), 645,924 (digital/electronic); Serial titles: 14,284 (digital/electronic). Students can reserve study rooms. *Research affiliation:* Cerro Tololo Interamerican Observatory (astronomy), Research Atlanta, Inc. (policy studies), Oak Ridge National Laboratory (environmental policy), Lowell Observatory (astronomy), Brookhaven National Laboratory (physics), Argonne National Laboratory, Advanced Photon Source (crystallography).

Computer facilities: 1,431 computers available on campus for general student use. A campuswide network can be accessed from student residence rooms and from off campus. Online class registration is available.
Website: http://www.gsu.edu/

GRADUATE UNITS

Andrew Young School of Policy Studies Students: 399 full-time (255 women), 100 part-time (59 women); includes 205 minority (143 Black or African American, non-Hispanic/Latino; 11 Asian, non-Hispanic/Latino; 34 Hispanic/Latino; 17 Two or more races, non-Hispanic/Latino), 99 international. Average age 30. 578 applicants, 56% accepted, 157 enrolled. *Faculty:* 74 full-time (30 women). Expenses: Contact institution. *Financial support:* Unspecified assistantships available. Financial award application deadline: 2/15; financial award applicants required to submit FAFSA. In 2016, 142 master's, 17 doctorates, 8 other advanced degrees awarded. *Program availability:* Part-time, evening/weekend. Offers criminal justice (MPA, MS, PhD); disaster management (Certificate); disaster policy (MPA); economics (MA); environmental economics (PhD); environmental policy (PhD); experimental economics (PhD); health policy (PhD); labor economics (PhD); management and finance (MPA); nonprofit management (MPA, Certificate); nonprofit policy (MPA); planning and economic development (MPP, Certificate); policy (MA); policy analysis and evaluation (MPA); policy studies (MA, MPA, MPP, MS, MSW, PhD, Certificate); public administration (MS); public and nonprofit management (PhD); public finance (PhD); public finance and budgeting (PhD); public finance policy (MPA); public health (MPA); urban and regional economics (PhD). *Application deadline:* For fall admission, 1/15 for domestic and international students. *Application fee:* $50. Electronic applications accepted. *Dean,* Dr. Mary Beth Walker, 404-413-0000, Fax: 404-413-0004.

School of Social Work Students: 123 full-time (111 women), 4 part-time (2 women); includes 83 minority (65 Black or African American, non-Hispanic/Latino; 12 Hispanic/Latino; 6 Two or more races, non-Hispanic/Latino), 1 international. Average age 30. 123 applicants, 70% accepted, 46 enrolled. *Faculty:* 17 full-time (12 women). Expenses: Contact institution. *Financial support:* In 2016–17, research assistantships with tuition reimbursements (averaging $4,000 per year), teaching assistantships with tuition reimbursements (averaging $4,000 per year) were awarded; career-related internships or fieldwork, institutionally sponsored loans, scholarships/grants, tuition waivers, and unspecified assistantships also available. Financial award application deadline: 2/1; financial award applicants required to submit FAFSA. In 2016, 49 master's awarded. *Program availability:* Part-time. Offers child welfare leadership (Certificate); community partnerships (MSW); forensic social work (Certificate). *Application deadline:* For fall admission, 2/1 priority date for domestic and international students. *Application fee:* $50. Electronic applications accepted. *Director of School of Social Work,* Brian Bride, 404-413-1052, Fax: 404-413-1075, E-mail: bbride@gsu.edu.

Byrdine F. Lewis School of Nursing Students: 280 full-time (202 women), 215 part-time (194 women); includes 204 minority (122 Black or African American, non-Hispanic/Latino; 45 Asian, non-Hispanic/Latino; 17 Hispanic/Latino; 20 Two or more races, non-Hispanic/Latino), 27 international. Average age 33. 242 applicants, 67% accepted, 103 enrolled. *Faculty:* 65 full-time (50 women). Expenses: Contact institution. *Financial support:* In 2016–17, research assistantships with tuition reimbursements (averaging $1,666 per year), teaching assistantships with tuition reimbursements (averaging $1,920 per year) were awarded; scholarships/grants, tuition waivers (full and partial), and unspecified assistantships also available. Support available to part-time students. Financial award application deadline: 8/1; financial award applicants required to submit FAFSA. In 2016, 139 master's, 41 doctorates, 13 other advanced degrees awarded. *Program availability:* Part-time, blended/hybrid learning. Offers adult health clinical nurse specialist/nurse practitioner (MS, Certificate); child health clinical nurse specialist/pediatric nurse practitioner (MS, Certificate); family nurse practitioner (MS, Certificate); family psychiatric mental health nurse practitioner (MS, Certificate); nursing (PhD); nursing leadership in healthcare innovations (MS); nutrition (MS); perinatal clinical nurse specialist/women's health nurse practitioner (MS, Certificate); physical therapy (DPT); respiratory therapy (MS). *Application deadline:* For fall admission, 2/1 priority date for domestic and international students; for spring admission, 9/15 for domestic and international students. Applications are processed on a rolling basis. *Application fee:* $50. Electronic applications accepted. *Dean of Nursing,* Nancy Kropf, 404-413-1101, Fax: 404-413-1090, E-mail: nkropf@gsu.edu.

Division of Nutrition Students: 33 full-time (30 women), 5 part-time (4 women); includes 8 minority (3 Asian, non-Hispanic/Latino; 1 Hispanic/Latino; 4 Two or more races, non-Hispanic/Latino). Average age 27. 42 applicants, 50% accepted, 14 enrolled. *Faculty:* 9 full-time (6 women). Expenses: Contact institution. *Financial support:* In 2016–17, research assistantships with tuition reimbursements (averaging $1,647 per year), teaching assistantships with full tuition reimbursements (averaging $2,666 per year) were awarded. Financial award application deadline: 4/1. In 2016, 25 master's awarded. *Program availability:* Part-time. Offers nutrition (MS). *Application deadline:* For fall admission, 5/15 for domestic and international students; for spring admission, 10/1 for domestic and international students. *Application fee:* $50. Electronic applications accepted. *Department Head,* Dr. Anita Nucci, 404-413-1234, Fax: 404-413-1228.

Division of Physical Therapy Students: 110 full-time (66 women); includes 35 minority (11 Black or African American, non-Hispanic/Latino; 17 Asian, non-Hispanic/Latino; 3 Hispanic/Latino; 4 Two or more races, non-Hispanic/Latino). Average age 27. 496 applicants, 17% accepted, 42 enrolled. *Faculty:* 10 full-time (5 women). Expenses: Contact institution. *Financial support:* In 2016–17, research assistantships with full tuition reimbursements (averaging $2,000 per year), teaching assistantships with full tuition reimbursements (averaging $2,000 per year) were awarded; scholarships/grants, tuition waivers (partial), and unspecified assistantships also available. Financial award application deadline: 4/1; financial award applicants required to submit FAFSA. In 2016, 35 doctorates awarded. Offers physical therapy (DPT). *Application deadline:* For fall admission, 11/15 for domestic and international students. *Application fee:* $50. Electronic applications accepted. *Department Head,* Dr. Andrew Butler, 404-413-1415, Fax: 404-413-1230, E-mail: andrewbutler@gsu.edu.

Division of Respiratory Therapy Students: 25 full-time (13 women), 5 part-time (2 women); includes 9 minority (5 Black or African American, non-Hispanic/Latino; 2 Asian, non-Hispanic/Latino; 2 Two or more races, non-Hispanic/Latino), 12 international. Average age 27. 49 applicants, 67% accepted, 30 enrolled. *Faculty:* 3 full-time (2 women). Expenses: Contact institution. *Financial support:* In 2016–17, research assistantships with full tuition reimbursements (averaging $2,000 per year), teaching assistantships with full tuition reimbursements (averaging $2,000 per year) were awarded; scholarships/grants and unspecified assistantships also available. Financial award application deadline: 6/1; financial award applicants required to submit FAFSA. In 2016, 9 master's awarded. Offers respiratory therapy (MS). *Application deadline:* For fall admission, 5/1 for domestic and international students; for spring admission, 9/15 for domestic and international students. *Application fee:* $50. Electronic applications accepted. *Department Head,* Dr. Douglas Gardenhire, 404-413-1270, Fax: 404-413-1230, E-mail: dgardenhire@gsu.edu.

College of Arts and Sciences Students: 1,754 full-time (968 women), 420 part-time (252 women); includes 643 minority (324 Black or African American, non-Hispanic/Latino; 3 American Indian or Alaska Native, non-Hispanic/Latino; 128 Asian, non-Hispanic/Latino; 100 Hispanic/Latino; 1 Native Hawaiian or other Pacific Islander, non-Hispanic/Latino; 87 Two or more races, non-Hispanic/Latino), 516 international. Average age 32. 2,443 applicants, 40% accepted, 567 enrolled. *Faculty:* 627 full-time (269 women). Expenses: Contact institution. *Financial support:* Fellowships with tuition reimbursements, research assistantships with tuition reimbursements, teaching assistantships with tuition reimbursements, career-related internships or fieldwork, scholarships/grants, health care benefits, tuition waivers (partial), and unspecified

assistantships available. Support available to part-time students. Financial award application deadline: 4/15; financial award applicants required to submit FAFSA. In 2016, 518 master's, 112 doctorates, 31 other advanced degrees awarded. *Program availability:* Part-time, evening/weekend. Offers African-American studies (MA); analytical chemistry (MS, PhD); anthropology (MA); applied and environmental microbiology (MS, PhD); applied linguistics (MA, PhD); applied linguistics and pedagogy (MA); arts and sciences (MA, MA Ed, MFA, MHP, MM, MS, PhD, Certificate, Graduate Certificate); astronomy (PhD); biochemistry (MS, PhD); bioinformatics (MS, PhD); biophysical chemistry (PhD); biostatistics (MS, PhD); cellular and molecular biology and physiology (MS, PhD); clinical (PhD); cognitive sciences (PhD); community (PhD); computational chemistry (MS, PhD); computer science (MS, PhD); creative writing (MA, MFA, PhD); developmental (PhD); discrete mathematics (MS); English (MA, PhD); fiction (MA, MFA); film, video, and digital imaging (MA); French (MA); French studies (MA); geochemistry (PhD); geographic information systems (Certificate); geography (MS); geology (MS); heritage preservation (MHP); historic preservation (MA); history (MA, PhD); human communication and social influence (MA); interpretation (Certificate); Latin American studies (Certificate); literary studies (MA, PhD); literature and culture (MA); mass communication (MA); mathematics (MS, PhD); media and society (PhD); molecular genetics and biochemistry (MS, PhD); moving image studies (PhD); neurobiology and behavior (MS, PhD); neuropsychology and behavioral neuroscience (PhD); organic/medicinal chemistry (MS, PhD); philosophy (MA); physical chemistry (MS); physics (MS, PhD); poetry (MA, MFA); political science (MA, PhD); public communication (PhD); public history (MA); religious studies (MA); rhetoric and composition (MA, PhD); rhetoric and politics (PhD); scientific computing (MS); sociology (MA, PhD); Spanish (MA); statistics (MS); translation (Certificate); translation and interpretation (Certificate); world history (MA). *Application deadline:* For fall admission, 7/1 for domestic and international students; for spring admission, 11/15 for domestic and international students. *Application fee:* $50. Electronic applications accepted. *Application Contact:* Amber Amari, Director, Graduate and Scheduling Services, 404-413-5037, E-mail: aamari@gsu.edu. *Dean,* Dr. William J. Long, 404-413-5114, Fax: 404-413-5117, E-mail: long@gsu.edu.

Ernest G. Welch School of Art and Design Students: 50 full-time (33 women), 11 part-time (9 women); includes 15 minority (4 Black or African American, non-Hispanic/Latino; 3 Asian, non-Hispanic/Latino; 5 Hispanic/Latino; 3 Two or more races, non-Hispanic/Latino), 4 international. Average age 33. 124 applicants, 30% accepted, 24 enrolled. *Faculty:* 35 full-time (17 women). Expenses: Contact institution. *Financial support:* In 2016–17, fellowships with full tuition reimbursements (averaging $11,000 per year), research assistantships with full tuition reimbursements (averaging $6,000 per year), teaching assistantships with full tuition reimbursements (averaging $7,000 per year) were awarded; scholarships/grants and unspecified assistantships also available. Financial award application deadline: 4/15; financial award applicants required to submit FAFSA. In 2016, 18 master's awarded. Offers art and design (MA, MA Ed, MFA); art education (MA Ed); art history (MA); ceramics (MFA); drawing and painting (MFA); graphic design (MFA); interior design (MFA); photography (MFA); printmaking (MFA); sculpture (MFA); textiles (MFA). *Application deadline:* For fall admission, 1/6 for domestic and international students; for spring admission, 1/15 priority date for domestic and international students. *Application fee:* $50. Electronic applications accepted. *Application Contact:* Hubert Stanley Anderson, Director of Graduate Studies, 404-413-5229, Fax: 404-413-5261, E-mail: artgrad@gsu.edu. *Director, Welch School of Art and Design,* Michael White, 404-413-5228, E-mail: mwhite@gsu.edu.

Gerontology Institute Students: 18 full-time (15 women), 17 part-time (14 women); includes 21 minority (15 Black or African American, non-Hispanic/Latino; 3 Asian, non-Hispanic/Latino; 2 Hispanic/Latino; 1 Two or more races, non-Hispanic/Latino), 1 international. Average age 45. 22 applicants, 100% accepted, 15 enrolled. *Faculty:* 4 full-time (all women). Expenses: Contact institution. *Financial support:* In 2016–17, research assistantships with full tuition reimbursements (averaging $6,000 per year) were awarded; career-related internships or fieldwork, scholarships/grants, and unspecified assistantships also available. Financial award application deadline: 4/15; financial award applicants required to submit FAFSA. In 2016, 10 master's, 3 other advanced degrees awarded. *Program availability:* Part-time. Offers gerontology (MA, Certificate). *Application deadline:* For fall admission, 4/15 for domestic and international students; for spring admission, 10/15 for domestic and international students. Applications are processed on a rolling basis. *Application fee:* $50. Electronic applications accepted. *Application Contact:* Dr. Candace L. Kemp, Director of Graduate Studies, 404-413-5210, Fax: 404-413-5219, E-mail: ckemp@gsu.edu. *Director,* Dr. Elizabeth O. Burgess, 404-413-5210, Fax: 404-413-5219, E-mail: eburgess@gsu.edu.

Institute for Women's, Gender, and Sexuality Studies Students: 12 full-time (all women), 2 part-time (both women); includes 9 minority (5 Black or African American, non-Hispanic/Latino; 2 Asian, non-Hispanic/Latino; 2 Two or more races, non-Hispanic/Latino), 1 international. Average age 32. 18 applicants, 89% accepted, 7 enrolled. *Faculty:* 6 full-time (5 women). Expenses: Contact institution. *Financial support:* In 2016–17, research assistantships with full tuition reimbursements (averaging $7,000 per year), teaching assistantships with full tuition reimbursements (averaging $7,500 per year) were awarded; career-related internships or fieldwork, health care benefits, and unspecified assistantships also available. Financial award application deadline: 2/15. In 2016, 8 master's, 2 other advanced degrees awarded. *Program availability:* Part-time. Offers women's, gender, and sexuality studies (MA, Graduate Certificate). *Application deadline:* For fall admission, 2/15 for domestic and international students. *Application fee:* $50. Electronic applications accepted. *Application Contact:* Dr. Amira Jarmakani, Director of Graduate Studies, 404-413-6583, Fax: 404-413-6585, E-mail: amira@gsu.edu. *Director,* Dr. Susan Talburt, 404-413-6581, Fax: 404-413-6585, E-mail: stalburt@gsu.edu.

Neuroscience Institute Students: 55 full-time (29 women), 1 (woman) part-time; includes 14 minority (1 Black or African American, non-Hispanic/Latino; 4 Asian, non-Hispanic/Latino; 5 Hispanic/Latino; 4 Two or more races, non-Hispanic/Latino), 11 international. Average age 29. 54 applicants, 31% accepted, 12 enrolled. *Faculty:* 20 full-time (8 women). Expenses: Contact institution. *Financial support:* In 2016–17, fellowships (averaging $22,000 per year), research assistantships (averaging $22,000 per year) were awarded. Financial award applicants required to submit FAFSA. In 2016, 4 doctorates awarded. Offers neuroscience (PhD). *Application deadline:* For fall admission, 12/10 for domestic and international students. *Application fee:* $50. Electronic applications accepted. *Application Contact:* Dr. Laura L. Carruth, Director of Graduate Studies, 404-413-5340, E-mail: lcarruth@gsu.edu. *Director,* Prof. Walter Wilczynski, 404-413-6307, E-mail: wwilczynski@gsu.edu.

School of Music Students: 80 full-time (36 women), 10 part-time (4 women); includes 32 minority (19 Black or African American, non-Hispanic/Latino; 5 Asian, non-Hispanic/Latino; 8 Hispanic/Latino), 13 international. Average age 30. 84 applicants, 69% accepted, 42 enrolled. *Faculty:* 40 full-time (13 women). Expenses: Contact institution. *Financial support:* In 2016–17, research assistantships with full tuition reimbursements (averaging $4,000 per year) were awarded; Federal Work-Study, scholarships/grants, health care benefits, tuition waivers (partial), and unspecified assistantships also available. Financial award application deadline: 3/1; financial award applicants required to submit FAFSA. In 2016, 25 master's, 2 other advanced degrees awarded. *Program availability:* Part-time, evening/weekend. Offers choral conducting (MM); jazz studies (MM); music (Certificate); music composition (MM); music education (PhD); orchestral conducting (MM); performance (MM); piano pedagogy (MM); wind band conducting (MM). *Application deadline:* For fall admission, 3/1 priority date for domestic and international students; for spring admission, 10/1 priority date for domestic and international students. Applications are processed on a rolling basis. *Application fee:* $50. Electronic applications accepted. *Application Contact:* Dr. Steven Andrew Harper, Graduate Director, 404-413-5943, Fax: 404-413-5910, E-mail: sharper@gsu.edu. *Director, School of Music,* William Dwight Coleman, 404-413-5953, Fax: 404-413-5910, E-mail: wcoleman@gsu.edu.

College of Education and Human Development Students: 785 full-time (573 women), 395 part-time (270 women); includes 521 minority (371 Black or African American, non-Hispanic/Latino; 1 American Indian or Alaska Native, non-Hispanic/Latino; 39 Asian, non-Hispanic/Latino; 74 Hispanic/Latino; 36 Two or more races, non-Hispanic/Latino; 44 international. Average age 32. 1,113 applicants, 34% accepted, 280 enrolled. *Faculty:* 148 full-time (98 women). Expenses: Contact institution. *Financial support:* In 2016–17, fellowships with full tuition reimbursements (averaging $25,000 per year), research assistantships with tuition reimbursements (averaging $4,867 per year), teaching assistantships with tuition reimbursements (averaging $4,683 per year) were awarded; career-related internships or fieldwork, Federal Work-Study, scholarships/grants, tuition waivers (partial), and unspecified assistantships also available. Support available to part-time students. Financial award applicants required to submit FAFSA. In 2016, 366 master's, 65 doctorates, 28 other advanced degrees awarded. *Program availability:* Part-time, evening/weekend, online learning. Offers autism spectrum disorders (PhD); behavior and learning disabilities (M Ed); behavior disorders (PhD); communication disorders (M Ed, PhD); counseling psychology (PhD); counselor education and practice (PhD); curriculum and instruction (Ed D); early childhood and elementary education (PhD); early childhood education (M Ed, Ed S); early childhood special education (M Ed, PhD); education and human development (M Ed, MAT, MS, Ed D, PhD, Ed S); education of students with exceptionalities (PhD); educational leadership (M Ed, Ed D, Ed S); educational psychology (MS, PhD); educational research (MS, PhD); English education (MAT); exercise science (MS); health and physical education (M Ed); kinesiology (PhD); learning disabilities (PhD); mathematics education (M Ed, MAT); mental health counseling (MS, Ed S); mental retardation (PhD); middle level education (MAT); multiple and severe disabilities (M Ed); orthopedic impairments (PhD); reading, language and literacy education (M Ed, MAT); rehabilitation counseling (MS); school counseling (M Ed, Ed S); school psychology (M Ed, PhD, Ed S); science education (M Ed, MAT); sensory impairments (PhD); social foundations of education (MS, PhD); social studies education (M Ed, MAT); special education adapted curriculum (intellectual disabilities) (M Ed); special education deaf education (M Ed); special education general and adapted curriculum (autism spectrum disorders) (M Ed); special education physical and health disabilities (orthopedic impairments) (M Ed); sports administration (MS); sports medicine (MS); teaching and learning (PhD); urban education (M Ed); urban teacher leadership (M Ed). *Application fee:* $50. Electronic applications accepted. *Application Contact:* Nancy Keita, Director, Office of Academic Assistance and Graduate Admissions, 404-413-8001, E-mail: nkeita@gsu.edu. *Interim Dean,* Dr. Paul A. Alberto, 404-413-8100, Fax: 404-413-8103, E-mail: palberto@gsu.edu.

Learning Technologies Division Students: 13 full-time (10 women), 34 part-time (19 women); includes 17 minority (11 Black or African American, non-Hispanic/Latino; 2 Asian, non-Hispanic/Latino; 1 Hispanic/Latino; 3 Two or more races, non-Hispanic/Latino), 1 international. Average age 39. 26 applicants, 38% accepted, 6 enrolled. *Faculty:* 7 full-time (3 women). Expenses: Contact institution. *Financial support:* Federal Work-Study and institutionally sponsored loans available. In 2016, 8 master's, 2 doctorates awarded. *Program availability:* Part-time, evening/weekend. Offers instructional design and technology (MS); instructional technology (PhD). *Application fee:* $50. Electronic applications accepted. *Application Contact:* Nancy Keita, Director, Office of Academic Assistance and Graduate Admissions, 404-413-8001, E-mail: nkeita@gsu.edu. *Interim Dean,* Dr. Paul A. Alberto, 404-413-8100, Fax: 404-413-8103, E-mail: palberto@gsu.edu.

College of Law Students: 647 full-time (321 women), 23 part-time (16 women); includes 195 minority (89 Black or African American, non-Hispanic/Latino; 1 American Indian or Alaska Native, non-Hispanic/Latino; 47 Asian, non-Hispanic/Latino; 46 Hispanic/Latino; 12 Two or more races, non-Hispanic/Latino), 15 international. Average age 29. 2,053 applicants, 30% accepted, 245 enrolled. *Faculty:* 56 full-time (32 women). Expenses: Contact institution. *Financial support:* In 2016–17, research assistantships with tuition reimbursements (averaging $2,500 per year), teaching assistantships (averaging $2,500 per year) were awarded; scholarships/grants, tuition waivers, and unspecified assistantships also available. Financial award application deadline: 4/1; financial award applicants required to submit FAFSA. In 2016, 203 doctorates awarded. *Program availability:* Part-time, evening/weekend. Offers law (JD). *Application deadline:* For fall admission, 3/15 for domestic students, 3/15 priority date for international students. Applications are processed on a rolling basis. *Application fee:* $50. Electronic applications accepted. *Application Contact:* Dr. Cheryl Jester-George, Senior Director of Admissions, 404-413-9004, Fax: 404-413-9203, E-mail: cjgeorge@gsu.edu. *Dean, College of Law,* Dr. Steven J. Kaminshine, 404-413-9035, Fax: 404-413-9227, E-mail: skaminshine@gsu.edu.

J. Mack Robinson College of Business Students: 1,083 full-time (512 women), 338 part-time (160 women); includes 500 minority (253 Black or African American, non-Hispanic/Latino; 1 American Indian or Alaska Native, non-Hispanic/Latino; 163 Asian, non-Hispanic/Latino; 50 Hispanic/Latino; 2 Native Hawaiian or other Pacific Islander, non-Hispanic/Latino; 31 Two or more races, non-Hispanic/Latino), 470 international. Average age 31. 2,011 applicants, 52% accepted, 571 enrolled. *Faculty:* 167 full-time (47 women). Expenses: Contact institution. *Financial support:* Research assistantships, teaching assistantships, scholarships/grants, tuition waivers, and unspecified assistantships available. Financial award applicants required to submit FAFSA. In 2016, 758 master's, 36 doctorates, 25 other advanced degrees awarded. *Program availability:* Part-time, evening/weekend. Offers actuarial science (MAS); business (EMBA, Exec MS, GMBA, M Tax, MAS, MBA, MIB, MPA, MPA, MS, MSCIS, MSHA, MSIS, MSRE, PMBA, EDB, PhD, Certificate); business administration (MBA); business analysis (MBA, MS); computer information systems (PhD); enterprise risk management (MBA, Certificate); entrepreneurship (MBA); executive business administration (EMBA); finance (MBA, MS, PhD); financial risk management (MBA); global business administration (GMBA); health informatics (MBA, MS); hotel real estate (MBA); human resources management (MBA, MS); information systems (MSIS, Certificate);

information systems development and project management (MBA); information systems management (MBA); managing information technology (Exec MS); marketing (MBA, MS, PhD); mathematical risk management (MS); operations management (MBA, MS); organization behavior/human resource management (PhD); organization management (MBA); organizational change (MS); professional business administration (PMBA); real estate (MBA, MS, PhD, Certificate); risk and insurance (MS); risk management and insurance (MBA, MS, PhD, Certificate); strategic management (PhD); the wireless organization (MBA). *Application deadline:* For fall admission, 5/1 priority date for domestic students, 2/1 priority date for international students; for spring admission, 9/15 priority date for domestic students, 4/1 priority date for international students. Applications are processed on a rolling basis. *Application fee:* $50. Electronic applications accepted. *Application Contact:* Toby McChesney, Assistant Dean for Graduate Recruiting and Student Services, 404-413-7167, Fax: 404-413-7162, E-mail: rcbgradadmissions@gsu.edu. *Dean of the J. Mack Robinson College of Business,* Dr. Richard D. Phillips, 404-413-7000, Fax: 404-413-7035.

Institute of Health Administration Students: 58 full-time (33 women), 14 part-time (6 women); includes 33 minority (11 Black or African American, non-Hispanic/Latino; 14 Asian, non-Hispanic/Latino; 3 Hispanic/Latino; 5 Two or more races, non-Hispanic/Latino), 8 international. Average age 30. 55 applicants, 42% accepted, 15 enrolled. *Faculty:* 8 full-time (2 women). Expenses: Contact institution. *Financial support:* Research assistantships, teaching assistantships, scholarships/grants, tuition waivers, and unspecified assistantships available. In 2016, 73 master's awarded. *Program availability:* Part-time, evening/weekend. Offers health administration (MBA, MSHA); health informatics (MBA, MSCIS). *Application deadline:* For fall admission, 5/1 priority date for domestic students, 2/1 priority date for international students; for spring admission, 9/15 priority date for domestic students, 4/1 priority date for international students. Applications are processed on a rolling basis. *Application fee:* $50. Electronic applications accepted. *Application Contact:* Toby McChesney, Assistant Dean for Graduate Recruiting and Student Services, 404-413-7167, Fax: 404-413-7162, E-mail: rcbgradadmissions@gsu.edu. *Chair in Health Administration/Director of the Institute of Health,* Dr. Andrew T. Sumner, 404-413-7630, Fax: 404-413-7631.

Institute of International Business Students: 22 full-time (14 women), 14 part-time (9 women); includes 20 minority (15 Black or African American, non-Hispanic/Latino; 4 Hispanic/Latino; 1 Two or more races, non-Hispanic/Latino), 5 international. Average age 31. 22 applicants, 27% accepted, 1 enrolled. *Faculty:* 11 full-time (4 women). Expenses: Contact institution. *Financial support:* Research assistantships, teaching assistantships, scholarships/grants, tuition waivers (partial), and unspecified assistantships available. Financial award application deadline: 5/1. In 2016, 31 master's awarded. *Program availability:* Part-time, evening/weekend. Offers international business (GMBA, MBA, MIB); international business and information technology (MBA); international entrepreneurship (MBA). *Application deadline:* For fall admission, 5/1 priority date for domestic students, 2/1 priority date for international students; for spring admission, 9/15 priority date for domestic students, 5/1 priority date for international students. Applications are processed on a rolling basis. *Application fee:* $50. Electronic applications accepted. *Application Contact:* Toby McChesney, Assistant Dean for Graduate Recruiting and Student Services, 404-413-7167, Fax: 404-413-7162, E-mail: rcbgradadmissions@gsu.edu. *Professor/Director of the Institute of International Business,* Dr. Daniel Bello, 404-413-7275, Fax: 404-413-7276.

School of Accountancy Students: 179 full-time (100 women), 97 part-time (54 women); includes 129 minority (58 Black or African American, non-Hispanic/Latino; 55 Asian, non-Hispanic/Latino; 11 Hispanic/Latino; 5 Two or more races, non-Hispanic/Latino), 50 international. Average age 30. 289 applicants, 68% accepted, 144 enrolled. *Faculty:* 16 full-time (5 women). Expenses: Contact institution. *Financial support:* Research assistantships, teaching assistantships, scholarships/grants, tuition waivers, and unspecified assistantships available. Financial award applicants required to submit FAFSA. In 2016, 153 master's, 2 doctorates awarded. *Program availability:* Part-time, evening/weekend. Offers accounting (MBA, PhD); information systems audit and control (MS); professional accountancy (MPA); taxation (M Tax). *Application deadline:* For fall admission, 5/1 priority date for domestic students, 2/1 priority date for international students; for spring admission, 9/15 priority date for domestic students, 4/1 priority date for international students. Applications are processed on a rolling basis. *Application fee:* $50. Electronic applications accepted. *Application Contact:* Toby McChesney, Assistant Dean for Graduate Recruiting and Student Services, 404-413-7167, Fax: 404-413-7162, E-mail: rcbgradadmissions@gsu.edu. *Director of the School of Accountancy,* Dr. Galen R. Sevcik, 404-413-7200, Fax: 404-413-7203.

School of Public Health Students: 232 full-time (177 women), 106 part-time (85 women); includes 205 minority (143 Black or African American, non-Hispanic/Latino; 11 Asian, non-Hispanic/Latino; 34 Hispanic/Latino; 17 Two or more races, non-Hispanic/Latino), 99 international. Average age 30. 578 applicants, 56% accepted, 157 enrolled. *Faculty:* 21 full-time (12 women). Expenses: Contact institution. *Financial support:* In 2016–17, fellowships (averaging $2,500 per year), research assistantships with full tuition reimbursements (averaging $22,000 per year), teaching assistantships with full tuition reimbursements (averaging $22,000 per year) were awarded; career-related internships or fieldwork, scholarships/grants, health care benefits, unspecified assistantships, and out-of-state tuition waivers also available. In 2016, 142 master's, 17 doctorates, 8 other advanced degrees awarded. *Program availability:* Part-time. Offers public health (MPH, PhD, Certificate). *Application deadline:* For fall admission, 2/1 for domestic and international students; for spring admission, 10/1 for domestic and international students. *Application fee:* $50. Electronic applications accepted. *Application Contact:* Courtney M. Burton, Graduate Coordinator, 404-413-1143, E-mail: cmburton@gsu.edu. *Dean,* Dr. Michael P. Eriksen, 404-413-1132, Fax: 404-413-1140, E-mail: meriksen@gsu.edu.

GERSTNER SLOAN KETTERING GRADUATE SCHOOL OF BIOMEDICAL SCIENCES, New York, NY 10021

General Information Independent, coed, graduate-only institution. *Enrollment by degree level:* 67 doctoral. *Graduate faculty:* 126 full-time (25 women). *Graduate housing:* Rooms and/or apartments available on a first-come, first-served basis to single and married students. Typical cost: $16,728 per year for single students; $20,928 per year for married students. Room charges vary according to housing facility selected. Housing application deadline: 5/5. *Student services:* Campus safety program, career counseling, child daycare facilities, grant writing training, international student services, low-cost health insurance, multicultural affairs office, services for students with disabilities, writing training. *Library facilities:* Memorial Sloan Kettering Cancer Center Library. *Collection:* Weekly public service hours: 53; students can reserve study rooms. *Research affiliation:* Memorial Sloan-Kettering Cancer Center (biomedical sciences).

Computer facilities: A campuswide network can be accessed from student residence rooms and from off campus. Online class registration is available.
Website: http://www.sloankettering.edu/

General Application Contact: Main Office, 646-888-6639, Fax: 646-422-2351, E-mail: gradstudies@sloankettering.edu.

GRADUATE UNITS

Program in Cancer Biology Students: 67 full-time (26 women); includes 11 minority (2 Black or African American, non-Hispanic/Latino; 5 Asian, non-Hispanic/Latino; 4 Hispanic/Latino), 27 international. 258 applicants, 17% accepted, 10 enrolled. *Faculty:* 126 full-time (25 women). Expenses: Contact institution. *Financial support:* In 2016–17, 67 students received support. Fellowship package including stipend ($33,773), full-tuition scholarship, first-year allowance, and comprehensive medical and dental insurance available. In 2016, 12 doctorates awarded. Offers cancer biology (PhD). *Application deadline:* For fall admission, 12/1 for domestic and international students. Electronic applications accepted. *Application Contact:* Main Office, 646-888-6639, Fax: 646-422-2351, E-mail: gradstudies@sloankettering.edu. *Associate Dean,* Linda Burnley, 646-888-6639, E-mail: burnleyl@sloankettering.edu.

GLION INSTITUTE OF HIGHER EDUCATION, CH-1823 Glion-sur-Montreux, Switzerland
General Information Proprietary, coed, comprehensive institution.

GRADUATE UNITS

Graduate Programs *Program availability:* Evening/weekend.

GLOBAL UNIVERSITY, Springfield, MO 65804
General Information Independent-religious, coed, comprehensive institution. *Graduate housing:* On-campus housing not available.

GRADUATE UNITS

Graduate School of Theology *Program availability:* Part-time, evening/weekend, online learning. Offers bible and theology (D Min); biblical language (M Div); biblical studies (MA); Christian ministry (M Div, D Min); ministerial studies (MA). Electronic applications accepted.

GODDARD COLLEGE, Plainfield, VT 05667-9432
General Information Independent, coed, comprehensive institution. *Graduate housing:* On-campus housing not available.

GRADUATE UNITS

Graduate Division *Program availability:* Part-time, online learning. Offers clinical mental health counseling (MA); community education (MA); consciousness studies (MA); creative writing (MFA); expressive arts therapy (MA); health arts and sciences (MA); interdisciplinary arts (MFA); psychology (MA); sexual orientation (MA); social innovation and sustainability (MA); teacher licensure (MA); transformative language arts (MA). Electronic applications accepted.

See Display on next page and Close-Up on page 881.

GOLDEN GATE UNIVERSITY, San Francisco, CA 94105-2968
General Information Independent, coed, university. *Enrollment:* 897 full-time matriculated graduate/professional students (528 women), 1,566 part-time matriculated graduate/professional students (822 women). *Enrollment by degree level:* 1,898 master's, 504 doctoral, 64 other advanced degrees. *Graduate faculty:* 55 full-time (19 women), 240 part-time/adjunct (116 women). *Tuition:* Full-time $29,250. One-time fee: $55 part-time. *Graduate housing:* On-campus housing not available. *Student services:* Campus employment opportunities, career counseling, international student services, low-cost health insurance, services for students with disabilities. *Library facilities:* Golden Gate University Library plus 1 other.

Computer facilities: Computer purchase and lease plans are available. 52 computers available on campus for general student use. A campuswide network can be accessed. Online class registration is available.
Website: http://www.ggu.edu/

General Application Contact: Angela Melero, Enrollment Services, 415-442-7800, Fax: 415-442-7807, E-mail: info@ggu.edu.

GRADUATE UNITS

Ageno School of Business Students: 458 full-time (254 women), 664 part-time (331 women); includes 346 minority (75 Black or African American, non-Hispanic/Latino; 2 American Indian or Alaska Native, non-Hispanic/Latino; 132 Asian, non-Hispanic/Latino; 105 Hispanic/Latino; 9 Native Hawaiian or other Pacific Islander, non-Hispanic/Latino; 23 Two or more races, non-Hispanic/Latino), 354 international. Average age 34. 905 applicants, 83% accepted, 165 enrolled. *Faculty:* 18 full-time (3 women), 117 part-time/adjunct (44 women). Expenses: Contact institution. *Financial support:* In 2016–17, 372 students received support. Career-related internships or fieldwork, Federal Work-Study, institutionally sponsored loans, and scholarships/grants available. Support available to part-time students. Financial award applicants required to submit FAFSA. In 2016, 350 master's, 2 doctorates awarded. *Program availability:* Part-time, evening/weekend. Offers accounting (MBA); business administration (EMBA, MBA, PMBA, DBA); business analytics (MS); finance (MBA, MS, Certificate); financial planning (MS, Certificate); healthcare information systems (Certificate); human resource management (MBA, MS); human resources management (Certificate); information systems (MS); information technology (MBA); information technology management (Certificate); integrated marketing and communications (MS, Certificate); international business (MBA); management (MBA); marketing (MBA, MS, Certificate); operations supply chain management (Certificate); psychology (MA, Certificate); public administration (EMPA); public relations (MS, Certificate); technical market analysis (Certificate). *Application deadline:* For fall admission, 5/15 for domestic and international students; for winter admission, 1/15 for domestic and international students; for spring admission, 9/15 for domestic and international students. Applications are processed on a rolling basis. *Application fee:* $70 ($110 for international students). Electronic applications accepted. *Application Contact:* Angela Melero, Enrollment Services, 415-442-7800, Fax: 415-442-7807, E-mail: info@ggu.edu. *Dean,* Dr. Gordon Swartz, 415-442-7027, Fax: 415-442-6579, E-mail: gswartz@ggu.edu.

School of Accounting Students: 121 full-time (88 women), 135 part-time (77 women); includes 68 minority (5 Black or African American, non-Hispanic/Latino; 1 American Indian or Alaska Native, non-Hispanic/Latino; 40 Asian, non-Hispanic/Latino; 20 Hispanic/Latino; 1 Native Hawaiian or other Pacific Islander, non-Hispanic/Latino; 1 Two or more races, non-Hispanic/Latino), 107 international. Average age 32. 128 applicants, 71% accepted, 48 enrolled. *Faculty:* 4 full-time (1 woman), 46 part-time/adjunct (14 women). Expenses: Contact institution. *Financial support:* In 2016–17, 38 students received support. Career-related internships or fieldwork, Federal Work-Study,

institutionally sponsored loans, and scholarships/grants available. Support available to part-time students. Financial award applicants required to submit FAFSA. In 2016, 80 master's awarded. *Program availability:* Part-time, evening/weekend. Offers accounting (M Ac, MSA, Graduate Certificate); forensic accounting (M Ac, MSA, Graduate Certificate); taxation (M Ac). *Application deadline:* For fall admission, 5/15 for international students; for winter admission, 1/15 for international students; for spring admission, 9/15 for international students. Applications are processed on a rolling basis. *Application fee:* $70 ($100 for international students). Electronic applications accepted. *Application Contact:* Angela Melero, Enrollment Services, 415-442-7800, Fax: 415-442-7807, E-mail: info@ggu.edu. *Dean,* Fred Sroka, 415-369-5285, Fax: 415-543-2607.

School of Law Students: 246 full-time (142 women), 228 part-time (133 women); includes 213 minority (28 Black or African American, non-Hispanic/Latino; 2 American Indian or Alaska Native, non-Hispanic/Latino; 68 Asian, non-Hispanic/Latino; 84 Hispanic/Latino; 7 Native Hawaiian or other Pacific Islander, non-Hispanic/Latino; 24 Two or more races, non-Hispanic/Latino), 58 international. Average age 31. 1,473 applicants, 65% accepted, 189 enrolled. *Faculty:* 41 full-time (19 women), 67 part-time/adjunct (27 women). Expenses: Contact institution. *Financial support:* In 2016–17, 315 students received support. Fellowships, research assistantships, teaching assistantships, career-related internships or fieldwork, Federal Work-Study, institutionally sponsored loans, scholarships/grants, tuition waivers (full and partial), and unspecified assistantships available. Support available to part-time students. Financial award applicants required to submit FAFSA. In 2016, 54 master's, 117 doctorates awarded. *Program availability:* Part-time, evening/weekend. Offers environmental law (LL M); estate planning (LL M); intellectual property law (LL M); international legal studies (LL M, SJD); law (JD); taxation (LL M); U.S. legal studies (LL M). *Application deadline:* For fall admission, 8/18 for domestic students, 4/1 for international students; for spring admission, 1/12 for domestic students; for summer admission, 6/4 for domestic students. Applications are processed on a rolling basis. Electronic applications accepted. *Application Contact:* Greg Egertson, Associate Dean and Director of Admissions, 415-442-6636, Fax: 415-442-6609, E-mail: lawadmit@ggu.edu. *Dean,* Rachel Van Cleave, 415-442-6601, Fax: 415-442-6609.

School of Taxation Students: 72 full-time (44 women), 539 part-time (281 women); includes 156 minority (17 Black or African American, non-Hispanic/Latino; 3 American Indian or Alaska Native, non-Hispanic/Latino; 100 Asian, non-Hispanic/Latino; 23 Hispanic/Latino; 7 Native Hawaiian or other Pacific Islander, non-Hispanic/Latino; 6 Two or more races, non-Hispanic/Latino), 82 international. Average age 36. 252 applicants, 84% accepted, 105 enrolled. *Faculty:* 7 full-time (1 woman), 65 part-time/adjunct (19 women). Expenses: Contact institution. *Financial support:* In 2016–17, 66 students received support. Career-related internships or fieldwork, Federal Work-Study, institutionally sponsored loans, and scholarships/grants available. Support available to part-time students. Financial award applicants required to submit FAFSA. In 2016, 193 master's awarded. *Program availability:* Part-time, evening/weekend. Offers advanced studies in taxation (Certificate); estate planning (Certificate); financial planning and taxation (MS); international tax (Certificate); state and local taxation (Certificate); tax (Certificate); taxation (MS). *Application deadline:* For fall admission, 5/15 for international students; for winter admission, 1/15 for international students; for spring admission, 9/15 for international students. Applications are processed on a rolling basis. *Application fee:* $70 ($100 for international students). Electronic applications accepted. *Application Contact:* Angela Melero, Enrollment Services, 415-442-7800, Fax: 415-442-7807, E-mail: info@ggu.edu. *Dean,* Fred Sroka, 415-369-5285, Fax: 415-442-7807.

GOLDEY-BEACOM COLLEGE, Wilmington, DE 19808-1999
General Information Independent, coed, comprehensive institution. *Graduate housing:* Room and/or apartments available on a first-come, first-served basis to single students; on-campus housing not available to married students.

GRADUATE UNITS

Graduate Program *Program availability:* Part-time, evening/weekend. Offers business administration (MBA); finance (MS); financial management (MBA); health care management (MBA); human resource management (MBA); information technology (MBA); international business management (MBA); major finance (MBA); major taxation (MBA); management (MM); marketing management (MBA); taxation (MBA, MS). Electronic applications accepted.

GOLDFARB SCHOOL OF NURSING AT BARNES-JEWISH COLLEGE, St. Louis, MO 63110
General Information Independent, coed, primarily women, comprehensive institution. *Enrollment:* 688 graduate, professional, and undergraduate students; 61 full-time matriculated graduate/professional students (52 women), 11 part-time matriculated graduate/professional students (9 women). *Enrollment by degree level:* 68 master's, 4 doctoral. *Graduate faculty:* 42 full-time (39 women), 6 part-time/adjunct (all women). *Tuition:* Full-time $3024; part-time $1512 per credit hour. *Required fees:* $30. Full-time tuition and fees vary according to program. *Graduate housing:* On-campus housing not available. *Student services:* Campus employment opportunities, campus safety program, international student services, services for students with disabilities. *Library facilities:* Goldfarb School of Nursing Library plus 2 others. *Collection:* Books: 1,100 (physical), 20,000 (digital/electronic); Serial titles: 40 (digital/electronic); Databases: 11.

Computer facilities: 160 computers available on campus for general student use. A campuswide network can be accessed from off campus. Software, research databases available.
Website: http://www.barnesjewishcollege.edu/

General Application Contact: Karen Sartorius, Admission Specialist, 314-454-7057, Fax: 314-362-9250, E-mail: karen.sartorius@bjc.org.

GRADUATE UNITS

Graduate Programs Students: 61 full-time (52 women), 11 part-time (9 women); includes 13 minority (8 Black or African American, non-Hispanic/Latino; 2 Asian, non-Hispanic/Latino; 1 Hispanic/Latino; 2 Two or more races, non-Hispanic/Latino). Average age 34. 44 applicants, 23% accepted, 7 enrolled. *Faculty:* 51 full-time (47 women), 6 part-time/adjunct (all women). Expenses: Contact institution. *Financial support:* Research assistantships, Federal Work-Study, institutionally sponsored loans, scholarships/grants, and traineeships available. Support available to part-time students. Financial award applicants required to submit FAFSA. In 2016, 35 master's awarded. *Program availability:* Part-time, online learning. Offers adult-gerontology (MSN); adult-gerontology nurse practitioner (MSN); nurse anesthesia (MSN); nurse educator (MSN); nurse executive (MSN). *Application deadline:* For fall admission, 2/1 priority date for international students; for spring admission, 10/1 priority date for international students. Applications are processed on a rolling basis. *Application fee:* $50. *Application Contact:* Karen Sartorius, Admissions Specialist, 314-454-7057, Fax: 314-362-9250, E-mail: ksartorius@bjc.org. *Interim Dean,* Dr. Gretchen Drinkard, 314-454-7540, Fax: 314-362-9222, E-mail: gld9643@bjc.org.

GONZAGA UNIVERSITY, Spokane, WA 99258

General Information Independent-religious, coed, comprehensive institution. *Enrollment:* 7,567 graduate, professional, and undergraduate students; 571 full-time matriculated graduate/professional students (297 women), 1,763 part-time matriculated graduate/professional students (1,217 women). *Enrollment by degree level:* 1,810 master's, 524 doctoral. *Graduate faculty:* 103 full-time (61 women), 121 part-time/adjunct (60 women). *Tuition:* Full-time $23,280; part-time $970 per credit. *Required fees:* $202 per semester. Tuition and fees vary according to course load, degree level and program. *Graduate housing:* Rooms and/or apartments available on a first-come, first-served basis to single and married students. Typical cost: $7461 per year ($12,911 including board) for single students; $7461 per year ($12,911 including board) for married students. Room and board charges vary according to board plan, campus/location and housing facility selected. Housing application deadline: 5/1. *Student services:* Campus employment opportunities, career counseling, exercise/wellness program, free psychological counseling, grant writing training, international student services, low-cost health insurance, multicultural affairs office, services for students with disabilities, writing training. *Library facilities:* Ralph E. and Helen Higgins Foley Center plus 1 other. *Collection:* Books: 264,009 (physical), 68,637 (digital/electronic); Serial titles: 7,690 (physical), 74,520 (digital/electronic); Databases: 206. Weekly public service hours: 112; study areas open 24 hours, 5–7 days a week; students can reserve study rooms.

Computer facilities: Computer purchase and lease plans are available. 500 computers available on campus for general student use. A campuswide network can be accessed from student residence rooms and from off campus. Online class registration is available.
Website: http://www.gonzaga.edu/

General Application Contact: Julie McCulloh, Dean of Admissions, 509-313-6592, Fax: 509-313-5780, E-mail: admissions@gonzaga.edu.

GRADUATE UNITS

College of Arts and Sciences Students: 31 part-time (17 women); includes 5 minority (2 Black or African American, non-Hispanic/Latino; 1 American Indian or Alaska Native, non-Hispanic/Latino; 1 Asian, non-Hispanic/Latino; 1 Hispanic/Latino), 1 international. Average age 39. *Faculty:* 9 full-time (3 women). Expenses: Contact institution. *Financial support:* In 2016–17, 27 students received support. Teaching assistantships, scholarships/grants, tuition waivers, and unspecified assistantships available. Support available to part-time students. Financial award applicants required to submit FAFSA. *Program availability:* Part-time, online with two required campus visits. Offers philosophy (MA); theology and leadership (MA). *Application deadline:* For fall admission, 7/15 priority date for domestic students; for spring admission, 11/1 for domestic students; for summer admission, 4/3 for domestic students. Applications are processed on a rolling basis. *Application fee:* $50. Electronic applications accepted. *Application Contact:* Carolyn Von Muller, Assistant to the Dean, 509-313-5522, E-mail: vonmuller@gonzaga.edu. *Dean,* Dr. Elisabeth Mermann-Jozwiak, 509-313-6603, Fax: 509-313-6684, E-mail: merrmann-jozwiak@gonzaga.edu.

English Language Center Students: 6 full-time (5 women), 21 part-time (16 women); includes 2 minority (1 Asian, non-Hispanic/Latino; 1 Hispanic/Latino), 14 international. Average age 34. 29 applicants, 66% accepted, 12 enrolled. *Faculty:* 8 full-time (7 women), 6 part-time/adjunct (all women). Expenses: Contact institution. *Financial support:* In 2016–17, 6 students received support. Scholarships/grants available. Support available to part-time students. Financial award applicants required to submit FAFSA. In 2016, 3 master's awarded. Offers teaching English as a second language (MA); teaching English as a second language: studies in language and culture (MA). *Application fee:* $50. Electronic applications accepted. *Manager of Student Services,* Melissa Heid, 509-313-6560, E-mail: heid@gonzaga.edu.

School of Business Administration Students: 80 full-time (32 women), 135 part-time (60 women); includes 37 minority (2 Black or African American, non-Hispanic/Latino; 10 American Indian or Alaska Native, non-Hispanic/Latino; 5 Asian, non-Hispanic/Latino; 10 Hispanic/Latino; 10 Two or more races, non-Hispanic/Latino), 14 international. Average age 29. 252 applicants, 131 enrolled. *Faculty:* 17 full-time (4 women), 14 part-time/adjunct (2 women). Expenses: Contact institution. *Financial support:* In 2016–17, 134 students received support. Scholarships/grants, tuition waivers, and unspecified assistantships available. Support available to part-time students. Financial award applicants required to submit FAFSA. In 2016, 113 master's awarded. *Program availability:* Part-time, evening/weekend. Offers accountancy (M Acc); American Indian entrepreneurship (MBA); business administration (MBA); taxation (MS). *Application deadline:* Applications are processed on a rolling basis. *Application fee:* $50. Electronic applications accepted. *Application Contact:* Stacey Chatman, Assistant Director for Admissions, 509-313-4622, E-mail: chatman@gonzaga.edu. *Interim Dean,* Dr. Ken Anderson, 509-313-5991, E-mail: anderson@gem.gonzaga.edu.

School of Education Students: 104 full-time (73 women), 275 part-time (184 women); includes 31 minority (5 Black or African American, non-Hispanic/Latino; 1 American Indian or Alaska Native, non-Hispanic/Latino; 3 Asian, non-Hispanic/Latino; 18 Hispanic/Latino; 4 Two or more races, non-Hispanic/Latino), 163 international. Average age 32. 419 applicants, 67% accepted, 165 enrolled. *Faculty:* 22 full-time (17 women), 38 part-time/adjunct (22 women). Expenses: Contact institution. *Financial support:* In 2016–17, 28 students received support. Scholarships/grants and tuition waivers available. Support available to part-time students. Financial award applicants required to submit FAFSA. In 2016, 39 master's awarded. *Program availability:* Part-time, evening/weekend, 100% online. Offers clinical mental health counseling (MA); elementary education (MIT); leadership and administration (MA); marriage and family counseling (MA); school counseling (MA); secondary education (MIT); special education (M Ed, MIT); sport and athletic administration (MA). *Application deadline:* Applications are processed on a rolling basis. *Application fee:* $50. Electronic applications accepted. *Application Contact:* Luke Cairney, Graduate Admissions Program Specialist, 509-313-3821, E-mail: cairney@gonzaga.edu. *Dean,* Dr. Vincent Alfonso, 509-313-3594, Fax: 509-313-5821, E-mail: alfonso@gonzaga.edu.

School of Engineering and Applied Science Students: 1 full-time (0 women), 17 part-time (1 woman); includes 3 minority (all Hispanic/Latino), 4 international. Average age 41. *Faculty:* 1 full-time (0 women), 4 part-time/adjunct (0 women). Expenses: Contact institution. *Financial support:* Available to part-time students. Applicants required to submit FAFSA. In 2016, 9 master's awarded. *Program availability:* Online only, 100% online. Offers transmission and distribution engineering (M Eng, Certificate). *Application fee:* $50. *Application Contact:* Jilliene McKinstry, Assistant Director, 509-313-5701, E-mail: mckinstry@gonzaga.edu. *Dean,* Dr. Stephen E. Silliman, 509-313-3522, E-mail: silliman@gonzaga.edu.

School of Law Students: 306 full-time (138 women), 2 part-time (1 woman); includes 49 minority (7 Black or African American, non-Hispanic/Latino; 2 American Indian or Alaska Native, non-Hispanic/Latino; 4 Asian, non-Hispanic/Latino; 20 Hispanic/Latino; 16 Two or more races, non-Hispanic/Latino), 5 international. Average age 27. 859 applicants,

57% accepted, 103 enrolled. *Faculty:* 17 full-time (11 women), 15 part-time/adjunct (3 women). Expenses: Contact institution. *Financial support:* In 2016–17, 279 students received support. Federal Work-Study and scholarships/grants available. Support available to part-time students. Financial award applicants required to submit FAFSA. In 2016, 113 doctorates awarded. *Program availability:* Part-time. Offers law (JD). *Application deadline:* For fall admission, 4/15 priority date for domestic students. *Application fee:* $50. Electronic applications accepted. *Application Contact:* Susan Lee, Director of Admissions, 509-313-3734, E-mail: slee@lawschool.gonzaga.edu. *Dean,* Jane Korn, 509-313-3700.

School of Nursing and Human Physiology Students: 42 full-time (27 women), 708 part-time (595 women); includes 111 minority (16 Black or African American, non-Hispanic/Latino; 4 American Indian or Alaska Native, non-Hispanic/Latino; 37 Asian, non-Hispanic/Latino; 27 Hispanic/Latino; 2 Native Hawaiian or other Pacific Islander, non-Hispanic/Latino; 25 Two or more races, non-Hispanic/Latino), 1 international. Average age 38. 360 applicants, 39% accepted, 100 enrolled. *Faculty:* 18 full-time (16 women), 26 part-time/adjunct (21 women). Expenses: Contact institution. *Financial support:* In 2016–17, 41 students received support. Scholarships/grants, traineeships, tuition waivers, and unspecified assistantships available. Support available to part-time students. Financial award applicants required to submit FAFSA. In 2016, 129 master's, 10 doctorates awarded. *Program availability:* Part-time, evening/weekend, immersion weekends. Offers nursing and human physiology (MSN, DNP, DNP-A). *Application deadline:* For spring admission, 9/11 for domestic students. Applications are processed on a rolling basis. *Application fee:* $50. Electronic applications accepted. *Application Contact:* Shannon Zaranski, Assistant to the Dean, 509-313-3569, E-mail: zaranski@gu.gonzaga.edu. *Interim Dean,* Dr. Lin Murphy, 509-313-3569, E-mail: murpheyl1@gonzaga.edu.

School of Professional Studies Students: 32 full-time (22 women), 574 part-time (343 women); includes 111 minority (33 Black or African American, non-Hispanic/Latino; 8 American Indian or Alaska Native, non-Hispanic/Latino; 11 Asian, non-Hispanic/Latino; 38 Hispanic/Latino; 3 Native Hawaiian or other Pacific Islander, non-Hispanic/Latino; 18 Two or more races, non-Hispanic/Latino), 22 international. Average age 38. 197 applicants, 96% accepted, 156 enrolled. *Faculty:* 16 full-time (6 women), 18 part-time/adjunct (6 women). Expenses: Contact institution. *Financial support:* In 2016–17, 61 students received support. Scholarships/grants, tuition waivers, and unspecified assistantships available. Support available to part-time students. Financial award applicants required to submit FAFSA. In 2016, 285 master's, 9 doctorates awarded. *Program availability:* Part-time, evening/weekend, blended/hybrid learning, immersion weekends. Offers communication and leadership (MA); leadership studies (PhD); organizational leadership (MA). *Application deadline:* For fall admission, 7/16 for domestic students; for spring admission, 11/16 for domestic students; for summer admission, 3/16 for domestic students. Applications are processed on a rolling basis. *Application fee:* $50. Electronic applications accepted. *Application Contact:* Teresa Crane, Program Specialist, 509-313-6645, E-mail: guonlinestudentservices@gonzaga.edu. *Interim Dean,* Dr. Jolanta Weber, 509-313-6595, E-mail: weberj@gonzaga.edu.

GORDON COLLEGE, Wenham, MA 01984-1899

General Information Independent-religious, coed, comprehensive institution. *Enrollment:* 2,004 graduate, professional, and undergraduate students; 110 full-time matriculated graduate/professional students (78 women), 164 part-time matriculated graduate/professional students (124 women). *Enrollment by degree level:* 274 master's. *Graduate faculty:* 19 full-time (10 women), 53 part-time/adjunct (40 women). *Tuition:* Full-time $4850; part-time $325 per credit. *Required fees:* $75 per term. Tuition and fees vary according to course load and program. *Graduate housing:* Room and/or apartments available on a first-come, first-served basis to single students; on-campus housing not available to married students. Housing application deadline: 6/15. *Student services:* Campus safety program, career counseling, exercise/wellness program, international student services, low-cost health insurance, multicultural affairs office, services for students with disabilities, teacher training, writing training. *Library facilities:* Jenks Learning Resource Center. *Collection:* Books: 132,914 (physical); Serial titles: 1,540 (physical). Weekly public service hours: 103; students can reserve study rooms. *Research affiliation:* National Association for Music Education (music education), Feierabend Association for Music Education (early childhood music education), American Choral Directors Association (choral music education), Embracing the New Music Educators Association (mentoring for new music teaching professionals).

Computer facilities: Computer purchase and lease plans are available. 100 computers available on campus for general student use. A campuswide network can be accessed from student residence rooms and from off campus. Online class registration is available.
Website: http://www.gordon.edu/

General Application Contact: Julie Lenocker, Program Administrator, 978-867-4322, Fax: 978-867-4663, E-mail: graduate-education@gordon.edu.

GRADUATE UNITS

Graduate Education Program Students: 81 full-time (61 women), 109 part-time (87 women); includes 28 minority (2 Black or African American, non-Hispanic/Latino; 11 Asian, non-Hispanic/Latino; 13 Hispanic/Latino; 2 Two or more races, non-Hispanic/Latino), 12 international. Average age 34. 190 applicants, 100% accepted, 141 enrolled. *Faculty:* 17 full-time (9 women), 41 part-time/adjunct (34 women). Expenses: Contact institution. *Financial support:* Applicants required to submit FAFSA. In 2016, 110 master's, 16 Ed Ss awarded. *Program availability:* Part-time, evening/weekend. Offers early childhood (M Ed); educational leadership (M Ed, Ed S); elementary education (M Ed); English as a second language (M Ed, Ed S); math specialist (M Ed); mathematics specialist (Ed S); middle school education (M Ed); moderate disabilities (M Ed); Montessori education (M Ed); reading (M Ed, Ed S); secondary education (M Ed). *Application deadline:* Applications are processed on a rolling basis. *Application fee:* $75. *Application Contact:* Julie Lenocker, Program Administrator, 978-867-4322, Fax: 978-867-4663, E-mail: graduate-education@gordon.edu. *Director of Graduate Studies,* Dr. Janet Arndt, 978-867-4355, Fax: 978-867-4663.

Graduate Leadership Program Students: 9 full-time (6 women), 10 part-time (all women); includes 2 minority (1 Asian, non-Hispanic/Latino; 1 Hispanic/Latino), 1 international. Average age 39. 13 applicants, 100% accepted, 10 enrolled. *Faculty:* 5 part-time/adjunct (2 women). Expenses: Contact institution. Offers leadership (MA, Ed S). *Application deadline:* For summer admission, 4/7 for domestic students. *Application fee:* $75. *Application Contact:* Julie Lenocker, Program Administrator, 978-867-4322, Fax: 978-867-4663, E-mail: graduate-education@gordon.edu. *Director of Graduate Studies,* Dr. Janet Arndt, 978-867-4663.

Graduate Music Education Program Students: 20 full-time (11 women), 45 part-time (27 women); includes 10 minority (2 Black or African American, non-Hispanic/Latino; 2 American Indian or Alaska Native, non-Hispanic/Latino; 3 Asian, non-Hispanic/Latino; 2 Hispanic/Latino; 1 Two or more races, non-Hispanic/Latino). Average age 35. 19

applicants, 100% accepted, 17 enrolled. *Faculty:* 2 full-time (1 woman), 7 part-time/adjunct (4 women). Expenses: Contact institution. *Financial support:* Applicants required to submit FAFSA. In 2016, 16 master's awarded. *Program availability:* Part-time. Offers music education (MM Ed). *Application deadline:* For summer admission, 4/1 for domestic and international students. Applications are processed on a rolling basis. *Application fee:* $50. *Application Contact:* Kristen Harrington, Program Administrator, 978-867-4429, Fax: 978-867-4663, E-mail: kristen.harrington@gordon.edu. *Associate Professor,* Dr. Sandra Doneski, 978-867-4818, E-mail: sandra.doneski@gordon.edu.

GORDON-CONWELL THEOLOGICAL SEMINARY, South Hamilton, MA 01982-2395

General Information Independent-religious, coed, graduate-only institution. *Graduate housing:* Rooms and/or apartments available to single and married students. Housing application deadline: 4/1.

GRADUATE UNITS

Graduate and Professional Programs *Program availability:* Part-time, evening/weekend. Offers Biblical languages (MABL); church history (MACH); counseling (MACO); ministry (D Min); missions/evangelism (MAME); New Testament (MANT); Old Testament (MAOT); religion (MAR); theology (M Div, MATH, Th M, Th D).

GOSHEN COLLEGE, Goshen, IN 46526-4794

General Information Independent-religious, coed, comprehensive institution. *Enrollment:* 870 graduate, professional, and undergraduate students; 67 full-time matriculated graduate/professional students (59 women), 3 part-time matriculated graduate/professional students (2 women). *Enrollment by degree level:* 70 master's. *Graduate faculty:* 14 full-time (5 women), 2 part-time/adjunct (1 woman). *Tuition:* Full-time $15,000; part-time $750 per credit hour. Tuition and fees vary according to program. *Graduate housing:* On-campus housing not available. *Student services:* Child daycare facilities, exercise/wellness program, international student services, multicultural affairs office, services for students with disabilities, writing training. *Library facilities:* The Harold and Wilma Good Library plus 1 other. *Collection:* Books: 106,274 (physical), 157,167 (digital/electronic); Serial titles: 2,769 (physical), 30,977 (digital/electronic); Databases: 69. Weekly public service hours: 81; students can reserve study rooms.

Computer facilities: 160 computers available on campus for general student use. A campuswide network can be accessed from student residence rooms and from off campus. Online class registration is available.
Website: http://www.goshen.edu/

General Application Contact: Kendra Ramseyer, Graduate and Continuing Studies Recruitment and Outreach Specialist, 574-535-7458, Fax: 574-535-7245, E-mail: kendramr@goshen.edu.

GRADUATE UNITS

Merry Lea Environmental Learning Center Students: 5 full-time (4 women). Average age 31. 17 applicants, 53% accepted, 5 enrolled. *Faculty:* 6 full-time (0 women). Expenses: Contact institution. *Financial support:* Application deadline: 9/10. In 2016, 3 master's awarded. Offers environmental education (MA). *Application deadline:* For fall admission, 4/30 for domestic students. Applications are processed on a rolling basis. *Application fee:* $25. Electronic applications accepted. *Application Contact:* Dr. David Ostergren, Director of the Graduate Program in Environmental Education, 260-799-5869, E-mail: daveo@goshen.edu. *Executive Director,* Dr. Luke Gascho, 260-799-5869, E-mail: lukeag@goshen.edu.

Program in Nursing Expenses: Contact institution. *Financial support:* Scholarships/grants available. *Program availability:* Part-time, evening/weekend. Offers family nurse practitioner (MSN). *Application deadline:* For fall admission, 3/15 priority date for domestic students. Electronic applications accepted. *Director,* Ruth Stoltzfus, 574-535-7973, E-mail: ruthas@goshen.edu.

GOUCHER COLLEGE, Baltimore, MD 21204-2794

General Information Independent, coed, comprehensive institution. *Enrollment:* 2,172 graduate, professional, and undergraduate students; 133 full-time matriculated graduate/professional students (98 women), 323 part-time matriculated graduate/professional students (251 women). *Enrollment by degree level:* 377 master's, 79 other advanced degrees. *Graduate faculty:* 7 full-time (5 women), 242 part-time/adjunct (165 women). *Graduate housing:* On-campus housing not available. *Student services:* Career counseling. *Library facilities:* Goucher College Library plus 1 other. *Collection:* Books: 250,000 (physical), 300,000 (digital/electronic); Serial titles: 96,000 (digital/electronic); Databases: 120. Weekly public service hours: 168; study areas open 24 hours, 5–7 days a week. *Research affiliation:* Sheppard-Pratt Hospital (education).

Computer facilities: Computer purchase and lease plans are available. 130 computers available on campus for general student use. A campuswide network can be accessed from student residence rooms and from off campus. Online class registration, transcripts, financial aid information, billing, ePortfolios, academic progress reports, study abroad plans are available.
Website: http://www.goucher.edu/

General Application Contact: Shelby Hillers, Admissions Coordinator, 410-337-6200, Fax: 410-337-6085, E-mail: shelby.hillers@goucher.edu.

GRADUATE UNITS

Graduate Programs in Education Students: 29 full-time (20 women), 285 part-time (217 women); includes 54 minority (41 Black or African American, non-Hispanic/Latino; 3 Asian, non-Hispanic/Latino; 7 Hispanic/Latino; 3 Two or more races, non-Hispanic/Latino), 1 international. Average age 34. 85 applicants, 100% accepted, 61 enrolled. *Faculty:* 3 full-time (all women), 52 part-time/adjunct (40 women). Expenses: Contact institution. *Financial support:* Career-related internships or fieldwork and unspecified assistantships available. Support available to part-time students. Financial award application deadline: 4/15; financial award applicants required to submit FAFSA. In 2016, 207 master's awarded. *Program availability:* Part-time, evening/weekend. Offers at-risk and diverse learners (M Ed, Certificate); athletic program leadership and administration (M Ed, Certificate); elementary and special education (MAT); elementary education (MAT); literacy strategies for content learning (M Ed, Certificate); middle school (M Ed, Certificate); Montessori studies (M Ed); reading instruction (M Ed, Certificate); school improvement leadership (M Ed, Certificate); school mediation (M Ed, Certificate); secondary and special education (MAT); secondary education (MAT); special education (MAT); special education for certified teachers (M Ed, Certificate); teacher as leader in technology (M Ed, Certificate). *Application deadline:* For fall admission, 9/1 for domestic students; for spring admission, 1/15 for domestic students. Applications are processed on a rolling basis. *Application fee:* $75. Electronic applications accepted. *Application Contact:* Shelby Hillers, Admissions Coordinator, 410-337-6200, Fax: 410-337-6085, E-mail: shelby.hillers@goucher.edu. *Assistant*

Provost, Dr. Phyllis Sunshine, 410-337-6047, Fax: 410-337-6394, E-mail: psunshin@goucher.edu.

MA and MFA Programs Students: 70 full-time (50 women), 69 part-time (52 women); includes 15 minority (7 Black or African American, non-Hispanic/Latino; 1 American Indian or Alaska Native, non-Hispanic/Latino; 1 Asian, non-Hispanic/Latino; 4 Hispanic/Latino; 2 Two or more races, non-Hispanic/Latino), 2 international. 74 applicants, 88% accepted, 42 enrolled. *Faculty:* 6 full-time (4 women), 100 part-time/adjunct (56 women). Expenses: Contact institution. *Financial support:* Scholarships/grants and unspecified assistantships available. Financial award application deadline: 4/15; financial award applicants required to submit FAFSA. In 2016, 83 master's awarded. *Program availability:* Part-time, evening/weekend, blended/hybrid learning. Offers arts administration (MA); creative nonfiction (MFA); cultural sustainability (MA); digital arts (MA, MFA); environmental studies (MA); historic preservation (MA); management (MA). *Application deadline:* Applications are processed on a rolling basis. *Application fee:* $75. Electronic applications accepted. *Application Contact:* Shelby Hillers, Admissions Coordinator, 410-337-6200, Fax: 410-337-6200, E-mail: shelby.hillers@goucher.edu. *Assistant Provost*, Leslie Rubinkowski, 410-337-6200, E-mail: leslie.rubinkowski@goucher.edu.

Post-Baccalaureate Premedical Program Students: 31 full-time (18 women); includes 5 minority (1 Black or African American, non-Hispanic/Latino; 3 Asian, non-Hispanic/Latino; 1 Hispanic/Latino). Average age 25. 339 applicants, 12% accepted, 30 enrolled. *Faculty:* 11 full-time (5 women). Expenses: Contact institution. *Financial support:* In 2016–17, 6 students received support, including 8 fellowships (averaging $4,000 per year); institutionally sponsored loans and scholarships/grants also available. Financial award application deadline: 3/1; financial award applicants required to submit FAFSA. Offers premedical studies (Certificate). *Application deadline:* Applications are processed on a rolling basis. *Application fee:* $60. Electronic applications accepted. *Application Contact:* Theresa Reifsnider, Program Assistant, 800-414-3437, Fax: 410-337-6461, E-mail: pbpm@goucher.edu. *Director*, Betsy Merideth, 800-414-3437, Fax: 410-337-6461, E-mail: bmerideth@goucher.edu.

GOVERNORS STATE UNIVERSITY, University Park, IL 60484

General Information State-supported, coed, university. CGS member. *Enrollment:* 5,819 graduate, professional, and undergraduate students; 927 full-time matriculated graduate/professional students (542 women), 1,212 part-time matriculated graduate/professional students (873 women). *Enrollment by degree level:* 1,928 master's, 211 doctoral. *Graduate faculty:* 217 full-time (130 women), 264 part-time/adjunct (156 women). Tuition, state resident: full-time $8472; part-time $353 per credit hour. Tuition, nonresident: full-time $16,944; part-time $706 per credit hour. *Required fees:* $1824; $76 per credit hour. $38 per term. Tuition and fees vary according to course load, degree level and program. *Graduate housing:* Rooms and/or apartments available on a first-come, first-served basis to single and married students. Housing application deadline: 6/1. *Student services:* Campus employment opportunities, career counseling, child daycare facilities, exercise/wellness program, free psychological counseling, international student services, multicultural affairs office, services for students with disabilities, writing training. *Library facilities:* University Library. *Collection:* Books: 296,238 (physical), 319,423 (digital/electronic); Serial titles: 2,187 (physical), 92,506 (digital/electronic); Databases: 176. Weekly public service hours: 75; students can reserve study rooms.

Computer facilities: Computer purchase and lease plans are available. 112 computers available on campus for general student use. A campuswide network can be accessed from student residence rooms. Online class registration, student portal are available. Website: http://www.govst.edu/

General Application Contact: Yakeea Daniels, Assistant Vice President for Enrollment Services/Director of Admission, 708-534-4510, E-mail: ydaniels@govst.edu.

GRADUATE UNITS

College of Arts and Sciences Students: 344 full-time (103 women), 324 part-time (172 women); includes 181 minority (159 Black or African American, non-Hispanic/Latino; 7 Asian, non-Hispanic/Latino; 13 Hispanic/Latino; 2 Two or more races, non-Hispanic/Latino), 345 international. Average age 31. 1,764 applicants, 52% accepted, 429 enrolled. *Faculty:* 91 full-time (43 women), 125 part-time/adjunct (64 women). Expenses: Contact institution. *Financial support:* Application deadline: 5/1; applicants required to submit FAFSA. In 2016, 299 master's awarded. *Program availability:* Part-time. Offers analytical chemistry (MS); art (MA); arts and sciences (MA, MFA, MPA, MS); communication studies (MA); computer science (MS); criminal justice (MA); English (MA); environmental biology (MS); independent film and digital imaging (MFA); media communication (MA); political and justice studies (MA); public administration (MPA). *Application deadline:* For fall admission, 4/1 for domestic students. Applications are processed on a rolling basis. *Application fee:* $50. Electronic applications accepted. *Application Contact:* Yakeea Daniels, Assistant Vice President for Enrollment Services/Director of Admission, 708-534-4510, E-mail: ydaniels@govst.edu. *Dean, College of Arts and Sciences*, Dr. Andre Marak, 708-534-4589, E-mail: amark@govst.edu.

College of Business Students: 62 full-time (26 women), 109 part-time (58 women); includes 90 minority (73 Black or African American, non-Hispanic/Latino; 3 Asian, non-Hispanic/Latino; 9 Hispanic/Latino; 5 Two or more races, non-Hispanic/Latino), 23 international. Average age 36. 515 applicants, 33% accepted, 94 enrolled. *Faculty:* 25 full-time (9 women), 30 part-time/adjunct (10 women). Expenses: Contact institution. *Financial support:* Application deadline: 5/1; applicants required to submit FAFSA. In 2016, 69 master's awarded. *Program availability:* Part-time. Offers accounting (MS); business (MBA, MS); business administration (MBA); management information systems (MS). *Application deadline:* For fall admission, 4/1 for domestic students. *Application fee:* $50. Electronic applications accepted. *Application Contact:* Yakeea Daniels, Assistant Vice President for Enrollment Services/Director of Admission, 708-534-4510, E-mail: ydaniels@govst.edu. *Dean, College of Business*, Dr. Jun Zhao, 708-534-4953, E-mail: jzhao@govst.edu.

College of Education Students: 139 full-time (119 women), 346 part-time (269 women); includes 235 minority (178 Black or African American, non-Hispanic/Latino; 4 Asian, non-Hispanic/Latino; 41 Hispanic/Latino; 12 Two or more races, non-Hispanic/Latino), 6 international. Average age 36. *Faculty:* 47 full-time (31 women), 49 part-time/adjunct (39 women). Expenses: Contact institution. *Financial support:* Application deadline: 5/1; applicants required to submit FAFSA. In 2016, 127 master's, 18 doctorates awarded. *Program availability:* Part-time. Offers counseling (MA); early childhood education (MA); education (MA, Ed D); educational administration and supervision (MA); higher education administration (Ed D); multi-categorical special education (MA); not-for-profit/social entrepreneurship (Ed D); psychology (MA); reading (MA); superintendent (P-12) (Ed D). *Application deadline:* For fall admission, 4/1 for domestic students. *Application fee:* $50. Electronic applications accepted. *Application Contact:* Yakeea Daniels, Assistant Vice President for Enrollment Services/Director of

Admission, 708-534-4510, E-mail: ydaniels@govst.edu. *Dean, College of Education*, Dr. Andrea Evans, 708-534-8396, E-mail: aevans6@govst.edu.

College of Health and Human Services Students: 382 full-time (294 women), 433 part-time (374 women); includes 424 minority (280 Black or African American, non-Hispanic/Latino; 2 American Indian or Alaska Native, non-Hispanic/Latino; 29 Asian, non-Hispanic/Latino; 96 Hispanic/Latino; 1 Native Hawaiian or other Pacific Islander, non-Hispanic/Latino; 16 Two or more races, non-Hispanic/Latino), 9 international. Average age 34. 1,009 applicants, 53% accepted, 372 enrolled. *Faculty:* 51 full-time (45 women), 60 part-time/adjunct (43 women). Expenses: Contact institution. *Financial support:* Application deadline: 5/1; applicants required to submit FAFSA. In 2016, 256 master's, 52 doctorates awarded. *Program availability:* Part-time. Offers addictions studies and behavioral health (MHS); communication disorders (MHS); health administration (MHA); health and human services (MHA, MHS, MOT, MSN, MSW, DPT); nursing (MSN); occupational therapy (MOT); physical therapy (DPT); social work (MSW). *Application deadline:* For fall admission, 4/1 for domestic students. *Application fee:* $50. Electronic applications accepted. *Application Contact:* Yakeea Daniels, Assistant Vice President for Enrollment Services/Director of Admission, 708-534-4510, E-mail: ydaniels@govst.edu. *Dean, College of Health and Human Services*, Dr. Elizabeth Cada, 708-534-7295, E-mail: bcada@govst.edu.

GRACE COLLEGE, Winona Lake, IN 46590-1294

General Information Independent-religious, coed, comprehensive institution. *Graduate housing:* On-campus housing not available.

GRADUATE UNITS

Department of Graduate Counseling *Program availability:* Part-time. Offers clinical mental health counseling (MA). Electronic applications accepted.

GRACE COLLEGE OF DIVINITY, Fayetteville, NC 28314

General Information Independent-religious, coed, comprehensive institution.

GRADUATE UNITS

Graduate Program Offers theology (MCL).

GRACELAND UNIVERSITY, Lamoni, IA 50140

General Information Independent-religious, coed, comprehensive institution. *Enrollment:* 2,230 graduate, professional, and undergraduate students; 394 full-time matriculated graduate/professional students (338 women), 346 part-time matriculated graduate/professional students (293 women). *Enrollment by degree level:* 733 master's, 26 doctoral, 39 other advanced degrees. *Graduate faculty:* 11 full-time (9 women), 29 part-time/adjunct (22 women). Tuition: Part-time $735 per credit hour. *Graduate housing:* On-campus housing not available. *Student services:* Campus safety program, career counseling, free psychological counseling, services for students with disabilities, teacher training, writing training. *Library facilities:* F. M. Smith Library. *Collection:* Books: 80,000 (physical); Serial titles: 153 (physical). Weekly public service hours: 80; students can reserve study rooms.

Computer facilities: A campuswide network can be accessed from student residence rooms and from off campus. Online class registration is available. Website: http://www.graceland.edu/

General Application Contact: Lisa Libich, Director of Retention Operations for College of Graduate and Continuing Studies, 816-423-4730, Fax: 816-833-2990, E-mail: libich@graceland.edu.

GRADUATE UNITS

Community of Christ Seminary Students: 14 full-time (7 women), 20 part-time (12 women); includes 1 minority (Native Hawaiian or other Pacific Islander, non-Hispanic/Latino), 5 international. 39 applicants, 64% accepted, 19 enrolled. Expenses: Contact institution. *Financial support:* Scholarships/grants available. Financial award application deadline: 12/15; financial award applicants required to submit FAFSA. In 2016, 1 master's awarded. *Program availability:* Part-time. Offers theology (MAR). *Application deadline:* For fall admission, 8/15 priority date for domestic students; for winter admission, 10/15 priority date for domestic students; for spring admission, 4/15 priority date for domestic students. Applications are processed on a rolling basis. *Application fee:* $50. Electronic applications accepted. *Application Contact:* Sharon Ward, Administrative Assistant, 816-423-4676, Fax: 816-423-4753, E-mail: ward@graceland.edu. *Dean*, Dr. Matthew Frizzell, 641-784-5276, E-mail: mfrizzel@graceland.edu.

Gleazer School of Education Students: 115 full-time (96 women), 20 part-time (17 women); includes 10 minority (5 Black or African American, non-Hispanic/Latino; 1 Asian, non-Hispanic/Latino; 1 Hispanic/Latino; 1 Native Hawaiian or other Pacific Islander, non-Hispanic/Latino; 2 Two or more races, non-Hispanic/Latino), 2 international. 155 applicants, 61% accepted, 85 enrolled. *Faculty:* 2 full-time (both women), 9 part-time/adjunct (5 women). Expenses: Contact institution. *Financial support:* Institutionally sponsored loans and scholarships/grants available. Financial award application deadline: 12/15; financial award applicants required to submit FAFSA. In 2016, 61 master's awarded. *Program availability:* Part-time, evening/weekend, online learning. Offers curriculum and instruction (M Ed); differentiated instruction (M Ed); instructional leadership (M Ed); literacy and instruction (M Ed); management in the inclusive classroom (M Ed); special education (M Ed); technology integration (M Ed). *Application deadline:* For fall admission, 10/1 for domestic students; for winter admission, 11/15 for domestic students; for spring admission, 2/15 priority date for domestic students; for summer admission, 6/1 for domestic students. Applications are processed on a rolling basis. *Application fee:* $50. Electronic applications accepted. *Application Contact:* Jeanette Calipetro, Admissions Representative, 816-423-4716, Fax: 816-833-2990, E-mail: jcali1@graceland.edu. *Interim Dean*, Dr. Lee Bash, 641-784-5072, E-mail: bash@graceland.edu.

School of Nursing Students: 275 full-time (246 women), 313 part-time (273 women); includes 79 minority (25 Black or African American, non-Hispanic/Latino; 4 American Indian or Alaska Native, non-Hispanic/Latino; 12 Asian, non-Hispanic/Latino; 23 Hispanic/Latino; 2 Native Hawaiian or other Pacific Islander, non-Hispanic/Latino; 13 Two or more races, non-Hispanic/Latino), 3 international. 140 applicants, 69% accepted, 69 enrolled. *Faculty:* 14 full-time (12 women), 21 part-time/adjunct (20 women). Expenses: Contact institution. *Financial support:* Institutionally sponsored loans available. Support available to part-time students. Financial award applicants required to submit FAFSA. In 2016, 137 master's, 11 doctorates awarded. *Program availability:* Part-time, online learning. Offers adult and gerontology acute care (MSN, PMC); family nurse practitioner (MSN, PMC); nurse educator (MSN, PMC); organizational leadership (DNP). *Application deadline:* For fall admission, 6/1 priority date for domestic students; for winter admission, 10/1 priority date for domestic students; for spring admission, 10/1 priority date for domestic students; for summer admission, 2/1 for domestic students. *Application fee:* $50. Electronic applications accepted. *Application Contact:* Nick Walker, Admissions Representative, 816-423-4717, Fax: 816-833-2990, E-mail: nowalker@

graceland.edu. *Dean*, Dr. Claudia D. Horton, 816-423-4670, Fax: 816-423-4753, E-mail: horton@graceland.edu.

GRACE MISSION UNIVERSITY, Fullerton, CA 92833
General Information Independent, coed, comprehensive institution.
GRADUATE UNITS
Graduate School Offers missions (M Div, MACE, MAICS, D Miss).

GRACE SCHOOL OF THEOLOGY, Conroe, TX 77384-4894
General Information Independent, coed, comprehensive institution.
GRADUATE UNITS
Graduate Programs Offers theology (M Div, MABS, MM, Th M).

GRACE THEOLOGICAL SEMINARY, Winona Lake, IN 46590-9907
General Information Independent-religious, coed, primarily men, graduate-only institution. *Graduate housing:* On-campus housing not available.
GRADUATE UNITS
Graduate and Professional Programs *Program availability:* Part-time, online learning. Offers biblical studies (Certificate); chaplaincy (M Div); exegetical studies (M Div); intercultural studies (M Div, MA, D Min); local church ministry (MA); pastoral counseling (M Div); pastoral studies (M Div, D Min); theology (Diploma). Electronic applications accepted.

GRACE UNIVERSITY, Omaha, NE 68108
General Information Independent-religious, coed, comprehensive institution. *Graduate housing:* Rooms and/or apartments available on a first-come, first-served basis to single and married students.
GRADUATE UNITS
College of Graduate Studies *Program availability:* Part-time, evening/weekend. Offers Bible (MA); counseling (MA). Electronic applications accepted.

THE GRADUATE CENTER, CITY UNIVERSITY OF NEW YORK, New York, NY 10016-4039
General Information State and locally supported, coed, graduate-only institution. CGS member. *Graduate housing:* Rooms and/or apartments available to single and married students. Housing application deadline: 5/1. *Research affiliation:* American Museum of Natural History (anthropology), Roche Institute of Molecular Biology (biological sciences), New York Botanical Gardens (biological sciences).
GRADUATE UNITS
Graduate Studies Offers accounting (PhD); anthropological linguistics (PhD); archaeology (PhD); architecture (PhD); audiology (Au D); basic applied neurocognition (PhD); behavioral science (PhD); biochemistry (PhD); biology (PhD); biomedical engineering (PhD); biopsychology (PhD); chemical engineering (PhD); chemistry (PhD); civil engineering (PhD); classics (MA, PhD); clinical psychology (PhD); comparative literature (MA, PhD); computer science (PhD); criminal justice (PhD); cultural anthropology (PhD); developmental psychology (PhD); earth and environmental sciences (PhD); economics (PhD); educational psychology (PhD); electrical engineering (PhD); English (PhD); environmental psychology (PhD); experimental psychology (PhD); finance (PhD); French (PhD); Germanic languages and literatures (MA, PhD); graphic arts (PhD); Hispanic and Luso-Brazilian literatures and languages (PhD); history (PhD); industrial psychology (PhD); learning processes (PhD); liberal studies (MA); linguistics (MA, PhD); management planning systems (PhD); mathematics (PhD); mechanical engineering (PhD); music (DMA, PhD); neuropsychology (PhD); nursing (PhD); painting (PhD); philosophy (MA, PhD); photography (PhD); physical anthropology (PhD); physical therapy (DPT); physics (PhD); political science (MA, PhD); psychology (PhD); public health (DPH); sculpture (PhD); social personality (PhD); social welfare (DSW, PhD); sociology (PhD); speech and hearing sciences (PhD); theatre (PhD); urban education (PhD). Electronic applications accepted.
Interdisciplinary Studies Offers language in social context (PhD); medieval studies (PhD); public policy (MA, PhD); urban studies (MA, PhD); women's studies (MA, PhD).

GRADUATE INSTITUTE OF APPLIED LINGUISTICS, Dallas, TX 75236
General Information Independent, coed, graduate-only institution.
GRADUATE UNITS
Graduate Programs *Program availability:* Part-time. Offers applied linguistics (MA, Certificate); language development (MA). Electronic applications accepted.

GRADUATE THEOLOGICAL UNION, Berkeley, CA 94709-1212
General Information Independent-religious, coed, graduate-only institution. *Graduate housing:* Rooms and/or apartments available on a first-come, first-served basis to single and married students. Housing application deadline: 6/1.
GRADUATE UNITS
Graduate Programs Offers art and religion (MA, PhD, Th D); biblical languages (MA); biblical studies (MA); Biblical studies (PhD, Th D); Buddhist studies (MA); Christian spirituality (MA, PhD, Th D); cultural and historical studies of religions (MA, PhD, Th D); ethics and social theory (Th D); history (MA, PhD, Th D); homiletics (MA, PhD, Th D); interdisciplinary studies (PhD, Th D); Jewish studies (MA, PhD, Th D, Certificate); liturgical studies (MA, PhD, Th D); Near Eastern religions (PhD, Th D); Orthodox Christian studies (MA); religion and psychology (MA, PhD, Th D); religion and society/ethics and social theory (MA); systematic and philosophical theology (MA, PhD, Th D). PhD programs in Jewish studies and Near Eastern religions offered jointly with University of California, Berkeley. Electronic applications accepted.

GRAMBLING STATE UNIVERSITY, Grambling, LA 71245
General Information State-supported, coed, university. CGS member. *Graduate housing:* On-campus housing not available. *Research affiliation:* U.S. Department of Defense (cyberspace technology, materials and manufacturing), National Institutes of Justice (technology and equipment in forensic science), U.S. Department of Housing and Urban Development (HUD) (housing preservation in low-income areas), National Science Foundation (science and engineering), NASA (aeronautics research), National Institutes of Health (biomedical sciences).
GRADUATE UNITS
School of Graduate Studies and Research *Program availability:* Part-time, evening/weekend. Electronic applications accepted.
College of Arts and Sciences *Program availability:* Part-time. Offers arts and sciences (MA, MPA); health services administration (MPA); human resource management

(MPA); public management (MPA); social sciences (MA); state and local government (MPA). Electronic applications accepted.
College of Education *Program availability:* Part-time, evening/weekend. Offers curriculum and instruction (MS); developmental education (MS, Ed D, PMC); education (M Ed, MAT, MS, Ed D, PMC); educational leadership (M Ed); special education (M Ed); sports administration (MS). Electronic applications accepted.
College of Professional Studies *Program availability:* Part-time. Offers criminal justice (MS); family nurse practitioner (PMC); mass communication (MA); nursing (MSN); social work (MSW). Electronic applications accepted.

GRAND CANYON UNIVERSITY, Phoenix, AZ 85017-1097
General Information Independent-religious, coed, comprehensive institution. *Enrollment by degree level:* 14,564 master's, 1,219 doctoral. *Graduate faculty:* 21 full-time (14 women), 696 part-time/adjunct (457 women). *Graduate housing:* Rooms and/or apartments available on a first-come, first-served basis to single and married students. *Student services:* Campus employment opportunities, campus safety program, career counseling, exercise/wellness program, free psychological counseling, international student services, low-cost health insurance, services for students with disabilities, teacher training, writing training. *Library facilities:* Fleming Library.
Computer facilities: 65 computers available on campus for general student use. A campuswide network can be accessed from student residence rooms and from off campus. Online class registration is available.
Website: http://www.gcu.edu/
General Application Contact: Becky Schildt, Online Enrollment Manager, 800-557-9551, Fax: 888-695-6316, E-mail: bschildt@online.gcu.edu.
GRADUATE UNITS
Colangelo College of Business Students: 1 full-time (0 women), 2,121 part-time (1,165 women); includes 341 minority (249 Black or African American, non-Hispanic/Latino; 17 American Indian or Alaska Native, non-Hispanic/Latino; 15 Asian, non-Hispanic/Latino; 29 Hispanic/Latino; 4 Native Hawaiian or other Pacific Islander, non-Hispanic/Latino; 27 Two or more races, non-Hispanic/Latino), 20 international. Average age 38. *Faculty:* 8 full-time (3 women), 147 part-time/adjunct (49 women). Expenses: Contact institution. *Financial support:* Federal Work-Study available. Support available to part-time students. Financial award applicants required to submit FAFSA. In 2016, 569 master's awarded. *Program availability:* Part-time, evening/weekend, online learning. Offers accounting (MBA, MS); business analytics (MS); disaster preparedness and executive fire service leadership (MS); finance (MBA); general management (MBA); health systems management (MBA); information technology management (MS); leadership (MBA, MS); marketing (MBA); organizational leadership and entrepreneurship (MS); project management (MBA); sports business (MBA); strategic human resource management (MBA). *Application deadline:* For fall admission, 8/21 for domestic students, 7/2 for international students; for spring admission, 12/24 for domestic students, 11/1 for international students. Applications are processed on a rolling basis. *Application fee:* $0. Electronic applications accepted. *Application Contact:* Matt Tidwell, Enrollment Manager, 602-639-6020, E-mail: mtidwell@gcu.edu. *Dean*, Kim Donaldson, 602-639-6597, E-mail: kdonaldson@gcu.edu.
College of Doctoral Studies Expenses: Contact institution. Offers data analytics (DBA); general psychology (PhD); management (DBA); marketing (DBA); organizational leadership (Ed D). *Application fee:* $0. *Application Contact:* Michael Berger, Dean, 602-639-7255. *Dean*, Michael Berger, 602-639-7255.
College of Education Expenses: Contact institution. *Financial support:* Federal Work-Study available. Support available to part-time students. Financial award applicants required to submit FAFSA. *Program availability:* Part-time, evening/weekend, online learning. Offers autism spectrum disorders (MA); curriculum and instruction (MA); early childhood education (M Ed); educational administration (M Ed); educational leadership (M Ed); elementary education (M Ed); gifted education (MA); instructional technology (MS); K-12 leadership (Ed S); reading (MA); secondary education (M Ed); secondary humanities education (M Ed); secondary STEM education (M Ed); special education (M Ed); teaching and learning (Ed D); teaching English to speakers of other languages (MA). *Application deadline:* For fall admission, 8/21 for domestic students, 7/2 for international students; for spring admission, 12/24 for domestic students, 11/1 for international students. Applications are processed on a rolling basis. *Application fee:* $100. Electronic applications accepted. *Application Contact:* Dr. Kimberly L. LaPrade, Dean, 602-639-6360, E-mail: kimberly.laprade@gcu.edu. *Dean*, Dr. Kimberly L. LaPrade, 602-639-6360, E-mail: kimberly.laprade@gcu.edu.
College of Nursing and Health Care Professions Expenses: Contact institution. *Financial support:* Federal Work-Study available. Support available to part-time students. Financial award applicants required to submit FAFSA. *Program availability:* Part-time, evening/weekend, online learning. Offers acute care nurse practitioner (MSN, PMC); family nurse practitioner (MSN, PMC); health care administration (MS); health care informatics (MS, MSN); leadership in health care systems (MSN); nursing (DNP); nursing education (MSN, PMC); public health (MPH, MSN). *Application fee:* $0. *Application Contact:* Lisa Smith, Dean, 602-639-6165, Fax: 602-589-2810. *Dean*, Lisa Smith, 602-639-6165, Fax: 602-589-2810.

GRAND RAPIDS THEOLOGICAL SEMINARY OF CORNERSTONE UNIVERSITY, Grand Rapids, MI 49525-5897
General Information Independent-religious, coed, graduate-only institution. *Graduate housing:* Rooms and/or apartments available on a first-come, first-served basis to single and married students. Housing application deadline: 6/1.
GRADUATE UNITS
Graduate Programs *Program availability:* Part-time, online learning. Offers Biblical counseling (M Div); biblical counseling (MA); chaplaincy (M Div); Christian education (M Div, MA); intercultural studies (M Div, MA); New Testament (MA, Th M); Old Testament (MA, Th M); pastoral studies (M Div); systematic theology (MA); theology (Th M). Electronic applications accepted.

GRAND VALLEY STATE UNIVERSITY, Allendale, MI 49401-9403
General Information State-supported, coed, comprehensive institution. CGS member. *Enrollment:* 25,460 graduate, professional, and undergraduate students; 1,419 full-time matriculated graduate/professional students (992 women), 1,627 part-time matriculated graduate/professional students (1,091 women). *Enrollment by degree level:* 2,728 master's, 286 doctoral, 32 other advanced degrees. *Graduate faculty:* 291 full-time (155 women), 107 part-time/adjunct (64 women). Tuition, state resident: full-time $11,304; part-time $5652 per credit hour. Tuition, nonresident: full-time $11,304; part-time $5652 per credit hour. Tuition and fees vary according to degree level and program. *Graduate housing:* Rooms and/or apartments available on a first-come, first-served basis to single and married students. Housing application deadline: 2/1. *Student services:* Campus employment opportunities, campus safety program, career counseling, child daycare

facilities, exercise/wellness program, free psychological counseling, grant writing training, international student services, low-cost health insurance, multicultural affairs office, services for students with disabilities, teacher training, writing training. *Library facilities:* Mary Idema Pew Library Learning and Information Commons plus 5 others. *Collection:* Books: 567,197 (physical), 1 million (digital/electronic). Students can reserve study rooms. *Research affiliation:* Van Andel Institute (life sciences/medical research), Spectrum Health (medical research), Elkins Innovations (life sciences), Progressive AE (water quality).

Computer facilities: 2,600 computers available on campus for general student use. A campuswide network can be accessed from student residence rooms and from off campus. Online class registration, transcript, degree audit, credit card payments are available.
Website: http://www.gvsu.edu/

General Application Contact: Tracey James-Heer, Associate Director for Graduate Recruitment, 616-331-2025, Fax: 616-486-6476, E-mail: james-ht@gvsu.edu.

GRADUATE UNITS

College of Community and Public Service Students: 276 full-time (225 women), 312 part-time (242 women); includes 115 minority (47 Black or African American, non-Hispanic/Latino; 1 American Indian or Alaska Native, non-Hispanic/Latino; 17 Asian, non-Hispanic/Latino; 27 Hispanic/Latino; 23 Two or more races, non-Hispanic/Latino), 17 international. Average age 29. 334 applicants, 88% accepted, 178 enrolled. *Faculty:* 34 full-time (19 women), 30 part-time/adjunct (19 women). Expenses: Contact institution. *Financial support:* In 2016–17, 88 students received support, including 42 fellowships, 56 research assistantships with full and partial tuition reimbursements available (averaging $8,000 per year); teaching assistantships, career-related internships or fieldwork, Federal Work-Study, institutionally sponsored loans, scholarships/grants, and unspecified assistantships also available. Financial award application deadline: 5/1. In 2016, 252 master's awarded. *Program availability:* Part-time, evening/weekend, online learning. Offers community and public service (MHA, MPA, MPNL, MS, MSW). *Application deadline:* For fall admission, 5/1 priority date for domestic students; for winter admission, 11/1 priority date for domestic students; for spring admission, 4/10 priority date for domestic students. Applications are processed on a rolling basis. *Application fee:* $30. Electronic applications accepted. *Application Contact:* Tracey James-Heer, Associate Director for Graduate Recruitment, 616-331-2025, Fax: 616-486-6476, E-mail: james-ht@gvsu.edu. *Dean,* George Grant, 616-331-6550.

School of Criminal Justice Students: 6 full-time (4 women), 22 part-time (12 women); includes 9 minority (3 Black or African American, non-Hispanic/Latino; 5 Hispanic/Latino; 1 Two or more races, non-Hispanic/Latino), 1 international. Average age 29. 11 applicants, 100% accepted, 10 enrolled. *Faculty:* 4 full-time (1 woman). Expenses: Contact institution. *Financial support:* In 2016–17, 10 students received support. Career-related internships or fieldwork, Federal Work-Study, scholarships/grants, and unspecified assistantships available. Financial award application deadline: 5/1. In 2016, 7 master's awarded. *Program availability:* Part-time, evening/weekend. Offers criminal justice (MS). *Application deadline:* For fall admission, 5/1 priority date for domestic students; for winter admission, 11/1 priority date for domestic students; for spring admission, 4/1 priority date for domestic students. Applications are processed on a rolling basis. *Application fee:* $30. Electronic applications accepted. *Application Contact:* Christopher Kierkus, Graduate Program Director/Recruiting Contact, 616-331-7132, Fax: 616-331-7155, E-mail: kierkusc@gvsu.edu. *Director,* Dr. Kathleen Bailey, 616-331-7148, Fax: 616-331-7155, E-mail: baileyk@gvsu.edu.

School of Public, Nonprofit and Health Administration Students: 44 full-time (27 women), 100 part-time (71 women); includes 27 minority (9 Black or African American, non-Hispanic/Latino; 5 Asian, non-Hispanic/Latino; 8 Hispanic/Latino; 4 Two or more races, non-Hispanic/Latino), 7 international. Average age 31. 65 applicants, 85% accepted, 32 enrolled. *Faculty:* 14 full-time (7 women), 5 part-time/adjunct (2 women). Expenses: Contact institution. *Financial support:* In 2016–17, 23 students received support, including 11 fellowships, 15 research assistantships with full and partial tuition reimbursements available (averaging $8,000 per year); career-related internships or fieldwork, Federal Work-Study, scholarships/grants, and unspecified assistantships also available. Financial award application deadline: 5/1. In 2016, 61 master's awarded. *Program availability:* Part-time, evening/weekend. Offers health administration (MHA); philanthropy and nonprofit leadership (MPNL); public, nonprofit and health administration (MHA, MPA, MPNL). *Application deadline:* For fall admission, 5/1 priority date for domestic students; for winter admission, 11/1 priority date for domestic students. Applications are processed on a rolling basis. *Application fee:* $30. Electronic applications accepted. *Application Contact:* Davia Downey, Graduate Program Director/Recruiting Contact, 616-331-6681, Fax: 616-331-7120, E-mail: downeyd@gvsu.edu. *Director,* Dr. Richard Jelier, 616-331-6575, Fax: 616-331-7120, E-mail: jelierr@gvsu.edu.

School of Social Work Students: 188 full-time (167 women), 138 part-time (116 women); includes 61 minority (31 Black or African American, non-Hispanic/Latino; 5 Asian, non-Hispanic/Latino; 13 Hispanic/Latino; 12 Two or more races, non-Hispanic/Latino), 1 international. Average age 28. 198 applicants, 91% accepted, 114 enrolled. *Faculty:* 15 full-time (11 women), 25 part-time/adjunct (17 women). Expenses: Contact institution. *Financial support:* In 2016–17, 40 students received support, including 22 fellowships, 23 research assistantships with full and partial tuition reimbursements available (averaging $8,000 per year); career-related internships or fieldwork, Federal Work-Study, institutionally sponsored loans, and unspecified assistantships also available. In 2016, 165 master's awarded. *Program availability:* Part-time. Offers social work (MSW). *Application deadline:* For fall admission, 5/1 priority date for domestic students; for winter admission, 10/1 priority date for domestic students; for spring admission, 3/15 priority date for domestic students. Applications are processed on a rolling basis. *Application fee:* $30. Electronic applications accepted. *Application Contact:* Cray Mulder, Graduate Program Director/Recruiting Contact, 616-331-6596, E-mail: mulderc@gvsu.edu. *Chair,* Dr. Dianne Green-Smith, 616-331-6565, Fax: 616-331-6550, E-mail: greensmd@gvsu.edu.

College of Education Students: 153 full-time (101 women), 755 part-time (568 women); includes 126 minority (64 Black or African American, non-Hispanic/Latino; 4 American Indian or Alaska Native, non-Hispanic/Latino; 11 Asian, non-Hispanic/Latino; 27 Hispanic/Latino; 20 Two or more races, non-Hispanic/Latino), 9 international. Average age 33. 284 applicants, 96% accepted, 124 enrolled. *Faculty:* 40 full-time (25 women), 17 part-time/adjunct (8 women). Expenses: Contact institution. *Financial support:* In 2016–17, 198 students received support, including 139 fellowships, 67 research assistantships with full and partial tuition reimbursements available (averaging $8,000 per year); career-related internships or fieldwork, Federal Work-Study, scholarships/grants, and unspecified assistantships also available. In 2016, 332 master's (plus 12 Ed Ss awarded. *Program availability:* Part-time, evening/weekend, 100% online. Offers adult and higher education (M Ed); cognitive impairment (M Ed); college student affairs leadership (M Ed); early childhood developmental delay (M Ed); early childhood education (M Ed); education (M Ed, Ed S); educational differentiation (M Ed); educational leadership (M Ed); educational technology (M Ed); educational technology integration (M Ed); elementary education (M Ed); emotional impairment (M Ed); higher education (M Ed); instruction and curriculum (M Ed); leadership (Ed S); learning disabilities (M Ed); literacy studies (M Ed); middle level education (M Ed); reading and language arts (M Ed); school counseling (M Ed); school library media services (M Ed); secondary level education (M Ed); special education (M Ed); teaching English to speakers of other languages (M Ed). *Application deadline:* Applications are processed on a rolling basis. *Application fee:* $30. Electronic applications accepted. *Application Contact:* Thomas Owens, Director, Student Information and Services Center, 616-331-6282, Fax: 616-331-6217, E-mail: owenst@gvsu.edu. *Dean,* Dr. Barry Kanpol, 616-331-6821, Fax: 616-331-6515, E-mail: kanpolb@gvsu.edu.

College of Health Professions Students: 627 full-time (474 women), 52 part-time (41 women); includes 60 minority (14 Black or African American, non-Hispanic/Latino; 8 Asian, non-Hispanic/Latino; 18 Hispanic/Latino; 20 Two or more races, non-Hispanic/Latino), 4 international. Average age 26. 1,096 applicants, 33% accepted, 283 enrolled. *Faculty:* 61 full-time (46 women), 16 part-time/adjunct (14 women). Expenses: Contact institution. *Financial support:* In 2016–17, 83 students received support, including 55 fellowships, 36 research assistantships with full and partial tuition reimbursements available (averaging $8,000 per year); career-related internships or fieldwork, Federal Work-Study, institutionally sponsored loans, and scholarships/grants also available. Financial award application deadline: 2/15. In 2016, 201 master's, 50 doctorates awarded. Offers clinical dietetics (MS); health professions (MPAS, MPH, MS, DPT); medical dosimetry (MS); occupational therapy (MS); physical therapy (DPT); physician assistant studies (MPAS); public health (MPH); speech-language pathology (MS). *Application deadline:* For winter admission, 1/15 priority date for domestic and international students. Applications are processed on a rolling basis. Electronic applications accepted. *Application Contact:* Darlene Zwart, Student Services Coordinator, 616-331-3958, E-mail: zwartda@gvsu.edu. *Dean,* Dr. Roy Olsson, 616-331-3356, Fax: 616-331-3350, E-mail: olssonr@gvsu.edu.

College of Liberal Arts and Sciences Students: 120 full-time (77 women), 141 part-time (89 women); includes 23 minority (8 Black or African American, non-Hispanic/Latino; 1 American Indian or Alaska Native, non-Hispanic/Latino; 7 Hispanic/Latino; 7 Two or more races, non-Hispanic/Latino), 34 international. Average age 27. 213 applicants, 71% accepted, 98 enrolled. *Faculty:* 78 full-time (32 women), 3 part-time/adjunct (1 woman). Expenses: Contact institution. *Financial support:* In 2016–17, 103 students received support, including 13 fellowships; career-related internships or fieldwork, Federal Work-Study, institutionally sponsored loans, scholarships/grants, and unspecified assistantships also available. In 2016, 80 master's awarded. *Program availability:* Part-time, evening/weekend. Offers applied linguistics (MA); biology (MS); biomedical sciences (MHS); biostatistics (MS); cell and molecular biology (MS); English (MA); liberal arts and sciences (MA, MHS, MS, Psy S); school psychology (MS, Psy S). *Application deadline:* Applications are processed on a rolling basis. *Application fee:* $30. Electronic applications accepted. *Application Contact:* Betty Schaner, Assistant Dean of Advising and Student Services, 616-331-2495, Fax: 616-331-3675, E-mail: schanerb@gvsu.edu. *Dean,* Dr. Frederick Antczak, 616-331-2495, Fax: 616-331-3675, E-mail: antczakf@gvsu.edu.

School of Communications Students: 11 full-time (8 women), 39 part-time (28 women); includes 10 minority (4 Black or African American, non-Hispanic/Latino; 4 Hispanic/Latino; 2 Two or more races, non-Hispanic/Latino), 4 international. Average age 30. 36 applicants, 94% accepted, 15 enrolled. *Faculty:* 8 full-time (2 women), 2 part-time/adjunct (0 women). Expenses: Contact institution. *Financial support:* In 2016–17, 11 students received support, including 7 fellowships, 4 research assistantships with full and partial tuition reimbursements available (averaging $8,000 per year); career-related internships or fieldwork, Federal Work-Study, and institutionally sponsored loans also available. Support available to part-time students. Financial award application deadline: 4/15. In 2016, 16 master's awarded. *Program availability:* Part-time, evening/weekend. Offers communications (MS). *Application deadline:* For fall admission, 8/15 priority date for domestic students; for winter admission, 12/15 priority date for domestic students; for spring admission, 4/15 priority date for domestic students. Applications are processed on a rolling basis. *Application fee:* $30. Electronic applications accepted. *Application Contact:* Dr. Alex Nesterenko, Graduate Program Director, 616-331-3668, Fax: 616-331-2700, E-mail: nesterea@gvsu.edu. *Director,* Dr. Vandana Pednekar Magal, 616-331-3606, Fax: 616-895-2700, E-mail: thompsoa@gvsu.edu.

Kirkhof College of Nursing Students: 67 full-time (56 women), 63 part-time (54 women); includes 16 minority (8 Black or African American, non-Hispanic/Latino; 3 Asian, non-Hispanic/Latino; 4 Hispanic/Latino; 1 Two or more races, non-Hispanic/Latino), 2 international. Average age 33. 44 applicants, 98% accepted, 27 enrolled. *Faculty:* 18 full-time (all women), 6 part-time/adjunct (3 women). Expenses: Contact institution. *Financial support:* In 2016–17, 48 students received support, including 25 fellowships, 30 research assistantships with partial tuition reimbursements available (averaging $4,000 per year); career-related internships or fieldwork, Federal Work-Study, institutionally sponsored loans, and traineeships also available. Financial award application deadline: 2/15. In 2016, 5 master's, 21 doctorates awarded. *Program availability:* Part-time. Offers advanced practice (MSN); case management (MSN); nursing administration (MSN); nursing education (MSN); nursing practice (DNP). *Application deadline:* For fall admission, 3/15 priority date for domestic students. Applications are processed on a rolling basis. *Application fee:* $30. Electronic applications accepted. *Application Contact:* Dr. Karen Burritt, Associate Dean for Graduate Programs, 616-331-5585, Fax: 616-331-7362, E-mail: coviakc@gvsu.edu. *Dean,* Dr. Cynthia McCurren, 616-331-7161, Fax: 616-331-7362.

Padnos College of Engineering and Computing Students: 69 full-time (17 women), 101 part-time (22 women); includes 18 minority (5 Black or African American, non-Hispanic/Latino; 6 Asian, non-Hispanic/Latino; 6 Hispanic/Latino; 1 Two or more races, non-Hispanic/Latino), 83 international. Average age 28. 242 applicants, 61% accepted, 46 enrolled. *Faculty:* 24 full-time (3 women), 1 part-time/adjunct (0 women). Expenses: Contact institution. *Financial support:* In 2016–17, 54 students received support, including 15 fellowships; unspecified assistantships also available. In 2016, 65 master's awarded. *Program availability:* Part-time. Offers engineering and computing (MS, MSE); medical and bioinformatics (MS). *Application deadline:* For fall admission, 2/1 for domestic students. Applications are processed on a rolling basis. *Application fee:* $30. Electronic applications accepted. *Application Contact:* Sara Wheeler, Director, Advising Center/Recruiting Contact, 616-331-6025, E-mail: wheelesa@gvsu.edu. *Dean,* Dr. Paul Plotkowski, 616-331-6260, Fax: 616-331-6770, E-mail: plotkowp@gvsu.edu.

School of Computing and Information Systems Students: 28 full-time (3 women), 57 part-time (14 women); includes 11 minority (3 Black or African American, non-Hispanic/Latino; 4 Asian, non-Hispanic/Latino; 3 Hispanic/Latino; 1 Two or more races, non-Hispanic/Latino), 32 international. Average age 30. 97 applicants, 59% accepted, 17 enrolled. *Faculty:* 10 full-time (3 women), 1 (woman) part-time/adjunct. Expenses: Contact institution. *Financial support:* In 2016–17, 11 students received support, including 3 fellowships, 10 research assistantships with full and partial tuition reimbursements available (averaging $8,000 per year). In 2016, 36 master's awarded. *Program availability:* Part-time, evening/weekend. Offers computer information systems (MS). *Application deadline:* For fall admission, 6/1 for international students; for winter admission, 9/1 for international students. Applications are processed on a rolling basis. *Application fee:* $30. Electronic applications accepted. *Application Contact:* Dr. D. Robert Adams, Graduate Program Director/Recruiting Contact, 616-331-3885, Fax: 616-331-2106, E-mail: adams@cis.gvsu.edu. *Director*, Dr. Paul Leidig, 616-331-2038, Fax: 616-331-2106. E-mail: leidigp@gvsu.edu.

School of Engineering Students: 29 full-time (8 women), 38 part-time (5 women); includes 5 minority (2 Black or African American, non-Hispanic/Latino; 1 Asian, non-Hispanic/Latino; 2 Hispanic/Latino), 37 international. Average age 26. 129 applicants, 58% accepted, 23 enrolled. *Faculty:* 16 full-time (3 women). Expenses: Contact institution. *Financial support:* In 2016–17, 32 students received support, including 8 fellowships; career-related internships or fieldwork, Federal Work-Study, institutionally sponsored loans, scholarships/grants, and unspecified assistantships also available. In 2016, 24 master's awarded. *Program availability:* Part-time, evening/weekend. Offers electrical and computer engineering (MSE); manufacturing operations (MSE); mechanical engineering (MSE); product design and manufacturing engineering (MSE). *Application deadline:* Applications are processed on a rolling basis. *Application fee:* $30. Electronic applications accepted. *Application Contact:* Dr. Shabbir Choudhuri, Graduate Program Director, 616-331-6845, Fax: 616-331-7215, E-mail: choudhus@gvsu.edu. *Director*, Dr. Wael Mokhtar, 616-331-6015, Fax: 616-331-7215, E-mail: mokhtarw@gvsu.edu.

Seidman College of Business Students: 107 full-time (42 women), 203 part-time (75 women); includes 17 minority (4 Black or African American, non-Hispanic/Latino; 5 Asian, non-Hispanic/Latino; 3 Hispanic/Latino; 5 Two or more races, non-Hispanic/Latino), 13 international. Average age 30. 120 applicants, 88% accepted, 82 enrolled. *Faculty:* 22 full-time (9 women), 15 part-time/adjunct (3 women). Expenses: Contact institution. *Financial support:* In 2016–17, 79 students received support, including 60 fellowships; Federal Work-Study, institutionally sponsored loans, and unspecified assistantships also available. Support available to part-time students. Financial award application deadline: 2/15; financial award applicants required to submit FAFSA. In 2016, 147 master's awarded. *Program availability:* Part-time, evening/weekend. Offers accounting (MSA); business (MBA, MSA, MST); business administration (MBA); taxation (MST). *Application deadline:* For fall admission, 8/1 priority date for domestic students, 5/1 priority date for international students; for winter admission, 12/1 priority date for domestic students, 11/1 priority date for international students; for spring admission, 4/1 priority date for domestic students, 3/1 priority date for international students. Applications are processed on a rolling basis. *Application fee:* $30. Electronic applications accepted. *Application Contact:* Koleta Moore, Assistant Director, Graduate Business Programs, 616-331-7400, Fax: 616-331-7389, E-mail: moorekol@gvsu.edu. *Dean*, Dr. Diana Lawson, 616-331-7385, Fax: 616-331-7380, E-mail: lawsond1@gvsu.edu.

GRAND VIEW UNIVERSITY, Des Moines, IA 50316-1599

General Information Independent-religious, coed, comprehensive institution.

GRADUATE UNITS

Graduate Studies *Program availability:* Part-time, evening/weekend. Offers athletic training (MS); clinical nurse leader (MSN, Post Master's Certificate); nursing education (MSN, Post Master's Certificate); organizational leadership (MS); sport management (MS); teacher leadership (M Ed); urban education (M Ed). Electronic applications accepted.

GRANITE STATE COLLEGE, Concord, NH 03301

General Information State and locally supported, coed, comprehensive institution. *Enrollment:* 2,136 graduate, professional, and undergraduate students; 57 full-time matriculated graduate/professional students (30 women), 65 part-time matriculated graduate/professional students (45 women). *Enrollment by degree level:* 122 master's. *Graduate faculty:* 2 full-time (both women), 23 part-time/adjunct (12 women). Tuition, state resident: full-time $9216; part-time $512 per credit. Tuition, nonresident: full-time $9810; part-time $545 per credit. *Graduate housing:* On-campus housing not available. *Student services:* Campus employment opportunities, campus safety program, career counseling, free psychological counseling, services for students with disabilities. *Library facilities:* GSC Library and Research Commons. *Collection:* Books: 200,000 (digital/electronic); Serial titles: 23,000 (digital/electronic); Databases: 20. Weekly public service hours: 126.

Computer facilities: 146 computers available on campus for general student use. A campuswide network can be accessed. Online class registration is available. Website: http://www.granite.edu/

General Application Contact: Ana Gonzalez, Administrative Assistant, Office of Graduate Studies, 603-513-1334, Fax: 603-513-1387, E-mail: gsc.graduatestudies@granite.edu.

GRADUATE UNITS

MS in Leadership Program Students: 25 full-time (11 women), 27 part-time (24 women); includes 1 minority (American Indian or Alaska Native, non-Hispanic/Latino). Average age 40. 11 applicants, 82% accepted, 6 enrolled. *Faculty:* 1 (woman) full-time, 7 part-time/adjunct (4 women). Expenses: Contact institution. *Financial support:* Federal Work-Study and National Guard course waivers available. Financial award applicants required to submit FAFSA. In 2016, 4 master's awarded. *Program availability:* Part-time, evening/weekend, 100% online, blended/hybrid learning. Offers leadership (MS). *Application deadline:* Applications are processed on a rolling basis. *Application fee:* $0. Electronic applications accepted. *Application Contact:* Ana Gonzalez, Administrative Assistant, Office of Graduate Studies, 603-822-5433, Fax: 603-513-1387, E-mail: gsc.graduatestudies@granite.edu. *Vice Provost of Academic Affairs*, Dr. Johnna Herrick-Phelps, 603-228-3000, E-mail: johnna.herrick-phelps@granite.edu.

MS in Management Program Students: 6 full-time (all women), 16 part-time (10 women); includes 2 minority (both Two or more races, non-Hispanic/Latino). Average age 35. 8 applicants, 88% accepted, 5 enrolled. *Faculty:* 1 (woman) full-time, 5 part-time/adjunct (1 woman). Expenses: Contact institution. *Financial support:* Federal Work-Study and National Guard course waivers available. Financial award applicants required to submit FAFSA. In 2016, 4 master's awarded. *Program availability:* Part-time, 100% online, blended/hybrid learning. Offers management (MS). *Application deadline:*

Applications are processed on a rolling basis. *Application fee:* $0. Electronic applications accepted. *Application Contact:* Ana Gonzalez, Administrative Assistant, Office of Graduate Studies, 603-822-5433, Fax: 603-513-1387, E-mail: gsc.graduatestudies@granite.edu. *Vice Provost of Academic Affairs*, Dr. Johnna Herrick-Phelps, 855-228-3000, E-mail: johnna.herrick-phelps@granite.edu.

MS in Project Management Program Students: 18 full-time (9 women), 19 part-time (11 women); includes 2 minority (1 American Indian or Alaska Native, non-Hispanic/Latino; 1 Hispanic/Latino). Average age 42. 12 applicants, 92% accepted, 9 enrolled. *Faculty:* 1 (woman) full-time, 10 part-time/adjunct (6 women). Expenses: Contact institution. *Financial support:* Federal Work-Study and National Guard course waivers available. Financial award applicants required to submit FAFSA. In 2016, 18 master's awarded. *Program availability:* Part-time, 100% online, blended/hybrid learning. Offers project management (MS). *Application deadline:* Applications are processed on a rolling basis. *Application fee:* $0. Electronic applications accepted. *Application Contact:* Ana Gonzalez, Administrative Assistant, Office of Graduate Studies, 603-513-1334, Fax: 603-513-1387, E-mail: gsc.graduatestudies@granite.edu. *Vice Provost for Academic Affairs*, Dr. Johnna Herrick-Phelps, 855-228-3000, E-mail: johnna.herrick-phelps@granite.edu.

GRANTHAM UNIVERSITY, Lenexa, KS 66219

General Information Proprietary, coed, comprehensive institution. *Enrollment:* 121 full-time matriculated graduate/professional students (68 women), 1,613 part-time matriculated graduate/professional students (713 women). *Enrollment by degree level:* 1,726 master's. *Graduate faculty:* 2 full-time, 68 part-time/adjunct. *Tuition:* Full-time $3900; part-time $325 per credit hour. *Required fees:* $45 per term. One-time fee: $100. *Student services:* Career counseling, international student services, services for students with disabilities, writing training. *Library facilities:* Grantham Online Library.

Computer facilities: Online class registration is available. Website: http://www.grantham.edu/

General Application Contact: Jared Parlette, Vice President of Student Enrollment, 888-947-2684, Fax: 866-908-2360, E-mail: admissions@grantham.edu.

GRADUATE UNITS

College of Engineering and Computer Science Students: 15 full-time (7 women), 244 part-time (56 women); includes 114 minority (81 Black or African American, non-Hispanic/Latino; 4 American Indian or Alaska Native, non-Hispanic/Latino; 8 Asian, non-Hispanic/Latino; 12 Hispanic/Latino; 9 Two or more races, non-Hispanic/Latino). Average age 40. 293 applicants, 96% accepted, 260 enrolled. *Faculty:* 12 part-time/adjunct. Expenses: Contact institution. *Financial support:* Scholarships/grants available. Financial award applicants required to submit FAFSA. In 2016, 78 master's awarded. *Program availability:* Part-time, online only, 100% online. Offers information management (MS); information technology (MS). *Application deadline:* Applications are processed on a rolling basis. Electronic applications accepted. *Application Contact:* Jared Parlette, Vice President of Student Enrollment, 888-947-2684, Fax: 866-908-2360, E-mail: admissions@grantham.edu. *Dean of the College of Engineering and Computer Sciences*, Dr. Nancy Miller, 913-309-4738, Fax: 855-681-5201, E-mail: nmiller@grantham.edu.

College of Nursing and Allied Health Students: 33 full-time (24 women), 310 part-time (230 women); includes 154 minority (98 Black or African American, non-Hispanic/Latino; 2 American Indian or Alaska Native, non-Hispanic/Latino; 25 Asian, non-Hispanic/Latino; 14 Hispanic/Latino; 3 Native Hawaiian or other Pacific Islander, non-Hispanic/Latino; 12 Two or more races, non-Hispanic/Latino). Average age 41. 422 applicants, 93% accepted, 343 enrolled. *Faculty:* 1 full-time, 18 part-time/adjunct. Expenses: Contact institution. *Financial support:* Scholarships/grants available. Financial award applicants required to submit FAFSA. In 2016, 127 master's awarded. *Program availability:* Part-time, online only, 100% online. Offers case management (MSN). *Application deadline:* Applications are processed on a rolling basis. Electronic applications accepted. *Application Contact:* Jared Parlette, Vice President of Student Enrollment, 888-947-2684, Fax: 866-908-2360, E-mail: admissions@grantham.edu. *Dean, College of Nursing and Allied Health*, Dr. Cheryl Rules, 913-309-4783, Fax: 844-897-6490, E-mail: crules@grantham.edu.

Mark Skousen School of Business Students: 73 full-time (37 women), 1,046 part-time (424 women); includes 442 minority (309 Black or African American, non-Hispanic/Latino; 8 American Indian or Alaska Native, non-Hispanic/Latino; 27 Asian, non-Hispanic/Latino; 63 Hispanic/Latino; 7 Native Hawaiian or other Pacific Islander, non-Hispanic/Latino; 28 Two or more races, non-Hispanic/Latino). Average age 40. 1,324 applicants, 95% accepted, 1123 enrolled. *Faculty:* 1 full-time, 36 part-time/adjunct. Expenses: Contact institution. *Financial support:* Scholarships/grants available. Financial award applicants required to submit FAFSA. In 2016, 331 master's awarded. *Program availability:* Part-time, online only, 100% online. Offers business administration (MBA); business intelligence (MS); human resources management (Certificate); information management (MBA); performance improvement (MS); project management (MBA, Certificate). *Application deadline:* Applications are processed on a rolling basis. Electronic applications accepted. *Application Contact:* Jared Parlette, Vice President of Student Enrollment, 800-955-2527, E-mail: admissions@grantham.edu. *Dean, Mark Skousen School of Business*, Dr. David Marker, 800-955-2527, E-mail: dmarker@grantham.edu.

GRATZ COLLEGE, Melrose Park, PA 19027

General Information Independent-religious, coed, graduate-only institution. *Graduate housing:* On-campus housing not available. *Student services:* Campus employment opportunities, career counseling, low-cost health insurance. *Library facilities:* Tuttleman Library. Website: http://www.gratz.edu/

General Application Contact: Joanna Boeing Bratton, Director of Admissions, 215-635-7300 Ext. 140, Fax: 215-635-7399, E-mail: admissions@gratz.edu.

GRADUATE UNITS

Graduate Programs Expenses: Contact institution. *Financial support:* Fellowships, career-related internships or fieldwork, Federal Work-Study, scholarships/grants, and tuition waivers (partial) available. Support available to part-time students. *Program availability:* Part-time, evening/weekend, online learning. Offers education (MA); education leadership (Ed D); Holocaust and genocide studies (MA, PhD); Jewish Christian studies (Graduate Certificate); Jewish communal service (MA, Certificate); Jewish instructional education (MA); Jewish studies (MA); nonprofit management (MS). *Application deadline:* Applications are processed on a rolling basis. *Application fee:* $50. *Application Contact:* Joanna Boeing Bratton, Director of Admissions, 215-635-7300 Ext. 140, Fax: 215-635-7399, E-mail: admissions@gratz.edu. *Dean for Academic Affairs*, Dr. Jerome Kutnick, 215-635-7300 Ext. 137, Fax: 215-635-7320, E-mail: jkutnick@gratz.edu.

GREEN MOUNTAIN COLLEGE, Poultney, VT 05764-1199

General Information Independent, coed, comprehensive institution.

GRADUATE UNITS

Program in Business Administration *Program availability:* Online learning. Offers business administration (MBA). Distance learning only. Electronic applications accepted.

Program in Environmental Studies *Program availability:* Part-time, evening/weekend, online learning. Offers environmental studies (MS). Distance learning only. Electronic applications accepted.

GREENSBORO COLLEGE, Greensboro, NC 27401-1875

General Information Independent-religious, coed, comprehensive institution. *Graduate housing:* Rooms and/or apartments guaranteed to single students and available on a first-come, first-served basis to married students. Housing application deadline: 6/1.

GRADUATE UNITS

Program in Education *Program availability:* Part-time, evening/weekend. Offers elementary education (M Ed); special education (M Ed). Electronic applications accepted.

Program in Teaching English to Speakers of Other Languages *Program availability:* Part-time, evening/weekend. Offers teaching English to speakers of other languages (MA). Electronic applications accepted.

GREENVILLE COLLEGE, Greenville, IL 62246-0159

General Information Independent-religious, coed, comprehensive institution. *Graduate housing:* On-campus housing not available.

GRADUATE UNITS

Program in Education Offers education (MAT); elementary education (MAE); secondary education (MAE). Electronic applications accepted.

Program in Leadership and Ministry *Program availability:* Part-time. Offers leadership and ministry (MA). Electronic applications accepted.

GWYNEDD MERCY UNIVERSITY, Gwynedd Valley, PA 19437-0901

General Information Independent-religious, coed, comprehensive institution. *Enrollment:* 2,667 graduate, professional, and undergraduate students; 562 full-time matriculated graduate/professional students (421 women), 70 part-time matriculated graduate/professional students (59 women). *Enrollment by degree level:* 443 master's, 144 doctoral, 45 other advanced degrees. *Graduate faculty:* 14 full-time (9 women), 97 part-time/adjunct (60 women). *Tuition:* Full-time $14,400; part-time $800 per credit hour. One-time fee: $165. Tuition and fees vary according to degree level and program. *Graduate housing:* On-campus housing not available. *Student services:* Campus employment opportunities, campus safety program, career counseling, exercise/wellness program, free psychological counseling, international student services, low-cost health insurance, services for students with disabilities, teacher training, writing training. *Library facilities:* Keiss Library plus 1 other. *Collection:* Books: 84,372 (physical), 150,948 (digital/electronic); Serial titles: 172 (physical), 32,373 (digital/electronic); Databases: 45. Weekly public service hours: 76; students can reserve study rooms.

Computer facilities: 250 computers available on campus for general student use. A campuswide network can be accessed from student residence rooms and from off campus. Online class registration is available.
Website: http://www.gmercyu.edu/

General Application Contact: Admission Counselor, 844-707-9060, E-mail: accelerate@gmercyu.edu.

GRADUATE UNITS

Frances M. Maguire School of Nursing and Health Professions Students: 22 full-time (18 women), 63 part-time (56 women); includes 26 minority (16 Black or African American, non-Hispanic/Latino; 8 Asian, non-Hispanic/Latino; 2 Hispanic/Latino). Average age 37. 72 applicants, 25% accepted, 16 enrolled. *Faculty:* 4 full-time (all women), 1 (woman) part-time/adjunct. Expenses: Contact institution. *Financial support:* In 2016–17, 21 students received support. Scholarships/grants, traineeships, and unspecified assistantships available. Financial award application deadline: 8/30. In 2016, 7 master's awarded. *Program availability:* Part-time, online learning. Offers clinical nurse specialist (MSN); nurse educator (MSN); nurse practitioner (MSN); nursing (DNP). *Application deadline:* For fall admission, 8/1 priority date for domestic students; for winter admission, 12/1 priority date for domestic students. Applications are processed on a rolling basis. Electronic applications accepted. *Application Contact:* Dr. Barbara A. Jones, Director, 215-646-7300 Ext. 407, Fax: 215-641-5564, E-mail: jones.b@gmc.edu. *Dean,* Dr. Andrea D. Hollingsworth, 215-646-7300 Ext. 539, Fax: 215-641-5517, E-mail: hollingsworth.a@gmc.edu.

School of Education Students: 466 full-time (355 women); includes 93 minority (66 Black or African American, non-Hispanic/Latino; 12 Asian, non-Hispanic/Latino; 15 Hispanic/Latino). Average age 36. 127 applicants, 18% accepted, 9 enrolled. *Faculty:* 8 full-time (5 women), 38 part-time/adjunct (24 women). Expenses: Contact institution. *Financial support:* In 2016–17, 2 research assistantships were awarded; career-related internships or fieldwork, Federal Work-Study, institutionally sponsored loans, tuition waivers (full and partial), and unspecified assistantships also available. Financial award applicants required to submit FAFSA. In 2016, 86 master's awarded. *Program availability:* Part-time, evening/weekend, 100% online. Offers educational administration (MS); master teacher (MS); school counseling (MS); special education (MS). *Application deadline:* Applications are processed on a rolling basis. *Application Contact:* Graduate Program Coordinator, 877-499-6333, E-mail: graduate@gmercyu.edu. *Dean,* Dr. Heather Pfleger, 215-646-7300 Ext. 21581, E-mail: pfleger.h@gmercyu.edu.

School of Graduate and Professional Studies Students: 73 full-time (48 women); includes 27 minority (20 Black or African American, non-Hispanic/Latino; 2 Asian, non-Hispanic/Latino; 5 Hispanic/Latino). Average age 39. *Faculty:* 5 full-time (all women), 22 part-time/adjunct (8 women). Expenses: Contact institution. *Financial support:* Career-related internships or fieldwork, Federal Work-Study, tuition waivers (full and partial), and unspecified assistantships available. Financial award application deadline: 8/31; financial award applicants required to submit FAFSA. In 2016, 80 master's awarded. *Program availability:* Part-time, evening/weekend. Offers health care administration (MBA); management (MSM); strategic management and leadership (MBA). *Application deadline:* Applications are processed on a rolling basis. *Application Contact:* Information Contact, 800-342-5462, Fax: 215-641-5556. *Dean,* Dr. Mary Sortino, 215-646-7300, E-mail: sortino.m@gmercyu.edu.

HALLMARK UNIVERSITY, San Antonio, TX 78230

General Information Independent, coed, comprehensive institution. *Enrollment:* 859 graduate, professional, and undergraduate students; 5 full-time matriculated graduate/professional students. *Enrollment by degree level:* 5 master's. *Graduate*

faculty: 2 full-time (0 women), 3 part-time/adjunct (1 woman). *Tuition:* Full-time $9653. *Graduate housing:* On-campus housing not available. *Library facilities:* Randall K. Williams Assessment Center/ Virtual Library plus 1 other.

Computer facilities: 250 computers available on campus for general student use. A campuswide network can be accessed from off campus. Online class registration is available.
Website: http://www.hallmarkuniversity.edu/

General Application Contact: Jennifer Sanchez, Director of Admissions, 210-690-9000 Ext. 212, Fax: 210-697-8225, E-mail: jsanchez@hallmarkuniversity.edu.

GRADUATE UNITS

School of Business Students: 5 full-time (0 women); includes 2 minority (1 Hispanic/Latino; 1 Two or more races, non-Hispanic/Latino). *Faculty:* 2 full-time (0 women), 3 part-time/adjunct (1 woman). Expenses: Contact institution. *Financial support:* Applicants required to submit FAFSA. In 2016, 1 master's awarded. Offers global management (MBA). *Application deadline:* Applications are processed on a rolling basis. *Application fee:* $60 ($0 for international students). *Application Contact:* Jennifer Sabchez, Director of Admissions, 210-690-9000 Ext. 212, Fax: 210-697-8225, E-mail: jsanchez@hallmarkuniversity.edu. *Dean of Academics,* Dr. Darla Kenward, 210-690-9000 Ext. 242, Fax: 210-697-8225, E-mail: dkenward@hallmarkuniversity.edu.

HAMLINE UNIVERSITY, St. Paul, MN 55104-1284

General Information Independent-religious, coed, comprehensive institution. *Enrollment:* 3,852 graduate, professional, and undergraduate students; 608 full-time matriculated graduate/professional students (380 women), 706 part-time matriculated graduate/professional students (515 women). *Enrollment by degree level:* 1,253 master's, 61 doctoral. *Graduate faculty:* 37 full-time (21 women), 109 part-time/adjunct (76 women). *Tuition:* Full-time $3728; part-time $466 per credit. *Required fees:* $14 per credit. One-time fee: $150 part-time. Tuition and fees vary according to degree level and program. *Graduate housing:* Rooms and/or apartments available on a first-come, first-served basis to single and married students. *Student services:* Campus employment opportunities, campus safety program, career counseling, exercise/wellness program, international student services, low-cost health insurance, multicultural affairs office, services for students with disabilities, teacher training, writing training. *Library facilities:* Bush Library. *Research affiliation:* Minnesota Women Elected Officials.

Computer facilities: 300 computers available on campus for general student use. A campuswide network can be accessed from student residence rooms and from off campus. Online class registration is available.
Website: http://www.hamline.edu/

General Application Contact: Shawn Skoog, Director of Graduate Recruitment and Admission, 651-523-2900, Fax: 651-523-3058, E-mail: sskoog03@hamline.edu.

GRADUATE UNITS

College of Liberal Arts Students: 89 full-time (65 women), 75 part-time (52 women); includes 14 minority (1 Black or African American, non-Hispanic/Latino; 1 American Indian or Alaska Native, non-Hispanic/Latino; 4 Asian, non-Hispanic/Latino; 3 Hispanic/Latino; 5 Two or more races, non-Hispanic/Latino), 2 international. Average age 37. 51 applicants, 55% accepted, 12 enrolled. *Faculty:* 9 full-time (8 women), 6 part-time/adjunct (5 women). Expenses: Contact institution. *Financial support:* Federal Work-Study and scholarships/grants available. Support available to part-time students. Financial award applicants required to submit FAFSA. In 2016, 46 master's awarded. *Program availability:* Part-time, evening/weekend. Offers creative writing (MFA); creative writing for children and young adults (MFA). *Application deadline:* For fall admission, 6/1 for domestic and international students; for spring admission, 11/1 for domestic students, 10/1 for international students; for summer admission, 3/1 for domestic students, 2/1 for international students. Applications are processed on a rolling basis. *Application fee:* $0 ($100 for international students). Electronic applications accepted. *Application Contact:* Shawn Skoog, Director of Graduate Admission and Recruitment, 651-523-2900, Fax: 651-523-3058, E-mail: gradprog@hamline.edu. *Interim Dean,* Dr. Marcela Kostihova, 651-523-2206, Fax: 651-523-3055, E-mail: cladean@hamline.edu.

School of Business Students: 272 full-time (137 women), 69 part-time (33 women); includes 76 minority (39 Black or African American, non-Hispanic/Latino; 2 American Indian or Alaska Native, non-Hispanic/Latino; 20 Asian, non-Hispanic/Latino; 10 Hispanic/Latino; 5 Two or more races, non-Hispanic/Latino), 19 international. Average age 34. 166 applicants, 64% accepted, 77 enrolled. *Faculty:* 21 full-time (7 women), 25 part-time/adjunct (4 women). Expenses: Contact institution. *Financial support:* Career-related internships or fieldwork, Federal Work-Study, scholarships/grants, and unspecified assistantships available. Support available to part-time students. Financial award applicants required to submit FAFSA. In 2016, 191 master's, 3 doctorates awarded. *Program availability:* Part-time, evening/weekend, blended/hybrid learning. Offers business administration (MBA); nonprofit management (MNM); public administration (MPA, DPA). *Application deadline:* For fall admission, 6/1 for domestic and international students; for spring admission, 11/1 for domestic students, 10/1 for international students; for summer admission, 3/1 for domestic students, 2/1 for international students. Applications are processed on a rolling basis. *Application fee:* $0 ($100 for international students). Electronic applications accepted. *Application Contact:* Shawn Skoog, Director of Graduate Recruitment and Admission, 651-523-2900, Fax: 651-523-3058, E-mail: gradprog@hamline.edu. *Dean,* Dr. Anne McCarthy, 651-523-2284, Fax: 651-523-3098, E-mail: hsb@hamline.edu.

School of Education Students: 277 full-time (201 women), 762 part-time (601 women); includes 122 minority (29 Black or African American, non-Hispanic/Latino; 1 American Indian or Alaska Native, non-Hispanic/Latino; 43 Asian, non-Hispanic/Latino; 29 Hispanic/Latino; 20 Two or more races, non-Hispanic/Latino), 12 international. Average age 34. 408 applicants, 77% accepted, 230 enrolled. *Faculty:* 29 full-time (23 women), 90 part-time/adjunct (70 women). Expenses: Contact institution. *Financial support:* Career-related internships or fieldwork, Federal Work-Study, and scholarships/grants available. Support available to part-time students. Financial award applicants required to submit FAFSA. In 2016, 279 master's, 14 doctorates awarded. *Program availability:* Part-time, evening/weekend, 100% online, blended/hybrid learning. Offers education (MA Ed, Ed D); English as a second language (MA); literacy education (MA); natural science and environmental education (MA Ed); teaching (MAT); teaching English to speakers of other languages (MA). *Application deadline:* For fall admission, 6/1 for domestic and international students; for spring admission, 11/1 for domestic and international students; for summer admission, 3/1 for domestic and international students. Applications are processed on a rolling basis. *Application fee:* $0 ($100 for international students). Electronic applications accepted. *Application Contact:* Shawn Skoog, Director of Graduate Recruitment and Admission, 651-523-2900, Fax: 651-523-3058, E-mail: gradprog@hamline.edu. *Dean,* Dr. Nancy Sorenson, 651-523-2600, Fax: 651-523-2489, E-mail: education@hamline.edu.

HAMPTON UNIVERSITY, Hampton, VA 23668

General Information Independent, coed, comprehensive institution. CGS member. *Enrollment:* 4,646 graduate, professional, and undergraduate students; 604 full-time matriculated graduate/professional students (447 women), 163 part-time matriculated graduate/professional students (106 women). *Enrollment by degree level:* 305 master's, 454 doctoral, 8 other advanced degrees. *Graduate faculty:* 120 full-time (55 women), 8 part-time/adjunct (2 women). *Tuition:* Full-time $10,776; part-time $548 per credit hour. *Required fees:* $35; $35 per credit hour. Tuition and fees vary according to course load and program. *Graduate housing:* Rooms and/or apartments available on a first-come, first-served basis to single and married students. Typical cost: $5556 per year ($10,684 including board) for single students. Room and board charges vary according to board plan. Housing application deadline: 6/1. *Student services:* Campus employment opportunities, campus safety program, career counseling, child daycare facilities, exercise/wellness program, free psychological counseling, international student services, services for students with disabilities, teacher training, writing training. *Library facilities:* William R. and Norma B. Harvey Library plus 4 others. *Collection:* Books: 307,143 (physical), 91,991 (digital/electronic); Serial titles: 8,240 (physical); Databases: 115. Study areas open 24 hours, 5–7 days a week; students can reserve study rooms. *Research affiliation:* NASA-Langley Research Center (physical sciences), Southeastern Universities Research Association (science), Continuous Electron Beam Accelerator Facility (science).

Computer facilities: Computer purchase and lease plans are available. 1,500 computers available on campus for general student use. A campuswide network can be accessed from student residence rooms and from off campus. Online class registration, learning management system are available.
Website: http://www.hamptonu.edu/

General Application Contact: Dr. Michelle Penn-Marshall, Dean, Graduate College, 757-727-5454, E-mail: hugrad@hamptonu.edu.

GRADUATE UNITS

Program in Business Administration Students: 39 full-time (27 women), 17 part-time (13 women); includes 53 minority (52 Black or African American, non-Hispanic/Latino; 1 Hispanic/Latino), 1 international. Average age 28. 29 applicants, 31% accepted, 9 enrolled. *Faculty:* 6 full-time (4 women). Expenses: Contact institution. *Financial support:* Teaching assistantships, career-related internships or fieldwork, Federal Work-Study, institutionally sponsored loans, scholarships/grants, unspecified assistantships, and stipends available. Support available to part-time students. Financial award application deadline: 6/30; financial award applicants required to submit FAFSA. In 2016, 22 master's, 1 doctorate awarded. *Program availability:* Part-time, online learning. Offers business administration (MBA, PhD). *Application deadline:* For fall admission, 6/1 priority date for domestic students, 4/1 priority date for international students; for spring admission, 11/1 priority date for domestic students, 9/1 priority date for international students; for summer admission, 4/1 priority date for domestic students, 2/1 priority date for international students. Applications are processed on a rolling basis. *Application fee:* $35. Electronic applications accepted. *Dean, School of Business,* Dr. Sid Credle, 757-727-5361.

School of Education and Human Development Students: 81 full-time (60 women), 80 part-time (44 women); includes 148 minority (all Black or African American, non-Hispanic/Latino), 2 international. Average age 33. 107 applicants, 59% accepted, 51 enrolled. *Faculty:* 18 full-time (11 women), 2 part-time/adjunct (both women). Expenses: Contact institution. *Financial support:* Fellowships, research assistantships, teaching assistantships, career-related internships or fieldwork, Federal Work-Study, institutionally sponsored loans, and scholarships/grants available. Support available to part-time students. Financial award application deadline: 5/1; financial award applicants required to submit FAFSA. In 2016, 54 master's, 12 doctorates awarded. *Program availability:* Part-time, evening/weekend. Offers college student development (MA); community agency counseling (MA); counseling (Ed S); counselor education and supervision (PhD); education and human development (MA, MS, MT, PhD, Ed S); educational leadership (MA); educational management (PhD); elementary education (MA); music education (MT); pastoral counseling (MA); school counseling (MA); secondary education (MT); sport administration (MS). *Application deadline:* For fall admission, 6/1 priority date for domestic students, 4/1 priority date for international students; for winter admission, 9/1 priority date for international students; for spring admission, 11/1 priority date for domestic students; for summer admission, 4/15 for domestic students, 2/1 priority date for international students. Applications are processed on a rolling basis. *Application fee:* $35. Electronic applications accepted. *Application Contact:* Dr. Michelle Penn-Marshall, Director, Graduate Programs, 757-727-5454, E-mail: hugrad@hamptonu.edu. *Dean,* Dr. Linda Malone-Colon, 757-727-5400.

School of Engineering and Technology Students: 12 full-time (7 women), 7 part-time (2 women); includes 16 minority (14 Black or African American, non-Hispanic/Latino; 2 Asian, non-Hispanic/Latino), 2 international. Average age 27. *Faculty:* 8 full-time (5 women), 2 part-time/adjunct (0 women). Expenses: Contact institution. *Financial support:* Applicants required to submit FAFSA. In 2016, 15 master's awarded. Offers architecture (M Arch). Electronic applications accepted. *Application Contact:* Robert Easter, Chair, Architecture Department, 757-727-5441, Fax: 757-728-6680. *Dean,* Dr. Joyce Shirazi, 757-728-6970, Fax: 757-728-6972, E-mail: joyce.shirazi@hamptonu.edu.

School of Nursing Students: 11 full-time (10 women), 28 part-time (26 women); includes 36 minority (32 Black or African American, non-Hispanic/Latino; 1 Asian, non-Hispanic/Latino; 3 Hispanic/Latino). Average age 47. 12 applicants, 58% accepted, 6 enrolled. *Faculty:* 6 full-time (all women), 2 part-time/adjunct (both women). Expenses: Contact institution. *Financial support:* In 2016–17, 2 students received support. Fellowships, research assistantships, teaching assistantships, career-related internships or fieldwork, Federal Work-Study, institutionally sponsored loans, and scholarships/grants available. Support available to part-time students. Financial award application deadline: 6/30; financial award applicants required to submit FAFSA. In 2016, 4 master's awarded. *Program availability:* Part-time, online learning. Offers advanced adult nursing (MS); community health nursing (MS); community mental health/psychiatric nursing (MS); family nursing (MS); gerontological nursing for the nurse practitioner (MS); nursing (PhD); women's health nursing (MS). *Application deadline:* For fall admission, 6/1 priority date for domestic students, 4/1 priority date for international students; for spring admission, 11/1 priority date for domestic students, 9/1 priority date for international students; for summer admission, 4/1 priority date for domestic students, 2/1 priority date for international students. Applications are processed on a rolling basis. *Application fee:* $35. Electronic applications accepted. *Chair,* Dr. Shevallanie Lott, 757-727-5654, E-mail: shevellanie.lott@hamptonu.edu.

School of Pharmacy Students: 237 full-time (188 women), 7 part-time (all women); includes 215 minority (201 Black or African American, non-Hispanic/Latino; 2 American Indian or Alaska Native, non-Hispanic/Latino; 12 Asian, non-Hispanic/Latino). Average age 25. 79 applicants, 44% accepted, 32 enrolled. *Faculty:* 22 full-time (10 women), 1 part-time/adjunct (0 women). Expenses: Contact institution. *Financial support:* In 2016–

17, 36 students received support. Scholarships/grants available. Financial award application deadline: 5/1; financial award applicants required to submit FAFSA. Offers pharmacy (Pharm D). *Application deadline:* For winter admission, 1/15 for domestic and international students. *Application fee:* $35. *Application Contact:* Denise James, Coordinator of Student Affairs, 757-728-6792, Fax: 757-727-5084, E-mail: denise.james@hamptonu.edu. *Dean,* Dr. Wayne T. Harris, 757-727-5071, Fax: 757-727-5840.

School of Science Students: 224 full-time (155 women), 24 part-time (14 women); includes 170 minority (141 Black or African American, non-Hispanic/Latino; 1 American Indian or Alaska Native, non-Hispanic/Latino; 15 Asian, non-Hispanic/Latino; 13 Hispanic/Latino), 10 international. Average age 26. 1,009 applicants, 12% accepted. *Faculty:* 56 full-time (20 women), 3 part-time/adjunct (1 woman). Expenses: Contact institution. *Financial support:* Fellowships, research assistantships, teaching assistantships, career-related internships or fieldwork, Federal Work-Study, institutionally sponsored loans, scholarships/grants, and stipends available. Support available to part-time students. Financial award application deadline: 6/30; financial award applicants required to submit FAFSA. In 2016, 63 master's, 25 doctorates awarded. *Program availability:* Part-time, evening/weekend, online learning. Offers atmospheric science (MS); biology (MS); chemistry and biochemistry (MS); computational mathematics (MS); computer science (MS); environmental science (MS); information assurance (MS); medical physics (MS, PhD); medical science (MS); nonlinear science (MS); nuclear physics (MS, PhD); optical physics (MS, PhD); physical therapy (DPT); planetary science (MS, PhD); science (MA, MS, MT, DPT, PhD); speech-language pathology (MA); statistics and probability (MS). *Application deadline:* For fall admission, 6/1 for domestic students, 4/1 for international students; for winter admission, 11/1 for domestic students, 9/1 for international students; for spring admission, 11/1 for domestic students, 9/1 for international students; for summer admission, 4/1 for domestic students, 2/1 for international students. Applications are processed on a rolling basis. *Application fee:* $35. Electronic applications accepted. *Dean,* Dr. Calvin Lowe, 757-722-5239.

HANNIBAL-LAGRANGE UNIVERSITY, Hannibal, MO 63401-1999

General Information Independent-religious, coed, comprehensive institution.

GRADUATE UNITS

Program in Education *Program availability:* Part-time, evening/weekend. Offers literacy (MS Ed); teaching and learning (MS Ed).

HARDING SCHOOL OF THEOLOGY, Memphis, TN 38117-5499

General Information Independent-religious, coed, primarily men, graduate-only institution. *Graduate housing:* Rooms and/or apartments available to single and married students.

GRADUATE UNITS

Graduate Programs *Program availability:* Part-time, online learning. Offers Christian ministry (MA); counseling (MA); ministry (M Div, D Min); religion (MA). Electronic applications accepted.

HARDING UNIVERSITY, Searcy, AR 72149-0001

General Information Independent-religious, coed, university. *Enrollment:* 5,904 graduate, professional, and undergraduate students; 672 full-time matriculated graduate/professional students (440 women), 811 part-time matriculated graduate/professional students (547 women). *Enrollment by degree level:* 884 master's, 376 doctoral, 36 other advanced degrees. *Graduate faculty:* 88 full-time (44 women), 96 part-time/adjunct (46 women). Tuition and fees vary according to degree level and program. *Graduate housing:* Rooms and/or apartments available on a first-come, first-served basis to single and married students. *Student services:* Campus employment opportunities, campus safety program, career counseling, exercise/wellness program, free psychological counseling, international student services, services for students with disabilities, writing training. *Library facilities:* Brackett Library plus 1 other. *Collection:* Books: 190,355 (physical), 129,853 (digital/electronic); Serial titles: 510 (physical), 81,906 (digital/electronic); Databases: 170. Students can reserve study rooms.

Computer facilities: 512 computers available on campus for general student use. A campuswide network can be accessed from student residence rooms and from off campus. Online class registration is available.
Website: http://www.harding.edu/

GRADUATE UNITS

Cannon-Clary College of Education Students: 130 full-time (94 women), 321 part-time (234 women); includes 83 minority (50 Black or African American, non-Hispanic/Latino; 4 American Indian or Alaska Native, non-Hispanic/Latino; 6 Asian, non-Hispanic/Latino; 13 Hispanic/Latino; 10 Two or more races, non-Hispanic/Latino), 11 international. Average age 35. 125 applicants, 88% accepted, 110 enrolled. *Faculty:* 22 full-time (9 women), 51 part-time/adjunct (37 women). Expenses: Contact institution. *Financial support:* In 2016–17, 31 students received support. Unspecified assistantships available. In 2016, 124 master's, 27 other advanced degrees awarded. *Program availability:* Part-time, evening/weekend. Offers advanced studies in teaching and learning (M Ed); art (MSE); behavioral science (MSE); counseling (MS, Ed S); early childhood special education (M Ed, MSE); education (MSE); educational leadership (M Ed, Ed S); elementary education (M Ed); English (MSE); French (MSE); history/social science (MSE); kinesiology (MSE); math (MSE); reading (M Ed); secondary education (M Ed); Spanish (MSE); teaching (MAT); teaching English as a second language (MSE). *Application deadline:* For fall admission, 8/1 for domestic and international students; for spring admission, 1/1 for domestic and international students. Applications are processed on a rolling basis. *Application fee:* $35. *Application Contact:* Information Contact, 501-279-4315, E-mail: gradstudiesedu@harding.edu. *Chair,* Dr. Clara Carroll, 501-279-4051, Fax: 501-279-4083, E-mail: ccarroll@harding.edu.

College of Allied Health Students: 244 full-time (169 women); includes 32 minority (7 Black or African American, non-Hispanic/Latino; 3 American Indian or Alaska Native, non-Hispanic/Latino; 8 Asian, non-Hispanic/Latino; 10 Hispanic/Latino; 4 Two or more races, non-Hispanic/Latino). Average age 25. 1,059 applicants, 17% accepted, 92 enrolled. *Faculty:* 27 full-time (16 women), 4 part-time/adjunct (2 women). Expenses: Contact institution. *Financial support:* In 2016–17, 6 students received support. In 2016, 57 master's, 32 doctorates awarded. Offers allied health (MS, DPT); communication sciences and disorders (MS); physical therapy (DPT); physician assistant (MS). *Application Contact:* Dr. Julie Hixson-Wallace, Vice Provost, 501-279-5205, Fax: 501-279-5192, E-mail: jahixson@harding.edu.

College of Bible and Ministry Students: 18 full-time (13 women), 19 part-time (2 women); includes 3 minority (all Black or African American, non-Hispanic/Latino). Average age 36. 12 applicants, 100% accepted, 12 enrolled. *Faculty:* 5 full-time (1 woman), 14 part-time/adjunct (1 woman). Expenses: Contact institution. *Financial support:* In 2016–17, 23 students received support. Scholarships/grants and unspecified assistantships available. Financial award applicants required to submit FAFSA. In 2016, 14 master's awarded. *Program availability:* Part-time, online learning. Offers Bible and ministry (M Min, MS); marriage and family therapy (MS); mental health counseling (MS); ministry (M Min). *Application Contact:* 501-279-4448, Fax: 501-279-5192, E-mail: bible@harding.edu. *Dean,* Dr. Monte Cox, 501-279-4448, Fax: 501-279-4042, E-mail: mcox@harding.edu.

College of Pharmacy Students: 211 full-time (136 women), 4 part-time (all women); includes 54 minority (17 Black or African American, non-Hispanic/Latino; 3 American Indian or Alaska Native, non-Hispanic/Latino; 31 Asian, non-Hispanic/Latino; 3 Hispanic/Latino), 8 international. Average age 27. 278 applicants, 37% accepted, 59 enrolled. *Faculty:* 34 full-time (18 women), 1 part-time/adjunct (0 women). Expenses: Contact institution. *Financial support:* In 2016–17, 35 students received support. Scholarships/grants available. Financial award applicants required to submit FAFSA. In 2016, 62 doctorates awarded. Offers pharmacy (Pharm D). *Application deadline:* For fall admission, 3/1 priority date for domestic and international students. Applications are processed on a rolling basis. *Application fee:* $50. Electronic applications accepted. *Application Contact:* Carol Jones, Director of Admissions, 501-279-5523, Fax: 501-279-5525, E-mail: ccjones@harding.edu. *Dean,* Dr. Jeff Mercer, 501-279-5205, Fax: 501-279-5525, E-mail: jmercer@harding.edu.

Paul R. Carter College of Business Administration Students: 36 full-time (15 women), 86 part-time (35 women); includes 17 minority (7 Black or African American, non-Hispanic/Latino; 5 Asian, non-Hispanic/Latino; 4 Hispanic/Latino; 1 Two or more races, non-Hispanic/Latino), 12 international. Average age 32. 22 applicants, 100% accepted, 22 enrolled. *Faculty:* 26 part-time/adjunct (6 women). Expenses: Contact institution. *Financial support:* Unspecified assistantships available. Financial award application deadline: 7/30; financial award applicants required to submit FAFSA. In 2016, 54 master's awarded. *Program availability:* Part-time, evening/weekend, 100% online. Offers international business (MBA); leadership and organizational management (MBA). *Application deadline:* For fall admission, 8/1 priority date for domestic and international students; for spring admission, 12/1 priority date for domestic and international students. Applications are processed on a rolling basis. *Application fee:* $40. *Application Contact:* Melanie Kiihnl, Recruiting Manager/Director of Marketing, 501-279-4523, Fax: 501-279-4805, E-mail: mba@harding.edu. *Director of Graduate Studies,* Glen Metheny, 501-279-5851, Fax: 501-279-4805, E-mail: gmetheny@harding.edu.

HARDIN-SIMMONS UNIVERSITY, Abilene, TX 79698-0001

General Information Independent-religious, coed, comprehensive institution. *Enrollment:* 2,205 graduate, professional, and undergraduate students; 249 full-time matriculated graduate/professional students (133 women), 235 part-time matriculated graduate/professional students (124 women). *Enrollment by degree level:* 340 master's, 144 doctoral. *Graduate faculty:* 81 full-time (33 women), 34 part-time/adjunct (8 women). *Tuition:* Full-time $12,510; part-time $695 per credit hour. *Required fees:* $325; $110 per semester. *Graduate housing:* Rooms and/or apartments available on a first-come, first-served basis to single and married students. Typical cost: $3750 per year ($8138 including board) for single students. Room and board charges vary according to board plan and housing facility selected. *Student services:* Campus employment opportunities, career counseling, free psychological counseling, services for students with disabilities. *Library facilities:* Richardson Library plus 1 other. *Collection:* Books: 515,254 (physical), 194,276 (digital/electronic); Serial titles: 1,040 (physical), 45,534 (digital/electronic); Databases: 137. Weekly public service hours: 89.

Computer facilities: 114 computers available on campus for general student use. A campuswide network can be accessed from student residence rooms and from off campus. Online class registration is available. Website: http://www.hsutx.edu/

General Application Contact: Dr. Nancy Kucinski, Dean of Graduate Studies, 325-670-1298, Fax: 325-670-1564, E-mail: gradoff@hsutx.edu.

GRADUATE UNITS

Graduate School Students: 137 full-time (68 women), 232 part-time (121 women); includes 95 minority (34 Black or African American, non-Hispanic/Latino; 6 Asian, non-Hispanic/Latino; 51 Hispanic/Latino; 4 Two or more races, non-Hispanic/Latino), 17 international. Average age 35. *Faculty:* 68 full-time (24 women), 33 part-time/adjunct (8 women). Expenses: Contact institution. *Financial support:* In 2016–17, 277 students received support, including 28 fellowships (averaging $2,735 per year); career-related internships or fieldwork, scholarships/grants, and recreation assistantships, coaching assistantships also available. Support available to part-time students. Financial award application deadline: 6/30; financial award applicants required to submit FAFSA. In 2016, 101 master's, 6 doctorates awarded. *Program availability:* Part-time. *Application deadline:* For fall admission, 8/15 priority date for domestic students, 4/1 for international students; for spring admission, 1/5 priority date for domestic students, 9/1 for international students. Applications are processed on a rolling basis. *Application fee:* $50. Electronic applications accepted. *Dean of Graduate Studies,* Dr. Nancy Kucinski, 325-670-1298, Fax: 325-670-1564, E-mail: gradoff@hsutx.edu.

College of Fine Arts Students: 4 full-time (2 women), 4 part-time (1 woman); includes 4 minority (1 Black or African American, non-Hispanic/Latino; 2 Hispanic/Latino; 1 Two or more races, non-Hispanic/Latino). Average age 28. *Faculty:* 9 full-time (3 women), 3 part-time/adjunct (1 woman). Expenses: Contact institution. *Financial support:* In 2016–17, 6 students received support, including 4 fellowships (averaging $2,700 per year); career-related internships or fieldwork and scholarships/grants also available. Support available to part-time students. Financial award application deadline: 6/30; financial award applicants required to submit FAFSA. In 2016, 2 master's awarded. *Program availability:* Part-time. Offers church music (MM); music education (MM); music performance (MM); theory and composition (MM). *Application deadline:* For fall admission, 8/15 priority date for domestic students, 4/1 for international students; for spring admission, 1/5 priority date for domestic students, 9/1 for international students. Applications are processed on a rolling basis. *Application fee:* $50. Electronic applications accepted. *Application Contact:* Dr. Nancy Kucinski, Dean of Graduate Studies, 325-670-1298, Fax: 325-670-1564, E-mail: gradoff@hsutx.edu. *Program Director,* Dr. Lynnette Chambers, 325-670-1430, Fax: 325-670-5873, E-mail: lchambers@hsutx.edu.

Cynthia Ann Parker College of Liberal Arts Students: 15 full-time (14 women), 8 part-time (5 women); includes 6 minority (5 Hispanic/Latino; 1 Two or more races, non-Hispanic/Latino). Average age 30. *Faculty:* 12 full-time (5 women). Expenses: Contact institution. *Financial support:* In 2016–17, 18 students received support, including 10 fellowships (averaging $1,975 per year); scholarships/grants also available. Support available to part-time students. Financial award application deadline: 6/30; financial award applicants required to submit FAFSA. In 2016, 16 master's awarded. *Program availability:* Part-time. Offers clinical counseling and marriage and family therapy (MA); English (MA); history (MA); liberal arts (MA). *Application deadline:* For fall admission, 8/15 priority date for domestic students, 4/1 for international students; for spring admission, 1/5 priority date for domestic students, 9/1 for international students. Applications are processed on a rolling basis. *Application fee:* $50. Electronic applications accepted. *Application Contact:* Dr. Nancy Kucinski, Dean of

Graduate Studies, 325-670-1298, Fax: 325-670-1564, E-mail: gradoff@hsutx.edu. *Dean,* Dr. Stephen Cook, 325-670-1487, E-mail: stephen.cook@hsutx.edu.

Holland School of Sciences and Mathematics Students: 4 full-time (2 women), 15 part-time (12 women); includes 3 minority (all Hispanic/Latino). Average age 35. *Faculty:* 5 full-time (2 women), 1 part-time/adjunct (0 women). Expenses: Contact institution. *Financial support:* In 2016–17, 9 students received support. Fellowships, career-related internships or fieldwork, and scholarships/grants available. Support available to part-time students. Financial award application deadline: 6/30; financial award applicants required to submit FAFSA. In 2016, 9 master's awarded. *Program availability:* Part-time. Offers environmental management (MS); mathematics (MS); physical therapy (DPT); sciences and mathematics (MS, DPT). *Application deadline:* For fall admission, 8/15 priority date for domestic students, 4/1 for international students; for spring admission, 1/5 priority date for domestic students, 9/1 for international students. Applications are processed on a rolling basis. *Application fee:* $50. Electronic applications accepted. *Application Contact:* Dr. Nancy Kucinski, Dean of Graduate Studies, 325-670-1298, Fax: 325-670-1564, E-mail: gradoff@hsutx.edu. *Dean,* Dr. Christopher McNair, 325-670-1401, Fax: 325-670-1385, E-mail: cmcnair@hsutx.edu.

Irvin School of Education Students: 29 full-time (20 women), 96 part-time (73 women); includes 27 minority (14 Black or African American, non-Hispanic/Latino; 12 Hispanic/Latino; 1 Two or more races, non-Hispanic/Latino), 4 international. Average age 36. *Faculty:* 16 full-time (8 women), 6 part-time/adjunct (3 women). Expenses: Contact institution. *Financial support:* In 2016–17, 71 students received support, including 14 fellowships (averaging $3,125 per year); career-related internships or fieldwork, scholarships/grants, and coaching assistantships also available. Support available to part-time students. Financial award application deadline: 6/30; financial award applicants required to submit FAFSA. In 2016, 31 master's, 3 doctorates awarded. *Program availability:* Part-time. Offers counseling and human development (M Ed); education (M Ed, Ed D); education leadership (Ed D); gifted education (M Ed); kinesiology, sport, and recreation (M Ed); reading specialist education (M Ed). *Application deadline:* For fall admission, 8/15 priority date for domestic students, 4/1 for international students; for spring admission, 1/5 priority date for domestic students, 9/1 for international students. Applications are processed on a rolling basis. *Application fee:* $50. Electronic applications accepted. *Application Contact:* Dr. Nancy Kucinski, Dean of Graduate Studies, 325-670-1298, Fax: 325-670-1564, E-mail: gradoff@hsutx.edu. *Dean,* Dr. Perry Kay Brown, 325-670-1021, Fax: 325-670-5859, E-mail: pkbrown@hsutx.edu.

Kelley College of Business Students: 16 full-time (7 women), 11 part-time (3 women); includes 2 minority (1 Hispanic/Latino; 1 Two or more races, non-Hispanic/Latino), 4 international. Average age 23. *Faculty:* 7 full-time (2 women), 1 part-time/adjunct (0 women). Expenses: Contact institution. *Financial support:* In 2016–17, 18 students received support. Fellowships and scholarships/grants available. Support available to part-time students. Financial award application deadline: 6/30; financial award applicants required to submit FAFSA. In 2016, 11 master's awarded. *Program availability:* Part-time. Offers business administration (MBA); sports management (MBA). *Application deadline:* For fall admission, 8/15 priority date for domestic students, 4/1 for international students; for spring admission, 1/5 priority date for domestic students, 9/1 for international students. Applications are processed on a rolling basis. *Application fee:* $50. Electronic applications accepted. *Application Contact:* Dr. Nancy Kucinski, Dean of Graduate Studies, 325-670-1298, Fax: 325-670-1564, E-mail: gradoff@hsutx.edu. *Program Director,* Dr. Jennifer Plantier, 325-671-2166, Fax: 325-670-1523, E-mail: jplantier@hsutx.edu.

Logsdon School of Theology Students: 69 full-time (23 women), 86 part-time (18 women); includes 50 minority (19 Black or African American, non-Hispanic/Latino; 5 Asian, non-Hispanic/Latino; 26 Hispanic/Latino), 8 international. Average age 36. *Faculty:* 16 full-time (1 woman), 20 part-time/adjunct (2 women). Expenses: Contact institution. *Financial support:* In 2016–17, 146 students received support. Fellowships and scholarships/grants available. Support available to part-time students. Financial award application deadline: 6/30; financial award applicants required to submit FAFSA. In 2016, 25 master's, 3 doctorates awarded. *Program availability:* Part-time, evening/weekend. Offers family ministry (MA); ministry (D Min); religion (MA); theology (M Div, MA, D Min). *Application deadline:* For fall admission, 8/15 priority date for domestic students, 4/1 for international students; for spring admission, 1/5 priority date for domestic students, 9/1 for international students. Applications are processed on a rolling basis. *Application fee:* $50. Electronic applications accepted. *Application Contact:* Dr. Nancy Kucinski, Dean of Graduate Studies, 325-670-1298, Fax: 325-670-1564, E-mail: gradoff@hsutx.edu. *Dean,* Dr. Don Williford, 325-670-1491, Fax: 325-671-2157, E-mail: willifrd@hsutx.edu.

Patty Hanks Shelton School of Nursing Students: 12 part-time (9 women); includes 3 minority (1 Asian, non-Hispanic/Latino; 2 Hispanic/Latino), 1 international. Average age 33. *Faculty:* 3 full-time (all women), 2 part-time/adjunct (both women). Expenses: Contact institution. *Financial support:* In 2016–17, 9 students received support. Career-related internships or fieldwork and scholarships/grants available. Support available to part-time students. Financial award application deadline: 6/30; financial award applicants required to submit FAFSA. In 2016, 7 master's awarded. *Program availability:* Part-time. Offers advanced healthcare delivery (MSN); family nurse practitioner (MSN). Programs offered jointly with McMurry University. *Application deadline:* For fall admission, 8/15 priority date for domestic students, 4/1 for international students; for spring admission, 1/5 priority date for domestic students, 9/1 for international students. Applications are processed on a rolling basis. *Application fee:* $50. Electronic applications accepted. *Application Contact:* Dr. Nancy Kucinski, Dean of Graduate Studies, 325-670-1298, Fax: 325-670-1564, E-mail: gradoff@hsutx.edu. *Dean,* Dr. Nina Ouimette, 325-671-2357, Fax: 325-671-2386, E-mail: nouimette@phssn.edu.

HARRISBURG UNIVERSITY OF SCIENCE AND TECHNOLOGY, Harrisburg, PA 17101

General Information Independent, coed, comprehensive institution. *Enrollment:* 2,520 full-time matriculated graduate/professional students (922 women), 81 part-time matriculated graduate/professional students (33 women). *Enrollment by degree level:* 2,601 master's. *Graduate faculty:* 32 full-time (3 women), 43 part-time/adjunct (12 women). *Tuition:* Full-time $4800; part-time $800 per semester hour. *Graduate housing:* On-campus housing not available. *Student services:* Campus employment opportunities, career counseling, international student services. *Library facilities:* Information Commons. *Collection:* Books: 4,130 (physical), 26 (digital/electronic); Serial titles: 103 (physical), 126 (digital/electronic); Databases: 24. Study areas open 24 hours, 5–7 days a week. *Research affiliation:* MistIQ Technologies (data analytics), WildFig Data Company (data analytics).

Computer facilities: Computer purchase and lease plans are available. 10 computers available on campus for general student use. A campuswide network can be accessed

from student residence rooms and from off campus.
Website: http://www.HarrisburgU.edu/

General Application Contact: Sruthy Chitturi, Admissions Counselor, 717-901-5100, E-mail: schitturi@harrisburgu.edu.

GRADUATE UNITS

Learning Technologies and Media Systems Program Students: 23 full-time (19 women), 13 part-time (7 women), 25 international. *Faculty:* 1 full-time (0 women), 5 part-time/adjunct (3 women). Expenses: Contact institution. *Financial support:* Applicants required to submit FAFSA. In 2016, 4 master's awarded. *Program availability:* Part-time, evening/weekend. Offers games and simulations (MS); instructional design (MS); instructional development (MS); instructional technology (MS); integration and leadership (MS). *Application deadline:* Applications are processed on a rolling basis. *Application fee:* $0. Electronic applications accepted. *Program Lead,* Dr. Richard Kordel, 717-901-5167, E-mail: rkordel@harrisburgu.edu.

Program in Information Systems Engineering and Management Students: 1,031 full-time (264 women), 35 part-time (10 women); includes 2 minority (1 Black or African American, non-Hispanic/Latino; 1 Asian, non-Hispanic/Latino), 1,060 international. *Faculty:* 9 full-time (0 women), 1 (woman) part-time/adjunct. Expenses: Contact institution. *Financial support:* In 2016–17, 2 students received support. Teaching assistantships available. Financial award applicants required to submit FAFSA. In 2016, 83 master's awarded. *Program availability:* Part-time, evening/weekend. Offers analytics (MS); digital government (MS); digital health (MS); entrepreneurship (MS); information security (MS); software engineering and systems development (MS). *Application deadline:* Applications are processed on a rolling basis. *Application fee:* $0. Electronic applications accepted. *Director and Professor,* Dr. Amjad Umar, 717-901-5141, Fax: 717-901-3141, E-mail: aumar@harrisburgu.edu.

Program in Project Management Students: 863 full-time (358 women), 15 part-time (7 women); includes 6 minority (3 Black or African American, non-Hispanic/Latino; 3 Asian, non-Hispanic/Latino), 868 international. *Faculty:* 2 full-time (0 women), 11 part-time/adjunct (1 woman). Expenses: Contact institution. *Financial support:* Applicants required to submit FAFSA. In 2016, 17 master's awarded. *Program availability:* Part-time, evening/weekend. Offers information technology (MS). *Application deadline:* Applications are processed on a rolling basis. *Application fee:* $0. Electronic applications accepted. *Program Lead/Associate Professor,* Dr. Thomas Sheives, 717-901-5158, E-mail: tsheives@harrisburgu.edu.

HARRISON MIDDLETON UNIVERSITY, Tempe, AZ 85282

General Information Independent, coed, comprehensive institution.

GRADUATE UNITS

Graduate Program *Program availability:* Part-time, evening/weekend, online learning. Offers education (MA, Ed D); humanities (MA); imaginative literature (MA); interdisciplinary studies (DA); jurisprudence (MA); natural science (MA); philosophy and religion (MA); social science (MA). Electronic applications accepted.

HARTFORD SEMINARY, Hartford, CT 06105-2279

General Information Independent-religious, coed, graduate-only institution. *Graduate housing:* Rooms and/or apartments available on a first-come, first-served basis to single and married students. Housing application deadline: 7/15.

GRADUATE UNITS

Graduate Programs *Program availability:* Part-time, evening/weekend, online learning. Offers Islamic studies (MA); ministry (D Min); religious studies (MA); spirituality (Certificate).

HARVARD UNIVERSITY, Cambridge, MA 02138

General Information Independent, coed, university. CGS member. *Graduate housing:* Rooms and/or apartments available on a first-come, first-served basis to single and married students. *Research affiliation:* Woods Hole Oceanographic Institution (biology).

GRADUATE UNITS

Cyprus International Institute for the Environment and Public Health in Association with Harvard School of Public Health Offers environmental health (MS); environmental/public health (PhD); epidemiology and biostatistics (MS). Electronic applications accepted.

Extension School *Program availability:* Part-time, evening/weekend. Offers applied sciences (CAS); biotechnology (ALM); educational technologies (ALM); educational technology (CET); English for graduate and professional studies (DGP); environmental management (ALM, CEM); information technology (ALM); journalism (ALM); liberal arts (ALM); management (ALM, CM); mathematics for teaching (ALM); museum studies (ALM); premedical studies (Diploma); publication and communication (CPC).

Graduate School of Arts and Sciences Offers African and African American studies (PhD); African history (PhD); Akkadian and Sumerian (AM, PhD); American history (PhD); ancient art (PhD); ancient Near Eastern art (PhD); ancient, medieval, early modern, and modern Europe (PhD); anthropology and Middle Eastern studies (PhD); Arabic (AM, PhD); archaeology (PhD); architecture (PhD); Armenian (AM, PhD); arts and sciences (AM, MDE, ME, MFS, SM, PhD); astronomy (PhD); astrophysics (PhD); Baroque art (PhD); biblical history (AM, PhD); biochemical chemistry (PhD); biological anthropology (PhD); biological sciences in dental medicine (PhD); biology (PhD); biophysics (PhD); biostatistics (PhD); business economics (PhD); Byzantine art (PhD); Byzantine Greek (PhD); chemical biology (PhD); chemical physics (PhD); Chinese (PhD); Chinese studies (AM); classical archaeology (PhD); classical art (PhD); classical philology (PhD); classical philosophy (PhD); comparative literature (PhD); composition (AM, PhD); critical theory (PhD); descriptive linguistics (PhD); diplomatic history (PhD); earth and planetary sciences (AM, PhD); East Asian history (PhD); economic and social history (PhD); economics (PhD); economics and Middle Eastern studies (PhD); eighteenth-century literature (PhD); experimental physics (PhD); fine arts and Middle Eastern studies (PhD); forest science (MFS); French (AM, PhD); German (PhD); health policy (PhD); Hebrew (AM, PhD); historical linguistics (PhD); history and Middle Eastern studies (PhD); history of American civilization (PhD); history of science (AM, PhD); Indian art (PhD); Indian philosophy (AM, PhD); Indo-Muslim culture (AM, PhD); information, technology and management (PhD); Inner Asian and Altaic studies (PhD); inorganic chemistry (PhD); intellectual history (PhD); Iranian (AM, PhD); Irish (PhD); Islamic art (PhD); Italian (AM, PhD); Japanese (PhD); Japanese and Chinese art (PhD); Japanese studies (AM); Jewish history and literature (AM, PhD); Korean (PhD); Korean studies (AM); landscape architecture (PhD); Latin American history (PhD); legal anthropology (AM); literature: nineteenth-century to the present (PhD); mathematics (PhD); medical anthropology (AM); medical engineering/medical physics (PhD); medieval art (PhD); medieval Latin (PhD); medieval literature and language (PhD); modern art (PhD); modern British and American literature (PhD); molecular and cellular biology (PhD); Mongolian (AM, PhD); Mongolian studies (AM); musicology (AM); musicology and ethnomusicology (PhD); Near Eastern history (PhD); neurobiology (PhD); oceanic

history (PhD); oral literature (PhD); organic chemistry (PhD); organizational behavior (PhD); Pali (AM, PhD); Persian (AM, PhD); philosophy (PhD); physical chemistry (PhD); Polish (PhD); political economy and government (PhD); political science (PhD); Portuguese (AM, PhD); psychology (PhD); public policy (PhD); regional studies–Middle East (AM); regional studies-Russia, Eastern Europe, and Central Asia (AM); Renaissance and modern architecture (PhD); Renaissance art (PhD); Renaissance literature (PhD); Russian (PhD); Sanskrit (AM, PhD); Scandinavian (PhD); Semitic philology (AM, PhD); Serbo-Croatian (PhD); Slavic philology (PhD); social anthropology (AM, PhD); social change and development (AM); social policy (PhD); social psychology (PhD); sociology (PhD); Spanish (AM, PhD); statistics (AM, PhD); study of religion (PhD); Syro-Palestinian archaeology (AM, PhD); systems biology (PhD); theoretical linguistics (PhD); theoretical physics (PhD); theory (AM, PhD); Tibetan (AM, PhD); Turkish (AM, PhD); Ukrainian (PhD); urban planning (PhD); Urdu (AM, PhD); Vietnamese (PhD); Vietnamese studies (AM); Welsh (PhD). Electronic applications accepted.

Division of Medical Sciences Offers biological chemistry and molecular pharmacology (PhD); cell biology (PhD); genetics (PhD); microbiology and molecular genetics (PhD); pathology (PhD).

Harvard John A. Paulson School of Engineering and Applied Sciences Students: 459 full-time (135 women), 19 part-time (7 women); includes 79 minority (2 Black or African American, non-Hispanic/Latino; 49 Asian, non-Hispanic/Latino; 15 Hispanic/Latino; 1 Native Hawaiian or other Pacific Islander, non-Hispanic/Latino; 12 Two or more races, non-Hispanic/Latino), 233 international. Average age 27. 2,486 applicants, 11% accepted, 126 enrolled. *Faculty:* 80 full-time (13 women), 47 part-time/adjunct (10 women). Expenses: Contact institution. *Financial support:* In 2016–17, 394 students received support, including 86 fellowships with full tuition reimbursements available (averaging $26,424 per year), 258 research assistantships with tuition reimbursements available (averaging $35,232 per year), 106 teaching assistantships with tuition reimbursements available (averaging $6,313 per year); health care benefits also available. In 2016, 37 master's, 48 doctorates awarded. *Program availability:* Part-time. Offers applied mathematics (PhD); applied physics (PhD); computational science and engineering (ME, SM); computer science (PhD); design engineering (MDE); engineering science (ME); engineering sciences (SM, PhD). MDE offered in collaboration with Graduate School of Design. *Application deadline:* For fall admission, 12/15 priority date for domestic and international students. *Application fee:* $105. Electronic applications accepted. *Application Contact:* Office of Admissions and Financial Aid, 617-495-5315, E-mail: admissions@seas.harvard.edu. *Dean,* Francis J. Doyle, III, 617-495-5829, Fax: 617-495-5264, E-mail: dean@seas.harvard.edu.

Graduate School of Design Offers architecture (M Arch); design (M Arch, M Des S, MAUD, MLA, MLAUD, MUP, Dr DES); design studies (M Des S); landscape architecture (MLA); urban planning (MUP); urban planning and design (MAUD, MLAUD). Electronic applications accepted.

Harvard Business School Offers accounting and management (DBA); business (MBA, DBA, PhD); business administration (MBA); business economics (PhD); health policy management (PhD); management (DBA); marketing (DBA); organizational behavior (PhD); science, technology and management (PhD); strategy (DBA); technology and operations management (DBA).

Harvard Divinity School Offers divinity (M Div, MTS, Th M). Electronic applications accepted.

Harvard Graduate School of Education *Program availability:* Part-time. Offers arts in education (Ed M); education (Ed M, Ed L D, PhD); education leadership (Ed L D); education policy and management (Ed M); higher education (Ed M); human development and psychology (Ed M); international education policy (Ed M); language and literacy (Ed M); learning and teaching (Ed M); mind, brain, and education (Ed M); prevention science and practice (Ed M); school leadership (Ed M); special studies (Ed M); teacher education (Ed M); technology, innovation, and education (Ed M). Electronic applications accepted.

Harvard Medical School Offers medicine (M Eng, SM, MD, PhD, Sc D). Electronic applications accepted.

Harvard T.H. Chan School of Public Health *Program availability:* Part-time. Offers biological sciences in public health (PhD); biostatistics (SM, PhD); cancer epidemiology (SM); cardiovascular epidemiology (SM, SD); clinical effectiveness (MPH); clinical epidemiology (SM, SD); computational biology and quantitative genetics (SM); environmental and occupational epidemiology (SM, SD); environmental health (SM, PhD, SD); epidemiologic methods (SD); epidemiology of aging (SM, SD); exposure, epidemiology, and risk (SM, SD); genetic epidemiology and statistical genetics (SD); global health (MPH); global health and population (SM, SD); health and social behavior (MPH); health management (MPH); health policy (MPH); health policy and management (SM); infectious disease epidemiology (SM, SD); neuroepidemiology (SD); nutrition (SD); nutritional epidemiology (SD); occupational and environmental health (MPH); occupational health (SM, SD); pharmacoepidemiology (SM, SD); physiology (PhD, SD); psychiatric epidemiology (SM); public health (MPH, SM, Dr PH, PhD, SD); public health nutrition (SD); quantitative methods (MPH); reproductive epidemiology (SM, SD); social and behavioral sciences (SM, SD). SM program offered jointly with Simmons College. Electronic applications accepted.

John F. Kennedy School of Government Students: 927 full-time (512 women), 6 part-time (2 women); includes 159 minority (34 Black or African American, non-Hispanic/Latino; 1 American Indian or Alaska Native, non-Hispanic/Latino; 69 Asian, non-Hispanic/Latino; 37 Hispanic/Latino; 1 Native Hawaiian or other Pacific Islander, non-Hispanic/Latino; 17 Two or more races, non-Hispanic/Latino), 430 international. Average age 31. 2,722 applicants, 33% accepted, 628 enrolled. Expenses: Contact institution. *Financial support:* Fellowships, research assistantships, teaching assistantships, career-related internships or fieldwork, Federal Work-Study, institutionally sponsored loans, scholarships/grants, and unspecified assistantships available. Support available to part-time students. Financial award application deadline: 2/24; financial award applicants required to submit CSS PROFILE or FAFSA. In 2016, 540 master's awarded. Offers government (MPA, MPAID, MPP, PhD); political economy and government (PhD); public administration (MPA); public administration in international development (MPAID); public policy (MPP). *Application deadline:* For fall admission, 12/1 for domestic students. *Application fee:* $100. Electronic applications accepted. *Application Contact:* 617-495-1155, Fax: 617-496-1165, E-mail: hks_admissions@harvard.edu. *Dean,* Douglas W. Elmendorf, 617-495-1122.

Law School Offers international and comparative law (JD); law (LL M, JD, SJD); law and business (JD); law and government (JD); law and social change (JD); law, science and technology (JD).

School of Dental Medicine Offers advanced general dentistry (Certificate); dental medicine (M Med Sc, D Med Sc, DMD, Certificate); dental public health (Certificate); endodontics (Certificate); general practice residency (Certificate); oral biology

(M Med Sc, D Med Sc); oral implantology (Certificate); oral medicine (Certificate); oral pathology (Certificate); oral surgery (Certificate); orthodontics (Certificate); pediatric dentistry (Certificate); periodontics (Certificate); prosthodontics (Certificate).

HASTINGS COLLEGE, Hastings, NE 68901

General Information Independent-religious, coed, comprehensive institution. *Graduate housing:* On-campus housing not available.

GRADUATE UNITS

Department of Teacher Education *Program availability:* Part-time. Offers teacher education (MAT). Electronic applications accepted.

HAWAI`I PACIFIC UNIVERSITY, Honolulu, HI 96813

General Information Independent, coed, comprehensive institution. *Enrollment:* 4,081 graduate, professional, and undergraduate students; 444 full-time matriculated graduate/professional students (256 women), 196 part-time matriculated graduate/professional students (104 women). *Enrollment by degree level:* 617 master's, 23 other advanced degrees. *Graduate faculty:* 63 full-time (24 women), 27 part-time/adjunct (12 women). *Tuition:* Full-time $17,190; part-time $955 per credit. *Required fees:* $150; $26 per credit. Tuition and fees vary according to course load and program. *Graduate housing:* Rooms and/or apartments available on a first-come, first-served basis to single and married students. Typical cost: $13,898 (including board) for single students. Room and board charges vary according to board plan, campus/location and housing facility selected. *Student services:* Campus employment opportunities, campus safety program, career counseling, exercise/wellness program, free psychological counseling, international student services, low-cost health insurance, multicultural affairs office, services for students with disabilities, writing training. *Library facilities:* Meader Library plus 2 others. *Collection:* Books: 103,021 (physical), 191,075 (digital/electronic); Serial titles: 64 (physical), 4,520 (digital/electronic); Databases: 101. Students can reserve study rooms. *Research affiliation:* Oceanic Institute (marine science).

Computer facilities: 200 computers available on campus for general student use. A campuswide network can be accessed from student residence rooms and from off campus. Online class registration is available.
Website: http://www.hpu.edu/

General Application Contact: Danny Lam, Assistant Director of Graduate Admissions, 808-544-1135, E-mail: graduate@hpu.edu.

GRADUATE UNITS

College of Business Students: 150 full-time (66 women), 72 part-time (29 women); includes 105 minority (10 Black or African American, non-Hispanic/Latino; 1 American Indian or Alaska Native, non-Hispanic/Latino; 32 Asian, non-Hispanic/Latino; 15 Hispanic/Latino; 4 Native Hawaiian or other Pacific Islander, non-Hispanic/Latino; 43 Two or more races, non-Hispanic/Latino), 56 international. Average age 33. 131 applicants, 81% accepted, 70 enrolled. *Faculty:* 18 full-time (6 women), 6 part-time/adjunct (0 women). Expenses: Contact institution. *Financial support:* In 2016–17, 30 students received support. Research assistantships, teaching assistantships, career-related internships or fieldwork, Federal Work-Study, scholarships/grants, tuition waivers, and unspecified assistantships available. Financial award application deadline: 3/1; financial award applicants required to submit FAFSA. In 2016, 148 master's awarded. *Program availability:* Part-time, evening/weekend, online learning. Offers accounting (MBA); business (MA, MBA, MSIS); economics (MBA); finance (MBA); hospitality and tourism management (MBA); human resource management (MBA); information systems (MBA); international business (MBA); management (MBA); marketing (MBA); organizational change (MBA); organizational change and development (MBA). *Application deadline:* For fall admission, 2/15 priority date for domestic students; for spring admission, 10/15 priority date for domestic students. Applications are processed on a rolling basis. *Application fee:* $50. Electronic applications accepted. *Application Contact:* Danny Lam, Assistant Director of Graduate Admissions, 808-544-1135, E-mail: graduate@hpu.edu. *Associate Dean/Associate Professor of Accounting,* Dr. Warren Wee, 808-544-9325, E-mail: wwee@hpu.edu.

College of Extended and Interdisciplinary Education Students: 45 full-time (25 women), 4 part-time (3 women); includes 28 minority (1 Black or African American, non-Hispanic/Latino; 10 Asian, non-Hispanic/Latino; 6 Hispanic/Latino; 11 Two or more races, non-Hispanic/Latino), 1 international. Average age 31. 32 applicants, 81% accepted, 21 enrolled. *Faculty:* 18 full-time (2 women), 6 part-time/adjunct (3 women). Expenses: Contact institution. *Financial support:* In 2016–17, 14 students received support. Career-related internships or fieldwork, Federal Work-Study, scholarships/grants, tuition waivers, and unspecified assistantships available. Financial award application deadline: 3/1; financial award applicants required to submit FAFSA. In 2016, 30 master's awarded. *Program availability:* Part-time, evening/weekend. Offers elementary education (M Ed); extended and interdisciplinary education (M Ed); secondary education (M Ed). *Application deadline:* For fall admission, 2/15 priority date for domestic students; for spring admission, 10/15 priority date for domestic students. Applications are processed on a rolling basis. *Application fee:* $50. Electronic applications accepted. *Application Contact:* Danny Lam, Assistant Director of Graduate Admissions, 808-544-1135, E-mail: graduate@hpu.edu. *Interim Dean,* Mani Sehgal, 808-543-8046, E-mail: msehgal@hpu.edu.

College of Health and Society Students: 96 full-time (73 women), 23 part-time (19 women); includes 72 minority (7 Black or African American, non-Hispanic/Latino; 16 Asian, non-Hispanic/Latino; 18 Hispanic/Latino; 4 Native Hawaiian or other Pacific Islander, non-Hispanic/Latino; 27 Two or more races, non-Hispanic/Latino), 8 international. Average age 33. 89 applicants, 84% accepted, 50 enrolled. *Faculty:* 9 full-time (6 women), 5 part-time/adjunct (4 women). Expenses: Contact institution. *Financial support:* In 2016–17, 16 students received support. Career-related internships or fieldwork, Federal Work-Study, scholarships/grants, traineeships, tuition waivers, and unspecified assistantships available. Financial award application deadline: 3/1; financial award applicants required to submit FAFSA. In 2016, 57 master's awarded. *Program availability:* Part-time, evening/weekend, online learning. Offers health and society (MPH, MSN, MSW); nursing (MSN); public health (MPH); social work (MSW). *Application deadline:* For fall admission, 2/15 priority date for domestic students; for spring admission, 10/15 priority date for domestic students. Applications are processed on a rolling basis. *Application fee:* $50. Electronic applications accepted. *Application Contact:* Danny Lam, Assistant Director of Graduate Admissions, 808-544-1135, E-mail: graduate@hpu.edu. *Dean,* Dr. Lynette Landry, 808-236-5811, E-mail: llandry@hpu.edu.

College of Liberal Arts Students: 109 full-time (61 women), 82 part-time (43 women); includes 83 minority (8 Black or African American, non-Hispanic/Latino; 23 Asian, non-Hispanic/Latino; 21 Hispanic/Latino; 2 Native Hawaiian or other Pacific Islander, non-Hispanic/Latino; 29 Two or more races, non-Hispanic/Latino), 27 international. Average age 33. 145 applicants, 86% accepted, 69 enrolled. *Faculty:* 22 full-time (6 women), 9 part-time/adjunct (4 women). Expenses: Contact institution. *Financial support:* In 2016–17, 37 students received support. Career-related internships or fieldwork, Federal Work-Study, scholarships/grants, tuition waivers, and unspecified assistantships available.

Financial award application deadline: 3/1; financial award applicants required to submit FAFSA. In 2016, 93 master's awarded. *Program availability:* Part-time, evening/weekend. Offers clinical mental health counseling (MA); communication (MA); diplomacy and military studies (MA); global leadership and sustainable development (MA); liberal arts (MA); teaching English to speakers of other languages (MA). *Application deadline:* For fall admission, 2/15 priority date for domestic students; for spring admission, 10/15 priority date for domestic students. Applications are processed on a rolling basis. *Application fee:* $50. Electronic applications accepted. *Application Contact:* Danny Lam, Assistant Director of Graduate Admissions, 808-544-1135, E-mail: graduate@hpu.edu. *Interim Dean,* Dr. William Potter, 808-544-0274, E-mail: wpotter@hpu.edu.

College of Natural and Computational Sciences Students: 20 full-time (15 women), 15 part-time (10 women); includes 5 minority (3 Asian, non-Hispanic/Latino; 2 Two or more races, non-Hispanic/Latino), 2 international. Average age 28. 28 applicants, 96% accepted, 16 enrolled. *Faculty:* 10 full-time (4 women). Expenses: Contact institution. *Financial support:* In 2016–17, 20 students received support. Career-related internships or fieldwork, Federal Work-Study, scholarships/grants, tuition waivers, and unspecified assistantships available. Financial award application deadline: 3/1; financial award applicants required to submit FAFSA. In 2016, 12 master's awarded. *Program availability:* Part-time. Offers marine science (MS); natural and computational sciences (MS). *Application deadline:* For fall admission, 1/15 for domestic students. *Application fee:* $50. Electronic applications accepted. *Application Contact:* Danny Lam, Assistant Director of Graduate Admissions, 808-544-1135, E-mail: graduate@hpu.edu. *Dean,* Dr. Brenda Jensen, 808-236-3533, E-mail: bjensen@hpu.edu.

HAZELDEN GRADUATE SCHOOL OF ADDICTION STUDIES, Center City, MN 55012

General Information Independent, coed, graduate-only institution. CGS member. *Graduate housing:* On-campus housing not available.

GRADUATE UNITS

Graduate Programs *Program availability:* Part-time. Offers addiction counseling (MA, Certificate).

HEBREW COLLEGE, Newton Centre, MA 02459

General Information Independent-religious, coed, graduate-only institution. *Graduate housing:* On-campus housing not available.

GRADUATE UNITS

Cantor Educator Program Offers cantor educator (MJ Ed).

Program in Jewish Studies *Program availability:* Part-time, evening/weekend, online learning. Offers Jewish liturgical music (Certificate); Jewish music education (Certificate); Jewish studies (MA).

Rabbinical School Offers rabbinics (MA).

Shoolman Graduate School of Jewish Education *Program availability:* Part-time, evening/weekend, online learning. Offers early childhood Jewish education (Certificate); Jewish day school education (Certificate); Jewish education (MJ Ed); Jewish family education (Certificate); Jewish special education (Certificate); Jewish youth education, informal education and camping (Certificate).

HEBREW UNION COLLEGE–JEWISH INSTITUTE OF RELIGION, New York, NY 10012-1186

General Information Independent-religious, coed, graduate-only institution. *Graduate housing:* On-campus housing not available.

GRADUATE UNITS

Rabbinical School Offers rabbinical studies (MAHL).

School of Education *Program availability:* Part-time. Offers education (MARE).

School of Graduate Studies *Program availability:* Part-time. Offers Hebrew letters (DHL); Judaic studies (MAJS); pastoral counseling (D Min).

School of Jewish Nonprofit Management Offers Jewish nonprofit management (MA).

School of Sacred Music Offers sacred music (MSM).

HEC MONTREAL, Montréal, QC H3T 2A7, Canada

General Information Province-supported, coed, comprehensive institution. *Enrollment:* 13,652 graduate, professional, and undergraduate students; 1,603 full-time matriculated graduate/professional students (815 women), 1,339 part-time matriculated graduate/professional students (751 women). *Enrollment by degree level:* 1,573 master's, 122 doctoral, 1,247 other advanced degrees. *Graduate faculty:* 289 full-time (96 women), 422 part-time/adjunct (136 women). *International tuition:* $19,131 Canadian dollars full-time. *Tuition, area resident:* Part-time $77.80 Canadian dollars per credit. Tuition, province resident: full-time $2797 Canadian dollars; part-time $240.92 Canadian dollars per credit. Tuition, Canadian resident: full-time $8673 Canadian dollars; part-time $531.43 Canadian dollars per credit. *Required fees:* $1699 Canadian dollars; $40.58 Canadian dollars per credit. $67.32 Canadian dollars per term. Tuition and fees vary according to degree level and program. *Graduate housing:* Rooms and/or apartments available on a first-come, first-served basis to single and married students. Typical cost: $3890 Canadian dollars per year for single students; $6330 Canadian dollars per year for married students. *Student services:* Campus employment opportunities, campus safety program, career counseling, child daycare facilities, exercise/wellness program, free psychological counseling, grant writing training, international student services, low-cost health insurance, multicultural affairs office, services for students with disabilities. *Library facilities:* Myriam et J.-Robert Ouimet Library plus 1 other. *Collection:* Books: 111,403 (physical), 299,595 (digital/electronic); Serial titles: 1,050 (physical), 118,890 (digital/electronic); Databases: 156. Weekly public service hours: 85; students can reserve study rooms. *Research affiliation:* CIRANO (Centre for Interuniversity Research and Analysis of Organizations), ACFAS (Association Francophone Pour Le Savoir), CRIAQ (Consortium of Synergetic Research and Innovation in Aerospace) (research in aerospace), UNIVALOR (Valorisation de la recherche universitaire et le transfert technologique).

Computer facilities: Computer purchase and lease plans are available. 161 computers available on campus for general student use. A campuswide network can be accessed from student residence rooms. Online class registration, learning management system, corporate calendar and Web sites for resources available for classes are available.
Website: http://www.hec.ca/

General Application Contact: Louise Champagne, Registrar, 514-340-6110, Fax: 514-340-6411, E-mail: registraire.info@hec.ca.

GRADUATE UNITS

School of Business Administration Students: 1,603 full-time (815 women), 1,339 part-time (751 women). Average age 29. 1,608 applicants, 59% accepted, 663 enrolled. *Faculty:* 293 full-time (99 women), 460 part-time/adjunct (156 women). Expenses:

Contact institution. *Financial support:* In 2016–17, 814 students received support. Research assistantships, teaching assistantships, and scholarships/grants available. Financial award application deadline: 9/2. In 2016, 580 master's, 18 doctorates, 599 other advanced degrees awarded. Offers administration (M Sc, PhD, Graduate Diploma); applied economics (M Sc); applied financial economics (M Sc); business administration (LL M, M Sc, MBA, MM, PhD, Graduate Certificate); business administration and management (MBA); business analytics (M Sc); business intelligence (M Sc); e-business (Graduate Diploma); electronic commerce (M Sc); finance (M Sc); financial engineering (M Sc); financial professions (Graduate Diploma); global supply chain management (M Sc); human resources management (M Sc); information technologies (M Sc); international business (M Sc); international logistics (M Sc); management (M Sc, Graduate Diploma); management and social innovations (M Sc); management and sustainable development (Graduate Diploma); management control (M Sc); management in cultural enterprises (MM); management of cultural organizations (Graduate Diploma); marketing (M Sc); marketing communication (Graduate Diploma); operations management (M Sc); organizational development (M Sc); professional accounting (M Sc, Graduate Diploma); strategy (M Sc); supply chain management (Graduate Diploma); taxation (Graduate Diploma). Most courses are given in French. *Application fee:* $86 Canadian dollars. Electronic applications accepted. *Application Contact:* Louise Champagne, Registrar, 514-340-6110, Fax: 514-340-6411, E-mail: registraire.info@hec.ca. *Director*, Dr. Michel Patry, 514-340-6110, Fax: 514-340-5640.

HEIDELBERG UNIVERSITY, Tiffin, OH 44883-2462

General Information Independent-religious, coed, comprehensive institution. *Enrollment:* 1,314 graduate, professional, and undergraduate students; 21 full-time matriculated graduate/professional students (13 women), 83 part-time matriculated graduate/professional students (51 women). *Enrollment by degree level:* 104 master's. *Graduate faculty:* 16 full-time (11 women), 11 part-time/adjunct (8 women). *Graduate housing:* On-campus housing not available. *Student services:* Campus employment opportunities, campus safety program, career counseling, exercise/wellness program, free psychological counseling, international student services, multicultural affairs office, services for students with disabilities, teacher training, writing training. *Library facilities:* Beeghly Library plus 1 other. *Collection:* Books: 86,891 (physical), 279,499 (digital/electronic); Serial titles: 1,293 (physical), 61,058 (digital/electronic); Databases: 198. Weekly public service hours: 83.

Computer facilities: 125 computers available on campus for general student use. A campuswide network can be accessed from student residence rooms and from off campus. Online class registration is available.
Website: http://www.heidelberg.edu/

General Application Contact: Katie Slosser, Graduate Admissions Coordinator, 419-448-2602, Fax: 419-448-2565, E-mail: kslosser@heidelberg.edu.

GRADUATE UNITS

Master of Arts in Counseling Program Students: 15 full-time (11 women), 31 part-time (26 women). Expenses: Contact institution. *Financial support:* Applicants required to submit FAFSA. In 2016, 12 master's awarded. *Program availability:* Part-time, evening/weekend. Offers clinical mental health counseling (MA); school counseling (MA). *Application deadline:* Applications are processed on a rolling basis. Electronic applications accepted. *Application Contact:* Katie Slosser, Graduate Admissions Coordinator, 419-448-2602, Fax: 419-448-2565, E-mail: kslosser@heidelberg.edu. *Associate Dean and Director of Master of Arts in Counseling*, Dr. Jo-Ann Lipford Sanders, 419-448-2312, E-mail: jsanders@heidelberg.edu.

Master of Arts in Education Program Expenses: Contact institution. *Financial support:* Applicants required to submit FAFSA. In 2016, 13 master's awarded. *Program availability:* Part-time, evening/weekend. Offers education (MAE). *Application deadline:* Applications are processed on a rolling basis. *Application fee:* $0. Electronic applications accepted. *Application Contact:* Katie Slosser, Graduate Admissions Coordinator, 419-448-2602, Fax: 419-448-2565, E-mail: kslosser@heidelberg.edu. *Associate Dean and Director of the School of Education*, Dr. Karen Jones, 419-448-2130, E-mail: kjones9@heidelberg.edu.

Master of Business Administration Program Students: 5 full-time (1 woman), 28 part-time (13 women). Expenses: Contact institution. *Financial support:* Scholarships/grants available. Financial award applicants required to submit FAFSA. In 2016, 8 master's awarded. *Program availability:* Part-time, evening/weekend. Offers business administration (MBA). *Application deadline:* Applications are processed on a rolling basis. Electronic applications accepted. *Application Contact:* Katie Slosser, Graduate Admissions Coordinator, 419-448-2602, Fax: 419-448-2565, E-mail: kslosser@heidelberg.edu. *Director of Graduate Studies in Business*, Allen Underwood, 419-448-2516, E-mail: aunderwo@heidelberg.edu.

Master of Music Education Program Expenses: Contact institution. *Financial support:* Applicants required to submit FAFSA. In 2016, 5 master's awarded. *Program availability:* Part-time. Offers music education (MME). Summer program only. *Application deadline:* For fall admission, 6/1 for domestic students. Applications are processed on a rolling basis. *Application fee:* $0. Electronic applications accepted. *Application Contact:* Katie Slosser, Graduate Studies Coordinator, 419-448-2602, Fax: 419-448-2565, E-mail: kslosser@heidelberg.edu. *Director*, Dr. Carol Dusdieker, 419-448-2080, E-mail: cdusdiek@heidelberg.edu.

HENDERSON STATE UNIVERSITY, Arkadelphia, AR 71999-0001

General Information State-supported, coed, comprehensive institution. CGS member. *Enrollment:* 3,565 graduate, professional, and undergraduate students; 88 full-time matriculated graduate/professional students (56 women), 368 part-time matriculated graduate/professional students (252 women). *Enrollment by degree level:* 426 master's, 30 other advanced degrees. *Graduate faculty:* 44 full-time (18 women), 6 part-time/adjunct (4 women). Tuition, state resident: full-time $6288; part-time $3144 per credit hour. Tuition, nonresident: full-time $12,888; part-time $6444 per credit hour. *Required fees:* $1429; $1024 per credit hour. Tuition and fees vary according to course load and student level. *Graduate housing:* Room and/or apartments available on a first-come, first-served basis to single students; on-campus housing not available to married students. Typical cost: $7500 (including board). Room and board charges vary according to board plan and housing facility selected. Housing application deadline: 8/1. *Student services:* Campus employment opportunities, career counseling, free psychological counseling, international student services, services for students with disabilities. *Library facilities:* Huie Library plus 1 other. *Collection:* Books: 225,859 (physical), 142,000 (digital/electronic); Databases: 223. Weekly public service hours: 80; students can reserve study rooms.

Computer facilities: 125 computers available on campus for general student use. A campuswide network can be accessed from student residence rooms and from off campus. Online class registration is available.
Website: http://www.hsu.edu/

General Application Contact: Dr. Ken Taylor, Graduate Dean, 870-230-5126, Fax: 870-230-5479, E-mail: taylorke@hsu.edu.

GRADUATE UNITS

Graduate Studies Students: 88 full-time (56 women), 368 part-time (252 women); includes 131 minority (98 Black or African American, non-Hispanic/Latino; 3 American Indian or Alaska Native, non-Hispanic/Latino; 3 Asian, non-Hispanic/Latino; 15 Hispanic/Latino; 12 Two or more races, non-Hispanic/Latino), 7 international. Average age 32. 134 applicants, 93% accepted, 124 enrolled. *Faculty:* 50 full-time (22 women), 6 part-time/adjunct (4 women). Expenses: Contact institution. *Financial support:* In 2016–17, 55 teaching assistantships with partial tuition reimbursements (averaging $4,000 per year) were awarded; scholarships/grants and unspecified assistantships also available. Financial award application deadline: 4/15; financial award applicants required to submit FAFSA. In 2016, 125 master's, 9 other advanced degrees awarded. *Program availability:* Part-time, 100% online. *Application deadline:* For fall admission, 8/1 priority date for domestic students, 6/30 priority date for international students; for spring admission, 1/1 priority date for domestic students, 11/30 priority date for international students. Applications are processed on a rolling basis. *Application fee:* $25 ($75 for international students). *Application Contact:* Yvette Bragg, Administrative Assistant I, 870-230-5126, Fax: 870-230-5479, E-mail: braggy@hsu.edu. *Graduate Dean*, Dr. Ken Taylor, 870-230-5126, Fax: 870-230-5479, E-mail: taylorke@hsu.edu.

Ellis College of Arts and Sciences Students: 6 full-time (3 women), 18 part-time (9 women); includes 8 minority (4 Black or African American, non-Hispanic/Latino; 2 Hispanic/Latino; 2 Two or more races, non-Hispanic/Latino). Average age 32. 7 applicants, 86% accepted, 6 enrolled. *Faculty:* 15 full-time (6 women). Expenses: Contact institution. *Financial support:* In 2016–17, 10 teaching assistantships with partial tuition reimbursements (averaging $4,000 per year) were awarded; scholarships/grants and unspecified assistantships also available. Financial award application deadline: 4/15; financial award applicants required to submit FAFSA. In 2016, 3 master's awarded. *Program availability:* Part-time. Offers arts and sciences (MLA). *Application deadline:* For fall admission, 8/1 priority date for domestic students, 6/30 priority date for international students; for spring admission, 1/1 priority date for domestic students, 11/30 priority date for international students. Applications are processed on a rolling basis. *Application fee:* $25 ($75 for international students). *Application Contact:* Dr. Ken Taylor, Graduate Dean, 870-230-5126, Fax: 870-230-5479, E-mail: taylorke@hsu.edu. *MLA Director*, Megan Hickerson, 870-230-5250, Fax: 870-230-5144, E-mail: hickerm@hsu.edu.

School of Business Students: 15 full-time (7 women), 38 part-time (19 women); includes 16 minority (7 Black or African American, non-Hispanic/Latino; 2 Asian, non-Hispanic/Latino; 5 Hispanic/Latino; 2 Two or more races, non-Hispanic/Latino), 3 international. Average age 29. 26 applicants, 92% accepted, 24 enrolled. *Faculty:* 9 full-time (1 woman). Expenses: Contact institution. *Financial support:* In 2016–17, 7 teaching assistantships with partial tuition reimbursements (averaging $4,000 per year) were awarded; scholarships/grants and unspecified assistantships also available. Financial award application deadline: 4/15; financial award applicants required to submit FAFSA. In 2016, 27 master's awarded. *Program availability:* Part-time, 100% online. Offers business (MBA). *Application deadline:* For fall admission, 8/1 priority date for domestic students, 6/30 priority date for international students; for spring admission, 1/1 priority date for domestic students, 11/30 priority date for international students. Applications are processed on a rolling basis. *Application fee:* $25 ($75 for international students). *Application Contact:* Dr. Ken Taylor, Graduate Dean, 870-230-5126, Fax: 870-230-5479, E-mail: taylorke@hsu.edu. *MBA Director*, Dr. Lonnie Jackson, 870-230-5311, Fax: 870-230-5286, E-mail: jacksol@hsu.edu.

Teachers College Students: 67 full-time (46 women), 306 part-time (218 women); includes 106 minority (86 Black or African American, non-Hispanic/Latino; 3 American Indian or Alaska Native, non-Hispanic/Latino; 1 Asian, non-Hispanic/Latino; 8 Hispanic/Latino; 8 Two or more races, non-Hispanic/Latino), 4 international. Average age 32. 79 applicants, 97% accepted, 77 enrolled. *Faculty:* 20 full-time (11 women), 6 part-time/adjunct (4 women). Expenses: Contact institution. *Financial support:* In 2016–17, 7 teaching assistantships with partial tuition reimbursements (averaging $4,000 per year) were awarded; scholarships/grants and unspecified assistantships also available. Financial award application deadline: 4/15; financial award applicants required to submit FAFSA. In 2016, 95 master's, 9 other advanced degrees awarded. *Program availability:* Part-time, 100% online. Offers clinical mental health counseling (MS); curriculum leadership (Ed S); developmental therapy (MS, MSE, Graduate Certificate); dyslexia therapy (Graduate Certificate); education (MAT); educational leadership (MSE, Ed S, Graduate Certificate); educational technology leadership (Graduate Certificate); English as a second language (MSE, Graduate Certificate); instructional facilitator (MSE, Graduate Certificate); middle level education (MAT); secondary school counseling (MSE); special education (K-12) (MAT, MSE); special education/early childhood (MAT); sports administration (MS). *Application deadline:* For fall admission, 8/1 priority date for domestic students, 6/30 priority date for international students; for spring admission, 1/1 priority date for domestic students, 11/30 priority date for international students. Applications are processed on a rolling basis. *Application fee:* $25 ($75 for international students). *Application Contact:* Dr. Ken Taylor, Graduate Dean, 870-230-5126, Fax: 870-230-5479, E-mail: taylorke@hsu.edu. *Dean*, Dr. Celya Taylor, 870-230-5363, Fax: 870-230-5455, E-mail: taylorc@hsu.edu.

HENDRIX COLLEGE, Conway, AR 72032-3080

General Information Independent-religious, coed, comprehensive institution. *Graduate housing:* Room and/or apartments available on a first-come, first-served basis to single students. Housing application deadline: 6/1.

GRADUATE UNITS

Program in Accounting *Program availability:* Part-time. Offers accounting (MA).

HENLEY-PUTNAM UNIVERSITY, San Jose, CA 95131

General Information Proprietary, coed, comprehensive institution.

GRADUATE UNITS

Doctorate Program in Strategic Security *Program availability:* Part-time, online learning. Offers strategic security (DSS).

Master of Science Program in Intelligence Management *Program availability:* Part-time, online learning. Offers intelligence management (MS).

Master of Science Program in Strategic Security and Protection Management *Program availability:* Part-time, online learning. Offers extremist organizations (MS).

Master of Science Program in Terrorism and Counterterrorism Studies *Program availability:* Part-time, online learning. Offers intelligence operations (MS); protective intelligence (MS).

HERITAGE CHRISTIAN UNIVERSITY, Florence, AL 35630

General Information Independent-religious, coed, primarily men, comprehensive institution.

GRADUATE UNITS

Graduate Programs Offers counseling (MM); Greek (MA); ministry (MM); New Testament (MA).

HERITAGE COLLEGE AND SEMINARY, Cambridge, ON N3C 3T2, Canada

General Information Independent-religious, coed, comprehensive institution. *Enrollment:* 22 full-time matriculated graduate/professional students (1 woman), 106 part-time matriculated graduate/professional students (30 women). *Enrollment by degree level:* 76 master's, 26 other advanced degrees. *Graduate faculty:* 1 full-time (0 women), 5 part-time/adjunct (1 woman). *Tuition:* Full-time $4800 Canadian dollars; part-time $320 Canadian dollars per credit hour. *Required fees:* $110 Canadian dollars; $65 Canadian dollars per term. One-time fee: $50 Canadian dollars. Tuition and fees vary according to course load and program. *Graduate housing:* Room and/or apartments available on a first-come, first-served basis to single students; on-campus housing not available to married students. Typical cost: $2020 Canadian dollars per year ($3015 Canadian dollars including board). Housing application deadline: 5/31. *Student services:* Free psychological counseling. *Library facilities:* Heritage Library.

Computer facilities: 6 computers available on campus for general student use. A campuswide network can be accessed from student residence rooms. Website: http://www.heritagecambridge.com/

General Application Contact: Theresa Beach, Registrar and Director of Admissions, 800-465-1961 Ext. 228, E-mail: tbeach@heritage-theo.edu.

GRADUATE UNITS

Graduate and Professional Programs Students: 22 full-time (1 woman), 106 part-time (30 women). *Faculty:* 1 full-time (0 women), 5 part-time/adjunct (1 woman). Expenses: Contact institution. Offers general (M Div); intercultural studies (M Div); pastoral (M Div); research (M Div); theological studies (MTS, CTS). *Application Contact:* Theresa Beach, Registrar/Director of Admissions, 800-465-1961. *Head,* 519-651-2869.

HERITAGE UNIVERSITY, Toppenish, WA 98948-9599

General Information Independent, coed, comprehensive institution. *Graduate housing:* On-campus housing not available.

GRADUATE UNITS

Graduate Programs in Education *Program availability:* Part-time, evening/weekend. Offers bilingual education/ESL (M Ed); biology (M Ed); counseling (M Ed); educational administration (M Ed); English and literature (M Ed); professional studies (M Ed); reading/literacy (M Ed); special education (M Ed); teaching (MIT).

HERZING UNIVERSITY ONLINE, Menomonee Falls, WI 53051

General Information Independent, coed, comprehensive institution. CGS member.

GRADUATE UNITS

Program in Business Administration *Program availability:* Online learning. Offers accounting (MBA); business administration (MBA); business management (MBA); healthcare management (MBA); human resources (MBA); marketing (MBA); project management (MBA); technology management (MBA).

Program in Nursing *Program availability:* Online learning. Offers nursing (MSN); nursing education (MSN); nursing management (MSN).

HIGH POINT UNIVERSITY, High Point, NC 27268

General Information Independent-religious, coed, comprehensive institution. *Graduate housing:* On-campus housing not available.

GRADUATE UNITS

Norcross Graduate School *Program availability:* Part-time, evening/weekend. Offers business administration (MBA); educational leadership (M Ed); elementary education (M Ed); history (MA); nonprofit management (MA); secondary math (M Ed); special education (M Ed); strategic communication (MA); teaching elementary education k-6 (MAT); teaching secondary mathematics 9-12 (MAT). Electronic applications accepted.

HILBERT COLLEGE, Hamburg, NY 14075-1597

General Information Independent-religious, coed, comprehensive institution. *Enrollment:* 866 graduate, professional, and undergraduate students; 44 full-time matriculated graduate/professional students (31 women), 13 part-time matriculated graduate/professional students (11 women). *Enrollment by degree level:* 57 master's. *Graduate faculty:* 6 full-time (3 women), 13 part-time/adjunct (6 women). *Tuition:* Full-time $18,600; part-time $775 per credit. *Required fees:* $160; $20 per course. One-time fee: $50. *Graduate housing:* On-campus housing not available. *Student services:* Campus safety program, career counseling, exercise/wellness program, free psychological counseling, multicultural affairs office, services for students with disabilities, writing training. *Library facilities:* McGrath Library. *Collection:* Books: 35,000 (physical), 1,484 (digital/electronic); Serial titles: 132 (physical), 83,818 (digital/electronic); Databases: 86. Weekly public service hours: 78; students can reserve study rooms.

Computer facilities: 146 computers available on campus for general student use. A campuswide network can be accessed from student residence rooms. Online class registration is available.
Website: http://www.hilbert.edu/

General Application Contact: Kim Chiarmonte, Director of Adult and Graduate Recruitment, 716-926-8949, Fax: 716-649-0702, E-mail: graduatestudies@hilbert.edu.

GRADUATE UNITS

Program in Criminal Justice Administration Students: 18 full-time (10 women), 3 part-time (2 women); includes 4 minority (2 Black or African American, non-Hispanic/Latino; 2 Two or more races, non-Hispanic/Latino). Average age 34. 7 applicants, 100% accepted, 6 enrolled. *Faculty:* 6 full-time (3 women), 5 part-time/adjunct (2 women). Expenses: Contact institution. *Financial support:* In 2016–17, 21 students received support. Scholarships/grants and tuition waivers (partial) available. Financial award application deadline: 7/1; financial award applicants required to submit FAFSA. In 2016, 11 master's awarded. *Program availability:* Evening/weekend, 100% online. Offers criminal justice administration (MS). *Application deadline:* Applications are processed on a rolling basis. *Application fee:* $25. Electronic applications accepted. *Application Contact:* Kim Chiarmonte, Director for Adult and Graduate Recruitment, 716-926-8948, Fax: 716-649-0702, E-mail: kchiarmonte@hilbert.edu. *Director for Adult and Graduate Studies,* Kathryn Eskew, 716-649-7900 Ext. 305, Fax: 716-649-0702, E-mail: keskew@hilbert.edu.

Program in Public Administration Students: 26 full-time (21 women), 10 part-time (9 women); includes 15 minority (8 Black or African American, non-Hispanic/Latino; 2 American Indian or Alaska Native, non-Hispanic/Latino; 1 Asian, non-Hispanic/Latino; 1 Hispanic/Latino; 3 Two or more races, non-Hispanic/Latino). Average age 32. 16 applicants, 100% accepted, 14 enrolled. *Faculty:* 1 full-time (0 women), 12 part-time/adjunct (6 women). Expenses: Contact institution. *Financial support:* In 2016–17, 25 students received support. Scholarships/grants and tuition waivers (partial) available. Financial award application deadline: 7/1; financial award applicants required to submit FAFSA. In 2016, 16 master's awarded. *Program availability:* Evening/weekend. Offers health administration (MPA); public administration (MPA). *Application deadline:* Applications are processed on a rolling basis. *Application fee:* $25. Electronic applications accepted. *Application Contact:* Kim Chiarmonte, Director for Adult and Graduate Recruitment, 716-926-8948, Fax: 716-649-0702, E-mail: kchiarmonte@hilbert.edu. *Director of Adult and Graduate Studies,* Kathryn Eskew, 716-649-7900 Ext. 305, Fax: 716-649-0702, E-mail: keskew@hilbert.edu.

HILLSDALE COLLEGE, Hillsdale, MI 49242-1298

General Information Independent, coed, comprehensive institution. *Tuition:* Full-time $23,420; part-time $1280 per credit hour. *Library facilities:* Michael Alex Mossey Library. *Collection:* Books: 268,001 (physical), 1.6 million (digital/electronic); Serial titles: 570 (physical), 86,771 (digital/electronic); Databases: 235. Weekly public service hours: 108.

Computer facilities: 181 computers available on campus for general student use. A campuswide network can be accessed from student residence rooms and from off campus. Online class registration is available.
Website: http://www.hillsdale.edu/

GRADUATE UNITS

Van Andel Graduate School of Statesmanship Expenses: Contact institution. Offers politics (MA, PhD). *Application deadline:* For fall admission, 12/15 priority date for domestic and international students; for spring admission, 10/15 priority date for domestic and international students. Electronic applications accepted. *Dean,* Dr. Ronald J. Pestritto, 517-607-2483, E-mail: gradschool@hillsdale.edu.

HIRAM COLLEGE, Hiram, OH 44234

General Information Independent, coed, comprehensive institution.

GRADUATE UNITS

Graduate Studies *Program availability:* Part-time, evening/weekend. Offers interdisciplinary studies (MAIS).

HODGES UNIVERSITY, Naples, FL 34119

General Information Independent, coed, comprehensive institution. *Graduate housing:* On-campus housing not available.

GRADUATE UNITS

Graduate Programs *Program availability:* Part-time, evening/weekend, 100% online, blended/hybrid learning. Offers accounting (M Acc); business administration (MBA); clinical mental health counseling (MS); health services administration (MS); information systems management (MIS); legal studies (MS); management (MSM). Electronic applications accepted.

HOFSTRA UNIVERSITY, Hempstead, NY 11549

General Information Independent, coed, university. CGS member. *Enrollment:* 11,145 graduate, professional, and undergraduate students; 2,987 full-time matriculated graduate/professional students (1,783 women), 1,137 part-time matriculated graduate/professional students (721 women). *Enrollment by degree level:* 2,637 master's, 1,410 doctoral, 77 other advanced degrees. *Graduate faculty:* 242 full-time (112 women), 262 part-time/adjunct (117 women). *Tuition:* Full-time $1240. *Required fees:* $970. Tuition and fees vary according to program. *Graduate housing:* Room and/or apartments available on a first-come, first-served basis to single students; on-campus housing not available to married students. Typical cost: $8150 (including board). Room and board charges vary according to board plan, campus/location and housing facility selected. Housing application deadline: 5/1. *Student services:* Campus employment opportunities, campus safety program, career counseling, child daycare facilities, exercise/wellness program, free psychological counseling, grant writing training, international student services, multicultural affairs office, services for students with disabilities, teacher training, writing training. *Library facilities:* Axinn Library plus 2 others. *Collection:* Books: 953,971 (physical), 175,393 (digital/electronic); Serial titles: 1,848 (physical), 14,521 (digital/electronic); Databases: 241. Weekly public service hours: 102; study areas open 24 hours, 5–7 days a week; students can reserve study rooms.

Computer facilities: Computer purchase and lease plans are available. 1,536 computers available on campus for general student use. Online class registration, emergency alert system, software tutoring, repair and rebuild after virus service, course management system, e-portfolio, card services balance update, printing services, support for specific technology-enhanced assignments are available.
Website: http://www.hofstra.edu/

General Application Contact: Sunil Samuel, Assistant Vice President of Admissions, 516-463-4723, Fax: 516-463-4664, E-mail: graduateadmission@hofstra.edu.

GRADUATE UNITS

College of Liberal Arts and Sciences Students: 280 full-time (179 women), 63 part-time (36 women); includes 80 minority (23 Black or African American, non-Hispanic/Latino; 3 American Indian or Alaska Native, non-Hispanic/Latino; 14 Asian, non-Hispanic/Latino; 35 Hispanic/Latino; 2 Native Hawaiian or other Pacific Islander, non-Hispanic/Latino; 3 Two or more races, non-Hispanic/Latino), 29 international. Average age 27. 434 applicants, 52% accepted, 94 enrolled. *Faculty:* 59 full-time (20 women), 52 part-time/adjunct (20 women). Expenses: Contact institution. *Financial support:* In 2016–17, 213 students received support, including 176 fellowships with full and partial tuition reimbursements available (averaging $6,869 per year), 7 research assistantships with full and partial tuition reimbursements available (averaging $7,139 per year); career-related internships or fieldwork, Federal Work-Study, institutionally sponsored loans, scholarships/grants, traineeships, tuition waivers (full and partial), and unspecified assistantships also available. Support available to part-time students. Financial award applicants required to submit FAFSA. In 2016, 112 master's, 36 doctorates awarded. *Program availability:* Part-time, evening/weekend, online learning. Offers applied linguistics (TESOL) (MA); applied organizational psychology (PhD); biology (MA, MS); clinical psychology (PhD); creative writing and English literature (MFA); industrial/organizational psychology (MA); liberal arts and sciences (MA, MFA, MS, PhD, Psy D); linguistics (MA); medical physics (MS); public advocacy (MA); school-community psychology (Psy D); sustainability studies (MA); urban ecology (MA, MS). *Application deadline:* Applications are processed on a rolling basis. *Application fee:* $75. Electronic applications accepted. *Application Contact:* Sunil Samuel, Assistant Vice

Hofstra University

President of Admissions, 516-463-4723, Fax: 516-463-4664, E-mail: graduateadmission@hofstra.edu. *Dean,* Dr. Bernard J. Firestone, 516-463-5411, Fax: 516-463-4861, E-mail: bernard.j.firestone@hofstra.edu.

Frank G. Zarb School of Business Students: 673 full-time (338 women), 289 part-time (122 women); includes 177 minority (41 Black or African American, non-Hispanic/Latino; 1 American Indian or Alaska Native, non-Hispanic/Latino; 75 Asian, non-Hispanic/Latino; 53 Hispanic/Latino; 1 Native Hawaiian or other Pacific Islander, non-Hispanic/Latino; 6 Two or more races, non-Hispanic/Latino; 454 international. Average age 28. 1,847 applicants, 68% accepted, 381 enrolled. *Faculty:* 52 full-time (14 women), 32 part-time/adjunct (8 women). Expenses: Contact institution. *Financial support:* In 2016–17, 252 students received support, including 211 fellowships with full and partial tuition reimbursements available (averaging $5,079 per year), 2 research assistantships with full and partial tuition reimbursements available (averaging $6,375 per year); career-related internships or fieldwork, Federal Work-Study, institutionally sponsored loans, scholarships/grants, tuition waivers (full and partial), and unspecified assistantships also available. Support available to part-time students. Financial award applicants required to submit FAFSA. In 2016, 415 master's awarded. *Program availability:* Part-time, evening/weekend, blended/hybrid learning. Offers accounting (MS, Advanced Certificate); business (EMBA, MBA, MS, Advanced Certificate); business administration (MBA); corporate finance (Advanced Certificate); finance (MS); general management (Advanced Certificate); human resource management (MS, Advanced Certificate); information systems (MS, Advanced Certificate); international business (Advanced Certificate); investment management (Advanced Certificate); marketing (MS, Advanced Certificate); marketing research (MS); quantitative finance (MS); taxation (MS, Advanced Certificate). *Application deadline:* Applications are processed on a rolling basis. *Application fee:* $75. Electronic applications accepted. *Application Contact:* Sunil Samuel, Assistant Vice President of Admissions, 516-463-4723, Fax: 516-463-4664, E-mail: graduateadmission@hofstra.edu. *Dean,* Dr. Herman Berliner, 516-463-5676, Fax: 516-463-5268, E-mail: herman.a.berliner@hofstra.edu.

Hofstra Northwell School of Graduate Nursing and Physician Assistant Studies Students: 132 full-time (102 women), 79 part-time (64 women); includes 55 minority (10 Black or African American, non-Hispanic/Latino; 1 American Indian or Alaska Native, non-Hispanic/Latino; 23 Asian, non-Hispanic/Latino; 17 Hispanic/Latino; 3 Native Hawaiian or other Pacific Islander, non-Hispanic/Latino; 1 Two or more races, non-Hispanic/Latino, 2 international. Average age 28. 1,609 applicants, 7% accepted, 92 enrolled. *Faculty:* 8 full-time (7 women), 2 part-time/adjunct (0 women). Expenses: Contact institution. *Financial support:* In 2016–17, 13 students received support, including 12 fellowships with full and partial tuition reimbursements available (averaging $7,465 per year); research assistantships with full and partial tuition reimbursements available, career-related internships or fieldwork, Federal Work-Study, institutionally sponsored loans, scholarships/grants, traineeships, tuition waivers (full and partial), and unspecified assistantships also available. Support available to part-time students. Financial award applicants required to submit FAFSA. In 2016, 50 master's awarded. Offers adult-gerontology acute care nurse practitioner (MS); family nurse practitioner (MS); nursing and physician assistant studies (MS); physician assistant studies (MS); psychiatric-mental health nurse practitioner (MS). *Application deadline:* Applications are processed on a rolling basis. *Application fee:* $50. Electronic applications accepted. *Application Contact:* Sunil Samuel, Assistant Vice President of Admissions, 516-463-4723, Fax: 516-463-4664, E-mail: graduateadmission@hofstra.edu. *Dean,* Dr. Kathleen Gallo, 516-463-7475, Fax: 516-463-7495, E-mail: kathleen.gallo@hofstra.edu.

Hofstra Northwell School of Medicine Students: 388 full-time (181 women); includes 160 minority (21 Black or African American, non-Hispanic/Latino; 76 Asian, non-Hispanic/Latino; 51 Hispanic/Latino; 4 Native Hawaiian or other Pacific Islander, non-Hispanic/Latino; 8 Two or more races, non-Hispanic/Latino), 2 international. Average age 25. *Faculty:* 19 full-time (12 women), 11 part-time/adjunct (4 women). Expenses: Contact institution. *Financial support:* In 2016–17, 293 students received support, including 275 fellowships with full and partial tuition reimbursements available (averaging $25,325 per year), 1 research assistantship with full and partial tuition reimbursement available (averaging $6,075 per year); career-related internships or fieldwork, Federal Work-Study, institutionally sponsored loans, scholarships/grants, tuition waivers (full and partial), and unspecified assistantships also available. Support available to part-time students. Financial award applicants required to submit FAFSA. In 2016, 58 doctorates awarded. Offers medicine (MD); molecular basis of medicine (PhD). *Application deadline:* For fall admission, 12/1 priority date for domestic students. *Application fee:* $100. Electronic applications accepted. *Application Contact:* Sunil Samuel, Assistant Vice President of Admissions, 516-463-4723, Fax: 516-463-4664. *Dean,* Dr. Lawrence Smith, 516-463-7517, Fax: 516-463-7543, E-mail: lawrence.smith@hofstra.edu.

Lawrence Herbert School of Communication Students: 58 full-time (43 women), 24 part-time (17 women); includes 38 minority (19 Black or African American, non-Hispanic/Latino; 3 Asian, non-Hispanic/Latino; 13 Hispanic/Latino; 3 Two or more races, non-Hispanic/Latino), 9 international. Average age 26. 89 applicants, 73% accepted, 33 enrolled. *Faculty:* 13 full-time (7 women), 7 part-time/adjunct (3 women). Expenses: Contact institution. *Financial support:* In 2016–17, 43 students received support, including 10 fellowships with full and partial tuition reimbursements available (averaging $3,045 per year), 3 research assistantships with full and partial tuition reimbursements available (averaging $7,125 per year); career-related internships or fieldwork, Federal Work-Study, institutionally sponsored loans, scholarships/grants, tuition waivers (full and partial), and unspecified assistantships also available. Support available to part-time students. Financial award applicants required to submit FAFSA. In 2016, 34 master's awarded. *Program availability:* Part-time, evening/weekend. Offers communication (MA); journalism (MA); public relations (MA). *Application deadline:* Applications are processed on a rolling basis. *Application fee:* $75. Electronic applications accepted. *Application Contact:* Sunil Samuel, Assistant Vice President of Admissions, 516-463-4664, E-mail: graduateadmission@hofstra.edu. *Dean,* Dr. Evan W. Cornog, 516-463-5215, Fax: 516-463-4866, E-mail: evan.w.cornog@hofstra.edu.

Maurice A. Deane School of Law Students: 692 full-time (377 women), 93 part-time (56 women); includes 216 minority (79 Black or African American, non-Hispanic/Latino; 3 American Indian or Alaska Native, non-Hispanic/Latino; 34 Asian, non-Hispanic/Latino; 87 Hispanic/Latino; 8 Native Hawaiian or other Pacific Islander, non-Hispanic/Latino; 5 Two or more races, non-Hispanic/Latino), 22 international. Average age 27. *Faculty:* 41 full-time (22 women), 47 part-time/adjunct (9 women). Expenses: Contact institution. *Financial support:* In 2016–17, 508 students received support, including 491 fellowships with full and partial tuition reimbursements available (averaging $31,765 per year), 3 research assistantships with full and partial tuition reimbursements available (averaging $6,675 per year); career-related internships or fieldwork, Federal Work-Study, institutionally sponsored loans, scholarships/grants, tuition waivers (full and partial), and unspecified assistantships also available. Support available to part-time students. Financial award applicants required to submit FAFSA. In 2016, 10 master's, 198 doctorates awarded. *Program availability:* Part-time, 100% online. Offers American legal studies (LL M); family law (LL M); health law and policy (LL M, MA); law (JD).

Application deadline: For fall admission, 4/15 priority date for domestic and international students. Applications are processed on a rolling basis. *Application fee:* $75. Electronic applications accepted. *Application Contact:* Sunil Samuel, Assistant Vice President of Admissions, 516-463-4723, Fax: 516-463-4664. *Dean,* Gail Prudenti, 516-463-4068, E-mail: gail.prudenti@hofstra.edu.

School of Education Students: 288 full-time (212 women), 403 part-time (293 women); includes 157 minority (65 Black or African American, non-Hispanic/Latino; 2 American Indian or Alaska Native, non-Hispanic/Latino; 23 Asian, non-Hispanic/Latino; 65 Hispanic/Latino; 1 Native Hawaiian or other Pacific Islander, non-Hispanic/Latino; 1 Two or more races, non-Hispanic/Latino), 26 international. Average age 31. 505 applicants, 87% accepted, 268 enrolled. Expenses: Contact institution. *Financial support:* In 2016–17, 367 students received support, including 165 fellowships with full and partial tuition reimbursements available (averaging $4,323 per year), 17 research assistantships with full and partial tuition reimbursements available (averaging $6,661 per year); Federal Work-Study, institutionally sponsored loans, scholarships/grants, traineeships, tuition waivers (full and partial), and unspecified assistantships also available. Support available to part-time students. Financial award applicants required to submit FAFSA. In 2016, 186 master's, 17 doctorates, 78 other advanced degrees awarded. *Program availability:* Part-time, evening/weekend, 100% online, blended/hybrid learning. Offers applied behavior analysis (Advanced Certificate); bilingual education (MA, Advanced Certificate); bilingual extension (Advanced Certificate); business education (MS Ed); early childhood and childhood education (MS Ed); early childhood education (MA, MS Ed); early childhood special education (MS Ed, Advanced Certificate); education (MA, MS, MS Ed, Ed D, PhD, Advanced Certificate); education technology (Advanced Certificate); educational and policy leadership (Ed D); educational leadership (Advanced Certificate); educational leadership and policy studies (MS Ed); elementary education (MA, MS Ed); English education (MS Ed); family and consumer science (MS Ed); fine arts and music education (Advanced Certificate); fine arts education (MS Ed); foreign language and TESOL (MS Ed); foreign language education (MS Ed); gifted education (Advanced Certificate); health education PK-12 teaching certification (MS); inclusive early childhood special education (MS Ed); inclusive elementary special education (MS Ed); inclusive secondary special education (MS Ed); learning and teaching (Ed D); literacy studies (MS Ed, Ed D, PhD, Advanced Certificate); mathematics education (MA, MS Ed); middle school extension (Advanced Certificate); music education (MA, MS Ed); physical education (MS); science education (MA, MS Ed); secondary education (Advanced Certificate); secondary education generalist (MS Ed); social studies education (MA, MS Ed); special education (MS Ed, Advanced Certificate); special education assessment and diagnosis (Advanced Certificate); special education generalist (MS Ed); sport science (MS); teaching languages other than English and TESOL (MS Ed); teaching students with severe or multiple disabilities (Advanced Certificate); TESOL (MS Ed, Advanced Certificate). *Application deadline:* Applications are processed on a rolling basis. *Application fee:* $75. Electronic applications accepted. *Application Contact:* Sunil Samuel, Assistant Vice President of Admissions, 516-463-4723, Fax: 516-463-4664, E-mail: graduateadmission@hofstra.edu. *Senior Associate Dean,* Dr. Karin Spencer, 516-463-5742, E-mail: karin.j.spencer@hofstra.edu.

School of Engineering and Applied Science Students: 34 full-time (8 women), 20 part-time (5 women); includes 13 minority (1 American Indian or Alaska Native, non-Hispanic/Latino; 6 Asian, non-Hispanic/Latino; 4 Hispanic/Latino; 1 Native Hawaiian or other Pacific Islander, non-Hispanic/Latino; 1 Two or more races, non-Hispanic/Latino), 20 international. Average age 30. 48 applicants, 90% accepted, 15 enrolled. *Faculty:* 10 full-time (3 women), 6 part-time/adjunct (1 woman). Expenses: Contact institution. *Financial support:* In 2016–17, 24 students received support, including 6 fellowships with full and partial tuition reimbursements available (averaging $2,647 per year); research assistantships with full and partial tuition reimbursements available, career-related internships or fieldwork, Federal Work-Study, institutionally sponsored loans, scholarships/grants, tuition waivers (full and partial), and unspecified assistantships also available. Support available to part-time students. Financial award applicants required to submit FAFSA. In 2016, 12 master's awarded. *Program availability:* Part-time, evening/weekend, blended/hybrid learning. Offers computer science (MS). *Application deadline:* Applications are processed on a rolling basis. *Application fee:* $75. Electronic applications accepted. *Application Contact:* Sunil Samuel, Assistant Vice President of Admissions, 516-463-4723, Fax: 516-463-4664, E-mail: graduateadmission@hofstra.edu. *Dean,* Dr. Sina Rabbany, 516-463-6672, E-mail: sina.y.rabbany@hofstra.edu.

School of Health Professions and Human Services Students: 442 full-time (343 women), 166 part-time (128 women); includes 221 minority (73 Black or African American, non-Hispanic/Latino; 1 American Indian or Alaska Native, non-Hispanic/Latino; 77 Asian, non-Hispanic/Latino; 60 Hispanic/Latino; 7 Native Hawaiian or other Pacific Islander, non-Hispanic/Latino; 3 Two or more races, non-Hispanic/Latino), 30 international. Average age 27. 1,139 applicants, 49% accepted, 255 enrolled. *Faculty:* 27 full-time (15 women), 59 part-time/adjunct (34 women). Expenses: Contact institution. *Financial support:* In 2016–17, 235 students received support, including 143 fellowships with full and partial tuition reimbursements available (averaging $3,814 per year), 11 research assistantships with full and partial tuition reimbursements available (averaging $7,681 per year); career-related internships or fieldwork, Federal Work-Study, institutionally sponsored loans, scholarships/grants, traineeships, tuition waivers (full and partial), and unspecified assistantships also available. Support available to part-time students. Financial award applicants required to submit FAFSA. In 2016, 223 master's, 5 doctorates, 9 other advanced degrees awarded. *Program availability:* Part-time, evening/weekend. Offers audiology (Au D); counseling (MS Ed, PD); creative arts therapy (MA); health administration (MHA); health informatics (MS); health professions and human services (MA, MHA, MPH, MS, MS Ed; Au D, Advanced Certificate, PD); interdisciplinary transition specialist (Advanced Certificate); marriage and family therapy (MA); mental health counseling (MA, Advanced Certificate); occupational therapy (MS); public health (MPH); rehabilitation administration (PD); rehabilitation counseling (MS Ed, Advanced Certificate); rehabilitation counseling in mental health (MS Ed, Advanced Certificate); school counselor bilingual extension (Advanced Certificate); speech-language pathology (MA); sport science (MS). *Application deadline:* Applications are processed on a rolling basis. *Application fee:* $75. Electronic applications accepted. *Application Contact:* Sunil Samuel, Assistant Vice President of Admissions, 516-463-4723, Fax: 516-463-4664, E-mail: graduateadmission@hofstra.edu. *Dean,* Dr. Holly Seirup, 516-463-5301, Fax: 516-463-5317, E-mail: holly.j.seirup@hofstra.edu.

HOLLINS UNIVERSITY, Roanoke, VA 24020

General Information Independent, Undergraduate: women only; graduate: coed, comprehensive institution. *Enrollment:* 827 graduate, professional, and undergraduate students; 50 full-time matriculated graduate/professional students (42 women), 124 part-time matriculated graduate/professional students (102 women). *Enrollment by degree level:* 173 master's, 1 other advanced degree. *Graduate faculty:* 17 full-time (10 women), 8 part-time/adjunct (5 women). *Graduate housing:* Room and/or apartments available on a first-come, first-served basis to single students; on-campus housing not available to married students. Typical cost: $8735 per year. Housing application deadline: 8/1. *Student services:* Campus safety program, career counseling, multicultural affairs office, services for students with disabilities, teacher training, writing training. *Library facilities:* Wyndham Robertson Library plus 1 other. *Collection:* Books: 315,214 (physical), 56,164 (digital/electronic); Serial titles: 682 (physical), 49,619 (digital/electronic); Databases: 131. Weekly public service hours: 94.

Computer facilities: Computer purchase and lease plans are available. 120 computers available on campus for general student use. A campuswide network can be accessed from student residence rooms. Online class registration is available. Website: http://www.hollins.edu/

General Application Contact: Cathy S. Koon, Manager of Graduate Services, 540-362-6326, Fax: 540-362-6288, E-mail: ckoon@hollins.edu.

GRADUATE UNITS

Graduate Programs Expenses: Contact institution. *Financial support:* Fellowships, teaching assistantships, Federal Work-Study, and scholarships/grants available. Support available to part-time students. Financial award application deadline: 7/15; financial award applicants required to submit FAFSA. *Program availability:* Part-time, evening/weekend. Offers children's book writing and illustrating (MFA); children's literature (MA, MFA); creative writing (MFA); dance (MFA); humanities (MALS); interdisciplinary studies (MALS); leadership (MALS); new play directing (Certificate); new play performance (Certificate); playwriting (MFA); screenwriting (MFA); screenwriting and film studies (MA); social sciences (MALS); teaching (MAT); visual and performing arts (MALS). *Application deadline:* For fall admission, 1/6 priority date for domestic and international students. Applications are processed on a rolling basis. *Application fee:* $40. Electronic applications accepted. *Application Contact:* Cathy S. Koon, Manager of Graduate Services, 540-362-6326, Fax: 540-362-6288, E-mail: ckoon@hollins.edu.

HOLMES INSTITUTE, Golden, CO 80401

General Information Independent-religious, coed, graduate-only institution. *Graduate housing:* On-campus housing not available.

GRADUATE UNITS

Graduate Program *Program availability:* Online learning. Offers consciousness studies (MS).

HOLY APOSTLES COLLEGE AND SEMINARY, Cromwell, CT 06416-2005

General Information Independent-religious, coed, comprehensive institution. *Graduate housing:* On-campus housing not available.

GRADUATE UNITS

Department of Theology *Program availability:* Part-time, evening/weekend, online learning. Offers bioethics (MA, Certificate, Post Master's Certificate); church history (MA, Certificate, Post Master's Certificate); dogmatic theology (MA, Certificate, Post Master's Certificate); liturgical music (MA, Certificate, Post Master's Certificate); liturgy (MA, Certificate, Post Master's Certificate); moral theology (MA, Certificate, Post Master's Certificate); philosophical theology (MA, Certificate, Post Master's Certificate); religious education (MA, Certificate, Post Master's Certificate); sacred scripture (MA, Post Master's Certificate); sacred scriptures (Certificate); theology (M Div). Electronic applications accepted.

HOLY CROSS GREEK ORTHODOX SCHOOL OF THEOLOGY, Brookline, MA 02445-7496

General Information Independent-religious, coed, primarily men, graduate-only institution. *Graduate housing:* Rooms and/or apartments available on a first-come, first-served basis to single and married students. *Student services:* Campus employment opportunities, career counseling, free psychological counseling, international student services, low-cost health insurance. *Library facilities:* Archbishop Iakovos Library and Learning Resource Center.

Computer facilities: 35 computers available on campus for general student use. Website: http://www.hchc.edu/

General Application Contact: Fr. Gregory Floor, Director of Admissions, 617-850-1285, Fax: 617-850-1460, E-mail: admissions@hchc.edu.

GRADUATE UNITS

Theological Programs Expenses: Contact institution. *Financial support:* Research assistantships, teaching assistantships, Federal Work-Study, scholarships/grants, and tuition waivers (partial) available. Financial award application deadline: 4/1; financial award applicants required to submit FAFSA. *Program availability:* Part-time. Offers theology (M Div, MTS, Th M). *Application deadline:* For fall admission, 6/1 for domestic students; for spring admission, 11/1 for domestic students. Applications are processed on a rolling basis. *Application fee:* $50. *Application Contact:* Fr. Gregory Floor, Director of Admissions, 617-850-1285, Fax: 617-850-1460, E-mail: gfloor@hchc.edu. *Dean,* James C. Skedros, 617-850-1254, Fax: 617-850-1460.

HOLY FAMILY UNIVERSITY, Philadelphia, PA 19114

General Information Independent-religious, coed, comprehensive institution. *Enrollment:* 2,737 graduate, professional, and undergraduate students; 329 full-time matriculated graduate/professional students (281 women), 458 part-time matriculated graduate/professional students (327 women). *Enrollment by degree level:* 479 master's, 26 doctoral, 282 other advanced degrees. *Graduate faculty:* 28 full-time (19 women), 66 part-time/adjunct (36 women). *Tuition:* Part-time $751 per hour. *Required fees:* $140 per semester. One-time fee: $165 part-time. Part-time tuition and fees vary according to degree level and program. *Graduate housing:* On-campus housing not available. *Student services:* Campus employment opportunities, campus safety program, career counseling, child daycare facilities, free psychological counseling, low-cost health insurance, services for students with disabilities, teacher training. *Library facilities:* Holy Family University Library plus 1 other. *Collection:* Books: 124,616 (physical), 18,080 (digital/electronic); Databases: 50. Weekly public service hours: 113; students can reserve study rooms.

Computer facilities: 300 computers available on campus for general student use. A campuswide network can be accessed from student residence rooms and from off campus. Online class registration, online course syllabi, online course evaluations are available. Website: http://www.holyfamily.edu/

General Application Contact: Robert McIntyre, Associate Director of Graduate Admissions, 267-341-3555, Fax: 215-637-1478, E-mail: rmcintyre01@holyfamily.edu.

GRADUATE UNITS

Division of Academic Affairs Students: 329 full-time (281 women), 458 part-time (327 women); includes 153 minority (83 Black or African American, non-Hispanic/Latino; 1 American Indian or Alaska Native, non-Hispanic/Latino; 27 Asian, non-Hispanic/Latino; 41 Hispanic/Latino; 1 Native Hawaiian or other Pacific Islander, non-Hispanic/Latino; 4 international. Average age 34. 467 applicants, 69% accepted, 262 enrolled. *Faculty:* 28 full-time (19 women), 66 part-time/adjunct (36 women). Expenses: Contact institution. *Financial support:* Available to part-time students. Applicants required to submit FAFSA. In 2016, 6 master's, 2 doctorates awarded. *Program availability:* Part-time, evening/weekend. Offers accountancy (MS); business administration (MBA); counseling psychology (MS); criminal justice (MA); education (M Ed); educational leadership (Ed D); nursing (MS). *Application deadline:* For fall admission, 7/1 priority date for domestic and international students; for spring admission, 11/1 priority date for domestic and international students; for summer admission, 4/1 priority date for domestic and international students. Applications are processed on a rolling basis. *Application fee:* $25. Electronic applications accepted. *Application Contact:* Don Reinmold, Director of Graduate Admissions, 267-341-5001 Ext. 3230, Fax: 215-633-0558, E-mail: dreinmold@holyfamily.edu. *Vice President of Academic Affairs,* Dr. Michael Markowitz, 267-341-3286, E-mail: mmarkowitz@holyfamily.edu.

Graduate and Professional Programs Expenses: Contact institution. *Financial support:* Research assistantships with partial tuition reimbursements and unspecified assistantships available. Support available to part-time students. Financial award application deadline: 2/15; financial award applicants required to submit FAFSA. *Program availability:* Part-time, evening/weekend. *Application deadline:* For fall admission, 7/1 priority date for domestic and international students; for spring admission, 11/1 priority date for domestic and international students; for summer admission, 4/1 priority date for domestic and international students. Applications are processed on a rolling basis. *Application fee:* $25. Electronic applications accepted. *Application Contact:* Robert McIntyre, Associate Director of Graduate Admissions, 267-341-3555, Fax: 215-637-1478, E-mail: rmcintyre01@holyfamily.edu. *Executive Director of Admissions,* Lauren Campbell, 215-637-3050, Fax: 215-281-1022, E-mail: lcampbell@holyfamily.edu.

School of Arts and Sciences Students: 141 full-time, 28 part-time. Average age 29. 92 applicants, 50% accepted, 32 enrolled. Expenses: Contact institution. *Financial support:* Available to part-time students. Application deadline: 5/1; applicants required to submit FAFSA. In 2016, 58 master's awarded. *Program availability:* Part-time, evening/weekend. Offers counseling psychology (MS); criminal justice (MA). *Application deadline:* For fall admission, 7/1 priority date for domestic and international students; for winter admission, 1/1 for domestic students; for spring admission, 11/1 priority date for domestic and international students; for summer admission, 4/1 priority date for domestic and international students. Applications are processed on a rolling basis. *Application fee:* $25. Electronic applications accepted. *Application Contact:* Robert McIntyre, Associate Director of Graduate Admissions, 267-341-3555, Fax: 215-637-1478, E-mail: rmcintyre01@holyfamily.edu. *Dean,* Dr. Rochelle Robbins, 267-341-3238, Fax: 215-827-0492, E-mail: srobbins@holyfamily.edu.

School of Business Administration Students: 140 part-time. 58 applicants, 78% accepted, 42 enrolled. Expenses: Contact institution. *Financial support:* Available to part-time students. Application deadline: 5/1; applicants required to submit FAFSA. In 2016, 44 master's awarded. *Program availability:* Part-time, evening/weekend. Offers accountancy (MS); finance (MBA); health care administration (MBA); human resource management (MBA); information systems management (MBA). *Application deadline:* For fall admission, 7/1 priority date for domestic and international students; for winter admission, 1/1 for domestic students; for spring admission, 11/1 priority date for domestic and international students; for summer admission, 4/1 priority date for domestic and international students. Applications are processed on a rolling basis. *Application fee:* $25. Electronic applications accepted. *Application Contact:* Gidget Marie Montelibano, Associate Director of Graduate Admissions, 267-341-3558, Fax: 215-637-1478, E-mail: gmontelibano@holyfamily.edu. *Dean,* Dr. Barry Dickinson, 267-341-3440, Fax: 215-637-5937, E-mail: bdickinson@holyfamily.edu.

School of Education Students: 65 full-time, 35 part-time. 87 applicants, 66% accepted, 36 enrolled. Expenses: Contact institution. *Financial support:* Research assistantships with partial tuition reimbursements available. Support available to part-time students. Financial award application deadline: 2/15; financial award applicants required to submit FAFSA. In 2016, 29 master's awarded. *Program availability:* Part-time, evening/weekend. Offers early elementary education (PreK-Grade 4) (M Ed); education (M Ed, Ed D); educational leadership (M Ed); educational leadership and professional studies (Ed D); general education (M Ed); reading specialist (M Ed); special education (M Ed); TESOL and literacy (M Ed). *Application deadline:* For fall admission, 7/1 priority date for domestic and international students; for winter admission, 1/1 for domestic students; for spring admission, 11/1 priority date for domestic and international students; for summer admission, 4/1 priority date for domestic and international students. Applications are processed on a rolling basis. *Application fee:* $25. Electronic applications accepted. *Application Contact:* Donald Reimold, Director of Graduate Admissions, 267-341-5001, Fax: 215-637-1478, E-mail: dreimold@holyfamily.edu. *Dean,* Dr. Kevin Zook, 267-341-3565, Fax: 215-824-2438, E-mail: kzook@holyfamily.edu.

School of Nursing and Allied Health Professions Students: 65 full-time, 35 part-time. Average age 36. 87 applicants, 66% accepted, 36 enrolled. Expenses: Contact institution. *Financial support:* Available to part-time students. Application deadline: 2/15; applicants required to submit FAFSA. In 2016, 29 master's awarded. *Program availability:* Part-time, evening/weekend. Offers nursing administration (MSN); nursing education (MSN). *Application deadline:* For fall admission, 7/1 priority date for domestic and international students; for winter admission, 1/1 for domestic students; for spring admission, 11/1 priority date for domestic and international students; for summer admission, 4/1 priority date for domestic and international students. Applications are processed on a rolling basis. *Application fee:* $25. Electronic applications accepted. *Application Contact:* Donald Reimold, Director of Graduate Admissions, 267-341-5001, Fax: 215-637-1478, E-mail: dreimold@holyfamily.edu. *Dean,* Dr. Cynthia Russell, 267-341-3293, Fax: 215-637-6598, E-mail: crussell@holyfamily.edu.

HOLY NAMES UNIVERSITY, Oakland, CA 94619-1699

General Information Independent-religious, coed, comprehensive institution. *Enrollment:* 866 graduate, professional, and undergraduate students; 104 full-time matriculated graduate/professional students (85 women), 236 part-time matriculated graduate/professional students (186 women). *Enrollment by degree level:* 291 master's, 49 other advanced degrees. *Tuition:* Full-time $17,532; part-time $974 per credit hour. *Required fees:* $500; $250 per credit hour. *Graduate housing:* Room and/or apartments available on a first-come, first-served basis to single students; on-campus housing not available to married students. Typical cost: $6614 per year ($12,808 including board). Room and board charges vary according to board plan. Housing application deadline: 8/15. *Student services:* Campus employment opportunities, campus safety program, career counseling, exercise/wellness program, free psychological counseling, international student services, low-cost health insurance, services for students with disabilities, writing training. *Library facilities:* Cushing Library. *Collection:* Books: 41,811 (physical), 137,046 (digital/electronic); Databases: 49. Students can reserve study rooms.

Computer facilities: 92 computers available on campus for general student use. A campuswide network can be accessed from student residence rooms. Online class registration is available.
Website: http://www.hnu.edu/

General Application Contact: Graduate Admissions Office, 510-436-1351, Fax: 510-436-1325, E-mail: graduateadmissions@hnu.edu.

GRADUATE UNITS

Graduate Division Students: 104 full-time (85 women), 236 part-time (186 women); includes 228 minority (108 Black or African American, non-Hispanic/Latino; 2 American Indian or Alaska Native, non-Hispanic/Latino; 56 Asian, non-Hispanic/Latino; 52 Hispanic/Latino; 6 Native Hawaiian or other Pacific Islander, non-Hispanic/Latino; 4 Two or more races, non-Hispanic/Latino), 7 international. Average age 35. 213 applicants, 71% accepted, 107 enrolled. Expenses: Contact institution. *Financial support:* Career-related internships or fieldwork, scholarships/grants, and unspecified assistantships available. Support available to part-time students. Financial award application deadline: 3/2; financial award applicants required to submit FAFSA. In 2016, 113 master's, 46 other advanced degrees awarded. *Program availability:* Part-time, evening/weekend. Offers administration/management (MSN, PMC); care transition management (MSN); counseling and forensic counseling (MA); counseling psychology (MA); creative writing (MA); educational therapy (Certificate); family nurse practitioner (MSN, PMC); finance (MBA); forensic psychology (MA); informatics (MSN); Kodaly (Certificate); management and leadership (MBA); marketing (MBA); mild/moderate disabilities (Ed S); multiple subject teaching (Credential); music education with Kodaly emphasis (MM); nurse educator (PMC); piano pedagogy (MM); single subject teaching (Credential); urban education: educational therapy (M Ed); urban education: K-12 education (M Ed); urban education: special education (M Ed); vocal pedagogy (MM). *Application deadline:* For fall admission, 8/1 priority date for domestic students, 7/15 for international students; for spring admission, 12/1 priority date for domestic students, 12/1 for international students; for summer admission, 5/1 priority date for domestic students, 5/1 for international students. Applications are processed on a rolling basis. *Application fee:* $65. Electronic applications accepted. *Application Contact:* Graduate Admissions Office. *Director of Admissions*, Chris Rascon, 510-436-1351, Fax: 510-436-1325, E-mail: graduateadmissions@hnu.edu.

HOOD COLLEGE, Frederick, MD 21701-8575

General Information Independent, coed, comprehensive institution. CGS member. *Enrollment:* 2,144 graduate, professional, and undergraduate students; 178 full-time matriculated graduate/professional students (90 women), 792 part-time matriculated graduate/professional students (540 women). *Enrollment by degree level:* 788 master's, 18 doctoral, 149 other advanced degrees. *Graduate faculty:* 42 full-time, 87 part-time/adjunct. *Tuition:* Part-time $450 per credit hour. *Required fees:* $105 per term. Part-time tuition and fees vary according to degree level, campus/location and program. *Graduate housing:* On-campus housing not available. *Student services:* Campus employment opportunities, campus safety program, career counseling, international student services, multicultural affairs office, services for students with disabilities, teacher training. *Library facilities:* Beneficial-Hodson Library and Information Technology Center plus 1 other. *Collection:* Books: 172,311 (physical), 295,531 (digital/electronic); Serial titles: 235 (physical), 42,000 (digital/electronic); Databases: 96. Students can reserve study rooms. *Research affiliation:* U.S. Department of Agriculture (USDA) (biomedical science and environmental biology), United States Army Medical Research Institute of Infectious Diseases (USAMRIID) (biomedical science), National Cancer Institute (biomedical science).

Computer facilities: Computer purchase and lease plans are available. 470 computers available on campus for general student use. A campuswide network can be accessed from student residence rooms and from off campus. Online class registration is available.
Website: http://www.hood.edu/

General Application Contact: Dr. April Boulton, Interim Dean of Graduate School, 301-696-3600, Fax: 301-696-3597, E-mail: gofurther@hood.edu.

GRADUATE UNITS

Graduate School Students: 178 full-time (90 women), 792 part-time (540 women); includes 161 minority (81 Black or African American, non-Hispanic/Latino; 31 Asian, non-Hispanic/Latino; 29 Hispanic/Latino; 20 Two or more races, non-Hispanic/Latino), 136 international. Average age 33. 422 applicants, 75% accepted, 226 enrolled. *Faculty:* 44 full-time, 85 part-time/adjunct. Expenses: Contact institution. *Financial support:* Research assistantships with full tuition reimbursements, tuition waivers (partial), and unspecified assistantships available. Financial award applicants required to submit FAFSA. In 2016, 263 master's, 58 other advanced degrees awarded. *Program availability:* Part-time, evening/weekend. Offers accounting (MBA); bioinformatics (MS, Certificate); biomedical science (MS); ceramic arts (Certificate); ceramics (MA, MFA); clinical mental health counseling (MS); computer science (MS); curriculum and instruction (MS); cyber security (Certificate); educational leadership (MS); environmental biology (MS); finance (MBA); human resource management (MBA); human sciences (MA); humanities (MA); information systems (MBA); information technology (MS); management of information technology (MS); marketing (MBA); organizational leadership (DBA); public management (MBA); reading specialization (MS); school counseling (MS); secondary mathematics education (Certificate); STEM education (Certificate). *Application deadline:* For fall admission, 8/15 priority date for domestic students, 8/5 for international students; for spring admission, 12/1 priority date for domestic students, 12/1 for international students; for summer admission, 5/1 priority date for domestic students, 4/15 for international students. Applications are processed on a rolling basis. *Application fee:* $35. Electronic applications accepted. *Interim Dean of the Graduate School*, April Boulton, 301-696-3600, E-mail: gofurther@hood.edu.

HOOD THEOLOGICAL SEMINARY, Salisbury, NC 28144

General Information Independent-religious, coed, graduate-only institution. *Tuition:* Part-time $500 per credit hour. Part-time tuition and fees vary according to degree level. *Graduate housing:* Rooms and/or apartments guaranteed to single students and available on a first-come, first-served basis to married students. Housing application deadline: 8/15. *Student services:* Campus employment opportunities, writing training. *Library facilities:* Hood Seminary Library.

Computer facilities: 7 computers available on campus for general student use.
Website: http://www.hoodseminary.edu/

General Application Contact: Reginald Boyd, Jr., Director of Recruitment and Admissions, 704-636-6455, Fax: 704-636-7685, E-mail: admissions@hoodseminary.edu.

GRADUATE UNITS

Graduate and Professional Programs Expenses: Contact institution. *Financial support:* Federal Work-Study, scholarships/grants, and resident assistantships available. Financial award application deadline: 7/1; financial award applicants required to submit FAFSA. *Program availability:* Part-time, evening/weekend, online learning. Offers theology (M Div, MTS, D Min). *Application deadline:* For fall admission, 7/15 for domestic students; for spring admission, 11/30 for domestic students. *Application fee:* $30. *Application Contact:* Reginald Boyd, Jr., Director of Recruitment and Admissions, 704-636-6455, Fax: 704-636-7685, E-mail: admissions@hoodseminary.edu. *President*, Vergel L. Lattimore, 704-636-6823, Fax: 704-636-7699, E-mail: president@hoodseminary.edu.

HOPE INTERNATIONAL UNIVERSITY, Fullerton, CA 92831-3138

General Information Independent-religious, coed, comprehensive institution. *Graduate housing:* Room and/or apartments available on a first-come, first-served basis to single students; on-campus housing not available to married students. Housing application deadline: 7/1.

GRADUATE UNITS

School of Graduate and Professional Studies *Program availability:* Part-time, evening/weekend, online learning. Offers Christian leadership (MCM); church music (MA); church music (Korean track) (MCM); church planting (MCM); education administration (MA); elementary education (ME); general management (MBA, MSM); intercultural studies (MCM); international development (MBA, MSM); marketing management (MBA, MSM); marriage and family therapy (MA, MFT); non-profit management (MBA, MSM); secondary education (ME); worship (MCM). Electronic applications accepted.

HOUGHTON COLLEGE, Houghton, NY 14744

General Information Independent-religious, coed, comprehensive institution. *Graduate housing:* On-campus housing not available.

GRADUATE UNITS

Greatbatch School of Music Offers collaborative performance (MMus); composition (MMus); conducting (MMus); music (MA); performance (MMus); world music with theology and intercultural studies (MA). Electronic applications accepted.

HOUSTON BAPTIST UNIVERSITY, Houston, TX 77074-3298

General Information Independent-religious, coed, comprehensive institution. *Enrollment:* 3,270 graduate, professional, and undergraduate students; 305 full-time matriculated graduate/professional students (202 women), 604 part-time matriculated graduate/professional students (420 women). *Enrollment by degree level:* 889 master's, 20 doctoral. *Graduate faculty:* 62 full-time (26 women), 22 part-time/adjunct (13 women). *Tuition:* Full-time $12,500; part-time $12,500 per year. *Required fees:* $2500; $2500 per unit. Tuition and fees vary according to campus/location and program. *Graduate housing:* Rooms and/or apartments available on a first-come, first-served basis to single and married students. Housing application deadline: 4/1. *Student services:* Campus employment opportunities, career counseling, exercise/wellness program, free psychological counseling, international student services, low-cost health insurance, services for students with disabilities, teacher training, writing training. *Library facilities:* Moody Library. *Collection:* Books: 109,121 (physical); Serial titles: 237 (physical), 41,354 (digital/electronic); Databases: 119. Weekly public service hours: 88; students can reserve study rooms.

Computer facilities: 100 computers available on campus for general student use. A campuswide network can be accessed from student residence rooms. Online class registration, office software for 5 devices for each student are available.
Website: http://www.hbu.edu/

General Application Contact: Allyson Cates, Director of Admissions, Graduate School, 281-649-3099, Fax: 281-649-3390, E-mail: acates@hbu.edu.

GRADUATE UNITS

Archie W. Dunham College of Business Students: 126 full-time (77 women), 125 part-time (75 women); includes 145 minority (76 Black or African American, non-Hispanic/Latino; 16 Asian, non-Hispanic/Latino; 47 Hispanic/Latino; 1 Native Hawaiian or other Pacific Islander, non-Hispanic/Latino; 5 Two or more races, non-Hispanic/Latino), 44 international. Average age 30. 502 applicants, 23% accepted, 70 enrolled. *Faculty:* 11 full-time (3 women), 7 part-time/adjunct (2 women). Expenses: Contact institution. *Financial support:* In 2016–17, 18 students received support. Federal Work-Study and scholarships/grants available. Support available to part-time students. Financial award application deadline: 4/1; financial award applicants required to submit FAFSA. In 2016, 101 master's awarded. *Program availability:* Part-time, evening/weekend. Offers business (MBA, MIB, MSHRM); business administration (MBA); human resources management (MSHRM); international business (MIB). *Application deadline:* For fall admission, 8/1 for domestic students, 6/1 for international students; for spring admission, 12/1 for domestic students, 10/1 for international students; for summer admission, 5/1 for domestic students, 3/1 for international students. Applications are processed on a rolling basis. *Application fee:* $0 ($100 for international students). Electronic applications accepted. *Application Contact:* Laurel Motal, Secretary, 281-649-3306, Fax: 281-649-3436, E-mail: lmotal@hbu.edu. *Dean, Archie W. Dunham College of Business*, Dr. Michael Weeks, 281-649-3014, E-mail: mweeks@hbu.edu.

College of Education and Behavioral Sciences Students: 127 full-time (104 women), 318 part-time (275 women); includes 294 minority (161 Black or African American, non-Hispanic/Latino; 2 American Indian or Alaska Native, non-Hispanic/Latino; 23 Asian, non-Hispanic/Latino; 104 Hispanic/Latino; 4 Two or more races, non-Hispanic/Latino), 9 international. Average age 32. 596 applicants, 30% accepted, 128 enrolled. *Faculty:* 25 full-time (18 women), 10 part-time/adjunct (all women). Expenses: Contact institution. *Financial support:* In 2016–17, 7 students received support. Career-related internships or fieldwork, Federal Work-Study, and scholarships/grants available. Support available to part-time students. Financial award application deadline: 4/1; financial award applicants required to submit FAFSA. In 2016, 162 master's awarded. *Program availability:* Part-time, evening/weekend. Offers bilingual education (M Ed); counseling (MAC); counselor education (M Ed); curriculum and instruction (M Ed); education and behavioral sciences (M Ed, MAC, MAP, Ed D, Postbaccalaureate Certificate); educational administration (M Ed); educational diagnostician (M Ed); executive educational leadership (Ed D); reading education (M Ed); school psychology (MAP). *Application deadline:* For fall admission, 8/1 for domestic students, 6/1 for international students; for spring admission,

1/1 for domestic students, 11/1 for international students; for summer admission, 5/1 for domestic students, 3/1 for international students. Applications are processed on a rolling basis. *Application fee:* $0 ($100 for international students). Electronic applications accepted. *Application Contact:* Kristy Wright, Administrative Assistant for Graduate Programs, 281-649-3094, Fax: 281-649-3361, E-mail: kwright@hbu.edu. *Dean,* Dr. Theresa McIntyre, 281-649-3127, Fax: 281-649-3361, E-mail: mmcintyre@hbu.edu.

School of Christian Thought Students: 21 full-time (5 women), 124 part-time (51 women); includes 44 minority (24 Black or African American, non-Hispanic/Latino; 1 American Indian or Alaska Native, non-Hispanic/Latino; 8 Asian, non-Hispanic/Latino; 7 Hispanic/Latino; 4 Two or more races, non-Hispanic/Latino), 4 international. Average age 38. 142 applicants, 67% accepted, 56 enrolled. *Faculty:* 11 full-time (2 women), 3 part-time/adjunct (0 women). Expenses: Contact institution. *Financial support:* In 2016–17, 15 students received support. Federal Work-Study and scholarships/grants available. Support available to part-time students. Financial award application deadline: 4/1; financial award applicants required to submit FAFSA. In 2016, 14 master's awarded. *Program availability:* Part-time, evening/weekend. Offers Biblical languages (M Div); Christian leadership (MA); Christian thought (M Div, MA); cultural apologetics (MA); English languages (M Div); philosophical apologetics (MA); theological studies (MA). *Application deadline:* For fall admission, 8/1 for domestic students, 6/1 for international students; for spring admission, 1/1 for international students, 11/1 for international students; for summer admission, 5/1 for domestic students, 3/1 for international students. Applications are processed on a rolling basis. *Application fee:* $0 ($100 for international students). Electronic applications accepted. *Application Contact:* Celeste Risteski, Administrative Assistant to the Dean, 281-649-3383, Fax: 281-649-3012, E-mail: cristeski@hbu.edu. *Interim Dean,* Dr. Jeffrey Gree, Fax: 281-649-3012, E-mail: jgreen@hbu.edu.

School of Fine Arts Students: 21 full-time (14 women); includes 7 minority (1 Black or African American, non-Hispanic/Latino; 1 Asian, non-Hispanic/Latino; 3 Hispanic/Latino; 2 Two or more races, non-Hispanic/Latino), 3 international. Average age 33. 44 applicants, 34% accepted, 9 enrolled. *Faculty:* 8 full-time (2 women), 2 part-time/adjunct (1 woman). Expenses: Contact institution. *Financial support:* In 2016–17, 5 students received support. Federal Work-Study and scholarships/grants available. Support available to part-time students. Financial award application deadline: 4/1; financial award applicants required to submit FAFSA. In 2016, 11 master's awarded. *Program availability:* Part-time, evening/weekend. Offers studio art (MFA). *Application deadline:* For fall admission, 4/1 for domestic students, 2/1 for international students. Applications are processed on a rolling basis. *Application fee:* $0 ($100 for international students). Electronic applications accepted. *Application Contact:* Dr. Michael Collins, Program Director, 281-649-3624, E-mail: mcollins@hbu.edu. *Dean,* Dr. Jason Lester, 281-649-3339, E-mail: jlester@hbu.edu.

School of Humanities Students: 10 full-time (2 women), 37 part-time (19 women); includes 20 minority (10 Black or African American, non-Hispanic/Latino; 2 American Indian or Alaska Native, non-Hispanic/Latino; 2 Asian, non-Hispanic/Latino; 6 Hispanic/Latino). Average age 32. 52 applicants, 37% accepted, 8 enrolled. *Faculty:* 8 full-time (1 woman). Expenses: Contact institution. *Financial support:* Federal Work-Study and scholarships/grants available. Financial award application deadline: 4/1; financial award applicants required to submit FAFSA. In 2016, 10 master's awarded. *Program availability:* Part-time, evening/weekend. Offers classical learning (MLA); general liberal arts (MLA); humanities (MA, MLA); philosophy (MA); research (MLA). *Application deadline:* For fall admission, 8/1 for domestic students, 6/1 for international students; for spring admission, 1/1 for international students, 11/1 for international students; for summer admission, 5/1 for domestic students, 3/1 for international students. Applications are processed on a rolling basis. *Application fee:* $0 ($100 for international students). Electronic applications accepted. *Application Contact:* Allyson Cates, Director of Admissions, Graduate School, 281-649-3099, Fax: 281-649-3390, E-mail: acates@hbu.edu. *Dean,* School of Humanities, Dr. Jodey Hinze, E-mail: jhinze@hbu.edu.

HOUSTON GRADUATE SCHOOL OF THEOLOGY, Houston, TX 77092

General Information Independent-religious, coed, graduate-only institution. *Graduate housing:* On-campus housing not available.

GRADUATE UNITS

Graduate Programs *Program availability:* Part-time, evening/weekend. Offers counseling (MA); pastoral ministry (M Div, D Min); theology (MA).

HOWARD PAYNE UNIVERSITY, Brownwood, TX 76801-2715

General Information Independent-religious, coed, comprehensive institution. *Enrollment:* 1,189 graduate, professional, and undergraduate students; 27 full-time matriculated graduate/professional students (13 women), 62 part-time matriculated graduate/professional students (21 women). *Enrollment by degree level:* 89 master's. *Graduate faculty:* 15 full-time (3 women), 7 part-time/adjunct (1 woman). *Graduate housing:* Room and/or apartments available on a first-come, first-served basis to single students; on-campus housing not available to married students. *Student services:* Campus employment opportunities, career counseling, exercise/wellness program, free psychological counseling, services for students with disabilities, writing training. *Library facilities:* Walker Memorial Library. *Collection:* Books: 125,784 (physical), 144,053 (digital/electronic); Serial titles: 27,347 (physical). Weekly public service hours: 84.

Computer facilities: 260 computers available on campus for general student use. A campuswide network can be accessed from student residence rooms and from off campus.
Website: http://www.hputx.edu/

General Application Contact: Dr. Gary Gramling, Director of Graduate Programs/Professor of Christian Studies, 325-649-8404, Fax: 325-649-8949, E-mail: ggramling@hputx.edu.

GRADUATE UNITS

Program in Business Administration Students: 12 full-time (4 women), 27 part-time (14 women); includes 16 minority (1 American Indian or Alaska Native, non-Hispanic/Latino; 15 Hispanic/Latino), 1 international. Average age 33. 23 applicants, 78% accepted, 11 enrolled. *Faculty:* 7 full-time (2 women), 2 part-time/adjunct (0 women). Expenses: Contact institution. *Financial support:* Application deadline: 3/15; applicants required to submit FAFSA. In 2016, 18 master's awarded. *Program availability:* Part-time, evening/weekend. Offers business administration (MBA). *Application deadline:* For fall admission, 7/1 for domestic students; for spring admission, 12/1 for domestic students. Applications are processed on a rolling basis. *Application fee:* $0. Electronic applications accepted. *Application Contact:* Mary Hill, Administrative Assistant, School of Business, 325-649-8704, E-mail: mhill@hputx.edu. *Director,* Dr. Brad Lemler, 325-649-8149, E-mail: blemler@hputx.edu.

Program in Criminal Justice *Faculty:* 2 full-time (1 woman). Expenses: Contact institution. *Financial support:* Veteran's Administration benefits available. Financial

award application deadline: 3/15; financial award applicants required to submit FAFSA. *Program availability:* Part-time, evening/weekend, online only, 100% online. Offers criminal justice (MS). *Application deadline:* Applications are processed on a rolling basis. Electronic applications accepted. *Director, Criminal Justice Program,* Lynn Humeniuk, 325-649-8703, E-mail: lhumeniuk@hputx.edu.

Program in Instructional Leadership Students: 9 full-time (8 women), 5 part-time (3 women); includes 3 minority (1 Black or African American, non-Hispanic/Latino; 2 Hispanic/Latino). Average age 34. 10 applicants, 80% accepted, 8 enrolled. *Faculty:* 1 full-time (0 women), 2 part-time/adjunct (1 woman). Expenses: Contact institution. *Financial support:* Application deadline: 3/15; applicants required to submit FAFSA. In 2016, 4 master's awarded. *Program availability:* Part-time, evening/weekend, online only. Offers instructional leadership (M Ed). *Application deadline:* For fall admission, 7/1 for domestic students; for spring admission, 12/1 for domestic students. Applications are processed on a rolling basis. *Application fee:* $0. Electronic applications accepted. *Application Contact:* Susan Sharp, Administrative Assistant, School of Education/Certification Officer, 325-649-8144, E-mail: ssharp@hputx.edu. *Director of Instructional Leadership Graduate Program/Professor of Education,* Dr. Joe Robinson, 325-649-8205, E-mail: jrobinson@hputx.edu.

Program in Sport and Wellness Leadership Students: 19 part-time (4 women); includes 4 minority (1 Black or African American, non-Hispanic/Latino; 3 Hispanic/Latino). Average age 30. *Faculty:* 2 full-time (0 women). Expenses: Contact institution. *Financial support:* Unspecified assistantships available. Financial award applicants required to submit FAFSA. *Program availability:* Part-time. Offers sport and wellness leadership (M Ed). Electronic applications accepted. *Professor and Chair, Exercise and Sport Science/Director, Graduate Program in Sport and Recreation Leadership,* Dr. Graham Hatcher, 325-649-8966, E-mail: ghatcher@hputx.edu.

Program in Theology and Ministry Students: 4 full-time (1 woman), 9 part-time (0 women); includes 1 minority (Hispanic/Latino). Average age 30. 9 applicants, 89% accepted, 5 enrolled. *Faculty:* 3 full-time (0 women), 2 part-time/adjunct (0 women). Expenses: Contact institution. *Financial support:* Applicants required to submit FAFSA. In 2016, 3 master's awarded. *Program availability:* Part-time. Offers theology and ministry (MA). *Application deadline:* For fall admission, 7/1 for domestic students; for spring admission, 12/1 for domestic students. Applications are processed on a rolling basis. *Application fee:* $0. Electronic applications accepted. *Application Contact:* Kristian Simpson, Administrative Assistant for Christian Studies Graduate Programs, 325-649-8039, E-mail: ksimpson@hputx.edu. *Director of Graduate Programs/Professor of Christian Studies,* Dr. Gary Gramling, 325-649-8404, E-mail: ggramling@hputx.edu.

Program in Youth Ministry Students: 2 full-time (0 women), 2 part-time (0 women). Average age 28. 5 applicants, 100% accepted, 4 enrolled. *Faculty:* 2 full-time (0 women), 1 part-time/adjunct (0 women). Expenses: Contact institution. *Financial support:* Application deadline: 3/15; applicants required to submit FAFSA. In 2016, 6 master's awarded. *Program availability:* Part-time. Offers youth ministry (MA). *Application deadline:* For fall admission, 7/1 for domestic students; for spring admission, 12/1 for domestic students. Applications are processed on a rolling basis. *Application fee:* $0. Electronic applications accepted. *Application Contact:* Kristian Simpson, Administrative Assistant for Christian Studies Graduate Programs, 325-649-8039, E-mail: ksimpson@hputx.edu. *Director,* Dr. Gary Gramling, 325-649-8404, E-mail: ggramling@hputx.edu.

HOWARD UNIVERSITY, Washington, DC 20059-0002

General Information Independent, coed, university. CGS member. *Graduate housing:* Rooms and/or apartments available on a first-come, first-served basis to single and married students. Housing application deadline: 4/1. *Research affiliation:* Ewing Marion Kauffman Foundation (science education), The Tokyo Foundation (women's studies, international affairs), National Oceanic and Atmospheric Administration (NOAA) (atmospheric science and nanotechnology), National Institute of Mental Health (NIMH) (genomics), Akilu Lamma Institute of Pathobiology (HIV/AIDS infection, water resources development, population movement), Labor Research Laboratories and Medical Center in Benin City, Nigeria (infectious diseases).

GRADUATE UNITS

College of Dentistry Expenses: Contact institution. *Financial support:* Federal Work-Study, institutionally sponsored loans, and scholarships/grants available. Financial award application deadline: 2/15; financial award applicants required to submit FAFSA. Offers advanced education in general dentistry (Certificate); dentistry (DDS); general dentistry practice (Certificate); oral and maxillofacial surgery (Certificate); orthodontics (Certificate); pediatric dentistry (Certificate). *Application deadline:* For fall admission, 3/1 for domestic and international students. Applications are processed on a rolling basis. *Application Contact:* Donna Grant-Mills, Associate Dean for Student Affairs and Admissions, 202-806-0400, Fax: 202-806-0354. *Dean,* Dr. Dexter A. Woods, 202-806-0440, Fax: 202-806-0354.

College of Engineering, Architecture, and Computer Sciences *Program availability:* Part-time. Offers engineering, architecture, and computer sciences (M Eng, MCS, MS, PhD). Electronic applications accepted.

School of Engineering and Computer Science *Program availability:* Part-time. Offers chemical engineering (MS); civil engineering (M Eng); electrical engineering (M Eng, PhD); engineering and computer science (M Eng, MCS, MS, PhD); mechanical engineering (M Eng, PhD); systems and computer science (MCS). Electronic applications accepted.

College of Medicine Offers biochemistry and molecular biology (PhD); biotechnology (MS); medicine (MPH, MS, MD, PhD); microbiology (PhD); pharmacology (MS, PhD); public health (MPH).

College of Nursing and Allied Health Sciences Expenses: Contact institution. *Financial support:* Research assistantships, teaching assistantships, career-related internships or fieldwork, Federal Work-Study, institutionally sponsored loans, and scholarships/grants available. Support available to part-time students. Financial award applicants required to submit FAFSA. *Program availability:* Part-time. Offers nursing and allied health sciences (MPA, MSN, MSOT, DPT, Certificate). Electronic applications accepted. *Application Contact:* Dr. Gina S. Brown, Dean, 202-806-5042, Fax: 202-234-1375. *Dean,* Dr. Gina S. Brown, 202-806-5042, Fax: 202-234-1375.

Division of Nursing Expenses: Contact institution. *Financial support:* Teaching assistantships, career-related internships or fieldwork, institutionally sponsored loans, and scholarships/grants available. Financial award application deadline: 4/1. *Program availability:* Part-time. Offers family nurse practitioner (MSN); nurse educator (MSN). *Application deadline:* For fall admission, 4/1 priority date for domestic students; for spring admission, 11/1 for domestic students. Applications are processed on a rolling basis. *Application Contact:* Tammi Damas, Associate Dean, 202-806-5021, Fax: 202-806-5958, E-mail: tammi.damas@howard.edu. *Associate Dean,* Dr. Tammi Damas, 202-806-5021, Fax: 202-806-5958, E-mail: tammi.damas@howard.edu.

College of Pharmacy *Program availability:* Online learning. Offers pharmacy (Pharm D). Electronic applications accepted.

Howard University

Graduate School *Program availability:* Part-time, evening/weekend. Offers African diaspora (MA, PhD); African history (MA, PhD); African studies (MA, PhD); analytical chemistry (MS, PhD); anatomy (MS, PhD); applied mathematics (MS, PhD); atmospheric (MS, PhD); atmospheric sciences (MS, PhD); biochemistry (MS, PhD); biology (MS, PhD); biophysics (PhD); clinical psychology (PhD); developmental psychology (PhD); economics (MA, PhD); English (MA, PhD); environmental (MS, PhD); exercise physiology (MS); experimental psychology (PhD); French (MA); health education (MS); inorganic chemistry (MS, PhD); Latin America and the Caribbean (MA, PhD); mathematics (MS, PhD); neuropsychology (PhD); nutrition (MS, PhD); organic chemistry (MS, PhD); personality psychology (PhD); philosophy (MA); physical chemistry (MS, PhD); physics (MS, PhD); physiology (PhD); political science (MA, MAPA, PhD); psychology (MS); public administration (MAPA); public history (MA); social psychology (PhD); sociology (MA, PhD); Spanish (MA); sports studies (MS); United States history (MA, PhD); urban recreation (MS). Electronic applications accepted.

Division of Fine Arts *Program availability:* Part-time. Offers 3D reality (sculpture and ceramics) (MFA); applied music (MM); art history (MA); design (MFA); electronic studio (MFA); fine arts (MFA); history of art and visual culture (MA); instrument (MM Ed); jazz studies (MM); organ (MM Ed); painting (MFA); photography (MFA); piano (MM Ed); voice (MM Ed).

School of Business *Program availability:* Part-time, evening/weekend, online learning. Offers accounting (MBA); business (MBA); entrepreneurship (MBA); finance (MBA); general management (MBA); human resources management (MBA); information systems (MBA); international business (MBA); marketing (MBA); supply chain management (MBA).

School of Communications *Program availability:* Part-time, evening/weekend. Offers communication sciences (PhD); communications (MA, MFA, MS, PhD); film (MFA); intercultural communication (MA, PhD); organizational communication (MA, PhD); speech pathology (MS). Electronic applications accepted.

Division of Mass Communication and Media Studies *Program availability:* Part-time, evening/weekend. Offers mass communication (MA, PhD); media studies (MA, PhD). Electronic applications accepted.

School of Divinity *Program availability:* Part-time, evening/weekend. Offers theology (M Div, MARS, D Min). Electronic applications accepted.

School of Education Offers counseling psychology (PhD); education (M Ed, Ed D, PhD, CAGS); educational administration (Ed D); educational administration and supervision (M Ed, CAGS); educational psychology (PhD); elementary education (M Ed); school psychology (PhD); school psychology and counseling services (M Ed); secondary education (M Ed); special education (M Ed). Electronic applications accepted.

School of Law Offers law (LL M, JD). Electronic applications accepted.

School of Social Work Expenses: Contact institution. *Financial support:* Fellowships, research assistantships, teaching assistantships, career-related internships or fieldwork, Federal Work-Study, institutionally sponsored loans, and scholarships/grants available. Financial award application deadline: 4/1. *Program availability:* Part-time. Offers social work (MSW, PhD). *Application deadline:* For fall admission, 4/1 for domestic students; for spring admission, 10/1 for domestic students. Applications are processed on a rolling basis. *Application fee:* $75. Electronic applications accepted. *Application Contact:* Sandra Gammons, Director of Admissions, 202-806-7300, Fax: 202-387-4309. *Dean,* Dr. Sandra Edmonds Crewe, 202-806-7311.

HULT INTERNATIONAL BUSINESS SCHOOL, Cambridge, MA 02141

General Information Independent, coed, comprehensive institution. *Enrollment by degree level:* 2,055 master's. *Graduate faculty:* 4 full-time (2 women), 28 part-time/adjunct (4 women). *Graduate housing:* On-campus housing not available. *Student services:* Campus employment opportunities, career counseling, international student services, low-cost health insurance, multicultural affairs office, services for students with disabilities, writing training.
Website: http://www.hult.edu/
General Application Contact: Boston Admissions Office, 617-746-1990, E-mail: postgraduate@hult.edu.

GRADUATE UNITS

Graduate Programs Average age 31. Expenses: Contact institution. *Financial support:* Scholarships/grants and tuition waivers (partial) available. Financial award application deadline: 6/1; financial award applicants required to submit FAFSA. Offers business administration (EMBA); business analytics (MBA, MIB); business statistics (MBS); disruptive innovation (MDI); entrepreneurship (MBA, MIB); family business (MBA, MIB); finance (MBA, MF, MIB); international marketing (MIM); marketing (MBA, MIB); project management (MBA, MIB). MDI and MBS offered in San Francisco; MBA also offered in Boston, San Francisco, Dubai, Shanghai, and New York. *Application deadline:* For fall admission, 9/1 priority date for domestic and international students; for winter admission, 11/1 priority date for domestic and international students; for spring admission, 12/1 priority date for domestic and international students; for summer admission, 6/1 for domestic and international students. Applications are processed on a rolling basis. *Application fee:* $150. Electronic applications accepted. *Application Contact:* Boston Admissions Office, 617-746-1990, E-mail: postgraduate@hult.edu.

HUMBOLDT STATE UNIVERSITY, Arcata, CA 95521-8299

General Information State-supported, coed, comprehensive institution. *Enrollment:* 8,503 graduate, professional, and undergraduate students; 310 full-time matriculated graduate/professional students (180 women), 242 part-time matriculated graduate/professional students (168 women). *Enrollment by degree level:* 552 master's. *Graduate faculty:* 241 full-time (106 women), 337 part-time/adjunct (200 women). Tuition, state resident: full-time $6738; part-time $1953 per semester. Tuition, nonresident: full-time $13,434; part-time $3813 per semester. *Required fees:* $1738; $653 per semester. Tuition and fees vary according to program. *Graduate housing:* Room and/or apartments available on a first-come, first-served basis to single students; on-campus housing not available to married students. Typical cost: $6610 per year ($13,056 including board). Room and board charges vary according to board plan, campus/location and housing facility selected. Housing application deadline: 2/1. *Student services:* Campus employment opportunities, campus safety program, career counseling, child daycare facilities, exercise/wellness program, free psychological counseling, international student services, low-cost health insurance, multicultural affairs office, services for students with disabilities, teacher training. *Library facilities:* Humboldt State University Library. *Research affiliation:* McIntire-Stennis (forestry), National Sea Grant, U.S. Fish and Wildlife Service-Wildlife Field Station, Redwood Sciences Laboratory of the Pacific Southwest Forest and Range Experiment Station, California Cooperative Fisheries Research Unit.
Computer facilities: Computer purchase and lease plans are available. 1,098 computers available on campus for general student use. A campuswide network can be accessed from student residence rooms and from off campus. Online class registration is available.
Website: http://www.humboldt.edu/
General Application Contact: Cynthia Werner, Admissions Coordinator, 707-826-6250, E-mail: apply@humboldt.edu.

GRADUATE UNITS

Academic Programs *Program availability:* Part-time, evening/weekend. Electronic applications accepted.

College of Arts, Humanities, and Social Sciences *Program availability:* Part-time. Offers applied anthropology (MA); arts, humanities, and social sciences (MA); English (MA); environment and community (MA); sociology (MA). Electronic applications accepted.

College of Natural Resources and Sciences *Program availability:* Part-time. Offers biological sciences (MS); environmental systems (MS); natural resources (MS); natural resources and sciences (MA, MS, Certificate).

College of Professional Studies *Program availability:* Part-time, evening/weekend. Offers business (MBA); education (MA); kinesiology (MS); psychology (MA); social work (MSW).

HUMPHREYS UNIVERSITY, Stockton, CA 95207-3896

General Information Independent, coed, comprehensive institution. *Enrollment:* 79 part-time matriculated graduate/professional students (49 women). *Enrollment by degree level:* 79 doctoral. *Graduate faculty:* 3 full-time (0 women), 17 part-time/adjunct (6 women). *Graduate housing:* On-campus housing not available. *Student services:* Campus employment opportunities, career counseling. *Library facilities:* Humphreys College Library plus 1 other.
Computer facilities: 40 computers available on campus for general student use.
Website: http://www.humphreys.edu/
General Application Contact: Santa Lopez-Minatre, Admission Counselor, 209-478-0800, Fax: 209-478-8721, E-mail: slopez@humphreys.edu.

GRADUATE UNITS

Drivon School of Law Students: 79 part-time (49 women); includes 34 minority (7 Black or African American, non-Hispanic/Latino; 7 Asian, non-Hispanic/Latino; 15 Hispanic/Latino; 5 Native Hawaiian or other Pacific Islander, non-Hispanic/Latino). Average age 36. 26 applicants, 81% accepted, 15 enrolled. *Faculty:* 3 full-time (0 women), 20 part-time/adjunct (6 women). Expenses: Contact institution. *Financial support:* In 2016–17, 63 students received support. Federal Work-Study available. Support available to part-time students. Financial award application deadline: 9/1; financial award applicants required to submit FAFSA. In 2016, 30 doctorates awarded. *Program availability:* Part-time, evening/weekend. Offers law (JD). *Application deadline:* For fall admission, 9/3 priority date for domestic students; for winter admission, 12/3 priority date for domestic students; for summer admission, 6/3 priority date for domestic students. Applications are processed on a rolling basis. *Application fee:* $40. Electronic applications accepted. *Application Contact:* Santa Lopez-Minatre, Admission Counselor, 209-478-0800 Ext. 202, Fax: 209-478-8721, E-mail: slopez@humphreys.edu. *Dean,* Leo Patrick Piggott, 209-235-2905, E-mail: ppiggott@humphreys.edu.

HUNTER COLLEGE OF THE CITY UNIVERSITY OF NEW YORK, New York, NY 10065-5085

General Information State and locally supported, coed, comprehensive institution. *Enrollment:* 22,993 graduate, professional, and undergraduate students; 1,454 full-time matriculated graduate/professional students (1,170 women), 4,461 part-time matriculated graduate/professional students (3,463 women). *Enrollment by degree level:* 5,647 master's, 10 doctoral, 258 other advanced degrees. *Graduate housing:* Room and/or apartments available on a first-come, first-served basis to single students; on-campus housing not available to married students. *Student services:* Campus employment opportunities, campus safety program, career counseling, child daycare facilities, exercise/wellness program, free psychological counseling, international student services, services for students with disabilities, teacher training, writing training. *Library facilities:* Hunter College Library plus 1 other. *Research affiliation:* Mount Sinai Medical Center, Bellevue Hospital Center, Cornell University Medical Center, New York Hospital.
Computer facilities: 600 computers available on campus for general student use. A campuswide network can be accessed. Online class registration is available.
Website: http://www.hunter.cuny.edu/
General Application Contact: Milena Solo, Director for Graduate Admissions, 212-772-4288, E-mail: gradadmissions@hunter.cuny.edu.

GRADUATE UNITS

Graduate School Students: 1,454 full-time (1,170 women), 4,461 part-time (3,463 women); includes 2,426 minority (894 Black or African American, non-Hispanic/Latino; 4 American Indian or Alaska Native, non-Hispanic/Latino; 542 Asian, non-Hispanic/Latino; 986 Hispanic/Latino; 218 international. 6,110 applicants, 50% accepted, 2080 enrolled. Expenses: Contact institution. *Financial support:* Fellowships with tuition reimbursements, research assistantships with partial tuition reimbursements, teaching assistantships, career-related internships or fieldwork, Federal Work-Study, institutionally sponsored loans, scholarships/grants, traineeships, tuition waivers (full and partial), unspecified assistantships, and lesson stipends available. Support available to part-time students. Financial award applicants required to submit FAFSA. In 2016, 1,910 master's, 30 doctorates, 237 other advanced degrees awarded. *Program availability:* Part-time, evening/weekend. *Application deadline:* For fall admission, 4/1 for domestic students; for spring admission, 11/1 for domestic students. *Application fee:* $125. *Application Contact:* Milena Solo, Director for Graduate Admissions, 212-772-4288, E-mail: milena.solo@hunter.cuny.edu.

Hunter-Bellevue School of Nursing Students: 17 full-time (11 women), 586 part-time (502 women); includes 287 minority (147 Black or African American, non-Hispanic/Latino; 98 Asian, non-Hispanic/Latino; 42 Hispanic/Latino), 28 international. Average age 34. 289 applicants, 61% accepted, 146 enrolled. Expenses: Contact institution. *Financial support:* Federal Work-Study, scholarships/grants, traineeships, and tuition waivers (partial) available. Support available to part-time students. Financial award application deadline: 5/1; financial award applicants required to submit FAFSA. In 2016, 123 master's, 7 other advanced degrees awarded. *Program availability:* Part-time. Offers adult-gerontology clinical nurse specialist (MS); community/public health nursing (MS); gerontological/adult nurse practitioner (MS); nursing (MS, AC); psychiatric-mental health nurse practitioner (MS, AC). *Application deadline:* For fall admission, 4/1 for domestic students; for spring admission, 11/1 for domestic students. Applications are processed on a rolling basis. *Application Contact:* Milena Solo, Director for Graduate Admissions, 212-772-4288, E-mail: milena.solo@hunter.cuny.edu. *Dean,* Gail C. McCain, 212-481-7596, Fax: 212-481-5078, E-mail: gmccain@hunter.cuny.edu.

School of Arts and Sciences Expenses: Contact institution. *Financial support:* Fellowships, research assistantships, teaching assistantships, career-related internships or fieldwork, Federal Work-Study, institutionally sponsored loans, scholarships/grants, tuition waivers (full and partial), unspecified assistantships, and lesson stipends available. Support available to part-time students. *Program availability:* Part-time, evening/weekend. Offers accounting (MS); adolescent mathematics education (MA); animal behavior and conservation (MA, Certificate); anthropology (MA); applied mathematics (MA); applied social research (MS); art history (MA); arts and sciences (MA, MFA, MS, MUP, PhD, Certificate); biochemistry (MA, PhD); bioinformatics (MA); biological sciences (MA, PhD); chemistry (PhD); composition (MFA); creative writing (MFA); economics (MA); ethnomusicology (MA); fiction (MFA); French (MA); general psychology (MA); geographic information science (Certificate); geography (MA); geoinformatics (MS); history (MA); integrated media arts (MFA); Italian (MA); literature, language, and theory (MA); memoir (MFA); music history (MA); music theory (MA); performance (MA); physics and astronomy (MA, PhD); playwriting (MFA); poetry (MFA); pure mathematics (MA); Spanish (MA); statistics (MA); studio art (MFA); teaching Chinese (MA); teaching Latin (MA); theatre (MA); urban affairs (MS); urban affairs and planning (MS, MUP); urban planning (MUP). *Application deadline:* For fall admission, 2/1 for domestic and international students; for spring admission, 11/1 for domestic students, 9/1 for international students. *Application Contact:* Milena Solo, Director of Graduate Admissions, 212-772-4288, E-mail: milena.solo@hunter.cuny.edu. *Dean,* Dr. Andrew J. Polsky, 212-772-5121, Fax: 212-772-5148, E-mail: apolsky@hunter.cuny.edu.

School of Education Students: 359 full-time (294 women), 2,554 part-time (2,089 women); includes 1,320 minority (355 Black or African American, non-Hispanic/Latino; 4 American Indian or Alaska Native, non-Hispanic/Latino; 250 Asian, non-Hispanic/Latino; 668 Hispanic/Latino; 3 Native Hawaiian or other Pacific Islander, non-Hispanic/Latino; 40 Two or more races, non-Hispanic/Latino), 75 international. Average age 31. 1,848 applicants, 73% accepted, 892 enrolled. *Faculty:* 66 full-time (46 women), 221 part-time/adjunct (175 women). Expenses: Contact institution. *Financial support:* Application deadline: 6/30; applicants required to submit FAFSA. In 2016, 879 master's, 214 other advanced degrees awarded. *Program availability:* Part-time, evening/weekend. Offers administration and supervision (AC); bilingual education (MS); biology education (MA); blind and visually impaired (MS Ed); chemistry education (MA); early childhood education (MS); earth science (MA); education (MA, MS, MS Ed, Ed D, AC); educational supervision and administration (Ed D, AC); elementary education (MS); English education (MA); French education (MA); instructional leadership (Ed D); Italian education (MA); mathematics education (MA); music education (MA); physics education (MA); rehabilitation counseling (MS Ed); school counseling (MS Ed); severe/multiple disabilities (MS Ed); social studies education (MA); Spanish education (MA); teaching English as a second language (MA). *Application deadline:* For fall admission, 3/15 for domestic students, 2/1 for international students; for spring admission, 10/15 for domestic students, 9/1 for international students. Applications are processed on a rolling basis. *Application fee:* $125. Electronic applications accepted. *Application Contact:* Milena Solo, Director for Graduate Admissions, 212-772-4482, E-mail: milena.solo@hunter.cuny.edu. *Dean,* Dr. Michael Middleton, 212-772-4622, E-mail: mm5378@hunter.cuny.edu.

School of Health Professions Students: 146 full-time (117 women), 2 part-time (1 woman); includes 33 minority (9 Black or African American, non-Hispanic/Latino; 12 Asian, non-Hispanic/Latino; 12 Hispanic/Latino), 2 international. Average age 27. 795 applicants, 13% accepted, 58 enrolled. Expenses: Contact institution. *Financial support:* Federal Work-Study and tuition waivers (partial) available. Support available to part-time students. In 2016, 18 master's, 24 doctorates awarded. *Program availability:* Part-time, evening/weekend. Offers health professions (MS, DPT, AC); physical therapy (DPT); speech-language pathology (MS). *Application deadline:* For fall admission, 4/1 for domestic students, 2/1 for international students; for spring admission, 11/1 for domestic students, 9/1 for international students. *Application Contact:* Milena Solo, Director for Graduate Admissions, 212-772-4288, E-mail: milena.solo@hunter.cuny.edu. *Dean,* Gail C. McCain, 212-481-7596.

School of Urban Public Health Expenses: Contact institution. *Financial support:* Application deadline: 3/1. *Program availability:* Part-time. Offers nutrition (MS). *Application deadline:* For fall admission, 4/1 for domestic students, 2/1 for international students; for spring admission, 11/1 for domestic students, 9/1 for international students. *Application Contact:* Milena Solo, Director for Graduate Admissions, 212-772-4288, E-mail: admissions@hunter.cuny.edu.

Silberman School of Social Work Students: 857 full-time (701 women), 231 part-time (178 women); includes 575 minority (242 Black or African American, non-Hispanic/Latino; 67 Asian, non-Hispanic/Latino; 266 Hispanic/Latino), 22 international. Average age 30. 1,488 applicants, 58% accepted, 569 enrolled. Expenses: Contact institution. *Financial support:* Fellowships, career-related internships or fieldwork, Federal Work-Study, and tuition waivers (partial) available. Support available to part-time students. In 2016, 523 master's awarded. Offers social work (MSW). *Application deadline:* For fall admission, 1/15 for domestic and international students. Applications are processed on a rolling basis. *Application Contact:* Raymond Montero, Coordinator of Admissions, 212-452-7005, E-mail: grad.socworkadvisor@hunter.cuny.edu. *Acting Dean,* Dr. Mary Cavanaugh, 212-452-7085, Fax: 212-452-7150, E-mail: mary.cavanaugh@hunter.cuny.edu.

HUNTINGTON COLLEGE OF HEALTH SCIENCES, Knoxville, TN 37918

General Information Proprietary, coed, comprehensive institution.

GRADUATE UNITS

Program in Nutrition *Program availability:* Part-time, evening/weekend, online learning. Offers clinical nutrition (DHS); nutrition (MS); personalized option (DHS). Electronic applications accepted.

HUNTINGTON UNIVERSITY, Huntington, IN 46750-1299

General Information Independent-religious, coed, comprehensive institution. *Graduate housing:* On-campus housing not available. *Research affiliation:* Link Institute (youth ministry).

GRADUATE UNITS

Graduate School *Program availability:* Part-time, online learning. Offers counseling (MA); early adolescent education (M Ed); education (M Ed); global missions leadership (MA); global youth ministry (MA); TESOL education (M Ed); youth ministry leadership (MA). Electronic applications accepted.

HUSSON UNIVERSITY, Bangor, ME 04401-2999

General Information Independent, coed, comprehensive institution. *Enrollment:* 3,669 graduate, professional, and undergraduate students; 437 full-time matriculated graduate/professional students (261 women), 383 part-time matriculated graduate/professional students (249 women). *Enrollment by degree level:* 524 master's, 287 doctoral, 9 other advanced degrees. *Graduate faculty:* 62 full-time (32 women), 43 part-time/adjunct (19 women). *Tuition:* Full-time $16,800; part-time $560 per credit. *Required fees:* $600; $220 per semester. Tuition and fees vary according to degree level and program. *Graduate housing:* Room and/or apartments available on a first-come, first-served basis to single students; on-campus housing not available to married students. Typical cost: $5400 per year ($10,000 including board). Room and board charges vary according to board plan and housing facility selected. Housing application deadline: 6/1. *Student services:* Campus employment opportunities, campus safety program, career counseling, exercise/wellness program, free psychological counseling, international student services, writing training. *Library facilities:* Sawyer Library. *Collection:* Books: 41,541 (physical), 27,592 (digital/electronic); Serial titles: 71 (physical), 39 (digital/electronic); Databases: 101. Weekly public service hours: 98; study areas open 24 hours, 5–7 days a week; students can reserve study rooms.

Computer facilities: 131 computers available on campus for general student use. A campuswide network can be accessed from student residence rooms and from off campus. Online class registration is available.
Website: http://www.husson.edu/

General Application Contact: Kristen Card, Director of Graduate Admissions, 207-404-5660, Fax: 207-941-7850, E-mail: cardk@husson.edu.

GRADUATE UNITS

Doctorate in Physical Therapy Program Students: 81 full-time (41 women); includes 3 minority (1 Black or African American, non-Hispanic/Latino; 1 Asian, non-Hispanic/Latino; 1 Two or more races, non-Hispanic/Latino), 2 international. Average age 25. 313 applicants, 12% accepted, 13 enrolled. *Faculty:* 10 full-time (7 women), 7 part-time/adjunct (3 women). Expenses: Contact institution. *Financial support:* Federal Work-Study, scholarships/grants, and unspecified assistantships available. Financial award application deadline: 4/15; financial award applicants required to submit FAFSA. In 2016, 30 doctorates awarded. Offers physical therapy (DPT). *Application deadline:* For fall admission, 4/15 for domestic and international students. *Application fee:* $50. Electronic applications accepted. *Application Contact:* Cecile Ferguson, Administrative Assistant, 207-941-7101, E-mail: fergusonc@husson.edu. *Director,* Dr. Karen Huhn, 207-941-7620, E-mail: huhnk@husson.edu.

Graduate Nursing Program Students: 60 part-time (52 women); includes 4 minority (1 Black or African American, non-Hispanic/Latino; 1 Asian, non-Hispanic/Latino; 1 Hispanic/Latino; 1 Two or more races, non-Hispanic/Latino). Average age 37. 70 applicants, 74% accepted, 49 enrolled. *Faculty:* 2 full-time (both women), 4 part-time/adjunct (3 women). Expenses: Contact institution. *Financial support:* Research assistantships, Federal Work-Study, institutionally sponsored loans, traineeships, and unspecified assistantships available. Financial award application deadline: 3/31; financial award applicants required to submit FAFSA. In 2016, 9 master's awarded. *Program availability:* Part-time. Offers family and community nurse practitioner (MSN, PMC). *Application deadline:* For fall admission, 3/31 for domestic students; for spring admission, 10/30 for domestic students. *Application fee:* $50. Electronic applications accepted. *Application Contact:* Kristen Card, Director of Graduate Admissions, 207-404-5660, Fax: 207-941-7935, E-mail: cardk@husson.edu. *Director, Graduate Nursing,* Prof. Mary Jude, 207-941-7769, Fax: 207-941-7198, E-mail: judem@husson.edu.

Graduate Programs in Counseling and Human Relations Students: 17 full-time (15 women), 55 part-time (48 women); includes 1 minority (Black or African American, non-Hispanic/Latino), 2 international. Average age 32. 50 applicants, 52% accepted, 20 enrolled. *Faculty:* 3 full-time (2 women), 5 part-time/adjunct (all women). Expenses: Contact institution. *Financial support:* Federal Work-Study, scholarships/grants, and unspecified assistantships available. Financial award application deadline: 4/15; financial award applicants required to submit FAFSA. In 2016, 16 master's awarded. *Program availability:* Part-time, evening/weekend. Offers clinical mental health counseling (MS); human relations (MS); school counseling (MS). *Application deadline:* For fall admission, 2/1 for domestic students. *Application fee:* $50. Electronic applications accepted. *Application Contact:* Kristen Card, Director of Graduate Admissions, 207-404-5660, Fax: 207-941-7935, E-mail: cardk@husson.edu. *Director, Graduate Counseling Programs,* Dr. Deborah Drew, 207-992-4912, Fax: 207-992-4952, E-mail: drewd@husson.edu.

Master of Business Administration Program Students: 81 full-time (47 women), 249 part-time (142 women); includes 32 minority (9 Black or African American, non-Hispanic/Latino; 2 American Indian or Alaska Native, non-Hispanic/Latino; 17 Asian, non-Hispanic/Latino; 3 Hispanic/Latino; 1 Two or more races, non-Hispanic/Latino), 11 international. Average age 34. 199 applicants, 78% accepted, 119 enrolled. *Faculty:* 8 full-time (4 women), 20 part-time/adjunct (5 women). Expenses: Contact institution. *Financial support:* Career-related internships or fieldwork, Federal Work-Study, scholarships/grants, and unspecified assistantships available. Financial award application deadline: 4/15; financial award applicants required to submit FAFSA. In 2016, 109 master's awarded. *Program availability:* Part-time, evening/weekend, 100% online, blended/hybrid learning. Offers athletic administration (MBA); biotechnology and innovation (MBA); general business administration (MBA); healthcare management (MBA); hospitality and tourism management (MBA); organizational management (MBA); risk management (MBA). *Application deadline:* Applications are processed on a rolling basis. *Application fee:* $50. Electronic applications accepted. *Application Contact:* Kristen Card, Director of Graduate Admissions, 207-404-5660, Fax: 207-941-7935, E-mail: cardk@husson.edu. *Director, Graduate and Online Programs,* Prof. Stephanie Shayne, 207-404-5632, Fax: 207-941-4987, E-mail: shaynes@husson.edu.

Master of Science in Criminal Justice Administration Program Students: 11 full-time (1 woman), 6 part-time (0 women); includes 1 minority (Two or more races, non-Hispanic/Latino). Average age 28. 8 applicants, 100% accepted, 5 enrolled. *Faculty:* 3 full-time (1 woman), 2 part-time/adjunct (1 woman). Expenses: Contact institution. *Financial support:* Career-related internships or fieldwork, scholarships/grants, and unspecified assistantships available. Financial award application deadline: 4/15; financial award applicants required to submit FAFSA. In 2016, 5 master's awarded. *Program availability:* Part-time. Offers criminal justice administration (MS). *Application deadline:* For fall admission, 8/1 for domestic students. Applications are processed on a rolling basis. *Application fee:* $50 ($0 for international students). Electronic applications accepted. *Application Contact:* Kristen Card, Director of Graduate Admissions, 207-404-5660, E-mail: cardk@husson.edu. *Director, School of Legal Studies,* John Michaud, 207-941-7037, E-mail: michaudj@husson.edu.

School of Pharmacy Students: 198 full-time (114 women), 8 part-time (5 women); includes 73 minority (31 Black or African American, non-Hispanic/Latino; 2 American Indian or Alaska Native, non-Hispanic/Latino; 32 Asian, non-Hispanic/Latino; 5 Hispanic/Latino; 1 Native Hawaiian or other Pacific Islander, non-Hispanic/Latino; 2 Two or more races, non-Hispanic/Latino), 7 international. Average age 26. 220 applicants, 35% accepted, 49 enrolled. *Faculty:* 28 full-time (9 women), 1 part-time/adjunct (0 women). Expenses: Contact institution. *Financial support:* Federal Work-Study, scholarships/grants, and unspecified assistantships available. Financial award application deadline: 3/1; financial award applicants required to submit FAFSA. In 2016, 55 doctorates awarded. Offers pharmacology (MS); pharmacy (Pharm D). *Application deadline:* For fall admission, 3/1 for domestic students. *Application fee:* $50 ($0 for international students). Electronic applications accepted. *Application Contact:* Kristen Card, Director of Graduate Admissions, 207-404-5660, E-mail: cardk@husson.edu. *Dean,* Dr. Rodney A. Larson, 207-941-7122, E-mail: larsonr@husson.edu.

HUSTON-TILLOTSON UNIVERSITY, Austin, TX 78702-2795
General Information Independent-religious, coed, comprehensive institution.
GRADUATE UNITS
Graduate Programs

ICAHN SCHOOL OF MEDICINE AT MOUNT SINAI, New York, NY 10029-6504
General Information Independent, coed, graduate-only institution. *Graduate housing:* Rooms and/or apartments guaranteed to single and married students. Housing application deadline: 6/1.

GRADUATE UNITS
The Bioethics Program Offers bioethics (MS). Program offered jointly with Union Graduate College.
Department of Medical Education Offers medical education (MD). Electronic applications accepted.
Graduate School of Biomedical Sciences Offers biomedical sciences (MS, PhD); clinical research education (MS, PhD); community medicine (MPH); genetic counseling (MS); neurosciences (PhD). Electronic applications accepted.

IDAHO STATE UNIVERSITY, Pocatello, ID 83209
General Information State-supported, coed, university. CGS member. *Graduate housing:* Rooms and/or apartments available on a first-come, first-served basis to single and married students. Housing application deadline: 5/1. *Research affiliation:* S.M. Stoller Corporation (ecology, waste management), ON Semiconductor (computer sciences, environmental management), Inland Northwest Research Alliance (INRA) (science), J.R. Simplot Company (plant sciences, environmental studies), Bechtel BWXT Idaho, LLC (environmental management, nuclear sciences), Environmental Science and Research Foundation (waste management, ecology).

GRADUATE UNITS
Office of Graduate Studies *Program availability:* Part-time. Offers general interdisciplinary (M Ed, MA, MNS); waste management and environmental science (MS). Electronic applications accepted.
College of Arts and Letters *Program availability:* Part-time. Offers anthropology (MA, MS); art (MFA); arts and letters (MA, MFA, MNS, MPA, MS, DA, PhD, Post-Master's Certificate, Postbaccalaureate Certificate); clinical psychology (PhD); communication and rhetorical studies (MA); English (MA, DA); English and the teaching of English (PhD); experimental psychology (PhD); historical resources management (MA); political science (MA, DA); public administration (MPA); sociology (MA); TESOL (Post-Master's Certificate); theatre (MA). Electronic applications accepted.
College of Business *Program availability:* Part-time. Offers business administration (MBA, Postbaccalaureate Certificate); computer information systems (MS, Postbaccalaureate Certificate). Electronic applications accepted.
College of Education *Program availability:* Part-time. Offers child and family studies (M Ed); curriculum leadership (M Ed); deaf education (M Ed); education (M Ed, MPE, Ed D, PhD, 5th Year Certificate, 6th Year Certificate, Ed S); educational administration (M Ed, 6th Year Certificate, Ed S); educational foundations (5th Year Certificate); educational leadership (Ed D); educational leadership and instructional design (PhD); elementary education (M Ed); human exceptionality (M Ed); instructional design (PhD); instructional technology (M Ed); literacy (M Ed); physical education (MPE); school psychology (Ed S); special education (M Ed). Electronic applications accepted.
College of Pharmacy *Program availability:* Part-time. Offers biopharmaceutical analysis (PhD); drug delivery (PhD); medicinal chemistry (PhD); pharmaceutical sciences (MS); pharmacology (PhD); pharmacy (MS, PhD, Pharm D); pharmacy administration (MS, PhD). Electronic applications accepted.
College of Science and Engineering *Program availability:* Part-time. Offers applied physics (PhD); biology (MNS, MS, DA, PhD); chemistry (MNS, MS); civil engineering (MS); clinical laboratory science (MS); environmental engineering (MS); environmental science and management (MS); geographic information science (MS); geology (MNS, MS); geology with emphasis in environmental geoscience (MS); geophysics/hydrology/geology (MS); geotechnology (Postbaccalaureate Certificate); health physics (MS); mathematics (MS, DA); mathematics for secondary teachers (MA); measurement and control engineering (MS); mechanical engineering (MS); microbiology (MS); nuclear science and engineering (MS, PhD); physics (MNS); science and engineering (MA, MNS, MS, DA, PhD, Postbaccalaureate Certificate). Electronic applications accepted.
College of Technology *Program availability:* Part-time, evening/weekend. Offers human resource training and development (MTD); technology (MTD). Electronic applications accepted.
Kasiska College of Health Professions *Program availability:* Part-time. Offers advanced general dentistry (Post-Doctoral Certificate); audiology (MS, Au D); communication sciences and disorders (Postbaccalaureate Certificate); communication sciences and disorders and education of the deaf (Certificate); counseling (M Coun, Ed S); counselor education and counseling (PhD); deaf education (MS); dental hygiene (MS); dietetics (Certificate); family medicine (Post-Master's Certificate); health education (MHE); health professions (M Coun, MHE, MOT, MPAS, MPH, MS, Au D, DPT, PhD, Certificate, Ed S, Post-Doctoral Certificate, Post-Master's Certificate, Postbaccalaureate Certificate); nursing (MS, Post-Master's Certificate); occupational therapy (MOT); physical therapy (DPT); physician assistant studies (MPAS); public health (MPH); speech language pathology (MS). Electronic applications accepted.

IGLOBAL UNIVERSITY, Vienna, VA 22182
General Information Proprietary, coed, comprehensive institution.
GRADUATE UNITS
Graduate Programs

ILIFF SCHOOL OF THEOLOGY, Denver, CO 80210-4798
General Information Independent-religious, coed, graduate-only institution. *Graduate housing:* Rooms and/or apartments available on a first-come, first-served basis to single and married students.

GRADUATE UNITS
Graduate and Professional Programs *Program availability:* Part-time, evening/weekend. Offers biblical studies (MA); church history (MA); religion (MA); religion and social change (MA); specialized ministry (MASM); theology (M Div, MTS, D Min, PhD); theology/ethics (MA). PhD offered jointly with University of Denver. Electronic applications accepted.

ILLINOIS COLLEGE, Jacksonville, IL 62650-2299
General Information Independent-religious, coed, comprehensive institution. *Enrollment:* 960 graduate, professional, and undergraduate students; 2 part-time matriculated graduate/professional students (both women). *Enrollment by degree level:* 2 master's. *Graduate faculty:* 8 part-time/adjunct (3 women). *Tuition:* Part-time $6400 per credit hour. *Required fees:* $35 per credit hour. Part-time tuition and fees vary according to course load, campus/location and program. *Graduate housing:* On-campus housing not available. *Student services:* Campus safety program, career counseling, exercise/wellness program, free psychological counseling, international student services, multicultural affairs office, services for students with disabilities, teacher training, writing training. *Library facilities:* Schewe Library.
Computer facilities: A campuswide network can be accessed from student residence rooms and from off campus. Online class registration is available. Website: http://www.ic.edu/
General Application Contact: Evan Wilson, Director of Admission, 217-245-3030, E-mail: evan.wilson@mail.ic.edu.

GRADUATE UNITS
Program in Education Students: 2 part-time (both women). Average age 39. *Faculty:* 8 part-time/adjunct (3 women). Expenses: Contact institution. *Financial support:* In 2016–17, 2 students received support. Applicants required to submit FAFSA. *Program availability:* Part-time-only, evening/weekend. Offers education (MA Ed). *Application deadline:* For fall admission, 5/31 priority date for domestic students. Applications are processed on a rolling basis. *Application fee:* $0. Electronic applications accepted. *Application Contact:* Evan Wilson, Director of Admission, 217-245-3030, E-mail: evan.wilson@mail.ic.edu. *Assistant Professor of Education,* Dr. Daniel Meyer, 217-291-1609, E-mail: daniel.meyer@mail.ic.edu.

ILLINOIS COLLEGE OF OPTOMETRY, Chicago, IL 60616-3878
General Information Independent, coed, graduate-only institution. *Graduate housing:* Rooms and/or apartments guaranteed to single students and available on a first-come, first-served basis to married students. Housing application deadline: 6/1. *Research affiliation:* University of Chicago (vision science), Rush University (cataract development), Ocular Science (contact lenses), University of Illinois at Chicago (neuropharmacology), Vision Service Plan (pediatric optometry), Ciba Vision (contact lenses).

GRADUATE UNITS
Professional Program Offers optometry (OD). Electronic applications accepted.

ILLINOIS INSTITUTE OF TECHNOLOGY, Chicago, IL 60616
General Information Independent, coed, university. CGS member. *Graduate housing:* Rooms and/or apartments available on a first-come, first-served basis to single and married students. Housing application deadline: 6/1.

GRADUATE UNITS
Chicago-Kent College of Law *Program availability:* Part-time, evening/weekend. Offers family law (LL M); financial services law (LL M); international intellectual property law (LL M); law (JD); legal studies (JSD); taxation (LL M); U.S., international, and transnational law (LL M). Electronic applications accepted.
Graduate College *Program availability:* Part-time, evening/weekend, online learning. Electronic applications accepted.
Armour College of Engineering *Program availability:* Part-time, evening/weekend, online learning. Offers architectural engineering (M Arch E); biological engineering (MAS); biomedical engineering (MAS, MS, PhD); biomedical imaging and signals (MAS); chemical engineering (MAS, MS, PhD); civil engineering (MS, PhD); computer engineering (MS, PhD); construction engineering and management (MCEM); electrical engineering (MS, PhD); electricity markets (MAS); engineering (M Arch E, M Env E, M Geoenv E, M Trans E, MAS, MCEM, MGE, MPW, MS, MSE, PhD); environmental engineering (M Env E, MAS, PhD); geoenvironmental engineering (M Geoenv E); geotechnical engineering (MGE); infrastructure engineering and management (MPW); manufacturing engineering (MAS, MS); materials science and engineering (MAS, MS, PhD); mechanical and aerospace engineering (MAS, MS, PhD); network engineering (MAS); power engineering (MAS); structural engineering (MSE); telecommunications and software engineering (MAS); transportation engineering (M Trans E); VLSI and microelectronics (MAS). Electronic applications accepted.
College of Architecture *Program availability:* Part-time. Offers architecture (M Arch, MLA, MS Arch, PhD). Electronic applications accepted.
College of Science *Program availability:* Part-time, evening/weekend, online learning. Offers analytical chemistry (MAS); applied mathematics (MS, PhD); applied physics (MS); biochemistry (MS); biology (MS, PhD); business (MCS); cell and molecular biology (MS); chemistry (MAS, MS, PhD); computational intelligence (MCS); computer science (MCS, MS, PhD); cyber-physical systems (MCS); data analytics (MCS); data science (MAS); database systems (MCS); distributed and cloud computing (MCS); education (MCS); finance (MCS); health physics (MAS); information security and assurance (MCS); materials chemistry (MAS); mathematical finance (MAS); mathematics education (MAS, PhD); microbiology (MS); molecular biochemistry and biophysics (MS, PhD); networking and communications (MCS); physics (MS, PhD); science (MAS, MCS, MS, PhD); science education (MAS, PhD); software engineering (MCS); telecommunications and software engineering (MAS). Electronic applications accepted.
Institute of Design *Program availability:* Part-time. Offers design (M Des, MDM, PhD). Electronic applications accepted.
Lewis College of Human Sciences Offers clinical psychology (PhD); human sciences (MS, PhD); industrial and organizational psychology (PhD); information architecture (MS); personnel and human resource development (MS); rehabilitation and mental health counseling (MS); rehabilitation counseling education (PhD); technical communication (PhD); technical communication and information design (MS).
School of Applied Technology *Program availability:* Part-time, evening/weekend, online learning. Offers applied technology (MAS, MFPE, MFST, MS); cyber forensics and security (MAS); food process engineering (MFPE, MS); food safety and technology (MFST, MS); industrial technology and management (MAS); information technology and management (MAS). Electronic applications accepted.

Stuart School of Business *Program availability:* Part-time, evening/weekend. Offers business (MBA, MMF, MPA, MS, PhD); environmental management and sustainability (MS); finance (MS); management science (PhD); marketing analytics and communication (MS); mathematical finance (MMF); public administration (MPA); sustainability (MBA); technological entrepreneurship (MTE). Electronic applications accepted.

ILLINOIS STATE UNIVERSITY, Normal, IL 61790-2200
General Information State-supported, coed, university. CGS member. *Graduate housing:* Rooms and/or apartments available to single and married students. Housing application deadline: 4/1.
GRADUATE UNITS
Graduate School *Program availability:* Part-time.
College of Applied Science and Technology *Program availability:* Part-time. Offers agribusiness (MS); applied science and technology (MA, MS, Certificate, Graduate Certificate); criminal justice sciences (MA, MS); family and consumer sciences (MA, MS); health education (MS); information technology (MS); technology (MS).
College of Arts and Sciences *Program availability:* Part-time. Offers animal behavior (MS); arts and sciences (MA, MS, MSW, PhD, SSP); bacteriology (MS); biochemistry (MS); biological sciences (MS); biology (PhD); biophysics (MS); biotechnology (MS); botany (MS, PhD); cell biology (MS); chemistry (MCE, MS, MSCE); communication (MA, MS); communication sciences and disorders (MA, MS); conservation biology (MS); developmental biology (MS); ecology (MS, PhD); economics (MA, MS); English (MA, MS, PhD); English studies (PhD); entomology (MS); evolutionary biology (MS); French (MA); French and German (MA); French and Spanish (MA); genetics (MS, PhD); geography-geology (Graduate Certificate); German (MA); German and Spanish (MA); historical archaeology (MA, MS); history (MA, MS); immunology (MS); mathematics (MA, MS); mathematics education (MA, PhD); microbiology (MS, PhD); molecular biology (MS); molecular genetics (MS); neurobiology (MS); neuroscience (MS); parasitology (MS); physiology (MS, PhD); plant biology (MS); plant molecular biology (MS); plant sciences (MS); politics and government (MA, MS); psychology (MA, MS); school psychology (PhD, SSP); social work (MSW); sociology (MA, MS); Spanish (MA); structural biology (MS); writing (MA, MS); zoology (MS, PhD).
College of Business *Program availability:* Part-time. Offers accounting (MPA, MS); business (MBA, MPA, MS); business administration (MBA).
College of Education *Program availability:* Part-time. Offers college student personnel administration (MS); curriculum and instruction (MS, MS Ed, Ed D); education (MS, MS Ed, Ed D, PhD, Certificate); educational administration (MS, MS Ed, Ed D, PhD); educational policies (Ed D); postsecondary education (Ed D); reading (MS Ed); special education (MS, MS Ed, Ed D, Certificate); supervision (Ed D).
College of Fine Arts *Program availability:* Part-time. Offers art history (MA, MS); arts technology (MS); ceramics (MFA, MS); drawing (MFA, MS); fibers (MFA, MS); fine arts (MA, MFA, MM, MM Ed, MS); glass (MFA, MS); graphic design (MFA, MS); metals (MFA, MS); music (MM, MM Ed); painting (MFA, MS); photography (MFA, MS); printmaking (MFA, MS); sculpture (MFA, MS); theatre (MA, MFA, MS).
Mennonite College of Nursing Offers family nurse practitioner (PMC); nursing (MSN, PhD).

IMCA–INTERNATIONAL MANAGEMENT CENTRES ASSOCIATION, Buckingham MK18 1BP, United Kingdom
General Information Independent, coed, graduate-only institution.
GRADUATE UNITS
Programs in Business Administration *Program availability:* Online learning. Offers business administration (M Mgt, M Phil, MBA, MS).

IMMACULATA UNIVERSITY, Immaculata, PA 19345
General Information Independent-religious, coed, university. CGS member. *Graduate housing:* Rooms and/or apartments available on a first-come, first-served basis to single and married students.
GRADUATE UNITS
College of Graduate Studies *Program availability:* Part-time, evening/weekend. Offers bilingual studies (MA); clinical mental health counseling (MA); clinical psychology (Psy D); educational leadership (MA, Ed D); forensic psychology (Graduate Certificate); integrative psychotherapy (Graduate Certificate); music therapy (MA); neuropsychology (Graduate Certificate); nutrition education for the registered dietitian (MA); nutrition education with dietetic internship (MA); nutrition education with wellness promotion (MA); organization leadership (MA); principal (Certificate); psychodynamic psychotherapy (Graduate Certificate); psychological testing (Graduate Certificate); school counseling (MA, Graduate Certificate); school psychology (MA); secondary education (Certificate); supervisor of special education (Certificate); TESOL (MA). Electronic applications accepted.
Division of Nursing *Program availability:* Part-time, evening/weekend. Offers nursing administration (MSN); nursing education (MSN).

INDEPENDENCE UNIVERSITY, Salt Lake City, UT 84107
General Information Proprietary, coed, comprehensive institution. *Graduate housing:* On-campus housing not available.
GRADUATE UNITS
Program in Business Administration Offers business administration (MBA).
Program in Business Administration in Health Care *Program availability:* Part-time, evening/weekend, online learning. Offers health care administration (MBA).
Program in Health Care Administration *Program availability:* Part-time, evening/weekend, online learning. Offers health care administration (MSHCA).
Program in Health Services *Program availability:* Part-time, evening/weekend, online learning. Offers community health (MSHS); wellness promotion (MSHS).
Program in Nursing Offers community health (MSN); gerontology (MSN); nursing administration (MSN); wellness promotion (MSN).
Program in Public Health *Program availability:* Part-time, evening/weekend, online learning. Offers public health (MPH).

INDIANA STATE UNIVERSITY, Terre Haute, IN 47809
General Information State-supported, coed, university. CGS member. *Graduate housing:* Rooms and/or apartments available on a first-come, first-served basis to single and married students. Housing application deadline: 4/18. *Research affiliation:* Indiana Space Grant (remote sensing), Indiana University School of Medicine (cancer and Lupus research), Cranberry Lake Biological Station (psychosocial impacts of cancer), Boston Museum of Science (remote sensing, biology), Great Lakes Northern Forest Cooperative Ecosystem Study Unit (biology, life sciences).

GRADUATE UNITS
College of Graduate and Professional Studies *Program availability:* Part-time, evening/weekend, online learning. Offers technology management (PhD). Electronic applications accepted.
Bayh College of Education *Program availability:* Part-time, evening/weekend. Offers clinical mental health counseling (MS); communication disorders (MS); curriculum and instruction (M Ed, PhD); education (M Ed, MS, PhD, Ed S); educational administration (PhD); educational technology (MS); higher education leadership (PhD); K-12 district leadership (PhD); school administration (Ed S); school administration and supervision (M Ed); school counseling (M Ed); school psychology (PhD, Ed S); student affairs and higher education (MS). Electronic applications accepted.
College of Arts and Sciences *Program availability:* Part-time, evening/weekend. Offers applied linguistics/teaching English as a second language (MA); arts and sciences (MA, MFA, MM, MPA, MS, PhD, Psy D, CAS); British and American literature (MA); cellular and molecular biology (PhD); ceramics (MA, MFA); clinical psychology (Psy D); communication studies (MA); computer science (MS); conducting (MM); criminology and criminal justice (MA, MS); drawing (MA, MFA); ecology, systematics and evolution (PhD); English (MA); general psychology (MA, MS); graphic design (MA, MFA); history (MA, MS); language education (PhD); life sciences (MS); mathematics (MA, MS); music education (MM); music performance (MM); painting (MA, MFA); photography (MA, MFA); physiology (PhD); printmaking (MA, MFA); public administration (MPA); radio, television and film (MA); science education (MS); sculpture (MA, MFA); Spanish/teaching english as a second language (MA); TESL/TEFL (CAS); writing (MA). Electronic applications accepted.
College of Nursing, Health, and Human Services Offers advanced practice nursing (DNP); applied health sciences (MS, DHS); athletic training (MS, DAT); family nurse practitioner (MS); nursing administration (MS); nursing education (MS); nursing, health, and human services (MA, MS, MSW, DAT, DNP, DPT, PhD); occupational therapy (MS); physical education (MS); physical therapy (DPT); physician assistant (MS); recreation and sport management (MS); social work (MSW); sport management (PhD). Electronic applications accepted.
College of Technology Offers career and technical education (MS); electronics and computer technology (MS); human resource development (MS); occupational safety management (MS); technology (MS); technology management (MS). Electronic applications accepted.
Scott College of Business *Program availability:* Part-time, evening/weekend. Offers business (MBA). Electronic applications accepted.
See Display on next page and Close-Up on page 883.

INDIANA TECH, Fort Wayne, IN 46803-1297
General Information Independent, coed, comprehensive institution. *Graduate housing:* Room and/or apartments available on a first-come, first-served basis to single students; on-campus housing not available to married students. Housing application deadline: 8/15.
GRADUATE UNITS
Program in Business Administration *Program availability:* Part-time, evening/weekend, online learning. Offers accounting (MBA); health care management (MBA); human resources (MBA); management (MBA); marketing (MBA). Electronic applications accepted.
Program in Engineering Management *Program availability:* Part-time, evening/weekend, online only, 100% online. Offers engineering management (MSE). Electronic applications accepted.
Program in Global Leadership *Program availability:* Part-time, evening/weekend, online only, 100% online. Offers global leadership (PhD). Electronic applications accepted.
Program in Management *Program availability:* Part-time, evening/weekend, 100% online. Offers management (MSM). Electronic applications accepted.
Program in Organizational Leadership *Program availability:* Part-time, evening/weekend, online only, 100% online. Offers organizational leadership (MS). Electronic applications accepted.
Program in Psychology Offers psychology (MS).

INDIANA UNIVERSITY BLOOMINGTON, Bloomington, IN 47405-7000
General Information State-supported, coed, university. CGS member. *Enrollment:* 49,695 graduate, professional, and undergraduate students; 8,331 full-time matriculated graduate/professional students (3,851 women), 2,076 part-time matriculated graduate/professional students (843 women). *Enrollment by degree level:* 5,314 master's, 4,495 doctoral, 537 other advanced degrees. *Graduate faculty:* 1,571 full-time (559 women), 10 part-time/adjunct (3 women). *Graduate housing:* Rooms and/or apartments available to single and married students. Housing application deadline: 5/11. *Student services:* Campus employment opportunities, campus safety program, career counseling, child daycare facilities, exercise/wellness program, free psychological counseling, international student services, low-cost health insurance, multicultural affairs office, services for students with disabilities, writing training. *Library facilities:* Indiana University Library plus 18 others. *Collection:* Books: 8.2 million (physical), 2 million (digital/electronic); Serial titles: 365,705 (physical), 33.4 million (digital/electronic); Databases: 1,871. Study areas open 24 hours, 5–7 days a week; students can reserve study rooms.
Computer facilities: Computer purchase and lease plans are available. 2,100 computers available on campus for general student use. A campuswide network can be accessed from student residence rooms and from off campus. Online class registration is available.
Website: http://www.iub.edu/
General Application Contact: Information Contact, 812-855-0661, Fax: 812-855-5102, E-mail: iuadmit@indiana.edu.
GRADUATE UNITS
Jacobs School of Music Students: 777 full-time (390 women), 72 part-time (39 women); includes 139 minority (17 Black or African American, non-Hispanic/Latino; 3 American Indian or Alaska Native, non-Hispanic/Latino; 54 Asian, non-Hispanic/Latino; 45 Hispanic/Latino; 1 Native Hawaiian or other Pacific Islander, non-Hispanic/Latino; 19 Two or more races, non-Hispanic/Latino), 254 international. Average age 28. 1,429 applicants, 42% accepted, 253 enrolled. *Faculty:* 143 full-time (43 women), 1 (woman) part-time/adjunct. *Expenses:* Contact institution. *Financial support:* Fellowships with full and partial tuition reimbursements, research assistantships with tuition reimbursements, teaching assistantships with full tuition reimbursements, Federal Work-Study, and health care benefits available. Financial award application deadline: 3/1. In 2016, 196 master's,

35 doctorates, 56 other advanced degrees awarded. Offers music (MA, MM, MME, MS, DM, DME, PhD, Artist Diploma, Performance Diploma, Spec). *Application deadline:* For fall admission, 12/1 for domestic and international students; for spring admission, 9/1 for domestic and international students. *Application fee:* $135 ($145 for international students). Electronic applications accepted. *Application Contact:* Rebecca Patrick Shipman, Music Admissions, 812-855-7998, E-mail: musicadm@indiana.edu. *Dean*, Gwyn Richards, 812-855-2435, E-mail: musdean@indiana.edu.

Kelley School of Business Students: 1,488 full-time (417 women), 1,045 part-time (312 women); includes 511 minority (100 Black or African American, non-Hispanic/Latino; 302 Asian, non-Hispanic/Latino; 69 Hispanic/Latino; 2 Native Hawaiian or other Pacific Islander, non-Hispanic/Latino; 38 Two or more races, non-Hispanic/Latino), 493 international. Average age 31. 3,169 applicants, 41% accepted, 744 enrolled. *Faculty:* 167 full-time (32 women). Expenses: Contact institution. *Financial support:* In 2016–17, 41 students received support, including 43 fellowships with full and partial tuition reimbursements available (averaging $5,430 per year), 55 teaching assistantships (averaging $15,003 per year); health care benefits, tuition waivers (full), and fee remissions also available. Financial award application deadline: 12/15; financial award applicants required to submit FAFSA. In 2016, 937 master's, 15 doctorates awarded. Offers business (MBA, MPA, MS, MBA, DBA, PhD). PhD offered through University Graduate School. *Application deadline:* For fall admission, 12/15 priority date for domestic and international students; for winter admission, 3/1 priority date for domestic students; for spring admission, 4/15 for domestic students, 9/1 for international students. *Application fee:* $55 ($65 for international students). Electronic applications accepted. *Application Contact:* Chrystyna Thorbecke, Assistant Director, Doctoral Programs, 812-855-3476, E-mail: chrythor@indiana.edu. *Dean*, Idalene Kesner, 812-855-8489, E-mail: business@indiana.edu.

Maurer School of Law Offers comparative law (MCL); juridical science (SJD); law (LL M, JD); law and social sciences (PhD); legal studies (Certificate). PhD offered through University Graduate School. Electronic applications accepted.

School of Education Students: 717 full-time (502 women), 308 part-time (213 women); includes 182 minority (86 Black or African American, non-Hispanic/Latino; 1 American Indian or Alaska Native, non-Hispanic/Latino; 33 Asian, non-Hispanic/Latino; 43 Hispanic/Latino; 1 Native Hawaiian or other Pacific Islander, non-Hispanic/Latino; 18 Two or more races, non-Hispanic/Latino), 205 international. Average age 34. 907 applicants, 46% accepted, 166 enrolled. Expenses: Contact institution. *Financial support:* Fellowships with full and partial tuition reimbursements, research assistantships with tuition reimbursements, teaching assistantships with tuition reimbursements, Federal Work-Study, scholarships/grants, tuition waivers (full and partial), and unspecified assistantships available. Financial award application deadline: 3/1; financial award applicants required to submit FAFSA. In 2016, 225 master's, 79 doctorates, 50 other advanced degrees awarded. *Program availability:* Part-time, 100% online, blended/hybrid learning. Offers art education (MS, Ed D, PhD); counseling (MS, PhD, Ed S); counselor education (MS, Ed S); curriculum studies (Ed D, PhD); education (MS, Ed D, PhD, Ed S, Graduate Certificate); educational leadership (MS, Ed D, Ed S); educational psychology (MS, PhD); elementary education (MS, Ed D, PhD, Ed S); higher education (Ed D, PhD); higher education and student affairs (MS); history and philosophy of education (MS); history, philosophy, and policy in education (PhD); inquiry methodology (PhD); instructional systems technology (MS, PhD); international and comparative education (MS); learning and developmental sciences (MS, PhD); literacy, culture, and language education (MS, Ed D, PhD, Ed S); mathematics education (MS,

Ed D, PhD); school psychology (PhD, Ed S); science education (MS, Ed D, PhD); secondary education (MS, Ed D, PhD); social studies education (MS, PhD); special education (PhD, Ed S). *Application deadline:* For fall admission, 1/15 priority date for domestic students, 12/1 priority date for international students; for spring admission, 11/1 priority date for domestic students, 9/1 priority date for international students. *Application fee:* $60 ($65 for international students). Electronic applications accepted. *Application Contact:* Christy Richards, Admissions Coordinator, 812-856-8504, Fax: 812-856-8505, E-mail: richarcj@indiana.edu. *Dean*, Dr. Terrence C. Mason, 812-856-8504, E-mail: educate@indiana.edu.

School of Informatics and Computing Students: 795 full-time (290 women), 76 part-time (41 women); includes 62 minority (15 Black or African American, non-Hispanic/Latino; 17 Asian, non-Hispanic/Latino; 17 Hispanic/Latino; 13 Two or more races, non-Hispanic/Latino), 538 international. Average age 27. 1,861 applicants, 55% accepted, 275 enrolled. *Faculty:* 103 full-time (35 women). Expenses: Contact institution. In 2016, 259 master's, 27 doctorates, 10 other advanced degrees awarded. *Program availability:* Part-time, online learning. Offers bioinformatics (MS); computer science (MS, PhD); cybersecurity risk management (MS); data science (MS, Graduate Certificate); informatics (MS, PhD); informatics and computing (MIS, MLS, MS, PhD, Graduate Certificate, Sp LIS); information architecture (Graduate Certificate); information science (MIS, PhD); intelligent systems engineering (PhD); library and information science (Sp LIS); library science (MLS); secure computing (MS, Graduate Certificate); visual heritage (PhD). PhD offered through University Graduate School. *Application deadline:* For fall admission, 1/15 for domestic students, 12/1 for international students. *Application fee:* $55 ($65 for international students). Electronic applications accepted. *Associate Dean for Graduate Studies*, Dr. Howard Rosenbaum, 812-855-3250, E-mail: hrosenba@indiana.edu.

School of Optometry Offers optometry (MS, OD, PhD). Electronic applications accepted.

School of Public and Environmental Affairs Average age 26. *Faculty:* 99 full-time (36 women), 12 part-time/adjunct (5 women). Expenses: Contact institution. *Financial support:* Fellowships with partial tuition reimbursements, research assistantships with partial tuition reimbursements, teaching assistantships with partial tuition reimbursements, Federal Work-Study, scholarships/grants, health care benefits, tuition waivers (partial), unspecified assistantships, and Service Corps Program; Educational Opportunity Fellowships available. Financial award application deadline: 2/1; financial award applicants required to submit FAFSA. *Program availability:* Part-time, 100% online. Offers applied ecology (MSES); arts administration (MAAA); economic development (MPA); energy (MPA, MSES); environmental chemistry, toxicology, and risk assessment (MSES); environmental policy (PhD); environmental policy and natural resource management (MPA); environmental science (PhD); hazardous materials management (Certificate); information systems (MPA); international development (MPA); local government management (MPA); nonprofit management (MPA, Certificate); policy analysis (MPA); public and environmental affairs (MAAA, MPA, MSES, PhD, Certificate); public budgeting and financial management (Certificate); public finance (PhD); public financial administration (MPA); public management (MPA, PhD, Certificate); public policy analysis (PhD); social entrepreneurship (Certificate); specialized environmental science (MSES); specialized public affairs (MPA); sustainability and sustainable development (MPA); water resources (MSES). *Application deadline:* For fall admission, 2/1 priority date for domestic students, 12/1 priority date for international students; for spring admission, 12/1 for domestic students, 10/1 for international students. Applications are processed on a rolling basis. *Application fee:* $55 ($65 for international students). Electronic applications accepted. *Application Contact:* Emily Miller, Assistant Director, Graduate Student Recruitment, 812-855-2840, E-mail: speainfo@indiana.edu. *Director, Graduate Student Services,* Megan Siehl, 812-855-2840, Fax: 812-856-3665, E-mail: speampo@indiana.edu.

School of Public Health *Program availability:* Part-time, online learning. Offers applied sport science (MS); athletic administration/sport management (MS); athletic training (MS); behavioral, social, and community health (MPH); biomechanics (MS); biostatistics (MPH); environmental health (MPH, PhD); epidemiology (MPH, PhD); ergonomics (MS); exercise physiology (MS); family health (MPH); health behavior (PhD); human performance (PhD); leisure behavior (PhD); motor learning/control (MS); nutrition science (MS); outdoor recreation (MS); park and public lands management (MS); physical activity (MPH); physical activity, fitness and wellness (MS); professional health education (MPH); public health (MPH, MS, PhD); public health administration (MPH); recreation administration (MS); recreational sports administration (MS); recreational therapy (MS); safety management (MS); school and college health education (MS); tourism management (MS). Electronic applications accepted.

University Graduate School Students: 3,734 full-time (1,866 women), 222 part-time (112 women); includes 562 minority (158 Black or African American, non-Hispanic/Latino; 4 American Indian or Alaska Native, non-Hispanic/Latino; 141 Asian, non-Hispanic/Latino; 181 Hispanic/Latino; 1 Native Hawaiian or other Pacific Islander, non-Hispanic/Latino; 77 Two or more races, non-Hispanic/Latino), 1,239 international. Average age 31. 5,089 applicants, 33% accepted, 694 enrolled. Expenses: Contact institution. *Financial support:* Fellowships with full and partial tuition reimbursements, research assistantships, teaching assistantships, career-related internships or fieldwork, Federal Work-Study, institutionally sponsored loans, scholarships/grants, health care benefits, and tuition waivers (full and partial) available. Support available to part-time students. In 2016, 410 master's, 405 doctorates, 2 other advanced degrees awarded. *Program availability:* Part-time. *Application deadline:* For fall admission, 1/15 for domestic students, 12/15 for international students; for spring admission, 9/1 for domestic and international students. *Application fee:* $55 ($65 for international students). Electronic applications accepted. *Application Contact:* Graduate School, 812-855-8853, E-mail: grdschl@indiana.edu. *Dean,* Dr. James Wimbush, 812-855-8853, E-mail: grdschl@indiana.edu.

College of Arts and Sciences Students: 2,543 full-time (1,275 women), 107 part-time (53 women); includes 376 minority (87 Black or African American, non-Hispanic/Latino; 4 American Indian or Alaska Native, non-Hispanic/Latino; 87 Asian, non-Hispanic/Latino; 138 Hispanic/Latino; 60 Two or more races, non-Hispanic/Latino), 690 international. Average age 30. 3,782 applicants, 31% accepted, 504 enrolled. *Faculty:* 620 full-time (184 women). Expenses: Contact institution. *Financial support:* Fellowships with full and partial tuition reimbursements, research assistantships, teaching assistantships, career-related internships or fieldwork, Federal Work-Study, institutionally sponsored loans, scholarships/grants, health care benefits, tuition waivers (full and partial), and unspecified assistantships available. Support available to part-time students. In 2016, 367 master's, 259 doctorates, 2 other advanced degrees awarded. *Program availability:* Part-time. Offers acting (MFA); African American and African diaspora studies (MA, PhD); African languages and linguistics (PhD); African studies (MA); analytical chemistry (PhD); anthropology (MA, PhD); apparel merchandising (MS); applied mathematics (MA); applied statistics (MS); arts and sciences (MA, MAT, MFA, MS, Au D, PhD, Certificate); astronomy (MA, PhD); astrophysics (PhD); audiology (Au D); auditory sciences (Au D, PhD); biochemistry (PhD); biogeochemistry (MS, PhD); biology teaching (MAT); biotechnology (MA); Central Eurasian studies (MA, PhD); chemical biology (PhD); chemistry (MAT); Chinese (MA, PhD); Chinese language pedagogy (MA); classical studies (MA, MAT, PhD); clinical science (PhD); cognitive neuroscience (PhD); cognitive psychology (PhD); cognitive science (PhD); comparative literature (MA, MAT, PhD); computational linguistics (MA, MS, PhD); creative writing (MA, MFA); crime and youth development (MA, PhD); crime, law and psychology (MA, PhD); criminal justice (MA, PhD); criminal justice institutions and practices (MA, PhD); criminology (MA, PhD); design and technology (MFA); developmental criminology (MA, PhD); developmental psychology (PhD); directing (MFA); East Asian studies (MA); economic geology (MS, PhD); economics (MS, PhD); ethnomusicology (MA, PhD); European studies (PhD); evolution, ecology, and behavior (MA, PhD); French (MA, PhD); gender studies (PhD); genetics (PhD); geobiology (MS, PhD); geography (PhD); geophysics, structural geology and tectonics (MS, PhD); German philology and linguistics (PhD); German studies (MA, PhD); global and international studies (MA, MS, PhD, Certificate); history (MA, MAT, PhD); history and philosophy of science (MA, PhD); hydrogeology (MS, PhD); inorganic chemistry (PhD); interdisciplinary studies in crime and punishment (PhD); interdisciplinary studies of crime and punishment (MA); international studies (MS); Italian (MA, PhD); Japanese (MA, PhD); Japanese language pedagogy (MA); Jewish studies (MA); Jewish studies and history (MA); language sciences (PhD); Latin American and Caribbean studies (MA); linguistics (MA, PhD); literature (PhD); materials chemistry (PhD); mathematical physics (PhD); mathematics education (MAT); media (MS); media arts and sciences (MA, PhD); medical physics (MS); medieval German studies (PhD); methods of behavior (PhD); microbiology (MA, PhD); mineralogy (MS, PhD); molecular systems neuroscience (PhD); molecular, cellular, and developmental biology (PhD); Near Eastern languages and cultures (MA, PhD); neuroscience (PhD); organic chemistry (PhD); philosophy (MA, PhD); physical chemistry (PhD); physics (MAT, MS, PhD); plant sciences (MA, PhD); playwriting (MFA); political science (MA, PhD); Portuguese (MA, PhD); pure mathematics (MA, PhD); religious studies (MA, PhD); rhetoric (PhD); Russian and East European studies (MA, Certificate); second language studies (MA, PhD); Slavic languages and literatures (MA, MAT, PhD); social psychology (PhD); sociology (MA, PhD); Spanish (MA, PhD); speech and hearing sciences (MA, Au D, PhD); speech and voice sciences (PhD); speech-language pathology (MA); statistical science (MS, PhD); stratigraphy and sedimentology (MS, PhD); studio art (MFA); teaching German (MAT); TESOL and applied linguistics (MA); the relationship between crime and gender, race and ethnicity (MA, PhD); theatre history, theory, and literature (MA, PhD); theoretical analyses of criminology (MA, PhD); zoology (MA, PhD). *Application deadline:* For fall admission, 1/15 for domestic students, 12/15 for international students; for spring admission, 9/1 for domestic and international students. *Application fee:* $55 ($65 for international students). Electronic applications accepted. *Application Contact:* Mitchell Byler, Assistant Dean, 812-855-4871, E-mail: mbyler@indiana.edu. *Executive Dean,* Dr. Larry Singell, 812-855-2392, E-mail: lsingell@indiana.edu.

INDIANA UNIVERSITY EAST, Richmond, IN 47374-1289

General Information State-supported, coed, comprehensive institution.

GRADUATE UNITS

School of Education Offers education (MS Ed).

School of Nursing Offers nursing (MSN).

School of Social Work Offers social work (MSW).

INDIANA UNIVERSITY KOKOMO, Kokomo, IN 46904-9003

General Information State-supported, coed, comprehensive institution. *Enrollment:* 4,106 graduate, professional, and undergraduate students; 37 full-time matriculated graduate/professional students (19 women), 93 part-time matriculated graduate/professional students (60 women). *Enrollment by degree level:* 101 master's, 17 other advanced degrees. *Graduate faculty:* 64 full-time (29 women). *Graduate housing:* On-campus housing not available. *Student services:* Career counseling, child daycare facilities, multicultural affairs office, services for students with disabilities, teacher training. *Library facilities:* IU Kokomo Library. *Collection:* Books: 129,040 (physical), 543,407 (digital/electronic); Serial titles: 4,210 (physical), 41,148 (digital/electronic); Databases: 317. Students can reserve study rooms.

Computer facilities: 325 computers available on campus for general student use. A campuswide network can be accessed from off campus. Online class registration is available.
Website: http://www.iuk.edu/

General Application Contact: Admissions Office, 765-455-9357.

GRADUATE UNITS

Department of Public Administration and Health Management Students: 11 full-time (9 women), 15 part-time (12 women); includes 4 minority (3 Black or African American, non-Hispanic/Latino; 1 Hispanic/Latino), 2 international. Average age 34. 13 applicants, 100% accepted, 8 enrolled. Expenses: Contact institution. *Financial support:* Scholarships/grants available. Financial award application deadline: 3/10; financial award applicants required to submit FAFSA. In 2016, 7 master's, 2 other advanced degrees awarded. *Program availability:* Part-time, evening/weekend. Offers health management (MPM, Graduate Certificate); public management (Graduate Certificate); public management and policy (MPM). *Application deadline:* For fall admission, 6/15 for domestic students, 6/1 for international students; for spring admission, 10/1 for domestic students, 10/1 for international students; for summer admission, 3/1 for domestic students. *Application fee:* $40 ($40 for international students). Electronic applications accepted. *Application Contact:* Gloria Preece, Director of the MPM Program, 765-455-9269, E-mail: gpreece@iuk.edu. *Dean,* Alan Krabbenhoff, 765-455-9275, E-mail: agkrabbe@iuk.edu.

School of Business Students: 21 full-time (7 women), 34 part-time (14 women); includes 1 minority (Black or African American, non-Hispanic/Latino), 23 international. Average age 31. 33 applicants, 70% accepted, 15 enrolled. *Faculty:* 14 full-time (6 women). Expenses: Contact institution. *Financial support:* Career-related internships or fieldwork and scholarships/grants available. Financial award application deadline: 3/10; financial award applicants required to submit FAFSA. In 2016, 36 master's awarded. *Program availability:* Part-time, evening/weekend. Offers accounting (Postbaccalaureate Certificate); business administration (MBA); business fundamentals (Postbaccalaureate Certificate). *Application deadline:* For fall admission, 6/15 for domestic students, 6/1 for international students; for spring admission, 11/1 for domestic students, 10/1 for international students; for summer admission, 3/1 for domestic students. *Application fee:* $40 ($60 for international students). Electronic applications accepted. *Application Contact:* Terri Butler, Administrative Secretary, 765-455-9275, E-mail: tbutler@iuk.edu. *Dean,* Dr. Alan Krabbenhoff, 756-455-9275, E-mail: agkrabbe@iuk.edu.

School of Nursing Students: 5 full-time (3 women), 17 part-time (15 women); includes 3 minority (all Black or African American, non-Hispanic/Latino), 5 international. Average age 42. 9 applicants. Expenses: Contact institution. *Financial support:* Scholarships/grants available. Financial award application deadline: 3/10; financial award applicants required to submit FAFSA. In 2016, 10 master's awarded. Offers family nurse practitioner (MSN); nurse administrator (MSN); nurse educator (MSN). *Application deadline:* For fall admission, 7/1 for domestic students; for spring admission, 12/1 for domestic students; for summer admission, 4/1 for domestic students. *Application fee:* $40 ($60 for international students). Electronic applications accepted. *Application Contact:* Stephanie Graves, 765-455-9308, Fax: 765-455-9421, E-mail: gravesst@iuk.edu. *Dean,* Dr. Linda Wallace, 765-455-9288, E-mail: lwallace@iuk.edu.

INDIANA UNIVERSITY NORTHWEST, Gary, IN 46408-1197

General Information State-supported, coed, comprehensive institution. *Enrollment:* 5,591 graduate, professional, and undergraduate students; 97 full-time matriculated graduate/professional students (64 women), 241 part-time matriculated graduate/professional students (165 women). *Enrollment by degree level:* 306 master's, 32 other advanced degrees. *Graduate faculty:* 126 full-time (54 women). *Graduate housing:* On-campus housing not available. *Student services:* Campus employment opportunities, campus safety program, career counseling, child daycare facilities, free psychological counseling, international student services, low-cost health insurance. *Library facilities:* IUN Library. *Collection:* Books: 251,000 (physical), 605,000 (digital/electronic); Serial titles: 7,500 (physical), 100 (digital/electronic); Databases: 325. Students can reserve study rooms.

Computer facilities: 605 computers available on campus for general student use. A campuswide network can be accessed from off campus. Online class registration is available.
Website: http://www.iun.edu/

General Application Contact: Admissions Counselor, 219-980-6760, Fax: 219-980-7103.

GRADUATE UNITS

College of Arts and Sciences Students: 4 full-time (all women), 18 part-time (10 women); includes 10 minority (9 Black or African American, non-Hispanic/Latino; 1 Hispanic/Latino). Average age 39. 22 applicants, 77% accepted, 13 enrolled. Expenses: Contact institution. *Financial support:* Applicants required to submit FAFSA. In 2016, 6 master's awarded. *Program availability:* Part-time, evening/weekend. Offers clinical counseling (MS); community development/urban studies (Graduate Certificate); computer information systems (Graduate Certificate); liberal studies (MLS); race-ethnic studies (Graduate Certificate); women's and gender studies (Graduate Certificate). *Application deadline:* For fall admission, 7/1 priority date for domestic and international students; for spring admission, 12/1 priority date for domestic and international students. *Application fee:* $40 ($60 for international students). Electronic applications accepted. *Dean,* Mark Hoyert, E-mail: mhoyert@iun.edu.

School of Business and Economics Students: 46 full-time (20 women), 53 part-time (24 women); includes 44 minority (22 Black or African American, non-Hispanic/Latino; 4 Asian, non-Hispanic/Latino; 15 Hispanic/Latino; 3 Two or more races, non-Hispanic/Latino), 2 international. Average age 35. 47 applicants, 94% accepted, 34 enrolled. *Faculty:* 11 full-time (4 women), 7 part-time/adjunct (1 woman). Expenses: Contact institution. *Financial support:* Institutionally sponsored loans and unspecified assistantships available. Support available to part-time students. Financial award application deadline: 3/10; financial award applicants required to submit FAFSA. In 2016, 30 master's, 5 other advanced degrees awarded. *Program availability:* Part-time, evening/weekend. Offers accounting (Graduate Certificate); management (Certificate); management and administrative studies (MBA). *Application deadline:* For fall admission, 7/15 priority date for domestic students; for spring admission, 11/15 for domestic students. Applications are processed on a rolling basis. *Application fee:* $40 ($60 for international students). Electronic applications accepted. *Dean,* Cynthia Roberts, PhD, 219-980-6552, Fax: 219-980-6916, E-mail: iunbiz@iun.edu.

School of Education Students: 11 full-time (8 women), 67 part-time (47 women); includes 32 minority (25 Black or African American, non-Hispanic/Latino; 7 Hispanic/Latino). Average age 38. 24 applicants, 96% accepted, 14 enrolled. *Faculty:* 10 full-time (5 women), 2 part-time/adjunct (both women). Expenses: Contact institution. *Financial support:* Applicants required to submit FAFSA. In 2016, 22 master's awarded. *Program availability:* Part-time, evening/weekend. Offers educational leadership (MS Ed); elementary education (MS Ed); K-12 online teaching (Graduate Certificate); secondary education (MS Ed). *Application deadline:* For fall admission, 7/15 priority date for domestic students; for spring admission, 11/15 for domestic students. *Application fee:* $40 ($60 for international students). Electronic applications accepted. *Application Contact:* Kelly Zieba, Director of Enrollment Management, Finance, and Operations, 219-980-6879, Fax: 219-980-4208, E-mail: kmzieba@iun.edu. *Interim Dean,* Dr. Charles Hobsen, 219-980-6903, Fax: 219-680-4208, E-mail: chobson@iun.edu.

School of Public and Environmental Affairs Students: 10 full-time (8 women), 39 part-time (28 women); includes 25 minority (18 Black or African American, non-Hispanic/Latino; 7 Hispanic/Latino), 1 international. Average age 37. 31 applicants, 97% accepted, 16 enrolled. *Faculty:* 5 full-time (3 women). Expenses: Contact institution. *Financial support:* Career-related internships or fieldwork, Federal Work-Study, and tuition waivers (partial) available. Support available to part-time students. Financial award application deadline: 3/1; financial award applicants required to submit FAFSA. In 2016, 13 master's, 9 other advanced degrees awarded. *Program availability:* Part-time. Offers criminal justice (MPA); environmental affairs (Graduate Certificate); health services (MPA); nonprofit management (Certificate); public management (MPA, Graduate Certificate). *Application deadline:* For fall admission, 8/15 priority date for domestic students. Applications are processed on a rolling basis. *Application fee:* $40 ($60 for international students). Electronic applications accepted. *Assistant Dean and Director,* Dr. Karl Besel, 219-980-6554, Fax: 219-980-6737, E-mail: kbesel@iun.edu.

School of Social Work Students: 26 full-time (24 women), 64 part-time (56 women); includes 36 minority (21 Black or African American, non-Hispanic/Latino; 13 Hispanic/Latino; 2 Two or more races, non-Hispanic/Latino). Average age 33. 65 applicants, 52% accepted, 24 enrolled. *Faculty:* 3 full-time (all women), 4 part-time/adjunct (3 women). Expenses: Contact institution. *Financial support:* Career-related internships or fieldwork, Federal Work-Study, and tuition waivers (partial) available. Support available to part-time students. Financial award application deadline: 6/1; financial award applicants required to submit FAFSA. In 2016, 27 master's awarded. *Program availability:* Part-time, evening/weekend. Offers health (MSW); mental health and addictions (MSW). *Application deadline:* For fall admission, 7/14 for domestic students; for spring admission, 2/1 priority date for domestic students. *Application fee:* $40 ($60 for international students). Electronic applications accepted. *Application Contact:* Elena Mrozinske, Clinical Assistant Professor, 219-980-6727, E-mail: emrozins@iun.edu. *Director,* Dr. Darlene Lynch, 219-980-7111, E-mail: darlynch@iun.edu.

INDIANA UNIVERSITY OF PENNSYLVANIA, Indiana, PA 15705

General Information State-supported, coed, university. CGS member. *Enrollment:* 12,853 graduate, professional, and undergraduate students; 1,009 full-time matriculated graduate/professional students (582 women), 1,226 part-time matriculated graduate/professional students (766 women). *Enrollment by degree level:* 1,353 master's, 807 doctoral, 75 other advanced degrees. *Graduate faculty:* 277 full-time (124 women), 13 part-time/adjunct (10 women). Tuition, state resident: full-time $8694; part-time $483 per credit. Tuition, nonresident: full-time $13,050; part-time $725 per credit. *Required fees:* $157 per credit. $50 per term. Tuition and fees vary according to course load and program. *Graduate housing:* Room and/or apartments available on a first-come, first-served basis to single students; on-campus housing not available to married students. Typical cost: $8950 per year ($12,402 including board). Housing application deadline: 4/15. *Student services:* Campus employment opportunities, campus safety program, career counseling, free psychological counseling, international student services, low-cost health insurance, multicultural affairs office, services for students with disabilities. *Library facilities:* Stapleton Library. *Collection:* Books: 547,640 (physical), 277,326 (digital/electronic); Serial titles: 125,517 (physical). Weekly public service hours: 134; study areas open 24 hours, 5–7 days a week; students can reserve study rooms.

Computer facilities: Computer purchase and lease plans are available. 2,363 computers available on campus for general student use. A campuswide network can be accessed from student residence rooms and from off campus. Online class registration is available.

Website: http://www.iup.edu/

General Application Contact: Paula Stossel, Assistant Dean for Administration, 724-357-2222, Fax: 724-357-4862, E-mail: graduate-admissions@iup.edu.

GRADUATE UNITS

School of Graduate Studies and Research Students: 1,009 full-time (582 women), 1,226 part-time (766 women); includes 223 minority (105 Black or African American, non-Hispanic/Latino; 4 American Indian or Alaska Native, non-Hispanic/Latino; 33 Asian, non-Hispanic/Latino; 44 Hispanic/Latino; 1 Native Hawaiian or other Pacific Islander, non-Hispanic/Latino; 36 Two or more races, non-Hispanic/Latino), 489 international. Average age 32. 2,527 applicants, 57% accepted, 854 enrolled. *Faculty:* 277 full-time (124 women), 13 part-time/adjunct (10 women). Expenses: Contact institution. *Financial support:* In 2016–17, 42 fellowships with full tuition reimbursements (averaging $954 per year), 426 research assistantships with tuition reimbursements (averaging $3,978 per year), 27 teaching assistantships with partial tuition reimbursements (averaging $17,551 per year) were awarded; career-related internships or fieldwork, Federal Work-Study, scholarships/grants, tuition waivers (full and partial), and unspecified assistantships also available. Support available to part-time students. Financial award application deadline: 3/15; financial award applicants required to submit FAFSA. In 2016, 561 master's, 126 doctorates, 15 other advanced degrees awarded. *Program availability:* Part-time, evening/weekend, blended/hybrid learning. *Application deadline:* Applications are processed on a rolling basis. *Application fee:* $50. Electronic applications accepted. *Application Contact:* Paula Stossel, Assistant Dean for Administration, 724-357-4511, Fax: 724-357-4862, E-mail: graduate-admissions@iup.edu. *Director of Graduate Marketing,* Simon Stuchlik, 724-357-2127, Fax: 724-357-4862, E-mail: stuchlik@iup.edu.

College of Education and Educational Technology Students: 282 full-time (223 women), 419 part-time (279 women); includes 76 minority (44 Black or African

American, non-Hispanic/Latino; 2 Asian, non-Hispanic/Latino; 14 Hispanic/Latino; 16 Two or more races, non-Hispanic/Latino), 31 international. Average age 33. 895 applicants, 53% accepted, 234 enrolled. *Faculty:* 62 full-time (38 women), 12 part-time/adjunct (9 women). Expenses: Contact institution. *Financial support:* In 2016–17, 22 fellowships (averaging $919 per year), 135 research assistantships with tuition reimbursements (averaging $4,373 per year), 8 teaching assistantships with tuition reimbursements (averaging $18,450 per year) were awarded; career-related internships or fieldwork, Federal Work-Study, scholarships/grants, and unspecified assistantships also available. Support available to part-time students. Financial award application deadline: 4/15; financial award applicants required to submit FAFSA. In 2016, 174 master's, 45 doctorates, 10 other advanced degrees awarded. *Program availability:* Part-time, evening/weekend. Offers administration and leadership studies (D Ed); adult and community education (MA); adult and community education/communications technology (MA); business/administrative (M Ed); business/business specialist (M Ed); business/workforce development (M Ed); clinical mental health counseling (MA); communications media and instructional technology (PhD); community counseling (MA); curriculum and instruction (D Ed); education (M Ed); education and educational technology (M Ed, MA, MS, D Ed, PhD, Certificate); educational psychology (M Ed, Certificate); literacy (M Ed, Certificate); principal (Certificate); reading (Certificate); school counseling (M Ed); school psychology (Certificate); special education (M Ed); speech-language pathology (MS); student affairs in higher education (MA). *Application deadline:* Applications are processed on a rolling basis. *Application fee:* $50. Electronic applications accepted. *Application Contact:* Paula Stossel, Assistant Dean for Administration, 724-357-4511, Fax: 724-357-4862, E-mail: graduate-admissions@iup.edu. *Dean,* Dr. Lara Luetkehans, 724-357-2480, Fax: 724-357-5595.

College of Fine Arts Students: 31 full-time (18 women), 14 part-time (10 women); includes 5 minority (2 Black or African American, non-Hispanic/Latino; 1 Asian, non-Hispanic/Latino; 2 Two or more races, non-Hispanic/Latino), 5 international. Average age 27. 38 applicants, 79% accepted, 22 enrolled. *Faculty:* 21 full-time (7 women). Expenses: Contact institution. *Financial support:* In 2016–17, 24 research assistantships with tuition reimbursements (averaging $2,955 per year) were awarded; fellowships with full tuition reimbursements, career-related internships or fieldwork, Federal Work-Study, scholarships/grants, and unspecified assistantships also available. Support available to part-time students. Financial award application deadline: 4/15; financial award applicants required to submit FAFSA. In 2016, 17 master's awarded. *Program availability:* Part-time. Offers art (MA, MFA); fine arts (MA, MFA); music education (MA); music performance (MA). *Application deadline:* Applications are processed on a rolling basis. *Application fee:* $50. Electronic applications accepted. *Application Contact:* Dr. Susan Palmisano, Graduate Coordinator, 724-357-2536, E-mail: palmisan@iup.edu. *Dean,* Michael Hood, 724-357-2397, E-mail: mhood@iup.edu.

College of Health and Human Services Students: 219 full-time (129 women), 278 part-time (193 women); includes 56 minority (26 Black or African American, non-Hispanic/Latino; 3 American Indian or Alaska Native, non-Hispanic/Latino; 6 Asian, non-Hispanic/Latino; 14 Hispanic/Latino; 7 Two or more races, non-Hispanic/Latino), 53 international. Average age 31. 489 applicants, 67% accepted, 210 enrolled. *Faculty:* 55 full-time (31 women), 1 (woman) part-time/adjunct. Expenses: Contact institution. *Financial support:* In 2016–17, 3 fellowships with full tuition reimbursements (averaging $2,018 per year), 89 research assistantships with tuition reimbursements (averaging $4,163 per year), 6 teaching assistantships with partial tuition reimbursements (averaging $23,305 per year) were awarded; career-related internships or fieldwork, Federal Work-Study, scholarships/grants, and unspecified assistantships also available. Support available to part-time students. Financial award application deadline: 4/15; financial award applicants required to submit FAFSA. In 2016, 180 master's, 11 doctorates awarded. *Program availability:* Part-time, evening/weekend, online learning. Offers criminology (MA, PhD); employment and labor relations (MA); food and nutrition (MS); health and human services (M Ed, MA, MS, PhD, Certificate); health and physical education (M Ed); health service administration (MS); health services administration (MS); nursing (PhD); nursing administration (MS); nursing education (MS); safety sciences (MS, PhD); sport science/exercise science (MS); sport science/sport management (MS); sport science/sport studies (MS). *Application deadline:* Applications are processed on a rolling basis. *Application fee:* $50. Electronic applications accepted. *Application Contact:* Paula Stossel, Assistant Dean, 724-357-4511, Fax: 724-357-4862, E-mail: graduate-admissions@iup.edu. *Acting Dean,* Dr. Mary Williams, 724-357-2560, Fax: 724-357-6205, E-mail: mary.e.williams@iup.edu.

College of Humanities and Social Sciences Students: 157 full-time (81 women), 308 part-time (185 women); includes 45 minority (21 Black or African American, non-Hispanic/Latino; 1 American Indian or Alaska Native, non-Hispanic/Latino; 9 Asian, non-Hispanic/Latino; 7 Hispanic/Latino; 7 Two or more races, non-Hispanic/Latino), 117 international. Average age 35. 407 applicants, 58% accepted, 102 enrolled. *Faculty:* 64 full-time (30 women). Expenses: Contact institution. *Financial support:* In 2016–17, 4 fellowships with full tuition reimbursements (averaging $1,760 per year), 87 research assistantships with tuition reimbursements (averaging $4,785 per year), 11 teaching assistantships with partial tuition reimbursements (averaging $12,712 per year) were awarded; career-related internships or fieldwork, Federal Work-Study, scholarships/grants, and unspecified assistantships also available. Support available to part-time students. Financial award application deadline: 4/15; financial award applicants required to submit FAFSA. In 2016, 56 master's, 40 doctorates, 6 other advanced degrees awarded. *Program availability:* Part-time, evening/weekend. Offers administration and leadership studies (PhD); applied archaeology (MA); composition and literature (MA); composition and teaching English to speakers of other languages (PhD); English: generalist (MA); English: literature (MA); English: TESOL (MA); environmental planning (MS); geographic information science and geospatial techniques (Certificate); geographic information science/cartography (MS); geography (MA); history (MA); humanities and social sciences (MA, MS, PhD, Certificate); literature and criticism (PhD); public affairs (MA); public history (MA); regional planning (MS); sociology (MA, PhD); Spanish/applied linguistics and teaching methodology (MA); Spanish/Hispanic literatures and cultures (MA); teaching English (MA). *Application deadline:* Applications are processed on a rolling basis. *Application fee:* $50. Electronic applications accepted. *Application Contact:* Paula Stossel, Assistant Dean, 724-357-4511, E-mail: graduate-admissions@iup.edu. *Dean,* Dr. Yaw Asamoah, 724-357-5764.

College of Natural Sciences and Mathematics Students: 93 full-time (58 women), 63 part-time (42 women); includes 19 minority (4 Black or African American, non-Hispanic/Latino; 6 Asian, non-Hispanic/Latino; 7 Hispanic/Latino; 2 Two or more races, non-Hispanic/Latino), 20 international. Average age 28. 352 applicants, 30% accepted, 56 enrolled. *Faculty:* 45 full-time (17 women). Expenses: Contact institution. *Financial support:* In 2016–17, 13 fellowships with full tuition reimbursements (averaging $522 per year), 67 research assistantships with tuition reimbursements (averaging $3,115 per year), 2 teaching assistantships (averaging $23,305 per year) were awarded; career-related internships or fieldwork, Federal Work-Study, scholarships/grants, and unspecified assistantships also available. Support available to part-time students. Financial award application deadline: 4/15; financial award applicants required to submit FAFSA. In 2016, 29 master's, 16 doctorates awarded. *Program availability:* Part-time. Offers applied and industrial chemistry (PSM); applied mathematics (MS); biology (MS); clinical psychology (Psy D); elementary and middle school mathematics education (M Ed); nanoscience/industrial materials (PSM); natural sciences and mathematics (M Ed, MA, MS, PSM, Psy D); physics (MA, PSM); psychology (MA); secondary mathematics education (M Ed). *Application deadline:* Applications are processed on a rolling basis. *Application fee:* $50. Electronic applications accepted. *Application Contact:* Paula Stossel, Assistant Dean of Administration, 724-357-4511, Fax: 724-357-4862, E-mail: graduate-admissions@iup.edu. *Dean,* Dr. Deanne Snavely, 724-357-2609, Fax: 724-357-5700, E-mail: snavely@iup.edu.

Eberly College of Business and Information Technology Students: 226 full-time (72 women), 126 part-time (47 women); includes 21 minority (8 Black or African American, non-Hispanic/Latino; 9 Asian, non-Hispanic/Latino; 2 Hispanic/Latino; 2 Two or more races, non-Hispanic/Latino), 253 international. Average age 27. 312 applicants, 73% accepted, 183 enrolled. *Faculty:* 27 full-time (4 women), 1 part-time/adjunct (0 women). Expenses: Contact institution. *Financial support:* In 2016–17, 24 research assistantships with tuition reimbursements (averaging $1,573 per year) were awarded; fellowships with full tuition reimbursements, career-related internships or fieldwork, Federal Work-Study, scholarships/grants, and unspecified assistantships also available. Support available to part-time students. Financial award application deadline: 4/15; financial award applicants required to submit FAFSA. In 2016, 228 master's awarded. *Program availability:* Part-time, evening/weekend. Offers business administration (MBA); business and information technology (M Ed, MBA). *Application deadline:* Applications are processed on a rolling basis. *Application fee:* $50. Electronic applications accepted. *Application Contact:* Paula Stossel, Assistant Dean, 724-357-4511, Fax: 724-357-4862, E-mail: graduate-admissions@iup.edu. *Dean,* Dr. Robert Camp, 724-357-7889, E-mail: bobcamp@iup.edu.

INDIANA UNIVERSITY–PURDUE UNIVERSITY FORT WAYNE, Fort Wayne, IN 46805-1499

General Information State-supported, coed, comprehensive institution. *Graduate housing:* Room and/or apartments available on a first-come, first-served basis to single students; on-campus housing not available to married students. *Research affiliation:* Regenstrief Institute, Inc. (nursing), Earthwatch (biology), PHD, Inc. (engineering), Bendix Commercial Vehicle Systems, LLC (engineering, technology, and computer science), Northeast Indiana Fund (education and public policy), Fort Wayne Metals (geosciences).

GRADUATE UNITS

College of Arts and Sciences *Program availability:* Part-time, evening/weekend. Offers applied mathematics (MS); applied statistics (Certificate); arts and sciences (MA, MAT, MS, Certificate); biology (MS); English (MA, MAT); mathematics (MS); operations research (MS); professional communication (MA, MS); teaching (MAT); TENL (teaching English as a new language) (Certificate).

College of Education and Public Policy *Program availability:* Part-time. Offers couple and family counseling (MS Ed); education and public policy (MPM, MS Ed, Certificate); educational leadership (MS Ed); elementary education (MS Ed); public management (MPM, Certificate); school counseling (MS Ed); secondary education (MS Ed); special education (MS Ed, Certificate).

College of Engineering, Technology, and Computer Science *Program availability:* Part-time. Offers applied computer science (MS); civil engineering (MSE); computer engineering (MSE); electrical engineering (MSE); engineering, technology, and computer science (MS, MSE, Certificate); facilities/construction management (MS); human resources (MS); industrial technology/manufacturing (MS); information technology/advanced computer applications (MS); leadership (MS); mechanical engineering (MSE); organizational leadership and supervision (Certificate); systems engineering (MSE). Electronic applications accepted.

College of Health and Human Services *Program availability:* Part-time. Offers adult-gerontology primary care nurse practitioner (MS); family nurse practitioner (MS); health and human services (MS, DNP, Certificate); nurse executive (MS); nursing administration (Certificate); nursing education (MS). Electronic applications accepted.

Doermer School of Business *Program availability:* Part-time. Offers business (MBA).

INDIANA UNIVERSITY–PURDUE UNIVERSITY INDIANAPOLIS, Indianapolis, IN 46202

General Information State-supported, coed, university. *Enrollment:* 29,804 graduate, professional, and undergraduate students; 5,334 full-time matriculated graduate/professional students (2,779 women), 2,389 part-time matriculated graduate/professional students (1,417 women). *Enrollment by degree level:* 3,905 master's, 3,583 doctoral, 234 other advanced degrees. *Graduate faculty:* 1,400 full-time (473 women), 6 part-time/adjunct (4 women). *Graduate housing:* Rooms and/or apartments available on a first-come, first-served basis to single and married students. Housing application deadline: 3/15. *Student services:* Campus employment opportunities, campus safety program, career counseling, child daycare facilities, exercise/wellness program, free psychological counseling, international student services, low-cost health insurance, multicultural affairs office, services for students with disabilities, writing training. *Library facilities:* University Library plus 4 others. *Collection:* Books: 1.4 million (physical), 700,000 (digital/electronic); Serial titles: 43,147 (physical), 1.8 million (digital/electronic); Databases: 600. Study areas open 24 hours, 5–7 days a week; students can reserve study rooms.

Computer facilities: 1,158 computers available on campus for general student use. A campuswide network can be accessed from student residence rooms and from off campus. Online class registration is available. Website: http://www.iupui.edu/

General Application Contact: Dr. Janice Blum, Associate Vice Chancellor for Graduate Education, 317-274-1577, E-mail: gradoff@iupui.edu.

GRADUATE UNITS

Herron School of Art and Design Students: 56 full-time (40 women), 1 (woman) part-time; includes 8 minority (4 Black or African American, non-Hispanic/Latino; 2 Asian, non-Hispanic/Latino; 2 Hispanic/Latino), 7 international. Average age 31. 72 applicants, 53% accepted, 25 enrolled. *Faculty:* 26 full-time (13 women), 16 part-time/adjunct (11 women). Expenses: Contact institution. *Financial support:* In 2016–17, 55 students received support, including 36 fellowships (averaging $2,830 per year), 11 teaching assistantships (averaging $3,609 per year); research assistantships, Federal Work-Study, scholarships/grants, health care benefits, tuition waivers, and unspecified assistantships also available. Financial award application deadline: 2/1. In 2016, 22 master's awarded. Offers art therapy (MA); visual art (MFA); visual communication design (MFA). *Application deadline:* For fall admission, 1/15 for domestic and international students; for spring admission, 11/1 for domestic students, 10/15 for international students. *Application fee:* $60 ($65 for international students). Electronic applications accepted. *Application Contact:* Abbey Chambers, Herron Office of Admissions and Student Services, 317-378-9400, E-mail: herron4u@iupui.edu. *Dean,* Prof. Valerie Eickmeier, 317-278-9470, Fax: 317-278-9471, E-mail: herron@iupui.edu.

Kelley School of Business Expenses: Contact institution. Offers accounting (MBA); business (MBA, MSA); business of medicine (MBA); entrepreneurship (MBA); finance (MBA); general administration (MBA); marketing (MBA); supply chain management (MBA). *Associate Dean of Academic Programs,* Philip T. Powell, 317-274-2481, E-mail: phpowell@iupui.edu.

Lilly Family School of Philanthropy Students: 55 full-time (39 women), 63 part-time (41 women); includes 16 minority (12 Black or African American, non-Hispanic/Latino; 3 Asian, non-Hispanic/Latino; 1 Two or more races, non-Hispanic/Latino), 20 international. Average age 36. 69 applicants, 65% accepted, 27 enrolled. *Faculty:* 52 full-time, 10 part-time/adjunct. Expenses: Contact institution. *Financial support:* In 2016–17, fellowships with partial tuition reimbursements (averaging $13,000 per year), research assistantships with partial tuition reimbursements (averaging $9,500 per year), teaching assistantships with partial tuition reimbursements (averaging $12,000 per year) were awarded; career-related internships or fieldwork, Federal Work-Study, institutionally sponsored loans, and scholarships/grants also available. Financial award application deadline: 3/1; financial award applicants required to submit FAFSA. In 2016, 24 master's, 4 doctorates awarded. Offers philanthropy (MA, XMA, PhD). *Application deadline:* For fall admission, 1/15 for domestic students, 1/1 for international students. *Application fee:* $55 ($65 for international students). *Director of Graduate Studies,* Dr. Gregory Witkowski, 317-278-8970, E-mail: gwitkows@iupui.edu.

Robert H. McKinney School of Law Students: 578 full-time (285 women), 328 part-time (154 women); includes 157 minority (71 Black or African American, non-Hispanic/Latino; 1 American Indian or Alaska Native, non-Hispanic/Latino; 17 Asian, non-Hispanic/Latino; 42 Hispanic/Latino; 3 Native Hawaiian or other Pacific Islander, non-Hispanic/Latino; 23 Two or more races, non-Hispanic/Latino), 59 international. Average age 29. 915 applicants, 58% accepted, 253 enrolled. *Faculty:* 47 full-time (24 women), 40 part-time/adjunct (17 women). Expenses: Contact institution. *Financial support:* In 2016–17, 528 students received support. Fellowships, research assistantships with full and partial tuition reimbursements available, career-related internships or fieldwork, Federal Work-Study, scholarships/grants, and tuition waivers available. Support available to part-time students. Financial award application deadline: 7/31; financial award applicants required to submit FAFSA. In 2016, 25 master's, 258 doctorates, 100 Certificates awarded. *Program availability:* Part-time. Offers advocacy skills (Certificate); American law for foreign lawyers (LL M); civil and human rights (Certificate); corporate and commercial law (LL M, Certificate); criminal law (Certificate); environmental and natural resources (Certificate); health law (Certificate); health law, policy and bioethics (LL M); intellectual property law (LL M, Certificate); international and comparative law (LL M, Certificate); international human rights law (LL M); law (MJ, JD, SJD). *Application deadline:* For fall admission, 7/31 for domestic students. Applications are processed on a rolling basis. *Application fee:* $0. Electronic applications accepted. *Application Contact:* Patricia Kinney, Assistant Dean of Admissions, 317-274-2459, E-mail: pkkinney@iupui.edu. *Dean,* Andrew R. Klein, 317-274-2099, E-mail: anrklein@iupui.edu.

School of Dentistry Students: 513 full-time (252 women), 47 part-time (20 women); includes 132 minority (18 Black or African American, non-Hispanic/Latino; 77 Asian, non-Hispanic/Latino; 22 Hispanic/Latino; 1 Native Hawaiian or other Pacific Islander, non-Hispanic/Latino; 14 Two or more races, non-Hispanic/Latino), 71 international. Average age 28. 2,099 applicants, 7% accepted, 160 enrolled. *Faculty:* 96 full-time (28 women). Expenses: Contact institution. *Financial support:* In 2016–17, 43 students received support, including 19 fellowships with full and partial tuition reimbursements available (averaging $12,000 per year). Financial award application deadline: 3/1; financial award applicants required to submit FAFSA. In 2016, 39 master's, 117 doctorates, 3 other advanced degrees awarded. Offers cariology and operative dentistry (MSD); dental materials (MS, MSD); dental sciences (PhD); dentistry (DDS, Certificate); endodontics (MSD); oral and maxillofacial surgery (MSD); orthodontics (MSD); pediatric dentistry (MSD); periodontics (MSD); prosthodontics (MSD). *Application deadline:* For winter admission, 11/1 for domestic and international students; for summer admission, 10/15 for domestic and international students. *Application fee:* $75. Electronic applications accepted. *Application Contact:* Dr. Melanie Peterson, Associate Dean for Admissions and Student Affairs, 317-274-8173, E-mail: oasamail@iupui.edu. *Dean,* Dr. John N. Williams, 317-274-7461, E-mail: jnwill01@iu.edu.

School of Education Students: 125 full-time (86 women), 181 part-time (139 women); includes 106 minority (78 Black or African American, non-Hispanic/Latino; 9 Asian, non-Hispanic/Latino; 12 Hispanic/Latino; 7 Two or more races, non-Hispanic/Latino), 3 international. Average age 32. 73 applicants, 93% accepted, 68 enrolled. *Faculty:* 35 full-time (27 women), 56 part-time/adjunct (42 women). Expenses: Contact institution. *Financial support:* Applicants required to submit FAFSA. In 2016, 73 master's awarded. *Program availability:* Part-time, evening/weekend. Offers curriculum and instruction (MS); early childhood (MS); educational leadership (MS, Certificate); English as a second language (Certificate); kindergarten (Certificate); language education (MS); reading (Certificate); school counseling (MS); special education (MS, Certificate). *Application deadline:* For fall admission, 5/1 for domestic students; for spring admission, 11/1 for domestic students. *Application fee:* $60 ($65 for international students). Electronic applications accepted. *Application Contact:* Ky Shaw, Graduate Admissions Coordinator, 317-278-6778, E-mail: kycshaw@iupui.edu. *Executive Associate Dean,* Dr. Robin Hughes, 317-274-6817, E-mail: roblhugh@iupui.edu.

School of Engineering and Technology Students: 236 full-time (35 women), 208 part-time (56 women); includes 41 minority (21 Black or African American, non-Hispanic/Latino; 11 Asian, non-Hispanic/Latino; 8 Hispanic/Latino; 1 Two or more races, non-Hispanic/Latino), 289 international. Average age 27. 454 applicants, 64% accepted, 158 enrolled. *Faculty:* 71 full-time (17 women), 20 part-time/adjunct (6 women). Expenses: Contact institution. *Financial support:* In 2016–17, 4 fellowships with full tuition reimbursements (averaging $17,250 per year), 62 research assistantships with full tuition reimbursements (averaging $15,000 per year), 38 teaching assistantships with full and partial tuition reimbursements (averaging $13,000 per year) were awarded; scholarships/grants, tuition waivers (full and partial), and unspecified assistantships also available. Financial award application deadline: 1/2. In 2016, 153 master's awarded. *Program availability:* Part-time, evening/weekend. Offers applied data management and analytics (MS); biomedical engineering (MS, PhD); electrical and computer engineering (MS, PhD); engineering (MSE); engineering and technology (MS, MS Bm E, MSE, MSME, PhD); facilities management (MS); information security and assurance (MS);

mechanical engineering (MSME, PhD); motorsports (MS); music technology (MS, PhD); music therapy (MS); organizational leadership (MS); technical communication (MS). *Application deadline:* For fall admission, 5/1 for domestic students. *Application fee:* $55 ($65 for international students). Electronic applications accepted. *Application Contact:* Valerie Lim Diemer, Director of Graduate Programs and Admissions, 317-278-4961, E-mail: wvlim@iupui.edu. *Dean*, Dr. David J. Russomanno, 317-274-0802, E-mail: drussoma@iupui.edu.

School of Liberal Arts Students: 115 full-time (72 women), 111 part-time (67 women); includes 41 minority (19 Black or African American, non-Hispanic/Latino; 1 American Indian or Alaska Native, non-Hispanic/Latino; 5 Asian, non-Hispanic/Latino; 14 Hispanic/Latino; 2 Two or more races, non-Hispanic/Latino), 29 international. Average age 33. 187 applicants, 61% accepted, 67 enrolled. Expenses: Contact institution. In 2016, 91 master's, 1 doctorate, 16 other advanced degrees awarded. Offers American philosophy (Certificate); applied communication (MA); bioethics (Certificate); economics (MA); English (MA); European history (MA); general sociology (MA); geographic information systems (MS, Certificate); health communication (PhD); liberal arts (MA, MS, PhD, Certificate); medical sociology (MA); museum studies (MA, Certificate); philosophy (MA); philosophy/bioethics (MA); political science (MA); public history (MA); teaching English to speakers of other languages (TESOL) (MA, Certificate); teaching literature (Certificate); teaching writing (Certificate); United States history (MA). *Application fee:* $55 ($65 for international students). *Application Contact:* Candice L. Smith, Coordinator of Academic and Graduate Programs, 317-274-8305, E-mail: canlsmit@iupui.edu. *Dean, School of Liberal Arts*, Dr. William Blomquist, 317-274-8448, E-mail: blomquis@iupui.edu.

School of Nursing Students: 54 full-time (49 women), 282 part-time (250 women); includes 45 minority (13 Black or African American, non-Hispanic/Latino; 1 American Indian or Alaska Native, non-Hispanic/Latino; 10 Asian, non-Hispanic/Latino; 14 Hispanic/Latino; 7 Two or more races, non-Hispanic/Latino), 5 international. Average age 38. 205 applicants, 78% accepted, 97 enrolled. *Faculty:* 38 full-time (all women), 13 part-time/adjunct (all women). Expenses: Contact institution. *Financial support:* In 2016–17, 123 students received support, including 165 fellowships (averaging $8,152 per year); research assistantships with full tuition reimbursements available, teaching assistantships, Federal Work-Study, institutionally sponsored loans, scholarships/grants, traineeships, tuition waivers (full and partial), and unspecified assistantships also available. Support available to part-time students. Financial award application deadline: 5/1; financial award applicants required to submit FAFSA. In 2016, 137 master's, 28 doctorates awarded. *Program availability:* Part-time, blended/hybrid learning. Offers adult/gerontology acute care nurse practitioner (MSN); adult/gerontology clinical nurse specialist (MSN); adult/gerontology primary care nurse practitioner (MSN); clinical nursing science (PhD); executive leadership (DNP); family nurse practitioner (MSN); health systems (PhD); nursing (MSN, DNP, PhD); nursing education (MSN); nursing leadership in health systems (MSN); pediatric clinical nurse specialist (MSN); pediatric nurse practitioner (MSN). *Application deadline:* For fall admission, 2/15 for domestic students; for spring admission, 9/15 for domestic students. *Application fee:* $60 ($65 for international students). Electronic applications accepted. *Dean/Professor*, Dr. Robin P. Newhouse, 317-274-1485, Fax: 317-278-1842, E-mail: newhouse@iu.edu.

School of Physical Education and Tourism Management Students: 18 full-time (9 women), 16 part-time (8 women); includes 4 minority (3 Black or African American, non-Hispanic/Latino; 1 Hispanic/Latino), 1 international. Average age 26. 22 applicants, 86% accepted, 13 enrolled. *Faculty:* 15 full-time (4 women). Expenses: Contact institution. *Financial support:* In 2016–17, 15 students received support. Teaching assistantships, unspecified assistantships, and assistantships with community partners available. Financial award application deadline: 3/15; financial award applicants required to submit FAFSA. In 2016, 11 master's awarded. Offers event tourism (MS); kinesiology (MS); public health (Graduate Certificate). *Application fee:* $60 ($65 for international students). Electronic applications accepted. *Assistant Professor and Director of Graduate Program*, Dr. Zachary Riley, 317-274-0600, Fax: 317-278-2041, E-mail: zariley@iupui.edu.

School of Public and Environmental Affairs *Program availability:* Part-time, evening/weekend, online learning. Offers criminal justice and public safety (MS); homeland security and emergency management (Graduate Certificate); library management (Graduate Certificate); nonprofit management (Graduate Certificate); public affairs (MPA); public management (Graduate Certificate); social entrepreneurship; nonprofit and public benefit organizations (Graduate Certificate). Electronic applications accepted.

School of Social Work Students: 366 full-time (306 women), 290 part-time (240 women); includes 134 minority (71 Black or African American, non-Hispanic/Latino; 9 Asian, non-Hispanic/Latino; 35 Hispanic/Latino; 19 Two or more races, non-Hispanic/Latino), 13 international. Average age 34. 343 applicants, 60% accepted, 167 enrolled. *Faculty:* 40 full-time. Expenses: Contact institution. *Financial support:* Fellowships with full tuition reimbursements, research assistantships with partial tuition reimbursements, teaching assistantships, Federal Work-Study, institutionally sponsored loans, scholarships/grants, and tuition waivers (partial) available. Support available to part-time students. Financial award applicants required to submit FAFSA. In 2016, 226 master's, 7 doctorates awarded. *Program availability:* Part-time, evening/weekend. Offers social work (MSW, PhD, Certificate). *Application fee:* $55 ($65 for international students). *Application Contact:* Marlo Dale, Information Contact for MSW, 317-274-6966. *Dean*, Dr. Margaret Adamek, 317-274-6730, Fax: 317-274-8630.

INDIANA UNIVERSITY SOUTH BEND, South Bend, IN 46634-7111

General Information State-supported, coed, comprehensive institution. *Enrollment:* 7,185 graduate, professional, and undergraduate students; 136 full-time matriculated graduate/professional students (92 women), 393 part-time matriculated graduate/professional students (261 women). *Enrollment by degree level:* 467 master's, 59 other advanced degrees. *Graduate faculty:* 199 full-time (82 women). *Graduate housing:* On-campus housing not available. *Student services:* Campus employment opportunities, campus safety program, career counseling, child daycare facilities, exercise/wellness program, free psychological counseling, international student services, low-cost health insurance, services for students with disabilities. *Library facilities:* Franklin D. Schurz Library. *Collection:* Books: 523,612 (physical), 364,427 (digital/electronic); Serial titles: 39,990 (physical), 16,293 (digital/electronic); Databases: 315. Students can reserve study rooms.

Computer facilities: 775 computers available on campus for general student use. A campuswide network can be accessed from student residence rooms and from off campus. Online class registration is available. Website: http://www.iusb.edu/

General Application Contact: Admissions Counselor, 574-520-4839, Fax: 574-520-4834, E-mail: graduate@iusb.edu.

GRADUATE UNITS

College of Liberal Arts and Sciences Students: 31 full-time (11 women), 92 part-time (53 women); includes 28 minority (9 Black or African American, non-Hispanic/Latino; 8 Asian, non-Hispanic/Latino; 5 Hispanic/Latino; 6 Two or more races, non-Hispanic/Latino), 19 international. Average age 38. 51 applicants, 84% accepted, 31 enrolled. *Faculty:* 79 full-time (33 women). Expenses: Contact institution. *Financial support:* In 2016–17, 5 teaching assistantships were awarded; Federal Work-Study also available. Support available to part-time students. Financial award application deadline: 3/10. In 2016, 30 master's, 6 other advanced degrees awarded. *Program availability:* Part-time, evening/weekend. Offers advanced computer programming (Graduate Certificate); applied informatics (Graduate Certificate); applied mathematics and computer science (MS); behavior modification (Graduate Certificate); computer applications (Graduate Certificate); computer programming (Graduate Certificate); correctional management and supervision (Graduate Certificate); English (MA); health systems management (Graduate Certificate); international studies (Graduate Certificate); liberal studies (MLS); nonprofit management (Graduate Certificate); paralegal studies (Graduate Certificate); professional writing (Graduate Certificate); public affairs (MPA); public management (Graduate Certificate); social and cultural diversity (Graduate Certificate); strategic sustainability leadership (Graduate Certificate); technology for administration (Graduate Certificate). *Application deadline:* For fall admission, 7/31 priority date for domestic students, 7/1 priority date for international students; for spring admission, 3/31 priority date for domestic students, 11/1 priority date for international students. Applications are processed on a rolling basis. *Application fee:* $40 ($60 for international students). *Application Contact:* Admissions Counselor, 574-520-4839, Fax: 574-520-4834, E-mail: graduate@iusb.edu. *Dean*, Dr. Elizabeth E. Dunn, 574-520-4290, E-mail: elizdunn@iusb.edu.

Ernestine M. Raclin School of the Arts Students: 2 full-time (1 woman), 11 part-time (3 women); includes 2 minority (1 Black or African American, non-Hispanic/Latino; 1 Hispanic/Latino), 3 international. Average age 32. 23 applicants, 65% accepted, 6 enrolled. *Faculty:* 1 full-time (0 women). Expenses: Contact institution. *Financial support:* Fellowships, teaching assistantships, and Federal Work-Study available. Support available to part-time students. Financial award application deadline: 3/1; financial award applicants required to submit FAFSA. In 2016, 4 master's awarded. *Program availability:* Part-time. Offers communication studies (MA); music (MM); music performance (AD). *Application deadline:* For fall admission, 7/1 priority date for domestic students; for spring admission, 11/1 for domestic students. Applications are processed on a rolling basis. *Application fee:* $40 ($60 for international students). Electronic applications accepted. *Application Contact:* Admissions Counselor, 574-520-4839, Fax: 574-520-4834, E-mail: graduate@iusb.edu. *Dean*, Dr. Marvin V. Curtis, 574-520-4170, E-mail: mvcurtis@iusb.edu.

Judd Leighton School of Business and Economics Students: 28 full-time (18 women), 85 part-time (36 women); includes 10 minority (3 Black or African American, non-Hispanic/Latino; 1 Asian, non-Hispanic/Latino; 5 Hispanic/Latino; 1 Two or more races, non-Hispanic/Latino), 22 international. Average age 32. 57 applicants, 68% accepted, 22 enrolled. *Faculty:* 17 full-time (2 women), 3 part-time/adjunct (1 woman). Expenses: Contact institution. *Financial support:* Fellowships, Federal Work-Study, and institutionally sponsored loans available. Support available to part-time students. Financial award application deadline: 7/1; financial award applicants required to submit FAFSA. In 2016, 67 master's, 7 other advanced degrees awarded. *Program availability:* Part-time, evening/weekend. Offers accounting (MSA); business (Graduate Certificate); business administration (MBA). *Application deadline:* For fall admission, 7/15 priority date for domestic and international students; for spring admission, 11/15 priority date for domestic and international students; for summer admission, 4/1 priority date for domestic and international students. Applications are processed on a rolling basis. *Application fee:* $40 ($60 for international students). Electronic applications accepted. *Application Contact:* 574-520-4839, Fax: 574-520-4834, E-mail: graduate@iusb.edu. *Dean*, Richard Kolbe, 574-520-4228, Fax: 574-520-4866, E-mail: rkolbe@iusb.edu.

School of Education Students: 26 full-time (19 women), 104 part-time (80 women); includes 22 minority (13 Black or African American, non-Hispanic/Latino; 5 Hispanic/Latino; 4 Two or more races, non-Hispanic/Latino). Average age 35. 51 applicants, 69% accepted, 22 enrolled. *Faculty:* 21 full-time (11 women), 9 part-time/adjunct (3 women). Expenses: Contact institution. *Financial support:* Career-related internships or fieldwork available. Support available to part-time students. Financial award application deadline: 3/1; financial award applicants required to submit FAFSA. In 2016, 31 master's, 2 other advanced degrees awarded. *Program availability:* Part-time, evening/weekend. Offers addiction counseling (MS Ed); alcohol and drug counseling (Graduate Certificate); clinical mental health counseling (MS Ed); educational leadership (MS Ed); elementary education (MS Ed); marriage, couple, and family counseling (MS Ed); school counseling (MS Ed); secondary education (MAT, MS Ed); special education (MAT, MS Ed). *Application deadline:* For fall admission, 7/1 for domestic students; for spring admission, 11/1 for domestic students. Applications are processed on a rolling basis. *Application fee:* $40 ($60 for international students). Electronic applications accepted. *Application Contact:* Yvonne Walker, Student Services Representative, 574-520-4185, E-mail: ydwalker@iusb.edu. *Dean*, Dr. Marvin Lynn, 574-520-4339, E-mail: lynnm@iusb.edu.

School of Social Work Students: 49 full-time (43 women), 74 part-time (62 women); includes 27 minority (19 Black or African American, non-Hispanic/Latino; 5 Hispanic/Latino; 3 Two or more races, non-Hispanic/Latino), 1 international. Average age 33. 68 applicants, 81% accepted, 49 enrolled. *Faculty:* 4 full-time (2 women). Expenses: Contact institution. *Financial support:* Career-related internships or fieldwork and Federal Work-Study available. Support available to part-time students. Financial award application deadline: 3/1; financial award applicants required to submit FAFSA. In 2016, 22 master's awarded. *Program availability:* Part-time, evening/weekend. Offers social work (MSW). *Application deadline:* For fall admission, 2/1 priority date for domestic students. Applications are processed on a rolling basis. *Application fee:* $40 ($60 for international students). *Application Contact:* Diane Banic, Administrative Assistant, 574-520-4880, E-mail: dbanic@iusb.edu. *Dean*, Dr. Michael A Patchner, 574-520-4880, Fax: 574-520-4876.

Vera Z. Dwyer College of Health Sciences Students: 27 part-time (all women); includes 7 minority (2 Black or African American, non-Hispanic/Latino; 1 American Indian or Alaska Native, non-Hispanic/Latino; 3 Hispanic/Latino; 1 Two or more races, non-Hispanic/Latino). Average age 35. 21 applicants, 90% accepted, 1 enrolled. Expenses: Contact institution. In 2016, 17 master's awarded. Offers health sciences (MSN). *Application fee:* $40 ($60 for international students). *Application Contact:* Admissions Counselor, 574-520-4839, Fax: 574-520-4834, E-mail: graduate@iusb.edu. *Interim Dean*, Dr. Karen R. Clark, 574-520-5511, Fax: 574-520-4461.

School of Nursing Students: 27 part-time (all women); includes 7 minority (2 Black or African American, non-Hispanic/Latino; 1 American Indian or Alaska Native, non-Hispanic/Latino; 3 Hispanic/Latino; 1 Two or more races, non-Hispanic/Latino). Average age 35. 21 applicants, 90% accepted, 1 enrolled. *Faculty:* 4 full-time (all women). Expenses: Contact institution. *Financial support:* Teaching assistantships and Federal Work-Study available. Support available to part-time students. Financial award application deadline: 3/1; financial award applicants required to submit FAFSA. In 2016, 17 master's awarded. *Program availability:* Part-time, evening/weekend. Offers family nurse practitioner (MSN). *Application deadline:* For fall admission, 4/1 for domestic students. *Application Contact:* Admissions Counselor, 574-520-4839, Fax: 574-520-4834, E-mail: graduate@iusb.edu. *Interim Dean,* Dr. Karen R. Clark, 574-520-5511.

INDIANA UNIVERSITY SOUTHEAST, New Albany, IN 47150-6405

General Information State-supported, coed, comprehensive institution. *Enrollment:* 5,874 graduate, professional, and undergraduate students; 28 full-time matriculated graduate/professional students (12 women), 361 part-time matriculated graduate/professional students (222 women). *Enrollment by degree level:* 324 master's. *Graduate faculty:* 144 full-time (69 women). *Graduate housing:* On-campus housing not available. *Student services:* Campus employment opportunities, campus safety program, career counseling, child daycare facilities, free psychological counseling, low-cost health insurance, multicultural affairs office, services for students with disabilities. *Library facilities:* IU Southeast Library. *Collection:* Books: 400,000 (physical), 590,000 (digital/electronic); Serial titles: 35,780 (physical), 60,000 (digital/electronic); Databases: 300. Students can reserve study rooms.

Computer facilities: 924 computers available on campus for general student use. A campuswide network can be accessed from student residence rooms and from off campus. Online class registration is available.
Website: http://www.ius.edu/

General Application Contact: Admissions Counselor, 812-941-2212, Fax: 812-941-2595, E-mail: admissions@ius.edu.

GRADUATE UNITS

Master of Interdisciplinary Studies Program Students: 1 full-time (0 women), 25 part-time (20 women); includes 5 minority (4 Black or African American, non-Hispanic/Latino; 1 American Indian or Alaska Native, non-Hispanic/Latino). Average age 40. 12 applicants, 83% accepted, 10 enrolled. Expenses: Contact institution. *Financial support:* Fellowships and scholarships/grants available. Financial award applicants required to submit FAFSA. In 2016, 2 master's, 3 other advanced degrees awarded. *Program availability:* Part-time. Offers interdisciplinary studies (MIS, Graduate Certificate). *Application deadline:* For fall admission, 8/10 for domestic and international students; for spring admission, 1/2 for domestic and international students; for summer admission, 4/15 for domestic and international students. *Application fee:* $40. Electronic applications accepted. *MLS Director,* Dr. Deborah Finkel, 812-941-2668, E-mail: dfinkel@ius.edu.

School of Business Students: 14 full-time (2 women), 145 part-time (51 women); includes 19 minority (5 Black or African American, non-Hispanic/Latino; 5 Asian, non-Hispanic/Latino; 4 Hispanic/Latino; 5 Two or more races, non-Hispanic/Latino), 2 international. Average age 32. 52 applicants, 69% accepted, 32 enrolled. *Faculty:* 11 full-time (2 women). Expenses: Contact institution. *Financial support:* In 2016–17, 2 teaching assistantships (averaging $4,500 per year) were awarded. Financial award applicants required to submit FAFSA. In 2016, 50 master's awarded. *Program availability:* Part-time. Offers business administration (MBA); strategic finance (MS). *Application deadline:* For fall admission, 7/20 for domestic and international students; for spring admission, 11/30 for domestic and international students; for summer admission, 4/15 for domestic and international students. *Application fee:* $40 ($60 for international students). Electronic applications accepted. *Application Contact:* Admissions Counselor, 812-941-2212, Fax: 812-941-2595, E-mail: admissions@ius.edu. *Director of Graduate Business Programs,* Sharon Allen, 812-941-2364, E-mail: allen81@ius.edu.

School of Education Students: 13 full-time (10 women), 190 part-time (150 women); includes 29 minority (21 Black or African American, non-Hispanic/Latino; 5 Hispanic/Latino; 3 Two or more races, non-Hispanic/Latino). Average age 33. 61 applicants, 84% accepted, 43 enrolled. Expenses: Contact institution. *Financial support:* Career-related internships or fieldwork, Federal Work-Study, and institutionally sponsored loans available. Support available to part-time students. Financial award applicants required to submit FAFSA. In 2016, 70 master's awarded. *Program availability:* Part-time, evening/weekend. Offers counselor education (MS Ed); elementary education (MS Ed); secondary education (MS Ed). *Application deadline:* Applications are processed on a rolling basis. *Application fee:* $40 ($60 for international students). Electronic applications accepted. *Application Contact:* Admissions Counselor, 812-941-2212, Fax: 812-941-2595, E-mail: admissions@ius.edu. *Director of Graduate Studies,* Dr. Faye Marsha Camahalan, 812-941-2136, Fax: 812-941-2667, E-mail: fcamahal@ius.edu.

INDIANA WESLEYAN UNIVERSITY, Marion, IN 46953-4974

General Information Independent-religious, coed, comprehensive institution. *Enrollment:* 3,687 full-time matriculated graduate/professional students (2,459 women), 384 part-time matriculated graduate/professional students (218 women). *Enrollment by degree level:* 3,866 master's, 205 doctoral. *Graduate faculty:* 92 full-time (37 women), 529 part-time/adjunct (248 women). *Graduate housing:* On-campus housing not available. *Student services:* Campus employment opportunities, campus safety program, career counseling, free psychological counseling, multicultural affairs office, services for students with disabilities, teacher training, writing training. *Library facilities:* Lewis A. Jackson Library. *Collection:* Students can reserve study rooms. *Research affiliation:* Eli Lilly and Company.

Computer facilities: A campuswide network can be accessed from student residence rooms and from off campus. Online class registration is available.
Website: http://www.indwes.edu/

General Application Contact: Graduate School, 866-IWU-4-YOU, Fax: 765-677-2541, E-mail: graduate@indwes.edu.

GRADUATE UNITS

College of Adult and Professional Studies *Program availability:* Part-time, evening/weekend, online learning. Offers accounting (MBA, Graduate Certificate); applied management (MBA); business administration (MBA); health care (MBA, Graduate Certificate); human resources (MBA, Graduate Certificate); management (MS); organizational leadership (Ed D). Electronic applications accepted.

School of Educational Leadership *Program availability:* Part-time, evening/weekend, online learning. Offers educational leadership (M Ed, Ed S). Electronic applications accepted.

Graduate School *Program availability:* Part-time, evening/weekend, online learning. Electronic applications accepted.

College of Arts and Sciences *Program availability:* Part-time. Offers addictions counseling (MS); clinical mental health counseling (MS); community counseling (MS);

marriage and family therapy (MS); school counseling (MS); student development counseling and administration (MS). Electronic applications accepted.

School of Nursing *Program availability:* Part-time, online learning. Offers nursing administration (MS); nursing education (MS); primary care nursing (MS).

Wesley Seminary Offers children, youth and family ministry (MA); divinity (M Div); ministerial leadership (MA); ministry (MA).

INSTITUTE FOR CHRISTIAN STUDIES, Toronto, ON M5T 1R4, Canada

General Information Independent-religious, coed, graduate-only institution. *Graduate housing:* On-campus housing not available.

GRADUATE UNITS

Graduate Programs *Program availability:* Part-time, online learning. Offers education (M Phil F, PhD); history of philosophy (M Phil F, PhD); philosophical aesthetics (M Phil F, PhD); philosophy of religion (M Phil F, PhD); political theory (M Phil F, PhD); systematic philosophy (M Phil F, PhD); theology (M Phil F, PhD); worldview studies (MWS).

INSTITUTE FOR CLINICAL SOCIAL WORK, Chicago, IL 60601

General Information Independent, coed, primarily women, graduate-only institution. *Graduate housing:* On-campus housing not available.

GRADUATE UNITS

Graduate Programs *Program availability:* Part-time. Offers clinical social work (PhD).

INSTITUTE FOR DOCTORAL STUDIES IN THE VISUAL ARTS, Portland, ME 04102

General Information Independent, coed, graduate-only institution. *Enrollment by degree level:* 56 doctoral. *Graduate faculty:* 3 full-time, 7 part-time/adjunct.
Website: http://www.idsva.org/

General Application Contact: Molly M. Davis, Director of Administration/Co-Director of Admissions, 207-771-8887, E-mail: info@idsva.edu.

GRADUATE UNITS

PhD Program in Visual Art: Philosophy, Aesthetics, and Art Theory Students: 56 full-time. *Faculty:* 3 full-time, 7 part-time/adjunct. Expenses: Contact institution. *Financial support:* Fellowships, teaching assistantships, and scholarships/grants available. Financial award applicants required to submit FAFSA. *Program availability:* Online learning. Offers aesthetics (PhD); art theory (PhD); philosophy (PhD). *Application deadline:* Applications are processed on a rolling basis. *Application fee:* $56. Electronic applications accepted. *Application Contact:* Molly M. Davis, Director of Administration/Co-Director of Admissions, 207-771-8887, E-mail: info@idsva.edu.

THE INSTITUTE FOR THE PSYCHOLOGICAL SCIENCES, Arlington, VA 30327

General Information Independent-religious, coed, graduate-only institution.

GRADUATE UNITS

Program in Clinical Psychology *Program availability:* Part-time. Offers clinical psychology (MS, Psy D).

INSTITUTE OF AMERICAN INDIAN ARTS, Santa Fe, NM 87508

General Information Federally supported, coed, comprehensive institution. *Enrollment:* 597 graduate, professional, and undergraduate students; 58 full-time matriculated graduate/professional students (34 women), 2 part-time matriculated graduate/professional students (both women). *Enrollment by degree level:* 60 master's. Tuition, state resident: full-time $10,680; part-time $445 per semester hour. Tuition, nonresident: full-time $10,680; part-time $445 per semester hour. *Required fees:* $720; $360 per semester. *Graduate housing:* On-campus housing not available. *Student services:* Campus safety program, career counseling, exercise/wellness program, services for students with disabilities. *Library facilities:* IAIA Library plus 1 other. *Collection:* Students can reserve study rooms.

Computer facilities: 50 computers available on campus for general student use. A campuswide network can be accessed from student residence rooms. Online class registration is available.
Website: http://www.iaia.edu/

General Application Contact: Jon Davis, Director, Low Residency MFA in Creative Writing, 505-424-2365, Fax: 505-424-3030, E-mail: jdavis@iaia.edu.

GRADUATE UNITS

Low Residency MFA in Creative Writing Program Students: 58 full-time (34 women), 2 part-time (both women); includes 38 minority (1 Black or African American, non-Hispanic/Latino; 27 American Indian or Alaska Native, non-Hispanic/Latino; 7 Hispanic/Latino; 3 Two or more races, non-Hispanic/Latino). Expenses: Contact institution. *Financial support:* Scholarships/grants available. Financial award application deadline: 1/31; financial award applicants required to submit FAFSA. In 2016, 26 master's awarded. *Program availability:* Low-residency. Offers creative writing (MFA). *Application deadline:* For fall admission, 1/31 for domestic and international students. *Application fee:* $25. Electronic applications accepted. *Director, Low Residency MFA in Creative Writing,* Jon Davis, 505-424-2365, Fax: 505-424-3030, E-mail: mfa@iaia.edu.

INSTITUTE OF CLINICAL ACUPUNCTURE AND ORIENTAL MEDICINE, Honolulu, HI 96817

General Information Proprietary, coed, graduate-only institution.

GRADUATE UNITS

Program in Oriental Medicine Offers Oriental medicine (MSOM).

INSTITUTE OF PUBLIC ADMINISTRATION, Dublin 4, Ireland

General Information Proprietary, coed, comprehensive institution.

GRADUATE UNITS

Programs in Public Administration Offers healthcare management (MA); local government management (MA); public management (MA, Diploma).

INSTITUTE OF TAOIST EDUCATION AND ACUPUNCTURE, Louisville, CO 80027

General Information Independent, coed, graduate-only institution.

GRADUATE UNITS

Graduate Program Offers classical five-element acupuncture (M Ac).

THE INSTITUTE OF WORLD POLITICS, Washington, DC 20036

General Information Independent, coed, graduate-only institution. *Graduate housing:* On-campus housing not available.

GRADUATE UNITS

Graduate Programs in National Security, Intelligence, and International Affairs *Program availability:* Part-time, evening/weekend. Offers American foreign policy (Certificate); comparative political culture (Certificate); counterintelligence (Certificate); democracy building (Certificate); intelligence (Certificate); international politics (Certificate); national security affairs (Certificate); public diplomacy and political warfare (Certificate); statecraft and national security affairs (MA); statecraft and world politics (MA); strategic intelligence studies (MA). Electronic applications accepted.

INSTITUT FRANCO-EUROPÉEN DE CHIROPRAXIE, F-94200 Ivry-sur-Seine, France

General Information Independent, coed, graduate-only institution.

GRADUATE UNITS

Professional Program Offers chiropractic (DC).

INSTITUTO CENTROAMERICANO DE ADMINISTRACIÓN DE EMPRESAS, La Garita, Alajuela, Costa Rica

General Information Independent, coed, graduate-only institution. *Graduate housing:* Rooms and/or apartments guaranteed to single students and available to married students. *Research affiliation:* Tropical Agricultural Research and Higher Education Center (agribusiness), Harvard Institute for International Development (macroeconomics and environment), Earth University (agribusiness), Inter-American Institute for Cooperation on Agriculture (agribusiness), David Rockefeller Center for Latin American Studies (competitiveness), Zamarano (agribusiness).

GRADUATE UNITS

Graduate Programs Offers agribusiness management (MIAM); business administration (EMBA); finance (MBA); real estate management (MGREM); sustainable development (MBA); technology (MBA). Electronic applications accepted.

INSTITUTO TECNOLÓGICO Y DE ESTUDIOS SUPERIORES DE MONTERREY, CAMPUS CENTRAL DE VERACRUZ, 94500 Córdoba, Veracruz, Mexico

General Information Independent, coed, comprehensive institution.

GRADUATE UNITS

Graduate Programs *Program availability:* Part-time, evening/weekend, online learning. Electronic applications accepted.

INSTITUTO TECNOLÓGICO Y DE ESTUDIOS SUPERIORES DE MONTERREY, CAMPUS CHIAPAS, 29000 Tuxtla Gutiérrez, Chiapas, Mexico

General Information Independent, coed, comprehensive institution.

INSTITUTO TECNOLÓGICO Y DE ESTUDIOS SUPERIORES DE MONTERREY, CAMPUS CHIHUAHUA, 31300 Chihuahua, Chihuahua, Mexico

General Information Independent, coed, comprehensive institution.

GRADUATE UNITS

Graduate Programs Offers computer systems engineering (Ingeniero); electrical engineering (Ingeniero); electromechanical engineering (Ingeniero); electronic engineering (Ingeniero); engineering administration (MEA); industrial engineering (MIE, Ingeniero); international trade (MIT); mechanical engineering (Ingeniero).

INSTITUTO TECNOLÓGICO Y DE ESTUDIOS SUPERIORES DE MONTERREY, CAMPUS CIUDAD DE MÉXICO, 14380 Ciudad de Mexico, DF, Mexico

General Information Independent, coed, comprehensive institution. *Graduate housing:* On-campus housing not available. *Research affiliation:* McGill University (management), Concordia University (business and management), Eli Lilly S. A. de C. U. (technological development), Ford Motor Company (industrial organizations), German Research Center on Artificial Intelligence (informatics), Brent University (telecommunications).

GRADUATE UNITS

School of Business Administration *Program availability:* Part-time, evening/weekend, online learning. Offers business administration (EMBA, MBA, PhD); economy (MBA); finance (MBA). EMBA program offered jointly with The University of Texas at Austin.

School of Design, Engineering and Architecture *Program availability:* Part-time, evening/weekend, online learning. Offers management (MA); telecommunications (MA).

School of Humanities and Social Sciences *Program availability:* Part-time, evening/weekend. Offers humanities and social sciences (LL B).

Virtual University Division *Program availability:* Part-time, evening/weekend, online learning.

INSTITUTO TECNOLÓGICO Y DE ESTUDIOS SUPERIORES DE MONTERREY, CAMPUS CIUDAD JUÁREZ, 32320 Ciudad Juárez, Chihuahua, Mexico

General Information Independent, coed, comprehensive institution.

GRADUATE UNITS

Program in Administration of Information Technology Offers administration of information technology (MAIT).

Program in Applied Public Management Offers applied public management (MPM).

Program in Business Administration *Program availability:* Part-time, online learning. Offers business administration (MBA).

Program in Education Offers education (M Ed).

Program in Educational Administration Offers educational administration (MEA).

Program in Educational Innovation Offers educational innovation (DE).

Program in Educational Technology Offers educational technology (MTE).

Program in Electronic Commerce Offers electronic commerce (MEC).

Program in Humanistic Studies Offers humanistic studies (MEH).

Program in Quality Management Offers quality management (MQM).

INSTITUTO TECNOLÓGICO Y DE ESTUDIOS SUPERIORES DE MONTERREY, CAMPUS CIUDAD OBREGÓN, 85000 Ciudad Obregón, Sonora, Mexico

General Information Independent, coed, comprehensive institution.

GRADUATE UNITS

Program in Administration Offers administration (MA).

Program in Administration of Information Technology Offers administration of information technology (MATI).

Program in Administration of Telecommunications Offers administration of telecommunications (MAT).

Program in Engineering Offers engineering (ME).

Program in Finance Offers finance (MF).

Program in International Relations Offers international relations (MIR).

Program in Marketing Technology Offers marketing technology (MMT).

Programs in Education Offers cognitive development (ME); communications (ME); mathematics (ME).

INSTITUTO TECNOLÓGICO Y DE ESTUDIOS SUPERIORES DE MONTERREY, CAMPUS COLIMA, 28010 Colima, Colima, Mexico

General Information Independent, coed, comprehensive institution.

INSTITUTO TECNOLÓGICO Y DE ESTUDIOS SUPERIORES DE MONTERREY, CAMPUS CUERNAVACA, 62000 Temixco, Morelos, Mexico

General Information Independent, coed, comprehensive institution.

GRADUATE UNITS

Programs in Business Administration Offers finance (MA); human resources management (MA); international business (MA); marketing (MA).

Programs in Information Science Offers administration of information technology (MATI); computer science (MCC, DCC); information technology (MTI).

INSTITUTO TECNOLÓGICO Y DE ESTUDIOS SUPERIORES DE MONTERREY, CAMPUS ESTADO DE MÉXICO, Estado de Mexico 52926, Mexico

General Information Independent, coed, comprehensive institution. *Graduate housing:* On-campus housing not available. *Research affiliation:* Transportadora San Marcos, S. A. de C. V. (quality control), Microsoft Visual Studio (computer science), Texas Instruments (semiconductors), Sony Electronics (new products), Kaltex (quality control).

GRADUATE UNITS

Professional and Graduate Division *Program availability:* Part-time, online learning. Offers administration of information technologies (MITA); architecture (M Arch); business administration (GMBA, MBA); computer sciences (MCS, PhD); education (M Ed); educational institution administration (MAD); educational technology and innovation (PhD); electronic commerce (MEC); environmental systems (MS); finance (MAF); humanistic studies (MHS); information sciences and knowledge management (MISKM); information systems (MS); manufacturing systems (MS); marketing (MEM); quality systems and productivity (MS); science and materials engineering (PhD); telecommunications management (MTM).

INSTITUTO TECNOLÓGICO Y DE ESTUDIOS SUPERIORES DE MONTERREY, CAMPUS GUADALAJARA, 45140 Zapopan, Jalisco, Mexico

General Information Independent, coed, comprehensive institution. *Graduate housing:* Rooms and/or apartments available to single and married students. Housing application deadline: 8/30.

GRADUATE UNITS

Program in Business Administration *Program availability:* Part-time, evening/weekend, online learning. Offers business administration (IEMBA, M Ad).

Program in Finance Offers finance (MF).

INSTITUTO TECNOLÓGICO Y DE ESTUDIOS SUPERIORES DE MONTERREY, CAMPUS HIDALGO, 42090 Pachuca, Hidalgo, Mexico

General Information Independent, coed, comprehensive institution.

INSTITUTO TECNOLÓGICO Y DE ESTUDIOS SUPERIORES DE MONTERREY, CAMPUS IRAPUATO, 36660 Irapuato, Guanajuato, Mexico

General Information Independent, coed, comprehensive institution.

GRADUATE UNITS

Graduate Programs Offers administration (MBA); administration of information technology (MAIT); administration of telecommunications (MAT); architecture (M Arch); computer science (MCS); education (M Ed); educational administration (MEA); educational innovation and technology (DEIT); educational technology (MET); electronic commerce (MBA); environmental administration and planning (MEAP); environmental systems (MES); finances (MBA); humanistic studies (MHS); international management for Latin American executives (MIMLAE); library and information science (MLIS); manufacturing quality management (MMQM); marketing research (MBA).

INSTITUTO TECNOLÓGICO Y DE ESTUDIOS SUPERIORES DE MONTERREY, CAMPUS LAGUNA, 27250 Torreón, Coahuila, Mexico

General Information Independent, coed, comprehensive institution. *Graduate housing:* On-campus housing not available.

GRADUATE UNITS

Graduate School *Program availability:* Part-time. Offers business administration (MBA); industrial engineering (MIE); management information systems (MS).

INSTITUTO TECNOLÓGICO Y DE ESTUDIOS SUPERIORES DE MONTERREY, CAMPUS LEÓN, 37120 León, Guanajuato, Mexico

General Information Independent, coed, comprehensive institution.

GRADUATE UNITS

Program in Business Administration *Program availability:* Part-time. Offers business administration (MBA).

INSTITUTO TECNOLÓGICO Y DE ESTUDIOS SUPERIORES DE MONTERREY, CAMPUS MONTERREY, 64849 Monterrey, Nuevo León, Mexico

General Information Independent, coed, comprehensive institution. *Graduate housing:* Room and/or apartments available to single students; on-campus housing not available to married students. *Research affiliation:* IBM de Mexico (computer science), Southwest Research Institute (environment), Hylsa (steel), Vitro (glass products), Cydsa (petrochemicals), Cemex (cement).

GRADUATE UNITS

Graduate and Research Division *Program availability:* Part-time, evening/weekend. Offers agricultural parasitology (PhD); agricultural sciences (MS); applied statistics (M Eng); artificial intelligence (PhD); automation engineering (M Eng); biotechnology (MS); chemical engineering (M Eng); chemistry (MS, PhD); civil engineering (M Eng); communications (MS); computer science (MS); education (MA); electrical engineering (M Eng); electronic engineering (M Eng); environmental engineering (M Eng); farming productivity (MS); food processing engineering (MS); industrial engineering (M Eng, PhD); informatics (PhD); information systems (MS); information technology (MS); manufacturing engineering (M Eng); mechanical engineering (M Eng); phytopathology (MS); systems and quality engineering (M Eng).

Graduate School of Business Administration and Leadership *Program availability:* Part-time. Offers business administration (MA, MBA); finance (M Sc); international business (M Sc); management (PhD); management and leadership (M Sc, MA, MBA, PhD); marketing (M Sc).

INSTITUTO TECNOLÓGICO Y DE ESTUDIOS SUPERIORES DE MONTERREY, CAMPUS QUERÉTARO, 76130 Querétaro, Querétaro, Mexico

General Information Independent, coed, comprehensive institution. *Graduate housing:* Room and/or apartments guaranteed to single students; on-campus housing not available to married students. Housing application deadline: 6/15. *Research affiliation:* Transmisiones y Equipos Mecanicos (manufacturing design).

GRADUATE UNITS

School of Business Offers business (MBA).

INSTITUTO TECNOLÓGICO Y DE ESTUDIOS SUPERIORES DE MONTERREY, CAMPUS SALTILLO, 25270 Saltillo, Coahuila, Mexico

General Information Independent, coed, comprehensive institution.

INSTITUTO TECNOLÓGICO Y DE ESTUDIOS SUPERIORES DE MONTERREY, CAMPUS SAN LUIS POTOSÍ, 78140 San Luis Potosí, SLP, Mexico

General Information Independent, coed, comprehensive institution.

INSTITUTO TECNOLÓGICO Y DE ESTUDIOS SUPERIORES DE MONTERREY, CAMPUS SINALOA, 80800 Culiacán, Sinaloa, Mexico

General Information Independent, coed, comprehensive institution.

INSTITUTO TECNOLÓGICO Y DE ESTUDIOS SUPERIORES DE MONTERREY, CAMPUS SONORA NORTE, 83000 Hermosillo, Sonora, Mexico

General Information Independent, coed, comprehensive institution. *Graduate housing:* On-campus housing not available. *Research affiliation:* National Council for Science and Technology (engineering).

GRADUATE UNITS

Program in Business Offers business (MA).

Program in Education Offers education (MA).

Program in Technological Information Management Offers technological information management (MA).

INSTITUTO TECNOLÓGICO Y DE ESTUDIOS SUPERIORES DE MONTERREY, CAMPUS TAMPICO, 89120 Altimira, Tamaulipas, Mexico

General Information Independent, coed, comprehensive institution.

INSTITUTO TECNOLÓGICO Y DE ESTUDIOS SUPERIORES DE MONTERREY, CAMPUS TOLUCA, 50252 Toluca, Estado de Mexico, Mexico

General Information Independent, coed, comprehensive institution.

GRADUATE UNITS

Graduate Programs *Program availability:* Part-time, evening/weekend.

INSTITUTO TECNOLÓGICO Y DE ESTUDIOS SUPERIORES DE MONTERREY, CAMPUS ZACATECAS, 98000 Zacatecas, Zacatecas, Mexico

General Information Independent, coed, comprehensive institution.

INTER AMERICAN UNIVERSITY OF PUERTO RICO, AGUADILLA CAMPUS, Aguadilla, PR 00605

General Information Independent, coed, comprehensive institution.

GRADUATE UNITS

Graduate School *Program availability:* Part-time, evening/weekend. Electronic applications accepted.

INTER AMERICAN UNIVERSITY OF PUERTO RICO, ARECIBO CAMPUS, Arecibo, PR 00614-4050

General Information Independent, coed, comprehensive institution.

GRADUATE UNITS

Program in Anesthesia Offers anesthesia (MS).

Program in Business Administration Offers accounting (MBA); finance (MBA); human resources (MBA).

Program in Nursing Offers critical care nursing (MSN); surgical nursing (MSN).

Programs in Education Offers administration and educational supervision (MA Ed); counseling and guidance (MA Ed); curriculum and teaching (MA Ed); elementary education (MA Ed).

INTER AMERICAN UNIVERSITY OF PUERTO RICO, BARRANQUITAS CAMPUS, Barranquitas, PR 00794

General Information Independent, coed, comprehensive institution. *Graduate housing:* Rooms and/or apartments available to single and married students.

GRADUATE UNITS

Program in Business Administration Offers accounting (IMBA); finance (IMBA).

Program in Education Offers curriculum and teaching (M Ed); educational leadership and management (MA); elementary education (M Ed); information and library service technology (M Ed); special education (MA). Electronic applications accepted.

INTER AMERICAN UNIVERSITY OF PUERTO RICO, BAYAMÓN CAMPUS, Bayamón, PR 00957

General Information Independent, coed, comprehensive institution. *Enrollment:* 4,450 graduate, professional, and undergraduate students; 7 full-time matriculated graduate/professional students (5 women), 115 part-time matriculated graduate/professional students (69 women). *Enrollment by degree level:* 122 master's. *Graduate faculty:* 12 full-time (5 women), 4 part-time/adjunct (2 women). *Tuition:* Part-time $207 per credit. *Required fees:* $328 per semester. *Graduate housing:* Room and/or apartments available on a first-come, first-served basis to single students; on-campus housing not available to married students. Typical cost: $3113 per year ($6114 including board). *Student services:* Career counseling, free psychological counseling, international student services, services for students with disabilities. *Library facilities:* Centro de Acceso a la Informacion plus 1 other. *Collection:* Books: 33,638 (physical), 224,713 (digital/electronic); Serial titles: 147 (physical), 2 (digital/electronic); Databases: 56. Weekly public service hours: 79; students can reserve study rooms. *Research affiliation:* Bayamon Central University.

Computer facilities: 730 computers available on campus for general student use. A campuswide network can be accessed from student residence rooms. Online class registration is available.
Website: http://bayamon.inter.edu/

General Application Contact: Hector Vargas, Interim Director of Admissions, 787-279-1912 Ext. 2017, Fax: 787-279-2205, E-mail: hvargas@bayamon.inter.edu.

GRADUATE UNITS

Graduate School Students: 7 full-time (5 women), 115 part-time (69 women); includes 119 minority (1 Black or African American, non-Hispanic/Latino; 118 Hispanic/Latino). Average age 28. 94 applicants, 72% accepted, 56 enrolled. *Faculty:* 12 full-time (5 women), 4 part-time/adjunct (2 women). Expenses: Contact institution. In 2016, 22 master's awarded. *Program availability:* Part-time, evening/weekend. Offers biology (MS); electrical engineering (ME); human resources (MBA); mechanical engineering (ME, MS). *Application deadline:* For fall admission, 7/1 for domestic students, 5/1 priority date for international students; for winter admission, 11/15 priority date for domestic and international students; for spring admission, 2/15 priority date for domestic and international students. *Application fee:* $31. *Application Contact:* Aurelis Báez, Director of Student Services, 787-279-1912 Ext. 2017, Fax: 787-279-2205, E-mail: abaez@bayamon.inter.edu. *Chancellor,* Prof. Juan F. Martinez, 787-279-1200 Ext. 2295, Fax: 787-279-2205, E-mail: jmartinez@bayamon.inter.edu.

INTER AMERICAN UNIVERSITY OF PUERTO RICO, FAJARDO CAMPUS, Fajardo, PR 00738-7003

General Information Independent, coed, comprehensive institution.

GRADUATE UNITS

Graduate Programs

INTER AMERICAN UNIVERSITY OF PUERTO RICO, GUAYAMA CAMPUS, Guayama, PR 00785

General Information Independent, coed, comprehensive institution.

GRADUATE UNITS

Department of Business Administration Offers marketing (MBA).

Department of Education and Social Sciences *Program availability:* Part-time. Offers early childhood education (0-4 years) (M Ed); elementary education (M Ed). Electronic applications accepted.

Department of Natural and Applied Sciences Offers computer security and networks (MS); networking and security (MCS).

INTER AMERICAN UNIVERSITY OF PUERTO RICO, METROPOLITAN CAMPUS, San Juan, PR 00919-1293

General Information Independent, coed, comprehensive institution. CGS member. *Graduate housing:* On-campus housing not available. *Research affiliation:* Innovation Technology (electronics).

GRADUATE UNITS

Graduate Programs *Program availability:* Part-time, evening/weekend. Offers accounting (MBA); administration of clinical laboratories (MS); advanced clinical services (MSW); advanced social work administration (MSW); American history (PhD); Christian education (PhD); clinical services (MSW); commercial education (MA); counseling psychology (MA, PhD); criminal justice (MA); curriculum and instruction (Ed D); educational administration (Ed D); educational computing (MA); elementary education (MA); English (MA); environmental evaluation and protection (MS); finance (MBA); general business (MBA); guidance and counseling (MA, Ed D); higher education administration (MA); history (MA, PhD); history education (MA); human resources (MBA); industrial management (MBA); industrial/organizational psychology (MA, PhD); international business (MIB); interregional and international business (PhD); labor relations (MA); management information systems (MA); marketing (MBA); molecular microbiology (MS); music education (MM); occupational education (MA); open information systems (MS); pastoral theology (PhD); school psychology (MA, PhD); social work administration (MSW); Spanish (MA); Spanish education (MA); special education (MA); special education administration (Ed D); teaching English as a second language (MA); teaching of math (MA); teaching of physical education (MA); teaching of science (MA); theological studies (PhD); training and sport performance (MA); women's and gender studies (MA). Electronic applications accepted.

INTER AMERICAN UNIVERSITY OF PUERTO RICO, PONCE CAMPUS, Mercedita, PR 00715-1602

General Information Independent, coed, comprehensive institution.

GRADUATE UNITS
Graduate School

INTER AMERICAN UNIVERSITY OF PUERTO RICO, SAN GERMÁN CAMPUS, San Germán, PR 00683-5008

General Information Independent, coed, university. *Graduate housing:* Room and/or apartments available on a first-come, first-served basis to single students; on-campus housing not available to married students. Housing application deadline: 6/15.

GRADUATE UNITS
Graduate Studies Center *Program availability:* Part-time, evening/weekend. Offers accounting (MBA); applied mathematics (MA); business education (MA); counseling psychology (MA, PhD); curriculum and instruction (Ed D); drawing (MFA); education: counseling (MA, PhD); elementary education (MA); environmental sciences (MS); finance (MBA); general business administration (MBA); graphic design (MFA); health and physical education (MA); human resources (MBA, PhD); industrial relations (MBA); information systems (MBA); international and interregional business (PhD); library sciences (MLS); management (MBA); marketing (MBA); music (MA); music teacher education (MA); painting (MFA); photography (MFA); printmaking (MFA); school psychology (MA, PhD); science education (MA); sculpture (MFA); special education (MA); teaching English as a second language (MA).

INTER AMERICAN UNIVERSITY OF PUERTO RICO SCHOOL OF LAW, San Juan, PR 00936-8351

General Information Independent, coed, graduate-only institution.

GRADUATE UNITS
Professional Program *Program availability:* Part-time, evening/weekend. Offers law (JD).

INTER AMERICAN UNIVERSITY OF PUERTO RICO SCHOOL OF OPTOMETRY, Bayamón, PR 00957

General Information Independent, coed, graduate-only institution. *Enrollment by degree level:* 231 doctoral. *Graduate faculty:* 22 full-time (11 women), 20 part-time/adjunct (10 women). *Tuition:* Full-time $26,750; part-time $1500 per credit. *Graduate housing:* Room and/or apartments available on a first-come, first-served basis to single students; on-campus housing not available to married students. *Student services:* Campus employment opportunities, career counseling, exercise/wellness program, international student services, multicultural affairs office. *Library facilities:* CAI Center for Access to Information (CAI). *Collection:* Weekly public service hours: 15; study areas open 24 hours, 5–7 days a week; students can reserve study rooms.

Computer facilities: 43 computers available on campus for general student use. A campuswide network can be accessed from student residence rooms. Online class registration is available.
Website: http://www.optonet.inter.edu/

General Application Contact: Fernando Acosta-Rosa, Director of Student Services, 787-765-1915 Ext. 1020, Fax: 787-756-7351, E-mail: facosta@opto.inter.edu.

GRADUATE UNITS
Professional Program Students: 231 full-time (156 women); includes 137 minority (12 Black or African American, non-Hispanic/Latino; 58 Asian, non-Hispanic/Latino; 67 Hispanic/Latino), 18 international. Average age 26. *Faculty:* 22 full-time (11 women), 20 part-time/adjunct (10 women). Expenses: Contact institution. *Financial support:* Scholarships/grants available. Financial award application deadline: 4/30; financial award applicants required to submit FAFSA. Offers optometry (OD). *Application deadline:* For fall admission, 6/1 priority date for domestic and international students. Applications are processed on a rolling basis. *Application fee:* $31. Electronic applications accepted. *Application Contact:* Fernando Acosta-Rosa, Director of Student Services, 787-765-1915 Ext. 1020, Fax: 787-756-7351, E-mail: facosta@opto.inter.edu. *Dean of Academic Affairs,* Dr. Angel Romero, 787-765-1915 Ext. 1005, Fax: 787-767-3920, E-mail: aromero@opto.inter.edu.

INTERDENOMINATIONAL THEOLOGICAL CENTER, Atlanta, GA 30314-4112

General Information Independent-religious, coed, graduate-only institution. *Enrollment by degree level:* 197 master's, 59 doctoral. *Graduate faculty:* 15 full-time (6 women), 12 part-time/adjunct (5 women). *Tuition:* Full-time $13,000; part-time $9324 per credit. *Required fees:* $938; $938 per credit. Full-time tuition and fees vary according to course load. *Graduate housing:* Room and/or apartments available on a first-come, first-served basis to single students; on-campus housing not available to married students. Typical cost: $2525 per year. Room charges vary according to housing facility selected. Housing application deadline: 8/1. *Student services:* Campus employment opportunities, campus safety program, career counseling, exercise/wellness program, free psychological counseling, services for students with disabilities. *Library facilities:* Robert W. Woodruff Library. *Collection:* Books: 364,010 (physical). Students can reserve study rooms. *Research affiliation:* Atlanta University Center, Inc., Columbia Theological Seminary Library, Candler School of Theology Library, Emory University Library.

Computer facilities: 50 computers available on campus for general student use. Online class registration is available.
Website: http://www.itc.edu/

General Application Contact: Michelle Davis, Office of Admission and Recruitment, 404-527-7793, E-mail: lmdavis@itc.edu.

GRADUATE UNITS
Graduate and Professional Programs Students: 119 full-time (45 women), 137 part-time (60 women); includes 249 minority (248 Black or African American, non-Hispanic/Latino; 1 Two or more races, non-Hispanic/Latino), 2 international. *Faculty:* 15 full-time (6 women), 12 part-time/adjunct (5 women). Expenses: Contact institution. *Financial support:* Research assistantships, career-related internships or fieldwork, and Federal Work-Study available. Support available to part-time students. Financial award application deadline: 6/15; financial award applicants required to submit FAFSA. *Program availability:* Part-time, evening/weekend, blended/hybrid learning. Offers Christian education (MACE); ministry (D Min); pastoral counseling (Th D); theology (M Div). D Min and Th D programs offered in collaboration with the Atlanta Theological Association. *Application deadline:* For fall admission, 7/1 for domestic and international students; for spring admission, 10/1 for domestic and international students. Applications are processed on a rolling basis. *Application fee:* $50. Electronic applications accepted. *Application Contact:* Michelle Davis, Office of Admission and Recruitment, 404-527-7793, E-mail: lmdavis@itc.edu. *President,* Edward Lorenza Wheeler, 404-527-7702, Fax: 404-527-7770.

INTERIOR DESIGNERS INSTITUTE, Newport Beach, CA 92660

General Information Proprietary, coed, comprehensive institution.

GRADUATE UNITS
Graduate Program Offers interior design (MA).

INTERNATIONAL BAPTIST COLLEGE AND SEMINARY, Chandler, AZ 85286

General Information Independent-religious, coed, comprehensive institution. *Graduate housing:* Room and/or apartments available on a first-come, first-served basis to single students; on-campus housing not available to married students.

GRADUATE UNITS
Program in Biblical Studies Offers Biblical studies (MA).
Program in Education Offers education (M Ed).
Program in Ministry Offers ministry (M Min, D Min).

INTERNATIONAL COLLEGE OF THE CAYMAN ISLANDS, Newlands, Grand Cayman, Cayman Islands

General Information Independent, coed, comprehensive institution. *Graduate housing:* Room and/or apartments available on a first-come, first-served basis to single students; on-campus housing not available to married students.

GRADUATE UNITS
Graduate Program in Management *Program availability:* Part-time, evening/weekend. Offers business administration (MBA); management (MS).

INTERNATIONAL INSTITUTE FOR RESTORATIVE PRACTICES, Bethlehem, PA 18018

General Information Independent, coed, graduate-only institution.

GRADUATE UNITS
Graduate Programs *Program availability:* Online learning. Offers restorative practices (MS, Certificate).

INTERNATIONAL TECHNOLOGICAL UNIVERSITY, San Jose, CA 95134

General Information Independent, coed, graduate-only institution. CGS member. *Research affiliation:* Linux Works, Inc. (software), @Channel (software), New Trends Technology, Inc. (hardware), Pico Turbo, Inc. (hardware).

GRADUATE UNITS
Program in Business Administration *Program availability:* Part-time, evening/weekend. Offers business administration (MBA, DBA). Electronic applications accepted.
Program in Computer Engineering *Program availability:* Part-time, evening/weekend. Offers computer engineering (MSCE). Electronic applications accepted.
Program in Digital Arts *Program availability:* Part-time. Offers digital arts (MA). Electronic applications accepted.
Program in Electrical Engineering *Program availability:* Part-time, evening/weekend. Offers electrical engineering (MSEE, PhD). Electronic applications accepted.
Program in Engineering Management *Program availability:* Part-time, evening/weekend. Offers engineering management (MSEM). Electronic applications accepted.
Program in Software Engineering *Program availability:* Part-time, evening/weekend. Offers software engineering (MSSE). Electronic applications accepted.

INTERNATIONAL UNIVERSITY IN GENEVA, CH-1215 Geneva 15, Switzerland

General Information Private, coed, comprehensive institution. *Graduate housing:* Room and/or apartments available on a first-come, first-served basis to single students; on-campus housing not available to married students. Housing application deadline: 7/31.

GRADUATE UNITS
Business Programs *Program availability:* Part-time, evening/weekend. Offers business administration (MBA, DBA); entrepreneurship (MBA); international business (MIB); international trade (MIT); sales and marketing (MBA). Electronic applications accepted.
Leadership Programs Offers international relations and diplomacy (MIRD); media and communication (MA); public administration (DPA). Electronic applications accepted.

THE INTERNATIONAL UNIVERSITY OF MONACO, MC-98000 Principality of Monaco, Monaco

General Information Independent, coed, comprehensive institution. *Graduate housing:* Rooms and/or apartments guaranteed to single and married students. *Research affiliation:* Alpstar (hedge funds).

GRADUATE UNITS
Graduate Programs *Program availability:* Part-time. Offers entrepreneurship (EMBA, MBA); financial engineering (M Sc); hedge fund and private equity (M Sc); international marketing (EMBA, MBA); international wealth management (M Sc); luxury goods and services (EMBA, M Sc, MBA); wealth and asset management (EMBA, MBA). Electronic applications accepted.

IONA COLLEGE, New Rochelle, NY 10801-1890

General Information Independent-religious, coed, comprehensive institution. *Enrollment:* 4,019 graduate, professional, and undergraduate students; 358 full-time matriculated graduate/professional students (222 women), 332 part-time matriculated graduate/professional students (170 women). *Enrollment by degree level:* 677 master's, 13 other advanced degrees. *Graduate faculty:* 83 full-time (31 women), 47 part-time/adjunct (25 women). *Tuition:* Full-time $19,692; part-time $1094 per credit. *Required fees:* $245 per term. Tuition and fees vary according to program. *Graduate housing:* On-campus housing not available. *Student services:* Campus employment opportunities, campus safety program, career counseling, exercise/wellness program, free psychological counseling, international student services, multicultural affairs office, services for students with disabilities, writing training. *Library facilities:* Ryan Library plus 1 other. *Collection:* Books: 269,396 (physical), 324,744 (digital/electronic); Serial titles: 112 (physical), 369 (digital/electronic); Databases: 150. Weekly public service hours: 101; students can reserve study rooms. *Research affiliation:* IBM (teacher preparation).

Computer facilities: Computer purchase and lease plans are available. A campuswide network can be accessed from student residence rooms and from off campus. Online class registration, bill payment are available.
Website: http://www.iona.edu/

General Application Contact: Katelyn Brunck, Associate Director of Graduate Admissions, 914-633-2451, Fax: 914-633-2277, E-mail: kbrunck@iona.edu.

GRADUATE UNITS

Hagan School of Business Students: 147 full-time (67 women), 205 part-time (92 women); includes 99 minority (31 Black or African American, non-Hispanic/Latino; 2 American Indian or Alaska Native, non-Hispanic/Latino; 12 Asian, non-Hispanic/Latino; 52 Hispanic/Latino; 1 Native Hawaiian or other Pacific Islander, non-Hispanic/Latino; 1 Two or more races, non-Hispanic/Latino), 68 international. Average age 28. 147 applicants, 99% accepted, 74 enrolled. *Faculty:* 35 full-time (8 women), 18 part-time/adjunct (7 women). Expenses: Contact institution. *Financial support:* In 2016–17, 151 students received support. Scholarships/grants, tuition waivers (partial), and unspecified assistantships available. Support available to part-time students. Financial award application deadline: 4/15; financial award applicants required to submit FAFSA. In 2016, 218 master's, 185 other advanced degrees awarded. *Program availability:* Part-time, evening/weekend, 100% online, blended/hybrid learning. Offers accounting and information systems (MS); business (MBA, MS, AC, PMC); business administration (MBA); business continuity and risk management (AC); finance (MS); financial management (MBA, PMC); financial services (MS); general accounting (MBA, AC); health care analytics (AC); health care management (MBA, AC); human resource management (MBA, PMC); information systems (MBA, MS, PMC); international business (AC, PMC); international finance (MS); long term care services management (AC); management (MBA, PMC); marketing (MBA); project management (MS); public accounting (MBA, MS, AC); sports and entertainment management (AC). *Application deadline:* For fall admission, 8/15 priority date for domestic students, 8/1 priority date for international students; for winter admission, 11/15 priority date for domestic students, 11/1 priority date for international students; for spring admission, 2/15 priority date for domestic students, 2/1 priority date for international students; for summer admission, 5/15 priority date for domestic students, 5/1 priority date for international students. Applications are processed on a rolling basis. *Application fee:* $50. Electronic applications accepted. *Application Contact:* Katelyn Brunck, Director of MBA Admissions, 914-633-2451, Fax: 914-633-2277, E-mail: kbrunck@iona.edu. *Interim Dean,* Dr. Charles J. Cante, 914-633-2258, E-mail: ccante@iona.edu.

School of Arts and Science Students: 211 full-time (155 women), 127 part-time (78 women); includes 125 minority (42 Black or African American, non-Hispanic/Latino; 7 Asian, non-Hispanic/Latino; 73 Hispanic/Latino; 1 Native Hawaiian or other Pacific Islander, non-Hispanic/Latino; 2 Two or more races, non-Hispanic/Latino), 20 international. Average age 27. 347 applicants, 62% accepted, 105 enrolled. *Faculty:* 48 full-time (23 women), 29 part-time/adjunct (18 women). Expenses: Contact institution. *Financial support:* In 2016–17, 177 students received support. Tuition waivers (partial) and unspecified assistantships available. Support available to part-time students. Financial award application deadline: 4/15; financial award applicants required to submit FAFSA. In 2016, 112 master's, 9 other advanced degrees awarded. *Program availability:* Part-time, evening/weekend. Offers adolescence education: biology (MS Ed, MST); adolescence education: English (MS Ed); adolescence education: mathematics (MST); adolescence education: social studies (MS Ed, MST); adolescence education: Spanish (MS Ed); adolescence special education 5-12 (MST); arts and science (MA, MS, MS Ed, MST, AC, Certificate); childhood and special education (MST); communication sciences and disorders (MA); computer science (MS); criminal justice (MS); cyber security (MS); cybercrime and security (AC); early childhood and childhood (MST); educational leadership (MS Ed); English (MA); forensic criminology and criminal justice systems (Certificate); game development (MS); general-experimental psychology (MA); history (MA); human resources (Certificate); industrial-organizational psychology (MA); marriage and family therapy (MS); mental health counseling (MA); non-profit public relations (Certificate); organizational behavior (Certificate); psychology (MA); public relations (MA); school psychology (MA); sports communication and media (MA). *Application deadline:* For fall admission, 8/1 priority date for domestic students, 5/1 priority date for international students; for winter admission, 12/1 priority date for domestic students, 8/1 priority date for international students; for spring admission, 1/1 priority date for domestic students, 9/1 priority date for international students; for summer admission, 5/1 priority date for domestic students, 1/1 priority date for international students. Applications are processed on a rolling basis. *Application fee:* $50. Electronic applications accepted. *Application Contact:* Dr. Katherine Zaromatidis, Director of Graduate Studies, School of Arts and Science, 914-633-2375, E-mail: kzaromatidis@iona.edu. *Dean, School of Arts and Science,* Sibdas Ghosh, PhD, 914-633-2112, Fax: 914-633-2023, E-mail: sghosh@iona.edu.

IOWA STATE UNIVERSITY OF SCIENCE AND TECHNOLOGY, Ames, IA 50011

General Information State-supported, coed, university. CGS member. *Graduate housing:* Rooms and/or apartments available on a first-come, first-served basis to single and married students. Housing application deadline: 6/15. *Student services:* Campus employment opportunities, campus safety program, career counseling, child daycare facilities, exercise/wellness program, free psychological counseling, grant writing training, international student services, low-cost health insurance, multicultural affairs office, services for students with disabilities, teacher training, writing training. *Library facilities:* University Library plus 1 other. *Collection:* Books: 2.9 million (physical), 457,967 (digital/electronic); Serial titles: 14,057 (physical), 96,398 (digital/electronic); Databases: 301. Weekly public service hours: 113; students can reserve study rooms. *Research affiliation:* National Veterinary Services Laboratories, National Animal Disease Center, National Soil Tilth Laboratory, North Central Regional Center for Rural Development, U.S. Department of Energy-Ames Laboratory.

Computer facilities: Computer purchase and lease plans are available. 2,400 computers available on campus for general student use. A campuswide network can be accessed from student residence rooms and from off campus. Online class registration, network services are available.
Website: http://www.iastate.edu/

General Application Contact: Information Contact, 515-294-5836, Fax: 515-294-2592, E-mail: grad_admissions@iastate.edu.

GRADUATE UNITS

Bioinformatics and Computational Biology Program Expenses: Contact institution. Offers bioinformatics and computational biology (MS, PhD). *Application deadline:* For fall admission, 1/15 priority date for domestic students, 1/15 for international students; for spring admission, 10/15 for domestic and international students. *Application fee:* $40 ($90 for international students). Electronic applications accepted. *Application Contact:* Trish Stauble, Information Contact, 515-294-5122, Fax: 515-294-2592, E-mail: bcb@iastate.edu.

Department of Accounting Expenses: Contact institution. Offers accounting (M Acc). *Application deadline:* For fall admission, 7/1 priority date for domestic students, 6/1 priority date for international students; for spring admission, 11/1 priority date for domestic students, 10/1 priority date for international students. *Application fee:* $60 ($90 for international students). Electronic applications accepted. *Application Contact:* Meleah Cue, Application Contact, 515-294-8118, Fax: 515-294-2446, E-mail: busgrad@iastate.edu.

Department of Aerospace Engineering and Engineering Mechanics Expenses: Contact institution. Offers aerospace engineering (M Eng, MS, PhD); engineering mechanics (M Eng, MS, PhD). *Application deadline:* For fall admission, 1/1 priority date for domestic and international students; for spring admission, 9/1 priority date for domestic and international students. *Application fee:* $60 ($90 for international students). Electronic applications accepted. *Application Contact:* Sara Goplin, Application Contact, 515-294-9669, Fax: 515-294-3262, E-mail: aere-info@iastate.edu.

Department of Agricultural Education and Studies Expenses: Contact institution. Offers agricultural education and studies (MS, PhD). *Application deadline:* For fall admission, 3/15 priority date for domestic and international students; for spring admission, 10/15 priority date for domestic and international students. *Application fee:* $60 ($90 for international students). Electronic applications accepted. *Application Contact:* Wendy Ortmann, Application Contact, 515-294-5872, Fax: 515-294-0530, E-mail: agedsinfo@iastate.edu.

Department of Agronomy Expenses: Contact institution. Offers agricultural meteorology (MS, PhD); agronomy (MS); crop production and physiology (MS, PhD); plant breeding (MS, PhD); soil science (MS, PhD). *Application deadline:* For fall admission, 4/15 priority date for domestic and international students; for spring admission, 10/1 priority date for domestic and international students. *Application fee:* $60 ($90 for international students). Electronic applications accepted. *Application Contact:* Jaci Severson, Application Contact, 515-294-1361, Fax: 515-294-5506, E-mail: msagron@iastate.edu.

Department of Animal Science Expenses: Contact institution. Offers animal breeding and genetics (MS, PhD); animal physiology (MS); animal psychology (MS); animal science (MS, PhD); meat science (MS, PhD). *Application deadline:* For fall admission, 2/1 priority date for domestic and international students; for spring admission, 9/1 priority date for domestic and international students. *Application fee:* $60 ($90 for international students). Electronic applications accepted. *Application Contact:* Jane Linn, Application Contact, 515-294-2160, Fax: 515-294-6994, E-mail: jlinn@iastate.edu.

Department of Anthropology Expenses: Contact institution. Offers anthropology (MA). *Application deadline:* For fall admission, 1/15 priority date for domestic and international students; for spring admission, 10/1 for domestic and international students. Applications are processed on a rolling basis. *Application fee:* $60 ($90 for international students). Electronic applications accepted. *Application Contact:* Amanda Runyan, Application Contact, 515-294-4910, E-mail: runyan@iastate.edu.

Department of Apparel, Events, and Hospitality Management Expenses: Contact institution. *Program availability:* Online learning. Offers apparel, merchandising, and design (MS, PhD); hospitality management (MS, PhD). *Application deadline:* For fall admission, 2/1 priority date for domestic and international students. *Application fee:* $40 ($90 for international students). Electronic applications accepted. *Application Contact:* Ann Marie Fiore, Director of Graduate Education, 515-294-9303, E-mail: amfiore@iastate.edu.

Department of Architecture Expenses: Contact institution. *Financial support:* In 2016–17, 30 students received support. Tuition waivers (partial) available. Financial award applicants required to submit FAFSA. Offers architectural studies (MSAS); architecture (M Arch, MS). *Application deadline:* For fall admission, 1/4 priority date for domestic and international students; for spring admission, 10/4 for domestic and international students. *Application fee:* $60 ($90 for international students). Electronic applications accepted. *Application Contact:* Meredith Foley, Application Contact, 515-294-0816, Fax: 515-294-2348, E-mail: merfoley@iastate.edu.

Department of Biomedical Sciences Expenses: Contact institution. Offers biomedical sciences (MS, PhD). *Application deadline:* For fall admission, 3/1 priority date for domestic and international students; for spring admission, 9/1 priority date for domestic and international students. *Application fee:* $60 ($90 for international students). Electronic applications accepted. *Application Contact:* Emma Hashman, Application Contact, 515-294-2440, E-mail: bmsgrad@iastate.edu.

Department of Chemical and Biological Engineering Expenses: Contact institution. Offers chemical and biological engineering (M Eng, MS, PhD). *Application deadline:* For fall admission, 1/15 priority date for domestic and international students; for spring admission, 10/1 for domestic and international students. *Application fee:* $60 ($100 for international students). Electronic applications accepted. *Application Contact:* Bellinda Hegelheimer, Application Contact, 515-294-1660, Fax: 515-294-2689, E-mail: chemengr@iastate.edu.

Department of Chemistry Expenses: Contact institution. Offers chemistry (MS, PhD). *Application deadline:* For fall admission, 2/1 priority date for domestic and international students. *Application fee:* $60 ($90 for international students). Electronic applications accepted. *Application Contact:* Lynette Edsall, Application Contact, 800-521-2436, Fax: 515-294-0105, E-mail: chemgrad@iastate.edu.

Department of Civil and Construction Engineering Expenses: Contact institution. Offers civil engineering (MS, PhD). *Application deadline:* For fall admission, 2/1 priority date for domestic students, 2/1 for international students; for spring admission, 8/1 priority date for domestic students, 8/1 for international students. *Application fee:* $60 ($90 for international students). Electronic applications accepted. *Application Contact:* Kathy Petersen, Application Contact, 515-294-4975, Fax: 515-294-8216, E-mail: ccee-grad-inquiry@iastate.edu.

Department of Community and Regional Planning Expenses: Contact institution. *Financial support:* Tuition waivers (partial) available. Financial award applicants required to submit FAFSA. Offers community and regional planning (MCRP); transportation (MS). *Application deadline:* For fall admission, 1/1 priority date for domestic and international students. Applications are processed on a rolling basis. *Application fee:* $60 ($90 for international students). Electronic applications accepted. *Application Contact:* Meredith Foley, Director of Graduate Education, 515-294-0816, Fax: 515-294-2348, E-mail: merfoley@iastate.edu.

Department of Computer Science Expenses: Contact institution. Offers computer science (MS, PhD). *Application deadline:* For fall admission, 1/15 priority date for domestic and international students; for spring admission, 9/1 priority date for domestic and international students. *Application fee:* $60 ($90 for international students). Electronic applications accepted. *Application Contact:* Carla Harris, Application Contact, 515-294-1224, Fax: 515-294-0258, E-mail: csadmissions@iastate.edu.

Department of Economics Expenses: Contact institution. Offers agricultural economics (MS, PhD); economics (MS, PhD). JD/MS and JD/PhD offered jointly with Drake University and The University of Iowa. *Application deadline:* For fall admission, 1/31 priority date for domestic and international students. *Application fee:* $40 ($90 for international students). Electronic applications accepted. *Application Contact:* Amy Bainum Emmett, Application Contact, 515-294-2702, E-mail: econgrad@iastate.edu.

Department of Education Expenses: Contact institution. Offers curriculum and instructional technology (M Ed, MS, PhD); elementary education (M Ed, MS); historical, philosophical, and comparative studies in education (M Ed, MS); special education (M Ed, MS, PhD). *Application deadline:* For fall admission, 1/1 priority date for domestic and international students; for spring admission, 9/1 for domestic and international students. *Application fee:* $60 ($90 for international students). Electronic applications accepted. *Application Contact:* Robyn Goldy, Application Contact, 515-294-1241, Fax: 515-294-4942, E-mail: rgoldy@iastate.edu.

Department of Educational Leadership and Policy Studies Expenses: Contact institution. Offers counselor education (M Ed, MS); educational administration (M Ed, MS); educational leadership (PhD); higher education (M Ed, MS); organizational learning and human resource development (M Ed, MS); research and evaluation (MS); student affairs (MS). *Application deadline:* For fall admission, 1/1 priority date for domestic and international students. *Application fee:* $60 ($90 for international students). Electronic applications accepted. *Application Contact:* Robyn Goldy, Application Contact, 515-294-1241, Fax: 515-294-4942, E-mail: rgoldy@iastate.edu.

Department of Electrical and Computer Engineering Expenses: Contact institution. Offers computer engineering (M Eng, MS, PhD); electrical engineering (M Eng, MS, PhD). *Application deadline:* For fall admission, 1/15 priority date for domestic and international students; for spring admission, 9/15 for domestic and international students. *Application fee:* $40 ($90 for international students). Electronic applications accepted. *Application Contact:* Vicky Thorland-Oster, Application Contact, 515-294-8403, E-mail: ecegrad@iastate.edu.

Department of English Expenses: Contact institution. Offers creative writing (MFA); English (MA); rhetoric and professional communication (PhD). *Application deadline:* For fall admission, 1/5 priority date for domestic and international students. *Application fee:* $60 ($90 for international students). Electronic applications accepted. *Application Contact:* Teresa Smiley, Application Contact, 515-294-2477, Fax: 515-294-6814, E-mail: englgrad@iastate.edu.

Department of Entomology Expenses: Contact institution. Offers entomology (MS, PhD). *Application deadline:* Applications are processed on a rolling basis. *Application fee:* $60 ($90 for international students). Electronic applications accepted. *Application Contact:* Kelly Kyle, Application Contact, 515-294-7400, Fax: 515-294-7406, E-mail: entomology@iastate.edu.

Department of Food Science and Human Nutrition Expenses: Contact institution. Offers food science and technology (MS, PhD); nutrition (MS, PhD). *Application deadline:* For fall admission, 1/15 priority date for domestic and international students. Applications are processed on a rolling basis. *Application fee:* $60 ($90 for international students). Electronic applications accepted. *Application Contact:* Brenda Emery, Director of Graduate Education, 515-294-6442, Fax: 515-294-6193, E-mail: fshngraduate@iastate.edu.

Department of Geological and Atmospheric Sciences Expenses: Contact institution. Offers earth science (MS); environmental science (MS, PhD); geology (MS, PhD); meteorology (MS, PhD). *Application deadline:* For fall admission, 1/1 priority date for domestic students. *Application fee:* $60 ($90 for international students). Electronic applications accepted. *Application Contact:* Deann Frisk, Application Contact, 515-294-4477, Fax: 515-294-6049, E-mail: geology@iastate.edu.

Department of History Expenses: Contact institution. Offers history (MA); rural, agricultural, technological, and environmental history (PhD). *Application deadline:* For fall admission, 1/15 priority date for domestic and international students. *Application fee:* $60 ($90 for international students). Electronic applications accepted. *Application Contact:* Jennifer Rivera, Application Contact, 515-294-7266, E-mail: rivera@iastate.edu.

Department of Horticulture Expenses: Contact institution. Offers horticulture (MS, PhD). *Application deadline:* Applications are processed on a rolling basis. *Application fee:* $60 ($90 for international students). Electronic applications accepted. *Application Contact:* Kim Gaul, Application Contact, 515-294-3718, Fax: 515-294-0730, E-mail: kimgaul@iastate.edu.

Department of Human Development and Family Studies Expenses: Contact institution. Offers human development and family studies (MFCS, MS, PhD). *Application deadline:* For fall admission, 1/15 priority date for domestic and international students. *Application fee:* $60 ($90 for international students). Electronic applications accepted. *Application Contact:* Brenda Nelson, Application Contact, 515-294-6321, Fax: 515-294-2502, E-mail: hdfs-grad-adm@iastate.edu.

Department of Industrial and Manufacturing Systems Engineering Expenses: Contact institution. Offers industrial engineering (M Eng, MS, PhD); operations research (MS); systems engineering (M Eng). *Application deadline:* For fall admission, 1/15 priority date for international students; for spring admission, 7/15 priority date for international students. *Application fee:* $60 ($90 for international students). Electronic applications accepted. *Application Contact:* Deborah McDonough, Application Contact, 515-294-0129, Fax: 515-294-3524, E-mail: imsegradprogram@iastate.edu.

Department of Kinesiology Expenses: Contact institution. Offers kinesiology (MS, PhD). *Application deadline:* For fall admission, 1/1 priority date for domestic students, 1/1 for international students. *Application fee:* $60 ($90 for international students). Electronic applications accepted. *Application Contact:* Dr. Jason Gillette, Application Contact, 515-294-8009, Fax: 515-294-8740, E-mail: gillette@iastate.edu.

Department of Landscape Architecture Expenses: Contact institution. *Financial support:* Institutionally sponsored loans available. Financial award application deadline: 2/15; financial award applicants required to submit FAFSA. *Program availability:* Part-time. Offers landscape architecture (MLA, MS). *Application deadline:* For fall admission, 2/1 priority date for domestic and international students. *Application fee:* $60 ($90 for international students). Electronic applications accepted. *Application Contact:* Meredith Foley, Application Contact, 515-294-0816, Fax: 515-294-2348, E-mail: landarch@iastate.edu.

Department of Materials Science and Engineering Expenses: Contact institution. *Financial support:* Teaching assistantships, scholarships/grants, health care benefits, and unspecified assistantships available. Offers materials science and engineering (M Eng, MS, PhD). *Application deadline:* For fall admission, 1/15 priority date for domestic and international students; for spring admission, 8/15 priority date for domestic and international students. *Application fee:* $60 ($90 for international students). Electronic applications accepted. *Application Contact:* Patrick Morton, Director of Graduate Education, 515-294-1214, Fax: 515-294-5444, E-mail: gradmse@iastate.edu.

Department of Mathematics Expenses: Contact institution. *Financial support:* Scholarships/grants, health care benefits, and unspecified assistantships available. Offers applied mathematics (MS, PhD); mathematics (MS, PhD); school mathematics (MSM). *Application deadline:* For fall admission, 2/1 priority date for domestic and international students. *Application fee:* $60 ($90 for international students). Electronic applications accepted. *Application Contact:* Melanie Erickson, Application Contact, 515-294-0393, Fax: 515-294-5454, E-mail: gradmath@iastate.edu.

Department of Mechanical Engineering Expenses: Contact institution. Offers mechanical engineering (M Eng, MS, PhD); systems engineering (M Eng). *Application deadline:* For fall admission, 1/10 priority date for domestic and international students; for spring admission, 8/10 priority date for domestic and international students. *Application fee:* $60 ($90 for international students). Electronic applications accepted. *Application Contact:* Hallie Golay, Application Contact, 515-294-0838, Fax: 515-294-6960, E-mail: megradinfo@iastate.edu.

Department of Natural Resource Ecology and Management Expenses: Contact institution. Offers forestry (MS, PhD); wildlife ecology (MS, PhD). *Application deadline:* For fall admission, 4/1 priority date for domestic and international students; for spring admission, 10/1 priority date for domestic and international students. *Application fee:* $60 ($90 for international students). Electronic applications accepted. *Application Contact:* Kelly Kyle, Director of Graduate Education, 515-294-7400, Fax: 515-294-7406, E-mail: nremgradinfo@iastate.edu.

Department of Physics and Astronomy Expenses: Contact institution. *Financial support:* Application deadline: 2/15. Offers applied physics (MS, PhD); astrophysics (MS, PhD); condensed matter physics (MS, PhD); high energy physics (MS, PhD); nuclear physics (MS, PhD); physics (MS, PhD). *Application deadline:* For fall admission, 2/15 priority date for domestic and international students; for spring admission, 10/15 for domestic and international students. Applications are processed on a rolling basis. *Application fee:* $60 ($90 for international students). Electronic applications accepted. *Application Contact:* Lori Hockett, Application Contact, 515-294-5870, Fax: 515-294-6027, E-mail: physastro@iastate.edu.

Department of Plant Pathology Expenses: Contact institution. Offers plant pathology (MS, PhD). *Application deadline:* For fall admission, 1/15 priority date for domestic and international students; for spring admission, 8/1 for domestic and international students. Applications are processed on a rolling basis. *Application fee:* $60 ($90 for international students). Electronic applications accepted. *Application Contact:* Dai Nguyen, Application Contact, 515-294-7159, Fax: 515-294-9420, E-mail: plantpath@iastate.edu.

Department of Political Science Expenses: Contact institution. Offers political science (MA); public administration (MPA). JD/MA offered jointly with Drake University. *Application deadline:* For fall admission, 1/1 priority date for domestic and international students; for spring admission, 10/1 for domestic and international students. *Application fee:* $60 ($90 for international students). Electronic applications accepted. *Application Contact:* Alex Tuckness, Application Contact, 515-294-8910, Fax: 515-294-1003, E-mail: tuckness@iastate.edu.

Department of Psychology Expenses: Contact institution. Offers cognitive psychology (PhD); counseling psychology (PhD); psychology (MS, PhD); social psychology (PhD). *Application deadline:* For fall admission, 1/2 priority date for domestic and international students. *Application fee:* $60 ($90 for international students). Electronic applications accepted. *Application Contact:* Sarah Kallsen, Application Contact, 515-294-1742, Fax: 515-294-6424, E-mail: psychadm@iastate.edu.

Department of Sociology Expenses: Contact institution. Offers rural sociology (MS, PhD); sociology (MS, PhD). *Application deadline:* For fall admission, 1/10 priority date for domestic and international students; for spring admission, 10/1 for domestic and international students. *Application fee:* $60 ($90 for international students). Electronic applications accepted. *Application Contact:* Rachel Burlingame, Application Contact, 515-294-2506, Fax: 515-294-8649, E-mail: rmb@iastate.edu.

Department of Statistics Expenses: Contact institution. Offers statistics (MS, PhD). *Application deadline:* For fall admission, 1/15 priority date for domestic and international students; for spring admission, 9/15 for domestic and international students. *Application fee:* $60 ($90 for international students). Electronic applications accepted. *Application Contact:* Jessica Higgins, Secretary II, 515-294-5044, Fax: 515-294-4040, E-mail: statistics@iastate.edu.

Department of Veterinary Clinical Sciences Expenses: Contact institution. Offers veterinary clinical sciences (MS). *Application deadline:* Applications are processed on a rolling basis. *Application fee:* $60 ($90 for international students). Electronic applications accepted. *Application Contact:* Lindsey Alley, Application Contact, 515-294-6411, Fax: 515-294-9281, E-mail: lindsey@iastate.edu.

Department of Veterinary Diagnostic and Production Animal Medicine Expenses: Contact institution. *Financial support:* Scholarships/grants available. Offers veterinary preventative medicine (MS). *Application deadline:* For fall admission, 2/1 for domestic and international students. Applications are processed on a rolling basis. *Application fee:* $60 ($90 for international students). Electronic applications accepted. *Application Contact:* Erica Hellmich, Application Contact, 515-294-1761, Fax: 515-294-1072, E-mail: eriah@iastate.edu.

Department of Veterinary Microbiology and Preventive Medicine Expenses: Contact institution. Offers veterinary microbiology (MS, PhD). *Application deadline:* For fall admission, 2/1 priority date for domestic and international students. Applications are processed on a rolling basis. *Application fee:* $60 ($90 for international students). Electronic applications accepted. *Application Contact:* Tammy Krock, Application Contact, 515-294-5776, Fax: 515-294-8500, E-mail: vetmicro@iastate.edu.

Department of Veterinary Pathology Expenses: Contact institution. Offers veterinary pathology (MS, PhD). *Application deadline:* Applications are processed on a rolling basis. *Application fee:* $60 ($90 for international students). Electronic applications accepted. *Application Contact:* Jesse M. Hostetter, Director of Graduate Education, 515-294-0953, E-mail: jesseh@iastate.edu.

Greenlee School of Journalism and Mass Communication Expenses: Contact institution. Offers journalism and mass communication (MS). *Application deadline:* For fall admission, 3/1 priority date for international students; for spring admission, 10/1 priority date for international students. Applications are processed on a rolling basis. *Application fee:* $60 ($90 for international students). Electronic applications accepted. *Application Contact:* Daniela Dimitrova, Application Contact, 515-294-5951, Fax: 515-294-5108, E-mail: danielad@iastate.edu.

Program in Agricultural and Biosystems Engineering Students: 55 full-time (21 women), 21 part-time (7 women); includes 7 minority (3 Black or African American, non-Hispanic/Latino; 1 American Indian or Alaska Native, non-Hispanic/Latino; 2 Asian, non-Hispanic/Latino; 1 Hispanic/Latino), 29 international. Expenses: Contact institution. Offers agricultural and biosystems engineering (M En, MS, PhD). *Application deadline:* For fall admission, 2/15 priority date for domestic students, 2/1 priority date for international students; for spring admission, 7/1 priority date for domestic and international students. *Application fee:* $40 ($90 for international students). Electronic applications accepted. *Application Contact:* Kris Bell, Graduate Secretary, 515-294-1033, E-mail: kabell@iastate.edu.

Program in Agricultural Economics Expenses: Contact institution. Offers agricultural economics (MS, PhD). *Application deadline:* For fall admission, 1/31 priority date for domestic and international students. *Application fee:* $60 ($90 for international students). Electronic applications accepted. *Application Contact:* Amy Bainum-Emmett, Application Contact, 515-294-2702, E-mail: econgrad@iastate.edu.

Program in Agricultural Meteorology Expenses: Contact institution. Offers agricultural meteorology (MS, PhD). *Application deadline:* Applications are processed on a rolling basis. Electronic applications accepted. *Application Contact:* Jaci Severson, Application Contact, 515-294-1361, Fax: 515-294-8146, E-mail: agrongradprograms@iastate.edu.

Program in Analytical Chemistry Expenses: Contact institution. Offers analytical chemistry (MS, PhD). *Application deadline:* For fall admission, 2/1 for domestic and international students. *Application fee:* $60 ($90 for international students). Electronic applications accepted. *Application Contact:* Lynette Edsall, Application Contact, 800-521-2436, Fax: 515-294-0105, E-mail: chemgrad@iastate.edu.

Program in Animal Breeding and Genetics Expenses: Contact institution. Offers animal breeding and genetics (MS); immunogenetics (PhD); molecular genetics (PhD); quantitative genetics (PhD). *Application deadline:* For fall admission, 2/1 for domestic and international students; for spring admission, 9/1 for domestic and international students. Electronic applications accepted. *Application Contact:* Jane Linn, Application Contact, 515-294-2160, Fax: 515-294-6994, E-mail: jlinn@iastate.edu.

Program in Animal Physiology Expenses: Contact institution. Offers animal physiology (MS, PhD). *Application deadline:* For fall admission, 2/1 for domestic and international students; for spring admission, 9/1 for domestic and international students. *Application fee:* $60 ($90 for international students). Electronic applications accepted. *Application Contact:* Jane Linn, Application Contact, 515-294-2160, Fax: 515-294-6994, E-mail: jlinn@iastate.edu.

Program in Apparel, Merchandising, and Design Expenses: Contact institution. Offers apparel, merchandising, and design (MS, PhD). *Application deadline:* For fall admission, 2/1 priority date for domestic and international students. *Application fee:* $60 ($90 for international students). Electronic applications accepted. *Application Contact:* Ann Marie Fiore, Application Contact, 515-294-9303, E-mail: amfiore@iastate.edu.

Program in Applied Linguistics and Technology Expenses: Contact institution. Offers applied linguistics and technology (PhD). *Application deadline:* For fall admission, 1/5 for domestic and international students. *Application fee:* $60 ($90 for international students). Electronic applications accepted. *Application Contact:* Teresa Smiley, Application Contact, 515-294-2477, Fax: 515-294-6814, E-mail: englgrad@iastate.edu.

Program in Applied Mathematics Expenses: Contact institution. Offers applied mathematics (MS, PhD). *Application deadline:* For fall admission, 2/1 for domestic and international students. Electronic applications accepted. *Application Contact:* Melanie Erickson, Application Contact, 515-294-0393, Fax: 515-294-5454, E-mail: gradmath@iastate.edu.

Program in Applied Physics Expenses: Contact institution. Offers applied physics (MS, PhD). *Application deadline:* For fall admission, 2/15 for domestic and international students; for spring admission, 10/15 for domestic and international students. Electronic applications accepted. *Application Contact:* Lori Hockett, Application Contact, 515-294-5870, Fax: 515-294-6027, E-mail: physastro@iastate.edu.

Program in Astrophysics Expenses: Contact institution. Offers astrophysics (MS, PhD). *Application deadline:* For fall admission, 2/15 for domestic students; for spring admission, 10/15 for domestic students. *Application Contact:* Lori Hockett, Application Contact, 515-294-5870, Fax: 515-294-6027, E-mail: physastro@iastate.edu.

Program in Biophysics Expenses: Contact institution. Offers biophysics (MS, PhD). *Application deadline:* For fall admission, 2/1 priority date for domestic students, 1/1 priority date for international students. Electronic applications accepted. *Application Contact:* Connie Garnett, Application Contact, 515-294-3317, Fax: 515-294-7629, E-mail: bbmbapps@iastate.edu.

Program in Biorenewable Resources and Technology Expenses: Contact institution. Offers biorenewable resources and technology (MS, PhD). *Application deadline:* For fall admission, 1/1 priority date for domestic and international students; for spring admission, 9/1 for domestic and international students. Applications are processed on a rolling basis. *Application fee:* $40 ($90 for international students). Electronic applications accepted. *Application Contact:* Laurie Engleen, Application Contact, 515-294-3759, Fax: 515-294-3091, E-mail: brtgrad@iastate.edu.

Program in Business Administration Expenses: Contact institution. Offers business administration (MBA). *Application deadline:* For fall admission, 7/1 priority date for domestic students, 3/1 priority date for international students; for winter admission, 12/1 for domestic and international students. *Application fee:* $60 ($90 for international students). Electronic applications accepted. *Application Contact:* Debbie Johnson, Application Contact, 515-294-5133, Fax: 515-294-2446, E-mail: busgrad@iastate.edu.

Program in Business Analytics *Program availability:* Online learning. Offers business analytics (MS).

Program in Business and Technology Expenses: Contact institution. Offers business and technology (PhD). *Application deadline:* For fall admission, 1/15 for domestic students. *Application fee:* $60 ($90 for international students). Electronic applications accepted. *Application Contact:* Debbie Johnson, Application Contact, 515-294-2474, Fax: 515-294-6060, E-mail: dljohns@iastate.edu.

Program in Computer Engineering Expenses: Contact institution. Offers computer engineering (M Eng, MS, PhD). *Application deadline:* For fall admission, 1/15 for domestic students; for spring admission, 9/15 for domestic students. *Application fee:* $60 ($90 for international students). Electronic applications accepted. *Application Contact:* Stacey Ross, Application Contact, 515-294-9162, E-mail: ecpe_grad_questions@iastate.edu.

Program in Condensed Matter Physics Expenses: Contact institution. Offers condensed matter physics (MS, PhD). *Application deadline:* For fall admission, 2/15 for domestic and international students; for spring admission, 10/15 for domestic and international students. *Application fee:* $60 ($90 for international students). Electronic applications accepted. *Application Contact:* Lori Hockett, Information Contact, 515-294-5870, Fax: 515-294-6027, E-mail: physastro@iastate.edu.

Program in Creative Writing and Environment Expenses: Contact institution. Offers creative writing and environment (MFA). *Application deadline:* For fall admission, 1/5 for domestic students. *Application fee:* $60 ($90 for international students). Electronic applications accepted. *Application Contact:* Teresa Smiley, Application Contact, 515-294-2477, Fax: 515-294-6814, E-mail: englgrad@iastate.edu.

Program in Crop Production and Physiology Expenses: Contact institution. Offers crop production and physiology (MS, PhD). *Application deadline:* Applications are processed on a rolling basis. *Application fee:* $60 ($90 for international students). Electronic applications accepted. *Application Contact:* Jaci Severson, Application Contact, 515-294-1361, Fax: 515-294-8146, E-mail: agrongradprograms@iastate.edu.

Program in Diet and Exercise Expenses: Contact institution. *Financial support:* Unspecified assistantships available. Offers diet and exercise (MS). *Application fee:* $60 ($90 for international students). Electronic applications accepted. *Application Contact:* Lorraine Lanningham-Foster, Application Contact, 515-294-4684, Fax: 515-294-6193, E-mail: lmlf@iastate.edu.

Program in Earth Science Expenses: Contact institution. Offers earth science (MS, PhD). *Application deadline:* For fall admission, 1/1 priority date for domestic students. *Application fee:* $60 ($90 for international students). Electronic applications accepted. *Application Contact:* Franek Hasiuk, Application Contact, 515-294-6610, Fax: 515-294-6049, E-mail: franek@iastate.edu.

Program in Ecology and Evolutionary Biology Expenses: Contact institution. Offers ecology and evolutionary biology (MS, PhD). *Application deadline:* For fall admission, 1/1 priority date for domestic and international students; for spring admission, 6/1 priority date for domestic and international students. *Application fee:* $60 ($90 for international students). Electronic applications accepted. *Application Contact:* Angela Stone, Application Contact, 515-294-1191, Fax: 515-294-6390, E-mail: eeb@iastate.edu.

Program in Engineering Mechanics Expenses: Contact institution. Offers engineering mechanics (M Eng, MS, PhD). *Application deadline:* For fall admission, 1/1 for domestic students; for spring admission, 9/1 for domestic students. *Application fee:* $60 ($90 for international students). Electronic applications accepted. *Application Contact:* Sara Goplin, Application Contact, 515-294-9669, Fax: 515-294-3262, E-mail: aere-info@iastate.edu.

Program in Environmental Sciences Expenses: Contact institution. Offers environmental sciences (MS, PhD). *Application deadline:* For fall admission, 2/1 for domestic and international students; for spring admission, 6/1 for domestic and international students. *Application fee:* $60 ($90 for international students). Electronic applications accepted. *Application Contact:* Melissa Stolt, Application Contact, 515-294-1170, Fax: 515-294-3003, E-mail: enscigrad@iastate.edu.

Program in Family and Consumer Sciences Expenses: Contact institution. Offers family and consumer sciences (MFCS). *Application deadline:* For fall admission, 4/15 priority date for domestic and international students; for spring admission, 10/15 priority date for domestic and international students. *Application fee:* $60 ($90 for international students). Electronic applications accepted. *Application Contact:* Karen Smidt, Application Contact, 515-294-5397, E-mail: mfcsinfo@iastate.edu.

Program in Finance Expenses: Contact institution. Offers finance (M Fin). *Application deadline:* For fall admission, 7/1 for domestic students; for spring admission, 11/1 for domestic students. *Application Contact:* Meleah Cue, Application Contact, 515-294-8118, Fax: 515-294-2592, E-mail: busgrad@iastate.edu.

Program in Fisheries Biology Expenses: Contact institution. Offers fisheries biology (MS, PhD). *Application deadline:* For fall admission, 4/1 for domestic students; for spring admission, 10/1 for domestic students. *Application fee:* $60 ($90 for international students). Electronic applications accepted. *Application Contact:* Kelly Kyle, Application Contact, 515-294-7400, Fax: 515-294-7406, E-mail: nremgradinfo@iastate.edu.

Program in Forestry Expenses: Contact institution. Offers forestry (MS, PhD). *Application deadline:* For fall admission, 4/1 for domestic students; for spring admission, 10/1 for domestic students. *Application fee:* $60 ($90 for international students). Electronic applications accepted. *Application Contact:* Kelly Kyle, Application Contact, 515-294-7400, Fax: 515-294-7406, E-mail: nremgradinfo@iastate.edu.

Program in Genetics Expenses: Contact institution. Offers genetics (MS, PhD). *Application deadline:* For fall admission, 2/1 priority date for domestic and international students; for spring admission, 9/1 priority date for domestic and international students. *Application fee:* $60 ($90 for international students). Electronic applications accepted. *Application Contact:* Linda Wild, Program Coordinator, 515-294-7697, Fax: 515-294-6669, E-mail: genetics@iastate.edu.

Program in Graphic Design Expenses: Contact institution. Offers graphic design (MA, MFA). *Application deadline:* For fall admission, 2/1 for domestic students; for spring admission, 4/15 for domestic students. *Application fee:* $60 ($90 for international students). Electronic applications accepted. *Application Contact:* Meredith Foley, Application Contact, 515-294-0816, Fax: 515-294-2725, E-mail: merfoley@iastate.edu.

Program in High Energy Physics Expenses: Contact institution. Offers high energy physics (MS, PhD). *Application deadline:* For fall admission, 2/15 for domestic students; for spring admission, 10/15 for domestic students. *Application fee:* $60 ($90 for international students). Electronic applications accepted. *Application Contact:* Lori Hockett, Application Contact, 515-294-5870, Fax: 515-294-6027, E-mail: physastro@iastate.edu.

Program in Human-Computer Interaction Expenses: Contact institution. Offers human-computer interaction (MS, PhD). *Application deadline:* For fall admission, 1/15 priority date for domestic and international students. *Application fee:* $40 ($90 for international students). Electronic applications accepted. *Application Contact:* Amy Carver, Application Contact, 515-294-2089, Fax: 515-294-5530, E-mail: info@hci.iastate.edu.

Program in Immunobiology Expenses: Contact institution. Offers immunobiology (MS, PhD). *Application deadline:* For fall admission, 1/15 priority date for domestic and international students. *Application fee:* $60 ($90 for international students). Electronic applications accepted. *Application Contact:* Katie Blair, Application Contact, 515-294-7252, Fax: 515-294-6790, E-mail: idgp@iastate.edu.

Program in Industrial Agriculture and Technology Expenses: Contact institution. Offers industrial agriculture and technology (MS, PhD). *Application deadline:* For fall admission, 2/1 priority date for domestic and international students; for spring admission, 7/1 for domestic and international students. *Application fee:* $60 ($90 for international students). Electronic applications accepted. *Application Contact:* Kris Bell, Application Contact, 515-294-1033, E-mail: kabell@iastate.edu.

Program in Industrial Design Expenses: Contact institution. Offers industrial design (MID). *Application deadline:* For fall admission, 3/15 for domestic students; for spring admission, 10/1 for domestic students. *Application fee:* $60 ($90 for international students). Electronic applications accepted. *Application Contact:* Meredith Foley, Application Contact, 515-294-0816, Fax: 515-294-2348, E-mail: merfoley@iastate.edu.

Program in Information Assurance Expenses: Contact institution. Offers information assurance (M Eng, MS). *Application deadline:* For fall admission, 5/1 priority date for domestic and international students; for spring admission, 11/1 priority date for domestic and international students. *Application fee:* $60 ($90 for international students). Electronic applications accepted. *Application Contact:* Virginia Anderson, Application Contact, 515-294-0659, Fax: 515-294-7582, E-mail: infas@iastate.edu.

Program in Information Systems Expenses: Contact institution. Offers information systems (MS). *Application deadline:* For fall admission, 6/1 priority date for domestic students, 3/1 priority date for international students; for spring admission, 11/1 priority date for domestic students, 3/1 priority date for international students. *Application fee:* $60 ($90 for international students). Electronic applications accepted. *Application Contact:* Meleah Cue, Application Contact, 515-294-8118, Fax: 515-294-2446, E-mail: busgrad@iastate.edu.

Program in Inorganic Chemistry Expenses: Contact institution. Offers inorganic chemistry (MS, PhD). *Application deadline:* For fall admission, 2/1 for domestic students. *Application fee:* $60 ($90 for international students). Electronic applications accepted.

Application Contact: Lynette Edsall, Application Contact, 515-294-7810, Fax: 515-294-0105, E-mail: chemgrad@iastate.edu.

Program in Integrated Visual Arts Expenses: Contact institution. Offers integrated visual arts (MFA). *Application deadline:* For fall admission, 2/1 priority date for domestic students. *Application Contact:* Meredith Foley, Application Contact, 515-294-0816, Fax: 515-294-2348, E-mail: merfoley@iastate.edu.

Program in Interdisciplinary Graduate Studies Expenses: Contact institution. Offers interdisciplinary graduate studies (MA, MS). *Application deadline:* For fall admission, 7/15 for domestic students; for spring admission, 11/15 for domestic students. *Application fee:* $60 ($90 for international students). Electronic applications accepted. *Application Contact:* Melissa Stolt, Application Contact, 515-294-1170, Fax: 515-294-3003, E-mail: mstolt@iastate.edu.

Program in Interior Design Expenses: Contact institution. Offers interior design (MA, MFA). *Application deadline:* For fall admission, 2/1 for domestic students. *Application fee:* $60 ($90 for international students). Electronic applications accepted. *Application Contact:* Meredith Foley, Application Contact, 515-294-0816, Fax: 515-294-2348, E-mail: merfoley@iastate.edu.

Program in Meat Science Expenses: Contact institution. Offers meat science (MS, PhD). *Application deadline:* For fall admission, 2/1 for domestic students; for spring admission, 9/1 for domestic students. Electronic applications accepted. *Application Contact:* Jane Linn, Application Contact, 515-294-2160, Fax: 515-294-6994, E-mail: jlinn@iastate.edu.

Program in Meteorology Expenses: Contact institution. Offers meteorology (MS, PhD). *Application deadline:* For fall admission, 12/1 priority date for domestic students. *Application fee:* $60 ($90 for international students). Electronic applications accepted. *Application Contact:* Jaci Severson, Application Contact, 515-294-1361, Fax: 515-294-8146, E-mail: meteorologygraduateprograms@iastate.edu.

Program in Microbiology Expenses: Contact institution. Offers microbiology (MS, PhD). *Application deadline:* For fall admission, 2/1 priority date for domestic and international students. *Application fee:* $60 ($90 for international students). Electronic applications accepted. *Application Contact:* Dai Nguyen, Information Contact, 515-294-9052, Fax: 515-294-6019, E-mail: microbiology@iastate.edu.

Program in Molecular, Cellular, and Developmental Biology Expenses: Contact institution. Offers molecular, cellular, and developmental biology (MS, PhD). *Application deadline:* For fall admission, 1/15 priority date for domestic and international students. *Application fee:* $60 ($90 for international students). Electronic applications accepted. *Application Contact:* Katie Blair, Application Contact, 515-294-7252, Fax: 515-924-6790, E-mail: idgp@iastate.edu.

Program in Neuroscience Expenses: Contact institution. Offers neuroscience (MS, PhD). *Application deadline:* For fall admission, 2/1 priority date for domestic students, 2/1 for international students. *Application fee:* $60 ($90 for international students). Electronic applications accepted. *Application Contact:* Katie Blair, Application Contact, 515-294-7252, Fax: 515-924-6790, E-mail: idgp@iastate.edu.

Program in Nuclear Physics Expenses: Contact institution. Offers nuclear physics (MS, PhD). *Application deadline:* For fall admission, 2/15 for domestic students; for spring admission, 10/15 for domestic students. *Application fee:* $60 ($90 for international students). Electronic applications accepted. *Application Contact:* Lori Hockett, Application Contact, 515-294-5870, Fax: 515-294-6027, E-mail: physastro@iastate.edu.

Program in Nutritional Sciences Expenses: Contact institution. Offers nutritional sciences (MS, PhD). *Application deadline:* For fall admission, 1/15 priority date for domestic and international students. Applications are processed on a rolling basis. *Application fee:* $60 ($90 for international students). Electronic applications accepted. *Application Contact:* Brenda Emery, Application Contact, 515-294-6442, Fax: 515-294-6193, E-mail: fshngraduate@iastate.edu.

Program in Organic Chemistry Expenses: Contact institution. Offers organic chemistry (MS, PhD). *Application deadline:* For fall admission, 2/1 for domestic students. *Application fee:* $60 ($90 for international students). Electronic applications accepted. *Application Contact:* Lynette Edsall, Application Contact, 800-521-2436, Fax: 515-294-0105, E-mail: chemgrad@iastate.edu.

Program in Physical Chemistry Expenses: Contact institution. Offers physical chemistry (MS, PhD). *Application deadline:* For fall admission, 2/1 for domestic students. *Application fee:* $60 ($90 for international students). Electronic applications accepted. *Application Contact:* Lynette Edsall, Application Contact, 800-521-2436, Fax: 515-294-0105, E-mail: chemgrad@iastate.edu.

Program in Plant Biology Expenses: Contact institution. Offers plant biology (MS, PhD). *Application deadline:* For fall admission, 1/16 priority date for domestic and international students. *Application fee:* $60 ($90 for international students). Electronic applications accepted. *Application Contact:* Dai Nguyen, Application Contact, 515-294-9052, Fax: 515-294-6019, E-mail: ipb@iastate.edu.

Program in Plant Breeding Expenses: Contact institution. Offers plant breeding (MS, PhD). *Application deadline:* Applications are processed on a rolling basis. *Application fee:* $60 ($90 for international students). Electronic applications accepted. *Application Contact:* Jaci Severson, Application Contact, 515-294-1361, Fax: 515-294-8146, E-mail: agrongradprograms@iastate.edu.

Program in Rhetoric and Professional Communication Expenses: Contact institution. Offers rhetoric and professional communication (PhD). *Application deadline:* For fall admission, 1/5 for domestic students. *Application fee:* $60 ($90 for international students). Electronic applications accepted. *Application Contact:* Teresa Smiley, Application Contact, 515-294-2477, Fax: 515-294-6814, E-mail: englgrad@iastate.edu.

Program in Rhetoric, Composition, and Professional Communication Expenses: Contact institution. Offers rhetoric, composition, and professional communication (MA). *Application deadline:* For fall admission, 1/5 for domestic students. *Application fee:* $60 ($90 for international students). Electronic applications accepted. *Application Contact:* Teresa Smiley, Application Contact, 515-294-2477, Fax: 515-294-6814, E-mail: englgrad@iastate.edu.

Program in Rural Sociology Expenses: Contact institution. Offers rural sociology (MS, PhD). *Application deadline:* For fall admission, 1/10 priority date for domestic and international students; for spring admission, 10/1 for domestic and international students. *Application fee:* $60 ($90 for international students). Electronic applications accepted. *Application Contact:* Rachel Burlingame, Application Contact, 515-294-2506, Fax: 515-294-8649, E-mail: rmb@iastate.edu.

Program in School Mathematics Expenses: Contact institution. Offers school mathematics (MSM). *Application fee:* $60 ($90 for international students). Electronic applications accepted. *Application Contact:* Melanie Erickson, Application Contact, 515-294-0393, Fax: 515-294-5454, E-mail: msm@iastate.edu.

Program in Science Education Expenses: Contact institution. Offers science education (MAT). *Application deadline:* For fall admission, 2/1 for domestic students.

Application fee: $60 ($90 for international students). Electronic applications accepted. *Application Contact:* Robyn Goldy, Application Contact, 515-294-1241, Fax: 515-294-6206, E-mail: rgoldy@iastate.edu.

Program in Seed Technology and Business Expenses: Contact institution. Offers seed technology and business (MS). *Application deadline:* For fall admission, 3/15 priority date for domestic students, 3/15 for international students. *Application fee:* $60 ($90 for international students). Electronic applications accepted. *Application Contact:* Lori Youngberg, Application Contact, 515-294-9137, Fax: 515-294-2014, E-mail: seedgrad@iastate.edu.

Program in Soil Science Expenses: Contact institution. Offers soil science (MS, PhD). *Application deadline:* Applications are processed on a rolling basis. *Application fee:* $60 ($90 for international students). Electronic applications accepted. *Application Contact:* Jaci Severson, Application Contact, 515-294-1361, Fax: 515-294-8146, E-mail: agrongradprograms@iastate.edu.

Program in Sustainable Agriculture Expenses: Contact institution. Offers sustainable agriculture (MS, PhD). *Application deadline:* For fall admission, 2/1 for domestic and international students; for spring admission, 6/1 priority date for domestic and international students. *Application fee:* $60 ($90 for international students). Electronic applications accepted. *Application Contact:* Angela Stone, Application Contact, 515-294-1191, Fax: 515-294-6390, E-mail: susag@iastate.edu.

Program in Systems Engineering Expenses: Contact institution. Offers systems engineering (M Eng). *Application deadline:* Applications are processed on a rolling basis. *Application fee:* $60 ($90 for international students). Electronic applications accepted. *Application Contact:* Holly Twedt, Application Contact, 515-294-4702. *Application Contact,* Laurie Hoifeldt, 515-294-4702, E-mail: systems-eng@iastate.edu.

Program in Teaching English as a Second Language/Applied Linguistics Expenses: Contact institution. Offers teaching English as a second language/applied linguistics (MA). *Application deadline:* For fall admission, 1/5 for domestic students. *Application fee:* $60 ($90 for international students). Electronic applications accepted. *Application Contact:* Teresa Smiley, Application Contact, 515-294-2477, Fax: 515-294-6814, E-mail: englgrad@iastate.edu.

Program in Toxicology Expenses: Contact institution. Offers toxicology (MS, PhD). *Application deadline:* For fall admission, 2/1 priority date for domestic and international students. Applications are processed on a rolling basis. *Application fee:* $60 ($90 for international students). Electronic applications accepted. *Application Contact:* Linda Wild, Application Contact, 515-294-7697, Fax: 515-294-6669, E-mail: toxmajor@iastate.edu.

Program in Transportation Expenses: Contact institution. Offers transportation (MS). *Application deadline:* For fall admission, 7/15 priority date for domestic students, 2/15 priority date for international students. *Application fee:* $60 ($90 for international students). Electronic applications accepted. *Application Contact:* Jing Dong, Application Contact, 515-294-3957, Fax: 515-294-0467, E-mail: jingdong@iastate.edu.

Rural, Agricultural, Technological, and Environmental History Program Expenses: Contact institution. Offers rural, agricultural, technological, and environmental history (PhD). *Application deadline:* For fall admission, 1/1 for domestic and international students. Electronic applications accepted. *Application Contact:* Michael Bailey, Application Contact, 515-294-1284, E-mail: mdbailey@iastate.edu.

IRELL & MANELLA GRADUATE SCHOOL OF BIOLOGICAL SCIENCES, Duarte, CA 91010

General Information Independent, coed, graduate-only institution. *Graduate housing:* Room and/or apartments available on a first-come, first-served basis to single students; on-campus housing not available to married students. Housing application deadline: 7/31.

GRADUATE UNITS

Graduate Program Offers brain metastatic cancer (PhD); cancer and stem cell metabolism (PhD); cancer biology (PhD); cancer biology and developmental therapeutics (PhD); cell biology (PhD); chemical biology (PhD); chromosomal break repair (PhD); diabetes and pancreatic progenitor cell biology (PhD); DNA repair and cancer biology (PhD); germline epigenetic remodeling and endocrine disruptors (PhD); hematology and hematopoietic cell transplantation (PhD); hematology and immunology (PhD); inflammation and cancer (PhD); micrornas and gene regulation in cardiovascular disease (PhD); mixed chimrism for reversal of autoimmunity (PhD); molecular and cellular biology (PhD); molecular biology and genetics (PhD); nanoparticle mediated twist1 silencing in metastatic cancer (PhD); neuro-oncology and stem cell biology (PhD); neuroscience (PhD); RNA directed therapies for HIV-1 (PhD); small RNA-induced transcriptional gene activation (PhD); stem cell regulation by the microenvironment (PhD); translational oncology and pharmaceutical sciences (PhD); tumor biology (PhD). Electronic applications accepted.

ITHACA COLLEGE, Ithaca, NY 14850

General Information Independent, coed, comprehensive institution. *Enrollment:* 6,678 graduate, professional, and undergraduate students; 391 full-time matriculated graduate/professional students (276 women), 65 part-time matriculated graduate/professional students (35 women). *Enrollment by degree level:* 282 master's, 174 doctoral. *Graduate faculty:* 165 full-time (79 women), 8 part-time/adjunct (4 women). Tuition and fees vary according to program. *Graduate housing:* On-campus housing not available. *Student services:* Campus employment opportunities, campus safety program, career counseling, exercise/wellness program, free psychological counseling, international student services, low-cost health insurance, multicultural affairs office, services for students with disabilities, teacher training, writing training. *Library facilities:* Ithaca College Library. *Collection:* Books: 311,396 (physical), 151,885 (digital/electronic); Databases: 151. Weekly public service hours: 148; study areas open 24 hours, 5–7 days a week. *Research affiliation:* National Science Foundation (Noyce Teacher Scholarship Program for students in STEM, computer science, physics), NASA (physics and astronomy), U.S. Department of Health and Human Services/National Institutes of Health (biology).

Computer facilities: Computer purchase and lease plans are available. 640 computers available on campus for general student use. A campuswide network can be accessed from student residence rooms and from off campus. Online class registration is available.

Website: http://www.ithaca.edu/

General Application Contact: Nicole Eversley Bradwell, Director, Office of Admission, 607-274-3124, Fax: 607-274-1263, E-mail: admission@ithaca.edu.

GRADUATE UNITS

Roy H. Park School of Communications Students: 18 part-time (8 women); includes 1 minority (Hispanic/Latino), 1 international. Average age 33. 25 applicants, 84% accepted, 13 enrolled. *Faculty:* 3 full-time (1 woman). Expenses: Contact institution. *Financial support:* In 2016–17, 13 students received support, including 11 fellowships (averaging $5,966 per year); career-related internships or fieldwork, Federal Work-Study, and scholarships/grants also available. Support available to part-time students. Financial award applicants required to submit CSS PROFILE or FAFSA. In 2016, 20 master's awarded. *Program availability:* Part-time. Offers communications innovation (MS); image text (MFA). *Application deadline:* For fall admission, 3/15 for domestic and international students; for spring admission, 12/1 for domestic and international students. Applications are processed on a rolling basis. *Application fee:* $40. Electronic applications accepted. *Application Contact:* Nicole Eversley Bradwell, Director, Office of Admission, 607-274-3124, Fax: 607-274-1263, E-mail: admission@ithaca.edu. *Dean,* Dr. Diane Gayeski, 607-274-3895, E-mail: gayeski@ithaca.edu.

School of Business Students: 20 full-time (6 women), 1 part-time (0 women); includes 3 minority (all Black or African American, non-Hispanic/Latino), 1 international. Average age 23. 23 applicants, 87% accepted, 16 enrolled. *Faculty:* 21 full-time (8 women), 3 part-time/adjunct (1 woman). Expenses: Contact institution. *Financial support:* In 2016–17, 18 students received support, including 17 fellowships (averaging $11,147 per year); career-related internships or fieldwork, Federal Work-Study, and scholarships/grants also available. Support available to part-time students. Financial award application deadline: 3/1; financial award applicants required to submit CSS PROFILE or FAFSA. In 2016, 10 master's awarded. *Program availability:* Part-time. Offers accounting (MS); business (MBA, MS); sport management (MBA). *Application deadline:* For fall admission, 5/15 for domestic and international students; for spring admission, 11/1 for domestic and international students. Applications are processed on a rolling basis. *Application fee:* $40. Electronic applications accepted. *Application Contact:* Nicole Eversley Bradwell, Director, Office of Admission, 607-274-3124, Fax: 607-274-1263, E-mail: admission@ithaca.edu. *Dean,* Sean Reid, 607-274-3341, E-mail: sreid@ithaca.edu.

School of Health Sciences and Human Performance Students: 325 full-time (248 women), 18 part-time (13 women); includes 37 minority (6 Black or African American, non-Hispanic/Latino; 10 Asian, non-Hispanic/Latino; 11 Hispanic/Latino; 10 Two or more races, non-Hispanic/Latino), 6 international. Average age 23. 506 applicants, 37% accepted, 201 enrolled. *Faculty:* 58 full-time (39 women), 1 part-time/adjunct (0 women). Expenses: Contact institution. *Financial support:* In 2016–17, 223 students received support, including 70 research assistantships (averaging $12,759 per year); career-related internships or fieldwork, Federal Work-Study, scholarships/grants, and unspecified assistantships also available. Support available to part-time students. Financial award applicants required to submit CSS PROFILE or FAFSA. In 2016, 97 master's, 85 doctorates awarded. *Program availability:* Part-time. Offers exercise and sport sciences (MS); health education (MS); health sciences and human performance (MS, DPT); occupational therapy (MS); physical education (MS); physical therapy (DPT); speech-language pathology (MS); speech-language pathology with teacher certification (MS). *Application deadline:* Applications are processed on a rolling basis. *Application fee:* $40. Electronic applications accepted. *Application Contact:* Nicole Eversley Bradwell, Interim Director, Office of Admission, 607-274-3124, Fax: 607-274-1263, E-mail: admission@ithaca.edu. *Acting Dean,* Dr. John Sigg, 607-274-3237, Fax: 607-274-1263, E-mail: sigg@ithaca.edu.

School of Humanities and Sciences Students: 24 full-time (15 women); includes 3 minority (all Hispanic/Latino). Average age 25. 41 applicants, 85% accepted, 23 enrolled. *Faculty:* 26 full-time (12 women). Expenses: Contact institution. *Financial support:* In 2016–17, 12 students received support, including 12 research assistantships (averaging $13,538 per year); career-related internships or fieldwork, Federal Work-Study, scholarships/grants, and unspecified assistantships also available. Support available to part-time students. Financial award application deadline: 2/15; financial award applicants required to submit CSS PROFILE or FAFSA. *Program availability:* Part-time. Offers agriculture education (MAT); biology (MAT); chemistry (MAT); childhood education (MS); earth science (MAT); English (MAT); French (MAT); humanities and sciences (MAT, MS); mathematics (MAT); physics (MAT); social studies (MAT); Spanish (MAT). *Application deadline:* For fall admission, 2/15 for domestic and international students; for spring admission, 12/1 for domestic and international students. Applications are processed on a rolling basis. *Application fee:* $40. Electronic applications accepted. *Application Contact:* Nicole Eversley Bradwell, Director, Office of Admission, 607-274-3124, Fax: 607-274-1263, E-mail: admission@ithaca.edu. *Dean,* Dr. Vincent Wang, 607-274-3102, E-mail: vwang@ithaca.edu.

School of Music Students: 22 full-time (7 women), 28 part-time (14 women); includes 11 minority (1 Black or African American, non-Hispanic/Latino; 6 Asian, non-Hispanic/Latino; 2 Hispanic/Latino; 2 Two or more races, non-Hispanic/Latino), 7 international. Average age 25. 155 applicants, 36% accepted, 25 enrolled. *Faculty:* 57 full-time (19 women), 4 part-time/adjunct (3 women). Expenses: Contact institution. *Financial support:* In 2016–17, 47 students received support, including 46 teaching assistantships (averaging $9,458 per year); career-related internships or fieldwork, Federal Work-Study, scholarships/grants, and unspecified assistantships also available. Support available to part-time students. Financial award application deadline: 1/15; financial award applicants required to submit CSS PROFILE or FAFSA. In 2016, 20 master's awarded. *Program availability:* Part-time, evening/weekend, online learning. Offers composition (MM); conducting (MM); music (MM, MS); music education (MM, MS); performance (MM); Suzuki pedagogy (MM). *Application deadline:* For fall admission, 1/15 for domestic and international students; for spring admission, 12/1 for domestic and international students. Applications are processed on a rolling basis. *Application fee:* $40. Electronic applications accepted. *Application Contact:* Nicole Eversley Bradwell, Director, Office of Admission, 607-274-3124, Fax: 607-274-1263, E-mail: admission@ithaca.edu. *Dean, School of Music,* Dr. Karl Paulnack, 607-274-3343, E-mail: kpaulnack@ithaca.edu.

JACKSON STATE UNIVERSITY, Jackson, MS 39217

General Information State-supported, coed, university. CGS member. *Enrollment:* 9,811 graduate, professional, and undergraduate students; 828 full-time matriculated graduate/professional students (617 women), 1,491 part-time matriculated graduate/professional students (1,095 women). *Enrollment by degree level:* 1,729 master's, 453 doctoral, 137 other advanced degrees. *Graduate faculty:* 207 full-time (85 women), 27 part-time/adjunct (9 women). Tuition, state resident: full-time $7141. Tuition, nonresident: full-time $17,494. *Required fees:* $1080. Tuition and fees vary according to class time, course level, course load, degree level, campus/location, program and student level. *Graduate housing:* Room and/or apartments available on a first-come, first-served basis to single students; on-campus housing not available to married students. Typical cost: $8226 (including board). Room and board charges vary according to board plan, campus/location and housing facility selected. Housing application deadline: 7/15. *Student services:* Campus employment opportunities, campus safety program, career counseling, child daycare facilities, exercise/wellness program, grant writing training, international student services, multicultural affairs office, services for students with disabilities, teacher training, writing training. *Library facilities:* H. T. Sampson Library plus 4 others. *Collection:* Books: 300,587 (physical), 339,368 (digital/electronic); Serial titles: 292,055 (digital/electronic); Databases: 68. *Research*

affiliation: Lawrence A. Berkeley Laboratories (biology, chemistry), U.S. Department of Energy (biology), National Science Foundation (biology, chemistry), Environmental Protection Agency, Oak Ridge Associated Universities (science), Raytheon Systems Company (computer science).

Computer facilities: 1,224 computers available on campus for general student use. A campuswide network can be accessed from student residence rooms and from off campus. Online class registration is available.
Website: http://www.jsums.edu/

General Application Contact: Dr. Darcie Bishop, Associate Dean of the Graduate School, 601-979-2455, Fax: 601-979-4321, E-mail: darcie.bishop@jsums.edu.

GRADUATE UNITS

Graduate School Students: 316 full-time (228 women), 344 part-time (269 women); includes 547 minority (534 Black or African American, non-Hispanic/Latino; 3 American Indian or Alaska Native, non-Hispanic/Latino; 2 Asian, non-Hispanic/Latino; 6 Hispanic/Latino; 2 Two or more races, non-Hispanic/Latino), 68 international. Average age 36. 1,687 applicants, 56% accepted, 568 enrolled. *Faculty:* 207 full-time (85 women), 27 part-time/adjunct (9 women). Expenses: Contact institution. *Financial support:* Fellowships, research assistantships, teaching assistantships, career-related internships or fieldwork, Federal Work-Study, institutionally sponsored loans, scholarships/grants, tuition waivers (full and partial), and unspecified assistantships available. Support available to part-time students. Financial award application deadline: 4/15; financial award applicants required to submit FAFSA. In 2016, 434 master's, 86 doctorates, 13 other advanced degrees awarded. *Program availability:* Part-time, evening/weekend, online only, 100% online, blended/hybrid learning. *Application deadline:* For fall admission, 9/5 for domestic students; for spring admission, 10/1 for domestic students. Applications are processed on a rolling basis. *Application fee:* $25. Electronic applications accepted. *Application Contact:* Dr. Darcie Bishop, Associate Dean of Graduate Studies, 601-979-2455, Fax: 601-979-4325, E-mail: darcie.bishop@jsums.edu. *Dean,* Dr. Dorris R. Robinson-Gardner, 601-979-2455, Fax: 601-979-4325, E-mail: dorris.r.gardner@jsums.edu.

College of Business Students: 60 full-time (41 women), 78 part-time (45 women); includes 107 minority (103 Black or African American, non-Hispanic/Latino; 4 Asian, non-Hispanic/Latino), 24 international. Average age 20. 214 applicants, 50% accepted, 88 enrolled. *Faculty:* 11 full-time (1 woman), 1 part-time/adjunct (0 women). Expenses: Contact institution. *Financial support:* Fellowships, research assistantships, teaching assistantships, career-related internships or fieldwork, Federal Work-Study, scholarships/grants, tuition waivers (full and partial), and unspecified assistantships available. Support available to part-time students. Financial award application deadline: 3/1; financial award applicants required to submit FAFSA. In 2016, 32 master's, 4 doctorates awarded. *Program availability:* Part-time, evening/weekend. Offers accounting (MPA); business (MBA, MPA, PhD); business administration (MBA, PhD). *Application deadline:* For fall admission, 3/1 priority date for domestic students, 3/1 for international students; for spring admission, 10/1 for domestic and international students. Applications are processed on a rolling basis. *Application fee:* $25. Electronic applications accepted. *Application Contact:* Dr. Kenneth Russ, Graduate Coordinator, 601-979-4327, Fax: 601-979-2690, E-mail: kenneth.russ@jsums.edu. *Dean,* Dr. Ramin Maysami, 601-979-2411, Fax: 601-979-2690, E-mail: ramin.c.maysami@jsums.edu.

College of Education and Human Development Students: 262 full-time (208 women), 669 part-time (526 women); includes 863 minority (853 Black or African American, non-Hispanic/Latino; 2 American Indian or Alaska Native, non-Hispanic/Latino; 4 Hispanic/Latino; 1 Native Hawaiian or other Pacific Islander, non-Hispanic/Latino; 3 Two or more races, non-Hispanic/Latino), 23 international. Average age 33. 1,687 applicants, 26% accepted, 269 enrolled. *Faculty:* 43 full-time (25 women), 9 part-time/adjunct (2 women). Expenses: Contact institution. *Financial support:* Teaching assistantships, career-related internships or fieldwork, Federal Work-Study, scholarships/grants, and unspecified assistantships available. Support available to part-time students. Financial award application deadline: 3/1; financial award applicants required to submit FAFSA. In 2016, 127 master's, 37 doctorates, 13 other advanced degrees awarded. *Program availability:* Part-time, evening/weekend, 100% online, blended/hybrid learning. Offers clinical mental health (MS); early childhood education (MS Ed, Ed D); education administration and supervision (Ed S); education and human development (MS, MS Ed, Ed D, PhD, Ed S); educational administration and supervision (MS Ed, PhD); elementary education (MS Ed, Ed S); higher education (Ed S); physical education (MS Ed); reading education (MS Ed); rehabilitation counseling (MS); school counseling (MS Ed); special education (MS Ed, Ed S); sport science (MS). *Application deadline:* For fall admission, 3/1 priority date for domestic students, 3/1 for international students; for spring admission, 10/1 for domestic and international students. Applications are processed on a rolling basis. *Application fee:* $25. Electronic applications accepted. *Application Contact:* Dr. Milliard Bingham, Associate Interim Dean, 601-979-1750, Fax: 601-979-3419, E-mail: millard.j.bingham@jsums.edu. *Interim Dean,* Dr. Daniel Watkins, 601-979-2433, E-mail: daniel.watkins@jsums.edu.

College of Liberal Arts Students: 49 full-time (29 women), 83 part-time (56 women); includes 108 minority (104 Black or African American, non-Hispanic/Latino; 1 Asian, non-Hispanic/Latino; 2 Hispanic/Latino; 1 Two or more races, non-Hispanic/Latino), 6 international. Average age 33. 680 applicants, 64% accepted, 269 enrolled. *Faculty:* 49 full-time (26 women), 2 part-time/adjunct (0 women). Expenses: Contact institution. *Financial support:* Fellowships, research assistantships, teaching assistantships, career-related internships or fieldwork, Federal Work-Study, scholarships/grants, tuition waivers (full and partial), and unspecified assistantships available. Support available to part-time students. Financial award application deadline: 3/1; financial award applicants required to submit FAFSA. In 2016, 37 master's, 9 doctorates awarded. *Program availability:* Part-time, evening/weekend. Offers clinical psychology (PhD); criminology and justice services (MA); English (MA); history (MA); liberal arts (MA, MAT, MM Ed, PhD); music education (MM Ed); political science (MA); sociology (MA); teaching English (MAT). *Application deadline:* For fall admission, 3/1 priority date for domestic students; for spring admission, 10/1 for domestic and international students. Applications are processed on a rolling basis. *Application fee:* $25. Electronic applications accepted. *Application Contact:* Courtney Brookins, Advisement and Enrollment Coordinator, 601-979-7036, Fax: 601-979-4325, E-mail: courtney.w.brookins@jsums.edu. *Dean,* Dr. Mario Azevedo, 601-979-7036, E-mail: mario.j.azevedo@jsums.edu.

College of Public Service Expenses: Contact institution. *Financial support:* Career-related internships or fieldwork, Federal Work-Study, scholarships/grants, tuition waivers (full), and unspecified assistantships available. Support available to part-time students. Financial award application deadline: 3/1; financial award applicants required to submit FAFSA. Offers public administration (PhD); public policy and administration (MPPA); public service (MA, MPPA, MSW, PhD); social work (MSW,

PhD); urban and regional planning (MA, PhD). *Application deadline:* For fall admission, 3/1 for domestic and international students; for spring admission, 10/1 for domestic and international students. *Application fee:* $25. *Application Contact:* Fatoumatta Sisay, Manager of Graduate Admissions, 601-979-0342, Fax: 601-979-4325, E-mail: fatoumatta.sisay@jsums.edu. *Dean,* Dr. Ricardo A. Brown, 601-979-8836, Fax: 601-979-3360, E-mail: deanofcps@jsums.edu.

College of Science, Engineering and Technology Expenses: Contact institution. *Financial support:* Career-related internships or fieldwork, Federal Work-Study, scholarships/grants, and unspecified assistantships available. Support available to part-time students. Financial award application deadline: 3/1; financial award applicants required to submit FAFSA. *Program availability:* Part-time, evening/weekend. Offers applied mathematics (MS); biology (MS); chemistry and biochemistry (MS, PhD); civil engineering (MS, PhD); coastal engineering (MS, PhD); computer science (MS); environmental engineering (MS, PhD); environmental science (MS); hazardous materials management (MS); mathematics education (MST); physical science (MS, PhD); pure mathematics (MS); science education (MST); science, engineering and technology (MS, MS Ed, MST, PhD); technology education (MS Ed). *Application deadline:* For fall admission, 3/1 priority date for domestic students, 3/1 for international students; for spring admission, 10/1 for domestic and international students. Applications are processed on a rolling basis. *Application fee:* $25. *Application Contact:* Fatoumatta Sisay, Manager of Graduate Admissions, 601-979-0342, Fax: 601-977-4325, E-mail: fatoumatta.sisay@jsums.edu. *Dean,* Dr. Richard Alo, 601-979-2153, E-mail: richard.a.alo@jsums.edu.

School of Public Health Expenses: Contact institution. Offers communicative disorders (MS); public health (MPH, MS, Dr PH). *Application Contact:* Fatoumatta Sisay, Manager of Graduate Admissions, 601-979-0342, Fax: 601-979-4325, E-mail: fatoumatta.sisay@jsums.edu. *Dean,* Dr. Mohammad Shahbazi, 601-979-6387, Fax: 601-979-4325, E-mail: mohammad.shahbazi@jsums.edu.

JACKSONVILLE STATE UNIVERSITY, Jacksonville, AL 36265-1602

General Information State-supported, coed, comprehensive institution. *Enrollment:* 8,514 graduate, professional, and undergraduate students; 248 full-time matriculated graduate/professional students (177 women), 705 part-time matriculated graduate/professional students (430 women). *Enrollment by degree level:* 799 master's, 40 doctoral, 114 other advanced degrees. *Graduate faculty:* 141 full-time (57 women), 24 part-time/adjunct (10 women). *Graduate housing:* Rooms and/or apartments available on a first-come, first-served basis to single and married students. Typical cost: $7128 (including board) for single students; $7128 (including board) for married students. Room and board charges vary according to board plan and housing facility selected. *Student services:* Campus employment opportunities, campus safety program, career counseling, child daycare facilities, exercise/wellness program, free psychological counseling, international student services, multicultural affairs office, services for students with disabilities, teacher training. *Library facilities:* Houston Cole Library. *Collection:* Books: 711,815 (physical), 32,128 (digital/electronic); Databases: 307. Weekly public service hours: 87.

Computer facilities: 350 computers available on campus for general student use. A campuswide network can be accessed from student residence rooms and from off campus. Online class registration is available.
Website: http://www.jsu.edu/

General Application Contact: Dr. Joe Walsh, Vice Provost and Interim Director, 256-782-5284, E-mail: ejwalsh@jsu.edu.

GRADUATE UNITS

College of Graduate Studies and Continuing Education Students: 248 full-time (177 women), 705 part-time (430 women); includes 149 minority (141 Black or African American, non-Hispanic/Latino; 4 American Indian or Alaska Native, non-Hispanic/Latino; 4 Hispanic/Latino), 44 international. Average age 40. 800 applicants, 58% accepted, 308 enrolled. *Faculty:* 141 full-time (57 women), 24 part-time/adjunct (10 women). Expenses: Contact institution. *Financial support:* In 2016–17, 219 students received support. Available to part-time students. Application deadline: 3/15; applicants required to submit FAFSA. In 2016, 288 master's, 1 doctorate, 49 other advanced degrees awarded. *Program availability:* Part-time, evening/weekend, 100% online, blended/hybrid learning. *Application deadline:* Applications are processed on a rolling basis. *Application fee:* $35. Electronic applications accepted. *Application Contact:* Dr. Jean Pugliese, Associate Dean, 256-782-8278, Fax: 256-782-5321, E-mail: pugliese@jsu.edu. *Vice Provost and Interim Director,* Dr. Joe Walsh, 256-782-5284, E-mail: ejwalsh@jsu.edu.

College of Arts and Sciences Students: 72 full-time (42 women), 241 part-time (127 women); includes 36 minority (34 Black or African American, non-Hispanic/Latino; 2 Hispanic/Latino), 26 international. Average age 32. 354 applicants, 54% accepted, 117 enrolled. *Faculty:* 86 full-time (29 women), 8 part-time/adjunct (2 women). Expenses: Contact institution. *Financial support:* In 2016–17, 104 students received support. Available to part-time students. Application deadline: 4/1; applicants required to submit FAFSA. In 2016, 70 master's, 1 doctorate awarded. *Program availability:* Part-time, evening/weekend, 100% online, blended/hybrid learning. Offers arts and sciences (MA, MPA, MS, D Sc); biology (MS); computer systems and software design (MS); criminal justice (MS); emergency management (MS, D Sc); English (MA); history (MA); liberal studies (MA); mathematics (MS); music (MA); political science (MPA); psychology (MS). *Application deadline:* Applications are processed on a rolling basis. *Application fee:* $35. *Application Contact:* Dr. Jean Pugliese, Associate Dean, 256-782-8278, Fax: 256-782-5321, E-mail: pugliese@jsu.edu. *Dean,* Dr. Earl Wade, 256-782-5649, E-mail: jwade@jsu.edu.

College of Commerce and Business Administration Students: 23 full-time (15 women), 56 part-time (20 women); includes 8 minority (all Black or African American, non-Hispanic/Latino), 9 international. Average age 32. 102 applicants, 34% accepted, 25 enrolled. *Faculty:* 11 full-time (1 woman). Expenses: Contact institution. *Financial support:* In 2016–17, 19 students received support. Available to part-time students. Application deadline: 4/1; applicants required to submit FAFSA. In 2016, 17 master's awarded. *Program availability:* Part-time, evening/weekend, 100% online, blended/hybrid learning. Offers commerce and business administration (MBA). *Application deadline:* Applications are processed on a rolling basis. *Application fee:* $35. Electronic applications accepted. *Application Contact:* Dr. Jean Pugliese, Associate Dean, 256-782-8278, Fax: 256-782-5321, E-mail: pugliese@jsu.edu. *Dean,* Dr. William Fielding, 256-782-5508, E-mail: fielding@jsu.edu.

College of Education and Professional Studies Students: 142 full-time (109 women), 359 part-time (243 women); includes 95 minority (90 Black or African American, non-Hispanic/Latino; 3 American Indian or Alaska Native, non-Hispanic/Latino; 2 Hispanic/Latino), 9 international. Average age 33. 319 applicants, 66% accepted, 150 enrolled. *Faculty:* 41 full-time (24 women), 15 part-time/adjunct (8 women). Expenses:

Contact institution. *Financial support:* In 2016–17, 92 students received support. Available to part-time students. Application deadline: 4/1; applicants required to submit FAFSA. In 2016, 181 master's, 37 other advanced degrees awarded. *Program availability:* Part-time, evening/weekend, 100% online, blended/hybrid learning. Offers early childhood education (MS Ed); education (Ed S); education and professional studies (MS, MS Ed, Ed S); elementary education (MS Ed); guidance and counseling (MS); instructional leadership (MS Ed, Ed S); library media (MS Ed); physical education (MS Ed, Ed S); reading specialist (MS Ed); secondary education (MS Ed); special education (MS Ed). *Application deadline:* Applications are processed on a rolling basis. *Application fee:* $35. Electronic applications accepted. *Application Contact:* Dr. Jean Pugliese, Associate Dean, 256-782-8278, Fax: 256-782-5321, E-mail: pugliese@jsu.edu. *Dean,* Dr. John Hammett, 256-782-8212, E-mail: jhammett@jsu.edu.

College of Nursing Students: 11 full-time (all women), 36 part-time (33 women); includes 9 minority (8 Black or African American, non-Hispanic/Latino; 1 American Indian or Alaska Native, non-Hispanic/Latino). Average age 40. 28 applicants, 50% accepted, 9 enrolled. *Faculty:* 3 full-time (all women), 1 part-time/adjunct (0 women). Expenses: Contact institution. *Financial support:* In 2016–17, 4 students received support. Available to part-time students. Application deadline: 4/1; applicants required to submit FAFSA. In 2016, 15 master's awarded. *Program availability:* Part-time, evening/weekend. Offers nursing (MSN). *Application deadline:* Applications are processed on a rolling basis. *Application fee:* $35. Electronic applications accepted. *Application Contact:* Dr. Jean Pugliese, Associate Dean, 256-782-8278, Fax: 256-782-5321, E-mail: pugliese@jsu.edu. *Dean,* Dr. Christie Shelton, 256-782-5431, E-mail: cshelton@jsu.edu.

JACKSONVILLE UNIVERSITY, Jacksonville, FL 32211

General Information Independent, coed, comprehensive institution. *Enrollment:* 4,060 graduate, professional, and undergraduate students; 377 full-time matriculated graduate/professional students (240 women), 784 part-time matriculated graduate/professional students (637 women). *Enrollment by degree level:* 982 master's, 134 doctoral, 45 other advanced degrees. *Graduate faculty:* 18 full-time (5 women), 27 part-time/adjunct (11 women). *Tuition:* Full-time $13,320. One-time fee: $50 part-time. Tuition and fees vary according to course load, degree level, campus/location and program. *Graduate housing:* Room and/or apartments available on a first-come, first-served basis to single students; on-campus housing not available to married students. Typical cost: $9150 per year ($13,550 including board). Room and board charges vary according to board plan and housing facility selected. Housing application deadline: 8/1. *Student services:* Campus employment opportunities, campus safety program, career counseling, free psychological counseling, international student services, low-cost health insurance, multicultural affairs office, services for students with disabilities, teacher training, writing training. *Library facilities:* Carl S. Swisher Library. *Collection:* Books: 156,688 (physical), 148,457 (digital/electronic); Serial titles: 183,530 (physical); Databases: 2. Weekly public service hours: 88; students can reserve study rooms.

Computer facilities: Computer purchase and lease plans are available. 400 computers available on campus for general student use. A campuswide network can be accessed from student residence rooms and from off campus. Online class registration, learning management systems are available.
Website: http://www.ju.edu/

General Application Contact: Allana Forte, Director of Admissions and Recruitment, 904-256-7000, E-mail: admissions@ju.edu.

GRADUATE UNITS

Brooks Rehabilitation College of Healthcare Sciences Offers healthcare sciences (MS, MSN, DNP, Certificate).

Keigwin School of Nursing Students: 54 full-time (50 women), 534 part-time (476 women); includes 144 minority (77 Black or African American, non-Hispanic/Latino; 4 American Indian or Alaska Native, non-Hispanic/Latino; 25 Asian, non-Hispanic/Latino; 33 Hispanic/Latino; 5 Two or more races, non-Hispanic/Latino), 2 international. Average age 40. 206 applicants, 55% accepted, 91 enrolled. *Faculty:* 22 full-time (19 women), 24 part-time/adjunct (19 women). Expenses: Contact institution. *Financial support:* Federal Work-Study and institutionally sponsored loans available. Support available to part-time students. Financial award application deadline: 3/15. In 2016, 191 master's, 10 doctorates awarded. *Program availability:* Part-time. Offers clinical nurse educator (MSN); family nurse practitioner (MSN); family nurse practitioner/emergency nurse practitioner (MSN); leadership in the healthcare system (MSN); nursing (MSN); nursing informatics (MSN); nursing practice (DNP); psychiatric nurse practitioner (MSN). *Application fee:* $50. Electronic applications accepted. *Application Contact:* Stephanie Bloom, Assistant Director, Enrollment and Advanced Graduate Nursing, 904-256-7286, E-mail: sstrick4@ju.edu. *Associate Dean, Keigwin School of Nursing,* Dr. Cheryl Bergman, 904-256-7282, E-mail: cbergma@ju.edu.

School of Applied Health Sciences Students: 116 full-time (97 women), 34 part-time (25 women); includes 51 minority (29 Black or African American, non-Hispanic/Latino; 3 Asian, non-Hispanic/Latino; 17 Hispanic/Latino; 2 Two or more races, non-Hispanic/Latino). Average age 30. 129 applicants, 74% accepted, 79 enrolled. *Faculty:* 11 full-time (8 women), 17 part-time/adjunct (4 women). Expenses: Contact institution. In 2016, 28 master's awarded. *Program availability:* Part-time, 100% online, blended/hybrid learning. Offers clinical mental health counseling (MS); health informatics (MS); kinesiological sciences (MS); mental health counseling (MS); speech language pathology (MS); speech-language pathology (MS); sport management (MS). *Application deadline:* For fall admission, 3/1 for domestic and international students. *Application fee:* $50. Electronic applications accepted. *Application Contact:* Ashlea Rieser, Assistant Director of Enrollment and Advising, 904-256-8934, E-mail: aquitte@ju.edu. *Associate Dean,* Dr. Heather Hausenblas.

School of Orthodontics Students: 30 full-time (21 women), 5 part-time (2 women); includes 9 minority (6 Asian, non-Hispanic/Latino; 3 Hispanic/Latino), 9 international. Average age 29. 241 applicants, 12% accepted, 20 enrolled. *Faculty:* 15 full-time (6 women). Expenses: Contact institution. *Financial support:* Scholarships/grants and health care benefits available. Financial award application deadline: 4/1. In 2016, 15 other advanced degrees awarded. Offers dentistry (MS); orthodontics (Certificate). *Application deadline:* For fall admission, 9/14 priority date for domestic students, 9/14 for international students. *Application fee:* $175. *Application Contact:* Nancy Srock, Academic Coordinator, Orthodontics, 904-256-7865, E-mail: nsrock@ju.edu. *Associate Dean of Health Sciences, Orthodontics Program,* Dr. Mark Alarbi, 904-256-7856, E-mail: malarab@ju.edu.

College of Arts and Sciences Offers arts and sciences (MA, MS); education leadership (MS); mathematics (MA).

Marine Science Research Institute Students: 7 full-time (6 women), 12 part-time (all women); includes 1 minority (Hispanic/Latino). Average age 25. 17 applicants, 100% accepted, 11 enrolled. *Faculty:* 3 full-time (1 woman), 1 part-time/adjunct (0 women).

Expenses: Contact institution. *Financial support:* In 2016–17, 2 teaching assistantships with partial tuition reimbursements (averaging $2,000 per year) were awarded; career-related internships or fieldwork, scholarships/grants, tuition waivers, and unspecified assistantships also available. Financial award application deadline: 4/1. In 2016, 6 master's awarded. *Program availability:* Part-time. Offers marine science (MA, MS). *Application deadline:* Applications are processed on a rolling basis. *Application fee:* $50. Electronic applications accepted. *Application Contact:* Heather Anderson, Assistant Director of Graduate Admissions, 904-256-7004, E-mail: handers6@ju.edu. *Executive Director,* Dr. A. Quinton White, Jr., 904-256-7100, E-mail: qwhite@ju.edu.

College of Fine Arts Students: 12 full-time (11 women), 13 part-time (10 women); includes 11 minority (4 Black or African American, non-Hispanic/Latino; 1 Asian, non-Hispanic/Latino; 5 Hispanic/Latino; 1 Two or more races, non-Hispanic/Latino). Average age 38. 1 applicant. *Faculty:* 7 full-time (4 women), 3 part-time/adjunct (2 women). Expenses: Contact institution. *Financial support:* In 2016–17, 2 fellowships (averaging $35,700 per year) were awarded; institutionally sponsored loans, scholarships/grants, and health care benefits also available. Support available to part-time students. Financial award application deadline: 3/1; financial award applicants required to submit FAFSA. In 2016, 12 master's awarded. *Program availability:* Blended/hybrid learning. Offers choreography (MFA); fine arts (MFA); visual arts (MFA). *Application deadline:* For spring admission, 5/1 priority date for domestic students, 2/1 priority date for international students. Applications are processed on a rolling basis. *Application fee:* $50. Electronic applications accepted. *Application Contact:* Cari Coble, MFA Co-Director, 904-256-7398, E-mail: ccoble@ju.edu. *MFA Co-Director,* Cari Coble, 904-256-7398, E-mail: ccoble@ju.edu.

Davis College of Business Students: 140 full-time (55 women), 118 part-time (56 women); includes 65 minority (37 Black or African American, non-Hispanic/Latino; 1 American Indian or Alaska Native, non-Hispanic/Latino; 8 Asian, non-Hispanic/Latino; 16 Hispanic/Latino; 3 Two or more races, non-Hispanic/Latino), 27 international. Average age 34. 269 applicants, 53% accepted, 110 enrolled. *Faculty:* 23 full-time (6 women), 5 part-time/adjunct (0 women). Expenses: Contact institution. *Financial support:* In 2016–17, 22 students received support, including 6 research assistantships with partial tuition reimbursements available (averaging $9,000 per year); scholarships/grants and unspecified assistantships also available. Financial award application deadline: 7/1; financial award applicants required to submit FAFSA. In 2016, 118 master's awarded. *Program availability:* Part-time, evening/weekend. Offers accounting and finance (MBA); business (MBA, MS, DBA); business administration (MBA, DBA); consumer goods and services marketing (MBA); leadership development (MBA); management (MBA); management accounting (MBA); organizational leadership (MS). JD/MBA offered jointly with Florida Coastal School of Law. *Application deadline:* For fall admission, 8/1 priority date for domestic students, 7/15 priority date for international students; for spring admission, 12/1 priority date for domestic students, 11/15 priority date for international students; for summer admission, 4/1 priority date for domestic students, 3/15 priority date for international students. Applications are processed on a rolling basis. *Application fee:* $50. Electronic applications accepted. *Application Contact:* AnnaMaria Murphy, Assistant Director of Graduate Admissions, 904-256-7426, Fax: 904-256-7012, E-mail: mba@ju.edu. *Dean,* Dr. Don Capener, 904-256-7431, Fax: 904-256-7467, E-mail: dcapene@ju.edu.

Public Policy Institute Students: 10 full-time (4 women), 19 part-time (10 women); includes 6 minority (2 Black or African American, non-Hispanic/Latino; 1 Asian, non-Hispanic/Latino; 2 Hispanic/Latino; 1 Two or more races, non-Hispanic/Latino). Average age 36. 43 applicants, 51% accepted, 19 enrolled. *Faculty:* 2 part-time/adjunct (0 women). Expenses: Contact institution. *Financial support:* In 2016–17, 11 students received support. Career-related internships or fieldwork, scholarships/grants, and unspecified assistantships available. Financial award application deadline: 4/1. In 2016, 10 master's awarded. *Program availability:* Part-time, evening/weekend. Offers public policy (MPP). MPP/JD offered in partnership with Florida Coastal School of Law; MBA/MPP with Davis College of Business; MPP/MS with Marine Science Research Institute. *Application deadline:* For fall admission, 4/1 priority date for domestic students. Applications are processed on a rolling basis. *Application fee:* $50. Electronic applications accepted. *Application Contact:* Allana Forte, Director of Admissions and Recruitment, 904-256-7000, E-mail: admiss@ju.edu. *Director,* Richard A. Mullaney, 904-256-7342, E-mail: rmullan1@ju.edu.

JAMES MADISON UNIVERSITY, Harrisonburg, VA 22807

General Information State-supported, coed, comprehensive institution. CGS member. *Enrollment:* 21,270 graduate, professional, and undergraduate students; 1,037 full-time matriculated graduate/professional students (748 women), 501 part-time matriculated graduate/professional students (316 women). *Enrollment by degree level:* 1,299 master's, 180 doctoral, 59 other advanced degrees. *Graduate faculty:* 539 full-time (261 women), 54 part-time/adjunct (29 women). *Graduate housing:* On-campus housing not available. *Student services:* Campus employment opportunities, campus safety program, career counseling, exercise/wellness program, free psychological counseling, international student services, multicultural affairs office, services for students with disabilities, teacher training, writing training. *Library facilities:* Carrier Library plus 2 others. *Collection:* Students can reserve study rooms. *Research affiliation:* National Institute of Standards and Technology (NIST) through George Mason University (network risk assessment), National Oceanic and Atmospheric Administration (NOAA) (applied meteorological research), National Science Foundation (development of a detector array for Compton Scattering using polarized beams and targets; quantitative skills in biology).

Computer facilities: Computer purchase and lease plans are available. A campuswide network can be accessed from student residence rooms and from off campus. Online class registration is available.
Website: http://www.jmu.edu/

General Application Contact: Dr. Jie Chen, Dean, The Graduate School, 540-568-4213, Fax: 540-568-7860, E-mail: grad@jmu.edu.

GRADUATE UNITS

The Graduate School Students: 1,037 full-time (748 women), 501 part-time (316 women); includes 213 minority (74 Black or African American, non-Hispanic/Latino; 2 American Indian or Alaska Native, non-Hispanic/Latino; 42 Asian, non-Hispanic/Latino; 53 Hispanic/Latino; 42 Two or more races, non-Hispanic/Latino), 37 international. Average age 30. 2,406 applicants, 55% accepted, 879 enrolled. *Faculty:* 539 full-time (261 women), 54 part-time/adjunct (29 women). Expenses: Contact institution. *Financial support:* In 2016–17, 425 students received support, including 289 fellowships with full tuition reimbursements available (averaging $7,911 per year), 40 teaching assistantships with full tuition reimbursements available (averaging $9,284 per year); career-related internships or fieldwork, Federal Work-Study, unspecified assistantships, and 10 athletic assistantships (averaging $9284), 7 service assistantships (averaging $7911), 76 doctoral assistantships (stipend varies) also available. Financial award application deadline: 3/1; financial award applicants required to submit FAFSA. In 2016, 729 master's, 38 doctorates, 19 other advanced degrees awarded. *Program availability:* Part-time, evening/weekend, 100% online, blended/hybrid learning. *Application fee:* $55. Electronic applications accepted. *Application Contact:* Lynette D. Michael, Director of Graduate Admissions, 540-568-6131 Ext. 6395, Fax: 540-568-7860, E-mail: michaeld@jmu.edu. *Dean, The Graduate School,* Dr. Jie Chen, 540-568-4213, Fax: 540-568-7860, E-mail: grad@jmu.edu.

College of Arts and Letters Students: 95 full-time (56 women), 34 part-time (13 women); includes 21 minority (10 Black or African American, non-Hispanic/Latino; 2 Asian, non-Hispanic/Latino; 4 Hispanic/Latino; 5 Two or more races, non-Hispanic/Latino), 2 international. Average age 30. 117 applicants, 90% accepted, 58 enrolled. *Faculty:* 110 full-time (54 women), 4 part-time/adjunct (all women). Expenses: Contact institution. *Financial support:* In 2016–17, 61 students received support, including 19 teaching assistantships with full tuition reimbursements available (averaging $9,284 per year); Federal Work-Study and 42 assistantships (averaging $7911) also available. Financial award application deadline: 3/1; financial award applicants required to submit FAFSA. In 2016, 54 master's awarded. *Program availability:* Part-time. Offers arts and letters (MA, MPA, MS); English (MA); environmental communication (MA); health communication (MA); individualized (MPA); local/regional/public history (MA); political science (MA); public management (MPA); strategic communication (MA); United States history (MA); world history (MA); writing, rhetoric, and technical communication (MA, MS). *Application fee:* $55. Electronic applications accepted. *Application Contact:* Lynette D. Michael, Director of Graduate Admissions, 540-568-6131 Ext. 6395, Fax: 540-568-7860, E-mail: michaeld@jmu.edu. *Dean,* Dr. David K. Jeffrey, 540-568-7044.

College of Business Students: 100 full-time (40 women), 102 part-time (37 women); includes 31 minority (15 Black or African American, non-Hispanic/Latino; 10 Asian, non-Hispanic/Latino; 3 Hispanic/Latino; 3 Two or more races, non-Hispanic/Latino), 5 international. Average age 30. 164 applicants, 80% accepted, 109 enrolled. *Faculty:* 48 full-time (12 women), 2 part-time/adjunct (1 woman). Expenses: Contact institution. *Financial support:* In 2016–17, 32 students received support. Career-related internships or fieldwork, Federal Work-Study, and 24 assistantships (averaging $7911), 5 doctoral assistantships available. Financial award application deadline: 3/1; financial award applicants required to submit FAFSA. In 2016, 117 master's, 5 doctorates awarded. *Program availability:* Part-time, evening/weekend, blended/hybrid learning. Offers accounting information systems (MS); business (MBA, MS, PhD); postsecondary analysis and leadership (PhD); taxation (MS). *Application fee:* $55. Electronic applications accepted. *Application Contact:* Lynette D. Michael, Director of Graduate Admissions, 540-568-6395, Fax: 540-568-7860, E-mail: michaeld@jmu.edu. *Dean,* Dr. Mary A. Gowan, 540-568-3254, E-mail: gowanma@jmu.edu.

College of Education Students: 290 full-time (258 women), 141 part-time (99 women); includes 52 minority (11 Black or African American, non-Hispanic/Latino; 7 Asian, non-Hispanic/Latino; 19 Hispanic/Latino; 15 Two or more races, non-Hispanic/Latino), 3 international. Average age 30. 415 applicants, 97% accepted, 360 enrolled. *Faculty:* 62 full-time (42 women), 14 part-time/adjunct (10 women). Expenses: Contact institution. *Financial support:* In 2016–17, 36 students received support. Career-related internships or fieldwork, Federal Work-Study, and 36 assistantships (averaging $7911), 1 athletic assistantship (averaging $9284) available. Financial award application deadline: 3/1; financial award applicants required to submit FAFSA. In 2016, 331 master's awarded. *Program availability:* Part-time, evening/weekend, 100% online, blended/hybrid learning. Offers adapted curriculum (MAT); autism (M Ed); behavior specialist (M Ed); early childhood education (MAT); early childhood education (preK-3) (MAT); early childhood special education (MAT); education (M Ed, MAT, MS Ed); educational leadership (M Ed); educational technology (M Ed); elementary education (MAT); equity and cultural diversity (M Ed); general curriculum K-12 special education (MAT); gifted education (M Ed); higher education (MS Ed); human resource management (MS Ed); inclusive early childhood education (MAT); inclusive early childhood special education (MAT); individualized (MS Ed); instructional design (MS Ed); instructional specialist (M Ed); K-12 special education (MAT); K-8 math specialist (M Ed); K-8 mathematics specialist (M Ed); leadership and facilitation (MS Ed); mathematics (M Ed); middle education (MAT); program evaluation and measurement (MS Ed); reading education (M Ed); secondary education (MAT); Spanish language and culture for educators (M Ed); TESOL (MAT); visual impairments (MAT). *Application fee:* $55. Electronic applications accepted. *Application Contact:* Lynette D. Michael, Director of Graduate Admissions, 540-568-6131 Ext. 6395, Fax: 540-568-7860, E-mail: michaeld@jmu.edu. *Dean,* Dr. Phillip M. Wishon, 540-568-6572, E-mail: wishonpm@jmu.edu.

College of Health and Behavioral Sciences Students: 464 full-time (348 women), 132 part-time (115 women); includes 84 minority (32 Black or African American, non-Hispanic/Latino; 2 American Indian or Alaska Native, non-Hispanic/Latino; 18 Asian, non-Hispanic/Latino; 17 Hispanic/Latino; 15 Two or more races, non-Hispanic/Latino), 6 international. Average age 30. 1,566 applicants, 25% accepted, 246 enrolled. *Faculty:* 177 full-time (99 women), 28 part-time/adjunct (14 women). Expenses: Contact institution. *Financial support:* In 2016–17, 222 students received support, including 17 teaching assistantships with full tuition reimbursements available (averaging $9,284 per year); career-related internships or fieldwork, Federal Work-Study, unspecified assistantships, and athletic assistantships (averaging $8837), service assistantships (averaging $7530), doctoral assistantships also available. Financial award application deadline: 3/1; financial award applicants required to submit FAFSA. In 2016, 209 master's, 15 doctorates, 18 other advanced degrees awarded. *Program availability:* Part-time, evening/weekend, 100% online, blended/hybrid learning. Offers adult/gerontology primary care nurse practitioner (MSN); applied research (MA); assessment and measurement (PhD); audiology (Au D); behavior analysis (MA); clinical and school psychology (Psy D); clinical exercise physiology (MS); clinical mental health counseling/clinical nurse leader (MSN); communication sciences and disorders (PhD); counseling and supervision (PhD); exercise physiology (MS); experimental psychology (MA); family nurse practitioner (MSN); health and behavioral sciences (M Ed, MA, MAT, MOT, MPAS, MS, MSN, Au D, DNP, PhD, Psy D, Ed S); kinesiology (MAT, MS); nurse administrator (MSN); nurse midwifery (MSN); nursing (MSN, DNP); nutrition and exercise (MS); nutrition and physical activity (MS); occupational therapy (MOT); physical and health education (MAT); physician assistant studies (MPAS); psychiatric mental health nurse practitioner (MSN); quantitative psychology (MA); school psychology (MA, Ed S); speech-language pathology (MS); sport and recreation leadership (MS). *Application fee:* $55. Electronic applications accepted. *Application Contact:* Lynette D. Michael, Director of Graduate Admissions, 540-568-6131 Ext. 6395, Fax: 540-568-7860, E-mail: michaeld@jmu.edu. *Dean,* Dr. Sharon E. Lovell, 540-568-2705, Fax: 540-568-2747, E-mail: lovellse@jmu.edu.

College of Integrated Science and Engineering Students: 24 full-time (14 women), 23 part-time (5 women); includes 9 minority (4 Black or African American, non-Hispanic/Latino; 1 Asian, non-Hispanic/Latino; 3 Hispanic/Latino; 1 Two or more races, non-Hispanic/Latino), 6 international. Average age 30. 29 applicants, 97% accepted, 18 enrolled. *Faculty:* 52 full-time (14 women), 4 part-time/adjunct (0 women). Expenses: Contact institution. *Financial support:* In 2016–17, 4 students received support. Career-related internships or fieldwork, Federal Work-Study, and 3 assistantships (averaging $7911) available. Financial award application deadline: 3/1; financial award applicants required to submit FAFSA. In 2016, 17 master's awarded. *Program availability:* Part-time, evening/weekend, 100% online, blended/hybrid learning, study abroad. Offers digital forensics (MS); environmental management and sustainability (MS); information security (MS); integrated science and engineering (MS). *Application fee:* $55. Electronic applications accepted. *Application Contact:* Lynette D. Michael, Director of Graduate Admissions, 540-568-6395, Fax: 540-568-7860, E-mail: michaeld@jmu.edu. *Dean,* Dr. Robert A. Kolvoord, 540-568-2752, E-mail: kolvoora@jmu.edu.

College of Science and Mathematics Students: 16 full-time (9 women), 14 part-time (7 women); includes 3 minority (1 Black or African American, non-Hispanic/Latino; 1 Asian, non-Hispanic/Latino; 1 Hispanic/Latino). Average age 30. 30 applicants, 47% accepted, 9 enrolled. *Faculty:* 63 full-time (25 women), 1 part-time/adjunct (0 women). Expenses: Contact institution. *Financial support:* In 2016–17, 16 students received support, including 4 fellowships; Federal Work-Study and 16 assistantships (averaging $7911) also available. Financial award application deadline: 3/1; financial award applicants required to submit FAFSA. In 2016, 8 master's awarded. *Program availability:* Part-time. Offers biology (MS); mathematics (M Ed); science and mathematics (M Ed, MS). *Application fee:* $55. Electronic applications accepted. *Application Contact:* Lynette D. Michael, Director of Graduate Admissions, 540-568-6131 Ext. 6395, Fax: 540-568-7860, E-mail: michaeld@jmu.edu. *Dean,* Dr. David F. Brakke, 540-568-3508, E-mail: brakkedf@jmu.edu.

College of Visual and Performing Arts Students: 48 full-time (23 women), 20 part-time (10 women); includes 8 minority (1 Black or African American, non-Hispanic/Latino; 6 Hispanic/Latino; 1 Two or more races, non-Hispanic/Latino), 15 international. Average age 30. 83 applicants, 65% accepted, 27 enrolled. *Faculty:* 64 full-time (27 women), 9 part-time/adjunct (3 women). Expenses: Contact institution. *Financial support:* In 2016–17, 41 students received support, including 4 teaching assistantships with full tuition reimbursements available (averaging $9,284 per year); fellowships, Federal Work-Study, and 19 assistantships (averaging $7911), 18 doctoral assistantships (stipend varies) also available. Financial award application deadline: 3/1; financial award applicants required to submit FAFSA. In 2016, 16 master's, 8 doctorates awarded. *Program availability:* Part-time. Offers art education (MA); composition (MM); conducting (MM, DMA); music education (MM); performance (MM, DMA); studio art (MA, MFA); visual and performing arts (MA, MFA, MM, DMA). *Application fee:* $55. Electronic applications accepted. *Application Contact:* Lynette D. Michael, Director of Graduate Admissions and Student Records, 540-568-6131 Ext. 6395, Fax: 540-568-7860, E-mail: michaeld@jmu.edu. *Dean,* Dr. George Sparks, 540-568-6247, E-mail: sparksge@jmu.edu.

JEFFERSON COLLEGE OF HEALTH SCIENCES, Roanoke, VA 24013

General Information Independent, coed, comprehensive institution. *Graduate housing:* Room and/or apartments available on a first-come, first-served basis to single students; on-campus housing not available to married students. *Research affiliation:* Carilion Clinic (hospital and medical services), Virginia Polytechnic Institute and State University/Carilion Medical School (medicine).

GRADUATE UNITS

Program in Nursing *Program availability:* Part-time. Offers nursing education (MSN); nursing management (MSN). Electronic applications accepted.

Program in Occupational Therapy *Program availability:* Part-time. Offers occupational therapy (MS). Electronic applications accepted.

Program in Physician Assistant Offers physician assistant (MS). Electronic applications accepted.

THE JEWISH THEOLOGICAL SEMINARY, New York, NY 10027-4649

General Information Independent-religious, coed, university. *Graduate housing:* Rooms and/or apartments available on a first-come, first-served basis to single and married students. Housing application deadline: 5/15.

GRADUATE UNITS

The Graduate School *Program availability:* Part-time. Offers ancient Judaism (MA, DHL, PhD); Bible and ancient Semitic languages (MA, DHL, PhD); interdepartmental studies (MA); Jewish art and visual culture (MA); Jewish gender and women's studies (MA); Jewish history (MA, DHL, PhD); Jewish literature (MA, DHL, PhD); Jewish philosophy (DHL); Jewish thought (MA, PhD); liturgy (MA, DHL, PhD); medieval Jewish studies (MA, DHL, PhD); Midrash (DHL); Midrash and scriptural interpretation (MA, PhD); modern Jewish studies (MA, DHL, PhD); Talmud and rabbinics (MA, DHL, PhD). MA/MSW offered jointly with Columbia University.

H. L. Miller Cantorial School and College of Jewish Music Offers Jewish music (MSM).

The Rabbinical School Offers theology (MA, Rabbi).

William Davidson Graduate School of Jewish Education *Program availability:* Part-time, online learning. Offers Jewish education (MA, Ed D). Offered in conjunction with The Rabbinical School; H. L. Miller Cantorial School and College of Jewish Music; Teacher's College, Columbia University; and Union Theological Seminary.

JOHN BROWN UNIVERSITY, Siloam Springs, AR 72761-2121

General Information Independent-religious, coed, comprehensive institution. *Enrollment:* 2,708 graduate, professional, and undergraduate students; 215 full-time matriculated graduate/professional students (162 women), 457 part-time matriculated graduate/professional students (289 women). *Enrollment by degree level:* 668 master's, 4 other advanced degrees. *Graduate faculty:* 13 full-time (4 women), 53 part-time/adjunct (17 women). *Tuition:* Full-time $13,000; part-time $6500 per credit hour. Part-time tuition and fees vary according to course load and program. *Graduate housing:* Rooms and/or apartments available on a first-come, first-served basis to single and married students. *Student services:* Campus employment opportunities, career counseling, exercise/wellness program, free psychological counseling, international student services, services for students with disabilities, teacher training. *Library facilities:* Arutunoff Learning Resource Center plus 4 others. *Collection:* Books: 104,100 (physical), 317,000 (digital/electronic); Serial titles: 1,000 (physical), 65,600

(digital/electronic); Databases: 134. Weekly public service hours: 110; students can reserve study rooms.

Computer facilities: 250 computers available on campus for general student use. A campuswide network can be accessed from student residence rooms and from off campus. Online class registration is available.
Website: http://www.jbu.edu/

General Application Contact: Kent Shaffer, Graduate Admissions Representative, 800-528-4723, E-mail: kents@jbu.edu.

GRADUATE UNITS

Graduate Counseling Programs Students: 157 full-time (124 women), 153 part-time (124 women); includes 94 minority (50 Black or African American, non-Hispanic/Latino; 7 American Indian or Alaska Native, non-Hispanic/Latino; 3 Asian, non-Hispanic/Latino; 21 Hispanic/Latino; 13 Two or more races, non-Hispanic/Latino), 1 international. Average age 32. 129 applicants, 74% accepted, 83 enrolled. *Faculty:* 9 full-time (2 women), 18 part-time/adjunct (6 women). Expenses: Contact institution. *Financial support:* Fellowships, institutionally sponsored loans, scholarships/grants, and unspecified assistantships available. Financial award applicants required to submit FAFSA. In 2016, 68 master's awarded. *Program availability:* Part-time, evening/weekend. Offers clinical mental health counseling (MS); marriage and family therapy (MS); play therapy (Graduate Certificate); school counseling (MS). *Application deadline:* Applications are processed on a rolling basis. *Application fee:* $35 ($100 for international students). Electronic applications accepted. *Application Contact:* Mark Bjornsen, Graduate Counseling Representative, 479-631-4665, E-mail: mbjornsen@jbu.edu. *Program Director,* Dr. John V. Carmack, 479-524-8630, E-mail: jcarmack@jbu.edu.

Graduate Education Programs Students: 17 part-time (8 women). Average age 32. 11 applicants, 64% accepted, 5 enrolled. *Faculty:* 1 (woman) full-time, 5 part-time/adjunct (3 women). Expenses: Contact institution. *Financial support:* Scholarships/grants and unspecified assistantships available. In 2016, 7 master's awarded. *Program availability:* Part-time, evening/weekend. Offers curriculum and instruction (M Ed); secondary education (MAT). *Application deadline:* Applications are processed on a rolling basis. *Application fee:* $35 ($100 for international students). Electronic applications accepted. *Application Contact:* Mark Bjornsen, Graduate Education Representative, 479-631-4665, E-mail: mbjornsen@jbu.edu. *Graduate Program Director,* Dr. Connie Matchell, 479-524-9500, E-mail: cmatchell@jbu.edu.

Soderquist College of Business Students: 42 full-time (27 women), 246 part-time (129 women); includes 65 minority (25 Black or African American, non-Hispanic/Latino; 7 American Indian or Alaska Native, non-Hispanic/Latino; 6 Asian, non-Hispanic/Latino; 15 Hispanic/Latino; 12 Two or more races, non-Hispanic/Latino), 6 international. Average age 33. 145 applicants, 80% accepted, 88 enrolled. *Faculty:* 4 full-time (2 women), 26 part-time/adjunct (7 women). Expenses: Contact institution. *Financial support:* Fellowships with full tuition reimbursements, scholarships/grants, and unspecified assistantships available. Financial award applicants required to submit FAFSA. In 2016, 114 master's awarded. *Program availability:* Part-time, evening/weekend, online only, 100% online, blended/hybrid learning. Offers international business (MBA); leadership and ethics (MBA, MS). *Application deadline:* Applications are processed on a rolling basis. *Application fee:* $35 ($100 for international students). Electronic applications accepted. *Application Contact:* Kent Shaffer, Graduate Business Representative, 479-631-4665, E-mail: kents@jbu.edu. *Program Director,* Kai Togami, 479-524-7370, E-mail: ktogami@jbu.edu.

JOHN CARROLL UNIVERSITY, University Heights, OH 44118-4581

General Information Independent-religious, coed, comprehensive institution. CGS member. *Enrollment:* 3,523 graduate, professional, and undergraduate students; 249 full-time matriculated graduate/professional students (166 women), 236 part-time matriculated graduate/professional students (146 women). *Enrollment by degree level:* 420 master's, 65 other advanced degrees. *Graduate faculty:* 62 full-time (23 women), 57 part-time/adjunct (21 women). *Tuition:* Full-time $10,425; part-time $695 per credit hour. One-time fee: $200 full-time. Tuition and fees vary according to course load, campus/location and program. *Graduate housing:* On-campus housing not available. *Student services:* Career counseling, exercise/wellness program, free psychological counseling, international student services, multicultural affairs office, services for students with disabilities, writing training. *Library facilities:* Grasselli Library. *Collection:* Books: 456,260 (physical), 91,554 (digital/electronic); Serial titles: 459,633 (physical), 115,548 (digital/electronic); Databases: 279. Weekly public service hours: 111; students can reserve study rooms.

Computer facilities: Computer purchase and lease plans are available. 396 computers available on campus for general student use. A campuswide network can be accessed from student residence rooms and from off campus. Online class registration, campus student online registration, billing, advising system, JCU mobile app, course management site (BlackBoard), online financial aid and billing; online course sites; online housing selection are available.
Website: http://www.jcu.edu/

General Application Contact: Dr. Anne Kugler, Associate Dean, 216-397-4770, E-mail: akugler@jcu.edu.

GRADUATE UNITS

Graduate Studies Expenses: Contact institution. *Financial support:* Research assistantships with full tuition reimbursements, teaching assistantships with full tuition reimbursements, career-related internships or fieldwork, institutionally sponsored loans, scholarships/grants, tuition waivers (partial), and unspecified assistantships available. Support available to part-time students. Financial award applicants required to submit FAFSA. *Program availability:* Part-time, evening/weekend. Offers biology (MA, MS); child and adolescent health and wellness (M Ed); clinical counseling (Certificate); community counseling (MA); educational psychology (M Ed); English (MA); humanities (MA); mathematics (MA); nonprofit administration (M Ed); professional teacher education (M Ed, MA); school counseling (M Ed); school psychology (M Ed, Ed S); secondary education (M Ed); theology and religious studies (MA). *Application deadline:* Applications are processed on a rolling basis. *Application fee:* $25 ($35 for international students). Electronic applications accepted. *Application Contact:* Terry Bradley, Records Management Assistant, 216-397-1925, Fax: 216-397-1835, E-mail: tbradley@jcu.edu. *Coordinator,* Dr. Anne Kugler, 216-397-4770, Fax: 216-397-1835, E-mail: akugler@jcu.edu.

John M. and Mary Jo Boler School of Business Expenses: Contact institution. *Financial support:* Research assistantships with full tuition reimbursements, scholarships/grants, and unspecified assistantships available. Financial award application deadline: 3/15; financial award applicants required to submit FAFSA. *Program availability:* Part-time, evening/weekend. Offers accountancy (MS); business (MBA); laboratory administration (MS). *Application deadline:* Applications are processed on a rolling basis. *Application fee:* $25 ($35 for international students).

Electronic applications accepted. *Application Contact:* Gayle T. Bruno-Gannon, Assistant to the Dean, 216-397-1970, Fax: 216-397-1728, E-mail: ggannon@jcu.edu. *Dean,* Dr. Alan R. Miciak, 216-397-4391, Fax: 216-397-1833.

JOHN F. KENNEDY UNIVERSITY, Pleasant Hill, CA 94523-4817
General Information Independent, coed, primarily women, upper-level institution. *Graduate housing:* On-campus housing not available.

GRADUATE UNITS
Graduate School of Holistic Studies *Program availability:* Part-time, evening/weekend. Offers consciousness and transformative studies (MA); counseling psychology (MA); dream studies (Certificate); holistic health education (MA); holistic studies (MA, MFA, Certificate); integral psychology (MA, Certificate); life coaching (Certificate); somatic psychology (MA); studio arts (MFA); transformative arts (MA); transpersonal psychology (MA).

Graduate School of Professional Psychology *Program availability:* Part-time, evening/weekend. Offers counseling psychology (MA); organizational psychology (MA, Certificate); professional psychology (MA, Psy D, Certificate); psychology (Psy D); sport psychology (MA).

School of Education and Liberal Arts *Program availability:* Part-time, evening/weekend. Offers education (MAT); education and liberal arts (MA, MAT, Certificate); museum studies (MA, Certificate).

School of Law *Program availability:* Part-time, evening/weekend. Offers law (JD).

School of Management *Program availability:* Part-time, evening/weekend. Offers business administration (MBA); career coaching (Certificate); career development (MA, Certificate); management (MA, MBA, Certificate); organizational leadership (Certificate).

JOHN JAY COLLEGE OF CRIMINAL JUSTICE OF THE CITY UNIVERSITY OF NEW YORK, New York, NY 10019
General Information State and locally supported, coed, comprehensive institution. CGS member. *Graduate housing:* On-campus housing not available. *Research affiliation:* Criminal Justice Center, Criminal Justice Research and Evaluation Center, Center on Violence and Human Survival, Center for Dispute Resolution, The Fire Science Institute, The Institute For Criminal Justice Ethics.

GRADUATE UNITS
Graduate Studies *Program availability:* Part-time, evening/weekend. Offers criminal justice (MA, PhD); criminology and deviance (PhD); forensic computing (MS); forensic psychology (PhD); forensic science (PhD); international crime and justice (MA); law and philosophy (PhD); organizational behavior (PhD); protection management (MS); public administration (MPA); public policy (PhD).

THE JOHN MARSHALL LAW SCHOOL, Chicago, IL 60604-3968
General Information Independent, coed, graduate-only institution. *Enrollment by degree level:* 166 master's, 1,038 doctoral. *Graduate faculty:* 55 full-time (23 women), 226 part-time/adjunct (79 women). *Tuition:* Full-time $46,200. *Required fees:* $2548. One-time fee: $1998 part-time. *Graduate housing:* On-campus housing not available. *Student services:* Campus employment opportunities, campus safety program, career counseling, exercise/wellness program, international student services, low-cost health insurance, multicultural affairs office, services for students with disabilities, writing training. *Library facilities:* Louis L. Biro Law Library. *Collection:* Books: 46,062 (physical), 25,821 (digital/electronic); Serial titles: 1,187 (physical), 73,555 (digital/electronic); Databases: 71. Weekly public service hours: 96; students can reserve study rooms. *Computer facilities:* 26 computers available on campus for general student use. A campuswide network can be accessed. Online class registration is available. Website: http://www.jmls.edu/

General Application Contact: Chante Spann, Interim Assistant Dean for Admissions, 800-537-4280, Fax: 312-427-5136, E-mail: admissions@jmls.edu.

GRADUATE UNITS
Graduate and Professional Programs Students: 839 full-time (415 women), 365 part-time (170 women); includes 380 minority (104 Black or African American, non-Hispanic/Latino; 24 American Indian or Alaska Native, non-Hispanic/Latino; 107 Asian, non-Hispanic/Latino; 117 Hispanic/Latino; 28 Two or more races, non-Hispanic/Latino), 63 international. Average age 27. 1,764 applicants, 73% accepted, 334 enrolled. *Faculty:* 55 full-time (23 women), 226 part-time/adjunct (79 women). Expenses: Contact institution. *Financial support:* In 2016–17, 798 students received support. Research assistantships, Federal Work-Study, scholarships/grants, and tuition waivers (full and partial) available. Support available to part-time students. Financial award application deadline: 4/1; financial award applicants required to submit FAFSA. In 2016, 66 master's, 296 doctorates awarded. *Program availability:* Part-time, evening/weekend, 100% online, blended/hybrid learning. Offers law (LL M, MJ, JD). *Application deadline:* For fall admission, 3/1 priority date for domestic and international students; for spring admission, 10/15 priority date for domestic and international students. Applications are processed on a rolling basis. *Application fee:* $0. Electronic applications accepted. *Application Contact:* Chante Spann, Interim Assistant Dean for Admissions, 800-537-4280, Fax: 312-427-5136, E-mail: admissions@jmls.edu. *Dean,* Darby Dickerson, 312-427-2737 Ext. 828, E-mail: ddickerson@jmls.edu.

JOHN PAUL THE GREAT CATHOLIC UNIVERSITY, Escondido, CA 92025
General Information Independent-religious, coed, comprehensive institution.

GRADUATE UNITS
School of Theology Offers biblical theology (MA).

JOHNS HOPKINS UNIVERSITY, Baltimore, MD 21218
General Information Independent, coed, university. CGS member. *Enrollment:* 23,992 graduate, professional, and undergraduate students; 8,155 full-time matriculated graduate/professional students (4,310 women), 9,213 part-time matriculated graduate/professional students (4,836 women). *Enrollment by degree level:* 13,068 master's, 3,778 doctoral, 522 other advanced degrees. *Graduate faculty:* 4,542 full-time (1,969 women), 226 part-time/adjunct (105 women). *Graduate housing:* On-campus housing not available. *Student services:* Campus employment opportunities, campus safety program, career counseling, exercise/wellness program, free psychological counseling, grant writing training, international student services, low-cost health insurance, multicultural affairs office, services for students with disabilities, teacher training, writing training. *Library facilities:* The Sheridan Libraries plus 2 others. *Collection:* Books: 4.1 million (physical). Study areas open 24 hours, 5–7 days a week; students can reserve study rooms. *Research affiliation:* Carnegie Institution of Washington (biological sciences), SmithKline Beecham (asthma and allergy), Bristol-Myers Squibb (human nutrition), Howard Hughes Medical Institute (biomedical sciences), Space Telescope Science Institute (astronomy), General Electric Company (GE) (medical technology).

Computer facilities: Computer purchase and lease plans are available. 200 computers available on campus for general student use. A campuswide network can be accessed from student residence rooms and from off campus. Online class registration is available.
Website: http://www.jhu.edu/

GRADUATE UNITS
Bloomberg School of Public Health Students: 1,405 full-time (985 women), 511 part-time (331 women); includes 563 minority (101 Black or African American, non-Hispanic/Latino; 2 American Indian or Alaska Native, non-Hispanic/Latino; 300 Asian, non-Hispanic/Latino; 97 Hispanic/Latino; 2 Native Hawaiian or other Pacific Islander, non-Hispanic/Latino; 61 Two or more races, non-Hispanic/Latino), 547 international. Average age 30. 4,234 applicants, 49% accepted, 1085 enrolled. *Faculty:* 670 full-time, 709 part-time/adjunct. Expenses: Contact institution. *Financial support:* In 2016–17, 1,605 students received support. Fellowships, research assistantships, teaching assistantships, career-related internships or fieldwork, Federal Work-Study, scholarships/grants, traineeships, health care benefits, and unspecified assistantships available. Support available to part-time students. In 2016, 758 master's, 140 doctorates awarded. *Program availability:* Part-time, 100% online, blended/hybrid learning. Offers biochemistry and molecular biology (MHS, Sc M, PhD); bioethics and policy (PhD); biostatistics (MHS, Sc M, PhD); cancer epidemiology (MHS, Sc M, PhD, Sc D); cardiovascular disease and clinical epidemiology (MHS, Sc M, PhD, Sc D); children's mental health services (PhD); clinical investigation (MHS, PhD); clinical trials (PhD, Sc D); clinical trials and evidence synthesis (MHS, Sc M, PhD, Sc D); demography (MHS); environmental epidemiology (MHS, Sc M, PhD, Sc D); environmental health (MHS, Sc M, Dr PH, PhD); epidemiology of aging (MHS, Sc M, PhD, Sc D); general epidemiology and methodology (MHS, Sc M); genetic counseling (Sc M); genetic epidemiology (MHS, Sc M, PhD, Sc D); global disease epidemiology and control (MSPH, PhD); health administration (MHA); health and public policy (PhD); health economics (MHS); health economics and policy (PhD); health education and health communication (MSPH); health finance and management (MHS); health policy (MSPH); health policy and management (Dr PH); health services research and policy (PhD); health systems (MSPH, PhD); human nutrition (MSPH, PhD); infectious disease epidemiology (MHS, Sc M, PhD, Sc D); mental health (MHS); molecular microbiology and immunology (MHS, Sc M, PhD); occupational and environmental hygiene (MSPH); population, family and reproductive health (MHS, MSPH, PhD); public health (MBE, MHA, MHS, MPH, MPP, MSPH, Sc M, Dr PH, PhD, Sc D); public policy (MPP); social and behavioral interventions (MSPH, PhD); social and behavioral sciences (PhD); social factors in health (MHS); toxicity testing and human health risk assessment of environmental agents (MSPH). *Application fee:* $135. Electronic applications accepted. *Application Contact:* Office of Admissions, 410-955-3543, Fax: 410-955-0464, E-mail: jhsph.admiss@jhu.edu. *Dean,* Dr. Michael J. Klag, 410-955-3540, Fax: 410-955-0121, E-mail: jhsph.admiss@jhu.edu.

Berman Institute of Bioethics Expenses: Contact institution. Offers bioethics (MBE). *Application deadline:* For fall admission, 7/15 for domestic students. Applications are processed on a rolling basis. Electronic applications accepted. *Application Contact:* Office of Admissions, 410-955-3543, Fax: 410-955-0464, E-mail: jhsph.admiss@jhu.edu. *Dean,* Dr. Michael J. Klag, 410-955-3540, Fax: 410-955-0121, E-mail: jhsph.admiss@jhu.edu.

Carey Business School Students: 923 full-time (502 women), 1,150 part-time (497 women); includes 447 minority (119 Black or African American, non-Hispanic/Latino; 1 American Indian or Alaska Native, non-Hispanic/Latino; 216 Asian, non-Hispanic/Latino; 76 Hispanic/Latino; 1 Native Hawaiian or other Pacific Islander, non-Hispanic/Latino; 34 Two or more races, non-Hispanic/Latino), 944 international. Average age 26. 4,563 applicants, 63% accepted, 1178 enrolled. *Faculty:* 87 full-time (32 women), 51 part-time/adjunct (8 women). Expenses: Contact institution. *Financial support:* In 2016–17, 217 students received support. Scholarships/grants available. Support available to part-time students. Financial award application deadline: 4/15; financial award applicants required to submit FAFSA. In 2016, 825 master's, 33 other advanced degrees awarded. *Program availability:* Part-time, evening/weekend, blended/hybrid learning, on-site residency requirement. Offers business (MBA, MS, Certificate); business administration (MBA); enterprise risk management (MS); finance (MS); health care management (MS); information systems (MS); investments (Certificate); marketing (MS); real estate and infrastructure (MS). *Application deadline:* For fall admission, 5/1 for domestic and international students. Applications are processed on a rolling basis. *Application fee:* $100. Electronic applications accepted. *Application Contact:* Office of Admissions, 410-234-9220, Fax: 443-529-1554, E-mail: carey.admissions@jhu.edu. *Dean,* Dr. Bernard T. Ferrari, 410-234-9210, E-mail: bferrari@jhu.edu.

Engineering Program for Professionals Students: 51 full-time (10 women), 2,076 part-time (503 women); includes 396 minority (88 Black or African American, non-Hispanic/Latino; 2 American Indian or Alaska Native, non-Hispanic/Latino; 140 Asian, non-Hispanic/Latino; 136 Hispanic/Latino; 3 Native Hawaiian or other Pacific Islander, non-Hispanic/Latino; 27 Two or more races, non-Hispanic/Latino), 60 international. Average age 30. 1,100 applicants, 95% accepted, 377 enrolled. *Faculty:* 6 full-time (0 women), 281 part-time/adjunct (45 women). Expenses: Contact institution. In 2016, 703 master's, 100 other advanced degrees awarded. *Program availability:* Part-time, evening/weekend, 100% online, blended/hybrid learning. Offers applied and computational mathematics (MS, Post-Master's Certificate); applied biomedical engineering (MS, Post-Master's Certificate); applied physics (MS, Post-Master's Certificate); chemical and biomolecular engineering (M Ch E); civil engineering (MCE, Graduate Certificate); communications and networking (MS); computer science (Post-Master's Certificate); cybersecurity (MS, Post-Master's Certificate); electrical and computer engineering (Graduate Certificate, Post-Master's Certificate); engineering (M Ch E, M Mat SE, MCE, MEE, MEM, MME, MS, MSE, Graduate Certificate, Post-Master's Certificate, Post-Master's Certificate); engineering management (MEM); environmental engineering (MS, Graduate Certificate, Post-Master's Certificate); environmental engineering and science (MEE, MS, Graduate Certificate, Post-Master's Certificate); environmental planning and management (MS, Graduate Certificate, Post-Master's Certificate); financial mathematics (MS); financial risk management (Graduate Certificate); information systems engineering (MS, Graduate Certificate, Post-Master's Certificate); mechanical engineering (MME, Post-Master's Certificate); nanotechnology (M Mat SE); photonics (MS); quantitative portfolio management (Graduate Certificate); securitization (Graduate Certificate); space systems engineering (MS); systems engineering (MS, MSE, Graduate Certificate, Post-Master's Certificate); technical management (MS, Graduate Certificate, Post-Master's Certificate). *Application deadline:* Applications are processed on a rolling basis. *Application fee:* $0. Electronic applications accepted. *Application Contact:* Doug Schiller, Admissions Director, 410-516-2300, Fax: 410-579-8049, E-mail: schiller@jhu.edu. *Assistant Dean,* Dr. Daniel Horn, 410-516-2300, Fax: 410-579-8049, E-mail: dhorn@jhu.edu.

G. W. C. Whiting School of Engineering Students: 1,159 full-time (323 women), 100 part-time (24 women); includes 155 minority (18 Black or African American, non-Hispanic/Latino; 88 Asian, non-Hispanic/Latino; 30 Hispanic/Latino; 19 Two or more races, non-Hispanic/Latino), 802 international. Average age 25. 4,631 applicants, 32% accepted, 552 enrolled. *Faculty:* 253 full-time (52 women), 96 part-time/adjunct (23 women). Expenses: Contact institution. *Financial support:* In 2016–17, 834 students received support, including 196 fellowships with full and partial tuition reimbursements available, 563 research assistantships with full and partial tuition reimbursements available, 75 teaching assistantships with full and partial tuition reimbursements available; Federal Work-Study, institutionally sponsored loans, scholarships/grants, health care benefits, tuition waivers (full and partial), and unspecified assistantships also available. Support available to part-time students. Financial award applicants required to submit FAFSA. In 2016, 328 master's, 82 doctorates, 12 other advanced degrees awarded. Offers bioengineering innovation and design (MSE); biomaterials (MSEM); biomedical engineering (MSE, PhD); chemical and biomolecular engineering (MSE, PhD); civil engineering (MSEM); communications science (MSEM); computational medicine (PhD); computer science (MSE, MSSI, PhD); discrete mathematics (MA, MSE, PhD); electrical and computer engineering (MSE, PhD); engineering (M Ch E, M Mat SE, MA, MEE, MME, MS, MSE, MSEM, MSSI, PhD, Certificate, Post-Master's Certificate); environmental health and engineering (MA, MS, MSE, PhD); environmental systems analysis, economics and public policy (MSEM); financial mathematics (MSE); fluid mechanics (MSEM); materials science and engineering (MSE); mechanical engineering (MSEM); mechanics and materials (MSEM); nano-biotechnology (MSEM); nanomaterials and nanotechnology (MSEM); operations research (MSEM); operations research/optimization (MA, MSE, PhD); probability and statistics (MSEM); robotics (MSE); security informatics (MSSI); smart product and device design (MSEM); statistics/probability (MA, MSE, PhD). *Application fee:* $75. Electronic applications accepted. *Application Contact:* Richard Helman, Director, Graduate Admissions and Enrollment, 410-516-8174, Fax: 410-516-8627, E-mail: graduateadmissions@jhu.edu. *Dean,* Dr. T. E. Schlesinger, 410-516-8350 Ext. 3, Fax: 410-516-8627.

National Institutes of Health Sponsored Programs Offers biology (PhD); cell, molecular, and developmental biology and biophysics (PhD). Electronic applications accepted.

Peabody Conservatory Students: 307 full-time (159 women), 9 part-time (5 women); includes 61 minority (4 Black or African American, non-Hispanic/Latino; 1 American Indian or Alaska Native, non-Hispanic/Latino; 34 Asian, non-Hispanic/Latino; 13 Hispanic/Latino; 9 Two or more races, non-Hispanic/Latino), 127 international. Average age 25. 933 applicants, 46% accepted, 184 enrolled. *Faculty:* 60 full-time (18 women), 50 part-time/adjunct (17 women). Expenses: Contact institution. *Financial support:* In 2016–17, 248 students received support, including 65 teaching assistantships (averaging $25,240 per year); fellowships, Federal Work-Study, institutionally sponsored loans, scholarships/grants, and unspecified assistantships also available. Financial award application deadline: 3/1; financial award applicants required to submit FAFSA. In 2016, 106 master's, 16 doctorates, 25 other advanced degrees awarded. Offers music (MA, MM, DMA, AD, GPD). *Application deadline:* For fall admission, 12/1 priority date for domestic and international students. *Application fee:* $120. Electronic applications accepted. *Application Contact:* John Huling, Director of Admissions, 800-368-2521, E-mail: admissions@peabody.jhu.edu. *Dean,* Dr. Fred Bronstein, 667-208-6500.

School of Advanced International Studies Students: 798 full-time (380 women), 43 part-time (27 women); includes 173 minority (28 Black or African American, non-Hispanic/Latino; 5 American Indian or Alaska Native, non-Hispanic/Latino; 60 Asian, non-Hispanic/Latino; 45 Hispanic/Latino; 1 Native Hawaiian or other Pacific Islander, non-Hispanic/Latino; 34 Two or more races, non-Hispanic/Latino), 283 international. Average age 27. 1,606 applicants, 214 enrolled. *Faculty:* 68 full-time (15 women), 130 part-time/adjunct (32 women). Expenses: Contact institution. *Financial support:* In 2016–17, 450 students received support, including 450 fellowships (averaging $12,000 per year), 32 teaching assistantships (averaging $3,906 per year); career-related internships or fieldwork, Federal Work-Study, and scholarships/grants also available. Financial award application deadline: 2/15; financial award applicants required to submit FAFSA. In 2016, 449 master's, 7 doctorates awarded. Offers global risk (MA); international development (MA, Certificate); international economics (Certificate); international economics and finance (MA); international public policy (MIPP); international relations (PhD); international studies (Certificate); Japan studies (MA); Korea studies (MA); South Asia studies (MA); Southeast Asia studies (MA). *Application deadline:* For fall admission, 1/7 for domestic and international students. *Application fee:* $85. Electronic applications accepted. *Application Contact:* Sidney Jackson, Director of Admissions, 202-663-5700, Fax: 202-663-7788, E-mail: admissions.sais@jhu.edu.

School of Education Students: 371 full-time (283 women), 2,008 part-time (1,557 women); includes 965 minority (456 Black or African American, non-Hispanic/Latino; 9 American Indian or Alaska Native, non-Hispanic/Latino; 158 Asian, non-Hispanic/Latino; 240 Hispanic/Latino; 7 Native Hawaiian or other Pacific Islander, non-Hispanic/Latino; 95 Two or more races, non-Hispanic/Latino), 79 international. Average age 29. 2,008 applicants, 66% accepted, 1044 enrolled. *Faculty:* 104 full-time (79 women), 224 part-time/adjunct (166 women). Expenses: Contact institution. *Financial support:* In 2016–17, 206 students received support, including 23 fellowships (averaging $25,500 per year); research assistantships, teaching assistantships, Federal Work-Study, and scholarships/grants also available. Support available to part-time students. Financial award application deadline: 4/1; financial award applicants required to submit FAFSA. In 2016, 642 master's, 11 doctorates, 167 other advanced degrees awarded. *Program availability:* Part-time, evening/weekend, 100% online, blended/hybrid learning. Offers advanced methods for differentiated instruction and inclusive education (Graduate Certificate); applied behavior analysis (Post-Master's Certificate); clinical mental health counseling (Post-Master's Certificate); counseling (MS, Advanced Certificate); data-based decision making and organizational improvement (Graduate Certificate); early intervention/preschool special education specialist (Graduate Certificate); education (M Ed, MAT, MS, Ed D, PhD, Advanced Certificate, Graduate Certificate, Post-Master's Certificate); education of students with autism and other pervasive developmental disorders (Graduate Certificate); educational leadership for independent schools (Graduate Certificate); elementary education (MAT); evidence-based teaching in the health professions (Post-Master's Certificate); gifted education (Graduate Certificate); health professions (M Ed); intelligence analysis (MS); leadership in technology integration (Graduate Certificate); mind, brain and teaching (Graduate Certificate); organizational leadership (MS); school administration and supervision (Graduate Certificate); secondary education (MAT); special education (MS); urban education (Graduate Certificate). *Application deadline:* For fall admission, 4/1 priority date for domestic students, 4/1 for international students; for spring admission, 10/1 priority date for domestic students, 10/1 for international students; for summer admission, 2/1 priority date for domestic students, 2/1 for international students. Applications are processed on a rolling basis. *Application fee:* $80. Electronic applications accepted. *Application*

Contact: Elisabeth Woodward, Director of Admissions, 410-516-9796, Fax: 410-516-9817, E-mail: soe.info@jhu.edu. *Dean,* Dr. Christopher C. Morphew.

School of Medicine Students: 1,239 full-time (630 women), 6 part-time (3 women); includes 454 minority (61 Black or African American, non-Hispanic/Latino; 4 American Indian or Alaska Native, non-Hispanic/Latino; 274 Asian, non-Hispanic/Latino; 77 Hispanic/Latino; 38 Two or more races, non-Hispanic/Latino), 226 international. Average age 26. Expenses: Contact institution. *Financial support:* Fellowships, research assistantships, teaching assistantships, career-related internships or fieldwork, Federal Work-Study, institutionally sponsored loans and tuition waivers (full) available. In 2016, 24 master's, 231 doctorates awarded. Offers medicine (MA, MS, MD, PhD, Certificate). *Application deadline:* Applications are processed on a rolling basis. *Application fee:* $85. Electronic applications accepted. *Application Contact:* Dr. Paul B. Rothman, Dean of Medical Faculty/Chief Executive Officer, 410-955-3180. *Dean of Medical Faculty/Chief Executive Officer,* Dr. Paul B. Rothman, 410-955-3180.

Division of Health Sciences Informatics Students: 7 full-time (2 women), 7 part-time (4 women); includes 4 minority (all Black or African American, non-Hispanic/Latino), 7 international. Average age 28. 64 applicants, 23% accepted, 8 enrolled. *Faculty:* 40 part-time/adjunct (10 women). Expenses: Contact institution. *Financial support:* Fellowships, career-related internships or fieldwork, and health care benefits available. In 2016, 2 master's awarded. Offers applied health sciences informatics (MS); clinical informatics (Certificate); health sciences informatics (PhD); health sciences informatics research (MS). *Application deadline:* For spring admission, 2/15 priority date for domestic students, 2/15 for international students. *Application fee:* $110. Electronic applications accepted. *Application Contact:* Kersti Winny, Academic Program Administrator, 410-502-3768, Fax: 410-614-2064, E-mail: kwinny@jhmi.edu. *Director, Training Program,* Dr. Harold P. Lehmann, 410-502-2569, Fax: 410-614-2064, E-mail: lehmann@jhmi.edu.

Graduate Programs in Medicine Expenses: Contact institution. *Financial support:* Fellowships, research assistantships, teaching assistantships, career-related internships or fieldwork, Federal Work-Study, institutionally sponsored loans, and tuition waivers (full) available. Financial award applicants required to submit FAFSA. Offers biochemistry, cellular and molecular biology (PhD); biological chemistry (PhD); cellular and molecular medicine (PhD); cellular and molecular physiology (PhD); functional anatomy and evolution (PhD); immunology (PhD); medical and biological illustration (MA); medicine (MA, PhD); neuroscience (PhD); pathobiology (PhD); pharmacology and molecular sciences (PhD); physiology (PhD). *Application deadline:* For fall admission, 1/10 for domestic students, 1/10 priority date for international students. *Application fee:* $85. Electronic applications accepted.

School of Nursing Students: 454 full-time (390 women), 333 part-time (307 women); includes 255 minority (85 Black or African American, non-Hispanic/Latino; 94 Asian, non-Hispanic/Latino; 51 Hispanic/Latino; 1 Native Hawaiian or other Pacific Islander, non-Hispanic/Latino; 24 Two or more races, non-Hispanic/Latino), 34 international. Average age 31. 790 applicants, 62% accepted, 289 enrolled. *Faculty:* 59 full-time (52 women), 161 part-time/adjunct (all women). Expenses: Contact institution. *Financial support:* In 2016–17, 424 students received support. Fellowships with partial tuition reimbursements available, research assistantships with full tuition reimbursements available, teaching assistantships with full tuition reimbursements available, Federal Work-Study, scholarships/grants, and tuition waivers (partial) available. Support available to part-time students. Financial award application deadline: 3/1; financial award applicants required to submit FAFSA. In 2016, 93 master's, 26 doctorates, 12 other advanced degrees awarded. *Program availability:* Part-time, 100% online, blended/hybrid learning. Offers adult-gerontological acute care nurse practitioner (DNP); adult-gerontological critical care clinical nurse specialist (DNP); adult-gerontological health clinical nurse specialist (DNP); adult-gerontological primary care nurse practitioner (DNP); family nurse practitioner (DNP); health systems management (MSN); nursing (MSN, DNP, PhD, Certificate); nursing practice (MSN); pediatric critical care clinical nurse specialist (DNP); pediatric primary care nurse practitioner (DNP); public health nursing (MSN). *Application deadline:* For fall admission, 1/1 priority date for domestic and international students; for spring admission, 7/1 priority date for domestic and international students; for summer admission, 11/1 priority date for domestic and international students. *Application fee:* $75. Electronic applications accepted. *Application Contact:* Cathy Wilson, Director of Admissions, 410-955-7548, Fax: 410-614-7086, E-mail: jhuson@jhu.edu. *Dean,* Dr. Patricia M. Davidson, 410-955-7544, Fax: 410-955-4890, E-mail: sondeansoffice@jhu.edu.

Zanvyl Krieger School of Arts and Sciences Offers anthropology (PhD); archaeology (PhD); arts and sciences (MA, MBEE, MFA, MS, PhD, Certificate); Assyriology (PhD); astronomy (PhD); biophysics (PhD); cell, molecular, developmental biology, and biophysics (PhD); chemical biology (PhD); chemistry (PhD); classics (PhD); cognitive science (PhD); earth and planetary sciences (MA, PhD); economics (PhD); Egyptology (PhD); English and American literature (PhD); fiction writing (MFA); French (PhD); German (PhD); Hebrew Bible/Northwest Semitics (PhD); history (PhD); history of art (MA, PhD); history of science and technology (MA, PhD); Italian (PhD); mathematics (PhD); philosophy (MA, PhD); physics (PhD); poetry (MFA); political science (MA, PhD); psychological and brain sciences (PhD); sociology (PhD); Spanish (PhD). Electronic applications accepted.

Advanced Academic Programs *Program availability:* Part-time, evening/weekend, online learning. Offers applied economics (MA); bioinformatics (MS); biotechnology (MS); biotechnology enterprise and entrepreneurship (MBEE); communication (MA); digital curation (Certificate); energy policy and climate (MS); environmental sciences (MS); film and media (MA); geographic information systems (MS, Certificate); global security studies (MA); government (MA); liberal arts (MA, Certificate); museum studies (MA); national securities study (Certificate); nonprofit management (Certificate); public management (MA); regulatory science (MS); research administration (MS); science writing (MA, Certificate); writing (MA). Electronic applications accepted.

Humanities Center Offers comparative literature (PhD); intellectual history (PhD). Electronic applications accepted.

JOHNSON & WALES UNIVERSITY, Providence, RI 02903-3703

General Information Independent, coed, comprehensive institution. *Graduate housing:* On-campus housing not available. *Research affiliation:* Consortium of Rhode Island Academic and Research Libraries, Association of Institutional Research.

GRADUATE UNITS

Graduate Studies *Program availability:* Part-time, evening/weekend. Offers accounting (MBA); addictions counseling (MS); business administration (MBA); business education and secondary special education (MAT); criminal justice (MS); culinary arts education (MAT); educational leadership (Ed D); elementary education and elementary special education (MAT); elementary education and elementary/secondary special education (MAT); elementary education and secondary special education (MAT); finance (MS); food service education (MAT); hospitality (MBA); human resource management (MS);

information security/assurance (MS); information technology (MBA); mental health counseling (MS); nonprofit management (MBA); operations and supply chain management (MBA); physician assistant studies (MS).

M Ed Program in Teaching and Learning *Program availability:* Evening/weekend. Offers teaching and learning (M Ed).

JOHNSON C. SMITH UNIVERSITY, Charlotte, NC 28216-5398

General Information Independent, coed, comprehensive institution. *Enrollment:* 1,428 graduate, professional, and undergraduate students; 84 full-time matriculated graduate/professional students (7 women), 18 part-time matriculated graduate/professional students (2 women). *Enrollment by degree level:* 102 master's. *Graduate faculty:* 6 full-time (2 women), 5 part-time/adjunct (all women). *Tuition:* Full-time $8640; part-time $576 per credit hour. *Graduate housing:* Room and/or apartments available on a first-come, first-served basis to single students; on-campus housing not available to married students. *Student services:* Exercise/wellness program, free psychological counseling, services for students with disabilities. *Library facilities:* James B. Duke Library. *Collection:* Books: 114,150 (physical), 184,548 (digital/electronic); Serial titles: 257 (physical); Databases: 78. Weekly public service hours: 79; study areas open 24 hours, 5–7 days a week; students can reserve study rooms.

Computer facilities: Computer purchase and lease plans are available. 125 computers available on campus for general student use. A campuswide network can be accessed from student residence rooms and from off campus. Online class registration is available.

Website: http://www.jcsu.edu/

GRADUATE UNITS

Program in Social Work Students: 84 full-time (77 women), 18 part-time (16 women); includes 97 minority (93 Black or African American, non-Hispanic/Latino; 1 Asian, non-Hispanic/Latino; 2 Hispanic/Latino; 1 Two or more races, non-Hispanic/Latino). Average age 30. 104 applicants, 98% accepted, 102 enrolled. *Faculty:* 6 full-time (2 women), 5 part-time/adjunct (all women). Expenses: Contact institution. *Financial support:* In 2016–17, 17 students received support. Federal Work-Study, scholarships/grants, and unspecified assistantships available. Financial award applicants required to submit FAFSA. In 2016, 34 master's awarded. *Program availability:* Part-time, evening/weekend. Offers social work (MSW). *Application fee:* $40. *Director of MSW Program*, Dr. Jeanne F. Cook, 704-378-1029, E-mail: jfcook@jcsu.edu.

JOHNSON STATE COLLEGE, Johnson, VT 05656

General Information State-supported, coed, comprehensive institution. *Enrollment:* 51 full-time matriculated graduate/professional students (44 women), 106 part-time matriculated graduate/professional students (88 women). *Enrollment by degree level:* 157 master's. *Graduate faculty:* 8 full-time (3 women), 11 part-time/adjunct (8 women). Tuition, state resident: part-time $555 per credit. Tuition, nonresident: part-time $800 per credit. *Graduate housing:* Rooms and/or apartments available on a first-come, first-served basis to single and married students. Housing application deadline: 3/15. *Student services:* Campus employment opportunities, career counseling, exercise/wellness program, free psychological counseling, international student services, services for students with disabilities. *Library facilities:* Willey Library plus 1 other. *Collection:* Books: 111,100 (physical), 6,500 (digital/electronic). Study areas open 24 hours, 5–7 days a week.

Computer facilities: 160 computers available on campus for general student use. A campuswide network can be accessed from student residence rooms and from off campus. Online class registration is available.

Website: http://www.jsc.edu/

General Application Contact: Catherine H. Higley, Administrative Assistant, Office of Graduate and Professional Learning, 800-635-2356 Ext. 1244, Fax: 802-635-1230, E-mail: catherine.higley@jsc.edu.

GRADUATE UNITS

Program in Counseling Expenses: Contact institution. *Financial support:* Career-related internships or fieldwork and unspecified assistantships available. Support available to part-time students. Financial award application deadline: 3/1; financial award applicants required to submit FAFSA. *Program availability:* Part-time. Offers addictions counseling (MA); clinical mental health counseling (MA); general counseling (MA); school counseling (MA). *Application deadline:* For fall admission, 7/1 for domestic students, 2/1 for international students; for spring admission, 11/1 for domestic students, 7/1 for international students; for summer admission, 4/1 for domestic students. Applications are processed on a rolling basis. Electronic applications accepted. *Application Contact:* Catherine H. Higley, Administrative Assistant, 800-635-2356 Ext. 1244, Fax: 802-635-1248, E-mail: catherine.higley@jsc.edu. *Coordinator*, Dr. David Fink, 802-635-1383, Fax: 802-635-1465, E-mail: david.fink@jsc.edu.

Program in Education Expenses: Contact institution. *Financial support:* Scholarships/grants and unspecified assistantships available. Financial award application deadline: 3/1; financial award applicants required to submit FAFSA. *Program availability:* Part-time. Offers applied behavior analysis (MA Ed); curriculum and instruction (MA Ed); foundations of education (MA Ed); special education (MA Ed). *Application deadline:* For fall admission, 5/1 for domestic students, 2/1 for international students. Applications are processed on a rolling basis. Electronic applications accepted. *Application Contact:* Catherine H. Higley, Administrative Assistant, 800-635-2356 Ext. 1244, Fax: 802-635-1248, E-mail: catherine.higley@jsc.edu. *Chair, Department of Education*, Dr. Kathleen Brinegar, 802-635-1472, Fax: 802-635-1465, E-mail: kathleen.brinegar@jsc.edu.

Program in Studio Arts Expenses: Contact institution. *Financial support:* Teaching assistantships and unspecified assistantships available. Support available to part-time students. Financial award application deadline: 3/1; financial award applicants required to submit FAFSA. *Program availability:* Part-time, online learning. Offers ceramics (MFA); digital media (MFA); drawing (MFA); painting (MFA); photography (MFA); printmaking (MFA); sculpture (MFA). *Application deadline:* For fall admission, 3/1 for domestic students, 2/1 for international students. Applications are processed on a rolling basis. Electronic applications accepted. *Application Contact:* Catherine H. Higley, Administrative Assistant, 800-635-2356 Ext. 1244, Fax: 802-635-1248, E-mail: catherine.higley@jsc.edu.

JOHNSON UNIVERSITY, Knoxville, TN 37998-1001

General Information Independent-religious, coed, comprehensive institution. *Enrollment:* 1,117 graduate, professional, and undergraduate students; 126 full-time matriculated graduate/professional students (46 women), 170 part-time matriculated graduate/professional students (65 women). *Enrollment by degree level:* 213 master's, 83 doctoral. *Graduate faculty:* 26 full-time (10 women), 32 part-time/adjunct (9 women). *Tuition:* Full-time $8437; part-time $5325 per semester hour. *Required fees:* $300; $300 per semester hour. $150 per semester. Tuition and fees vary according to degree level,

campus/location and program. *Graduate housing:* Rooms and/or apartments available on a first-come, first-served basis to single and married students. Typical cost: $4620 per year ($8040 including board) for single students; $5428 per year ($8668 including board) for married students. Room and board charges vary according to board plan, campus/location and housing facility selected. Housing application deadline: 8/1. *Student services:* Campus employment opportunities, career counseling, child daycare facilities, exercise/wellness program, free psychological counseling, multicultural affairs office, services for students with disabilities, teacher training, writing training. *Library facilities:* Glass Memorial Library plus 1 other. *Collection:* Books: 117,967 (physical), 245,630 (digital/electronic); Serial titles: 4,698 (physical), 27 (digital/electronic); Databases: 125. Weekly public service hours: 80.

Computer facilities: 70 computers available on campus for general student use. A campuswide network can be accessed from student residence rooms and from off campus. Online class registration is available.

Website: http://www.johnsonu.edu/

General Application Contact: Lisa Tarwater, Director of Graduate Admissions, 865-251-3400, Fax: 865-251-2336, E-mail: ltarwater@johnsonu.edu.

GRADUATE UNITS

Graduate and Professional Programs Students: 126 full-time (46 women), 170 part-time (65 women); includes 33 minority (13 Black or African American, non-Hispanic/Latino; 1 American Indian or Alaska Native, non-Hispanic/Latino; 4 Asian, non-Hispanic/Latino; 8 Hispanic/Latino; 7 Two or more races, non-Hispanic/Latino), 21 international. Average age 35. *Faculty:* 26 full-time (10 women), 32 part-time/adjunct (9 women). Expenses: Contact institution. *Financial support:* Scholarships/grants available. Financial award application deadline: 4/15; financial award applicants required to submit FAFSA. In 2016, 106 master's, 3 doctorates awarded. *Program availability:* Part-time, evening/weekend, 100% online, blended/hybrid learning. Offers biblical interpretation (Graduate Certificate); business administration (MBA); Christian ministries (Graduate Certificate); clinical mental health counseling (MA); educational technology (MA); intercultural studies (MA); leadership (MBA); leadership studies (PhD); New Testament (MA); nonprofit management (MBA); school counseling (MA); spiritual formation and leadership (Graduate Certificate); strategic ministry (MA); teacher education (MA). *Application deadline:* For fall admission, 7/1 for domestic students; for spring admission, 11/1 for domestic students; for summer admission, 4/1 for domestic students. *Application fee:* $50. Electronic applications accepted. *Application Contact:* Lisa Tarwater, Director of Graduate Admissions, 865-251-3400, E-mail: ltarwater@johnsonu.edu. *Vice President for External Relations*, Richard Clark, 865-251-2327, E-mail: rclark@johnsonu.edu.

JOHN WESLEY UNIVERSITY, High Point, NC 27265

General Information Independent-religious, coed, comprehensive institution. *Enrollment:* 150 graduate, professional, and undergraduate students; 21 full-time matriculated graduate/professional students (13 women), 3 part-time matriculated graduate/professional students (all women). *Enrollment by degree level:* 9 master's, 15 doctoral. *Graduate faculty:* 1 full-time (0 women), 9 part-time/adjunct (3 women). *Tuition:* Full-time $3780; part-time $2520 per semester. *Required fees:* $365; $365 per semester. Tuition and fees vary according to degree level. *Graduate housing:* On-campus housing not available. *Student services:* Campus employment opportunities, campus safety program, services for students with disabilities. *Library facilities:* Temple Library. *Collection:* Books: 3,885 (physical), 26 (digital/electronic); Serial titles: 38 (physical), 164 (digital/electronic); Databases: 4.

Computer facilities: 7 computers available on campus for general student use. Online class registration is available.

Website: http://www.johnwesley.edu/

General Application Contact: Rosalie Seitz, Admissions, 336-821-2474, Fax: 336-889-2261, E-mail: admissions@johnwesley.edu.

GRADUATE UNITS

Graduate Programs Students: 21 full-time (13 women), 3 part-time (all women). *Faculty:* 1 full-time (0 women), 9 part-time/adjunct (3 women). Expenses: Contact institution. *Program availability:* 100% online. Offers Christian leadership (D Min); organizational leadership (MBA); theological studies (MTS). *Application fee:* $50. Electronic applications accepted. *Application Contact:* Rosalie Seitz, Admissions, 336-821-2474, Fax: 336-889-2261, E-mail: admissions@johnwesley.edu.

JOSE MARIA VARGAS UNIVERSITY, Pembroke Pines, FL 33026

General Information Proprietary, coed, comprehensive institution.

GRADUATE UNITS

Program in Preschool Education Offers preschool education (MS).

THE JUDGE ADVOCATE GENERAL'S SCHOOL, U.S. ARMY, Charlottesville, VA 22903-1781

General Information Federally supported, coed, primarily men, graduate-only institution. *Graduate housing:* On-campus housing not available.

GRADUATE UNITS

Graduate Programs Offers military law (LL M). Program available only to active duty military lawyers.

JUDSON UNIVERSITY, Elgin, IL 60123-1498

General Information Independent-religious, coed, comprehensive institution. *Enrollment:* 1,285 graduate, professional, and undergraduate students; 75 full-time matriculated graduate/professional students (48 women), 87 part-time matriculated graduate/professional students (66 women). *Enrollment by degree level:* 124 master's, 37 doctoral, 1 other advanced degree. *Graduate housing:* Rooms and/or apartments available on a first-come, first-served basis to single and married students. Housing application deadline: 8/1. *Student services:* Campus employment opportunities, campus safety program, career counseling, exercise/wellness program, free psychological counseling, international student services, low-cost health insurance, multicultural affairs office, services for students with disabilities, writing training. *Library facilities:* Benjamin P. Browne Library. *Collection:* Books: 120,524 (physical), 2,243 (digital/electronic); Serial titles: 291 (physical), 46,254 (digital/electronic); Databases: 57. Weekly public service hours: 83; students can reserve study rooms.

Computer facilities: 181 computers available on campus for general student use. A campuswide network can be accessed from student residence rooms and from off campus. Online class registration is available.

Website: http://www.judsonu.edu/

General Application Contact: Maria Aguirre, Student Academic Advisor, 847-628-1160, E-mail: maguirre@judsonu.edu.

GRADUATE UNITS

Doctor of Education in Literacy Program Students: 37 full-time (32 women); includes 2 minority (1 Black or African American, non-Hispanic/Latino; 1 Two or more races, non-Hispanic/Latino). Average age 40. 10 applicants, 90% accepted, 8 enrolled. *Faculty:* 6 full-time, 8 part-time/adjunct. Expenses: Contact institution. *Financial support:* Application deadline: 4/1; applicants required to submit FAFSA. *Program availability:* Evening/weekend. Offers literacy (Ed D). *Application deadline:* For fall admission, 11/1 for domestic and international students. *Application fee:* $200. *Application Contact:* Maria Aguirre, Student Academic Advisor, 847-628-1160, E-mail: maguirre@judsonu.edu. *Director,* Dr. Steven L. Layne, 847-628-1093, E-mail: slayne@judsonu.edu.

Master of Architecture Program Students: 19 full-time (5 women); includes 5 minority (1 Black or African American, non-Hispanic/Latino; 3 Hispanic/Latino; 1 Two or more races, non-Hispanic/Latino). Average age 22. 24 applicants, 83% accepted, 19 enrolled. *Faculty:* 9 full-time (3 women), 3 part-time/adjunct (1 woman). Expenses: Contact institution. *Financial support:* In 2016–17, 19 students received support, including 1 fellowship with partial tuition reimbursement available (averaging $5,000 per year), 1 research assistantship with partial tuition reimbursement available (averaging $5,000 per year), 12 teaching assistantships with partial tuition reimbursements available (averaging $2,500 per year); unspecified assistantships also available. Financial award application deadline: 7/1; financial award applicants required to submit FAFSA. In 2016, 16 master's awarded. *Program availability:* Part-time. Offers architecture (M Arch); sustainable design (M Arch); traditional architecture and urbanism (M Arch). *Application deadline:* For fall admission, 2/15 priority date for domestic and international students; for winter admission, 11/15 for domestic students; for spring admission, 11/15 for domestic and international students. Applications are processed on a rolling basis. *Application fee:* $100. Electronic applications accepted. *Application Contact:* Molly Smith, Director of Admissions, 847-628-2521, E-mail: molly.smith@judsonu.edu. *Chair,* Ian Hoffman, 847-628-1014, E-mail: ihoffman@judsonu.edu.

Master of Arts in Clinical Mental Health Counseling Program *Faculty:* 1 (woman) full-time. Expenses: Contact institution. *Program availability:* Evening/weekend. Offers clinical mental health counseling (MA). *Application deadline:* Applications are processed on a rolling basis. Electronic applications accepted. *Application Contact:* Maria Aguirre, Student Academic Advisor, 847-628-1160, E-mail: maguirre@judsonu.edu. *Chair, Professional Studies,* Dr. Susan Wesner, 847-628-1544, E-mail: susan.wesner@judsonu.edu.

Master of Arts in Human Services Administration Program Students: 12 part-time (9 women). *Faculty:* 1 (woman) full-time. Expenses: Contact institution. Offers human services administration (MA). *Application deadline:* Applications are processed on a rolling basis. Electronic applications accepted. *Application Contact:* Maria Aguirre, Student Academic Advisor, 847-628-1160, E-mail: maguirre@judsonu.edu.

Master of Arts in Organizational Leadership Program Students: 23 full-time, 14 part-time; includes 13 minority (6 Black or African American, non-Hispanic/Latino; 5 Hispanic/Latino; 2 Two or more races, non-Hispanic/Latino), 2 international. Average age 37. *Faculty:* 4 full-time (2 women), 20 part-time/adjunct (10 women). Expenses: Contact institution. *Financial support:* Institutionally sponsored loans and scholarships/grants available. Financial award applicants required to submit FAFSA. *Program availability:* Part-time, evening/weekend, 100% online, blended/hybrid learning. Offers organizational leadership (MA). *Application deadline:* For fall admission, 8/1 for domestic students, 7/1 for international students; for spring admission, 3/1 for domestic students, 1/2 for international students. Applications are processed on a rolling basis. *Application fee:* $35. Electronic applications accepted. *Application Contact:* Eric Downs, Enrollment Manager, 847-628-5026, Fax: 847-628-1007, E-mail: eric.downs@info.judsonu.edu. *Chair,* Dr. Teri Stein, 847-628-1524, E-mail: tstein@judsonu.edu.

Master of Business Administration Program Students: 31 full-time, 22 part-time; includes 20 minority (12 Black or African American, non-Hispanic/Latino; 7 Hispanic/Latino; 1 Two or more races, non-Hispanic/Latino), 2 international. 25 applicants, 80% accepted, 18 enrolled. Expenses: Contact institution. *Financial support:* Applicants required to submit FAFSA. *Program availability:* Evening/weekend, 100% online. Offers business administration (MBA). *Application deadline:* Applications are processed on a rolling basis. *Application fee:* $35. Electronic applications accepted. *Application Contact:* Maria Aguirre, Student Academic Advisor, 847-628-1160, E-mail: maguirre@judsonu.edu. *Chair,* Dr. Michelle L. Kilbourne, 847-268-1515, E-mail: mkilbourne@judsonu.edu.

Master of Education in Literacy Program Students: 14 full-time (13 women). Average age 33. 17 applicants, 100% accepted, 17 enrolled. *Faculty:* 4 full-time (2 women), 9 part-time/adjunct (all women). Expenses: Contact institution. *Financial support:* Application deadline: 4/15; applicants required to submit FAFSA. In 2016, 17 master's awarded. Offers literacy (M Ed). *Application deadline:* Applications are processed on a rolling basis. *Application fee:* $40. *Application Contact:* Maria Aguirre, Student Academic Advisor, 847-628-1160, E-mail: maguirre@judsonu.edu. *Director,* Dr. Steven L. Layne, 847-628-1093, E-mail: slayne@judsonu.edu.

Master of Leadership in Ministry Program Students: 1 (woman) part-time; includes 3 minority (all Black or African American, non-Hispanic/Latino). Average age 37. *Faculty:* 3 full-time (1 woman), 5 part-time/adjunct (2 women). Expenses: Contact institution. *Financial support:* In 2016–17, 5 students received support. Scholarships/grants available. Financial award application deadline: 10/31; financial award applicants required to submit FAFSA. *Program availability:* Evening/weekend, online only, blended/hybrid learning. Offers leadership in ministry (MLM). *Application deadline:* Applications are processed on a rolling basis. *Application fee:* $35. Electronic applications accepted. *Application Contact:* Debbie Sanders, Assistant, Department of Christian Ministries, 847-628-1124, E-mail: deborah.sanders@judsonu.edu. *Director,* Dr. Keith Krispin, Jr., 847-628-1057, E-mail: kkrispin@judsonu.edu.

THE JUILLIARD SCHOOL, New York, NY 10023-6588

General Information Independent, coed, comprehensive institution. *Tuition:* Full-time $41,310. *Graduate housing:* Room and/or apartments available on a first-come, first-served basis to single students; on-campus housing not available to married students. Typical cost: $19,970 (including board). Housing application deadline: 5/15. *Student services:* Campus employment opportunities, campus safety program, career counseling, exercise/wellness program, free psychological counseling, international student services, low-cost health insurance. *Library facilities:* Lila Acheson Wallace Library.

Computer facilities: A campuswide network can be accessed from off campus.
Website: http://www.juilliard.edu/

General Application Contact: Ekaterina Lawson, Director of Admissions and Academic Affairs, 212-799-5000 Ext. 223, Fax: 212-724-6420, E-mail: admissions@juilliard.edu.

GRADUATE UNITS

Graduate Programs Expenses: Contact institution. *Financial support:* In 2016–17, 308 students received support. Fellowships, research assistantships, teaching assistantships, Federal Work-Study, institutionally sponsored loans, scholarships/grants, and unspecified assistantships available. Support available to part-time students. Financial award application deadline: 3/1; financial award applicants required to submit FAFSA. Offers acting (MFA); jazz studies (Artist Diploma); music (MM, DMA, Diploma); music performance (Artist Diploma); opera studies (Artist Diploma); string quartet (Artist Diploma). *Application deadline:* For fall admission, 12/1 for domestic and international students. *Application fee:* $110. Electronic applications accepted. *Application Contact:* Ekaterina Lawson, Director of Admissions and Academic Affairs, 212-799-5000 Ext. 223, Fax: 212-724-6420. *Provost and Dean,* Ara Guzelimian, 212-799-5204, Fax: 212-724-0263.

JUNIATA COLLEGE, Huntingdon, PA 16652-2119

General Information Independent-religious, coed, comprehensive institution. *Enrollment:* 3,935 graduate, professional, and undergraduate students; 3 full-time matriculated graduate/professional students (1 woman), 2 part-time matriculated graduate/professional students (both women). *Enrollment by degree level:* 5 master's. *Tuition:* Full-time $24,800; part-time $775 per credit. *Required fees:* $560. *Graduate housing:* On-campus housing not available. *Library facilities:* Beeghly Library. *Collection:* Books: 52,000 (physical); Serial titles: 12,000 (physical). Weekly public service hours: 107.

Computer facilities: 150 computers available on campus for general student use. A campuswide network can be accessed from student residence rooms and from off campus. Online class registration, access to bills are available.
Website: http://www.juniata.edu/

General Application Contact: Michelle Bartol, Dean of Enrollment, 814-641-3432, E-mail: bartolm@juniata.edu.

GRADUATE UNITS

Department of Accounting, Business, and Economics Students: 3 full-time (1 woman); includes 1 minority (Black or African American, non-Hispanic/Latino). Average age 22. Expenses: Contact institution. In 2016, 8 master's awarded. Offers accounting (M Acc). *Chair,* Dr. Dominick Peruso, 814-641-3661, E-mail: peruso@juniata.edu.

KANSAS CITY UNIVERSITY OF MEDICINE AND BIOSCIENCES, Kansas City, MO 64106-1453

General Information Independent, coed, graduate-only institution. CGS member. *Graduate housing:* On-campus housing not available. *Research affiliation:* Boehringer Ingelheim (HIV/AIDS), Mylanta-Bertek (hypertension), Covance (hypertension), Novartis Pharmaceuticals (Chronic Obstructive Pulmonary Disease (COPD)).

GRADUATE UNITS

College of Biosciences *Program availability:* Part-time. Offers bioethics (MA); biomedical sciences (MS).

College of Osteopathic Medicine Offers osteopathic medicine (DO).

KANSAS STATE UNIVERSITY, Manhattan, KS 66506

General Information State-supported, coed, university. CGS member. *Enrollment:* 23,779 graduate, professional, and undergraduate students; 2,078 full-time matriculated graduate/professional students (1,016 women), 1,639 part-time matriculated graduate/professional students (941 women). *Faculty:* 977 full-time (298 women), 190 part-time/adjunct (49 women). *Tuition:* state resident: full-time $9670. *Tuition,* nonresident: full-time $21,828. *Required fees:* $862. *Graduate housing:* Rooms and/or apartments available on a first-come, first-served basis to single and married students. Housing application deadline: 2/1. *Student services:* Campus employment opportunities, campus safety program, career counseling, child daycare facilities, exercise/wellness program, free psychological counseling, grant writing training, international student services, low-cost health insurance, multicultural affairs office, services for students with disabilities, teacher training, writing training. *Library facilities:* Hale Library plus 3 others. *Collection:* Books: 1.4 million (physical), 1.5 million (digital/electronic); Serial titles: 162,581 (physical), 101,651 (digital/electronic); Databases: 309. Weekly public service hours: 80; study areas open 24 hours, 5–7 days a week; students can reserve study rooms. *Research affiliation:* Visteon Corporation, Midwest Research Institute, NASA-Research Center, U.S. Grain Marketing Research Laboratory.

Computer facilities: A campuswide network can be accessed from student residence rooms and from off campus. Online class registration is available.
Website: http://www.k-state.edu/

General Application Contact: Dr. Carol W. Shanklin, Dean of Graduate School, 785-532-7927, Fax: 785-532-2983, E-mail: shanklin@ksu.edu.

GRADUATE UNITS

Graduate School Students: 1,957 full-time (933 women), 1,578 part-time (896 women); includes 502 minority (151 Black or African American, non-Hispanic/Latino; 15 American Indian or Alaska Native, non-Hispanic/Latino; 76 Asian, non-Hispanic/Latino; 182 Hispanic/Latino; 4 Native Hawaiian or other Pacific Islander, non-Hispanic/Latino; 74 Two or more races, non-Hispanic/Latino), 792 international. Average age 31. 2,860 applicants, 50% accepted, 912 enrolled. *Faculty:* 868 full-time (289 women), 179 part-time/adjunct (44 women). Expenses: Contact institution. *Financial support:* Research assistantships, teaching assistantships, career-related internships or fieldwork, Federal Work-Study, institutionally sponsored loans, scholarships/grants, and tuition waivers (full and partial) available. Support available to part-time students. Financial award application deadline: 3/1; financial award applicants required to submit FAFSA. In 2016, 948 master's, 162 doctorates, 125 other advanced degrees awarded. *Program availability:* Part-time, evening/weekend, online learning. *Application deadline:* For fall admission, 2/1 for domestic and international students; for spring admission, 7/1 for domestic students, 8/1 for international students. Applications are processed on a rolling basis. *Application fee:* $65 ($75 for international students). Electronic applications accepted. *Application Contact:* Camila Haselwood, Graduate Admissions Coordinator, 785-532-3218, Fax: 785-532-2983, E-mail: grad@k-state.edu. *Dean,* Dr. Carol W. Shanklin, 785-532-6191, Fax: 785-532-2983, E-mail: shanklin@ksu.edu.

College of Agriculture Students: 337 full-time (144 women), 215 part-time (114 women); includes 42 minority (10 Black or African American, non-Hispanic/Latino; 1 American Indian or Alaska Native, non-Hispanic/Latino; 8 Asian, non-Hispanic/Latino; 20 Hispanic/Latino; 3 Two or more races, non-Hispanic/Latino), 179 international. Average age 29. 316 applicants, 43% accepted, 90 enrolled. *Faculty:* 172 full-time (37 women), 45 part-time/adjunct (4 women). Expenses: Contact institution. *Financial support:* In 2016–17, 278 research assistantships (averaging $16,545 per year), 48 teaching assistantships (averaging $9,850 per year) were awarded; career-related internships or fieldwork, Federal Work-Study, institutionally sponsored loans, scholarships/grants, and tuition waivers (partial) also available. Support available to part-time students. Financial award application deadline: 3/1; financial award applicants required to submit FAFSA. In 2016, 127 master's, 38 doctorates, 4 other advanced degrees awarded. *Program availability:* Part-time, online learning. Offers agricultural economics (MAB, MS, PhD); agricultural education and communication (MS); agriculture (MAB, MS, PhD, Certificate); crop science (MS, PhD); entomology (MS, PhD); food science (MS, PhD); genetics (MS, PhD); grain science and industry (MS, PhD); grassland management (Certificate); horticulture and natural resources (MS, PhD); meat science (MS, PhD); monogastric nutrition (MS, PhD); physiology (MS, PhD); plant breeding and genetics (MS, PhD); plant pathology (MS, PhD); range and forage science (MS, PhD); ruminant nutrition (MS, PhD); soil and environmental science (MS, PhD); weed science (MS, PhD). *Application deadline:* For fall admission, 2/1 priority date for domestic and international students; for spring admission, 8/1 priority date for domestic and international students. Applications are processed on a rolling basis. *Application fee:* $50 ($75 for international students). Electronic applications accepted. *Application Contact:* Camila Haselwood, Admissions Coordinator, 785-532-3218, Fax: 785-532-2983, E-mail: grad@ksu.edu. *Dean,* Dr. John Floros, 785-532-6151, Fax: 785-532-6897, E-mail: floros@ksu.edu.

College of Architecture, Planning and Design Students: 252 full-time (128 women), 28 part-time (16 women); includes 54 minority (10 Black or African American, non-Hispanic/Latino; 11 Asian, non-Hispanic/Latino; 21 Hispanic/Latino; 12 Two or more races, non-Hispanic/Latino), 37 international. Average age 24. 227 applicants, 70% accepted, 133 enrolled. *Faculty:* 50 full-time (16 women), 4 part-time/adjunct (2 women). Expenses: Contact institution. *Financial support:* In 2016–17, 5 research assistantships (averaging $4,640 per year), 41 teaching assistantships with full tuition reimbursements (averaging $7,054 per year) were awarded; career-related internships or fieldwork and scholarships/grants also available. Financial award application deadline: 3/1; financial award applicants required to submit FAFSA. In 2016, 115 master's, 4 doctorates awarded. *Program availability:* Part-time. Offers architecture (M Arch, MS Arch); architecture, planning and design (M Arch, MIAPD, MLA, MRCP, MS, MS Arch, PhD); community development (MS); environmental design and planning (PhD); interior architecture and product design (MIAPD); landscape architecture (MLA); regional and community planning (MRCP). *Application deadline:* For fall admission, 2/1 priority date for domestic students, 1/1 priority date for international students; for spring admission, 8/1 priority date for domestic and international students. Applications are processed on a rolling basis. *Application fee:* $90 ($100 for international students). Electronic applications accepted. *Application Contact:* Susan Lannou, Director of Student Recruitment, 785-532-5047, E-mail: myapd@ksu.edu. *Dean,* Tim de Noble, 785-532-5950, Fax: 785-532-6722, E-mail: tdenoble@ksu.edu.

College of Arts and Sciences Students: 614 full-time (302 women), 222 part-time (108 women); includes 96 minority (25 Black or African American, non-Hispanic/Latino; 3 American Indian or Alaska Native, non-Hispanic/Latino; 13 Asian, non-Hispanic/Latino; 42 Hispanic/Latino; 13 Two or more races, non-Hispanic/Latino), 260 international. Average age 30. 844 applicants, 39% accepted, 203 enrolled. *Faculty:* 356 full-time (121 women), 62 part-time/adjunct (10 women). Expenses: Contact institution. *Financial support:* In 2016–17, 131 research assistantships (averaging $14,645 per year), 425 teaching assistantships with full tuition reimbursements (averaging $12,635 per year) were awarded; career-related internships or fieldwork, Federal Work-Study, institutionally sponsored loans, scholarships/grants, and tuition waivers also available. Support available to part-time students. Financial award application deadline: 3/1; financial award applicants required to submit FAFSA. In 2016, 168 master's, 55 doctorates, 16 other advanced degrees awarded. *Program availability:* Part-time, online learning. Offers advertising (MS); art (MFA); arts and sciences (MA, MFA, MM, MPA, MS, PhD, Graduate Certificate); biochemistry and molecular biophysics (MS, PhD); biology (MS); chemistry (MS, PhD); communication studies (MA); community journalism (MS); economics (MA, PhD); English (MA); gender, women and sexuality studies (Graduate Certificate); geographic information science (Graduate Certificate); geography (MA, PhD); geology (MS); global communication (MS); health communication (MS); history (MA, PhD); mathematics (MS, PhD, Graduate Certificate); media management (MS); modern languages (MA); music, theatre and dance (MA, MM); physics (MS, PhD); political science (MA); psychological sciences (MS, PhD); public administration (MPA); public relations (MS); security studies (MA, PhD); sociology (MS, PhD); statistics (MS, PhD, Graduate Certificate); technical writing and professional communication (Graduate Certificate). *Application deadline:* For fall admission, 2/1 priority date for domestic and international students; for spring admission, 8/1 priority date for domestic and international students. Applications are processed on a rolling basis. *Application fee:* $50 ($75 for international students). Electronic applications accepted. *Application Contact:* Camila Haselwood, Admissions Coordinator, 785-532-3218, Fax: 785-532-2983, E-mail: grad@ksu.edu. *Interim Dean,* Dr. Amit Chakrabarti, 785-532-6900, E-mail: artsci@ksu.edu.

College of Business Students: 108 full-time (55 women), 92 part-time (38 women); includes 29 minority (9 Black or African American, non-Hispanic/Latino; 7 Asian, non-Hispanic/Latino; 5 Hispanic/Latino; 8 Two or more races, non-Hispanic/Latino), 22 international. Average age 30. 136 applicants, 91% accepted, 65 enrolled. *Faculty:* 33 full-time (9 women), 7 part-time/adjunct (4 women). Expenses: Contact institution. *Financial support:* In 2016–17, 19 research assistantships with partial tuition reimbursements (averaging $5,604 per year), 18 teaching assistantships with partial tuition reimbursements (averaging $5,528 per year) were awarded; scholarships/grants also available. Financial award application deadline: 3/1; financial award applicants required to submit FAFSA. In 2016, 53 master's, 3 other advanced degrees awarded. *Program availability:* Part-time. Offers accounting (M Acc); business (M Acc, MBA, Certificate); data analytics (MBA); finance (MBA); management (MBA); marketing (MBA); technology entrepreneurship (MBA). *Application deadline:* For fall admission, 2/1 priority date for domestic and international students; for spring admission, 8/1 priority date for domestic and international students. Applications are processed on a rolling basis. *Application fee:* $65 ($80 for international students). Electronic applications accepted. *Application Contact:* Lynn S. Waugh, Graduate Program Coordinator, 785-532-7190, E-mail: lwaugh@ksu.edu. *Dean,* Kevin Gwinner, 785-532-7227, E-mail: kgwinner@ksu.edu.

College of Education Students: 209 full-time (123 women), 646 part-time (452 women); includes 169 minority (62 Black or African American, non-Hispanic/Latino; 10 American Indian or Alaska Native, non-Hispanic/Latino; 13 Asian, non-Hispanic/Latino; 60 Hispanic/Latino; 3 Native Hawaiian or other Pacific Islander, non-Hispanic/Latino; 21 Two or more races, non-Hispanic/Latino), 27 international. Average age 36. 439 applicants, 84% accepted, 258 enrolled. *Faculty:* 43 full-time (28 women), 14 part-time/adjunct (7 women). Expenses: Contact institution. *Financial support:* In 2016–17, 10 research assistantships (averaging $14,458 per year), 16 teaching assistantships with full tuition reimbursements (averaging $13,015 per year)

were awarded; career-related internships or fieldwork, Federal Work-Study, institutionally sponsored loans, and scholarships/grants also available. Support available to part-time students. Financial award application deadline: 3/1; financial award applicants required to submit FAFSA. In 2016, 305 master's, 18 doctorates, 81 other advanced degrees awarded. *Program availability:* Part-time, evening/weekend, online learning. Offers academic advising (MS, Certificate); adult learning (Certificate); counseling and student development (MS); curriculum and instruction (Ed D, PhD); digital teaching and learning (MS); education (MS, Ed D, PhD, Certificate); educational computing, design and online learning (MS); educational leadership (MS, Ed D, PhD); elementary/middle level curriculum and instruction (MS); leadership dynamics for adult learners (Certificate); online learning (Certificate); qualitative research (Certificate); reading specialist endorsement (MS); reading/language arts (MS); social justice education (Certificate); special education (MS, Ed D); special education, counseling, and student affairs (PhD); teacher leader/school improvement (MS); teaching and learning (Certificate); teaching English as a second language for adult learners (Certificate). *Application deadline:* For fall admission, 2/1 priority date for domestic and international students; for spring admission, 8/1 priority date for domestic and international students. Applications are processed on a rolling basis. *Application fee:* $50 ($75 for international students). Electronic applications accepted. *Application Contact:* Dr. Linda P. Thurston, Associate Dean for Research and Graduate Studies, 785-532-5765, E-mail: coegrads@ksu.edu. *Dean,* Dr. Debbie Mercer, 785-532-5525, Fax: 785-532-7304, E-mail: edcoll@ksu.edu.

College of Engineering Students: 286 full-time (76 women), 194 part-time (32 women); includes 57 minority (18 Black or African American, non-Hispanic/Latino; 19 Asian, non-Hispanic/Latino; 11 Hispanic/Latino; 9 Two or more races, non-Hispanic/Latino), 220 international. Average age 29. 598 applicants, 37% accepted, 95 enrolled. *Faculty:* 123 full-time (20 women), 24 part-time/adjunct (4 women). Expenses: Contact institution. *Financial support:* In 2016–17, 126 research assistantships (averaging $16,448 per year), 83 teaching assistantships (averaging $14,697 per year) were awarded; career-related internships or fieldwork, Federal Work-Study, institutionally sponsored loans, and scholarships/grants also available. Support available to part-time students. Financial award application deadline: 3/1; financial award applicants required to submit FAFSA. In 2016, 98 master's, 29 doctorates, 1 other advanced degree awarded. *Program availability:* Part-time, online learning. Offers architectural engineering and construction science (MS); biological and agricultural engineering (MS, PhD); chemical engineering (MS, PhD, Graduate Certificate); civil engineering (MS, PhD); computer science (MS, MSE, PhD); electrical engineering (MS); engineering (MEM, MS, MSE, PhD, Graduate Certificate); engineering management (MEM); environmental engineering (MS, PhD); geotechnical engineering (MS, PhD); industrial engineering (MS); mechanical engineering (MS); nuclear engineering (PhD); operations research (MS); structural engineering (MS, PhD); transportation engineering (MS, PhD); water resources engineering (MS, PhD). *Application deadline:* For fall admission, 2/1 priority date for domestic students, 1/1 priority date for international students; for spring admission, 8/1 priority date for domestic and international students. Applications are processed on a rolling basis. *Application fee:* $50 ($75 for international students). Electronic applications accepted. *Application Contact:* Maureen Lockhart, Administrative Assistant to the Dean, 785-532-5441, E-mail: maureen@k-state.edu. *Dean,* Dr. Darren Dawson, 785-532-5590, E-mail: dmdawson@k-state.edu.

College of Human Ecology Students: 147 full-time (104 women), 167 part-time (131 women); includes 53 minority (17 Black or African American, non-Hispanic/Latino; 1 American Indian or Alaska Native, non-Hispanic/Latino; 5 Asian, non-Hispanic/Latino; 23 Hispanic/Latino; 1 Native Hawaiian or other Pacific Islander, non-Hispanic/Latino; 6 Two or more races, non-Hispanic/Latino), 45 international. Average age 33. 285 applicants, 35% accepted, 63 enrolled. *Faculty:* 64 full-time (41 women), 10 part-time/adjunct (7 women). Expenses: Contact institution. *Financial support:* In 2016–17, 71 research assistantships (averaging $13,454 per year), 50 teaching assistantships with full and partial tuition reimbursements (averaging $13,202 per year) were awarded; career-related internships or fieldwork, Federal Work-Study, institutionally sponsored loans, scholarships/grants, and tuition waivers (full) also available. Support available to part-time students. Financial award application deadline: 3/1; financial award applicants required to submit FAFSA. In 2016, 82 master's, 18 doctorates, 20 other advanced degrees awarded. *Program availability:* Part-time, online learning. Offers apparel and textiles (MS, PhD); applied family sciences (MS, PhD); communication sciences and disorders (MS); conflict resolution (Graduate Certificate); couple and family therapy (MS, PhD); dietetics (MS); early childhood education (MS); family and community service (MS); gerontology (MS, Graduate Certificate); hospitality administration (PhD); hospitality and dietetics administration (MS); human ecology (MS, PhD, Graduate Certificate); human nutrition (PhD); kinesiology (MS, PhD); life-span human development (MS, PhD); nutrition, dietetics and sensory sciences (MS); nutritional sciences (PhD); personal financial planning (MS, PhD, Graduate Certificate); public health nutrition (PhD); public health physical activity (PhD); sensory analysis and consumer behavior (PhD); youth development (MS, Graduate Certificate). *Application deadline:* For fall admission, 2/1 priority date for domestic and international students; for spring admission, 8/1 priority date for domestic and international students. Applications are processed on a rolling basis. *Application fee:* $50 ($75 for international students). Electronic applications accepted. *Application Contact:* Mary Anne Andrews, Director, Academic and Student Services, 785-532-5500, Fax: 785-532-5504, E-mail: mandrews@ksu.edu. *Dean,* Dr. John Buckwalter, 785-532-5500, Fax: 785-532-5504, E-mail: jbb3@ksu.edu.

College of Technology and Aviation Students: 4 full-time (1 woman), 8 part-time (4 women); includes 2 minority (both Two or more races, non-Hispanic/Latino), 2 international. Average age 35. 6 applicants, 33% accepted, 1 enrolled. *Faculty:* 4 full-time (1 woman), 1 part-time/adjunct (0 women). Expenses: Contact institution. In 2016, 1 master's awarded. *Program availability:* Part-time, evening/weekend, 100% online. Offers technology and aviation (MT). *Application deadline:* For fall admission, 3/1 for domestic students, 1/1 for international students; for spring admission, 10/1 for domestic students, 8/1 for international students. *Application fee:* $50 ($75 for international students). Electronic applications accepted. *Application Contact:* Dr. Don Von Bergen, Graduate Program Director, 785-826-2904, E-mail: salgrad@k-state.edu. *Dean,* Dr. Verna Fitzsimmons, 785-826-2601, E-mail: vfitzsimmons@ksu.edu.

College of Veterinary Medicine Students: 573 full-time (451 women), 70 part-time (51 women); includes 73 minority (5 Black or African American, non-Hispanic/Latino; 2 American Indian or Alaska Native, non-Hispanic/Latino; 20 Asian, non-Hispanic/Latino; 28 Hispanic/Latino; 18 Two or more races, non-Hispanic/Latino), 40 international. Average age 28. *Faculty:* 81 full-time (24 women), 18 part-time/adjunct (11 women). Expenses: Contact institution. *Financial support:* In 2016–17, 53 research assistantships (averaging $19,235 per year), 1 teaching assistantship (averaging $30,760 per year) were awarded; Federal Work-Study, institutionally sponsored loans, and scholarships/grants also available. Financial award application deadline: 3/1; financial award applicants required to submit FAFSA. In 2016, 24 master's, 113 doctorates, 5 other advanced degrees awarded. Offers biomedical science (MS); clinical sciences (MPH, Graduate Certificate); diagnostic medicine/pathobiology (PhD); physiology (PhD); veterinary medicine (MPH, MS, DVM, PhD, Graduate Certificate). *Application deadline:* For fall admission, 2/1 priority date for domestic and international students; for spring admission, 8/1 priority date for domestic and international students. Applications are processed on a rolling basis. *Application fee:* $50 ($75 for international students). Electronic applications accepted. *Application Contact:* Gail Eyestone, Administrative Assistant, 785-532-4005, Fax: 785-532-5884, E-mail: geyestone@vet.ksu.edu. *Dean,* Tammy R. Beckham, 785-532-5660, E-mail: vetdean@ksu.edu.

School of Applied and Interdisciplinary Studies Students: 8 part-time (2 women); includes 1 minority (Black or African American, non-Hispanic/Latino). Average age 35. 9 applicants, 100% accepted, 8 enrolled. *Faculty:* 22 full-time (16 women), 2 part-time/adjunct (1 woman). Expenses: Contact institution. *Financial support:* In 2016–17, 8 students received support. Scholarships/grants available. *Program availability:* Part-time, 100% online, blended/hybrid learning. Offers applied science and technology (PSM); professional interdisciplinary sciences (Graduate Certificate); professional skills for STEM practitioners (Graduate Certificate). *Application deadline:* Applications are processed on a rolling basis. *Application fee:* $65 ($75 for international students). Electronic applications accepted. *Application Contact:* Dr. Janice Barrow, Associate Dean for Academic Affairs and Executive Education, 913-541-1220, E-mail: jbarrow@k-state.edu. *Dean and CEO,* Dr. Ralph Richardson, 913-541-1220, Fax: 913-541-1488, E-mail: olatheinfo@ksu.edu.

See Display below and Close-Up on page 885.

KANSAS WESLEYAN UNIVERSITY, Salina, KS 67401-6196

General Information Independent-religious, coed, comprehensive institution. *Graduate housing:* Rooms and/or apartments available to single and married students.

GRADUATE UNITS

Program in Business Administration *Program availability:* Part-time, evening/weekend. Offers business administration (MBA); sports management (MBA).

KAPLAN UNIVERSITY, DAVENPORT CAMPUS, Davenport, IA 52807

General Information Proprietary, coed, comprehensive institution.

GRADUATE UNITS

School of Business *Program availability:* Part-time, evening/weekend, online learning. Offers business administration (MBA); change leadership (MS); entrepreneurship (MBA); finance (MBA); health care management (MBA, MS); human resource (MBA); international business (MBA); management (MS); marketing (MBA); project management (MBA, MS); supply chain management and logistics (MBA, MS). Electronic applications accepted.

School of Criminal Justice *Program availability:* Part-time, evening/weekend, online learning. Offers corrections (MSCJ); global issues in criminal justice (MSCJ); law (MSCJ); leadership and executive management (MSCJ); policing (MSCJ). Electronic applications accepted.

School of Higher Education Studies *Program availability:* Part-time, evening/weekend, online learning. Offers college administration and leadership (MS); college teaching and learning (MS); student services (MS).

School of Information Technology *Program availability:* Part-time, evening/weekend, online learning. Offers decision support systems (MS); information security and assurance (MS).

School of Legal Studies *Program availability:* Part-time, evening/weekend, online learning. Offers health care delivery (MS); pathway to paralegal (Postbaccalaureate Certificate); state and local government (MS).

School of Nursing *Program availability:* Part-time, evening/weekend, online learning. Offers nurse administrator (MS); nurse educator (MS).

School of Teacher Education *Program availability:* Part-time, evening/weekend, online learning. Offers education (M Ed); secondary education (M Ed); teaching and learning (MA); teaching literacy and language: grades 6-12 (MA); teaching literacy and language: grades K-6 (MA); teaching mathematics: grades 6-8 (MA); teaching mathematics: grades 9-12 (MA); teaching mathematics: grades K-5 (MA); teaching science: grades 6-12 (MA); teaching science: grades K-6 (MA); teaching students with special needs (MA); teaching with technology (MA).

KEAN UNIVERSITY, Union, NJ 07083

General Information State-supported, coed, university. *Enrollment:* 14,070 graduate, professional, and undergraduate students; 886 full-time matriculated graduate/professional students (690 women), 874 part-time matriculated graduate/professional students (658 women). *Enrollment by degree level:* 1,586 master's, 130 doctoral, 44 other advanced degrees. *Graduate faculty:* 247 full-time (130 women). Tuition, state resident: full-time $13,156; part-time $640 per credit. Tuition, nonresident: full-time $17,831; part-time $785 per credit. *Required fees:* $3316; $151 per credit. Tuition and fees vary according to course level, course load, degree level and program. *Graduate housing:* Room and/or apartments available on a first-come, first-served basis to single students; on-campus housing not available to married students. Housing application deadline: 5/1. *Student services:* Campus employment opportunities, campus safety program, career counseling, exercise/wellness program, free psychological counseling, grant writing training, international student services, low-cost health insurance, multicultural affairs office, services for students with disabilities, teacher training, writing training. *Library facilities:* Nancy Thompson Library. *Collection:* Books: 201,146 (physical), 10,966 (digital/electronic); Serial titles: 56,478 (digital/electronic); Databases: 246. Weekly public service hours: 102. *Research affiliation:* Robert Wood Johnson Foundation (the effect of tobacco control policy), Institute of Vertebrate Paleontology and Paleoanthropology (paleoanthropology), Shodor Foundation (intelligent Internet search engines for science research and education), New Jersey Institute of Technology (partitioning to support auditing and extending the UMLS), National Bureau of Economic Research (alcoholic advertising and youth).

Computer facilities: 1,700 computers available on campus for general student use. A campuswide network can be accessed from student residence rooms and from off campus. Online class registration is available.
Website: http://www.kean.edu/

General Application Contact: Helen Ramirez, Associate Director, 908-737-7137, E-mail: hramirez@kean.edu.

GRADUATE UNITS

College of Business and Public Management Students: 156 full-time (98 women), 112 part-time (67 women); includes 166 minority (92 Black or African American, non-Hispanic/Latino; 23 Asian, non-Hispanic/Latino; 49 Hispanic/Latino; 2 Two or more races, non-Hispanic/Latino), 28 international. Average age 31. *Faculty:* 29 full-time (7 women). Expenses: Contact institution. *Financial support:* Federal Work-Study, scholarships/grants, and unspecified assistantships available. Financial award applicants required to submit FAFSA. In 2016, 111 master's awarded. *Program availability:* Part-time. Offers accounting (MS); business and public management (MA, MBA, MPA, MS); criminal justice (MA); executive management (MBA); global management (MBA); health services administration (MPA); non-profit management (MPA); public administration (MPA). *Application deadline:* For fall admission, 6/1 for domestic and international students; for spring admission, 12/1 for domestic and international students. Applications are processed on a rolling basis. *Application fee:* $75. Electronic applications accepted. *Application Contact:* Pedro Lopes, Admissions Counselor, 908-737-7100, E-mail: grad-adm@kean.edu. *Dean,* Dr. Michael Cooper, 908-737-4707, Fax: 908-737-4765, E-mail: mrcooper@kean.edu.

College of Education Students: 30 full-time (21 women), 145 part-time (115 women); includes 72 minority (14 Black or African American, non-Hispanic/Latino; 14 Asian, non-Hispanic/Latino; 43 Hispanic/Latino; 1 Two or more races, non-Hispanic/Latino), 2 international. Average age 33. 272 applicants, 55% accepted, 151 enrolled. *Faculty:* 46 full-time (29 women). Expenses: Contact institution. *Financial support:* Scholarships/grants and unspecified assistantships available. Financial award applicants required to submit FAFSA. In 2016, 91 master's awarded. *Program availability:* Part-time. Offers administration in early childhood and family studies (MA); advanced curriculum and teaching (MA); autism and developmental disabilities (MA); bilingual/bicultural education (MA); classroom instruction - P-3 certification (MA); education (MA, MS); exercise science (MS); Hindi and Urdu language pedagogy (MA); learning and behavioral disabilities (MA); reading specialization (MA); teaching English as a second language (MA). *Application deadline:* For fall admission, 6/1 for domestic and international students; for spring admission, 12/1 for domestic and international students. Applications are processed on a rolling basis. *Application fee:* $75. Electronic applications accepted. *Application Contact:* Brittany Gerstenhaber, Admissions Counselor, 908-737-7100, E-mail: grad-adm@kean.edu. *Acting Dean,* Dr. Anthony Pitmann, 908-737-3750, Fax: 908-737-3760, E-mail: polirsts@kean.edu.

College of Liberal Arts Students: 110 full-time (91 women), 106 part-time (73 women); includes 104 minority (52 Black or African American, non-Hispanic/Latino; 9 Asian, non-Hispanic/Latino; 39 Hispanic/Latino; 1 Native Hawaiian or other Pacific Islander, non-Hispanic/Latino; 3 Two or more races, non-Hispanic/Latino), 2 international. Average age 30. 146 applicants, 49% accepted, 62 enrolled. *Faculty:* 78 full-time (39 women). Expenses: Contact institution. *Financial support:* Scholarships/grants and unspecified assistantships available. Financial award applicants required to submit FAFSA. In 2016, 89 master's, 9 other advanced degrees awarded. *Program availability:* Part-time. Offers communication studies (MA); English writing studies (MA); forensic psychology (MA); Holocaust and genocide studies (MA); human behavior and organizational psychology (MA); initial teaching certification (MA); liberal arts (MA, Diploma); marriage and family therapy (MA, Diploma); psychological services (MA); studio (MA); supervision (MA). *Application deadline:* For fall admission, 6/1 for domestic and international students; for spring admission, 12/1 for domestic and international students. Applications are processed on a rolling basis. *Application fee:* $75. Electronic applications accepted. *Application Contact:* Amy Hadjusek, Program Assistant, 908-737-7100, E-mail: grad-adm@kean.edu. *Dean,* Dr. Susan Bousequet, 908-737-0430, Fax: 908-737-0435, E-mail: sbousque@kean.edu.

College of Natural, Applied and Health Sciences Students: 28 full-time (19 women), 130 part-time (120 women); includes 72 minority (50 Black or African American, non-Hispanic/Latino; 18 Asian, non-Hispanic/Latino; 2 Hispanic/Latino; 2 Two or more races, non-Hispanic/Latino), 12 international. Average age 44. 100 applicants, 31% accepted, 28 enrolled. *Faculty:* 32 full-time (17 women). Expenses: Contact institution. *Financial support:* Scholarships/grants and unspecified assistantships available. Financial award applicants required to submit FAFSA. In 2016, 62 master's awarded. *Program availability:* Part-time. Offers clinical management (MSN); community health nursing (MSN); computer information systems (MS); educational leadership (PhD); natural, applied and health sciences (MS, MSN, PhD). *Application deadline:* For fall admission, 6/1 for domestic and international students; for spring admission, 12/1 for domestic and international students. Applications are processed on a rolling basis. *Application fee:* $75. Electronic applications accepted. *Application Contact:* Pedro Lopes, Admissions Counselor, 908-737-7100, E-mail: grad-adm@kean.edu. *Dean,* Dr. George Chang, 908-737-3600, Fax: 908-737-3606, E-mail: gchang@kean.edu.

Nathan Weiss Graduate College Students: 529 full-time (441 women), 376 part-time (279 women); includes 377 minority (161 Black or African American, non-Hispanic/Latino; 2 American Indian or Alaska Native, non-Hispanic/Latino; 33 Asian, non-Hispanic/Latino; 165 Hispanic/Latino; 1 Native Hawaiian or other Pacific Islander, non-Hispanic/Latino; 15 Two or more races, non-Hispanic/Latino), 7 international. Average age 30. 1,650 applicants, 25% accepted, 385 enrolled. *Faculty:* 45 full-time (33 women). Expenses: Contact institution. *Financial support:* Scholarships/grants and unspecified assistantships available. Financial award applicants required to submit FAFSA. In 2016, 252 master's, 20 doctorates, 9 other advanced degrees awarded. *Program availability:* Part-time. Offers alcohol and drug abuse counseling (MA); clinical mental health counseling (MA); combined school and clinical psychology (Psy D); educational leadership (Ed D); occupational therapy (MS); physical therapy (DPT); school business administrator (MA); school counseling (MA); school psychology (Diploma); social work (MSW); speech language pathology (MA); supervisor and principal (MA); supervisors, principals, and school business administrators (MA). *Application deadline:* For fall admission, 6/1 for domestic and international students; for spring admission, 12/1 for domestic and international students. Applications are processed on a rolling basis. *Application fee:* $75. Electronic applications accepted. *Application Contact:* Ann-Marie Kay, Associate Director, Graduate Admissions, 908-737-7100, E-mail: grad-adm@kean.edu. *Dean,* Dr. Jeffrey Beck, 908-737-5902, Fax: 908-737-5905, E-mail: jbeck@kean.edu.

New Jersey Center for Science, Technology and Mathematics Students: 33 full-time (20 women), 5 part-time (4 women); includes 21 minority (2 Black or African American, non-Hispanic/Latino; 10 Asian, non-Hispanic/Latino; 9 Hispanic/Latino), 4 international. Average age 26. 17 applicants, 41% accepted, 7 enrolled. *Faculty:* 8 full-time (1 woman). Expenses: Contact institution. *Financial support:* Scholarships/grants and unspecified assistantships available. Financial award applicants required to submit FAFSA. In 2016, 20 master's awarded. Offers biotechnology science (MS); instruction and curriculum (MA). *Application deadline:* For fall admission, 6/1 for domestic and international students; for spring admission, 12/1 for domestic and international students. Applications are processed on a rolling basis. *Application fee:* $75. Electronic applications accepted. *Application Contact:* Pedro Lopes, Admissions Counselor, 908-

737-7100, E-mail: grad-adm@kean.edu. *Program Coordinator,* Dr. Salvatore Coniglio, 908-737-7216, E-mail: coniglsa@kean.edu.

KECK GRADUATE INSTITUTE, Claremont, CA 91711

General Information Independent, coed, graduate-only institution. CGS member.

GRADUATE UNITS

School of Applied Life Sciences Offers applied life sciences (PhD); bioscience (MBS); bioscience management (Certificate). Electronic applications accepted.

School of Pharmacy Offers pharmacy (Pharm D).

KEENE STATE COLLEGE, Keene, NH 03435

General Information State-supported, coed, comprehensive institution. *Enrollment:* 4,282 graduate, professional, and undergraduate students; 24 full-time matriculated graduate/professional students (17 women), 66 part-time matriculated graduate/professional students (38 women). *Enrollment by degree level:* 90 master's. *Graduate faculty:* 9 full-time (4 women), 8 part-time/adjunct (3 women). Tuition, state resident: full-time $9180; part-time $510 per credit. Tuition, nonresident: full-time $10,080; part-time $560 per credit. *Required fees:* $1908; $106 per credit. Tuition and fees vary according to course load. *Graduate housing:* Room and/or apartments available on a first-come, first-served basis to single students; on-campus housing not available to married students. Typical cost: $6882 per year ($10,390 including board). Room and board charges vary according to board plan and housing facility selected. Housing application deadline: 5/1. *Student services:* Campus employment opportunities, campus safety program, career counseling, exercise/wellness program, free psychological counseling, grant writing training, international student services, multicultural affairs office, services for students with disabilities, teacher training, writing training. *Library facilities:* Mason Library. *Collection:* Books: 259,538 (physical), 275,694 (digital/electronic); Serial titles: 245 (physical), 68,825 (digital/electronic); Databases: 92. Weekly public service hours: 102; students can reserve study rooms.

Computer facilities: Computer purchase and lease plans are available. 600 computers available on campus for general student use. A campuswide network can be accessed from student residence rooms and from off campus. Online class registration is available.

Website: http://www.keene.edu/

General Application Contact: Peter Tandy, Assistant Director for Graduate Studies, 603-358-2497, E-mail: kscgraduatestudies@keene.edu.

GRADUATE UNITS

School of Professional and Graduate Studies Students: 24 full-time (17 women), 66 part-time (38 women); includes 3 minority (1 Black or African American, non-Hispanic/Latino; 1 Hispanic/Latino; 1 Two or more races, non-Hispanic/Latino), 1 international. Average age 33. 24 applicants, 100% accepted, 24 enrolled. *Faculty:* 9 full-time (4 women), 8 part-time/adjunct (3 women). Expenses: Contact institution. *Financial support:* In 2016–17, 27 students received support. Career-related internships or fieldwork, Federal Work-Study, institutionally sponsored loans, scholarships/grants, and unspecified assistantships available. Support available to part-time students. Financial award application deadline: 3/1; financial award applicants required to submit FAFSA. In 2016, 26 master's, 1 other advanced degree awarded. *Program availability:* Part-time, evening/weekend. Offers curriculum and instruction (M Ed); education leadership (PMC); educational leadership (M Ed); safety and occupational health applied science (MS); school counselor (M Ed, PMC); special education (M Ed). *Application deadline:* For fall admission, 4/1 for domestic and international students; for spring admission, 11/1 for domestic and international students; for summer admission, 3/1 for domestic and international students. Applications are processed on a rolling basis. *Application fee:* $50. Electronic applications accepted. *Application Contact:* Peter Tandy, Assistant Director for Graduate Studies, 603-358-2332, E-mail: kscgraduatestudies@keene.edu. *Dean of Professional and Graduate Studies,* Dr. Karrie Kalich, 603-358-2885, E-mail: kkalich@keene.edu.

KEHILATH YAKOV RABBINICAL SEMINARY, Ossining, NY 10562

General Information Independent-religious, men only, comprehensive institution.

GRADUATE UNITS

Graduate Programs

KEISER UNIVERSITY, Fort Lauderdale, FL 33309

General Information Independent, coed, university.

GRADUATE UNITS

Doctor of Business Administration Program Offers global business (DBA); global organizational leadership (DBA); marketing (DBA).

EdS in Educational Leadership Program Offers educational leadership (Ed S).

EdS in Instructional Design and Technology Program Offers instructional design and technology (Ed S).

Joint MS Ed/MBA Program

MA in Criminal Justice-Homeland Security Program Offers criminal justice-homeland security (MA).

MA in Criminal Justice Program *Program availability:* Part-time, online learning. Offers criminal justice (MA).

Master of Accountancy Program Offers forensic accounting (M Acc); general accounting (M Acc).

Master of Business Administration Program *Program availability:* Part-time, online learning. Offers accounting (MBA); health services management (MBA); information security management (MBA); international business (MBA); leadership for managers (MBA); marketing (MBA). All concentrations except information security management also offered in Mandarin; leadership for managers and international business also offered in Spanish.

Master of Science in Education Program *Program availability:* Part-time, online learning. Offers allied health teaching and leadership (MS Ed); career college administration (MS Ed); leadership (MS Ed); online teaching and learning (MS Ed); teaching and learning (MS Ed).

Master of Science in Nursing Program Offers nursing (MSN).

MS in Information Security Program Offers information security (MS).

MS in Information Technology Leadership Program Offers information technology leadership (MS).

MS in Management Program Offers management (MS). Program also offered in Spanish.

MS in Organizational Psychology Program Offers organizational psychology (MS).

MS in Physician Assistant Program Offers physician assistant (MS).

MS in Psychology Program Offers psychology (MS).

PhD in Educational Leadership Program Offers educational leadership (PhD).

PhD in Industrial and Organizational Psychology Program Offers industrial and organizational psychology (PhD).

PhD in Instructional Design and Technology Program Offers instructional design and technology (PhD).

PhD in Psychology Program Offers psychology (PhD).

KENNESAW STATE UNIVERSITY, Kennesaw, GA 30144

General Information State-supported, coed, comprehensive institution. CGS member. *Graduate housing:* Room and/or apartments available on a first-come, first-served basis to single students; on-campus housing not available to married students.

GRADUATE UNITS

College of Architecture and Construction Management *Program availability:* Part-time, evening/weekend. Offers architecture (MS Arch); architecture and construction management (MS, MS Arch); construction management (MS). Electronic applications accepted.

College of Computing and Software Engineering *Program availability:* Part-time, evening/weekend, online learning. Offers computer science (MS); computing and software engineering (MS, MSIT, MSSWE, Graduate Certificate, Graduate Transition Certificate, Postbaccalaureate Certificate); health information technology (Postbaccalaureate Certificate); information security and assurance (Graduate Certificate); information technology (MSIT, Graduate Certificate); information technology fundamentals (Postbaccalaureate Certificate); software engineering (MSSWE, Graduate Certificate); software engineering foundations (Graduate Certificate). Electronic applications accepted.

College of Humanities and Social Sciences *Program availability:* Part-time, evening/weekend. Offers American studies (MA); conflict management (MSCM); criminal justice (MS); humanities and social sciences (MA, MAPW, MPA, MS, MSCM, PhD); integrated global communication (MA); international conflict management (PhD); international policy management (MS); professional writing (MAPW); public administration (MPA). Electronic applications accepted.

College of Science and Mathematics *Program availability:* Part-time, online learning. Offers applied statistics (MSAS); biochemistry (MS); chemistry (MS); integrative biology (MS); science and mathematics (MS, MSAS). Electronic applications accepted.

Leland and Clarice C. Bagwell College of Education *Program availability:* Part-time. Offers art education (MAT); biology (MAT); chemistry (MAT); education (M Ed, MAT, Ed D, Ed S); educational leadership (M Ed); educational leadership technology (M Ed); elementary and early childhood education (M Ed); foreign language education (Chinese and Spanish) (MAT); instructional technology (M Ed); leadership for learning (Ed D, Ed S); middle grades education (M Ed); physics (MAT); reading (M Ed); secondary education (M Ed); secondary English (MAT); secondary mathematics (MAT); special education (M Ed, MAT); teaching English to speakers of other languages (M Ed, MAT). Electronic applications accepted.

Michael J. Coles College of Business *Program availability:* Part-time, evening/weekend. Offers accounting (M Acc); business (M Acc, MBA, MSIS, DBA); business administration (MBA, DBA); information systems (MSIS). Electronic applications accepted.

Siegel Institute for Leadership, Ethics and Character *Program availability:* Part-time, evening/weekend, online learning. Offers leadership and ethics (Graduate Certificate). Electronic applications accepted.

Southern Polytechnic College of Engineering and Engineering Technology *Program availability:* Part-time, evening/weekend, online learning. Offers electrical engineering technology (M Ed); engineering and engineering technology (MBA, MS, MSA, Graduate Certificate, Graduate Transition Certificate); quality assurance (MS); systems engineering (MS, Graduate Certificate). Electronic applications accepted.

WellStar College of Health and Human Services *Program availability:* Part-time, evening/weekend, online learning. Offers advanced care management and leadership (MSN); applied exercise and health science (MS); health and human services (MS, MSN, MSW, DNS); nursing science (DNS); primary care nurse practitioner (MSN); social work (MSW). Electronic applications accepted.

KENRICK-GLENNON SEMINARY, St. Louis, MO 63119-4330

General Information Independent-religious, men only, graduate-only institution. *Graduate housing:* Room and/or apartments available to single students; on-campus housing not available to married students.

GRADUATE UNITS

Graduate and Professional Programs Offers theology (M Div, MA).

KENT STATE UNIVERSITY, Kent, OH 44242-0001

General Information State-supported, coed, university. CGS member. *Enrollment:* 29,911 graduate, professional, and undergraduate students; 3,769 full-time matriculated graduate/professional students (2,036 women), 2,494 part-time matriculated graduate/professional students (1,747 women). *Enrollment by degree level:* 4,402 master's, 1,732 doctoral, 129 other advanced degrees. *Graduate faculty:* 856. Tuition, state resident: full-time $10,864; part-time $495 per credit hour. Tuition, nonresident: full-time $18,380; part-time $837 per credit hour. *Graduate housing:* Room and/or apartments available on a first-come, first-served basis to single students; on-campus housing not available to married students. *Student services:* Campus employment opportunities, campus safety program, career counseling, child daycare facilities, exercise/wellness program, free psychological counseling, grant writing training, international student services, multicultural affairs office, services for students with disabilities, teacher training, writing training. *Library facilities:* Kent State University Main Library plus 4 others. *Collection:* Books: 2.5 million (physical), 220,834 (digital/electronic); Serial titles: 35,857 (physical), 14,996 (digital/electronic); Databases: 454. Weekly public service hours: 141; study areas open 24 hours, 5–7 days a week; students can reserve study rooms.

Computer facilities: Computer purchase and lease plans are available. 2,000 computers available on campus for general student use. A campuswide network can be accessed from student residence rooms and from off campus. Online class registration is available.
Website: http://www.kent.edu/

General Application Contact: Lana Whitehead, Director, Graduate Admissions, 330-672-2661, Fax: 330-672-6262, E-mail: gradapps@kent.edu.

GRADUATE UNITS

College of Applied Engineering, Sustainability and Technology Students: 144 full-time (34 women), 32 part-time (7 women); includes 7 minority (3 Black or African American, non-Hispanic/Latino; 3 Asian, non-Hispanic/Latino; 1 Hispanic/Latino), 182 international. Average age 27. 306 applicants, 56% accepted, 36 enrolled. *Faculty:* 27 full-time (0 women). Expenses: Contact institution. *Financial support:* Research assistantships with full tuition reimbursements, teaching assistantships with full tuition reimbursements, career-related internships or fieldwork, Federal Work-Study, and unspecified assistantships available. Financial award application deadline: 2/3. In 2016, 23 master's awarded. *Program availability:* Part-time. Offers technology (MTC). *Application deadline:* For fall admission, 7/12 for domestic students, 5/1 for international students; for spring admission, 11/29 for domestic students, 10/1 for international students. Applications are processed on a rolling basis. *Application fee:* $45 ($70 for international students). Electronic applications accepted. *Application Contact:* Richard Mangrum, Coordinator, Graduate Program, 330-672-1933, E-mail: rmangum@kent.edu. *Interim Dean,* Robert G. Sines, Jr., 330-672-9780, E-mail: rsines@kent.edu.

College of Architecture and Environmental Design Students: 75 full-time (31 women), 7 part-time (2 women); includes 6 minority (3 Black or African American, non-Hispanic/Latino; 1 American Indian or Alaska Native, non-Hispanic/Latino; 2 Hispanic/Latino), 10 international. Average age 25. 125 applicants, 56% accepted, 58 enrolled. *Faculty:* 20 full-time (3 women). Expenses: Contact institution. *Financial support:* Research assistantships with full tuition reimbursements, teaching assistantships with full tuition reimbursements, Federal Work-Study, scholarships/grants, and unspecified assistantships available. Financial award application deadline: 2/1. In 2016, 55 master's awarded. *Program availability:* Part-time. Offers architecture (M Arc); architecture and environmental design (MS); health care design (MHCD); landscape architecture (MLA); urban design (MUD). *Application deadline:* For fall admission, 1/15 for domestic and international students. Applications are processed on a rolling basis. *Application fee:* $45 ($70 for international students). Electronic applications accepted. *Application Contact:* Johnathan Fleming, Assistant Professor and Director, Master of Architecture, 330-672-0934, E-mail: jpflemi1@kent.edu. *Dean,* Mark Mistur, E-mail: mmistur1@kent.edu.

College of Arts and Sciences Students: 971 full-time (481 women), 300 part-time (161 women); includes 121 minority (47 Black or African American, non-Hispanic/Latino; 1 American Indian or Alaska Native, non-Hispanic/Latino; 19 Asian, non-Hispanic/Latino; 29 Hispanic/Latino; 25 Two or more races, non-Hispanic/Latino), 495 international. Average age 30. 1,911 applicants, 35% accepted, 300 enrolled. *Faculty:* 380 full-time (166 women). Expenses: Contact institution. *Financial support:* Fellowships with full tuition reimbursements, research assistantships with full tuition reimbursements, teaching assistantships with full tuition reimbursements, career-related internships or fieldwork, Federal Work-Study, institutionally sponsored loans, scholarships/grants, health care benefits, tuition waivers (full), and unspecified assistantships available. In 2016, 294 master's, 101 doctorates awarded. *Program availability:* Part-time, online learning. Offers anthropology (MA); applied geology (PhD); applied mathematics (MA, MS, PhD); arts and sciences (MA, MFA, MGIS, MLS, MPA, MS, PhD); biological sciences (MA, MS, PhD); chemical physics (MS, PhD); chemistry (MA, MS, PhD); clinical psychology (MA, PhD); computer science (MA, MS, PhD); creative writing (MFA); criminology and criminal justice (MA); English (MA, PhD); English for teachers (MA); experimental psychology (MA, PhD); French (MA); geographic information science (MGIS); geography (MA, PhD); geology (MS); history (MA, PhD); Latin (MA); literature and writing (MA, MS, PhD); mathematics for secondary teachers (MA); philosophy (MA); physics (MA, MS, PhD); political science (MA, PhD); public administration (MPA); pure mathematics (MA, MS, PhD); rhetoric and composition (PhD); sociology (MA, PhD); Spanish (MA); teaching English as a second language (MA); translation (MA); translation studies (PhD). *Application deadline:* Applications are processed on a rolling basis. *Application fee:* $45 ($70 for international students). Electronic applications accepted. *Application Contact:* Office of Graduate Studies, 330-672-2661, E-mail: gradapps@kent.edu. *Dean, College of Arts and Sciences,* Dr. James L. Blank, 330-672-2650, E-mail: jblank@kent.edu.

Center for Comparative and Integrative Programs Students: 9 part-time (7 women); includes 1 minority (Black or African American, non-Hispanic/Latino). Average age 40. 7 applicants, 43% accepted, 3 enrolled. *Faculty:* 11 full-time (2 women). Expenses: Contact institution. *Financial support:* Career-related internships or fieldwork and Federal Work-Study available. In 2016, 2 master's awarded. *Program availability:* Part-time, evening/weekend, online learning. Offers comparative and integrative programs (MLS). *Application deadline:* For fall admission, 6/15 for domestic and international students; for spring admission, 11/29 for domestic and international students. Applications are processed on a rolling basis. *Application fee:* $45 ($70 for international students). Electronic applications accepted. *Application Contact:* Richard M. Berrong, Director of Liberal Studies, E-mail: rberrong@kent.edu. *Associate Dean,* Dr. David W. Odell-Scott, 330-672-0271, E-mail: dodellsc@kent.edu.

School of Biomedical Sciences Students: 72 full-time (47 women), 1 part-time (0 women); includes 6 minority (2 Asian, non-Hispanic/Latino; 1 Hispanic/Latino; 3 Two or more races, non-Hispanic/Latino), 25 international. Average age 30. 111 applicants, 22% accepted, 16 enrolled. Expenses: Contact institution. *Financial support:* Research assistantships with full tuition reimbursements, teaching assistantships, health care benefits, and unspecified assistantships available. Financial award application deadline: 1/1. In 2016, 2 master's, 19 doctorates awarded. Offers biological anthropology (PhD); biomedical mathematics (PhD); cellular and molecular biology (MS, PhD); neurosciences (MS, PhD); pharmacology (MS, PhD); physiology (MS, PhD). *Application deadline:* For fall admission, 1/1 for domestic and international students. Applications are processed on a rolling basis. *Application fee:* $45 ($70 for international students). Electronic applications accepted. *Application Contact:* School of Biomedical Sciences, 330-672-2263, Fax: 330-672-9391, E-mail: efreema2@kent.edu. *Director, School of Biomedical Sciences,* Dr. Ernest J. Freeman, 330-672-2363, E-mail: efreema2@kent.edu.

College of Business Administration Students: 269 (116 women); includes 15 minority (8 Black or African American, non-Hispanic/Latino; 4 Asian, non-Hispanic/Latino; 1 Hispanic/Latino; 2 Two or more races, non-Hispanic/Latino), 95 international. Average age 30. 291 applicants, 60% accepted, 74 enrolled. Expenses: Contact institution. *Financial support:* In 2016–17, 13 research assistantships with full tuition reimbursements (averaging $4,500 per year), 47 teaching assistantships with full tuition reimbursements (averaging $23,000 per year) were awarded; fellowships with full tuition reimbursements, career-related internships or fieldwork, Federal Work-Study, and unspecified assistantships also available. Financial award applicants required to submit FAFSA. In 2016, 72 master's, 2 doctorates awarded. *Program availability:* Part-time, evening/weekend. Offers accounting (MS, PhD); business administration (MA, MBA, MS, MSBA, PhD); business analytics (MS); economics (MA); finance (PhD); management systems (PhD); marketing (PhD). *Application fee:* $45 ($70 for international students). Electronic applications accepted. *Application Contact:* Louise M. Ditchey, Administrative Director, 330-672-2282, Fax: 330-672-7303, E-mail: gradbus@kent.edu. *Associate Dean,* Dr. Robert D. Hisrich, 330-672-2772, Fax: 330-672-1231, E-mail: rhisric1@kent.edu.

College of Communication and Information Students: 239 full-time (172 women), 779 part-time (568 women); includes 144 minority (60 Black or African American, non-

Hispanic/Latino; 2 American Indian or Alaska Native, non-Hispanic/Latino; 17 Asian, non-Hispanic/Latino; 40 Hispanic/Latino; 2 Native Hawaiian or other Pacific Islander, non-Hispanic/Latino; 23 Two or more races, non-Hispanic/Latino), 44 international. Average age 30. 431 applicants, 72% accepted, 230 enrolled. *Faculty:* 76 full-time (45 women). Expenses: Contact institution. *Financial support:* Fellowships with full tuition reimbursements, research assistantships with full tuition reimbursements, teaching assistantships with full tuition reimbursements, career-related internships or fieldwork, Federal Work-Study, scholarships/grants, health care benefits, and unspecified assistantships available. Financial award application deadline: 1/15. In 2016, 386 master's awarded. *Program availability:* Part-time, online learning. Offers communication and information (MA, MFA, MLIS, MS). *Application deadline:* For fall admission, 1/15 for domestic students, 12/15 for international students; for spring admission, 11/25 for domestic students, 10/25 for international students. Applications are processed on a rolling basis. *Application fee:* $45 ($70 for international students). Electronic applications accepted. *Application Contact:* Nzinga Hart, Graduate Academic Program Coordinator, 330-672-2285, E-mail: nbodden@kent.edu. *Professor and Dean,* Amy Reynolds, 330-672-2950, E-mail: areyno24@kent.edu.

School of Communication Studies Students: 30 full-time (24 women), 10 part-time (9 women); includes 4 minority (3 Asian, non-Hispanic/Latino; 1 Hispanic/Latino), 12 international. Average age 30. 44 applicants, 55% accepted, 14 enrolled. *Faculty:* 16 full-time (9 women). Expenses: Contact institution. *Financial support:* Research assistantships with full tuition reimbursements, teaching assistantships with full tuition reimbursements, career-related internships or fieldwork, health care benefits, and unspecified assistantships available. Financial award application deadline: 1/15. In 2016, 10 master's awarded. *Program availability:* Part-time. Offers communication studies (MA). *Application deadline:* For fall admission, 1/15 for domestic students, 12/25 for international students; for spring admission, 11/15 for domestic students, 10/25 for international students. Applications are processed on a rolling basis. *Application fee:* $45 ($70 for international students). Electronic applications accepted. *Application Contact:* Dr. Nichole Egbert, Professor and Graduate Coordinator, 330-672-3314, E-mail: negbert@kent.edu. *Director,* Dr. Elizabeth E. Graham, 330-672-3087, E-mail: egraha18@kent.edu.

School of Journalism and Mass Communication Students: 12 full-time (7 women), 102 part-time (68 women); includes 19 minority (14 Black or African American, non-Hispanic/Latino; 3 Hispanic/Latino; 2 Two or more races, non-Hispanic/Latino), 5 international. Average age 30. 46 applicants, 67% accepted, 20 enrolled. *Faculty:* 25 full-time (13 women). Expenses: Contact institution. *Financial support:* Research assistantships with full tuition reimbursements, teaching assistantships with full tuition reimbursements, scholarships/grants, and unspecified assistantships available. Financial award application deadline: 3/1. In 2016, 79 master's awarded. *Program availability:* Part-time, online learning. Offers journalism and mass communication (MA). *Application deadline:* For fall admission, 7/1 for domestic and international students. Applications are processed on a rolling basis. *Application fee:* $45 ($70 for international students). Electronic applications accepted. *Application Contact:* Mark Goodman, Graduate Coordinator/Professor, 330-672-5256, E-mail: mgoodm10@kent.edu. *Director and Professor,* Thor Wasbotten, 330-672-4066, E-mail: thor@kent.edu.

School of Library and Information Science Students: 208 full-time (163 women), 633 part-time (459 women); includes 112 minority (41 Black or African American, non-Hispanic/Latino; 2 American Indian or Alaska Native, non-Hispanic/Latino; 12 Asian, non-Hispanic/Latino; 36 Hispanic/Latino; 1 Native Hawaiian or other Pacific Islander, non-Hispanic/Latino; 20 Two or more races, non-Hispanic/Latino), 10 international. Average age 33. 269 applicants, 80% accepted, 175 enrolled. *Faculty:* 19 full-time (16 women). Expenses: Contact institution. *Financial support:* Fellowships with full tuition reimbursements, research assistantships with full tuition reimbursements, teaching assistantships with full tuition reimbursements, scholarships/grants, and unspecified assistantships available. Financial award application deadline: 3/1. In 2016, 294 master's awarded. *Program availability:* Part-time, online learning. Offers information architecture and knowledge management (MS); library and information science (MLIS). *Application deadline:* For fall admission, 3/15 for domestic and international students; for spring admission, 9/15 for domestic and international students; for summer admission, 1/15 for domestic students. Applications are processed on a rolling basis. *Application fee:* $45 ($70 for international students). Electronic applications accepted. *Application Contact:* Dr. Karen Gracy, Graduate Co-Coordinator/Associate Professor, 330-672-2782, E-mail: kgracy@kent.edu. *Director and Professor,* Dr. Kendra Albright, 330-672-8535, E-mail: kalbrig7@kent.edu.

School of Visual Communication Design Students: 27 full-time (15 women), 8 part-time (5 women); includes 6 minority (4 Black or African American, non-Hispanic/Latino; 1 Asian, non-Hispanic/Latino; 1 Two or more races, non-Hispanic/Latino), 11 international. Average age 28. 25 applicants, 88% accepted, 12 enrolled. *Faculty:* 16 full-time (7 women). Expenses: Contact institution. *Financial support:* Scholarships/grants and unspecified assistantships available. Financial award application deadline: 3/1. In 2016, 7 master's awarded. *Program availability:* Part-time. Offers visual communication design (MA, MFA). *Application deadline:* For fall admission, 3/1 for domestic and international students; for spring admission, 10/1 for domestic and international students. Applications are processed on a rolling basis. *Application fee:* $45 ($70 for international students). Electronic applications accepted. *Application Contact:* Ken Visocky O'Grady, Graduate Coordinator and Associate Professor, 330-672-1353, E-mail: kogrady@kent.edu. *Interim Director,* Dr. David Robins, 330-672-2782, E-mail: drobins@kent.edu.

College of Education, Health and Human Services *Program availability:* Part-time, evening/weekend, online learning. Offers education, health and human services (M Ed, MA, MAT, MS, Au D, PhD, Ed S). Electronic applications accepted.

School of Foundations, Leadership and Administration Offers cultural foundations (M Ed, MA, PhD); evaluation and measurement (M Ed, PhD); higher education (PhD, Ed S); higher education and student personnel (M Ed); hospitality and tourism management (MS); K-12 leadership (M Ed, PhD, Ed S); sport and recreation management (MA); sports recreation and management (MA); sports studies (MA). Electronic applications accepted.

School of Health Sciences *Program availability:* Part-time, evening/weekend. Offers athletic training (MS); audiology (Au D, PhD); exercise physiology (MS, PhD); health education and promotion (M Ed, PhD); nutrition (MS); speech language pathology (MA, PhD). Electronic applications accepted.

School of Lifespan Development and Educational Sciences *Program availability:* Part-time, evening/weekend. Offers clinical mental health counseling (M Ed); computer technology (M Ed); counseling (Ed S); counseling and human development services (PhD); deaf education (M Ed); early childhood education (M Ed); educational interpreter K-12 (M Ed); educational psychology (M Ed, MA, PhD); general instructional technology (M Ed); general special education (M Ed); human development and family studies (MA); instructional technology (M Ed, PhD);

mild/moderate intervention (M Ed); rehabilitation counseling (M Ed); school counseling (M Ed); school psychology (PhD, Ed S); special education (M Ed, PhD, Ed S); transition to work (M Ed). Electronic applications accepted.

School of Teaching, Learning and Curriculum Studies *Program availability:* Part-time, evening/weekend. Offers career technical teacher education (M Ed); curriculum and instruction (M Ed, PhD, Ed S); early childhood education (M Ed, MA, MAT); junior high/middle school (M Ed, MA); math specialization (M Ed, MA); reading specialization (M Ed, MA); secondary education (MAT). Electronic applications accepted.

College of Nursing Students: 350 full-time (264 women), 1,195 part-time (931 women); includes 207 minority (94 Black or African American, non-Hispanic/Latino; 3 American Indian or Alaska Native, non-Hispanic/Latino; 29 Asian, non-Hispanic/Latino; 53 Hispanic/Latino; 2 Native Hawaiian or other Pacific Islander, non-Hispanic/Latino; 26 Two or more races, non-Hispanic/Latino), 60 international. Average age 36. 352 applicants, 47% accepted, 148 enrolled. Expenses: Contact institution. *Financial support:* Scholarships/grants available. Financial award application deadline: 3/17. In 2016, 123 master's, 3 doctorates awarded. *Program availability:* Part-time, online learning. Offers advanced nursing practice (DNP); nursing (MSN, PhD). PhD program offered jointly with The University of Akron. *Application deadline:* For fall admission, 3/1 for domestic and international students; for spring admission, 10/1 for domestic and international students. Applications are processed on a rolling basis. *Application fee:* $45 ($70 for international students). Electronic applications accepted. *Application Contact:* Dr. Wendy A. Umberger, Associate Dean for Graduate Programs/Professor, 330-672-8813, E-mail: wlewando@kent.edu. *Dean,* Dr. Barbara Broome, 330-672-3777, E-mail: bbroome1@kent.edu.

College of Podiatric Medicine Offers podiatric medicine (DPM). Electronic applications accepted.

College of Public Health Students: 131 full-time (104 women), 133 part-time (102 women); includes 56 minority (36 Black or African American, non-Hispanic/Latino; 1 American Indian or Alaska Native, non-Hispanic/Latino; 5 Asian, non-Hispanic/Latino; 8 Hispanic/Latino; 6 Two or more races, non-Hispanic/Latino), 35 international. Average age 33. 216 applicants, 59% accepted, 80 enrolled. *Faculty:* 28 full-time (16 women). Expenses: Contact institution. *Financial support:* Unspecified assistantships available. In 2016, 55 master's, 1 doctorate awarded. *Program availability:* Part-time, online learning. Offers public health (MPH, PhD). *Application deadline:* For fall admission, 6/15 for domestic and international students; for spring admission, 10/15 for domestic and international students; for summer admission, 3/15 for domestic and international students. Applications are processed on a rolling basis. *Application fee:* $45 ($70 for international students). Electronic applications accepted. *Application Contact:* Dr. Mark A. James, Professor/Chair/Graduate Advisor, 330-672-6506, E-mail: mjames22@kent.edu. *Dean and Professor of Health Policy and Management,* Dr. Sonia Alemagno, 330-672-6500, E-mail: salemagn@kent.edu.

College of the Arts Students: 97 full-time (44 women), 189 part-time (138 women); includes 22 minority (11 Black or African American, non-Hispanic/Latino; 1 American Indian or Alaska Native, non-Hispanic/Latino; 2 Asian, non-Hispanic/Latino; 3 Hispanic/Latino; 1 Native Hawaiian or other Pacific Islander, non-Hispanic/Latino; 4 Two or more races, non-Hispanic/Latino), 35 international. Average age 32. 173 applicants, 69% accepted, 80 enrolled. *Faculty:* 106 full-time (65 women). Expenses: Contact institution. *Financial support:* Research assistantships with full tuition reimbursements, teaching assistantships with full tuition reimbursements, and unspecified assistantships available. Financial award application deadline: 2/2. In 2016, 131 master's, 2 doctorates awarded. *Program availability:* Part-time, online learning. Offers arts (MA, MFA, MM, PhD). *Application deadline:* For fall admission, 2/2 for domestic and international students; for spring admission, 10/15 for domestic and international students. Applications are processed on a rolling basis. *Application fee:* $45 ($70 for international students). Electronic applications accepted. *Application Contact:* 330-672-2760, E-mail: collegeofthearts@kent.edu. *Dean,* Dr. John R. Crawford-Spinelli, 330-672-2760, E-mail: jcrawfo1@kent.edu.

Hugh A. Glauser School of Music Students: 51 full-time (23 women), 167 part-time (120 women); includes 18 minority (8 Black or African American, non-Hispanic/Latino; 1 American Indian or Alaska Native, non-Hispanic/Latino; 1 Asian, non-Hispanic/Latino; 4 Hispanic/Latino; 1 Native Hawaiian or other Pacific Islander, non-Hispanic/Latino; 3 Two or more races, non-Hispanic/Latino), 25 international. Average age 32. 90 applicants, 86% accepted, 51 enrolled. *Faculty:* 33 full-time (12 women). Expenses: Contact institution. *Financial support:* Unspecified assistantships available. Financial award application deadline: 4/1. In 2016, 95 master's, 2 doctorates awarded. *Program availability:* Part-time, online learning. Offers conducting (MM); ethnomusicology (MA); music composition (MA); music education (MM, PhD); music theory (MA); music theory-composition (PhD); performance (MM). *Application deadline:* Applications are processed on a rolling basis. *Application fee:* $45 ($70 for international students). Electronic applications accepted. *Application Contact:* Michael Chunn, Graduate Coordinator/Trumpet Professor, 330-672-9234, Fax: 330-672-7837, E-mail: mchunn@kent.edu. *Interim Director,* Dr. Ralph Lorenz, 330-672-2172, E-mail: rlorenz@kent.edu.

School of Art Students: 51 full-time (23 women), 167 part-time (120 women); includes 18 minority (8 Black or African American, non-Hispanic/Latino; 1 American Indian or Alaska Native, non-Hispanic/Latino; 1 Asian, non-Hispanic/Latino; 4 Hispanic/Latino; 1 Native Hawaiian or other Pacific Islander, non-Hispanic/Latino; 3 Two or more races, non-Hispanic/Latino), 25 international. Average age 31. 57 applicants, 53% accepted, 21 enrolled. *Faculty:* 23 full-time (15 women). Expenses: Contact institution. *Financial support:* Career-related internships or fieldwork, scholarships/grants, and unspecified assistantships available. Financial award application deadline: 2/2. In 2016, 30 master's awarded. *Program availability:* Part-time, online learning. Offers art education (MA); art history (MA); crafts (MA, MFA); fine arts (MA, MFA). *Application deadline:* For fall admission, 2/2 for domestic and international students; for spring admission, 10/15 for domestic and international students. Applications are processed on a rolling basis. *Application fee:* $45 ($70 for international students). Electronic applications accepted. *Application Contact:* Linda Hoeptner Poling, Graduate Coordinator and Associate Professor of Art Education, 330-672-7895, E-mail: lhoeptne@kent.edu. *Interim Director/Professor, Print Media and Photography,* Michael J. Loderstedt, 330-672-2192, E-mail: mloderst@kent.edu.

School of Theatre and Dance Students: 15 full-time (7 women), 1 (woman) part-time, 1 international. Average age 34. 17 applicants, 53% accepted, 7 enrolled. *Faculty:* 18 full-time (11 women). Expenses: Contact institution. *Financial support:* Teaching assistantships with full tuition reimbursements, career-related internships or fieldwork, Federal Work-Study, scholarships/grants, and unspecified assistantships available. Financial award application deadline: 5/1. In 2016, 6 master's awarded. *Program availability:* Part-time. Offers theatre studies (MFA). *Application deadline:* Applications are processed on a rolling basis. *Application fee:* $45 ($70 for international students). Electronic applications accepted. *Application Contact:* Yuko Kurahashi, Graduate

Kent State University

Coordinator and Associate Professor of Theatre, 330-672-9483, E-mail: ykurahas@kent.edu. *Director and Associate Professor*, Eric van Baars, 330-672-0102, E-mail: fvanbaar@kent.edu.

School of Digital Sciences Students: 409 full-time (153 women), 156 part-time (51 women); includes 1 minority (Asian, non-Hispanic/Latino), 539 international. Average age 24. 617 applicants, 67% accepted, 94 enrolled. Expenses: Contact institution. *Financial support:* Career-related internships or fieldwork available. In 2016, 231 master's awarded. *Program availability:* Part-time. Offers digital sciences (MDS); digital sciences management (MDS); digital sciences software development (MDS); digital sciences telecommunication network (MDS); digital sciences training technology (MDS); enterprise architecture (MDS). *Application deadline:* For fall admission, 7/1 for domestic students, 5/15 for international students; for spring admission, 11/15 for domestic students, 10/15 for international students; for summer admission, 4/15 for domestic students, 3/15 for international students. Applications are processed on a rolling basis. *Application fee:* $45 ($70 for international students). Electronic applications accepted. *Application Contact:* Amy Copus, Academic Advisor II for Graduate Students, 330-672-9105, E-mail: acopus@kent.edu. *Interim Director*, Jeffery Fruit, 330-672-9105, E-mail: jfruit@kent.edu.

KENT STATE UNIVERSITY AT STARK, Canton, OH 44720-7599
General Information State-supported, coed, comprehensive institution.

GRADUATE UNITS

Graduate School of Education, Health and Human Services Offers curriculum and instruction studies (M Ed, MA).

Professional MBA Program Offers business administration (MBA).

KENTUCKY CHRISTIAN UNIVERSITY, Grayson, KY 41143-2205
General Information Independent-religious, coed, comprehensive institution. *Graduate housing:* Rooms and/or apartments available on a first-come, first-served basis to single and married students.

GRADUATE UNITS

Graduate School *Program availability:* Part-time. Offers Biblical studies (MA); Christian leadership (MA). Electronic applications accepted.

KENTUCKY STATE UNIVERSITY, Frankfort, KY 40601
General Information State-related, coed, comprehensive institution. *Enrollment:* 1,736 graduate, professional, and undergraduate students; 94 full-time matriculated graduate/professional students (44 women), 73 part-time matriculated graduate/professional students (48 women). *Enrollment by degree level:* 153 master's, 14 doctoral. *Graduate faculty:* 26 full-time (6 women), 8 part-time/adjunct (6 women). Tuition, state resident: full-time $7524; part-time $418 per credit hour. Tuition, nonresident: full-time $11,322; part-time $629 per credit hour. Tuition and fees vary according to course load. *Graduate housing:* Rooms and/or apartments available on a first-come, first-served basis to single and married students. Typical cost: $4440 per year ($7790 including board) for single students; $4440 per year ($7790 including board) for married students. Room and board charges vary according to campus/location and housing facility selected. Housing application deadline: 6/30. *Student services:* Campus employment opportunities, campus safety program, career counseling, child daycare facilities, exercise/wellness program, free psychological counseling, international student services, services for students with disabilities, writing training. *Library facilities:* Paul G. Blazer Library. *Collection:* Books: 170,726 (physical), 23,417 (digital/electronic); Serial titles: 1,894 (physical), 38,647 (digital/electronic); Databases: 56. Weekly public service hours: 101; study areas open 24 hours, 5–7 days a week. *Research affiliation:* Alltech (aquaculture nutrition).

Computer facilities: 142 computers available on campus for general student use. A campuswide network can be accessed from student residence rooms and from off campus. Online class registration, student bill-pay, address verification, ability to accept financial aid awards are available.
Website: http://www.kysu.edu/

General Application Contact: Dr. James Obielodan, Director of Graduate Studies, 502-597-4723, E-mail: james.obielodan@kysu.edu.

GRADUATE UNITS

College of Agriculture, Food Science and Sustainable Systems Students: 31 full-time (13 women), 14 part-time (9 women); includes 10 minority (7 Black or African American, non-Hispanic/Latino; 1 Asian, non-Hispanic/Latino; 1 Hispanic/Latino; 1 Two or more races, non-Hispanic/Latino), 6 international. Average age 31. 21 applicants, 76% accepted, 14 enrolled. *Faculty:* 9 full-time (0 women). Expenses: Contact institution. *Financial support:* In 2016–17, 41 students received support, including 31 research assistantships (averaging $21,112 per year); scholarships/grants, tuition waivers (partial), and unspecified assistantships also available. Financial award application deadline: 4/15; financial award applicants required to submit FAFSA. In 2016, 9 master's awarded. *Program availability:* Part-time, evening/weekend. Offers aquaculture (MS); environmental studies (MS). *Application deadline:* For fall admission, 7/1 for domestic students, 4/1 for international students; for spring admission, 11/15 for domestic students, 8/15 for international students; for summer admission, 5/1 for domestic students, 2/1 for international students. Applications are processed on a rolling basis. *Application fee:* $30 ($100 for international students). Electronic applications accepted. *Application Contact:* Dr. James Obielodan, Director of Graduate Studies, 502-597-4723, E-mail: james.obielodan@kysu.edu. *Interim Director of Land Grant Programs*, Dr. Kirk Pomper, 502-597-5942, E-mail: kirk.pomper@kysu.edu.

College of Arts and Sciences Students: 2 full-time (1 woman), 4 part-time (all women); includes 3 minority (all Black or African American, non-Hispanic/Latino). Average age 29. 5 applicants, 40% accepted, 2 enrolled. *Faculty:* 3 full-time (2 women). Expenses: Contact institution. *Financial support:* In 2016–17, 5 students received support. Research assistantships, scholarships/grants, tuition waivers (partial), and unspecified assistantships available. Financial award application deadline: 4/15; financial award applicants required to submit FAFSA. In 2016, 2 master's awarded. *Program availability:* Part-time, evening/weekend, blended/hybrid learning. Offers interdisciplinary behavioral sciences (MA). *Application deadline:* For fall admission, 7/1 for domestic students, 4/1 for international students; for spring admission, 11/15 for domestic students, 8/15 for international students; for summer admission, 5/1 for domestic students, 2/1 for international students. Applications are processed on a rolling basis. *Application fee:* $30 ($100 for international students). Electronic applications accepted. *Application Contact:* Dr. James Obielodan, Director of Graduate Studies, 502-597-4723, E-mail: james.obielodan@kysu.edu. *Chair of Behavioral and Social Sciences*, Dr. Tierra Freeman, 502-597-5932, E-mail: tierra.freeman@kysu.edu.

College of Business and Computer Science Students: 29 full-time (8 women), 18 part-time (5 women); includes 18 minority (13 Black or African American, non-Hispanic/Latino; 5 Asian, non-Hispanic/Latino), 10 international. Average age 33. 39 applicants, 72% accepted, 20 enrolled. *Faculty:* 8 full-time (1 woman), 1 part-time/adjunct (0 women). Expenses: Contact institution. *Financial support:* In 2016–17, 43 students received support, including 5 research assistantships (averaging $9,200 per year); scholarships/grants, tuition waivers (partial), and unspecified assistantships also available. Financial award application deadline: 4/15; financial award applicants required to submit FAFSA. In 2016, 15 master's awarded. *Program availability:* Part-time, evening/weekend. Offers business administration (MBA); computer science technology (MS). *Application deadline:* For fall admission, 7/1 for domestic students, 4/1 for international students; for spring admission, 11/15 for domestic students, 8/15 for international students; for summer admission, 5/1 for domestic students, 2/1 for international students. Applications are processed on a rolling basis. *Application fee:* $30 ($100 for international students). Electronic applications accepted. *Application Contact:* Dr. James Obielodan, Director of Graduate Studies, 502-597-4723, E-mail: james.obielodan@kysu.edu. *Vice President of Academic Affairs*, Dr. Candice L. Jackson, 502-597-6442, E-mail: candice.jackson@kysu.edu.

College of Professional Studies Students: 32 full-time (22 women), 37 part-time (30 women); includes 48 minority (47 Black or African American, non-Hispanic/Latino; 1 Asian, non-Hispanic/Latino). Average age 34. 42 applicants, 79% accepted, 24 enrolled. *Faculty:* 6 full-time (3 women), 7 part-time/adjunct (6 women). Expenses: Contact institution. *Financial support:* In 2016–17, 57 students received support, including 3 research assistantships (averaging $10,083 per year); scholarships/grants, tuition waivers (partial), and unspecified assistantships also available. Financial award application deadline: 4/15; financial award applicants required to submit FAFSA. In 2016, 19 master's awarded. *Program availability:* Part-time, evening/weekend, 100% online, blended/hybrid learning. Offers nursing (DNP); public administration (MPA); special education (MA). *Application deadline:* For fall admission, 7/1 for domestic students, 4/1 for international students; for spring admission, 11/15 for domestic students, 8/15 for international students; for summer admission, 5/1 for domestic students, 2/1 for international students. Applications are processed on a rolling basis. *Application fee:* $30 ($100 for international students). Electronic applications accepted. *Application Contact:* Dr. James Obielodan, Director of Graduate Studies, 502-597-4723, E-mail: james.obielodan@kysu.edu. *Vice President of Academic Affairs*, Dr. Candice L. Jackson, 502-597-6442, E-mail: candice.jackson@kysu.edu.

KETTERING COLLEGE, Kettering, OH 45429-1299
General Information Independent-religious, coed, primarily women, comprehensive institution.

GRADUATE UNITS

Program in Physician Assistant Studies Offers physician assistant studies (MPAS).

KETTERING UNIVERSITY, Flint, MI 48504
General Information Independent, coed, comprehensive institution. *Graduate housing:* Rooms and/or apartments available on a first-come, first-served basis to single students and available to married students. Housing application deadline: 7/15. *Research affiliation:* McLaren Foundation (orthopedic surgery biomechanics), Shin-Estu Chemical Company (atmospheric plasma technology), Broad-Ocean Technologies (electric vehicle battery systems), Landaal Packaging Systems (space utilization and process flow of operations), Mahindra Tractor Assembly, dba Mahindra GenZe (electric power and control boards), TRW (crash safety).

GRADUATE UNITS

Graduate School *Program availability:* Part-time, evening/weekend, online learning. Offers business (MBA, MS); engineering (MS). Electronic applications accepted.

KEUKA COLLEGE, Keuka Park, NY 14478
General Information Independent-religious, coed, comprehensive institution. *Enrollment:* 2,003 graduate, professional, and undergraduate students; 199 full-time matriculated graduate/professional students (164 women), 74 part-time matriculated graduate/professional students (58 women). *Enrollment by degree level:* 255 master's, 18 doctoral. *Graduate faculty:* 29 full-time (20 women), 124 part-time/adjunct (50 women). *Tuition:* Full-time $28,244; part-time $761 per credit hour. Part-time tuition and fees vary according to course load, campus/location and program. *Graduate housing:* Room and/or apartments available on a first-come, first-served basis to single students; on-campus housing not available to married students. Typical cost: $9492 per year ($13,506 including board). Room and board charges vary according to board plan and housing facility selected. Housing application deadline: 5/1. *Student services:* Career counseling, exercise/wellness program, free psychological counseling, grant writing training, international student services, low-cost health insurance, multicultural affairs office, services for students with disabilities, teacher training, writing training. *Library facilities:* Lightner Library plus 1 other. *Collection:* Books: 79,009 (physical), 1,083 (digital/electronic); Serial titles: 687 (physical), 112 (digital/electronic); Databases: 89. Weekly public service hours: 96.

Computer facilities: Computer purchase and lease plans are available. 185 computers available on campus for general student use. A campuswide network can be accessed from student residence rooms and from off campus. Online class registration, phone app for cancellations are available.
Website: http://www.keuka.edu/

General Application Contact: Megan Perkins, Director of Admissions, 315-279-5254, Fax: 315-279-5386, E-mail: admissions@keuka.edu.

GRADUATE UNITS

Program in Childhood Education/Literacy Students: 9 full-time (8 women); includes 1 minority (Hispanic/Latino). Average age 23. 9 applicants, 100% accepted, 9 enrolled. *Faculty:* 7 full-time (5 women). Expenses: Contact institution. *Financial support:* In 2016–17, 8 students received support. Scholarships/grants and tuition waivers (full and partial) available. Financial award applicants required to submit FAFSA. In 2016, 8 master's awarded. Offers literacy 5-12 (MS); literacy B-6 (MS). *Application deadline:* For fall admission, 8/15 priority date for domestic students; for winter admission, 12/15 priority date for domestic students; for spring admission, 4/15 priority date for domestic students. Applications are processed on a rolling basis. *Application fee:* $50. Electronic applications accepted. *Application Contact:* Anna Decker, Secretary, Graduate Education, 315-279-5510, E-mail: adecker@keuka.edu. *Director of Graduate Program in Education*, Dr. Andrew Beigel, 315-279-5442 Ext. 5662, E-mail: abeigel@keuka.edu.

Program in Criminal Justice Administration Students: 16 full-time (8 women), 1 (woman) part-time; includes 8 minority (6 Black or African American, non-Hispanic/Latino; 2 Two or more races, non-Hispanic/Latino). Average age 36. 11 applicants, 82% accepted, 6 enrolled. *Faculty:* 2 full-time (0 women), 6 part-time/adjunct (2 women). Expenses: Contact institution. *Financial support:* Scholarships/grants and tuition waivers (full and partial) available. Financial award applicants required to submit FAFSA. In 2016, 5 master's awarded. *Program availability:* Part-time, evening/weekend. Offers criminal justice administration (MS). *Application deadline:* For fall admission, 8/15 for domestic students; for winter admission, 12/15 for domestic students; for spring admission, 4/15 for domestic students. Applications are processed on a rolling basis. *Application fee:* $50. Electronic applications accepted. *Application Contact:* Fred Hoyle, Graduate Admissions, 866-255-3852, Fax: 315-279-5386, E-mail: asapadvisor@keuka.edu. *Program Director*, Dr. Tom Tremer, 315-279-5672, E-mail: ttremer@mail.keuka.edu.

Program in Management Students: 32 full-time (21 women), 32 part-time (18 women); includes 18 minority (8 Black or African American, non-Hispanic/Latino; 5 Asian, non-Hispanic/Latino; 3 Hispanic/Latino; 2 Two or more races, non-Hispanic/Latino). Average age 35. 56 applicants, 66% accepted, 27 enrolled. *Faculty:* 4 full-time (1 woman), 20 part-time/adjunct (7 women). Expenses: Contact institution. *Financial support:* Scholarships/grants and tuition waivers (full and partial) available. Financial award applicants required to submit FAFSA. In 2016, 53 master's awarded. *Program availability:* Part-time, evening/weekend, 100% online, blended/hybrid learning. Offers management (MS). *Application deadline:* For fall admission, 8/15 priority date for domestic students; for winter admission, 12/15 priority date for domestic students; for spring admission, 4/15 priority date for domestic students. Applications are processed on a rolling basis. *Application fee:* $50. *Application Contact:* Graduate Admissions, 866-255-3852, Fax: 315-279-5386, E-mail: asapadvisor@keuka.edu. *Chair, Division of Business and Management*, Ann Tuttle, 315-279-5286, E-mail: atuttle@keuka.edu.

Program in Nursing Students: 59 full-time (56 women), 40 part-time (38 women); includes 7 minority (6 Black or African American, non-Hispanic/Latino; 1 Asian, non-Hispanic/Latino). Average age 40. 113 applicants, 64% accepted, 52 enrolled. *Faculty:* 8 full-time (all women), 23 part-time/adjunct (22 women). Expenses: Contact institution. *Financial support:* Scholarships/grants and tuition waivers (full and partial) available. Financial award applicants required to submit FAFSA. In 2016, 22 master's awarded. Offers adult gerontology (MS); nursing education (MS). *Application deadline:* For fall admission, 8/15 for domestic students; for winter admission, 9/15 for domestic students; for spring admission, 4/15 for domestic students. Applications are processed on a rolling basis. *Application fee:* $50. Electronic applications accepted. *Application Contact:* Graduate Admissions, 866-255-3852, Fax: 315-279-5386, E-mail: asapadvisor@keuka.edu. *Chair*, Dr. Debra Gates, 315-279-5115 Ext. 5273, E-mail: dgates@keuka.edu.

Program in Occupational Therapy Students: 34 full-time (29 women); includes 3 minority (1 Black or African American, non-Hispanic/Latino; 1 Hispanic/Latino; 1 Native Hawaiian or other Pacific Islander, non-Hispanic/Latino). Average age 24. 34 applicants, 100% accepted, 34 enrolled. *Faculty:* 4 full-time (3 women). Expenses: Contact institution. *Financial support:* Research assistantships, scholarships/grants, and tuition waivers (full and partial) available. Financial award applicants required to submit FAFSA. In 2016, 37 master's awarded. Offers occupational therapy (MS). *Application deadline:* For fall admission, 8/15 priority date for domestic students; for winter admission, 12/15 priority date for domestic students; for spring admission, 4/15 priority date for domestic students. Applications are processed on a rolling basis. *Application fee:* $50. Electronic applications accepted. *Application Contact:* Jennifer Nielsen, Transfer Counselor, Admissions, 315-279-5203, Fax: 315-279-5386, E-mail: jnielsen@keuka.edu. *Associate Professor/Chair/Program Director*, Dr. Dianne Trickey-Rokenbrok, 315-279-5608, Fax: 315-279-5439, E-mail: dtrickey@keuka.edu.

Program in Social Work Students: 50 full-time (43 women); includes 13 minority (6 Black or African American, non-Hispanic/Latino; 3 Hispanic/Latino; 4 Two or more races, non-Hispanic/Latino). Average age 33. 125 applicants, 53% accepted, 27 enrolled. *Faculty:* 5 full-time (4 women), 6 part-time/adjunct (5 women). Expenses: Contact institution. *Financial support:* Scholarships/grants and tuition waivers (full and partial) available. Financial award applicants required to submit FAFSA. In 2016, 6 master's awarded. Offers social work (MSW). *Application deadline:* For fall admission, 8/15 for domestic students; for winter admission, 12/15 for domestic students; for spring admission, 4/15 for domestic students. Applications are processed on a rolling basis. *Application fee:* $50. Electronic applications accepted. *Application Contact:* Jennifer Nielsen, Admissions, 315-279-5203, Fax: 315-279-5386, E-mail: admissions@keuka.edu. *Division Chair*, Dr. Ed Silverman, 315-279-5120, E-mail: esilverman@keuka.edu.

KEYSTONE COLLEGE, La Plume, PA 18440

General Information Independent, coed, comprehensive institution. *Enrollment:* 6 full-time matriculated graduate/professional students (4 women), 45 part-time matriculated graduate/professional students (38 women). *Enrollment by degree level:* 51 master's. *Graduate faculty:* 7 full-time (5 women), 8 part-time/adjunct (5 women). *Tuition:* Full-time $19,500; part-time $650 per credit. One-time fee: $175. *Graduate housing:* On-campus housing not available. *Student services:* Campus employment opportunities, campus safety program, career counseling, child daycare facilities, exercise/wellness program, free psychological counseling, grant writing training, international student services, services for students with disabilities, writing training. *Library facilities:* Miller Library.

Computer facilities: 100 computers available on campus for general student use. A campuswide network can be accessed from student residence rooms and from off campus. Online class registration is available. Website: http://www.keystone.edu/

General Application Contact: Jennifer Sekol, Director of Admissions, 570-945-8117, Fax: 570-945-7916, E-mail: jennifer.sekol@keystone.edu.

GRADUATE UNITS

Program in Accountancy 2 applicants, 50% accepted. *Faculty:* 2 full-time (1 woman), 3 part-time/adjunct (1 woman). Expenses: Contact institution. *Financial support:* Unspecified assistantships available. Financial award application deadline: 5/1; financial award applicants required to submit FAFSA. *Program availability:* Part-time, online only, 100% online. Offers accountancy (M Acc). *Application deadline:* For fall admission, 8/1 for domestic students; for spring admission, 12/1 for domestic students; for summer admission, 5/1 for domestic students. Applications are processed on a rolling basis. *Application fee:* $50. Electronic applications accepted. *Application Contact:* Jennifer Sekol, Director of Admissions, 570-945-8117, Fax: 570-945-7916, E-mail: jennifer.sekol@keystone.edu. *Professor*, Patricia Davis, PhD, 570-945-8424, E-mail: patricia.davis@keystone.edu.

Program in Early Childhood Education Leadership Students: 44 part-time (37 women). 35 applicants, 77% accepted, 23 enrolled. *Faculty:* 3 full-time (all women), 2 part-time/adjunct (both women). Expenses: Contact institution. *Financial support:* Unspecified assistantships available. Financial award application deadline: 5/1; financial award applicants required to submit FAFSA. *Program availability:* Part-time, blended/hybrid learning. Offers early childhood education leadership (M Ed). *Application deadline:* For fall admission, 8/1 for domestic students; for spring admission, 12/1 for domestic students; for summer admission, 5/1 for domestic students. Applications are processed on a rolling basis. *Application fee:* $50. Electronic applications accepted. *Application Contact:* Jennifer Sekol, Director of Admissions, 570-945-8117, Fax: 570-

945-7916, E-mail: jennifer.sekol@keystone.edu. *Dean, School of Professional Studies*, Fran Langan, PhD, 570-945-8472, E-mail: fran.langan@keystone.edu.

Program in Sport Leadership and Management 8 applicants, 88% accepted, 4 enrolled. *Faculty:* 2 full-time (1 woman), 3 part-time/adjunct (2 women). Expenses: Contact institution. *Financial support:* In 2016–17, 1 student received support. Unspecified assistantships available. Financial award application deadline: 5/1; financial award applicants required to submit FAFSA. *Program availability:* Part-time, online only, 100% online. Offers sport leadership and management (MS). *Application deadline:* For fall admission, 8/1 for domestic students; for spring admission, 12/1 for domestic students; for summer admission, 5/1 for domestic students. Applications are processed on a rolling basis. *Application fee:* $50. Electronic applications accepted. *Application Contact:* Jennifer Sekol, Director of Admissions, 570-945-8117, Fax: 570-945-7916, E-mail: jennifer.sekol@keystone.edu. *Assistant Professor*, Mac Ross, PhD, 570-945-8434, E-mail: mac.ross@keystone.edu.

KING'S COLLEGE, Wilkes-Barre, PA 18711-0801

General Information Independent-religious, coed, comprehensive institution. *Graduate housing:* On-campus housing not available.

GRADUATE UNITS

Program in Education *Program availability:* Part-time, evening/weekend. Offers education (M Ed).

Program in Physician Assistant Studies Offers physician assistant studies (MSPAS). Electronic applications accepted.

William G. McGowan School of Business *Program availability:* Part-time. Offers health care administration (MS).

THE KING'S UNIVERSITY, Southlake, TX 76092

General Information Independent-religious, coed, comprehensive institution.

GRADUATE UNITS

Graduate and Professional Programs Offers Biblical studies (Graduate Certificate); Christian ministry (Graduate Certificate); ministry (M Div, MPT, D Min).

KINGSWOOD UNIVERSITY, Sussex, NB E4E 5L2, Canada

General Information Independent-religious, coed, comprehensive institution.

GRADUATE UNITS

Program in Pastoral Theology Offers pastoral theology (MA).

KING UNIVERSITY, Bristol, TN 37620-2699

General Information Independent-religious, coed, comprehensive institution. *Graduate housing:* Room and/or apartments available on a first-come, first-served basis to single students; on-campus housing not available to married students.

GRADUATE UNITS

School of Business and Economics *Program availability:* Part-time, evening/weekend, online learning. Offers accounting (MBA); finance (MBA); healthcare management (MBA); human resources management (MBA); leadership (MBA); management (MBA); marketing (MBA); project management (MBA). Electronic applications accepted.

School of Nursing Offers family nurse practitioner (MSN); nurse educator (MSN); nursing (DNP); nursing administration (MSN); pediatric nurse practitioner (MSN).

KNOWLEDGE SYSTEMS INSTITUTE, Skokie, IL 60076

General Information Independent, coed, graduate-only institution. *Graduate housing:* On-campus housing not available.

GRADUATE UNITS

Program in Computer and Information Sciences *Program availability:* Part-time, evening/weekend, online learning. Offers computer and information sciences (MS). Electronic applications accepted.

KNOX COLLEGE, Toronto, ON M5S 2E6, Canada

General Information Independent-religious, coed, graduate-only institution. *Graduate housing:* Room and/or apartments available on a first-come, first-served basis to single students; on-campus housing not available to married students. Housing application deadline: 5/31.

GRADUATE UNITS

College of Theology *Program availability:* Part-time. Offers theology (M Div, MRE, MTS, Th M, D Min, Th D). Applicants for D Min, Th M, and Th D must apply to Toronto School of Theology; MRE, M Div, MTS, Th D, and Th M programs offered jointly with University of Toronto.

KNOX THEOLOGICAL SEMINARY, Fort Lauderdale, FL 33308

General Information Independent-religious, coed, primarily men, graduate-only institution. *Graduate housing:* On-campus housing not available.

GRADUATE UNITS

Graduate Programs *Program availability:* Part-time, blended/hybrid learning. Offers Biblical and theological studies (MA); Christian and classical studies (MA); divinity (M Div); ministry (D Min).

KUTZTOWN UNIVERSITY OF PENNSYLVANIA, Kutztown, PA 19530-0730

General Information State-supported, coed, comprehensive institution. CGS member. *Enrollment:* 8,513 graduate, professional, and undergraduate students; 274 full-time matriculated graduate/professional students (209 women), 495 part-time matriculated graduate/professional students (380 women). *Enrollment by degree level:* 753 master's, 16 doctoral. *Graduate faculty:* 73 full-time (46 women), 6 part-time/adjunct (2 women). Tuition, state resident: full-time $4347; part-time $483 per credit. Tuition, nonresident: full-time $6525; part-time $725 per credit. *Required fees:* $88 per credit. One-time fee: $50 full-time. *Graduate housing:* Rooms and/or apartments available on a first-come, first-served basis to single and married students. Typical cost: $5552 per year for married students. *Student services:* Campus employment opportunities, campus safety program, career counseling, exercise/wellness program, free psychological counseling, international student services, low-cost health insurance, multicultural affairs office, services for students with disabilities. *Library facilities:* Rohrbach Library. *Collection:* Books: 379,570 (physical), 385,501 (digital/electronic); Serial titles: 5,277 (physical), 142,078 (digital/electronic); Databases: 119. Weekly public service hours: 92; students can reserve study rooms.

Computer facilities: Computer purchase and lease plans are available. 1,075 computers available on campus for general student use. A campuswide network can be accessed from student residence rooms. Online class registration is available. Website: http://www.kutztown.edu/

Kutztown University of Pennsylvania

General Application Contact: Kelly Hish, Admissions Clerk, 610-683-4190, Fax: 610-683-1375, E-mail: graduate@kutztown.edu.

GRADUATE UNITS

College of Business Students: 16 full-time (6 women), 18 part-time (7 women); includes 3 minority (2 Black or African American, non-Hispanic/Latino; 1 Asian, non-Hispanic/Latino), 4 international. Average age 30. 31 applicants, 77% accepted, 15 enrolled. *Faculty:* 7 full-time (4 women). Expenses: Contact institution. *Financial support:* Career-related internships or fieldwork, Federal Work-Study, scholarships/grants, and unspecified assistantships available. Financial award application deadline: 3/1; financial award applicants required to submit FAFSA. In 2016, 16 master's awarded. *Program availability:* Part-time, evening/weekend. Offers business (MBA); business administration (MBA). *Application deadline:* For fall admission, 8/1 priority date for domestic and international students; for spring admission, 12/1 priority date for domestic and international students. *Application fee:* $35. Electronic applications accepted. *Interim Dean,* Dr. Ernest Clary, 610-683-4575, Fax: 610-683-4573, E-mail: clary@kutztown.edu.

College of Education Students: 168 full-time (139 women), 348 part-time (277 women); includes 51 minority (19 Black or African American, non-Hispanic/Latino; 5 Asian, non-Hispanic/Latino; 22 Hispanic/Latino; 5 Two or more races, non-Hispanic/Latino), 1 international. Average age 30. 373 applicants, 88% accepted, 187 enrolled. *Faculty:* 25 full-time (17 women), 3 part-time/adjunct (1 woman). Expenses: Contact institution. *Financial support:* Career-related internships or fieldwork, Federal Work-Study, scholarships/grants, and unspecified assistantships available. Financial award application deadline: 3/1; financial award applicants required to submit FAFSA. In 2016, 161 master's awarded. *Program availability:* Part-time, evening/weekend. Offers biology (M Ed); clinical mental health counseling (MA); curriculum and instruction (M Ed); education (M Ed, MA, MLS, MS); elementary education (M Ed); English (M Ed); instructional technology (M Ed); library science (MLS); marriage, couple and family counseling (MA); mathematics (M Ed); middle level (M Ed); reading (M Ed); school counseling (MS); social studies (M Ed); student affairs in higher education (M Ed); teaching (M Ed). *Application deadline:* For fall admission, 8/1 for domestic and international students; for spring admission, 12/1 for domestic and international students. *Application fee:* $35. Electronic applications accepted. *Dean,* Dr. Kenneth Teitelbaum, 610-683-4253, Fax: 610-683-4255, E-mail: teitelba@kutztown.edu.

College of Liberal Arts and Sciences Students: 73 full-time (50 women), 92 part-time (60 women); includes 33 minority (19 Black or African American, non-Hispanic/Latino; 2 Asian, non-Hispanic/Latino; 10 Hispanic/Latino; 2 Two or more races, non-Hispanic/Latino), 3 international. Average age 31. 168 applicants, 87% accepted, 70 enrolled. *Faculty:* 27 full-time (14 women), 1 part-time/adjunct (0 women). Expenses: Contact institution. *Financial support:* Career-related internships or fieldwork, Federal Work-Study, scholarships/grants, and unspecified assistantships available. Financial award application deadline: 3/1; financial award applicants required to submit FAFSA. In 2016, 62 master's awarded. *Program availability:* Part-time, evening/weekend. Offers computer science (MS); English (MA); liberal arts and sciences (MA, MPA, MS, MSW, DSW); public administration (MPA); social work (MSW, DSW). *Application deadline:* For fall admission, 8/1 for domestic and international students; for spring admission, 12/1 for domestic and international students. *Application fee:* $35. Electronic applications accepted. *Dean,* Dr. David Beougher, 610-683-4305, Fax: 610-683-4633, E-mail: clas@kutztown.edu.

College of Visual and Performing Arts Students: 17 full-time (14 women), 37 part-time (36 women), 2 international. Average age 33. 36 applicants, 89% accepted, 15 enrolled. *Faculty:* 16 full-time (13 women), 1 (woman) part-time/adjunct. Expenses: Contact institution. *Financial support:* Career-related internships or fieldwork, Federal Work-Study, scholarships/grants, and unspecified assistantships available. Financial award application deadline: 3/1; financial award applicants required to submit FAFSA. In 2016, 16 master's awarded. *Program availability:* Part-time. Offers art education (M Ed); communication design (MFA); visual and performing arts (M Ed, MFA). *Application deadline:* For fall admission, 8/1 for domestic and international students; for spring admission, 12/1 for domestic and international students. *Application fee:* $35. Electronic applications accepted. *Dean,* Dr. William Mowder, 610-683-4500, Fax: 610-683-4547, E-mail: mowder@kutztown.edu.

LAGRANGE COLLEGE, LaGrange, GA 30240-2999

General Information Independent-religious, coed, comprehensive institution. *Graduate housing:* Room and/or apartments available on a first-come, first-served basis to single students; on-campus housing not available to married students. Housing application deadline: 5/1.

GRADUATE UNITS

Graduate Programs *Program availability:* Part-time, evening/weekend. Offers clinical mental health counseling (MS); curriculum and instruction (M Ed, Ed S); middle grades (MAT); organizational leadership (MA); secondary education (MAT). Electronic applications accepted.

LAGUNA COLLEGE OF ART & DESIGN, Laguna Beach, CA 92651-1136

General Information Independent, coed, comprehensive institution.

GRADUATE UNITS

Graduate Program Electronic applications accepted.

LAKE ERIE COLLEGE, Painesville, OH 44077-3389

General Information Independent, coed, comprehensive institution. *Graduate housing:* On-campus housing not available.

GRADUATE UNITS

School of Business *Program availability:* Part-time, evening/weekend. Offers general management (MBA); health care administration (MBA); information technology management (MBA). Electronic applications accepted.

School of Education and Professional Studies *Program availability:* Part-time, evening/weekend. Offers education and professional studies (M Ed). Electronic applications accepted.

LAKE ERIE COLLEGE OF OSTEOPATHIC MEDICINE, Erie, PA 16509-1025

General Information Independent, coed, graduate-only institution. *Graduate housing:* On-campus housing not available. *Research affiliation:* West Virginia University (neurology), Neuro Structural Research Laboratories (neurology), Cornelli Consulting (CORCON) (neurology), University of Maryland (neurology), Duke University (neurology).

GRADUATE UNITS

Professional Programs Offers biomedical sciences (Postbaccalaureate Certificate); medical education (MS); osteopathic medicine (DO); pharmacy (Pharm D). Electronic applications accepted.

LAKE FOREST COLLEGE, Lake Forest, IL 60045

General Information Independent, coed, comprehensive institution. *Graduate housing:* On-campus housing not available. *Research affiliation:* Argonne National Laboratory (physics), Merck & Company, Inc., Chicago History Museum (Chicago history), Lake Forest Hospital (genomes), The Art Institute of Chicago (Asian art), Newberry Library (medieval and Renaissance history, American West).

GRADUATE UNITS

Graduate Program in Liberal Studies Students: 1 full-time (0 women), 38 part-time (20 women); includes 5 minority (1 Black or African American, non-Hispanic/Latino; 2 Asian, non-Hispanic/Latino; 2 Hispanic/Latino). Average age 38. 19 applicants, 53% accepted, 7 enrolled. *Faculty:* 9 full-time (3 women), 1 part-time/adjunct (0 women). Expenses: Contact institution. *Financial support:* In 2016–17, 2 students received support. Partial tuition grants for full-time teachers available. In 2016, 4 master's awarded. *Program availability:* Part-time, evening/weekend. Offers American studies (MLS); environmental studies (MLS); history (MLS); Medieval and Renaissance art (MLS); philosophy (MLS); Spanish (MLS); writing (MLS). *Application deadline:* For fall admission, 7/15 priority date for domestic students, 6/1 priority date for international students; for spring admission, 12/1 priority date for domestic students, 10/1 priority date for international students. Applications are processed on a rolling basis. *Application fee:* $30. *Application Contact:* Prof. Carol Gayle, Associate Director, 847-735-5083, Fax: 847-735-6291, E-mail: gayle@lakeforest.edu. *Director,* Prof. D. L. LeMahieu, 847-735-5133, Fax: 847-735-6291, E-mail: lemahieu@lakeforest.edu.

Master of Arts in Teaching Program Offers elementary education (MAT); K-12 French (MAT); K-12 music (MAT); K-12 Spanish (MAT); K-12 visual art (MAT); secondary biology (MAT); secondary chemistry (MAT); secondary English (MAT); secondary history (MAT); secondary mathematics (MAT).

LAKE FOREST GRADUATE SCHOOL OF MANAGEMENT, Lake Forest, IL 60045

General Information Independent, coed, graduate-only institution. *Graduate housing:* On-campus housing not available.

GRADUATE UNITS

The Immersion MBA Program (iMBA) *Program availability:* Online learning. Offers global business (MBA).

The Leadership MBA Program *Program availability:* Part-time, evening/weekend. Offers finance (MBA); global business (MBA); healthcare management (MBA); management (MBA); marketing (MBA); organizational behavior (MBA). Electronic applications accepted.

LAKEHEAD UNIVERSITY, Thunder Bay, ON P7B 5E1, Canada

General Information Province-supported, coed, comprehensive institution. *Graduate housing:* Rooms and/or apartments available to single students and available on a first-come, first-served basis to married students. Housing application deadline: 3/10. *Research affiliation:* Falcon Bridge (biology), Placer Dome (biology), Bowater Inc. (engineering), Centre for Northern Forest Ecosystem Research (biology, forestry, tourism), Thunder Bay Regional Cancer Centre (psychosocial oncology), Bowater Inc. (chemistry).

GRADUATE UNITS

Graduate Studies *Program availability:* Part-time, evening/weekend. Offers clinical psychology (PhD); experimental psychology (MA); geology (M Sc); gerontology (M Ed, M Sc, MA, MSW); history (MA); physics (M Sc); women's studies (MA).

Faculty of Education *Program availability:* Part-time, evening/weekend. Offers educational studies (PhD); gerontology (M Ed); women's studies (M Ed).

Faculty of Engineering *Program availability:* Part-time. Offers control engineering (M Sc Engr); electrical/computer engineering (M Sc Engr); environmental engineering (M Sc Engr).

Faculty of Natural Resources Management *Program availability:* Part-time. Offers forest sciences (PhD); forestry (M Sc F).

Faculty of Social Sciences and Humanities *Program availability:* Part-time, evening/weekend. Offers biology (M Sc); chemistry (M Sc); economics (MA); English (MA); gerontology (MA); health services and policy research (MA); social sciences and humanities (M Sc, MA, MSW, PhD); sociology (MA); women's studies (MA).

School of Kinesiology *Program availability:* Part-time. Offers kinesiology (M Sc); kinesiology and gerontology (M Sc).

School of Mathematical Sciences *Program availability:* Part-time, evening/weekend. Offers computer science (M Sc); mathematical science (MA).

School of Social Work *Program availability:* Part-time. Offers gerontology (MSW); social work (MSW); women's studies (MSW).

LAKELAND UNIVERSITY, Plymouth, WI 53073

General Information Independent-religious, coed, comprehensive institution. *Graduate housing:* On-campus housing not available.

GRADUATE UNITS

Graduate Studies Division *Program availability:* Part-time, evening/weekend. Offers accounting (MBA); counseling (MA); education (M Ed); finance (MBA); healthcare management (MBA); project management (MBA); theology (MAT).

LAMAR UNIVERSITY, Beaumont, TX 77710

General Information State-supported, coed, university. CGS member. *Enrollment:* 15,001 graduate, professional, and undergraduate students; 845 full-time matriculated graduate/professional students (290 women), 4,784 part-time matriculated graduate/professional students (3,466 women). *Enrollment by degree level:* 4,578 master's, 380 doctoral, 708 other advanced degrees. *Graduate faculty:* 234 full-time (101 women), 34 part-time/adjunct (20 women). Tuition, state resident: full-time $6174; part-time $343 per credit. Tuition, nonresident: full-time $15,604; part-time $758 per credit. *Required fees:* $1960; $729 per semester. Tuition and fees vary according to course load and program. *Graduate housing:* Rooms and/or apartments available to single students and available on a first-come, first-served basis to married students. Typical cost: $5252 (including board) for single students; $7878 (including board) for married students. Room and board charges vary according to board plan. Housing application deadline: 6/30. *Student services:* Campus employment opportunities, campus safety program, career counseling, exercise/wellness program, free psychological counseling, grant writing training, international student services, low-cost health insurance, multicultural affairs office, services for students with disabilities, teacher training, writing training. *Library facilities:* Mary and John Gray Library plus 1 other. *Collection:* Books: 529,806 (physical), 83,153 (digital/electronic); Serial titles: 42,694 (physical), 47,629 (digital/electronic); Databases: 141. Weekly public service hours: 94; students can reserve study rooms. *Research affiliation:* Grants Resource Center, National Council of Research Administrators, BASF.

Computer facilities: 644 computers available on campus for general student use. A campuswide network can be accessed from student residence rooms and from off campus. Online class registration is available.
Website: http://www.lamar.edu/

General Application Contact: Deidre Mayer, Interim Director, Admissions and Academic Services, 409-880-8888, Fax: 409-880-7419, E-mail: gradmissions@lamar.edu.

GRADUATE UNITS

College of Graduate Studies Students: 1,090 full-time (351 women), 4,090 part-time (2,952 women); includes 1,648 minority (774 Black or African American, non-Hispanic/Latino; 20 American Indian or Alaska Native, non-Hispanic/Latino; 77 Asian, non-Hispanic/Latino; 700 Hispanic/Latino; 77 Two or more races, non-Hispanic/Latino), 1,139 international. Average age 29. 2,975 applicants, 93% accepted, 1405 enrolled. *Faculty:* 235 full-time (108 women), 73 part-time/adjunct (42 women). Expenses: Contact institution. *Financial support:* Fellowships with partial tuition reimbursements, research assistantships, teaching assistantships, career-related internships or fieldwork, Federal Work-Study, institutionally sponsored loans, scholarships/grants, and tuition waivers (partial) available. Support available to part-time students. Financial award application deadline: 4/1; financial award applicants required to submit FAFSA. In 2016, 2,594 master's, 100 doctorates, 17 other advanced degrees awarded. *Program availability:* Part-time, evening/weekend. *Application deadline:* For fall admission, 8/1 for domestic students, 7/1 for international students; for spring admission, 1/5 for domestic students, 12/5 for international students. Applications are processed on a rolling basis. *Application fee:* $25 ($50 for international students). Electronic applications accepted. *Application Contact:* Melissa Gallien, Director, Admissions and Academic Services, 409-880-8888, Fax: 409-880-7419, E-mail: gradmissions@lamar.edu. *Dean,* Dr. William E. Harn, 409-880-8229, Fax: 409-880-1723, E-mail: lugradstudies@lamar.edu.

College of Arts and Sciences Students: 256 full-time (71 women), 316 part-time (192 women); includes 156 minority (94 Black or African American, non-Hispanic/Latino; 11 Asian, non-Hispanic/Latino; 45 Hispanic/Latino; 6 Two or more races, non-Hispanic/Latino), 284 international. Average age 31. 408 applicants, 95% accepted, 114 enrolled. *Faculty:* 68 full-time (29 women). Expenses: Contact institution. *Financial support:* Fellowships, research assistantships, teaching assistantships with tuition reimbursements, career-related internships or fieldwork, Federal Work-Study, institutionally sponsored loans, scholarships/grants, and tuition waivers (partial) available. Support available to part-time students. Financial award application deadline: 4/1; financial award applicants required to submit FAFSA. In 2016, 269 master's awarded. *Program availability:* Part-time, evening/weekend. Offers arts and sciences (MA, MPA, MS, MSN); biology (MS); chemistry (MS); clinical psychology (MS); computer science (MS); criminal justice (MS); English (MA); history (MA); industrial/organizational psychology (MS); mathematics (MS); nursing administration (MSN); nursing education (MSN); public administration (MPA); teaching Spanish (MA). *Application deadline:* For fall admission, 8/10 for domestic students, 7/1 for international students; for spring admission, 1/15 for domestic students, 12/1 for international students. Applications are processed on a rolling basis. *Application fee:* $25 ($50 for international students). Electronic applications accepted. *Application Contact:* Deidre Mayer, Interim Director, Admissions and Academic Services, 409-880-8888, E-mail: gradmissions@lamar.edu. *Interim Dean,* Dr. Joe Nordgren, 409-880-8508, Fax: 409-880-8007.

College of Business Students: 23 full-time (12 women), 209 part-time (109 women); includes 96 minority (46 Black or African American, non-Hispanic/Latino; 11 Asian, non-Hispanic/Latino; 32 Hispanic/Latino; 7 Two or more races, non-Hispanic/Latino), 33 international. Average age 33. 151 applicants, 99% accepted, 81 enrolled. *Faculty:* 22 full-time (5 women). Expenses: Contact institution. *Financial support:* Fellowships with tuition reimbursements, research assistantships with partial tuition reimbursements, career-related internships or fieldwork, Federal Work-Study, institutionally sponsored loans, scholarships/grants, and tuition waivers (partial) available. Support available to part-time students. Financial award application deadline: 4/1; financial award applicants required to submit FAFSA. In 2016, 104 master's awarded. *Program availability:* Part-time, evening/weekend. Offers accounting (MBA); experiential business and entrepreneurship (MBA); healthcare administration (MBA). *Application deadline:* For fall admission, 8/10 for domestic students, 7/1 for international students; for spring admission, 1/5 for domestic students, 12/1 for international students. Applications are processed on a rolling basis. *Application fee:* $25 ($50 for international students). Electronic applications accepted. *Application Contact:* Deidre Mayer, Interim Director, Admissions and Academic Services, 409-880-8888, Fax: 409-880-7419, E-mail: gradmissions@lamar.edu. *Dean,* Dr. Enrique R. Venta, 409-880-8603, Fax: 409-880-8088, E-mail: henry.venta@lamar.edu.

College of Education and Human Development Students: 95 full-time (65 women), 4,039 part-time (3,122 women); includes 1,731 minority (829 Black or African American, non-Hispanic/Latino; 14 American Indian or Alaska Native, non-Hispanic/Latino; 56 Asian, non-Hispanic/Latino; 754 Hispanic/Latino; 3 Native Hawaiian or other Pacific Islander, non-Hispanic/Latino; 75 Two or more races, non-Hispanic/Latino), 18 international. Average age 37. 1,904 applicants, 93% accepted, 1051 enrolled. *Faculty:* 72 full-time (51 women), 29 part-time/adjunct (17 women). Expenses: Contact institution. *Financial support:* Fellowships, research assistantships, teaching assistantships, career-related internships or fieldwork, Federal Work-Study, institutionally sponsored loans, and scholarships/grants available. Support available to part-time students. Financial award application deadline: 4/1; financial award applicants required to submit FAFSA. In 2016, 1,849 master's, 82 doctorates, 17 other advanced degrees awarded. *Program availability:* Part-time, evening/weekend, online learning. Offers clinical mental health counseling (M Ed); digital learning and leading (M Ed); education administration (M Ed); education and human development (M Ed, MS, Ed D, Certificate); educational leadership (Ed D); educational technology (M Ed); family and consumer sciences (MS); public health (MS); school counseling (M Ed); science of kinesiology promotion (MS); special education (M Ed); teacher leadership (M Ed). *Application deadline:* For fall admission, 8/10 for domestic students, 7/1 for international students; for spring admission, 1/5 for domestic students, 12/1 for international students. Applications are processed on a rolling basis. *Application fee:* $25 ($50 for international students). Electronic applications accepted. *Application Contact:* Deidre Mayer, Interim Director, Admissions and Academic Services, 409-880-8888, Fax: 409-880-7419, E-mail: gradmissions@lamar.edu. *Dean,* Dr. Robert Spina, 409-880-8661.

College of Engineering Students: 361 full-time (52 women), 190 part-time (24 women); includes 19 minority (3 Black or African American, non-Hispanic/Latino; 1 American Indian or Alaska Native, non-Hispanic/Latino; 11 Asian, non-Hispanic/Latino; 3 Hispanic/Latino; 1 Two or more races, non-Hispanic/Latino), 511 international. Average age 26. 444 applicants, 87% accepted, 109 enrolled. *Faculty:* 48 full-time (5 women), 1 part-time/adjunct (0 women). Expenses: Contact institution. *Financial support:* Fellowships with partial tuition reimbursements, research assistantships with partial tuition reimbursements, teaching assistantships with partial tuition reimbursements, career-related internships or fieldwork, Federal Work-Study, institutionally sponsored loans, scholarships/grants, tuition waivers (full and partial), and laboratory assistantships available. Support available to part-time students. Financial award application deadline: 4/1; financial award applicants required to submit FAFSA. In 2016, 330 master's, 11 doctorates awarded. *Program availability:* Part-time, evening/weekend. Offers chemical engineering (ME, PhD); civil engineering (ME, MES); electrical engineering (ME, MES, DE); engineering (ME, MEM, MES, MS, DE, PhD); engineering management (MEM); environmental engineering (ME); environmental studies (MS, DE); industrial engineering (ME, MES, DE); mechanical engineering (ME, MES, DE). *Application deadline:* For fall admission, 8/1 for domestic students, 7/1 for international students; for spring admission, 1/5 for domestic students, 12/1 for international students. Applications are processed on a rolling basis. *Application fee:* $25 ($50 for international students). Electronic applications accepted. *Application Contact:* Deidre Mayer, Interim Director, Admissions and Academic Services, 409-880-8888, Fax: 409-880-7419, E-mail: gradmissions@lamar.edu. *Dean,* Dr. Srinivas Palanki, 409-880-8784, Fax: 409-880-2197.

College of Fine Arts and Communication Students: 110 full-time (90 women), 30 part-time (19 women); includes 45 minority (14 Black or African American, non-Hispanic/Latino; 4 Asian, non-Hispanic/Latino; 23 Hispanic/Latino; 4 Two or more races, non-Hispanic/Latino), 10 international. Average age 29. 68 applicants, 99% accepted, 50 enrolled. *Faculty:* 24 full-time (11 women), 4 part-time/adjunct (3 women). Expenses: Contact institution. *Financial support:* Fellowships, research assistantships, teaching assistantships, career-related internships or fieldwork, Federal Work-Study, institutionally sponsored loans, and tuition waivers (partial) available. Support available to part-time students. Financial award application deadline: 4/1; financial award applicants required to submit FAFSA. In 2016, 42 master's, 7 doctorates awarded. *Program availability:* Part-time, evening/weekend. Offers audiology (Au D); deaf studies and deaf education (MS, Ed D); fine arts and communication (MM, MS, Au D, Ed D); music (MM); speech language pathology (MS). *Application deadline:* For fall admission, 8/10 for domestic students, 7/1 for international students; for spring admission, 1/5 for domestic students, 12/1 for international students. Applications are processed on a rolling basis. *Application fee:* $25 ($50 for international students). Electronic applications accepted. *Application Contact:* Deidre Mayer, Interim Director, Admissions and Academic Services, 409-880-8888, Fax: 409-880-7419, E-mail: gradmissions@lamar.edu. *Dean,* Dr. Derina Holtzhausen, 409-880-8137, Fax: 409-880-2286.

LANCASTER BIBLE COLLEGE, Lancaster, PA 17601
General Information Independent-religious, coed, comprehensive institution. *Graduate housing:* On-campus housing not available.
GRADUATE UNITS
Capital Bible Seminary *Program availability:* Part-time, evening/weekend. Offers biblical studies (MA, Certificate); Christian counseling and discipleship (MA, Certificate); ministry (MA); theology (M Div).

Graduate School *Program availability:* Part-time, evening/weekend. Offers adult ministries (MA); Bible (MA); children and family ministry (MA); church planting (MA); consulting resource teacher (M Ed); elementary school counseling (M Ed); leadership (PhD); leadership studies (MA); marriage and family counseling (MA); mental health counseling (MA); pastoral studies (MA); secondary school counseling (M Ed); sports ministry (MA); student ministry (MA); town and country ministry (MA).

LANCASTER THEOLOGICAL SEMINARY, Lancaster, PA 17603-2812
General Information Independent-religious, coed, graduate-only institution. *Graduate housing:* Rooms and/or apartments available on a first-come, first-served basis to single and married students. Housing application deadline: 8/1.
GRADUATE UNITS
Graduate and Professional Programs Offers biblical studies (MAR); Christian education (MAR); Christianity and the arts (MAR); church history (MAR); congregational life (MAR); lay leadership (Certificate); theological studies (M Div); theology (D Min); theology and ethics (MAR).

LANDER UNIVERSITY, Greenwood, SC 29649-2099
General Information State-supported, coed, comprehensive institution. *Graduate housing:* Room and/or apartments available on a first-come, first-served basis to single students; on-campus housing not available to married students.
GRADUATE UNITS
Graduate Studies *Program availability:* Part-time, online learning. Offers clinical nurse leader (MSN); emergency management (MS); Montessori education (M Ed); teaching and learning (M Ed). Electronic applications accepted.

LANGSTON UNIVERSITY, Langston, OK 73050
General Information State-supported, coed, comprehensive institution. CGS member. *Graduate housing:* Rooms and/or apartments available on a first-come, first-served basis to single and married students.
GRADUATE UNITS
School of Education and Behavioral Sciences *Program availability:* Part-time. Offers bilingual/multicultural (M Ed); elementary education (M Ed); English as a second language (M Ed); rehabilitation counseling (M Sc); urban education (M Ed).
School of Physical Therapy Offers physical therapy (DPT).

LA ROCHE COLLEGE, Pittsburgh, PA 15237-5898
General Information Independent-religious, coed, comprehensive institution. *Enrollment:* 1,555 graduate, professional, and undergraduate students; 87 full-time matriculated graduate/professional students (66 women), 62 part-time matriculated graduate/professional students (41 women). *Enrollment by degree level:* 129 master's, 5 doctoral, 15 other advanced degrees. *Graduate faculty:* 10 full-time (9 women), 16 part-time/adjunct (4 women). *Tuition:* Full-time $12,600; part-time $700 per credit. *Required fees:* $25 per semester. *Graduate housing:* On-campus housing not available. *Student services:* Campus employment opportunities, career counseling, free psychological counseling, international student services, low-cost health insurance, multicultural affairs

office, services for students with disabilities. *Library facilities:* John J. Wright Library plus 1 other. *Collection:* Books: 75,803 (physical), 221,000 (digital/electronic); Databases: 1,248.

Computer facilities: Computer purchase and lease plans are available. A campuswide network can be accessed. Online class registration is available. Website: http://www.laroche.edu/

General Application Contact: Hope Schiffgens, Director of Graduate Studies and Adult Education, 412-536-1266, Fax: 412-536-1283, E-mail: schombh1@laroche.edu.

GRADUATE UNITS

School of Graduate Studies and Adult Education Students: 87 full-time (66 women), 62 part-time (41 women); includes 2 minority (1 Black or African American, non-Hispanic/Latino; 1 Hispanic/Latino), 27 international. Average age 33. *Faculty:* 10 full-time (9 women), 16 part-time/adjunct (4 women). Expenses: Contact institution. *Financial support:* Unspecified assistantships available. Financial award application deadline: 3/31; financial award applicants required to submit FAFSA. In 2016, 45 master's awarded. *Program availability:* Part-time, evening/weekend, 100% online. Offers accounting (MS); human resources management (MS, Certificate); nurse anesthesia (MS, DNAP); nursing education (MSN); nursing management (MSN). *Application deadline:* For fall admission, 8/15 for domestic and international students; for spring admission, 12/15 for domestic and international students. Applications are processed on a rolling basis. *Application fee:* $50. Electronic applications accepted. *Application Contact:* Hope Schiffgens, Director of Graduate Studies and Adult Education, 412-536-1266, Fax: 412-536-1283, E-mail: schombh1@laroche.edu. *Dean,* Dr. Rosemary McCarthy, 412-536-1193, Fax: 412-536-1763, E-mail: rosemary.mccarthy@laroche.edu.

LA SALLE UNIVERSITY, Philadelphia, PA 19141-1199

General Information Independent-religious, coed, comprehensive institution. *Enrollment:* 5,197 graduate, professional, and undergraduate students; 294 full-time matriculated graduate/professional students (211 women), 1,251 part-time matriculated graduate/professional students (877 women). *Enrollment by degree level:* 1,282 master's, 175 doctoral, 88 other advanced degrees. *Graduate faculty:* 71 full-time (45 women), 108 part-time/adjunct (61 women). *Tuition:* Full-time $23,020; part-time $970 per credit. *Required fees:* $570; $210 per semester. Tuition and fees vary according to course load, degree level, program and reciprocity agreements. *Graduate housing:* Room and/or apartments available on a first-come, first-served basis to single students; on-campus housing not available to married students. Typical cost: $9410 per year. Room charges vary according to board plan and housing facility selected. *Student services:* Campus employment opportunities, campus safety program, career counseling, exercise/wellness program, free psychological counseling, international student services, multicultural affairs office, services for students with disabilities, teacher training, writing training. *Library facilities:* Connelly Library. *Collection:* Books: 274,998 (physical), 172,068 (digital/electronic); Serial titles: 1,470 (physical), 127,163 (digital/electronic); Databases: 88. Weekly public service hours: 96; students can reserve study rooms.

Computer facilities: 1,100 computers available on campus for general student use. A campuswide network can be accessed from student residence rooms and from off campus. Online class registration, course management system are available. Website: http://www.lasalle.edu/

General Application Contact: Elizabeth Heenan, Director, Graduate and Adult Enrollment, 215-951-1100, Fax: 215-951-1462, E-mail: heenan@lasalle.edu.

GRADUATE UNITS

School of Arts and Sciences Students: 185 full-time (138 women), 553 part-time (382 women); includes 223 minority (121 Black or African American, non-Hispanic/Latino; 2 American Indian or Alaska Native, non-Hispanic/Latino; 18 Asian, non-Hispanic/Latino; 66 Hispanic/Latino; 16 Two or more races, non-Hispanic/Latino), 20 international. Average age 32. 783 applicants, 60% accepted, 271 enrolled. *Faculty:* 34 full-time (23 women), 65 part-time/adjunct (32 women). Expenses: Contact institution. *Financial support:* In 2016–17, 116 students received support. Career-related internships or fieldwork, Federal Work-Study, scholarships/grants, and unspecified assistantships available. Support available to part-time students. Financial award application deadline: 8/31; financial award applicants required to submit FAFSA. In 2016, 313 master's, 22 doctorates, 16 other advanced degrees awarded. *Program availability:* Part-time, evening/weekend, 100% online, blended/hybrid learning. Offers American history (Certificate); application development (Certificate); arts and sciences (MA, MS, Psy D, Certificate); autism spectrum disorders (MA, Certificate); bilingual/bicultural studies (MA); child clinical psychology (Psy D); classroom management (MA); clinical health psychology (Psy D); clinical psychology (MA); communication consulting and development (MA); communication management (MA); computer information science (MS); corporate fraud (MS); dual early childhood and special education (MA); dual middle-level science and math and special education (MA); education (MA); English (MA); English as a second language (Certificate); European history (Certificate); fraud and forensic accounting (Certificate); general practice psychology (Psy D); general professional communication (MA); history (MA); history for educators (MA); industrial/organizational management and human resources (MA); information technology leadership (MS); instructional coach (Certificate); instructional leadership (MA); instructional technology management (MS, Certificate); marriage and family therapy (MA); network security (MS); pastoral counseling (MA); professional and business communication (Certificate); professional clinical counseling (MA); public history (MA); public relations (MA); reading specialist (MA, Certificate); secondary education (MA); social and new media (Certificate); software project leadership (Certificate); special education (MA, Certificate); teaching advanced placement history (Certificate); world history (Certificate). *Application fee:* $35. Electronic applications accepted. *Application Contact:* Elizabeth Heenan, Director, Graduate and Adult Enrollment, 215-951-1100, Fax: 215-951-1886, E-mail: heenan@lasalle.edu. *Interim Dean,* Dr. Lynne A. Texter, 215-951-1043, E-mail: texter@lasalle.edu.

Hispanic Institute Students: 1 (woman) full-time, 26 part-time (18 women); includes 15 minority (5 Black or African American, non-Hispanic/Latino; 10 Hispanic/Latino), 1 international. Average age 37. 17 applicants, 76% accepted, 7 enrolled. *Faculty:* 2 full-time (1 woman), 6 part-time/adjunct (3 women). Expenses: Contact institution. *Financial support:* In 2016–17, 3 students received support. Scholarships/grants available. Support available to part-time students. Financial award application deadline: 8/31; financial award applicants required to submit FAFSA. In 2016, 7 master's, 4 other advanced degrees awarded. *Program availability:* Part-time, evening/weekend. Offers bilingual/bicultural studies (MA); ESL program specialist (Certificate); interpretation: English/Spanish-Spanish/English (Certificate); teaching English to speakers of other languages (MA); translation and interpretation (MA); translation: English/Spanish-Spanish/English (Certificate). *Application deadline:* For fall admission, 8/15 priority date for domestic students, 7/15 for international students;

for spring admission, 12/15 priority date for domestic students, 11/15 for international students; for summer admission, 4/15 priority date for domestic students, 3/15 for international students. Applications are processed on a rolling basis. *Application fee:* $35. Electronic applications accepted. *Application Contact:* Elizabeth Heenan, Director, Graduate and Adult Enrollment, 215-951-1100, Fax: 215-951-1462, E-mail: heenan@lasalle.edu. *Director,* Guadalupe Da Costa Montesinos, 215-951-1209, Fax: 215-991-3506, E-mail: montesin@lasalle.edu.

School of Business Students: 57 full-time (25 women), 295 part-time (161 women); includes 95 minority (57 Black or African American, non-Hispanic/Latino; 17 Asian, non-Hispanic/Latino; 15 Hispanic/Latino; 6 Two or more races, non-Hispanic/Latino), 17 international. Average age 32. 232 applicants, 64% accepted, 91 enrolled. *Faculty:* 19 full-time (6 women), 20 part-time/adjunct (8 women). Expenses: Contact institution. *Financial support:* In 2016–17, 63 students received support. Scholarships/grants and unspecified assistantships available. Support available to part-time students. Financial award application deadline: 8/31; financial award applicants required to submit FAFSA. In 2016, 201 master's, 2 other advanced degrees awarded. *Program availability:* Part-time, evening/weekend, 100% online, blended/hybrid learning. Offers accounting (MBA, Post-MBA Certificate); business administration (MBA, Post-MBA Certificate); business systems and analytics (MBA, Post-MBA Certificate); finance (MBA, Post-MBA Certificate); general business administration (MBA, Post-MBA Certificate); human capital development (MS, Certificate); human resource management (MBA, Post-MBA Certificate); international business (MBA, Post-MBA Certificate); management (MBA, Post-MBA Certificate); marketing (Post-MBA Certificate); nonprofit leadership (MS). *Application deadline:* For fall admission, 8/15 priority date for domestic students, 7/15 for international students; for spring admission, 12/15 priority date for domestic students, 11/15 for international students; for summer admission, 4/15 priority date for domestic students, 3/15 for international students. Applications are processed on a rolling basis. *Application fee:* $35. Electronic applications accepted. *Application Contact:* Elizabeth Heenan, Director, Graduate and Adult Enrollment, 215-951-1100, Fax: 215-951-1462, E-mail: heenan@lasalle.edu. *Interim Dean,* Dr. MarySheila McDonald, 215-951-1040, Fax: 215-951-1886, E-mail: mcdonaldms@lasalle.edu.

School of Nursing and Health Sciences Students: 52 full-time (48 women), 403 part-time (333 women); includes 133 minority (76 Black or African American, non-Hispanic/Latino; 1 American Indian or Alaska Native, non-Hispanic/Latino; 27 Asian, non-Hispanic/Latino; 18 Hispanic/Latino; 1 Native Hawaiian or other Pacific Islander, non-Hispanic/Latino; 10 Two or more races, non-Hispanic/Latino), 9 international. Average age 35. 486 applicants, 31% accepted, 75 enrolled. *Faculty:* 18 full-time (16 women), 26 part-time/adjunct (22 women). Expenses: Contact institution. *Financial support:* In 2016–17, 21 students received support. Scholarships/grants, tuition waivers (partial), and unspecified assistantships available. Support available to part-time students. Financial award application deadline: 8/31; financial award applicants required to submit FAFSA. In 2016, 126 master's, 2 doctorates, 9 other advanced degrees awarded. *Program availability:* Part-time, evening/weekend. Offers gerontology primary care nurse practitioner (MSN, Certificate); adult health and illness clinical nurse specialist (MSN); adult-gerontology clinical nurse specialist (MSN, Certificate); clinical nurse leader (MSN); family primary care nurse practitioner (MSN, Certificate); gerontology (Certificate); nurse anesthetist (MSN, Certificate); nursing (MSN, Certificate); nursing administration (MSN, Certificate); nursing and health sciences (MPH, MS, MSN, DNP, Certificate); nursing education (Certificate); nursing practice (DNP); nursing service administration (MSN); public health (MPH); public health nursing (MSN, Certificate); school nursing (Certificate); speech-language pathology (MS). *Application deadline:* Applications are processed on a rolling basis. *Application fee:* $35. Electronic applications accepted. *Application Contact:* Elizabeth Heenan, Director, Graduate and Adult Enrollment, 215-951-1100, Fax: 215-951-1462, E-mail: heenan@lasalle.edu. *Dean,* Dr. Kathleen Czekanski, 215-951-1430, Fax: 215-951-1896, E-mail: czekanski@lasalle.edu.

LASELL COLLEGE, Newton, MA 02466-2709

General Information Independent, coed, comprehensive institution. *Enrollment:* 2,104 graduate, professional, and undergraduate students; 82 full-time matriculated graduate/professional students (52 women), 224 part-time matriculated graduate/professional students (162 women). *Enrollment by degree level:* 301 master's, 5 other advanced degrees. *Graduate faculty:* 17 full-time (7 women), 12 part-time/adjunct (8 women). *Tuition:* Full-time $10,800; part-time $600 per credit hour. *Required fees:* $160; $160 per credit hour. One-time fee: $40. *Graduate housing:* On-campus housing not available. *Student services:* Campus employment opportunities, career counseling, exercise/wellness program, international student services, multicultural affairs office, services for students with disabilities. *Library facilities:* Brennan Library. *Collection:* Study areas open 24 hours, 5–7 days a week. *Research affiliation:* Lasell Village (elder care).

Computer facilities: Computer purchase and lease plans are available. 219 computers available on campus for general student use. A campuswide network can be accessed from student residence rooms and from off campus. Online class registration, online tutoring are available. Website: http://www.lasell.edu/

General Application Contact: Adrienne Franciosi, Director of Graduate Enrollment, 617-243-2400, Fax: 617-243-2450, E-mail: gradinfo@lasell.edu.

GRADUATE UNITS

Graduate and Professional Studies in Communication Students: 12 full-time (9 women), 38 part-time (28 women); includes 11 minority (8 Black or African American, non-Hispanic/Latino; 1 Asian, non-Hispanic/Latino; 2 Hispanic/Latino), 8 international. Average age 31. 60 applicants, 43% accepted, 13 enrolled. *Faculty:* 4 full-time (2 women), 5 part-time/adjunct (2 women). Expenses: Contact institution. *Financial support:* In 2016–17, 6 students received support. Federal Work-Study, scholarships/grants, and tuition discounts available. Support available to part-time students. Financial award application deadline: 8/31; financial award applicants required to submit FAFSA. In 2016, 71 master's, 3 other advanced degrees awarded. *Program availability:* Part-time, evening/weekend, 100% online, blended/hybrid learning. Offers health communication (MSC, Graduate Certificate); integrated marketing communication (MSC, Graduate Certificate); public relations (MSC, Graduate Certificate). *Application deadline:* For fall admission, 8/31 priority date for domestic students, 6/30 priority date for international students; for spring admission, 12/31 priority date for domestic students, 10/31 priority date for international students. Applications are processed on a rolling basis. Electronic applications accepted. *Application Contact:* Adrienne Franciosi, Director of Graduate Enrollment, 617-243-2214, Fax: 617-243-2450, E-mail: gradinfo@lasell.edu. *Dean of Graduate and Professional Studies,* Dr. Joan Dolamore, 617-243-2485, Fax: 617-243-2450, E-mail: gradinfo@lasell.edu.

Graduate and Professional Studies in Criminal Justice Students: 5 full-time (2 women), 11 part-time (5 women); includes 2 minority (1 Black or African American, non-Hispanic/Latino; 1 Asian, non-Hispanic/Latino). Average age 30. 23 applicants, 52%

accepted, 8 enrolled. *Faculty:* 1 full-time (0 women), 2 part-time/adjunct (both women). Expenses: Contact institution. *Financial support:* In 2016–17, 6 students received support. Federal Work-Study, scholarships/grants, and tuition discounts available. Support available to part-time students. Financial award application deadline: 8/31; financial award applicants required to submit FAFSA. *Program availability:* Part-time, evening/weekend, online only, 100% online. Offers emergency and crisis management (MS, Certificate); homeland security and global justice (MS, Certificate); violence prevention and advocacy (MS, Certificate). *Application deadline:* For fall admission, 8/31 priority date for domestic students, 6/30 priority date for international students; for spring admission, 12/31 priority date for domestic students, 10/31 priority date for international students. Applications are processed on a rolling basis. Electronic applications accepted. *Application Contact:* Adrienne Franciosi, Director of Graduate Enrollment, 617-243-2214, Fax: 617-243-2450, E-mail: gradinfo@lasell.edu. *Dean of Graduate and Professional Studies*, Dr. Joan Dolamore, 617-243-2485, Fax: 617-243-2450, E-mail: gradinfo@lasell.edu.

Graduate and Professional Studies in Education Students: 4 full-time (3 women), 45 part-time (40 women); includes 2 minority (1 Hispanic/Latino; 1 Two or more races, non-Hispanic/Latino). Average age 28. 31 applicants, 58% accepted, 9 enrolled. *Faculty:* 3 full-time (all women), 6 part-time/adjunct (5 women). Expenses: Contact institution. *Financial support:* In 2016–17, 13 students received support. Federal Work-Study, scholarships/grants, and tuition discounts available. Support available to part-time students. Financial award application deadline: 8/31; financial award applicants required to submit FAFSA. In 2016, 12 master's awarded. *Program availability:* Part-time-only, evening/weekend, blended/hybrid learning. Offers elementary education (M Ed); special education (M Ed). *Application deadline:* For fall admission, 8/31 priority date for domestic students, 6/30 priority date for international students; for spring admission, 12/31 priority date for domestic students, 10/31 priority date for international students. Applications are processed on a rolling basis. Electronic applications accepted. *Application Contact:* Adrienne Franciosi, Director of Graduate Enrollment, 617-243-2214, Fax: 617-243-2450, E-mail: gradinfo@lasell.edu. *Dean of Graduate and Professional Studies*, Dr. Joan Dolamore, 617-243-2485, Fax: 617-243-2450, E-mail: gradinfo@lasell.edu.

Graduate and Professional Studies in Management Students: 47 full-time (34 women), 93 part-time (72 women); includes 28 minority (20 Black or African American, non-Hispanic/Latino; 4 Asian, non-Hispanic/Latino; 3 Hispanic/Latino; 1 Two or more races, non-Hispanic/Latino), 24 international. Average age 31. 121 applicants, 55% accepted, 32 enrolled. *Faculty:* 3 full-time (2 women), 16 part-time/adjunct (10 women). Expenses: Contact institution. *Financial support:* In 2016–17, 12 students received support. Federal Work-Study, scholarships/grants, and tuition discounts available. Support available to part-time students. Financial award application deadline: 8/31; financial award applicants required to submit FAFSA. In 2016, 61 master's, 3 other advanced degrees awarded. *Program availability:* Part-time, evening/weekend, 100% online, blended/hybrid learning. Offers business administration (PMBA); elder care management (MSM, Graduate Certificate); hospitality and event management (MSM, Graduate Certificate); human resources management (MSM, Graduate Certificate); management (MSM, Graduate Certificate); marketing (MSM, Graduate Certificate); non-profit management (MSM, Graduate Certificate); project management (MSM, Graduate Certificate). *Application deadline:* For fall admission, 8/31 priority date for domestic students, 6/30 priority date for international students; for spring admission, 12/31 priority date for domestic students, 10/31 priority date for international students. Applications are processed on a rolling basis. Electronic applications accepted. *Application Contact:* Adrienne Franciosi, Director of Graduate Enrollment, 617-243-2214, Fax: 617-243-2450, E-mail: gradinfo@lasell.edu. *Dean of Graduate and Professional Studies*, Dr. Joan Dolamore, 617-243-2485, Fax: 617-243-2450, E-mail: gradinfo@lasell.edu.

Graduate and Professional Studies in Rehabilitation Science Students: 6 part-time (all women); includes 1 minority (Two or more races, non-Hispanic/Latino). Average age 26. 14 applicants, 71% accepted, 5 enrolled. *Faculty:* 2 full-time (0 women). Expenses: Contact institution. *Financial support:* In 2016–17, 2 students received support. Federal Work-Study, scholarships/grants, and tuition discounts available. Support available to part-time students. Financial award application deadline: 8/31; financial award applicants required to submit FAFSA. *Program availability:* Part-time, evening/weekend, online only, 100% online. Offers rehabilitation science (MS). *Application deadline:* For fall admission, 8/31 priority date for domestic students, 6/30 priority date for international students; for spring admission, 12/31 priority date for domestic students, 10/31 priority date for international students. Applications are processed on a rolling basis. Electronic applications accepted. *Application Contact:* Adrienne Franciosi, Director of Graduate Enrollment, 617-243-2214, Fax: 617-243-2450, E-mail: gradinfo@lasell.edu. *Dean of Graduate and Professional Studies*, Dr. Joan Dolamore, 617-243-2485, Fax: 617-243-2450, E-mail: gradinfo@lasell.edu.

Graduate and Professional Studies in Sport Management Students: 14 full-time (4 women), 30 part-time (10 women); includes 10 minority (9 Black or African American, non-Hispanic/Latino; 1 Hispanic/Latino). Average age 30. 40 applicants, 43% accepted, 9 enrolled. *Faculty:* 4 full-time (0 women), 3 part-time/adjunct (1 woman). Expenses: Contact institution. *Financial support:* In 2016–17, 4 students received support. Federal Work-Study, scholarships/grants, and tuition discounts available. Support available to part-time students. Financial award application deadline: 8/31; financial award applicants required to submit FAFSA. In 2016, 21 master's, 2 other advanced degrees awarded. *Program availability:* Part-time, evening/weekend, online only, 100% online. Offers sport hospitality management (MS, Graduate Certificate); sport leadership (MS, Graduate Certificate); sport non-profit management (MS, Graduate Certificate). *Application deadline:* For fall admission, 8/31 priority date for domestic students, 6/30 priority date for international students; for spring admission, 12/31 priority date for domestic students, 10/31 priority date for international students. Applications are processed on a rolling basis. Electronic applications accepted. *Application Contact:* Adrienne Franciosi, Director of Graduate Enrollment, 617-243-2214, Fax: 617-243-2450, E-mail: gradinfo@lasell.edu. *Dean of Graduate and Professional Studies*, Dr. Joan Dolamore, 617-243-2485, Fax: 617-243-2450, E-mail: gradinfo@lasell.edu.

LA SIERRA UNIVERSITY, Riverside, CA 92515

General Information Independent-religious, coed, comprehensive institution. CGS member. *Graduate housing:* Rooms and/or apartments available on a first-come, first-served basis to single students and available to married students.

GRADUATE UNITS

College of Arts and Sciences *Program availability:* Part-time. Offers arts and sciences (MA); communication (MA); English (MA).

School of Business and Management Offers accounting (MBA); finance (MBA); general management (MBA); human resources management (MBA); leadership, values, and ethics for business and management (Certificate); marketing (MBA).

School of Education *Program availability:* Part-time, evening/weekend. Offers administration and leadership (MA, Ed D, Ed S); counseling (MA); curriculum and instruction (MA, Ed D, Ed S); education (MA, MAT, Ed D, Ed S); educational psychology (Ed S); school psychology (Ed S); teaching (MAT).

School of Religion *Program availability:* Part-time. Offers pastoral ministry (M Div); religion (MA); religious education (MA); religious studies (MA).

LAURENTIAN UNIVERSITY, Sudbury, ON P3E 2C6, Canada

General Information Province-supported, coed, comprehensive institution. *Graduate housing:* Rooms and/or apartments available on a first-come, first-served basis to single and married students.

GRADUATE UNITS

School of Graduate Studies and Research *Program availability:* Part-time, evening/weekend. Offers analytical chemistry (M Sc); applied psychology (MA); applied social research (MA); biochemistry (M Sc); biology (M Sc); boreal ecology (PhD); environmental chemistry (M Sc); European history (MA); experimental psychology (MA); geology (M Sc); history of Northern Ontario (MA); human development (M Sc, MA); humanities: interpretation and values (MA); mineral deposits and precambrian geology (PhD); mineral exploration (M Sc); North American history (MA); nursing (M Sc N); organic chemistry (M Sc); physical/theoretical chemistry (M Sc); physics (M Sc); rural and Northern health (PhD); science communication (G Dip).

School of Commerce and Administration *Program availability:* Part-time, evening/weekend. Offers commerce and administration (MBA).

School of Engineering *Program availability:* Part-time. Offers mineral resources engineering (M Eng, MA Sc); natural resources engineering (PhD).

School of Social Work *Program availability:* Part-time. Offers social work (MSW). Open only to French-speaking students.

LAWRENCE TECHNOLOGICAL UNIVERSITY, Southfield, MI 48075-1058

General Information Independent, coed, university. *Enrollment:* 3,309 graduate, professional, and undergraduate students; 37 full-time matriculated graduate/professional students (13 women), 1,108 part-time matriculated graduate/professional students (288 women). *Enrollment by degree level:* 1,068 master's, 49 doctoral, 28 other advanced degrees. *Graduate faculty:* 58 full-time (15 women), 58 part-time/adjunct (12 women). *Tuition:* Full-time $14,868; part-time $1062 per credit. *Required fees:* $75 per semester. Tuition and fees vary according to campus/location. *Graduate housing:* Rooms and/or apartments available on a first-come, first-served basis to single and married students. Typical cost: $5907 per year ($10,107 including board) for single students; $5907 per year ($10,107 including board) for married students. Room and board charges vary according to board plan, campus/location and housing facility selected. Housing application deadline: 5/1. *Student services:* Campus employment opportunities, campus safety program, career counseling, exercise/wellness program, free psychological counseling, international student services, low-cost health insurance, multicultural affairs office, services for students with disabilities, writing training. *Library facilities:* Lawrence Technological University Library plus 1 other. *Collection:* Books: 64,982 (physical), 267,794 (digital/electronic); Serial titles: 1,829 (physical), 43,887 (digital/electronic); Databases: 171. Weekly public service hours: 73. *Research affiliation:* Ford Motor Company (engineering), Clinton River Watershed Council (storm water analysis), Detroit Economic Growth Association (Great Lakes Shoreline Cities Green Infrastructure Project), Hyundai-KIA America Technical Center, Inc. (improvement of built-in hands-free cell phone performance), Johnson Controls Battery Group, Inc. (vehicle system power management testing), Meijer Foundation (engineering).

Computer facilities: Computer purchase and lease plans are available. 72 computers available on campus for general student use. A campuswide network can be accessed from student residence rooms and from off campus. Online class registration, degree audit, learning management system, learning management system, personal websites, document collection, placement are available.
Website: http://www.ltu.edu/

General Application Contact: Jane Rohrback, Director of Admissions, 248-204-3160, Fax: 248-204-2228, E-mail: admissions@ltu.edu.

GRADUATE UNITS

College of Architecture and Design Students: 8 full-time (3 women), 159 part-time (69 women); includes 15 minority (2 Black or African American, non-Hispanic/Latino; 4 Asian, non-Hispanic/Latino; 7 Hispanic/Latino; 2 Two or more races, non-Hispanic/Latino), 50 international. Average age 30. 119 applicants, 58% accepted, 43 enrolled. *Faculty:* 14 full-time (2 women), 13 part-time/adjunct (3 women). Expenses: Contact institution. *Financial support:* In 2016–17, 43 students received support, including 8 research assistantships with partial tuition reimbursements available (averaging $6,000 per year), 24 teaching assistantships (averaging $5,000 per year); career-related internships or fieldwork, scholarships/grants, and unspecified assistantships also available. Financial award application deadline: 4/1; financial award applicants required to submit FAFSA. In 2016, 78 master's awarded. *Program availability:* Part-time, evening/weekend. Offers architecture (M Arch); build information modeling (Graduate Certificate); interior design (MID); transportation design (Graduate Certificate); urban design (MUD). *Application deadline:* For fall admission, 5/22 for international students; for spring admission, 10/11 for international students; for summer admission, 2/16 for international students. Applications are processed on a rolling basis. *Application fee:* $50. Electronic applications accepted. *Application Contact:* Jane Rohrback, Director of Admissions, 248-204-3160, Fax: 248-204-2228, E-mail: admissions@ltu.edu. *Dean/Professor,* Prof. Karl Daubmann, 248-204-2805, E-mail: archdean@ltu.edu.

College of Arts and Sciences Students: 37 part-time (18 women); includes 4 minority (1 Black or African American, non-Hispanic/Latino; 1 Asian, non-Hispanic/Latino; 2 Hispanic/Latino), 8 international. Average age 33. 301 applicants, 23% accepted, 9 enrolled. *Faculty:* 6 full-time (2 women), 10 part-time/adjunct (5 women). Expenses: Contact institution. *Financial support:* In 2016–17, 9 students received support. Scholarships/grants and tuition reduction available. Financial award application deadline: 4/1; financial award applicants required to submit FAFSA. In 2016, 22 master's, 2 other advanced degrees awarded. *Program availability:* Part-time, evening/weekend. Offers bioinformatics (Graduate Certificate); computer science (MS); instructional design, communication, and presentation (Graduate Certificate); instructional technology (Graduate Certificate); premedical studies (Graduate Certificate); technical and professional communication (MS, Graduate Certificate); writing for the digital age (Graduate Certificate). *Application deadline:* For fall admission, 5/22 for international students; for spring admission, 10/11 for international students; for summer admission, 2/16 for international students. Applications are processed on a rolling basis. *Application fee:* $50. Electronic applications accepted. *Application Contact:* Jane Rohrback, Director of Admissions, 248-204-3160, Fax: 248-204-2228,

E-mail: admissions@ltu.edu. *Dean*, Dr. Hsiao-Ping Moore, 248-204-3500, Fax: 248-204-3518, E-mail: scidean@itu.edu.

College of Engineering Students: 22 full-time (7 women), 588 part-time (81 women); includes 23 minority (11 Black or African American, non-Hispanic/Latino; 4 Asian, non-Hispanic/Latino; 7 Hispanic/Latino; 1 Two or more races, non-Hispanic/Latino), 469 international. Average age 27. 1,186 applicants, 39% accepted, 99 enrolled. *Faculty:* 24 full-time (5 women), 26 part-time/adjunct (2 women). Expenses: Contact institution. *Financial support:* In 2016–17, 25 students received support, including 5 research assistantships with full tuition reimbursements available; unspecified assistantships also available. Financial award application deadline: 4/1; financial award applicants required to submit FAFSA. In 2016, 293 master's, 3 doctorates awarded. *Program availability:* Part-time, evening/weekend. Offers architectural engineering (MS); automotive engineering (MS); biomedical engineering (MS); civil engineering (MA, MS, PhD); construction engineering management (MA); electrical and computer engineering (MS); engineering management (MA); engineering technology (MS); fire engineering (MS); industrial engineering (MS); manufacturing systems (ME); mechanical engineering (MS, DE, PhD); mechatronic systems engineering (MS). *Application deadline:* For fall admission, 5/22 for international students; for spring admission, 10/11 for international students; for summer admission, 2/16 for international students. Applications are processed on a rolling basis. *Application fee:* $50. Electronic applications accepted. *Application Contact:* Jane Rohrback, Director of Admissions, 248-204-3160, Fax: 248-204-2228, E-mail: admissions@ltu.edu. *Dean*, Dr. Nabil Grace, 248-204-2500, Fax: 248-204-2509, E-mail: engrdean@ltu.edu.

College of Management Students: 7 full-time (3 women), 323 part-time (120 women); includes 60 minority (29 Black or African American, non-Hispanic/Latino; 2 American Indian or Alaska Native, non-Hispanic/Latino; 17 Asian, non-Hispanic/Latino; 8 Hispanic/Latino; 4 Two or more races, non-Hispanic/Latino), 118 international. Average age 33. 275 applicants, 56% accepted, 72 enrolled. *Faculty:* 14 full-time (6 women), 10 part-time/adjunct (2 women). Expenses: Contact institution. *Financial support:* In 2016–17, 35 students received support, including 8 research assistantships with partial tuition reimbursements available (averaging $3,250 per year); career-related internships or fieldwork, unspecified assistantships, and corporate tuition incentives also available. Financial award application deadline: 4/1; financial award applicants required to submit FAFSA. In 2016, 167 master's, 12 other advanced degrees awarded. *Program availability:* Part-time, evening/weekend, 100% online. Offers business administration (MBA); information technology (MS); project management (Graduate Certificate). *Application deadline:* For fall admission, 5/22 for international students; for spring admission, 10/11 for international students; for summer admission, 2/16 for international students. Applications are processed on a rolling basis. *Application fee:* $50. Electronic applications accepted. *Application Contact:* Jane Rohrback, Director of Admissions, 248-204-3160, Fax: 248-204-2228, E-mail: admissions@ltu.edu. *Dean*, Dr. Bahman Mirshab, 248-204-3050, E-mail: mgtdean@ltu.edu.

LEBANESE AMERICAN UNIVERSITY, Beirut, Lebanon

General Information Private, coed, comprehensive institution.

GRADUATE UNITS

School of Arts and Sciences Offers computer science (MS); international affairs (MA).

School of Business Offers business (MBA).

School of Pharmacy Offers pharmacy (Pharm D).

LEBANON VALLEY COLLEGE, Annville, PA 17003-1400

General Information Independent-religious, coed, comprehensive institution. *Enrollment:* 1,916 graduate, professional, and undergraduate students; 95 full-time matriculated graduate/professional students (63 women), 109 part-time matriculated graduate/professional students (59 women). *Enrollment by degree level:* 123 master's, 78 doctoral, 3 other advanced degrees. *Graduate faculty:* 17 full-time (7 women), 17 part-time/adjunct (6 women). Tuition and fees vary according to program. *Graduate housing:* Room and/or apartments available on a first-come, first-served basis to single students; on-campus housing not available to married students. Typical cost: $10,980 (including board). Room and board charges vary according to board plan and housing facility selected. Housing application deadline: 3/3. *Student services:* Campus safety program, career counseling, exercise/wellness program, free psychological counseling, international student services, multicultural affairs office, services for students with disabilities, teacher training, writing training. *Library facilities:* Vernon and Doris Bishop Library. *Collection:* Books: 158,734 (physical), 198,403 (digital/electronic); Databases: 129. Weekly public service hours: 101; students can reserve study rooms.

Computer facilities: Computer purchase and lease plans are available. 198 computers available on campus for general student use. A campuswide network can be accessed from student residence rooms and from off campus. Online class registration is available.
Website: http://www.lvc.edu/

General Application Contact: Christine Martin, Enrollment and Operations Specialist, 717-867-6486, E-mail: cmartin@lvc.edu.

GRADUATE UNITS

Program in Athletic Training 65 applicants, 85% accepted, 13 enrolled. *Faculty:* 4 full-time (2 women), 4 part-time/adjunct (2 women). Expenses: Contact institution. *Financial support:* Career-related internships or fieldwork, Federal Work-Study, and scholarships/grants available. Financial award applicants required to submit FAFSA. Offers athletic training (MAT). *Application deadline:* Applications are processed on a rolling basis. Electronic applications accepted. *Application Contact:* Dr. Joseph M. Murphy, Assistant Professor/Director of Athletic Training, 717-867-6845, Fax: 717-867-6849, E-mail: jmurphy@lvc.edu. *Assistant Professor/Director of Athletic Training*, Dr. Joseph M. Murphy, 717-867-6845, Fax: 717-867-6849, E-mail: jmurphy@lvc.edu.

Program in Business Administration Students: 17 full-time (12 women), 79 part-time (42 women); includes 14 minority (2 Black or African American, non-Hispanic/Latino; 3 Asian, non-Hispanic/Latino; 8 Hispanic/Latino; 1 Two or more races, non-Hispanic/Latino), 5 international. Average age 34. 23 applicants, 87% accepted, 18 enrolled. *Faculty:* 8 full-time (1 woman), 8 part-time/adjunct (1 woman). Expenses: Contact institution. *Financial support:* Career-related internships or fieldwork and scholarships/grants available. Financial award applicants required to submit FAFSA. In 2016, 49 master's awarded. *Program availability:* Part-time, evening/weekend, 100% online, blended/hybrid learning. Offers business administration (MBA); healthcare management (MBA); leadership and ethics (MBA). *Application deadline:* Applications are processed on a rolling basis. *Application fee:* $0. *Application Contact:* Christine M. Martin, Enrollment and Operations Specialist, 717-867-6486, Fax: 717-867-6013, E-mail: cmartin@lvc.edu. *Associate Professor/Chair of Business Administration/Director of the MBA Program*, Dr. David Setley, 717-867-6104, Fax: 717-867-6018, E-mail: setley@lvc.edu.

Program in Music Education Students: 18 part-time (11 women); includes 1 minority (Black or African American, non-Hispanic/Latino). Average age 34. 4 applicants, 100% accepted, 4 enrolled. *Faculty:* 10 part-time/adjunct (2 women). Expenses: Contact institution. *Financial support:* Career-related internships or fieldwork and scholarships/grants available. Financial award application deadline: 3/1; financial award applicants required to submit FAFSA. In 2016, 16 master's awarded. *Program availability:* Part-time-only, evening/weekend. Offers music education (MME). *Application deadline:* Applications are processed on a rolling basis. *Application fee:* $0. Electronic applications accepted. *Application Contact:* Cherie VanZant, Graduate and Community Programs Administrator, 717-867-6383, E-mail: vanzant@lvc.edu. *Graduate and Community Programs Administrator*, Cherie Van Zant, 717-867-6383, E-mail: vanzant@lvc.edu.

Program in Physical Therapy Students: 76 full-time (50 women), 1 part-time (0 women); includes 5 minority (1 Black or African American, non-Hispanic/Latino; 2 Asian, non-Hispanic/Latino; 2 Two or more races, non-Hispanic/Latino). Average age 23. 108 applicants, 90% accepted, 52 enrolled. *Faculty:* 8 full-time (4 women), 3 part-time/adjunct (2 women). Expenses: Contact institution. *Financial support:* In 2016–17, 100 students received support. Scholarships/grants available. Financial award application deadline: 3/1; financial award applicants required to submit FAFSA. In 2016, 40 doctorates awarded. Offers physical therapy (DPT). *Application deadline:* For fall admission, 2/1 for domestic and international students. *Application fee:* $50. Electronic applications accepted. *Application Contact:* EJ Smith, Assistant Director of Admission, 717-867-6183, E-mail: ejsmith@lvc.edu. *Co-Chair/Professor of Physical Therapy*, Dr. Katie Oriel, 717-867-6852, E-mail: oriel@lvc.edu.

Program in Science Education Students: 1 full-time (0 women), 14 part-time (9 women). Average age 35. 10 applicants, 70% accepted, 7 enrolled. *Faculty:* 11 part-time/adjunct (6 women). Expenses: Contact institution. *Financial support:* Scholarships/grants available. Financial award application deadline: 3/1; financial award applicants required to submit FAFSA. In 2016, 6 master's awarded. *Program availability:* Part-time-only, evening/weekend. Offers Integrative STEM Education (Certificate); STEM education (MSE). *Application deadline:* Applications are processed on a rolling basis. *Application fee:* $0. Electronic applications accepted. *Director of MSE and STEM-based programs*, Carrie Coryer, 717-867-6190, Fax: 717-867-6018, E-mail: coryer@lvc.edu.

LEE UNIVERSITY, Cleveland, TN 37320-3450

General Information Independent-religious, coed, comprehensive institution. *Enrollment:* 5,302 graduate, professional, and undergraduate students; 215 full-time matriculated graduate/professional students (128 women), 233 part-time matriculated graduate/professional students (111 women). *Enrollment by degree level:* 443 master's, 5 other advanced degrees. *Graduate faculty:* 62 full-time (18 women), 19 part-time/adjunct (6 women). *Tuition:* Full-time $11,367; part-time $632 per credit hour. *Required fees:* $35 per term. One-time fee: $25. Tuition and fees vary according to program. *Graduate housing:* Rooms and/or apartments available on a first-come, first-served basis to single and married students. Typical cost: $4330 per year ($7880 including board) for single students; $7200 per year ($10,890 including board) for married students. Room and board charges vary according to board plan, campus/location and housing facility selected. Housing application deadline: 9/1. *Student services:* Campus employment opportunities, campus safety program, career counseling, exercise/wellness program, free psychological counseling, international student services, services for students with disabilities, teacher training, writing training. *Library facilities:* William G. Squires Library plus 2 others. *Collection:* Books: 158,647 (physical), 231,120 (digital/electronic); Serial titles: 242 (physical), 23,216 (digital/electronic); Databases: 137. Weekly public service hours: 91; students can reserve study rooms.

Computer facilities: 350 computers available on campus for general student use. A campuswide network can be accessed from student residence rooms and from off campus. Online class registration is available.
Website: http://www.leeuniversity.edu/

General Application Contact: Jeffery McGirt, Director of Graduate Enrollment, 423-614-8691, Fax: 423-614-8317, E-mail: jmcgirt@leeuniversity.edu.

GRADUATE UNITS

Graduate Studies in Counseling Students: 86 full-time (65 women), 27 part-time (18 women); includes 46 minority (9 Black or African American, non-Hispanic/Latino; 1 American Indian or Alaska Native, non-Hispanic/Latino; 1 Asian, non-Hispanic/Latino; 33 Hispanic/Latino; 2 Two or more races, non-Hispanic/Latino). Average age 31. 34 applicants, 65% accepted, 18 enrolled. *Faculty:* 8 full-time (3 women), 3 part-time/adjunct (0 women). Expenses: Contact institution. *Financial support:* In 2016–17, 25 students received support. Career-related internships or fieldwork, Federal Work-Study, institutionally sponsored loans, scholarships/grants, and unspecified assistantships available. Financial award application deadline: 3/1; financial award applicants required to submit FAFSA. In 2016, 31 master's awarded. *Program availability:* Part-time, 100% online. Offers holistic child development (MS); marriage and family studies (MS); marriage and family therapy (MS); school counseling (MS). *Application deadline:* For fall admission, 4/1 priority date for domestic and international students; for spring admission, 11/1 priority date for domestic and international students. Applications are processed on a rolling basis. *Application fee:* $25. Electronic applications accepted. *Director*, Dr. Trevor Milliron, 423-614-8126, Fax: 423-614-8124, E-mail: tmilliron@leeuniversity.edu.

MBA Program Students: 12 full-time (4 women), 55 part-time (26 women); includes 9 minority (3 Black or African American, non-Hispanic/Latino; 2 American Indian or Alaska Native, non-Hispanic/Latino; 1 Asian, non-Hispanic/Latino; 3 Hispanic/Latino), 9 international. Average age 30. 41 applicants, 71% accepted, 26 enrolled. *Faculty:* 7 full-time (2 women). Expenses: Contact institution. *Financial support:* In 2016–17, 26 students received support. Scholarships/grants available. Financial award application deadline: 3/1; financial award applicants required to submit FAFSA. In 2016, 26 master's awarded. *Program availability:* Part-time, evening/weekend, 100% online. Offers business administration (MBA). *Application deadline:* For fall admission, 4/1 priority date for domestic and international students; for spring admission, 10/1 priority date for domestic and international students. Applications are processed on a rolling basis. *Application fee:* $25. Electronic applications accepted. *Director*, Dr. Shane Griffith, 423-614-8694, E-mail: mba@leeuniversity.edu.

Program in Education Students: 35 full-time (27 women), 50 part-time (32 women); includes 12 minority (5 Black or African American, non-Hispanic/Latino; 5 Hispanic/Latino; 2 Two or more races, non-Hispanic/Latino), 4 international. Average age 30. 43 applicants, 79% accepted, 28 enrolled. *Faculty:* 13 full-time (6 women), 9 part-time/adjunct (4 women). Expenses: Contact institution. *Financial support:* In 2016–17, 42 students received support. Career-related internships or fieldwork, Federal Work-Study, institutionally sponsored loans, scholarships/grants, and unspecified assistantships available. Financial award application deadline: 3/1; financial award applicants required to submit FAFSA. In 2016, 42 master's, 6 other advanced degrees awarded. *Program availability:* Part-time. Offers art (MAT); curriculum and instruction (M Ed, Ed S); early childhood (MAT); educational leadership (M Ed, Ed S); elementary education (MAT); English and math (MAT); English and science (MAT); English and social studies (MAT); higher education administration (MS); history (MAT); history and economics (MAT); math and science (MAT); math and social studies (MAT); middle grades (MAT); science and social studies (MASW); secondary education (MAT); Spanish (MAT); special education (M Ed, MAT); TESOL (MAT). *Application deadline:* For fall admission, 6/1 priority date for domestic and international students; for spring admission, 11/1 priority date for domestic and international students; for summer admission, 4/1 priority date for domestic and international students. Applications are processed on a rolling basis. *Application fee:* $25. Electronic applications accepted. *Application Contact:* Crystal Keeter, Graduate Education Secretary, 423-614-8544, E-mail: ckeeter@leeuniversity.edu. *Director,* Dr. William Kamm, 423-614-8544, E-mail: wkamm@leeuniversity.edu.

Program in Music Students: 25 full-time (13 women), 9 part-time (7 women); includes 5 minority (3 Black or African American, non-Hispanic/Latino; 2 Asian, non-Hispanic/Latino), 10 international. Average age 28. 21 applicants, 67% accepted, 8 enrolled. *Faculty:* 21 full-time (5 women), 5 part-time/adjunct (2 women). Expenses: Contact institution. *Financial support:* In 2016–17, 30 students received support. Career-related internships or fieldwork, Federal Work-Study, institutionally sponsored loans, scholarships/grants, and unspecified assistantships available. Financial award application deadline: 3/1; financial award applicants required to submit FAFSA. In 2016, 17 master's awarded. *Program availability:* Part-time. Offers conducting (MM); music education (MM); music performance (MM); religious studies (MCM); sacred music (MCM). *Application deadline:* For fall admission, 4/1 priority date for domestic and international students; for spring admission, 10/1 priority date for domestic and international students. Applications are processed on a rolling basis. *Application fee:* $25. Electronic applications accepted. *Director,* Dr. Brad J. Moffett, 423-614-8240, Fax: 423-614-8245, E-mail: gradmusic@leeuniversity.edu.

Programs in Religion Students: 57 full-time (19 women), 92 part-time (28 women); includes 72 minority (16 Black or African American, non-Hispanic/Latino; 2 Asian, non-Hispanic/Latino; 53 Hispanic/Latino; 1 Two or more races, non-Hispanic/Latino), 4 international. Average age 37. 19 applicants, 79% accepted, 12 enrolled. *Faculty:* 13 full-time (2 women), 2 part-time/adjunct (0 women). Expenses: Contact institution. *Financial support:* In 2016–17, 25 students received support, including 7 teaching assistantships (averaging $2,031 per year); career-related internships or fieldwork, Federal Work-Study, institutionally sponsored loans, scholarships/grants, and unspecified assistantships also available. Financial award application deadline: 3/1; financial award applicants required to submit FAFSA. In 2016, 9 master's awarded. *Program availability:* Part-time, 100% online. Offers biblical studies (MA); ministry studies (MA); ministry studies/leadership (MA); ministry studies/worship (MA); ministry studies/youth and family (MA); theological studies (MA). *Application deadline:* For fall admission, 4/1 priority date for domestic and international students; for spring admission, 10/1 priority date for domestic and international students. Applications are processed on a rolling basis. *Application fee:* $25. Electronic applications accepted. *Director,* Dr. Lisa Long, 423-303-5100, E-mail: llong@leeuniversity.edu.

LEHIGH UNIVERSITY, Bethlehem, PA 18015-3094

General Information Independent, coed, university. CGS member. *Enrollment:* 7,059 graduate, professional, and undergraduate students; 1,225 full-time matriculated graduate/professional students (517 women), 671 part-time matriculated graduate/professional students (335 women). *Enrollment by degree level:* 1,170 master's, 713 doctoral, 13 other advanced degrees. *Graduate faculty:* 371 full-time (107 women), 48 part-time/adjunct (26 women). Tuition and fees vary according to program. *Graduate housing:* Rooms and/or apartments available on a first-come, first-served basis to single and married students. *Student services:* Campus employment opportunities, campus safety program, career counseling, child daycare facilities, exercise/wellness program, free psychological counseling, international student services, low-cost health insurance, multicultural affairs office, services for students with disabilities, teacher training, writing training. *Library facilities:* E. W. Fairchild-Martindale Library plus 1 other. *Collection:* Books: 887,151 (physical), 402,005 (digital/electronic); Serial titles: 2,010 (physical), 61,305 (digital/electronic); Databases: 189. Weekly public service hours: 80; students can reserve study rooms.

Computer facilities: Computer purchase and lease plans are available. 597 computers available on campus for general student use. A campuswide network can be accessed from student residence rooms and from off campus. Online class registration is available.
Website: http://www.lehigh.edu/

GRADUATE UNITS

College of Arts and Sciences Students: 275 full-time (132 women), 77 part-time (41 women); includes 36 minority (14 Black or African American, non-Hispanic/Latino; 8 Asian, non-Hispanic/Latino; 10 Hispanic/Latino; 4 Two or more races, non-Hispanic/Latino), 76 international. Average age 28. 544 applicants, 37% accepted, 85 enrolled. *Faculty:* 165 full-time (61 women), 9 part-time/adjunct (3 women). Expenses: Contact institution. *Financial support:* In 2016–17, 26 fellowships with full tuition reimbursements (averaging $25,000 per year) were awarded; scholarships/grants, tuition waivers (full and partial), and unspecified assistantships also available. Financial award application deadline: 1/1. In 2016, 93 master's, 32 doctorates awarded. *Program availability:* Part-time, online learning. Offers American studies (MA); applied mathematics (MS, PhD); arts and sciences (MA, MS, PhD, Graduate Certificate); Atlantic world (PhD); biochemistry (PhD); British history (PhD); cell and molecular biology (PhD); chemistry (MS, PhD); documentary film (Graduate Certificate); earth and environmental sciences (MS, PhD); English (MA, PhD); environmental policy and law (Graduate Certificate); environmental policy design (MA); history (MA); industrial and modern America (PhD); integrative biology (PhD); mathematics (MS, PhD); molecular biology (MS); photonics (MS); physics (MS, PhD); politics and policy (MA); psychology (MS, PhD); public history (MA); sociology (MA); statistics (MS); sustainable development (Graduate Certificate); urban environmental policy (Graduate Certificate). *Application deadline:* For fall admission, 7/1 for domestic students, 7/15 for international students; for spring admission, 12/1 for domestic and international students. *Application fee:* $75. Electronic applications accepted. *Application Contact:* Gary Burgess, Administrative Clerk, 610-758-4281, Fax: 610-758-6232, E-mail: glb215@lehigh.edu. *Associate Dean of Graduate Studies,* Dr. Dominic Packer, 610-758-4282, Fax: 610-758-6232, E-mail: dlp208@lehigh.edu.

College of Business and Economics Students: 184 full-time (102 women), 164 part-time (43 women); includes 37 minority (6 Black or African American, non-Hispanic/Latino; 18 Asian, non-Hispanic/Latino; 11 Hispanic/Latino; 2 Two or more races, non-Hispanic/Latino), 143 international. Average age 29. 706 applicants, 50%

accepted, 111 enrolled. *Faculty:* 29 full-time (3 women), 7 part-time/adjunct (4 women). Expenses: Contact institution. *Financial support:* In 2016–17, 93 students received support, including 10 fellowships with partial tuition reimbursements available, 1 research assistantship with full tuition reimbursement available (averaging $18,000 per year), 15 teaching assistantships with full tuition reimbursements available (averaging $18,000 per year); career-related internships or fieldwork, scholarships/grants, health care benefits, and unspecified assistantships also available. Support available to part-time students. Financial award application deadline: 1/15. In 2016, 177 master's, 5 doctorates awarded. *Program availability:* Part-time, evening/weekend, online learning. Offers accounting and information analysis (MS); analytical finance (MS); business administration (MBA); business and economics (MBA, MS, PhD); economics (MS, PhD); project management (MBA). *Application deadline:* For fall admission, 7/15 for domestic students, 5/1 for international students; for spring admission, 12/1 for domestic and international students. *Application fee:* $75. Electronic applications accepted. *Application Contact:* Michael Tarantino, Director of Recruitment and Admissions, 610-758-3418, Fax: 610-758-5283, E-mail: mgt215@lehigh.edu. *Dean,* Georgette Chapman-Phillips, 610-758-6725, Fax: 610-758-4499, E-mail: gcp214@lehigh.edu.

College of Education Students: 159 full-time (137 women), 291 part-time (212 women); includes 50 minority (13 Black or African American, non-Hispanic/Latino; 12 Asian, non-Hispanic/Latino; 22 Hispanic/Latino; 1 Native Hawaiian or other Pacific Islander, non-Hispanic/Latino; 2 Two or more races, non-Hispanic/Latino), 43 international. Average age 32. 496 applicants, 55% accepted, 74 enrolled. *Faculty:* 36 full-time (22 women), 23 part-time/adjunct (16 women). Expenses: Contact institution. *Financial support:* In 2016–17, 162 students received support, including 3 fellowships with tuition reimbursements available (averaging $21,556 per year), 47 research assistantships with tuition reimbursements available (averaging $12,882 per year); teaching assistantships, career-related internships or fieldwork, institutionally sponsored loans, scholarships/grants, tuition waivers (partial), and unspecified assistantships also available. Financial award application deadline: 3/1. In 2016, 138 master's, 18 doctorates, 5 other advanced degrees awarded. *Program availability:* Part-time, evening/weekend, 100% online, blended/hybrid learning. Offers comparative and international education (MA, PhD); counseling and human services (M Ed); counseling psychology (PhD); education (M Ed, MA, MS, Ed D, PhD, Certificate, Ed S, Graduate Certificate); educational leadership (M Ed, Ed D, Certificate); elementary education (M Ed); globalization and educational change (M Ed); instructional technology (MS); international counseling (M Ed, Certificate); international development in education (Certificate); school counseling (M Ed); school psychology (PhD, Ed S); special education (M Ed, PhD); teaching, learning and technology (PhD); technology use in the schools (Graduate Certificate). *Application deadline:* For fall admission, 1/1 for domestic and international students; for spring admission, 11/1 for domestic and international students; for summer admission, 5/1 for domestic and international students. *Application fee:* $65. Electronic applications accepted. *Application Contact:* Donna M. Johnson, Manager of Admissions and Recruitment, 610-758-3231, Fax: 610-758-6223, E-mail: dmj4@lehigh.edu. *Dean,* Dr. Gary M. Sasso, 610-758-3221, Fax: 610-758-6223, E-mail: gary.sasso@lehigh.edu.

P.C. Rossin College of Engineering and Applied Science Students: 607 full-time (146 women), 139 part-time (39 women); includes 65 minority (9 Black or African American, non-Hispanic/Latino; 28 Asian, non-Hispanic/Latino; 24 Hispanic/Latino; 2 Native Hawaiian or other Pacific Islander, non-Hispanic/Latino; 2 Two or more races, non-Hispanic/Latino), 448 international. Average age 26. 1,925 applicants, 33% accepted, 201 enrolled. *Faculty:* 141 full-time (21 women), 13 part-time/adjunct (3 women). Expenses: Contact institution. *Financial support:* In 2016–17, 279 students received support, including 26 fellowships with tuition reimbursements available (averaging $21,105 per year), 185 research assistantships with tuition reimbursements available (averaging $28,140 per year), 68 teaching assistantships with tuition reimbursements available (averaging $21,530 per year); scholarships/grants, tuition waivers (full and partial), and unspecified assistantships also available. Financial award application deadline: 1/15. In 2016, 224 master's, 66 doctorates awarded. *Program availability:* Part-time, 100% online, blended/hybrid learning. Offers analytical finance (MS); bioengineering (MS, PhD); biological chemical engineering (M Eng); chemical energy engineering (M Eng); chemical engineering (M Eng, MS, PhD); civil and environmental engineering (M Eng, MS, PhD); computational and engineering mechanics (MS, PhD); computer engineering (M Eng, MS, PhD); computer science (M Eng, MS, PhD); electrical engineering (MS, PhD); energy systems engineering (M Eng); engineering and applied science (M Eng, MS, PhD); healthcare systems engineering (M Eng, Certificate); industrial and systems engineering (M Eng, MS, PhD); management science and engineering (M Eng, MS); manufacturing systems engineering (MS); materials science and engineering (M Eng, MS, PhD); mechanical engineering (M Eng, MS, PhD); photonics (MS); polymer science/engineering (M Eng, MS, PhD); technical entrepreneurship (M Eng); wireless network engineering (MS). *Application deadline:* For fall admission, 7/15 for domestic and international students; for spring admission, 12/1 for domestic and international students. *Application fee:* $75. Electronic applications accepted. *Application Contact:* Brianne Lisk, Manager of Graduate Programs, 610-758-6310, Fax: 610-758-5623, E-mail: brie.lisk@lehigh.edu. *Dean,* Dr. Stephen P. DeWeerth, 610-758-5308, Fax: 610-758-5623, E-mail: steve.deweerth@lehigh.edu.

Center for Polymer Science and Engineering Students: 5 full-time (4 women), 22 part-time (5 women); includes 8 minority (1 Black or African American, non-Hispanic/Latino; 6 Asian, non-Hispanic/Latino; 1 Native Hawaiian or other Pacific Islander, non-Hispanic/Latino), 4 international. Average age 31. 48 applicants, 21% accepted, 6 enrolled. *Faculty:* 24 full-time (4 women). Expenses: Contact institution. *Financial support:* In 2016–17, 1 student received support, including 1 research assistantship (averaging $27,106 per year); teaching assistantships, scholarships/grants, and health care benefits also available. Financial award application deadline: 1/15. In 2016, 4 master's awarded. *Program availability:* Part-time, evening/weekend, 100% online, blended/hybrid learning. Offers polymer science and engineering (M Eng, MS, PhD). *Application deadline:* For fall admission, 7/15 for domestic students, 1/15 for international students; for spring admission, 12/1 for domestic and international students. Applications are processed on a rolling basis. *Application fee:* $75. Electronic applications accepted. *Application Contact:* James E. Roberts, Chair, Polymer Education Committee, 610-758-4841, Fax: 610-758-6536, E-mail: jer1@lehigh.edu. *Director,* Dr. Raymond A. Pearson, 610-758-3857, Fax: 610-758-3526, E-mail: rp02@lehigh.edu.

LEHMAN COLLEGE OF THE CITY UNIVERSITY OF NEW YORK, Bronx, NY 10468-1589

General Information State and locally supported, coed, comprehensive institution. *Graduate housing:* On-campus housing not available. *Research affiliation:* New York Botanical Gardens, Montefiore Hospital and Medical Center.

Lehman College of the City University of New York

GRADUATE UNITS

School of Arts and Humanities *Program availability:* Part-time, evening/weekend. Offers art (MA, MFA); arts and humanities (MA, MAT, MFA); English (MA); history (MA); music (MAT); Spanish (MA).

School of Education *Program availability:* Part-time, evening/weekend. Offers bilingual special education (MS Ed); business education (MS Ed); early childhood education (MS Ed); early special education (MS Ed); education (MA, MS Ed); elementary education (MS Ed); emotional handicaps (MS Ed); English education (MS Ed); guidance and counseling (MS Ed); learning disabilities (MS Ed); mathematics 7–12 (MS Ed); mental retardation (MS Ed); music education (MS Ed); reading teacher (MS Ed); science education (MS Ed); social studies 7–12 (MA); teachers of special education (MS Ed); teaching English to speakers of other languages (MS Ed).

School of Health Sciences, Human Services and Nursing Offers adult health nursing (MS); clinical nutrition (MS); community nutrition (MS); dietetic internship (MS); health education and promotion (MA); health N–12 teacher (MS Ed); health sciences, human services and nursing (MA, MS, MS Ed, MSN, MSW); nursing of older adults (MS); nutrition (MS); parent-child nursing (MS); pediatric nurse practitioner (MS); recreation (MA, MS Ed); recreation education (MA, MS Ed); speech-language pathology (MA).

School of Natural and Social Sciences *Program availability:* Part-time, evening/weekend. Offers accounting (MS); biology (MA); businesscomputer science (MS); mathematics (MA); natural and social sciences (MA, MS, MS Ed, PhD); plant sciences (PhD).

LE MOYNE COLLEGE, Syracuse, NY 13214

General Information Independent-religious, coed, comprehensive institution. *Enrollment:* 3,549 graduate, professional, and undergraduate students; 345 full-time matriculated graduate/professional students (242 women), 270 part-time matriculated graduate/professional students (189 women). *Enrollment by degree level:* 563 master's, 52 other advanced degrees. *Graduate faculty:* 33 full-time (20 women), 53 part-time/adjunct (31 women). *Tuition:* Full-time $14,346; part-time $797 per credit hour. Tuition and fees vary according to program. *Graduate housing:* On-campus housing not available. *Student services:* Campus employment opportunities, campus safety program, career counseling, exercise/wellness program, free psychological counseling, international student services, low-cost health insurance, multicultural affairs office, services for students with disabilities, writing tutoring. *Library facilities:* Noreen Reale Falcone Library. *Collection:* Books: 259,932 (physical), 31,050 (digital/electronic); Serial titles: 1,991 (physical), 1,143 (digital/electronic); Databases: 260. Weekly public service hours: 109; study areas open 24 hours, 5–7 days a week; students can reserve study rooms. *Research affiliation:* Blue Highway, Inc. (medical technology).

Computer facilities: 330 computers available on campus for general student use. A campuswide network can be accessed from student residence rooms and from off campus. Online class registration, ECHO (campus-wide portal), some virtual access from off campus are available.
Website: http://www.lemoyne.edu/

General Application Contact: Kristen P. Richards, Senior Director of Enrollment Management, 315-445-5444, Fax: 315-445-6092, E-mail: trapaskp@lemoyne.edu.

GRADUATE UNITS

Department of Education Students: 66 full-time (40 women), 155 part-time (117 women); includes 13 minority (4 Black or African American, non-Hispanic/Latino; 2 American Indian or Alaska Native, non-Hispanic/Latino; 2 Asian, non-Hispanic/Latino; 5 Hispanic/Latino), 3 international. Average age 30. 74 applicants, 99% accepted, 66 enrolled. *Faculty:* 8 full-time (5 women), 20 part-time/adjunct (12 women). Expenses: Contact institution. *Financial support:* In 2016–17, 21 students received support. Career-related internships or fieldwork, scholarships/grants, and health care benefits available. Support available to part-time students. Financial award applicants required to submit FAFSA. In 2016, 81 master's, 53 CASs awarded. *Program availability:* Part-time, evening/weekend. Offers adolescent education (MS Ed, MST); adolescent education/special education (MS Ed, MST); adolescent English (MST); adolescent English/special education (MST); adolescent foreign language (MST); adolescent history (MST); childhood education (MS Ed); childhood education/special education (MS Ed); elementary education (MS Ed); general education (MS Ed); inclusive childhood education (MST); literacy education (MS Ed); school building leader (MS Ed); school building leadership (CAS); school district business leader (MS Ed, CAS); school district leader (MS Ed); school district leadership (CAS); secondary education (MS Ed); special education (MS Ed); teaching English to speakers of other languages (MS Ed); urban studies (MS Ed). *Application deadline:* For fall admission, 4/1 priority date for domestic and international students; for spring admission, 10/1 priority date for domestic and international students; for summer admission, 3/1 priority date for domestic and international students. Applications are processed on a rolling basis. *Application fee:* $50. Electronic applications accepted. *Application Contact:* Kristen P. Richards, Senior Director of Enrollment Management, 315-445-5444, Fax: 315-445-6092, E-mail: trapaskp@lemoyne.edu. *Chair, Department of Education*, Dr. Stephen C. Fleury, 315-445-4376, Fax: 315-445-4744, E-mail: fleurysc@lemoyne.edu.

Department of Nursing Students: 21 full-time (16 women), 51 part-time (44 women); includes 9 minority (5 Black or African American, non-Hispanic/Latino; 2 Asian, non-Hispanic/Latino; 1 Hispanic/Latino; 1 Two or more races, non-Hispanic/Latino), 1 international. Average age 34. 51 applicants, 92% accepted, 43 enrolled. *Faculty:* 6 full-time (all women), 4 part-time/adjunct (3 women). Expenses: Contact institution. *Financial support:* In 2016–17, 24 students received support. Career-related internships or fieldwork, scholarships/grants, health care benefits, and unspecified assistantships available. Support available to part-time students. Financial award applicants required to submit FAFSA. In 2016, 4 master's awarded. *Program availability:* Part-time, evening/weekend. Offers family nurse practitioner (MS, CAS); informatics (MS, CAS); nursing administration (MS, CAS); nursing education (MS, CAS). *Application deadline:* For fall admission, 8/1 priority date for domestic students, 8/1 for international students; for spring admission, 12/15 priority date for domestic students, 12/15 for international students; for summer admission, 5/1 priority date for domestic students, 5/1 for international students. Applications are processed on a rolling basis. *Application fee:* $50. Electronic applications accepted. *Application Contact:* Kristen P. Richards, Senior Director of Enrollment Management, 315-445-5444, Fax: 315-445-6092, E-mail: trapaskp@lemoyne.edu. *Professor/Chair of Nursing*, Dr. Margaret M. Wells, 315-445-5435, Fax: 315-445-6024, E-mail: wellsmm@lemoyne.edu.

Department of Occupational Therapy Students: 67 full-time (60 women); includes 6 minority (2 Black or African American, non-Hispanic/Latino; 2 Asian, non-Hispanic/Latino; 2 Hispanic/Latino), 1 international. Average age 25. 80 applicants, 79% accepted, 42 enrolled. *Faculty:* 3 full-time (all women), 6 part-time/adjunct (3 women). Expenses: Contact institution. *Financial support:* In 2016–17, 2 students received support. Career-related internships or fieldwork, scholarships/grants, and health care benefits available. Financial award applicants required to submit FAFSA. Offers occupational therapy (MS). *Application deadline:* For fall admission, 3/30 for domestic and international students. Applications are processed on a rolling basis. *Application fee:* $125. Electronic applications accepted. *Application Contact:* Kristen P. Richards, Senior Director of Enrollment Management, 315-445-5444, Fax: 315-445-6092, E-mail: trapaskp@lemoyne.edu. *Chair*, Dr. Ivelisse Lazzarini, 315-445-5432, E-mail: occupationaltherapy@lemoyne.edu.

Department of Physician Assistant Studies Students: 139 full-time (101 women); includes 25 minority (5 Black or African American, non-Hispanic/Latino; 12 Asian, non-Hispanic/Latino; 7 Hispanic/Latino; 1 Two or more races, non-Hispanic/Latino). Average age 26. 1,269 applicants, 8% accepted, 77 enrolled. *Faculty:* 6 full-time (4 women), 15 part-time/adjunct (9 women). Expenses: Contact institution. *Financial support:* In 2016–17, 54 students received support. Career-related internships or fieldwork, scholarships/grants, and health care benefits available. Financial award applicants required to submit FAFSA. In 2016, 54 master's awarded. Offers physician assistant studies (MS). *Application deadline:* For fall admission, 10/1 priority date for domestic and international students. *Application fee:* $177. Electronic applications accepted. *Application Contact:* Kristen P. Richards, Senior Director of Enrollment Management, 315-445-5444, Fax: 315-445-6092, E-mail: trapaskp@lemoyne.edu. *Clinical Assistant Professor/Director of Department of Physician Assistant Studies*, Mary E. Springston, 315-445-4163, Fax: 315-445-4602, E-mail: springme@lemoyne.edu.

Madden School of Business Students: 42 full-time (19 women), 58 part-time (23 women); includes 7 minority (3 Black or African American, non-Hispanic/Latino; 1 Asian, non-Hispanic/Latino; 3 Hispanic/Latino), 1 international. Average age 28. 82 applicants, 88% accepted, 67 enrolled. *Faculty:* 9 full-time (2 women), 6 part-time/adjunct (2 women). Expenses: Contact institution. *Financial support:* In 2016–17, 27 students received support. Career-related internships or fieldwork, scholarships/grants, health care benefits, and unspecified assistantships available. Support available to part-time students. Financial award applicants required to submit FAFSA. In 2016, 61 master's awarded. *Program availability:* Part-time, evening/weekend. Offers business administration (MBA); information systems (MS). *Application deadline:* For fall admission, 7/1 priority date for domestic and international students; for spring admission, 11/1 priority date for domestic and international students; for summer admission, 4/1 priority date for domestic and international students. Applications are processed on a rolling basis. *Application fee:* $0. Electronic applications accepted. *Application Contact:* Kristen P. Richards, Senior Director of Enrollment Management, 315-445-5444, Fax: 315-445-6092, E-mail: trapaskp@lemoyne.edu. *Dean of Madden School of Business*, James Joseph, 315-445-4280, Fax: 315-445-4787, E-mail: josepjae@lemoyne.edu.

Program in Arts Administration Students: 10 full-time (6 women), 6 part-time (5 women); includes 3 minority (1 Black or African American, non-Hispanic/Latino; 1 American Indian or Alaska Native, non-Hispanic/Latino; 1 Hispanic/Latino). Average age 29. 16 applicants, 94% accepted, 14 enrolled. *Faculty:* 1 full-time (0 women), 2 part-time/adjunct (both women). Expenses: Contact institution. *Financial support:* In 2016–17, 3 students received support. Career-related internships or fieldwork, scholarships/grants, and health care benefits available. Financial award applicants required to submit FAFSA. *Program availability:* Part-time, evening/weekend. Offers arts administration (MS). *Application deadline:* For fall admission, 7/1 priority date for domestic and international students; for spring admission, 11/1 priority date for domestic and international students; for summer admission, 4/1 priority date for domestic and international students. Applications are processed on a rolling basis. *Application fee:* $50. Electronic applications accepted. *Application Contact:* Kristen P. Richards, Senior Director of Enrollment Management, 315-445-5444, Fax: 315-445-6092, E-mail: trapaskp@lemoyne.edu. *Assistant Professor and Director of Arts Administration*, Travis Newton, 315-445-4201, E-mail: newtontm@lemoyne.edu.

LENOIR-RHYNE UNIVERSITY, Hickory, NC 28601

General Information Independent-religious, coed, comprehensive institution. *Enrollment:* 2,523 graduate, professional, and undergraduate students; 370 full-time matriculated graduate/professional students (257 women), 399 part-time matriculated graduate/professional students (294 women). *Enrollment by degree level:* 769 master's. *Graduate faculty:* 66 full-time (39 women), 41 part-time/adjunct (20 women). *Tuition:* Full-time $9900; part-time $550 per credit hour. Tuition and fees vary according to program. *Graduate housing:* Room and/or apartments available on a first-come, first-served basis to single students; on-campus housing not available to married students. Housing application deadline: 5/1. *Student services:* Campus employment opportunities, campus safety program, career counseling, exercise/wellness program, free psychological counseling, international student services, multicultural affairs office, services for students with disabilities, teacher training, writing tutoring. *Library facilities:* Carl Rudisill Library. *Collection:* Books: 124,059 (physical), 487,733 (digital/electronic); Serial titles: 56 (physical), 29,949 (digital/electronic); Databases: 134. Weekly public service hours: 89.

Computer facilities: Computer purchase and lease plans are available. 150 computers available on campus for general student use. A campuswide network can be accessed from student residence rooms and from off campus. Online class registration is available.
Website: http://www.lr.edu/

General Application Contact: Mary Ann Gosnell, Director of Graduate Recruiting, 828-328-7111, Fax: 828-328-7378, E-mail: admission@lr.edu.

GRADUATE UNITS

Graduate Programs *Program availability:* Part-time, evening/weekend, online learning. Electronic applications accepted.

Charles M. Snipes School of Business *Program availability:* Part-time, evening/weekend, online learning. Offers accounting (MBA); business analytics and information technology (MBA); entrepreneurship (MBA); global business (MBA); healthcare administration (MBA); innovation and change management (MBA); leadership development (MBA). Electronic applications accepted.

Lutheran Theological Southern Seminary *Program availability:* Part-time. Offers theology (M Div, MACM, MAR, STM).

School of Arts and Letters Offers arts and letters (MA); writing (MA). Electronic applications accepted.

School of Counseling and Human Services *Program availability:* Part-time, evening/weekend. Offers clinical mental health counseling (MA); counseling and human services (MA); school counseling (MA). Electronic applications accepted.

School of Education *Program availability:* Part-time, evening/weekend, online learning. Offers community and nonprofit leadership (MA); community college administration (MA); education (MA, MAT, MS); general management (MA); higher education leadership (MA); management (MA); online teaching and instructional design (MS); second language community services (MA); secondary education (MAT); substance abuse (MA); vocational strategies (MA). Electronic applications accepted.

School of Health, Exercise and Sport Science *Program availability:* Part-time. Offers athletic training (MS); public health (MPH).

School of Natural Sciences *Program availability:* Part-time, evening/weekend, online learning. Offers natural sciences (MS); sustainability studies (MS). Electronic applications accepted.

School of Nursing *Program availability:* Online only. Offers nursing (MSN); nursing administration (MSN); nursing education (MSN). Electronic applications accepted.

School of Occupational Therapy Offers occupational therapy (MS).

School of Physician Assistant Studies Offers physician assistant studies (MS).

LESLEY UNIVERSITY, Cambridge, MA 02138-2790

General Information Independent, coed, primarily women, comprehensive institution. *Graduate housing:* Room and/or apartments available to single students; on-campus housing not available to married students. *Research affiliation:* TERC (education research and development).

GRADUATE UNITS

College of Art and Design *Program availability:* Part-time. Offers photography (MFA); visual arts (MFA). Electronic applications accepted.

Graduate School of Arts and Social Sciences *Program availability:* Part-time, online learning. Offers clinical mental health counseling (MA); counseling psychology (MA, CAGS); creative writing (MFA); expressive therapies (MA, PhD, CAGS); independent studies (CAGS); independent study (MA); intercultural relations (MA, CAGS); interdisciplinary studies (MA); urban environmental leadership (MA). Electronic applications accepted.

Graduate School of Education *Program availability:* Part-time, evening/weekend, online learning. Offers arts, community, and education (M Ed); autism studies (Certificate); curriculum and instruction (M Ed, CAGS); early childhood education (M Ed); ecological teaching and learning (MS); educational studies (PhD); elementary education (M Ed); emergent technologies for educators (Certificate); ESLArts: language learning through the arts (M Ed); high school education (M Ed); individually designed (M Ed); integrated teaching through the arts (M Ed); literacy for K–8 classroom teachers (M Ed); mathematics education (M Ed); middle school education (M Ed); moderate disabilities (M Ed); online learning (Certificate); reading (CAGS); science in education (M Ed); severe disabilities (M Ed); special needs (CAGS); specialist teacher of reading (M Ed); teacher of visual art (M Ed); technology in education (M Ed, CAGS). Electronic applications accepted.

LES ROCHES INTERNATIONAL SCHOOL OF HOTEL MANAGEMENT, CH-3975 Bluche, Switzerland

General Information Private, coed, comprehensive institution.

GRADUATE UNITS

Program in Hospitality Management Offers hospitality management (MBA). Available only at Switzerland campus.

LETOURNEAU UNIVERSITY, Longview, TX 75607-7001

General Information Independent-religious, coed, comprehensive institution. *Enrollment:* 2,721 graduate, professional, and undergraduate students; 82 full-time matriculated graduate/professional students (48 women), 428 part-time matriculated graduate/professional students (331 women). *Enrollment by degree level:* 510 master's. *Graduate faculty:* 24 full-time (7 women), 40 part-time/adjunct (15 women). *Graduate housing:* Rooms and/or apartments available on a first-come, first-served basis to single and married students. *Student services:* Campus employment opportunities, campus safety program, career counseling, exercise/wellness program, free psychological counseling, international student services, low-cost health insurance, multicultural affairs office, services for students with disabilities, writing training. *Library facilities:* Margaret Estes Library plus 1 other. *Collection:* Books: 46,700 (physical), 234,328 (digital/electronic); Serial titles: 200 (physical), 46,450 (digital/electronic); Databases: 90.

Computer facilities: Computer purchase and lease plans are available. 210 computers available on campus for general student use. A campuswide network can be accessed from student residence rooms and from off campus. Online class registration is available.
Website: http://www.letu.edu/

General Application Contact: Chris Fontaine, Assistant Vice President, Enrollment Services and Global Admissions, 903-233-4312, E-mail: chrisfontaine@letu.edu.

GRADUATE UNITS

Graduate Programs Students: 82 full-time (48 women), 428 part-time (331 women); includes 234 minority (138 Black or African American, non-Hispanic/Latino; 5 American Indian or Alaska Native, non-Hispanic/Latino; 5 Asian, non-Hispanic/Latino; 50 Hispanic/Latino; 36 Two or more races, non-Hispanic/Latino), 15 international. Average age 37. 257 applicants, 60% accepted, 141 enrolled. *Faculty:* 24 full-time (7 women), 40 part-time/adjunct (15 women). Expenses: Contact institution. *Financial support:* Research assistantships, institutionally sponsored loans, and unspecified assistantships available. Financial award applicants required to submit FAFSA. In 2016, 136 master's awarded. *Program availability:* Part-time, 100% online, blended/hybrid learning. Offers business (MBA); counseling (MA); curriculum and instruction (M Ed); educational administration (M Ed); engineering (ME, MS); engineering management (MEM); health care administration (MS); marriage and family therapy (MA); psychology (MA); strategic leadership (MSL); teacher leadership (M Ed); teaching and learning (M Ed). *Application deadline:* For fall admission, 8/22 for domestic students, 8/29 for international students; for winter admission, 10/10 for domestic students; for spring admission, 1/2 for domestic students, 1/10 for international students; for summer admission, 5/1 for domestic and international students. Applications are processed on a rolling basis. Electronic applications accepted. *Application Contact:* Chris Fontaine, Assistant Vice President for Enrollment Services and Global Admissions, 903-233-4312, E-mail: chrisfontaine@letu.edu.

LEWIS & CLARK COLLEGE, Portland, OR 97219-7899

General Information Independent, coed, comprehensive institution. *Graduate housing:* On-campus housing not available. *Student services:* Campus employment opportunities, campus safety program, career counseling, free psychological counseling, international student services, low-cost health insurance, multicultural affairs office, services for students with disabilities, writing training. *Library facilities:* Aubrey Watzek Library plus 1 other. *Collection:* Books: 523,517 (physical), 275,318 (digital/electronic); Serial titles:

7,568 (physical), 6,299 (digital/electronic); Databases: 327. Weekly public service hours: 141; study areas open 24 hours, 5–7 days a week; students can reserve study rooms.

Computer facilities: 440 computers available on campus for general student use. A campuswide network can be accessed from student residence rooms and from off campus. Online class registration is available.
Website: http://www.lclark.edu/

General Application Contact: Becky Haas, Director of Admissions, 503-768-6200, Fax: 503-768-6205, E-mail: gseadmit@lclark.edu.

GRADUATE UNITS

Graduate School of Education and Counseling Expenses: Contact institution. *Financial support:* Career-related internships or fieldwork, Federal Work-Study, institutionally sponsored loans, scholarships/grants, health care benefits, and tuition waivers (partial) available. Support available to part-time students. Financial award application deadline: 3/1; financial award applicants required to submit FAFSA. *Program availability:* Part-time, evening/weekend. Offers curriculum and instruction (M Ed); education and counseling (M Ed, MA, MAT, MS, Ed D, Ed S); educational administration (M Ed, Ed S); educational leadership (M Ed, MA, Ed D, Ed S); elementary education (MAT); marriage, couple, and family therapy (MA, MS); professional mental health counseling (MA, MS); professional mental health counseling - addictions (MA, MS); school counseling (M Ed); school psychology (Ed S); secondary education (MAT); special education (MA); student affairs administration (MA). *Application deadline:* For fall admission, 2/1 for domestic and international students; for spring admission, 10/1 for domestic and international students. Applications are processed on a rolling basis. *Application fee:* $50. Electronic applications accepted. *Application Contact:* Becky Haas, Director of Admissions, 503-768-6200, Fax: 503-768-6205, E-mail: gseadmit@lclark.edu. *Dean,* Dr. Scott Fletcher, 503-768-6004, Fax: 503-768-6005, E-mail: graddean@lclark.edu.

Lewis & Clark Law School Expenses: Contact institution. *Financial support:* Research assistantships, teaching assistantships, career-related internships or fieldwork, Federal Work-Study, scholarships/grants, and tuition waivers (partial) available. Support available to part-time students. Financial award application deadline: 3/1; financial award applicants required to submit FAFSA. *Program availability:* Part-time, evening/weekend. Offers animal law (LL M); environmental, natural resources, and energy law (LL M, MSL); law (JD). *Application deadline:* For fall admission, 3/1 for domestic students, 1/15 priority date for international students. Applications are processed on a rolling basis. *Application fee:* $50. Electronic applications accepted. *Application Contact:* Office of Admissions, 503-768-6613, Fax: 503-768-6793, E-mail: lawadmss@lclark.edu. *Dean,* Jennifer Johnson, 503-768-6601, Fax: 503-768-6671.

LEWIS UNIVERSITY, Romeoville, IL 60446

General Information Independent-religious, coed, comprehensive institution. CGS member. *Enrollment:* 6,544 graduate, professional, and undergraduate students; 422 full-time matriculated graduate/professional students (225 women), 1,489 part-time matriculated graduate/professional students (993 women). *Enrollment by degree level:* 1,801 master's, 83 doctoral, 27 other advanced degrees. *Tuition:* Full-time $13,860; part-time $770 per credit hour. *Required fees:* $75 per semester. Tuition and fees vary according to degree level and program. *Graduate housing:* Room and/or apartments available on a first-come, first-served basis to single students; on-campus housing not available to married students. Housing application deadline: 7/1. *Student services:* Campus employment opportunities, campus safety program, career counseling, exercise/wellness program, free psychological counseling, international student services, low-cost health insurance, multicultural affairs office, services for students with disabilities, teacher training, writing training. *Library facilities:* Lewis University Library. *Collection:* Books: 141,150 (physical), 204,209 (digital/electronic); Serial titles: 13,419 (physical), 140,108 (digital/electronic); Databases: 121. Weekly public service hours: 102; students can reserve study rooms.

Computer facilities: 600 computers available on campus for general student use. A campuswide network can be accessed from student residence rooms and from off campus. Online class registration, online help, online billing, online financial aid, online payments, online housing application, online application for graduation, course management system are available.
Website: http://www.lewisu.edu/

General Application Contact: Dr. Leslie Jacobson, Assistant Director, Graduate and Adult Admission, 815-836-5610, Fax: 815-836-5578, E-mail: grad@lewisu.edu.

GRADUATE UNITS

College of Arts and Sciences Students: 196 full-time (103 women), 617 part-time (344 women); includes 218 minority (113 Black or African American, non-Hispanic/Latino; 3 American Indian or Alaska Native, non-Hispanic/Latino; 11 Asian, non-Hispanic/Latino; 68 Hispanic/Latino; 2 Native Hawaiian or other Pacific Islander, non-Hispanic/Latino; 21 Two or more races, non-Hispanic/Latino), 35 international. Average age 33. Expenses: Contact institution. *Financial support:* Federal Work-Study, scholarships/grants, tuition waivers (partial), and unspecified assistantships available. Financial award application deadline: 5/1; financial award applicants required to submit FAFSA. *Program availability:* Part-time, evening/weekend, 100% online, blended/hybrid learning. Offers administration (MS); arts and sciences (MA, MS); child and adolescent counseling (MA); criminal/social justice (MS); higher education/student services (MA); management (MS); mental health counseling (MA); non-profit management (MA); organizational management (MA); professional and executive coaching (MA); public safety administration (MS); safety and security (MS); school counseling (MA); technical (MS); training and development (MA). *Application deadline:* For fall admission, 5/1 priority date for international students; for spring admission, 11/15 priority date for international students. Applications are processed on a rolling basis. *Application fee:* $40. Electronic applications accepted. *Application Contact:* Dr. Leslie Jacobson, Director, Graduate and Adult Admission, 815-836-5610, Fax: 815-836-5578, E-mail: grad@lewisu.edu. *Dean,* Dr. Bonnie Bondavalli, 815-838-0500 Ext. 5240, Fax: 815-836-5240, E-mail: bondavbo@lewisu.edu.

College of Business Students: 175 full-time (85 women), 303 part-time (159 women); includes 136 minority (62 Black or African American, non-Hispanic/Latino; 2 American Indian or Alaska Native, non-Hispanic/Latino; 10 Asian, non-Hispanic/Latino; 55 Hispanic/Latino; 1 Native Hawaiian or other Pacific Islander, non-Hispanic/Latino; 6 Two or more races, non-Hispanic/Latino), 60 international. Average age 32. Expenses: Contact institution. *Financial support:* Career-related internships or fieldwork, Federal Work-Study, scholarships/grants, tuition waivers (full), and unspecified assistantships available. Support available to part-time students. Financial award application deadline: 5/1; financial award applicants required to submit FAFSA. *Program availability:* Part-time, evening/weekend, 100% online, blended/hybrid learning. Offers business (MBA, MS). *Application deadline:* For fall admission, 5/1 priority date for international students; for spring admission, 11/15 priority date for international students. Applications are processed on a rolling basis. *Application fee:* $40. Electronic applications accepted.

Application Contact: Michele Ryan, Director of Admission, 815-836-5384, E-mail: gsm@lewisu.edu. *Dean,* Dr. Rami Khasawneh, 800-838-0500 Ext. 5360, E-mail: khasawra@lewisu.edu.

Graduate School of Management Students: 2 part-time (1 woman). Average age 32. Expenses: Contact institution. *Financial support:* Career-related internships or fieldwork, Federal Work-Study, and unspecified assistantships available. Financial award application deadline: 5/1; financial award applicants required to submit FAFSA. *Program availability:* Part-time, evening/weekend, 100% online, blended/hybrid learning. Offers accounting (MBA); business administration (MBA); business analytics (MS); custom elective option (MBA); e-business (MBA); finance (MS); financial analytics (MS); healthcare analytics (MS); healthcare management (MBA); human resources management (MBA); information security (MBA); international business (MBA); management information systems (MBA); marketing (MBA); marketing analytics (MS); operations analytics (MS); project management (MBA, MS); technology and operations management (MBA). *Application deadline:* Applications are processed on a rolling basis. *Application fee:* $40. Electronic applications accepted. *Application Contact:* Michele Ryan, Director of Admission, 815-836-5384, E-mail: gsm@lewisu.edu. *Dean,* Dr. Rami Khasawneh, 800-838-0500 Ext. 5360, E-mail: khasawra@lewisu.edu.

College of Education Students: 38 full-time (25 women), 187 part-time (135 women); includes 54 minority (26 Black or African American, non-Hispanic/Latino; 1 Asian, non-Hispanic/Latino; 26 Hispanic/Latino; 1 Two or more races, non-Hispanic/Latino), 11 international. Expenses: Contact institution. *Financial support:* Career-related internships or fieldwork, Federal Work-Study, scholarships/grants, tuition waivers (partial), and unspecified assistantships available. Financial award application deadline: 5/1; financial award applicants required to submit FAFSA. *Program availability:* Part-time, evening/weekend. Offers biology (MA); chemistry (MA); curriculum and instruction: instructional technology (M Ed); education (M Ed, MA, Ed D); educational leadership (M Ed, MA); educational leadership for teaching and learning (Ed D); elementary education (MA); English (MA); English as a second language (M Ed); history (MA); math (MA); physics (MA); psychology and social science (MA); reading and literacy (M Ed, MA); special education (MA). *Application deadline:* For fall admission, 5/1 priority date for international students; for spring admission, 11/15 priority date for international students. Applications are processed on a rolling basis. *Application fee:* $40. Electronic applications accepted. *Application Contact:* Linda Campbell, Graduate Admission Counselor, 815-836-5704, Fax: 815-836-5578, E-mail: campbeli@lewisu.edu. *Dean,* Dr. Pamela Jessee, 815-836-5316, E-mail: jesseepa@lewisu.edu.

College of Nursing and Health Professions Students: 13 full-time (12 women), 382 part-time (355 women); includes 103 minority (37 Black or African American, non-Hispanic/Latino; 32 Asian, non-Hispanic/Latino; 29 Hispanic/Latino; 5 Two or more races, non-Hispanic/Latino). Expenses: Contact institution. *Financial support:* Federal Work-Study, scholarships/grants, tuition waivers (full and partial), and unspecified assistantships available. Financial award application deadline: 5/1; financial award applicants required to submit FAFSA. *Program availability:* Part-time, evening/weekend, 100% online, blended/hybrid learning. Offers adult gerontology acute care nurse practitioner (MSN); adult gerontology clinical nurse specialist (MSN); adult gerontology primary care nurse practitioner (MSN); family nurse practitioner (MSN); healthcare systems leadership (MSN); nursing (DNP); nursing and health professions (MSN, DNP); nursing education (MSN); school nurse (MSN). *Application deadline:* For fall admission, 5/1 priority date for international students; for spring admission, 11/15 priority date for international students. Applications are processed on a rolling basis. *Application fee:* $40. Electronic applications accepted. *Application Contact:* Nancy Wiksten, Graduate Admission Counselor, 815-836-5628, Fax: 815-836-5578, E-mail: wikstena@lewisu.edu. *Dean,* Dr. Peggy Rice, 815-838-0500 Ext. 5245, E-mail: ricema@lewisu.edu.

LEXINGTON THEOLOGICAL SEMINARY, Lexington, KY 40508-3218

General Information Independent-religious, coed, graduate-only institution. *Graduate housing:* Rooms and/or apartments available on a first-come, first-served basis to single and married students. Housing application deadline: 6/15.

GRADUATE UNITS

Graduate and Professional Programs *Program availability:* Part-time, evening/weekend. Offers theology (M Div, MA, MAPS, D Min). M Div/MSW offered jointly with University of Kentucky.

LIBERTY UNIVERSITY, Lynchburg, VA 24515

General Information Independent-religious, coed, comprehensive institution. *Enrollment:* 9,417 full-time matriculated graduate/professional students (5,555 women), 18,991 part-time matriculated graduate/professional students (11,573 women). *Enrollment by degree level:* 24,536 master's, 2,646 doctoral, 1,226 other advanced degrees. *Graduate housing:* Room and/or apartments available on a first-come, first-served basis to single students; on-campus housing not available to married students. *Student services:* Campus employment opportunities, career counseling, exercise/wellness program, free psychological counseling, international student services, multicultural affairs office, services for students with disabilities, writing training. *Library facilities:* Jerry Falwell Library plus 1 other. *Collection:* Books: 405,620 (physical), 283,195 (digital/electronic); Serial titles: 120 (physical), 78,253 (digital/electronic); Databases: 589. Students can reserve study rooms.

Computer facilities: 820 computers available on campus for general student use. A campuswide network can be accessed from student residence rooms and from off campus. Online class registration is available. Website: http://www.liberty.edu/

General Application Contact: Jay Bridge, Director of Admissions, 800-424-9595, Fax: 800-628-7977, E-mail: gradadmissions@liberty.edu.

GRADUATE UNITS

College of Arts and Sciences Students: 59 full-time (28 women), 58 part-time (26 women); includes 9 minority (2 Black or African American, non-Hispanic/Latino; 1 American Indian or Alaska Native, non-Hispanic/Latino; 1 Asian, non-Hispanic/Latino; 2 Hispanic/Latino; 3 Two or more races, non-Hispanic/Latino), 1 international. Average age 33. 206 applicants, 35% accepted, 52 enrolled. Expenses: Contact institution. *Financial support:* Teaching assistantships with tuition reimbursements and Federal Work-Study available. In 2016, 36 master's awarded. *Program availability:* Part-time, online learning. Offers English (MA); history (MA); professional writing (MA). *Application deadline:* For fall admission, 6/1 for domestic students; for spring admission, 11/1 for domestic students. Applications are processed on a rolling basis. *Application fee:* $50. Electronic applications accepted. *Application Contact:* Dr. Terry Elam, Director of Graduate Admissions, 434-592-3966, Fax: 434-522-0430, E-mail: gradadmissions@liberty.edu. *Dean,* Dr. Roger Schultz, 434-592-4031, Fax: 434-522-0430, E-mail: rschultz@liberty.edu.

College of Osteopathic Medicine Students: 464 full-time (219 women), 1 part-time (0 women); includes 30 minority (4 Black or African American, non-Hispanic/Latino; 15 Asian, non-Hispanic/Latino; 3 Hispanic/Latino; 8 Two or more races, non-Hispanic/Latino), 17 international. Average age 27. 1,483 applicants, 11% accepted, 156 enrolled. Expenses: Contact institution. Offers osteopathic medicine (DO). *Application deadline:* Applications are processed on a rolling basis. Electronic applications accepted. *Application Contact:* Jay Bridge, Director of Admissions, 800-424-9595, Fax: 800-628-7977, E-mail: gradadmissions@liberty.edu. *Dean,* Dr. Ronnie B. Martin, 434-592-6400.

Helms School of Government Students: 279 full-time (128 women), 626 part-time (233 women); includes 223 minority (163 Black or African American, non-Hispanic/Latino; 10 American Indian or Alaska Native, non-Hispanic/Latino; 10 Asian, non-Hispanic/Latino; 11 Hispanic/Latino; 1 Native Hawaiian or other Pacific Islander, non-Hispanic/Latino; 28 Two or more races, non-Hispanic/Latino), 12 international. Average age 35. 713 applicants, 51% accepted, 182 enrolled. Expenses: Contact institution. In 2016, 256 master's awarded. *Program availability:* Part-time, online learning. Offers public administration (MS). *Application deadline:* Applications are processed on a rolling basis. *Application fee:* $50. Electronic applications accepted. *Application Contact:* Jay Bridge, Director of Admissions, 800-424-9595, Fax: 800-628-7977, E-mail: gradadmissions@liberty.edu. *Dean,* Shawn D. Akers, 434-592-4986.

School of Behavioral Sciences Students: 2,041 full-time (1,612 women), 4,970 part-time (3,875 women); includes 1,991 minority (1,678 Black or African American, non-Hispanic/Latino; 33 American Indian or Alaska Native, non-Hispanic/Latino; 48 Asian, non-Hispanic/Latino; 80 Hispanic/Latino; 8 Native Hawaiian or other Pacific Islander, non-Hispanic/Latino; 144 Two or more races, non-Hispanic/Latino), 127 international. Average age 39. 5,496 applicants, 41% accepted, 1257 enrolled. Expenses: Contact institution. *Financial support:* Applicants required to submit FAFSA. In 2016, 2,813 master's, 11 doctorates, 20 other advanced degrees awarded. *Program availability:* Part-time, online learning. Offers clinical mental health counseling (MA); counselor education and supervision (PhD); human services counseling (MA); marriage and family therapy (MA); military resilience (Certificate); professional counseling (MA). *Application deadline:* Applications are processed on a rolling basis. *Application fee:* $50. Electronic applications accepted. *Application Contact:* Jay Bridge, Director of Admissions, 800-424-9595, Fax: 800-628-7977, E-mail: gradadmissions@liberty.edu. *Founding Dean, School of Behavioral Sciences,* Dr. Ronald Hawkins.

School of Business Students: 1,458 full-time (807 women), 4,188 part-time (2,041 women); includes 1,372 minority (1,060 Black or African American, non-Hispanic/Latino; 19 American Indian or Alaska Native, non-Hispanic/Latino; 85 Asian, non-Hispanic/Latino; 75 Hispanic/Latino; 10 Native Hawaiian or other Pacific Islander, non-Hispanic/Latino; 123 Two or more races, non-Hispanic/Latino), 124 international. Average age 35. 5,424 applicants, 45% accepted, 1242 enrolled. Expenses: Contact institution. *Financial support:* Applicants required to submit FAFSA. In 2016, 1,859 master's, 87 other advanced degrees awarded. *Program availability:* Part-time, online learning. Offers accounting (MBA, MS); business administration (MBA); criminal justice (MBA); cyber security (MS); executive leadership (MA); information systems (MS); international business (MBA, DBA); leadership (DBA); marketing (MBA, MS, DBA); project management (MBA, DBA); public administration (MBA); public relations (MBA). *Application deadline:* Applications are processed on a rolling basis. *Application fee:* $50. Electronic applications accepted. *Application Contact:* Jay Bridge, Director of Graduate Admissions, 800-424-9595, Fax: 800-628-7977, E-mail: gradadmissions@liberty.edu. *Dean,* Dr. Scott Hicks, 434-592-4808, Fax: 434-582-2366, E-mail: smhicks@liberty.edu.

School of Communication and Creative Arts Students: 120 full-time (82 women), 142 part-time (90 women); includes 56 minority (45 Black or African American, non-Hispanic/Latino; 1 Asian, non-Hispanic/Latino; 1 Hispanic/Latino; 9 Two or more races, non-Hispanic/Latino), 12 international. Average age 32. 384 applicants, 33% accepted, 66 enrolled. Expenses: Contact institution. *Financial support:* Federal Work-Study and unspecified assistantships available. Financial award applicants required to submit FAFSA. In 2016, 58 master's awarded. *Program availability:* Part-time. Offers strategic communication (MA); studio and digital arts (MFA). *Application deadline:* For fall admission, 6/1 for domestic students; for spring admission, 11/1 for domestic students. Applications are processed on a rolling basis. *Application fee:* $50. Electronic applications accepted. *Application Contact:* Dr. Terry Elam, Director of Graduate Admissions, 434-582-2111, Fax: 434-582-7836, E-mail: gradadmissions@liberty.edu. *Dean,* Dr. Norman Mintle, 434-582-2077, E-mail: cvkramer@liberty.edu.

School of Divinity Students: 2,140 full-time (615 women), 3,020 part-time (906 women); includes 1,312 minority (1,016 Black or African American, non-Hispanic/Latino; 9 American Indian or Alaska Native, non-Hispanic/Latino; 100 Asian, non-Hispanic/Latino; 90 Hispanic/Latino; 7 Native Hawaiian or other Pacific Islander, non-Hispanic/Latino; 90 Two or more races, non-Hispanic/Latino), 158 international. Average age 42. 3,651 applicants, 37% accepted, 909 enrolled. Expenses: Contact institution. *Financial support:* Teaching assistantships with tuition reimbursements, career-related internships or fieldwork, and Federal Work-Study available. Financial award applicants required to submit FAFSA. In 2016, 1,551 master's, 39 doctorates, 168 other advanced degrees awarded. *Program availability:* Part-time, online learning. Offers Biblical studies (M Div); church history (MAR, Th M); discipleship and church ministry (M Div, MAR, MCM); evangelism and church planting (M Div, MAR, MCM); global studies (M Div, MCM, MGS); homiletics (M Div, MAR, Th M, D Min); leadership (M Div, D Min); marketplace chaplaincy (M Div, MCM); ministry (D Min); pastoral counseling (M Div, MA, MAR, D Min); pastoral ministries (M Div, MCM); religious education (MRE); theology (M Div, MAR, MTS); theology and apologetics (PhD); worship (M Div, MAR, MCM, D Min). *Application deadline:* For fall admission, 6/1 for domestic students; for spring admission, 11/1 for domestic students. Applications are processed on a rolling basis. *Application fee:* $50. Electronic applications accepted. *Application Contact:* Jay Bridge, Director of Graduate Admissions, 800-424-9595, Fax: 800-628-7977, E-mail: gradadmissions@liberty.edu. *Dean,* Dr. Ed Hindson, 434-592-4140, Fax: 434-522-0415, E-mail: ehindson@liberty.edu.

School of Education Students: 1,910 full-time (1,427 women), 4,420 part-time (3,311 women); includes 1,451 minority (1,182 Black or African American, non-Hispanic/Latino; 33 American Indian or Alaska Native, non-Hispanic/Latino; 44 Asian, non-Hispanic/Latino; 46 Hispanic/Latino; 11 Native Hawaiian or other Pacific Islander, non-Hispanic/Latino; 135 Two or more races, non-Hispanic/Latino), 87 international. Average age 37. 5,120 applicants, 44% accepted, 1193 enrolled. Expenses: Contact institution. *Financial support:* Federal Work-Study and tuition waivers (partial) available. In 2016, 1,378 master's, 151 doctorates, 497 other advanced degrees awarded. *Program availability:* Part-time, online learning. Offers educational leadership (Ed D); gifted education (Certificate); math specialist (M Ed); middle grades (MAT, Certificate); reading specialist (M Ed); school leadership (Certificate); secondary education (MAT); sport management (MS). *Application deadline:* For fall admission, 6/1 for domestic students; for spring admission, 11/1 for domestic students. Applications are processed on a rolling basis. *Application fee:* $50. Electronic applications accepted. *Application Contact:* Jay

Bridge, Director of Graduate Admissions, 800-424-9595, Fax: 800-628-7977, E-mail: gradadmissions@liberty.edu. *Dean*, Dr. Heather Schoffstall, 434-582-2445, Fax: 434-582-2468, E-mail: awgunter@liberty.edu.

School of Engineering and Computational Sciences Students: 44 full-time (10 women), 145 part-time (18 women); includes 53 minority (38 Black or African American, non-Hispanic/Latino; 1 American Indian or Alaska Native, non-Hispanic/Latino; 6 Asian, non-Hispanic/Latino; 1 Hispanic/Latino; 1 Native Hawaiian or other Pacific Islander, non-Hispanic/Latino; 6 Two or more races, non-Hispanic/Latino), 3 international. Average age 37. 223 applicants, 24% accepted, 24 enrolled. Expenses: Contact institution. *Financial support:* Applicants required to submit FAFSA. In 2016, 27 master's awarded. *Program availability:* Part-time, online learning. Offers cyber security (MS). *Application deadline:* Applications are processed on a rolling basis. *Application fee:* $50. Electronic applications accepted. *Application Contact:* Jay Bridge, Director of Admissions, 800-424-9595, Fax: 800-628-7977, E-mail: gradadmissions@liberty.edu. *Dean*, David Donahoo, 434-592-7150.

School of Health Sciences Students: 518 full-time (401 women), 676 part-time (512 women); includes 353 minority (276 Black or African American, non-Hispanic/Latino; 5 American Indian or Alaska Native, non-Hispanic/Latino; 30 Asian, non-Hispanic/Latino; 15 Hispanic/Latino; 1 Native Hawaiian or other Pacific Islander, non-Hispanic/Latino; 26 Two or more races, non-Hispanic/Latino), 66 international. Average age 32. 1,639 applicants, 41% accepted, 332 enrolled. Expenses: Contact institution. *Financial support:* Applicants required to submit FAFSA. In 2016, 190 master's awarded. *Program availability:* Part-time, online learning. Offers biomedical sciences (MS); global health (MPH); health promotion (MPH); nutrition (MPH). *Application fee:* $50. *Application Contact:* Jay Bridge, Director of Admissions, 800-424-9595, Fax: 800-628-7977, E-mail: gradadmissions@liberty.edu. *Dean*, Dr. Ralph Linstra.

School of Law Students: 209 full-time (91 women), 61 part-time (30 women); includes 51 minority (27 Black or African American, non-Hispanic/Latino; 3 American Indian or Alaska Native, non-Hispanic/Latino; 7 Asian, non-Hispanic/Latino; 8 Hispanic/Latino; 6 Two or more races, non-Hispanic/Latino), 4 international. Average age 31. 305 applicants, 55% accepted, 113 enrolled. Expenses: Contact institution. *Financial support:* Applicants required to submit FAFSA. In 2016, 18 doctorates awarded. *Program availability:* Online learning. Offers law (JD). *Application deadline:* For fall admission, 6/1 for domestic students. *Application Contact:* Joleen Thaxton, Assistant Director of Admissions, 434-592-5300, Fax: 434-592-5400, E-mail: lawadmissions@liberty.edu. *Dean*, B. Keith Faulkner, 434-592-5300, Fax: 434-592-5400, E-mail: law@liberty.edu.

School of Music Students: 58 full-time (26 women), 184 part-time (90 women); includes 52 minority (42 Black or African American, non-Hispanic/Latino; 3 Asian, non-Hispanic/Latino; 2 Hispanic/Latino; 5 Two or more races, non-Hispanic/Latino), 8 international. Average age 38. 323 applicants, 24% accepted, 49 enrolled. Expenses: Contact institution. *Financial support:* Applicants required to submit FAFSA. In 2016, 39 master's, 1 doctorate awarded. *Program availability:* Part-time, online learning. Offers ethnomusicology (MA); music and worship (MA); music education (MA); worship studies (MA, DWS). *Application deadline:* Applications are processed on a rolling basis. *Application fee:* $50. Electronic applications accepted. *Application Contact:* Jay Bridge, Director of Admissions, 800-424-9595, Fax: 800-628-7977, E-mail: gradadmissions@liberty.edu. *Dean*, Dr. Vernon Whaley, 434-592-3463, E-mail: vwhaley@liberty.edu.

School of Nursing Students: 117 full-time (109 women), 500 part-time (441 women); includes 90 minority (63 Black or African American, non-Hispanic/Latino; 5 American Indian or Alaska Native, non-Hispanic/Latino; 10 Asian, non-Hispanic/Latino; 1 Hispanic/Latino; 2 Native Hawaiian or other Pacific Islander, non-Hispanic/Latino; 9 Two or more races, non-Hispanic/Latino), 6 international. Average age 39. 486 applicants, 33% accepted, 106 enrolled. Expenses: Contact institution. *Financial support:* Applicants required to submit FAFSA. In 2016, 115 master's awarded. *Program availability:* Part-time, online learning. Offers family nurse practitioner (DNP); nurse educator (MSN); nursing administration (MSN). *Application deadline:* Applications are processed on a rolling basis. *Application fee:* $50. Electronic applications accepted. *Application Contact:* Jay Bridge, Director of Admissions, 800-424-9595, Fax: 800-628-7977, E-mail: gradadmissions@liberty.edu. *Dean*, Dr. Deanna Britt, 434-582-2519, E-mail: dbritt@liberty.edu.

LIFE CHIROPRACTIC COLLEGE WEST, Hayward, CA 94545

General Information Independent, coed, graduate-only institution. *Graduate housing:* On-campus housing not available. *Research affiliation:* National Center for Complimentary Medicine, National Center for Complementary and Alternative Medicine/University Cancer Research Fund, Advanced Orthogonality, San Jose State University, University of Calgary.

GRADUATE UNITS

Professional Program Offers chiropractic (DC). Electronic applications accepted.

LIFE UNIVERSITY, Marietta, GA 30060-2903

General Information Independent, coed, comprehensive institution. *Graduate housing:* Rooms and/or apartments available on a first-come, first-served basis to single and married students.

GRADUATE UNITS

College of Chiropractic *Program availability:* Part-time. Offers chiropractic (DC). Electronic applications accepted.

Graduate Programs *Program availability:* Part-time, 100% online, blended/hybrid learning. Offers athletic training (MAT); chiropractic sport science (MS); clinical nutrition (MS); nutrition and sport science (MS); sport coaching (MS); sport injury management (MS); sports health science (MS). Electronic applications accepted.

LIM COLLEGE, New York, NY 10022-5268

General Information Proprietary, coed, primarily women, comprehensive institution. *Graduate housing:* Room and/or apartments available on a first-come, first-served basis to single students; on-campus housing not available to married students.

GRADUATE UNITS

MBA Program Offers entrepreneurship (MBA); fashion management (MBA).

MPS Program Offers fashion marketing (MPS); fashion merchandising and retail management (MPS); visual merchandising (MPS).

LIMESTONE COLLEGE, Gaffney, SC 29340-3799

General Information Independent, coed, comprehensive institution. *Enrollment:* 1,280 graduate, professional, and undergraduate students; 41 full-time matriculated graduate/professional students (28 women), 28 part-time matriculated graduate/professional students (16 women). *Enrollment by degree level:* 69 master's. *Graduate faculty:* 10 full-time (2 women), 1 (woman) part-time/adjunct. *Tuition:* Part-time $1875 per course. *Graduate housing:* On-campus housing not available. *Student*

services: Career counseling, free psychological counseling, services for students with disabilities. *Library facilities:* A. J. Eastwood Library plus 1 other. *Collection:* Books: 67,000 (physical), 239,537 (digital/electronic). Serial titles: 111 (physical), 482,082 (digital/electronic); Databases: 156. Weekly public service hours: 70.

Computer facilities: 137 computers available on campus for general student use. A campuswide network can be accessed from student residence rooms and from off campus. Online class registration is available. Website: http://www.limestone.edu/

General Application Contact: Adair Haynes, Administrative Assistant, MBA Program, 800-795-7151 Ext. 4370, Fax: 864-487-8706, E-mail: ahaynes@limestone.edu.

GRADUATE UNITS

MBA Program Students: 41 full-time (28 women), 28 part-time (16 women); includes 30 minority (25 Black or African American, non-Hispanic/Latino; 3 Asian, non-Hispanic/Latino; 2 Two or more races, non-Hispanic/Latino). Average age 40. 74 applicants, 33 enrolled. *Faculty:* 10 full-time (2 women), 1 (woman) part-time/adjunct. Expenses: Contact institution. *Financial support:* Scholarships/grants available. Financial award application deadline: 6/15; financial award applicants required to submit FAFSA. In 2016, 20 master's awarded. *Program availability:* Part-time, evening/weekend, online learning. Offers business administration (MBA). *Application deadline:* For fall admission, 8/1 priority date for domestic and international students; for winter admission, 12/12 priority date for domestic and international students; for spring admission, 4/1 priority date for domestic and international students. Applications are processed on a rolling basis. *Application fee:* $25. Electronic applications accepted. *Application Contact:* Adair Haynes, Administrative Assistant, MBA Program, 800-795-7151 Ext. 4370, Fax: 864-467-8706, E-mail: ahaynes@limestone.edu. *Director, MBA Program*, Shannon Creighton, 864-488-4371, Fax: 864-487-8706, E-mail: screighton@limestone.edu.

LINCOLN CHRISTIAN SEMINARY, Lincoln, IL 62656-2167

General Information Independent-religious, coed, graduate-only institution. *Graduate housing:* Rooms and/or apartments available on a first-come, first-served basis to single and married students.

GRADUATE UNITS

Graduate and Professional Programs *Program availability:* Part-time. Offers Bible and theology (MA); Christian ministries (MA); counseling (MA); divinity (M Div); leadership ministry (D Min); religious education (MRE). Electronic applications accepted.

LINCOLN CHRISTIAN UNIVERSITY, Lincoln, IL 62656-2167

General Information Independent-religious, coed, comprehensive institution. *Enrollment:* 886 graduate, professional, and undergraduate students; 89 full-time matriculated graduate/professional students (45 women), 225 part-time matriculated graduate/professional students (91 women). *Enrollment by degree level:* 294 master's, 20 doctoral. *Graduate faculty:* 22 full-time (6 women), 27 part-time/adjunct (9 women). *Tuition:* Full-time $7812; part-time $5208 per credit hour. *Required fees:* $1000 ($1000 per credit hour. One-time fee: $150. Full-time tuition and fees vary according to campus/location and program. *Graduate housing:* Rooms and/or apartments available on a first-come, first-served basis to single and married students. Typical cost: $5340 per year ($7564 including board) for single students; $5340 per year ($7564 including board) for married students. Room and board charges vary according to board plan, campus/location and housing facility selected. *Student services:* Campus employment opportunities, campus safety program, free psychological counseling, international student services, services for students with disabilities. *Library facilities:* Jessie Eury Library. *Collection:* Books: 92,813 (physical), 55,082 (digital/electronic); Serial titles: 719 (physical), 15,442 (digital/electronic); Databases: 52. Weekly public service hours: 82.

Computer facilities: 51 computers available on campus for general student use. A campuswide network can be accessed from student residence rooms and from off campus. Online class registration is available. Website: http://www.lincolnchristian.edu/

General Application Contact: Lindsey Clark, Associate Director of Graduate and Seminary Enrollment, 217-732-3168 Ext. 2398, E-mail: lclark@lincolnchristian.edu.

GRADUATE UNITS

Graduate Programs Students: 89 full-time (45 women), 225 part-time (91 women). Average age 39. *Faculty:* 22 full-time (6 women), 27 part-time/adjunct (9 women). Expenses: Contact institution. *Financial support:* Applicants required to submit FAFSA. *Program availability:* Online learning. Offers Biblical studies (MA); church history/historical theology (MA); intercultural studies (MA); ministry (MA); organizational leadership (MA); philosophy and apologetics (MA); spiritual formation (MA); theology (MA). MA in spiritual formation offered in Normal, IL. *Application deadline:* For fall admission, 8/1 for domestic students, 3/1 for international students; for spring admission, 11/15 for domestic students, 11/1 for international students. *Application fee:* $25 ($50 for international students). *Application Contact:* Lindsey Clark, Associate Director of Graduate and Seminary Enrollment, 217-732-3168 Ext. 2398, E-mail: lclark@lincolnchristian.edu.

LINCOLN MEMORIAL UNIVERSITY, Harrogate, TN 37752-1901

General Information Independent, coed, comprehensive institution. *Graduate housing:* Rooms and/or apartments available on a first-come, first-served basis to single and married students.

GRADUATE UNITS

Carter and Moyers School of Education *Program availability:* Part-time, evening/weekend, online learning. Offers administration and supervision (M Ed, Ed S); counseling and guidance (M Ed); curriculum and instruction (M Ed, Ed D, Ed S); English (M Ed); executive leadership (Ed D); higher education administration (Ed D); human resource development (Ed D); leadership and administration (Ed D).

Caylor School of Nursing *Program availability:* Part-time. Offers family nurse practitioner (MSN); nurse anesthesia (MSN); psychiatric mental health nurse practitioner (MSN).

DeBusk College of Osteopathic Medicine Offers osteopathic medicine (DO).

Duncan School of Law *Program availability:* Part-time. Offers law (JD). Electronic applications accepted.

School of Business *Program availability:* Part-time, evening/weekend. Offers business (MBA).

LINCOLN UNIVERSITY, Oakland, CA 94612

General Information Independent, coed, comprehensive institution. *Enrollment:* 1,059 graduate, professional, and undergraduate students; 796 full-time matriculated graduate/professional students (328 women), 32 part-time matriculated graduate/professional students (22 women). *Enrollment by degree level:* 600 master's,

44 doctoral, 139 other advanced degrees. *Graduate faculty:* 14 full-time (2 women), 18 part-time/adjunct (6 women). *Tuition:* Full-time $7920. *Required fees:* $400. Tuition and fees vary according to course level, course load, degree level and program. *Student services:* Campus employment opportunities, career counseling, international student services, low-cost health insurance, writing training. *Library facilities:* Lincoln University Library. *Collection:* Books: 14,400 (physical), 128,000 (digital/electronic); Serial titles: 350 (physical), 5,050 (digital/electronic); Databases: 19.

Computer facilities: 39 computers available on campus for general student use. A campuswide network can be accessed. Website: http://www.lincolnuca.edu/

General Application Contact: Peggy Au, Director of Admissions and Records, 510-628-8010, Fax: 510-628-8012, E-mail: admissions@lincolnuca.edu.

GRADUATE UNITS

Graduate Studies Students: 542 full-time (215 women), 3 part-time (1 woman); includes 10 minority (8 Asian, non-Hispanic/Latino; 1 Hispanic/Latino; 1 Two or more races, non-Hispanic/Latino), 531 international. Average age 26. 800 applicants, 71% accepted, 81 enrolled. *Faculty:* 13 full-time (1 woman), 16 part-time/adjunct (3 women). Expenses: Contact institution. *Financial support:* Teaching assistantships, career-related internships or fieldwork, and scholarships/grants available. Financial award applicants required to submit FAFSA. In 2016, 109 master's, 1 doctorate awarded. *Program availability:* Part-time. Offers finance and investments (DBA); finance management (MS); finance management and investments (MBA); general business (MBA); human resource management (MBA, DBA); international business (MBA, MS); management information systems (MBA). *Application deadline:* For fall admission, 8/7 for domestic students, 7/14 for international students; for spring admission, 11/30 for domestic students, 10/31 for international students; for summer admission, 5/29 for domestic students, 5/5 for international students. Applications are processed on a rolling basis. *Application fee:* $75. Electronic applications accepted. *Application Contact:* Reenu Shrestha, Assistant to the President, 510-628-8017, Fax: 510-208-2826, E-mail: sreenu@lincolnuca.edu. *Director of Graduate Programs,* Dr. Marshall Burak, 510-628-8016, Fax: 510-628-8012, E-mail: mburak@lincolnuca.edu.

LINCOLN UNIVERSITY, Jefferson City, MO 65101

General Information State-supported, coed, comprehensive institution. *Enrollment:* 2,738 graduate, professional, and undergraduate students; 50 full-time matriculated graduate/professional students (29 women), 68 part-time matriculated graduate/professional students (39 women). *Enrollment by degree level:* 118 master's. Tuition, state resident: full-time $6840; part-time $5130 per year. Tuition, nonresident: full-time $12,720; part-time $9540 per year. *Required fees:* $852; $811 per unit. Tuition and fees vary according to course load. *Graduate housing:* Room and/or apartments available on a first-come, first-served basis to single students; on-campus housing not available to married students. Typical cost: $4076 per year ($7080 including board). Room and board charges vary according to board plan and housing facility selected. Housing application deadline: 7/1. *Student services:* Campus employment opportunities, career counseling, international student services, services for students with disabilities. *Library facilities:* Inman E. Page Library. *Collection:* Books: 99,126 (physical), 197,476 (digital/electronic); Serial titles: 1,194 (physical), 19,000 (digital/electronic); Databases: 39. Weekly public service hours: 90. *Research affiliation:* National Science Foundation (STEM research), Ceres Trust (agriculture), Missouri Department of Agriculture (agriculture), Center for Rural Affairs (sustainable agriculture), U.S. Department of Education (DOE) (defense, government), U.S. Department of Agriculture (USDA) (agriculture, government).

Computer facilities: Computer purchase and lease plans are available. 365 computers available on campus for general student use. A campuswide network can be accessed from student residence rooms and from off campus. Online class registration is available. Website: http://www.lincolnu.edu/

General Application Contact: Dr. Rolundus Rice, Dean, 573-681-5247, Fax: 573-681-5106, E-mail: gradschool@lincolnu.edu.

GRADUATE UNITS

Graduate Studies Students: 50 full-time (29 women), 68 part-time (39 women); includes 40 minority (37 Black or African American, non-Hispanic/Latino; 1 Asian, non-Hispanic/Latino; 2 Two or more races, non-Hispanic/Latino), 14 international. Average age 33. 75 applicants, 80% accepted, 34 enrolled. Expenses: Contact institution. *Financial support:* In 2016–17, 2 fellowships with tuition reimbursements, 8 research assistantships with tuition reimbursements were awarded; Federal Work-Study, scholarships/grants, and unspecified assistantships also available. Support available to part-time students. Financial award application deadline: 3/1; financial award applicants required to submit FAFSA. In 2016, 51 master's awarded. *Program availability:* Part-time, evening/weekend, 100% online, blended/hybrid learning. Offers business administration (MBA); elementary teaching (M Ed); environmental science (MS); guidance and counseling (M Ed); higher education (MA); history (MA); integrated agricultural systems (MS); middle school (M Ed); natural sciences (MS); secondary teaching (M Ed); sociology (MA); sociology/criminal justice (MA). *Application deadline:* For fall admission, 7/1 priority date for domestic students, 5/1 priority date for international students; for spring admission, 11/1 priority date for domestic students, 10/1 priority date for international students; for summer admission, 6/1 priority date for domestic students. Applications are processed on a rolling basis. *Application fee:* $30. Electronic applications accepted. *Application Contact:* Irasema Steck, Administrative Assistant, 573-681-5247, Fax: 573-681-5106, E-mail: gradschool@lincolnu.edu. *Dean,* Dr. Rolundus R. Rice, 573-681-5247, Fax: 573-681-5106, E-mail: gradschool@lincolnu.edu.

LINCOLN UNIVERSITY, Lincoln University, PA 19352

General Information State-related, coed, comprehensive institution. *Enrollment:* 2,092 graduate, professional, and undergraduate students; 191 full-time matriculated graduate/professional students (131 women), 77 part-time matriculated graduate/professional students (60 women). *Enrollment by degree level:* 268 master's. *Graduate faculty:* 11 full-time (5 women), 45 part-time/adjunct (24 women). Tuition, state resident: full-time $12,264; part-time $511 per credit hour. Tuition, nonresident: full-time $21,264; part-time $886 per credit hour. *Required fees:* $1344; $56 per credit hour. Tuition and fees vary according to course load. *Graduate housing:* On-campus housing not available. *Student services:* Campus employment opportunities, campus safety program, career counseling, free psychological counseling, international student services, low-cost health insurance, services for students with disabilities, teacher training, writing training. *Library facilities:* Langston Hughes Memorial Library. *Collection:* Books: 179,155 (physical), 161,264 (digital/electronic); Databases: 17. Weekly public service hours: 80; study areas open 24 hours, 5–7 days a week; students can reserve study rooms. *Research affiliation:* The Treatment Research Institute (addictive disorders).

Computer facilities: 155 computers available on campus for general student use. A campuswide network can be accessed from student residence rooms and from off campus. Online class registration is available. Website: http://www.lincoln.edu/

General Application Contact: Jernice Lea, Director, Graduate Student Services and Admissions, 215-590-8231, Fax: 215-387-3859, E-mail: jlea@lincoln.edu.

GRADUATE UNITS

Graduate Programs Students: 191 full-time (131 women), 77 part-time (60 women); includes 245 minority (236 Black or African American, non-Hispanic/Latino; 1 American Indian or Alaska Native, non-Hispanic/Latino; 7 Hispanic/Latino; 1 Two or more races, non-Hispanic/Latino), 4 international. Average age 34. 221 applicants, 58% accepted, 55 enrolled. *Faculty:* 11 full-time (5 women), 45 part-time/adjunct (24 women). Expenses: Contact institution. *Financial support:* In 2016–17, 9 students received support. Scholarships/grants available. Financial award application deadline: 8/1; financial award applicants required to submit FAFSA. In 2016, 97 master's awarded. *Program availability:* Part-time, evening/weekend. Offers counseling (MSC); early childhood education (M Ed); early childhood education and special education (M Ed); educational leadership (M Ed); finance (MSB); human resources management (MSB); human services (MAHS). *Application deadline:* For fall admission, 6/1 priority date for domestic and international students. Applications are processed on a rolling basis. *Application fee:* $50. Electronic applications accepted. *Application Contact:* Jernice Lea, Director of Graduate Admissions, 215-590-8231, Fax: 215-387-3859, E-mail: jlea@lincoln.edu. *Dean, College of Professional, Graduate and Extended Studies,* Dr. Patricia Joseph, 484-365-7659, E-mail: joseph@lincoln.edu.

LINDENWOOD UNIVERSITY, St. Charles, MO 63301-1695

General Information Independent-religious, coed, comprehensive institution. *Enrollment:* 10,750 graduate, professional, and undergraduate students; 1,162 full-time matriculated graduate/professional students (741 women), 2,039 part-time matriculated graduate/professional students (1,511 women). *Enrollment by degree level:* 2,725 master's, 313 doctoral, 163 other advanced degrees. *Graduate faculty:* 83 full-time (42 women), 238 part-time/adjunct (144 women). *Tuition:* Full-time $15,672; part-time $453 per credit hour. *Required fees:* $205 per semester. Tuition and fees vary according to course level, course load and degree level. *Graduate housing:* Rooms and/or apartments available on a first-come, first-served basis to single and married students. Housing application deadline: 8/28. *Student services:* Campus employment opportunities, campus safety program, career counseling, exercise/wellness program, free psychological counseling, international student services, services for students with disabilities, teacher training, writing training. *Library facilities:* Butler Library plus 1 other. *Collection:* Books: 93,916 (physical), 200,752 (digital/electronic); Serial titles: 272 (physical), 139 (digital/electronic); Databases: 96. Study areas open 24 hours, 5–7 days a week.

Computer facilities: 286 computers available on campus for general student use. A campuswide network can be accessed from student residence rooms and from off campus. Online class registration is available. Website: http://www.lindenwood.edu/

General Application Contact: Tyler Kostich, Director, Evening and Graduate Admissions, 636-949-4138, Fax: 636-949-4109, E-mail: adultadmissions@lindenwood.edu.

GRADUATE UNITS

Graduate Programs Students: 1,162 full-time (741 women), 2,039 part-time (1,511 women); includes 766 minority (612 Black or African American, non-Hispanic/Latino; 9 American Indian or Alaska Native, non-Hispanic/Latino; 21 Asian, non-Hispanic/Latino; 78 Hispanic/Latino; 2 Native Hawaiian or other Pacific Islander, non-Hispanic/Latino; 44 Two or more races, non-Hispanic/Latino), 138 international. Average age 35. 1,281 applicants, 65% accepted, 735 enrolled. *Faculty:* 83 full-time (42 women), 238 part-time/adjunct (144 women). Expenses: Contact institution. *Financial support:* In 2016–17, 1,820 students received support. Career-related internships or fieldwork, Federal Work-Study, institutionally sponsored loans, scholarships/grants, tuition waivers (full), and unspecified assistantships available. Financial award application deadline: 6/30; financial award applicants required to submit FAFSA. In 2016, 1,271 master's, 72 doctorates, 111 other advanced degrees awarded. *Program availability:* Part-time, evening/weekend, 100% online. *Application deadline:* For fall admission, 8/28 priority date for domestic and international students; for spring admission, 1/8 priority date for domestic and international students; for summer admission, 6/6 priority date for domestic and international students. Applications are processed on a rolling basis. *Application fee:* $30 ($100 for international students). Electronic applications accepted. *Application Contact:* Tyler Kostich, Director, Evening and Graduate Admissions, 636-949-4138, Fax: 636-949-4109, E-mail: adultadmissions@lindenwood.edu. *Provost and Vice President of Academic Affairs,* Dr. Marilyn Abbott, 636-949-4846, Fax: 636-949-4912, E-mail: mabbott@lindenwood.edu.

Plaster School of Business and Entrepreneurship Students: 197 full-time (97 women), 213 part-time (132 women); includes 81 minority (62 Black or African American, non-Hispanic/Latino; 1 American Indian or Alaska Native, non-Hispanic/Latino; 4 Asian, non-Hispanic/Latino; 9 Hispanic/Latino; 5 Two or more races, non-Hispanic/Latino), 83 international. Average age 31. 279 applicants, 54% accepted, 133 enrolled. *Faculty:* 15 full-time (6 women), 25 part-time/adjunct (7 women). Expenses: Contact institution. *Financial support:* In 2016–17, 256 students received support. Career-related internships or fieldwork, Federal Work-Study, institutionally sponsored loans, scholarships/grants, tuition waivers (partial), and unspecified assistantships available. Financial award application deadline: 6/30; financial award applicants required to submit FAFSA. In 2016, 269 master's awarded. *Program availability:* Part-time, evening/weekend, 100% online. Offers accountancy (M Acc); accounting (MBA); business administration (MBA); entrepreneurial studies (MBA); finance (MBA, MS); human resource management (MBA); international business (MBA); leadership (MA); management (MBA); marketing (MBA, MS); nonprofit administration (MA); public administration (MBA); sport management (MA); supply chain management (MBA). *Application deadline:* For fall admission, 8/28 priority date for domestic and international students; for winter admission, 1/8 priority date for domestic and international students; for spring admission, 3/5 for domestic students, 3/5 priority date for international students; for summer admission, 6/4 priority date for international students. Applications are processed on a rolling basis. *Application fee:* $30 ($100 for international students). Electronic applications accepted. *Application Contact:* Tyler Kostich, Director, Evening and Graduate Admissions, 636-949-4138, Fax: 636-949-4109, E-mail: adultadmissions@lindenwood.edu. *Dean, School of Business and Entrepreneurship,* Roger Ellis, 636-949-4839, E-mail: rellis@lindenwood.edu.

School of Accelerated Degree Programs Students: 609 full-time (386 women), 179 part-time (121 women); includes 257 minority (202 Black or African American, non-

Hispanic/Latino; 4 American Indian or Alaska Native, non-Hispanic/Latino; 5 Asian, non-Hispanic/Latino; 28 Hispanic/Latino; 1 Native Hawaiian or other Pacific Islander, non-Hispanic/Latino; 17 Two or more races, non-Hispanic/Latino; 28 international. Average age 36. 332 applicants, 70% accepted, 205 enrolled. *Faculty:* 16 full-time (7 women), 75 part-time/adjunct (27 women). Expenses: Contact institution. *Financial support:* In 2016–17, 467 students received support. Career-related internships or fieldwork, institutionally sponsored loans, scholarships/grants, tuition waivers (partial), and unspecified assistantships available. Financial award application deadline: 6/30; financial award applicants required to submit FAFSA. In 2016, 479 master's awarded. *Program availability:* Part-time, evening/weekend, 100% online. Offers administration (MSA); business administration (MBA); communications (MA); criminal justice and administration (MS); healthcare administration (MS); human resource management (MS); information technology (Certificate); managing information security (MS); managing information technology (MS); managing virtualization and cloud computing (MS); writing (MFA). *Application deadline:* For fall admission, 9/26 priority date for domestic and international students; for winter admission, 1/3 priority date for domestic and international students; for spring admission, 3/31 priority date for domestic and international students; for summer admission, 7/3 priority date for domestic and international students. Applications are processed on a rolling basis. *Application fee:* $30 ($100 for international students). Electronic applications accepted. *Application Contact:* Tyler Kostich, Director, Evening and Graduate Admissions, 636-949-4138, Fax: 636-949-4109, E-mail: adultadmissions@lindenwood.edu. *Dean, Accelerated Degree Programs,* Dr. Gina Ganahl, 636-949-4501, Fax: 636-949-4505, E-mail: gganahl@lindenwood.edu.

School of Arts, Media, and Communications Students: 15 full-time (8 women), 5 part-time (3 women); includes 4 minority (2 Black or African American, non-Hispanic/Latino; 1 Hispanic/Latino; 1 Two or more races, non-Hispanic/Latino), 3 international. Average age 30. 16 applicants, 56% accepted, 6 enrolled. *Faculty:* 17 full-time (6 women), 6 part-time/adjunct (5 women). Expenses: Contact institution. *Financial support:* In 2016–17, 12 students received support. Career-related internships or fieldwork, institutionally sponsored loans, scholarships/grants, tuition waivers (partial), and unspecified assistantships available. Financial award application deadline: 6/30; financial award applicants required to submit FAFSA. In 2016, 8 master's awarded. *Program availability:* Part-time. Offers cinema and media arts (MFA). *Application deadline:* For fall admission, 8/28 priority date for domestic and international students; for spring admission, 1/8 for domestic students, 1/8 priority date for international students; for summer admission, 6/5 priority date for domestic and international students. Applications are processed on a rolling basis. *Application fee:* $30 ($100 for international students). Electronic applications accepted. *Application Contact:* Tyler Kostich, Director, Evening and Graduate Admissions, 636-949-4138, Fax: 636-949-4109, E-mail: adultadmissions@lindenwood.edu. *Dean, School of Arts, Media, and Communications,* Dr. Joseph Alsobrook, 636-949-4164, Fax: 636-949-4910, E-mail: jalsobrook@lindenwood.edu.

School of Education Students: 292 full-time (227 women), 1,580 part-time (1,203 women); includes 404 minority (333 Black or African American, non-Hispanic/Latino; 4 American Indian or Alaska Native, non-Hispanic/Latino; 10 Asian, non-Hispanic/Latino; 36 Hispanic/Latino; 1 Native Hawaiian or other Pacific Islander, non-Hispanic/Latino; 20 Two or more races, non-Hispanic/Latino), 20 international. Average age 36. 558 applicants, 72% accepted, 353 enrolled. *Faculty:* 39 full-time (27 women), 210 part-time/adjunct (136 women). Expenses: Contact institution. *Financial support:* In 2016–17, 334 students received support. Career-related internships or fieldwork, Federal Work-Study, institutionally sponsored loans, scholarships/grants, tuition waivers (partial), and unspecified assistantships available. Financial award application deadline: 6/30; financial award applicants required to submit FAFSA. In 2016, 491 master's, 72 doctorates, 111 other advanced degrees awarded. *Program availability:* Part-time, evening/weekend, 100% online, blended/hybrid learning. Offers education (MA); educational administration (MA, Ed D, Ed S); English to speakers of other languages (MA); instructional leadership (Ed D, Ed S); library media (MA); professional counseling (MA); school administration (MA, Ed S); school counseling (MA); teaching (MA). *Application deadline:* For fall admission, 8/28 priority date for domestic and international students; for spring admission, 1/8 priority date for domestic and international students; for summer admission, 6/5 priority date for domestic and international students. Applications are processed on a rolling basis. *Application fee:* $30 ($100 for international students). Electronic applications accepted. *Application Contact:* Tyler Kostich, Director, Evening and Graduate Admissions, 636-949-4138, Fax: 636-949-4109, E-mail: adultadmissions@lindenwood.edu. *Dean, School of Education,* Dr. Cynthia Bice, 636-949-4618, Fax: 636-949-4197, E-mail: cbice@lindenwood.edu.

School of Health Sciences Students: 31 full-time (12 women), 54 part-time (47 women); includes 11 minority (4 Black or African American, non-Hispanic/Latino; 2 Asian, non-Hispanic/Latino; 4 Hispanic/Latino; 1 Two or more races, non-Hispanic/Latino), 4 international. Average age 35. 76 applicants, 43% accepted, 30 enrolled. *Faculty:* 10 full-time (5 women), 4 part-time/adjunct (all women). Expenses: Contact institution. *Financial support:* In 2016–17, 67 students received support. Career-related internships or fieldwork, Federal Work-Study, institutionally sponsored loans, scholarships/grants, tuition waivers (partial), and unspecified assistantships available. Financial award application deadline: 6/30; financial award applicants required to submit FAFSA. In 2016, 13 master's awarded. *Program availability:* Part-time, blended/hybrid learning. Offers human performance (MS); nursing (MS). *Application deadline:* For fall admission, 8/28 priority date for domestic and international students; for spring admission, 1/8 priority date for domestic and international students; for summer admission, 6/5 priority date for domestic and international students. Applications are processed on a rolling basis. *Application fee:* $30 ($100 for international students). Electronic applications accepted. *Application Contact:* Tyler Kostich, Director, Evening and Graduate Admissions, 636-949-4138, Fax: 636-949-4109, E-mail: adultadmissions@lindenwood.edu. *Dean, School of Health Sciences,* Dr. Cynthia Schroeder, 636-949-4318, E-mail: cschroeder@lindenwood.edu.

LINDENWOOD UNIVERSITY–BELLEVILLE, Belleville, IL 62226

General Information Independent-religious, coed, comprehensive institution.

GRADUATE UNITS

Graduate Programs

LINDSEY WILSON COLLEGE, Columbia, KY 42728

General Information Independent-religious, coed, comprehensive institution. *Graduate housing:* Rooms and/or apartments available on a first-come, first-served basis to single and married students.

GRADUATE UNITS

Division of Education *Program availability:* Online learning. Offers teacher as leader (M Ed).

Louisville Center for Design *Program availability:* Online learning. Offers interactive design (MA).

School of Professional Counseling *Program availability:* Part-time, evening/weekend, online learning. Offers counseling and human development (M Ed); counselor education and supervision (PhD).

LIPSCOMB UNIVERSITY, Nashville, TN 37204-3951

General Information Independent-religious, coed, comprehensive institution. CGS member. *Enrollment:* 4,632 graduate, professional, and undergraduate students; 857 full-time matriculated graduate/professional students (507 women), 642 part-time matriculated graduate/professional students (442 women). *Enrollment by degree level:* 967 master's, 428 doctoral, 104 other advanced degrees. *Graduate faculty:* 111 full-time (44 women), 100 part-time/adjunct (50 women). *Tuition:* Full-time $18,522; part-time $1029 per credit hour. Tuition and fees vary according to degree level and program. *Graduate housing:* Room and/or apartments available on a first-come, first-served basis to single students; on-campus housing not available to married students. Housing application deadline: 7/15. *Student services:* Campus employment opportunities, campus safety program, career counseling, exercise/wellness program, free psychological counseling, international student services, multicultural affairs office, services for students with disabilities, teacher training. *Library facilities:* Beaman Library plus 1 other. *Collection:* Books: 157,824 (physical), 167,520 (digital/electronic); Serial titles: 253 (physical), 489 (digital/electronic); Databases: 100. Students can reserve study rooms.

Computer facilities: 150 computers available on campus for general student use. A campuswide network can be accessed from student residence rooms and from off campus. Online class registration is available.
Website: http://www.lipscomb.edu/

General Application Contact: Barbara Blackman, Coordinator of Graduate Studies, 615-966-6287, Fax: 615-966-7619, E-mail: graduatestudies@lipscomb.edu.

GRADUATE UNITS

College of Business Students: 112 full-time (51 women), 69 part-time (34 women); includes 30 minority (17 Black or African American, non-Hispanic/Latino; 3 Asian, non-Hispanic/Latino; 8 Hispanic/Latino; 2 Two or more races, non-Hispanic/Latino), 5 international. Average age 32. 244 applicants, 55% accepted, 54 enrolled. *Faculty:* 22 full-time (4 women), 12 part-time/adjunct (4 women). Expenses: Contact institution. *Financial support:* Career-related internships or fieldwork, scholarships/grants, tuition waivers (partial), and unspecified assistantships available. Support available to part-time students. Financial award application deadline: 7/1; financial award applicants required to submit FAFSA. In 2016, 164 master's awarded. *Program availability:* Part-time, evening/weekend. Offers accountancy (M Acc); accounting (MBA); business administration (MM); conflict management (MBA); financial services (MBA); health care informatics (MBA); healthcare management (MBA); information security (MBA); leadership (MBA); nonprofit management (MBA); professional accountancy (Certificate); sports management (MBA); strategic human resources (MBA); sustainability (MBA). *Application deadline:* For fall admission, 6/15 for domestic students, 2/1 for international students; for winter admission, 6/1 for international students; for spring admission, 11/15 for domestic students. Applications are processed on a rolling basis. *Application fee:* $50 ($75 for international students). Electronic applications accepted. *Application Contact:* Karen Risley, Manager, Graduate Business Recruiting, 615-966-5145, E-mail: karen.risley@lipscomb.edu. *Associate Dean of Graduate Business Programs,* Allison Duke, 615-966-5732, Fax: 615-966-1818, E-mail: allison.duke@lipscomb.edu.

College of Computing and Technology Students: 21 full-time (10 women), 10 part-time (3 women); includes 9 minority (5 Black or African American, non-Hispanic/Latino; 4 Asian, non-Hispanic/Latino), 1 international. Average age 34. 47 applicants, 49% accepted, 12 enrolled. *Faculty:* 7 full-time (0 women), 6 part-time/adjunct (1 woman). Expenses: Contact institution. *Financial support:* Scholarships/grants and employer agreements available. Financial award applicants required to submit FAFSA. In 2016, 26 degrees awarded. *Program availability:* Part-time, evening/weekend. Offers data science (MS); information technology (MS); software engineering (MS). *Application deadline:* Applications are processed on a rolling basis. *Application fee:* $50 ($75 for international students). Electronic applications accepted. *Application Contact:* Brett Ramsey, Enrollment Management Specialist, 615-966-1193, E-mail: brett.ramsey@lipscomb.edu. *Dean,* Dr. Fortune S. Mhlanga, 615-966-5073, E-mail: fortune.mhlanga@lipscomb.edu.

College of Education Students: 111 full-time (80 women), 345 part-time (292 women); includes 104 minority (70 Black or African American, non-Hispanic/Latino; 1 American Indian or Alaska Native, non-Hispanic/Latino; 3 Asian, non-Hispanic/Latino; 20 Hispanic/Latino; 10 Two or more races, non-Hispanic/Latino), 1 international. Average age 33. *Faculty:* 21 full-time (15 women), 38 part-time/adjunct (26 women). Expenses: Contact institution. *Financial support:* Scholarships/grants, unspecified assistantships, and partnerships with local school districts available. Financial award applicants required to submit FAFSA. In 2016, 201 master's, 36 doctorates, 86 other advanced degrees awarded. *Program availability:* Part-time, evening/weekend, 100% online. Offers applied behavior analysis (MS, Certificate); educational leadership (M Ed, Ed S); English language learning (M Ed, Ed S); instructional coaching (M Ed, Certificate, Ed S); instructional practice (M Ed); learning organizations and strategic change (Ed D); literacy coaching (Certificate); reading specialty (M Ed, Ed S); special education (M Ed); teaching, learning, and leading (M Ed); technology integration (M Ed, Ed S); technology integration specialist (Certificate). *Application deadline:* For fall admission, 8/29 priority date for domestic students; for spring admission, 1/15 priority date for domestic students. Applications are processed on a rolling basis. *Application fee:* $50 ($75 for international students). Electronic applications accepted. *Application Contact:* Amanda Logsdon, Director of Enrollment and Outreach, 615-966-7199, E-mail: amanda.logsdon@lipscomb.edu. *Director of Graduate Studies,* Dr. Deborah Boyd, 615-966-6263, E-mail: deborah.boyd@lipscomb.edu.

College of Pharmacy Students: 297 full-time (172 women); includes 74 minority (26 Black or African American, non-Hispanic/Latino; 4 American Indian or Alaska Native, non-Hispanic/Latino; 30 Asian, non-Hispanic/Latino; 7 Hispanic/Latino; 1 Native Hawaiian or other Pacific Islander, non-Hispanic/Latino; 6 Two or more races, non-Hispanic/Latino). Average age 26. *Faculty:* 32 full-time (14 women), 6 part-time/adjunct (4 women). Expenses: Contact institution. *Financial support:* Application deadline: 2/15; applicants required to submit FAFSA. In 2016, 3 master's, 69 doctorates awarded. Offers healthcare informatics (MS); pharmacy (Pharm D). *Application deadline:* For fall admission, 2/7 for domestic students. Applications are processed on a rolling basis. *Application fee:* $50 ($75 for international students). Electronic applications accepted. *Application Contact:* Laura Ward, Director of Admissions and Student Affairs, 615-966-

7173, E-mail: laura.ward@lipscomb.edu. *Dean/Professor of Pharmacy Practice*, Dr. Roger Davis, 615-966-7161.

Department of Graduate Psychology and Counseling Students: 120 full-time (92 women), 30 part-time (27 women); includes 38 minority (22 Black or African American, non-Hispanic/Latino; 1 American Indian or Alaska Native, non-Hispanic/Latino; 1 Asian, non-Hispanic/Latino; 11 Hispanic/Latino; 3 Two or more races, non-Hispanic/Latino), 2 international. Average age 28. *Faculty*: 13 full-time (5 women), 10 part-time/adjunct (6 women). Expenses: Contact institution. *Financial support*: Scholarships/grants and unspecified assistantships available. Financial award applicants required to submit FAFSA. In 2016, 44 master's, 1 other advanced degree awarded. *Program availability*: Part-time, evening/weekend. Offers clinical mental health counseling (MS); counseling psychology (Certificate); marriage and family therapy (MMFT); psychology (MS). *Application deadline*: For fall admission, 7/1 for domestic students; for spring admission, 11/1 for domestic students. Applications are processed on a rolling basis. *Application fee*: $50 ($75 for international students). Electronic applications accepted. *Application Contact*: Kathi Johnson, Recruiting and Marketing Coordinator, 615-966-5237, E-mail: kathi.johnson@lipscomb.edu. *Director/Professor of Psychology*, Dr. Shanna Ray, 615-966-5833, E-mail: shanna.ray@lipscomb.edu.

Hazelip School of Theology Students: 52 full-time (12 women), 90 part-time (18 women); includes 17 minority (13 Black or African American, non-Hispanic/Latino; 2 Hispanic/Latino; 2 Two or more races, non-Hispanic/Latino), 4 international. Average age 38. *Faculty*: 13 full-time (0 women), 4 part-time/adjunct (1 woman). Expenses: Contact institution. *Financial support*: Scholarships/grants and unspecified assistantships available. Financial award application deadline: 3/1; financial award applicants required to submit FAFSA. In 2016, 16 master's, 8 doctorates awarded. *Program availability*: Part-time, evening/weekend, online learning. Offers Christian practice (MA); missional and spiritual formation (D Min); student ministry (Certificate); theology (M Div). *Application deadline*: For fall admission, 8/1 priority date for domestic students; for spring admission, 12/15 for domestic students. Applications are processed on a rolling basis. *Application fee*: $50 ($75 for international students). Electronic applications accepted. *Application Contact*: Kellye McCool, Coordinator of Student Services, 615-966-5458, Fax: 615-966-6052, E-mail: kellye.mccool@lipscomb.edu. *Director*, Frank Guertin, 615-966-5709, Fax: 615-966-5352, E-mail: frank.guertin@lipscomb.edu.

Institute for Conflict Management Students: 15 full-time (8 women), 24 part-time (17 women); includes 9 minority (8 Black or African American, non-Hispanic/Latino; 1 Two or more races, non-Hispanic/Latino). Average age 40. *Faculty*: 3 full-time (1 woman), 6 part-time/adjunct (4 women). Expenses: Contact institution. *Financial support*: Tuition waivers (full) available. Financial award applicants required to submit FAFSA. In 2016, 13 master's, 9 other advanced degrees awarded. *Program availability*: Part-time, evening/weekend. Offers conflict management (MA, Certificate). *Application deadline*: For fall admission, 7/15 for domestic students; for spring admission, 12/15 for domestic students. Applications are processed on a rolling basis. *Application fee*: $50 ($75 for international students). Electronic applications accepted. *Application Contact*: Dr. Phyllis Hildreth, Academic Director, 615-966-5695, Fax: 615-966-7143, E-mail: phyllis.hildreth@lipscomb.edu. *Director*, Dr. Steve Joiner, 615-966-7141, Fax: 615-966-7143, E-mail: phyllis.hildreth@lipscomb.edu.

Institute for Sustainable Practice Students: 8 full-time (5 women), 10 part-time (7 women); includes 5 minority (3 Black or African American, non-Hispanic/Latino; 2 Hispanic/Latino). Average age 31. 24 applicants, 71% accepted, 8 enrolled. *Faculty*: 2 full-time (0 women), 3 part-time/adjunct (1 woman). Expenses: Contact institution. *Financial support*: Unspecified assistantships available. Financial award applicants required to submit FAFSA. In 2016, 13 master's awarded. *Program availability*: Part-time, evening/weekend, online learning. Offers sustainable practice (MS, Certificate). *Application deadline*: For fall admission, 7/15 for domestic students; for spring admission, 12/15 for domestic students. Applications are processed on a rolling basis. *Application fee*: $50 ($75 for international students). Electronic applications accepted. *Application Contact*: Emily Stutzman Jones, Academic Director, 615-966-5076, E-mail: emily.jones@lipscomb.edu. *Executive Director*, G. Dodd Galbreath, 615-966-1771, E-mail: dodd.galbreath@lipscomb.edu.

Nelson and Sue Andrews Institute for Civic Leadership Students: 10 full-time (7 women), 15 part-time (10 women); includes 17 minority (15 Black or African American, non-Hispanic/Latino; 2 Two or more races, non-Hispanic/Latino). Average age 37. *Faculty*: 1 (woman) full-time, 1 (woman) part-time/adjunct. Expenses: Contact institution. *Financial support*: Applicants required to submit FAFSA. In 2016, 10 master's awarded. *Program availability*: Part-time, evening/weekend. Offers civic leadership (MA). *Application deadline*: Applications are processed on a rolling basis. *Application fee*: $50 ($75 for international students). Electronic applications accepted. *Application Contact*: Dr. MIchelle Steele, Academic Director, 615-966-5181, E-mail: michelle.steele@lipscomb.edu. *Executive Director*, Linda Peek Schacht, 615-966-1341, E-mail: linda.schacht@lipscomb.edu.

Program in Biomolecular Science Students: 27 full-time (16 women), 3 part-time (1 woman); includes 6 minority (4 Black or African American, non-Hispanic/Latino; 2 Asian, non-Hispanic/Latino). Average age 26. 63 applicants, 65% accepted, 9 enrolled. *Faculty*: 6 full-time (4 women), 1 part-time/adjunct (0 women). Expenses: Contact institution. *Financial support*: Unspecified assistantships available. Financial award applicants required to submit FAFSA. In 2016, 27 master's awarded. *Program availability*: Part-time, evening/weekend. Offers biomolecular science (MS). *Application deadline*: For fall admission, 8/1 for domestic students; for winter admission, 12/14 for domestic students; for spring admission, 5/14 for domestic students. Applications are processed on a rolling basis. *Application fee*: $50 ($75 for international students). Electronic applications accepted. *Application Contact*: Tina Fulford, Administrative Assistant, 615-966-5330, E-mail: tina.fulford@lipscomb.edu. *Director*, Dr. Kent Gallaher, 615-966-5721, E-mail: kent.gallaher@lipscomb.edu.

Program in Exercise and Nutrition Science Students: 25 full-time (16 women), 15 part-time (12 women); includes 7 minority (4 Black or African American, non-Hispanic/Latino; 3 Hispanic/Latino). Average age 27. *Faculty*: 7 full-time (4 women). Expenses: Contact institution. *Financial support*: Unspecified assistantships available. Financial award applicants required to submit FAFSA. In 2016, 31 master's awarded. *Program availability*: Part-time, evening/weekend. Offers exercise and nutrition science (MS). *Application deadline*: For fall admission, 6/1 for domestic students; for spring admission, 12/1 for domestic students. Applications are processed on a rolling basis. *Application fee*: $50 ($75 for international students). Electronic applications accepted. *Application Contact*: Julie Lillicrap, Administrative Assistant, 615-966-5700, E-mail: julie.lillicrap@lipscomb.edu. *Director*, Dr. Karen Robichaud, 615-966-5602, E-mail: karen.robichaud@lipscomb.edu.

Program in Film and Creative Media Students: 21 full-time (14 women), 6 part-time (5 women); includes 12 minority (10 Black or African American, non-Hispanic/Latino; 1 Hispanic/Latino; 1 Two or more races, non-Hispanic/Latino), 1 international. Average age 30. 21 applicants, 48% accepted, 8 enrolled. *Faculty*: 5 full-time (1 woman), 4 part-time/adjunct (1 woman). Expenses: Contact institution. *Financial support*: Unspecified assistantships available. Financial award applicants required to submit FAFSA. In 2016, 7 master's awarded. *Program availability*: Part-time, evening/weekend. Offers writer/director (MFA). *Application deadline*: Applications are processed on a rolling basis. *Application fee*: $50 ($75 for international students). Electronic applications accepted. *Application Contact*: Josh Link, Recruiting and Marketing Coordinator, 615-966-6005, E-mail: josh.link@lipscomb.edu. *Director*, David DeBorde, 615-966-7111, E-mail: david.deborde@lipscomb.edu.

Program in Organizational Leadership Students: 4 full-time (1 woman), 16 part-time (11 women); includes 2 minority (1 Black or African American, non-Hispanic/Latino; 1 Hispanic/Latino). Average age 42. *Faculty*: 2 full-time (both women), 2 part-time/adjunct (1 woman). Expenses: Contact institution. *Program availability*: Part-time, online only, blended/hybrid learning. Offers organizational leadership (MPS). *Application deadline*: For fall admission, 8/1 for domestic students. Applications are processed on a rolling basis. *Application fee*: $50 ($75 for international students). Electronic applications accepted. *Application Contact*: Barbara Blackman, Coordinator of Graduate Studies, 615-966-6287, Fax: 615-966-7619, E-mail: graduatestudies@lipscomb.edu. *Director*, Dr. Hope Nordstrom, 615-966-1107, E-mail: hope.nordstrom@lipscomb.edu.

School of Public Policy Students: 22 full-time (15 women); includes 8 minority (7 Black or African American, non-Hispanic/Latino; 1 Hispanic/Latino). Average age 28. *Faculty*: 6 full-time (2 women), 3 part-time/adjunct (1 woman). Expenses: Contact institution. Offers leadership and public service (MA). *Application deadline*: Applications are processed on a rolling basis. *Application fee*: $50 ($75 for international students). Electronic applications accepted. *Application Contact*: Amy Goode, New Student Enrollment Manager, 615-966-6691, E-mail: amy.goode@lipscomb.edu. *Academic Director*, Dr. Kristine LaLonde, 615-966-6692, E-mail: kristine.lalonde@lipscomb.edu.

LOCK HAVEN UNIVERSITY OF PENNSYLVANIA, Lock Haven, PA 17745-2390

General Information State-supported, coed, comprehensive institution. *Graduate housing*: Room and/or apartments available on a first-come, first-served basis to single students; on-campus housing not available to married students. Housing application deadline: 6/1.

GRADUATE UNITS

College of Liberal Arts and Education *Program availability*: Part-time, evening/weekend, online learning. Offers alternative education (M Ed); educational leadership (M Ed); teaching and learning (M Ed). Electronic applications accepted.

College of Natural, Behavioral and Health Sciences Offers actuarial science (PSM); athletic training (MS); health promotion/education (MHS); healthcare management (MHS); physician assistant (MS). Program also offered at the Clearfield, Coudersport, and Harrisburg campuses. Electronic applications accepted.

The Stephen Poorman College of Business, Information Systems, and Human Services *Program availability*: Online learning. Offers clinical mental health counseling (MS); sport science (MS). Electronic applications accepted.

LOGAN UNIVERSITY, Chesterfield, MO 63017

General Information Independent, coed, upper-level institution. *Enrollment*: 1,136 graduate, professional, and undergraduate students; 749 full-time matriculated graduate/professional students (310 women), 256 part-time matriculated graduate/professional students (183 women). *Enrollment by degree level*: 299 master's, 696 doctoral. *Graduate faculty*: 59 full-time (21 women), 45 part-time/adjunct (16 women). *Graduate housing*: On-campus housing not available. *Student services*: Campus employment opportunities, campus safety program, career counseling, free psychological counseling, services for students with disabilities. *Library facilities*: Learning Resources Center. *Collection*: Books: 12,651 (physical), 3,044 (digital/electronic); Serial titles: 23 (physical), 20,360 (digital/electronic); Databases: 87. Weekly public service hours: 84. *Research affiliation*: BTE-Multi-Cervical Unit (cervical spine analysis), Cadwell (electrophysiological diagnosis), Standard Process (nutrition and lipid management), Biofreeze (topical analgesics), Foot Levelers, Inc. (orthotics).

Computer facilities: 100 computers available on campus for general student use. A campuswide network can be accessed. Online class registration, student portal, learning management system, online storage, specialty health care software, high-speed printing are available.

Website: http://www.logan.edu/

General Application Contact: Natacha Douglas, Executive Director of Admissions, 636-227-2100 Ext. 1718, Fax: 636-207-2431, E-mail: admissions@logan.edu.

GRADUATE UNITS

College of Chiropractic Students: 695 full-time (270 women), 1 (woman) part-time; includes 74 minority (27 Black or African American, non-Hispanic/Latino; 3 American Indian or Alaska Native, non-Hispanic/Latino; 20 Asian, non-Hispanic/Latino; 15 Hispanic/Latino; 9 Two or more races, non-Hispanic/Latino), 14 international. Average age 26. 240 applicants, 124 enrolled. *Faculty*: 45 full-time (19 women), 31 part-time/adjunct (10 women). Expenses: Contact institution. *Financial support*: In 2016–17, 129 students received support. Federal Work-Study and scholarships/grants available. Support available to part-time students. Financial award applicants required to submit FAFSA. In 2016, 132 doctorates awarded. Offers chiropractic (DC). *Application deadline*: Applications are processed on a rolling basis. *Application fee*: $50. Electronic applications accepted. *Application Contact*: Natacha Douglas, Executive Director of Admissions, 636-227-2100 Ext. 1718, Fax: 636-207-2425, E-mail: admissions@logan.edu. *Dean of the College of Chiropractic*, Dr. Vincent DeBono, 636-227-2100 Ext. 2701, Fax: 636-207-2431, E-mail: vincent.debono@logan.edu.

College of Health Sciences Students: 54 full-time (40 women), 255 part-time (182 women); includes 38 minority (16 Black or African American, non-Hispanic/Latino; 4 Asian, non-Hispanic/Latino; 10 Hispanic/Latino; 8 Two or more races, non-Hispanic/Latino), 14 international. Average age 35. 229 applicants, 88% accepted, 164 enrolled. *Faculty*: 2 full-time (1 woman), 14 part-time/adjunct (6 women). Expenses: Contact institution. *Financial support*: In 2016–17, 4 students received support. Federal Work-Study and scholarships/grants available. Support available to part-time students. Financial award applicants required to submit FAFSA. In 2016, 89 master's awarded. *Program availability*: Part-time, online only, 100% online. Offers health informatics (MS); health professionals education (DHPE); nutrition and human performance (MS); sports science and rehabilitation (MS). *Application deadline*: Applications are processed on a rolling basis. *Application fee*: $50. Electronic applications accepted. *Application Contact*: Jordan LaMarca, Assistant Director of Admissions, 636-227-2100 Ext. 1973, Fax: 636-207-2425, E-mail: admissions@logan.edu. *Dean, College of Health Sciences*, Dr. Sherri Cole, 636-227-2100 Ext. 2702, Fax: 636-207-2418, E-mail: sherri.cole@logan.edu.

LOGOS EVANGELICAL SEMINARY, El Monte, CA 91731

General Information Independent-religious, coed, graduate-only institution. *Enrollment by degree level:* 141 master's, 40 doctoral, 4 other advanced degrees. *Graduate faculty:* 13 full-time (4 women), 11 part-time/adjunct (3 women). *Tuition:* Full-time $8624; part-time $308 per unit. *Required fees:* $50 per term. Tuition and fees vary according to degree level. *Graduate housing:* Rooms and/or apartments available on a first-come, first-served basis to single and married students. Typical cost: $6840 per year for single students; $9360 per year for married students. Room charges vary according to housing facility selected. Housing application deadline: 7/15. *Student services:* Campus employment opportunities, campus safety program, career counseling, exercise/wellness program, free psychological counseling, international student services, low-cost health insurance. *Library facilities:* Logos Library plus 1 other. *Collection:* Books: 57,516 (physical); Serial titles: 157 (physical). Weekly public service hours: 65; students can reserve study rooms.

Computer facilities: 17 computers available on campus for general student use. A campuswide network can be accessed. Online class registration is available. Website: http://www.les.edu/?lang=zh

General Application Contact: Becky Perng, Admission Specialist, 626-571-5110 Ext. 112, Fax: 626-571-5119, E-mail: admission@les.edu.

GRADUATE UNITS

Graduate Programs Students: 78 full-time (31 women), 107 part-time (57 women); includes 111 minority (all Asian, non-Hispanic/Latino), 74 international. Average age 48. 58 applicants, 95% accepted, 47 enrolled. *Faculty:* 13 full-time (4 women), 11 part-time/adjunct (3 women). Expenses: Contact institution. In 2016, 26 master's, 16 doctorates, 3 other advanced degrees awarded. *Program availability:* Part-time, 100% online. Offers theology (M Div, MA, Th M, D Min, PhD, Diploma). *Application deadline:* For fall admission, 6/15 for domestic students, 5/15 for international students; for spring admission, 12/15 for domestic students, 10/15 for international students. Applications are processed on a rolling basis. *Application fee:* $75. Electronic applications accepted. *Application Contact:* Becky Perng, Admission Specialist, 626-571-5110 Ext. 112, Fax: 626-571-5119, E-mail: admission@les.edu. *Academic Dean,* Rev. Ekron Chen, PhD, 626-571-5110 Ext. 120, Fax: 626-571-5119, E-mail: ekron@les.edu.

LOMA LINDA UNIVERSITY, Loma Linda, CA 92350

General Information Independent-religious, coed, university. CGS member. *Graduate housing:* Room and/or apartments available on a first-come, first-served basis to single students; on-campus housing not available to married students. *Research affiliation:* City of Hope Hospital (cancer research), Children's Hospital Los Angeles (cancer research), Children's Hospital Orange County (cancer research).

GRADUATE UNITS

School of Allied Health Professions Offers allied health professions (MOT, MPA, MS, DPT, OTD, PhD, SLPD); occupational therapy (MOT, OTD); physical therapy (DPT, PhD); physician assistant sciences (MPA); rehabilitation (MS); speech-language pathology (MS, SLPD). Electronic applications accepted.

School of Behavioral Health Offers behavioral health (MS, MSW, DMFT, PhD, Psy D, Certificate); child life specialist (MS); clinical mediation (Certificate); clinical psychology (PhD, Psy D); counseling (MS); criminal justice (MS); drug and alcohol counseling (Certificate); family life education (Certificate); gerontology (MS); marital and family therapy (DMFT); school counseling (Certificate); social policy and social research (PhD); social work (MSW). Electronic applications accepted.

School of Dentistry Offers dentistry (MS, DDS, Certificate); endodontics (MS, Certificate); implant dentistry (MS, Certificate); oral and maxillofacial surgery (MS, Certificate); orthodontics and dentofacial orthopedics (MS, Certificate); periodontics (MS).

School of Medicine Offers biochemistry (MS, PhD); human anatomy (PhD); medicine (MS, MD, PhD); microbiology (PhD); pathology (PhD); pharmacology (PhD); physiology (PhD).

School of Nursing *Program availability:* Part-time. Offers adult/gerontology (MS); nursing (MS, DNP, PhD); nursing administration (MS); obstetrics-pediatrics (MS). Electronic applications accepted.

School of Pharmacy Offers pharmacy (Pharm D).

School of Public Health *Program availability:* Part-time. Offers biostatistics (MPH); environmental and occupational health (MPH); epidemiology (MPH, Dr PH, PhD); global health (MPH); health education (MPH, Dr PH); healthcare administration (MBA); public health (MBA, MPH, MS, Dr PH, PhD); public health nutrition (MPH, Dr PH). Electronic applications accepted.

School of Religion Offers bioethics (MA, Certificate); chaplaincy (MS); religion (MA, MS, Certificate); religion and society (MA). Electronic applications accepted.

LONDON METROPOLITAN UNIVERSITY, London N7 8DB, United Kingdom

General Information Private, coed, university.

GRADUATE UNITS
Graduate Programs

LONG ISLAND UNIVERSITY–BRENTWOOD CAMPUS, Brentwood, NY 11717

General Information Independent, coed, upper-level institution. *Enrollment:* 98 full-time matriculated graduate/professional students (80 women), 57 part-time matriculated graduate/professional students (47 women). *Enrollment by degree level:* 141 master's, 13 other advanced degrees. *Graduate faculty:* 54 part-time/adjunct (30 women). *Tuition:* Full-time $28,272; part-time $1178 per credit. *Required fees:* $451 per term. *Graduate housing:* On-campus housing not available. *Student services:* Career counseling, services for students with disabilities, teacher training. *Library facilities:* Brentwood Campus Library.

Computer facilities: Computer purchase and lease plans are available. 50 computers available on campus for general student use. A campuswide network can be accessed from off campus. Online class registration is available. Website: http://www.liu.edu/

General Application Contact: Jean Conroy, Associate Dean, 631-287-8500, Fax: 631-287-8575, E-mail: jean.conroy@liu.edu.

GRADUATE UNITS

Graduate Programs Students: 98 full-time (80 women), 57 part-time (47 women); includes 28 minority (7 Black or African American, non-Hispanic/Latino; 1 Asian, non-Hispanic/Latino; 20 Hispanic/Latino). 85 applicants, 89% accepted, 43 enrolled. *Faculty:* 54 part-time/adjunct (30 women). Expenses: Contact institution. *Financial support:* Scholarships/grants and unspecified assistantships available. Support available to part-

time students. Financial award applicants required to submit FAFSA. In 2016, 99 master's, 11 other advanced degrees awarded. *Program availability:* Part-time. Offers childhood education (grades 1-6) (MS); childhood education/literacy (grades 1-6) (MS); childhood education/special education (grades 1-6) (MS); clinical mental health counseling (MS, Advanced Certificate); early childhood education (B-2) (MS); literacy (B-6) (MS Ed); school counselor (MS); special education (grades 1-6) (MS Ed); students with disabilities generalist (grades 7-12) (Advanced Certificate). *Application deadline:* Applications are processed on a rolling basis. *Application fee:* $50. Electronic applications accepted. *Application Contact:* Scott Aug, Associate Director of Enrollment Management, 631-287-8500, Fax: 631-287-8575, E-mail: scott.aug@liu.edu. *Dean and Chief Operating Officer,* Donna Di Donato, 631-287-8010, Fax: 631-287-8575, E-mail: donna.didonato@liu.edu.

LONG ISLAND UNIVERSITY–HUDSON, Purchase, NY 10577

General Information Independent, coed, graduate-only institution. *Enrollment by degree level:* 167 master's, 42 other advanced degrees. *Graduate faculty:* 7 full-time (5 women), 42 part-time/adjunct (25 women). *Tuition:* Full-time $28,272; part-time $1178 per credit. *Required fees:* $451 per term. *Graduate housing:* On-campus housing not available. *Student services:* Career counseling, services for students with disabilities, teacher training. *Library facilities:* Long Island University Library System.

Computer facilities: A campuswide network can be accessed from off campus. Online class registration is available. Website: http://liu.edu/Hudson

General Application Contact: Dr. Sylvia Blake, Dean/Chief Operating Officer, 914-831-2700, E-mail: westchester@liu.edu.

GRADUATE UNITS

Graduate School Students: 55 full-time (41 women), 158 part-time (123 women); includes 40 minority (8 Black or African American, non-Hispanic/Latino; 1 Asian, non-Hispanic/Latino; 31 Hispanic/Latino). Average age 35. *Faculty:* 7 full-time (5 women), 42 part-time/adjunct (25 women). Expenses: Contact institution. *Program availability:* Part-time, evening/weekend, online learning. Offers autism (Advanced Certificate); childhood education (MS Ed); early childhood education (MS Ed); educational leadership (MS Ed); finance (MBA); health administration (MPA); healthcare sector management (MBA); literacy (MS Ed); management (MBA); marriage and family therapy (MS); mental health counseling (MS); middle childhood and adolescence education (MS Ed); pharmaceutics (MS); public administration (MPA); school counseling (MS Ed, Advanced Certificate); school psychology (MS Ed); special education (MS Ed); TESOL (all grades) (Advanced Certificate); TESOL and bilingual education (MS Ed); the business of pharmaceutics and biotechnology (MBA). *Application deadline:* Applications are processed on a rolling basis. *Application fee:* $50. Electronic applications accepted. *Application Contact:* Cindy Pagnotta, Director of Marketing and Enrollment, 914-831-2701, Fax: 914-251-5959, E-mail: cindy.pagnotta@liu.edu. *Dean and Chief Operating Officer,* Dr. Sylvia Blake, 914-831-2700, E-mail: westchester@liu.edu.

LONG ISLAND UNIVERSITY–LIU BROOKLYN, Brooklyn, NY 11201-8423

General Information Independent, coed, university. *Enrollment:* 1,878 full-time matriculated graduate/professional students (1,249 women), 1,342 part-time matriculated graduate/professional students (1,023 women). *Enrollment by degree level:* 2,503 master's, 645 doctoral, 72 other advanced degrees. *Graduate faculty:* 213 full-time (112 women), 325 part-time/adjunct (178 women). *Tuition:* Full-time $28,272; part-time $1178 per credit. *Required fees:* $451 per term. Tuition and fees vary according to degree level, program and student level. *Graduate housing:* Room and/or apartments available on a first-come, first-served basis to single students; on-campus housing not available to married students. Typical cost: $20,718 (including board). Room and board charges vary according to board plan and housing facility selected. Housing application deadline: 5/1. *Student services:* Campus employment opportunities, career counseling, exercise/wellness program, international student services, low-cost health insurance, services for students with disabilities, teacher training, writing training. *Library facilities:* Salena Library. *Collection:* Books: 217,633 (physical), 170,074 (digital/electronic); Serial titles: 327,932 (physical), 94,194 (digital/electronic); Databases: 396. *Research affiliation:* California Table Grape Commission (pharmacy), Latitude Pharmaceuticals, Inc. (pharmacy), National Institute for Pharmaceutical Technology and Education (pharmacy), Natoli Engineering Company (pharmacy), Onconova Therapeutics, Inc. (pharmacy), Transdermal Research Pharm Laboratories, LLC (pharmacy).

Computer facilities: 580 computers available on campus for general student use. A campuswide network can be accessed from student residence rooms and from off campus. Online class registration is available. Website: http://www.liu.edu/

General Application Contact: Gabrielle Gannon, Director of Graduate Admissions, 718-488-1011, Fax: 718-780-6110, E-mail: bkln-admissions@liu.edu.

GRADUATE UNITS

Arnold and Marie Schwartz College of Pharmacy and Health Sciences Students: 562 full-time (337 women), 42 part-time (24 women); includes 197 minority (26 Black or African American, non-Hispanic/Latino; 1 American Indian or Alaska Native, non-Hispanic/Latino; 138 Asian, non-Hispanic/Latino; 21 Hispanic/Latino; 11 Two or more races, non-Hispanic/Latino), 180 international. 297 applicants, 58% accepted, 44 enrolled. *Faculty:* 18 full-time (6 women), 6 part-time/adjunct (1 woman). Expenses: Contact institution. *Financial support:* In 2016–17, 66 students received support, including 11 research assistantships with partial tuition reimbursements available (averaging $5,090 per year), 54 teaching assistantships with partial tuition reimbursements available (averaging $2,140 per year); career-related internships or fieldwork, Federal Work-Study, institutionally sponsored loans, scholarships/grants, tuition waivers (full and partial), and unspecified assistantships also available. Support available to part-time students. Financial award application deadline: 2/15; financial award applicants required to submit FAFSA. In 2016, 114 master's, 206 doctorates awarded. *Program availability:* Part-time. Offers drug regulatory affairs (MS); pharmaceutics (MS, PhD); pharmacology and toxicology (MS); pharmacy (Pharm D). *Application deadline:* Applications are processed on a rolling basis. *Application fee:* $50. Electronic applications accepted. *Application Contact:* Michael Young, Senior Assistant Director of Admissions, 718-488-3308, E-mail: michael.young@liu.edu. *Dean,* Dr. John M. Pezzuto, 718-488-1004, Fax: 718-488-0628, E-mail: john.pezzuto@liu.edu.

Harriet Rothkopf Heilbrunn School of Nursing Students: 2 full-time (both women), 183 part-time (167 women); includes 116 minority (73 Black or African American, non-Hispanic/Latino; 27 Asian, non-Hispanic/Latino; 12 Hispanic/Latino; 4 Two or more races, non-Hispanic/Latino), 1 international. 185 applicants, 38% accepted, 52 enrolled. *Faculty:* 4 full-time (3 women), 9 part-time/adjunct (7 women). Expenses: Contact institution. *Financial support:* In 2016–17, 24 students received support. Career-related internships or fieldwork, Federal Work-Study, institutionally sponsored loans, scholarships/grants, and unspecified assistantships available. Support available to part-time students. Financial award application deadline: 2/15; financial award applicants required to submit FAFSA. In 2016, 65 master's awarded. *Program availability:* Part-time, evening/weekend, blended/hybrid learning. Offers adult nurse practitioner (MS, Advanced Certificate); family nurse practitioner (MS, Advanced Certificate); nurse educator (MS). *Application deadline:* Applications are processed on a rolling basis. *Application fee:* $50. Electronic applications accepted. *Application Contact:* Richard Sunday, Dean of Admissions, 718-488-1011, Fax: 718-780-6110, E-mail: bkln-admissions@liu.edu. *Dean,* Dr. David Keepnews, 718-488-1059, E-mail: david.keepnews@liu.edu.

Richard L. Conolly College of Liberal Arts and Sciences Students: 355 full-time (276 women), 220 part-time (161 women); includes 245 minority (119 Black or African American, non-Hispanic/Latino; 32 Asian, non-Hispanic/Latino; 80 Hispanic/Latino; 1 Native Hawaiian or other Pacific Islander, non-Hispanic/Latino; 13 Two or more races, non-Hispanic/Latino), 85 international. 792 applicants, 41% accepted, 141 enrolled. *Faculty:* 90 full-time (35 women), 125 part-time/adjunct (67 women). Expenses: Contact institution. *Financial support:* In 2016–17, 120 fellowships with full and partial tuition reimbursements (averaging $915 per year), 5 research assistantships with full and partial tuition reimbursements (averaging $2,300 per year), 136 teaching assistantships with full and partial tuition reimbursements (averaging $2,300 per year) were awarded; career-related internships or fieldwork, Federal Work-Study, institutionally sponsored loans, scholarships/grants, tuition waivers (full and partial), and unspecified assistantships also available. Support available to part-time students. Financial award application deadline: 2/15; financial award applicants required to submit FAFSA. In 2016, 154 master's, 18 doctorates, 4 other advanced degrees awarded. *Program availability:* Part-time, evening/weekend. Offers biology (MS); chemistry (MS); clinical psychology (PhD); communication sciences and disorders (MS); creative writing (MFA); English (MA); media arts (MA, MFA); political science (MA); psychology (MS); social science (MS); sociology (MA); speech-language pathology (MS); United Nations (Advanced Certificate); urban studies (MA); writing and production for television (MFA). *Application deadline:* Applications are processed on a rolling basis. *Application fee:* $50. Electronic applications accepted. *Application Contact:* Gabrielle Gannon, Director of Graduate Admissions, 718-488-1011, Fax: 718-780-6110, E-mail: bkln-admissions@liu.edu. *Acting Dean,* Dr. Kevin Lauth, 718-488-1347, E-mail: kevin.lauth@liu.edu.

School of Business, Public Administration and Information Sciences Students: 275 full-time (150 women), 238 part-time (161 women); includes 281 minority (200 Black or African American, non-Hispanic/Latino; 2 American Indian or Alaska Native, non-Hispanic/Latino; 38 Asian, non-Hispanic/Latino; 36 Hispanic/Latino; 1 Native Hawaiian or other Pacific Islander, non-Hispanic/Latino; 4 Two or more races, non-Hispanic/Latino), 140 international. 796 applicants, 66% accepted, 143 enrolled. *Faculty:* 18 full-time (9 women), 32 part-time/adjunct (10 women). Expenses: Contact institution. *Financial support:* In 2016–17, 94 students received support. Career-related internships or fieldwork, Federal Work-Study, institutionally sponsored loans, scholarships/grants, and unspecified assistantships available. Support available to part-time students. Financial award application deadline: 2/15; financial award applicants required to submit FAFSA. In 2016, 185 master's, 17 other advanced degrees awarded. *Program availability:* Part-time, evening/weekend, blended/hybrid learning. Offers accounting (MBA); accounting (MS); business administration (MBA); computer science (MS); gerontology (Advanced Certificate); health administration (MPA); human resources management (MS); not-for-profit management (Advanced Certificate); public administration (MPA); taxation (MS). *Application deadline:* Applications are processed on a rolling basis. *Application fee:* $50. Electronic applications accepted. *Application Contact:* Gabrielle Gannon, Director of Graduate Admissions, 718-488-1011, Fax: 718-780-6110, E-mail: bkln-admissions@liu.edu. *Dean,* Dr. Edward Rogoff, 718-488-1159, E-mail: edward.rogoff@liu.edu.

School of Education Students: 161 full-time (144 women), 594 part-time (461 women); includes 493 minority (229 Black or African American, non-Hispanic/Latino; 1 American Indian or Alaska Native, non-Hispanic/Latino; 30 Asian, non-Hispanic/Latino; 218 Hispanic/Latino; 2 Native Hawaiian or other Pacific Islander, non-Hispanic/Latino; 13 Two or more races, non-Hispanic/Latino), 9 international. 513 applicants, 73% accepted, 272 enrolled. *Faculty:* 23 full-time (17 women), 44 part-time/adjunct (32 women). Expenses: Contact institution. *Financial support:* In 2016–17, 81 students received support. Career-related internships or fieldwork, Federal Work-Study, institutionally sponsored loans, scholarships/grants, and unspecified assistantships available. Support available to part-time students. Financial award application deadline: 2/15; financial award applicants required to submit FAFSA. In 2016, 262 master's, 18 other advanced degrees awarded. *Program availability:* Part-time, evening/weekend. Offers adolescence urban education (MS Ed); applied behavior analysis (Advanced Certificate); bilingual education (Advanced Certificate); bilingual school counselor (MS Ed, Advanced Certificate); childhood urban education (MS Ed); childhood/early childhood urban education (MS Ed); early childhood urban education (MS Ed, Advanced Certificate); educational leadership (Advanced Certificate); marriage and family therapy (MS, Advanced Certificate); mental health counseling (MS, Advanced Certificate); school building district leader (Advanced Certificate); school counselor (MS Ed, Advanced Certificate); school psychologist (MS Ed); teaching urban children/adolescents with disabilities (MS Ed); TESOL (MS Ed). *Application deadline:* Applications are processed on a rolling basis. *Application fee:* $50. Electronic applications accepted. *Application Contact:* Gabrielle Gannon, Director of Graduate Admissions, 718-488-1011, Fax: 718-780-6110, E-mail: bkln-admissions@liu.edu. *Dean,* Dr. Amy Ginsberg, 718-246-6308, E-mail: amy.ginsberg@liu.edu.

School of Health Professions Students: 603 full-time (405 women), 69 part-time (52 women); includes 219 minority (117 Black or African American, non-Hispanic/Latino; 1 American Indian or Alaska Native, non-Hispanic/Latino; 38 Asian, non-Hispanic/Latino; 48 Hispanic/Latino; 15 Two or more races, non-Hispanic/Latino), 68 international. 1,127 applicants, 43% accepted, 213 enrolled. *Faculty:* 60 full-time (42 women), 109 part-time/adjunct (62 women). Expenses: Contact institution. *Financial support:* Research assistantships, teaching assistantships, career-related internships or fieldwork, Federal Work-Study, institutionally sponsored loans, scholarships/grants, tuition waivers (partial), and unspecified assistantships available. Support available to part-time students. Financial award application deadline: 2/15; financial award applicants required to submit FAFSA. In 2016, 192 master's, 24 doctorates awarded. Offers athletic training and sport sciences (MS); community health (MS Ed); exercise science (MS); forensic social work (Advanced Certificate); occupational therapy (MS); physical therapy (DPT); physician assistant (MS); public health (MPH); social work (MSW). *Application deadline:* Applications are processed on a rolling basis. *Application fee:* $50. Electronic applications accepted. *Application Contact:* Dr. Dominick Fortugno, Dean of Admissions, 718-780-6578, Fax: 718-780-4561, E-mail: dominick.fortugno@liu.edu. *Dean,* Dr. Barry S. Eckert, 718-780-6578, Fax: 718-780-4561, E-mail: barry.eckert@liu.edu.

LONG ISLAND UNIVERSITY–LIU POST, Brookville, NY 11548-1300
General Information Independent, coed, comprehensive institution. *Enrollment:* 1,103 full-time matriculated graduate/professional students (823 women), 1,192 part-time matriculated graduate/professional students (896 women). *Enrollment by degree level:* 1,758 master's, 264 doctoral, 273 other advanced degrees. *Graduate faculty:* 221 full-time (116 women), 336 part-time/adjunct (182 women). *Tuition:* Full-time $28,272; part-time $1178 per credit. *Required fees:* $451 per term. Tuition and fees vary according to degree level and program. *Graduate housing:* Room and/or apartments available on a first-come, first-served basis to single students; on-campus housing not available to married students. Typical cost: $18,220 (including board). Room and board charges vary according to board plan and housing facility selected. Housing application deadline: 5/1. *Student services:* Campus employment opportunities, career counseling, exercise/wellness program, international student services, low-cost health insurance, services for students with disabilities, teacher training, writing training. *Library facilities:* B. Davis Schwartz Memorial Library. *Collection:* Books: 1.6 million (physical), 170,023 (digital/electronic); Serial titles: 459,188 (physical), 94,194 (digital/electronic); Databases: 383. *Research affiliation:* Structure-ase Inc. (biology).

Computer facilities: 580 computers available on campus for general student use. A campuswide network can be accessed from student residence rooms and from off campus. Online class registration is available. Website: http://www.liu.edu/

General Application Contact: William Martinov, Chief of Admissions and Enrollment Strategy, 516-299-2900, Fax: 516-299-2137, E-mail: post-enroll@liu.edu.

GRADUATE UNITS

College of Arts, Communications and Design Students: 123 full-time (91 women), 21 part-time (18 women); includes 25 minority (6 Black or African American, non-Hispanic/Latino; 1 American Indian or Alaska Native, non-Hispanic/Latino; 6 Asian, non-Hispanic/Latino; 11 Hispanic/Latino; 1 Two or more races, non-Hispanic/Latino), 32 international. 175 applicants, 73% accepted, 46 enrolled. *Faculty:* 36 full-time (19 women), 144 part-time/adjunct (74 women). Expenses: Contact institution. *Financial support:* In 2016–17, 6 research assistantships with partial tuition reimbursements (averaging $1,020 per year), 14 teaching assistantships with partial tuition reimbursements (averaging $670 per year) were awarded; career-related internships or fieldwork, Federal Work-Study, institutionally sponsored loans, scholarships/grants, tuition waivers (full and partial), and unspecified assistantships also available. Support available to part-time students. Financial award application deadline: 2/15; financial award applicants required to submit FAFSA. In 2016, 68 master's awarded. Offers art (MA); clinical art therapy (MA); clinical art therapy and counseling (MA); digital game design and development (MA); fine arts and design (MFA); interactive multimedia arts (MA); music (MA); theater (MA); theatre (MFA). *Application deadline:* Applications are processed on a rolling basis. *Application fee:* $50. Electronic applications accepted. *Application Contact:* Carol Zerah, Director of Graduate Admissions, 516-299-2900, Fax: 516-299-2137, E-mail: post-enroll@liu.edu. *Acting Dean,* Dr. Christine Kerr, 516-299-2309, E-mail: christine.kerr@liu.edu.

College of Education, Information and Technology Students: 464 full-time (390 women), 740 part-time (580 women); includes 265 minority (99 Black or African American, non-Hispanic/Latino; 45 Asian, non-Hispanic/Latino; 113 Hispanic/Latino; 1 Native Hawaiian or other Pacific Islander, non-Hispanic/Latino; 7 Two or more races, non-Hispanic/Latino), 33 international. 928 applicants, 76% accepted, 406 enrolled. *Faculty:* 55 full-time (35 women), 104 part-time/adjunct (57 women). Expenses: Contact institution. *Financial support:* Career-related internships or fieldwork, Federal Work-Study, institutionally sponsored loans, scholarships/grants, tuition waivers (partial), and unspecified assistantships available. Support available to part-time students. Financial award application deadline: 2/15; financial award applicants required to submit FAFSA. In 2016, 334 master's, 10 doctorates, 137 other advanced degrees awarded. *Program availability:* Part-time, 100% online, blended/hybrid learning. Offers adolescence education (MS); adolescence education 7-12 (MS); archives and records management (AC); art education (MS); childhood education (MS); childhood teaching literacy B-6 (MS); childhood/special education (MS); clinical mental health counseling (MS, AC); early childhood education (MS); early childhood education/childhood education (MS); educational leadership (AC); educational technology (MS); information studies (PhD); interdisciplinary educational studies (Ed D); middle childhood education (MS); music education (MS); school counselor (MS Ed); special education (MS Ed); speech-language pathology (MA); students with disabilities, 7-12 generalist (AC); TESOL (MA). *Application deadline:* Applications are processed on a rolling basis. *Application fee:* $50. Electronic applications accepted. *Application Contact:* Carol Zerah, Director of Graduate Admissions, 516-299-2900, Fax: 516-299-2137, E-mail: post-enroll@liu.edu. *Dean,* Dr. Albert Inserra, 516-299-2210, E-mail: albert.inserra@liu.edu.

College of Liberal Arts and Sciences Students: 155 full-time (117 women), 125 part-time (82 women); includes 65 minority (17 Black or African American, non-Hispanic/Latino; 14 Asian, non-Hispanic/Latino; 27 Hispanic/Latino; 7 Two or more races, non-Hispanic/Latino), 19 international. 485 applicants, 36% accepted, 77 enrolled. *Faculty:* 68 full-time (30 women), 20 part-time/adjunct (13 women). Expenses: Contact institution. *Financial support:* In 2016–17, 24 teaching assistantships with partial tuition reimbursements (averaging $410 per year) were awarded; fellowships, research assistantships, career-related internships or fieldwork, Federal Work-Study, institutionally sponsored loans, scholarships/grants, tuition waivers (partial), and unspecified assistantships also available. Support available to part-time students. Financial award application deadline: 2/15; financial award applicants required to submit FAFSA. In 2016, 91 master's, 15 other advanced degrees awarded. *Program availability:* Part-time, evening/weekend, blended/hybrid learning. Offers applied mathematics (MS); behavior analysis (MA); biology (MS); criminal justice (MS); earth science (MS); English (MA); environmental sustainability (MS); genetic counseling (MS); history (MS); interdisciplinary studies (MA, MS); mathematics for secondary school teachers (MS); mobile GIS application development (Advanced Certificate); political science (MA); psychology (MA). *Application deadline:* Applications are processed on a rolling basis. *Application fee:* $50. Electronic applications accepted. *Application Contact:* Carol Zerah, Director of Graduate Admissions, 516-299-2900, Fax: 516-299-2137, E-mail: post-enroll@liu.edu. *Acting Dean,* Dr. Jeffrey Belnap, 516-299-2233, Fax: 516-299-4140, E-mail: jeffrey.belnap@liu.edu.

College of Management Students: 153 full-time (61 women), 68 part-time (22 women); includes 44 minority (8 Black or African American, non-Hispanic/Latino; 24 Asian, non-Hispanic/Latino; 11 Hispanic/Latino; 1 Two or more races, non-Hispanic/Latino), 79 international. 429 applicants, 58% accepted, 74 enrolled. *Faculty:* 35 full-time (12 women), 25 part-time/adjunct (6 women). Expenses: Contact institution. *Financial support:* In 2016–17, 68 students received support. Career-related internships or fieldwork, Federal Work-Study, institutionally sponsored loans, and scholarships/grants available. Support available to part-time students. Financial award application deadline: 2/15; financial award applicants required to submit FAFSA. In 2016, 124 master's awarded. *Program availability:* Part-time, 100% online, blended/hybrid learning. Offers accountancy (MS); finance (MBA); information systems (MS); international business (MBA); management (MBA); management engineering (MS); marketing (MBA); taxation (MS); technical project management (MS). *Application deadline:* Applications are processed on a rolling basis. *Application fee:* $50. Electronic applications accepted. *Application Contact:* Carol Zerah, Director of Graduate and International Admissions, 516-299-2900, Fax: 516-299-2137, E-mail: post-enroll@liu.edu. *Dean:* Dr. Robert M. Valli, 516-299-4192, E-mail: rob.valli@liu.edu.

School of Health Professions and Nursing Students: 251 full-time (184 women), 243 part-time (197 women); includes 179 minority (76 Black or African American, non-Hispanic/Latino; 55 Asian, non-Hispanic/Latino; 42 Hispanic/Latino; 1 Native Hawaiian or other Pacific Islander, non-Hispanic/Latino; 5 Two or more races, non-Hispanic/Latino), 79 international. 581 applicants, 67% accepted, 168 enrolled. *Faculty:* 27 full-time (20 women), 43 part-time/adjunct (32 women). Expenses: Contact institution. *Financial support:* In 2016–17, 5 research assistantships with partial tuition reimbursements (averaging $725 per year), 3 teaching assistantships with partial tuition reimbursements (averaging $800 per year) were awarded; career-related internships or fieldwork, Federal Work-Study, institutionally sponsored loans, scholarships/grants, and unspecified assistantships also available. Support available to part-time students. Financial award application deadline: 2/15; financial award applicants required to submit FAFSA. In 2016, 185 master's, 29 other advanced degrees awarded. *Program availability:* Part-time, evening/weekend, blended/hybrid learning. Offers cardiovascular perfusion (MS); clinical lab sciences (MS); clinical laboratory management (MS); dietetic internship (Advanced Certificate); family nurse practitioner (MS, Advanced Certificate); forensic social work (Advanced Certificate); gerontology (Advanced Certificate); health administration (MPA); medical biology (MS); non-profit management (Advanced Certificate); nursing education (MS); nutrition (MS); public administration (MPA); social work (MSW). *Application deadline:* Applications are processed on a rolling basis. *Application fee:* $50. Electronic applications accepted. *Application Contact:* Carol Zerah, Director of Graduate Admissions, 516-299-2900, Fax: 516-299-2137, E-mail: post-enroll@liu.edu. *Dean:* Dr. Stacy Gropack, 516-299-2485, Fax: 516-299-2527, E-mail: post-shpn@liu.edu.

LONG ISLAND UNIVERSITY–RIVERHEAD, Riverhead, NY 11901

General Information Independent, coed, graduate-only institution. *Enrollment by degree level:* 85 master's, 7 other advanced degrees. *Graduate faculty:* 1 full-time (1 woman), 19 part-time/adjunct (10 women). *Tuition:* Full-time $28,272; part-time $1178 per credit. *Required fees:* $451 per term. *Graduate housing:* On-campus housing not available. *Student services:* Career counseling, services for students with disabilities, teacher training. *Library facilities:* LIU Riverhead Library.

Computer facilities: A campuswide network can be accessed from off campus. Online class registration is available.
Website: http://www.liu.edu/Riverhead/

General Application Contact: Jean Conroy, Associate Dean, 631-287-8301, Fax: 631-287-8253, E-mail: jean.conroy@liu.edu.

GRADUATE UNITS

Graduate Programs Expenses: Contact institution. *Financial support:* Institutionally sponsored loans, scholarships/grants, tuition waivers (partial), and unspecified assistantships available. Support available to part-time students. Financial award application deadline: 2/15; financial award applicants required to submit FAFSA. *Program availability:* Part-time. Offers childhood education (MS); homeland security management (MS); literacy education (MS); teaching students with disabilities (MS); TESOL (Advanced Certificate). *Application deadline:* Applications are processed on a rolling basis. *Application fee:* $50. Electronic applications accepted. *Application Contact:* Christina Seifert, Director of Admission, LIU Brentwood and LIU Riverhead, 631-287-8505, Fax: 631-287-8253, E-mail: christina.seifert@liu.edu. *Dean and Chief Operating Officer, LIU Brentwood and LIU Riverhead,* Donna Di Donato, 631-287-8010, Fax: 631-287-8575, E-mail: donna.didonato@liu.edu.

LONGWOOD UNIVERSITY, Farmville, VA 23909

General Information State-supported, coed, comprehensive institution. CGS member. *Graduate housing:* On-campus housing not available.

GRADUATE UNITS

College of Graduate and Professional Studies *Program availability:* Part-time, evening/weekend. Electronic applications accepted.

College of Business and Economics *Program availability:* Part-time, online only, 100% online. Offers general business (MBA); real estate (MBA); retail management (MBA). Electronic applications accepted.

College of Education and Human Services *Program availability:* Part-time, evening/weekend. Offers communication sciences and disorders (MS); education (MS); reading, literacy and learning (M Ed); school librarianship (M Ed); social work and communication sciences and disorders (MS). Electronic applications accepted.

LORAS COLLEGE, Dubuque, IA 52004-0178

General Information Independent-religious, coed, comprehensive institution. *Graduate housing:* On-campus housing not available.

GRADUATE UNITS

Graduate Division *Program availability:* Part-time, evening/weekend. Offers applied psychology (MA); educational leadership (MA); instructional strategist I K-6 and 7-12 (MA); ministry (MA); theology (MA).

LOUISIANA COLLEGE, Pineville, LA 71359-0001

General Information Independent-religious, coed, comprehensive institution.

GRADUATE UNITS

Caskey School of Divinity Offers biblical and theological studies (MA); pastoral ministry (MA).

Graduate Programs

LOUISIANA STATE UNIVERSITY AND AGRICULTURAL & MECHANICAL COLLEGE, Baton Rouge, LA 70803

General Information State-supported, coed, university. CGS member. *Graduate housing:* Rooms and/or apartments available on a first-come, first-served basis to single and married students. Housing application deadline: 3/15. *Research affiliation:* Arctic Research Consortium of the U.S., Organization for Tropical Studies, Coalition for Academic Scientific Computing, Albert Einstein Institute, Inter-University Consortium for Political and Social Research, Laser Interferometer Gravitational Wave Observatory.

GRADUATE UNITS

Graduate School Students: 3,572 full-time (1,899 women), 1,143 part-time (687 women); includes 925 minority (537 Black or African American, non-Hispanic/Latino; 12 American Indian or Alaska Native, non-Hispanic/Latino; 101 Asian, non-Hispanic/Latino; 210 Hispanic/Latino; 1 Native Hawaiian or other Pacific Islander, non-Hispanic/Latino; 64 Two or more races, non-Hispanic/Latino), 1,088 international. Average age 28. 4,288 applicants, 37% accepted, 988 enrolled. *Faculty:* 1,197 full-time (347 women), 16 part-time/adjunct (5 women). Expenses: Contact institution. *Financial support:* In 2016–17, 2,174 students received support, including 117 fellowships with full tuition reimbursements available (averaging $27,000 per year), 901 research assistantships with full tuition reimbursements available (averaging $19,000 per year), 1,273 teaching assistantships with full tuition reimbursements available (averaging $15,000 per year); scholarships/grants, tuition waivers (full), and unspecified assistantships also available. Financial award application deadline: 3/1; financial award applicants required to submit FAFSA. In 2016, 1,134 master's, 429 doctorates, 23 other advanced degrees awarded. *Program availability:* Part-time, evening/weekend. *Application deadline:* For fall admission, 5/15 for domestic students, 6/15 for international students; for spring admission, 11/1 for domestic and international students; for summer admission, 5/15 for domestic students, 4/15 for international students. Applications are processed on a rolling basis. *Application fee:* $50 ($70 for international students). Electronic applications accepted. *Application Contact:* E-mail: gradsvcs@lsu.edu.

College of Agriculture Offers agricultural economics and agribusiness (MS, PhD); agriculture (M App St, MS, PhD); animal sciences (MS, PhD); applied statistics (M App St); entomology (MS, PhD); fisheries (MS); food science (MS, PhD); forestry (MS, PhD); human ecology (MS, PhD); plant health (MS, PhD); plant, environmental and soil sciences (MS, PhD); wildlife (MS); wildlife and fisheries science (PhD).

College of Art and Design Offers architecture (M Arch); art and design (M Arch, M Sc, MA, MFA, MLA); art history (MA); ceramics (MFA); digital media arts and engineering (M Sc); graphic design (MFA); landscape architecture (MLA); painting and drawing (MFA); photography (MFA); printmaking (MFA); sculpture (MFA); studio art (MFA).

College of Engineering Offers biological and agricultural engineering (MSBAE); chemical engineering (MS Ch E, PhD); computer science (MSSS, PhD); construction management (MS, PhD); electrical and computer engineering (MSEE, PhD); engineering (MS, MS Ch E, MS Pet E, MSBAE, MSCE, MSEE, MSES, MSME, MSSS, PhD); engineering science (MS); environmental engineering (MSCE, PhD); geotechnical engineering (MSCE, PhD); mechanical and industrial engineering (MSME, PhD); petroleum engineering (MS Pet E, PhD); structural engineering and mechanics (MSCE, PhD); systems science (MSSS); transportation engineering (MSCE, PhD); water resources (MSCE, PhD).

College of Humanities and Social Sciences Offers biological psychology (MA, PhD); clinical psychology (MA, PhD); cognitive psychology (MA, PhD); communication sciences and disorders (MA, PhD); communication studies (MA, PhD); comparative literature (MA, PhD); creative writing (MFA); developmental psychology (MA, PhD); English (MA, PhD); French literature and linguistics (MA, PhD); geography (MA, MS); geography and anthropology (PhD); Hispanic studies (MA); history (MA, PhD); humanities and social sciences (MA, MALA, MFA, MS, PhD); liberal arts (MALA); philosophy (MA); political science (MA, PhD); school psychology (MA, PhD); sociology (MA, PhD).

College of Human Sciences and Education Offers agriculture and extension education and youth development (MS, PhD); career and technical education (MS, PhD); comprehensive vocational education (MS, PhD); counseling (M Ed, MA, Ed S); educational administration (M Ed, MA, PhD, Ed S); educational technology (MA); elementary education (M Ed, MAT); extension and international education (MS, PhD); higher education (PhD); human resource and leadership development (MS, PhD); human sciences and education (M Ed, MA, MAT, MLIS, MS, MSW, PhD, Ed S); industrial education (MS); kinesiology (MS, PhD); library and information science (MLIS); research methodology (PhD); secondary education (M Ed, MAT); social work (MSW, PhD); vocational agriculture education (MS, PhD); vocational business education (MS); vocational home economics education (MS).

College of Music and Dramatic Arts Offers acting (MFA); directing (MFA); music (MM, DMA, PhD); music and dramatic arts (MFA, MM, DMA, PhD); music education (PhD); theatre (PhD); theatre design/technology (MFA).

College of Science Offers astronomy (PhD); astrophysics (PhD); biochemistry (MS, PhD); biological science (MS, PhD); chemistry (MS, PhD); geology and geophysics (MS, PhD); mathematics (MS, PhD); medical physics (MS); natural sciences (MNS); physics (MS, PhD); science (MNS).

E. J. Ourso College of Business Offers accounting (MS, PhD); business (EMBA, MBA, MPA, MS, PMBA, PhD); business administration (PhD); economics (MS, PhD); finance (MS); information systems and decision sciences (MS, PhD); public administration (MPA).

Manship School of Mass Communication Offers mass communication (MMC, PhD).

School of the Coast and Environment Offers environmental planning and management (MS); environmental science (PhD); environmental toxicology (MS); oceanography and coastal sciences (MS, PhD); the coast and environment (MS, PhD).

Paul M. Hebert Law Center Students: 544 full-time (247 women), 11 part-time (5 women); includes 78 minority (28 Black or African American, non-Hispanic/Latino; 1 American Indian or Alaska Native, non-Hispanic/Latino; 8 Asian, non-Hispanic/Latino; 25 Hispanic/Latino; 16 Two or more races, non-Hispanic/Latino), 10 international. Average age 26. 847 applicants, 60% accepted, 198 enrolled. *Faculty:* 36 full-time (12 women), 20 part-time/adjunct (2 women). Expenses: Contact institution. *Financial support:* In 2016–17, 454 students received support. Scholarships/grants and tuition waivers (full and partial) available. Financial award application deadline: 7/1; financial award applicants required to submit FAFSA. In 2016, 4 master's awarded. Offers law (LL M, JD). *Application deadline:* For fall admission, 3/1 priority date for domestic and international students. Applications are processed on a rolling basis. *Application fee:* $50. Electronic applications accepted. *Application Contact:* Jake T. Henry, III, Director of Admissions, 225-578-8646, Fax: 225-578-8647, E-mail: jake.henry@law.lsu.edu. *Dean:* Thomas Galligan, 225-578-8491, Fax: 225-578-8202, E-mail: thomas.galligan@law.lsu.edu.

School of Veterinary Medicine Offers comparative biomedical sciences (MS, PhD); pathobiological sciences (MS, PhD); veterinary clinical sciences (MS, PhD); veterinary medicine (MS, DVM, PhD).

LOUISIANA STATE UNIVERSITY HEALTH SCIENCES CENTER, New Orleans, LA 70112-2223

General Information State-supported, coed, university. CGS member. *Enrollment:* 2,758 graduate, professional, and undergraduate students; 1,803 full-time matriculated graduate/professional students (995 women), 82 part-time matriculated

Louisiana State University Health Sciences Center

graduate/professional students (60 women). *Enrollment by degree level:* 347 master's, 1,526 doctoral, 12 other advanced degrees. *Graduate faculty:* 906 full-time (404 women). Tuition, state resident: full-time $11,835. Tuition, nonresident: full-time $25,361. *Required fees:* $1254. *Graduate housing:* Rooms and/or apartments available on a first-come, first-served basis to single and married students. Housing application deadline: 5/1. *Student services:* Campus safety program, exercise/wellness program, free psychological counseling, grant writing training, international student services, low-cost health insurance, multicultural affairs office, services for students with disabilities, teacher training, writing training. *Library facilities:* John P. Ische Library plus 1 other.

Computer facilities: Computer purchase and lease plans are available. 120 computers available on campus for general student use. A campuswide network can be accessed from student residence rooms and from off campus.
Website: http://www.lsuhsc.edu/

General Application Contact: Leigh Smith-Vaniz, Coordinator of Student Affairs, 504-568-2211, Fax: 504-568-5588, E-mail: lsmi30@lsuhsc.edu.

GRADUATE UNITS

School of Allied Health Professions Students: 361 full-time (285 women); includes 46 minority (18 Black or African American, non-Hispanic/Latino; 2 American Indian or Alaska Native, non-Hispanic/Latino; 10 Asian, non-Hispanic/Latino; 9 Hispanic/Latino; 7 Two or more races, non-Hispanic/Latino). Average age 25. 1,236 applicants, 12% accepted, 148 enrolled. *Faculty:* 31 full-time (23 women), 11 part-time/adjunct (8 women). Expenses: Contact institution. *Financial support:* In 2016–17, 13 students received support. Work assistantships available. Financial award application deadline: 4/15; financial award applicants required to submit FAFSA. In 2016, 98 master's, 46 doctorates awarded. Offers allied health professions (MCD, MHS, MOT, MPAS, Au D, DPT); audiology (Au D); clinical rehabilitation and counseling (MHS); occupational therapy (MOT); physical therapy (DPT); physician assistant studies (MPAS); speech pathology (MCD). *Application deadline:* For fall admission, 4/15 priority date for domestic students. Applications are processed on a rolling basis. Electronic applications accepted. *Application Contact:* Yudialys Delgado Cazanas, Student Affairs Director, 504-568-4253, Fax: 504-568-3185, E-mail: ydelga@lsuhsc.edu. *Dean,* Dr. Jimmy M. Cairo, 504-556-3400, Fax: 504-568-4249, E-mail: jcairo@lsuhsc.edu.

School of Dentistry Offers dentistry (DDS).

School of Graduate Studies in New Orleans Students: 70 full-time (38 women); includes 18 minority (7 Black or African American, non-Hispanic/Latino; 9 Asian, non-Hispanic/Latino; 2 Hispanic/Latino), 9 international. Average age 26. 60 applicants, 27% accepted, 14 enrolled. *Faculty:* 159 full-time (45 women). Expenses: Contact institution. *Financial support:* In 2016–17, 61 students received support. Tuition waivers (full) and unspecified assistantships available. Financial award application deadline: 4/1. In 2016, 14 doctorates awarded. Offers cell biology and anatomy (PhD); human genetics (PhD); medicine (PhD); microbiology and immunology (PhD); neuroscience (PhD); pharmacology and experimental therapeutics (PhD); physiology (PhD). *Application deadline:* For fall admission, 4/1 for domestic and international students. Applications are processed on a rolling basis. *Application fee:* $30. *Application Contact:* Leigh A. Smith-Vaniz, Coordinator of Student Affairs, 504-568-2211, Fax: 504-568-5588, E-mail: lsmi30@lsuhsc.edu. *Head,* Dr. Joseph M. Moerschbaecher, III, 504-568-2211, Fax: 504-568-2361.

School of Medicine in New Orleans Offers medicine (MPH, MD). Open only to Louisiana residents. Electronic applications accepted.

School of Nursing Students: 202 (140 women); includes 61 minority (37 Black or African American, non-Hispanic/Latino; 11 Asian, non-Hispanic/Latino; 13 Hispanic/Latino). Average age 28. 162 applicants, 42% accepted, 68 enrolled. *Faculty:* 26 full-time (23 women), 22 part-time/adjunct (10 women). Expenses: Contact institution. *Financial support:* Federal Work-Study, institutionally sponsored loans, scholarships/grants, and traineeships available. Financial award applicants required to submit FAFSA. In 2016, 52 master's, 46 doctorates awarded. *Program availability:* Part-time. Offers adult gerontology acute care nurse practitioner (DNP, Post-Master's Certificate); adult gerontology clinical nurse specialist (DNP, Post-Master's Certificate); adult gerontology primary care nurse practitioner (DNP, Post-Master's Certificate); clinical nurse leader (MSN); executive nurse leader (DNP, Post-Master's Certificate); neonatal nurse practitioner (DNP, Post-Master's Certificate); nurse anesthesia (DNP, Post-Master's Certificate); nurse educator (MSN); nursing (DNS); primary care family nurse practitioner (DNP, Post-Master's Certificate); public/community health nursing (DNP, Post-Master's Certificate). *Application deadline:* Applications are processed on a rolling basis. *Application fee:* $100. Electronic applications accepted. *Application Contact:* Tracie Gravolet, Director, Office of Student Affairs, 504-568-4114, Fax: 504-568-5711, E-mail: tgravo@lsuhsc.edu. *Dean,* Dr. Demetrius James Porche, 504-568-4106, Fax: 504-599-0573, E-mail: dporch@lsuhsc.edu.

School of Public Health *Program availability:* Part-time. Offers behavioral and community health sciences (MPH); biostatistics (MPH, MS, PhD); community health sciences (PhD); environmental and occupational health sciences (MPH); epidemiology (MPH, PhD); health policy and systems management (MPH).

LOUISIANA STATE UNIVERSITY HEALTH SCIENCES CENTER AT SHREVEPORT, Shreveport, LA 71130-3932

General Information State-supported, coed, university. *Research affiliation:* Pennington Biomedical Research Center (metabolic disorders/obesity).

GRADUATE UNITS

Department of Biochemistry and Molecular Biology Offers biochemistry and molecular biology (MS, PhD). Electronic applications accepted.

Department of Cellular Biology and Anatomy Offers cellular biology and anatomy (MS, PhD).

Department of Microbiology and Immunology Offers microbiology and immunology (MS, PhD). Electronic applications accepted.

Department of Molecular and Cellular Physiology Offers physiology (MS, PhD).

Department of Pharmacology, Toxicology and Neuroscience Offers pharmacology (PhD).

Master of Science in Biomedical Sciences Program Offers biomedical sciences (MS).

School of Medicine Offers medicine (MD).

LOUISIANA STATE UNIVERSITY IN SHREVEPORT, Shreveport, LA 71115-2399

General Information State-supported, coed, comprehensive institution. *Enrollment:* 414 full-time matriculated graduate/professional students (279 women), 1,605 part-time matriculated graduate/professional students (924 women). *Enrollment by degree level:* 1,999 master's, 56 doctoral, 20 other advanced degrees. Tuition, state resident: full-time $5163; part-time $350 per credit hour. Tuition, nonresident: full-time $15,578; part-time

$1038 per credit hour. *Required fees:* $63 per credit hour. Tuition and fees vary according to course load and program. *Student services:* Campus employment opportunities, career counseling, exercise/wellness program, free psychological counseling, multicultural affairs office, services for students with disabilities, teacher training. *Library facilities:* Noel Memorial Library. *Collection:* Databases: 142. Weekly public service hours: 71; students can reserve study rooms. *Research affiliation:* Micromanufacturing Institute (manufacturing technology), U.S. Department of Agriculture (USDA) (crop science), Louisiana Manufacturing Science Center (robotics), Biomedical Research Institute, Cotton, Incorporated (plant physiology).

Computer facilities: A campuswide network can be accessed from off campus. Online class registration is available.
Website: http://www.lsus.edu

General Application Contact: Jolie Banks, Data Coordinator, 318-798-4112, Fax: 318-798-4120, E-mail: jolie.banks@lsus.edu.

GRADUATE UNITS

College of Arts and Sciences Students: 54 full-time (26 women), 82 part-time (55 women); includes 52 minority (33 Black or African American, non-Hispanic/Latino; 5 Asian, non-Hispanic/Latino; 6 Hispanic/Latino; 8 Two or more races, non-Hispanic/Latino). Average age 32. 215 applicants, 93% accepted, 53 enrolled. Expenses: Contact institution. *Financial support:* Unspecified assistantships available. Financial award applicants required to submit FAFSA. In 2016, 34 master's awarded. *Program availability:* Part-time, evening/weekend. Offers arts and sciences (MA, MS); biological sciences (MS); computer systems technology (MS); liberal arts (MA); nonprofit administration (MS). *Application deadline:* For fall admission, 6/30 for domestic and international students; for spring admission, 11/30 for domestic and international students; for summer admission, 4/30 for domestic and international students. Applications are processed on a rolling basis. *Application fee:* $20 ($30 for international students). Electronic applications accepted. *Application Contact:* Mary Catherine Harvison, Director of Admissions, 318-797-2400, Fax: 318-797-5286, E-mail: mary.harvison@lsus.edu. *Dean,* Dr. Larry Anderson, 318-797-5371, Fax: 318-797-5358, E-mail: larry.anderson@lsus.edu.

College of Business, Education, and Human Development Students: 363 full-time (253 women), 1,523 part-time (869 women); includes 668 minority (464 Black or African American, non-Hispanic/Latino; 8 American Indian or Alaska Native, non-Hispanic/Latino; 62 Asian, non-Hispanic/Latino; 94 Hispanic/Latino; 1 Native Hawaiian or other Pacific Islander, non-Hispanic/Latino; 39 Two or more races, non-Hispanic/Latino). Average age 33. 1,437 applicants, 92% accepted, 565 enrolled. Expenses: Contact institution. *Financial support:* Research assistantships available. Financial award applicants required to submit FAFSA. In 2016, 320 master's, 2 other advanced degrees awarded. *Program availability:* Part-time. Offers business administration (MBA); business, education, and human development (M Ed, MBA, MHA, MPH, MS, Ed D, SSP); counseling (MS); curriculum and instruction (M Ed); health administration (MHA); leadership (M Ed); leadership studies (Ed D); public health (MPH); school psychology (SSP). *Application deadline:* For fall admission, 6/30 for domestic and international students; for spring admission, 10/30 for domestic students, 11/30 for international students; for summer admission, 4/30 for domestic and international students. Applications are processed on a rolling basis. *Application fee:* $20 ($30 for international students). Electronic applications accepted. *Application Contact:* Mary Catherine Harvison, Director, Admissions, 318-797-2400, Fax: 318-797-5286, E-mail: mary.harvison@lsus.edu. *Dean,* Dr. Nancy Miller, 318-797-5383, Fax: 318-797-5176, E-mail: nancy.miller@lsus.edu.

LOUISIANA TECH UNIVERSITY, Ruston, LA 71272

General Information State-supported, coed, university. *Enrollment:* 12,672 graduate, professional, and undergraduate students; 826 full-time matriculated graduate/professional students (457 women), 565 part-time matriculated graduate/professional students (388 women). *Enrollment by degree level:* 1,238 master's, 153 doctoral. *Graduate housing:* Rooms and/or apartments available on a first-come, first-served basis to single and married students. Housing application deadline: 7/15. *Student services:* Campus employment opportunities, career counseling, exercise/wellness program, free psychological counseling, international student services, low-cost health insurance, multicultural affairs office, services for students with disabilities. *Library facilities:* Prescott Memorial Library.

Computer facilities: A campuswide network can be accessed from student residence rooms and from off campus.
Website: http://www.latech.edu/

General Application Contact: Dr. Sheryl S. Shoemaker, Dean of the Graduate School, 318-257-2924, Fax: 318-257-4487, E-mail: sshoemaker@latech.edu.

GRADUATE UNITS

Graduate School Students: 826 full-time (457 women), 565 part-time (388 women); includes 512 minority (436 Black or African American, non-Hispanic/Latino; 15 American Indian or Alaska Native, non-Hispanic/Latino; 48 Asian, non-Hispanic/Latino; 13 Hispanic/Latino), 206 international. Expenses: Contact institution. *Financial support:* Fellowships, research assistantships, teaching assistantships, career-related internships or fieldwork, Federal Work-Study, institutionally sponsored loans, tuition waivers (partial), and unspecified assistantships available. In 2016, 457 master's, 49 doctorates awarded. *Program availability:* Part-time. *Application deadline:* For fall admission, 8/1 for domestic students, 6/1 for international students; for winter admission, 11/1 for domestic students, 9/1 for international students; for spring admission, 2/1 for domestic students, 12/1 for international students; for summer admission, 5/1 for domestic students, 3/1 for international students. *Application fee:* $40 ($50 for international students). *Application Contact:* Marilyn J. Robinson, Assistant to the Dean, 318-257-2924, Fax: 318-257-4487. *Dean,* Dr. Sheryl S. Shoemaker, 318-257-2924, Fax: 318-257-4487, E-mail: sshoemaker@latech.edu.

College of Applied and Natural Sciences Expenses: Contact institution. *Financial support:* Fellowships, research assistantships, teaching assistantships, career-related internships or fieldwork, and Federal Work-Study available. Financial award application deadline: 2/1. *Program availability:* Part-time. Offers applied and natural sciences (MHI, MS); biology (MS); health informatics (MHI); molecular sciences and nanotechnology (MS); nutrition and dietetics (MS). *Application deadline:* For fall admission, 7/29 priority date for domestic students; for spring admission, 2/3 for domestic students. Applications are processed on a rolling basis. *Application fee:* $20 ($30 for international students). *Dean,* Dr. Gary A. Kennedy, 318-257-4287, Fax: 318-257-5060, E-mail: kennedy@latech.edu.

College of Business Expenses: Contact institution. *Financial support:* Fellowships, research assistantships, and teaching assistantships available. *Program availability:* Part-time. Offers accounting (MPA, DBA); business (MBA, MPA, DBA); finance (MBA, DBA); finance and economics (DBA). *Application deadline:* For fall admission, 7/29 for domestic students; for spring admission, 2/3 for domestic students. *Application fee:*

$20 ($30 for international students). *Application Contact:* Marilyn J. Robinson, Assistant to the Dean, 318-257-2924, Fax: 318-257-4487. *Dean,* Dr. Christopher D. Martin, 318-257-4526, Fax: 318-257-4253.

College of Education Expenses: Contact institution. *Financial support:* Fellowships, research assistantships, teaching assistantships, and career-related internships or fieldwork available. Financial award application deadline: 2/1. *Program availability:* Part-time. Offers administration of sport and physical activity (MS); counseling and guidance (MA); counseling psychology (PhD); curriculum and instruction (M Ed); education (M Ed, MA, MS, Ed D, PhD); educational leadership (M Ed, Ed D); industrial and organizational psychology (MA, PhD); sports performance (MS). *Application deadline:* For fall admission, 7/29 for domestic students; for spring admission, 2/3 for domestic students. *Application fee:* $20 ($30 for international students). *Application Contact:* Dr. Cathy Stockton, Associate Dean of Graduate Studies, 318-257-3229, Fax: 318-257-2379, E-mail: cstock@latech.edu. *Dean,* Don Schillinger, 318-257-3712.

College of Engineering and Science Expenses: Contact institution. *Financial support:* Fellowships, research assistantships, teaching assistantships, career-related internships or fieldwork, Federal Work-Study, tuition waivers (partial), and unspecified assistantships available. Financial award application deadline: 4/1. *Program availability:* Part-time. Offers applied physics (MS); biomedical engineering (PhD); chemical engineering (MS); civil engineering (MS); computational analysis and modeling (PhD); computer science (MS); electrical engineering (MS, PhD); engineering and science (MS, PhD); industrial engineering (MS); mathematics and statistics (MS); molecular sciences and nanotechnology (MS, PhD). *Application deadline:* For fall admission, 8/1 for domestic students; for spring admission, 2/1 for domestic students. Applications are processed on a rolling basis. *Application fee:* $20 ($30 for international students). *Application Contact:* Marilyn J. Robinson, Assistant to the Dean, 318-257-2924, Fax: 318-257-4487. *Dean,* Dr. Hisham Hegab, 318-257-4647, Fax: 318-257-5562, E-mail: hhegab@latech.edu.

College of Liberal Arts Expenses: Contact institution. *Financial support:* Fellowships, research assistantships, teaching assistantships, career-related internships or fieldwork, Federal Work-Study, institutionally sponsored loans, tuition waivers (partial), and unspecified assistantships available. Financial award application deadline: 2/1. *Program availability:* Part-time. Offers architecture (M Arch); audiology (Au D); English (MA); graphic design (MFA); history (MA); liberal arts (M Arch, MA, MFA, Au D, Graduate Certificate); photography (MFA); speech-language pathology (MA); studio (MFA); technical writing (Graduate Certificate); theatre (MA). *Application deadline:* For fall admission, 7/29 for domestic students; for spring admission, 2/3 for domestic students. Applications are processed on a rolling basis. *Application fee:* $40 ($50 for international students). *Application Contact:* Mary Green, Administrative Assistant, 318-257-2924, Fax: 318-257-4487, E-mail: meg@latech.edu. *Dean,* Dr. Donald P. Kaczvinsky, 318-257-4805, Fax: 318-257-3935, E-mail: dkaczv@latech.edu.

LOUISVILLE PRESBYTERIAN THEOLOGICAL SEMINARY, Louisville, KY 40205-1798

General Information Independent-religious, coed, graduate-only institution. *Enrollment by degree level:* 108 master's, 44 doctoral. *Graduate faculty:* 18 full-time (9 women), 8 part-time/adjunct (5 women). *Tuition:* Full-time $11,400; part-time $380 per credit hour. *Required fees:* $286; $286 per credit hour. $143 per semester. *Graduate housing:* Rooms and/or apartments available on a first-come, first-served basis to single and married students. *Typical cost:* $6132 per year for single students; $7644 per year for married students. Room charges vary according to housing facility selected. Housing application deadline: 4/15. *Student services:* Campus employment opportunities, career counseling, international student services, services for students with disabilities, writing training. *Library facilities:* E.M. White Library. *Collection:* Books: 194,503 (physical), 10,586 (digital/electronic). Students can reserve study rooms. *Research affiliation:* Louisville Institute (American religion).

Computer facilities: 22 computers available on campus for general student use. A campuswide network can be accessed.
Website: http://www.lpts.edu/

General Application Contact: Rev. Emily Miller, Director of Admissions, 502-895-3411 Ext. 371, Fax: 502-895-1096, E-mail: emiller@lpts.edu.

GRADUATE UNITS

Graduate and Professional Programs Students: 99 full-time (54 women), 53 part-time (34 women); includes 42 minority (31 Black or African American, non-Hispanic/Latino; 3 Asian, non-Hispanic/Latino; 6 Hispanic/Latino; 2 Two or more races, non-Hispanic/Latino), 2 international. Average age 40. *Faculty:* 18 full-time (9 women), 8 part-time/adjunct (5 women). Expenses: Contact institution. *Financial support:* Career-related internships or fieldwork, Federal Work-Study, institutionally sponsored loans, and scholarships/grants available. Financial award application deadline: 2/1. In 2016, 27 master's, 17 doctorates awarded. *Program availability:* Part-time. Offers Bible (MAR); divinity (M Div); ministry (D Min); religious thought (MAR). JD/M Div, M Div/MBA, and M Div/MSSW offered jointly with University of Louisville. *Application deadline:* For fall admission, 6/1 priority date for domestic students, 2/1 priority date for international students; for spring admission, 11/1 priority date for domestic students. Applications are processed on a rolling basis. *Application fee:* $50. Electronic applications accepted. *Application Contact:* Rev. Emily Miller, Director of Admissions, 502-895-3411, Fax: 502-895-1096, E-mail: emiller@lpts.edu. *Dean,* Dr. Susan R. Garrett, 502-895-3411, Fax: 502-895-1096, E-mail: sgarrett@lpts.edu.

LOURDES UNIVERSITY, Sylvania, OH 43560-2898

General Information Independent-religious, coed, comprehensive institution. CGS member. *Graduate housing:* Rooms and/or apartments available to single and married students. Housing application deadline: 5/1.

GRADUATE UNITS

Graduate School *Program availability:* Evening/weekend. Offers business (MBA); leadership (M Ed); nurse anesthesia (MSN); nurse educator (MSN); nurse leader (MSN); organizational leadership (MOL); reading (M Ed); teaching and curriculum (M Ed); theology (MA).

LOYOLA MARYMOUNT UNIVERSITY, Los Angeles, CA 90045-2659

General Information Independent-religious, coed, comprehensive institution. CGS member. *Enrollment:* 9,330 graduate, professional, and undergraduate students; 2,142 full-time matriculated graduate/professional students (1,352 women), 894 part-time matriculated graduate/professional students (579 women). *Enrollment by degree level:* 1,592 master's, 1,011 doctoral, 433 other advanced degrees. *Graduate faculty:* 342 full-time (145 women), 129 part-time/adjunct (67 women). *Graduate housing:* Room and/or apartments available on a first-come, first-served basis to single students; on-campus

housing not available to married students. *Student services:* Campus employment opportunities, career counseling, child daycare facilities, exercise/wellness program, free psychological counseling, international student services, low-cost health insurance, multicultural affairs office, services for students with disabilities, teacher training. *Library facilities:* William H. Hannon Library. *Collection:* Books: 516,463 (physical), 491,084 (digital/electronic); Serial titles: 974 (physical), 44,816 (digital/electronic); Databases: 275. Weekly public service hours: 146; study areas open 24 hours, 5–7 days a week; students can reserve study rooms.

Computer facilities: Computer purchase and lease plans are available. 820 computers available on campus for general student use. A campuswide network can be accessed from student residence rooms and from off campus. Online class registration is available.
Website: http://www.lmu.edu/

General Application Contact: Chake H. Kouyoumjian, Associate Dean of Graduate Studies, 310-338-2721, Fax: 310-338-6086, E-mail: ckouyou@lmu.edu.

GRADUATE UNITS

College of Business Administration *Faculty:* 37 full-time (7 women), 12 part-time/adjunct (1 woman). Expenses: Contact institution. Offers accounting (MS); business administration (MBA, MS); executive business administration (MBA). *Application Contact:* Chake H Kouyoumjian, Associate Dean of Graduate Studies, 310-338-2721, E-mail: ckouyou@lmu.edu. Interim Associate Dean and Director, MBA Program, Bill Semos, 310-338-2848, Fax: 310-338-2899, E-mail: william.semos@lmu.edu.

College of Fine Arts *Faculty:* 15 full-time (12 women), 5 part-time/adjunct (4 women). Expenses: Contact institution. Offers fine arts (MA); marital and family therapy (MA). *Application Contact:* Chake H. Kouyoumjian, Associate Dean of Graduate Studies, 310-338-2721, E-mail: ckouyou@lmu.edu. *Dean,* Dr. Bryant Keith Alexander, 310-338-7430, E-mail: bryantkeithalexander@lmu.edu.

College of Liberal Arts *Faculty:* 28 full-time (8 women), 2 part-time/adjunct (1 woman). Expenses: Contact institution. Offers English (MA); liberal arts (MA); pastoral theology (MA); philosophy (MA); theology (MA); yoga studies (MA). *Application Contact:* Chake H. Kouyoumjian, Associate Dean of Graduate Studies, 310-338-2721, E-mail: ckouyou@lmu.edu. *Dean,* Dr. Robin D. Crabtree, 310-338-2716, E-mail: rcrabtr1@lmu.edu.

The Bioethics Institute Expenses: Contact institution. Offers bioethics (MA). *Application Contact:* Chake H. Kouyoumjian, Associate Dean of Graduate Studies, 310-338-2721, E-mail: ckouyou@lmu.edu. *Director, Bioethics Institute,* Dr. Roberto Dell'Oro, 310-338-2752, E-mail: rdelloro@lmu.edu.

College of Science and Engineering Students: 23 full-time (2 women), 15 part-time (5 women). Expenses: Contact institution. Offers civil engineering (MSE); electrical engineering (MS); environmental science (MS); healthcare systems engineering (MS); mechanical engineering (MSE); science and engineering (MAT, MS, MSE); system engineering leadership (MS); systems engineering (MS); teaching in mathematics (MAT). *Application Contact:* Chake H. Kouyoumjian, Associate Dean of Graduate Studies, 310-338-2721, E-mail: ckouyou@lmu.edu. *Dean,* Dr. Tina Choe, 310-338-2834, E-mail: tchoe@lmu.edu.

Loyola Law School Los Angeles Students: 771 full-time (439 women), 167 part-time (82 women); includes 387 minority (46 Black or African American, non-Hispanic/Latino; 6 American Indian or Alaska Native, non-Hispanic/Latino; 112 Asian, non-Hispanic/Latino; 183 Hispanic/Latino; 40 Two or more races, non-Hispanic/Latino), 45 international. Average age 25. 4,048 applicants, 37% accepted, 306 enrolled. *Faculty:* 57 full-time (27 women), 60 part-time/adjunct (21 women). Expenses: Contact institution. *Financial support:* Research assistantships, Federal Work-Study, and scholarships/grants available. Financial award application deadline: 3/15; financial award applicants required to submit FAFSA. In 2016, 36 master's, 355 doctorates awarded. *Program availability:* Part-time, evening/weekend. Offers law (LL M, MLS, JD, JSD); tax (LL M in Tax, MT). *Application deadline:* For fall admission, 2/23 priority date for domestic students, 2/1 for international students. Applications are processed on a rolling basis. *Application fee:* $0. Electronic applications accepted. *Application Contact:* Jannell Lundy Roberts, Assistant Dean, Admissions, 213-736-1074, Fax: 213-736-6523, E-mail: admissions@lls.edu. *Dean,* Michael Waterstone, 213-736-2243, Fax: 213-487-6736, E-mail: michael.waterstone@lls.edu.

School of Education Students: 64 full-time (37 women), 112 part-time (61 women). Expenses: Contact institution. Offers bilingual elementary education (MA); bilingual secondary education (MA); Catholic inclusive education (MA); Catholic school administration (MA); counseling (MA); education (MA, Ed D); educational leadership (MA); educational leadership for social justice (Ed D); educational studies (MA); elementary education (MA); guidance and counseling (MA); higher education administration (MA); literacy education (MA); literacy/language arts (MA); reading instruction (MA); school administration (MA); school counseling (MA); school psychology (MA); secondary education (MA); special education (MA); urban education (MA). *Application Contact:* Chake H. Kouyoumjian, Associate Dean of Graduate Studies, 310-338-2721, E-mail: ckouyou@lmu.edu. *Dean,* Dr. Shane P. Martin, 310-338-7301, E-mail: smartin@lmu.edu.

School of Film and Television Expenses: Contact institution. *Financial support:* Applicants required to submit FAFSA. Offers film and television (MFA); film and television production (MFA); writing and producing for television (MFA); writing for the screen (MFA). Electronic applications accepted. *Application Contact:* Chake H. Kouyoumjian, Associate Dean of Graduate Studies, 310-338-2721, E-mail: ckouyou@lmu.edu. *Dean,* Stephen Ujlaki, 310-338-5800, E-mail: sujlaki@lmu.edu.

LOYOLA UNIVERSITY CHICAGO, Chicago, IL 60660

General Information Independent-religious, coed, university. CGS member. *Enrollment:* 16,422 graduate, professional, and undergraduate students; 3,920 full-time matriculated graduate/professional students (2,475 women), 1,318 part-time matriculated graduate/professional students (960 women). *Enrollment by degree level:* 3,096 master's, 2,011 doctoral, 131 other advanced degrees. *Graduate faculty:* 898 full-time (420 women), 727 part-time/adjunct (371 women). *Tuition:* Full-time $18,594. *Required fees:* $848. Part-time tuition and fees vary according to course load, degree level and program. *Graduate housing:* Room and/or apartments available on a first-come, first-served basis to single students; on-campus housing not available to married students. *Typical cost:* $13,770 (including board). Room and board charges vary according to housing facility selected. Housing application deadline: 5/1. *Student services:* Campus employment opportunities, campus safety program, career counseling, exercise/wellness program, free psychological counseling, international student services, low-cost health insurance, services for students with disabilities, teacher training, writing training. *Library facilities:* Cudahy Library plus 7 others. *Collection:* Books: 1.2 million (physical), 669,326 (digital/electronic); Serial titles: 2,310 (physical), 57,961 (digital/electronic); Databases: 534. Weekly public service hours: 144; study

Loyola University Chicago

areas open 24 hours, 5–7 days a week; students can reserve study rooms. *Research affiliation:* Center for Community Arts Partnerships (arts integration), Aspire of Illinois (inclusion of children with disabilities), Illinois Institutions of Higher Education Partnership (preservice educator program curricula), Big Shoulders/Opening Doors to All/Greeley Center for Catholic Education (classroom teachers addressing the varied needs of all learners), Collaboration for Effective Educator Development, Accountability, and Reform Center (CEEDAR Center) (improving core and specialized instruction in settings that enable students with disabilities to achieve college ready standards), Illinois School Board of Education (student behavior and learning).

Computer facilities: Computer purchase and lease plans are available. 1,300 computers available on campus for general student use. A campuswide network can be accessed from student residence rooms and from off campus. Online class registration is available.
Website: http://www.luc.edu/

General Application Contact: Ron Martin, Associate Director, Graduate and Professional Enrollment Management Operations, 312-915-8951, E-mail: rmarti7@luc.edu.

GRADUATE UNITS

Graduate School Students: 939 full-time (554 women), 281 part-time (153 women); includes 312 minority (80 Black or African American, non-Hispanic/Latino; 1 American Indian or Alaska Native, non-Hispanic/Latino; 98 Asian, non-Hispanic/Latino; 100 Hispanic/Latino; 2 Native Hawaiian or other Pacific Islander, non-Hispanic/Latino; 31 Two or more races, non-Hispanic/Latino), 141 international. Average age 31. 1,534 applicants, 35% accepted, 257 enrolled. Expenses: Contact institution. *Financial support:* Fellowships with full tuition reimbursements, research assistantships with full tuition reimbursements, teaching assistantships with tuition reimbursements, career-related internships or fieldwork, Federal Work-Study, institutionally sponsored loans, scholarships/grants, and unspecified assistantships available. Support available to part-time students. Financial award application deadline: 2/1; financial award applicants required to submit FAFSA. In 2016, 402 master's, 91 doctorates, 19 other advanced degrees awarded. *Program availability:* Part-time, evening/weekend, 100% online, blended/hybrid learning. Offers applied and public sociology (MA); applied statistics (MS); biochemistry and molecular biology (MA, PhD); biology (MA, MS); cell and molecular physiology (MS, PhD); chemistry and biochemistry (MS, PhD); clinical psychology (MA, PhD); clinical research methods (MS); computer science (MS); criminal justice and criminology (MA); developmental psychology (PhD); digital humanities (MA); English (MA, PhD); history (PhD); infectious disease and immunology (MS); information technology (MS); integrative cell biology (MS, PhD); mathematics (MS); microbiology and immunology (MS, PhD); molecular pharmacology and therapeutics (MS, PhD); neuroscience (MS, PhD); philosophy (MA, PhD); political science (MA, PhD); public health (MPH, Certificate); public history (MA); public policy (MPP); sociology (MA, PhD); software engineering (MS); Spanish (MA); theology (MA, PhD); urban affairs (MA). *Application deadline:* Applications are processed on a rolling basis. *Application fee:* $50. Electronic applications accepted. *Application Contact:* Ron Martin, Associate Director of Enrollment Management, 312-915-8950, Fax: 312-915-8905, E-mail: gradapp@luc.edu. *Dean,* Dr. Thomas Regan, 773-508-3505, Fax: 773-508-3514, E-mail: tregan1@luc.edu.

Marcella Niehoff School of Nursing Students: 189 full-time (180 women), 223 part-time (211 women); includes 113 minority (26 Black or African American, non-Hispanic/Latino; 2 American Indian or Alaska Native, non-Hispanic/Latino; 44 Asian, non-Hispanic/Latino; 31 Hispanic/Latino; 4 Native Hawaiian or other Pacific Islander, non-Hispanic/Latino; 6 Two or more races, non-Hispanic/Latino), 4 international. Average age 35. 191 applicants, 58% accepted, 110 enrolled. *Faculty:* 24 full-time (22 women), 12 part-time/adjunct (11 women). Expenses: Contact institution. *Financial support:* In 2016–17, 10 students received support, including 3 research assistantships with full tuition reimbursements available (averaging $18,000 per year), 1 teaching assistantship with full tuition reimbursement available (averaging $18,000 per year); scholarships/grants, unspecified assistantships, and nurse faculty loan program also available. Financial award application deadline: 5/1; financial award applicants required to submit FAFSA. In 2016, 78 master's, 15 doctorates, 24 other advanced degrees awarded. *Program availability:* Part-time, blended/hybrid learning. Offers nursing (MS, MSN, DNP, PhD, Certificate). *Application deadline:* For fall admission, 6/1 priority date for domestic and international students; for spring admission, 11/15 priority date for domestic and international students; for summer admission, 3/15 priority date for domestic and international students. Applications are processed on a rolling basis. *Application fee:* $50. Electronic applications accepted. *Application Contact:* Toni Topalova, Enrollment Advisor, 708-216-3751, Fax: 708-216-9555, E-mail: atopalova@luc.edu. *Dean,* Dr. Vicky Keough, 708-216-5448, Fax: 708-216-9555, E-mail: vkeough@luc.edu.

Neiswanger Institute for Bioethics Students: 24 full-time (18 women), 81 part-time (49 women); includes 18 minority (5 Black or African American, non-Hispanic/Latino; 5 Asian, non-Hispanic/Latino; 4 Hispanic/Latino; 1 Native Hawaiian or other Pacific Islander, non-Hispanic/Latino; 3 Two or more races, non-Hispanic/Latino). Average age 48. 44 applicants, 73% accepted, 23 enrolled. *Faculty:* 7 full-time (4 women), 6 part-time/adjunct (2 women). Expenses: Contact institution. *Financial support:* Scholarships/grants available. In 2016, 38 master's, 12 doctorates, 13 other advanced degrees awarded. *Program availability:* Online learning. Offers bioethics (MA, D Be, Certificate). *Application Contact:* Robbin Hiller, Coordinator, Bioethics Education, 708-321-9219, Fax: 708-327-9209, E-mail: rhiller@luc.edu. *Director, Neiswanger Institute for Bioethics,* Dr. Mark Kuczewski, 708-327-9200, Fax: 708-327-9209, E-mail: mkuczew@luc.edu.

School of Communication Students: 39 full-time (26 women), 15 part-time (10 women); includes 24 minority (17 Black or African American, non-Hispanic/Latino; 1 American Indian or Alaska Native, non-Hispanic/Latino; 6 Hispanic/Latino), 7 international. Average age 29. 96 applicants, 45% accepted, 25 enrolled. Expenses: Contact institution. In 2016, 17 master's awarded. Offers digital storytelling (MC); global strategic communication (MS). *Application Contact:* Ron Martin, Associate Director of Enrollment Management, 312-915-8950, Fax: 312-915-8905, E-mail: gradapp@luc.edu. *Dean,* Dr. Don Heider, 312-915-6548, E-mail: dheider@luc.edu.

Institute of Pastoral Studies Students: 79 full-time (58 women), 120 part-time (76 women); includes 54 minority (22 Black or African American, non-Hispanic/Latino; 1 American Indian or Alaska Native, non-Hispanic/Latino; 6 Asian, non-Hispanic/Latino; 23 Hispanic/Latino; 2 Two or more races, non-Hispanic/Latino), 23 international. Average age 42. 116 applicants, 83% accepted, 71 enrolled. *Faculty:* 11 full-time (4 women), 25 part-time/adjunct (11 women). Expenses: Contact institution. *Financial support:* In 2016–17, 84 students received support. Career-related internships or fieldwork, Federal Work-Study, institutionally sponsored loans, scholarships/grants, tuition waivers (partial), and unspecified assistantships available. Support available to part-time students. Financial award application deadline: 3/1; financial award applicants required to submit FAFSA. In 2016, 63 master's, 4 other advanced degrees awarded.

Program availability: Part-time, evening/weekend, 100% online, blended/hybrid learning. Offers Christian spirituality (MA); church management (Certificate); counseling for ministry (MA); health care ministry leadership (Certificate); health care mission leadership (MA); pastoral counseling (MA, Certificate); pastoral studies (M Div, MA); religious education (Certificate); social justice (MA, Certificate); spiritual direction (Certificate). MSW/MA offered with School of Social Work. *Application deadline:* Applications are processed on a rolling basis. *Application fee:* $50. Electronic applications accepted. *Application Contact:* Dr. M. Therese Lysaught, Associate Dean, 312-915-7485, Fax: 312-915-7410, E-mail: mlysaught@luc.edu. *Dean,* Dr. Brian J. Schmisek, 312-915-7400, Fax: 312-915-7410, E-mail: bschmisek@luc.edu.

Quinlan School of Business Students: 484 full-time (273 women), 106 part-time (52 women); includes 109 minority (33 Black or African American, non-Hispanic/Latino; 36 Asian, non-Hispanic/Latino; 34 Hispanic/Latino; 6 Two or more races, non-Hispanic/Latino), 180 international. Average age 28. 969 applicants, 56% accepted, 218 enrolled. *Faculty:* 79 full-time (22 women), 10 part-time/adjunct (4 women). Expenses: Contact institution. *Financial support:* Federal Work-Study, scholarships/grants, health care benefits, and unspecified assistantships available. Support available to part-time students. In 2016, 336 master's, 40 other advanced degrees awarded. *Program availability:* Part-time, evening/weekend. Offers accountancy (MSA); accounting (MBA); asset management (MSF); business (EMBA, MBA, MSA, MSF, MSHR, MSIMC, MSSCM, Certificate); business administration (EMBA); business ethics (MBA); corporate finance (MSF); data warehousing (Certificate); economics (MBA); entrepreneurship (MBA); finance (MBA); healthcare management (MBA); human resources (MSHR); human resources management (MBA); information systems and supply chain management (MSSCM); integrated marketing communications (MSIMC); international business (MBA); management (MBA); marketing (MBA); operation management (MBA); risk management (MBA, MSF); supply chain management (MBA). *Application deadline:* For fall admission, 7/15 for domestic and international students; for winter admission, 10/1 for domestic and international students; for spring admission, 1/15 for domestic and international students; for summer admission, 4/1 for domestic and international students. Applications are processed on a rolling basis. *Application fee:* $50. Electronic applications accepted. *Application Contact:* Lauren Griffin, Enrollment Advisor, Quinlan School of Business Graduate Programs, 312-915-8908, Fax: 312-915-7207, E-mail: lgriffin3@luc.edu. *Assistant Dean for Graduate Programs,* Katherine Acles, 312-915-6124, Fax: 312-915-7207, E-mail: kacles@luc.edu.

School of Education Students: 430 full-time (329 women), 211 part-time (167 women); includes 242 minority (101 Black or African American, non-Hispanic/Latino; 1 American Indian or Alaska Native, non-Hispanic/Latino; 30 Asian, non-Hispanic/Latino; 88 Hispanic/Latino; 1 Native Hawaiian or other Pacific Islander, non-Hispanic/Latino; 21 Two or more races, non-Hispanic/Latino), 22 international. Average age 30. 718 applicants, 62% accepted, 280 enrolled. *Faculty:* 59 full-time (40 women), 71 part-time/adjunct (48 women). Expenses: Contact institution. *Financial support:* In 2016–17, 392 students received support, including 132 fellowships with partial tuition reimbursements available, 87 research assistantships with full tuition reimbursements available (averaging $14,000 per year), 96 teaching assistantships (averaging $4,000 per year); career-related internships or fieldwork, Federal Work-Study, institutionally sponsored loans, scholarships/grants, traineeships, health care benefits, and unspecified assistantships also available. Support available to part-time students. Financial award application deadline: 2/1; financial award applicants required to submit FAFSA. In 2016, 145 master's, 45 doctorates, 9 other advanced degrees awarded. *Program availability:* Part-time, evening/weekend, blended/hybrid learning. Offers administration and supervision (M Ed, Ed D, Certificate); community counseling (M Ed, MA, Ed S); counseling psychology (PhD); cultural and educational policy studies (M Ed, MA, PhD); curriculum and instruction (M Ed, Ed D); education (M Ed, MA, Ed D, PhD, Certificate, Ed S); elementary education (M Ed); English language teaching and learning (M Ed); higher education (M Ed, PhD); research methods (MA, PhD); school counseling (M Ed, Certificate); school psychology (Ed D, PhD, Ed S); secondary education (M Ed). *Application fee:* $50. Electronic applications accepted. *Application Contact:* Thomas Ott, Information Contact, 312-915-8907, E-mail: tott@luc.edu. *Interim Dean,* Dr. David Slavsky, 312-915-6992, Fax: 312-915-6980, E-mail: dslavsk@luc.edu.

School of Law Students: 788 full-time (432 women), 283 part-time (217 women); includes 328 minority (139 Black or African American, non-Hispanic/Latino; 3 American Indian or Alaska Native, non-Hispanic/Latino; 53 Asian, non-Hispanic/Latino; 94 Hispanic/Latino; 2 Native Hawaiian or other Pacific Islander, non-Hispanic/Latino; 37 Two or more races, non-Hispanic/Latino), 39 international. Average age 31. 2,581 applicants, 53% accepted, 377 enrolled. *Faculty:* 54 full-time (27 women), 178 part-time/adjunct (82 women). Expenses: Contact institution. *Financial support:* In 2016–17, 549 students received support, including 72 fellowships; Federal Work-Study and scholarships/grants also available. Financial award application deadline: 3/1; financial award applicants required to submit FAFSA. In 2016, 152 master's, 212 doctorates awarded. *Program availability:* Part-time, evening/weekend, 100% online, blended/hybrid learning. Offers law (LL M, MJ, JD, SJD). *Application deadline:* For fall admission, 4/1 for domestic and international students. Applications are processed on a rolling basis. *Application fee:* $0. Electronic applications accepted. *Application Contact:* Ron Martin, Associate Director, Graduate and Professional Enrollment Management Operations, 312-915-8951, E-mail: rmarti7@luc.edu. *Associate Dean for Administration, Law School,* James Faught, JD, 312-915-7131, Fax: 312-915-6911, E-mail: law-admissions@luc.edu.

School of Social Work *Program availability:* Part-time. Offers social work (MSW, PhD, PGC).

LOYOLA UNIVERSITY MARYLAND, Baltimore, MD 21210-2699

General Information Independent-religious, coed, university. CGS member. Enrollment: 6,084 graduate, professional, and undergraduate students; 932 full-time matriculated graduate/professional students (728 women), 1,163 part-time matriculated graduate/professional students (927 women). *Enrollment by degree level:* 1,921 master's, 88 doctoral, 86 other advanced degrees. *Graduate faculty:* 58 full-time (34 women), 73 part-time/adjunct (43 women). *Graduate housing:* On-campus housing not available. *Student services:* Campus employment opportunities, campus safety program, career counseling, exercise/wellness program, free psychological counseling, international student services, low-cost health insurance, multicultural affairs office, services for students with disabilities. *Library facilities:* Loyola/Notre Dame Library plus 1 other.

Computer facilities: Computer purchase and lease plans are available. 690 computers available on campus for general student use. A campuswide network can be accessed from student residence rooms and from off campus. Online class registration is available.
Website: http://www.loyola.edu/

General Application Contact: Maureen Faux, Executive Director, Graduate Admissions, 410-617-5020, Fax: 410-617-2002, E-mail: graduate@loyola.edu.

GRADUATE UNITS

Graduate Programs Students: 932 full-time (728 women), 1,163 part-time (927 women); includes 424 minority (238 Black or African American, non-Hispanic/Latino; 7 American Indian or Alaska Native, non-Hispanic/Latino; 63 Asian, non-Hispanic/Latino; 75 Hispanic/Latino; 3 Native Hawaiian or other Pacific Islander, non-Hispanic/Latino; 38 Two or more races, non-Hispanic/Latino), 45 international. Average age 32. 1,158 applicants, 36% accepted, 191 enrolled. *Faculty:* 58 full-time (34 women), 73 part-time/adjunct (43 women). Expenses: Contact institution. *Financial support:* In 2016–17, 125 students received support. Scholarships/grants and unspecified assistantships available. Financial award application deadline: 4/15; financial award applicants required to submit FAFSA. In 2016, 665 master's, 24 doctorates awarded. *Program availability:* Part-time, evening/weekend. *Application deadline:* For fall admission, 3/1 for domestic and international students. Applications are processed on a rolling basis. *Application fee:* $60. Electronic applications accepted. *Application Contact:* Maureen Faux, Executive Director, Graduate Admissions, 410-617-5020, Fax: 410-617-2002, E-mail: graduate@loyola.edu. *Associate Dean for Graduate Programs,* Dr. Cindy Moore, 410-617-2830, E-mail: clmoore1@loyola.edu.

Loyola College of Arts and Sciences Students: 41 full-time (9 women); includes 9 minority (4 Black or African American, non-Hispanic/Latino; 2 Asian, non-Hispanic/Latino; 3 Two or more races, non-Hispanic/Latino). Average age 31. *Faculty:* 65 full-time (40 women), 26 part-time/adjunct (18 women). Expenses: Contact institution. *Financial support:* In 2016–17, 30 students received support. Scholarships/grants and unspecified assistantships available. Financial award application deadline: 4/15; financial award applicants required to submit FAFSA. In 2016, 206 master's, 20 doctorates awarded. *Program availability:* Part-time, evening/weekend. Offers arts and sciences (MA, MS, MTS, PhD, Psy D, CAS, Certificate); clinical psychology (MS, Psy D, CAS); counseling psychology (MS, CAS); emerging media (MA); liberal studies (MA); speech-language pathology (MS); theology (MTS). *Application deadline:* For fall admission, 8/1 for domestic students. *Application fee:* $60. Electronic applications accepted.

School of Education Students: 126 full-time (110 women), 618 part-time (516 women); includes 247 minority (165 Black or African American, non-Hispanic/Latino; 1 American Indian or Alaska Native, non-Hispanic/Latino; 22 Asian, non-Hispanic/Latino; 36 Hispanic/Latino; 2 Native Hawaiian or other Pacific Islander, non-Hispanic/Latino; 21 Two or more races, non-Hispanic/Latino), 7 international. Average age 31. 549 applicants, 66% accepted, 171 enrolled. *Faculty:* 34 full-time (22 women), 30 part-time/adjunct (24 women). Expenses: Contact institution. *Financial support:* In 2016–17, 30 students received support. Research assistantships, scholarships/grants, and unspecified assistantships available. Financial award application deadline: 4/15; financial award applicants required to submit FAFSA. In 2016, 275 master's awarded. *Program availability:* Part-time, evening/weekend. Offers curriculum and instruction (MA); education (M Ed, MA, MAT, CAS); educational leadership (M Ed, CAS); educational technology (M Ed, MA); elementary education (M Ed, MAT); Kodaly music education (M Ed); literacy teacher (M Ed); Montessori education (CAS); reading specialist (M Ed); school counseling (M Ed, MA, CAS); secondary education (MAT). *Application deadline:* For fall admission, 6/15 for domestic students. Applications are processed on a rolling basis. *Application fee:* $60. Electronic applications accepted. *Application Contact:* Mechelle Palmer, Senior Associate Director of Graduate Admission, 410-617-7741, E-mail: mjpalmer@loyola.edu. *Dean, School of Education,* Dr. Joshua Smith, 410-617-5343.

Sellinger School of Business Students: 42 full-time (17 women), 408 part-time (149 women); includes 74 minority (23 Black or African American, non-Hispanic/Latino; 20 Asian, non-Hispanic/Latino; 19 Hispanic/Latino; 1 Native Hawaiian or other Pacific Islander, non-Hispanic/Latino; 11 Two or more races, non-Hispanic/Latino), 3 international. Average age 32. 137 applicants, 85% accepted, 96 enrolled. *Faculty:* 26 full-time (8 women), 13 part-time/adjunct (5 women). Expenses: Contact institution. *Financial support:* In 2016–17, 65 students received support. Scholarships/grants available. Financial award application deadline: 4/15; financial award applicants required to submit FAFSA. In 2016, 146 master's awarded. *Program availability:* Part-time, evening/weekend. Offers accounting (MBA); business (M Acc, MBA, MSF); business administration (MBA); executive business administration (MBA); finance (MSF); information systems operations management (MBA). *Application deadline:* For fall admission, 8/1 priority date for domestic students; for winter admission, 12/1 priority date for domestic students; for spring admission, 5/1 priority date for domestic students. *Application fee:* $60. Electronic applications accepted. *Application Contact:* Maureen Faux, Executive Director, Graduate Admissions, 410-617-5020, Fax: 410-617-2002, E-mail: graduate@loyola.edu. *Dean,* Kathleen A. Getz, 410-617-2301.

LOYOLA UNIVERSITY NEW ORLEANS, New Orleans, LA 70118-6195

General Information Independent-religious, coed, comprehensive institution. *Enrollment:* 3,679 graduate, professional, and undergraduate students; 958 full-time matriculated graduate/professional students (647 women), 372 part-time matriculated graduate/professional students (284 women). *Enrollment by degree level:* 635 master's, 561 doctoral, 134 other advanced degrees. *Graduate faculty:* 52 full-time (30 women), 31 part-time/adjunct (18 women). *Graduate housing:* Room and/or apartments available on a first-come, first-served basis to single students; on-campus housing not available to married students. Housing application deadline: 8/1. *Student services:* Campus employment opportunities, campus safety program, career counseling, child daycare facilities, exercise/wellness program, free psychological counseling, international student services, low-cost health insurance, multicultural affairs office, services for students with disabilities. *Library facilities:* Monroe Library plus 1 other. *Collection:* Books: 387,652 (physical), 42,637 (digital/electronic); Serial titles: 221,718 (physical). Weekly public service hours: 114; students can reserve study rooms. *Research affiliation:* New Orleans Museum of Art (communications, history, visual arts).

Computer facilities: Computer purchase and lease plans are available. 300 computers available on campus for general student use. A campuswide network can be accessed from student residence rooms and from off campus. Online class registration is available.
Website: http://www.loyno.edu/

General Application Contact: Melissa L. Lightell, Director, Office of Professional and Continuing Studies, 504-865-2157, Fax: 504-865-2787, E-mail: malandr2@loyno.edu.

GRADUATE UNITS

College of Arts and Sciences Students: 10 full-time (8 women), 16 part-time (10 women); includes 9 minority (5 Black or African American, non-Hispanic/Latino; 2 American Indian or Alaska Native, non-Hispanic/Latino; 1 Asian, non-Hispanic/Latino; 2 Hispanic/Latino). Average age 31. 46 applicants, 39% accepted, 15 enrolled. *Faculty:* 5 full-time (2 women), 3 part-time/adjunct (1 woman). Expenses: Contact institution. *Financial support:* Research assistantships, teaching assistantships, career-related internships or fieldwork, Federal Work-Study, scholarships/grants, and tuition waivers (partial) available. Support available to part-time students. Financial award application deadline: 5/1; financial award applicants required to submit FAFSA. In 2016, 33 master's awarded. *Program availability:* Part-time, evening/weekend. Offers arts and sciences (MAT, MCJ); criminal justice (MCJ); teaching (MAT). *Application fee:* $20. Electronic applications accepted. *Application Contact:* Melissa Lightell, Director of Professional and Continuing Studies, 504-865-2157, Fax: 504-865-3383, E-mail: malandr2@loyno.wsu. *Dean,* Maria Calzada, 504-865-3244, Fax: 5048652059.

College of Law Students: 466 full-time (246 women), 13 part-time (9 women); includes 140 minority (64 Black or African American, non-Hispanic/Latino; 8 American Indian or Alaska Native, non-Hispanic/Latino; 9 Asian, non-Hispanic/Latino; 49 Hispanic/Latino; 10 Two or more races, non-Hispanic/Latino), 9 international. Average age 28. 729 applicants, 82% accepted, 173 enrolled. *Faculty:* 40 full-time (22 women), 19 part-time/adjunct (5 women). Expenses: Contact institution. *Financial support:* Fellowships, research assistantships, teaching assistantships, career-related internships or fieldwork, institutionally sponsored loans, scholarships/grants, traineeships, health care benefits, tuition waivers, and unspecified assistantships available. Support available to part-time students. Financial award applicants required to submit FAFSA. In 2016, 217 doctorates awarded. *Program availability:* Part-time, evening/weekend, online learning. Offers law (LL M, JD). *Application deadline:* For fall admission, 8/1 priority date for domestic and international students. Applications are processed on a rolling basis. *Application fee:* $0. Electronic applications accepted. *Application Contact:* Kimberly Jones, Director of Law Admissions, 504-861-5575, Fax: 504-861-5772, E-mail: ladmit@loyno.edu. *Interim Dean,* Dr. Lawrence W. Moore, 504-861-5575, Fax: 504-861-5677, E-mail: lmoore@loyno.edu.

College of Music and Fine Arts Students: 37 full-time (25 women), 8 part-time (6 women); includes 16 minority (6 Black or African American, non-Hispanic/Latino; 1 Asian, non-Hispanic/Latino; 6 Hispanic/Latino; 3 Two or more races, non-Hispanic/Latino), 3 international. Average age 28. 55 applicants, 44% accepted, 17 enrolled. *Faculty:* 15 full-time (7 women), 7 part-time/adjunct (5 women). Expenses: Contact institution. *Financial support:* Career-related internships or fieldwork, Federal Work-Study, institutionally sponsored loans, scholarships/grants, unspecified assistantships, and talent-based music scholarships available. Support available to part-time students. Financial award application deadline: 5/1; financial award applicants required to submit FAFSA. In 2016, 5 master's awarded. *Program availability:* Part-time. Offers music therapy (MMT); performance (MM). *Application deadline:* For fall admission, 8/15 priority date for domestic and international students; for spring admission, 1/1 priority date for domestic and international students. Applications are processed on a rolling basis. *Application fee:* $20. Electronic applications accepted. *Application Contact:* Melissa L. Lightell, Director, Office of Professional and Continuing Studies, 504-865-3530, Fax: 504-865-2787, E-mail: evening@loyno.edu. *Associate Dean,* Dr. Victoria P. Vega, 504-865-3037, Fax: 504-865-2852, E-mail: vpvega@loyno.edu.

Department of Counseling Students: 44 full-time (42 women), 17 part-time (15 women); includes 9 minority (5 Black or African American, non-Hispanic/Latino; 1 Asian, non-Hispanic/Latino; 3 Hispanic/Latino). Average age 28. 26 applicants, 58% accepted, 13 enrolled. *Faculty:* 5 full-time (2 women), 2 part-time/adjunct (1 woman). Expenses: Contact institution. *Financial support:* Research assistantships, career-related internships or fieldwork, and tuition waivers (partial) available. Support available to part-time students. Financial award application deadline: 5/1; financial award applicants required to submit FAFSA. In 2016, 23 master's awarded. *Program availability:* Part-time, evening/weekend. Offers clinical mental health counseling (MS). *Application deadline:* For fall admission, 12/1 priority date for domestic and international students. Applications are processed on a rolling basis. *Application fee:* $0. Electronic applications accepted. *Application Contact:* Dianna Whitfield, Department Assistant, 504-864-7848, Fax: 504-864-7844, E-mail: counselingdept@loyno.edu. *Chair,* Dr. Thomas Foster, 504-864-7867, Fax: 504-864-7844, E-mail: counselingdept@loyno.edu.

Joseph A. Butt, S.J., College of Business Students: 69 full-time (39 women), 15 part-time (10 women); includes 27 minority (14 Black or African American, non-Hispanic/Latino; 1 American Indian or Alaska Native, non-Hispanic/Latino; 3 Asian, non-Hispanic/Latino; 8 Hispanic/Latino; 1 Two or more races, non-Hispanic/Latino), 3 international. Average age 29. 52 applicants, 96% accepted, 28 enrolled. *Faculty:* 11 full-time (6 women), 3 part-time/adjunct (0 women). Expenses: Contact institution. *Financial support:* Research assistantships, scholarships/grants, tuition waivers (partial), and unspecified assistantships available. Financial award applicants required to submit FAFSA. In 2016, 39 master's awarded. *Program availability:* Part-time, evening/weekend, online learning. Offers business (MBA); entrepreneurship and marketing innovation (MBA); organizational performance excellence (MBA). *Application deadline:* For fall admission, 6/15 priority date for domestic students, 5/15 priority date for international students; for spring admission, 11/15 priority date for domestic students, 10/15 priority date for international students. Applications are processed on a rolling basis. *Application fee:* $50. Electronic applications accepted. *Application Contact:* Ashley Francis, Director of Graduate Programs, 504-864-7979, Fax: 504-864-7970, E-mail: mba@loyno.edu. *Dean,* Dr. William B. Locander, 504-864-7990, Fax: 504-864-7970, E-mail: mba@loyno.edu.

Loyola Institute for Ministry Students: 23 full-time (16 women), 119 part-time (77 women); includes 20 minority (7 Black or African American, non-Hispanic/Latino; 1 Asian, non-Hispanic/Latino; 11 Hispanic/Latino; 1 Two or more races, non-Hispanic/Latino). Average age 46. 37 applicants, 92% accepted, 25 enrolled. *Faculty:* 3 full-time (1 woman), 4 part-time/adjunct (2 women). Expenses: Contact institution. *Financial support:* Career-related internships or fieldwork, scholarships/grants, health care benefits, and tuition waivers (partial) available. Support available to part-time students. Financial award application deadline: 5/1; financial award applicants required to submit FAFSA. In 2016, 38 master's awarded. *Program availability:* Part-time, evening/weekend, online learning. Offers pastoral studies (MPS); religious education (MRE); theology and ministry (Certificate). *Application deadline:* For fall admission, 8/15 for domestic and international students; for spring admission, 1/1 for domestic and international students. Applications are processed on a rolling basis. *Application fee:* $20. Electronic applications accepted. *Application Contact:* Diane Blair, Manager of Admissions, 504-865-3728, Fax: 504-865-2066, E-mail: lim@loyno.edu. *Director,* Dr. Tom Ryan, 504-865-2069, Fax: 504-865-2066, E-mail: tfryan@loyno.edu.

School of Nursing Students: 257 full-time (239 women), 69 part-time (63 women); includes 91 minority (58 Black or African American, non-Hispanic/Latino; 1 American Indian or Alaska Native, non-Hispanic/Latino; 19 Asian, non-Hispanic/Latino; 11 Hispanic/Latino; 1 Native Hawaiian or other Pacific Islander, non-Hispanic/Latino; 1 Two or more races, non-Hispanic/Latino). Average age 41. 154 applicants, 83% accepted, 82 enrolled. *Faculty:* 16 full-time (14 women), 13 part-time/adjunct (9 women). Expenses: Contact institution. *Financial support:* Traineeships and Incumbent Workers Training Program grants available. Financial award application deadline: 5/1; financial award applicants required to submit FAFSA. In 2016, 164 master's, 37 doctorates awarded.

Program availability: Part-time, evening/weekend, online learning. Offers family nurse practitioner (DNP); health care systems management (MSN); nursing (MSN, DNP); nursing educator (MSN). *Application deadline:* For fall admission, 8/1 priority date for domestic and international students; for winter admission, 12/15 priority date for domestic and international students; for spring admission, 5/15 priority date for domestic and international students. Applications are processed on a rolling basis. *Application fee:* $40. Electronic applications accepted. *Application Contact:* Elizabeth Wadsworth, Executive Assistant to the Director, 504-865-2307, Fax: 504-865-3254, E-mail: edwadswo@loyno.edu. *Interim Director,* Dr. Laurie Ann Ferguson, 504-865-2880, Fax: 504-865-3254, E-mail: nursing@loyno.edu.

LUBBOCK CHRISTIAN UNIVERSITY, Lubbock, TX 79407-2099

General Information Independent-religious, coed, comprehensive institution. *Graduate housing:* Rooms and or apartments available to single and married students. Housing application deadline: 8/15.

GRADUATE UNITS

Graduate Biblical Studies *Program availability:* Part-time. Offers Bible and ministry (MS); biblical interpretation (MA).

LUTHERAN SCHOOL OF THEOLOGY AT CHICAGO, Chicago, IL 60615-5199

General Information Independent-religious, coed, graduate-only institution. *Graduate housing:* Rooms and/or apartments available on a first-come, first-served basis to single and married students. Housing application deadline: 5/15. *Research affiliation:* Chicago Center for Public Ministry, Zygon Center for Religion and Science.

GRADUATE UNITS

Graduate and Professional Programs *Program availability:* Part-time. Offers ministry (MAM, D Min); theological studies (MATS, PhD); theology (M Div).

LUTHERAN THEOLOGICAL SEMINARY AT GETTYSBURG, Gettysburg, PA 17325-1795

General Information Independent-religious, coed, graduate-only institution. *Graduate housing:* Rooms and/or apartments available on a first-come, first-served basis to single and married students. Housing application deadline: 4/1.

GRADUATE UNITS

Graduate and Professional Programs *Program availability:* Part-time, online learning. Offers divinity (M Div); ministerial studies (MAMS); outdoor ministry (MAR); parish ministry (D Min); theology (STM). Electronic applications accepted.

THE LUTHERAN THEOLOGICAL SEMINARY AT PHILADELPHIA, Philadelphia, PA 19119-1794

General Information Independent-religious, coed, graduate-only institution. *Graduate housing:* Rooms and/or apartments available on a first-come, first-served basis to single and married students. Housing application deadline: 5/15.

GRADUATE UNITS

Graduate School *Program availability:* Part-time, evening/weekend. Offers divinity (M Div); ministry (D Min); public leadership (MA); religion (MAR); social ministry and church (Certificate); theology (STM, PhD). Electronic applications accepted.

LUTHERAN THEOLOGICAL SEMINARY SASKATOON, Saskatoon, SK S7N 0X3, Canada

General Information Independent-religious, coed, graduate-only institution. *Graduate housing:* Room and/or apartments available to single students; on-campus housing not available to married students. Housing application deadline: 4/30.

GRADUATE UNITS

Graduate and Professional Programs *Program availability:* Part-time. Offers Biblical studies (MTS); church history (MTS); ethics/church and society (MTS); history of Christianity (STM); New Testament (STM); Old Testament (STM); pastoral studies (STM); pastoral theology (MTS); systematic theology (MTS); systematic theology and philosophy of religion (STM); theology (M Div, D Div). STM programs offered jointly with College of Emmanuel and St. Chad and St. Andrew's College.

LUTHER RICE COLLEGE & SEMINARY, Lithonia, GA 30038-2454

General Information Independent-religious, coed, comprehensive institution. *Graduate housing:* On-campus housing not available.

GRADUATE UNITS

Graduate Programs *Program availability:* Part-time, evening/weekend, online learning. Offers apologetics (MA); Bible languages (M Div); Biblical counseling (MA); Christian ministry (M Div, D Min); Christian studies (MA); leadership (MA). Electronic applications accepted.

LUTHER SEMINARY, St. Paul, MN 55108-1445

General Information Independent-religious, coed, graduate-only institution. *Graduate housing:* Rooms and/or apartments available on a first-come, first-served basis to single and married students.

GRADUATE UNITS

Graduate and Professional Programs *Program availability:* Part-time, online learning. Offers aging and health (MA); Biblical preaching (D Min); children, youth and family (M Div, MA); congregational mission and leadership (M Th, MA, D Min); history of Christianity (M Th, MA); missions and world religions (M Th); New Testament (M Th, MA); Old Testament (M Th, MA); pastoral care: clinical pastoral theology (M Th); pastoral theology and ministry (M Th); systematic theology (M Th, MA). Electronic applications accepted.

LYNCHBURG COLLEGE, Lynchburg, VA 24501-3199

General Information Independent-religious, coed, comprehensive institution. *Enrollment:* 2,720 graduate, professional, and undergraduate students; 301 full-time matriculated graduate/professional students (220 women), 292 part-time matriculated graduate/professional students (212 women). *Enrollment by degree level:* 399 master's, 168 doctoral, 26 other advanced degrees. *Graduate faculty:* 56 full-time (34 women), 14 part-time/adjunct (9 women). *Tuition:* Full-time $17,640; part-time $490 per credit hour. *Required fees:* $120; $5.10 per credit hour. Tuition and fees vary according to course load, degree level and program. *Graduate housing:* On-campus housing not available. *Student services:* Campus employment opportunities, career counseling, exercise/wellness program, free psychological counseling, international student services, multicultural affairs office, services for students with disabilities, teacher training, writing training. *Library facilities:* Knight-Capron Library. *Collection:* Books: 122,870 (physical), 306,584 (digital/electronic). Study areas open 24 hours, 5–7 days a week.

Computer facilities: 300 computers available on campus for general student use. A campuswide network can be accessed from student residence rooms and from off campus. Online class registration is available.
Website: http://www.lynchburg.edu/

General Application Contact: Dr. Atul Gupta, Associate Dean for Academic Affairs, Graduate Studies, 434-544-8651, E-mail: gupta@lynchburg.edu.

GRADUATE UNITS

Graduate Studies Students: 301 full-time (220 women), 292 part-time (212 women); includes 69 minority (44 Black or African American, non-Hispanic/Latino; 1 American Indian or Alaska Native, non-Hispanic/Latino; 6 Asian, non-Hispanic/Latino; 9 Hispanic/Latino; 1 Native Hawaiian or other Pacific Islander, non-Hispanic/Latino; 8 Two or more races, non-Hispanic/Latino), 15 international. Average age 31. *Faculty:* 56 full-time (31 women), 14 part-time/adjunct (8 women). Expenses: Contact institution. *Financial support:* Career-related internships or fieldwork, Federal Work-Study, scholarships/grants, and unspecified assistantships available. Financial award applicants required to submit FAFSA. In 2016, 151 master's, 53 doctorates awarded. *Program availability:* Part-time, evening/weekend. Offers business administration (MBA); clinical mental health counseling (M Ed); clinical nurse leader (MS); higher education (M Ed); instructional leadership (M Ed); leadership studies (Ed D); music (MA); physical therapy (DPT); PK-12 administrative and supervisory (M Ed); reading instruction (M Ed); reading specialist (M Ed); school counseling (M Ed); science education (M Ed); special education (M Ed); teacher licensure (M Ed). *Application deadline:* Applications are processed on a rolling basis. *Application fee:* $30. Electronic applications accepted. *Dean of Graduate Studies,* Dr. Atul Gupta, 434-544-8651, E-mail: gupta@lynchburg.edu.

LYNDON STATE COLLEGE, Lyndonville, VT 05851-0919

General Information State-supported, coed, comprehensive institution. *Graduate housing:* On-campus housing not available.

GRADUATE UNITS

Graduate Programs in Education *Program availability:* Part-time, evening/weekend. Offers curriculum and instruction (M Ed); education (M Ed); natural sciences (MST); reading specialist (M Ed); science education (MST); special education (M Ed); teaching and counseling (M Ed).

LYNN UNIVERSITY, Boca Raton, FL 33431-5598

General Information Independent, coed, comprehensive institution. *Enrollment:* 2,842 graduate, professional, and undergraduate students; 476 full-time matriculated graduate/professional students (278 women), 271 part-time matriculated graduate/professional students (154 women). *Enrollment by degree level:* 653 master's, 68 doctoral, 26 other advanced degrees. *Graduate faculty:* 107 full-time (46 women), 70 part-time/adjunct (30 women). *Tuition:* Full-time $17,400; part-time $725 per course. One-time fee: $100. Tuition and fees vary according to class time, course load and degree level. *Graduate housing:* Room and/or apartments available on a first-come, first-served basis to single students; on-campus housing not available to married students. Typical cost: $11,970 (including board). Room and board charges vary according to board plan and housing facility selected. *Student services:* Campus employment opportunities, campus safety program, career counseling, exercise/wellness program, free psychological counseling, international student services, low-cost health insurance, multicultural affairs office, services for students with disabilities. *Library facilities:* Eugene M. and Christine E. Lynn Library. *Collection:* Books: 58,957 (physical), 186,437 (digital/electronic); Serial titles: 209 (physical), 36,193 (digital/electronic); Databases: 109. Weekly public service hours: 96.

Computer facilities: Computer purchase and lease plans are available. 150 computers available on campus for general student use. A campuswide network can be accessed from student residence rooms and from off campus. Online registration with advisor approval for juniors, seniors and MBA students available.
Website: http://www.lynn.edu/

General Application Contact: Steven Pruitt, Assistant Director of Graduate Admissions, 561-237-7834, Fax: 561-237-7100, E-mail: admission@lynn.edu.

GRADUATE UNITS

College of Arts and Sciences Students: 74 full-time (57 women), 39 part-time (28 women); includes 32 minority (20 Black or African American, non-Hispanic/Latino; 2 Asian, non-Hispanic/Latino; 9 Hispanic/Latino; 1 Native Hawaiian or other Pacific Islander, non-Hispanic/Latino), 10 international. Average age 29. 77 applicants, 77% accepted, 39 enrolled. *Faculty:* 52 full-time (22 women), 19 part-time/adjunct (11 women). Expenses: Contact institution. *Financial support:* In 2016–17, 25 students received support. Career-related internships or fieldwork, Federal Work-Study, scholarships/grants, tuition waivers (full and partial), and unspecified assistantships available. Support available to part-time students. Financial award application deadline: 3/1; financial award applicants required to submit FAFSA. In 2016, 65 master's awarded. *Program availability:* Part-time, evening/weekend, blended/hybrid learning. Offers administration (MS); applied psychology (MS); mental health counseling (MS). *Application deadline:* For fall admission, 8/18 for domestic students, 8/4 for international students; for spring admission, 12/15 for domestic students, 12/1 for international students; for summer admission, 4/17 for domestic students, 4/3 for international students. Applications are processed on a rolling basis. *Application fee:* $45. Electronic applications accepted. *Application Contact:* Steven Pruitt, Director of Graduate Admission, 561-237-7834, Fax: 561-237-7100, E-mail: admissionpm@lynn.edu. *Dean,* Dr. Katrina Carter-Tellison, 561-237-7412, E-mail: kcartertellison@lynn.edu.

College of Business and Management Students: 265 full-time (125 women), 182 part-time (96 women); includes 100 minority (41 Black or African American, non-Hispanic/Latino; 11 Asian, non-Hispanic/Latino; 42 Hispanic/Latino; 6 Two or more races, non-Hispanic/Latino), 119 international. Average age 28. 280 applicants, 94% accepted, 181 enrolled. *Faculty:* 24 full-time (9 women), 24 part-time/adjunct (4 women). Expenses: Contact institution. *Financial support:* In 2016–17, 115 students received support. Career-related internships or fieldwork, Federal Work-Study, scholarships/grants, tuition waivers (full and partial), and unspecified assistantships available. Support available to part-time students. Financial award application deadline: 3/1; financial award applicants required to submit FAFSA. In 2016, 219 master's awarded. *Program availability:* Part-time, evening/weekend, 100% online, blended/hybrid learning. Offers business administration (MBA). *Application deadline:* For fall admission, 8/18 for domestic students, 8/4 for international students; for spring admission, 12/15 for domestic students, 12/1 for international students; for summer admission, 4/17 for domestic students, 4/3 for international students. Applications are processed on a rolling basis. *Application fee:* $45. Electronic applications accepted. *Application Contact:* Steven Pruitt, Director of Graduate and Undergraduate Evening Admission, 561-237-7834, Fax: 561-237-7100, E-mail: spruitt@lynn.edu. *Dean of the College of Business and Management,* Dr. RT Good, 561-237-7458, E-mail: rgood@lynn.edu.

Conservatory of Music Students: 32 full-time (14 women), 21 part-time (9 women); includes 8 minority (3 Black or African American, non-Hispanic/Latino; 5 Hispanic/Latino), 29 international. Average age 24. 88 applicants, 93% accepted, 31 enrolled. *Faculty:* 11 full-time (3 women), 20 part-time/adjunct (11 women). Expenses: Contact institution. *Financial support:* In 2016–17, 53 students received support. Federal Work-Study, scholarships/grants, and unspecified assistantships available. Support available to part-time students. Financial award application deadline: 3/1; financial award applicants required to submit FAFSA. In 2016, 16 master's, 9 Certificates awarded. *Program availability:* Part-time, evening/weekend. Offers collaborative piano (MM); composition (MM); performance (MM); professional performance (Certificate). *Application deadline:* For fall admission, 8/18 for domestic students, 8/4 for international students; for spring admission, 12/15 for domestic students, 12/1 for international students; for summer admission, 4/17 for domestic students, 4/3 for international students. Applications are processed on a rolling basis. *Application fee:* $50. Electronic applications accepted. *Application Contact:* Steven Pruitt, Director of Graduate Admissions, 561-237-7834, Fax: 561-237-7100, E-mail: admission@lynn.edu. *Dean,* Dr. Jon Robertson, 561-237-7702, Fax: 561-237-9002, E-mail: jrobertson@lynn.edu.

Donald E. and Helen L. Ross College of Education Students: 85 full-time (63 women), 10 part-time (6 women); includes 27 minority (19 Black or African American, non-Hispanic/Latino; 7 Hispanic/Latino; 1 Two or more races, non-Hispanic/Latino), 4 international. Average age 36. 17 applicants, 94% accepted, 11 enrolled. *Faculty:* 5 full-time (4 women), 8 part-time/adjunct (all women). Expenses: Contact institution. *Financial support:* In 2016–17, 74 students received support. Career-related internships or fieldwork, Federal Work-Study, scholarships/grants, tuition waivers (partial), and unspecified assistantships available. Support available to part-time students. Financial award application deadline: 3/1; financial award applicants required to submit FAFSA. In 2016, 24 master's, 22 doctorates awarded. *Program availability:* Part-time, evening/weekend, online learning. Offers educational leadership (M Ed, Ed D); exceptional student education (M Ed). *Application deadline:* For fall admission, 8/18 for domestic students, 8/4 for international students; for spring admission, 12/15 for domestic students, 12/1 for international students; for summer admission, 4/17 for domestic students, 4/3 for international students. Applications are processed on a rolling basis. *Application fee:* $45. Electronic applications accepted. *Application Contact:* Steven Pruitt, Director of Graduate and Undergraduate Evening Admission, 561-237-7834, Fax: 561-237-7100, E-mail: spruitt@lynn.edu. *Dean, College of Education,* Dr. Kathleen Weigel, 561-237-7441, E-mail: kweigel@lynn.edu.

Eugene M. and Christine E. Lynn College of International Communication Students: 24 full-time (20 women), 15 part-time (14 women); includes 11 minority (9 Black or African American, non-Hispanic/Latino; 2 Asian, non-Hispanic/Latino; 2 Hispanic/Latino), 14 international. Average age 27. 38 applicants, 87% accepted, 17 enrolled. *Faculty:* 15 full-time (8 women), 6 part-time/adjunct (3 women). Expenses: Contact institution. *Financial support:* In 2016–17, 7 students received support. Career-related internships or fieldwork, Federal Work-Study, institutionally sponsored loans, scholarships/grants, tuition waivers (partial), and unspecified assistantships available. Support available to part-time students. Financial award application deadline: 8/1; financial award applicants required to submit FAFSA. In 2016, 18 master's, 1 other advanced degree awarded. *Program availability:* Part-time, evening/weekend. Offers communication and media (MS); digital media (Certificate). *Application deadline:* For fall admission, 8/18 for domestic students, 8/4 for international students; for spring admission, 12/15 for domestic students, 12/1 for international students; for summer admission, 4/17 for domestic students, 4/3 for international students. Applications are processed on a rolling basis. *Application fee:* $45. Electronic applications accepted. *Application Contact:* Steven Pruitt, Director of Graduate Admission, 561-237-7834, Fax: 561-237-7100, E-mail: admission@lynn.edu. *Dean,* Dr. David L. Jaffe, 561-237-7099, Fax: 561-237-7097, E-mail: djaffe@lynn.edu.

MAASTRICHT SCHOOL OF MANAGEMENT, 6201 BE Maastricht, Netherlands

General Information Private, coed, graduate-only institution.

GRADUATE UNITS

Graduate Programs Offers business administration (MBA, DBA, PhD); facility management (Exec MBA); management (M Sc); sustainability (Exec MBA).

MACHZIKEI HADATH RABBINICAL COLLEGE, Brooklyn, NY 11204-1805

General Information Independent-religious, men only, comprehensive institution. *Graduate housing:* Room and/or apartments available to single students; on-campus housing not available to married students.

GRADUATE UNITS

Graduate Programs

MADONNA UNIVERSITY, Livonia, MI 48150-1173

General Information Independent-religious, coed, comprehensive institution. *Graduate housing:* Room and/or apartments available on a first-come, first-served basis to single students; on-campus housing not available to married students. Housing application deadline: 4/29.

GRADUATE UNITS

Department of Psychology *Program availability:* Part-time, evening/weekend. Offers clinical psychology (MSCP). Electronic applications accepted.

Program in Health Services *Program availability:* Part-time. Offers health services (MSHS). Electronic applications accepted.

Program in Hospice *Program availability:* Part-time, evening/weekend. Offers hospice (MSH). Electronic applications accepted.

Program in Liberal Studies Offers liberal studies (MALS).

Program in Nursing *Program availability:* Part-time. Offers adult health: chronic health conditions (MSN); adult nurse practitioner (MSN); nursing administration (MSN). Electronic applications accepted.

Program in Religious Studies Offers pastoral ministry (MA).

Program in Teaching English to Speakers of Other Languages *Program availability:* Part-time, evening/weekend. Offers teaching English to speakers of other languages (MATESOL). Electronic applications accepted.

Programs in Education *Program availability:* Part-time, evening/weekend. Offers Catholic school leadership (MSA); educational leadership (MSA); learning disabilities

(MAT); literacy education (MAT); teaching and learning (MAT). Electronic applications accepted.

School of Business *Program availability:* Part-time, evening/weekend, online learning. Offers business administration (MBA); international business (MSBA); leadership studies (MSBA); leadership studies in criminal justice (MSBA); quality and operations management (MSBA). Electronic applications accepted.

MAHARISHI UNIVERSITY OF MANAGEMENT, Fairfield, IA 52557

General Information Independent, coed, university. *Graduate housing:* Room and/or apartments guaranteed to single students; on-campus housing not available to married students. Housing application deadline: 8/1. *Research affiliation:* National Institutes of Health (stress reduction/disease prevention), U.S. Department of Defense (therapy/education/PTSD in veterans), Columbia University Medical Center (natural medicine and prevention), Institute of Noetic Sciences (psychophysiological correlates of consciousness), San Diego VA Healthcare System (veterans' health/PTSD stress reduction), Howard University Medical Center (stress reduction/hypertension prevention).

GRADUATE UNITS

Graduate Studies *Program availability:* Evening/weekend, online learning. Offers accounting (MBA); computer science (MS); Maharishi Vedic science (MA, PhD); management (PhD); physiology (PhD); screenwriting (MFA); sustainability (MBA). Electronic applications accepted.

MAINE COLLEGE OF ART, Portland, ME 04101

General Information Independent, coed, comprehensive institution.

GRADUATE UNITS

Program in Studio Art Offers studio art (MA, MFA). Electronic applications accepted.

MAINE MARITIME ACADEMY, Castine, ME 04420

General Information State-supported, coed, primarily men, comprehensive institution. *Graduate housing:* Rooms and/or apartments available on a first-come, first-served basis to single and married students. Housing application deadline: 4/15.

GRADUATE UNITS

Loeb-Sullivan School of International Business and Logistics *Program availability:* Part-time. Offers global logistics and maritime management (MS); international logistics management (MS).

MALONE UNIVERSITY, Canton, OH 44709

General Information Independent-religious, coed, comprehensive institution. *Graduate housing:* On-campus housing not available.

GRADUATE UNITS

Graduate Program in Business *Program availability:* Part-time, evening/weekend, online learning. Offers business (MBA).

Graduate Program in Counseling and Human Development *Program availability:* Part-time, evening/weekend. Offers clinical counseling (MA); school counseling (MA).

Graduate Program in Education *Program availability:* Part-time, evening/weekend. Offers curriculum and instruction (MA); curriculum, instruction, and professional development (MA); educational leadership (principal license) (MA); intervention specialist (MA).

Graduate Program in Nursing *Program availability:* Part-time, evening/weekend. Offers family nurse practitioner (MSN).

Graduate Program in Organizational Leadership *Program availability:* Part-time, evening/weekend. Offers organizational leadership (MAOL).

Graduate Program in Theological Studies *Program availability:* Part-time, evening/weekend. Offers theological studies (MA).

MANCHESTER UNIVERSITY, North Manchester, IN 46962-1225

General Information Independent-religious, coed, comprehensive institution. *Enrollment:* 1,598 graduate, professional, and undergraduate students; 319 full-time matriculated graduate/professional students (199 women), 6 part-time matriculated graduate/professional students (4 women). *Enrollment by degree level:* 32 master's, 293 doctoral. *Graduate faculty:* 37 full-time (18 women), 1 part-time/adjunct (0 women). *Graduate housing:* On-campus housing not available. *Student services:* Campus safety program, career counseling, multicultural affairs office. *Library facilities:* Funderburg Library.

Computer facilities: Computer purchase and lease plans are available. 226 computers available on campus for general student use. A campuswide network can be accessed from student residence rooms and from off campus. Online class registration is available.
Website: http://www.manchester.edu/

General Application Contact: Dr. Mark Huntington, Graduate Program Director, 260-982-5033, E-mail: mwhuntington@manchester.edu.

GRADUATE UNITS

Doctor of Pharmacy Program Students: 287 full-time (176 women), 6 part-time (4 women); includes 112 minority (39 Black or African American, non-Hispanic/Latino; 2 American Indian or Alaska Native, non-Hispanic/Latino; 63 Asian, non-Hispanic/Latino; 7 Hispanic/Latino; 1 Native Hawaiian or other Pacific Islander, non-Hispanic/Latino). Average age 24. 594 applicants, 21% accepted, 73 enrolled. *Faculty:* 31 full-time (16 women). Expenses: Contact institution. Offers pharmacy (Pharm D). *Application deadline:* For fall admission, 3/1 for domestic students. *Application fee:* $180. *Associate Dean for Student Affairs,* Dr. Joseph K. Bonnarens, 260-470-2655, E-mail: jkbonnarens@manchester.edu.

Master of Athletic Training Program Students: 21 full-time (16 women); includes 4 minority (3 Black or African American, non-Hispanic/Latino; 1 Hispanic/Latino). Average age 23. 31 applicants, 74% accepted, 15 enrolled. *Faculty:* 6 full-time (2 women), 1 part-time/adjunct (0 women). Expenses: Contact institution. *Financial support:* In 2016–17, 21 students received support, including 21 fellowships (averaging $7,850 per year). Financial award application deadline: 5/1; financial award applicants required to submit FAFSA. In 2016, 7 master's awarded. Offers athletic training (MAT). *Application deadline:* For fall admission, 1/1 priority date for domestic students. Applications are processed on a rolling basis. *Application fee:* $60. Electronic applications accepted. *Program Director, Graduate Athletic Training Education,* Mark Huntington, 260-982-5033, E-mail: mwhuntington@manchester.edu.

Master of Science in Pharmacogenomics Program Students: 11 full-time (7 women); includes 3 minority (2 Asian, non-Hispanic/Latino; 1 Hispanic/Latino). Average age 25. 13 applicants, 85% accepted, 11 enrolled. *Faculty:* 10 full-time (4 women). Expenses: Contact institution. *Program availability:* Part-time, 100% online, blended/hybrid learning. Offers pharmacogenomics (MS). *Application deadline:* Applications are processed on a rolling basis. *Application fee:* $25. Electronic applications accepted. *Application Contact:* Dr. Joseph Bonnarens, Assistant Dean for Student and Alumni Experience, 260-470-2655, E-mail: jkbonnarens@manchester.edu. *Director,* Dr. David F. Kisor, 260-470-2747, E-mail: dfkisor@manchester.edu.

MANHATTAN COLLEGE, Riverdale, NY 10471

General Information Independent-religious, coed, comprehensive institution. *Enrollment:* 4,214 graduate, professional, and undergraduate students; 216 full-time matriculated graduate/professional students (142 women), 265 part-time matriculated graduate/professional students (143 women). *Graduate faculty:* 36 full-time (12 women), 55 part-time/adjunct (24 women). *Graduate housing:* Rooms and/or apartments available on a first-come, first-served basis to single and married students. *Student services:* Career counseling, free psychological counseling, low-cost health insurance, services for students with disabilities. *Library facilities:* Mary Alice and Tom O'Malley Library. *Collection:* Books: 259,987 (physical), 191,706 (digital/electronic); Serial titles: 379 (physical), 186,500 (digital/electronic). Weekly public service hours: 168; study areas open 24 hours, 5–7 days a week.

Computer facilities: 450 computers available on campus for general student use. A campuswide network can be accessed from student residence rooms and from off campus. Online class registration, course management system, degree audit/planning tool, campus card access are available.
Website: http://www.manhattan.edu/

General Application Contact: William Bisset, Vice President for Enrollment Management, 718-862-7199, Fax: 718-862-8019,
E-mail: william.bisset@manhattan.edu.

GRADUATE UNITS

Graduate Programs Expenses: Contact institution. *Financial support:* Fellowships with full tuition reimbursements, research assistantships with full tuition reimbursements, teaching assistantships with partial tuition reimbursements, career-related internships or fieldwork, Federal Work-Study, scholarships/grants, tuition waivers (full and partial), and laboratory assistantships available. Support available to part-time students. Financial award application deadline: 2/1. *Program availability:* Part-time, evening/weekend. *Application deadline:* For fall admission, 8/10 priority date for domestic and international students; for winter admission, 1/7 for domestic and international students; for spring admission, 1/7 priority date for domestic and international students. Applications are processed on a rolling basis. *Application fee:* $60. *Application Contact:* William Bisset, Vice President for Enrollment Management, 718-862-7199, Fax: 718-862-8019, E-mail: william.bisset@manhattan.edu. *Executive Vice President/Provost,* Dr. William Clyde, 718-862-7303, Fax: 718-862-7929, E-mail: william.clyde@manhattan.edu.

School of Business Students: 45 full-time (24 women), 7 part-time (4 women). Average age 24. *Faculty:* 35 full-time (19 women), 2 part-time/adjunct (1 woman). Expenses: Contact institution. *Financial support:* Research assistantships, career-related internships or fieldwork, scholarships/grants, and unspecified assistantships available. In 2016, 36 master's awarded. *Program availability:* Part-time, 100% online, blended/hybrid learning. Offers business (MBA). *Application deadline:* For fall admission, 8/1 for domestic and international students; for spring admission, 1/1 for domestic and international students; for summer admission, 4/1 for domestic and international students. Applications are processed on a rolling basis. *Application fee:* $75. Electronic applications accepted. *Application Contact:* Dr. Marc Waldman, MBA Program Director, 718-862-3856, E-mail: marc.waldman@manhattan.edu. *Dean,* Dr. Salwa Ammar, 718-862-7440, Fax: 718-862-8032, E-mail: salwa.ammar@manhattan.edu.

School of Continuing and Professional Studies Expenses: Contact institution. Offers organizational leadership (MS). *Application deadline:* For fall admission, 8/1 for domestic students; for spring admission, 11/15 for domestic students. Electronic applications accepted. *Application Contact:* William Bisset, Vice President for Enrollment Management, 718-862-7199, Fax: 718-862-8019, E-mail: william.bisset@manhattan.edu. *Dean,* Cheryl Harrison, 718-862-7862, E-mail: cheryl.harrison@manhattan.edu.

School of Education and Health Students: 140 full-time (124 women), 139 part-time (111 women). 218 applicants, 81% accepted, 145 enrolled. *Faculty:* 8 full-time (6 women), 35 part-time/adjunct (20 women). Expenses: Contact institution. *Financial support:* In 2016–17, 1 research assistantship was awarded; scholarships/grants and tuition waivers (partial) also available. Financial award application deadline: 2/1. In 2016, 75 master's, 24 other advanced degrees awarded. *Program availability:* Part-time, evening/weekend, online learning. Offers adolescence education students with disabilities generalist extension in English or math or social studies - grades 7-12 (MS Ed); advanced leadership studies (MS Ed, Advanced Certificate); bilingual education (Advanced Certificate); bilingual pupil personnel services (Professional Diploma); dual childhood/students with disabilities - grades 1-6 (MS Ed); education and health (MA, MS, MS Ed, Advanced Certificate, Certificate, Professional Diploma); instructional design and delivery (MS); mental health counseling (MS, Professional Diploma); school building leadership (MS Ed, Advanced Certificate); school counseling (MA, Professional Diploma); students with disabilities - grades 1-6 (MS Ed). *Application deadline:* For fall admission, 8/10 priority date for domestic students, 4/10 for international students; for spring admission, 1/7 priority date for domestic students, 8/1 for international students. Applications are processed on a rolling basis. *Application fee:* $60. *Application Contact:* William Bisset, Vice President for Enrollment, 718-862-7199, Fax: 718-862-8019, E-mail: william.bisset@manhattan.edu. *Program Director,* Dr. Remigia Kushner, 718-862-7473, Fax: 718-862-7816, E-mail: sr.remigia.kushner@manhattan.edu.

School of Engineering Expenses: Contact institution. *Financial support:* Fellowships with full tuition reimbursements, research assistantships with full tuition reimbursements, teaching assistantships with partial tuition reimbursements, career-related internships or fieldwork, Federal Work-Study, scholarships/grants, unspecified assistantships, and laboratory assistantships available. Support available to part-time students. Financial award application deadline: 2/1. *Program availability:* Part-time, evening/weekend. Offers chemical engineering (MS); civil engineering (MS); computer engineering (MS); electrical engineering (MS); environmental engineering (ME, MS); mechanical engineering (MS). *Application deadline:* For fall admission, 8/10 priority date for domestic students, 8/10 for international students; for spring admission, 1/7 for domestic and international students. Applications are processed on a rolling basis. *Application fee:* $60. *Application Contact:* Erica Reubel, Office Manager, 718-862-7281, Fax: 718-862-8015, E-mail: deanengr@manhattan.edu. *Dean,* Dr. Tim J. Ward, 718-862-7307, Fax: 718-862-8015, E-mail: deanengr@manhattan.edu.

School of Science Students: 8 full-time (3 women); includes 1 minority (Hispanic/Latino), 2 international. Average age 24. 8 applicants, 75% accepted, 5 enrolled. *Faculty:* 23 full-time (10 women). Expenses: Contact institution. Offers

applied mathematics - data analytics (MS); mathematics (MS). *Application Contact:* William Bisset, Vice President for Enrollment Management, 718-862-7199, Fax: 718-862-8019, E-mail: william.bisset@manhattan.edu. *Dean,* Dr. Constantine Theodosiou, 718-862-7368, E-mail: constantine.theodosiou@manhattan.edu.

MANHATTAN SCHOOL OF MUSIC, New York, NY 10027-4698

General Information Independent, coed, comprehensive institution. *Graduate housing:* Room and/or apartments available on a first-come, first-served basis to single students; on-campus housing not available to married students. Housing application deadline: 6/15.

GRADUATE UNITS

Graduate Programs Offers composition (MM, DMA); jazz (MM, DMA); music performance (MM, DMA); orchestral performance (MM). Electronic applications accepted.

Professional Studies Certificate Program Offers instrumental music (CPS); vocal music (CPS). Electronic applications accepted.

MANHATTANVILLE COLLEGE, Purchase, NY 10577-2132

General Information Independent, coed, comprehensive institution. *Enrollment:* 2,834 graduate, professional, and undergraduate students; 268 full-time matriculated graduate/professional students (170 women), 772 part-time matriculated graduate/professional students (548 women). *Enrollment by degree level:* 819 master's, 83 doctoral, 138 other advanced degrees. *Graduate faculty:* 23 full-time (15 women), 99 part-time/adjunct (49 women). *Tuition:* Full-time $16,470; part-time $915 per credit. *Required fees:* $60 per semester. Part-time tuition and fees vary according to course load and program. *Graduate housing:* Room and/or apartments available on a first-come, first-served basis to single students; on-campus housing not available to married students. Typical cost: $8680 per year ($14,520 including board). Room and board charges vary according to board plan. Housing application deadline: 7/22. *Student services:* Campus employment opportunities, campus safety program, career counseling, exercise/wellness program, international student services, multicultural affairs office, services for students with disabilities, teacher training, writing training. *Library facilities:* Manhattanville College Library. *Collection:* Books: 229,036 (physical), 152,619 (digital/electronic); Serial titles: 949 (physical), 58,002 (digital/electronic); Databases: 117. Weekly public service hours: 139; study areas open 24 hours, 5–7 days a week.

Computer facilities: 150 computers available on campus for general student use. A campuswide network can be accessed from student residence rooms and from off campus. Online class registration, mobile apps are available.
Website: http://www.mville.edu/

GRADUATE UNITS

Master of Fine Arts in Creative Writing Program Students: 11 full-time (7 women), 7 part-time (3 women). Average age 29. 21 applicants, 76% accepted, 5 enrolled. *Faculty:* 3 full-time (1 woman), 5 part-time/adjunct (4 women). Expenses: Contact institution. *Financial support:* Fellowships, Federal Work-Study, scholarships/grants, tuition waivers (partial), and unspecified assistantships available. Financial award application deadline: 7/15; financial award applicants required to submit FAFSA. *Program availability:* Part-time. Offers creative writing (MFA). *Application deadline:* Applications are processed on a rolling basis. *Application fee:* $0. Electronic applications accepted. *Application Contact:* Jeanine Pardey-Levine, Director of Graduate Enrollment Management, 914-323-3208, E-mail: jeanine.pardey@mville.edu. *Program Director,* Lori Soderlind, 914-323-5239, E-mail: mfa@mville.edu.

School of Business Students: 142 (91 women); includes 59 minority (26 Black or African American, non-Hispanic/Latino; 8 Asian, non-Hispanic/Latino; 20 Hispanic/Latino; 5 Two or more races, non-Hispanic/Latino). Average age 30. 154 applicants, 39% accepted, 40 enrolled. *Faculty:* 32 part-time/adjunct (10 women). Expenses: Contact institution. *Financial support:* Federal Work-Study, institutionally sponsored loans, scholarships/grants, and unspecified assistantships available. Financial award applicants required to submit FAFSA. In 2016, 44 master's awarded. *Program availability:* Part-time, evening/weekend. Offers accounting (MS); business (MS); business leadership (MS); corporate finance (MS); finance (MS); human resource management (MS); investment management (MS); marketing communication management (MS); organizational effectiveness (MS); sport business management (MS). *Application deadline:* Applications are processed on a rolling basis. *Application fee:* $75. Electronic applications accepted. *Application Contact:* Monika Pottgen, Assistant Director, Recruitment and Admissions, 914-323-5150, E-mail: business@mville.edu. *Interim Dean,* Steve Albanese, 914-323-5469, E-mail: steve.albanese@mville.edu.

School of Education Students: 137 full-time (92 women), 741 part-time (537 women); includes 100 minority (32 Black or African American, non-Hispanic/Latino; 2 American Indian or Alaska Native, non-Hispanic/Latino; 11 Asian, non-Hispanic/Latino; 55 Hispanic/Latino). Average age 33. 315 applicants, 64% accepted, 161 enrolled. *Faculty:* 23 full-time (15 women), 67 part-time/adjunct (39 women). Expenses: Contact institution. *Financial support:* Teaching assistantships, career-related internships or fieldwork, Federal Work-Study, institutionally sponsored loans, scholarships/grants, and unspecified assistantships available. Financial award applicants required to submit FAFSA. In 2016, 192 master's, 8 doctorates, 13 other advanced degrees awarded. *Program availability:* Part-time, evening/weekend. Offers adult and international settings (MPS); biology (MAT); biology and special education (MPS); chemistry (MAT); chemistry and special education (MPS); childhood and special education (MPS); childhood education (MPS); childhood education (grades 1-6) (MAT); early childhood and special education (birth-grade 2) (MPS); early childhood education (MPS); early childhood education (birth-grade 2) (MAT); education (Advanced Certificate); education entrepreneurship (M Ed); education leadership (Ed D); educational studies (M Ed); English (MAT); English and special education (MPS); health and wellness specialist (Advanced Certificate); higher education leadership (Ed D); literacy and special education (MPS); literacy specialist (MPS); literacy specialist (MPS); math and special education (MPS); mathematics (MAT); music education (MAT); physical education and sport pedagogy (MAT); physics (MAT); school building leader (MPS); school district leader (PD); secondary education (MPS); secondary subject areas and special education (MPS); social studies (MAT); social studies and special education (MPS); special education (birth-grade 2) (MPS); special education (birth-grade 6) (MPS); special education generalist (MPS); teaching English as a second language (MPS); teaching languages other than English (MAT); TESOL (MPS); visual arts education (MAT). *Application deadline:* For fall admission, 7/1 priority date for domestic and international students; for spring admission, 11/1 priority date for domestic and international students; for summer admission, 4/1 priority date for domestic and international students. Applications are processed on a rolling basis. *Application fee:* $75. Electronic applications accepted. *Application Contact:* Jeanine Pardey-Levine,

Director of Graduate Enrollment Management, 914-323-3208, Fax: 914-694-1732, E-mail: edschool@mville.edu. *Dean,* Dr. Shelley Wepner, 914-323-3153, Fax: 914-323-5493, E-mail: shelley.wepner@mville.edu.

MANSFIELD UNIVERSITY OF PENNSYLVANIA, Mansfield, PA 16933

General Information State-supported, coed, comprehensive institution. *Graduate housing:* Room and/or apartments available on a first-come, first-served basis to single students; on-campus housing not available to married students.

GRADUATE UNITS

Graduate Studies *Program availability:* Part-time, evening/weekend, online learning. Offers art education (M Ed); band conducting (MA); choral conducting (MA); elementary education (M Ed); library science (M Ed); nursing (MSN); organizational leadership (MA); performance (MA); secondary education (MS); special education (M Ed). Electronic applications accepted.

MAPLE SPRINGS BAPTIST BIBLE COLLEGE AND SEMINARY, Capitol Heights, MD 20743

General Information Independent-religious, coed, comprehensive institution. *Graduate housing:* On-campus housing not available.

GRADUATE UNITS

Graduate and Professional Programs Offers biblical studies (MA, Certificate); Christian counseling (MA); church administration (MA); divinity (M Div); ministry (D Min); religious education (MRE).

MARANATHA BAPTIST UNIVERSITY, Watertown, WI 53094

General Information Independent-religious, coed, comprehensive institution. *Enrollment:* 1,118 graduate, professional, and undergraduate students; 20 full-time matriculated graduate/professional students (3 women), 127 part-time matriculated graduate/professional students (39 women). *Enrollment by degree level:* 147 master's. *Tuition:* Full-time $6300; part-time $3150 per credit. *Required fees:* $210; $35 per course. Tuition and fees vary according to course load and degree level. *Graduate housing:* Room and/or apartments available to single students; on-campus housing not available to married students. *Student services:* Campus employment opportunities, campus safety program, child daycare facilities, teacher training. *Library facilities:* Cedarholm Library and Resource Center.

Computer facilities: A campuswide network can be accessed from student residence rooms and from off campus. Online class registration is available.
Website: http://www.mbu.edu/

General Application Contact: Dr. Jim Harrison, Director of Admissions, 920-206-2327, Fax: 920-261-9109, E-mail: admissions@mbbc.edu.

GRADUATE UNITS

Master of Arts in English Bible Program Expenses: Contact institution. *Program availability:* Part-time, 100% online. Offers English Bible (MA). *Application fee:* $50. *Application Contact:* Dr. Jim Harrison, Director of Admissions, 920-206-2327, Fax: 920-261-9109, E-mail: admissions@mbu.edu. *Dean of Maranatha Baptist Seminary,* Dr. Larry Oats, 920-206-2324, Fax: 920-261-9109, E-mail: larry.oats@mbu.edu.
Master of Arts in Intercultural Studies Program Expenses: Contact institution. *Financial support:* Scholarships/grants and tuition waivers (full and partial) available. Support available to part-time students. *Program availability:* Part-time. Offers intercultural studies (MA). *Application deadline:* Applications are processed on a rolling basis. *Application fee:* $50. *Application Contact:* Dr. Jim Harrison, Director of Admissions, 920-206-2327, Fax: 920-261-9109, E-mail: admissions@mbu.edu. *Dean of Maranatha Baptist Seminary,* Dr. Larry Oats, 920-206-2324, Fax: 920-261-9109, E-mail: larry.oats@mbu.edu.
Master of Divinity Program Expenses: Contact institution. *Financial support:* Scholarships/grants and tuition waivers (full and partial) available. Support available to part-time students. *Program availability:* Part-time. Offers divinity (M Div). *Application deadline:* Applications are processed on a rolling basis. *Application fee:* $50. *Application Contact:* Dr. Jim Harrison, Director of Admissions, 920-206-2327, Fax: 920-261-9109, E-mail: admissions@mbu.edu. *Dean of Maranatha Baptist Seminary,* Dr. Larry Oats, 920-206-2324, Fax: 920-261-9109, E-mail: larry.oats@mbu.edu.
Program in Biblical Counseling Expenses: Contact institution. *Financial support:* Scholarships/grants and tuition waivers (full and partial) available. Support available to part-time students. Financial award applicants required to submit FAFSA. *Program availability:* Part-time. Offers Biblical counseling (MA). *Application deadline:* Applications are processed on a rolling basis. *Application fee:* $50. *Application Contact:* Dr. Jim Harrison, Director of Admissions, 920-206-2327, Fax: 920-261-9109, E-mail: admissions@mbbc.edu. *Dean of Maranatha Baptist Seminary,* Dr. Larry Oats, 920-206-2324, Fax: 920-261-9109, E-mail: larry.oats@mbu.edu.
Program in Biblical Studies Expenses: Contact institution. *Financial support:* Scholarships/grants and tuition waivers (full and partial) available. Support available to part-time students. *Program availability:* Part-time. Offers Biblical studies (MA). *Application deadline:* Applications are processed on a rolling basis. *Application fee:* $50. *Application Contact:* Dr. Jim Harrison, Director of Admissions, 920-206-2327, Fax: 920-261-9109, E-mail: admissions@mbu.edu. *Dean of Maranatha Baptist Seminary,* Dr. Larry Oats, 920-206-2324, Fax: 920-261-9109, E-mail: larry.oats@mbu.edu.
Program in Teaching and Learning Expenses: Contact institution. *Financial support:* Scholarships/grants, tuition waivers (full and partial), and unspecified assistantships available. Support available to part-time students. Financial award applicants required to submit FAFSA. *Program availability:* Part-time, evening/weekend, 100% online. Offers teaching and learning (M Ed). *Application Contact:* Dr. Jim Harrison, Director of Admissions, 920-206-2327, Fax: 920-261-9109, E-mail: admissions@mbu.edu. *Director of the School of Education,* David Handyside, 920-261-6987, Fax: 920-261-9109, E-mail: david.handyside@mbu.edu.

MARCONI INTERNATIONAL UNIVERSITY, Pembroke Pines, FL 33028

General Information Proprietary, coed, comprehensive institution.
GRADUATE UNITS
Graduate Programs

MARIAN UNIVERSITY, Indianapolis, IN 46222-1997

General Information Independent-religious, coed, comprehensive institution. *Enrollment:* 3,165 graduate, professional, and undergraduate students; 677 full-time matriculated graduate/professional students (323 women), 288 part-time matriculated graduate/professional students (196 women). *Enrollment by degree level:* 343 master's, 622 doctoral. *Graduate faculty:* 38 full-time (17 women), 36 part-time/adjunct (25

women). *Tuition:* Full-time $47,200; part-time $945 per credit hour. *Required fees:* $1500. Tuition and fees vary according to degree level and program. *Graduate housing:* Rooms and/or apartments available on a first-come, first-served basis to single and married students. Typical cost: $10,596 per year ($15,506 including board) for single students; $13,500 per year ($18,410 including board) for married students. Room and board charges vary according to housing facility selected. Housing application deadline: 3/1. *Student services:* Campus safety program, career counseling, exercise/wellness program, free psychological counseling, international student services, low-cost health insurance, services for students with disabilities, teacher training, writing training. *Library facilities:* Mother Theresa Hackelmeier Memorial Library. *Collection:* Books: 79,801 (physical); Serial titles: 150 (physical). Weekly public service hours: 95.

Computer facilities: Computer purchase and lease plans are available. 118 computers available on campus for general student use. A campuswide network can be accessed from student residence rooms. Online class registration is available.
Website: http://www.marian.edu/

General Application Contact: Bryan Moody, Executive Director of Graduate Admission, 317-955-6284, E-mail: bmoody@marian.edu.

GRADUATE UNITS

College of Osteopathic Medicine Students: 665 full-time (314 women), 1 part-time (0 women); includes 130 minority (13 Black or African American, non-Hispanic/Latino; 1 American Indian or Alaska Native, non-Hispanic/Latino; 80 Asian, non-Hispanic/Latino; 27 Hispanic/Latino; 9 Two or more races, non-Hispanic/Latino), 20 international. Average age 26. 4,592 applicants, 9% accepted, 205 enrolled. *Faculty:* 28 full-time (10 women), 1 part-time/adjunct (0 women). Expenses: Contact institution. *Financial support:* Applicants required to submit FAFSA. Offers osteopathic medicine (MS, DO). *Application deadline:* For fall admission, 3/1 for domestic and international students. Applications are processed on a rolling basis. *Application fee:* $100. Electronic applications accepted. *Application Contact:* Bryan Moody, Director of Enrollment Management, 317-955-6284, E-mail: bmoody@marian.edu. *Vice President of Health Professions/Dean of the College of Osteopathic Medicine,* Dr. Donald Sefcik, 317-955-6289, E-mail: dsefcik@marian.edu.

Educators College Students: 10 full-time (9 women), 287 part-time (196 women); includes 71 minority (44 Black or African American, non-Hispanic/Latino; 6 Asian, non-Hispanic/Latino; 14 Hispanic/Latino; 7 Two or more races, non-Hispanic/Latino). Average age 29. 351 applicants, 53% accepted, 152 enrolled. *Faculty:* 6 full-time (4 women), 33 part-time/adjunct (24 women). Expenses: Contact institution. *Financial support:* Application deadline: 3/10; applicants required to submit FAFSA. In 2016, 138 master's awarded. *Program availability:* Part-time, evening/weekend. Offers educators (MA, MA Ed, MAT). *Application deadline:* For fall admission, 3/1 priority date for domestic students. Applications are processed on a rolling basis. *Application fee:* $35. Electronic applications accepted. *Senior Vice President of Teacher Learning Excellence/Dean,* Dr. Kenith Britt, 317-955-6209, Fax: 317-955-6406, E-mail: kbritt@marian.edu.

MARIAN UNIVERSITY, Fond du Lac, WI 54935-4699

General Information Independent-religious, coed, comprehensive institution. CGS member. *Enrollment:* 1,974 graduate, professional, and undergraduate students; 25 full-time matriculated graduate/professional students (21 women), 346 part-time matriculated graduate/professional students (239 women). *Enrollment by degree level:* 306 master's, 65 doctoral. *Graduate faculty:* 19 full-time (15 women), 35 part-time/adjunct (17 women). *Tuition:* Full-time $5130; part-time $570 per credit hour. *Graduate housing:* On-campus housing not available. *Student services:* Campus employment opportunities, campus safety program, career counseling, exercise/wellness program, free psychological counseling, international student services, multicultural affairs office, services for students with disabilities, teacher training, writing training. *Library facilities:* Cardinal Meyer Library plus 1 other. *Collection:* Books: 210,079 (physical), 147,236 (digital/electronic); Databases: 1,805.

Computer facilities: Computer purchase and lease plans are available. 500 computers available on campus for general student use. A campuswide network can be accessed from student residence rooms and from off campus. Online class registration is available.
Website: http://www.marianuniversity.edu/

General Application Contact: Shannon LaLuzerne, Dean of Admission, 920-923-7650, E-mail: admission@marianuniversity.edu.

GRADUATE UNITS

School of Business and Public Safety Students: 60 part-time (32 women); includes 9 minority (6 Black or African American, non-Hispanic/Latino; 1 Asian, non-Hispanic/Latino; 2 Hispanic/Latino). Average age 36. *Faculty:* 4 part-time/adjunct (2 women). Expenses: Contact institution. *Financial support:* Application deadline: 3/1; applicants required to submit FAFSA. In 2016, 26 master's awarded. *Program availability:* Part-time, evening/weekend. Offers organizational leadership (MS). *Application deadline:* Applications are processed on a rolling basis. *Application fee:* $25. Electronic applications accepted. *Dean, Marian School of Business,* Dr. Jeffrey G. Reed, 920-923-8759, Fax: 920-923-7167, E-mail: jreed@marianuniversity.edu.

School of Education Students: 13 full-time (9 women), 179 part-time (113 women); includes 16 minority (6 Black or African American, non-Hispanic/Latino; 3 American Indian or Alaska Native, non-Hispanic/Latino; 2 Asian, non-Hispanic/Latino; 3 Hispanic/Latino; 2 Two or more races, non-Hispanic/Latino). Average age 39. *Faculty:* 11 full-time (7 women), 14 part-time/adjunct (8 women). Expenses: Contact institution. *Financial support:* In 2016–17, 3 students received support. Federal Work-Study available. Support available to part-time students. Financial award application deadline: 3/1; financial award applicants required to submit FAFSA. In 2016, 72 master's, 8 doctorates awarded. *Program availability:* Part-time, evening/weekend, online learning. Offers curriculum and instruction leadership (PhD); educational administration (PhD); educational leadership (MAE); educational technology (MAE); leadership studies (PhD); special education (MAE); teacher education (MAE). *Application deadline:* Applications are processed on a rolling basis. *Application fee:* $50. *Dean,* Dr. Kelly Chaney, 920-923-8610, Fax: 920-923-7663, E-mail: kachaney01@marianuniversity.edu.

School of Nursing and Health Professions Students: 12 full-time (all women), 107 part-time (94 women); includes 14 minority (7 Black or African American, non-Hispanic/Latino; 4 Asian, non-Hispanic/Latino; 3 Hispanic/Latino). Average age 41. *Faculty:* 5 full-time (all women), 4 part-time/adjunct (2 women). Expenses: Contact institution. *Financial support:* In 2016–17, 3 students received support. Scholarships/grants available. Support available to part-time students. Financial award application deadline: 3/1; financial award applicants required to submit FAFSA. In 2016, 28 master's awarded. *Program availability:* Part-time, evening/weekend. Offers adult nurse practitioner (MSN); nurse educator (MSN); thanatology (MS). *Application* *deadline:* Applications are processed on a rolling basis. *Application fee:* $50. Electronic applications accepted. *Dean,* Dr. Linda Matheson, 920-923-7668, Fax: 920-923-8770, E-mail: lkmatheson85@marianuniversity.edu.

MARIETTA COLLEGE, Marietta, OH 45750-4000

General Information Independent, coed, comprehensive institution. *Enrollment:* 1,224 graduate, professional, and undergraduate students; 75 full-time matriculated graduate/professional students (57 women), 5 part-time matriculated graduate/professional students (3 women). *Enrollment by degree level:* 80 master's. *Graduate faculty:* 5 full-time (2 women), 7 part-time/adjunct (2 women). *Tuition:* Full-time $36,433; part-time $750 per credit hour. One-time fee: $500 full-time. Tuition and fees vary according to program. *Graduate housing:* On-campus housing not available. *Student services:* Campus safety program, career counseling, free psychological counseling, international student services, services for students with disabilities, teacher training, writing training. *Library facilities:* Legacy Library. *Collection:* Books: 163,843 (physical), 126,903 (digital/electronic); Serial titles: 246 (physical), 15,186 (digital/electronic); Databases: 167. Weekly public service hours: 95; students can reserve study rooms.

Computer facilities: 475 computers available on campus for general student use. A campuswide network can be accessed from student residence rooms and from off campus. Online class registration is available. Website: http://www.marietta.edu/

General Application Contact: Scott McVicar, Director of Admissions, 740-376-4606, E-mail: scott.mcvicar@marietta.edu.

GRADUATE UNITS

Program in Physician Assistant Studies Students: 71 full-time (53 women); includes 11 minority (1 Black or African American, non-Hispanic/Latino; 1 American Indian or Alaska Native, non-Hispanic/Latino; 7 Asian, non-Hispanic/Latino; 2 Hispanic/Latino). Average age 25. 862 applicants, 7% accepted, 36 enrolled. *Faculty:* 5 full-time (2 women), 2 part-time/adjunct (0 women). Expenses: Contact institution. *Financial support:* Scholarships/grants available. In 2016, 36 master's awarded. Offers physician assistant studies (MS). *Application deadline:* For fall admission, 11/1 for domestic students. *Application fee:* $175. Electronic applications accepted. *Director,* Miranda Collins, 740-376-4953, E-mail: miranda.collins@marietta.edu.

Program in Psychology Students: 10 full-time (6 women), 1 (woman) part-time; includes 1 minority (Black or African American, non-Hispanic/Latino), 1 international. Average age 24. 12 applicants, 83% accepted, 7 enrolled. *Faculty:* 5 part-time/adjunct (2 women). Expenses: Contact institution. *Financial support:* Unspecified assistantships available. In 2016, 1 master's awarded. *Program availability:* Part-time. Offers psychology (MAP). *Application deadline:* Applications are processed on a rolling basis. *Application fee:* $25. *Director,* Dr. Chris Klein, 740-376-4795, E-mail: clk002@marietta.edu.

MARIST COLLEGE, Poughkeepsie, NY 12601-1387

General Information Independent, coed, comprehensive institution. *Graduate housing:* On-campus housing not available. *Research affiliation:* Center for Advanced Brain Imaging Psychology (psychology), New York State Office of Technology and Academic Research (NYSTAR) (technology), Hudson Valley Technology Development Corporation (HVTDC) (technology), Hudson River Psychiatric Center (psychology), St. Francis Hospital, Dutchess County Community Mental Health Center (mental health).

GRADUATE UNITS

Graduate Programs *Program availability:* Part-time, evening/weekend, online learning. Electronic applications accepted.

School of Communication and the Arts *Program availability:* Part-time, online learning. Offers communication (MA); integrated marketing communication (MA); museum studies (MA). Electronic applications accepted.

School of Computer Science and Mathematics *Program availability:* Part-time, evening/weekend, online learning. Offers computer science/software development (MS); information systems (MS, Adv C); technology management (MS). Electronic applications accepted.

School of Management *Program availability:* Part-time, evening/weekend, online learning. Offers business administration (MBA, Adv C); executive leadership (Adv C); public administration (MPA); technology management (MS). Electronic applications accepted.

School of Social and Behavioral Sciences *Program availability:* Part-time, evening/weekend, online learning. Offers education (M Ed, MA); mental health counseling (MA); school psychology (MA, Adv C). Electronic applications accepted.

MARLBORO COLLEGE, Marlboro, VT 05344

General Information Independent, coed, comprehensive institution. *Enrollment:* 274 graduate, professional, and undergraduate students; 22 full-time matriculated graduate/professional students (14 women), 50 part-time matriculated graduate/professional students (29 women). *Enrollment by degree level:* 64 master's, 8 other advanced degrees. *Graduate faculty:* 3 full-time (2 women), 42 part-time/adjunct (27 women). *Tuition:* Full-time $22,950; part-time $765 per credit. Tuition and fees vary according to course load. *Graduate housing:* On-campus housing not available. *Student services:* Career counseling, international student services, services for students with disabilities, teacher training, writing training. *Library facilities:* Rice-Aron Library. *Collection:* Books: 88,500 (physical), 137,548 (digital/electronic); Serial titles: 5,400 (physical), 150 (digital/electronic); Databases: 75. Study areas open 24 hours, 5–7 days a week.

Computer facilities: Computer purchase and lease plans are available. 47 computers available on campus for general student use. A campuswide network can be accessed from student residence rooms and from off campus. Online class registration is available. Website: http://www.marlboro.edu/

General Application Contact: Don Parker, Admissions Assistant, 802-451-7505, Fax: 802-258-9201, E-mail: graduateadmissions@marlboro.edu.

GRADUATE UNITS

Graduate and Professional Studies Students: 22 full-time (14 women), 50 part-time (29 women); includes 11 minority (1 Black or African American, non-Hispanic/Latino; 3 American Indian or Alaska Native, non-Hispanic/Latino; 2 Hispanic/Latino; 5 Two or more races, non-Hispanic/Latino). Average age 39. 32 applicants, 81% accepted, 24 enrolled. *Faculty:* 3 full-time (2 women), 41 part-time/adjunct (27 women). Expenses: Contact institution. *Financial support:* In 2016–17, 6 students received support. Scholarships/grants available. Financial award applicants required to submit FAFSA. In 2016, 34 master's awarded. *Program availability:* Part-time, evening/weekend, blended/hybrid learning. Offers collaborative leadership (MBA, MS); conscious business

(MBA, MS); educational technology (Certificate); mission driven organizations (MBA, MS); project management (MBA, MS); social innovation (MBA, MS); sustainable food systems (MBA, MS); teaching English to speakers of other languages (MAT); teaching for social justice (MAT); teaching with technology (MAT). *Application deadline:* For fall admission, 8/5 for domestic and international students; for winter admission, 12/5 for domestic and international students; for spring admission, 4/5 for domestic and international students. Applications are processed on a rolling basis. *Application fee:* $0. Electronic applications accepted. *Application Contact:* Don Parker, Admissions Assistant, 802-451-7505, Fax: 802-258-9201, E-mail: graduateadmissions@marlboro.edu. *Associate Dean for Graduate and Professional Studies,* Kate Jellema, 802-258-9203, Fax: 802-258-9201, E-mail: katej@gradschool.marlboro.edu.

MARQUETTE UNIVERSITY, Milwaukee, WI 53201-1881

General Information Independent-religious, coed, university. CGS member. *Enrollment:* 11,294 graduate, professional, and undergraduate students; 2,090 full-time matriculated graduate/professional students (1,097 women), 887 part-time matriculated graduate/professional students (468 women). *Graduate faculty:* 598 full-time (249 women), 493 part-time/adjunct (239 women). *Graduate housing:* Rooms and/or apartments available on a first-come, first-served basis to single and married students. *Student services:* Campus employment opportunities, campus safety program, career counseling, child daycare facilities, exercise/wellness program, free psychological counseling, grant writing training, international student services, low-cost health insurance, multicultural affairs office, services for students with disabilities, teacher training, writing training. *Library facilities:* Raynor Memorial Libraries plus 1 other. *Collection:* Books: 1.3 million (physical), 2.5 million (digital/electronic); Serial titles: 1,562 (physical), 50,539 (digital/electronic); Databases: 464. Weekly public service hours: 166; study areas open 24 hours, 5–7 days a week; students can reserve study rooms. *Research affiliation:* Shriners Hospital for Children in Chicago, Rehabilitation Institute of Chicago, Froedtert Memorial Lutheran Hospital, Children's Hospital of Wisconsin, Blood Center of Wisconsin, Department of Orthopedic Surgery, Medical College of Wisconsin.

Computer facilities: 1,720 computers available on campus for general student use. A campuswide network can be accessed from student residence rooms and from off campus. Online class registration, AV Software, MATLAB, Printwise are available. Website: http://www.marquette.edu/

GRADUATE UNITS

Graduate School Students: 997 full-time (607 women), 598 part-time (364 women); includes 196 minority (33 Black or African American, non-Hispanic/Latino; 4 American Indian or Alaska Native, non-Hispanic/Latino; 56 Asian, non-Hispanic/Latino; 75 Hispanic/Latino; 28 Two or more races, non-Hispanic/Latino), 171 international. Average age 28. 1,705 applicants, 59% accepted, 495 enrolled. *Faculty:* 437 full-time (197 women), 268 part-time/adjunct (170 women). Expenses: Contact institution. *Financial support:* In 2016–17, 56 fellowships, 73 research assistantships with full tuition reimbursements, 217 teaching assistantships with full tuition reimbursements were awarded; career-related internships or fieldwork, Federal Work-Study, institutionally sponsored loans, scholarships/grants, and tuition waivers (full and partial) also available. Support available to part-time students. Financial award application deadline: 2/15. In 2016, 429 master's, 151 doctorates, 5 other advanced degrees awarded. *Program availability:* Part-time, evening/weekend, online learning. Offers interdisciplinary studies (PhD); transfusion medicine (MSTM). *Application deadline:* Applications are processed on a rolling basis. Electronic applications accepted. *Vice Provost for Research/Dean,* Dr. Douglas Woods, 414-288-1532, Fax: 414-288-1578.

College of Arts and Sciences Students: 327 full-time (131 women), 142 part-time (51 women); includes 48 minority (5 Black or African American, non-Hispanic/Latino; 11 Asian, non-Hispanic/Latino; 22 Hispanic/Latino; 10 Two or more races, non-Hispanic/Latino), 102 international. Average age 30. 600 applicants, 42% accepted, 127 enrolled. *Faculty:* 236 full-time (92 women), 58 part-time/adjunct (21 women). Expenses: Contact institution. *Financial support:* In 2016–17, 309 students received support, including 33 fellowships with partial tuition reimbursements available, 43 research assistantships with full tuition reimbursements available, 166 teaching assistantships with full tuition reimbursements available; scholarships/grants, health care benefits, tuition waivers (full and partial), and unspecified assistantships also available. Support available to part-time students. Financial award application deadline: 2/15. In 2016, 88 master's, 56 doctorates awarded. *Program availability:* Part-time. Offers American literature (PhD); analytical chemistry (MS, PhD); ancient philosophy (PhD); arts and sciences (MA, MACD, MS, PhD); bioanalytical chemistry (MS, PhD); bioinformatics (MS); biophysical chemistry (MS, PhD); British and American literature (MA); British empiricism and analytic philosophy (PhD); British literature (PhD); cell biology (MS, PhD); chemical physics (MS, PhD); Christian philosophy (PhD); computational sciences (MS, PhD); computing (MS, PhD); developmental biology (MS, PhD); early modern European philosophy (PhD); ecology (MS, PhD); epithelial physiology (MS, PhD); ethics (PhD); European history (MA, PhD); genetics (MS, PhD); German philosophy (PhD); global studies (MA); history of philosophy (MA); inorganic chemistry (MS, PhD); international affairs (MA); mathematics education (MS); medieval philosophy (PhD); microbiology (MS, PhD); molecular biology (MS, PhD); muscle and exercise physiology (MS, PhD); neuroscience (PhD); organic chemistry (MS, PhD); phenomenology and existentialism (PhD); philosophy of religion (PhD); physical chemistry (MS, PhD); political science (MA); psychology (PhD); public service (MA); social and applied philosophy (MA); Spanish (MA); theology (MA, PhD); United States history (MA, PhD). *Application deadline:* Applications are processed on a rolling basis. Electronic applications accepted. *Dean,* Dr. Richard Holz, 414-288-7230.

College of Communication Students: 25 full-time (22 women), 23 part-time (16 women); includes 9 minority (3 Black or African American, non-Hispanic/Latino; 1 American Indian or Alaska Native, non-Hispanic/Latino; 4 Hispanic/Latino; 1 Two or more races, non-Hispanic/Latino), 4 international. Average age 28. 55 applicants, 62% accepted, 21 enrolled. *Faculty:* 36 full-time (18 women), 45 part-time/adjunct (20 women). Expenses: Contact institution. *Financial support:* Fellowships, research assistantships, teaching assistantships, career-related internships or fieldwork, scholarships/grants, health care benefits, tuition waivers (full and partial), and unspecified assistantships available. Support available to part-time students. Financial award application deadline: 2/15. In 2016, 10 master's, 1 other advanced degree awarded. *Program availability:* Part-time, evening/weekend. Offers advertising and public relations (MA); communication studies (MA); digital storytelling (Certificate); journalism (MA); mass communication (MA); science, health and environmental communication (MA). *Application deadline:* Applications are processed on a rolling basis. Electronic applications accepted. *Application Contact:* Dr. Sarah Bonewits Feldner. *Associate Dean,* Dr. Sarah Feldner.

College of Education Students: 100 full-time (76 women), 116 part-time (76 women); includes 40 minority (13 Black or African American, non-Hispanic/Latino; 1 American Indian or Alaska Native, non-Hispanic/Latino; 9 Asian, non-Hispanic/Latino; 13

Hispanic/Latino; 4 Two or more races, non-Hispanic/Latino), 3 international. Average age 29. 218 applicants, 67% accepted, 99 enrolled. *Faculty:* 23 full-time (17 women), 33 part-time/adjunct (26 women). Expenses: Contact institution. *Financial support:* Fellowships, research assistantships, scholarships/grants, health care benefits, tuition waivers (partial), and unspecified assistantships available. Support available to part-time students. Financial award application deadline: 2/15. In 2016, 71 master's, 2 doctorates, 3 other advanced degrees awarded. *Program availability:* Part-time. Offers clinical mental health counseling (MS); college student personnel administration (M Ed); community counseling (MA); counseling psychology (PhD); curriculum and instruction (MA); education (M Ed, MA, MS, PhD, Certificate); educational administration (M Ed); educational policy and foundations (MA); elementary education (Certificate); literacy (MA); principal (Certificate); reading specialist (Certificate); reading teacher (Certificate); school counseling (MA); secondary education (Certificate); superintendent (Certificate). *Application deadline:* For fall admission, 1/15 for domestic and international students.

College of Engineering Students: 113 full-time (26 women), 80 part-time (16 women); includes 24 minority (4 Black or African American, non-Hispanic/Latino; 9 Asian, non-Hispanic/Latino; 8 Hispanic/Latino; 3 Two or more races, non-Hispanic/Latino), 54 international. Average age 27. 312 applicants, 61% accepted, 45 enrolled. *Faculty:* 66 full-time (10 women), 18 part-time/adjunct (4 women). Expenses: Contact institution. *Financial support:* Fellowships, research assistantships, teaching assistantships, scholarships/grants, health care benefits, tuition waivers (partial), and unspecified assistantships available. Support available to part-time students. Financial award application deadline: 2/15. In 2016, 49 master's, 15 doctorates awarded. *Program availability:* Part-time, evening/weekend. Offers biocomputing (ME); bioimaging (ME); bioinstrumentation (ME); bioinstrumentation/computers (MS, PhD); biomechanics (ME); biomechanics/biomaterials (MS, PhD); biorehabilitation (ME); construction engineering and management (MS, PhD, Certificate); digital signal processing (Certificate); electric machines, drives, and controls (Certificate); electrical and computer engineering (MS, PhD); engineering (ME, MS, MSEM, PhD, Certificate); engineering innovation (Certificate); engineering management (MSEM); environmental engineering (MS, PhD); functional imaging (PhD); healthcare technologies management (MS); mechanical engineering (MS, PhD); microwaves and antennas (Certificate); new product and process development (Certificate); rehabilitation bioengineering (PhD); sensors and smart systems (Certificate); structural design (Certificate); structural engineering and structural mechanics (MS, PhD); systems physiology (MS, PhD); transportation (Certificate); transportation engineering and materials (MS, PhD); waste and wastewater treatment processes (Certificate); water resources engineering (Certificate). *Application deadline:* Applications are processed on a rolling basis. Electronic applications accepted. *Dean,* Dr. Kris Ropella, 414-288-6591, Fax: 414-288-7082.

College of Health Sciences Students: 265 full-time (210 women), 39 part-time (28 women); includes 44 minority (3 Black or African American, non-Hispanic/Latino; 17 Asian, non-Hispanic/Latino; 16 Hispanic/Latino; 8 Two or more races, non-Hispanic/Latino), 4 international. Average age 24. 310 applicants, 58% accepted, 99 enrolled. *Faculty:* 38 full-time (24 women), 38 part-time/adjunct (27 women). Expenses: Contact institution. *Financial support:* Fellowships and research assistantships available. In 2016, 90 master's, 63 doctorates awarded. Offers bilingual English/Spanish (Certificate); clinical and translational rehabilitation science (MS, PhD); health sciences (MPAS, MS, DPT, PhD, Certificate); physical therapy (DPT); physician assistant studies (MPAS); speech-language pathology (MS). Electronic applications accepted. *Dean,* Dr. William C. Cullinan, 414-288-5053, E-mail: jack.brooks@mu.edu.

College of Nursing Students: 165 full-time (141 women), 193 part-time (173 women); includes 35 minority (9 Black or African American, non-Hispanic/Latino; 2 American Indian or Alaska Native, non-Hispanic/Latino; 10 Asian, non-Hispanic/Latino; 12 Hispanic/Latino; 2 Two or more races, non-Hispanic/Latino), 4 international. Average age 30. 208 applicants, 100% accepted, 98 enrolled. *Faculty:* 38 full-time (36 women), 76 part-time/adjunct (72 women). Expenses: Contact institution. *Financial support:* Fellowships, research assistantships, teaching assistantships, career-related internships or fieldwork, Federal Work-Study, scholarships/grants, health care benefits, tuition waivers (partial), and unspecified assistantships available. Support available to part-time students. Financial award application deadline: 2/15. In 2016, 118 master's, 14 doctorates, 1 other advanced degree awarded. Offers acute care nurse practitioner (Certificate); adult clinical nurse specialist (Certificate); adult nurse practitioner (Certificate); advanced practice nursing (MSN, DNP); family nurse practitioner (Certificate); nurse-midwifery (Certificate); nursing (PhD); pediatric acute care (Certificate); pediatric primary care (Certificate); systems leadership and healthcare quality (Certificate). *Application deadline:* For fall admission, 2/15 for domestic and international students. Electronic applications accepted. *Application Contact:* Dr. Kerry Kosmoski-Geopfert. *Dean,* Dr. Janet Krejci.

Graduate School of Management Students: 144 full-time (69 women), 227 part-time (68 women); includes 32 minority (11 Black or African American, non-Hispanic/Latino; 10 Asian, non-Hispanic/Latino; 7 Hispanic/Latino; 1 Native Hawaiian or other Pacific Islander, non-Hispanic/Latino; 3 Two or more races, non-Hispanic/Latino), 61 international. Average age 30. 365 applicants, 82% accepted, 212 enrolled. *Faculty:* 72 full-time (22 women), 32 part-time/adjunct (12 women). Expenses: Contact institution. *Financial support:* Fellowships, research assistantships, teaching assistantships, Federal Work-Study, institutionally sponsored loans, scholarships/grants, and tuition waivers (full and partial) available. Support available to part-time students. Financial award application deadline: 2/15. In 2016, 198 master's, 5 other advanced degrees awarded. *Program availability:* Part-time, evening/weekend. Offers accounting (MSA); business administration (MBA); business economics (MSAE); economics (MBA); entrepreneurship (Certificate); finance (MBA); financial economics (MSAE); human resources (MBA); international business (MBA); international economics (MSAE); management (MBA, MSA, MSAE, MSHR, Certificate); management information systems (MBA); marketing (MBA); marketing research (MSAE); operations and supply chain management (MBA); real estate economics (MSAE); sports business (MBA). *Application deadline:* For fall admission, 2/15 for domestic and international students. Applications are processed on a rolling basis. Electronic applications accepted. *Application Contact:* Dr. Jeanne Simmons. *Dean,* Dr. Brian Till, 414-288-5724.

Law School Students: 520 full-time (207 women), 55 part-time (32 women); includes 105 minority (22 Black or African American, non-Hispanic/Latino; 1 American Indian or Alaska Native, non-Hispanic/Latino; 16 Asian, non-Hispanic/Latino; 51 Hispanic/Latino; 15 Two or more races, non-Hispanic/Latino), 2 international. Average age 26. 2,259 applicants, 100% accepted, 810 enrolled. *Faculty:* 32 full-time (13 women), 36 part-time/adjunct (19 women). Expenses: Contact institution. *Financial support:* Career-related internships or fieldwork, Federal Work-Study, and scholarships/grants available. Support available to part-time students. Financial award application deadline: 3/1; financial award applicants required to submit FAFSA. In 2016, 573 doctorates awarded.

Program availability: Part-time, evening/weekend. Offers law (JD). *Application deadline:* For fall admission, 4/1 for domestic students. Applications are processed on a rolling basis. *Application fee:* $50. Electronic applications accepted. *Dean,* Joseph D. Kearney, 414-288-7090, Fax: 414-288-6403.

School of Dentistry Students: 429 full-time (214 women), 7 part-time (4 women); includes 115 minority (9 Black or African American, non-Hispanic/Latino; 2 American Indian or Alaska Native, non-Hispanic/Latino; 48 Asian, non-Hispanic/Latino; 45 Hispanic/Latino; 11 Two or more races, non-Hispanic/Latino), 13 international. Average age 25. 354 applicants, 40% accepted, 85 enrolled. *Faculty:* 57 full-time (17 women), 157 part-time/adjunct (38 women). Expenses: Contact institution. *Financial support:* Fellowships, career-related internships or fieldwork, Federal Work-Study, institutionally sponsored loans, scholarships/grants, and tuition waivers (full and partial) available. Support available to part-time students. Financial award application deadline: 3/1; financial award applicants required to submit FAFSA. In 2016, 10 master's, 81 doctorates, 4 other advanced degrees awarded. Offers advanced training in general dentistry (MS, Certificate); dental biomaterials (MS); dentistry (MS, DDS, Certificate); endodontics (MS, Certificate); orthodontics (MS, Certificate); periodontics (MS, Certificate); prosthodontics (MS, Certificate). *Application deadline:* For spring admission, 3/1 priority date for domestic and international students. Applications are processed on a rolling basis. *Application Contact:* Dr. T. Gerry Bradley. *Dean,* Dr. William K. Lobb, 414-288-6546, Fax: 414-288-3586, E-mail: william.lobb@marquette.edu.

MARSHALL B. KETCHUM UNIVERSITY, Fullerton, CA 92831-1615

General Information Independent, coed, graduate-only institution. *Graduate housing:* On-campus housing not available. *Research affiliation:* Alcon Laboratories (ophthalmic products), Essilor (spectacle lenses), Allergan (ophthalmic products).

GRADUATE UNITS

Graduate and Professional Programs Offers optometry (OD); vision science (MS). Electronic applications accepted.

MARSHALL UNIVERSITY, Huntington, WV 25755

General Information State-supported, coed, university. *Graduate housing:* Rooms and/or apartments available on a first-come, first-served basis to single and married students. *Research affiliation:* Bayer Corporation, Kanawha Valley Local Port District, Greenbrier County Commission, Dominion Power, Wyeth-Ayerst (clinical pharmaceutical study).

GRADUATE UNITS

Academic Affairs Division *Program availability:* Part-time, evening/weekend.

College of Arts and Media *Program availability:* Evening/weekend. Offers arts and media (MA, MAJ); journalism (MAJ); music (MA).

College of Business *Program availability:* Part-time, evening/weekend. Offers accountancy (MS); business (MBA, MS, DMPNA, Graduate Certificate); business administration (MBA); health care administration (MS); human resource management (MS); nurse anesthesia (DMPNA).

College of Education and Professional Development *Program availability:* Part-time, evening/weekend. Offers adult and technical education (MS); counseling (MA, Ed S, Graduate Certificate); early childhood education (MA); education and professional development (MA, MAT, MS, Ed D, Certificate, Ed S, Graduate Certificate); elementary education (MA, Graduate Certificate); leadership studies (MA, MS, Ed D, Certificate, Ed S); literacy education (MA, Ed S); school psychology (Ed S); secondary education (MA); special education (MA); teaching (MAT). Electronic applications accepted.

College of Health Professions Offers athletic training (MS); communication disorders (MS); dietetics (MS); exercise science (MS); health informatics (MS); health professions (MPH, MS, MSN, MSW, DPT); kinesiology (MS); nursing (MSN); physical therapy (DPT); public health (MPH); social work (MSW); sport administration (MS).

College of Information Technology and Engineering *Program availability:* Part-time, evening/weekend. Offers applied science and technology (MS); computer science (MS); engineering (MSME); engineering management (MSE); environmental engineering (MSE); environmental science (MS); information systems (MS); information technology and engineering (MS, MSE, MSME); safety (MS); technology management (MS); transportation and infrastructure engineering (MSE).

College of Liberal Arts *Program availability:* Evening/weekend. Offers clinical psychology (Certificate); communication studies (MA); English (MA, Graduate Certificate); geography (MA, MS, Certificate); history (MA, Certificate); humanities (MA, Certificate); Latin (MA, Certificate); liberal arts (MA, MPA, MS, Psy D, Certificate, Graduate Certificate); political science (MA, MPA); psychology (MA, Psy D); sociology (MA).

College of Science Offers biological science (MA, MS); chemistry (MS); criminal justice (MS); mathematics (MA); physical and applied science (MS); science (MA, MS).

Forensic Science Center Offers forensic science (MS, Graduate Certificate).

School of Pharmacy Offers pharmacy (Pharm D).

Joan C. Edwards School of Medicine Offers biomedical sciences (MS, PhD); medicine (MS, MD, PhD). Electronic applications accepted.

MARS HILL UNIVERSITY, Mars Hill, NC 28754

General Information Independent-religious, coed, comprehensive institution.

GRADUATE UNITS

Adult and Graduate Studies

MARTIN LUTHER COLLEGE, New Ulm, MN 56073

General Information Independent-religious, coed, comprehensive institution. *Enrollment:* 937 graduate, professional, and undergraduate students; 1 (woman) full-time matriculated graduate/professional student, 77 part-time matriculated graduate/professional students (30 women). *Enrollment by degree level:* 78 master's. *Graduate faculty:* 9 full-time (1 woman), 21 part-time/adjunct (10 women). *Tuition:* Full-time $5400; part-time $300 per credit. *Required fees:* $105; $105 per credit. $35 per semester. Tuition and fees vary according to course load. *Graduate housing:* On-campus housing not available. *Library facilities:* Martin Luther College Library.

Computer facilities: A campuswide network can be accessed from student residence rooms.
Website: http://www.mlc.edu/

General Application Contact: John E. Meyer, Director of Graduate Studies, 507-354-8221 Ext. 398, Fax: 507-354-8225, E-mail: meyerjd@mlc-wels.edu.

GRADUATE UNITS

Graduate Studies Students: 1 (woman) full-time, 77 part-time (30 women); includes 2 minority (1 Asian, non-Hispanic/Latino; 1 Two or more races, non-Hispanic/Latino), 4 international. Average age 37. 6 applicants, 100% accepted, 6 enrolled. *Faculty:* 9 full-time (1 woman), 21 part-time/adjunct (10 women). Expenses: Contact institution. *Financial support:* In 2016–17, 2 students received support. Scholarships/grants available. Financial award application deadline: 9/1. In 2016, 15 master's awarded. *Program availability:* Part-time, evening/weekend. Offers early childhood director (MS Ed Admin); educational technology (MS Ed); instruction (MS Ed); leadership (MS Ed); principal (MS Ed Admin); special education (MS Ed). *Application deadline:* Applications are processed on a rolling basis. *Application fee:* $35. Electronic applications accepted. *Director of Graduate Studies,* John E. Meyer, 507-354-8221 Ext. 398, E-mail: meyerjd@mlc-wels.edu.

MARTIN UNIVERSITY, Indianapolis, IN 46218-3867

General Information Independent, coed, comprehensive institution. *Graduate housing:* On-campus housing not available.

GRADUATE UNITS

Division of Psychology *Program availability:* Part-time, evening/weekend. Offers community psychology (MS).

Graduate School of Urban Ministry *Program availability:* Part-time, evening/weekend. Offers urban ministry studies (MA).

MARY BALDWIN UNIVERSITY, Staunton, VA 24401-3610

General Information Independent, coed, primarily women, comprehensive institution. *Graduate housing:* On-campus housing not available.

GRADUATE UNITS

Graduate Studies *Program availability:* Part-time, evening/weekend, online learning. Offers acting (M Litt); directing (M Litt); elementary education (MAT); middle grades education (MAT); occupational therapy (OTD); Shakespeare and Renaissance literature in performance (M Litt, MFA); teaching (M Litt, MAT).

MARYGROVE COLLEGE, Detroit, MI 48221-2599

General Information Independent-religious, coed, primarily women, graduate-only institution. *Graduate housing:* Room and/or apartments available to single students; on-campus housing not available to married students.

GRADUATE UNITS

Graduate Division *Program availability:* Part-time, evening/weekend, online learning. Offers art of teaching (MAT); educational leadership (MA); educational technology (M Ed); English (MA); Griot (M Ed); human resource management (MA); modern language translation (Certificate); reading and literacy (M Ed); Sage (M Ed); social justice (MA). Electronic applications accepted.

MARYLAND INSTITUTE COLLEGE OF ART, Baltimore, MD 21217

General Information Independent, coed, comprehensive institution. *Enrollment:* 2,076 graduate, professional, and undergraduate students; 367 full-time matriculated graduate/professional students (241 women). *Enrollment by degree level:* 299 master's, 68 other advanced degrees. *Graduate faculty:* 26 full-time (18 women), 56 part-time/adjunct (23 women). *Tuition:* Full-time $45,290; part-time $1510 per credit. *Required fees:* $1700. One-time fee: $335 full-time. Full-time tuition and fees vary according to course load. *Graduate housing:* Room and/or apartments available on a first-come, first-served basis to single students; on-campus housing not available to married students. Typical cost: $11,700 per year ($13,900 including board). Housing application deadline: 5/15. *Student services:* Campus employment opportunities, campus safety program, career counseling, exercise/wellness program, free psychological counseling, grant writing training, international student services, low-cost health insurance, multicultural affairs office, services for students with disabilities, teacher training, writing training. *Library facilities:* Decker Library. *Collection:* Books: 75,000 (physical), 163,918 (digital/electronic); Serial titles: 671 (physical), 71 (digital/electronic); Databases: 47. Weekly public service hours: 70; students can reserve study rooms.

Computer facilities: 1,100 computers available on campus for general student use. A campuswide network can be accessed from student residence rooms and from off campus. Online class registration, campus portal, online gallery space, network storage space, personal websites, online software training tutorials, learning management system are available.
Website: http://www.mica.edu/

General Application Contact: Chris D. Harring, Director of Graduate Admission, 410-225-2256, Fax: 410-225-5275, E-mail: graduate@mica.edu.

GRADUATE UNITS

Graduate Studies Students: 367 full-time (241 women); includes 86 minority (16 Black or African American, non-Hispanic/Latino; 1 American Indian or Alaska Native, non-Hispanic/Latino; 28 Asian, non-Hispanic/Latino; 18 Hispanic/Latino; 1 Native Hawaiian or other Pacific Islander, non-Hispanic/Latino; 22 Two or more races, non-Hispanic/Latino), 46 international. Average age 27. 1,100 applicants, 36% accepted, 215 enrolled. *Faculty:* 26 full-time (18 women), 56 part-time/adjunct (23 women). Expenses: Contact institution. *Financial support:* In 2016–17, 303 students received support, including 367 fellowships (averaging $11,000 per year), 328 teaching assistantships (averaging $3,200 per year); career-related internships or fieldwork and scholarships/grants also available. Financial award application deadline: 1/15. In 2016, 175 master's, 23 other advanced degrees awarded. *Program availability:* Part-time, online learning. Offers art education (MA); business of art and design (MPS); community arts (MFA); curatorial practice (MFA); filmmaking (MFA); fine arts (Postbaccalaureate Certificate); graphic design (MA, MFA); illustration practice (MFA); information visualization (MPS); photographic and electronic media (MFA); social design (MA); studio art (MFA); teaching (MAT). *Application deadline:* For fall admission, 1/15 for domestic and international students. *Application fee:* $75. Electronic applications accepted. *Application Contact:* Chris D. Harring, Director of Graduate Admission, 410-225-2256, Fax: 410-225-5275, E-mail: graduate@mica.edu. *Vice Provost for Graduate Studies and Research,* Gwynne Keathley, 410-225-5274, Fax: 410-225-5275, E-mail: graduate@mica.edu.

LeRoy E. Hoffberger School of Painting Students: 20 full-time (12 women); includes 4 minority (1 Black or African American, non-Hispanic/Latino; 1 Asian, non-Hispanic/Latino; 1 Hispanic/Latino; 1 Two or more races, non-Hispanic/Latino), 4 international. Average age 27. 200 applicants, 10% accepted, 10 enrolled. *Faculty:* 1 (woman) full-time, 2 part-time/adjunct (0 women). Expenses: Contact institution. *Financial support:* In 2016–17, 20 students received support, including 20 fellowships (averaging $13,000 per year), 20 teaching assistantships (averaging $3,200 per year); career-related internships or fieldwork and scholarships/grants also available. Financial award application deadline: 1/15; financial award applicants required to submit FAFSA. In 2016, 10 master's awarded. Offers painting (MFA). *Application deadline:* For fall admission, 1/15 for domestic and international students. *Application fee:* $75. Electronic applications accepted. *Application Contact:* Chris D. Harring,

Director of Graduate Admission, 410-225-2256, Fax: 410-225-5275, E-mail: graduate@mica.edu. *Director,* Joan Waltemath, 410-225-5274, Fax: 410-225-5275, E-mail: graduate@mica.edu.

Mount Royal School of Art Students: 28 full-time (17 women); includes 3 minority (1 Asian, non-Hispanic/Latino; 2 Two or more races, non-Hispanic/Latino), 5 international. Average age 27. 175 applicants, 11% accepted, 15 enrolled. *Faculty:* 1 full-time (0 women), 6 part-time/adjunct (3 women). Expenses: Contact institution. *Financial support:* In 2016–17, 28 students received support, including 28 fellowships (averaging $13,000 per year), 28 teaching assistantships (averaging $3,200 per year); career-related internships or fieldwork and scholarships/grants also available. Financial award application deadline: 1/15. In 2016, 15 master's awarded. Offers painting (MFA). *Application deadline:* For fall admission, 1/15 for domestic and international students. *Application fee:* $75. Electronic applications accepted. *Application Contact:* Chris D. Harring, Director, Graduate Admission, 410-225-2256, Fax: 410-225-5275, E-mail: graduate@mica.edu. *Director,* Luca Buvoli, 410-225-5274, Fax: 410-225-5275, E-mail: graduate@mica.edu.

Rinehart School of Sculpture Students: 15 full-time (9 women); includes 4 minority (3 Asian, non-Hispanic/Latino; 1 Native Hawaiian or other Pacific Islander, non-Hispanic/Latino). Average age 27. 80 applicants, 25% accepted, 8 enrolled. *Faculty:* 3 full-time (2 women), 2 part-time/adjunct (both women). Expenses: Contact institution. *Financial support:* In 2016–17, 11 students received support, including 15 fellowships with partial tuition reimbursements available (averaging $13,000 per year), 11 teaching assistantships (averaging $3,200 per year); career-related internships or fieldwork and scholarships/grants also available. Financial award application deadline: 1/15; financial award applicants required to submit FAFSA. In 2016, 5 master's awarded. Offers sculpture (MFA). *Application deadline:* For fall admission, 1/15 for domestic and international students. *Application fee:* $75. Electronic applications accepted. *Application Contact:* Chris D. Harring, Director of Graduate Admission, 410-225-2256, Fax: 410-225-2408, E-mail: graduate@mica.edu. *Director,* Maren Hassinger, 410-225-2271, Fax: 410-225-2408.

MARYLHURST UNIVERSITY, Marylhurst, OR 97036-0261

General Information Independent-religious, coed, comprehensive institution. *Enrollment:* 808 graduate, professional, and undergraduate students; 261 full-time matriculated graduate/professional students (168 women), 149 part-time matriculated graduate/professional students (108 women). *Enrollment by degree level:* 410 master's. *Tuition:* Full-time $16,681. *Graduate housing:* On-campus housing not available. *Student services:* Campus employment opportunities, career counseling, free psychological counseling, international student services, low-cost health insurance, services for students with disabilities, teacher training, writing training. *Library facilities:* Shoen Library. *Collection:* Books: 105,004 (physical), 11,479 (digital/electronic); Serial titles: 156 (physical).

Computer facilities: A campuswide network can be accessed from student residence rooms and from off campus. Online class registration is available.
Website: http://www.marylhurst.edu/

General Application Contact: Office of Admissions, 503-699-6268, Fax: 503-699-6320, E-mail: admissions@marylhurst.edu.

GRADUATE UNITS

Applied Pastoral Theology Program Students: 3 (1 woman). Average age 50. Expenses: Contact institution. *Financial support:* Scholarships/grants available. Support available to part-time students. Financial award applicants required to submit FAFSA. In 2016, 5 master's awarded. *Program availability:* Part-time, evening/weekend. Offers applied pastoral theology (MA). *Application deadline:* Applications are processed on a rolling basis. *Application fee:* $0. Electronic applications accepted. *Application Contact:* Maruska Lynch, Graduate Admissions Counselor, 800-699-6322, E-mail: admissions@marylhurst.edu. *Chair,* Dr. Jerry Roussell, Jr., E-mail: jroussell@marylhurst.edu.

Department of Art Therapy Counseling Students: 36 (34 women); includes 10 minority (2 Hispanic/Latino; 8 Two or more races, non-Hispanic/Latino). Average age 32. Expenses: Contact institution. *Financial support:* Career-related internships or fieldwork and scholarships/grants available. Support available to part-time students. Financial award application deadline: 2/1; financial award applicants required to submit FAFSA. In 2016, 15 master's awarded. *Program availability:* Part-time. Offers art therapy counseling (MA, PGC). *Application deadline:* For fall admission, 1/31 priority date for domestic and international students. Applications are processed on a rolling basis. *Application fee:* $0. Electronic applications accepted. *Application Contact:* Maruska Lynch, Graduate Admissions Counselor, 503-699-6322, E-mail: admissions@marylhurst.edu. *Director of Art Therapy Counseling,* Mary Andrus, 503-534-7046, E-mail: mandrus@marylhurst.edu.

Department of Education Students: 46 (39 women); includes 10 minority (1 Asian, non-Hispanic/Latino; 5 Hispanic/Latino; 4 Two or more races, non-Hispanic/Latino), 1 international. Average age 35. Expenses: Contact institution. *Financial support:* Career-related internships or fieldwork and scholarships/grants available. Support available to part-time students. Financial award applicants required to submit FAFSA. In 2016, 21 master's awarded. *Program availability:* Part-time. Offers education (M Ed); teaching (MA). *Application deadline:* Applications are processed on a rolling basis. *Application fee:* $0. Electronic applications accepted. *Application Contact:* Maruska Lynch, Graduate Admissions Counselor, 800-699-6322, E-mail: admissions@marylhurst.edu. *Chair,* Dr. Jan Carpenter, 503-675-3975, E-mail: jcarpenter@marylhurst.edu.

Department of Food Systems and Society Students: 21 (20 women); includes 3 minority (1 Black or African American, non-Hispanic/Latino; 1 Hispanic/Latino; 1 Two or more races, non-Hispanic/Latino). Average age 35. Expenses: Contact institution. *Financial support:* Career-related internships or fieldwork and scholarships/grants available. Support available to part-time students. Financial award applicants required to submit FAFSA. *Program availability:* Part-time, blended/hybrid learning. Offers food systems and society (MS). *Application deadline:* For fall admission, 3/15 priority date for domestic students. Applications are processed on a rolling basis. *Application fee:* $0. Electronic applications accepted. *Application Contact:* Maruska Lynch, Graduate Admissions Counselor, 503-699-6268, E-mail: admissions@marylhurst.edu. *Chair, Department of Interdisciplinary and Applied Liberal Arts,* Dr. Sean Gillon, 503-534-4037, E-mail: sgillon@marylhurst.edu.

Department of Interdisciplinary Studies Students: 15 (13 women); includes 4 minority (1 Hispanic/Latino; 2 Native Hawaiian or other Pacific Islander, non-Hispanic/Latino; 1 Two or more races, non-Hispanic/Latino). Average age 50. Expenses: Contact institution. *Financial support:* Scholarships/grants available. Support available to part-time students. Financial award applicants required to submit FAFSA. In 2016, 23 master's awarded. *Program availability:* Part-time, evening/weekend. Offers interdisciplinary studies (MA). *Application deadline:* Applications are processed on a rolling basis. *Application fee:* $0. Electronic applications accepted. *Application Contact:* Maruska Lynch, Graduate Admissions Counselor, 800-699-6322, E-mail: admissions@

marylhurst.edu. *Chair, Department of Interdisciplinary and Applied Liberal Arts*, Dr. Sean Gillon, 503-534-4037, E-mail: sgillon@marylhurst.edu.

Divinity Program Students: 22 (16 women). Average age 46. Expenses: Contact institution. *Financial support:* Scholarships/grants available. Support available to part-time students. Financial award applicants required to submit FAFSA. In 2016, 4 master's awarded. *Program availability:* Part-time, evening/weekend. Offers divinity (M Div). *Application deadline:* Applications are processed on a rolling basis. *Application fee:* $0. Electronic applications accepted. *Application Contact:* Maruska Lynch, Graduate Admissions Counselor, 503-699-6322, Fax: 503-699-6320, E-mail: admissions@marylhurst.edu. *Chair*, Dr. Jerry Roussell, Jr., 503-636-8141, E-mail: jroussell@marylhurst.edu.

Master of Business Administration Program Students: 153 (82 women); includes 34 minority (5 Black or African American, non-Hispanic/Latino; 1 American Indian or Alaska Native, non-Hispanic/Latino; 12 Asian, non-Hispanic/Latino; 12 Hispanic/Latino; 4 Two or more races, non-Hispanic/Latino), 1 international. Average age 38. Expenses: Contact institution. *Financial support:* Career-related internships or fieldwork and scholarships/grants available. Support available to part-time students. Financial award applicants required to submit FAFSA. In 2016, 173 master's awarded. *Program availability:* Part-time, evening/weekend, 100% online, blended/hybrid learning. Offers health care management (MBA); real estate (MBA); sustainable business (MBA). *Application deadline:* Applications are processed on a rolling basis. *Application fee:* $0. Electronic applications accepted. *Application Contact:* Laura Sequeira, Graduate Admissions Counselor, 503-699-6268, E-mail: lsequeira@marylhurst.edu. *School of Business Director*, Stuart Noble-Goodman, 503-699-6315, E-mail: snoblegoodman@marylhurst.edu.

MARYMOUNT CALIFORNIA UNIVERSITY, Rancho Palos Verdes, CA 90275-6299

General Information Independent-religious, coed, comprehensive institution.

GRADUATE UNITS

Program in Business Administration Offers business administration (MBA).

Program in Community Psychology Offers community psychology (MS).

Program in Leadership and Global Development Offers leadership and global development (MS).

MARYMOUNT UNIVERSITY, Arlington, VA 22207-4299

General Information Independent-religious, coed, comprehensive institution. *Enrollment:* 3,369 graduate, professional, and undergraduate students; 540 full-time matriculated graduate/professional students (421 women), 465 part-time matriculated graduate/professional students (351 women). *Enrollment by degree level:* 838 master's, 147 doctoral, 20 other advanced degrees. *Graduate faculty:* 64 full-time (49 women), 51 part-time/adjunct (29 women). *Tuition:* Full-time $8460; part-time $940 per credit hour. *Required fees:* $10 per credit hour. One-time fee: $240 part-time. Tuition and fees vary according to program. *Graduate housing:* Room and/or apartments available on a first-come, first-served basis to single students; on-campus housing not available to married students. Typical cost: $13,430 (including board). Room and board charges vary according to board plan and housing facility selected. Housing application deadline: 5/1. *Student services:* Campus employment opportunities, campus safety program, career counseling, free psychological counseling, international student services, low-cost health insurance, services for students with disabilities, teacher training. *Library facilities:* Emerson C. Reinsch Library plus 1 other. *Collection:* Books: 242,577 (physical), 330,705 (digital/electronic); *Databases:* 227. Weekly public service hours: 104; students can reserve study rooms.

Computer facilities: 250 computers available on campus for general student use. A campuswide network can be accessed from student residence rooms and from off campus. Online class registration, online drive space are available. Website: http://www.marymount.edu/

General Application Contact: Francesca Reed, Director, Graduate Admissions, 703-284-5901, Fax: 703-527-3815, E-mail: grad.admissions@marymount.edu.

GRADUATE UNITS

Malek School of Health Professions Students: 134 full-time (96 women), 63 part-time (58 women); includes 61 minority (29 Black or African American, non-Hispanic/Latino; 16 Asian, non-Hispanic/Latino; 11 Hispanic/Latino; 5 Two or more races, non-Hispanic/Latino), 3 international. Average age 30. 389 applicants, 40% accepted, 61 enrolled. *Faculty:* 39 full-time (32 women), 18 part-time/adjunct (15 women). Expenses: Contact institution. *Financial support:* In 2016–17, 24 students received support, including 4 research assistantships with tuition reimbursements available, 12 teaching assistantships with tuition reimbursements available; career-related internships or fieldwork, Federal Work-Study, scholarships/grants, and unspecified assistantships also available. Support available to part-time students. Financial award applicants required to submit FAFSA. In 2016, 26 master's, 37 doctorates, 2 other advanced degrees awarded. *Program availability:* Part-time, evening/weekend. Offers family nurse practitioner (MSN, Certificate); health education and promotion (MS); health professions (MS, MSN, DNP, DPT, Certificate); nursing (DNP); physical therapy (DPT). *Application deadline:* For fall admission, 3/1 priority date for domestic and international students; for spring admission, 11/1 priority date for domestic and international students. Applications are processed on a rolling basis. *Application fee:* $40. Electronic applications accepted. *Application Contact:* Francesca Reed, Director, Graduate Admissions, 703-284-5901, Fax: 703-527-3815, E-mail: grad.admissions@marymount.edu. *Dean*, Dr. Jeanne Matthews, 703-284-1580, Fax: 703-284-3819, E-mail: jeanne.matthews@marymount.edu.

School of Arts and Sciences Students: 37 full-time (35 women), 33 part-time (28 women); includes 17 minority (7 Black or African American, non-Hispanic/Latino; 1 Asian, non-Hispanic/Latino; 6 Hispanic/Latino; 1 Native Hawaiian or other Pacific Islander, non-Hispanic/Latino; 2 Two or more races, non-Hispanic/Latino), 14 international. Average age 32. 42 applicants, 98% accepted, 28 enrolled. *Faculty:* 16 full-time (11 women), 7 part-time/adjunct (6 women). Expenses: Contact institution. *Financial support:* In 2016–17, 11 students received support, including 1 research assistantship with tuition reimbursement available, 6 teaching assistantships with tuition reimbursements available; career-related internships or fieldwork, Federal Work-Study, scholarships/grants, and unspecified assistantships also available. Support available to part-time students. Financial award applicants required to submit FAFSA. In 2016, 10 master's, 2 other advanced degrees awarded. *Program availability:* Part-time, evening/weekend. Offers arts and sciences (MA, Certificate); English and humanities (MA); interior design (MA); teaching English at the community college (Certificate). *Application deadline:* For fall admission, 7/15 priority date for domestic and international students; for spring admission, 11/1 priority date for domestic and international students; for summer admission, 4/15 priority date for domestic and international students. Applications are processed on a rolling basis. *Application fee:* $40. Electronic

applications accepted. *Application Contact:* Francesca Reed, Director, Graduate Admissions, 703-284-5901, Fax: 703-527-3815, E-mail: grad.admissions@marymount.edu. *Dean*, Dr. Christina Clark, 703-284-1560, Fax: 703-284-3859, E-mail: christina.clark@marymount.edu.

School of Business Administration Students: 118 full-time (69 women), 184 part-time (113 women); includes 125 minority (65 Black or African American, non-Hispanic/Latino; 1 American Indian or Alaska Native, non-Hispanic/Latino; 24 Asian, non-Hispanic/Latino; 29 Hispanic/Latino; 1 Native Hawaiian or other Pacific Islander, non-Hispanic/Latino; 5 Two or more races, non-Hispanic/Latino), 57 international. Average age 32. 214 applicants, 97% accepted, 98 enrolled. *Faculty:* 37 full-time (27 women), 18 part-time/adjunct (4 women). Expenses: Contact institution. *Financial support:* In 2016–17, 29 students received support, including 9 research assistantships with tuition reimbursements available, 3 teaching assistantships with tuition reimbursements available; career-related internships or fieldwork, Federal Work-Study, scholarships/grants, and unspecified assistantships also available. Support available to part-time students. Financial award applicants required to submit FAFSA. In 2016, 118 master's, 20 other advanced degrees awarded. *Program availability:* Part-time, evening/weekend. Offers association and nonprofit management (Certificate); business administration (MA, MBA, MS, Certificate); cybersecurity (MS, Certificate); health care informatics (Certificate); health care management (MS); human resource management (MA, Certificate); information technology (MS, Certificate); information technology project management and technology leadership (Certificate); leadership and management (MS); management studies (Certificate); organization development (Certificate). *Application deadline:* For fall admission, 7/16 priority date for domestic and international students; for spring admission, 11/16 priority date for domestic and international students; for summer admission, 4/16 for domestic and international students. Applications are processed on a rolling basis. *Application fee:* $40. Electronic applications accepted. *Application Contact:* Francesca Reed, Director, Graduate Admissions, 703-284-5901, Fax: 703-527-3815, E-mail: grad.admissions@marymount.edu. *Dean*, James Ryerson, 703-284-5910, Fax: 703-527-3830, E-mail: james.ryerson@marymount.edu.

School of Education and Human Services Students: 251 full-time (221 women), 185 part-time (152 women); includes 119 minority (45 Black or African American, non-Hispanic/Latino; 3 American Indian or Alaska Native, non-Hispanic/Latino; 11 Asian, non-Hispanic/Latino; 41 Hispanic/Latino; 19 Two or more races, non-Hispanic/Latino), 16 international. Average age 29. 253 applicants, 83% accepted, 138 enrolled. *Faculty:* 74 full-time (58 women), 27 part-time/adjunct (22 women). Expenses: Contact institution. *Financial support:* In 2016–17, 33 students received support, including 15 research assistantships with tuition reimbursements available, 11 teaching assistantships with tuition reimbursements available; career-related internships or fieldwork, Federal Work-Study, scholarships/grants, and unspecified assistantships also available. Support available to part-time students. Financial award applicants required to submit FAFSA. In 2016, 196 master's awarded. *Program availability:* Part-time, evening/weekend. Offers clinical mental health counseling (MA); education and human services (M Ed, MA); elementary education (M Ed); English as a second language (M Ed); forensic and legal psychology (MA); intelligence studies (MA); pastoral counseling (MA); professional studies (M Ed); school counseling (MA); secondary education (M Ed); special education: general curriculum (M Ed). *Application deadline:* For fall admission, 1/15 priority date for domestic and international students; for spring admission, 10/5 for domestic and international students. Applications are processed on a rolling basis. *Application fee:* $40. Electronic applications accepted. *Application Contact:* Francesca Reed, Director, Graduate Admissions, 703-284-5901, Fax: 703-527-3815, E-mail: grad.admissions@marymount.edu. *Dean*, Dr. Lois Stover, 703-284-1620, Fax: 703-284-1631, E-mail: lois.stover@marymount.edu.

MARYVILLE UNIVERSITY OF SAINT LOUIS, St. Louis, MO 63141-7299

General Information Independent, coed, comprehensive institution. *Enrollment:* 6,828 graduate, professional, and undergraduate students; 335 full-time matriculated graduate/professional students (236 women), 3,526 part-time matriculated graduate/professional students (2,996 women). *Enrollment by degree level:* 3,334 master's, 527 doctoral. *Graduate faculty:* 78 full-time (49 women), 233 part-time/adjunct (176 women). *Tuition:* Full-time $25,558; part-time $781 per credit hour. *Required fees:* $2400. Part-time tuition and fees vary according to course load and degree level. *Graduate housing:* Room and/or apartments available on a first-come, first-served basis to single students; on-campus housing not available to married students. Typical cost: $11,088 (including board). Room and board charges vary according to board plan and housing facility selected. Housing application deadline: 5/1. *Student services:* Campus employment opportunities, campus safety program, career counseling, exercise/wellness program, free psychological counseling, international student services, low-cost health insurance, multicultural affairs office, services for students with disabilities, teacher training, writing training. *Library facilities:* Maryville University Library. *Collection:* Books: 60,082 (physical), 224,165 (digital/electronic); Serial titles: 94,642 (digital/electronic); Databases: 122. Weekly public service hours: 101; study areas open 24 hours, 5–7 days a week. *Research affiliation:* Monsanto Fund (early childhood, science, mathematics curriculum development and teacher enrichment), Southwestern Bell Foundation (secondary education curriculum and teacher education).

Computer facilities: Computer purchase and lease plans are available. 575 computers available on campus for general student use. A campuswide network can be accessed from student residence rooms and from off campus. Online class registration, specialized software, university catalog are available. Website: http://www.maryville.edu/

General Application Contact: Jeannie DeLuca, Director of Admissions and Advising, 314-529-9355, Fax: 314-529-9927, E-mail: jdeluca@maryville.edu.

GRADUATE UNITS

College of Arts and Sciences Students: 37 full-time (16 women), 28 part-time (22 women); includes 10 minority (4 Black or African American, non-Hispanic/Latino; 1 American Indian or Alaska Native, non-Hispanic/Latino; 4 Asian, non-Hispanic/Latino; 1 Two or more races, non-Hispanic/Latino), 22 international. Average age 30. *Faculty:* 7 full-time (4 women), 10 part-time/adjunct (7 women). Expenses: Contact institution. *Financial support:* Application deadline: 3/1; applicants required to submit FAFSA. In 2016, 22 master's awarded. *Program availability:* Part-time. Offers actuarial science (MS); organizational leadership and development (MA); strategic communication and leadership (MA). *Application deadline:* Applications are processed on a rolling basis. Electronic applications accepted. *Application Contact:* Crystal Jacobsmeyer, Assistant Director, Graduate Enrollment Advising, 314-529-9654, Fax: 314-529-9927, E-mail: cjacobsmeyer@maryville.edu. *Dean*, Cherie Fister, 314-529-9563, Fax: 314-529-9965, E-mail: cfister@maryville.edu.

The John E. Simon School of Business Students: 84 full-time (40 women), 223 part-time (118 women); includes 67 minority (40 Black or African American, non-

Hispanic/Latino; 2 American Indian or Alaska Native, non-Hispanic/Latino; 8 Asian, non-Hispanic/Latino; 12 Hispanic/Latino; 1 Native Hawaiian or other Pacific Islander, non-Hispanic/Latino; 4 Two or more races, non-Hispanic/Latino, 15 international. Average age 32. *Faculty:* 7 full-time (3 women), 34 part-time/adjunct (9 women). Expenses: Contact institution. *Financial support:* Career-related internships or fieldwork, Federal Work-Study, tuition waivers (partial), and campus employment available. Financial award application deadline: 3/1; financial award applicants required to submit FAFSA. In 2016, 67 master's awarded. *Program availability:* Part-time, evening/weekend, 100% online, blended/hybrid learning. Offers accounting (MBA, Certificate); business studies (Certificate); cyber security (MBA); cybersecurity (Certificate); financial services (MBA, Certificate); healthcare practice management (MBA, Certificate); human resource management (MBA); information technology (MBA, Certificate); management (MBA, Certificate); management and leadership (MA); marketing (MBA, Certificate); project management (MBA); sport business management (MBA); supply chain management/logistics (MBA). *Application deadline:* Applications are processed on a rolling basis. Electronic applications accepted. *Application Contact:* Dustin Loeffler, Director for Graduate Studies in Business, 314-529-9571, Fax: 314-529-9975, E-mail: dloeffler@maryville.edu. *Interim Dean,* Pam Horwitz, 314-529-9680, Fax 314-529-9975.

School of Education Students: 12 full-time (11 women), 297 part-time (208 women); includes 92 minority (79 Black or African American, non-Hispanic/Latino; 4 Asian, non-Hispanic/Latino; 4 Hispanic/Latino; 5 Two or more races, non-Hispanic/Latino, 4 international. Average age 38. *Faculty:* 17 full-time (11 women), 21 part-time/adjunct (17 women). Expenses: Contact institution. *Financial support:* Career-related internships or fieldwork, Federal Work-Study, tuition waivers (partial), and professional educator discounts available. Financial award application deadline: 3/1; financial award applicants required to submit FAFSA. In 2016, 32 master's, 61 doctorates awarded. *Program availability:* Part-time, evening/weekend. Offers early childhood education (MA Ed); educational leadership (Ed D); educational leadership: principal certification (MA Ed); elementary education (MA Ed); gifted education (MA Ed); higher education leadership (Ed D); literacy specialist (MA Ed); middle grades education (MA Ed); secondary teaching and inquiry (MA Ed); teacher as leader (MA Ed); teacher leadership (Ed D). *Application deadline:* Applications are processed on a rolling basis. Electronic applications accepted. *Application Contact:* Stacey Ruffin, Coordinator of Clinical Experiences and Graduate Programs, 314-529-9542, Fax: 314-529-9921, E-mail: teachered@maryville.edu. *Dean,* Dr. Cathy Bear, 314-529-9692, Fax: 314-529-9921, E-mail: cbear@maryville.edu.

Walker College of Health Professions Students: 202 full-time (169 women), 2,977 part-time (2,648 women); includes 723 minority (355 Black or African American, non-Hispanic/Latino; 36 American Indian or Alaska Native, non-Hispanic/Latino; 129 Hispanic/Latino; 4 Native Hawaiian or other Pacific Islander, non-Hispanic/Latino; 59 Two or more races, non-Hispanic/Latino, 43 international. Average age 35. *Faculty:* 73 full-time (59 women), 155 part-time/adjunct (135 women). Expenses: Contact institution. *Financial support:* Career-related internships or fieldwork, Federal Work-Study, and campus employment available. Financial award application deadline: 3/1; financial award applicants required to submit FAFSA. In 2016, 902 master's, 89 doctorates awarded. *Program availability:* Part-time, evening/weekend, 100% online. Offers health professions (MARC, MMT, MOT, MS, MSN, DNP, DPT); marriage and family therapy (MARC); music therapy (MARC); occupational therapy (MOT); physical therapy (DPT); speech-language pathology (MS); substance abuse (MARC). *Application deadline:* Applications are processed on a rolling basis. Electronic applications accepted. *Application Contact:* Jeannie DeLuca, Director of Admissions and Advising, 314-529-9355, Fax: 314-529-9927, E-mail: jdeluca@maryville.edu. *Dean,* Dr. Charles Gulas, 314-529-9625, Fax: 314-529-9495, E-mail: hlthprofessions@maryville.edu.

The Catherine McAuley School of Nursing Students: 35 full-time (33 women), 2,881 part-time (2,562 women); includes 694 minority (344 Black or African American, non-Hispanic/Latino; 36 American Indian or Alaska Native, non-Hispanic/Latino; 139 Asian, non-Hispanic/Latino; 117 Hispanic/Latino; 4 Native Hawaiian or other Pacific Islander, non-Hispanic/Latino; 54 Two or more races, non-Hispanic/Latino, 40 international. Average age 36. *Faculty:* 18 full-time (all women), 136 part-time/adjunct (121 women). Expenses: Contact institution. *Financial support:* Federal Work-Study and campus employment available. Support available to part-time students. Financial award application deadline: 3/1; financial award applicants required to submit FAFSA. In 2016, 858 master's, 50 doctorates awarded. *Program availability:* 100% online. Offers acute care nurse practice (MSN); adult gerontology nurse practitioner (MSN); advanced practice nursing (DNP); family nurse practitioner (MSN); pediatric nurse practice (MSN). *Application deadline:* Applications are processed on a rolling basis. Electronic applications accepted. *Application Contact:* Jeannie DeLuca, Director of Admissions and Advising, 314-929-9355, Fax: 314-529-9927, E-mail: cjacobsmeyer@maryville.edu. *Assistant Dean/Director of Online Nursing,* Dr. Elizabeth Buck, 314-529-9453, Fax: 314-529-9139, E-mail: ebuck@maryville.edu.

MARYWOOD UNIVERSITY, Scranton, PA 18509-1598

General Information Independent-religious, coed, comprehensive institution. *Graduate housing:* Room and/or apartments available on a first-come, first-served basis to single students; on-campus housing not available to married students.

GRADUATE UNITS

Academic Affairs *Program availability:* Part-time, evening/weekend, online learning. Electronic applications accepted.

Center for Interdisciplinary Studies *Program availability:* Part-time. Offers human development (PhD). Electronic applications accepted.

College of Health and Human Services *Program availability:* Part-time, online learning. Offers dietetic internship (Certificate); gerontology (MS); health and human services (MHSA, MPA, MS, MSW, Certificate); health services administration (MHSA); nutrition (MS); physician assistant studies (MS); public administration (MPA); social work (MHSA, MPA, MS, MSW); sports nutrition and exercise science (MS). Electronic applications accepted.

Insalaco College of Creative and Performing Arts *Program availability:* Part-time. Offers art (Graduate Certificate); art education (MA); art therapy (MA, Graduate Certificate); clay (MA, MFA); communication arts (MA); creative and performing arts (MA, MFA, MMT, Graduate Certificate); graphic design (MFA); illustration (MFA); music education (MA); painting (MA, MFA); photography (MA, MFA); printmaking (MA, MFA); sculpture (MA, MFA); studio art (MA); visual arts (MFA). Electronic applications accepted.

Munley College of Liberal Arts and Sciences *Program availability:* Part-time, online learning. Offers biotechnology (MS); criminal justice (MS); finance/investment (MBA); general management (MBA); information security (MS); liberal arts and sciences (MBA, MS); management information systems (MBA, MS). Electronic applications accepted.

Reap College of Education and Human Development *Program availability:* Part-time. Offers clinical psychology (Psy D); clinical services (MA); counselor education (MS); early childhood intervention (MS); education and human development (M Ed, MA, MAT, MS, Psy D, Certificate, Post-Master's Certificate); general theoretical psychology (MA); higher education administration (MS); instructional leadership (M Ed); mental health counseling (MA); PK-4 education (MAT); psychology (MA); reading education (MS); school leadership (MS); secondary/K-12 education (MAT); special education (MS); special education administration and supervision (MS); speech-language pathology (MS).

School of Architecture *Program availability:* Part-time. Offers architecture (M Arch, MA); interior architecture/design (MA). Electronic applications accepted.

★ MASSACHUSETTS COLLEGE OF ART AND DESIGN, Boston, MA 02115-5882

General Information State-supported, coed, comprehensive institution. *Enrollment:* 1,982 graduate, professional, and undergraduate students; 113 full-time matriculated graduate/professional students (71 women), 27 part-time matriculated graduate/professional students (22 women). *Enrollment by degree level:* 133 master's, 7 other advanced degrees. *Graduate faculty:* 50 full-time (24 women), 84 part-time/adjunct (34 women). Tuition, state resident: full-time $23,400; part-time $780 per credit. Tuition, nonresident: full-time $23,400; part-time $780 per credit. Tuition and fees vary according to course load, degree level and program. *Graduate housing:* Room and/or apartments available on a first-come, first-served basis to single students; on-campus housing not available to married students. Typical cost: $12,807 per year ($15,978 including board). Room and board charges vary according to board plan and housing facility selected. Housing application deadline: 5/1. *Student services:* Campus employment opportunities, campus safety program, career counseling, exercise/wellness program, free psychological counseling, international student services, low-cost health insurance, multicultural affairs office, services for students with disabilities, teacher training, writing training. *Library facilities:* Morton R. Godine Library. *Collection:* Books: 106,885 (physical), 173,498 (digital/electronic); Databases: 75.

Computer facilities: Computer purchase and lease plans are available. 370 computers available on campus for general student use. A campuswide network can be accessed from student residence rooms and from off campus. Online class registration is available.

Website: http://www.massart.edu/

General Application Contact: Lauren O'Neill, Assistant Director of Graduate Admissions, 617-879-7222, E-mail: gradadmissions@massart.edu.

GRADUATE UNITS

Graduate Programs Students: 113 full-time (71 women), 27 part-time (22 women); includes 19 minority (4 Black or African American, non-Hispanic/Latino; 9 Asian, non-Hispanic/Latino; 5 Hispanic/Latino; 1 Native Hawaiian or other Pacific Islander, non-Hispanic/Latino), 40 international. 358 applicants, 57% accepted, 77 enrolled. *Faculty:* 50 full-time (24 women), 84 part-time/adjunct (34 women). Expenses: Contact institution. *Financial support:* In 2016–17, 94 students received support, including 2 research assistantships (averaging $2,160 per year), 42 teaching assistantships (averaging $2,160 per year); fellowships, career-related internships or fieldwork, scholarships/grants, tuition waivers (partial), unspecified assistantships, and 6-8 one-term adjunct co-teaching positions; 37 2-term general assistantships also available. Support available to part-time students. Financial award application deadline: 1/4; financial award applicants required to submit FAFSA. In 2016, 48 master's, 5 other advanced degrees awarded. Offers 2D fine arts (MFA); 3D fine arts (MFA); architecture (M Arch); art education (MAT, Postbaccalaureate Certificate); design (MFA, Postbaccalaureate Certificate); design innovation (M Des); fine arts (MFA); media arts (MFA, Postbaccalaureate Certificate). *Application deadline:* For fall admission, 1/4 priority date for domestic and international students; for summer admission, 1/4 priority date for domestic and international students. *Application fee:* $90. Electronic applications accepted. *Application Contact:* Lauren O'Neill, Assistant Director of Graduate Admissions, 617-879-7203, E-mail: gradadmissions@massart.edu. *Dean of Graduate Studies,* Paul Paturzo, 617-879-7166, E-mail: pjpaturzo@massart.edu.

See Display on next page and Close-Up on page 887.

MASSACHUSETTS COLLEGE OF LIBERAL ARTS, North Adams, MA 01247-4100

General Information State-supported, coed, comprehensive institution. *Graduate housing:* On-campus housing not available.

GRADUATE UNITS

Graduate Programs *Program availability:* Part-time, evening/weekend. Offers business (MBA); educational administration (M Ed); educational leadership (CAGS); instruction and curriculum (M Ed); instructional technology (M Ed); physical education and health (M Ed); reading (M Ed); special education (M Ed).

MASSACHUSETTS INSTITUTE OF TECHNOLOGY, Cambridge, MA 02139-4307

General Information Independent, coed, university. CGS member. *Enrollment:* 11,376 graduate, professional, and undergraduate students; 6,681 full-time matriculated graduate/professional students (2,273 women), 15 part-time matriculated graduate/professional students (3 women). *Enrollment by degree level:* 2,818 master's, 3,878 doctoral. *Graduate faculty:* 1,030 full-time (223 women), 10 part-time/adjunct (4 women). *Tuition:* Full-time $46,400; part-time $725 per credit. One-time fee: $312 full-time. Full-time tuition and fees vary according to course load and program. *Graduate housing:* Rooms and/or apartments available to single and married students. Housing application deadline: 5/15. *Student services:* Campus employment opportunities, campus safety program, career counseling, child daycare facilities, exercise/wellness program, free psychological counseling, grant writing training, international student services, low-cost health insurance, services for students with disabilities, teacher training, writing training. *Library facilities:* MIT Libraries plus 5 others. *Collection:* Books: 1.7 million (physical), 698,043 (digital/electronic); Serial titles: 51,946 (physical), 55,502 (digital/electronic); Databases: 351. Weekly public service hours: 95; study areas open 24 hours, 5–7 days a week; students can reserve study rooms. *Research affiliation:* Novartis Pharmaceuticals (pharmaceutical manufacturing), Singapore National Research Foundation (infectious diseases, environmental sensing, biosystems, urban transportation, low power electronics), Woods Hole Oceanographic Institution (applied ocean science and engineering), Broad Institute (genomics and biomedical research),

Whitehead Institute for Biomedical Research (developmental biology), Eni S.p.A (renewable energy).

Computer facilities: Computer purchase and lease plans are available. 1,050 computers available on campus for general student use. A campuswide network can be accessed from student residence rooms and from off campus. Online class registration is available.
Website: http://www.mit.edu/

General Application Contact: Graduate Admissions, 617-324-6730, E-mail: gradadmissions@mit.edu.

GRADUATE UNITS

MIT Sloan School of Management Expenses: Contact institution. *Financial support:* Fellowships with tuition reimbursements, research assistantships with tuition reimbursements, teaching assistantships with tuition reimbursements, Federal Work-Study, institutionally sponsored loans, scholarships/grants, health care benefits, and unspecified assistantships available. Support available to part-time students. Offers management (M Fin, MBA, MS, SM, PhD). Electronic applications accepted. *Application Contact:* Rod Garcia, Director of Admissions, 617-253-5434, Fax: 617-253-6405, E-mail: mbaadmissions@sloan.mit.edu. *Dean,* David C. Schmittlein, 617-253-2804, Fax: 617-258-6617, E-mail: dschmitt@mit.edu.

Operations Research Center Students: 86 full-time (21 women); includes 8 minority (7 Asian, non-Hispanic/Latino; 1 Two or more races, non-Hispanic/Latino), 48 international. Average age 26. 335 applicants, 9% accepted, 20 enrolled. *Faculty:* 48 full-time (9 women). Expenses: Contact institution. *Financial support:* In 2016–17, 81 students received support, including 5 fellowships (averaging $45,400 per year), 62 research assistantships (averaging $38,100 per year), 11 teaching assistantships (averaging $39,600 per year); Federal Work-Study, institutionally sponsored loans, scholarships/grants, traineeships, health care benefits, unspecified assistantships, and resident tutors also available. Support available to part-time students. Financial award application deadline: 5/1; financial award applicants required to submit FAFSA. In 2016, 5 master's, 9 doctorates awarded. Offers operations research (SM, PhD). *Application deadline:* For fall admission, 12/15 for domestic and international students. *Application fee:* $75. Electronic applications accepted. *Application Contact:* Laura A. Rose, Graduate Admissions Coordinator, 617-253-9303, E-mail: lrose@mit.edu. *Co-Director,* Dr. Dimitris J. Bertsimas, 617-253-3601, Fax: 617-258-9214, E-mail: orc_staff@mit.edu.

School of Architecture and Planning Students: 640 full-time (297 women), 1 part-time (0 women); includes 138 minority (20 Black or African American, non-Hispanic/Latino; 50 Asian, non-Hispanic/Latino; 50 Hispanic/Latino; 18 Two or more races, non-Hispanic/Latino), 284 international. Average age 29. 2,752 applicants, 13% accepted, 261 enrolled. *Faculty:* 84 full-time (24 women). Expenses: Contact institution. *Financial support:* In 2016–17, 549 students received support, including 242 fellowships (averaging $26,800 per year), 269 research assistantships (averaging $33,200 per year), 56 teaching assistantships (averaging $35,700 per year); Federal Work-Study, institutionally sponsored loans, scholarships/grants, health care benefits, unspecified assistantships, and resident tutors also available. Support available to part-time students. Financial award application deadline: 5/1; financial award applicants required to submit FAFSA. In 2016, 185 master's, 32 doctorates awarded. Offers architecture (M Arch, PhD); architecture and planning (M Arch, MCP, MSRED, SM, SM Arch S, SMACT, SMBT, PhD); architecture studies (SM Arch S); art, culture and technology (SMACT); building technology (SMBT); city planning (MCP); media arts and sciences (SM, PhD); media technology (SM); urban and regional planning (PhD); urban and regional studies (PhD); urban studies and planning (SM). *Application fee:* $75. Electronic applications accepted. *Application Contact:* Graduate Admissions, 617-324-6730, E-mail: gradadmissions@mit.edu. *Dean,* Prof. Hashim Sarkis, 617-253-4401, Fax: 617-253-9417, E-mail: sap-info@mit.edu.

Center for Real Estate Students: 35 full-time (13 women); includes 5 minority (3 Asian, non-Hispanic/Latino; 1 Hispanic/Latino; 1 Two or more races, non-Hispanic/Latino), 20 international. Average age 32. 125 applicants, 33% accepted, 30 enrolled. *Faculty:* 3 full-time (0 women), 11 part-time/adjunct (3 women). Expenses: Contact institution. *Financial support:* In 2016–17, 9 students received support, including 12 fellowships (averaging $29,100 per year); research assistantships, teaching assistantships, Federal Work-Study, institutionally sponsored loans, scholarships/grants, traineeships, health care benefits, and unspecified assistantships also available. Support available to part-time students. Financial award application deadline: 5/1; financial award applicants required to submit FAFSA. In 2016, 26 master's awarded. Offers real estate development (MSRED). *Application deadline:* For fall admission, 1/15 for domestic and international students. *Application fee:* $75. Electronic applications accepted. *Application Contact:* 617-253-4373, E-mail: msredadmissions@mit.edu. *Director,* Prof. Albert Saiz, 617-253-4373, Fax: 617-258-6991, E-mail: mit-cre@mit.edu.

School of Engineering Students: 3,112 full-time (914 women), 12 part-time (3 women); includes 661 minority (33 Black or African American, non-Hispanic/Latino; 3 American Indian or Alaska Native, non-Hispanic/Latino; 395 Asian, non-Hispanic/Latino; 154 Hispanic/Latino; 76 Two or more races, non-Hispanic/Latino), 1,380 international. Average age 26. 8,785 applicants, 16% accepted, 929 enrolled. *Faculty:* 377 full-time (68 women), 2 part-time/adjunct (0 women). Expenses: Contact institution. *Financial support:* In 2016–17, 2,537 students received support, including 615 fellowships (averaging $39,100 per year), 1,664 research assistantships (averaging $37,300 per year), 331 teaching assistantships (averaging $37,900 per year); Federal Work-Study, institutionally sponsored loans, scholarships/grants, traineeships, health care benefits, unspecified assistantships, and resident tutors also available. Support available to part-time students. Financial award application deadline: 5/1; financial award applicants required to submit FAFSA. In 2016, 750 master's, 334 doctorates, 10 other advanced degrees awarded. Offers aerospace computational engineering (PhD, Sc D); air transportation systems (PhD, Sc D); air-breathing propulsion (PhD, Sc D); aircraft systems engineering (PhD, Sc D); applied biosciences (PhD, Sc D); archaeological materials (PhD, Sc D); autonomous systems (PhD, Sc D); bioengineering (PhD, Sc D); biological engineering (PhD, Sc D); biological oceanography (PhD, Sc D); biomedical engineering (M Eng); chemical engineering (PhD, Sc D); chemical engineering practice (SM, PhD); chemical oceanography (PhD, Sc D); civil and environmental engineering (M Eng, SM, PhD, Sc D); civil and environmental systems (PhD, Sc D); civil engineering (PhD, Sc D, CE); civil engineering and computation (PhD); coastal engineering (PhD, Sc D); communications and networks (PhD, Sc D); computation for design and optimization (SM); computational and systems biology (PhD); computer science (PhD, Sc D, ECS); computer science and engineering (PhD, Sc D); computer science and molecular biology (M Eng); construction engineering and management (PhD, Sc D); controls (PhD, Sc D); electrical engineering (PhD, Sc D, EE); electrical engineering and computer science (M Eng, SM, PhD, Sc D, CE, EAA, ECS, EE, Mat E, Mech E, NE, Naval E); engineering and management (SM); environmental biology (PhD, Sc D); environmental chemistry (PhD, Sc D); environmental engineering (PhD, Sc D); environmental engineering and computation (PhD); environmental fluid mechanics (PhD, Sc D); geotechnical and geoenvironmental engineering (PhD, Sc D); health sciences and technology (SM, PhD, Sc D); humans in aerospace (PhD, Sc D); hydrology (PhD, Sc D); information technology (PhD, Sc D); logistics (M Eng); manufacturing (M Eng); materials and structures (PhD, Sc D); materials engineering (Mat E); materials science and engineering (SM, PhD, Sc D); mechanical engineering (SM, PhD, Sc D, Mech E); naval architecture and marine engineering (SM, PhD, Sc D); naval engineering (Naval E); nuclear science and engineering (SM, PhD, Sc D, NE); ocean engineering (SM, PhD, Sc D); oceanographic engineering (SM, PhD, Sc D); space propulsion (PhD, Sc D); space systems (PhD, Sc D); structures and materials (PhD, Sc D); toxicology (SM); transportation (PhD, Sc D). *Application fee:* $75. Electronic applications accepted. *Application Contact:* 617-324-6730, E-mail: gradadmission@mit.edu. *Dean of Engineering*, Prof. Ian A. Waitz, 617-253-3291, Fax: 617-253-8549.

Institute for Data, Systems, and Society Students: 112 full-time (43 women), 1 part-time (0 women); includes 15 minority (1 Black or African American, non-Hispanic/Latino; 8 Asian, non-Hispanic/Latino; 3 Hispanic/Latino; 3 Two or more races, non-Hispanic/Latino), 54 international. Average age 27. 659 applicants, 18% accepted, 84 enrolled. *Faculty:* 4 full-time (2 women). Expenses: Contact institution. *Financial support:* In 2016–17, 97 students received support, including fellowships (averaging $38,400 per year), 66 research assistantships (averaging $36,100 per year), 8 teaching assistantships (averaging $38,300 per year); Federal Work-Study, institutionally sponsored loans, traineeships, health care benefits, unspecified assistantships, and resident tutors also available. Support available to part-time students. Financial award application deadline: 5/1; financial award applicants required to submit FAFSA. In 2016, 82 master's, 8 doctorates awarded. Offers social and engineering systems (PhD); technology and policy (SM). *Application deadline:* For fall admission, 12/15 for domestic and international students. *Application fee:* $75. Electronic applications accepted. *Application Contact:* 617-253-1182, E-mail: idss_academic_office@mit.edu. *Department Head*, Munther A. Dahleh, 617-253-3300, E-mail: idss-info@mit.edu.

School of Humanities, Arts, and Social Sciences Students: 328 full-time (136 women), 2 part-time (0 women); includes 49 minority (1 Black or African American, non-Hispanic/Latino; 2 American Indian or Alaska Native, non-Hispanic/Latino; 20 Asian, non-Hispanic/Latino; 14 Hispanic/Latino; 12 Two or more races, non-Hispanic/Latino), 147 international. Average age 28. 1,791 applicants, 7% accepted, 69 enrolled. *Faculty:* 173 full-time (58 women), 5 part-time/adjunct (2 women). Expenses: Contact institution. *Financial support:* In 2016–17, 296 students received support, including fellowships (averaging $40,300 per year), 101 research assistantships (averaging $38,200 per year), 58 teaching assistantships (averaging $44,500 per year); Federal Work-Study, institutionally sponsored loans, traineeships, health care benefits, unspecified assistantships, and resident tutors also available. Support available to part-time students. Financial award application deadline: 5/1; financial award applicants required to submit FAFSA. In 2016, 20 master's, 42 doctorates awarded. Offers comparative media studies (SM); economics (SM, PhD); history, anthropology, and science, technology and society (PhD); humanities, arts, and social sciences (SM, PhD); linguistics (PhD); philosophy (PhD); political science (SM, PhD); science writing (SM). *Application fee:* $75. Electronic applications accepted. *Application Contact:* 617-324-6730, E-mail: gradadmissions@mit.edu. *Dean*, Prof. Melissa Nobles, 617-253-3450, Fax: 617-253-3451, E-mail: shass-www@mit.edu.

School of Science Students: 1,132 full-time (385 women); includes 230 minority (7 Black or African American, non-Hispanic/Latino; 1 American Indian or Alaska Native, non-Hispanic/Latino; 112 Asian, non-Hispanic/Latino; 76 Hispanic/Latino; 34 Two or more races, non-Hispanic/Latino), 393 international. Average age 26. 3,568 applicants, 12% accepted, 213 enrolled. *Faculty:* 269 full-time (49 women), 1 (woman) part-time/adjunct. Expenses: Contact institution. *Financial support:* In 2016–17, 996 students received support, including 386 fellowships (averaging $41,400 per year), 541 research assistantships (averaging $39,600 per year), 173 teaching assistantships (averaging $40,700 per year); Federal Work-Study, institutionally sponsored loans, scholarships/grants, traineeships, health care benefits, unspecified assistantships, and resident tutors also available. Support available to part-time students. Financial award application deadline: 5/1; financial award applicants required to submit FAFSA. In 2016, 16 master's, 217 doctorates awarded. Offers atmospheric chemistry (PhD, Sc D); atmospheric science (SM, PhD, Sc D); biochemistry (PhD); biological chemistry (PhD); biological oceanography (PhD); biology (PhD); biophysical chemistry and molecular structure (PhD); cell biology (PhD); chemical oceanography (SM, PhD, Sc D); climate physics and chemistry (SM, PhD, Sc D); cognitive science (PhD); computational and systems biology (PhD); developmental biology (PhD); earth and planetary sciences (SM); genetics (PhD); geochemistry (PhD, Sc D); geology (PhD, Sc D); geophysics (PhD, Sc D); immunology (PhD); inorganic chemistry (PhD); marine geology and geophysics (SM, PhD, Sc D); mathematics (PhD); microbiology (PhD); molecular biology (PhD); neurobiology (PhD); neuroscience (PhD); organic chemistry (PhD); physical chemistry (PhD); physical oceanography (SM, PhD, Sc D); physics (SM, PhD); planetary sciences (PhD, Sc D); science (SM, PhD, Sc D). *Application fee:* $75. Electronic applications accepted. *Application Contact:* 617-324-6730, E-mail: gradadmissions@mit.edu. *Dean*, Michael Sipser, 617-253-8900, Fax: 617-253-8901, E-mail: scninfo@mit.edu.

MASSACHUSETTS MARITIME ACADEMY, Buzzards Bay, MA 02532-1803

General Information State-supported, coed, comprehensive institution.

GRADUATE UNITS

Program in Emergency Management *Program availability:* Part-time-only, evening/weekend. Offers emergency management (MS). Electronic applications accepted.

Program in Facilities Management *Program availability:* Part-time-only, evening/weekend. Offers facilities management (MS). Electronic applications accepted.

MASSACHUSETTS SCHOOL OF LAW AT ANDOVER, Andover, MA 01810

General Information Independent, coed, graduate-only institution. *Graduate housing:* On-campus housing not available.

GRADUATE UNITS

Professional Program *Program availability:* Part-time, evening/weekend. Offers law (JD). Electronic applications accepted.

THE MASTER'S UNIVERSITY, Santa Clarita, CA 91321-1200

General Information Independent-religious, coed, comprehensive institution. *Graduate housing:* On-campus housing not available.

GRADUATE UNITS

The Master's Seminary *Program availability:* Part-time. Offers biblical counseling (MABC); New Testament (Th D); Old Testament (Th D); preaching (D Min); theology (M Div, M Th, Th D).

MAYO CLINIC GRADUATE SCHOOL OF BIOMEDICAL SCIENCES, Rochester, MN 55905

General Information Independent, coed, graduate-only institution. *Graduate housing:* On-campus housing not available.

GRADUATE UNITS

Graduate Programs in Biomedical Sciences Offers biochemistry and structural biology (PhD); biomedical engineering (PhD); biomedical sciences (PhD); cell biology and genetics (PhD); immunology (PhD); molecular biology (PhD); molecular neuroscience (PhD); molecular pharmacology and experimental therapeutics (PhD); tumor biology (PhD); virology and gene therapy (PhD). Electronic applications accepted.

MAYO CLINIC SCHOOL OF HEALTH SCIENCES, Rochester, MN 55905

General Information Independent, coed, graduate-only institution. *Enrollment:* 207 full-time matriculated graduate/professional students (136 women). *Enrollment by degree level:* 27 master's, 180 doctoral. *Graduate faculty:* 18 full-time (9 women). Full-time tuition and fees vary according to course load and program. *Student services:* Campus employment opportunities, campus safety program, career counseling, exercise/wellness program, free psychological counseling, international student services, multicultural affairs office, services for students with disabilities. *Library facilities:* Venables Health Sciences Library plus 1 other. *Collection:* Study areas open 24 hours, 5–7 days a week; students can reserve study rooms.

Computer facilities: A campuswide network can be accessed. Online class registration is available.

Website: http://www.mayo.edu/mayo-clinic-school-of-health-sciences

General Application Contact: Kammi Englund, Education Coordinator, 507-284-3678, Fax: 507-284-0656, E-mail: englund.kammi@mayo.edu.

GRADUATE UNITS

Doctor of Nurse Anesthesia Practice Program Expenses: Contact institution. *Financial support:* Institutionally sponsored loans, scholarships/grants, health care benefits, and stipends available. Financial award applicants required to submit FAFSA. Offers nurse anesthesia practice (DNAP). *Application deadline:* For fall admission, 9/1 for domestic students. *Application fee:* $50. Electronic applications accepted. *Application Contact:* Julie Predmore, Administrative Assistant, 507-286-4163, Fax: 507-284-2818, E-mail: predmore.julie@mayo.edu. *Director*, Dr. Mary E. Marienau, 507-284-8331, Fax: 507-284-2818, E-mail: marienau.mary@mayo.edu.

Program in Physical Therapy Expenses: Contact institution. *Financial support:* Scholarships/grants available. Financial award applicants required to submit FAFSA. Offers physical therapy (DPT). *Application deadline:* For fall admission, 10/16 for domestic and international students. Applications are processed on a rolling basis. Electronic applications accepted. *Application Contact:* Carol Cooper, Administrative Assistant, 507-284-2054, Fax: 507-284-0656, E-mail: cooper.carol@mayo.edu. *Director*, Dr. John Hollman, 507-284-2054, Fax: 507-284-0656, E-mail: hollman.john@mayo.edu.

MAYO CLINIC SCHOOL OF MEDICINE, Rochester, MN 55905

General Information Independent, coed, graduate-only institution. *Graduate housing:* On-campus housing not available.

GRADUATE UNITS

Professional Program Offers medicine (MD). MD offered through the Mayo Foundation's Division of Education; MD/PhD, MD/Certificate with Mayo Graduate School. Electronic applications accepted.

MCCORMICK THEOLOGICAL SEMINARY, Chicago, IL 60615

General Information Independent-religious, coed, graduate-only institution. *Graduate housing:* Rooms and/or apartments available on a first-come, first-served basis to single and married students. Housing application deadline: 7/1.

GRADUATE UNITS

Graduate and Professional Programs *Program availability:* Part-time, evening/weekend. Offers ministry (D Min); theological studies (MATS, Certificate); theology (M Div). M Div/MSW offered jointly with Loyola University Chicago, University of Chicago, and University of Illinois at Chicago.

MCDANIEL COLLEGE, Westminster, MD 21157-4390

General Information Independent, coed, comprehensive institution. *Enrollment:* 2,903 graduate, professional, and undergraduate students; 122 full-time matriculated graduate/professional students (85 women), 1,336 part-time matriculated graduate/professional students (1,079 women). *Enrollment by degree level:* 898 master's, 401 other advanced degrees. *Graduate faculty:* 30 full-time (21 women), 124 part-time/adjunct (79 women). *Tuition:* Full-time $8370; part-time $465 per credit. *Required fees:* $75 per semester. Tuition and fees vary according to course load, program and reciprocity agreements. *Graduate housing:* On-campus housing not available. *Student services:* Campus safety program, career counseling, free psychological counseling, international student services, multicultural affairs office, services for students with disabilities. *Library facilities:* Hoover Library. *Collection:* Books: 179,112 (physical), 152,246 (digital/electronic); Serial titles: 1,422 (physical), 64,815 (digital/electronic); Databases: 79. Study areas open 24 hours, 5–7 days a week; students can reserve study rooms.

Computer facilities: 138 computers available on campus for general student use. A campuswide network can be accessed from student residence rooms and from off campus. Online class registration, online billing summaries, financial aid letter, tax information are available.

Website: http://www.mcdaniel.edu/

General Application Contact: Crystal L. Perry, Assistant Director of Graduate Enrollment Management, 410-857-2516, Fax: 410-857-2515, E-mail: cperry@mcdaniel.edu.

GRADUATE UNITS

Graduate and Professional Studies Students: 120 full-time (83 women), 1,179 part-time (939 women); includes 244 minority (157 Black or African American, non-Hispanic/Latino; 4 American Indian or Alaska Native, non-Hispanic/Latino; 33 Asian, non-Hispanic/Latino; 39 Hispanic/Latino; 3 Native Hawaiian or other Pacific Islander, non-Hispanic/Latino; 8 Two or more races, non-Hispanic/Latino), 9 international. Average age 34. 485 applicants, 96% accepted. *Faculty:* 30 full-time (21 women), 124 part-time/adjunct (79 women). Expenses: Contact institution. *Financial support:* In

2016–17, 1 student received support. Career-related internships or fieldwork, institutionally sponsored loans, scholarships/grants, and unspecified assistantships available. Support available to part-time students. Financial award application deadline: 3/1; financial award applicants required to submit FAFSA. In 2016, 298 master's, 128 other advanced degrees awarded. *Program availability:* Part-time, evening/weekend, 100% online, blended/hybrid learning. Offers counseling (MS); curriculum and instruction (MS); deaf education (MS); educational leadership (MS); elementary education (MS); elementary STEM instructional leader (Postbaccalaureate Certificate); equity and excellence in education (Postbaccalaureate Certificate); exercise science and physical education (MS); gerontology (MS, Postbaccalaureate Certificate); human resources development (MS); human services management (MS); learning technology specialist (Postbaccalaureate Certificate); liberal arts (MLA); reading specialists: literacy leadership (MS); school librarianship (MS); secondary education (MS); special education (MS); teaching of English to speakers of other languages (MS); writing for children and young adults (Postbaccalaureate Certificate). *Application deadline:* For fall admission, 6/1 priority date for domestic students; for spring admission, 11/1 priority date for domestic students; for summer admission, 3/1 priority date for domestic students. Applications are processed on a rolling basis. *Application fee:* $75. Electronic applications accepted. *Application Contact:* Penny Pfeiffer, Senior Graduate Enrollment Management Specialist, 410-857-2513, Fax: 410-857-2515, E-mail: ppfeiffer@mcdaniel.edu. *Dean, Graduate and Professional Studies,* Dr. J. Michael Tyler, 410-857-2525, Fax: 410-857-2515, E-mail: mtyler@mcdaniel.edu.

MCGILL UNIVERSITY, Montréal, QC H3A 2T5, Canada

General Information Province-supported, coed, university. CGS member. *Graduate housing:* Room and/or apartments available to married students; on-campus housing not available to single students.

GRADUATE UNITS

Faculty of Graduate and Postdoctoral Studies

Desautels Faculty of Management Offers administration (PhD); entrepreneurial studies (MBA); finance (MBA); general management (Post Master's Certificate); information systems (MBA); international business (MBA); international practicing management (MM); management (MBA); management for development (MBA); manufacturing management (MMM); marketing (MBA); operations management (MBA); public accountancy (Diploma); strategic management (MBA). MMM offered jointly with Faculty of Engineering; PhD with Concordia University, HEC Montreal, Université de Montréal, Université du Québec à Montréal.

Faculty of Agricultural and Environmental Sciences Offers agricultural and environmental sciences (M Sc, M Sc A, PhD, Certificate, Graduate Diploma); agricultural economics (M Sc); animal science (M Sc, M Sc A, PhD); biotechnology (M Sc A, Certificate); computer applications (M Sc, M Sc A, PhD); dietetics (M Sc A, Graduate Diploma); entomology (M Sc, PhD); environmental assessment (M Sc); food engineering (M Sc, M Sc A, PhD); food science and agricultural chemistry (M Sc, PhD); forest science (M Sc, PhD); grain drying (M Sc, M Sc A, PhD); human nutrition (M Sc, M Sc A, PhD); irrigation and drainage (M Sc, M Sc A, PhD); machinery (M Sc, M Sc A, PhD); microbiology (M Sc, PhD); micrometeorology (M Sc, PhD); neotropical environment (M Sc, PhD); parasitology (M Sc, M Sc A, PhD); plant science (M Sc, M Sc A, PhD, Certificate); pollution control (M Sc, M Sc A, PhD); post-harvest technology (M Sc, M Sc A, PhD); soil dynamics (M Sc, M Sc A, PhD); soil science (M Sc, PhD); structure and environment (M Sc, M Sc A, PhD); vegetable and fruit storage (M Sc, M Sc A, PhD); wildlife biology (M Sc, PhD).

Faculty of Arts Offers anthropology (MA, PhD); art history and communication studies (MA, PhD); arts (MA, MSW, PhD, Diploma); bioethics (MA); East Asian studies (MA, PhD); economics (MA, PhD); English (MA, PhD); French language and literature (MA, PhD); German studies (MA, PhD); Hispanic studies (MA, PhD); history (MA, PhD); history of medicine (MA); Islamic studies (MA, PhD, Diploma); Italian studies (MA, PhD); Jewish studies (MA, PhD); language acquisition (MA, PhD); linguistics (MA, PhD); medical anthropology (MA); medical sociology (MA); neo-tropical environment (MA); philosophy (PhD); political science (MA, PhD); Russian literature (MA, PhD); social statistics (MA); social work (MSW, PhD, Diploma); sociology (MA, PhD, Diploma).

Faculty of Dentistry Offers forensic dentistry (Certificate); oral and maxillofacial surgery (M Sc, PhD).

Faculty of Education Offers counseling psychology (MA, PhD); culture and values in education (MA, PhD); curriculum studies (MA); education (M Ed, M Sc, MA, MLIS, PhD, Certificate, Diploma); educational leadership (MA, Certificate); educational psychology (M Ed, MA, PhD); educational studies (PhD); information studies (MLIS, PhD, Certificate, Diploma); integrated studies in education (M Ed); kinesiology and physical education (M Sc, MA, PhD, Certificate, Diploma); school/applied child psychology and applied developmental psychology (M Ed, MA, PhD, Diploma); second language education (MA, PhD).

Faculty of Engineering Offers aerospace (M Eng); affordable homes (M Arch II, Diploma); architectural history and theory (M Arch II); architecture (PhD); chemical engineering (M Eng, PhD); domestic environment (M Arch II); domestic environments (Diploma); electrical and computer engineering (M Eng, PhD); engineering (M Arch I, M Arch II, M Eng, M Sc, MMM, MUP, PhD, Diploma); environmental engineering (M Eng, M Sc, PhD); environmental planning (MUP); fluid mechanics (M Sc); fluid mechanics and hydraulic engineering (M Eng, PhD); housing (MUP); manufacturing management (MMM); materials engineering (M Eng, PhD); mechanical engineering (M Eng, M Sc, PhD); minimum cost housing in developing countries (M Arch II, Diploma); mining engineering (M Eng, M Sc, PhD, Diploma); professional architecture (M Arch I); rehabilitation of urban infrastructure (M Eng, PhD); soil behavior (M Eng, PhD); soil mechanics and foundations (M Eng, PhD); structures and structural mechanics (M Eng, PhD); transportation (MUP); urban design (MUP); urban planning, policy and design (PhD); water resources (M Sc); water resources engineering (M Eng, PhD).

Faculty of Law Offers air and space law (LL M, DCL, Graduate Certificate); bioethics (LL M); comparative law (LL M, DCL, Graduate Certificate); law (LL M, DCL). Applications for LL M with specialization in bioethics are made initially through the Biomedical Ethics Unit in the Faculty of Medicine.

Faculty of Medicine Offers anatomy and cell biology (M Sc, PhD); assessing driving capability (PGC); biochemistry (M Sc, PhD); biomedical engineering (M Eng, PhD); communication science and disorders (M Sc); communication sciences and disorders (PhD); community health (M Sc); environmental health (M Sc); epidemiology and biostatistics (M Sc, PhD, Diploma); experimental medicine (M Sc, PhD); genetic counseling (M Sc); health care evaluation (M Sc); human genetics (M Sc, PhD); medical anthropology (MA, PhD); medical history (MA, PhD); medical physics (M Sc, PhD); medical sociology (MA, PhD); medical statistics (M Sc); medicine (M Eng, M Sc, M Sc A, MA, PhD, Diploma, Graduate Diploma, PGC); microbiology and immunology (M Sc, M Sc A, PhD); neurology and neurosurgery (M Sc, PhD); nurse practitioner (Graduate Diploma); nursing (M Sc A, PhD); occupational health (M Sc, PhD); otolaryngology (M Sc); pathology (M Sc, PhD); pharmacology and therapeutics (M Sc, PhD); physiology (M Sc, PhD); psychiatry (M Sc); rehabilitation science (M Sc, PhD); speech-language pathology (M Sc A); surgery (M Sc, PhD).

Faculty of Religious Studies Offers religious studies (MA, STM, PhD).

Faculty of Science Offers atmospheric science (M Sc, PhD); bioinformatics (M Sc, PhD); chemical biology (M Sc, PhD); chemistry (M Sc, PhD); clinical psychology (PhD); computational science and engineering (M Sc); computer science (M Sc, PhD); earth and planetary sciences (M Sc, PhD); environment (M Sc, PhD); experimental psychology (M Sc, MA, PhD); geography (M Sc, MA, PhD); mathematics and statistics (M Sc, MA, PhD); neo-tropical environment (M Sc, MA, PhD); physical oceanography (M Sc, PhD); physics (M Sc, PhD); science (M Sc, MA, PhD); social statistics (MA).

Schulich School of Music Offers composition (M Mus, D Mus, PhD); music education (MA, PhD); music technology (MA, PhD); musicology (MA, PhD); performance (M Mus); performance studies (D Mus); sound recording (M Mus, PhD); theory (MA, PhD).

Professional Program in Dentistry Offers dentistry (DMD). Electronic applications accepted.

Professional Program in Medicine Offers medicine.

MCKENDREE UNIVERSITY, Lebanon, IL 62254-1299

General Information Independent-religious, coed, comprehensive institution. *Graduate housing:* On-campus housing not available.

GRADUATE UNITS

Graduate Programs *Program availability:* Part-time, evening/weekend. Offers business administration (MBA); clinical mental health counseling (MA); curriculum design and instruction (Ed D, Ed S); educational administration and leadership (MA Ed); educational studies (MA Ed); higher education administrative services (MA Ed); human resource management (MBA); international business (MBA); music education (MA Ed); nursing education (MSN); nursing management/administration (MSN); reading (MA Ed); special education (MA Ed); teacher leadership (MA Ed); teaching certification (MA Ed). Electronic applications accepted.

MCMASTER UNIVERSITY, Hamilton, ON L8S 4M2, Canada

General Information Province-supported, coed, university. CGS member. *Graduate housing:* Room and/or apartments available to single students; on-campus housing not available to married students. Housing application deadline: 6/30. *Research affiliation:* Commonwealth Development (telecommunications), Canadian Centre for Inland Waters (chemical and civil engineering).

GRADUATE UNITS

Faculty of Health Sciences *Program availability:* Part-time, online learning. Offers biochemistry and biomedical sciences (M Sc, PhD); blood and vascular (M Sc, PhD); genetics and cancer (M Sc, PhD); health research methodology (M Sc, PhD); health sciences (M Sc, PhD); immunity and infection (M Sc, PhD); metabolism and nutrition (M Sc, PhD); neurosciences and behavioral sciences (M Sc, PhD); nursing (M Sc, PhD); occupational therapy (M Sc); physiology/pharmacology (M Sc, PhD); physiotherapy (M Sc); rehabilitation science (M Sc, PhD); rehabilitation science (course-based) (M Sc).

McMaster Divinity College *Program availability:* Part-time. Offers Biblical studies (MA, MTS, Diploma); biblical studies (M Div); Christian interpretation/history (M Div, MA, MTS, Diploma); Christian ministry (M Div, MA, MTS, Diploma); Christian Studies (Certificate); Christian theology (PhD). Affiliated with the Toronto School of Theology.

School of Graduate Studies *Program availability:* Part-time.

DeGroote School of Business *Program availability:* Part-time. Offers business (MBA, PhD); human resources and management (MBA, PhD); information systems (PhD).

Faculty of Engineering *Program availability:* Part-time. Offers chemical engineering (M Eng, MA Sc, PhD); civil engineering (M Eng, MA Sc, PhD); computer science (M Sc, PhD); electrical engineering (M Eng, MA Sc, PhD); engineering (M Eng, M Sc, MA Sc, PhD); engineering physics (M Eng, MA Sc, PhD); materials engineering (M Eng, MA Sc, PhD); materials science (M Eng, PhD); mechanical engineering (M Eng, MA Sc, PhD); nuclear engineering (PhD); software engineering (M Eng, MA Sc, PhD).

Faculty of Humanities *Program availability:* Part-time, evening/weekend. Offers classics (MA, PhD); cultural studies and critical theory (MA); English (MA, PhD); French (MA, PhD); globalization studies (MA); history (MA, PhD); humanities (MA, PhD); philosophy (MA, PhD).

Faculty of Science *Program availability:* Part-time, evening/weekend. Offers analytical chemistry (M Sc, PhD); applied statistics (M Sc); astrophysics (PhD); biology (M Sc, PhD); chemical physics (M Sc, PhD); chemistry (M Sc, PhD); geochemistry (PhD); geology (M Sc, PhD); health and radiation physics (M Sc); human geography (MA, PhD); inorganic chemistry (M Sc, PhD); mathematics (M Sc, PhD); medical physics (M Sc, PhD); medical statistics (M Sc); organic chemistry (M Sc, PhD); physical chemistry (M Sc, PhD); physical geography (M Sc, PhD); physics (PhD); polymer chemistry (M Sc, PhD); psychology (M Sc, PhD); science (M Sc, MA, PhD); statistical theory (M Sc); statistics (M Sc).

Faculty of Social Sciences *Program availability:* Part-time, evening/weekend. Offers analysis of social welfare policy (MSW); analysis of social work practice (MSW); anthropology (MA, PhD); economics (MA, PhD); human biodynamics (MA); international relations (MA); political science (MA); public and the global economy (MA); public policy (PhD); public policy and administration (MA); religious studies (MA, PhD); social sciences (M Sc, MA, MSW, PhD); sociology (MA, PhD); work and society (MA).

MCMURRY UNIVERSITY, Abilene, TX 79697

General Information Independent-religious, coed, comprehensive institution.

GRADUATE UNITS

Graduate Studies

MCNALLY SMITH COLLEGE OF MUSIC, Saint Paul, MN 55101

General Information Proprietary, coed, comprehensive institution. *Graduate housing:* On-campus housing not available.

GRADUATE UNITS

Master of Music in Performance Program *Program availability:* Part-time, evening/weekend. Offers bass performance (MM); brass and woodwind performance (MM); guitar performance (MM); keyboard performance (MM); percussion performance (MM); string performance (MM); vocal performance (MM). Electronic applications accepted.

MCNEESE STATE UNIVERSITY, Lake Charles, LA 70609

General Information State-supported, coed, comprehensive institution. *Graduate housing:* Room and/or apartments available on a first-come, first-served basis to single students. Housing application deadline: 8/15.

GRADUATE UNITS

Doré School of Graduate Studies *Program availability:* Part-time, evening/weekend.

Burton College of Education *Program availability:* Part-time, evening/weekend. Offers addiction treatment (MA); advanced professional (M Ed); applied behavior analysis (MA); autism (M Ed); counseling psychology (MA); counseling, grades K-12 (Graduate Certificate); curriculum and instruction (M Ed); early childhood education (M Ed); early childhood education grades PK-3 (Postbaccalaureate Certificate); education (M Ed, MA, MAT, MS, Ed S, Graduate Certificate, Postbaccalaureate Certificate); educational diagnostician (M Ed, Graduate Certificate); educational leadership (M Ed, Ed S); educational technology (Ed S); educational technology leadership (M Ed); elementary education (M Ed, MAT); elementary education grades 1-5 (Postbaccalaureate Certificate); exercise physiology (MS); general/experimental psychology (MA); health promotion (MS); instructional technology (MS); middle school education grades 4-8 (Postbaccalaureate Certificate); multiple levels grades K-12 (Postbaccalaureate Certificate); nutrition and wellness (MS); reading (M Ed); reading specialist (Graduate Certificate); school counseling (M Ed); school librarian (Postbaccalaureate Certificate); secondary education (MAT); secondary education grades 6-12 (Postbaccalaureate Certificate); special education (M Ed); special education - mild/moderate grades 1-12 (MAT); special education intervention birth-5 (Postbaccalaureate Certificate); special education, mild/moderate for elementary education grades 1-5 (Postbaccalaureate Certificate); special education, mild/moderate for secondary education grades 6-12 (Postbaccalaureate Certificate).

College of Business *Program availability:* Part-time, evening/weekend. Offers business (MBA); business administration (MBA).

College of Engineering and Engineering Technology *Program availability:* Part-time, evening/weekend. Offers chemical engineering (M Eng); civil engineering (M Eng); electrical (M Eng); electrical engineering (M Eng); engineering (M Eng); engineering and engineering technology (M Eng, Graduate Certificate, Postbaccalaureate Certificate); engineering management (M Eng); mechanical engineering (M Eng); pump reliability engineering (Graduate Certificate, Postbaccalaureate Certificate).

College of Liberal Arts *Program availability:* Part-time, evening/weekend. Offers creative writing (MFA); criminal justice (MS); English (MA); liberal arts (MA, MFA, MS, Postbaccalaureate Certificate); music education (Postbaccalaureate Certificate).

College of Nursing Offers family nurse practitioner (PMC); family psychiatric/mental health nurse practitioner (PMC); nurse educator (MSN); nurse executive (MSN); nursing (MSN); nursing case management (Postbaccalaureate Certificate). Program offered jointly with Southeastern Louisiana University and Southern University and Agricultural and Mechanical College.

College of Science *Program availability:* Part-time, evening/weekend. Offers agricultural sciences (MS); chemistry (MS); chemistry/environmental science education (MS); computer science (MS); environmental and chemical sciences (MS); environmental science (MS); mathematics (MS); science (MS); statistics (MS).

MCPHERSON COLLEGE, McPherson, KS 67460-1402

General Information Independent-religious, coed, comprehensive institution. *Graduate housing:* On-campus housing not available.

GRADUATE UNITS

Program in Education Offers education (M Ed).

MCPHS UNIVERSITY, Boston, MA 02115-5896

General Information Independent, coed, university. *Enrollment:* 7,095 graduate, professional, and undergraduate students; 2,766 full-time matriculated graduate/professional students (1,799 women), 486 part-time matriculated graduate/professional students (374 women). *Enrollment by degree level:* 1,189 master's, 2,018 doctoral, 45 other advanced degrees. *Graduate housing:* Room and/or apartments available on a first-come, first-served basis to single students; on-campus housing not available to married students. Housing application deadline: 5/1. *Student services:* Campus employment opportunities, campus safety program, career counseling, exercise/wellness program, free psychological counseling, grant writing training, international student services, low-cost health insurance, multicultural affairs office, services for students with disabilities, writing training. *Library facilities:* Henrietta DeBenedictis Library plus 2 others. *Research affiliation:* Cephrim Biosciences, Inc. (pharmaceutics), Center for Analytical Science (analytical medicinal chemistry).

Computer facilities: 507 computers available on campus for general student use. A campuswide network can be accessed from student residence rooms and from off campus. Online class registration is available.

Website: http://www.mcphs.edu/

General Application Contact: Julie George, Director of Graduate, Transfer and Online Admission, 617-732-2988, E-mail: admissions@mcphs.edu.

GRADUATE UNITS

Graduate Studies Students: 2,766 full-time (1,799 women), 477 part-time (365 women); includes 1,022 minority (229 Black or African American, non-Hispanic/Latino; 3 American Indian or Alaska Native, non-Hispanic/Latino; 644 Asian, non-Hispanic/Latino; 112 Hispanic/Latino; 5 Native Hawaiian or other Pacific Islander, non-Hispanic/Latino; 29 Two or more races, non-Hispanic/Latino), 426 international. Average age 28. Expenses: Contact institution. *Financial support:* Fellowships with partial tuition reimbursements, research assistantships with partial tuition reimbursements, teaching assistantships with partial tuition reimbursements, scholarships/grants, tuition waivers (partial), and unspecified assistantships available. Financial award application deadline: 3/15. In 2016, 422 master's, 739 doctorates awarded. *Program availability:* Part-time. Offers drug regulatory affairs and health policy (MS); medicinal chemistry (MS, PhD); nursing (MS); pharmaceutics/industrial pharmacy (MS, PhD); pharmacology (MS, PhD); pharmacy (Pharm D); pharmacy and health sciences (MPAS, MS, PhD, Pharm D); physician assistant studies (MPAS). *Application Contact:* Julie George, Director of Graduate, Transfer and Online Admission, 617-732-2988, E-mail: admissions@mcphs.edu. *Assistant Dean of Graduate Studies,* Dr. Timothy Maher, 617-732-2757, E-mail: barbara.leduc@mcphs.edu.

New England School of Acupuncture Students: 127 full-time (102 women), 12 part-time (11 women); includes 29 minority (2 Black or African American, non-Hispanic/Latino; 19 Asian, non-Hispanic/Latino; 6 Hispanic/Latino; 2 Two or more races, non-Hispanic/Latino), 8 international. Average age 37. 100 applicants, 91% accepted, 61 enrolled. *Faculty:* 1 (woman) full-time, 76 part-time/adjunct (46 women). Expenses: Contact institution. *Financial support:* In 2016–17, 124 students received support. Available to part-time students. Application deadline: 7/1; applicants required to submit FAFSA. In 2016, 11 master's awarded. *Program availability:* Part-time. Offers acupuncture (M Ac); acupuncture and Oriental medicine (MAOM). *Application deadline:* For fall admission, 5/1 priority date for domestic and international students. Applications are processed on a rolling basis. *Application fee:* $75. *Application Contact:* Anna B. Di Vasta, Admissions Coordinator, 617-558-1788 Ext. 125, Fax: 617-924-4167, E-mail: adivasta@nesa.edu. *Academic Dean,* Amy Hull, 617-558-1788 Ext. 118, Fax: 617-924-4167, E-mail: ahull@nesa.edu.

School of Optometry Students: 259 full-time (177 women), 4 part-time (3 women); includes 82 minority (6 Black or African American, non-Hispanic/Latino; 1 American Indian or Alaska Native, non-Hispanic/Latino; 74 Asian, non-Hispanic/Latino; 1 Hispanic/Latino), 21 international. Average age 25. Expenses: Contact institution. In 2016, 59 doctorates awarded. Offers optometry (OD). *Application Contact:* Julie George, Director of Graduate, Transfer and Online Admission, 617-732-2988, E-mail: admissions@mcphs.edu.

School of Pharmacy–Worcester/Manchester Students: 887 full-time (512 women), 4 part-time (3 women); includes 440 minority (144 Black or African American, non-Hispanic/Latino; 248 Asian, non-Hispanic/Latino; 39 Hispanic/Latino; 1 Native Hawaiian or other Pacific Islander, non-Hispanic/Latino; 8 Two or more races, non-Hispanic/Latino), 120 international. Average age 27. Expenses: Contact institution. In 2016, 278 doctorates awarded. Offers pharmacy (Pharm D). *Application fee:* $0. *Application Contact:* Director of Admissions, Worcester and Manchester, 508-373-5623. *Dean,* Dr. Anna Morin, 508-373-5603.

School of Physical Therapy Students: 128 full-time (71 women), 1 part-time (0 women); includes 19 minority (4 Black or African American, non-Hispanic/Latino; 10 Asian, non-Hispanic/Latino; 4 Hispanic/Latino; 1 Native Hawaiian or other Pacific Islander, non-Hispanic/Latino), 2 international. Average age 25. Expenses: Contact institution. In 2016, 39 doctorates awarded. Offers physical therapy (DPT). *Application Contact:* Julie George, Director of Graduate, Transfer and Online Admission, 617-732-2988, E-mail: admissions@mcphs.edu. *Program Director,* 508-373-5872.

MEADVILLE LOMBARD THEOLOGICAL SCHOOL, Chicago, IL 60637-1602

General Information Independent-religious, coed, graduate-only institution. *Graduate housing:* Rooms and/or apartments available on a first-come, first-served basis to single and married students. Housing application deadline: 3/15.

GRADUATE UNITS

Graduate and Professional Programs *Program availability:* Part-time, online learning. Offers divinity (M Div); ministry (D Min); religion (MA). M Div/MSW offered jointly with University of Chicago.

MEDAILLE COLLEGE, Buffalo, NY 14214-2695

General Information Independent, coed, comprehensive institution. *Graduate housing:* Rooms and/or apartments available on a first-come, first-served basis to single and married students. Housing application deadline: 8/15.

GRADUATE UNITS

Program in Business Administration - Amherst *Program availability:* Evening/weekend. Offers business administration (MBA); organizational leadership (MA). Electronic applications accepted.

Program in Business Administration - Rochester *Program availability:* Evening/weekend. Offers business administration (MBA); organizational leadership (MA).

Program in Education *Program availability:* Part-time, evening/weekend. Offers adolescent education (MS Ed); curriculum and instruction (MS Ed); education preparation (MS Ed); literacy (MS Ed); special education (MS). Electronic applications accepted.

Programs in Psychology *Program availability:* Part-time, evening/weekend. Offers clinical psychology (Psy D); marriage and family therapy (MA); mental health counseling (MA); psychology (MA). Electronic applications accepted.

MEDICAL COLLEGE OF WISCONSIN, Milwaukee, WI 53226-0509

General Information Independent, coed, graduate-only institution. CGS member. *Graduate housing:* On-campus housing not available. *Research affiliation:* General Electric Medical Systems (biophysics, radiology).

GRADUATE UNITS

Graduate School *Program availability:* Part-time, evening/weekend, online learning. Offers biochemistry (PhD); biomedical sciences (MA, MPH, MS, PhD, Graduate Certificate); biophysics (PhD); biostatistics (PhD); clinical and translational science (MS); microbiology and molecular genetics (MS, PhD); neuroscience (PhD); pharmacology and toxicology (PhD); physiology (PhD); public and community health (PhD); public health (MPH, Graduate Certificate). Electronic applications accepted.

Center for Bioethics and Medical Humanities *Program availability:* Part-time. Offers bioethics (MA); clinical bioethics (Graduate Certificate); research ethics (Graduate Certificate).

Medical Scientist Training Program

Interdisciplinary Program in Biomedical Sciences Offers biomedical sciences (PhD). **Medical School** *Program availability:* Part-time, online learning. Offers medicine (MPH, MD).

MEDICAL UNIVERSITY OF SOUTH CAROLINA, Charleston, SC 29425

General Information State-supported, coed, upper-level institution. CGS member. *Research affiliation:* Novartis Pharmaceuticals (cancer), Boston Scientific Corporation (cardiovascular diseases), Genentech (Alzheimer's disease), AstraZeneca (cancer/cardiovascular diseases), Merck & Company, Inc. (neuroscience), Eli Lilly and Company (substance abuse).

GRADUATE UNITS

College of Dental Medicine Offers dental medicine (DMD). Electronic applications accepted.

College of Graduate Studies Offers biochemistry and molecular biology (MS, PhD); cancer biology (PhD); cardiovascular biology (PhD); cardiovascular imaging (PhD); cell and molecular pharmacology and experimental therapeutics (MS, PhD); cell injury and repair (PhD); cell regulation (PhD); craniofacial biology (PhD); drug discovery (PhD); genetics and development (PhD); marine biomedicine (PhD); medicinal chemistry (PhD); microbiology and immunology (MS, PhD); neurosciences (MS, PhD); pathology and laboratory medicine (MS, PhD); toxicology (PhD). Electronic applications accepted.

Division of Biostatistics and Epidemiology Offers biostatistics (MS, PhD); epidemiology (MS, PhD). Electronic applications accepted.

South Carolina Clinical and Translational Research Institute *Program availability:* Online learning. Offers clinical and translational research (MS). Electronic applications accepted.

College of Health Professions *Program availability:* Part-time. Offers anesthesia for nurses (MSNA); health administration (DHA); health administration-executive (MHA); health administration-global (MHA); health administration-residential (MHA); health and rehabilitation science (PhD); health professions (MHA, MS, MSNA, MSOT, DHA, DPT, PhD); occupational therapy (MSOT); physical therapy (DPT); physician assistant studies (MS). Electronic applications accepted.

College of Medicine Offers medicine (MD). Electronic applications accepted.

College of Nursing *Program availability:* Part-time, online learning. Offers adult-gerontology health nurse practitioner (MSN, DNP); advanced practice nursing (DNP); family nurse practitioner (MSN, DNP); nurse administrator (MSN); nurse educator (MSN); nursing (MSN, DNP, PhD); pediatric nurse practitioner (MSN, DNP). Electronic applications accepted.

South Carolina College of Pharmacy Offers pharmacy (Pharm D). Electronic applications accepted.

MEHARRY MEDICAL COLLEGE, Nashville, TN 37208-9989

General Information Independent-religious, coed, graduate-only institution. CGS member. *Graduate faculty:* 273 full-time (69 women), 46 part-time/adjunct (11 women). *Graduate housing:* Rooms and/or apartments available on a first-come, first-served basis to single and married students. *Student services:* Campus employment opportunities, campus safety program, career counseling, child daycare facilities, exercise/wellness program, free psychological counseling, international student services, low-cost health insurance. *Library facilities:* Meharry Medical College Library.

Computer facilities: 100 computers available on campus for general student use. Website: http://www.mmc.edu/

General Application Contact: April Curry, Director of Admissions and Recruitment, 615-327-6453, Fax: 615-327-6228, E-mail: acurry@mmc.edu.

GRADUATE UNITS

School of Dentistry Expenses: Contact institution. *Financial support:* Career-related internships or fieldwork, Federal Work-Study, and institutionally sponsored loans available. Financial award application deadline: 4/15; financial award applicants required to submit FAFSA. Offers dentistry (DDS, PhD). *Application deadline:* For winter admission, 1/15 for domestic and international students. Applications are processed on a rolling basis. *Application fee:* $65. *Application Contact:* Cherae M. Farmer-Dixon, DDS, Dean, 615-327-6207, E-mail: cdixon@mmc.edu. *Dean,* Cherae M. Farmer-Dixon, DDS, 615-327-6207, E-mail: cdixon@mmc.edu.

School of Graduate Studies Expenses: Contact institution. *Financial support:* Fellowships, research assistantships, teaching assistantships, career-related internships or fieldwork, Federal Work-Study, institutionally sponsored loans, scholarships/grants, and tuition waivers (full) available. Support available to part-time students. Financial award applicants required to submit FAFSA. *Program availability:* Online learning. Offers biochemistry and cancer biology (PhD); microbiology and immunology (PhD); neuroscience (PhD); pharmacology (PhD). *Application deadline:* For fall admission, 6/1 for domestic students. Applications are processed on a rolling basis. *Application fee:* $65. Electronic applications accepted. *Application Contact:* Dr. Evangeline Motley-Johnson, Associate Dean, 615-327-6533, Fax: 615-321-2933, E-mail: emotley@mmc.edu. *Dean,* Dr. Maria Fatima Lima, 615-327-6533, Fax: 615-321-2933, E-mail: mflima@mmc.edu.

Division of Public Health Practice Expenses: Contact institution. *Financial support:* Career-related internships or fieldwork, Federal Work-Study, institutionally sponsored loans, and scholarships/grants available. Support available to part-time students. Financial award application deadline: 7/15; financial award applicants required to submit FAFSA. *Program availability:* Part-time, evening/weekend. Offers occupational medicine (MSPH); public health administration (MSPH). *Application deadline:* For fall admission, 6/1 for domestic students. Applications are processed on a rolling basis. *Application fee:* $65. *Application Contact:* Kendric D. Dartis, Program Coordinator, 615-327-5897, E-mail: kdartis@mmc.edu. *Senior Associate Dean,* Stephanie Bailey, MD, 615-327-6069, E-mail: sbailey@mmc.edu.

School of Medicine Expenses: Contact institution. *Financial support:* Federal Work-Study, institutionally sponsored loans, and tuition waivers (partial) available. Financial award applicants required to submit FAFSA. Offers medicine (MD). *Application deadline:* For fall admission, 12/15 for domestic students. Applications are processed on a rolling basis. *Application fee:* $65. Electronic applications accepted. *Application Contact:* Dr. Veronica T. Mallett, Dean, 615-327-6204, E-mail: vmallett@mmc.edu. *Dean,* Dr. Veronica T. Mallett, 615-327-6204, E-mail: vmallett@mmc.edu.

MELBOURNE BUSINESS SCHOOL, Carlton, Victoria 3053, Australia

General Information Independent, coed, graduate-only institution.

GRADUATE UNITS

Graduate Programs Offers business administration (Exec MBA, MBA); management (PhD); management science (PhD); marketing (PhD); social impact (Graduate Certificate).

MEMORIAL UNIVERSITY OF NEWFOUNDLAND, St. John's, NL A1C 5S7, Canada

General Information Province-supported, coed, university. CGS member. *Graduate housing:* Rooms and/or apartments available on a first-come, first-served basis to single and married students. *Research affiliation:* Eastern Regional Health Authority (health research).

GRADUATE UNITS

Faculty of Medicine *Program availability:* Part-time, online learning. Offers medicine (M Sc, PhD, Diploma). Electronic applications accepted.

Graduate Programs in Medicine *Program availability:* Part-time. Offers applied health services research (M Sc); cancer (M Sc, PhD); cardiovascular (M Sc, PhD); clinical epidemiology (M Sc, PhD, Diploma); community health (M Sc, PhD, Diploma); human genetics (M Sc, PhD); immunology (M Sc, PhD); medicine (M Sc, PhD, Diploma); neuroscience (M Sc, PhD). Electronic applications accepted.

School of Graduate Studies *Program availability:* Part-time, evening/weekend, 100% online, blended/hybrid learning. Offers applied psychological sciences (MAPS); aquaculture (M Sc); archaeology and physical anthropology (MA, PhD); atomic and molecular physics (PhD); biochemistry (M Sc, PhD); biology (M Sc, PhD); chemistry (M Sc, PhD); classics (MA); clinical psychology (Psy D); cognitive and behavioral ecology (M Sc, PhD); computer engineering (MA Sc); computer science (M Sc, PhD); condensed matter physics (PhD); economics (MA); employment relations (MER); English (MA, PhD); environmental science (M Env Sc, M Sc, PhD); environmental systems engineering and management (MA Sc); ethnomusicology (MA, PhD); experimental psychology (M Sc, PhD); fisheries resource management (MMS, Graduate Diploma); folklore (MA, PhD); food science (M Sc, PhD); French studies (MA); gender (PhD); gender studies (MGS); geography (M Sc, MA, PhD); geology (M Sc, PhD); geophysics (M Sc, PhD); German language and literature (M Phil, MA); history (MA, PhD); humanities (M Phil); instrumental analysis (M Sc); linguistics (M Sc); marine spatial planning and management (MMS); maritime sociology (PhD); mathematics (M Sc, PhD); philosophy (MA, PhD); physical oceanography (M Sc, PhD); physics (M Sc); political science (MA); religious studies (MA); scientific computing (M Sc); social and cultural anthropology (MA, PhD); sociology (M Phil, MA); statistics (M Sc, MAS, PhD); work and development (PhD). Electronic applications accepted.

Faculty of Business Administration *Program availability:* Part-time. Offers business administration (MBA). Electronic applications accepted.

Faculty of Education *Program availability:* Part-time. Offers counseling psychology (M Ed); curriculum, teaching, and learning studies (M Ed); education (PhD); educational leadership studies (M Ed, Graduate Diploma); information technology (M Ed); post-secondary studies (M Ed, Diploma). Electronic applications accepted.

Faculty of Engineering and Applied Science *Program availability:* Part-time. Offers civil engineering (M Eng, PhD); electrical and computer engineering (M Eng, PhD); mechanical engineering (M Eng, PhD); ocean and naval architecture engineering (M Eng, PhD). Electronic applications accepted.

School of Human Kinetics and Recreation *Program availability:* Part-time. Offers administration, curriculum and supervision (MPE); biomechanics/ergonomics (MS Kin); exercise and work physiology (MS Kin); psychology of sport, exercise and recreation (MS Kin); socio-cultural studies of physical activity and health (MS Kin). Electronic applications accepted.

School of Music Offers conducting (MMus); performance pedagogy (MMus); performing (MMus). Electronic applications accepted.

School of Nursing *Program availability:* Part-time. Offers nursing (MN, PhD). Electronic applications accepted.

School of Pharmacy *Program availability:* Part-time. Offers pharmacy (MSCPharm, PhD). Electronic applications accepted.

School of Social Work Offers social work (MSW, PhD). Electronic applications accepted.

MEMPHIS COLLEGE OF ART, Memphis, TN 38104-2764

General Information Independent, coed, comprehensive institution. *Enrollment:* 435 graduate, professional, and undergraduate students; 17 full-time matriculated graduate/professional students (13 women), 23 part-time matriculated graduate/professional students (14 women). *Enrollment by degree level:* 40 master's, 9 other advanced degrees. *Graduate faculty:* 27 full-time (16 women), 25 part-time/adjunct (13 women). *Tuition:* Full-time $32,400; part-time $3875 per course. *Required fees:* $700; $250 per course. Tuition and fees vary according to program. *Graduate housing:* Room and/or apartments available on a first-come, first-served basis to single students; on-campus housing not available to married students. Typical cost: $6750 per year ($8750 including board). Room and board charges vary according to housing facility selected. Housing application deadline: 6/1. *Student services:* Campus employment opportunities, campus safety program, career counseling, free psychological counseling, international student services, services for students with disabilities. *Library facilities:* G. Pillow Lewis Library. *Collection:* Books: 20,972 (physical); Serial titles: 162 (physical); Databases: 66.

Computer facilities: 100 computers available on campus for general student use. A campuswide network can be accessed from student residence rooms. Website: http://www.mca.edu/

General Application Contact: Katey Henriksen, Director of Admissions, 901-272-5151, Fax: 901-272-5158, E-mail: khenriksen@mca.edu.

GRADUATE UNITS

Graduate Programs Students: 17 full-time (13 women), 23 part-time (14 women); includes 14 minority (10 Black or African American, non-Hispanic/Latino; 2 Hispanic/Latino; 2 Two or more races, non-Hispanic/Latino), 2 international. Average age 32. 39 applicants, 51% accepted, 13 enrolled. *Faculty:* 27 full-time (16 women), 25 part-time/adjunct (13 women). Expenses: Contact institution. *Financial support:* In 2016–17, 40 students received support, including 8 teaching assistantships (averaging $3,000 per year); career-related internships or fieldwork, Federal Work-Study, scholarships/grants, unspecified assistantships, and teaching professional tuition discounts also available. Financial award application deadline: 8/1; financial award applicants required to submit FAFSA. In 2016, 17 master's awarded. *Program availability:* Part-time, evening/weekend. Offers art education (MA, MAT); illustration (MFA); metals (MFA); painting/drawing (MFA); photography (MFA); studio art (MFA). *Application deadline:* For fall admission, 2/1 for domestic students, 3/1 for international students; for spring admission, 11/1 for domestic and international students. *Application fee:* $50. Electronic applications accepted. *Application Contact:* Katey Henriksen, Director of Admissions, 901-272-5151, Fax: 901-272-5158, E-mail: khenriksen@mca.edu. *Interim Vice President for Academic Affairs,* Haley Cafiero, 901-272-5100, Fax: 901-272-5104, E-mail: hcafiero@mca.edu.

MEMPHIS THEOLOGICAL SEMINARY, Memphis, TN 38104-4395

General Information Independent-religious, coed, graduate-only institution. *Graduate housing:* Rooms and/or apartments available on a first-come, first-served basis to single and married students. Housing application deadline: 7/15. *Research affiliation:* Lilly Foundation (technology, religion), Wabash Center for Teaching and Learning (theology, religion).

GRADUATE UNITS

Graduate and Professional Programs *Program availability:* Part-time. Offers theology (M Div, MAR, D Min).

MERCER UNIVERSITY, Macon, GA 31207

General Information Independent-religious, coed, university. *Enrollment:* 6,955 graduate, professional, and undergraduate students; 2,772 full-time matriculated graduate/professional students (1,704 women), 1,098 part-time matriculated graduate/professional students (793 women). *Enrollment by degree level:* 1,850 master's, 1,961 doctoral, 59 other advanced degrees. *Graduate faculty:* 233 full-time (108 women), 116 part-time/adjunct (64 women). Tuition and fees vary according to degree level, campus/location and program. *Graduate housing:* Rooms and/or apartments available on a first-come, first-served basis to single and married students. *Student services:* Campus employment opportunities, campus safety program, career counseling, exercise/wellness program, free psychological counseling, international student services, low-cost health insurance, services for students with disabilities.

Library facilities: Jack Tarver Library plus 3 others. *Collection:* Books: 668,465 (physical), 40,482 (digital/electronic); Serial titles: 20,131 (physical), 40,707 (digital/electronic); Databases: 225. Study areas open 24 hours, 5–7 days a week. *Research affiliation:* Memorial Health Care (medical research), Piedmont (medical research), Total Therapeutic Management (pharmaceuticals), The Coca Cola Company (pharmaceutical research), Georgia Neurological Institute (medical research), Medical Center of Central Georgia (medical research).

Computer facilities: A campuswide network can be accessed from student residence rooms and from off campus. Online class registration is available. Website: http://www.mercer.edu/

General Application Contact: Tracey M. Wofford, Director of Graduate Admissions, 678-547-6422, Fax: 678-547-6422, E-mail: wofford_tm@mercer.edu.

GRADUATE UNITS

Graduate Studies, Cecil B. Day Campus Students: 1,622 full-time (1,137 women), 784 part-time (584 women); includes 1,247 minority (834 Black or African American, non-Hispanic/Latino; 5 American Indian or Alaska Native, non-Hispanic/Latino; 267 Asian, non-Hispanic/Latino; 96 Hispanic/Latino; 3 Native Hawaiian or other Pacific Islander, non-Hispanic/Latino; 42 Two or more races, non-Hispanic/Latino), 91 international. Average age 30. *Faculty:* 125 full-time (71 women), 70 part-time/adjunct (50 women). Expenses: Contact institution. *Financial support:* Teaching assistantships, career-related internships or fieldwork, Federal Work-Study, and scholarships/grants available. Support available to part-time students. Financial award applicants required to submit FAFSA. In 2016, 513 master's, 198 doctorates, 17 other advanced degrees awarded. *Program availability:* Part-time, evening/weekend, 100% online, blended/hybrid learning. *Application Contact:* Tracey M. Wofford, Director of Admissions, 678-547-6422, E-mail: wofford_tm@mercer.edu. *Provost,* Scott Davis, 478-301-2110, E-mail: davis_ds@mercer.edu.

College of Health Professions Students: 313 full-time (242 women), 52 part-time (43 women); includes 133 minority (96 Black or African American, non-Hispanic/Latino; 20 Asian, non-Hispanic/Latino; 16 Hispanic/Latino; 1 Two or more races, non-Hispanic/Latino), 4 international. Average age 26. *Faculty:* 20 full-time (13 women), 8 part-time/adjunct (6 women). Expenses: Contact institution. *Financial support:* Federal Work-Study, traineeships, and unspecified assistantships available. In 2016, 77 master's, 36 doctorates awarded. Offers clinical medical psychology (Psy D); physical therapy (DPT); physician assistant studies (MM Sc); public health (MPH). *Application Contact:* Laura Ellison, Director of Admissions and Student Affairs, 678-547-6391, E-mail: ellison_la@mercer.edu. *Dean/Clinical Professor,* Dr. Lisa Lundquist, 678-547-6308, E-mail: lundquist_lm@mercer.edu.

College of Pharmacy Students: 669 full-time (437 women), 8 part-time (2 women); includes 385 minority (142 Black or African American, non-Hispanic/Latino; 1 American Indian or Alaska Native, non-Hispanic/Latino; 188 Asian, non-Hispanic/Latino; 27 Two or more races, non-Hispanic/Latino), 40 international. Average age 26. 1,895 applicants, 18% accepted, 176 enrolled. *Faculty:* 24 full-time (14 women), 1 part-time/adjunct (0 women). Expenses: Contact institution. *Financial support:* In 2016–17, 350 students received support. Teaching assistantships with tuition reimbursements available, career-related internships or fieldwork, Federal Work-Study, institutionally sponsored loans, scholarships/grants, tuition waivers, and unspecified assistantships available. Support available to part-time students. Financial award application deadline: 5/1; financial award applicants required to submit FAFSA. In 2016, 150 doctorates awarded. Offers pharmacy (Pharm D). *Application deadline:* Applications are processed on a rolling basis. Electronic applications accepted. *Application Contact:* Dr. James W. Bartling, Associate Dean for Student Affairs and Admissions, 678-547-6181, Fax: 678-547-6518, E-mail: bartling_jw@mercer.edu. *Dean,* Dr. Hewitt W. Matthews, 678-547-6306, Fax: 678-547-6315, E-mail: matthews_h@mercer.edu.

Eugene W. Stetson School of Business and Economics (Atlanta) Students: 183 full-time (91 women), 129 part-time (69 women); includes 136 minority (99 Black or African American, non-Hispanic/Latino; 2 American Indian or Alaska Native, non-Hispanic/Latino; 22 Asian, non-Hispanic/Latino; 10 Hispanic/Latino; 3 Two or more races, non-Hispanic/Latino), 43 international. Average age 32. 207 applicants, 77% accepted, 110 enrolled. *Faculty:* 19 full-time (7 women), 7 part-time/adjunct (1 woman). Expenses: Contact institution. *Financial support:* Federal Work-Study available. Financial award application deadline: 5/1; financial award applicants required to submit FAFSA. In 2016, 176 master's awarded. *Program availability:* Part-time, evening/weekend, 100% online, blended/hybrid learning. Offers accounting (M Acc); business analytics (MS); innovation (PMBA); international business (MBA). *Application deadline:* For fall admission, 6/15 priority date for domestic and international students; for spring admission, 11/1 priority date for domestic and international students; for summer admission, 3/15 priority date for domestic and international students. Applications are processed on a rolling basis. *Application fee:* $50 ($100 for international students). Electronic applications accepted. *Application Contact:* Lael Whiteside, Director of Admissions, 678-547-6300, Fax: 678-547-6160, E-mail: whiteside_l@mercer.edu. *Dean,* Dr. Susan P. Gilbert, 678-547-6438, Fax: 678-547-6337, E-mail: gilbert_sp@mercer.edu.

Georgia Baptist College of Nursing Students: 70 full-time (65 women), 37 part-time (34 women); includes 54 minority (28 Black or African American, non-Hispanic/Latino; 17 Asian, non-Hispanic/Latino; 5 Hispanic/Latino; 1 Native Hawaiian or other Pacific Islander, non-Hispanic/Latino; 3 Two or more races, non-Hispanic/Latino), 5 international. Average age 36. 65 applicants, 66% accepted, 30 enrolled. *Faculty:* 10 full-time (all women), 4 part-time/adjunct (3 women). Expenses: Contact institution. *Financial support:* In 2016–17, 59 students received support. Scholarships/grants and traineeships available. Financial award application deadline: 6/30; financial award applicants required to submit FAFSA. In 2016, 49 master's, 7 doctorates awarded. *Program availability:* Part-time, blended/hybrid learning. Offers adult gerontology acute care nurse practitioner (MSN, Certificate); family nurse practitioner (MSN); nursing (PhD); nursing practice (DNP). *Application deadline:* For fall admission, 5/1 for domestic students, 3/1 for international students; for winter admission, 11/1 for domestic students, 9/1 for international students; for spring admission, 11/1 for domestic students, 10/1 for international students; for summer admission, 3/1 for domestic and international students. Applications are processed on a rolling basis. *Application fee:* $50. Electronic applications accepted. *Application Contact:* Janda Anderson, Director of Admissions, 678-547-6700, Fax: 678-547-6794, E-mail: anderson_j@mercer.edu. *Dean/Professor,* Dr. Linda Streit, 678-547-6793, Fax: 678-547-6796, E-mail: streit_la@mercer.edu.

James and Carolyn McAfee School of Theology Students: 106 full-time (65 women), 84 part-time (35 women); includes 100 minority (89 Black or African American, non-Hispanic/Latino; 2 American Indian or Alaska Native, non-Hispanic/Latino; 1 Asian, non-Hispanic/Latino; 5 Hispanic/Latino; 1 Native Hawaiian or other Pacific Islander, non-Hispanic/Latino; 2 Two or more races, non-Hispanic/Latino), 1 international.

Average age 37. 66 applicants, 71% accepted, 40 enrolled. *Faculty:* 14 full-time (7 women), 5 part-time/adjunct (0 women). Expenses: Contact institution. *Financial support:* In 2016–17, 70 students received support. Career-related internships or fieldwork, Federal Work-Study, institutionally sponsored loans, and scholarships/grants available. Support available to part-time students. Financial award application deadline: 10/1; financial award applicants required to submit FAFSA. In 2016, 53 master's, 2 doctorates awarded. *Program availability:* Part-time. Offers Christian ministry (MACM); Christian spirituality (D Min); divinity (M Div); preaching (D Min). *Application deadline:* For fall admission, 7/1 for domestic and international students; for spring admission, 11/15 for domestic and international students. Applications are processed on a rolling basis. *Application fee:* $50. Electronic applications accepted. *Application Contact:* L. Nikki Hardeman, Director of Admissions, 678-547-6357, Fax: 678-547-6478, E-mail: hardeman_ln@mercer.edu. *Dean,* Dr. Jeffrey Willetts, 678-547-6470, Fax: 678-547-6478, E-mail: willetts_jg@mercer.edu.

Penfield College Students: 168 full-time (136 women), 242 part-time (201 women); includes 231 minority (192 Black or African American, non-Hispanic/Latino; 1 American Indian or Alaska Native, non-Hispanic/Latino; 15 Asian, non-Hispanic/Latino; 19 Hispanic/Latino; 1 Native Hawaiian or other Pacific Islander, non-Hispanic/Latino; 3 Two or more races, non-Hispanic/Latino), 1 international. Average age 32. 300 applicants, 45% accepted, 114 enrolled. *Faculty:* 15 full-time (8 women), 22 part-time/adjunct (18 women). Expenses: Contact institution. *Financial support:* In 2016–17, 32 students received support. Federal Work-Study, scholarships/grants, and unspecified assistantships available. Financial award applicants required to submit FAFSA. In 2016, 92 master's, 8 doctorates awarded. *Program availability:* Part-time, evening/weekend, 100% online, blended/hybrid learning. Offers certified rehabilitation counseling (MS); clinical mental health (MS); counselor education and supervision (PhD); criminal justice and public safety leadership (MS); health informatics (MS); human services (MS); organizational leadership (MS); school counseling (MS). *Application deadline:* For fall admission, 7/1 priority date for domestic and international students; for spring admission, 11/1 priority date for domestic and international students; for summer admission, 4/1 priority date for domestic and international students. *Application fee:* $35. Electronic applications accepted. *Dean,* Dr. Priscilla R. Danheiser, 678-547-6028, Fax: 678-547-6008, E-mail: danheiser_p@mercer.edu.

Tift College of Education (Atlanta) Students: 177 full-time (150 women), 324 part-time (264 women); includes 288 minority (256 Black or African American, non-Hispanic/Latino; 1 American Indian or Alaska Native, non-Hispanic/Latino; 7 Asian, non-Hispanic/Latino; 17 Hispanic/Latino; 1 Native Hawaiian or other Pacific Islander, non-Hispanic/Latino; 6 Two or more races, non-Hispanic/Latino), 1 international. Average age 35. *Faculty:* 28 full-time (15 women), 30 part-time/adjunct (27 women). Expenses: Contact institution. *Financial support:* Federal Work-Study and unspecified assistantships available. Support available to part-time students. Financial award application deadline: 5/1; financial award applicants required to submit FAFSA. In 2016, 173 master's, 34 doctorates, 54 other advanced degrees awarded. *Program availability:* Part-time, evening/weekend. Offers curriculum and instruction (PhD); early childhood education (M Ed, MAT, Ed S); educational leadership (PhD); educational leadership P-12 (M Ed, Ed S); higher education leadership (PhD); independent and charter school leadership (M Ed); middle grades education (M Ed, MAT); reading specialist (M Ed); secondary education (M Ed, MAT); teacher leadership (Ed S). *Application deadline:* For fall admission, 8/1 for domestic and international students; for spring admission, 12/1 for domestic and international students; for summer admission, 5/1 for domestic and international students. Applications are processed on a rolling basis. *Application fee:* $25 ($50 for international students). Electronic applications accepted. *Application Contact:* Renee Slaton, Associate Director of Graduate Admissions, 678-547-6084, Fax: 678-547-6055, E-mail: mcereducation@mercer.edu. *Dean,* Dr. James Barta, 478-301-5355, Fax: 478-301-2280, E-mail: barta_jj@mercer.edu.

Graduate Studies, Macon Campus Students: 168 full-time (68 women), 131 part-time (61 women); includes 87 minority (60 Black or African American, non-Hispanic/Latino; 2 American Indian or Alaska Native, non-Hispanic/Latino; 10 Asian, non-Hispanic/Latino; 8 Hispanic/Latino; 1 Native Hawaiian or other Pacific Islander, non-Hispanic/Latino; 6 Two or more races, non-Hispanic/Latino), 6 international. Average age 30. *Faculty:* 95 full-time (34 women), 18 part-time/adjunct (9 women). Expenses: Contact institution. *Financial support:* Career-related internships or fieldwork, Federal Work-Study, and institutionally sponsored loans available. Support available to part-time students. In 2016, 157 master's, 13 doctorates, 4 other advanced degrees awarded. *Program availability:* Part-time, evening/weekend. *Application Contact:* Tracey M. Wofford, Director of Graduate Admissions, 678-547-6422, E-mail: wofford_tm@mercer.edu. *Interim Dean of Graduate Studies/Professor of Mathematics,* Keith Howard, 478-301-5983, E-mail: howard_ke@mercer.edu.

Eugene W. Stetson School of Business and Economics (Macon) Students: 51 full-time (14 women), 31 part-time (18 women); includes 31 minority (21 Black or African American, non-Hispanic/Latino; 1 American Indian or Alaska Native, non-Hispanic/Latino; 5 Asian, non-Hispanic/Latino; 2 Hispanic/Latino; 2 Two or more races, non-Hispanic/Latino), 1 international. Average age 30. *Faculty:* 7 full-time (2 women), 3 part-time/adjunct (1 woman). Expenses: Contact institution. In 2016, 56 master's awarded. *Program availability:* Part-time, evening/weekend. Offers business and economics (MBA). *Application deadline:* For fall admission, 8/1 for domestic students; for spring admission, 12/1 for domestic students; for summer admission, 4/1 for domestic students. Applications are processed on a rolling basis. *Application fee:* $50 ($100 for international students). Electronic applications accepted. *Application Contact:* Dr. James L. Hunt, Professor/Associate Dean, 478-301-2833, Fax: 478-301-2635, E-mail: maconmba@mercer.edu. *Dean,* Dr. Susan P. Gilbert, 478-301-6438, E-mail: gilbert_sp@mercer.edu.

School of Engineering Students: 44 full-time (9 women), 60 part-time (12 women); includes 14 minority (3 Black or African American, non-Hispanic/Latino; 1 American Indian or Alaska Native, non-Hispanic/Latino; 4 Asian, non-Hispanic/Latino; 3 Hispanic/Latino; 3 Two or more races, non-Hispanic/Latino), 2 international. Average age 27. *Faculty:* 21 full-time (5 women), 1 part-time/adjunct (0 women). Expenses: Contact institution. *Financial support:* Applicants required to submit FAFSA. In 2016, 64 master's awarded. *Program availability:* Part-time-only, evening/weekend, online learning. Offers biomedical engineering (MSE); computer engineering (MSE); electrical engineering (MSE); engineering management (MSE); environmental engineering (MSE); environmental systems (MS); mechanical engineering (MSE); software engineering (MSE); software systems (MS); technical communications management (MS); technical management (MS). *Application deadline:* For fall admission, 4/1 priority date for domestic and international students; for spring admission, 11/1 priority date for domestic and international students. Applications are processed on a rolling basis. *Application fee:* $75. *Application Contact:* Dr. Richard O.

Mines, Jr., Program Director, 478-301-2347, Fax: 478-301-5433, E-mail: mines_ro@mercer.edu. *Dean,* Dr. Laura W. Lackey, 478-301-4106, Fax: 478-301-5593, E-mail: lackey_l@mercer.edu.

Tift College of Education (Macon) Students: 61 full-time (39 women), 39 part-time (30 women); includes 39 minority (34 Black or African American, non-Hispanic/Latino; 1 Asian, non-Hispanic/Latino; 2 Hispanic/Latino; 1 Native Hawaiian or other Pacific Islander, non-Hispanic/Latino; 1 Two or more races, non-Hispanic/Latino), 3 international. Average age 33. *Faculty:* 14 full-time (11 women), 1 part-time/adjunct (0 women). Expenses: Contact institution. *Financial support:* Federal Work-Study, institutionally sponsored loans, and unspecified assistantships available. Support available to part-time students. Financial award application deadline: 5/1; financial award applicants required to submit FAFSA. In 2016, 23 master's, 13 doctorates awarded. *Program availability:* Part-time, evening/weekend, 100% online, blended/hybrid learning. Offers early childhood education (M Ed, Ed S); educational leadership (M Ed, PhD, Ed S); higher education leadership (M Ed); teacher leadership (Ed S). *Application deadline:* For fall admission, 8/1 for domestic and international students; for spring admission, 12/1 for domestic and international students. Applications are processed on a rolling basis. *Application fee:* $35. Electronic applications accepted. *Application Contact:* Tracey M. Wofford, Associate Director of Admissions, 678-547-6422, Fax: 678-547-6367, E-mail: wofford_tm@mercer.edu. *Dean,* Dr. James Barta, 478-301-5397, Fax: 478-301-2280, E-mail: barta_jj@mercer.edu.

Townsend School of Music Students: 12 full-time (6 women), 1 (woman) part-time; includes 3 minority (2 Black or African American, non-Hispanic/Latino; 1 Hispanic/Latino). Average age 25. 25 applicants, 48% accepted, 9 enrolled. *Faculty:* 9 full-time (3 women), 3 part-time/adjunct (2 women). Expenses: Contact institution. *Financial support:* In 2016–17, 14 students received support. Tuition waivers (full) and unspecified assistantships available. Financial award application deadline: 6/1; financial award applicants required to submit FAFSA. In 2016, 11 master's awarded. Offers choral conducting (MM); church music (MM); collaborative piano (MM); instrumental conducting (MM); performance (MM). *Application deadline:* For fall admission, 6/1 for domestic students, 5/1 for international students. Applications are processed on a rolling basis. *Application fee:* $100. *Application Contact:* Director, 912-301-2700. *Director of Graduate Studies,* Dr. Richard G. Kosowski, 478-301-4167, Fax: 478-301-5633, E-mail: keith_cd@mercer.edu.

School of Medicine Offers medicine (MFT, MPH, MSA, MD).

Walter F. George School of Law *Program availability:* Part-time. Offers law (JD). Electronic applications accepted.

MERCY COLLEGE, Dobbs Ferry, NY 10522-1189

General Information Independent, coed, comprehensive institution. CGS member. *Enrollment:* 10,099 graduate, professional, and undergraduate students; 1,334 full-time matriculated graduate/professional students (1,017 women), 1,432 part-time matriculated graduate/professional students (1,175 women). *Enrollment by degree level:* 2,610 master's, 111 doctoral, 45 other advanced degrees. *Tuition:* Full-time $15,156; part-time $842 per credit hour. *Required fees:* $620; $155 per term. Tuition and fees vary according to course load and program. *Graduate housing:* Room and/or apartments available on a first-come, first-served basis to single students; on-campus housing not available to married students. Typical cost: $9150 per year ($13,700 including board). Room and board charges vary according to board plan. Housing application deadline: 7/1. *Student services:* Campus employment opportunities, campus safety program, career counseling, exercise/wellness program, free psychological counseling, international student services, services for students with disabilities, teacher training, writing training. *Library facilities:* Mercy College Library plus 3 others. *Collection:* Books: 85,689 (digital/electronic); Serial titles: 21,126 (digital/electronic). Students can reserve study rooms.

Computer facilities: Computer purchase and lease plans are available. 972 computers available on campus for general student use. A campuswide network can be accessed from student residence rooms and from off campus. Online class registration is available.

Website: http://www.mercy.edu/

General Application Contact: Allison Gurdineer, Senior Director of Admissions, 877-637-2946, Fax: 914-674-7382, E-mail: admissions@mercy.edu.

GRADUATE UNITS

School of Business Students: 234 full-time (200 women), 292 part-time (240 women); includes 388 minority (169 Black or African American, non-Hispanic/Latino; 1 American Indian or Alaska Native, non-Hispanic/Latino; 19 Asian, non-Hispanic/Latino; 190 Hispanic/Latino; 2 Native Hawaiian or other Pacific Islander, non-Hispanic/Latino; 7 Two or more races, non-Hispanic/Latino), 5 international. Average age 32. 354 applicants, 68% accepted, 134 enrolled. Expenses: Contact institution. *Financial support:* Career-related internships or fieldwork, Federal Work-Study, scholarships/grants, and unspecified assistantships available. Support available to part-time students. Financial award applicants required to submit FAFSA. In 2016, 199 master's awarded. *Program availability:* Part-time, evening/weekend, 100% online, blended/hybrid learning. Offers accounting (MS); business (MBA, MS); business administration (MBA); human resource management (MS); organizational leadership (MS). *Application deadline:* For fall admission, 8/1 for international students. Applications are processed on a rolling basis. *Application fee:* $40. Electronic applications accepted. *Application Contact:* Allison Gurdineer, Senior Director of Admissions, 877-637-2946, E-mail: admissions@mercy.edu. *Dean, School of Business,* Ed Weis, 914-674-7490, E-mail: eweis@mercy.edu.

School of Education Students: 329 full-time (300 women), 714 part-time (598 women); includes 489 minority (215 Black or African American, non-Hispanic/Latino; 8 American Indian or Alaska Native, non-Hispanic/Latino; 21 Asian, non-Hispanic/Latino; 233 Hispanic/Latino; 1 Native Hawaiian or other Pacific Islander, non-Hispanic/Latino; 11 Two or more races, non-Hispanic/Latino). Average age 32. 344 applicants, 40% accepted, 76 enrolled. Expenses: Contact institution. *Financial support:* Career-related internships or fieldwork, Federal Work-Study, scholarships/grants, and unspecified assistantships available. Support available to part-time students. Financial award applicants required to submit FAFSA. In 2016, 476 master's, 38 other advanced degrees awarded. *Program availability:* Part-time, evening/weekend, 100% online, blended/hybrid learning. Offers adolescence education (MS); childhood education (MS); early childhood education (MS); education (MS, Advanced Certificate); educational leadership (Advanced Certificate); teaching English to speakers of other languages (TESOL) (MS, Advanced Certificate); teaching literacy (Advanced Certificate); teaching literacy, birth-6 (MS); teaching literacy, grades 5-12 (MS). *Application deadline:* For fall admission, 8/1 for international students. Applications are processed on a rolling basis. *Application fee:* $40. Electronic applications accepted. *Application Contact:* Allison Gurdineer, Senior

Director of Admissions, 877-637-2946, Fax: 914-674-7382, E-mail: admissions@mercy.edu. *Dean for the School of Education,* 914-674-7350.

School of Health and Natural Sciences Students: 356 full-time (278 women), 245 part-time (217 women); includes 291 minority (113 Black or African American, non-Hispanic/Latino; 1 American Indian or Alaska Native, non-Hispanic/Latino; 82 Asian, non-Hispanic/Latino; 82 Hispanic/Latino; 4 Native Hawaiian or other Pacific Islander, non-Hispanic/Latino; 9 Two or more races, non-Hispanic/Latino), 1 international. Average age 33. 1,117 applicants, 20% accepted, 151 enrolled. Expenses: Contact institution. *Financial support:* Career-related internships or fieldwork, Federal Work-Study, scholarships/grants, and unspecified assistantships available. Support available to part-time students. Financial award applicants required to submit FAFSA. In 2016, 178 master's, 18 doctorates awarded. *Program availability:* Part-time, evening/weekend, blended/hybrid learning. Offers communication disorders (MS); nursing (MS); nursing administration (MS); nursing education (MS); occupational therapy (MS); physical therapy (DPT); physician assistant studies (MS). *Application deadline:* For fall admission, 8/1 for international students. Applications are processed on a rolling basis. *Application fee:* $40. Electronic applications accepted. *Application Contact:* Allison Gurdineer, Senior Director of Admissions, 877-637-2946, Fax: 914-674-7382, E-mail: admissions@mercy.edu. *Dean, School of Health and Natural Sciences,* Dr. Joan Toglia, 914-674-7837, E-mail: jtoglia@mercy.edu.

School of Liberal Arts Students: 33 full-time (12 women), 70 part-time (45 women); includes 19 minority (16 Black or African American, non-Hispanic/Latino; 1 American Indian or Alaska Native, non-Hispanic/Latino; 2 Asian, non-Hispanic/Latino; 13 Hispanic/Latino), 8 international. Average age 35. 79 applicants, 63% accepted, 30 enrolled. Expenses: Contact institution. *Financial support:* Career-related internships or fieldwork, Federal Work-Study, scholarships/grants, and unspecified assistantships available. Support available to part-time students. Financial award applicants required to submit FAFSA. In 2016, 43 master's awarded. *Program availability:* Part-time, evening/weekend, 100% online, blended/hybrid learning. Offers cybersecurity (MS); English literature (MA). *Application deadline:* For fall admission, 8/1 for international students. Applications are processed on a rolling basis. *Application fee:* $40. Electronic applications accepted. *Application Contact:* Allison Gurdineer, Senior Director of Admissions, 877-637-2946, Fax: 914-674-7382, E-mail: admissions@mercy.edu. *Dean, School of Liberal Arts,* 914-674-7593.

School of Social and Behavioral Sciences Students: 234 full-time (200 women), 292 part-time (240 women); includes 388 minority (169 Black or African American, non-Hispanic/Latino; 1 American Indian or Alaska Native, non-Hispanic/Latino; 19 Asian, non-Hispanic/Latino; 190 Hispanic/Latino; 2 Native Hawaiian or other Pacific Islander, non-Hispanic/Latino; 7 Two or more races, non-Hispanic/Latino), 5 international. Average age 34. 448 applicants, 48% accepted, 150 enrolled. Expenses: Contact institution. *Financial support:* Career-related internships or fieldwork, Federal Work-Study, scholarships/grants, and unspecified assistantships available. Support available to part-time students. Financial award applicants required to submit FAFSA. In 2016, 150 master's, 2 other advanced degrees awarded. *Program availability:* Part-time, evening/weekend, 100% online, blended/hybrid learning. Offers counseling (MS, Certificate); family counseling (Certificate); health services management (MPA, MS); marriage and family therapy (MS); mental health counseling (MS); psychology (MS); school counseling (Certificate); school psychology (MS). *Application deadline:* For fall admission, 8/1 for international students. Applications are processed on a rolling basis. *Application fee:* $40. Electronic applications accepted. *Application Contact:* Allison Gurdineer, Senior Director of Admissions, 877-637-2946, Fax: 914-674-7382, E-mail: admissions@mercy.edu. *Dean, School of Social and Behavioral Sciences,* Dr. Karol Dean, 914-674-7517, E-mail: kdean@mercy.edu.

MERCYHURST UNIVERSITY, Erie, PA 16546

General Information Independent-religious, coed, comprehensive institution. *Graduate housing:* On-campus housing not available.

GRADUATE UNITS

Graduate Studies *Program availability:* Part-time, evening/weekend. Offers accounting (MS); administration of justice (MS); applied behavior analysis (MS); applied intelligence (MS, Certificate); archaeology and geological archaeology (MS); autism (MS); data science (MS); forensic and biological anthropology (MS); generalist (MS); higher education administration (MS); higher education leadership and disabilities (MS); human resources (MS); organizational leadership (MS, Certificate); physician assistant studies (MS); secondary education: pedagogy and practice (MS); sports leadership (MS); strategy and innovation (MS). Electronic applications accepted.

MEREDITH COLLEGE, Raleigh, NC 27607-5298

General Information Independent, Undergraduate: women only; graduate: coed, comprehensive institution. *Graduate housing:* On-campus housing not available.

GRADUATE UNITS

School of Business *Program availability:* Part-time, evening/weekend. Offers business administration (MBA). Electronic applications accepted.

School of Education, Health and Human Sciences *Program availability:* Part-time, evening/weekend. Offers academically and intellectually gifted (M Ed); curriculum instruction specialist (M Ed); dietetic internship (Postbaccalaureate Certificate); elementary education (M Ed, MAT); English as a second language (M Ed, MAT); health and physical education (MAT); nutrition (MS); nutrition, health and human performance (MS, Postbaccalaureate Certificate); reading (M Ed); special education (MAT). Electronic applications accepted.

MERRIMACK COLLEGE, North Andover, MA 01845-5800

General Information Independent-religious, coed, comprehensive institution. CGS member. *Enrollment:* 4,029 graduate, professional, and undergraduate students; 415 full-time matriculated graduate/professional students (265 women), 133 part-time matriculated graduate/professional students (86 women). *Enrollment by degree level:* 548 master's. *Graduate faculty:* 45 full-time, 57 part-time/adjunct. Tuition and fees vary according to course load and program. *Graduate housing:* On-campus housing not available. *Student services:* Campus employment opportunities, campus safety program, career counseling, exercise/wellness program, free psychological counseling, international student services, low-cost health insurance, multicultural affairs office, services for students with disabilities, teacher training, writing training. *Library facilities:* McQuade Library.

Computer facilities: Computer purchase and lease plans are available. A campuswide network can be accessed from student residence rooms and from off campus. Online class registration is available.

Website: http://www.merrimack.edu/

General Application Contact: Megan Goddard, Office of Graduate Studies, 978-837-3563, E-mail: graduate@merrimack.edu.

GRADUATE UNITS

Girard School of Business Students: 101 full-time (45 women), 35 part-time (13 women); includes 6 minority (2 Asian, non-Hispanic/Latino; 3 Hispanic/Latino; 1 Two or more races, non-Hispanic/Latino), 55 international. Average age 27. 116 applicants, 81% accepted, 53 enrolled. *Faculty:* 7 full-time, 17 part-time/adjunct. Expenses: Contact institution. *Financial support:* Career-related internships or fieldwork, scholarships/grants, health care benefits, and unspecified assistantships available. Support available to part-time students. Financial award application deadline: 5/1; financial award applicants required to submit FAFSA. In 2016, 57 master's awarded. *Program availability:* Part-time, evening/weekend, 100% online. Offers accounting (MS); business analytics (MS); management (MS). *Application deadline:* For fall admission, 8/13 for domestic students, 7/15 for international students; for spring admission, 1/10 for domestic and international students; for summer admission, 5/10 for domestic students, 4/10 for international students. Applications are processed on a rolling basis. *Application fee:* $0. Electronic applications accepted. *Application Contact:* Jennifer Greenwood, Graduate Admission Counselor, 978-837-3563, E-mail: graduate@merrimack.edu.

School of Education and Social Policy Students: 204 full-time (172 women), 83 part-time (67 women); includes 32 minority (4 Black or African American, non-Hispanic/Latino; 2 Asian, non-Hispanic/Latino; 23 Hispanic/Latino; 3 Two or more races, non-Hispanic/Latino), 1 international. Average age 27. 261 applicants, 89% accepted, 200 enrolled. *Faculty:* 17 full-time, 34 part-time/adjunct. Expenses: Contact institution. *Financial support:* Fellowships with full tuition reimbursements, career-related internships or fieldwork, scholarships/grants, and health care benefits available. Support available to part-time students. Financial award application deadline: 5/1; financial award applicants required to submit FAFSA. In 2016, 153 master's, 2 other advanced degrees awarded. *Program availability:* Part-time, evening/weekend, 100% online courses with immersion events and in-classroom practicum close to home. Offers community engagement (M Ed); criminology and criminal justice (MS); curriculum and instruction (M Ed); early childhood education (M Ed); educational leadership (CAGS); elementary education (M Ed); English as a second language (PreK-6) (M Ed); high school education (M Ed); higher education (M Ed); middle school education (M Ed); moderate disabilities (PreK-8) (M Ed); school counseling (M Ed). *Application deadline:* For fall admission, 8/14 for domestic students, 7/14 for international students; for spring admission, 1/10 for domestic students, 12/10 for international students; for summer admission, 5/10 for domestic students, 4/10 for international students. Applications are processed on a rolling basis. *Application fee:* $0. Electronic applications accepted. *Application Contact:* Alyssa Frey, Graduate Admissions Counselor, 978-837-3563, E-mail: freya@merrimack.edu.

School of Liberal Arts Students: 22 full-time (16 women), 2 part-time (0 women); includes 3 minority (2 Black or African American, non-Hispanic/Latino; 1 Hispanic/Latino), 1 international. Average age 32. 22 applicants, 95% accepted, 16 enrolled. *Faculty:* 6 full-time, 4 part-time/adjunct. Expenses: Contact institution. *Financial support:* Career-related internships or fieldwork, scholarships/grants, and health care benefits available. Support available to part-time students. Financial award application deadline: 5/1; financial award applicants required to submit FAFSA. *Program availability:* Part-time, evening/weekend. Offers clinical mental health counseling (MS); public affairs (MPA). *Application deadline:* For fall admission, 8/14 for domestic students, 7/14 for international students; for spring admission, 1/10 for domestic students, 12/10 for international students; for summer admission, 5/10 for domestic students, 4/10 for international students. Applications are processed on a rolling basis. Electronic applications accepted. *Application Contact:* Jennifer Greenwood, Graduate Admissions Counselor, 978-837-3563, E-mail: greenwoodjl@merrimack.edu.

School of Science and Engineering Students: 88 full-time (32 women), 13 part-time (6 women); includes 6 minority (4 Hispanic/Latino; 2 Two or more races, non-Hispanic/Latino), 39 international. Average age 25. 156 applicants, 67% accepted, 59 enrolled. *Faculty:* 16 full-time, 2 part-time/adjunct. Expenses: Contact institution. *Financial support:* Fellowships with full tuition reimbursements, career-related internships or fieldwork, scholarships/grants, and health care benefits available. Support available to part-time students. Financial award application deadline: 5/1; financial award applicants required to submit FAFSA. In 2016, 46 master's awarded. *Program availability:* Part-time, evening/weekend, 100% online. Offers athletic training (MS); civil engineering (MS); community health education (MS); computer science (MS); data science (MS); exercise and sport science (MS); health and wellness management (MS); mechanical engineering (MS). *Application deadline:* For fall admission, 8/14 for domestic students, 7/14 for international students; for spring admission, 1/10 for domestic students, 12/10 for international students; for summer admission, 5/10 for domestic students, 4/10 for international students. Applications are processed on a rolling basis. *Application fee:* $0. Electronic applications accepted. *Application Contact:* Allison Pena, Graduate Admissions Counselor, 978-837-3563, E-mail: penaa@merrimack.edu.

MESIVTA OF EASTERN PARKWAY–YESHIVA ZICHRON MEILECH, Brooklyn, NY 11218-5559

General Information Independent-religious, men only, comprehensive institution.

GRADUATE UNITS
Graduate Programs

MESIVTA TORAH VODAATH RABBINICAL SEMINARY, Brooklyn, NY 11218-5299

General Information Independent-religious, men only, comprehensive institution.

GRADUATE UNITS
Graduate Programs

MESIVTHA TIFERETH JERUSALEM OF AMERICA, New York, NY 10002-6301

General Information Independent-religious, men only, comprehensive institution.

GRADUATE UNITS
Graduate Programs

MESSIAH COLLEGE, Mechanicsburg, PA 17055

General Information Independent-religious, coed, comprehensive institution.

GRADUATE UNITS

Program in Business and Leadership *Program availability:* Online learning. Offers leadership (MBA, Certificate); management (Certificate); strategic leadership (MA).

Program in Conducting *Program availability:* Part-time, online learning. Offers choral conducting (MM); orchestral conducting (MM); wind conducting (MM). Electronic applications accepted.

Program in Counseling *Program availability:* Part-time, online learning. Offers clinical mental health counseling (MAC); counseling (CAGS); marriage, couple, and family counseling (MAC); school counseling (MAC). Electronic applications accepted.

Program in Education *Program availability:* Part-time, online learning. Offers curriculum and instruction (M Ed); special education (M Ed); teaching English to speakers of other languages (M Ed). Electronic applications accepted.

Program in Higher Education *Program availability:* Part-time. Offers college athletics management (MA); self-designed concentration (MA); student affairs (MA). Electronic applications accepted.

Program in Nursing Offers nurse educator (MSN).

METHODIST THEOLOGICAL SCHOOL IN OHIO, Delaware, OH 43015-8004

General Information Independent-religious, coed, graduate-only institution. *Graduate housing:* Rooms and/or apartments available on a first-come, first-served basis to single students and available to married students. Housing application deadline: 8/15.

GRADUATE UNITS

Graduate and Professional Programs *Program availability:* Part-time. Offers theology (M Div, MACE, MACM, MTS, D Min).

METHODIST UNIVERSITY, Fayetteville, NC 28311-1498

General Information Independent-religious, coed, comprehensive institution. *Graduate housing:* Room and/or apartments available on a first-come, first-served basis to single students; on-campus housing not available to married students. Housing application deadline: 6/1.

GRADUATE UNITS

School of Graduate Studies *Program availability:* Part-time, evening/weekend. Offers business administration (MBA); justice administration (MJA); physician assistant studies (MMS). Electronic applications accepted.

METROPOLITAN COLLEGE OF NEW YORK, New York, NY 10006

General Information Independent, coed, comprehensive institution. *Enrollment:* 1,059 graduate, professional, and undergraduate students; 308 full-time matriculated graduate/professional students (221 women), 54 part-time matriculated graduate/professional students (35 women). *Enrollment by degree level:* 362 master's. *Tuition:* Full-time $26,460; part-time $882 per credit hour. *Required fees:* $790; $790 per year. $395 per semester. One-time fee: $45. *Graduate housing:* On-campus housing not available. *Student services:* Career counseling, free psychological counseling, grant writing training, international student services. *Library facilities:* Main Library plus 1 other. *Collection:* Books: 26,191 (physical), 156,497 (digital/electronic); Serial titles: 29,206 (digital/electronic); Databases: 91. Weekly public service hours: 72. *Research affiliation:* U.S. Department of Homeland Security (homeland security), U.S. Federal Emergency Management Administration (higher education).

Computer facilities: 120 computers available on campus for general student use. A campuswide network can be accessed from off campus. Online class registration is available.
Website: http://www.mcny.edu/

General Application Contact: Steebo Varghese, Associate Director of Admissions, 212-343-1234 Ext. 2708, Fax: 212-343-8470, E-mail: svarghese@mcny.edu.

GRADUATE UNITS

Program in Business Administration Students: 167 full-time (117 women), 43 part-time (30 women); includes 161 minority (114 Black or African American, non-Hispanic/Latino; 3 American Indian or Alaska Native, non-Hispanic/Latino; 10 Asian, non-Hispanic/Latino; 32 Hispanic/Latino; 2 Two or more races, non-Hispanic/Latino), 26 international. Average age 37. Expenses: Contact institution. *Financial support:* Scholarships/grants available. Financial award application deadline: 8/15; financial award applicants required to submit FAFSA. In 2016, 111 master's awarded. *Program availability:* Evening/weekend. Offers financial services (MBA); general management (MBA); health services and risk management (MBA); media management (MBA). *Application deadline:* For fall admission, 7/15 priority date for domestic students; for winter admission, 11/15 priority date for domestic students; for spring admission, 3/30 priority date for domestic students. Applications are processed on a rolling basis. *Application fee:* $45. Electronic applications accepted. *Application Contact:* Steebo Varghese, Assistant Director of Admissions, 212-343-1234 Ext. 2708, Fax: 212-343-8470. *Dean and Professor, School for Business,* Dr. Tilokie Depoo, 212-343-1234 Ext. 2204.

Program in Childhood/Special Education Students: 21 full-time (19 women), 1 (woman) part-time; includes 15 minority (13 Black or African American, non-Hispanic/Latino; 2 Hispanic/Latino), 1 international. Average age 32. Expenses: Contact institution. *Financial support:* Career-related internships or fieldwork, Federal Work-Study, institutionally sponsored loans, and scholarships/grants available. Financial award application deadline: 8/15; financial award applicants required to submit FAFSA. In 2016, 21 master's awarded. Offers dual childhood 1-6 special education (MS). *Application deadline:* Applications are processed on a rolling basis. *Application fee:* $45. Electronic applications accepted. *Application Contact:* Sylvia Cameron, Graduate Admissions Coordinator, 212-343-1234 Ext. 2704, Fax: 212-343-7900, E-mail: scameron@mcny.edu. *Director,* Dr. Patrick Ianniello, 212-343-1234 Ext. 2424, E-mail: pianniello@metropolitan.edu.

Program in Public Administration Students: 120 full-time (85 women), 10 part-time (4 women); includes 108 minority (76 Black or African American, non-Hispanic/Latino; 5 Asian, non-Hispanic/Latino; 26 Hispanic/Latino; 1 Native Hawaiian or other Pacific Islander, non-Hispanic/Latino), 2 international. Average age 37. Expenses: Contact institution. *Financial support:* Fellowships with tuition reimbursements, career-related internships or fieldwork, scholarships/grants, and tuition waivers (partial) available. Financial award application deadline: 8/15; financial award applicants required to submit FAFSA. In 2016, 118 master's awarded. *Program availability:* Evening/weekend. Offers emergency and disaster management (MPA); public affairs and administration (MPA). *Application deadline:* For fall admission, 7/30 priority date for domestic students, 7/1 for international students; for winter admission, 11/30 priority date for domestic students, 11/1 for international students; for spring admission, 3/30 priority date for domestic students, 3/1 for international students. Applications are processed on a rolling basis. *Application fee:* $45. Electronic applications accepted. *Application Contact:* Steebo Varghese, Assistant Director of Admissions, 212-343-1234 Ext. 2708, Fax: 212-343-8474, E-mail: svarghese@mcny.edu. *Dean, Graduate School for Public Affairs Administration,* Prof. Humphrey Crookendale, 212-343-1234 Ext. 2209, E-mail: hcrookendale@mcny.edu.

METROPOLITAN STATE UNIVERSITY, St. Paul, MN 55106-5000

General Information State-supported, coed, comprehensive institution. *Graduate housing:* On-campus housing not available.

GRADUATE UNITS

College of Arts and Sciences *Program availability:* Part-time, evening/weekend. Offers computer science (MS); liberal studies (MA); technical communication (MS). Electronic applications accepted.

College of Health, Community and Professional Studies *Program availability:* Part-time. Offers advanced dental therapy (MS); leadership and management (MSN); nurse educator (MSN); nursing (DNP); psychology (MA).

College of Management *Program availability:* Part-time, evening/weekend. Offers business administration (MBA, DBA); database administration (Graduate Certificate); healthcare information technology management (Graduate Certificate); information assurance security (Graduate Certificate); management information systems (MMIS); MIS generalist (Graduate Certificate); MIS systems analysis and design (Graduate Certificate); project management (Graduate Certificate); public and nonprofit administration (MPNA). Electronic applications accepted.

School of Law Enforcement and Criminal Justice *Program availability:* Part-time, evening/weekend. Offers criminal justice (MS). Electronic applications accepted.

METROPOLITAN STATE UNIVERSITY OF DENVER, Denver, CO 80204

General Information State-supported, coed, comprehensive institution. CGS member. *Enrollment:* 20,474 graduate, professional, and undergraduate students; 452 full-time matriculated graduate/professional students (351 women), 68 part-time matriculated graduate/professional students (41 women). *Enrollment by degree level:* 520 master's. *Graduate faculty:* 51 full-time (35 women), 22 part-time/adjunct (19 women). Tuition, state resident: full-time $7568; part-time $420 per credit hour. Tuition, nonresident: full-time $11,873; part-time $660 per credit hour. *Required fees:* $1073. Tuition and fees vary according to program. *Student services:* Campus employment opportunities, campus safety program, career counseling, child daycare facilities, international student services, low-cost health insurance, multicultural affairs office, services for students with disabilities. *Library facilities:* Auraria Library.

Computer facilities: 808 computers available on campus for general student use. A campuswide network can be accessed from off campus. Online class registration is available.
Website: http://www.msudenver.edu/

General Application Contact: Adrienne Perucca, Graduate Admissions Coordinator, 303-352-4147, Fax: 303-556-6345, E-mail: aperucca@msudenver.edu.

GRADUATE UNITS

College of Letters, Arts and Sciences Students: 255 full-time (215 women), 13 part-time (12 women); includes 69 minority (13 Black or African American, non-Hispanic/Latino; 2 American Indian or Alaska Native, non-Hispanic/Latino; 8 Asian, non-Hispanic/Latino; 37 Hispanic/Latino; 2 Native Hawaiian or other Pacific Islander, non-Hispanic/Latino; 7 Two or more races, non-Hispanic/Latino). Average age 33. *Faculty:* 17 full-time (15 women), 20 part-time/adjunct (18 women). Expenses: Contact institution. In 2016, 85 master's awarded. Offers individual and families (MSW); macro practice (MSW); social work (MSW). *Application deadline:* For fall admission, 1/23 for domestic students. *Application fee:* $50. *Application Contact:* Bailee Bannon, Assistant Director, Graduate Program, 303-556-3474, E-mail: bbannon1@msudenver.edu. *Dean,* Dr. Joan Laura Foster, 303-556-4453.

School of Business Students: 76 full-time (41 women), 36 part-time (16 women); includes 22 minority (4 Black or African American, non-Hispanic/Latino; 1 American Indian or Alaska Native, non-Hispanic/Latino; 11 Asian, non-Hispanic/Latino; 6 Hispanic/Latino). Average age 34. *Faculty:* 11 full-time (2 women), 1 (woman) part-time/adjunct. Expenses: Contact institution. In 2016, 38 master's awarded. Offers accounting (MP Acc); fraud exam and forensic auditing (MP Acc); internal audit (MP Acc); public accounting (MP Acc); taxation (MP Acc). *Application deadline:* For fall admission, 6/5 for domestic and international students; for spring admission, 10/2 for domestic and international students. *Application fee:* $50. *Application Contact:* Kim Bernie, Graduate Student Outreach, CBUS Graduate Programs, 303-556-5161, E-mail: kbernie1@msudenver.edu. *Dean,* Ann Murphy, 303-556-4695, E-mail: murphann@msudenver.edu.

School of Education Students: 115 full-time (90 women), 14 part-time (11 women); includes 23 minority (7 Black or African American, non-Hispanic/Latino; 2 American Indian or Alaska Native, non-Hispanic/Latino; 1 Asian, non-Hispanic/Latino; 9 Hispanic/Latino; 4 Two or more races, non-Hispanic/Latino). Average age 32. *Faculty:* 20 full-time (16 women), 1 part-time/adjunct (0 women). Expenses: Contact institution. In 2016, 59 master's awarded. Offers elementary education (MAT); special education (MAT). *Application deadline:* For fall admission, 2/1 for domestic and international students; for spring admission, 10/1 for domestic and international students; for summer admission, 2/1 for domestic and international students. *Application fee:* $50. *Application Contact:* Ellen Sunbury, Graduate Admissions Coordinator, 303-556-6228, E-mail: esunbury@msudenver.edu. *Interim Dean,* Kathy Heyl, 303-556-2978, E-mail: heyl@msudenver.edu.

MGH INSTITUTE OF HEALTH PROFESSIONS, Boston, MA 02129

General Information Independent, coed, primarily women, graduate-only institution. *Graduate housing:* On-campus housing not available. *Research affiliation:* Health and Disability Research Institute, Boston University (efficacy of a post-rehabilitation exercise intervention in patients after hip fracture), Eunice Kennedy Shriver National Institute of Child and Health Development (dyadic intervention for women at risk for postpartum depression and their infants), National Institutes of Health (postnatal parental depression family dynamics in early parenting), Robert Wood Johnson Foundation (mother-infant intervention for the prevention of postpartum depression and associated mother-infant relationship dysfunction), U.S. Department of Defense (robotic nursing assistant to H-star technology), The American Academy of Nursing/John W. Hartford Foundation (building academic geriatric nursing capacity).

GRADUATE UNITS

School of Health and Rehabilitation Sciences *Program availability:* Part-time. Offers health and rehabilitation sciences (MPAS, MS, DPT, OTD, Certificate); occupational therapy (OTD); physical therapy (MS, DPT, Certificate); physician assistant studies (MPAS); reading (Certificate); speech-language pathology (MS). Electronic applications accepted.

School of Nursing Offers advanced practice nursing (MSN); gerontological nursing (MSN); nursing (DNP); pediatric nursing (MSN); psychiatric nursing (MSN); teaching and learning for health care education (Certificate); women's health nursing (MSN). Electronic applications accepted.

MIAMI INTERNATIONAL UNIVERSITY OF ART & DESIGN, Miami, FL 33132-1418

General Information Proprietary, coed, comprehensive institution.

GRADUATE UNITS

Program in Design and Media Management Offers design and media management (MA).

Program in Film *Program availability:* Online learning. Offers film (MFA).

MIAMI REGIONAL UNIVERSITY, Miami Springs, FL 33166

General Information Proprietary, coed, comprehensive institution.

GRADUATE UNITS

School of Nursing and Health Sciences Offers nursing (MSN); nursing education (MSN); nursing leadership (MSN).

MIAMI UNIVERSITY, Oxford, OH 45056

General Information State-related, coed, university. CGS member. *Enrollment:* 19,697 graduate, professional, and undergraduate students; 963 full-time matriculated graduate/professional students (552 women), 1,341 part-time matriculated graduate/professional students (1,014 women). *Enrollment by degree level:* 1,957 master's, 347 doctoral. *Graduate faculty:* 687 full-time (300 women). Tuition, state resident: full-time $12,890; part-time $564 per credit hour. Tuition, nonresident: full-time $29,604; part-time $1260 per credit hour. *Required fees:* $638. Part-time tuition and fees vary according to course load and program. *Graduate housing:* Rooms and/or apartments available on a first-come, first-served basis to single and married students. *Student services:* Campus employment opportunities, campus safety program, career counseling, child daycare facilities, exercise/wellness program, free psychological counseling, grant writing training, international student services, low-cost health insurance, multicultural affairs office, services for students with disabilities, teacher training, writing training. *Library facilities:* King Library plus 3 others. *Collection:* Books: 2.4 million (physical), 658,343 (digital/electronic); Serial titles: 1,019 (physical), 25,772 (digital/electronic); Databases: 743. Weekly public service hours: 168; study areas open 24 hours, 5–7 days a week; students can reserve study rooms.

Computer facilities: Computer purchase and lease plans are available. A campuswide network can be accessed from student residence rooms and from off campus. Online class registration is available.
Website: http://miamioh.edu/

General Application Contact: Graduate Admission Coordinator, 513-529-3734, E-mail: applygrad@miamioh.edu.

GRADUATE UNITS

College of Arts and Science Expenses: Contact institution. *Program availability:* Part-time. Offers arts and science (M Env, MA, MAT, MGS, MPSG, MS, MS Stat, PhD); biology (MA, MAT, MS, PhD); chemistry and biochemistry (MS, PhD); English (MA, MAT, PhD); French (MA); geography (MA); geology (MA, MS, PhD); gerontology (MGS); history (MA); mathematics (MA, MAT, MS); microbiology (MS, PhD); philosophy (MA); physics (MS); political science (MA); population and social gerontology (MPSG); psychology (MA, PhD); social gerontology (PhD); speech pathology and audiology (MA, MS); statistics (MS Stat). *Application Contact:* Admission Coordinator, 513-529-3734, E-mail: applygrad@miamioh.edu. *Dean,* Dr. Chris Makaroff, 513-529-1234, E-mail: cas@miamioh.edu.

College of Creative Arts Expenses: Contact institution. Offers architecture and interior design (M Arch); art education (MA); creative arts (M Arch, MA, MFA, MM); music education (MM); music performance (MM); studio art (MFA); theatre (MA). *Application Contact:* Graduate Admission Coordinator, 513-529-3734, E-mail: applygrad@miamioh.edu. *Dean,* Dr. Liz Mullenix, 513-529-6010, E-mail: cca@miamioh.edu.

College of Education, Health and Society Expenses: Contact institution. Offers education, health and society (M Ed, MA, MAT, MS, Ed D, PhD, Ed S); educational leadership (M Ed, MS, Ed D, PhD); educational psychology (M Ed, MA, MS, Ed S); family studies and social work (MA); kinesiology and health (MS); teacher education (M Ed, MAT). *Application Contact:* Graduate Admission Coordinator, 513-529-3734, E-mail: applygrad@miamioh.edu. *Dean,* Dr. Michael Dantley, 513-529-6317, E-mail: ehs@miamioh.edu.

College of Engineering and Computing Expenses: Contact institution. Offers chemical, paper and biomedical engineering (MS); computer science (MCS); electrical and computer engineering (MS); engineering and computing (MCS, MS); mechanical and manufacturing engineering (MS). *Application Contact:* Graduate Admission Coordinator, 513-529-3734, E-mail: applygrad@miamioh.edu. *Dean,* Dr. Marek Dollar, 513-529-0700, E-mail: cec@miamioh.edu.

Farmer School of Business Expenses: Contact institution. Offers accountancy (M Acc); business (M Acc, MA, MBA); business administration (MBA); economics (MA). *Application Contact:* Admission Coordinator, 513-529-3734, E-mail: applygrad@miamioh.edu. *Dean/Chair of Business Leadership,* Dr. Matthew Myers, 513-529-3631, E-mail: deanofbusiness@miamioh.edu.

Institute for the Environment and Sustainability Students: 31 full-time (18 women), 18 part-time (10 women); includes 4 minority (1 American Indian or Alaska Native, non-Hispanic/Latino; 2 Hispanic/Latino; 1 Two or more races, non-Hispanic/Latino), 4 international. Average age 27. Expenses: Contact institution. In 2016, 9 master's awarded. Offers environment and sustainability (M Env). Electronic applications accepted. *Application Contact:* 513-529-5811, E-mail: ies@miamioh.edu. *Director/Associate Professor of Geology and Environmental Earth Science,* Dr. Jonathan Levy, 513-529-1947, E-mail: levyj@miamioh.edu.

MICHIGAN SCHOOL OF PROFESSIONAL PSYCHOLOGY, Farmington Hills, MI 48334

General Information Independent, coed, graduate-only institution. *Enrollment by degree level:* 70 master's, 70 doctoral. *Graduate faculty:* 8 full-time (4 women), 13 part-time/adjunct (11 women). *Tuition:* Full-time $21,405; part-time $15,000 per year. *Required fees:* $725; $460 per semester. One-time fee: $75. Tuition and fees vary according to course load, degree level and program. *Graduate housing:* On-campus housing not available. *Student services:* Campus employment opportunities, campus safety program, international student services, multicultural affairs office, services for students with disabilities, writing training. *Library facilities:* Moustakas Johnson Library plus 1 other. *Collection:* Books: 7,247 (physical), 4,299 (digital/electronic); Serial titles: 2 (physical); Databases: 70. Weekly public service hours: 47.

Computer facilities: 16 computers available on campus for general student use. A campuswide network can be accessed.
Website: http://www.mispp.edu/

General Application Contact: Carrie Hauser, Coordinator of Admissions and Student Engagement, 248-476-1122 Ext. 117, Fax: 248-476-1125, E-mail: chauser@mispp.edu.

GRADUATE UNITS

MA and Psy D Programs in Clinical Psychology Students: 84 full-time (66 women), 56 part-time (46 women); includes 42 minority (29 Black or African American, non-Hispanic/Latino; 2 Asian, non-Hispanic/Latino; 5 Hispanic/Latino; 6 Two or more races, non-Hispanic/Latino), 1 international. Average age 34. 155 applicants, 54% accepted, 61 enrolled. *Faculty:* 8 full-time (4 women), 13 part-time/adjunct (11 women). Expenses: Contact institution. *Financial support:* In 2016–17, 6 students received support, including 1 research assistantship, 5 teaching assistantships (averaging $14,436 per year); institutionally sponsored loans, scholarships/grants, and unspecified assistantships also available. Financial award application deadline: 8/30; financial award applicants required to submit FAFSA. In 2016, 42 master's, 17 doctorates awarded. *Program availability:* Part-time. Offers clinical psychology (MA, Psy D). *Application deadline:* For fall admission, 8/15 for domestic students; for winter admission, 12/1 for domestic students; for spring admission, 4/3 for domestic students. Applications are processed on a rolling basis. *Application fee:* $75. Electronic applications accepted. *Application Contact:* Carrie Hauser, Coordinator of Admissions and Student Engagement, 248-476-1122 Ext. 117, Fax: 248-476-1125, E-mail: chauser@mispp.edu. *Program Director,* Dr. Frances Brown, 248-476-1122, Fax: 248-476-1125.

MICHIGAN STATE UNIVERSITY, East Lansing, MI 48824

General Information State-supported, coed, university. CGS member. *Graduate housing:* Rooms and/or apartments available on a first-come, first-served basis to single and married students. *Research affiliation:* Argonne National Laboratory (high-energy physics and structural biology), Association of Sea Grant Programs (fresh water ecosystems), Fraunhofer Center (manufacturing), Michigan Economic Development Corporation (life sciences, homeland security, automotive technologies), Oak Ridge Associated Universities (scientific research and education), Southern Astrophysical Research (SOAR) Telescope (astronomy).

GRADUATE UNITS

College of Human Medicine Offers biochemistry and molecular biology (MS, PhD); epidemiology (MS, PhD); human medicine (MD); human medicine/medical scientist training program (MD); microbiology (MS); microbiology and molecular genetics (PhD); pharmacology and toxicology (MS, PhD); physiology (MS, PhD); public health (MPH).

College of Osteopathic Medicine Offers biochemistry and molecular biology (MS, PhD); integrative pharmacology (MS); microbiology (MS); microbiology and molecular genetics (PhD); osteopathic medicine (MS, DO, PhD); pharmacology and toxicology (MS, PhD); pharmacology and toxicology-environmental toxicology (PhD); physiology (MS, PhD).

College of Veterinary Medicine Offers animal science–environmental toxicology (PhD); biochemistry and molecular biology–environmental toxicology (PhD); chemistry–environmental toxicology (PhD); comparative medicine and integrative biology (MS, PhD); comparative medicine and integrative biology–environmental toxicology (PhD); crop and soil sciences–environmental toxicology (PhD); environmental engineering–environmental toxicology (PhD); environmental geosciences–environmental toxicology (PhD); fisheries and wildlife–environmental toxicology (PhD); food safety (MS); food safety and toxicology (MS); food science–environmental toxicology (PhD); forestry–environmental toxicology (PhD); genetics–environmental toxicology (PhD); human nutrition–environmental toxicology (PhD); industrial microbiology (MS, PhD); integrative toxicology (PhD); large animal clinical sciences (MS); microbiology (MS, PhD); microbiology and molecular genetics (MS, PhD); microbiology–environmental toxicology (PhD); pathobiology and diagnostic investigation (MS, PhD); pathology (MS, PhD); pathology–environmental toxicology (PhD); pharmacology and toxicology (MS, PhD); pharmacology and toxicology–environmental toxicology (PhD); physiology (MS, PhD); small animal clinical sciences (MS); veterinary medicine (DVM); veterinary medicine/medical scientist training program (DVM); zoology–environmental toxicology (PhD).

The Graduate School *Program availability:* Part-time, evening/weekend, online learning. Electronic applications accepted.

College of Agriculture and Natural Resources Offers agricultural economics (MS, PhD); agricultural, food, and resource economics (MS, PhD); agriculture and natural resources (MA, MIPS, MS, MURP, PhD); animal science (MS, PhD); animal science–environmental toxicology (PhD); biochemistry and molecular biology (PhD); biosystems engineering (MS, PhD); cellular and molecular biology (PhD); community, agriculture, recreation, and resource studies (MS, PhD); construction management (MS, PhD); crop and soil sciences (MS, PhD); crop and soil sciences-environmental toxicology (PhD); entomology (MS, PhD); environmental design (MA); fisheries and wildlife (MS, PhD); fisheries and wildlife - environmental toxicology (PhD); food science (MS, PhD); food science - environmental toxicology (PhD); forestry (MS, PhD); forestry-environmental toxicology (PhD); genetics (PhD); horticulture (MS, PhD); human nutrition (MS, PhD); human nutrition-environmental toxicology (PhD); integrated pest management (MS); interior design and facilities management (MA); international planning studies (MIPS); microbiology and molecular genetics (PhD); packaging (MS, PhD); plant biology (PhD); plant breeding and genetics (MS, PhD); plant breeding and genetics-crop and soil sciences (MS); plant breeding, genetics and biotechnology-crop and soil sciences (PhD); plant breeding, genetics and biotechnology-forestry (MS, PhD); plant breeding, genetics and biotechnology-horticulture (MS, PhD); plant pathology (MS, PhD); plant physiology (PhD); urban and regional planning (MURP).

College of Arts and Letters Offers African American and African studies (MA, PhD); American studies (MA, PhD); applied Spanish linguistics (MA); arts and letters (MA, MFA, PhD); critical studies in literacy and pedagogy (MA); digital rhetoric and professional writing (MA); English (PhD); French (MA); French language and literature (PhD); German studies (MA, PhD); Hispanic cultural studies (PhD); Hispanic literatures (MA); linguistics (MA, PhD); literature in English (MA); philosophy (MA, PhD); rhetoric and writing (PhD); second language studies (PhD); studio art (MFA); teaching English to speakers of other languages (MA); theatre (MA, MFA). Electronic applications accepted.

College of Communication Arts and Sciences Offers advertising (MA); communication (MA, PhD); communication arts and sciences (MA, MS, PhD); communication arts and sciences–media and information studies (PhD); communicative sciences and disorders (MA, PhD); digital media arts and technology (MA); health communication (MA); information and telecommunication management (MA); information, policy and society (MA); journalism (MA); public relations (MA); retailing (MS); serious game design (MA).

College of Education Offers counseling (MA); curriculum, instruction and teacher education (PhD, Ed S); education (MA, MS, PhD, Ed S); educational policy (PhD); educational psychology and educational technology (PhD); educational technology (MA); higher, adult and lifelong education (MA, PhD); K–12 educational administration (MA, PhD, Ed S); kinesiology (MS, PhD); literacy instruction (MA); measurement and quantitative methods (PhD); rehabilitation counseling (MA); rehabilitation counselor

education (PhD); school psychology (MA, PhD, Ed S); special education (MA, PhD); student affairs administration (MA); teaching and curriculum (MA). Electronic applications accepted.

College of Engineering *Program availability:* Part-time. Offers chemical engineering (MS, PhD); civil engineering (MS, PhD); computer science (MS, PhD); electrical engineering (MS, PhD); engineering (MS, PhD); engineering mechanics (MS, PhD); environmental engineering (MS, PhD); environmental engineering-environmental toxicology (PhD); materials science and engineering (MS, PhD); mechanical engineering (MS, PhD). Electronic applications accepted.

College of Music Offers collaborative piano (M Mus); jazz studies (M Mus); music (PhD); music composition (M Mus, DMA); music conducting (M Mus, DMA); music education (M Mus); music performance (M Mus, DMA); music theory (M Mus); music therapy (M Mus); musicology (MA); piano pedagogy (M Mus). Electronic applications accepted.

College of Natural Science Offers applied mathematics (MS, PhD); applied statistics (MS); astrophysics and astronomy (MS, PhD); biochemistry and molecular biology (MS, PhD); biochemistry and molecular biology/environmental toxicology (PhD); biological, physical and general science for teachers (MAT, MS); biomedical laboratory operations (MS); cell and molecular biology (MS, PhD); cell and molecular biology/environmental toxicology (PhD); chemical physics (PhD); chemistry (MS, PhD); chemistry-environmental toxicology (PhD); clinical laboratory sciences (MS); computational chemistry (MS); ecology, evolutionary biology and behavior (PhD); environmental geosciences (MS, PhD); environmental geosciences-environmental toxicology (PhD); genetics (MS, PhD); genetics–environmental toxicology (PhD); geological sciences (MS, PhD); industrial mathematics (MS); mathematics (MAT, MS, PhD); mathematics education (MS, PhD); natural science (MAT, MS, PhD); neuroscience (MS, PhD); physics (MS, PhD); physiology (MS, PhD); plant biology (MS, PhD); plant breeding, genetics and biotechnology - plant biology (MS, PhD); quantitative biology (PhD); statistics (MS, PhD); zoo and aquarium management (MS); zoology (MS, PhD); zoology-environmental toxicology (PhD). Electronic applications accepted.

College of Nursing *Program availability:* Part-time, online learning. Offers nursing (MSN, PhD). Electronic applications accepted.

College of Social Science Offers anthropology (MA, PhD); Chicano/Latino studies (PhD); child development (MA); clinical social work (MSW); community services (MS); criminal justice (MS, PhD); economics (MA); family and child ecology (PhD); family studies (MA); forensic science (MS); geographic information science (MS); geography (MS, PhD); history (MA, PhD); history-secondary school teaching (MA); human resources and labor relations (MLRHR); industrial relations and human resources (PhD); law enforcement intelligence and analysis (MS); marriage and family therapy (MA); organizational and community practice (MSW); political science (MA, PhD); professional applications in anthropology (MA); psychology (MA, PhD); public policy (MPP); social science (MA, MIPS, MLRHR, MPP, MS, MSW, MURP, PhD); social work (PhD); sociology (MA, PhD); youth development (MA). Electronic applications accepted.

Eli Broad College of Business *Program availability:* Evening/weekend. Offers accounting (MS, PhD); business (MBA, MS, PhD); business analytics (MS); business information systems (PhD); finance (MS, PhD); foodservice business management (MS); hospitality business management (MS); human resource management (MBA); integrative management (MBA); logistics (PhD); management (PhD); management, strategy, and leadership (MS); marketing (MBA, PhD); marketing research (MS); operations and sourcing management (PhD); supply chain management (MBA, MS). Electronic applications accepted.

National Superconducting Cyclotron Laboratory Offers chemistry (PhD); physics (PhD).

MICHIGAN STATE UNIVERSITY COLLEGE OF LAW, East Lansing, MI 48824-1300

General Information Independent, coed, graduate-only institution. *Enrollment by degree level:* 86 master's, 760 doctoral. *Graduate faculty:* 52 full-time (22 women), 74 part-time/adjunct (17 women). *Graduate housing:* Rooms and/or apartments available on a first-come, first-served basis to single and married students. Housing application deadline: 4/1. *Student services:* Campus employment opportunities, campus safety program, career counseling, exercise/wellness program, international student services, low-cost health insurance, multicultural affairs office, services for students with disabilities, writing training. *Library facilities:* John F. Schaefer Law Library plus 5 others. *Collection:* Books: 43,813 (physical), 40,255 (digital/electronic); Serial titles: 4,421 (physical), 14,667 (digital/electronic); Databases: 32. Weekly public service hours: 71; students can reserve study rooms.

Computer facilities: 100 computers available on campus for general student use. A campuswide network can be accessed from student residence rooms. Online class registration is available.
Website: http://www.law.msu.edu/

General Application Contact: Charles Roboski, Assistant Dean of Admissions, 517-432-0222, Fax: 517-432-0098, E-mail: roboski@law.msu.edu.

GRADUATE UNITS

Professional Program Students: 723 full-time (362 women), 123 part-time (70 women); includes 173 minority (57 Black or African American, non-Hispanic/Latino; 9 American Indian or Alaska Native, non-Hispanic/Latino; 28 Asian, non-Hispanic/Latino; 40 Hispanic/Latino; 2 Native Hawaiian or other Pacific Islander, non-Hispanic/Latino; 37 Two or more races, non-Hispanic/Latino), 91 international. Average age 24. 2,362 applicants, 45% accepted, 259 enrolled. *Faculty:* 55 full-time (22 women), 85 part-time/adjunct (32 women). Expenses: Contact institution. *Financial support:* In 2016–17, 559 students received support. Career-related internships or fieldwork, Federal Work-Study, scholarships/grants, and tuition waivers (full and partial) available. Support available to part-time students. Financial award application deadline: 4/1; financial award applicants required to submit FAFSA. In 2016, 45 master's, 265 doctorates awarded. *Program availability:* Part-time. Offers American legal system (LL M, MJ); global food law (LL M, MJ); intellectual property (LL M, MJ); law (JD); legal doctrine and analysis (MJ). *Application deadline:* For fall admission, 4/30 priority date for domestic students, 7/1 priority date for international students. Applications are processed on a rolling basis. *Application fee:* $60. Electronic applications accepted. *Application Contact:* Charles Roboski, Assistant Dean of Admissions, 517-432-0222, Fax: 517-432-0098, E-mail: roboski@law.msu.edu. *Dean/Professor of Law,* Lawrence Ponoroff, 517-432-6993, Fax: 517-432-6801, E-mail: lponoroff@law.msu.edu.

MICHIGAN TECHNOLOGICAL UNIVERSITY, Houghton, MI 49931

General Information State-supported, coed, university. CGS member. *Enrollment:* 7,270 graduate, professional, and undergraduate students; 1,098 full-time matriculated graduate/professional students (284 women), 322 part-time matriculated graduate/professional students (92 women). *Enrollment by degree level:* 904 master's, 514 doctoral, 2 other advanced degrees. *Graduate faculty:* 520 full-time (134 women), 289 part-time/adjunct (47 women). Tuition, state resident: full-time $16,290; part-time $905 per credit. Tuition, nonresident: full-time $16,290; part-time $905 per credit. *Required fees:* $248; $124 per term. Tuition and fees vary according to course load and program. *Graduate housing:* Rooms and/or apartments available on a first-come, first-served basis to single and married students. Typical cost: $5970 per year ($10,465 including board) for single students; $5970 per year ($10,465 including board) for married students. Room and board charges vary according to board plan and housing facility selected. *Student services:* Campus employment opportunities, campus safety program, career counseling, child daycare facilities, exercise/wellness program, free psychological counseling, grant writing training, international student services, low-cost health insurance, multicultural affairs office, services for students with disabilities, teacher training, writing training. *Library facilities:* J. R. Van Pelt and John and Ruanne Opie Library. *Collection:* Books: 478,976 (physical), 133,000 (digital/electronic); Databases: 152. Weekly public service hours: 119; study areas open 24 hours, 5–7 days a week; students can reserve study rooms. *Research affiliation:* E3 Spark Plugs (automotive technology and design), IR Telemetrics (automotive technology and design), Nostrum Energy, LLC (control system design), ACG Materials (materials testing), MAHLE Powertrain LLC (control system design), General Motors Holdings LLC (vehicle engine research).

Computer facilities: 1,079 computers available on campus for general student use. A campuswide network can be accessed from student residence rooms and from off campus. Online class registration is available.
Website: http://www.mtu.edu/

General Application Contact: Carol T. Wingerson, Administrative Aide, 906-487-2328, Fax: 906-487-2284, E-mail: gradadms@mtu.edu.

GRADUATE UNITS

Graduate School Students: 1,098 full-time (284 women), 322 part-time (92 women); includes 62 minority (15 Black or African American, non-Hispanic/Latino; 3 American Indian or Alaska Native, non-Hispanic/Latino; 10 Asian, non-Hispanic/Latino; 16 Hispanic/Latino; 18 Two or more races, non-Hispanic/Latino; 873 international. Average age 28. 5,213 applicants, 24% accepted, 383 enrolled. *Faculty:* 520 full-time (134 women), 289 part-time/adjunct (47 women). *Expenses:* Contact institution. *Financial support:* In 2016–17, 969 students received support, including 73 fellowships with tuition reimbursements available (averaging $15,242 per year), 198 research assistantships with tuition reimbursements available (averaging $15,242 per year), 223 teaching assistantships with tuition reimbursements available (averaging $15,242 per year); career-related internships or fieldwork, Federal Work-Study, scholarships/grants, traineeships, health care benefits, unspecified assistantships, and cooperative program also available. Financial award applicants required to submit FAFSA. In 2016, 416 master's, 86 doctorates, 71 other advanced degrees awarded. *Program availability:* Part-time, 100% online, blended/hybrid learning. Offers atmospheric sciences (PhD); biochemistry and molecular biology (PhD); computational science and engineering (PhD); data science (MS, Graduate Certificate); engineering (M Eng); environmental engineering (PhD); international profile (Graduate Certificate); nanotechnology (Graduate Certificate); sustainability (Graduate Certificate); sustainable water resources systems (Graduate Certificate). *Application deadline:* Applications are processed on a rolling basis. Electronic applications accepted. *Application Contact:* Carol T. Wingerson, Administrative Aide, 906-487-2328, Fax: 906-487-2284, E-mail: gradadms@mtu.edu. *Dean of the Graduate School/Associate Provost for Graduate Education,* Dr. Pushpalatha Murthy, 906-487-3007, Fax: 906-487-2284, E-mail: pprmurthy@mtu.edu.

College of Engineering Students: 730 full-time (134 women), 184 part-time (37 women); includes 39 minority (7 Black or African American, non-Hispanic/Latino; 9 Asian, non-Hispanic/Latino; 14 Hispanic/Latino; 9 Two or more races, non-Hispanic/Latino; 651 international. Average age 27. 3,452 applicants, 25% accepted, 244 enrolled. *Expenses:* Contact institution. *Financial support:* In 2016–17, 614 students received support, including 38 fellowships with tuition reimbursements available (averaging $15,242 per year), 114 research assistantships with tuition reimbursements available (averaging $15,242 per year), 86 teaching assistantships with tuition reimbursements available (averaging $15,242 per year); career-related internships or fieldwork, Federal Work-Study, scholarships/grants, health care benefits, unspecified assistantships, and cooperative program also available. Financial award applicants required to submit FAFSA. In 2016, 295 master's, 34 doctorates, 63 other advanced degrees awarded. *Program availability:* Part-time, 100% online, blended/hybrid learning. Offers advanced electric power engineering (Graduate Certificate); automotive systems and controls (Graduate Certificate); biomedical engineering (MS, PhD); chemical engineering (MS, PhD); civil engineering (MS, PhD); computer engineering (MS, PhD); electrical engineering (MS, PhD); engineering (MS, PhD, Graduate Certificate); engineering mechanics (MS); environmental engineering (MS, PhD); environmental engineering science (MS); geological engineering (MS, PhD); geology (MS, PhD); geophysics (MS, PhD); hybrid electric drive vehicle engineering (Graduate Certificate); materials science and engineering (MS, PhD); mechanical engineering (MS); mechanical engineering-engineering mechanics (PhD); mining engineering (MS, PhD). *Application deadline:* Applications are processed on a rolling basis. Electronic applications accepted. *Application Contact:* Carol T. Wingerson, Administrative Aide, 906-487-2328, Fax: 906-487-2284, E-mail: gradadms@mtu.edu. *Dean,* Dr. Wayne D. Pennington, 906-487-2005, Fax: 906-487-2782, E-mail: wayne@mtu.edu.

College of Sciences and Arts Students: 231 full-time (98 women), 71 part-time (29 women); includes 15 minority (5 Black or African American, non-Hispanic/Latino; 2 American Indian or Alaska Native, non-Hispanic/Latino; 1 Hispanic/Latino; 7 Two or more races, non-Hispanic/Latino; 132 international. Average age 31. 1,096 applicants, 19% accepted, 79 enrolled. *Faculty:* 257 full-time (89 women), 84 part-time/adjunct (17 women). *Expenses:* Contact institution. *Financial support:* In 2016–17, 231 students received support, including 23 fellowships with tuition reimbursements available (averaging $15,242 per year), 46 research assistantships with tuition reimbursements available (averaging $15,242 per year), 124 teaching assistantships with tuition reimbursements available (averaging $15,242 per year); career-related internships or fieldwork, Federal Work-Study, scholarships/grants, traineeships, health care benefits, unspecified assistantships, and cooperative program also available. Financial award applicants required to submit FAFSA. In 2016, 65 master's, 37 doctorates awarded. *Program availability:* Part-time, blended/hybrid learning. Offers applied cognitive science and human factors (MS, PhD); applied physics (MS, PhD); applied science education (MS); biological sciences (MS, PhD); chemistry (MS, PhD); computational science and engineering (PhD); computer science (MS, PhD); cybersecurity (MS); environmental and energy policy (MS, PhD); industrial archaeology (MS); industrial heritage and archaeology (PhD);

kinesiology (MS); mathematics (MS, PhD); physics (MS, PhD); post-secondary STEM education (Graduate Certificate); rhetoric, theory and culture (MS, PhD); sciences and arts (MS, PhD, Graduate Certificate). *Application deadline:* For fall admission, 4/1 for domestic and international students; for spring admission, 9/1 for domestic and international students. Applications are processed on a rolling basis. Electronic applications accepted. *Application Contact:* Carol T. Wingerson, Administrative Aide, 906-487-2328, Fax: 906-487-2284, E-mail: gradadms@mtu.edu. *Dean,* Dr. Bruce E. Seely, 906-487-2156, Fax: 906-487-3347, E-mail: bseely@mtu.edu.

School of Business and Economics Students: 18 full-time (8 women), 23 part-time (12 women); includes 3 minority (1 Black or African American, non-Hispanic/Latino; 1 Asian, non-Hispanic/Latino; 1 Hispanic/Latino), 10 international. Average age 29. 122 applicants, 30% accepted, 16 enrolled. *Faculty:* 23 full-time (7 women), 1 part-time/adjunct. *Expenses:* Contact institution. *Financial support:* In 2016–17, 13 students received support. Health care benefits and unspecified assistantships available. Financial award application deadline: 2/1; financial award applicants required to submit FAFSA. In 2016, 27 master's awarded. *Program availability:* Part-time, evening/weekend. Offers accounting (MS); applied natural resource economics (MS); business administration (MBA). *Application deadline:* For fall admission, 7/1 for domestic and international students; for spring admission, 12/1 for domestic and international students. Applications are processed on a rolling basis. Electronic applications accepted. *Application Contact:* Carol T. Wingerson, Administrative Aide, 906-487-2328, Fax: 906-487-2284, E-mail: gradadms@mtu.edu. *Dean,* Dr. Dean Johnson, 906-487-2668, Fax: 906-487-1863, E-mail: dean@mtu.edu.

School of Forest Resources and Environmental Science Students: 50 full-time (20 women), 18 part-time (5 women); includes 1 minority (Two or more races, non-Hispanic/Latino), 16 international. Average age 31. 95 applicants, 28% accepted, 15 enrolled. *Faculty:* 44 full-time (12 women), 55 part-time/adjunct (17 women). *Expenses:* Contact institution. *Financial support:* In 2016–17, 51 students received support, including 4 fellowships with tuition reimbursements available (averaging $15,242 per year), 18 research assistantships with tuition reimbursements available (averaging $15,242 per year), 5 teaching assistantships with tuition reimbursements available (averaging $15,242 per year); career-related internships or fieldwork, Federal Work-Study, scholarships/grants, health care benefits, unspecified assistantships, and cooperative program also available. Financial award applicants required to submit FAFSA. In 2016, 20 master's, 8 doctorates awarded. *Program availability:* Part-time. Offers applied ecology (MS); forest molecular genetics and biotechnology (MS, PhD); forest resources and environmental science (MF, MGIS); forest science (PhD); forestry (MS); forestry ecology and management (MS). *Application deadline:* Applications are processed on a rolling basis. Electronic applications accepted. *Application Contact:* Dr. Andrew J. Storer, Associate Dean, 906-487-3470, Fax: 906-487-2915, E-mail: storer@mtu.edu. *Dean,* Dr. Terry Sharik, 906-487-2352, Fax: 906-487-2915, E-mail: tlsharik@mtu.edu.

School of Technology Students: 11 full-time (6 women), 9 part-time (4 women); includes 2 minority (1 Black or African American, non-Hispanic/Latino; 1 American Indian or Alaska Native, non-Hispanic/Latino), 8 international. Average age 36. 53 applicants, 43% accepted, 7 enrolled. *Faculty:* 26 full-time, 4 part-time/adjunct. *Expenses:* Contact institution. *Financial support:* In 2016–17, 6 students received support, including 1 research assistantship (averaging $15,242 per year); career-related internships or fieldwork, Federal Work-Study, scholarships/grants, and health care benefits also available. Financial award applicants required to submit FAFSA. In 2016, 6 master's awarded. *Program availability:* Part-time, 100% online, blended/hybrid learning. Offers integrated geospatial technology (MS); medical informatics (MS). *Application deadline:* Applications are processed on a rolling basis. Electronic applications accepted. *Application Contact:* Peggy A. Gorton, Executive Assistant, 906-487-2260, E-mail: pagorton@mtu.edu. *Dean,* Dr. James O. Frendewey, 906-487-2260, Fax: 906-487-2583, E-mail: jimf@mtu.edu.

MID-AMERICA BAPTIST THEOLOGICAL SEMINARY, Cordova, TN 38016

General Information Independent-religious, men only, comprehensive institution. *Graduate housing:* Rooms and/or apartments available on a first-come, first-served basis to single and married students.

GRADUATE UNITS

Graduate and Professional Programs Offers theology (M Div, MACE, MCE, MM, D Min, PhD). Electronic applications accepted.

MID-AMERICA BAPTIST THEOLOGICAL SEMINARY NORTHEAST BRANCH, Schenectady, NY 12303-3463

General Information Independent-religious, coed, primarily men, graduate-only institution. *Graduate housing:* Rooms and/or apartments available on a first-come, first-served basis to single and married students.

GRADUATE UNITS

Program in Theology *Program availability:* Part-time, evening/weekend. Offers theology (M Div). Electronic applications accepted.

MID-AMERICA CHRISTIAN UNIVERSITY, Oklahoma City, OK 73170-4504

General Information Independent-religious, coed, comprehensive institution.

GRADUATE UNITS

Program in Business Administration Offers business administration (MBA).

Program in Counseling Offers marital and family therapy (MS); pastoral/spiritual direction (MS); professional counselor (MS).

Program in Leadership Offers leadership (MA).

Program in Public Administration Offers public administration (MA).

MIDAMERICA NAZARENE UNIVERSITY, Olathe, KS 66062-1899

General Information Independent-religious, coed, comprehensive institution. *Enrollment:* 1,876 graduate, professional, and undergraduate students; 151 full-time matriculated graduate/professional students (124 women), 362 part-time matriculated graduate/professional students (291 women). *Enrollment by degree level:* 466 master's, 47 other advanced degrees. *Graduate faculty:* 29 full-time (16 women), 47 part-time/adjunct (24 women). Tuition and fees vary according to program. *Graduate housing:* On-campus housing not available. *Student services:* Campus employment opportunities, campus safety program, career counseling, free psychological counseling, international student services, multicultural affairs office, services for students with disabilities, teacher training. *Library facilities:* Mabee Library. *Collection:* Books: 88,000 (physical), 249,000 (digital/electronic); Serial titles: 397 (physical), 25 (digital/electronic); Databases: 35. Weekly public service hours: 81; study areas open 24 hours, 5–7 days a week; students can reserve study rooms.

Computer facilities: 85 computers available on campus for general student use. A campuswide network can be accessed from student residence rooms and from off campus. Online class registration is available.
Website: http://www.mnu.edu/

General Application Contact: E-mail: pgadmissions@mnu.edu.

GRADUATE UNITS

Professional and Graduate Studies in Education Students: 22 full-time (16 women), 43 part-time (38 women); includes 6 minority (3 Black or African American, non-Hispanic/Latino; 1 Asian, non-Hispanic/Latino; 2 Two or more races, non-Hispanic/Latino). Average age 32. 18 applicants, 22% accepted, 2 enrolled. *Faculty:* 5 full-time (3 women), 12 part-time/adjunct (7 women). Expenses: Contact institution. *Financial support:* Scholarships/grants available. Financial award applicants required to submit FAFSA. In 2016, 41 master's awarded. *Program availability:* Part-time, evening/weekend, online only, 100% online. Offers ESOL (M Ed); reading specialist (M Ed); technology enhanced teaching (M Ed). *Application deadline:* For fall admission, 8/6 for domestic students; for spring admission, 12/15 for domestic students; for summer admission, 5/7 for domestic students. Applications are processed on a rolling basis. Electronic applications accepted. *Application Contact:* Glenna Murray, Administrative Assistant, 913-971-3292, Fax: 913-971-3002, E-mail: gkmurray@mnu.edu. *Chair,* Dr. Ramona Stowe, 913-971-3524, Fax: 913-791-3407, E-mail: rsstowe@mnu.edu.

School of Behavioral Sciences and Counseling Students: 109 full-time (92 women), 100 part-time (87 women); includes 39 minority (21 Black or African American, non-Hispanic/Latino; 3 Asian, non-Hispanic/Latino; 5 Hispanic/Latino; 1 Native Hawaiian or other Pacific Islander, non-Hispanic/Latino; 9 Two or more races, non-Hispanic/Latino). 97 applicants, 79% accepted, 61 enrolled. *Faculty:* 10 full-time (4 women), 13 part-time/adjunct (9 women). Expenses: Contact institution. *Financial support:* Applicants required to submit FAFSA. In 2016, 55 master's awarded. *Program availability:* Evening/weekend. Offers counseling (MA). *Application deadline:* For winter admission, 2/15 for domestic and international students; for spring admission, 4/1 for domestic and international students. Electronic applications accepted. *Application Contact:* Jean Blades, Administrative Assistant, 913-971-3730, E-mail: jmblades@mnu.edu. *Dean, School of Behavioral Sciences and Counseling,* Dr. Todd Frye, 913-971-3449, Fax: 913-971-3402, E-mail: tmfrye@mnu.edu.

School of Business Students: 3 full-time (1 woman), 106 part-time (55 women); includes 32 minority (21 Black or African American, non-Hispanic/Latino; 1 Asian, non-Hispanic/Latino; 3 Hispanic/Latino; 7 Two or more races, non-Hispanic/Latino). Average age 30. 54 applicants, 100% accepted, 52 enrolled. *Faculty:* 7 full-time (2 women), 17 part-time/adjunct (5 women). Expenses: Contact institution. *Financial support:* Scholarships/grants and unspecified assistantships available. Financial award applicants required to submit FAFSA. In 2016, 50 master's awarded. *Program availability:* Part-time, evening/weekend, 100% online, blended/hybrid learning. Offers management (MBA, MSM). *Application deadline:* Applications are processed on a rolling basis. Electronic applications accepted. *Application Contact:* Piper Childs, Director of School of Professional and Graduate Studies Enrollment Services, 913-971-3804, E-mail: pmchilds@mnu.edu. *Professor and Chair, Graduate Studies in Management,* Dr. Graydon Dawson, 913-971-3873, Fax: 913-791-3409, E-mail: rgdawson@mnu.edu.

School of Nursing and Health Science Students: 17 full-time (15 women), 111 part-time (109 women); includes 21 minority (14 Black or African American, non-Hispanic/Latino; 1 American Indian or Alaska Native, non-Hispanic/Latino; 2 Asian, non-Hispanic/Latino; 2 Hispanic/Latino; 2 Two or more races, non-Hispanic/Latino). Average age 38. 62 applicants, 50% accepted, 18 enrolled. *Faculty:* 7 full-time (all women), 5 part-time/adjunct (3 women). Expenses: Contact institution. *Financial support:* Unspecified assistantships available. Financial award applicants required to submit FAFSA. In 2016, 23 master's awarded. *Program availability:* Part-time, evening/weekend, 100% online, blended/hybrid learning. Offers healthcare administration (MSN); healthcare quality management (MSN); nursing education (MSN); public health (MSN). *Application deadline:* Applications are processed on a rolling basis. Electronic applications accepted. *Application Contact:* pgadmissions@mnu.edu. *Dean,* Dr. Karen Wiegman, 913-971-3839, E-mail: kdwiegman@mnu.edu.

MID-AMERICA REFORMED SEMINARY, Dyer, IN 46311

General Information Independent-religious, men only, graduate-only institution.

GRADUATE UNITS

Graduate Programs Offers theology (M Div, MTS).

MIDDLEBURY COLLEGE, Middlebury, VT 05753-6002

General Information Independent, coed, comprehensive institution. Full-time tuition and fees vary according to program. *Graduate housing:* Room and/or apartments guaranteed to single students; on-campus housing not available to married students. Typical cost: $3215 (including board). *Student services:* Campus safety program, career counseling, free psychological counseling, international student services, services for students with disabilities, teacher training. *Library facilities:* Davis Family Library plus 2 others. *Collection:* Books: 764,667 (physical), 644,056 (digital/electronic); Databases: 695. Weekly public service hours: 112; students can reserve study rooms.

Computer facilities: Computer purchase and lease plans are available. 250 computers available on campus for general student use. A campuswide network can be accessed from student residence rooms and from off campus. Online class registration, personal Web pages, file servers are available.
Website: http://www.middlebury.edu/

General Application Contact: Admissions Office, 802-443-3000, Fax: 802-443-2056, E-mail: admissions@middlebury.edu.

GRADUATE UNITS

Language Schools Students: 393 full-time (276 women); includes 101 minority (8 Black or African American, non-Hispanic/Latino; 29 Asian, non-Hispanic/Latino; 54 Hispanic/Latino; 10 Two or more races, non-Hispanic/Latino). Average age 33. *Faculty:* 257 full-time (142 women). Expenses: Contact institution. *Financial support:* Fellowships and scholarships/grants available. Financial award applicants required to submit FAFSA. Offers language (MA, DML). *Application deadline:* For summer admission, 5/1 for domestic and international students. Applications are processed on a rolling basis. *Application fee:* $75. Electronic applications accepted. *Application Contact:* Kara Gennarelli, Technical and Lead Coordinator, Language Schools Office, 802-443-5727, Fax: 802-443-2075, E-mail: languages@middlebury.edu. *Dean,* Dr. Stephen B. Snyder, 802-443-5979, Fax: 802-443-2075, E-mail: ssnyder@middlebury.edu.

Arabic School Students: 27 full-time (11 women); includes 3 minority (2 Hispanic/Latino; 1 Two or more races, non-Hispanic/Latino). Average age 34. Expenses: Contact institution. *Financial support:* Fellowships and scholarships/grants available. Financial award application deadline: 3/14; financial award applicants required to submit FAFSA. Offers Arabic language pedagogy (MA); Arabic studies (MA). *Application deadline:* For summer admission, 5/1 for domestic and international

students. Applications are processed on a rolling basis. *Application fee:* $75. Electronic applications accepted. *Application Contact:* Barbara Walter, Coordinator, 802-443-5230, Fax: 802-443-2075, E-mail: bwalter@middlebury.edu. *Director,* Dr. Mahmoud Abdalla, 802-443-5230, Fax: 802-443-2075, E-mail: mabdalla@miis.edu.

Chinese School Expenses: Contact institution. *Financial support:* Fellowships and scholarships/grants available. Financial award application deadline: 3/15; financial award applicants required to submit FAFSA. Offers Chinese (MA). *Application deadline:* Applications are processed on a rolling basis. *Application fee:* $75. Electronic applications accepted. *Application Contact:* Mimi Clark, Coordinator, 802-443-5520, Fax: 802-443-2075, E-mail: chineseschool@middlebury.edu. *Director,* Dr. Jianhua Bai, 802-443-5520, Fax: 802-443-2075, E-mail: jbai@middlebury.edu.

French School Expenses: Contact institution. *Financial support:* Fellowships and scholarships/grants available. Financial award application deadline: 3/10; financial award applicants required to submit FAFSA. Offers French (MA, DML). *Application deadline:* Applications are processed on a rolling basis. *Application fee:* $75. Electronic applications accepted. *Application Contact:* Sheila Schwaneflugel, Coordinator, 802-443-5526, Fax: 802-443-2075, E-mail: sschwaneflugel@middlebury.edu. *Director,* Dr. Philippe France, 802-443-5526, Fax: 802-443-2075.

German School Expenses: Contact institution. *Financial support:* Fellowships and scholarships/grants available. Financial award application deadline: 3/9; financial award applicants required to submit FAFSA. Offers German (MA, DML). *Application deadline:* Applications are processed on a rolling basis. *Application fee:* $75. Electronic applications accepted. *Application Contact:* Christina Ellison, Coordinator, 802-443-5203, Fax: 802-443-2075, E-mail: germanschool@middlebury.edu. *Director,* Dr. Bettina Matthias, 802-443-3527, Fax: 802-443-2075, E-mail: bmatthia@middlebury.edu.

Hebrew School Expenses: Contact institution. *Financial support:* Fellowships and scholarships/grants available. Financial award application deadline: 3/28; financial award applicants required to submit FAFSA. *Program availability:* Blended/hybrid learning. Offers Hebrew (MA). *Application deadline:* Applications are processed on a rolling basis. *Application fee:* $75. Electronic applications accepted. *Application Contact:* Vardit Ringvald, Director, 802-443-3574, E-mail: vringval@middlebury.edu. *Director,* Vardit Ringvald, 802-443-3574, E-mail: vringval@middlebury.edu.

Italian School Students: 29 full-time (23 women); includes 6 minority (1 Asian, non-Hispanic/Latino; 3 Hispanic/Latino; 2 Two or more races, non-Hispanic/Latino). Average age 34. Expenses: Contact institution. *Financial support:* Fellowships and scholarships/grants available. Financial award application deadline: 3/10; financial award applicants required to submit FAFSA. Offers Italian (MA, DML). *Application deadline:* Applications are processed on a rolling basis. *Application fee:* $75. Electronic applications accepted. *Application Contact:* Joseph Tamagni, Coordinator, 802-443-5727, Fax: 802-443-2075, E-mail: italianschool@middlebury.edu. *Director,* Dr. Antonio Vitti, 802-443-5727, Fax: 802-443-2075, E-mail: acvitti@middlebury.edu.

Russian School Expenses: Contact institution. *Financial support:* Fellowships and scholarships/grants available. Financial award application deadline: 3/14; financial award applicants required to submit FAFSA. Offers Russian (MA, DML). *Application deadline:* Applications are processed on a rolling basis. *Application fee:* $75. Electronic applications accepted. *Application Contact:* Oliver Carling, Coordinator, 802-443-2006, Fax: 802-443-2075, E-mail: ocarling@middlebury.edu. *Director,* Dr. Jason Merrill, 802-443-5230, Fax: 802-443-2075, E-mail: jmerrill@middlebury.edu.

Spanish School Expenses: Contact institution. *Financial support:* Fellowships and scholarships/grants available. Financial award application deadline: 3/8; financial award applicants required to submit FAFSA. Offers Spanish (MA, DML). *Application deadline:* Applications are processed on a rolling basis. *Application fee:* $75. Electronic applications accepted. *Application Contact:* Audrey LaRock, Coordinator, 802-443-5539, Fax: 802-443-2075, E-mail: larock@middlebury.edu. *Director,* Dr. Jacobo Sefami, 802-443-5539, Fax: 802-443-2075, E-mail: jsefami@middlebury.edu.

Middlebury Bread Loaf School of English *Program availability:* Part-time. Offers English (M Litt, MA). Offered during summer only. Electronic applications accepted.

MIDDLEBURY INSTITUTE OF INTERNATIONAL STUDIES AT MONTEREY, Monterey, CA 93940-2691

General Information Independent, coed, graduate-only institution. *Enrollment:* 657 full-time matriculated graduate/professional students (432 women), 96 part-time matriculated graduate/professional students (70 women). *Enrollment by degree level:* 752 master's, 1 other advanced degree. *Graduate faculty:* 82 full-time (41 women), 75 part-time/adjunct (40 women). *Tuition:* Full-time $38,250; part-time $1820 per credit. *Required fees:* $78 per semester. *Graduate housing:* On-campus housing not available. *Student services:* Campus employment opportunities, career counseling, exercise/wellness program, international student services, low-cost health insurance, services for students with disabilities, writing training. *Library facilities:* William Tell Coleman Library. *Collection:* Books: 100,000 (physical), 21,799 (digital/electronic); Serial titles: 400 (physical), 18,258 (digital/electronic); Databases: 50. Students can reserve study rooms.

Computer facilities: 91 computers available on campus for general student use. Online class registration is available.
Website: http://www.miis.edu/

General Application Contact: Madeline Aiello, Admissions Office, 831-647-4662, Fax: 831-647-4188, E-mail: info@miis.edu.

GRADUATE UNITS

Graduate School of International Policy and Management Offers corporate risk management and compliance (MBA); international education management (MA); international environmental policy (MA); international policy and development (MA); international policy and management (MA, MBA, MPA); international trade and economic diplomacy (MA); nonproliferation and terrorism studies (MA); public administration (MPA). Electronic applications accepted.

Graduate School of Translation, Interpretation and Language Education Offers conference interpretation (MA); teaching English to speakers of other languages (MATESOL); teaching foreign language (MATFL); translation (MA); translation and interpretation (MA); translation and localization management (MA); translation, interpretation and language education (MA, MATESOL, MATFL). Electronic applications accepted.

MIDDLE GEORGIA STATE UNIVERSITY, Macon, GA 31206

General Information State-supported, coed, comprehensive institution.

GRADUATE UNITS

Office of Graduate Studies Offers adult/gerontology acute care nurse practitioner (MSN); information technology (MS).

MIDDLE TENNESSEE SCHOOL OF ANESTHESIA, Madison, TN 37116

General Information Independent-religious, coed, graduate-only institution. *Graduate housing:* On-campus housing not available.

GRADUATE UNITS

Graduate Programs Offers anesthesia (MS, DNAP).

MIDDLE TENNESSEE STATE UNIVERSITY, Murfreesboro, TN 37132

General Information State-supported, coed, university. CGS member. *Graduate housing:* Rooms and/or apartments available on a first-come, first-served basis to single and married students.

GRADUATE UNITS

College of Graduate Studies *Program availability:* Part-time, evening/weekend, online learning. Offers mathematics and science education (PhD). Electronic applications accepted.

College of Basic and Applied Sciences *Program availability:* Part-time, evening/weekend, online learning. Offers actuarial sciences (MS); aerospace education (M Ed); aviation administration (MS); basic and applied sciences (M Ed, MS, MSN, MST, PhD, Graduate Certificate); biology (MS); biostatistics (MS); biotechnology (MS); chemistry (MS); computational science (PhD); computer science (MS); engineering management (MS); engineering technology (MS); health care informatics (MS); horse science (MS); mathematics (MS, MST); molecular biosciences (PhD). Electronic applications accepted.

College of Behavioral and Health Sciences Offers behavioral and health sciences (MA, MCJ, MS, MSN, MSW, PhD, Ed S, Graduate Certificate); clinical psychology (MA); criminal justice administration (MCJ); exercise science (MS); experimental psychology (MA); family nurse practitioner (MSN, Graduate Certificate); health and human performance (MS); health, physical education and recreation (MS); human performance (PhD); industrial/organizational psychology (MA); leisure and sport management (MS); nursing (MSN, Graduate Certificate); psychology (MA, Ed S); quantitative psychology (MA); school psychology (MA); social work (MSW). Electronic applications accepted.

College of Education *Program availability:* Part-time, evening/weekend, online learning. Offers administration and supervision (M Ed, Ed S); curriculum and instruction (M Ed, Ed S); early childhood education (M Ed); education (M Ed, PhD, Ed S); elementary education (M Ed, Ed S); English as a second language (M Ed, Ed S); literacy studies (PhD); mental health counseling (M Ed); middle school education (M Ed); professional counseling (M Ed); reading (M Ed); school counseling (M Ed); secondary education (M Ed); special education (M Ed); technology and curriculum design (Ed S). Electronic applications accepted.

College of Liberal Arts *Program availability:* Part-time, evening/weekend, online learning. Offers archival management (Graduate Certificate); English (MA, PhD); foreign languages (MAT); geosciences (Graduate Certificate); gerontology (Graduate Certificate); history (MA); international affairs (MA); liberal arts (MA, MAT, MSW, PhD, Graduate Certificate); music (MA); public history (PhD); sociology (MA); women's and gender studies (Graduate Certificate). Electronic applications accepted.

College of Mass Communication *Program availability:* Part-time, evening/weekend, online learning. Offers mass communication (MFA, MS); recording arts and technologies (MFA). Electronic applications accepted.

Jennings A. Jones College of Business *Program availability:* Part-time, evening/weekend, online learning. Offers accounting (M Acc); business (M Acc, MA, MBA, MBE, MS, PhD); business administration (MBA); business education (MBE); computer information systems (MS); economics (MA, PhD); management (MS). Electronic applications accepted.

University College *Program availability:* Part-time, evening/weekend, online learning. Offers advanced studies in teaching and learning (M Ed); human resources leadership (MPS); nursing administration (MSN); nursing education (MSN); strategic leadership (MPS); training and development (MPS).

MIDWAY UNIVERSITY, Midway, KY 40347-1120

General Information Independent-religious, coed, comprehensive institution. *Graduate housing:* On-campus housing not available.

GRADUATE UNITS

Graduate Programs Offers education (MAT); leadership (MBA).

MIDWEST COLLEGE OF ORIENTAL MEDICINE, Racine, WI 53403-9747

General Information Proprietary, coed, graduate-only institution. *Graduate housing:* On-campus housing not available. *Research affiliation:* Guangzhou University of Traditional Chinese Medicine (pharmacology).

GRADUATE UNITS

Graduate Programs *Program availability:* Part-time, evening/weekend. Offers acupuncture (Certificate); Oriental medicine (MSOM).

Graduate Programs-Chicago *Program availability:* Part-time, evening/weekend.

MIDWESTERN BAPTIST THEOLOGICAL SEMINARY, Kansas City, MO 64118-4697

General Information Independent-religious, coed, graduate-only institution. *Graduate housing:* Rooms and/or apartments guaranteed to single and married students.

GRADUATE UNITS

Graduate and Professional Programs *Program availability:* Part-time, online learning. Offers Christian education (MACE); Christian foundations (Graduate Certificate); church music (MCM); counseling (MA); ministry (D Ed Min, D Min); Old or New Testament studies (PhD); theology (M Div). Electronic applications accepted.

MIDWESTERN STATE UNIVERSITY, Wichita Falls, TX 76308

General Information State-supported, coed, comprehensive institution. *Graduate housing:* Rooms and/or apartments available on a first-come, first-served basis to single and married students.

GRADUATE UNITS

Billie Doris McAda Graduate School *Program availability:* Part-time, evening/weekend. Electronic applications accepted.

College of Science and Mathematics *Program availability:* Part-time, evening/weekend. Offers biology (MS); computer science (MS); science and mathematics (MS). Electronic applications accepted.

Dillard College of Business Administration *Program availability:* Part-time, evening/weekend. Offers business administration (MBA). Electronic applications accepted.

Prothro-Yeager College of Humanities and Social Sciences *Program availability:* Part-time, evening/weekend. Offers clinical/counseling psychology (MA); English (MA); history (MA); humanities and social sciences (MA, PhD); philosophy (PhD); political science (MA). Electronic applications accepted.

Robert D. and Carol Gunn College of Health Sciences and Human Services *Program availability:* Part-time, evening/weekend. Offers criminal justice (MA); exercise physiology (MS); family nurse practitioner (MSN); family psychiatric mental health nurse practitioner (MSN); health information management (MHA); health sciences and human services (MA, MHA, MS, MSN, Graduate Certificate); health services administration (Graduate Certificate); medical practice management (MHA); nurse educator (MSN); public and community sector health care management (MHA); radiologic sciences (MS); rural and urban hospital management (MHA). Electronic applications accepted.

West College of Education *Program availability:* Part-time, evening/weekend. Offers counseling (MA); curriculum and instruction (M Ed); education (M Ed, MA); educational leadership (M Ed); educational technology (M Ed); human resource development (MA); reading (M Ed); school counseling (M Ed); special education (M Ed); sport administration (M Ed); training and development (MA). Electronic applications accepted.

MIDWESTERN UNIVERSITY, DOWNERS GROVE CAMPUS, Downers Grove, IL 60515-1235

General Information Independent, coed, graduate-only institution. *Graduate housing:* Rooms and/or apartments available on a first-come, first-served basis to single and married students.

GRADUATE UNITS

Chicago College of Optometry Offers optometry (OD).

Chicago College of Osteopathic Medicine Offers osteopathic medicine (DO).

Chicago College of Pharmacy *Program availability:* Part-time, online learning. Offers pharmacy (Pharm D).

College of Dental Medicine-Illinois Offers dental medicine (DMD).

College of Health Sciences, Illinois Campus Offers biomedical sciences (MA, MBS); clinical psychology (MA, Psy D); health science (DHS); health sciences (MA, MBS, MMS, MOT, DHS, DPT, Psy D); occupational therapy (MOT); physical therapy (DPT); physician assistant studies (MMS); speech-language pathology (MS).

MIDWESTERN UNIVERSITY, GLENDALE CAMPUS, Glendale, AZ 85308

General Information Independent, coed, graduate-only institution. *Graduate housing:* Rooms and/or apartments available on a first-come, first-served basis to single and married students.

GRADUATE UNITS

Arizona College of Optometry Offers optometry (OD).

Arizona College of Osteopathic Medicine Offers osteopathic medicine (DO). Electronic applications accepted.

College of Dental Medicine Offers dental medicine (DMD).

College of Health Sciences, Arizona Campus *Program availability:* Part-time. Offers biomedical sciences (MA, MBS); cardiovascular science (MCVS); clinical psychology (Psy D); health sciences (MA, MBS, MCVS, MMS, MOT, MS, DPM, DPT, Psy D); nurse anesthesia (MS); occupational therapy (MOT); physical therapy (DPT); physician assistant studies (MMS); podiatric medicine (DPM); speech-language pathology (MS).

College of Pharmacy-Glendale Offers pharmacy (Pharm D).

MIDWEST UNIVERSITY, Wentzville, MO 63385

General Information Independent-religious, coed, university. *Graduate housing:* Rooms and/or apartments available on a first-come, first-served basis to single and married students. Housing application deadline: 1/21.

MIDWIVES COLLEGE OF UTAH, Salt Lake City, UT 84106

General Information Independent, women only, comprehensive institution.

GRADUATE UNITS

Graduate Program Offers midwifery (MS).

MILLENNIA ATLANTIC UNIVERSITY, Doral, FL 33178

General Information Proprietary, coed, comprehensive institution.

GRADUATE UNITS

Graduate Programs *Program availability:* Online learning.

MILLERSVILLE UNIVERSITY OF PENNSYLVANIA, Millersville, PA 17551-0302

General Information State-supported, coed, comprehensive institution. CGS member. *Enrollment:* 7,927 graduate, professional, and undergraduate students; 157 full-time matriculated graduate/professional students (125 women), 589 part-time matriculated graduate/professional students (436 women). *Enrollment by degree level:* 698 master's, 32 doctoral, 16 other advanced degrees. *Graduate faculty:* 172 full-time (95 women), 6 part-time/adjunct (4 women). *Tuition, state resident:* full-time $8694; part-time $483 per credit. *Tuition, nonresident:* full-time $13,050; part-time $725 per credit. *Required fees:* $2480; $137.75 per credit. Tuition and fees vary according to course load, degree level and program. *Graduate housing:* Room and/or apartments available on a first-come, first-served basis to single students; on-campus housing not available to married students. *Typical cost:* $8274 per year ($12,288 including board). Room and board charges vary according to board plan and housing facility selected. *Student services:* Campus employment opportunities, campus safety program, career counseling, exercise/wellness program, free psychological counseling, grant writing training, international student services, low-cost health insurance, multicultural affairs office, services for students with disabilities, teacher training, writing training. *Library facilities:* The Francine G. McNairy Library and Learning Forum at Ganser Hall. Collection: Books: 317,945 (physical), 53,341 (digital/electronic); Serial titles: 4,191 (physical), 372,826 (digital/electronic); Databases: 179. Weekly public service hours: 94; students can reserve study rooms. *Research affiliation:* Chincoteague Bay Field Station of the Marine Science Consortium (biology).

Computer facilities: 430 computers available on campus for general student use. A campuswide network can be accessed from student residence rooms and from off campus. Online class registration is available.
Website: http://www.millersville.edu/

Millersville University of Pennsylvania

General Application Contact: Dr. Victor S. DeSantis, Dean of College of Graduate Studies and Adult Education/Associate Provost for Civic and Community Engagement, 717-871-5154, Fax: 717-871-7955, E-mail: victor.desantis@millersville.edu.

GRADUATE UNITS

College of Graduate Studies and Adult Learning Students: 157 full-time (125 women), 589 part-time (436 women); includes 98 minority (33 Black or African American, non-Hispanic/Latino; 3 American Indian or Alaska Native, non-Hispanic/Latino; 16 Asian, non-Hispanic/Latino; 38 Hispanic/Latino; 2 Native Hawaiian or other Pacific Islander, non-Hispanic/Latino; 6 Two or more races, non-Hispanic/Latino), 7 international. Average age 31. 407 applicants, 81% accepted, 215 enrolled. *Faculty:* 172 full-time (95 women), 6 part-time/adjunct (4 women). Expenses: Contact institution. *Financial support:* In 2016–17, 109 students received support. Unspecified assistantships available. Financial award application deadline: 3/15; financial award applicants required to submit FAFSA. In 2016, 266 master's awarded. *Program availability:* Part-time, evening/weekend, 100% online, blended/hybrid learning. *Application fee:* $40. Electronic applications accepted. *Application Contact:* Chad E. Baker, Director of Graduate Admissions and Recruitment, 717-871-7644, E-mail: chad.baker@millersville.edu. *Dean of College of Graduate Studies and Adult Learning/Associate Provost for Civic and Community Engagement,* Dr. Victor S. DeSantis, 717-871-7619, Fax: 717-871-7954, E-mail: victor.desantis@millersville.edu.

College of Arts, Humanities and Social Sciences Students: 16 full-time (9 women), 54 part-time (34 women); includes 11 minority (2 Black or African American, non-Hispanic/Latino; 6 Asian, non-Hispanic/Latino; 3 Hispanic/Latino), 1 international. Average age 33. 23 applicants, 91% accepted, 13 enrolled. *Faculty:* 58 full-time (36 women), 3 part-time/adjunct (2 women). Expenses: Contact institution. *Financial support:* In 2016–17, 9 students received support. Unspecified assistantships available. Financial award application deadline: 3/15; financial award applicants required to submit FAFSA. In 2016, 21 master's awarded. *Program availability:* Part-time. Offers art education (M Ed); arts, humanities and social sciences (M Ed, MA, Postbaccalaureate Certificate); English (M Ed, MA); history (MA); languages and cultures: French (MA); languages and cultures: German (MA); languages and cultures: Spanish (MA); writing (Postbaccalaureate Certificate). *Application deadline:* Applications are processed on a rolling basis. *Application fee:* $40. Electronic applications accepted. *Application Contact:* Dr. Victor S. DeSantis, Dean of College of Graduate Studies and Adult Learning/Associate Provost for Civic and Community Engagement, 717-871-7619, Fax: 717-871-7954, E-mail: victor.desantis@millersville.edu. *Dean,* Dr. Diane M. Umble, 717-871-7160, Fax: 717-871-7947, E-mail: diane.umble@millersville.edu.

College of Education and Human Services Students: 121 full-time (104 women), 369 part-time (300 women); includes 62 minority (26 Black or African American, non-Hispanic/Latino; 2 American Indian or Alaska Native, non-Hispanic/Latino; 4 Asian, non-Hispanic/Latino; 25 Hispanic/Latino; 5 Two or more races, non-Hispanic/Latino), 2 international. Average age 30. 272 applicants, 88% accepted, 150 enrolled. *Faculty:* 60 full-time (38 women), 2 part-time/adjunct (both women). Expenses: Contact institution. *Financial support:* In 2016–17, 80 students received support. Unspecified assistantships available. Financial award application deadline: 3/15; financial award applicants required to submit FAFSA. In 2016, 167 master's awarded. *Program availability:* Part-time, 100% online, blended/hybrid learning. Offers assessment, curriculum and teaching - online teaching (M Ed); assessment, curriculum and teaching - STEM education (M Ed); clinical psychology (MS); coaching education (Post-Master's Certificate); early childhood education (M Ed); education (M Ed, MS, MSW, DSW, Ed D, Post-Master's Certificate, Postbaccalaureate Certificate); educational leadership (Ed D); gifted education (M Ed, Postbaccalaureate Certificate); language and literacy: ESL (M Ed); language and literacy: reading specialist (M Ed); leadership for teaching and learning (M Ed); school counseling (M Ed); school psychology (MS); social work (MSW, DSW); special education (M Ed); special education: 7-12 (M Ed); special education: PreK-8 (M Ed); sport management: athletic coaching (M Ed, Post-Master's Certificate); sport management: athletic management (M Ed). *Application fee:* $40. Electronic applications accepted. *Application Contact:* Dr. Victor S. DeSantis, Dean of College of Graduate Studies and Adult Learning/Associate Provost for Civic and Community Engagement, 717-871-7619, Fax: 717-871-7954, E-mail: victor.desantis@millersville.edu. *Dean,* Dr. George Drake, 717-871-7333, E-mail: george.drake@millersville.edu.

College of Science and Technology Students: 20 full-time (12 women), 166 part-time (102 women); includes 25 minority (5 Black or African American, non-Hispanic/Latino; 1 American Indian or Alaska Native, non-Hispanic/Latino; 6 Asian, non-Hispanic/Latino; 10 Hispanic/Latino; 2 Native Hawaiian or other Pacific Islander, non-Hispanic/Latino; 1 Two or more races, non-Hispanic/Latino), 4 international. Average age 34. 112 applicants, 64% accepted, 52 enrolled. *Faculty:* 54 full-time (21 women), 1 part-time/adjunct (0 women). Expenses: Contact institution. *Financial support:* In 2016–17, 20 students received support. Unspecified assistantships available. Financial award application deadline: 3/15; financial award applicants required to submit FAFSA. In 2016, 78 master's awarded. *Program availability:* Part-time, evening/weekend, 100% online. Offers emergency management (MS); family nurse practitioner (MSN, Post-Master's Certificate); integrated scientific applications: climate science applications (MS); integrated scientific applications: environmental systems management (MS); integrated scientific applications: geoinformatics (MS); integrated scientific applications: weather intelligence and risk management (MS); mathematics (M Ed); nursing education (MSN, Post-Master's Certificate); nursing practice (DNP); science and technology (M Ed, MS, MSN, DNP); technology and innovation (M Ed). *Application deadline:* Applications are processed on a rolling basis. *Application fee:* $40. Electronic applications accepted. *Application Contact:* Dr. Victor S. DeSantis, Dean of College of Graduate Studies and Adult Learning/Associate Provost for Civic and Community Engagement, 717-871-7619, Fax: 717-871-7954, E-mail: victor.desantis@millersville.edu. *Dean, College of Science and Technology,* Dr. Michael Jackson, 717-871-4292, E-mail: michael.jackson@millersville.edu.

MILLIGAN COLLEGE, Milligan College, TN 37682

General Information Independent-religious, coed, comprehensive institution. Enrollment: 1,194 graduate, professional, and undergraduate students; 204 full-time matriculated graduate/professional students (124 women), 119 part-time matriculated graduate/professional students (58 women). Enrollment by degree level: 317 master's, 6 doctoral. Graduate faculty: 17 full-time (11 women), 8 part-time/adjunct (4 women). One-time fee: $75 part-time. Full-time tuition and fees vary according to degree level and program. Graduate housing: Rooms and/or apartments available on a first-come, first-served basis to single and married students. Typical cost: $2500 per year for single students; $2500 per year for married students. Room charges vary according to campus/location and housing facility selected. Housing application deadline: 4/1. Student services: Campus employment opportunities, career counseling, exercise/wellness program, free psychological counseling, international student services, services for students with disabilities, teacher training, writing training. Library facilities: P. H. Welshimer Memorial Library plus 1 other. Collection: Books: 171,308 (physical), 224,015 (digital/electronic); Serial titles: 945 (physical), 33,520 (digital/electronic); Databases: 83. Weekly public service hours: 89; students can reserve study rooms.

Computer facilities: 97 computers available on campus for general student use. A campuswide network can be accessed from student residence rooms and from off campus. Online class registration is available.
Website: http://www.milligan.edu/

General Application Contact: Brenda Bourn, Operations Manager, 423-461-8482, Fax: 423-461-8789, E-mail: bsbourn@milligan.edu.

GRADUATE UNITS

Area of Business Administration Students: 38 full-time (19 women), 12 part-time (5 women); includes 2 minority (1 Black or African American, non-Hispanic/Latino; 1 Hispanic/Latino). Average age 37. 25 applicants, 100% accepted, 19 enrolled. *Faculty:* 3 full-time (1 woman), 1 part-time/adjunct (0 women). Expenses: Contact institution. *Financial support:* Scholarships/grants available. Financial award application deadline: 12/1; financial award applicants required to submit FAFSA. In 2016, 32 master's awarded. *Program availability:* Blended/hybrid learning. Offers health sector management (MBA, Graduate Certificate); leadership (MBA, Graduate Certificate); operations management (MBA, Graduate Certificate). *Application deadline:* For fall admission, 8/1 for domestic students, 6/1 for international students; for spring admission, 1/15 for domestic students, 12/1 for international students. Applications are processed on a rolling basis. *Application fee:* $30. Electronic applications accepted. *Application Contact:* Rebecca Banton, Graduate Admissions Recruiter, Business Area, 423-461-8662, Fax: 423-461-8789, E-mail: rbbanton@milligan.edu. *Area Chair of Business,* Dr. David Campbell, 423-461-8674, Fax: 423-461-8677, E-mail: dacampbell@milligan.edu.

Area of Education Students: 26 full-time (19 women), 20 part-time (10 women); includes 2 minority (1 Black or African American, non-Hispanic/Latino; 1 Hispanic/Latino), 2 international. Average age 28. 16 applicants, 81% accepted, 11 enrolled. *Faculty:* 5 full-time (3 women), 3 part-time/adjunct (1 woman). Expenses: Contact institution. *Financial support:* Scholarships/grants available. Financial award application deadline: 12/1; financial award applicants required to submit FAFSA. In 2016, 19 master's awarded. *Program availability:* Part-time. Offers combined preK-3/K-5 education (M Ed); educational leadership (Ed D, Ed S); K-5 education (M Ed); middle grades education (M Ed); preK-3 education (M Ed); preK-3 special education (M Ed); secondary education (M Ed). *Application deadline:* For fall admission, 8/1 priority date for domestic students, 6/1 for international students; for spring admission, 11/15 priority date for domestic students, 12/1 for international students; for summer admission, 4/1 for domestic students. Applications are processed on a rolling basis. *Application fee:* $30. Electronic applications accepted. *Application Contact:* Melissa Dillow, Graduate Admissions Recruiter, Education, 423-461-8306, Fax: 423-461-8982, E-mail: msdillow@milligan.edu. *Area Chair of Education,* Dr. Angela Hilton-Prillhart, 423-461-8769, Fax: 423-461-3103, E-mail: anhilton-prillhart@milligan.edu.

Area of Physician Assistant Studies *Faculty:* 4 full-time (2 women). Expenses: Contact institution. *Financial support:* Scholarships/grants available. Financial award application deadline: 12/1; financial award applicants required to submit FAFSA. Offers physician assistant studies (MSPAS). *Application deadline:* For spring admission, 8/1 for domestic students, 6/1 for international students. *Application fee:* $30. Electronic applications accepted. *Application Contact:* Rebekah Bess, Program Secretary, 423-461-1557, Fax: 423-461-1518, E-mail: rbess@milligan.edu. *Area Chair and Director,* Andrew Hull, 423-461-1558, Fax: 423-461-1518, E-mail: awhull@milligan.edu.

Area of Social Learning Students: 25 full-time (22 women), 3 part-time (2 women); includes 2 minority (1 Black or African American, non-Hispanic/Latino; 1 Two or more races, non-Hispanic/Latino), 1 international. Average age 31. 29 applicants, 72% accepted, 14 enrolled. *Faculty:* 3 full-time (all women), 2 part-time/adjunct (0 women). Expenses: Contact institution. *Financial support:* Scholarships/grants available. Financial award application deadline: 12/1; financial award applicants required to submit FAFSA. In 2016, 15 master's awarded. *Program availability:* Part-time. Offers clinical mental health counseling (MSC); counseling ministry (Graduate Certificate); school counseling (MSC). *Application deadline:* For fall admission, 8/1 for domestic students, 6/1 for international students. Applications are processed on a rolling basis. *Application fee:* $30. Electronic applications accepted. *Application Contact:* Jenni Duran, Graduate Admissions Recruiter, Healthcare Programs, 423-461-8424, Fax: 423-461-8789, E-mail: jduran@milligan.edu. *Director of Master of Science in Counseling Program,* Dr. Christine Browning, 423-461-3513, Fax: 423-461-8777, E-mail: cmbrowning@milligan.edu.

Emmanuel Christian Seminary at Milligan College Students: 55 full-time (16 women), 44 part-time (17 women); includes 7 minority (6 Black or African American, non-Hispanic/Latino; 1 Hispanic/Latino), 6 international. Average age 33. *Faculty:* 9 full-time (1 woman), 11 part-time/adjunct (0 women). Expenses: Contact institution. *Financial support:* In 2016–17, 124 students received support. Scholarships/grants and unspecified assistantships available. Financial award application deadline: 12/1; financial award applicants required to submit FAFSA. In 2016, 21 master's, 3 doctorates awarded. *Program availability:* Part-time, blended/hybrid learning. Offers Christian care and counseling (M Div); Christian education (M Div); Christian ministries (MACM, Graduate Certificate); Christian ministry (M Div); Christian theology (M Div, MAR); church history (MAR); church history/historical theology (M Div); general studies (M Div); ministry (D Min); New Testament (M Div, MAR); Old Testament (M Div, MAR); urban ministry (M Div); world missions (M Div). *Application deadline:* For fall admission, 8/1 for domestic students, 6/1 for international students; for spring admission, 12/15 for domestic students, 8/1 for international students. Applications are processed on a rolling basis. *Application fee:* $30 ($0 for international students). Electronic applications accepted. *Application Contact:* Lauren Gullett, Director of Admissions and Recruitment for Emmanuel Christian Seminary, 423-461-1535, Fax: 423-926-6198, E-mail: lwgullett@milligan.edu. *Academic Dean, Emmanuel Christian Seminary,* Dr. Rollin Ramsaran, 423-461-1524, Fax: 423-926-6198, E-mail: raramsaran@milligan.edu.

Program in Occupational Therapy Offers occupational therapy (MSOT). Electronic applications accepted.

MILLIKIN UNIVERSITY, Decatur, IL 62522-2084

General Information Independent-religious, coed, comprehensive institution. Enrollment: 2,056 graduate, professional, and undergraduate students; 63 full-time matriculated graduate/professional students (36 women), 22 part-time matriculated graduate/professional students (17 women). Enrollment by degree level: 47 master's, 38 doctoral. Graduate faculty: 18 full-time (12 women), 14 part-time/adjunct (8 women). Tuition: Part-time $750 per credit hour. Tuition and fees vary according to course load, degree level and program. Student services: Campus employment opportunities, career counseling, exercise/wellness program, grant writing training, international student services, multicultural affairs office, services for students with disabilities, writing training.

Library facilities: Staley Library. *Collection:* Books: 167,802 (physical), 22,272 (digital/electronic); Serial titles: 1,000 (physical), 53,000 (digital/electronic); Databases: 133. Weekly public service hours: 89.

Computer facilities: 255 computers available on campus for general student use. A campuswide network can be accessed from student residence rooms. Online class registration, online degree audit, online financials (view and pay bills, financial aid) are available.

Website: http://www.millikin.edu/

General Application Contact: Marianne Taylor, Director of Graduate Admission, 217-420-6771, Fax: 217-425-4669, E-mail: mgtaylor@millikin.edu.

GRADUATE UNITS

School of Nursing Students: 32 full-time (25 women), 22 part-time (17 women); includes 10 minority (7 Black or African American, non-Hispanic/Latino; 1 Asian, non-Hispanic/Latino; 1 Hispanic/Latino; 1 Two or more races, non-Hispanic/Latino), 1 international. Average age 30. 76 applicants, 45% accepted, 19 enrolled. *Faculty:* 13 full-time (11 women). Expenses: Contact institution. *Financial support:* Traineeships and unspecified assistantships available. Financial award applicants required to submit FAFSA. In 2016, 22 master's, 2 doctorates awarded. *Program availability:* Part-time. Offers entry into nursing practice (MSN); nurse anesthesia (DNP); nurse educator (MSN); nursing practice (DNP). *Application deadline:* For spring admission, 7/1 priority date for domestic and international students; for summer admission, 11/1 priority date for domestic and international students. Applications are processed on a rolling basis. *Application fee:* $0. Electronic applications accepted. *Application Contact:* Bonnie Niemeyer, Administrative Assistant, 800-373-7733 Ext. 5034, Fax: 217-420-6677, E-mail: bniemeyer@millikin.edu. *Director,* Dr. Pamela Lindsey, 217-424-6348, Fax: 217-420-6731, E-mail: plindsey@millikin.edu.

Tabor School of Business Students: 31 full-time (11 women); includes 10 minority (3 Black or African American, non-Hispanic/Latino; 2 Hispanic/Latino; 5 Two or more races, non-Hispanic/Latino). Average age 31. 66 applicants, 55% accepted, 33 enrolled. *Faculty:* 5 full-time (1 woman), 9 part-time/adjunct (3 women). Expenses: Contact institution. *Financial support:* In 2016–17, 6 students received support, including 1 research assistantship with partial tuition reimbursement available (averaging $6,000 per year), 1 teaching assistantship with partial tuition reimbursement available (averaging $6,000 per year). Financial award applicants required to submit FAFSA. In 2016, 16 master's awarded. *Program availability:* Evening/weekend. Offers business (MBA). *Application deadline:* For fall admission, 6/1 priority date for domestic students, 4/1 for international students; for spring admission, 11/1 priority date for domestic students, 8/1 priority date for international students. Applications are processed on a rolling basis. *Application fee:* $0. Electronic applications accepted. *MBA Director/Associate Professor,* Dr. Anthony Liberatore, 217-424-6338, E-mail: aliberatore@millikin.edu.

MILLSAPS COLLEGE, Jackson, MS 39210-0001

General Information Independent-religious, coed, comprehensive institution. *Graduate housing:* Room and/or apartments available to single students; on-campus housing not available to married students. Housing application deadline: 6/1. *Research affiliation:* Downtown Jackson Partners Group (real estate development), Oxbow Ventures (commercialization of renewable energy), Midtown Partners (economic development).

GRADUATE UNITS

Else School of Management *Program availability:* Part-time. Offers accounting (M Acc); business administration (MBA). Electronic applications accepted.

MILLS COLLEGE, Oakland, CA 94613-1000

General Information Independent, Undergraduate: women only; graduate: coed, comprehensive institution. *Enrollment:* 1,367 graduate, professional, and undergraduate students; 424 full-time matriculated graduate/professional students (340 women), 100 part-time matriculated graduate/professional students (76 women). *Enrollment by degree level:* 411 master's, 40 doctoral, 73 other advanced degrees. *Graduate faculty:* 55 full-time (36 women), 71 part-time/adjunct (48 women). *Tuition:* Full-time $31,620. *Required fees:* $1118. Tuition and fees vary according to course load, degree level and program. *Graduate housing:* Rooms and/or apartments available on a first-come, first-served basis to single and married students. Typical cost: $6926 per year ($13,124 including board) for single students; $9506 per year ($15,704 including board) for married students. Room and board charges vary according to board plan and housing facility selected. Housing application deadline: 6/15. *Student services:* Campus employment opportunities, campus safety program, career counseling, exercise/wellness program, free psychological counseling, international student services, low-cost health insurance, multicultural affairs office, services for students with disabilities, teacher training, writing training. *Library facilities:* F. W. Olin Library. *Collection:* Books: 188,132 (physical), 136,684 (digital/electronic); Serial titles: 166 (physical), 46,007 (digital/electronic); Databases: 97. Weekly public service hours: 89; students can reserve study rooms.

Computer facilities: Computer purchase and lease plans are available. 335 computers available on campus for general student use. A campuswide network can be accessed from student residence rooms and from off campus. Online class registration, online degree audit are available.

Website: http://www.mills.edu/

General Application Contact: Robynne Lofton, Director of Admissions, 510-430-3295, Fax: 510-430-2159, E-mail: grad-studies@mills.edu.

GRADUATE UNITS

Graduate Studies Students: 427 full-time (343 women), 97 part-time (73 women); includes 237 minority (65 Black or African American, non-Hispanic/Latino; 2 American Indian or Alaska Native, non-Hispanic/Latino; 44 Asian, non-Hispanic/Latino; 91 Hispanic/Latino; 35 Two or more races, non-Hispanic/Latino), 24 international. Average age 30. 700 applicants, 85% accepted, 274 enrolled. *Faculty:* 55 full-time (36 women), 71 part-time/adjunct (48 women). Expenses: Contact institution. *Financial support:* In 2016–17, 642 students received support, including 481 fellowships with tuition reimbursements available (averaging $8,233 per year), 161 teaching assistantships with tuition reimbursements available (averaging $6,221 per year); research assistantships, career-related internships or fieldwork, institutionally sponsored loans, scholarships/grants, and unspecified assistantships also available. Support available to part-time students. Financial award application deadline: 2/1; financial award applicants required to submit FAFSA. In 2016, 188 master's, 9 doctorates, 66 other advanced degrees awarded. *Program availability:* Part-time, evening/weekend. Offers art (MFA); book art and creative writing (MFA); ceramics (MFA); composition (MA); computer science (Certificate); dance (MA, MFA); electronic music and recording media (MFA); infant mental health (MA); interdisciplinary computer science (MA); intermedia (MFA); literature (MA); music performance and literature (MFA); painting (MFA); photography (MFA); poetry (MFA); pre-medical studies (Certificate); prose (MFA); public policy (MPP); sculpture (MFA); Spanish creative writing (Certificate); translation (MFA).

Application deadline: For fall admission, 12/15 priority date for domestic students, 12/15 for international students; for spring admission, 11/1 priority date for domestic students, 10/1 for international students. Applications are processed on a rolling basis. *Application fee:* $50. Electronic applications accepted. *Director of Admissions,* Robynne Lofton, 510-430-3295, Fax: 510-430-2159, E-mail: grad-admissions@mills.edu.

Lorry I. Lokey Graduate School of Business Students: 38 full-time (34 women), 20 part-time (16 women); includes 38 minority (15 Black or African American, non-Hispanic/Latino; 3 Asian, non-Hispanic/Latino; 15 Hispanic/Latino; 5 Two or more races, non-Hispanic/Latino), 3 international. Average age 33. 47 applicants, 81% accepted, 22 enrolled. *Faculty:* 3 full-time (all women), 9 part-time/adjunct (5 women). Expenses: Contact institution. *Financial support:* In 2016–17, 62 students received support, including 62 fellowships with tuition reimbursements available (averaging $8,048 per year); teaching assistantships with tuition reimbursements available, scholarships/grants, and unspecified assistantships also available. Support available to part-time students. Financial award application deadline: 2/1; financial award applicants required to submit FAFSA. In 2016, 35 master's awarded. *Program availability:* Part-time. Offers applied economics (MA); management (MBA). *Application deadline:* For fall admission, 2/1 priority date for domestic students, 12/15 for international students; for spring admission, 10/1 for domestic students. Applications are processed on a rolling basis. *Application fee:* $50. *Application Contact:* Robynne Lofton, Director of Admissions, 510-430-3295, Fax: 510-430-2159, E-mail: grad-admission@mills.edu. *Department Chair,* Dr. Carolyn Sherwood Call, 510-430-3365, Fax: 510-430-2159, E-mail: csherwoodcall@mills.edu.

School of Education Students: 131 full-time (116 women), 49 part-time (36 women); includes 85 minority (25 Black or African American, non-Hispanic/Latino; 1 American Indian or Alaska Native, non-Hispanic/Latino; 16 Asian, non-Hispanic/Latino; 33 Hispanic/Latino; 10 Two or more races, non-Hispanic/Latino), 7 international. Average age 31. 231 applicants, 84% accepted, 99 enrolled. *Faculty:* 11 full-time (9 women), 13 part-time/adjunct (10 women). Expenses: Contact institution. *Financial support:* In 2016–17, 205 students received support, including 177 fellowships with tuition reimbursements available (averaging $7,171 per year), 28 teaching assistantships with tuition reimbursements available (averaging $3,700 per year); career-related internships or fieldwork and scholarships/grants also available. Support available to part-time students. Financial award application deadline: 2/1; financial award applicants required to submit FAFSA. In 2016, 31 master's, 15 doctorates, 71 other advanced degrees awarded. *Program availability:* Part-time, evening/weekend. Offers education (MA, Ed D, Certificate). *Application deadline:* For fall admission, 12/31 priority date for domestic students, 12/15 for international students; for spring admission, 11/1 priority date for domestic students, 10/1 for international students. Applications are processed on a rolling basis. *Application fee:* $50. Electronic applications accepted. *Application Contact:* Robynne Lofton, Director of Admissions, 510-430-3295, Fax: 510-430-2159, E-mail: grad-admission@mills.edu. *Department Head,* Dr. Diane Ketelle, 510-430-3190, Fax: 510-430-2159, E-mail: dketelle@mills.edu.

MILWAUKEE SCHOOL OF ENGINEERING, Milwaukee, WI 53202-3109

General Information Independent, coed, primarily men, comprehensive institution. *Enrollment:* 2,880 graduate, professional, and undergraduate students; 59 full-time matriculated graduate/professional students (22 women), 146 part-time matriculated graduate/professional students (40 women). *Enrollment by degree level:* 205 master's. *Graduate faculty:* 28 full-time (13 women), 48 part-time/adjunct (18 women). *Tuition:* Full-time $31,440; part-time $655 per credit. *Graduate housing:* Room and/or apartments available on a first-come, first-served basis to single students; on-campus housing not available to married students. Typical cost: $5718 per year ($9102 including board). Room and board charges vary according to board plan. Housing application deadline: 7/1. *Student services:* Campus employment opportunities, campus safety program, career counseling, exercise/wellness program, international student services, multicultural affairs office, services for students with disabilities, writing training. *Library facilities:* Walter Schroeder. *Collection:* Books: 68,970 (physical), 305,378 (digital/electronic); Serial titles: 2,000 (physical), 2,431 (digital/electronic); Databases: 98. Weekly public service hours: 96; students can reserve study rooms. *Research affiliation:* Keen Foundation (entrepreneurship and engineering education), National Fluid Power Association (hydraulics and pneumatics), 3dMD (biomolecular modeling), National Additive Manufacturing Innovation Institute (rapid prototyping), Caterpillar, Inc. (electrohydraulics), Clinical Translational Science Institute (medical and healthcare innovation and transfer).

Computer facilities: Computer purchase and lease plans are available. 50 computers available on campus for general student use. A campuswide network can be accessed from student residence rooms and from off campus. Online class registration is available.

Website: http://www.msoe.edu/

General Application Contact: Ian Dahlinghaus, Graduate Admissions Counselor, 414-277-7208, E-mail: dahlinghaus@msoe.edu.

GRADUATE UNITS

Civil and Architectural Engineering and Construction Management Department Students: 1 full-time (0 women), 7 part-time (4 women); includes 1 minority (Black or African American, non-Hispanic/Latino), 2 international. Average age 25. 15 applicants, 60% accepted, 9 enrolled. *Faculty:* 3 full-time (0 women), 2 part-time/adjunct (0 women). Expenses: Contact institution. *Financial support:* Research assistantships, career-related internships or fieldwork, institutionally sponsored loans, and scholarships/grants available. Financial award application deadline: 3/15; financial award applicants required to submit FAFSA. In 2016, 4 master's awarded. *Program availability:* Part-time, evening/weekend. Offers architectural engineering (MSAE); civil engineering (MS). *Application deadline:* Applications are processed on a rolling basis. *Application fee:* $0. Electronic applications accepted. *Application Contact:* Ian Dahlinghaus, Graduate Program Associate, 414-277-7208, E-mail: dahlinghaus@msoe.edu. *Chair,* Dr. Blake E. Wentz, 414-277-2204, E-mail: wentz@msoe.edu.

Department of Electrical Engineering and Computer Science Students: 20 full-time (6 women), 26 part-time (3 women); includes 5 minority (1 Black or African American, non-Hispanic/Latino; 1 American Indian or Alaska Native, non-Hispanic/Latino; 2 Asian, non-Hispanic/Latino; 1 Hispanic/Latino), 8 international. Average age 28. 86 applicants, 21% accepted, 14 enrolled. *Faculty:* 3 full-time (0 women), 12 part-time/adjunct (4 women). Expenses: Contact institution. *Financial support:* In 2016–17, 10 students received support, including 3 research assistantships (averaging $8,043 per year); career-related internships or fieldwork, institutionally sponsored loans, scholarships/grants, and tuition waivers (partial) also available. Financial award application deadline: 3/15; financial award applicants required to submit FAFSA. In 2016, 19 master's awarded. *Program availability:* Part-time, evening/weekend. Offers electrical engineering and computer science (MS); engineering (MS); perfusion (MS).

Application deadline: Applications are processed on a rolling basis. *Application fee:* $0. Electronic applications accepted. *Application Contact:* Ian Dahlinghaus, Graduate Program Associate, 414-277-7208, E-mail: dahlinghaus@msoe.edu. *Chairman,* Dr. Steven Williams, 414-277-7420, E-mail: williams@msoe.edu.

Program in Health Care Systems Management Students: 5 part-time (all women); includes 1 minority (Hispanic/Latino). Average age 24. 1 applicant. *Faculty:* 1 (woman) full-time, 2 part-time/adjunct (both women). Expenses: Contact institution. *Financial support:* In 2016–17, 2 students received support. Scholarships/grants available. Financial award application deadline: 3/15; financial award applicants required to submit FAFSA. In 2016, 3 master's awarded. Offers health care systems management (MSN). *Application deadline:* Applications are processed on a rolling basis. Electronic applications accepted. *Application Contact:* Ian Dahlinghaus, Graduate Admissions Counselor, 414-277-7208, E-mail: dahlinghaus@msoe.edu. *Department Chair,* Dr. Debra Jenks, 414-277-4516, E-mail: jenks@msoe.edu.

Rader School of Business Students: 39 full-time (16 women), 107 part-time (24 women); includes 21 minority (7 Black or African American, non-Hispanic/Latino; 4 Asian, non-Hispanic/Latino; 10 Hispanic/Latino), 9 international. Average age 31. 66 applicants, 52% accepted, 25 enrolled. *Faculty:* 6 full-time (3 women), 23 part-time/adjunct (10 women). Expenses: Contact institution. *Financial support:* In 2016–17, 15 fellowships (averaging $45,552 per year) were awarded; career-related internships or fieldwork, institutionally sponsored loans, scholarships/grants, traineeships, and tuition waivers (partial) also available. Financial award application deadline: 3/15; financial award applicants required to submit FAFSA. In 2016, 55 master's awarded. *Program availability:* Part-time, evening/weekend. Offers business administration (MBA); construction and business management (MS); education leadership (MBA); engineering management (MS); marketing and export management (MS); medical informatics (MS); new product management (MS); STEM leadership (MBA). *Application deadline:* Applications are processed on a rolling basis. *Application fee:* $0. Electronic applications accepted. *Application Contact:* Ian Dahlinghaus, Graduate Program Associate, 414-277-7208, E-mail: dahlinghaus@msoe.edu. *Chairman,* Dr. Steven Bialek, 414-277-7364, Fax: 414-277-7479, E-mail: bialek@msoe.edu.

MINNEAPOLIS COLLEGE OF ART AND DESIGN, Minneapolis, MN 55404-4347

General Information Independent, coed, comprehensive institution. *Graduate housing:* On-campus housing not available.

GRADUATE UNITS

Certificate Programs *Program availability:* Part-time, online learning. Offers design (Certificate); fine arts (Certificate); graphic design (Certificate); media (Certificate); sustainable design (Certificate). Electronic applications accepted.

Program in Visual Studies *Program availability:* Part-time. Offers animation (MFA); comic art (MFA); drawing (MFA); filmmaking (MFA); fine arts (MFA); furniture design (MFA); graphic design (MFA); illustration (MFA); interactive media (MFA); painting (MFA); photography (MFA); printmaking (MFA); sculpture (MFA). Electronic applications accepted.

MINNESOTA STATE UNIVERSITY MANKATO, Mankato, MN 56001

General Information State-supported, coed, university. CGS member. *Enrollment:* 15,407 graduate, professional, and undergraduate students; 691 full-time matriculated graduate/professional students (455 women), 1,212 part-time matriculated graduate/professional students (786 women). *Graduate housing:* Room and/or apartments available on a first-come, first-served basis to single students; on-campus housing not available to married students. *Student services:* Campus employment opportunities, campus safety program, career counseling, child daycare facilities, exercise/wellness program, free psychological counseling, international student services, low-cost health insurance, multicultural affairs office, services for students with disabilities, teacher training, writing training. *Library facilities:* Memorial Library.

Computer facilities: Computer purchase and lease plans are available. 900 computers available on campus for general student use. A campuswide network can be accessed from student residence rooms and from off campus. Online class registration is available.

Website: http://www.mnsu.edu/

General Application Contact: Joni H. Miller, Information Contact, 507-389-2321, E-mail: grad@mnsu.edu.

GRADUATE UNITS

College of Graduate Studies and Research Students: 691 full-time (455 women), 1,212 part-time (786 women). Expenses: Contact institution. *Financial support:* Fellowships with full tuition reimbursements, research assistantships with tuition reimbursements, teaching assistantships with tuition reimbursements, career-related internships or fieldwork, Federal Work-Study, institutionally sponsored loans, scholarships/grants, and unspecified assistantships available. Support available to part-time students. Financial award application deadline: 3/15; financial award applicants required to submit FAFSA. *Program availability:* Part-time, online learning. Offers cross-disciplinary studies (MS). *Application deadline:* For fall admission, 7/1 for domestic students, 5/1 for international students; for spring admission, 11/1 for domestic students, 10/1 for international students. Applications are processed on a rolling basis. *Application fee:* $42. Electronic applications accepted. *Associate Vice President of Research/Dean of Graduate Studies,* Dr. Barry J. Ries, 507-389-1242, E-mail: barry.ries@mnsu.edu.

College of Allied Health and Nursing Students: 116 full-time (77 women), 73 part-time (46 women). Expenses: Contact institution. *Financial support:* Research assistantships with full tuition reimbursements, teaching assistantships with full tuition reimbursements, career-related internships or fieldwork, Federal Work-Study, institutionally sponsored loans, and unspecified assistantships available. Support available to part-time students. Financial award application deadline: 3/15; financial award applicants required to submit FAFSA. *Program availability:* Part-time. Offers allied health and nursing (MA, MS, MSN, DNP, Postbaccalaureate Certificate); communication disorders (MS); community health education (MS); family nurse practitioner (MSN); nurse educator (MSN); nursing (DNP); physical education (MA, MS); public health education (Postbaccalaureate Certificate); rehabilitation counseling (MS); school health education (MS, Postbaccalaureate Certificate). *Application deadline:* Applications are processed on a rolling basis. *Application fee:* $40. Electronic applications accepted. *Dean,* Kristine Retherford, 507-389-6315, E-mail: kristine.retherford@mnsu.edu.

College of Arts and Humanities Students: 94 full-time (64 women), 172 part-time (107 women). Expenses: Contact institution. *Financial support:* Research assistantships with full tuition reimbursements, teaching assistantships with full tuition reimbursements, career-related internships or fieldwork, Federal Work-Study, institutionally sponsored loans, and unspecified assistantships available. Support

available to part-time students. Financial award application deadline: 3/15; financial award applicants required to submit FAFSA. *Program availability:* Part-time, evening/weekend. Offers art (MA); art education (MAT); arts and humanities (MA, MAT, MFA, MM, MS, Certificate); choral conducting (MM); communication and composition (MA); communication education (Certificate); communication studies (MA, MS); creative writing (MFA); English studies (MA); forensics (MFA); French (MS); French education (MS); music education (MAT); piano performance (MM); professional communication (Certificate); Spanish (MS); Spanish education (MS); Spanish for the professions (MS); teaching English as a second language (MA, Certificate); technical communication (MA, Certificate); theatre arts (MA, MFA); wind band conducting (MM). *Application deadline:* For fall admission, 7/1 for domestic students, 5/1 for international students; for spring admission, 11/1 for domestic students, 10/1 for international students. Applications are processed on a rolling basis. *Application fee:* $40. *Dean,* Dr. Matthew Cecil, 507-389-1712, E-mail: matt.cecil@mnsu.edu.

College of Business Students: 21 full-time (5 women), 73 part-time (31 women). Expenses: Contact institution. Offers accounting (MSA); business (MBA). *Application deadline:* For fall admission, 7/1 for domestic students, 5/1 for international students; for spring admission, 11/1 for domestic students, 10/1 for international students. Electronic applications accepted. *Dean,* Dr. Brenda Flannery, 507-389-5420, E-mail: brenda.flannery@mnsu.edu.

College of Education Students: 153 full-time (121 women), 289 part-time (183 women). Expenses: Contact institution. *Financial support:* Fellowships with partial tuition reimbursements, research assistantships with full tuition reimbursements, teaching assistantships with full tuition reimbursements, career-related internships or fieldwork, Federal Work-Study, institutionally sponsored loans, and unspecified assistantships available. Support available to part-time students. Financial award application deadline: 3/15; financial award applicants required to submit FAFSA. *Program availability:* Part-time, evening/weekend. Offers college student affairs (MS); counselor education and supervision (Ed D); education (MAT, MS, Ed D, Certificate); educational leadership (MS, Ed D); emotional and behavioral disorders (MS, Certificate); experiential education (MS); learning disabilities (MS, Certificate); mental health counseling (MS); professional school counseling (K-12) (MS). *Application deadline:* Applications are processed on a rolling basis. *Application fee:* $40. Electronic applications accepted. *Dean,* Dr. Jean Haar, 507-389-5445.

College of Science, Engineering and Technology Students: 88 full-time (38 women), 92 part-time (28 women). Expenses: Contact institution. *Financial support:* Research assistantships with full tuition reimbursements, teaching assistantships with full tuition reimbursements, career-related internships or fieldwork, Federal Work-Study, institutionally sponsored loans, and unspecified assistantships available. Support available to part-time students. Financial award application deadline: 3/15; financial award applicants required to submit FAFSA. *Program availability:* Part-time. Offers applied statistics (MS); biology (MS); biology education (MS); environmental sciences (MS); information technology (MS); manufacturing engineering technology (MS); mathematics (MA, MS); mathematics education (MS); physics (MS); physics education (MS); science, engineering and technology (MA, MAT, MS, Certificate); statistics (MS). *Application deadline:* For fall admission, 7/1 priority date for domestic students; for spring admission, 11/1 for domestic students. Applications are processed on a rolling basis. *Application fee:* $40. Electronic applications accepted. *Dean,* Dr. Brian Martensen, 507-389-5998.

College of Social and Behavioral Sciences Students: 136 full-time (107 women), 108 part-time (61 women). Expenses: Contact institution. *Financial support:* Fellowships with partial tuition reimbursements, research assistantships with full tuition reimbursements, teaching assistantships with full tuition reimbursements, career-related internships or fieldwork, Federal Work-Study, institutionally sponsored loans, and unspecified assistantships available. Support available to part-time students. Financial award application deadline: 3/15; financial award applicants required to submit FAFSA. *Program availability:* Part-time. Offers aging studies (MS); applied anthropology (MS); clinical psychology (MA); ethnic studies (MS); gender and women's studies (MS); geography (MS); history (MA, MS); industrial/organizational psychology (MA); local government management (Certificate); non-profit leadership (Certificate); public administration (MPA); school psychology (Psy D); social and behavioral sciences (MA, MAT, MPA, MS, MSW, Psy D, Certificate); social studies (MAT); social work (MSW); sociology (MA); sociology: college teaching (MA); sociology: corrections (MS); sociology: human services planning and administration (MS); urban and regional studies (MA); urban planning (MA, Certificate). *Application deadline:* Applications are processed on a rolling basis. *Application fee:* $40. Electronic applications accepted. *Interim Dean,* Dr. Maria Bevacqua, 507-389-6307, E-mail: maria.bevacqua@mnsu.edu.

MINNESOTA STATE UNIVERSITY MOORHEAD, Moorhead, MN 56563

General Information State-supported, coed, comprehensive institution. *Enrollment:* 5,924 graduate, professional, and undergraduate students; 182 full-time matriculated graduate/professional students (153 women), 535 part-time matriculated graduate/professional students (399 women). *Enrollment by degree level:* 625 master's, 92 other advanced degrees. *Graduate faculty:* 81. Tuition, state resident: full-time $9000; part-time $4500 per credit. Tuition, nonresident: full-time $18,000; part-time $9000 per credit. *Required fees:* $42; $39.25 per credit. One-time fee: $90 full-time. Full-time tuition and fees vary according to course load, degree level, program and reciprocity agreements. *Graduate housing:* Room and/or apartments available on a first-come, first-served basis to single students; on-campus housing not available to married students. Typical cost: $5824 per year ($7450 including board). Room and board charges vary according to board plan and housing facility selected. Housing application deadline: 3/1. *Student services:* Campus employment opportunities, campus safety program, career counseling, child daycare facilities, exercise/wellness program, free psychological counseling, grant writing training, international student services, low-cost health insurance, multicultural affairs office, services for students with disabilities, teacher training, writing training. *Library facilities:* Livingston Lord Library plus 1 other. *Collection:* Books: 319,033 (physical), 20,127 (digital/electronic); Serial titles: 1,746 (physical), 21,919 (digital/electronic); Databases: 97. Weekly public service hours: 79; students can reserve study rooms. *Research affiliation:* West Central Minnesota Business Innovation Center.

Computer facilities: Computer purchase and lease plans are available. 2,200 computers available on campus for general student use. A campuswide network can be accessed from student residence rooms and from off campus. Online class registration is available.

Website: http://www.mnstate.edu/

General Application Contact: Karla Wenger, Graduate Studies Office, 218-477-2344, Fax: 218-477-2344, E-mail: wengerk@mnstate.edu.

GRADUATE UNITS

Graduate Studies Students: 182 full-time (153 women), 535 part-time (399 women). Average age 33. *Faculty:* 81. Expenses: Contact institution. *Financial support:* Federal Work-Study and unspecified assistantships available. Financial award application deadline: 10/1; financial award applicants required to submit FAFSA. In 2016, 191 master's, 18 other advanced degrees awarded. *Program availability:* Part-time, evening/weekend, 100% online, blended/hybrid learning. *Application deadline:* Applications are processed on a rolling basis. *Application fee:* $20. Electronic applications accepted. *Application Contact:* Karla Wenger, Graduate Studies Office Manager, 218-236-2344, Fax: 218-236-2482, E-mail: wengerk@mnstate.edu. *Director of Graduate Studies,* Dr. Lisa Karch, 218-477-2699, Fax: 218-236-2482, E-mail: lisa.karch@mnstate.edu.

College of Business and Innovation Students: 15 full-time (8 women), 27 part-time (11 women). Average age 32. 20 applicants, 100% accepted. Expenses: Contact institution. *Financial support:* Federal Work-Study and unspecified assistantships available. Financial award application deadline: 10/1; financial award applicants required to submit FAFSA. In 2016, 9 master's awarded. *Program availability:* Part-time. Offers accounting and finance (MS); business administration (MBA); health care management (MBA). *Application deadline:* For fall admission, 3/15 for domestic students; for spring admission, 10/15 for domestic students. Applications are processed on a rolling basis. *Application fee:* $20. Electronic applications accepted. *Application Contact:* Karla Wenger, Coordinator, 218-477-2344, E-mail: wengerk@mnstate.edu. *Dean,* Dr. Marsha Weber, 218-477-2076, E-mail: marsha.weber@mnstate.edu.

College of Education and Human Services Students: 133 full-time (116 women), 363 part-time (274 women). Average age 32. 273 applicants, 49% accepted. Expenses: Contact institution. *Financial support:* Federal Work-Study and unspecified assistantships available. Financial award application deadline: 10/1; financial award applicants required to submit FAFSA. In 2016, 114 master's awarded. *Program availability:* Part-time, 100% online, blended/hybrid learning. Offers counseling and student affairs (MS); curriculum and instruction (MS); educational leadership (MS, Ed S); special education (MS); speech-language pathology (MS). *Application deadline:* For fall admission, 4/15 priority date for domestic students; for spring admission, 11/1 priority date for domestic students. Applications are processed on a rolling basis. *Application fee:* $20. Electronic applications accepted. *Application Contact:* Karla Wenger, Office Manager, 218-477-2344, Fax: 218-477-2482, E-mail: wengerk@mnstate.edu. *Dean,* Dr. Ok-Hee Lee, 218-477-2095, E-mail: okheelee@mnstate.edu.

College of Humanities and Social Sciences Students: 13 part-time (9 women). Average age 32. 4 applicants, 100% accepted. Expenses: Contact institution. *Financial support:* Federal Work-Study and unspecified assistantships available. Financial award application deadline: 10/1; financial award applicants required to submit FAFSA. In 2016, 3 master's awarded. *Program availability:* Part-time, evening/weekend. Offers teaching English as a second language (MA). *Application deadline:* For fall admission, 4/15 for domestic students; for spring admission, 11/15 for domestic students. Applications are processed on a rolling basis. *Application fee:* $20. Electronic applications accepted. *Application Contact:* Karla Wenger, Graduate Studies Office Manager, 218-477-2344, Fax: 218-477-2482, E-mail: wengerk@mnstate.edu. *Dean,* Dr. Randy Cagle, 218-477-2477, E-mail: caglera@mnstate.edu.

College of Science, Health and the Environment Students: 34 full-time (29 women), 88 part-time (76 women). Average age 33. 85 applicants, 51% accepted. Expenses: Contact institution. *Financial support:* Federal Work-Study and unspecified assistantships available. Financial award application deadline: 10/1; financial award applicants required to submit FAFSA. In 2016, 29 master's awarded. *Program availability:* Part-time. Offers healthcare administration (MHA); nursing (MS); school psychology (MS, Psy S). *Application deadline:* For fall admission, 4/15 for domestic students; for spring admission, 11/15 for domestic students. Applications are processed on a rolling basis. *Application fee:* $20. Electronic applications accepted. *Application Contact:* Karla Wenger, Graduate Studies Office Manager, 218-477-2344, Fax: 218-477-2482, E-mail: wengerk@mnstate.edu. *Dean,* Dr. Jeffrey Bodwin, 218-477-5892, E-mail: jeffrey.bodwin@mnstate.edu.

MINOT STATE UNIVERSITY, Minot, ND 58707-0002

General Information State-supported, coed, comprehensive institution. *Graduate housing:* Rooms and/or apartments available on a first-come, first-served basis to single and married students. Housing application deadline: 6/30. *Research affiliation:* Rural Crime and Justice Center (criminal justice research), North Dakota Center for Persons with Disabilities (NDCPD).

GRADUATE UNITS

Graduate School *Program availability:* Part-time, 100% online, blended/hybrid learning. Offers deaf/hard of hearing education (MS); elementary education (M Ed); information systems (MSIS); management (MSM); mathematics (MAT); school psychology (Ed Sp); science (MAT); specific learning disabilities (MS); speech-language pathology (MS). Electronic applications accepted.

MIRRER YESHIVA, Brooklyn, NY 11223-2010

General Information Independent-religious, men only, comprehensive institution.

GRADUATE UNITS

Graduate Programs

MISERICORDIA UNIVERSITY, Dallas, PA 18612-1098

General Information Independent-religious, coed, comprehensive institution. *Graduate housing:* On-campus housing not available. *Student services:* Campus employment opportunities, campus safety program, career counseling, exercise/wellness program, free psychological counseling, international student services, low-cost health insurance, multicultural affairs office, services for students with disabilities, writing training. *Library facilities:* Mary Kintz Bevevino Library. *Collection:* Books: 80,036 (physical), 13,154 (digital/electronic); Serial titles: 8,153 (physical), 28,230 (digital/electronic); Databases: 111. Students can reserve study rooms.

Computer facilities: Computer purchase and lease plans are available. 150 computers available on campus for general student use. A campuswide network can be accessed from student residence rooms and from off campus. Online class registration is available.
Website: http://www.misericordia.edu/

General Application Contact: Maureen Sheridan, Assistant Director of Admissions, Part-Time and Graduate Programs, 570-674-6451, E-mail: msherida@misericordia.edu.

GRADUATE UNITS

College of Business Students: 158 part-time (90 women); includes 7 minority (1 Black or African American, non-Hispanic/Latino; 1 Asian, non-Hispanic/Latino; 3 Hispanic/Latino; 2 Native Hawaiian or other Pacific Islander, non-Hispanic/Latino). Average age 34. *Faculty:* 11 full-time (2 women), 11 part-time/adjunct (4 women). Expenses: Contact institution. *Financial support:* Career-related internships or fieldwork and scholarships/grants available. Support available to part-time students. Financial award application deadline: 6/30; financial award applicants required to submit FAFSA. *Program availability:* Part-time, evening/weekend. Offers accounting (MBA); business (MBA, MS); healthcare management (MBA, MS); human resource management (MBA, MS); management (MBA, MS); sport management (MBA). *Application deadline:* Applications are processed on a rolling basis. *Application fee:* $35. Electronic applications accepted. *Application Contact:* Karen Cefalo, Assistant Director of Admissions, 570-674-8094, Fax: 570-674-6232, E-mail: kcefalo@misericordia.edu. *Interim Dean,* Dr. Corina Slaff, 570-674-8022, E-mail: cslaff@misericordia.edu.

College of Health Sciences and Education Students: 228 full-time (167 women), 151 part-time (132 women); includes 21 minority (3 Black or African American, non-Hispanic/Latino; 5 Asian, non-Hispanic/Latino; 8 Hispanic/Latino; 5 Two or more races, non-Hispanic/Latino). Average age 28. Expenses: Contact institution. *Financial support:* Teaching assistantships, career-related internships or fieldwork, Federal Work-Study, scholarships/grants, traineeships, and tuition waivers (partial) available. Support available to part-time students. Financial award application deadline: 6/30; financial award applicants required to submit FAFSA. *Program availability:* Part-time, evening/weekend. Offers health sciences and education (MSN, MSOT, MSSLP, DNP, DPT, OTD); instructional technology (MS); nursing (MSN, DNP); occupational therapy (MSOT, OTD); physical therapy (DPT); reading specialist (MS); special education (MS); speech-language pathology (MSSLP). *Application deadline:* Applications are processed on a rolling basis. *Application fee:* $35. Electronic applications accepted. *Application Contact:* Maureen Sheridan, Assistant Director of Admissions, Part-Time Undergraduate and Graduate Programs, 570-674-6451, Fax: 570-674-6232, E-mail: msherida@misericordia.edu. *Dean,* Dr. Leamor Kahanov, 570-674-6471, E-mail: lkahanov@misericordia.edu.

MISSISSIPPI COLLEGE, Clinton, MS 39058

General Information Independent-religious, coed, comprehensive institution. *Graduate housing:* Room and/or apartments available on a first-come, first-served basis to single students; on-campus housing not available to married students. Housing application deadline: 8/15. *Research affiliation:* Gulf Coast Research Laboratory (marine biology).

GRADUATE UNITS

Graduate School *Program availability:* Part-time, evening/weekend, online learning. Offers health services administration (MHSA); liberal studies (MLS). Electronic applications accepted.

College of Arts and Sciences *Program availability:* Part-time, evening/weekend. Offers administration of justice (MSS); applied communication (MSC); applied music performance (MM); art (M Ed, MA, MFA); arts and sciences (M Ed, MA, MCS, MFA, MM, MS, MSC, MSS, Certificate); biological science (M Ed); biology (MCS); biology-biological sciences (MS); biology-medical sciences (MS); chemistry and biochemistry (MCS, MS); Christian studies and the arts (M Ed, MA, MFA, MM, MSC); computer science (M Ed, MS); conducting (MM); English (M Ed, MA); history (M Ed, MA, MSS); humanities and social sciences (M Ed, MA, MS, MSS, Certificate); mathematics (M Ed, MCS, MS); music education (MM); music performance: organ (MM); paralegal studies (Certificate); political science (MSS); public relations and corporate communication (MSC); science and mathematics (M Ed, MCS, MS); social sciences (M Ed, MSS); teaching English to speakers of other languages (MA, MS); vocal pedagogy (MM). Electronic applications accepted.

School of Business *Program availability:* Part-time, evening/weekend. Offers accounting (Certificate); business administration (MBA); business education (M Ed); finance (MBA, Certificate). Electronic applications accepted.

School of Education *Program availability:* Part-time, evening/weekend, online learning. Offers art (M Ed); athletic administration (MS); biological science (M Ed); business education (M Ed); computer science (M Ed); counseling (Ed S); dyslexia therapy (M Ed); education (M Ed, MS, Ed D, Ed S); educational leadership (M Ed, Ed D, Ed S); elementary education (M Ed, Ed S); English (M Ed); higher education administration (MS); marriage and family counseling (MS); mathematics (M Ed); mental health counseling (MS); school counseling (M Ed); secondary education (M Ed); social studies (history) (M Ed); teaching arts (M Ed). Electronic applications accepted.

School of Law Offers civil law studies (Certificate); law (JD). Electronic applications accepted.

MISSISSIPPI STATE UNIVERSITY, Mississippi State, MS 39762

General Information State-supported, coed, university. CGS member. *Enrollment:* 21,622 graduate, professional, and undergraduate students; 1,905 full-time matriculated graduate/professional students (961 women), 1,496 part-time matriculated graduate/professional students (718 women). *Enrollment by degree level:* 1,845 master's, 1,494 doctoral, 63 other advanced degrees. *Graduate faculty:* 868 full-time (277 women), 23 part-time/adjunct (7 women). Tuition, state resident: full-time $7670; part-time $852.50 per credit hour. Tuition, nonresident: full-time $20,790; part-time $2310.50 per credit hour. Part-time tuition and fees vary according to course load. *Graduate housing:* Room and/or apartments available on a first-come, first-served basis to single students; on-campus housing not available to married students. Typical cost: $12,288 (including board). Housing application deadline: 8/1. *Student services:* Campus employment opportunities, campus safety program, career counseling, child daycare facilities, exercise/wellness program, free psychological counseling, grant writing training, international student services, low-cost health insurance, multicultural affairs office, services for students with disabilities, teacher training, writing training. *Library facilities:* Mitchell Memorial Library plus 2 others. *Collection:* Books: 2.5 million (physical), 52,173 (digital/electronic); Serial titles: 4,400 (physical), 114,771 (digital/electronic); Databases: 102. Weekly public service hours: 110; students can reserve study rooms. *Research affiliation:* Southeastern Universities Research Association (interdisciplinary research), Oak Ridge Associated Universities (interdisciplinary energy-related research), Mississippi Research and Technology Park (interdisciplinary engineering), Mississippi Mineral Resources Institute (geology sciences and engineering), NASA-Stennis Space Center (interdisciplinary research), Mississippi Research Consortium (interdisciplinary research).

Computer facilities: 1,000 computers available on campus for general student use. A campuswide network can be accessed from student residence rooms and from off campus. Online class registration is available.
Website: http://www.msstate.edu/

General Application Contact: Forest Sparks, Admissions Manager, 662-325-7400, Fax: 662-325-1967, E-mail: grad@grad.msstate.edu.

GRADUATE UNITS

Bagley College of Engineering Students: 359 full-time (93 women), 306 part-time (61 women); includes 98 minority (41 Black or African American, non-Hispanic/Latino; 19 Asian, non-Hispanic/Latino; 32 Hispanic/Latino; 1 Native Hawaiian or other Pacific Islander, non-Hispanic/Latino; 5 Two or more races, non-Hispanic/Latino), 215 international. Average age 30. 665 applicants, 44% accepted, 161 enrolled. *Faculty:* 115 full-time (14 women), 8 part-time/adjunct (1 woman). Expenses: Contact institution. *Financial support:* In 2016–17, 72 research assistantships with full tuition reimbursements (averaging $17,082 per year), 63 teaching assistantships with full tuition reimbursements (averaging $15,709 per year) were awarded; Federal Work-Study, institutionally sponsored loans, scholarships/grants, and unspecified assistantships also available. Financial award application deadline: 4/1; financial award applicants required to submit FAFSA. In 2016, 121 master's, 46 doctorates awarded. *Program availability:* Part-time, 100% online. Offers aerospace engineering (MS); civil and environmental engineering (MS, PhD); computer science and engineering (MS, PhD); electrical and computer engineering (MS, PhD); engineering (M Eng, MS, PhD); human factors and ergonomics (MS); industrial and systems engineering (PhD); industrial systems (MS); management systems (MS); manufacturing systems (MS); mechanical engineering (MS); operations research (MS). *Application deadline:* For fall admission, 7/1 for domestic students, 5/1 for international students; for spring admission, 11/1 for domestic students, 9/1 for international students. Applications are processed on a rolling basis. *Application fee:* $60. Electronic applications accepted. *Application Contact:* Doretta Martin, Senior Admissions Assistant, 662-325-9514, E-mail: dmartin@grad.msstate.edu. *Dean*, Dr. Jason Keith, 662-325-2270, Fax: 662-325-8573, E-mail: keith@bagley.msstate.edu.

Dave C. Swalm School of Chemical Engineering Students: 14 full-time (4 women), 5 part-time (1 woman); includes 1 minority (Black or African American, non-Hispanic/Latino), 16 international. Average age 29. 26 applicants, 31% accepted, 5 enrolled. *Faculty:* 9 full-time (1 woman). Expenses: Contact institution. *Financial support:* In 2016–17, 10 research assistantships with full tuition reimbursements (averaging $16,589 per year), 4 teaching assistantships with full tuition reimbursements (averaging $16,288 per year) were awarded; Federal Work-Study, institutionally sponsored loans, and unspecified assistantships also available. Financial award application deadline: 4/1; financial award applicants required to submit FAFSA. In 2016, 5 master's, 1 doctorate awarded. Offers chemical engineering (MS, PhD). *Application deadline:* For fall admission, 4/1 priority date for domestic students, 5/1 for international students; for spring admission, 8/1 priority date for domestic students, 9/1 for international students. Applications are processed on a rolling basis. *Application fee:* $60. Electronic applications accepted. *Application Contact:* Doretta Martin, Senior Admissions Assistant, 662-325-9514, E-mail: dmartin@grad.msstate.edu. *Interim Director*, Dr. Bill Elmore, 662-325-2480, Fax: 662-325-2482, E-mail: elmore@che.msstate.edu.

College of Agriculture and Life Sciences Students: 261 full-time (143 women), 145 part-time (86 women); includes 55 minority (35 Black or African American, non-Hispanic/Latino; 3 Asian, non-Hispanic/Latino; 14 Hispanic/Latino; 3 Two or more races, non-Hispanic/Latino), 81 international. Average age 30. 259 applicants, 42% accepted, 74 enrolled. *Faculty:* 194 full-time (52 women), 2 part-time/adjunct (1 woman). Expenses: Contact institution. *Financial support:* In 2016–17, 172 research assistantships with full tuition reimbursements (averaging $14,986 per year), 12 teaching assistantships with full tuition reimbursements (averaging $12,094 per year) were awarded; career-related internships or fieldwork, Federal Work-Study, institutionally sponsored loans, scholarships/grants, tuition waivers (partial), and unspecified assistantships also available. Financial award application deadline: 4/1; financial award applicants required to submit FAFSA. In 2016, 81 master's, 26 doctorates awarded. *Program availability:* Blended/hybrid learning. Offers agricultural economics (MS); agricultural life sciences (MS); agricultural science (PhD); agricultural sciences (PhD); agriculture (MS); agriculture and life sciences (MABM, MLA, MS, PhD); biochemistry (MS, PhD); biological engineering (MS, PhD); biomedical engineering (MS, PhD); entomology (MS, PhD); food science and technology (MS, PhD); health promotion (MS); horticulture (MS); landscape architecture (MLA); life sciences (PhD); nutrition (MS, PhD); plant pathology (MS, PhD); weed science (PhD). *Application deadline:* For fall admission, 7/1 for domestic students, 5/1 for international students; for spring admission, 11/1 for domestic students, 9/1 for international students. Applications are processed on a rolling basis. *Application fee:* $60. Electronic applications accepted. *Application Contact:* Marina Hunt, Admissions and Enrollment Assistant, 662-325-5188, Fax: 662-325-1967, E-mail: mhunt@grad.msstate.edu. *Dean of Agriculture and Life Sciences/Director of Mississippi Agricultural and Forestry Experiment Station*, Dr. George Hopper, 662-325-2110, Fax: 662-325-8880, E-mail: dean@cfr.msstate.edu.

School of Human Sciences Students: 35 full-time (25 women), 61 part-time (45 women); includes 19 minority (15 Black or African American, non-Hispanic/Latino; 2 Hispanic/Latino; 2 Two or more races, non-Hispanic/Latino), 5 international. Average age 35. 22 applicants, 73% accepted, 12 enrolled. *Faculty:* 23 full-time (13 women), 1 part-time/adjunct (0 women). Expenses: Contact institution. *Financial support:* Federal Work-Study, institutionally sponsored loans, and unspecified assistantships available. Financial award application deadline: 4/1; financial award applicants required to submit FAFSA. In 2016, 8 master's, 4 doctorates awarded. *Program availability:* Part-time. Offers agriculture and extension education (MS, PhD); human development and family studies (MS, PhD). *Application deadline:* For fall admission, 7/1 for domestic students, 5/1 for international students; for spring admission, 11/1 for domestic students, 9/1 for international students. Applications are processed on a rolling basis. *Application fee:* $60. Electronic applications accepted. *Application Contact:* Marina Hunt, Admissions and Enrollment Assistant, 662-325-5188, Fax: 662-325-1967, E-mail: mhunt@grad.msstate.edu. *Director and Professor*, Dr. Michael Newman, 662-325-2950, E-mail: mnewman@humansci.msstate.edu.

College of Arts and Sciences Students: 420 full-time (201 women), 304 part-time (156 women); includes 115 minority (60 Black or African American, non-Hispanic/Latino; 2 American Indian or Alaska Native, non-Hispanic/Latino; 10 Asian, non-Hispanic/Latino; 30 Hispanic/Latino; 1 Native Hawaiian or other Pacific Islander, non-Hispanic/Latino; 12 Two or more races, non-Hispanic/Latino), 130 international. Average age 31. 597 applicants, 52% accepted, 223 enrolled. *Faculty:* 240 full-time (87 women), 5 part-time/adjunct (1 woman). Expenses: Contact institution. *Financial support:* In 2016–17, 52 research assistantships with full tuition reimbursements (averaging $14,851 per year), 295 teaching assistantships with full tuition reimbursements (averaging $13,869 per year) were awarded; Federal Work-Study, institutionally sponsored loans, scholarships/grants, tuition waivers (partial), and unspecified assistantships also available. Financial award application deadline: 4/1; financial award applicants required to submit FAFSA. In 2016, 176 master's, 34 doctorates awarded. *Program availability:* Part-time, evening/weekend. Offers anthropology and Middle Eastern cultures (MA); applied cognitive science (PhD); applied meteorology (MS); arts and sciences (MA,

MPPA, MS, PhD); biological sciences (MS, PhD); broadcast meteorology (MS); chemistry (MA, MS, PhD); classical and modern languages and literatures (MA); clinical psychology (PhD); earth and atmospheric science (PhD); English (MA); environmental geosciences (MS); general biology (MS); geography (MS); geology (MS); geospatial sciences (MS); mathematical sciences (PhD); mathematics (MS); physics (MS, PhD); political science (MA); professional meteorology (MS); psychology (MS); public policy and administration (MPPA, PhD); sociology (MS, PhD); statistics (MS); teachers in geosciences (MS); U.S. and European history (MA). *Application deadline:* For fall admission, 7/1 for domestic students, 5/1 for international students; for spring admission, 11/1 for domestic students, 9/1 for international students. Applications are processed on a rolling basis. *Application fee:* $60. Electronic applications accepted. *Application Contact:* Linda Boomer, Admissions and Enrollment Assistant, 662-325-3363, E-mail: lbonner@grad.msstate.edu. *Interim Dean*, Dr. Rick Travis, 662-325-8071, Fax: 662-325-8740, E-mail: rtravis@deanas.msstate.edu.

College of Business Students: 127 full-time (45 women), 204 part-time (41 women); includes 27 minority (11 Black or African American, non-Hispanic/Latino; 1 American Indian or Alaska Native, non-Hispanic/Latino; 5 Asian, non-Hispanic/Latino; 6 Hispanic/Latino; 4 Two or more races, non-Hispanic/Latino), 28 international. Average age 30. 238 applicants, 40% accepted, 73 enrolled. *Faculty:* 61 full-time (17 women), 1 part-time/adjunct (0 women). Expenses: Contact institution. *Financial support:* In 2016–17, 2 research assistantships (averaging $10,634 per year), 43 teaching assistantships (averaging $11,781 per year) were awarded; career-related internships or fieldwork, Federal Work-Study, institutionally sponsored loans, scholarships/grants, and unspecified assistantships also available. Financial award application deadline: 4/1; financial award applicants required to submit FAFSA. In 2016, 123 master's, 2 doctorates awarded. *Program availability:* Part-time, evening/weekend, blended/hybrid learning. Offers business (MA, MBA, MPA, MSIS, MTX, PhD); business administration (MBA, PhD); finance and economics (MA, PhD); information systems (MSIS, PhD); management (PhD); project management (MBA). *Application deadline:* For fall admission, 3/1 priority date for domestic students, 5/1 for international students; for spring admission, 11/1 for domestic students, 9/1 for international students. Applications are processed on a rolling basis. *Application fee:* $60. Electronic applications accepted. *Application Contact:* Lakan Drinker, Admissions and Enrollment Assistant, 662-325-8951, E-mail: ldrinker@grad.msstate.edu. *Dean and Professor*, Dr. Sharon Oswald, 662-325-2580, Fax: 662-325-2410, E-mail: slo49@msstate.edu.

Adkerson School of Accountancy Students: 49 full-time (23 women), 1 (woman) part-time; includes 1 minority (Asian, non-Hispanic/Latino), 3 international. Average age 23. 37 applicants, 54% accepted, 18 enrolled. *Faculty:* 10 full-time (2 women). Expenses: Contact institution. *Financial support:* Career-related internships or fieldwork, Federal Work-Study, institutionally sponsored loans, scholarships/grants, and unspecified assistantships available. Support available to part-time students. Financial award application deadline: 4/1; financial award applicants required to submit FAFSA. In 2016, 39 master's awarded. Offers accountancy (MPA, MTX); systems (MPA). *Application deadline:* For fall admission, 7/1 for domestic students, 5/1 for international students; for spring admission, 11/1 for domestic students, 9/1 for international students. Applications are processed on a rolling basis. *Application fee:* $60. Electronic applications accepted. *Application Contact:* Lakan Drinker, Admissions and Enrollment Assistant, 662-325-8951, E-mail: ldrinker@grad.msstate.edu. *Director and Professor*, Dr. Shawn Mauldin, 662-325-3710, Fax: 662-325-1646, E-mail: smauldin@business.msstate.edu.

College of Education Students: 267 full-time (163 women), 455 part-time (333 women); includes 246 minority (215 Black or African American, non-Hispanic/Latino; 4 American Indian or Alaska Native, non-Hispanic/Latino; 6 Asian, non-Hispanic/Latino; 9 Hispanic/Latino; 1 Native Hawaiian or other Pacific Islander, non-Hispanic/Latino; 11 Two or more races, non-Hispanic/Latino), 16 international. Average age 33. 401 applicants, 59% accepted, 189 enrolled. *Faculty:* 99 full-time (53 women), 4 part-time/adjunct (3 women). Expenses: Contact institution. *Financial support:* In 2016–17, 13 research assistantships (averaging $12,017 per year), 28 teaching assistantships (averaging $9,736 per year) were awarded; career-related internships or fieldwork, Federal Work-Study, institutionally sponsored loans, scholarships/grants, and unspecified assistantships also available. Financial award application deadline: 4/1; financial award applicants required to submit FAFSA. In 2016, 180 master's, 27 doctorates, 24 other advanced degrees awarded. *Program availability:* Part-time, evening/weekend, online learning. Offers clinical mental health (MS); college counseling (MS); college/post secondary student counseling and personnel services (PhD); community college education (MAT, PhD); counselor education (Ed S); counselor education/student counseling and guidance services (PhD); distance education (MSIT); early childhood education (PhD); education (MAT, MS, MSIT, MST, PhD, Ed S); elementary education (MS, PhD, Ed S); elementary, middle and secondary education administration (PhD); exercise physiology (MS); exercise science (PhD); general curriculum and instruction (PhD); general educational psychology (MS); instructional design (MSIT); instructional systems and workforce development (MST, PhD); middle level (MAT); multimedia (MSIT); psychometry (MS); reading education (PhD); rehabilitation (MS); school administration (MS, Ed S); school counseling (MS); school psychology (PhD, Ed S); secondary education (MAT, MS, PhD, Ed S); special education (MAT, MS, PhD, Ed S); sport administration (MS); sport pedagogy (MS); sport studies (PhD); student affairs (MS); technology (Ed S); workforce education leadership (MS). *Application deadline:* For fall admission, 7/1 for domestic students, 5/1 for international students; for spring admission, 11/1 for domestic students, 9/1 for international students. Applications are processed on a rolling basis. *Application fee:* $60. Electronic applications accepted. *Application Contact:* Linda Bonner, Senior Admissions Assistant, 662-325-3363, E-mail: lbonner@grad.msstate.edu. *Dean*, Dr. Richard Blackbourn, 662-325-3717, Fax: 662-325-8784, E-mail: rlb277@msstate.edu.

College of Forest Resources Students: 100 full-time (38 women), 42 part-time (15 women); includes 11 minority (4 Black or African American, non-Hispanic/Latino; 1 American Indian or Alaska Native, non-Hispanic/Latino; 2 Asian, non-Hispanic/Latino; 2 Hispanic/Latino; 2 Two or more races, non-Hispanic/Latino), 43 international. Average age 29. 82 applicants, 74% accepted, 56 enrolled. *Faculty:* 58 full-time (12 women), 1 part-time/adjunct (0 women). Expenses: Contact institution. *Financial support:* In 2016–17, 95 research assistantships with full tuition reimbursements (averaging $14,883 per year) were awarded; career-related internships or fieldwork, Federal Work-Study, institutionally sponsored loans, and unspecified assistantships also available. Financial award application deadline: 4/1; financial award applicants required to submit FAFSA. In 2016, 25 master's, 17 doctorates awarded. *Program availability:* Part-time. Offers forest resources (MS, PhD); forestry (MS); sustainable bioproducts (MS, PhD); wildlife, fisheries and aquaculture (MS, PhD). *Application deadline:* For fall admission, 7/1 for domestic students, 5/1 for international students; for spring admission, 11/1 for domestic students, 9/1 for international students. Applications are processed on a rolling basis. *Application fee:* $60. Electronic applications accepted. *Application Contact:* Nathan

Drake, Admissions Assistant, 662-325-3804, E-mail: ndrake@grad.msstate.edu. *Dean,* Dr. George Hopper, 662-325-2953, Fax: 662-325-8726, E-mail: ghopper@cfr.msstate.edu.

College of Veterinary Medicine Students: 346 full-time (270 women), 36 part-time (21 women); includes 21 minority (5 Black or African American, non-Hispanic/Latino; 3 American Indian or Alaska Native, non-Hispanic/Latino; 1 Asian, non-Hispanic/Latino; 10 Hispanic/Latino; 2 Two or more races, non-Hispanic/Latino). Average age 24. 957 applicants, 10% accepted, 92 enrolled. *Faculty:* 112 full-time (36 women). Expenses: Contact institution. *Financial support:* In 2016–17, 33 research assistantships with full tuition reimbursements (averaging $15,933 per year) were awarded; career-related internships or fieldwork, Federal Work-Study, and institutionally sponsored loans also available. Financial award application deadline: 6/30; financial award applicants required to submit FAFSA. In 2016, 84 doctorates awarded. Offers veterinary medical science (MS, PhD); veterinary medicine (MS, DVM, PhD). *Application deadline:* For fall admission, 9/15 for domestic and international students. *Application fee:* $55. Electronic applications accepted. *Application Contact:* Missy Hadaway, Admissions and Student Affairs Coordinator, 662-325-9065, Fax: 663-325-1027, E-mail: missy.hadaway@msstate.edu. *Dean,* Dr. Kent H. Hoblet, 662-325-1131, Fax: 662-325-1498, E-mail: hoblet@cvm.msstate.edu.

MISSISSIPPI UNIVERSITY FOR WOMEN, Columbus, MS 39701-9998

General Information State-supported, coed, comprehensive institution. *Graduate housing:* Rooms and/or apartments available on a first-come, first-served basis to single and married students.

GRADUATE UNITS

Graduate School *Program availability:* Part-time. Offers health education (MS).

College of Education and Human Sciences *Program availability:* Part-time. Offers differentiated instruction (M Ed); educational leadership (M Ed); gifted studies (M Ed); reading/literacy (M Ed); teaching (MAT).

College of Nursing and Speech Language Pathology *Program availability:* Part-time. Offers nursing (MSN, PMC); speech-language pathology (MS).

MISSISSIPPI VALLEY STATE UNIVERSITY, Itta Bena, MS 38941-1400

General Information State-supported, coed, comprehensive institution. *Enrollment:* 2,455 graduate, professional, and undergraduate students; 152 full-time matriculated graduate/professional students (118 women), 292 part-time matriculated graduate/professional students (186 women). *Enrollment by degree level:* 444 master's. *Graduate faculty:* 38 full-time (18 women), 8 part-time/adjunct (3 women). Tuition, state resident: full-time $6858; part-time $381 per credit hour. Tuition, nonresident: full-time $6858; part-time $381 per credit hour. *Required fees:* $150; $150 per credit hour. $75 per semester. *Graduate housing:* On-campus housing not available. *Student services:* Career counseling, child daycare facilities, exercise/wellness program, international student services, low-cost health insurance, writing training. *Library facilities:* James Herbert White Library. *Collection:* Books: 127,541 (physical), 53,358 (digital/electronic); Databases: 62. Weekly public service hours: 84; students can reserve study rooms.

Computer facilities: 285 computers available on campus for general student use. A campuswide network can be accessed from student residence rooms and from off campus. Online class registration is available. Website: http://www.mvsu.edu/

General Application Contact: Jacqueline Williams, Office of Admissions, 662-254-3344, Fax: 662-254-3759, E-mail: jawill@mvsu.edu.

GRADUATE UNITS

College of Education Students: 6 full-time (4 women), 132 part-time (89 women); includes 133 minority (132 Black or African American, non-Hispanic/Latino; 1 Asian, non-Hispanic/Latino). Average age 34. *Faculty:* 7 full-time (6 women), 2 part-time/adjunct (both women). Expenses: Contact institution. *Financial support:* Institutionally sponsored loans available. Financial award application deadline: 8/1; financial award applicants required to submit FAFSA. In 2016, 17 master's awarded. *Program availability:* Part-time, evening/weekend. Offers education (MAT, MS). *Application deadline:* Applications are processed on a rolling basis. *Application fee:* $0. *Application Contact:* Office of Admissions, 601-254-3344. *Chair,* Dr. Chukwuma Ahanonu, 601-254-3619.

Department of Criminal Justice Students: 8 full-time (4 women), 46 part-time (27 women); includes 52 minority (all Black or African American, non-Hispanic/Latino). Average age 33. 13 applicants, 100% accepted. *Faculty:* 5 full-time (2 women), 5 part-time/adjunct (all women). Expenses: Contact institution. *Financial support:* In 2016–17, 12 students received support, including research assistantships with full tuition reimbursements available (averaging $3,640 per year); Federal Work-Study and scholarships/grants also available. Support available to part-time students. Financial award application deadline: 4/15; financial award applicants required to submit FAFSA. In 2016, 26 master's awarded. *Program availability:* Part-time, evening/weekend. Offers criminal justice (MS). *Application deadline:* For fall admission, 4/1 priority date for domestic students; for spring admission, 12/15 priority date for domestic students. Applications are processed on a rolling basis. *Application fee:* $0. Electronic applications accepted. *Chair,* Dr. Emmanuel Amadi, 601-254-3363, Fax: 601-254-3646.

Department of Natural Science and Environmental Health Students: 19 full-time (16 women), 6 part-time (4 women); includes 23 minority (19 Black or African American, non-Hispanic/Latino; 2 Asian, non-Hispanic/Latino; 2 Hispanic/Latino). Average age 27. *Faculty:* 5 full-time (2 women), 1 part-time/adjunct (0 women). Expenses: Contact institution. *Financial support:* Research assistantships, teaching assistantships, career-related internships or fieldwork, Federal Work-Study, scholarships/grants, and unspecified assistantships available. Financial award application deadline: 4/1; financial award applicants required to submit FAFSA. In 2016, 9 master's awarded. *Program availability:* Part-time, evening/weekend. Offers natural science and environmental health (MS). *Application deadline:* For fall admission, 4/1 for domestic students; for spring admission, 12/15 for domestic students. Applications are processed on a rolling basis. *Application fee:* $0. *Application Contact:* Office of Admissions, 601-254-3344. *Chair,* Julius Ikenga, 662-254-3377.

MISSOURI BAPTIST UNIVERSITY, St. Louis, MO 63141-8660

General Information Independent-religious, coed, comprehensive institution.

GRADUATE UNITS

Graduate Programs

MISSOURI SOUTHERN STATE UNIVERSITY, Joplin, MO 64801-1595

General Information State-supported, coed, comprehensive institution.

GRADUATE UNITS

Program in Business Administration *Program availability:* Online learning. Offers business administration (MBA). Program offered jointly with Northwest Missouri State University.

Program in Criminal Justice Administration *Program availability:* Online learning. Offers criminal justice administration (MS). Program offered jointly with Southeast Missouri State University.

Program in Dental Hygiene *Program availability:* Part-time. Offers dental hygiene (MS). Program offered jointly with University of Missouri–Kansas City. Electronic applications accepted.

Program in Early Childhood Education Offers early childhood education (MS Ed). Program offered jointly with Northwest Missouri State University.

Program in Instructional Technology Offers instructional technology (MS Ed). Program offered jointly with Northwest Missouri State University.

Program in Nursing *Program availability:* Part-time. Offers nursing (MSN). Program offered jointly with University of Missouri–Kansas City. Electronic applications accepted.

Program in Teaching Offers teaching (MAT). Program offered jointly with Missouri State University.

★ MISSOURI STATE UNIVERSITY, Springfield, MO 65897

General Information State-supported, coed, comprehensive institution. CGS member. *Enrollment:* 23,538 graduate, professional, and undergraduate students; 1,577 full-time matriculated graduate/professional students (962 women), 1,844 part-time matriculated graduate/professional students (1,187 women). *Enrollment by degree level:* 2,458 master's, 338 doctoral, 90 other advanced degrees. *Graduate faculty:* 370 full-time (150 women), 74 part-time/adjunct (36 women). Tuition, state resident: full-time $5830. Tuition, nonresident: full-time $10,708. *Required fees:* $1130. Tuition and fees vary according to class time, course level, course load and program. *Graduate housing:* Rooms and/or apartments available on a first-come, first-served basis to single and married students. Typical cost: $9316 (including board) for single students; $7854 per year ($10,254 including board) for married students. Room and board charges vary according to board plan, campus/location and housing facility selected. Housing application deadline: 7/1. *Student services:* Campus employment opportunities, campus safety program, career counseling, child daycare facilities, exercise/wellness program, free psychological counseling, grant writing training, international student services, multicultural affairs office, services for students with disabilities, teacher training, writing training. *Library facilities:* Meyer Library.

Computer facilities: A campuswide network can be accessed from student residence rooms and from off campus. Online class registration is available. Website: http://www.missouristate.edu/

General Application Contact: Michael Edwards, Coordinator of Graduate Admissions, 417-836-5330, Fax: 417-836-6200, E-mail: graduateadmissions@missouristate.edu.

GRADUATE UNITS

Graduate College Students: 1,473 full-time (914 women), 1,413 part-time (890 women); includes 283 minority (75 Black or African American, non-Hispanic/Latino; 9 American Indian or Alaska Native, non-Hispanic/Latino; 38 Asian, non-Hispanic/Latino; 86 Hispanic/Latino; 1 Native Hawaiian or other Pacific Islander, non-Hispanic/Latino; 74 Two or more races, non-Hispanic/Latino), 489 international. Average age 32. 1,368 applicants, 75% accepted, 762 enrolled. *Faculty:* 743 full-time (364 women), 392 part-time/adjunct (210 women). Expenses: Contact institution. *Financial support:* In 2016–17, 44 research assistantships with full tuition reimbursements (averaging $8,772 per year), 195 teaching assistantships with full tuition reimbursements (averaging $8,772 per year) were awarded; Federal Work-Study, institutionally sponsored loans, scholarships/grants, and unspecified assistantships also available. Financial award application deadline: 3/31; financial award applicants required to submit FAFSA. In 2016, 1,416 master's, 184 doctorates, 22 other advanced degrees awarded. *Program availability:* Part-time, 100% online, blended/hybrid learning. Offers administrative studies (Certificate); applied communication (MS); criminal justice (MS); environmental management (MS); homeland security (MS); individualized (MS); screenwriting and producing (MS); sports management (MS). *Application deadline:* For fall admission, 7/20 priority date for domestic students, 5/1 for international students; for spring admission, 12/20 priority date for domestic students, 9/1 for international students. Applications are processed on a rolling basis. *Application fee:* $35 ($50 for international students). Electronic applications accepted. *Application Contact:* Michael Edwards, Coordinator of Graduate Admissions, 417-836-5330, Fax: 417-836-6200, E-mail: michaeledwards@missouristate.edu. *Associate Provost/Dean,* Dr. Julie Masterson, 417-836-5335, Fax: 417-836-6888, E-mail: juliemasterson@missouristate.edu.

College of Arts and Letters Students: 98 full-time (71 women), 111 part-time (76 women); includes 17 minority (3 Black or African American, non-Hispanic/Latino; 2 Asian, non-Hispanic/Latino; 4 Hispanic/Latino; 1 Native Hawaiian or other Pacific Islander, non-Hispanic/Latino; 7 Two or more races, non-Hispanic/Latino), 40 international. Average age 34. 184 applicants, 61% accepted, 66 enrolled. *Faculty:* 74 full-time (32 women), 7 part-time/adjunct (5 women). Expenses: Contact institution. *Financial support:* In 2016–17, 61 teaching assistantships with full tuition reimbursements (averaging $8,772 per year) were awarded; Federal Work-Study, institutionally sponsored loans, scholarships/grants, and unspecified assistantships also available. Financial award application deadline: 3/31; financial award applicants required to submit FAFSA. In 2016, 102 master's awarded. *Program availability:* Part-time, evening/weekend, 100% online, blended/hybrid learning. Offers applied second language acquisition (MASLA); arts and letters (MA, MASLA, MFA, MM, MS Ed, Certificate); communication and mass media (MA); English (MA); English education (MS Ed); music (MM, MS Ed); speech and theatre education (MS Ed); teaching English to speakers of other languages (Certificate); visual studies (MFA); writing (MA). *Application deadline:* For fall admission, 7/20 priority date for domestic students, 5/1 for international students; for spring admission, 12/20 priority date for domestic students, 9/1 for international students; for summer admission, 5/20 priority date for domestic students. Applications are processed on a rolling basis. *Application fee:* $35 ($50 for international students). Electronic applications accepted. *Application Contact:* Michael Edwards, Coordinator of Graduate Admissions, 417-836-5330, Fax: 417-836-6200, E-mail: michaeledwards@missouristate.edu. *Dean,* Dr. Gloria Galanes, 417-836-5247, Fax: 417-836-6940, E-mail: gloriagalanes@missouristate.edu.

College of Business Administration Students: 395 full-time (194 women), 339 part-time (134 women); includes 71 minority (20 Black or African American, non-Hispanic/Latino; 13 Asian, non-Hispanic/Latino; 22 Hispanic/Latino; 16 Two or more races, non-Hispanic/Latino), 299 international. Average age 33. 581 applicants, 52% accepted, 195 enrolled. *Faculty:* 50 full-time (13 women), 8 part-time/adjunct (1 woman). Expenses: Contact institution. *Financial support:* In 2016–17, 4 teaching assistantships with full tuition reimbursements (averaging $10,672 per year) were awarded; Federal Work-Study, institutionally sponsored loans, scholarships/grants, and unspecified assistantships also available. Financial award application deadline: 3/31; financial award applicants required to submit FAFSA. In 2016, 1,115 master's awarded. *Program availability:* Part-time, evening/weekend, 100% online, blended/hybrid learning. Offers accountancy (M Acc); business administration (M Acc, MBA, MHA, MS, MS Ed); cybersecurity (MS); health administration (MHA); project management (MS). *Application deadline:* For fall admission, 7/20 priority date for domestic students, 5/1 for international students; for spring admission, 12/20 priority date for domestic students, 9/1 for international students; for summer admission, 5/20 priority date for domestic students. Applications are processed on a rolling basis. *Application fee:* $35 ($50 for international students). Electronic applications accepted. *Application Contact:* Michael Edwards, Coordinator of Graduate Admissions, 417-836-5330, Fax: 417-836-6200, E-mail: michaeledwards@missouristate.edu. *Dean,* Dr. Stephanie Bryant, 417-836-5646, Fax: 417-836-4407, E-mail: coba@missouristate.edu.

College of Education Students: 205 full-time (162 women), 546 part-time (458 women); includes 65 minority (18 Black or African American, non-Hispanic/Latino; 1 American Indian or Alaska Native, non-Hispanic/Latino; 1 Asian, non-Hispanic/Latino; 30 Hispanic/Latino; 1 Native Hawaiian or other Pacific Islander, non-Hispanic/Latino; 14 Two or more races, non-Hispanic/Latino), 21 international. Average age 33. 266 applicants, 66% accepted, 126 enrolled. *Faculty:* 43 full-time (26 women), 11 part-time/adjunct (6 women). Expenses: Contact institution. *Financial support:* Teaching assistantships, Federal Work-Study, institutionally sponsored loans, scholarships/grants, and unspecified assistantships available. Financial award application deadline: 3/31; financial award applicants required to submit FAFSA. In 2016, 195 master's, 16 other advanced degrees awarded. *Program availability:* Part-time. Offers alternative certification (MS Ed); autism spectrum disorder (MS Ed); blindness and low vision (MS Ed); counseling (MS); counseling and assessment (Ed S); early childhood and family development (MS); education (MAT, MS, MS Ed, Ed S); educational administration (MS Ed, Ed S); educational technology (MS Ed); elementary education (MS Ed); elementary principal (MS Ed, Ed S); elementary school counseling (MS); literacy (MS Ed); mental health counseling (MS); orientation and mobility (MS Ed); secondary principal (MS Ed, Ed S); secondary school counseling (MS); special education (MS Ed); student affairs in higher education (MS); superintendent (Ed S); teacher leadership (Certificate, Ed S); teaching (MAT); teaching and learning (MA, Certificate). *Application deadline:* For fall admission, 7/20 for domestic students, 5/1 for international students; for spring admission, 12/20 for domestic students, 9/1 for international students; for summer admission, 5/20 for domestic students. Applications are processed on a rolling basis. *Application fee:* $35 ($50 for international students). Electronic applications accepted. *Application Contact:* Michael Edwards, Coordinator of Graduate Admissions, 417-836-5330, Fax: 417-836-6200, E-mail: michaeledwards@missouristate.edu. *Dean,* Dr. David Hough, 417-836-5254, Fax: 417-836-4884, E-mail: collegeofeducation@missouristate.edu.

College of Health and Human Services Students: 610 full-time (425 women), 160 part-time (130 women); includes 81 minority (17 Black or African American, non-Hispanic/Latino; 7 American Indian or Alaska Native, non-Hispanic/Latino; 16 Asian, non-Hispanic/Latino; 18 Hispanic/Latino; 23 Two or more races, non-Hispanic/Latino), 31 international. Average age 28. 549 applicants, 42% accepted, 180 enrolled. *Faculty:* 89 full-time (58 women), 33 part-time/adjunct (21 women). Expenses: Contact institution. *Financial support:* In 2016–17, 9 research assistantships with full tuition reimbursements (averaging $8,772 per year), 33 teaching assistantships with full tuition reimbursements (averaging $8,772 per year) were awarded; Federal Work-Study, institutionally sponsored loans, scholarships/grants, and unspecified assistantships also available. Financial award application deadline: 3/31; financial award applicants required to submit FAFSA. In 2016, 189 master's, 78 doctorates awarded. *Program availability:* Part-time. Offers applied behavior analysis (MS); athletic training (MS); cell and molecular biology (MS); clinical psychology (MS); communication sciences and disorders (Au D); dietetic internship (Certificate); experimental psychology (MS); forensic child psychology (Certificate); health and human services (MOT, MPH, MS, MS Ed, MSN, MSW, Au D, DNAP, DNP, DPT, Certificate); health promotion and wellness management (MS); industrial/organizational psychology (MS); nurse anesthesia (DNAP); nursing (MSN); nursing practice (DNP); occupational therapy (MOT); physical therapy (DPT); physician assistant studies (MS); public health (MPH); secondary education (MS Ed); social work (MSW); speech language pathology (MS). *Application fee:* $35 ($50 for international students). Electronic applications accepted. *Application Contact:* Michael Edwards, Coordinator of Graduate Admissions, 417-836-5330, Fax: 417-836-6200, E-mail: michaeledwards@missouristate.edu. *Dean,* Dr. Helen Reid, 417-836-4176, Fax: 417-836-6905, E-mail: chhs@missouristate.edu.

College of Humanities and Public Affairs Students: 73 full-time (30 women), 151 part-time (58 women); includes 31 minority (11 Black or African American, non-Hispanic/Latino; 1 American Indian or Alaska Native, non-Hispanic/Latino; 4 Asian, non-Hispanic/Latino; 7 Hispanic/Latino; 8 Two or more races, non-Hispanic/Latino), 13 international. Average age 32. 157 applicants, 65% accepted, 69 enrolled. *Faculty:* 66 full-time (20 women), 21 part-time/adjunct (5 women). Expenses: Contact institution. *Financial support:* In 2016–17, 3 teaching assistantships with partial tuition reimbursements (averaging $2,150 per year) were awarded; Federal Work-Study, institutionally sponsored loans, scholarships/grants, and unspecified assistantships also available. Financial award application deadline: 3/31; financial award applicants required to submit FAFSA. In 2016, 82 master's awarded. *Program availability:* Part-time. Offers community corrections (Certificate); criminology and criminal justice (MS); defense and strategic studies (Certificate); general weapons of mass destruction (MS); global studies (MGS); history (MA); history education (MS Ed); history for teachers (Certificate); homeland security and defense (Certificate); humanities and public affairs (MA, MGS, MIAA, MPA, MS, MS Ed, Certificate); public administration (MPA); public management (Certificate); religious studies (MA, Certificate). *Application deadline:* For fall admission, 7/20 priority date for domestic students, 5/1 for international students; for spring admission, 12/20 priority date for domestic students, 9/1 for international students; for summer admission, 5/20 priority date for domestic students. Applications are processed on a rolling basis. *Application fee:* $35 ($50 for international students). Electronic applications accepted. *Application Contact:* Michael Edwards, Coordinator of Graduate Admissions, 417-836-5330, Fax: 417-836-6200, E-mail: michaeledwards@missouristate.edu. *Dean,* Dr. Victor Matthews, 417-836-5529, Fax: 417-836-8472, E-mail: victormatthews@missouristate.edu.

College of Natural and Applied Sciences Students: 63 full-time (20 women), 78 part-time (43 women); includes 6 minority (1 Asian, non-Hispanic/Latino; 4 Hispanic/Latino; 1 Two or more races, non-Hispanic/Latino), 39 international. Average age 27. 161 applicants, 43% accepted, 43 enrolled. *Faculty:* 87 full-time (14 women), 8 part-time/adjunct (2 women). Expenses: Contact institution. *Financial support:* In 2016–17, 11 research assistantships with full tuition reimbursements (averaging $10,672 per year), 81 teaching assistantships with full tuition reimbursements (averaging $9,483 per year) were awarded; Federal Work-Study, institutionally sponsored loans, scholarships/grants, and unspecified assistantships also available. Financial award application deadline: 3/31; financial award applicants required to submit FAFSA. In 2016, 60 master's awarded. *Program availability:* Part-time, evening/weekend. Offers biology (MS); chemistry (MS); materials science (MS); mathematics (MS); natural and applied science (MNAS); natural and applied sciences (MNAS, MS, MS Ed); secondary education (MS Ed). *Application deadline:* For fall admission, 7/20 priority date for domestic students, 5/1 for international students; for spring admission, 12/20 priority date for domestic students, 9/1 for international students; for summer admission, 5/20 priority date for domestic students. Applications are processed on a rolling basis. *Application fee:* $35 ($50 for international students). Electronic applications accepted. *Application Contact:* Michael Edwards, Coordinator of Graduate Admissions, 417-836-5330, Fax: 417-836-6200, E-mail: michaeledwards@missouristate.edu. *Dean,* Dr. Tamera Jahnke, 417-836-5249, Fax: 417-836-6934, E-mail: tamerajahnke@missouristate.edu.

Darr College of Agriculture Students: 20 full-time (16 women), 26 part-time (10 women); includes 4 minority (1 Black or African American, non-Hispanic/Latino; 3 Two or more races, non-Hispanic/Latino), 2 international. Average age 27. 28 applicants, 64% accepted, 17 enrolled. *Faculty:* 16 full-time (5 women), 1 part-time/adjunct (0 women). Expenses: Contact institution. *Financial support:* In 2016–17, 7 research assistantships with full tuition reimbursements (averaging $9,365 per year), 6 teaching assistantships with full tuition reimbursements (averaging $8,450 per year) were awarded; Federal Work-Study, institutionally sponsored loans, scholarships/grants, and unspecified assistantships also available. Financial award application deadline: 3/31; financial award applicants required to submit FAFSA. In 2016, 26 master's awarded. *Program availability:* Part-time. Offers plant science (MS); secondary education (MS Ed). *Application deadline:* For fall admission, 7/20 priority date for domestic students, 5/1 for international students; for spring admission, 12/20 priority date for domestic students, 9/1 for international students; for summer admission, 5/20 priority date for domestic students. Applications are processed on a rolling basis. *Application fee:* $35 ($50 for international students). Electronic applications accepted. *Application Contact:* Michael Edwards, Coordinator of Graduate Admissions, 417-836-5330, Fax: 417-836-6200, E-mail: michaeledwards@missouristate.edu. *Dean,* Dr. Ronald Del Vecchio, 417-836-5050, E-mail: darr@missouristate.edu.

See Close-Up on page 889.

MISSOURI UNIVERSITY OF SCIENCE AND TECHNOLOGY, Rolla, MO 65409

General Information State-supported, coed, university. CGS member. *Graduate housing:* Rooms and/or apartments available on a first-come, first-served basis to single and married students. *Research affiliation:* Geoengineers, Inc. (rock mechanics and explosives research), Caterpillar, Inc. (mining and nuclear engineering), Idaho National Laboratory (material research), Hussmann, Corp (mining and nuclear engineering), Samsung (material research), Cisco (material research).

GRADUATE UNITS

Graduate School *Program availability:* Part-time, evening/weekend. Offers aerospace engineering (MS, PhD); applied and environmental biology (MS); applied mathematics (MS); business and management systems (MBA); ceramic engineering (MS, DE, PhD); chemical engineering (MS, DE, PhD); chemistry (MS, MST, PhD); civil engineering (MS, DE, PhD); computer engineering (MS, DE, PhD); computer science (MS, PhD); construction engineering (MS, DE, PhD); electrical engineering (MS, DE, PhD); engineering management (MS, DE, PhD); environmental engineering (MS); fluid mechanics (MS, DE, PhD); geological engineering (MS, DE, PhD); geology and geophysics (MS, PhD); geotechnical engineering (MS, DE, PhD); hydrology and hydraulic engineering (MS, DE, PhD); information science and technology (MS); manufacturing engineering (M Eng, MS); mathematics (MST, PhD); mechanical engineering (MS, DE, PhD); metallurgical engineering (MS, PhD); mining engineering (MS, DE, PhD); nuclear engineering (MS, DE, PhD); petroleum engineering (MS, DE, PhD); physics (MS, MST, PhD); systems engineering (MS, PhD). Electronic applications accepted.

MISSOURI VALLEY COLLEGE, Marshall, MO 65340-3197

General Information Independent-religious, coed, comprehensive institution.

GRADUATE UNITS

Graduate Studies

★ MISSOURI WESTERN STATE UNIVERSITY, St. Joseph, MO 64507-2294

General Information State-supported, coed, comprehensive institution. CGS member. *Enrollment:* 5,363 graduate, professional, and undergraduate students; 92 full-time matriculated graduate/professional students (37 women), 142 part-time matriculated graduate/professional students (96 women). *Enrollment by degree level:* 227 master's, 7 other advanced degrees. *Graduate faculty:* 45 full-time (17 women), 6 part-time/adjunct (4 women). Tuition, state resident: full-time $6548; part-time $327.39 per credit hour. Tuition, nonresident: full-time $11,848; part-time $592.39 per credit hour. *Required fees:* $542; $99 per credit hour. $176 per semester. One-time fee: $50. Tuition and fees vary according to course load and program. *Graduate housing:* Room and/or apartments available on a first-come, first-served basis to single students; on-campus housing not available to married students. Typical cost: $6676 per year ($10,002 including board). Room and board charges vary according to board plan and housing facility selected. *Student services:* Campus employment opportunities, campus safety program, career counseling, child daycare facilities, exercise/wellness program, free psychological counseling, international student services, low-cost health insurance, multicultural affairs office, services for students with disabilities. *Library facilities:* Missouri Western State University Library. *Collection:* Books: 229,238 (physical), 431,211 (digital/electronic); Serial titles: 13,079 (physical), 6,056 (digital/electronic); Databases: 68.

Computer facilities: Computer purchase and lease plans are available. A campuswide network can be accessed from student residence rooms and from off campus. Online class registration, personal online storage are available.

Website: http://www.missouriwestern.edu/

General Application Contact: Dr. Benjamin D. Caldwell, Dean of the Graduate School, 816-271-4525, Fax: 816-271-4525, E-mail: graduate@missouriwestern.edu.

GRADUATE UNITS

Program in Applied Science Students: 41 full-time (18 women), 27 part-time (11 women); includes 7 minority (6 Black or African American, non-Hispanic/Latino; 1 Two or more races, non-Hispanic/Latino), 15 international. Average age 29. 43 applicants, 88% accepted, 30 enrolled. Expenses: Contact institution. *Financial support:* Scholarships/grants and unspecified assistantships available. Support available to part-time students. In 2016, 34 master's awarded. *Program availability:* Part-time. Offers chemistry (MAS); engineering technology management (MAS); human factors and usability testing (MAS); industrial life science (MAS); sport and fitness management (MAS). *Application deadline:* For fall admission, 7/15 for domestic and international students; for spring admission, 10/1 for domestic and international students; for summer admission, 3/15 for domestic students. Applications are processed on a rolling basis. *Application fee:* $50. Electronic applications accepted. *Dean of the Graduate School,* Dr. Benjamin D. Caldwell, 816-271-4394, Fax: 816-271-4525, E-mail: graduate@missouriwestern.edu.

Program in Assessment Students: 1 (woman) full-time, 33 part-time (25 women). Average age 37. 9 applicants, 100% accepted, 5 enrolled. Expenses: Contact institution. *Financial support:* Scholarships/grants and unspecified assistantships available. Support available to part-time students. In 2016, 6 master's, 1 other advanced degree awarded. *Program availability:* Part-time. Offers autism spectrum disorders (MAS, Graduate Certificate); TESOL (MAS, Graduate Certificate); writing (MAS). *Application deadline:* For fall admission, 7/15 for domestic and international students; for spring admission, 10/1 for domestic and international students; for summer admission, 3/15 for domestic students. Applications are processed on a rolling basis. *Application fee:* $50. Electronic applications accepted. *Application Contact:* Dr. Benjamin D. Caldwell, Dean of the Graduate School, 816-271-4394, Fax: 816-271-4525, E-mail: graduate@missouriwestern.edu. *Director of Graduate Programs in Education,* Dr. Susan Bashinski, 816-271-5629, E-mail: sbashinski@missouriwestern.edu.

Program in Business Administration Expenses: Contact institution. *Financial support:* Scholarships/grants and unspecified assistantships available. Support available to part-time students. *Program availability:* Part-time. Offers animal and life sciences (MBA); enterprise resource planning (MBA); forensic accounting (MBA); general business (MBA). *Application deadline:* For fall admission, 7/15 for domestic and international students; for spring admission, 10/1 for domestic and international students; for summer admission, 3/15 for domestic students. Applications are processed on a rolling basis. *Application fee:* $50. Electronic applications accepted. *Application Contact:* Dr. Benjamin D. Caldwell, Dean of the Graduate School, 816-271-4394, Fax: 816-271-4525, E-mail: graduate@missouriwestern.edu. *Director,* Dr. Logan Jones, 816-271-4351, E-mail: jjones81@missouriwestern.edu.

Program in Digital Media Students: 12 full-time (5 women), 5 part-time (1 woman), 9 international. Average age 30. 9 applicants, 56% accepted, 3 enrolled. Expenses: Contact institution. *Financial support:* Scholarships/grants and unspecified assistantships available. Support available to part-time students. In 2016, 1 master's awarded. *Program availability:* Part-time. Offers digital media (MAA). *Application deadline:* For fall admission, 7/15 for domestic and international students; for spring admission, 10/1 for domestic and international students; for summer admission, 3/15 for domestic students. Applications are processed on a rolling basis. *Application fee:* $50. Electronic applications accepted. *Application Contact:* Dr. Benjamin D. Caldwell, Dean of the Graduate School, 816-271-4394, Fax: 816-271-4525, E-mail: graduate@missouriwestern.edu. *Professor,* Dr. Bob Bergland, 816-271-4446, E-mail: bergland@missouriwestern.edu.

Program in Forensic Investigations Students: 4 full-time (all women), 15 part-time (12 women); includes 5 minority (4 Black or African American, non-Hispanic/Latino; 1 Two or more races, non-Hispanic/Latino), 1 international. Average age 30. 7 applicants, 100% accepted, 6 enrolled. Expenses: Contact institution. *Financial support:* Scholarships/grants and unspecified assistantships available. Support available to part-time students. In 2016, 1 master's, 1 other advanced degree awarded. *Program availability:* Part-time. Offers forensic investigations (MAS, Graduate Certificate). *Application deadline:* For fall admission, 7/15 for domestic and international students; for spring admission, 10/1 for domestic and international students; for summer admission, 3/15 for domestic students. Applications are processed on a rolling basis. *Application fee:* $50. Electronic applications accepted. *Application Contact:* Dr. Benjamin D. Caldwell, Dean of the Graduate School, 816-271-4394, Fax: 816-271-4525, E-mail: graduate@missouriwestern.edu. *Forensics Graduate Program Director,* Dr. Monty Smith, 816-271-4434, E-mail: msmith84@missouriwestern.edu.

Program in Information Management Students: 21 full-time (8 women), 18 part-time (9 women); includes 3 minority (1 Black or African American, non-Hispanic/Latino; 1 Asian, non-Hispanic/Latino; 1 Two or more races, non-Hispanic/Latino), 25 international. Average age 30. 10 applicants, 80% accepted, 5 enrolled. Expenses: Contact institution. *Financial support:* Scholarships/grants and unspecified assistantships available. Support available to part-time students. In 2016, 2 master's awarded. *Program availability:* Part-time. Offers enterprise resource planning (MIM). *Application deadline:* For fall admission, 7/15 for domestic and international students; for spring admission, 10/1 for domestic and international students; for summer admission, 3/15 for domestic students. Applications are processed on a rolling basis. *Application fee:* $50. Electronic applications accepted. *Application Contact:* Dr. Benjamin D. Caldwell, Dean of the Graduate School, 816-271-4394, Fax: 816-271-4525, E-mail: graduate@missouriwestern.edu. *Professor,* Dr. Peggy Lane, 816-271-5832, E-mail: plane3@missouriwestern.edu.

Program in Information Technology Assurance Administration Students: 12 full-time (1 woman), 4 part-time (0 women), 13 international. Average age 26. 17 applicants, 47% accepted, 3 enrolled. Expenses: Contact institution. *Financial support:* Scholarships/grants and unspecified assistantships available. Support available to part-time students. In 2016, 9 master's awarded. *Program availability:* Part-time. Offers information technology assurance administration (MS). *Application deadline:* For fall admission, 7/15 for domestic and international students; for spring admission, 10/1 for domestic and international students; for summer admission, 3/15 for domestic students. Applications are processed on a rolling basis. *Application fee:* $50. Electronic applications accepted. *Application Contact:* Dr. Benjamin D. Caldwell, Dean of the Graduate School, 816-271-4394, Fax: 816-271-4525, E-mail: graduate@missouriwestern.edu. *Associate Professor,* Dr. Baoqiang Yan, 816-271-4372, E-mail: byan@missouriwestern.edu.

Program in Nursing Students: 34 part-time (32 women). Average age 34. 6 applicants, 100% accepted, 5 enrolled. Expenses: Contact institution. *Financial support:* Scholarships/grants and unspecified assistantships available. Support available to part-time students. In 2016, 3 master's awarded. *Program availability:* Part-time. Offers health care leadership (MSN); nurse educator (MSN, Graduate Certificate). *Application deadline:* For fall admission, 7/15 for domestic and international students; for spring

admission, 10/1 for domestic and international students; for summer admission, 3/15 for domestic students. Applications are processed on a rolling basis. *Application fee:* $50. Electronic applications accepted. *Application Contact:* Dr. Benjamin D. Caldwell, Dean of the Graduate School, 816-271-4394, Fax: 816-271-4525, E-mail: graduate@missouriwestern.edu. *Associate Professor,* Dr. Carolyn Brose, 816-271-5912, E-mail: brose@missouriwestern.edu.

Program in Written Communication Students: 1 full-time (0 women), 8 part-time (7 women). Average age 33. Expenses: Contact institution. *Financial support:* Scholarships/grants and unspecified assistantships available. Support available to part-time students. In 2016, 7 master's, 1 other advanced degree awarded. *Program availability:* Part-time. Offers teaching of writing (Graduate Certificate); technical communication (MAA); writing studies (MAA). *Application deadline:* For fall admission, 7/15 for domestic and international students; for spring admission, 10/1 for domestic and international students; for summer admission, 3/15 for domestic students. Applications are processed on a rolling basis. *Application fee:* $50. Electronic applications accepted. *Application Contact:* Dr. Benjamin D. Caldwell, Dean of the Graduate School, 816-271-4394, Fax: 816-271-4525, E-mail: graduate@missouriwestern.edu. *Associate Professor/Interim Director of Graduate Studies,* Dr. Cynthia Jeney, 816-271-4447, E-mail: jeney@missouriwestern.edu.

See Display on next page and Close-Up on page 891.

MITCHELL HAMLINE SCHOOL OF LAW, Saint Paul, MN 55105-3076

General Information Independent, coed, graduate-only institution. *Enrollment by degree level:* 987 doctoral. *Graduate faculty:* 44 full-time (20 women), 215 part-time/adjunct (129 women). *Tuition:* Full-time $40,570. *Student services:* Campus employment opportunities, campus safety program, career counseling, multicultural affairs office, services for students with disabilities. *Library facilities:* Warren E. Burger Library. *Collection:* Books: 64,606 (physical), 1,615 (digital/electronic); Serial titles: 3,623 (physical), 20,859 (digital/electronic); Databases: 139. Weekly public service hours: 109; students can reserve study rooms.

Computer facilities: 15 computers available on campus for general student use. A campuswide network can be accessed from off campus. Online class registration is available.
Website: http://www.mitchellhamline.edu/

General Application Contact: Emily Dunsworth, Dean of Admissions, 651-290-6434, E-mail: admissions@mitchellhamline.edu.

GRADUATE UNITS

Graduate and Professional Programs Students: 477 full-time (243 women), 510 part-time (264 women); includes 93 minority (22 Black or African American, non-Hispanic/Latino; 6 American Indian or Alaska Native, non-Hispanic/Latino; 19 Asian, non-Hispanic/Latino; 20 Hispanic/Latino; 1 Native Hawaiian or other Pacific Islander, non-Hispanic/Latino; 25 Two or more races, non-Hispanic/Latino), 12 international. Average age 28. *Faculty:* 44 full-time (20 women), 215 part-time/adjunct (129 women). Expenses: Contact institution. *Financial support:* Research assistantships, Federal Work-Study, and scholarships/grants available. Financial award application deadline: 4/15; financial award applicants required to submit FAFSA. *Program availability:* Part-time, evening/weekend, blended/hybrid learning. Offers law (LL M, JD). *Application deadline:* For fall admission, 8/1 for domestic and international students; for spring admission, 11/1 for domestic and international students. Applications are processed on a rolling basis. *Application fee:* $0. Electronic applications accepted. *Application Contact:* Emily Dunsworth, Dean of Admissions, 651-290-6434, E-mail: admissions@mitchellhamline.edu. *President/Dean,* Mark C. Gordon, 651-290-6310, Fax: 651-290-6426.

MOLLOY COLLEGE, Rockville Centre, NY 11571-5002

General Information Independent, coed, comprehensive institution. *Enrollment:* 5,069 graduate, professional, and undergraduate students; 285 full-time matriculated graduate/professional students (216 women), 1,008 part-time matriculated graduate/professional students (814 women). *Enrollment by degree level:* 1,201 master's, 77 doctoral, 15 other advanced degrees. *Graduate faculty:* 66 full-time (57 women), 61 part-time/adjunct (41 women). *Tuition:* Full-time $19,170; part-time $1065 per credit. *Required fees:* $950; $790 per credit. Tuition and fees vary according to course load. *Graduate housing:* On-campus housing not available. *Student services:* Campus employment opportunities, campus safety program, career counseling, free psychological counseling, international student services, low-cost health insurance, services for students with disabilities, teacher training, writing training. *Library facilities:* James Edward Tobin Library plus 1 other. *Collection:* Books: 45,477 (physical), 247,157 (digital/electronic); Serial titles: 55 (physical), 59,417 (digital/electronic); Databases: 180.

Computer facilities: 784 computers available on campus for general student use. A campuswide network can be accessed from student residence rooms and from off campus. Online class registration is available.
Website: http://www.molloy.edu/

General Application Contact: Jaclyn Machowicz, Assistant Director for Admissions, 516-323-4010, E-mail: jmachowicz@molloy.edu.

GRADUATE UNITS

The Barbara H. Hagan School of Nursing Students: 19 full-time (17 women), 542 part-time (499 women); includes 319 minority (172 Black or African American, non-Hispanic/Latino; 1 American Indian or Alaska Native, non-Hispanic/Latino; 93 Asian, non-Hispanic/Latino; 51 Hispanic/Latino; 1 Native Hawaiian or other Pacific Islander, non-Hispanic/Latino; 1 Two or more races, non-Hispanic/Latino), 2 international. Average age 44. 249 applicants, 57% accepted, 100 enrolled. *Faculty:* 25 full-time (all women), 11 part-time/adjunct (8 women). Expenses: Contact institution. *Financial support:* Research assistantships with partial tuition reimbursements, teaching assistantships with partial tuition reimbursements, institutionally sponsored loans, scholarships/grants, and unspecified assistantships available. Support available to part-time students. Financial award application deadline: 4/1; financial award applicants required to submit FAFSA. In 2016, 127 master's, 10 doctorates, 7 other advanced degrees awarded. *Program availability:* Part-time, evening/weekend. Offers adult - gerontology nurse practitioner (MS); clinical nurse specialist: adult - gerontology (MS); family nurse practitioner (MS); family psychiatric/mental health nurse practitioner (MS); nursing (DNP, PhD, Advanced Certificate); nursing administration with informatics (MS); nursing education (MS); pediatric nurse practitioner (MS). *Application deadline:* For fall admission, 9/2 priority date for domestic students; for spring admission, 1/20 priority date for domestic students. Applications are processed on a rolling basis. *Application fee:* $60. Electronic applications accepted. *Application Contact:* Jaclyn Machowicz, Assistant Director for Admissions, 516-323-4010, E-mail: jmachowicz@molloy.edu. *Dean of Nursing,* Dr. Jeannine Muldoon, 516-323-3651, E-mail: jmuldoon@molloy.edu.

Criminal Justice Program Students: 17 full-time (8 women), 18 part-time (8 women); includes 14 minority (7 Black or African American, non-Hispanic/Latino; 2 Asian, non-Hispanic/Latino; 5 Hispanic/Latino). Average age 34. 18 applicants, 78% accepted, 11 enrolled. *Faculty:* 5 full-time (2 women), 2 part-time/adjunct (0 women). Expenses: Contact institution. In 2016, 17 master's awarded. *Program availability:* Part-time, evening/weekend. Offers criminal justice (MS). *Application deadline:* Applications are processed on a rolling basis. *Application fee:* $60. Electronic applications accepted. *Application Contact:* Jaclyn Machowicz, Assistant Director for Admissions, 516-323-4010, E-mail: jmachowicz@molloy.edu. *Associate Dean/Graduate Program Director*, Dr. John Eterno, 516-323-3806, E-mail: jeterno@molloy.edu.

Graduate Business Program Students: 66 full-time (32 women), 178 part-time (92 women); includes 96 minority (38 Black or African American, non-Hispanic/Latino; 24 Asian, non-Hispanic/Latino; 32 Hispanic/Latino; 1 Native Hawaiian or other Pacific Islander, non-Hispanic/Latino; 1 Two or more races, non-Hispanic/Latino), 5 international. Average age 40. 198 applicants, 69% accepted, 108 enrolled. *Faculty:* 6 full-time (3 women), 14 part-time/adjunct (5 women). Expenses: Contact institution. *Financial support:* Applicants required to submit FAFSA. In 2016, 55 master's awarded. *Program availability:* Part-time, evening/weekend. Offers accounting (MBA); finance (MBA, Advanced Certificate); healthcare (MBA, Advanced Certificate); management (MBA); marketing (MBA, Advanced Certificate); personal financial planning (MBA). *Application deadline:* Applications are processed on a rolling basis. *Application fee:* $60. Electronic applications accepted. *Application Contact:* Jaclyn Machowicz, Assistant Director for Admissions, 516-323-4010, E-mail: jmachowicz@molloy.edu. *Dean, Division of Business/Director of Graduate Programs*, Dr. Maureen Mackenzie, 516-323-3080, E-mail: mmackenzie@molloy.edu.

Graduate Education Program Students: 95 full-time (75 women), 221 part-time (177 women); includes 59 minority (14 Black or African American, non-Hispanic/Latino; 6 Asian, non-Hispanic/Latino; 38 Hispanic/Latino; 1 Two or more races, non-Hispanic/Latino), 1 international. Average age 42. 214 applicants, 66% accepted, 125 enrolled. *Faculty:* 17 full-time (16 women), 23 part-time/adjunct (19 women). Expenses: Contact institution. *Financial support:* Applicants required to submit FAFSA. In 2016, 95 master's, 4 Advanced Certificates awarded. *Program availability:* Part-time, evening/weekend. Offers adolescent education in biology (MS Ed); adolescent special education (Advanced Certificate); bilingual extension (Advanced Certificate); childhood education (MS Ed); childhood special education (Advanced Certificate); early childhood education (MS Ed); educational technology (MS Ed); English (MS Ed); mathematics (MS Ed); social studies (MS Ed); Spanish (MS Ed); special education on both childhood and adolescent levels (MS Ed); teaching English to speakers of other languages (TESOL) in grades Pre-K to 12 (MS Ed); TESOL (Advanced Certificate). *Application deadline:* Applications are processed on a rolling basis. *Application fee:* $60. Electronic applications accepted. *Application Contact:* Jaclyn Machowicz, Assistant Director for Admissions, 516-323-4010, E-mail: jmachowicz@molloy.edu. *Associate Dean/Director*, Joanne O'Brien, 516-323-3116, E-mail: jobrien@molloy.edu.

Graduate Music Therapy Program Students: 9 full-time (6 women), 20 part-time (12 women); includes 5 minority (1 Black or African American, non-Hispanic/Latino; 1 Asian, non-Hispanic/Latino; 3 Hispanic/Latino), 5 international. Average age 33. 28 applicants, 39% accepted, 9 enrolled. *Faculty:* 4 full-time (3 women), 6 part-time/adjunct (5 women). Expenses: Contact institution. *Financial support:* Applicants required to submit FAFSA. In 2016, 12 master's awarded. *Program availability:* Part-time, evening/weekend. Offers music therapy (MS). *Application deadline:* Applications are processed on a rolling basis.

Application fee: $60. Electronic applications accepted. *Application Contact:* Jaclyn Machowicz, Assistant Director for Admissions, 516-323-4010, E-mail: jmachowicz@molloy.edu. *Associate Dean/Director of Graduate Music Therapy*, Suzanne Sorel, 516-323-3322, E-mail: ssorel@molloy.edu.

Program in Clinical Mental Health Counseling Students: 27 part-time (24 women); includes 8 minority (3 Black or African American, non-Hispanic/Latino; 1 American Indian or Alaska Native, non-Hispanic/Latino; 3 Hispanic/Latino; 1 Two or more races, non-Hispanic/Latino). Average age 37. 35 applicants, 54% accepted, 12 enrolled. *Faculty:* 2 full-time (both women), 1 part-time/adjunct (0 women). Expenses: Contact institution. *Financial support:* Applicants required to submit FAFSA. *Program availability:* Part-time-only, evening/weekend. Offers clinical mental health counseling (MS). *Application deadline:* Applications are processed on a rolling basis. *Application fee:* $60. Electronic applications accepted. *Application Contact:* Jaclyn Machowicz, Assistant Director for Admissions, 516-323-4010, E-mail: jmachowicz@molloy.edu. *Associate Dean and Director for Department of Clinical Mental Health Counseling*, Dr. Laura B. Kestemberg, 516-323-3842, E-mail: lkestemberg@molloy.edu.

Program in Speech Language Pathology Students: 79 full-time (78 women), 2 part-time (both women); includes 13 minority (1 American Indian or Alaska Native, non-Hispanic/Latino; 4 Asian, non-Hispanic/Latino; 7 Hispanic/Latino; 1 Two or more races, non-Hispanic/Latino). Average age 30. 286 applicants, 34% accepted, 40 enrolled. *Faculty:* 7 full-time (6 women), 4 part-time/adjunct (all women). Expenses: Contact institution. *Financial support:* Applicants required to submit FAFSA. In 2016, 26 master's awarded. *Program availability:* Part-time, evening/weekend. Offers speech language pathology (MS). *Application deadline:* Applications are processed on a rolling basis. *Application fee:* $60. Electronic applications accepted. *Application Contact:* Jaclyn Machowicz, Assistant Director for Admissions, 516-323-4010, E-mail: jmachowicz@molloy.edu. *Associate Dean of Speech-Language Pathology*, Dr. Barbara Schmidt, 516-323-3519, E-mail: bschmidt@molloy.edu.

MONMOUTH UNIVERSITY, West Long Branch, NJ 07764-1898

General Information Independent, coed, comprehensive institution. CGS member. *Enrollment:* 6,371 graduate, professional, and undergraduate students; 695 full-time matriculated graduate/professional students (529 women), 894 part-time matriculated graduate/professional students (674 women). *Enrollment by degree level:* 1,521 master's, 17 doctoral, 51 other advanced degrees. *Graduate faculty:* 111 full-time (65 women), 104 part-time/adjunct (61 women). *Tuition:* Full-time $19,764; part-time $1098 per credit hour. *Required fees:* $175 per semester. Tuition and fees vary according to program. *Graduate housing:* On-campus housing not available. *Student services:* Campus employment opportunities, campus safety program, career counseling, exercise/wellness program, free psychological counseling, international student services, low-cost health insurance, multicultural affairs office, services for students with disabilities, writing training. *Library facilities:* Monmouth University Library. *Collection:* Books: 275,000 (physical), 40,416 (digital/electronic); Serial titles: 1,622 (physical), 73,909 (digital/electronic); Databases: 189. Weekly public service hours: 111; students can reserve study rooms. *Research affiliation:* The Nature Conservancy, Ecotrust (healthy oceans and coastal communities), National Institute of Standards and Technology (NIST), National Oceanic and Atmospheric Administration (NOAA), Substance Abuse and Mental Health Services Administration (SAMHSA) (campus suicide prevention), Gordon and Betty Moore Foundation (environmental conservation, patient care).

Computer facilities: Computer purchase and lease plans are available. 1,000 computers available on campus for general student use. A campuswide network can be accessed from student residence rooms and from off campus. Online class registration is available.
Website: http://www.monmouth.edu/

General Application Contact: Lauren Vento-Cifelli, Associate Vice President of Undergraduate and Graduate Admission, 732-571-3562, Fax: 732-263-5123, E-mail: gradadm@monmouth.edu.

GRADUATE UNITS

Graduate Studies Students: 737 full-time (566 women), 898 part-time (673 women); includes 317 minority (109 Black or African American, non-Hispanic/Latino; 3 American Indian or Alaska Native, non-Hispanic/Latino; 73 Asian, non-Hispanic/Latino; 113 Hispanic/Latino; 4 Native Hawaiian or other Pacific Islander, non-Hispanic/Latino; 15 Two or more races, non-Hispanic/Latino), 96 international. Average age 30. 1,739 applicants, 60% accepted, 633 enrolled. *Faculty:* 111 full-time (65 women), 104 part-time/adjunct (61 women). Expenses: Contact institution. *Financial support:* In 2016–17, 1,341 students received support, including 1,265 fellowships (averaging $3,165 per year), 177 teaching assistantships (averaging $8,386 per year); research assistantships, career-related internships or fieldwork, institutionally sponsored loans, scholarships/grants, and unspecified assistantships also available. Support available to part-time students. Financial award applicants required to submit FAFSA. In 2016, 658 master's, 6 doctorates, 34 other advanced degrees awarded. *Program availability:* Part-time, evening/weekend, 100% online, blended/hybrid learning. Offers addiction studies (MA); anthropology (MA); clinical mental health counseling (MS); computer science (MS); corporate and public communication (MA); creative writing (MA); criminal justice (MA); criminal justice administration (Certificate); European history (MA); human resources management and communication (Certificate); literature (MA); professional counseling (PMC); public policy (MA); public service communication specialist (Certificate); rhetoric and writing (MA); software development (Certificate); software engineering (MS); strategic public relations and new media (Certificate); United States history (MA); world history (MA). *Application deadline:* For fall admission, 7/15 priority date for domestic students, 6/1 for international students; for spring admission, 12/1 priority date for domestic students, 11/1 for international students; for summer admission, 5/1 for domestic students. Applications are processed on a rolling basis. *Application fee:* $50. Electronic applications accepted. *Application Contact:* Laurie Kuhn, Associate Director of Graduate Admission, 732-571-3452, Fax: 732-263-5123, E-mail: gradadm@monmouth.edu. *Vice Provost for Graduate Studies,* Dr. Michael A. Palladino, 732-571-7550, Fax: 732-263-5142.

Leon Hess Business School Students: 76 full-time (37 women), 94 part-time (43 women); includes 17 minority (2 Black or African American, non-Hispanic/Latino; 6 Asian, non-Hispanic/Latino; 6 Hispanic/Latino; 1 Native Hawaiian or other Pacific Islander, non-Hispanic/Latino; 2 Two or more races, non-Hispanic/Latino), 8 international. Average age 30. 105 applicants, 90% accepted, 67 enrolled. *Faculty:* 20 full-time (4 women), 8 part-time/adjunct (0 women). Expenses: Contact institution. *Financial support:* In 2016–17, 191 students received support, including 137 fellowships (averaging $2,643 per year), 20 teaching assistantships with full and partial tuition reimbursements available (averaging $10,034 per year); research assistantships, institutionally sponsored loans, scholarships/grants, and unspecified assistantships also available. Support available to part-time students. Financial award application deadline: 2/1; financial award applicants required to submit FAFSA. In 2016, 93 master's, 1 other advanced degree awarded. *Program availability:* Part-time, evening/weekend. Offers accounting (MBA, Certificate); business administration (MBA); finance (MBA); management (MBA); marketing (MBA); real estate (MBA). *Application deadline:* For fall admission, 7/15 priority date for domestic students, 6/1 for international students; for spring admission, 12/1 priority date for domestic students, 11/1 for international students; for summer admission, 5/1 for domestic students. Applications are processed on a rolling basis. *Application fee:* $50. Electronic applications accepted. *Application Contact:* Laurie Kuhn, Associate Director of Graduate Admission, 732-571-3452, Fax: 732-263-5123, E-mail: gradadm@monmouth.edu. *MBA Program Director,* Dr. Susan Gupta, 732-571-3639, Fax: 732-263-5517, E-mail: sgupta@monmouth.edu.

Marjorie K. Unterberg School of Nursing and Health Studies Students: 76 full-time (54 women), 302 part-time (276 women); includes 117 minority (39 Black or African American, non-Hispanic/Latino; 43 Asian, non-Hispanic/Latino; 28 Hispanic/Latino; 2 Native Hawaiian or other Pacific Islander, non-Hispanic/Latino; 5 Two or more races, non-Hispanic/Latino), 2 international. Average age 35. 380 applicants, 41% accepted, 128 enrolled. *Faculty:* 12 full-time (all women), 20 part-time/adjunct (12 women). Expenses: Contact institution. *Financial support:* In 2016–17, 302 students received support, including 254 fellowships (averaging $2,962 per year), 13 teaching assistantships with full and partial tuition reimbursements available (averaging $5,163 per year); research assistantships, institutionally sponsored loans, scholarships/grants, and unspecified assistantships also available. Support available to part-time students. Financial award application deadline: 2/1; financial award applicants required to submit FAFSA. In 2016, 69 master's, 6 doctorates, 12 other advanced degrees awarded. *Program availability:* Part-time, evening/weekend, 100% online, blended/hybrid learning. Offers adult-gerontological primary care nurse practitioner (MSN, Post-Master's Certificate); family nurse practitioner (MSN, Post-Master's Certificate); forensic nursing (MSN, Certificate); nursing (MSN); nursing administration (MSN); nursing education (MSN, Post-Master's Certificate); nursing practice (DNP); physician assistant (MS); psychiatric and mental health nurse practitioner (MSN, Post-Master's Certificate); school nursing (MSN, Certificate). *Application deadline:* For fall admission, 7/15 priority date for domestic students, 6/1 for international students; for spring admission, 12/1 priority date for domestic students, 11/1 for international students; for summer admission, 5/1 for domestic students. Applications are processed on a rolling basis. *Application fee:* $50. Electronic applications accepted. *Application Contact:* Lucia Fedele, Graduate Admission Counselor, 732-571-3452, Fax: 732-263-5123, E-mail: gradadm@monmouth.edu. *Dean,* Dr. Janet Mahoney, 732-571-3443, Fax: 732-263-5131, E-mail: jmahoney@monmouth.edu.

School of Education Students: 191 full-time (172 women), 141 part-time (122 women); includes 56 minority (10 Black or African American, non-Hispanic/Latino; 9 Asian, non-Hispanic/Latino; 31 Hispanic/Latino; 6 Two or more races, non-Hispanic/Latino). Average age 26. 423 applicants, 53% accepted, 139 enrolled. *Faculty:* 23 full-time (19 women), 33 part-time/adjunct (25 women). Expenses: Contact institution. *Financial support:* In 2016–17, 349 students received support, including 305 fellowships (averaging $3,558 per year), 48 teaching assistantships (averaging $9,619 per year); research assistantships, institutionally sponsored loans, scholarships/grants, and unspecified assistantships also available. Support available to part-time students. Financial award application deadline: 2/1; financial award applicants required to submit FAFSA. In 2016, 148 master's, 4 other advanced degrees awarded. *Program*

availability: Part-time, evening/weekend, 100% online, blended/hybrid learning. Offers applied behavior analysis (Certificate); autism (Certificate); director of school counseling services (Post-Master's Certificate); early childhood (M Ed); educational leadership (Ed D); elementary education (MAT); English as a second language (M Ed); learning disabilities teacher-consultant (Post-Master's Certificate); literacy (MS Ed); school counseling (MS Ed); special education (MS Ed); speech-language pathology (MS Ed); student affairs and college counseling (MS Ed); supervisor (Post-Master's Certificate); teaching English to speakers of other languages (Certificate). *Application deadline:* For fall admission, 7/15 priority date for domestic students, 7/1 for international students; for spring admission, 12/1 priority date for domestic students, 11/1 for international students; for summer admission, 5/1 for domestic students. Applications are processed on a rolling basis. *Application fee:* $50. Electronic applications accepted. *Application Contact:* Laurie Kuhn, Associate Director of Graduate Admission, 732-571-3452, Fax: 732-263-5123, E-mail: gradadm@monmouth.edu. *Dean,* Dr. John E. Henning, 732-263-5513, Fax: 732-263-5277.

School of Social Work Students: 136 full-time (123 women), 86 part-time (69 women); includes 75 minority (38 Black or African American, non-Hispanic/Latino; 1 American Indian or Alaska Native, non-Hispanic/Latino; 2 Asian, non-Hispanic/Latino; 30 Hispanic/Latino; 4 Two or more races, non-Hispanic/Latino), 1 international. Average age 30. 206 applicants, 94% accepted, 122 enrolled. *Faculty:* 12 full-time (8 women), 22 part-time/adjunct (18 women). Expenses: Contact institution. *Financial support:* In 2016–17, 128 students received support, including 137 fellowships (averaging $4,502 per year), 12 teaching assistantships (averaging $11,637 per year); research assistantships, institutionally sponsored loans, scholarships/grants, and unspecified assistantships also available. Support available to part-time students. Financial award application deadline: 2/1; financial award applicants required to submit FAFSA. In 2016, 135 master's, 1 other advanced degree awarded. *Program availability:* Part-time, evening/weekend. Offers clinical practice with families and children (MSW); international and community development (MSW); play therapy (Certificate). *Application deadline:* For fall admission, 3/15 for domestic and international students. Applications are processed on a rolling basis. *Application fee:* $50. Electronic applications accepted. *Application Contact:* Lucia Fedele, Graduate Admission Counselor, 732-571-3452, Fax: 732-263-5123, E-mail: gradm@monmouth.edu. *Dean,* Dr. Robin Mama, 732-571-3543, Fax: 732-263-5217, E-mail: swdept@monmouth.edu.

Monmouth University (International Student Information)

MONROE COLLEGE, Bronx, NY 10468

General Information Proprietary, coed, comprehensive institution. *Enrollment:* 618 full-time matriculated graduate/professional students (328 women), 312 part-time matriculated graduate/professional students (226 women). *Enrollment by degree level:* 930 master's. *Graduate housing:* Rooms and/or apartments available on a first-come, first-served basis to single and married students. Housing application deadline: 5/1. *Student services:* Campus employment opportunities, career counseling, international student services, multicultural affairs office, services for students with disabilities, teacher training, writing training. *Library facilities:* Main library plus 1 other. *Collection:* Books: 44,109 (physical), 2,466 (digital/electronic); Serial titles: 739 (physical), 8 (digital/electronic); Databases: 73.

Computer facilities: 800 computers available on campus for general student use. A campuswide network can be accessed from student residence rooms and from off campus. Online class registration is available.
Website: http://www.monroecollege.edu/

General Application Contact: Craig Patrick, Vice President for Admissions, 718-933-6700, E-mail: cpatrick@monroecollege.edu.

GRADUATE UNITS

King Graduate School Expenses: Contact institution. *Program availability:* Online learning. Offers accounting (MS); business administration (MBA); computer science (MS); criminal justice (MS); hospitality management (MS); public health (MPH). *Application fee:* $50.

MONTANA STATE UNIVERSITY, Bozeman, MT 59717

General Information State-supported, coed, university. CGS member. *Graduate housing:* Rooms and/or apartments available on a first-come, first-served basis to single and married students. *Research affiliation:* Phillips Environmental (microbial technology), Microvision (information transmission systems), LigoCyte Pharmaceuticals, Inc. (pharmaceuticals), Eli Lilly and Company (antifungal technology), S2 Corporation (instrumentation), ILX Lightwave (laser diodes, electro-optical test equipment).

GRADUATE UNITS

The Graduate School *Program availability:* Part-time, online learning. Electronic applications accepted.

College of Agriculture *Program availability:* Part-time, online learning. Offers agricultural education (MS); agriculture (MS, PhD); animal and range sciences (MS, PhD); immunology and infectious diseases (MS, PhD); land rehabilitation (interdisciplinary) (MS); land resources and environmental sciences (MS); plant pathology (MS); plant sciences (MS, PhD). Electronic applications accepted.

College of Arts and Architecture *Program availability:* Part-time. Offers architecture (M Arch); art (MFA); art history (MA); arts and architecture (M Arch, MA, MFA); science and natural history filmmaking (MFA). Electronic applications accepted.

College of Business *Program availability:* Part-time. Offers professional accountancy (MP Ac). Electronic applications accepted.

College of Education, Health, and Human Development *Program availability:* Part-time, online learning. Offers adult and higher education (Ed D); curriculum and instruction (M Ed, Ed D); education (M Ed); education, health, and human development (M Ed, MS, Ed D, Ed S); educational leadership (Ed D, Ed S); family and consumer sciences (MS). Electronic applications accepted.

College of Engineering *Program availability:* Part-time. Offers chemical engineering (MS); civil engineering (MS); computer science (MS, PhD); construction engineering management (MCEM); electrical engineering (MS); engineering (PhD); environmental engineering (MS); industrial and management engineering (MS); mechanical engineering (MS). Electronic applications accepted.

College of Letters and Science *Program availability:* Part-time, online learning. Offers biochemistry (MS, PhD); biological sciences (PhD); chemistry (MS, PhD); earth sciences (MS, PhD); ecological and environmental statistics (MS); ecology and environmental sciences (PhD); English (MA); fish and wildlife biology (PhD); fish and wildlife management (MS); history (MA, PhD); letters and science (MA, MPA, MS, PhD); mathematics (MS, PhD); microbiology (MS, PhD); Native American studies (MA); neuroscience (MS, PhD); physics (MS, PhD); psychology (MS); public administration (MPA); statistics (MS, PhD). Electronic applications accepted.

College of Nursing *Program availability:* Part-time, online learning. Offers clinical nurse leader (MN); family and individual nurse practitioner (DNP); family nurse practitioner (MN, Post-Master's Certificate); nursing education (Certificate, Post-Master's Certificate); psychiatric mental health nurse practitioner (MN); psychiatric/mental health nurse practitioner (DNP). Electronic applications accepted.

MONTANA STATE UNIVERSITY BILLINGS, Billings, MT 59101
General Information State-supported, coed, comprehensive institution. *Enrollment:* 4,388 graduate, professional, and undergraduate students; 38 full-time matriculated graduate/professional students (25 women), 260 part-time matriculated graduate/professional students (207 women). *Enrollment by degree level:* 394 master's, 76 other advanced degrees. *Graduate faculty:* 57 full-time (36 women), 3 part-time/adjunct (2 women). *International tuition:* \$19,295 full-time. Tuition, state resident: full-time \$5265; part-time \$3436 per year. Tuition, nonresident: full-time \$14,030; part-time \$9280 per year. Tuition and fees vary according to degree level, campus/location and program. *Graduate housing:* Rooms and/or apartments available on a first-come, first-served basis to single and married students. Typical cost: \$2160 per year (\$3660 including board) for single students; \$2200 per year (\$3700 including board) for married students. Room and board charges vary according to board plan. Housing application deadline: 5/1. *Student services:* Campus employment opportunities, campus safety program, career counseling, child daycare facilities, exercise/wellness program, free psychological counseling, grant writing training, international student services, low-cost health insurance, multicultural affairs office, services for students with disabilities, teacher training, writing training. *Library facilities:* Montana State University Billings Library plus 2 others. *Collection:* Books: 138,650 (physical), 351,351 (digital/electronic); Serial titles: 1,368 (physical), 669,204 (digital/electronic); Databases: 170. Weekly public service hours: 82; students can reserve study rooms.

Computer facilities: Computer purchase and lease plans are available. 1,500 computers available on campus for general student use. A campuswide network can be accessed from student residence rooms and from off campus. Online class registration, online degree programs are available. Website: http://www.msubillings.edu/

General Application Contact: David M. Sullivan, Graduate Studies Counselor, 406-657-2053, Fax: 406-657-2299, E-mail: dsullivan@msubillings.edu.

GRADUATE UNITS
College of Allied Health Professions Students: 91. *Faculty:* 11 full-time (5 women), 1 (woman) part-time/adjunct. Expenses: Contact institution. *Financial support:* Research assistantships with partial tuition reimbursements, teaching assistantships with partial tuition reimbursements, career-related internships or fieldwork, institutionally sponsored loans, scholarships/grants, and unspecified assistantships available. Support available to part-time students. Financial award application deadline: 5/1; financial award applicants required to submit FAFSA. *Program availability:* Part-time, evening/weekend, 100% online, blended/hybrid learning. Offers allied health professions (MHA, MS); athletic training (MS); clinical rehabilitation and mental health counseling (MS); health administration (MHA). *Application deadline:* For fall admission, 7/15 priority date for domestic students; for spring admission, 12/1 priority date for domestic students. Applications are processed on a rolling basis. *Application fee:* \$40. Electronic applications accepted. *Application Contact:* David M. Sullivan, Graduate Studies Counselor, 406-657-2053, Fax: 406-657-2299, E-mail: dsullivan@msubillings.edu. *Dean*, Dr. Diane Duin, 406-896-5841, E-mail: dduin@msubillings.edu.

College of Arts and Sciences Students: 35. *Faculty:* 21 full-time (11 women). Expenses: Contact institution. *Financial support:* Research assistantships with partial tuition reimbursements, teaching assistantships with partial tuition reimbursements, career-related internships or fieldwork, Federal Work-Study, institutionally sponsored loans, scholarships/grants, tuition waivers (partial), and unspecified assistantships available. Support available to part-time students. Financial award application deadline: 5/1; financial award applicants required to submit FAFSA. *Program availability:* Part-time, 100% online, blended/hybrid learning. Offers arts and sciences (MS); psychology (MS); public relations (MS). *Application deadline:* For fall admission, 7/15 for international students; for spring admission, 12/1 for international students. Applications are processed on a rolling basis. *Application fee:* \$40. Electronic applications accepted. *Application Contact:* David M. Sullivan, Graduate Studies Counselor, 406-657-2053, Fax: 406-657-2299, E-mail: dsullivan@msubillings.edu. *Dean*, Dr. Christine Shearer-Cremean, 406-657-2177, E-mail: c.shearercremean@msubillings.edu.

College of Education Students: 158. *Faculty:* 16 full-time (11 women), 1 (woman) part-time/adjunct. Expenses: Contact institution. *Financial support:* In 2016–17, research assistantships with partial tuition reimbursements (averaging \$2,500 per year), teaching assistantships with partial tuition reimbursements (averaging \$2,500 per year) were awarded; career-related internships or fieldwork, Federal Work-Study, institutionally sponsored loans, scholarships/grants, tuition waivers (partial), and unspecified assistantships also available. Support available to part-time students. Financial award application deadline: 5/1; financial award applicants required to submit FAFSA. *Program availability:* Part-time, 100% online, blended/hybrid learning. Offers advanced studies (MS Sp Ed); applied behavior analysis (MS Sp Ed); education (M Ed, MS Sp Ed, Certificate); general curriculum (M Ed); generalist (MS Sp Ed); interdisciplinary studies (M Ed); K-8 (M Ed); online instructional technologies (M Ed); reading (M Ed); school counseling (M Ed); secondary (M Ed); special education (MS Sp Ed); teaching (Certificate). *Application deadline:* For fall admission, 7/15 for international students; for spring admission, 12/1 for international students. Applications are processed on a rolling basis. *Application fee:* \$40. Electronic applications accepted. *Application Contact:* David M. Sullivan, Graduate Studies Counselor, 406-657-2053, Fax: 406-657-2299, E-mail: dsullivan@msubillings.edu. *Dean*, Dr. Mary Susan Fishbaugh, 406-657-2285, Fax: 406-657-2299, E-mail: mfishbaugh@msubillings.edu.

MONTANA STATE UNIVERSITY–NORTHERN, Havre, MT 59501-7751
General Information State-supported, coed, comprehensive institution. *Enrollment:* 1,273 graduate, professional, and undergraduate students; 71 part-time matriculated graduate/professional students (52 women). *Enrollment by degree level:* 71 master's. *Graduate faculty:* 3 full-time (1 woman), 6 part-time/adjunct (3 women). *Graduate housing:* Rooms and/or apartments available on a first-come, first-served basis to single students and available to married students. Housing application deadline: 8/22. *Student services:* Campus employment opportunities, career counseling, child daycare facilities, exercise/wellness program, low-cost health insurance, multicultural affairs office, teacher training. *Library facilities:* Vande Bogart Libraries.

Computer facilities: A campuswide network can be accessed from student residence rooms and from off campus. Online class registration is available. Website: http://www.msun.edu/

General Application Contact: Norton Pease, Chair, College of Education, Arts and Sciences, and Nursing, 406-265-3735, E-mail: norton.pease@msun.edu.

GRADUATE UNITS
Graduate Programs Expenses: Contact institution. *Financial support:* Research assistantships with partial tuition reimbursements, teaching assistantships with partial tuition reimbursements, career-related internships or fieldwork, Federal Work-Study, institutionally sponsored loans, and unspecified assistantships available. Support available to part-time students. Financial award application deadline: 4/1; financial award applicants required to submit FAFSA. *Program availability:* Part-time, evening/weekend, online learning. Offers counselor education (M Ed); instruction and learning (MS Ed). *Application deadline:* For fall admission, 9/20 priority date for domestic students. Applications are processed on a rolling basis. *Application fee:* \$30. Electronic applications accepted. *Application Contact:* Robert Kurtz, Program Advisor, 406-265-3700. *Interim Provost*, Larry Strizich, 406-265-3726, Fax: 406-265-3530, E-mail: strizich@msun.edu.

MONTANA TECH OF THE UNIVERSITY OF MONTANA, Butte, MT 59701-8997
General Information State-supported, coed, comprehensive institution. CGS member. *Enrollment:* 2,809 graduate, professional, and undergraduate students; 87 full-time matriculated graduate/professional students (23 women), 155 part-time matriculated graduate/professional students (60 women). *Enrollment by degree level:* 228 master's, 12 doctoral, 2 other advanced degrees. *Graduate faculty:* 138 full-time (49 women), 78 part-time/adjunct (35 women). Tuition, state resident: full-time \$2901; part-time \$1450.68 per degree program. Tuition, nonresident: full-time \$8432; part-time \$4215.84 per degree program. *Required fees:* \$668; \$354 per degree program. Tuition and fees vary according to course load and program. *Graduate housing:* Rooms and/or apartments available on a first-come, first-served basis to single and married students. Typical cost: \$4098 per year (\$7128 including board) for single students; \$4950 per year for married students. Room and board charges vary according to board plan, campus/location and housing facility selected. Housing application deadline: 7/1. *Student services:* Campus employment opportunities, campus safety program, career counseling, exercise/wellness program, free psychological counseling, grant writing training, international student services, low-cost health insurance, multicultural affairs office, services for students with disabilities, writing training. *Library facilities:* Montana Tech Library. *Collection:* Books: 80,864 (physical), 91,830 (digital/electronic); Serial titles: 1,859 (physical), 67,191 (digital/electronic); Databases: 148. Weekly public service hours: 80; students can reserve study rooms. *Research affiliation:* Newmont Mining (mining and mineral processing), Stillwater Mining (mineral production and training), NorthWestern Energy (electric efficiency), Edison Welding Institute (fuel cell design), Montana Resources, Inc. (mine reclamation and revegetation), QualTech, Inc. (battery monitor technology).

Computer facilities: 660 computers available on campus for general student use. A campuswide network can be accessed from student residence rooms and from off campus. Online class registration is available. Website: http://www.mtech.edu/

General Application Contact: Daniel Stirling, Graduate School Program Manager, 406-496-4304, Fax: 406-496-4710, E-mail: gradschool@mtech.edu.

GRADUATE UNITS
Department of Environmental Engineering Students: 8 full-time (2 women), 3 part-time (0 women); includes 3 minority (2 Black or African American, non-Hispanic/Latino; 1 American Indian or Alaska Native, non-Hispanic/Latino), 1 international. Average age 26. 5 applicants, 100% accepted, 5 enrolled. *Faculty:* 7 full-time (2 women). Expenses: Contact institution. *Financial support:* In 2016–17, 3 students received support, including 4 teaching assistantships with partial tuition reimbursements available (averaging \$4,000 per year); research assistantships with full tuition reimbursements available, career-related internships or fieldwork, tuition waivers (full and partial), and unspecified assistantships also available. Financial award application deadline: 4/1; financial award applicants required to submit FAFSA. In 2016, 3 master's awarded. *Program availability:* Part-time. Offers environmental engineering (MS). *Application deadline:* For fall admission, 4/1 priority date for domestic students, 3/1 priority date for international students; for spring admission, 10/1 priority date for domestic students, 6/1 priority date for international students. Applications are processed on a rolling basis. *Application fee:* \$50. Electronic applications accepted. *Application Contact:* Daniel Stirling, Administrator, Graduate School, 406-496-4304, Fax: 406-496-4710, E-mail: gradschool@mtech.edu. *Head*, Dr. Kumar Ganesan, 406-496-4239, Fax: 406-496-4650, E-mail: kganesan@mtech.edu.

Department of General Engineering Students: 5 full-time (0 women), 2 part-time (0 women); includes 2 minority (both Black or African American, non-Hispanic/Latino). Average age 25. 5 applicants, 60% accepted, 3 enrolled. *Faculty:* 7 full-time (0 women), 4 part-time/adjunct (0 women). Expenses: Contact institution. *Financial support:* In 2016–17, 9 students received support, including 11 teaching assistantships with partial tuition reimbursements available (averaging \$3,500 per year); research assistantships with partial tuition reimbursements available, career-related internships or fieldwork, tuition waivers (full and partial), and unspecified assistantships also available. Financial award application deadline: 4/1; financial award applicants required to submit FAFSA. In 2016, 8 master's awarded. *Program availability:* Part-time. Offers general engineering (MS). *Application deadline:* For fall admission, 4/1 priority date for domestic students, 3/1 priority date for international students; for spring admission, 10/1 priority date for domestic students, 6/1 priority date for international students. Applications are processed on a rolling basis. *Application fee:* \$50. Electronic applications accepted. *Application Contact:* Daniel Stirling, Administrator, Graduate School, 406-496-4304, Fax: 406-496-4710, E-mail: gradschool@mtech.edu. *Department Head*, Dr. Bruce Madigan, 406-496-4109, Fax: 406-496-4650, E-mail: bmadigan@mtech.edu.

Department of Industrial Hygiene Students: 9 full-time (4 women), 75 part-time (28 women); includes 13 minority (3 Black or African American, non-Hispanic/Latino; 1 Asian, non-Hispanic/Latino; 8 Hispanic/Latino; 1 Native Hawaiian or other Pacific Islander, non-Hispanic/Latino), 1 international. 30 applicants, 70% accepted, 19 enrolled. *Faculty:* 8 full-time (3 women). Expenses: Contact institution. *Financial support:* In 2016–17, 15 students received support, including 9 teaching assistantships with partial tuition reimbursements available (averaging \$2,400 per year); research assistantships with partial tuition reimbursements available, career-related internships or fieldwork, institutionally sponsored loans, and tuition waivers (full and partial) also available. Financial award application deadline: 4/1; financial award applicants required to submit FAFSA. In 2016, 23 master's awarded. *Program availability:* Part-time, online learning. Offers industrial hygiene (MS). *Application deadline:* For fall admission, 4/1 priority date for domestic students; for spring admission, 10/1 priority date for domestic students. Applications are processed on a rolling basis. *Application fee:* \$50. Electronic applications accepted. *Application Contact:* Daniel Stirling, Administrator, Graduate

School, 406-496-4304, Fax: 406-496-4710, E-mail: gradschool@mtech.edu. *Head*, Dr. Terry Spear, 406-496-4445, Fax: 406-496-4650, E-mail: tspear@mtech.edu.

Department of Metallurgical/Mineral Processing Engineering Students: 6 full-time (4 women), 2 part-time (0 women); includes 2 minority (both Black or African American, non-Hispanic/Latino), 3 international. 4 applicants, 75% accepted, 3 enrolled. *Faculty:* 6 full-time (0 women). Expenses: Contact institution. *Financial support:* In 2016–17, 4 students received support, including 2 teaching assistantships with partial tuition reimbursements available (averaging $5,000 per year); research assistantships with partial tuition reimbursements available, career-related internships or fieldwork, tuition waivers (full and partial), and unspecified assistantships also available. Financial award application deadline: 4/1; financial award applicants required to submit FAFSA. In 2016, 2 master's awarded. *Program availability:* Part-time. Offers metallurgical/mineral processing engineering (MS). *Application deadline:* For fall admission, 4/1 priority date for domestic students, 3/1 priority date for international students; for spring admission, 10/1 priority date for domestic students, 6/1 priority date for international students. Applications are processed on a rolling basis. *Application fee:* $50. Electronic applications accepted. *Application Contact:* Daniel Stirling, Administrator, Graduate School, 406-496-4304, Fax: 406-496-4710, E-mail: gradschool@mtech.edu. *Department Head*, Dr. Courtney Young, 406-496-4158, Fax: 406-496-4664, E-mail: cyoung@mtech.edu.

Department of Petroleum Engineering Students: 7 full-time (0 women), 1 part-time (0 women); includes 1 minority (American Indian or Alaska Native, non-Hispanic/Latino), 2 international. 23 applicants, 9% accepted, 2 enrolled. *Faculty:* 8 full-time (2 women), 1 part-time/adjunct (0 women). Expenses: Contact institution. *Financial support:* In 2016–17, 6 students received support, including 5 teaching assistantships with partial tuition reimbursements available (averaging $4,800 per year); research assistantships, career-related internships or fieldwork, institutionally sponsored loans, tuition waivers (full and partial), and unspecified assistantships also available. Financial award application deadline: 4/1; financial award applicants required to submit FAFSA. In 2016, 4 master's awarded. *Program availability:* Part-time, evening/weekend. Offers petroleum engineering (MS). *Application deadline:* For fall admission, 4/1 priority date for domestic students, 3/1 priority date for international students; for spring admission, 10/1 priority date for domestic students, 6/1 priority date for international students. Applications are processed on a rolling basis. *Application fee:* $50. Electronic applications accepted. *Application Contact:* Daniel Stirling, Administrator, Graduate School, 406-496-4304, Fax: 406-496-4710, E-mail: gradschool@mtech.edu. *Head*, Burt Todd, 406-496-4834, Fax: 406-496-4417, E-mail: btodd@mtech.edu.

Department of Technical Communication Students: 2 full-time (1 woman), 6 part-time (3 women); includes 1 minority (Asian, non-Hispanic/Latino). Average age 26. 4 applicants, 100% accepted, 3 enrolled. *Faculty:* 8 full-time (4 women), 2 part-time/adjunct (1 woman). Expenses: Contact institution. *Financial support:* In 2016–17, 6 students received support, including 5 teaching assistantships with partial tuition reimbursements available (averaging $4,000 per year); research assistantships with partial tuition reimbursements available, career-related internships or fieldwork, tuition waivers (partial), and unspecified assistantships also available. Financial award application deadline: 4/1; financial award applicants required to submit FAFSA. In 2016, 4 master's awarded. *Program availability:* Part-time. Offers technical communication (MS). *Application deadline:* For fall admission, 4/1 priority date for domestic students, 3/1 priority date for international students; for spring admission, 10/1 priority date for domestic students, 6/1 priority date for international students. Applications are processed on a rolling basis. *Application fee:* $50. Electronic applications accepted. *Application Contact:* Daniel Stirling, Administrator, Graduate School, 406-496-4304, Fax: 406-496-4710, E-mail: gradschool@mtech.edu. *Head*, Dr. Nicholas Hawthorne, 406-496-4224, Fax: 406-496-4510, E-mail: nhawthorne@mtech.edu.

Electrical Engineering Program Students: 5 full-time (1 woman), 2 part-time (1 woman); includes 1 minority (Asian, non-Hispanic/Latino), 2 international. Average age 25. 5 applicants, 40% accepted. *Faculty:* 4 full-time (0 women). Expenses: Contact institution. *Financial support:* In 2016–17, 3 students received support, including 5 teaching assistantships with partial tuition reimbursements available (averaging $4,000 per year); research assistantships with full tuition reimbursements available, career-related internships or fieldwork, tuition waivers (full and partial), and unspecified assistantships also available. Financial award application deadline: 4/1. In 2016, 3 master's awarded. *Program availability:* Part-time. Offers electrical engineering (MS). *Application deadline:* For fall admission, 4/1 priority date for domestic students, 3/1 priority date for international students; for spring admission, 10/1 priority date for domestic students, 6/1 priority date for international students. Applications are processed on a rolling basis. *Application fee:* $50. Electronic applications accepted. *Application Contact:* Daniel Stirling, Administrator, Graduate School, 406-496-4304, Fax: 406-496-4710, E-mail: gradschool@mtech.edu. *Professor*, Dr. Daniel Trudnowski, 406-496-4681, Fax: 406-496-4849, E-mail: dtrudnowski@mtech.edu.

Geosciences Programs Students: 25 full-time (8 women), 13 part-time (4 women); includes 5 minority (3 Black or African American, non-Hispanic/Latino; 2 Hispanic/Latino), 8 international. Average age 28. 24 applicants, 50% accepted, 10 enrolled. *Faculty:* 17 full-time (5 women), 6 part-time/adjunct (2 women). Expenses: Contact institution. *Financial support:* In 2016–17, 15 students received support, including 10 teaching assistantships with partial tuition reimbursements available (averaging $5,000 per year); research assistantships with partial tuition reimbursements available, career-related internships or fieldwork, tuition waivers (full and partial), and unspecified assistantships also available. Financial award application deadline: 4/1; financial award applicants required to submit FAFSA. In 2016, 12 master's awarded. *Program availability:* Part-time. Offers geochemistry (MS); geological engineering (MS); geology (MS); geophysical engineering (MS); hydrogeological engineering (MS); hydrogeology (MS). *Application deadline:* For fall admission, 4/1 priority date for domestic students, 3/1 priority date for international students; for spring admission, 10/1 priority date for domestic students, 7/1 priority date for international students. Applications are processed on a rolling basis. *Application fee:* $50. Electronic applications accepted. *Application Contact:* Daniel Stirling, Administrator, Graduate School, 406-496-4304, Fax: 406-496-4710, E-mail: gradschool@mtech.edu. *Department Head*, Dr. Larry Smith, 406-496-4859, Fax: 406-496-4260, E-mail: lsmith@mtech.edu.

Health Care Informatics Program Students: 7 part-time (5 women). 1 applicant. *Faculty:* 4 full-time (2 women). Expenses: Contact institution. *Financial support:* Scholarships/grants available. Financial award application deadline: 4/1; financial award applicants required to submit FAFSA. In 2016, 4 Certificates awarded. *Program availability:* Part-time, evening/weekend, online learning. Offers health care informatics (Certificate). *Application deadline:* For fall admission, 4/1 priority date for domestic students, 3/1 priority date for international students; for spring admission, 10/1 priority date for domestic students, 6/1 priority date for international students. Applications are processed on a rolling basis. *Application fee:* $50. Electronic applications accepted. *Application Contact:* Daniel Stirling, Administrator, Graduate School, 406-496-4304, Fax:

406-496-4710, E-mail: gradschool@mtech.edu. *Department Head*, Dr. Charie Faught, 406-496-4884, Fax: 406-496-4435, E-mail: cfaught@mtech.edu.

Interdisciplinary Program Students: 8 full-time (3 women), 2 part-time (1 woman); includes 3 minority (2 Black or African American, non-Hispanic/Latino; 1 Hispanic/Latino). 3 applicants, 67% accepted, 2 enrolled. *Faculty:* 7 full-time (4 women), 4 part-time/adjunct (2 women). Expenses: Contact institution. *Financial support:* In 2016–17, 3 students received support. Research assistantships, teaching assistantships, career-related internships or fieldwork, tuition waivers (full and partial), and unspecified assistantships available. In 2016, 3 master's awarded. *Program availability:* Part-time. Offers interdisciplinary studies (MS). *Application deadline:* For fall admission, 4/1 for domestic students, 3/1 priority date for international students; for spring admission, 10/1 for domestic students, 6/1 priority date for international students. *Application fee:* $50. *Application Contact:* Daniel Stirling, Administrator, Graduate School, 406-496-4304, Fax: 406-496-4710, E-mail: gradschool@mtech.edu. *Vice Chancellor of Research/Dean of the Graduate School*, Dr. Beverly Hartline, 406-496-4456, E-mail: graduatedean@mtech.edu.

Mining Engineering Program Students: 6 full-time (2 women), 1 part-time (0 women), 4 international. Average age 26. 9 applicants, 67% accepted, 6 enrolled. *Faculty:* 4 full-time (0 women). Expenses: Contact institution. *Financial support:* In 2016–17, 2 students received support, including 2 teaching assistantships with partial tuition reimbursements available (averaging $4,000 per year); research assistantships, career-related internships or fieldwork, tuition waivers (full and partial), and unspecified assistantships also available. Financial award application deadline: 4/1; financial award applicants required to submit FAFSA. In 2016, 3 master's awarded. *Program availability:* Part-time. Offers mining engineering (MS). *Application deadline:* For fall admission, 4/1 priority date for domestic students, 3/1 priority date for international students; for spring admission, 10/1 priority date for domestic students, 6/1 priority date for international students. Applications are processed on a rolling basis. *Application fee:* $50. Electronic applications accepted. *Application Contact:* Daniel Stirling, Administrator, Graduate School, 406-496-4304, Fax: 406-496-4710, E-mail: gradschool@mtech.edu. *Department Head*, Dr. Scott Rosenthal, 406-496-4867, Fax: 406-496-4260, E-mail: srosenthal@mtech.edu.

Program in Materials Science Students: 8 full-time (0 women), 5 part-time (2 women), 2 international. Average age 29. 9 applicants, 56% accepted, 5 enrolled. *Faculty:* 11 full-time (1 woman), 3 part-time/adjunct (0 women). Expenses: Contact institution. *Financial support:* In 2016–17, 4 research assistantships with full tuition reimbursements (averaging $24,000 per year) were awarded; teaching assistantships, Federal Work-Study, health care benefits, tuition waivers (full), and unspecified assistantships also available. Financial award applicants required to submit FAFSA. Offers materials science (PhD). *Application deadline:* For fall admission, 4/1 for domestic students, 6/1 for international students; for spring admission, 9/1 for domestic and international students. *Application fee:* $50. *Application Contact:* Daniel Stirling, Administrator, Graduate School, 406-496-4304, Fax: 406-496-4723, E-mail: gradschool@mtech.edu. *Associate Professor, Metallurgical and Materials Engineering*, Dr. Jerry Downey, 406-496-4578, Fax: 406-496-4723, E-mail: jdowney@mtech.edu.

Project Engineering and Management Program Students: 10 part-time (5 women); includes 2 minority (both Black or African American, non-Hispanic/Latino). Average age 28. 10 applicants, 90% accepted, 5 enrolled. *Faculty:* 1 full-time (0 women), 8 part-time/adjunct (2 women). Expenses: Contact institution. *Financial support:* Application deadline: 4/1; applicants required to submit FAFSA. In 2016, 4 master's awarded. *Program availability:* Part-time, evening/weekend, online learning. Offers project engineering and management (MPEM). *Application deadline:* For fall admission, 4/1 priority date for domestic students, 3/1 priority date for international students; for spring admission, 10/1 priority date for domestic students, 8/1 priority date for international students. Applications are processed on a rolling basis. *Application fee:* $50. Electronic applications accepted. *Application Contact:* Daniel Stirling, Administrator, Graduate School, 406-496-4304, Fax: 406-496-4710, E-mail: gradschool@mtech.edu. *Director*, Dr. Kumar Ganesan, 406-496-4239, Fax: 406-496-4650, E-mail: kganesan@mtech.edu.

MONTCLAIR STATE UNIVERSITY, Montclair, NJ 07043-1624

General Information State-supported, coed, university. CGS member. *Enrollment:* 20,987 graduate, professional, and undergraduate students; 1,373 full-time matriculated graduate/professional students (955 women), 2,194 part-time matriculated graduate/professional students (1,562 women). *Enrollment by degree level:* 3,068 master's, 231 doctoral, 268 other advanced degrees. *Graduate faculty:* 604 full-time (292 women), 1,210 part-time/adjunct (648 women). Tuition, state resident: part-time $553 per credit. Tuition, nonresident: part-time $854 per credit. *Required fees:* $91 per credit. Tuition and fees vary according to program. *Graduate housing:* Room and/or apartments available on a first-come, first-served basis to single students; on-campus housing not available to married students. Typical cost: $10,466 (including board). Housing application deadline: 3/1. *Student services:* Campus employment opportunities, campus safety program, career counseling, child daycare facilities, exercise/wellness program, free psychological counseling, grant writing training, international student services, low-cost health insurance, multicultural affairs office, services for students with disabilities, teacher training, writing training. *Library facilities:* Sprague Library. *Collection:* Books: 441,470 (physical), 145,833 (digital/electronic); Serial titles: 9,751 (physical), 40,969 (digital/electronic); Databases: 165. Weekly public service hours: 93; students can reserve study rooms. *Research affiliation:* Spencer Foundation (education improvement), The International Society for Optical Engineering (optics and photonics), Deafness Research Foundation (heating science).

Computer facilities: Computer purchase and lease plans are available. 1,850 computers available on campus for general student use. A campuswide network can be accessed from student residence rooms and from off campus. Online class registration, online storage, online course delivery, online computing lab, student online portal are available.

Website: http://www.montclair.edu/

General Application Contact: Amy Aiello, Executive Director of The Graduate School, 973-655-5147, Fax: 973-655-7869, E-mail: aielloa@mail.montclair.edu.

GRADUATE UNITS

The Graduate School *Program availability:* Part-time, evening/weekend. Electronic applications accepted.

College of Education and Human Services *Program availability:* Part-time, evening/weekend. Offers art (MAT); biology (MAT); certified alcohol and drug counselor (Certificate); chemistry (MAT); counseling (MA); counselor education (PhD); developmental models of autism intervention (Certificate); dietetics (Postbaccalaureate Certificate); earth science (MAT); education and human services (M Ed, MA, MAT, MPH, MS, Ed D, PhD, Certificate, Post Master's Certificate, Postbaccalaureate Certificate); educational leadership (MA); English (MAT); exercise science (MA); family and child studies (MA); family studies (PhD); French (MAT);

health and physical education (MAT); health education (MAT); inclusive early childhood education (M Ed); infant and early childhood mental health (Certificate); learning disabilities (M Ed); mathematics (MAT); music (MAT); nutrition and exercise science (Certificate); nutrition and food science (MS); physical education (MAT); physical science (MAT); program evaluation (Certificate); public health (MPH); reading (MA); social studies (MAT); Spanish (MAT); sports administration and coaching (MA); teacher education and teacher development (PhD); teacher of English as a second language (MAT); teaching and supervision in physical education (MA). Electronic applications accepted.

College of Humanities and Social Sciences *Program availability:* Part-time, evening/weekend. Offers adolescent advocacy (Certificate); applied linguistics (MA); audiology (Sc D); child advocacy and policy (MA, Certificate); clinical psychology (MA); communication sciences and disorders (MA); computational linguistics (Certificate); conflict management and peace studies (MA); conflict management in the workplace (Certificate); data collection and management (Certificate); English (MA); family/civil forensic psychology (Certificate); forensic psychology (Certificate); French literature (MA); French studies (MA); governance, compliance and regulation (MA); humanities and social sciences (MA, Sc D, Certificate); industrial and organizational psychology (MA); intellectual property (MA); law and governance (MA); legal management (MA); paralegal studies (Certificate); psychology (MA); Spanish (MA); teaching English to speakers of other languages (Certificate); teaching writing (Certificate); translation and interpreting in Spanish (Certificate). Electronic applications accepted.

College of Science and Mathematics *Program availability:* Part-time, evening/weekend. Offers biological science/education (MS); biology (MS); chemistry (MS); computer networking (Certificate); computer science (MS); earth and environmental science (MS); ecology and evolution (MS); environmental education (MA); environmental forensics (Certificate); environmental management (MA); environmental science (MA); geographic information science (Certificate); geoscience (MS); information technology (MS); marine biology and coastal sciences (MS); mathematics education (Ed D); molecular biology (MS, Certificate); pharmaceutical biochemistry (MS); physiology (MS); pure and applied mathematics (MS); science and mathematics (MA, MAT, MS, Ed D, PhD, Certificate); statistics (MS); sustainability science (MS); teaching middle grades mathematics (MA, Certificate); teaching physical education (MAT); water resource management (Certificate). Electronic applications accepted.

College of the Arts *Program availability:* Part-time, evening/weekend. Offers arts (MA, MFA, AD, Performer's Certificate, Postbaccalaureate Certificate); arts management (MA); museum management (MA); music (MA, AD, Performer's Certificate); music education (MA); music therapy (MA, Postbaccalaureate Certificate); performance (MA); production/stage management (MA); public and organizational relations (MA); studio (MA); studio art (MFA); theatre studies (MA); theory/composition (MA). Electronic applications accepted.

Feliciano School of Business *Program availability:* Part-time, evening/weekend. Offers accounting (MS, Post Master's Certificate); business (MBA, MS, Graduate Certificate, Post Master's Certificate); business administration (MBA); forensic accounting (Graduate Certificate). Electronic applications accepted.

MONTREAT COLLEGE, Montreat, NC 28757-1267

General Information Independent-religious, coed, comprehensive institution. *Graduate housing:* On-campus housing not available.

GRADUATE UNITS

School of Professional and Adult Studies *Program availability:* Part-time, evening/weekend, online learning. Electronic applications accepted.

MOODY BIBLE INSTITUTE, Chicago, IL 60610-3284

General Information Independent-religious, coed, comprehensive institution. *Graduate housing:* Rooms and/or apartments guaranteed to single students and available on a first-come, first-served basis to married students. Housing application deadline: 6/1.

GRADUATE UNITS

Graduate School *Program availability:* Part-time. Offers biblical studies (MABS, Graduate Certificate); intercultural studies (MAIS, Graduate Certificate); ministry (M Div, M Min); spiritual formation and discipleship (MASF, Graduate Certificate); urban studies (MA, Graduate Certificate).

MOODY THEOLOGICAL SEMINARY—MICHIGAN, Plymouth, MI 48170

General Information Independent-religious, coed, graduate-only institution. *Graduate housing:* On-campus housing not available.

GRADUATE UNITS

Graduate Programs *Program availability:* Part-time, evening/weekend. Offers Bible (Graduate Certificate); Christian education (MA); counseling psychology (MA); divinity (M Div); theological studies (MA).

MOORE COLLEGE OF ART & DESIGN, Philadelphia, PA 19103

General Information Independent, Undergraduate: women only; graduate: coed, comprehensive institution.

GRADUATE UNITS

Program in Art Education *Program availability:* Part-time. Offers art education (MA).
Program in Community Practice Offers community practice (MFA).
Program in Interior Design *Program availability:* Evening/weekend. Offers interior design (MFA).
Program in Social Engagement *Program availability:* Part-time. Offers social engagement (MA).
Program in Studio Art Offers studio art (MFA).

MORAVIAN COLLEGE, Bethlehem, PA 18018-6650

General Information Independent-religious, coed, comprehensive institution. *Enrollment:* 2,448 graduate, professional, and undergraduate students; 23 full-time matriculated graduate/professional students (13 women), 244 part-time matriculated graduate/professional students (180 women). *Enrollment by degree level:* 240 master's, 27 other advanced degrees. *Graduate faculty:* 17 full-time (10 women), 37 part-time/adjunct (23 women). *Tuition:* Full-time $2619. Tuition and fees vary according to course load and program. *Graduate housing:* On-campus housing not available. *Student services:* Campus employment opportunities, campus safety program, career counseling, exercise/wellness program, international student services, multicultural affairs office, services for students with disabilities, teacher training, writing training. *Library facilities:* Reeves Library. *Collection:* Books: 253,908 (physical), 154,565

(digital/electronic); Serial titles: 3 (physical), 75,717 (digital/electronic); Databases: 50. Weekly public service hours: 86.

Computer facilities: Computer purchase and lease plans are available. 306 computers available on campus for general student use. A campuswide network can be accessed from student residence rooms and from off campus. Online class registration is available.
Website: http://www.moravian.edu/

General Application Contact: Scott Dams, Executive Director of Graduate and Adult Admission, 610-861-1400, E-mail: graduate@moravian.edu.

GRADUATE UNITS

Graduate and Continuing Studies Students: 23 full-time (13 women), 244 part-time (180 women); includes 30 minority (8 Black or African American, non-Hispanic/Latino; 1 American Indian or Alaska Native, non-Hispanic/Latino; 5 Asian, non-Hispanic/Latino; 15 Hispanic/Latino; 1 Two or more races, non-Hispanic/Latino), 1 international. Average age 34. 66 applicants, 88% accepted, 47 enrolled. *Faculty:* 17 full-time (10 women), 37 part-time/adjunct (23 women). Expenses: Contact institution. *Financial support:* In 2016–17, 1 teaching assistantship with full tuition reimbursement was awarded. Financial award applicants required to submit FAFSA. In 2016, 31 master's awarded. *Program availability:* Part-time, evening/weekend. Offers accounting (MBA); athletic training (MS); business analytics (MBA); curriculum and instruction (M Ed); education (MAT); general management (MBA); health administration (MHA); healthcare management (MBA); human resource management (MBA); leadership (MSHRM); learning and performance management (MSHRM); supply chain management (MBA). *Application deadline:* For fall admission, 8/1 priority date for domestic and international students; for spring admission, 1/1 priority date for domestic and international students; for summer admission, 5/1 priority date for domestic and international students. Applications are processed on a rolling basis. Electronic applications accepted. *Application Contact:* Kristy Sullivan, Director of Student Recruitment Operations, 610-861-1400, Fax: 610-861-1466, E-mail: graduate@moravian.edu. *Executive Director of Graduate Admission,* Scott Dams, 610-861-1400, Fax: 610-861-1466, E-mail: graduate@moravian.edu.

Helen S. Breidegam School of Nursing Students: 1 (woman) full-time, 71 part-time (66 women); includes 5 minority (1 Black or African American, non-Hispanic/Latino; 1 Asian, non-Hispanic/Latino; 3 Hispanic/Latino). Average age 39. 17 applicants, 82% accepted, 11 enrolled. *Faculty:* 4 full-time (all women), 11 part-time/adjunct (7 women). Expenses: Contact institution. *Financial support:* Applicants required to submit FAFSA. In 2016, 7 master's awarded. *Program availability:* Part-time, evening/weekend. Offers clinical nurse leader (MS); nurse administrator (MS); nurse educator (MS); nurse practitioner - acute care (MS); nurse practitioner - primary care (MS). *Application deadline:* For fall admission, 8/1 priority date for domestic and international students; for spring admission, 1/1 priority date for domestic and international students; for summer admission, 5/1 priority date for domestic and international students. Applications are processed on a rolling basis. Electronic applications accepted. *Application Contact:* Kristy Sullivan, Director of Student Recruiting Operations, 610-861-1400, Fax: 610-861-1466, E-mail: graduate@moravian.edu. *Professor/Chairperson,* Dr. Kerry Cheever, 610-861-1412, Fax: 610-861-1466, E-mail: nursing@moravian.edu.

MORAVIAN THEOLOGICAL SEMINARY, Bethlehem, PA 18018-6614

General Information Independent-religious, coed, graduate-only institution. *Enrollment by degree level:* 71 master's, 23 other advanced degrees. *Graduate faculty:* 8 full-time (3 women), 10 part-time/adjunct (6 women). *Tuition:* Full-time $13,680; part-time $7596 per year. *Required fees:* $430; $430 per unit. Tuition and fees vary according to course load. *Graduate housing:* Rooms and/or apartments available on a first-come, first-served basis to single and married students. Typical cost: $9912 per year for single students; $13,980 per year for married students. Room charges vary according to housing facility selected. Housing application deadline: 7/31. *Student services:* Campus employment opportunities, campus safety program, exercise/wellness program, international student services, low-cost health insurance, multicultural affairs office, services for students with disabilities, writing training. *Library facilities:* Reeves Library. *Collection:* Books: 192,017 (physical), 137,800 (digital/electronic); Serial titles: 6,082 (physical), 2,168 (digital/electronic); Databases: 62. Weekly public service hours: 100; students can reserve study rooms.

Computer facilities: 227 computers available on campus for general student use. A campuswide network can be accessed from student residence rooms and from off campus. Online class registration is available.
Website: http://www.moravianseminary.edu/

General Application Contact: Dr. David H. DeRemer, Director of Enrollment, 610-861-1512, Fax: 610-861-1569, E-mail: deremerd@moravian.edu.

GRADUATE UNITS

Graduate and Certificate Programs Students: 26 full-time (12 women), 68 part-time (51 women); includes 17 minority (11 Black or African American, non-Hispanic/Latino; 5 Hispanic/Latino; 1 Two or more races, non-Hispanic/Latino), 1 international. Average age 48. 37 applicants, 73% accepted, 25 enrolled. *Faculty:* 8 full-time (3 women), 10 part-time/adjunct (6 women). Expenses: Contact institution. *Financial support:* In 2016–17, 71 students received support. Career-related internships or fieldwork, Federal Work-Study, and scholarships/grants available. Support available to part-time students. Financial award application deadline: 5/1; financial award applicants required to submit FAFSA. In 2016, 20 master's, 8 other advanced degrees awarded. *Program availability:* Part-time. Offers chaplaincy (MACH); clinical counseling (MACC); divinity (M Div); formative spirituality (M Div, MATS, Graduate Certificate); spiritual direction (Graduate Certificate). *Application deadline:* For fall admission, 4/1 priority date for international students; for spring admission, 9/1 priority date for international students. Applications are processed on a rolling basis. *Application fee:* $50. Electronic applications accepted. *Application Contact:* Rev. Dr. David H. DeRemer, Director of Enrollment, 610-861-1512, Fax: 610-861-1569, E-mail: deremerd@moravian.edu. *Dean and Vice President,* Rev. Dr. Frank L. Crouch, 610-861-1516, E-mail: crouchf@moravian.edu.

MOREHEAD STATE UNIVERSITY, Morehead, KY 40351

General Information State-supported, coed, comprehensive institution. *Graduate housing:* Room and/or apartments available on a first-come, first-served basis to single students; on-campus housing not available to married students. Housing application deadline: 3/12.

GRADUATE UNITS

Graduate Programs *Program availability:* Part-time, evening/weekend, online learning. Electronic applications accepted.

Caudill College of Arts, Humanities and Social Sciences Program availability: Part-time, evening/weekend, online learning. Offers art education (MA); arts, humanities and social sciences (MA, MM); communication (MA); criminology (MA); English (MA); general sociology (MA); gerontology (MA); graphic design (MA); music education (MM); music performance (MM); sociology regional analysis (MA); sociology/chemical dependency (MA); studio art (MA). Electronic applications accepted.

College of Business and Public Affairs Program availability: Part-time, evening/weekend, online learning. Offers business administration (MA, MBA, MSIS); business and public affairs (MA, MBA, MPA, MSIS); information systems (MSIS); public policy (MPA); sport management (MA). Electronic applications accepted.

College of Education Program availability: Part-time, evening/weekend. Offers adult and higher education (MA, Ed S); business and marketing education (MAT); certified professional counselor (Ed S); counseling P-12 (MA); curriculum and instruction (Ed S); education (MA, MA Ed, MAT, Ed S); educational technology (MA Ed); elementary education (MA Ed); English/language arts 5-9 (MAT); French (MAT); health P-12 (MAT); instructional leadership (Ed S); learning and behavioral disorders P-12 (MAT); mathematics 5-9 (MAT); moderate and severe disabilities P-12 (MAT); physical education P-12 (MAT); school administration (MA); school counseling (Ed S); science 5-9 (MAT); secondary biology (MAT); secondary chemistry (MAT); secondary earth science (MAT); secondary education (MA Ed); secondary English (MAT); secondary math (MAT); secondary physics (MAT); secondary social studies (MAT); social studies 5-9 (MAT); Spanish (MAT); special education (MA Ed); teacher leader business and marketing content (MA Ed); teacher leader business and marketing technology (MA Ed); teacher leader educational technology (MA Ed); teacher leader English (MA Ed); teacher leader gifted education (MA Ed); teacher leader IECE certification (MA Ed); teacher leader interdisciplinary education P-5 (MA Ed); teacher leader middle grades (MA Ed); teacher leader non IECE certification (MA Ed); teacher leader reading/writing - non-certification (MA Ed); teacher leader reading/writing certification (MA Ed); teacher leader school communication - certification (MA Ed); teacher leader school communication - non-certification (MA Ed); teacher leader social studies (MA Ed); teacher leader special education (MA Ed); teaching (MAT). Electronic applications accepted.

College of Science and Technology Program availability: Part-time, evening/weekend. Offers biology (MS); biology regional analysis (MS); career and technical agricultural education (MS); career and technical education (MS); clinical/counseling psychology (MS); engineering technology (MS); general/experimental psychology (MS); health/physical education (MA); science and technology (MA, MS). Electronic applications accepted.

Institute for Regional Analysis and Public Policy Offers public administration (MPA). Electronic applications accepted.

MOREHOUSE SCHOOL OF MEDICINE, Atlanta, GA 30310-1495

General Information Independent, coed, graduate-only institution. CGS member. *Graduate housing:* On-campus housing not available. *Research affiliation:* Merck & Company, Inc. (hypotension), CareStat (renal insufficiency), Wyeth (helicobacter pylori study), Bristol-Myers Squibb (pharmacokinetics), Parke-Davis (cardiovascular risk factors), NitroMel, Inc. (heart failure).

GRADUATE UNITS

Graduate Programs in Biomedical Sciences Offers biomedical research (MS); biomedical sciences (PhD); biomedical technology (MS); medical sciences (MS). Electronic applications accepted.

Master of Public Health Program Program availability: Part-time. Offers public health (MPH). Electronic applications accepted.

Master of Science in Clinical Research Program Program availability: Part-time. Offers clinical research (MS). Electronic applications accepted.

Professional Program Offers medicine (MD). Electronic applications accepted.

MORGAN STATE UNIVERSITY, Baltimore, MD 21251

General Information State-supported, coed, university. CGS member. *Graduate housing:* Rooms and/or apartments available on a first-come, first-served basis to single and married students.

GRADUATE UNITS

School of Graduate Studies Program availability: Part-time, evening/weekend.

Clarence M. Mitchell, Jr. School of Engineering Program availability: Part-time, evening/weekend. Offers civil engineering (M Eng, D Eng); electrical and computer engineering (M Eng, MS, D Eng); industrial and systems engineering (M Eng, D Eng); transportation (MS).

College of Liberal Arts Program availability: Part-time. Offers African-American studies (MA); economics (MA); English (MA, PhD); fine and performing arts (MA); history (MA, PhD); international studies (MA); liberal arts (MA, MS, PhD); museum studies and historic preservation (MA); psychometrics (MS, PhD); sociology (MA, MS).

Earl G. Graves School of Business and Management Program availability: Part-time, evening/weekend. Offers business administration (MBA, PhD); business and management (MBA, PhD).

Institute of Architecture and Planning Offers architecture (M Arch); city and regional planning (MCRP); landscape architecture (MLA).

School of Community Health and Policy Offers nursing (MS); public health (MPH, Dr PH).

School of Computer, Mathematical, and Natural Sciences Offers bioenvironmental science (PhD); bioinformatics (MS); biology (MS); chemistry (MS); computer, mathematical, and natural sciences (MA, MS, PhD); mathematics (MS); science education (MS).

School of Education and Urban Studies Program availability: Part-time. Offers community college leadership (Ed D); education and urban studies (MA, MAT, MS, Ed D, PhD); educational administration and supervision (Ed D); elementary education (MAT); high school education (MAT); higher education (PhD); higher education administration (MA, MA, PhD); mathematics education (MS, Ed D); middle school education (MAT); science education (MS, Ed D); urban educational leadership (Ed D).

School of Social Work Offers social work (MSW, PhD).

MORNINGSIDE COLLEGE, Sioux City, IA 51106

General Information Independent-religious, coed, comprehensive institution. CGS member. *Enrollment:* 2,902 graduate, professional, and undergraduate students; 1 full-time matriculated graduate/professional student, 179 part-time matriculated graduate/professional students. *Enrollment by degree level:* 180 master's. *Graduate faculty:* 33. *Tuition:* Part-time $240 per credit. *Graduate housing:* On-campus housing not available. *Student services:* Career counseling, free psychological counseling, writing training. *Library facilities:* Hickman-Johnson-Furrow Learning Center. *Collection:*

Books: 47,802 (physical), 285,794 (digital/electronic); Serial titles: 170 (physical); Databases: 34. Weekly public service hours: 93. *Research affiliation:* Iowa Public Service Company (biology, chemistry, physics).

Computer facilities: Computer purchase and lease plans are available. 150 computers available on campus for general student use. A campuswide network can be accessed from student residence rooms and from off campus. Online class registration, academic and financial records are available.
Website: http://www.morningside.edu/

General Application Contact: Tracy Sursely, Student Records Enrollment Coordinator, 712-274-5576, Fax: 712-274-5101, E-mail: surselyt@morningside.edu.

GRADUATE UNITS

Graduate Division Students: 34 full-time (30 women), 1,547 part-time (1,263 women); includes 54 minority (5 Black or African American, non-Hispanic/Latino; 4 American Indian or Alaska Native, non-Hispanic/Latino; 11 Asian, non-Hispanic/Latino; 28 Hispanic/Latino; 1 Native Hawaiian or other Pacific Islander, non-Hispanic/Latino; 5 Two or more races, non-Hispanic/Latino), 1 international. Average age 35. *Faculty:* 5 full-time (2 women), 108 part-time/adjunct (80 women). Expenses: Contact institution. *Financial support:* Institutionally sponsored loans and tuition waivers (partial) available. Support available to part-time students. Financial award applicants required to submit FAFSA. In 2016, 316 master's awarded. *Program availability:* Part-time, evening/weekend, online only, 100% online. *Application deadline:* Applications are processed on a rolling basis. Electronic applications accepted. *Application Contact:* Barbara Chambers, Director, 712-274-5465, Fax: 712-274-5101, E-mail: chambersb@morningside.edu. *Director,* Barbara Chambers, 712-274-5465, Fax: 712-274-5101, E-mail: chambersb@morningside.edu.

Sharon Walker School of Education Students: 23 full-time (20 women), 1,468 part-time (1,191 women); includes 51 minority (5 Black or African American, non-Hispanic/Latino; 4 American Indian or Alaska Native, non-Hispanic/Latino; 9 Asian, non-Hispanic/Latino; 27 Hispanic/Latino; 1 Native Hawaiian or other Pacific Islander, non-Hispanic/Latino; 5 Two or more races, non-Hispanic/Latino), 1 international. Average age 35. *Faculty:* 4 full-time (1 woman), 108 part-time/adjunct (80 women). Expenses: Contact institution. *Financial support:* Institutionally sponsored loans and tuition waivers (partial) available. Support available to part-time students. In 2016, 316 master's awarded. *Program availability:* Part-time, evening/weekend, online only, 100% online. Offers professional educator (MAT); special education (MAT). *Application deadline:* Applications are processed on a rolling basis. *Application fee:* $15. Electronic applications accepted. *Application Contact:* Tracy Sursely, Student Records Enrollment Coordinator, 712-274-5576, Fax: 712-274-5101, E-mail: surselyt@morningside.edu. *Director,* Barbara Chambers, 712-274-5465, Fax: 712-274-5488, E-mail: chambersb@morningside.edu.

MOUNT ALLISON UNIVERSITY, Sackville, NB E4L 1E4, Canada

General Information Province-supported, coed, comprehensive institution. *Graduate housing:* Room and/or apartments available to single students; on-campus housing not available to married students. Housing application deadline: 5/15. *Research affiliation:* Atlantic Cancer Institute (medical research), Moncton Hospital (medical research), Huntsman Marine Science Centre (marine biology).

GRADUATE UNITS

Department of Biology Offers biology (M Sc).

Department of Chemistry Offers chemistry (M Sc).

MOUNT ALOYSIUS COLLEGE, Cresson, PA 16630-1999

General Information Independent-religious, coed, comprehensive institution. *Enrollment:* 1,785 graduate, professional, and undergraduate students; 38 full-time matriculated graduate/professional students, 27 part-time matriculated graduate/professional students. *Enrollment by degree level:* 65 master's. *Graduate faculty:* 12 full-time (10 women), 18 part-time/adjunct (7 women). *Tuition:* Full-time $6750; part-time $750 per credit. *Required fees:* $285 per semester. *Graduate housing:* On-campus housing not available. *Student services:* Campus employment opportunities, campus safety program, career counseling, child daycare facilities, exercise/wellness program, free psychological counseling, international student services, services for students with disabilities, writing training. *Library facilities:* Mount Aloysius College Library.

Computer facilities: Computer purchase and lease plans are available. A campuswide network can be accessed from student residence rooms and from off campus. Online class registration is available.
Website: http://www.mtaloy.edu/

General Application Contact: Matthew P. Bodenschatz, Director of Graduate and Continuing Education Admissions, 814-886-6556, Fax: 814-886-6441, E-mail: mbodenschatz@mtaloy.edu.

GRADUATE UNITS

Program in Business Administration Expenses: Contact institution. *Financial support:* Unspecified assistantships available. Financial award applicants required to submit FAFSA. *Program availability:* Part-time, evening/weekend. Offers accounting (MBA); health and human services administration (MBA); non-profit management (MBA); project management (MBA). *Application deadline:* For fall admission, 8/1 for domestic students; for spring admission, 12/1 for domestic students. Applications are processed on a rolling basis. *Application fee:* $30. Electronic applications accepted. *Application Contact:* Matthew P. Bodenschatz, Director of Graduate and Continuing Education Admissions, 814-886-6556, Fax: 814-886-6441, E-mail: mbodenschatz@mtaloy.edu.

Program in Community Counseling Expenses: Contact institution. *Financial support:* Unspecified assistantships available. *Program availability:* Part-time. Offers community counseling (MS). *Application deadline:* For fall admission, 8/1 for domestic students; for spring admission, 12/1 for domestic students. Applications are processed on a rolling basis. *Application fee:* $30. Electronic applications accepted. *Application Contact:* Matthew P. Bodenschatz, Director of Graduate and Continuing Education Admissions, 814-886-6556, Fax: 814-886-6441, E-mail: mbodenschatz@mtaloy.edu.

Program in Psychology Expenses: Contact institution. *Financial support:* Unspecified assistantships available. *Program availability:* Part-time, evening/weekend. Offers psychology (MS). *Application deadline:* Applications are processed on a rolling basis. *Application fee:* $30. Electronic applications accepted. *Application Contact:* Matthew P. Bodenschatz, Director of Graduate and Continuing Education Admissions, 814-886-6556, Fax: 814-886-6441, E-mail: mbodenschatz@mtaloy.edu.

MOUNT ANGEL SEMINARY, Saint Benedict, OR 97373

General Information Independent-religious, Undergraduate: men only; graduate: coed, comprehensive institution. *Graduate housing:* Room and/or apartments guaranteed to single students; on-campus housing not available to married students.

GRADUATE UNITS

Program in Theology *Program availability:* Part-time. Offers theology (M Div, MA).

MOUNT CARMEL COLLEGE OF NURSING, Columbus, OH 43222

General Information Independent, coed, primarily women, comprehensive institution. *Enrollment:* 1,105 graduate, professional, and undergraduate students; 97 full-time matriculated graduate/professional students (83 women), 75 part-time matriculated graduate/professional students (65 women). *Enrollment by degree level:* 172 master's, 4 doctoral, 6 other advanced degrees. *Graduate faculty:* 9 full-time (all women), 6 part-time/adjunct (4 women). *Tuition:* Full-time $10,920; part-time $520 per credit. One-time fee: $110. Tuition and fees vary according to course load, degree level and program. *Graduate housing:* Rooms and/or apartments available on a first-come, first-served basis to single and married students. Typical cost: $5000 per year for single students. *Student services:* Free psychological counseling, grant writing training, multicultural affairs office, teacher training, writing training. *Library facilities:* The Mount Carmel Health Sciences Library plus 1 other. *Collection:* Books: 8,187 (physical), 237,569 (digital/electronic); Serial titles: 1,951 (physical), 61,543 (digital/electronic); Databases: 50. Weekly public service hours: 65; study areas open 24 hours, 5–7 days a week; students can reserve study rooms.

Computer facilities: 25 computers available on campus for general student use. A campuswide network can be accessed from student residence rooms. Online class registration is available.
Website: http://www.mccn.edu/

General Application Contact: Dr. Kim Campbell, Director of Recruitment and Admissions, 614-234-5144, Fax: 614-234-5427, E-mail: kcampbell@mccn.edu.

GRADUATE UNITS

Nursing Program Students: 97 full-time (83 women), 75 part-time (65 women); includes 18 minority (13 Black or African American, non-Hispanic/Latino; 3 Asian, non-Hispanic/Latino; 1 Hispanic/Latino; 1 Two or more races, non-Hispanic/Latino). Average age 34. 158 applicants, 77% accepted, 104 enrolled. *Faculty:* 9 full-time (all women), 6 part-time/adjunct (4 women). Expenses: Contact institution. *Financial support:* In 2016–17, 3 students received support. Institutionally sponsored loans and scholarships/grants available. Financial award applicants required to submit FAFSA. In 2016, 52 master's awarded. *Program availability:* Part-time. Offers adult gerontology acute care nurse practitioner (MS); adult health clinical nurse specialist (MS); family nurse practitioner (MS); nursing (DNP). *Application deadline:* For fall admission, 2/1 priority date for domestic students; for spring admission, 11/1 priority date for domestic students. Applications are processed on a rolling basis. *Application fee:* $30. Electronic applications accepted. *Application Contact:* Dr. Kim Campbell, Director of Recruitment and Admissions, 614-234-5144, Fax: 614-234-5427, E-mail: kcampbell@mccn.edu.

MOUNT HOLYOKE COLLEGE, South Hadley, MA 01075

General Information Independent, women only, comprehensive institution. *Enrollment:* 2,330 graduate, professional, and undergraduate students; 23 full-time matriculated graduate/professional students (21 women), 84 part-time matriculated graduate/professional students (76 women). *Enrollment by degree level:* 107 master's. *Graduate faculty:* 4 full-time (3 women), 12 part-time/adjunct (10 women). *Tuition:* Full-time $24,500; part-time $770 per credit hour. *Required fees:* $117. Tuition and fees vary according to course load and program. *Graduate housing:* On-campus housing not available. *Student services:* Campus employment opportunities, career counseling, free psychological counseling, low-cost health insurance, services for students with disabilities. *Library facilities:* Williston Memorial Library plus 2 others. *Collection:* Books: 662,010 (physical), 853,290 (digital/electronic); Serial titles: 603 (physical), 8,098 (digital/electronic); Databases: 227. Weekly public service hours: 115; students can reserve study rooms.

Computer facilities: Computer purchase and lease plans are available. 364 computers available on campus for general student use. A campuswide network can be accessed from student residence rooms and from off campus. Online class registration, personal Web pages are available.
Website: http://www.mtholyoke.edu/

General Application Contact: Dr. Tiffany Espinosa, Executive Director of Professional and Graduate Education, 413-538-3478, Fax: 413-538-3098.

GRADUATE UNITS

Professional and Graduate Education (PaGE) Students: 23 full-time (21 women), 84 part-time (76 women); includes 11 minority (4 Black or African American, non-Hispanic/Latino; 2 Asian, non-Hispanic/Latino; 5 Two or more races, non-Hispanic/Latino), 7 international. Average age 37. *Faculty:* 4 full-time (3 women), 12 part-time/adjunct (10 women). Expenses: Contact institution. *Financial support:* Scholarships/grants available. Financial award applicants required to submit FAFSA. In 2016, 30 master's awarded. *Program availability:* Part-time, 100% online, blended/hybrid learning. Offers mathematics teaching (MAMT); teacher leadership (MATL); teaching (MAT). *Application deadline:* Applications are processed on a rolling basis. *Application fee:* $0. Electronic applications accepted. *Application Contact:* Executive Director of Professional and Graduate Education, Dr. Tiffany Espinosa, 413-538-3478, Fax: 413-538-3098.

MOUNT IDA COLLEGE, Newton, MA 02459-3310

General Information Independent, coed, comprehensive institution. *Graduate housing:* On-campus housing not available.

GRADUATE UNITS

Program in Management *Program availability:* Part-time, evening/weekend, online learning. Offers healthcare management (MSM); human resource management (MSM); interior architecture (MSM); leadership in sport (MSM); management (MSM). Electronic applications accepted.

MOUNT MARTY COLLEGE, Yankton, SD 57078-3724

General Information Independent-religious, coed, comprehensive institution. *Graduate housing:* On-campus housing not available.

GRADUATE UNITS

Graduate Studies Division Offers business administration (MBA); nurse anesthesia (MS); nursing (MSN); pastoral ministries (MPM). Electronic applications accepted.

MOUNT MARY UNIVERSITY, Milwaukee, WI 53222-4597

General Information Independent-religious, Undergraduate: women only; graduate: coed, comprehensive institution. CGS member. *Enrollment:* 1,404 graduate, professional, and undergraduate students; 419 full-time matriculated graduate/professional students (389 women), 178 part-time matriculated graduate/professional students (155 women). *Enrollment by degree level:* 404 master's, 27 doctoral, 10 other advanced degrees. *Graduate faculty:* 24 full-time (21 women), 44 part-time/adjunct (30 women). *Tuition:* Full-time $12,308; part-time $684 per credit. *Required fees:* $440; $220 per semester. Tuition and fees vary according to course load, degree level and program. *Graduate housing:* Room and/or apartments available on a first-come, first-served basis to single students; on-campus housing not available to married students. Typical cost: $8530 (including board). *Student services:* Campus employment opportunities, campus safety program, career counseling, exercise/wellness program, free psychological counseling, international student services, low-cost health insurance, services for students with disabilities, teacher training, writing training. *Library facilities:* The Patrick and Beatrice Haggerty Library. *Collection:* Books: 65,458 (physical), 130,464 (digital/electronic); Serial titles: 5,483 (physical), 160,422 (digital/electronic); Databases: 89. Students can reserve study rooms.

Computer facilities: 177 computers available on campus for general student use. A campuswide network can be accessed from student residence rooms and from off campus. Online class registration is available.
Website: http://www.mtmary.edu/

General Application Contact: Kirk Heller de Messer, Director, Graduate Admissions, 414-930-3221, E-mail: hellerk@mtmary.edu.

GRADUATE UNITS

Graduate Programs Students: 393 full-time (364 women), 165 part-time (143 women); includes 99 minority (31 Black or African American, non-Hispanic/Latino; 3 American Indian or Alaska Native, non-Hispanic/Latino; 13 Asian, non-Hispanic/Latino; 32 Hispanic/Latino; 1 Native Hawaiian or other Pacific Islander, non-Hispanic/Latino; 19 Two or more races, non-Hispanic/Latino), 6 international. Average age 33. 674 applicants, 32% accepted, 167 enrolled. *Faculty:* 28 full-time (25 women), 49 part-time/adjunct (34 women). Expenses: Contact institution. *Financial support:* Career-related internships or fieldwork, Federal Work-Study, and unspecified assistantships available. Support available to part-time students. Financial award application deadline: 5/1; financial award applicants required to submit FAFSA. In 2016, 193 master's, 6 doctorates, 2 other advanced degrees awarded. *Program availability:* Part-time, evening/weekend, 100% online, blended/hybrid learning. Offers art therapy (MS, DAT); clinical mental health counseling (MS, Certificate); clinical rehabilitation counseling (MS, Certificate); creative writing (MA); dietetics (MS); dietetics internship (MS); general management (MBA); health systems leadership (MBA); occupational therapy (MS, OTD); professional and new media writing (MA); professional development (MA); school counseling (MS, Certificate); vocational rehabilitation counseling (MS, Certificate). *Application deadline:* For fall admission, 8/1 for domestic and international students; for winter admission, 8/15 for domestic students, 9/15 for international students; for spring admission, 12/1 for domestic and international students; for summer admission, 5/1 for domestic and international students. Applications are processed on a rolling basis. *Application fee:* $45. Electronic applications accepted. *Application Contact:* Kirk Heller de Messer, Director, Graduate Admissions, 414-930-3221, E-mail: hellerk@mtmary.edu.

MOUNT MERCY UNIVERSITY, Cedar Rapids, IA 52402-4797

General Information Independent-religious, coed, comprehensive institution.

GRADUATE UNITS

Program in Business Administration *Program availability:* Evening/weekend. Offers human resource (MBA); quality management (MBA). Electronic applications accepted.

Program in Criminal Justice *Program availability:* Evening/weekend, online learning. Offers criminal justice (MA).

Program in Education Offers reading (MA Ed); special education (MA Ed); teacher leadership (MA Ed). Electronic applications accepted.

Program in Marriage and Family Therapy *Program availability:* Evening/weekend. Offers marriage and family therapy (MA).

Program in Nursing *Program availability:* Evening/weekend. Offers health advocacy (MSN); nurse administration (MSN); nurse education (MSN).

Program in Strategic Leadership *Program availability:* Evening/weekend. Offers strategic leadership (MSL).

MOUNT ST. JOSEPH UNIVERSITY, Cincinnati, OH 45233-1670

General Information Independent-religious, coed, comprehensive institution. CGS member. *Enrollment:* 2,045 graduate, professional, and undergraduate students; 223 full-time matriculated graduate/professional students (160 women), 486 part-time matriculated graduate/professional students (411 women). *Enrollment by degree level:* 560 master's, 149 doctoral. *Graduate faculty:* 36 full-time (29 women), 65 part-time/adjunct (59 women). *Tuition:* Full-time $9525; part-time $635 per credit hour. *Required fees:* $250 per credit hour. $125 per semester. Tuition and fees vary according to course load, degree level and program. *Graduate housing:* Room and/or apartments available on a first-come, first-served basis to single students; on-campus housing not available to married students. Typical cost: $9266 (including board). Room and board charges vary according to board plan and housing facility selected. Housing application deadline: 4/1. *Student services:* Campus employment opportunities, campus safety program, career counseling, child daycare facilities, exercise/wellness program, free psychological counseling, international student services, low-cost health insurance, services for students with disabilities, teacher training, writing training. *Library facilities:* Archbishop Alter Library. *Collection:* Books: 58,604 (physical), 149,341 (digital/electronic); Serial titles: 80 (physical), 30,599 (digital/electronic); Databases: 113. Weekly public service hours: 93.

Computer facilities: 172 computers available on campus for general student use. A campuswide network can be accessed from student residence rooms and from off campus. Online class registration, wireless printing, storage space are available.
Website: http://www.msj.edu/

General Application Contact: Mary Brigham, Assistant Director for Graduate Recruitment, 513-244-4233, Fax: 513-244-4629, E-mail: mary.brigham@msj.edu.

GRADUATE UNITS

Doctor of Nursing Practice Program Students: 38 part-time (35 women); includes 3 minority (all Black or African American, non-Hispanic/Latino). Average age 48. *Faculty:* 8 full-time (6 women), 10 part-time/adjunct (8 women). Expenses: Contact institution. *Financial support:* Applicants required to submit FAFSA. In 2016, 15 doctorates awarded. *Program availability:* Part-time-only. Offers health systems leadership (DNP). *Application deadline:* Applications are processed on a rolling basis. *Application fee:* $50. Electronic applications accepted. *Application Contact:* Shawn Adkins, Admission Counselor for Graduate Studies, 513-244-4723, Fax: 513-244-4629, E-mail: shawn.adkins@msj.edu. *Assistant Dean of Nursing,* Dr. Nancy Hinzman, 513-244-4325, Fax: 513-451-2547, E-mail: nancy.hinzman@msj.edu.

Graduate Education Program Students: 44 full-time (33 women), 112 part-time (104 women); includes 16 minority (15 Black or African American, non-Hispanic/Latino; 1 Two or more races, non-Hispanic/Latino). Average age 34. *Faculty:* 7 full-time (5 women), 12 part-time/adjunct (10 women). Expenses: Contact institution. *Financial support:*

Applicants required to submit FAFSA. In 2016, 60 master's awarded. *Program availability:* Part-time, evening/weekend, online learning. Offers adolescent to young adult education (MA); dyslexia (Certificate); inclusive early childhood education (MA); middle childhood education (MA); multicultural special education (MA); reading science (MA). *Application deadline:* Applications are processed on a rolling basis. *Application fee:* $50. Electronic applications accepted. *Application Contact:* Mary Brigham, Assistant Director of Graduate Recruitment, 513-244-4233, Fax: 513-244-4629, E-mail: mary.brigham@msj.edu. *Dean,* Dr. Laura Saylor, 513-244-3263, E-mail: laura.saylor@msj.edu.

Graduate Program in Religious Studies Students: 1 (woman) full-time, 6 part-time (4 women); includes 2 minority (1 Black or African American, non-Hispanic/Latino; 1 Hispanic/Latino). Average age 42. *Faculty:* 3 full-time (1 woman), 4 part-time/adjunct (2 women). Expenses: Contact institution. *Financial support:* In 2016–17, 5 students received support. Scholarships/grants available. Financial award applicants required to submit FAFSA. In 2016, 5 master's awarded. *Program availability:* Part-time, evening/weekend. Offers religious studies (MA); spirituality and wellness (Certificate). *Application deadline:* Applications are processed on a rolling basis. Electronic applications accepted. *Application Contact:* Mary Brigham, Assistant Director of Graduate Recruitment, 513-244-4233, Fax: 513-244-4629, E-mail: mary.brigham@msj.edu. *Associate Professor of Religious and Pastoral Studies/Director of Graduate Program,* Dr. John Trokan, 513-244-4272, Fax: 513-244-4222, E-mail: john.trokan@msj.edu.

Master of Business Administration Program Students: 11 full-time (3 women), 41 part-time (23 women); includes 6 minority (4 Black or African American, non-Hispanic/Latino; 1 Asian, non-Hispanic/Latino; 1 Two or more races, non-Hispanic/Latino). Average age 32. *Faculty:* 8 full-time (4 women), 2 part-time/adjunct (0 women). Expenses: Contact institution. *Financial support:* Applicants required to submit FAFSA. In 2016, 28 master's awarded. *Program availability:* Part-time, evening/weekend. Offers business administration (MBA). *Application deadline:* Applications are processed on a rolling basis. *Application fee:* $50. Electronic applications accepted. *Application Contact:* Amy Wolf, Senior Admissions Counselor for Graduate Studies, 513-244-4204, Fax: 513-745-4629, E-mail: amy.wolf@msj.edu. *Interim Dean,* Dr. Anna Goldhahn, 513-244-4924, Fax: 513-244-4270, E-mail: anna.goldhahn@msj.edu.

Master of Science in Nursing Program Students: 1 (woman) full-time, 109 part-time (102 women); includes 1 minority (Black or African American, non-Hispanic/Latino). Average age 39. *Faculty:* 12 full-time (11 women), 5 part-time/adjunct (all women). Expenses: Contact institution. *Financial support:* Applicants required to submit FAFSA. In 2016, 14 master's awarded. *Program availability:* Part-time. Offers administration (MSN); clinical nurse leader (MSN); education (MSN). *Application deadline:* Applications are processed on a rolling basis. *Application fee:* $50. Electronic applications accepted. *Application Contact:* Mary Brigham, Assistant Director for Graduate Recruitment, 513-244-4233, Fax: 513-244-4629, E-mail: mary.brigham@msj.edu. *MSN/DNP Director,* Dr. Nancy Hinzman, 513-244-4325, E-mail: nancy.hinzman@msj.edu.

Master of Science in Organizational Leadership Program Students: 57 part-time (32 women); includes 11 minority (9 Black or African American, non-Hispanic/Latino; 1 Hispanic/Latino; 1 Two or more races, non-Hispanic/Latino). Average age 43. Expenses: Contact institution. *Financial support:* Applicants required to submit FAFSA. In 2016, 10 master's awarded. *Program availability:* Part-time, evening/weekend. Offers organizational leadership (MS). *Application deadline:* Applications are processed on a rolling basis. *Application fee:* $50. Electronic applications accepted. *Application Contact:* Mary Brigham, Assistant Director of Graduate Recruitment, 513-244-4233, Fax: 513-244-4629, E-mail: mary.brigham@msj.edu. *Interim Dean,* Dr. Anna Goldhahn, 513-244-4924, Fax: 513-244-4270, E-mail: anna.goldhahn@msj.edu.

Master's Graduate Entry-Level into Nursing (MAGELIN) Program Students: 84 full-time (69 women); includes 22 minority (17 Black or African American, non-Hispanic/Latino; 3 Asian, non-Hispanic/Latino; 2 Two or more races, non-Hispanic/Latino). Average age 28. *Faculty:* 12 full-time (11 women), 20 part-time/adjunct (all women). Expenses: Contact institution. *Financial support:* In 2016–17, 3 students received support. Scholarships/grants available. Financial award applicants required to submit FAFSA. In 2016, 66 master's awarded. Offers nursing (MSN). *Application deadline:* Applications are processed on a rolling basis. *Application fee:* $50. Electronic applications accepted. *Application Contact:* Mary Brigham, Assistant Director of Graduate Recruitment, 513-244-4233, Fax: 513-244-4629, E-mail: mary.brigham@msj.edu. *Program Director,* Donna Glankler, 513-244-4321, Fax: 513-451-2547, E-mail: donna.glankler@msj.edu.

Physical Therapy Program Students: 81 full-time (52 women), 30 part-time (18 women); includes 3 minority (2 Black or African American, non-Hispanic/Latino; 1 Two or more races, non-Hispanic/Latino). Average age 24. *Faculty:* 7 full-time (5 women), 10 part-time/adjunct (8 women). Expenses: Contact institution. *Financial support:* Applicants required to submit FAFSA. In 2016, 33 doctorates awarded. Offers physical therapy (DPT). *Application deadline:* For fall admission, 11/1 for domestic students. *Application fee:* $50. Electronic applications accepted. *Application Contact:* Mary Brigham, Assistant Director of Graduate Recruitment, 513-244-4233, Fax: 513-244-4629, E-mail: mary.brigham@msj.edu. *Chair,* Dr. Rosanne Thomas, 513-244-4519, Fax: 513-451-2547, E-mail: rosanne.thomas@msj.edu.

MOUNT SAINT MARY COLLEGE, Newburgh, NY 12550-3494

General Information Independent, coed, comprehensive institution. *Enrollment:* 2,468 graduate, professional, and undergraduate students; 82 full-time matriculated graduate/professional students (45 women), 252 part-time matriculated graduate/professional students (211 women). *Enrollment by degree level:* 327 master's, 7 other advanced degrees. *Graduate faculty:* 23 full-time (17 women), 16 part-time/adjunct (9 women). *Tuition:* Full-time $13,914; part-time $773 per credit. *Required fees:* $82 per semester. *Graduate housing:* Room and/or apartments guaranteed to single students; on-campus housing not available to married students. Typical cost: $9400 per year ($15,512 including board). Housing application deadline: 5/1. *Student services:* Campus employment opportunities, campus safety program, career counseling, free psychological counseling, international student services, services for students with disabilities. *Library facilities:* Kaplan Family Library and Learning Center. *Collection:* Books: 86,692 (physical), 11,600 (digital/electronic); Serial titles: 208 (physical), 61,954 (digital/electronic); Databases: 85. Students can reserve study rooms.

Computer facilities: Computer purchase and lease plans are available. 470 computers available on campus for general student use. A campuswide network can be accessed from student residence rooms and from off campus. Online class registration is available.
Website: http://www.msmc.edu/

General Application Contact: Lisa Gallina, Director of Admissions for Graduate Programs and Adult Degree Completion, 845-569-3166, Fax: 845-569-3450, E-mail: lisa.gallina@msmc.edu.

GRADUATE UNITS
Division of Education Students: 27 full-time (19 women), 78 part-time (59 women); includes 12 minority (1 Black or African American, non-Hispanic/Latino; 1 Asian, non-Hispanic/Latino; 7 Hispanic/Latino; 3 Two or more races, non-Hispanic/Latino). Average age 28. 30 applicants, 100% accepted, 16 enrolled. *Faculty:* 12 full-time (10 women), 3 part-time/adjunct (all women). Expenses: Contact institution. *Financial support:* In 2016–17, 18 students received support. Unspecified assistantships available. Financial award application deadline: 4/15; financial award applicants required to submit FAFSA. In 2016, 62 master's awarded. *Program availability:* Part-time, evening/weekend. Offers adolescence and special education (MS Ed); childhood education (MS Ed); literacy education (MS Ed); middle school (7-9) (MS Ed). *Application deadline:* Applications are processed on a rolling basis. *Application fee:* $45. Electronic applications accepted. *Application Contact:* Lisa Gallina, Director of Admissions for Graduate Programs and Adult Degree Completion, 845-569-3166, Fax: 845-569-3450, E-mail: lisa.gallina@msmc.edu. *Graduate Coordinator,* Dr. Monica Merritt, 845-569-3430, Fax: 845-569-3535, E-mail: monica.merritt@msmc.edu.

School of Business Students: 55 full-time (26 women), 28 part-time (17 women); includes 20 minority (7 Black or African American, non-Hispanic/Latino; 12 Hispanic/Latino; 1 Native Hawaiian or other Pacific Islander, non-Hispanic/Latino; 1 international. Average age 32. 21 applicants, 100% accepted, 15 enrolled. *Faculty:* 6 full-time (2 women), 8 part-time/adjunct (2 women). Expenses: Contact institution. *Financial support:* In 2016–17, 18 students received support. Unspecified assistantships available. Financial award application deadline: 4/15; financial award applicants required to submit FAFSA. In 2016, 47 master's awarded. *Program availability:* Part-time, evening/weekend. Offers business (MBA); financial planning (MBA); health care management (MBA). *Application deadline:* Applications are processed on a rolling basis. *Application fee:* $45. Electronic applications accepted. *Application Contact:* Lisa Gallina, Director of Admissions for Graduate Programs and Adult Degree Completion, 845-569-3166, Fax: 845-569-3450, E-mail: lisa.gallina@msmc.edu. *Graduate Coordinator,* Dr. Moira Tolan, 845-569-3121, Fax: 845-562-6762, E-mail: moira.tolan@msmc.edu.

School of Nursing Students: 146 part-time (135 women); includes 52 minority (22 Black or African American, non-Hispanic/Latino; 2 American Indian or Alaska Native, non-Hispanic/Latino; 11 Asian, non-Hispanic/Latino; 16 Hispanic/Latino; 1 Native Hawaiian or other Pacific Islander, non-Hispanic/Latino). Average age 37. 30 applicants, 87% accepted, 16 enrolled. *Faculty:* 5 full-time (all women), 5 part-time/adjunct (4 women). Expenses: Contact institution. *Financial support:* In 2016–17, 11 students received support. Unspecified assistantships available. Financial award application deadline: 4/15; financial award applicants required to submit FAFSA. In 2016, 19 master's, 3 other advanced degrees awarded. *Program availability:* Part-time, evening/weekend, blended/hybrid learning. Offers adult nurse practitioner (MS, Advanced Certificate); family nurse practitioner (Advanced Certificate). *Application deadline:* For fall admission, 6/3 priority date for domestic students; for spring admission, 10/31 priority date for domestic students. Applications are processed on a rolling basis. *Application fee:* $45. Electronic applications accepted. *Application Contact:* Lisa Gallina, Director of Admissions for Graduate Programs and Adult Degree Completion, 845-569-3166, Fax: 845-569-3450, E-mail: lisa.gallina@msmc.edu. *Graduate Coordinator,* Christine Berte, 845-569-3141, Fax: 845-562-6762, E-mail: christine.berte@msmc.edu.

MOUNT SAINT MARY'S UNIVERSITY, Los Angeles, CA 90049

General Information Independent-religious, coed, primarily women, comprehensive institution. CGS member. *Enrollment:* 3,541 graduate, professional, and undergraduate students; 379 full-time matriculated graduate/professional students (264 women), 129 part-time matriculated graduate/professional students (100 women). *Enrollment by degree level:* 363 master's, 99 doctoral, 43 other advanced degrees. *Graduate faculty:* 50 full-time (35 women), 116 part-time/adjunct (81 women). *Tuition:* Full-time $9983; part-time $829 per unit. One-time fee: $135. Tuition and fees vary according to degree level and program. *Graduate housing:* Room and/or apartments available on a first-come, first-served basis to single students; on-campus housing not available to married students. *Student services:* Campus employment opportunities, career counseling, exercise/wellness program, free psychological counseling, low-cost health insurance, services for students with disabilities, writing training. *Library facilities:* Charles Willard Coe Library plus 2 others. *Collection:* Books: 310,130 (physical), 363,514 (digital/electronic); Serial titles: 615 (physical), 37,727 (digital/electronic); Databases: 217. Weekly public service hours: 89; study areas open 24 hours, 5–7 days a week. *Research affiliation:* John Tracy Clinic (education - deaf and hard of hearing teacher preparation).

Computer facilities: 170 computers available on campus for general student use. A campuswide network can be accessed from student residence rooms and from off campus. Online class registration is available.
Website: http://www.msmu.edu/

General Application Contact: Albert Ramos, Director of Graduate Admissions, 213-477-2800, Fax: 213-477-2797, E-mail: gradprograms@msmu.edu.

GRADUATE UNITS
Graduate Division Students: 670 full-time (518 women), 147 part-time (116 women); includes 414 minority (73 Black or African American, non-Hispanic/Latino; 4 American Indian or Alaska Native, non-Hispanic/Latino; 60 Asian, non-Hispanic/Latino; 259 Hispanic/Latino; 7 Native Hawaiian or other Pacific Islander, non-Hispanic/Latino; 11 Two or more races, non-Hispanic/Latino), 4 international. Average age 32. 1,398 applicants, 21% accepted, 242 enrolled. *Faculty:* 50 full-time (35 women), 116 part-time/adjunct (81 women). Expenses: Contact institution. *Financial support:* Career-related internships or fieldwork, Federal Work-Study, institutionally sponsored loans, and tuition waivers (full and partial) available. Support available to part-time students. Financial award application deadline: 3/15; financial award applicants required to submit FAFSA. In 2016, 170 master's, 28 doctorates, 35 other advanced degrees awarded. *Program availability:* Part-time, evening/weekend. Offers business administration (MBA); counseling psychology (MS); creative writing (MFA); education (MS, Certificate); film and television (MFA); health policy and management (MS); humanities (MA); nursing (MSN, Certificate); physical therapy (DPT); religious studies (MA). *Application deadline:* For fall admission, 6/30 priority date for domestic and international students; for spring admission, 10/30 priority date for domestic and international students; for summer admission, 3/30 priority date for domestic and international students. Applications are processed on a rolling basis. *Application fee:* $50. Electronic applications accepted. *Application Contact:* Shawn Peters, Graduate Admission Counselor, 213-477-2676, E-mail: gradprograms@msmu.edu. *Director of Graduate Admissions,* Albert Ramos, 213-477-2800, E-mail: gradprograms@msmu.edu.

MOUNT ST. MARY'S UNIVERSITY, Emmitsburg, MD 21727-7799

General Information Independent-religious, coed, comprehensive institution. *Enrollment:* 2,186 graduate, professional, and undergraduate students; 184 full-time matriculated graduate/professional students (36 women), 268 part-time matriculated graduate/professional students (155 women). *Enrollment by degree level:* 440 master's, 12 other advanced degrees. *Graduate faculty:* 34 full-time (12 women), 27 part-time/adjunct (13 women). *Tuition:* Full-time \$10,980; part-time \$610 per credit hour. Tuition and fees vary according to program. *Graduate housing:* Room and/or apartments available on a first-come, first-served basis to single students; on-campus housing not available to married students. Typical cost: \$6280 per year (\$12,610 including board). *Student services:* Campus employment opportunities, campus safety program, career counseling, exercise/wellness program, free psychological counseling, international student services, low-cost health insurance, multicultural affairs office, services for students with disabilities, teacher training, writing training. *Library facilities:* Phillips Library. *Collection:* Books: 149,287 (physical), 227,412 (digital/electronic); Serial titles: 233 (physical), 26,544 (digital/electronic); Databases: 130.

Computer facilities: 80 computers available on campus for general student use. A campuswide network can be accessed from student residence rooms. Online class registration, tuition payment, course management system are available. Website: http://www.msmary.edu/

General Application Contact: Carol Rinkoff, Director, Graduate Business Programs, 301-447-5840, E-mail: rinkoff@msmary.edu.

GRADUATE UNITS

Graduate Seminary Students: 115 full-time (0 women); includes 8 minority (1 Black or African American, non-Hispanic/Latino; 1 Asian, non-Hispanic/Latino; 6 Hispanic/Latino), 7 international. Average age 29. 49 applicants, 86% accepted, 36 enrolled. *Faculty:* 12 full-time (2 women), 6 part-time/adjunct (2 women). Expenses: Contact institution. *Financial support:* Applicants required to submit FAFSA. In 2016, 28 master's awarded. Offers theology (M Div, MA). *Application deadline:* For fall admission, 8/1 for domestic and international students. *Application fee:* \$0. *Application Contact:* Susan Nield, Seminary Admissions, 301-447-7423, Fax: 301-447-7402, E-mail: nield@msmary.edu. *Vice President/Rector,* Rev. Andrew R. Baker, 301-447-5295, Fax: 301-447-5636, E-mail: baker@msmary.edu.

Program in Biotechnology and Management Students: 2 full-time (1 woman), 21 part-time (13 women); includes 11 minority (7 Black or African American, non-Hispanic/Latino; 1 Asian, non-Hispanic/Latino; 2 Hispanic/Latino; 1 Two or more races, non-Hispanic/Latino), 2 international. Average age 30. 24 applicants, 54% accepted, 6 enrolled. *Faculty:* 1 (woman) full-time, 1 part-time/adjunct (0 women). Expenses: Contact institution. *Financial support:* Unspecified assistantships available. Financial award applicants required to submit FAFSA. *Program availability:* Part-time-only, evening/weekend. Offers biotechnology and management (MS). *Application deadline:* Applications are processed on a rolling basis. Electronic applications accepted. *Director of Graduate Programs in Science,* Dr. Connie E. Dudley, 301-447-5090, E-mail: cdudley@msmary.edu.

Program in Business Administration Students: 38 full-time (17 women), 111 part-time (53 women); includes 37 minority (13 Black or African American, non-Hispanic/Latino; 2 American Indian or Alaska Native, non-Hispanic/Latino; 3 Asian, non-Hispanic/Latino; 14 Hispanic/Latino; 2 Native Hawaiian or other Pacific Islander, non-Hispanic/Latino; 3 Two or more races, non-Hispanic/Latino), 6 international. Average age 31. 109 applicants, 89% accepted, 55 enrolled. *Faculty:* 11 full-time (4 women), 9 part-time/adjunct (3 women). Expenses: Contact institution. *Financial support:* Career-related internships or fieldwork and unspecified assistantships available. Financial award applicants required to submit FAFSA. In 2016, 95 master's awarded. *Program availability:* Part-time, evening/weekend. Offers business administration (MBA). *Application deadline:* Applications are processed on a rolling basis. Electronic applications accepted. *Application Contact:* Melissa Flohr, Assistant Director of Graduate Programs, Business, 301-447-5908, E-mail: mflohr@msmary.edu. *Director of Graduate Business Programs,* Carol Rinkoff, 301-447-5840, E-mail: rinkoff@msmary.edu.

Program in Education Students: 18 full-time (13 women), 78 part-time (57 women); includes 7 minority (2 Black or African American, non-Hispanic/Latino; 2 American Indian or Alaska Native, non-Hispanic/Latino; 1 Asian, non-Hispanic/Latino; 1 Hispanic/Latino; 1 Two or more races, non-Hispanic/Latino), 3 international. Average age 32. *Faculty:* 5 full-time (4 women), 7 part-time/adjunct (all women). Expenses: Contact institution. *Financial support:* Unspecified assistantships available. Financial award applicants required to submit FAFSA. In 2016, 15 master's awarded. Offers education (M Ed, MAT). *Application deadline:* Applications are processed on a rolling basis. Electronic applications accepted. *Dean of School of Education and Human Services,* Dr. Barbara Martin-Palmer, 301-447-5371, Fax: 301-447-5250, E-mail: palmer@msmary.edu.

Program in Health Administration Students: 2 full-time (0 women), 43 part-time (27 women); includes 17 minority (9 Black or African American, non-Hispanic/Latino; 1 American Indian or Alaska Native, non-Hispanic/Latino; 3 Asian, non-Hispanic/Latino; 4 Hispanic/Latino), 1 international. Average age 34. 20 applicants, 90% accepted, 12 enrolled. *Faculty:* 4 part-time/adjunct (1 woman). Expenses: Contact institution. *Financial support:* Unspecified assistantships available. Financial award applicants required to submit FAFSA. In 2016, 25 master's awarded. *Program availability:* Part-time, evening/weekend. Offers health administration (MHA). *Application deadline:* Applications are processed on a rolling basis. Electronic applications accepted. *Application Contact:* Melissa Flohr, Assistant Director of Graduate Programs, Business, 301-447-5451, E-mail: mflohr@msmary.edu. *Director of Graduate Business Programs,* Carol Rinkoff, 301-447-5840, E-mail: rinkoff@msmary.edu.

Program in Philosophical Studies Students: 1 full-time (0 women), 1 part-time (0 women). Average age 38. *Faculty:* 3 full-time (0 women). Expenses: Contact institution. *Financial support:* Unspecified assistantships available. Financial award applicants required to submit FAFSA. In 2016, 5 master's awarded. *Program availability:* Part-time. Offers philosophical studies (MA). *Application deadline:* For fall admission, 8/1 for domestic students; for spring admission, 12/1 for domestic students. *Director,* Dr. Christopher Anadale, 301-447-5307 Ext. 4307, E-mail: anadale@msmary.edu.

Program in Sport Management Students: 8 full-time (5 women), 8 part-time (2 women); includes 3 minority (2 Black or African American, non-Hispanic/Latino; 1 Hispanic/Latino), 1 international. Average age 25. 15 applicants, 80% accepted, 8 enrolled. *Faculty:* 2 full-time (1 woman). Expenses: Contact institution. *Financial support:* Unspecified assistantships available. Financial award applicants required to submit FAFSA. *Program availability:* Part-time, evening/weekend. Offers sport management (MS). *Application deadline:* Applications are processed on a rolling basis. Electronic applications accepted. *Application Contact:* Melissa Flohr, Assistant Director of Graduate Programs, Business, 301-447-5451, E-mail: mflohr@msmary.edu. *Director of Graduate Business Program,* Carol Rinkoff, 301-447-5840, E-mail: rinkoff@msmary.edu.

MOUNT SAINT VINCENT UNIVERSITY, Halifax, NS B3M 2J6, Canada

General Information Province-supported, coed, primarily women, comprehensive institution. *Graduate housing:* Room and/or apartments available on a first-come, first-served basis to single students; on-campus housing not available to married students. Housing application deadline: 5/15.

GRADUATE UNITS

Graduate Programs *Program availability:* Part-time, evening/weekend, online learning. Offers applied human nutrition (M Sc AHN, MAHN); child and youth study (MA); family studies and gerontology (MA); women's studies (MA). Electronic applications accepted.

Faculty of Education *Program availability:* Part-time, evening/weekend, online learning. Offers adult education (M Ed, MA Ed, MA-R); curriculum studies (M Ed, MA Ed, MA-R); education of the blind or visually impaired (M Ed, MA Ed); education of the deaf or hard of hearing (M Ed, MA Ed); education of young adolescents (M Ed, MA Ed, MA-R); educational foundations (M Ed, MA Ed, MA-R); educational psychology (M Ed, MA Ed, MA-R); elementary education (M Ed, MA Ed, MA-R); general studies (M Ed, MA Ed, MA-R); human relations (M Ed, MA Ed); literacy education (M Ed, MA Ed, MA-R); school psychology (MASP); teaching English as a second language (M Ed, MA Ed, MA-R). Electronic applications accepted.

MOUNT VERNON NAZARENE UNIVERSITY, Mount Vernon, OH 43050-9500

General Information Independent-religious, coed, comprehensive institution. *Graduate housing:* On-campus housing not available.

GRADUATE UNITS

Department of Education *Program availability:* Part-time, evening/weekend. Offers education (MA Ed); professional educator's license (MA Ed).

Program in Management *Program availability:* Part-time, evening/weekend. Offers management (MSM).

Program in Ministry *Program availability:* Part-time, evening/weekend. Offers ministry (M Min).

MULTNOMAH UNIVERSITY, Portland, OR 97220-5898

General Information Independent-religious, coed, comprehensive institution. *Enrollment:* 714 graduate, professional, and undergraduate students; 244 full-time matriculated graduate/professional students (106 women), 85 part-time matriculated graduate/professional students (33 women). *Enrollment by degree level:* 302 master's, 27 doctoral. *Graduate faculty:* 20 full-time (9 women), 16 part-time/adjunct (3 women). *Tuition:* Full-time \$10,000; part-time \$6000 per semester. *Required fees:* \$230; \$120 per semester. Tuition and fees vary according to course load, degree level and program. *Graduate housing:* Rooms and/or apartments available on a first-come, first-served basis to single and married students. Typical cost: \$5180 per year (\$8290 including board) for single students; \$8050 per year for married students. Room and board charges vary according to board plan and housing facility selected. Housing application deadline: 7/15. *Student services:* Campus employment opportunities, career counseling, free psychological counseling, low-cost health insurance, teacher training. *Library facilities:* John Mitchell Library. *Collection:* Books: 109,731 (physical), 133,470 (digital/electronic); Serial titles: 294 (physical), 20,000 (digital/electronic); Databases: 42. Weekly public service hours: 88; students can reserve study rooms.

Computer facilities: 36 computers available on campus for general student use. A campuswide network can be accessed from student residence rooms and from off campus. Online class registration is available. Website: http://www.multnomah.edu/

General Application Contact: Mindy Kate Hasenkamp, Director of Admissions, 503-251-6483, Fax: 503-254-1268, E-mail: admiss@multnomah.edu.

GRADUATE UNITS

Graduate Programs Students: 120 full-time (80 women), 31 part-time (23 women); includes 35 minority (15 Black or African American, non-Hispanic/Latino; 2 Asian, non-Hispanic/Latino; 9 Hispanic/Latino; 1 Native Hawaiian or other Pacific Islander, non-Hispanic/Latino; 8 Two or more races, non-Hispanic/Latino), 3 international. Average age 30. 69 applicants, 55% accepted, 24 enrolled. *Faculty:* 6 full-time (4 women), 16 part-time/adjunct (10 women). Expenses: Contact institution. *Financial support:* Career-related internships or fieldwork and scholarships/grants available. Support available to part-time students. Financial award application deadline: 7/1; financial award applicants required to submit FAFSA. In 2016, 55 degrees awarded. *Program availability:* Part-time, evening/weekend. Offers counseling (MA); global development and justice (MA); teaching (MA); TESOL (MA). *Application deadline:* For fall admission, 8/1 for domestic students, 12/1 for international students; for spring admission, 12/1 for domestic and international students. *Application fee:* \$40. Electronic applications accepted. *Application Contact:* Mindy Kate Hasenkamp, Director of Admissions, 503-251-6483, Fax: 503-254-1268, E-mail: admiss@multnomah.edu. *Academic Dean,* Dr. Daniel Scalberg, 503-251-6441, E-mail: dscalberg@multnomah.edu.

Multnomah Biblical Seminary Students: 95 full-time (27 women), 56 part-time (10 women); includes 26 minority (3 Black or African American, non-Hispanic/Latino; 1 American Indian or Alaska Native, non-Hispanic/Latino; 8 Asian, non-Hispanic/Latino; 8 Hispanic/Latino; 2 Native Hawaiian or other Pacific Islander, non-Hispanic/Latino; 4 Two or more races, non-Hispanic/Latino), 2 international. Average age 35. 75 applicants, 79% accepted, 50 enrolled. *Faculty:* 9 full-time (3 women), 6 part-time/adjunct (0 women). Expenses: Contact institution. *Financial support:* Career-related internships or fieldwork and scholarships/grants available. Support available to part-time students. Financial award application deadline: 7/1; financial award applicants required to submit FAFSA. In 2016, 51 master's awarded. *Program availability:* Part-time. Offers theology (M Div, MABS, MACL, MATS, Th M, D Min). *Application deadline:* For fall and spring admission, 12/1 priority date for domestic and international students. Applications are processed on a rolling basis. *Application fee:* \$40. *Application Contact:* Mindy Kate Hasenkamp, Director of Admissions, 503-251-6483, Fax: 503-254-1268, E-mail: admiss@multnomah.edu. *Dean,* Dr. Derek Chinn, 503-252-6731, Fax: 503-251-6444, E-mail: dchinn@multnomah.edu.

MURRAY STATE UNIVERSITY, Murray, KY 42071

General Information State-supported, coed, university. *Graduate housing:* Rooms and/or apartments available on a first-come, first-served basis to single and married students.

GRADUATE UNITS

College of Business and Public Affairs *Program availability:* Part-time, evening/weekend. Offers business administration (MBA); business and public affairs (MA, MBA, MPAC, MS); economics (MS); mass communications (MA, MS);

organizational communication (MA, MS); professional accountancy (MPAC); telecommunications systems management (MS).

College of Education *Program availability:* Part-time. Offers advanced learning behavior disorders (MA Ed); community and agency counseling (Ed S); early childhood education (MA Ed); education (MA Ed, MS, Ed D, PhD, Ed S); elementary education (MA Ed, Ed S); elementary education/reading and writing (MA Ed, Ed S); health, physical education, and recreation (MA); human development and leadership (MS); industrial and technical education (MS); learning disabilities (MA Ed); middle school education (MA Ed, Ed S); moderate/severe disorders (MA Ed); reading and writing (MA Ed); school administration (MA Ed, Ed S); school guidance and counseling (MA Ed, Ed S); secondary education (MA Ed, Ed S); special education (MA Ed). PhD, Ed D offered jointly with University of Kentucky.

College of Health Sciences and Human Services *Program availability:* Part-time. Offers clinical nurse specialist (MSN); environmental science (MS); exercise and leisure studies (MS); family nurse practitioner (MSN); health sciences and human services (MS, MSN); industrial hygiene (MS); nurse anesthesia (MSN); safety management (MS); speech-language pathology (MS).

College of Humanities and Fine Arts *Program availability:* Part-time. Offers clinical psychology (MA, MS); creative writing (MFA); English (MA); history (MA); humanities and fine arts (MA, MFA, MME, MPA, MS); music education (MME); psychology (MA, MS); public administration (MPA); public affairs (MPA); teaching English to speakers of other languages (MA).

College of Science, Engineering and Technology *Program availability:* Part-time. Offers biological sciences (MAT, MS, PhD); chemistry (MS); geosciences (MS); management of technology (MS); mathematics (MA, MAT, MS); science, engineering and technology (MA, MAT, MS, PhD); water science (MS).

School of Agriculture *Program availability:* Evening/weekend, online learning. Offers agriculture (MS); agriculture education (MS).

MUSKINGUM UNIVERSITY, New Concord, OH 43762

General Information Independent-religious, coed, comprehensive institution. *Graduate housing:* On-campus housing not available.

GRADUATE UNITS

Graduate Programs in Education *Program availability:* Part-time. Offers education (MAE, MAT).

NAROPA UNIVERSITY, Boulder, CO 80302-6697

General Information Independent, coed, comprehensive institution. *Enrollment:* 373 full-time matriculated graduate/professional students (270 women), 176 part-time matriculated graduate/professional students (112 women). *Enrollment by degree level:* 549 master's. *Graduate faculty:* 36 full-time (21 women), 69 part-time/adjunct (53 women). *Tuition:* Full-time $23,880; part-time $995 per credit hour. *Required fees:* $335 per semester. Tuition and fees vary according to course load. *Graduate housing:* Room and/or apartments available on a first-come, first-served basis to single students; on-campus housing not available to married students. Typical cost: $11,880 (including board). Room and board charges vary according to housing facility selected. Housing application deadline: 7/1. *Student services:* Campus employment opportunities, campus safety program, career counseling, free psychological counseling, international student services, low-cost health insurance, multicultural affairs office, services for students with disabilities, writing training. *Library facilities:* Allen Ginsberg Library plus 2 others. *Collection:* Books: 34,909 (physical), 150,000 (digital/electronic); Serial titles: 47 (physical), 12 (digital/electronic); Databases: 29. Weekly public service hours: 69.

Computer facilities: 48 computers available on campus for general student use. A campuswide network can be accessed from student residence rooms and from off campus. Online class registration is available. Website: http://www.naropa.edu/

General Application Contact: Office of Admissions, 303-546-3572, Fax: 303-546-3583, E-mail: admissions@naropa.edu.

GRADUATE UNITS

Graduate Programs Students: 373 full-time (270 women), 176 part-time (112 women); includes 99 minority (7 Black or African American, non-Hispanic/Latino; 5 American Indian or Alaska Native, non-Hispanic/Latino; 10 Asian, non-Hispanic/Latino; 50 Hispanic/Latino; 27 Two or more races, non-Hispanic/Latino), 16 international. Average age 32. 472 applicants, 79% accepted, 203 enrolled. *Faculty:* 36 full-time (21 women), 69 part-time/adjunct (53 women). Expenses: Contact institution. *Financial support:* In 2016–17, 260 students received support, including 4 fellowships with full tuition reimbursements available (averaging $3,000 per year), 8 research assistantships with partial tuition reimbursements available (averaging $2,156 per year), 14 teaching assistantships with partial tuition reimbursements available (averaging $2,207 per year); career-related internships or fieldwork, Federal Work-Study, scholarships/grants, tuition waivers (partial), and unspecified assistantships also available. Support available to part-time students. Financial award application deadline: 3/1; financial award applicants required to submit FAFSA. In 2016, 185 master's awarded. *Program availability:* Part-time, blended/hybrid learning. Offers contemplative education (MA); contemplative psychotherapy and Buddhist psychology (MA); creative writing (MFA); creative writing and poetics (MFA); divinity (M Div); ecopsychology (MA); mindfulness-based transpersonal counseling (MA); religious studies (MA); religious studies with language (MA); resilient leadership (MA); somatic counseling: body psychotherapy (MA); somatic counseling: dance/movement therapy (MA); theater: contemporary performance (MFA); transpersonal art therapy (MA); transpersonal wilderness therapy (MA). *Application deadline:* For fall admission, 1/15 priority date for domestic and international students; for spring admission, 10/15 priority date for domestic and international students. Applications are processed on a rolling basis. *Application fee:* $60. Electronic applications accepted. *Application Contact:* Office of Admissions, 303-546-3572, Fax: 303-546-3583, E-mail: admissions@naropa.edu. *Dean of Admissions,* Janet Erickson, 303-245-4725, Fax: 303-546-3583, E-mail: jerickson@naropa.edu.

NASHOTAH HOUSE THEOLOGICAL SEMINARY, Nashotah, WI 53058-9793

General Information Independent-religious, coed, primarily men, graduate-only institution. *Enrollment by degree level:* 8 master's, 45 doctoral, 3 other advanced degrees. *Graduate faculty:* 8 full-time (0 women), 6 part-time/adjunct (0 women). *Graduate housing:* Rooms and/or apartments available on a first-come, first-served basis to single and married students. Housing application deadline: 5/1. *Student services:* Campus employment opportunities, career counseling. *Library facilities:* Frances Donaldson Library. *Collection:* Study areas open 24 hours, 5–7 days a week.

Computer facilities: 6 computers available on campus for general student use. Online class registration is available. Website: http://www.nashotah.edu/

General Application Contact: Fr. Dr. Rick Hartley, Associate Dean of Students/Registrar, 262-646-6547, Fax: 262-646-6504, E-mail: rhartley@nashotah.edu.

GRADUATE UNITS

Graduate Programs Students: 78 full-time (14 women), 5 part-time (2 women); includes 3 minority (2 Black or African American, non-Hispanic/Latino; 1 Asian, non-Hispanic/Latino). Average age 37. *Faculty:* 8 full-time (0 women), 6 part-time/adjunct (0 women). Expenses: Contact institution. *Financial support:* Teaching assistantships, career-related internships or fieldwork, scholarships/grants, and tuition waivers (partial) available. Support available to part-time students. Financial award application deadline: 1/15; financial award applicants required to submit FAFSA. *Program availability:* Part-time. Offers Anglican studies (Certificate); Biblical studies (STM); Christian spirituality (STM); church history (STM); liturgy (STM); ministry (M Div, MM); pastoral ministry (MPM); theological studies (MTS); theology (STM, D Min). *Application deadline:* For fall admission, 6/15 for domestic students. Applications are processed on a rolling basis. *Application fee:* $0. Electronic applications accepted. *Application Contact:* Fr. Dr. Rick Hartley, Associate Dean of Students/Registrar, 262-646-6547, Fax: 262-646-6504, E-mail: rhartley@nashotah.edu. *Dean/President,* Very Rev. Steven A. Peay, 262-646-6512, Fax: 262-646-6504, E-mail: speay@nashotah.edu.

NATIONAL AMERICAN UNIVERSITY, Rapid City, SD 57701

General Information Proprietary, coed, comprehensive institution. *Graduate housing:* Room and/or apartments available on a first-come, first-served basis to single students. Housing application deadline: 6/1.

GRADUATE UNITS

Graduate Programs *Program availability:* Part-time, evening/weekend, online learning. Offers business (MBA, MM). Programs also offered in Wichita, KS; Albuquerque, NM; Bloomington, MN; Brooklyn Center, MN; Colorado Springs, CO; Denver, CO; Independence, MO; Overland Park, KS; Rio Rancho, NM; Roseville, MN; Zona Rosa, MO. Electronic applications accepted.

NATIONAL COLLEGE OF MIDWIFERY, Taos, NM 87571

General Information Independent, women only, comprehensive institution.

GRADUATE UNITS

Graduate Programs *Program availability:* Part-time, evening/weekend, online learning. Offers midwifery (MS, PhD). Electronic applications accepted.

NATIONAL DEFENSE UNIVERSITY, Washington, DC 20319-5066

General Information Federally supported, coed, graduate-only institution. *Graduate housing:* On-campus housing not available.

GRADUATE UNITS

College of International Security Affairs *Program availability:* Part-time, evening/weekend. Offers strategic security studies (MA).

The Dwight D. Eisenhower School for National Security and Resource Strategy Offers national resource strategy (MS). Open only to Department of Defense employees and specific federal agencies.

Joint Advanced Warfighting School Offers joint campaign planning and strategy (MS). Open only to Department of Defense employees and specific federal agencies.

National War College Offers national security strategy (MS). Open only to Department of Defense employees and specific federal agencies.

THE NATIONAL GRADUATE SCHOOL OF QUALITY MANAGEMENT, Falmouth, MA 02541

General Information Independent, coed, graduate-only institution.

GRADUATE UNITS

Graduate Programs Offers homeland security (MS); quality systems management (MS, DBA).

NATIONAL INTELLIGENCE UNIVERSITY, Washington, DC 20340-5100

General Information Federally supported, coed, upper-level institution. *Graduate housing:* On-campus housing not available.

GRADUATE UNITS

Graduate Program *Program availability:* Part-time, evening/weekend. Offers strategic intelligence (MSSI). Open only to federal government employees.

NATIONAL LOUIS UNIVERSITY, Chicago, IL 60603

General Information Independent, coed, university.

GRADUATE UNITS

College of Arts and Sciences *Program availability:* Part-time, evening/weekend, online learning. Offers adult education (Ed D); counseling and human services (MS); language and academic development (M Ed, Certificate); psychology (MA, PhD, Certificate); public policy (MA); written communication (MS, Certificate). Electronic applications accepted.

College of Management and Business *Program availability:* Part-time, evening/weekend. Offers business administration (MBA); human resource management and development (MS); management (MS).

National College of Education *Program availability:* Part-time, evening/weekend. Offers administration and supervision (M Ed, Ed D, CAS, Ed S); curriculum and instruction (M Ed, MS Ed, CAS); early childhood administration (M Ed, CAS); early childhood education (M Ed, MAT, MS Ed, CAS); education (Ed D); educational psychology/human learning and development (M Ed, MS Ed, CAS, Ed S); elementary education (MAT); interdisciplinary curriculum and instruction (M Ed); mathematics education (M Ed, MS Ed, CAS); middle grades education (MAT); reading and language (M Ed, MS Ed, CAS); school psychology (M Ed, Ed S); science education (M Ed, MS Ed, CAS); secondary education (MAT); special education (M Ed, MAT, CAS); technology in education (M Ed, CAS).

NATIONAL PARALEGAL COLLEGE, Phoenix, AZ 85014

General Information Proprietary, coed, comprehensive institution.

GRADUATE UNITS

Graduate Programs *Program availability:* Part-time. Offers compliance law (MS); legal studies (MS); taxation (MS). Electronic applications accepted.

NATIONAL TEST PILOT SCHOOL, Mojave, CA 93502-0658

General Information Independent, coed, graduate-only institution.

GRADUATE UNITS

National Flight Institute Offers flight test and evaluation (MS); flight test engineering (MS).

NATIONAL UNIVERSITY, La Jolla, CA 92037-1011

General Information Independent, coed, comprehensive institution. CGS member. *Enrollment:* 17,173 graduate, professional, and undergraduate students; 5,494 full-time matriculated graduate/professional students (3,636 women), 3,225 part-time matriculated graduate/professional students (2,097 women). *Enrollment by degree level:* 7,609 master's, 1,110 other advanced degrees. *Graduate faculty:* 248 full-time (123 women), 659 part-time/adjunct (349 women). *Graduate housing:* On-campus housing not available. *Student services:* Campus employment opportunities, campus safety program, career counseling, international student services, services for students with disabilities, teacher training, writing training. *Library facilities:* National University Library. *Collection:* Books: 216,574 (physical), 289,279 (digital/electronic); Serial titles: 1,630 (physical), 77,230 (digital/electronic); Databases: 190. Weekly public service hours: 72; students can reserve study rooms.

Computer facilities: 2,800 computers available on campus for general student use. A campuswide network can be accessed from off campus. Online class registration is available.
Website: http://www.nu.edu/

General Application Contact: Brandon Jouganatos, Vice President for Enrollment Services, 800-628-8648, E-mail: advisor@nu.edu.

GRADUATE UNITS

Academic Affairs Students: 5,494 full-time (3,636 women), 3,225 part-time (2,097 women); includes 4,162 minority (823 Black or African American, non-Hispanic/Latino; 38 American Indian or Alaska Native, non-Hispanic/Latino; 633 Asian, non-Hispanic/Latino; 2,249 Hispanic/Latino; 78 Native Hawaiian or other Pacific Islander, non-Hispanic/Latino; 341 Two or more races, non-Hispanic/Latino), 235 international. Average age 34. *Faculty:* 248 full-time (123 women), 659 part-time/adjunct (349 women). Expenses: Contact institution. *Financial support:* Career-related internships or fieldwork, institutionally sponsored loans, scholarships/grants, and tuition waivers (partial) available. Support available to part-time students. Financial award application deadline: 6/30; financial award applicants required to submit FAFSA. In 2016, 2,982 master's awarded. *Program availability:* Part-time, evening/weekend, 100% online, blended/hybrid learning. *Application deadline:* Applications are processed on a rolling basis. *Application fee:* $60 ($65 for international students). Electronic applications accepted. *Application Contact:* Brandon Jouganatos, Vice President for Enrollment Services, 916-855-4101, E-mail: advisor@nu.edu. Provost, Gangaram Singh, 858-642-8130, E-mail: instresearch@nu.edu.

College of Letters and Sciences Students: 566 full-time (408 women), 287 part-time (197 women); includes 394 minority (101 Black or African American, non-Hispanic/Latino; 3 American Indian or Alaska Native, non-Hispanic/Latino; 47 Asian, non-Hispanic/Latino; 185 Hispanic/Latino; 8 Native Hawaiian or other Pacific Islander, non-Hispanic/Latino; 50 Two or more races, non-Hispanic/Latino), 3 international. Average age 34. *Faculty:* 68 full-time (33 women), 70 part-time/adjunct (34 women). Expenses: Contact institution. *Financial support:* Career-related internships or fieldwork, institutionally sponsored loans, scholarships/grants, and tuition waivers (partial) available. Support available to part-time students. Financial award application deadline: 6/30; financial award applicants required to submit FAFSA. In 2016, 450 master's awarded. *Program availability:* Part-time, evening/weekend, 100% online, blended/hybrid learning. Offers biology (MS); counseling psychology (MA); creative writing (MFA). *Application deadline:* Applications are processed on a rolling basis. *Application fee:* $60 ($65 for international students). Electronic applications accepted. *Application Contact:* Brandon Jouganatos, Interim Vice President for Enrollment Services, 800-628-8648, E-mail: advisor@nu.edu. College of Letters and Sciences, 800-628-8648, E-mail: cols@nu.edu.

School of Business and Management Students: 624 full-time (322 women), 217 part-time (104 women); includes 432 minority (136 Black or African American, non-Hispanic/Latino; 2 American Indian or Alaska Native, non-Hispanic/Latino; 89 Asian, non-Hispanic/Latino; 164 Hispanic/Latino; 15 Native Hawaiian or other Pacific Islander, non-Hispanic/Latino; 26 Two or more races, non-Hispanic/Latino), 110 international. Average age 34. *Faculty:* 34 full-time (10 women), 73 part-time/adjunct (20 women). Expenses: Contact institution. *Financial support:* Career-related internships or fieldwork, scholarships/grants, and tuition waivers (partial) available. Support available to part-time students. Financial award application deadline: 6/30; financial award applicants required to submit FAFSA. In 2016, 637 master's awarded. *Program availability:* Part-time, evening/weekend, 100% online, blended/hybrid learning. Offers business and management (GMBA, M Acc, MA, MBA, MGM, MS, Certificate). *Application deadline:* Applications are processed on a rolling basis. *Application fee:* $60 ($65 for international students). Electronic applications accepted. *Application Contact:* Brandon Jouganatos, Vice President for Enrollment Services, 800-628-8648, Fax: 858-642-8719, E-mail: advisor@nu.edu. School of Business and Management, 800-628-8648, Fax: 858-642-8719, E-mail: sobm@nu.edu.

School of Education Students: 3,376 full-time (2,418 women), 2,410 part-time (1,641 women); includes 2,652 minority (357 Black or African American, non-Hispanic/Latino; 29 American Indian or Alaska Native, non-Hispanic/Latino; 337 Asian, non-Hispanic/Latino; 1,680 Hispanic/Latino; 45 Native Hawaiian or other Pacific Islander, non-Hispanic/Latino; 204 Two or more races, non-Hispanic/Latino). Average age 33. *Faculty:* 74 full-time (48 women), 422 part-time/adjunct (260 women). Expenses: Contact institution. *Financial support:* Career-related internships or fieldwork, institutionally sponsored loans, scholarships/grants, and tuition waivers (partial) available. Support available to part-time students. Financial award application deadline: 6/30. In 2016, 1,456 master's awarded. *Program availability:* Part-time, evening/weekend, 100% online, blended/hybrid learning. Offers e-teaching and learning (Certificate); educational administration (MS). *Application deadline:* Applications are processed on a rolling basis. *Application fee:* $60 ($65 for international students). Electronic applications accepted. *Application Contact:* Brandon Jouganatos, Vice President for Enrollment Services, 800-628-8648, E-mail: advisor@nu.edu. School of Education, 800-628-8648, E-mail: soe@nu.edu.

School of Engineering and Computing Students: 285 full-time (70 women), 107 part-time (33 women); includes 155 minority (49 Black or African American, non-Hispanic/Latino; 2 American Indian or Alaska Native, non-Hispanic/Latino; 44 Asian, non-Hispanic/Latino; 47 Hispanic/Latino; 2 Native Hawaiian or other Pacific Islander, non-Hispanic/Latino; 11 Two or more races, non-Hispanic/Latino), 90 international. Average age 33. *Faculty:* 21 full-time (4 women), 24 part-time/adjunct (5 women). Expenses: Contact institution. *Financial support:* Career-related internships or fieldwork, institutionally sponsored loans, scholarships/grants, and tuition waivers (partial) available. Support available to part-time students. Financial award application deadline: 6/30; financial award applicants required to submit FAFSA. In 2016, 273 master's awarded. *Program availability:* Part-time, evening/weekend, 100% online, blended/hybrid learning. Offers computer science (MS). *Application deadline:* Applications are processed on a rolling basis. *Application fee:* $60 ($65 for

international students). Electronic applications accepted. *Application Contact:* Brandon Jouganatos, Vice President for Enrollment Services, 800-628-8648, E-mail: advisor@nu.edu. *School of Engineering and Computing*, 800-628-8648, E-mail: soec@nu.edu.

School of Health and Human Services Students: 363 full-time (263 women), 104 part-time (68 women); includes 303 minority (104 Black or African American, non-Hispanic/Latino; 1 American Indian or Alaska Native, non-Hispanic/Latino; 89 Asian, non-Hispanic/Latino; 71 Hispanic/Latino; 5 Native Hawaiian or other Pacific Islander, non-Hispanic/Latino; 33 Two or more races, non-Hispanic/Latino), 29 international. Average age 33. *Faculty:* 30 full-time (20 women), 35 part-time/adjunct (21 women). Expenses: Contact institution. *Financial support:* Career-related internships or fieldwork, institutionally sponsored loans, scholarships/grants, and tuition waivers (partial) available. Support available to part-time students. Financial award application deadline: 6/30; financial award applicants required to submit FAFSA. In 2016, 145 master's awarded. *Program availability:* Part-time, evening/weekend, 100% online, blended/hybrid learning. Offers clinical affairs (MS); healthcare administration (MHA); nursing informatics (Certificate); nursing practice (DNP); public health (MPH). *Application deadline:* Applications are processed on a rolling basis. *Application fee:* $60 ($65 for international students). Electronic applications accepted. *Application Contact:* Brandon Jouganatos, Vice President for Enrollment Services, 800-628-8648, E-mail: advisor@nu.edu. *School of Health and Human Services*, 800-628-8648, E-mail: shhs@nu.edu.

School of Professional Studies Students: 280 full-time (155 women), 100 part-time (54 women); includes 226 minority (76 Black or African American, non-Hispanic/Latino; 1 American Indian or Alaska Native, non-Hispanic/Latino; 27 Asian, non-Hispanic/Latino; 102 Hispanic/Latino; 3 Native Hawaiian or other Pacific Islander, non-Hispanic/Latino; 17 Two or more races, non-Hispanic/Latino), 3 international. Average age 37. *Faculty:* 21 full-time (8 women), 35 part-time/adjunct (9 women). Expenses: Contact institution. *Financial support:* Career-related internships or fieldwork, institutionally sponsored loans, scholarships/grants, and tuition waivers (partial) available. Support available to part-time students. Financial award application deadline: 6/30; financial award applicants required to submit FAFSA. In 2016, 21 master's awarded. *Program availability:* Part-time, evening/weekend, 100% online, blended/hybrid learning. Offers criminal justice (MCJ); digital cinema (MFA); digital journalism (MA); juvenile justice (MS); public administration (MPA). *Application deadline:* Applications are processed on a rolling basis. *Application fee:* $60 ($65 for international students). Electronic applications accepted. *Application Contact:* Brandon Jouganatos, Vice President for Enrollment Services, 800-628-8648, E-mail: advisor@nu.edu. *School of Professional Studies*, 800-628-8648, E-mail: sops@nu.edu.

NATIONAL UNIVERSITY COLLEGE, Bayamón, PR 00960

General Information Proprietary, coed, comprehensive institution.

GRADUATE UNITS
Graduate Programs

NATIONAL UNIVERSITY OF HEALTH SCIENCES, Lombard, IL 60148-4583

General Information Independent, coed, graduate-only institution. *Enrollment:* 587 full-time matriculated graduate/professional students (328 women), 21 part-time matriculated graduate/professional students (17 women). *Enrollment by degree level:* 73 master's, 535 doctoral. *Tuition:* Full-time $7664; part-time $479 per credit hour. *Required fees:* $136 per trimester. *Graduate housing:* Rooms and/or apartments available on a first-come, first-served basis to single and married students. Typical cost: $7420 per year for single students; $7420 per year for married students. Room charges vary according to housing facility selected. *Student services:* Campus employment opportunities, campus safety program, career counseling, international student services, services for students with disabilities. *Library facilities:* Learning Resource Center. *Collection:* Books: 15,000 (physical), 109,823 (digital/electronic); Databases: 32. Weekly public service hours: 93; students can reserve study rooms. *Research affiliation:* University of Illinois at Chicago (public health), Canadian Memorial Chiropractic College (mechanisms of CAM), Cox Technic F/D Enterprise LLC (mechanisms of CAM), Logan Chiropractic College (behavior research), Foot Levelers, Inc. (orthotics/biomechanics), Auburn University (mechanisms of CAM).

Computer facilities: 38 computers available on campus for general student use. Online class registration is available.
Website: http://www.nuhs.edu/

General Application Contact: Teri Hatfield, Assistant Director of Admissions, 800-826-6285, Fax: 630-889-6566, E-mail: thatfield@nuhs.edu.

GRADUATE UNITS

Graduate Programs Students: 587 full-time (328 women), 21 part-time (17 women). Expenses: Contact institution. Offers acupuncture (MSAC); chiropractic (DC); diagnostic imaging (MS); naturopathic medicine (ND); Oriental medicine (MSOM). *Application Contact:* Teri Hatfield, Assistant Director of Admissions, 800-826-6285, Fax: 630-889-6566, E-mail: thatfield@nuhs.edu.

NATIONAL UNIVERSITY OF NATURAL MEDICINE, Portland, OR 97201

General Information Independent, coed, primarily women, graduate-only institution. *Graduate housing:* On-campus housing not available. *Research affiliation:* Kaiser Center for Health Research, Oregon Health & Science University, Bob's Red Mill, Oregon College of Oriental Medicine.

GRADUATE UNITS
College of Classical Chinese Medicine *Program availability:* Evening/weekend. Offers classical Chinese medicine (M Ac, MSOM).
College of Naturopathic Medicine Offers integrative medicine research (MS); naturopathic medicine (ND).

NAVAJO TECHNICAL UNIVERSITY, Crownpoint, NM 87313
General Information Independent, coed, comprehensive institution.
GRADUATE UNITS
Program in Dine Studies Offers dine studies (MA).

NAVAL POSTGRADUATE SCHOOL, Monterey, CA 93943
General Information Federally supported, coed, graduate-only institution. *Graduate housing:* Rooms and/or apartments available to single and married students. *Research affiliation:* U.S. Department of Homeland Security, National Reconnaissance Office, National Oceanic and Atmospheric Administration (NOAA), National Security Agency, Federal Law Enforcement Training.

GRADUATE UNITS

Departments and Academic Groups *Program availability:* Part-time, online learning. Offers applied mathematics (MS); applied physics (MS, PhD); applied science (MS); astronautical engineer (AstE); astronautical engineering (MS); combat systems technology (MS); command and control (MS); communications (MS); computer engineering (MS); computer science (MS, PhD); cost estimating analysis (MS); defense analysis (MS); electrical engineer (EE); electrical engineering (MS, PhD); electronic warfare systems engineering (MS); engineering acoustics (MS, PhD); engineering science (MS); engineering systems (MS); financial management (MS); human systems integration (MS); identity management and cyber security (MA); information operations (MS); information sciences (PhD); information systems and operations (MS); information technology management (MS); information warfare systems engineering (MS); irregular warfare (MS); knowledge superiority (Certificate); mechanical and aerospace engineering (PhD); mechanical engineer (ME); mechanical engineering (MS, MSME); meteorology (MS, PhD); meteorology and physical oceanography (MS); modeling of virtual environments and simulations (MS, PhD); national security affairs (MA, MS); operations analysis (MS); operations research (MS, PhD); physical oceanography (MS, PhD); physics (MS, PhD); product development (MS); remote sensing intelligence (MS); security studies (MA); software engineering (MS, PhD); space systems (Engr); space systems operations (MS); special operations (MA, MS); stability, security, and development in complex operations (Certificate); system technology (command, control and communications) (MS); systems analysis (MS); systems engineering (MS, PhD, Certificate); systems engineering analysis (MS, PhD); systems engineering management (MS, PhD); tactile missiles (MS); terrorist operations and financing (MS). Programs only open to commissioned officers of the United States and friendly nations and selected United States federal civilian employees.

Graduate School of Business and Public Policy *Program availability:* Part-time, online learning. Offers acquisition and contract management (MBA); business administration (EMBA, MBA); contract management (MS); defense business management (MBA); defense systems analysis (MS); defense systems management (international) (MBA); financial management (MBA); information management (MBA); manpower systems analysis (MS); material logistics support management (MBA); program management (MS); resource planning and management for international defense (MBA); supply chain management (MBA); systems acquisition management (MBA); transportation management (MBA). Program only open to commissioned officers of the United States and friendly nations and selected United States federal civilian employees.

NAVAL WAR COLLEGE, Newport, RI 02841-1207
General Information Federally supported, coed, primarily men, graduate-only institution.

GRADUATE UNITS
Program in National Security and Strategic Studies Offers national security and strategic studies (MA). Program open only to full-time military personnel.

NAZARENE THEOLOGICAL SEMINARY, Kansas City, MO 64131-1263
General Information Independent-religious, coed, graduate-only institution. *Enrollment by degree level:* 205 master's, 38 doctoral, 17 other advanced degrees. *Graduate faculty:* 11 full-time (2 women), 26 part-time/adjunct (4 women). *Graduate housing:* Rooms and/or apartments available on a first-come, first-served basis to single and married students. *Student services:* Campus employment opportunities, career counseling, free psychological counseling, international student services, low-cost health insurance. *Library facilities:* William Broadhurst Library. *Collection:* Students can reserve study rooms. *Research affiliation:* University of Missouri-Kansas City (religious studies).

Computer facilities: 14 computers available on campus for general student use.
Website: http://www.nts.edu/

General Application Contact: Pamala J. Asher, Registrar/Director of Admissions, 816-268-5442, Fax: 816-268-5500, E-mail: pjasher@nts.edu.

GRADUATE UNITS
Graduate and Professional Programs Students: 105 full-time (33 women), 155 part-time (45 women); includes 22 minority (7 Black or African American, non-Hispanic/Latino; 1 American Indian or Alaska Native, non-Hispanic/Latino; 1 Asian, non-Hispanic/Latino; 9 Hispanic/Latino; 4 Two or more races, non-Hispanic/Latino), 29 international. *Faculty:* 11 full-time (2 women), 26 part-time/adjunct (4 women). Expenses: Contact institution. *Financial support:* Teaching assistantships, institutionally sponsored loans, and scholarships/grants available. Support available to part-time students. Financial award application deadline: 3/1; financial award applicants required to submit FAFSA. *Program availability:* Part-time. Offers Christian formation and discipleship (MA); intercultural studies (MA); theological studies (MA); theology (M Div, D Min). *Application deadline:* For fall admission, 3/1 for domestic and international students; for spring admission, 11/1 for domestic and international students. Applications are processed on a rolling basis. *Application fee:* $50. Electronic applications accepted. *Application Contact:* Pamala J. Asher, Registrar/Director of Admissions, 816-268-5442, Fax: 816-268-5500, E-mail: pjasher@nts.edu. *Dean of the Faculty,* Dr. Josh Sweeden, 816-268-5412, Fax: 816-268-5500, E-mail: jsweeden@nts.edu.

NAZARETH COLLEGE OF ROCHESTER, Rochester, NY 14618
General Information Independent, coed, comprehensive institution. *Enrollment:* 2,883 graduate, professional, and undergraduate students; 400 full-time matriculated graduate/professional students (324 women), 295 part-time matriculated graduate/professional students (238 women). *Tuition:* Part-time $880 per credit hour. *Graduate housing:* Room and/or apartments available on a first-come, first-served basis to single students; on-campus housing not available to married students. Housing application deadline: 5/15. *Student services:* Campus safety program, career counseling, free psychological counseling, international student services, multicultural affairs office, services for students with disabilities, teacher training, writing training. *Library facilities:* Lorette Wilmot Library. *Collection:* Books: 45,000 (physical), 137,000 (digital/electronic); Databases: 137,000. Students can reserve study rooms.

Computer facilities: 240 computers available on campus for general student use. A campuswide network can be accessed from student residence rooms and from off campus. Online class registration is available.
Website: http://www.naz.edu/

General Application Contact: Judith Baker, Director, Transfer and Graduate Admissions, 585-531-1154, Fax: 585-389-2826, E-mail: gradstudies@naz.edu.

GRADUATE UNITS
Graduate Studies Students: 400 full-time (324 women), 295 part-time (238 women); includes 77 minority (38 Black or African American, non-Hispanic/Latino; 4 American Indian or Alaska Native, non-Hispanic/Latino; 21 Asian, non-Hispanic/Latino; 1 Native Hawaiian or other Pacific Islander, non-Hispanic/Latino; 13 Two or more races, non-Hispanic/Latino). Average age 27. 1,153 applicants, 39% accepted, 272 enrolled. Expenses: Contact institution. *Financial support:* Career-related internships or fieldwork and unspecified assistantships available. Financial award application deadline: 3/1; financial award applicants required to submit FAFSA. *Program availability:* Part-time, evening/weekend. Offers art education (MS Ed); art therapy (MS); communication sciences and disorders (MS); educational technology (MS); human resource management (MS); inclusive adolescence education (MS Ed); inclusive childhood education (MS Ed); inclusive early childhood education (MS Ed); literacy education (MS Ed); management (MS); music education (MS Ed); music performance and pedagogy (MM); music therapy (MS); physical therapy (DPT); social work (MSW); teaching English to speakers of other languages (MS Ed). *Application fee:* $0. *Application Contact:* Judith Baker, Director, Transfer and Graduate Admissions, 585-531-1154, Fax: 585-389-2826, E-mail: gradadmissions@naz.edu.

NEBRASKA METHODIST COLLEGE, Omaha, NE 68114
General Information Independent-religious, coed, comprehensive institution. *Graduate housing:* Rooms and/or apartments available on a first-come, first-served basis to single students and available to married students. Housing application deadline: 4/1.

GRADUATE UNITS
Program in Healthcare Operations Management *Program availability:* Part-time, evening/weekend, online learning. Offers healthcare operations management (MS).
Program in Health Promotion Management *Program availability:* Part-time, evening/weekend, online learning. Offers health promotion management (MS).
Program in Nursing *Program availability:* Evening/weekend, online learning. Offers nurse educator (MSN); nurse executive (MSN).

NEBRASKA WESLEYAN UNIVERSITY, Lincoln, NE 68504-2796
General Information Independent-religious, coed, comprehensive institution.

GRADUATE UNITS
University College *Program availability:* Part-time. Offers forensic science (MFS); historical studies (MA); nursing (MSN).

NER ISRAEL RABBINICAL COLLEGE, Baltimore, MD 21208
General Information Independent-religious, men only, comprehensive institution. *Graduate housing:* Rooms and/or apartments guaranteed to single students and available on a first-come, first-served basis to married students.

GRADUATE UNITS
Graduate Programs Offers rabbinics (MTL, DTL, Professional Certificate).

NER ISRAEL YESHIVA COLLEGE OF TORONTO, Thornhill, ON L4J 8A7, Canada
General Information Independent-religious, men only, comprehensive institution.
GRADUATE UNITS
Graduate Programs

NEUMANN UNIVERSITY, Aston, PA 19014-1298
General Information Independent-religious, coed, comprehensive institution. *Enrollment:* 3,011 graduate, professional, and undergraduate students; 188 full-time matriculated graduate/professional students (124 women), 394 part-time matriculated graduate/professional students (271 women). *Enrollment by degree level:* 425 master's, 157 doctoral. *Graduate faculty:* 26 full-time (19 women), 41 part-time/adjunct (18 women). *Tuition:* Full-time $15,400; part-time $700 per credit. Tuition and fees vary according to degree level, campus/location and program. *Graduate housing:* On-campus housing not available. *Student services:* Campus safety program, career counseling, child daycare facilities, exercise/wellness program, free psychological counseling, international student services, services for students with disabilities, teacher training, writing training. *Library facilities:* Neumann University Library plus 1 other. *Collection:* Books: 46,200 (physical), 160,882 (digital/electronic); Serial titles: 25 (physical), 100,000 (digital/electronic); Databases: 51. Weekly public service hours: 80; students can reserve study rooms.

Computer facilities: Computer purchase and lease plans are available. 550 computers available on campus for general student use. A campuswide network can be accessed from student residence rooms and from off campus. Online class registration is available.
Website: http://www.neumann.edu/

General Application Contact: Dr. Erika Davis, Director of Adult and Graduate Admissions, 610-361-5208, Fax: 610-361-2548, E-mail: davise@neumann.edu.

GRADUATE UNITS
Graduate Program in Education Students: 80 full-time (64 women), 108 part-time (91 women); includes 40 minority (30 Black or African American, non-Hispanic/Latino; 6 Hispanic/Latino; 4 Two or more races, non-Hispanic/Latino), 1 international. Average age 34. 152 applicants, 67% accepted, 82 enrolled. *Faculty:* 6 full-time (5 women), 18 part-time/adjunct (7 women). Expenses: Contact institution. *Financial support:* Scholarships/grants and health care benefits available. Support available to part-time students. Financial award application deadline: 3/15; financial award applicants required to submit FAFSA. In 2016, 42 master's awarded. *Program availability:* Part-time, evening/weekend, 100% online, blended/hybrid learning. Offers education (MS). *Application deadline:* Applications are processed on a rolling basis. *Application fee:* $0. Electronic applications accepted. *Application Contact:* Dr. Erika Davis, Director of Adult and Graduate Admissions, 800-9-NEUMANN Ext. 5208, Fax: 610-361-2548, E-mail: gradadultadmiss@neumann.edu. *Director of Graduate Education,* Dr. Stephanie Smith-Budhai, 610-358-4249, E-mail: budhais@neumann.edu.
Graduate Program in Nursing Students: 32 part-time (29 women); includes 12 minority (7 Black or African American, non-Hispanic/Latino; 2 Asian, non-Hispanic/Latino; 3 Two or more races, non-Hispanic/Latino), 1 international. Average age 39. 37 applicants, 32% accepted, 11 enrolled. *Faculty:* 2 full-time (both women), 3 part-time/adjunct (2 women). Expenses: Contact institution. *Financial support:* Scholarships/grants, traineeships, and health care benefits available. Support available to part-time students. Financial award application deadline: 3/15; financial award applicants required to submit FAFSA. In 2016, 11 master's awarded. *Program availability:* Part-time, evening/weekend. Offers adult-gerontology nurse practitioner (MS); adult/gerontology nurse practitioner (Certificate). *Application deadline:* Applications are processed on a rolling basis. *Application fee:* $0. Electronic applications accepted. *Application Contact:* Dr. Erika Davis, Director of Adult and Graduate Admissions, 800-9-NEUMANN Ext.

5208, Fax: 610-361-2548, E-mail: gradadultadmiss@neumann.edu. *Dean, Division of Nursing and Health Sciences*, Dr. Kathleen Hoover, 610-558-5560, Fax: 610-361-5265, E-mail: hooverk@neumann.edu.

Graduate Programs in Business and Information Management Students: 9 full-time (2 women), 33 part-time (12 women); includes 14 minority (11 Black or African American, non-Hispanic/Latino; 1 Asian, non-Hispanic/Latino; 2 Hispanic/Latino). Average age 31. 58 applicants, 50% accepted, 26 enrolled. *Faculty:* 3 full-time (2 women), 4 part-time/adjunct (1 woman). Expenses: Contact institution. *Financial support:* Scholarships/grants and health care benefits available. Support available to part-time students. Financial award application deadline: 3/15; financial award applicants required to submit FAFSA. In 2016, 16 master's awarded. *Program availability:* Part-time, evening/weekend. Offers accounting (MS); sport business (MS). *Application deadline:* Applications are processed on a rolling basis. *Application fee:* $0. Electronic applications accepted. *Application Contact:* Dr. Erika Davis, Director of Adult and Graduate Admissions, 800-9-NEUMANN Ext. 5208, Fax: 610-361-2548, E-mail: gradadultadmiss@neumann.edu. *Dean of Business and Information Management*, Dr. Eric Wellington, 610-558-5596, Fax: 610-558-5574, E-mail: wellinge@neumann.edu.

Program in Educational Leadership Students: 43 part-time (25 women); includes 12 minority (11 Black or African American, non-Hispanic/Latino; 1 Asian, non-Hispanic/Latino). Average age 41. 27 applicants, 44% accepted, 8 enrolled. *Faculty:* 3 full-time (1 woman), 2 part-time/adjunct (1 woman). Expenses: Contact institution. *Financial support:* Scholarships/grants and health care benefits available. Support available to part-time students. Financial award application deadline: 3/15; financial award applicants required to submit FAFSA. In 2016, 6 doctorates awarded. *Program availability:* Part-time, evening/weekend. Offers educational leadership (Ed D). *Application deadline:* For fall admission, 7/1 for domestic and international students. Applications are processed on a rolling basis. *Application fee:* $0. Electronic applications accepted. *Application Contact:* Dr. Erika Davis, Director of Adult and Graduate Admissions, 800-9-NEUMANN Ext. 5208, Fax: 610-361-2548, E-mail: gradadultadmiss@neumann.edu. *Director of Ed D Program*, Dr. Cynthia Speace, 610-358-4243, E-mail: speacec@neumann.edu.

Program in Organizational and Strategic Leadership Students: 5 full-time (3 women), 88 part-time (50 women); includes 27 minority (21 Black or African American, non-Hispanic/Latino; 5 Hispanic/Latino; 1 Two or more races, non-Hispanic/Latino; 1 international. Average age 37. 83 applicants, 75% accepted, 52 enrolled. *Faculty:* 9 part-time/adjunct (3 women). Expenses: Contact institution. *Financial support:* Scholarships/grants and health care benefits available. Support available to part-time students. Financial award application deadline: 3/15; financial award applicants required to submit FAFSA. In 2016, 49 master's awarded. *Program availability:* Part-time, evening/weekend, 100% online, blended/hybrid learning. Offers organizational and strategic leadership (MS). *Application deadline:* Applications are processed on a rolling basis. *Application fee:* $0. Electronic applications accepted. *Application Contact:* Janice Sackawicz, Coordinator of Student Services, Division of Continuing Adult and Professional Studies, 610-558-5629, Fax: 610-361-5235, E-mail: caps@neumann.edu. *Program Director, Master of Science in Organizational and Strategic Leadership Program*, Dr. Samuel Lemon, 610-361-5239, Fax: 610-361-5235, E-mail: lemons@neumann.edu.

Program in Pastoral Clinical Mental Health Counseling Students: 15 full-time (14 women), 90 part-time (64 women); includes 15 minority (10 Black or African American, non-Hispanic/Latino; 1 Asian, non-Hispanic/Latino; 2 Hispanic/Latino; 2 Two or more races, non-Hispanic/Latino). Average age 47. 61 applicants, 52% accepted, 27 enrolled. *Faculty:* 7 full-time (5 women), 3 part-time/adjunct (2 women). Expenses: Contact institution. *Financial support:* Scholarships/grants and health care benefits available. Support available to part-time students. Financial award application deadline: 3/15; financial award applicants required to submit FAFSA. In 2016, 22 master's, 1 doctorate awarded. *Program availability:* Part-time, evening/weekend. Offers pastoral care specialist (Certificate); pastoral clinical mental health counseling (MS); pastoral clinical mental health counseling certificate of advanced study (Certificate); pastoral counseling (PhD); spiritual formation and direction (CSD); spiritual formation and direction supervision certificate of advanced study (Certificate). *Application deadline:* For fall admission, 8/1 for domestic students; for spring admission, 12/1 for domestic students. Applications are processed on a rolling basis. *Application fee:* $0. Electronic applications accepted. *Application Contact:* Dr. Erika Davis, Director of Adult and Graduate Admissions, 800-9-NEUMANN Ext. 5208, Fax: 610-361-2548, E-mail: gradadultadmiss@neumann.edu. *Director of Pastoral Clinical Mental Health Counseling Program*, Sr. Suzanne Mayer, 610-361-2292, Fax: 610-358-4525, E-mail: mayers@neumann.edu.

Program in Physical Therapy Students: 79 full-time (41 women); includes 18 minority (7 Black or African American, non-Hispanic/Latino; 2 American Indian or Alaska Native, non-Hispanic/Latino; 3 Asian, non-Hispanic/Latino; 4 Hispanic/Latino; 2 Two or more races, non-Hispanic/Latino). Average age 27. 148 applicants, 23% accepted, 30 enrolled. *Faculty:* 6 full-time (5 women), 3 part-time/adjunct (2 women). Expenses: Contact institution. *Financial support:* Scholarships/grants and health care benefits available. Support available to part-time students. Financial award application deadline: 3/15; financial award applicants required to submit FAFSA. In 2016, 25 doctorates awarded. *Program availability:* Evening/weekend. Offers physical therapy (DPT). *Application deadline:* For fall admission, 8/31 for domestic students. Applications are processed on a rolling basis. *Application fee:* $0. Electronic applications accepted. *Application Contact:* Dr. Erika Davis, Director of Adult and Graduate Admissions, 800-9-NEUMANN Ext. 5208, Fax: 610-361-2548, E-mail: gradadultadmiss@neumann.edu. *Program Director, Physical Therapy*, Dr. Robert Post, 610-558-5233, Fax: 610-459-1370, E-mail: postr@neumann.edu.

NEW BRUNSWICK THEOLOGICAL SEMINARY, New Brunswick, NJ 08901-1196

General Information Independent-religious, coed, graduate-only institution. *Graduate housing:* Rooms and/or apartments available on a first-come, first-served basis to single and married students. Housing application deadline: 6/30.

GRADUATE UNITS

Graduate and Professional Programs *Program availability:* Part-time, evening/weekend. Offers pastoral care and counseling (D Min). Electronic applications accepted.

NEW CHARTER UNIVERSITY, Salt Lake City, UT 84101

General Information Proprietary, coed, comprehensive institution. *Graduate housing:* On-campus housing not available.

GRADUATE UNITS

College of Business *Program availability:* Part-time, evening/weekend, online learning. Offers finance (MBA); health care management (MBA); management (MBA). Electronic applications accepted.

College of Public Policy and Administration *Program availability:* Part-time, evening/weekend, online learning. Offers criminal justice (MS); public administration (MPA); public policy and administration (MPA, MS). Electronic applications accepted.

NEW COLLEGE OF FLORIDA, Sarasota, FL 34243

General Information State-supported, coed, comprehensive institution.

GRADUATE UNITS

Program in Data Science Offers data science (MDS).

NEW ENGLAND COLLEGE, Henniker, NH 03242-3293

General Information Independent, coed, comprehensive institution. *Graduate housing:* Room and/or apartments available on a first-come, first-served basis to single students; on-campus housing not available to married students. Housing application deadline: 5/1.

GRADUATE UNITS

Program in Community Mental Health Counseling *Program availability:* Part-time, evening/weekend. Offers human services (MS); mental health counseling (MS).

Program in Education *Program availability:* Part-time, evening/weekend. Offers higher education administration (MS, Ed D); K-12 leadership (Ed D); literacy and language arts (M Ed); meeting the needs of all learners/special education (M Ed); teacher leadership/school reform (M Ed).

Program in Management *Program availability:* Part-time, evening/weekend. Offers accounting (MSA); healthcare administration (MS); international relations (MA); marketing management (MS); nonprofit leadership (MS); project management (MS); strategic leadership (MS). Electronic applications accepted.

Program in Public Policy *Program availability:* Part-time, evening/weekend, online learning. Offers public policy (MA). Electronic applications accepted.

Program in Sports and Recreation Management: Coaching Offers sports and recreation management: coaching (MS).

Programs in Writing *Program availability:* Part-time, evening/weekend. Offers poetry (MFA); professional writing (MA). Electronic applications accepted.

NEW ENGLAND COLLEGE OF BUSINESS AND FINANCE, Boston, MA 02111-2645

General Information Independent, coed, primarily women, comprehensive institution.

GRADUATE UNITS

Program in Business Ethics and Compliance *Program availability:* Online learning. Offers business ethics and compliance (MS).

Program in Finance *Program availability:* Online learning. Offers finance (MSF).

NEW ENGLAND COLLEGE OF OPTOMETRY, Boston, MA 02115-1100

General Information Independent, coed, graduate-only institution. *Graduate housing:* On-campus housing not available. *Research affiliation:* Vistakon-Johnson & Johnson (contact lenses), Boston University School of Medicine (vision science).

GRADUATE UNITS

Graduate and Professional Programs Offers optometry (OD); vision science (MS). Electronic applications accepted.

NEW ENGLAND CONSERVATORY OF MUSIC, Boston, MA 02115-5000

General Information Independent, coed, comprehensive institution. *Enrollment:* 380 full-time matriculated graduate/professional students (182 women), 26 part-time matriculated graduate/professional students (14 women). *Enrollment by degree level:* 305 master's, 37 doctoral, 64 other advanced degrees. *Graduate faculty:* 92 full-time (31 women), 106 part-time/adjunct (37 women). *Tuition:* Full-time $44,300. *Graduate housing:* Room and/or apartments available on a first-come, first-served basis to single students; on-campus housing not available to married students. Typical cost: $15,700 (including board). Housing application deadline: 6/15. *Student services:* Campus employment opportunities, career counseling, free psychological counseling, international student services, low-cost health insurance, services for students with disabilities. *Library facilities:* Spaulding Library plus 3 others. *Collection:* Books: 103,097 (physical), 248,432 (digital/electronic); Serial titles: 161 (physical), 98 (digital/electronic); Databases: 109. Weekly public service hours: 85.

Computer facilities: 70 computers available on campus for general student use. A campuswide network can be accessed. Online class registration is available. Website: http://necmusic.edu/

General Application Contact: Alex Powell, Assistant Dean for Admissions, 617-585-1101, Fax: 617-585-1115, E-mail: alex.powell@necmusic.edu.

GRADUATE UNITS

Graduate Program in Music Students: 380 full-time (182 women), 26 part-time (14 women); includes 70 minority (4 Black or African American, non-Hispanic/Latino; 37 Asian, non-Hispanic/Latino; 16 Hispanic/Latino; 13 Two or more races, non-Hispanic/Latino), 175 international. Average age 22. 1,369 applicants, 33% accepted, 195 enrolled. *Faculty:* 92 full-time (31 women), 106 part-time/adjunct (37 women). Expenses: Contact institution. *Financial support:* In 2016-17, 392 students received support. Fellowships with partial tuition reimbursements available, teaching assistantships, Federal Work-Study, scholarships/grants, and tuition waivers (partial) available. Support available to part-time students. Financial award application deadline: 12/1; financial award applicants required to submit FAFSA. In 2016, 167 master's, 7 doctorates awarded. Offers music (MM, DMA, Diploma). *Application deadline:* For fall admission, 12/1 priority date for domestic and international students; for spring admission, 10/15 for domestic and international students. Applications are processed on a rolling basis. *Application fee:* $115. Electronic applications accepted. *Application Contact:* Alex Powell, Assistant Dean for Admissions, 617-585-1101, Fax: 617-585-1115, E-mail: alex.powell@newenglandconservatory.edu. *Provost/Dean of the College*, Tom Novak, 617-585-1308, Fax: 617-585-1303, E-mail: tom.novak@necmusic.edu.

NEW ENGLAND INSTITUTE OF TECHNOLOGY, East Greenwich, RI 02818

General Information Independent, coed, comprehensive institution. *Enrollment:* 2,962 graduate, professional, and undergraduate students; 61 full-time matriculated graduate/professional students (52 women), 48 part-time matriculated graduate/professional students (14 women). *Enrollment by degree level:* 109 master's. *Graduate housing:* On-campus housing not available. *Student services:* Campus safety program, career counseling, exercise/wellness program. *Library facilities:* New England Institute of Technology Library. *Collection:* Books: 46,744 (physical), 24,454 (digital/electronic); Serial titles: 109 (physical), 30,789 (digital/electronic); Databases: 64. Weekly public service hours: 67; students can reserve study rooms.

Computer facilities: 1,000 computers available on campus for general student use. A campuswide network can be accessed from off campus. Online class registration is available.
Website: http://www.neit.edu/

General Application Contact: Michael Caruso, Director of Admissions, 800-736-7744 Ext. 3411, Fax: 401-886-0868, E-mail: neitadmissions@neit.edu.

GRADUATE UNITS

Program in Construction Management Expenses: Contact institution. *Financial support:* Applicants required to submit FAFSA. *Program availability:* Part-time-only, evening/weekend, 100% online, blended/hybrid learning. Offers construction management (MS). *Application deadline:* Applications are processed on a rolling basis. *Application fee:* $25. Electronic applications accepted. *Application Contact:* Michael Caruso, Director of Admissions, 800-736-7744 Ext. 3411, Fax: 401-886-0868, E-mail: mcaruso@neit.edu.

Program in Information Technology Expenses: Contact institution. *Financial support:* Applicants required to submit FAFSA. *Program availability:* Part-time-only, evening/weekend, 100% online, blended/hybrid learning. Offers information technology (MS). *Application deadline:* Applications are processed on a rolling basis. *Application fee:* $25. Electronic applications accepted. *Application Contact:* Michael Caruso, Director of Admissions, 800-736-7744 Ext. 3411, Fax: 401-886-0868, E-mail: mcaruso@neit.edu.

Program in Occupational Therapy Students: 55 full-time (47 women), 9 part-time (6 women); includes 4 minority (1 Black or African American, non-Hispanic/Latino; 2 Asian, non-Hispanic/Latino; 1 Two or more races, non-Hispanic/Latino), 6 international. Average age 33. Expenses: Contact institution. *Financial support:* Applicants required to submit FAFSA. *Program availability:* Part-time-only, evening/weekend, blended/hybrid learning. Offers occupational therapy (MS). *Application deadline:* Applications are processed on a rolling basis. *Application fee:* $25. Electronic applications accepted. *Application Contact:* Michael Caruso, Director of Admissions, 800-736-7744 Ext. 3411, Fax: 401-886-0868, E-mail: mcaruso@neit.edu.

Program in Public Health Expenses: Contact institution. *Program availability:* Part-time-only, evening/weekend, online only, 100% online. Offers public health (MPH). *Application deadline:* Applications are processed on a rolling basis. *Application fee:* $25. Electronic applications accepted. *Application Contact:* Michael Caruso, Director of Admissions, 800-736-7744 Ext. 3411, Fax: 401-886-0868, E-mail: mcaruso@neit.edu.

NEW ENGLAND LAW–BOSTON, Boston, MA 02116-5687

General Information Independent, coed, graduate-only institution. *Enrollment by degree level:* 622 doctoral. *Graduate faculty:* 42 full-time (16 women), 85 part-time/adjunct (38 women). *Tuition:* Full-time $46,974; part-time $35,250 per year. *Required fees:* $80; $80 per unit. Tuition and fees vary according to class time, course load and degree level. *Graduate housing:* On-campus housing not available. *Student services:* Campus employment opportunities, career counseling, low-cost health insurance, services for students with disabilities, writing training. *Library facilities:* New England Law | Boston Law Library. *Collection:* Books: 100,889 (physical), 42,701 (digital/electronic); Serial titles: 2,157 (physical), 21,704 (digital/electronic); Databases: 96. Weekly public service hours: 104; students can reserve study rooms.

Computer facilities: 36 computers available on campus for general student use. A campuswide network can be accessed. Online class registration is available.
Website: http://www.nesl.edu/

General Application Contact: Michelle L'Etoile, Director of Admissions, 617-422-7210, Fax: 617-422-7201, E-mail: admit@nesl.edu.

GRADUATE UNITS

Graduate Programs Students: 433 full-time (258 women), 189 part-time (98 women); includes 195 minority (65 Black or African American, non-Hispanic/Latino; 1 American Indian or Alaska Native, non-Hispanic/Latino; 32 Asian, non-Hispanic/Latino; 69 Hispanic/Latino; 28 Two or more races, non-Hispanic/Latino), 15 international. *Faculty:* 42 full-time (16 women), 85 part-time/adjunct (38 women). Expenses: Contact institution. *Financial support:* In 2016–17, 416 students received support, including 80 fellowships (averaging $3,500 per year); Federal Work-Study, scholarships/grants, and tuition waivers (full and partial) also available. Financial award application deadline: 3/19; financial award applicants required to submit FAFSA. In 2016, 335 doctorates awarded. *Program availability:* Part-time, evening/weekend. Offers American law (LL M); law (JD). *Application deadline:* For fall admission, 3/15 priority date for domestic students. Applications are processed on a rolling basis. *Application fee:* $65. Electronic applications accepted. *Application Contact:* Michelle L'Etoile, Director of Admissions, 617-422-7210, Fax: 617-422-7201, E-mail: admit@nesl.edu. *Dean,* John F. O'Brien, 617-422-7221, Fax: 617-422-7333.

NEW HAMPSHIRE INSTITUTE OF ART, Manchester, NH 03104

General Information Independent, coed, comprehensive institution. *Enrollment:* 402 graduate, professional, and undergraduate students; 59 full-time matriculated graduate/professional students (42 women), 6 part-time matriculated graduate/professional students (3 women). *Enrollment by degree level:* 65 master's. *Graduate faculty:* 31 part-time/adjunct (14 women). *Graduate housing:* Room and/or apartments available on a first-come, first-served basis to single students; on-campus housing not available to married students. Housing application deadline: 6/15. *Student services:* Campus employment opportunities, career counseling, free psychological counseling, services for students with disabilities, teacher training. *Library facilities:* Teti Library. *Collection:* Books: 17,000 (physical), 144,463 (digital/electronic); Serial titles: 80 (physical), 7,800 (digital/electronic); Databases: 30. Weekly public service hours: 63.

Computer facilities: 100 computers available on campus for general student use. A campuswide network can be accessed from student residence rooms and from off campus. Online class registration is available.
Website: http://www.nhia.edu/

General Application Contact: Graduate Admissions, 603-836-2122, E-mail: gradadmissions@nhia.edu.

GRADUATE UNITS

Graduate Studies Students: 59 full-time (42 women), 6 part-time (3 women); includes 2 minority (1 Asian, non-Hispanic/Latino; 1 Hispanic/Latino). Average age 43. 36 applicants, 58% accepted, 12 enrolled. *Faculty:* 31 part-time/adjunct (14 women). Expenses: Contact institution. *Financial support:* In 2016–17, 2 teaching assistantships (averaging $1,200 per year) were awarded; scholarships/grants and unspecified assistantships also available. Support available to part-time students. Financial award application deadline: 6/1; financial award applicants required to submit FAFSA. In 2016, 2 master's awarded. Offers art education (MA); creative writing (MFA); photography (MFA); teaching visual arts (MAT); visual arts (MFA); writing for stage and screen (MFA). *Application deadline:* For fall admission, 5/1 priority date for domestic students; for

spring admission, 11/1 priority date for domestic students. Applications are processed on a rolling basis. *Application fee:* $75. Electronic applications accepted. *Application Contact:* Moriah Billups, Graduate Admissions Coordinator, 603-836 2588, E-mail: gradadmissions@nhia.edu. *Dean of Graduate Studies,* Lucinda Bliss, 603-836 2522, E-mail: lucindabliss@nhia.edu.

NEW JERSEY CITY UNIVERSITY, Jersey City, NJ 07305-1597

General Information State-supported, coed, comprehensive institution. *Graduate housing:* On-campus housing not available.

GRADUATE UNITS

College of Professional Studies *Program availability:* Part-time, evening/weekend. Offers civil security leadership (D Sc); community health education (MS); criminal justice (MS); health administration (MS); national security studies (MS, Certificate); school health education (MS).

Debra Cannon Partridge Wolfe College of Education *Program availability:* Part-time, evening/weekend. Offers bilingual/bicultural education (MA); counselor education (MA); early childhood education (MAT); education (MA, MAT, Ed D); educational administration and supervision (MA); educational technology (MA); educational technology leadership (Ed D); elementary education (MAT); English as a second language (MA); secondary education (MAT); special education (MA); urban education (MA); urban education world language (MA).

Graduate Studies and Continuing Education *Program availability:* Part-time, evening/weekend, online learning.

School of Business *Program availability:* Part-time, evening/weekend. Offers accounting (MS, Graduate Certificate); business (MBA, MS, Graduate Certificate); finance (MBA, MS, Graduate Certificate); marketing (MBA); organizational management and leadership (MBA).

William J. Maxwell College of Arts and Sciences *Program availability:* Part-time, evening/weekend. Offers art (MFA); art education (MA); arts and sciences (MA, MFA, MM); mathematics education (MA); music education (MA); performance (MM); studio art (MFA).

NEW JERSEY INSTITUTE OF TECHNOLOGY, Newark, NJ 07102

General Information State-supported, coed, university. CGS member. *Enrollment:* 1,948 full-time matriculated graduate/professional students (561 women), 996 part-time matriculated graduate/professional students (268 women). *Enrollment by degree level:* 2,518 master's, 425 doctoral, 1 other advanced degree. *Graduate faculty:* 436 full-time (87 women), 317 part-time/adjunct (68 women). *Tuition, state resident:* full-time $19,008; part-time $1034 per credit. *Tuition, nonresident:* full-time $28,092; part-time $1484 per credit. *Required fees:* $2806; $165 per credit. Tuition and fees vary according to degree level. *Graduate housing:* Room and/or apartments available on a first-come, first-served basis to single students; on-campus housing not available to married students. Typical cost: $13,700 (including board). Housing application deadline: 3/31. *Student services:* Campus employment opportunities, campus safety program, career counseling, child daycare facilities, exercise/wellness program, free psychological counseling, grant writing training, international student services, low-cost health insurance, services for students with disabilities, teacher training, writing training. *Library facilities:* Van Houten Library plus 1 other. *Collection:* Books: 170,618 (physical), 27,759 (digital/electronic); Serial titles: 59 (physical), 33,674 (digital/electronic); Databases: 33. Weekly public service hours: 105; students can reserve study rooms. *Research affiliation:* UT-Battelle, LLC c/o ORNL, Brookhaven National Laboratory, Booz Allen Hamilton, Inc., The Wistar Institute, EPRI - Electronic Power Research Insitue, ExxonMobil.

Computer facilities: Computer purchase and lease plans are available. 1,938 computers available on campus for general student use. A campuswide network can be accessed from student residence rooms and from off campus. Online class registration is available.
Website: http://www.njit.edu/

General Application Contact: Stephen Eck, Director of Admissions, 973-596-3300, Fax: 973-596-3461, E-mail: admissions@njit.edu.

GRADUATE UNITS

College of Architecture and Design Students: 40 full-time (23 women), 6 part-time (0 women); includes 10 minority (1 Black or African American, non-Hispanic/Latino; 3 Asian, non-Hispanic/Latino; 5 Hispanic/Latino; 1 Two or more races, non-Hispanic/Latino), 19 international. Average age 30. 129 applicants, 37% accepted, 10 enrolled. *Faculty:* 31 full-time (8 women), 37 part-time/adjunct (14 women). Expenses: Contact institution. *Financial support:* In 2016–17, 21 students received support, including 6 teaching assistantships (averaging $22,500 per year); fellowships, career-related internships or fieldwork, Federal Work-Study, institutionally sponsored loans, scholarships/grants, traineeships, unspecified assistantships, and studio assistantships (1 averaging $10,000) also available. Financial award application deadline: 1/15. In 2016, 16 master's, 4 doctorates awarded. *Program availability:* Part-time, evening/weekend. Offers architecture (M Arch, MS Arch); infrastructure planning (MIP); urban systems (PhD). *Application deadline:* For fall admission, 6/1 priority date for domestic students, 5/1 priority date for international students; for spring admission, 11/15 priority date for domestic and international students. Applications are processed on a rolling basis. *Application fee:* $75. Electronic applications accepted. *Application Contact:* Stephen Eck, Director of Admissions, 973-596-3300, Fax: 973-596-3461, E-mail: admissions@njit.edu. *Interim Dean,* Anthony W. Schuman, 973-596-6370, E-mail: anthony.w.schuman@njit.edu.

College of Science and Liberal Arts Students: 196 full-time (71 women), 68 part-time (33 women); includes 55 minority (15 Black or African American, non-Hispanic/Latino; 19 Asian, non-Hispanic/Latino; 15 Hispanic/Latino; 6 Two or more races, non-Hispanic/Latino), 140 international. Average age 28. 504 applicants, 64% accepted, 65 enrolled. *Faculty:* 166 full-time (39 women), 87 part-time/adjunct (32 women). Expenses: Contact institution. *Financial support:* In 2016–17, 106 students received support, including 32 research assistantships (averaging $17,108 per year), 74 teaching assistantships (averaging $21,368 per year); fellowships, scholarships/grants, traineeships and unspecified assistantships also available. Financial award application deadline: 1/15. In 2016, 81 master's, 18 doctorates, 1 other advanced degree awarded. *Program availability:* Part-time, evening/weekend. Offers applied mathematics (MS); applied physics (M Sc, PhD); applied statistics (MS, Certificate); biology (MS, PhD); biostatistics (MS); chemistry (MS, PhD); computational biology (MS); environmental and sustainability policy (MS); environmental science (MS, PhD); history (MA, MAT); materials science and engineering (MS, PhD); mathematical and computational finance (MS); mathematics science (PhD); pharmaceutical chemistry (MS); practice of technical communications (Certificate); professional and technical communications (MS). *Application deadline:* For fall admission, 6/1 priority date for domestic students, 5/1 priority date for international students; for spring admission, 11/15 priority date for domestic and international students. Applications are processed on a rolling basis.

New Jersey Institute of Technology

Application fee: $75. Electronic applications accepted. *Application Contact:* Stephen Eck, Director of Admissions, 973-596-3300, Fax: 973-596-3461, E-mail: admissions@njit.edu. *Dean,* Dr. Kevin Belfield, 973-596-3676, Fax: 973-565-0586, E-mail: kevin.d.belfield@njit.edu.

Martin Tuchman School of Management Students: 90 full-time (35 women), 147 part-time (53 women); includes 104 minority (30 Black or African American, non-Hispanic/Latino; 30 Asian, non-Hispanic/Latino; 38 Hispanic/Latino; 6 Two or more races, non-Hispanic/Latino), 57 international. Average age 31. 385 applicants, 52% accepted, 80 enrolled. *Faculty:* 29 full-time (9 women), 21 part-time/adjunct (3 women). Expenses: Contact institution. *Financial support:* In 2016–17, 7 students received support, including 3 research assistantships (averaging $9,088 per year), 4 teaching assistantships (averaging $19,250 per year); fellowships, career-related internships or fieldwork, Federal Work-Study, institutionally sponsored loans, and unspecified assistantships also available. Financial award application deadline: 1/15. In 2016, 81 master's, 11 other advanced degrees awarded. *Program availability:* Part-time, evening/weekend. Offers business administration (MBA); business data science (PhD); finance for managers (Certificate); international business (MS); management (MS); management essentials (Certificate); management of technology (Certificate). *Application deadline:* For fall admission, 6/1 priority date for domestic students, 5/1 priority date for international students; for spring admission, 11/15 priority date for domestic and international students. Applications are processed on a rolling basis. *Application fee:* $75. Electronic applications accepted. *Application Contact:* Stephen Eck, Director of Admissions, 973-596-3300, Fax: 973-596-3461, E-mail: admissions@njit.edu. *Interim Dean,* Dr. Reggie Caudill, 973-596-5856, Fax: 973-596-3074, E-mail: reggie.j.caudill@njit.edu.

Newark College of Engineering Students: 804 full-time (191 women), 550 part-time (129 women); includes 357 minority (82 Black or African American, non-Hispanic/Latino; 1 American Indian or Alaska Native, non-Hispanic/Latino; 138 Asian, non-Hispanic/Latino; 114 Hispanic/Latino; 22 Two or more races, non-Hispanic/Latino), 675 international. Average age 27. 2,959 applicants, 51% accepted, 442 enrolled. *Faculty:* 146 full-time (21 women), 119 part-time/adjunct (10 women). Expenses: Contact institution. *Financial support:* In 2016–17, 172 students received support, including 1 fellowship (averaging $1,528 per year), 79 research assistantships (averaging $13,336 per year), 92 teaching assistantships (averaging $20,619 per year); scholarships/grants also available. Financial award application deadline: 1/15. In 2016, 595 master's, 29 doctorates awarded. *Program availability:* Part-time, evening/weekend. Offers biomedical engineering (MS, PhD); chemical engineering (MS, PhD); computer engineering (MS, PhD); electrical engineering (MS, PhD); engineering management (MS); environmental engineering (PhD); healthcare systems management (MS); industrial engineering (MS, PhD); Internet engineering (MS); manufacturing engineering (MS); mechanical engineering (MS, PhD); occupational safety and health engineering (MS); pharmaceutical bioprocessing (MS); pharmaceutical engineering (MS); pharmaceutical systems management (MS); power and energy systems (MS); telecommunications (MS); transportation (MS, PhD). *Application deadline:* For fall admission, 6/1 priority date for domestic students, 5/1 priority date for international students; for spring admission, 11/15 priority date for domestic and international students. Applications are processed on a rolling basis. *Application fee:* $75. Electronic applications accepted. *Application Contact:* Stephen Eck, Director of Admissions, 973-596-3300, Fax: 973-596-3461, E-mail: admissions@njit.edu. *Dean,* Dr. Moshe Kam, 973-596-5534, E-mail: moshe.kam@njit.edu.

Ying Wu College of Computing Students: 818 full-time (241 women), 225 part-time (53 women); includes 162 minority (35 Black or African American, non-Hispanic/Latino; 77 Asian, non-Hispanic/Latino; 41 Hispanic/Latino; 9 Two or more races, non-Hispanic/Latino), 772 international. Average age 27. 2,666 applicants, 51% accepted, 377 enrolled. *Faculty:* 64 full-time (10 women), 38 part-time/adjunct (4 women). Expenses: Contact institution. *Financial support:* In 2016–17, 57 students received support, including 18 research assistantships (averaging $16,073 per year), 39 teaching assistantships (averaging $20,194 per year); fellowships, career-related internships or fieldwork, Federal Work-Study, institutionally sponsored loans, and unspecified assistantships also available. Financial award application deadline: 1/15. In 2016, 398 master's, 10 doctorates, 9 other advanced degrees awarded. *Program availability:* Part-time, evening/weekend. Offers big data management and mining (Certificate); business and information systems (Certificate); computer science (MS, PhD); data mining (Certificate); information security (Certificate); information systems (MS, PhD); information technology administration and security (MS); IT administration (Certificate); network security and information assurance (Certificate); software engineering analysis/design (Certificate); Web systems development (Certificate). *Application deadline:* For fall admission, 6/1 priority date for domestic students, 5/1 priority date for international students; for spring admission, 11/15 priority date for domestic and international students. Applications are processed on a rolling basis. *Application fee:* $75. Electronic applications accepted. *Application Contact:* Stephen Eck, Director of Admissions, 973-596-3300, Fax: 973-596-3461, E-mail: admissions@njit.edu. *Dean,* Dr. Craig Gotsman, 973-542-5488, Fax: 973-596-5777, E-mail: marek.rusinkiewicz@njit.edu.

NEWMAN THEOLOGICAL COLLEGE, Edmonton, AB T6V 1H3, Canada

General Information Independent-religious, coed, graduate-only institution. *Enrollment:* 34 full-time matriculated graduate/professional students (2 women), 103 part-time matriculated graduate/professional students (71 women). *Enrollment by degree level:* 116 master's, 11 other advanced degrees. *Graduate faculty:* 13 full-time (3 women), 15 part-time/adjunct (2 women). *Tuition:* Full-time $6390 Canadian dollars; part-time $639 Canadian dollars per credit. *Required fees:* $160 Canadian dollars; $70 Canadian dollars per credit. $35 Canadian dollars per semester. One-time fee: $45 Canadian dollars. Tuition and fees vary according to course level and campus/location. *Graduate housing:* On-campus housing not available. *Student services:* Campus employment opportunities, career counseling, free psychological counseling, services for students with disabilities. *Library facilities:* Sophyshyn Family Library. *Collection:* Books: 70,415 (physical); Serial titles: 7,859 (physical); Databases: 12. Weekly public service hours: 42; students can reserve study rooms.
Computer facilities: 6 computers available on campus for general student use. A campuswide network can be accessed from student residence rooms. Website: http://www.newman.edu/
General Information Contact: Maria Saulnier, Registrar, 780-392-2451, Fax: 780-462-4013, E-mail: registrar@newman.edu.
GRADUATE UNITS
Religious Education Programs Students: 87 part-time (61 women). 20 applicants, 100% accepted, 20 enrolled. *Faculty:* 2 full-time (1 woman), 11 part-time/adjunct (3 women). Expenses: Contact institution. *Financial support:* In 2016–17, 9,041 students received support. Tuition bursaries available. Support available to part-time students.

Financial award application deadline: 5/31. In 2016, 8 master's awarded. *Program availability:* Part-time, blended/hybrid learning. Offers religious education (MRE, Graduate Certificate). *Application deadline:* For fall admission, 8/21 priority date for domestic students; for winter admission, 11/22 priority date for domestic students; for spring admission, 4/18 priority date for domestic students. Applications are processed on a rolling basis. *Application fee:* $45 ($250 for international students). *Application Contact:* Maria Saulnier, Registrar, 780-392-2451, Fax: 780-462-4013, E-mail: registrar@newman.edu. *Director,* Sandra Talarico, 780-392-2450 Ext. 2214, Fax: 780-462-4013, E-mail: sandra.talarico@newman.edu.
Theology Programs Students: 34 full-time (2 women), 16 part-time (10 women). 22 applicants, 100% accepted, 19 enrolled. *Faculty:* 16 full-time (3 women), 7 part-time/adjunct (0 women). Expenses: Contact institution. *Financial support:* Tuition bursaries available. Support available to part-time students. Financial award application deadline: 5/31. In 2016, 8 master's awarded. *Program availability:* Part-time. Offers theology (M Div, M Th, MTS). *Application deadline:* For fall admission, 8/21 priority date for domestic students; for winter admission, 11/22 priority date for domestic students; for spring admission, 4/21 priority date for domestic students. Applications are processed on a rolling basis. *Application fee:* $45 ($250 for international students). *Application Contact:* Maria Saulnier, Registrar, 780-392-2451, Fax: 780-462-4013, E-mail: registrar@newman.edu. *Academic Dean/Vice President,* Sr. Zoe Bernatsky, 780-392-2450 Ext. 2213, Fax: 780-462-4013, E-mail: zoe.bernatsky@newman.edu.

NEWMAN UNIVERSITY, Wichita, KS 67213-2097

General Information Independent-religious, coed, comprehensive institution. *Graduate housing:* Rooms and/or apartments available on a first-come, first-served basis to single and married students. Housing application deadline: 8/1.
GRADUATE UNITS
Graduate Theology Program *Program availability:* Part-time, online learning. Offers theological studies (MTS); theology (MA).
Master of Science in Education Program *Program availability:* Part-time, evening/weekend, online learning. Offers building leadership (MS Ed); curriculum and instruction (MS Ed); organizational leadership (MS Ed). Electronic applications accepted.
MBA Program *Program availability:* Part-time. Offers finance (MBA); international business (MBA); leadership (MBA); management (MBA); management information technology (MBA). Electronic applications accepted.
School of Nursing and Allied Health Offers nurse anesthesia (MS). Electronic applications accepted.
School of Social Work *Program availability:* Online learning. Offers social work (MSW).

NEW MEXICO HIGHLANDS UNIVERSITY, Las Vegas, NM 87701

General Information State-supported, coed, comprehensive institution. CGS member. *Graduate housing:* Rooms and/or apartments guaranteed to single and married students. *Research affiliation:* Spectra Gases, Inc. (chemistry), Los Alamos National Laboratory (chemistry), Sigma Aldrich (chemistry).
GRADUATE UNITS
Graduate Studies *Program availability:* Part-time.
College of Arts and Sciences *Program availability:* Part-time. Offers arts and sciences (MA, MS); chemistry (MS); English (MA); human performance and sport (MA); media arts and computer science (MS); natural science (MS); psychology (MS); public affairs (MA); Southwest studies (MA). Electronic applications accepted.
School of Business, Media and Technology Offers business administration (MBA); media arts and computer science (MA); media arts and technology (MA).
School of Education *Program availability:* Part-time. Offers curriculum and instruction (MA); educational leadership (MA); professional counseling (MA); special education (MA).
School of Social Work *Program availability:* Part-time. Offers bilingual/bicultural clinical practice (MSW); clinical practice (MSW).

NEW MEXICO INSTITUTE OF MINING AND TECHNOLOGY, Socorro, NM 87801

General Information State-supported, coed, university. CGS member. *Graduate housing:* Rooms and/or apartments available on a first-come, first-served basis to single and married students. Housing application deadline: 6/1. *Research affiliation:* National Center for Atmospheric Research (atmosphere research), National Radio Astronomy Observatory (astronomy), Joint Center for Materials Research (materials engineering, metallurgy), Gas Technology Institute (natural gas recovery), Optical Surface Technologies LLC (custom optical components).
GRADUATE UNITS
Center for Graduate Studies Offers applied and industrial mathematics (PhD); astrophysics (PhD); atmospheric physics (PhD); biology (MS); chemistry (MS, PhD); computer science (MS, PhD); electrical engineering (MS); environmental engineering (MS); explosives engineering (MS); fluid and thermal sciences (MS); geobiology (PhD); geochemistry (MS, PhD); geology (MS, PhD); geophysics (MS, PhD); geotechnical engineering (MS); hydrology (MS, PhD); industrial mathematics (MS); instrumentation (MS); materials engineering (MS, PhD); mathematical physics (PhD); mathematics (MS); mechatronics systems engineering (MS); mining engineering (MS); operations research and statistics (MS); petroleum engineering (MS, PhD); physics (MS); science teaching (MST); solid mechanics (MS); STEM education (MEM). Electronic applications accepted.

NEW MEXICO STATE UNIVERSITY, Las Cruces, NM 88003-8001

General Information State-supported, coed, university. CGS member. *Enrollment:* 14,852 graduate, professional, and undergraduate students; 1,481 full-time matriculated graduate/professional students (799 women), 1,244 part-time matriculated graduate/professional students (746 women). *Enrollment by degree level:* 1,894 master's, 802 doctoral, 29 other advanced degrees. *Graduate faculty:* 523 full-time (212 women), 34 part-time/adjunct (19 women). *Tuition:* state resident: full-time $4086. Tuition, nonresident: full-time $14,254. *Required fees:* $853. Tuition and fees vary according to course load. *Graduate housing:* Rooms and/or apartments available on a first-come, first-served basis to single and married students. Typical cost: $3692 per year ($4296 including board) for single students; $6120 per year ($8896 including board) for married students. Room and board charges vary according to board plan and housing facility selected. Housing application deadline: 7/1. *Student services:* Campus employment opportunities, campus safety program, career counseling, child daycare facilities, exercise/wellness program, free psychological counseling, grant writing training, international student services, low-cost health insurance, multicultural affairs office, services for students with disabilities, teacher training, writing training. *Library facilities:* New Mexico State University Library - Zuhl plus 1 other. *Collection:* Books: 1.5

million (physical), 159,632 (digital/electronic); Serial titles: 474 (physical), 1,055 (digital/electronic); Databases: 401. Weekly public service hours: 112; students can reserve study rooms. *Research affiliation:* Sandia National Laboratories (energy research, computation), NASA (STEM education research), Fred Hutchinson Cancer Research Center (cancer research), U.S. Air Force Research Laboratory (AFRL) (space weather, high energy research), U.S. Bureau of Land Management (BLM) (resource management research), Los Alamos National Laboratory (energy research, environmental sciences, information sciences).

Computer facilities: Computer purchase and lease plans are available. 354 computers available on campus for general student use. A campuswide network can be accessed from student residence rooms and from off campus. Online class registration, antivirus software; student portal online with file share/storage space, student employee clock-in, payments system, hardware rentals, short-term tablet checkout, software discounts are available.
Website: http://www.nmsu.edu/

General Application Contact: Dr. Loui Reyes, Dean, 575-646-5745, Fax: 575-646-7758, E-mail: gradinfo@nmsu.edu.

GRADUATE UNITS

College of Agricultural, Consumer and Environmental Sciences Students: 147 full-time (88 women), 54 part-time (32 women); includes 50 minority (2 Black or African American, non-Hispanic/Latino; 5 American Indian or Alaska Native, non-Hispanic/Latino; 41 Hispanic/Latino; 2 Two or more races, non-Hispanic/Latino), 37 international. Average age 29. 114 applicants, 66% accepted, 58 enrolled. *Faculty:* 72 full-time (24 women), 1 (woman) part-time/adjunct. Expenses: Contact institution. *Financial support:* In 2016–17, 155 students received support, including 2 fellowships (averaging $4,088 per year), 73 research assistantships (averaging $19,479 per year), 65 teaching assistantships (averaging $15,447 per year); career-related internships or fieldwork, Federal Work-Study, scholarships/grants, traineeships, health care benefits, and unspecified assistantships also available. Support available to part-time students. Financial award application deadline: 3/1. In 2016, 56 master's, 7 doctorates awarded. *Program availability:* Part-time, evening/weekend. Offers agribusiness (MBA); agricultural and extension education (MA); agricultural, consumer and environmental sciences (M Ag, MA, MBA, MS, DED, PhD); agriculture (M Ag); animal science (MS, PhD); clothing, textiles, and merchandising (MS); economic development (DED); entomology, plant pathology and weed science (MS); family and child science (MS); family and consumer science education (MS); family and consumer sciences (MS); fish, wildlife and conservation ecology (MS); food science and technology (MS); horticulture (MS); hotel, restaurant, and tourism management (MS); human nutrition and dietetic sciences (MS); plant and environmental sciences (MS, PhD); range science (MS, PhD); water science management (MS). *Application deadline:* For fall admission, 7/1 priority date for domestic students; for spring admission, 11/1 for domestic students. Applications are processed on a rolling basis. *Application fee:* $40 ($50 for international students). Electronic applications accepted. *Application Contact:* Dr. Jerry Hawkes, Interim Associate Dean/Director of Academic Program, 575-646-3210, Fax: 575-646-5975, E-mail: jhawkes@nmsu.edu. *Dean,* Dr. Rolando A. Flores, 575-646-3748, Fax: 575-646-5975, E-mail: agdean@nmsu.edu.

College of Arts and Sciences Students: 504 full-time (230 women), 288 part-time (171 women); includes 255 minority (15 Black or African American, non-Hispanic/Latino; 4 American Indian or Alaska Native, non-Hispanic/Latino; 11 Asian, non-Hispanic/Latino; 205 Hispanic/Latino; 1 Native Hawaiian or other Pacific Islander, non-Hispanic/Latino; 19 Two or more races, non-Hispanic/Latino), 185 international. Average age 32. 764 applicants, 57% accepted, 175 enrolled. *Faculty:* 225 full-time (87 women), 9 part-time/adjunct (4 women). Expenses: Contact institution. *Financial support:* In 2016–17, 469 students received support, including 38 fellowships (averaging $3,921 per year), 74 research assistantships (averaging $19,927 per year), 301 teaching assistantships (averaging $15,577 per year); career-related internships or fieldwork, Federal Work-Study, scholarships/grants, traineeships, health care benefits, and unspecified assistantships also available. Support available to part-time students. Financial award application deadline: 3/1. In 2016, 189 master's, 29 doctorates, 7 other advanced degrees awarded. *Program availability:* Part-time, online learning. Offers anthropology (MA); applied geography (MAG); art history (MA); arts and sciences (MA, MAG, MCJ, MFA, MM, MPA, MS, PhD, Graduate Certificate); astronomy (MS, PhD); bioinformatics (MS); biology (MS, PhD); biotechnology (MS); chemistry (MS, PhD); communication studies (MA); computer science (MS, PhD); conducting (MM); creative writing (MFA); criminal justice (MCJ); cultural resource management (Graduate Certificate); engineering psychology (PhD); English (MA); geological sciences (MS); government (MA); history (MA); mathematical sciences (MS, PhD); museum studies (Graduate Certificate); music education (MM); performance (MM); psychology (MA); public administration (MPA); public history (MA); rhetoric and professional communication (PhD); sociology (MA); space physics (MS); Spanish (MA); studio art (MFA). *Application fee:* $40 ($50 for international students). Electronic applications accepted. *Application Contact:* Dr. James Murphy, Associate Dean, 575-646-3500, Fax: 575-646-6096, E-mail: admissions@nmsu.edu. *Interim Dean,* Dr. Enrico Pontelli, 575-646-3500, Fax: 575-646-6096, E-mail: epontell@nmsu.edu.

College of Business Students: 150 full-time (71 women), 147 part-time (79 women); includes 144 minority (6 Black or African American, non-Hispanic/Latino; 7 American Indian or Alaska Native, non-Hispanic/Latino; 6 Asian, non-Hispanic/Latino; 118 Hispanic/Latino; 7 Two or more races, non-Hispanic/Latino), 46 international. Average age 32. 277 applicants, 53% accepted, 57 enrolled. *Faculty:* 59 full-time (16 women). Expenses: Contact institution. *Financial support:* In 2016–17, 123 students received support, including 6 fellowships (averaging $4,088 per year), 63 teaching assistantships (averaging $15,359 per year); career-related internships or fieldwork, Federal Work-Study, scholarships/grants, traineeships, health care benefits, and unspecified assistantships also available. Support available to part-time students. Financial award application deadline: 3/1. In 2016, 85 master's, 5 doctorates, 6 other advanced degrees awarded. *Program availability:* Part-time. Offers accountancy (MACCT); agribusiness (MBA); applied statistics (MS); business (MA, MACCT, MBA, MS, DED, PhD, Graduate Certificate); business administration (PhD); economic development (DED); economics (MA); finance (MBA, Graduate Certificate); information systems (MBA); management (PhD); public utility regulation and economics (Graduate Certificate). *Application deadline:* For fall admission, 7/1 priority date for domestic students; for spring admission, 11/1 for domestic students. Applications are processed on a rolling basis. *Application fee:* $40 ($50 for international students). Electronic applications accepted. *Application Contact:* Graduate Admissions, 575-646-3121, E-mail: admissions@nmsu.edu. *Dean,* Dr. James Hoffman, 575-646-2821, Fax: 575-646-6155, E-mail: jhoffman@nmsu.edu.

College of Education Students: 268 full-time (204 women), 412 part-time (307 women); includes 404 minority (23 Black or African American, non-Hispanic/Latino; 12 American Indian or Alaska Native, non-Hispanic/Latino; 18 Asian, non-Hispanic/Latino; 338 Hispanic/Latino; 1 Native Hawaiian or other Pacific Islander, non-Hispanic/Latino; 12 Two or more races, non-Hispanic/Latino), 44 international. Average age 36. 445

applicants, 40% accepted, 127 enrolled. *Faculty:* 66 full-time (46 women), 16 part-time/adjunct (10 women). Expenses: Contact institution. *Financial support:* In 2016–17, 233 students received support, including 8 fellowships (averaging $4,085 per year), 17 research assistantships (averaging $13,906 per year), 63 teaching assistantships (averaging $13,051 per year); career-related internships or fieldwork, Federal Work-Study, scholarships/grants, traineeships, health care benefits, and unspecified assistantships also available. Support available to part-time students. Financial award application deadline: 3/1. In 2016, 171 master's, 32 doctorates, 18 other advanced degrees awarded. *Program availability:* Part-time, evening/weekend, blended/hybrid learning. Offers bilingual education (MA); communication disorders (MA); counseling psychology (PhD); curriculum and instruction (Ed D, Ed S); early childhood education (MA); education (MA, MAT, Ed D, PhD, Ed S, Graduate Certificate); educational administration (MA); educational diagnostics (MA, Ed S); educational leadership (Ed D, PhD); kinesiology (PhD); language, literacy and culture (MA); learning design and technologies (MA); online teaching and learning (Graduate Certificate); school psychology (Ed S); special education (Ed D, PhD); teaching (MAT); teaching English to speakers of other languages (MA). *Application deadline:* Applications are processed on a rolling basis. *Application fee:* $40 ($50 for international students). Electronic applications accepted. *Application Contact:* Dr. David Rutledge, Graduate Education Advising, 575-646-5411, Fax: 575-646-6032, E-mail: rutledge@nmsu.edu. *Dean,* Dr. Donald Pope Davis, 575-646-5858, Fax: 575-646-6032, E-mail: dpd@nmsu.edu.

College of Engineering Students: 225 full-time (48 women), 172 part-time (40 women); includes 115 minority (16 Black or African American, non-Hispanic/Latino; 5 American Indian or Alaska Native, non-Hispanic/Latino; 5 Asian, non-Hispanic/Latino; 80 Hispanic/Latino; 9 Two or more races, non-Hispanic/Latino), 167 international. Average age 31. 397 applicants, 48% accepted, 98 enrolled. *Faculty:* 62 full-time (12 women), 1 part-time/adjunct (0 women). Expenses: Contact institution. *Financial support:* In 2016–17, 227 students received support, including 9 fellowships (averaging $3,402 per year), 71 research assistantships (averaging $14,746 per year), 77 teaching assistantships (averaging $12,577 per year); career-related internships or fieldwork, Federal Work-Study, scholarships/grants, traineeships, health care benefits, and unspecified assistantships also available. Support available to part-time students. Financial award application deadline: 3/1. In 2016, 134 master's, 24 doctorates, 2 other advanced degrees awarded. *Program availability:* Part-time. Offers aerospace engineering (MSAE); chemical and materials engineering (MS Ch E, PhD); civil and geological engineering (MSCE, PhD); engineering (MS Ch E, MS Env E, MSAE, MSCE, MSEE, MSIE, MSME, PhD, Graduate Certificate); environmental engineering (MS Env E); industrial engineering (MSIE, PhD); mechanical engineering (MSME, PhD); systems engineering (Graduate Certificate). *Application deadline:* For fall admission, 7/1 priority date for domestic students; for spring admission, 11/1 for domestic students. Applications are processed on a rolling basis. *Application fee:* $40 ($50 for international students). Electronic applications accepted. *Application Contact:* Graduate Admissions, 575-646-3121, E-mail: admissions@nmsu.edu. *Associate Dean of Research and Graduate Studies,* Dr. Phillip De Leon, 575-646-3422, Fax: 575-646-3549, E-mail: oer@nmsu.edu.

Klipsch School of Electrical and Computer Engineering Students: 73 full-time (11 women), 44 part-time (10 women); includes 30 minority (4 Black or African American, non-Hispanic/Latino; 1 American Indian or Alaska Native, non-Hispanic/Latino; 1 Asian, non-Hispanic/Latino; 22 Hispanic/Latino; 2 Two or more races, non-Hispanic/Latino), 55 international. Average age 30. 125 applicants, 48% accepted, 26 enrolled. *Faculty:* 18 full-time (1 woman), 1 part-time/adjunct (0 women). Expenses: Contact institution. *Financial support:* In 2016–17, 66 students received support, including 1 fellowship (averaging $4,088 per year), 23 research assistantships (averaging $13,395 per year), 20 teaching assistantships (averaging $11,971 per year); career-related internships or fieldwork, Federal Work-Study, scholarships/grants, traineeships, health care benefits, and unspecified assistantships also available. Support available to part-time students. Financial award application deadline: 3/1. In 2016, 37 master's, 6 doctorates awarded. *Program availability:* Part-time, evening/weekend, 100% online. Offers electrical and computer engineering (MSEE, PhD, Graduate Certificate). *Application deadline:* For fall admission, 3/1 priority date for domestic and international students; for spring admission, 8/1 priority date for domestic and international students. Applications are processed on a rolling basis. *Application fee:* $40 ($50 for international students). Electronic applications accepted. *Application Contact:* 575-646-3115, Fax: 575-646-1435, E-mail: eceoffice@nmsu.edu. *Department Head,* Dr. Satishkuma Ranade, 575-646-3115, Fax: 575-646-1435, E-mail: sranade@nmsu.edu.

College of Health and Social Services Students: 160 full-time (143 women), 150 part-time (109 women); includes 179 minority (22 Black or African American, non-Hispanic/Latino; 6 American Indian or Alaska Native, non-Hispanic/Latino; 10 Asian, non-Hispanic/Latino; 134 Hispanic/Latino; 7 Two or more races, non-Hispanic/Latino), 10 international. Average age 36. 180 applicants, 79% accepted, 84 enrolled. *Faculty:* 34 full-time (27 women), 7 part-time/adjunct (4 women). Expenses: Contact institution. *Financial support:* In 2016–17, 86 students received support, including 1 fellowship (averaging $4,088 per year), 4 research assistantships (averaging $16,022 per year), 24 teaching assistantships (averaging $10,572 per year); career-related internships or fieldwork, Federal Work-Study, scholarships/grants, traineeships, health care benefits, and unspecified assistantships also available. Support available to part-time students. Financial award application deadline: 3/1. In 2016, 90 master's, 17 doctorates, 5 other advanced degrees awarded. *Program availability:* Part-time, evening/weekend, online learning. Offers health and social services (MPH, MSN, MSW, DNP, PhD, Graduate Certificate); public health (MPH, Graduate Certificate). *Application deadline:* For fall admission, 7/1 priority date for domestic students. Applications are processed on a rolling basis. *Application fee:* $40 ($50 for international students). Electronic applications accepted. *Application Contact:* Graduate Admissions, 575-646-3121, E-mail: admissions@nmsu.edu. *Dean,* Dr. Donna Wagner, 575-646-3526, Fax: 575-646-6166, E-mail: dlwagner@nmsu.edu.

School of Nursing Students: 20 full-time (all women), 81 part-time (64 women); includes 51 minority (11 Black or African American, non-Hispanic/Latino; 1 American Indian or Alaska Native, non-Hispanic/Latino; 6 Asian, non-Hispanic/Latino; 32 Hispanic/Latino; 1 Two or more races, non-Hispanic/Latino), 2 international. Average age 43. 48 applicants, 90% accepted, 25 enrolled. *Faculty:* 11 full-time (all women). Expenses: Contact institution. *Financial support:* In 2016–17, 22 students received support, including 6 teaching assistantships (averaging $11,160 per year); career-related internships or fieldwork, Federal Work-Study, scholarships/grants, traineeships, health care benefits, and unspecified assistantships also available. Support available to part-time students. Financial award application deadline: 3/1. In 2016, 13 master's, 17 doctorates awarded. *Program availability:* Blended/hybrid learning. Offers adult/geriatric nursing practitioner (DNP); family nurse practitioner (DNP, Graduate Certificate); family/psychiatric mental health nurse practitioner (DNP, Graduate Certificate); nursing administration (MSN); nursing science (PhD);

public/community health nursing (DNP). *Application deadline:* For fall admission, 1/15 for domestic students; for spring admission, 1/15 priority date for domestic students; for summer admission, 1/15 for domestic students. *Application fee:* $40 ($50 for international students). Electronic applications accepted. *Application Contact:* Dr. Teresa Keller, Director of Graduate Studies, 575-646-4370, Fax: 575-646-2167, E-mail: tkeller@nmsu.edu. *Department Head,* Dr. Kathleen Huttlinger, 575-646-3812, Fax: 575-646-2167, E-mail: khuttlin@nmsu.edu.

School of Social Work Students: 111 full-time (101 women), 19 part-time (11 women); includes 94 minority (6 Black or African American, non-Hispanic/Latino; 3 American Indian or Alaska Native, non-Hispanic/Latino; 2 Asian, non-Hispanic/Latino; 80 Hispanic/Latino; 3 Two or more races, non-Hispanic/Latino), 2 international. Average age 32. 82 applicants, 72% accepted, 49 enrolled. *Faculty:* 12 full-time (10 women), 6 part-time/adjunct (4 women). Expenses: Contact institution. *Financial support:* In 2016–17, 42 students received support, including 9 teaching assistantships (averaging $8,455 per year); career-related internships or fieldwork, Federal Work-Study, scholarships/grants, traineeships, health care benefits, and unspecified assistantships also available. Support available to part-time students. Financial award application deadline: 3/1. In 2016, 64 master's awarded. *Program availability:* Part-time. Offers social work (MSW). *Application deadline:* For fall admission, 1/16 priority date for domestic students, 2/16 priority date for international students. Applications are processed on a rolling basis. *Application fee:* $40 ($50 for international students). Electronic applications accepted. *Application Contact:* Dr. Wanda Whittlesey-Jerome, Coordinator, MSW Program Coordinator, 575-646-0322, Fax: 575-646-4116, E-mail: wkjerome@nmsu.edu. *Interim Department Head,* Dr. Stephen Anderson, 575-646-3043, Fax: 575-646-4116, E-mail: stephean@nmsu.edu.

Graduate School Students: 43 full-time (23 women), 29 part-time (14 women); includes 18 minority (2 Black or African American, non-Hispanic/Latino; 16 Hispanic/Latino), 27 international. Average age 38. 33 applicants, 61% accepted, 9 enrolled. *Faculty:* 5 full-time (0 women). Expenses: Contact institution. *Financial support:* In 2016–17, 43 students received support, including 1 fellowship (averaging $4,088 per year), 7 research assistantships (averaging $20,367 per year), 5 teaching assistantships (averaging $13,894 per year); career-related internships or fieldwork, Federal Work-Study, scholarships/grants, traineeships, health care benefits, and unspecified assistantships also available. Support available to part-time students. Financial award application deadline: 3/1. In 2016, 10 master's, 6 doctorates awarded. *Program availability:* Part-time, evening/weekend, online learning. Offers interdisciplinary studies (MA, MS, PhD); molecular biology (MS, PhD); water science management (MS, PhD). *Application fee:* $40 ($50 for international students). Electronic applications accepted. *Application Contact:* Graduate Admissions, 575-646-3121, E-mail: admissions@nmsu.edu. *Dean,* Dr. Loui Reyes, 575-646-5746, Fax: 575-646-7758, E-mail: gradinfo@nmsu.edu.

NEW ORLEANS BAPTIST THEOLOGICAL SEMINARY, New Orleans, LA 70126-4858

General Information Independent-religious, coed, primarily men, comprehensive institution. *Graduate housing:* Rooms and/or apartments available to single and married students.

GRADUATE UNITS

Graduate and Professional Programs *Program availability:* Evening/weekend. Offers theology (M Div, MA, MACE, MAMFC, MMCM, D Min, DEM, DMA, PhD).

Division of Biblical Studies Offers biblical studies (M Div, MA, PhD).

Division of Christian Education Ministries *Program availability:* Evening/weekend, online learning. Offers Christian education (M Div, MACE, D Min, DEM, PhD).

Division of Church Music Ministries *Program availability:* Online learning. Offers church music ministries (M Div, MMCM, DMA).

Division of Pastoral Ministries *Program availability:* Online learning. Offers pastoral ministries (M Div, MAMFC, D Min, PhD).

Division of Theological and Historical Studies *Program availability:* Online learning. Offers theological and historical studies (M Div, MA, D Min, PhD).

NEW SAINT ANDREWS COLLEGE, Moscow, ID 83843

General Information Independent-religious, coed, comprehensive institution. *Enrollment:* 158 graduate, professional, and undergraduate students; 12 full-time matriculated graduate/professional students (3 women), 8 part-time matriculated graduate/professional students (5 women). *Enrollment by degree level:* 19 master's, 1 other advanced degree. *Graduate faculty:* 12 part-time/adjunct (0 women). *Tuition:* Full-time $7200; part-time $475 per credit. One-time fee: $160. *Graduate housing:* On-campus housing not available. *Student services:* Campus employment opportunities, career counseling, international student services. *Library facilities:* Tyndale Library plus 1 other.

Computer facilities: 4 computers available on campus for general student use. A campuswide network can be accessed from off campus. Online class registration is available.
Website: http://www.nsa.edu/

General Application Contact: Brenda Schlect, Director of Admissions, 208-882-1566 Ext. 113, Fax: 208-882-4293, E-mail: admissions@nsa.edu.

GRADUATE UNITS

Graduate School Students: 12 full-time (3 women), 8 part-time (5 women), 1 international. Average age 25. 15 applicants, 53% accepted, 7 enrolled. *Faculty:* 12 part-time/adjunct (0 women). Expenses: Contact institution. In 2016, 3 master's awarded. *Program availability:* Part-time, blended/hybrid learning. Offers classical Christian studies (Graduate Certificate); theology and letters (MA). *Application deadline:* For fall admission, 12/1 for domestic students. Applications are processed on a rolling basis. *Application fee:* $50. Electronic applications accepted. *Application Contact:* Brenda Schlect, Director of Admissions, 208-882-1566 Ext. 113, Fax: 208-882-4293, E-mail: admissions@nsa.edu. *Academic Dean,* Benjamin Merkle, 208-882-1566 Ext. 104, E-mail: bmerkle@nsa.edu.

THE NEW SCHOOL, New York, NY 10011

General Information Independent, coed, university. *Enrollment by degree level:* 2,563 master's, 484 doctoral, 107 other advanced degrees. *Graduate faculty:* 285 full-time (134 women), 357 part-time/adjunct (167 women). *Tuition:* Full-time $42,610; part-time $1685 per credit. *Required fees:* $276; $138 per semester. Full-time tuition and fees vary according to degree level and program. Part-time tuition and fees vary according to course load and program. *Graduate housing:* Room and/or apartments available on a first-come, first-served basis to single students; on-campus housing not available to married students. Typical cost: $30,404 per year ($30,720 including board). Room and board charges vary according to board plan, campus/location and housing facility selected. Housing application deadline: 6/15. *Student services:* Campus employment

opportunities, campus safety program, career counseling, exercise/wellness program, free psychological counseling, grant writing training, international student services, low-cost health insurance, multicultural affairs office, services for students with disabilities, teacher training, writing training. *Research affiliation:* The Goldman Sachs Group, Inc., Siemens, Raytheon Corporation, National Geospatial-Intelligence Agency, Environmental Systems Research Institute, Dow Jones & Company, Inc.
Website: http://www.newschool.edu/

General Application Contact: Heather Fomin, Assistant Vice President of Enrollment, 212-229-5155 Ext. 3230, E-mail: fominh@newschool.edu.

GRADUATE UNITS

College of Performing Arts Students: 265 full-time (156 women), 36 part-time (19 women); includes 50 minority (10 Black or African American, non-Hispanic/Latino; 17 Asian, non-Hispanic/Latino; 19 Hispanic/Latino; 4 Two or more races, non-Hispanic/Latino), 134 international. Average age 26. 1,026 applicants, 47% accepted, 146 enrolled. *Faculty:* 20 full-time (10 women), 42 part-time/adjunct (22 women). Expenses: Contact institution. *Financial support:* Fellowships, teaching assistantships, career-related internships or fieldwork, Federal Work-Study, scholarships/grants, and unspecified assistantships available. Support available to part-time students. Financial award application deadline: 3/1; financial award applicants required to submit FAFSA. In 2016, 107 master's, 18 other advanced degrees awarded. Offers performing arts (MFA, MM, Advanced Diploma). *Application deadline:* For fall admission, 12/1 priority date for domestic and international students; for spring admission, 11/1 priority date for domestic and international students. Applications are processed on a rolling basis. *Application fee:* $50. Electronic applications accepted. *Application Contact:* Taryn Wolf, Senior Director of Recruitment and Outreach, 212-229-5150, E-mail: copaadmissions@newschool.edu. *Executive Dean, College of Performing Arts,* Richard Kessler, 212-580-0210 Ext. 4848, E-mail: richardkessler@newschool.edu.

Mannes School of Music Students: 206 full-time (124 women), 35 part-time (18 women); includes 38 minority (7 Black or African American, non-Hispanic/Latino; 15 Asian, non-Hispanic/Latino; 12 Hispanic/Latino; 1 Native Hawaiian or other Pacific Islander, non-Hispanic/Latino; 3 Two or more races, non-Hispanic/Latino), 129 international. Average age 25. 835 applicants, 53% accepted, 127 enrolled. *Faculty:* 9 full-time (4 women), 2 part-time/adjunct (0 women). Expenses: Contact institution. *Financial support:* Fellowships, research assistantships, teaching assistantships, Federal Work-Study, scholarships/grants, and unspecified assistantships available. Support available to part-time students. Financial award application deadline: 2/1; financial award applicants required to submit FAFSA. In 2016, 91 master's, 18 Advanced Diplomas awarded. *Program availability:* Part-time. Offers composition (MM, Advanced Diploma); guitar (MM, Advanced Diploma); harpsichord (MM, Advanced Diploma); music theory (MM); orchestral conducting (MM, Advanced Diploma); orchestral instruments (MM, Advanced Diploma); piano (MM, Advanced Diploma); piano and collaborative piano (MM, Advanced Diploma); theory (Advanced Diploma); voice (MM, Advanced Diploma). *Application deadline:* For fall admission, 1/15 priority date for domestic and international students; for spring admission, 11/1 priority date for domestic and international students. Applications are processed on a rolling basis. *Application fee:* $50. Electronic applications accepted. *Application Contact:* Taryn Wolf, Senior Director of Recruitment and Outreach, 212-229-5150 Ext. 3007, E-mail: performingarts@newschool.edu. *Executive Dean, College of Performing Arts,* Richard Kessler, 212-580-0210 Ext. 4848, E-mail: richardkessler@newschool.edu.

School of Drama Students: 59 full-time (32 women), 1 (woman) part-time; includes 13 minority (3 Black or African American, non-Hispanic/Latino; 2 Asian, non-Hispanic/Latino; 7 Hispanic/Latino; 1 Two or more races, non-Hispanic/Latino), 5 international. Average age 27. 226 applicants, 17% accepted, 19 enrolled. *Faculty:* 35 part-time/adjunct (19 women). Expenses: Contact institution. *Financial support:* Fellowships, teaching assistantships, career-related internships or fieldwork, Federal Work-Study, scholarships/grants, and unspecified assistantships available. Support available to part-time students. Financial award application deadline: 2/1; financial award applicants required to submit FAFSA. In 2016, 16 master's awarded. *Program availability:* Part-time. Offers acting (MFA); directing (MFA); playwriting (MFA). *Application deadline:* For fall admission, 1/10 priority date for domestic and international students. Applications are processed on a rolling basis. *Application fee:* $50. Electronic applications accepted. *Application Contact:* Taryn Wolf, Senior Director of Recruitment and Outreach, 212-229-5150 Ext. 3007, E-mail: wolft@newschool.edu. *Dean, School of Drama,* Pippin Parker, 212-229-5859 Ext. 2636, E-mail: parkerp@newschool.edu.

The New School for Social Research Students: 606 full-time (309 women), 184 part-time (107 women); includes 116 minority (24 Black or African American, non-Hispanic/Latino; 1 American Indian or Alaska Native, non-Hispanic/Latino; 24 Asian, non-Hispanic/Latino; 48 Hispanic/Latino; 19 Two or more races, non-Hispanic/Latino), 266 international. Average age 31. 979 applicants, 76% accepted, 161 enrolled. *Faculty:* 50 full-time (18 women), 12 part-time/adjunct (4 women). Expenses: Contact institution. *Financial support:* Fellowships, research assistantships, teaching assistantships, career-related internships or fieldwork, Federal Work-Study, scholarships/grants, and tuition waivers (full and partial) available. Support available to part-time students. Financial award application deadline: 3/1; financial award applicants required to submit FAFSA. In 2016, 195 master's, 57 doctorates awarded. *Program availability:* Part-time. Offers anthropology (M Phil, MA, PhD); clinical psychology (PhD); cognitive, social, and developmental psychology (PhD); economics (M Phil, MA, MS, PhD); global political economy and finance (MA); historical studies (PhD); liberal studies (MA); philosophy (M Phil, MA); politics (M Phil, MA, PhD); psychoanalysis (MA); psychology (MA); social research (M Phil, MA, MS, PhD); sociology (MA). *Application deadline:* For fall admission, 8/1 priority date for domestic students, 6/1 priority date for international students; for spring admission, 10/15 priority date for domestic and international students. Applications are processed on a rolling basis. *Application fee:* $50. Electronic applications accepted. *Application Contact:* Dana Messinger, Director of Graduate Admission, 212-229-5150 Ext. 2300, E-mail: messingd@newschool.edu. *Dean,* Dr. William Milberg, 212-229-5777, E-mail: milbergw@newschool.edu.

Parsons Paris Students: 27 full-time (22 women), 1 (woman) part-time; includes 6 minority (1 Black or African American, non-Hispanic/Latino; 2 Asian, non-Hispanic/Latino; 1 Hispanic/Latino; 2 Two or more races, non-Hispanic/Latino), 16 international. Average age 27. 46 applicants, 96% accepted, 16 enrolled. *Faculty:* 5 full-time (2 women), 43 part-time/adjunct (26 women). Expenses: Contact institution. *Financial support:* Scholarships/grants available. Financial award applicants required to submit FAFSA. In 2016, 5 master's awarded. *Program availability:* Part-time. Offers art and design (MA); fashion studies (MA); history of design and curatorial studies (MA). *Application deadline:* Applications are processed on a rolling basis. *Application fee:* $50. Electronic applications accepted. *Application Contact:* Mike Fakih, Director of

Admissions, Parsons Paris, 33 176 21 76 67, E-mail: thinkparsonsparis@newschool.edu. *Dean*, Prof. Susan Taylor-Leduc, 33-176217661, E-mail: leducs@newschool.edu.

Parsons School of Design Students: 839 full-time (619 women), 91 part-time (71 women); includes 170 minority (41 Black or African American, non-Hispanic/Latino; 2 American Indian or Alaska Native, non-Hispanic/Latino; 50 Asian, non-Hispanic/Latino; 59 Hispanic/Latino; 2 Native Hawaiian or other Pacific Islander, non-Hispanic/Latino; 16 Two or more races, non-Hispanic/Latino), 513 international. Average age 27. 1,943 applicants, 56% accepted, 458 enrolled. *Faculty:* 161 full-time (83 women), 179 part-time/adjunct (91 women). Expenses: Contact institution. *Financial support:* Research assistantships, teaching assistantships, career-related internships or fieldwork, Federal Work-Study, scholarships/grants, unspecified assistantships, and travel funding; tuition waivers for students who are also New School employees available. Support available to part-time students. Financial award application deadline: 2/1; financial award applicants required to submit FAFSA. In 2016, 406 master's, 5 other advanced degrees awarded. Offers architecture (M Arch); business of design (Advanced Certificate); data visualization (MS); design (M Arch, MA, MFA, MS, Advanced Certificate); design and technology (MFA); design and urban ecologies (MS); design studies (MFA); fashion design and society (MFA); fashion studies (MA); fine arts (MFA); history of design and curatorial studies (MA); industrial design (MFA); interior design (MFA); lighting design (MFA); photography (MFA); strategic design management (MS); theories of urban practice (MA); transdisciplinary design (MFA). *Application deadline:* For fall admission, 1/1 for domestic and international students. Applications are processed on a rolling basis. *Application fee:* $50. Electronic applications accepted. *Application Contact:* Courtney Malenius, Director of Graduate Admission, 212-229-5150 Ext. 4011, E-mail: thinkparsonsgrad@newschool.edu. *Executive Dean, Parsons School of Design*, Joel Towers, 212-229-8950 Ext. 4393, E-mail: towersj@newschool.edu.

Schools of Public Engagement Students: 737 full-time (519 women), 396 part-time (270 women); includes 391 minority (149 Black or African American, non-Hispanic/Latino; 3 American Indian or Alaska Native, non-Hispanic/Latino; 57 Asian, non-Hispanic/Latino; 146 Hispanic/Latino; 1 Native Hawaiian or other Pacific Islander, non-Hispanic/Latino; 35 Two or more races, non-Hispanic/Latino), 265 international. Average age 30. 1,254 applicants, 85% accepted, 374 enrolled. *Faculty:* 59 full-time (28 women), 123 part-time/adjunct (50 women). Expenses: Contact institution. *Financial support:* Fellowships, research assistantships, teaching assistantships, career-related internships or fieldwork, Federal Work-Study, scholarships/grants, and unspecified assistantships available. Support available to part-time students. Financial award application deadline: 2/1; financial award applicants required to submit FAFSA. In 2016, 564 master's, 6 doctorates, 46 other advanced degrees awarded. *Program availability:* Part-time, online learning. Offers creative writing (MFA); documentary media studies (Graduate Certificate); environmental policy and sustainability management (MS); international affairs (MA, MS); leadership and change (Graduate Certificate); media management (MS, Graduate Certificate); media studies (MA); nonprofit management (MS); organizational change management (MS); organizational development (Graduate Certificate); public and urban policy (PhD); public engagement (MA, MFA, MS, PhD, Certificate, Graduate Certificate); sustainability strategies (Certificate); teaching English to speakers of other languages (MA); urban policy analysis and management (MS). *Application deadline:* For fall admission, 1/15 priority date for domestic and international students; for spring admission, 10/15 priority date for domestic and international students. Applications are processed on a rolling basis. *Application fee:* $50. Electronic applications accepted. *Application Contact:* Merida Gasbarro, Senior Director of Admissions, 212-229-5150 Ext. 3230, E-mail: escandom@newschool.edu. *Executive Dean, Schools of Public Engagement*, Mary Watson, 212-229-5613 Ext. 2130, E-mail: watsonm@newschool.edu.

NEWSCHOOL OF ARCHITECTURE AND DESIGN, San Diego, CA 92101-6634

General Information Proprietary, coed, primarily men, comprehensive institution. *Research affiliation:* Academy of Neuroscience for Architecture (neuroscience and architecture).

GRADUATE UNITS

Program in Architecture *Program availability:* Part-time, online learning. Offers architecture (M Arch, MS).

Program in Construction Management *Program availability:* Part-time, online learning. Offers construction management (MCM). Electronic applications accepted.

NEW YORK ACADEMY OF ART, New York, NY 10013-2911

General Information Independent, coed, graduate-only institution. *Enrollment by degree level:* 109 master's, 10 other advanced degrees. *Graduate faculty:* 5 full-time (1 woman), 31 part-time/adjunct (13 women). *Tuition:* Full-time $37,436; part-time $1248 per credit hour. *Required fees:* $1500; $750 per degree program. Tuition and fees vary according to student level. *Graduate housing:* On-campus housing not available. *Student services:* Campus employment opportunities, campus safety program, career counseling, grant writing training, international student services, services for students with disabilities. *Library facilities:* New York Academy of Art Library. *Collection:* Books: 9,937 (physical); Serial titles: 6 (digital/electronic); Databases: 37. Weekly public service hours: 65.

Computer facilities: 12 computers available on campus for general student use. Online class registration, X are available.
Website: http://www.nyaa.edu/

General Application Contact: Jessica Augier, Admissions Officer, 212-842-5972, E-mail: admissions@nyaa.edu.

GRADUATE UNITS

Master of Fine Arts Program Students: 119 full-time (76 women); includes 22 minority (4 Black or African American, non-Hispanic/Latino; 1 American Indian or Alaska Native, non-Hispanic/Latino; 4 Asian, non-Hispanic/Latino; 8 Hispanic/Latino; 2 Native Hawaiian or other Pacific Islander, non-Hispanic/Latino; 3 Two or more races, non-Hispanic/Latino), 33 international. Average age 30. 115 applicants, 77% accepted, 55 enrolled. *Faculty:* 5 full-time (1 woman), 31 part-time/adjunct (13 women). Expenses: Contact institution. *Financial support:* In 2016–17, 92 students received support, including 3 fellowships (averaging $10,000 per year); career-related internships or fieldwork, Federal Work-Study, and scholarships/grants also available. Financial award application deadline: 9/1; financial award applicants required to submit FAFSA. In 2016, 49 master's awarded. Offers drawing (MFA); painting (MFA); sculpture (MFA). *Application deadline:* For fall admission, 1/17 priority date for domestic and international students. *Application fee:* $80. Electronic applications accepted. *Application Contact:* Katie Hemmer, Director of Admissions/Registrar, 212-842-5961, E-mail: khemmer@nyaa.edu. *President*, David Kratz, 212-966-0300.

NEW YORK CHIROPRACTIC COLLEGE, Seneca Falls, NY 13148-0800

General Information Independent, coed, graduate-only institution. *Graduate housing:* Rooms and/or apartments available on a first-come, first-served basis to single and married students. *Research affiliation:* Foot Levelers, Inc. (orthotics research), Atrium Innovations (nutrition), Nimmo Education Foundation (muscle physiology).

GRADUATE UNITS

Doctor of Chiropractic Program Offers chiropractic (DC). Electronic applications accepted.

Finger Lakes School of Acupuncture and Oriental Medicine Offers acupuncture (MS); acupuncture and Oriental medicine (MS). Electronic applications accepted.

Program in Applied Clinical Nutrition *Program availability:* Part-time, evening/weekend. Offers applied clinical nutrition (MS). Electronic applications accepted.

Program in Clinical Anatomy Offers clinical anatomy (MS). Electronic applications accepted.

Program in Human Anatomy and Physiology Instruction *Program availability:* Online learning. Offers human anatomy and physiology (MS).

NEW YORK COLLEGE OF HEALTH PROFESSIONS, Syosset, NY 11791-4413

General Information Independent, coed, comprehensive institution. *Graduate housing:* On-campus housing not available. *Research affiliation:* North Shore Hospital (acupuncture).

GRADUATE UNITS

Graduate School of Oriental Medicine *Program availability:* Part-time. Offers acupuncture (MS); Oriental medicine (MS).

NEW YORK COLLEGE OF PODIATRIC MEDICINE, New York, NY 10035

General Information Independent, coed, graduate-only institution. *Graduate housing:* Rooms and/or apartments available on a first-come, first-served basis to single and married students. Housing application deadline: 8/15. *Research affiliation:* Cyberlogics (ultrasound use), Novartis Pharmaceuticals (fungal diseases of nail), Prescription Dispensing Laboratories (topical verapamil), Anodyne Corporation (light energy applications).

GRADUATE UNITS

Professional Program Offers podiatric medicine (DPM).

NEW YORK COLLEGE OF TRADITIONAL CHINESE MEDICINE, Mineola, NY 11501

General Information Independent, coed, graduate-only institution. *Enrollment by degree level:* 180 master's, 4 other advanced degrees. *Graduate faculty:* 30.
Website: http://www.nyctcm.edu

General Application Contact: Lynn Bai, Admissions Manager, 516-739-1545 Ext. 23, Fax: 516-873-9622, E-mail: admissions@nyctcm.edu.

GRADUATE UNITS

Graduate Programs Students: 184. *Faculty:* 30. Expenses: Contact institution. Offers Oriental medicine (MAOM). *Application deadline:* For fall admission, 3/31 for domestic students. *Application fee:* $70 ($170 for international students). *Application Contact:* Lynn Bai, Admissions Manager, 516-739-1545 Ext. 23, Fax: 516-873-9622, E-mail: admissions@nyctcm.edu. *Administrative Dean*, Jim Bare, 516-739-1545 Ext. 216, Fax: 516-873-9622, E-mail: admin_dean@nyctcm.edu.

NEW YORK FILM ACADEMY, Burbank, CA 91505

General Information Independent, coed, comprehensive institution.

GRADUATE UNITS

Program in Filmmaking–Los Angeles Offers acting for film (MFA); cinematography (MFA); documentary film (MFA); film and media production (MFA); game design (MFA); photography (MFA); producing (MA, MFA); screenwriting (MA, MFA).

Program in Filmmaking–South Beach, Florida Offers acting for film (MFA); cinematography (MFA); documentary film (MFA); film and media production (MA); filmmaking (MFA); game design (MFA); photography (MFA); producing (MA, MFA); screenwriting (MA, MFA).

NEW YORK INSTITUTE OF TECHNOLOGY, Old Westbury, NY 11568-8000

General Information Independent, coed, university. *Enrollment:* 7,662 graduate, professional, and undergraduate students; 3,158 full-time matriculated graduate/professional students (1,525 women), 865 part-time matriculated graduate/professional students (458 women). *Enrollment by degree level:* 2,463 master's, 1,473 doctoral, 87 other advanced degrees. *Graduate faculty:* 177 full-time (66 women), 210 part-time/adjunct (81 women). *Tuition:* Full-time $21,870; part-time $1215 per credit. *Required fees:* $100; $80 per term. Full-time tuition and fees vary according to degree level, campus/location and program. Part-time tuition and fees vary according to course load, campus/location and program. *Graduate housing:* Room and/or apartments available on a first-come, first-served basis to single students; on-campus housing not available to married students. Typical cost: $8790 per year ($13,570 including board). Room and board charges vary according to board plan, campus/location and housing facility selected. *Student services:* Campus employment opportunities, campus safety program, career counseling, exercise/wellness program, free psychological counseling, international student services, low-cost health insurance, services for students with disabilities, writing training. *Library facilities:* George and Gertrude Wisser Memorial Library plus 3 others. *Collection:* Books: 177,496 (physical), 64,280 (digital/electronic); Serial titles: 424 (physical), 80,477 (digital/electronic); Databases: 200. Weekly public service hours: 78; students can reserve study rooms.

Computer facilities: 1,250 computers available on campus for general student use. A campuswide network can be accessed from student residence rooms and from off campus. Online class registration is available.
Website: http://www.nyit.edu/

General Application Contact: Alice Dolitsky, Director, Graduate Admissions, 516-686-7520, Fax: 516-686-1116, E-mail: nyitgrad@nyit.edu.

GRADUATE UNITS

College of Arts and Sciences Students: 156 full-time (99 women), 63 part-time (35 women); includes 22 minority (12 Black or African American, non-Hispanic/Latino; 2

Asian, non-Hispanic/Latino; 8 Hispanic/Latino), 160 international. Average age 26. 129 applicants, 79% accepted, 45 enrolled. *Faculty:* 17 full-time (8 women), 24 part-time/adjunct (9 women). Expenses: Contact institution. *Financial support:* Career-related internships or fieldwork, Federal Work-Study, scholarships/grants, tuition waivers (full and partial), and unspecified assistantships available. Support available to part-time students. Financial award application deadline: 3/1; financial award applicants required to submit FAFSA. In 2016, 102 master's awarded. *Program availability:* Part-time, evening/weekend. Offers arts and sciences (MA, MFA); communication arts (MA); computer graphics (MFA). *Application deadline:* For fall admission, 6/1 for domestic and international students. Applications are processed on a rolling basis. *Application fee:* $50. Electronic applications accepted. *Application Contact:* Alice Dolitsky, Director, Graduate Admissions, 516-686-1316, Fax: 516-686-1116, E-mail: nyitgrad@nyit.edu. *Dean*, Dr. Jim Simon, 516-686-7665, E-mail: james.simon@nyit.edu.

College of Osteopathic Medicine Students: 1,354 full-time (659 women); includes 584 minority (41 Black or African American, non-Hispanic/Latino; 498 Asian, non-Hispanic/Latino; 30 Hispanic/Latino; 1 Native Hawaiian or other Pacific Islander, non-Hispanic/Latino; 14 Two or more races, non-Hispanic/Latino). Average age 27. 6,515 applicants, 7% accepted, 272 enrolled. *Faculty:* 69 full-time, 24 part-time/adjunct. Expenses: Contact institution. *Financial support:* Federal Work-Study and scholarships/grants available. Financial award application deadline: 3/1; financial award applicants required to submit FAFSA. In 2016, 16 master's, 298 doctorates awarded. Offers medical/healthcare simulation (MS); osteopathic medicine (DO). *Application deadline:* For fall admission, 2/1 for domestic students. Applications are processed on a rolling basis. *Application fee:* $80. Electronic applications accepted. *Application Contact:* Gina Moses, Director, Admissions, 516-686-3997, E-mail: gmoses@nyit.edu. *Dean*, Dr. Wolfgang Gilliar, 516-686-3722, Fax: 516-686-3830, E-mail: wgilliar@nyit.edu.

School of Architecture and Design Students: 20 full-time (14 women), all international. Average age 26. 55 applicants, 25% accepted, 9 enrolled. *Faculty:* 3 full-time (1 woman), 3 part-time/adjunct (0 women). Expenses: Contact institution. *Financial support:* Career-related internships or fieldwork, Federal Work-Study, institutionally sponsored loans, scholarships/grants, tuition waivers (full and partial), and unspecified assistantships available. Support available to part-time students. Financial award application deadline: 3/1; financial award applicants required to submit FAFSA. In 2016, 7 master's awarded. *Program availability:* Part-time. Offers architecture, urban and regional design (MS). *Application deadline:* For fall admission, 3/1 for domestic and international students. Applications are processed on a rolling basis. *Application fee:* $50. Electronic applications accepted. *Application Contact:* Alice Dolitsky, Director, Graduate Admissions, 516-686-7520, Fax: 516-686-1116, E-mail: nyitgrad@nyit.edu. *Graduate Director*, Jeffrey Raven, 212-261-1547, E-mail: jraven@nyit.edu.

School of Engineering and Computing Sciences Students: 798 full-time (254 women), 320 part-time (77 women); includes 93 minority (25 Black or African American, non-Hispanic/Latino; 1 American Indian or Alaska Native, non-Hispanic/Latino; 41 Asian, non-Hispanic/Latino; 25 Hispanic/Latino; 1 Two or more races, non-Hispanic/Latino), 949 international. Average age 25. 2,577 applicants, 64% accepted, 283 enrolled. *Faculty:* 26 full-time (6 women), 38 part-time/adjunct (3 women). Expenses: Contact institution. *Financial support:* Fellowships with partial tuition reimbursements, teaching assistantships with partial tuition reimbursements, career-related internships or fieldwork, Federal Work-Study, scholarships/grants, tuition waivers (full and partial), and unspecified assistantships available. Support available to part-time students. Financial award application deadline: 3/1; financial award applicants required to submit FAFSA. In 2016, 614 master's awarded. *Program availability:* Part-time, evening/weekend, 100% online, blended/hybrid learning. Offers computer science (MS); electrical and computer engineering (MS); energy management (MS); energy technology (Advanced Certificate); engineering and computing sciences (MS, Advanced Certificate); environmental management (Advanced Certificate); environmental technology and sustainability (MS); facilities management (Advanced Certificate); information, network, and computer security (MS); infrastructure security management (Advanced Certificate). *Application deadline:* For fall admission, 7/1 for domestic students, 6/1 for international students; for spring admission, 12/1 for domestic and international students. Applications are processed on a rolling basis. *Application fee:* $50. Electronic applications accepted. *Application Contact:* Alice Dolitsky, Director, Graduate Admissions, 516-686-7520, Fax: 516-686-1116, E-mail: nyitgrad@nyit.edu. *Dean*, Dr. Nada Anid, 516-686-7931, Fax: 516-625-7933, E-mail: nanid@nyit.edu.

School of Health Professions Students: 362 full-time (263 women), 51 part-time (44 women); includes 127 minority (21 Black or African American, non-Hispanic/Latino; 62 Asian, non-Hispanic/Latino; 35 Hispanic/Latino; 1 Native Hawaiian or other Pacific Islander, non-Hispanic/Latino; 8 Two or more races, non-Hispanic/Latino), 2 international. Average age 25. 3,045 applicants, 9% accepted, 160 enrolled. *Faculty:* 23 full-time (15 women), 25 part-time/adjunct (16 women). Expenses: Contact institution. *Financial support:* Career-related internships or fieldwork, Federal Work-Study, scholarships/grants, tuition waivers (full and partial), and unspecified assistantships available. Support available to part-time students. Financial award application deadline: 3/1; financial award applicants required to submit FAFSA. In 2016, 94 master's, 36 doctorates awarded. *Program availability:* Part-time, evening/weekend, 100% online. Offers clinical nutrition (MS); health professions (MS, DPT); occupational therapy (MS); physical therapy (DPT); physician assistant studies (MS). *Application fee:* $50. Electronic applications accepted. *Application Contact:* Alice Dolitsky, Director, Graduate Admissions, 516-686-7520, Fax: 516-686-1116, E-mail: nyitgrad@nyit.edu. *Dean*, Dr. Sheldon Fields, 516-686-3939, E-mail: shp@nyit.edu.

School of Interdisciplinary Studies and Education Students: 58 full-time (48 women), 284 part-time (210 women); includes 95 minority (33 Black or African American, non-Hispanic/Latino; 1 American Indian or Alaska Native, non-Hispanic/Latino; 13 Asian, non-Hispanic/Latino; 42 Hispanic/Latino; 6 Two or more races, non-Hispanic/Latino), 4 international. Average age 33. 247 applicants, 74% accepted, 135 enrolled. *Faculty:* 12 full-time (7 women), 19 part-time/adjunct (11 women). Expenses: Contact institution. *Financial support:* Career-related internships or fieldwork, Federal Work-Study, scholarships/grants, tuition waivers (full and partial), and unspecified assistantships available. Support available to part-time students. Financial award application deadline: 3/1; financial award applicants required to submit FAFSA. In 2016, 76 master's, 13 other advanced degrees awarded. *Program availability:* Part-time, evening/weekend, 100% online, blended/hybrid learning. Offers adolescence education (MS); arts and entertainment leadership (Advanced Certificate); childhood education (MS); early childhood (MS); emerging technologies for trainers (Advanced Certificate); instructional design for global e-learning (Advanced Certificate); instructional technology (MS); interdisciplinary studies and education (MA, MS, Advanced Certificate, Advanced Diploma); leadership in the arts and entertainment industries (MA); school counseling (MS); school leadership and technology (Advanced Diploma); STEM education (Advanced Certificate); student behavior management (Advanced Certificate). *Application deadline:* Applications are processed on a rolling basis. *Application fee:* $50. Electronic applications accepted. *Application Contact:* Alice Dolitsky, Director, Graduate

Admissions, 516-686-7520, Fax: 516-686-1116, E-mail: nyitgrad@nyit.edu. *Interim Dean*, Dr. Jess Boronico, 516-686-7403, E-mail: soeinfo@nyit.edu.

School of Management Students: 410 full-time (188 women), 172 part-time (110 women); includes 60 minority (17 Black or African American, non-Hispanic/Latino; 1 American Indian or Alaska Native, non-Hispanic/Latino; 28 Asian, non-Hispanic/Latino; 11 Hispanic/Latino; 2 Native Hawaiian or other Pacific Islander, non-Hispanic/Latino; 1 Two or more races, non-Hispanic/Latino), 446 international. Average age 26. 873 applicants, 68% accepted, 235 enrolled. *Faculty:* 30 full-time (5 women), 24 part-time/adjunct (7 women). Expenses: Contact institution. *Financial support:* Career-related internships or fieldwork, Federal Work-Study, scholarships/grants, tuition waivers (full and partial), and unspecified assistantships available. Support available to part-time students. Financial award application deadline: 3/1; financial award applicants required to submit FAFSA. In 2016, 215 master's, 1 other advanced degree awarded. *Program availability:* Part-time, evening/weekend. Offers executive (MBA); human resource management (Advanced Certificate); human resource management and labor relations (MS); management (MBA, MS, Advanced Certificate); professional accounting (MBA). *Application deadline:* Applications are processed on a rolling basis. *Application fee:* $50. Electronic applications accepted. *Application Contact:* Alice Dolitsky, Director, Graduate Admissions, 516-686-7520, Fax: 516-686-1116, E-mail: nyitgrad@nyit.edu. *Dean*, Dr. Jess Boronico, 516-686-7838, Fax: 516-686-7430, E-mail: jboronic@nyit.edu.

NEW YORK LAW SCHOOL, New York, NY 10013

General Information Independent, coed, graduate-only institution. *Enrollment by degree level:* 27 master's, 863 doctoral. *Graduate faculty:* 59 full-time (27 women), 63 part-time/adjunct (16 women). *Tuition:* Full-time $47,600; part-time $36,680 per year. *Required fees:* $1640; $1200 per unit. Tuition and fees vary according to course load and degree level. *Graduate housing:* Room and/or apartments available on a first-come, first-served basis to single students; on-campus housing not available to married students. Typical cost: $22,200 per year. Room charges vary according to housing facility selected. Housing application deadline: 7/1. *Student services:* Campus employment opportunities, campus safety program, career counseling, exercise/wellness program, free psychological counseling, international student services, low-cost health insurance, multicultural affairs office, services for students with disabilities, writing training. *Library facilities:* Mendik Library. *Collection:* Books: 281,237 (physical), 246,854 (digital/electronic); Serial titles: 5,461 (physical), 247,568 (digital/electronic); Databases: 137. Weekly public service hours: 93.

Computer facilities: 64 computers available on campus for general student use. A campuswide network can be accessed from off campus. Online class registration is available.
Website: http://www.nyls.edu/

General Application Contact: Ella Mae Estrada, Associate Dean for Enrollment Management, Financial Aid and Diversity Initiatives, 212-431-2888, Fax: 212-966-1522, E-mail: admissions@nyls.edu.

GRADUATE UNITS

Graduate Programs Students: 633 full-time (379 women), 257 part-time (127 women); includes 308 minority (69 Black or African American, non-Hispanic/Latino; 66 Asian, non-Hispanic/Latino; 143 Hispanic/Latino; 30 Two or more races, non-Hispanic/Latino), 35 international. Average age 27. 2,694 applicants, 56% accepted, 326 enrolled. *Faculty:* 59 full-time (27 women), 63 part-time/adjunct (16 women). Expenses: Contact institution. *Financial support:* In 2016–17, 698 students received support, including 100 fellowships (averaging $3,010 per year), 22 research assistantships (averaging $4,663 per year), 19 teaching assistantships (averaging $4,661 per year); career-related internships or fieldwork, Federal Work-Study, and scholarships/grants also available. Support available to part-time students. Financial award application deadline: 7/1; financial award applicants required to submit FAFSA. In 2016, 20 master's, 304 doctorates awarded. *Program availability:* Part-time, evening/weekend. Offers law (LL M, JD). JD/MBA offered jointly with Baruch College of the City University of New York; JD/MA in forensic psychology offered jointly with John Jay College of Criminal Justice of the City University of New York. *Application deadline:* For fall admission, 7/1 priority date for domestic and international students; for winter admission, 11/15 priority date for domestic and international students. Applications are processed on a rolling basis. *Application fee:* $0. Electronic applications accepted. *Application Contact:* Ella Mae Estrada, Associate Dean for Enrollment Management, Financial Aid and Diversity Initiatives, 212-431-2888, Fax: 212-966-1522, E-mail: admissions@nyls.edu. *Dean and President*, Anthony W. Crowell, 212-431-2840, Fax: 212-219-3752, E-mail: acrowell@nyls.edu.

NEW YORK MEDICAL COLLEGE, Valhalla, NY 10595

General Information Independent, coed, graduate-only institution. CGS member. *Enrollment by degree level:* 411 master's, 1,028 doctoral, 29 other advanced degrees. *Graduate faculty:* 1,066 full-time (421 women), 1,494 part-time/adjunct (562 women). *Tuition:* Full-time $44,937; part-time $1070 per credit. *Required fees:* $500; $105 per year. One-time fee: $150. Tuition and fees vary according to course load and program. *Graduate housing:* Rooms and/or apartments available on a first-come, first-served basis to single and married students. Typical cost: $10,900 per year for single students; $17,720 per year for married students. Room charges vary according to housing facility selected. Housing application deadline: 7/15. *Student services:* Campus employment opportunities, career counseling, exercise/wellness program, free psychological counseling, international student services, low-cost health insurance, multicultural affairs office, services for students with disabilities. *Library facilities:* Health Sciences Library plus 1 other. *Collection:* Books: 44,311 (physical), 147,979 (digital/electronic); Serial titles: 58,654 (physical), 19,979 (digital/electronic); Databases: 121. Weekly public service hours: 75; study areas open 24 hours, 5–7 days a week; students can reserve study rooms. *Research affiliation:* Touro College & University System (biomedical research), Westchester Medical Center (biomedical research), Metropolitan Hospital (biomedical research), Westchester Institute for Human Development (biomedical research), Columbia University College of Physicians and Surgeons (neurosciences), Seattle Children's Hospital (pediatric pulmonary disease).

Computer facilities: 19 computers available on campus for general student use. A campuswide network can be accessed. Online class registration is available.
Website: http://www.nymc.edu/

General Application Contact: Pamela Suett, Director of Recruitment, School of Health Sciences and Practice, 914-594-4510, Fax: 914-594-4292, E-mail: shsp_admissions@nymc.edu.

GRADUATE UNITS

Graduate School of Basic Medical Sciences Students: 116 full-time (66 women), 27 part-time (14 women); includes 61 minority (22 Black or African American, non-Hispanic/Latino; 1 American Indian or Alaska Native, non-Hispanic/Latino; 18 Asian, non-Hispanic/Latino; 18 Hispanic/Latino; 2 Two or more races, non-Hispanic/Latino), 24 international. Average age 26. 279 applicants, 50% accepted, 58 enrolled. Expenses: Contact institution. *Financial support:* Fellowships, research assistantships, Federal Work-Study, institutionally sponsored loans, scholarships/grants, tuition waivers (full), and health benefits (for PhD candidates only) available. Support available to part-time students. Financial award applicants required to submit FAFSA. In 2016, 42 master's, 6 doctorates awarded. *Program availability:* Part-time, evening/weekend. Offers biochemistry and molecular biology (MS, PhD); cell biology (MS, PhD); microbiology and immunology (MS, PhD); pathology (MS, PhD); pharmacology (MS, PhD); physiology (MS, PhD). *Application deadline:* For fall admission, 7/1 priority date for domestic students, 5/1 priority date for international students; for spring admission, 12/1 priority date for domestic students, 9/15 priority date for international students. Applications are processed on a rolling basis. *Application fee:* $135. Electronic applications accepted. *Application Contact:* Valerie Romeo-Messana, Director of Admissions, 914-594-4110, Fax: 914-594-4944, E-mail: v_romeomessana@nymc.edu. *Dean,* Dr. Francis L. Belloni, 914-594-4110, Fax: 914-594-4944, E-mail: francis_belloni@nymc.edu.

School of Health Sciences and Practice Students: 235 full-time (165 women), 252 part-time (185 women); includes 188 minority (83 Black or African American, non-Hispanic/Latino; 1 American Indian or Alaska Native, non-Hispanic/Latino; 62 Asian, non-Hispanic/Latino; 36 Hispanic/Latino; 6 Two or more races, non-Hispanic/Latino; 26 international. Average age 27. *Faculty:* 42 full-time (31 women), 236 part-time/adjunct (138 women). Expenses: Contact institution. In 2016, 110 master's, 37 doctorates awarded. *Program availability:* Part-time, evening/weekend, 100% online, blended/hybrid learning. Offers behavioral sciences and health promotion (MPH); biostatistics (MS); children with special health care (Graduate Certificate); emergency preparedness (Graduate Certificate); environmental health science (MPH); epidemiology (MPH, MS); global health (Graduate Certificate); health education (Graduate Certificate); health policy and management (MPH, Dr PH); industrial hygiene (Graduate Certificate); pediatric dysphagia (Post-Graduate Certificate); physical therapy (DPT); public health (Graduate Certificate); speech-language pathology (MS). *Application Contact:* Veronica Jarek-Prinz, Associate Dean for Admissions and Enrollment Management, 914-594-3941, E-mail: veronica_jarekprinz@nymc.edu. *Vice Dean,* Ben Watson, PhD, 914-594-4531, E-mail: ben_watson@nymc.edu.

School of Medicine Students: 844 full-time (428 women); includes 380 minority (73 Black or African American, non-Hispanic/Latino; 1 American Indian or Alaska Native, non-Hispanic/Latino; 198 Asian, non-Hispanic/Latino; 91 Hispanic/Latino; 17 Two or more races, non-Hispanic/Latino), 8 international. Average age 27. 12,738 applicants, 5% accepted, 213 enrolled. *Faculty:* 1,024 full-time (390 women), 1,258 part-time/adjunct (424 women). Expenses: Contact institution. *Financial support:* In 2016–17, 390 students received support. Federal Work-Study, scholarships/grants, and health care benefits available. Support available to part-time students. Financial award application deadline: 4/30; financial award applicants required to submit FAFSA. In 2016, 193 doctorates awarded. Offers medicine (MD). *Application deadline:* For fall admission, 1/31 for domestic and international students. Applications are processed on a rolling basis. *Application fee:* $120. Electronic applications accepted. *Application Contact:* Fern Juster, MD, Associate Dean of Admissions, 914-594-4507, Fax: 914-594-4613, E-mail: mdadmit@nymc.edu. *Senior Associate Dean for Medical Education,* Jennifer Koestler, MD, 914-594-4500, E-mail: jennifer_koestler@nymc.edu.

NEW YORK SCHOOL OF INTERIOR DESIGN, New York, NY 10021-5110

General Information Independent, coed, primarily women, comprehensive institution. *Graduate housing:* Room and/or apartments available on a first-come, first-served basis to single students; on-campus housing not available to married students. Housing application deadline: 5/1. *Research affiliation:* Metropolitan New York Library Council-Research Consortium.

GRADUATE UNITS

Program in Healthcare Interior Design Offers healthcare interior design (MPS). Electronic applications accepted.

Program in Interior Design (Post-Professional Level) Offers interior design (MFA). Electronic applications accepted.

Program in Interior Design (Professional-Level) Offers interior design (MFA). Electronic applications accepted.

Program in Interior Lighting Design Offers interior lighting design (MPS). Electronic applications accepted.

Program in Sustainable Interior Environments Offers sustainable interior environments (MPS). Electronic applications accepted.

NEW YORK STUDIO SCHOOL OF DRAWING, PAINTING AND SCULPTURE, New York, NY 10011

General Information Independent, coed, comprehensive institution.

GRADUATE UNITS

Certificate Program Offers studio art (Certificate).

MFA Program Offers painting (MFA); sculpture (MFA).

NEW YORK THEOLOGICAL SEMINARY, New York, NY 10115

General Information Independent-religious, coed, graduate-only institution. *Graduate housing:* On-campus housing not available. *Research affiliation:* Bellevue Hospital Center, Goldwater Memorial Hospital, Institutes of Religion and Health, Lutheran Medical Center, Postgraduate Center for Mental Health.

GRADUATE UNITS

Graduate and Professional Programs *Program availability:* Part-time. Offers theology (M Div, MPS, MSW, D Min). MSW offered jointly with Fordham University.

NEW YORK UNIVERSITY, New York, NY 10012-1019

General Information Independent, coed, university. CGS member. *Graduate housing:* Room and/or apartments available on a first-come, first-served basis to single students; on-campus housing not available to married students. Housing application deadline: 5/1. *Research affiliation:* Center for the Study of Complex Malaria in India, National Institutes of Health (biology), Materials Research Science and Engineering Centers: Semantophoretic Assemblies, NSF (chemistry), Training in Systems and Integrative Neuroscience, National Institutes of Health (neural science), Research Network on Opening Governance, MacArthur Foundation (technology management and innovation), Assessment of Learning Outcomes and Social Effects in Community-Based Education in Afghanistan (human development and social change), Data Science Environments Program, Gordon and Betty Moore Foundation (data science).

GRADUATE UNITS

College of Dentistry Offers biomaterials science (MS); clinical research (MS); dentistry (MS, DDS, Advanced Certificate); endodontics (Advanced Certificate); oral and maxillofacial surgery (Advanced Certificate); orthodontics (Advanced Certificate); pediatric dentistry (Advanced Certificate); periodontics (Advanced Certificate); prosthodontics (Advanced Certificate). Electronic applications accepted.

College of Global Public Health *Program availability:* Part-time, online learning. Offers biological basis of public health (PhD); community and international health (MPH); global health leadership (MPH); health systems and health services research (PhD); population and community health (PhD); public health nutrition (MPH); social and behavioral sciences (MPH); socio-behavioral health (PhD). Electronic applications accepted.

Gallatin School of Individualized Study *Program availability:* Part-time, evening/weekend. Offers individualized study (MA). Electronic applications accepted.

Graduate School of Arts and Science *Program availability:* Part-time, evening/weekend. Offers African diaspora (PhD); African history (PhD); Africana studies (MA); American studies (MA, PhD); anthropology (MA, PhD); anthropology and French studies (PhD); applied economic analysis (Advanced Certificate); archival management (Advanced Certificate); arts and science (MA, MFA, MS, PhD, Advanced Certificate); Atlantic history (PhD); bioethics (MA); biology (PhD); biomedical journalism (MS); cancer and molecular biology (PhD); chemistry (MS, PhD); classics (MA, PhD); cognition and perception (PhD); community psychology (PhD); comparative literature (MA, PhD); composition and theory (MA, PhD); computational biology (PhD); computers in biological research (MS); creative writing (MA, MFA); cultural reporting and criticism (MA); data science (MS); developmental genetics (PhD); early music performance (Advanced Certificate); East Asian studies (MA, PhD); economics (MA, PhD); English and American literature (MA, PhD); environmental health sciences (MS, PhD); ethnomusicology (MA, PhD); French studies and sociology (PhD); French studies/history (PhD); French studies/journalism (MA); general biology (MS); general psychology (MA); German studies and critical thought (MA, PhD); Hebrew and Judaic studies (MA, PhD); Hebrew and Judaic studies/history (PhD); Hebrew and Judaic studies/museum studies (MA); historical and sustainable architecture (MA); history (MA, PhD); humanities and social thought (MA); immunology and microbiology (MA, PhD); industrial/organizational psychology (PhD); Irish and Irish American studies (MA); Italian (MA, PhD); Italian studies (MA); journalism (MA); Latin American and Caribbean studies/journalism (MA); linguistics (MA, PhD); Middle Eastern history (MA); Middle Eastern studies/history (PhD); molecular genetics (PhD); museum studies (MA, Advanced Certificate); Near Eastern studies/journalism (MA); neurobiology (PhD); oral biology (MS); philosophy (MA, PhD); physics (MS, PhD); plant biology (PhD); poetics and theory (Advanced Certificate); political campaign management (MA); politics (MA, PhD); Portuguese (MA, PhD); psychotherapy and psychoanalysis (Advanced Certificate); public history (Advanced Certificate); recombinant DNA technology (MS); religion (Advanced Certificate); religious studies (MA); Russian literature (MA); science and environmental reporting (Advanced Certificate); Slavic literature (MA); social theory (Advanced Certificate); social/personality psychology (PhD); sociology (MA, PhD); Spanish (PhD); Spanish and Latin American literatures and cultures (MA); Spanish language and translation (MA); world history (MA). Electronic applications accepted.

Center for European Studies Offers European studies (MA). Electronic applications accepted.

Center for French Civilization and Culture *Program availability:* Part-time, evening/weekend. Offers French (PhD); French civilization (PhD); French civilization and culture (MA, PhD, Advanced Certificate); French language and civilization (MA); French literature (MA); French studies (MA, PhD, Advanced Certificate); French studies and anthropology (PhD); French studies and history (PhD); French studies and journalism (MA); French studies and sociology (PhD); Romance languages and literatures (MA).

Center for Latin American and Caribbean Studies *Program availability:* Part-time. Offers Latin American and Caribbean studies (MA).

Center for Neural Science Offers neural science (PhD).

Courant Institute of Mathematical Sciences *Program availability:* Part-time, evening/weekend. Offers atmosphere ocean science and mathematics (PhD); computer science (MS, PhD); information systems (MS); mathematics (MS, PhD); mathematics and statistics/operations research (MS); mathematics in finance (MS); scientific computing (MS).

Hagop Kevorkian Center for Near Eastern Studies *Program availability:* Part-time, evening/weekend. Offers Middle Eastern and Islamic studies (MA, PhD); Middle Eastern and Islamic studies/history (PhD); Near Eastern studies (MA); Near Eastern studies/journalism (MA); Near Eastern studies/museum studies (MA).

Institute for Law and Society Offers law and society (MA, PhD).

Institute for the Study of the Ancient World Offers study of the ancient world (PhD). Electronic applications accepted.

Institute of Fine Arts *Program availability:* Part-time. Offers architectural studies (PhD); art history and archaeology (MA, PhD); classical art and archaeology (PhD); curatorial studies (MA); East and South Asian art (PhD); Near Eastern art and archaeology (PhD).

Leonard N. Stern School of Business *Program availability:* Part-time, evening/weekend. Offers accounting (MBA, PhD); business (MBA, PhD); economics (MBA, PhD); entertainment, media and technology (MBA); finance (MBA, PhD); general marketing (MBA); information systems (MBA, PhD); management organizations (MBA); marketing (PhD); operations management (MBA, PhD); organization theory (PhD); organizational behavior (PhD); product management (MBA); statistics (MBA, PhD); strategy (PhD). Electronic applications accepted.

Polytechnic School of Engineering Offers applied physics (MS, PhD); bioinformatics (MS); biomedical engineering (MS, PhD); biotechnology (MS); biotechnology and entrepreneurship (MS); chemical engineering (MS, PhD); chemistry (MS); civil engineering (MS, PhD); computer engineering (MS, Certificate); computer science (MS, PhD); construction management (MS); cyber security (Graduate Certificate); electrical engineering (MS, PhD); electronic business management (Advanced Certificate); engineering (MS, PhD, Advanced Certificate, Certificate, Graduate Certificate); entrepreneurship (Advanced Certificate); environmental engineering (MS); environmental science (MS); financial engineering (MS, Advanced Certificate); financial technology management (Advanced Certificate); human resources management (Advanced Certificate); industrial engineering (MS); information management (Advanced Certificate); integrated digital media (MS, Graduate Certificate); management (MS); management of technology (MS); manufacturing engineering (MS); materials chemistry (PhD); mathematics (MS, PhD); mechanical engineering (MS, PhD); organizational behavior (MS); project management (Advanced Certificate); risk management (Advanced Certificate); software engineering (Graduate Certificate); systems engineering (MS); technology management (MBA, PhD, Advanced Certificate);

telecommunications management (Advanced Certificate); transportation management (MS); transportation planning and engineering (MS, PhD); urban systems engineering and management (MS). Electronic applications accepted.

Robert F. Wagner Graduate School of Public Service *Program availability:* Part-time. Offers global public policy and management (EMPA); health finance (MPA); health policy analysis (MPA); health services management (MPA); international health (MPA); public administration (PhD); public and nonprofit management and policy (MPA, Advanced Certificate); public service (EMPA, MPA, MUP, PhD, Advanced Certificate); urban planning (MUP). Electronic applications accepted.

Rory Meyers College of Nursing Students: 65 full-time (60 women), 646 part-time (581 women); includes 256 minority (70 Black or African American, non-Hispanic/Latino; 2 American Indian or Alaska Native, non-Hispanic/Latino; 128 Asian, non-Hispanic/Latino; 45 Hispanic/Latino; 2 Native Hawaiian or other Pacific Islander, non-Hispanic/Latino; 9 Two or more races, non-Hispanic/Latino), 34 international. Average age 33. 455 applicants, 64% accepted, 172 enrolled. Faculty: 73 full-time (69 women), 63 part-time/adjunct (54 women). Expenses: Contact institution. *Financial support:* In 2016–17, 196 students received support, including 7 research assistantships with full tuition reimbursements available (averaging $26,988 per year); career-related internships or fieldwork, Federal Work-Study, and scholarships/grants also available. Support available to part-time students. Financial award application deadline: 3/1; financial award applicants required to submit FAFSA. In 2016, 171 master's, 10 doctorates, 15 other advanced degrees awarded. *Program availability:* Part-time, evening/weekend. Offers adult-gerontology acute care nurse practitioner (MS, Advanced Certificate); adult-gerontology primary care nurse practitioner (MS, Advanced Certificate); family nurse practitioner (MS, Advanced Certificate); gerontology nurse practitioner (Advanced Certificate); nurse-midwifery (MS, Advanced Certificate); nursing (MS, DNP, PhD, Advanced Certificate); nursing administration (MS, Advanced Certificate); nursing education (MS, Advanced Certificate); nursing informatics (MS, Advanced Certificate); pediatrics nurse practitioner (MS, Advanced Certificate); psychiatric-mental health nurse practitioner (MS, Advanced Certificate); research and theory development in nursing science (PhD). *Application deadline:* For fall admission, 6/15 for domestic and international students; for spring admission, 12/1 for domestic and international students; for summer admission, 3/1 for domestic and international students. *Application fee:* $80. Electronic applications accepted. *Application Contact:* Matthew Burke, Assistant Director, Graduate Student Affairs and Admissions, 212-998-7397, E-mail: mb6060@nyu.edu. *Senior Associate Dean for Academic Programs*, Dr. James Pace, 212-992-7343, E-mail: james.pace@nyu.edu.

School of Continuing and Professional Studies *Program availability:* Part-time, evening/weekend, online learning. Electronic applications accepted.

Center for Foreign Languages, Translation and Interpretation Program availability: Part-time, evening/weekend. Offers translation (MS). Electronic applications accepted.

Center for Global Affairs Program availability: Part-time, evening/weekend. Offers global affairs (MS); global energy (Advanced Certificate); peacebuilding (Advanced Certificate); transnational security (Advanced Certificate). Electronic applications accepted.

Center for Publishing Program availability: Part-time, evening/weekend. Offers digital and print media (MS). Electronic applications accepted.

Division of Humanities, Arts, and Writing Program availability: Part-time, evening/weekend, online learning. Offers professional writing (MS). Electronic applications accepted.

Division of Programs in Business Program availability: Part-time, evening/weekend, online learning. Offers benefits and compensation (Advanced Certificate); brand management (MS); core business competencies (Advanced Certificate); corporate and organizational communication (MS); database technologies (MS); digital marketing (MS); enterprise risk management (MS, Advanced Certificate); graphic communications management and technology (MA); human resource management (Advanced Certificate); human resource management and development (MS); information technologies (Advanced Certificate); integrated marketing (MS); interactive motion graphics and visual effects (MS); leadership and human capital management (MS, Advanced Certificate); management and systems (MS, Advanced Certificate); marketing analytics (MS); marketing and public relations (MS); organizational and executive coaching (Advanced Certificate); public relations management (MS); strategy and leadership (MS, Advanced Certificate); systems management (MS). Electronic applications accepted.

The George Heyman Jr. Center for Philanthropy and Fundraising Program availability: Part-time, evening/weekend. Offers fundraising and grantmaking (MS). Electronic applications accepted.

Schack Institute of Real Estate Program availability: Part-time, evening/weekend. Offers construction management (MS, Advanced Certificate); finance and investment (MS); global real estate (MS); real estate (MS, Advanced Certificate); real estate development (MS); real estate management (MS); sustainable development (MS); the business of development (MS). Electronic applications accepted.

Tisch Center for Hospitality and Tourism Program availability: Part-time, evening/weekend. Offers brand strategy (MS); hospitality industry studies (MS, Advanced Certificate); hotel finance (MS); lodging operations (MS); revenue management (MS); tourism management (MS, Advanced Certificate). Electronic applications accepted.

Tisch Institute for Sports Management, Media, and Business Program availability: Part-time, evening/weekend. Offers global sports media (MS); professional and collegiate sports operations (MS); sports business (Advanced Certificate); sports law (MS); sports marketing and sales (MS). Electronic applications accepted.

School of Law *Program availability:* Part-time, online learning. Offers law (LL M, JD, JSD); law and business (Advanced Certificate); taxation (MSL, Advanced Certificate). Electronic applications accepted.

School of Medicine Offers medicine (MS, MD, PhD).

Sackler Institute of Graduate Biomedical Sciences Offers biomedical imaging (PhD); biomedical informatics (PhD); cellular and molecular biology (PhD); computational biology (PhD); developmental genetics (PhD); genome integrity (PhD); immunology (PhD); immunology and inflammation (PhD); microbiology (PhD); molecular biophysics (PhD); molecular oncology (PhD); molecular oncology and tumor immunology (PhD); molecular pharmacology (PhD); neuroscience and physiology (PhD); pathobiology and translational medicine (PhD); stem cell biology (PhD). Electronic applications accepted.

Silver School of Social Work *Program availability:* Part-time, evening/weekend. Offers social work (MSW, PhD). Electronic applications accepted.

Steinhardt School of Culture, Education, and Human Development *Program availability:* Part-time. Offers advanced occupational therapy (MA); applied statistics for social science research (MS); art education (MA); art therapy (MA); art, education, and community practice (MA); bilingual education (MA, PhD, Advanced Certificate); business and workplace education (MA, Advanced Certificate); business education (MA, Advanced Certificate); childhood (MA); childhood education (MA); clinical nutrition (MS); clinically rich integrated science (MA); clinically-based English education, grades 7-12 (MA); communication sciences and disorders (MS, PhD); costume studies (MA); counseling (MA, PhD, Advanced Certificate); counseling and guidance (MA, Advanced Certificate); counseling for mental health and wellness (MA); counseling psychology (PhD); culture, education, and human development (MA, MFA, MM, MPH, MS, DPS, DPT, Ed D, PhD, Advanced Certificate, Post Master's Certificate, Postbaccalaureate Certificate); dance education (MA, Advanced Certificate); developmental psychology (PhD); digital media design for learning (MA, Advanced Certificate); drama therapy (MA); early childhood (MA); early childhood and childhood education (MA); early childhood education (MA); early childhood education/early childhood special education (MA); education and Jewish studies (MA, PhD); education policy (MA); educational and developmental psychology (MA, PhD); educational communication and technology (MA, MS, PhD, Advanced Certificate); educational leadership (MA, Ed D, PhD, Advanced Certificate); educational leadership, politics and advocacy (MA); educational theatre (MA, Ed D, PhD); educational theatre and English 7-12 (MA); educational theatre and social studies 7-12 (MA); educational theatre in colleges and communities (MA, Ed D, PhD); educational theatre, all grades (MA); English education (MA, PhD, Advanced Certificate); English education, grades 7-12 (MA); environmental conservation education (MA); food studies (MA, PhD); foreign language education (MA); games for learning (MS); higher and postsecondary education (PhD); higher education (MA, Ed D, PhD); higher education administration (Ed D); higher education and student affairs (MA); history of education (MA, PhD); human development and social intervention (MA); instrumental performance (MM); international education (MA, PhD, Advanced Certificate); LGBT health, education, and social services (Advanced Certificate); literacy education (MA); mathematics education (MA); media, culture and communication (MA, PhD); multilingual/multicultural studies (MA, PhD, Advanced Certificate); music business (MA); music education (MA); music performance and composition (MM, PhD, Advanced Certificate); music technology (MA, MM, PhD); music theatre (MM); music theory and composition (MM); music therapy (MA); nutrition and dietetics (MS, PhD); occupational therapy (MS, DPS); orthopedic physical therapy (Advanced Certificate); performing arts administration (MA); physical therapy (MA, DPT, PhD); piano performance (MM); psychology and social intervention (PhD); rehabilitation sciences (PhD); research in occupational therapy (PhD); school building leader (MA); school district leader (Advanced Certificate); social and cultural studies of education (MA); social studies education (MA); sociology of education (MA, PhD); special education (MA); studio art (MA, MFA, Advanced Certificate); teachers of art, all grades (MA); teaching and learning (Ed D, PhD); teaching art/social studies 7-12 (MA); teaching dance in the professions (MA); teaching dance, all grades (MA, Advanced Certificate); teaching English to speakers of other languages (MA, PhD); teaching foreign languages, 7-12 (MA); teaching French as a foreign language (MA); teaching social studies 7-12 (MA); teaching Spanish as a foreign language (MA); visual arts administration (MA); visual culture (MA); vocal pedagogy (Advanced Certificate); vocal performance (MM); workplace learning (Advanced Certificate). Electronic applications accepted.

Tisch School of the Arts Offers acting (MFA); arts (MA, MFA, MPS, PhD); arts politics (MA); dance (MFA); design for stage and film (MFA); dramatic writing (MFA); interactive telecommunications (MPS); moving image archiving and preservation (MA); musical theatre writing (MFA); performance studies (MA, PhD). Electronic applications accepted.

Game Center Offers game design (MFA).

Kanbar Institute of Film and Television Offers film and television (MFA). Electronic applications accepted.

NIAGARA UNIVERSITY, Niagara University, NY 14109

General Information Independent-religious, coed, comprehensive institution. *Enrollment:* 4,017 graduate, professional, and undergraduate students; 450 full-time matriculated graduate/professional students (282 women), 388 part-time matriculated graduate/professional students (278 women). *Enrollment by degree level:* 708 master's, 51 doctoral, 78 other advanced degrees. Tuition and fees vary according to course load and program. *Graduate housing:* Room and/or apartments available to single students; on-campus housing not available to married students. Typical cost: $12,700 (including board). Room and board charges vary according to housing facility selected. Housing application deadline: 8/1. *Student services:* Campus employment opportunities, campus safety program, career counseling, exercise/wellness program, free psychological counseling, international student services, low-cost health insurance, multicultural affairs office, services for students with disabilities. *Library facilities:* Our Lady of Angels Library. *Collection:* Books: 171,911 (physical), 322,812 (digital/electronic); Serial titles: 160 (physical), 31,384 (digital/electronic); Databases: 85. Weekly public service hours: 106; study areas open 24 hours, 5–7 days a week; students can reserve study rooms. *Research affiliation:* Roswell Park Memorial Institute.

Computer facilities: 81 computers available on campus for general student use. A campuswide network can be accessed from student residence rooms. Online class registration is available.
Website: http://www.niagara.edu/

General Application Contact: Evan Pierce, Associate Director for Academic Affairs, Graduate Studies, 716-286-8327, Fax: 716-286-8710, E-mail: epierce@niagara.edu.

GRADUATE UNITS

Graduate Division of Arts and Sciences Students: 26 full-time (13 women), 20 part-time (8 women); includes 8 minority (5 Black or African American, non-Hispanic/Latino; 2 Hispanic/Latino; 1 Two or more races, non-Hispanic/Latino), 13 international. Average age 31. Expenses: Contact institution. *Financial support:* Research assistantships with tuition reimbursements, teaching assistantships with tuition reimbursements, career-related internships or fieldwork, Federal Work-Study, scholarships/grants, and unspecified assistantships available. Support available to part-time students. Financial award application deadline: 4/15; financial award applicants required to submit FAFSA. In 2016, 22 master's awarded. *Program availability:* Part-time, evening/weekend. Offers criminal justice (MS); criminal justice administration (MS); interdisciplinary studies (MA). *Application deadline:* For fall admission, 8/1 for domestic students. Applications are processed on a rolling basis. *Application Contact:* Evan Pierce, Associate Dean for Graduate Recruitment, 716-286-8769, Fax: 716-286-8170. *Interim Dean*, Dr. Peter Butera, 716-286-8060, Fax: 716-286-8601, E-mail: pbutera@niagara.edu.

Graduate Division of Business Administration Students: 172 full-time (69 women), 65 part-time (36 women); includes 25 minority (4 Black or African American, non-Hispanic/Latino; 7 Asian, non-Hispanic/Latino; 7 Hispanic/Latino; 1 Native Hawaiian or other Pacific Islander, non-Hispanic/Latino; 6 Two or more races, non-Hispanic/Latino), 76 international. Average age 27. Expenses: Contact institution. *Financial support:* Fellowships, research assistantships, career-related internships or fieldwork, and Federal Work-Study available. Support available to part-time students. Financial award application deadline: 4/15; financial award applicants required to submit FAFSA. In 2016, 107 master's awarded. *Program availability:* Part-time, evening/weekend. Offers accounting (MBA); business administration (MBA); finance (MBA, MS); financial planning (MBA); healthcare administration (MBA, MHA); human resources (MBA); international business (MBA); marketing (MBA); professional accountancy (MBA); strategic management (MBA); supply chain management (MBA). *Application deadline:* For fall admission, 8/1 for domestic students; for spring admission, 11/1 for domestic students. Applications are processed on a rolling basis. Electronic applications accepted. *Application Contact:* Evan Pierce, Associate Director for Graduate Recruitment, 716-286-8769, Fax: 716-286-8170, E-mail: epierce@niagara.edu. *MBA Director/Chair of the Marketing Department,* Dr. Paul Richardson, 716-286-8169, Fax: 716-286-8206, E-mail: psr@niagara.edu.

Graduate Division of Education Students: 239 full-time (195 women), 302 part-time (234 women); includes 53 minority (26 Black or African American, non-Hispanic/Latino; 1 American Indian or Alaska Native, non-Hispanic/Latino; 3 Asian, non-Hispanic/Latino; 15 Hispanic/Latino; 8 Two or more races, non-Hispanic/Latino), 79 international. Average age 31. Expenses: Contact institution. *Financial support:* Research assistantships with tuition reimbursements, teaching assistantships with tuition reimbursements, career-related internships or fieldwork, Federal Work-Study, scholarships/grants, and unspecified assistantships available. Financial award application deadline: 4/15; financial award applicants required to submit FAFSA. In 2016, 159 master's, 35 other advanced degrees awarded. *Program availability:* Part-time, evening/weekend. Offers early childhood and childhood education (MS Ed, Certificate); early childhood special education (MS); educational leadership (MS Ed, Certificate); literacy instruction (MS Ed); mental health counseling (MS, Certificate); middle and adolescence education (MS Ed); school building leader (MS Ed); school counseling (MS Ed, Certificate); school district business leader (Certificate); school district leader (MS Ed, Certificate); school psychology (MS); special education (MS Ed); special education (grades 1-12) (Certificate); teacher education (MS, MS Ed, Certificate); teaching English to speakers of other languages (MS Ed, Certificate). *Application deadline:* For fall admission, 8/1 for domestic students. Applications are processed on a rolling basis. *Application fee:* $30. *Application Contact:* Evan Pierce, Associate Director for Graduate Recruitment, 716-286-8769, Fax: 716-286-8170, E-mail: epierce@niagara.edu. *Dean, College of Education,* Dr. Chandra Foote, 716-286-8549, Fax: 716-286-8561, E-mail: cjf@niagara.edu.

NICHOLLS STATE UNIVERSITY, Thibodaux, LA 70310
General Information State-supported, coed, comprehensive institution. *Graduate housing:* Rooms and/or apartments available on a first-come, first-served basis to single and married students. Housing application deadline: 4/15.

GRADUATE UNITS

Graduate Studies *Program availability:* Part-time, evening/weekend, online learning.

College of Arts and Sciences *Program availability:* Part-time, evening/weekend. Offers arts and sciences (MS); marine and environmental biology (MS). Electronic applications accepted.

College of Business Administration *Program availability:* Part-time, evening/weekend. Offers business administration (MBA). Electronic applications accepted.

College of Education *Program availability:* Part-time, evening/weekend. Offers clinical mental health counseling (MA); curriculum and instruction (M Ed); education (M Ed, MA, MAT, SSP); educational leadership (M Ed); elementary education (MAT); human performance education (MAT); middle school education (MAT); school counseling (M Ed); school psychology (SSP); secondary education (MAT). Electronic applications accepted.

College of Nursing and Allied Health Offers family nurse practitioner (MSN); nurse executive (MSN); nursing education (MSN); psychiatric/mental health nurse practitioner (MSN).

NICHOLS COLLEGE, Dudley, MA 01571-5000
General Information Independent, coed, comprehensive institution. *Graduate housing:* On-campus housing not available.

GRADUATE UNITS

Graduate and Professional Studies *Program availability:* Part-time, evening/weekend, online learning. Offers business administration (MBA); organizational leadership (MSOL). Electronic applications accepted.

NIPISSING UNIVERSITY, North Bay, ON P1B 8L7, Canada
General Information Province-supported, coed, comprehensive institution. *Graduate housing:* Room and/or apartments available to single students; on-campus housing not available to married students. Housing application deadline: 6/13. *Research affiliation:* Canada Space Agency (CSA) and MacDonald, Dettwiler and Associates Ltd. (MDA–RADARSAT-2) (remote sensing), Education Quality and Accountability Office (EQAO) (assessing educational quality), Ontario Association of Deans of Education (OADE) (assessing pre-service practicum processes), Tembec (forestry restoration), Metals in the Human Environment Research Network (MITHE-RN) (assessing environmental pollutants on aquatic ecosystems).

GRADUATE UNITS

Faculty of Education *Program availability:* Part-time, evening/weekend. Offers education (M Ed, Certificate).

NORFOLK STATE UNIVERSITY, Norfolk, VA 23504
General Information State-supported, coed, comprehensive institution. CGS member. *Graduate housing:* Room and/or apartments available to single students; on-campus housing not available to married students. Housing application deadline: 3/1. *Research affiliation:* U.S. Department of Energy/NASA (fundamental and applied research studies), NASA-Langley Research Center (aerospace applications, lidar application), National Science Foundation (fundamental and applied research studies), U.S. Department of Education (DOE) (Title III projects, No Child Left Behind Initiative), University of Virginia's Integrative Graduate Education and Research Traineeship (IGERT) (science and engineering interactions with matter), Applied Research Center (technology transfer).

GRADUATE UNITS

School of Graduate Studies *Program availability:* Part-time. Electronic applications accepted.

Ethelyn R. Strong School of Social Work *Program availability:* Part-time. Offers social work (MSW, PhD).

School of Education *Program availability:* Part-time. Offers early childhood education (MAT); education (MA, MAT); pre-elementary education (MA); principal preparation (MA); secondary education (MAT); severe disabilities (MA); teaching (MA); urban education/administration (MA).

School of Liberal Arts *Program availability:* Part-time. Offers community/clinical psychology (MA); criminal justice (MA); liberal arts (MA, MFA, MM, Psy D); media and communication (MA); music (MM); music education (MM); performance (MM); psychology (Psy D); theory and composition (MM); urban affairs (MA); visual studies (MA, MFA).

School of Science and Technology Offers computer science (MS); electronics engineering (MS); materials science (MS); optical engineering (MS); science and technology (MS).

NORTH AMERICAN UNIVERSITY, Stafford, TX 77477
General Information Independent, coed, comprehensive institution.

GRADUATE UNITS

Program in Educational Leadership Offers educational leadership (M Ed).

NORTH CAROLINA AGRICULTURAL AND TECHNICAL STATE UNIVERSITY, Greensboro, NC 27411
General Information State-supported, coed, university. CGS member. *Graduate housing:* Room and/or apartments available on a first-come, first-served basis to single students; on-campus housing not available to married students. Housing application deadline: 5/8. *Research affiliation:* North Carolina Biotechnology Research Center (biotechnology), Boeing (aerospace engineering), Northrop Grumman Corporation (high performance computing), Research Triangle Institute (environmental protection, advanced technology), Rockwell, Inc. (avionics technology, communications technology), Honeywell (industrial automation control).

GRADUATE UNITS

School of Graduate Studies *Program availability:* Part-time, evening/weekend. Electronic applications accepted.

College of Arts and Sciences *Program availability:* Part-time, evening/weekend. Offers applied mathematics (MS); arts and sciences (MA, MAT, MS, MSW); biology (MS); biology education (MAT); chemistry (MS, PhD); computational sciences (MS) English (MA); English and African-American literature (MA); English education (MAT, MS); physics (MS); sociology and social work (MSW).

College of Engineering *Program availability:* Part-time. Offers bioengineering (MS); biological engineering (MS); chemical engineering (MS); civil engineering (MSCE); computer science (MSCS); electrical engineering (MSEE, PhD); engineering (MS, MSCE, MSCS, MSE, MSEE, MSIE, MSME, PhD); industrial engineering (MSIE, PhD); mechanical engineering (MSME, PhD).

School of Agriculture and Environmental Sciences *Program availability:* Part-time, evening/weekend. Offers agricultural economics (MS); agricultural education (MS); agriculture and environmental sciences (MAT, MS); animal health science (MS); child development early education and family studies (MAT); family and consumer sciences (MAT); food and nutrition (MS); plant, soil and environmental science (MS).

School of Business and Economics Offers accounting (MBA); business education (MAT); human resources management (MBA); supply chain systems (MBA).

School of Education *Program availability:* Part-time, evening/weekend. Offers adult education (MS); counseling (MS); education (MA Ed, MAT, MS); elementary education (MA Ed); instructional technology (MS); physical education (MAT, MS); reading education (MA Ed); school administration (MS); teaching (MAT).

School of Technology *Program availability:* Part-time, evening/weekend. Offers construction management (MSTM); electronics and computer technology (MSIT, MSTM); environmental and occupational safety (MSTM); graphic communication systems (MSTM); information technology (MSIT, MSTM); manufacturing (MSTM); occupational safety and health (MSTM); technology (MAT, MSIT, MSTM); technology education (MAT).

NORTH CAROLINA CENTRAL UNIVERSITY, Durham, NC 27707-3129
General Information State-supported, coed, comprehensive institution. CGS member. *Graduate housing:* Room and/or apartments available on a first-come, first-served basis to single students; on-campus housing not available to married students. Housing application deadline: 7/1.

GRADUATE UNITS

College of Behavioral and Social Sciences Offers athletic administration (MS); behavioral and social sciences (MA, MPA, MS); criminal justice (MS); physical education (MS); psychology (MA); public administration (MPA); recreation administration (MS); therapeutic recreation (MS).

College of Liberal Arts *Program availability:* Part-time, evening/weekend. Offers English (MA); history (MA); jazz studies (MM); liberal arts (MA, MM).

College of Science and Technology Offers applied mathematics (MS); biology (MS); chemistry (MS); earth sciences (MS); mathematics education (MS); physics (MS); pure mathematics (MS); science and technology (MS).

School of Business *Program availability:* Part-time, evening/weekend. Offers business (MBA).

School of Education *Program availability:* Part-time, evening/weekend. Offers career counseling (MA); communication disorders (M Ed); education (M Ed, MA, MSA); educational technology (MA); instructional technology (M Ed); school administration (MSA); school counseling (MA); special education (M Ed).

School of Law *Program availability:* Part-time, evening/weekend. Offers law (JD).

School of Library and Information Sciences *Program availability:* Part-time, evening/weekend. Offers library and information sciences (MIS, MLS).

NORTH CAROLINA STATE UNIVERSITY, Raleigh, NC 27695
General Information State-supported, coed, university. CGS member. *Graduate housing:* Rooms and/or apartments available on a first-come, first-served basis to single and married students. *Research affiliation:* Triangle Universities Nuclear Laboratory, Research Triangle Institute, Highlands Biological Station, National Humanities Center, Microelectronics Center of North Carolina, North Carolina–Japan Center.

GRADUATE UNITS

College of Veterinary Medicine *Program availability:* Part-time. Offers cell biology (MS, PhD); infectious disease (MS, PhD); pathology (MS, PhD); pharmacology (MS, PhD); population medicine (MS, PhD); veterinary medicine (MS, MSpVM, MVPH, DVM, PhD); veterinary public health (MVPH). Electronic applications accepted.

Graduate School *Program availability:* Part-time, evening/weekend, online learning. Electronic applications accepted.

College of Agriculture and Life Sciences *Program availability:* Part-time. Offers agricultural and extension education (Ed D); agricultural and resource economics (MS); agricultural education (MAE, MS, Certificate); agriculture and life sciences

(M Tox, MAE, MB, MBAE, MFG, MFM, MFS, MG, MMB, MN, MP, MS, MZS, Ed D, PhD, Certificate); animal and poultry science (PhD); animal science (MS); biochemistry (PhD); bioinformatics (MB, PhD); biological and agricultural engineering (MBAE, MS, PhD, Certificate); crop science (MS, PhD); entomology (MS, PhD); environmental and molecular toxicology (M Tox, MS, PhD); extension education (MS); financial mathematics (MFM); food science (MFS, MS, PhD); functional genomics (MFG, MS, PhD); genetics (MG, MS, PhD); genomic sciences (PhD); horticultural science (MS, PhD, Certificate); microbial biotechnology (MMB); microbiology (MMB, MS, PhD); nutrition (MN, MS, PhD); physiology (MP, MS, PhD); plant biology (MS, PhD); plant pathology (MS, PhD); poultry science (MS); soil science (MS, PhD); zoology (MS, MZS, PhD). Electronic applications accepted.

College of Design Program availability: Part-time. Offers architecture (M Arch); art and design (MAD); design (M Arch, MAD, MGD, MID, MLA, PhD); graphic design (MGD); industrial design (MID); landscape architecture (MLA). Electronic applications accepted.

College of Education Program availability: Part-time. Offers adult and community college education (M Ed, MS, Ed D); agency counseling (M Ed, MS); business and marketing education (M Ed, MS); counselor education (M Ed, MS); curriculum and instruction (M Ed, MS, PhD); education (M Ed, MS, MS Ed, MSA, Ed D, PhD, Certificate); educational administration and supervision (Ed D); educational research and policy analysis (PhD); elementary education (M Ed); higher education administration (M Ed, MS, Ed D); human resource development (MS); instructional technology (M Ed, MS); mathematics education (M Ed, MS, PhD); middle grades education (M Ed, MS); school administration (MSA); science education (M Ed, MS, PhD); secondary English education (M Ed, MS Ed); social studies education (M Ed); special education (M Ed, MS); technology education (M Ed, MS, Ed D); training and development (M Ed, Ed D, Certificate). Electronic applications accepted.

College of Engineering Program availability: Part-time. Offers aerospace engineering (MS, PhD); biomedical engineering (MS, PhD); chemical engineering (M Ch E, MS, PhD); civil engineering (MCE, MS, PhD); computer engineering (MS, PhD); computer networking (MS); computer science (MC Sc, MS, PhD); electrical engineering (MS, PhD); engineering (M Ch E, M Eng, MC Sc, MCE, MIE, MIMS, MMSE, MNE, MOR, MS, PhD); industrial engineering (MIE, MS, PhD); integrated manufacturing systems engineering (MIMS); materials science and engineering (MMSE, MS, PhD); mechanical engineering (MS, PhD); nuclear engineering (MNE, MS, PhD); operations research (MOR, MS, PhD). Electronic applications accepted.

College of Humanities and Social Sciences Program availability: Part-time, evening/weekend. Offers anthropology (MA); bioarchaeology (MA); communication (MS); communication, rhetoric, and digital media (PhD); creative writing (MFA); cultural anthropology (MA); developmental psychology (PhD); English (MA); environmental anthropology (MA); ergonomics and experimental psychology (PhD); French language and literature (MA); history (MA); humanities and social sciences (M Soc, MA, MFA, MIS, MPA, MS, MSW, PhD, Certificate); industrial/organizational psychology (PhD); international studies (MIS); liberal studies (MA); nonprofit management (Certificate); psychology in the public interest (PhD); public administration (MPA, PhD); public history (MA); school psychology (PhD); social work (MSW); sociology (M Soc, MS, PhD); Spanish language and literature (MA); technical communication (MS). Electronic applications accepted.

College of Natural Resources Program availability: Part-time. Offers fisheries and wildlife sciences (MFWS, MS, PhD); forestry and environmental resources (MF, MS, PhD); natural resource management (MPRTM, MS); natural resources (MF, MFWS, MNR, MPRTM, MS, MWPS, PhD); park and recreation management (MPRTM, MS); parks, recreation and tourism management (PhD); recreational sport management (MPRTM, MS); spatial information science (MPRTM, MS); tourism policy and development (MPRTM, MS); wood and paper science (MS, MWPS, PhD). Electronic applications accepted.

College of Physical and Mathematical Sciences Program availability: Part-time. Offers applied mathematics (MS, PhD); biomathematics (M Biomath, MS, PhD); chemistry (MS, PhD); marine, earth, and atmospheric sciences (PhD); mathematics (MS, PhD); meteorology (MS, PhD); oceanography (MS, PhD); physical and mathematical sciences (M Biomath, M Stat, MS, PhD); physics (MS, PhD); statistics (M Stat, MS, PhD). Electronic applications accepted.

College of Textiles Program availability: Part-time, evening/weekend, online learning. Offers fiber and polymer science (PhD); textile and apparel technology and management (MS, MT); textile chemistry (MS); textile engineering (MS); textile technology management (PhD); textiles (MS, MT, PhD). Electronic applications accepted.

Institute for Advanced Analytics Offers analytics (MS). Electronic applications accepted.

Poole College of Management Program availability: Part-time. Offers accounting (MAC); biosciences management (MBA); economics (M Econ, MA, PhD); entrepreneurship and technology commercialization (MBA); financial management (MBA); innovation management (MBA); management (M Econ, MA, MAC, MBA, MS, PhD); marketing management (MBA); services management (MBA); supply chain management (MBA). Electronic applications accepted.

NORTH CENTRAL COLLEGE, Naperville, IL 60566-7063

General Information Independent-religious, coed, comprehensive institution. CGS member. *Enrollment:* 2,949 graduate, professional, and undergraduate students; 85 full-time matriculated graduate/professional students (44 women), 148 part-time matriculated graduate/professional students (91 women). *Enrollment by degree level:* 232 master's. *Graduate faculty:* 20 full-time (11 women), 17 part-time/adjunct (6 women). *Tuition:* Full-time $19,800; part-time $825 per credit hour. Tuition and fees vary according to program. *Graduate housing:* Room and/or apartments available on a first-come, first-served basis to single students; on-campus housing not available to married students. Typical cost: $7173 per year ($10,356 including board). Room and board charges vary according to board plan and housing facility selected. Housing application deadline: 4/15. *Student services:* Campus employment opportunities, campus safety program, career counseling, free psychological counseling, international student services, multicultural affairs office, services for students with disabilities, teacher training, writing training. *Library facilities:* Oesterle Library. *Collection:* Books: 124,616 (physical), 77,180 (digital/electronic); Databases: 214.

Computer facilities: 350 computers available on campus for general student use. A campuswide network can be accessed from student residence rooms and from off campus. Online class registration, software packages are available.
Website: http://www.northcentralcollege.edu/

General Application Contact: Wendy Kulpinski, Director of Graduate Admission, 630-637-5808, Fax: 630-637-5819, E-mail: wekulpinski@noctrl.edu.

GRADUATE UNITS

School of Graduate and Professional Studies Students: 85 full-time (44 women), 147 part-time (90 women); includes 44 minority (14 Black or African American, non-Hispanic/Latino; 5 Asian, non-Hispanic/Latino; 20 Hispanic/Latino; 1 Native Hawaiian or other Pacific Islander, non-Hispanic/Latino; 4 Two or more races, non-Hispanic/Latino), 8 international. Average age 29. 316 applicants, 48% accepted, 93 enrolled. *Faculty:* 20 full-time (11 women), 17 part-time/adjunct (6 women). Expenses: Contact institution. *Financial support:* Unspecified assistantships available. Support available to part-time students. Financial award applicants required to submit FAFSA. In 2016, 104 master's awarded. *Program availability:* Part-time, evening/weekend. Offers change management (MBA); computer science (MS); culture and society (MALS); education (MA Ed); finance (MBA); human resource management (MBA); leadership studies (MLD); management (MBA). *Application deadline:* For fall admission, 8/15 for domestic students, 7/15 for international students; for winter admission, 12/1 for domestic students, 11/1 for international students; for spring admission, 2/1 for domestic students, 12/1 for international students. Applications are processed on a rolling basis. *Application fee:* $25. Electronic applications accepted. *Application Contact:* Wendy Kulpinski, Director of Graduate and Professional Studies Admission, 630-637-5808, Fax: 630-637-5819, E-mail: wekulpinski@noctrl.edu. *Dean of Graduate and Professional Studies,* Dr. Pamela Monaco, 630-637-5384, Fax: 630-637-5844, E-mail: pjmonaco@noctrl.edu.

NORTHCENTRAL UNIVERSITY, San Diego, CA 92106

General Information Proprietary, coed, upper-level institution. CGS member. *Enrollment:* 10,916 graduate, professional, and undergraduate students; 5,036 full-time matriculated graduate/professional students (3,291 women), 5,747 part-time matriculated graduate/professional students (3,977 women). *Enrollment by degree level:* 3,652 master's, 6,870 doctoral, 261 other advanced degrees. *Graduate faculty:* 98 full-time (63 women), 385 part-time/adjunct (203 women). *Tuition:* Full-time $16,821; part-time $935 per credit hour. One-time fee: $350. Tuition and fees vary according to degree level and program. *Student services:* Services for students with disabilities, writing training. *Library facilities:* Northcentral University Library (Virtual). *Research affiliation:* Coalition for Research to Practice (mental health services; aligning academic training with workforce demands).

Computer facilities: Online class registration is available.
Website: http://www.ncu.edu/

General Application Contact: Enrollment Advisor, 866-776-0331, Fax: 928-541-7817, E-mail: admissions@ncu.edu.

GRADUATE UNITS

Graduate Studies Students: 5,036 full-time (3,291 women), 5,747 part-time (3,977 women); includes 3,777 minority (2,550 Black or African American, non-Hispanic/Latino; 76 American Indian or Alaska Native, non-Hispanic/Latino; 192 Asian, non-Hispanic/Latino; 603 Hispanic/Latino; 39 Native Hawaiian or other Pacific Islander, non-Hispanic/Latino; 317 Two or more races, non-Hispanic/Latino). Average age 45. *Faculty:* 98 full-time (63 women), 385 part-time/adjunct (203 women). Expenses: Contact institution. *Financial support:* Scholarships/grants available. In 2016, 799 master's, 399 doctorates, 230 other advanced degrees awarded. *Program availability:* Part-time, evening/weekend, online only, 100% online. Offers business (MBA, DBA, PhD, Postbaccalaureate Certificate); education (M Ed, Ed D, PhD, Ed S, Post-Master's Certificate, Postbaccalaureate Certificate); marriage and family therapy (MA, DMFT, PhD, Post-Master's Certificate, Postbaccalaureate Certificate); psychology (MA, PhD, Post-Master's Certificate, Postbaccalaureate Certificate). *Application deadline:* Applications are processed on a rolling basis. *Application fee:* $0. Electronic applications accepted. *Application Contact:* Ken Boutelle, Vice President, Enrollment Services, 888-628-4979, E-mail: enrollmentservices@ncu.edu. *Acting Provost,* Dr. David Harpool, 888-327-2877 Ext. 8181, E-mail: provost@ncu.edu.

NORTH DAKOTA STATE UNIVERSITY, Fargo, ND 58102

General Information State-supported, coed, university. CGS member. *Graduate housing:* Rooms and/or apartments available on a first-come, first-served basis to single and married students. *Research affiliation:* U.S. Department of Agriculture (USDA), Metabolism and Radiation Laboratory.

GRADUATE UNITS

College of Graduate and Interdisciplinary Studies Students: 665 full-time (330 women), 1,417 part-time (706 women); includes 161 minority (37 Black or African American, non-Hispanic/Latino; 28 American Indian or Alaska Native, non-Hispanic/Latino; 46 Asian, non-Hispanic/Latino; 28 Hispanic/Latino; 3 Native Hawaiian or other Pacific Islander, non-Hispanic/Latino; 19 Two or more races, non-Hispanic/Latino), 585 international. Average age 28. 1,619 applicants, 37% accepted, 446 enrolled. *Faculty:* 445 full-time (151 women), 34 part-time/adjunct (11 women). Expenses: Contact institution. *Financial support:* Fellowships with full tuition reimbursements, research assistantships with full tuition reimbursements, teaching assistantships with full tuition reimbursements, career-related internships or fieldwork, Federal Work-Study, institutionally sponsored loans, scholarships/grants, traineeships, tuition waivers (full and partial), and unspecified assistantships available. Support available to part-time students. In 2016, 319 master's, 81 doctorates, 82 other advanced degrees awarded. *Program availability:* Part-time, evening/weekend, 100% online, blended/hybrid learning. Offers cellular and molecular biology (PhD); college teaching (Certificate); environmental and conservation sciences (MS, PhD); food protection (Certificate); food safety (MS, PhD); genomics and bioinformatics (MS, PhD); managerial logistics (MML); materials and nanotechnology (MS, PhD); science, technology, engineering, and mathematics education (PhD); transportation and logistics (PhD); transportation and urban systems (MS). *Application fee:* $35. Electronic applications accepted. *Application Contact:* Elizabeth Worth, Student Recruitment Coordinator, 701-231-8476, Fax: 701-231-6524, E-mail: elizabeth.worth@ndsu.edu. *Dean,* Dr. Claudia Tomany, 701-231-7033, Fax: 701-231-6524.

College of Agriculture, Food Systems, and Natural Resources Program availability: Part-time. Offers agribusiness and applied economics (MS); agriculture, food systems, and natural resources (MS, PhD); animal sciences (MS, PhD); cereal science (MS, PhD); entomology (MS, PhD); horticulture (MS); international agribusiness (MS); microbiology (MS); molecular pathogenesis (PhD); natural resources management (MS, PhD); plant pathology (MS, PhD); plant sciences (MS, PhD); soil sciences (MS, PhD). Electronic applications accepted.

College of Arts, Humanities and Social Sciences Program availability: Part-time, evening/weekend. Offers anthropology (MA, MS); architecture (M Arch); arts, humanities and social sciences (M Arch, M Ed, MM, MS, DMA, PhD); communication (PhD); community development (MA, MS); composition (MA); conducting (MM, DMA); criminal justice (PhD); criminal justice administration (MS); history (MA, MS, PhD); literature (MA); mass communication (MA, MS); music education (MM); performance (MM, DMA); rhetoric, writing and culture (PhD); social science (MA, MS); sociology (MS); speech communication (MA, MS). Electronic applications accepted.

College of Business *Program availability:* Part-time, evening/weekend. Offers accountancy (M Acc); business administration (MBA). Electronic applications accepted.

College of Engineering *Program availability:* Part-time. Offers civil and environmental engineering (PhD); civil engineering (MS, PhD); construction management (MCM, MS, Graduate Certificate); electrical and computer engineering (ME, MS, PhD); engineering (MCM, ME, MS, PhD, Graduate Certificate); environmental and conservation science (PhD); environmental engineering (MS); industrial and manufacturing engineering (PhD); industrial engineering and management (MS); manufacturing engineering (MS); materials and nanotechnology (PhD); mechanical engineering (MS, PhD); natural resource management (PhD); science, technology, engineering, mathematics education (STEM) (PhD); transportation and logistics (PhD). Electronic applications accepted.

College of Health Professions *Program availability:* Part-time. Offers American Indian public health (MPH); health professions (MPH, MS, DNP, PhD, Pharm D); health promotion (MPH); management of infectious diseases (MPH); nursing (MS, DNP); pharmacy (MS, PhD, Pharm D); public health in clinical systems (MPH). Electronic applications accepted.

College of Human Development and Education *Program availability:* Part-time, evening/weekend, online learning. Offers agricultural education (M Ed, MS); athletic training (MAT, MS); clinical mental health counseling (M Ed, MS); counselor education (M Ed, MS, PhD); counselor education and supervision (PhD); couple and family therapy (PhD); curriculum and instruction (M Ed, MS); developmental science (PhD); dietetics (MS); education (PhD); educational leadership (M Ed, MS, Ed S); exercise science and nutrition (PhD); exercise/nutrition science (MS); family and consumer sciences education (M Ed, MS); family financial planning (MS, Certificate); gerontology (MS, Certificate); health promotion (MPH); history education (M Ed, MS); human development and education (M Ed, MAT, MPH, MS, Ed D, PhD, Certificate, Ed S); institutional analysis (Ed D); leadership in physical education and sport (MS); mathematics education (M Ed, MS); merchandising (MS, Certificate); music education (M Ed, MS); occupational and adult education (Ed D); school counseling (M Ed, MS); science education (M Ed, MS); youth development (MS). Electronic applications accepted.

College of Science and Mathematics *Program availability:* Part-time. Offers applied mathematics (MS, PhD); biochemistry (MS, PhD); biology (MS); botany (MS, PhD); cellular and molecular biology (PhD); chemistry (MS, PhD); clinical psychology (MS); coatings and polymeric materials (MS, PhD); computer science (MS, PhD); genomics (PhD); health and social psychology (PhD); mathematics (MS, PhD); physics (MS, PhD); psychological clinical science (PhD); psychology (MS); science and mathematics (MS, PhD, Certificate); software engineering (MS, MSE, PhD, Certificate); sports statistics (PhD); statistics (MS, PhD, Certificate); visual and cognitive neuroscience (PhD); zoology (MS, PhD). Electronic applications accepted.

NORTHEASTERN ILLINOIS UNIVERSITY, Chicago, IL 60625-4699

General Information State-supported, coed, comprehensive institution. *Graduate housing:* On-campus housing not available. *Research affiliation:* Advocate Health Care Network (health care cost containment), Lutheran General Hospital (clinical cardiology), Advocate Medical Group (health care outcomes research).

GRADUATE UNITS

College of Graduate Studies and Research *Program availability:* Part-time, evening/weekend. Electronic applications accepted.

College of Arts and Sciences *Program availability:* Part-time, evening/weekend. Offers applied mathematics (MS); arts and sciences (MA, MS); biology (MS); chemistry (MS); communication, media and theatre (MA); composition/writing (MA); computer science (MS); geography and environmental studies (MA); gerontology (MA); history (MA); Latin American literatures and cultures (MA); linguistics (MA); literature (MA); mathematics (MS); music (MA); pedagogical content knowledge for teaching elementary and middle school mathematics (MA); political science (MA); secondary education mathematics (MS); teaching English as a second/foreign language (MA); TESL (MA). Electronic applications accepted.

College of Business and Management *Program availability:* Part-time, evening/weekend. Offers accounting (MSA); business administration (MBA); finance (MBA); management (MBA); marketing (MBA). Electronic applications accepted.

College of Education *Program availability:* Part-time, evening/weekend. Offers bicultural/bilingual education (MAT); bilingual/bicultural education (MAT, MSI); community counseling (MA); early childhood education (MAT); education (MA, MAT, MS, MSI); educational administration and supervision (MA); educational leadership (MA); exercise science (MS); family counseling (MA); gifted education (MA); human resource development (MA); inner city studies (MA); language arts - elementary education (MAT, MSI); language arts - secondary education (MAT, MSI); learning behavior specialist (MA); literacy education (MA); rehabilitation counseling (MA); school counseling (MA). Electronic applications accepted.

NORTHEASTERN SEMINARY AT ROBERTS WESLEYAN COLLEGE, Rochester, NY 14624

General Information Independent-religious, coed, graduate-only institution. *Enrollment by degree level:* 89 master's. *Graduate faculty:* 6 full-time (2 women), 23 part-time/adjunct (4 women). One-time fee: $400 full-time. Tuition and fees vary according to course load. *Graduate housing:* On-campus housing not available. *Student services:* Campus employment opportunities, campus safety program, career counseling, exercise/wellness program, international student services, low-cost health insurance, services for students with disabilities, teacher training, writing training. *Library facilities:* B. Thomas Golisano Library plus 2 others. *Collection:* Study areas open 24 hours, 5–7 days a week; students can reserve study rooms.

Computer facilities: 104 computers available on campus for general student use. A campuswide network can be accessed from student residence rooms and from off campus. Online class registration is available.
Website: http://www.nes.edu/

General Application Contact: Caleb Matthews, Director of Recruitment, 585-594-6832, Fax: 585-594-6801, E-mail: matthews_caleb@nes.edu.

GRADUATE UNITS

Graduate and Professional Programs Students: 81 full-time (42 women), 40 part-time (9 women); includes 34 minority (28 Black or African American, non-Hispanic/Latino; 1 American Indian or Alaska Native, non-Hispanic/Latino; 2 Asian, non-Hispanic/Latino; 3 Hispanic/Latino). *Faculty:* 6 full-time (2 women), 23 part-time/adjunct (4 women). Expenses: Contact institution. *Financial support:* Teaching assistantships with partial

tuition reimbursements, career-related internships or fieldwork, institutionally sponsored loans, scholarships/grants, and tuition waivers (partial) available. Financial award applicants required to submit FAFSA. *Program availability:* Evening/weekend. Offers ministry (D Min); theological studies (MA); theology (M Div); theology and social justice (MA); transformational leadership (MA). M Div/MSW offered jointly with Roberts Wesleyan College. *Application deadline:* For fall admission, 8/1 priority date for domestic and international students; for spring admission, 12/15 priority date for domestic and international students. Applications are processed on a rolling basis. *Application fee:* $35. Electronic applications accepted. *Application Contact:* Douglas Cullum, Dean, 585-594-6331, Fax: 585-594-6801. *Dean*, Douglas Cullum, 585-594-6331, Fax: 585-594-6801.

NORTHEASTERN STATE UNIVERSITY, Tahlequah, OK 74464-2399

General Information State-supported, coed, comprehensive institution. *Enrollment:* 8,100 graduate, professional, and undergraduate students; 479 full-time matriculated graduate/professional students (331 women), 698 part-time matriculated graduate/professional students (515 women). *Enrollment by degree level:* 1,064 master's, 113 doctoral. *Graduate faculty:* 138 full-time (73 women), 11 part-time/adjunct (8 women). Tuition, state resident: full-time $2816; part-time $216.60 per credit hour. Tuition, nonresident: full-time $6365; part-time $489.60 per credit hour. *Required fees:* $37.40 per credit hour. *Graduate housing:* Rooms and/or apartments available on a first-come, first-served basis to single and married students. Typical cost: $2900 per year ($6650 including board) for single students; $6300 per year ($10,050 including board) for married students. Room and board charges vary according to board plan and housing facility selected. Housing application deadline: 6/1. *Student services:* Campus employment opportunities, campus safety program, career counseling, exercise/wellness program, free psychological counseling, international student services, low-cost health insurance, multicultural affairs office, services for students with disabilities, teacher training. *Library facilities:* John Vaughn Library. *Collection:* Books: 407,981 (physical), 56,335 (digital/electronic); Serial titles: 27,983 (physical), 58,449 (digital/electronic); Databases: 130. Weekly public service hours: 114.

Computer facilities: Computer purchase and lease plans are available. 1,160 computers available on campus for general student use. A campuswide network can be accessed from student residence rooms and from off campus. Online class registration is available.
Website: http://www.nsuok.edu/

General Application Contact: Dr. Donna Trout, Graduate Program Coordinator, 918-449-6123, Fax: 918-449-6120, E-mail: troutdk@nsuok.edu.

GRADUATE UNITS

College of Business and Technology Students: 44 full-time (16 women), 136 part-time (63 women); includes 73 minority (11 Black or African American, non-Hispanic/Latino; 33 American Indian or Alaska Native, non-Hispanic/Latino; 6 Asian, non-Hispanic/Latino; 10 Hispanic/Latino; 13 Two or more races, non-Hispanic/Latino), 15 international. Average age 33. *Faculty:* 16 full-time (5 women). Expenses: Contact institution. *Financial support:* Teaching assistantships and Federal Work-Study available. Financial award application deadline: 3/1. In 2016, 61 degrees awarded. *Program availability:* Part-time, evening/weekend. Offers accounting and financial analysis (MS); business administration (MBA, PMBA); business and technology (MBA, MEHS, MS, PMBA); environmental, health, and safety management (MEHS). *Application deadline:* For fall admission, 6/1 priority date for domestic students. Applications are processed on a rolling basis. *Application fee:* $0 ($25 for international students). Electronic applications accepted. *Application Contact:* Josh McCollum, Graduate Coordinator, 918-444-2093, E-mail: mccolluj@nsuok.edu. *Dean*, Dr. Roger Collier, 918-444-2900, E-mail: colliere@nsuok.edu.

College of Education Students: 145 full-time (112 women), 336 part-time (285 women); includes 193 minority (17 Black or African American, non-Hispanic/Latino; 89 American Indian or Alaska Native, non-Hispanic/Latino; 8 Asian, non-Hispanic/Latino; 10 Hispanic/Latino; 69 Two or more races, non-Hispanic/Latino), 6 international. Average age 34. *Faculty:* 43 full-time (28 women). Expenses: Contact institution. *Financial support:* Teaching assistantships, career-related internships or fieldwork, and Federal Work-Study available. Financial award application deadline: 3/1. In 2016, 167 master's awarded. *Program availability:* Part-time, evening/weekend. Offers counseling psychology (MS); early childhood education (M Ed); education (M Ed, MS, MS Ed); health and kinesiology (MS); higher education leadership (MS); instructional leadership (M Ed); library media and information technology (MS); reading (M Ed); school administration (M Ed); school counseling (M Ed); special education-autism spectrum disorders (M Ed); substance abuse counseling (MS). *Application deadline:* For fall admission, 6/1 priority date for domestic students. Applications are processed on a rolling basis. *Application fee:* $25. Electronic applications accepted. *Application Contact:* Josh McCollum, Graduate Coordinator, 918-444-2093, E-mail: mccolluj@nsuok.edu. *Dean of the College of Education*, Dr. Deborah Landry, 918-444-3700, E-mail: landryd@nsuok.edu.

College of Liberal Arts Students: 36 full-time (25 women), 68 part-time (45 women); includes 41 minority (3 Black or African American, non-Hispanic/Latino; 20 American Indian or Alaska Native, non-Hispanic/Latino; 6 Hispanic/Latino; 12 Two or more races, non-Hispanic/Latino), 1 international. Average age 33. *Faculty:* 18 full-time (7 women). Expenses: Contact institution. *Financial support:* Teaching assistantships and Federal Work-Study available. Financial award application deadline: 3/1. In 2016, 30 master's awarded. *Program availability:* Part-time, evening/weekend. Offers American studies (MA); communication (MS); criminal justice (MS); English (MA); liberal arts (MA, MS). *Application deadline:* For fall admission, 6/1 priority date for domestic students. Applications are processed on a rolling basis. *Application fee:* $25. Electronic applications accepted. *Application Contact:* Josh McCollum, Graduate Coordinator, 918-444-2093, E-mail: mccolluj@nsuok.edu. *Dean of Liberal Arts Administration*, Dr. Phillip Bridgmon, 918-444-3618, Fax: 918-458-2348, E-mail: bridgmon@nsuok.edu.

College of Optometry Students: 113 full-time (61 women); includes 32 minority (3 Black or African American, non-Hispanic/Latino; 11 American Indian or Alaska Native, non-Hispanic/Latino; 7 Asian, non-Hispanic/Latino; 5 Hispanic/Latino; 6 Two or more races, non-Hispanic/Latino). Average age 26. *Faculty:* 31 full-time (13 women), 2 part-time/adjunct (1 woman). Expenses: Contact institution. *Financial support:* Federal Work-Study, institutionally sponsored loans, scholarships/grants, tuition waivers (partial), and residencies available. Financial award application deadline: 5/1; financial award applicants required to submit FAFSA. In 2016, 28 doctorates awarded. Offers optometry (OD). *Application deadline:* For fall admission, 2/1 for domestic students. Applications are processed on a rolling basis. *Application fee:* $45. Electronic applications accepted. *Application Contact:* Sandy Medearis, Optometric Student and Alumni Services Director, 918-444-4006, Fax: 918-458-2104, E-mail: medearis@nsuok.edu. *Dean of Oklahoma College of Optometry*, Dr. Douglas Penisten, 918-444-4025, E-mail: penisten@nsuok.edu.

College of Science and Health Professions Students: 132 full-time (109 women), 69 part-time (57 women); includes 60 minority (2 Black or African American, non-Hispanic/Latino; 22 American Indian or Alaska Native, non-Hispanic/Latino; 2 Asian, non-Hispanic/Latino; 11 Hispanic/Latino; 23 Two or more races, non-Hispanic/Latino), 1 international. Average age 31. *Faculty:* 28 full-time (19 women). Expenses: Contact institution. In 2016, 73 master's awarded. Offers mathematics education (M Ed); natural sciences (MS); nursing education (MSN); occupational therapy (MS); science and health professions (M Ed, MS, MSN); science education (M Ed); speech-language pathology (MS). *Application fee:* $25. *Application Contact:* Josh McCollum, Graduate Coordinator, 918-444-2093, E-mail: mccolluj@nsuok.edu. *Dean,* Dr. Pamela Hathorn, 918-444-3800, E-mail: hathorn@nsuok.edu.

NORTHEASTERN UNIVERSITY, Boston, MA 02115-5096

General Information Independent, coed, university. CGS member. *Enrollment:* 25,466 graduate, professional, and undergraduate students; 7,604 full-time matriculated graduate/professional students (3,462 women), 6,777 part-time matriculated graduate/professional students (3,942 women). *Enrollment by degree level:* 10,461 master's, 3,545 doctoral, 375 other advanced degrees. *Graduate faculty:* 1,380 full-time (591 women), 1,411 part-time/adjunct (655 women). Tuition and fees vary according to course load and program. *Student services:* Campus employment opportunities, campus safety program, career counseling, child daycare facilities, exercise/wellness program, free psychological counseling, grant writing training, international student services, low-cost health insurance, multicultural affairs office, services for students with disabilities, teacher training. *Library facilities:* Snell Library plus 3 others. *Collection:* Books: 829,604 (physical), 548,629 (digital/electronic); Databases: 292. Study areas open 24 hours, 5–7 days a week; students can reserve study rooms. *Research affiliation:* Jobs for America's Graduates (labor studies), Cytyc Corporation (medical technology), BBN Technologies (information technology), Analog Devices, Inc. (electronics), General Electric Company (GE) (engineering).

Computer facilities: Computer purchase and lease plans are available. A campuswide network can be accessed from student residence rooms and from off campus. Online class registration is available.
Website: http://www.northeastern.edu/

GRADUATE UNITS

Bouvé College of Health Sciences Students: 1,371 full-time (1,009 women), 262 part-time (219 women). *Faculty:* 192 full-time (119 women), 194 part-time/adjunct (156 women). Expenses: Contact institution. *Financial support:* Fellowships, research assistantships, teaching assistantships, career-related internships or fieldwork, scholarships/grants, health care benefits, tuition waivers, and unspecified assistantships available. Support available to part-time students. Financial award applicants required to submit FAFSA. In 2016, 352 master's, 312 doctorates, 25 other advanced degrees awarded. *Program availability:* Part-time, evening/weekend, online learning. Offers applied behavior analysis (MS); audiology (Au D); counseling psychology (MS, PhD, CAGS); exercise science (MS); nursing (MS, PhD, CAGS); nursing practice (DNP); pharmaceutical sciences (MS, PhD); pharmacology (MS); pharmacy (Pharm D); school psychology (PhD); urban health (MPH). *Application fee:* $75. Electronic applications accepted. *Application Contact:* E-mail: bouvegrad@northeastern.edu. *Dean,* Bouvé College of Health Sciences, Susan L. Parish, 617-373-3323, Fax: 617-373-3030.

College of Arts, Media and Design Students: 239 full-time (147 women), 16 part-time (12 women). *Faculty:* 142 full-time (55 women), 80 part-time/adjunct (34 women). Expenses: Contact institution. *Financial support:* Applicants required to submit FAFSA. In 2016, 83 master's awarded. Offers architecture (M Arch); game science and design (MS); information design and visualization (MFA); interdisciplinary arts (MFA); journalism (MA); music industry leadership (MS); studio art (MFA); sustainable building systems (MS); sustainable urban environments (M Des). *Application fee:* $75. Electronic applications accepted. *Application Contact:* Jane Amidon, Associate Dean for Graduate Programs and Research, 617-373-4614, E-mail: gscamd@northeastern.edu. *Dean,* Dr. Elizabeth Hudson.

College of Computer and Information Science Students: 1,064 full-time (306 women), 34 part-time (10 women). *Faculty:* 79 full-time (21 women), 34 part-time/adjunct (7 women). Expenses: Contact institution. *Financial support:* Research assistantships, teaching assistantships, scholarships/grants, health care benefits, and unspecified assistantships available. Financial award applicants required to submit FAFSA. In 2016, 322 master's, 8 doctorates awarded. *Program availability:* Part-time, evening/weekend. Offers computer science (MS, PhD); data science (MS); game science and design (MS); health informatics (MS); information assurance (MS); network science (PhD); personal health informatics (PhD). *Application fee:* $75. Electronic applications accepted. *Application Contact:* Dr. Rajmohan Rajaraman, Professor/Associate Dean/Director of the Graduate School, 617-373-8493, E-mail: gradschool@ccs.neu.edu. *Professor and Dean,* Dr. Carla Brodley.

College of Engineering Students: 2,982 full-time (954 women), 192 part-time (38 women). *Faculty:* 202 full-time (59 women), 53 part-time/adjunct (9 women). Expenses: Contact institution. *Financial support:* Fellowships, research assistantships, teaching assistantships, career-related internships or fieldwork, scholarships/grants, health care benefits, tuition waivers, and unspecified assistantships available. Support available to part-time students. Financial award applicants required to submit FAFSA. In 2016, 851 master's, 74 doctorates awarded. *Program availability:* Part-time, online learning. Offers bioengineering (MS, PhD); chemical engineering (MS, PhD); civil engineering (MS, PhD); computer engineering (PhD); computer systems engineering (MS); electrical and computer engineering (MS); electrical and computer engineering leadership (MS); electrical engineering (PhD); energy systems (MS); engineering and public policy (PhD); engineering management (MS, Certificate); environmental engineering (MS); industrial engineering (MS, PhD); information assurance (PhD); information systems (MS); interdisciplinary engineering (PhD); mechanical engineering (PhD); operations research (MS); telecommunication systems management (MS). *Application fee:* $75. Electronic applications accepted. *Application Contact:* Jeffery Hengel, Director of Graduate Admissions, 617-373-2711, E-mail: j.hengel@northeastern.edu. *Dean,* College of Engineering, Dr. Nadine Aubry.

College of Professional Studies Students: 4,947 full-time (3,076 women), *Faculty:* 82 full-time (51 women), 853 part-time/adjunct (366 women). Expenses: Contact institution. *Financial support:* Applicants required to submit FAFSA. In 2016, 1,456 master's awarded. *Program availability:* Part-time, evening/weekend, 100% online, blended/hybrid learning. Offers applied nutrition (MS); college athletics administration (MSL); commerce and economic development (MS); corporate and organizational communication (MS); criminal justice (MS); digital media (MPS); elearning and instructional design (M Ed); elementary education (MAT); geographic information technology (MPS); global studies and international relations (MS); higher education administration (M Ed); homeland security (MA); human services (MS); informatics (MPS); leadership (MS); learning analytics (M Ed); learning and instruction (M Ed); nonprofit management (MS); professional sports administration (MSL); project management (MS); regulatory affairs

for drugs, biologics, and medical devices (MS); respiratory care leadership (MS); special education (M Ed); technical communication (MS). *Application deadline:* Applications are processed on a rolling basis. *Application fee:* $0. Electronic applications accepted. *Interim Dean of the College of Professional Studies,* Dr. Mary Loeffelholz.

College of Science Students: 578 full-time (268 women), 63 part-time (27 women). *Faculty:* 217 full-time (76 women), 58 part-time/adjunct (20 women). Expenses: Contact institution. *Financial support:* Fellowships with tuition reimbursements, research assistantships with tuition reimbursements, teaching assistantships with tuition reimbursements, career-related internships or fieldwork, scholarships/grants, health care benefits, tuition waivers (full and partial), and unspecified assistantships available. Support available to part-time students. Financial award applicants required to submit FAFSA. In 2016, 121 master's, 50 doctorates awarded. *Program availability:* Part-time. Offers applied mathematics (MS); bioinformatics (MS); biology (PhD); biotechnology (MS); chemistry (MS, PhD); ecology, evolution, and marine biology (PhD); marine biology (MS); mathematics (MS, PhD); network science (PhD); operations research (MSOR); physics (MS, PhD); psychology (PhD). *Application deadline:* Applications are processed on a rolling basis. *Application fee:* $75. Electronic applications accepted. *Application Contact:* Graduate Student Services, 617-373-4275, E-mail: gradcos@northeastern.edu. *Dean,* Dr. Kenneth Henderson.

College of Social Sciences and Humanities Students: 427 full-time (239 women), 77 part-time (42 women). *Faculty:* 234 full-time (114 women), 55 part-time/adjunct (34 women). Expenses: Contact institution. *Financial support:* Teaching assistantships, career-related internships or fieldwork, scholarships/grants, health care benefits, tuition waivers (full and partial), and unspecified assistantships available. Support available to part-time students. Financial award applicants required to submit FAFSA. In 2016, 143 master's, 38 doctorates awarded. *Program availability:* Online learning. Offers criminology and criminal justice (MSCJ); criminology and justice policy (PhD); economics (MA, PhD); English (MA, PhD); international affairs (MA); law and public policy (PhD); political science (MA, PhD); public administration (MPA); public history (MA); public policy (MPP); security and resilience studies (MS); sociology (MA, PhD); urban and regional policy (MS); urban informatics (MS); world history (MA, PhD). *Application fee:* $75. Electronic applications accepted. *Application Contact:* Amber Crowe, Administrative Coordinator, 617-373-5990, Fax: 617-373-7281, E-mail: gradcssh@northeastern.edu. *Dean,* Dr. Uta Poiger, 617-373-5173.

D'Amore-McKim School of Business Students: 379 full-time (180 women), 1,182 part-time (514 women). *Faculty:* 185 full-time (66 women), 57 part-time/adjunct (13 women). Expenses: Contact institution. *Financial support:* Scholarships/grants available. Financial award applicants required to submit FAFSA. In 2016, 800 master's awarded. *Program availability:* Part-time, evening/weekend, online learning. Offers accounting (MS); business administration (EMBA, MBA); finance (MS); innovation (MS); international business (MS); international management (MS); taxation (MS); technological entrepreneurship (MS). *Application fee:* $75. Electronic applications accepted. *Application Contact:* Evelyn Tate, Director, Graduate Recruitment and Admissions, 617-373-3258, Fax: 617-373-8564, E-mail: e.tate@northeastern.edu. *Dean, D'Amore-McKim School of Business,* Dr. Hugh Courtney.

School of Law Students: 564 full-time (359 women), 4 part-time (all women). *Faculty:* 46 full-time (30 women), 26 part-time/adjunct (16 women). Expenses: Contact institution. *Financial support:* Scholarships/grants available. Financial award applicants required to submit FAFSA. In 2016, 32 master's, 175 doctorates awarded. *Program availability:* Online learning. Offers law (LL M, MLS, JD). JD/MPH offered jointly with Tufts University; JD/MSA/MBA with Graduate School of Professional Accounting; JD/MS with Program in Law and Public Policy; JD/MELP with Vermont Law School; and JD/MA with Brandeis University. *Application deadline:* Applications are processed on a rolling basis. *Application fee:* $75. Electronic applications accepted. *Application Contact:* Information Contact, 617-373-2395, Fax: 617-373-8865, E-mail: lawadmissions@northeastern.edu. *Dean,* Jeremy R. Paul, 617-373-3307, Fax: 617-373-8793, E-mail: j.paul@northeastern.edu.

NORTHEAST OHIO MEDICAL UNIVERSITY, Rootstown, OH 44272-0095

General Information State-supported, coed, graduate-only institution. *Enrollment by degree level:* 24 master's, 936 doctoral, 19 other advanced degrees. *Graduate faculty:* 517 full-time (201 women), 2,187 part-time/adjunct (758 women). Tuition, state resident: part-time $576 per credit hour. Tuition, nonresident: part-time $587 per credit hour. Full-time tuition and fees vary according to program and student level. *Graduate housing:* Rooms and/or apartments guaranteed to single and married students. *Student services:* Campus employment opportunities, campus safety program, career counseling, free psychological counseling, low-cost health insurance, multicultural affairs office, services for students with disabilities. *Library facilities:* Oliver Ocasek Regional Medical Information Center. *Collection:* Books: 47,900 (physical), 122,231 (digital/electronic); Serial titles: 7,455 (physical), 11,060 (digital/electronic); Databases: 131. Weekly public service hours: 74; study areas open 24 hours, 5–7 days a week. *Research affiliation:* American Heart Association (physiology, biochemistry), National Science Foundation (anatomy), National Institutes of Health (anatomy, biochemistry, immunology, neurobiology, microbiology), Summa Health Systems (orthopedics, anatomy), Margaret Clark Morgan Foundation (schizophrenia, mental illness), Austen BioInnovation Institute in Akron (pharmacology, drug delivery, biotechnology, community health).

Computer facilities: 50 computers available on campus for general student use. A campuswide network can be accessed from student residence rooms and from off campus. Online class registration is available.
Website: http://www.neomed.edu/

General Application Contact: Heidi Terry, Director, Admissions and Student Services, 330-325-6270, E-mail: admission@neomed.edu.

GRADUATE UNITS

College of Graduate Studies Students: 15 full-time (7 women), 26 part-time (11 women); includes 7 minority (5 Asian, non-Hispanic/Latino; 2 Hispanic/Latino). Average age 27. Expenses: Contact institution. *Program availability:* Part-time. Offers bioethics (Certificate); health-system pharmacy administration (MS); integrated pharmaceutical medicine (MS, PhD); public health (MS). *Application deadline:* For fall admission, 9/1 priority date for domestic students; for winter admission, 1/5 priority date for domestic students. Applications are processed on a rolling basis. Electronic applications accepted. *Application Contact:* Heidi Terry, Executive Director, Enrollment Services, 330-325-6479, E-mail: htterry@neomed.edu. *Dean,* Dr. Steven Schmidt, 330-325-6290.

College of Medicine Expenses: Contact institution. *Financial support:* Institutionally sponsored loans and scholarships/grants available. Financial award application deadline: 4/15; financial award applicants required to submit FAFSA. Offers medicine (MD). *Application deadline:* For fall admission, 8/1 priority date for domestic students; for winter admission, 10/1 for domestic students. Applications are processed on a rolling basis. *Application fee:* $40. Electronic applications accepted. *Application Contact:* Heidi Terry, Executive Director, Enrollment Services, 330-325-6479, E-mail: htterry@neomed.edu. *Dean,* Dr. Jeffrey L. Susman, 330-325-6101.

College of Pharmacy Expenses: Contact institution. *Financial support:* Scholarships/grants available. Financial award application deadline: 4/15; financial award applicants required to submit FAFSA. Offers pharmacy (Pharm D). *Application deadline:* For fall admission, 9/1 priority date for domestic students; for winter admission, 1/5 for domestic students. Applications are processed on a rolling basis. *Application fee:* $50. Electronic applications accepted. *Application Contact:* Heidi Terry, Executive Director, Enrollment Services, 330-325-6479, E-mail: htterry@neomed.edu. *Dean,* Dr. Charles Taylor, 330-325-6461, Fax: 330-325-5930.

NORTHERN ARIZONA UNIVERSITY, Flagstaff, AZ 86011

General Information State-supported, coed, university. CGS member. *Enrollment:* 30,368 graduate, professional, and undergraduate students; 1,848 full-time matriculated graduate/professional students (1,216 women), 1,909 part-time matriculated graduate/professional students (1,356 women). *Enrollment by degree level:* 2,898 master's, 740 doctoral, 119 other advanced degrees. *Graduate faculty:* 1,078 full-time (537 women), 522 part-time/adjunct (328 women). Tuition, state resident: full-time $8971; part-time $444 per credit hour. Tuition, nonresident: full-time $20,958; part-time $1164 per credit hour. *Required fees:* $1018; $644 per credit hour. Tuition and fees vary according to course load, campus/location and program. *Graduate housing:* Rooms and/or apartments available on a first-come, first-served basis to single and married students. Housing application deadline: 5/15. *Student services:* Campus employment opportunities, campus safety program, career counseling, exercise/wellness program, free psychological counseling, grant writing training, international student services, low-cost health insurance, multicultural affairs office, services for students with disabilities, teacher training, writing training. *Library facilities:* Cline Library plus 1 other. *Collection:* Books: 574,723 (physical), 232,571 (digital/electronic); Serial titles: 6,264 (physical), 88,412 (digital/electronic); Databases: 141. Weekly public service hours: 117; students can reserve study rooms. *Research affiliation:* W.L. Gore and Associates, Inc. (biomedical engineering), Museum of Northern Arizona (anthropology), Lowell Observatory (physics and astronomy), Rocky Mountain Forest and Range Experiment Station (forestry), U.S. Naval Observatory (physics and astronomy), U.S. Geological Survey (USGS) (geology).

Computer facilities: Computer purchase and lease plans are available. A campuswide network can be accessed from student residence rooms and from off campus. Online class registration, computer repair service available on campus are available. Website: http://www.nau.edu/

General Application Contact: Graduate Admissions, 928-523-4348, Fax: 928-523-8950, E-mail: graduate@nau.edu.

GRADUATE UNITS

Graduate College *Program availability:* Part-time, 100% online, blended/hybrid learning. Electronic applications accepted.

College of Arts and Letters Program availability: Part-time. Offers applied linguistics (PhD); arts and letters (MA, MAT, MFA, MM, PhD, Certificate); choral conducting (MM); composition (MM); creative writing (MFA); English (MA); history (MA); instrumental conducting (MM); instrumental performance (MM); musicology (MM); performance (Certificate); piano accompanying and chamber music (MM); professional writing (Certificate); Spanish (MAT); Spanish education (MAT); Suzuki violin/viola (MM); teaching English as a second language (MA, Certificate); theory (MM); vocal performance (MM). Electronic applications accepted.

College of Education Program availability: Part-time, evening/weekend, online learning. Offers autism spectrum disorders (Certificate); bilingual/multicultural education (M Ed); career and technical education (M Ed, Certificate); community college teaching and learning (Certificate); community college/higher education (M Ed); counseling (MA); culturally and linguistically diverse special education (Certificate); curriculum and instruction (Ed D); early childhood education (M Ed); early childhood special education (M Ed); education (M Ed, MA, Ed D, PhD, Certificate, Ed S); educational foundations (M Ed); educational leadership (M Ed, Ed D); educational psychology (PhD); educational technology (M Ed, Certificate); elementary education (M Ed); English as a second language (Certificate); human relations (M Ed); mild/moderate disabilities (M Ed); positive behavior support (Certificate); principal (Certificate); principal K-12 (M Ed); school counseling (M Ed); school leadership K-12 (M Ed); school psychology (Ed S); secondary education (M Ed); special education (M Ed); student affairs (M Ed); superintendent (Certificate). Electronic applications accepted.

College of Engineering, Forestry, and Natural Sciences Offers applied physics (MS); applied statistics (Certificate); astronomy (PhD); biological sciences (MS, PhD); chemistry (MS); civil engineering (M Eng, MSE); climate science and solutions (MS); computer science (MSE); earth sciences and environmental sustainability (PhD); electrical and computer engineering (M Eng, MSE); engineering (M Eng, MSE); engineering, forestry, and natural sciences (M Eng, MAST, MAT, MF, MS, MSE, MSF, PhD, Certificate); environmental engineering (M Eng, MSE); environmental sciences and policy (MS); forest science (PhD); forestry (MF, MSF); geology (MS); mathematics (MS); mathematics education (MS); mechanical engineering (M Eng, MSE); science teaching (MAST, Certificate); statistics (MS); teaching science (MAT).

College of Health and Human Services Program availability: Part-time. Offers clinical speech-language pathology (MS); family nurse practitioner (MSN, Certificate); health and human services (MPAS, MS, MSN, DNP, DPT, Certificate); nurse generalist (MSN); nursing practice (DNP); occupational therapy (OTD); physical therapy (DPT); physician assistant (MPAS).

College of Social and Behavioral Sciences Program availability: Part-time. Offers applied criminology (MS); applied geospatial sciences (MS); applied sociology (MA); archaeology (MA); assistive technology (Certificate); clinical health psychology (MA); communication (MA); community planning (Certificate); disability policy and practice (Certificate); ethnic studies (Graduate Certificate); general psychology (MA); geographic information systems (Certificate); linguistic anthropology (MA); political science (MA, PhD); public administration (MPA); public management (Certificate); social and behavioral sciences (MA, MPA, MS, PhD, Certificate, Graduate Certificate); sociocultural anthropology (MA); sustainable communities (MA); teaching psychology (MA); women's and gender studies (Graduate Certificate). Electronic applications accepted.

NAU-Yuma Offers administration (M Adm); global business administration (MGBA). Electronic applications accepted.

The W. A. Franke College of Business Program availability: Part-time. Offers business (MBA). Electronic applications accepted.

NORTHERN ILLINOIS UNIVERSITY, De Kalb, IL 60115-2854

General Information State-supported, coed, university. CGS member. *Enrollment:* 19,015 graduate, professional, and undergraduate students; 2,245 full-time matriculated graduate/professional students (1,071 women), 2,160 part-time matriculated graduate/professional students (1,205 women). *Enrollment by degree level:* 3,462 master's, 906 doctoral, 37 other advanced degrees. *Graduate faculty:* 672 full-time (248 women), 66 part-time/adjunct (17 women). *Graduate housing:* Rooms and/or apartments available on a first-come, first-served basis to single and married students. *Student services:* Campus employment opportunities, campus safety program, career counseling, child daycare facilities, exercise/wellness program, free psychological counseling, grant writing training, international student services, low-cost health insurance, services for students with disabilities, teacher training, writing training. *Library facilities:* Founders Memorial Library plus 4 others. *Collection:* Books: 1.8 million (physical), 471,409 (digital/electronic); Serial titles: 600 (physical), 76,936 (digital/electronic); Databases: 318. Students can reserve study rooms. *Research affiliation:* Field Museum of Natural History, Burpee Museum of Natural History, Argonne National Laboratory, Fermi National Accelerator Laboratory.

Computer facilities: 1,500 computers available on campus for general student use. A campuswide network can be accessed from student residence rooms and from off campus. Online class registration is available. Website: http://www.niu.edu/

General Application Contact: Dr. Bradley G. Bond, Dean, Graduate School, 815-753-0395, Fax: 815-753-6366, E-mail: gradsch@niu.edu.

GRADUATE UNITS

College of Law Students: 229 full-time (110 women), 35 part-time (17 women); includes 66 minority (26 Black or African American, non-Hispanic/Latino; 12 Asian, non-Hispanic/Latino; 23 Hispanic/Latino; 2 Native Hawaiian or other Pacific Islander, non-Hispanic/Latino; 3 Two or more races, non-Hispanic/Latino), 1 international. Average age 28. 564 applicants, 63% accepted, 106 enrolled. *Faculty:* 22 full-time (11 women). Expenses: Contact institution. *Financial support:* In 2016–17, 8 teaching assistantships were awarded; research assistantships, career-related internships or fieldwork, Federal Work-Study, tuition waivers (full and partial), and unspecified assistantships also available. Support available to part-time students. Financial award application deadline: 3/1; financial award applicants required to submit FAFSA. In 2016, 88 doctorates awarded. *Program availability:* Offers law (JD). *Application deadline:* For fall admission, 4/1 priority date for domestic and international students. Applications are processed on a rolling basis. Electronic applications accepted. *Application Contact:* Amanda Noascono, Director of Admissions and Financial Aid, 815-753-8595, Fax: 815-753-5680, E-mail: law-admit@niu.edu. *Dean,* Eric Dannenmaier, 815-753-5300, Fax: 815-753-8552, E-mail: edan@niu.edu.

Graduate School Students: 2,016 full-time (961 women), 2,125 part-time (1,188 women); includes 785 minority (234 Black or African American, non-Hispanic/Latino; 2 American Indian or Alaska Native, non-Hispanic/Latino; 196 Asian, non-Hispanic/Latino; 251 Hispanic/Latino; 102 Two or more races, non-Hispanic/Latino), 855 international. Average age 31. 3,995 applicants, 53% accepted, 899 enrolled. *Faculty:* 672 full-time (248 women), 66 part-time/adjunct (17 women). Expenses: Contact institution. *Financial support:* In 2016–17, 397 research assistantships with full tuition reimbursements, 825 teaching assistantships with full tuition reimbursements were awarded; fellowships with full tuition reimbursements, career-related internships or fieldwork, Federal Work-Study, scholarships/grants, tuition waivers (full), and staff assistantships also available. Support available to part-time students. Financial award applicants required to submit FAFSA. In 2016, 1,545 master's, 162 doctorates, 22 other advanced degrees awarded. *Program availability:* Part-time, evening/weekend, online learning. *Application deadline:* For fall admission, 8/1 for domestic students, 5/1 for international students; for spring admission, 12/1 for domestic students, 10/1 for international students. Applications are processed on a rolling basis. *Application fee:* $40. Electronic applications accepted. *Application Contact:* Graduate School Information, 815-753-0395, E-mail: gradsch@niu.edu. *Dean,* Dr. Bradley G. Bond, 815-753-9403, Fax: 815-753-6366, E-mail: bbond@niu.edu.

College of Business Students: 434 full-time (158 women), 486 part-time (165 women); includes 226 minority (48 Black or African American, non-Hispanic/Latino; 97 Asian, non-Hispanic/Latino; 59 Hispanic/Latino; 22 Two or more races, non-Hispanic/Latino), 240 international. Average age 31. 807 applicants, 63% accepted, 243 enrolled. *Faculty:* 53 full-time (17 women), 3 part-time/adjunct (0 women). Expenses: Contact institution. *Financial support:* In 2016–17, 5 research assistantships with full tuition reimbursements were awarded; fellowships with full tuition reimbursements, teaching assistantships with full tuition reimbursements, career-related internships or fieldwork, Federal Work-Study, scholarships/grants, tuition waivers (full), and unspecified assistantships also available. Support available to part-time students. Financial award applicants required to submit FAFSA. In 2016, 537 master's awarded. *Program availability:* Part-time, evening/weekend. Offers accountancy (MAS, MST); business (MAS, MBA, MST); business administration (MBA); management information systems (MS). *Application deadline:* For fall admission, 6/1 for domestic students, 5/1 for international students; for spring admission, 11/1 for domestic students, 10/1 for international students. Applications are processed on a rolling basis. *Application fee:* $40. Electronic applications accepted. *Application Contact:* Office of Graduate Studies in Business, 815-753-6301. *Dean,* Balaji Rajagopalan, 815-753-6225, Fax: 815-753-5305, E-mail: brajagopalan@niu.edu.

College of Education Students: 320 full-time (193 women), 882 part-time (637 women); includes 275 minority (122 Black or African American, non-Hispanic/Latino; 2 American Indian or Alaska Native, non-Hispanic/Latino; 27 Asian, non-Hispanic/Latino; 90 Hispanic/Latino; 34 Two or more races, non-Hispanic/Latino), 66 international. Average age 35. 544 applicants, 67% accepted, 195 enrolled. *Faculty:* 110 full-time (66 women), 5 part-time/adjunct (3 women). Expenses: Contact institution. *Financial support:* Fellowships with full tuition reimbursements, research assistantships with full tuition reimbursements, teaching assistantships with full tuition reimbursements, career-related internships or fieldwork, Federal Work-Study, scholarships/grants, tuition waivers (full), and staff assistantships available. Support available to part-time students. Financial award applicants required to submit FAFSA. In 2016, 331 master's, 69 doctorates, 17 other advanced degrees awarded. *Program availability:* Part-time, evening/weekend, online learning. Offers adult and higher education (MS Ed, Ed D); counseling (MS Ed, Ed D); curriculum and instruction (MS Ed, Ed D); early childhood education (MS Ed); education (MS, MS Ed, Ed D, Ed S); educational administration (MS Ed, Ed D, Ed S); educational psychology (MS Ed, Ed D); educational research and evaluation (MS); elementary education (MS Ed); foundations of education (MS Ed); instructional technology (MS Ed, Ed D); kinesiology and physical education (MS, MS Ed); literacy education (MS Ed); school business management (MS Ed); special education (MS Ed). *Application deadline:* For fall admission, 6/1 for domestic students, 5/1 for international students; for spring admission, 11/1 for domestic students, 10/1 for international students. Applications are processed on a rolling basis. *Application fee:* $40. Electronic applications accepted. *Application Contact:* Graduate School Office, 815-753-0395, E-mail: gradsch@niu.edu. *Dean,* Laurie Elish-Piper, 815-753-1949, Fax: 851-753-2100.

College of Engineering and Engineering Technology Students: 169 full-time (27 women), 143 part-time (21 women); includes 32 minority (8 Black or African American, non-Hispanic/Latino; 7 Asian, non-Hispanic/Latino; 12 Hispanic/Latino; 5 Two or more races, non-Hispanic/Latino), 210 international. Average age 26. 527 applicants, 52% accepted, 68 enrolled. *Faculty:* 36 full-time (2 women), 2 part-time/adjunct (0 women). Expenses: Contact institution. *Financial support:* In 2016–17, 1 research assistantship with full tuition reimbursement, 1 teaching assistantship with full tuition reimbursement were awarded; fellowships with full tuition reimbursements, career-related internships or fieldwork, Federal Work-Study, scholarships/grants, tuition waivers (full), and unspecified assistantships also available. Support available to part-time students. Financial award applicants required to submit FAFSA. In 2016, 133 master's awarded. *Program availability:* Part-time, evening/weekend. Offers electrical engineering (MS); engineering and engineering technology (MS); industrial engineering (MS); industrial management (MS); mechanical engineering (MS). *Application deadline:* For fall admission, 6/1 for domestic students, 5/1 for international students; for spring admission, 11/1 for domestic students, 10/1 for international students. Applications are processed on a rolling basis. *Application fee:* $40. Electronic applications accepted. *Application Contact:* Graduate School Office, 815-753-0395, E-mail: gradsch@niu.edu. *Acting Dean,* Dr. Omar A. Ghrayeb, 815-753-1281, Fax: 815-753-1310, E-mail: oghrayeb@niu.edu.

College of Health and Human Sciences Students: 291 full-time (214 women), 198 part-time (169 women); includes 99 minority (24 Black or African American, non-Hispanic/Latino; 28 Asian, non-Hispanic/Latino; 30 Hispanic/Latino; 17 Two or more races, non-Hispanic/Latino), 8 international. Average age 30. 431 applicants, 38% accepted, 88 enrolled. *Faculty:* 46 full-time (37 women), 5 part-time/adjunct (3 women). Expenses: Contact institution. *Financial support:* In 2016–17, 4 research assistantships with full tuition reimbursements were awarded; fellowships with full tuition reimbursements, teaching assistantships with full tuition reimbursements, career-related internships or fieldwork, Federal Work-Study, scholarships/grants, tuition waivers (full), and staff assistantships also available. Support available to part-time students. Financial award applicants required to submit FAFSA. In 2016, 141 master's, 41 doctorates awarded. *Program availability:* Part-time, evening/weekend. Offers allied health and communicative disorders (MA, MPT, Au D, DPT, TDPT); applied family and child studies (MS); communicative disorders (MA, Au D); health and human sciences (MA, MPT, MS, Au D, DPT, TDPT); nursing (MS); nutrition and dietetics (MS); physical therapy (MPT, DPT, TDPT). *Application deadline:* For fall admission, 6/1 for domestic students, 5/1 for international students; for spring admission, 11/1 for domestic students, 10/1 for international students. Applications are processed on a rolling basis. *Application fee:* $40. Electronic applications accepted. *Application Contact:* Graduate School Office, 815-753-0395, E-mail: gradsch@niu.edu. *Dean,* Dr. Derryl Block, 815-753-6157.

College of Liberal Arts and Sciences Students: 684 full-time (304 women), 365 part-time (168 women); includes 118 minority (27 Black or African American, non-Hispanic/Latino; 21 Asian, non-Hispanic/Latino; 51 Hispanic/Latino; 19 Two or more races, non-Hispanic/Latino), 297 international. Average age 29. 1,469 applicants, 47% accepted, 224 enrolled. *Faculty:* 342 full-time (99 women), 36 part-time/adjunct (7 women). Expenses: Contact institution. *Financial support:* In 2016–17, 1 research assistantship with full tuition reimbursement was awarded; fellowships with full tuition reimbursements, teaching assistantships with full tuition reimbursements, career-related internships or fieldwork, Federal Work-Study, scholarships/grants, tuition waivers (full), and unspecified assistantships also available. Support available to part-time students. Financial award applicants required to submit FAFSA. In 2016, 337 master's, 52 doctorates awarded. *Program availability:* Part-time, evening/weekend. Offers anthropology (MA); biological sciences (MS, PhD); chemistry and biochemistry (MS, PhD); communication studies (MA); computer science (MS); economics (MA, PhD); English (MA, PhD); French (MA); geography (MS, PhD); geology and environmental geosciences (MS, PhD); history (MA, PhD); liberal arts and sciences (MA, MPA, MS, PhD); mathematical sciences (PhD); mathematics (MS); philosophy (MA); physics (MS, PhD); political science (MA, PhD); psychology (MA, PhD); public administration (MPA); sociology (MA); Spanish (MA); statistics (MS). *Application deadline:* For fall admission, 6/1 for international students; for spring admission, 11/1 for domestic students, 10/1 for international students. Applications are processed on a rolling basis. *Application fee:* $40. Electronic applications accepted. *Application Contact:* Graduate School Office, 815-753-0395, E-mail: gradsch@niu.edu. *Acting Dean,* Dr. Christopher McCord, 815-753-1061, Fax: 815-753-7950, E-mail: mccord@niu.edu.

College of Visual and Performing Arts Students: 118 full-time (65 women), 51 part-time (28 women); includes 24 minority (5 Black or African American, non-Hispanic/Latino; 5 Asian, non-Hispanic/Latino; 9 Hispanic/Latino; 5 Two or more races, non-Hispanic/Latino), 34 international. Average age 30. 216 applicants, 54% accepted, 63 enrolled. *Faculty:* 85 full-time (27 women), 15 part-time/adjunct (4 women). Expenses: Contact institution. *Financial support:* Fellowships with full tuition reimbursements, research assistantships with full tuition reimbursements, teaching assistantships with full tuition reimbursements, career-related internships or fieldwork, Federal Work-Study, scholarships/grants, tuition waivers (full), and staff assistantships available. Support available to part-time students. Financial award applicants required to submit FAFSA. In 2016, 79 master's, 5 other advanced degrees awarded. *Program availability:* Part-time, evening/weekend. Offers art (MA, MFA, MS); music (MM, Performer's Certificate); theatre and dance (MFA); visual and performing arts (MA, MFA, MM, MS, Performer's Certificate). *Application deadline:* For fall admission, 5/1 for international students; for spring admission, 10/1 for international students. Applications are processed on a rolling basis. *Application fee:* $40. Electronic applications accepted. *Application Contact:* Graduate School Office, 815-753-0395, E-mail: gradsch@niu.edu. *Dean,* Dr. Paul Bauer, 815-753-1138, Fax: 815-753-8372, E-mail: paulbauer@niu.edu.

NORTHERN KENTUCKY UNIVERSITY, Highland Heights, KY 41099

General Information State-supported, coed, comprehensive institution. CGS member. *Graduate housing:* Room and/or apartments available on a first-come, first-serve basis to single students; on-campus housing not available to married students. Housing application deadline: 5/1.

GRADUATE UNITS

Chase College of Law *Program availability:* Part-time, evening/weekend. Offers law (JD). Electronic applications accepted.

Office of Graduate Programs *Program availability:* Part-time, evening/weekend, online learning. Electronic applications accepted.

College of Arts and Sciences *Program availability:* Part-time, evening/weekend, online learning. Offers arts and sciences (MA, MPA, MS, Certificate); composition and rhetoric (Certificate); creative writing (Certificate); cultural studies and discourses (Certificate); English (MA); industrial psychology (Certificate); industrial-organizational psychology (MS); integrative studies (MA); non-profit management (Certificate); occupational health psychology (Certificate); organizational psychology (Certificate); professional writing (Certificate); public administration (MPA); public history (MA). Electronic applications accepted.

College of Business *Program availability:* Part-time, evening/weekend. Offers accountancy (M Acc); advanced taxation (Certificate); business (M Acc, MBA, MS, Certificate); business administration (MBA, Certificate); executive leadership and organizational change (MS). Electronic applications accepted.

College of Education and Human Services *Program availability:* Part-time, evening/weekend. Offers clinical mental health counseling (MS); education (MA, Certificate); education and human services (MA, MAT, MS, MSW, Ed D, Certificate, Ed S); educational leadership (Ed D, Ed S); school counseling (MA); social work (MSW); special education (Certificate); teaching (MAT). Electronic applications accepted.

College of Informatics *Program availability:* Part-time, evening/weekend. Offers business informatics (MS, Certificate); communication (MA); communication teaching (Certificate); computer information technology (MSCIT); computer science (MSCS); corporate information security (Certificate); documentary studies (Certificate); enterprise resource planning (Certificate); geographic information systems (Certificate); health informatics (MS, Certificate); informatics (MA, MS, MSCIT, MSCS, Certificate); public relations (Certificate); relationships (Certificate); secure software engineering (Certificate). Electronic applications accepted.

School of Nursing and Health Professions *Program availability:* Part-time, evening/weekend, online learning. Offers health science (MS); nursing (MSHS, MSN, DNP, Certificate, Post-Master's Certificate); nursing and health professions (MS, MSHS, MSN, DNP, Certificate, Post-Master's Certificate). Electronic applications accepted.

NORTHERN MICHIGAN UNIVERSITY, Marquette, MI 49855-5301

General Information State-supported, coed, comprehensive institution. CGS member. *Graduate housing:* Rooms and/or apartments available on a first-come, first-served basis to single and married students. Housing application deadline: 6/30.

GRADUATE UNITS

Office of Graduate Education and Research Students: 177 full-time (93 women), 413 part-time (226 women); includes 52 minority (10 Black or African American, non-Hispanic/Latino; 16 American Indian or Alaska Native, non-Hispanic/Latino; 7 Asian, non-Hispanic/Latino; 8 Hispanic/Latino; 11 Two or more races, non-Hispanic/Latino), 10 international. *Faculty:* 63 full-time (31 women), 1 part-time/adjunct (0 women). Expenses: Contact institution. *Financial support:* In 2016–17, 100 teaching assistantships with full tuition reimbursements (averaging $9,076 per year) were awarded; career-related internships or fieldwork, Federal Work-Study, institutionally sponsored loans, and unspecified assistantships also available. Support available to part-time students. Financial award applicants required to submit FAFSA. *Program availability:* Part-time, evening/weekend, online learning. *Application deadline:* For fall admission, 7/1 for domestic students; for winter admission, 11/15 for domestic students; for spring admission, 3/17 for domestic students. Applications are processed on a rolling basis. *Application fee:* $50. Electronic applications accepted. *Application Contact:* Helen Bicigo, 906-227-2300, Fax: 906-227-2315, E-mail: graduate@nmu.edu. *Interim Director of Graduate Education,* Dr. Lisa Eckert, 906-227-2300, E-mail: graduate@nmu.edu.

College of Arts and Sciences *Program availability:* Part-time, online learning. Offers applied behavior analysis (MS); arts and sciences (MA, MFA, MS, Graduate Certificate); biochemistry (MS); biology (MS); creative writing (MFA); literature (MA); pedagogy (MA); performance improvement (Graduate Certificate); psychology (MS); teaching English to speakers of other languages (Graduate Certificate); theater (MA); training and performance improvement (MS); writing (MA). Electronic applications accepted.

College of Business *Program availability:* Part-time. Offers business (MBA). Electronic applications accepted.

College of Health Sciences and Professional Studies *Program availability:* Part-time. Offers administration and supervision (MAE); clinical molecular genetics (MS); elementary education (MAE); exercise science (MS); health sciences and professional studies (MA, MA Ed, MAE, MPA, MS, MSN, DNP); higher education in student affairs (MA); instruction (MAE); learning disabilities (MAE); nursing (MSN, DNP); public administration (MPA); reading education (MAE); science education (MS); secondary education (MAE).

NORTHERN SEMINARY, Lombard, IL 60148-5698

General Information Independent-religious, coed, primarily men, graduate-only institution. *Enrollment by degree level:* 141 master's, 67 doctoral. *Graduate faculty:* 6 full-time (1 woman), 33 part-time/adjunct (8 women). *Tuition:* Full-time $18,000; part-time $9000 per quarter. *Required fees:* $375; $375 per unit. $125 per quarter. One-time fee: $475. Tuition and fees vary according to degree level. *Graduate housing:* Room and/or apartments available on a first-come, first-served basis to single students; on-campus housing not available to married students. Housing application deadline: 1/30. *Student services:* Campus employment opportunities, low-cost health insurance. *Library facilities:* Brimson Grow Library. *Collection:* Books: 53,200 (physical). Weekly public service hours: 30; students can reserve study rooms.

Computer facilities: 8 computers available on campus for general student use. Online class registration, X are available.
Website: http://www.seminary.edu/

General Application Contact: Greg Armstrong, Director of Admissions, 630-620-2175, Fax: 630-620-2190, E-mail: admissions@seminary.edu.

GRADUATE UNITS

Graduate and Professional Programs Students: 126 full-time (34 women), 80 part-time (32 women); includes 89 minority (73 Black or African American, non-Hispanic/Latino; 6 Asian, non-Hispanic/Latino; 8 Hispanic/Latino; 2 Two or more races, non-Hispanic/Latino), 3 international. Average age 44. *Faculty:* 6 full-time (1 woman), 33 part-time/adjunct (8 women). Expenses: Contact institution. *Financial support:* In 2016–17, 3 teaching assistantships with partial tuition reimbursements were awarded; Federal Work-Study and scholarships/grants also available. Support available to part-time students. Financial award application deadline: 9/1; financial award applicants required to submit FAFSA. In 2016, 18 master's, 14 doctorates awarded. *Program availability:* Part-time, evening/weekend. Offers Biblical studies (M Div); Christian community development (D Min); Christian ministry (MACM); contextual theology (D Min); New Testament (MANT); New Testament context (D Min); theology (M Div); theology and mission (MA); urban leadership (MA); worship (MAW). *Application deadline:* For fall admission, 8/25 for domestic students, 2/1 for international students; for winter admission, 12/10 for domestic students, 2/1 for international students; for spring admission, 3/15 for domestic students, 2/1 for international students. Applications are processed on a rolling basis. *Application fee:* $35. Electronic applications accepted. *Application Contact:* Greg Armstrong, Director of Admissions, 630-620-2175, Fax: 630-620-2190, E-mail: admissions@seminary.edu. *President,* Dr. William Shiell, 630-620-2101, Fax: 630-620-2190.

NORTHERN STATE UNIVERSITY, Aberdeen, SD 57401-7198

General Information State-supported, coed, comprehensive institution. *Graduate housing:* Room and/or apartments available on a first-come, first-served basis to single students; on-campus housing not available to married students. Housing application deadline: 8/1. *Research affiliation:* AASCU–Grants Resource Center.

GRADUATE UNITS

MME Program in Music Education *Program availability:* Part-time, online learning. Offers music education (MME). Electronic applications accepted.

MS Ed Program in Counseling *Program availability:* Part-time, online learning. Offers clinical mental health counseling (MS Ed); school counseling (MS Ed). Electronic applications accepted.

MS Ed Program in Educational Studies *Program availability:* Part-time, online learning. Offers educational studies (MS Ed). Electronic applications accepted.

MS Ed Program in Instructional Design in E-learning *Program availability:* Part-time, online learning. Offers instructional design in e-learning (MS Ed). Electronic applications accepted.

MS Ed Program in Leadership and Administration *Program availability:* Part-time, evening/weekend, online learning. Offers leadership and administration (MS Ed). Electronic applications accepted.

MS Ed Program in Sport Performance and Leadership *Program availability:* Part-time. Offers sport performance and leadership (MS Ed). Electronic applications accepted.

MS Ed Program in Teaching and Learning *Program availability:* Part-time, evening/weekend, online learning. Offers teaching and learning (MS Ed). Electronic applications accepted.

MS Program in Banking and Financial Services *Program availability:* Part-time, online learning. Offers banking and financial services (MS). Electronic applications accepted.

MS Program in Training and Development in E-learning *Program availability:* Part-time, online learning. Offers training and development in e-learning (MS). Electronic applications accepted.

NORTH GREENVILLE UNIVERSITY, Tigerville, SC 29688-1892

General Information Independent-religious, coed, comprehensive institution. *Graduate housing:* Room and/or apartments available on a first-come, first-served basis to single students; on-campus housing not available to married students. Housing application deadline: 8/1.

GRADUATE UNITS

T. Walter Brashier Graduate School *Program availability:* Part-time, evening/weekend, online learning. Offers Christian ministry (MCM, D Min); education (M Ed, MAT); financial planning (MBA); human resources (MBA). Electronic applications accepted.

NORTH PARK THEOLOGICAL SEMINARY, Chicago, IL 60625-4895

General Information Independent-religious, coed, graduate-only institution. *Graduate housing:* Rooms and/or apartments available to single and married students. Housing application deadline: 9/1. *Research affiliation:* Northside Chicago Theological Institute, Covenant Archives and Historical Society, American Theological Library Association.

GRADUATE UNITS

Graduate and Professional Programs *Program availability:* Part-time. Offers adult ministry (Certificate); camping and retreat ministry (Certificate); children and family ministry (Certificate); Christian formation (MA); Christian ministry (MACM); faith and health (Certificate); intercultural studies (Certificate); justice ministry (Certificate); leadership and administration (Certificate); preaching (D Min); spiritual direction (Certificate); theological studies (MATS); theology (M Div); youth ministry (Certificate).

NORTH PARK UNIVERSITY, Chicago, IL 60625-4895

General Information Independent-religious, coed, comprehensive institution. *Graduate housing:* Rooms and/or apartments available to single and married students.

GRADUATE UNITS

School of Business and Nonprofit Management *Program availability:* Part-time, evening/weekend, online learning. Offers business and nonprofit management (MBA, MHEA, MHRM, MM, MNA).

School of Education Offers education (MA).

School of Music Offers vocal performance (MM).

School of Nursing and Health Sciences *Program availability:* Part-time, evening/weekend. Offers advanced practice nursing (MS); leadership and management (MS).

NORTHWEST CHRISTIAN UNIVERSITY, Eugene, OR 97401-3745

General Information Independent-religious, coed, comprehensive institution. *Enrollment:* 766 graduate, professional, and undergraduate students; 109 full-time matriculated graduate/professional students (75 women), 91 part-time matriculated graduate/professional students (52 women). *Enrollment by degree level:* 199 master's. *Graduate faculty:* 12 full-time (5 women), 27 part-time/adjunct (16 women). *Tuition:* Full-time $7620; part-time $3810 per semester. *Required fees:* $90 per semester. Tuition and fees vary according to course load and program. *Graduate housing:* On-campus housing not available. *Student services:* Campus employment opportunities, career counseling, free psychological counseling, services for students with disabilities, teacher training, writing training. *Library facilities:* Edward P. Kellenberger Library. *Collection:* Books: 59,536 (physical), 14 (digital/electronic); Serial titles: 156 (physical), 105,706 (digital/electronic); Databases: 105. Weekly public service hours: 70.

Computer facilities: 16 computers available on campus for general student use. A campuswide network can be accessed from student residence rooms and from off campus. Online class registration is available.

Website: http://www.nwcu.edu/

General Application Contact: Heath Alexander, Recruiter, 541-684-7348, E-mail: halexander@nwcu.edu.

GRADUATE UNITS

School of Business and Management Students: 22 full-time (11 women), 38 part-time (11 women); includes 18 minority (3 Black or African American, non-Hispanic/Latino; 2

American Indian or Alaska Native, non-Hispanic/Latino; 4 Asian, non-Hispanic/Latino; 6 Hispanic/Latino; 3 Two or more races, non-Hispanic/Latino). Average age 33. *Faculty:* 4 full-time (1 woman), 5 part-time/adjunct (2 women). Expenses: Contact institution. In 2016, 32 master's awarded. *Program availability:* Part-time, evening/weekend, online only, 100% online. Offers accounting (MBA); management (MBA). *Application deadline:* Applications are processed on a rolling basis. Electronic applications accepted. *Application Contact:* Billy Dorsch, Admission Counselor for Graduate Studies, 541-684-7279, Fax: 541-349-5281, E-mail: wdorsch@nwcu.edu. *Assistant Dean,* Dr. Peter Diffenderfer, 541-684-7441, Fax: 541-684-7336, E-mail: pdiffenderfer@nwcu.edu.

School of Education and Counseling Students: 87 full-time (64 women), 52 part-time (40 women); includes 22 minority (5 Black or African American, non-Hispanic/Latino; 2 American Indian or Alaska Native, non-Hispanic/Latino; 2 Asian, non-Hispanic/Latino; 7 Hispanic/Latino; 2 Native Hawaiian or other Pacific Islander, non-Hispanic/Latino; 4 Two or more races, non-Hispanic/Latino). Average age 36. *Faculty:* 9 full-time (5 women), 21 part-time/adjunct (14 women). Expenses: Contact institution. In 2016, 76 master's awarded. *Program availability:* Part-time, evening/weekend, online learning. Offers clinical mental health counseling (MA); elementary teaching (MAT); English for speakers of other languages (ESOL) (MAT); school counseling (MA); secondary teaching (MAT). *Application deadline:* Applications are processed on a rolling basis. Electronic applications accepted. *Application Contact:* Billy Dorsch, Admission Counselor for Graduate Studies, 541-684-7279, Fax: 541-349-5281, E-mail: wdorsch@nwcu.edu. *Dean of Counseling,* Gene James, 541-684-7261, Fax: 541-684-7310, E-mail: gjames@nwcu.edu.

NORTHWESTERN COLLEGE, Orange City, IA 51041-1996

General Information Independent-religious, coed, comprehensive institution.

GRADUATE UNITS

Program in Education *Program availability:* Online learning. Offers early childhood (M Ed); master teacher (M Ed); teacher leadership (M Ed, Graduate Certificate).

NORTHWESTERN HEALTH SCIENCES UNIVERSITY, Bloomington, MN 55431-1599

General Information Independent, coed, graduate-only institution. *Graduate housing:* On-campus housing not available. *Research affiliation:* University of Minnesota, Center for Spirituality and Healing (education research), University of Western States (clinical research), University of Pittsburgh (education research).

GRADUATE UNITS

College of Acupuncture and Oriental Medicine Offers acupuncture (M Ac); Oriental medicine (MOM). Electronic applications accepted.

College of Chiropractic Offers chiropractic (DC). Electronic applications accepted.

NORTHWESTERN OKLAHOMA STATE UNIVERSITY, Alva, OK 73717-2799

General Information State-supported, coed, comprehensive institution. *Graduate housing:* Room and/or apartments available to single students; on-campus housing not available to married students.

GRADUATE UNITS

Program in American Studies *Program availability:* Part-time. Offers American studies (MA).

School of Professional Studies *Program availability:* Part-time. Offers adult education management and administration (M Ed); counseling psychology (MCP); curriculum and instruction (M Ed); educational leadership (M Ed); elementary education (M Ed); reading specialist (M Ed); school counseling (M Ed); secondary education (M Ed).

NORTHWESTERN POLYTECHNIC UNIVERSITY, Fremont, CA 94539-7482

General Information Independent, coed, comprehensive institution. *Graduate housing:* Room and/or apartments available on a first-come, first-served basis to single students; on-campus housing not available to married students. Housing application deadline: 7/15.

GRADUATE UNITS

School of Business and Information Technology *Program availability:* Part-time, evening/weekend. Offers business and information technology (MBA, DBA).

School of Engineering *Program availability:* Part-time, evening/weekend. Offers computer engineering (DCE); computer science (MS); computer systems engineering (MS); electrical engineering (MS).

NORTHWESTERN STATE UNIVERSITY OF LOUISIANA, Natchitoches, LA 71497

General Information State-supported, coed, comprehensive institution. CGS member. *Graduate housing:* Room and/or apartments available on a first-come, first-served basis to single students; on-campus housing not available to married students. Housing application deadline: 3/1. *Research affiliation:* NASA (Strategic Defense Initiative), Central State Hospital, Federal Records and Archives Services.

GRADUATE UNITS

Graduate Studies and Research *Program availability:* Part-time, evening/weekend, online learning. Offers clinical psychology (MS); English (MA); health and human performance (MS); homeland security (MS). Electronic applications accepted.

College of Education and Human Development Offers adult and continuing education (MA); counseling (Ed S); curriculum and instruction (M Ed); early childhood education and teaching (M Ed, MAT); education and human development (M Ed, MA, MAT, Ed S); educational leadership (M Ed, Ed S); educational technology (Ed S); educational technology leadership (M Ed); elementary education (MAT); elementary teaching (Ed S); middle school education (MAT); reading (Ed S); school counseling (MA); secondary education (MAT); secondary teaching (Ed S); special education (Ed S); student affairs in higher education (MA). Electronic applications accepted.

College of Nursing and School of Allied Health *Program availability:* Part-time. Offers nursing and allied health (MS, MSN); radiologic sciences (MS). Electronic applications accepted.

School of Creative and Performing Arts Offers art (MA); fine and graphic arts (MA); music (MM). Electronic applications accepted.

NORTHWESTERN UNIVERSITY, Evanston, IL 60208

General Information Independent, coed, university. CGS member. *Graduate housing:* Rooms and/or apartments available on a first-come, first-served basis to single students and available to married students. Housing application deadline: 9/1. *Research affiliation:* Dow Chemical Company (materials science and engineering), E.I. du Pont de

Nemours and Company (physics), Exxon Chemical Company (chemical engineering), Ford Motor Company (mechanical engineering), Medtronics, Inc. (cardiology), Amoco Oil Company (materials science and engineering).

GRADUATE UNITS

Feinberg School of Medicine Offers biostatistics (PhD); clinical investigation (MSCI); epidemiology (PhD); health and biomedical informatics (PhD); health services and outcomes research (PhD); healthcare quality and patient safety (PhD); medicine (MS, MSCI, DPT, MD, PhD); neuroscience (PhD); physical therapy (DPT); public health (MPH); translational outcomes in science (PhD). Electronic applications accepted.

The Graduate School *Program availability:* Part-time, evening/weekend. Offers biochemistry (PhD); bioengineering and biotechnology (PhD); biotechnology (PhD); cell and molecular biology (PhD); clinical investigation (MSCI, Certificate); clinical psychology (PhD); developmental and systems biology (PhD); gender and sexuality studies (Graduate Certificate); genetic counseling (MS); marital and family therapy (MS); nanotechnology (PhD); neurobiology (PhD); neuroscience (PhD); structural biology and biophysics (PhD). Electronic applications accepted.

Center for International and Comparative Studies Offers international and comparative studies (Certificate).

Judd A. and Marjorie Weinberg College of Arts and Sciences *Program availability:* Part-time, evening/weekend. Offers African American studies (PhD); African studies (Graduate Certificate); ancient philosophy (PhD); anthropology (PhD); applied physics (PhD); art history (PhD); arts and sciences (MA, MFA, MS, PhD, Graduate Certificate); brain, behavior and cognition (PhD); chemistry (PhD); clinical psychology (PhD); cognitive psychology (PhD); comparative literary studies (PhD); earth and planetary sciences (PhD); economics (PhD); English (MA, PhD); French/Francophone studies (PhD); German literature and critical thought (PhD); history (PhD); Italian studies (Graduate Certificate); linguistics (PhD); mathematics (PhD); neurobiology and physiology (MS); personality psychology (PhD); philosophy (PhD); physics and astronomy (PhD); plant biology and conservation (MA, PhD); political science (PhD); religious studies (PhD); Slavic languages and literature (PhD); social psychology (PhD); sociology (PhD); Spanish and Portuguese (PhD); statistics (MS, PhD); visual arts (MFA).

Kellogg School of Management *Program availability:* Part-time, evening/weekend. Offers accounting information and management (MBA, PhD); analytical finance (MBA); business administration (MBA); decision sciences (MBA); entrepreneurship and innovation (MBA); finance (PhD); health enterprise management (MBA); human resources management (MBA); international business (MBA); management (MBA, MS, PhD); management and organizations (MBA, PhD); management and organizations and sociology (PhD); management and strategy (PhD); management studies (MS); managerial analytics (MBA); managerial economics (MBA); managerial economics and decision sciences (PhD); managerial economics and strategy (PhD); marketing (MBA, PhD); marketing management (MBA); media management (MBA); operations management (MBA, PhD); real estate (MBA); social enterprise at Kellogg (MBA). PhD admissions and degree offered through The Graduate School. Electronic applications accepted.

School of Communication *Program availability:* Part-time. Offers audiology (Au D); communication (MA, MFA, MS, MSC, Au D, PhD); communication sciences and disorders (PhD); communication studies (PhD); directing (MFA); documentary media (MFA); leadership for creative enterprises (MS); managerial communication (MSC); media, technology and society (PhD); performance studies (MA, PhD); screen cultures (MA, PhD); speech, language, and learning (MS); stage design (MFA); technology and social behavior (PhD); theatre and drama (PhD); writing for the screen and stage (MFA). MA, MFA, and PhD admissions and degrees offered through The Graduate School; MSC admissions and degrees offered through the School of Communication.

School of Education and Social Policy *Program availability:* Part-time, evening/weekend. Offers education (MS); elementary teaching (MS); human development and social policy (PhD); learning and organizational change (MS); learning sciences (MA, PhD); secondary teaching (MS); teacher leadership (MS). MA and PhD admissions and degrees offered through The Graduate School. Electronic applications accepted.

Henry and Leigh Bienen School of Music Offers brass performance (MM, DMA); composition (DMA); conducting (MM, DMA); jazz studies (MM); music education (MME, PhD); music theory (MM); music theory and cognition (PhD); musicology (MM, PhD); percussion performance (MM, DMA); performance (MM); piano pedagogy (MME); piano performance (MM, DMA); piano performance and collaborative arts (MM, DMA); piano performance and pedagogy (MM, DMA); string performance (MM, DMA); theory (MM); voice and opera performance (MM, DMA); woodwind performance (MM, DMA). PhD admissions and degree offered through The Graduate School. Electronic applications accepted.

McCormick School of Engineering and Applied Science *Program availability:* Part-time, evening/weekend. Offers analytics (MS); biomedical engineering (MS, PhD); biotechnology (MS); chemical engineering (MS, PhD); computer engineering (MS, PhD); computer science (MS, PhD); design innovation (MBA, MS); electrical engineering (MS, PhD); engineering and applied science (MBA, MEM, MIT, MME, MMM, MPD, MS, PhD, Certificate); engineering management (MEM); engineering sciences and applied mathematics (MS, PhD); environmental engineering and science (MS, PhD); geotechnical engineering (MS, PhD); industrial engineering and management science (MS, PhD); information technology (MS); integrated computational materials engineering (Certificate); materials science and engineering (MS, PhD); mechanical engineering (MS, PhD); mechanics of materials and solids (MS, PhD); product design and development management (MS); project management (MS); robotics (MS); structural engineering and materials (MS, PhD); theoretical and applied mechanics (MS, PhD); transportation systems analysis and planning (MS, PhD). MS and PhD admissions and degrees offered through The Graduate School. Electronic applications accepted.

Segal Design Institute Offers engineering design and innovation (MS).

Medill School of Journalism, Media, and Integrated Marketing Communications Offers brand strategy (MSIMC); content marketing (MSIMC); direct and interactive marketing (MSIMC); integrated marketing communications (MSIMC); interactive publishing (MSJ); magazine writing/editing (MSJ); marketing analytics (MSIMC); reporting (MSJ); strategic communications (MSIMC); video/broadcast (MSJ). Electronic applications accepted.

Pritzker School of Law Offers international human rights (LL M); law (JD); law and business (LL M); science law (MSL); tax (LL M in Tax). Executive LL M programs offered in Madrid (Spain), Seoul (South Korea), and Tel Aviv (Israel). Electronic applications accepted.

School of Professional Studies Offers American literature (MA); American studies (MA); analytics and business intelligence (MS); British literature (MA); clinical research (MS); comparative and world literature (MA); computer-based data mining (MS); creative writing (MA, MFA); database and Internet technologies (MS); global health (MS); global policy (MA); health services policy (MA); healthcare compliance (MS); history (MA); information systems (MS); information systems management (MS); information systems security (MS); marketing analytics (MS); medical informatics (MS); predictive modeling (MS); public administration (MA); public policy (MA); quality systems (MS); religious and ethical studies (MA); risk analytics (MS); software project management and development (MS); sports administration (MA); Web analytics (MS).

NORTHWEST MISSOURI STATE UNIVERSITY, Maryville, MO 64468-6001

General Information State-supported, coed, comprehensive institution. *Enrollment:* 6,530 graduate, professional, and undergraduate students; 441 full-time matriculated graduate/professional students (158 women), 461 part-time matriculated graduate/professional students (247 women). *Enrollment by degree level:* 810 master's, 18 doctoral, 38 other advanced degrees. *Graduate faculty:* 252 full-time (114 women), 69 part-time/adjunct (50 women). Tuition, state resident: full-time $3447; part-time $383 per credit hour. Tuition, nonresident: full-time $5724; part-time $636 per credit hour. *Required fees:* $130 per credit hour. *Graduate housing:* Rooms and/or apartments available on a first-come, first-served basis to single and married students. Housing application deadline: 6/1. *Student services:* Campus employment opportunities, campus safety program, career counseling, exercise/wellness program, free psychological counseling, international student services, low-cost health insurance, multicultural affairs office, services for students with disabilities, teacher training, writing training. *Library facilities:* Owens Library. *Collection:* Books: 240,370 (physical), 240,370 (digital/electronic); Serial titles: 33,868 (digital/electronic). Students can reserve study rooms.

Computer facilities: Computer purchase and lease plans are available. 6,500 computers available on campus for general student use. A campuswide network can be accessed from student residence rooms and from off campus. Online class registration, online courses with library and databases are available. Website: http://www.nwmissouri.edu/

General Application Contact: Dr. Gregory Haddock, Dean of Graduate School, 660-562-1145, Fax: 660-562-1096, E-mail: gradsch@nwmissouri.edu.

GRADUATE UNITS

Graduate School Students: 446 full-time (156 women), 529 part-time (307 women). Expenses: Contact institution. *Financial support:* Research assistantships with full tuition reimbursements, teaching assistantships with full tuition reimbursements, career-related internships or fieldwork, Federal Work-Study, institutionally sponsored loans, scholarships/grants, and administrative assistantships, tutorial assistantships available. Financial award application deadline: 4/1; financial award applicants required to submit FAFSA. *Program availability:* Part-time, evening/weekend. *Application deadline:* For fall admission, 7/1 for domestic and international students; for spring admission, 11/15 for domestic and international students. Applications are processed on a rolling basis. *Application fee:* $0 ($50 for international students). Electronic applications accepted. *Application Contact:* Terry Immel, Executive Secretary, 660-562-1145, Fax: 660-562-1096, E-mail: gradsch@nwmissouri.edu. *Dean,* Dr. Gregory Haddock, 660-562-1145, Fax: 660-562-1096, E-mail: gradsch@nwmissouri.edu.

College of Arts and Sciences Students: 12 full-time (8 women), 69 part-time (31 women). Expenses: Contact institution. *Financial support:* Research assistantships with full tuition reimbursements, teaching assistantships with full tuition reimbursements, and administrative assistantships, tutorial assistantships available. Financial award application deadline: 4/1; financial award applicants required to submit FAFSA. *Program availability:* Part-time. Offers biology (MS); elementary mathematics specialist (MS Ed); English (MA); English education (MS Ed); English pedagogy (MA); geographic information science (MS, Certificate); history (MS Ed); mathematics (MS); mathematics education (MS Ed); teaching: science (MS Ed). *Application deadline:* For fall admission, 7/1 for domestic and international students; for spring admission, 11/15 for domestic and international students. Applications are processed on a rolling basis. *Application fee:* $0 ($50 for international students). Electronic applications accepted. *Dean,* Dr. Michael Steiner, 660-562-1197.

Melvin and Valorie Booth College of Business and Professional Studies Students: 50 full-time (18 women), 50 part-time (27 women); includes 10 minority (5 Black or African American, non-Hispanic/Latino; 2 Asian, non-Hispanic/Latino; 3 Hispanic/Latino), 16 international. Expenses: Contact institution. *Financial support:* Research assistantships with full tuition reimbursements, teaching assistantships with full tuition reimbursements, career-related internships or fieldwork, and administrative assistantships, tutorial assistantships available. Financial award application deadline: 4/1; financial award applicants required to submit FAFSA. In 2016, 55 master's awarded. *Program availability:* Part-time. Offers agricultural economics (MBA); general management (MBA); human resource management (MBA); marketing (MBA). *Application deadline:* For fall admission, 7/1 for domestic and international students; for spring admission, 11/15 for domestic and international students; for summer admission, 4/1 for domestic and international students. Applications are processed on a rolling basis. *Application fee:* $0 ($50 for international students). Electronic applications accepted. *Dean of Graduate School,* Dr. Gregory Haddock, 660-562-1145, Fax: 660-562-1096, E-mail: gradsch@nwmissouri.edu.

School of Agricultural Sciences Students: 4 full-time (1 woman), 8 part-time (3 women). Expenses: Contact institution. *Financial support:* Research assistantships with full tuition reimbursements, teaching assistantships with full tuition reimbursements, and unspecified assistantships available. Financial award application deadline: 4/1; financial award applicants required to submit FAFSA. In 2016, 3 master's awarded. *Program availability:* Part-time. Offers agricultural economics (MBA); agricultural education (MS Ed); agriculture (MS); teaching: agriculture (MS Ed). *Application deadline:* For fall admission, 7/1 for domestic and international students; for spring admission, 11/15 for domestic and international students. Applications are processed on a rolling basis. *Application fee:* $0 ($50 for international students). *Director,* Rodney Barr, 660-562-1620.

School of Computer Science and Information Systems Students: 291 full-time (81 women), 122 part-time (39 women), 403 international. Expenses: Contact institution. *Financial support:* Research assistantships, teaching assistantships with full tuition reimbursements, and unspecified assistantships available. Financial award application deadline: 4/1; financial award applicants required to submit FAFSA. In 2016, 292 master's awarded. *Program availability:* Part-time. Offers applied computer science (MS); information systems (MS); instructional technology (MS). *Application deadline:* Applications are processed on a rolling basis. *Application fee:* $0 ($50 for international students). *Application Contact:* Dr. Gregory Haddock, Dean of Graduate School, 660-562-1145, Fax: 660-562-1096, E-mail: gradsch@nwmissouri.edu. *Director,* Dr. Carol Spradling, 660-562-1588.

School of Education Students: 15 full-time (11 women), 150 part-time (103 women). Expenses: Contact institution. *Financial support:* Research assistantships with full tuition reimbursements, teaching assistantships with full tuition reimbursements, and unspecified assistantships available. Financial award application deadline: 4/1; financial award applicants required to submit FAFSA. In 2016, 46 master's awarded. *Program availability:* Part-time. Offers early childhood education (MS Ed); education leadership (MS Ed); educational leadership (Ed S); educational leadership and policy analysis (Ed D); elementary education (MS Ed); elementary mathematics (MS Ed); higher education leadership (MS Ed); middle school education (MS Ed); reading (MS Ed); special education (MS Ed); teacher leadership (MS Ed); teaching English language learners (MS Ed). *Application deadline:* For fall admission, 7/1 for domestic and international students; for spring admission, 11/15 for domestic and international students. Applications are processed on a rolling basis. *Application fee:* $0 ($50 for international students). Electronic applications accepted. *Dean*, Dr. Tim Wall, 660-562-1179, E-mail: timwall@nwmissouri.edu.

School of Health Science and Wellness Students: 68 full-time (38 women), 27 part-time (19 women). Expenses: Contact institution. *Financial support:* Teaching assistantships with full tuition reimbursements and unspecified assistantships available. Financial award application deadline: 4/1; financial award applicants required to submit FAFSA. *Program availability:* Part-time. Offers applied health and sport sciences (MS); recreation (MS). *Application deadline:* For fall admission, 7/1 for domestic and international students; for spring admission, 11/15 for domestic and international students. Applications are processed on a rolling basis. *Application fee:* $0 ($50 for international students). *Application Contact:* Cathie Hannigan, Office Manager, 660-562-1297, Fax: 660-562-1483, E-mail: channig@nwmissouri.edu. *Director, School of Health Science and Wellness*, Dr. Terry Long, 660-562-1706, E-mail: tlong@nwmissouri.edu.

NORTHWEST NAZARENE UNIVERSITY, Nampa, ID 83686-5897

General Information Independent-religious, coed, comprehensive institution. *Enrollment:* 541 full-time matriculated graduate/professional students (354 women), 187 part-time matriculated graduate/professional students (97 women). *Graduate faculty:* 20 full-time (13 women), 117 part-time/adjunct (57 women). *Tuition:* Full-time $9315; part-time $4658 per credit hour. *Required fees:* $120. *Graduate housing:* On-campus housing not available. *Student services:* Career counseling, free psychological counseling, multicultural affairs office, services for students with disabilities, teacher training, writing training. *Library facilities:* John E. Riley Library.

Computer facilities: Computer purchase and lease plans are available. A campuswide network can be accessed from student residence rooms. Online class registration is available.
Website: http://www.nnu.edu/

General Application Contact: Dr. Paula Kellerer, Dean, College of Adult and Graduate Studies, 208-467-8729, Fax: 208-467-8252, E-mail: pkellerer@nnu.edu.

GRADUATE UNITS

Graduate Education Program Students: 112 full-time (72 women), 73 part-time (36 women); includes 19 minority (3 Black or African American, non-Hispanic/Latino; 2 Asian, non-Hispanic/Latino; 6 Hispanic/Latino; 1 Native Hawaiian or other Pacific Islander, non-Hispanic/Latino; 7 Two or more races, non-Hispanic/Latino), 5 international. Average age 39. 96 applicants, 72% accepted, 67 enrolled. *Faculty:* 4 full-time (3 women), 17 part-time/adjunct (6 women). Expenses: Contact institution. *Financial support:* In 2016–17, research assistantships (averaging $5,000 per year) were awarded. Financial award application deadline: 1/15; financial award applicants required to submit FAFSA. In 2016, 59 master's, 13 doctorates, 33 other advanced degrees awarded. *Program availability:* Part-time, online only, 100% online, 2-week face-to-face residency (for doctoral programs). Offers curriculum and instruction (M Ed); educational leadership (M Ed, Ed D, PhD, Ed S). *Application deadline:* Applications are processed on a rolling basis. *Application fee:* $50. Electronic applications accepted. *Application Contact:* Charlene Brown, Admissions Counselor, 208-467-8492, Fax: 208-467-8384, E-mail: hlcurtis@nnu.edu. *Chair*, Dr. Heidi Curtis, 208-467-8250, E-mail: hlcurtis@nnu.edu.

Program in Business Administration Students: 57 full-time (27 women), 30 part-time (10 women); includes 11 minority (1 Black or African American, non-Hispanic/Latino; 2 American Indian or Alaska Native, non-Hispanic/Latino; 2 Asian, non-Hispanic/Latino; 5 Hispanic/Latino; 1 Two or more races, non-Hispanic/Latino), 2 international. Average age 34. 26 applicants, 62% accepted, 11 enrolled. *Faculty:* 12 full-time (4 women), 14 part-time/adjunct (2 women). Expenses: Contact institution. In 2016, 41 master's awarded. *Program availability:* Part-time, evening/weekend, 100% online, blended/hybrid learning. Offers business administration (MBA). *Application deadline:* Applications are processed on a rolling basis. *Application fee:* $50. Electronic applications accepted. *Application Contact:* Heather Beam, MBA Program Coordinator, 208-467-8100, Fax: 208-467-8440, E-mail: nnu-mba@nnu.edu. *Director*, Dr. Brenda Johnson, 208-467-8415, Fax: 208-467-8440, E-mail: mba@nnu.edu.

Program in Counselor Education Students: 92 full-time (74 women), 26 part-time (19 women); includes 10 minority (2 Black or African American, non-Hispanic/Latino; 6 Hispanic/Latino; 2 Two or more races, non-Hispanic/Latino), 1 international. Average age 35. 47 applicants, 66% accepted, 25 enrolled. *Faculty:* 6 full-time (4 women), 10 part-time/adjunct (6 women). Expenses: Contact institution. In 2016, 33 master's awarded. *Program availability:* Part-time. Offers clinical counseling (MS); marriage and family counseling (MS); school counseling (MS). *Application deadline:* For fall admission, 2/15 for domestic and international students; for spring admission, 9/15 for domestic and international students. *Application fee:* $50. Electronic applications accepted. *Application Contact:* Lynette Kingsmore, Graduate Admissions Counselor, 208-467-8107, E-mail: lkingsmore@nnu.edu. *Chair*, Dr. Michael Pitts, 208-467-8040, Fax: 208-467-8339.

Program in Nursing Students: 53 full-time (45 women), 2 part-time (1 woman). Average age 40. 24 applicants, 88% accepted, 12 enrolled. *Faculty:* 1 (woman) full-time, 6 part-time/adjunct (all women). Expenses: Contact institution. In 2016, 10 master's awarded. *Program availability:* Online learning. Offers nursing (MSN). *Application fee:* $50. *Application Contact:* Sandy Blom, Graduate Nursing Coordinator, 208-467-8642, Fax: 208-467-8651, E-mail: sblom@nnu.edu. *Director*, Dr. Leonie Sutherland, 208-467-8679, E-mail: lsutherland@nnu.edu.

Program in Religion Students: 65 full-time (23 women), 25 part-time (11 women); includes 11 minority (4 Black or African American, non-Hispanic/Latino; 1 American Indian or Alaska Native, non-Hispanic/Latino; 2 Asian, non-Hispanic/Latino; 3 Hispanic/Latino; 1 Native Hawaiian or other Pacific Islander, non-Hispanic/Latino), 1 international. Average age 39. 37 applicants, 76% accepted, 24 enrolled. *Faculty:* 11 full-time (3 women), 18 part-time/adjunct (0 women). Expenses: Contact institution. *Financial support:* In 2016–17, 3 students received support. Scholarships/grants available. In 2016, 40 master's awarded. *Program availability:* Part-time, online only,

100% online. Offers missional leadership (M Div, MA); pastoral ministry (MA); spiritual formation (M Div, MA); youth, children, and family ministry (M Div, MA). *Application deadline:* For fall admission, 7/31 for domestic students, 7/1 for international students; for spring admission, 2/1 for domestic students, 1/5 for international students. Applications are processed on a rolling basis. *Application fee:* $50. Electronic applications accepted. *Application Contact:* Vicki Funk, Program Coordinator, 208-467-8432, Fax: 208-467-8252, E-mail: vlfunk@nnu.edu. *Director, Graduate Studies*, Dr. Jay Akkerman, 208-467-8437, Fax: 208-467-8252.

Program in Social Work Students: 123 full-time (85 women), 24 part-time (13 women); includes 23 minority (3 Black or African American, non-Hispanic/Latino; 1 American Indian or Alaska Native, non-Hispanic/Latino; 12 Hispanic/Latino; 7 Two or more races, non-Hispanic/Latino). Average age 27. 152 applicants, 54% accepted, 73 enrolled. *Faculty:* 7 full-time (4 women), 9 part-time/adjunct (5 women). Expenses: Contact institution. In 2016, 54 master's awarded. *Program availability:* Part-time-only, evening/weekend. Offers clinical mental health and addictions practice (MSW). *Application deadline:* Applications are processed on a rolling basis. *Application fee:* $50. Electronic applications accepted. *Application Contact:* Jodie Rodriguez-Engel, Program Coordinator, 208-467-8679, Fax: 208-467-8879, E-mail: jrodriguez-engel@nnu.edu. *Director/Department Chair*, Dr. Lawanna Lancaster, 208-467-8372, Fax: 208-467-8879, E-mail: mswinfo@nnu.edu.

NORTHWEST UNIVERSITY, Kirkland, WA 98033

General Information Independent-religious, coed, comprehensive institution. *Graduate housing:* Rooms and/or apartments available on a first-come, first-served basis to single and married students.

GRADUATE UNITS

College of Business *Program availability:* Part-time, evening/weekend. Offers business administration (MBA); international business (MBA); project management (MBA); social entrepreneurship (MBA). Electronic applications accepted.

College of Ministry *Program availability:* Part-time, evening/weekend, online learning. Offers ministry (MIM); missional leadership (MA); theology and culture (MA). Electronic applications accepted.

College of Social and Behavioral Sciences *Program availability:* Evening/weekend. Offers counseling psychology (MA, Psy D); international community development (MA).

School of Education *Program availability:* Part-time, evening/weekend. Offers education (M Ed); teaching (MIT). Electronic applications accepted.

NORTHWOOD UNIVERSITY, MICHIGAN CAMPUS, Midland, MI 48640-2398

General Information Independent, coed, comprehensive institution. *Graduate housing:* Room and/or apartments available on a first-come, first-served basis to single students. Housing application deadline: 8/30. *Research affiliation:* Motor & Equipment Manufacturers Association (automotive engineering), Specialized Equipment Manufacturers Association (automotive engineering), Automotive Aftermarket Industry Association (automotive engineering), Automotive Warehouse Distributors Association (automotive engineering).

GRADUATE UNITS

DeVos Graduate School *Program availability:* Part-time, evening/weekend, online learning. Offers management (MBA, MSOL). MBA also offered on Florida and Texas campuses; MSOL offered online only. Electronic applications accepted.

NORWICH UNIVERSITY, Northfield, VT 05663

General Information Independent, coed, comprehensive institution. *Enrollment:* 1,050 full-time matriculated graduate/professional students (320 women). *Enrollment by degree level:* 1,003 master's, 47 other advanced degrees. *Graduate faculty:* 3 full-time (1 woman), 131 part-time/adjunct (29 women). *Student services:* Services for students with disabilities. *Library facilities:* Kreitzberg Library.

Computer facilities: A campuswide network can be accessed from student residence rooms and from off campus.
Website: http://www.norwich.edu/

General Application Contact: Admissions Advisor, 800-460-5597, Fax: 802-485-2533, E-mail: masters@online.norwich.edu.

GRADUATE UNITS

College of Graduate and Continuing Studies Students: 1,050 full-time (320 women); includes 204 minority (99 Black or African American, non-Hispanic/Latino; 3 American Indian or Alaska Native, non-Hispanic/Latino; 31 Asian, non-Hispanic/Latino; 44 Hispanic/Latino; 2 Native Hawaiian or other Pacific Islander, non-Hispanic/Latino; 25 Two or more races, non-Hispanic/Latino), 16 international. Average age 37. 375 applicants, 97% accepted, 268 enrolled. *Faculty:* 2 full-time (0 women), 132 part-time/adjunct (30 women). Expenses: Contact institution. *Financial support:* In 2016–17, 432 students received support. Scholarships/grants available. Financial award application deadline: 8/4; financial award applicants required to submit FAFSA. In 2016, 566 master's awarded. *Program availability:* Evening/weekend, online only, mostly all online with a week-long residency requirement. Offers construction management (MBA, MCE); criminal justice (MS); criminal justice and public safety (MPA); diplomacy (MA); energy management (MBA); executive leadership (MS); finance (MBA); fiscal management (MPA); geotechnical (MCE); history (MA); information security and assurance (MS); international development and influence (MPA); international relations (MA); leadership (MS); logistics (MBA); military history (MA); municipal governance (MPA); nonprofit management (MPA); nursing administration (MSN); nursing education (MSN); organizational leadership (MBA); policy analysis and analytics (MPA); project management (MBA); public administration leadership and crisis management (MPA); public works and sustainability (MPA); structural (MCE); supply chain management (MBA). *Application deadline:* For fall admission, 8/14 for domestic and international students; for winter admission, 11/13 for domestic and international students; for spring admission, 2/13 for domestic and international students; for summer admission, 5/15 for domestic and international students. Electronic applications accepted. *Application Contact:* Admissions Office, 800-460-5597, Fax: 802-485-2533, E-mail: masters@online.norwich.edu. *Vice President and Dean*, Dr. William H. Clements, 802-485-2567, Fax: 802-485-2533, E-mail: cgcsdean@norwich.edu.

NOTRE DAME COLLEGE, South Euclid, OH 44121-4293

General Information Independent-religious, coed, comprehensive institution. *Graduate housing:* On-campus housing not available.

GRADUATE UNITS

Graduate Programs *Program availability:* Part-time, evening/weekend. Offers mild/moderate needs (M Ed); reading (M Ed); security policy studies (MA, Graduate Certificate); technology (M Ed).

NOTRE DAME DE NAMUR UNIVERSITY, Belmont, CA 94002-1908

General Information Independent-religious, coed, comprehensive institution. *Graduate housing:* Room and/or apartments available on a first-come, first-served basis to single students; on-campus housing not available to married students. Housing application deadline: 6/1.

GRADUATE UNITS

Division of Academic Affairs *Program availability:* Part-time, evening/weekend, online learning. Electronic applications accepted.

College of Arts and Sciences *Program availability:* Part-time, online learning. Offers art therapy (MA); arts and sciences (MA, MFA, MS); clinical psychology (MS); clinical psychology: marital and family therapy (MS); English (MA); musical performance (MFA, Certificate). Electronic applications accepted.

School of Business and Management *Program availability:* Part-time, online learning. Offers business administration (MBA); business and management (MBA, MPA, MSM); entrepreneurship (MBA); finance (MBA); human resource management (MBA, MPA); marketing (MBA); media and promotion (MBA); public administration (MPA); public affairs administration (MPA); social enterprise (MPA); systems management (MSM); technology and operations management (MBA). Electronic applications accepted.

School of Education and Leadership *Program availability:* Part-time, evening/weekend. Offers curriculum and instruction (MA); education and leadership (MA, Ed D); school administration (MA); special education (MA). Electronic applications accepted.

NOTRE DAME OF MARYLAND UNIVERSITY, Baltimore, MD 21210-2476

General Information Independent-religious, coed, primarily women, comprehensive institution. *Graduate housing:* On-campus housing not available.

GRADUATE UNITS

Graduate Studies *Program availability:* Part-time, evening/weekend. Offers contemporary communication (MA); instructional leadership for changing populations (PhD); leadership in teaching (MA); liberal studies (MA); management (MA); nonprofit management (MA); pharmacy (Pharm D); teaching (MA); teaching English to speakers of other languages (MA). Electronic applications accepted.

NOTRE DAME SEMINARY, New Orleans, LA 70118-4391

General Information Independent-religious, coed, primarily men, graduate-only institution. *Graduate housing:* Room and/or apartments guaranteed to single students; on-campus housing not available to married students. Housing application deadline: 7/31.

GRADUATE UNITS

Graduate School of Theology *Program availability:* Part-time. Offers theology (M Div, MA).

NOVA SOUTHEASTERN UNIVERSITY, Fort Lauderdale, FL 33314-7796

General Information Independent, coed, university. *Enrollment:* 21,625 graduate, professional, and undergraduate students; 10,518 full-time matriculated graduate/professional students (6,897 women), 6,775 part-time matriculated graduate/professional students (5,140 women). *Enrollment by degree level:* 8,499 master's, 4,597 doctoral, 483 other advanced degrees. Tuition and fees vary according to degree level and program. *Graduate housing:* Rooms and/or apartments guaranteed to single and married students. *Student services:* Campus employment opportunities, campus safety program, career counseling, exercise/wellness program, free psychological counseling, international student services, low-cost health insurance, services for students with disabilities, teacher training. *Library facilities:* Alvin Sherman Library, Research, and Information Technology Center plus 4 others. *Collection:* Books: 498,823 (physical), 379,928 (digital/electronic); Serial titles: 6,035 (physical), 20,738 (digital/electronic); Databases: 577. Study areas open 24 hours, 5–7 days a week; students can reserve study rooms.

Computer facilities: 3,000 computers available on campus for general student use. A campuswide network can be accessed from student residence rooms and from off campus. Online class registration is available. Website: http://www.nova.edu/

General Application Contact: Information Contact, 800-541-6682, E-mail: nsuinfo@nsu.nova.edu.

GRADUATE UNITS

Abraham S. Fischler College of Education Students: 1,841 full-time (1,435 women), 1,705 part-time (1,336 women); includes 2,584 minority (1,389 Black or African American, non-Hispanic/Latino; 8 American Indian or Alaska Native, non-Hispanic/Latino; 44 Asian, non-Hispanic/Latino; 1,078 Hispanic/Latino; 2 Native Hawaiian or other Pacific Islander, non-Hispanic/Latino; 63 Two or more races, non-Hispanic/Latino), 26 international. Average age 41. 1,753 applicants, 47% accepted, 581 enrolled. *Faculty:* 94 full-time (58 women), 204 part-time/adjunct (145 women). Expenses: Contact institution. *Financial support:* In 2016–17, 67 students received support. Career-related internships or fieldwork and Federal Work-Study available. Support available to part-time students. Financial award application deadline: 4/15; financial award applicants required to submit FAFSA. In 2016, 654 master's, 387 doctorates, 119 other advanced degrees awarded. *Program availability:* Part-time, evening/weekend, 100% online, blended/hybrid learning. Offers education (MS, Ed D, PhD, Ed S); instructional technology and distance education (MS); teaching and learning (MA). *Application deadline:* Applications are processed on a rolling basis. *Application fee:* $50. Electronic applications accepted. *Application Contact:* Adriana Garay, Executive Director for Marketing, Recruitment and Admissions, 800-986-3223 Ext. 8500, E-mail: fserecruit@nova.edu. *Interim Dean,* Dr. Kim Durham, 954-262-8731, Fax: 954-262-3894, E-mail: durham@nova.edu.

College of Arts, Humanities, and Social Sciences Students: 306 full-time (242 women), 889 part-time (683 women); includes 677 minority (403 Black or African American, non-Hispanic/Latino; 2 American Indian or Alaska Native, non-Hispanic/Latino; 20 Asian, non-Hispanic/Latino; 224 Hispanic/Latino; 1 Native Hawaiian or other Pacific Islander, non-Hispanic/Latino; 27 Two or more races, non-Hispanic/Latino), 53 international. Average age 37. 624 applicants, 61% accepted, 285 enrolled. *Faculty:* 29 full-time (18 women), 27 part-time/adjunct (21 women). Expenses: Contact institution. *Financial support:* In 2016–17, 170 students received support. Career-related internships or fieldwork, Federal Work-Study, scholarships/grants, and unspecified assistantships available. Financial award application deadline: 4/1; financial award applicants required to submit CSS PROFILE. In 2016, 303 master's, 71 doctorates, 34 other advanced degrees awarded. *Program availability:* Part-time, evening/weekend, 100% online, blended/hybrid learning. Offers advanced conflict

resolution practice (Graduate Certificate); college student affairs (MS); conflict analysis and resolution (MS, PhD); cross-disciplinary studies (MA); family studies (Graduate Certificate); family systems health care (Graduate Certificate); family therapy (MS, PhD); marriage and family therapy (DMFT); peace studies (Graduate Certificate); qualitative research (Graduate Certificate); solution focused coaching (Graduate Certificate). *Application deadline:* For fall admission, 5/17 priority date for domestic and international students; for winter admission, 12/1 priority date for domestic and international students; for spring admission, 4/1 priority date for domestic and international students. Applications are processed on a rolling basis. *Application fee:* $50. Electronic applications accepted. *Application Contact:* Marcia Arango, Student Recruitment Coordinator, 954-262-3006, Fax: 954-262-3968, E-mail: marango@nsu.nova.edu. *Dean,* Dr. Honggang Yang, 954-262-3016, Fax: 954-262-3968, E-mail: yangh@nova.edu.

College of Dental Medicine Students: 604 full-time (293 women), 7 part-time (3 women); includes 278 minority (4 Black or African American, non-Hispanic/Latino; 105 Asian, non-Hispanic/Latino; 155 Hispanic/Latino; 14 Two or more races, non-Hispanic/Latino), 77 international. Average age 28. 2,274 applicants, 11% accepted, 124 enrolled. *Faculty:* 106 full-time (38 women), 163 part-time/adjunct (31 women). Expenses: Contact institution. *Financial support:* Application deadline: 4/15; applicants required to submit FAFSA. In 2016, 18 master's, 116 doctorates awarded. Offers dental medicine (DMD); dentistry (MS). *Application deadline:* For fall admission, 12/31 for domestic students, 1/1 for international students. Applications are processed on a rolling basis. *Application fee:* $50. Electronic applications accepted. *Application Contact:* Su-Ann Zarrett, Associate Director of HPD Admissions, 954-262-1108, Fax: 954-262-2282, E-mail: zarrett@nsu.nova.edu. *Dean,* Dr. Linda C. Niessen, 954-262-7334, Fax: 954-262-3293, E-mail: lniessen@nova.edu.

College of Engineering and Computing Students: 309 full-time (87 women), 407 part-time (125 women); includes 321 minority (139 Black or African American, non-Hispanic/Latino; 2 American Indian or Alaska Native, non-Hispanic/Latino; 52 Asian, non-Hispanic/Latino; 117 Hispanic/Latino; 11 Two or more races, non-Hispanic/Latino), 160 international. Average age 40. 390 applicants, 74% accepted. *Faculty:* 18 full-time (4 women), 11 part-time/adjunct (2 women). Expenses: Contact institution. *Financial support:* In 2016–17, 43 students received support. Federal Work-Study, scholarships/grants, and traineeships available. Financial award application deadline: 4/15; financial award applicants required to submit FAFSA. In 2016, 188 master's, 53 doctorates awarded. *Program availability:* Part-time, evening/weekend, blended/hybrid learning. Offers computer science (MS, PhD); information assurance (PhD); information assurance and cybersecurity (MS); information systems (PhD); information technology (MS); management information systems (MS). *Application deadline:* Applications are processed on a rolling basis. *Application fee:* $50. Electronic applications accepted. *Application Contact:* Nancy Azoulay, Director, Admissions, 954-262-2026, Fax: 954-262-2752, E-mail: azoulayn@nova.edu. *Dean,* Dr. Yong X. Tao, 954-262-2063, Fax: 954-262-2752, E-mail: ytao@nova.edu.

College of Health Care Sciences Students: 501 full-time (407 women); includes 131 minority (18 Black or African American, non-Hispanic/Latino; 2 American Indian or Alaska Native, non-Hispanic/Latino; 45 Asian, non-Hispanic/Latino; 65 Hispanic/Latino; 1 Two or more races, non-Hispanic/Latino). Average age 24. 7,683 applicants, 7% accepted, 452 enrolled. *Faculty:* 54 full-time (31 women), 15 part-time/adjunct (7 women). Expenses: Contact institution. *Financial support:* Federal Work-Study, institutionally sponsored loans, and scholarships/grants available. Financial award application deadline: 4/15; financial award applicants required to submit FAFSA. In 2016, 670 master's, 258 doctorates awarded. Offers anesthesiologist assistant (MSA); audiology (Au D); health science (MH Sc, DHSc, PhD); occupational therapy (MOT, Dr OT, PhD); physical therapy (DPT, TDPT); physician assistant (MMS). *Application deadline:* For spring admission, 2/15 for domestic and international students; for summer admission, 12/1 for domestic and international students. Applications are processed on a rolling basis. *Application fee:* $50. Electronic applications accepted. *Application Contact:* Joey Jankie, Admissions Counselor, 954-262-7249, E-mail: joey@nova.edu. *Dean,* Dr. Stanley Wilson, 954-262-1203, E-mail: swilson@nova.edu.

College of Medical Sciences Students: 46 full-time (30 women); includes 32 minority (6 Black or African American, non-Hispanic/Latino; 7 Asian, non-Hispanic/Latino; 18 Hispanic/Latino; 1 Two or more races, non-Hispanic/Latino). Average age 25. 350 applicants, 11% accepted, 40 enrolled. *Faculty:* 30 full-time (12 women), 1 part-time/adjunct (0 women). Expenses: Contact institution. *Financial support:* Application deadline: 4/15; applicants required to submit FAFSA. In 2016, 4 master's awarded. Offers biomedical sciences (MBS). *Application deadline:* For fall admission, 4/15 for domestic students. Applications are processed on a rolling basis. *Application fee:* $50. *Application Contact:* Dr. Lori B. Dribin, Assistant Dean for Student Affairs, 954-262-1341, Fax: 954-262-1802, E-mail: lorib@nova.edu. *Dean,* Dr. Harold E. Laubach, 954-262-1303, Fax: 954-262-1802, E-mail: harold@nova.edu.

College of Nursing Students: 535 full-time (496 women); includes 330 minority (143 Black or African American, non-Hispanic/Latino; 3 American Indian or Alaska Native, non-Hispanic/Latino; 45 Asian, non-Hispanic/Latino; 138 Hispanic/Latino; 1 Native Hawaiian or other Pacific Islander, non-Hispanic/Latino), 1 international. Average age 40. 345 applicants, 63% accepted, 104 enrolled. *Faculty:* 8 full-time (all women), 47 part-time/adjunct (43 women). Expenses: Contact institution. *Financial support:* In 2016–17, 41 students received support. Traineeships available. Financial award application deadline: 4/15; financial award applicants required to submit FAFSA. In 2016, 131 master's, 25 doctorates awarded. *Program availability:* Part-time, evening/weekend, 100% online, blended/hybrid learning, annual one-week summer institute delivered face-to-face on main campus. Offers advanced practice registered nurse (APRN) (MSN); nursing (PhD); nursing (MSN); nursing practice (DNP). *Application deadline:* For fall admission, 3/1 priority date for domestic students, 3/1 for international students; for winter admission, 11/1 for domestic and international students. Applications are processed on a rolling basis. *Application fee:* $50. Electronic applications accepted. *Dean,* Dr. Marcella Rutherford, 954-262-1963, E-mail: rmarcell@nova.edu.

College of Optometry Students: 433 full-time (305 women), 9 part-time (3 women); includes 196 minority (33 Black or African American, non-Hispanic/Latino; 2 American Indian or Alaska Native, non-Hispanic/Latino; 74 Asian, non-Hispanic/Latino; 72 Hispanic/Latino; 15 Two or more races, non-Hispanic/Latino), 51 international. Average age 26. Expenses: Contact institution. *Financial support:* Federal Work-Study, institutionally sponsored loans, and scholarships/grants available. Support available to part-time students. Financial award application deadline: 4/15; financial award applicants required to submit FAFSA. In 2016, 2 master's, 103 doctorates awarded. *Program availability:* Online learning. Offers optometry (MS, OD). *Application deadline:* For fall admission, 4/1 for domestic and international students. Applications are processed on a rolling basis. *Application fee:* $50. Electronic applications accepted. *Application Contact:* Juan Saavedra, Admissions Counselor, 954-262-1132, Fax: 954-262-2282, E-mail: jsaavedra@nova.edu. *Dean,* Dr. David Loshin, 954-262-1404, Fax: 954-262-1818, E-mail: loshin@nova.edu.

College of Osteopathic Medicine Students: 1,040 full-time (476 women), 196 part-time (135 women); includes 635 minority (95 Black or African American, non-Hispanic/Latino; 298 Asian, non-Hispanic/Latino; 208 Hispanic/Latino; 1 Native Hawaiian or other Pacific Islander, non-Hispanic/Latino; 33 Two or more races, non-Hispanic/Latino), 54 international. Average age 27. 5,383 applicants, 7% accepted, 248 enrolled. *Faculty:* 126 full-time (64 women), 1,411 part-time/adjunct (352 women). Expenses: Contact institution. *Financial support:* In 2016–17, 46 students received support, including 8 fellowships (averaging $30,690 per year); research assistantships, teaching assistantships, Federal Work-Study, and scholarships/grants also available. Financial award application deadline: 6/1; financial award applicants required to submit FAFSA. In 2016, 94 master's, 231 doctorates, 2 other advanced degrees awarded. Offers biomedical informatics (MS, Graduate Certificate); disaster and emergency management (MS); medical education (MS); nutrition (MS, Graduate Certificate); osteopathic medicine (DO); public health (MPH, Graduate Certificate); social medicine (Graduate Certificate). *Application deadline:* For fall admission, 1/15 for domestic students. Applications are processed on a rolling basis. *Application fee:* $50. Electronic applications accepted. *Application Contact:* HPD Admissions, 877-640-0218, E-mail: hpdinfo@nova.edu. *Dean,* Elaine M. Wallace, 954-262-1457, Fax: 954-262-2250, E-mail: ewallace@nova.edu.

College of Pharmacy Students: 972 full-time (671 women), 49 part-time (21 women); includes 725 minority (57 Black or African American, non-Hispanic/Latino; 169 Asian, non-Hispanic/Latino; 483 Hispanic/Latino; 1 Native Hawaiian or other Pacific Islander, non-Hispanic/Latino; 15 Two or more races, non-Hispanic/Latino), 96 international. Average age 27. 1,024 applicants, 41% accepted, 255 enrolled. *Faculty:* 67 full-time (31 women), 3 part-time/adjunct (1 woman). Expenses: Contact institution. *Financial support:* In 2016–17, 70 students received support, including 12 teaching assistantships with full tuition reimbursements available (averaging $18,000 per year); career-related internships or fieldwork, Federal Work-Study, scholarships/grants, tuition waivers (full), and unspecified assistantships also available. Financial award application deadline: 4/15; financial award applicants required to submit FAFSA. In 2016, 228 doctorates awarded. Offers pharmaceutical affairs (MS); pharmaceutical sciences (MS, PhD); pharmacy (Pharm D). *Application deadline:* For fall admission, 3/15 for domestic and international students. Applications are processed on a rolling basis. *Application fee:* $50. Electronic applications accepted. *Application Contact:* Jennifer Gundersen, Admissions Counselor, 954-262-1112, Fax: 954-262-2282, E-mail: nsupharmacyinfo@nova.edu. *Dean,* Dr. Lisa Deziel, 954-262-1304, Fax: 954-262-2278, E-mail: copdean@nova.edu.

College of Psychology Students: 724 full-time (596 women), 918 part-time (792 women); includes 797 minority (276 Black or African American, non-Hispanic/Latino; 1 American Indian or Alaska Native, non-Hispanic/Latino; 44 Asian, non-Hispanic/Latino; 427 Hispanic/Latino; 2 Native Hawaiian or other Pacific Islander, non-Hispanic/Latino; 47 Two or more races, non-Hispanic/Latino), 41 international. Average age 31. 1,349 applicants, 61% accepted, 651 enrolled. *Faculty:* 51 full-time (21 women), 120 part-time/adjunct (70 women). Expenses: Contact institution. *Financial support:* In 2016–17, 197 students received support, including 15 research assistantships (averaging $5,600 per year), 68 teaching assistantships (averaging $2,000 per year); career-related internships or fieldwork, Federal Work-Study, institutionally sponsored loans, scholarships/grants, and unspecified assistantships also available. Support available to part-time students. Financial award application deadline: 4/15; financial award applicants required to submit FAFSA. In 2016, 377 master's, 177 doctorates, 26 other advanced degrees awarded. *Program availability:* 100% online, blended/hybrid learning. Offers clinical psychology (PhD, Psy D); counseling (MS); experimental psychology (MS); forensic psychology (MS); general psychology (MS); mental health counseling (MS); school counseling (MS); school psychology (Psy D, Psy S). *Application deadline:* Applications are processed on a rolling basis. *Application fee:* $50. Electronic applications accepted. *Application Contact:* Carlos Perez, Senior Manager of Outreach, 954-262-5702, Fax: 954-262-3893, E-mail: gradschool@nova.edu. *Dean,* Dr. Karen Grosby, 954-262-5790, Fax: 954-262-3859, E-mail: grosby@nova.edu.

Halmos College of Natural Sciences and Oceanography Students: 44 full-time (32 women), 139 part-time (89 women); includes 31 minority (2 Black or African American, non-Hispanic/Latino; 6 Asian, non-Hispanic/Latino; 15 Hispanic/Latino; 8 Two or more races, non-Hispanic/Latino), 4 international. Average age 30. 85 applicants, 60% accepted, 39 enrolled. *Faculty:* 17 full-time (3 women), 21 part-time/adjunct (11 women). Expenses: Contact institution. *Financial support:* In 2016–17, 157 students received support, including 14 fellowships with tuition reimbursements available (averaging $25,000 per year), 42 research assistantships with tuition reimbursements available (averaging $19,000 per year), 8 teaching assistantships with tuition reimbursements available (averaging $15,000 per year); career-related internships or fieldwork, Federal Work-Study, scholarships/grants, health care benefits, tuition waivers (full and partial), and unspecified assistantships also available. Support available to part-time students. Financial award application deadline: 4/15; financial award applicants required to submit FAFSA. In 2016, 58 master's, 2 doctorates awarded. *Program availability:* Part-time, evening/weekend, blended/hybrid learning. Offers biological sciences (MS); coastal zone management (MS); marine biology (MS); marine biology and oceanography (PhD); marine environmental sciences (MS). *Application deadline:* Applications are processed on a rolling basis. *Application fee:* $50. Electronic applications accepted. *Application Contact:* Dr. Bernhard Riegl, Chair, Department of Marine and Environmental Sciences, 954-262-3600, Fax: 954-262-4020, E-mail: rieglb@nova.edu. *Dean,* Dr. Richard Dodge, 954-262-3600, Fax: 954-262-4020, E-mail: dodge@nsu.nova.edu.

H. Wayne Huizenga College of Business and Entrepreneurship Students: 2,242 full-time (1,400 women), 425 part-time (239 women); includes 1,798 minority (734 Black or African American, non-Hispanic/Latino; 5 American Indian or Alaska Native, non-Hispanic/Latino; 110 Asian, non-Hispanic/Latino; 890 Hispanic/Latino; 2 Native Hawaiian or other Pacific Islander, non-Hispanic/Latino; 57 Two or more races, non-Hispanic/Latino), 255 international. Average age 34. 1,422 applicants, 64% accepted, 672 enrolled. *Faculty:* 65 full-time (26 women), 111 part-time/adjunct (74 women). Expenses: Contact institution. *Financial support:* In 2016–17, 325 students received support. Federal Work-Study and scholarships/grants available. Support available to part-time students. Financial award application deadline: 4/15; financial award applicants required to submit FAFSA. In 2016, 971 master's awarded. *Program availability:* Part-time, evening/weekend, 100% online, blended/hybrid learning. Offers accounting (M Acc); business intelligence/analytics (MBA); entrepreneurship (MBA); finance (MBA); human resource management (MBA); international business (MBA); management (MBA); marketing (MBA); process improvement (MBA); public administration (MPA); real estate development (MS); sport revenue generation (MBA); supply chain management (MBA); taxation (M Tax). *Application deadline:* For fall admission, 8/5 priority date for domestic students, 7/29 priority date for international students; for winter admission, 12/16 priority date for domestic students, 12/9 priority date for international students; for summer admission, 4/21 priority date for domestic and international students. Applications are processed on a rolling basis. *Application*

fee: $50. Electronic applications accepted. *Application Contact:* Zeida Rodriguez, Associate Director of Enrollment Services, 954-262-5163, Fax: 954-262-3822, E-mail: zeida@nova.edu. *Dean,* Dr. J. Preston Jones, 954-262-5127, E-mail: prestonj@nova.edu.

Shepard Broad College of Law Students: 554 full-time (298 women), 325 part-time (230 women); includes 351 minority (71 Black or African American, non-Hispanic/Latino; 3 American Indian or Alaska Native, non-Hispanic/Latino; 17 Asian, non-Hispanic/Latino; 251 Hispanic/Latino; 2 Native Hawaiian or other Pacific Islander, non-Hispanic/Latino; 7 Two or more races, non-Hispanic/Latino), 36 international. Average age 29. 1,414 applicants, 49% accepted, 256 enrolled. *Faculty:* 42 full-time (23 women), 35 part-time/adjunct (14 women). Expenses: Contact institution. *Financial support:* In 2016–17, 231 students received support, including 221 fellowships (averaging $12,680 per year); Federal Work-Study, institutionally sponsored loans, scholarships/grants, and unspecified assistantships also available. Support available to part-time students. Financial award application deadline: 4/15; financial award applicants required to submit FAFSA. In 2016, 46 master's, 236 doctorates awarded. *Program availability:* Part-time, evening/weekend, 100% online, blended/hybrid learning. Offers education law (MS); employment law (MS); health law (MS, JD); international law (JD); law and policy (MS). *Application deadline:* For fall admission, 5/1 priority date for domestic and international students; for winter admission, 12/12 for domestic and international students; for spring admission, 3/31 for domestic and international students; for summer admission, 4/1 for domestic and international students. Applications are processed on a rolling basis. *Application fee:* $0. Electronic applications accepted. *Application Contact:* William Daniel Perez, Assistant Dean of Admissions, 954-262-5163, Fax: 954-262-3844, E-mail: wperez1@nova.edu. *Dean,* Jon M. Garon, 954-262-6101, Fax: 954-262-2862, E-mail: garon@nova.edu.

NSCAD UNIVERSITY, Halifax, NS B3J 3J6, Canada

General Information Province-supported, coed, comprehensive institution. *Graduate housing:* On-campus housing not available.

GRADUATE UNITS

Program in Fine Arts Offers craft (MFA); design (M Des); fine and media arts (MFA).

NYACK COLLEGE, Nyack, NY 10960

General Information Independent-religious, coed, comprehensive institution. *Enrollment:* 2,502 graduate, professional, and undergraduate students; 467 full-time matriculated graduate/professional students (257 women), 584 part-time matriculated graduate/professional students (351 women). *Enrollment by degree level:* 978 master's, 73 doctoral. *Graduate faculty:* 26 full-time (10 women), 61 part-time/adjunct (23 women). *Graduate housing:* Rooms and/or apartments available on a first-come, first-served basis to single and married students. Housing application deadline: 9/1. *Student services:* Campus employment opportunities, career counseling, free psychological counseling, international student services, low-cost health insurance, services for students with disabilities, writing training. *Library facilities:* Bailey Library plus 3 others.

Computer facilities: A campuswide network can be accessed. Online class registration is available.
Website: http://www.nyack.edu/

General Application Contact: 800-541-6891, Fax: 845-348-3912, E-mail: admissions.grad@nyack.edu.

GRADUATE UNITS

Alliance Graduate School of Counseling Students: 84 full-time (69 women), 123 part-time (103 women); includes 152 minority (64 Black or African American, non-Hispanic/Latino; 44 Asian, non-Hispanic/Latino; 41 Hispanic/Latino; 3 Two or more races, non-Hispanic/Latino), 9 international. Average age 37. Expenses: Contact institution. *Financial support:* Career-related internships or fieldwork and scholarships/grants available. Financial award applicants required to submit FAFSA. In 2016, 70 master's awarded. *Program availability:* Part-time, evening/weekend, 100% online. Offers marriage and family therapy (MA); mental health counseling (MA). *Application deadline:* For fall admission, 8/1 for domestic students, 2/15 for international students; for spring admission, 12/15 for domestic students, 7/15 for international students. Applications are processed on a rolling basis. *Application fee:* $30. Electronic applications accepted. *Application Contact:* Esther Guzman, Admissions Associate, 800-541-6891, E-mail: admissions.grad@nyack.edu. *Associate Dean,* Dr. Carol Robles, 845-770-5735.

Alliance Theological Seminary Students: 275 full-time (111 women), 370 part-time (175 women); includes 505 minority (177 Black or African American, non-Hispanic/Latino; 128 Asian, non-Hispanic/Latino; 190 Hispanic/Latino; 10 Two or more races, non-Hispanic/Latino), 32 international. Average age 43. Expenses: Contact institution. *Financial support:* Career-related internships or fieldwork, Federal Work-Study, and scholarships/grants available. Financial award applicants required to submit FAFSA. In 2016, 117 master's, 14 doctorates awarded. *Program availability:* Part-time, evening/weekend, 100% online, blended/hybrid learning. Offers Biblical literature (MA); Biblical studies (MA); Christian ministry (MPS); intercultural studies (MA); ministry (D Min); theology and missions (M Div); urban ministry (MPS). *Application deadline:* Applications are processed on a rolling basis. *Application fee:* $30. Electronic applications accepted. *Application Contact:* Julian Williams, Associate Director of Admissions, 800-541-6891, Fax: 845-348-3912, E-mail: admissions.ats@nyack.edu. *Dean,* Dr. Ronald Walborn, 845-770-5715, Fax: 845-358-1663.

College of Bible and Christian Ministry Students: 2 full-time (1 woman), 6 part-time (0 women); includes 5 minority (2 Black or African American, non-Hispanic/Latino; 2 Hispanic/Latino; 1 Two or more races, non-Hispanic/Latino). Average age 39. Expenses: Contact institution. *Financial support:* Applicants required to submit FAFSA. In 2016, 2 master's awarded. *Program availability:* Part-time, evening/weekend, 100% online, blended/hybrid learning. Offers ancient Judaism and Christian origins (MA). *Application deadline:* Applications are processed on a rolling basis. *Application fee:* $30. Electronic applications accepted. *Application Contact:* 800-541-6891, Fax: 845-348-3912, E-mail: admissions.grad@nyack.edu. *Director,* Dr. Steven Notley, 646-378-6148, E-mail: steven.notley@nyack.edu.

School of Business and Leadership Students: 45 full-time (21 women), 20 part-time (15 women); includes 40 minority (26 Black or African American, non-Hispanic/Latino; 1 American Indian or Alaska Native, non-Hispanic/Latino; 4 Asian, non-Hispanic/Latino; 9 Hispanic/Latino), 5 international. Average age 38. Expenses: Contact institution. *Financial support:* Scholarships/grants available. Financial award applicants required to submit FAFSA. In 2016, 40 master's awarded. *Program availability:* Part-time, evening/weekend, 100% online, blended/hybrid learning. Offers business administration (MBA); organizational leadership (MS). *Application deadline:* Applications are processed on a rolling basis. *Application fee:* $50. Electronic applications accepted. *Application*

Contact: Joseph M. Williams, Graduate Admissions Associate, 800-541-6891, Fax: 845-348-3912, E-mail: admissions.grad@nyack.edu. *Dean,* Dr. Anita Underwood, 845-675-4511, Fax: 845-353-5812.

School of Education Students: 21 full-time (20 women), 36 part-time (31 women); includes 34 minority (7 Black or African American, non-Hispanic/Latino; 3 Asian, non-Hispanic/Latino; 22 Hispanic/Latino; 1 Native Hawaiian or other Pacific Islander, non-Hispanic/Latino; 1 Two or more races, non-Hispanic/Latino), 5 international. Average age 33. Expenses: Contact institution. *Financial support:* Scholarships/grants available. Financial award applicants required to submit FAFSA. In 2016, 23 master's awarded. *Program availability:* Part-time, 100% online, blended/hybrid learning. Offers childhood education (MS); childhood special education (MS); inclusive education (MA); TESOL (MAT, MS). *Application deadline:* For fall admission, 8/4 for domestic students, 7/4 for international students; for spring admission, 12/15 for domestic students, 11/15 for international students; for summer admission, 4/7 for domestic students, 3/7 for international students. Applications are processed on a rolling basis. *Application fee:* $30. Electronic applications accepted. *Application Contact:* Joseph Kim, Admissions Associate, 845-675-4400 Ext. 5708, Fax: 845-348-3912, E-mail: admissions.grad@nyack.edu. *Dean,* Dr. JoAnn Looney, 845-675-4538, Fax: 845-358-0874.

School of Social Work Students: 40 full-time (35 women), 29 part-time (27 women); includes 58 minority (32 Black or African American, non-Hispanic/Latino; 1 American Indian or Alaska Native, non-Hispanic/Latino; 5 Asian, non-Hispanic/Latino; 18 Hispanic/Latino; 2 Two or more races, non-Hispanic/Latino), 1 international. Average age 35. Expenses: Contact institution. *Financial support:* Institutionally sponsored loans available. Financial award applicants required to submit FAFSA. In 2016, 8 master's awarded. *Program availability:* Part-time, evening/weekend. Offers clinical social work practice (MSW); leadership in organizations and communities (MSW). *Application deadline:* Applications are processed on a rolling basis. *Application fee:* $45. Electronic applications accepted. *Application Contact:* Apryll Campbell, Admissions Associate, 646-378-6195, E-mail: admissions.grad@nyack.edu. *Director of MSW Program,* Dr. Janet Furness, 646-378-6169, E-mail: janet.furness@nyack.edu.

OAKLAND CITY UNIVERSITY, Oakland City, IN 47660-1099

General Information Independent-religious, coed, comprehensive institution. *Graduate housing:* Rooms and/or apartments guaranteed to single students and available on a first-come, first-served basis to married students. Housing application deadline: 7/1.

GRADUATE UNITS

Chapman Seminary *Program availability:* Part-time. Offers religious studies (M Div, D Min).

School of Adult and Extended Learning *Program availability:* Part-time, evening/weekend. Offers adult and extended learning (MBA).

School of Education Offers educational leadership (Ed D); teaching (MA).

OAKLAND UNIVERSITY, Rochester, MI 48309-4401

General Information State-supported, coed, university. CGS member. *Graduate housing:* Rooms and/or apartments available on a first-come, first-served basis to single and married students. Housing application deadline: 9/1. *Research affiliation:* Beaumont Hospital Corporation (eye research, nursing), Henry Ford Health Systems (medical physics).

GRADUATE UNITS

Graduate Study and Lifelong Learning *Program availability:* Part-time, evening/weekend. Electronic applications accepted.

College of Arts and Sciences *Program availability:* Part-time, evening/weekend. Offers applied mathematical sciences (PhD); applied statistics (MS); arts and sciences (MA, MM, MPA, MS, PhD, Certificate, Graduate Certificate, PMC); biology (MA, MS); biomedical sciences (Graduate Certificate); biomedical sciences: biological communication (PhD); biomedical sciences: health and environmental chemistry (PhD); chemistry (MS); English (MA); history (MA); industrial applied mathematics (MS); liberal studies (MA); linguistics (MA); local government management (Graduate Certificate); mathematical statistics (MS); mathematics (MA); medical physics (PhD); music (MM); music education (PhD); non-profit and organizational management (PMC); physics (MS); public administration (MPA); statistical methods (Certificate); teaching English as a second language (Certificate). Electronic applications accepted.

School of Business Administration *Program availability:* Part-time, evening/weekend. Offers accounting (M Acc, Certificate); business administration (EMBA, M Acc, MBA, MS, Certificate); economics (MBA, Certificate); entrepreneurship (Certificate); finance (Certificate); general management (Certificate); human resource management (Certificate); information technology management (MS); international business (Certificate); management and marketing (EMBA); management information systems (Certificate); marketing (Certificate); production and operations management (Certificate). Electronic applications accepted.

School of Education and Human Services *Program availability:* Part-time, evening/weekend. Offers advanced microcomputer applications (Graduate Certificate); applied behavior analysis (Graduate Certificate); autism spectrum disorder (Graduate Certificate); counseling (MA, PhD, Certificate); digital literacies and learning (Graduate Certificate); early childhood education (M Ed, PhD, Ed S); early education and intervention (Ed S); education and human services (M Ed, MA, MAT, PhD, Certificate, Ed S, Graduate Certificate, PMC); educational leadership (M Ed, PhD); educational studies (M Ed); elementary education (MAT); emotional impairment (Graduate Certificate); higher education (Certificate); microcomputer applications (Graduate Certificate); reading and language arts (MAT); reading education (PhD); reading, language arts and literature (PMC); school administration (Ed S); secondary education (MAT); special education (M Ed, Graduate Certificate); specific learning disabilities (Graduate Certificate); teaching and learning (Graduate Certificate). Electronic applications accepted.

School of Engineering and Computer Science *Program availability:* Part-time, evening/weekend. Offers computer science (MS); computer science and informatics (PhD); electrical and computer engineering (MS, PhD); embedded systems (MS); engineering and computer science (MS, PhD, Graduate Certificate); engineering management (MS); industrial and systems engineering (MS); mechanical engineering (MS, PhD); mechatronics (MS); productivity improvement (Graduate Certificate); software engineering and information technology (MS); systems engineering (PhD). Electronic applications accepted.

School of Health Sciences Offers clinical exercise science (Dr Sc PT); complementary medicine and wellness (Dr Sc PT); corporate worksite wellness (Dr Sc PT); exercise science (MS, Graduate Certificate); health sciences (MS, DPT, Dr Sc PT, TDPT, Graduate Certificate); neurological rehabilitation (Dr Sc PT, TDPT); orthopedic manual physical therapy (Dr Sc PT, TDPT, Graduate Certificate); orthopedic physical therapy (Graduate Certificate); orthopedics (Dr Sc PT, TDPT); pediatric rehabilitation (Dr Sc PT, TDPT); physical therapy (DPT); safety management (MS); teaching and learning for rehabilitation professionals (Dr Sc PT, TDPT). Electronic applications accepted.

School of Nursing *Program availability:* Part-time, evening/weekend. Offers adult gerontological nurse practitioner (MSN, PMC); family nurse practitioner (MSN, PMC); nurse anesthesia (MSN, PMC); nursing (MSN, DNP, PMC); nursing practice (DNP). Electronic applications accepted.

OAKWOOD UNIVERSITY, Huntsville, AL 35896

General Information Independent-religious, coed, comprehensive institution. *Graduate housing:* On-campus housing not available.

GRADUATE UNITS

Program in Pastoral Studies Offers pastoral studies (MA).

OBERLIN COLLEGE, Oberlin, OH 44074

General Information Independent, coed, comprehensive institution. *Enrollment:* 2,912 graduate, professional, and undergraduate students; 16 full-time matriculated graduate/professional students (5 women). *Enrollment by degree level:* 16 master's. *Graduate housing:* Room and/or apartments available on a first-come, first-served basis to single students; on-campus housing not available to married students. Housing application deadline: 6/15. *Student services:* Campus employment opportunities, campus safety program, career counseling, exercise/wellness program, free psychological counseling, international student services, multicultural affairs office, services for students with disabilities, writing training. *Library facilities:* Mudd Center Library plus 3 others. *Collection:* Books: 1.4 million (physical), 676,883 (digital/electronic); Serial titles: 181,044 (physical), 115,097 (digital/electronic). Students can reserve study rooms.

Computer facilities: Computer purchase and lease plans are available. 340 computers available on campus for general student use. A campuswide network can be accessed from student residence rooms and from off campus. Online class registration is available.
Website: http://www.oberlin.edu/

General Application Contact: Michael Manderen, Director of Conservatory Admissions, 440-775-8413, Fax: 440-775-6972, E-mail: conservatory.admissions@oberlin.edu.

GRADUATE UNITS

Conservatory of Music Students: 16 full-time (5 women). 102 applicants, 23% accepted, 14 enrolled. Expenses: Contact institution. *Financial support:* Career-related internships or fieldwork, Federal Work-Study, and scholarships/grants available. Financial award application deadline: 2/15; financial award applicants required to submit CSS PROFILE or FAFSA. Offers conducting (MM); contemporary chamber music (MM); historical performance (MM); performance (AD); piano technology (AD). *Application deadline:* For fall admission, 12/1 for domestic and international students. *Application fee:* $100. Electronic applications accepted. *Application Contact:* Michael Manderen, Director of Conservatory Admissions, 440-775-8413, Fax: 440-775-6972, E-mail: conservatory.admissions@oberlin.edu. *Dean,* Andrea Kalyn, 440-775-8200.

OBLATE SCHOOL OF THEOLOGY, San Antonio, TX 78216-6693

General Information Independent-religious, coed, graduate-only institution. *Enrollment by degree level:* 110 master's, 17 doctoral. *Graduate faculty:* 24 full-time (8 women), 4 part-time/adjunct (0 women). *Tuition:* Full-time $10,530; part-time $585 per credit. *Required fees:* $970. One-time fee: $110. Tuition and fees vary according to course load, degree level and program. *Graduate housing:* On-campus housing not available. *Student services:* Campus employment opportunities, international student services, services for students with disabilities, writing training. *Library facilities:* Donald E. O'Shaughnessy Library. *Collection:* Books: 90,554 (physical), 28,470 (digital/electronic); Serial titles: 300 (physical), 25 (digital/electronic); Databases: 15. Weekly public service hours: 60.

Computer facilities: 10 computers available on campus for general student use. A campuswide network can be accessed from student residence rooms. Online class registration is available.
Website: http://www.ost.edu/

General Application Contact: Mario A. Porter, Registrar, 210-341-1366 Ext. 226, Fax: 210-341-4519, E-mail: registrar@ost.edu.

GRADUATE UNITS

Graduate and Professional Programs Students: 76 full-time (10 women), 51 part-time (32 women); includes 56 minority (8 Black or African American, non-Hispanic/Latino; 9 Asian, non-Hispanic/Latino; 39 Hispanic/Latino), 41 international. Average age 40. *Faculty:* 24 full-time (8 women), 4 part-time/adjunct (0 women). Expenses: Contact institution. *Financial support:* In 2016–17, 25 students received support. Scholarships/grants available. Support available to part-time students. Financial award application deadline: 8/1; financial award applicants required to submit FAFSA. In 2016, 31 master's, 3 doctorates awarded. *Program availability:* Part-time, online learning. Offers African-American pastoral leadership (D Min); divinity (M Div); pastoral leadership (D Min); pastoral ministry (MAP Min); pastoral studies (Certificate); spiritual formation in the local community (D Min); spirituality (MA Sp, PhD); spirituality and ministry (D Min); theology (MA Th); U.S. Hispanic/Latino ministry (D Min). *Application deadline:* For fall admission, 6/15 priority date for domestic and international students; for winter admission, 11/30 for domestic and international students; for spring admission, 11/30 for domestic and international students; for summer admission, 4/1 for domestic and international students. Applications are processed on a rolling basis. *Application fee:* $65. *Application Contact:* Mario A. Porter, Registrar, 210-341-1366 Ext. 226, Fax: 210-341-4519, E-mail: registrar@ost.edu. *Academic Dean,* Dr. R. Scott Woodward, 210-341-1366, Fax: 210-341-4519, E-mail: rsw@ost.edu.

OCCIDENTAL COLLEGE, Los Angeles, CA 90041-3314

General Information Independent, coed, comprehensive institution. *Enrollment:* 2,062 graduate, professional, and undergraduate students. *Tuition:* Full-time $42,080; part-time $2104 per unit. *Required fees:* $578; $289 per semester. *Graduate housing:* On-campus housing not available. *Student services:* Campus employment opportunities, campus safety program, career counseling, child daycare facilities, free psychological counseling, low-cost health insurance, multicultural affairs office. *Library facilities:* Mary Norton Clapp Library and Academic Commons plus 2 others. *Collection:* Study areas open 24 hours, 5–7 days a week; students can reserve study rooms.

Computer facilities: Computer purchase and lease plans are available. 200 computers available on campus for general student use. A campuswide network can be accessed from student residence rooms and from off campus. Online class registration is available.
Website: http://www.oxy.edu/

General Application Contact: Susan Molik, Academic Services Assistant, Graduate Office, 323-259-2921, Fax: 323-341-4988, E-mail: molik@oxy.edu.

GRADUATE UNITS

Department of Biology *Faculty:* 11 full-time (6 women), 8 part-time/adjunct (4 women). *Expenses:* Contact institution. *Financial support:* Fellowships, Federal Work-Study, institutionally sponsored loans, and scholarships/grants available. Support available to part-time students. Financial award application deadline: 3/1; financial award applicants required to submit FAFSA. *Program availability:* Part-time. Offers biology (MA). *Application deadline:* For fall admission, 3/1 for domestic students; for spring admission, 10/1 for domestic students. Applications are processed on a rolling basis. *Application fee:* $60. *Application Contact:* Susan Molik, Academic Services Assistant, Graduate Office, 323-259-2921, Fax: 323-341-4988, E-mail: molik@oxy.edu. *Department Chair*, 323-259-2697, E-mail: biology@oxy.edu.

OGLALA LAKOTA COLLEGE, Kyle, SD 57752-0490

General Information State and locally supported, coed, comprehensive institution. *Graduate housing:* On-campus housing not available.

GRADUATE UNITS

Graduate Studies *Program availability:* Part-time, evening/weekend. Offers educational administration (MA); Lakota leadership and management (MA).

OHIO CHRISTIAN UNIVERSITY, Circleville, OH 43113-9487

General Information Independent-religious, coed, comprehensive institution.

GRADUATE UNITS
Graduate Programs

OHIO DOMINICAN UNIVERSITY, Columbus, OH 43219-2099

General Information Independent-religious, coed, comprehensive institution. *Enrollment:* 2,406 graduate, professional, and undergraduate students; 189 full-time matriculated graduate/professional students (109 women), 338 part-time matriculated graduate/professional students (220 women). *Enrollment by degree level:* 527 master's, 2 other advanced degrees. *Graduate faculty:* 32 full-time (15 women), 33 part-time/adjunct (15 women). *Tuition:* Full-time $10,620; part-time $590 per credit hour. *Required fees:* $450; $450 per credit hour. Tuition and fees vary according to program. *Graduate housing:* Room and/or apartments available on a first-come, first-served basis to single students; on-campus housing not available to married students. Typical cost: $10,928 (including board). Room and board charges vary according to board plan. Housing application deadline: 8/20. *Student services:* Campus employment opportunities, campus safety program, career counseling, exercise/wellness program, free psychological counseling, international student services, multicultural affairs office, services for students with disabilities, writing training. *Library facilities:* Ohio Dominican Library. *Collection:* Books: 78,234 (physical), 149,341 (digital/electronic); Serial titles: 611 (physical), 29,195 (digital/electronic); Databases: 264. Students can reserve study rooms.

Computer facilities: 350 computers available on campus for general student use. A campuswide network can be accessed from student residence rooms and from off campus. Online class registration is available.
Website: http://www.ohiodominican.edu/

General Application Contact: John W. Naughton, Director for Graduate Admissions, 614-251-4721, Fax: 614-251-6654, E-mail: grad@ohiodominican.edu.

GRADUATE UNITS

Division of Arts and Letters Students: 1 (woman) full-time, 50 part-time (32 women); includes 4 minority (2 Black or African American, non-Hispanic/Latino; 1 Hispanic/Latino; 1 Two or more races, non-Hispanic/Latino), 1 international. Average age 40. 22 applicants, 77% accepted, 15 enrolled. *Faculty:* 4 full-time (1 woman), 2 part-time/adjunct (1 woman). *Expenses:* Contact institution. *Financial support:* Applicants required to submit FAFSA. *Program availability:* Part-time, evening/weekend, 100% online. Offers English (MA); theology (MA). *Application deadline:* For fall admission, 8/15 for domestic students, 6/10 for international students; for spring admission, 1/4 for domestic students, 11/2 for international students; for summer admission, 5/30 for domestic students. Applications are processed on a rolling basis. *Application fee:* $25. Electronic applications accepted. *Application Contact:* John W. Naughton, Director for Graduate Admissions, 614-251-4721, Fax: 614-251-6654, E-mail: grad@ohiodominican.edu. *Chair*, Dr. Bruce Gartner, 614-251-4604, Fax: 614-253-3656, E-mail: gartnerb@ohiodominican.edu.

Division of Business Students: 80 full-time (34 women), 128 part-time (68 women); includes 63 minority (40 Black or African American, non-Hispanic/Latino; 2 American Indian or Alaska Native, non-Hispanic/Latino; 7 Asian, non-Hispanic/Latino; 6 Hispanic/Latino; 2 Native Hawaiian or other Pacific Islander, non-Hispanic/Latino; 6 Two or more races, non-Hispanic/Latino), 9 international. Average age 31. 91 applicants, 53% accepted, 37 enrolled. *Faculty:* 11 full-time (5 women), 22 part-time/adjunct (8 women). *Expenses:* Contact institution. *Financial support:* Applicants required to submit FAFSA. *Program availability:* Part-time, evening/weekend, 100% online, blended/hybrid learning. Offers accounting (MBA); business administration (MBA); data analytics (MBA); finance (MBA); healthcare administration (MS); leadership (MBA); risk management (MBA); sport management (MBA, MS). *Application deadline:* For fall admission, 8/15 for domestic students, 6/10 for international students; for spring admission, 1/4 for domestic students, 11/2 for international students; for summer admission, 5/30 for domestic students. Applications are processed on a rolling basis. *Application fee:* $25. Electronic applications accepted. *Application Contact:* John W. Naughton, Director for Graduate Admissions, 614-251-4721, Fax: 614-251-6654, E-mail: grad@ohiodominican.edu. *Chair*, Dr. Kenneth C. Fah, 614-251-4566, E-mail: fahk@ohiodominican.edu.

Division of Education Students: 10 full-time (9 women), 111 part-time (87 women); includes 14 minority (6 Black or African American, non-Hispanic/Latino; 2 Asian, non-Hispanic/Latino; 4 Hispanic/Latino; 2 Two or more races, non-Hispanic/Latino), 5 international. Average age 32. 49 applicants, 67% accepted, 30 enrolled. *Faculty:* 7 full-time (4 women), 8 part-time/adjunct (1 woman). *Expenses:* Contact institution. *Financial support:* Tuition waivers and tuition discount for Diocesan teachers available. Financial award applicants required to submit FAFSA. *Program availability:* Part-time, evening/weekend, 100% online, blended/hybrid learning. Offers curriculum and instruction (M Ed); educational leadership (M Ed); teaching English to speakers of other languages (MA). *Application deadline:* For fall admission, 8/15 for domestic students, 6/10 for international students; for spring admission, 1/4 for domestic students, 11/2 for international students; for summer admission, 5/30 for domestic students. Applications are processed on a rolling basis. *Application fee:* $25. Electronic applications accepted. *Application Contact:* John W. Naughton, Director for Graduate Admissions, 614-251-4721, Fax: 614-251-6654, E-mail: grad@ohiodominican.edu. *Chair*, Dr. JoAnn Hohenbrink, 614-251-4759, E-mail: hohenbrj@ohiodominican.edu.

Division of Physician Assistant Studies Students: 98 full-time (65 women), 48 part-time (32 women); includes 11 minority (2 Black or African American, non-Hispanic/Latino; 1 American Indian or Alaska Native, non-Hispanic/Latino; 5 Asian, non-Hispanic/Latino; 2 Hispanic/Latino; 1 Two or more races, non-Hispanic/Latino). Average age 26. 499 applicants, 17% accepted, 50 enrolled. *Faculty:* 7 full-time (4 women), 2 part-time/adjunct (0 women). *Expenses:* Contact institution. *Financial support:* Applicants required to submit FAFSA. In 2016, 53 master's awarded. Offers physician assistant studies (MS). *Application deadline:* For fall admission, 10/1 for domestic and international students. Applications are processed on a rolling basis. Electronic applications accepted. *Application Contact:* John W. Naughton, Director for Graduate Admissions, 614-251-4721, Fax: 614-251-6654, E-mail: grad@ohiodominican.edu. *Program Director*, Prof. Shonna Riedlinger, 614-251-8988, E-mail: riedlins@ohiodominican.edu.

OHIO NORTHERN UNIVERSITY, Ada, OH 45810-1599

General Information Independent-religious, coed, comprehensive institution. *Graduate housing:* Room and/or apartments available on a first-come, first-served basis to single students; on-campus housing not available to married students.

GRADUATE UNITS

Claude W. Pettit College of Law Offers law (LL M, JD). Electronic applications accepted.

College of Business Offers business (MSA).

Raabe College of Pharmacy Offers pharmacy (Pharm D). Students enter the program as undergraduates.

THE OHIO STATE UNIVERSITY, Columbus, OH 43210

General Information State-supported, coed, university. CGS member. *Enrollment:* 59,482 graduate, professional, and undergraduate students; 11,715 full-time matriculated graduate/professional students (6,251 women), 1,399 part-time matriculated graduate/professional students (842 women). *Enrollment by degree level:* 5,080 master's, 8,014 doctoral, 20 other advanced degrees. *Graduate faculty:* 4,076. *Graduate housing:* Rooms and/or apartments available on a first-come, first-served basis to single and married students. *Student services:* Campus employment opportunities, campus safety program, career counseling, child daycare facilities, exercise/wellness program, free psychological counseling, grant writing training, international student services, low-cost health insurance, multicultural affairs office, services for students with disabilities, teacher training, writing training. *Library facilities:* Thompson Library plus 12 others. *Collection:* Study areas open 24 hours, 5–7 days a week; students can reserve study rooms. *Research affiliation:* Transportation Research Center, Midwest Universities Consortium for International Activities, Children's Hospital (pediatrics), Ohio Learning Network (education).

Computer facilities: A campuswide network can be accessed from student residence rooms and from off campus. Online class registration, admission applications, fee payment are available.
Website: http://www.osu.edu/

General Application Contact: Graduate and Professional Admissions, 614-292-9444, Fax: 614-292-3895, E-mail: gpadmissions@osu.edu.

GRADUATE UNITS

College of Dentistry Students: 504 full-time (199 women), 7 part-time (5 women). Average age 26. *Faculty:* 86. *Expenses:* Contact institution. *Financial support:* Fellowships with tuition reimbursements, research assistantships with tuition reimbursements, teaching assistantships with tuition reimbursements, Federal Work-Study, institutionally sponsored loans, and health care benefits available. Financial award application deadline: 2/15. In 2016, 30 master's, 112 doctorates awarded. Offers dental anesthesiology (MS); dental hygiene (MDH); dentistry (DDS); endodontics (MS); oral and maxillofacial pathology (MS), oral and maxillofacial surgery (MS); oral biology (PhD); orthodontics (MS); pediatric dentistry (MS); periodontology (MS); prosthodontics (MS). *Application deadline:* For fall admission, 10/1 for domestic and international students; for summer admission, 4/11 for domestic students, 3/10 for international students. Applications are processed on a rolling basis. Electronic applications accepted. *Application Contact:* Graduate and Professional Admissions, 614-292-9444, Fax: 614-292-3895, E-mail: gpadmissions@osu.edu. *Dean*, Dr. Patrick M. Lloyd, 614-292-9755, E-mail: lloyd.256@osu.edu.

College of Medicine Students: 1,268 full-time (728 women), 28 part-time (21 women); includes 420 minority (76 Black or African American, non-Hispanic/Latino; 196 Asian, non-Hispanic/Latino; 99 Hispanic/Latino; 49 Two or more races, non-Hispanic/Latino), 5 international. Average age 25. *Faculty:* 1,701. *Expenses:* Contact institution. *Financial support:* Fellowships with tuition reimbursements, research assistantships with tuition reimbursements, teaching assistantships with tuition reimbursements, Federal Work-Study, institutionally sponsored loans, and scholarships/grants available. Support available to part-time students. Financial award application deadline: 2/15; financial award applicants required to submit FAFSA. In 2016, 88 master's, 258 doctorates awarded. Offers biomedical sciences (PhD); medicine (MOT, MS, DPT, MD, PhD). *Application deadline:* Applications are processed on a rolling basis. Electronic applications accepted. *Application Contact:* Graduate and Professional Admissions, 614-292-9444, Fax: 614-292-3895, E-mail: gpadmissions@osu.edu. *Dean and Vice President of Health Sciences*, Dr. K. Craig Kent, MD, 614-292-2600, Fax: 614-292-1301.

School of Health and Rehabilitation Sciences Students: 356 full-time (279 women), 18 part-time (13 women); includes 33 minority (14 Asian, non-Hispanic/Latino; 11 Hispanic/Latino; 8 Two or more races, non-Hispanic/Latino). Average age 25. *Faculty:* 39. *Expenses:* Contact institution. *Financial support:* Fellowships with tuition reimbursements, research assistantships with full tuition reimbursements, teaching assistantships with full tuition reimbursements, traineeships, unspecified assistantships, and administrative assistantships available. Financial award application deadline: 3/1. In 2016, 60 master's, 52 doctorates awarded. *Program availability:* Part-time. Offers allied health (MS); anatomy (MS, PhD); health and rehabilitation sciences (MOT, MS, DPT, PhD); occupational therapy (MOT); physical therapy (DPT). *Application deadline:* Applications are processed on a rolling basis. *Application fee:* $60 ($70 for international students). Electronic applications accepted. *Application Contact:* Graduate and Professional Admissions, 614-292-9444, Fax: 614-292-3895, E-mail: gpadmissions@osu.edu. *Associate Dean and Director*, Dr. Deborah S. Larsen, 614-292-5645, Fax: 614-292-0210, E-mail: larsen.64@osu.edu.

College of Optometry Students: 266 full-time (180 women); includes 39 minority (8 Black or African American, non-Hispanic/Latino; 18 Asian, non-Hispanic/Latino; 8 Hispanic/Latino; 5 Two or more races, non-Hispanic/Latino), 2 international. Average age 25. *Faculty:* 34. *Expenses:* Contact institution. *Financial support:* Research assistantships with full tuition reimbursements, teaching assistantships with full tuition reimbursements, institutionally sponsored loans, and scholarships/grants available. Financial award application deadline: 2/15; financial award applicants required to submit

FAFSA. In 2016, 13 master's, 58 doctorates awarded. Offers optometry (OD); vision science (MS, PhD). *Application deadline:* For fall admission, 3/31 for domestic and international students; for spring admission, 12/1 for domestic students, 11/1 for international students. Applications are processed on a rolling basis. *Application fee:* $60 ($70 for international students). Electronic applications accepted. *Application Contact:* Office of Student Affairs, College of Optometry, 614-292-2647, Fax: 614-292-7493, E-mail: admissions@optometry.osu.edu. *Dean,* Dr. Karla Zadnik, 614-292-6603, E-mail: zadnik.4@osu.edu.

College of Pharmacy Students: 596 full-time (326 women), 3 part-time (2 women); includes 167 minority (36 Black or African American, non-Hispanic/Latino; 99 Asian, non-Hispanic/Latino; 20 Hispanic/Latino; 12 Two or more races, non-Hispanic/Latino), 55 international. Average age 25. *Faculty:* 56. Expenses: Contact institution. *Financial support:* Fellowships with full tuition reimbursements, research assistantships with full tuition reimbursements, teaching assistantships with full tuition reimbursements, career-related internships or fieldwork, Federal Work-Study, institutionally sponsored loans, scholarships/grants, and traineeships available. In 2016, 8 master's, 123 doctorates awarded. Offers pharmacy (MS, PhD, Pharm D). *Application deadline:* For fall admission, 12/15 for domestic and international students. *Application fee:* $60 ($70 for international students). Electronic applications accepted. *Application Contact:* E-mail: admissions@pharmacy.ohio-state.edu. *Dean and Professor,* Dr. Henry J. Mann, 614-292-5711, Fax: 614-292-2588, E-mail: mann.414@osu.edu.

College of Public Health Students: 260 full-time (198 women), 71 part-time (47 women); includes 71 minority (24 Black or African American, non-Hispanic/Latino; 23 Asian, non-Hispanic/Latino; 14 Hispanic/Latino; 10 Two or more races, non-Hispanic/Latino), 19 international. Average age 28. *Faculty:* 50. Expenses: Contact institution. *Financial support:* Fellowships with tuition reimbursements and research assistantships with tuition reimbursements available. In 2016, 133 master's, 15 doctorates awarded. *Program availability:* Part-time. Offers public health (MHA, MPH, MS, PhD). *Application deadline:* For fall admission, 12/1 priority date for domestic students, 11/1 priority date for international students. Applications are processed on a rolling basis. *Application fee:* $60 ($70 for international students). Electronic applications accepted. *Application Contact:* 614-292-8350, Fax: 614-247-1846, E-mail: cph@cph.osu.edu. *Dean and Professor,* Dr. William J. Martin, II, 614-292-8350, E-mail: martin.3047@osu.edu.

College of Veterinary Medicine Students: 712 full-time (571 women), 31 part-time (21 women). Average age 26. *Faculty:* 113. Expenses: Contact institution. In 2016, 17 master's, 168 doctorates awarded. Offers comparative and veterinary medicine (MS, PhD); veterinary medicine (MS, DVM, PhD). *Application deadline:* For fall admission, 9/15 for domestic and international students. Applications are processed on a rolling basis. *Application fee:* $60 ($70 for international students). Electronic applications accepted. *Application Contact:* Graduate and Professional Admissions, 614-292-9444, Fax: 614-292-3895, E-mail: gpadmissions@osu.edu. *Dean/Chair/Professor,* Dr. Rustin M. Moore, 614-688-8749, Fax: 614-292-3544, E-mail: moore.66@osu.edu.

Graduate School Students: 7,567 full-time (3,783 women), 1,254 part-time (741 women); includes 1,178 minority (372 Black or African American, non-Hispanic/Latino; 13 American Indian or Alaska Native, non-Hispanic/Latino; 305 Asian, non-Hispanic/Latino; 303 Hispanic/Latino; 3 Native Hawaiian or other Pacific Islander, non-Hispanic/Latino; 182 Two or more races, non-Hispanic/Latino), 2,581 international. Average age 29. Expenses: Contact institution. *Financial support:* Fellowships with tuition reimbursements, research assistantships with tuition reimbursements, teaching assistantships with tuition reimbursements, career-related internships or fieldwork, Federal Work-Study, institutionally sponsored loans, and unspecified assistantships available. Support available to part-time students. In 2016, 2,305 master's, 696 doctorates, 7 other advanced degrees awarded. *Program availability:* Part-time, evening/weekend. Offers biostatistics (PhD). *Application deadline:* For fall admission, 8/12 for domestic students, 7/1 for international students; for spring admission, 3/1 for domestic students, 2/1 for international students. Applications are processed on a rolling basis. *Application fee:* $60 ($70 for international students). Electronic applications accepted. *Application Contact:* Graduate and Professional Admissions, 614-292-9444, Fax: 614-292-3895, E-mail: gpadmissions@osu.edu. *Interim Vice Provost and Dean,* Dr. M. Scott Herness, 614-292-9490, E-mail: herness.1@osu.edu.

Center for Applied Plant Sciences Students: 10 full-time (6 women). Average age 28. Expenses: Contact institution. *Financial support:* Fellowships with tuition reimbursements and research assistantships with tuition reimbursements available. Offers applied plant sciences (PhD). *Application deadline:* For fall admission, 11/15 priority date for domestic and international students. Applications are processed on a rolling basis. *Application fee:* $60 ($70 for international students). Electronic applications accepted. *Application Contact:* Graduate and Professional Admissions, 614-292-9444, Fax: 614-292-3895, E-mail: gpadmissions@osu.edu. *Graduate Studies Committee Chair,* Dr. Thomas Mitchell, E-mail: mitchell.815@osu.edu.

Center for Latin American Studies Students: 1 full-time. Expenses: Contact institution. *Financial support:* Fellowships with tuition reimbursements available. In 2016, 1 master's awarded. Offers Latin American studies (MA). *Application deadline:* For fall admission, 12/13 priority date for domestic students, 11/30 priority date for international students; for spring admission, 12/12 for domestic students, 11/10 for international students; for summer admission, 4/10 for domestic students, 3/13 for international students. Applications are processed on a rolling basis. *Application fee:* $60 ($70 for international students). Electronic applications accepted. *Application Contact:* Graduate and Professional Admissions, 614-292-9444, Fax: 614-292-3895, E-mail: gpadmissions@osu.edu. *Director,* Dr. Abril Trigo, 614-292-8695, E-mail: trigo.1@osu.edu.

Center for Slavic and East European Studies Students: 10 full-time (2 women). Average age 25. Expenses: Contact institution. *Financial support:* Fellowships, Federal Work-Study, and institutionally sponsored loans available. Support available to part-time students. In 2016, 5 master's awarded. Offers Slavic and East European studies (MA). *Application deadline:* For fall admission, 12/13 priority date for domestic students, 11/30 priority date for international students; for spring admission, 11/10 for domestic and international students; for summer admission, 3/13 for domestic and international students. Applications are processed on a rolling basis. *Application fee:* $60 ($70 for international students). Electronic applications accepted. *Application Contact:* Graduate and Professional Admissions, 614-292-9444, Fax: 614-292-3895, E-mail: gpadmissions@osu.edu. *Director,* Dr. Yana Hashamova, E-mail: hashamova.1@osu.edu.

College of Arts and Sciences Students: 2,688 full-time (1,336 women), 62 part-time (38 women); includes 362 minority (77 Black or African American, non-Hispanic/Latino; 88 Asian, non-Hispanic/Latino; 131 Hispanic/Latino; 66 Two or more races, non-Hispanic/Latino), 760 international. Average age 28. *Faculty:* 959. Expenses: Contact institution. *Financial support:* Fellowships, research assistantships, teaching assistantships, career-related internships or fieldwork, Federal Work-Study, institutionally sponsored loans, and unspecified assistantships

available. Support available to part-time students. In 2016, 397 master's, 374 doctorates awarded. *Program availability:* Part-time. Offers acting (MFA); actuarial and quantitative risk management (MAQRM); African-American and African studies (MA, PhD); ancient Greek and Latin (MA, PhD); anthropology (MA, PhD); art (MFA); art education (MA); arts administration, education and policy (PhD); arts and humanities (MA, MFA, MM, DMA, PhD); arts and sciences (M Mus, MA, MAQRM, MFA, MMS, MS, DMA, PhD); arts policy and administration (MA); astronomy (MS, PhD); atmospheric sciences (MS, PhD); audiology (Au D); behavioral neuroscience (PhD); biochemistry (PhD); biophysics (MS, PhD); biostatistics (PhD); cell and developmental biology (MS, PhD); chemical physics (MS, PhD); chemistry (MS, PhD); Chinese (MA, PhD); choreography (MFA); clinical psychology (PhD); cognitive psychology (PhD); communication (MA, PhD); comparative studies (MA, PhD); computational sciences (MMS); dance (MFA, PhD); dance and technology (MFA); dance studies (PhD); design (MA, MFA); design research and development (MFA); developmental psychology (PhD); digital animation and interactive media (MFA); earth sciences (MS, PhD); economics (MA, PhD); English (MA, MFA, PhD); evolution, ecology, and organismal biology (MS, PhD); French (MA, PhD); genetics (PhD); geodetic science (MS, PhD); geography (MA, PhD); geological sciences (MS, PhD); Germanic languages and literatures (MA, PhD); Greek studies (MA); hearing science (PhD); history (MA, PhD); history of art (MA, PhD); history, theory and literature (MFA); intellectual and developmental disabilities psychology (PhD); Italian (MA); Italian studies (PhD); Japanese (MA, PhD); Latin studies (MA, PhD); lighting and production (MFA); linguistics (MA, PhD); mathematical biosciences (MMS); mathematics (PhD); mathematics for educators (MMS); microbiology (MS, PhD); modern Greek (MA, PhD); molecular biology (MS, PhD); molecular, cellular and developmental biology (MS, PhD); movement analysis, Laban studies, notation and dance documentation (MFA); music (MA, MM, DMA, PhD); natural and mathematical sciences (M Appl Stat, MAQRM, MMS, MS, PhD); Near Eastern languages and cultures (MA); neuroscience (PhD); performance (MFA); philosophy (MA, PhD); physics (MS, PhD); political science (PhD); quantitative psychology (PhD); Slavic linguistics (MA, PhD); Slavic literature, film, and cultural studies (MA, PhD); social and behavioral sciences (MA, MS, Au D, PhD); social psychology (PhD); sociology (PhD); Spanish and Portuguese (MA, PhD); speech-language pathology (MA); speech-language science (PhD); statistics (M Appl Stat, MS, PhD); theatre (PhD); theatre studies (MA); women's, gender and sexuality studies (MA, PhD). *Application deadline:* For fall admission, 8/1 for domestic students, 7/1 for international students; for spring admission, 3/1 for domestic students, 2/1 for international students. Applications are processed on a rolling basis. *Application fee:* $60 ($70 for international students). Electronic applications accepted. *Application Contact:* Graduate and Professional Admissions, 614-292-9444, Fax: 614-292-3895, E-mail: gpadmissions@osu.edu. *Executive Dean and Vice Provost,* Dr. David C. Manderscheid, 614-292-3236, E-mail: manderscheid.1@osu.edu.

College of Education and Human Ecology Students: 810 full-time (545 women), 239 part-time (175 women); includes 171 minority (82 Black or African American, non-Hispanic/Latino; 29 Asian, non-Hispanic/Latino; 38 Hispanic/Latino; 22 Two or more races, non-Hispanic/Latino), 202 international. Average age 31. *Faculty:* 144. Expenses: Contact institution. *Financial support:* Fellowships with tuition reimbursements, research assistantships with tuition reimbursements, teaching assistantships with tuition reimbursements, career-related internships or fieldwork, Federal Work-Study, institutionally sponsored loans, scholarships/grants, traineeships, health care benefits, and unspecified assistantships available. Support available to part-time students. In 2016, 281 master's, 72 doctorates, 7 other advanced degrees awarded. Offers consumer sciences (MS, PhD); education and human ecology (M Ed, MA, MS, PhD, Ed S); educational studies (M Ed, MA, PhD, Ed S); human development and family science (PhD); human nutrition (MS, PhD); kinesiology (MA, PhD); teaching and learning (M Ed, MA, PhD, Ed S). *Application deadline:* Applications are processed on a rolling basis. *Application fee:* $60 ($70 for international students). Electronic applications accepted. *Application Contact:* Graduate and Professional Admissions, 614-292-9444, Fax: 614-292-3895, E-mail: gpadmissions@osu.edu. *Dean,* Dr. Cheryl Achterberg, 614-292-2461, Fax: 614-292-8052, E-mail: achterberg.1@osu.edu.

College of Engineering Students: 1,766 full-time (415 women), 139 part-time (28 women); includes 145 minority (32 Black or African American, non-Hispanic/Latino; 4 American Indian or Alaska Native, non-Hispanic/Latino; 49 Asian, non-Hispanic/Latino; 37 Hispanic/Latino; 23 Two or more races, non-Hispanic/Latino), 1,097 international. Average age 26. *Faculty:* 351. Expenses: Contact institution. *Financial support:* Fellowships with tuition reimbursements, research assistantships with tuition reimbursements, teaching assistantships with tuition reimbursements, career-related internships or fieldwork, Federal Work-Study, institutionally sponsored loans, and unspecified assistantships available. Support available to part-time students. In 2016, 523 master's, 166 doctorates awarded. *Program availability:* Part-time, evening/weekend. Offers aerospace engineering (MS, PhD); architecture (M Arch); biomedical engineering (MS, PhD); chemical engineering (MS, PhD); city and regional planning (MCRP, PhD); civil engineering (MS, PhD); computer science and engineering (MS, PhD); electrical and computer engineering (MS, PhD); electrical engineering (MS, PhD); engineering (M Arch, M Land Arch, MCRP, MS, PhD); industrial and systems engineering (MS, PhD); landscape architecture (M Land Arch); materials science and engineering (MS, PhD); mechanical engineering (MS, PhD); nuclear engineering (MS, PhD); welding engineering (MS, PhD). *Application deadline:* For fall admission, 11/30 priority date for domestic and international students. Applications are processed on a rolling basis. *Application fee:* $60 ($70 for international students). Electronic applications accepted. *Application Contact:* Graduate and Professional Admissions, 614-292-9444, Fax: 614-292-3895, E-mail: gpadmissions@osu.edu. *Dean,* Dr. David B. Williams, 614-292-2836, Fax: 614-292-9615, E-mail: williams.4219@osu.edu.

College of Food, Agricultural, and Environmental Sciences Students: 488 full-time (273 women), 55 part-time (31 women); includes 58 minority (9 Black or African American, non-Hispanic/Latino; 16 Asian, non-Hispanic/Latino; 24 Hispanic/Latino; 9 Two or more races, non-Hispanic/Latino), 187 international. Average age 28. *Faculty:* 327. Expenses: Contact institution. *Financial support:* Fellowships with tuition reimbursements, research assistantships with tuition reimbursements, teaching assistantships with tuition reimbursements, career-related internships or fieldwork, Federal Work-Study, institutionally sponsored loans, and unspecified assistantships available. Support available to part-time students. In 2016, 112 master's, 42 doctorates awarded. *Program availability:* Part-time. Offers agricultural and extension education (M Ed, MS, PhD); agricultural, environmental, and development economics (MS, PhD); animal sciences (MAS, MS, PhD); ecological restoration (MS, PhD); ecosystem science (MS, PhD); entomology (MPHM, MS, PhD); environment and natural resources (MENR); environmental science (MS, PhD); environmental social sciences (MS, PhD); fisheries and wildlife science (MS, PhD); food science and technology (MS, PhD); food, agricultural, and biological engineering (MS, PhD); food, agricultural, and environmental sciences (M Ed, MAS, MENR, MPHM, MS, PhD); forest science (MS, PhD); horticulture and crop science (MS, PhD); plant pathology (MPHM, MS, PhD); rural sociology (MS, PhD); soil science (MS, PhD). *Application deadline:* Applications are processed on a rolling basis. *Application fee:* $60 ($70 for international students). Electronic applications accepted. *Application Contact:* Graduate and Professional Admissions, 614-292-9444, Fax: 614-292-3895, E-mail: gpadmissions@osu.edu. *Vice President and Dean,* Dr. Cathann A. Kress, 614-292-6164, E-mail: kress.98@osu.edu.

College of Nursing Students: 571 full-time (484 women), 216 part-time (185 women); includes 130 minority (56 Black or African American, non-Hispanic/Latino; 32 Asian, non-Hispanic/Latino; 25 Hispanic/Latino; 17 Two or more races, non-Hispanic/Latino), 5 international. Average age 32. *Faculty:* 45. Expenses: Contact institution. *Financial support:* Fellowships, research assistantships, teaching assistantships, Federal Work-Study, institutionally sponsored loans, and unspecified assistantships available. Support available to part-time students. In 2016, 185 master's, 22 doctorates awarded. *Program availability:* Part-time. Offers nursing (MS, DNP, PhD). *Application deadline:* For fall admission, 12/13 priority date for domestic students, 11/30 priority date for international students; for summer admission, 10/12 for domestic and international students. Applications are processed on a rolling basis. *Application fee:* $60 ($70 for international students). Electronic applications accepted. *Application Contact:* Graduate and Professional Admissions, 614-292-9444, Fax: 614-292-3895, E-mail: gpadmissions@osu.edu. *Dean,* Dr. Bernadette M. Melnyk, 614-292-4844, Fax: 614-292-4535, E-mail: melnyk.15@osu.edu.

College of Social Work Students: 413 full-time (353 women), 95 part-time (79 women); includes 97 minority (55 Black or African American, non-Hispanic/Latino; 7 Asian, non-Hispanic/Latino; 17 Hispanic/Latino; 18 Two or more races, non-Hispanic/Latino), 14 international. Average age 29. *Faculty:* 32. Expenses: Contact institution. *Financial support:* Fellowships, research assistantships, teaching assistantships, Federal Work-Study, institutionally sponsored loans, and unspecified assistantships available. Support available to part-time students. In 2016, 215 master's, 3 doctorates awarded. *Program availability:* Part-time. Offers social work (MSW, PhD). *Application deadline:* For fall admission, 12/13 priority date for domestic students, 11/30 priority date for international students; for summer admission, 4/1 for domestic students, 3/1 for international students. Applications are processed on a rolling basis. *Application fee:* $60 ($70 for international students). Electronic applications accepted. *Application Contact:* Graduate and Professional Admissions, 614-292-6031, Fax: 614-292-3656, E-mail: gpadmissions@osu.edu. *Dean,* Dr. Tom Gregoire, 614-292-9426, E-mail: gregoire.5@osu.edu.

East Asian Studies Center Students: 12 full-time (7 women). Average age 27. Expenses: Contact institution. In 2016, 2 master's awarded. Offers East Asian studies (MA). *Application deadline:* For fall admission, 12/13 priority date for domestic students, 11/30 priority date for international students; for spring admission, 12/1 for domestic students, 11/1 for international students; for summer admission, 4/10 for domestic students, 3/13 for international students. Applications are processed on a rolling basis. *Application fee:* $60 ($70 for international students). Electronic applications accepted. *Application Contact:* Graduate and Professional Admissions, 614-292-9444, Fax: 614-292-3895, E-mail: gpadmissions@osu.edu. *Associate Professor,* Dr. Etsuyo Yuasa, 614-292-5816, E-mail: yuasa.1@osu.edu.

John Glenn College of Public Affairs Students: 122 full-time (58 women), 41 part-time (30 women). Average age 31. *Faculty:* 20. Expenses: Contact institution. *Financial support:* Fellowships, research assistantships, teaching assistantships, Federal Work-Study, institutionally sponsored loans, and unspecified assistantships available. Support available to part-time students. In 2016, 78 master's, 2 doctorates awarded. *Program availability:* Part-time. Offers public administration (MA, MPA); public policy and management (PhD). *Application deadline:* For fall admission, 12/1 priority date for domestic students, 11/30 priority date for international students; for spring admission, 11/15 for domestic and international students; for summer admission, 4/1 for domestic and international students. Applications are processed on a rolling basis. *Application fee:* $60 ($70 for international students). Electronic applications accepted. *Application Contact:* Graduate and Professional Admissions, 614-292-6031, Fax: 614-292-3656, E-mail: gpadmissions@osu.edu. *Dean,* Dr. Trevor Brown, 614-292-4533, Fax: 614-292-4868, E-mail: brown.2296@osu.edu.

Max M. Fisher College of Business Students: 629 full-time (270 women), 321 part-time (108 women); includes 141 minority (36 Black or African American, non-Hispanic/Latino; 64 Asian, non-Hispanic/Latino; 23 Hispanic/Latino; 18 Two or more races, non-Hispanic/Latino), 278 international. Average age 29. *Faculty:* 95. Expenses: Contact institution. *Financial support:* Fellowships, research assistantships, teaching assistantships, career-related internships or fieldwork, Federal Work-Study, institutionally sponsored loans, and unspecified assistantships available. Support available to part-time students. In 2016, 494 master's, 7 doctorates awarded. *Program availability:* Part-time, evening/weekend. Offers accounting (M Acc); accounting and management information systems (M Acc, PhD); business (M Acc, MA, MBA, MBLE, MBOE, MF, MHRM, PhD); business administration (MA, MBA, PhD); business logistics engineering (MBLE); business operational excellence (MBOE); finance (MF); human resource management (MHRM, PhD); labor and human resources (PhD). *Application deadline:* Applications are processed on a rolling basis. *Application fee:* $60 ($70 for international students). Electronic applications accepted. *Application Contact:* Graduate and Professional Admissions, 614-292-9444, Fax: 614-292-3656, E-mail: gpadmissions@osu.edu. *Dean/Chair,* Dr. Anil K. Makhija, 614-292-2666, E-mail: makhija.1@osu.edu.

Moritz College of Law Students: 546 full-time (267 women); includes 100 minority (36 Black or African American, non-Hispanic/Latino; 1 American Indian or Alaska Native, non-Hispanic/Latino; 22 Asian, non-Hispanic/Latino; 28 Hispanic/Latino; 1 Native Hawaiian or other Pacific Islander, non-Hispanic/Latino; 12 Two or more races, non-Hispanic/Latino), 7 international. Average age 25. 1,574 applicants, 49% accepted, 166 enrolled. *Faculty:* 48 full-time (21 women). Expenses: Contact institution. *Financial support:* In 2016–17, 516 students received support. Career-related internships or fieldwork, institutionally sponsored loans, and scholarships/grants available. Financial award application deadline: 4/1; financial award applicants required to submit FAFSA. In 2016, 179 doctorates awarded. Offers law (LL M, MSL, JD). *Application deadline:* For fall admission, 4/1 priority date for domestic students. Applications are processed on a rolling basis. *Application fee:* $60 ($70 for international students). Electronic applications accepted. *Application Contact:* Moritz College of Law Admissions, 614-292-8810, Fax: 614-292-3895, E-mail: lawadmit@osu.edu. *Dean,* Alan Michaels, 614-292-0574, Fax: 614-292-1492.

THE OHIO STATE UNIVERSITY AT LIMA, Lima, OH 45804

General Information State-supported, coed, comprehensive institution. *Enrollment:* 1,010 graduate, professional, and undergraduate students; 6 matriculated graduate/professional students (all women). *Enrollment by degree level:* 6 master's.

Graduate faculty: 36. *Graduate housing:* On-campus housing not available. *Student services:* Campus safety program, career counseling, child daycare facilities, exercise/wellness program, free psychological counseling, grant writing training, international student services, low-cost health insurance, multicultural affairs office, services for students with disabilities, teacher training, writing training. *Library facilities:* Lima Campus Library plus 1 other. *Collection:* Study areas open 24 hours, 5–7 days a week; students can reserve study rooms.

Computer facilities: Computer purchase and lease plans are available. A campuswide network can be accessed from student residence rooms and from off campus. Online class registration is available.
Website: http://lima.osu.edu/

General Application Contact: Graduate and Professional Admissions, 614-292-9444, Fax: 614-292-3895, E-mail: gpadmissions@osu.edu.

GRADUATE UNITS

Graduate Programs Students: 6 (all women); includes 1 minority (Black or African American, non-Hispanic/Latino). Average age 32. *Faculty:* 36. Expenses: Contact institution. *Financial support:* Application deadline: 2/15. *Program availability:* Part-time. Offers social work (MSW). *Application deadline:* For fall admission, 4/1 for domestic students, 3/1 for international students; for spring admission, 10/15 for domestic and international students; for summer admission, 4/10 for domestic students, 3/1 for international students. Applications are processed on a rolling basis. *Application fee:* $60 ($70 for international students). Electronic applications accepted. *Application Contact:* Graduate and Professional Admissions, 614-292-9444, Fax: 614-292-3895, E-mail: gpadmissions@osu.edu. *Dean and Director,* Dr. Charlene Gilbert, 419-995-8481, E-mail: gilbert.583@osu.edu.

THE OHIO STATE UNIVERSITY AT MARION, Marion, OH 43302-5695

General Information State-supported, coed, comprehensive institution. *Graduate faculty:* 38. *Graduate housing:* On-campus housing not available. *Student services:* Campus employment opportunities, campus safety program, career counseling, child daycare facilities, exercise/wellness program, free psychological counseling, grant writing training, international student services, low-cost health insurance, multicultural affairs office, services for students with disabilities, teacher training, writing training. *Library facilities:* Marion Campus Library plus 1 other.

Computer facilities: Computer purchase and lease plans are available. A campuswide network can be accessed. Online class registration is available.
Website: http://osumarion.osu.edu/

General Application Contact: Graduate and Professional Admissions, 614-292-9444, Fax: 614-292-3985, E-mail: gpadmissions@osu.edu.

GRADUATE UNITS

Graduate Programs *Faculty:* 38. Expenses: Contact institution. *Financial support:* Application deadline: 2/15; applicants required to submit FAFSA. *Program availability:* Part-time. Offers education (MA). *Application deadline:* Applications are processed on a rolling basis. *Application fee:* $60 ($70 for international students). Electronic applications accepted. *Application Contact:* Graduate and Professional Admissions, 614-292-9444, Fax: 614-292-3895, E-mail: gpadmissions@osu.edu. *Dean/Director,* Dr. Gregory S. Rose, 740-725-6218, E-mail: rose.9@osu.edu.

THE OHIO STATE UNIVERSITY–MANSFIELD CAMPUS, Mansfield, OH 44906-1599

General Information State-supported, coed, comprehensive institution. *Enrollment:* 1,199 graduate, professional, and undergraduate students; 3 matriculated graduate/professional students (all women). *Enrollment by degree level:* 3 master's. *Graduate faculty:* 40. *Graduate housing:* On-campus housing not available. *Student services:* Campus employment opportunities, campus safety program, career counseling, child daycare facilities, exercise/wellness program, free psychological counseling, grant writing training, international student services, low-cost health insurance, multicultural affairs office, services for students with disabilities, teacher training, writing training. *Library facilities:* Bromfield Library plus 1 other.

Computer facilities: Computer purchase and lease plans are available. A campuswide network can be accessed. Online class registration is available.
Website: http://www.mansfield.osu.edu/

General Application Contact: Graduate and Professional Admissions, 614-292-9444, Fax: 614-292-3895, E-mail: gpadmissions@osu.edu.

GRADUATE UNITS

Graduate Programs Students: 3 (all women). *Faculty:* 40. Expenses: Contact institution. *Financial support:* Teaching assistantships with full tuition reimbursements, Federal Work-Study, and scholarships/grants available. Support available to part-time students. Financial award application deadline: 2/15; financial award applicants required to submit FAFSA. *Program availability:* Part-time. Offers education (MA); social work (MSW). *Application deadline:* For fall admission, 4/1 for domestic students, 3/1 for international students; for spring admission, 10/15 for domestic and international students. Applications are processed on a rolling basis. *Application fee:* $60 ($70 for international students). Electronic applications accepted. *Application Contact:* Graduate and Professional Admissions, 614-292-9444, Fax: 614-292-3895, E-mail: gpadmissions@osu.edu.

THE OHIO STATE UNIVERSITY–NEWARK CAMPUS, Newark, OH 43055-1797

General Information State-supported, coed, comprehensive institution. *Enrollment:* 2,476 graduate, professional, and undergraduate students; 15 matriculated graduate/professional students (all women). *Enrollment by degree level:* 15 master's. *Graduate faculty:* 52. *Graduate housing:* Rooms and/or apartments available on a first-come, first-served basis to single and married students. *Student services:* Campus safety program, career counseling, child daycare facilities, exercise/wellness program, free psychological counseling, grant writing training, international student services, low-cost health insurance, multicultural affairs office, services for students with disabilities, teacher training, writing training. *Library facilities:* Newark Campus Library plus 1 other.

Computer facilities: Computer purchase and lease plans are available. A campuswide network can be accessed from student residence rooms. Online class registration is available.
Website: http://www.newark.osu.edu/

General Application Contact: Graduate and Professional Admissions, 614-292-9444, Fax: 614-292-3985, E-mail: gpadmissions@osu.edu.

GRADUATE UNITS

Graduate Programs Students: 15 (all women); includes 2 minority (1 Black or African American, non-Hispanic/Latino; 1 Hispanic/Latino). Average age 32. *Faculty:* 51. Expenses: Contact institution. *Financial support:* Application deadline: 2/15. *Program availability:* Part-time. Offers education - teaching and learning (MA); social work (MSW). *Application deadline:* For fall admission, 3/1 for domestic and international students. Applications are processed on a rolling basis. *Application fee:* $60 ($70 for international students). Electronic applications accepted. *Application Contact:* Graduate and Professional Admissions, 614-292-9444, Fax: 614-292-3985, E-mail: gpadmissions@osu.edu. *Dean/Director*, Dr. William L. MacDonald, 740-366-9333 Ext. 330, E-mail: macdonald.24@osu.edu.

OHIO UNIVERSITY, Athens, OH 45701-2979

General Information State-supported, coed, university. CGS member. *Graduate housing:* Rooms and/or apartments available on a first-come, first-served basis to single and married students. Housing application deadline: 5/1.

GRADUATE UNITS

Graduate College Expenses: Contact institution. *Financial support:* Fellowships with full tuition reimbursements, research assistantships with full and partial tuition reimbursements, teaching assistantships with full and partial tuition reimbursements, career-related internships or fieldwork, Federal Work-Study, institutionally sponsored loans, scholarships/grants, traineeships, tuition waivers (full and partial), and unspecified assistantships available. Financial award applicants required to submit FAFSA. *Program availability:* Part-time, evening/weekend, online learning. *Application fee:* $50 ($55 for international students). Electronic applications accepted. *Application Contact:* Marnie Miller, Student Services Coordinator, 740-593-2800, Fax: 740-593-4625, E-mail: graduate@ohio.edu. *Vice President for Research and Creative Activity/Dean of the Graduate College*, Dr. Joseph Shields, 740-593-2800, Fax: 740-593-4625, E-mail: graduate@ohio.edu.

Center for International Studies Expenses: Contact institution. *Financial support:* Fellowships with full tuition reimbursements, research assistantships with full and partial tuition reimbursements, teaching assistantships with full and partial tuition reimbursements, career-related internships or fieldwork, Federal Work-Study, institutionally sponsored loans, scholarships/grants, tuition waivers (partial), and unspecified assistantships available. Financial award application deadline: 1/1. *Program availability:* Part-time. Offers African studies (MA); Asian studies (MA); communications and development studies (MA); international development studies (MA); international studies (MA); Latin American studies (MA). *Application deadline:* For fall admission, 1/1 for domestic and international students. *Application fee:* $50 ($55 for international students). Electronic applications accepted. *Application Contact:* Gloria Balch, Administrative Assistant, 740-597-1618, Fax: 740-593-1837, E-mail: balchg@ohio.edu. *Interim Executive Director*, Dr. Ming Li, 740-593-1840, Fax: 740-593-1837, E-mail: lim1@ohio.edu.

College of Arts and Sciences Expenses: Contact institution. *Financial support:* Fellowships with full tuition reimbursements, research assistantships with full tuition reimbursements, teaching assistantships with full tuition reimbursements, career-related internships or fieldwork, Federal Work-Study, institutionally sponsored loans, scholarships/grants, traineeships, tuition waivers (full and partial), and unspecified assistantships available. *Program availability:* Part-time, evening/weekend. Offers applied economics (MA); applied linguistics (MA); arts and sciences (MA, MFE, MS, MSS, PhD); astronomy (MS, PhD); biological sciences (MS, PhD); cell biology and physiology (MS, PhD); chemistry and biochemistry (MS, PhD); clinical psychology (PhD); ecology and evolutionary biology (MS, PhD); English language and literature (MA, PhD); environmental and plant biology (MS, PhD); environmental geochemistry (MS); exercise physiology and muscle biology (MS, PhD); experimental psychology (PhD); financial economics (MFE); French (MA); geography (MA, MS); history (MA, PhD); mathematics (MS, PhD); microbiology (MS, PhD); molecular and cellular biology (PhD); neuroscience (MS, PhD); organizational psychology (PhD); philosophy (MA); physics (MS, PhD); political science (MA); social sciences (MSS); sociology (MA); Spanish (MA). *Application fee:* $50 ($55 for international students). Electronic applications accepted. *Application Contact:* Marnie Miller, Student Services Coordinator, 740-593-2800, Fax: 740-593-4625, E-mail: graduate@ohio.edu. *Dean*, Dr. Robert Frank, 740-593-1833, E-mail: frank@ohio.edu.

College of Business Expenses: Contact institution. *Financial support:* Research assistantships with full and partial tuition reimbursements, career-related internships or fieldwork, Federal Work-Study, institutionally sponsored loans, and unspecified assistantships available. Financial award application deadline: 2/1. *Program availability:* Part-time, evening/weekend, online learning. Offers athletic administration (MS); business (MBA, MS); executive management (MBA). *Application deadline:* For fall admission, 2/1 for domestic and international students. *Application fee:* $50 ($55 for international students). Electronic applications accepted. *Application Contact:* Marnie Miller, Student Services Coordinator, 740-593-2800, Fax: 740-593-4625, E-mail: graduate@ohio.edu. *Dean*, Dr. Hugh Sherman, 740-593-2001, Fax: 740-593-1388, E-mail: shermanh@ohio.edu.

College of Fine Arts Expenses: Contact institution. *Financial support:* Research assistantships with full and partial tuition reimbursements, teaching assistantships with full and partial tuition reimbursements, career-related internships or fieldwork, Federal Work-Study, institutionally sponsored loans, scholarships/grants, tuition waivers (full and partial), and unspecified assistantships available. *Program availability:* Part-time, evening/weekend, online learning. Offers accompanying (MM); art history (MA); ceramics (MFA); composition (MM); conducting (MM); film (MFA); film studies (MA); fine arts (MA, MFA, MM, PhD, Certificate); graphic design (MFA); history/literature (MM); interdisciplinary arts (PhD); music education (MM); music therapy (MM); painting (MFA); performance (MM, Certificate); performance/pedagogy (MM); photography (MFA); printmaking (MFA); sculpture (MFA); theater (MA, MFA); theory (MM). *Application fee:* $50 ($55 for international students). Electronic applications accepted. *Application Contact:* Dr. Jody Lamb, Associate Dean, 740-593-1811, E-mail: lambj@ohio.edu. *Dean*, Dr. Margaret Kennedy-Dygas, 740-593-1808, Fax: 740-593-0570, E-mail: kennedm1@ohio.edu.

College of Health Sciences and Professions Expenses: Contact institution. *Financial support:* Fellowships with tuition reimbursements, research assistantships with full and partial tuition reimbursements, teaching assistantships with full and partial tuition reimbursements, career-related internships or fieldwork, Federal Work-Study, institutionally sponsored loans, scholarships/grants, tuition waivers (partial), unspecified assistantships, and stipends available. *Program availability:* Part-time, evening/weekend, online learning. Offers advanced clinical practice (DNP); athletic training (MS); clinical audiology (Au D); communication sciences and disorders (MA, Au D, PhD); early child development and family life (MS); executive practice (DNP); family nurse practitioner (MSN); family studies (MS); food and nutrition (MS); health administration (MHA); health sciences and professions (MA, MHA, MPH, MS, MSN,

MSW, Au D, DNP, DPT, PhD); hearing science (PhD); human and consumer sciences (MS); nurse educator (MSN); physical therapy (DPT); physiology of exercise (MS); public health (MPH); social work (MSW); speech language pathology (MA); speech language science (PhD). *Application deadline:* Applications are processed on a rolling basis. *Application fee:* $50 ($55 for international students). Electronic applications accepted. *Application Contact:* Marnie Miller, Student Services Coordinator, 740-593-2800, Fax: 740-593-4625, E-mail: graduate@ohio.edu. *Interim Dean*, Dr. Randy Leite, 740-593-4756, Fax: 740-593-0285, E-mail: leite@ohio.edu.

Gladys W. and David H. Patton College of Education and Human Services Expenses: Contact institution. *Financial support:* Research assistantships with full and partial tuition reimbursements, teaching assistantships with full and partial tuition reimbursements, Federal Work-Study, institutionally sponsored loans, tuition waivers (full and partial), and unspecified assistantships available. Financial award application deadline: 3/15. *Program availability:* Part-time, evening/weekend. Offers adolescent to young adult education (M Ed); coaching education (MS); college student personnel (M Ed); community/agency counseling (M Ed); computer education and technology (M Ed); counselor education (PhD); curriculum and instruction (M Ed, PhD); early childhood/special education (M Ed); education and human services (M Ed, MS, MSA, Ed D, PhD); educational administration (M Ed, Ed D); educational research and evaluation (M Ed, PhD); higher education (PhD); instructional technology (PhD); intervention specialist/mild-moderate needs (M Ed); intervention specialist/moderate-intensive needs (M Ed); middle childhood education (M Ed); reading education (M Ed); recreation studies (MS); rehabilitation counseling (M Ed); school counseling (M Ed). *Application deadline:* Applications are processed on a rolling basis. *Application fee:* $50 ($55 for international students). Electronic applications accepted. *Application Contact:* Floyd J. Doney, Director of Student Affairs, 740-593-4400, Fax: 740-593-9310, E-mail: doney@ohio.edu. *Dean*, Dr. Renee A. Middleton, 740-593-4403, E-mail: middletonr@ohio.edu.

Russ College of Engineering and Technology Expenses: Contact institution. *Financial support:* Fellowships with full tuition reimbursements, research assistantships with full tuition reimbursements, teaching assistantships with full tuition reimbursements, career-related internships or fieldwork, Federal Work-Study, institutionally sponsored loans, and unspecified assistantships available. Financial award application deadline: 3/15. *Program availability:* Part-time. Offers biomedical engineering (MS); chemical engineering (MS, PhD); civil engineering (PhD); construction engineering and management (MS); electrical engineering (MS); electrical engineering and computer science (PhD); engineering and technology (M Eng Mgt, MS, PhD); environmental (MS); geoenvironmental (MS); geotechnical (MS); industrial and systems engineering (MS); mechanical and systems engineering (PhD); mechanical engineering (MS); mechanics (MS); structures (MS); transportation (MS); water resources (MS). *Application deadline:* Applications are processed on a rolling basis. *Application fee:* $50 ($55 for international students). Electronic applications accepted. *Application Contact:* Dr. Shawn Ostermann, Associate Dean, 740-593-1482, Fax: 740-593-0659, E-mail: ostermann@ohio.edu. *Dean*, Dr. Dennis Irwin, 740-593-1482, Fax: 740-593-0659, E-mail: irwind@ohio.edu.

Scripps College of Communication Expenses: Contact institution. *Financial support:* Fellowships with tuition reimbursements, research assistantships with full and partial tuition reimbursements, teaching assistantships with full tuition reimbursements, career-related internships or fieldwork, Federal Work-Study, institutionally sponsored loans, tuition waivers (full and partial), and unspecified assistantships available. Financial award applicants required to submit FAFSA. *Program availability:* Part-time. Offers communication (MA, MCTP, MS, PhD); health communication (PhD); information and telecommunication systems (MCTP); journalism (MS, PhD); mass communication (PhD); media arts and studies (MA); organizational communication (MA); relating and organizing (PhD); rhetoric and public culture (PhD); visual communication (MA). *Application fee:* $50 ($55 for international students). Electronic applications accepted. *Application Contact:* Dr. Eric Rothenbuhler, Associate Dean, 740-593-4885, Fax: 740-593-0459. *Interim Dean*, Dr. Scott Titsworth, 740-593-4882, Fax: 740-593-0459, E-mail: titswort@ohio.edu.

Voinovich School of Leadership and Public Affairs Expenses: Contact institution. Offers environmental studies (MS, Certificate); public administration (MPA). *Application fee:* $50 ($55 for international students). Electronic applications accepted. *Application Contact:* Dr. Ani Ruhil, Associate Director of Academic Affairs, 740-597-1949, E-mail: ruhil@ohio.edu. *Head*, Dr. Mark Weinberg, 740-593-4390, Fax: 740-593-9758, E-mail: weinberm@ohio.edu.

Heritage College of Osteopathic Medicine Students: 815 full-time (384 women); includes 197 minority (68 Black or African American, non-Hispanic/Latino; 4 American Indian or Alaska Native, non-Hispanic/Latino; 68 Asian, non-Hispanic/Latino; 34 Hispanic/Latino; 23 Two or more races, non-Hispanic/Latino). Average age 26. 4,830 applicants, 7% accepted, 246 enrolled. *Faculty:* 106 full-time (54 women), 42 part-time/adjunct (16 women). Expenses: Contact institution. *Financial support:* In 2016–17, 249 students received support, including 19 fellowships (averaging $25,439 per year); Federal Work-Study, institutionally sponsored loans, scholarships/grants, and tuition waivers (partial) also available. Financial award applicants required to submit FAFSA. In 2016, 136 doctorates awarded. Offers osteopathic medicine (DO). Applicants must be U.S. residents to apply. *Application deadline:* For fall admission, 2/1 for domestic students. Applications are processed on a rolling basis. *Application fee:* $60. Electronic applications accepted. *Application Contact:* Jill Harman, Senior Director of Admissions and Recruitment, 740-593-2147, Fax: 740-593-2256, E-mail: harmanj@ohio.edu. *Executive Dean*, Dr. Kenneth Johnson, 740-593-9350, Fax: 740-593-0761, E-mail: wilcox@ohio.edu.

OHIO VALLEY UNIVERSITY, Vienna, WV 26105-8000

General Information Independent-religious, coed, comprehensive institution.

GRADUATE UNITS

School of Graduate Education *Program availability:* Online learning. Offers curriculum and instruction (M Ed).

OHR HAMEIR THEOLOGICAL SEMINARY, Cortlandt Manor, NY 10567

General Information Independent-religious, men only, comprehensive institution.

GRADUATE UNITS
Graduate Programs

OKLAHOMA BAPTIST UNIVERSITY, Shawnee, OK 74804

General Information Independent-religious, coed, comprehensive institution. *Graduate housing:* Rooms and/or apartments available on a first-come, first-served basis to single and married students. Housing application deadline: 4/15.

GRADUATE UNITS

Program in Business Administration *Program availability:* Online learning. Offers business administration (MBA); energy management (MBA).

Program in Marriage and Family Therapy *Program availability:* Part-time, evening/weekend. Offers marriage and family therapy (MS). Electronic applications accepted.

Program in Nursing Offers global nursing (MSN); nursing education (MSN).

OKLAHOMA CHRISTIAN UNIVERSITY, Oklahoma City, OK 73136-1100

General Information Independent-religious, coed, comprehensive institution. *Enrollment:* 2,570 graduate, professional, and undergraduate students; 315 full-time matriculated graduate/professional students (96 women), 267 part-time matriculated graduate/professional students (90 women). *Enrollment by degree level:* 582 master's. *Graduate faculty:* 28 full-time (5 women), 26 part-time/adjunct (2 women). *Tuition:* Full-time $4995; part-time $3300 per semester hour. Tuition and fees vary according to program. *Graduate housing:* Rooms and/or apartments available on a first-come, first-served basis to single and married students. Typical cost: $3870 per year ($7030 including board) for single students; $3870 per year ($7030 including board) for married students. Room and board charges vary according to board plan and housing facility selected. Housing application deadline: 8/31. *Student services:* Campus employment opportunities, campus safety program, exercise/wellness program, free psychological counseling, international student services, writing training. *Library facilities:* Tom and Ada Beam Library plus 1 other. *Collection:* Books: 107,541 (physical), 65,297 (digital/electronic); Serial titles: 83 (physical), 42,000 (digital/electronic); Databases: 66. Weekly public service hours: 83; students can reserve study rooms.

Computer facilities: 101 computers available on campus for general student use. A campuswide network can be accessed from student residence rooms and from off campus. Online class registration is available.
Website: http://www.oc.edu/

General Application Contact: Angie Ricketts, Admissions Counselor, 405-425-5587, E-mail: angie.ricketts@oc.edu.

GRADUATE UNITS

Graduate School of Business Students: 156 full-time (68 women), 137 part-time (73 women). Average age 30. 374 applicants, 213 enrolled. *Faculty:* 10 full-time (2 women), 21 part-time/adjunct (2 women). Expenses: Contact institution. In 2016, 114 master's awarded. *Program availability:* Part-time, 100% online. Offers accounting (M Acc, MBA); financial services (MBA); general business (MBA); health services management (MBA); human resources (MBA); international business (MBA); leadership and organizational development (MBA); marketing (MBA); nonprofit management (MBA); project management (MBA). *Application fee:* $25. Electronic applications accepted. *Application Contact:* Angie Ricketts, Graduate School Admissions Counselor, 405-425-5587, Fax: 405-425-5585, E-mail: angie.ricketts@oc.edu. Chair, Dr. Ken Johnson, 405-425-5567, Fax: 405-425-5585, E-mail: ken.johnson@oc.edu.

Graduate School of Engineering and Computer Science Students: 187 full-time (27 women), 85 part-time (12 women). Average age 25. 255 applicants, 33% accepted, 69 enrolled. *Faculty:* 8 full-time (1 woman), 7 part-time/adjunct (0 women). Expenses: Contact institution. In 2016, 188 master's awarded. *Program availability:* Part-time. Offers electrical and computer engineering (MSE); engineering management (MSE); mechanical engineering (MSE); software engineering (MSCS, MSE). *Application deadline:* Applications are processed on a rolling basis. *Application fee:* $25. Electronic applications accepted. *Application Contact:* Angie Ricketts, Admissions Counselor, 405-425-5587, E-mail: angie.ricketts@oc.edu. *Director for Graduate School Engineering,* Mary Ann Brown, 405-425-5579.

Graduate School of Theology Students: 12 full-time (0 women), 30 part-time (4 women). Average age 32. 12 applicants, 100% accepted, 10 enrolled. *Faculty:* 8 full-time (0 women). Expenses: Contact institution. *Financial support:* In 2016–17, 38 students received support. Scholarships/grants available. Financial award application deadline: 8/15; financial award applicants required to submit FAFSA. In 2016, 8 master's awarded. *Program availability:* Part-time. Offers scripture (MTS); theology (M Div, MACM, MTS). *Application deadline:* For fall admission, 8/15 priority date for domestic and international students; for spring admission, 1/3 priority date for domestic and international students. Applications are processed on a rolling basis. *Application fee:* $25. Electronic applications accepted. *Application Contact:* Josh Bailey, Program Director, 405-425-5389, Fax: 405-425-5379, E-mail: josh.bailey@oc.edu. *Dean,* Dr. Charles Rix, 405-425-5379, E-mail: charles.rix@oc.edu.

OKLAHOMA CITY UNIVERSITY, Oklahoma City, OK 73106-1402

General Information Independent-religious, coed, comprehensive institution. *Enrollment:* 2,939 graduate, professional, and undergraduate students; 850 full-time matriculated graduate/professional students (468 women), 327 part-time matriculated graduate/professional students (162 women). *Enrollment by degree level:* 845 master's, 539 doctoral. *Graduate faculty:* 89 full-time (35 women), 73 part-time/adjunct (33 women). *Tuition:* Full-time $7080; part-time $590 per credit hour. One-time fee: $250 full-time. Tuition and fees vary according to degree level and program. *Graduate housing:* Rooms and/or apartments available on a first-come, first-served basis to single and married students. Typical cost: $4100 per year ($8624 including board) for single students; $4100 per year ($8624 including board) for married students. Room and board charges vary according to board plan and housing facility selected. Housing application deadline: 6/15. *Student services:* Campus employment opportunities, campus safety program, career counseling, exercise/wellness program, free psychological counseling, international student services, low-cost health insurance, multicultural affairs office, services for students with disabilities, teacher training, writing training. *Library facilities:* Dulaney Browne Library plus 1 other. *Collection:* Books: 326,514 (physical), 240,741 (digital/electronic); Serial titles: 581 (physical), 3,060 (digital/electronic); Databases: 142. Weekly public service hours: 99; students can reserve study rooms.

Computer facilities: Computer purchase and lease plans are available. 368 computers available on campus for general student use. A campuswide network can be accessed from student residence rooms and from off campus. Online class registration is available.
Website: http://www.okcu.edu/

General Application Contact: Michael Harrington, Director of Graduate Admissions, 800-633-7242, Fax: 405-208-5916, E-mail: gadmissions@okcu.edu.

GRADUATE UNITS

Kramer School of Nursing Students: 119 full-time (106 women), 32 part-time (28 women); includes 51 minority (13 Black or African American, non-Hispanic/Latino; 13 American Indian or Alaska Native, non-Hispanic/Latino; 9 Asian, non-Hispanic/Latino; 6 Hispanic/Latino; 10 Two or more races, non-Hispanic/Latino), 16 international. Average age 38. 59 applicants, 76% accepted, 31 enrolled. *Faculty:* 8 full-time (all women), 10 part-time/adjunct (8 women). Expenses: Contact institution. *Financial support:* In 2016–17, 95 students received support. Federal Work-Study, institutionally sponsored loans, scholarships/grants, and tuition waivers (full and partial) available. Support available to part-time students. Financial award application deadline: 3/1; financial award applicants required to submit FAFSA. In 2016, 25 master's, 5 doctorates awarded. *Program availability:* Part-time, evening/weekend, online learning. Offers clinical nurse leader (MSN); nursing (DNP, PhD); nursing education (MSN). *Application deadline:* Applications are processed on a rolling basis. *Application fee:* $50. Electronic applications accepted. *Application Contact:* Michael Harrington, Director of Graduate Admissions, 800-633-7242, Fax: 405-208-5916, E-mail: gadmissions@okcu.edu. *Dean,* Kramer School of Nursing, Dr. Lois Salmeron, 405-208-5900, Fax: 405-208-5914, E-mail: lsalmeron@okcu.edu.

Meinders School of Business Students: 170 full-time (68 women), 218 part-time (90 women); includes 82 minority (17 Black or African American, non-Hispanic/Latino; 10 American Indian or Alaska Native, non-Hispanic/Latino; 16 Asian, non-Hispanic/Latino; 24 Hispanic/Latino; 15 Two or more races, non-Hispanic/Latino), 103 international. Average age 30. 592 applicants, 50% accepted, 138 enrolled. *Faculty:* 17 full-time (3 women), 5 part-time/adjunct (1 woman). Expenses: Contact institution. *Financial support:* In 2016–17, 262 students received support. Career-related internships or fieldwork, Federal Work-Study, institutionally sponsored loans, scholarships/grants, and tuition waivers (full and partial) available. Support available to part-time students. Financial award application deadline: 6/1; financial award applicants required to submit FAFSA. In 2016, 171 master's awarded. *Program availability:* Part-time, evening/weekend, 100% online. Offers business (MBA, MSA); computer science (MS); energy legal studies (MS); energy management (MS). *Application deadline:* Applications are processed on a rolling basis. *Application fee:* $50. Electronic applications accepted. *Application Contact:* Michael Harrington, Director of Graduate Admission, 800-633-7242, Fax: 405-208-5916, E-mail: gadmissions@okcu.edu. *Dean,* Dr. Steve Agee, 405-208-5275, Fax: 405-208-5008, E-mail: sagee@okcu.edu.

Petree College of Arts and Sciences Students: 77 full-time (55 women), 46 part-time (30 women); includes 32 minority (13 Black or African American, non-Hispanic/Latino; 1 American Indian or Alaska Native, non-Hispanic/Latino; 2 Asian, non-Hispanic/Latino; 12 Hispanic/Latino; 4 Two or more races, non-Hispanic/Latino), 37 international. Average age 34. 92 applicants, 74% accepted, 46 enrolled. *Faculty:* 11 full-time (5 women), 15 part-time/adjunct (6 women). Expenses: Contact institution. *Financial support:* In 2016–17, 16 students received support. Federal Work-Study, institutionally sponsored loans, scholarships/grants, and tuition waivers (full and partial) available. Support available to part-time students. Financial award application deadline: 6/1; financial award applicants required to submit FAFSA. In 2016, 72 master's awarded. *Program availability:* Part-time, evening/weekend. Offers applied behavioral studies (M Ed); applied sociology: nonprofit leadership (MA); creative writing (MFA); criminology (MS); early childhood education (M Ed); elementary education (M Ed); general studies (MLA); leadership/management (MLA); moving image arts (MFA); professional counseling (M Ed); teaching (MA); teaching English to speakers of other languages (MA). *Application deadline:* Applications are processed on a rolling basis. *Application fee:* $50. Electronic applications accepted. *Application Contact:* Michael Harrington, Director of Graduate Admissions, 800-633-7242, Fax: 405-208-5356, E-mail: gadmissions@okcu.edu. *Dean,* Dr. Amy Cataldi, 405-208-5446, Fax: 405-208-5447, E-mail: acataldi@okcu.edu.

School of Law Students: 385 full-time (189 women), 28 part-time (12 women); includes 141 minority (25 Black or African American, non-Hispanic/Latino; 28 American Indian or Alaska Native, non-Hispanic/Latino; 18 Asian, non-Hispanic/Latino; 42 Hispanic/Latino; 2 Native Hawaiian or other Pacific Islander, non-Hispanic/Latino; 26 Two or more races, non-Hispanic/Latino), 4 international. Average age 28. *Faculty:* 20 full-time (6 women), 31 part-time/adjunct (8 women). Expenses: Contact institution. *Financial support:* In 2016–17, 304 students received support. Career-related internships or fieldwork, Federal Work-Study, institutionally sponsored loans, scholarships/grants, and tuition waivers (full and partial) available. Support available to part-time students. Financial award application deadline: 2/1; financial award applicants required to submit FAFSA. In 2016, 139 doctorates awarded. *Program availability:* Part-time, evening/weekend. Offers law (LL M, JD). *Application deadline:* For fall admission, 8/1 for domestic and international students. *Application fee:* $50. Electronic applications accepted. *Application Contact:* Dr. Laurie W. Jones, Associate Dean of Admissions, Law School, 405-208-5354, Fax: 405-208-5814, E-mail: ljones@okcu.edu. *Dean,* Dr. Valerie K. Couch, 405-208-5440, Fax: 405-208-6041, E-mail: vcouch@okcu.edu.

Wanda L. Bass School of Music Students: 62 full-time (21 women), 3 part-time (2 women); includes 15 minority (4 Black or African American, non-Hispanic/Latino; 2 American Indian or Alaska Native, non-Hispanic/Latino; 3 Asian, non-Hispanic/Latino; 3 Hispanic/Latino; 3 Two or more races, non-Hispanic/Latino), 14 international. Average age 25. 98 applicants, 70% accepted, 35 enrolled. *Faculty:* 25 full-time (9 women), 10 part-time/adjunct (5 women). Expenses: Contact institution. *Financial support:* In 2016–17, 63 students received support. Career-related internships or fieldwork, Federal Work-Study, institutionally sponsored loans, scholarships/grants, and tuition waivers (full and partial) available. Support available to part-time students. Financial award application deadline: 6/1; financial award applicants required to submit FAFSA. In 2016, 22 master's awarded. *Program availability:* Part-time. Offers composition (MM); conducting (MM); musical theatre (MM); opera performance (MM); performance (MM); vocal coaching (MM). *Application deadline:* Applications are processed on a rolling basis. *Application fee:* $50. Electronic applications accepted. *Application Contact:* Michael Harrington, Director of Graduate Admission, 800-633-7242, Fax: 405-208-5916, E-mail: gadmissions@okcu.edu. *Dean,* Mark Parker, 405-208-5474, Fax: 405-208-5971, E-mail: mparker@okcu.edu.

OKLAHOMA STATE UNIVERSITY, Stillwater, OK 74078

General Information State-supported, coed, university. CGS member. *Enrollment:* 25,594 graduate, professional, and undergraduate students; 1,815 full-time matriculated graduate/professional students (925 women), 2,686 part-time matriculated graduate/professional students (1,199 women). *Enrollment by degree level:* 2,517 master's, 1,757 doctoral, 227 other advanced degrees. *Graduate faculty:* 1,240 full-time (461 women), 167 part-time/adjunct (91 women). *Tuition, state resident:* full-time $3775; part-time $209.70 per credit hour. *Tuition, nonresident:* full-time $14,851; part-time $825.05 per credit hour. *Required fees:* $2027; $112.60 per credit hour. Tuition and fees vary according to campus/location. *Graduate housing:* Rooms and/or apartments available on a first-come, first-served basis to single and married students. Typical cost: $4743 per year ($8443 including board) for single students; $10,200 per year for married students. Room and board charges vary according to board plan and housing facility selected. *Student services:* Campus employment opportunities, campus safety program, career counseling, exercise/wellness program, free psychological counseling, grant writing training, international student services, low-cost health insurance, multicultural affairs office, services for students with disabilities, teacher training, writing training.

Oklahoma State University

Library facilities: Edmon Low Library plus 3 others. *Collection:* Weekly public service hours: 146; study areas open 24 hours, 5–7 days a week; students can reserve study rooms. *Research affiliation:* Allens, Inc. (horticulture and landscape architecture), General Motors (industrial engineering and management), Simons Foundation (mathematics), Howard Hughes Medical Institute (educational studies), California Strawberry Commission (nutritional sciences), LiteCure, LLC (veterinary clinical sciences).

Computer facilities: Computer purchase and lease plans are available. A campuswide network can be accessed from student residence rooms and from off campus. Online class registration is available.
Website: http://www.okstate.edu/

General Application Contact: Dr. Sheryl Tucker, Dean, 405-744-6368, Fax: 405-744-0355, E-mail: gradi@okstate.edu.

GRADUATE UNITS

Center for Veterinary Health Sciences *Program availability:* Online learning. Offers veterinary biomedical sciences (MS, PhD); veterinary health sciences (MS, DVM, PhD); veterinary medicine (DVM).

College of Agricultural Science and Natural Resources Students: 129 full-time (67 women), 303 part-time (144 women); includes 48 minority (6 Black or African American, non-Hispanic/Latino; 8 American Indian or Alaska Native, non-Hispanic/Latino; 5 Asian, non-Hispanic/Latino; 17 Hispanic/Latino; 12 Two or more races, non-Hispanic/Latino), 120 international. Average age 28. 250 applicants, 44% accepted, 88 enrolled. *Faculty:* 220 full-time (53 women), 11 part-time/adjunct (3 women). Expenses: Contact institution. *Financial support:* In 2016–17, 261 research assistantships (averaging $17,761 per year), 43 teaching assistantships (averaging $15,702 per year) were awarded; fellowships, career-related internships or fieldwork, Federal Work-Study, scholarships/grants, health care benefits, tuition waivers (partial), and unspecified assistantships also available. Support available to part-time students. Financial award application deadline: 3/1; financial award applicants required to submit FAFSA. In 2016, 99 master's, 41 doctorates awarded. *Program availability:* Online learning. Offers agricultural economics (M Ag, MS, PhD); agricultural education, communications and leadership (M Ag, MS, PhD); agricultural science and natural resources (M Ag, MS, PhD); animal sciences (M Ag, MS); biochemistry and molecular biology (MS, PhD); biosystems engineering (MS, PhD); crop science (PhD); entomology (PhD); entomology and plant pathology (MS); environmental and natural resources (MS, PhD); environmental science (PhD); food science (MS, PhD); horticulture (M Ag, MS); natural resource ecology and management (M Ag, MS, PhD); plant and soil sciences (MS); plant pathology (PhD); plant science (PhD); soil science (M Ag, PhD). *Application deadline:* For fall admission, 3/1 priority date for domestic and international students; for spring admission, 8/1 priority date for domestic and international students. Applications are processed on a rolling basis. *Application fee:* $40 ($75 for international students). Electronic applications accepted. *Vice President/Dean,* Dr. Thomas Coon, 405-744-2474, E-mail: thomas.coon@okstate.edu.

College of Arts and Sciences Students: 315 full-time (156 women), 588 part-time (236 women); includes 117 minority (20 Black or African American, non-Hispanic/Latino; 14 American Indian or Alaska Native, non-Hispanic/Latino; 12 Asian, non-Hispanic/Latino; 34 Hispanic/Latino; 2 Native Hawaiian or other Pacific Islander, non-Hispanic/Latino; 35 Two or more races, non-Hispanic/Latino), 261 international. Average age 30. 1,316 applicants, 27% accepted, 231 enrolled. *Faculty:* 470 full-time (179 women), 51 part-time/adjunct (29 women). Expenses: Contact institution. *Financial support:* In 2016–17, 122 research assistantships (averaging $14,749 per year), 564 teaching assistantships (averaging $15,430 per year) were awarded; career-related internships or fieldwork, Federal Work-Study, scholarships/grants, health care benefits, tuition waivers (partial), and unspecified assistantships also available. Support available to part-time students. Financial award application deadline: 3/1; financial award applicants required to submit FAFSA. In 2016, 192 master's, 61 doctorates awarded. Offers applied mathematics (MS, PhD); art history (MA); arts and sciences (MA, MFA, MM, MS, PhD); botany (MS); chemistry (MS, PhD); clinical psychology (PhD); communication sciences and disorders (MS); computer science (MS, PhD); creative writing (MFA); English (MA, PhD); environmental science (MS); fire and emergency management administration (MS, PhD); general psychology (MS); geography (MS, PhD); graphic design (MA); history (MA, PhD); integrative biology (MS, PhD); lifespan development psychology (PhD); mathematics education (MS, PhD); microbiology and molecular genetics (MS, PhD); pedagogy and performance (MM); philosophy (MA); photonics (MS, PhD); physics (MS, PhD); plant science (PhD); political science (MA); pure mathematics (MS, PhD); sociology (MS, PhD); statistics (MS, PhD); theatre (MA). *Application deadline:* For fall admission, 3/1 priority date for domestic and international students; for spring admission, 8/1 priority date for domestic and international students. Applications are processed on a rolling basis. *Application fee:* $40 ($75 for international students). Electronic applications accepted. *Dean,* Dr. Bret Danilowicz, 405-744-5663, Fax: 405-744-1797, E-mail: bret.danilowicz@okstate.edu.

School of Geology Students: 40 full-time (8 women), 46 part-time (12 women); includes 14 minority (2 Black or African American, non-Hispanic/Latino; 1 American Indian or Alaska Native, non-Hispanic/Latino; 1 Asian, non-Hispanic/Latino; 2 Hispanic/Latino; 1 Native Hawaiian or other Pacific Islander, non-Hispanic/Latino; 7 Two or more races, non-Hispanic/Latino), 21 international. Average age 30. 95 applicants, 22% accepted, 18 enrolled. *Faculty:* 14 full-time (4 women). Expenses: Contact institution. *Financial support:* In 2016–17, 22 research assistantships (averaging $14,121 per year), 34 teaching assistantships (averaging $9,447 per year) were awarded; career-related internships or fieldwork, Federal Work-Study, scholarships/grants, health care benefits, tuition waivers (partial), and unspecified assistantships also available. Support available to part-time students. Financial award application deadline: 3/1; financial award applicants required to submit FAFSA. In 2016, 21 master's, 1 doctorate awarded. Offers geology (MS, PhD). *Application deadline:* For fall admission, 3/1 priority date for international students; for spring admission, 8/1 priority date for international students. Applications are processed on a rolling basis. *Application fee:* $40 ($75 for international students). Electronic applications accepted. *Department Head,* Dr. Estella Atekwana, 405-744-6358, Fax: 405-744-7841, E-mail: estella.atekwana@okstate.edu.

School of Media and Strategic Communications Students: 10 full-time (7 women), 27 part-time (17 women); includes 10 minority (6 Black or African American, non-Hispanic/Latino; 2 American Indian or Alaska Native, non-Hispanic/Latino; 1 Hispanic/Latino; 1 Two or more races, non-Hispanic/Latino), 1 international. Average age 27. 23 applicants, 65% accepted, 13 enrolled. *Faculty:* 17 full-time (4 women), 5 part-time/adjunct (2 women). Expenses: Contact institution. *Financial support:* In 2016–17, 2 research assistantships (averaging $14,489 per year), 7 teaching assistantships (averaging $15,033 per year) were awarded; career-related internships or fieldwork, Federal Work-Study, scholarships/grants, health care benefits, tuition waivers (partial), and unspecified assistantships also available. Support available to

part-time students. Financial award application deadline: 3/1; financial award applicants required to submit FAFSA. In 2016, 7 master's awarded. Offers mass communication (MS). *Application deadline:* For fall admission, 3/1 priority date for international students; for spring admission, 8/1 priority date for international students. Applications are processed on a rolling basis. *Application fee:* $40 ($75 for international students). Electronic applications accepted. *Director,* Dr. Craig Freem, 405-744-7676, Fax: 405-744-7104, E-mail: freemanc@okstate.edu.

College of Education Students: 264 full-time (182 women), 543 part-time (347 women); includes 216 minority (56 Black or African American, non-Hispanic/Latino; 38 American Indian or Alaska Native, non-Hispanic/Latino; 12 Asian, non-Hispanic/Latino; 52 Hispanic/Latino; 1 Native Hawaiian or other Pacific Islander, non-Hispanic/Latino; 57 Two or more races, non-Hispanic/Latino), 25 international. Average age 35. 312 applicants, 59% accepted, 163 enrolled. *Faculty:* 95 full-time (67 women), 73 part-time/adjunct (40 women). Expenses: Contact institution. *Financial support:* In 2016–17, 56 research assistantships (averaging $9,206 per year), 78 teaching assistantships (averaging $11,175 per year) were awarded; career-related internships or fieldwork, Federal Work-Study, scholarships/grants, health care benefits, tuition waivers (partial), and unspecified assistantships also available. Support available to part-time students. Financial award application deadline: 3/1; financial award applicants required to submit FAFSA. In 2016, 170 master's, 55 doctorates awarded. *Program availability:* Part-time, online learning. Offers education (MS, Ed D, PhD, Ed S). *Application deadline:* For fall admission, 3/1 priority date for domestic and international students; for spring admission, 8/1 priority date for domestic and international students. Applications are processed on a rolling basis. *Application fee:* $40 ($75 for international students). Electronic applications accepted. *Interim Dean,* Dr. Robert Davis, 405-744-6350, Fax: 405-744-6350, E-mail: robert.davis@okstate.edu.

School of Applied Health and Educational Psychology Students: 168 full-time (122 women), 140 part-time (80 women); includes 86 minority (21 Black or African American, non-Hispanic/Latino; 10 American Indian or Alaska Native, non-Hispanic/Latino; 3 Asian, non-Hispanic/Latino; 24 Hispanic/Latino; 28 Two or more races, non-Hispanic/Latino), 13 international. Average age 30. 157 applicants, 51% accepted, 73 enrolled. *Faculty:* 38 full-time (22 women), 11 part-time/adjunct (6 women). Expenses: Contact institution. *Financial support:* In 2016–17, 31 research assistantships (averaging $9,791 per year), 64 teaching assistantships (averaging $11,347 per year) were awarded; career-related internships or fieldwork, Federal Work-Study, scholarships/grants, health care benefits, tuition waivers (partial), and unspecified assistantships also available. Support available to part-time students. Financial award application deadline: 3/1; financial award applicants required to submit FAFSA. In 2016, 73 master's, 21 doctorates awarded. *Program availability:* Part-time. Offers applied behavioral studies (Ed D); applied health and educational psychology (MS, PhD, Ed S). *Application deadline:* For fall admission, 3/1 priority date for international students; for spring admission, 8/1 priority date for international students. Applications are processed on a rolling basis. *Application fee:* $40 ($75 for international students). Electronic applications accepted. *Head,* Dr. Aric Warren, 405-744-6040, Fax: 405-744-6779, E-mail: aric.warren@okstate.edu.

School of Educational Studies Students: 56 full-time (28 women), 224 part-time (122 women); includes 77 minority (21 Black or African American, non-Hispanic/Latino; 19 American Indian or Alaska Native, non-Hispanic/Latino; 7 Asian, non-Hispanic/Latino; 18 Hispanic/Latino; 1 Native Hawaiian or other Pacific Islander, non-Hispanic/Latino; 11 Two or more races, non-Hispanic/Latino), 5 international. Average age 38. 117 applicants, 67% accepted, 70 enrolled. *Faculty:* 26 full-time (15 women), 34 part-time/adjunct (10 women). Expenses: Contact institution. *Financial support:* In 2016–17, 19 research assistantships (averaging $8,716 per year), 7 teaching assistantships (averaging $9,086 per year) were awarded; career-related internships or fieldwork, Federal Work-Study, scholarships/grants, health care benefits, tuition waivers (partial), and unspecified assistantships also available. Support available to part-time students. Financial award application deadline: 3/1; financial award applicants required to submit FAFSA. In 2016, 39 master's, 24 doctorates awarded. *Program availability:* Part-time. Offers higher education (Ed D). *Application deadline:* For fall admission, 3/1 priority date for international students; for spring admission, 8/1 priority date for international students. Applications are processed on a rolling basis. *Application fee:* $40 ($75 for international students). Electronic applications accepted. *Head,* Dr. Jesse Mendez, 405-744-9447, Fax: 405-744-7758, E-mail: jesse.perez.mendez@okstate.edu.

School of Teaching and Curriculum Leadership Students: 23 full-time (all women), 129 part-time (107 women); includes 40 minority (10 Black or African American, non-Hispanic/Latino; 4 American Indian or Alaska Native, non-Hispanic/Latino; 1 Asian, non-Hispanic/Latino; 7 Hispanic/Latino; 18 Two or more races, non-Hispanic/Latino), 5 international. Average age 37. 35 applicants, 89% accepted, 27 enrolled. *Faculty:* 31 full-time (30 women), 28 part-time/adjunct (24 women). Expenses: Contact institution. *Financial support:* In 2016–17, 5 research assistantships (averaging $8,240 per year), 7 teaching assistantships (averaging $11,691 per year) were awarded; career-related internships or fieldwork, Federal Work-Study, scholarships/grants, health care benefits, tuition waivers (partial), and unspecified assistantships also available. Support available to part-time students. Financial award application deadline: 3/1; financial award applicants required to submit FAFSA. In 2016, 58 master's, 10 doctorates awarded. *Program availability:* Part-time. Offers teaching and curriculum leadership (MS, PhD). *Application deadline:* For fall admission, 3/1 priority date for international students; for spring admission, 8/1 priority date for international students. Applications are processed on a rolling basis. *Application fee:* $40 ($75 for international students). Electronic applications accepted. *Interim Department Head,* Dr. Jennifer Sanders, 405-744-9214, Fax: 405-744-6290, E-mail: jenn.sanders10@okstate.edu.

College of Engineering, Architecture and Technology Students: 251 full-time (45 women), 366 part-time (75 women); includes 50 minority (9 Black or African American, non-Hispanic/Latino; 2 American Indian or Alaska Native, non-Hispanic/Latino; 9 Asian, non-Hispanic/Latino; 12 Hispanic/Latino; 18 Two or more races, non-Hispanic/Latino), 337 international. Average age 28. 1,110 applicants, 21% accepted, 154 enrolled. *Faculty:* 127 full-time (15 women), 5 part-time/adjunct (2 women). Expenses: Contact institution. *Financial support:* In 2016–17, 160 research assistantships (averaging $11,340 per year), 129 teaching assistantships (averaging $7,778 per year) were awarded; career-related internships or fieldwork, Federal Work-Study, scholarships/grants, health care benefits, tuition waivers (partial), and unspecified assistantships also available. Support available to part-time students. Financial award application deadline: 3/1; financial award applicants required to submit FAFSA. In 2016, 218 master's, 41 doctorates awarded. *Program availability:* Online learning. Offers engineering, architecture and technology (MS, PhD). *Application deadline:* For fall admission, 3/1 priority date for domestic and international students; for spring admission, 8/1 priority date for domestic and international students. Applications are processed on a rolling basis. *Application fee:* $40 ($75 for international students). Electronic applications accepted. *Dean,* Dr. Paul Tikalsky, 405-744-5140, E-mail: paul.tikalsky@okstate.edu.

School of Chemical Engineering Students: 22 full-time (4 women), 22 part-time (6 women); includes 4 minority (1 American Indian or Alaska Native, non-Hispanic/Latino; 2 Asian, non-Hispanic/Latino; 1 Two or more races, non-Hispanic/Latino), 26 international. Average age 29. 65 applicants, 17% accepted, 11 enrolled. *Faculty:* 17 full-time (3 women), 1 part-time/adjunct (0 women). Expenses: Contact institution. *Financial support:* In 2016–17, 26 research assistantships (averaging $15,000 per year), 7 teaching assistantships (averaging $14,143 per year) were awarded; career-related internships or fieldwork, Federal Work-Study, scholarships/grants, health care benefits, tuition waivers (partial), and unspecified assistantships also available. Support available to part-time students. Financial award application deadline: 3/1; financial award applicants required to submit FAFSA. In 2016, 7 master's, 6 doctorates awarded. Offers chemical engineering (MS, PhD). *Application deadline:* For fall admission, 3/1 priority date for international students; for spring admission, 8/1 priority date for international students. Applications are processed on a rolling basis. *Application fee:* $40 ($75 for international students). Electronic applications accepted. *Head,* Dr. Rob Whiteley, 405-744-5280, Fax: 405-744-6338, E-mail: rob.whiteley@okstate.edu.

School of Civil and Environmental Engineering Students: 28 full-time (5 women), 49 part-time (12 women); includes 1 minority (Black or African American, non-Hispanic/Latino), 52 international. Average age 28. 112 applicants, 32% accepted, 22 enrolled. *Faculty:* 20 full-time (1 woman), 1 part-time/adjunct (0 women). Expenses: Contact institution. *Financial support:* In 2016–17, 41 research assistantships (averaging $11,139 per year), 2 teaching assistantships (averaging $8,500 per year) were awarded; career-related internships or fieldwork, Federal Work-Study, scholarships/grants, health care benefits, tuition waivers (partial), and unspecified assistantships also available. Support available to part-time students. Financial award application deadline: 3/1; financial award applicants required to submit FAFSA. In 2016, 28 master's, 7 doctorates awarded. Offers civil engineering (MS, PhD); environmental engineering (MS). *Application deadline:* For fall admission, 3/1 priority date for international students; for spring admission, 8/1 priority date for international students. Applications are processed on a rolling basis. *Application fee:* $40 ($75 for international students). Electronic applications accepted. *Department Head,* Dr. Norb Delatte, 405-744-5190, Fax: 405-744-7554, E-mail: norb.delatte@okstate.edu.

School of Electrical and Computer Engineering Students: 53 full-time (12 women), 48 part-time (11 women); includes 8 minority (1 Black or African American, non-Hispanic/Latino; 2 Asian, non-Hispanic/Latino; 4 Hispanic/Latino; 1 Two or more races, non-Hispanic/Latino), 69 international. Average age 28. 285 applicants, 18% accepted, 24 enrolled. *Faculty:* 22 full-time (2 women). Expenses: Contact institution. *Financial support:* In 2016–17, 18 research assistantships (averaging $10,061 per year), 21 teaching assistantships (averaging $6,318 per year) were awarded; career-related internships or fieldwork, Federal Work-Study, scholarships/grants, health care benefits, tuition waivers (partial), and unspecified assistantships also available. Support available to part-time students. Financial award application deadline: 3/1; financial award applicants required to submit FAFSA. In 2016, 88 master's, 11 doctorates awarded. *Program availability:* Online learning. Offers electrical and computer engineering (MS, PhD). *Application deadline:* For fall admission, 3/1 priority date for international students; for spring admission, 8/1 priority date for international students. Applications are processed on a rolling basis. *Application fee:* $40 ($75 for international students). Electronic applications accepted. *Application Contact:* Dr. R. G. Ramakumar, Graduate Coordinator, 405-744-5157, Fax: 405-744-9198, E-mail: ramakum@okstate.edu. *Department Head,* Dr. Jeffrey Young, 405-744-5151, Fax: 405-744-9198, E-mail: jl.young@okstate.edu.

School of Industrial Engineering and Management Students: 98 full-time (11 women), 138 part-time (26 women); includes 18 minority (5 Black or African American, non-Hispanic/Latino; 2 Asian, non-Hispanic/Latino; 6 Hispanic/Latino; 5 Two or more races, non-Hispanic/Latino), 114 international. Average age 29. 364 applicants, 25% accepted, 67 enrolled. *Faculty:* 14 full-time (4 women). Expenses: Contact institution. *Financial support:* In 2016–17, 12 research assistantships (averaging $8,253 per year), 27 teaching assistantships (averaging $7,819 per year) were awarded; career-related internships or fieldwork, Federal Work-Study, scholarships/grants, health care benefits, tuition waivers (partial), and unspecified assistantships also available. Support available to part-time students. Financial award application deadline: 3/1; financial award applicants required to submit FAFSA. In 2016, 69 master's, 5 doctorates awarded. *Program availability:* Online learning. Offers industrial engineering and management (MS, PhD). *Application deadline:* For fall admission, 3/1 priority date for international students; for spring admission, 8/1 priority date for international students. Applications are processed on a rolling basis. *Application fee:* $40 ($75 for international students). Electronic applications accepted. *Application Contact:* Dr. Baski Balasundaram, Director of Graduate Program, 405-744-6055, Fax: 405-744-4654, E-mail: baski@okstate.edu. *Head,* Dr. Sunderesh Heragu, 405-744-6055, Fax: 405-744-4654, E-mail: sunderesh.heragu@okstate.edu.

School of Materials Science and Engineering Students: 3 full-time (1 woman), 17 part-time (5 women); includes 3 minority (1 Asian, non-Hispanic/Latino; 2 Two or more races, non-Hispanic/Latino), 13 international. Average age 28. 16 applicants, 38% accepted, 5 enrolled. *Faculty:* 7 full-time (0 women). Expenses: Contact institution. *Financial support:* In 2016–17, 13 research assistantships (averaging $18,193 per year), 4 teaching assistantships (averaging $10,229 per year) were awarded. Offers materials science and engineering (MS, PhD). *Application deadline:* For fall admission, 3/1 for domestic students; for spring admission, 8/1 for domestic students. *Application fee:* $40 ($75 for international students). Electronic applications accepted. *Head,* Dr. Raj N. Singh, 918-594-8650, E-mail: rajns@okstate.edu.

School of Mechanical and Aerospace Engineering Students: 27 full-time (5 women), 81 part-time (12 women); includes 13 minority (2 Black or African American, non-Hispanic/Latino; 1 American Indian or Alaska Native, non-Hispanic/Latino; 2 Asian, non-Hispanic/Latino; 8 Two or more races, non-Hispanic/Latino), 49 international. Average age 27. 236 applicants, 10% accepted, 20 enrolled. *Faculty:* 31 full-time (1 woman), 2 part-time/adjunct (1 woman). Expenses: Contact institution. *Financial support:* In 2016–17, 50 research assistantships (averaging $9,022 per year), 60 teaching assistantships (averaging $5,796 per year) were awarded; career-related internships or fieldwork, Federal Work-Study, scholarships/grants, health care benefits, tuition waivers (partial), and unspecified assistantships also available. Support available to part-time students. Financial award application deadline: 3/1; financial award applicants required to submit FAFSA. In 2016, 24 master's, 12 doctorates awarded. *Program availability:* Online learning. Offers mechanical and aerospace engineering (MS, PhD); mechanical engineering (MS, PhD). *Application deadline:* For fall admission, 3/1 priority date for international students; for spring admission, 8/1 priority date for international students. Applications are processed on a

rolling basis. *Application fee:* $40 ($75 for international students). Electronic applications accepted. *Application Contact:* Dr. Charlotte Fore, Manager of Graduate Studies and Research Development, 405-744-5900, Fax: 405-744-7873, E-mail: charlotte.fore@okstate.edu. *Department Head,* Dr. Daniel E. Fisher, 405-744-5900, Fax: 405-744-7873, E-mail: maehead@okstate.edu.

College of Human Sciences Students: 86 full-time (62 women), 123 part-time (99 women); includes 36 minority (15 Black or African American, non-Hispanic/Latino; 3 American Indian or Alaska Native, non-Hispanic/Latino; 6 Asian, non-Hispanic/Latino; 8 Hispanic/Latino; 4 Two or more races, non-Hispanic/Latino), 48 international. Average age 30. 150 applicants, 42% accepted, 53 enrolled. *Faculty:* 81 full-time (59 women), 17 part-time/adjunct (12 women). Expenses: Contact institution. *Financial support:* In 2016–17, 76 research assistantships (averaging $8,049 per year), 67 teaching assistantships (averaging $7,889 per year) were awarded; career-related internships or fieldwork, Federal Work-Study, scholarships/grants, health care benefits, tuition waivers (partial), and unspecified assistantships also available. Support available to part-time students. Financial award application deadline: 3/1; financial award applicants required to submit FAFSA. In 2016, 60 master's, 13 doctorates awarded. *Program availability:* Online learning. Offers design, housing and merchandising (MS, PhD); human development and family science (MS, PhD); human sciences (MS, PhD); marriage and family therapy (MS); nutritional sciences (MS, PhD). *Application deadline:* For fall admission, 3/1 priority date for domestic and international students; for spring admission, 8/1 priority date for domestic and international students. Applications are processed on a rolling basis. *Application fee:* $40 ($75 for international students). Electronic applications accepted. *Dean,* Dr. Stephan M. Wilson, 405-744-9805, Fax: 405-744-7113, E-mail: stephan.m.wilson@okstate.edu.

School of Hotel and Restaurant Administration Students: 10 full-time (6 women), 12 part-time (10 women); includes 7 minority (3 Black or African American, non-Hispanic/Latino; 3 Asian, non-Hispanic/Latino; 1 Hispanic/Latino), 13 international. Average age 30. 9 applicants, 67% accepted, 6 enrolled. *Faculty:* 14 full-time (8 women), 4 part-time/adjunct (1 woman). Expenses: Contact institution. *Financial support:* In 2016–17, 10 research assistantships (averaging $13,429 per year), 16 teaching assistantships (averaging $12,342 per year) were awarded; career-related internships or fieldwork, Federal Work-Study, scholarships/grants, health care benefits, tuition waivers (partial), and unspecified assistantships also available. Support available to part-time students. Financial award application deadline: 3/1; financial award applicants required to submit FAFSA. In 2016, 5 master's, 6 doctorates awarded. Offers hotel and restaurant administration (MS, PhD). *Application deadline:* For fall admission, 3/1 priority date for international students; for spring admission, 8/1 priority date for international students. Applications are processed on a rolling basis. *Application fee:* $40 ($75 for international students). Electronic applications accepted. *Application Contact:* Dr. Li Miao, Graduate Coordinator, 405-744-1277, Fax: 405-744-6299, E-mail: lm@okstate.edu. *Director,* Dr. Ben Goh, 405-744-7651, Fax: 405-744-6299, E-mail: ben.goh@okstate.edu.

Graduate College Students: 50 full-time (28 women), 109 part-time (63 women); includes 23 minority (4 Black or African American, non-Hispanic/Latino; 5 American Indian or Alaska Native, non-Hispanic/Latino; 4 Asian, non-Hispanic/Latino; 4 Hispanic/Latino; 6 Two or more races, non-Hispanic/Latino), 58 international. Average age 29. 363 applicants, 81% accepted, 71 enrolled. Expenses: Contact institution. *Financial support:* Research assistantships, career-related internships or fieldwork, Federal Work-Study, scholarships/grants, health care benefits, tuition waivers (partial), and unspecified assistantships available. Support available to part-time students. Financial award application deadline: 3/1; financial award applicants required to submit FAFSA. In 2016, 56 master's, 9 doctorates awarded. Offers aerospace security (Graduate Certificate); bioenergy and sustainable technology (Graduate Certificate); business data mining (Graduate Certificate); business sustainability (Graduate Certificate); environmental science (MS); international studies (MS); non-profit management (Graduate Certificate); teaching English to speakers of other languages (Graduate Certificate); telecommunications management (MS). Programs are interdisciplinary. *Application deadline:* For fall admission, 3/1 priority date for domestic and international students; for spring admission, 8/1 priority date for domestic and international students. Applications are processed on a rolling basis. *Application fee:* $40 ($75 for international students). Electronic applications accepted. *Application Contact:* Dr. Susan Mathew, Assistant Director of Graduate Admissions, 405-744-6368, Fax: 405-744-0355, E-mail: gradi@okstate.edu. *Dean,* Dr. Sheryl Tucker, 405-744-6368, Fax: 405-744-0355, E-mail: gradi@okstate.edu.

Spears School of Business Students: 372 full-time (114 women), 449 part-time (118 women); includes 122 minority (25 Black or African American, non-Hispanic/Latino; 11 American Indian or Alaska Native, non-Hispanic/Latino; 22 Asian, non-Hispanic/Latino; 30 Hispanic/Latino; 2 Native Hawaiian or other Pacific Islander, non-Hispanic/Latino; 32 Two or more races, non-Hispanic/Latino), 265 international. Average age 29. 1,337 applicants, 24% accepted, 257 enrolled. *Faculty:* 139 full-time (35 women), 25 part-time/adjunct (11 women). Expenses: Contact institution. *Financial support:* In 2016–17, 67 research assistantships (averaging $11,793 per year), 115 teaching assistantships (averaging $7,847 per year) were awarded; career-related internships or fieldwork, Federal Work-Study, scholarships/grants, health care benefits, tuition waivers (partial), and unspecified assistantships also available. Support available to part-time students. Financial award application deadline: 3/1; financial award applicants required to submit FAFSA. In 2016, 368 master's, 28 doctorates awarded. *Program availability:* Part-time, online learning. Offers business (MBA, MS, PhD); business administration (PhD); economics and legal studies in business (MS, PhD); entrepreneurship (MBA, MS, PhD); finance (MS, PhD); management (MBA, MS, PhD); management information systems (MS); management science and information systems (PhD); marketing (MBA); telecommunications management (MS). *Application deadline:* For fall admission, 3/1 priority date for domestic and international students; for spring admission, 8/1 priority date for domestic and international students. Applications are processed on a rolling basis. *Application fee:* $40 ($75 for international students). Electronic applications accepted. *Dean,* Dr. Ken Eastman, 405-744-5064, Fax: 405-744-8956, E-mail: ken.eastman@okstate.edu.

School of Accounting Students: 39 full-time (15 women), 11 part-time (5 women); includes 10 minority (1 Black or African American, non-Hispanic/Latino; 2 American Indian or Alaska Native, non-Hispanic/Latino; 1 Asian, non-Hispanic/Latino; 1 Hispanic/Latino; 5 Two or more races, non-Hispanic/Latino), 3 international. Average age 23. 33 applicants, 21% accepted, 7 enrolled. *Faculty:* 17 full-time (8 women), 5 part-time/adjunct (4 women). Expenses: Contact institution. *Financial support:* In 2016–17, 6 research assistantships (averaging $15,818 per year), 23 teaching assistantships (averaging $5,404 per year) were awarded; career-related internships or fieldwork, Federal Work-Study, scholarships/grants, health care benefits, tuition waivers (partial), and unspecified assistantships also available. Support available to part-time students. Financial award application deadline: 3/1; financial award applicants required to submit FAFSA. In 2016, 42 master's, 4 doctorates awarded.

Program availability: Part-time. Offers accounting (MS, PhD). *Application deadline:* For fall admission, 3/1 priority date for international students; for spring admission, 8/1 priority date for international students. Applications are processed on a rolling basis. *Application fee:* $40 ($75 for international students). Electronic applications accepted. *Application Contact:* Dr. Alyssa Vowell, Graduate Coordinator, 405-744-6635, Fax: 405-744-1680, E-mail: alyssa.vowell@okstate.edu. *Department Head:* Dr. Rick Wilson, 405-744-3551, Fax: 405-744-1680, E-mail: rick.wilson@okstate.edu.

OKLAHOMA STATE UNIVERSITY CENTER FOR HEALTH SCIENCES, Tulsa, OK 74107-1898

General Information State-supported, coed, graduate-only institution. *Enrollment by degree level:* 187 master's, 449 doctoral. *Graduate faculty:* 105 full-time (23 women), 830 part-time/adjunct (204 women). *Graduate housing:* On-campus housing not available. *Student services:* Campus employment opportunities, campus safety program, career counseling, exercise/wellness program, free psychological counseling, low-cost health insurance, services for students with disabilities. *Library facilities:* Oklahoma State University Center for Health Sciences Medical Library. *Collection:* Books: 42,831 (physical), 1,985 (digital/electronic); Serial titles: 483 (physical), 14,658 (digital/electronic); Databases: 72. Weekly public service hours: 105; students can reserve study rooms. *Research affiliation:* Viropharma, Inc. (pharmaceutical sciences), Ingenex (pharmaceutical sciences), The Procter & Gamble Company (pharmaceutical sciences), Glaxo-Smith Kline (pharmaceutical sciences), Sun River, Inc. (cognitive rehabilitation), Merck & Company, Inc. (pharmaceutical sciences).

Computer facilities: 56 computers available on campus for general student use. A campuswide network can be accessed. Online class registration is available. Website: http://www.healthsciences.okstate.edu/

General Application Contact: Lindsey Yoder, Director of Admissions and Recruitment, 800-677-1972, Fax: 918-561-8243.

GRADUATE UNITS

College of Osteopathic Medicine Offers osteopathic medicine (DO). Electronic applications accepted.

Graduate Program in Forensic Sciences *Program availability:* Part-time, evening/weekend, 100% online, blended/hybrid learning. Offers forensic sciences (MS). Electronic applications accepted.

Program in Biomedical Sciences Offers biomedical sciences (MS, PhD). Electronic applications accepted.

Program in Health Care Administration *Program availability:* Part-time, evening/weekend, 100% online. Offers health care administration (MS).

OKLAHOMA WESLEYAN UNIVERSITY, Bartlesville, OK 74006-6299

General Information Independent-religious, coed, comprehensive institution.

GRADUATE UNITS
Professional Studies Division

OLD DOMINION UNIVERSITY, Norfolk, VA 23529

General Information State-supported, coed, university. CGS member. *Enrollment:* 24,322 graduate, professional, and undergraduate students; 1,504 full-time matriculated graduate/professional students (943 women), 2,193 part-time matriculated graduate/professional students (1,182 women). *Enrollment by degree level:* 2,371 master's, 1,235 doctoral, 91 other advanced degrees. *Graduate faculty:* 698 full-time (259 women), 150 part-time/adjunct (84 women). *Tuition, state resident:* full-time $8604; part-time $478 per credit hour. *Tuition, nonresident:* full-time $21,510; part-time $1195 per credit hour. *Required fees:* $66 per semester. Tuition and fees vary according to campus/location, program and reciprocity agreements. *Graduate housing:* Room and/or apartments available on a first-come, first-served basis to single students; on-campus housing not available to married students. Typical cost: $6094 per year ($10,864 including board). Room and board charges vary according to board plan and housing facility selected. Housing application deadline: 5/1. *Student services:* Campus employment opportunities, campus safety program, career counseling, exercise/wellness program, free psychological counseling, grant writing training, international student services, low-cost health insurance, multicultural affairs office, services for students with disabilities, teacher training, writing training. *Library facilities:* Patricia W. and Douglas Perry Library plus 3 others. *Collection:* Books: 1.3 million (physical), 1.3 million (digital/electronic); Serial titles: 18,082 (physical), 70,169 (digital/electronic); Databases: 383. Weekly public service hours: 146; study areas open 24 hours, 5–7 days a week; students can reserve study rooms. *Research affiliation:* Commonwealth Center for Advanced Manufacturing (CCAM) (advanced engineering and manufacturing), Joint Staff J7 (modeling and simulation for training), Thomas Jefferson National Accelerator Facility (high energy physics and laser processing), NASA Langley Research Center (aeronautics and data analytics), Eastern Virginia Medical School (medicine), Virginia Institute of Marine Science (marine science and coastal resilience).

Computer facilities: 2,025 computers available on campus for general student use. A campuswide network can be accessed from student residence rooms and from off campus. Online class registration, online courses are available. Website: http://www.odu.edu/

General Application Contact: William Heffelfinger, Director of Graduate Admissions, 757-683-5554, Fax: 757-683-3255, E-mail: gradadmit@odu.edu.

GRADUATE UNITS

College of Arts and Letters Students: 135 full-time (73 women), 202 part-time (132 women); includes 81 minority (40 Black or African American, non-Hispanic/Latino; 1 American Indian or Alaska Native, non-Hispanic/Latino; 9 Asian, non-Hispanic/Latino; 12 Hispanic/Latino; 19 Two or more races, non-Hispanic/Latino), 22 international. Average age 34. 276 applicants, 66% accepted, 117 enrolled. *Faculty:* 135 full-time (61 women), 11 part-time/adjunct (4 women). Expenses: Contact institution. *Financial support:* In 2016–17, 122 students received support, including 5 fellowships with full tuition reimbursements available (averaging $15,000 per year), 54 research assistantships (averaging $10,000 per year), 60 teaching assistantships with full tuition reimbursements available (averaging $15,000 per year); institutionally sponsored loans, scholarships/grants, and unspecified assistantships also available. Support available to part-time students. Financial award application deadline: 2/15; financial award applicants required to submit CSS PROFILE or FAFSA. In 2016, 85 master's, 20 doctorates awarded. *Program availability:* Part-time, evening/weekend, online learning. Offers arts and letters (MA, MFA, MME, PhD); conflict and cooperation (MA, PhD); creative writing (MFA); criminal justice (MA); criminology and criminal justice (PhD); English (MA, PhD); general sociology (MA); history (MA); humanities (MA); interdependence and transnationalism (MA, PhD); international cultural studies (MA,

PhD); international political economy and development (MA, PhD); lifespan and digital communication (MA); modeling and simulation (MA, PhD); music education (MME); sociolinguistics (MA); TESOL (MA); U.S. foreign policy and international relations (MA, PhD); women's studies (MA). *Application deadline:* For fall admission, 6/1 priority date for domestic students, 2/15 for international students; for spring admission, 11/1 priority date for domestic students, 10/1 for international students. *Application fee:* $50. Electronic applications accepted. *Application Contact:* Dr. David C. Earnest, Associate Dean, 757-683-6077, Fax: 757-683-5746, E-mail: dearnest@odu.edu. *Dean,* Dr. Charles E. Wilson, Jr., 757-683-3925, Fax: 757-683-5746, E-mail: cwilson@odu.edu.

College of Health Sciences Students: 305 full-time (219 women), 102 part-time (91 women); includes 80 minority (34 Black or African American, non-Hispanic/Latino; 2 American Indian or Alaska Native, non-Hispanic/Latino; 14 Asian, non-Hispanic/Latino; 17 Hispanic/Latino; 13 Two or more races, non-Hispanic/Latino), 6 international. Average age 32. 1,047 applicants, 25% accepted, 202 enrolled. *Faculty:* 64 full-time (42 women), 2 part-time/adjunct (0 women). Expenses: Contact institution. *Financial support:* In 2016–17, 37 students received support, including 7 fellowships with full tuition reimbursements available (averaging $15,000 per year), 12 research assistantships with partial tuition reimbursements available (averaging $15,000 per year), 9 teaching assistantships with partial tuition reimbursements available (averaging $13,000 per year); career-related internships or fieldwork, institutionally sponsored loans, scholarships/grants, health care benefits, tuition waivers (full and partial), and unspecified assistantships also available. Support available to part-time students. Financial award application deadline: 2/15; financial award applicants required to submit FAFSA. In 2016, 81 master's, 91 doctorates awarded. *Program availability:* Part-time, evening/weekend, 100% online, blended/hybrid learning. Offers advanced practice (DNP); health sciences (MS, MSAT, MSN, DNP, DPT, PhD); health services research (PhD); nurse executive (DNP). *Application deadline:* Applications are processed on a rolling basis. *Application fee:* $50. Electronic applications accepted. *Application Contact:* William Heffelfinger, Director of Graduate Admissions, 757-683-5554, Fax: 757-683-3255, E-mail: gradadmit@odu.edu. *Dean,* Dr. Shelley Mishoe, 757-683-4960, Fax: 757-683-5674, E-mail: smishoe@odu.edu.

School of Community and Environmental Health Students: 17 full-time (9 women), 9 part-time (6 women); includes 11 minority (9 Black or African American, non-Hispanic/Latino; 2 Hispanic/Latino). Average age 29. 12 applicants, 83% accepted, 8 enrolled. *Faculty:* 5 full-time (2 women), 4 part-time/adjunct (2 women). Expenses: Contact institution. *Financial support:* In 2016–17, 4 students received support, including 4 teaching assistantships with partial tuition reimbursements available (averaging $10,000 per year); scholarships/grants and tuition waivers (partial) also available. Financial award application deadline: 4/30; financial award applicants required to submit FAFSA. In 2016, 7 master's awarded. Offers industrial hygiene (MS); occupational health and safety (MS). *Application deadline:* For fall admission, 8/1 priority date for domestic students, 7/1 priority date for international students; for winter admission, 11/1 priority date for domestic students, 10/1 priority date for international students; for spring admission, 4/1 priority date for domestic students, 3/1 priority date for international students. Applications are processed on a rolling basis. *Application fee:* $50. Electronic applications accepted. *Application Contact:* William Heffelfinger, Director of Graduate Admissions, 757-683-5554, Fax: 757-683-3255, E-mail: gradadmit@odu.edu. *Graduate Program Director,* Dr. Anna Jeng, 757-683-4594, Fax: 757-683-4410, E-mail: hjeng@odu.edu.

School of Dental Hygiene Students: 4 full-time (all women), 16 part-time (15 women); includes 2 minority (both Asian, non-Hispanic/Latino), 2 international. Average age 35. 12 applicants, 25% accepted, 2 enrolled. *Faculty:* 10 full-time (9 women). Expenses: Contact institution. *Financial support:* In 2016–17, 4 students received support, including 4 teaching assistantships with partial tuition reimbursements available (averaging $13,000 per year); scholarships/grants and health care benefits also available. Support available to part-time students. Financial award application deadline: 2/15; financial award applicants required to submit CSS PROFILE or FAFSA. In 2016, 7 master's awarded. *Program availability:* Part-time, evening/weekend, blended/hybrid learning. Offers dental hygiene (MS). *Application deadline:* For fall admission, 7/1 for domestic students, 4/15 for international students; for spring admission, 12/1 for domestic students, 10/1 for international students; for summer admission, 3/1 for domestic students, 2/1 for international students. Applications are processed on a rolling basis. *Application fee:* $50. Electronic applications accepted. *Application Contact:* William Heffelfinger, Director of Graduate Admissions, 757-683-5554, Fax: 757-683-3255, E-mail: gradadmit@odu.edu. *Assistant Dean/Graduate Program Director,* Deborah B. Bauman, 757-683-6079, Fax: 757-683-4753, E-mail: dbauman@odu.edu.

School of Nursing Students: 121 full-time (107 women), 59 part-time (53 women); includes 38 minority (17 Black or African American, non-Hispanic/Latino; 2 American Indian or Alaska Native, non-Hispanic/Latino; 5 Asian, non-Hispanic/Latino; 6 Hispanic/Latino; 8 Two or more races, non-Hispanic/Latino). Average age 39. 199 applicants, 42% accepted, 74 enrolled. *Faculty:* 6 full-time (5 women), 17 part-time/adjunct (15 women). Expenses: Contact institution. *Financial support:* In 2016–17, 18 students received support, including 2 research assistantships with partial tuition reimbursements available (averaging $10,000 per year), 1 teaching assistantship (averaging $2,500 per year); career-related internships or fieldwork, scholarships/grants, traineeships, and tuition waivers (partial) also available. Support available to part-time students. Financial award application deadline: 2/15; financial award applicants required to submit FAFSA. In 2016, 57 master's, 44 doctorates awarded. *Program availability:* Part-time, 100% online, blended/hybrid learning. Offers adult gerontology clinical nurse specialist/administrator (MSN); adult gerontology clinical nurse specialist/educator (MSN); adult gerontology nursing (MSN, DNP); advanced practice (DNP); family nurse practitioner (MSN, DNP); neonatal clinical nurse specialist (MSN); neonatal nurse practitioner (MSN); neonatal nursing (MSN, DNP); nurse administrator (MSN, DNP); nurse anesthesia (DNP); nurse executive (DNP); nurse midwifery (MSN); pediatric clinical nurse specialist (MSN); pediatric nurse practitioner (MSN); pediatric nursing (MSN, DNP). MSN in nurse midwifery offered in cooperation with Shenandoah University. *Application deadline:* For fall admission, 3/1 for domestic students, 4/15 for international students; for spring admission, 9/15 for domestic students. *Application fee:* $50. Electronic applications accepted. *Application Contact:* Sue Parker, Coordinator, Graduate Student Services, 757-683-4298, Fax: 757-683-5253, E-mail: sparker@odu.edu. *Chair,* Dr. Karen Karlowicz, 757-683-5262, Fax: 757-683-5253, E-mail: nursgpd@odu.edu.

School of Physical Therapy and Athletic Training Students: 130 full-time (80 women); includes 16 minority (6 Black or African American, non-Hispanic/Latino; 3 Asian, non-Hispanic/Latino; 3 Hispanic/Latino; 2 Native Hawaiian or other Pacific Islander, non-Hispanic/Latino; 2 Two or more races, non-Hispanic/Latino). Average age 23. 536 applicants, 15% accepted, 43 enrolled. *Faculty:* 11 full-time (7 women), 7 part-time/adjunct (5 women). Expenses: Contact institution. *Financial support:* In 2016–17, 2 students received support, including 2 teaching assistantships with partial tuition reimbursements available (averaging $5,000 per year); scholarships/grants also available. Financial award applicants required to submit FAFSA. In 2016, 44 doctorates awarded. Offers athletic training (MSAT); kinesiology and rehabilitation (PhD); physical therapy (DPT). *Application deadline:* For fall admission, 11/1 for domestic and international students. *Application fee:* $50. Electronic applications accepted. *Application Contact:* William Heffelfinger, Director of Graduate Admissions, 757-683-5554, Fax: 757-683-3255, E-mail: gradadmit@odu.edu. *Graduate Program Director,* Dr. Martha Walker, 757-683-4519, Fax: 757-683-4410, E-mail: ptgpd@odu.edu.

College of Sciences Students: 249 full-time (119 women), 196 part-time (75 women); includes 65 minority (24 Black or African American, non-Hispanic/Latino; 20 Asian, non-Hispanic/Latino; 13 Hispanic/Latino; 8 Two or more races, non-Hispanic/Latino), 140 international. Average age 29. *Faculty:* 143 full-time (31 women), 33 part-time/adjunct (7 women). Expenses: Contact institution. *Financial support:* In 2016–17, 262 students received support, including 3 fellowships with full tuition reimbursements available (averaging $5,000 per year), 158 research assistantships with full and partial tuition reimbursements available (averaging $18,000 per year), 101 teaching assistantships with tuition reimbursements available (averaging $16,000 per year); career-related internships or fieldwork, scholarships/grants, and tuition waivers (partial) also available. Support available to part-time students. Financial award application deadline: 2/15; financial award applicants required to submit FAFSA. In 2016, 89 master's, 32 doctorates awarded. *Program availability:* Part-time, evening/weekend, 100% online. Offers analytical (MS, PhD); applied mathematics (MS, PhD); applied psychological sciences (PhD); biochemistry (MS, PhD); biology (MS); biomedical sciences (PhD); biostatistics (MS); clinical psychology (PhD); computer information systems (MS); computer science (MS, PhD); ecological sciences (PhD); environmental (MS, PhD); human factors psychology (PhD); industrial/organizational psychology (PhD); inorganic (MS, PhD); ocean and earth sciences (MS); oceanography (PhD); organic (MS, PhD); physical (MS, PhD); physics (MS, PhD); psychology (MS, PhD); sciences (MS, PhD); statistics (MS); statistics/biostatistics (PhD). *Application fee:* $50. Electronic applications accepted. *Application Contact:* William Heffelfinger, Director of Graduate Admissions, 757-683-5554, Fax: 757-683-3255, E-mail: gradadmit@odu.edu. *Dean,* Dr. Chris Platsoucas, 757-683-3274, Fax: 757-683-3034, E-mail: cplatsoucas@odu.edu.

Darden College of Education Students: 529 full-time (427 women), 794 part-time (599 women); includes 378 minority (251 Black or African American, non-Hispanic/Latino; 4 American Indian or Alaska Native, non-Hispanic/Latino; 21 Asian, non-Hispanic/Latino; 60 Hispanic/Latino; 42 Two or more races, non-Hispanic/Latino), 28 international. Average age 34. 808 applicants, 58% accepted, 309 enrolled. *Faculty:* 94 full-time (55 women), 62 part-time/adjunct (40 women). Expenses: Contact institution. *Financial support:* In 2016–17, 141 students received support, including 4 fellowships with tuition reimbursements available (averaging $15,000 per year), 60 research assistantships with tuition reimbursements available (averaging $15,000 per year), 72 teaching assistantships with tuition reimbursements available (averaging $15,000 per year); career-related internships or fieldwork, Federal Work-Study, institutionally sponsored loans, scholarships/grants, tuition waivers (partial), and unspecified assistantships also available. Support available to part-time students. Financial award application deadline: 2/15; financial award applicants required to submit CSS PROFILE or FAFSA. In 2016, 420 master's, 53 doctorates, 56 other advanced degrees awarded. *Program availability:* Part-time, evening/weekend, 100% online, blended/hybrid learning. Offers adapted curriculum K-12 (MS Ed); adapted physical education (MS Ed); chemistry (MS Ed); clinical mental health counseling (MS Ed); coaching education (MS Ed); college counseling (MS Ed); community college leadership (PhD); community college teaching (MS); counseling (Ed S); counselor education (PhD); curriculum and instruction (MS Ed, PhD); early childhood education (MS Ed, PhD); early childhood special education (MS Ed); education (MS, MS Ed, PhD, Ed S, Postbaccalaureate Certificate); educational leadership (MS Ed, PhD, Ed S); elementary education (Postbaccalaureate Certificate); English (MS Ed); exercise and wellness (MS Ed); general curriculum K-12 (MS Ed); higher education (MS Ed, PhD, Ed S); human movement science (PhD); human movement sciences (PhD); human resources training (PhD); instructional design and technology (PhD); instructional technology (MS Ed); library science (MS Ed); literacy leadership (PhD); physical education (MS Ed); reading specialist (MS Ed); school counseling (MS Ed); secondary education (MS Ed); special education (PhD); speech-language pathology (MS Ed); sport management (MS Ed); technology education (PhD). *Application deadline:* For fall admission, 6/1 priority date for domestic and international students; for spring admission, 11/1 priority date for domestic and international students. Applications are processed on a rolling basis. *Application fee:* $50. Electronic applications accepted. *Application Contact:* William Heffelfinger, Director of Graduate Admissions, 757-683-5554, Fax: 757-683-3255, E-mail: gradadmit@odu.edu. *Dean,* Dr. Jane S. Bray, 757-683-3938, Fax: 757-683-5083, E-mail: jsbray@odu.edu.

Frank Batten College of Engineering and Technology Students: 157 full-time (44 women), 569 part-time (125 women); includes 167 minority (72 Black or African American, non-Hispanic/Latino; 36 Asian, non-Hispanic/Latino; 42 Hispanic/Latino; 1 Native Hawaiian or other Pacific Islander, non-Hispanic/Latino; 16 Two or more races, non-Hispanic/Latino), 167 international. Average age 32. 558 applicants, 63% accepted, 144 enrolled. *Faculty:* 93 full-time (12 women), 32 part-time/adjunct (5 women). Expenses: Contact institution. *Financial support:* In 2016–17, 168 students received support, including 8 fellowships with tuition reimbursements available (averaging $15,000 per year), 92 research assistantships with tuition reimbursements available (averaging $15,000 per year), 68 teaching assistantships with tuition reimbursements available (averaging $15,000 per year); career-related internships or fieldwork, Federal Work-Study, institutionally sponsored loans, scholarships/grants, and unspecified assistantships also available. Support available to part-time students. Financial award applicants required to submit FAFSA. In 2016, 199 master's, 31 doctorates awarded. *Program availability:* Part-time, evening/weekend, 100% online, blended/hybrid learning. Offers aerospace engineering (ME, MS, D Eng, PhD); biomedical engineering (ME, MS, PhD); civil and environmental engineering (D Eng, PhD); civil engineering (ME, MS); electrical and computer engineering (ME, MS, D Eng, PhD); engineering and technology (ME, MS, D Eng, PhD); engineering management and systems engineering (D Eng, PhD); environmental engineering (ME, MS); mechanical engineering (ME, MS, D Eng, PhD); modeling and simulation (ME, MS, D Eng, PhD); systems engineering (ME). *Application deadline:* For fall admission, 6/1 for domestic students, 2/15 priority date for international students; for spring admission, 11/1 for domestic students, 10/1 for international students. Applications are processed on a rolling basis. *Application fee:* $50. Electronic applications accepted. *Application Contact:* Dr. Rafael E. Landaeta, Associate Dean, 757-683-4478, Fax: 757-683-4898, E-mail: rlandaet@odu.edu. *Dean,* Dr. Stephanie G. Adams, 757-683-3789, Fax: 757-683-4898, E-mail: sgadams@odu.edu.

Strome College of Business Students: 129 full-time (61 women), 330 part-time (160 women); includes 137 minority (79 Black or African American, non-Hispanic/Latino; 16 Asian, non-Hispanic/Latino; 18 Hispanic/Latino; 24 Two or more races, non-Hispanic/Latino), 76 international. Average age 34. 306 applicants, 63% accepted, 142 enrolled. *Faculty:* 80 full-time (19 women), 13 part-time/adjunct (7 women). Expenses: Contact institution. *Financial support:* In 2016–17, 94 students received support, including 4 fellowships with partial tuition reimbursements available (averaging $7,500 per year), 12 teaching assistantships with full tuition reimbursements available (averaging $15,000 per year); career-related internships or fieldwork, Federal Work-Study, scholarships/grants, tuition waivers (partial), and unspecified assistantships also available. Financial award application deadline: 2/15; financial award applicants required to submit FAFSA. In 2016, 121 master's, 13 doctorates awarded. *Program availability:* Part-time, evening/weekend, online learning. Offers accounting (MS); business (MA, MBA, MPA, MS, PhD); business administration (MBA, PhD); economics (MA); finance (PhD); information technology (PhD); maritime trade and supply chain management (MS); marketing (PhD); multi sector public service (MPA); public administration (MPA); public administration and urban policy (PhD); strategic management (PhD). *Application deadline:* For fall admission, 6/1 priority date for domestic and international students; for winter admission, 11/1 priority date for domestic and international students. Applications are processed on a rolling basis. *Application fee:* $50. Electronic applications accepted. *Application Contact:* Dr. Kiran Karande, Associate Dean, 757-683-3520, Fax: 757-683-4076, E-mail: kkarande@odu.edu. *Dean,* Dr. Jeff Tanner, 757-683-3520, Fax: 757-683-4076, E-mail: jtanner@odu.edu.

OLIVET COLLEGE, Olivet, MI 49076-9701

General Information Independent-religious, coed, comprehensive institution. *Enrollment:* 1,078 graduate, professional, and undergraduate students; 33 part-time matriculated graduate/professional students (8 women). *Enrollment by degree level:* 33 master's. *Graduate faculty:* 5 part-time/adjunct (2 women). *Tuition:* Part-time $760 per semester hour. *Required fees:* $100 per semester hour. *Library facilities:* Burrage Library plus 1 other. *Collection:* Books: 61,268 (physical); Serial titles: 211 (physical), 68,401 (digital/electronic); Databases: 14. Students can reserve study rooms.

Computer facilities: 125 computers available on campus for general student use. A campuswide network can be accessed from student residence rooms and from off campus. Online class registration is available.
Website: http://www.olivetcollege.edu/

General Application Contact: Kelly Parker, Associate Director of Graduate Business Programs, 269-749-7626, E-mail: kparker@olivetcollege.edu.

GRADUATE UNITS

Master of Business Administration in Insurance Program Students: 33 part-time (8 women). Average age 37. *Faculty:* 5 part-time/adjunct (2 women). Expenses: Contact institution. In 2016, 7 master's awarded. *Program availability:* Part-time, online only, 100% online, blended/hybrid learning. Offers insurance (MBA). *Application deadline:* For fall admission, 9/15 for domestic students. Applications are processed on a rolling basis. *Application fee:* $0. Electronic applications accepted. *Application Contact:* Kelly M. Parker, Associate Director of Graduate Business Programs, 269-749-7626, E-mail: kparker@olivetcollege.edu. *MBA Program Director,* John S. Homer, PhD, 269-749-7150, E-mail: jhomer@olivetcollege.edu.

OLIVET NAZARENE UNIVERSITY, Bourbonnais, IL 60914

General Information Independent-religious, coed, comprehensive institution. *Graduate housing:* Room and/or apartments available to single students; on-campus housing not available to married students. Housing application deadline: 8/15.

GRADUATE UNITS

Graduate School *Program availability:* Part-time, evening/weekend. Offers business administration (MBA); familly nurse practitioner (MSN); nursing (MSN); practical ministries (MPM).

Division of Education *Program availability:* Evening/weekend. Offers curriculum and instruction (MAE); elementary education (MAT); library information specialist (MAE); reading specialist (MAE); school leadership (MAE); secondary education (MAT).

Division of Religion *Program availability:* Part-time. Offers biblical literature (MA); religion (MA); theology (MA).

Program in Organizational Leadership Offers organizational leadership (MOL).

OPEN UNIVERSITY, Milton Keynes MK7 6AA, United Kingdom

General Information Public, coed, comprehensive institution.

GRADUATE UNITS

Graduate Programs

ORAL ROBERTS UNIVERSITY, Tulsa, OK 74171

General Information Independent-religious, coed, comprehensive institution. *Graduate housing:* Room and/or apartments available on a first-come, first-served basis to single students; on-campus housing not available to married students.

GRADUATE UNITS

School of Business *Program availability:* Part-time, online learning. Offers accounting (MBA); entrepreneurship (MBA); finance (MBA); international business (MBA); management (MBA); marketing (MBA); non-profit management (MBA); not for profit management (MNM). Electronic applications accepted.

School of Education *Program availability:* Part-time, online learning. Offers Christian school administration (K-12) (MA Ed, Ed D); Christian school curriculum development (MA Ed); college and higher education administration (Ed D); public school administration (K-12) (MA Ed, Ed D); public school teaching (MA Ed).

School of Theology and Missions *Program availability:* Part-time, online learning. Offers biblical literature (MA); Christian counseling (MA); divinity (M Div); missions (MA); practical theology (MA); theological/historical studies (MA); theology (D Min). Electronic applications accepted.

OREGON COLLEGE OF ART AND CRAFT, Portland, OR 97225

General Information Independent, coed, comprehensive institution.

GRADUATE UNITS

MFA Program Offers craft (MFA).

OREGON COLLEGE OF ORIENTAL MEDICINE, Portland, OR 97216

General Information Independent, coed, graduate-only institution. *Graduate housing:* On-campus housing not available.

GRADUATE UNITS

Graduate Program in Acupuncture and Oriental Medicine *Program availability:* Part-time. Offers acupuncture and Oriental medicine (M Ac OM, MAcOM, DAOM).

OREGON HEALTH & SCIENCE UNIVERSITY, Portland, OR 97239-3098

General Information State-related, coed, upper-level institution. CGS member. *Graduate housing:* On-campus housing not available. *Research affiliation:* Oregon Regional Primate Research Center.

GRADUATE UNITS

School of Dentistry Offers biomaterials and biomechanics (MS); dentistry (MS, DMD, Certificate); endodontics (Certificate); oral and maxillofacial surgery (Certificate); oral molecular biology (MS); orthodontics (MS, Certificate); pediatric dentistry (Certificate); periodontology (MS, Certificate); restorative dentistry (MS). Electronic applications accepted.

School of Medicine Students: 916 full-time (504 women), 425 part-time (223 women); includes 252 minority (30 Black or African American, non-Hispanic/Latino; 8 American Indian or Alaska Native, non-Hispanic/Latino; 161 Asian, non-Hispanic/Latino; 1 Hispanic/Latino; 1 Native Hawaiian or other Pacific Islander, non-Hispanic/Latino; 51 Two or more races, non-Hispanic/Latino), 63 international. Average age 30. *Faculty:* 2,708. Expenses: Contact institution. *Financial support:* Fellowships, research assistantships, teaching assistantships, career-related internships or fieldwork, Federal Work-Study, institutionally sponsored loans, scholarships/grants, health care benefits, and full-tuition and stipends (for PhD students) available. Support available to part-time students. Financial award application deadline: 3/1; financial award applicants required to submit FAFSA. In 2016, 153 master's, 161 doctorates, 78 other advanced degrees awarded. *Program availability:* Part-time. Offers medicine (MBA, MBI, MBST, MCR, MPAS, MS, MSCNU, MD, PhD, Certificate, Graduate Certificate). *Application deadline:* Applications are processed on a rolling basis. Electronic applications accepted. *Application Contact:* Registrar's Office, 503-494-7800. *Interim Dean*, Dr. John Hunter, 503-494-8220, Fax: 503-494-3400.

Graduate Programs in Medicine Students: 370 full-time (214 women), 396 part-time (215 women); includes 173 minority (18 Black or African American, non-Hispanic/Latino; 5 American Indian or Alaska Native, non-Hispanic/Latino; 86 Asian, non-Hispanic/Latino; 38 Hispanic/Latino; 26 Two or more races, non-Hispanic/Latino), 61 international. Average age 30. *Faculty:* 333 full-time (124 women), 605 part-time/adjunct (187 women). Expenses: Contact institution. *Financial support:* Fellowships, research assistantships, teaching assistantships, scholarships/grants, health care benefits, and full-tuition and stipends (for PhD students) available. Financial award application deadline: 3/1; financial award applicants required to submit FAFSA. In 2016, 153 master's, 34 doctorates, 78 other advanced degrees awarded. *Program availability:* Part-time. Offers behavioral neuroscience (PhD); biochemistry and molecular biology (PhD); bioinformatics (MS, PhD); biomedical engineering (PhD); cancer biology (PhD); cell and developmental biology (PhD); clinical informatics (MBI, MS, PhD, Certificate); clinical research (MCR, Certificate); computer science and engineering (MS, PhD); dietetics (Certificate); electrical engineering (MS, PhD); environmental science and engineering (MS, PhD); health information management (Certificate); healthcare management (MBA, MS, Certificate); human nutrition (MS); medicine (MBA, MBI, MCR, MPAS, MS, MSCNU, PhD, Certificate); molecular and cellular biosciences (PhD); molecular and medical genetics (PhD); molecular microbiology and immunology (PhD); neuroscience (PhD); physician assistant studies (MPAS); physiology and pharmacology (PhD). *Application Contact:* Lorie Gookin, Admissions Coordinator, 503-494-6222, E-mail: somgrad@ohsu.edu. *Associate Dean for Graduate Studies*, Dr. Allison Fryer, 503-494-6222, E-mail: somgrad@ohsu.edu.

School of Nursing Students: 204 full-time (175 women), 44 part-time (37 women); includes 51 minority (4 Black or African American, non-Hispanic/Latino; 2 American Indian or Alaska Native, non-Hispanic/Latino; 14 Asian, non-Hispanic/Latino; 18 Hispanic/Latino; 13 Two or more races, non-Hispanic/Latino), 6 international. Average age 35. 294 applicants, 47% accepted, 118 enrolled. *Faculty:* 45 full-time (40 women), 28 part-time/adjunct (25 women). Expenses: Contact institution. *Financial support:* Fellowships, research assistantships, teaching assistantships, career-related internships or fieldwork, Federal Work-Study, institutionally sponsored loans, scholarships/grants, and traineeships available. Financial award application deadline: 3/1; financial award applicants required to submit FAFSA. In 2016, 85 master's, 42 doctorates awarded. *Program availability:* Part-time, 100% online, blended/hybrid learning. Offers adult gerontology acute care nurse practitioner (MN); family nurse practitioner (MN); health systems and organizational leadership (MN); nurse anesthesia (MN); nurse midwifery (MN); nursing (MN, DNP, PhD, Post Master's Certificate); nursing education (MN, Post Master's Certificate); pediatric nurse practitioner (MN); psychiatric mental health nurse practitioner (MN). *Application deadline:* For fall admission, 1/5 for domestic and international students; for summer admission, 1/5 for domestic and international students. Applications are processed on a rolling basis. *Application fee:* $65. Electronic applications accepted. *Application Contact:* Office of Recruitment, 503-494-7725, Fax: 503-494-4350, E-mail: proginfo@ohsu.edu. *Senior Associate Dean for Academic Affairs*, Dr. Sarah Shannon, E-mail: shannons@ohsu.edu.

OREGON INSTITUTE OF TECHNOLOGY, Klamath Falls, OR 97601-8801

General Information State-supported, coed, comprehensive institution. *Graduate housing:* Room and/or apartments available on a first-come, first-served basis to single students; on-campus housing not available to married students. Housing application deadline: 3/1.

GRADUATE UNITS

Program in Manufacturing Engineering Technology *Program availability:* Part-time, online learning. Offers manufacturing engineering technology (MS). Electronic applications accepted.

OREGON STATE UNIVERSITY, Corvallis, OR 97331

General Information State-supported, coed, university. CGS member. *Enrollment:* 30,354 graduate, professional, and undergraduate students; 3,525 full-time matriculated graduate/professional students (1,669 women), 733 part-time matriculated graduate/professional students (401 women). *Enrollment by degree level:* 2,061 master's, 2,197 doctoral. *Graduate faculty:* 970 full-time (347 women), 134 part-time/adjunct (60 women). Tuition, state resident: full-time $12,150; part-time $450 per credit. Tuition, nonresident: full-time $21,789; part-time $807 per credit. *Required fees:* $1651; $1507 per credit. One-time fee: $350. Tuition and fees vary according to course load, campus/location and program. *Graduate housing:* Rooms and/or apartments guaranteed to single students and available on a first-come, first-served basis to married students. Typical cost: $10,710 per year ($13,560 including board) for single students; $5715 per year ($8565 including board) for married students. Room and board charges vary according to board plan and housing facility selected. Housing application deadline: 5/1. *Student services:* Campus employment opportunities, campus safety program, career counseling, child daycare facilities, exercise/wellness program, free psychological counseling, grant writing training, international student services, low-cost health insurance, multicultural affairs office, services for students with disabilities, teacher training, writing training. *Library facilities:* Valley Library plus 2 others. *Collection:* Books: 1.8 million (physical), 403,777 (digital/electronic); Databases: 196. Weekly public service hours: 144; study areas open 24 hours, 5–7 days a week; students can reserve study rooms. *Research affiliation:* W.M. Keck Foundation (science, engineering), David and Lucille Packard Foundation (science, environmental science), William and Flora Hewlett Foundation (science, engineering), George and Betty Moore Foundation (medical research, science education), Comer Science and Educational Foundation (science).

Computer facilities: Computer purchase and lease plans are available. 2,179 computers available on campus for general student use. A campuswide network can be accessed from student residence rooms and from off campus. Online class registration is available.

Website: http://www.oregonstate.edu/

General Application Contact: Graduate School, 541-737-4881, Fax: 541-737-3313, E-mail: graduate.admissions@oregonstate.edu.

GRADUATE UNITS

College of Agricultural Sciences Students: 313 full-time (158 women), 35 part-time (21 women); includes 43 minority (3 Black or African American, non-Hispanic/Latino; 1 American Indian or Alaska Native, non-Hispanic/Latino; 4 Asian, non-Hispanic/Latino; 27 Hispanic/Latino; 8 Two or more races, non-Hispanic/Latino), 75 international. Average age 30. *Faculty:* 158 full-time (48 women), 31 part-time/adjunct (9 women). Expenses: Contact institution. *Financial support:* Fellowships, research assistantships, teaching assistantships, career-related internships or fieldwork, Federal Work-Study, and institutionally sponsored loans available. Support available to part-time students. In 2016, 75 master's, 26 doctorates awarded. *Program availability:* Part-time, online learning. Offers agricultural sciences (M Ag, MA, MS, PSM, PhD); agroforestry (MS, PhD); animal nutrition (PhD); animal-habitat relationships (MS, PhD); aquaculture (MS); behavior (MS, PhD); biology of big game and small mammals (MS, PhD); breeding, genetics and biotechnology (MS, PhD); brewing (MS, PhD); community and landscape horticultural systems (MS, PhD); community studies (MS, PhD); conservation biology (MS, PhD); crop science (M Ag, MS, PhD); dairy production (MS); ecology (MA); ecology of avian and mammalian predators (MS, PhD); ecology of rangelands (MS, PhD); ecology of waterfowl and upland gamebirds (MS, PhD); effects of parasites, diseases, and environmental contaminants (MS, PhD); embryo physiology (MS, PhD); endocrinology (MS, PhD); enology (MS, PhD); environmental chemistry and ecotoxicology (MS, PhD); environmental soil science (MS, PhD); fish genetics (MS, PhD); fisheries and wildlife administration (PSM); flavor chemistry (MS, PhD); food and seafood processing (MS, PhD); food chemistry/biochemistry (MS, PhD); food engineering (MS, PhD); food microbiology/biotechnology (MS, PhD); forest soils (MS, PhD); genetics (MA, MS, PhD); genomics and computational biology (MA, MS, PhD); growth and development (MS, PhD); ichthyology (MS, PhD); leadership and communication in agriculture (MS); limnology (MS, PhD); livestock management (MS); mechanistic toxicology (MS, PhD); molecular and cellular biology (MA, MS, PhD); molecular and cellular toxicology (MS, PhD); mycology (MA, MS, PhD); neurotoxicology (MS, PhD); nutrient cycling (MS, PhD); nutrition (MS, PhD); nutritional biochemistry (MS, PhD); parasites and diseases (MS, PhD); physiology and ecology of marine and freshwater fishes (MS, PhD); physiology of range plants (MS, PhD); plant pathology (MA, MS, PhD); plant physiology (MA, MS, PhD); population (MS, PhD); population dynamics (MS, PhD); public health economics (MA, MS, PhD); range improvement (MS, PhD); range nutrition (MS, PhD); reproductive biology (MS, PhD); reproductive physiology (MS, PhD); resource and environmental economics (MA); restoration ecology (MS, PhD); riparian zone management (MS, PhD); sensory evaluation (MS, PhD); soil conservation and land use (MS, PhD); soil fertility and plant nutrition (MS, PhD); soil genesis and classification (MS, PhD); soil geochemistry (MS, PhD); soil microbiology (MS, PhD); soil physics (MS, PhD); stream ecology (MS, PhD); sustainable crop production (MS); systematics (MA, MS, PhD); teacher preparation (MS); toxicology (MS, PhD); trade and development (MA, MS); transportation economics (MA, MS); water pollution biology (MS, PhD); watershed management (MS, PhD). *Application fee:* $75 ($85 for international students). *Dean*, Dr. Dan Arp.

College of Business Students: 143 full-time (62 women), 90 part-time (43 women); includes 28 minority (3 Black or African American, non-Hispanic/Latino; 13 Asian, non-Hispanic/Latino; 9 Hispanic/Latino; 1 Native Hawaiian or other Pacific Islander, non-Hispanic/Latino; 2 Two or more races, non-Hispanic/Latino), 100 international. Average age 30. *Faculty:* 53 full-time (19 women), 10 part-time/adjunct (3 women). Expenses: Contact institution. *Financial support:* Fellowships, teaching assistantships, career-related internships or fieldwork, Federal Work-Study, and institutionally sponsored loans available. In 2016, 99 master's, 1 doctorate awarded. *Program availability:* Part-time, blended/hybrid learning. Offers accounting (MBA); business (MA, MBA, MS, PhD); business administration (PhD); business analytics (MBA); corporate finance (MBA); design and human environment (MA, MS, PhD); innovation management (MBA); organizational leadership (MBA); research thesis (MBA); supply chain and logistics management (MBA). *Application fee:* $75 ($85 for international students). *Application Contact:* Dr. Jim Coakley, Associate Dean for Academic Programs, 541-737-5510, E-mail: jim.coakley@bus.oregonstate.edu. *Dean*, Dr. Mitzi Montoya.

College of Earth, Ocean, and Atmospheric Sciences Students: 122 full-time (66 women), 7 part-time (2 women); includes 12 minority (3 Asian, non-Hispanic/Latino; 6 Hispanic/Latino; 3 Two or more races, non-Hispanic/Latino), 17 international. Average age 29. *Faculty:* 66 full-time (18 women), 11 part-time/adjunct (4 women). Expenses: Contact institution. *Financial support:* Fellowships, research assistantships, teaching assistantships, career-related internships or fieldwork, Federal Work-Study, and institutionally sponsored loans available. Support available to part-time students. Financial award application deadline: 1/5. In 2016, 32 master's, 15 doctorates awarded. Offers atmospheric sciences (MA, MS, PhD); earth, ocean, and atmospheric sciences (MA, MS, PhD); geographic information science (MA, MS, PhD); geological oceanography (MA, MS, PhD); geophysics (MA, MS, PhD); marine resource management (MA, MS); ocean ecology and biogeochemistry (MA, MS, PhD); physical geography (MA, MS, PhD); physical oceanography (MA, MS, PhD); resource geography (MA, MS, PhD); solid earth processes and history (MA, MS, PhD); surface earth processes and history (MA, MS, PhD). *Application deadline:* For fall admission, 1/5 for domestic students. *Application fee:* $75 ($85 for international students). *Application Contact:* Robert Allan, Director of Graduate Student Services and Development, 541-737-1340, E-mail: rallan@coas.oregonstate.edu. *Dean and Professor*, Dr. Roberta Marinelli.

College of Education Students: 163 full-time (122 women), 256 part-time (190 women); includes 88 minority (14 Black or African American, non-Hispanic/Latino; 3 American Indian or Alaska Native, non-Hispanic/Latino; 15 Asian, non-Hispanic/Latino; 32 Hispanic/Latino; 2 Native Hawaiian or other Pacific Islander, non-Hispanic/Latino; 22 Two or more races, non-Hispanic/Latino), 4 international. Average age 36. *Faculty:* 47

full-time (29 women), 37 part-time/adjunct (23 women). Expenses: Contact institution. *Financial support:* Fellowships, research assistantships, teaching assistantships, career-related internships or fieldwork, Federal Work-Study, and institutionally sponsored loans available. Support available to part-time students. In 2016, 162 master's, 32 doctorates awarded. *Program availability:* Part-time, 100% online, blended/hybrid learning. Offers adult and higher education (Ed M, Ed D, PhD); advanced science and mathematics education (Ed M); agricultural education (PhD); clinical mental health (M Coun); clinically based elementary education (MAT); counseling (MS, PhD); education (Ed M, M Coun, MAT, MS, Ed D, PhD); elementary education (MAT); free-choice learning (Ed M); language arts (MAT); language equity and educational policy (PhD); mathematics (MAT); mathematics education (MS); music education (MAT); pre-K-12 English to speakers of other languages (ESOL) (Ed M); school counseling (M Coun); science (MAT); science education (MS); science/mathematics education (PhD); social justice in education (Ed M); social studies (MAT). *Application fee:* $75 ($85 for international students). *Dean,* Dr. Larry Flick.

College of Engineering Students: 1,068 full-time (239 women), 188 part-time (53 women); includes 115 minority (8 Black or African American, non-Hispanic/Latino; 1 American Indian or Alaska Native, non-Hispanic/Latino; 48 Asian, non-Hispanic/Latino; 33 Hispanic/Latino; 1 Native Hawaiian or other Pacific Islander, non-Hispanic/Latino; 24 Two or more races, non-Hispanic/Latino, 700 international. Average age 28. *Faculty:* 193 full-time (37 women), 12 part-time/adjunct (3 women). Expenses: Contact institution. *Financial support:* Fellowships with full tuition reimbursements, research assistantships with full tuition reimbursements, teaching assistantships with full tuition reimbursements, and instructorships available. In 2016, 290 master's, 48 doctorates awarded. *Program availability:* Part-time, 100% online. Offers advanced manufacturing (M Eng, MS, PhD); algorithms and cryptography (M Eng, MS, PhD); analog and mixed signal (M Eng, MS, PhD); application of nuclear techniques (M Eng, MHP, MS, PhD); arms control technology (M Eng, MS, PhD); artificial intelligence and machine learning (M Eng, MS, PhD); artificial intelligence, machine learning and data science (M Eng, PhD); assistive robots (M Eng, MS, PhD); autonomous robots (M Eng, MS, PhD); bio-based products and fuels (M Eng, MS, PhD); biological systems analysis (M Eng, MS, PhD); biomaterials (M Eng, MS, PhD); biomedical devices and instrumentation (M Eng, MS, PhD); bioprocessing (M Eng, MS, PhD); bioremediation (M Eng, MS, PhD); boron neutron capture therapy (MHP, MS, PhD); chemical engineering (MS, PhD); chemistry (MS, PhD); civil engineering (M Eng, MS, PhD); coastal and ocean engineering (M Eng, MS, PhD); communications and signal processing (M Eng, MS, PhD); computer graphics, visualization, and vision (M Eng, MS, PhD); computer systems (M Eng, MS, PhD); computer systems and networking (M Eng, MS, PhD); construction engineering management (M Eng, MS, PhD); ecosystems analysis and modeling (M Eng, MS, PhD); electrical and computer engineering (MS, PhD); emergency response planning (MHP, MS, PhD); energy systems (M Eng, MS, PhD); engineering (M Eng, MHP, MMP, MS, PhD); engineering education (M Eng, MS, PhD); engineering management (M Eng); environmental fluid mechanics (M Eng, MS, PhD); environmental microbiology (M Eng, MS, PhD); environmental modeling (M Eng, MS, PhD); environmental monitoring (MHP, MS, PhD); environmental pathways assessment (MHP, MS, PhD); forest products (MS, PhD); geomatics (M Eng, MS, PhD); geotechnical engineering (M Eng, MS, PhD); human performance engineering (M Eng, MS, PhD); human systems engineering (M Eng, MS, PhD); human-computer interaction (M Eng, MS, PhD); human-robot interaction (M Eng, MS, PhD); information systems engineering (M Eng, MS, PhD); infrastructure materials (M Eng, MS, PhD); legged locomotion (M Eng, MS, PhD); manipulation (M Eng, MS); materials and devices (M Eng, MS, PhD); mathematics (MS, PhD); mechanical engineering (M Eng, MS, PhD); medical health physics (MMP, MS, PhD); medical imaging (M Eng, MS, PhD); mobile robots (M Eng, MS, PhD); multi-robot coordination (M Eng, MS, PhD); multiphase phenomena (M Eng, MS, PhD); nuclear engineering (MS); nuclear instrumentation and applications (M Eng, MS, PhD); nuclear medicine (M Eng, MHP, MS, PhD); nuclear power generation (M Eng, PhD); nuclear reactor engineering (M Eng, MS, PhD); nuclear systems design and modeling (M Eng, MS, PhD); nuclear waste management (M Eng, MS, PhD); numerical methods for reactor analysis (M Eng); physics (MS, PhD); programming languages (M Eng, MS, PhD); radiation detection and instrumentation (MHP, MS, PhD); radiation dosimetry (MHP, MS, PhD); radiation shielding (M Eng, MHP); radio frequencies/microwaves/optoelectronics (M Eng, MS, PhD); software engineering (M Eng, MS, PhD); structural engineering (M Eng, MS, PhD); subsurface flow and transport (M Eng, MS, PhD); systems and computation biology (M Eng, MS, PhD); therapeutic radiologic physics (MS, PhD); transportation engineering (M Eng); water and wastewater treatment (M Eng, MS, PhD); water quality (M Eng, MS, PhD); water resources (M Eng, MS, PhD). *Application fee:* $75 ($85 for international students). *Application Contact:* Dr. Dorthe Wildenschild, Associate Dean for Graduate Programs, E-mail: info@engr.oregonstate.edu. *Dean,* Scott Ashford.

College of Forestry Students: 145 full-time (59 women), 55 part-time (29 women); includes 19 minority (2 American Indian or Alaska Native, non-Hispanic/Latino; 5 Asian, non-Hispanic/Latino; 8 Hispanic/Latino; 4 Two or more races, non-Hispanic/Latino), 38 international. Average age 32. *Faculty:* 54 full-time (12 women), 9 part-time/adjunct (2 women). Expenses: Contact institution. *Financial support:* Fellowships, research assistantships, teaching assistantships, career-related internships or fieldwork, Federal Work-Study, institutionally sponsored loans, and unspecified assistantships available. Support available to part-time students. In 2016, 41 master's, 11 doctorates awarded. *Program availability:* Part-time, 100% online. Offers biodeterioration and materials protection (MS, PhD); chemistry and chemical processing (MS, PhD); engineering for sustainable forestry (MF, MS, PhD); fisheries management (MNR); forest biology (MF); forest biometrics and geomatics (MF, MS, PhD); forest operations planning and management (MF, MS, PhD); forest policy analysis and economics (MF, MS, PhD); forest products business and marketing (MS, PhD); forest watershed management (MF, MS, PhD); forest, wildlife and landscape ecology (MS, PhD); forestry (MF, MNR, MS, PhD); forests and climate change (MNR); genetics and physiology (MS, PhD); geographic information science (MNR); integrated social and ecological systems (MS, PhD); physics and moisture relations (MS, PhD); process modeling and analysis (MS, PhD); renewable materials sciences and engineered composites (MS, PhD); science of conservation, restoration and sustainable management (MS, PhD); silviculture (MF); silviculture, fire, and forest health (MF, MS, PhD); social science, policy, and natural resources (MS, PhD); soil-plant-atmosphere continuum (MS, PhD); sustainable natural resources (MNR); sustainable recreation and tourism (MS); urban forestry (MNR); water conflict management and transformation (MNR); wildlife management (MNR); wood anatomy and quality (MS, PhD); wood engineering and mechanics (MS, PhD). *Application fee:* $75 ($85 for international students). *Application Contact:* Helene Serewis, College of Forestry Graduate Programs Manager, E-mail: forestry.gradprograms@oregonstate.edu. *Dean,* Dr. Thomas Maness.

College of Liberal Arts Students: 249 full-time (175 women), 34 part-time (21 women); includes 63 minority (5 Black or African American, non-Hispanic/Latino; 3 American Indian or Alaska Native, non-Hispanic/Latino; 10 Asian, non-Hispanic/Latino; 28 Hispanic/Latino; 1 Native Hawaiian or other Pacific Islander, non-Hispanic/Latino; 16 Two or more races, non-Hispanic/Latino), 43 international. Average age 31. *Faculty:* 141 full-time (66 women), 20 part-time/adjunct (14 women). Expenses: Contact institution. *Financial support:* Fellowships, research assistantships, teaching assistantships, career-related internships or fieldwork, Federal Work-Study, and institutionally sponsored loans available. Support available to part-time students. In 2016, 92 master's, 4 doctorates awarded. *Program availability:* Part-time. Offers applied anthropology (MA, PhD); applied cognition (MS, PhD); biomedical ethics (MA); college student services administration (Ed M, MS); contemporary Hispanic studies (MA); development of the physical, biological, and environmental sciences (MA, MS, PhD); energy policy (MPP, PhD); engineering psychology (MS, PhD); environmental action (MA); environmental ethics (MA); environmental imagination (MA); environmental policy (MPP, PhD); environmental thinking (MA); ethics and religion (MA); feminist leadership (PhD); fiction (MFA); gender, rhetoric, and representation (PhD); global justice, peace, and war (MA); health and gender justice (PhD); health psychology (MS, PhD); history of science and medicine (MA, MS, PhD); intellectual and social history of science in Europe and the U.S. (MA, MS, PhD); international policy (MPP, PhD); law, crime, and policy (MPP, PhD); liberal arts (Ed M, MA, MFA, MPP, MS, PhD); literature and culture (MA); nonfiction writing (MFA); poetry (MFA); rhetoric, writing, and culture (MA); rural policy (MPP, PhD); science and technology policy (MPP, PhD); social justice (MA); social justice theory and practice (PhD); social policy (MPP, PhD). *Application fee:* $60. *Dean,* Dr. Larry Rodgers.

College of Pharmacy Students: 367 full-time (202 women), 4 part-time (2 women); includes 181 minority (6 Black or African American, non-Hispanic/Latino; 134 Asian, non-Hispanic/Latino; 20 Hispanic/Latino; 1 Native Hawaiian or other Pacific Islander, non-Hispanic/Latino; 20 Two or more races, non-Hispanic/Latino), 20 international. Average age 27. *Faculty:* 32 full-time (15 women). Expenses: Contact institution. *Financial support:* Career-related internships or fieldwork available. In 2016, 3 master's, 95 doctorates awarded. Offers biopharmaceutics (MS, PhD); medicinal chemistry (MS, PhD); natural products chemistry (MS, PhD); pharmaceutics (MS, PhD); pharmacoeconomics (MS, PhD); pharmacokinetics (MS, PhD); pharmacology (MS, PhD); pharmacy (MS, PhD, Pharm D); toxicology (MS, PhD). *Application Contact:* Angela Austin Haney, Director of Student Services/Head Advisor, 541-737-5784, E-mail: angela.austinhaney@oregonstate.edu. *Dean,* Dr. Mark Zabriskie.

College of Public Health and Human Sciences Students: 214 full-time (158 women), 21 part-time (15 women); includes 72 minority (3 Black or African American, non-Hispanic/Latino; 3 American Indian or Alaska Native, non-Hispanic/Latino; 15 Asian, non-Hispanic/Latino; 33 Hispanic/Latino; 18 Two or more races, non-Hispanic/Latino), 27 international. Average age 30. *Faculty:* 76 full-time (42 women), 8 part-time/adjunct (5 women). Expenses: Contact institution. *Financial support:* Institutionally sponsored loans available. In 2016, 69 master's, 22 doctorates awarded. Offers athletic training (MATRN); biophysical kinesiology (MS, PhD); biostatistics (MPH); environmental and occupational health and safety (MPH, PhD); epidemiology (MPH, PhD); health management and policy (MPH); health policy (PhD); health promotion and health behavior (MPH, PhD); human development and family studies (MS, PhD); international health (MPH); nutrition (MS, PhD); psychosocial kinesiology (MS, PhD); public health and human sciences (MATRN, MPH, MS, PhD). Electronic applications accepted. *Application Contact:* Suzanna Chase, Manager of Admissions, Applications and Recruitment of Graduate Students, E-mail: suzanna.chase@oregonstate.edu. *Dean and Professor,* Dr. F. Javier Nieto.

College of Science Students: 401 full-time (159 women), 11 part-time (5 women); includes 60 minority (4 Black or African American, non-Hispanic/Latino; 1 American Indian or Alaska Native, non-Hispanic/Latino; 22 Asian, non-Hispanic/Latino; 19 Hispanic/Latino; 14 Two or more races, non-Hispanic/Latino), 110 international. Average age 28. *Faculty:* 124 full-time (44 women), 13 part-time/adjunct (7 women). Expenses: Contact institution. In 2016, 44 master's, 39 doctorates awarded. *Program availability:* Part-time. Offers actuarial science (MA, MS, PhD); algebra (MA, MS, PhD); analysis (MA, MS, PhD); analytical chemistry (MA, MS, PhD); applied mathematics (MA, MS, PhD); atomic physics (MA, MS, PhD); behavioral ecology (MA, MS, PhD); behavioral endocrinology (MA, MS, PhD); biochemistry and biophysics (MA, MS, PhD); cell biology (MA, MS, PhD); chemical ecology (MA, MS); computational mathematics (MA, MS, PhD); computational physics (MA, MS, PhD); conservation biology (MA, MS, PhD); data analytics (MA); developmental biology (MA, MS, PhD); differential equations (MA, MS, PhD); environmental microbiology (MA, MS, PhD); evolutionary biology (MA, MS, PhD); financial mathematics (MA, MS, PhD); food microbiology (MA, MS, PhD); genetics (MA, MS, PhD); genomics (MA, MS, PhD); geometry (MA, MS, PhD); immunology (MA, MS, PhD); inorganic chemistry (MA, MS, PhD); materials chemistry (MA, MS, PhD); mathematics education (MA); microbial ecology (MA, MS, PhD); microbial evolution (MA, MS, PhD); nuclear chemistry (MA, MS, PhD); nuclear physics (MA, MS, PhD); optical physics (MA, MS, PhD); organic chemistry (MA, MS, PhD); parasitology (MA, MS, PhD); particle physics (MA, MS, PhD); pathogenic microbiology (MA, MS, PhD); physical chemistry (MA, MS, PhD); physics education (MA, MS, PhD); relativity (MA, MS, PhD); science (MA, MS, PhD); solid state physics (MA, MS, PhD); statistics (MA, MS, PhD); virology (MA). *Application fee:* $75 ($85 for international students). *Application Contact:* E-mail: science@oregonstate.edu. *Dean,* Dr. Sastry Pantula.

College of Veterinary Medicine Students: 218 full-time (185 women), 3 part-time (2 women); includes 34 minority (1 American Indian or Alaska Native, non-Hispanic/Latino; 11 Asian, non-Hispanic/Latino; 16 Hispanic/Latino; 6 Two or more races, non-Hispanic/Latino), 2 international. Average age 27. *Faculty:* 43 full-time (20 women), 6 part-time/adjunct (all women). Expenses: Contact institution. *Financial support:* Fellowships and research assistantships available. In 2016, 59 doctorates awarded. Offers veterinary medicine (DVM). DVM admissions open only to residents of Oregon and other states participating in the Western Interstate Commission for Higher Education. *Application deadline:* For fall admission, 9/15 for domestic and international students. *Application Contact:* Admissions, 541-737-2098, E-mail: cvmproginfo@oregonstate.edu. *Dean,* Dr. Susan J. Tornquist.

Interdisciplinary/Institutional Programs Students: 162 full-time (96 women), 32 part-time (19 women); includes 33 minority (6 Black or African American, non-Hispanic/Latino; 1 American Indian or Alaska Native, non-Hispanic/Latino; 9 Asian, non-Hispanic/Latino; 12 Hispanic/Latino; 5 Two or more races, non-Hispanic/Latino), 34 international. Average age 31. Expenses: Contact institution. In 2016, 37 master's, 13 doctorates awarded. *Program availability:* Part-time. Offers biogeochemistry (MA, MS, PhD); bioinformatics (PhD); biomedical sciences (MS, PhD); biotechnology (PhD); cell biology (PhD); developmental biology (PhD); ecology (MA, MS, PhD); environmental education (MA, MS, PhD); environmental sciences (PSM); genome biology (PhD); groundwater engineering (MS, PhD); interdisciplinary studies (MAIS); molecular biology (PhD); molecular pathogenesis (PhD); molecular virology (PhD); natural resources (MA, MS, PhD); plant molecular biology (PhD); quantitative analysis (MA, MS, PhD); social science (MA, MS, PhD); structural biology (PhD); surface water engineering (MS, PhD); water resources (MA, MS, PhD); water resources policy and management (MS); water resources science (MS, PhD); watershed engineering (MS, PhD). *Application fee:* $75 ($85 for international students). *Application Contact:* E-mail: graduate.admissions@oregonstate.edu. *Vice Provost/Dean,* Dr. Jennifer Brown.

OREGON STATE UNIVERSITY–CASCADES, Bend, OR 97701
General Information State-supported, coed, comprehensive institution.

GRADUATE UNITS

Program in Counseling Offers community counseling (MS); school counseling (MS).
Program in Education Offers education (MAT).

OTIS COLLEGE OF ART AND DESIGN, Los Angeles, CA 90045-9785
General Information Independent, coed, comprehensive institution. *Graduate housing:* On-campus housing not available.

GRADUATE UNITS

Program in Fine Arts Offers new genres (MFA); painting (MFA); photography (MFA); sculpture (MFA). Electronic applications accepted.
Program in Graphic Design Offers graphic design (MFA). Electronic applications accepted.
Program in Public Practice Offers public practice (MFA). Electronic applications accepted.
Program in Writing Offers writing (MFA). Electronic applications accepted.

OTTAWA UNIVERSITY, Ottawa, KS 66067-3399
General Information Independent-religious, coed, comprehensive institution. *Graduate housing:* On-campus housing not available.

GRADUATE UNITS

Graduate Studies-Arizona *Program availability:* Part-time, evening/weekend, online learning. Offers business administration (MBA); Christian counseling (MA); community college counseling (MA); curriculum and instruction (MA); early childhood (MA); education intervention (MA); education leadership (MA); education technology (MA); expressive arts therapy (MA); finance (MBA); human resources (MA, MBA); leadership (MBA); marketing (MBA); marriage and family therapy (MA); Montessori early childhood education (MA); Montessori elementary education (MA); professional development (MA); school guidance counseling (MA); special education - cross categorical (MA); treatment of trauma, abuse and deprivation (MA). Electronic applications accepted.
Graduate Studies-International *Program availability:* Online learning. Offers business administration (MBA). Electronic applications accepted.
Graduate Studies-Kansas City *Program availability:* Part-time, evening/weekend, online learning. Offers business administration (MBA); human resources (MA). Electronic applications accepted.
Graduate Studies-Wisconsin *Program availability:* Part-time, evening/weekend, online learning. Offers business administration (MBA). Electronic applications accepted.

OTTERBEIN UNIVERSITY, Westerville, OH 43081
General Information Independent-religious, coed, comprehensive institution. CGS member. *Graduate housing:* On-campus housing not available.

GRADUATE UNITS

Department of Business, Accounting and Economics *Program availability:* Part-time, evening/weekend. Offers business, accounting and economics (MBA).
Department of Education Offers education (MAE, MAT).
Department of Nursing *Program availability:* Part-time, evening/weekend, online learning. Offers advanced practice nurse educator (Certificate); clinical nurse leader (MSN); family nurse practitioner (MSN, Certificate); nurse anesthesia (MSN, Certificate); nursing (DNP); nursing service administration (MSN).

OUR LADY OF THE LAKE COLLEGE, Baton Rouge, LA 70808
General Information Independent-religious, coed, comprehensive institution. *Graduate housing:* On-campus housing not available.

GRADUATE UNITS

School of Arts, Sciences and Health Professions Offers health administration (MHA); physician assistant studies (MMS).
School of Nursing Offers administration (MS); education (MS); nurse anesthesia (MS); nursing (MS).

OUR LADY OF THE LAKE UNIVERSITY, San Antonio, TX 78207-4689
General Information Independent-religious, coed, comprehensive institution. *Enrollment:* 3,130 graduate, professional, and undergraduate students; 1,654 full-time matriculated graduate/professional students (1,314 women), 122 part-time matriculated graduate/professional students (93 women). *Graduate faculty:* 72 full-time (51 women), 118 part-time/adjunct (66 women). *Tuition:* Full-time $14,796. Tuition and fees vary according to course load, degree level, campus/location and program. *Graduate housing:* Room and/or apartments available on a first-come, first-served basis to single students; on-campus housing not available to married students. Typical cost: $4300 per year ($7872 including board). Room and board charges vary according to housing facility selected. Housing application deadline: 7/15. *Student services:* Campus employment opportunities, campus safety program, career counseling, exercise/wellness program, free psychological counseling, international student services, low-cost health insurance, services for students with disabilities, teacher training. *Library facilities:* The Sueltenfuss Library. *Collection:* Books: 71,610 (physical), 51,161 (digital/electronic); Serial titles: 416 (physical), 60,823 (digital/electronic); Databases: 53. Weekly public service hours: 95; study areas open 24 hours, 5–7 days a week. *Research affiliation:* Texas Higher Education Coordinating Board: Teacher Quality (education), Texas Regional Collaborative (education).

Computer facilities: 230 computers available on campus for general student use. A campuswide network can be accessed from student residence rooms and from off campus. Online class registration is available.
Website: http://www.ollusa.edu/

General Application Contact: Graduate Admissions Office, 210-431-3995, Fax: 210-431-3945, E-mail: gradadm@ollusa.edu.

GRADUATE UNITS

College of Arts and Sciences Expenses: Contact institution. *Financial support:* Federal Work-Study, scholarships/grants, unspecified assistantships, and tuition discounts available. Support available to part-time students. Financial award application deadline: 5/1; financial award applicants required to submit FAFSA. *Program availability:* Part-time, evening/weekend. Offers arts and sciences (MA); literature, creative writing, and

social justice (MA). *Application deadline:* For fall admission, 4/15 for domestic and international students; for spring admission, 11/15 for domestic and international students; for summer admission, 2/15 for domestic and international students. Electronic applications accepted. *Application Contact:* Graduate Admission, 210-431-3995, Fax: 210-431-3945, E-mail: gradadm@lake.ollusa.edu. *Dean for the College of Arts and Science,* Dr. Michael Laney, 210-431-4170, E-mail: mjlaney@lake.ollusa.edu.
College of Professional Studies Students: 1,059 full-time (950 women), 59 part-time (51 women); includes 713 minority (253 Black or African American, non-Hispanic/Latino; 8 American Indian or Alaska Native, non-Hispanic/Latino; 9 Asian, non-Hispanic/Latino; 426 Hispanic/Latino; 3 Native Hawaiian or other Pacific Islander, non-Hispanic/Latino; 14 Two or more races, non-Hispanic/Latino), 1 international. Average age 34. 565 applicants, 66% accepted, 226 enrolled. *Faculty:* 36 full-time (30 women), 73 part-time/adjunct (54 women). Expenses: Contact institution. *Financial support:* In 2016–17, 111 students received support. Research assistantships, teaching assistantships, Federal Work-Study, scholarships/grants, unspecified assistantships, and tuition discounts available. Support available to part-time students. Financial award application deadline: 5/1; financial award applicants required to submit FAFSA. In 2016, 251 master's, 9 doctorates awarded. *Program availability:* Part-time, evening/weekend, 100% online, blended/hybrid learning. Offers communication and learning disorders (MA); counseling psychology (Psy D); integrated science teaching (M Ed); marriage and family therapy (MS); school counseling (M Ed); school psychology (MS); sociology (MA). *Application fee:* $40 ($50 for international students). Electronic applications accepted. *Application Contact:* Graduate Admissions, 210-431-3995 Ext. 2314, Fax: 210-431-3945, E-mail: gradadm@lake.ollusa.edu. *Dean,* Dr. Marcheta Evans, 210-431-4140, E-mail: sps@ollusa.edu.
School of Business and Leadership Students: 585 full-time (357 women), 53 part-time (32 women); includes 477 minority (62 Black or African American, non-Hispanic/Latino; 3 American Indian or Alaska Native, non-Hispanic/Latino; 11 Asian, non-Hispanic/Latino; 392 Hispanic/Latino; 2 Native Hawaiian or other Pacific Islander, non-Hispanic/Latino; 7 Two or more races, non-Hispanic/Latino), 5 international. Average age 39. 229 applicants, 79% accepted, 134 enrolled. *Faculty:* 15 full-time (all women), 42 part-time/adjunct (10 women). Expenses: Contact institution. *Financial support:* In 2016–17, 128 students received support. Teaching assistantships, Federal Work-Study, unspecified assistantships, and tuition discounts available. Support available to part-time students. Financial award application deadline: 5/1; financial award applicants required to submit FAFSA. In 2016, 131 master's, 25 doctorates awarded. *Program availability:* Part-time, evening/weekend, 100% online, blended/hybrid learning. Offers accounting (MS); finance (MBA); healthcare management (MBA); information systems and security (MS); leadership studies (PhD); management (MBA); nonprofit management (MS); organizational leadership (MS). *Application fee:* $40 ($50 for international students). Electronic applications accepted. *Dean for the School of Business and Leadership,* Dr. Dwayne Banks, 210-434-6711 Ext. 5561, E-mail: sbdean@ollusa.edu.
Worden School of Social Service Students: 776 full-time (694 women), 8 part-time (7 women); includes 490 minority (220 Black or African American, non-Hispanic/Latino; 8 American Indian or Alaska Native, non-Hispanic/Latino; 5 Asian, non-Hispanic/Latino; 241 Hispanic/Latino; 3 Native Hawaiian or other Pacific Islander, non-Hispanic/Latino; 13 Two or more races, non-Hispanic/Latino). Average age 34. 248 applicants, 93% accepted, 121 enrolled. *Faculty:* 9 full-time (all women), 45 part-time/adjunct (34 women). Expenses: Contact institution. *Financial support:* In 2016–17, 35 students received support, including 1 research assistantship (averaging $15,300 per year); teaching assistantships, Federal Work-Study, scholarships/grants, unspecified assistantships, and tuition discounts also available. Support available to part-time students. Financial award application deadline: 5/1; financial award applicants required to submit FAFSA. In 2016, 185 master's awarded. *Program availability:* Part-time, evening/weekend, 100% online, blended/hybrid learning. Offers social work (MSW). *Application deadline:* For fall admission, 6/15 for domestic and international students; for spring admission, 11/15 for domestic and international students; for summer admission, 4/15 for domestic and international students. Applications are processed on a rolling basis. *Application fee:* $40 ($50 for international students). Electronic applications accepted. *Application Contact:* Office of Graduate Admissions, 210-431-3995, Fax: 210-431-3945, E-mail: gradadm@lake.ollusa.edu. *Program Director,* Rebecca Gomez, 210-434-6711 Ext. 5578, E-mail: rjgomez@ollusa.edu.

OXFORD GRADUATE SCHOOL, Dayton, TN 37321-6736
General Information Independent-religious, coed, graduate-only institution. *Enrollment by degree level:* 20 master's, 85 doctoral. *Graduate faculty:* 10 full-time (2 women), 22 part-time/adjunct (7 women). *Graduate housing:* Rooms and/or apartments guaranteed to single students and available on a first-come, first-served basis to married students. *Student services:* Campus employment opportunities, campus safety program, international student services, services for students with disabilities, teacher training, writing training. *Collection:* Study areas open 24 hours, 5–7 days a week; students can reserve study rooms.

Computer facilities: 4 computers available on campus for general student use. A campuswide network can be accessed from student residence rooms and from off campus. Online class registration is available.
Website: http://www.ogs.edu/

General Application Contact: Gwen Bollant, Director of Admissions, 423-775-6596, Fax: 423-775-6599, E-mail: oxfordgraduateschool@ogs.edu.

GRADUATE UNITS

Graduate Programs Students: 105 full-time (40 women). *Faculty:* 10 full-time (2 women), 22 part-time/adjunct (7 women). Expenses: Contact institution. Offers family life education (M Litt); integration of religion and society (D Phil); organizational leadership (M Litt). *Application Contact:* Gwen Ballant, Director of Admissions, 423-775-6596, Fax: 423-775-6599, E-mail: oxfordgraduateschool@ogs.edu.

PACE UNIVERSITY, New York, NY 10038
General Information Independent, coed, university. *Enrollment:* 9,149 graduate, professional, and undergraduate students; 2,346 full-time matriculated graduate/professional students (1,285 women), 1,985 part-time matriculated graduate/professional students (1,314 women). *Enrollment by degree level:* 3,369 master's, 920 doctoral, 42 other advanced degrees. *Tuition:* Part-time $1195 per credit. *Required fees:* $260 per semester. Tuition and fees vary according to degree level, campus/location and program. *Graduate housing:* Room and/or apartments available on a first-come, first-served basis to single students; on-campus housing not available to married students. *Student services:* Campus employment opportunities, career counseling, free psychological counseling, grant writing training, international student services, low-cost health insurance, multicultural affairs office, services for students with disabilities, teacher training, writing training. *Library facilities:* Henry Birnbaum Library.

Collection: Books: 176,661 (physical), 193,680 (digital/electronic); Serial titles: 75 (physical), 143,640 (digital/electronic); Databases: 208. Weekly public service hours: 93; students can reserve study rooms.

Computer facilities: 156 computers available on campus for general student use. A campuswide network can be accessed from student residence rooms and from off campus. Online class registration, administrative functions (tuition, student records, financial aid, health insurance waiver) are available. Website: http://www.pace.edu/nyc

General Application Contact: Susan Ford-Goldschein, Director of Graduate Admissions, 212-346-1531, Fax: 212-346-1585, E-mail: graduateadmission@pace.edu.

GRADUATE UNITS

College of Health Professions Students: 153 full-time (118 women), 441 part-time (405 women); includes 260 minority (110 Black or African American, non-Hispanic/Latino; 4 American Indian or Alaska Native, non-Hispanic/Latino; 92 Asian, non-Hispanic/Latino; 43 Hispanic/Latino; 11 Two or more races, non-Hispanic/Latino). Average age 32. 1,300 applicants, 11% accepted, 121 enrolled. *Faculty:* 22 full-time (20 women), 31 part-time/adjunct (27 women). Expenses: Contact institution. *Financial support:* Research assistantships, teaching assistantships, career-related internships or fieldwork, institutionally sponsored loans, scholarships/grants, and unspecified assistantships available. Financial award application deadline: 2/15; financial award applicants required to submit FAFSA. In 2016, 248 master's, 20 doctorates awarded. *Program availability:* Part-time. Offers health professions (MS, DNP, PhD, CAGS); physician assistant studies (MS). *Application deadline:* For fall admission, 3/1 for domestic students; for spring admission, 9/1 for domestic students. Applications are processed on a rolling basis. *Application fee:* $70. Electronic applications accepted. *Application Contact:* Susan Ford-Goldschein, Dean of Graduate Admissions, 212-346-1531, Fax: 212-346-1585, E-mail: graduateadmission@pace.edu. *Dean, College of Health Professions,* Dr. Harriet R. Feldman, 914-773-3341, Fax: 914-773-3341, E-mail: hfeldman@pace.edu.

Lienhard School of Nursing Students: 403 part-time (374 women); includes 207 minority (103 Black or African American, non-Hispanic/Latino; 3 American Indian or Alaska Native, non-Hispanic/Latino; 66 Asian, non-Hispanic/Latino; 30 Hispanic/Latino; 5 Two or more races, non-Hispanic/Latino). Average age 34. 291 applicants, 69% accepted, 129 enrolled. *Faculty:* 11 full-time (10 women), 31 part-time/adjunct (27 women). Expenses: Contact institution. *Financial support:* Research assistantships, teaching assistantships, career-related internships or fieldwork, Federal Work-Study, institutionally sponsored loans, tuition waivers (partial), and unspecified assistantships available. Support available to part-time students. Financial award application deadline: 2/15; financial award applicants required to submit FAFSA. In 2016, 117 master's, 17 doctorates, 4 other advanced degrees awarded. *Program availability:* Part-time. Offers adult acute care nurse practitioner (MS, CAGS); family nurse practitioner (MS, CAGS); nursing (DNP, PhD); professional nursing leadership (MS, CAGS). *Application deadline:* For fall admission, 3/1 for domestic and international students. Applications are processed on a rolling basis. *Application fee:* $70. Electronic applications accepted. *Application Contact:* Susan Ford-Goldschein, Director of Graduate Admissions, 212-346-1531, Fax: 212-346-1585, E-mail: graduateadmission@pace.edu. *Dean, College of Health Professions,* Dr. Harriet R. Feldman, 914-773-3341, E-mail: hfeldman@pace.edu.

Dyson College of Arts and Sciences Students: 455 full-time (325 women), 267 part-time (213 women); includes 277 minority (119 Black or African American, non-Hispanic/Latino; 1 American Indian or Alaska Native, non-Hispanic/Latino; 39 Asian, non-Hispanic/Latino; 97 Hispanic/Latino; 1 Native Hawaiian or other Pacific Islander, non-Hispanic/Latino; 20 Two or more races, non-Hispanic/Latino), 75 international. Average age 28. Expenses: Contact institution. *Financial support:* In 2016–17, 34 research assistantships with partial tuition reimbursements (averaging $2,918 per year) were awarded; teaching assistantships, career-related internships or fieldwork, Federal Work-Study, scholarships/grants, and tuition waivers (partial) also available. Support available to part-time students. Financial award application deadline: 2/15; financial award applicants required to submit FAFSA. In 2016, 250 master's, 20 doctorates awarded. *Program availability:* Part-time, evening/weekend, 100% online, blended/hybrid learning. Offers acting (MFA); arts and sciences (MA, MFA, MPA, MS, MS Ed, PhD, Psy D, Certificate); biochemistry and molecular biology (MS); book publishing (Certificate); business side of publishing (Certificate); digital publishing (Certificate); directing (MFA); environmental science (MS); forensic science (MS); government management (MPA); grief and loss (MS); health care administration (MPA); magazine publishing (Certificate); management for public safety and homeland security professionals (MA); media and communication arts (MA); mental health counseling (MS, PhD); not-for-profit management (MPA); playwriting (MFA); psychology (MA, MS, MS Ed, PhD, Psy D); publishing (MS); school psychology (MS Ed); school-clinical child psychology (MS Ed, Psy D); substance abuse (MS). *Application deadline:* For fall admission, 8/1 for domestic students, 6/1 for international students; for spring admission, 12/1 for domestic students, 10/1 for international students. Applications are processed on a rolling basis. *Application fee:* $70. Electronic applications accepted. *Application Contact:* Susan Ford-Goldschein, Director of Admissions, 212-346-1531, Fax: 212-346-1585, E-mail: graduateadmission@pace.edu. *Dean,* Dr. Nira Herrmann, 212-346-1517, Fax: 212-346-1725, E-mail: nherrmann@pace.edu.

Elisabeth Haub School of Law Students: 516 full-time (274 women), 63 part-time (36 women); includes 150 minority (30 Black or African American, non-Hispanic/Latino; 2 American Indian or Alaska Native, non-Hispanic/Latino; 23 Asian, non-Hispanic/Latino; 58 Hispanic/Latino; 37 Two or more races, non-Hispanic/Latino), 2 international. Average age 26. 1,423 applicants, 56% accepted, 206 enrolled. *Faculty:* 26 full-time (11 women), 52 part-time/adjunct (19 women). Expenses: Contact institution. *Financial support:* In 2016–17, 430 students received support. Fellowships, research assistantships, career-related internships or fieldwork, Federal Work-Study, institutionally sponsored loans, scholarships/grants, and unspecified assistantships available. Support available to part-time students. Financial award application deadline: 2/1; financial award applicants required to submit FAFSA. In 2016, 20 master's, 171 doctorates awarded. *Program availability:* Part-time. Offers comparative legal studies (LL M); environmental law (LL M, SJD); law (JD). JD/MA offered jointly with Sarah Lawrence College; JD/MEM offered jointly with Yale University School of Forestry and Environmental Studies. *Application deadline:* For fall admission, 6/1 priority date for domestic students; for winter admission, 11/15 priority date for domestic students. Applications are processed on a rolling basis. *Application fee:* $65. Electronic applications accepted. *Application Contact:* Cathy Alexander, Assistant Dean, 914-422-4210, Fax: 914-989-8714, E-mail: calexander@law.pace.edu. *Dean,* David Yassky, 914-422-4407, E-mail: dyassky@law.pace.edu.

Lubin School of Business Students: 525 full-time (274 women), 409 part-time (216 women); includes 235 minority (59 Black or African American, non-Hispanic/Latino; 2 American Indian or Alaska Native, non-Hispanic/Latino; 109 Asian, non-Hispanic/Latino;

52 Hispanic/Latino; 1 Native Hawaiian or other Pacific Islander, non-Hispanic/Latino; 12 Two or more races, non-Hispanic/Latino), 432 international. Average age 29. 1,148 applicants, 64% accepted, 300 enrolled. Expenses: Contact institution. *Financial support:* Research assistantships, career-related internships or fieldwork, Federal Work-Study, and tuition waivers (full and partial) available. Support available to part-time students. Financial award application deadline: 2/15; financial award applicants required to submit FAFSA. In 2016, 409 master's, 4 doctorates awarded. *Program availability:* Part-time, evening/weekend, blended/hybrid learning. Offers analytics and customer intelligence (MS); business (MBA, MS, DPS, APC); business economics (APC); change management (MBA); e-business (APC); entrepreneurial studies (MBA); entrepreneurship (MS); finance (DPS); financial management (MBA, MS, APC); financial risk management (MS); human resource management (MBA, MS); information systems (MBA); international business (MBA); international economics (APC); international finance (MBA); investment management (MBA, MS, APC); management (DPS); marketing (DPS, APC); marketing management (MBA); public accounting (MBA, MS, APC); social media and mobile marketing (MS); strategic management (MBA, MS); taxation (MBA, MS). *Application deadline:* For fall admission, 8/1 priority date for domestic students, 6/1 for international students; for spring admission, 12/1 priority date for domestic students, 10/1 for international students; for summer admission, 5/1 priority date for domestic students, 3/1 for international students. Applications are processed on a rolling basis. *Application fee:* $70. Electronic applications accepted. *Application Contact:* Susan Ford-Goldschein, Director of Graduate Admissions, 212-346-1531, Fax: 212-346-1585, E-mail: graduateadmission@pace.edu. *Dean, Lubin School of Business,* Neil S. Braun, 212-618-6600, Fax: 212-618-6603, E-mail: nbraun@pace.edu.

School of Education Students: 115 full-time (97 women), 543 part-time (381 women); includes 280 minority (137 Black or African American, non-Hispanic/Latino; 1 American Indian or Alaska Native, non-Hispanic/Latino; 40 Asian, non-Hispanic/Latino; 87 Hispanic/Latino; 15 Two or more races, non-Hispanic/Latino), 13 international. Average age 30. 181 applicants, 78% accepted, 72 enrolled. *Faculty:* 19 full-time (13 women), 86 part-time/adjunct (49 women). Expenses: Contact institution. *Financial support:* In 2016–17, 17 students received support, including 17 research assistantships with partial tuition reimbursements available (averaging $6,020 per year); career-related internships or fieldwork and Federal Work-Study also available. Financial award application deadline: 9/1; financial award applicants required to submit FAFSA. In 2016, 193 master's, 9 other advanced degrees awarded. *Program availability:* Part-time, evening/weekend, blended/hybrid learning. Offers adolescent education (MST); childhood education (MST); early childhood development, learning and intervention (MST); educational technology studies (MS); inclusive adolescent education (MST); integrated instruction for educational technology (Certificate); integrated instruction for literacy and technology (Certificate); literacy (MS Ed); special education (MS Ed). *Application deadline:* For fall admission, 8/1 priority date for domestic students, 6/1 for international students; for spring admission, 12/1 priority date for domestic students, 10/1 for international students. Applications are processed on a rolling basis. *Application fee:* $70. Electronic applications accepted. *Application Contact:* Susan Ford-Goldschein, Director of Graduate Admissions, 212-346-1531, Fax: 212-346-1585, E-mail: graduateadmission@pace.edu. *Dean, School of Education,* Dr. Xiao-Lei Wang, 914-773-3876, E-mail: xwang@pace.edu.

Seidenberg School of Computer Science and Information Systems Students: 537 full-time (175 women), 303 part-time (85 women); includes 192 minority (79 Black or African American, non-Hispanic/Latino; 3 American Indian or Alaska Native, non-Hispanic/Latino; 53 Asian, non-Hispanic/Latino; 49 Hispanic/Latino; 8 Two or more races, non-Hispanic/Latino), 486 international. Average age 32. 599 applicants, 89% accepted, 248 enrolled. *Faculty:* 26 full-time (7 women), 7 part-time/adjunct (2 women). Expenses: Contact institution. *Financial support:* In 2016–17, 45 students received support. Research assistantships, career-related internships or fieldwork, scholarships/grants, and unspecified assistantships available. Support available to part-time students. Financial award application deadline: 2/15; financial award applicants required to submit FAFSA. In 2016, 180 master's, 19 doctorates, 1 other advanced degree awarded. *Program availability:* Part-time, evening/weekend, online only, 100% online, blended/hybrid learning. Offers chief information security officer (APC); computer science (MS, PhD); enterprise analytics (MS); information and communication technology strategy and innovation (APC); information systems (MS, APC); Internet technology (MS); professional studies in computing (DPS); secure software and information engineering (APC); security and information assurance (Certificate); software development and engineering (MS, Certificate); telecommunications systems and networks (MS, Certificate). *Application deadline:* For fall admission, 8/1 priority date for domestic students, 6/1 for international students; for spring admission, 12/1 for domestic students, 10/1 for international students. Applications are processed on a rolling basis. *Application fee:* $70. Electronic applications accepted. *Application Contact:* Susan Ford-Goldschein, Director of Graduate Admissions, 914-422-4283, Fax: 212-346-1585, E-mail: graduateadmission@pace.edu. *Dean, Seidenberg School of Computer Science and Information Systems,* Dr. Jonathan Hill, 212-346-1864, E-mail: jhill@pace.edu.

PACIFICA GRADUATE INSTITUTE, Carpinteria, CA 93013

General Information Proprietary, coed, graduate-only institution. *Graduate housing:* Rooms and/or apartments guaranteed to single and married students. Housing application deadline: 8/15. *Research affiliation:* Elton B. Stevens Company (EBSCO) (journal management), American Psychological Association (psychology), North California Consortium of Psychology Libraries (psychology).

GRADUATE UNITS

Graduate Programs Offers clinical psychology (PhD); counseling psychology (MA); depth psychology (MA, PhD); mythological studies (MA, PhD).

PACIFIC COLLEGE OF ORIENTAL MEDICINE, San Diego, CA 92108

General Information Proprietary, coed, graduate-only institution. *Graduate housing:* On-campus housing not available. *Research affiliation:* National Institutes of Health (complimentary and alternative medicine).

GRADUATE UNITS

Graduate Program *Program availability:* Part-time, evening/weekend. Offers Oriental medicine (MSTOM, DAOM).

PACIFIC COLLEGE OF ORIENTAL MEDICINE–CHICAGO, Chicago, IL 60601

General Information Proprietary, coed, graduate-only institution. *Graduate housing:* On-campus housing not available. *Research affiliation:* Children's Memorial Hospital of Chicago (pediatric research).

GRADUATE UNITS

Graduate Program *Program availability:* Part-time, evening/weekend. Offers oriental medicine (MTOM).

PACIFIC COLLEGE OF ORIENTAL MEDICINE-NEW YORK, New York, NY 10010

General Information Proprietary, coed, graduate-only institution. *Graduate housing:* On-campus housing not available.

GRADUATE UNITS

Graduate Program *Program availability:* Part-time, evening/weekend. Offers Oriental medicine (MSTOM).

PACIFIC LUTHERAN UNIVERSITY, Tacoma, WA 98447

General Information Independent-religious, coed, comprehensive institution. *Graduate housing:* Rooms and/or apartments available on a first-come, first-served basis to single and married students. Housing application deadline: 5/1.

GRADUATE UNITS

Division of Humanities *Program availability:* Part-time, blended/hybrid learning. Offers creative writing (MFA). Electronic applications accepted.

Division of Social Sciences Offers marriage and family therapy (MA). Electronic applications accepted.

School of Business *Program availability:* Part-time, evening/weekend. Offers accounting (MSA); business (MBA, MS, MSA, MSF); business administration (MBA); finance (MSF); market research (MS). Electronic applications accepted.

School of Education and Kinesiology *Program availability:* Part-time, evening/weekend. Offers education and kinesiology (MAE); initial teaching certification (MAE). Electronic applications accepted.

School of Nursing Offers entry level nursing (MSN); nursing (MSN, DNP). Electronic applications accepted.

PACIFIC NORTHWEST COLLEGE OF ART, Portland, OR 97209

General Information Independent, coed, comprehensive institution.

GRADUATE UNITS

Program in Applied Craft and Design Offers applied craft and design (MFA). Program offered in collaboration with Oregon College of Art & Craft.

Program in Collaborative Design Offers collaborative design (MFA).

Program in Critical Theory and Creative Research Offers critical theory and creative research (MA).

Program in Visual Studies Offers visual studies (MFA).

PACIFIC NORTHWEST UNIVERSITY OF HEALTH SCIENCES, Yakima, WA 98901

General Information Independent, coed, graduate-only institution. *Enrollment by degree level:* 569 doctoral. *Graduate faculty:* 19 full-time (7 women), 27 part-time/adjunct (7 women). *Tuition:* Full-time $51,500. *Graduate housing:* On-campus housing not available. *Student services:* Campus employment opportunities, campus safety program, career counseling, exercise/wellness program, free psychological counseling. *Library facilities:* PNWU Library. *Collection:* Books: 970 (physical), 240 (digital/electronic); Serial titles: 64 (physical), 33,915 (digital/electronic); Databases: 9. Weekly public service hours: 45; study areas open 24 hours, 5–7 days a week. *Research affiliation:* Yakima Valley Community Foundation (health care), Arnold P. Gold Foundation (health care), Health Resources and Services Administration (health care).

Computer facilities: 20 computers available on campus for general student use. A campuswide network can be accessed. Online class registration is available. Website: http://www.pnwu.edu/

General Application Contact: Mike Riggin, Assistant Director, Student Recruitment, 509-249-7740, Fax: 509-249-7907, E-mail: admission@pnwu.edu.

GRADUATE UNITS

College of Osteopathic Medicine Students: 567 full-time (270 women), 2 part-time (both women); includes 165 minority (4 Black or African American, non-Hispanic/Latino; 2 American Indian or Alaska Native, non-Hispanic/Latino; 86 Asian, non-Hispanic/Latino; 40 Hispanic/Latino; 1 Native Hawaiian or other Pacific Islander, non-Hispanic/Latino; 32 Two or more races, non-Hispanic/Latino). Average age 28. 4,270 applicants, 6% accepted, 146 enrolled. *Faculty:* 19 full-time (7 women), 27 part-time/adjunct (7 women). Expenses: Contact institution. *Financial support:* In 2016–17, 25 students received support. Scholarships/grants and tuition waivers (full and partial) available. Financial award applicants required to submit FAFSA. In 2016, 71 doctorates awarded. Offers osteopathic medicine (DO). *Application deadline:* For fall admission, 2/1 for domestic and international students. *Application fee:* $85. Electronic applications accepted. *Dean,* Dr. Thomas Scandalis, 509-249-7803, E-mail: vkoch@pnwu.edu.

PACIFIC OAKS COLLEGE, Pasadena, CA 91103

General Information Independent, coed, primarily women, upper-level institution. *Graduate housing:* Room and/or apartments available to single students; on-campus housing not available to married students.

GRADUATE UNITS

Graduate School *Program availability:* Part-time, evening/weekend, online learning. Offers early childhood education (MA); human development (MA); marriage, family and child counseling (MA); preliminary education specialist (MA); preliminary multiple subject (MA).

PACIFIC RIM CHRISTIAN UNIVERSITY, Honolulu, HI 96819

General Information Independent-religious, coed, comprehensive institution.

GRADUATE UNITS

Program in Christian Ministry Offers Christian ministry (MA).

PACIFIC SCHOOL OF RELIGION, Berkeley, CA 94709-1323

General Information Independent, coed, graduate-only institution. *Graduate housing:* Rooms and/or apartments guaranteed to single and married students. Housing application deadline: 4/1. *Research affiliation:* Center for Women and Religion (women's studies), Center for Ethics and Social Policy (business ethics), Disciples Seminary Foundation (theology), Swedenborgian House of Studies (theology), Bay Area Faith and Health Consortium (public health).

GRADUATE UNITS

Graduate and Professional Programs *Program availability:* Part-time. Offers religion (M Div, MA, MTS, D Min, PhD, Th D, CAPS, CMS, CSS, CTS). MA, PhD, Th D offered jointly with Graduate Theological Union; D Min with Church Divinity School of the Pacific. Electronic applications accepted.

PACIFIC STATES UNIVERSITY, Los Angeles, CA 90010

General Information Independent, coed, comprehensive institution. *Graduate housing:* Room and/or apartments available on a first-come, first-served basis to single students; on-campus housing not available to married students.

GRADUATE UNITS

College of Business *Program availability:* Part-time, evening/weekend, online learning. Offers accounting (MBA); finance (MBA); international business (MBA, DBA); management of information technology (MBA); real estate management (MBA).

College of Computer Science and Information Systems *Program availability:* Part-time, evening/weekend. Offers computer science (MS); information systems (MS).

PACIFIC UNION COLLEGE, Angwin, CA 94508-9707

General Information Independent-religious, coed, comprehensive institution. *Enrollment:* 1 (woman) full-time matriculated graduate/professional student, 5 part-time matriculated graduate/professional students (3 women). *Enrollment by degree level:* 6 master's. *Graduate faculty:* 3 full-time (1 woman), 1 (woman) part-time/adjunct. *Tuition:* Part-time $405 per quarter hour. *Required fees:* $210 per quarter. Tuition and fees vary according to student's religious affiliation. *Graduate housing:* On-campus housing not available. *Student services:* Teacher training. *Library facilities:* W.E. Nelson Memorial Library.

Computer facilities: A campuswide network can be accessed from student residence rooms and from off campus. Online class registration, student financial information are available.
Website: http://www.puc.edu/

General Application Contact: Cherith Mundy, Credential Analyst, 707-965-6643, Fax: 707-965-6645, E-mail: teachingcredentials@puc.edu.

GRADUATE UNITS

Education Department Students: 1 (woman) full-time, 5 part-time (3 women); includes 1 minority (Hispanic/Latino). Average age 41. *Faculty:* 3 full-time (1 woman), 1 (woman) part-time/adjunct. Expenses: Contact institution. *Financial support:* Scholarships/grants available. Support available to part-time students. In 2016, 1 master's awarded. *Program availability:* Part-time. Offers education (M Ed); elementary teaching (MAT); secondary teaching (MAT). *Application deadline:* For summer admission, 6/1 for domestic students. Applications are processed on a rolling basis. *Application fee:* $0. *Application Contact:* Cherith Mundy, Credential Analyst, 707-965-6643, Fax: 707-965-6645, E-mail: teachingcredentials@puc.edu. *Department Chair,* Prof. Thomas Lee, 707-965-6646, Fax: 707-965-6645, E-mail: tdlee@puc.edu.

PACIFIC UNIVERSITY, Forest Grove, OR 97116-1797

General Information Independent, coed, comprehensive institution. *Graduate housing:* On-campus housing not available. *Research affiliation:* NEI/PEDIG–JAEB Center of Health Research (amblyopia treatment), BSK, CIBA Vision (contact lenses), Cooper Vision (contact lenses), The Ohio State University/Vistakon-Johnson & Johnson (adolescent and child vision care).

GRADUATE UNITS

College of Business Offers business administration (MBA); finance (MSF).

College of Education *Program availability:* Part-time, evening/weekend. Offers early childhood education (MAT); education (MAE); elementary education (MAT); ESOL (MAT); high school education (MAT); middle school education (MAT); special education (MAT); speech-language pathology (MS); STEM education (MAT); talented and gifted (M Ed); visual function in learning (M Ed). Electronic applications accepted.

College of Optometry Offers optometry (OD); vision science (MS, PhD). Electronic applications accepted.

Healthcare Administration Program Offers healthcare administration (MHA).

Program in Social Work Offers social work (MSW).

Program in Writing *Program availability:* Part-time. Offers writing (MFA).

School of Audiology Offers audiology (Au D).

School of Occupational Therapy Offers occupational therapy (OTD). Electronic applications accepted.

School of Pharmacy Offers pharmacy (Pharm D). Electronic applications accepted.

School of Physical Therapy Offers athletic training (MSAT); physical therapy (DPT). Electronic applications accepted.

School of Physician Assistant Studies Offers physician assistant studies (MS).

School of Professional Psychology *Program availability:* Part-time. Offers applied psychological science (MA, MS); clinical psychology (PhD, Psy D). Electronic applications accepted.

PALM BEACH ATLANTIC UNIVERSITY, West Palm Beach, FL 33416-4708

General Information Independent-religious, coed, comprehensive institution. *Enrollment:* 3,764 graduate, professional, and undergraduate students; 741 full-time matriculated graduate/professional students (513 women), 97 part-time matriculated graduate/professional students (59 women). *Enrollment by degree level:* 520 master's, 318 doctoral. *Graduate faculty:* 35 full-time (18 women), 65 part-time/adjunct (36 women). *Tuition:* Full-time $6600; part-time $550 per credit hour. Full-time tuition and fees vary according to degree level, campus/location and program. *Graduate housing:* On-campus housing not available. *Student services:* Campus employment opportunities, campus safety program, career counseling, exercise/wellness program, services for students with disabilities, writing training. *Library facilities:* Warren Library plus 1 other. *Collection:* Books: 141,300 (physical), 123,825 (digital/electronic); Serial titles: 142 (physical), 133,086 (digital/electronic); Databases: 90. Weekly public service hours: 97; students can reserve study rooms.

Computer facilities: 350 computers available on campus for general student use. A campuswide network can be accessed from student residence rooms and from off campus. Online class registration is available.
Website: http://www.pba.edu/

General Application Contact: Joseph Bryan, Assistant Vice President for Admissions, 888-468-6722, E-mail: grad@pba.edu.

GRADUATE UNITS

Gregory School of Pharmacy Students: 268 full-time (163 women), 28 part-time (17 women); includes 168 minority (43 Black or African American, non-Hispanic/Latino; 44

Asian, non-Hispanic/Latino; 65 Hispanic/Latino; 1 Native Hawaiian or other Pacific Islander, non-Hispanic/Latino; 15 Two or more races, non-Hispanic/Latino; 9 international. Average age 27. 554 applicants, 29% accepted, 75 enrolled. *Faculty:* 24 full-time (14 women), 14 part-time/adjunct (9 women). Expenses: Contact institution. *Financial support:* In 2016–17, 51 students received support. Scholarships/grants and employee education grants available. Financial award application deadline: 5/1; financial award applicants required to submit FAFSA. In 2016, 67 doctorates awarded. Offers pharmacy (Pharm D). *Application deadline:* For fall admission, 3/1 priority date for domestic and international students. Applications are processed on a rolling basis. *Application fee:* $150. Electronic applications accepted. *Application Contact:* Lucas Whittaker, Director of Pharmacy Admissions, 561-803-2751, E-mail: lucas_whittaker@pba.edu. *Dean,* Dr. Jeff Lewis, 561-803-2701, E-mail: jeff_lewis@pba.edu.

MacArthur School of Leadership Students: 59 full-time (40 women), 16 part-time (8 women); includes 49 minority (24 Black or African American, non-Hispanic/Latino; 2 Asian, non-Hispanic/Latino; 18 Hispanic/Latino; 5 Two or more races, non-Hispanic/Latino; 2 international. Average age 39. 27 applicants, 96% accepted, 19 enrolled. *Faculty:* 8 part-time/adjunct (1 woman). Expenses: Contact institution. *Financial support:* Scholarships/grants and employee education grants available. Financial award application deadline: 5/1; financial award applicants required to submit FAFSA. In 2016, 37 master's awarded. *Program availability:* Part-time, evening/weekend, blended/hybrid learning. Offers leadership (MS). *Application deadline:* Applications are processed on a rolling basis. *Application fee:* $50. Electronic applications accepted. *Application Contact:* Graduate Admissions, 888-468-6722, E-mail: grad@pba.edu. *Dean,* Dr. Craig Domeck, 561-803-2318, E-mail: craig_domeck@pba.edu.

Rinker School of Business Students: 71 full-time (37 women), 21 part-time (7 women); includes 34 minority (15 Black or African American, non-Hispanic/Latino; 4 Asian, non-Hispanic/Latino; 13 Hispanic/Latino; 1 Native Hawaiian or other Pacific Islander, non-Hispanic/Latino; 1 Two or more races, non-Hispanic/Latino), 22 international. Average age 31. 32 applicants, 97% accepted, 25 enrolled. *Faculty:* 1 full-time (0 women), 9 part-time/adjunct (4 women). Expenses: Contact institution. *Financial support:* Scholarships/grants and employee education grants available. Financial award application deadline: 5/1; financial award applicants required to submit FAFSA. In 2016, 34 master's awarded. *Program availability:* Part-time, evening/weekend. Offers business (MACC, MBA). *Application deadline:* Applications are processed on a rolling basis. *Application fee:* $50. Electronic applications accepted. *Application Contact:* Graduate Admissions, 888-468-6722, Fax: 561-803-2115, E-mail: grad@pba.edu. *MBA Program Director,* Dr. David Smith, 561-803-2473, E-mail: david_smith@pba.edu.

School of Education and Behavioral Studies Students: 243 full-time (206 women), 29 part-time (24 women); includes 147 minority (67 Black or African American, non-Hispanic/Latino; 4 Asian, non-Hispanic/Latino; 60 Hispanic/Latino; 1 Native Hawaiian or other Pacific Islander, non-Hispanic/Latino; 15 Two or more races, non-Hispanic/Latino), 6 international. Average age 35. 81 applicants, 89% accepted, 53 enrolled. *Faculty:* 8 full-time (2 women), 17 part-time/adjunct (13 women). Expenses: Contact institution. *Financial support:* In 2016–17, 11 students received support. Career-related internships or fieldwork, scholarships/grants, and employee education grants available. Financial award application deadline: 5/1; financial award applicants required to submit FAFSA. In 2016, 122 master's awarded. *Program availability:* Part-time, evening/weekend. Offers counseling psychology (MS). *Application deadline:* Applications are processed on a rolling basis. *Application fee:* $50. Electronic applications accepted. *Application Contact:* Graduate Admissions, 888-468-6722, E-mail: grad@pba.edu. *Program Director,* Dr. Gene Sale, 561-803-2352.

School of Ministry Students: 36 full-time (12 women), 1 part-time (0 women); includes 10 minority (2 Black or African American, non-Hispanic/Latino; 7 Hispanic/Latino; 1 Two or more races, non-Hispanic/Latino), 1 international. Average age 28. 26 applicants, 88% accepted, 16 enrolled. *Faculty:* 10 part-time/adjunct (2 women). Expenses: Contact institution. *Financial support:* In 2016–17, 25 students received support. Scholarships/grants, unspecified assistantships, and employee education grants available. Financial award application deadline: 5/1; financial award applicants required to submit FAFSA. In 2016, 7 master's awarded. *Program availability:* Part-time. Offers Christian studies (MA); ministry (M Div). *Application deadline:* Applications are processed on a rolling basis. *Application fee:* $50. Electronic applications accepted. *Application Contact:* Graduate Admissions, 888-468-6722, E-mail: grad@pba.edu. *Director of the M Div Program,* Dr. Jonathan Grenz, 561-803-2622.

School of Nursing Students: 63 full-time (55 women), 2 part-time (both women); includes 28 minority (16 Black or African American, non-Hispanic/Latino; 2 Asian, non-Hispanic/Latino; 9 Hispanic/Latino; 1 Two or more races, non-Hispanic/Latino). Average age 32. 35 applicants, 91% accepted, 14 enrolled. *Faculty:* 2 full-time (both women), 7 part-time/adjunct (all women). Expenses: Contact institution. *Financial support:* In 2016–17, 13 students received support. Scholarships/grants and employee education grants available. Financial award application deadline: 5/1; financial award applicants required to submit FAFSA. In 2016, 3 doctorates awarded. *Program availability:* Part-time. Offers family nurse practitioner (DNP); health systems leadership (MSN). *Application deadline:* Applications are processed on a rolling basis. *Application fee:* $50. Electronic applications accepted. *Application Contact:* Graduate Admissions, 888-468-6722, E-mail: grad@pba.edu. *Dean,* Joanne Masella, 561-803-2827.

PALMER COLLEGE OF CHIROPRACTIC, Davenport, IA 52803-5287

General Information Independent, coed, comprehensive institution. *Enrollment:* 2,225 full-time matriculated graduate/professional students (797 women), 18 part-time matriculated graduate/professional students (5 women). *Enrollment by degree level:* 14 master's, 2,229 doctoral. *Graduate faculty:* 135 full-time (55 women), 35 part-time/adjunct (18 women). One-time fee: $150 part-time. Tuition and fees vary according to campus/location. *Student services:* Campus employment opportunities, campus safety program, career counseling, child daycare facilities, exercise/wellness program, free psychological counseling, international student services, low-cost health insurance, services for students with disabilities. *Library facilities:* David D. Palmer Health Sciences Library.

Computer facilities: 94 computers available on campus for general student use. A campuswide network can be accessed.
Website: http://www.palmer.edu/

General Application Contact: Karen Eden, Director of Admissions, 563-884-5656, Fax: 563-884-5414, E-mail: pcadmit@palmer.edu.

GRADUATE UNITS

Division of Graduate Studies Students: 7 full-time (2 women), 1 (woman) part-time; includes 1 minority (Black or African American, non-Hispanic/Latino). 3 applicants, 100% accepted, 3 enrolled. *Faculty:* 8 full-time (3 women), 3 part-time/adjunct (2 women). Expenses: Contact institution. *Financial support:* In 2016–17, 7 students

received support, including 7 research assistantships with full tuition reimbursements available (averaging $30,000 per year), teaching assistantships with tuition reimbursements available (averaging $6,269 per year); tuition waivers (full) and unspecified assistantships also available. Financial award application deadline: 8/1; financial award applicants required to submit FAFSA. In 2016, 3 master's awarded. *Program availability:* Part-time. Offers clinical research (MS). *Application deadline:* For fall admission, 8/1 for domestic and international students; for spring admission, 5/28 for domestic students. Applications are processed on a rolling basis. *Application fee:* $50. Electronic applications accepted. *Application Contact:* Lori Byrd, Program Coordinator, 563-884-5198, Fax: 563-884-5227, E-mail: lori.byrd@plamer.edu. *Interim Vice President for Academic Affairs,* Dr. Dan Weinert, 563-884-5761, Fax: 563-884-5624, E-mail: weinert_d@palmer.edu.

Professional Program Expenses: Contact institution. *Financial support:* In 2016–17, 391 students received support. Career-related internships or fieldwork, Federal Work-Study, and scholarships/grants available. Financial award application deadline: 4/1; financial award applicants required to submit FAFSA. *Program availability:* Part-time. Offers chiropractic (DC). *Application deadline:* Applications are processed on a rolling basis. *Application fee:* $50. Electronic applications accepted. *Application Contact:* Karen Eden, Senior Director of Admissions, 563-884-5656, Fax: 563-884-5414, E-mail: pcadmit@palmer.edu. *Chancellor,* Dr. Dennis Marchiori, 563-884-5466, Fax: 563-884-5624, E-mail: marchiori_d@palmer.edu.

Professional Program–Florida Campus Expenses: Contact institution. *Financial support:* In 2016–17, 140 students received support. Career-related internships or fieldwork, Federal Work-Study, and scholarships/grants available. Financial award application deadline: 4/1; financial award applicants required to submit FAFSA. In 2016, 225 doctorates awarded. *Program availability:* Part-time. Offers chiropractic (DC). *Application fee:* $50. *Application Contact:* Admissions Representative, 866-585-9677, Fax: 386-763-2620, E-mail: pcaf_admiss@palmer.edu. *Chancellor,* Dr. Dennis Marchiori, 563-884-5511, Fax: 563-884-5409, E-mail: marchiori_d@palmer.edu.

Professional Program–West Campus Expenses: Contact institution. *Financial support:* In 2016–17, 231 students received support. Career-related internships or fieldwork, Federal Work-Study, and scholarships/grants available. Financial award application deadline: 4/1; financial award applicants required to submit FAFSA. In 2016, 117 doctorates awarded. *Program availability:* Part-time. Offers chiropractic (DC). *Application deadline:* Applications are processed on a rolling basis. *Application fee:* $50. Electronic applications accepted. *Application Contact:* Julie Behn, Campus Enrollment Director, 408-944-6121, Fax: 408-944-6032, E-mail: julie.behn@palmer.edu.

PALO ALTO UNIVERSITY, Palo Alto, CA 94304

General Information Independent, coed, upper-level institution. *Enrollment:* 740 full-time matriculated graduate/professional students (589 women), 233 part-time matriculated graduate/professional students (193 women). *Enrollment by degree level:* 355 master's, 450 doctoral. *Graduate faculty:* 48 full-time (31 women), 79 part-time/adjunct (51 women). *Tuition:* Full-time $44,919; part-time $1048 per unit. *Required fees:* $5076. Tuition and fees vary according to degree level and program. *Graduate housing:* On-campus housing not available. *Student services:* Campus employment opportunities, international student services, services for students with disabilities.
Website: http://www.paloaltou.edu/

General Application Contact: Eirian Williams, Director of Admissions, 800-818-6136, E-mail: admissions@paloaltou.edu.

GRADUATE UNITS

MA in Counseling Program Students: 38 full-time (34 women), 28 part-time (22 women); includes 29 minority (3 Black or African American, non-Hispanic/Latino; 9 Asian, non-Hispanic/Latino; 14 Hispanic/Latino; 3 Two or more races, non-Hispanic/Latino), 1 international. Average age 32. 111 applicants, 91% accepted, 89 enrolled. *Faculty:* 6 full-time (4 women), 5 part-time/adjunct (4 women). Expenses: Contact institution. *Financial support:* In 2016–17, 12 students received support. Federal Work-Study and scholarships/grants available. Financial award application deadline: 1/15; financial award applicants required to submit FAFSA. In 2016, 91 master's awarded. *Program availability:* Part-time, 100% online, blended/hybrid learning. Offers clinical mental health (MA); marriage, family and child (MA). *Application deadline:* For fall admission, 6/30 priority date for domestic and international students; for spring admission, 3/21 for domestic and international students. Applications are processed on a rolling basis. *Application fee:* $40. Electronic applications accepted. *Application Contact:* Deanna Berger, Assistant Director of Admissions, 650-417-2023, E-mail: dberger@paloaltou.edu. *Director of Counseling,* Dr. William Snow, 831-246-2440, E-mail: wsnow@paloaltou.edu.

MS in Psychology (PhD Prep) Program Students: 9 full-time (6 women), 38 part-time (31 women); includes 19 minority (3 Black or African American, non-Hispanic/Latino; 7 Asian, non-Hispanic/Latino; 8 Hispanic/Latino; 1 Two or more races, non-Hispanic/Latino), 1 international. Average age 31. 46 applicants, 25 enrolled. *Faculty:* 6 full-time (5 women), 4 part-time/adjunct (3 women). Expenses: Contact institution. *Financial support:* In 2016–17, 1 student received support. Federal Work-Study and scholarships/grants available. Financial award application deadline: 1/15; financial award applicants required to submit FAFSA. In 2016, 12 master's awarded. *Program availability:* Part-time, online learning. Offers psychology (MS). *Application deadline:* For fall admission, 6/30 priority date for domestic and international students. Applications are processed on a rolling basis. *Application fee:* $40. Electronic applications accepted. *Application Contact:* Deanna Berger, Assistant Director of Admissions, 650-417-2023, E-mail: dberger@paloaltou.edu. *Associate Director,* Dr. Kristel Nazzal, 650-417-2022, E-mail: knazzal@paloaltou.edu.

PGSP-Stanford Psy D Consortium Program Students: 155 full-time (129 women), 4 part-time (all women); includes 47 minority (5 Black or African American, non-Hispanic/Latino; 25 Asian, non-Hispanic/Latino; 14 Hispanic/Latino; 3 Two or more races, non-Hispanic/Latino), 3 international. Average age 29. 339 applicants, 17% accepted, 32 enrolled. *Faculty:* 16 full-time (12 women), 31 part-time/adjunct (22 women). Expenses: Contact institution. *Financial support:* In 2016–17, 48 students received support, including fellowships (averaging $4,000 per year), research assistantships (averaging $1,000 per year), teaching assistantships (averaging $3,000 per year); Federal Work-Study and scholarships/grants also available. Financial award application deadline: 1/15; financial award applicants required to submit FAFSA. In 2016, 29 doctorates awarded. Offers psychology (Psy D). Program offered jointly with Stanford University. *Application deadline:* For fall admission, 12/2 priority date for domestic and international students. Applications are processed on a rolling basis. *Application fee:* $50. Electronic applications accepted. *Application Contact:* Dr. Kimberly Hill, Co-Director of Clinical Training, PGSP-Stanford Psy D Consortium, 650-725-5582, E-mail: khill@paloaltou.edu. *Co-Director of Clinical Training, PGSP-Stanford Psy D Consortium,* Dr. Steve Smith, E-mail: stevesmith@paloaltou.edu.

PhD in Clinical Psychology Program Students: 427 full-time (326 women), 9 part-time (all women); includes 132 minority (20 Black or African American, non-Hispanic/Latino; 2

American Indian or Alaska Native, non-Hispanic/Latino; 57 Asian, non-Hispanic/Latino; 41 Hispanic/Latino; 2 Native Hawaiian or other Pacific Islander, non-Hispanic/Latino; 10 Two or more races, non-Hispanic/Latino), 22 international. Average age 32. 251 applicants, 76 enrolled. *Faculty:* 33 full-time (19 women), 39 part-time/adjunct (25 women). Expenses: Contact institution. *Financial support:* In 2016–17, 115 students received support, including fellowships (averaging $7,500 per year), research assistantships (averaging $4,000 per year), teaching assistantships (averaging $3,000 per year); Federal Work-Study and scholarships/grants also available. Financial award application deadline: 1/15; financial award applicants required to submit FAFSA. In 2016, 62 doctorates awarded. Offers clinical psychology (PhD). *Application deadline:* For fall admission, 12/2 priority date for domestic and international students. Applications are processed on a rolling basis. *Application fee:* $50. Electronic applications accepted. *Application Contact:* Eirian Williams, Vice President of Enrollment Management, 800-818-6136, E-mail: admissions@paloaltou.edu. *Director of Clinical Training,* Dr. Rowena Gomez, 650-433-3823, E-mail: rgomez@paloaltou.edu.

PARIS COLLEGE OF ART, 75010 Paris, France
General Information Independent, coed, comprehensive institution.

GRADUATE UNITS

Graduate Programs Offers accessories design (MA); fashion design: new materials and technologies (MA); fashion film and photography (MA); interior design (MA); transdisciplinary new media (MA, MFA).

PARKER UNIVERSITY, Dallas, TX 75229-5668
General Information Independent, coed, graduate-only institution. *Graduate housing:* On-campus housing not available.

GRADUATE UNITS

Doctor of Chiropractic Program *Program availability:* Part-time. Offers chiropractic (DC). Electronic applications accepted.

PARK UNIVERSITY, Parkville, MO 64152-3795
General Information Independent, coed, comprehensive institution. CGS member.

GRADUATE UNITS

School of Graduate and Professional Studies *Program availability:* Part-time, evening/weekend, online learning. Offers adult education (M Ed); business and government leadership (Graduate Certificate); business, government, and global society (MPA); communication and leadership (MA); creative and life writing (Graduate Certificate); disaster and emergency management (MPA, Graduate Certificate); educational leadership (M Ed); finance (MBA, Graduate Certificate); general business (MBA); global business (Graduate Certificate); healthcare administration (MHA); healthcare services management and leadership (Graduate Certificate); international business (MBA); language and literacy (M Ed); leadership of international healthcare organizations (Graduate Certificate); management information systems (MBA, Graduate Certificate); music performance (ADP, Graduate Certificate); nonprofit and community services management (MPA); nonprofit leadership (Graduate Certificate); performance (MM); public management (MPA); social work (MSW); teacher leadership (M Ed). Electronic applications accepted.

PAYNE THEOLOGICAL SEMINARY, Wilberforce, OH 45384-3474
General Information Independent-religious, coed, graduate-only institution. *Graduate housing:* Rooms and/or apartments available on a first-come, first-served basis to single and married students. Housing application deadline: 8/15.

GRADUATE UNITS

Program in Theology *Program availability:* Part-time, evening/weekend, online learning. Offers theology (M Div).

PEIRCE COLLEGE, Philadelphia, PA 19102-4699
General Information Independent, coed, primarily women, comprehensive institution.

GRADUATE UNITS

Program in Organizational Leadership and Management Offers organizational leadership and management (MS).

PENN STATE ERIE, THE BEHREND COLLEGE, Erie, PA 16563
General Information State-related, coed, comprehensive institution. *Enrollment:* 4,566 graduate, professional, and undergraduate students; 28 full-time matriculated graduate/professional students (9 women), 118 part-time matriculated graduate/professional students (31 women). *Enrollment by degree level:* 146 master's. *Graduate housing:* Room and/or apartments available on a first-come, first-served basis to single students; on-campus housing not available to married students. *Student services:* Campus employment opportunities, campus safety program, career counseling, child daycare facilities, exercise/wellness program, free psychological counseling, grant writing training, international student services, low-cost health insurance, multicultural affairs office, services for students with disabilities. *Library facilities:* John M. Lilley Library.

Computer facilities: Computer purchase and lease plans are available. A campuswide network can be accessed from student residence rooms and from off campus. Online class registration is available.
Website: http://www.psbehrend.psu.edu/

General Application Contact: Ann M. Burbules, Assistant Director of Graduate Admissions, 814-898-7255, Fax: 814-898-6044, E-mail: behrend.admissions@psu.edu.

GRADUATE UNITS

Graduate School Students: 28 full-time (9 women), 118 part-time (31 women); includes 11 minority (5 Black or African American, non-Hispanic/Latino; 2 Asian, non-Hispanic/Latino; 1 Hispanic/Latino; 3 Two or more races, non-Hispanic/Latino), 2 international. Average age 32. 91 applicants, 74% accepted, 55 enrolled. Expenses: Contact institution. *Financial support:* Federal Work-Study available. Financial award application deadline: 3/1; financial award applicants required to submit FAFSA. In 2016, 59 master's awarded. *Program availability:* Part-time. Offers accounting (MPAC); business administration (MBA); project management (MPM); quality and manufacturing management (MMM). *Application deadline:* Applications are processed on a rolling basis. *Application fee:* $65. Electronic applications accepted. *Application Contact:* Ann M. Burbules, Assistant Director, Graduate Admissions, 866-374-3378, Fax: 814-898-6044, E-mail: behrend.admissions@psu.edu. *Chancellor,* Dr. Ralph M. Ford, 814-898-6160, Fax: 814-898-6461.

PENN STATE GREAT VALLEY, Malvern, PA 19355-1488
General Information State-related, coed, graduate-only institution. *Enrollment by degree level:* 413 master's. *Graduate housing:* On-campus housing not available.

Student services: Campus employment opportunities, campus safety program, career counseling, grant writing training, international student services, low-cost health insurance, multicultural affairs office, services for students with disabilities. *Library facilities:* Great Valley Library.

Computer facilities: Online class registration is available.
Website: http://www.gv.psu.edu/

General Application Contact: JoAnn Kelly, Director of Admissions, 610-648-3315, Fax: 610-725-5296, E-mail: gvadmiss@psu.edu.

GRADUATE UNITS

Graduate Studies Students: 78 full-time (31 women), 348 part-time (114 women); includes 87 minority (20 Black or African American, non-Hispanic/Latino; 44 Asian, non-Hispanic/Latino; 15 Hispanic/Latino; 1 Native Hawaiian or other Pacific Islander, non-Hispanic/Latino; 7 Two or more races, non-Hispanic/Latino), 58 international. Average age 33. 280 applicants, 56% accepted, 106 enrolled. Expenses: Contact institution. *Financial support:* Fellowships, research assistantships, teaching assistantships, Federal Work-Study, scholarships/grants, health care benefits, and unspecified assistantships available. Support available to part-time students. Financial award application deadline: 3/1; financial award applicants required to submit FAFSA. In 2016, 167 master's awarded. *Program availability:* Part-time, evening/weekend. *Application deadline:* Applications are processed on a rolling basis. *Application fee:* $65. Electronic applications accepted. *Application Contact:* JoAnn Kelly, Director of Admissions, 610-648-3315, Fax: 610-725-5296, E-mail: gvadmiss@psu.edu. *Chancellor,* Dr. James A. Nemes, 610-648-3202, Fax: 610-725-5296.

Engineering Division Expenses: Contact institution. Offers engineering management (MEM); software engineering (MSE); systems engineering (M Eng, Certificate). *Application Contact:* JoAnn Kelly, Director of Admissions, 610-648-3315, Fax: 610-725-5296, E-mail: jek2@psu.edu. *Chancellor,* Dr. James A. Nemes, 610-648-3202 Ext. 610, Fax: 610-725-5296, E-mail: cse1@psu.edu.

Management Division Expenses: Contact institution. Offers business administration (MBA); cyber security (Certificate); data analytics (Certificate); distributed energy and grid modernization (Certificate); finance (M Fin, Certificate); health sector management (Certificate); human resource management (Certificate); information science (MSIS); leadership development (MLD); new ventures and entrepreneurship (Certificate); professional studies in data analytics (MPS); sustainable management practices (Certificate). *Application Contact:* JoAnn Kelly, Director of Admissions, 610-648-3315, Fax: 610-725-5296, E-mail: jek2@psu.edu. *Chancellor,* Dr. James A. Nemes, 610-648-3202, Fax: 610-725-5296.

PENN STATE HARRISBURG, Middletown, PA 17057
General Information State-related, coed, comprehensive institution. *Enrollment:* 5,046 graduate, professional, and undergraduate students; 239 full-time matriculated graduate/professional students (123 women), 607 part-time matriculated graduate/professional students (363 women). *Enrollment by degree level:* 712 master's. *Graduate housing:* Room and/or apartments available on a first-come, first-served basis to single students; on-campus housing not available to married students. *Student services:* Campus employment opportunities, campus safety program, career counseling, child daycare facilities, exercise/wellness program, free psychological counseling, grant writing training, international student services, low-cost health insurance, multicultural affairs office, services for students with disabilities, teacher training, writing training. *Library facilities:* Penn State Harrisburg Library.

Computer facilities: Computer purchase and lease plans are available. A campuswide network can be accessed from student residence rooms and from off campus. Online class registration is available.
Website: http://www.hbg.psu.edu/

General Application Contact: Robert W. Coffman, Jr., Director of Enrollment Management, Recruitment and Admissions, 717-948-6250, Fax: 717-948-6325, E-mail: hbgadmit@psu.edu.

GRADUATE UNITS

Graduate School Students: 239 full-time (123 women), 607 part-time (363 women); includes 118 minority (39 Black or African American, non-Hispanic/Latino; 1 American Indian or Alaska Native, non-Hispanic/Latino; 36 Asian, non-Hispanic/Latino; 30 Hispanic/Latino; 12 Two or more races, non-Hispanic/Latino), 108 international. Average age 32. 731 applicants, 52% accepted, 267 enrolled. Expenses: Contact institution. *Financial support:* Fellowships, research assistantships, teaching assistantships, career-related internships or fieldwork, Federal Work-Study, and unspecified assistantships available. Support available to part-time students. Financial award application deadline: 3/1; financial award applicants required to submit FAFSA. In 2016, 253 master's, 8 doctorates awarded. *Program availability:* Part-time, evening/weekend. *Application deadline:* Applications are processed on a rolling basis. *Application fee:* $65. Electronic applications accepted. *Application Contact:* Robert W. Coffman, Jr., Director of Enrollment Management, Recruitment and Admissions, 717-948-6250, Fax: 717-948-6325, E-mail: hbgadmit@psu.edu. *Chancellor,* Dr. Mukund S. Kulkarni, 717-948-6105, Fax: 717-948-6452.

School of Behavioral Sciences and Education Expenses: Contact institution. *Program availability:* Part-time, evening/weekend. Offers adult education in the health and medical professions (Certificate); applied behavior analysis (MA); applied clinical psychology (MA); applied psychological research (MA); community psychology and social change (MA); English as a second language (ESL) program specialist and leadership (Certificate); folklore and ethnography (Certificate); health education (M Ed); lifelong learning and adult education (M Ed, D Ed); literacy education (M Ed); literacy leadership (Certificate); psychology: applications in clinical psychology (Certificate); psychology: health psychology (Certificate); teaching and curriculum (M Ed); training and development (M Ed, Certificate). *Application Contact:* Robert W. Coffman, Jr., Director of Enrollment Management, Recruitment and Admissions, 717-948-6250, Fax: 717-948-6325, E-mail: hbgadmit@psu.edu. *Chancellor,* Dr. Mukund S. Kulkarni, 717-948-6105, Fax: 717-948-6452.

School of Business Administration Expenses: Contact institution. *Program availability:* Part-time, evening/weekend. Offers accounting (MPAC, Certificate); business administration (MBA); information systems (MS); operations and supply chain management (Certificate). *Application Contact:* Robert W. Coffman, Jr., Director of Enrollment Management, Admissions, 717-948-6250, Fax: 717-948-6325, E-mail: hbgadmit@psu.edu. *Chancellor,* Dr. Mukund S. Kulkarni, 717-948-6105, Fax: 717-948-6452.

School of Humanities Expenses: Contact institution. *Program availability:* Evening/weekend. Offers American studies (MA, PhD); communications (MA); heritage and museum practice (Certificate); humanities (MA); writing instruction specialist (Certificate). *Application Contact:* Robert W. Coffman, Jr., Director of

Enrollment Management, Admissions, 717-948-6250, Fax: 717-948-6325, E-mail: hbgadmit@psu.edu. *Chancellor,* Dr. Mukund S. Kulkarni, 717-948-6105, Fax: 717-948-6452.

School of Public Affairs Expenses: Contact institution. Offers criminal justice (MA); health administration (MHA); health administration: long term care (Certificate); homeland security (Certificate); public administration (MPA, PhD); public administration: non-profit administration (Certificate); public budgeting and financial management (Certificate); public sector human resource management (Certificate). *Application Contact:* Robert W. Coffman, Jr., Director of Enrollment Management, Admissions, 717-948-6250, Fax: 717-948-6325, E-mail: hbgadmit@psu.edu. *Chancellor,* Dr. Mukund S. Kulkarni, 717-948-6105, Fax: 717-948-6452.

School of Science, Engineering and Technology Expenses: Contact institution. *Program availability:* Part-time, evening/weekend. Offers computer science (MS); electrical engineering (M Eng, MS); engineering management (MPS); engineering science (M Eng); environmental engineering (M Eng); environmental pollution control (MEPC, MS); structural engineering (Certificate). *Application Contact:* Robert W. Coffman, Jr., Director of Enrollment Management, Admissions, 717-948-6250, Fax: 717-948-6325, E-mail: hbgadmit@psu.edu. *Chancellor,* Dr. Mukund S. Kulkarni, 717-948-6105, Fax: 717-948-6452.

PENN STATE HERSHEY MEDICAL CENTER, Hershey, PA 17033-2360

General Information State-related, coed, graduate-only institution. *Graduate faculty:* 209 full-time (47 women), 7 part-time/adjunct (3 women). *Graduate housing:* Rooms and/or apartments available on a first-come, first-served basis to single and married students. *Student services:* Campus safety program, career counseling, child daycare facilities, exercise/wellness program, free psychological counseling, grant writing training, international student services, low-cost health insurance, multicultural affairs office, services for students with disabilities, teacher training, writing training. *Library facilities:* George T. Harrell Health Sciences Library.

Computer facilities: Online class registration is available.
Website: http://www.hmc.psu.edu/college/

General Application Contact: Dr. Michael F. Verderame, Associate Dean of Graduate Studies, 717-531-8892, Fax: 717-531-0786, E-mail: grad-hmc@psu.edu.

GRADUATE UNITS

College of Medicine Expenses: Contact institution. *Financial support:* In 2016–17, 99 students received support, including research assistantships with full tuition reimbursements available (averaging $22,260 per year); fellowships with full tuition reimbursements available, career-related internships or fieldwork, scholarships/grants, health care benefits, and unspecified assistantships also available. Offers medicine (MPAS, MPH, MS, Dr PH, MD, PhD). *Application deadline:* Applications are processed on a rolling basis. *Application fee:* $65. Electronic applications accepted. *Application Contact:* Dr. Sheila L. Vrana, Interim Vice Dean for Research and Graduate Studies, 717-531-7199, Fax: 717-531-0786, E-mail: grad-hmc@psu.edu. *Dean,* Dr. A. Craig Hillemeier, 717-531-8323, Fax: 717-531-0786, E-mail: grad-hmc@psu.edu.

Graduate School Programs in the Biomedical Sciences Expenses: Contact institution. *Financial support:* In 2016–17, 3 fellowships with full tuition reimbursements (averaging $27,250 per year), 30 research assistantships with full tuition reimbursements (averaging $26,196 per year) were awarded; career-related internships or fieldwork, scholarships/grants, health care benefits, tuition waivers (full), and unspecified assistantships also available. Offers anatomy (MS, PhD); biochemistry and molecular genetics (MS, PhD); biomedical sciences (MS, PhD); biostatistics (PhD); cell and developmental biology (PhD); cellular and integrative physiology (MS, PhD); laboratory animal medicine (MS); life sciences (MS, PhD); molecular medicine (PhD); molecular toxicology (PhD); neurobiology (PhD); neuroscience (MS, PhD); public health (MPH, Dr PH); public health sciences (MS); translational therapeutics (MS, PhD); virology and immunology (MS, PhD). *Application deadline:* Applications are processed on a rolling basis. *Application fee:* $65. Electronic applications accepted. *Application Contact:* Kristin E. Smith, Director of Graduate Admissions, 717-531-1045, Fax: 717-531-0786, E-mail: kec17@psu.edu. *Associate Dean of Graduate Studies,* Dr. Charles Lang, 717-531-8892, Fax: 717-531-0786, E-mail: grad-hmc@psu.edu.

PENN STATE UNIVERSITY–DICKINSON LAW, Carlisle, PA 17013

General Information State-related, coed, graduate-only institution. *Enrollment by degree level:* 2 master's, 184 doctoral. *Graduate faculty:* 24 full-time (15 women), 15 part-time/adjunct (4 women). Tuition, state resident: full-time $46,176. Tuition, nonresident: full-time $46,176. *Required fees:* $678. *Student services:* Campus employment opportunities, career counseling, exercise/wellness program, free psychological counseling, international student services, low-cost health insurance, services for students with disabilities. *Library facilities:* H. Laddie Montague Jr. Law Library. *Collection:* Books: 105,737 (physical), 50,244 (digital/electronic); Serial titles: 7,320 (physical), 127,906 (digital/electronic); Databases: 167. Weekly public service hours: 43; study areas open 24 hours, 5–7 days a week; students can reserve study rooms.

Computer facilities: 21 computers available on campus for general student use. A campuswide network can be accessed. Online class registration is available.
Website: http://law.psu.edu/

General Application Contact: Bekah A. Saidman-Krauss, Assistant Dean of Admissions and Financial Aid, 717-240-5207, E-mail: ras1075@psu.edu.

GRADUATE UNITS

Graduate and Professional Programs Students: 186 full-time (84 women). *Faculty:* 24 full-time (15 women), 15 part-time/adjunct (4 women). Expenses: Contact institution. *Financial support:* Research assistantships, Federal Work-Study, and scholarships/grants available. Financial award application deadline: 4/15; financial award applicants required to submit FAFSA. Offers law (LL M, JD). *Application deadline:* Applications are processed on a rolling basis. Electronic applications accepted. *Application Contact:* Bekah A. Saidman-Krauss, Assistant Dean of Admissions and Financial Aid, 717-240-5207, E-mail: ras1075@psu.edu. *Dean,* Gary S. Gildin, 717-240-5238, Fax: 717-240-5213, E-mail: gsg2@psu.edu.

PENN STATE UNIVERSITY PARK, University Park, PA 16802

General Information State-related, coed, university. CGS member. *Enrollment:* 47,789 graduate, professional, and undergraduate students; 5,735 full-time matriculated graduate/professional students (2,568 women), 695 part-time matriculated graduate/professional students (345 women). *Enrollment by degree level:* 1,851 master's, 4,579 doctoral. *Graduate housing:* Rooms and/or apartments available on a first-come, first-served basis to single and married students. *Student services:* Campus employment opportunities, campus safety program, career counseling, child daycare facilities, exercise/wellness program, free psychological counseling, grant writing training, international student services, low-cost health insurance, multicultural affairs office, services for students with disabilities, teacher training, writing training. *Library facilities:* Pattee and Paterno Libraries plus 4 others. *Collection:* Books: 4.2 million (physical), 421,000 (digital/electronic); Serial titles: 85,765 (physical), 115,000 (digital/electronic); Databases: 779. Weekly public service hours: 148; study areas open 24 hours, 5–7 days a week; students can reserve study rooms.

Computer facilities: Computer purchase and lease plans are available. 6,200 computers available on campus for general student use. A campuswide network can be accessed from student residence rooms and from off campus. Online class registration is available.
Website: http://www.psu.edu/

General Application Contact: Lori Hawn, Director, Graduate Student Services, 814-865-1795, Fax: 814-863-4627, E-mail: l-gswww@lists.psu.edu.

GRADUATE UNITS

Graduate School Students: 5,221 full-time (2,329 women), 681 part-time (339 women); includes 718 minority (162 Black or African American, non-Hispanic/Latino; 2 American Indian or Alaska Native, non-Hispanic/Latino; 181 Asian, non-Hispanic/Latino; 262 Hispanic/Latino; 6 Native Hawaiian or other Pacific Islander, non-Hispanic/Latino; 105 Two or more races, non-Hispanic/Latino), 2,533 international. Average age 29. 15,170 applicants, 23% accepted, 1907 enrolled. Expenses: Contact institution. *Financial support:* Fellowships, research assistantships, teaching assistantships, career-related internships or fieldwork, Federal Work-Study, scholarships/grants, traineeships, health care benefits, and unspecified assistantships available. Support available to part-time students. Financial award application deadline: 3/1; financial award applicants required to submit FAFSA. In 2016, 1,327 master's, 659 doctorates awarded. *Program availability:* Part-time, evening/weekend, online learning. *Application deadline:* Applications are processed on a rolling basis. *Application fee:* $65. Electronic applications accepted. *Application Contact:* Lori Hawn, Director, Graduate Student Services, 814-865-1795, Fax: 814-863-4627, E-mail: l-gswww@lists.psu.edu. *Vice Provost for Graduate Education/Dean, Graduate School,* Dr. Regina Vasilatos-Younken, 814-865-2516, Fax: 814-863-4627.

College of Agricultural Sciences Students: 308 full-time (177 women), 23 part-time (15 women). Average age 28. 569 applicants, 21% accepted, 84 enrolled. Expenses: Contact institution. *Financial support:* Fellowships, research assistantships, teaching assistantships, career-related internships or fieldwork, Federal Work-Study, scholarships/grants, traineeships, health care benefits, and unspecified assistantships available. Support available to part-time students. Financial award application deadline: 3/1; financial award applicants required to submit FAFSA. In 2016, 36 master's, 36 doctorates awarded. Offers agricultural and biological engineering (MS, PhD); agricultural and extension education (M Ed, MS, PhD, Certificate); agricultural sciences (M Ed, MPS, MS, PhD, Certificate); agricultural, environmental and regional economics (MS, PhD); agronomy (MS, PhD); animal science (MPS, MS, PhD); applied youth, family and community education (M Ed); biorenewable systems (MS, PhD); community and economic development (MPS); entomology (MS, PhD); food science (MS, PhD); forest resources (MS, PhD); horticulture (MS, PhD); pathobiology (MS, PhD); plant pathology (MS, PhD); rural sociology (MS, PhD); soil science (MS, PhD); turfgrass management (MPS); wildlife and fisheries science (MS, PhD). *Application deadline:* Applications are processed on a rolling basis. *Application fee:* $65. Electronic applications accepted. *Application Contact:* Lori Hawn, Director, Graduate Student Services, 814-865-1795, Fax: 814-863-4627, E-mail: l-gswww@lists.psu.edu. *Dean,* Dr. Richard T. Roush, 814-865-2541, Fax: 814-865-3103.

College of Arts and Architecture Students: 208 full-time (136 women), 20 part-time (13 women). Average age 30. 558 applicants, 41% accepted, 101 enrolled. Expenses: Contact institution. *Financial support:* Fellowships, research assistantships, teaching assistantships, career-related internships or fieldwork, Federal Work-Study, scholarships/grants, traineeships, health care benefits, and unspecified assistantships available. Support available to part-time students. Financial award application deadline: 3/1; financial award applicants required to submit FAFSA. In 2016, 81 master's, 10 doctorates awarded. Offers architecture (M Arch, MS, PhD); art (MFA); art education (MPS, MS, PhD, Certificate); art history (MA, PhD); arts and architecture (M Arch, M Ed, M Mus, MA, MFA, MLA, MME, MPS, MS, DMA, PhD, Certificate); composition-theory (M Mus); conducting (M Mus); geodesign (MPS); landscape architecture (MLA, MS); music (MA); music education (MME, PhD, Certificate); pedagogy and performance (M Mus); performance (M Mus); piano performance (DMA); theatre (MFA). *Application deadline:* Applications are processed on a rolling basis. *Application fee:* $65. Electronic applications accepted. *Application Contact:* Lori Hawn, Director, Graduate Student Services, 814-865-1795, Fax: 814-863-4627, E-mail: l-gswww@lists.psu.edu. *Dean,* Dr. Barbara O. Korner, 814-865-2592, Fax: 814-865-2018.

College of Communications Students: 42 full-time (31 women), 8 part-time (6 women). Average age 29. 155 applicants, 23% accepted, 11 enrolled. Expenses: Contact institution. *Financial support:* Fellowships, research assistantships, teaching assistantships, career-related internships or fieldwork, Federal Work-Study, scholarships/grants, traineeships, health care benefits, and unspecified assistantships available. Support available to part-time students. Financial award application deadline: 3/1; financial award applicants required to submit FAFSA. In 2016, 1 master's, 7 doctorates awarded. Offers communications (MA, PhD); mass communications (PhD); media studies (MA). *Application deadline:* Applications are processed on a rolling basis. *Application fee:* $65. Electronic applications accepted. *Application Contact:* Lori Hawn, Director, Graduate Student Services, 814-865-1795, Fax: 814-863-4627, E-mail: l-gswww@lists.psu.edu. *Dean,* Dr. Marie C. Hardin, 814-863-1484, Fax: 814-863-8044.

College of Earth and Mineral Sciences Students: 281 full-time (112 women), 24 part-time (7 women). Average age 28. 779 applicants, 16% accepted, 65 enrolled. Expenses: Contact institution. *Financial support:* Fellowships, research assistantships, teaching assistantships, career-related internships or fieldwork, Federal Work-Study, scholarships/grants, traineeships, health care benefits, and unspecified assistantships available. Support available to part-time students. Financial award application deadline: 3/1; financial award applicants required to submit FAFSA. In 2016, 70 master's, 44 doctorates awarded. Offers earth and mineral sciences (M Ed, MGIS, MS, PhD); earth sciences (M Ed); energy and mineral engineering (MS, PhD); geographic information systems (MGIS); geography (MS, PhD); geosciences (MS, PhD); meteorology (MS, PhD). *Application deadline:* Applications are processed on a rolling basis. *Application fee:* $65. Electronic applications accepted. *Application Contact:* Lori Hawn, Director, Graduate Student Services, 814-865-1795, Fax: 814-863-4627, E-mail: l-gswww@lists.psu.edu. *Dean,* Dr. William E. Easterling, III, 814-865-7482, Fax: 814-863-7708.

College of Education Students: 476 full-time (346 women), 221 part-time (130 women). Average age 33. 714 applicants, 42% accepted, 167 enrolled. Expenses: Contact institution. *Financial support:* Fellowships, research assistantships, teaching assistantships, career-related internships or fieldwork, Federal Work-Study, scholarships/grants, traineeships, health care benefits, and unspecified assistantships available. Support available to part-time students. Financial award application deadline: 3/1; financial award applicants required to submit FAFSA. In 2016, 160 master's, 85 doctorates awarded. Offers adult education (M Ed, D Ed, PhD, Certificate); corporate training (MPS); counselor education (M Ed, D Ed, PhD, Certificate); curriculum and instruction (M Ed, MS, PhD, Certificate); education (M Ed, MA, MPS, MS, D Ed, PhD, Certificate); educational leadership (M Ed, D Ed, PhD, Certificate); educational psychology (MS, PhD, Certificate); educational theory and policy (MA, PhD); higher education (M Ed, MS, D Ed, PhD); learning, design, and technology (M Ed, MS, PhD, Certificate); lifelong learning and adult education (M Ed, D Ed, PhD, Certificate); organization development and change (MPS); school psychology (M Ed, MS, PhD, Certificate); special education (M Ed, MS, PhD, Certificate); workforce education and development (M Ed, MS, PhD). *Application deadline:* Applications are processed on a rolling basis. *Application fee:* $65. Electronic applications accepted. *Application Contact:* Lori Hawn, Director, Graduate Student Services, 814-865-1795, Fax: 814-863-4627, E-mail: l-gswww@lists.psu.edu. *Dean,* Dr. David H. Monk, 814-865-2523, Fax: 814-865-0555.

College of Engineering Students: 1,252 full-time (273 women), 125 part-time (22 women). Average age 26. 4,634 applicants, 23% accepted, 521 enrolled. Expenses: Contact institution. *Financial support:* Fellowships, research assistantships, teaching assistantships, career-related internships or fieldwork, Federal Work-Study, scholarships/grants, traineeships, health care benefits, and unspecified assistantships available. Support available to part-time students. Financial award application deadline: 3/1; financial award applicants required to submit FAFSA. In 2016, 305 master's, 149 doctorates awarded. Offers aerospace engineering (M Eng, MS, PhD); architectural engineering (M Eng, MAE, MS, PhD); chemical engineering (MS, PhD); civil engineering (M Eng, MS, PhD); computer science and engineering (M Eng, MS, PhD); electrical engineering (M Eng, MS, PhD); engineering (M Eng, MA, MAE, MFR, MS, PhD); engineering design (M Eng, MS); engineering mechanics (M Eng); engineering science (M Eng); engineering science and mechanics (MS, PhD); environmental engineering (M Eng, MS, PhD); facilities engineering and management (M Eng); industrial engineering (MS, PhD); mechanical engineering (MS, PhD); nuclear engineering (M Eng, MS, PhD). *Application deadline:* Applications are processed on a rolling basis. *Application fee:* $65. Electronic applications accepted. *Application Contact:* Lori Hawn, Director, Graduate Student Services, 814-865-1795, Fax: 814-863-4627, E-mail: l-gswww@lists.psu.edu. *Dean,* Dr. Amr S. Elnashai, 814-865-7537, Fax: 814-863-4749.

College of Health and Human Development Students: 294 full-time (209 women), 22 part-time (17 women). Average age 28. 586 applicants, 27% accepted, 93 enrolled. Expenses: Contact institution. *Financial support:* Fellowships, research assistantships, teaching assistantships, career-related internships or fieldwork, Federal Work-Study, scholarships/grants, traineeships, health care benefits, and unspecified assistantships available. Support available to part-time students. Financial award application deadline: 3/1; financial award applicants required to submit FAFSA. In 2016, 59 master's, 41 doctorates awarded. Offers biobehavioral health (MS, PhD); communication sciences and disorders (MS, PhD, Certificate); health and human development (MHA, MS, PhD, Certificate); health policy and administration (MHA, MS, PhD); hospitality management (MS, PhD); human development and family studies (MS, PhD); kinesiology (MS, PhD, Certificate); nutritional sciences (MS, PhD); recreation, park and tourism management (MS, PhD). *Application deadline:* Applications are processed on a rolling basis. *Application fee:* $65. Electronic applications accepted. *Application Contact:* Lori Hawn, Director, Graduate Student Services, 814-865-1795, Fax: 814-863-4627, E-mail: l-gswww@lists.psu.edu. *Dean,* Dr. Ann C. Crouter, 814-865-1420, Fax: 814-865-3282.

College of Information Sciences and Technology Students: 108 full-time (41 women), 9 part-time (0 women). Average age 28. 262 applicants, 28% accepted, 38 enrolled. Expenses: Contact institution. *Financial support:* Fellowships, research assistantships, teaching assistantships, career-related internships or fieldwork, Federal Work-Study, scholarships/grants, traineeships, health care benefits, and unspecified assistantships available. Support available to part-time students. Financial award application deadline: 3/1; financial award applicants required to submit FAFSA. In 2016, 19 master's, 12 doctorates awarded. Offers enterprise architecture (MPS); information sciences (MPS); information sciences and technology (MS, PhD). *Application deadline:* For fall admission, 12/15 for domestic and international students. Applications are processed on a rolling basis. *Application fee:* $65. Electronic applications accepted. *Application Contact:* Lori Hawn, Director, Graduate Student Services, 814-865-1795, Fax: 814-863-4627, E-mail: l-gswww@lists.psu.edu. *Dean,* Dr. Andrew L. Sears, 814-865-3528, Fax: 814-865-7485.

College of Nursing Students: 53 full-time (43 women), 61 part-time (53 women). Average age 32. 57 applicants, 47% accepted, 21 enrolled. Expenses: Contact institution. *Financial support:* Fellowships, research assistantships, teaching assistantships, career-related internships or fieldwork, Federal Work-Study, scholarships/grants, traineeships, health care benefits, and unspecified assistantships available. Support available to part-time students. Financial award application deadline: 3/1; financial award applicants required to submit FAFSA. In 2016, 37 master's, 3 doctorates awarded. Offers nursing (MS, MSN, DNP, PhD). *Application deadline:* Applications are processed on a rolling basis. *Application fee:* $65. Electronic applications accepted. *Application Contact:* Lori Hawn, Director, Graduate Student Services, 814-865-1795, Fax: 814-863-4627, E-mail: l-gswww@lists.psu.edu. *Dean,* Dr. Paula F. Milone-Nuzzo, 814-863-0245, Fax: 814-865-3779.

College of the Liberal Arts Students: 752 full-time (412 women), 52 part-time (30 women). Average age 28. 2,576 applicants, 17% accepted, 250 enrolled. Expenses: Contact institution. *Financial support:* Fellowships, research assistantships, teaching assistantships, career-related internships or fieldwork, Federal Work-Study, scholarships/grants, traineeships, health care benefits, and unspecified assistantships available. Support available to part-time students. Financial award application deadline: 3/1; financial award applicants required to submit FAFSA. In 2016, 143 master's, 90 doctorates awarded. Offers anthropology (MA, PhD); applied linguistics (PhD); communication arts and sciences (MA, PhD); comparative literature (MA, PhD); criminology (MA, PhD); economics (MA, PhD); English (MA, MFA, PhD); French (MA, PhD); German (MA, PhD); history (MA, PhD); human resources and employment relations (MPS, MS); labor and global workers' rights (MPS); liberal arts (MA, MFA, MPS, MS, PhD); philosophy (MA, PhD); political science (MA, PhD); psychology (MS, PhD); psychology of leadership at work (MPS); Russian and comparative literature (MA); sociology (MA, PhD); Spanish (MA, PhD); teaching English as a second language (MA). *Application deadline:* Applications are processed

on a rolling basis. *Application fee:* $65. Electronic applications accepted. *Application Contact:* Lori Hawn, Director, Graduate Student Services, 814-865-1795, Fax: 814-863-4627, E-mail: l-gswww@lists.psu.edu. *Dean,* Dr. Susan Welch, 814-865-7691, Fax: 814-863-2085.

Eberly College of Science Students: 656 full-time (226 women), 23 part-time (11 women). Average age 26. 1,816 applicants, 19% accepted, 163 enrolled. Expenses: Contact institution. *Financial support:* Fellowships, research assistantships, teaching assistantships, career-related internships or fieldwork, Federal Work-Study, scholarships/grants, traineeships, health care benefits, and unspecified assistantships available. Support available to part-time students. Financial award application deadline: 3/1; financial award applicants required to submit FAFSA. In 2016, 73 master's, 106 doctorates awarded. Offers applied statistics (MAS); astronomy and astrophysics (MS, PhD); biochemistry, microbiology, and molecular biology (MS, PhD); biology (MS, PhD); biotechnology (MBIOT); chemistry (MS, PhD); forensic science (MPS); mathematics (M Ed, MA, D Ed, PhD); physics (M Ed, MS, PhD); science (M Ed, MA, MAS, MBIOT, MPS, MS, D Ed, PhD); statistics (MA, MS, PhD). *Application deadline:* Applications are processed on a rolling basis. *Application fee:* $65. Electronic applications accepted. *Application Contact:* Lori Hawn, Director, Graduate Student Services, 814-865-1795, Fax: 814-863-4627, E-mail: l-gswww@lists.psu.edu. *Dean,* Dr. Douglas R. Cavener, 814-865-9591, Fax: 814-865-3634.

Intercollege Graduate Programs Students: 423 full-time (178 women), 13 part-time (1 woman). Average age 26. 1,055 applicants, 16% accepted, 84 enrolled. Expenses: Contact institution. *Financial support:* Fellowships, research assistantships, teaching assistantships, career-related internships or fieldwork, Federal Work-Study, scholarships/grants, traineeships, health care benefits, and unspecified assistantships available. Support available to part-time students. Financial award application deadline: 3/1; financial award applicants required to submit FAFSA. Offers acoustics (PhD); bioengineering (MS, PhD); ecology (MS, PhD); environmental pollution control (MEPC, MS); materials science and engineering (MS, PhD); molecular, cellular, and integrative biosciences (MS, PhD); physiology (MS, PhD); plant biology (MS, PhD); renewable energy and sustainability systems (MPS). *Application deadline:* Applications are processed on a rolling basis. *Application fee:* $65. Electronic applications accepted. *Application Contact:* Lori Hawn, Director, Graduate Student Services, 814-865-1795, Fax: 814-863-4627, E-mail: l-gswww@lists.psu.edu. *Vice Provost for Graduate Education and Dean of the Graduate School,* Dr. Regina Vasilatos-Younken, 814-865-2516, Fax: 814-863-4627.

School of International Affairs Students: 83 full-time (47 women), 4 part-time (3 women). Average age 25. 166 applicants, 82% accepted, 49 enrolled. Expenses: Contact institution. *Financial support:* Fellowships, research assistantships, teaching assistantships, career-related internships or fieldwork, Federal Work-Study, scholarships/grants, traineeships, health care benefits, and unspecified assistantships available. Support available to part-time students. Financial award application deadline: 3/1; financial award applicants required to submit FAFSA. In 2016, 40 master's awarded. Offers international affairs (MIA). *Application deadline:* Applications are processed on a rolling basis. *Application fee:* $65. Electronic applications accepted. *Application Contact:* Lori Hawn, Director, Graduate Student Services, 814-865-1795, Fax: 814-863-4627, E-mail: l-gswww@lists.psu.edu. *Dean,* Hari M. Osofsky, 814-863-1521, Fax: 814-863-7274.

Smeal College of Business Students: 276 full-time (90 women). Average age 30. 1,243 applicants, 26% accepted, 260 enrolled. Expenses: Contact institution. *Financial support:* Fellowships, research assistantships, teaching assistantships, career-related internships or fieldwork, Federal Work-Study, scholarships/grants, traineeships, health care benefits, and unspecified assistantships available. Support available to part-time students. Financial award application deadline: 3/1; financial award applicants required to submit FAFSA. In 2016, 274 master's, 11 doctorates awarded. Offers accounting (M Acc); business administration (MBA, MS, PhD); management and organizational leadership (MPS); supply chain management (MPS). *Application deadline:* Applications are processed on a rolling basis. *Application fee:* $65. Electronic applications accepted. *Application Contact:* Lori Hawn, Director, Graduate Student Services, 814-865-1795, Fax: 814-863-4627, E-mail: l-gswww@lists.psu.edu. *Dean,* Dr. Charles H. Whiteman, 814-863-0448, Fax: 814-865-7064.

Penn State Law Students: 533 full-time (247 women). 2,214 applicants, 42% accepted, 242 enrolled. *Faculty:* 42 full-time (18 women), 7 part-time/adjunct (3 women). Expenses: Contact institution. Offers law (LL M, JD, SJD). *Application deadline:* For fall admission, 3/31 for domestic students. Applications are processed on a rolling basis. *Application fee:* $60. Electronic applications accepted. *Application Contact:* Amanda DiPolvere, Assistant Dean, Admissions and Financial Aid, 800-840-1122, E-mail: admissions@pennstatelaw.psu.edu. *Dean,* Hari M. Osofsky, 814-863-1521.

PENN STATE YORK, York, PA 17403

General Information State-related, coed, comprehensive institution. *Enrollment:* 1,066 graduate, professional, and undergraduate students; 6 part-time matriculated graduate/professional students (all women). *Enrollment by degree level:* 6 master's.

Computer facilities: Computer purchase and lease plans are available. A campuswide network can be accessed from off campus. Online class registration is available. Website: http://www.yk.psu.edu/

GRADUATE UNITS

Graduate School Students: 6 part-time (all women). Average age 33. 3 applicants, 33% accepted, 1 enrolled. Expenses: Contact institution. Offers ESL specialist (Certificate); teaching and curriculum (M Ed). *Application Contact:* Lori Hawn, Director, Graduate Student Services, 814-865-1795, Fax: 814-863-4627, E-mail: l-gswww@lists.psu.edu. *Vice Provost for Graduate Education/Dean, Graduate School,* Dr. Regina Vasilatos-Younken, 814-865-2516, Fax: 814-863-4627.

PENNSYLVANIA ACADEMY OF THE FINE ARTS, Philadelphia, PA 19102

General Information Independent, coed, comprehensive institution. *Graduate housing:* On-campus housing not available.

GRADUATE UNITS

Division of Graduate Studies Offers drawing (MFA, Postbaccalaureate Certificate); painting (MFA, Postbaccalaureate Certificate); printmaking (MFA, Postbaccalaureate Certificate); sculpture (MFA, Postbaccalaureate Certificate). MFA program also available in a low-residency format. Electronic applications accepted.

PENNSYLVANIA COLLEGE OF HEALTH SCIENCES, Lancaster, PA 17601

General Information Independent, coed, primarily women, comprehensive institution.

GRADUATE UNITS

Graduate Programs Offers administration (MSN); education (MSHS, MSN); healthcare administration (MHA).

PENSACOLA CHRISTIAN COLLEGE, Pensacola, FL 32503-2267

General Information Independent-religious, coed, comprehensive institution.

GRADUATE UNITS

Graduate Studies

PENTECOSTAL THEOLOGICAL SEMINARY, Cleveland, TN 37320-3330

General Information Independent-religious, coed, graduate-only institution. *Graduate housing:* Rooms and/or apartments available to single and married students.

GRADUATE UNITS

Graduate and Professional Programs *Program availability:* Part-time. Offers biblical studies (MTS); church ministries (MA); counseling (MA); discipleship and Christian formation (MA); ministry (D Min); Pentecostal theology (MTS); theology (M Div).

PEPPERDINE UNIVERSITY, Malibu, CA 90263

General Information Independent-religious, coed, university. *Enrollment:* 7,826 graduate, professional, and undergraduate students; 2,420 full-time matriculated graduate/professional students (1,401 women), 1,836 part-time matriculated graduate/professional students (1,132 women). *Enrollment by degree level:* 3,029 master's, 1,544 doctoral, 16 other advanced degrees. *Graduate faculty:* 170 full-time (108 women), 200 part-time/adjunct (93 women). *Graduate housing:* Rooms and/or apartments available on a first-come, first-served basis to single and married students. *Student services:* Campus employment opportunities, campus safety program, career counseling, exercise/wellness program, free psychological counseling, international student services, low-cost health insurance, multicultural affairs office, services for students with disabilities, teacher training. *Library facilities:* Payson Library plus 5 others. *Collection:* Books: 348,364 (physical), 237,133 (digital/electronic); Serial titles: 411 (physical), 61,042 (digital/electronic); Databases: 150. Weekly public service hours: 112; students can reserve study rooms.

Computer facilities: Computer purchase and lease plans are available. 218 computers available on campus for general student use. A campuswide network can be accessed from student residence rooms and from off campus. Online class registration is available.

Website: http://www.pepperdine.edu/

General Application Contact: Kristy Collins, Dean of Admission and Enrollment Management, Seaver College, 310-506-4392, Fax: 310-506-4861, E-mail: admission-seaver@pepperdine.edu.

GRADUATE UNITS

Graduate School of Education and Psychology Students: 751 full-time (577 women), 817 part-time (612 women); includes 690 minority (215 Black or African American, non-Hispanic/Latino; 8 American Indian or Alaska Native, non-Hispanic/Latino; 136 Asian, non-Hispanic/Latino; 275 Hispanic/Latino; 11 Native Hawaiian or other Pacific Islander, non-Hispanic/Latino; 45 Two or more races, non-Hispanic/Latino; 92 international. Average age 34. 931 applicants, 85% accepted, 479 enrolled. *Faculty:* 44 full-time (26 women), 128 part-time/adjunct (85 women). Expenses: Contact institution. *Financial support:* Research assistantships, teaching assistantships, career-related internships or fieldwork, Federal Work-Study, institutionally sponsored loans, scholarships/grants, and unspecified assistantships available. Support available to part-time students. Financial award applicants required to submit FAFSA. In 2016, 407 master's, 103 doctorates awarded. *Program availability:* Part-time, evening/weekend, online learning. Offers education and psychology (MA, MS, Ed D, PhD, Psy D). *Application deadline:* Applications are processed on a rolling basis. *Application fee:* $55. Electronic applications accepted. *Application Contact:* Chris Costa, Director of Enrollment, 310-568-2850, E-mail: chris.costa@pepperdine.edu. *Dean,* Dr. Helen Williams, 310-568-5615, E-mail: helen.williams@pepperdine.edu.

Division of Education Students: 262 full-time (169 women), 385 part-time (264 women); includes 286 minority (123 Black or African American, non-Hispanic/Latino; 4 American Indian or Alaska Native, non-Hispanic/Latino; 59 Asian, non-Hispanic/Latino; 77 Hispanic/Latino; 6 Native Hawaiian or other Pacific Islander, non-Hispanic/Latino; 17 Two or more races, non-Hispanic/Latino; 46 international. Average age 38. 372 applicants, 95% accepted, 200 enrolled. Expenses: Contact institution. *Financial support:* Research assistantships, teaching assistantships, career-related internships or fieldwork, institutionally sponsored loans, and scholarships/grants available. Support available to part-time students. Financial award application deadline: 7/1; financial award applicants required to submit FAFSA. In 2016, 142 master's, 66 doctorates awarded. *Program availability:* Part-time, evening/weekend, online learning. Offers administration and preliminary administrative services (MA); education (MA); educational leadership, administration, and policy (Ed D); global leadership and change (PhD); learning technologies (MA, Ed D); organizational leadership (Ed D); social entrepreneurship and change (MA); teaching (MA); teaching: TESOL (MA). *Application deadline:* Applications are processed on a rolling basis. *Application fee:* $55. *Application Contact:* Chris Costa, Director of Enrollment, 310-568-2850, E-mail: chris.costa@pepperdine.edu. *Associate Dean, Education Division,* Dr. Martine Jago, 310-568-2828, E-mail: martine.jago@pepperdine.edu.

Division of Psychology Students: 489 full-time (408 women), 432 part-time (348 women); includes 404 minority (92 Black or African American, non-Hispanic/Latino; 4 American Indian or Alaska Native, non-Hispanic/Latino; 77 Asian, non-Hispanic/Latino; 198 Hispanic/Latino; 5 Native Hawaiian or other Pacific Islander, non-Hispanic/Latino; 28 Two or more races, non-Hispanic/Latino; 46 international. Average age 31. 559 applicants, 77% accepted, 279 enrolled. Expenses: Contact institution. *Financial support:* Research assistantships, teaching assistantships, career-related internships or fieldwork, and scholarships/grants available. Support available to part-time students. Financial award application deadline: 7/1; financial award applicants required to submit FAFSA. In 2016, 265 master's, 27 doctorates awarded. *Program availability:* Part-time, evening/weekend. Offers behavioral psychology (MS); clinical psychology (Psy D); clinical psychology (MA); clinical psychology with Latinos (MA); psychology (MA). *Application deadline:* For fall admission, 2/1 for domestic students. Applications are processed on a rolling basis. *Application fee:* $55. *Application Contact:* Chris Costa, Director of Enrollment, 310-568-2850, E-mail: chris.costa@pepperdine.edu. *Associate Dean, Psychology Division,* Dr. Robert A. deMayo, 310-568-5747, E-mail: robert.demayo@pepperdine.edu.

Graziadio School of Business and Management Students: 956 full-time (441 women), 847 part-time (422 women); includes 463 minority (121 Black or African

American, non-Hispanic/Latino; 7 American Indian or Alaska Native, non-Hispanic/Latino; 240 Asian, non-Hispanic/Latino; 93 Hispanic/Latino; 2 Two or more races, non-Hispanic/Latino; 385 international. Average age 31. 2,568 applicants, 62% accepted, 520 enrolled. *Faculty:* 86 full-time (23 women), 30 part-time/adjunct (10 women). Expenses: Contact institution. *Financial support:* Career-related internships or fieldwork, institutionally sponsored loans, scholarships/grants, and unspecified assistantships available. Support available to part-time students. Financial award applicants required to submit FAFSA. In 2016, 728 master's awarded. *Program availability:* Part-time. Offers accounting (MS); applied analytics (MS); applied finance (MS); business administration (MBA, MS); business and management (MBA, MS); global business (MS); human resources (MS); international business administration (MBA); management and leadership (MS); organization development (MS); real estate investment and finance (MS). *Application fee:* $75. Electronic applications accepted. *Application Contact:* Morag Knapp, Assistant Director of Admission, Graziadio School of Business and Management, 310-568-5527, E-mail: morag.knapp@pepperdine.edu. *Dean,* Dr. Deryck J. Rensburg, 310-568-5689, Fax: 310-568-5500, E-mail: deryck.rensburg@pepperdine.edu.

School of Law Students: 634 full-time (344 women), 74 part-time (39 women); includes 224 minority (34 Black or African American, non-Hispanic/Latino; 3 American Indian or Alaska Native, non-Hispanic/Latino; 61 Asian, non-Hispanic/Latino; 85 Hispanic/Latino; 41 Two or more races, non-Hispanic/Latino; 69 international. Average age 27. 2,492 applicants, 50% accepted, 257 enrolled. *Faculty:* 36 full-time (12 women), 37 part-time/adjunct (12 women). Expenses: Contact institution. *Financial support:* Fellowships, research assistantships, teaching assistantships, career-related internships or fieldwork, Federal Work-Study, institutionally sponsored loans, and scholarships/grants available. Support available to part-time students. Financial award application deadline: 4/1; financial award applicants required to submit FAFSA. In 2016, 71 master's, 179 doctorates awarded. Offers dispute resolution (LL M, MDR); law (LL M, MDR, JD). *Application deadline:* For fall admission, 3/1 for domestic and international students. Applications are processed on a rolling basis. *Application fee:* $60. Electronic applications accepted. *Application Contact:* Shannon Phillips, Assistant Dean, 310-506-4631, Fax: 310-506-4266, E-mail: shannon.phillips@pepperdine.edu. *Dean/Professor of Law,* Dr. Tacha Deanell, 310-506-4611, E-mail: deanell.tacha@pepperdine.edu.

School of Public Policy Students: 57 full-time (27 women), 7 part-time (5 women); includes 22 minority (9 Black or African American, non-Hispanic/Latino; 2 American Indian or Alaska Native, non-Hispanic/Latino; 6 Asian, non-Hispanic/Latino; 4 Hispanic/Latino; 1 Two or more races, non-Hispanic/Latino; 10 international. Average age 25. 174 applicants, 55% accepted, 29 enrolled. *Faculty:* 4 full-time (1 woman), 5 part-time/adjunct (0 women). Expenses: Contact institution. *Financial support:* Institutionally sponsored loans and scholarships/grants available. Financial award application deadline: 5/1; financial award applicants required to submit FAFSA. In 2016, 34 master's awarded. Offers American politics (MPP); economics (MPP); international relations (MPP); state and local policy (MPP). *Application deadline:* For fall admission, 6/15 for domestic students. Applications are processed on a rolling basis. *Application fee:* $50. Electronic applications accepted. *Application Contact:* Carson Bruno, Assistant Dean for Admission and Program Relations, 310-506-7493, E-mail: carson.bruno@pepperdine.edu. *Dean, School of Public Policy,* Dr. Pete Peterson, 310-506-7490, Fax: 310-506-7494, E-mail: pete.n.peterson@pepperdine.edu.

Seaver College Students: 22 full-time (12 women), 91 part-time (54 women); includes 32 minority (10 Black or African American, non-Hispanic/Latino; 2 American Indian or Alaska Native, non-Hispanic/Latino; 8 Asian, non-Hispanic/Latino; 9 Hispanic/Latino; 1 Native Hawaiian or other Pacific Islander, non-Hispanic/Latino; 2 Two or more races, non-Hispanic/Latino; 10 international. Average age 29. 162 applicants, 51% accepted, 42 enrolled. Expenses: Contact institution. *Financial support:* Fellowships, research assistantships, teaching assistantships, career-related internships or fieldwork, Federal Work-Study, institutionally sponsored loans, scholarships/grants, and tuition waivers (partial) available. Support available to part-time students. Financial award application deadline: 2/15; financial award applicants required to submit FAFSA. In 2016, 36 master's awarded. *Program availability:* Part-time, evening/weekend. Offers business (MS); communication (MA, MFA); humanities (MA, MFA); religion (M Div, MA, MS). *Application deadline:* For fall admission, 2/1 priority date for domestic students. Applications are processed on a rolling basis. *Application fee:* $55. *Application Contact:* Joy Brown, Admission Counselor, 310-506-4392, E-mail: joy.brown@pepperdine.edu. *Assistant Dean, Special Academic and Graduate Programs for Seaver College,* Dr. Dana Dudley, 310-506-6047, Fax: 310-506-4816, E-mail: dana.dudley@pepperdine.edu.

Division of Business Students: 1 full-time (0 women), 1 (woman) part-time, 1 international. Average age 22. Expenses: Contact institution. In 2016, 2 master's awarded. Offers accounting (MS). *Application deadline:* For fall admission, 2/1 priority date for domestic students. *Application fee:* $55. Electronic applications accepted. *Application Contact:* Hayley Wolf, Director of Admission, 310-506-4392, E-mail: hayley.wolf@pepperdine.edu. *Divisional Dean/Professor of Economics and Finance,* Dr. Dean Baim, 310-506-4237, E-mail: dean.baim@pepperdine.edu.

Division of Communication Students: 7 full-time (3 women), 26 part-time (16 women); includes 11 minority (4 Black or African American, non-Hispanic/Latino; 1 American Indian or Alaska Native, non-Hispanic/Latino; 3 Asian, non-Hispanic/Latino; 2 Hispanic/Latino; 1 Native Hawaiian or other Pacific Islander, non-Hispanic/Latino; 4 international. Average age 27. Expenses: Contact institution. *Financial support:* Research assistantships, teaching assistantships, career-related internships or fieldwork, and scholarships/grants available. Support available to part-time students. Financial award applicants required to submit FAFSA. In 2016, 8 master's awarded. *Program availability:* Part-time. Offers cinematic media production (MFA); strategic communication (MA). *Application deadline:* For fall admission, 2/1 priority date for domestic students, 2/1 for international students. Applications are processed on a rolling basis. *Application fee:* $65. Electronic applications accepted. *Application Contact:* Hayley Wolf, Director of Admission, 310-506-4392, E-mail: hayley.wolf@pepperdine.edu. *Divisional Dean/Professor of Journalism,* Dr. Kenneth E. Waters, 310-506-4245, E-mail: ken.waters@pepperdine.edu.

Division of Humanities Students: 9 full-time (7 women), 41 part-time (23 women); includes 12 minority (3 Black or African American, non-Hispanic/Latino; 2 Asian, non-Hispanic/Latino; 5 Hispanic/Latino; 2 Two or more races, non-Hispanic/Latino; 3 international. Average age 31. Expenses: Contact institution. *Financial support:* Applicants required to submit FAFSA. In 2016, 15 master's awarded. *Program availability:* Part-time. Offers American studies (MA); writing for screen and television (MFA). *Application deadline:* For fall admission, 2/1 priority date for domestic students. Applications are processed on a rolling basis. *Application fee:* $65. *Application Contact:* Hayley Wolf, Director of Admission, 310-506-4392, E-mail: hayley.wolf@pepperdine.edu. *Chair/Professor of English,* Dr. Michael G. Ditmore, 310-506-4182, Fax: 310-506-7307, E-mail: michael.ditmore@pepperdine.edu.

Division of Religion Students: 5 full-time (2 women), 13 part-time (4 women); includes 7 minority (3 Black or African American, non-Hispanic/Latino; 2 Asian, non-

Hispanic/Latino; 2 Hispanic/Latino). Average age 32. Expenses: Contact institution. *Financial support:* Applicants required to submit FAFSA. In 2016, 7 master's awarded. *Program availability:* Part-time, evening/weekend. Offers ministry (MS); religion (M Div, MA). *Application deadline:* For fall admission, 2/1 priority date for domestic students. Applications are processed on a rolling basis. *Application fee:* $65. Electronic applications accepted. *Application Contact:* Hayley Wolf, Director of Admission, 310-506-4392, E-mail: hayley.wolf@pepperdine.edu. *Chair/Professor*, Dr. Timothy Willis, 310-506-4352, Fax: 310-506-7271, E-mail: timothy.willis@pepperdine.edu.

PERU STATE COLLEGE, Peru, NE 68421

General Information State-supported, coed, comprehensive institution. *Graduate housing:* Rooms and/or apartments available to single and married students.

GRADUATE UNITS

Graduate Programs *Program availability:* Part-time, online learning. Offers curriculum and instruction (MS Ed); organizational management (MS).

PFEIFFER UNIVERSITY, Misenheimer, NC 28109-0960

General Information Independent-religious, coed, comprehensive institution. *Graduate housing:* On-campus housing not available.

GRADUATE UNITS

Program in Business Administration *Program availability:* Part-time, evening/weekend, online learning. Offers business administration (MBA).

Program in Elementary Education Offers elementary education (MAT, MS).

Program in Health Administration Offers health administration (MHA).

Program in Leadership and Organizational Change Offers leadership and organizational change (MS).

Program in Practical Theology *Program availability:* Part-time, evening/weekend. Offers practical theology (MA).

PHILADELPHIA COLLEGE OF OSTEOPATHIC MEDICINE, Philadelphia, PA 19131-1694

General Information Independent, coed, graduate-only institution. *Enrollment by degree level:* 421 master's, 1,275 doctoral, 43 other advanced degrees. *Graduate faculty:* 152 full-time (67 women), 1,639 part-time/adjunct (435 women). Tuition and fees vary according to course load, degree level and program. *Graduate housing:* On-campus housing not available. *Student services:* Campus employment opportunities, campus safety program, career counseling, exercise/wellness program, free psychological counseling, low-cost health insurance, multicultural affairs office, services for students with disabilities, writing training. *Library facilities:* PCOM Library plus 1 other. *Collection:* Study areas open 24 hours, 5–7 days a week; students can reserve study rooms. *Research affiliation:* Intracell (biotechnology inflammation), Proteapex (biotechnology), Novartis Pharmaceuticals (drug development), Theramunex (biotechnology inflammation), Lankenau Institute for Medical Research (cell biology), Cleveland Museum Natural History (developmental biology).

Computer facilities: 142 computers available on campus for general student use. Online class registration is available. Website: http://www.pcom.edu/

General Application Contact: Kari A. Shotwell, Director of Admissions, 215-871-6700, Fax: 215-871-6719, E-mail: karis@pcom.edu.

GRADUATE UNITS

Graduate and Professional Programs Students: 1,737 full-time (1,003 women); includes 520 minority (168 Black or African American, non-Hispanic/Latino; 2 American Indian or Alaska Native, non-Hispanic/Latino; 61 Asian, non-Hispanic/Latino; 33 Hispanic/Latino; 256 Two or more races, non-Hispanic/Latino), 7 international. 19,020 applicants, 8% accepted, 882 enrolled. *Faculty:* 87 full-time (37 women), 927 part-time/adjunct (146 women). Expenses: Contact institution. *Financial support:* Fellowships, research assistantships, career-related internships or fieldwork, Federal Work-Study, institutionally sponsored loans, and scholarships/grants available. Financial award application deadline: 3/15; financial award applicants required to submit FAFSA. In 2016, 207 master's, 519 doctorates, 13 other advanced degrees awarded. Offers applied behavior analysis (Certificate); biomedical sciences (MS); clinical health psychology (Post-Doctoral Certificate); clinical neuropsychology (Post-Doctoral Certificate); clinical psychology (Psy D); forensic medicine (MS); health sciences (MS); mental health counseling (MS); organizational development and leadership (MS); osteopathic medicine (DO); psychology (Certificate); school psychology (MS, Psy D, Ed S). *Application deadline:* Applications are processed on a rolling basis. *Application fee:* $75. Electronic applications accepted. *Application Contact:* Kari A. Shotwell, Director of Admissions, 215-871-6700, Fax: 215-871-6719, E-mail: karis@pcom.edu.

PHILADELPHIA UNIVERSITY, Philadelphia, PA 19144

General Information Independent, coed, comprehensive institution. *Graduate housing:* On-campus housing not available.

GRADUATE UNITS

College of Architecture and the Built Environment Offers architecture (M Arch); architecture and the built environment (MS); construction management (MS); geodesign (MS); high performance building (MS); interior architecture (MS); real estate development (MS); sustainable design (MS).

College of Science, Health and the Liberal Arts *Program availability:* Part-time, evening/weekend, online learning. Offers athletic training (MS); community and trauma counseling (MS); disaster medicine and management (MS); midwifery (MS); nurse midwifery (Postbaccalaureate Certificate); occupational therapy (MS, OTD); physician assistant studies (MS); science, health and the liberal arts (MS, Postbaccalaureate Certificate). Electronic applications accepted.

School of Business Administration *Program availability:* Part-time, evening/weekend, online learning. Offers business administration (MBA, MS); general business (MBA); global fashion enterprise (MS); innovation (MBA); management (MBA); marketing (MBA); strategic design (MBA); strategic design business administration (MBA); taxation (MS). Electronic applications accepted.

School of Design and Engineering *Program availability:* Part-time. Offers design and engineering (MS, PhD); industrial design (MS); interactive design and media (MS); modeling, simulation and data analytics (MS); surface imaging (MS); textile design (MS); textile engineering (MS); textile engineering and sciences (PhD). Electronic applications accepted.

PHILLIPS GRADUATE UNIVERSITY, Chatsworth, CA 91311

General Information Independent, coed, graduate-only institution. *Graduate housing:* On-campus housing not available.

GRADUATE UNITS

Program in Organizational Management and Consulting *Program availability:* Evening/weekend. Offers organizational management and consulting (Psy D). Electronic applications accepted.

Programs in Marriage and Family Therapy and School Counseling *Program availability:* Evening/weekend. Offers art therapy (MA); marriage and family therapy (MA); school counseling (MA). Electronic applications accepted.

PHILLIPS THEOLOGICAL SEMINARY, Tulsa, OK 74116

General Information Independent-religious, coed, graduate-only institution. *Graduate housing:* On-campus housing not available.

GRADUATE UNITS

Programs in Theology *Program availability:* Part-time, online learning. Offers administration of church agencies (M Div); campus ministry (M Div); church-related social work (M Div); college and seminary teaching (M Div); global mission work (M Div); institutional chaplaincy (M Div); ministerial vocations in Christian education (M Div); ministry (D Min); ministry and culture (MAMC); ministry of music (M Div); parish ministry (D Min); pastoral care and counseling (M Div); pastoral counseling (D Min); pastoral ministry (M Div); practices of ministry (D Min); theological studies (MTS).

PHOENIX INSTITUTE OF HERBAL MEDICINE & ACUPUNCTURE, Phoenix, AZ 85018

General Information Proprietary, coed, graduate-only institution.

GRADUATE UNITS

Graduate Programs Offers acupuncture (MSAC); Oriental medicine (MSOM).

PHOENIX SEMINARY, Phoenix, AZ 85018

General Information Independent-religious, coed, graduate-only institution.

GRADUATE UNITS

Graduate Programs *Program availability:* Part-time, evening/weekend. Offers Biblical and theological studies (Graduate Diploma); Biblical communication (M Div); Biblical leadership (MA); Christian counseling (Graduate Diploma); counseling and family (M Div); leadership development (M Div); ministry (D Min); professional counseling (MA).

PIEDMONT COLLEGE, Demorest, GA 30535

General Information Independent-religious, coed, comprehensive institution. *Enrollment:* 2,266 graduate, professional, and undergraduate students; 380 full-time matriculated graduate/professional students (284 women), 591 part-time matriculated graduate/professional students (477 women). *Enrollment by degree level:* 478 master's, 91 doctoral, 402 other advanced degrees. *Tuition:* Full-time $8910. *Graduate housing:* Room and/or apartments available on a first-come, first-served basis to single students; on-campus housing not available to married students. Typical cost: $5940 per year ($9400 including board). *Student services:* Campus employment opportunities, campus safety program, career counseling, exercise/wellness program, services for students with disabilities, teacher training, writing training. *Library facilities:* Arrendale Library plus 2 others. *Collection:* Books: 99,693 (physical), 416,680 (digital/electronic); Serial titles: 24,272 (digital/electronic). Students can reserve study rooms.

Computer facilities: 150 computers available on campus for general student use. A campuswide network can be accessed from student residence rooms and from off campus. Online class registration is available. Website: http://www.piedmont.edu/

General Application Contact: Kathleen Carter, Director of Graduate Enrollment Management, 706-778-8500 Ext. 1181, Fax: 706-776-0150, E-mail: kanderson@piedmont.edu.

GRADUATE UNITS

School of Business Students: 44 full-time (23 women), 16 part-time (9 women); includes 6 minority (4 Black or African American, non-Hispanic/Latino; 2 Hispanic/Latino). Average age 29. 29 applicants, 62% accepted, 15 enrolled. Expenses: Contact institution. *Financial support:* Federal Work-Study and unspecified assistantships available. Financial award applicants required to submit FAFSA. In 2016, 35 master's awarded. *Program availability:* Part-time, evening/weekend. Offers business (MBA). *Application deadline:* For fall admission, 7/15 for domestic students; for spring admission, 12/1 for domestic students. Applications are processed on a rolling basis. Electronic applications accepted. *Application Contact:* Kathleen Carter, Director of Graduate Enrollment Management, 706-778-3000, E-mail: kcarter@piedmont.edu. *Dean*, Dr. Edward Taylor, 706-778-3000, E-mail: etaylor@piedmont.edu.

School of Education Students: 290 full-time (217 women), 614 part-time (508 women); includes 131 minority (97 Black or African American, non-Hispanic/Latino; 4 American Indian or Alaska Native, non-Hispanic/Latino; 5 Asian, non-Hispanic/Latino; 11 Hispanic/Latino; 6 Native Hawaiian or other Pacific Islander, non-Hispanic/Latino; 8 Two or more races, non-Hispanic/Latino), 6 international. Average age 37. 257 applicants, 64% accepted, 160 enrolled. Expenses: Contact institution. *Financial support:* Career-related internships or fieldwork, Federal Work-Study, and unspecified assistantships available. Support available to part-time students. Financial award applicants required to submit FAFSA. In 2016, 288 master's, 243 other advanced degrees awarded. *Program availability:* Part-time, evening/weekend. Offers art education (MAT); curriculum and instruction (Ed S); early childhood education (MA, MAT); instructional technology (MAT); middle grades education (MA, MAT); music education (MA, MAT); secondary education (MA, MAT); special education (MA, MAT). *Application deadline:* For fall admission, 7/15 for domestic students; for spring admission, 12/1 for domestic students. Applications are processed on a rolling basis. Electronic applications accepted. *Application Contact:* Kathleen Anderson, Director of Graduate Enrollment Management, 706-778-8500 Ext. 1181, Fax: 706-778-0150, E-mail: kanderson@piedmont.edu. *Dean*, Dr. Don Gnecco, 706-778-3000 Ext. 1201, Fax: 706-776-9608, E-mail: dgnecco@piedmont.edu.

PIEDMONT INTERNATIONAL UNIVERSITY, Winston-Salem, NC 27101-5197

General Information Independent-religious, coed, comprehensive institution. *Graduate housing:* Rooms and/or apartments available on a first-come, first-served basis to single and married students. Housing application deadline: 5/1.

GRADUATE UNITS

Graduate School *Program availability:* Part-time, online learning. Offers Biblical studies (PhD); curriculum and instruction (M Div); divinity (M Div); educational leadership (M Ed); leadership (MA, PhD); ministry (MA Min, D Min); non-language track (MABS); PhD preparation track (MABS). Electronic applications accepted.

Temple Baptist Seminary *Program availability:* Part-time, evening/weekend, online learning. Offers theology (M Div, D Min).

PITTSBURGH THEOLOGICAL SEMINARY, Pittsburgh, PA 15206-2596

General Information Independent-religious, coed, graduate-only institution. *Enrollment by degree level:* 123 master's, 77 doctoral. *Graduate faculty:* 16 full-time (5 women), 6 part-time/adjunct (2 women). *Tuition:* Full-time $11,520; part-time $358 per credit. *Required fees:* $300. One-time fee: $125. *Graduate housing:* Rooms and/or apartments available on a first-come, first-served basis to single and married students. Typical cost: $5175 per year for single students; $6244 per year for married students. Housing application deadline: 6/1. *Student services:* Campus employment opportunities, campus safety program, career counseling, exercise/wellness program, free psychological counseling, international student services, low-cost health insurance, services for students with disabilities, writing training. *Library facilities:* Clifford E. Barbour Library. *Collection:* Books: 304,623 (physical), 71 (digital/electronic); Serial titles: 779 (physical), 156 (digital/electronic); Databases: 23. Weekly public service hours: 67.

Computer facilities: 15 computers available on campus for general student use. A campuswide network can be accessed from student residence rooms. Online class registration is available.
Website: http://www.pts.edu/

General Application Contact: Rev. Anthony Rivera, Associate Director of Recruiting and Admissions, 412-924-1450, Fax: 412-924-1383, E-mail: arivera@pts.edu.

GRADUATE UNITS

Graduate and Professional Programs Students: 153 full-time (56 women), 47 part-time (28 women); includes 57 minority (49 Black or African American, non-Hispanic/Latino; 3 Asian, non-Hispanic/Latino; 3 Hispanic/Latino; 1 Native Hawaiian or other Pacific Islander, non-Hispanic/Latino; 1 Two or more races, non-Hispanic/Latino), 9 international. Average age 35. 57 applicants, 93% accepted, 44 enrolled. *Faculty:* 16 full-time (5 women), 6 part-time/adjunct (2 women). Expenses: Contact institution. *Financial support:* In 2016–17, 104 students received support. Career-related internships or fieldwork, scholarships/grants, and institutional work-study available. Financial award application deadline: 5/1; financial award applicants required to submit FAFSA. In 2016, 34 master's, 16 doctorates awarded. *Program availability:* Part-time, evening/weekend. Offers divinity (M Div); theological studies (MA); theology (Th M); theology and ministry (MA, D Min). M Div/MSW offered jointly with University of Pittsburgh; JD/M Div with Duquesne University; M Div/MSPPM with Carnegie Mellon University. *Application deadline:* For fall admission, 6/30 priority date for domestic students, 12/1 for international students; for winter admission, 10/15 priority date for domestic students; for spring admission, 1/15 priority date for domestic students. Applications are processed on a rolling basis. *Application fee:* $50. Electronic applications accepted. *Application Contact:* Dr. Heather Vacek, Dean of Faculty and Vice President for Academic Affairs, 412-924-1374, Fax: 412-924-1774, E-mail: hvacek@pts.edu. *Dean of Faculty and Vice President for Academic Affairs,* Dr. Heathear H. Vacek, 412-924-1374, Fax: 412-924-1774, E-mail: hvacek@pts.edu.

PITTSBURG STATE UNIVERSITY, Pittsburg, KS 66762

General Information State-supported, coed, comprehensive institution. CGS member. *Enrollment:* 7,102 graduate, professional, and undergraduate students; 367 full-time matriculated graduate/professional students (183 women), 831 part-time matriculated graduate/professional students (577 women). *Enrollment by degree level:* 1,133 master's, 35 doctoral, 39 other advanced degrees. *Graduate faculty:* 126 full-time (40 women), 35 part-time/adjunct (14 women). Tuition, state resident: full-time $7732; part-time $323 per credit hour. Tuition, nonresident: full-time $17,816; part-time $743 per credit hour. Tuition and fees vary according to course load, degree level and campus/location. *Graduate housing:* Rooms and/or apartments available on a first-come, first-served basis to single and married students. Typical cost: $12,972 per year ($15,864 including board) for single students; $15,864 (including board) for married students. Room and board charges vary according to board plan, campus/location and housing facility selected. Housing application deadline: 8/15. *Student services:* Campus employment opportunities, campus safety program, career counseling, exercise/wellness program, free psychological counseling, international student services, low-cost health insurance, multicultural affairs office, services for students with disabilities, teacher training, writing training. *Library facilities:* Leonard H. Axe Library plus 2 others. *Research affiliation:* Cargill, Inc. (vegetable oil).

Computer facilities: A campuswide network can be accessed from student residence rooms and from off campus. Online class registration is available.
Website: http://www.pittstate.edu/

General Application Contact: Lisa Allen, Assistant Director, 620-235-4218, Fax: 620-235-4219, E-mail: lallen@pittstate.edu.

GRADUATE UNITS

Graduate School Students: 387 full-time (223 women), 764 part-time (518 women); includes 130 minority (30 Black or African American, non-Hispanic/Latino; 25 American Indian or Alaska Native, non-Hispanic/Latino; 6 Asian, non-Hispanic/Latino; 31 Hispanic/Latino; 38 Two or more races, non-Hispanic/Latino), 165 international. 836 applicants, 83% accepted, 362 enrolled. *Faculty:* 223 full-time (74 women), 129 part-time/adjunct (68 women). Expenses: Contact institution. *Financial support:* In 2016–17, 6 research assistantships with partial tuition reimbursements (averaging $5,000 per year), 104 teaching assistantships with full tuition reimbursements (averaging $5,500 per year) were awarded; career-related internships or fieldwork, Federal Work-Study, and unspecified assistantships also available. Financial award application deadline: 2/1; financial award applicants required to submit FAFSA. In 2016, 512 master's, 13 other advanced degrees awarded. *Program availability:* Part-time, evening/weekend, 100% online, blended/hybrid learning. *Application deadline:* For fall admission, 7/15 for domestic students, 6/1 for international students; for spring admission, 12/15 for domestic students, 10/15 for international students; for summer admission, 5/15 for domestic students, 4/1 for international students. Applications are processed on a rolling basis. *Application fee:* $35 ($60 for international students). Electronic applications accepted. *Application Contact:* Lisa Allen, Assistant Director of Graduate and Continuing Studies, 620-235-4223, Fax: 620-235-4219, E-mail: lallen@pittstate.edu. *Dean of Graduate and Continuing Studies,* Dr. Pawan Kahol, 620-235-4222, Fax: 620-235-4219, E-mail: pkahol@pittstate.edu.

College of Arts and Sciences Students: 191 (116 women); includes 31 minority (5 Black or African American, non-Hispanic/Latino; 6 American Indian or Alaska Native, non-Hispanic/Latino; 1 Asian, non-Hispanic/Latino; 6 Hispanic/Latino; 13 Two or more races, non-Hispanic/Latino), 33 international. Expenses: Contact institution. *Financial support:* In 2016–17, 6 research assistantships with partial tuition reimbursements (averaging $5,000 per year), 48 teaching assistantships with full tuition reimbursements (averaging $5,500 per year) were awarded; career-related internships or fieldwork, Federal Work-Study, and unspecified assistantships also available. Financial award application deadline: 2/1; financial award applicants required to submit FAFSA. In 2016, 88 master's awarded. *Program availability:* Part-

time, 100% online, blended/hybrid learning. Offers arts and sciences (MA, MM, MS, MSN, DNP); biology (MS); chemistry (MS); communication (MA); conducting (MM); education (MM); English (MA); history (MA); mathematics (MS); nursing (MSN, DNP); performance (MM); physics (MS); polymer chemistry (MS). *Application deadline:* For fall admission, 7/15 for domestic students, 6/1 for international students; for spring admission, 12/15 for domestic students, 10/15 for international students; for summer admission, 5/15 for domestic students, 4/1 for international students. Applications are processed on a rolling basis. *Application fee:* $35 ($60 for international students). Electronic applications accepted. *Application Contact:* Lisa Allen, Assistant Director of Graduate and Continuing Studies, 620-235-4223, Fax: 620-235-4219, E-mail: lallen@pittstate.edu. *Dean,* Dr. Mary Carol Pomatto, 620-235-4432, E-mail: mpomatto@pittstate.edu.

College of Education Students: 550 (409 women); includes 61 minority (17 Black or African American, non-Hispanic/Latino; 12 American Indian or Alaska Native, non-Hispanic/Latino; 2 Asian, non-Hispanic/Latino; 16 Hispanic/Latino; 14 Two or more races, non-Hispanic/Latino), 8 international. Expenses: Contact institution. *Financial support:* In 2016–17, 25 teaching assistantships with full tuition reimbursements (averaging $5,500 per year) were awarded; career-related internships or fieldwork, Federal Work-Study, and unspecified assistantships also available. Financial award application deadline: 2/1; financial award applicants required to submit FAFSA. In 2016, 266 master's, 13 other advanced degrees awarded. *Program availability:* Part-time, 100% online, blended/hybrid learning. Offers advanced studies in leadership (Ed S); counselor education (MS); education (MS, Ed S); educational leadership (MS); educational technology (MS); general school administration (Ed S); health, human performance, and recreation (MS); psychology (MS); school counseling (MS); school psychology (Ed S); special education (MAT, MS). *Application deadline:* For fall admission, 6/1 for international students; for spring admission, 10/15 for international students; for summer admission, 4/1 for international students. Applications are processed on a rolling basis. *Application fee:* $35 ($60 for international students). Electronic applications accepted. *Application Contact:* Lisa Allen, Assistant Director of Graduate and Continuing Studies, 620-235-4223, Fax: 620-235-4219, E-mail: lallen@pittstate.edu. *Interim Dean,* Dr. Jan Smith, 620-235-4518, Fax: 620-235-4520, E-mail: jsmith@pittstate.edu.

College of Technology Students: 230 (88 women); includes 24 minority (6 Black or African American, non-Hispanic/Latino; 5 American Indian or Alaska Native, non-Hispanic/Latino; 3 Asian, non-Hispanic/Latino; 4 Hispanic/Latino; 6 Two or more races, non-Hispanic/Latino), 96 international. Expenses: Contact institution. *Financial support:* In 2016–17, 14 teaching assistantships with full tuition reimbursements (averaging $5,500 per year) were awarded; career-related internships or fieldwork, Federal Work-Study, and unspecified assistantships also available. Financial award application deadline: 2/1; financial award applicants required to submit FAFSA. In 2016, 104 master's, 2 other advanced degrees awarded. *Program availability:* Part-time, 100% online, blended/hybrid learning. Offers career and technical education (MS); construction engineering technology (MET); electrical engineering technology (MET); general engineering technology (MET); human resource development (MS); manufacturing engineering technology (MET); mechanical engineering technology (MET); plastics engineering technology (MET); technology (MS); workforce development and education (Ed S). *Application deadline:* For fall admission, 7/15 for domestic students, 6/1 for international students; for spring admission, 12/15 for domestic students, 10/15 for international students; for summer admission, 5/15 for domestic students, 4/1 for international students. Applications are processed on a rolling basis. *Application fee:* $35 ($60 for international students). Electronic applications accepted. *Application Contact:* Lisa Allen, Assistant Director of Graduate and Continuing Studies, 620-235-4223, Fax: 620-235-4219, E-mail: lallen@pittstate.edu. *Dean,* Dr. Tim Dawsey, 620-235-4366.

Kelce College of Business Students: 62 (30 women); includes 7 minority (1 Black or African American, non-Hispanic/Latino; 2 American Indian or Alaska Native, non-Hispanic/Latino; 1 Hispanic/Latino; 3 Two or more races, non-Hispanic/Latino), 19 international. Expenses: Contact institution. *Financial support:* In 2016–17, 15 teaching assistantships with full tuition reimbursements (averaging $5,500 per year) were awarded; research assistantships, career-related internships or fieldwork, Federal Work-Study, and unspecified assistantships also available. Financial award application deadline: 2/1; financial award applicants required to submit FAFSA. In 2016, 55 master's awarded. Offers accounting (MBA); business (MBA); general administration (MBA); international business (MBA). *Application deadline:* For fall admission, 7/15 for domestic students, 6/1 for international students; for spring admission, 12/15 for domestic students, 10/15 for international students; for summer admission, 5/15 for domestic students, 4/1 for international students. Applications are processed on a rolling basis. *Application fee:* $35 ($60 for international students). Electronic applications accepted. *Application Contact:* Lisa Allen, Assistant Director of Graduate and Continuing Studies, 620-235-4218, Fax: 620-235-4219, E-mail: lallen@pittstate.edu. *Dean,* Dr. Paul Grimes, 620-235-4590, Fax: 620-235-4578, E-mail: pgrimes@pittstate.edu.

PLYMOUTH STATE UNIVERSITY, Plymouth, NH 03264-1595

General Information State-supported, coed, comprehensive institution. *Graduate housing:* Rooms and/or apartments available on a first-come, first-served basis to single students and guaranteed to married students. Housing application deadline: 5/1. *Research affiliation:* Hubbard Brook Experimental Forest (science), New Hampshire Department of Environmental Services (science), White Mountain National Forest (science), National Oceanic and Atmospheric Administration (NOAA) (science).

GRADUATE UNITS

College of Graduate Studies *Program availability:* Part-time, evening/weekend, online learning.

Graduate Studies in Business *Program availability:* Part-time, evening/weekend, online learning. Offers general management (MBA).

Graduate Studies in Education *Program availability:* Part-time, evening/weekend, online learning. Offers applied meteorology (MS); art education (MAT); athletic training (MS); biology (MS); clinical mental health counseling (MS, CAGS); counseling (M Ed); curriculum and instruction (M Ed); education (CAGS); educational leadership (M Ed, CAGS); elementary education (M Ed); English education (M Ed); environmental science and policy (MS); health education (M Ed); heritage studies (M Ed); higher education (Ed D); human relations (M Ed); integrated arts (M Ed); language education (M Ed); learning, leadership and community (Ed D); library media (M Ed); mathematics education (M Ed); music education (M Ed); physical education (M Ed); reading and writing (M Ed); school counseling (M Ed); school psychology (M Ed, CAGS); science (MS); science education (MAT, MS); secondary education (M Ed); social studies education (M Ed); special education (M Ed); teaching (MAT).

Program in Historic Preservation Offers historic preservation (MA).

Program in Personal and Organizational Wellness Offers personal and organizational wellness (MA).

POINT LOMA NAZARENE UNIVERSITY, San Diego, CA 92106-2899

General Information Independent-religious, coed, comprehensive institution. *Enrollment:* 4,156 graduate, professional, and undergraduate students; 377 full-time matriculated graduate/professional students (261 women), 640 part-time matriculated graduate/professional students (469 women). *Enrollment by degree level:* 1,017 master's. *Graduate faculty:* 32 full-time (18 women), 110 part-time/adjunct (70 women). Tuition and fees vary according to campus/location and program. *Graduate housing:* On-campus housing not available. *Student services:* Campus employment opportunities, campus safety program, career counseling, free psychological counseling, international student services, low-cost health insurance, services for students with disabilities, teacher training. *Library facilities:* Ryan Library.

Computer facilities: 346 computers available on campus for general student use. A campuswide network can be accessed from student residence rooms and from off campus. Online class registration is available.
Website: http://www.pointloma.edu/

General Application Contact: Claire Buckley, Director, Graduate Admissions, 866-692-4723, E-mail: gradinfo@pointloma.edu.

GRADUATE UNITS

Department of Biology Students: 14 part-time (10 women); includes 8 minority (1 Black or African American, non-Hispanic/Latino; 3 Asian, non-Hispanic/Latino; 2 Hispanic/Latino; 2 Two or more races, non-Hispanic/Latino). Average age 31. 3 applicants, 67% accepted, 2 enrolled. *Faculty:* 3 full-time (2 women). Expenses: Contact institution. *Financial support:* Available to part-time students. Applicants required to submit FAFSA. In 2016, 5 master's awarded. *Program availability:* Part-time. Offers biology (MS). *Application deadline:* For fall admission, 7/26 priority date for domestic students; for spring admission, 11/29 priority date for domestic students; for summer admission, 5/23 priority date for domestic students. *Application fee:* $50. *Application Contact:* Claire Buckley, Director of Graduate Admissions, 866-563-2846, E-mail: gradinfo@pointloma.edu. *Director of Master's Program in Biology*, Dr. Dianne Anderson, 619-849-2705, E-mail: dianneanderson@pointloma.edu.

Department of Kinesiology Students: 48 full-time (21 women), 4 part-time (1 woman); includes 21 minority (3 Black or African American, non-Hispanic/Latino; 2 Asian, non-Hispanic/Latino; 13 Hispanic/Latino; 3 Two or more races, non-Hispanic/Latino), 4 international. Average age 26. 84 applicants, 80% accepted, 49 enrolled. *Faculty:* 3 full-time (1 woman), 6 part-time/adjunct (1 woman). Expenses: Contact institution. *Financial support:* Teaching assistantships, scholarships/grants, and unspecified assistantships available. *Program availability:* Part-time, online learning. Offers integrative wellness (MS); sport performance (MS). *Application fee:* $50. *Application Contact:* Claire Buckley, Director, Graduate Admissions, 866-563-2846, E-mail: gradinfo@pointloma.edu. *Chair*, Jeff Sullivan, 619-849-2629, E-mail: jeffsullivan@pointloma.edu.

Fermanian School of Business Students: 33 full-time (14 women), 64 part-time (30 women); includes 32 minority (6 Black or African American, non-Hispanic/Latino; 4 Asian, non-Hispanic/Latino; 19 Hispanic/Latino; 3 Two or more races, non-Hispanic/Latino), 7 international. Average age 31. 71 applicants, 79% accepted, 47 enrolled. *Faculty:* 8 full-time (1 woman), 8 part-time/adjunct (4 women). Expenses: Contact institution. *Financial support:* Applicants required to submit FAFSA. In 2016, 37 master's awarded. *Program availability:* Part-time, evening/weekend. Offers general business (MBA); healthcare management (MBA); innovation and entrepreneurship (MBA); organizational leadership (MBA); project management (MBA). *Application deadline:* For fall admission, 7/26 priority date for domestic students; for spring admission, 11/29 priority date for domestic students; for summer admission, 4/2 priority date for domestic students. Applications are processed on a rolling basis. *Application fee:* $50. Electronic applications accepted. *Application Contact:* Claire Buckley, Director of Graduate Admission, 866-692-4723, E-mail: gradinfo@pointloma.edu. *Associate Dean, Graduate Business*, Jamie Ressler, 619-849-2721, E-mail: jamieressler@pointloma.edu.

Program in Clinical Counseling Students: 10 full-time (8 women), 7 part-time (4 women); includes 8 minority (1 Asian, non-Hispanic/Latino; 6 Hispanic/Latino; 1 Native Hawaiian or other Pacific Islander, non-Hispanic/Latino). Average age 27. 21 applicants, 86% accepted, 17 enrolled. *Faculty:* 1 full-time, 1 part-time/adjunct. Expenses: Contact institution. *Financial support:* Scholarships/grants available. Financial award applicants required to submit FAFSA. Offers clinical counseling (MA). *Application Contact:* Claire Buckley, Director of Graduate Admissions, 866-692-4723, E-mail: gradinfo@pointloma.edu.

Program in Organizational Leadership Students: 1 full-time (0 women), 68 part-time (47 women); includes 30 minority (5 Black or African American, non-Hispanic/Latino; 1 American Indian or Alaska Native, non-Hispanic/Latino; 1 Asian, non-Hispanic/Latino; 20 Hispanic/Latino; 3 Two or more races, non-Hispanic/Latino), 1 international. Average age 35. 35 applicants, 94% accepted, 25 enrolled. *Faculty:* 11 part-time/adjunct (2 women). Expenses: Contact institution. *Program availability:* Online learning. Offers organizational leadership (MA). *Application deadline:* For fall admission, 8/8 priority date for domestic students. *Application Contact:* Claire Buckley, Director, Graduate Admissions, 866-692-4723, E-mail: gradinfo@pointloma.edu.

School of Education Students: 283 full-time (216 women), 404 part-time (314 women); includes 320 minority (24 Black or African American, non-Hispanic/Latino; 2 American Indian or Alaska Native, non-Hispanic/Latino; 25 Asian, non-Hispanic/Latino; 233 Hispanic/Latino; 4 Native Hawaiian or other Pacific Islander, non-Hispanic/Latino; 32 Two or more races, non-Hispanic/Latino), 4 international. Average age 31. 236 applicants, 84% accepted, 166 enrolled. *Faculty:* 10 full-time (8 women), 81 part-time/adjunct (61 women). Expenses: Contact institution. *Financial support:* Career-related internships or fieldwork and scholarships/grants available. Support available to part-time students. Financial award application deadline: 4/10; financial award applicants required to submit FAFSA. In 2016, 151 master's awarded. *Program availability:* Part-time, evening/weekend. Offers counseling and guidance (MA); education (MA, MAT); education specialist mild to moderate (MAT); education specialist moderate to severe (MAT); educational administration (MA); leadership in learning (MA); multiple subject (MAT); single subject (MAT); special education (MA). *Application deadline:* For fall admission, 8/4 priority date for domestic students; for spring admission, 12/8 priority date for domestic students; for summer admission, 4/13 priority date for domestic students. Applications are processed on a rolling basis. *Application fee:* $50. Electronic applications accepted. *Application Contact:* Claire Buckley, Director of Graduate Admission, 866-692-4723, E-mail: gradinfo@pointloma.edu. *Dean*, Dr. Deborah Erickson, 619-849-2332, Fax: 619-849-2579, E-mail: deberickson@pointloma.edu.

School of Nursing Students: 2 full-time (both women), 66 part-time (58 women); includes 35 minority (5 Black or African American, non-Hispanic/Latino; 11 Asian, non-Hispanic/Latino; 10 Hispanic/Latino; 3 Native Hawaiian or other Pacific Islander, non-Hispanic/Latino; 6 Two or more races, non-Hispanic/Latino), 1 international. Average age 36. 28 applicants, 93% accepted, 18 enrolled. *Faculty:* 6 full-time (5 women), 2 part-time/adjunct (both women). Expenses: Contact institution. *Financial support:* Scholarships/grants available. Financial award applicants required to submit FAFSA. In 2016, 32 master's awarded. *Program availability:* Part-time. Offers adult/gerontology nursing (MSN); family/individual health (MSN); general nursing (MSN); nursing (Post-MSN Certificate); pediatric nursing (MSN). *Application deadline:* For fall admission, 7/5 priority date for domestic students; for spring admission, 11/1 priority date for domestic students; for summer admission, 3/22 priority date for domestic students. Applications are processed on a rolling basis. *Application fee:* $50. *Application Contact:* Claire Buckley, Director of Graduate Admissions, 866-692-4723, E-mail: gradinfo@pointloma.edu. *Dean of the School of Nursing*, Dr. Barb Taylor, 619-849-2766, E-mail: bataylor@pointloma.edu.

School of Theology and Christian Ministry Students: 13 part-time (5 women); includes 5 minority (1 American Indian or Alaska Native, non-Hispanic/Latino; 4 Hispanic/Latino). Average age 41. 6 applicants, 83% accepted, 3 enrolled. *Faculty:* 1 part-time/adjunct (0 women). Expenses: Contact institution. *Financial support:* Scholarships/grants available. Financial award application deadline: 6/5; financial award applicants required to submit FAFSA. In 2016, 7 master's awarded. *Program availability:* Part-time, online only, nine-week quads with eight weeks of online coursework and a one-week intensive. Offers theology and Christian ministry (M Min). *Application deadline:* For fall admission, 8/30 priority date for domestic students; for spring admission, 4/4 priority date for domestic students; for summer admission, 6/20 priority date for domestic students. Applications are processed on a rolling basis. *Application fee:* $0. Electronic applications accepted. *Application Contact:* Claire Buckley, Director of Graduate Admissions, 866-692-4723, E-mail: gradinfo@pointloma.edu. *Dean*, Dr. Mark Maddix, 619-849-2234, E-mail: markmaddix@pointloma.edu.

POINT PARK UNIVERSITY, Pittsburgh, PA 15222-1984

General Information Independent, coed, comprehensive institution. CGS member. *Graduate housing:* Room and/or apartments available on a first-come, first-served basis to single students; on-campus housing not available to married students. Housing application deadline: 7/31. *Student services:* Campus employment opportunities, career counseling, free psychological counseling, international student services, low-cost health insurance, services for students with disabilities. *Library facilities:* Point Park University Library.

Computer facilities: Computer purchase and lease plans are available. 309 computers available on campus for general student use. A campuswide network can be accessed from student residence rooms. Online class registration is available.
Website: http://www.pointpark.edu/

General Application Contact: Kathy Ballas, Director, Office of Graduate Admission, 412-392-3812, Fax: 412-392-6164, E-mail: kballas@pointpark.edu.

GRADUATE UNITS

Center for Innovative Learning Expenses: Contact institution. Offers community engagement (PhD). *Application Contact:* Kathy Ballas, Director, Office of Graduate Admission, 412-392-3812, Fax: 412-392-6164, E-mail: kballas@pointpark.edu.

Conservatory of Performing Arts Expenses: Contact institution. *Financial support:* Teaching assistantships with full tuition reimbursements and scholarships/grants available. Financial award application deadline: 3/31; financial award applicants required to submit FAFSA. *Program availability:* Blended/hybrid learning. Offers screenwriting and playwriting (MFA). *Application deadline:* Applications are processed on a rolling basis. *Application fee:* $30. Electronic applications accepted. *Application Contact:* Lynn C. Ribar, Associate Director, Office of Graduate Admission, 412-392-3908, Fax: 412-392-6164, E-mail: lribar@pointpark.edu. *Director*, Ronald Allan-Lindblom, 412-392-6132, Fax: 412-392-2424, E-mail: rlindblom@pointpark.edu.

Rowland School of Business Expenses: Contact institution. *Financial support:* Teaching assistantships with full tuition reimbursements and scholarships/grants available. Financial award application deadline: 3/31; financial award applicants required to submit FAFSA. *Program availability:* Part-time, evening/weekend, 100% online. Offers business (MBA); business analytics (MBA); global management and administration (MBA); health care administration and management (MS); health systems management (MBA); international business (MBA); leadership (MA); management (MBA); management information systems (MBA); organizational leadership (MA); sports, arts and entertainment management (MBA). *Application deadline:* Applications are processed on a rolling basis. *Application fee:* $30. Electronic applications accepted. *Application Contact:* Dayna Coleman, Admissions Counselor, Office of Graduate Admission, 412-392-3807, Fax: 412-392-6164, E-mail: dcoleman@pointpark.edu. *Dean*, Steve Tanzilli, JD, 412-392-4742, Fax: 412-392-8048, E-mail: stanzilli@pointpark.edu.

School of Arts and Sciences Expenses: Contact institution. *Financial support:* Teaching assistantships with full tuition reimbursements and scholarships/grants available. Financial award application deadline: 3/31; financial award applicants required to submit FAFSA. *Program availability:* Part-time, evening/weekend, online learning. Offers adult learning and training (MA); arts and sciences (M Ed, MA, MS, Ed D, Psy D); athletic coaching (M Ed); clinical-community psychology (MA, Psy D); criminal justice administration (MS); curriculum and instruction (MA); educational administration (MA); engineering management (MS); environmental studies (MS); intelligence and global security (MA); leadership and administration (Ed D); secondary education (M Ed); special education grades 7-12 (M Ed); special education PreK-grade 8 (M Ed). *Application deadline:* Applications are processed on a rolling basis. *Application fee:* $30. Electronic applications accepted. *Application Contact:* Kathy Ballas, Director, Office of Graduate Admission, 412-392-3812, Fax: 412-392-6164, E-mail: kballas@pointpark.edu. *Acting Dean*, Dr. Robert Fessler, 412-392-3479, E-mail: rfessler@pointpark.edu.

School of Communication Expenses: Contact institution. *Financial support:* Teaching assistantships with full tuition reimbursements, scholarships/grants, and unspecified assistantships available. Financial award application deadline: 3/31; financial award applicants required to submit FAFSA. *Program availability:* Part-time, evening/weekend. Offers communication technology (MA); media communication (MA). *Application deadline:* Applications are processed on a rolling basis. *Application fee:* $30. Electronic applications accepted. *Application Contact:* Dayna Coleman, Admissions Counselor, Office of Graduate Admission, 412-392-3807, Fax: 412-392-6164, E-mail: dcoleman@pointpark.edu.

POLYTECHNIC UNIVERSITY OF PUERTO RICO, Hato Rey, PR 00918

General Information Independent, coed, comprehensive institution. CGS member. *Graduate housing:* On-campus housing not available. *Research affiliation:* University of Missouri (engineering, mathematics and science), University of Puerto Rico, Mayaguez

Campus (electrical engineering), Virginia Polytechnic Institute and State University (mechanical and electrical engineering), Naval Research Laboratories (mechanical and electrical engineering), U.S. Department of Energy Laboratories (electrical engineering).

GRADUATE UNITS

Graduate School *Program availability:* Part-time, evening/weekend.

POLYTECHNIC UNIVERSITY OF PUERTO RICO, MIAMI CAMPUS, Miami, FL 33166

General Information Independent, coed, comprehensive institution.

GRADUATE UNITS

Graduate School *Program availability:* Part-time, evening/weekend, online learning. Electronic applications accepted.

POLYTECHNIC UNIVERSITY OF PUERTO RICO, ORLANDO CAMPUS, Orlando, FL 32825

General Information Independent, coed, comprehensive institution. *Graduate housing:* On-campus housing not available.

GRADUATE UNITS

Graduate School *Program availability:* Part-time, evening/weekend, online learning. Electronic applications accepted.

PONCE HEALTH SCIENCES UNIVERSITY, Ponce, PR 00732-7004

General Information Independent, coed, graduate-only institution. *Research affiliation:* The University of Texas at San Antonio (health disparities, proteomics, bioinformatics), H.L. Moffitt Cancer Center (cancer biology, oncology), Oregon Health & Science University (neurosciences, cancer, inflammation), University of Puerto Rico, Mayaguez Campus (cancer biology, molecular genetics), University of Puerto Rico, Medical Sciences Campus (translational research), University of Maryland–Institute of Human Virology (HIV/AIDS research).

GRADUATE UNITS

Professional Program Offers medicine (MD).

Program in Biomedical Sciences Offers biomedical sciences (PhD).

Program in Clinical Psychology Offers clinical psychology (PhD, Psy D).

Program in Public Health Offers epidemiology (Dr PH); public health (MPH).

PONTIFICAL CATHOLIC UNIVERSITY OF PUERTO RICO, Ponce, PR 00717-0777

General Information Independent-religious, coed, university. *Graduate housing:* Room and/or apartments available to single students; on-campus housing not available to married students. Housing application deadline: 7/15.

GRADUATE UNITS

College of Arts and Humanities *Program availability:* Part-time, evening/weekend. Offers arts and humanities (MA, Professional Certificate); grammar and writing (Professional Certificate); Hispanic studies (MA); history (MA); painting and drawing (MA); theology and philosophy (M Div).

College of Business Administration *Program availability:* Part-time, evening/weekend. Offers accounting (MBA); business administration (MBA, DBA, PhD, Professional Certificate); finance (MBA); general business (MBA, Professional Certificate); human resources (MBA, Professional Certificate); international business (MBA); management (MBA); management and accounting (Professional Certificate); management information systems (MBA, Professional Certificate); maritime logistics and transportation (Professional Certificate); marketing (MBA); office administration (MBA, MS).

College of Education *Program availability:* Part-time, evening/weekend. Offers business teacher education (M Ed, PhD); counselor education (M Ed); curriculum and instruction (M Ed, PhD); education (M Ed, MA Ed, MRE, PhD); education-general (M Ed, MA Ed); educational leadership and administration (PhD); educational psychology (M Ed); English as a second language (M Ed).

College of Graduate Studies in Behavioral Science and Community Affairs *Program availability:* Part-time, evening/weekend. Offers clinical psychology (PhD, Psy D); clinical social work (MSW); criminology (MA); industrial psychology (PhD); psychology (PhD); public administration (MSS); rehabilitation counseling (MA).

College of Sciences *Program availability:* Part-time, evening/weekend. Offers chemistry (MS); environmental sciences (MS); medical-surgical nursing (MSN); mental health and psychiatric nursing (MSN); sciences (MS, Certificate).

School of Medical Technology Offers medical technology (Certificate).

School of Law *Program availability:* Part-time, evening/weekend. Offers law (JD).

PONTIFICAL COLLEGE JOSEPHINUM, Columbus, OH 43235

General Information Independent-religious, men only, comprehensive institution. *Graduate housing:* Room and/or apartments guaranteed to single students; on-campus housing not available to married students. Housing application deadline: 8/15.

GRADUATE UNITS

School of Theology *Program availability:* Part-time. Offers theology (M Div, MA). All students are sponsored/selected by their diocese.

PONTIFICAL JOHN PAUL II INSTITUTE FOR STUDIES ON MARRIAGE AND FAMILY, Washington, DC 20064

General Information Independent-religious, coed, graduate-only institution.

GRADUATE UNITS

Graduate Programs Offers biotechnology and ethics (MTS); marriage and family (MTS, STD, STL); theology (PhD).

POPE ST. JOHN XXIII NATIONAL SEMINARY, Weston, MA 02493-2618

General Information Independent-religious, men only, graduate-only institution. *Graduate housing:* Room and/or apartments available to single students; on-campus housing not available to married students. Housing application deadline: 8/1.

GRADUATE UNITS

Graduate Program Offers theology (M Div).

PORTLAND STATE UNIVERSITY, Portland, OR 97207-0751

General Information State-supported, coed, university. CGS member. *Enrollment:* 27,229 graduate, professional, and undergraduate students; 2,671 full-time matriculated graduate/professional students (1,569 women), 2,440 part-time matriculated graduate/professional students (1,485 women). *Enrollment by degree level:* 3,901 master's, 694 doctoral, 516 other advanced degrees. *Graduate faculty:* 848 full-time (398 women), 651 part-time/adjunct (321 women). Tuition, state resident: full-time $10,040. Tuition, nonresident: full-time $14,063. *Graduate housing:* Rooms and/or apartments available on a first-come, first-served basis to single and married students. Housing application deadline: 8/30. *Student services:* Campus employment opportunities, campus safety program, career counseling, child daycare facilities, exercise/wellness program, free psychological counseling, international student services, low-cost health insurance, multicultural affairs office, services for students with disabilities, teacher training, writing training. *Library facilities:* Branford P. Millar Library plus 1 other. *Collection:* Students can reserve study rooms. *Research affiliation:* City of Portland (civil engineering, urban planning), Bonneville Power Administration (civil and mechanical engineering, geology, urban studies), Battelle–Pacific Northwest National Laboratory (computer science, geographic information systems, mechanical engineering, science education), Intel Corporation (electronic cooling, engineering), Tri-County Metropolitan Transportation District of Oregon, Tektronix (electrical engineering).

Computer facilities: A campuswide network can be accessed from student residence rooms and from off campus. Online class registration is available. Website: http://www.pdx.edu/

General Application Contact: 503-725-3511, Fax: 503-725-5525, E-mail: admissions@pdx.edu.

GRADUATE UNITS

Graduate Studies Students: 2,671 full-time (1,569 women), 2,440 part-time (1,485 women); includes 1,079 minority (122 Black or African American, non-Hispanic/Latino; 73 American Indian or Alaska Native, non-Hispanic/Latino; 252 Asian, non-Hispanic/Latino; 403 Hispanic/Latino; 16 Native Hawaiian or other Pacific Islander, non-Hispanic/Latino; 213 Two or more races, non-Hispanic/Latino), 676 international. Average age 33. 4,793 applicants, 39% accepted, 1410 enrolled. *Faculty:* 878 full-time (403 women), 727 part-time/adjunct (365 women). Expenses: Contact institution. *Financial support:* In 2016–17, 251 research assistantships with tuition reimbursements (averaging $7,934 per year), 472 teaching assistantships with tuition reimbursements (averaging $6,747 per year) were awarded; fellowships, career-related internships or fieldwork, Federal Work-Study, scholarships/grants, tuition waivers (partial), and unspecified assistantships also available. Support available to part-time students. Financial award application deadline: 3/1; financial award applicants required to submit FAFSA. In 2016, 1,537 master's, 82 doctorates, 163 other advanced degrees awarded. *Program availability:* Part-time, evening/weekend, online learning. *Application deadline:* For fall admission, 6/1 for domestic students, 3/1 for international students; for winter admission, 10/1 for domestic students, 7/1 for international students; for spring admission, 2/1 for domestic students, 11/1 for international students. Applications are processed on a rolling basis. *Application fee:* $65. *Application Contact:* Kelly Doherty, Director of Graduate Admissions, 503-725-5391, Fax: 503-725-3416, E-mail: dohertyk@pdx.edu. *Dean of Graduate Studies,* Dr. Margaret Everett, 503-725-5258, Fax: 503-725-3416, E-mail: everettm@pdx.edu.

College of Liberal Arts and Sciences Students: 692 full-time (420 women), 378 part-time (190 women); includes 170 minority (15 Black or African American, non-Hispanic/Latino; 8 American Indian or Alaska Native, non-Hispanic/Latino; 36 Asian, non-Hispanic/Latino; 66 Hispanic/Latino; 3 Native Hawaiian or other Pacific Islander, non-Hispanic/Latino; 42 Two or more races, non-Hispanic/Latino), 66 international. Average age 32. 1,492 applicants, 26% accepted, 303 enrolled. *Faculty:* 339 full-time (147 women), 191 part-time/adjunct (96 women). Expenses: Contact institution. *Financial support:* In 2016–17, 71 research assistantships with tuition reimbursements (averaging $9,949 per year), 288 teaching assistantships with tuition reimbursements (averaging $8,160 per year) were awarded; career-related internships or fieldwork, Federal Work-Study, scholarships/grants, and tuition waivers (partial) also available. Support available to part-time students. Financial award application deadline: 3/1; financial award applicants required to submit FAFSA. In 2016, 262 master's, 37 doctorates, 46 other advanced degrees awarded. *Program availability:* Part-time, evening/weekend. Offers anthropology (MA); biology (MA, MS, PhD); chemistry (MA, MS, PhD); computational intelligence (Certificate); computer modeling and simulation (Certificate); conflict resolution (MA, MS); English (MA, MFA); environmental management (MEM); environmental sciences and resources (PhD); environmental sciences/biology (PhD); environmental sciences/chemistry (PhD); environmental sciences/civil engineering (PhD); environmental sciences/geography (PhD); environmental sciences/geology (PhD); environmental sciences/physics (PhD); environmental studies (MS); French (MA); general arts and letters education (MAT, MST); general science education (MAT, MST); general social science education (MAT, MST); general speech communication (MA, MS, Certificate); geography (MA, MAT, MS, MST, PhD); geology (MA, MS); German (MA); history (MA); Japanese (MA); liberal arts and sciences (MA, MAT, MEM, MFA, MS, MST, MST, PhD, Certificate); mathematical sciences (PhD); mathematics education (PhD); physics (MA, MS, PhD); psychology (MA, MS, PhD); science/environmental science (MST); science/geology (MAT, MST); sociology (MA, MS, PhD); Spanish (MA); speech-language pathology (MA, MS); statistics (MS); systems science (MS); systems science/anthropology (PhD); systems science/business administration (PhD); systems science/civil engineering (PhD); systems science/economics (PhD); systems science/engineering management (PhD); systems science/general (PhD); systems science/mathematical sciences (PhD); systems science/mechanical engineering (PhD); systems science/psychology (PhD); systems science/sociology (PhD); teaching English to speakers of other languages (MA); world literature and language (MA). *Application deadline:* Applications are processed on a rolling basis. *Application fee:* $65. *Application Contact:* Dr. Todd Rosenstiel, Associate Dean for Research and Graduate Programs, 503-725-8503, Fax: 503-725-3693. *Dean,* Dr. Karen Marrongelle, 503-725-5061, Fax: 503-725-3693.

College of the Arts Students: 104 full-time (55 women), 23 part-time (15 women); includes 16 minority (3 Black or African American, non-Hispanic/Latino; 1 Asian, non-Hispanic/Latino; 6 Hispanic/Latino; 6 Two or more races, non-Hispanic/Latino), 15 international. Average age 31. 161 applicants, 48% accepted, 46 enrolled. *Faculty:* 75 full-time (37 women), 141 part-time/adjunct (64 women). Expenses: Contact institution. *Financial support:* In 2016–17, 12 research assistantships with partial tuition reimbursements (averaging $3,799 per year), 19 teaching assistantships with partial tuition reimbursements (averaging $3,550 per year) were awarded; career-related internships or fieldwork, Federal Work-Study, scholarships/grants, tuition waivers (partial), and unspecified assistantships also available. Support available to part-time students. Financial award application deadline: 3/1; financial award applicants required to submit FAFSA. In 2016, 45 master's awarded. *Program availability:* Part-time. Offers architecture (M Arch); conducting (MMC); drawing (MFA); mixed media (MFA); music education (MAT, MST); painting (MFA); performance (MMP); printmaking (MFA); sculpture (MFA); the arts (M Arch, MA, MAT, MFA, MMC, MMP, MS, MST); theater (MA, MS). *Application deadline:* For fall admission, 3/1 for domestic and international students. Applications are processed on a rolling basis. *Application fee:* $65. *Dean,* Sue Taylor, 503-725-3408, E-mail: taylorsc@pdx.edu.

College of Urban and Public Affairs Students: 253 full-time (143 women), 185 part-time (110 women); includes 92 minority (10 Black or African American, non-Hispanic/Latino; 7 American Indian or Alaska Native, non-Hispanic/Latino; 13 Asian, non-Hispanic/Latino; 40 Hispanic/Latino; 1 Native Hawaiian or other Pacific Islander, non-Hispanic/Latino; 21 Two or more races, non-Hispanic/Latino), 39 international. Average age 34. 430 applicants, 57% accepted, 182 enrolled. *Faculty:* 75 full-time (29 women), 50 part-time/adjunct (21 women). Expenses: Contact institution. *Financial support:* In 2016–17, 46 research assistantships with tuition reimbursements (averaging $6,032 per year), 32 teaching assistantships with full tuition reimbursements (averaging $7,032 per year) were awarded; fellowships, career-related internships or fieldwork, Federal Work-Study, scholarships/grants, tuition waivers (partial), and unspecified assistantships also available. Support available to part-time students. Financial award application deadline: 3/1; financial award applicants required to submit FAFSA. In 2016, 164 master's, 6 doctorates awarded. *Program availability:* Part-time, evening/weekend. Offers applied economics (MA, MS); criminology and criminal justice (MS, PhD); general economics (MA, MS); government (MA, MAT, MPA, MS, MST, PhD); political science (MA, MAT, MS, MST, PhD); public administration (MPA); public affairs and policy (PhD); urban and public affairs (MA, MAT, MPA, MPH, MS, MST, MURP, MUS, PhD, Certificate); urban and regional planning (MURP); urban studies (MUS, PhD); urban studies and planning (MURP, MUS, PhD). *Application fee:* $65. *Dean,* Dr. Stephen Percy, 503-725-5143, Fax: 503-725-5199, E-mail: spercy@pdx.edu.

Maseeh College of Engineering and Computer Science Students: 414 full-time (117 women), 373 part-time (106 women); includes 101 minority (8 Black or African American, non-Hispanic/Latino; 54 Asian, non-Hispanic/Latino; 19 Hispanic/Latino; 20 Two or more races, non-Hispanic/Latino), 409 international. Average age 31. 960 applicants, 40% accepted, 225 enrolled. *Faculty:* 103 full-time (16 women), 40 part-time/adjunct (7 women). Expenses: Contact institution. *Financial support:* In 2016–17, 67 research assistantships with tuition reimbursements (averaging $6,608 per year), 81 teaching assistantships with tuition reimbursements (averaging $3,922 per year) were awarded; career-related internships or fieldwork, Federal Work-Study, scholarships/grants, and unspecified assistantships also available. Support available to part-time students. Financial award application deadline: 3/1; financial award applicants required to submit FAFSA. In 2016, 251 master's, 17 doctorates awarded. *Program availability:* Part-time, evening/weekend. Offers civil and environmental engineering (M Eng, MS, PhD); civil and environmental engineering management (M Eng); computer science (MS, PhD); electrical and computer engineering (M Eng, MS, PhD); engineering and computer science (M Eng, ME, MS, MSE, PhD, Certificate); engineering and technology management (M Eng); engineering management (MS); environmental sciences and resources (PhD); manufacturing engineering (ME); manufacturing management (M Eng); mechanical engineering (M Eng, MS, PhD); software engineering (MSE); systems science (PhD); systems science/engineering management (PhD). *Application deadline:* For fall admission, 4/1 for domestic students, 3/1 for international students; for winter admission, 9/1 for domestic and international students; for spring admission, 2/1 for domestic and international students. *Application fee:* $65. *Dean,* Dr. Renjeng Su, 503-725-8393, Fax: 503-725-2825, E-mail: renjengs@pdx.edu.

OHSU-PSU School of Public Health Expenses: Contact institution. Offers community health (PhD); health management and policy (MPH); health promotion (MPH); health studies (MA, MS); health systems and policy (PhD); public health (MA, MPH, MS, PhD). *Application Contact:* Kelly Doherty, Director of Graduate Admissions, 503-725-5391, Fax: 503-725-3416, E-mail: dohertyk@pdx.edu. *Dean,* David Bangsberg, 503-494-8257.

School of Business Administration Students: 240 full-time (118 women), 187 part-time (80 women); includes 92 minority (16 Black or African American, non-Hispanic/Latino; 4 American Indian or Alaska Native, non-Hispanic/Latino; 40 Asian, non-Hispanic/Latino; 20 Hispanic/Latino; 12 Two or more races, non-Hispanic/Latino), 99 international. Average age 33. 407 applicants, 64% accepted, 189 enrolled. *Faculty:* 43 full-time (20 women), 72 part-time/adjunct (18 women). Expenses: Contact institution. *Financial support:* In 2016–17, 16 research assistantships with partial tuition reimbursements (averaging $7,987 per year) were awarded; career-related internships or fieldwork, Federal Work-Study, scholarships/grants, tuition waivers (partial), and unspecified assistantships also available. Support available to part-time students. Financial award application deadline: 3/1; financial award applicants required to submit FAFSA. In 2016, 164 master's awarded. *Program availability:* Part-time, evening/weekend. Offers business administration (MBA, MIM, MRED, MS, MSFA, PhD); financial analysis (MSFA); global supply chain management (MS); international management (MIM); real estate development (MRED). *Application deadline:* For fall admission, 4/1 for domestic students, 3/1 for international students. *Application fee:* $65. Electronic applications accepted. *Application Contact:* Pam Mitchell, Director, 503-725-4733, E-mail: mitchep@pdx.edu. *Dean,* Dr. Cliff Allen, 503-725-5053, Fax: 503-725-5850, E-mail: cliffa@pdx.edu.

School of Education Students: 480 full-time (342 women), 756 part-time (590 women); includes 311 minority (29 Black or African American, non-Hispanic/Latino; 22 American Indian or Alaska Native, non-Hispanic/Latino; 54 Asian, non-Hispanic/Latino; 150 Hispanic/Latino; 6 Native Hawaiian or other Pacific Islander, non-Hispanic/Latino; 50 Two or more races, non-Hispanic/Latino), 38 international. Average age 36. 455 applicants, 51% accepted, 205 enrolled. *Faculty:* 67 full-time (44 women), 94 part-time/adjunct (69 women). Expenses: Contact institution. *Financial support:* In 2016–17, 6 research assistantships with tuition reimbursements (averaging $7,366 per year), 5 teaching assistantships with tuition reimbursements (averaging $5,621 per year) were awarded; career-related internships or fieldwork, Federal Work-Study, institutionally sponsored loans, scholarships/grants, and unspecified assistantships also available. Support available to part-time students. Financial award application deadline: 3/1; financial award applicants required to submit FAFSA. In 2016, 412 master's, 16 doctorates awarded. *Program availability:* Part-time, evening/weekend. Offers education (M Ed, MA, MAT, MS, MST, Ed D). *Application deadline:* For fall admission, 4/1 for domestic and international students; for winter admission, 9/1 for domestic and international students; for spring admission, 11/1 for domestic and international students. *Application fee:* $65. Electronic applications accepted. *Application Contact:* Information Contact, 503-725-4619, Fax: 503-725-5599, E-mail: gseinfo@pdx.edu. *Dean,* Dr. Randy Hitz, 503-725-4697, Fax: 503-725-5399, E-mail: hitz@pdx.edu.

School of Social Work Students: 358 full-time (284 women), 270 part-time (222 women); includes 188 minority (33 Black or African American, non-Hispanic/Latino; 22 American Indian or Alaska Native, non-Hispanic/Latino; 20 Asian, non-Hispanic/Latino; 75 Hispanic/Latino; 1 Native Hawaiian or other Pacific Islander, non-

Hispanic/Latino; 37 Two or more races, non-Hispanic/Latino), 2 international. Average age 35. 794 applicants, 33% accepted, 239 enrolled. *Faculty:* 35 full-time (26 women), 41 part-time/adjunct (32 women). Expenses: Contact institution. *Financial support:* In 2016–17, 6 research assistantships with tuition reimbursements (averaging $7,366 per year), 5 teaching assistantships with tuition reimbursements (averaging $5,621 per year) were awarded; career-related internships or fieldwork, Federal Work-Study, scholarships/grants, tuition waivers (partial), and unspecified assistantships also available. Support available to part-time students. Financial award application deadline: 3/1; financial award applicants required to submit FAFSA. In 2016, 221 master's, 6 doctorates awarded. *Program availability:* Part-time. Offers social work (MSW); social work and social research (PhD). *Application deadline:* For fall admission, 2/1 for domestic and international students. *Application fee:* $65. *Application Contact:* Prof. Sarah Bradley, Director of MSW Program, 503-725-8028, Fax: 503-725-5545, E-mail: bradles@pdx.edu. *Dean,* Dr. Laura B. Nissen, 503-725-3997, Fax: 503-725-5545, E-mail: nissen@pdx.edu.

POST UNIVERSITY, Waterbury, CT 06723-2540

General Information Independent, coed, comprehensive institution.

GRADUATE UNITS

Program in Business Administration *Program availability:* Online learning. Offers accounting (MSA); business administration (MBA); corporate innovation (MBA); entrepreneurship (MBA); finance (MBA); healthcare (MBA); leadership (MBA); marketing (MBA); project management (MBA).

Program in Education *Program availability:* Online learning. Offers education (M Ed); higher education administration (M Ed); instructional design and technology (M Ed); online teaching (M Ed); teaching and learning (M Ed); TESOL (teaching English to speakers of other languages) (M Ed).

Program in Human Services *Program availability:* Part-time, evening/weekend, online learning. Offers human services (MS); human services/alcohol and drug counseling (MS); human services/clinical counseling (MS); human services/non-profit management (MS).

Program in Public Administration *Program availability:* Online learning. Offers public administration (MPA).

PRAIRIE VIEW A&M UNIVERSITY, Prairie View, TX 77446

General Information State-supported, coed, university. *Enrollment:* 8,762 graduate, professional, and undergraduate students; 617 full-time matriculated graduate/professional students (379 women), 728 part-time matriculated graduate/professional students (518 women). *Enrollment by degree level:* 1,182 master's, 125 doctoral, 38 other advanced degrees. *Graduate faculty:* 109 full-time (48 women), 25 part-time/adjunct (18 women). Tuition, state resident: full-time $4362; part-time $273.48 per credit hour. Tuition, nonresident: full-time $12,390; part-time $534.10 per credit hour. *Required fees:* $2782; $178.26 per credit hour. *Graduate housing:* Rooms and/or apartments available on a first-come, first-served basis to single and married students. Typical cost: $8754 (including board) for single students. Housing application deadline: 4/16. *Student services:* Campus employment opportunities, campus safety program, career counseling, exercise/wellness program, free psychological counseling, grant writing training, international student services, low-cost health insurance, multicultural affairs office, services for students with disabilities, teacher training, writing training. *Library facilities:* John B. Coleman Library plus 4 others. *Collection:* Books: 345,971 (physical), 16,626 (digital/electronic); Serial titles: 199 (physical); Databases: 81. Weekly public service hours: 97; students can reserve study rooms. *Research affiliation:* U.S. Department of Education (DOE) (engineering), U.S. Department of Energy (engineering and sciences), Science and Engineering Alliance, NASA (space radiation on material systems and devices), Sandia National Laboratories (engineering and chemistry), Lawrence Livermore National Laboratory (engineering and sciences).

Computer facilities: 341 computers available on campus for general student use. A campuswide network can be accessed from student residence rooms and from off campus. Online class registration is available.
Website: http://www.pvamu.edu/

General Application Contact: Pauline Walker, Office of Graduate Admissions, 936-261-3521, Fax: 936-261-3529, E-mail: gradadmissions@pvamu.edu.

GRADUATE UNITS

College of Agriculture and Human Sciences Students: 53 full-time (43 women), 24 part-time (20 women); includes 70 minority (62 Black or African American, non-Hispanic/Latino; 4 Asian, non-Hispanic/Latino; 3 Hispanic/Latino; 1 Two or more races, non-Hispanic/Latino), 1 international. Average age 33. 45 applicants, 93% accepted, 37 enrolled. *Faculty:* 5 full-time (3 women). Expenses: Contact institution. *Financial support:* Research assistantships, career-related internships or fieldwork, Federal Work-Study, institutionally sponsored loans, scholarships/grants, tuition waivers (full and partial), and unspecified assistantships available. Support available to part-time students. Financial award application deadline: 4/1; financial award applicants required to submit FAFSA. In 2016, 24 master's awarded. *Program availability:* Part-time, evening/weekend. Offers agriculture and human sciences (MS). *Application deadline:* For fall admission, 5/1 priority date for domestic and international students; for spring admission, 10/11 priority date for domestic students, 9/1 priority date for international students; for summer admission, 3/1 priority date for domestic students, 2/1 priority date for international students. Applications are processed on a rolling basis. *Application fee:* $50. Electronic applications accepted. *Application Contact:* Pauline Walker, Administrative Assistant II, 936-261-3521, Fax: 936-261-3529, E-mail: gradadmissions@pvamu.edu. *Interim Dean and Director of Land-Grant Programs,* Dr. James Palmer, 936-261-2214, E-mail: jmpalmer@pvamu.edu.

College of Arts and Sciences Students: 11 full-time (9 women), 5 part-time (2 women); includes 10 minority (11 Black or African American, non-Hispanic/Latino; 1 Asian, non-Hispanic/Latino), 3 international. Average age 29. 11 applicants, 91% accepted, 8 enrolled. *Faculty:* 8 full-time (1 woman). Expenses: Contact institution. *Financial support:* Fellowships, research assistantships, teaching assistantships, career-related internships or fieldwork, Federal Work-Study, institutionally sponsored loans, and tuition waivers (full and partial) available. Support available to part-time students. Financial award application deadline: 4/1; financial award applicants required to submit FAFSA. In 2016, 13 master's awarded. *Program availability:* Part-time, evening/weekend. Offers arts and sciences (MA, MS); chemistry (MS). *Application deadline:* For fall admission, 5/1 priority date for domestic and international students; for spring admission, 10/11 priority date for domestic students, 9/1 priority date for international students; for summer admission, 3/1 priority date for domestic students, 2/1 priority date for international students. Applications are processed on a rolling basis. *Application fee:* $50. Electronic applications accepted. *Application Contact:* Pauline Walker, Administrative Assistant II,

Research and Graduate Studies, 936-261-3521, Fax: 936-261-3529, E-mail: gradadmissions@pvamu.edu. *Dean*, Dr. Danny R. Kelley, 936-261-3180, Fax: 936-261-3188, E-mail: drkelley@pvamu.edu.

Division of Social Work, Behavioral and Political Sciences Students: 2 full-time (both women), 1 part-time (0 women); all minorities (all Black or African American, non-Hispanic/Latino). Average age 41. 3 applicants, 100% accepted, 2 enrolled. *Faculty:* 4 full-time (1 woman). Expenses: Contact institution. *Financial support:* Career-related internships or fieldwork, Federal Work-Study, institutionally sponsored loans, and tuition waivers available. Financial award application deadline: 4/1; financial award applicants required to submit FAFSA. In 2016, 7 master's awarded. *Program availability:* Part-time, evening/weekend. Offers sociology (MA). *Application deadline:* For fall admission, 5/1 priority date for domestic and international students; for spring admission, 10/1 priority date for domestic students, 9/1 priority date for international students; for summer admission, 3/1 priority date for domestic students, 2/1 priority date for international students. Applications are processed on a rolling basis. *Application fee:* $50. Electronic applications accepted. *Application Contact:* Pauline Walker, Administrative Assistant II, Research and Graduate Studies, 936-261-3521, Fax: 936-261-3529, E-mail: gradadmissions@pvamu.edu. *Division Head*, Dr. Walle Engedayehu, 936-261-3202, Fax: 936-261-3229, E-mail: waengedayehu@pvamu.edu.

College of Business Students: 81 full-time (49 women), 157 part-time (89 women); includes 205 minority (181 Black or African American, non-Hispanic/Latino; 14 Asian, non-Hispanic/Latino; 10 Hispanic/Latino), 18 international. Average age 32. 172 applicants, 94% accepted, 104 enrolled. Expenses: Contact institution. *Financial support:* In 2016–17, 5 students received support, including 2 research assistantships (averaging $24,000 per year), 5 teaching assistantships (averaging $60,000 per year); scholarships/grants and unspecified assistantships also available. Financial award application deadline: 4/1; financial award applicants required to submit FAFSA. In 2016, 87 master's awarded. *Program availability:* Part-time, evening/weekend. Offers accounting (MS); business administration (MBA). *Application deadline:* For fall admission, 5/1 for domestic students, 5/1 priority date for international students; for spring admission, 10/1 for domestic students, 9/1 priority date for international students; for summer admission, 3/1 for domestic students, 2/1 for international students. Applications are processed on a rolling basis. *Application fee:* $50. Electronic applications accepted. *Application Contact:* Gabriel Crosby, Director, Graduate Programs in Business, 936-261-9217, Fax: 936-261-9232, E-mail: mba@pvamu.edu. *Dean*, Dr. Munir Quddus, 936-261-9200, Fax: 936-261-9241, E-mail: cob@pvamu.edu.

College of Education Students: 150 full-time (119 women), 351 part-time (273 women); includes 468 minority (442 Black or African American, non-Hispanic/Latino; 2 American Indian or Alaska Native, non-Hispanic/Latino; 1 Asian, non-Hispanic/Latino; 19 Hispanic/Latino; 4 Two or more races, non-Hispanic/Latino), 8 international. Average age 39. 329 applicants, 85% accepted, 213 enrolled. *Faculty:* 24 full-time (13 women), 11 part-time/adjunct (9 women). Expenses: Contact institution. *Financial support:* Career-related internships or fieldwork, institutionally sponsored loans, scholarships/grants, and unspecified assistantships available. Support available to part-time students. Financial award application deadline: 4/1; financial award applicants required to submit FAFSA. In 2016, 146 master's, 6 doctorates awarded. *Program availability:* Part-time, evening/weekend, blended/hybrid learning. Offers curriculum and instruction (M Ed, MA Ed, MS Ed); education (M Ed, MA, MA Ed, MS, MS Ed, PhD); educational leadership and counseling (M Ed, MA, MS Ed, PhD); health and kinesiology (M Ed, MS). *Application deadline:* For fall admission, 5/1 priority date for domestic and international students; for spring admission, 10/1 priority date for domestic students, 9/1 priority date for international students; for summer admission, 3/1 priority date for domestic students, 2/1 priority date for international students. Applications are processed on a rolling basis. *Application fee:* $50. Electronic applications accepted. *Application Contact:* Pauline Walker, Administrative Assistant II, Research and Graduate Studies, 936-261-3521, Fax: 936-261-3529, E-mail: gradadmissions@pvamu.edu. *Dean*, Dr. Phyllis Metcalf-Turner, 936-261-3600, Fax: 936-261-3621, E-mail: pmmetcalf@pvamu.edu.

College of Engineering Students: 171 full-time (45 women), 50 part-time (17 women); includes 89 minority (70 Black or African American, non-Hispanic/Latino; 16 Asian, non-Hispanic/Latino; 3 Hispanic/Latino), 115 international. Average age 30. 155 applicants, 94% accepted, 85 enrolled. *Faculty:* 27 full-time (7 women), 2 part-time/adjunct (both women). Expenses: Contact institution. *Financial support:* In 2016–17, 1 fellowship with full tuition reimbursement (averaging $14,000 per year), 33 research assistantships with full and partial tuition reimbursements (averaging $17,260 per year), 3 teaching assistantships with full and partial tuition reimbursements (averaging $15,000 per year) were awarded; career-related internships or fieldwork, institutionally sponsored loans, scholarships/grants, health care benefits, tuition waivers (full), and unspecified assistantships also available. Financial award application deadline: 4/1; financial award applicants required to submit FAFSA. In 2016, 43 master's, 3 doctorates awarded. *Program availability:* Part-time, evening/weekend. Offers computer information systems (MSCIS); computer science (MSCS); electrical engineering (MSEE, PhDEE); general engineering (MS Engr). *Application deadline:* For fall admission, 5/1 priority date for domestic and international students; for spring admission, 10/1 priority date for domestic students, 9/1 priority date for international students; for summer admission, 3/1 priority date for domestic students, 2/1 priority date for international students. Applications are processed on a rolling basis. *Application fee:* $50. Electronic applications accepted. *Application Contact:* Pauline Walker, Administrative Assistant II, Research and Graduate Studies, 936-261-3521, Fax: 936-261-3529, E-mail: gradadmissions@pvamu.edu. *Dean*, Dr. Kendall T. Harris, 936-261-9900, Fax: 936-261-9868, E-mail: tharris@pvamu.edu.

College of Juvenile Justice and Psychology Students: 29 full-time (24 women), 31 part-time (22 women); includes 53 minority (49 Black or African American, non-Hispanic/Latino; 3 Hispanic/Latino; 1 Two or more races, non-Hispanic/Latino), 5 international. Average age 30. 37 applicants, 92% accepted, 25 enrolled. *Faculty:* 6 full-time (2 women), 6 part-time/adjunct (3 women). Expenses: Contact institution. *Financial support:* In 2016–17, 20 students received support, including 20 research assistantships; teaching assistantships, scholarships/grants, and unspecified assistantships also available. Financial award application deadline: 4/1; financial award applicants required to submit FAFSA. In 2016, 16 master's, 2 doctorates awarded. *Program availability:* Part-time, evening/weekend, online only, 100% online. Offers clinical adolescent psychology (PhD); juvenile forensic psychology (MSJFP); juvenile justice (MSJJ, PhD). *Application deadline:* For fall admission, 5/1 priority date for domestic and international students; for spring admission, 10/1 priority date for domestic students, 9/1 priority date for international students; for summer admission, 3/1 priority date for domestic students, 2/1 priority date for international students. Applications are processed on a rolling basis. *Application fee:* $50. Electronic applications accepted.

Application Contact: Pauline Walker, Executive Secretary, Graduate Program, 936-261-3521, Fax: 936-261-3529, E-mail: gradadmissions@pvamu.edu. *Dean*, Dr. Tamara L. Brown, 936-261-5206, Fax: 936-261-5253, E-mail: tlbrown@pvamu.edu.

College of Nursing Students: 74 full-time (65 women), 57 part-time (52 women); includes 119 minority (90 Black or African American, non-Hispanic/Latino; 20 Asian, non-Hispanic/Latino; 9 Hispanic/Latino), 5 international. Average age 35. 35 applicants, 97% accepted, 32 enrolled. *Faculty:* 14 full-time (13 women), 3 part-time/adjunct (all women). Expenses: Contact institution. *Financial support:* Career-related internships or fieldwork, Federal Work-Study, institutionally sponsored loans, scholarships/grants, and traineeships available. Support available to part-time students. Financial award application deadline: 4/1; financial award applicants required to submit FAFSA. In 2016, 41 master's, 8 doctorates awarded. *Program availability:* Part-time, evening/weekend. Offers nursing (MSN, DNP). *Application deadline:* For fall admission, 5/1 priority date for domestic and international students; for spring admission, 10/1 priority date for domestic students, 9/1 priority date for international students; for summer admission, 3/1 priority date for domestic students, 2/1 priority date for international students. Applications are processed on a rolling basis. *Application fee:* $50. Electronic applications accepted. *Application Contact:* Dr. Forest Smith, Director of Student Services and Admissions, 713-797-7031, Fax: 713-797-7012, E-mail: fdsmith@pvamu.edu. *Dean*, Dr. Betty N. Adams, 713-797-7009, Fax: 713-797-7013, E-mail: bnadams@pvamu.edu.

School of Architecture Students: 45 full-time (23 women), 18 part-time (12 women); includes 54 minority (46 Black or African American, non-Hispanic/Latino; 1 American Indian or Alaska Native, non-Hispanic/Latino; 7 Hispanic/Latino), 8 international. Average age 30. 46 applicants, 91% accepted, 36 enrolled. *Faculty:* 3 full-time (0 women), 3 part-time/adjunct (1 woman). Expenses: Contact institution. *Financial support:* Career-related internships or fieldwork, Federal Work-Study, institutionally sponsored loans, scholarships/grants, tuition waivers (full and partial), and unspecified assistantships available. Support available to part-time students. Financial award application deadline: 4/1; financial award applicants required to submit FAFSA. In 2016, 24 master's awarded. *Program availability:* Part-time, evening/weekend. Offers architecture (M Arch, MCD). *Application deadline:* For fall admission, 5/1 priority date for domestic and international students; for spring admission, 10/1 priority date for domestic students, 9/1 priority date for international students; for summer admission, 3/1 priority date for domestic students, 2/1 priority date for international students. Applications are processed on a rolling basis. *Application fee:* $50. Electronic applications accepted. *Application Contact:* Pauline Walker, Administrative Assistant II, Research and Graduate Studies, 936-261-3521, Fax: 936-261-3529, E-mail: pmwalker@pvamu.edu. *Dean*, Dr. Ikhlas Sabouni, 936-261-9800, Fax: 936-261-2350, E-mail: isabouni@pvamu.edu.

PRATT INSTITUTE, Brooklyn, NY 11205-3899

General Information Independent, coed, comprehensive institution. *Enrollment:* 4,659 graduate, professional, and undergraduate students; 1,248 full-time matriculated graduate/professional students (915 women), 96 part-time matriculated graduate/professional students (69 women). *Enrollment by degree level:* 1,342 master's, 2 other advanced degrees. *Tuition:* Full-time $29,646. *Required fees:* $1938. *Graduate housing:* Room and/or apartments available on a first-come, first-served basis to single students; on-campus housing not available to married students. Typical cost: $18,880 per year ($23,006 including board). Room and board charges vary according to board plan and housing facility selected. Housing application deadline: 5/1. *Student services:* Campus employment opportunities, campus safety program, career counseling, exercise/wellness program, free psychological counseling, grant writing training, international student services, low-cost health insurance, multicultural affairs office, services for students with disabilities, teacher training, writing training. *Library facilities:* Pratt Institute Library. *Research affiliation:* The Procter & Gamble Company (product design), General Motors (transportation), Ford Motor Company (transportation).

Computer facilities: A campuswide network can be accessed from student residence rooms and from off campus. Online class registration is available.
Website: http://www.pratt.edu/

General Application Contact: Natalie Capannelli, Director of Graduate Admissions, 718-636-3551, Fax: 718-636-3670, E-mail: ncapanne@pratt.edu.

GRADUATE UNITS

School of Architecture Students: 348 full-time (200 women), 17 part-time (6 women); includes 84 minority (19 Black or African American, non-Hispanic/Latino; 24 Asian, non-Hispanic/Latino; 35 Hispanic/Latino; 6 Two or more races, non-Hispanic/Latino), 153 international. Average age 27. 728 applicants, 74% accepted, 127 enrolled. *Faculty:* 10 full-time (4 women), 99 part-time/adjunct (31 women). Expenses: Contact institution. *Financial support:* Career-related internships or fieldwork, Federal Work-Study, institutionally sponsored loans, scholarships/grants, health care benefits, and unspecified assistantships available. Support available to part-time students. Financial award application deadline: 2/1; financial award applicants required to submit FAFSA. In 2016, 137 master's awarded. Offers architecture (M Arch, MS, MS Arch, MSCRP); architecture (first-professional) (M Arch); architecture (post-professional) (MS Arch); architecture and urban design (MS); city and regional planning (MSCRP); facilities management (MS); historic preservation (MS); real estate practice (MS); sustainable environmental systems (MS); urban placemaking and management (MS). *Application deadline:* For fall admission, 1/5 for domestic and international students; for spring admission, 10/1 for domestic and international students. *Application fee:* $50 ($90 for international students). Electronic applications accepted. *Application Contact:* Natalie Capannelli, Director of Graduate Admissions, 718-636-3551, Fax: 718-399-4242, E-mail: ncapanne@pratt.edu. *Dean*, Thomas Hanrahan, 718-399-4304, Fax: 718-399-4315, E-mail: hanrahan@pratt.edu.

School of Art Students: 346 full-time (289 women), 8 part-time (6 women); includes 81 minority (26 Black or African American, non-Hispanic/Latino; 1 American Indian or Alaska Native, non-Hispanic/Latino; 16 Asian, non-Hispanic/Latino; 30 Hispanic/Latino; 8 Two or more races, non-Hispanic/Latino), 146 international. Average age 27. 858 applicants, 47% accepted, 144 enrolled. *Faculty:* 22 full-time (13 women), 141 part-time/adjunct (68 women). Expenses: Contact institution. *Financial support:* Career-related internships or fieldwork, Federal Work-Study, institutionally sponsored loans, scholarships/grants, health care benefits, and unspecified assistantships available. Support available to part-time students. Financial award application deadline: 2/1; financial award applicants required to submit FAFSA. In 2016, 170 master's awarded. *Program availability:* Part-time. Offers art (MFA, MPS, MS, Adv C); art and design education (MS, Adv C); art therapy and creativity development (MPS); arts and cultural management (MPS); dance/movement therapy (MS); design management (MPS); digital arts (MFA); fine arts (MFA). *Application deadline:* For fall admission, 1/5 for domestic and international students; for spring admission, 10/1 for domestic and international students. *Application fee:* $50 ($90 for international students). Electronic applications accepted. *Application Contact:* Natalie Capannelli, Director of Graduate Admissions, 718-636-3551, Fax: 718-399-4242, E-mail: ncapanne@pratt.edu. *Dean*, Gerry Snyder, 718-636-3619, E-mail: gsnyder@pratt.edu.

Pratt Institute

School of Design Students: 367 full-time (278 women), 7 part-time (6 women); includes 55 minority (8 Black or African American, non-Hispanic/Latino; 27 Asian, non-Hispanic/Latino; 17 Hispanic/Latino; 1 Native Hawaiian or other Pacific Islander, non-Hispanic/Latino; 2 Two or more races, non-Hispanic/Latino), 233 international. Average age 26. 947 applicants, 45% accepted, 133 enrolled. *Faculty:* 12 full-time (5 women), 136 part-time/adjunct (56 women). Expenses: Contact institution. *Financial support:* Career-related internships or fieldwork, Federal Work-Study, institutionally sponsored loans, scholarships/grants, health care benefits, and unspecified assistantships available. Support available to part-time students. Financial award application deadline: 2/1; financial award applicants required to submit FAFSA. In 2016, 151 master's awarded. *Program availability:* Part-time. Offers communications design (MFA); design (MFA, MID, MS); industrial design (MID); interior design (MFA); package design (MS). *Application deadline:* For fall admission, 1/5 for domestic and international students; for spring admission, 10/1 for domestic and international students. *Application fee:* $50 ($90 for international students). Electronic applications accepted. *Application Contact:* Natalie Capannelli, Director of Graduate Admissions, 718-636-3551, Fax: 718-636-3670, E-mail: ncapanne@pratt.edu. *Dean, School of Design,* Anita Cooney, 718-687-5744, Fax: 718-636-3410, E-mail: acooney@pratt.edu.

School of Information Students: 95 full-time (77 women), 62 part-time (50 women); includes 43 minority (11 Black or African American, non-Hispanic/Latino; 12 Asian, non-Hispanic/Latino; 17 Hispanic/Latino; 3 Two or more races, non-Hispanic/Latino), 11 international. Average age 31. 129 applicants, 88% accepted, 59 enrolled. *Faculty:* 9 full-time (4 women), 26 part-time/adjunct (13 women). Expenses: Contact institution. *Financial support:* Career-related internships or fieldwork, Federal Work-Study, institutionally sponsored loans, scholarships/grants, health care benefits, and unspecified assistantships available. Support available to part-time students. Financial award application deadline: 2/1; financial award applicants required to submit FAFSA. In 2016, 64 master's, 1 other advanced degree awarded. *Program availability:* Part-time. Offers information (MS, Adv C). *Application deadline:* For fall admission, 1/5 for domestic and international students; for spring admission, 10/1 for domestic and international students. Applications are processed on a rolling basis. *Application fee:* $50 ($90 for international students). Electronic applications accepted. *Application Contact:* Natalie Capannelli, Director of Graduate Admissions, 718-636-3551, Fax: 718-399-4242, E-mail: ncapanne@pratt.edu. *Dean,* Dr. Tula Giannini, 212-647-7682, Fax: 212-367-2492, E-mail: giannini@pratt.edu.

School of Liberal Arts and Sciences Students: 92 full-time (71 women), 2 part-time (1 woman); includes 37 minority (15 Black or African American, non-Hispanic/Latino; 2 American Indian or Alaska Native, non-Hispanic/Latino; 2 Asian, non-Hispanic/Latino; 11 Hispanic/Latino; 7 Two or more races, non-Hispanic/Latino), 15 international. Average age 28. 178 applicants, 72% accepted, 42 enrolled. Expenses: Contact institution. *Financial support:* Career-related internships or fieldwork, Federal Work-Study, institutionally sponsored loans, scholarships/grants, health care benefits, and unspecified assistantships available. Support available to part-time students. Financial award application deadline: 2/1; financial award applicants required to submit FAFSA. In 2016, 31 master's awarded. Offers history of art and design (MS); liberal arts and sciences (MA, MFA, MS); media studies (MA); performance and performance studies (MFA); writing (MFA). *Application deadline:* For fall admission, 1/5 for domestic and international students; for spring admission, 10/1 for domestic and international students. *Application fee:* $50 ($90 for international students). Electronic applications accepted. *Application Contact:* Natalie Capannelli, Director of Graduate Admissions, 718-636-3551, Fax: 718-399-4242, E-mail: ncapanne@pratt.edu. *Dean,* Andrew W. Barnes, 718-636-3570, Fax: 718-399-4586, E-mail: awbarnes@pratt.edu.

PRESCOTT COLLEGE, Prescott, AZ 86301

General Information Independent, coed, comprehensive institution. *Enrollment:* 703 graduate, professional, and undergraduate students; 89 full-time matriculated graduate/professional students (71 women), 258 part-time matriculated graduate/professional students (196 women). *Enrollment by degree level:* 283 master's, 54 doctoral, 5 other advanced degrees. *Graduate faculty:* 15 full-time (11 women), 19 part-time/adjunct (12 women). *Tuition:* Full-time $19,680. One-time fee: $260 part-time. *Graduate housing:* Room and/or apartments available on a first-come, first-served basis to single students; on-campus housing not available to married students. Typical cost: $8900 per year ($9300 including board). Room and board charges vary according to housing facility selected. Housing application deadline: 5/1. *Student services:* Campus employment opportunities, low-cost health insurance, services for students with disabilities, teacher training. *Library facilities:* Prescott College Library. *Research affiliation:* Marshall Foundation (youth and wilderness), U.S. Department of Agriculture (USDA) (agro-ecology), National Park Service (forest health), Packard Foundation (Kino Bay research).

Computer facilities: 100 computers available on campus for general student use. A campuswide network can be accessed from student residence rooms. Learning management system, free e-portfolios available.
Website: http://www.prescott.edu/

General Application Contact: Amber Harris, Assistant Director for Graduate Admissions, 928-350-2100, Fax: 928-776-5242, E-mail: admissions@prescott.edu.

GRADUATE UNITS

Graduate Programs Students: 58 full-time (51 women), 221 part-time (168 women); includes 41 minority (4 Black or African American, non-Hispanic/Latino; 7 American Indian or Alaska Native, non-Hispanic/Latino; 2 Asian, non-Hispanic/Latino; 14 Hispanic/Latino; 2 Native Hawaiian or other Pacific Islander, non-Hispanic/Latino; 12 Two or more races, non-Hispanic/Latino), 8 international. Average age 37. 254 applicants, 81% accepted, 129 enrolled. *Faculty:* 11 full-time (5 women), 18 part-time/adjunct (14 women). Expenses: Contact institution. *Financial support:* Fellowships, research assistantships, teaching assistantships, career-related internships or fieldwork, Federal Work-Study, institutionally sponsored loans, scholarships/grants, traineeships, health care benefits, tuition waivers, and unspecified assistantships available. Support available to part-time students. Financial award applicants required to submit FAFSA. In 2016, 76 master's, 8 doctorates awarded. *Program availability:* Part-time, online learning. Offers adventure education (MA); adventure-based environmental education (MA); adventure-based psychotherapy (MA); counseling psychology (MA); early childhood education (MA); early childhood special education (MA); ecopsychology (MA); ecotherapy (MA); education (MA); elementary education (MA); environmental education leadership and administration (MA); environmental studies (MA); equine-assisted learning (MA); equine-assisted mental health (MA); expressive arts therapy (MA); humanities (MA); school guidance counseling (MA); secondary education (MA); social justice and human rights (MA); somatic psychology (MA); special education: learning disabilities (MA); special education: mental retardation (MA); special education: serious emotional disabilities (MA); student-directed concentration (MA); student-directed independent study (MA); sustainability education (PhD). *Application deadline:* For fall admission, 4/15 priority date for domestic and international students; for spring

admission, 9/15 priority date for domestic and international students. Applications are processed on a rolling basis. *Application fee:* $0. Electronic applications accepted. *Application Contact:* Amber Harris, Assistant Director, Graduate Admissions, 928-615-8446, Fax: 928-776-5242, E-mail: amber.harris@prescott.edu. *Dean,* Dr. Jan Kempster, 928-350-3213, Fax: 928-776-5151, E-mail: jkempster@prescott.edu.

PRESIDIO GRADUATE SCHOOL, San Francisco, CA 94129

General Information Independent, coed, graduate-only institution.

GRADUATE UNITS

Graduate Programs - San Francisco Offers sustainable management (MBA, MPA, Certificate). MBA/JD offered in conjunction with the University of California, Hastings College of the Law.

MBA Programs - Seattle Average age 34. Expenses: Contact institution. *Financial support:* Scholarships/grants available. Financial award application deadline: 6/15; financial award applicants required to submit FAFSA. *Program availability:* Part-time, evening/weekend, blended/hybrid learning. Offers co-operative management (Certificate); food and agriculture systems (Certificate); sustainable business (MBA); sustainable systems (MBA). *Application deadline:* For fall admission, 6/1 priority date for domestic and international students. Applications are processed on a rolling basis. *Application fee:* $75. Electronic applications accepted. *Application Contact:* Kari Dorth, Director of Admissions, 415-655-8912, E-mail: admissions@presidio.edu. *Provost,* Steven Crane, 415-651-6555, E-mail: info@presidio.edu.

PRINCETON THEOLOGICAL SEMINARY, Princeton, NJ 08542-0803

General Information Independent-religious, coed, graduate-only institution. *Graduate housing:* Rooms and/or apartments available on a first-come, first-served basis to single and married students. *Research affiliation:* Center of Theological Inquiry.

GRADUATE UNITS

Graduate and Professional Programs *Program availability:* Part-time. Offers theology (M Div, MA, Th M, D Min, PhD). Electronic applications accepted.

PRINCETON UNIVERSITY, Princeton, NJ 08544-1019

General Information Independent, coed, university. CGS member. *Graduate housing:* Rooms and/or apartments available to single and married students. Housing application deadline: 4/15. *Research affiliation:* Institute for Advanced Study (physics and mathematics), Brookhaven National Laboratory (experimental physics), Textile Research Institute (polymer research), National Oceanic and Atmospheric Administration (NOAA)–GFD Laboratory (weather prediction).

GRADUATE UNITS

Graduate School Offers anthropology (PhD); applied and computational mathematics (PhD); astronomy (PhD); atmospheric and oceanic sciences (PhD); chemistry (PhD); classical and hellenic studies (PhD); classical art and archaeology (PhD); classical philosophy (PhD); comparative literature (PhD); composition (PhD); demography (PhD, Certificate); East Asian art and archaeology (PhD); East Asian studies (PhD); ecology and evolutionary biology (PhD); economics (PhD); economics and demography (PhD); English (PhD); French language and literature (PhD); geosciences (PhD); German (PhD); history (PhD); history (the ancient world) (PhD); history of science (PhD); industrial chemistry (MS); literature and philology (PhD); mathematics (PhD); molecular biology (PhD); musicology (PhD); Near Eastern studies (MA, PhD); neuroscience (PhD); ocean sciences and marine biology (PhD); philosophy (PhD); philosophy of science (PhD); physics (PhD); plasma physics (PhD); political philosophy (PhD); politics (PhD); psychology (PhD); public affairs and demography (PhD); religion (PhD); Russian and Slavic linguistics (PhD); Russian literature (PhD); sociology (PhD); sociology and demography (PhD); Spanish and Portuguese languages and cultures (PhD). Electronic applications accepted.

Bendheim Center for Finance Offers finance (M Fin). Electronic applications accepted.

School of Architecture Offers architecture (M Arch, PhD). Electronic applications accepted.

School of Engineering and Applied Science Offers chemical engineering (M Eng, MSE, PhD); civil and environmental engineering (M Eng, MSE, PhD); computer science (MSE, PhD); electrical engineering (M Eng, PhD); engineering and applied science (M Eng, MSE, PhD); mechanical and aerospace engineering (M Eng, MSE, PhD); operations research and financial engineering (M Eng, MSE, PhD). Electronic applications accepted.

Woodrow Wilson School of Public and International Affairs Offers public affairs (MPA); public policy (MPP). JD/MPA offered jointly with Columbia University, New York University, Stanford University. Electronic applications accepted.

Princeton Institute for the Science and Technology of Materials (PRISM) Offers materials (PhD).

Princeton Neuroscience Institute Offers neuroscience (PhD). Electronic applications accepted.

PROVIDENCE COLLEGE, Providence, RI 02918

General Information Independent-religious, coed, comprehensive institution. *Enrollment:* 4,804 graduate, professional, and undergraduate students; 214 full-time matriculated graduate/professional students (120 women), 276 part-time matriculated graduate/professional students (166 women). *Enrollment by degree level:* 490 master's. *Graduate faculty:* 29 full-time (10 women), 44 part-time/adjunct (23 women). *Tuition:* Part-time $1260 per course. One-time fee: $265. Tuition and fees vary according to course load and program. *Graduate housing:* On-campus housing not available. *Student services:* Campus employment opportunities, campus safety program, career counseling, exercise/wellness program, international student services, low-cost health insurance, multicultural affairs office, services for students with disabilities, teacher training, writing training. *Library facilities:* Phillips Memorial Library. *Collection:* Books: 391,000 (physical), 1.3 million (digital/electronic); Serial titles: 565 (physical), 42,609 (digital/electronic); Databases: 394. Weekly public service hours: 116; students can reserve study rooms.

Computer facilities: Computer purchase and lease plans are available. 440 computers available on campus for general student use. A campuswide network can be accessed from student residence rooms and from off campus. Online class registration is available.
Website: http://www.providence.edu/

General Application Contact: Rev. Mark D. Nowel, Dean of Undergraduate and Graduate Studies, 401-865-2649, Fax: 401-865-1496, E-mail: mnowel@providence.edu.

GRADUATE UNITS

Department of History Students: 13 full-time (6 women), 19 part-time (2 women); includes 1 minority (Two or more races, non-Hispanic/Latino). Average age 33. 14

applicants, 100% accepted, 11 enrolled. *Faculty:* 6 full-time (1 woman), 4 part-time/adjunct (0 women). Expenses: Contact institution. *Financial support:* Career-related internships or fieldwork, institutionally sponsored loans, and unspecified assistantships available. Support available to part-time students. Financial award application deadline: 8/1; financial award applicants required to submit FAFSA. In 2016, 20 master's awarded. *Program availability:* Part-time, evening/weekend. Offers American history (MA); modern European history (MA). *Application deadline:* For fall admission, 7/15 priority date for domestic and international students; for spring admission, 11/15 priority date for domestic and international students; for summer admission, 3/15 priority date for domestic students, 3/15 for international students. *Application fee:* $55.

Department of Theology Students: 8 full-time (2 women), 13 part-time (4 women); includes 1 minority (Black or African American, non-Hispanic/Latino), 5 international. Average age 38. 9 applicants, 100% accepted, 7 enrolled. *Faculty:* 7 full-time (2 women), 2 part-time/adjunct (0 women). Expenses: Contact institution. *Financial support:* Career-related internships or fieldwork, institutionally sponsored loans, and unspecified assistantships available. Support available to part-time students. Financial award application deadline: 8/1; financial award applicants required to submit FAFSA. In 2016, 6 master's awarded. *Program availability:* Part-time, evening/weekend. Offers Biblical studies (MA); theology (MA, MTS). *Application deadline:* For fall admission, 7/15 priority date for domestic and international students; for spring admission, 11/15 priority date for domestic and international students; for summer admission, 3/15 priority date for domestic students, 3/15 for international students. *Application fee:* $55.

Program in Counseling Students: 60 full-time (40 women), 49 part-time (38 women); includes 18 minority (7 Black or African American, non-Hispanic/Latino; 6 Hispanic/Latino; 1 Native Hawaiian or other Pacific Islander, non-Hispanic/Latino; 4 Two or more races, non-Hispanic/Latino), 7 international. Average age 29. 50 applicants, 100% accepted, 46 enrolled. *Faculty:* 6 full-time (4 women), 33 part-time/adjunct (21 women). Expenses: Contact institution. *Financial support:* Career-related internships or fieldwork, institutionally sponsored loans, and unspecified assistantships available. Support available to part-time students. Financial award application deadline: 8/1; financial award applicants required to submit FAFSA. In 2016, 46 master's awarded. *Program availability:* Part-time, evening/weekend. Offers counseling (M Ed). *Application deadline:* For fall admission, 7/15 priority date for domestic and international students; for spring admission, 11/15 priority date for domestic and international students; for summer admission, 3/15 priority date for domestic students, 3/15 for international students. *Application fee:* $55.

Program in Literacy Students: 7 full-time (all women), 27 part-time (26 women). Average age 29. 16 applicants, 88% accepted, 11 enrolled. *Faculty:* 6 full-time (4 women), 33 part-time/adjunct (21 women). Expenses: Contact institution. *Financial support:* Career-related internships or fieldwork, institutionally sponsored loans, and unspecified assistantships available. Support available to part-time students. Financial award application deadline: 8/1; financial award applicants required to submit FAFSA. In 2016, 10 master's awarded. *Program availability:* Part-time, evening/weekend. Offers literacy (M Ed). *Application deadline:* For fall admission, 7/15 priority date for domestic and international students; for spring admission, 11/15 priority date for domestic and international students; for summer admission, 3/15 priority date for domestic students, 3/15 for international students. *Application fee:* $55.

Program in Special Education Students: 3 full-time (2 women), 25 part-time (22 women); includes 2 minority (1 Asian, non-Hispanic/Latino; 1 Hispanic/Latino). Average age 28. 13 applicants, 100% accepted, 12 enrolled. *Faculty:* 6 full-time (4 women), 33 part-time/adjunct (21 women). Expenses: Contact institution. *Financial support:* Career-related internships or fieldwork, institutionally sponsored loans, and unspecified assistantships available. Support available to part-time students. Financial award application deadline: 8/1; financial award applicants required to submit FAFSA. In 2016, 14 master's awarded. *Program availability:* Part-time, evening/weekend. Offers special education (M Ed). *Application deadline:* For fall admission, 7/15 priority date for domestic and international students; for spring admission, 11/15 priority date for domestic and international students; for summer admission, 3/15 priority date for domestic students, 3/15 for international students. *Application fee:* $55.

Program in Teaching Mathematics Students: 9 part-time (5 women); includes 1 minority (Black or African American, non-Hispanic/Latino). Average age 33. 1 applicant, 100% accepted, 1 enrolled. *Faculty:* 6 full-time (4 women), 33 part-time/adjunct (21 women). Expenses: Contact institution. *Financial support:* Career-related internships or fieldwork, institutionally sponsored loans, and unspecified assistantships available. Support available to part-time students. Financial award application deadline: 8/1; financial award applicants required to submit FAFSA. In 2016, 13 master's awarded. *Program availability:* Part-time, evening/weekend. Offers teaching mathematics (MA). *Application deadline:* For fall admission, 7/15 priority date for domestic and international students; for spring admission, 11/15 priority date for domestic and international students; for summer admission, 3/15 priority date for domestic students, 3/15 for international students. *Application fee:* $55.

Program in Urban Teaching Students: 9 full-time (7 women), 21 part-time (16 women); includes 7 minority (4 Black or African American, non-Hispanic/Latino; 1 Asian, non-Hispanic/Latino; 1 Hispanic/Latino; 1 Two or more races, non-Hispanic/Latino). Average age 31. 18 applicants, 100% accepted, 16 enrolled. *Faculty:* 6 full-time (4 women), 33 part-time/adjunct (21 women). Expenses: Contact institution. *Financial support:* Career-related internships or fieldwork, institutionally sponsored loans, and unspecified assistantships available. Support available to part-time students. Financial award application deadline: 8/1; financial award applicants required to submit FAFSA. In 2016, 7 master's awarded. *Program availability:* Part-time, evening/weekend. Offers urban teaching (M Ed). *Application deadline:* For fall admission, 7/15 priority date for domestic students, 7/15 for international students; for spring admission, 11/15 for international students; for summer admission, 3/15 priority date for domestic students, 3/15 for international students. *Application fee:* $55.

Programs in Administration Students: 2 full-time (both women), 47 part-time (30 women); includes 3 minority (1 Asian, non-Hispanic/Latino; 2 Hispanic/Latino). Average age 37. 23 applicants, 100% accepted, 13 enrolled. *Faculty:* 6 full-time (4 women), 33 part-time/adjunct (21 women). Expenses: Contact institution. *Financial support:* Career-related internships or fieldwork, institutionally sponsored loans, and unspecified assistantships available. Support available to part-time students. Financial award application deadline: 8/1; financial award applicants required to submit FAFSA. In 2016, 16 master's awarded. *Program availability:* Part-time, evening/weekend. Offers elementary administration (M Ed); secondary administration (M Ed). *Application deadline:* For fall admission, 7/15 priority date for domestic and international students; for spring admission, 11/15 priority date for domestic and international students; for summer admission, 3/15 priority date for domestic students, 3/15 for international students. *Application fee:* $55. *Application Contact:* Rev. Mark D. Nowel, Dean of Undergraduate and Graduate Studies, 401-865-2649, Fax: 401-865-1496, E-mail: mnowel@providence.edu.

Providence Alliance for Catholic Teachers (PACT) Program Students: 28 full-time (15 women); includes 2 minority (1 Hispanic/Latino; 1 Native Hawaiian or other Pacific Islander, non-Hispanic/Latino). Average age 23. 25 applicants, 92% accepted, 15 enrolled. *Faculty:* 6 full-time (4 women), 33 part-time/adjunct (21 women). Expenses: Contact institution. *Financial support:* Career-related internships or fieldwork, institutionally sponsored loans, and unspecified assistantships available. Support available to part-time students. Financial award application deadline: 8/1; financial award applicants required to submit FAFSA. In 2016, 14 master's awarded. Offers secondary education (M Ed). *Application deadline:* For fall admission, 3/10 priority date for domestic and international students. Applications are processed on a rolling basis. *Application fee:* $55.

School of Business Students: 84 full-time (39 women), 66 part-time (23 women); includes 15 minority (6 Black or African American, non-Hispanic/Latino; 1 Asian, non-Hispanic/Latino; 8 Hispanic/Latino), 5 international. Average age 26. 116 applicants, 96% accepted, 94 enrolled. *Faculty:* 10 full-time (3 women), 5 part-time/adjunct (2 women). Expenses: Contact institution. *Financial support:* Career-related internships or fieldwork, institutionally sponsored loans, and unspecified assistantships available. Support available to part-time students. Financial award application deadline: 8/1; financial award applicants required to submit FAFSA. In 2016, 80 master's awarded. *Program availability:* Part-time, evening/weekend. Offers accounting (MBA); finance (MBA); international business (MBA); management (MBA); marketing (MBA). *Application deadline:* For fall admission, 5/1 priority date for domestic and international students; for spring admission, 11/1 priority date for domestic and international students; for summer admission, 3/15 priority date for domestic students, 3/15 for international students. Applications are processed on a rolling basis. *Application fee:* $55.

PROVIDENCE UNIVERSITY COLLEGE & THEOLOGICAL SEMINARY, Otterburne, MB R0A 1G0, Canada

General Information Independent-religious, coed, comprehensive institution. *Graduate housing:* Rooms and/or apartments guaranteed to single students and available on a first-come, first-served basis to married students. Housing application deadline: 8/15.

GRADUATE UNITS

Theological Seminary *Program availability:* Part-time. Offers children's ministry (Certificate); Christian studies (MA, Certificate); counseling (MA); cross-cultural discipleship (Certificate); divinity (M Div); educational studies (MA); global studies (MA); lay counseling (Diploma); ministry (D Min); teaching English to speakers of other languages (Certificate); theological studies (MA); training teacher of English to speakers of other languages (Certificate); youth ministry (Certificate).

PURCHASE COLLEGE, STATE UNIVERSITY OF NEW YORK, Purchase, NY 10577-1400

General Information State-supported, coed, comprehensive institution. *Enrollment:* 4,224 graduate, professional, and undergraduate students; 95 full-time matriculated graduate/professional students (50 women), 8 part-time matriculated graduate/professional students (5 women). *Enrollment by degree level:* 103 master's. Tuition, state resident: full-time $10,870; part-time $453 per credit. Tuition, nonresident: full-time $22,210; part-time $925 per credit. *Required fees:* $1737. *Graduate housing:* Rooms and/or apartments available on a first-come, first-served basis to single and married students. *Student services:* Campus employment opportunities, campus safety program, career counseling, child daycare facilities, exercise/wellness program, free psychological counseling, international student services, low-cost health insurance, services for students with disabilities. *Library facilities:* Purchase College Library.

Computer facilities: 600 computers available on campus for general student use. A campuswide network can be accessed from student residence rooms and from off campus. Online class registration is available. Website: http://www.purchase.edu/

General Application Contact: Sabrina Johnston, Admissions Counselor, 914-251-6479, Fax: 914-251-6314, E-mail: admissn@purchase.edu.

GRADUATE UNITS

Conservatory of Music Expenses: Contact institution. *Financial support:* Fellowships, teaching assistantships, career-related internships or fieldwork, Federal Work-Study, scholarships/grants, and tuition waivers (partial) available. Support available to part-time students. Financial award application deadline: 3/15; financial award applicants required to submit FAFSA. Offers classical composition (MM); instrumental performance (MM); jazz studies (MM); studio composition (MM); voice and opera studies (MM). *Application deadline:* For fall admission, 1/15 for domestic students; for spring admission, 10/15 for domestic students. *Application fee:* $85. Electronic applications accepted. *Application Contact:* Sabrina Johnston, Admission Counselor, 914-251-6479, Fax: 914-251-6314, E-mail: admissn@purchase.edu. *Interim Director,* James Undercofler, 914-251-6700, Fax: 914-251-6739, E-mail: james.undercofler@purchase.edu.

School of Art and Design Expenses: Contact institution. *Financial support:* Fellowships, teaching assistantships, Federal Work-Study, scholarships/grants, and tuition waivers (partial) available. Support available to part-time students. Financial award application deadline: 3/15; financial award applicants required to submit FAFSA. Offers visual arts (MFA). *Application deadline:* For fall admission, 2/15 for domestic students. Applications are processed on a rolling basis. *Application fee:* $85. Electronic applications accepted. *Application Contact:* Sabrina Johnston, Admission Counselor, 914-251-6479, Fax: 914-251-6314, E-mail: admissn@purchase.edu. *Director,* Steven Lam, 914-251-6750, Fax: 914-251-6793, E-mail: steven.lam@purchase.edu.

School of Humanities Expenses: Contact institution. *Financial support:* Fellowships, Federal Work-Study, scholarships/grants, and tuition waivers (partial) available. Support available to part-time students. Financial award application deadline: 3/15; financial award applicants required to submit FAFSA. Offers art history (MA). *Application deadline:* For fall admission, 3/1 for domestic students. *Application fee:* $80. Electronic applications accepted. *Application Contact:* Sabrina Johnston, Admissions Counselor, 914-251-6479, Fax: 914-251-6314, E-mail: admissn@purchase.edu. *Chair,* Ross Daly, 914-251-6550.

PURDUE UNIVERSITY, West Lafayette, IN 47907

General Information State-supported, coed, university. CGS member. *Enrollment:* 40,451 graduate, professional, and undergraduate students; 6,046 full-time matriculated graduate/professional students (2,350 women), 3,415 part-time matriculated graduate/professional students (1,468 women). *Enrollment by degree level:* 4,373 master's, 4,722 doctoral, 59 other advanced degrees. *Graduate faculty:* 2,168 full-time (675 women), 114 part-time/adjunct (45 women). *Graduate housing:* Rooms and/or apartments available on a first-come, first-served basis to single and married students. Housing application deadline: 3/1. *Student services:* Campus employment opportunities, campus safety program, career counseling, child daycare facilities, exercise/wellness program, free psychological counseling, grant writing training, international student services, low-cost health insurance, multicultural affairs office, services for students with disabilities, teacher training, writing training. *Library facilities:* Purdue University Libraries plus 12 others. *Collection:* Books: 1.1 million (physical), 2.3 million (digital/electronic); Serial titles: 1,100 (physical), 177,006 (digital/electronic); Databases: 450. Weekly public service hours: 168; study areas open 24 hours, 5–7 days a week; students can reserve study rooms.

Computer facilities: Computer purchase and lease plans are available. 5,237 computers available on campus for general student use. A campuswide network can be accessed from student residence rooms and from off campus. Online class registration is available.
Website: http://www.purdue.edu/

General Application Contact: Marcia Fritzlen, Graduate School Admissions, 765-494-2600, Fax: 765-494-0136, E-mail: gradinfo@purdue.edu.

GRADUATE UNITS

College of Engineering Students: 3,463. *Faculty:* 636. Expenses: Contact institution. *Financial support:* Fellowships with full and partial tuition reimbursements, research assistantships with full and partial tuition reimbursements, teaching assistantships with full and partial tuition reimbursements, career-related internships or fieldwork, scholarships/grants, health care benefits, and unspecified assistantships available. In 2016, 672 master's, 284 doctorates awarded. *Program availability:* Part-time, 100% online, blended/hybrid learning. Offers biomedical engineering (MSBME, PhD); engineering (MS, MSABE, MSBME, MSCE, MSChE, MSE, MSECE, MSIE, MSME, MSMSE, MSNE, PhD, Certificate); interdisciplinary engineering (MS, MSE). *Application deadline:* Applications are processed on a rolling basis. *Application fee:* $60 ($75 for international students). Electronic applications accepted. *Application Contact:* Dr. Janet Beagle, Director of Graduate Programs, E-mail: engrgrad@purdue.edu. *Associate Dean,* Dr. Audeen Fentiman, E-mail: engrgrad@purdue.edu.

Davidson School of Chemical Engineering Students: 158. *Faculty:* 43. Expenses: Contact institution. *Financial support:* Fellowships with full and partial tuition reimbursements, research assistantships with full and partial tuition reimbursements, teaching assistantships with full and partial tuition reimbursements, career-related internships or fieldwork, scholarships/grants, health care benefits, and unspecified assistantships available. Financial award applicants required to submit FAFSA. In 2016, 10 master's, 31 doctorates awarded. Offers chemical engineering (MSChE, PhD). *Application deadline:* For fall admission, 12/15 for domestic and international students. Applications are processed on a rolling basis. *Application fee:* $60 ($75 for international students). Electronic applications accepted. *Application Contact:* Beverly Johnson, Graduate Program Administrator, 765-494-4057, E-mail: bevjohnson@purdue.edu. *Head of Chemical Engineering/Professor,* Dr. Sangtae Kim, E-mail: kim55@purdue.edu.

Division of Environmental and Ecological Engineering Students: 18. *Faculty:* 59. Expenses: Contact institution. *Financial support:* Fellowships with full and partial tuition reimbursements, research assistantships with full and partial tuition reimbursements, teaching assistantships with full and partial tuition reimbursements, career-related internships or fieldwork, scholarships/grants, health care benefits, and unspecified assistantships available. Financial award applicants required to submit FAFSA. Offers environmental and ecological engineering (MS, PhD). *Application deadline:* For fall admission, 1/1 for domestic and international students. *Application fee:* $60 ($75 for international students). *Application Contact:* Patricia Finney, Graduate Administrative Assistant, 765-496-0545, E-mail: eee@purdue.edu. *Professor/Head of Environmental and Ecological Engineering,* Dr. John W. Sutherland, E-mail: jwsuther@purdue.edu.

Lyles School of Civil Engineering Students: 356. *Faculty:* 73. Expenses: Contact institution. *Financial support:* Fellowships with full and partial tuition reimbursements, research assistantships with full and partial tuition reimbursements, teaching assistantships with full and partial tuition reimbursements, scholarships/grants, health care benefits, and unspecified assistantships available. Support available to part-time students. Financial award applicants required to submit FAFSA. In 2016, 105 master's, 28 doctorates awarded. *Program availability:* Part-time. Offers civil engineering (MS, MSCE, MSE, PhD). *Application deadline:* For fall admission, 1/1 priority date for domestic and international students; for spring admission, 9/15 for domestic and international students. Applications are processed on a rolling basis. *Application fee:* $60 ($75 for international students). Electronic applications accepted. *Application Contact:* Jenny Ricksy, Graduate Program Coordinator, 765-494-2436, E-mail: jricksy@purdue.edu. *Head/Professor,* Dr. Rao Govindaraju, E-mail: govind@purdue.edu.

School of Aeronautics and Astronautics Students: 525. *Faculty:* 63. Expenses: Contact institution. *Financial support:* Fellowships with full and partial tuition reimbursements, research assistantships with full and partial tuition reimbursements, teaching assistantships with full and partial tuition reimbursements, career-related internships or fieldwork, scholarships/grants, health care benefits, and unspecified assistantships available. In 2016, 28 doctorates awarded. *Program availability:* Part-time, 100% online. Offers aeronautics and astronautics (PhD). *Application deadline:* For fall admission, 1/1 priority date for domestic and international students; for spring admission, 9/15 priority date for domestic and international students. Applications are processed on a rolling basis. *Application fee:* $60 ($75 for international students). Electronic applications accepted. *Application Contact:* Xiaomin Qian, Graduate Program Coordinator, E-mail: xiaomin@purdue.edu. *Head/Professor of Aeronautics and Astronautics,* Dr. Tom Shih, E-mail: tomshih@purdue.edu.

School of Agricultural and Biological Engineering Students: 97. *Faculty:* 61. Expenses: Contact institution. *Financial support:* Fellowships with full and partial tuition reimbursements, research assistantships with full and partial tuition reimbursements, teaching assistantships with full and partial tuition reimbursements, career-related internships or fieldwork, scholarships/grants, health care benefits, unspecified assistantships, and instructorships available. Financial award applicants required to submit FAFSA. In 2016, 8 master's, 21 doctorates awarded. *Program availability:* Part-time. Offers agricultural and biological engineering (MS, MSABE, MSE, PhD). *Application deadline:* For fall admission, 12/1 for domestic and international students; for spring admission, 10/1 for domestic and international students; for summer admission, 12/1 for domestic and international students. Applications are processed on a rolling basis. *Application fee:* $60 ($74 for international students). Electronic applications accepted. *Application Contact:* Daniel Taylor, Assistant to Department Head, 765-494-1181, E-mail: taylordc@purdue.edu. *Department Head/Professor, Agricultural and Biological Engineering,* Dr. Bernard Engel, 765-494-1162, E-mail: engrad@purdue.edu.

School of Electrical and Computer Engineering Students: 675. *Faculty:* 129. Expenses: Contact institution. *Financial support:* Fellowships with full and partial tuition reimbursements, research assistantships with full and partial tuition reimbursements, teaching assistantships with full and partial tuition reimbursements,

scholarships/grants, health care benefits, and unspecified assistantships available. Financial award application deadline: 12/15. In 2016, 127 master's, 80 doctorates awarded. *Program availability:* Part-time, online learning. Offers electrical and computer engineering (MSECE, PhD). MS and PhD degree programs in biomedical engineering offered jointly with School of Mechanical Engineering and School of Chemical Engineering. *Application deadline:* For fall admission, 12/15 priority date for domestic and international students; for spring admission, 9/15 for domestic and international students. *Application fee:* $60 ($75 for international students). Electronic applications accepted. *Application Contact:* Debra Bowman, Graduate Admissions, E-mail: ecegrad@purdue.edu. *Head/Professor,* Ragu Balakrishnan, E-mail: ragu@ecn.purdue.edu.

School of Engineering Education Students: 62. *Faculty:* 34. Expenses: Contact institution. *Financial support:* Fellowships with full and partial tuition reimbursements, research assistantships with full and partial tuition reimbursements, teaching assistantships with full and partial tuition reimbursements, health care benefits, and unspecified assistantships available. Financial award applicants required to submit FAFSA. In 2016, 12 doctorates awarded. Offers engineering education (PhD). *Application deadline:* For fall admission, 12/15 for domestic and international students. Applications are processed on a rolling basis. *Application fee:* $60 ($75 for international students). Electronic applications accepted. *Application Contact:* Loretta McKinniss, Secretary V, E-mail: enegrad@purdue.edu.

School of Industrial Engineering Students: 287. *Faculty:* 38. Expenses: Contact institution. *Financial support:* Fellowships with full and partial tuition reimbursements, research assistantships with full and partial tuition reimbursements, teaching assistantships with full and partial tuition reimbursements, scholarships/grants, health care benefits, and unspecified assistantships available. Financial award applicants required to submit FAFSA. In 2016, 52 master's, 13 doctorates awarded. *Program availability:* Part-time, online learning. Offers industrial engineering (MS, MSIE, PhD). *Application deadline:* For fall admission, 1/5 for domestic and international students; for spring admission, 9/15 for domestic and international students. Applications are processed on a rolling basis. *Application fee:* $60 ($75 for international students). Electronic applications accepted. *Application Contact:* Cheryl Barnhart, Graduate Program Administrator, E-mail: iego@purdue.edu. *Head/Professor of Industrial Engineering,* Dr. Abhijit Deshmukh, E-mail: abhi@purdue.edu.

School of Materials Engineering Students: 142. *Faculty:* 52. Expenses: Contact institution. *Financial support:* Fellowships with full and partial tuition reimbursements, research assistantships with full and partial tuition reimbursements, teaching assistantships with full and partial tuition reimbursements, career-related internships or fieldwork, scholarships/grants, health care benefits, and unspecified assistantships available. Support available to part-time students. Financial award applicants required to submit FAFSA. In 2016, 7 master's, 8 doctorates awarded. *Program availability:* Part-time. Offers materials engineering (MSMSE, PhD). *Application deadline:* For fall admission, 1/1 for domestic and international students. Applications are processed on a rolling basis. *Application fee:* $60 ($75 for international students). Electronic applications accepted. *Application Contact:* Vicki Cline, Academic Program Administrator, E-mail: msegrad@purdue.edu. *Head and Professor of Materials Engineering,* Dr. David Bahr, E-mail: dfbahr@purdue.edu.

School of Mechanical Engineering Students: 569. *Faculty:* 113. Expenses: Contact institution. *Financial support:* Fellowships with full and partial tuition reimbursements, research assistantships with full and partial tuition reimbursements, teaching assistantships with full and partial tuition reimbursements, career-related internships or fieldwork, scholarships/grants, health care benefits, and unspecified assistantships available. In 2016, 119 master's, 42 doctorates awarded. *Program availability:* Part-time, online learning. Offers mechanical engineering (MS, MSE, MSME, PhD, Certificate). MS and PhD degree programs in biomedical engineering offered jointly with School of Electrical and Computer Engineering and School of Chemical Engineering. *Application deadline:* For fall admission, 12/15 for domestic and international students; for spring admission, 11/1 for domestic and international students. Applications are processed on a rolling basis. *Application fee:* $60 ($75 for international students). Electronic applications accepted. *Application Contact:* Julayne Moser, Director of Graduate Programs, E-mail: megradoffice@purdue.edu. *Head/Professor,* Anil K. Bajaj.

School of Nuclear Engineering Students: 53. *Faculty:* 25. Expenses: Contact institution. *Financial support:* Fellowships with full and partial tuition reimbursements, research assistantships with full and partial tuition reimbursements, teaching assistantships with full and partial tuition reimbursements, career-related internships or fieldwork, scholarships/grants, and unspecified assistantships available. Support available to part-time students. Financial award applicants required to submit FAFSA. In 2016, 12 master's, 8 doctorates awarded. *Program availability:* Part-time. Offers nuclear engineering (MS, MSNE, PhD). *Application deadline:* For fall admission, 1/15 priority date for domestic and international students; for spring admission, 9/30 for domestic and international students. Applications are processed on a rolling basis. *Application fee:* $60 ($75 for international students). Electronic applications accepted. *Application Contact:* Tiffany Stergar, Academic Program Administrator, E-mail: nuclss@purdue.edu.

College of Pharmacy and Pharmacal Sciences Students: 709 full-time (462 women), 10 part-time (6 women); includes 157 minority (29 Black or African American, non-Hispanic/Latino; 1 American Indian or Alaska Native, non-Hispanic/Latino; 90 Asian, non-Hispanic/Latino; 22 Hispanic/Latino; 15 Two or more races, non-Hispanic/Latino), 88 international. Average age 24. 748 applicants, 28% accepted, 173 enrolled. *Faculty:* 72 full-time (29 women), 5 part-time/adjunct (3 women). Expenses: Contact institution. *Financial support:* Fellowships, research assistantships, teaching assistantships, career-related internships or fieldwork, Federal Work-Study, scholarships/grants, and traineeships available. Support available to part-time students. Financial award applicants required to submit FAFSA. In 2016, 10 master's, 29 doctorates, 142 other advanced degrees awarded. *Program availability:* Part-time. Offers biophysical and computational chemistry (PhD); cancer research (PhD); clinical pharmacy (MS, PhD); immunology and infectious disease (PhD); industrial and physical pharmacy (MS, PhD, Certificate); medicinal biochemistry and molecular biology (PhD); medicinal chemistry and chemical biology (PhD); medicinal chemistry and molecular pharmacology (MS, PhD); molecular pharmacology (PhD); neuropharmacology, neurodegeneration, and neurotoxicity (PhD); pharmaceutics (PhD); pharmacy administration (MS, PhD); pharmacy and pharmacal sciences (MS, PhD, Pharm D, Certificate); pharmacy practice (MS, PhD); regulatory quality compliance (MS, Certificate); systems biology and functional genomics (PhD). *Application deadline:* Applications are processed on a rolling basis. *Application fee:* $60 ($75 for international students). Electronic applications accepted. *Application Contact:* G. Marc Loudon, Associate Dean for Research and Graduate Programs, 765-494-1362. *Dean,* Dr. Craig K. Svensson, 765-494-1368, E-mail: svensson@purdue.edu.

Graduate School Students: 5,925 full-time (2,291 women), 3,120 part-time (1,315 women); includes 1,144 minority (277 Black or African American, non-Hispanic/Latino; 20 American Indian or Alaska Native, non-Hispanic/Latino; 358 Asian, non-Hispanic/Latino; 333 Hispanic/Latino; 9 Native Hawaiian or other Pacific Islander, non-Hispanic/Latino; 147 Two or more races, non-Hispanic/Latino), 4,026 international. Average age 29. 16,245 applicants, 31% accepted, 2381 enrolled. *Faculty:* 2,096 full-time (646 women), 109 part-time/adjunct (42 women). Expenses: Contact institution. *Financial support:* Fellowships with tuition reimbursements, research assistantships with tuition reimbursements, teaching assistantships with tuition reimbursements, career-related internships or fieldwork, scholarships/grants, tuition waivers (full and partial), and instructorships available. Support available to part-time students. Financial award applicants required to submit FAFSA. In 2016, 1,859 master's, 698 doctorates, 160 other advanced degrees awarded. *Program availability:* Part-time, evening/weekend, online learning. Offers biomedical sciences (PhD); biomolecular structure and biophysics (PhD); biotechnology (PhD); chemical biology (PhD); chromatin and regulation of gene expression (PhD); ecological sciences and engineering (MS, PhD); food science (MS, PhD); information security (MS); integrative neuroscience (PhD); integrative plant sciences (PhD); membrane biology (PhD); microbiology (PhD); molecular evolutionary and cancer biology (PhD); molecular evolutionary genetics (PhD); molecular virology (PhD); philosophy and literature (PhD). MD/PhD offered jointly with Indiana University–Purdue University Indianapolis. *Application deadline:* Applications are processed on a rolling basis. *Application fee:* $60 ($75 for international students). Electronic applications accepted. *Application Contact:* Graduate School Admissions, 765-494-2600, Fax: 765-494-0136, E-mail: gradinfo@purdue.edu. *Dean,* Dr. M. Smith, 765-494-2604, Fax: 765-494-0136, E-mail: gradinfo@purdue.edu.

College of Agriculture Students: 542 full-time (262 women), 124 part-time (48 women); includes 72 minority (21 Black or African American, non-Hispanic/Latino; 5 American Indian or Alaska Native, non-Hispanic/Latino; 15 Asian, non-Hispanic/Latino; 19 Hispanic/Latino; 12 Two or more races, non-Hispanic/Latino), 288 international. Average age 28. 529 applicants, 38% accepted, 139 enrolled. *Faculty:* 310 full-time (69 women), 11 part-time/adjunct (3 women). Expenses: Contact institution. *Financial support:* Fellowships with tuition reimbursements, research assistantships with tuition reimbursements, teaching assistantships with tuition reimbursements, career-related internships or fieldwork, and tuition waivers (partial) available. Support available to part-time students. Financial award applicants required to submit FAFSA. In 2016, 107 master's, 68 doctorates awarded. *Program availability:* Part-time. Offers agricultural economics (MS, PhD); agriculture (EMBA, M Agr, MA, MS, MSF, PhD); agronomy (MS, PhD); animal sciences (MS, PhD); biochemistry (MS, PhD); botany and plant pathology (MS, PhD); entomology (MS, PhD); fisheries and aquatic sciences (MS, MSF, PhD); food and agricultural business (EMBA); food science (MS, PhD); forest biology (MS, MSF, PhD); horticulture (M Agr, MS, PhD); natural resource social science (MS, PhD); natural resources social science (MSF); quantitative ecology (MS, MSF, PhD); wildlife science (MS, MSF, PhD); wood products and wood products manufacturing (MS, MSF, PhD); youth development and agricultural education (MA, PhD). *Application deadline:* Applications are processed on a rolling basis. *Application fee:* $60 ($75 for international students). Electronic applications accepted. *Application Contact:* Graduate School Admissions, 765-494-2600, Fax: 765-494-0136, E-mail: gradinfo@purdue.edu. *Dean,* Dr. Jay W. Akridge, 765-494-8391, E-mail: akridge@purdue.edu.

College of Education Students: 156 full-time (110 women), 530 part-time (370 women); includes 114 minority (41 Black or African American, non-Hispanic/Latino; 3 American Indian or Alaska Native, non-Hispanic/Latino; 18 Asian, non-Hispanic/Latino; 38 Hispanic/Latino; 1 Native Hawaiian or other Pacific Islander, non-Hispanic/Latino; 13 Two or more races, non-Hispanic/Latino), 97 international. Average age 34. 377 applicants, 64% accepted, 151 enrolled. *Faculty:* 70 full-time (51 women), 2 part-time/adjunct (1 woman). Expenses: Contact institution. *Financial support:* Fellowships with full tuition reimbursements, research assistantships with full tuition reimbursements, teaching assistantships with full tuition reimbursements, career-related internships or fieldwork, and tuition waivers (full) available. Support available to part-time students. Financial award application deadline: 3/1; financial award applicants required to submit FAFSA. In 2016, 40 master's, 145 doctorates, 6 other advanced degrees awarded. *Program availability:* Part-time, evening/weekend. Offers administration (MS Ed, PhD, Ed S); agricultural and extension education (MS, MS Ed, PhD, Ed S); art education (PhD); career and technical education (MS Ed, PhD, Ed S); counseling and development (MS Ed, PhD); curriculum studies (MS Ed, PhD, Ed S); education (MS, MS Ed, PhD, Ed S); education of the gifted (MS Ed); educational psychology (MS Ed, PhD); educational technology (MS Ed, PhD, Ed S); elementary education (MS Ed); family and consumer sciences education (MS Ed, PhD, Ed S); foreign language education (MS Ed, PhD, Ed S); foundations of education (MS Ed, PhD); higher education administration (MS Ed, PhD); industrial technology (PhD, Ed S); language arts (MS Ed, PhD, Ed S); literacy (MS Ed, PhD, Ed S); mathematics education (MS, MS Ed, PhD, Ed S); science education (MS, MS Ed, PhD, Ed S); social studies education (MS Ed, PhD, Ed S); special education (MS Ed, PhD). *Application deadline:* For fall admission, 12/15 for domestic students, 3/1 for international students; for spring admission, 9/15 for domestic students, 8/1 for international students. *Application fee:* $60 ($75 for international students). Electronic applications accepted. *Application Contact:* Graduate School Admissions, 765-494-2600, Fax: 765-494-0136, E-mail: gradinfo@purdue.edu. *Dean,* Dr. M. Smith, 765-494-2604, Fax: 765-494-0136, E-mail: gradinfo@purdue.edu.

College of Health and Human Sciences Students: 417 full-time (312 women), 97 part-time (71 women); includes 64 minority (16 Black or African American, non-Hispanic/Latino; 1 American Indian or Alaska Native, non-Hispanic/Latino; 17 Asian, non-Hispanic/Latino; 17 Hispanic/Latino; 13 Two or more races, non-Hispanic/Latino), 121 international. Average age 28. 1,035 applicants, 34% accepted, 168 enrolled. *Faculty:* 212 full-time (119 women), 16 part-time/adjunct (11 women). Expenses: Contact institution. *Financial support:* Fellowships, research assistantships, teaching assistantships, and career-related internships or fieldwork available. Support available to part-time students. Financial award applicants required to submit FAFSA. In 2016, 53 master's, 118 doctorates, 8 other advanced degrees awarded. *Program availability:* Part-time. Offers adult gerontology primary care nurse practitioner (MS, Post Master's Certificate); animal health (MS, PhD); athletic training education administration (MS, PhD); audiology clinic (MS, Au D, PhD); behavioral neuroscience (PhD); biochemical and molecular nutrition (MS, PhD); biomechanics (MS, PhD); clinical psychology (PhD); cognitive psychology (PhD); consumer behavior (MS, PhD); developmental studies (MS, PhD); exercise physiology (MS, PhD); family and consumer economics (MS, PhD); family studies (MS, PhD); growth and development (MS, PhD); health and human sciences (MS, Au D, DNP, PhD, Post Master's Certificate); health education (MS, PhD); health physics (MS, PhD); history/philosophy of sport (MS, PhD); hospitality and tourism management (MS, PhD); human and clinical nutrition (MS, PhD); industrial/organizational psychology (PhD); linguistics (MS, PhD); marriage and family therapy (MS, PhD); mathematical and computational cognitive science (PhD); medical physics (MS, PhD); motor control and development (MS, PhD); nursing (DNP, PhD); occupational and environmental health science (MS, PhD); physical education pedagogy (PhD); physical education teacher education (MS); primary care family nurse practitioner (MS, Post Master's Certificate); primary care pediatric nurse practitioner (MS, Post Master's Certificate); public health and education (MS, PhD); radiation biology (PhD); recreation and sport management (MS, PhD); speech and hearing science (MS, PhD); speech-language pathology (MS, PhD); sport and exercise psychology (MS, PhD); toxicology (PhD). *Application deadline:* Applications are processed on a rolling basis. *Application fee:* $60 ($75 for international students). Electronic applications accepted. *Application Contact:* Graduate School Admissions, 765-494-2600, Fax: 765-494-0136, E-mail: gradinfo@purdue.edu. *Inaugural Dean,* Dr. Christine M. Ladisch, 765-494-8210.

College of Liberal Arts Students: 487 full-time (286 women), 601 part-time (410 women); includes 201 minority (75 Black or African American, non-Hispanic/Latino; 2 American Indian or Alaska Native, non-Hispanic/Latino; 25 Asian, non-Hispanic/Latino; 72 Hispanic/Latino; 3 Native Hawaiian or other Pacific Islander, non-Hispanic/Latino; 24 Two or more races, non-Hispanic/Latino), 196 international. Average age 32. 1,107 applicants, 35% accepted, 284 enrolled. *Faculty:* 291 full-time (134 women), 20 part-time/adjunct (13 women). Expenses: Contact institution. *Financial support:* Fellowships, research assistantships, teaching assistantships, career-related internships or fieldwork, scholarships/grants, and tuition waivers (full) available. Support available to part-time students. Financial award applicants required to submit FAFSA. In 2016, 74 doctorates awarded. *Program availability:* Part-time, evening/weekend. Offers American studies (MA, PhD); anthropology (MS, PhD); art education (MA, PhD); communication (MA, MS, PhD); comparative literature (MA, PhD); creative writing (MFA); French (MA, MAT, PhD); German (MA, MAT, PhD); history (MA, PhD); industrial design (MFA); integrated studio arts (MFA); interior design (MFA); Japanese pedagogy (MA); liberal arts (MA, MAT, MFA, MS, Au D, PhD); linguistics (MS, PhD); literature (MA, PhD); philosophy (MA, PhD); photography (MFA); political science (MA, PhD); sociology (MS, PhD); Spanish (MA, MAT, PhD); theatre (MFA); visual communications design (MFA). *Application deadline:* Applications are processed on a rolling basis. *Application fee:* $60 ($75 for international students). Electronic applications accepted. *Application Contact:* Graduate School Admissions, 765-494-2600, Fax: 765-494-0136, E-mail: gradinfo@purdue.edu. *Dean,* Dr. Irwin Weiser, 765-494-3661, E-mail: iweiser@purdue.edu.

College of Science Students: 1,066 full-time (359 women), 173 part-time (36 women); includes 142 minority (27 Black or African American, non-Hispanic/Latino; 3 American Indian or Alaska Native, non-Hispanic/Latino; 43 Asian, non-Hispanic/Latino; 51 Hispanic/Latino; 2 Native Hawaiian or other Pacific Islander, non-Hispanic/Latino; 16 Two or more races, non-Hispanic/Latino), 678 international. Average age 27. 3,411 applicants, 19% accepted, 246 enrolled. *Faculty:* 340 full-time (60 women), 14 part-time/adjunct (3 women). Expenses: Contact institution. *Financial support:* Fellowships with tuition reimbursements, research assistantships with tuition reimbursements, teaching assistantships with tuition reimbursements, career-related internships or fieldwork, and tuition waivers (partial) available. Support available to part-time students. Financial award applicants required to submit FAFSA. In 2016, 127 master's, 156 doctorates, 3 other advanced degrees awarded. *Program availability:* Part-time. Offers analytical chemistry (MS, PhD); biochemistry (MS, PhD); biophysics (PhD); cell and developmental biology (PhD); chemical education (PhD); computer sciences (MS, PhD); earth and atmospheric sciences (MS, PhD); ecology, evolutionary and population biology (MS, PhD); genetics (MS, PhD); inorganic chemistry (MS, PhD); mathematics (MS, PhD); microbiology (MS, PhD); molecular biology (PhD); neurobiology (MS, PhD); organic chemistry (MS, PhD); physical chemistry (MS, PhD); physics (MS, PhD); plant physiology (PhD); science (MS, PhD, Certificate); statistics (MS, PhD). *Application fee:* $60 ($75 for international students). Electronic applications accepted. *Application Contact:* Graduate School Admissions, 765-494-2600, Fax: 765-494-0136, E-mail: gradinfo@purdue.edu. *Dean,* Dr. Jeffrey Roberts, 765-494-1730, E-mail: jtrob@purdue.edu.

College of Technology Students: 301 full-time (116 women), 287 part-time (101 women); includes 84 minority (23 Black or African American, non-Hispanic/Latino; 2 American Indian or Alaska Native, non-Hispanic/Latino; 25 Asian, non-Hispanic/Latino; 24 Hispanic/Latino; 2 Native Hawaiian or other Pacific Islander, non-Hispanic/Latino; 8 Two or more races, non-Hispanic/Latino), 233 international. Average age 31. 490 applicants, 57% accepted, 171 enrolled. *Faculty:* 201 full-time (46 women), 3 part-time/adjunct (1 woman). Expenses: Contact institution. *Financial support:* In 2016–17, 37 teaching assistantships were awarded; fellowships also available. Support available to part-time students. Financial award applicants required to submit FAFSA. In 2016, 144 master's, 21 doctorates awarded. *Program availability:* Online learning. Offers aviation and aerospace management (MS); building construction management (MS); computer and information technology (MS); computer graphics technology (MS, PhD); leadership (MS, PhD); organizational leadership (MS); technology (MS, PhD); technology innovation (MS). *Application deadline:* Applications are processed on a rolling basis. *Application fee:* $60 ($75 for international students). Electronic applications accepted. *Application Contact:* Graduate School Admissions, 765-494-2600, Fax: 765-494-0136, E-mail: gradinfo@purdue.edu. *Dean,* Dr. Gary R. Bertoline, 765-496-6071, E-mail: bertoline@purdue.edu.

Krannert School of Management Offers business administration (EMBA, MBA); economics (PhD); finance (MSF); global executive business administration (MBA); human resource management (MSHRM); management (EMBA, MBA, MSF, MSHRM, MSIA, PhD); organizational behavior and human resource management (PhD). Electronic applications accepted.

School of Veterinary Medicine *Program availability:* Part-time, evening/weekend. Offers anatomy (MS, PhD); basic medical sciences (MS, PhD); comparative epidemiology and public health (MS); comparative epidemiology and public heath (PhD); comparative microbiology and immunology (MS, PhD); comparative pathobiology (MS, PhD); interdisciplinary studies (MS); lab animal medicine (MS); pharmacology (MS, PhD); physiology (MS, PhD); veterinary anatomic pathology (MS); veterinary clinical pathology (MS); veterinary clinical sciences (MS, PhD); veterinary medicine (MS, DVM, PhD).

PURDUE UNIVERSITY NORTHWEST, Hammond, IN 46323-2094

General Information State-supported, coed, comprehensive institution. *Graduate housing:* Room and/or apartments available on a first-come, first-served basis to single students; on-campus housing not available to married students.

GRADUATE UNITS

Graduate Studies Office *Program availability:* Part-time, evening/weekend, online learning. Electronic applications accepted.

School of Education Offers counseling (MS Ed); educational administration (MS Ed); human services (MS Ed); instructional technology (MS Ed); mental health counseling (MS Ed); school counseling (MS Ed); special education (MS Ed).

School of Engineering, Mathematics, and Science *Program availability:* Part-time, evening/weekend, online learning. Offers biology (MS); biology teaching (MS); biotechnology (MS); computer engineering (MSE); computer science (MS); electrical engineering (MSE); engineering (MS); engineering, mathematics, and science (MAT, MS, MSE); mathematics (MAT, MS); mechanical engineering (MSE). Electronic applications accepted.

School of Liberal Arts and Social Sciences *Program availability:* Part-time. Offers child development and family studies (MS); communication (MA); English (MA); history (MA); liberal arts and social sciences (MA, MS); marriage and family therapy (MS).

School of Management *Program availability:* Part-time, evening/weekend. Offers accountancy (M Acc); business administration (MBA); business administration for executives (EMBA). Electronic applications accepted.

School of Nursing *Program availability:* Part-time, online learning. Offers adult health clinical nurse specialist (MS); critical care clinical nurse specialist (MS); family nurse practitioner (MS); nurse executive (MS). Electronic applications accepted.

School of Technology Offers technology (MS).

QUEENS COLLEGE OF THE CITY UNIVERSITY OF NEW YORK, Queens, NY 11367-1597

General Information State and locally supported, coed, comprehensive institution. *Enrollment:* 19,632 graduate, professional, and undergraduate students; 463 full-time matriculated graduate/professional students (345 women), 2,669 part-time matriculated graduate/professional students (1,816 women). *Enrollment by degree level:* 2,678 master's, 454 other advanced degrees. *Graduate faculty:* 527 full-time (240 women), 854 part-time/adjunct (443 women). Tuition, state resident: full-time $5065; part-time $425 per credit. Tuition, nonresident: part-time $780 per credit. *Required fees:* $522; $397 per credit. Part-time tuition and fees vary according to course load and program. *Graduate housing:* Room and/or apartments available on a first-come, first-served basis to single students; on-campus housing not available to married students. Typical cost: $15,074 per year ($17,424 including board). Room and board charges vary according to housing facility selected. *Student services:* Campus employment opportunities, career counseling, child daycare facilities, free psychological counseling, international student services, low-cost health insurance, services for students with disabilities, teacher training, writing training. *Library facilities:* The Benjamin S. Rosenthal Library plus 1 other. *Collection:* Books: 1.1 million (physical), 341,721 (digital/electronic); Serial titles: 303 (physical), 123,332 (digital/electronic); Databases: 274. Weekly public service hours: 90; students can reserve study rooms. *Research affiliation:* Hudson River Foundation (earth and environmental sciences), Consortium for Ocean Leadership (earth and environmental sciences), Institute for New Economic Thinking (economics), Social Explorer (sociology), Wildlife Conservation Society (biology), IBM (computer science).

Computer facilities: 2,448 computers available on campus for general student use. A campuswide network can be accessed from student residence rooms and from off campus. Online class registration is available. Website: http://www.qc.cuny.edu/

General Application Contact: Richard Alvarez, Vice President for Enrollment and Student Retention, 718-997-5929, Fax: 718-997-5193, E-mail: graduate_admissions@qc.cuny.edu.

GRADUATE UNITS

Arts and Humanities Division Students: 80 full-time (57 women), 431 part-time (265 women); includes 187 minority (38 Black or African American, non-Hispanic/Latino; 48 Asian, non-Hispanic/Latino; 86 Hispanic/Latino; 15 Two or more races, non-Hispanic/Latino), 66 international. Average age 31. 795 applicants, 40% accepted, 203 enrolled. *Faculty:* 154 full-time (76 women), 266 part-time/adjunct (159 women). Expenses: Contact institution. *Financial support:* Career-related internships or fieldwork available. Financial award application deadline: 4/1; financial award applicants required to submit FAFSA. In 2016, 119 master's, 12 other advanced degrees awarded. *Program availability:* Part-time. Offers applied linguistics (MA); art history (MA); arts and humanities (MA, MFA, MM, MS Ed, AC, Advanced Certificate, Advanced Diploma); creative writing and literary translation (MFA); early childhood birth-2nd grade (Advanced Certificate); English (MA); English language teaching (Advanced Certificate); French (MA); Italian (MA); media studies (MA); Spanish (MA); speech-language pathology (MA); studio art (MFA); teaching English to speakers of other languages (MS Ed); TESOL (MS Ed); TESOL and bilingual education (MS Ed). *Application deadline:* For fall admission, 4/1 for domestic students; for spring admission, 11/1 for domestic students. Applications are processed on a rolling basis. *Application fee:* $125. Electronic applications accepted. *Dean,* Dr. William McClure, 718-997-5790, E-mail: william.mcclure@qc.cuny.edu.

Aaron Copland School of Music Students: 17 full-time (4 women), 166 part-time (73 women); includes 58 minority (8 Black or African American, non-Hispanic/Latino; 19 Asian, non-Hispanic/Latino; 23 Hispanic/Latino; 8 Two or more races, non-Hispanic/Latino), 54 international. Average age 30. 197 applicants, 57% accepted, 61 enrolled. *Faculty:* 26 full-time (7 women), 67 part-time/adjunct (32 women). Expenses: Contact institution. *Financial support:* Career-related internships or fieldwork, Federal Work-Study, institutionally sponsored loans, and tuition waivers (partial) available. Support available to part-time students. Financial award application deadline: 4/1; financial award applicants required to submit FAFSA. In 2016, 97 master's, 16 other advanced degrees awarded. *Program availability:* Part-time. Offers classical performance (MM, Advanced Diploma); jazz studies (MM); music (MA); music (PreK-12) (MS Ed); performance (Advanced Certificate). *Application deadline:* For fall admission, 4/1 for domestic students; for spring admission, 11/1 for domestic students. Applications are processed on a rolling basis. *Application fee:* $125. Electronic applications accepted. *Chair/Director,* Dr. Edward Smaldone, 718-997-3800, E-mail: edward.smaldone@qc.cuny.edu.

Division of Education Students: 266 full-time (225 women), 1,189 part-time (943 women); includes 645 minority (121 Black or African American, non-Hispanic/Latino; 4 American Indian or Alaska Native, non-Hispanic/Latino; 182 Asian, non-Hispanic/Latino; 312 Hispanic/Latino; 1 Native Hawaiian or other Pacific Islander, non-Hispanic/Latino; 25 Two or more races, non-Hispanic/Latino), 26 international. Average age 29. 1,069 applicants, 68% accepted, 540 enrolled. *Faculty:* 67 full-time (47 women), 123 part-time/adjunct (80 women). Expenses: Contact institution. *Financial support:* Career-related internships or fieldwork available. Financial award application deadline: 4/1; financial award applicants required to submit FAFSA. In 2016, 425 master's, 130 other advanced degrees awarded. *Program availability:* Part-time, evening/weekend. Offers adolescent biology (MAT); art (MS Ed); bilingual education (MS Ed); bilingual pupil personnel (AC); biology (MS Ed, AC); chemistry (MS Ed, AC); child development psychology (AC); childhood education (MAT, MS Ed); childhood education and special education (MAT); childhood education-bilingual education (MAT, MS Ed, AC); children's literacy (AC); counselor education (MS Ed); early childhood education (MAT); early childhood education birth-2 (MS Ed, AC); earth sciences (MS Ed, AC); education (MA, MAT, MS Ed, AC); elementary education (MS Ed); English (MS Ed, AC); French (MS Ed); Italian (MS Ed, AC); literacy birth-grade 6 (AC); literacy education (MS Ed); literacy technology birth-grade 6 (MS Ed); mathematics (MS Ed, AC); mental health counseling (MS); music (MS Ed, AC); physics (MS Ed, AC); school building leader (AC); school district leader (AC); school psychologist (MS Ed); social studies (MS Ed, AC); social studies education grades 1-6 (AC); Spanish (MS Ed, AC); special education-childhood education (AC); special education-early childhood (MS Ed); teacher of special education 1-6 (MS Ed); teacher of special education birth-2 (MS Ed); teaching students with disabilities, grades 7-12 (MS Ed, AC). *Application deadline:* For fall admission, 4/1 for domestic students; for spring admission, 11/1 for domestic students. Applications are processed on a rolling basis. *Application fee:* $125. Electronic applications accepted. *Dean,* Dr. Craig Michaels, 718-997-5220, E-mail: craig.michaels@qc.cuny.edu.

Division of Social Sciences Students: 73 full-time (44 women), 588 part-time (347 women); includes 353 minority (89 Black or African American, non-Hispanic/Latino; 123 Asian, non-Hispanic/Latino; 120 Hispanic/Latino; 42 Two or more races, non-Hispanic/Latino), 42 international. Average age 32. 441 applicants, 60% accepted, 219 enrolled. *Faculty:* 143 full-time (60 women), 193 part-time/adjunct (68 women). Expenses: Contact institution. *Financial support:* Career-related internships or fieldwork available. Financial award application deadline: 4/1; financial award applicants required to submit FAFSA. In 2016, 207 master's awarded. *Program availability:* Part-time, evening/weekend. Offers accounting (MA); data analytics and applied social research (MA); history (MA); liberal studies (MA); risk management-accounting (MS); risk management-dynamic finance analysis (MS); risk management-finance (MS); social science (MA, MLS, MS, AC); sociology (MA); urban affairs (MA). *Application deadline:* For fall admission, 4/1 for domestic students; for spring admission, 11/1 for domestic students. Applications are processed on a rolling basis. *Application fee:* $125. Electronic applications accepted. *Dean,* Dr. Michael Wolfe, 718-997-5211, E-mail: michael.wolfe@qc.cuny.edu.

Graduate School of Library and Information Studies Students: 28 full-time (22 women), 230 part-time (153 women); includes 106 minority (35 Black or African American, non-Hispanic/Latino; 21 Asian, non-Hispanic/Latino; 38 Hispanic/Latino; 12 Two or more races, non-Hispanic/Latino), 5 international. Average age 33. 163 applicants, 82% accepted, 92 enrolled. *Faculty:* 12 full-time (7 women), 15 part-time/adjunct (11 women). Expenses: Contact institution. *Financial support:* Career-related internships or fieldwork and unspecified assistantships available. Financial award application deadline: 4/1; financial award applicants required to submit FAFSA. In 2016, 74 master's, 4 other advanced degrees awarded. *Program availability:* Part-time, evening/weekend. Offers archives, records management and preservation (AC); children's and young adult services in the public library (AC); library media specialist (MLS, AC); library science (MLS, AC); school media specialist (MLS). *Application deadline:* For fall admission, 4/1 for domestic students; for spring admission, 11/1 for domestic students. Applications are processed on a rolling basis. *Application fee:* $125. Electronic applications accepted. *Director/Chair,* Dr. Roberta Brody, 718-997-3790, E-mail: roberta.brody@qc.cuny.edu.

Mathematics and Natural Sciences Division Students: 44 full-time (19 women), 461 part-time (261 women); includes 206 minority (44 Black or African American, non-Hispanic/Latino; 2 American Indian or Alaska Native, non-Hispanic/Latino; 63 Asian, non-Hispanic/Latino; 80 Hispanic/Latino; 1 Native Hawaiian or other Pacific Islander, non-Hispanic/Latino; 16 Two or more races, non-Hispanic/Latino), 57 international. Average age 29. 454 applicants, 60% accepted, 183 enrolled. *Faculty:* 163 full-time (57 women), 272 part-time/adjunct (136 women). Expenses: Contact institution. *Financial support:* Career-related internships or fieldwork available. Financial award application deadline: 4/1; financial award applicants required to submit FAFSA. In 2016, 83 master's, 7 other advanced degrees awarded. *Program availability:* Part-time. Offers applied behavior analysis (MA, AC); behavioral neuroscience (MA); biology (MA); chemistry (MA); computer science (MA); exercise science specialist (MS); family and consumer science (K-12) (AC); family and consumer science/teaching curriculum (K-12) (MS Ed); mathematics (MA); mathematics and natural sciences (MA, MAT, MS, MS Ed, AC); nutrition and exercise science (MS); nutrition specialist (MS); photonics (MS); physical education (K-12) (AC); physical education/teaching curriculum (pre K-12) (MS Ed); physics (MA); psychology (MA). *Application deadline:* For fall admission, 4/1 for domestic students; for spring admission, 11/1 for domestic students. Applications are processed on a rolling basis. *Application fee:* $125. Electronic applications accepted. *Dean,* Dr. Martin Klotz, 718-997-4105, E-mail: martin.klotz@qc.cuny.edu.

School of Earth and Environmental Sciences Students: 18 part-time (11 women); includes 5 minority (3 Hispanic/Latino; 2 Two or more races, non-Hispanic/Latino), 3 international. Average age 26. 16 applicants, 81% accepted, 7 enrolled. *Faculty:* 17 full-time (2 women), 11 part-time/adjunct (4 women). Expenses: Contact institution. *Financial support:* Career-related internships or fieldwork and unspecified assistantships available. Financial award application deadline: 4/1; financial award applicants required to submit FAFSA. *Program availability:* Part-time, evening/weekend. Offers applied environmental geoscience (MS); geological and environmental science (MA). *Application deadline:* For fall admission, 4/1 for domestic students; for spring admission, 11/1 for domestic students. Applications are processed on a rolling basis. *Application fee:* $125. Electronic applications accepted. *Chairperson,* Dr. George Hendrey, 718-997-3300, E-mail: george.hendrey@qc.cuny.edu.

QUEEN'S UNIVERSITY AT KINGSTON, Kingston, ON K7L 3N6, Canada

General Information Province-supported, coed, university. CGS member. *Graduate housing:* Rooms and/or apartments available to single students and available on a first-come, first-served basis to married students. Housing application deadline: 6/15.

GRADUATE UNITS

Faculty of Law *Program availability:* Part-time. Offers law (LL M, JD).

Queens School of Business Offers business (M Sc, MBA, PhD); consulting and project management (MBA); finance (MBA); innovation and entrepreneurship (MBA); marketing (MBA).

Queen's School of Religion *Program availability:* Part-time. Offers religion (M Div, MTS, Certificate).

School of Graduate Studies *Program availability:* Part-time.

Faculty of Applied Science *Program availability:* Part-time. Offers applied science (M Eng, M Sc, M Sc Eng, PhD); chemical engineering (M Sc, PhD); civil engineering (M Eng, M Sc Eng, PhD); electrical and computer engineering (M Eng, M Sc,

M Sc Eng, PhD); mechanical and materials engineering (M Eng, M Sc, M Sc Eng, PhD); mining engineering (M Eng, M Sc, M Sc Eng, PhD). Electronic applications accepted.

Faculty of Arts and Sciences *Program availability:* Part-time. Offers arts and sciences (M Sc, M Sc Eng, MA, PhD); biology (M Sc, PhD); brain behavior and cognitive science (MA, PhD); Canadian politics (PhD); chemistry (M Sc, PhD); classics, Greek, Latin (MA); clinical psychology (MA, PhD); communication and Information technology (MA, PhD); comparative politics (PhD); computing (M Sc, PhD); developmental psychology (MA, PhD); English language and literature (MA, PhD); feminist sociology (MA, PhD); French studies (MA, PhD); gender and politics (PhD); geography (M Sc, MA, PhD); geological sciences and geological engineering (M Sc, M Sc Eng, PhD); German (MA, PhD); international relations (MA, PhD); mathematics (M Sc, M Sc Eng, PhD); philosophy (MA, PhD); physics (M Sc, M Sc Eng, PhD); political theory (PhD); religious studies (MA); social personality psychology (MA, PhD); socio-legal studies (MA, PhD); sociological theory (MA, PhD); Spanish language and literature (MA); statistics (M Sc, M Sc Eng, PhD). Electronic applications accepted.

Faculty of Education *Program availability:* Part-time. Offers education (M Ed, PhD).

Faculty of Health Sciences *Program availability:* Part-time. Offers biochemistry (M Sc, PhD); biology of reproduction (M Sc, PhD); cancer (M Sc, PhD); cardiovascular pathophysiology (M Sc, PhD); cell and molecular biology (M Sc, PhD); drug metabolism (M Sc, PhD); endocrinology (M Sc, PhD); epidemiology (PhD); epidemiology and population health (M Sc); health and chronic illness (M Sc); health sciences (M Sc, M Sc OT, M Sc PT, MPH, PhD, Certificate); health services (M Sc); microbiology and immunology (M Sc, PhD); motor control (M Sc, PhD); neural regeneration (M Sc, PhD); neurophysiology (M Sc, PhD); nurse scientist (PhD); occupational therapy (M Sc OT); pathology and molecular medicine (M Sc, PhD); pharmacology and toxicology (M Sc, PhD); physical therapy (M Sc PT); physiology (M Sc, PhD); policy research and clinical epidemiology (M Sc); primary health care nurse practitioner (Certificate); public health (MPH); rehabilitation science (M Sc, PhD); women's and children's health (M Sc). Electronic applications accepted.

School of Industrial Relations *Program availability:* Part-time. Offers industrial relations (MIR).

School of Kinesiology and Health Studies *Program availability:* Part-time. Offers applied exercise science (PhD); biomechanics/ergonomics (M Sc); exercise physiology (M Sc); social psychology of sport and exercise rehabilitation (MA); sociology of sport (MA). Electronic applications accepted.

School of Policy Studies *Program availability:* Part-time. Offers policy studies (MIR, MPA).

School of Urban and Regional Planning *Program availability:* Part-time. Offers urban and regional planning (M Pl).

School of Medicine Offers medicine (MD). Electronic applications accepted.

QUEENS UNIVERSITY OF CHARLOTTE, Charlotte, NC 28274-0002
General Information Independent-religious, coed, comprehensive institution. *Graduate housing:* On-campus housing not available.

GRADUATE UNITS

College of Arts and Sciences *Program availability:* Part-time, online learning. Offers creative writing (MFA); interior design (MA). Electronic applications accepted.

Knight School of Communication *Program availability:* Part-time, evening/weekend, online learning. Offers organizational and strategic communication (MA).

McColl School of Business *Program availability:* Part-time, evening/weekend, online learning. Offers business administration (EMBA, MBA, PMBA); organization development (MSOD). Electronic applications accepted.

Presbyterian School of Nursing Offers clinical nurse leader (MSN); nurse educator (MSN); nursing administrator (MSN). Electronic applications accepted.

Wayland H. Cato, Jr. School of Education *Program availability:* Part-time, evening/weekend, online learning. Offers educational leadership (MA); K-6 (MAT); literacy K-12 (M Ed).

QUINCY UNIVERSITY, Quincy, IL 62301-2699
General Information Independent-religious, coed, comprehensive institution. *Graduate housing:* Room and/or apartments available to single students; on-campus housing not available to married students.

GRADUATE UNITS

Master of Arts in Communication Program *Program availability:* Part-time, evening/weekend, online learning. Offers communication (MA). Electronic applications accepted.

Master of Science in Education Counseling Program *Program availability:* Part-time, evening/weekend, online learning. Offers college personnel (MS Ed); counseling (MS Ed); school counseling (MS Ed). Electronic applications accepted.

Master of Science in Education Programs *Program availability:* Part-time, evening/weekend, online learning. Offers curriculum and instruction (MS Ed); leadership (MS Ed); reading education (MS Ed); special education (MS Ed); teacher leader (MS Ed). Electronic applications accepted.

MBA Program *Program availability:* Part-time, evening/weekend, online learning. Offers business administration (MBA). Electronic applications accepted.

QUINNIPIAC UNIVERSITY, Hamden, CT 06518-1940
General Information Independent, coed, comprehensive institution. *Enrollment:* 9,900 graduate, professional, and undergraduate students; 670 full-time matriculated graduate/professional students (429 women); 967 part-time matriculated graduate/professional students (654 women). *Enrollment by degree level:* 1,386 master's, 211 doctoral, 60 other advanced degrees. *Graduate faculty:* 112 full-time (62 women), 131 part-time/adjunct (53 women). *Tuition:* Part-time $985 per credit. *Required fees:* $40 per credit. $150 per semester. Tuition and fees vary according to program. *Graduate housing:* Rooms and/or apartments available on a first-come, first-served basis to single and married students. *Student services:* Campus employment opportunities, campus safety program, career counseling, exercise/wellness program, free psychological counseling, international student services, low-cost health insurance, multicultural affairs office, services for students with disabilities. *Library facilities:* Arnold Bernhard Library plus 3 others. *Collection:* Books: 135,000 (physical), 500,000 (digital/electronic); Databases: 190. Weekly public service hours: 93; study areas open 24 hours, 5–7 days a week; students can reserve study rooms.

Computer facilities: Computer purchase and lease plans are available. 600 computers available on campus for general student use. A campuswide network can be accessed from student residence rooms and from off campus. Online class registration, e-commerce and "Q" card for local merchants, food service, dorm card access are available.
Website: http://www.qu.edu/

General Application Contact: Graduate Admissions, 800-462-1944, Fax: 203-582-3443, E-mail: graduate@qu.edu.

GRADUATE UNITS

College of Arts and Sciences Students: 14 full-time (7 women), 12 part-time (7 women); includes 3 minority (2 Black or African American, non-Hispanic/Latino; 1 Hispanic/Latino), 5 international. 52 applicants, 58% accepted, 10 enrolled. *Faculty:* 7 full-time (5 women), 2 part-time/adjunct (0 women). Expenses: Contact institution. *Financial support:* Federal Work-Study, scholarships/grants, and unspecified assistantships available. Financial award application deadline: 6/1; financial award applicants required to submit FAFSA. In 2016, 14 master's awarded. *Program availability:* Part-time, evening/weekend. Offers arts and sciences (MS); molecular and cell biology (MS). *Application deadline:* For fall admission, 7/30 priority date for domestic students, 4/30 for international students; for spring admission, 12/15 priority date for domestic students, 9/15 for international students. Applications are processed on a rolling basis. *Application fee:* $45. Electronic applications accepted. *Application Contact:* The Office of Graduate Admissions, 800-462-1944, Fax: 203-582-3443, E-mail: graduate@qu.edu.

Frank H. Netter MD School of Medicine Students: 328 full-time (144 women); includes 132 minority (18 Black or African American, non-Hispanic/Latino; 1 American Indian or Alaska Native, non-Hispanic/Latino; 94 Asian, non-Hispanic/Latino; 17 Hispanic/Latino; 2 Native Hawaiian or other Pacific Islander, non-Hispanic/Latino). Average age 25. 5,025 applicants, 8% accepted, 90 enrolled. *Faculty:* 30 full-time (9 women), 6 part-time/adjunct (3 women). Expenses: Contact institution. *Financial support:* In 2016–17, 187 students received support. Scholarships/grants available. Financial award application deadline: 3/28; financial award applicants required to submit FAFSA. Offers anesthesiologist assistant (MMS); medicine (MMS, MD). *Application deadline:* For fall admission, 12/15 for domestic students. Applications are processed on a rolling basis. *Application fee:* $100. Electronic applications accepted. *Application Contact:* Michael Cole, Director of Admissions for Operations, 203-582-7766, E-mail: medicine@qu.edu. *Dean,* Dr. Bruce Koeppen, 203-582-5301.

School of Business and Engineering Students: 204 full-time (95 women), 485 part-time (276 women); includes 121 minority (40 Black or African American, non-Hispanic/Latino; 24 Asian, non-Hispanic/Latino; 44 Hispanic/Latino; 13 Two or more races, non-Hispanic/Latino), 23 international. 403 applicants, 83% accepted, 298 enrolled. *Faculty:* 34 full-time (11 women), 8 part-time/adjunct (2 women). Expenses: Contact institution. *Financial support:* Career-related internships or fieldwork, Federal Work-Study, scholarships/grants, and unspecified assistantships available. Financial award application deadline: 6/1; financial award applicants required to submit FAFSA. In 2016, 271 master's awarded. *Program availability:* Part-time, evening/weekend, 100% online, blended/hybrid learning. Offers business and engineering (MBA, MS); chartered financial analyst (MBA); health care management (MBA); organizational leadership (MS); supply chain management (MBA). *Application deadline:* For fall admission, 7/30 priority date for domestic students, 4/30 priority date for international students; for spring admission, 12/15 priority date for domestic students, 9/30 priority date for international students. Applications are processed on a rolling basis. *Application fee:* $45. Electronic applications accepted. *Application Contact:* Office of Graduate Admissions, 800-462-1944, Fax: 203-582-3443, E-mail: graduate@qu.edu.

School of Communications Students: 34 full-time (15 women), 99 part-time (61 women); includes 40 minority (20 Black or African American, non-Hispanic/Latino; 2 Asian, non-Hispanic/Latino; 14 Hispanic/Latino; 4 Two or more races, non-Hispanic/Latino), 3 international. 112 applicants, 84% accepted, 65 enrolled. *Faculty:* 13 full-time (7 women), 32 part-time/adjunct (8 women). Expenses: Contact institution. *Financial support:* Career-related internships or fieldwork, Federal Work-Study, scholarships/grants, and unspecified assistantships available. Financial award application deadline: 6/1; financial award applicants required to submit FAFSA. In 2016, 69 master's awarded. *Program availability:* Part-time, evening/weekend, online learning. Offers communications (MS); interactive media (MS); journalism (MS); media design (MS); public relations (MS); social media (MS); sports journalism (MS); UX design (MS). *Application deadline:* For fall admission, 7/30 priority date for domestic students, 4/30 priority date for international students; for spring admission, 12/15 priority date for domestic students, 9/30 priority date for international students. Applications are processed on a rolling basis. *Application fee:* $45. Electronic applications accepted. *Program Director,* Phillip Simon.

School of Education Students: 93 full-time (77 women), 145 part-time (113 women); includes 21 minority (3 Black or African American, non-Hispanic/Latino; 1 American Indian or Alaska Native, non-Hispanic/Latino; 1 Asian, non-Hispanic/Latino; 14 Hispanic/Latino; 5 Two or more races, non-Hispanic/Latino). 149 applicants, 93% accepted, 123 enrolled. *Faculty:* 11 full-time (7 women), 35 part-time/adjunct (21 women). Expenses: Contact institution. *Financial support:* Career-related internships or fieldwork, Federal Work-Study, and unspecified assistantships available. Financial award application deadline: 6/1; financial award applicants required to submit FAFSA. In 2016, 81 master's, 23 other advanced degrees awarded. Offers biology (MAT); education (MAT, MS, Diploma); educational leadership (Diploma); elementary education (MAT); English (MAT); history/social studies (MAT); instructional design (MS); mathematics (MAT); Spanish (MAT); teacher leadership (MS). *Application deadline:* Applications are processed on a rolling basis. *Application fee:* $45. Electronic applications accepted.

School of Health Sciences Students: 271 full-time (187 women), 38 part-time (27 women); includes 75 minority (21 Black or African American, non-Hispanic/Latino; 1 American Indian or Alaska Native, non-Hispanic/Latino; 24 Asian, non-Hispanic/Latino; 26 Hispanic/Latino; 3 Two or more races, non-Hispanic/Latino), 17 international. 1,453 applicants, 18% accepted, 152 enrolled. *Faculty:* 30 full-time (16 women), 44 part-time/adjunct (16 women). Expenses: Contact institution. *Financial support:* Federal Work-Study, scholarships/grants, and unspecified assistantships available. Financial award applicants required to submit FAFSA. In 2016, 143 master's awarded. Offers cardiovascular perfusion (MHS); health sciences (MHS, MHS, MSW); medical laboratory sciences (MHS); pathologists' assistant (MHS); physician assistant (MHS); radiologist assistant (MHS); social work (MSW). *Application deadline:* Applications are processed on a rolling basis. *Application fee:* $45. Electronic applications accepted. *Application Contact:* Office of Graduate Admissions, 800-462-1944, Fax: 203-582-3443, E-mail: graduate@qu.edu.

School of Law *Program availability:* Part-time, evening/weekend. Offers law (LL M, JD). Electronic applications accepted.

School of Nursing Students: 54 full-time (48 women), 188 part-time (170 women); includes 72 minority (36 Black or African American, non-Hispanic/Latino; 1 American Indian or Alaska Native, non-Hispanic/Latino; 20 Asian, non-Hispanic/Latino; 11 Hispanic/Latino; 4 Two or more races, non-Hispanic/Latino), 1 international. 225 applicants, 64% accepted, 104 enrolled. *Faculty:* 17 full-time (16 women), 10 part-time/adjunct (6 women). Expenses: Contact institution. *Financial support:* Federal Work-Study, scholarships/grants, and unspecified assistantships available. Financial award application deadline: 6/1; financial award applicants required to submit FAFSA. In 2016, 38 doctorates awarded. Offers adult nurse practitioner (DNP); care of populations (DNP); family nurse practitioner (DNP); nurse anesthesia (DNP); nursing (DNP); nursing leadership (DNP). *Application deadline:* Applications are processed on a rolling basis. *Application fee:* $45. Electronic applications accepted.

See Display below and Close-Up on page 893.

RABBINICAL ACADEMY MESIVTA RABBI CHAIM BERLIN, Brooklyn, NY 11230-4715

General Information Independent-religious, men only, comprehensive institution. *Graduate housing:* Room and/or apartments available to single students; on-campus housing not available to married students. Housing application deadline: 9/30.

GRADUATE UNITS

Graduate Program Offers Talmudic law and rabbinics (Advanced Talmudic Degree, Second Talmudic Degree).

RABBINICAL COLLEGE BETH SHRAGA, Monsey, NY 10952-3035

General Information Independent-religious, men only, comprehensive institution.
GRADUATE UNITS
Graduate Programs Offers theology.

RABBINICAL COLLEGE BOBOVER YESHIVA B'NEI ZION, Brooklyn, NY 11219

General Information Independent-religious, men only, comprehensive institution. *Graduate housing:* Room and/or apartments available to single students; on-campus housing not available to married students.

GRADUATE UNITS

Graduate Programs Offers theology.

RABBINICAL COLLEGE OF LONG ISLAND, Long Beach, NY 11561-3305

General Information Independent-religious, men only, comprehensive institution.

GRADUATE UNITS

Graduate Programs Offers theology.

RABBINICAL SEMINARY OF AMERICA, Flushing, NY 11367

General Information Independent-religious, men only, comprehensive institution. *Graduate housing:* Room and/or apartments available to single students; on-campus housing not available to married students. Housing application deadline: 6/15.

GRADUATE UNITS

Graduate Programs School offers a master's and first professional degree.

RADFORD UNIVERSITY, Radford, VA 24142

General Information State-supported, coed, comprehensive institution. CGS member. *Enrollment:* 9,401 graduate, professional, and undergraduate students; 556 full-time matriculated graduate/professional students (437 women), 345 part-time matriculated graduate/professional students (254 women). *Enrollment by degree level:* 706 master's, 146 doctoral, 49 other advanced degrees. *Graduate faculty:* 152 full-time (96 women), 39 part-time/adjunct (29 women). Tuition, state resident: full-time $7868; part-time $328 per credit hour. Tuition, nonresident: full-time $16,394; part-time $683 per credit hour. *Required fees:* $3090; $130 per credit hour. Tuition and fees vary according to course load and program. *Graduate housing:* On-campus housing not available. *Student services:* Campus employment opportunities, campus safety program, career counseling, exercise/wellness program, free psychological counseling, international student services, multicultural affairs office, services for students with disabilities, teacher training, writing training. *Library facilities:* McConnell Library. *Collection:* Books: 271,383 (physical), 332,165 (digital/electronic); Serial titles: 558 (physical), 28,298 (digital/electronic); Databases: 535. Students can reserve study rooms. *Research affiliation:* U.S. Department of Health and Human Services (nursing, psychology), Virginia Department of Social Services (social work), Virginia Department of Education (teacher education and leadership), Verizon Foundation (communication sciences and disorders), National Science Foundation (communication sciences and disorders, nursing, criminal justice, psychology, mathematics, biology, computer science), U.S. Department of Education (DOE) (teacher education and leadership).

Computer facilities: Computer purchase and lease plans are available. 900 computers available on campus for general student use. A campuswide network can be accessed from student residence rooms and from off campus. Online class registration, online financial aid status and student accounts payable are available. Website: http://www.radford.edu/

General Application Contact: Rebecca Conner, Director of Graduate Enrollment, 540-831-5431, Fax: 540-831-6061, E-mail: gradcollege@radford.edu.

GRADUATE UNITS

College of Graduate Studies and Research Students: 556 full-time (437 women), 345 part-time (254 women); includes 127 minority (69 Black or African American, non-Hispanic/Latino; 3 American Indian or Alaska Native, non-Hispanic/Latino; 13 Asian, non-Hispanic/Latino; 22 Hispanic/Latino; 2 Native Hawaiian or other Pacific Islander, non-Hispanic/Latino; 18 Two or more races, non-Hispanic/Latino), 12 international. Average age 29. 1,229 applicants, 53% accepted, 366 enrolled. *Faculty:* 152 full-time (96 women), 39 part-time/adjunct (29 women). Expenses: Contact institution. *Financial support:* In 2016–17, 347 students received support, including 19 research assistantships (averaging $9,295 per year), 68 teaching assistantships (averaging $10,412 per year); career-related internships or fieldwork, scholarships/grants, and unspecified assistantships also available. Support available to part-time students. Financial award application deadline: 3/1; financial award applicants required to submit FAFSA. In 2016, 317 master's, 44 doctorates, 6 other advanced degrees awarded. *Program availability:* Part-time, evening/weekend, 100% online, blended/hybrid learning. Offers art (MFA); business administration (MBA); communication sciences and disorders (MA, MS); corporate and professional communication (MS); counseling psychology (Psy D); counselor education (MS); criminal justice (MA, MS, Certificate); early childhood education (MS); educational leadership (MS); English (MA, MS); literacy education (MS); math education content area studies (MS); music (MA, MS); nursing practice (DNP); occupational therapy (MOT); physical therapy (DPT); psychology (MA, MS); school psychology (Ed S); social work (MSW); special education (MS, Certificate). *Application deadline:* Applications are processed on a rolling basis. *Application fee:* $50. Electronic applications accepted. *Application Contact:* Rebecca Conner, Director,

Graduate Enrollment, 540-831-5431, Fax: 540-831-6061, E-mail: gradcollege@radford.edu. *Dean*, Dr. Laura Jacobsen, 540-831-5724, Fax: 540-831-6061, E-mail: gradcollege@radford.edu.

Program in Data and Information Management Students: 3 full-time (1 woman); includes 2 minority (both Asian, non-Hispanic/Latino), 1 international. Average age 27. 5 applicants, 80% accepted, 3 enrolled. *Faculty:* 2 full-time (0 women). Expenses: Contact institution. *Financial support:* In 2016–17, 2 students received support, including 1 research assistantship (averaging $11,000 per year); teaching assistantships, scholarships/grants, and unspecified assistantships also available. Support available to part-time students. *Program availability:* Part-time, evening/weekend. Offers data and information management (MS). *Application deadline:* Applications are processed on a rolling basis. *Application fee:* $50. Electronic applications accepted. *Chair, Department of Information Technology*, Dr. Jeff Pittges, 540-831-5381, E-mail: jpittges@radford.edu.

RAMAPO COLLEGE OF NEW JERSEY, Mahwah, NJ 07430-1680

General Information State-supported, coed, comprehensive institution. *Enrollment:* 6,234 graduate, professional, and undergraduate students; 112 full-time matriculated graduate/professional students (83 women), 350 part-time matriculated graduate/professional students (252 women). *Enrollment by degree level:* 462 master's. *Graduate faculty:* 17 full-time (14 women), 27 part-time/adjunct (10 women). Tuition, state resident: part-time $606.05 per credit. Tuition, nonresident: part-time $606.05 per credit. *Required fees:* $130.45 per credit. *Graduate housing:* On-campus housing not available. *Student services:* Career counseling, services for students with disabilities. *Library facilities:* George T. Potter Library. *Research affiliation:* The Valley Hospital (nursing), New Jersey Association of State Colleges and Universities (veterans' issues), New Jersey Meadowlands Commission (environment).

Computer facilities: A campuswide network can be accessed from student residence rooms and from off campus. Online class registration is available.
Website: http://www.ramapo.edu/

General Application Contact: Anthony Dovi, Associate Director of Admissions, Adult Learners and Graduate Programs, 201-684-7305, Fax: 201-684-7964, E-mail: adovi@ramapo.edu.

GRADUATE UNITS

Master of Arts in Educational Leadership Program Students: 39 full-time (22 women), 30 part-time (21 women); includes 9 minority (3 Black or African American, non-Hispanic/Latino; 1 Asian, non-Hispanic/Latino; 4 Hispanic/Latino; 1 Two or more races, non-Hispanic/Latino). Average age 36. 57 applicants, 91% accepted, 35 enrolled. *Faculty:* 2 full-time (0 women), 10 part-time/adjunct (2 women). Expenses: Contact institution. *Financial support:* Career-related internships or fieldwork available. Financial award application deadline: 3/1; financial award applicants required to submit FAFSA. In 2016, 23 master's awarded. *Program availability:* Part-time. Offers educational leadership (MA). *Application deadline:* For fall admission, 5/1 for domestic and international students; for spring admission, 12/1 for domestic and international students. Applications are processed on a rolling basis. *Application fee:* $60. Electronic applications accepted. *Application Contact:* M. Joyce Wilson, Secretarial Assistant, 201-684-7721, Fax: 201-684-6699, E-mail: jwilson@ramapo.edu. *Associate Professor, Educational Leadership*, Dr. Brian P. Chinni, 201-684-7613, E-mail: bchinni@ramapo.edu.

Master of Arts in Special Education Program Students: 39 part-time (34 women); includes 4 minority (all Hispanic/Latino). Average age 27. 35 applicants, 74% accepted, 21 enrolled. *Faculty:* 1 (woman) full-time, 3 part-time/adjunct (2 women). Expenses: Contact institution. *Financial support:* Career-related internships or fieldwork available. Financial award application deadline: 3/1; financial award applicants required to submit FAFSA. In 2016, 23 master's awarded. *Program availability:* Part-time. Offers special education (MA). *Application deadline:* For fall admission, 5/1 for domestic and international students. Applications are processed on a rolling basis. *Application fee:* $60. Electronic applications accepted. *Application Contact:* M. Joyce Wilson, Secretarial Assistant, 201-684-7721, Fax: 201-684-6699, E-mail: jwilson@ramapo.edu. *Director*, Dr. Julie Norflus-Good, 201-684-7246, E-mail: jgood@ramapo.edu.

Master of Business Administration Program Students: 66 part-time (29 women); includes 17 minority (6 Black or African American, non-Hispanic/Latino; 1 American Indian or Alaska Native, non-Hispanic/Latino; 4 Asian, non-Hispanic/Latino; 5 Hispanic/Latino; 1 Two or more races, non-Hispanic/Latino). Average age 32. 115 applicants, 40% accepted, 32 enrolled. *Faculty:* 3 full-time (all women). Expenses: Contact institution. *Financial support:* Career-related internships or fieldwork and scholarships/grants available. Financial award application deadline: 3/1; financial award applicants required to submit FAFSA. In 2016, 28 master's awarded. *Program availability:* Part-time, evening/weekend. Offers leadership (MBA). *Application deadline:* For fall admission, 5/1 for domestic and international students. Applications are processed on a rolling basis. *Application fee:* $60. Electronic applications accepted. *Application Contact:* Timothy Landers, Assistant Dean/Director of the MBA Program, 201-684-7771, E-mail: tlanders@ramapo.edu. *Dean of the Anisfield School of Business*, Dr. Edward Petkus, 201-684-7377, E-mail: epetkus@ramapo.edu.

Master of Science in Educational Technology Program Students: 2 full-time (both women), 142 part-time (103 women); includes 18 minority (2 Black or African American, non-Hispanic/Latino; 3 Asian, non-Hispanic/Latino; 13 Hispanic/Latino), 3 international. Average age 34. 72 applicants, 93% accepted, 55 enrolled. *Faculty:* 12 part-time/adjunct (5 women). Expenses: Contact institution. *Financial support:* Career-related internships or fieldwork available. Financial award application deadline: 3/1; financial award applicants required to submit FAFSA. In 2016, 37 master's awarded. *Program availability:* Part-time, evening/weekend. Offers educational technology (MS). *Application deadline:* For fall admission, 5/1 for domestic and international students; for spring admission, 12/1 for domestic and international students. Applications are processed on a rolling basis. *Application fee:* $60. Electronic applications accepted. *Application Contact:* M. Joyce Wilson, Administrative Assistant, 201-684-7721, Fax: 201-684-6699, E-mail: jwilson@ramapo.edu. *Director of the Master in Educational Technology Program*, Dr. Richard Russo, 201-684-7899, Fax: 201-684-6699, E-mail: rrusso@ramapo.edu.

Master of Science in Nursing Program Students: 1 full-time (0 women), 50 part-time (45 women); includes 20 minority (3 Black or African American, non-Hispanic/Latino; 9 Asian, non-Hispanic/Latino; 7 Hispanic/Latino; 1 Two or more races, non-Hispanic/Latino). Average age 36. 28 applicants, 79% accepted, 16 enrolled. *Faculty:* 3 full-time (all women), 1 part-time/adjunct (0 women). Expenses: Contact institution. *Financial support:* Career-related internships or fieldwork available. Financial award application deadline: 3/1; financial award applicants required to submit FAFSA. In 2016, 12 master's awarded. *Program availability:* Part-time. Offers family nurse practitioner (MSN); nursing administrator (MSN); nursing education (MSN). *Application deadline:* For fall admission, 5/1 for domestic and international students; for spring admission, 12/1 for

domestic and international students. Applications are processed on a rolling basis. *Application fee:* $60. Electronic applications accepted. *Application Contact:* Anthony Dovi, Associate Director of Admissions, Adult Learners and Graduate Programs, 201-684-7305, Fax: 201-684-7964, E-mail: adovi@ramapo.edu. *Assistant Dean in Charge of Nursing Programs/Professor*, Dr. Kathleen M. Burke, 201-684-7737, Fax: 201-684-7954, E-mail: kmburke@ramapo.edu.

Master of Social Work Program Students: 70 full-time (59 women), 14 part-time (all women); includes 24 minority (10 Black or African American, non-Hispanic/Latino; 13 Hispanic/Latino; 1 Two or more races, non-Hispanic/Latino). Average age 31. 167 applicants, 59% accepted, 51 enrolled. *Faculty:* 4 full-time (all women), 5 part-time/adjunct (4 women). Expenses: Contact institution. *Financial support:* Scholarships/grants available. Financial award application deadline: 3/1; financial award applicants required to submit FAFSA. *Program availability:* Part-time. Offers social work (MSW). *Application deadline:* For fall admission, 3/1 for domestic and international students. Applications are processed on a rolling basis. *Application fee:* $60. Electronic applications accepted. *Assistant Dean/Director*, Ann Marie Moreno, 201-684-7191, E-mail: amoreno@ramapo.edu.

RANDALL UNIVERSITY, Moore, OK 73160-1208

General Information Independent-religious, coed, comprehensive institution. *Graduate housing:* Room and/or apartments available on a first-come, first-served basis to single students.

GRADUATE UNITS

Department of Bible Studies *Program availability:* Part-time, evening/weekend. Offers ministry (MA).

RANDOLPH COLLEGE, Lynchburg, VA 24503

General Information Independent-religious, coed, comprehensive institution.

GRADUATE UNITS

Programs in Education Offers curriculum and instruction (MAT); special education-learning disabilities (M Ed, MAT).

RECONSTRUCTIONIST RABBINICAL COLLEGE, Wyncote, PA 19095-1898

General Information Independent-religious, coed, graduate-only institution. *Graduate housing:* On-campus housing not available.

GRADUATE UNITS

Graduate Programs *Program availability:* Part-time. Offers Jewish studies (MAJS); rabbinics (MAHL, DHL); women's studies (Certificate). Certificate offered jointly with Temple University.

REED COLLEGE, Portland, OR 97202-8199

General Information Independent, coed, comprehensive institution. *Enrollment:* 1,427 graduate, professional, and undergraduate students; 23 part-time matriculated graduate/professional students (13 women). *Enrollment by degree level:* 23 master's. *Graduate faculty:* 13 part-time/adjunct (7 women). *Graduate housing:* On-campus housing not available. *Student services:* Campus employment opportunities, campus safety program, career counseling, exercise/wellness program, free psychological counseling, low-cost health insurance, multicultural affairs office, services for students with disabilities, writing training. *Library facilities:* Eric V. Hauser Memorial Library plus 1 other.

Computer facilities: Computer purchase and lease plans are available. 434 computers available on campus for general student use. A campuswide network can be accessed from student residence rooms. Online class registration is available.
Website: http://www.reed.edu/

General Application Contact: Barbara A. Amen, Director, Graduate Studies, 503-777-7259, Fax: 503-517-7345, E-mail: bamen@reed.edu.

GRADUATE UNITS

Graduate Program in Liberal Studies Students: 23 part-time (13 women); includes 2 minority (both Black or African American, non-Hispanic/Latino). Average age 45. 5 applicants, 20% accepted, 1 enrolled. *Faculty:* 13 part-time/adjunct (7 women). Expenses: Contact institution. *Financial support:* In 2016–17, 5 students received support. Scholarships/grants and health care benefits available. Support available to part-time students. Financial award application deadline: 5/1; financial award applicants required to submit CSS PROFILE or FAFSA. In 2016, 3 master's awarded. *Program availability:* Part-time-only, evening/weekend. Offers liberal studies (MALS). *Application deadline:* For fall admission, 7/1 priority date for domestic students, 5/1 for international students; for spring admission, 12/1 priority date for domestic students, 9/1 for international students; for summer admission, 4/1 for domestic students, 2/1 for international students. Applications are processed on a rolling basis. *Application fee:* $75. Electronic applications accepted. *Director, Graduate Studies*, Barbara A. Amen, 503-777-7259, Fax: 503-517-7345, E-mail: bamen@reed.edu.

REFORMED EPISCOPAL SEMINARY, Blue Bell, PA 19422

General Information Independent-religious, coed, graduate-only institution. *Graduate housing:* Room and/or apartments available on a first-come, first-served basis to single students; on-campus housing not available to married students.

GRADUATE UNITS

Graduate Program Offers theology (M Div).

REFORMED PRESBYTERIAN THEOLOGICAL SEMINARY, Pittsburgh, PA 15208-2594

General Information Independent-religious, coed, primarily men, graduate-only institution. *Graduate housing:* Rooms and/or apartments available on a first-come, first-served basis to single and married students.

GRADUATE UNITS

Graduate and Professional Programs *Program availability:* Part-time, evening/weekend. Offers theology (M Div, MTS, D Min). Electronic applications accepted.

REFORMED THEOLOGICAL SEMINARY–ATLANTA CAMPUS, Marietta, GA 30067

General Information Independent-religious, coed, primarily men, graduate-only institution.

GRADUATE UNITS

Graduate Programs Offers theology (M Div, MABS, MAR, D Min, Certificate).

REFORMED THEOLOGICAL SEMINARY–CHARLOTTE CAMPUS, Charlotte, NC 28226-6318

General Information Independent-religious, coed, primarily men, graduate-only institution. *Graduate housing:* On-campus housing not available.

GRADUATE UNITS

Graduate and Professional Programs *Program availability:* Part-time. Offers biblical studies (MA); ministry (D Min); pastoral ministry (M Div); theological studies (MA). Electronic applications accepted.

REFORMED THEOLOGICAL SEMINARY–HOUSTON CAMPUS, Houston, TX 77024

General Information Independent-religious, coed, primarily men, graduate-only institution. *Graduate housing:* On-campus housing not available.

GRADUATE UNITS

Graduate Program Offers Biblical studies (MA). Electronic applications accepted.

REFORMED THEOLOGICAL SEMINARY–JACKSON CAMPUS, Jackson, MS 39209-3004

General Information Independent-religious, coed, primarily men, graduate-only institution. *Graduate housing:* Rooms and/or apartments available on a first-come, first-served basis to single and married students.

GRADUATE UNITS

Graduate and Professional Programs Offers Bible, theology, and missions (Certificate); Biblical exegesis (M Div); biblical studies (MA); Christian education (MA); counseling (M Div); marriage and family therapy (MA); ministry (D Min); missions (M Div, MA, D Min); theological studies (MA).

REFORMED THEOLOGICAL SEMINARY–ORLANDO CAMPUS, Oviedo, FL 32765

General Information Independent-religious, coed, primarily men, graduate-only institution. *Enrollment by degree level:* 272 master's, 61 doctoral, 7 other advanced degrees. *Graduate faculty:* 12 full-time (0 women), 11 part-time/adjunct (2 women). *Tuition:* Full-time $17,325. *Required fees:* $160. Tuition and fees vary according to course load. *Graduate housing:* Rooms and/or apartments available on a first-come, first-served basis to single and married students. *Student services:* Campus employment opportunities, career counseling, free psychological counseling, international student services, writing training. *Library facilities:* RTS Library. *Collection:* Books: 88,348 (physical), 73,000 (digital/electronic); Serial titles: 125 (physical). Weekly public service hours: 69.

Computer facilities: 6 computers available on campus for general student use. Online class registration is available.
Website: http://www.rts.edu/

General Application Contact: Winston J. Miller, Director of Admissions, 800-752-4382, Fax: 407-366-9425, E-mail: applications.orlando@rts.edu.

GRADUATE UNITS

Graduate Programs Students: 340. *Faculty:* 12 full-time (0 women), 11 part-time/adjunct (2 women). Expenses: Contact institution. *Program availability:* Part-time, online learning. Offers Bible (Certificate); biblical studies (MA); counseling (MA); missions (Certificate); reformed expository preaching (D Min); reformed theology and ministry (D Min); theological studies (MA); theology (M Div, Certificate). *Application deadline:* Applications are processed on a rolling basis. *Application fee:* $75. Electronic applications accepted. *Application Contact:* Winston J. Miller, Director of Admissions, 800-752-4382, Fax: 407-366-9425, E-mail: applications.orlando@rts.edu. *President,* Dr. Scott R. Swain, 407-278-4406, Fax: 407-366-9425.

REFORMED THEOLOGICAL SEMINARY–WASHINGTON D.C., McLean, VA 22102

General Information Independent-religious, coed, primarily men, graduate-only institution. *Enrollment by degree level:* 88 master's, 62 other advanced degrees. *Graduate faculty:* 4 full-time (0 women), 10 part-time/adjunct (2 women). *Tuition:* Full-time $11,880; part-time $5940 per credit. *Required fees:* $60 per term. Tuition and fees vary according to course load. *Graduate housing:* On-campus housing not available. *Student services:* Campus employment opportunities, campus safety program, career counseling, international student services, writing training. *Library facilities:* RTS Library plus 1 other. *Collection:* Books: 2,500 (physical). Study areas open 24 hours, 5–7 days a week.

Computer facilities: 1 computer available on campus for general student use. Online class registration is available.
Website: http://www.rts.edu/

General Application Contact: Geoff M. Sackett, Director of Admissions/Dean of Students, 703-448-3393 Ext. 104, E-mail: gsackett@rts.edu.

GRADUATE UNITS

Graduate and Professional Programs Students: 5 full-time (0 women), 86 part-time (7 women); includes 25 minority (4 Black or African American, non-Hispanic/Latino; 18 Asian, non-Hispanic/Latino; 3 Hispanic/Latino), 1 international. Average age 35. 73 applicants, 95% accepted, 67 enrolled. *Faculty:* 4 full-time (0 women), 10 part-time/adjunct (2 women). Expenses: Contact institution. *Financial support:* In 2016–17, 116 students received support. Scholarships/grants and tuition waivers (partial) available. Support available to part-time students. Financial award application deadline: 5/1. In 2016, 8 master's awarded. *Program availability:* Part-time, evening/weekend. Offers Bible (M Div); biblical studies (MA); practical theology (M Div); religion (MA); theology (M Div). *Application deadline:* Applications are processed on a rolling basis. *Application fee:* $75. Electronic applications accepted. *Application Contact:* Geoff M. Sackett, Director of Admissions, 703-448-3393 Ext. 5104, E-mail: gsackett@rts.edu. *President,* Dr. John S. Redd, Jr., 703-448-3393 Ext. 5107, E-mail: sredd@rts.edu.

REGENT COLLEGE, Vancouver, BC V6T 2E4, Canada

General Information Independent-religious, coed, graduate-only institution. *Enrollment by degree level:* 455 master's. *Graduate faculty:* 16 full-time (2 women), 26 part-time/adjunct (7 women). *Tuition:* Full-time $8640 Canadian dollars; part-time $480 Canadian dollars per credit hour. *Required fees:* $800 Canadian dollars; $800 Canadian dollars per credit hour. *Graduate housing:* On-campus housing not available. *Student services:* Campus employment opportunities, campus safety program, career counseling, international student services, low-cost health insurance, services for students with disabilities, writing training. *Library facilities:* The John Richard Allison Library plus 15 others. *Collection:* Books: 200,000 (physical); Databases: 12. Students can reserve study rooms. *Research affiliation:* University of British Columbia (theology, religion).

Computer facilities: 8 computers available on campus for general student use. Online class registration is available.
Website: http://www.regent-college.edu/

General Application Contact: Admissions, 604-224-3245, Fax: 604-224-3097, E-mail: admissions@regent-college.edu.

GRADUATE UNITS

Program in Theology Students: 187 full-time (53 women), 268 part-time (103 women). 173 applicants, 65% accepted, 102 enrolled. *Faculty:* 16 full-time (2 women), 23 part-time/adjunct (6 women). Expenses: Contact institution. *Financial support:* Teaching assistantships, career-related internships or fieldwork, scholarships/grants, and health care benefits available. Financial award application deadline: 3/1. *Program availability:* Part-time. Offers Christian history and theology (M Div, MATS); Christian studies (MATS, G Dip); Christianity, church and culture (M Div, MATS); scripture (M Div, MATS); theology (Th M). *Application deadline:* For fall admission, 2/1 priority date for domestic students, 1/1 priority date for international students; for winter admission, 7/2 priority date for domestic and international students; for spring admission, 2/1 for domestic students, 1/1 for international students. Applications are processed on a rolling basis. *Application fee:* $60 Canadian dollars. Electronic applications accepted. *Application Contact:* Admissions, 604-224-3245, Fax: 604-224-3097, E-mail: admissions@regent-college.edu. *President,* Dr. Jeff Greenman, 604-221-3318, Fax: 604-224-3097, E-mail: presidentsoffice@regent-college.edu.

REGENT'S UNIVERSITY LONDON, London NW1 4NS, United Kingdom

General Information Independent, coed, comprehensive institution.

GRADUATE UNITS

Webster Graduate School *Program availability:* Part-time. Offers business (MBA); finance (MS); human resources (MA); information technology management (MA); international business (MA); international non-governmental organizations (MA); international relations (MA); management and leadership (MA); marketing (MA).

REGENT UNIVERSITY, Virginia Beach, VA 23464-9800

General Information Independent-religious, coed, comprehensive institution. *Enrollment:* 8,868 graduate, professional, and undergraduate students; 1,128 full-time matriculated graduate/professional students (716 women), 3,794 part-time matriculated graduate/professional students (2,336 women). *Enrollment by degree level:* 3,438 master's, 1,336 doctoral, 148 other advanced degrees. *Graduate faculty:* 121 full-time (42 women), 303 part-time/adjunct (112 women). *Required fees:* $750. Tuition and fees vary according to course load, degree level and program. *Graduate housing:* Rooms and/or apartments available on a first-come, first-served basis to single and married students. *Typical cost:* $8885 per year ($11,405 including board) for single students; $11,925 per year ($14,445 including board) for married students. Room and board charges vary according to board plan and housing facility selected. Housing application deadline: 5/1. *Student services:* Campus employment opportunities, campus safety program, career counseling, free psychological counseling, international student services, low-cost health insurance, services for students with disabilities, teacher training, writing training. *Library facilities:* Regent University Library plus 1 other. *Collection:* Books: 321,520 (physical), 454,079 (digital/electronic); Serial titles: 133 (physical), 380,580 (digital/electronic); Databases: 174. Weekly public service hours: 102; students can reserve study rooms.

Computer facilities: 70 computers available on campus for general student use. A campuswide network can be accessed from student residence rooms and from off campus. Online class registration is available.
Website: http://www.regent.edu/

General Application Contact: Heidi Cece, Assistant Vice President of Enrollment Management, 800-373-5504, Fax: 757-352-4381, E-mail: admissions@regent.edu.

GRADUATE UNITS

Graduate School Students: 1,128 full-time (716 women), 3,794 part-time (2,336 women); includes 2,227 minority (1,749 Black or African American, non-Hispanic/Latino; 22 American Indian or Alaska Native, non-Hispanic/Latino; 103 Asian, non-Hispanic/Latino; 258 Hispanic/Latino; 4 Native Hawaiian or other Pacific Islander, non-Hispanic/Latino; 91 Two or more races, non-Hispanic/Latino), 229 international. Average age 39. 4,161 applicants, 88% accepted, 1444 enrolled. *Faculty:* 121 full-time (42 women), 303 part-time/adjunct (112 women). Expenses: Contact institution. In 2016, 792 master's, 251 doctorates, 5 other advanced degrees awarded. *Program availability:* Part-time, evening/weekend, 100% online, blended/hybrid learning. *Application deadline:* Applications are processed on a rolling basis. *Application fee:* $50. Electronic applications accepted. *Application Contact:* Heidi Cece, Assistant Vice President of Enrollment Management, 800-373-5504, Fax: 757-352-4381, E-mail: admissions@regent.edu. *Executive Vice President for Academic Affairs,* Dr. Gerson Moreno-Riano, 757-352-4448, E-mail: gmorenoriano@regent.edu.

Robertson School of Government Students: 40 full-time (27 women), 119 part-time (69 women); includes 73 minority (47 Black or African American, non-Hispanic/Latino; 3 Asian, non-Hispanic/Latino; 15 Hispanic/Latino; 8 Two or more races, non-Hispanic/Latino), 6 international. Average age 35. 253 applicants, 41% accepted, 70 enrolled. *Faculty:* 8 full-time (1 woman), 19 part-time/adjunct (3 women). Expenses: Contact institution. *Financial support:* In 2016–17, 78 students received support. Career-related internships or fieldwork, scholarships/grants, and unspecified assistantships available. Support available to part-time students. In 2016, 34 master's awarded. *Program availability:* Part-time, evening/weekend, 100% online, blended/hybrid learning. Offers government (MA); public administration (MPA). *Application deadline:* For fall admission, 5/1 priority date for domestic students; for spring admission, 11/1 priority date for domestic students. Applications are processed on a rolling basis. *Application fee:* $50. Electronic applications accepted. *Application Contact:* Heidi Cece, Assistant Vice President of Enrollment Management, 800-373-5504, Fax: 757-352-4381, E-mail: admissions@regent.edu. *Dean,* Dr. Eric Patterson, 757-352-4616, Fax: 757-352-4735, E-mail: epatterson@regent.edu.

School of Business and Leadership Students: 100 full-time (56 women), 1,008 part-time (528 women); includes 562 minority (453 Black or African American, non-Hispanic/Latino; 7 American Indian or Alaska Native, non-Hispanic/Latino; 30 Asian, non-Hispanic/Latino; 51 Hispanic/Latino; 1 Native Hawaiian or other Pacific Islander, non-Hispanic/Latino; 20 Two or more races, non-Hispanic/Latino), 76 international. Average age 40. 1,240 applicants, 45% accepted, 352 enrolled. *Faculty:* 9 full-time (2 women), 28 part-time/adjunct (10 women). Expenses: Contact institution. *Financial support:* In 2016–17, 631 students received support. Career-related internships or fieldwork, scholarships/grants, and unspecified assistantships available. Support available to part-time students. In 2016, 95 master's, 71 doctorates awarded. *Program availability:* Part-time, evening/weekend, 100% online, blended/hybrid learning. Offers business administration (MBA); leadership (Certificate); organizational leadership (MA, PhD); strategic leadership (DSL). *Application deadline:* For fall admission, 5/1 priority date for domestic students; for spring admission, 10/1 priority date for domestic students. Applications are processed on a rolling basis. *Application fee:* $50. Electronic applications accepted. *Application Contact:* Heidi Cece, Assistant Vice President of Enrollment Management, 800-373-5504, Fax: 757-352-4381, E-mail: admissions@regent.edu. *Dean,* Dr. Doris Gomez, 757-352-4686, Fax: 757-352-4634, E-mail: dorigom@regent.edu.

School of Communication and the Arts Students: 92 full-time (52 women), 344 part-time (225 women); includes 163 minority (116 Black or African American, non-Hispanic/Latino; 6 American Indian or Alaska Native, non-Hispanic/Latino; 7 Asian, non-Hispanic/Latino; 25 Hispanic/Latino; 1 Native Hawaiian or other Pacific Islander, non-Hispanic/Latino; 8 Two or more races, non-Hispanic/Latino), 8 international. Average age 37. 368 applicants, 52% accepted, 124 enrolled. *Faculty:* 19 full-time (3 women), 51 part-time/adjunct (17 women). *Expenses:* Contact institution. *Financial support:* In 2016–17, 178 students received support, including 2 fellowships (averaging $10,000 per year); career-related internships or fieldwork, scholarships/grants, and unspecified assistantships also available. Support available to part-time students. In 2016, 91 master's, 7 doctorates awarded. *Program availability:* Part-time, 100% online, blended/hybrid learning. Offers communication (MA, PhD); directing for cinema/television (MFA); film and TV (MA); journalism (MA); producing for cinema/television (MFA); script and screenwriting (MFA); theatre (MA). *Application deadline:* For fall admission, 3/1 priority date for domestic students; for spring admission, 10/1 priority date for domestic students. Applications are processed on a rolling basis. *Application fee:* $50. Electronic applications accepted. *Application Contact:* Heidi Cece, Assistant Vice President of Enrollment Management, 800-373-5504, Fax: 757-352-4381, E-mail: admissions@regent.edu. *Dean,* Dr. Mitch Land, 757-352-4916, Fax: 757-352-4291, E-mail: mland@regent.edu.

School of Divinity Students: 148 full-time (60 women), 787 part-time (321 women); includes 506 minority (416 Black or African American, non-Hispanic/Latino; 1 American Indian or Alaska Native, non-Hispanic/Latino; 23 Asian, non-Hispanic/Latino; 54 Hispanic/Latino; 1 Native Hawaiian or other Pacific Islander, non-Hispanic/Latino; 11 Two or more races, non-Hispanic/Latino), 31 international. Average age 43. 1,020 applicants, 42% accepted, 276 enrolled. *Faculty:* 15 full-time (3 women), 51 part-time/adjunct (6 women). *Expenses:* Contact institution. *Financial support:* In 2016–17, 602 students received support. Career-related internships or fieldwork, scholarships/grants, and unspecified assistantships available. Support available to part-time students. In 2016, 127 master's, 25 doctorates awarded. *Program availability:* Part-time, evening/weekend, 100% online, blended/hybrid learning. Offers divinity (M Div); leadership and renewal (D Min); practical theology (MA); theological studies (MTS, PhD). *Application deadline:* For fall admission, 5/1 priority date for domestic students. Applications are processed on a rolling basis. *Application fee:* $50. Electronic applications accepted. *Application Contact:* Heidi Cece, Assistant Vice President of Enrollment Management, 800-373-5504, Fax: 757-352-4381, E-mail: admissions@regent.edu. *Dean,* Dr. Cornelius Bekker, 757-352-4401, Fax: 757-352-4597, E-mail: clbekker@regent.edu.

School of Education Students: 89 full-time (62 women), 1,035 part-time (823 women); includes 466 minority (381 Black or African American, non-Hispanic/Latino; 3 American Indian or Alaska Native, non-Hispanic/Latino; 19 Asian, non-Hispanic/Latino; 50 Hispanic/Latino; 13 Two or more races, non-Hispanic/Latino), 11 international. Average age 39. 976 applicants, 59% accepted, 449 enrolled. *Faculty:* 22 full-time (10 women), 42 part-time/adjunct (31 women). *Expenses:* Contact institution. *Financial support:* In 2016–17, 622 students received support, including 1 fellowship (averaging $5,000 per year); career-related internships or fieldwork, scholarships/grants, and unspecified assistantships also available. Support available to part-time students. In 2016, 241 master's, 22 doctorates, 4 other advanced degrees awarded. *Program availability:* Part-time, evening/weekend, 100% online, blended/hybrid learning. Offers adult education (Ed D, PhD, Ed S); advanced educational leadership (Ed D, PhD, Ed S); career switcher (M Ed); character education (Ed D, PhD, Ed S); Christian education leadership (Ed D, PhD, Ed S); Christian school administration (M Ed); curriculum and instruction (M Ed); educational leadership (M Ed); educational psychology (Ed D, PhD, Ed S); educational technology and online learning (Ed D, PhD, Ed S); elementary education (M Ed); exceptional education executive leadership (Ed D, PhD, Ed S); higher education (Ed D, PhD, Ed S); higher education leadership and management (Ed D, PhD, Ed S); individualized degree plan (Ed D, PhD, Ed S); K-12 school leadership (Ed D, PhD, Ed S); K-12 special education (M Ed); K-8 leadership in mathematics education (M Ed); leadership in mathematics education (Ed S); reading specialist (M Ed); special education (Ed D, PhD, Ed S); student affairs (M Ed); TESOL (M Ed). *Application deadline:* For fall admission, 4/1 priority date for domestic students; for spring admission, 10/15 priority date for domestic students. Applications are processed on a rolling basis. *Application fee:* $50. Electronic applications accepted. *Application Contact:* Heidi Cece, Assistant Vice President of Enrollment Management, 800-373-5504, Fax: 757-352-4381, E-mail: admissions@regent.edu. *Dean,* Dr. Donald Finn, 757-352-4278, Fax: 757-352-4318, E-mail: dfinn@regent.edu.

School of Law Students: 364 full-time (219 women), 170 part-time (118 women); includes 213 minority (150 Black or African American, non-Hispanic/Latino; 1 American Indian or Alaska Native, non-Hispanic/Latino; 10 Asian, non-Hispanic/Latino; 34 Hispanic/Latino; 1 Native Hawaiian or other Pacific Islander, non-Hispanic/Latino; 17 Two or more races, non-Hispanic/Latino), 87 international. Average age 34. 834 applicants, 45% accepted, 174 enrolled. *Faculty:* 20 full-time (6 women), 67 part-time/adjunct (19 women). *Expenses:* Contact institution. *Financial support:* In 2016–17, 319 students received support. Career-related internships or fieldwork, scholarships/grants, and unspecified assistantships available. Support available to part-time students. In 2016, 48 master's, 85 doctorates awarded. *Program availability:* Part-time, 100% online, blended/hybrid learning. Offers American legal studies (LL M); human rights (LL M); law (MA, JD). *Application deadline:* For fall admission, 3/1 for domestic students. Applications are processed on a rolling basis. *Application fee:* $50. Electronic applications accepted. *Application Contact:* Katie Kerley, Director of Law Admissions, 877-267-5072, Fax: 757-352-4139, E-mail: lawschool@regent.edu. *Dean,* Michael Hernandez, 757-352-4040, Fax: 757-352-4595, E-mail: michher@regent.edu.

School of Psychology and Counseling Students: 295 full-time (240 women), 331 part-time (252 women); includes 244 minority (186 Black or African American, non-Hispanic/Latino; 4 American Indian or Alaska Native, non-Hispanic/Latino; 11 Asian, non-Hispanic/Latino; 29 Hispanic/Latino; 14 Two or more races, non-Hispanic/Latino), 10 international. Average age 36. 1,192 applicants, 29% accepted, 235 enrolled.

Faculty: 28 full-time (17 women), 45 part-time/adjunct (26 women). *Expenses:* Contact institution. *Financial support:* In 2016–17, 446 students received support, including 5 fellowships (averaging $4,000 per year), 10 research assistantships (averaging $3,200 per year); career-related internships or fieldwork, scholarships/grants, and unspecified assistantships also available. Support available to part-time students. In 2016, 156 master's, 41 doctorates, 1 other advanced degree awarded. *Program availability:* Part-time, evening/weekend, 100% online, blended/hybrid learning. Offers clinical mental health counseling (MA); clinical psychology (Psy D); counseling and psychological studies (PhD); counseling studies (CAGS); counselor education and supervision (PhD); general psychology (MS); marriage, couple, and family counseling (MA); pastoral counseling (MA); school counseling (MA). *Application deadline:* For fall admission, 4/1 priority date for domestic students; for spring admission, 11/1 priority date for domestic students. Applications are processed on a rolling basis. *Application fee:* $50. Electronic applications accepted. *Application Contact:* Heidi Cece, Assistant Vice President of Enrollment Management, 800-373-5504, Fax: 757-352-4381, E-mail: admissions@regent.edu. *Dean,* Dr. William Hathaway, 757-352-4294, Fax: 757-352-4282, E-mail: willhat@regent.edu.

REGIS COLLEGE, Toronto, ON M5S 2Z5, Canada

General Information Independent-religious, coed, graduate-only institution. *Graduate housing:* Room and/or apartments available on a first-come, first-served basis to single students; on-campus housing not available to married students. *Research affiliation:* Lonergan Research Institute (theology/philosophy), Lupina Foundation (research and innovation related to health/society issues).

GRADUATE UNITS

Graduate and Professional Programs Offers eastern Christian studies (Certificate); Ignatian spirituality (Diploma); ministry (D Min); ministry and spirituality (MAMS); philosophical studies (Diploma); retreat direction (Certificate); sacred theology (STM, STD, STB, STL); spiritual direction (Diploma); theological studies (MTS, Diploma); theology (M Div, MA, Th M, PhD, Th D).

REGIS COLLEGE, Weston, MA 02493

General Information Independent-religious, coed, comprehensive institution. *Enrollment:* 1,954 graduate, professional, and undergraduate students; 200 full-time matriculated graduate/professional students, 900 part-time matriculated graduate/professional students. *Graduate housing:* Room and/or apartments available on a first-come, first-served basis to single students; on-campus housing not available to married students. *Student services:* Campus employment opportunities, campus safety program, career counseling, exercise/wellness program, international student services, low-cost health insurance, multicultural affairs office, services for students with disabilities, teacher training, writing training. *Library facilities:* Regis College Library. *Collection:* Books: 108,313 (physical), 421,975 (digital/electronic); Serial titles: 126 (physical), 153 (digital/electronic); Databases: 58. Weekly public service hours: 108. *Research affiliation:* Beth Israel Deaconess Medical Center (nursing), Caritas Norwood Hospital (nursing), Boston Medical Center (nursing), Lahey Clinic Medical Center (nursing).

Computer facilities: 196 computers available on campus for general student use. A campuswide network can be accessed from student residence rooms and from off campus. Online class registration, online bills, financial aid award letters and check-in requirements are available.

Website: http://www.regiscollege.edu/

General Application Contact: Shelagh Tomaino, Director of Graduate Admission, 781-768-7330, Fax: 781-768-7071, E-mail: graduatedepartment@regiscollege.edu.

GRADUATE UNITS

Department of Education *Expenses:* Contact institution. *Financial support:* Federal Work-Study, scholarships/grants, and unspecified assistantships available. Financial award applicants required to submit FAFSA. *Program availability:* Part-time, evening/weekend, blended/hybrid learning. Offers elementary teacher (MAT); higher education leadership (Ed D); reading (MAT); special education (MAT). *Application deadline:* Applications are processed on a rolling basis. *Application fee:* $50. Electronic applications accepted. *Department Chair/Graduate Program Director,* Dr. Priscilla Boerger, 781-768-7422, E-mail: priscilla.boerger@regiscollege.edu.

Program in Heritage Studies for a Global Society *Expenses:* Contact institution. *Financial support:* Federal Work-Study and unspecified assistantships available. Financial award applicants required to submit FAFSA. *Program availability:* Part-time, blended/hybrid learning. Offers heritage studies for a global society (MA). *Application deadline:* Applications are processed on a rolling basis. *Application fee:* $65. Electronic applications accepted. *Director,* Kathryn Edney, 781-768-7196.

Program in Organizational and Professional Communication *Expenses:* Contact institution. *Financial support:* Federal Work-Study and unspecified assistantships available. Financial award applicants required to submit FAFSA. *Program availability:* Part-time, evening/weekend, blended/hybrid learning. Offers organizational and professional communication (MS). *Application deadline:* Applications are processed on a rolling basis. *Application fee:* $65. Electronic applications accepted. *Director,* Colleen Malachowski, 781-768-7373, E-mail: colleen.malachowski@regiscollege.edu.

Program in Regulatory and Clinical Research Management *Expenses:* Contact institution. *Financial support:* Career-related internships or fieldwork, scholarships/grants, and unspecified assistantships available. Financial award applicants required to submit FAFSA. *Program availability:* Part-time, evening/weekend, blended/hybrid learning. Offers regulatory and clinical research management (MS). *Application deadline:* Applications are processed on a rolling basis. *Application fee:* $65. Electronic applications accepted. *Director,* Joni Beshansky, 781-768-7008, E-mail: joni.beshansky@regiscollege.edu.

School of Nursing and Health Sciences *Expenses:* Contact institution. *Financial support:* Federal Work-Study, scholarships/grants, traineeships, and unspecified assistantships available. Support available to part-time students. Financial award applicants required to submit FAFSA. *Program availability:* Part-time, evening/weekend, 100% online, blended/hybrid learning. Offers applied behavior analysis (MS); counseling psychology (MA); health administration (MS); nurse practitioner (Certificate); nursing (MS, DNP); nursing education (Certificate); occupational therapy (MS). *Application deadline:* Applications are processed on a rolling basis. *Application fee:* $75. Electronic applications accepted. *Application Contact:* Catherine Hamilton, Senior Assistant Director, Graduate Admission, 781-768-7101, E-mail: catherine.hamilton@regiscollege.edu.

REGIS UNIVERSITY, Denver, CO 80221-1099

General Information Independent-religious, coed, comprehensive institution. *Enrollment:* 8,368 graduate, professional, and undergraduate students; 2,697 full-time matriculated graduate/professional students (1,714 women), 1,601 part-time matriculated graduate/professional students (1,054 women). *Enrollment by degree level:* 3,737 master's, 2,064 doctoral. *Graduate faculty:* 124 full-time (68 women), 362 part-time/adjunct (218 women). *Graduate housing:* Room and/or apartments available on a first-come, first-served basis to single students; on-campus housing not available to married students. Housing application deadline: 5/1. *Student services:* Campus employment opportunities, campus safety program, career counseling, exercise/wellness program, grant writing training, international student services, services for students with disabilities, writing training. *Library facilities:* Dayton Memorial Library. *Collection:* Books: 393,000 (physical), 118,000 (digital/electronic); Databases: 248. Weekly public service hours: 101; students can reserve study rooms. *Research affiliation:* Commission for Accelerated Programs, Learning Anytime Anywhere Partnership (Internet-based technology), Transparency by Design (online programs, best practices).

Computer facilities: Computer purchase and lease plans are available. 600 computers available on campus for general student use. A campuswide network can be accessed from student residence rooms and from off campus. Online class registration is available.

Website: http://www.regis.edu/

General Application Contact: Cate Clark, Director of Admissions, 303-458-4900, Fax: 303-964-5534, E-mail: regisadm@regis.edu.

GRADUATE UNITS

College of Business and Economics Students: 622 full-time (350 women), 460 part-time (170 women); includes 317 minority (88 Black or African American, non-Hispanic/Latino; 7 American Indian or Alaska Native, non-Hispanic/Latino; 44 Asian, non-Hispanic/Latino; 151 Hispanic/Latino; 1 Native Hawaiian or other Pacific Islander, non-Hispanic/Latino; 26 Two or more races, non-Hispanic/Latino), 44 international. Average age 36. 307 applicants, 73% accepted, 134 enrolled. *Faculty:* 15 full-time (5 women), 43 part-time/adjunct (16 women). Expenses: Contact institution. *Financial support:* Scholarships/grants available. Financial award application deadline: 4/15; financial award applicants required to submit FAFSA. In 2016, 394 master's awarded. *Program availability:* Part-time, evening/weekend, 100% online, blended/hybrid learning. Offers accounting (MS); executive leadership (Certificate); finance (MS); finance and accounting (MBA); health industry leadership (MBA); human resource management and leadership (MSOL); management (MBA); marketing (MBA); nonprofit leadership (Post-Graduate Certificate); nonprofit management (MNM); nonprofit organizational capacity building (Certificate); operations management (MBA); organizational leadership and management (MSOL); project leadership and management (MS, MSOL); strategic business management (Certificate); strategic human resource integration (Certificate); strategic management (MBA). Programs offered at Colorado Springs Campus, Northwest Denver Campus, Southeast Denver Campus, Fort Collins Campus, Broomfield Campus, Henderson (Nevada) Campus, and Summerlin (Nevada) Campus. *Application deadline:* For fall admission, 8/15 priority date for domestic students, 8/13 for international students; for winter admission, 10/10 priority date for domestic students, 9/8 for international students; for spring admission, 1/10 priority date for domestic students, 11/17 for international students; for summer admission, 5/1 priority date for domestic students. Applications are processed on a rolling basis. *Application fee:* $75. Electronic applications accepted. *Application Contact:* Cate Clark, Director of Admissions, 303-458-4900, Fax: 303-964-5534, E-mail: ruadmissions@regis.edu. *Academic Dean,* Dr. Timothy Keane.

College of Computer and Information Sciences Students: 341 full-time (95 women), 318 part-time (98 women); includes 186 minority (56 Black or African American, non-Hispanic/Latino; 2 American Indian or Alaska Native, non-Hispanic/Latino; 48 Asian, non-Hispanic/Latino; 63 Hispanic/Latino; 17 Two or more races, non-Hispanic/Latino), 57 international. Average age 37. 342 applicants, 79% accepted, 174 enrolled. *Faculty:* 11 full-time (3 women), 30 part-time/adjunct (10 women). Expenses: Contact institution. *Financial support:* Scholarships/grants available. Financial award application deadline: 4/15; financial award applicants required to submit FAFSA. In 2016, 192 master's awarded. *Program availability:* Part-time, evening/weekend, 100% online, blended/hybrid learning. Offers agile technologies (Certificate); cybersecurity (Certificate); data science (M Sc); database administration with Oracle (Certificate); database development (Certificate); database technologies (M Sc); enterprise Java software development (Certificate); enterprise resource planning (Certificate); executive information technology (Certificate); health care informatics (Certificate); health care informatics and information management (M Sc); information assurance (M Sc); information assurance policy management (Certificate); information technology management (M Sc); mobile software development (Certificate); software engineering (M Sc, Certificate); software engineering and database technology (M Sc); storage area networks (Certificate); systems engineering (M Sc, Certificate). *Application deadline:* For fall admission, 8/15 priority date for domestic students, 7/13 for international students; for winter admission, 10/10 priority date for domestic students, 9/8 for international students; for spring admission, 1/10 priority date for domestic students, 11/17 for international students; for summer admission, 5/1 priority date for domestic students. Applications are processed on a rolling basis. *Application fee:* $75. Electronic applications accepted. *Application Contact:* Cate Clark, Director of Admissions, 303-458-4900, Fax: 303-964-5534, E-mail: ruadmissions@regis.edu. *Academic Dean,* Shari Plantz-Masters.

College of Contemporary Liberal Studies Students: 302 full-time (234 women), 270 part-time (218 women); includes 148 minority (33 Black or African American, non-Hispanic/Latino; 3 American Indian or Alaska Native, non-Hispanic/Latino; 13 Asian, non-Hispanic/Latino; 83 Hispanic/Latino; 16 Two or more races, non-Hispanic/Latino), 3 international. Average age 36. 431 applicants, 90% accepted, 110 enrolled. *Faculty:* 18 full-time (12 women), 42 part-time/adjunct (26 women). Expenses: Contact institution. *Financial support:* Scholarships/grants available. Financial award application deadline: 4/15; financial award applicants required to submit FAFSA. In 2016, 308 master's awarded. *Program availability:* Part-time, evening/weekend, 100% online, blended/hybrid learning. Offers creative writing (MFA); criminology (M Sc); curriculum, instruction and assessment (M Ed); education - teacher leadership (M Ed); educational leadership (M Ed); elementary education (M Ed); literacy (Certificate); reading (M Ed); secondary education (M Ed); special education (M Ed); teacher academic leadership (Certificate); teacher leadership (MA); teacher/educational leadership (M Ed); teaching the linguistically diverse (M Ed). *Application deadline:* For fall admission, 8/15 priority date for domestic students, 7/13 for international students; for winter admission, 10/10 priority date for domestic students, 9/8 for international students; for spring admission, 1/10 priority date for domestic students, 11/17 for international students; for summer admission, 5/1 priority date for domestic students. Applications are processed on a rolling basis. *Application fee:* $75. Electronic applications accepted. *Application Contact:* Cate Clark, Director of Admissions, 303-458-4900, Fax: 303-964-5534, E-mail: ruadmissions@regis.edu. *Academic Dean,* Dr. Elisa Robyn.

Regis College Students: 109 full-time (64 women), 15 part-time (13 women); includes 29 minority (7 Black or African American, non-Hispanic/Latino; 8 Asian, non-Hispanic/Latino; 7 Hispanic/Latino; 7 Two or more races, non-Hispanic/Latino), 25

international. Average age 30. 390 applicants, 71% accepted, 45 enrolled. *Faculty:* 2 full-time (1 woman), 22 part-time/adjunct (12 women). Expenses: Contact institution. *Financial support:* Federal Work-Study and scholarships/grants available. Financial award application deadline: 4/15; financial award applicants required to submit FAFSA. In 2016, 29 master's awarded. *Program availability:* Part-time. Offers biomedical sciences (MS); developmental practice (MDP); education (MA); environmental biology (MS). *Application deadline:* For fall admission, 5/15 priority date for domestic students, 4/1 priority date for international students; for spring admission, 12/15 priority date for domestic students. Applications are processed on a rolling basis. *Application fee:* $75. Electronic applications accepted. *Application Contact:* Sarah Engel, Director of Admissions, 303-458-4900, Fax: 303-964-5534, E-mail: ruadmissions@regis.edu. *Academic Dean,* Dr. Thomas Bowie.

Rueckert-Hartman College for Health Professions Students: 1,088 full-time (788 women), 316 part-time (253 women); includes 403 minority (59 Black or African American, non-Hispanic/Latino; 5 American Indian or Alaska Native, non-Hispanic/Latino; 101 Asian, non-Hispanic/Latino; 187 Hispanic/Latino; 51 Two or more races, non-Hispanic/Latino), 11 international. Average age 33. 2,199 applicants, 25% accepted, 277 enrolled. *Faculty:* 66 full-time (44 women), 33 part-time/adjunct (25 women). Expenses: Contact institution. *Financial support:* In 2016–17, 102 students received support. Federal Work-Study and scholarships/grants available. Financial award application deadline: 4/15; financial award applicants required to submit FAFSA. In 2016, 428 master's, 160 doctorates awarded. *Program availability:* Part-time, evening/weekend, 100% online, blended/hybrid learning. Offers advanced practice nurse (DNP); counseling (MA); counseling children and adolescents (Post-Graduate Certificate); counseling military families (Post-Graduate Certificate); depth psychotherapy (Post-Graduate Certificate); fellowship in orthopedic manual physical therapy (Certificate); health care business management (Certificate); health care quality and patient safety (Certificate); health industry leadership (MBA); health services administration (MS); marriage and family therapy (MA, Post-Graduate Certificate); neonatal nurse practitioner (MSN); nursing education (MSN); nursing leadership (MSN); occupational therapy (OTD); pharmacy (Pharm D); physical therapy (DPT). *Application deadline:* For fall admission, 8/15 priority date for domestic students; for spring admission, 1/10 priority date for domestic students; for summer admission, 5/1 priority date for domestic students. Applications are processed on a rolling basis. *Application fee:* $75. Electronic applications accepted. *Application Contact:* Cate Clark, Director of Admissions, 303-458-4900, Fax: 303-964-5534, E-mail: ruadmissions@regis.edu. *Academic Dean,* Dr. Janet Houser.

REINHARDT UNIVERSITY, Waleska, GA 30183-2981

General Information Independent-religious, coed, comprehensive institution. *Tuition:* Part-time $475 per credit hour. *Required fees:* $100 per semester. Part-time tuition and fees vary according to program. *Graduate housing:* Room and/or apartments available on a first-come, first-served basis to single students; on-campus housing not available to married students. *Student services:* Campus safety program, career counseling, exercise/wellness program, free psychological counseling, international student services, low-cost health insurance, services for students with disabilities, teacher training, writing training. *Library facilities:* Hill Freeman Library/Spruill Learning Center.

Computer facilities: Computer purchase and lease plans are available. A campuswide network can be accessed from student residence rooms and from off campus. Online class registration is available.

Website: http://www.reinhardt.edu/

General Application Contact: Nydia Patrick, Administrative Assistant for the Office of Graduate Studies, 770-720-5797, Fax: 770-720-9236, E-mail: nsp@reinhardt.edu.

GRADUATE UNITS

McCamish School of Business Expenses: Contact institution. *Financial support:* Application deadline: 5/1; applicants required to submit FAFSA. *Program availability:* Part-time, evening/weekend. Offers business (MBA). Program offered at the Chattahoochee Technical College campus in downtown Woodstock, GA. *Application deadline:* For fall admission, 5/7 for domestic and international students; for spring admission, 8/9 for domestic and international students. Applications are processed on a rolling basis. *Application fee:* $25. Electronic applications accepted. *Application Contact:* Dr. Dana L. Hall, Program Coordinator, 770-720-5756, Fax: 770-720-9236, E-mail: dlh@reinhardt.edu.

Price School of Education Expenses: Contact institution. *Financial support:* Application deadline: 5/1; applicants required to submit FAFSA. *Program availability:* Part-time, evening/weekend, online learning. Offers education (M Ed, MAT). *Application deadline:* For fall admission, 5/7 for domestic and international students. Applications are processed on a rolling basis. *Application fee:* $25. Electronic applications accepted. *Application Contact:* Dr. Nancy Marsh, Interim Dean, 770-720-5657, Fax: 770-720-9173, E-mail: njm@reinhardt.edu. *Interim Dean,* Dr. Nancy Marsh, 770-720-5657, Fax: 770-720-9173, E-mail: njm@reinhardt.edu.

RELAY GRADUATE SCHOOL OF EDUCATION, New York, NY 10011

General Information Independent, coed, graduate-only institution.

GRADUATE UNITS

Graduate Programs *Program availability:* Online learning. Offers education (MAT). Program also offered at Chicago, Delaware, Houston, Memphis, New Orleans, and Newark campuses.

RENSSELAER AT HARTFORD, Hartford, CT 06120-2991

General Information Independent, coed, graduate-only institution. *Graduate housing:* On-campus housing not available.

GRADUATE UNITS

Department of Computer and Information Science *Program availability:* Part-time, evening/weekend. Offers computer science (MS); information technology (MS). Electronic applications accepted.

Department of Engineering *Program availability:* Part-time, evening/weekend. Offers computer and systems engineering (ME); electrical engineering (ME, MS); engineering (ME, MS); engineering science (MS); mechanical engineering (ME, MS). Electronic applications accepted.

Lally School of Management and Technology *Program availability:* Part-time, evening/weekend, online learning. Offers management and technology (MBA, MS). Electronic applications accepted.

RENSSELAER POLYTECHNIC INSTITUTE, Troy, NY 12180-3590

General Information Independent, coed, university. CGS member. *Enrollment:* 7,442 graduate, professional, and undergraduate students; 1,018 full-time matriculated graduate/professional students (327 women), 150 part-time matriculated graduate/professional students (39 women). *Enrollment by degree level:* 377 master's, 791 doctoral. *Graduate faculty:* 444 full-time (110 women), 44 part-time/adjunct (9 women). *Tuition:* Full-time $49,520; part-time $2060 per credit hour. *Required fees:* $2617. *Graduate housing:* Rooms and/or apartments available on a first-come, first-served basis to single and married students. *Student services:* Campus employment opportunities, campus safety program, career counseling, exercise/wellness program, free psychological counseling, grant writing training, international student services, low-cost health insurance, multicultural affairs office, services for students with disabilities, teacher training, writing training. *Library facilities:* Folsom Library plus 2 others. *Collection:* Students can reserve study rooms. *Research affiliation:* Disney (synthetic characters), General Electric Company (GE) (renewable energy, power electronic, and imaging research), IBM (high performance computing, advanced modeling and simulation research), Boeing (flow control, computational fluid dynamics), Skidmore, Owings & Merrill (SOM) (built environment (solar concentrators, phytoremediation, integrated hybrid flow control, parametric design)), Mount Sinai School of Medicine (biomedical and clinical research (healthcare analytics, orthopedic-musculoskeletal research, imaging, brain-machine interfaces)).

Computer facilities: Computer purchase and lease plans are available. A campuswide network can be accessed from student residence rooms and from off campus. Online class registration, billing, downloadable software, webpages are available. Website: http://www.rpi.edu/

General Application Contact: Jarron Decker, Director of Graduate Admissions, 518-276-6216, Fax: 518-276-4072, E-mail: gradadmissions@rpi.edu.

GRADUATE UNITS

Graduate School Students: 1,066 full-time (345 women), 96 part-time (17 women). Expenses: Contact institution. *Financial support:* In 2016–17, 968 students received support, including research assistantships with full tuition reimbursements available (averaging $22,000 per year), teaching assistantships with full tuition reimbursements available (averaging $22,000 per year); fellowships with full tuition reimbursements available, career-related internships or fieldwork, scholarships/grants, health care benefits, and tuition waivers (partial) also available. Financial award application deadline: 1/1. *Program availability:* Part-time, evening/weekend. *Application deadline:* For fall admission, 1/1 priority date for domestic and international students; for spring admission, 8/15 priority date for domestic and international students. Applications are processed on a rolling basis. *Application fee:* $75. Electronic applications accepted. *Application Contact:* Graduate Admissions, 518-276-6216, E-mail: gradadmissions@rpi.edu.

Lally School of Management Students: 172 full-time (84 women), 1,019 applicants, 38% accepted, 104 enrolled. *Faculty:* 35 full-time (10 women), 7 part-time/adjunct (0 women). Expenses: Contact institution. *Financial support:* In 2016–17, 64 students received support. Scholarships/grants available. Financial award application deadline: 1/1; financial award applicants required to submit FAFSA. In 2016, 79 master's, 7 doctorates awarded. *Program availability:* Part-time, evening/weekend. Offers business analytics (MS); management (MBA, MS, PhD); quantitative finance and risk analytics (MS); supply chain management (MS); technology commercialization and entrepreneurship (MS). *Application deadline:* For fall admission, 1/1 priority date for domestic and international students; for spring admission, 8/15 priority date for domestic and international students. Applications are processed on a rolling basis. *Application fee:* $75. Electronic applications accepted. *Application Contact:* Office of Graduate Admissions, 518-276-6216, E-mail: gradadmissions@rpi.edu. *Associate Dean, Lally School of Management,* Dr. Gina O'Connor, 518-276-6842, E-mail: oconng@rpi.edu.

School of Architecture Students: 55 full-time (26 women). 108 applicants, 67% accepted. *Faculty:* 34 full-time (8 women), 11 part-time/adjunct (2 women). Expenses: Contact institution. *Financial support:* In 2016–17, research assistantships (averaging $22,000 per year), teaching assistantships (averaging $22,000 per year) were awarded; fellowships and scholarships/grants also available. Financial award application deadline: 1/1. In 2016, 17 master's, 14 doctorates awarded. Offers architectural acoustics (PhD); architectural sciences (MS, PhD); architecture (M Arch, MS, PhD); built ecologies (PhD); lighting (PhD). *Application deadline:* For fall admission, 1/1 priority date for domestic and international students; for spring admission, 8/15 for domestic and international students; for summer admission, 1/1 for domestic and international students. Applications are processed on a rolling basis. *Application fee:* $75. Electronic applications accepted. *Application Contact:* Office of Graduate Admissions, 518-276-2716, E-mail: gradadmissions@rpi.edu. *Graduate Program Director,* Chris Perry, 518-276-4785, E-mail: perryc3@rpi.edu.

School of Engineering Students: 452 full-time (112 women), 96 part-time (17 women). 1,366 applicants, 26% accepted, 121 enrolled. *Faculty:* 392 full-time (62 women), 19 part-time/adjunct (0 women). Expenses: Contact institution. *Financial support:* In 2016–17, 462 students received support, including research assistantships (averaging $22,000 per year), teaching assistantships (averaging $22,000 per year); fellowships also available. Financial award application deadline: 1/1. *Program availability:* Part-time. Offers aeronautical engineering (M Eng, MS, D Eng, PhD); biomedical engineering (MS, D Eng, PhD); chemical engineering (M Eng, MS, D Eng, PhD); civil engineering (M Eng, MS, D Eng, PhD); computer and systems engineering (M Eng, MS, D Eng, PhD); decision sciences and engineering systems (PhD); electrical engineering (M Eng, MS, D Eng, PhD); engineering (M Eng, MS, D Eng, PhD); engineering physics (MS, PhD); environmental engineering (M Eng, MS, D Eng, PhD); industrial and management engineering (M Eng, MS); materials science and engineering (M Eng, MS, D Eng, PhD); mechanical engineering (M Eng, MS, D Eng, PhD); nuclear engineering (M Eng, MS, D Eng, PhD); systems engineering and technology management (M Eng); transportation engineering (M Eng, MS, D Eng, PhD). *Application deadline:* For fall admission, 1/1 priority date for domestic and international students; for spring admission, 8/15 priority date for domestic and international students. Applications are processed on a rolling basis. *Application fee:* $75. Electronic applications accepted. *Application Contact:* Office of Graduate Admissions, 518-276-6216, E-mail: gradadmissions@rpi.edu. *Dean,* Shekhar Garde, 518-276-6298, E-mail: gardes@rpi.edu.

School of Humanities, Arts, and Social Sciences Students: 71 full-time (35 women). Expenses: Contact institution. *Financial support:* In 2016–17, research assistantships (averaging $22,000 per year), teaching assistantships (averaging $22,000 per year) were awarded; fellowships and scholarships/grants also available. Financial award application deadline: 1/1. *Program availability:* Part-time, evening/weekend, online learning. Offers cognitive science (PhD); communication and rhetoric (MS, PhD); electronic arts (PhD); humanities, arts, and social sciences (MS, PhD); science and technology studies (MS, PhD). *Application deadline:* For fall admission, 1/1 priority date for domestic students, 1/15 priority date for international students; for spring admission, 8/15 priority date for domestic and international students. Applications are processed on a rolling basis. *Application fee:* $75. Electronic applications accepted.

Application Contact: Office of Graduate Admissions, 518-276-6216, E-mail: gradadmissions@rpi.edu. *Associate Dean for Research and Graduate Studies,* Dr. Curtis Bahn, 518-276-6065, E-mail: crb@rpi.edu.

School of Science Students: 316 full-time (88 women). 856 applicants, 31% accepted, 73 enrolled. *Faculty:* 134 full-time (37 women). Expenses: Contact institution. *Financial support:* In 2016–17, research assistantships (averaging $22,000 per year), teaching assistantships (averaging $22,000 per year) were awarded; fellowships also available. Financial award application deadline: 1/1. In 2016, 68 master's, 41 doctorates awarded. Offers applied mathematics (MS); biochemistry and biophysics (MS, PhD); biology (MS, PhD); chemistry (MS, PhD); computer science (MS, PhD); geology (MS, PhD); information technology and Web science (MS); mathematics (MS, PhD); physics, applied physics and astronomy (MS, PhD); science (MS, PhD). *Application deadline:* For fall admission, 1/1 priority date for domestic and international students; for spring admission, 8/15 priority date for domestic and international students. Applications are processed on a rolling basis. *Application fee:* $75. Electronic applications accepted. *Application Contact:* Office of Graduate Admissions, 518-276-6216, E-mail: gradadmissions@rpi.edu. *Associate Dean, School of Science,* Dr. Christian Wetzel, 518-276-3755, E-mail: wetzel@rpi.edu.

RESEARCH COLLEGE OF NURSING, Kansas City, MO 64132

General Information Independent, coed, primarily women, comprehensive institution. *Enrollment:* 474 graduate, professional, and undergraduate students; 8 full-time matriculated graduate/professional students (7 women), 135 part-time matriculated graduate/professional students (116 women). *Enrollment by degree level:* 143 master's. *Graduate faculty:* 10 full-time (all women), 4 part-time/adjunct (2 women). *Tuition:* Part-time $525 per credit hour. *Required fees:* $25 per credit hour. *Graduate housing:* Rooms and/or apartments available on a first-come, first-served basis to single and married students. Typical cost: $7500 per year for single students. Room charges vary according to housing facility selected. *Student services:* Campus safety program, child daycare facilities. *Library facilities:* Greenlease Library.

Computer facilities: 125 computers available on campus for general student use. A campuswide network can be accessed from student residence rooms and from off campus. Online class registration is available. Website: http://www.researchcollege.edu/

General Application Contact: Leslie Burry, Director of Transfer and Graduate Recruitment, 816-995-2820, Fax: 816-995-2813, E-mail: leslie.burry@researchcollege.edu.

GRADUATE UNITS

Nursing Program Students: 1 full-time (0 women), 169 part-time (148 women); includes 14 minority (7 Black or African American, non-Hispanic/Latino; 1 American Indian or Alaska Native, non-Hispanic/Latino; 2 Asian, non-Hispanic/Latino; 2 Hispanic/Latino; 1 Native Hawaiian or other Pacific Islander, non-Hispanic/Latino; 1 Two or more races, non-Hispanic/Latino). *Faculty:* 9 full-time (all women), 5 part-time/adjunct (2 women). Expenses: Contact institution. *Financial support:* Applicants required to submit FAFSA. In 2016, 38 master's awarded. *Program availability:* Part-time-only, 100% online. Offers adult-gerontological nurse practitioner (MSN); executive practice and healthcare leadership (MSN); family nurse practitioner (MSN). *Application deadline:* Applications are processed on a rolling basis. *Application fee:* $65. Electronic applications accepted. *Application Contact:* Leslie Burry, Director of Transfer and Graduate Recruitment, 816-995-2820, Fax: 816-995-2813, E-mail: leslie.burry@researchcollege.edu. *President and Dean,* Dr. Nancy O. DeBasio, 816-995-2815, Fax: 816-995-2817, E-mail: nancy.debasio@researchcollege.edu.

RESURRECTION UNIVERSITY, Chicago, IL 60622

General Information Independent, coed, upper-level institution.

GRADUATE UNITS

Nursing Program Offers nursing (MSN).

RHODE ISLAND COLLEGE, Providence, RI 02908-1991

General Information State-supported, coed, comprehensive institution. *Enrollment:* 8,446 graduate, professional, and undergraduate students; 167 full-time matriculated graduate/professional students (128 women), 513 part-time matriculated graduate/professional students (417 women). *Enrollment by degree level:* 587 master's, 57 doctoral, 36 other advanced degrees. *Graduate faculty:* 97 full-time (57 women), 73 part-time/adjunct (59 women). *Tuition:* state resident: full-time $8928; part-time $372 per credit. Tuition, nonresident: full-time $17,376; part-time $724 per credit. *Required fees:* $604; $22 per credit. *One-time fee:* $74. *Graduate housing:* On-campus housing not available. *Student services:* Campus employment opportunities, career counseling, free psychological counseling, international student services, low-cost health insurance, multicultural affairs office, services for students with disabilities. *Library facilities:* Adams Library. *Collection:* Books: 545,755 (physical), 151,873 (digital/electronic); Serial titles: 1,195 (physical), 54,116 (digital/electronic); Databases: 101. Weekly public service hours: 79.

Computer facilities: Computer purchase and lease plans are available. 250 computers available on campus for general student use. A campuswide network can be accessed from student residence rooms and from off campus. Online class registration is available. Website: http://www.ric.edu/

General Application Contact: Dr. Leslie Schuster, Interim Dean of Graduate Studies, 401-456-9723, E-mail: graduatestudies@ric.edu.

GRADUATE UNITS

School of Graduate Studies Students: 167 full-time (128 women), 513 part-time (417 women); includes 102 minority (29 Black or African American, non-Hispanic/Latino; 3 American Indian or Alaska Native, non-Hispanic/Latino; 19 Asian, non-Hispanic/Latino; 48 Hispanic/Latino; 1 Native Hawaiian or other Pacific Islander, non-Hispanic/Latino; 2 Two or more races, non-Hispanic/Latino), 1 international. Average age 34. *Faculty:* 97 full-time (57 women), 73 part-time/adjunct (59 women). Expenses: Contact institution. *Financial support:* In 2016–17, 32 teaching assistantships with full tuition reimbursements (averaging $2,184 per year) were awarded; career-related internships or fieldwork, Federal Work-Study, traineeships, health care benefits, tuition waivers (partial), and unspecified assistantships also available. Support available to part-time students. Financial award application deadline: 5/15; financial award applicants required to submit FAFSA. In 2016, 263 master's, 3 doctorates, 56 other advanced degrees awarded. *Program availability:* Part-time, evening/weekend. *Application deadline:* For fall admission, 3/1 priority date for domestic students; for spring admission, 11/1 for domestic students. Applications are processed on a rolling basis. *Application fee:* $50. Electronic applications accepted. *Application Contact:* Graduate Studies, 401-456-8700. *Interim Dean of Graduate Studies,* Dr. Leslie Schuster, 401-456-9723, E-mail: graduatestudies@ric.edu.

Faculty of Arts and Sciences Students: 16 full-time (9 women), 22 part-time (13 women); includes 2 minority (1 American Indian or Alaska Native, non-Hispanic/Latino; 1 Hispanic/Latino). Average age 30. *Faculty:* 52 full-time (23 women), 4 part-time/adjunct (1 woman). Expenses: Contact institution. *Financial support:* In 2016–17, 16 teaching assistantships with full tuition reimbursements (averaging $2,586 per year) were awarded; research assistantships with tuition reimbursements, career-related internships or fieldwork, Federal Work-Study, scholarships/grants, health care benefits, and unspecified assistantships also available. Support available to part-time students. Financial award application deadline: 5/15; financial award applicants required to submit FAFSA. In 2016, 25 master's, 1 other advanced degree awarded. *Program availability:* Part-time, evening/weekend. Offers art education (MA, MAT); arts and sciences (MA, MAT, MM Ed, MPA, CGS); biology (MA); creative writing (MA, CGS); English (MA); health psychology (CGS); history (MA); literature (CGS); mathematics (MA); mathematics content specialist (CGS); media studies (MA); modern biological sciences (CGS); music education (MAT, MM Ed); psychology (MA); public administration (MPA). *Application deadline:* For fall admission, 3/1 for domestic students; for spring admission, 11/1 for domestic students. Applications are processed on a rolling basis. *Application fee:* $50. Electronic applications accepted. *Application Contact:* Graduate Studies, 401-456-8700. *Dean,* Dr. Earl Simson, 401-456-8107, E-mail: esimson@ric.edu.

Feinstein School of Education and Human Development Students: 56 full-time (46 women), 272 part-time (225 women); includes 43 minority (12 Black or African American, non-Hispanic/Latino; 10 Asian, non-Hispanic/Latino; 20 Hispanic/Latino; 1 Two or more races, non-Hispanic/Latino). Average age 35. *Faculty:* 29 full-time (21 women), 36 part-time/adjunct (30 women). Expenses: Contact institution. *Financial support:* In 2016–17, 5 teaching assistantships with full tuition reimbursements (averaging $2,400 per year) were awarded; career-related internships or fieldwork, Federal Work-Study, scholarships/grants, health care benefits, and unspecified assistantships also available. Support available to part-time students. Financial award application deadline: 5/15; financial award applicants required to submit FAFSA. In 2016, 134 master's, 3 doctorates, 41 other advanced degrees awarded. *Program availability:* Part-time, evening/weekend. Offers advanced counseling (CGS); advanced studies in teaching and learning (M Ed); agency counseling (MA); autism education (CGS); clinical mental health counseling (MS); co-occurring disorders (MA, CGS); early childhood education (M Ed); education (PhD); education and human development (M Ed, MA, MAT, MS, PhD, CAGS, CGS); educational leadership (M Ed); elementary education (M Ed, MAT); English (MAT); French (MAT); health education (M Ed); history (MAT); math (MAT); mental health counseling (CAGS); physical education (CGS); reading (M Ed); school counseling (MA); school psychology (CAGS); secondary education (MAT); severe intellectual disabilities (CGS); Spanish (MAT); special education (M Ed); teacher leadership (CGS); teaching English as a second language (M Ed). *Application deadline:* For fall admission, 3/1 for domestic students; for spring admission, 11/1 for domestic students. Applications are processed on a rolling basis. *Application fee:* $50. Electronic applications accepted. *Application Contact:* Graduate Studies, 401-456-8700. *Dean,* Dr. Donald Halquist, 401-456-8110, E-mail: dhalquist@ric.edu.

School of Management Students: 6 full-time (2 women), 17 part-time (10 women); includes 3 minority (1 Black or African American, non-Hispanic/Latino; 2 Asian, non-Hispanic/Latino). Average age 31. *Faculty:* 1 (woman) full-time, 2 part-time/adjunct (1 woman). Expenses: Contact institution. *Financial support:* In 2016–17, 3 teaching assistantships (averaging $1,500 per year) were awarded; Federal Work-Study, scholarships/grants, health care benefits, and unspecified assistantships also available. Support available to part-time students. Financial award application deadline: 5/15; financial award applicants required to submit FAFSA. In 2016, 10 master's awarded. *Program availability:* Part-time, evening/weekend. Offers accounting (MP Ac); financial planning (CGS); health care administration (MS); management (MP Ac, MS, CGS). *Application deadline:* For fall admission, 3/1 for domestic students. Applications are processed on a rolling basis. *Application fee:* $50. Electronic applications accepted. *Application Contact:* Graduate Studies, 401-456-8700. *Dean,* Dr. Jeffrey Mello, 401-456-9650, E-mail: jmello@ric.edu.

School of Nursing Students: 14 full-time (9 women), 76 part-time (63 women); includes 15 minority (4 Black or African American, non-Hispanic/Latino; 6 Asian, non-Hispanic/Latino; 4 Hispanic/Latino; 1 Native Hawaiian or other Pacific Islander, non-Hispanic/Latino), 1 international. Average age 37. *Faculty:* 6 full-time (all women), 14 part-time/adjunct (13 women). Expenses: Contact institution. *Financial support:* In 2016–17, 8 teaching assistantships with full tuition reimbursements (averaging $1,500 per year) were awarded; Federal Work-Study, scholarships/grants, health care benefits, and unspecified assistantships also available. Support available to part-time students. Financial award application deadline: 5/15; financial award applicants required to submit FAFSA. In 2016, 21 master's awarded. *Program availability:* Part-time. Offers nursing (MSN, DNP). *Application deadline:* For fall admission, 2/15 for domestic students. Applications are processed on a rolling basis. *Application fee:* $50. Electronic applications accepted. *Application Contact:* Graduate Studies, 401-456-8700. *Dean,* Dr. Jane Williams, 401-456-8013, Fax: 401-456-9608, E-mail: jwilliams@ric.edu.

School of Social Work Students: 75 full-time (62 women), 126 part-time (106 women); includes 39 minority (12 Black or African American, non-Hispanic/Latino; 2 American Indian or Alaska Native, non-Hispanic/Latino; 1 Asian, non-Hispanic/Latino; 23 Hispanic/Latino; 1 Two or more races, non-Hispanic/Latino). Average age 32. *Faculty:* 9 full-time (6 women), 17 part-time/adjunct (14 women). Expenses: Contact institution. *Financial support:* Career-related internships or fieldwork, Federal Work-Study, scholarships/grants, health care benefits, and unspecified assistantships available. Support available to part-time students. Financial award application deadline: 5/15; financial award applicants required to submit FAFSA. In 2016, 73 master's awarded. *Program availability:* Part-time. Offers social work (MSW). *Application deadline:* For fall admission, 2/1 for domestic students. Applications are processed on a rolling basis. *Application fee:* $50. Electronic applications accepted. *Application Contact:* Graduate Studies, 401-456-8700. *Dean,* Dr. Sue Pearlmutter, 401-456-8042, E-mail: spearlmutter@ric.edu.

RHODE ISLAND SCHOOL OF DESIGN, Providence, RI 02903-2784

General Information Independent, coed, comprehensive institution. *Enrollment:* 2,478 graduate, professional, and undergraduate students; 478 full-time matriculated graduate/professional students (332 women). *Enrollment by degree level:* 468 master's. *Graduate faculty:* 78 full-time (29 women), 132 part-time/adjunct (46 women). *Tuition:* Full-time $46,800. *Required fees:* $310. *Graduate housing:* Rooms and/or apartments available on a first-come, first-served basis to single and married students. *Typical cost:* $8000 per year for single students; $10,000 per year for married students. Room charges vary according to board plan and housing facility selected. *Student services:* Campus employment opportunities, campus safety program, career counseling, exercise/wellness program, free psychological counseling, grant writing training, international student services, low-cost health insurance, multicultural affairs office, services for students with disabilities, teacher training, writing training. *Library facilities:* Fleet Library. *Collection:* Books: 160,296 (physical), 144,887 (digital/electronic); Serial titles: 1,200 (digital/electronic); Databases: 62. Weekly public service hours: 89; students can reserve study rooms.

Computer facilities: Computer purchase and lease plans are available. 65 computers available on campus for general student use. A campuswide network can be accessed from student residence rooms and from off campus. Online class registration is available.

Website: http://www.risd.edu/

General Application Contact: Molly Pettengil, Assistant Director for Graduate Recruitment, 401-454-6312, Fax: 401-454-6309, E-mail: admissions@risd.edu.

GRADUATE UNITS

Division of Architecture and Design Students: 339 full-time (230 women); includes 46 minority (5 Black or African American, non-Hispanic/Latino; 27 Asian, non-Hispanic/Latino; 13 Hispanic/Latino; 1 Two or more races, non-Hispanic/Latino), 210 international. Average age 28. 1,166 applicants, 33% accepted, 143 enrolled. *Faculty:* 53 full-time (20 women), 114 part-time/adjunct (37 women). Expenses: Contact institution. *Financial support:* Fellowships, research assistantships, teaching assistantships, Federal Work-Study, scholarships/grants, and unspecified assistantships available. Financial award application deadline: 2/15; financial award applicants required to submit FAFSA. In 2016, 132 master's awarded. Offers adaptive reuse (MA); architecture (M Arch); architecture and design (M Arch, M Des, MA, MFA, MID, MLA); furniture design (MFA); graphic design (MFA); industrial design (MID); interior studies/adaptive reuse (M Des); interior studies/exhibition and narrative environments (M Des); landscape architecture (MLA). *Application deadline:* For fall admission, 2/1 for domestic and international students. *Application fee:* $60. Electronic applications accepted. *Dean,* Nancy Skolos, 401-454-6280, Fax: 401-454-6718, E-mail: nskolos@risd.edu.

Division of Fine Arts Students: 49 full-time (40 women); includes 7 minority (5 Asian, non-Hispanic/Latino; 1 Hispanic/Latino; 1 Two or more races, non-Hispanic/Latino), 18 international. Average age 27. 591 applicants, 16% accepted, 49 enrolled. *Faculty:* 33 full-time (13 women), 36 part-time/adjunct (16 women). Expenses: Contact institution. *Financial support:* Fellowships, research assistantships, teaching assistantships, Federal Work-Study, scholarships/grants, and unspecified assistantships available. Financial award application deadline: 2/15; financial award applicants required to submit FAFSA. In 2016, 49 master's awarded. Offers ceramics (MFA); glass (MFA); jewelry and metalsmithing (MFA); painting (MFA); photography (MFA); printmaking (MFA); sculpture (MFA); textiles (MFA). *Application deadline:* For fall admission, 2/1 for domestic and international students. *Application fee:* $60. Electronic applications accepted. *Dean,* Sheri Wills, 401-454-6183, Fax: 401-454-6198, E-mail: swills@risd.edu.

Graduate Studies Students: 49 full-time (40 women); includes 7 minority (5 Asian, non-Hispanic/Latino; 1 Hispanic/Latino; 1 Two or more races, non-Hispanic/Latino), 18 international. Average age 27. 182 applicants, 32% accepted, 32 enrolled. *Faculty:* 14 full-time (5 women), 23 part-time/adjunct (9 women). Expenses: Contact institution. *Financial support:* Fellowships, research assistantships, teaching assistantships, Federal Work-Study, scholarships/grants, and unspecified assistantships available. Financial award application deadline: 2/15; financial award applicants required to submit FAFSA. In 2016, 31 master's awarded. Offers art education (MA, MAT); digital and media (MFA). *Application deadline:* For fall admission, 2/1 for domestic and international students. *Application fee:* $60. Electronic applications accepted.

RHODES COLLEGE, Memphis, TN 38112-1690

General Information Independent, coed, comprehensive institution. *Graduate housing:* Room and/or apartments available on a first-come, first-served basis to single students; on-campus housing not available to married students. Housing application deadline: 3/1.

GRADUATE UNITS

Department of Commerce and Business *Program availability:* Part-time. Offers accounting (MS).

RICE UNIVERSITY, Houston, TX 77251-1892

General Information Independent, coed, university. CGS member. *Graduate housing:* Rooms and/or apartments available on a first-come, first-served basis to single and married students. Housing application deadline: 7/15. *Research affiliation:* Fermi National Accelerator Laboratory, Los Alamos National Laboratory, Brookhaven National Laboratory, Arecibo Observatory, Houston Area Research Center.

GRADUATE UNITS

Graduate Programs *Program availability:* Part-time. Offers education (MAT). Electronic applications accepted.

George R. Brown School of Engineering *Program availability:* Part-time. Offers bioengineering (MS, PhD); bioinformatics (PhD); biostatistics (PhD); chemical and biomolecular engineering (MS, PhD); chemical engineering (M Ch E); circuits, controls, and communication systems (MS, PhD); civil engineering (MCE, MS, PhD); computational and applied mathematics (MA, MCAM, PhD); computational finance (PhD); computational science and engineering (PhD); computer science (MCS, MS, PhD); computer science and engineering (MS, PhD); electrical engineering (MEE); engineering (M Ch E, M Stat, MA, MBE, MCAM, MCE, MCS, MEE, MEE, MES, MME, MMS, MS, PhD); environmental engineering (MEE, MES, MS, PhD); environmental science (MEE, MES, MS, PhD); general statistics (PhD); lasers, microwaves, and solid-state electronics (MS, PhD); materials science (MMS, MS, PhD); mechanical engineering (MME, MS, PhD); statistics (M Stat, MA). MD/PhD offered jointly with Baylor College of Medicine, The University of Texas Health Science Center at Houston. Electronic applications accepted.

Jesse H. Jones Graduate School of Business Students: 110 full-time (27 women), 145 part-time (25 women); includes 66 minority (5 Black or African American, non-Hispanic/Latino; 3 American Indian or Alaska Native, non-Hispanic/Latino; 39 Asian, non-Hispanic/Latino; 19 Hispanic/Latino), 52 international. Average age 28. 840 applicants, 53% accepted, 296 enrolled. *Faculty:* 64 full-time, 68 part-time/adjunct. Expenses: Contact institution. *Financial support:* In 2016–17, 97 students received support. Fellowships, career-related internships or fieldwork, Federal Work-Study, institutionally sponsored loans, scholarships/grants, and tuition waivers (full and partial) available. Financial award applicants required to submit FAFSA. In 2016, 217 master's awarded. *Program availability:* Evening/weekend. Offers business administration (EMBA, MBA, PMBA). *Application deadline:* For fall admission, 10/5 priority date for domestic students; for winter admission, 1/9 priority date for domestic students; for spring admission, 4/7 priority date for domestic students. Applications are processed on a rolling basis. *Application fee:* $200. Electronic applications accepted. *Application Contact:* Sue Oldham, Executive Director of Recruiting and

Admissions, 713-348-6153, E-mail: ricemba@rice.edu. *Dean,* Dr. Peter Rodriguez, E-mail: prod@rice.edu.

School of Architecture Offers architecture (M Arch, D Arch); urban design (M Arch). Electronic applications accepted.

School of Humanities Offers African religions (PhD); African-American religions (PhD); art history (PhD); contemplative studies (PhD); English (MA, PhD); ghosticism, esotericism, mysticism (PhD); history (MA, PhD); humanities (MA, PhD); Islam (PhD); Jewish thought and philosophy (PhD); linguistics (MA, PhD); modern Christianity in thought and popular culture (PhD); philosophy (MA, PhD); psychology of religion (PhD); the Bible and beyond (PhD).

School of Social Sciences Offers archaeology (MA, PhD); cognitive sciences (MA, PhD); economics (PhD); energy economics (MEECON); industrial-organizational/social psychology (MA, PhD); political science (PhD); psychology (MA, PhD); social sciences (MA, MEECON, PhD); social-cultural anthropology (MA, PhD); sociology (PhD).

Shepherd School of Music Offers composition (MM, DMA); conducting (MM); musicology (MM); performance (MM, DMA); theory (MM).

Susanne M. Glasscock School of Continuing Studies *Program availability:* Part-time, evening/weekend. Offers liberal studies (MLS).

Wiess School of Natural Sciences *Program availability:* Part-time. Offers biochemistry and cell biology (MA, PhD); chemistry (MA); earth science (MS, PhD); ecology and evolutionary biology (MA, MS, PhD); inorganic chemistry (PhD); mathematics (PhD); nanoscale physics (MS); natural sciences (MA, MS, MST, PhD); organic chemistry (PhD); physical chemistry (PhD); physics and astronomy (PhD); science teaching (MST). Electronic applications accepted.

Wiess School–Professional Science Master's Programs Offers bioscience research and health policy (MS); environmental analysis and decision making (MS); geophysics (MS); nanoscale physics (MS); professional science (MS).

Rice Quantum Institute Offers quantum physics (MS, PhD). Electronic applications accepted.

RICHMOND, THE AMERICAN INTERNATIONAL UNIVERSITY IN LONDON, Richmond, Surrey TW10 6JP, United Kingdom

General Information Independent, coed, comprehensive institution. *Graduate housing:* Room and/or apartments available on a first-come, first-served basis to single students; on-campus housing not available to married students. Housing application deadline: 8/1.

GRADUATE UNITS

MA in Art History Program *Program availability:* Part-time. Offers art history (MA). Electronic applications accepted.

MA in International Relations Program *Program availability:* Part-time. Offers international relations (MA). Electronic applications accepted.

RICHMONT GRADUATE UNIVERSITY, Atlanta, GA 30339

General Information Independent-religious, coed, graduate-only institution. *Enrollment by degree level:* 281 master's. *Graduate faculty:* 18 full-time (8 women), 40 part-time/adjunct (16 women). *Tuition:* Part-time $665 per credit hour. *Required fees:* $200 per semester. One-time fee: $250. *Student services:* Campus employment opportunities, campus safety program, career counseling, free psychological counseling, services for students with disabilities, writing training. *Library facilities:* Richmont Graduate University Library plus 1 other. *Collection:* Books: 40,000 (physical), 22,000 (digital/electronic); Serial titles: 43 (physical), 1,100 (digital/electronic); Databases: 274. Weekly public service hours: 59.

Computer facilities: 10 computers available on campus for general student use. A campuswide network can be accessed from off campus. Online class registration is available.
Website: http://www.richmont.edu/

General Application Contact: Admissions, 888-924-6774, Fax: 866-363-4323, E-mail: admissions@richmont.edu.

GRADUATE UNITS

School of Counseling Expenses: Contact institution. *Financial support:* Career-related internships or fieldwork, scholarships/grants, and unspecified assistantships available. Financial award application deadline: 5/1. *Program availability:* Part-time, evening/weekend. Offers clinical mental health counseling (MA); marriage and family therapy (MA). *Application deadline:* Applications are processed on a rolling basis. *Application fee:* $50. Electronic applications accepted. *Application Contact:* Admissions, 888-924-6774, Fax: 866-363-4323, E-mail: admissions@richmont.edu. *Dean,* Dr. Stephen P. Bradshaw, E-mail: sbradshaw@richmont.edu.

School of Ministry Expenses: Contact institution. *Financial support:* Scholarships/grants, tuition waivers (partial), and unspecified assistantships available. Financial award application deadline: 5/1; financial award applicants required to submit FAFSA. *Program availability:* Part-time, evening/weekend, 100% online, blended/hybrid learning. Offers ministry (MA); spiritual direction (Graduate Certificate); spiritual formation and direction (MA). *Application deadline:* For fall admission, 5/1 priority date for domestic students. Applications are processed on a rolling basis. *Application fee:* $50. Electronic applications accepted. *Application Contact:* Scottie Blackburn, Admissions Counselor, 404-835-6118, Fax: 404-239-9460, E-mail: sblackburn@richmont.edu. *Dean,* Dr. Michael Stewart, 404-835-6129, Fax: 404-239-9460, E-mail: mstewart@richmont.edu.

RIVIER UNIVERSITY, Nashua, NH 03060

General Information Independent-religious, coed, comprehensive institution. *Graduate housing:* On-campus housing not available.

GRADUATE UNITS

School of Graduate Studies *Program availability:* Part-time. Offers business administration (MBA); clinical psychology (MS); computer information systems (MS); computer science (MS); curriculum and instruction (M Ed); early childhood education (M Ed); educational administration (M Ed); educational studies (M Ed); elementary education (M Ed); elementary education and general special education (M Ed); emotional and behavioral disorders (M Ed); English (MAT); experimental psychology (MS); general social education (M Ed); leadership and learning (Ed D, CAGS); learning disabilities (M Ed); learning disabilities and reading (M Ed); mathematics (MAT); mental health counseling (MA); reading (M Ed); school counseling (M Ed); social studies

education (MAT); Spanish (MAT); writing and literature (MA). Electronic applications accepted.

Division of Nursing and Health Professions *Program availability:* Part-time, evening/weekend. Offers family nurse practitioner (MS); leadership in health systems management (MS); nursing education (MS); nursing practice (DNP); psychiatric/mental health nurse practitioner (MS); public health (MPH). Electronic applications accepted.

THE ROBERT E. WEBBER INSTITUTE FOR WORSHIP STUDIES, Orange Park, FL 32073

General Information Independent-religious, coed, graduate-only institution.

GRADUATE UNITS

Doctor of Worship Studies Program Offers worship studies (DWS).

Master of Worship Studies Program Offers worship studies (MWS).

ROBERT MORRIS UNIVERSITY, Moon Township, PA 15108-1189

General Information Independent, coed, university. *Enrollment:* 5,199 graduate, professional, and undergraduate students; 815 part-time matriculated graduate/professional students (479 women). *Enrollment by degree level:* 645 master's, 235 doctoral. *Graduate faculty:* 85 full-time (39 women), 27 part-time/adjunct (19 women). *Tuition:* Part-time $925 per credit. Part-time tuition and fees vary according to degree level and program. *Graduate housing:* On-campus housing not available. *Student services:* Campus employment opportunities, campus safety program, career counseling, exercise/wellness program, international student services, multicultural affairs office, services for students with disabilities. *Library facilities:* Robert Morris University Library. *Collection:* Books: 87,233 (physical), 172,931 (digital/electronic); Serial titles: 244 (physical), 2,810 (digital/electronic); Databases: 75. Weekly public service hours: 101; study areas open 24 hours, 5–7 days a week; students can reserve study rooms.

Computer facilities: Computer purchase and lease plans are available. 300 computers available on campus for general student use. A campuswide network can be accessed from student residence rooms and from off campus. Online class registration, online payment are available.
Website: http://www.rmu.edu/

General Application Contact: Kellie L. Laurenzi, Associate Vice President, 412-397-5200, Fax: 412-397-2425, E-mail: graduateadmissions@rmu.edu.

GRADUATE UNITS

School of Business Students: 148 part-time (64 women); includes 9 minority (3 Black or African American, non-Hispanic/Latino; 6 Asian, non-Hispanic/Latino), 1 international. Average age 27. 147 applicants, 23% accepted, 32 enrolled. *Faculty:* 24 full-time (8 women), 4 part-time/adjunct (3 women). Expenses: Contact institution. *Financial support:* Institutionally sponsored loans available. Support available to part-time students. Financial award application deadline: 5/1; financial award applicants required to submit FAFSA. In 2016, 96 master's awarded. *Program availability:* Part-time-only, evening/weekend, 100% online. Offers business administration (MBA); human resource management (MS); taxation (MS). *Application deadline:* For fall admission, 7/1 priority date for domestic and international students; for spring admission, 11/1 priority date for domestic and international students. Applications are processed on a rolling basis. *Application fee:* $35. Electronic applications accepted. *Application Contact:* E-mail: graduateadmissions@rmu.edu. *Dean,* Dr. Michelle L. Patrick, 412-397-5445, Fax: 412-397-2585, E-mail: patrick@rmu.edu.

School of Communications and Information Systems Students: 269 part-time (110 women); includes 49 minority (29 Black or African American, non-Hispanic/Latino; 10 Asian, non-Hispanic/Latino; 5 Hispanic/Latino; 5 Two or more races, non-Hispanic/Latino), 49 international. Average age 34. 239 applicants, 46% accepted, 83 enrolled. *Faculty:* 28 full-time (11 women), 6 part-time/adjunct (0 women). Expenses: Contact institution. *Financial support:* Institutionally sponsored loans available. Support available to part-time students. Financial award application deadline: 5/1. In 2016, 110 master's, 15 doctorates awarded. *Program availability:* Part-time, evening/weekend, online learning. Offers communication and information systems (MS); cyber security (MS); data analytics (MS); information security and assurance (MS); information systems and communications (D Sc); information systems management (MS); information technology project management (MS); Internet information systems (MS); organizational leadership (MS). *Application deadline:* For fall admission, 7/1 priority date for domestic and international students; for spring admission, 11/1 priority date for domestic and international students. Applications are processed on a rolling basis. *Application fee:* $35. Electronic applications accepted. *Application Contact:* Kellie L. Laurenzi, Associate Vice President, 412-397-5200, Fax: 412-397-5915, E-mail: graduateadmissions@rmu.edu. *Dean,* Ann Marie M. Le Blanc, 412-397-6433, Fax: 412-397-6469, E-mail: leblanc@rmu.edu.

School of Education and Social Sciences Students: 154 part-time (104 women); includes 18 minority (11 Black or African American, non-Hispanic/Latino; 2 Hispanic/Latino; 5 Two or more races, non-Hispanic/Latino), 1 international. Average age 26. 69 applicants, 26% accepted, 18 enrolled. *Faculty:* 17 full-time (9 women), 4 part-time/adjunct (3 women). Expenses: Contact institution. In 2016, 40 master's, 15 doctorates awarded. *Program availability:* Part-time, evening/weekend, online learning. Offers business education (MS); counseling psychology (MS); education (Postbaccalaureate Certificate); higher education (MS); instructional leadership (MS); instructional management and leadership (PhD); literacy (MS); special education (MS). *Application deadline:* For fall admission, 7/1 priority date for domestic and international students; for spring admission, 11/1 priority date for domestic and international students. Applications are processed on a rolling basis. *Application fee:* $35. Electronic applications accepted. *Dean,* Dr. Mary Ann Rafoth, 412-397-6020, Fax: 412-397-6044, E-mail: rafoth@rmu.edu.

School of Engineering, Mathematics and Science Students: 17 part-time (6 women); includes 2 minority (1 Asian, non-Hispanic/Latino; 1 Hispanic/Latino), 6 international. Average age 36. 40 applicants, 28% accepted, 4 enrolled. *Faculty:* 7 full-time (1 woman). Expenses: Contact institution. *Financial support:* Federal Work-Study, institutionally sponsored loans, and unspecified assistantships available. Financial award application deadline: 5/1; financial award applicants required to submit FAFSA. In 2016, 20 master's awarded. *Program availability:* Part-time, evening/weekend. Offers engineering management (MS). *Application deadline:* For fall admission, 7/1 priority date for domestic and international students; for spring admission, 11/1 priority date for domestic and international students. Applications are processed on a rolling basis. *Application fee:* $35. Electronic applications accepted. *Dean,* Dr. Maria V. Kalevitch, 412-397-4020, Fax: 412-397-2472, E-mail: kalevitch@rmu.edu.

School of Nursing and Health Sciences Students: 227 part-time (192 women); includes 17 minority (12 Black or African American, non-Hispanic/Latino; 1 Asian, non-Hispanic/Latino; 2 Hispanic/Latino; 2 Two or more races, non-Hispanic/Latino). Average

age 36. 144 applicants, 61% accepted, 80 enrolled. *Faculty:* 16 full-time (15 women), 8 part-time/adjunct (all women). Expenses: Contact institution. *Financial support:* Federal Work-Study, institutionally sponsored loans, and unspecified assistantships available. Financial award application deadline: 5/1; financial award applicants required to submit FAFSA. In 2016, 74 master's, 16 doctorates awarded. *Program availability:* Part-time, evening/weekend. Offers nursing and health sciences (MSN, DNP). *Application deadline:* For fall admission, 7/1 priority date for domestic and international students; for spring admission, 11/1 priority date for domestic and international students. Applications are processed on a rolling basis. *Application fee:* $35. Electronic applications accepted. *Dean,* Dr. Valerie M. Howard, 412-397-6801, Fax: 412-397-3277, E-mail: howardv@rmu.edu.

ROBERT MORRIS UNIVERSITY ILLINOIS, Chicago, IL 60605

General Information Independent, coed, comprehensive institution. *Enrollment:* 2,703 graduate, professional, and undergraduate students; 196 full-time matriculated graduate/professional students (98 women), 151 part-time matriculated graduate/professional students (85 women). *Enrollment by degree level:* 347 master's. *Graduate faculty:* 4 full-time (1 woman), 25 part-time/adjunct (5 women). *Tuition:* Full-time $16,500; part-time $2750 per course. *Graduate housing:* Room and/or apartments available to single students. *Student services:* Campus employment opportunities, career counseling, exercise/wellness program, free psychological counseling, international student services, services for students with disabilities, writing training. *Library facilities:* Information Technology Library. *Collection:* Books: 163,851 (physical), 62,525 (digital/electronic); Databases: 40. Weekly public service hours: 74; students can reserve study rooms.

Computer facilities: 1,360 computers available on campus for general student use. A campuswide network can be accessed from student residence rooms. Online class registration, online credentials, online payments, online student accounts, online degree audit are available.
Website: http://www.robertmorris.edu/

General Application Contact: Danielle Naffziger, Vice President of Marketing and Enrollment, 312-935-4812, Fax: 312-935-6020, E-mail: dnaffziger@robertmorris.edu.

GRADUATE UNITS

Morris Graduate School of Management Students: 196 full-time (98 women), 151 part-time (85 women); includes 200 minority (114 Black or African American, non-Hispanic/Latino; 17 Asian, non-Hispanic/Latino; 67 Hispanic/Latino; 2 Two or more races, non-Hispanic/Latino), 23 international. Average age 33. 174 applicants, 61% accepted, 97 enrolled. *Faculty:* 4 full-time (1 woman), 25 part-time/adjunct (5 women). Expenses: Contact institution. *Financial support:* In 2016–17, 444 students received support. Federal Work-Study, scholarships/grants, and unspecified assistantships available. Support available to part-time students. Financial award applicants required to submit FAFSA. In 2016, 190 master's awarded. *Program availability:* Part-time, evening/weekend. Offers accounting (MBA); accounting/finance (MBA); business analytics (MIS); design and media (MM); design management (MM); educational technology (MM); health care administration (MM); higher education administration (MM); human resource management (MBA); information security (MIS); information systems (MBA, MIS); law enforcement administration (MM); management (MBA); management/finance (MBA); management/human resource management (MBA); mobile computing (MIS); sports administration (MM). *Application deadline:* Applications are processed on a rolling basis. *Application fee:* $20 ($100 for international students). Electronic applications accepted. *Application Contact:* Danielle Naffziger, Vice President of Marketing and Enrollment, 312-935-4812, Fax: 312-935-6020, E-mail: dnaffziger@robertmorris.edu. *Dean,* Kayed Akkawi, 312-935-6050, Fax: 312-935-6020, E-mail: kakkawi@robertmorris.edu.

ROBERTS WESLEYAN COLLEGE, Rochester, NY 14624-1997

General Information Independent-religious, coed, comprehensive institution. *Graduate housing:* Rooms and/or apartments available on a first-come, first-served basis to single and married students.

GRADUATE UNITS

Department of Nursing *Program availability:* Evening/weekend, online learning. Offers nursing education (MSN); nursing leadership and administration (MSN). Electronic applications accepted.

Department of Social Work Offers child and family practice (MSW); mental health practice (MSW).

Graduate Business Programs *Program availability:* Evening/weekend. Offers strategic leadership (MS); strategic marketing (MS).

Graduate Psychology Programs *Program availability:* Part-time, evening/weekend. Offers clinical/school psychology (Psy D); school counseling (MS); school psychology (MS). Electronic applications accepted.

Graduate Teacher Education Programs *Program availability:* Part-time, evening/weekend. Offers adolescence and special education (M Ed); childhood and special education (M Ed); literacy education (M Ed); special education (M Ed). Electronic applications accepted.

Health Administration Programs *Program availability:* Evening/weekend, online learning. Offers health administration (MS); healthcare informatics administration (MS).

ROCHESTER COLLEGE, Rochester Hills, MI 48307-2764

General Information Independent-religious, coed, comprehensive institution.

GRADUATE UNITS

Center for Missional Leadership Offers missional leadership (MRE).

ROCHESTER INSTITUTE OF TECHNOLOGY, Rochester, NY 14623-5603

General Information Independent, coed, comprehensive institution. CGS member. *Enrollment:* 16,507 graduate, professional, and undergraduate students; 2,259 full-time matriculated graduate/professional students (823 women), 903 part-time matriculated graduate/professional students (326 women). *Enrollment by degree level:* 2,893 master's, 246 doctoral, 23 other advanced degrees. *Tuition:* Full-time $41,804; part-time $1742 per credit hour. *Required fees:* $274. Tuition and fees vary according to course load and program. *Graduate housing:* Rooms and/or apartments available on a first-come, first-served basis to single and married students. *Student services:* Campus employment opportunities, career counseling, child daycare facilities, exercise/wellness program, free psychological counseling, grant writing training, international student services, low-cost health insurance, multicultural affairs office, services for students with disabilities, teacher training, writing training. *Library facilities:* Wallace Memorial Library. *Collection:* Books: 429,176 (physical), 240,712 (digital/electronic); Serial titles: 58,293 (digital/electronic); Databases: 113. Weekly public service hours: 147; study areas open 24 hours, 5–7 days a week; students can reserve study rooms. *Research affiliation:*

Ortho Clinical Diagnostics (simulation and mathematical modeling), Hewlett Packard (printing and packaging research and testing), Delphi (fuel cell technology), Toyota Motor Company (systems engineering, supply chain, manufacturing), Corning Inc. (thin-film transistor (TFT) fabrication, device modeling, and performance), Library of Congress (image permanence, storage, and sustainable preservation).

Computer facilities: Computer purchase and lease plans are available. 2,500 computers available on campus for general student use. A campuswide network can be accessed from student residence rooms and from off campus. Online class registration, student account information are available.
Website: http://www.rit.edu/

General Application Contact: Diane Ellison, Associate Vice President, Graduate Enrollment Services, 585-475-2229, Fax: 585-475-7164, E-mail: gradinfo@rit.edu.

GRADUATE UNITS

Graduate Enrollment Services Students: 2,259 full-time (823 women), 903 part-time (326 women); includes 212 minority (57 Black or African American, non-Hispanic/Latino; 5 American Indian or Alaska Native, non-Hispanic/Latino; 62 Asian, non-Hispanic/Latino; 61 Hispanic/Latino; 27 Two or more races, non-Hispanic/Latino), 1,876 international. Average age 27. Expenses: Contact institution. *Financial support:* Research assistantships, teaching assistantships, career-related internships or fieldwork, scholarships/grants, health care benefits, and unspecified assistantships available. Support available to part-time students. Financial award applicants required to submit FAFSA. *Program availability:* Part-time, evening/weekend, online learning. *Application deadline:* Applications are processed on a rolling basis. Electronic applications accepted. *Associate Vice President,* Diane Ellison, 585-475-2229, Fax: 585-475-7164, E-mail: gradinfo@rit.edu.

College of Applied Science and Technology Students: 212 full-time (63 women), 148 part-time (54 women); includes 28 minority (10 Black or African American, non-Hispanic/Latino; 7 Asian, non-Hispanic/Latino; 8 Hispanic/Latino; 3 Two or more races, non-Hispanic/Latino), 234 international. Average age 28. 518 applicants, 61% accepted, 106 enrolled. Expenses: Contact institution. *Financial support:* In 2016–17, 229 students received support. Research assistantships with partial tuition reimbursements available, teaching assistantships with partial tuition reimbursements available, career-related internships or fieldwork, scholarships/grants, and unspecified assistantships available. Support available to part-time students. Financial award applicants required to submit FAFSA. In 2016, 102 master's awarded. *Program availability:* Part-time, evening/weekend, 100% online, blended/hybrid learning. Offers applied science and technology (MS, Advanced Certificate); engineering technology (MS); environmental, health and safety management (MS); hospitality and tourism management (MS); human resources development (MS); international hospitality and service innovation (MS, Advanced Certificate); manufacturing and mechanical systems integration (MS); organizational learning (Advanced Certificate); packaging science (MS); service leadership and innovation (MS); telecommunications engineering technology (MS); workplace learning and instruction (Advanced Certificate). *Application deadline:* Applications are processed on a rolling basis. *Application fee:* $60. Electronic applications accepted. *Application Contact:* Diane Ellison, Associate Vice President, Graduate Enrollment Services, 585-475-2229, Fax: 585-475-7164, E-mail: gradinfo@rit.edu. *Dean,* Dr. H. Fred Walker, 585-475-6439, E-mail: hfwast@rit.edu.

College of Health Sciences and Technology Students: 45 full-time (32 women), 22 part-time (13 women); includes 11 minority (6 Black or African American, non-Hispanic/Latino; 2 Asian, non-Hispanic/Latino; 3 Hispanic/Latino), 3 international. Average age 26. 47 applicants, 30% accepted, 10 enrolled. Expenses: Contact institution. *Financial support:* In 2016–17, 10 students received support. Research assistantships with partial tuition reimbursements available, teaching assistantships with partial tuition reimbursements available, career-related internships or fieldwork, scholarships/grants, and unspecified assistantships available. Support available to part-time students. Financial award applicants required to submit FAFSA. In 2016, 40 master's awarded. *Program availability:* Part-time, evening/weekend, 100% online. Offers health care finance (Advanced Certificate); health sciences and technology (MFA, MS, Advanced Certificate); health systems administration (MS); medical illustration (MFA). *Application deadline:* Applications are processed on a rolling basis. *Application fee:* $60. Electronic applications accepted. *Application Contact:* Diane Ellison, Associate Vice President, Graduate Enrollment Services, 585-475-2229, Fax: 585-475-7164, E-mail: gradinfo@rit.edu. *Vice President and Dean, Institute and College of Health Sciences and Technology,* Dr. Daniel Ornt, 585-475-4017, Fax: 585-475-4330, E-mail: daniel.ornt@rit.edu.

College of Imaging Arts and Sciences Students: 210 full-time (134 women), 78 part-time (46 women); includes 21 minority (2 Black or African American, non-Hispanic/Latino; 10 Asian, non-Hispanic/Latino; 6 Hispanic/Latino; 3 Two or more races, non-Hispanic/Latino), 197 international. Average age 26. 706 applicants, 41% accepted, 97 enrolled. Expenses: Contact institution. *Financial support:* In 2016–17, 166 students received support. Teaching assistantships with partial tuition reimbursements available, career-related internships or fieldwork, scholarships/grants, and unspecified assistantships available. Support available to part-time students. Financial award applicants required to submit FAFSA. In 2016, 70 master's, 7 other advanced degrees awarded. *Program availability:* Part-time, 100% online. Offers American crafts (MFA); ceramics (MFA); design (MFA, Advanced Certificate); film and animation (MFA); fine arts studio (MFA); furniture design (MFA); glass (MFA); imaging arts and sciences (MFA, MS, MST, Advanced Certificate); imaging arts, photography and related media (MFA); industrial design (MFA); media arts and technology (MS); media sciences (MS); metals and jewelry design (MFA); photographic arts and sciences (MFA); print media (MS); user experience design and development (Advanced Certificate); visual arts-all grades (MST); visual communication design (MFA). *Application deadline:* For fall admission, 2/15 priority date for domestic and international students. Applications are processed on a rolling basis. *Application fee:* $60. Electronic applications accepted. *Application Contact:* Diane Ellison, Associate Vice President, Graduate Enrollment Services, 585-475-2229, Fax: 585-475-7164, E-mail: gradinfo@rit.edu. *Dean,* Dr. Lorraine Justice, 585-475-2733, E-mail: glg8801@rit.edu.

College of Liberal Arts Students: 48 full-time (34 women), 23 part-time (13 women); includes 13 minority (7 Black or African American, non-Hispanic/Latino; 1 American Indian or Alaska Native, non-Hispanic/Latino; 3 Asian, non-Hispanic/Latino; 2 Hispanic/Latino), 10 international. Average age 27. 117 applicants, 37% accepted, 22 enrolled. Expenses: Contact institution. *Financial support:* In 2016–17, 44 students received support. Research assistantships with partial tuition reimbursements available, teaching assistantships with partial tuition reimbursements available, career-related internships or fieldwork, scholarships/grants, and unspecified assistantships available. Support available to part-time students. Financial award applicants required to submit FAFSA. In 2016, 27 master's, 10 other advanced degrees awarded. *Program availability:* Part-time, 100% online. Offers communication and digital media (Advanced Certificate); communication and media technologies (MS); criminal justice (MS); engineering psychology (Advanced Certificate); experimental psychology (MS); liberal arts (MS, Advanced Certificate); public policy (MS); school psychology (MS, Advanced Certificate); science, technology and public policy (MS). *Application deadline:* For fall admission, 2/15 priority date for domestic and international students; for spring admission, 12/15 priority date for domestic and international students. Applications are processed on a rolling basis. *Application fee:* $60. Electronic applications accepted. *Application Contact:* Diane Ellison, Associate Vice President, Graduate Enrollment Services, 585-475-2229, Fax: 585-475-7164, E-mail: gradinfo@rit.edu. *Dean,* Dr. James Winebrake, 585-475-2929, Fax: 585-475-7120, E-mail: libarts@rit.edu.

College of Science Students: 188 full-time (75 women), 104 part-time (38 women); includes 22 minority (5 Black or African American, non-Hispanic/Latino; 7 Asian, non-Hispanic/Latino; 3 Hispanic/Latino; 7 Two or more races, non-Hispanic/Latino), 125 international. Average age 28. 381 applicants, 47% accepted, 85 enrolled. Expenses: Contact institution. *Financial support:* In 2016–17, 188 students received support. Research assistantships with tuition reimbursements available, teaching assistantships with tuition reimbursements available, career-related internships or fieldwork, institutionally sponsored loans, scholarships/grants, unspecified assistantships, and health care benefits (for PhD program only) available. Support available to part-time students. Financial award applicants required to submit FAFSA. In 2016, 65 master's, 10 doctorates, 7 other advanced degrees awarded. *Program availability:* Part-time, evening/weekend, 100% online. Offers applied and computational mathematics (MS); applied statistics (MS, Advanced Certificate); astrophysical science and technology (MS, PhD); bioinformatics (MS); chemistry (MS); color science (MS, PhD); environmental science (MS); imaging science (MS, PhD); life sciences (MS); materials science and engineering (MS); mathematical modeling (PhD); physics and astronomy (MS, PhD); science (MS, PhD, Advanced Certificate). *Application deadline:* For fall admission, 2/15 priority date for domestic and international students; for spring admission, 12/15 priority date for domestic and international students. Applications are processed on a rolling basis. *Application fee:* $60. Electronic applications accepted. *Application Contact:* Diane Ellison, Associate Vice President, Graduate Enrollment Services, 585-475-2229, Fax: 585-475-7164, E-mail: gradinfo@rit.edu. *Dean,* Dr. Sophia Maggelakis, 585-475-5221, Fax: 585-475-2398, E-mail: science@rit.edu.

Golisano College of Computing and Information Sciences Students: 691 full-time (199 women), 149 part-time (39 women); includes 27 minority (5 Black or African American, non-Hispanic/Latino; 2 American Indian or Alaska Native, non-Hispanic/Latino; 11 Asian, non-Hispanic/Latino; 5 Hispanic/Latino; 4 Two or more races, non-Hispanic/Latino), 720 international. Average age 25. 2,369 applicants, 42% accepted, 262 enrolled. Expenses: Contact institution. *Financial support:* In 2016–17, 655 students received support. Research assistantships with tuition reimbursements available, teaching assistantships with tuition reimbursements available, career-related internships or fieldwork, scholarships/grants, unspecified assistantships, and health care benefits (for PhD program only) available. Support available to part-time students. Financial award applicants required to submit FAFSA. In 2016, 250 master's, 3 doctorates, 51 other advanced degrees awarded. *Program availability:* Part-time, evening/weekend, 100% online. Offers big data analytics (Advanced Certificate); computer science (MS, Advanced Certificate); computing and information sciences (MS, PhD, Advanced Certificate); computing security (MS); game design and development (MS); human computer interaction (MS); information assurance (cybersecurity) (Advanced Certificate); information sciences and technologies (MS); networking and systems administration (MS); networking, planning and design (Advanced Certificate); software engineering (MS); Web development (Advanced Certificate). *Application deadline:* For fall admission, 2/15 priority date for domestic and international students; for spring admission, 12/15 priority date for domestic and international students. Applications are processed on a rolling basis. *Application fee:* $60. Electronic applications accepted. *Application Contact:* Diane Ellison, Associate Vice President, Graduate Enrollment Services, 585-475-2229, Fax: 585-475-7164, E-mail: gradinfo@rit.edu. *Interim Dean,* Dr. Anne Haake, 585-475-7203, Fax: 585-475-4775, E-mail: gccis-email@rit.edu.

Golisano Institute for Sustainability Students: 71 full-time (33 women), 18 part-time (7 women); includes 4 minority (1 Black or African American, non-Hispanic/Latino; 2 Hispanic/Latino; 1 Two or more races, non-Hispanic/Latino), 50 international. Average age 29. 145 applicants, 62% accepted, 21 enrolled. Expenses: Contact institution. *Financial support:* In 2016–17, 61 students received support. Research assistantships with tuition reimbursements available, teaching assistantships with tuition reimbursements available, career-related internships or fieldwork, scholarships/grants, unspecified assistantships, and health care benefits (for PhD program only) available. Support available to part-time students. Financial award applicants required to submit FAFSA. In 2016, 9 master's, 4 doctorates awarded. *Program availability:* Part-time. Offers architecture (M Arch); sustainability (PhD); sustainable systems (MS). *Application deadline:* For fall admission, 2/15 priority date for domestic and international students; for spring admission, 12/15 priority date for domestic and international students. Applications are processed on a rolling basis. *Application fee:* $60. Electronic applications accepted. *Application Contact:* Diane Ellison, Associate Vice President, Graduate Enrollment Services, 585-475-2229, Fax: 585-475-7164, E-mail: gradinfo@rit.edu. *Associate Provost and Director,* Dr. Nabil Nasr, 585-475-5101, E-mail: info@sustainability.rit.edu.

Kate Gleason College of Engineering Students: 473 full-time (98 women), 220 part-time (36 women); includes 45 minority (7 Black or African American, non-Hispanic/Latino; 19 Asian, non-Hispanic/Latino; 15 Hispanic/Latino; 4 Two or more races, non-Hispanic/Latino), 393 international. Average age 26. 1,731 applicants, 35% accepted, 193 enrolled. Expenses: Contact institution. *Financial support:* In 2016–17, 409 students received support. Fellowships with tuition reimbursements available, research assistantships with tuition reimbursements available, teaching assistantships with tuition reimbursements available, career-related internships or fieldwork, scholarships/grants, tuition waivers (full and partial), unspecified assistantships, and health care benefits (for PhD program only) available. Support available to part-time students. Financial award applicants required to submit FAFSA. In 2016, 218 master's, 4 doctorates, 1 other advanced degree awarded. *Program availability:* Part-time, evening/weekend, 100% online. Offers computer engineering (MS); electrical and microelectronic engineering (ME, MS); electrical engineering (MS); engineering (ME, MS, PhD, Advanced Certificate); engineering management (ME); industrial and systems engineering (ME, MS); Lean Six Sigma (Advanced Certificate); manufacturing leadership (MS); mechanical engineering (ME, MS); microelectronic engineering (MS); microelectronic manufacturing engineering (ME); microsystems engineering (PhD); product development (MS); quality and applied statistics (Advanced Certificate); sustainable engineering (ME, MS). *Application*

deadline: For fall admission, 2/15 priority date for domestic and international students. Applications are processed on a rolling basis. *Application fee:* $60. Electronic applications accepted. *Application Contact:* Diane Ellison, Associate Vice President, Graduate Enrollment Services, 585-475-2229, Fax: 585-475-7164, E-mail: gradinfo@rit.edu. *Dean,* Dr. Doreen Edwards, 585-475-2145, Fax: 585-475-6879, E-mail: coe@rit.edu.

National Technical Institute for the Deaf Students: 32 full-time (25 women), 6 part-time (all women); includes 10 minority (3 Black or African American, non-Hispanic/Latino; 4 Hispanic/Latino; 3 Two or more races, non-Hispanic/Latino), 6 international. Average age 30. 44 applicants, 43% accepted, 17 enrolled. Expenses: Contact institution. *Financial support:* In 2016–17, 1 student received support. Fellowships with partial tuition reimbursements available, research assistantships with partial tuition reimbursements available, career-related internships or fieldwork, scholarships/grants, and unspecified assistantships available. Support available to part-time students. Financial award applicants required to submit FAFSA. In 2016, 20 master's awarded. *Program availability:* Part-time, evening/weekend, blended/hybrid learning. Offers deaf studies (MS); health care interpretation (MS); secondary education for the deaf and hard of hearing (MS). *Application deadline:* For fall admission, 2/15 priority date for domestic and international students. Applications are processed on a rolling basis. *Application fee:* $60. Electronic applications accepted. *Application Contact:* Diane Ellison, Assistant Vice President, Graduate Enrollment Services, 585-475-2229, Fax: 585-475-7164, E-mail: gradinfo@rit.edu. *President,* Dr. Gerard J. Buckley, 585-475-6317, Fax: 585-475-5978, E-mail: gbuckley@ntid.rit.edu.

Saunders College of Business Students: 251 full-time (112 women), 95 part-time (54 women); includes 21 minority (6 Black or African American, non-Hispanic/Latino; 1 American Indian or Alaska Native, non-Hispanic/Latino; 2 Asian, non-Hispanic/Latino; 10 Hispanic/Latino; 2 Two or more races, non-Hispanic/Latino), 117 international. Average age 27. 687 applicants, 55% accepted, 157 enrolled. Expenses: Contact institution. *Financial support:* In 2016–17, 192 students received support. Research assistantships with partial tuition reimbursements available, teaching assistantships with partial tuition reimbursements available, career-related internships or fieldwork, Federal Work-Study, scholarships/grants, and unspecified assistantships available. Support available to part-time students. Financial award applicants required to submit FAFSA. In 2016, 109 master's awarded. *Program availability:* Part-time, evening/weekend, 100% online, blended/hybrid learning. Offers accounting (MBA, MS); business (Exec MBA, MBA, MS); business administration (MBA); computational finance (MS); entrepreneurship and innovative ventures (MS); executive business administration (Exec MBA); finance (MS); management (MS); marketing (MBA). *Application deadline:* Applications are processed on a rolling basis. *Application fee:* $60. Electronic applications accepted. *Application Contact:* Diane Ellison, Associate Vice President, Graduate Enrollment Services, 585-475-2229, Fax: 585-475-7164, E-mail: gradinfo@rit.edu. *Dean,* Dr. Jacqueline Mozrall, 585-475-6025, E-mail: gradbus@saunders.rit.edu.

School of Individualized Study Students: 38 full-time (18 women), 40 part-time (20 women); includes 10 minority (5 Black or African American, non-Hispanic/Latino; 1 American Indian or Alaska Native, non-Hispanic/Latino; 1 Asian, non-Hispanic/Latino; 3 Hispanic/Latino), 21 international. Average age 35. 47 applicants, 55% accepted, 16 enrolled. Expenses: Contact institution. *Financial support:* In 2016–17, 8 students received support. Career-related internships or fieldwork, scholarships/grants, and unspecified assistantships available. Support available to part-time students. Financial award applicants required to submit FAFSA. In 2016, 28 master's, 13 other advanced degrees awarded. *Program availability:* Part-time, evening/weekend, 100% online, blended/hybrid learning. Offers individualized studies (MS, Advanced Certificate); professional studies (MS); project management (Advanced Certificate). *Application deadline:* Applications are processed on a rolling basis. *Application fee:* $60. Electronic applications accepted. *Application Contact:* Diane Ellison, Associate Vice President, Graduate Enrollment Services, 585-475-2229, Fax: 585-475-7164, E-mail: gradinfo@rit.edu. *Executive Director,* Dr. James Hall, 585-475-2295, Fax: 585-475-6292, E-mail: sois@rit.edu.

THE ROCKEFELLER UNIVERSITY, New York, NY 10021-6399

General Information Independent, coed, graduate-only institution. CGS member. *Enrollment by degree level:* 17 master's, 199 doctoral. *Graduate faculty:* 76 full-time (9 women). *Graduate housing:* Rooms and/or apartments guaranteed to single and married students. Typical cost: $9465 (including board) for single students. Room and board charges vary according to campus/location and housing facility selected. Housing application deadline: 6/1. *Student services:* Campus safety program, career counseling, child daycare facilities, exercise/wellness program, free psychological counseling, grant writing training, low-cost health insurance, teacher training. *Library facilities:* Rita and Frits Markus Library. *Collection:* Books: 44,701 (physical), 51,768 (digital/electronic); Serial titles: 6,067 (digital/electronic); Databases: 9. Weekly public service hours: 40; study areas open 24 hours, 5–7 days a week; students can reserve study rooms.

Computer facilities: 32 computers available on campus for general student use. Online class registration is available.
Website: http://www.rockefeller.edu/

General Application Contact: Kristen Cullen, Graduate Admissions Administrator/Registrar, 212-327-8086, Fax: 212-327-8505, E-mail: phd@rockefeller.edu.

GRADUATE UNITS

The David Rockefeller Graduate Program in Bioscience Students: 216 full-time (88 women); includes 46 minority (5 Black or African American, non-Hispanic/Latino; 20 Asian, non-Hispanic/Latino; 20 Hispanic/Latino; 1 Native Hawaiian or other Pacific Islander, non-Hispanic/Latino), 74 international. Average age 25. 786 applicants, 10% accepted, 26 enrolled. *Faculty:* 76 full-time (9 women). Expenses: Contact institution. *Financial support:* In 2016–17, 216 students received support. Fellowships with full tuition reimbursements available, institutionally sponsored loans, scholarships/grants, traineeships, and health care benefits available. In 2016, 8 master's, 31 doctorates awarded. Offers bioscience (MS, PhD). *Application deadline:* For fall and winter admission, 12/1 for domestic and international students. *Application fee:* $50. Electronic applications accepted. *Application Contact:* Kristen Cullen, Graduate Admissions Administrator/Registrar, 212-327-8086, Fax: 212-327-8505, E-mail: phd@rockefeller.edu. *Dean of Graduate and Postgraduate Studies/Vice President,* Dr. Sidney Strickland, 212-327-8086, Fax: 212-327-8505, E-mail: phd@rockefeller.edu.

ROCKFORD UNIVERSITY, Rockford, IL 61108-2393

General Information Independent, coed, comprehensive institution. *Enrollment:* 1,298 graduate, professional, and undergraduate students; 60 full-time matriculated graduate/professional students (26 women), 138 part-time matriculated graduate/professional students (73 women). *Enrollment by degree level:* 313 master's. *Graduate faculty:* 15 full-time (7 women), 24 part-time/adjunct (20 women). *Tuition:* Part-time $710 per credit. *Required fees:* $50 per semester. *Graduate housing:* Room and/or apartments available on a first-come, first-served basis to single students; on-campus housing not available to married students. *Student services:* Campus employment opportunities, campus safety program, career counseling, free psychological counseling, grant writing training, international student services, low-cost health insurance, multicultural affairs office, services for students with disabilities, teacher training, writing training. *Library facilities:* Howard Colman Library. *Collection:* Books: 134,831 (physical), 140,140 (digital/electronic); Serial titles: 157 (physical), 23,000 (digital/electronic); Databases: 27. Weekly public service hours: 85; students can reserve study rooms.

Computer facilities: 94 computers available on campus for general student use. A campuswide network can be accessed from student residence rooms and from off campus. Online class registration, online bill payment are available. Website: http://www.rockford.edu/

General Application Contact: Michele Mehren, Office Manager for Graduate Studies, 815-226-4041, Fax: 815-394-3706, E-mail: mmehren@rockford.edu.

GRADUATE UNITS

Graduate Studies Expenses: Contact institution. *Financial support:* Scholarships/grants and unspecified assistantships available. Support available to part-time students. Financial award application deadline: 3/1; financial award applicants required to submit FAFSA. *Program availability:* Part-time, evening/weekend. Offers business administration (MBA); early childhood education (MAT); elementary education (MAT); instructional strategies (MAT); reading (MAT); secondary education (MAT); special education (MAT). *Application deadline:* Applications are processed on a rolling basis. *Application fee:* $50. Electronic applications accepted. *Application Contact:* Michele Mehren, Assistant Director, Office of Graduate Studies, 815-226-4040, Fax: 815-394-3706, E-mail: mmehren@rockford.edu.

ROCKHURST UNIVERSITY, Kansas City, MO 64110-2561

General Information Independent-religious, coed, comprehensive institution. *Graduate housing:* Room and/or apartments available on a first-come, first-served basis to single students; on-campus housing not available to married students.

GRADUATE UNITS

College of Health and Human Services *Program availability:* Part-time, evening/weekend. Offers communication sciences and disorders (MS); education (M Ed); health and human services (M Ed, MOT, MS, DPT); occupational therapy (MOT); physical therapy (DPT). Electronic applications accepted.

Helzberg School of Management *Program availability:* Part-time, evening/weekend. Offers accounting (MBA); business intelligence (MBA, Certificate); data science (MBA, Certificate); entrepreneurship (MBA); finance (MBA); fundraising leadership (MBA, Certificate); healthcare management (MBA, Certificate); human capital (Certificate); international business (Certificate); management (MBA, Certificate); nonprofit administration (Certificate); organizational development (Certificate); science leadership (Certificate). Electronic applications accepted.

ROCKY MOUNTAIN COLLEGE, Billings, MT 59102-1796

General Information Independent-religious, coed, comprehensive institution. *Enrollment:* 1,000 graduate, professional, and undergraduate students; 90 full-time matriculated graduate/professional students (57 women), 1 (woman) part-time matriculated graduate/professional student. *Enrollment by degree level:* 91 master's. *Graduate faculty:* 8 full-time (4 women), 7 part-time/adjunct (3 women). *Graduate housing:* Rooms and/or apartments available on a first-come, first-served basis to single and married students. Typical cost: $6938 per year for single students; $4972 per year for married students. Room charges vary according to board plan and housing facility selected. *Student services:* Campus employment opportunities, campus safety program, career counseling, free psychological counseling, international student services, services for students with disabilities, teacher training. *Library facilities:* Paul M. Adams Memorial Library. *Collection:* Books: 46,317 (physical), 4,156 (digital/electronic); Serial titles: 402 (physical), 50,020 (digital/electronic); Databases: 64. Weekly public service hours: 89.

Computer facilities: 113 computers available on campus for general student use. A campuswide network can be accessed from student residence rooms and from off campus. Online class registration is available. Website: http://www.rocky.edu/

General Application Contact: Austin Mapston, Dean of Enrollment Services, 406-657-1026, Fax: 406-657-1189, E-mail: admissions@rocky.edu.

GRADUATE UNITS

Program in Accountancy Students: 1 (woman) part-time. Average age 27. *Faculty:* 2 full-time (0 women). Expenses: Contact institution. *Financial support:* Applicants required to submit FAFSA. In 2016, 3 master's awarded. *Program availability:* Part-time-only. Offers accountancy (M Acc). *Application deadline:* Applications are processed on a rolling basis. *Application fee:* $35 ($40 for international students). Electronic applications accepted. *Application Contact:* Austin Mapston, Dean of Enrollment Services, 406-657-1026, Fax: 406-657-1189, E-mail: admissions@rocky.edu. *Professor of Business Administration and Economics*, Anthony Piltz, 406-657-1069, E-mail: piltza@rocky.edu.

Program in Educational Leadership Students: 18 full-time (10 women); includes 1 minority (Hispanic/Latino). Average age 36. *Faculty:* 2 full-time (both women), 3 part-time/adjunct (1 woman). Expenses: Contact institution. *Financial support:* In 2016–17, 18 students received support. Scholarships/grants available. Financial award applicants required to submit FAFSA. In 2016, 22 master's awarded. Offers educational leadership (M Ed). *Application deadline:* Applications are processed on a rolling basis. *Application fee:* $35 ($40 for international students). Electronic applications accepted. *Director of Educational Leadership and Distance Education,* Dr. Stevie Schmitz, 406-657-1134, E-mail: schmitzs@rocky.edu.

Program in Physician Assistant Studies Students: 72 full-time (47 women); includes 7 minority (2 Asian, non-Hispanic/Latino; 1 Hispanic/Latino; 4 Two or more races, non-Hispanic/Latino). Average age 28. *Faculty:* 4 full-time (2 women), 4 part-time/adjunct (2 women). Expenses: Contact institution. *Financial support:* Applicants required to submit FAFSA. In 2016, 32 master's awarded. Offers physician assistant studies (MPAS). *Application deadline:* Applications are processed on a rolling basis. *Application fee:* $35. Electronic applications accepted. *Application Contact:* Calley Thompson, PA Admissions Counselor, 406-657-1198, E-mail: calley.thompson@rocky.edu. *Program Director,* Heather Heggem, 406-657-1190, E-mail: heather.heggem@rocky.edu.

ROCKY MOUNTAIN COLLEGE OF ART + DESIGN, Lakewood, CO 80214

General Information Proprietary, coed, comprehensive institution.

GRADUATE UNITS

Program in Education, Leadership + Emerging Technologies *Program availability:* Online learning. Offers education, leadership and emerging technologies (MA).

ROCKY MOUNTAIN UNIVERSITY OF HEALTH PROFESSIONS, Provo, UT 84606

General Information Proprietary, coed, graduate-only institution. *Research affiliation:* Aegis Corporation.

GRADUATE UNITS

Doctor of Nursing Practice Program Offers nursing practice (DNP).

Doctor of Science Program in Clinical Electrophysiology *Program availability:* Online learning. Offers clinical electrophysiology (D Sc).

Program in Occupational Therapy *Program availability:* Online learning. Offers occupational therapy (OTD). Electronic applications accepted.

Program in Physician Assistant Studies Offers physician assistant studies (MPAS).

Program in Speech-Language Pathology Offers speech-language pathology (Clin Sc D).

Programs in Physical Therapy Offers physical therapy (DPT, TDPT).

ROCKY VISTA UNIVERSITY, Parker, CO 80134

General Information Proprietary, coed, graduate-only institution.

GRADUATE UNITS

College of Osteopathic Medicine Offers osteopathic medicine (DO).

Program in Biomedical Sciences Offers biomedical sciences (MS).

ROGERS STATE UNIVERSITY, Claremore, OK 74017-3252

General Information State-supported, coed, comprehensive institution.

GRADUATE UNITS

Program in Business Administration Offers business administration (MBA).

ROGER WILLIAMS UNIVERSITY, Bristol, RI 02809

General Information Independent, coed, comprehensive institution. *Enrollment:* 5,193 graduate, professional, and undergraduate students; 207 full-time matriculated graduate/professional students (120 women), 81 part-time matriculated graduate/professional students (42 women). *Enrollment by degree level:* 280 master's, 8 other advanced degrees. *Graduate faculty:* 36 full-time (15 women), 11 part-time/adjunct (4 women). *Tuition:* Part-time $809 per credit hour. Tuition and fees vary according to program. *Graduate housing:* On-campus housing not available. *Student services:* Campus employment opportunities, campus safety program, career counseling, exercise/wellness program, free psychological counseling, international student services, low-cost health insurance, multicultural affairs office, services for students with disabilities, teacher training. *Library facilities:* Roger Williams University Library plus 1 other. *Collection:* Books: 201,390 (physical), 236,803 (digital/electronic); Databases: 104. Weekly public service hours: 111; students can reserve study rooms.

Computer facilities: 105 computers available on campus for general student use. A campuswide network can be accessed from student residence rooms and from off campus. Online class registration is available. Website: http://www.rwu.edu/

General Application Contact: Marcus Hanscom, Director of Graduate Admissions, 401-254-3345, Fax: 401-254-3557, E-mail: mhanscom@rwu.edu.

GRADUATE UNITS

Feinstein College of Arts and Sciences Students: 34 full-time (27 women); includes 3 minority (1 Asian, non-Hispanic/Latino; 2 Hispanic/Latino). Average age 25. 73 applicants, 75% accepted, 18 enrolled. *Faculty:* 9 full-time (4 women). Expenses: Contact institution. *Financial support:* In 2016–17, 9 students received support. Federal Work-Study and scholarships/grants available. Financial award application deadline: 6/15; financial award applicants required to submit FAFSA. In 2016, 16 master's awarded. *Program availability:* Part-time, evening/weekend, online learning. Offers clinical psychology (MA); forensic psychology (MA). *Application deadline:* For fall admission, 3/15 priority date for domestic students. *Application fee:* $50. Electronic applications accepted. *Application Contact:* Lori Vales, Director of Graduate Admissions, 401-254-6200, Fax: 401-254-3557, E-mail: gradadmit@rwu.edu. *Dean,* Robert Eisinger, 401-254-3149, E-mail: reisinger@rwu.edu.

School of Architecture, Art and Historic Preservation Students: 100 full-time (43 women), 1 part-time (0 women); includes 14 minority (3 Black or African American, non-Hispanic/Latino; 1 Asian, non-Hispanic/Latino; 4 Two or more races, non-Hispanic/Latino), 4 international. Average age 25. 77 applicants, 95% accepted, 48 enrolled. *Faculty:* 15 full-time (4 women), 4 part-time/adjunct (2 women). Expenses: Contact institution. *Financial support:* In 2016–17, 95 students received support, including 91 research assistantships (averaging $2,753 per year); scholarships/grants and unspecified assistantships also available. Financial award application deadline: 4/1; financial award applicants required to submit FAFSA. In 2016, 43 master's awarded. Offers architecture (M Arch); art and architectural history (MA); historical preservation (MS). *Application deadline:* For fall admission, 4/1 for domestic students; for spring admission, 1/1 for domestic students. *Application fee:* $50. Electronic applications accepted. *Application Contact:* Marcus Hanscom, Director of Graduate Admissions, 401-254-6200, Fax: 401-254-3345, E-mail: gradadmit@rwu.edu. *Dean,* Stephen White, 401-254-3607, E-mail: swhite@rwu.edu.

School of Education Students: 7 full-time (all women), 10 part-time (all women); includes 1 minority (Hispanic/Latino). Average age 34. 4 applicants, 100% accepted, 2 enrolled. *Faculty:* 1 (woman) full-time, 2 part-time/adjunct (1 woman). Expenses: Contact institution. *Financial support:* Application deadline: 4/1; applicants required to submit FAFSA. In 2016, 3 master's awarded. *Program availability:* Part-time, evening/weekend. Offers literacy education (MA). *Application deadline:* Applications are processed on a rolling basis. *Application fee:* $50. Electronic applications accepted. *Application Contact:* Marcus Hanscom, Director of Graduate Admissions, 401-254-3345, Fax: 401-254-3557, E-mail: gradadmit@rwu.edu. *Interim Dean of School of Education,* Robert McKenna, 401-254-3715, Fax: 401-254-3710, E-mail: rmckenna@rwu.edu.

School of Justice Studies Students: 63 full-time (37 women), 67 part-time (30 women); includes 30 minority (13 Black or African American, non-Hispanic/Latino; 1 American Indian or Alaska Native, non-Hispanic/Latino; 2 Asian, non-Hispanic/Latino; 13 Hispanic/Latino; 1 Native Hawaiian or other Pacific Islander, non-Hispanic/Latino), 3 international. Average age 36. 67 applicants, 96% accepted, 34 enrolled. *Faculty:* 10 full-time (5 women), 4 part-time/adjunct (0 women). Expenses: Contact institution. *Financial support:* Research assistantships, scholarships/grants, and unspecified assistantships available. Financial award application deadline: 4/1; financial award applicants required to submit FAFSA. In 2016, 27 master's awarded. *Program availability:* Part-time, evening/weekend, 100% online, blended/hybrid learning. Offers criminal justice (MS);

cybersecurity (MS); leadership (MS); public administration (MPA). *Application deadline:* For fall admission, 8/1 for domestic students; for spring admission, 1/1 for domestic students. Applications are processed on a rolling basis. *Application fee:* $50. Electronic applications accepted. *Application Contact:* Marcus Hanscom, Director of Graduate Admissions, 401-254-6200, Fax: 401-254-3557, E-mail: gradadmit@rwu.edu. *Dean*, Dr. Stephanie Manzi, 401-254-3021, Fax: 401-254-3431, E-mail: smanzi@rwu.edu.

School of Law Students: 420 full-time (217 women), 5 part-time (4 women); includes 105 minority (32 Black or African American, non-Hispanic/Latino; 2 American Indian or Alaska Native, non-Hispanic/Latino; 14 Asian, non-Hispanic/Latino; 40 Hispanic/Latino; 2 Native Hawaiian or other Pacific Islander, non-Hispanic/Latino; 15 Two or more races, non-Hispanic/Latino), 1 international. Average age 26. 856 applicants, 69% accepted, 158 enrolled. *Faculty:* 25 full-time (15 women), 52 part-time/adjunct (20 women). Expenses: Contact institution. *Financial support:* In 2016–17, 289 students received support, including 12 fellowships (averaging $623 per year), 37 research assistantships (averaging $695 per year); Federal Work-Study also available. Financial award application deadline: 3/31; financial award applicants required to submit FAFSA. In 2016, 86 doctorates awarded. *Program availability:* Part-time. Offers law (MSL, JD). JD/MMA and JD/MLRHR offered jointly with University of Rhode Island. *Application deadline:* For fall admission, 4/1 priority date for domestic and international students. Applications are processed on a rolling basis. *Application fee:* $60. Electronic applications accepted. *Application Contact:* Michael W. Donnelly-Boylen, Assistant Dean of Admissions, 401-254-4555, Fax: 401-254-4516, E-mail: mdonnelly-boylen@rwu.edu. *Dean*, Michael Yelnosky, 401-254-4500, Fax: 401-254-3525, E-mail: myelnosky@rwu.edu.

ROLLINS COLLEGE, Winter Park, FL 32789-4499

General Information Independent, coed, comprehensive institution. Enrollment: 2,540 graduate, professional, and undergraduate students; 332 full-time matriculated graduate/professional students (190 women), 266 part-time matriculated graduate/professional students (151 women). Enrollment by degree level: 553 master's, 45 doctoral. *Graduate faculty:* 43 full-time (15 women), 26 part-time/adjunct (13 women). *Graduate housing:* Room and/or apartments available on a first-come, first-served basis to single students; on-campus housing not available to married students. *Student services:* Campus employment opportunities, campus safety program, career counseling, exercise/wellness program, free psychological counseling, international student services, low-cost health insurance, multicultural affairs office, services for students with disabilities, writing training. *Library facilities:* Olin Library. *Collection:* Books: 259,302 (physical), 200,491 (digital/electronic); Serial titles: 2,358 (physical), 134,353 (digital/electronic); Databases: 80. Study areas open 24 hours, 5–7 days a week; students can reserve study rooms.

Computer facilities: 254 computers available on campus for general student use. A campuswide network can be accessed from student residence rooms and from off campus. Online class registration is available.
Website: http://www.rollins.edu/

General Application Contact: Faye Tydlaska, Vice President for Enrollment Management and Marketing, 407-646-2161 Ext. 2532, E-mail: eveningadmission@rollins.edu.

GRADUATE UNITS

Crummer Graduate School of Business Students: 254 full-time (105 women), 83 part-time (36 women); includes 63 minority (15 Black or African American, non-Hispanic/Latino; 9 Asian, non-Hispanic/Latino; 35 Hispanic/Latino; 4 Two or more races, non-Hispanic/Latino), 48 international. Average age 31. 360 applicants, 74% accepted, 207 enrolled. *Faculty:* 22 full-time (5 women), 4 part-time/adjunct (3 women). Expenses: Contact institution. *Financial support:* In 2016–17, 125 students received support. Federal Work-Study and scholarships/grants available. Support available to part-time students. Financial award applicants required to submit FAFSA. In 2016, 159 master's awarded. *Program availability:* Part-time, evening/weekend, online learning. Offers business administration (EDBA); entrepreneurship (MBA); finance (MBA); international business (MBA); management (MBA); marketing (MBA); operations and technology management (MBA). *Application deadline:* Applications are processed on a rolling basis. *Application fee:* $50. Electronic applications accepted. *Application Contact:* Maralyn E. Graham, Admissions Coordinator, 407-646-2405, Fax: 407-646-1550, E-mail: mbaadmissions@rollins.edu. *Dean*, Deborah Crown, 407-646-2249, Fax: 407-646-1550, E-mail: dcrown@rollins.edu.

Hamilton Holt School Students: 123 full-time (100 women), 138 part-time (100 women); includes 78 minority (24 Black or African American, non-Hispanic/Latino; 4 American Indian or Alaska Native, non-Hispanic/Latino; 10 Asian, non-Hispanic/Latino; 33 Hispanic/Latino; 1 Native Hawaiian or other Pacific Islander, non-Hispanic/Latino; 6 Two or more races, non-Hispanic/Latino), 8 international. Average age 34. 174 applicants, 78% accepted, 108 enrolled. *Faculty:* 14 full-time (6 women), 12 part-time/adjunct (8 women). Expenses: Contact institution. *Financial support:* In 2016–17, 56 students received support. Federal Work-Study, scholarships/grants, and unspecified assistantships available. Support available to part-time students. Financial award applicants required to submit FAFSA. In 2016, 48 master's awarded. *Program availability:* Part-time, evening/weekend. Offers applied behavior analysis and clinical science (MA); clinical mental health counseling (MA); elementary education (M Ed, MAT); health services administration (MHSA); human resources (MHR); liberal studies (MLS). *Application fee:* $50. *Application Contact:* Nick Georgoudiou, Director of Admission, 407-691-1781, Fax: 407-646-1551, E-mail: ngeorgoudiou@rollins.edu. *Dean*, Dr. David Richard, 407-646-2292, Fax: 407-646-1551, E-mail: dcrichard@rollins.edu.

ROOSEVELT UNIVERSITY, Chicago, IL 60605

General Information Independent, coed, comprehensive institution. CGS member. Enrollment: 967 full-time matriculated graduate/professional students (634 women), 928 part-time matriculated graduate/professional students (647 women). Enrollment by degree level: 1,534 master's, 361 doctoral. *Graduate faculty:* 210 full-time (86 women), 543 part-time/adjunct (247 women). *Tuition:* Full-time $19,566; part-time $880 per credit hour. *Required fees:* $175 per semester. One-time fee: $200. Part-time tuition and fees vary according to course load, degree level and program. *Graduate housing:* Room and/or apartments available on a first-come, first-served basis to single students; on-campus housing not available to married students. Typical cost: $9227 per year ($12,927 including board). Room and board charges vary according to board plan and housing facility selected. Housing application deadline: 7/1. *Student services:* Campus employment opportunities, campus safety program, career counseling, child daycare facilities, exercise/wellness program, free psychological counseling, international student

services, low-cost health insurance, services for students with disabilities, teacher training, writing training. *Library facilities:* Murray-Green Library plus 4 others.

Computer facilities: 646 computers available on campus for general student use. A campuswide network can be accessed from student residence rooms and from off campus. Online class registration is available.
Website: http://www.roosevelt.edu/

General Application Contact: Angela Ryan, Director of Graduate Enrollment, 312-341-2420, Fax: 312-281-3356, E-mail: applyru@roosevelt.edu.

GRADUATE UNITS

Graduate Division Students: 967 full-time (634 women), 928 part-time (647 women); includes 787 minority (378 Black or African American, non-Hispanic/Latino; 2 American Indian or Alaska Native, non-Hispanic/Latino; 157 Asian, non-Hispanic/Latino; 193 Hispanic/Latino; 2 Native Hawaiian or other Pacific Islander, non-Hispanic/Latino; 55 Two or more races, non-Hispanic/Latino), 218 international. Average age 30. 1,293 applicants, 82% accepted, 494 enrolled. *Faculty:* 216 full-time (86 women), 415 part-time/adjunct (193 women). Expenses: Contact institution. *Financial support:* Research assistantships with full tuition reimbursements, career-related internships or fieldwork, Federal Work-Study, scholarships/grants, tuition waivers (full and partial), and unspecified assistantships available. Support available to part-time students. Financial award application deadline: 5/1; financial award applicants required to submit FAFSA. In 2016, 739 master's, 88 doctorates, 8 other advanced degrees awarded. *Program availability:* Part-time, evening/weekend. *Application deadline:* For fall admission, 6/1 priority date for domestic students; for spring admission, 12/1 for domestic students. Applications are processed on a rolling basis. *Application fee:* $25. Electronic applications accepted. *Application Contact:* Angela Ryan, Director of Graduate Enrollment, 312-341-2420, Fax: 312-281-3356, E-mail: applyru@roosevelt.edu. *Dean of Graduate Studies*, Dr. Janett Trubatch, 312-341-2440, Fax: 312-341-2013.

Chicago College of Performing Arts Students: 136 full-time (80 women), 1 part-time (0 women); includes 12 minority (1 Black or African American, non-Hispanic/Latino; 2 Asian, non-Hispanic/Latino; 5 Hispanic/Latino; 4 Two or more races, non-Hispanic/Latino), 41 international. Average age 25. 201 applicants, 84% accepted, 70 enrolled. Expenses: Contact institution. *Financial support:* Research assistantships, career-related internships or fieldwork, Federal Work-Study, scholarships/grants, and tuition waivers (full and partial) available. Support available to part-time students. In 2016, 62 master's, 8 advanced degrees awarded. *Program availability:* Part-time, evening/weekend. Offers brass (Diploma); brass performance (MM); classical guitar (MM, Diploma); music (MM); music composition (MM); opera (Diploma); orchestral studies (MM, Diploma); percussion (MM, Diploma); performing arts (MA, MM, Diploma); performing arts administration (MA); piano (Diploma); piano performance (MM); strings (MM, Diploma); theatre directing (MA); voice (MM); woodwinds (MM, Diploma). *Application deadline:* For fall admission, 6/1 priority date for domestic students. Applications are processed on a rolling basis. *Application fee:* $25 ($35 for international students). *Application Contact:* Angela Ryan, Director of Graduate Enrollment, 312-341-2420, Fax: 312-281-3356, E-mail: applyru@roosevelt.edu. *Interim Dean*, Rudy Marcozzi, 312-341-3782.

College of Arts and Sciences Students: 394 full-time (275 women), 258 part-time (189 women); includes 256 minority (112 Black or African American, non-Hispanic/Latino; 1 American Indian or Alaska Native, non-Hispanic/Latino; 51 Asian, non-Hispanic/Latino; 68 Hispanic/Latino; 24 Two or more races, non-Hispanic/Latino), 75 international. Average age 28. 611 applicants, 75% accepted, 195 enrolled. Expenses: Contact institution. *Financial support:* Research assistantships, teaching assistantships, career-related internships or fieldwork, Federal Work-Study, institutionally sponsored loans, scholarships/grants, and tuition waivers (full and partial) available. Support available to part-time students. Financial award application deadline: 2/15. In 2016, 293 master's, 16 doctorates awarded. *Program availability:* Part-time, evening/weekend. Offers actuarial science (MS); arts and sciences (MA, MFA, MPA, MS, MSIMC, PhD, Psy D); biology (MS); biotechnology and chemical science (MS); clinical psychology (MA, Psy D); clinical psychology - counseling practice (MA); computer science (MS); creative writing (MFA); economics (MA); history (MA); industrial/organizational psychology (MA, PhD); integrated marketing communications (MSIMC); mathematics (MS); public administration (MPA). *Application deadline:* For fall admission, 6/1 priority date for domestic students. Applications are processed on a rolling basis. *Application fee:* $25 ($35 for international students). *Application Contact:* Angela Ryan, Director of Graduate Enrollment, 312-341-2420, Fax: 312-281-3356, E-mail: applyru@roosevelt.edu. *Dean*, Lynn Weiner, 312-341-2134, E-mail: lweiner@roosevelt.edu.

College of Education Students: 79 full-time (62 women), 178 part-time (135 women); includes 92 minority (55 Black or African American, non-Hispanic/Latino; 1 American Indian or Alaska Native, non-Hispanic/Latino; 7 Asian, non-Hispanic/Latino; 25 Hispanic/Latino; 4 Two or more races, non-Hispanic/Latino), 4 international. Average age 32. 176 applicants, 97% accepted, 74 enrolled. Expenses: Contact institution. *Financial support:* Federal Work-Study available. Support available to part-time students. Financial award application deadline: 2/15. In 2016, 99 master's awarded. *Program availability:* Part-time, evening/weekend. Offers clinical mental health counseling (MA); early childhood education (MA); education (MA); elementary education (MA); instructional leadership (MA); organizational development (MA); reading teacher education (MA); school counseling (MA); secondary education (MA); special education (MA). *Application deadline:* For fall admission, 6/1 priority date for domestic students. Applications are processed on a rolling basis. *Application fee:* $25 ($35 for international students). *Application Contact:* Angela Ryan, Director of Graduate Enrollment, 312-341-2420, Fax: 312-281-3356, E-mail: aryan@roosevelt.edu. *Interim Dean*, George Olson, 312-341-3700.

College of Pharmacy Students: 194 full-time (117 women), 2 part-time (1 woman); includes 87 minority (12 Black or African American, non-Hispanic/Latino; 52 Asian, non-Hispanic/Latino; 15 Hispanic/Latino; 1 Native Hawaiian or other Pacific Islander, non-Hispanic/Latino; 7 Two or more races, non-Hispanic/Latino), 11 international. Average age 26. Expenses: Contact institution. In 2016, 61 doctorates awarded. Offers pharmacy (Pharm D). *Application Contact:* Angela Ryan, Director of Graduate Enrollment, 312-341-2420, Fax: 312-281-3356, E-mail: aryan@roosevelt.edu. *Dean*, Dr. George E. MacKinnon, III, 847-619-7300, E-mail: cop@roosevelt.edu.

College of Professional Studies Students: 24 full-time (21 women), 104 part-time (81 women); includes 74 minority (52 Black or African American, non-Hispanic/Latino; 4 Asian, non-Hispanic/Latino; 14 Hispanic/Latino; 4 Two or more races, non-Hispanic/Latino), 7 international. Average age 38. 55 applicants, 89% accepted, 29 enrolled. Expenses: Contact institution. *Financial support:* Federal Work-Study available. Support available to part-time students. Financial award application deadline: 2/15. In 2016, 56 master's awarded. *Program availability:* Part-time, evening/weekend. Offers hospitality and tourism management (MS); training and development (MA). *Application deadline:* For fall admission, 6/1 priority date for domestic students. Applications are processed on a rolling basis. *Application fee:* $25 ($35 for international students). *Application Contact:* Angela Ryan, Director of Graduate Enrollment, 877-APPLY RU, Fax: 312-281-3356, E-mail: applyru@roosevelt.edu. *Dean,* 312-281-3376.

Walter E. Heller College of Business Students: 140 full-time (79 women), 385 part-time (241 women); includes 266 minority (146 Black or African American, non-Hispanic/Latino; 41 Asian, non-Hispanic/Latino; 66 Hispanic/Latino; 1 Native Hawaiian or other Pacific Islander, non-Hispanic/Latino; 12 Two or more races, non-Hispanic/Latino), 80 international. Average age 31. 279 applicants, 94% accepted, 126 enrolled. *Expenses:* Contact institution. *Financial support:* Career-related internships or fieldwork, Federal Work-Study, and tuition waivers (partial) available. Support available to part-time students. Financial award application deadline: 2/15. In 2016, 229 master's awarded. *Program availability:* Part-time, evening/weekend. Offers accounting (MSA); business (MBA, MS, MSA, MSHRM, Certificate); business administration (MBA); commercial real estate development (Certificate); human resource management (MSHRM); real estate (MS). *Application deadline:* For fall admission, 6/1 priority date for domestic students. Applications are processed on a rolling basis. *Application fee:* $40. *Application Contact:* Angela Ryan, Director of Graduate Enrollment, 877-APPLY RU, Fax: 312-281-3356, E-mail: applyru@roosevelt.edu. *Dean,* Dr. Asghar Sabbaghi, 312-281-3350.

ROSALIND FRANKLIN UNIVERSITY OF MEDICINE AND SCIENCE, North Chicago, IL 60064-3095

General Information Independent, coed, graduate-only institution. CGS member. *Graduate housing:* Rooms and/or apartments available on a first-come, first-served basis to single and married students. Housing application deadline: 3/13. *Research affiliation:* Argonne National Laboratory (medical physics), Veterans Administration Hospital (pulmonary medicine).

GRADUATE UNITS

Chicago Medical School Offers medicine (MD).

College of Health Professions *Program availability:* Part-time, online learning. Offers biomedical sciences (MS); clinical nutrition (MS); clinical psychology (MS); health professions (MS, D Sc, DNAP, DPT, PhD, TDPT, Certificate); health professions education (MS); health promotion and wellness (MS); healthcare administration and management (MS, Certificate); interprofessional studies (D Sc, PhD); nurse anesthesia (DNAP); nutrition education (MS); pathologists' assistant (MS); physical therapy (MS, DPT, TDPT); physician assistant (MS).

College of Pharmacy Offers pharmacy (Pharm D).

Dr. William M. Scholl College of Podiatric Medicine Offers podiatric medicine (DPM).

School of Graduate and Postdoctoral Studies - Interdisciplinary Graduate Program in Biomedical Sciences Offers biochemistry and molecular biology (PhD); cell biology and anatomy (PhD); cellular and molecular pharmacology (MS, PhD); microbiology and immunology (PhD); neuroscience (PhD); physiology and biophysics (MS, PhD). Electronic applications accepted.

ROSE-HULMAN INSTITUTE OF TECHNOLOGY, Terre Haute, IN 47803-3999

General Information Independent, coed, primarily men, comprehensive institution. *Enrollment:* 2,278 graduate, professional, and undergraduate students; 48 full-time matriculated graduate/professional students (12 women), 28 part-time matriculated graduate/professional students (3 women). *Enrollment by degree level:* 76 master's. *Graduate faculty:* 121 full-time (25 women), 5 part-time/adjunct (1 woman). *Tuition:* Full-time $43,122. *Graduate housing:* On-campus housing not available. *Student services:* Campus employment opportunities, career counseling, exercise/wellness program, free psychological counseling, international student services, low-cost health insurance, services for students with disabilities. *Library facilities:* John A. Logan Library. *Collection:* Books: 25,985 (physical), 283,399 (digital/electronic); Serial titles: 46 (physical), 41,278 (digital/electronic); Databases: 34. Weekly public service hours: 101; students can reserve study rooms.

Computer facilities: Computer purchase and lease plans are available. 48 computers available on campus for general student use. A campuswide network can be accessed from student residence rooms and from off campus. Online class registration is available.
Website: http://www.rose-hulman.edu/

General Application Contact: Dr. Azad Siahmakoun, Associate Dean of the Faculty, 812-877-8400, Fax: 812-877-8061, E-mail: siahmako@rose-hulman.edu.

GRADUATE UNITS

Faculty of Engineering and Applied Sciences Students: 48 full-time (12 women), 28 part-time (3 women); includes 8 minority (2 Black or African American, non-Hispanic/Latino; 2 Asian, non-Hispanic/Latino; 2 Hispanic/Latino; 2 Two or more races, non-Hispanic/Latino), 36 international. Average age 24. 97 applicants, 75% accepted, 37 enrolled. *Faculty:* 121 full-time (25 women), 5 part-time/adjunct (1 woman). *Expenses:* Contact institution. *Financial support:* In 2016–17, 68 students received support. Fellowships with tuition reimbursements available, research assistantships with tuition reimbursements available, institutionally sponsored loans, scholarships/grants, and tuition waivers (full and partial) available. In 2016, 39 master's awarded. *Program availability:* Part-time, evening/weekend. Offers biology and biomedical engineering (MS); chemical engineering (M Eng, MS); civil engineering (MS); electrical and computer engineering (M Eng); electrical engineering (MS); engineering and applied sciences (M Eng, MS); engineering management (M Eng, MS); environmental engineering (MS); mechanical engineering (M Eng, MS); optical engineering (MS); software engineering (MS); systems engineering and management (MS). *Application deadline:* For fall admission, 2/1 priority date for domestic students. Applications are processed on a rolling basis. *Application fee:* $0. Electronic applications accepted. *Application Contact:* Dr. Azad Siahmakoun, Associate Dean of the Faculty, 812-877-8400, Fax: 812-877-8061, E-mail: siahmako@rose-hulman.edu.

ROSEMAN UNIVERSITY OF HEALTH SCIENCES, Henderson, NV 89014

General Information Private, coed, graduate-only institution. *Enrollment by degree level:* 25 master's, 1,046 doctoral, 30 other advanced degrees. *Graduate faculty:* 96 full-time (30 women), 51 part-time/adjunct (8 women). *Tuition:* Full-time $30,069; part-time $771 per credit. *Required fees:* $469 per credit. Tuition and fees vary according to program. *Graduate housing:* On-campus housing not available. *Student services:* Campus employment opportunities, career counseling, international student services, services for students with disabilities. *Library facilities:* Roseman University Library plus 1 other. *Collection:* Books: 8,601 (physical), 5 (digital/electronic); Serial titles: 14 (physical), 111 (digital/electronic); Databases: 27. Weekly public service hours: 82; students can reserve study rooms.

Computer facilities: 28 computers available on campus for general student use. A campuswide network can be accessed. X available.
Website: http://www.roseman.edu/

General Application Contact: Dr. Okeleke Nzeogwu, Director, MBA Program, 702-968-1659, E-mail: onzeogwu@roseman.edu.

GRADUATE UNITS

College of Dental Medicine - Henderson Campus Students: 30 full-time (10 women); includes 14 minority (13 Asian, non-Hispanic/Latino; 1 Hispanic/Latino). Average age 30. 132 applicants, 8% accepted, 10 enrolled. *Faculty:* 6 full-time (2 women), 5 part-time/adjunct (0 women). *Expenses:* Contact institution. *Financial support:* Application deadline: 6/15; applicants required to submit FAFSA. In 2016, 12 other advanced degrees awarded. Offers business administration (MBA); dental medicine (Post-Doctoral Certificate). *Application deadline:* For fall admission, 1/31 for domestic and international students. *Application fee:* $50. *Application Contact:* Rochelle Sharp, Administrative Assistant to the Dean, 702-968-1682, E-mail: rsharp@roseman.edu. *Dean,* Dr. Jaleh Pourhamidi, 702-968-1652, Fax: 702-968-5277, E-mail: jpourhamidi@roseman.edu.

College of Dental Medicine - South Jordan, Utah Campus Students: 326 full-time (128 women); includes 116 minority (2 Black or African American, non-Hispanic/Latino; 1 American Indian or Alaska Native, non-Hispanic/Latino; 88 Asian, non-Hispanic/Latino; 15 Hispanic/Latino; 3 Native Hawaiian or other Pacific Islander, non-Hispanic/Latino; 7 Two or more races, non-Hispanic/Latino), 6 international. Average age 28. 2,217 applicants, 8% accepted, 84 enrolled. *Faculty:* 40 full-time (6 women), 35 part-time/adjunct (3 women). *Expenses:* Contact institution. *Financial support:* In 2016–17, 10 students received support. Federal Work-Study and tuition waivers (partial) available. Financial award application deadline: 6/15; financial award applicants required to submit FAFSA. In 2016, 77 doctorates awarded. Offers dental medicine (DMD). *Application deadline:* For fall admission, 12/1 for domestic and international students. Applications are processed on a rolling basis. *Application fee:* $75. Electronic applications accepted. *Application Contact:* Alicia Spittle, Admissions Coordinator, 801-878-1405, E-mail: aspittle@roseman.edu. *Dean, College of Dental Medicine,* Dr. Frank W. Licari, 801-878-1400, E-mail: flicari@roseman.edu.

College of Pharmacy Students: 720 full-time (391 women); includes 414 minority (41 Black or African American, non-Hispanic/Latino; 4 American Indian or Alaska Native, non-Hispanic/Latino; 313 Asian, non-Hispanic/Latino; 30 Hispanic/Latino; 8 Native Hawaiian or other Pacific Islander, non-Hispanic/Latino; 18 Two or more races, non-Hispanic/Latino), 3 international. Average age 28. 653 applicants, 52% accepted, 248 enrolled. *Faculty:* 37 full-time (16 women), 2 part-time/adjunct (0 women). *Expenses:* Contact institution. *Financial support:* In 2016–17, 116 students received support. Federal Work-Study and scholarships/grants available. Financial award application deadline: 7/15; financial award applicants required to submit FAFSA. In 2016, 239 doctorates awarded. Offers pharmacy (Pharm D). *Application deadline:* For fall admission, 2/1 for domestic and international students. Applications are processed on a rolling basis. *Application fee:* $60. Electronic applications accepted. *Application Contact:* Dr. Helen Park, Assistant Dean for Admissions and Student Affairs, 702-968-5248, Fax: 702-968-1644, E-mail: hpark@roseman.edu. *Interim Dean,* Dr. Larry Fannin, 702-968-5944, Fax: 702-990-4435, E-mail: lfannin@roseman.edu.

MBA Program Students: 2 full-time (1 woman), 23 part-time (14 women); includes 10 minority (4 Black or African American, non-Hispanic/Latino; 5 Asian, non-Hispanic/Latino; 1 Hispanic/Latino). Average age 37. 10 applicants, 100% accepted, 7 enrolled. *Faculty:* 2 full-time (1 woman), 11 part-time/adjunct (5 women). *Expenses:* Contact institution. *Financial support:* Application deadline: 5/1; applicants required to submit FAFSA. In 2016, 68 master's awarded. *Program availability:* Part-time, evening/weekend. Offers business administration (MBA). *Application deadline:* For fall admission, 5/15 for domestic and international students. *Application fee:* $100. *Program Director,* Dr. Okeleke Nzeogwu, 702-968-1659, Fax: 702-968-1685, E-mail: onzeogwu@roseman.edu.

ROSEMONT COLLEGE, Rosemont, PA 19010-1699

General Information Independent-religious, coed, comprehensive institution. *Graduate housing:* Room and/or apartments available on a first-come, first-served basis to single students; on-campus housing not available to married students. Housing application deadline: 8/1.

GRADUATE UNITS

Schools of Graduate and Professional Studies *Program availability:* Part-time, evening/weekend, online learning. Offers business administration (MBA); creative writing (MFA); elementary certification (MA); human services (MS); leadership (MS); management (MS); PreK-4 (MA); publishing (MA); school counseling (MA). Electronic applications accepted.

ROWAN UNIVERSITY, Glassboro, NJ 08028-1701

General Information State-supported, coed, comprehensive institution. CGS member. *Enrollment:* 17,355 graduate, professional, and undergraduate students; 1,347 full-time matriculated graduate/professional students (714 women), 1,638 part-time matriculated graduate/professional students (1,143 women). *Enrollment by degree level:* 1,310 master's, 938 doctoral, 414 other advanced degrees. *Graduate faculty:* 227 full-time (98 women), 204 part-time/adjunct (112 women). *Tuition, state resident:* full-time $8710; part-time $871 per credit. *Tuition, nonresident:* full-time $8710; part-time $871 per credit. *Required fees:* $1510; $151 per credit. *Graduate housing:* Room and/or apartments available on a first-come, first-served basis to single students; on-campus housing not available to married students. Typical cost: $7608 per year ($11,948 including board). Housing application deadline: 5/1. *Student services:* Campus employment opportunities, campus safety program, career counseling, child daycare facilities, exercise/wellness program, free psychological counseling, international student services, low-cost health insurance, multicultural affairs office, services for students with disabilities, teacher training, writing training. *Library facilities:* Keith and Shirley Campbell Library plus 4 others. *Collection:* Books: 328,891 (physical), 249,282 (digital/electronic); Databases: 739. Students can reserve study rooms.

Computer facilities: 900 computers available on campus for general student use. A campuswide network can be accessed from student residence rooms and from off campus. Online class registration is available.
Website: http://www.rowan.edu/

General Application Contact: Jeffrey Fields, College of Graduate and Continuing Education, 856-256-4747, E-mail: cgce@rowan.edu.

GRADUATE UNITS

Graduate School *Expenses:* Contact institution. *Financial support:* Research assistantships with full and partial tuition reimbursements, career-related internships or fieldwork, Federal Work-Study, scholarships/grants, traineeships, health care benefits, tuition waivers, and unspecified assistantships available. Support available to part-time students. Financial award applicants required to submit FAFSA. *Program availability:*

Part-time, evening/weekend. *Application deadline:* For fall admission, 10/15 for domestic and international students; for spring admission, 2/15 for domestic and international students. Applications are processed on a rolling basis. *Application fee:* $65. Electronic applications accepted. *Application Contact:* Admissions and Enrollment Services, 856-256-5435, Fax: 856-256-5637, E-mail: cgceadmissions@rowan.edu. *Dean, College of Graduate and Continuing Education,* Dr. Horacio Sosa, 856-256-4747, Fax: 856-256-5638, E-mail: sosa@rowan.edu.

College of Communication and Creative Arts Expenses: Contact institution. *Financial support:* Career-related internships or fieldwork and unspecified assistantships available. Support available to part-time students. *Program availability:* Part-time, evening/weekend. Offers communication and creative arts (MA, CGS); editing and publishing (CGS); integrated marketing communication and new media (CGS); public relations/advertising (MA); writing (MA); writing, composition, and rhetoric (CGS). *Application deadline:* For fall admission, 8/1 for domestic and international students; for spring admission, 12/1 for domestic and international students; for summer admission, 4/1 for domestic and international students. Applications are processed on a rolling basis. *Application fee:* $65. Electronic applications accepted. *Application Contact:* Admissions and Enrollment Services, 856-256-5435, Fax: 856-256-5637, E-mail: cgceadmissions@rowan.edu. *Dean, College of Graduate and Continuing Education,* Dr. Horacio Sosa, 856-256-4747, Fax: 856-256-5638, E-mail: sosa@rowan.edu.

College of Education Expenses: Contact institution. *Financial support:* Career-related internships or fieldwork, Federal Work-Study, scholarships/grants, health care benefits, and unspecified assistantships available. Support available to part-time students. *Program availability:* Part-time, evening/weekend. Offers counseling in educational settings (MA); education (M Ed, MA, MST, Ed D, CAGS, CGS, Ed S, Postbaccalaureate Certificate); educational leadership (Ed D, CAGS); ESL education (CGS); higher education administration (MA); learning disabilities (MA); principal preparation (CAGS); reading education (MA, CGS); reading/writing literacy (CGS); school administration (MA); school and public librarianship (MA); school nursing (Postbaccalaureate Certificate); school psychology (MA, Ed S); special education (MA, CGS); subject matter education (MST); supervisor (CAGS); teacher of reading (Postbaccalaureate Certificate); teacher of students with disabilities (Postbaccalaureate Certificate); teaching STEM (MA); theatre education (MST). *Application deadline:* Applications are processed on a rolling basis. *Application fee:* $65. Electronic applications accepted.

College of Engineering Expenses: Contact institution. *Financial support:* Career-related internships or fieldwork, Federal Work-Study, and unspecified assistantships available. Support available to part-time students. *Program availability:* Part-time, evening/weekend. Offers chemical engineering (MS); civil engineering (MEM, MS); electrical engineering (MS); engineering (MEM, MS, MSE); mechanical engineering (MS). *Application deadline:* Applications are processed on a rolling basis. *Application fee:* $65. Electronic applications accepted.

College of Humanities and Social Sciences Expenses: Contact institution. Offers criminal justice (MA); history (MA, CGS); humanities and social sciences (MA, CGS). *Application fee:* $65. *Application Contact:* Admissions and Enrollment Services, 856-256-4747, Fax: 856-256-5637, E-mail: globaladmissions@rowan.edu. *Dean,* Dr. Cindy Vitto, 856-256-5840, E-mail: vitto@rowan.edu.

College of Performing Arts Expenses: Contact institution. *Financial support:* Career-related internships or fieldwork, scholarships/grants, health care benefits, and unspecified assistantships available. *Program availability:* Part-time, evening/weekend. Offers performance (MM); performing arts (MA, MM, MST); theatre arts administration (MA). *Application deadline:* For fall admission, 8/1 for domestic and international students; for spring admission, 11/1 for domestic and international students. Applications are processed on a rolling basis. *Application fee:* $65. Electronic applications accepted.

College of Science and Mathematics Expenses: Contact institution. *Financial support:* Career-related internships or fieldwork, Federal Work-Study, scholarships/grants, health care benefits, and unspecified assistantships available. Support available to part-time students. *Program availability:* Part-time, evening/weekend. Offers applied behavioral analysis (MA, CAGS); bioinformatics (MS); biological science (MS); clinical mental health counseling (MA, CAGS); computer science (MS); mathematics (MA); middle grades math education (CGS); networks (CGS); nursing (MS); pharmaceutical sciences (MS); psychology (MA, CAGS); science and mathematics (MA, MS, CAGS, CGS). *Application deadline:* Applications are processed on a rolling basis. *Application fee:* $65. Electronic applications accepted.

Rohrer College of Business Expenses: Contact institution. *Financial support:* Career-related internships or fieldwork, scholarships/grants, health care benefits, and unspecified assistantships available. *Program availability:* Part-time, evening/weekend. Offers business (MBA, CAGS, CGS); business administration (MBA). *Application deadline:* For fall admission, 8/1 for domestic and international students; for spring admission, 12/1 for domestic and international students; for summer admission, 4/1 for domestic and international students. Applications are processed on a rolling basis. *Application fee:* $65. Electronic applications accepted. *Application Contact:* Admissions and Enrollment Services, 856-256-5435, Fax: 856-256-5637, E-mail: cgceadmissions@rowan.edu. *Dean, College of Graduate and Continuing Education,* Dr. Horacio Sosa, 856-256-4747, E-mail: sosa@rowan.edu.

School of Biomedical Science and Health Professions Expenses: Contact institution. *Financial support:* Career-related internships or fieldwork, Federal Work-Study, health care benefits, and unspecified assistantships available. Support available to part-time students. *Program availability:* Part-time, evening/weekend, online learning. Offers health and exercise science (MA); wellness and lifestyle management (MA). *Application deadline:* For fall admission, 6/1 for domestic and international students. Applications are processed on a rolling basis. *Application fee:* $65. Electronic applications accepted. *Application Contact:* Admissions and Enrollment Services, 856-256-5435, Fax: 856-256-5637, E-mail: cgceadmissions@rowan.edu. *Senior Associate Dean,* Dr. Carl E. Hock, E-mail: hock@rowan.edu.

School of Osteopathic Medicine Expenses: Contact institution. *Financial support:* Federal Work-Study and scholarships/grants available. Financial award applicants required to submit FAFSA. Offers osteopathic medicine (DO). *Application deadline:* For fall admission, 2/1 for domestic and international students. Applications are processed on a rolling basis. *Application fee:* $90. Electronic applications accepted. *Application Contact:* Paula Watkins, Director of Enrollment Management, 856-566-7050, Fax: 856-566-6895, E-mail: fennerpa@rowan.edu. *Assistant Dean of Admissions,* Paula Watkins, E-mail: fennerpa@rowan.edu.

ROYAL MILITARY COLLEGE OF CANADA, Kingston, ON K7K 7B4, Canada

General Information Federally supported, coed, university.

GRADUATE UNITS

Division of Graduate Studies and Research *Program availability:* Part-time, online learning. Electronic applications accepted.

Continuing Studies Offers business administration (MBA); defense management and policy (MA); history (PhD); war studies (MA). Electronic applications accepted.

Engineering Division Offers chemical and materials (M Eng); chemical and materials science (M Sc, PhD); chemistry (M Eng); civil engineering (M Eng, MA Sc, PhD); computer engineering (M Eng, PhD); electrical engineering (M Eng, PhD); engineering (M Eng, M Sc, MA Sc, PhD); environmental (PhD); environmental engineering (M Eng, PhD); environmental science (M Sc, PhD); mechanical engineering (M Eng, MA Sc, PhD); nuclear (PhD); nuclear engineering (M Eng, MA Sc, PhD); nuclear science (M Sc, PhD); software engineering (M Eng, PhD). Electronic applications accepted.

Science Division Offers chemical engineering (M Eng, MA Sc, PhD); chemistry (M Sc, PhD); computer science (M Sc); mathematics (M Sc); physics (M Sc); science (M Eng, M Sc, MA Sc, PhD). Electronic applications accepted.

ROYAL ROADS UNIVERSITY, Victoria, BC V9B 5Y2, Canada

General Information Province-supported, coed, upper-level institution. *Graduate housing:* Room and/or apartments available on a first-come, first-served basis to single students; on-campus housing not available to married students.

GRADUATE UNITS

Graduate Studies *Program availability:* Online learning. Offers conflict analysis (G Dip); conflict analysis and management (MA); destination development (Graduate Certificate); disaster and emergency management (MA); environment and management (M Sc, MA); environmental education and communication (MA, G Dip, Graduate Certificate); executive coaching (Graduate Certificate); health systems leadership (Graduate Certificate); human security and peacebuilding (MA); international hotel management (MA); project management (Graduate Certificate); public relations management (Graduate Certificate); strategic human resources management (Graduate Certificate); sustainable tourism (Graduate Certificate); tourism leadership (Graduate Certificate); tourism management (MA). Electronic applications accepted.

Faculty of Management *Program availability:* Online learning. Offers digital technologies management (MBA); executive management (MBA); human resources management (MBA). Electronic applications accepted.

RUDOLF STEINER COLLEGE, Fair Oaks, CA 95628-6811

General Information Independent, coed, graduate-only institution.

GRADUATE UNITS

Waldorf Teacher Education Programs Offers early childhood education (MA); elementary education (MA).

RUSH UNIVERSITY, Chicago, IL 60612-3832

General Information Independent, coed, upper-level institution. CGS member. *Graduate housing:* Rooms and/or apartments available on a first-come, first-served basis to single and married students.

GRADUATE UNITS

College of Health Sciences Expenses: Contact institution. *Financial support:* Career-related internships or fieldwork, Federal Work-Study, institutionally sponsored loans, and scholarships/grants available. Support available to part-time students. Financial award application deadline: 4/1; financial award applicants required to submit FAFSA. *Program availability:* Part-time. Offers audiology (Au D); clinical laboratory management (MS); clinical nutrition (MS); health sciences (MS, Au D, PhD); health systems management (MS, PhD); medical laboratory science (MS); occupational therapy (MS); perfusion technology (MS); physician assistant studies (MS); respiratory care (MS); speech-language pathology (MS). Electronic applications accepted. *Application Contact:* 312-942-7120, E-mail: chs_admissions@rush.edu.

College of Nursing Students: 403 full-time (333 women), 682 part-time (628 women); includes 257 minority (68 Black or African American, non-Hispanic/Latino; 1 American Indian or Alaska Native, non-Hispanic/Latino; 69 Asian, non-Hispanic/Latino; 99 Hispanic/Latino; 20 Two or more races, non-Hispanic/Latino). Average age 32. 807 applicants, 50% accepted, 291 enrolled. *Faculty:* 80 full-time (75 women), 46 part-time/adjunct (42 women). Expenses: Contact institution. *Financial support:* Research assistantships, teaching assistantships, Federal Work-Study, scholarships/grants, traineeships, and health care benefits available. Support available to part-time students. Financial award application deadline: 3/1; financial award applicants required to submit FAFSA. In 2016, 162 master's, 178 doctorates, 12 other advanced degrees awarded. *Program availability:* 100% online, blended/hybrid learning. Offers adult gerontology acute care clinical nurse specialist (DNP); adult gerontology acute care nurse practitioner (DNP); adult gerontology primary care nurse practitioner (DNP); advanced public health nursing (DNP); clinical nurse leader (MSN); family nurse practitioner (DNP); neonatal clinical nurse specialist (DNP); neonatal nurse practitioner (DNP, Post-Graduate Certificate); nurse anesthesia (DNP); nursing (MSN, DNP, PhD, Post-Graduate Certificate); nursing science (PhD); pediatric acute care nurse practitioner (DNP, Post-Graduate Certificate); pediatric clinical nurse specialist (DNP); pediatric primary care nurse practitioner (DNP); psychiatric mental health nurse practitioner (DNP); transformative leadership: population health (DNP); transformative leadership: systems (DNP). *Application deadline:* For fall admission, 1/2 for domestic students; for spring admission, 8/1 for domestic students; for summer admission, 12/1 for domestic students. Applications are processed on a rolling basis. *Application fee:* $100. Electronic applications accepted. *Application Contact:* Jennifer Thorndyke, Director of Admissions for the College of Nursing, 312-563-7526, E-mail: jennifer_thorndyke@rush.edu. *Dean,* Dr. Marquis Foreman, 312-942-7117, E-mail: marquis_d_foreman@rush.edu.

Graduate College *Program availability:* Part-time. Offers physiology (PhD). Electronic applications accepted.

Division of Anatomy and Cell Biology Offers anatomy and cell biology (MS, PhD). Electronic applications accepted.

Division of Biochemistry Offers biochemistry (MS, PhD). Electronic applications accepted.

Division of Immunology and Microbiology Offers immunology (MS, PhD); microbiology (PhD); virology (MS, PhD).

Division of Medical Physics Offers medical physics (MS, PhD). Electronic applications accepted.

Division of Neuroscience Offers neuroscience (MS, PhD). Electronic applications accepted.

Division of Pharmacology Offers clinical research (MS); pharmacology (MS, PhD).

Rush Medical College Students: 515 full-time (255 women); includes 211 minority (27 Black or African American, non-Hispanic/Latino; 134 Asian, non-Hispanic/Latino; 33 Hispanic/Latino; 17 Two or more races, non-Hispanic/Latino). Average age 26. 7,013 applicants, 5% accepted, 136 enrolled. *Faculty:* 698 full-time (333 women), 174 part-time/adjunct (66 women). Expenses: Contact institution. *Financial support:* Federal Work-Study, institutionally sponsored loans, and scholarships/grants available. Financial award application deadline: 3/1; financial award applicants required to submit FAFSA. In 2016, 130 doctorates awarded. Offers medicine (MD). *Application deadline:* For fall admission, 11/1 for domestic students. Applications are processed on a rolling basis. *Application fee:* $100. Electronic applications accepted. *Application Contact:* E-mail: rmc_admissions@rush.edu. *Assistant Dean, Admissions and Recruitment,* Dr. Cynthia E. Boyd, E-mail: rmc_admissions@rush.edu.

RUTGERS UNIVERSITY–CAMDEN, Camden, NJ 08102-1401

General Information State-supported, coed, university. *Graduate housing:* Rooms and/or apartments available to single and married students.

GRADUATE UNITS

Graduate School of Arts and Sciences *Program availability:* Part-time, evening/weekend. Offers American and public history (MA); biology (MS); chemistry (MS); childhood studies (MA); computational and integrative biology (MS, PhD); computer science (MS); creative writing (MFA); criminal justice (MA); education policy and leadership (MPA); English (MA); industrial mathematics (MBS); industrial/applied mathematics (MS); international public service and development (MPA); liberal studies (MALS); mathematical computer science (MS); physical therapy (DPT); psychology (MA); public management (MPA); pure mathematics (MS); teaching in mathematical sciences (MS). Electronic applications accepted.

School of Business *Program availability:* Part-time, evening/weekend. Offers business (MBA). Electronic applications accepted.

School of Law *Program availability:* Part-time, evening/weekend. Offers law (JD). JD/MCRP, JD/MA, JD/MPA, JD/MSW, JD/MS offered jointly with Rutgers, The State University of New Jersey, New Brunswick; JD/MPA, JD/MD, JD/DO with University of Medicine and Dentistry of New Jersey. Electronic applications accepted.

School of Nursing–Camden Offers adult gerontology primary care nurse practitioner (DNP); family nurse practitioner (DNP).

School of Public Health *Program availability:* Part-time, evening/weekend. Offers general public health (Certificate); health systems and policy (MPH). Electronic applications accepted.

RUTGERS UNIVERSITY–NEWARK, Newark, NJ 07102

General Information State-supported, coed, university. CGS member. *Graduate housing:* Room and/or apartments available to single students; on-campus housing not available to married students. Housing application deadline: 5/15.

GRADUATE UNITS

Graduate School *Program availability:* Part-time, evening/weekend. Offers accounting (PhD); accounting information systems (PhD); American political system (MA); American studies (MA, PhD); analytical chemistry (MS, PhD); applied physics (MS, PhD); biochemistry (MS, PhD); biology (MS, PhD); cognitive neuroscience (PhD); cognitive science (PhD); computational biology (MS); computer information systems (PhD); creative writing (MFA); economics (MA); English (MA); environmental geology (MS); environmental science (MS, PhD); finance (PhD); health care administration (MPA); history (MA, MAT); human resources administration (MPA); information technology (PhD); inorganic chemistry (MS, PhD); international business (PhD); international relations (MA); jazz history and research (MA); management science (PhD); marketing (PhD); mathematical sciences (PhD); organic chemistry (MS, PhD); organization management (PhD); perception (PhD); physical chemistry (MS, PhD); psychobiology (PhD); public administration (PhD); public management (MPA); public policy analysis (MPA); social cognition (PhD); urban systems (PhD); urban systems and issues (MPA). Electronic applications accepted.

Division of Global Affairs *Program availability:* Part-time, evening/weekend. Offers global affairs (MS, PhD). Electronic applications accepted.

Graduate School of Biomedical Sciences *Program availability:* Part-time, evening/weekend. Offers biochemistry and molecular biology (MS, PhD); biodefense (Certificate); biomedical engineering (PhD); biomedical sciences (interdisciplinary) (PhD); biomedical sciences (multidisciplinary) (PhD); cell biology and molecular medicine (PhD); cellular biology, neuroscience and physiology (PhD); infection, immunity and inflammation (PhD); integrative neuroscience (PhD); microbiology and molecular genetics (PhD); molecular biology, genetics and cancer (PhD); molecular pathology and immunology (PhD); neuroscience (Certificate); pharmacological sciences (Certificate); pharmacology and physiology (PhD); stem cell (Certificate). PhD in biomedical engineering offered jointly with New Jersey Institute of Technology. Electronic applications accepted.

School of Criminal Justice Offers criminal justice (MA, PhD). Electronic applications accepted.

New Jersey Medical School Offers medicine (MD). Electronic applications accepted.

Rutgers Business School–Newark and New Brunswick *Program availability:* Part-time, evening/weekend. Offers accountancy (M Accy); accounting (PhD); accounting information systems (PhD); business (MBA, MFA, MHSM, MIT, MRE); business administration (MBA); business of fashion (MBA); economics (PhD); finance (PhD); financial analysis (MFA); healthcare services management (MHSM); individualized study (PhD); information technology (PhD); international business (PhD); management science (PhD); marketing science (PhD); organizational management (PhD); pharmaceutical management (MBA); professional accounting (MBA); quantitative finance (MQF); real estate and logistics (MRE); science, technology and management (PhD); supply chain management (PhD). Electronic applications accepted.

Rutgers School of Dental Medicine Offers dental science (MS); dentistry (DMD); endodontics (Certificate); oral medicine (Certificate); orthodontics (Certificate); pediatric dentistry (Certificate); periodontics (Certificate); prosthodontics (Certificate). DMD/MPH offered jointly with New Jersey Institute of Technology, Rutgers, The State University of New Jersey, Camden. Electronic applications accepted.

Rutgers School of Nursing *Program availability:* Part-time. Offers adult health (MSN); adult occupational health (MSN); advanced practice nursing (MSN, Post Master's Certificate); family nurse practitioner (MSN); nurse anesthesia (MSN); nursing (MSN); nursing informatics (MSN); urban health (PhD); women's health practitioner (MSN). Electronic applications accepted.

School of Health Related Professions *Program availability:* Part-time. Offers biomedical informatics (MS, PhD); clinical laboratory sciences (MS); clinical nutrition (MS, DCN); community counseling (MS); dietetic internship (Certificate); health care informatics (Certificate); health care management (MS); health related professions (MS, DCN, DPT, PhD, Certificate); health sciences (MS); nutrition (PhD); physical

therapy (DPT); physician assistant (MS); psychiatric rehabilitation (MS, PhD); radiologist assistant (MS); rehabilitation counseling (MS). Electronic applications accepted.

School of Law *Program availability:* Part-time, evening/weekend. Offers law (JD). JD/MCRP, JD/PhD offered jointly with Rutgers, The State University of New Jersey, New Brunswick.

School of Public Health *Program availability:* Part-time, evening/weekend. Offers clinical epidemiology (Certificate); dental public health (MPH); general public health (Certificate); public policy and oral health services administration (Certificate); quantitative methods (MPH); urban health (MPH). Electronic applications accepted.

RUTGERS UNIVERSITY–NEW BRUNSWICK, Piscataway, NJ 08854-8097

General Information State-supported, coed, university. CGS member. *Graduate housing:* Rooms and/or apartments available to single and married students.

GRADUATE UNITS

Edward J. Bloustein School of Planning and Public Policy *Program availability:* Part-time, evening/weekend, online learning. Offers planning and public policy (MCRP, MCRS, MPAP, MPH, MPP, Dr PH, PhD); public policy (MPAP, MPP); urban planning and policy development (MCRP, MCRS). Electronic applications accepted.

Ernest Mario School of Pharmacy Offers medicinal chemistry (MS, PhD); pharmaceutical science (MS, PhD); pharmacy (Pharm D). Electronic applications accepted.

Graduate School-New Brunswick *Program availability:* Part-time, evening/weekend, online learning. Offers African-American history (PhD); air pollution and resources (MS, PhD); American politics (PhD); anthropology (PhD); applied mathematics (MS, PhD); applied statistics (MS); aquatic biology (MS, PhD); aquatic chemistry (MS, PhD); art history (MA, PhD); astronomy (MS, PhD); atmospheric science (MS, PhD); behavioral neuroscience (PhD); bilingualism and second language acquisition (MA, PhD); biochemistry (PhD); biological chemistry (MS, PhD); biophysics (PhD); biostatistics (MS); cell and developmental biology (MS, PhD); chemical and biochemical engineering (MS, PhD); chemistry and physics of aerosol and hydrosol systems (MS, PhD); civil and environmental engineering (MS, PhD); classics (MA, MAT, PhD); clinical psychology (PhD); cognitive psychology (PhD); communications and solid-state electronics (MS, PhD); comparative literature (MA, PhD); comparative politics (PhD); computational biology and molecular biophysics (PhD); computer engineering (MS, PhD); computer science (MS, PhD); condensed matter physics (MS, PhD); control systems (MS, PhD); cultural heritage and preservation studies (MA); curatorial studies (Certificate); data mining (MS); design and control (MS, PhD); digital signal processing (MS, PhD); early American history (PhD); early modern European history (PhD); east Asian history (PhD); East Asian languages and cultures (MA); ecology and evolution (MS, PhD); economics (MA, PhD); elementary particle physics (MS, PhD); endocrinology and animal biosciences (MS, PhD); entomology (MS, PhD); environmental chemistry (MS, PhD); environmental microbiology (MS, PhD); environmental toxicology (MS, PhD); exposure assessment (PhD); fate and effects of pollutants (MS, PhD); fluid mechanics (MS, PhD); food and business economics (MS); food science (M Phil, MS, PhD); French (MA, PhD); French studies (MAT); geography (MA, MS, PhD); geological sciences (MS, PhD); German (MAT, PhD); German literature (MA, PhD); global and comparative history (PhD); historic preservation (Certificate); history (PhD); history of diplomacy and foreign relations (PhD); history of technology, environment and health (PhD); history of the Atlantic cultures and African diaspora (PhD); horticulture and plant technology (MS, PhD); industrial and systems engineering (MS, PhD); industrial-occupational toxicology (MS, PhD); information technology (MS, PhD); inorganic chemistry (MS, PhD); interdisciplinary classical studies and ancient history (MA, PhD); interdisciplinary health psychology (PhD); intermediate energy nuclear physics (MS); international relations (PhD); Italian (MA, PhD); Italian literature and literary criticism (MA); Jewish studies (MA, Certificate); language, literature and culture (MAT); Latin American history (PhD); linguistics (PhD); literatures in English (PhD); manufacturing systems engineering (MS); materials science and engineering (MS, PhD); mathematics (MS, PhD); mechanics (MS, PhD); medieval history (PhD); microbiology and molecular genetics (MS, PhD); modern European history (PhD); molecular and cellular biology (MS, PhD); nineteenth and twentieth century American history (PhD); nuclear physics (MS, PhD); nutritional sciences (MS, PhD); nutritional toxicology (MS, PhD); oceanography (MS, PhD); operations research (PhD); organic chemistry (MS, PhD); organismal and population biology (MS, PhD); pharmaceutical toxicology (MS, PhD); philosophy (PhD); physical chemistry (MS, PhD); physics (MST); plant pathology (MS, PhD); political theory (PhD); pollution prevention and control (MS, PhD); public law (PhD); quality and productivity management (MS); quality and reliability engineering (MS); religious studies (MA, Graduate Certificate); social psychology (PhD); sociology (MA, PhD); solid mechanics (MS, PhD); Spanish (MA, MAT, PhD); Spanish literature (MA, PhD); statistics (MS, PhD); surface science (PhD); theoretical physics (MS, PhD); thermal sciences (MS, PhD); translation (MA); United Nations and global policy studies (MA); water and wastewater treatment (MS, PhD); water resources (MS, PhD); women and politics (PhD); women's and gender history (PhD); women's and gender studies (MA, PhD).

Graduate School of Applied and Professional Psychology Offers applied and professional psychology (Psy M, Psy D); clinical psychology (Psy M, Psy D); school psychology (Psy M, Psy D). Electronic applications accepted.

Graduate School of Biomedical Sciences Offers biochemistry (MS, PhD); biochemistry and molecular biology (MS, PhD); biomedical engineering (MS, PhD); biomedical science (MS); biomedical sciences (MBS, MS, PhD); cellular and molecular pharmacology (MS, PhD); clinical and translational science (MS); environmental sciences/exposure assessment (PhD); exposure science and assessment (PhD); microbiology and molecular genetics (MS, PhD); molecular genetics, microbiology and immunology (MS, PhD); neuroscience (MS, PhD); physiology and integrative biology (MS, PhD); toxicology (PhD). Electronic applications accepted.

Graduate School of Education *Program availability:* Part-time, evening/weekend. Offers college student affairs (Ed M); early childhood/elementary education (Ed M, Ed D); education (Ed M, Ed D, PhD); educational administration and supervision (Ed M, Ed D); educational policy (PhD); educational psychology (PhD); educational statistics, measurement and evaluation (Ed M); English as a second language education (Ed M); English education (Ed M); language education (Ed M, Ed D); learning, cognition and development (Ed M); literacy education (Ed M, Ed D, PhD); mathematics education (Ed M, Ed D, PhD); reading education (Ed M); school counseling and counseling psychology (Ed M); science education (Ed M, Ed D); social and philosophical foundations of education (Ed M, Ed D); social studies education (Ed M, Ed D); special education (Ed M, Ed D). Electronic applications accepted.

Mason Gross School of the Arts *Program availability:* Part-time. Offers acting (MFA); arts (MFA, MM, DMA, AD); collaborative piano (MM, DMA); conducting: choral (MM, DMA); conducting: instrumental (MM, DMA); conducting: orchestral (MM, DMA); design

(MFA); drawing (MFA); jazz studies (MM); music (DMA, AD); music education (MM, DMA); music performance (MM); painting (MFA); playwriting (MFA); sculpture (MFA); stage management (MFA); technical direction (MFA); visual arts (MFA).

Robert Wood Johnson Medical School Offers medicine (MD). Electronic applications accepted.

School of Communication and Information *Program availability:* Part-time, online learning. Offers communication and information (MCIS, MI, MLS, PhD); communication and information studies (MCIS); communication, information and library studies (PhD); information (MI). Electronic applications accepted.

School of Management and Labor Relations *Program availability:* Part-time, evening/weekend. Offers human resource management (MHRM); industrial relations and human resources (PhD); labor and employment relations (MLER). Electronic applications accepted.

School of Public Health *Program availability:* Part-time, evening/weekend. Offers biostatistics (MPH, MS, Dr PH, PhD); clinical epidemiology (Certificate); environmental and occupational health (MPH, Dr PH, PhD, Certificate); epidemiology (MPH, Dr PH, PhD); general public health (Certificate); health education and behavioral science (MPH, Dr PH, PhD); health systems and policy (MPH, PhD); public health (MPH, MS, Dr PH, PhD, Certificate); public health preparedness (Certificate). Electronic applications accepted.

School of Social Work *Program availability:* Part-time. Offers social work (MSW, PhD). Electronic applications accepted.

RYERSON UNIVERSITY, Toronto, ON M5B 2K3, Canada

General Information Province-supported, coed, comprehensive institution. CGS member.

GRADUATE UNITS

School of Graduate Studies Offers photographic preservation and collections management (MA).

Ted Rogers School of Management Offers global business administration (MBA); management (MSM); management of technology and innovation (MBA).

SACRED HEART MAJOR SEMINARY, Detroit, MI 48206-1799

General Information Independent-religious, coed, comprehensive institution. *Graduate housing:* Room or apartments guaranteed to single students; on-campus housing not available to married students. Housing application deadline: 8/1.

GRADUATE UNITS

School of Theology *Program availability:* Part-time, evening/weekend. Offers pastoral studies (MAPS); theology (M Div, MA).

SACRED HEART SCHOOL OF THEOLOGY, Hales Corners, WI 53130-0429

General Information Independent-religious, coed, primarily men, graduate-only institution. *Graduate housing:* Room and/or apartments guaranteed to single students; on-campus housing not available to married students.

GRADUATE UNITS

Graduate and Professional Programs *Program availability:* Part-time. Offers priestly formation (Certificate); theology (M Div, MA).

SACRED HEART UNIVERSITY, Fairfield, CT 06825

General Information Independent-religious, coed, comprehensive institution. *Enrollment:* 8,532 graduate, professional, and undergraduate students; 1,150 full-time matriculated graduate/professional students (734 women), 1,849 part-time matriculated graduate/professional students (1,416 women). *Enrollment by degree level:* 2,365 master's, 235 doctoral, 399 other advanced degrees. *Graduate faculty:* 130 full-time (73 women), 155 part-time/adjunct (91 women). *Tuition:* Part-time $654 per credit hour. *Graduate housing:* On-campus housing not available. *Student services:* Campus employment opportunities, campus safety program, career counseling, exercise/wellness program, free psychological counseling, international student services, low-cost health insurance, multicultural affairs office, services for students with disabilities, teacher training, writing training. *Library facilities:* Ryan Matura Library plus 1 other. *Collection:* Books: 122,977 (physical), 183,824 (digital/electronic); Serial titles: 436 (physical), 51,535 (digital/electronic); Databases: 132. Weekly public service hours: 119; students can reserve study rooms.

Computer facilities: 424 computers available on campus for general student use. A campuswide network can be accessed from student residence rooms and from off campus. Online class registration is available. Website: http://www.sacredheart.edu/

General Application Contact: William Sweeney, Director of Graduate Admissions Operations, 203-365-4727, E-mail: gradstudies@sacredheart.edu.

GRADUATE PROGRAMS

Graduate Programs Students: 1,150 full-time (734 women), 1,849 part-time (1,416 women); includes 493 minority (187 Black or African American, non-Hispanic/Latino; 6 American Indian or Alaska Native, non-Hispanic/Latino; 75 Asian, non-Hispanic/Latino; 205 Hispanic/Latino; 2 Native Hawaiian or other Pacific Islander, non-Hispanic/Latino; 18 Two or more races, non-Hispanic/Latino), 473 international. Average age 32. 4,320 applicants, 48% accepted, 874 enrolled. *Faculty:* 134 full-time (74 women), 158 part-time/adjunct (92 women). Expenses: Contact institution. *Financial support:* Unspecified assistantships available. Financial award applicants required to submit FAFSA. In 2016, 1,101 master's, 74 doctorates, 92 other advanced degrees awarded. *Program availability:* Part-time, evening/weekend, online learning. *Application deadline:* Applications are processed on a rolling basis. *Application fee:* $75. Electronic applications accepted. *Application Contact:* William Sweeney, Director of Graduate Admissions Operations, 203-365-4827, E-mail: sweeneyw@sacredheart.edu. *Acting Provost and Vice President for Academic Affairs,* Rupendra Paliwal, 203-371-7851, E-mail: paliwalr@sacredheart.edu.

College of Arts and Sciences Students: 388 full-time (172 women), 311 part-time (159 women); includes 103 minority (49 Black or African American, non-Hispanic/Latino; 5 Asian, non-Hispanic/Latino; 43 Hispanic/Latino; 6 Two or more races, non-Hispanic/Latino), 318 international. Average age 27. 1,479 applicants, 69% accepted, 194 enrolled. *Faculty:* 34 full-time (13 women), 27 part-time/adjunct (6 women). Expenses: Contact institution. *Financial support:* Unspecified assistantships available. Financial award applicants required to submit FAFSA. In 2016, 445 master's awarded. *Program availability:* Part-time, evening/weekend, online learning. Offers applied psychology (MS); arts and sciences (MA, MA Comm, MAT, MS, MSW, PhD); bioinformatics (MS); biology (MS, PhD); chemistry (MS); computer science (MS); computer science gaming (MS); corporate communications and public relations (MA Comm); criminal justice (MA); cybersecurity (MS); digital multimedia journalism

(MA Comm); digital multimedia production (MA Comm); film and television production (MA); information technology (MS); media literacy and digital culture (MA); molecular biology (MS); social work (MSW); sports communication and media (MA). *Application deadline:* Applications are processed on a rolling basis. *Application fee:* $75. Electronic applications accepted. *Application Contact:* William Sweeney, Director of Graduate Admissions Operations, 203-365-4827, E-mail: gradstudies@sacredheart.edu. *Dean of College of Arts and Sciences,* Robin Cautin, 203-396-8020, E-mail: cautinr@sacredheart.edu.

College of Health Professions Students: 423 full-time (333 women), 31 part-time (24 women); includes 71 minority (18 Black or African American, non-Hispanic/Latino; 1 American Indian or Alaska Native, non-Hispanic/Latino; 21 Asian, non-Hispanic/Latino; 26 Hispanic/Latino; 1 Native Hawaiian or other Pacific Islander, non-Hispanic/Latino; 4 Two or more races, non-Hispanic/Latino), 41 international. Average age 25. 2,091 applicants, 22% accepted, 212 enrolled. *Faculty:* 37 full-time (24 women), 51 part-time/adjunct (41 women). Expenses: Contact institution. *Financial support:* Research assistantships and unspecified assistantships available. Financial award applicants required to submit FAFSA. In 2016, 93 master's, 62 doctorates awarded. *Program availability:* Part-time, evening/weekend, online learning. Offers exercise science and nutrition (MS); health professions (MPAS, MS, MSOT, DPT); health science and leadership (MS); occupational therapy (MSOT); physical therapy (DPT); physician assistant studies (MPAS); speech-language pathology (MS). *Application deadline:* Applications are processed on a rolling basis. *Application fee:* $75. Electronic applications accepted. *Application Contact:* William Sweeney, Director of Graduate Admissions Operations, 203-365-4827, Fax: 203-365-4732, E-mail: gradstudies@sacredheart.edu. *Dean,* Dr. Patricia Walker, 203-396-8024, Fax: 203-396-8075, E-mail: walkerp@sacredheart.edu.

College of Nursing Students: 16 full-time (14 women), 777 part-time (723 women); includes 155 minority (63 Black or African American, non-Hispanic/Latino; 3 American Indian or Alaska Native, non-Hispanic/Latino; 38 Asian, non-Hispanic/Latino; 39 Hispanic/Latino; 1 Native Hawaiian or other Pacific Islander, non-Hispanic/Latino; 11 Two or more races, non-Hispanic/Latino). Average age 37. 145 applicants, 42% accepted, 41 enrolled. *Faculty:* 17 full-time (all women), 28 part-time/adjunct (24 women). Expenses: Contact institution. *Financial support:* Unspecified assistantships available. Financial award applicants required to submit FAFSA. In 2016, 220 master's, 12 doctorates, 1 other advanced degree awarded. *Program availability:* Part-time, evening/weekend, online learning. Offers clinical (DNP); clinical nurse leader (MSN); family nurse practitioner (MSN, Post-Master's Certificate); leadership (DNP); nursing education (MSN); nursing management and executive leadership (MSN). *Application deadline:* For fall admission, 2/15 for domestic and international students. Applications are processed on a rolling basis. *Application fee:* $75. Electronic applications accepted. *Application Contact:* William Sweeney, Director of Graduate Admissions Operations, 203-365-4716, Fax: 203-365-4732, E-mail: gradstudies@sacredheart.edu. *Dean of Nursing,* Mary Alice Donius, 203-365-4508, E-mail: donium@sacredheart.edu.

Isabelle Farrington College of Education Students: 203 full-time (155 women), 510 part-time (398 women); includes 98 minority (30 Black or African American, non-Hispanic/Latino; 1 American Indian or Alaska Native, non-Hispanic/Latino; 12 Asian, non-Hispanic/Latino; 50 Hispanic/Latino; 5 Two or more races, non-Hispanic/Latino). Average age 34. 306 applicants, 97% accepted, 263 enrolled. *Faculty:* 21 full-time (10 women), 28 part-time/adjunct (14 women). Expenses: Contact institution. *Financial support:* Teaching assistantships with partial tuition reimbursements and unspecified assistantships available. Financial award applicants required to submit FAFSA. In 2016, 241 master's, 91 other advanced degrees awarded. *Program availability:* Part-time, evening/weekend. Offers advanced educational studies for teachers (CAS); advanced studies in administration (Professional Certificate); advanced studies in literacy (Professional Certificate); education (MAT, CAS, Professional Certificate); teaching: education (MAT); TESOL (MAT). *Application deadline:* Applications are processed on a rolling basis. *Application fee:* $75. Electronic applications accepted. *Application Contact:* William Sweeney, Director of Graduate Admissions Operations, 203-365-4827, E-mail: sweeneyw@sacredheart.edu. *Dean,* Dr. Jim Carl, 203-396-8454, Fax: 203-365-7513, E-mail: carlj@sacredheart.edu.

Jack Welch College of Business Students: 120 full-time (60 women), 220 part-time (112 women); includes 88 minority (27 Black or African American, non-Hispanic/Latino; 1 American Indian or Alaska Native, non-Hispanic/Latino; 10 Asian, non-Hispanic/Latino; 47 Hispanic/Latino; 3 Two or more races, non-Hispanic/Latino), 51 international. Average age 31. 299 applicants, 80% accepted, 164 enrolled. *Faculty:* 25 full-time (10 women), 24 part-time/adjunct (7 women). Expenses: Contact institution. *Financial support:* Unspecified assistantships available. Financial award applicants required to submit FAFSA. In 2016, 102 master's awarded. *Program availability:* Part-time, evening/weekend. Offers accounting (MS); administration (MBA, DBA); business (MBA, MS, DBA, Graduate Certificate); digital marketing (MS); finance and investment management (MS); human resource management (MS); marketing (MBA, Graduate Certificate). *Application deadline:* Applications are processed on a rolling basis. *Application fee:* $75. Electronic applications accepted. *Application Contact:* William Sweeney, Director of Graduate Admissions Operations, 203-365-4827, E-mail: sweeneyw@sacredheart.edu. *Dean,* Dr. John Chalykoff, 203-396-8084, Fax: 203-365-7538, E-mail: chalykoffj@sacredheart.edu.

SAGE GRADUATE SCHOOL, Troy, NY 12180-4115

General Information Independent, coed, graduate-only institution. *Enrollment by degree level:* 910 master's, 236 doctoral, 72 other advanced degrees. *Graduate faculty:* 51 full-time (44 women), 70 part-time/adjunct (51 women). *Tuition:* Full-time $12,240; part-time $680 per credit hour. Tuition and fees vary according to degree level and program. *Graduate housing:* Room and/or apartments available on a first-come, first-served basis to single students; on-campus housing not available to married students. Housing application deadline: 5/1. *Student services:* Career counseling, low-cost health insurance. *Library facilities:* James Wheelock Clark Library plus 1 other. *Collection:* Weekly public service hours: 65; students can reserve study rooms. *Research affiliation:* Rensselaer Polytechnic Institute (education), St. Peter's Hospital (health care services), University at Albany, State University of New York (public health, health and the environment), Albany Medical College (health care services), National Center for Adaptive Neurotechnologies (NCAN).

Computer facilities: 452 computers available on campus for general student use. A campuswide network can be accessed. Online class registration is available. Website: http://www.sage.edu/

General Application Contact: Wendy D. Diefendorf, Director of Graduate and Adult Admission, 518-244-2443, Fax: 518-244-6880, E-mail: sgsadm@sage.edu.

GRADUATE UNITS

Esteves School of Education Students: 121 full-time (107 women), 289 part-time (215 women); includes 115 minority (55 Black or African American, non-Hispanic/Latino; 1

American Indian or Alaska Native, non-Hispanic/Latino; 15 Asian, non-Hispanic/Latino; 35 Hispanic/Latino; 9 Two or more races, non-Hispanic/Latino). Average age 33. 475 applicants, 45% accepted, 142 enrolled. *Faculty:* 17 full-time (13 women), 18 part-time/adjunct (12 women). Expenses: Contact institution. *Financial support:* Fellowships, research assistantships, Federal Work-Study, scholarships/grants, tuition waivers (partial), and unspecified assistantships available. Support available to part-time students. Financial award application deadline: 3/1; financial award applicants required to submit FAFSA. In 2016, 135 master's, 26 doctorates, 16 other advanced degrees awarded. *Program availability:* Part-time, evening/weekend. Offers applied behavior analysis and autism (MS, Post Master's Certificate); childhood education/literacy (MS); childhood special education (MS Ed); education (MS, MS Ed, Ed D, Post Master's Certificate); educational leadership (Ed D); literacy (MS Ed); literacy/childhood special education (MS Ed); school counseling (MS, Post Master's Certificate); school health education (MS); special education (MS Ed). *Application deadline:* Applications are processed on a rolling basis. *Application fee:* $40. Electronic applications accepted. *Application Contact:* Wendy D. Diefendorf, Director of Graduate and Adult Admission, 518-244-2443, Fax: 518-244-6880, E-mail: diefew@sage.edu. *Interim Dean, Esteves School of Education,* Dr. John Pelizza, 518-244-2051, Fax: 518-244-2334, E-mail: pelizj@sage.edu.

School of Health Sciences Students: 314 full-time (264 women), 324 part-time (294 women); includes 111 minority (43 Black or African American, non-Hispanic/Latino; 3 American Indian or Alaska Native, non-Hispanic/Latino; 24 Asian, non-Hispanic/Latino; 21 Hispanic/Latino; 20 Two or more races, non-Hispanic/Latino), 4 international. Average age 30. 1,050 applicants, 24% accepted, 177 enrolled. *Faculty:* 31 full-time (29 women), 39 part-time/adjunct (35 women). Expenses: Contact institution. *Financial support:* Fellowships, research assistantships, Federal Work-Study, scholarships/grants, and unspecified assistantships available. Support available to part-time students. Financial award application deadline: 3/1; financial award applicants required to submit FAFSA. In 2016, 121 master's, 40 doctorates, 40 other advanced degrees awarded. *Program availability:* Part-time, evening/weekend. Offers adult gerontology nurse practitioner (MS, Certificate); applied nutrition (MS); community psychology (MA); counseling and community psychology (MA); dietetic internship (Certificate); education and leadership (DNS); family nurse practitioner (MS); forensic mental health (MS, Certificate); health sciences (MA, MS, DNS, DPT, Certificate, Post Master's Certificate, Postbaccalaureate Certificate); nursing (MS, DNS, Certificate, Post Master's Certificate); nutrition (Certificate); occupational therapy (DPT); physical therapy (DPT); psychiatric mental health nurse practitioner (MS, Post Master's Certificate); psychology (MA, Certificate). *Application deadline:* Applications are processed on a rolling basis. *Application fee:* $40. Electronic applications accepted. *Application Contact:* Wendy D. Diefendorf, Director of Graduate and Adult Admission, 518-244-2443, Fax: 518-244-6880, E-mail: diefew@sage.edu. *Dean, School of Health Sciences,* Dr. Theresa Hand, 518-244-2264, Fax: 518-244-4571, E-mail: handt@sage.edu.

School of Management Students: 41 full-time (all women), 129 part-time (80 women); includes 43 minority (16 Black or African American, non-Hispanic/Latino; 1 American Indian or Alaska Native, non-Hispanic/Latino; 11 Asian, non-Hispanic/Latino; 5 Hispanic/Latino; 10 Two or more races, non-Hispanic/Latino), 8 international. Average age 32. 156 applicants, 46% accepted, 49 enrolled. *Faculty:* 3 full-time (2 women), 13 part-time/adjunct (4 women). Expenses: Contact institution. *Financial support:* Fellowships, research assistantships, Federal Work-Study, scholarships/grants, and unspecified assistantships available. Support available to part-time students. Financial award application deadline: 3/1; financial award applicants required to submit FAFSA. In 2016, 47 master's awarded. *Program availability:* Part-time, evening/weekend. Offers business administration (MBA); gerontology (MS); management (MBA, MS); organization management (MS). *Application deadline:* Applications are processed on a rolling basis. *Application fee:* $40. Electronic applications accepted. *Application Contact:* Wendy D. Diefendorf, Director of Graduate and Adult Admission, 518-244-2443, Fax: 518-244-6880, E-mail: diefew@sage.edu. *Dean, School of Management,* Dr. Kimberly Fredericks, 518-292-1782, Fax: 518-292-1964, E-mail: fredek1@sage.edu.

SAGINAW VALLEY STATE UNIVERSITY, University Center, MI 48710

General Information State-supported, coed, comprehensive institution. *Enrollment:* 9,165 graduate, professional, and undergraduate students; 236 full-time matriculated graduate/professional students (166 women), 532 part-time matriculated graduate/professional students (395 women). *Enrollment by degree level:* 720 master's, 44 doctoral, 4 other advanced degrees. *Graduate faculty:* 47 full-time (30 women), 34 part-time/adjunct (23 women). Tuition, state resident: full-time $9652; part-time $536 per credit hour. Tuition, nonresident: full-time $12,259; part-time $1022 per credit hour. *Required fees:* $263; $14.60 per credit hour. Tuition and fees vary according to degree level. *Graduate housing:* Room and/or apartments available on a first-come, first-served basis to single students; on-campus housing not available to married students. *Student services:* Campus employment opportunities, career counseling, exercise/wellness program, free psychological counseling, international student services, multicultural affairs office, services for students with disabilities, writing training. *Library facilities:* Zahnow Library. *Collection:* Books: 217,900 (physical), 107,479 (digital/electronic); Serial titles: 127 (physical), 50,164 (digital/electronic); Databases: 63. Weekly public service hours: 95.

Computer facilities: Computer purchase and lease plans are available. 424 computers available on campus for general student use. A campuswide network can be accessed from student residence rooms and from off campus. Online class registration is available.
Website: http://www.svsu.edu/

General Application Contact: Jenna Briggs, Director, Graduate and International Admissions, 989-964-6096, Fax: 989-964-2788, E-mail: gradadm@svsu.edu.

GRADUATE UNITS

College of Arts and Behavioral Sciences Students: 40 full-time (22 women), 32 part-time (21 women); includes 11 minority (8 Black or African American, non-Hispanic/Latino; 2 Asian, non-Hispanic/Latino; 1 Two or more races, non-Hispanic/Latino), 25 international. Average age 29. 47 applicants, 68% accepted, 24 enrolled. *Faculty:* 7 full-time (2 women), 4 part-time/adjunct (1 woman). Expenses: Contact institution. *Financial support:* Federal Work-Study and scholarships/grants available. Support available to part-time students. Financial award applicants required to submit FAFSA. In 2016, 36 master's awarded. *Program availability:* Part-time, evening/weekend. Offers arts and behavioral sciences (MA); communication and media administration (MA); public administration (MA). *Application deadline:* For fall admission, 7/15 for international students; for winter admission, 11/15 for international students; for spring admission, 4/15 for international students. Applications are processed on a rolling basis. *Application fee:* $30 ($90 for international students). Electronic applications accepted. *Application Contact:* Jenna Briggs, Director, Graduate and International Admissions, 989-964-6096, E-mail: gradadm@svsu.edu. *Interim Dean,* Dr. Marc Peretz, 989-964-4062, Fax: 989-964-7232, E-mail: mhp@svsu.edu.

College of Business and Management Students: 29 full-time (8 women), 37 part-time (13 women); includes 3 minority (2 Black or African American, non-Hispanic/Latino; 1 Asian, non-Hispanic/Latino), 36 international. Average age 28. 53 applicants, 51% accepted, 12 enrolled. *Faculty:* 10 full-time (3 women). Expenses: Contact institution. *Financial support:* Federal Work-Study and scholarships/grants available. Support available to part-time students. Financial award application deadline: 4/1; financial award applicants required to submit FAFSA. In 2016, 48 master's awarded. *Program availability:* Part-time, evening/weekend, online only, 100% online, blended/hybrid learning. Offers business administration (MBA); business and management (MBA). *Application deadline:* For fall admission, 7/15 for international students; for winter admission, 11/15 for international students; for spring admission, 4/15 for international students. Applications are processed on a rolling basis. *Application fee:* $30 ($90 for international students). Electronic applications accepted. *Application Contact:* Jenna Briggs, Director, Graduate and International Admissions, 989-964-6096, Fax: 989-964-2788, E-mail: gradadm@svsu.edu. *MBA Program Coordinator,* Dr. Mark McCartney, 989-964-4064.

College of Education Students: 15 full-time (12 women), 233 part-time (188 women); includes 17 minority (8 Black or African American, non-Hispanic/Latino; 6 Hispanic/Latino; 3 Two or more races, non-Hispanic/Latino), 5 international. Average age 34. 83 applicants, 89% accepted, 47 enrolled. *Faculty:* 12 full-time (9 women), 23 part-time/adjunct (17 women). Expenses: Contact institution. *Financial support:* Federal Work-Study and scholarships/grants available. Support available to part-time students. Financial award applicants required to submit FAFSA. In 2016, 143 master's, 24 other advanced degrees awarded. *Program availability:* Part-time, evening/weekend, online learning. Offers e-learning (MA); early childhood education (MAT); education (M Ed, MA, MAT, Ed S); educational leadership (M Ed, Ed S); elementary classroom teaching (MAT); instructional technology (MA); K-12 literacy specialist (MAT); middle school classroom teaching (MAT); natural science teaching (MAT); reading education (MAT); secondary classroom teaching (MAT); special education (MAT); teaching Chinese as a foreign language (MAT). *Application deadline:* For fall admission, 7/15 for international students; for winter admission, 11/15 for international students; for spring admission, 4/15 for international students. Applications are processed on a rolling basis. *Application fee:* $30 ($90 for international students). Electronic applications accepted. *Application Contact:* Jenna Briggs, Director, Graduate and International Admissions, 989-964-6096, Fax: 989-964-2788, E-mail: gradadm@svsu.edu. *Dean,* Dr. Craig Douglas, 989-964-4057, Fax: 989-964-4563, E-mail: coeconnect@svsu.edu.

College of Health and Human Services Students: 151 full-time (124 women), 226 part-time (171 women); includes 34 minority (11 Black or African American, non-Hispanic/Latino; 6 Asian, non-Hispanic/Latino; 8 Two or more races, non-Hispanic/Latino), 11 international. Average age 30. 109 applicants, 69% accepted, 57 enrolled. *Faculty:* 17 full-time (16 women), 8 part-time/adjunct (6 women). Expenses: Contact institution. *Financial support:* Federal Work-Study and scholarships/grants available. Support available to part-time students. Financial award application deadline: 4/1; financial award applicants required to submit FAFSA. In 2016, 96 master's awarded. *Program availability:* Part-time, evening/weekend. Offers clinical nurse specialist (MSN); health and human services (MS, MSN, MSOT, DNP); health leadership (MS); health system nurse specialist (MSN); nurse practitioner (MSN, DNP); nursing (MSN); occupational therapy (MSOT). *Application deadline:* For fall admission, 7/15 for international students; for winter admission, 11/15 for international students; for spring admission, 4/15 for international students. Applications are processed on a rolling basis. *Application fee:* $30 ($90 for international students). Electronic applications accepted. *Application Contact:* Jenna Briggs, Director, Graduate and International Admissions, 989-964-6096, Fax: 989-964-2788, E-mail: gradadm@svsu.edu. *Dean,* Dr. Judith Ruland, 989-964-4145, Fax: 989-964-4024, E-mail: jruland@svsu.edu.

College of Science, Engineering, and Technology Students: 1 full-time (0 women), 4 part-time (2 women), 2 international. Average age 31. 33 applicants, 12% accepted, 1 enrolled. *Faculty:* 2 full-time (0 women). Expenses: Contact institution. *Financial support:* Federal Work-Study and scholarships/grants available. Support available to part-time students. Financial award application deadline: 4/1; financial award applicants required to submit FAFSA. *Program availability:* Part-time, evening/weekend. Offers science, engineering, and technology (MS). *Application deadline:* For fall admission, 7/15 for international students; for winter admission, 11/15 for international students; for spring admission, 4/15 for international students. Applications are processed on a rolling basis. *Application fee:* $30 ($90 for international students). Electronic applications accepted. *Application Contact:* Jenna Briggs, Director, Graduate and International Admissions, 989-964-6096, Fax: 989-964-2788, E-mail: gradadm@svsu.edu. *Program Coordinator,* Dr. Robert Tuttle, 989-964-4144, Fax: 989-964-2717.

ST. AMBROSE UNIVERSITY, Davenport, IA 52803-2898

General Information Independent-religious, coed, comprehensive institution. CGS member. *Graduate housing:* Room and/or apartments available on a first-come, first-served basis to single students; on-campus housing not available to married students. Housing application deadline: 3/1.

GRADUATE UNITS

College of Arts and Sciences *Program availability:* Part-time, evening/weekend. Offers arts and sciences (MCJ, MP Th, MSITM); criminal justice (MCJ); information technology management (MSITM); juvenile justice education (MCJ); pastoral theology (MP Th). Electronic applications accepted.

College of Business *Program availability:* Part-time, evening/weekend. Offers accounting (MAC); business (MAC, MBA, MOL, DBA); business administration (DBA); health care (MBA); human resources (MBA); organizational leadership (MOL). Electronic applications accepted.

College of Education and Health Sciences *Program availability:* Part-time, evening/weekend, online learning. Offers education and health sciences (M Ed, MEA, MOT, MSLP, MSN, MSW, DPT); educational administration (MEA); nursing (MSN); occupational therapy (MOT); physical therapy (DPT); social work (MSW); special education (M Ed); speech-language pathology (MSLP); teaching (M Ed). Electronic applications accepted.

ST. ANDREW'S COLLEGE, Saskatoon, SK S7N 0W3, Canada

General Information Independent-religious, coed, graduate-only institution.

GRADUATE UNITS

Graduate Programs in Theology Offers theology (M Div, MTS, STM, D Min, Diploma).

ST. ANDREW'S COLLEGE IN WINNIPEG, Winnipeg, MB R3T 2M7, Canada

General Information Independent-religious, coed, primarily men, graduate-only institution. *Graduate housing:* Rooms and/or apartments available to single and married students. Housing application deadline: 7/31.

GRADUATE UNITS

Graduate Programs Offers theology (M Div).

SAINT ANTHONY COLLEGE OF NURSING, Rockford, IL 61108

General Information Independent-religious, coed, primarily women, upper-level institution.

GRADUATE UNITS

Graduate Program *Program availability:* Part-time. Offers nursing (MSN).

ST. AUGUSTINE'S SEMINARY OF TORONTO, Scarborough, ON M1M 1M3, Canada

General Information Independent-religious, coed, primarily men, graduate-only institution. *Graduate housing:* On-campus housing not available.

GRADUATE UNITS

Graduate and Professional Programs *Program availability:* Part-time, evening/weekend. Offers divinity (M Div); lay ministry (Diploma); religious education (MRE); theological studies (MTS, Diploma).

ST. BERNARD'S SCHOOL OF THEOLOGY AND MINISTRY, Rochester, NY 14618

General Information Independent-religious, coed, graduate-only institution. *Enrollment by degree level:* 96 master's, 5 other advanced degrees. *Graduate faculty:* 4 full-time (3 women), 4 part-time/adjunct (1 woman). *Tuition:* Full-time $10,644; part-time $3548 per year. *Required fees:* $40 per semester. *Graduate housing:* On-campus housing not available. *Student services:* Services for students with disabilities, writing training. *Library facilities:* Rush Rhees Library at University of Rochester plus 1 other. *Research affiliation:* Colgate Rochester Crozer Divinity School.

Computer facilities: 3 computers available on campus for general student use. A campuswide network can be accessed. Online class registration is available. Website: http://www.stbernards.edu/

General Application Contact: Mark R. Capellazzi, Director of Recruitment and Financial Aid, 585-271-3657 Ext. 289, Fax: 585-271-2045, E-mail: admissions@ stbernards.edu.

GRADUATE UNITS

Graduate and Professional Programs Students: 1 (woman) full-time, 102 part-time (59 women); includes 6 minority (1 Black or African American, non-Hispanic/Latino; 3 Asian, non-Hispanic/Latino; 2 Hispanic/Latino). *Faculty:* 4 full-time (3 women), 4 part-time/adjunct (1 woman). *Expenses:* Contact institution. *Financial support:* In 2016–17, 30 students received support. Fellowships, research assistantships, teaching assistantships, career-related internships or fieldwork, scholarships/grants, and tuition waivers (partial) available. Support available to part-time students. *Financial award application deadline:* 4/1; financial award applicants required to submit FAFSA. *Program availability:* Part-time, evening/weekend. Offers pastoral studies (MA, Certificate); theological studies (MA); theology (M Div). *Application deadline:* Applications are processed on a rolling basis. *Application fee:* $75. *Application Contact:* Mark R. Capellazzi, Director of Recruitment and Financial Aid, 585-271-3657 Ext. 289, Fax: 585-271-2045, E-mail: admissions@stbernards.edu. *President,* Rev. George Heyman, 585-271-3657 Ext. 292, Fax: 585-271-2045, E-mail: george.heyman@stbernards.edu.

ST. BONAVENTURE UNIVERSITY, St. Bonaventure, NY 14778-2284

General Information Independent-religious, coed, comprehensive institution. CGS member. *Enrollment:* 2,052 graduate, professional, and undergraduate students; 186 full-time matriculated graduate/professional students (110 women), 194 part-time matriculated graduate/professional students (126 women). *Enrollment by degree level:* 361 master's, 19 other advanced degrees. *Graduate faculty:* 35 full-time (16 women), 30 part-time (21 women). *Tuition:* Full-time $13,194; part-time $733 per credit. One-time fee: $100. *Graduate housing:* Room and/or apartments available on a first-come, first-served basis to single students; on-campus housing not available to married students. Typical cost: $6031 per year ($11,906 including board). Room and board charges vary according to board plan. Housing application deadline: 3/19. *Student services:* Career counseling, international student services, low-cost health insurance, multicultural affairs office. *Library facilities:* Friedsam Memorial Library. *Collection:* Books: 369,279 (physical), 1.6 million (digital/electronic); Serial titles: 253 (physical), 269,989 (digital/electronic); Databases: 64. Weekly public service hours: 109; students can reserve study rooms.

Computer facilities: 300 computers available on campus for general student use. A campuswide network can be accessed from student residence rooms and from off campus. Online class registration is available. Website: http://www.sbu.edu/

General Application Contact: Bruce Campbell, Director of Graduate Admissions, 716-375-2429, Fax: 716-375-4015, E-mail: gradsch@sbu.edu.

GRADUATE UNITS

School of Graduate Studies Students: 185 full-time (110 women), 195 part-time (126 women); includes 47 minority (16 Black or African American, non-Hispanic/Latino; 3 American Indian or Alaska Native, non-Hispanic/Latino; 6 Asian, non-Hispanic/Latino; 16 Hispanic/Latino; 6 Two or more races, non-Hispanic/Latino), 9 international. Average age 29. 316 applicants, 79% accepted, 173 enrolled. *Faculty:* 35 full-time (16 women), 30 part-time/adjunct (21 women). *Expenses:* Contact institution. *Financial support:* Unspecified assistantships available. Financial award application deadline: 4/15; financial award applicants required to submit FAFSA. In 2016, 161 master's, 12 other advanced degrees awarded. *Program availability:* Part-time, evening/weekend, 100% online, blended/hybrid learning. *Application deadline:* For fall admission, 3/15 priority date for domestic students, 2/1 priority date for international students; for spring admission, 10/15 priority date for domestic students, 7/1 priority date for international students. Applications are processed on a rolling basis. *Application fee:* $0. Electronic applications accepted. *Application Contact:* Bruce Campbell, Director of Graduate Admissions, 716-375-2429, Fax: 716-375-4015, E-mail: gradsch@sbu.edu. *Dean,* Dr. Nancy Casey, 716-375-2394, Fax: 716-375-2360, E-mail: ncasey@sbu.edu.

Jandoli School of Communication Students: 33 full-time (18 women), 44 part-time (30 women); includes 15 minority (6 Black or African American, non-Hispanic/Latino; 1 Asian, non-Hispanic/Latino; 7 Hispanic/Latino; 1 Two or more races, non-

Hispanic/Latino), 4 international. Average age 31. 88 applicants, 78% accepted, 42 enrolled. *Faculty:* 6 full-time (3 women), 8 part-time/adjunct (7 women). Expenses: Contact institution. *Financial support:* Federal Work-Study, scholarships/grants, health care benefits, and unspecified assistantships available. Support available to part-time students. Financial award application deadline: 4/15; financial award applicants required to submit FAFSA. In 2016, 37 master's awarded. *Program availability:* Part-time, evening/weekend, 100% online. Offers communication (MA); integrated marketing communications (MA); strategic leadership (MA). *Application deadline:* For fall admission, 6/15 priority date for domestic students, 2/1 priority date for international students; for spring admission, 10/15 priority date for domestic students, 7/1 priority date for international students. Applications are processed on a rolling basis. *Application fee:* $0. Electronic applications accepted. *Application Contact:* Bruce Campbell, Director of Graduate Admissions, 716-375-2429, Fax: 716-375-4015, E-mail: gradsch@sbu.edu. *Dean,* Dr. Pauline Hoffmann, 716-375-2578, Fax: 716-375-2588, E-mail: hoffmann@sbu.edu.

School of Business Students: 60 full-time (19 women), 58 part-time (29 women); includes 19 minority (4 Black or African American, non-Hispanic/Latino; 3 American Indian or Alaska Native, non-Hispanic/Latino; 4 Asian, non-Hispanic/Latino; 7 Hispanic/Latino; 1 Two or more races, non-Hispanic/Latino), 3 international. Average age 28. 123 applicants, 84% accepted, 73 enrolled. *Faculty:* 6 full-time (1 woman), 14 part-time/adjunct (4 women). Expenses: Contact institution. *Financial support:* Career-related internships or fieldwork, Federal Work-Study, scholarships/grants, health care benefits, and unspecified assistantships available. Support available to part-time students. Financial award application deadline: 4/15; financial award applicants required to submit FAFSA. In 2016, 68 master's awarded. *Program availability:* Part-time, evening/weekend, 100% online. Offers general business (MBA); professional accountancy (MBA). *Application deadline:* For fall admission, 6/15 priority date for domestic students, 2/1 priority date for international students; for spring admission, 11/1 priority date for domestic students, 7/1 priority date for international students. Applications are processed on a rolling basis. *Application fee:* $0. Electronic applications accepted. *Application Contact:* Bruce Campbell, Director of Graduate Admissions, 716-375-2429, Fax: 716-375-4015, E-mail: gradsch@sbu.edu. *Dean,* Dr. Matrecia James, 716-375-2200, Fax: 716-372-2191, E-mail: mjames@ sbu.edu.

School of Education Students: 90 full-time (70 women), 83 part-time (63 women); includes 11 minority (5 Black or African American, non-Hispanic/Latino; 2 Hispanic/Latino; 4 Two or more races, non-Hispanic/Latino), 2 international. Average age 29. 99 applicants, 76% accepted, 54 enrolled. *Faculty:* 12 full-time (8 women), 16 part-time/adjunct (13 women). Expenses: Contact institution. *Financial support:* Career-related internships or fieldwork, Federal Work-Study, scholarships/grants, health care benefits, and unspecified assistantships available. Support available to part-time students. Financial award application deadline: 4/15; financial award applicants required to submit FAFSA. In 2016, 55 master's, 12 Adv Cs awarded. *Program availability:* Part-time, evening/weekend. Offers adolescence education (MS Ed); adolescent literacy 5-12 (MS Ed); childhood literacy B-6 (MS Ed); community mental health counseling (MS Ed); education (MS Ed, Adv C); educational leadership (MS Ed); gifted education (MS Ed, Adv C); gifted education and students with disabilities (MS Ed); rehabilitation counseling (MS Ed); school building leader (Adv C); school counseling (MS Ed); school counselor (Adv C); school district leader (Adv C). *Application deadline:* For fall admission, 6/15 priority date for domestic students, 2/1 priority date for international students; for spring admission, 11/15 priority date for domestic students, 7/1 priority date for international students. Applications are processed on a rolling basis. *Application fee:* $0. Electronic applications accepted. *Application Contact:* Bruce Campbell, Director of Graduate Admissions, 716-375-2429, Fax: 716-375-4015, E-mail: gradsch@sbu.edu. *Interim Dean,* Dr. Nancy Casey, 716-375-2394, Fax: 716-375-2360, E-mail: jezimmer@ sbu.edu.

School of Franciscan Studies *Faculty:* 3 full-time (0 women). Expenses: Contact institution. *Financial support:* Federal Work-Study, scholarships/grants, health care benefits, and unspecified assistantships available. Support available to part-time students. Financial award application deadline: 4/15; financial award applicants required to submit FAFSA. In 2016, 2 other advanced degrees awarded. *Program availability:* Part-time. Offers Franciscan studies (MA, Adv C). *Application deadline:* For fall admission, 3/15 priority date for domestic students, 2/1 priority date for international students. Applications are processed on a rolling basis. *Application fee:* $0. Electronic applications accepted. *Application Contact:* Bruce Campbell, Director of Graduate Admissions, 716-375-2429, Fax: 716-375-4015, E-mail: gradsch@sbu.edu. *Dean,* Fr. David Couturier, OFM, 716-375-2160, E-mail: dcouturi@sbu.edu.

ST. CATHERINE UNIVERSITY, St. Paul, MN 55105

General Information Independent-religious, Undergraduate: women only; graduate: coed, comprehensive institution. CGS member. *Enrollment:* 4,686 graduate, professional, and undergraduate students; 671 full-time matriculated graduate/professional students (583 women), 939 part-time matriculated graduate/professional students (839 women). *Enrollment by degree level:* 1,301 master's, 195 doctoral, 114 other advanced degrees. *Graduate faculty:* 70 full-time (59 women), 57 part-time/adjunct (44 women). Tuition and fees vary according to program. *Graduate housing:* Rooms and/or apartments available on a first-come, first-served basis to single and married students. Typical cost: $9250 per year ($11,310 including board) for single students; $9250 per year ($11,310 including board) for married students. Room and board charges vary according to housing facility selected. Housing application deadline: 5/1. *Student services:* Campus employment opportunities, campus safety program, career counseling, child daycare facilities, exercise/wellness program, free psychological counseling, international student services, low-cost health insurance, multicultural affairs office, services for students with disabilities. *Library facilities:* St. Catherine Library.

Computer facilities: Computer purchase and lease plans are available. A campuswide network can be accessed from student residence rooms and from off campus. Online class registration, transcript are available. Website: http://www.stkate.edu/

General Application Contact: Kristina Sande, Director of Graduate Admissions, 651-690-6933, Fax: 651-690-6064, E-mail: graduate_study@stkate.edu.

GRADUATE UNITS

Graduate Programs *Program availability:* Part-time, evening/weekend, online learning. Offers adult gerontological nurse practitioner (Certificate); catechetical ministry (Certificate); education - initial licensure (MA); education - Montessori education (MA); education–curriculum and instruction (MA); healthcare (MBA); holistic health studies (MA); integrated marketing communications (MBA); library and information science (MLIS); management (MBA); neonatal nurse practitioner (MS); nurse educator (MS); nursing (DNP); nursing: entry-level (MS); occupational therapy (MA, OTD); organizational leadership (MA); pastoral ministry (Certificate); pediatric nurse practitioner (MS); physical therapy (DPT); physician assistant studies (MPAS); social work (MSW, DSW); spiritual direction (Certificate); theology (MA).

SAINT CHARLES BORROMEO SEMINARY, OVERBROOK, Wynnewood, PA 19096

General Information Independent-religious, coed, primarily men, comprehensive institution. *Graduate housing:* Room and/or apartments guaranteed to single students; on-campus housing not available to married students. Housing application deadline: 7/15.

GRADUATE UNITS

Graduate and Professional Programs *Program availability:* Part-time, evening/weekend. Offers Catholic studies (MA).
Division of Theology Offers theology (M Div, MA).

ST. CLOUD STATE UNIVERSITY, St. Cloud, MN 56301-4498

General Information State-supported, coed, comprehensive institution. CGS member. *Graduate housing:* Room and/or apartments available on a first-come, first-served basis to single students; on-campus housing not available to married students. Housing application deadline: 4/15.

GRADUATE UNITS

School of Graduate Studies *Program availability:* Part-time, evening/weekend, online learning. Electronic applications accepted.
College of Liberal Arts Offers conducting and literature (MM); English (MA, MS); history (MA, MS); industrial-organizational psychology (MS); liberal arts (MA, MM, MS); mass communications (MS); music education (MM); piano pedagogy (MM); teaching English as a second language (MA).
College of Science and Engineering Offers applied statistics (MS); biology (MA, MS); computer science (MS); electrical engineering (MS); engineering management (MEM); environmental and technological studies (MS); information assurance (MS); mathematics (MS); mechanical engineering (MS); regulatory affairs and services (MS); science and engineering (MA, MEM, MS). Electronic applications accepted.
College of Social Sciences *Program availability:* Part-time. Offers applied economics (MS); criminal justice (MS); criminal justice administration (MS); cultural resource management archeology (MS); geography and planning (MS); public and nonprofit institutions (MS); public safety executive leadership (MS); social sciences (MA, MS, MSW). Electronic applications accepted.
Herberger Business School *Program availability:* Part-time, evening/weekend. Offers business (MBA, MS); business administration (MBA); information assurance (MS). Electronic applications accepted.
School of Education *Program availability:* Part-time, evening/weekend, online learning. Offers child and family studies (MS); college counseling and student development (MS); curriculum and instruction (MS); developmental/cognitive disabilities (MS); education (MS, Ed D); emotional/behavioral disorders (MS); gifted and talented (MS); higher education administration (MS, Ed D); information media (MS); learning disabilities (MS); rehabilitation counseling (MS); school counseling (MS); social responsibility (MS); special education (MS).
School of Health and Human Services Offers applied behavior analysis (MS); communication sciences and disorders (MS); community counseling (MS); educational administration and leadership (MS); educational leadership and community psychology (Spt); exercise science (MS); gerontology (MS); health and human services (MS, MSW, Spt); marriage and family therapy (MS); social work (MSW); sports management (MS).

ST. EDWARD'S UNIVERSITY, Austin, TX 78704

General Information Independent-religious, coed, comprehensive institution. *Enrollment:* 4,601 graduate, professional, and undergraduate students; 190 full-time matriculated graduate/professional students (127 women), 355 part-time matriculated graduate/professional students (240 women). *Enrollment by degree level:* 545 master's. *Tuition:* Full-time $25,092; part-time $1394 per credit hour. *Required fees:* $75 per trimester. Full-time tuition and fees vary according to course load and program. *Graduate housing:* On-campus housing not available. *Student services:* Campus employment opportunities, campus safety program, career counseling, exercise/wellness program, free psychological counseling, international student services, low-cost health insurance, services for students with disabilities, writing training. *Library facilities:* Munday Library. *Collection:* Books: 71,983 (physical), 273,440 (digital/electronic); Serial titles: 202 (physical), 121,477 (digital/electronic); Databases: 230. Weekly public service hours: 103; students can reserve study rooms.

Computer facilities: 928 computers available on campus for general student use. A campuswide network can be accessed from student residence rooms and from off campus. Online class registration, access to address and biographical data, transcripts, statements of account, online progress reports and degree audit, campus job postings, student timesheets, financial aid information are available. Website: http://www.stedwards.edu/

General Application Contact: Dave Bralower, Director of Graduate Admission, 512-233-1424, Fax: 512-464-8877, E-mail: davidcb@stedwards.edu.

GRADUATE UNITS

Bill Munday School of Business Students: 53 full-time (19 women), 183 part-time (103 women); includes 100 minority (19 Black or African American, non-Hispanic/Latino; 14 Asian, non-Hispanic/Latino; 59 Hispanic/Latino; 1 Native Hawaiian or other Pacific Islander, non-Hispanic/Latino; 10 Two or more races, non-Hispanic/Latino), 16 international. Average age 32. 221 applicants, 58% accepted, 80 enrolled. Expenses: Contact institution. In 2016, 78 master's awarded. *Program availability:* Part-time, evening/weekend. Offers accounting (M Ac, MBA); business (Certificate); business administration (MBA); leadership and change (MS). *Application deadline:* For fall admission, 6/1 priority date for domestic and international students; for spring admission, 10/1 priority date for domestic and international students; for summer admission, 3/1 priority date for domestic and international students. Applications are processed on a rolling basis. *Application fee:* $50. Electronic applications accepted. *Application Contact:* Mike Leveriza, Graduate Recruiter, 512-448-8745, Fax: 512-464-8877, E-mail: mleveriz@stedwards.edu. *Dean,* Dr. Nancy Schreiber, 512-428-1287, Fax: 512-428-1217, E-mail: nschreib@stedwards.edu.

New College Students: 11 full-time (7 women), 49 part-time (37 women); includes 26 minority (5 Black or African American, non-Hispanic/Latino; 1 American Indian or Alaska Native, non-Hispanic/Latino; 1 Asian, non-Hispanic/Latino; 16 Hispanic/Latino; 3 Two or more races, non-Hispanic/Latino), 1 international. Average age 35. 42 applicants, 74% accepted, 15 enrolled. Expenses: Contact institution. In 2016, 18 master's awarded. *Program availability:* Part-time, evening/weekend. Offers college student development

(MA); humanities (MLA); liberal arts (MLA, Certificate). *Application deadline:* For fall admission, 6/1 priority date for domestic and international students; for spring admission, 10/1 priority date for domestic and international students; for summer admission, 3/1 priority date for domestic and international students. Applications are processed on a rolling basis. *Application fee:* $50. Electronic applications accepted. *Application Contact:* Dave Bralower, Director of Graduate Admission, 512-233-1421, Fax: 512-464-8877, E-mail: davidcb@stedwards.edu. *Interim Dean,* Dr. Ramsey Fowler, 512-448-8736, Fax: 512-448-8492, E-mail: ramseyf@stedwards.edu.
School of Behavioral and Social Sciences Students: 33 full-time (26 women); includes 9 minority (1 Asian, non-Hispanic/Latino; 7 Hispanic/Latino; 1 Native Hawaiian or other Pacific Islander, non-Hispanic/Latino). Average age 26. 75 applicants, 51% accepted, 14 enrolled. Expenses: Contact institution. In 2016, 15 master's awarded. Offers environmental management and sustainability (PSM). *Application deadline:* For fall admission, 2/15 priority date for domestic and international students. Applications are processed on a rolling basis. *Application fee:* $50. Electronic applications accepted. *Application Contact:* Dave Bralower, Director of Graduate Admission, 512-233-1424, Fax: 512-464-8877, E-mail: davidcb@stedwards.edu. *Program Director/Associate Professor,* Dr. Peter Beck, 512-428-1249, Fax: 512-233-1664, E-mail: peterab@stedwards.edu.
School of Education Students: 93 full-time (75 women), 123 part-time (100 women); includes 80 minority (16 Black or African American, non-Hispanic/Latino; 1 American Indian or Alaska Native, non-Hispanic/Latino; 5 Asian, non-Hispanic/Latino; 53 Hispanic/Latino; 5 Two or more races, non-Hispanic/Latino), 2 international. Average age 34. 126 applicants, 60% accepted, 45 enrolled. Expenses: Contact institution. In 2016, 79 master's awarded. *Program availability:* Part-time, evening/weekend. Offers counseling (MA); education (Certificate). *Application deadline:* For fall admission, 6/1 for domestic students, 6/1 priority date for international students; for spring admission, 10/1 for domestic students, 10/1 priority date for international students; for summer admission, 3/1 for domestic students, 3/1 priority date for international students. Applications are processed on a rolling basis. *Application fee:* $50. Electronic applications accepted. *Application Contact:* Dave Bralower, Director of Graduate Admission, 512-233-1424, Fax: 512-464-8877, E-mail: davidcb@stedwards.edu. *MAC Program Director/Associate Professor of Counseling,* Dr. Elizabeth Katz, 512-464-8833, E-mail: elizk@stedwards.edu.

ST. FRANCIS COLLEGE, Brooklyn Heights, NY 11201-4398

General Information Independent-religious, coed, comprehensive institution.

GRADUATE UNITS

Program in Professional Accountancy Offers professional accountancy (MS).

SAINT FRANCIS MEDICAL CENTER COLLEGE OF NURSING, Peoria, IL 61603-3783

General Information Independent-religious, coed, primarily women, upper-level institution. *Enrollment:* 638 graduate, professional, and undergraduate students; 13 full-time matriculated graduate/professional students (12 women), 257 part-time matriculated graduate/professional students (228 women). *Enrollment by degree level:* 234 master's, 27 doctoral, 9 other advanced degrees. *Graduate faculty:* 14 full-time (all women), 5 part-time/adjunct (all women). *Tuition:* Full-time $7728; part-time $644 per credit hour. *Required fees:* $540. *Graduate housing:* Room and/or apartments available on a first-come, first-served basis to single students; on-campus housing not available to married students. Housing application deadline: 3/15. *Student services:* Campus safety program, exercise/wellness program, free psychological counseling, multicultural affairs office. *Library facilities:* Sister Mary Ludgera Pieperbeck Learning and Resource Center plus 1 other. *Collection:* Books: 4,054 (physical), 298 (digital/electronic); Serial titles: 126 (physical); Databases: 57. Students can reserve study rooms.

Computer facilities: 62 computers available on campus for general student use. A campuswide network can be accessed from student residence rooms and from off campus. Online class registration is available.
Website: http://www.sfmccon.edu/

General Application Contact: Dr. Kim A. Mitchell, Dean, Graduate Program, 309-655-2201, Fax: 309-624-8973, E-mail: kim.a.mitchell@osfhealthcare.org.

GRADUATE UNITS

Graduate Programs Students: 13 full-time (12 women), 257 part-time (228 women); includes 23 minority (14 Black or African American, non-Hispanic/Latino; 3 Asian, non-Hispanic/Latino; 4 Hispanic/Latino; 2 Two or more races, non-Hispanic/Latino). Average age 37. 103 applicants, 90% accepted, 68 enrolled. *Faculty:* 14 full-time (all women), 5 part-time/adjunct (all women). Expenses: Contact institution. *Financial support:* In 2016-17, 13 students received support. Scholarships/grants and tuition waivers (partial) available. Support available to part-time students. Financial award application deadline: 6/15; financial award applicants required to submit FAFSA. In 2016, 65 master's, 6 doctorates awarded. *Program availability:* Part-time, online only, 100% online, blended/hybrid learning. Offers adult gerontology (MSN); clinical nurse leader (MSN); family nurse practitioner (MSN); family psychiatric mental health nurse practitioner (MSN); neonatal nurse practitioner (MSN); nurse clinician (Post-Graduate Certificate); nurse educator (MSN, Post-Graduate Certificate); nursing (DNP); nursing management leadership (MSN). *Application deadline:* For fall admission, 6/1 priority date for domestic and international students; for spring admission, 11/15 priority date for domestic and international students. Applications are processed on a rolling basis. *Application fee:* $50. *Application Contact:* Dr. Kim A. Mitchell, Dean, Graduate Program, 309-655-2201, Fax: 309-624-8973, E-mail: kim.a.mitchell@osfhealthcare.org. *President of the College,* Dr. Patti A. Stockert, 309-655-4124, Fax: 309-624-8973, E-mail: patricia.a.stockert@osfhealthcare.org.

SAINT FRANCIS UNIVERSITY, Loretto, PA 15940-0600

General Information Independent-religious, coed, comprehensive institution. *Graduate housing:* On-campus housing not available.

GRADUATE UNITS

Department of Occupational Therapy Offers occupational therapy (MOT).
Department of Physical Therapy Offers physical therapy (DPT). Electronic applications accepted.
Department of Physician Assistant Sciences Offers physician assistant sciences (MPAS). Electronic applications accepted.
Graduate Education Program *Program availability:* Part-time, 100% online, blended/hybrid learning. Offers education (M Ed); leadership (M Ed); reading (M Ed).
Health Science Program *Program availability:* Part-time, evening/weekend, online learning. Offers health science (MHS). Electronic applications accepted.
Medical Science Program *Program availability:* Part-time, evening/weekend, online learning. Offers medical science (MMS). Electronic applications accepted.

School of Business *Program availability:* Part-time, evening/weekend. Offers business administration (MBA); human resource management (MHRM).

ST. FRANCIS XAVIER UNIVERSITY, Antigonish, NS B2G 2W5, Canada

General Information Independent-religious, coed, comprehensive institution. *Enrollment:* 88 full-time matriculated graduate/professional students (69 women), 464 part-time matriculated graduate/professional students (327 women). *Enrollment by degree level:* 386 master's, 9 doctoral, 157 other advanced degrees. *Graduate faculty:* 32 full-time (8 women), 22 part-time/adjunct (10 women). *Tuition:* Full-time $9060 Canadian dollars; part-time $725 Canadian dollars per credit. *Required fees:* $789 Canadian dollars; $78.84 Canadian dollars per credit. Tuition and fees vary according to course load, degree level and program. *Graduate housing:* Room and/or apartments guaranteed to single students; on-campus housing not available to married students. *Student services:* Campus employment opportunities, campus safety program, career counseling, child daycare facilities, exercise/wellness program, free psychological counseling, international student services, low-cost health insurance, multicultural affairs office, services for students with disabilities, teacher training, writing training. *Library facilities:* Angus L. Macdonald Library plus 1 other.

Computer facilities: 500 computers available on campus for general student use. A campuswide network can be accessed from student residence rooms and from off campus. Online class registration, online financial account, personal network storage, personal Web publishing, WirelessSynch iPods, Smartphones are available. Website: http://www.stfx.ca/

General Application Contact: Dr. Richard Isnor, Associate Vice-President, Research and Graduate Studies, 902-867-2393.

GRADUATE UNITS

Graduate Studies Expenses: Contact institution. *Financial support:* Teaching assistantships, scholarships/grants, and tuition waivers (partial) available. *Program availability:* Part-time, online learning. Offers adult education (M Ad Ed); biology (M Sc); Celtic studies (MA); chemistry (M Sc); community development (M Ad Ed); computer science (M Sc); curriculum and instruction (M Ed); earth sciences (M Sc); educational administration and leadership (M Ed). *Application deadline:* For fall admission, 7/1 priority date for domestic students. Applications are processed on a rolling basis. *Application fee:* $40. *Application Contact:* 902-867-2219, Fax: 902-867-2329, E-mail: admit@stfx.ca. *Associate Vice-President, Research and Graduate Studies,* Dr. Richard Isnor, 902-867-2324, Fax: 902-867-2414.

ST. JOHN FISHER COLLEGE, Rochester, NY 14618-3597

General Information Independent-religious, coed, comprehensive institution. *Enrollment:* 3,787 graduate, professional, and undergraduate students; 631 full-time matriculated graduate/professional students (404 women), 370 part-time matriculated graduate/professional students (277 women). *Enrollment by degree level:* 502 master's, 499 doctoral. *Graduate faculty:* 83 full-time (52 women), 24 part-time/adjunct (18 women). *Tuition:* Part-time $885 per credit hour. *Required fees:* $10 per credit hour. Tuition and fees vary according to degree level and program. *Graduate housing:* On-campus housing not available. *Student services:* Campus employment opportunities, campus safety program, career counseling, child daycare facilities, exercise/wellness program, free psychological counseling, international student services, low-cost health insurance, multicultural affairs office, services for students with disabilities, teacher training, writing training. *Library facilities:* Charles J. Lavery Library plus 1 other. *Collection:* Books: 162,694 (physical), 137,162 (digital/electronic); Databases: 197. Students can reserve study rooms.

Computer facilities: 550 computers available on campus for general student use. A campuswide network can be accessed from student residence rooms and from off campus. Online class registration is available. Website: http://www.sjfc.edu/

General Application Contact: Michelle Gosier, Associate Director of Transfer and Graduate Admissions, 585-385-8064, Fax: 585-385-8344, E-mail: mgosier@sjfc.edu.

GRADUATE UNITS

Ralph C. Wilson Jr. School of Education Students: 168 full-time (121 women), 89 part-time (67 women); includes 87 minority (62 Black or African American, non-Hispanic/Latino; 3 American Indian or Alaska Native, non-Hispanic/Latino; 2 Asian, non-Hispanic/Latino; 16 Hispanic/Latino; 4 Two or more races, non-Hispanic/Latino). Average age 37. 168 applicants, 71% accepted, 90 enrolled. *Faculty:* 26 full-time (20 women), 12 part-time/adjunct (11 women). Expenses: Contact institution. *Financial support:* Scholarships/grants available. Financial award applicants required to submit FAFSA. In 2016, 41 doctorates awarded. *Program availability:* Part-time, evening/weekend. Offers adolescence education: biology with special education (MS Ed); adolescence education: chemistry with special education (MS Ed); adolescence education: English with special education (MS Ed); adolescence education: French with special education (MS Ed); adolescence education: math with special education (MS Ed); adolescence education: physics with special education (MS Ed); adolescence education: social studies with special education (MS Ed); adolescence education: Spanish with special education (MS Ed); childhood education (MS); childhood education/special education (Certificate); education (MS, MS Ed, Ed D, Certificate); educational leadership (MS Ed); executive leadership (Ed D); literacy birth to grade 6 (MS); literacy grades 5 to 12 (MS). *Application deadline:* Applications are processed on a rolling basis. *Application fee:* $30. Electronic applications accepted. *Application Contact:* Michelle Gosier, Associate Director of Transfer and Graduate Admissions, 585-385-8064, E-mail: mgosier@sjfc.edu. *Dean,* Dr. Michael Wischnowski, 585-385-7361, E-mail: mwischnowski@sjfc.edu.

School of Business Students: 69 full-time (32 women), 83 part-time (41 women); includes 14 minority (4 Black or African American, non-Hispanic/Latino; 4 Asian, non-Hispanic/Latino; 5 Hispanic/Latino; 1 Two or more races, non-Hispanic/Latino; 3 international. Average age 28. 112 applicants, 85% accepted, 61 enrolled. *Faculty:* 14 full-time (3 women), 5 part-time/adjunct (2 women). Expenses: Contact institution. *Financial support:* Scholarships/grants available. Financial award applicants required to submit FAFSA. In 2016, 73 master's awarded. *Program availability:* Part-time, evening/weekend. Offers business (MBA, MS); business administration (MBA); management (MS). *Application deadline:* Applications are processed on a rolling basis. *Application fee:* $30. Electronic applications accepted. *Application Contact:* Michelle Gosier, Associate Director of Transfer and Graduate Admissions, 585-385-8064, E-mail: mgosier@sjfc.edu. *Dean, School of Business,* Rama Yelkur, 585-385-8446, E-mail: ryelkur@sjfc.edu.

Wegmans School of Nursing Students: 63 full-time (53 women), 186 part-time (164 women); includes 42 minority (19 Black or African American, non-Hispanic/Latino; 1 American Indian or Alaska Native, non-Hispanic/Latino; 7 Asian, non-Hispanic/Latino; 11 Hispanic/Latino; 4 Two or more races, non-Hispanic/Latino). Average age 30. 198

applicants, 54% accepted, 78 enrolled. *Faculty:* 21 full-time (18 women), 7 part-time/adjunct (5 women). Expenses: Contact institution. *Financial support:* Scholarships/grants available. Financial award applicants required to submit FAFSA. In 2016, 72 master's, 6 doctorates awarded. *Program availability:* Part-time, evening/weekend. Offers advanced practice nursing (MS, Certificate); mental health counseling (MS); nursing (MS, DNP, Certificate); nursing practice (DNP). *Application deadline:* Applications are processed on a rolling basis. Electronic applications accepted. *Application Contact:* Michelle Gosier, Associate Director of Transfer and Graduate Admissions, 585-385-8064, E-mail: mgosier@sjfc.edu. *Dean,* Dr. Diane Cooney-Miner, 585-385-8241, Fax: 585-385-8466, E-mail: dcooney-miner@sjfc.edu.

Wegmans School of Pharmacy Students: 331 full-time (198 women), 3 part-time (1 woman); includes 63 minority (12 Black or African American, non-Hispanic/Latino; 37 Asian, non-Hispanic/Latino; 10 Hispanic/Latino; 4 Two or more races, non-Hispanic/Latino), 5 international. Average age 24. 497 applicants, 30% accepted, 85 enrolled. *Faculty:* 33 full-time (21 women). Expenses: Contact institution. *Financial support:* Scholarships/grants available. Financial award applicants required to submit FAFSA. In 2016, 82 doctorates awarded. Offers pharmacy (Pharm D). *Application deadline:* For fall admission, 3/1 for domestic students. Applications are processed on a rolling basis. Electronic applications accepted. *Application Contact:* Michelle Gosier, Associate Director of Transfer and Graduate Admissions, 585-385-8064, E-mail: mgosier@sjfc.edu. *Dean,* Dr. Christine Birnie, 585-385-7202, E-mail: cbirnie@sjfc.edu.

ST. JOHN'S COLLEGE, Annapolis, MD 21401

General Information Independent, coed, comprehensive institution. *Graduate housing:* On-campus housing not available.

GRADUATE UNITS

Graduate Institute *Program availability:* Evening/weekend. Offers liberal arts (MALA). Electronic applications accepted.

ST. JOHN'S COLLEGE, Santa Fe, NM 87505

General Information Independent, coed, comprehensive institution. *Graduate housing:* Rooms and/or apartments available on a first-come, first-served basis to single and married students. Housing application deadline: 4/1.

GRADUATE UNITS

Graduate Institute in Liberal Education *Program availability:* Evening/weekend. Offers Eastern classics (MA); liberal arts (MA); liberal education (MA).

ST. JOHN'S SEMINARY, Camarillo, CA 93012-2598

General Information Independent-religious, coed, primarily men, graduate-only institution. *Graduate housing:* Room and/or apartments guaranteed to single students; on-campus housing not available to married students.

GRADUATE UNITS

Graduate and Professional Programs *Program availability:* Part-time. Offers divinity (M Div); pastoral ministry (MAPM); theology (MA). Electronic applications accepted.

SAINT JOHN'S SEMINARY, Brighton, MA 02135

General Information Independent-religious, coed, graduate-only institution. *Graduate housing:* Room and/or apartments available to single students; on-campus housing not available to married students. Housing application deadline: 8/1.

GRADUATE UNITS

Graduate Programs Offers theology (M Div, MA Th, MAM).

SAINT JOHN'S UNIVERSITY, Collegeville, MN 56321

General Information Independent-religious, Undergraduate: men only; graduate: coed, comprehensive institution. *Graduate housing:* Rooms and/or apartments available on a first-come, first-served basis to single and married students. *Research affiliation:* Hill Monastic Manuscript Library (monastic studies, liturgy, spirituality), Center for Ecumenical and Cultural Research, Arca Artium (visual and book arts).

GRADUATE UNITS

Saint John's School of Theology and Seminary *Program availability:* Part-time, online learning. Offers divinity (M Div); liturgical music (MA); liturgical studies (MA); pastoral ministry (MA); theology (MA). Electronic applications accepted.

ST. JOSEPH'S COLLEGE, LONG ISLAND CAMPUS, Patchogue, NY 11772-2399

General Information Independent, coed, comprehensive institution. *Enrollment:* 3,914 graduate, professional, and undergraduate students; 133 full-time matriculated graduate/professional students (87 women), 618 part-time matriculated graduate/professional students (484 women). *Enrollment by degree level:* 751 master's. *Graduate faculty:* 2 full-time (1 woman), 34 part-time/adjunct (18 women). *Tuition:* Full-time $16,182; part-time $899 per credit. *Required fees:* $440. *Graduate housing:* On-campus housing not available. *Student services:* Campus employment opportunities, campus safety program, career counseling, exercise/wellness program, free psychological counseling, low-cost health insurance, multicultural affairs office, services for students with disabilities, teacher training, writing training. *Library facilities:* Callahan Library plus 1 other. *Collection:* Books: 95,674 (physical), 121,688 (digital/electronic); Serial titles: 224 (physical), 60,197 (digital/electronic); Databases: 116. Weekly public service hours: 80; students can reserve study rooms.

Computer facilities: 265 computers available on campus for general student use. A campuswide network can be accessed from off campus. Online class registration, learning management system, course evaluations, print management, virtual application labs, office software, student suggestion box are available. Website: http://www.sjcny.edu/

General Application Contact: Jodi A. Duffy, Director of Graduate and Professional Studies Admissions, 631-687-4525, E-mail: jduffy@sjcny.edu.

GRADUATE UNITS

Program in Nursing Students: 3 full-time (all women), 24 part-time (22 women); includes 10 minority (7 Black or African American, non-Hispanic/Latino; 2 Asian, non-Hispanic/Latino; 1 Hispanic/Latino). Average age 44. 28 applicants, 64% accepted, 17 enrolled. *Faculty:* 1 part-time/adjunct (0 women). Expenses: Contact institution. *Financial support:* In 2016–17, 16 students received support. In 2016, 4 master's awarded. *Program availability:* Part-time, evening/weekend. Offers nursing (MS). *Application deadline:* Applications are processed on a rolling basis. *Application fee:* $25. Electronic applications accepted. *Director/Associate Professor,* Dr. Maria Fletcher, RN, 631-687-5180, E-mail: mfletcher@sjcny.edu.

Programs in Business Management and Administration Students: 59 full-time (27 women), 138 part-time (72 women); includes 49 minority (14 Black or African American, non-Hispanic/Latino; 13 Asian, non-Hispanic/Latino; 20 Hispanic/Latino; 1 Native Hawaiian or other Pacific Islander, non-Hispanic/Latino; 1 Two or more races, non-

Hispanic/Latino). Average age 35. 136 applicants, 79% accepted, 75 enrolled. *Faculty:* 1 (woman) full-time, 12 part-time/adjunct (3 women). Expenses: Contact institution. *Financial support:* In 2016–17, 50 students received support. In 2016, 42 master's awarded. *Program availability:* Part-time, evening/weekend, 100% online, blended/hybrid learning. Offers accounting (MBA); business administration (MBA); business management and administration (EMBA, MBA). *Application deadline:* Applications are processed on a rolling basis. *Application fee:* $25. Electronic applications accepted. *Professor and Chair*, Eileen White Jahn, 631-687-1296, E-mail: ejahn@sjcny.edu.

Field of Executive Business Administration Students: 19 full-time (6 women), 81 part-time (50 women); includes 34 minority (13 Black or African American, non-Hispanic/Latino; 7 Asian, non-Hispanic/Latino; 13 Hispanic/Latino; 1 Two or more races, non-Hispanic/Latino). Average age 35. 72 applicants, 75% accepted, 38 enrolled. *Faculty:* 1 (woman) full-time, 12 part-time/adjunct (3 women). Expenses: Contact institution. *Financial support:* In 2016–17, 27 students received support. In 2016, 20 master's awarded. *Program availability:* Part-time, evening/weekend, 100% online, blended/hybrid learning. Offers executive business administration (EMBA). *Application deadline:* Applications are processed on a rolling basis. *Application fee:* $25. Electronic applications accepted. *Application Contact:* Jodi A. Duffy, Senior Associate Director of Graduate Admissions, 631-687-4501, E-mail: jduffy@sjcny.edu. *Director and Assistant Professor*, Charles Pendola, 631-687-1297, E-mail: cpendola@sjcny.edu.

Programs in Education Students: 39 full-time (34 women), 289 part-time (258 women); includes 23 minority (3 Black or African American, non-Hispanic/Latino; 3 Asian, non-Hispanic/Latino; 14 Hispanic/Latino; 3 Two or more races, non-Hispanic/Latino). Average age 25. 262 applicants, 73% accepted, 154 enrolled. *Faculty:* 1 full-time (0 women), 21 part-time/adjunct (15 women). Expenses: Contact institution. *Financial support:* In 2016–17, 125 students received support. In 2016, 157 master's awarded. Offers education (MA); educational leadership (MA); mathematics education (MA). *Application fee:* $25. *Application Contact:* Jodi A. Duffy, Senior Associate Director of Graduate Admissions, 631-687-4525, E-mail: jduffy@sjcny.edu. *Associate Professor and Department Chair*, Sr. Nancy Gilchriest, 631-687-1472, E-mail: ngilchriest@sjcny.edu.

Field in Special Education Students: 21 full-time (16 women), 107 part-time (87 women); includes 10 minority (4 Black or African American, non-Hispanic/Latino; 1 Asian, non-Hispanic/Latino; 5 Hispanic/Latino; 3 Two or more races, non-Hispanic/Latino). Average age 25. 104 applicants, 65% accepted, 60 enrolled. *Faculty:* 1 full-time (0 women), 8 part-time/adjunct (5 women). Expenses: Contact institution. *Financial support:* In 2016–17, 41 students received support. In 2016, 90 master's awarded. *Program availability:* Evening/weekend. Offers special education (MA). *Application fee:* $25. *Application Contact:* Sr. Nancy Gilchriest, Associate Professor/Department Chair, 631-687-1472, E-mail: ngilchriest@sjcny.edu. *Associate Professor/Department Chair*, Sr. Nancy Gilchriest, 631-687-1472, E-mail: ngilchriest@sjcny.edu.

Field of Infant/Toddler Early Childhood Special Education Students: 15 full-time (all women), 70 part-time (66 women); includes 9 minority (1 Black or African American, non-Hispanic/Latino; 1 Asian, non-Hispanic/Latino; 7 Hispanic/Latino). Average age 26. 83 applicants, 81% accepted, 50 enrolled. *Faculty:* 1 full-time (0 women), 10 part-time/adjunct (7 women). Expenses: Contact institution. *Financial support:* In 2016–17, 24 students received support. Applicants required to submit FAFSA. In 2016, 15 master's awarded. *Program availability:* Part-time, evening/weekend. Offers infant/toddler early childhood special education (MA). *Application deadline:* For fall admission, 8/1 for domestic students, 5/1 for international students. Applications are processed on a rolling basis. *Application fee:* $25. Electronic applications accepted. *Application Contact:* Jodi A. Duffy, Senior Associate Director of Graduate Admissions, 631-687-4525, E-mail: jduffy@sjcny.edu. *Assistant Professor and Chair*, Sr. Mary Ann Cashin, 631-687-1235, E-mail: mcashin@sjcny.edu.

Field of Literacy and Cognition Students: 3 full-time (all women), 112 part-time (105 women); includes 4 minority (1 Black or African American, non-Hispanic/Latino; 1 Asian, non-Hispanic/Latino; 2 Hispanic/Latino). Average age 25. 75 applicants, 73% accepted, 44 enrolled. *Faculty:* 2 part-time/adjunct (both women). Expenses: Contact institution. *Financial support:* In 2016–17, 59 students received support. In 2016, 52 master's awarded. *Program availability:* Part-time, evening/weekend. Offers literacy and cognition (MA). *Application deadline:* Applications are processed on a rolling basis. *Application fee:* $25. Electronic applications accepted. *Application Contact:* Jodi A. Duffy, Senior Associate Director of Graduate Admissions, 631-687-4525, E-mail: jduffy@sjcny.edu. *Assistant Professor and Chair*, Sr. Mary Ann Cashin, 631-687-1235, E-mail: mcashin@sjcny.edu.

Programs in Health Care Administration Students: 3 full-time (2 women), 20 part-time (18 women); includes 7 minority (4 Black or African American, non-Hispanic/Latino; 3 Hispanic/Latino). Average age 37. 12 applicants, 67% accepted, 7 enrolled. *Faculty:* 1 (woman) full-time, 13 part-time/adjunct (3 women). Expenses: Contact institution. *Financial support:* In 2016–17, 2 students received support. In 2016, 8 master's awarded. *Program availability:* Part-time, evening/weekend, 100% online, blended/hybrid learning. Offers health care administration (MBA); health care management (MBA); health care management - health information systems (MBA). *Application fee:* $25. *Application Contact:* Jodi A. Duffy, Senior Associate Director of Graduate Admissions, 631-687-4525, E-mail: jduffy@sjcny.edu. *Director and Assistant Professor*, Charles Pendola, 631-687-1297, E-mail: cpendola@sjcny.edu.

Programs in Management Students: 25 full-time (18 women), 122 part-time (93 women); includes 49 minority (23 Black or African American, non-Hispanic/Latino; 4 Asian, non-Hispanic/Latino; 21 Hispanic/Latino; 1 Two or more races, non-Hispanic/Latino). Average age 36. 129 applicants, 61% accepted, 60 enrolled. *Faculty:* 1 (woman) full-time, 13 part-time/adjunct (3 women). Expenses: Contact institution. *Financial support:* In 2016–17, 25 students received support. In 2016, 33 master's awarded. *Program availability:* Part-time, evening/weekend. Offers health care management (MS); human resources management (MS); human services leadership (MS); organizational management (MS). *Application deadline:* Applications are processed on a rolling basis. *Application fee:* $25. Electronic applications accepted. *Application Contact:* Jodi A. Duffy, Senior Associate Director of Graduate Admissions, E-mail: tsaladino@sjcny.edu. *Director and Assistant Professor*, Charles Pendola, 631-687-1297, E-mail: cpendola@sjcny.edu.

ST. JOSEPH'S COLLEGE, NEW YORK, Brooklyn, NY 11205-3688

General Information Independent, coed, comprehensive institution. *Enrollment:* 1,205 graduate, professional, and undergraduate students; 67 full-time matriculated graduate/professional students (48 women), 165 part-time matriculated graduate/professional students (131 women). *Enrollment by degree level:* 232 master's. *Graduate faculty:* 13 part-time/adjunct (8 women). *Tuition:* Full-time $16,182; part-time $899 per credit. *Required fees:* $351. *Graduate housing:* On-campus housing not available. *Student services:* Campus employment opportunities, campus safety

program, career counseling, exercise/wellness program, free psychological counseling, low-cost health insurance, multicultural affairs office, services for students with disabilities, teacher training, writing training. *Library facilities:* McEntegart Hall Library plus 1 other. *Collection:* Books: 81,405 (physical), 121,688 (digital/electronic); Serial titles: 35 (physical), 60,197 (digital/electronic); Databases: 116. Weekly public service hours: 83; students can reserve study rooms.

Computer facilities: 238 computers available on campus for general student use. A campuswide network can be accessed from off campus. Online class registration, learning management system, course evaluations, print management, virtual application labs, office software, student suggestion box are available.
Website: http://www.sjcny.edu/

General Application Contact: Roberto Figueroa, Director, Adult, Transfer and Graduate Admissions, 718-940-5828, E-mail: rfigueroa@sjcny.edu.

GRADUATE UNITS

Program in Creative Writing Students: 34 full-time (25 women); includes 12 minority (4 Black or African American, non-Hispanic/Latino; 3 Asian, non-Hispanic/Latino; 4 Hispanic/Latino; 1 Two or more races, non-Hispanic/Latino). Average age 35. 34 applicants, 82% accepted, 19 enrolled. *Faculty:* 4 part-time/adjunct (1 woman). Expenses: Contact institution. *Financial support:* In 2016–17, 27 students received support. In 2016, 11 master's awarded. *Program availability:* Part-time, evening/weekend. Offers creative writing (MFA). *Application deadline:* Applications are processed on a rolling basis. Electronic applications accepted. *Associate Professor/Chair*, Ted Hamm, 718-940-5307, E-mail: thamm@sjcny.edu.

Program in Forensic Computing Students: 3 full-time (all women), 5 part-time (4 women); includes 3 minority (1 Asian, non-Hispanic/Latino; 2 Hispanic/Latino). Average age 27. 9 applicants, 89% accepted, 8 enrolled. *Faculty:* 2 part-time/adjunct (1 woman). Expenses: Contact institution. *Financial support:* In 2016–17, 2 students received support. *Program availability:* Part-time, evening/weekend. Offers forensic computing (MS). *Application deadline:* Applications are processed on a rolling basis. Electronic applications accepted. *Application Contact:* Roberto Figueroa, Director, Graduate and Adult Admissions, 718-940-5828, E-mail: rfigueroa@sjcny.edu. *Associate Professor*, Dr. Joseph Pascarella, 718-940-5775, E-mail: jpascarella2@sjcny.edu.

Program in Nursing Students: 1 (woman) full-time, 34 part-time (all women); includes 28 minority (25 Black or African American, non-Hispanic/Latino; 1 Hispanic/Latino; 2 Two or more races, non-Hispanic/Latino). Average age 44. 39 applicants, 54% accepted, 19 enrolled. *Faculty:* 3 part-time/adjunct (2 women). Expenses: Contact institution. *Financial support:* In 2016–17, 2 students received support. In 2016, 16 master's awarded. *Program availability:* Part-time, evening/weekend. Offers nursing (MS). *Application deadline:* Applications are processed on a rolling basis. *Application fee:* $25. Electronic applications accepted. *Associate Professor/Director*, Maria Fletcher, 718-940-5891, E-mail: mfletcher@sjcny.edu.

Programs in Business Management and Administration Students: 8 full-time (6 women), 23 part-time (15 women); includes 21 minority (6 Black or African American, non-Hispanic/Latino; 3 Asian, non-Hispanic/Latino; 9 Hispanic/Latino; 3 Two or more races, non-Hispanic/Latino). Average age 39. 24 applicants, 63% accepted, 10 enrolled. *Faculty:* 2 part-time/adjunct (both women). Expenses: Contact institution. *Financial support:* In 2016–17, 11 students received support. In 2016, 17 master's awarded. *Program availability:* Part-time, evening/weekend, 100% online, blended/hybrid learning. Offers accounting (MBA); business administration (MBA); executive business administration (EMBA); management (MS). *Application deadline:* Applications are processed on a rolling basis. *Application fee:* $25. Electronic applications accepted. *Chair and Professor*, Eileen Jahn, 631-687-1296, E-mail: ejahn@sjcny.edu.

Field of Executive Business Administration Students: 8 full-time (6 women), 22 part-time (14 women); includes 14 minority (6 Black or African American, non-Hispanic/Latino; 3 Asian, non-Hispanic/Latino; 2 Hispanic/Latino; 3 Two or more races, non-Hispanic/Latino). Average age 38. 24 applicants, 63% accepted, 10 enrolled. *Faculty:* 2 full-time (both women), 6 part-time/adjunct (3 women). Expenses: Contact institution. *Financial support:* In 2016–17, 9 students received support. In 2016, 15 master's awarded. *Program availability:* Part-time, evening/weekend, 100% online, blended/hybrid learning. Offers executive business administration (EMBA). *Application deadline:* Applications are processed on a rolling basis. *Application fee:* $25. Electronic applications accepted. *Co-Director of Graduate Management Studies/Assistant Professor*, Sharon Didier, 718-940-5790, E-mail: sdidier@sjcny.edu.

Programs in Education Students: 34 part-time (29 women); includes 6 minority (1 Black or African American, non-Hispanic/Latino; 5 Hispanic/Latino). Average age 23. 37 applicants, 70% accepted, 18 enrolled. *Faculty:* 2 part-time/adjunct (both women). Expenses: Contact institution. *Financial support:* In 2016–17, 30 students received support. In 2016, 22 master's awarded. Offers educational leadership (MA); literacy and cognition (MA); special education (MA). *Application deadline:* Applications are processed on a rolling basis. *Application fee:* $25. Electronic applications accepted. *Professor/Department Chair*, Sr. Nancy Gilchriest, 631-687-1472, E-mail: ngilchriest@sjcny.edu.

Field of Literacy and Cognition Students: 17 part-time (all women); includes 3 minority (all Hispanic/Latino). Average age 23. 17 applicants, 76% accepted, 9 enrolled. *Faculty:* 2 part-time/adjunct (both women). Expenses: Contact institution. *Financial support:* In 2016–17, 16 students received support. In 2016, 15 master's awarded. *Program availability:* Part-time, evening/weekend. Offers literacy and cognition (MA). *Application deadline:* Applications are processed on a rolling basis. *Application fee:* $25. Electronic applications accepted. *Professor/Associate Chair/Director of the Special Education Program*, Susan Straut-Collard, 718-940-5689, E-mail: sstrautcollard@sjcny.edu.

Field of Special Education Students: 17 part-time (12 women); includes 3 minority (1 Black or African American, non-Hispanic/Latino; 2 Hispanic/Latino). Average age 23. 20 applicants, 65% accepted, 9 enrolled. *Faculty:* 2 part-time/adjunct (both women). Expenses: Contact institution. *Financial support:* In 2016–17, 14 students received support. In 2016, 7 master's awarded. *Program availability:* Part-time, evening/weekend. Offers severe and multiple disabilities (MA). *Application deadline:* Applications are processed on a rolling basis. *Application fee:* $25. Electronic applications accepted. *Professor/Department Chair*, Sr. Nancy Gilchriest, 631-687-1472, E-mail: ngilchriest@sjcny.edu.

Programs in Health Care Administration Students: 4 full-time (3 women), 16 part-time (11 women); includes 16 minority (13 Black or African American, non-Hispanic/Latino; 2 Asian, non-Hispanic/Latino; 1 Hispanic/Latino). Average age 36. 7 applicants, 71% accepted, 5 enrolled. *Faculty:* 2 full-time (both women), 6 part-time/adjunct (3 women). Expenses: Contact institution. *Financial support:* In 2016–17, 3 students received support. In 2016, 3 master's awarded. *Program availability:* Part-time, evening/weekend. Offers health care management (MBA); health care management - health information systems (MBA). *Application deadline:* Applications are processed on a rolling basis. *Application fee:* $25. Electronic applications accepted. *Application Contact:* John

Fitzgerald, Associate Director, Admissions, 718-940-5810, Fax: 718-636-8303, E-mail: jfitzgerald3@sjcny.edu. *Associate Professor and Chair,* Lauren Pete, 718-940-5890, E-mail: lpete@sjcny.edu.

Field in Health Care Management - Health Information Systems Students: 4 full-time (3 women), 12 part-time (7 women); includes 13 minority (10 Black or African American, non-Hispanic/Latino; 2 Asian, non-Hispanic/Latino; 1 Hispanic/Latino). Average age 37. 5 applicants, 60% accepted, 3 enrolled. *Faculty:* 2 full-time (both women), 6 part-time/adjunct (3 women). Expenses: Contact institution. *Financial support:* In 2016–17, 3 students received support. In 2016, 4 master's awarded. *Program availability:* Part-time, evening/weekend, 100% online, blended/hybrid learning. Offers health care management - health information systems (MS). *Application fee:* $25. *Application Contact:* John Fitzgerald, Associate Director, Admissions, 718-940-5810, E-mail: jfitzgerald3@sjcny.edu. *Chair,* Lauren Pete, 718-940-5890, E-mail: lpete@sjcny.edu.

Programs in Management Students: 12 full-time (9 women), 52 part-time (40 women); includes 48 minority (29 Black or African American, non-Hispanic/Latino; 6 Asian, non-Hispanic/Latino; 13 Hispanic/Latino). Average age 39. 43 applicants, 51% accepted, 8 enrolled. *Faculty:* 5 part-time/adjunct (1 woman). Expenses: Contact institution. *Financial support:* In 2016–17, 7 students received support. Federal Work-Study available. In 2016, 19 master's awarded. *Program availability:* Part-time, evening/weekend, 100% online, blended/hybrid learning. Offers human resources management (MS); management (MS); organizational management (MS). *Application deadline:* Applications are processed on a rolling basis. *Application fee:* $25. Electronic applications accepted. *Application Contact:* John Fitzgerald, Associate Director, Admissions, 718-940-5810, Fax: 718-636-8303, E-mail: jfitzgerald3@sjcny.edu. *Chair and Professor,* Eileen Jahn, 631-687-1296, E-mail: ejahn@sjcny.edu.

Field in Health Care Management Students: 5 full-time (4 women), 24 part-time (18 women); includes 13 minority (3 Black or African American, non-Hispanic/Latino; 4 Asian, non-Hispanic/Latino; 6 Hispanic/Latino). Average age 40. 22 applicants, 41% accepted, 2 enrolled. *Faculty:* 5 part-time/adjunct (1 woman). Expenses: Contact institution. *Financial support:* In 2016–17, 2 students received support. In 2016, 9 master's awarded. *Program availability:* Part-time, evening/weekend, 100% online, blended/hybrid learning. Offers health care management (MBA, MS). *Application deadline:* Applications are processed on a rolling basis. *Application fee:* $25. Electronic applications accepted. *Associate Professor/Chair,* Lauren Pete, 718-940-5890, E-mail: lpete@sjcny.edu.

Field in Human Services Management and Leadership Students: 11 part-time (9 women); includes 9 minority (4 Black or African American, non-Hispanic/Latino; 5 Hispanic/Latino). Average age 43. 8 applicants, 63% accepted, 1 enrolled. *Faculty:* 5 part-time/adjunct (4 women). Expenses: Contact institution. *Financial support:* In 2016–17, 1 student received support. Federal Work-Study available. In 2016, 5 master's awarded. *Program availability:* Part-time, evening/weekend. Offers human services management and leadership (MS). *Application deadline:* Applications are processed on a rolling basis. *Application fee:* $25. Electronic applications accepted. *Associate Professor/Associate Chair,* Candis Best, 718-940-5849, E-mail: cbest@sjcny.edu.

SAINT JOSEPH'S COLLEGE OF MAINE, Standish, ME 04084

General Information Independent-religious, coed, comprehensive institution. *Graduate housing:* On-campus housing not available.

GRADUATE UNITS

Master of Accountancy Program *Program availability:* Part-time, online learning. Offers accountancy (M Acc). Electronic applications accepted.

Master of Arts in Pastoral Theology Program *Program availability:* Part-time, online learning. Offers pastoral theology (MA).

Master of Business Administration in Leadership Program *Program availability:* Part-time, online learning. Offers leadership (MBA).

Master of Health Administration Program *Program availability:* Part-time, online learning. Offers health administration (MHA). Degree program is external; available only by correspondence and online. Electronic applications accepted.

Master of Science in Education Program *Program availability:* Part-time, online learning. Offers adult education and training (MS Ed); Catholic school leadership (MS Ed); health care educator (MS Ed); school educator (MS Ed). Program available by correspondence. Electronic applications accepted.

Master of Science in Nursing Program *Program availability:* Part-time, online learning. Offers administration (MSN); education (MSN); family nurse practitioner (MSN); nursing administration and leadership (Certificate); nursing and health care education (Certificate). Electronic applications accepted.

ST. JOSEPH'S SEMINARY, Yonkers, NY 10704

General Information Independent-religious, coed, graduate-only institution. *Graduate housing:* Room and/or apartments guaranteed to single students; on-campus housing not available to married students.

GRADUATE UNITS

Graduate and Professional Programs Offers Catholic philosophical studies (MA); divinity (M Div); pastoral studies (MAPS); theology (MA).

SAINT JOSEPH'S UNIVERSITY, Philadelphia, PA 19131-1395

General Information Independent-religious, coed, comprehensive institution. *Enrollment:* 8,415 graduate, professional, and undergraduate students; 532 full-time matriculated graduate/professional students (291 women), 2,502 part-time matriculated graduate/professional students (1,600 women). *Enrollment by degree level:* 2,816 master's, 78 doctoral, 140 other advanced degrees. *Graduate faculty:* 111 full-time (53 women), 193 part-time/adjunct (89 women). Tuition and fees vary according to program. *Graduate housing:* On-campus housing not available. *Student services:* Campus employment opportunities, campus safety program, career counseling, exercise/wellness program, free psychological counseling, international student services, low-cost health insurance, multicultural affairs office, services for students with disabilities, teacher training, writing training. *Library facilities:* Post Learning Commons and Drexel Library. *Collection:* Books: 260,000 (physical), 9,511 (digital/electronic); Serial titles: 590 (physical), 57,790 (digital/electronic); Databases: 203. Weekly public service hours: 107; students can reserve study rooms.

Computer facilities: Computer purchase and lease plans are available. 521 computers available on campus for general student use. A campuswide network can be accessed from student residence rooms and from off campus. Online class registration is available.
Website: http://www.sju.edu/

General Application Contact: Office of Graduate Operations, 610-660-1101, E-mail: graduate@sju.edu.

GRADUATE UNITS

College of Arts and Sciences Students: 271 full-time (177 women), 1,741 part-time (1,270 women); includes 490 minority (332 Black or African American, non-Hispanic/Latino; 5 American Indian or Alaska Native, non-Hispanic/Latino; 56 Asian, non-Hispanic/Latino; 74 Hispanic/Latino; 4 Native Hawaiian or other Pacific Islander, non-Hispanic/Latino; 19 Two or more races, non-Hispanic/Latino), 113 international. Average age 32. 918 applicants, 69% accepted, 395 enrolled. *Faculty:* 65 full-time (41 women), 149 part-time/adjunct (78 women). Expenses: Contact institution. *Financial support:* In 2016–17, 85 students received support. Scholarships/grants and unspecified assistantships available. Financial award application deadline: 5/1; financial award applicants required to submit FAFSA. In 2016, 841 master's, 16 doctorates, 61 other advanced degrees awarded. *Program availability:* Part-time, evening/weekend, 100% online, blended/hybrid learning. Offers arts and sciences (MA, MS, Ed D, Certificate, Post-Master's Certificate); behavior analysis (MS, Post-Master's Certificate); behavior management (MS); biology (MA, MS); computer science (MS); criminal justice (MS); curriculum supervisor (Certificate); educational leadership (MS, Ed D); elementary education (MS, Certificate); elementary/middle school education (Certificate); federal law (MS); health administration (MS); health education (MS); informatics (MS); instructional technology (MS, Certificate); intelligence and crime (MS); mathematics and computer science (Post-Master's Certificate); organizational development and leadership (MS); organizations development and leadership (MS); principal (Certificate); professional education (MS); psychology (MS); reading specialist (MS, Certificate); reading supervisor (Certificate); secondary education (MS, Certificate); special education (MS); special education 7-12 (Certificate); special education PK-8 (Certificate); superintendent's letter of eligibility (Certificate); supervisor of special education (Certificate); teacher of the deaf and hard of hearing (Certificate); writing studies (MA). *Application deadline:* For fall admission, 3/15 for international students; for spring admission, 11/1 for international students. Applications are processed on a rolling basis. *Application fee:* $35. Electronic applications accepted. *Application Contact:* Marketing and Admissions, Graduate Arts and Sciences, 610-660-3131, E-mail: gradstudies@sju.edu. *Dean,* Dr. Richard Warren, 610-660-3131, E-mail: gradstudies@sju.edu.

Erivan K. Haub School of Business Students: 261 full-time (114 women), 761 part-time (330 women); includes 188 minority (96 Black or African American, non-Hispanic/Latino; 52 Asian, non-Hispanic/Latino; 31 Hispanic/Latino; 1 Native Hawaiian or other Pacific Islander, non-Hispanic/Latino; 8 Two or more races, non-Hispanic/Latino), 221 international. Average age 32. 742 applicants, 65% accepted, 236 enrolled. *Faculty:* 51 full-time (15 women), 46 part-time/adjunct (11 women). Expenses: Contact institution. *Financial support:* In 2016–17, 293 students received support, including research assistantships with partial tuition reimbursements available (averaging $2,000 per year); scholarships/grants and unspecified assistantships also available. Support available to part-time students. Financial award application deadline: 5/1; financial award applicants required to submit FAFSA. In 2016, 401 master's, 3 other advanced degrees awarded. *Program availability:* Part-time, evening/weekend, 100% online, blended/hybrid learning. Offers accounting (MBA, Postbaccalaureate Certificate); business (MBA, MS, Post Master's Certificate, Postbaccalaureate Certificate); business intelligence (MBA); business intelligence and analytics (MS); executive business administration (MBA); finance (MBA); financial services (MBA); food marketing (MBA, MS); general business (MBA); health and medical services administration (MBA); international business (MBA); international marketing (MS); managing human capital (MBA); marketing (MBA); pharmaceutical and healthcare marketing (MBA, Post Master's Certificate). *Application deadline:* For fall admission, 7/15 priority date for domestic students, 5/15 priority date for international students; for spring admission, 11/15 priority date for domestic students, 10/15 priority date for international students; for summer admission, 4/15 priority date for domestic students, 2/15 priority date for international students. Applications are processed on a rolling basis. *Application fee:* $35. Electronic applications accepted. *Application Contact:* Dr. Patricia Rafferty, Director, MBA Program, 610-660-1318, Fax: 610-660-1599, E-mail: praffert@sju.edu. *Dean,* Dr. Joseph A. DiAngelo, 610-660-1645, Fax: 610-660-1649, E-mail: jodiange@sju.edu.

ST. LAWRENCE UNIVERSITY, Canton, NY 13617

General Information Independent, coed, comprehensive institution. *Graduate housing:* Room and/or apartments available on a first-come, first-served basis to single students; on-campus housing not available to married students. Housing application deadline: 4/1.

GRADUATE UNITS

Department of Education *Program availability:* Part-time, evening/weekend. Offers combined school building leadership/school district leadership (CAS); counseling and human development (M Ed, MS, CAS); educational leadership (M Ed, CAS); general studies in education (M Ed); mental health counseling (MS); school building leadership (M Ed); school counseling (M Ed, CAS); school district leadership (CAS).

SAINT LEO UNIVERSITY, Saint Leo, FL 33574-6665

General Information Independent-religious, coed, comprehensive institution. *Enrollment:* 5,898 graduate, professional, and undergraduate students; 159 full-time matriculated graduate/professional students (129 women), 3,458 part-time matriculated graduate/professional students (2,126 women). *Enrollment by degree level:* 3,492 master's, 78 doctoral, 47 other advanced degrees. *Graduate faculty:* 88 full-time (35 women), 140 part-time/adjunct (64 women). *Tuition:* Full-time $12,510; part-time $695 per semester hour. Tuition and fees vary according to degree level, campus/location and program. *Graduate housing:* Room and/or apartments available on a first-come, first-served basis to single students; on-campus housing not available to married students. *Student services:* Campus employment opportunities, career counseling, exercise/wellness program, free psychological counseling, international student services, low-cost health insurance, multicultural affairs office, services for students with disabilities, teacher training, writing training. *Library facilities:* Cannon Memorial Library plus 1 other. *Collection:* Books: 97,155 (physical), 403,383 (digital/electronic); Serial titles: 265 (physical), 170,845 (digital/electronic); Databases: 72. Weekly public service hours: 119. *Research affiliation:* American Jewish Committee (religion).

Computer facilities: Computer purchase and lease plans are available. 150 computers available on campus for general student use. A campuswide network can be accessed from student residence rooms and from off campus. Online class registration is available.
Website: http://www.saintleo.edu/

General Application Contact: Jennifer Shelley, Senior Associate Director of Graduate Admissions, 800-707-8846, Fax: 352-588-7873, E-mail: grad.admissions@saintleo.edu.

GRADUATE UNITS

Graduate Business Studies Students: 8 full-time (4 women), 2,001 part-time (1,160 women); includes 928 minority (650 Black or African American, non-Hispanic/Latino; 5 American Indian or Alaska Native, non-Hispanic/Latino; 43 Asian, non-Hispanic/Latino; 193 Hispanic/Latino; 2 Native Hawaiian or other Pacific Islander, non-Hispanic/Latino; 35

Two or more races, non-Hispanic/Latino), 51 international. Average age 37. 922 applicants, 85% accepted, 517 enrolled. *Faculty:* 53 full-time (18 women), 53 part-time/adjunct (19 women). Expenses: Contact institution. *Financial support:* In 2016–17, 118 students received support. Career-related internships or fieldwork, scholarships/grants, and health care benefits available. Financial award application deadline: 3/1; financial award applicants required to submit FAFSA. In 2016, 874 master's, 17 other advanced degrees awarded. *Program availability:* Part-time, evening/weekend, 100% online, blended/hybrid learning. Offers accounting (M Acc, MBA, Certificate); cybersecurity (MS); health care management (MBA, Certificate); human resource management (MBA, Certificate); information security management (MBA, Certificate); management (MBA, DBA); marketing (MBA, Certificate); marketing research and social media analytics (MBA, Certificate); project management (MBA, Certificate); sport business (MBA); supply chain global integration management (MBA, Certificate). *Application deadline:* For fall admission, 7/1 priority date for domestic and international students; for spring admission, 11/12 priority date for domestic students, 11/1 for international students. Applications are processed on a rolling basis. *Application fee:* $80. Electronic applications accepted. *Application Contact:* Jennifer Shelley, Senior Associate Director of Graduate Admissions, 800-707-8846, Fax: 352-588-7873, E-mail: grad.admissions@saintleo.edu. *Associate Dean, School of Business,* Dr. Lorrie McGovern, 352-588-7869, Fax: 352-588-8912, E-mail: mbaslu@saintleo.edu.

Graduate Studies in Creative Writing Students: 15 part-time (8 women); includes 2 minority (both Black or African American, non-Hispanic/Latino). Average age 40. 23 applicants, 87% accepted, 13 enrolled. *Faculty:* 2 full-time (0 women). Expenses: Contact institution. *Financial support:* Scholarships/grants and health care benefits available. *Program availability:* Part-time. Offers creative writing (MA); war literature and writing for veterans (MA). *Application deadline:* For fall admission, 7/1 priority date for domestic and international students; for spring admission, 11/1 priority date for domestic and international students. Applications are processed on a rolling basis. *Application fee:* $80. Electronic applications accepted. *Application Contact:* Jennifer Shelley, Senior Associate Director of Graduate Admissions, 800-707-8846, Fax: 352-588-7873, E-mail: grad.admissions@saintleo.edu. *Director,* Dr. Steve Kistulentz, 352-588-7218, Fax: 352-588-8300, E-mail: steven.kistulentz@saintleo.edu.

Graduate Studies in Education Students: 424 part-time (335 women); includes 94 minority (54 Black or African American, non-Hispanic/Latino; 2 Asian, non-Hispanic/Latino; 32 Hispanic/Latino; 6 Two or more races, non-Hispanic/Latino), 1 international. Average age 37. 260 applicants, 76% accepted, 107 enrolled. *Faculty:* 11 full-time (10 women), 22 part-time/adjunct (15 women). Expenses: Contact institution. *Financial support:* In 2016–17, 17 students received support. Career-related internships or fieldwork, scholarships/grants, and health care benefits available. Financial award application deadline: 3/1; financial award applicants required to submit FAFSA. In 2016, 166 master's, 6 other advanced degrees awarded. *Program availability:* Part-time, evening/weekend, online learning. Offers educational leadership (M Ed); exceptional student education (M Ed); instructional design (MS, Certificate); instructional leadership (M Ed); reading (M Ed, Certificate); school leadership (Ed S). *Application deadline:* For fall admission, 7/1 priority date for domestic students, 7/1 for international students; for winter admission, 7/1 for international students; for spring admission, 11/1 priority date for domestic students. Applications are processed on a rolling basis. *Application fee:* $80. Electronic applications accepted. *Application Contact:* Jennifer Shelley, Senior Associate Director of Graduate Admissions, 800-707-8846, Fax: 352-588-7873, E-mail: grad.admissions@saintleo.edu. *Director of Graduate Studies in Education,* Dr. Fern Aefsky, 352-588-8309, Fax: 352-588-8861, E-mail: kara.winkler@saintleo.edu.

Graduate Studies in Human Services Students: 20 part-time (19 women); includes 15 minority (14 Black or African American, non-Hispanic/Latino; 1 Two or more races, non-Hispanic/Latino). Average age 42. 12 applicants, 100% accepted, 11 enrolled. *Faculty:* 2 full-time (both women), 2 part-time/adjunct (both women). Expenses: Contact institution. *Financial support:* Career-related internships or fieldwork, scholarships/grants, and health care benefits available. Financial award applicants required to submit FAFSA. *Program availability:* Part-time, evening/weekend. Offers human services (MS). *Application deadline:* For fall admission, 7/1 for domestic and international students; for spring admission, 11/1 for domestic and international students. *Application fee:* $80. *Application Contact:* Mary Martinez-Drovie, Graduate Enrollment Counselor, 352-588-5802, Fax: 352-588-8289, E-mail: mary.martinez-drovie@saintleo.edu. *Dean, School of Education and Social Services,* Dr. Susan Kinsella, 352-588-8272, Fax: 352-588-8289, E-mail: susan.kinsella@saintleo.edu.

Graduate Studies in Public Safety Administration Students: 3 full-time (1 woman), 667 part-time (446 women); includes 355 minority (275 Black or African American, non-Hispanic/Latino; 6 American Indian or Alaska Native, non-Hispanic/Latino; 4 Asian, non-Hispanic/Latino; 56 Hispanic/Latino; 3 Native Hawaiian or other Pacific Islander, non-Hispanic/Latino; 11 Two or more races, non-Hispanic/Latino). Average age 37. 361 applicants, 87% accepted, 177 enrolled. *Faculty:* 7 full-time (2 women), 32 part-time/adjunct (8 women). Expenses: Contact institution. *Financial support:* In 2016–17, 14 students received support. Scholarships/grants and health care benefits available. Financial award application deadline: 3/1; financial award applicants required to submit FAFSA. In 2016, 265 master's awarded. *Program availability:* Part-time, evening/weekend, 100% online, blended/hybrid learning. Offers criminal justice (MS); emergency and disaster management (MS). *Application deadline:* For fall admission, 7/1 priority date for domestic and international students; for spring admission, 11/1 priority date for domestic and international students. Applications are processed on a rolling basis. *Application fee:* $80. Electronic applications accepted. *Application Contact:* Jennifer Shelley, Senior Associate Director of Graduate Admissions, 800-707-8846, Fax: 352-588-7873, E-mail: grad.admissions@saintleo.edu. *Director of Graduate Studies in Safety Administration,* Dr. Robert Diemer, 352-588-8974, Fax: 352-588-8289, E-mail: graduatepublicsafety@saintleo.edu.

Graduate Studies in Social Work Students: 143 full-time (123 women), 83 part-time (68 women); includes 94 minority (67 Black or African American, non-Hispanic/Latino; 1 Asian, non-Hispanic/Latino; 22 Hispanic/Latino; 4 Two or more races, non-Hispanic/Latino). Average age 36. 275 applicants, 73% accepted, 126 enrolled. *Faculty:* 8 full-time (6 women), 21 part-time/adjunct (17 women). Expenses: Contact institution. *Financial support:* In 2016–17, 2 students received support. Career-related internships or fieldwork and health care benefits available. Financial award application deadline: 3/1. In 2016, 73 master's awarded. *Program availability:* Online only, blended/hybrid learning. Offers advanced clinical practice (MSW). *Application deadline:* For fall admission, 6/1 for domestic and international students. *Application fee:* $80. Electronic applications accepted. *Application Contact:* Jennifer Shelley, Senior Associate Director of Graduate Admissions, 800-707-8846, Fax: 352-588-7873, E-mail: grad.admissions@saintleo.edu. *Director of Graduate Studies in Social Work,* Dr. Cindy Lee, 352-588-8869, Fax: 352-588-8289, E-mail: cindy.lee@saintleo.edu.

Graduate Studies in Theology Students: 253 full-time (91 women); includes 54 minority (35 Black or African American, non-Hispanic/Latino; 1 Asian, non-Hispanic/Latino; 13 Hispanic/Latino; 1 Native Hawaiian or other Pacific Islander, non-

Hispanic/Latino; 4 Two or more races, non-Hispanic/Latino), 3 international. Average age 50. 115 applicants, 83% accepted, 55 enrolled. *Faculty:* 10 full-time (0 women), 10 part-time/adjunct (3 women). Expenses: Contact institution. *Financial support:* In 2016–17, 3 students received support. Scholarships/grants and health care benefits available. Financial award application deadline: 3/1; financial award applicants required to submit FAFSA. In 2016, 73 master's, 2 other advanced degrees awarded. *Program availability:* Part-time, evening/weekend, 100% online, blended/hybrid learning. Offers theology (MA, Certificate). *Application deadline:* For fall admission, 7/1 priority date for domestic and international students; for spring admission, 11/1 priority date for domestic and international students. Applications are processed on a rolling basis. *Application fee:* $80. Electronic applications accepted. *Application Contact:* Jennifer Shelley, Senior Associate Director of Graduate Admission, 800-707-8846, Fax: 352-588-7873, E-mail: grad.admissions@saintleo.edu. *Director, Graduate Theology,* Dr. Randall Woodard, 352-588-8239, Fax: 352-588-8404, E-mail: randall.woodard@saintleo.edu.

ST. LOUIS COLLEGE OF PHARMACY, St. Louis, MO 63110-1088

General Information Independent, coed, comprehensive institution. *Enrollment:* 1,384 graduate, professional, and undergraduate students; 840 full-time matriculated graduate/professional students (502 women), 5 part-time matriculated graduate/professional students (2 women). *Enrollment by degree level:* 845 doctoral. *Graduate faculty:* 54 full-time (35 women), 25 part-time/adjunct (13 women). *Tuition:* Full-time $32,957; part-time $1084 per credit hour. *Required fees:* $463; $463 per credit hour. Tuition and fees vary according to student level. *Graduate housing:* Room and/or apartments available on a first-come, first-served basis to single students; on-campus housing not available to married students. Typical cost: $5880 per year ($10,901 including board). Room and board charges vary according to board plan. Housing application deadline: 6/1. *Student services:* Campus employment opportunities, campus safety program, career counseling, exercise/wellness program, free psychological counseling, international student services, low-cost health insurance, multicultural affairs office, services for students with disabilities, writing training. *Library facilities:* O. J. Cloughly Alumni Library. *Collection:* Books: 56,675 (physical), 175,165 (digital/electronic); Serial titles: 63 (physical), 217 (digital/electronic); Databases: 64. Weekly public service hours: 101; study areas open 24 hours, 5–7 days a week; students can reserve study rooms. *Research affiliation:* Express Scripts (pharmacy), Strategic Biomedical, Inc.

Computer facilities: Computer purchase and lease plans are available. 1,390 computers available on campus for general student use. A campuswide network can be accessed from student residence rooms and from off campus. Online class registration is available.
Website: http://www.stlcop.edu/

General Application Contact: Chase Davis, Director of Admissions, 314-446-8140, Fax: 314-446-8309, E-mail: chase.davis@stlcop.edu.

GRADUATE UNITS

Professional Program Students: 840 full-time (502 women), 5 part-time (2 women); includes 266 minority (61 Black or African American, non-Hispanic/Latino; 3 American Indian or Alaska Native, non-Hispanic/Latino; 181 Asian, non-Hispanic/Latino; 5 Hispanic/Latino; 2 Native Hawaiian or other Pacific Islander, non-Hispanic/Latino; 14 Two or more races, non-Hispanic/Latino), 21 international. Average age 23. 294 applicants, 52% accepted, 74 enrolled. *Faculty:* 54 full-time (35 women), 25 part-time/adjunct (13 women). Expenses: Contact institution. *Financial support:* In 2016–17, 388 students received support. Federal Work-Study and scholarships/grants available. Support available to part-time students. Financial award application deadline: 3/15; financial award applicants required to submit FAFSA. In 2016, 213 doctorates awarded. Offers pharmacy (Pharm D). *Application deadline:* For fall admission, 3/1 for domestic and international students. Applications are processed on a rolling basis. *Application fee:* $55. Electronic applications accepted. *Application Contact:* Chase Davis, Director of Admissions, 314-446-8140, Fax: 314-446-8309, E-mail: chase.davis@stlcop.edu. *Dean of Pharmacy,* Dr. Bruce Canaday.

SAINT LOUIS UNIVERSITY, St. Louis, MO 63103

General Information Independent-religious, coed, university. CGS member. *Graduate housing:* Rooms and/or apartments available to single and married students. Housing application deadline: 5/1. *Research affiliation:* AT&T Foundation (communication), National Center for Atmospheric Research (earth and atmospheric sciences), Argonne National Laboratory (energy, physics, chemistry, mathematics and computer science), Small Business Administration (business, administration and entrepreneurship), Monsanto Chemical Corporation (chemistry), Missouri Botanical Garden (biology, plant science).

GRADUATE UNITS

Graduate Education *Program availability:* Part-time, evening/weekend, online learning. Offers anatomy (MS-R, PhD); biochemistry and molecular biology (PhD); biomedical sciences (MS-R, PhD); molecular microbiology and immunology (PhD); pathology (PhD); pharmacological and physiological science (PhD). Electronic applications accepted.

Center for Advanced Dental Education Offers endodontics (MSD); orthodontics (MSD); periodontics (MSD). Electronic applications accepted.

Center for Health Care Ethics Offers clinical health care ethics (Certificate); health care ethics (PhD). Electronic applications accepted.

College of Arts and Sciences *Program availability:* Part-time, evening/weekend. Offers American studies (MA, MA-R, PhD); arts and sciences (M Pr Met, MA, MA-R, MS, MS-R, PhD); biology (MS, MS-R, PhD); chemistry (MS, MS-R, PhD); clinical psychology (MS-R, PhD); communication (MA, MA-R); communication sciences and disorders (MA, MA-R); English (MA, MA-R, PhD); experimental psychology (MS-R, PhD); French (MA); geophysics (PhD); geoscience (MS); historical theology (MA, PhD); history (MA, MA-R, PhD); industrial-organizational psychology (PhD); mathematics (MA, MA-R, PhD); meteorology (M Pr Met, MS-R, PhD); philosophy (MA, MA-R, PhD); political science (MA); psychology (PhD); Spanish (MA); theology (MA). Electronic applications accepted.

College of Education and Public Service *Program availability:* Part-time. Offers Catholic school leadership (MA); counseling and family therapy (PhD); curriculum and instruction (MA, Ed D, PhD); education and public service (MA, MA-R, MAPA, MAT, MAUA, MSW, MUPRED, Ed D, PhD, Certificate, Ed S); educational administration (MA, Ed D, PhD, Ed S); educational foundations (MA, Ed D, PhD); geographic information systems (Certificate); higher education (MA, Ed D, PhD); human development counseling (MA); marriage and family therapy (Certificate); organizational development (Certificate); public administration (MAPA); public policy analysis (PhD); school counseling (MA, MA-R); social work (MSW); special education (MA); student personnel administration (MA); teaching (MAT); urban affairs (MAUA);

urban planning and real estate development (MUPRED). Electronic applications accepted.

Doisy College of Health Sciences *Program availability:* Part-time. Offers athletic training (MAT); health sciences (MAT, MMS, MOT, MS, MSN, DNP, DPT, PhD, Certificate); medical dietetics (MS); nursing (MSN, DNP, PhD, Certificate); nutrition and physical performance (MS); occupational science and occupational therapy (MOT); physical therapy (DPT); physician assistant education (MMS).

John Cook School of Business *Program availability:* Part-time, evening/weekend. Offers accounting (M Acct, MBA); business (EMIB, M Acct, MBA, MSF, PhD); business administration (MBA); executive international business (EMIB); finance (MBA, MSF); international business (MBA). Electronic applications accepted.

Parks College of Engineering, Aviation, and Technology *Program availability:* Part-time, online learning. Offers biomedical engineering (MS, MS-R, PhD); engineering, aviation, and technology (MS, MS-R, PhD).

School of Medicine Offers medicine (MD). Electronic applications accepted.

School of Public Health *Program availability:* Part-time. Offers biosecurity (Certificate); community health (MPH, MS, MSPH); health administration (MHA); health management and policy (MHA, MPH, PhD); health policy (MPH); public health (PhD); public health studies (PhD).

School of Law *Program availability:* Part-time, evening/weekend. Offers law (LL M, JD). Electronic applications accepted.

SAINT LOUIS UNIVERSITY–MADRID CAMPUS, 28003 Madrid, Spain

General Information Independent-religious, coed, comprehensive institution. *Graduate housing:* Room and/or apartments guaranteed to single students. *Research affiliation:* Universidad Autonoma de Madrid (English philology), Pontificia Universidade Catolica do Rio de Janeiro, Sogang University, Korea.

GRADUATE UNITS

Graduate Programs *Program availability:* Part-time. Offers English (MA); Spanish (MA).

SAINT MARTIN'S UNIVERSITY, Lacey, WA 98503

General Information Independent-religious, coed, comprehensive institution. *Enrollment:* 1,585 graduate, professional, and undergraduate students; 221 full-time matriculated graduate/professional students (139 women), 60 part-time matriculated graduate/professional students (40 women). *Enrollment by degree level:* 266 master's, 15 other advanced degrees. *Graduate faculty:* 21 full-time (10 women), 35 part-time/adjunct (19 women). *Tuition:* Full-time $13,800; part-time $1150 per credit hour. *Required fees:* $720; $60 per credit hour. Tuition and fees vary according to course level and program. *Graduate housing:* Room and/or apartments available on a first-come, first-served basis to single students; on-campus housing not available to married students. Typical cost: $10,700 (including board). Room and board charges vary according to board plan and housing facility selected. Housing application deadline: 3/15. *Student services:* Campus employment opportunities, campus safety program, career counseling, exercise/wellness program, free psychological counseling, international student services, low-cost health insurance, multicultural affairs office, services for students with disabilities, writing training. *Library facilities:* O'Grady Library. *Collection:* Books: 82,453 (physical), 199,324 (digital/electronic); Serial titles: 100 (physical), 46,874 (digital/electronic); Databases: 110. Weekly public service hours: 88; students can reserve study rooms.

Computer facilities: 80 computers available on campus for general student use. A campuswide network can be accessed from student residence rooms. Online class registration is available.
Website: http://www.stmartin.edu/

General Application Contact: Casey Caronna, Administrative Assistant III, 360-412-6128, E-mail: ccaronna@stmartin.edu.

GRADUATE UNITS

Office of Graduate Studies Students: 225 full-time (134 women), 54 part-time (37 women); includes 85 minority (19 Black or African American, non-Hispanic/Latino; 2 American Indian or Alaska Native, non-Hispanic/Latino; 9 Asian, non-Hispanic/Latino; 33 Hispanic/Latino; 3 Native Hawaiian or other Pacific Islander, non-Hispanic/Latino; 19 Two or more races, non-Hispanic/Latino), 26 international. Average age 33. 143 applicants, 57% accepted, 59 enrolled. *Faculty:* 19 full-time (5 women), 27 part-time/adjunct (13 women). Expenses: Contact institution. *Financial support:* Career-related internships or fieldwork, institutionally sponsored loans, and scholarships/grants available. Support available to part-time students. Financial award application deadline: 3/1; financial award applicants required to submit FAFSA. In 2016, 113 master's awarded. *Program availability:* Part-time, evening/weekend. Offers civil engineering (MCE); counseling psychology (MAC); engineering management (M Eng Mgt); mechanical engineering (MME). *Application deadline:* For fall admission, 4/1 priority date for domestic and international students; for spring admission, 11/1 for domestic students, 11/1 priority date for international students. Applications are processed on a rolling basis. *Application fee:* $50. Electronic applications accepted. *Application Contact:* Casey Caronna, Administrative Assistant, 360-412-6142, E-mail: ccaronna@stmartin.edu.

College of Education Students: 50 full-time (29 women), 14 part-time (11 women); includes 14 minority (2 Black or African American, non-Hispanic/Latino; 1 American Indian or Alaska Native, non-Hispanic/Latino; 9 Hispanic/Latino; 2 Two or more races, non-Hispanic/Latino). Average age 33. 31 applicants, 61% accepted, 13 enrolled. *Faculty:* 10 full-time (7 women), 12 part-time/adjunct (8 women). Expenses: Contact institution. *Financial support:* Career-related internships or fieldwork, Federal Work-Study, institutionally sponsored loans, and unspecified assistantships available. Support available to part-time students. Financial award application deadline: 3/1; financial award applicants required to submit FAFSA. In 2016, 30 master's awarded. *Program availability:* Part-time, evening/weekend. Offers education (M Ed, MIT). *Application deadline:* For fall admission, 4/1 priority date for domestic and international students; for spring admission, 11/1 priority date for domestic and international students. Applications are processed on a rolling basis. *Application fee:* $50. Electronic applications accepted. *Application Contact:* Casey Caronna, Administrative Assistant, 360-412-6128, E-mail: ccaronna@stmartin.edu. *College of Education and Counseling Psychology,* Dr. Kathleen M. Boyle, 360-438-4333, Fax: 360-438-4486, E-mail: kboyle@stmartin.edu.

School of Business Students: 72 full-time (30 women), 9 part-time (3 women); includes 28 minority (8 Black or African American, non-Hispanic/Latino; 5 Asian, non-Hispanic/Latino; 8 Hispanic/Latino; 1 Native Hawaiian or other Pacific Islander, non-Hispanic/Latino; 6 Two or more races, non-Hispanic/Latino), 21 international. Average age 31. 46 applicants, 74% accepted, 25 enrolled. *Faculty:* 6 full-time (4 women), 8 part-time/adjunct (3 women). Expenses: Contact institution. *Financial support:* Career-related internships or fieldwork and scholarships/grants available. Support

available to part-time students. Financial award application deadline: 3/1; financial award applicants required to submit FAFSA. In 2016, 38 master's awarded. *Program availability:* Part-time, evening/weekend. Offers business (MBA). *Application deadline:* For fall admission, 7/1 priority date for domestic and international students; for spring admission, 12/1 for domestic students, 12/1 priority date for international students. Applications are processed on a rolling basis. *Application fee:* $50. Electronic applications accepted. *Application Contact:* Casey Caronna, Administrative Assistant, 360-412-6128, E-mail: ccaronna@stmartin.edu. *Director, MBA Program,* Dr. Donald Conant, 360-556-7359, E-mail: dconant@stmartin.edu.

SAINT MARY-OF-THE-WOODS COLLEGE, Saint Mary of the Woods, IN 47876

General Information Independent-religious, coed, primarily women, comprehensive institution. *Enrollment:* 883 graduate, professional, and undergraduate students; 230 full-time matriculated graduate/professional students (216 women). *Enrollment by degree level:* 230 master's. *Graduate faculty:* 18 full-time (13 women), 8 part-time/adjunct (7 women). *Tuition:* Full-time $10,000. *Required fees:* $2000. Full-time tuition and fees vary according to program. *Graduate housing:* On-campus housing not available. *Student services:* Campus employment opportunities, campus safety program, career counseling, exercise/wellness program, international student services, services for students with disabilities, teacher training, writing training. *Library facilities:* Rooney Library.

Computer facilities: Computer purchase and lease plans are available. A campuswide network can be accessed from student residence rooms.
Website: http://www.smwc.edu/

General Application Contact: Marie Elliott, Assistant Director of Admissions, 812-535-5106, E-mail: graduate@smwc.edu.

GRADUATE UNITS

Master of Arts in Art Therapy Program Students: 144 full-time (139 women); includes 20 minority (all Two or more races, non-Hispanic/Latino). Average age 37. *Faculty:* 2 full-time (both women). Expenses: Contact institution. *Financial support:* Scholarships/grants available. Financial award applicants required to submit FAFSA. *Program availability:* Evening/weekend, online learning. Offers art therapy (MA, Post-Master's Certificate). *Application fee:* $0. Electronic applications accepted. *Director,* Dr. Jill McNutt, 812-535-5160, E-mail: jmcnutt@smwc.edu.

Master of Arts in Music Therapy Program Students: 24 full-time (22 women). Average age 32. Expenses: Contact institution. *Financial support:* Career-related internships or fieldwork, scholarships/grants, and unspecified assistantships available. *Program availability:* Blended/hybrid learning. Offers music therapy (MA). *Application deadline:* Applications are processed on a rolling basis. *Application fee:* $0. Electronic applications accepted. *Director,* Dr. Tracy Richardson, 812-535-5154, E-mail: trichardson@smwc.edu.

Master of Leadership Development Program Students: 47 full-time (41 women); includes 4 minority (all Black or African American, non-Hispanic/Latino). Average age 35. Expenses: Contact institution. *Financial support:* Scholarships/grants available. *Program availability:* Part-time, blended/hybrid learning. Offers not-for-profit leadership (MLD); organizational leadership (MLD). *Application deadline:* Applications are processed on a rolling basis. *Application fee:* $0. Electronic applications accepted. *Director, Master of Leadership Development,* Susan Decker, 812-535-5206, E-mail: sdecker2@smwc.edu.

SAINT MARY'S COLLEGE, Notre Dame, IN 46556

General Information Independent-religious, women only, comprehensive institution. *Enrollment:* 1,701 graduate, professional, and undergraduate students; 50 full-time matriculated graduate/professional students (46 women), 26 part-time matriculated graduate/professional students (20 women). *Enrollment by degree level:* 58 master's, 18 doctoral. *Graduate faculty:* 18 full-time (15 women), 2 part-time/adjunct (both women). *Tuition:* Full-time $17,825; part-time $775 per credit hour. *Required fees:* $400 per credit hour. Tuition and fees vary according to program. *Graduate housing:* Room and/or apartments available on a first-come, first-served basis to single students; on-campus housing not available to married students. Typical cost: $7250 per year ($11,720 including board). Room and board charges vary according to board plan, campus/location and housing facility selected. Housing application deadline: 5/1. *Student services:* Campus employment opportunities, campus safety program, career counseling, child daycare facilities, exercise/wellness program, international student services, multicultural affairs office, services for students with disabilities, writing training. *Library facilities:* Cushwa-Leighton Library. *Collection:* Books: 260,077 (physical), 140,170 (digital/electronic); Serial titles: 4,136 (physical), 205,506 (digital/electronic); Databases: 74. Weekly public service hours: 54; study areas open 24 hours, 5–7 days a week; students can reserve study rooms.

Computer facilities: Computer purchase and lease plans are available. 291 computers available on campus for general student use. A campuswide network can be accessed from student residence rooms and from off campus. Online class registration is available.
Website: http://www.saintmarys.edu/

General Application Contact: Melissa Fruscione, Associate Director of Admission, Graduate Programs, 574-284-5098, E-mail: mfruscione@saintmarys.edu.

GRADUATE UNITS

Graduate Programs Students: 50 full-time (46 women), 26 part-time (20 women); includes 11 minority (3 Black or African American, non-Hispanic/Latino; 5 Asian, non-Hispanic/Latino; 3 Hispanic/Latino). Average age 30. 229 applicants, 42% accepted, 43 enrolled. *Faculty:* 19 full-time (16 women), 2 part-time/adjunct (both women). Expenses: Contact institution. Offers data science (MS); nursing (DNP); speech language pathology (MS). *Application Contact:* Melissa Fruscione, Associate Director of Graduate Admissions, 574-284-5098, E-mail: graduateadmission@saintmarys.edu.

SAINT MARY'S COLLEGE OF CALIFORNIA, Moraga, CA 94575

General Information Independent-religious, coed, upper-level institution. CGS member. *Graduate housing:* Room and/or apartments available on a first-come, first-served basis to single students; on-campus housing not available to married students. Housing application deadline: 6/1.

GRADUATE UNITS

Kalmanovitz School of Education *Program availability:* Part-time, evening/weekend. Offers career counseling (MA); coaching and facilitation (MA); college student services (Credential); education (M Ed, MA, MA Ed, Ed D, Credential); educational administration (MA); educational leadership (Ed D); general counseling (MA); marriage and family therapy (MA); Montessori education (MA); organizational leadership and change (MA); peacebuilding and conflict transformation (MA); preliminary administrative services (Credential); pupil personnel services (Credential); school counseling (MA); school psychology (MA); social justice (MA); special education (M Ed); supervision and leadership (MA); teaching (MA Ed); teaching leadership (MA).

School of Economics and Business Administration *Program availability:* Part-time, evening/weekend. Offers accounting (MS); business analytics (MS); executive business administration (MBA); financial analysis and investment management (MS); management (MS); professional business administration (MBA).

School of Liberal Arts *Program availability:* Part-time. Offers creative writing (MFA); dance: creative practice (MFA); dance: design and production (MFA); fitness management (MA); liberal arts (MA, MFA); sport management (MA); sport studies (MA).

ST. MARY'S COLLEGE OF MARYLAND, St. Mary's City, MD 20686-3001

General Information State-supported, coed, comprehensive institution. *Graduate housing:* Room and/or apartments available on a first-come, first-served basis to single students; on-campus housing not available to married students. Housing application deadline: 5/1.

GRADUATE UNITS

Department of Educational Studies Offers educational studies (MAT). Electronic applications accepted.

SAINT MARY SEMINARY AND GRADUATE SCHOOL OF THEOLOGY, Wickliffe, OH 44092-2527

General Information Independent-religious, coed, primarily men, graduate-only institution. *Graduate housing:* Room and/or apartments available to single students; on-campus housing not available to married students.

GRADUATE UNITS

Graduate and Professional Programs *Program availability:* Part-time. Offers theology (M Div, MA, D Min).

ST. MARY'S SEMINARY AND UNIVERSITY, Baltimore, MD 21210-1994

General Information Independent-religious, coed, primarily men, graduate-only institution. *Graduate housing:* Room and/or apartments guaranteed to single students; on-campus housing not available to married students. Housing application deadline: 8/15.

GRADUATE UNITS

Ecumenical Institute of Theology *Program availability:* Part-time, evening/weekend. Offers church ministries (MA); theology (MA Th, Certificate).

School of Theology *Program availability:* Part-time. Offers theology (M Div, MA Th, STD, STB, STL).

SAINT MARY'S UNIVERSITY, Halifax, NS B3H 3C3, Canada

General Information Province-supported, coed, comprehensive institution. *Graduate housing:* Rooms and/or apartments available on a first-come, first-served basis to single students and available to married students.

GRADUATE UNITS

Faculty of Arts *Program availability:* Part-time, evening/weekend. Offers arts (MA, Certificate, Graduate Diploma); Atlantic Canada studies (MA, Certificate); criminology (MA); history (MA); international development studies (MA, Graduate Diploma); philosophy (MA); theology and religious studies (MA); women and gender studies (MA).

Faculty of Science *Program availability:* Part-time. Offers applied psychology (M Sc, PhD); applied science (M Sc); astronomy (M Sc, PhD); science (M Sc, PhD).

Sobey School of Business *Program availability:* Part-time, evening/weekend. Offers business (MBA, MF, PhD).

ST. MARY'S UNIVERSITY, San Antonio, TX 78228-8507

General Information Independent-religious, coed, comprehensive institution. *Enrollment:* 878 full-time matriculated graduate/professional students (416 women), 391 part-time matriculated graduate/professional students (208 women). *Enrollment by degree level:* 409 master's, 858 doctoral, 2 other advanced degrees. *Graduate faculty:* 58 full-time (21 women). *Tuition:* Full-time $15,600; part-time $865 per credit hour. *Required fees:* $148 per semester. *Graduate housing:* Room and/or apartments available on a first-come, first-served basis to single students; on-campus housing not available to married students. Typical cost: $2905 per year. Room charges vary according to board plan. Housing application deadline: 5/1. *Student services:* Campus employment opportunities, career counseling, exercise/wellness program, free psychological counseling, international student services, low-cost health insurance, services for students with disabilities. *Library facilities:* Louis J. Blume Library plus 1 other. *Collection:* Books: 195,486 (physical), 84,385 (digital/electronic); Serial titles: 498 (physical), 32,005 (digital/electronic); Databases: 137. Weekly public service hours: 100. *Research affiliation:* Southeast Research Consortium (behavioral science, biomedical engineering, social science).

Computer facilities: Computer purchase and lease plans are available. 200 computers available on campus for general student use. A campuswide network can be accessed from student residence rooms and from off campus. Online class registration is available.
Website: http://www.stmarytx.edu/

General Application Contact: Kim Thornton, Director, Graduate and Adult Enrollment Services, 210-436-3101, E-mail: akthornton@stmarytx.edu.

GRADUATE UNITS

Graduate Studies Students: 878 full-time (416 women), 391 part-time (208 women); includes 211 minority (27 Black or African American, non-Hispanic/Latino; 16 Asian, non-Hispanic/Latino; 166 Hispanic/Latino; 2 Two or more races, non-Hispanic/Latino; 110 international. Average age 33. 683 applicants, 40% accepted, 126 enrolled. *Faculty:* 54 full-time (22 women), 52 part-time/adjunct (14 women). Expenses: Contact institution. *Financial support:* Fellowships, research assistantships, career-related internships or fieldwork, Federal Work-Study, institutionally sponsored loans, scholarships/grants, health care benefits, tuition waivers, and unspecified assistantships available. Financial award application deadline: 3/31; financial award applicants required to submit FAFSA. In 2016, 118 master's, 14 doctorates, 8 other advanced degrees awarded. *Program availability:* Part-time, evening/weekend, 100% online. Offers Catholic school leadership (MA); clinical mental health counseling (MA); communication studies (MA); conflict transformation (Certificate); counselor education and supervision (PhD); education (MA); educational leadership (MA); English literature and language (MA); industrial/organizational psychology (MA, MS); international conflict resolution (MA); international development (MA); international relations (MA); marriage and family therapy (MA, PhD); public administration (MPA); public communication, public policy and

public leadership (Certificate); security policy (MA); theology (MA). *Application deadline:* For fall admission, 7/1 for domestic students; for spring admission, 11/15 for domestic students; for summer admission, 4/1 for domestic students. Applications are processed on a rolling basis. Electronic applications accepted. *Application Contact:* Kim Thornton, Director, Graduate and Adult Enrollment Services, 210-436-3101, E-mail: kthornton@stmarytx.edu. *Interim Dean of Graduate Studies,* Dr. Megan Mustain, 210-436-3554, E-mail: mmustain@stmarytx.edu.

Greehey School of Business Students: 51 full-time (21 women); includes 23 minority (3 Black or African American, non-Hispanic/Latino; 1 Asian, non-Hispanic/Latino; 19 Hispanic/Latino), 10 international. Average age 27. 133 applicants, 39% accepted, 40 enrolled. Expenses: Contact institution. *Financial support:* Research assistantships, institutionally sponsored loans, scholarships/grants, and unspecified assistantships available. Financial award application deadline: 3/31; financial award applicants required to submit FAFSA. In 2016, 22 master's awarded. *Program availability:* Part-time, evening/weekend. Offers business administration (MBA). *Application deadline:* For fall admission, 7/1 for domestic students; for spring admission, 11/15 for domestic students; for summer admission, 4/1 for domestic students. *Application fee:* $0. Electronic applications accepted. *Application Contact:* Jeremy Grace, Director, Master of Business Administration Programs, 210-431-2027, E-mail: jmgrace@stmarytx.edu.

School of Law Students: 610 full-time (276 women), 170 part-time (71 women); includes 415 minority (37 Black or African American, non-Hispanic/Latino; 11 American Indian or Alaska Native, non-Hispanic/Latino; 20 Asian, non-Hispanic/Latino; 346 Hispanic/Latino; 1 Native Hawaiian or other Pacific Islander, non-Hispanic/Latino). Average age 29. 1,338 applicants, 64% accepted, 242 enrolled. *Faculty:* 39 full-time (18 women), 43 part-time/adjunct (11 women). Expenses: Contact institution. *Financial support:* Application deadline: 2/15; applicants required to submit FAFSA. In 2016, 38 master's, 242 doctorates awarded. Offers American legal studies (LL M); international and comparative law (LL M); international criminal law (LL M); law (LL M, MJ, JD). *Application deadline:* For fall admission, 3/1 for domestic students. *Application fee:* $0. *Application Contact:* Kim Thornton, Director, Graduate and Adult Enrollment Services, 210-436-3101, E-mail: akthornton@stmarytx.edu. *Dean,* Stephen Sheppard, 210-436-3684, E-mail: sheppard@stmarytx.edu.

School of Science, Engineering and Technology Students: 87 full-time (21 women); includes 23 minority (2 Black or African American, non-Hispanic/Latino; 2 Asian, non-Hispanic/Latino; 19 Hispanic/Latino), 50 international. Average age 30. Expenses: Contact institution. *Financial support:* Application deadline: 3/31; applicants required to submit FAFSA. In 2016, 79 master's awarded. *Program availability:* Part-time, evening/weekend, blended/hybrid learning. Offers computer engineering (MS); computer information systems (MS); computer science (MS); cybersecurity (MS); electrical engineering (MS); engineering systems management (MS); industrial engineering (MS); science, engineering and technology (MS, Certificate); software engineering (MS, Certificate). *Application deadline:* For fall admission, 7/1 for domestic students; for spring admission, 11/15 for domestic students; for summer admission, 4/1 for domestic students. Applications are processed on a rolling basis. Electronic applications accepted. *Dean,* Dr. Winston F. Erevelles, 210-436-3996, E-mail: werevelles@stmarytx.edu.

SAINT MARY'S UNIVERSITY OF MINNESOTA, Winona, MN 55987-1399

General Information Independent-religious, coed, comprehensive institution. *Enrollment:* 5,640 graduate, professional, and undergraduate students; 2,678 full-time matriculated graduate/professional students (1,825 women), 1,158 part-time matriculated graduate/professional students (794 women). *Enrollment by degree level:* 3,294 master's, 316 doctoral, 226 other advanced degrees. *Graduate faculty:* 12 full-time (7 women), 332 part-time/adjunct (187 women). Tuition and fees vary according to degree level and program. *Student services:* Campus safety program, services for students with disabilities, teacher training, writing training. *Library facilities:* Fitzgerald Library plus 1 other. *Collection:* Books: 210,639 (physical), 10,144 (digital/electronic); Serial titles: 169 (physical), 82,154 (digital/electronic); Databases: 77. Weekly public service hours: 97; students can reserve study rooms.

Computer facilities: 200 computers available on campus for general student use. A campuswide network can be accessed from student residence rooms and from off campus. Online class registration is available.
Website: http://www.smumn.edu/

General Application Contact: James Callinan, Director of Admission for Graduate and Professional Programs, 612-728-5158, Fax: 612-728-5121, E-mail: jcallina@smumn.edu.

GRADUATE UNITS

Schools of Graduate and Professional Programs Students: 2,678 full-time (1,825 women), 1,158 part-time (794 women); includes 425 minority (201 Black or African American, non-Hispanic/Latino; 8 American Indian or Alaska Native, non-Hispanic/Latino; 101 Asian, non-Hispanic/Latino; 89 Hispanic/Latino; 2 Native Hawaiian or other Pacific Islander, non-Hispanic/Latino; 24 Two or more races, non-Hispanic/Latino), 120 international. Average age 35. *Faculty:* 12 full-time (7 women), 332 part-time/adjunct (187 women). Expenses: Contact institution. *Financial support:* Applicants required to submit FAFSA. In 2016, 919 master's, 13 doctorates, 245 other advanced degrees awarded. *Program availability:* Part-time, evening/weekend, 100% online, blended/hybrid learning. *Application deadline:* Applications are processed on a rolling basis. Electronic applications accepted. *Application Contact:* James Callinan, Director of Admissions for Graduate and Professional Programs, 612-728-5158, Fax: 612-728-5121, E-mail: jcallina@smumn.edu. *Vice President and Chief Academic Officer,* Br. Robert Smith, 612-728-5201, Fax: 612-728-5169, E-mail: rsmith@smumn.edu.

Graduate School of Business and Technology Students: 841 full-time (482 women), 302 part-time (183 women); includes 161 minority (83 Black or African American, non-Hispanic/Latino; 2 American Indian or Alaska Native, non-Hispanic/Latino; 37 Asian, non-Hispanic/Latino; 31 Hispanic/Latino; 1 Native Hawaiian or other Pacific Islander, non-Hispanic/Latino; 7 Two or more races, non-Hispanic/Latino), 94 international. Average age 36. Expenses: Contact institution. *Program availability:* Part-time, evening/weekend, 100% online, blended/hybrid learning. Offers accountancy (MS); arts and cultural management (MA); business administration (MBA, DBA); business and technology (MA, MBA, MS, DBA, Certificate); geographic information science (MS, Certificate); human development (MA); human resource management (MA); information technology management (MS); international business (MA); international development (MA); management (MA); organizational leadership (MA); philanthropy and development (MA); project management (MS, Certificate). *Application deadline:* Applications are processed on a rolling basis. Electronic applications accepted. *Application Contact:* James Callinan, Director of Admissions for Graduate and Professional Programs, 612-728-5158, Fax: 612-728-5121, E-mail: jcallina@smumn.edu. *Dean,* Dr. Thomas Marpe, 612-457-6967, E-mail: tmarpe@smumn.edu.

Graduate School of Education Students: 1,060 full-time (734 women), 628 part-time (442 women); includes 115 minority (43 Black or African American, non-Hispanic/Latino; 3 American Indian or Alaska Native, non-Hispanic/Latino; 26 Asian, non-Hispanic/Latino; 34 Hispanic/Latino; 1 Native Hawaiian or other Pacific Islander, non-Hispanic/Latino; 8 Two or more races, non-Hispanic/Latino), 15 international. Average age 35. Expenses: Contact institution. *Program availability:* Part-time, evening/weekend, 100% online, blended/hybrid learning. Offers behavioral disorders (Certificate); culturally responsive teaching (Certificate); education (M Ed, MA, Ed D, Certificate, Ed S); educational administration (Certificate, Ed S); educational leadership (MA, Ed D); gifted inclusive education (Certificate); instruction (MA); K-12 reading teacher (Certificate); LaSallian leadership (MA); LaSallian studies (MA); learning design and technology (M Ed); learning disabilities (Certificate); literacy education (MA); special education (MA); teaching and learning (M Ed). *Application deadline:* Applications are processed on a rolling basis. Electronic applications accepted. *Application Contact:* James Callinan, Director of Admissions for Graduate and Professional Programs, 612-728-5185, Fax: 612-728-5121, E-mail: jcallina@smumn.edu. *Dean,* Dr. Rebecca Hopkins, 507-457-6620, E-mail: rhopkins@smumn.edu.

Graduate School of Health and Human Services Students: 777 full-time (609 women), 228 part-time (169 women); includes 149 minority (75 Black or African American, non-Hispanic/Latino; 3 American Indian or Alaska Native, non-Hispanic/Latino; 38 Asian, non-Hispanic/Latino; 24 Hispanic/Latino; 9 Two or more races, non-Hispanic/Latino), 11 international. Average age 33. Expenses: Contact institution. *Program availability:* Part-time, evening/weekend, 100% online, blended/hybrid learning. Offers addiction studies (Certificate); counseling and psychological services (MA); counseling psychology (Psy D); health and human services (MA, MS, Psy D, Certificate); health and human services administration (MA); marriage and family therapy (MA); nurse anesthesia (MS). *Application deadline:* Applications are processed on a rolling basis. Electronic applications accepted. *Application Contact:* James Callinan, Director of Admissions for Graduate and Professional Programs, 612-728-5185, Fax: 612-728-5121, E-mail: jcallina@smumn.edu. *Dean,* Dr. Todd Reinhart, 507-457-1758, E-mail: treinhar@smumn.edu.

SAINT MEINRAD SCHOOL OF THEOLOGY, Saint Meinrad, IN 47577

General Information Independent-religious, coed, primarily men, graduate-only institution. *Enrollment by degree level:* 181 master's, 31 other advanced degrees. *Graduate faculty:* 18 full-time (2 women), 5 part-time/adjunct (1 woman). *Tuition:* Full-time $25,137; part-time $475 per credit hour. *Required fees:* $2900; $34 per course. *Graduate housing:* On-campus housing not available. *Student services:* Campus employment opportunities, campus safety program, exercise/wellness program, free psychological counseling, low-cost health insurance, writing training. *Library facilities:* Archabbey Library. *Collection:* Students can reserve study rooms.

Computer facilities: 30 computers available on campus for general student use. A campuswide network can be accessed from student residence rooms and from off campus.
Website: http://www.saintmeinrad.edu/

General Application Contact: Dr. John Schlachter, Director of Admissions, 812-357-6142, Fax: 812-357-6462, E-mail: apply@saintmeinrad.edu.

GRADUATE UNITS

Master of Arts (Catholic Philosophical Studies) Program Students: 17 full-time (0 women), 2 international. Average age 32. *Faculty:* 7 full-time (2 women), 2 part-time/adjunct (0 women). Expenses: Contact institution. *Financial support:* Federal Work-Study and scholarships/grants available. Financial award applicants required to submit FAFSA. In 2016, 8 master's awarded. Offers Catholic philosophical studies (MA). *Application deadline:* For fall admission, 7/31 for domestic and international students; for winter admission, 11/15 for domestic and international students. Applications are processed on a rolling basis. Electronic applications accepted. *Application Contact:* Dr. John Schlachter, Director of Admissions, 812-357-6142, Fax: 812-357-6816, E-mail: jschlachter@saintmeinrad.edu. *Academic Dean,* Dr. Robert Alvis, 812-357-6543, Fax: 812-357-6816, E-mail: ralvis@saintmeinrad.edu.

Master of Arts (Theology) Program Students: 1 full-time (0 women), 27 part-time (10 women), 1 international. Average age 45. *Faculty:* 19 full-time (2 women), 6 part-time/adjunct (1 woman). Expenses: Contact institution. *Financial support:* Federal Work-Study, institutionally sponsored loans, and scholarships/grants available. Support available to part-time students. Financial award application deadline: 7/31; financial award applicants required to submit FAFSA. In 2016, 15 master's awarded. *Program availability:* Part-time, evening/weekend. Offers theology (MA). *Application deadline:* For fall admission, 7/31 for domestic and international students; for winter admission, 11/15 for domestic and international students. Applications are processed on a rolling basis. *Application fee:* $30. Electronic applications accepted. *Application Contact:* Dr. John Schlachter, Director of Admissions, 812-357-6142, Fax: 812-357-6816, E-mail: apply@saintmeinrad.edu. *Director of Graduate Theology Programs,* Sr. Jeana Visel, OSB, 812-357-6721, Fax: 812-357-6816.

Master of Divinity Program Students: 106 full-time (0 women); includes 7 minority (1 Black or African American, non-Hispanic/Latino; 3 Asian, non-Hispanic/Latino; 3 Hispanic/Latino), 22 international. Average age 31. *Faculty:* 19 full-time (2 women), 6 part-time/adjunct (1 woman). Expenses: Contact institution. *Financial support:* Federal Work-Study, institutionally sponsored loans, and scholarships/grants available. Support available to part-time students. Financial award application deadline: 7/31; financial award applicants required to submit FAFSA. In 2016, 20 master's awarded. Offers divinity (M Div). *Application deadline:* For fall admission, 7/31 for domestic and international students; for winter admission, 11/15 for domestic and international students. Applications are processed on a rolling basis. *Application fee:* $0. Electronic applications accepted. *Application Contact:* Dr. John Schlachter, Director of Admissions, 812-357-6142, Fax: 812-357-6816, E-mail: apply@saintmeinrad.edu. *Academic Dean,* Dr. Robert Alvis, 812-357-6543, Fax: 812-357-6816, E-mail: ralvis@saintmeinrad.edu.

SAINT MICHAEL'S COLLEGE, Colchester, VT 05439

General Information Independent-religious, coed, comprehensive institution. *Enrollment:* 2,226 graduate, professional, and undergraduate students; 37 full-time matriculated graduate/professional students (30 women), 121 part-time matriculated graduate/professional students (93 women). *Enrollment by degree level:* 158 master's. *Tuition:* Full-time $10,620; part-time $590 per credit. Part-time tuition and fees vary according to course load and program. *Graduate housing:* Rooms and/or apartments available on a first-come, first-served basis to single and married students. Housing application deadline: 5/1. *Student services:* Campus employment opportunities, campus

safety program, career counseling, international student services, multicultural affairs office. *Library facilities:* Durick Library. *Collection:* Books: 231,540 (physical), 230,090 (digital/electronic); Serial titles: 1,621 (physical), 128,515 (digital/electronic); Databases: 142. Weekly public service hours: 102.

Computer facilities: Computer purchase and lease plans are available. 79 computers available on campus for general student use. A campuswide network can be accessed from student residence rooms and from off campus. Online class registration is available. Website: http://www.smcvt.edu/

General Application Contact: Lindsay A. Damici, Marketing Communications Manager, 802-654-2556.

GRADUATE UNITS

Graduate Programs Students: 37 full-time (30 women), 121 part-time (93 women). Expenses: Contact institution. *Financial support:* Fellowships, research assistantships, teaching assistantships with full tuition reimbursements, career-related internships or fieldwork, Federal Work-Study, institutionally sponsored loans, scholarships/grants, tuition waivers (partial), and unspecified assistantships available. Financial award application deadline: 2/1; financial award applicants required to submit FAFSA. In 2016, 64 master's awarded. *Program availability:* Part-time, evening/weekend. Offers arts in education (CAGS); clinical psychology (MA); literacy (M Ed); school leadership (CAGS); special education (M Ed); teaching English to speakers of other languages (MATESOL, Certificate). *Application deadline:* For fall admission, 6/1 for domestic students, 6/1 for international students; for spring admission, 12/1 for domestic students, 10/1 for international students; for summer admission, 4/1 for domestic students, 2/1 for international students. Applications are processed on a rolling basis. *Application fee:* $50. Electronic applications accepted. *Application Contact:* Lindsay A. Damici, Marketing Communications Manager, 802-654-2556, Fax: 802-654-2732.

ST. NORBERT COLLEGE, De Pere, WI 54115-2099

General Information Independent-religious, coed, comprehensive institution. *Enrollment:* 2,211 graduate, professional, and undergraduate students; 123 part-time matriculated graduate/professional students (75 women). *Enrollment by degree level:* 123 master's. *Graduate faculty:* 9 full-time (3 women), 14 part-time/adjunct (6 women). *Tuition:* Part-time $675 per credit. Tuition and fees vary according to program. *Graduate housing:* On-campus housing not available. *Student services:* Campus safety program, career counseling, child daycare facilities, exercise/wellness program, free psychological counseling, international student services, multicultural affairs office, services for students with disabilities, teacher training, writing training. *Library facilities:* Miriam B. and James J. Mulva Library plus 1 other. *Collection:* Books: 246,257 (physical), 89,569 (digital/electronic); Serial titles: 100,047 (physical), 99,843 (digital/electronic). Weekly public service hours: 116; students can reserve study rooms.

Computer facilities: Computer purchase and lease plans are available. 214 computers available on campus for general student use. A campuswide network can be accessed from student residence rooms and from off campus. Online class registration is available.
Website: http://www.snc.edu/

General Application Contact: Brenda Busch, Associate Director of Graduate Recruitment, 920-403-3942, Fax: 920-403-4072, E-mail: brenda.busch@snc.edu.

GRADUATE UNITS

Master of Arts in Liberal Studies Program Students: 14 part-time (11 women); includes 1 minority (Hispanic/Latino). Average age 40. 2 applicants, 100% accepted, 1 enrolled. *Faculty:* 4 part-time/adjunct (3 women). Expenses: Contact institution. *Financial support:* Applicants required to submit FAFSA. In 2016, 4 master's awarded. *Program availability:* Part-time-only, evening/weekend. Offers liberal studies (MA). *Application deadline:* Applications are processed on a rolling basis. *Application fee:* $50. Electronic applications accepted. *Application Contact:* Dinah Grassel, Program Coordinator, 920-403-3957, Fax: 920-403-4086, E-mail: dlnah.grassel@snc.edu. *Director,* Dr. Howard Ebert, 920-403-3956, Fax: 920-403-4086, E-mail: howard.ebert@snc.edu.

Master of Business Administration Program Students: 64 part-time (33 women); includes 6 minority (1 American Indian or Alaska Native, non-Hispanic/Latino; 2 Asian, non-Hispanic/Latino; 2 Hispanic/Latino; 1 Two or more races, non-Hispanic/Latino), 1 international. Average age 33. 17 applicants, 100% accepted, 16 enrolled. *Faculty:* 9 full-time (3 women), 3 part-time/adjunct (0 women). Expenses: Contact institution. *Financial support:* Federal Work-Study available. Financial award application deadline: 1/1; financial award applicants required to submit FAFSA. *Program availability:* Part-time. Offers business (MBA); health care (MBA); supply chain and management (MBA). *Application deadline:* For fall admission, 8/5 for domestic students; for winter admission, 12/16 for domestic students; for spring admission, 3/3 for domestic students; for summer admission, 4/22 for domestic students. Applications are processed on a rolling basis. *Application fee:* $50. Electronic applications accepted. *Application Contact:* Brenda Busch, Associate Director of Graduate Recruitment, 920-403-3942, Fax: 920-403-4072, E-mail: brenda.busch@snc.edu. *Executive Assistant,* Lisa Gray, 920-403-3449, E-mail: lisa.gray@snc.edu.

Master of Theological Studies Program Students: 45 part-time (31 women); includes 10 minority (9 Hispanic/Latino; 1 Two or more races, non-Hispanic/Latino). Average age 51. 4 applicants, 100% accepted, 4 enrolled. *Faculty:* 7 part-time/adjunct (3 women). Expenses: Contact institution. *Financial support:* In 2016–17, 10 students received support. Scholarships/grants available. Support available to part-time students. In 2016, 2 master's awarded. *Program availability:* Part-time-only, evening/weekend. Offers theological studies (MTS). *Application deadline:* Applications are processed on a rolling basis. *Application fee:* $50. Electronic applications accepted. *Application Contact:* Dinah Grassel, Program Coordinator, 920-403-3957, Fax: 920-403-4086, E-mail: dinah.grassel@snc.edu. *Director,* Dr. Howard Ebert, 920-403-3956, Fax: 920-403-4086, E-mail: howard.ebert@snc.edu.

ST. PATRICK'S SEMINARY & UNIVERSITY, Menlo Park, CA 94025-3596

General Information Independent-religious, coed, primarily men, graduate-only institution. *Graduate housing:* Room and/or apartments guaranteed to single students; on-campus housing not available to married students. Housing application deadline: 8/15.

GRADUATE UNITS

School of Theology *Program availability:* Part-time. Offers theology (M Div, MA, STB). STB offered jointly with St. Mary's Seminary and University.

SAINT PAUL SCHOOL OF THEOLOGY, Overland Park, KS 66211

General Information Independent-religious, coed, graduate-only institution. *Graduate housing:* Rooms and/or apartments available to single and married students. Housing application deadline: 5/31.

GRADUATE UNITS

Graduate and Professional Programs *Program availability:* Part-time. Offers theology (M Div, MA, MTS, D Min).

SAINT PAUL UNIVERSITY, Ottawa, ON K1S 1C4, Canada
General Information Province-supported, coed, university. *Graduate housing:* Room and/or apartments available to single students; on-campus housing not available to married students.

GRADUATE UNITS

Faculty of Canon Law *Program availability:* Part-time. Offers canon law (MCL, JCD, PhD, Graduate Certificate, JCL); canonical practice (Graduate Certificate); ecclesiastical administration (Graduate Certificate).

Faculty of Human Sciences Offers conflict studies (MA); counseling and spirituality (MA); individual and/or marital/couple counseling (MA Past St); individual or marital/couple counseling (MA); mission and interreligious studies (MA); pastoral care in health care services (MA Past St); spiritual care (MA). Programs offered in French and English.

Faculty of Theology Offers theology (MA Th, MP Th, MRE, D Min, D Th, PhD, L Th).

ST. PETER'S SEMINARY, London, ON N6A 3Y1, Canada
General Information Independent-religious, coed, primarily men, graduate-only institution.

GRADUATE UNITS

Department of Theology Offers theology (M Div, MTS).

SAINT PETER'S UNIVERSITY, Jersey City, NJ 07306-5997
General Information Independent-religious, coed, comprehensive institution. *Graduate housing:* On-campus housing not available.

GRADUATE UNITS

Graduate Business Programs *Program availability:* Part-time, evening/weekend. Offers accountancy (MS); business (MBA, MS); business analytics (MS); finance (MBA); health care administration (MBA); human resource management (MBA); international business (MBA); management (MBA); management information systems (MBA); marketing (MBA); risk management (MBA). Electronic applications accepted.

Graduate Programs in Education *Program availability:* Part-time, evening/weekend. Offers 6-8 middle school education (MA Ed, Certificate); director of school counseling services (Certificate); educational leadership (MA Ed, Ed D); higher education (Ed D); K-12 secondary education (MA Ed, Certificate); K-5 elementary education (MA Ed, Certificate); literacy (MA Ed); middle school mathematics (Certificate); professional/associate counselor (Certificate); reading (MA Ed); school business administrator (Certificate); school counseling (MA, Certificate); special education (MA Ed, Certificate); teaching (MA Ed, Certificate). Electronic applications accepted.

Program in Criminal Justice Administration *Program availability:* Part-time, evening/weekend. Offers federal law enforcement administration (MA); police administration (MA). Electronic applications accepted.

Program in Public Administration Offers public administration (MPA).

School of Nursing *Program availability:* Part-time, evening/weekend. Offers adult nurse practitioner (MSN, Certificate); advanced practice (DNP); case management (MSN, DNP); nursing (MSN, DNP, Certificate). Electronic applications accepted.

SAINTS CYRIL AND METHODIUS SEMINARY, Orchard Lake, MI 48324
General Information Independent-religious, coed, graduate-only institution. *Graduate housing:* Room and/or apartments guaranteed to single students; on-campus housing not available to married students. Housing application deadline: 7/1.

GRADUATE UNITS

Graduate and Professional Programs *Program availability:* Part-time. Offers pastoral ministry (MAPM); religious education (MARE); theology (M Div, MA).

ST. STEPHEN'S COLLEGE, Edmonton, AB T6G 2J6, Canada
General Information Independent-religious, coed, graduate-only institution. *Graduate housing:* On-campus housing not available.

GRADUATE UNITS

Programs in Theology *Program availability:* Part-time, evening/weekend, online learning. Offers ministry (D Min); pastoral counseling (MA); social transformation ministry (MA); spirituality and liturgy (MA); theological studies (MTS); theology (M Th). Electronic applications accepted.

ST. THOMAS AQUINAS COLLEGE, Sparkill, NY 10976
General Information Independent, coed, comprehensive institution. *Graduate housing:* On-campus housing not available. *Research affiliation:* Lederle Laboratories (science education), Lamont Doherty Laboratories (science education).

GRADUATE UNITS

Division of Business Administration *Program availability:* Part-time, evening/weekend. Offers business administration (MBA); finance (MBA); management (MBA); marketing (MBA). Electronic applications accepted.

Division of Teacher Education *Program availability:* Part-time, evening/weekend. Offers adolescence education (MST); childhood and special education (MST); childhood education (MST); educational leadership (MS Ed); reading (MS Ed, PMC); special education (MS Ed, PMC); teaching (MS Ed). Electronic applications accepted.

ST. THOMAS UNIVERSITY, Miami Gardens, FL 33054-6459
General Information Independent-religious, coed, university. *Graduate housing:* Room and/or apartments available on a first-come, first-served basis to single students; on-campus housing not available to married students. Housing application deadline: 7/1.

GRADUATE UNITS

Biscayne College Offers guidance and counseling (MS, Post-Master's Certificate); marriage and family therapy (MS, Post-Master's Certificate); mental health counseling (MS).

School of Business Offers accounting (MBA); business (M Acc, MBA, MIB, MS, MSM, Certificate); business administration (M Acc, MBA, Certificate); general management (MSM, Certificate); health management (MBA, MSM, Certificate); human resource management (MBA, MSM, Certificate); international business (MBA, MIB, MSM, Certificate); justice administration (MSM, Certificate); management accounting (MSM, Certificate); public management (MSM, Certificate); sports administration (MS).

School of Law *Program availability:* Online learning. Offers international human rights (LL M); international taxation (LL M); law (JD). Electronic applications accepted.

School of Leadership Studies *Program availability:* Part-time, evening/weekend. Offers art management (MA); electronic media (MA); executive management (MPS); Hispanic media (MA, Certificate); leadership studies (MA, MPS, MS, Ed D, Certificate).

Institute for Education *Program availability:* Part-time, evening/weekend. Offers earth/space science (Certificate); educational administration (MS, Certificate); educational leadership (Ed D); elementary education (MS); ESOL (Certificate); gifted education (Certificate); instructional technology (MS, Certificate); professional/studies (Certificate); reading (MS, Certificate); special education (MS). Electronic applications accepted.

School of Theology and Ministry Offers theology and ministry (MA, PhD, Certificate).

Institute for Pastoral Ministries *Program availability:* Part-time, evening/weekend. Offers pastoral ministries (MA, Certificate); practical theology (PhD). Electronic applications accepted.

ST. TIKHON'S ORTHODOX THEOLOGICAL SEMINARY, South Canaan, PA 18459
General Information Independent-religious, men only, graduate-only institution. *Enrollment by degree level:* 29 master's. *Graduate faculty:* 8 full-time (1 woman), 6 part-time/adjunct (0 women). *Tuition:* Full-time $6500; part-time $2260 per year. *Required fees:* $720; $720 per unit. One-time fee: $215. *Graduate housing:* Room and/or apartments guaranteed to single students; on-campus housing not available to married students. Typical cost: $3600 (including board). *Student services:* Career counseling. *Library facilities:* St. Tikhon's Seminary Library. *Collection:* Books: 41,000 (physical); Serial titles: 700 (physical); Databases: 4. Weekly public service hours: 6; study areas open 24 hours, 5–7 days a week.

Computer facilities: 10 computers available on campus for general student use. Website: http://www.stots.edu/

General Application Contact: Steven Voytovich, Dean and Director of Admissions, 570-561-1818 Ext. 101, E-mail: steven.voytovich@stots.edu.

GRADUATE UNITS

Divinity Program Students: 29 full-time (1 woman); includes 1 minority (Black or African American, non-Hispanic/Latino), 2 international. Average age 35. 16 applicants, 100% accepted, 12 enrolled. *Faculty:* 8 full-time (1 woman), 6 part-time/adjunct (0 women). Expenses: Contact institution. *Financial support:* Scholarships/grants and tuition waivers (full and partial) available. In 2016, 15 master's awarded. *Program availability:* Part-time. Offers divinity (M Div). *Application deadline:* For fall admission, 7/30 for domestic students, 6/30 for international students. Applications are processed on a rolling basis. *Application fee:* $15. *Dean/Director of Admissions,* Steven Voytovich, 570-561-1818 Ext. 101, Fax: 570-937-4139, E-mail: steven.voytovich@stots.edu.

SAINT VINCENT COLLEGE, Latrobe, PA 15650-2690
General Information Independent-religious, coed, comprehensive institution. *Graduate housing:* Room and/or apartments available on a first-come, first-served basis to single students; on-campus housing not available to married students.

GRADUATE UNITS

Program in Business Offers business (MS).

Program in Education *Program availability:* Part-time, evening/weekend. Offers curriculum and instruction (MS); instructional design and technology (MS); school administration and supervision (MS); special education (MS).

Program in Health Science Offers nurse anesthesia (MS).

ST. VINCENT DE PAUL REGIONAL SEMINARY, Boynton Beach, FL 33436-4899
General Information Independent-religious, coed, primarily men, graduate-only institution. *Graduate housing:* Room and/or apartments guaranteed to single students; on-campus housing not available to married students.

GRADUATE UNITS

Graduate and Professional Programs *Program availability:* Part-time. Offers theology (M Div, MA Th).

SAINT VINCENT SEMINARY, Latrobe, PA 15650-2690
General Information Independent-religious, coed, primarily men, graduate-only institution. *Enrollment by degree level:* 45 master's. *Graduate faculty:* 6 full-time (2 women), 16 part-time/adjunct (2 women). *Tuition:* Full-time $26,320; part-time $874 per credit. *Graduate housing:* Room and/or apartments guaranteed to single students; on-campus housing not available to married students. Typical cost: $6610 per year ($13,010 including board). Housing application deadline: 8/15. *Student services:* Campus safety program, exercise/wellness program, free psychological counseling, international student services, services for students with disabilities, writing training. *Library facilities:* Latimer Family Library. *Collection:* Books: 289,773 (physical), 4 (digital/electronic); Serial titles: 269 (physical); Databases: 29. Weekly public service hours: 84.

Computer facilities: 150 computers available on campus for general student use. A campuswide network can be accessed from student residence rooms and from off campus. Online class registration, X are available. Website: http://www.saintvincentseminary.edu/

General Application Contact: Rev. Patrick T. Cronauer, OSB, Academic Dean, 724-805-2324, Fax: 724-805-2880, E-mail: patrick.cronauer@stvincent.edu.

GRADUATE UNITS

School of Theology Students: 44 full-time (0 women), 1 part-time (0 women); includes 5 minority (1 American Indian or Alaska Native, non-Hispanic/Latino; 2 Asian, non-Hispanic/Latino; 1 Hispanic/Latino; 1 Two or more races, non-Hispanic/Latino), 7 international. Average age 33. 12 applicants, 100% accepted, 12 enrolled. *Faculty:* 6 full-time (2 women), 16 part-time/adjunct (2 women). Expenses: Contact institution. *Financial support:* In 2016–17, 45 students received support. Scholarships/grants available. Support available to part-time students. Financial award application deadline: 8/15. In 2016, 12 master's awarded. *Program availability:* Part-time, evening/weekend. Offers Catholic philosophical studies (MA); ecclesial ministry (MA); ministry (M Div); monastic studies (MA); sacred scripture (MA); systematic theology (MA). *Application deadline:* For fall admission, 8/15 for domestic and international students. Applications are processed on a rolling basis. *Application fee:* $34. *Application Contact:* Rev. Patrick T. Cronauer, OSB, Academic Dean, 724-805-2324, Fax: 724-805-2880, E-mail: patrick.cronauer@stvincent.edu. *President/Rector,* Very Rev. Edward M. Mazich, OSB, 724-805-2845, Fax: 724-532-5052, E-mail: edward.mazich@stvincent.edu.

ST. VLADIMIR'S ORTHODOX THEOLOGICAL SEMINARY, Crestwood, NY 10707-1699
General Information Independent-religious, coed, primarily men, graduate-only institution. *Enrollment by degree level:* 71 master's, 17 doctoral. *Graduate faculty:* 8 full-

time (1 woman), 21 part-time/adjunct (2 women). *Tuition:* Full-time $12,000; part-time $500 per credit. *Required fees:* $375; $300 per semester. Part-time tuition and fees vary according to course load and campus/location. *Graduate housing:* Rooms and/or apartments available on a first-come, first-served basis to single and married students. Typical cost: $6700 (including board) for single students; $8100 per year ($12,100 including board) for married students. Room and board charges vary according to housing facility selected. Housing application deadline: 5/1. *Student services:* Exercise/wellness program, international student services, services for students with disabilities. *Library facilities:* Father Georges Florovsky Library. *Collection:* Books: 100,000 (physical); Serial titles: 330 (physical); Databases: 3.

Computer facilities: 5 computers available on campus for general student use. Website: http://www.svots.edu/

General Application Contact: Rev. David Mezynski, Director of Admissions, 914-961-8313 Ext. 322, Fax: 914-961-4507, E-mail: admissions@svots.edu.

GRADUATE UNITS

Graduate School of Theology Students: 71 full-time (6 women), 4 part-time (0 women); includes 8 minority (2 Black or African American, non-Hispanic/Latino; 6 Asian, non-Hispanic/Latino), 15 international. Average age 29. 41 applicants, 95% accepted, 37 enrolled. *Faculty:* 8 full-time (1 woman), 21 part-time/adjunct (2 women). *Expenses:* Contact institution. *Financial support:* In 2016–17, 75 students received support. Fellowships, research assistantships, teaching assistantships, and scholarships/grants available. Financial award application deadline: 4/1; financial award applicants required to submit FAFSA. In 2016, 26 master's awarded. *Program availability:* Part-time. Offers theology (M Div, M Th, MA, D Min). MA in general theological studies and M Div offered jointly with St. Nersess Seminary. *Application deadline:* For fall admission, 5/1 priority date for domestic and international students. Applications are processed on a rolling basis. *Application fee:* $50. Electronic applications accepted. *Application Contact:* Gabrielle Russin, Student Affairs Administrator, 914-961-8313 Ext. 348, Fax: 914-961-4507, E-mail: grussin@svots.edu. *Dean,* Rev. Dr. John Behr, 914-961-8313, Fax: 914-961-4507, E-mail: jbehr@svots.edu.

SAINT XAVIER UNIVERSITY, Chicago, IL 60655-3105

General Information Independent-religious, coed, comprehensive institution. CGS member. *Graduate housing:* Room and/or apartments available on a first-come, first-served basis to single students; on-campus housing not available to married students. Housing application deadline: 8/15. *Research affiliation:* Alexian Brothers Hospital, Holy Cross Hospital, Little Company of Mary Hospital, Mercy Center for Health Care Services.

GRADUATE UNITS

Graduate Studies *Program availability:* Part-time, evening/weekend. Electronic applications accepted.

College of Arts and Sciences *Program availability:* Part-time, evening/weekend. Offers arts and sciences (MA, MACS, MS); computer science (MACS); speech-language pathology (MS).

Graham School of Management *Program availability:* Part-time, evening/weekend. Offers employee health benefits (Certificate); finance (MBA); financial fraud examination and management (MBA, Certificate); financial planning (MBA, Certificate); generalist/individualized (MBA); health administration (MBA); managed care (Certificate); management (MBA); marketing (MBA); project management (MBA, Certificate). Electronic applications accepted.

School of Education *Program availability:* Part-time, evening/weekend. Offers counseling (MA); curriculum and instruction (MA); early childhood education (MA); educational administration (MA); elementary education (MA); individualized studies (MA); music education (MA); reading (MA); secondary education (MA); Spanish education (MA); special education (MA); teaching and leadership (MA).

School of Nursing *Program availability:* Part-time, evening/weekend. Offers nursing (MSN, Certificate).

SALEM COLLEGE, Winston-Salem, NC 27101

General Information Independent-religious, coed, primarily women, comprehensive institution. *Graduate housing:* On-campus housing not available.

GRADUATE UNITS

Department of Education *Program availability:* Part-time, evening/weekend, online learning. Offers art education (MAT); elementary education (M Ed, MAT); language and literacy (M Ed); middle school education (MAT); school counseling (M Ed); second language studies (MAT); secondary education (MAT); special education (M Ed, MAT).

SALEM INTERNATIONAL UNIVERSITY, Salem, WV 26426-0500

General Information Independent, coed, comprehensive institution. *Graduate housing:* Rooms and/or apartments available on a first-come, first-served basis to single students and available to married students.

GRADUATE UNITS

School of Business *Program availability:* Part-time, online learning. Offers information security (MBA); international business (MBA). Electronic applications accepted.

School of Education *Program availability:* Part-time, evening/weekend, online learning. Offers curriculum and instruction (M Ed); educational leadership (M Ed). Electronic applications accepted.

SALEM STATE UNIVERSITY, Salem, MA 01970-5353

General Information State-supported, coed, comprehensive institution. CGS member. *Graduate housing:* On-campus housing not available.

GRADUATE UNITS

School of Graduate Studies *Program availability:* Part-time, evening/weekend. Offers adult-gerontology primary care nursing (MSN); advanced professional studies in counseling (Graduate Certificate); art (MAT); business administration (MBA); chemistry (MAT); counseling and psychological services (MS, Graduate Certificate); criminal justice (MS); early childhood education (M Ed); education (CAGS); elementary education (M Ed); English (MA, MAT); geo-information science (MS); higher education in student affairs (M Ed); history (MA, MAT); humanities (M Ed); library media studies (M Ed); math/science (MAT); mathematics (MAT, MS); middle school general education (MAT); middle school math (MAT); nursing administration (MSN); nursing education (MSN); occupational therapy (MS); physical education (M Ed); reading (M Ed); school counseling (M Ed); secondary education (MAT); social work (MSW); Spanish (MAT); special education (M Ed); teaching English as a second language (MAT).

SALISBURY UNIVERSITY, Salisbury, MD 21801-6837

General Information State-supported, coed, comprehensive institution. CGS member. *Enrollment:* 8,748 graduate, professional, and undergraduate students; 485 full-time matriculated graduate/professional students (379 women), 320 part-time matriculated graduate/professional students (234 women). *Enrollment by degree level:* 738 master's, 66 doctoral, 1 other advanced degree. *Graduate faculty:* 103 full-time (54 women), 37 part-time/adjunct (30 women). Tuition, state resident: part-time $381 per credit hour. Tuition, nonresident: part-time $670 per credit hour. *Required fees:* $84 per credit hour. Tuition and fees vary according to degree level and program. *Graduate housing:* On-campus housing not available. *Student services:* Campus employment opportunities, campus safety program, career counseling, exercise/wellness program, free psychological counseling, international student services, multicultural affairs office, services for students with disabilities, teacher training, writing training. *Library facilities:* SU Libraries plus 1 other. *Collection:* Books: 205,155 (physical), 225 (digital/electronic); Serial titles: 722 (physical), 146 (digital/electronic); Databases: 106. Weekly public service hours: 111; study areas open 24 hours, 5–7 days a week; students can reserve study rooms. *Research affiliation:* Maryland Department of Labor (program effectiveness and efficiency research), Talbot County Senior Center (market research for demand analysis), Maryland Association of Boards of Education (statewide economic impact analysis for K-12 public education), Trinity Sterile (expansion feasibility and scenario analysis), Town of Annapolis (mixed use development economic impact analysis), Konsyl Pharmaceuticals (compensation research).

Computer facilities: 750 computers available on campus for general student use. A campuswide network can be accessed from student residence rooms and from off campus. Online class registration, university accounts, student Web hosting are available.

Website: http://www.salisbury.edu/

General Application Contact: Lacie Doyle, Graduate Enrollment Management Specialist, 410-548-3546, Fax: 410-677-0052, E-mail: lhdoyle@salisbury.edu.

GRADUATE UNITS

Department of Conflict Analysis and Dispute Resolution Students: 38 full-time (26 women), 4 part-time (1 woman); includes 15 minority (10 Black or African American, non-Hispanic/Latino; 1 Asian, non-Hispanic/Latino; 3 Hispanic/Latino; 1 Two or more races, non-Hispanic/Latino), 1 international. Average age 31. 29 applicants, 72% accepted, 16 enrolled. *Faculty:* 6 full-time. *Expenses:* Contact institution. *Financial support:* In 2016–17, 8 teaching assistantships with full tuition reimbursements (averaging $8,219 per year) were awarded; career-related internships or fieldwork and scholarships/grants also available. Support available to part-time students. Financial award application deadline: 3/1; financial award applicants required to submit FAFSA. In 2016, 18 master's awarded. *Program availability:* Part-time. Offers conflict analysis and dispute resolution (MA). *Application deadline:* For fall admission, 4/14 priority date for domestic and international students. Applications are processed on a rolling basis. *Application fee:* $65. Electronic applications accepted. *Graduate Program Director, Conflict Analysis and Dispute Resolution,* Dr. Vitus Ozoke, 410-677-0276, E-mail: vaozoke@salisbury.edu.

Department of English Students: 11 full-time (9 women), 24 part-time (19 women); includes 1 minority (Black or African American, non-Hispanic/Latino), 4 international. Average age 33. 18 applicants, 67% accepted, 9 enrolled. *Faculty:* 11 full-time (5 women), 1 (woman) part-time/adjunct. *Expenses:* Contact institution. *Financial support:* In 2016–17, 2 students received support, including 11 teaching assistantships with full tuition reimbursements available (averaging $9,395 per year); career-related internships or fieldwork and scholarships/grants also available. Support available to part-time students. Financial award application deadline: 3/1; financial award applicants required to submit FAFSA. In 2016, 17 master's awarded. *Program availability:* Part-time. Offers English (MA). *Application deadline:* For fall admission, 8/1 for domestic and international students; for spring admission, 1/1 for domestic and international students. *Application fee:* $65. Electronic applications accepted. *Graduate Program Director, English,* Dr. Christopher Vilmar, 410-677-6511, E-mail: csvilmar@salisbury.edu.

Department of History Students: 4 full-time (2 women), 9 part-time (2 women); includes 1 minority (Black or African American, non-Hispanic/Latino). Average age 27. 4 applicants, 100% accepted, 2 enrolled. *Faculty:* 8 full-time (2 women). *Expenses:* Contact institution. *Financial support:* In 2016–17, 2 teaching assistantships with full tuition reimbursements (averaging $8,000 per year) were awarded; career-related internships or fieldwork and scholarships/grants also available. Support available to part-time students. Financial award application deadline: 3/1; financial award applicants required to submit FAFSA. In 2016, 3 master's awarded. *Program availability:* Part-time, evening/weekend. Offers history (MA). *Application deadline:* For fall admission, 4/15 priority date for domestic and international students; for spring admission, 10/15 priority date for domestic and international students. Applications are processed on a rolling basis. *Application fee:* $65. Electronic applications accepted. *Graduate Program Director,* Dr. Celine Carayon, 410-677-3251, E-mail: cxcarayon@salisbury.edu.

Department of Social Work Students: 281 full-time (251 women), 55 part-time (49 women); includes 59 minority (32 Black or African American, non-Hispanic/Latino; 15 Hispanic/Latino; 12 Two or more races, non-Hispanic/Latino). Average age 31. 242 applicants, 70% accepted, 144 enrolled. *Faculty:* 19 full-time (16 women), 28 part-time/adjunct (24 women). *Expenses:* Contact institution. *Financial support:* In 2016–17, 18 students received support, including 6 teaching assistantships with full tuition reimbursements available (averaging $8,042 per year); career-related internships or fieldwork and scholarships/grants also available. Support available to part-time students. Financial award application deadline: 3/1; financial award applicants required to submit FAFSA. In 2016, 119 master's awarded. *Program availability:* Part-time, 100% online, blended/hybrid learning. Offers social work (MSW). *Application deadline:* For fall admission, 2/3 for domestic and international students. *Application fee:* $65. Electronic applications accepted. *Application Contact:* Susan Mareski, Administrative Assistant, 410-677-5363, E-mail: smmareski@salisbury.edu. *Graduate Program Director, Social Work,* Dr. Vicki Root, 410-543-6307, E-mail: vbroot@salisbury.edu.

DNP Program Students: 28 full-time (25 women), 5 part-time (all women); includes 7 minority (6 Black or African American, non-Hispanic/Latino; 1 Asian, non-Hispanic/Latino). Average age 34. 24 applicants, 58% accepted, 14 enrolled. *Faculty:* 5 full-time (all women). *Expenses:* Contact institution. *Financial support:* In 2016–17, 16 students received support. Career-related internships or fieldwork and scholarships/grants available. Support available to part-time students. Financial award application deadline: 3/1; financial award applicants required to submit FAFSA. *Program availability:* Part-time. Offers family nurse practitioner (DNP); nursing leadership (DNP). *Application deadline:* For fall admission, 3/1 priority date for domestic and international students. Applications are processed on a rolling basis. *Application fee:* $65. Electronic applications accepted. *Application Contact:* Carmel Boger, Administrative Assistant, 410-543-6420, E-mail: ciboger@salisbury.edu. *Graduate Program Director, Nursing DNP,* Dr. Erica Alessandrini, 410-548-1497, E-mail: eaalessandrini@salisbury.edu.

MS in Nursing Program Students: 1 (woman) part-time. Average age 53. 1 applicant. *Faculty:* 5 full-time (4 women), 1 (woman) part-time/adjunct. *Expenses:* Contact institution. *Financial support:* Career-related internships or fieldwork and scholarships/grants available. Support available to part-time students. Financial award application deadline: 3/1; financial award applicants required to submit FAFSA. In 2016, 3 master's awarded. *Program availability:* Part-time. Offers nursing (MS). *Application deadline:* For fall admission, 5/15 priority date for domestic and international students. Applications are processed on a rolling basis. *Application fee:* $65. Electronic applications accepted. *Application Contact:* Carmel Boger, Administrative Assistant, 410-543-6420, Fax: 410-548-3313, E-mail: ciboger@salisbury.edu. *Graduate Program Director, Nursing MS,* Dr. Erica Alessandrini, 410-548-1497, E-mail: eaalessandrini@salisbury.edu.

Perdue School of Business Students: 38 full-time (15 women), 25 part-time (13 women); includes 8 minority (4 Black or African American, non-Hispanic/Latino; 3 Asian, non-Hispanic/Latino; 1 Two or more races, non-Hispanic/Latino), 5 international. Average age 29. 64 applicants, 64% accepted, 36 enrolled. *Faculty:* 6 full-time (2 women). Expenses: Contact institution. *Financial support:* In 2016–17, 2 students received support, including 6 teaching assistantships with full tuition reimbursements available (averaging $8,208 per year); career-related internships or fieldwork and scholarships/grants also available. Support available to part-time students. Financial award application deadline: 3/1; financial award applicants required to submit FAFSA. In 2016, 27 master's awarded. *Program availability:* Part-time, evening/weekend, 100% online, blended/hybrid learning. Offers business administration (MBA). *Application deadline:* For fall admission, 3/1 priority date for domestic and international students. Applications are processed on a rolling basis. *Application fee:* $65. Electronic applications accepted. *Graduate Program Director, Business Administration,* Yvonne Downie Hanley, 410-548-3983, E-mail: yxdownie@salisbury.edu.

Program in Applied Biology Students: 8 full-time (3 women), 1 part-time (0 women). Average age 26. 6 applicants, 50% accepted, 3 enrolled. *Faculty:* 10 full-time (5 women). Expenses: Contact institution. *Financial support:* In 2016–17, 9 teaching assistantships with full tuition reimbursements (averaging $13,000 per year) were awarded; career-related internships or fieldwork and scholarships/grants also available. Support available to part-time students. Financial award application deadline: 3/1; financial award applicants required to submit FAFSA. In 2016, 5 master's awarded. *Program availability:* Part-time. Offers applied biology (MS). *Application deadline:* For fall admission, 3/1 for domestic and international students; for spring admission, 10/1 for domestic and international students. *Application fee:* $65. Electronic applications accepted. *Application Contact:* Valerie Butler, Administrative Assistant, 410-543-6490, E-mail: vwbutler@salisbury.edu. *Graduate Program Director, Applied Biology,* Dr. Dana Price, 410-543-6498, E-mail: dlprice@salisbury.edu.

Program in Applied Health Physiology Students: 31 full-time (15 women), 7 part-time (3 women); includes 6 minority (2 Black or African American, non-Hispanic/Latino; 2 Asian, non-Hispanic/Latino; 1 Native Hawaiian or other Pacific Islander, non-Hispanic/Latino; 1 Two or more races, non-Hispanic/Latino), 1 international. Average age 25. 27 applicants, 56% accepted, 15 enrolled. *Faculty:* 6 full-time. Expenses: Contact institution. *Financial support:* In 2016–17, 3 students received support, including 17 teaching assistantships with full tuition reimbursements available (averaging $8,118 per year); career-related internships or fieldwork and scholarships/grants also available. Support available to part-time students. Financial award application deadline: 3/1; financial award applicants required to submit FAFSA. In 2016, 27 master's awarded. *Program availability:* Part-time. Offers applied health physiology (MS). *Application deadline:* For fall admission, 8/1 for domestic and international students; for spring admission, 12/1 for domestic and international students. *Application fee:* $65. Electronic applications accepted. *Application Contact:* Dr. Thomas Pellinger, Faculty, Applied Health Physiology, 410-677-0144, E-mail: tkpellinger@salisbury.edu. *Graduate Program Director, Applied Health Physiology,* Dr. Carlton Insley, 410-677-0145, E-mail: rcinsley@salisbury.edu.

Program in Athletic Training Students: 5 full-time (4 women); includes 1 minority (Hispanic/Latino). Average age 22. 1 applicant, 100% accepted. *Faculty:* 2 full-time (both women). Expenses: Contact institution. *Financial support:* Career-related internships or fieldwork and scholarships/grants available. Support available to part-time students. Financial award application deadline: 3/1; financial award applicants required to submit FAFSA. Offers athletic training (MSAT). *Application deadline:* For summer admission, 3/15 priority date for domestic and international students. Applications are processed on a rolling basis. *Application fee:* $65. Electronic applications accepted. *Graduate Program Director, Athletic Training,* Dr. Jenny Toonstra, 410-677-5493, E-mail: jltoonstra@salisbury.edu.

Program in Contemporary Curriculum Theory and Instruction: Literacy Students: 18 full-time (16 women), 15 part-time (11 women); includes 1 minority (Two or more races, non-Hispanic/Latino). Average age 37. 17 applicants, 88% accepted, 13 enrolled. *Faculty:* 4 full-time (2 women). Expenses: Contact institution. *Financial support:* In 2016–17, 9 students received support, including 1 teaching assistantship with full tuition reimbursement available (averaging $10,000 per year); career-related internships or fieldwork and scholarships/grants also available. Support available to part-time students. Financial award application deadline: 3/1; financial award applicants required to submit FAFSA. *Program availability:* Part-time. Offers contemporary curriculum theory and instruction: literacy (Ed D). *Application deadline:* For fall admission, 3/31 priority date for domestic and international students. Applications are processed on a rolling basis. *Application fee:* $65. Electronic applications accepted. *Application Contact:* Stefani Hoffman, Administrative Assistant II, 410-677-0236, E-mail: slhoffman@salisbury.edu. *Graduate Program Director,* Dr. Judith Franzak, 410-677-0238, E-mail: jkfranzak@salisbury.edu.

Program in Curriculum and Instruction Students: 10 full-time (6 women), 87 part-time (73 women); includes 11 minority (9 Black or African American, non-Hispanic/Latino; 2 Two or more races, non-Hispanic/Latino). Average age 30. 29 applicants, 41% accepted, 10 enrolled. *Faculty:* 11 full-time (6 women), 3 part-time/adjunct (2 women). Expenses: Contact institution. *Financial support:* In 2016–17, 1 student received support, including 5 teaching assistantships with full tuition reimbursements available (averaging $8,250 per year); career-related internships or fieldwork and scholarships/grants also available. Support available to part-time students. Financial award application deadline: 3/1; financial award applicants required to submit FAFSA. In 2016, 28 master's awarded. *Program availability:* Part-time, evening/weekend. Offers curriculum and instruction (M Ed). *Application deadline:* For fall admission, 3/1 priority date for domestic and international students; for spring admission, 10/1 priority date for domestic and international students; for summer admission, 3/1 priority date for domestic and international students. Applications are processed on a rolling basis. *Application fee:* $65. Electronic applications accepted. *Graduate Program Director, Curriculum and Instruction,* Dr. Diana Wagner, 410-677-5490, E-mail: dmwagner@salisbury.edu.

Program in Educational Leadership Students: 1 (woman) full-time, 31 part-time (17 women); includes 3 minority (1 Black or African American, non-Hispanic/Latino; 1 Hispanic/Latino; 1 Two or more races, non-Hispanic/Latino). Average age 32. 5 applicants, 40% accepted, 2 enrolled. *Faculty:* 2 full-time (0 women), 2 part-time/adjunct (1 woman). Expenses: Contact institution. *Financial support:* In 2016–17, 1 student received support. Career-related internships or fieldwork and scholarships/grants

available. Support available to part-time students. Financial award application deadline: 3/1; financial award applicants required to submit FAFSA. In 2016, 10 master's awarded. *Program availability:* Part-time, evening/weekend. Offers educational leadership (M Ed). *Application deadline:* For fall admission, 3/1 priority date for domestic and international students; for spring admission, 10/1 priority date for domestic and international students; for summer admission, 3/1 priority date for domestic and international students. Applications are processed on a rolling basis. *Application fee:* $65. Electronic applications accepted. *Application Contact:* Claire Williams, Program Management Specialist, 410-677-0001, E-mail: clwilliams@salisbury.edu. *Graduate Program Director, Educational Leadership,* Dr. Douglas DeWitt, 410-543-6286, Fax: 410-677-0249, E-mail: dmdewitt@salisbury.edu.

Program in Geographic Information Systems Management Students: 4 full-time (2 women), 14 part-time (4 women); includes 1 minority (Black or African American, non-Hispanic/Latino), 2 international. Average age 34. 2 applicants, 50% accepted, 1 enrolled. *Faculty:* 2 full-time. Expenses: Contact institution. *Financial support:* In 2016–17, 2 teaching assistantships with full tuition reimbursements (averaging $9,000 per year) were awarded; career-related internships or fieldwork and scholarships/grants also available. Support available to part-time students. Financial award application deadline: 3/1; financial award applicants required to submit FAFSA. In 2016, 3 master's awarded. *Program availability:* Part-time, evening/weekend, online only, 100% online. Offers geographic information systems management (MS). *Application deadline:* For fall admission, 7/1 priority date for domestic and international students; for spring admission, 10/1 priority date for domestic and international students; for summer admission, 3/1 priority date for domestic and international students. Applications are processed on a rolling basis. *Application fee:* $65. Electronic applications accepted. *Application Contact:* Jennifer Gordy, Program Management Specialist, 410-543-6460, E-mail: jlgordy@salisbury.edu. *Graduate Program Director, Geographic Information Systems Management,* Dr. Stuart Hamilton, 410-543-6456, E-mail: sehamilton@salisbury.edu.

Program in Mathematics Education Students: 2 full-time (1 woman), 8 part-time (5 women); includes 1 minority (Two or more races, non-Hispanic/Latino). Average age 27. 2 applicants, 100% accepted, 2 enrolled. *Faculty:* 3 full-time (1 woman). Expenses: Contact institution. *Financial support:* In 2016–17, 1 teaching assistantship with full tuition reimbursement (averaging $8,000 per year) was awarded; career-related internships or fieldwork and scholarships/grants also available. Support available to part-time students. Financial award application deadline: 3/1; financial award applicants required to submit FAFSA. In 2016, 2 master's awarded. *Program availability:* Part-time. Offers mathematics (MSME). *Application deadline:* For fall admission, 5/15 priority date for domestic and international students; for spring admission, 10/1 priority date for domestic and international students. Applications are processed on a rolling basis. *Application fee:* $65. Electronic applications accepted. *Graduate Program Director, Mathematics Education,* Dr. Jennifer Bergner, 410-677-5429, E-mail: jabergner@salisbury.edu.

Program in Reading Specialist Students: 32 part-time (29 women); includes 3 minority (2 Black or African American, non-Hispanic/Latino; 1 Asian, non-Hispanic/Latino). Average age 30. 8 applicants, 75% accepted, 6 enrolled. *Faculty:* 2 full-time (both women), 1 part-time/adjunct. Expenses: Contact institution. *Financial support:* In 2016–17, 3 students received support, including 4 teaching assistantships with full tuition reimbursements available (averaging $8,500 per year); career-related internships or fieldwork and scholarships/grants also available. Support available to part-time students. Financial award application deadline: 3/1; financial award applicants required to submit FAFSA. In 2016, 3 master's awarded. *Program availability:* Part-time, evening/weekend. Offers reading specialist (M Ed). *Application deadline:* For fall admission, 3/1 priority date for domestic and international students; for spring admission, 10/1 priority date for domestic and international students; for summer admission, 3/1 priority date for domestic and international students. Applications are processed on a rolling basis. *Application fee:* $65. Electronic applications accepted. *Graduate Program Director, Reading Specialist,* Dr. Patricia Richards, 410-543-6379, E-mail: porichards@salisbury.edu.

Program in Teaching Students: 6 full-time (3 women), 1 (woman) part-time. Average age 29. *Faculty:* 3 full-time (2 women). Expenses: Contact institution. *Financial support:* Career-related internships or fieldwork and scholarships/grants available. Support available to part-time students. Financial award application deadline: 3/1; financial award applicants required to submit FAFSA. In 2016, 6 master's awarded. Offers secondary education (MAT). *Application deadline:* For winter admission, 12/15 priority date for domestic and international students. *Application fee:* $65. Electronic applications accepted. *Graduate Program Director, Teaching,* Dr. Regina Royer, 410-548-3949, E-mail: rdroyer@salisbury.edu.

See Display on next page and Close-Up on page 895.

SALUS UNIVERSITY, Elkins Park, PA 19027-1598

General Information Independent, coed, graduate-only institution. *Graduate housing:* On-campus housing not available. *Research affiliation:* Dynamis Pharmaceuticals (diabetes research), DakDak (photobiology).

GRADUATE UNITS

College of Education and Rehabilitation *Program availability:* Part-time, online learning. Offers education of children and youth with visual and multiple impairments (M Ed, Certificate); low vision rehabilitation (MS, Certificate); orientation and mobility therapy (MS, Certificate); vision rehabilitation therapy (MS, Certificate).

College of Health Sciences Offers physician assistant (MMS); public health (MPH). Electronic applications accepted.

Osborne College of Audiology Offers audiology (Au D). Electronic applications accepted.

Pennsylvania College of Optometry Offers optometry (OD). Electronic applications accepted.

SALVE REGINA UNIVERSITY, Newport, RI 02840-4192

General Information Independent-religious, coed, comprehensive institution. *Graduate housing:* On-campus housing not available. *Student services:* Campus employment opportunities, campus safety program, career counseling, international student services, multicultural affairs office, services for students with disabilities. *Library facilities:* McKillop Library. *Collection:* Books: 158,092 (physical), 266,078 (digital/electronic); Serial titles: 18,762 (physical), 46,067 (digital/electronic); Databases: 53. Weekly public service hours: 52; students can reserve study rooms.

Computer facilities: Computer purchase and lease plans are available. 163 computers available on campus for general student use. A campuswide network can be accessed from student residence rooms and from off campus. Online class registration is available.

Website: http://www.salve.edu/

General Application Contact: Laurie Reilly, Graduate Admissions Manager, 401-341-2153, Fax: 401-341-2973, E-mail: laurie.reilly@salve.edu.

GRADUATE UNITS

Program in Administration of Justice and Homeland Security Expenses: Contact institution. *Financial support:* Career-related internships or fieldwork and Federal Work-Study available. Support available to part-time students. Financial award application deadline: 3/1; financial award applicants required to submit FAFSA. *Program availability:* Part-time, evening/weekend, online learning. Offers administration of justice and homeland security (MS); cybersecurity and intelligence (CGS); digital forensics (CGS); leadership in justice (CGS). *Application deadline:* For fall admission, 3/5 priority date for domestic students, 3/15 priority date for international students; for spring admission, 9/15 priority date for domestic students, 9/5 priority date for international students. Applications are processed on a rolling basis. *Application fee:* $60. Electronic applications accepted. *Application Contact:* Laurie Reilly, Graduate Admissions Manager, 401-341-2153, Fax: 401-341-2973, E-mail: laurie.reilly@salve.edu. *Director,* David Smith, 401-341-3210, E-mail: david.smith@salve.edu.

Program in Business Administration Expenses: Contact institution. *Financial support:* Career-related internships or fieldwork and Federal Work-Study available. Support available to part-time students. Financial award applicants required to submit FAFSA. *Program availability:* Part-time, evening/weekend, online learning. Offers cybersecurity issues in business (MBA); entrepreneurial enterprise (MBA); health care administration and management (MBA); nonprofit management (MBA); social ventures (MBA). *Application deadline:* For fall admission, 3/15 priority date for domestic and international students; for spring admission, 9/15 priority date for domestic and international students. Applications are processed on a rolling basis. *Application fee:* $60. Electronic applications accepted. *Application Contact:* Laurie Reilly, Graduate Admissions Manager, 401-341-2153, Fax: 401-341-2973, E-mail: laurie.reilly@salve.edu. *Director,* Dr. Arlene Nicholas, 401-341-3280, E-mail: arlene.nicholas@salve.edu.

Program in Healthcare Administration and Management Expenses: Contact institution. *Financial support:* Career-related internships or fieldwork and Federal Work-Study available. Support available to part-time students. Financial award application deadline: 3/1; financial award applicants required to submit FAFSA. *Program availability:* Part-time, evening/weekend, online learning. Offers healthcare administration and management (MS, CGS). *Application deadline:* For fall admission, 3/15 priority date for domestic and international students; for spring admission, 9/15 priority date for domestic and international students. Applications are processed on a rolling basis. *Application fee:* $60. Electronic applications accepted. *Application Contact:* Laurie Reilly, Graduate Admissions Manager, 401-341-2153, Fax: 401-341-2973, E-mail: laurie.reilly@salve.edu. *Director,* Mark Hough, 401-341-3123, E-mail: mark.hough@salve.edu.

Program in Humanities Expenses: Contact institution. *Financial support:* Career-related internships or fieldwork and Federal Work-Study available. Support available to part-time students. Financial award application deadline: 3/1; financial award applicants required to submit FAFSA. *Program availability:* Part-time, evening/weekend, online learning. Offers humanitarian assistance (MA); humanities (PhD); public humanities (MA); religion, peace and justice (MA). *Application deadline:* For fall admission, 3/15 priority date for domestic and international students; for spring admission, 9/15 priority date for domestic and international students. Applications are processed on a rolling basis. *Application fee:* $60. Electronic applications accepted. *Application Contact:* Laurie Reilly, Graduate Admissions Manager, 401-341-2153, Fax: 401-341-2973, E-mail: laurie.reilly@salve.edu. *Director,* Dr. Michael Budd, 401-341-3284, E-mail: michael.budd@salve.edu.

Program in International Relations Expenses: Contact institution. *Financial support:* Career-related internships or fieldwork and Federal Work-Study available. Support available to part-time students. Financial award application deadline: 3/1; financial award applicants required to submit FAFSA. *Program availability:* Part-time, evening/weekend, online learning. Offers international relations (MA, CGS). *Application deadline:* For fall admission, 3/15 priority date for domestic and international students; for spring admission, 9/15 priority date for domestic and international students. Applications are processed on a rolling basis. *Application fee:* $60. Electronic applications accepted. *Application Contact:* Laurie Reilly, Graduate Admissions Manager, 401-341-2153, Fax: 401-341-2973, E-mail: laurie.reilly@salve.edu. *Director,* Dr. Symeon Giannakos, 401-341-3177, E-mail: symeon.giannakos@salve.edu.

Program in Management Expenses: Contact institution. *Financial support:* Career-related internships or fieldwork and Federal Work-Study available. Support available to part-time students. Financial award application deadline: 3/1; financial award applicants required to submit FAFSA. *Program availability:* Part-time, evening/weekend, online learning. Offers business studies (CGS); human resource management (CGS); innovation and strategic management (MS); management (CGS); nonprofit management (CGS); social entrepreneurship (CGS). *Application deadline:* For fall admission, 3/15 priority date for domestic students, 3/5 priority date for international students; for spring admission, 9/15 priority date for domestic and international students. Applications are processed on a rolling basis. *Application fee:* $60. Electronic applications accepted. *Application Contact:* Laurie Reilly, Graduate Admissions Manager, 401-341-2153, Fax: 401-341-2973, E-mail: laurie.reilly@salve.edu. *Director,* Dr. Arlene Nicholas, 401-341-3280, E-mail: arlene.nicholas@salve.edu.

Program in Nursing Expenses: Contact institution. *Financial support:* Application deadline: 3/1; applicants required to submit FAFSA. *Program availability:* Part-time, evening/weekend. Offers nursing (DNP). *Application deadline:* For fall admission, 5/1 for domestic students, 3/15 priority date for international students; for spring admission, 9/15 priority date for domestic and international students. Applications are processed on a rolling basis. *Application fee:* $60. Electronic applications accepted. *Application Contact:* Laurie Reilly, Graduate Admissions Manager, 401-341-2153, Fax: 401-341-2973, E-mail: laurie.reilly@salve.edu. *Director,* Dr. Sharon Stager, 401-341-3297, E-mail: sharon.stager@salve.edu.

Program in Rehabilitation Counseling Expenses: Contact institution. *Financial support:* Career-related internships or fieldwork and Federal Work-Study available. Support available to part-time students. Financial award application deadline: 3/1; financial award applicants required to submit FAFSA. *Program availability:* Part-time, evening/weekend. Offers clinical rehabilitation and mental health counseling (MA); mental health (CAGS); rehabilitation (CAGS); rehabilitation counseling (MA); substance abuse and treatment (CAGS). *Application deadline:* For fall admission, 3/15 priority date for domestic and international students; for spring admission, 9/15 priority date for domestic and international students. Applications are processed on a rolling basis. *Application fee:* $60. Electronic applications accepted. *Application Contact:* Laurie Reilly, Graduate Admissions Manager, 401-341-2153, Fax: 401-341-2973, E-mail: laurie.reilly@salve.edu. *Director,* Dr. Judith Drew, 401-341-3189, E-mail: judith.drew@salve.edu.

SAMFORD UNIVERSITY, Birmingham, AL 35229

General Information Independent-religious, coed, university. *Enrollment:* 5,471 graduate, professional, and undergraduate students; 1,897 full-time matriculated graduate/professional students (1,140 women), 176 part-time matriculated graduate/professional students (118 women). *Enrollment by degree level:* 839 master's, 1,203 doctoral, 31 other advanced degrees. *Graduate faculty:* 164 full-time (90 women), 52 part-time/adjunct (23 women). *Tuition:* Full-time $18,530; part-time $789 per credit hour. *Required fees:* $610. Tuition and fees vary according to course load, degree level, program and student level. *Graduate housing:* Room and/or apartments available on a first-come, first-served basis to single students; on-campus housing not available to married students. Typical cost: $12,104 per year ($9682 including board). Room and board charges vary according to board plan, campus/location and housing facility selected. Housing application deadline: 5/1. *Student services:* Campus employment opportunities, campus safety program, career counseling, exercise/wellness program, free psychological counseling, grant writing training, international student services, low-cost health insurance, services for students with disabilities, teacher training, writing training. *Library facilities:* University Library plus 2 others. *Collection:* Books: 636,268 (physical), 196,223 (digital/electronic); Serial titles: 5,960 (physical), 117,223 (digital/electronic); Databases: 291. Weekly public service hours: 99; students can reserve study rooms. *Research affiliation:* Cystic Fibrosis Foundation (Bethesda, MD) (drug discovery research), Independent Insitiute, Heartland Institute, Beacon Center of Tennessee, Institute for Faith, Work, and Economics, Jack Miller Center.

Computer facilities: 330 computers available on campus for general student use. A campuswide network can be accessed from student residence rooms and from off campus. Online class registration, free online storage and tech support are available. Website: http://www.samford.edu/

General Application Contact: Brian L. Kennedy, Director of Recruitment, 205-726-4176, Fax: 205-726-2171, E-mail: blkenned@samford.edu.

GRADUATE UNITS

Beeson School of Divinity Students: 159 full-time (28 women), 8 part-time (4 women); includes 24 minority (19 Black or African American, non-Hispanic/Latino; 1 Asian, non-Hispanic/Latino; 2 Hispanic/Latino; 2 Two or more races, non-Hispanic/Latino), 2 international. Average age 29. 65 applicants, 94% accepted, 45 enrolled. *Faculty:* 14 full-time (1 woman), 1 part-time/adjunct (0 women). Expenses: Contact institution. *Financial support:* In 2016–17, 140 students received support. Federal Work-Study, institutionally sponsored loans, scholarships/grants, and tuition waivers (full and partial) available. Financial award application deadline: 2/15; financial award applicants required to submit FAFSA. In 2016, 36 master's, 8 doctorates awarded. *Program availability:* Part-time. Offers divinity (M Div, MATS, D Min). *Application deadline:* For fall admission, 2/15 for domestic and international students; for spring admission, 10/1 for domestic and international students. *Application fee:* $35. Electronic applications accepted. *Application Contact:* Sherri S. Brown, Director of Admission, 205-726-2066, E-mail: sbrown5@samford.edu. *Dean,* Dr. Timothy George, 205-726-2632, E-mail: tfgeorge@samford.edu.

Brock School of Business Students: 87 full-time (33 women), 14 part-time (6 women); includes 10 minority (7 Black or African American, non-Hispanic/Latino; 1 Asian, non-Hispanic/Latino; 1 Hispanic/Latino; 1 Two or more races, non-Hispanic/Latino), 6 international. Average age 28. 148 applicants, 41% accepted, 32 enrolled. *Faculty:* 9 full-time (2 women), 3 part-time/adjunct (0 women). Expenses: Contact institution. *Financial support:* In 2016–17, 55 students received support. Career-related internships or fieldwork, institutionally sponsored loans, scholarships/grants, and tuition waivers (partial) available. Support available to part-time students. Financial award application deadline: 3/1; financial award applicants required to submit FAFSA. In 2016, 63 master's awarded. *Program availability:* Part-time-only, evening/weekend, 100% online, blended/hybrid learning. Offers accounting (M Acc); business administration (MBA); entrepreneurship (MBA); finance (MBA); marketing (MBA). *Application deadline:* For fall admission, 7/1 for domestic and international students; for spring admission, 12/1 for domestic and international students; for summer admission, 4/1 for domestic and international students. Applications are processed on a rolling basis. *Application fee:* $35. Electronic applications accepted. *Application Contact:* Elizabeth Anne Gambrell, Assistant Director of Academic Programs, 205-726-2040, Fax: 205-726-2540, E-mail: eagambre@samford.edu. *Assistant Dean,* Dr. Barbara Cartledge, 205-726-2935, Fax: 205-726-2540, E-mail: bhcartle@samford.edu.

Cumberland School of Law Students: 456 full-time (221 women), 9 part-time (7 women); includes 78 minority (40 Black or African American, non-Hispanic/Latino; 5 American Indian or Alaska Native, non-Hispanic/Latino; 6 Asian, non-Hispanic/Latino; 18 Hispanic/Latino; 1 Native Hawaiian or other Pacific Islander, non-Hispanic/Latino; 8 Two or more races, non-Hispanic/Latino), 7 international. Average age 26. 579 applicants, 68% accepted, 149 enrolled. *Faculty:* 22 full-time (7 women), 20 part-time/adjunct (8 women). Expenses: Contact institution. *Financial support:* In 2016–17, 345 students received support. Career-related internships or fieldwork, Federal Work-Study, institutionally sponsored loans, and scholarships/grants available. Financial award application deadline: 3/1; financial award applicants required to submit FAFSA. In 2016, 158 doctorates awarded. Offers law (MCL, JD). JD/MPH, JD/MPA offered jointly with The University of Alabama at Birmingham; JD/MS offered with Albany Medical College. *Application deadline:* For fall admission, 6/1 for domestic students, 6/1 priority date for international students. Applications are processed on a rolling basis. Electronic applications accepted. *Application Contact:* Jen Hartzog, Director of Admissions, 205-726-2701, Fax: 205-726-2057, E-mail: jhartzog@samford.edu. *Dean/Professor of Law,* Henry C. Strickland, 205-726-2704, Fax: 205-726-4457, E-mail: hcstrick@samford.edu.

Howard College of Arts and Sciences Students: 7 full-time (2 women), 4 part-time (0 women); includes 1 minority (Black or African American, non-Hispanic/Latino), 7 international. Average age 27. *Faculty:* 6 full-time (3 women), 3 part-time/adjunct (0 women). Expenses: Contact institution. *Financial support:* Application deadline: 3/1; applicants required to submit FAFSA. In 2016, 14 master's awarded. *Program availability:* Part-time, evening/weekend. Offers energy management and policy (MSEM). *Application deadline:* For fall admission, 8/1 for domestic and international students; for winter admission, 12/1 for domestic and international students; for spring admission, 12/1 for domestic and international students; for summer admission, 5/1 for domestic and international students. Applications are processed on a rolling basis. *Application fee:* $35. *Application Contact:* Dr. Ronald N. Hunsinger, Professor/Chair, Biological and Environmental Sciences, 205-726-2944, Fax: 205-726-2479, E-mail: rnhunsin@samford.edu. *Dean of Howard College of Arts and Sciences,* Tim Hall, E-mail: thall5@samford.edu.

Ida Moffett School of Nursing Students: 299 full-time (229 women), 43 part-time (38 women); includes 55 minority (26 Black or African American, non-Hispanic/Latino; 1 American Indian or Alaska Native, non-Hispanic/Latino; 7 Asian, non-Hispanic/Latino; 13 Hispanic/Latino; 8 Two or more races, non-Hispanic/Latino). Average age 35. 93 applicants, 52% accepted, 35 enrolled. *Faculty:* 19 full-time (17 women), 3 part-

time/adjunct (1 woman). Expenses: Contact institution. *Financial support:* In 2016–17, 28 students received support. Institutionally sponsored loans, scholarships/grants, and traineeships available. Financial award application deadline: 3/1; financial award applicants required to submit FAFSA. In 2016, 124 master's, 33 doctorates awarded. *Program availability:* Part-time, evening/weekend, blended/hybrid learning. Offers administration (DNP); advanced practice (DNP); family nurse practitioner (MSN, DNP); health systems and administration (DNP); nurse anesthesia (MSN). *Application deadline:* For fall admission, 4/1 for domestic and international students; for spring admission, 8/1 for domestic and international students; for summer admission, 2/1 for domestic and international students. *Application fee:* $65. Electronic applications accepted. *Application Contact:* Allyson Maddox, Director of Graduate Student Services, 205-726-2047, E-mail: amaddox@samford.edu. *Vice Provost, College of Health Sciences/Dean/Professor,* Dr. Nena F. Sanders, 205-726-2612, E-mail: nfsander@samford.edu.

McWhorter School of Pharmacy Students: 474 full-time (310 women), 10 part-time (7 women); includes 100 minority (49 Black or African American, non-Hispanic/Latino; 3 American Indian or Alaska Native, non-Hispanic/Latino; 35 Asian, non-Hispanic/Latino; 6 Hispanic/Latino; 7 Two or more races, non-Hispanic/Latino), 9 international. Average age 24. *Faculty:* 37 full-time (25 women), 2 part-time/adjunct (1 woman). Expenses: Contact institution. *Financial support:* In 2016–17, 197 students received support. Research assistantships, teaching assistantships, Federal Work-Study, institutionally sponsored loans, and scholarships/grants available. Financial award application deadline: 3/1; financial award applicants required to submit FAFSA. In 2016, 105 doctorates awarded. Offers pharmacy (Pharm D). *Application deadline:* For spring admission, 3/1 for domestic and international students. Applications are processed on a rolling basis. *Application fee:* $25. Electronic applications accepted. *Application Contact:* Jon M. Parker, Assistant Director of Pharmacy Admissions, 205-726-4242, Fax: 205-726-4141, E-mail: jmparker@samford.edu. *Dean/Professor,* Dr. Michael A. Crouch, 205-726-2820, Fax: 205-726-2759, E-mail: macrouch@samford.edu.

Orlean Beeson School of Education Students: 219 full-time (161 women), 86 part-time (55 women); includes 97 minority (86 Black or African American, non-Hispanic/Latino; 5 American Indian or Alaska Native, non-Hispanic/Latino; 1 Asian, non-Hispanic/Latino; 1 Hispanic/Latino; 4 Two or more races, non-Hispanic/Latino), 2 international. Average age 38. 244 applicants, 52% accepted, 112 enrolled. *Faculty:* 15 full-time (9 women), 12 part-time/adjunct (12 women). Expenses: Contact institution. *Financial support:* In 2016–17, 246 students received support. Scholarships/grants available. Financial award application deadline: 3/1; financial award applicants required to submit FAFSA. In 2016, 84 master's, 22 doctorates, 12 Certificates awarded. *Program availability:* Part-time, evening/weekend, 100% online, blended/hybrid learning. Offers education (Ed D, Certificate); educational leadership: policy, organizations, leadership (MSE); elementary education (MS Ed); gifted certification (MSE); instructional design and technology (MSE); instructional leadership (MSE, Ed S); K-12 collaborative special education (MSE); teacher leader (Ed S). *Application deadline:* For fall admission, 7/15 for domestic students, 7/1 for international students; for spring admission, 11/15 for domestic and international students; for summer admission, 4/15 for domestic and international students. *Application fee:* $35. Electronic applications accepted. *Application Contact:* Brooke Karr, Graduate Admissions Coordinator, 205-729-2783, Fax: 205-726-4233, E-mail: kbglenna@samford.edu. *Dean,* Dr. Jean Box, 205-726-2565, Fax: 205-726-4233, E-mail: jabox@samford.edu.

School of Health Professions Students: 102 full-time (74 women); includes 5 minority (1 Asian, non-Hispanic/Latino; 2 Hispanic/Latino; 2 Two or more races, non-Hispanic/Latino). Average age 24. 244 applicants, 44% accepted, 58 enrolled. *Faculty:* 19 full-time (12 women). Expenses: Contact institution. *Financial support:* In 2016–17, 7 students received support. Application deadline: 3/1; applicants required to submit FAFSA. Offers athletic training (MAT); physical therapy (DPT); respiratory care (MS); speech language pathology (MS). *Application deadline:* For fall admission, 6/1 for domestic students; for spring admission, 10/1 for domestic students. *Application fee:* $120. Electronic applications accepted. *Application Contact:* Dr. Marian Carter, Assistant Dean of Enrollment Management and Student Services, 205-726-2611, E-mail: mwcarter@samford.edu. *Dean, School of Health Professions,* Dr. Alan P. Jung, 205-726-2716, E-mail: apjung@samford.edu.

School of Public Health Students: 83 full-time (77 women), 2 part-time (1 woman); includes 7 minority (1 American Indian or Alaska Native, non-Hispanic/Latino; 2 Asian, non-Hispanic/Latino; 2 Hispanic/Latino; 2 Two or more races, non-Hispanic/Latino). Average age 27. 47 applicants, 100% accepted, 37 enrolled. *Faculty:* 14 full-time (10 women). Expenses: Contact institution. *Financial support:* In 2016–17, 28 students received support. Scholarships/grants available. Financial award application deadline: 3/1; financial award applicants required to submit FAFSA. In 2016, 3 master's awarded. *Program availability:* Part-time, evening/weekend, 100% online, blended/hybrid learning. Offers clinical social work (MSW); global community development (MSW); public health (MPH). *Application deadline:* For fall admission, 6/1 for domestic and international students; for spring admission, 10/1 for domestic and international students. *Application fee:* $75. Electronic applications accepted. *Application Contact:* Dr. Marian Carter, Assistant Dean of Enrollment Management and Student Services, 205-726-2611, E-mail: mwcarter@samford.edu. *Dean, School of Public Health,* Dr. Keith Elder, 205-726-4655, E-mail: kelder@samford.edu.

School of the Arts Students: 11 full-time (5 women); includes 4 minority (all Black or African American, non-Hispanic/Latino), 1 international. Average age 30. 9 applicants, 100% accepted, 5 enrolled. *Faculty:* 9 full-time (4 women), 3 part-time/adjunct (1 woman). Expenses: Contact institution. *Financial support:* In 2016–17, 10 students received support. Federal Work-Study, scholarships/grants, and unspecified assistantships available. Financial award application deadline: 3/1; financial award applicants required to submit FAFSA. In 2016, 7 master's awarded. *Program availability:* Part-time, evening/weekend, online learning. Offers design studies (MS); music (MM); music education (MME). MME program offered in traditional, fifth year non-traditional, and national board cohort formats. *Application deadline:* For fall admission, 11/15 for domestic and international students; for spring admission, 4/15 for domestic and international students; for summer admission, 8/1 for domestic and international students. Applications are processed on a rolling basis. *Application fee:* $35. Electronic applications accepted. *Application Contact:* Dr. Demondrae L. Thurman, Director of Graduate Studies/Professor of Music, 205-726-2389, Fax: 205-726-2615, E-mail: dthurman@samford.edu. *Dean of the School of the Arts/Professor,* Dr. Joseph Hopkin, 205-726-2778, Fax: 205-726-2615, E-mail: jhopkins@samford.edu.

SAM HOUSTON STATE UNIVERSITY, Huntsville, TX 77341

General Information State-supported, coed, university. CGS member. *Graduate housing:* Room and/or apartments available on a first-come, first-served basis to single students; on-campus housing not available to married students. Housing application deadline: 8/20. *Research affiliation:* Texas Criminal Justice Division, Texas Department of Corrections, Research Division.

GRADUATE UNITS

College of Business Administration *Program availability:* Part-time, evening/weekend, online learning. Offers accounting (MS); banking and financial institutions (EMBA); business administration (EMBA, MBA, MS); project management (MS). Electronic applications accepted.

College of Criminal Justice *Program availability:* Part-time, evening/weekend, online learning. Offers criminal justice (MS, PhD); criminal justice and criminology (MA); criminal justice leadership and management (MS); forensic science (MS); homeland security studies (MS); victim services management (MS). Electronic applications accepted.

College of Education *Program availability:* Part-time, evening/weekend, online learning. Offers administration (M Ed); counseling (M Ed, MA, PhD); curriculum and instruction (M Ed); developmental education administration (Ed D); education (M Ed, MA, MLS, Ed D, PhD); educational leadership (Ed D); higher education administration (MA); instructional leadership (M Ed, MA); international literacy (M Ed); library science (MLS); reading (M Ed); special education (M Ed, MA). Electronic applications accepted.

College of Fine Arts and Mass Communication *Program availability:* Part-time. Offers dance (MFA); digital media (MA); fine arts and mass communication (MA, MFA, MM). Electronic applications accepted.

School of Music *Program availability:* Part-time. Offers music (MM). Electronic applications accepted.

College of Health Sciences *Program availability:* Part-time. Offers dietetics (MS); family and consumer sciences (MS); health (MA); health sciences (MA, MS); sport and human performance (MA); sport management (MA). Electronic applications accepted.

College of Humanities and Social Sciences *Program availability:* Part-time, online learning. Offers communication studies (MA); creative writing, editing, and publishing (MFA); English (MA); history (MA); humanities and social sciences (MA, MFA, MPA, PhD, SSP); political science (MA); psychology (MA, PhD, SSP); public administration (MPA); sociology (MA); Spanish (MA). Electronic applications accepted.

College of Sciences *Program availability:* Part-time, evening/weekend. Offers agriculture (MS); applied geographic information science (MS); biological sciences (MA, MS); chemistry (MS); computing and information science (MS); digital forensics (MS); geographic information science (Certificate); information assurance and security (MS); mathematics (MA, MS); sciences (MA, MS, PhD, Certificate); statistics (MS). Electronic applications accepted.

SAMUEL MERRITT UNIVERSITY, Oakland, CA 94609-3108

General Information Independent, coed, primarily women, upper-level institution. *Enrollment:* 1,907 graduate, professional, and undergraduate students; 1,105 full-time matriculated graduate/professional students (793 women), 64 part-time matriculated graduate/professional students (47 women). *Enrollment by degree level:* 820 master's, 331 doctoral, 18 other advanced degrees. *Graduate faculty:* 105 full-time (75 women), 107 part-time/adjunct (78 women). *Tuition:* Full-time $20,016; part-time $1251 per unit. *Required fees:* $50 per unit. One-time fee: $300. Tuition and fees vary according to degree level and program. *Graduate housing:* On-campus housing not available. *Student services:* Campus employment opportunities, campus safety program, career counseling, free psychological counseling, low-cost health insurance, services for students with disabilities. *Library facilities:* John A. Graziano Memorial Library. *Collection:* Books: 11,777 (physical), 242 (digital/electronic); Serial titles: 719 (physical), 16,204 (digital/electronic); Databases: 24. Weekly public service hours: 86; students can reserve study rooms. *Research affiliation:* Summit Medical Center (nursing).

Computer facilities: 160 computers available on campus for general student use. A campuswide network can be accessed. Online class registration is available. Website: http://www.samuelmerritt.edu/

General Application Contact: Timothy Cranford, Dean of Admissions, 510-869-1550, Fax: 510-869-6525, E-mail: admission@samuelmerritt.edu.

GRADUATE UNITS

California School of Podiatric Medicine Students: 186 full-time (80 women), 1 part-time (0 women); includes 101 minority (6 Black or African American, non-Hispanic/Latino; 61 Asian, non-Hispanic/Latino; 19 Hispanic/Latino; 15 Two or more races, non-Hispanic/Latino), 3 international. Average age 27. 316 applicants, 34% accepted, 42 enrolled. *Faculty:* 17 full-time (5 women), 7 part-time/adjunct (4 women). Expenses: Contact institution. *Financial support:* Federal Work-Study, institutionally sponsored loans, and scholarships/grants available. Financial award application deadline: 3/2; financial award applicants required to submit FAFSA. In 2016, 42 degrees awarded. Offers podiatric medicine (DPM). *Application deadline:* For fall admission, 4/1 priority date for domestic and international students. Applications are processed on a rolling basis. *Application fee:* $160. Electronic applications accepted. *Application Contact:* Dr. David Tran, Assistant Director of Admission, 510-869-6789, Fax: 510-869-6525, E-mail: dtran@samuelmerritt.edu. *Associate Dean for Administrative Affairs,* Irma Walker-Adame, 510-869-8742, E-mail: iadame@samuelmerritt.edu.

Department of Occupational Therapy Students: 119 full-time (100 women); includes 59 minority (4 Black or African American, non-Hispanic/Latino; 1 American Indian or Alaska Native, non-Hispanic/Latino; 26 Asian, non-Hispanic/Latino; 24 Hispanic/Latino; 4 Two or more races, non-Hispanic/Latino). Average age 29. 284 applicants, 25% accepted, 42 enrolled. *Faculty:* 12 full-time (10 women), 10 part-time/adjunct (9 women). Expenses: Contact institution. *Financial support:* In 2016–17, 3 students received support. Career-related internships or fieldwork, Federal Work-Study, and scholarships/grants available. Support available to part-time students. Financial award application deadline: 3/2; financial award applicants required to submit FAFSA. Offers occupational therapy (OTD). *Application deadline:* For fall admission, 10/1 priority date for domestic students. *Application fee:* $140. Electronic applications accepted. *Application Contact:* Timothy Cranford, Dean of Admission, 510-869-1550, Fax: 510-869-6525, E-mail: admission@samuelmerritt.edu. *Chair,* Kate Hayner, 510-869-4780, E-mail: khayner@samuelmerritt.edu.

Department of Physical Therapy Students: 110 full-time (71 women), 1 part-time (0 women); includes 58 minority (3 Asian, non-Hispanic/Latino; 21 Hispanic/Latino; 1 Native Hawaiian or other Pacific Islander, non-Hispanic/Latino; 6 Two or more races, non-Hispanic/Latino). Average age 28. 593 applicants, 15% accepted, 41 enrolled. *Faculty:* 11 full-time (9 women), 17 part-time/adjunct (5 women). Expenses: Contact institution. *Financial support:* In 2016–17, 25 students received support. Career-related internships or fieldwork, Federal Work-Study, and scholarships/grants available. Financial award application deadline: 3/2; financial award applicants required to submit FAFSA. In 2016, 36 doctorates awarded. Offers physical therapy (DPT). *Application deadline:* For fall admission, 10/1 priority date for domestic students. *Application fee:* $140. Electronic applications accepted. *Application Contact:* Timothy Cranford, Dean of Admissions, 510-869-1550, Fax: 510-869-6525, E-mail: admission@samuelmerritt.edu. *Co-Chair,* Dr. Nicole Christensen, 510-869-6567, Fax: 510-869-6282, E-mail: nchristensen@samuelmerritt.edu.

Department of Physician Assistant Studies Students: 129 full-time (95 women), 2 part-time (1 woman); includes 67 minority (4 Black or African American, non-Hispanic/Latino; 30 Asian, non-Hispanic/Latino; 27 Hispanic/Latino; 1 Native Hawaiian or other Pacific Islander, non-Hispanic/Latino; 5 Two or more races, non-Hispanic/Latino). Average age 31. 2,013 applicants, 3% accepted, 44 enrolled. *Faculty:* 9 full-time (5 women), 11 part-time/adjunct (6 women). Expenses: Contact institution. *Financial support:* In 2016–17, 27 students received support. Federal Work-Study, institutionally sponsored loans, and scholarships/grants available. Financial award application deadline: 3/2; financial award applicants required to submit FAFSA. In 2016, 43 master's awarded. Offers physician assistant studies (MPA). *Application deadline:* For fall admission, 10/1 priority date for domestic students. *Application fee:* $175. Electronic applications accepted. *Application Contact:* Timothy Cranford, Dean of Admission, 510-869-1550, Fax: 510-869-6525, E-mail: admission@samuelmerritt.edu.

School of Nursing Students: 561 full-time (447 women), 60 part-time (46 women); includes 403 minority (44 Black or African American, non-Hispanic/Latino; 4 American Indian or Alaska Native, non-Hispanic/Latino; 212 Asian, non-Hispanic/Latino; 98 Hispanic/Latino; 9 Native Hawaiian or other Pacific Islander, non-Hispanic/Latino; 36 Two or more races, non-Hispanic/Latino), 1 international. Average age 34. 464 applicants, 47% accepted, 143 enrolled. *Faculty:* 56 full-time (46 women), 62 part-time/adjunct (54 women). Expenses: Contact institution. *Financial support:* In 2016–17, 48 students received support. Career-related internships or fieldwork, Federal Work-Study, scholarships/grants, and traineeships available. Support available to part-time students. Financial award application deadline: 3/2; financial award applicants required to submit FAFSA. In 2016, 128 master's, 9 doctorates, 1 other advanced degree awarded. *Program availability:* Part-time, evening/weekend, 100% online, blended/hybrid learning. Offers case management (MSN); family nurse practitioner (MSN, DNP, Certificate); nurse anesthetist (MSN, Certificate); nursing (DNP). *Application deadline:* For fall admission, 1/1 priority date for domestic students; for spring admission, 7/1 priority date for domestic students; for summer admission, 10/1 priority date for domestic students. Applications are processed on a rolling basis. *Application fee:* $65. Electronic applications accepted. *Application Contact:* Timothy Cranford, Dean of Admission, 510-869-6576, Fax: 510-869-6525, E-mail: admission@samuelmerritt.edu. *Dean of Nursing,* Dr. Audrey Berman, 510-869-6733, Fax: 510-869-6525.

SAN DIEGO CHRISTIAN COLLEGE, Santee, CA 92071
General Information Independent-religious, coed, comprehensive institution.
GRADUATE UNITS
Graduate Programs

SAN DIEGO STATE UNIVERSITY, San Diego, CA 92182
General Information State-supported, coed, university. CGS member. *Graduate housing:* Room and/or apartments available on a first-come, first-served basis to single students; on-campus housing not available to married students. Housing application deadline: 5/1. *Research affiliation:* Robert Wood Johnson Foundation (public health), General Atomics (technical student services), William and Flora Hewlett Foundation (teacher education), American Heart Association (biology), Children's Hospital and Research Center (children's health), Qualcomm (wireless and telecommunications).

GRADUATE UNITS

Graduate and Research Affairs *Program availability:* Part-time, evening/weekend. Offers interdisciplinary studies (MA, MS). Electronic applications accepted.

College of Arts and Letters *Program availability:* Part-time, evening/weekend. Offers anthropology (MA); applied linguistics and English as a second language (CAL); arts and letters (MA, MFA, PhD, CAL); Asian studies (MA); computational linguistics (MA); creative writing (MFA); economics (MA); English (MA); English as a second language/applied linguistics (MA); European studies (MA); general linguistics (MA); geography (MA, PhD); history (MA); Latin American studies (MA); lesbian, gay, bisexual and transgender studies (Graduate Certificate); liberal arts and sciences (MA); philosophy (MA); political science (MA); rhetoric and writing studies (MA); sociology (MA); Spanish (MA); women's studies (MA). Electronic applications accepted.

College of Business Administration *Program availability:* Part-time, evening/weekend. Offers accountancy (MS); business administration (MBA, MS); entrepreneurship (MS); finance (MS); human resources management (MS); information systems (MS); management science (MS); marketing (MS); sports business management (MBA). Electronic applications accepted.

College of Education *Program availability:* Part-time, evening/weekend. Offers child development (MS); counseling and school psychology (MS); education (MA, MS, Ed D, PhD); educational leadership (MA); educational leadership in post-secondary education (MA); educational technology (MA); educational technology and teaching and learning (Ed D); elementary curriculum and instruction (MA); multi-cultural emphasis (PhD); policy studies in language and cross cultural education (MA); reading education (MA); rehabilitation counseling (MS); secondary curriculum and instruction (MA); special education (MA). Electronic applications accepted.

College of Engineering *Program availability:* Part-time, evening/weekend. Offers aerospace engineering (MS); civil engineering (MS); electrical engineering (MS); engineering (MS, PhD); engineering mechanics (MS); engineering sciences and applied mechanics (PhD); flight dynamics (MS); fluid dynamics (MS); manufacture and design (MS); mechanical engineering (MS). Electronic applications accepted.

College of Health and Human Services *Program availability:* Part-time, evening/weekend. Offers audiology (Au D); biometry (MPH); communicative disorders (MA); environmental health (MPH); epidemiology (MPH, PhD); exercise physiology (MS); gerontology (MS); global emergency preparedness and response (MS); global health (PhD); health and human services (MA, MPH, MS, MSW, Au D, DPT, PhD); health behavior (PhD); health promotion (MPH); health services administration (MPH); kinesiology (MA); language and communicative disorders (PhD); nursing (MS); nutritional sciences (MS); physical therapy (DPT); social work (MSW); toxicology (MS). Electronic applications accepted.

College of Professional Studies and Fine Arts *Program availability:* Part-time. Offers advertising and public relations (MA); art history (MA); city planning (MCP); composition (acoustic and electronic) (MM); conducting (MM); criminal justice administration (MPA); criminal justice and criminology (MA); critical-cultural studies (MA); ethnomusicology (MA); interaction studies (MA); intercultural and international studies (MA); jazz studies (MM); musicology (MA); new media studies (MA); news and information studies (MA); performance (MM); piano pedagogy (MA); professional studies and fine arts (MA, MCP, MFA, MM, MPA, MS); public administration (MPA); studio arts (MA, MFA); telecommunications and media management (MA); television, film, and new media production (MA); theatre arts (MA, MFA); theory (MA).

College of Sciences *Program availability:* Part-time. Offers applied mathematics (MS); astronomy (MS); biology (MA, MS); cell and molecular biology (PhD); chemistry and biochemistry (MA, MS, PhD); clinical psychology (MS, PhD); computational science (MS, PhD); computer science (MS); ecology (MS, PhD); geological sciences (MS); industrial and organizational psychology (MS); mathematics (MA); mathematics and science education (PhD); microbiology (MS); molecular biology (MA, MS); physics (MA, MS); program evaluation (MS); psychology (MA); radiological physics (MS); regulatory affairs (MS); sciences (MA, MS, PhD); statistics (MS). Electronic applications accepted.

SANFORD BURNHAM PREBYS MEDICAL DISCOVERY INSTITUTE, La Jolla, CA 92037

General Information Independent, coed, graduate-only institution. *Enrollment by degree level:* 32 doctoral. *Graduate faculty:* 52. *Student services:* Career counseling, grant writing training, international student services.
Website: http://www.sbpdiscovery.org/trainingandeducation/gradschool/pages/home.aspx
GRADUATE UNITS
Graduate School of Biomedical Sciences Students: 32 full-time (20 women). *Faculty:* 52. Expenses: Contact institution. *Financial support:* Fellowships, scholarships/grants, and health care benefits available. In 2016, 4 doctorates awarded. Offers biomedical sciences (PhD). *Application deadline:* For fall admission, 12/1 for domestic students. *Application fee:* $80. *Application Contact:* Mary Bradley, Manager, Graduate School Administration, 858-646-3100, E-mail: gradoffice@sbp.edu. *Dean,* Dr. Guy Salvesen.

SAN FRANCISCO ART INSTITUTE, San Francisco, CA 94133

General Information Independent, coed, comprehensive institution. *Enrollment:* 506 graduate, professional, and undergraduate students; 141 full-time matriculated graduate/professional students (90 women), 27 part-time matriculated graduate/professional students (19 women). *Enrollment by degree level:* 160 master's, 8 other advanced degrees. *Graduate faculty:* 21 full-time (11 women), 53 part-time/adjunct (27 women). *Tuition:* Full-time $46,010; part-time $2020 per credit. *Required fees:* $870; $870 per credit. *Graduate housing:* Room and/or apartments available on a first-come, first-served basis to single students; on-campus housing not available to married students. Typical cost: $11,500 (including board). Housing application deadline: 6/1. *Student services:* Campus employment opportunities, campus safety program, career counseling, free psychological counseling, grant writing training, international student services, low-cost health insurance, services for students with disabilities, writing training. *Library facilities:* Anne Bremer Memorial Library plus 1 other. *Collection:* Books: 31,831 (physical); Serial titles: 126 (physical), 791 (digital/electronic); Databases: 6. Weekly public service hours: 59. *Research affiliation:* Headlands Center for the Arts (multidisciplinary art exhibition), Kadist Art Foundation (contemporary art exhibition), San Francisco Museum of Modern Art (art history, museum studies, contemporary art), Yerba Buena Center for the Arts (art exhibits), Tremaine Foundation (education; art, environment, and learning disabilities), Prelinger Library (library).

Computer facilities: 150 computers available on campus for general student use. A campuswide network can be accessed. Online class registration is available.
Website: http://www.sfai.edu/

General Application Contact: Jana Rumberger, Director of Graduate Admissions, 415-351-3507, Fax: 415-749-4592, E-mail: jrumberger@sfai.edu.
GRADUATE UNITS
Master of Arts Programs Students: 6 full-time (all women), 3 part-time (all women); includes 1 minority (Asian, non-Hispanic/Latino), 3 international. Average age 27. 20 applicants, 60% accepted, 5 enrolled. *Faculty:* 3 full-time (all women), 12 part-time/adjunct (7 women). Expenses: Contact institution. *Financial support:* Fellowships, teaching assistantships, career-related internships or fieldwork, Federal Work-Study, scholarships/grants, and unspecified assistantships available. Support available to part-time students. Financial award application deadline: 3/1; financial award applicants required to submit FAFSA. In 2016, 9 master's awarded. Offers exhibition and museum studies (MA); history and theory of contemporary art (MA). *Application deadline:* Applications are processed on a rolling basis. *Application fee:* $85. Electronic applications accepted. *Application Contact:* Jana Rumberger, Director of Graduate Admissions, 415-351-3507, Fax: 415-749-4592, E-mail: jrumberger@sfai.edu. *Chair, Master of Arts Department,* Claire Daigle, 415-351-3573, Fax: 415-641-1205, E-mail: cdaigle@sfai.edu.
Master of Fine Arts Programs Students: 135 full-time (84 women), 24 part-time (16 women); includes 36 minority (2 Black or African American, non-Hispanic/Latino; 6 Asian, non-Hispanic/Latino; 21 Hispanic/Latino; 1 Native Hawaiian or other Pacific Islander, non-Hispanic/Latino; 6 Two or more races, non-Hispanic/Latino), 61 international. Average age 30. 295 applicants, 66% accepted, 64 enrolled. *Faculty:* 18 full-time (8 women), 41 part-time/adjunct (20 women). Expenses: Contact institution. *Financial support:* Fellowships, teaching assistantships, career-related internships or fieldwork, Federal Work-Study, scholarships/grants, and unspecified assistantships available. Support available to part-time students. Financial award application deadline: 3/1; financial award applicants required to submit FAFSA. In 2016, 78 master's, 8 other advanced degrees awarded. Offers studio art (MFA, Certificate). *Application deadline:* For spring admission, 11/1 priority date for domestic and international students. Applications are processed on a rolling basis. *Application fee:* $85. Electronic applications accepted. *Application Contact:* Jana Rumberger, Director of Graduate Admissions, 415-351-3507, Fax: 415-749-4592, E-mail: jrumberger@sfai.edu. *Chair, Master of Fine Arts Department,* Tony Labat, 415-351-3574, Fax: 415-641-1205, E-mail: tlabat@sfai.edu.

SAN FRANCISCO CONSERVATORY OF MUSIC, San Francisco, CA 94102

General Information Independent, coed, comprehensive institution. *Enrollment:* 401 graduate, professional, and undergraduate students; 211 full-time matriculated graduate/professional students (122 women), 2 part-time matriculated graduate/professional students. *Enrollment by degree level:* 171 master's, 42 other advanced degrees. *Graduate faculty:* 26 full-time (7 women), 94 part-time/adjunct (31 women). *Tuition:* Full-time $42,400; part-time $1868 per credit. *Required fees:* $1010; $1010 per credit. *One-time fee:* $50 full-time. Tuition and fees vary according to course load. *Graduate housing:* Rooms and/or apartments available on a first-come, first-served basis to single and married students. Typical cost: $13,980 per year ($20,730 including board) for single students; $24,200 per year ($37,700 including board) for married students. Room and board charges vary according to board plan, campus/location and housing facility selected. Housing application deadline: 5/31. *Student services:* Campus employment opportunities, campus safety program, career counseling, free psychological counseling, grant writing training, low-cost health insurance, services for students with disabilities, teacher training, writing training. *Library facilities:* San Francisco Conservatory of Music Library. *Collection:* Books: 22,873 (physical), 3,073 (digital/electronic); Serial titles: 70 (physical), 374 (digital/electronic); Databases: 13. Weekly public service hours: 72.

Computer facilities: 12 computers available on campus for general student use. A campuswide network can be accessed from student residence rooms. Online class registration is available.
Website: http://www.sfcm.edu/

General Application Contact: Melissa Cocco-Mitten, Director of Admissions, 415-503-6231, Fax: 415-503-6299, E-mail: admit@sfcm.edu.
GRADUATE UNITS
Graduate Division Students: 211 full-time (122 women), 2 part-time (0 women); includes 42 minority (6 Black or African American, non-Hispanic/Latino; 1 American Indian or Alaska Native, non-Hispanic/Latino; 20 Asian, non-Hispanic/Latino; 8 Hispanic/Latino; 1 Native Hawaiian or other Pacific Islander, non-Hispanic/Latino; 6 Two or more races, non-Hispanic/Latino), 83 international. Average age 25. 684 applicants, 39% accepted, 131 enrolled. *Faculty:* 26 full-time (7 women), 94 part-time/adjunct (31 women). Expenses: Contact institution. *Financial support:* In 2016–17, 212 students received support. Federal Work-Study, scholarships/grants, tuition waivers (partial), and unspecified assistantships available. Financial award application deadline: 2/15; financial award applicants required to submit FAFSA. In 2016, 99 master's, 29 other advanced degrees awarded. Offers brass (MM); chamber music (MM, Artist Certificate); composition (MM); conducting (MM); guitar (MM); harp (MM); percussion (MM); piano (MM, MM). *Application deadline:* For fall admission, 12/1 for domestic and international students; for spring admission, 10/1 for domestic and international students. *Application fee:* $110. Electronic applications accepted. *Application Contact:* Melissa Cocco-Mitten, Director of Admission, 415-503-6231, Fax: 415-503-6299, E-mail: admit@sfcm.edu. *Provost and Dean,* Kate Sheeran, 415-503-6251, Fax: 415-503-6205, E-mail: lnickels@sfcm.edu.

SAN FRANCISCO STATE UNIVERSITY, San Francisco, CA 94132-1722

General Information State-supported, coed, university. *Enrollment:* 29,045 graduate, professional, and undergraduate students; 1,683 full-time matriculated graduate/professional students (1,109 women), 1,123 part-time matriculated graduate/professional students (678 women). *Tuition,* state resident: full-time $6738. Tuition, nonresident: full-time $15,666. *Required fees:* $1012. Tuition and fees vary according to degree level and program. *Graduate housing:* Room and/or apartments available on a first-come, first-served basis to single students; on-campus housing not available to married students. *Student services:* Campus employment opportunities, campus safety program, career counseling, child daycare facilities, exercise/wellness program, free psychological counseling, international student services, low-cost health insurance, multicultural affairs office, services for students with disabilities, teacher training. *Library facilities:* J. Paul Leonard Library. *Collection:* Study areas open 24 hours, 5–7 days a week; students can reserve study rooms.

Computer facilities: Computer purchase and lease plans are available. 2,000 computers available on campus for general student use. A campuswide network can be accessed from student residence rooms and from off campus. Online class registration is available.
Website: http://www.sfsu.edu/

General Application Contact: Noah Price, Director of Graduate Admissions, 415-405-3506, Fax: 415-405-0340, E-mail: nprice@sfsu.edu.
GRADUATE UNITS
Division of Graduate Studies Expenses: Contact institution. *Financial support:* Fellowships, research assistantships, teaching assistantships, career-related internships or fieldwork, Federal Work-Study, institutionally sponsored loans, tuition waivers (partial), and unspecified assistantships available. Support available to part-time students. Financial award application deadline: 3/1; financial award applicants required to submit FAFSA. *Program availability:* Part-time, evening/weekend. *Application fee:* $55. *Application Contact:* Noah Price, Director, Graduate Admissions, 415-405-3506, Fax: 415-405-0340, E-mail: nprice@sfsu.edu. *Interim Dean,* Dr. Mi-Sook Kim, 415-338-2231, Fax: 415-405-0340.
College of Business Expenses: Contact institution. Offers accounting (MSA); business (EMBA, MA, MBA, MSA); decision sciences/operations research (MBA); economics (MA); ethics and compliance (MBA); finance (MBA); global business and innovation (MBA); healthcare administration (MBA); hospitality and tourism management (MBA); information systems (MBA); leadership (MBA); marketing (MBA); nonprofit and social enterprise leadership (MBA); sustainable business (MBA). *Application Contact:* Dr. Yim-Yu Wong, Associate Dean, 415-338-1276, Fax: 415-338-6237, E-mail: yywong@sfsu.edu. *Dean,* Linda Oubre, 415-338-3650, Fax: 415-338-6237, E-mail: loubre@sfsu.edu.
College of Education Expenses: Contact institution. Offers adult education (MA); augmentative and alternative communication (AC); autism spectrum (AC); communicative disorders (MS); early childhood education (MA); early childhood special education (AC); education (MA, MS, Ed D, PhD, AC, Certificate, Credential); education specialist (Credential); educational administration (MA, Credential); educational leadership (Ed D); elementary education (MA, Certificate, Credential); equity and social justice (MA); instructional technologies (MA); language and literacy education (MA, Certificate, Credential); mathematics education (MA); orientation and mobility (MA, Credential); reading (Certificate); reading and literacy leadership (Credential); secondary education (MA, Credential); special education (MA, PhD); special interest (MA). *Application Contact:* Victoria Narkewicz, Executive Assistant, 415-338-2687, Fax: 415-338-7019, E-mail: toria@sfsu.edu. *Interim Dean,* Dr. Nancy Robinson, 415-338-2687, Fax: 415-338-7019, E-mail: nancyr@sfsu.edu.
College of Ethnic Studies Expenses: Contact institution. *Program availability:* Part-time. Offers Asian American studies (MA); ethnic studies (MA). *Application Contact:* Dr. Amy H. Sueyoshi, Associate Dean, 415-338-1693, Fax: 415-338-1739, E-mail: sueyoshi@sfsu.edu. *Dean,* Dr. Kenneth P. Monteiro, 415-338-1693, Fax: 415-338-1739, E-mail: ethnicst@sfsu.edu.
College of Health and Social Sciences Expenses: Contact institution. *Financial support:* Fellowships, research assistantships, teaching assistantships, career-related internships or fieldwork, Federal Work-Study, institutionally sponsored loans, and unspecified assistantships available. *Program availability:* Part-time. Offers adult acute care (MS); clinical nurse specialist (MS); clinical rehabilitation and mental health counseling (MS); community/public health nursing (MS); consumer and family studies/dietetics (MA); counseling (MS); criminal justice administration (MPA); environmental administration and policy (MPA); family nurse practitioner (MS, Certificate); gerontology (MA); health and social sciences (MA, MPA, MPH, MS, MSC, MSW, DPT, Certificate, Credential); health education (MPH); human sexuality studies (MA); kinesiology (MS); marriage, family, and child counseling (MSC); nonprofit administration (MPA); nursing administration (MS); pediatrics (MS); physical therapy (DPT); public management (MPA); public policy (MPA); recreation, parks, and tourism (MS); school counseling (Credential); social work (MSW); urban administration (MPA);

women's health (MS). *Application Contact:* Christina Alcantara, Assistant to the Dean, 415-338-3327, Fax: 415-338-0586, E-mail: cba@sfsu.edu. *Dean,* Dr. Alvin Alvarez, 415-338-3326, Fax: 415-338-0586, E-mail: aalvarez@sfsu.edu.

College of Liberal and Creative Arts Expenses: Contact institution. *Financial support:* Teaching assistantships, career-related internships or fieldwork, and Federal Work-Study available. *Program availability:* Part-time, evening/weekend. Offers archaeology (MA); art (MFA); art history (MA); biological/physical anthropology (MA); broadcast and electronic communication arts (MA); chamber music (MM); Chinese (MA); cinema (MA, MFA); classical performance (MM); classics (MA); communication studies (MA); comparative literature (MA); composition (MA, Certificate); conducting (MM); creative writing (MA, MFA); drama (MA); French (MA); German (MA); history (MA); humanities and liberal studies (MA); immigrant literacies (Certificate); industrial arts (MA); international relations (MA); Italian (MA); Japanese (MA); liberal and creative arts (MA, MFA, MM, Certificate); linguistics (MA); literature (MA); museum studies (MA); music education (MA); music history (MA); philosophy (MA); political science (MA); social/cultural anthropology (MA); Spanish (MA); teaching English to speakers of other languages (MA); teaching post-secondary reading (Certificate); theatre arts (MFA); visual anthropology (MA); women and gender studies (MA). *Application Contact:* Florence Tu, Executive Assistant to the Dean, 415-338-7692, Fax: 415-338-6159, E-mail: ftu@sfsu.edu. *Dean,* Dr. Andrew Harris, 415-338-1471, Fax: 415-338-6159, E-mail: a1harris@sfsu.edu.

College of Science and Engineering Expenses: Contact institution. *Program availability:* Part-time. Offers astronomy (MS); biochemistry (MS); biotechnology (PSM); cell and molecular biology (MS); chemistry (MS); clinical psychology (MS); computer science (MS); developmental psychology (MA); ecology, evolution, and conservation biology (MS); embedded electrical and computer systems (MS); energy systems (MS); geographic information science (MS); geography (MA); geosciences (MS); industrial/organizational psychology (MS); marine biology (MS); marine science (MS); mathematics (MA); microbiology (MS); mind, brain, and behavior (MA); physics (MS); physiology and behavioral biology (MS); resource management and environmental planning (MA); school psychology (MS, Credential); science (PSM); science and engineering (MA, MS, PSM, Credential); social psychology (MS); stem cell science (PSM); structural/earthquake engineering (MS). *Application deadline:* Applications are processed on a rolling basis. Electronic applications accepted. *Application Contact:* Nadia Chan, Executive Assistant to the Dean, 415-338-1571, Fax: 415-338-6136, E-mail: nadiach@sfsu.edu. *Dean,* Dr. Keith Bowman, 415-338-1571, Fax: 415-338-6136, E-mail: kjbowman@sfsu.edu.

SAN FRANCISCO THEOLOGICAL SEMINARY, San Anselmo, CA 94960

General Information Independent-religious, coed, graduate-only institution. *Graduate housing:* Rooms and/or apartments available on a first-come, first-served basis to single and married students. Housing application deadline: 5/1.

GRADUATE UNITS

Graduate and Professional Programs *Program availability:* Part-time. Offers theology (M Div, MA, MATS, D Min, PhD, Th D). MA, Th D, PhD, M Div/MA offered jointly with Graduate Theological Union.

SAN JOAQUIN COLLEGE OF LAW, Clovis, CA 93612-1312

General Information Independent, coed, graduate-only institution. *Graduate housing:* On-campus housing not available.

GRADUATE UNITS

Law Program *Program availability:* Part-time, evening/weekend. Offers law (JD).

SAN JOSE STATE UNIVERSITY, San Jose, CA 95192-0001

General Information State-supported, coed, comprehensive institution. CGS member. *Graduate housing:* Room and/or apartments available on a first-come, first-served basis to single students; on-campus housing not available to married students. *Research affiliation:* Moss Landing Marine Laboratories.

GRADUATE UNITS

Graduate Studies and Research *Program availability:* Part-time, evening/weekend, online learning. Electronic applications accepted.

Charles W. Davidson College of Engineering *Program availability:* Part-time. Offers engineering (MS). Electronic applications accepted.

College of Applied Sciences and Arts *Program availability:* Part-time, evening/weekend. Offers big data (Certificate); California library media teacher services (Credential); collaborative response to family violence (Certificate); justice studies (MS); kinesiology (MA); library and information science (MLIS, Certificate); mass communication (MS); nutritional science (MS); occupational therapy (MS); public health (MPH); pupil personnel services (Credential); recreation (MS); social work (MSW); Spanish language counseling (Certificate); strategic management of digital assets and services (Certificate). Electronic applications accepted.

College of Humanities and the Arts Offers art (MA, MFA); computational linguistics (Certificate); English (MA, MFA); French (MA); humanities and arts (Certificate); linguistics (MA); music (MA); philosophy (MA); professional and technical communication (Certificate); Spanish (MA); teaching English to speakers of other languages (MA); TESOL (Certificate); theatre arts (MA). Electronic applications accepted.

College of Science *Program availability:* Part-time, evening/weekend. Offers biological sciences (MA, MS); biotechnology (MBT); chemistry (MA, MS); computer science (MS); cybersecurity (Certificate); cybersecurity: core technologies (Certificate); geology (MS); marine science (MS); mathematics (MA, MS); meteorology (MS); physics (MS); science education (MS); statistics (MS); Unix system administration (Certificate). Electronic applications accepted.

College of Social Sciences *Program availability:* Part-time, evening/weekend. Offers applications of technology in planning (Certificate); applied anthropology (MA); communication studies (MS); community design and development (Certificate); economics (MA); environmental planning (Certificate); geographic information science (Certificate); geography (MA); global citizenship (Certificate); history (MA); Mexican American studies (MA); psychology (MA, MS); public administration (MPA); real estate development (Certificate); social sciences (MPA, MS); sociology (MA); transportation and land use planning (Certificate). Electronic applications accepted.

Connie L. Lurie College of Education *Program availability:* Evening/weekend. Offers child and adolescent development (MA); common core mathematics (K-8) (Certificate, Credential); education (MA, Credential); educational leadership (MA, Ed D, Credential); elementary education (MA); K-12 school counseling (Credential); K-12 school counseling internship (Credential); school child welfare attendance (Credential); single subject (Credential). Electronic applications accepted.

Lucas Graduate School of Business *Program availability:* Part-time, evening/weekend, online learning. Offers accountancy (MS); business administration (MBA); taxation (MS); transportation management (MS). Electronic applications accepted.

SAN JUAN BAUTISTA SCHOOL OF MEDICINE, Caguas, PR 00726-4968

General Information Independent, coed, graduate-only institution. *Graduate housing:* On-campus housing not available. *Research affiliation:* Universidad Central del Caribe (molecular biology), Fundacion de Investigacion de Puerto Rico (clinical and translational research), University of Puerto Rico, Medical Sciences Campus (molecular biology, microbiology, neurosciences, pediatrics, public health), Ponce School of Medicine and Health Sciences (virology, immunology), Veteran Affairs (clinical research).

GRADUATE UNITS

Graduate and Professional Programs

THE SANTA BARBARA AND VENTURA COLLEGES OF LAW–SANTA BARBARA, Santa Barbara, CA 93101

General Information Independent, coed, graduate-only institution.

GRADUATE UNITS

Graduate and Professional Programs Offers law (MLS, JD).

THE SANTA BARBARA AND VENTURA COLLEGES OF LAW–VENTURA, Ventura, CA 93003

General Information Independent, coed, graduate-only institution.

GRADUATE UNITS

Graduate and Professional Programs Offers law (MLS, JD).

SANTA CLARA UNIVERSITY, Santa Clara, CA 95053

General Information Independent-religious, coed, university. *Enrollment:* 8,422 graduate, professional, and undergraduate students; 1,822 full-time matriculated graduate/professional students (965 women), 1,102 part-time matriculated graduate/professional students (590 women). *Enrollment by degree level:* 2,093 master's, 713 doctoral, 118 other advanced degrees. *Graduate faculty:* 269 full-time (107 women), 192 part-time/adjunct (82 women). Tuition and fees vary according to course load, degree level and program. *Graduate housing:* Rooms and/or apartments available on a first-come, first-served basis to single and married students. Housing application deadline: 6/1. *Student services:* Campus employment opportunities, campus safety program, career counseling, child daycare facilities, exercise/wellness program, free psychological counseling, international student services, low-cost health insurance, multicultural affairs office, services for students with disabilities, teacher training, writing training. *Library facilities:* University Library plus 1 other. *Collection:* Books: 603,388 (physical), 612,072 (digital/electronic); Serial titles: 15,262 (physical), 77,789 (digital/electronic); Databases: 373. Weekly public service hours: 121; students can reserve study rooms.

Computer facilities: Computer purchase and lease plans are available. A campuswide network can be accessed from student residence rooms and from off campus. Online class registration is available.
Website: http://www.scu.edu/

GRADUATE UNITS

College of Arts and Sciences Students: 12 full-time (9 women), 50 part-time (35 women); includes 34 minority (1 Black or African American, non-Hispanic/Latino; 6 Asian, non-Hispanic/Latino; 24 Hispanic/Latino; 1 Native Hawaiian or other Pacific Islander, non-Hispanic/Latino; 2 Two or more races, non-Hispanic/Latino), 2 international. Average age 46. 8 applicants, 88% accepted, 5 enrolled. *Faculty:* 3 full-time (1 woman), 5 part-time/adjunct (1 woman). Expenses: Contact institution. *Financial support:* Fellowships, research assistantships, teaching assistantships, career-related internships or fieldwork, Federal Work-Study, scholarships/grants, traineeships, health care benefits, tuition waivers, and unspecified assistantships available. Support available to part-time students. Financial award applicants required to submit FAFSA. In 2016, 7 master's awarded. *Program availability:* Part-time, evening/weekend. Offers pastoral ministries (MA). *Application deadline:* For fall admission, 7/1 for domestic students; for winter admission, 10/1 for domestic students; for spring admission, 2/14 for domestic students. Applications are processed on a rolling basis. *Application fee:* $50. Electronic applications accepted. *Application Contact:* Saralynn Ferrara, Associate Director, 408-554-4322, E-mail: sferrara@scu.edu. *Director, Graduate Program in Pastoral Ministries,* Gary Macy, 408-554-2357, E-mail: gmacy@scu.edu.

Jesuit School of Theology Students: 125 full-time (29 women), 9 part-time (5 women); includes 71 minority (22 Black or African American, non-Hispanic/Latino; 27 Asian, non-Hispanic/Latino; 19 Hispanic/Latino; 2 Native Hawaiian or other Pacific Islander, non-Hispanic/Latino; 1 Two or more races, non-Hispanic/Latino). Average age 36. 93 applicants, 92% accepted, 56 enrolled. *Faculty:* 20 full-time (5 women), 6 part-time/adjunct (3 women). Expenses: Contact institution. *Financial support:* Scholarships/grants and unspecified assistantships available. Financial award application deadline: 3/1; financial award applicants required to submit FAFSA. In 2016, 55 master's, 5 doctorates awarded. *Program availability:* Part-time, evening/weekend, 100% online. Offers Biblical languages (MABL); Biblical studies (MTS); Christian spirituality (MTS); church history (MTS); cultural and historical studies of Catholicism (MTS); ethics and social theory/religion and society (MTS); history of art and religion (MTS); liturgical studies (MTS); pastoral ministry (M Div); systematic and philosophical theology (MTS); theology (MA, MTS, Th M, STD, STB, STL). *Application deadline:* For fall admission, 3/1 priority date for domestic students; for spring admission, 10/1 priority date for domestic students. Applications are processed on a rolling basis. *Application fee:* $50 ($0 for international students). Electronic applications accepted. *Application Contact:* Barbara Godoy, Assistant Dean of Enrollment Management, 510-549-5016, E-mail: bgodoy@scu.edu. *Associate Dean,* Alison Benders, 510-549-5055, E-mail: ambenders@scu.edu.

Leavey School of Business Students: 330 full-time (192 women), 323 part-time (136 women); includes 190 minority (7 Black or African American, non-Hispanic/Latino; 140 Asian, non-Hispanic/Latino; 28 Hispanic/Latino; 2 Native Hawaiian or other Pacific Islander, non-Hispanic/Latino; 13 Two or more races, non-Hispanic/Latino), 275 international. Average age 30. 388 applicants, 53% accepted, 107 enrolled. *Faculty:* 92 full-time (27 women), 44 part-time/adjunct (18 women). Expenses: Contact institution. *Financial support:* Fellowships, research assistantships, teaching assistantships, career-related internships or fieldwork, Federal Work-Study, scholarships/grants, traineeships, health care benefits, tuition waivers, and unspecified assistantships available. Support available to part-time students. Financial award applicants required to submit FAFSA. In 2016, 339 master's awarded. *Program availability:* Part-time, evening/weekend. Offers business administration (MBA); business analytics (MS); finance (MS); information systems (MS); supply chain management and analytics (MS). *Application fee:* $100 ($150 for international students). Electronic applications accepted. *Application Contact:* Taryn Upchurch, Director, Graduate Admissions and Recruitment, 408-551-7858, E-mail: upchurch@scu.edu. *Dean,* Caryn Beck-Dudley.

School of Education and Counseling Psychology Students: 265 full-time (213 women), 333 part-time (270 women); includes 282 minority (16 Black or African American, non-Hispanic/Latino; 1 American Indian or Alaska Native, non-Hispanic/Latino; 78 Asian, non-Hispanic/Latino; 156 Hispanic/Latino; 31 Two or more races, non-Hispanic/Latino), 46 international. Average age 30. 266 applicants, 74% accepted, 126 enrolled. *Faculty:* 32 full-time (22 women), 40 part-time/adjunct (25 women). Expenses: Contact institution. *Financial support:* Fellowships, research assistantships, teaching assistantships, career-related internships or fieldwork, Federal Work-Study, scholarships/grants, traineeships, health care benefits, and tuition waivers available. Support available to part-time students. Financial award applicants required to submit FAFSA. In 2016, 253 master's awarded. *Program availability:* Part-time, evening/weekend. Offers Catholic school teaching (MA); counseling (MA); counseling psychology (MA); educational leadership (MA); interdisciplinary education (MA); teaching multiple subjects (MA); teaching single subjects (MA). *Application deadline:* Applications are processed on a rolling basis. *Application fee:* $50. Electronic applications accepted. *Application Contact:* Victoria Rodriguez, Graduate Admissions Advisor, 408-554-4723, E-mail: v1rodriguez@scu.edu. *Dean,* Dr. Sabrina Zirkel, 408-551-3074, Fax: 408-554-4367, E-mail: szirkel@scu.edu.

School of Engineering Students: 449 full-time (188 women), 315 part-time (114 women); includes 197 minority (3 Black or African American, non-Hispanic/Latino; 144 Asian, non-Hispanic/Latino; 33 Hispanic/Latino; 1 Native Hawaiian or other Pacific Islander, non-Hispanic/Latino; 16 Two or more races, non-Hispanic/Latino), 418 international. Average age 28. 1,217 applicants, 45% accepted, 293 enrolled. *Faculty:* 66 full-time (22 women), 59 part-time/adjunct (12 women). Expenses: Contact institution. *Financial support:* Fellowships, research assistantships, teaching assistantships, career-related internships or fieldwork, Federal Work-Study, scholarships/grants, traineeships, health care benefits, tuition waivers, and unspecified assistantships available. Support available to part-time students. Financial award applicants required to submit FAFSA. In 2016, 466 master's awarded. *Program availability:* Part-time, evening/weekend. Offers applied mathematics (MS); bioengineering (MS); civil engineering (MS); computer science and engineering (MS, PhD); electrical engineering (MS, PhD); engineering (Engineer); engineering management and leadership (MS); mechanical engineering (MS, PhD); software engineering (MS); sustainable energy (MS). *Application deadline:* For fall admission, 4/1 for domestic and international students; for winter admission, 9/9 for domestic students, 9/2 for international students; for spring admission, 2/17 for domestic students, 12/9 for international students. *Application fee:* $60. Electronic applications accepted. *Application Contact:* Stacey Tinker, Director of Admissions and Marketing, 408-554-4313, Fax: 408-554-4323, E-mail: stinker@scu.edu. *Dean,* Dr. Alfonso Ortega.

School of Law Students: 641 full-time (334 women), 72 part-time (30 women); includes 304 minority (29 Black or African American, non-Hispanic/Latino; 128 Asian, non-Hispanic/Latino; 108 Hispanic/Latino; 2 Native Hawaiian or other Pacific Islander, non-Hispanic/Latino; 37 Two or more races, non-Hispanic/Latino), 81 international. Average age 27. 2,235 applicants, 75% accepted, 305 enrolled. *Faculty:* 56 full-time (30 women), 38 part-time/adjunct (23 women). Expenses: Contact institution. *Financial support:* Fellowships, research assistantships, teaching assistantships, career-related internships or fieldwork, Federal Work-Study, scholarships/grants, traineeships, health care benefits, tuition waivers, and unspecified assistantships available. Support available to part-time students. Financial award application deadline: 3/1; financial award applicants required to submit FAFSA. In 2016, 27 master's, 218 doctorates awarded. *Program availability:* Part-time, evening/weekend. Offers intellectual property (LL M); international and comparative law (LL M); law (JD); United States law (LL M). LL M in United States law track only open to non-U.S. attorneys; JD/MBA, JD/MSIS are joint programs with the Leavey School of Business. *Application deadline:* Applications are processed on a rolling basis. *Application fee:* $75. Electronic applications accepted. *Application Contact:* Nanette Cannon, Director of Admissions, 408-551-1846, E-mail: ncannon@scu.edu. *Dean,* Lisa Kloppenberg, 408-554-4362.

SARAH LAWRENCE COLLEGE, Bronxville, NY 10708-5999

General Information Independent, coed, comprehensive institution. CGS member. *Graduate housing:* On-campus housing not available. *Research affiliation:* Westchester Medical Center/New York Medical College, New York Hospital–Cornell Medical Center, Albert Einstein College of Medicine, New York University Medical Center, Columbia University Medical Center.

GRADUATE UNITS

Graduate Studies *Program availability:* Part-time. Offers art of teaching (MS Ed); child development (MA); creative non-fiction (MFA); dance (MFA); dance/movement therapy (MS); fiction (MFA); health advocacy (MA); human genetics (MS); poetry (MFA); theater (MFA); women's history (MA). Electronic applications accepted.

SAVANNAH COLLEGE OF ART AND DESIGN, Savannah, GA 31402-3146

General Information Independent, coed, comprehensive institution. CGS member. *Enrollment:* 12,951 graduate, professional, and undergraduate students; 1,707 full-time matriculated graduate/professional students (1,088 women), 670 part-time matriculated graduate/professional students (426 women). *Enrollment by degree level:* 2,377 master's. *Graduate faculty:* 532 full-time (213 women), 154 part-time/adjunct (80 women). *Tuition:* Full-time $36,045. Tuition and fees vary according to course load. *Graduate housing:* Room and/or apartments available on a first-come, first-served basis to single students; on-campus housing not available to married students. Typical cost: $9528 per year ($14,244 including board). Room and board charges vary according to board plan, campus/location and housing facility selected. Housing application deadline: 4/1. *Student services:* Campus employment opportunities, campus safety program, career counseling, exercise/wellness program, free psychological counseling, international student services, multicultural affairs office, services for students with disabilities, writing training. *Library facilities:* Jen Library plus 4 others. *Collection:* Books: 260,652 (physical), 191,604 (digital/electronic); Serial titles: 936 (physical), 45,815 (digital/electronic); Databases: 92. Weekly public service hours: 105; students can reserve study rooms.

Computer facilities: Computer purchase and lease plans are available. 3,450 computers available on campus for general student use. A campuswide network can be accessed from student residence rooms and from off campus. Online class registration is available. Website: http://www.scad.edu/

General Application Contact: Jenny Jaquillard, Executive Director of Admissions, Recruitment and Events, 912-525-5100, Fax: 912-525-5985, E-mail: admission@scad.edu.

GRADUATE UNITS

Graduate School Expenses: Contact institution. *Financial support:* Fellowships, career-related internships or fieldwork, Federal Work-Study, and scholarships/grants available. Financial award application deadline: 4/1; financial award applicants required to submit FAFSA. *Program availability:* Part-time, online learning. Offers accessory design (MA, MFA); advertising (MA, MFA); animation (MA, MFA); architectural history (MFA); architecture (M Arch); art and design (M Arch, MA, MFA, MUD); art history (MA); business design and arts leadership (MA); cinema studies (MA); design for sustainability (MA, MFA); design management (MA, MFA); dramatic writing (MFA); fashion (MA, MFA); fibers (MA, MFA); film and television (MA, MFA); furniture design (MA, MFA); graphic design and visual experience (MA, MFA); illustration (MA, MFA); industrial design (MA, MFA); interactive design and game development (MA, MFA); interior design (MA, MFA); jewelry (MA, MFA); luxury and fashion management (MA, MFA); motion media design (MA, MFA); painting (MA, MFA); performing arts (MFA); photography (MA, MFA); preservation design (MA, MFA); printmaking (MFA); production design (MA, MFA); sculpture (MA, MFA); sequential art (MA, MFA); service design (MFA); sound design (MA, MFA); themed entertainment design (MFA); urban design (MUD); visual effects (MA, MFA); writing (MFA). *Application deadline:* For fall admission, 4/1 for domestic and international students. Applications are processed on a rolling basis. *Application fee:* $40. Electronic applications accepted. *Application Contact:* Jenny Jaquillard, Executive Director of Admissions, Recruitment and Events, 912-525-5100, Fax: 912-525-5985, E-mail: admission@scad.edu. *Director of Graduate Programs,* Sarah McCarn.

SAVANNAH LAW SCHOOL, Savannah, GA 31401

General Information Proprietary, coed, graduate-only institution. Website: http://www.savannahlawschool.org/

General Application Contact: 525-912-3913, E-mail: admissions@savannahlawschool.org.

GRADUATE UNITS

JD Program Expenses: Contact institution. *Financial support:* Fellowships and scholarships/grants available. Financial award application deadline: 6/1; financial award applicants required to submit FAFSA. *Program availability:* Part-time. Offers law (JD). Electronic applications accepted. *Application Contact:* Rebecca Milter, Director of Admissions, E-mail: rmilter@savannahlawschool.org. *Dean,* Malcolm L. Morris, 912-525-3910, E-mail: mmorris@savannahlawschool.org.

SAVANNAH STATE UNIVERSITY, Savannah, GA 31404

General Information State-supported, coed, comprehensive institution. CGS member. *Graduate housing:* Room and/or apartments available on a first-come, first-served basis to single students; on-campus housing not available to married students. Housing application deadline: 5/1. *Research affiliation:* Office of Naval Research (ONR) (marine science), Living Marine Resources Cooperative Science Center (LMRCSC) (marine science), National Institute of Mental Health (NIMH) (social work), U.S. Department of Homeland Security (urban studies and planning), Skidaway Institute of Oceanography (marine science), University of Georgia Marine Education Center & Aquarium (marine science).

GRADUATE UNITS

Master of Business Administration Program *Program availability:* Part-time, evening/weekend. Offers business administration (MBA). Electronic applications accepted.

Master of Public Administration Program *Program availability:* Part-time. Offers city management (MPA); human resources (MPA). Electronic applications accepted.

Master of Science in Marine Sciences Program *Program availability:* Part-time. Offers applied marine science (MSMS); marine science research (MSMS); professional advancement (MSMS). Electronic applications accepted.

Master of Science in Urban Studies and Planning Program *Program availability:* Part-time. Offers urban studies and planning (MSUS). Electronic applications accepted.

Master of Social Work Program Offers social work (MSW).

SAYBROOK UNIVERSITY, San Francisco, CA 94612

General Information Independent, coed, graduate-only institution. *Research affiliation:* Rollo May Center for Humanistic Studies.

GRADUATE UNITS

LIOS MA Residential Programs Offers leadership and organization development (MA); psychology counseling (MA).

School of Clinical Psychology Offers clinical psychology (MA). Program offered jointly with Bastyr University.

School of Mind-Body Medicine Offers mind-body medicine (MS, PhD, Certificate). Electronic applications accepted.

School of Organizational Leadership and Transformation Offers organizational leadership and transformation (MA). Program offered jointly with Bastyr University.

School of Psychology and Interdisciplinary Inquiry *Program availability:* Online learning. Offers human science (MA, PhD); organizational systems (MA, PhD); psychology (MA, PhD). Electronic applications accepted.

SCHILLER INTERNATIONAL UNIVERSITY, 69115 Heidelberg, Germany

General Information Independent, coed, comprehensive institution. *Graduate housing:* Room and/or apartments available on a first-come, first-served basis to single students; on-campus housing not available to married students.

GRADUATE UNITS

MBA Programs, Heidelberg, Germany *Program availability:* Part-time, evening/weekend. Offers international business (MBA, MIM); management of information technology (MBA).

SCHILLER INTERNATIONAL UNIVERSITY, F-75015 Paris, France

General Information Independent, coed, comprehensive institution. *Graduate housing:* On-campus housing not available.

GRADUATE UNITS

MBA Program Paris, France *Program availability:* Part-time, evening/weekend, online learning. Offers international business (MBA). Bilingual French/English MBA available for native French speakers.

Program in International Relations and Diplomacy *Program availability:* Part-time, evening/weekend. Offers international relations and diplomacy (MA).

SCHILLER INTERNATIONAL UNIVERSITY, 28002 Madrid, Spain

General Information Independent, coed, comprehensive institution. *Graduate housing:* On-campus housing not available.

GRADUATE UNITS

MBA Program, Madrid, Spain *Program availability:* Part-time. Offers international business (MBA).

SCHILLER INTERNATIONAL UNIVERSITY, Largo, FL 33771

General Information Independent, coed, comprehensive institution. *Graduate housing:* Room and/or apartments available on a first-come, first-served basis to single students; on-campus housing not available to married students. Housing application deadline: 8/1.

GRADUATE UNITS

MBA Programs, Florida *Program availability:* Part-time, evening/weekend, online learning. Offers financial planning (MBA); information technology (MBA); international business (MBA); international hotel and tourism management (MBA).

SCHOOL OF ADVANCED AIR AND SPACE STUDIES, Maxwell AFB, AL 36112-6424

General Information Federally supported, coed, primarily men, graduate-only institution.

GRADUATE UNITS

Program in Airpower Art and Science Offers airpower art and science (MA). Available to active duty military officers only.

SCHOOL OF ARCHITECTURE AT TALIESIN, Scottsdale, AZ 85261-4430

General Information Independent, coed, graduate-only institution. *Enrollment by degree level:* 16 master's. *Graduate faculty:* 3 full-time (1 woman), 17 part-time/adjunct (4 women). *Tuition:* Full-time $40,800. *Graduate housing:* Rooms and/or apartments guaranteed to single students and available on a first-come, first-served basis to married students. Typical cost: $6500 (including board) for single students; $8900 (including board) for married students. Housing application deadline: 3/20. *Student services:* Campus employment opportunities, campus safety program, career counseling, free psychological counseling, international student services, writing training. *Library facilities:* William Wesley Peters Library plus 1 other. *Collection:* Books: 30,000 (physical). Study areas open 24 hours, 5–7 days a week.

Computer facilities: 30 computers available on campus for general student use. A campuswide network can be accessed from student residence rooms. Website: http://www.taliesin.edu/

General Application Contact: Jerry Kavalieratos, Director of Admissions and Student Services, 480-627-5345, E-mail: jkavalieratos@taliesin.edu.

GRADUATE UNITS

Graduate Program Students: 16 full-time (4 women); includes 1 minority (Hispanic/Latino), 5 international. Average age 29. 27 applicants, 44% accepted, 8 enrolled. *Faculty:* 3 full-time (1 woman), 17 part-time/adjunct (4 women). Expenses: Contact institution. *Financial support:* In 2016–17, 1 student received support. Career-related internships or fieldwork, scholarships/grants, and traineeships available. Financial award application deadline: 7/1; financial award applicants required to submit FAFSA. In 2016, 12 master's awarded. Offers architecture (M Arch). Summer session held in Spring Green, WI. *Application deadline:* For fall admission, 3/1 for domestic and international students. Applications are processed on a rolling basis. *Application fee:* $50. Electronic applications accepted. *Application Contact:* Jerry Kavalieratos, Director of Admissions and Student Services, 480-627-5345, E-mail: jkavalieratos@taliesin.edu. *Dean,* Aaron A. Betsky, 480-860-2700, Fax: 480-391-4009, E-mail: abetsky@taliesin.edu.

SCHOOL OF THE ART INSTITUTE OF CHICAGO, Chicago, IL 60603-3103

General Information Independent, coed, comprehensive institution. *Graduate housing:* Room and/or apartments available on a first-come, first-served basis to single students; on-campus housing not available to married students. Housing application deadline: 3/21.

GRADUATE UNITS

Graduate Division *Program availability:* Part-time. Offers architecture (M Arc); art and technology studies (MFA); art education and art teaching (MAAE, MAT); art therapy (MAAT); arts administration (MAAAP); ceramics (MFA); design for emerging technologies (MFA); designed objects (M Des); fashion, body, and garment (M Des, Certificate); fiber and material studies (MFA); film, video, and new media (MFA); historic preservation (MSHP); interior architecture (M Arc); modern art history, theory, and criticism (MA); new arts journalism (MA); painting and drawing (MFA); performance (MFA); photography (MFA); printmaking (MFA); sculpture (MFA); sound (MFA); visual and critical studies (MA); visual communication (MFA); writing (MFA, Certificate).

SCHOOL OF VISUAL ARTS, New York, NY 10010-3994

General Information Proprietary, coed, comprehensive institution. *Graduate housing:* Room and/or apartments available on a first-come, first-served basis to single students; on-campus housing not available to married students.

GRADUATE UNITS

Graduate Programs Offers art education (MAT); art practice (MFA); art therapy (MPS); art writing (MFA); branding (MPS); computer art (MFA); critical theory and the arts (MA); curatorial practice (MA); design (MFA); design for social innovation (MFA); design research, writing and criticism (MA); digital photography (MPS); directing (MPS); fashion photography (MPS); fine arts (MFA); illustration as visual essay (MFA); interaction design (MFA); photography, video and related media (MFA); products of design (MFA); social documentary film (MFA); visual narrative (MFA). Electronic applications accepted.

SCHREINER UNIVERSITY, Kerrville, TX 78028-5697

General Information Independent-religious, coed, comprehensive institution. *Graduate housing:* Room and/or apartments available on a first-come, first-served basis to single students; on-campus housing not available to married students.

GRADUATE UNITS

Department of Education *Program availability:* Part-time, evening/weekend, online learning. Offers education (M Ed); principal (Certificate). Electronic applications accepted.

MBA Program *Program availability:* Part-time, online learning. Offers ethical leadership (MBA). Electronic applications accepted.

THE SCRIPPS RESEARCH INSTITUTE, La Jolla, CA 92037

General Information Independent, coed, graduate-only institution. *Graduate housing:* On-campus housing not available.

GRADUATE UNITS

Kellogg School of Science and Technology Offers chemical and biological sciences (PhD). Electronic applications accepted.

SEATTLE INSTITUTE OF ORIENTAL MEDICINE, Seattle, WA 98115

General Information Proprietary, coed, primarily women, graduate-only institution. *Graduate housing:* On-campus housing not available.

GRADUATE UNITS

Graduate Program Offers Oriental medicine (M Ac OM).

SEATTLE PACIFIC UNIVERSITY, Seattle, WA 98119-1997

General Information Independent-religious, coed, comprehensive institution. *Enrollment:* 4,061 graduate, professional, and undergraduate students; 361 full-time matriculated graduate/professional students (288 women), 559 part-time matriculated graduate/professional students (412 women). *Enrollment by degree level:* 747 master's, 173 doctoral. *Graduate housing:* Rooms and/or apartments available on a first-come, first-served basis to single and married students. Housing application deadline: 8/1. *Student services:* Campus employment opportunities, campus safety program, career counseling, exercise/wellness program, free psychological counseling, international student services, low-cost health insurance, multicultural affairs office, services for students with disabilities, teacher training, writing training. *Library facilities:* University Library. *Research affiliation:* Washington Research Center/Gates Foundation (education effectiveness), Fred Hutchinson Cancer Research Center (cancer and tumors), Battelle Research Center (business marketing).

Computer facilities: 150 computers available on campus for general student use. A campuswide network can be accessed from student residence rooms and from off campus. Online class registration is available. Website: http://www.spu.edu/

General Application Contact: 206-281-2091, E-mail: gradadmissions@spu.edu.

GRADUATE UNITS

Doctoral Program in Education Offers education (Ed D, PhD).

Educational Leadership Programs *Program availability:* Part-time, evening/weekend. Offers educational leadership (M Ed, Ed D); principal (Certificate); program administrator (Certificate); superintendent (Certificate). Electronic applications accepted.

Industrial Organizational Psychology Program Offers industrial organizational psychology (MA, PhD). Electronic applications accepted.

MA in Teaching English to Speakers of Other Languages Program *Program availability:* Part-time. Offers K-12 (MA); teaching English to speakers of other languages (MA). Electronic applications accepted.

Master of Arts in Management Program Offers faith and business (MA); human resources (MA); social and sustainable management (MA).

Master of Arts in Teaching Program *Program availability:* Part-time, evening/weekend. Offers teaching (MAT). Electronic applications accepted.

Master of Arts in Theology Program Offers Asian American ministry (MA); business and applied theology (MA); Christian leadership (MA); Christian scripture (MA); Christian studies (Graduate Certificate); reconciliation and intercultural studies (MA); theology (MA). Electronic applications accepted.

Master of Business Administration Program *Program availability:* Part-time. Offers business administration (MBA); social and sustainable enterprise (MBA). Electronic applications accepted.

The Master of Divinity Program Offers divinity (M Div).

Master of Education in Literacy Program *Program availability:* Part-time. Offers literacy (M Ed).

Master of Education in School Counseling Program *Program availability:* Part-time. Offers school counseling (M Ed, Certificate). Electronic applications accepted.

Master of Education in Teacher Leadership Program *Program availability:* Part-time, evening/weekend. Offers teacher leadership (M Ed). Electronic applications accepted.

Master of Fine Arts in Creative Writing Program *Program availability:* Part-time. Offers creative writing (MFA). Electronic applications accepted.

Master of Science in Information Systems Management Program *Program availability:* Part-time. Offers information systems management (MS). Electronic applications accepted.

MS in Marriage and Family Therapy Program *Program availability:* Part-time. Offers marriage and family therapy (MS); medical family therapy (Certificate). Electronic applications accepted.

MS in Nursing Program *Program availability:* Part-time. Offers administration (MSN); adult/gerontology nurse practitioner (MSN); clinical nurse specialist (MSN); family nurse practitioner (MSN, Certificate); informatics (MSN); nurse educator (MSN). Electronic applications accepted.

PhD in Clinical Psychology Program Offers clinical psychology (PhD). Electronic applications accepted.

PhD in Counselor Education Program Offers counselor education (PhD).

Program in Digital Education Leadership Offers digital education leadership (M Ed).

Program in Teaching Mathematics and Science Offers teaching mathematics and science (MTMS).

THE SEATTLE SCHOOL OF THEOLOGY AND PSYCHOLOGY, Seattle, WA 98121

General Information Independent-religious, coed, graduate-only institution.

GRADUATE UNITS

Graduate Programs *Program availability:* Part-time.

SEATTLE UNIVERSITY, Seattle, WA 98122-1090

General Information Independent-religious, coed, comprehensive institution. *Enrollment:* 7,477 graduate, professional, and undergraduate students; 1,355 full-time matriculated graduate/professional students (862 women), 1,398 part-time matriculated graduate/professional students (823 women). *Graduate faculty:* 149 full-time (77 women), 75 part-time/adjunct (51 women). *Graduate housing:* Room and/or apartments available on a first-come, first-served basis to single students; on-campus housing not available to married students. *Student services:* Campus employment opportunities, campus safety program, career counseling, exercise/wellness program, free psychological counseling, international student services, low-cost health insurance,

Seattle University

multicultural affairs office, services for students with disabilities, teacher training, writing training. *Library facilities:* Lemieux Library & McGoldrick Learning Commons plus 1 other. *Collection:* Books: 472,572 (physical), 257,641 (digital/electronic); Serial titles: 118,353 (physical), 8,597 (digital/electronic); Databases: 235. Students can reserve study rooms. *Research affiliation:* Swedish Medical Centers (nursing).

Computer facilities: Computer purchase and lease plans are available. 467 computers available on campus for general student use. A campuswide network can be accessed from student residence rooms and from off campus. Online class registration is available.

Website: http://www.seattleu.edu/

General Application Contact: Janet Shandley, Director of Graduate Admissions, 206-296-5900, Fax: 206-298-5656, E-mail: grad_admissions@seattleu.edu.

GRADUATE UNITS

Albers School of Business and Economics Students: 283 full-time (156 women), 335 part-time (137 women); includes 252 minority (10 Black or African American, non-Hispanic/Latino; 2 American Indian or Alaska Native, non-Hispanic/Latino; 196 Asian, non-Hispanic/Latino; 26 Hispanic/Latino; 2 Native Hawaiian or other Pacific Islander, non-Hispanic/Latino; 16 Two or more races, non-Hispanic/Latino), 157 international. Average age 31. 490 applicants, 59% accepted, 188 enrolled. *Faculty:* 45 full-time (17 women), 12 part-time/adjunct (5 women). Expenses: Contact institution. *Financial support:* In 2016–17, 172 students received support. Fellowships with partial tuition reimbursements available, research assistantships, career-related internships or fieldwork, Federal Work-Study, scholarships/grants, and unspecified assistantships available. Support available to part-time students. Financial award application deadline: 6/1; financial award applicants required to submit FAFSA. In 2016, 246 master's, 244 other advanced degrees awarded. *Program availability:* Part-time, evening/weekend. Offers business administration (MBA, Certificate); business analytics (MSBA, Certificate); business and economics (EMBA, MBA, MPAC, MSBA, MSF, Certificate); finance (MSF, Certificate); professional accounting (MPAC). *Application deadline:* For fall admission, 8/20 priority date for domestic students, 4/1 priority date for international students; for winter admission, 11/20 priority date for domestic students, 9/1 priority date for international students; for spring admission, 2/20 priority date for domestic students, 12/1 priority date for international students; for summer admission, 5/20 priority date for domestic students, 1/1 priority date for international students. Applications are processed on a rolling basis. *Application fee:* $55. Electronic applications accepted. *Application Contact:* Jeff Millard, Assistant Dean of Graduate Programs, 206-296-5700, E-mail: albersgrad@seattleu.edu. *Dean,* Dr. Joseph M. Phillips, Jr., 206-296-5700, Fax: 206-296-5795, E-mail: phillipsj@seattleu.edu.

Center for Leadership Formation Students: 65 full-time (28 women); includes 14 minority (2 Black or African American, non-Hispanic/Latino; 8 Asian, non-Hispanic/Latino; 1 Two or more races, non-Hispanic/Latino). Average age 42. 42 applicants, 93% accepted, 34 enrolled. *Faculty:* 14 full-time (7 women), 4 part-time/adjunct (all women). Expenses: Contact institution. *Financial support:* In 2016–17, 15 students received support. Scholarships/grants available. Financial award applicants required to submit FAFSA. In 2016, 14 master's, 7 other advanced degrees awarded. *Program availability:* Evening/weekend. Offers leadership (EMBA, Certificate). *Application deadline:* Applications are processed on a rolling basis. *Application fee:* $55. Electronic applications accepted. *Application Contact:* Sommer Harrison, Manager, Graduate Programs Outreach, 206-296-2529, E-mail: emba@seattleu.edu. *Associate Dean of Executive Education,* Dr. Marilyn Gist, 206-296-5413, E-mail: gistm@seattleu.edu.

College of Arts and Sciences Students: 103 full-time (71 women), 315 part-time (222 women); includes 139 minority (37 Black or African American, non-Hispanic/Latino; 3 American Indian or Alaska Native, non-Hispanic/Latino; 36 Asian, non-Hispanic/Latino; 34 Hispanic/Latino; 2 Native Hawaiian or other Pacific Islander, non-Hispanic/Latino; 27 Two or more races, non-Hispanic/Latino), 29 international. Average age 30. 362 applicants, 66% accepted, 150 enrolled. *Faculty:* 36 full-time (17 women), 17 part-time/adjunct (9 women). Expenses: Contact institution. *Financial support:* In 2016–17, 145 students received support. Career-related internships or fieldwork, Federal Work-Study, scholarships/grants, and unspecified assistantships available. Support available to part-time students. Financial award application deadline: 3/15; financial award applicants required to submit FAFSA. In 2016, 175 master's, 29 other advanced degrees awarded. *Program availability:* Part-time, evening/weekend. Offers arts and sciences (MA Psych, MACJ, MFA, MNPL, MPA, MSAL, MSW, Certificate); arts leadership (MFA); crime analysis (Certificate); criminal justice (MACJ); existential and phenomenological therapeutic psychology (MA Psych); social work (MSW). *Application deadline:* For fall admission, 1/15 for domestic and international students; for winter admission, 10/15 for domestic and international students; for spring admission, 2/15 for domestic and international students. Applications are processed on a rolling basis. *Application fee:* $55. Electronic applications accepted. *Application Contact:* Janet Shandley, Director of Graduate Admissions, 206-296-5900, Fax: 206-298-5656, E-mail: grad_admissions@seattleu.edu. *Dean,* Dr. David Powers, 206-296-5300, E-mail: powersda@seattleu.edu.

Center for the Study of Sport and Exercise Students: 7 full-time (4 women), 35 part-time (12 women); includes 9 minority (3 Black or African American, non-Hispanic/Latino; 4 Asian, non-Hispanic/Latino; 1 Hispanic/Latino; 1 Two or more races, non-Hispanic/Latino), 6 international. Average age 26. 5 applicants, 100% accepted, 5 enrolled. *Faculty:* 2 full-time (1 woman). Expenses: Contact institution. *Financial support:* In 2016–17, 24 students received support. Research assistantships and scholarships/grants available. Financial award applicants required to submit FAFSA. In 2016, 14 master's awarded. *Program availability:* Part-time, evening/weekend. Offers sport and exercise (MSAL). *Application deadline:* For fall admission, 2/15 for domestic and international students. *Application fee:* $55. Electronic applications accepted. *Application Contact:* Janet Shandley, Associate Dean of Graduate Admissions, 206-296-5900, Fax: 206-298-5656, E-mail: grad_admissions@seattleu.edu. *Director,* Dr. Dan Tripps, 206-398-4605, E-mail: trippsd@seattleu.edu.

Institute of Public Service Students: 19 full-time (11 women), 127 part-time (91 women); includes 56 minority (16 Black or African American, non-Hispanic/Latino; 2 American Indian or Alaska Native, non-Hispanic/Latino; 16 Asian, non-Hispanic/Latino; 11 Hispanic/Latino; 11 Two or more races, non-Hispanic/Latino), 8 international. Average age 31. 64 applicants, 72% accepted, 31 enrolled. *Faculty:* 11 full-time (6 women), 4 part-time/adjunct (2 women). Expenses: Contact institution. *Financial support:* In 2016–17, 22 students received support. Career-related internships or fieldwork, Federal Work-Study, and unspecified assistantships available. Support available to part-time students. Financial award applicants required to submit FAFSA. In 2016, 58 master's awarded. *Program availability:* Part-time, evening/weekend. Offers public service (MNPL, MPA). *Application deadline:* For fall admission, 7/20 priority date for domestic students, 7/20 for international students; for winter admission, 10/20 priority date for domestic students, 10/20 for international

students; for spring admission, 2/20 priority date for domestic students, 2/20 for international students. Applications are processed on a rolling basis. *Application fee:* $55. Electronic applications accepted. *Application Contact:* Janet Shandley, Associate Dean of Graduate Admissions, 206-296-5900, Fax: 206-298-5656, E-mail: grad_admissions@seattleu.edu. *Interim Director, Institute of Public Service,* Dr. John Collins, 206-296-5442, Fax: 206-296-5997, E-mail: collinsj@seattleu.edu.

College of Education Students: 196 full-time (144 women), 300 part-time (221 women); includes 165 minority (24 Black or African American, non-Hispanic/Latino; 7 American Indian or Alaska Native, non-Hispanic/Latino; 46 Asian, non-Hispanic/Latino; 61 Hispanic/Latino; 1 Native Hawaiian or other Pacific Islander, non-Hispanic/Latino; 26 Two or more races, non-Hispanic/Latino), 17 international. Average age 32. 487 applicants, 50% accepted, 141 enrolled. *Faculty:* 27 full-time (13 women), 11 part-time/adjunct (14 women). Expenses: Contact institution. *Financial support:* In 2016–17, 89 students received support. Career-related internships or fieldwork, Federal Work-Study, scholarships/grants, and unspecified assistantships available. Support available to part-time students. Financial award applicants required to submit FAFSA. In 2016, 184 master's, 19 doctorates, 48 other advanced degrees awarded. *Program availability:* Part-time, evening/weekend. Offers adult education and training (M Ed, MA, Certificate); counseling and school psychology (MA, Certificate, Ed S); education (M Ed, MA, MIT, Ed D, Certificate, Ed S, Post-Master's Certificate); educational administration (M Ed, MA, Certificate, Ed S); educational leadership (Ed D); special education (M Ed, MA, Certificate); student development administration (M Ed, MA); teacher education (MIT); teaching English to speakers of other languages (M Ed, MA, Certificate). *Application deadline:* Applications are processed on a rolling basis. *Application fee:* $55. Electronic applications accepted. *Application Contact:* Janet Shandley, Director of Graduate Admissions, 206-296-5900, Fax: 206-298-5656, E-mail: grad_admissions@seattleu.edu. *Dean,* Dr. Deanna Sands, 206-296-5758, E-mail: sandsd@seattleu.edu.

College of Nursing Students: 182 full-time (155 women), 41 part-time (36 women); includes 53 minority (4 Black or African American, non-Hispanic/Latino; 27 Asian, non-Hispanic/Latino; 14 Hispanic/Latino; 8 Two or more races, non-Hispanic/Latino), 1 international. Average age 34. 72 applicants, 72% accepted, 37 enrolled. *Faculty:* 35 full-time (29 women), 15 part-time/adjunct (12 women). Expenses: Contact institution. *Financial support:* In 2016–17, 74 students received support. Fellowships, research assistantships, career-related internships or fieldwork, Federal Work-Study, and scholarships/grants available. Support available to part-time students. Financial award applicants required to submit FAFSA. In 2016, 57 master's awarded. *Program availability:* Part-time, evening/weekend. Offers adult/gerontological nurse practitioner (MSN); advanced community public health (MSN); advanced community public health nursing (MSN); family nurse practitioner (MSN); family psychiatric mental health nurse practitioner (MSN); nurse midwifery (MSN); nursing (MSN, DNP); psychiatric mental health nurse practitioner (MSN). *Application deadline:* For fall admission, 7/1 for domestic students. *Application fee:* $55. *Application Contact:* Janet Shandley, Director of Graduate Admissions, 206-296-5900, Fax: 206-298-5656, E-mail: grad_admissions@seattleu.edu. *Interim Dean,* Dr. Janiece DeSocio, 206-296-5676.

College of Science and Engineering Students: 49 full-time (19 women), 61 part-time (16 women); includes 31 minority (1 Black or African American, non-Hispanic/Latino; 22 Asian, non-Hispanic/Latino; 5 Hispanic/Latino; 3 Two or more races, non-Hispanic/Latino), 31 international. Average age 28. 130 applicants, 52% accepted, 45 enrolled. *Faculty:* 11 full-time (5 women), 6 part-time/adjunct (0 women). Expenses: Contact institution. *Financial support:* In 2016–17, 7 students received support. Career-related internships or fieldwork and Federal Work-Study available. Support available to part-time students. Financial award applicants required to submit FAFSA. In 2016, 39 master's awarded. *Program availability:* Part-time, evening/weekend. Offers computer science (MSCS); science and engineering (MSCS, MSE); software engineering (MSE). *Application deadline:* For fall admission, 7/1 for domestic students. *Application fee:* $55. *Application Contact:* Janet Shandley, Director of Graduate Admissions, 206-296-5900, Fax: 206-298-5656, E-mail: grad_admissions@seattleu.edu. *Dean,* Dr. Michael Quinn, 206-296-5500, Fax: 206-296-2071.

School of Law *Program availability:* Part-time. Offers law (JD). Electronic applications accepted.

School of Theology and Ministry Students: 40 full-time (33 women), 124 part-time (89 women); includes 45 minority (14 Black or African American, non-Hispanic/Latino; 1 American Indian or Alaska Native, non-Hispanic/Latino; 12 Asian, non-Hispanic/Latino; 13 Hispanic/Latino; 5 Two or more races, non-Hispanic/Latino), 8 international. Average age 44. 50 applicants, 64% accepted, 24 enrolled. *Faculty:* 12 full-time (7 women), 10 part-time/adjunct (5 women). Expenses: Contact institution. *Financial support:* In 2016–17, 108 students received support. Career-related internships or fieldwork, Federal Work-Study, and scholarships/grants available. Support available to part-time students. Financial award application deadline: 6/1; financial award applicants required to submit FAFSA. In 2016, 43 master's, 43 other advanced degrees awarded. *Program availability:* Part-time, online learning. Offers couples and family therapy (MA); divinity (M Div, D Min); pastoral studies (MAPS); theology and ministry (M Div, MA, MAPS, MATL, MATS, D Min, Certificate); transformational leadership (MATL); transforming spirituality (MATS, Certificate). *Application deadline:* For fall admission, 6/1 priority date for domestic students, 4/1 for international students. *Application fee:* $55. Electronic applications accepted. *Application Contact:* Colette Meda Casavant, Admissions Coordinator, 206-296-5333, Fax: 206-296-5329, E-mail: casavant@seattleu.edu. *Dean,* Dr. Mark Markuly, 206-296-5330, Fax: 206-296-5329, E-mail: stm@seattleu.edu.

SELMA UNIVERSITY, Selma, AL 36701-5299

General Information Independent-religious, coed, comprehensive institution.

GRADUATE UNITS

Graduate Programs Offers Bible and Christian education (MA); Bible and pastoral ministry (MA).

SEMINARY OF THE SOUTHWEST, Austin, TX 78768-2247

General Information Independent-religious, coed, graduate-only institution. *Enrollment by degree level:* 109 master's, 8 other advanced degrees. *Graduate faculty:* 10 full-time (4 women), 13 part-time/adjunct (5 women). *Tuition:* Full-time $14,400; part-time $600 per credit hour. *Required fees:* $95; $55 per credit hour. $234 per semester. Tuition and fees vary according to class time. *Graduate housing:* Rooms and/or apartments available on a first-come, first-served basis to single and married students. Typical cost: $5400 per year for single students; $15,060 per year for married students. Room charges vary according to housing facility selected. Housing application deadline: 8/1. *Student services:* Exercise/wellness program, writing training. *Library facilities:* Booher Library. *Collection:* Books: 144,425 (physical), 35,702 (digital/electronic); Serial titles: 794 (physical), 48 (digital/electronic); Databases: 67. Weekly public service hours: 86; students can reserve study rooms.

Computer facilities: 8 computers available on campus for general student use. Online class registration is available.
Website: http://www.ssw.edu/

General Application Contact: Beth Jordan, Enrollment Manager, 512-472-4133 Ext. 357, Fax: 512-472-3098, E-mail: beth.jordan@ssw.edu.

GRADUATE UNITS

Graduate and Professional Programs Students: 59 full-time (28 women), 58 part-time (44 women); includes 22 minority (11 Black or African American, non-Hispanic/Latino; 1 American Indian or Alaska Native, non-Hispanic/Latino; 4 Hispanic/Latino; 6 Two or more races, non-Hispanic/Latino). Average age 46. 47 applicants, 98% accepted, 43 enrolled. *Faculty:* 10 full-time (4 women), 13 part-time/adjunct (5 women). Expenses: Contact institution. *Financial support:* In 2016–17, 110 students received support. Career-related internships or fieldwork and scholarships/grants available. Support available to part-time students. Financial award application deadline: 6/15; financial award applicants required to submit FAFSA. In 2016, 20 master's, 4 other advanced degrees awarded. *Program availability:* Part-time, evening/weekend. Offers theology (M Div, MAC, MAR, MCPC, MSF, Advanced Diploma). *Application deadline:* For fall admission, 6/30 priority date for domestic and international students; for spring admission, 12/1 priority date for domestic and international students. Applications are processed on a rolling basis. *Application fee:* $50. *Application Contact:* Hope Benko, Director of Enrollment Management, 512-472-4133 Ext. 375, Fax: 512-472-3098, E-mail: hope.benko@ssw.edu. *Dean and President,* Rev. Dr. Cynthia Briggs Kittredge, 512-472-4133 Ext. 332, Fax: 512-472-3098, E-mail: cynthia.kittredge@ssw.edu.

SETON HALL UNIVERSITY, South Orange, NJ 07079-2697

General Information Independent-religious, coed, university. CGS member. *Graduate housing:* On-campus housing not available.

GRADUATE UNITS

College of Arts and Sciences *Program availability:* Part-time, evening/weekend, online learning. Offers analytical chemistry (MS, PhD); arts and sciences (MA, MPA, MS, PhD, Graduate Certificate); Asian studies (MA); biochemistry (MS, PhD); biology (MS); biology/business administration (MS); chemistry (MS); experimental psychology (MS); history (MA); inorganic chemistry (MS, PhD); Jewish-Christian studies (MA); literature (MA); microbiology (MS); molecular bioscience (PhD); molecular bioscience/neuroscience (PhD); nonprofit organization management (Graduate Certificate); organic chemistry (MS, PhD); physical chemistry (MS, PhD); public administration (MPA); social work (MSW). Electronic applications accepted.

College of Communication and the Arts *Program availability:* Part-time, evening/weekend, online learning. Offers museum professions (MA); public relations (MA); strategic communication (MA). Electronic applications accepted.

College of Education and Human Services Students: 72 full-time (53 women), 989 part-time (589 women); includes 319 minority (181 Black or African American, non-Hispanic/Latino; 3 American Indian or Alaska Native, non-Hispanic/Latino; 22 Asian, non-Hispanic/Latino; 106 Hispanic/Latino; 2 Native Hawaiian or other Pacific Islander, non-Hispanic/Latino; 5 Two or more races, non-Hispanic/Latino), 23 international. Average age 33. 539 applicants, 61% accepted, 221 enrolled. *Faculty:* 45 full-time (24 women), 71 part-time/adjunct (38 women). Expenses: Contact institution. *Financial support:* In 2016–17, 30 students received support. Fellowships, research assistantships, career-related internships or fieldwork, institutionally sponsored loans, and unspecified assistantships available. Financial award application deadline: 2/1; financial award applicants required to submit FAFSA. In 2016, 327 master's, 57 doctorates, 136 other advanced degrees awarded. *Program availability:* Part-time, evening/weekend, 100% online, blended/hybrid learning. Offers college student personnel administration (MA); counseling psychology (MA, PhD); education and human services (MA, MS, Ed D, Exec Ed D, PhD, Ed S); education research, assessment and program evaluation (PhD); higher education administration (Ed D, PhD); human resource training and development (MA); individualized (MA); instructional design and technology (MA); K–12 administration and supervision (Ed D, Exec Ed D, Ed S); K–12 leadership, management and policy (Ed D, Exec Ed D, Ed S); marriage and family therapy (MA); psychological studies (MA); school counseling (MA); school psychology (MA); special education (MA); sport and exercise psychology (MA). *Application deadline:* Applications are processed on a rolling basis. *Application fee:* $75. Electronic applications accepted. *Application Contact:* Dr. Joseph J. Martinelli, Associate Dean for Academic Affairs, 973-275-2733, Fax: 973-275-2187, E-mail: joseph.martinelli@shu.edu. *Dean,* Dr. Maureen D. Gillette, 973-761-9025, E-mail: maureen.gillette@shu.edu.

College of Nursing *Program availability:* Part-time, online learning. Offers advanced practice in primary health care (MSN, DNP); entry into practice (MSN); health systems administration (MSN, DNP); nursing (PhD); nursing case management (MSN); nursing education (MSN); school nurse (MSN). Electronic applications accepted.

Immaculate Conception Seminary School of Theology *Program availability:* Part-time, evening/weekend. Offers Christian spirituality (Certificate); great spiritual books (Certificate); pastoral ministry (M Div, MA, Certificate); scripture studies (Certificate); Seminary's Theological Education for Parish Services (STEPS) (Certificate); theology (MA). Electronic applications accepted.

School of Diplomacy and International Relations *Program availability:* Part-time, evening/weekend, 100% online, blended/hybrid learning. Offers diplomacy and international relations (MA); global health management (Graduate Certificate); post-conflict state reconstruction and sustainability (Graduate Certificate); United Nations studies (Graduate Certificate). Electronic applications accepted.

School of Health and Medical Sciences *Program availability:* Part-time, evening/weekend. Offers athletic training (MS); health and medical sciences (MS, DPT, PhD); health sciences (PhD); occupational therapy (MS); physician assistant (MS); professional physical therapy (DPT); speech-language pathology (MS). Electronic applications accepted.

School of Law *Program availability:* Part-time, evening/weekend. Offers health law (LL M, JD); intellectual property (LL M, JD); law (MSJ). MD/JD, MD/MSJ offered jointly with University of Medicine and Dentistry of New Jersey. Electronic applications accepted.

Stillman School of Business Students: 95 full-time (36 women), 158 part-time (57 women); includes 65 minority (22 Black or African American, non-Hispanic/Latino; 20 Asian, non-Hispanic/Latino; 21 Hispanic/Latino; 2 Two or more races, non-Hispanic/Latino), 58 international. Average age 31. *Faculty:* 26 full-time (5 women), 19 part-time/adjunct (1 woman). Expenses: Contact institution. *Financial support:* Research assistantships with full tuition reimbursements, career-related internships or fieldwork, scholarships/grants, and unspecified assistantships available. Financial award application deadline: 6/30; financial award applicants required to submit FAFSA. *Program availability:* Part-time, evening/weekend. Offers accounting (MBA, MS,

Certificate); business (MBA, MS, Certificate); entrepreneurial studies (Certificate); finance (MBA); financial decision making (Certificate); information technology management (MBA); international business (Certificate); management (MBA); marketing (MBA); professional accounting (MS); sport management (MBA); supply chain management (MBA, Certificate); taxation (Certificate). *Application deadline:* For fall admission, 5/31 priority date for domestic students, 3/31 priority date for international students; for spring admission, 10/31 priority date for domestic students, 9/30 priority date for international students; for summer admission, 4/30 priority date for domestic students, 3/31 priority date for international students. Applications are processed on a rolling basis. *Application fee:* $75. Electronic applications accepted. *Application Contact:* Alfred Ayoub, Director of Graduate Admissions, 973-761-9262, Fax: 973-761-9208, E-mail: alfred.ayoub@shu.edu. *Dean,* Dr. Joyce Strawser, 973-761-9013, Fax: 973-275-2465, E-mail: joyce.strawser@shu.edu.

SETON HILL UNIVERSITY, Greensburg, PA 15601

General Information Independent-religious, coed, comprehensive institution. *Graduate housing:* Room and/or apartments available on a first-come, first-served basis to single students; on-campus housing not available to married students. Housing application deadline: 7/1.

GRADUATE UNITS

Program in Art Therapy *Program availability:* Part-time. Offers art therapy (MA). Electronic applications accepted.

Program in Business Administration *Program availability:* Part-time, evening/weekend. Offers accounting (MBA); entrepreneurship (MBA, Certificate); management (MBA). Electronic applications accepted.

Program in Elementary Education/Middle Level Education *Program availability:* Part-time, evening/weekend, online learning. Offers elementary education/middle level education (MA, Certificate). Electronic applications accepted.

Program in Genocide and Holocaust Studies *Program availability:* Part-time, evening/weekend, online learning. Offers genocide and Holocaust studies (Certificate). Electronic applications accepted.

Program in Marriage and Family Therapy *Program availability:* Part-time, evening/weekend. Offers marriage and family therapy (MA). Electronic applications accepted.

Program in Orthodontics Offers orthodontics (MS, Certificate).

Program in Physician Assistant Offers physician assistant (MS). Electronic applications accepted.

Program in Special Education *Program availability:* Part-time, evening/weekend, online learning. Offers special education (MA). Electronic applications accepted.

Program in Writing Popular Fiction *Program availability:* Part-time. Offers writing popular fiction (MFA, Certificate).

SEWANEE: THE UNIVERSITY OF THE SOUTH, Sewanee, TN 37383-1000

General Information Independent-religious, coed, comprehensive institution. *Enrollment:* 1,815 graduate, professional, and undergraduate students; 72 full-time matriculated graduate/professional students (28 women), 8 part-time matriculated graduate/professional students (5 women). *Enrollment by degree level:* 76 master's, 4 other advanced degrees. *Graduate faculty:* 10 full-time (3 women), 12 part-time/adjunct (2 women). *Graduate housing:* Rooms and/or apartments available on a first-come, first-served basis to single and married students. Housing application deadline: 4/15. *Student services:* Campus employment opportunities, campus safety program, career counseling, child daycare facilities, free psychological counseling, international student services, multicultural affairs office, writing training. *Library facilities:* Jessie Ball duPont Library. *Collection:* Books: 784,306 (physical), 622,710 (digital/electronic); Serial titles: 4,508 (physical), 10,570 (digital/electronic); Databases: 342. Study areas open 24 hours, 5–7 days a week; students can reserve study rooms.

Computer facilities: A campuswide network can be accessed from student residence rooms and from off campus. Online class registration is available.
Website: http://www.sewanee.edu/

GRADUATE UNITS

School of Theology Students: 72 full-time (28 women), 5 part-time (3 women); includes 5 minority (3 Black or African American, non-Hispanic/Latino; 1 American Indian or Alaska Native, non-Hispanic/Latino; 1 Two or more races, non-Hispanic/Latino), 5 international. Average age 37. *Faculty:* 10 full-time (3 women), 12 part-time/adjunct (2 women). Expenses: Contact institution. *Financial support:* Institutionally sponsored loans and scholarships/grants available. Support available to part-time students. Financial award application deadline: 4/30. In 2016, 29 master's, 7 doctorates awarded. *Program availability:* Part-time. Offers theology (M Div, MA, STM, D Min). *Application deadline:* For fall admission, 7/15 for domestic and international students. Applications are processed on a rolling basis. *Application fee:* $0. Electronic applications accepted. *Application Contact:* Rev. Annwn H. Myers, Associate Dean for Recruiting and Admission, 931-598-1373, E-mail: amyers@sewanee.edu. *Dean,* Very Rev. Dr. J. Neil Alexander, 931-598-1288, Fax: 931-598-1412, E-mail: deansot@sewanee.edu.

Sewanee School of Letters Students: 54 part-time (31 women); includes 4 minority (1 Black or African American, non-Hispanic/Latino; 3 Two or more races, non-Hispanic/Latino), 1 international. Average age 41. *Faculty:* 1 full-time (0 women), 10 part-time/adjunct (7 women). Expenses: Contact institution. *Financial support:* Institutionally sponsored loans and scholarships/grants available. Financial award applicants required to submit FAFSA. In 2016, 10 master's awarded. *Program availability:* Part-time. Offers American and English literature (MA); creative writing (MFA). *Application deadline:* Applications are processed on a rolling basis. *Application fee:* $40. Electronic applications accepted. *Application Contact:* April R. Alvarez, Coordinator, 931-598-1636, Fax: 931-598-3303. *Director,* Dr. John M. Grammer, 931-598-1483, Fax: 931-598-3303, E-mail: jgrammer@sewanee.edu.

SHASTA BIBLE COLLEGE, Redding, CA 96002

General Information Independent-religious, coed, comprehensive institution. *Graduate housing:* Rooms and/or apartments available on a first-come, first-served basis to single and married students.

GRADUATE UNITS

Program in Biblical Counseling *Program availability:* Part-time. Offers biblical counseling and Christian family life education (MA).

Program in Christian Ministry *Program availability:* Part-time, online learning. Offers Christian ministry (MA).

Program in School and Church Administration *Program availability:* Part-time, evening/weekend. Offers school and church administration (MS).

SHAWNEE STATE UNIVERSITY, Portsmouth, OH 45662

General Information State-supported, coed, comprehensive institution.

GRADUATE UNITS

Program in Curriculum and Instruction Offers curriculum and instruction (M Ed).

Program in Occupational Therapy Offers occupational therapy (MOT).

SHAW UNIVERSITY, Raleigh, NC 27601-2399

General Information Independent-religious, coed, comprehensive institution. *Graduate housing:* Room and/or apartments available on a first-come, first-served basis to single students; on-campus housing not available to married students. *Research affiliation:* The Louisville Institute (book writing, theology), Wabash Center (philosophy of religious education), The Society of Biblical Literature (biblical studies), The American Academy of Religion (theology, ethics, Church history, contemporary issues), Society for the Study of Black Religion (African American churches), The Association of Theological Schools (theological research).

GRADUATE UNITS

Department of Education *Program availability:* Part-time, evening/weekend. Offers curriculum and instruction (MS). Electronic applications accepted.

Divinity School *Program availability:* Part-time, evening/weekend. Offers divinity (M Div, MACE). Electronic applications accepted.

SHENANDOAH UNIVERSITY, Winchester, VA 22601-5195

General Information Independent-religious, coed, comprehensive institution. *Enrollment:* 3,918 graduate, professional, and undergraduate students; 939 full-time matriculated graduate/professional students (690 women), 708 part-time matriculated graduate/professional students (477 women). *Enrollment by degree level:* 662 master's, 882 doctoral, 103 other advanced degrees. *Graduate faculty:* 146 full-time (87 women), 86 part-time/adjunct (62 women). *Tuition:* Full-time $20,304; part-time $846 per credit hour. *Required fees:* $780; $240 per semester. Tuition and fees vary according to course load and program. *Graduate housing:* Rooms and/or apartments available on a first-come, first-served basis to single and married students. Typical cost: $9990 (including board) for single students; $6600 per year for married students. Room and board charges vary according to board plan and housing facility selected. Housing application deadline: 3/3. *Student services:* Campus employment opportunities, campus safety program, career counseling, child daycare facilities, exercise/wellness program, free psychological counseling, international student services, low-cost health insurance, multicultural affairs office, services for students with disabilities, teacher training, writing training. *Library facilities:* Alson H. Smith, Jr. Library plus 1 other. *Collection:* Books: 122,422 (physical), 217,000 (digital/electronic); Serial titles: 700 (physical), 86,500 (digital/electronic); Databases: 135. Weekly public service hours: 96; students can reserve study rooms. *Research affiliation:* Inova Center for Personalized Health (pharmacogenomics and precision medicine).

Computer facilities: 32 computers available on campus for general student use. A campuswide network can be accessed from student residence rooms and from off campus. Online class registration, online student account information are available. Website: http://www.su.edu/

General Application Contact: Andrew Woodall, Executive Dean of Admissions, 540-665-4581, Fax: 540-665-4627, E-mail: admit@su.edu.

GRADUATE UNITS

Bernard J. Dunn School of Pharmacy Students: 333 full-time (225 women), 175 part-time (101 women); includes 230 minority (90 Black or African American, non-Hispanic/Latino; 116 Asian, non-Hispanic/Latino; 17 Hispanic/Latino; 1 Native Hawaiian or other Pacific Islander, non-Hispanic/Latino; 6 Two or more races, non-Hispanic/Latino), 21 international. Average age 32. 508 applicants, 52% accepted, 131 enrolled. *Faculty:* 39 full-time (23 women), 2 part-time/adjunct (both women). Expenses: Contact institution. *Financial support:* In 2016–17, 38 students received support. Scholarships/grants available. Financial award applicants required to submit FAFSA. In 2016, 160 doctorates awarded. *Program availability:* Part-time, evening/weekend, 100% online. Offers pharmacy (Pharm D). *Application deadline:* For fall admission, 3/1 for domestic and international students. *Application fee:* $30. Electronic applications accepted. *Application Contact:* Andrew Woodall, Executive Director of Recruitment and Admissions, 540-665-4581, Fax: 540-665-4627, E-mail: admit@su.edu. *Dean*, Robert DiCenzo, PhD, 540-665-1282, Fax: 540-665-1283, E-mail: rdicenzo@su.edu.

College of Arts and Sciences Students: 14 full-time (13 women), 2 part-time (both women); includes 1 minority (Black or African American, non-Hispanic/Latino). Average age 28. 19 applicants, 84% accepted, 7 enrolled. *Faculty:* 1 full-time (0 women), 3 part-time/adjunct (all women). Expenses: Contact institution. *Financial support:* In 2016–17, 1 student received support. Scholarships/grants and unspecified assistantships available. Financial award applicants required to submit FAFSA. In 2016, 9 master's awarded. *Program availability:* Part-time, evening/weekend. Offers applied behavior analysis (MS). *Application deadline:* For fall admission, 7/15 for domestic and international students. *Application fee:* $30. Electronic applications accepted. *Application Contact:* Andrew Woodall, Executive Director of Recruitment and Admissions, 540-665-4581, Fax: 540-665-4627, E-mail: admit@su.edu. *Dean*, Jeff W. Coker, PhD, 540-665-4587, Fax: 540-665-4644, E-mail: jcoker2@su.edu.

Eleanor Wade Custer School of Nursing Students: 36 full-time (34 women), 47 part-time (44 women); includes 19 minority (14 Black or African American, non-Hispanic/Latino; 3 Asian, non-Hispanic/Latino; 1 Hispanic/Latino; 1 Two or more races, non-Hispanic/Latino), 3 international. Average age 35. 50 applicants, 90% accepted, 36 enrolled. *Faculty:* 7 full-time (all women), 3 part-time/adjunct (all women). Expenses: Contact institution. *Financial support:* In 2016–17, 32 students received support. Scholarships/grants and unspecified assistantships available. Financial award applicants required to submit FAFSA. In 2016, 26 master's, 2 doctorates, 19 other advanced degrees awarded. Offers adult gerontology primary care nurse practitioner (Graduate Certificate); family nurse practitioner (MSN, DNP, Graduate Certificate); health systems leadership (DNP); nurse midwifery (MSN); nurse-midwifery (Graduate Certificate); nursing education (Graduate Certificate); nursing practice (DNP); primary care adult-geriatric nurse practitioner (MSN); psychiatric mental health nurse practitioner (MSN, DNP, Graduate Certificate). *Application deadline:* For fall admission, 4/15 priority date for domestic and international students; for spring admission, 11/1 for domestic and international students; for summer admission, 3/1 for domestic and international students. *Application fee:* $30. Electronic applications accepted. *Application Contact:* Andrew Woodall, Executive Director of Recruitment and Admissions, 540-665-4581, Fax: 540-665-4627, E-mail: admit@su.edu. *Dean*, Dr. Kathleen LaSala, RN, 540-678-4381, Fax: 540-665-5519, E-mail: klasala@su.edu.

Harry F. Byrd, Jr. School of Business Students: 35 full-time (19 women), 46 part-time (23 women); includes 16 minority (9 Black or African American, non-Hispanic/Latino; 1 American Indian or Alaska Native, non-Hispanic/Latino; 2 Asian, non-Hispanic/Latino; 3 Hispanic/Latino; 1 Native Hawaiian or other Pacific Islander, non-Hispanic/Latino), 18 international. Average age 31. 46 applicants, 63% accepted, 20 enrolled. *Faculty:* 17 full-time (7 women), 4 part-time/adjunct (1 woman). Expenses: Contact institution. *Financial support:* In 2016–17, 21 students received support. Scholarships/grants and unspecified assistantships available. Financial award applicants required to submit FAFSA. In 2016, 28 master's awarded. *Program availability:* Part-time, evening/weekend. Offers business administration (MBA); healthcare management (Certificate). *Application deadline:* For fall admission, 5/1 for domestic students, 4/15 for international students; for spring admission, 11/15 for domestic students, 10/15 for international students; for summer admission, 2/15 for domestic students, 3/1 for international students. *Application fee:* $30. Electronic applications accepted. *Application Contact:* Andrew Woodall, Executive Director of Recruitment and Admissions, 540-665-4581, Fax: 540-665-4627, E-mail: admit@su.edu. *Dean*, Miles K. Davis, PhD, 540-665-4572, Fax: 540-665-5437, E-mail: mdavi3@su.edu.

School of Education and Human Development Students: 31 full-time (25 women), 236 part-time (160 women); includes 39 minority (19 Black or African American, non-Hispanic/Latino; 1 American Indian or Alaska Native, non-Hispanic/Latino; 10 Asian, non-Hispanic/Latino; 7 Hispanic/Latino; 1 Native Hawaiian or other Pacific Islander, non-Hispanic/Latino; 1 Two or more races, non-Hispanic/Latino), 4 international. Average age 37. 90 applicants, 97% accepted, 56 enrolled. *Faculty:* 9 full-time (7 women), 43 part-time/adjunct (33 women). Expenses: Contact institution. *Financial support:* In 2016–17, 18 students received support. Scholarships/grants and unspecified assistantships available. Financial award applicants required to submit FAFSA. In 2016, 113 master's, 13 doctorates, 38 other advanced degrees awarded. *Program availability:* Part-time, evening/weekend. Offers administrative leadership (D Ed); educational administration (MSE); emphasis in teaching (MSE); health and physical education (Certificate); individual focus (MSE); literacy education (MS); middle school teacher education (Certificate); organizational leadership (MS, D Prof); secondary school teacher education (Certificate); special education (MSE). *Application deadline:* For fall admission, 5/1 priority date for domestic students, 5/1 for international students; for spring admission, 10/15 priority date for domestic students, 10/15 for international students; for summer admission, 3/15 priority date for domestic students, 3/15 for international students. *Application fee:* $30. Electronic applications accepted. *Application Contact:* Andrew Woodall, Executive Director of Recruitment and Admissions, 540-665-4581, Fax: 540-665-4627, E-mail: admit@su.edu. *Director*, Dennis William Kellison, PhD, 540-535-7324, Fax: 540-665-4726, E-mail: dkelliso@su.edu.

School of Health Professions Students: 420 full-time (334 women), 131 part-time (104 women); includes 90 minority (16 Black or African American, non-Hispanic/Latino; 36 Asian, non-Hispanic/Latino; 26 Hispanic/Latino; 1 Native Hawaiian or other Pacific Islander, non-Hispanic/Latino; 11 Two or more races, non-Hispanic/Latino), 17 international. Average age 28. 1,511 applicants, 27% accepted, 227 enrolled. *Faculty:* 34 full-time (27 women), 28 part-time/adjunct (16 women). Expenses: Contact institution. *Financial support:* In 2016–17, 51 students received support. Scholarships/grants and unspecified assistantships available. Financial award applicants required to submit FAFSA. In 2016, 91 master's, 77 doctorates awarded. *Program availability:* Online learning. Offers athletic training (MS); occupational therapy (MS); performing arts medicine (Certificate); physical therapy (DPT); physician assistant studies (MS). *Application deadline:* For fall admission, 7/1 for domestic and international students; for summer admission, 4/1 for domestic and international students. *Application fee:* $30. Electronic applications accepted. *Application Contact:* Andrew Woodall, Executive Director of Recruitment and Admissions, 540-665-4581, Fax: 540-665-4627, E-mail: admit@su.edu. *Interim Dean of Health Professions*, Karen Abraham, PhD, 540-545-5209, Fax: 540-665.5564, E-mail: kabraham@su.edu.

Shenandoah Conservatory Students: 70 full-time (40 women), 71 part-time (43 women); includes 25 minority (7 Black or African American, non-Hispanic/Latino; 2 American Indian or Alaska Native, non-Hispanic/Latino; 5 Asian, non-Hispanic/Latino; 11 Hispanic/Latino), 21 international. Average age 31. 121 applicants, 79% accepted, 47 enrolled. *Faculty:* 36 full-time (13 women), 12 part-time/adjunct (6 women). Expenses: Contact institution. *Financial support:* In 2016–17, 43 students received support. Scholarships/grants and unspecified assistantships available. Financial award applicants required to submit FAFSA. In 2016, 29 master's, 7 doctorates, 9 other advanced degrees awarded. *Program availability:* Part-time. Offers church music (MM, Certificate); collaborative piano (MM); composition (MM); conducting (MM); music (Artist Diploma); music education (MME); music therapy (MMT); pedagogy - voice (MM, DMA); performance (MM, DMA); performing arts leadership and management (MS). *Application deadline:* For fall and spring admission, 1/15 for domestic and international students; for summer admission, 4/15 for domestic and international students. *Application fee:* $30. Electronic applications accepted. *Application Contact:* Andrew Woodall, Executive Director of Recruitment and Advancement, 540-665-4581, Fax: 540-665-4627, E-mail: admit@su.edu. *Dean*, Dr. Michael J. Stepniak, 540-542.6201, Fax: 540-665-5402, E-mail: mstepnia@su.edu.

SHEPHERDS THEOLOGICAL SEMINARY, Cary, NC 27518

General Information Independent-religious, coed, graduate-only institution. *Graduate faculty:* 6 full-time (0 women), 14 part-time/adjunct (3 women). *Tuition:* Full-time $5400; part-time $300 per credit hour. Tuition and fees vary according to program. *Graduate housing:* On-campus housing not available. *Student services:* Campus employment opportunities, campus safety program, career counseling, international student services, writing training. *Library facilities:* Jackson Library plus 1 other. *Collection:* Books: 30,000 (physical), 1,000 (digital/electronic); Serial titles: 800 (digital/electronic); Databases: 10. Weekly public service hours: 40.

Computer facilities: 10 computers available on campus for general student use. A campuswide network can be accessed from off campus. Online class registration, X are available.
Website: http://www.shepherds.edu/

General Application Contact: Ann Clampett, Admissions Coordinator, 919-573-1571, Fax: 919-573-1438, E-mail: lburggraff@shepherds.edu.

GRADUATE UNITS

Graduate Programs Expenses: Contact institution. Offers Biblical literature and languages (MA); church ministry (MA); ministry (MTS); New Testament (M Div); Old Testament (M Div); theology (M Div). *Application fee:* $40. *Application Contact:* Lucy Burggraff, Registrar, 919-573-1572, Fax: 919-573-1438, E-mail: lburggraff@shepherds.edu.

SHEPHERD UNIVERSITY, Los Angeles, CA 90065

General Information Independent-religious, coed, comprehensive institution.

GRADUATE UNITS

Cornel School of Contemporary Music Offers contemporary music (MM). Electronic applications accepted.

Hollywood CG School of Digital Arts Offers game art and design (MSIT); visual effects and animation (MSIT).

School of Theology Offers theology (M Div, D Min).

SHEPHERD UNIVERSITY, Shepherdstown, WV 25443

General Information State-supported, coed, comprehensive institution.

GRADUATE UNITS

Program in Curriculum and Instruction Offers curriculum and instruction (MA).

SHERMAN COLLEGE OF CHIROPRACTIC, Spartanburg, SC 29304-1452

General Information Independent, coed, graduate-only institution. *Graduate housing:* Room and/or apartments available to single students. *Research affiliation:* American Public Health Service (chiropractic research), Upper Cervical Research Foundation (chiropractic).

GRADUATE UNITS

Professional Program Offers chiropractic (DC). Electronic applications accepted.

SHILOH UNIVERSITY, Kalona, IA 52247

General Information Independent, coed, comprehensive institution. *Enrollment:* 59 graduate, professional, and undergraduate students; 7 full-time matriculated graduate/professional students (3 women), 29 part-time matriculated graduate/professional students (10 women). *Enrollment by degree level:* 28 master's, 8 doctoral. *Graduate faculty:* 2 full-time (0 women), 12 part-time/adjunct (2 women). *Tuition:* Full-time $3000; part-time $167 per credit hour. Tuition and fees vary according to degree level. *Student services:* Writing training. *Library facilities:* University e-Library. *Collection:* Databases: 2.
Website: http://www.shilohuniversity.edu/

General Application Contact: Andrew Thompson, Admissions Coordinator, 319-656-2447, Fax: 319-656-2448, E-mail: admissions@shilohuniversity.edu.

GRADUATE UNITS

Graduate Programs Students: 7 full-time (3 women), 29 part-time (10 women); includes 8 minority (4 Black or African American, non-Hispanic/Latino; 3 Hispanic/Latino; 1 Native Hawaiian or other Pacific Islander, non-Hispanic/Latino), 1 international. Average age 50. 29 applicants, 86% accepted, 17 enrolled. *Faculty:* 2 full-time (0 women), 12 part-time/adjunct (2 women). Expenses: Contact institution. *Financial support:* In 2016–17, 2 students received support. Scholarships/grants available. Financial award applicants required to submit FAFSA. In 2016, 2 master's awarded. *Program availability:* Part-time, evening/weekend, online only, 100% online. Offers Christian ministries (M Div); leadership of church and spiritual formation (D Min); theological studies (MA). *Application deadline:* For fall admission, 7/3 priority date for domestic and international students; for spring admission, 11/6 priority date for domestic and international students; for summer admission, 3/4 priority date for domestic and international students. Applications are processed on a rolling basis. *Application fee:* $0. Electronic applications accepted. *Application Contact:* Andrew Thompson, Admissions Coordinator, 319-656-2447, Fax: 319-656-2448, E-mail: admissions@shilohuniversity.edu. *President,* Christopher Reeves, 319-656-2447, Fax: 319-656-2448, E-mail: chris.reeves@shilohuniversity.edu.

SHIPPENSBURG UNIVERSITY OF PENNSYLVANIA, Shippensburg, PA 17257-2299

General Information State-supported, coed, comprehensive institution. CGS member. *Enrollment:* 6,989 graduate, professional, and undergraduate students; 354 full-time matriculated graduate/professional students (214 women), 596 part-time matriculated graduate/professional students (328 women). *Enrollment by degree level:* 919 master's, 23 doctoral, 8 other advanced degrees. *Graduate faculty:* 146 full-time (55 women), 33 part-time/adjunct (22 women). Tuition, state resident: part-time $483 per credit. Tuition, nonresident: part-time $725 per credit. *Required fees:* $141 per credit. *Graduate housing:* On-campus housing not available. *Student services:* Campus employment opportunities, campus safety program, career counseling, child daycare facilities, exercise/wellness program, free psychological counseling, grant writing training, international student services, low-cost health insurance, multicultural affairs office, services for students with disabilities, teacher training, writing training. *Library facilities:* Ezra Lehman Memorial Library plus 1 other. *Collection:* Books: 357,662 (physical), 57,973 (digital/electronic); Serial titles: 50 (physical), 255 (digital/electronic); Databases: 109. Weekly public service hours: 97.

Computer facilities: 1,100 computers available on campus for general student use. A campuswide network can be accessed from student residence rooms and from off campus. Online class registration, personal Web pages are available.
Website: http://www.ship.edu/

General Application Contact: Megan N. Luft, Assistant Dean of Graduate Admissions, 717-477-1231, Fax: 717-477-4016, E-mail: mnluft@ship.edu.

GRADUATE UNITS

School of Graduate Studies Students: 354 full-time (214 women), 596 part-time (328 women); includes 112 minority (65 Black or African American, non-Hispanic/Latino; 12 Asian, non-Hispanic/Latino; 25 Hispanic/Latino; 10 Two or more races, non-Hispanic/Latino), 80 international. Average age 30. 967 applicants, 60% accepted, 366 enrolled. *Faculty:* 146 full-time (55 women), 33 part-time/adjunct (22 women). Expenses: Contact institution. *Financial support:* In 2016–17, 153 students received support. Career-related internships or fieldwork, scholarships/grants, unspecified assistantships, and resident hall director and student payroll positions available. Support available to part-time students. Financial award application deadline: 3/1; financial award applicants required to submit FAFSA. In 2016, 370 master's awarded. *Program availability:* Part-time, evening/weekend, 100% online, blended/hybrid learning. *Application deadline:* For fall admission, 4/30 for international students; for spring admission, 9/30 for international students. Applications are processed on a rolling basis. *Application fee:* $45. Electronic applications accepted. *Application Contact:* Megan N. Luft, Assistant Dean of Graduate Admissions, 717-477-1231, Fax: 717-477-4016, E-mail: mnluft@ship.edu. *Associate Provost and Dean of Graduate Studies,* Dr. Tracy A. Schoolcraft, 717-477-1148, Fax: 717-477-4038, E-mail: tascho@ship.edu.

College of Arts and Sciences Students: 127 full-time (58 women), 104 part-time (60 women); includes 22 minority (15 Black or African American, non-Hispanic/Latino; 4 Hispanic/Latino; 3 Two or more races, non-Hispanic/Latino), 34 international. Average age 28. 321 applicants, 61% accepted, 94 enrolled. *Faculty:* 78 full-time (30 women), 5 part-time/adjunct (3 women). Expenses: Contact institution. *Financial support:* In 2016–17, 60 students received support. Career-related internships or fieldwork, scholarships/grants, unspecified assistantships, and resident hall director and student payroll positions available. Support available to part-time students. Financial award

application deadline: 3/1; financial award applicants required to submit FAFSA. In 2016, 125 master's awarded. *Program availability:* Part-time, evening/weekend. Offers agile software engineering (Certificate); applied history (MA); arts and sciences (MA, MPA, MS, Certificate); biology (MS); communication studies (MS); computer science (MS); geoenvironmental studies (MS); IT leadership (Certificate); organizational development and leadership (MS); psychological science (MS); public administration (MPA). *Application deadline:* For fall admission, 4/30 for international students; for spring admission, 9/30 for international students. Applications are processed on a rolling basis. *Application fee:* $45. Electronic applications accepted. *Application Contact:* Megan N. Luft, Assistant Dean of Graduate Admissions, 717-477-1231, Fax: 717-477-4016, E-mail: mnluft@ship.edu. *Dean,* Dr. James H. Mike, 717-477-1151, Fax: 717-477-4026, E-mail: jhmike@ship.edu.

College of Education and Human Services Students: 169 full-time (139 women), 297 part-time (209 women); includes 64 minority (38 Black or African American, non-Hispanic/Latino; 4 Asian, non-Hispanic/Latino; 16 Hispanic/Latino; 6 Two or more races, non-Hispanic/Latino), 20 international. Average age 30. 422 applicants, 61% accepted, 202 enrolled. *Faculty:* 45 full-time (21 women), 24 part-time/adjunct (18 women). Expenses: Contact institution. *Financial support:* In 2016–17, 81 students received support. Career-related internships or fieldwork, scholarships/grants, unspecified assistantships, and resident hall director and student payroll positions available. Support available to part-time students. Financial award application deadline: 3/1; financial award applicants required to submit FAFSA. In 2016, 144 master's awarded. *Program availability:* Part-time, evening/weekend, blended/hybrid learning. Offers administration of justice (MS); clinical mental health (MS); college counseling (MS); college student personnel (MS); counselor education and supervision (Ed D); couple and family counseling (Certificate); curriculum and instruction (M Ed); education and human services (M Ed, MAT, MS, MSW, Ed D, Certificate); educational leadership (M Ed, Ed D); literacy studies (Certificate); online instruction, learning, and technology (Certificate); reading (M Ed); school counseling (M Ed); social work (MSW); special education (M Ed); STEM education (MAT); teaching English as a second language (Certificate). *Application deadline:* For fall admission, 4/30 for international students; for spring admission, 9/30 for international students. Applications are processed on a rolling basis. *Application fee:* $45. Electronic applications accepted. *Application Contact:* Megan N. Luft, Assistant Dean of Graduate Admissions, 717-477-1231, Fax: 717-477-4016, E-mail: mnluft@ship.edu. *Dean of the College of Education and Human Services,* Dr. James R. Johnson, 717-477-1373, Fax: 717-477-4012, E-mail: jrjohnson@ship.edu.

John L. Grove College of Business Students: 58 full-time (17 women), 195 part-time (59 women); includes 26 minority (12 Black or African American, non-Hispanic/Latino; 8 Asian, non-Hispanic/Latino; 5 Hispanic/Latino; 1 Two or more races, non-Hispanic/Latino), 26 international. Average age 32. 224 applicants, 55% accepted, 70 enrolled. *Faculty:* 23 full-time (4 women), 4 part-time/adjunct (1 woman). Expenses: Contact institution. *Financial support:* In 2016–17, 12 students received support. Career-related internships or fieldwork, scholarships/grants, unspecified assistantships, and resident hall director and student payroll positions available. Support available to part-time students. Financial award application deadline: 3/1; financial award applicants required to submit FAFSA. In 2016, 101 master's awarded. *Program availability:* Part-time, evening/weekend, 100% online, blended/hybrid learning. Offers advanced studies in business (Certificate); advanced supply chain and logistics management (Certificate); business administration (MBA); finance (Certificate); health care management (Certificate); management information systems (Certificate). *Application deadline:* For fall admission, 4/30 for international students; for spring admission, 9/30 for international students. Applications are processed on a rolling basis. *Application fee:* $45. Electronic applications accepted. *Application Contact:* Megan N. Luft, Associate Dean of Graduate Admissions, 717-477-1231, Fax: 717-477-4016, E-mail: mnluft@ship.edu. *Dean of the College of Business,* Dr. John G. Kooti, 717-477-1435, Fax: 717-477-4003, E-mail: jgkooti@ship.edu.

SHORTER UNIVERSITY, Rome, GA 30165

General Information Independent-religious, coed, comprehensive institution. *Graduate housing:* Room and/or apartments available on a first-come, first-served basis to single students; on-campus housing not available to married students. Housing application deadline: 3/30.

GRADUATE UNITS

Professional Studies *Program availability:* Evening/weekend. Offers accountancy (MAC); business administration (MBA); management (MM). Electronic applications accepted.

SH'OR YOSHUV RABBINICAL COLLEGE, Lawrence, NY 11559-1714

General Information Independent-religious, men only, comprehensive institution.

GRADUATE UNITS

Graduate Programs

SIENA COLLEGE, Loudonville, NY 12211-1462

General Information Independent-religious, coed, comprehensive institution. *Graduate housing:* On-campus housing not available.

GRADUATE UNITS

School of Business *Program availability:* Evening/weekend. Offers accounting (MS).

SIENA HEIGHTS UNIVERSITY, Adrian, MI 49221-1796

General Information Independent-religious, coed, comprehensive institution. *Graduate housing:* Rooms and/or apartments available on a first-come, first-served basis to single and married students. Housing application deadline: 5/1.

GRADUATE UNITS

Graduate College *Program availability:* Part-time, evening/weekend. Offers clinical mental health counseling (MA); educational leadership (Specialist); leadership (MA); teacher education (MA). Electronic applications accepted.

SIERRA NEVADA COLLEGE, Incline Village, NV 89451

General Information Independent, coed, comprehensive institution. *Graduate housing:* On-campus housing not available.

GRADUATE UNITS

Teacher Education Program *Program availability:* Part-time, evening/weekend, online learning. Offers advanced teaching and leadership (M Ed); elementary education (MAT); secondary education (MAT). Electronic applications accepted.

SILICON VALLEY UNIVERSITY, San Jose, CA 95131

General Information Proprietary, coed, comprehensive institution.

GRADUATE UNITS
Graduate Programs

SILVER LAKE COLLEGE OF THE HOLY FAMILY, Manitowoc, WI 54220-9319

General Information Independent-religious, coed, comprehensive institution. *Enrollment:* 429 graduate, professional, and undergraduate students; 41 full-time matriculated graduate/professional students (24 women), 31 part-time matriculated graduate/professional students (26 women). *Enrollment by degree level:* 61 master's, 1 other advanced degrees. *Graduate faculty:* 6 full-time (4 women), 8 part-time/adjunct (4 women). *Tuition:* Full-time $9720; part-time $540 per credit. One-time fee: $220. *Graduate housing:* Room and/or apartments guaranteed to single students; on-campus housing not available to married students. Typical cost: $6050 per year ($9610 including board). Room and board charges vary according to board plan and housing facility selected. Housing application deadline: 6/1. *Student services:* Campus employment opportunities, career counseling, exercise/wellness program, free psychological counseling, low-cost health insurance, multicultural affairs office, services for students with disabilities, teacher training, writing training. *Library facilities:* The Erma M. and Theodore M. Zigmunt Library. *Collection:* Study areas open 24 hours, 5–7 days a week; students can reserve study rooms.

Computer facilities: Computer purchase and lease plans are available. 120 computers available on campus for student use. A campuswide network can be accessed from student residence rooms. Online class registration is available.
Website: http://www.sl.edu/

General Application Contact: Jamie A. Grant, Executive Director of Enrollment Management, 800-236-4752 Ext. 206, Fax: 920-686-6322, E-mail: jamie.grant@sl.edu.

GRADUATE UNITS

Graduate School Students: 41 full-time (24 women), 31 part-time (26 women); includes 7 minority (4 Black or African American, non-Hispanic/Latino; 2 American Indian or Alaska Native, non-Hispanic/Latino; 1 Asian, non-Hispanic/Latino). Average age 40. 7 applicants, 14% accepted. *Faculty:* 6 full-time (4 women), 8 part-time/adjunct (4 women). Expenses: Contact institution. *Financial support:* Career-related internships or fieldwork, Federal Work-Study, scholarships/grants, and unspecified assistantships available. Support available to part-time students. Financial award application deadline: 6/1; financial award applicants required to submit FAFSA. In 2016, 53 master's awarded. *Program availability:* Part-time. Offers administrative leadership (MA Ed); leadership and organizational development (MS); music education-Kodaly emphasis (MM); teacher leadership (MA Ed). *Application deadline:* For fall admission, 8/1 priority date for domestic students, 8/1 for international students; for spring admission, 12/1 priority date for domestic students, 12/1 for international students. Applications are processed on a rolling basis. *Application fee:* $50. Electronic applications accepted. *Application Contact:* Jamie A. Grant, Executive Director of Enrollment Management, 920-686-6175, Fax: 920-686-6322, E-mail: jamie.grant@sl.edu. *Vice President for Academic Affairs,* Matthew R. Soucy, 920-686-6190, Fax: 920-686-6322, E-mail: matthew.soucy@sl.edu.

SIMMONS COLLEGE, Boston, MA 02115

General Information Independent, Undergraduate: women only; graduate: coed, university. CGS member. *Enrollment:* 6,213 graduate, professional, and undergraduate students; 1,460 full-time matriculated graduate/professional students (1,287 women), 2,852 part-time matriculated graduate/professional students (2,512 women). *Enrollment by degree level:* 3,935 master's, 262 doctoral, 115 other advanced degrees. *Graduate faculty:* 120 full-time (90 women), 461 part-time/adjunct (400 women). Tuition and fees vary according to course load and program. *Graduate housing:* Room and/or apartments available on a first-come, first-served basis to single students; on-campus housing not available to married students. Typical cost: $14,500 (including board). Housing application deadline: 3/31. *Student services:* Campus employment opportunities, campus safety program, career counseling, exercise/wellness program, free psychological counseling, grant writing training, international student services, low-cost health insurance, multicultural affairs office, services for students with disabilities, writing training. *Library facilities:* Beatley Library. *Collection:* Books: 253,094 (physical), 33,326 (digital/electronic); Serial titles: 25,707 (physical), 291,590 (digital/electronic); Databases: 96. Weekly public service hours: 105; students can reserve study rooms. *Research affiliation:* Carnegie Corporation of New York (gender equality in higher education in Sub-Saharan African universities), Harvard Medical School (women in academic medicine), Institute for Quantitative Social Science, Harvard University (usability), Boston Children's Hospital (scholarly communication), University College London (cultural heritage and informatics), Oxfam America (gender mainstreaming).

Computer facilities: Computer purchase and lease plans are available. 350 computers available on campus for general student use. A campuswide network can be accessed from student residence rooms and from off campus. Online class registration is available.
Website: http://www.simmons.edu/

General Application Contact: Kristen Haack, Assistant Vice President, Enrollment Management and Graduate Admission, 617-521-2917, Fax: 617-521-3058, E-mail: kristen.haack@simmons.edu.

GRADUATE UNITS

College of Arts and Sciences Students: 6 full-time (all women), 38 part-time (27 women); includes 10 minority (4 Black or African American, non-Hispanic/Latino; 1 Asian, non-Hispanic/Latino; 2 Hispanic/Latino; 3 Two or more races, non-Hispanic/Latino; 1 international. Average age 26. 50 applicants, 88% accepted, 17 enrolled. *Faculty:* 19 full-time (12 women), 1 (woman) part-time/adjunct. Expenses: Contact institution. *Financial support:* In 2016–17, 4 fellowships with partial tuition reimbursements, 22 teaching assistantships with partial tuition reimbursements were awarded; scholarships/grants and unspecified assistantships also available. Support available to part-time students. Financial award applicants required to submit FAFSA. In 2016, 19 master's awarded. *Program availability:* Part-time. Offers elementary education (MAT); English (MA); gender/cultural studies (MA); history (MA); public health (MPH); public policy (MPP). *Application deadline:* For fall admission, 8/1 for domestic and international students; for spring admission, 12/15 for domestic and international students; for summer admission, 5/1 for domestic and international students. Applications are processed on a rolling basis. *Application fee:* $35. Electronic applications accepted. *Application Contact:* Patricia Flaherty, Director, Graduate Studies Admission, 617-521-3902, Fax: 617-521-3058, E-mail: gsa@simmons.edu. *Dean,* Dr. Renee White, 617-521-2079.

School of Library and Information Science Students: 313 full-time (262 women), 511 part-time (420 women); includes 88 minority (13 Black or African American, non-Hispanic/Latino; 10 Asian, non-Hispanic/Latino; 41 Hispanic/Latino; 24 Two or more races, non-Hispanic/Latino), 19 international. Average age 30. 568 applicants, 98% accepted, 319 enrolled. *Faculty:* 23 full-time (17 women), 23 part-time/adjunct (16 women). Expenses: Contact institution. *Financial support:* In 2016–17, 10 fellowships with partial tuition reimbursements were awarded; scholarships/grants, tuition waivers, and unspecified assistantships also available. Support available to part-time students. Financial award application deadline: 2/1; financial award applicants required to submit FAFSA. In 2016, 245 master's, 3 doctorates, 4 other advanced degrees awarded. *Program availability:* Part-time, evening/weekend, 100% online, blended/hybrid learning. Offers children's literature (MA); library and information science (MS, PhD, Certificate); writing for children (MFA). *Application deadline:* For fall admission, 3/1 for domestic and international students; for spring admission, 9/1 for domestic and international students; for summer admission, 2/1 for domestic and international students. Applications are processed on a rolling basis. *Application fee:* $65. Electronic applications accepted. *Application Contact:* Sarah Petrakos, Assistant Dean for Admission and Recruitment, 617-521-2868, Fax: 617-521-3192, E-mail: gslisadm@simmons.edu. *Dean,* Dr. Eileen G. Abels, 617-521-2869.

School of Management Students: 23 full-time (20 women), 141 part-time (126 women); includes 41 minority (20 Black or African American, non-Hispanic/Latino; 7 Asian, non-Hispanic/Latino; 13 Hispanic/Latino; 1 Two or more races, non-Hispanic/Latino), 7 international. Average age 32. 62 applicants, 74% accepted, 32 enrolled. *Faculty:* 14 full-time (10 women), 5 part-time/adjunct (3 women). Expenses: Contact institution. *Financial support:* Scholarships/grants and unspecified assistantships available. Financial award applicants required to submit FAFSA. In 2016, 58 master's awarded. *Program availability:* Part-time, evening/weekend. Offers business administration (MBA); health care (MBA); management (MS, MSM). *Application deadline:* For fall admission, 7/18 priority date for domestic students; for summer admission, 4/24 priority date for domestic students. Applications are processed on a rolling basis. *Application fee:* $75. Electronic applications accepted. *Associate Dean for Graduate Programs,* Patricia Deyton, 617-521-3876.

School of Nursing and Health Sciences Students: 321 full-time (294 women), 1,211 part-time (1,110 women); includes 310 minority (119 Black or African American, non-Hispanic/Latino; 5 American Indian or Alaska Native, non-Hispanic/Latino; 71 Asian, non-Hispanic/Latino; 81 Hispanic/Latino; 4 Native Hawaiian or other Pacific Islander, non-Hispanic/Latino; 30 Two or more races, non-Hispanic/Latino), 8 international. Average age 34. 1,056 applicants, 86% accepted, 429 enrolled. *Faculty:* 25 full-time (21 women), 243 part-time/adjunct (226 women). Expenses: Contact institution. *Financial support:* In 2016–17, 15 research assistantships with partial tuition reimbursements were awarded; scholarships/grants and unspecified assistantships also available. In 2016, 181 master's, 28 doctorates, 40 other advanced degrees awarded. *Program availability:* Part-time, blended/hybrid learning. Offers didactic dietetics (Certificate); dietetic internship (Certificate); health professions education (PhD, CAGS); nursing (MS, MSN); nursing practice (DNP); nutrition and health promotion (MS); physical therapy (DPT); sports nutrition (Certificate). *Application deadline:* For fall admission, 6/1 for international students. *Application fee:* $50. Electronic applications accepted. *Application Contact:* Brett DiMarzo, Director of Graduate Admission, 617-521-2651, Fax: 617-521-3137, E-mail: brett.dimarzo@simmons.edu. *Dean,* Dr. Judy Beal, 617-521-2139.

School of Social Work Students: 797 full-time (705 women), 951 part-time (829 women); includes 420 minority (200 Black or African American, non-Hispanic/Latino; 5 American Indian or Alaska Native, non-Hispanic/Latino; 46 Asian, non-Hispanic/Latino; 122 Hispanic/Latino; 4 Native Hawaiian or other Pacific Islander, non-Hispanic/Latino; 43 Two or more races, non-Hispanic/Latino), 13 international. Average age 31. 1,356 applicants, 78% accepted, 592 enrolled. *Faculty:* 37 full-time (28 women), 62 part-time/adjunct (44 women). Expenses: Contact institution. *Financial support:* In 2016–17, 12 fellowships with partial tuition reimbursements were awarded; scholarships/grants and unspecified assistantships also available. Support available to part-time students. In 2016, 342 master's, 2 doctorates, 1 other advanced degree awarded. *Program availability:* Part-time, 100% online. Offers behavior analysis (MS, PhD, Ed S); education (MS Ed); social work (MSW, PhD); special education (MS Ed); teaching (MAT). *Application deadline:* For fall admission, 8/1 for domestic students; for spring admission, 12/15 for domestic students; for summer admission, 5/1 for domestic students. Applications are processed on a rolling basis. *Application fee:* $35. Electronic applications accepted. *Application Contact:* Carlos D. Frontado, Director of Admissions, 617-521-3920, Fax: 617-521-3980, E-mail: ssw@simmons.edu. *Dean,* Dr. Cheryl Parks, 617-521-3293, E-mail: cheryl.parks@simmons.edu.

SIMON FRASER UNIVERSITY, Burnaby, BC V5A 1S6, Canada

General Information Province-supported, coed, university. CGS member. *Enrollment:* 29,879 graduate, professional, and undergraduate students; 3,913 full-time matriculated graduate/professional students (2,137 women), 621 part-time matriculated graduate/professional students (414 women). *Graduate housing:* Room and/or apartments available on a first-come, first-served basis to single students; on-campus housing not available to married students. Housing application deadline: 12/1. *Student services:* Campus employment opportunities, campus safety program, career counseling, child daycare facilities, exercise/wellness program, free psychological counseling, grant writing training, international student services, low-cost health insurance, multicultural affairs office, services for students with disabilities, teacher training, writing training. *Library facilities:* Bennett Library plus 2 others. *Collection:* Books: 1.5 million (physical), 1.1 million (digital/electronic); Serial titles: 2,500 (physical), 98,000 (digital/electronic). Weekly public service hours: 103; students can reserve study rooms. *Research affiliation:* BC Cancer Agency (health sciences, biomedical sciences, physiology, kinesiology), TRIUMF (physics), Ballard Power Systems (mechatronics), Bamfield Marine Research Station (marine biology, ecology, archaeology).

Computer facilities: 200 computers available on campus for general student use. A campuswide network can be accessed from student residence rooms and from off campus. Online class registration is available.
Website: http://www.sfu.ca/

General Application Contact: Deena Coburn, Director of Administrative Services, 778-782-6830, Fax: 778-782-3080, E-mail: gradstdy@sfu.ca.

GRADUATE UNITS

Office of Graduate Studies and Postdoctoral Fellows Students: 3,913 full-time (2,137 women), 621 part-time (414 women). 6,112 applicants, 33% accepted, 1244 enrolled. Expenses: Contact institution. *Financial support:* In 2016–17, 1,482 students received support, including 759 fellowships (averaging $5,537 per year), teaching assistantships (averaging $5,608 per year); research assistantships, career-related internships or fieldwork, Federal Work-Study, institutionally sponsored loans, and scholarships/grants also available. Support available to part-time students. *Program availability:* Part-time, evening/weekend, online learning. *Application fee:* $90 ($125 for international students). Electronic applications accepted. *Application Contact:* Deena Coburn, Administrative Director, Graduate Studies and Postdoctoral Fellows Office, 778-782-6830, Fax: 778-782-3080, E-mail: gradstudies@sfu.ca. *Dean,* Dr. Wade Parkhouse, 778-782-4255, Fax: 778-782-3080, E-mail: parkhous@sfu.ca.

Faculty of Applied Sciences Students: 506 full-time (141 women), 7 part-time (0 women). 1,217 applicants, 21% accepted, 129 enrolled. Expenses: Contact institution. *Financial support:* In 2016–17, fellowships (averaging $6,500 per year) were awarded; research assistantships, teaching assistantships, career-related internships or fieldwork, Federal Work-Study, institutionally sponsored loans, and scholarships/grants also available. In 2016, 99 master's, 42 doctorates awarded. Offers applied sciences (M Eng, M Sc, MA Sc, PhD, Graduate Certificate); computing science (M Sc, PhD); engineering science (M Eng, MA Sc, PhD); mechatronic systems engineering (MA Sc, PhD). *Application fee:* $90 ($125 for international students). Electronic applications accepted. *Associate Dean,* Dr. Faisal Beg, 778-782-5696, E-mail: mfbeg@sfu.ca.

Faculty of Arts and Social Sciences Students: 705 full-time (427 women), 85 part-time (49 women). 1,294 applicants, 33% accepted, 240 enrolled. *Faculty:* 304 full-time (131 women). Expenses: Contact institution. *Financial support:* In 2016–17, fellowships (averaging $6,500 per year), teaching assistantships (averaging $5,608 per year) were awarded; research assistantships, career-related internships or fieldwork, and scholarships/grants also available. In 2016, 208 master's, 33 doctorates, 3 other advanced degrees awarded. *Program availability:* Part-time, evening/weekend. Offers anthropology (MA, PhD); applied legal studies (MA); arts and social sciences (M Pub, M Sc, M Urb, MA, MALS, MPP, PhD, Graduate Certificate, Graduate Diploma); criminology (MA, PhD); economics (MA, PhD); English (MA, PhD); French (MA); gender, sexuality and women's studies (MA); gerontology (MA, PhD); history (MA, PhD); humanities (MA); international studies (MA); Latin American studies (MA, Graduate Certificate); liberal studies (MALS); linguistics (MA, PhD); philosophy (MA, PhD); political science (MA, PhD); psychology (MA, PhD); public policy (MPP); sociology (MA, PhD); teachers of English (MA); urban studies (M Urb, Graduate Diploma). *Application deadline:* Applications are processed on a rolling basis. *Application fee:* $90 ($125 for international students). Electronic applications accepted. *Dean,* Dr. Jane Pulkingham, 778-782-4415, Fax: 778-782-3033, E-mail: fassdean@sfu.ca.

Faculty of Business Administration Students: 554 full-time (252 women), 161 part-time (58 women). 928 applicants, 45% accepted, 279 enrolled. *Faculty:* 33 full-time (33 women). Expenses: Contact institution. *Financial support:* In 2016–17, 71 students received support, including 9 fellowships (averaging $6,139 per year), teaching assistantships (averaging $5,608 per year); research assistantships, career-related internships or fieldwork, and scholarships/grants also available. In 2016, 178 master's, 3 doctorates, 78 other advanced degrees awarded. *Program availability:* Online learning. Offers business administration (EMBA, PhD, Graduate Diploma); finance (M Sc); management of technology (MBA); management of technology/biotechnology (MBA). *Application deadline:* For fall admission, 4/2 for domestic students; for winter admission, 10/1 for domestic students; for spring admission, 2/2 for domestic students. *Application fee:* $90 ($125 for international students). *Application Contact:* Graduate Secretary, 778-782-5013, Fax: 778-782-5122, E-mail: grad-business@sfu.ca. *Associate Dean, Graduate Programs,* Dr. Ian McCarthy, 778-782-9255, Fax: 778-782-4920, E-mail: grad-business@sfu.ca.

Faculty of Communication, Art and Technology Expenses: Contact institution. Offers communication (MA, PhD); communication, art and technology (M Pub, M Sc, MA, MFA, PhD); contemporary arts (MA, MFA); interactive arts and technology (M Sc, MA, PhD); publishing (M Pub). *Application Contact:* Deena Coburn, Administrative Director, Graduate Studies and Postdoctoral Fellows Office, 778-782-6830, Fax: 778-782-3080, E-mail: gradstudies@sfu.ca. *Dean,* Aoife Mac Namara, 778-782-8790, Fax: 778-782-8789, E-mail: fcatdean@sfu.ca.

Faculty of Education Students: 712 full-time (528 women), 361 part-time (303 women). 880 applicants, 41% accepted, 225 enrolled. *Faculty:* 70 full-time (44 women). Expenses: Contact institution. *Financial support:* In 2016–17, 70 students received support, including 30 fellowships (averaging $6,500 per year), teaching assistantships (averaging $5,608 per year); research assistantships, career-related internships or fieldwork, and scholarships/grants also available. Support available to part-time students. In 2016, 245 master's, 29 doctorates, 42 other advanced degrees awarded. Offers arts education (M Ed, MA, Ed D, PhD); counseling psychology (M Ed, MA); curriculum and instruction (M Ed); curriculum and instruction foundations (M Ed, MA); curriculum theory and implementation (PhD); education (M Ed, M Sc, MA, Ed D, PhD, Graduate Diploma); educational leadership (M Ed, MA, Ed D); educational practice (M Ed); educational psychology (M Ed, MA, PhD); educational technology and learning design (M Ed, MA, PhD); languages, cultures, and literacies (PhD); mathematics education (M Ed, MA, PhD); philosophy of education (PhD); secondary mathematics education (M Ed, M Sc); teaching English as a second/foreign language (M Ed). *Application fee:* $90 ($125 for international students). Electronic applications accepted. *Application Contact:* Kim Peterson, Administrative Assistant, 778-782-9488, Fax: 778-782-4320, E-mail: fenvoa@sfu.ca. *Graduate Chair,* Dr. Shawn Bullock, 778-782-4102.

Faculty of Environment Students: 256 full-time (147 women), 1 part-time (0 women). 307 applicants, 35% accepted, 68 enrolled. Expenses: Contact institution. Offers archaeology (MA, PhD); environment (M Sc, MA, MRM, PhD, Graduate Diploma); geography (M Sc, MA, PhD); quantitative methods in fisheries management (Graduate Diploma); resource and environmental management (MRM, PhD); resource and environmental planning (MRM). *Application Contact:* Angie Van Vliet, Dean's Secretary, 778-782-8787, Fax: 778-782-3080, E-mail: envadgrd@sfu.ca. *Associate Dean,* Dr. Sean Markey, 778-782-9606, Fax: 778-782-3080, E-mail: envadgrd@sfu.ca.

Faculty of Health Sciences Students: 157 full-time (129 women), 3 part-time (2 women). 373 applicants, 26% accepted, 51 enrolled. *Faculty:* 42 full-time (18 women). Expenses: Contact institution. *Financial support:* In 2016–17, 91 students received support, including 42 fellowships (averaging $5,262 per year), teaching assistantships (averaging $5,608 per year); research assistantships, career-related internships or fieldwork, and scholarships/grants also available. In 2016, 51 master's, 5 doctorates, 1 other advanced degree awarded. Offers global health (Graduate Diploma); health sciences (M Sc, PhD); public health (MPH). *Application fee:* $90 ($125 for international students). Electronic applications accepted. *Application Contact:* Jennifer Van Rassel, Graduate Secretary, 778-782-7036, Fax: 778-782-5927, E-mail: fhsgrads@sfu.ca. *Graduate Chair,* Dr. Tim Takaro, 778-782-7186, Fax: 778-782-5927, E-mail: msc-phd-grad-chair@sfu.ca.

Faculty of Science Students: 618 full-time (261 women). 549 applicants, 30% accepted, 109 enrolled. *Faculty:* 240 full-time (68 women). Expenses: Contact institution. *Financial support:* In 2016–17, fellowships (averaging $6,500 per year), teaching assistantships (averaging $5,608 per year) were awarded; research assistantships, career-related internships or fieldwork, and scholarships/grants also available. In 2016, 72 master's, 45 doctorates awarded. Offers actuarial science (M Sc); applied and computational mathematics (M Sc, PhD); bioinformatics (Graduate Diploma); biological sciences (M Sc, PhD); biomedical physiology and

kinesiology (M Sc, PhD); chemistry (M Sc, PhD); earth sciences (M Sc, PhD); environmental toxicology (MET); mathematics (M Sc, PhD); molecular biology and biochemistry (M Sc, PhD); operations research (M Sc, PhD); pest management (MPM); physics (M Sc, PhD); science (M Sc, MET, MPM, PhD, Graduate Diploma); statistics (M Sc, PhD). *Application fee:* $90 ($125 for international students). Electronic applications accepted. *Associate Dean, Research and Graduate Studies,* Dr. Peter Ruben, 778-782-9351, Fax: 778-782-3424, E-mail: pruben@sfu.ca.

SIMPSON COLLEGE, Indianola, IA 50125-1297

General Information Independent-religious, coed, comprehensive institution.

GRADUATE UNITS

Department of Education Offers secondary education (MAT).

Department of Social Sciences *Program availability:* Evening/weekend. Offers criminal justice (MACJ).

SIMPSON UNIVERSITY, Redding, CA 96003-8606

General Information Independent-religious, coed, comprehensive institution. *Enrollment:* 1,012 graduate, professional, and undergraduate students; 47 full-time matriculated graduate/professional students (33 women), 42 part-time matriculated graduate/professional students (20 women). *Enrollment by degree level:* 89 master's. *Graduate faculty:* 4 full-time (1 woman), 28 part-time/adjunct (11 women). Tuition and fees vary according to program. *Graduate housing:* On-campus housing not available. *Student services:* Campus employment opportunities, campus safety program, career counseling, international student services, services for students with disabilities, teacher training. *Library facilities:* Start-Kilgour Memorial Library. *Collection:* Books: 103,721 (physical), 369,714 (digital/electronic); Serial titles: 340 (physical), 28,286 (digital/electronic); Databases: 54. Weekly public service hours: 93; students can reserve study rooms.

Computer facilities: 50 computers available on campus for general student use. A campuswide network can be accessed from student residence rooms. Online class registration is available.

Website: http://www.simpsonu.edu/

General Application Contact: Stacy Burgess, Director of Admissions for Adult and Graduate Studies, 530-226-4961, Fax: 530-226-4861, E-mail: sburgess@simpsonu.edu.

GRADUATE UNITS

A.W. Tozer Theological Seminary Students: 9 full-time (2 women), 30 part-time (7 women); includes 9 minority (1 Black or African American, non-Hispanic/Latino; 3 Asian, non-Hispanic/Latino; 4 Hispanic/Latino; 1 Two or more races, non-Hispanic/Latino), 1 international. Average age 36. *Faculty:* 9 part-time/adjunct (0 women). Expenses: Contact institution. *Financial support:* Scholarships/grants available. Support available to part-time students. Financial award application deadline: 7/1; financial award applicants required to submit FAFSA. In 2016, 12 master's awarded. *Program availability:* Part-time, evening/weekend, 100% online, blended/hybrid learning. Offers ministry leadership (MA). *Application deadline:* For fall admission, 8/1 for domestic and international students; for spring admission, 12/1 for domestic and international students; for summer admission, 4/1 for domestic and international students. Applications are processed on a rolling basis. *Application fee:* $35. Electronic applications accepted. *Application Contact:* Stacy Burgess, Director of Admissions for Adult and Graduate Studies, 530-226-4961, Fax: 530-226-4861, E-mail: admissions@simpsonu.edu. *Dean,* Dr. Patrick Blewett, 530-226-4144, Fax: 530-226-4871, E-mail: pblewett@simpsonu.edu.

School of Education Students: 8 full-time (7 women), 10 part-time (7 women); includes 1 minority (Two or more races, non-Hispanic/Latino), 1 international. Average age 37. *Faculty:* 4 full-time (1 woman), 9 part-time/adjunct (3 women). Expenses: Contact institution. *Financial support:* Scholarships/grants available. Financial award application deadline: 7/15; financial award applicants required to submit FAFSA. In 2016, 16 master's awarded. *Program availability:* Part-time, evening/weekend. Offers education (MA); education and preliminary administrative services credential (MA); education and preliminary teaching credential (MA); teaching (MA). *Application deadline:* Applications are processed on a rolling basis. *Application fee:* $35. Electronic applications accepted. *Application Contact:* Stacy Burgess, Director of Admissions for Adult and Graduate Studies, 530-226-4961, E-mail: sburgess@simpsonu.edu. *Dean of Education,* Dr. Craig Cook, 530-226-4188, Fax: 530-226-4872, E-mail: ccook@simpsonu.edu.

School of Graduate Studies Students: 16 full-time (24 women), 9 part-time (7 women); includes 11 minority (1 Black or African American, non-Hispanic/Latino; 2 Asian, non-Hispanic/Latino; 7 Hispanic/Latino; 1 Two or more races, non-Hispanic/Latino), 1 international. Average age 35. *Faculty:* 10 part-time/adjunct (8 women). Expenses: Contact institution. *Financial support:* Applicants required to submit FAFSA. In 2016, 17 master's awarded. *Program availability:* Evening/weekend, 100% online, blended/hybrid learning. Offers counseling psychology (MA); organizational leadership (MA). *Application deadline:* For fall admission, 3/1 for domestic and international students; for spring admission, 11/1 for domestic and international students. *Application fee:* $35. Electronic applications accepted. *Application Contact:* Stacy Burgess, Director of Admissions for Adult and Graduate Studies, 530-226-4961, E-mail: sburgess@simpsonu.edu. *Dean,* Adeline Jackson, 530-226-4788, E-mail: ajackson@simpsonu.edu.

SINTE GLESKA UNIVERSITY, Mission, SD 57555

General Information Independent, coed, comprehensive institution. *Graduate housing:* Rooms and/or apartments available on a first-come, first-served basis to single and married students.

GRADUATE UNITS

Graduate Education Program *Program availability:* Part-time, evening/weekend. Offers elementary education (M Ed).

SIOUX FALLS SEMINARY, Sioux Falls, SD 57105-1599

General Information Independent-religious, coed, graduate-only institution. *Graduate faculty:* 5 full-time (1 woman), 12 part-time/adjunct (3 women). *Graduate housing:* On-campus housing not available. *Student services:* Campus employment opportunities, career counseling, free psychological counseling, international student services. *Library facilities:* Mikkelsen Library, Sioux Falls Seminary Theological Collection. *Collection:* Students can reserve study rooms.

Website: http://www.sfseminary.edu/

General Application Contact: Nathan M. Helling, Vice President for Enrollment and Development, 605-336-6588, Fax: 605-335-9090, E-mail: nhelling@sfseminary.edu.

GRADUATE UNITS

Graduate and Professional Programs Expenses: Contact institution. *Financial support:* Career-related internships or fieldwork and scholarships/grants available. Support available to part-time students. *Program availability:* Part-time. Offers Bible and theology (MA); Christian leadership (MA); counseling (MA); marriage and family therapy

(M Div); ministry (D Min); pastoral care and counseling (M Div); theological studies (Certificate). *Application deadline:* Applications are processed on a rolling basis. *Application fee:* $25. *Application Contact:* Dustin Brouwer, Director of Enrollment Management, 605-336-6588, Fax: 605-335-9090, E-mail: dbrouwer@sfseminary.edu. *Chief Academic Officer/Dean,* Larry Caldwell, 605-336-6588, Fax: 605-335-9090, E-mail: lcaldwell@sfseminary.edu.

 SIT GRADUATE INSTITUTE, Brattleboro, VT 05302-0676
General Information Independent, coed, graduate-only institution. *Graduate housing:* Rooms and/or apartments available on a first-come, first-served basis to single and married students. Housing application deadline: 7/1.

GRADUATE UNITS
Graduate Programs *Program availability:* Part-time, online learning. Offers global youth development and leadership (M Ed); intercultural service, leadership, and management (self-designed) (MA); international education (MA); peace and justice leadership (MA); sustainable development (MA); teaching English as a second language (MAT). Electronic applications accepted.

See Display below and Close-Up on page 897.

SITTING BULL COLLEGE, Fort Yates, ND 58538-9701
General Information Independent, coed, comprehensive institution.

GRADUATE UNITS
Program in Environmental Science Offers environmental science (MS).

SLIPPERY ROCK UNIVERSITY OF PENNSYLVANIA, Slippery Rock, PA 16057-1383
General Information State-supported, coed, comprehensive institution. *Enrollment:* 8,881 graduate, professional, and undergraduate students; 456 full-time matriculated graduate/professional students (313 women), 650 part-time matriculated graduate/professional students (503 women). *Enrollment by degree level:* 917 master's, 189 doctoral. *Graduate faculty:* 84 full-time (54 women), 7 part-time/adjunct (5 women). Tuition, state resident: full-time $8694; part-time $483 per credit. Tuition, nonresident: full-time $13,050; part-time $725 per credit. *Required fees:* $2476; $164 per credit. Tuition and fees vary according to course load. *Graduate housing:* Room and/or apartments available on a first-come, first-served basis to single students; on-campus housing not available to married students. Typical cost: $6620 per year ($10,110 including board). Room and board charges vary according to board plan and housing facility selected. *Student services:* Campus employment opportunities, campus safety program, career counseling, child daycare facilities, exercise/wellness program, free psychological counseling, international student services, multicultural affairs office, services for students with disabilities, writing training. *Library facilities:* Bailey Library. *Collection:* Books: 314,860 (physical), 280,458 (digital/electronic); Serial titles: 248 (physical), 46,495 (digital/electronic); Databases: 125. Weekly public service hours: 96; students can reserve study rooms.

Computer facilities: Computer purchase and lease plans are available. 1,654 computers available on campus for general student use. A campuswide network can be accessed from student residence rooms and from off campus. Online class registration is available.
Website: http://www.sru.edu/

General Application Contact: Brandi Weber-Mortimer, Director of Graduate Admissions, 724-738-2051, Fax: 724-738-2146, E-mail: graduate.admissions@sru.edu.

GRADUATE UNITS
Graduate Studies (Recruitment) Students: 456 full-time (313 women), 650 part-time (503 women); includes 66 minority (33 Black or African American, non-Hispanic/Latino; 8 Asian, non-Hispanic/Latino; 13 Hispanic/Latino; 1 Native Hawaiian or other Pacific Islander, non-Hispanic/Latino; 11 Two or more races, non-Hispanic/Latino), 2 international. Average age 29. 1,478 applicants, 56% accepted, 475 enrolled. *Faculty:* 84 full-time (54 women), 7 part-time/adjunct (5 women). Expenses: Contact institution. *Financial support:* In 2016–17, 168 students received support. Career-related internships or fieldwork, Federal Work-Study, institutionally sponsored loans, scholarships/grants, tuition waivers (partial), and unspecified assistantships available. Support available to part-time students. Financial award application deadline: 5/1; financial award applicants required to submit FAFSA. In 2016, 371 master's, 50 doctorates awarded. *Program availability:* Part-time, evening/weekend, 100% online, blended/hybrid learning. *Application deadline:* For fall admission, 1/15 priority date for domestic and international students; for spring admission, 10/1 priority date for domestic students, 9/1 priority date for international students. Applications are processed on a rolling basis. *Application fee:* $25 ($30 for international students). Electronic applications accepted. *Director of Graduate Admissions,* Brandi Weber-Mortimer, 724-738-4340, Fax: 724-738-2146, E-mail: graduate.admissions@sru.edu.

College of Business Students: 16 full-time (9 women), 9 part-time (6 women); includes 1 minority (Black or African American, non-Hispanic/Latino). Average age 29. 109 applicants, 26% accepted, 13 enrolled. *Faculty:* 6 full-time (4 women), 1 part-time/adjunct (0 women). Expenses: Contact institution. *Financial support:* In 2016–17, 5 students received support. Career-related internships or fieldwork, Federal Work-Study, institutionally sponsored loans, scholarships/grants, tuition waivers (partial), and unspecified assistantships available. Support available to part-time students. Financial award application deadline: 5/1; financial award applicants required to submit FAFSA. In 2016, 26 master's awarded. *Program availability:* Part-time, evening/weekend. Offers accounting/finance (MBA); business (MBA); general (MBA); marketing/management (MBA). *Application deadline:* For fall admission, 3/1 priority date for domestic students, 5/1 priority date for international students; for spring admission, 10/1 priority date for domestic students, 9/1 priority date for international students. Applications are processed on a rolling basis. *Application fee:* $25 ($30 for international students). Electronic applications accepted. *Application Contact:* Brandi Weber-Mortimer, Director of Graduate Admissions, 724-738-2051, Fax: 724-738-2146, E-mail: graduate.admissions@sru.edu. *Dean,* Dr. Lawrence Shao, 724-738-2687, Fax: 724-738-4767, E-mail: lawrence.shao@sru.edu.

College of Education Students: 198 full-time (137 women), 466 part-time (396 women); includes 26 minority (13 Black or African American, non-Hispanic/Latino; 1 Asian, non-Hispanic/Latino; 7 Hispanic/Latino; 5 Two or more races, non-Hispanic/Latino), 1 international. Average age 30. 552 applicants, 73% accepted, 248 enrolled. *Faculty:* 39 full-time (24 women), 2 part-time/adjunct (1 woman). Expenses: Contact institution. *Financial support:* In 2016–17, 88 students received support. Career-related internships or fieldwork, Federal Work-Study, institutionally sponsored loans, scholarships/grants, tuition waivers (partial), and unspecified assistantships available. Support available to part-time students. Financial award application deadline: 5/1; financial award applicants required to submit FAFSA. In 2016, 283 master's awarded. *Program availability:* Part-time, evening/weekend, 100% online.

Offers adapted physical activity (MS); autism (M Ed); clinical mental health (MA); education (M Ed, MA, MS, Ed D); instructional coach (M Ed); K-12 reading (M Ed); K-12 science and math (M Ed); master teacher (M Ed); reading specialist (M Ed); school counseling (M Ed); secondary education (M Ed); special education (Ed D); student affairs in higher education (MA); student affairs in higher education with college counseling (MA); supervision (M Ed); technology for online instruction (M Ed). *Application deadline:* For fall admission, 3/1 priority date for domestic students, 5/1 priority date for international students; for spring admission, 10/1 priority date for domestic students, 9/1 priority date for international students. Applications are processed on a rolling basis. *Application fee:* $25 ($30 for international students). Electronic applications accepted. *Application Contact:* Brandi Weber-Mortimer, Director of Graduate Admissions, 724-738-2051, Fax: 724-738-2146, E-mail: graduate.admissions@sru.edu. *Dean,* Dr. A. Keith Dils, 724-738-2007, Fax: 724-738-2880, E-mail: keith.dils@sru.edu.

College of Health, Environment, and Science Students: 229 full-time (157 women), 110 part-time (67 women); includes 29 minority (15 Black or African American, non-Hispanic/Latino; 6 Asian, non-Hispanic/Latino; 5 Hispanic/Latino; 3 Two or more races, non-Hispanic/Latino), 1 international. Average age 28. 713 applicants, 45% accepted, 171 enrolled. *Faculty:* 24 full-time (16 women), 4 part-time/adjunct (all women). Expenses: Contact institution. *Financial support:* In 2016–17, 65 students received support. Career-related internships or fieldwork, Federal Work-Study, institutionally sponsored loans, scholarships/grants, tuition waivers (partial), and unspecified assistantships available. Support available to part-time students. Financial award application deadline: 5/1; financial award applicants required to submit FAFSA. In 2016, 42 master's, 50 doctorates awarded. *Program availability:* Part-time, evening/weekend, 100% online. Offers data analytics (MS); environmental education (M Ed); health informatics (MS); health, environment, and science (M Ed, MPH, MS, DPT); park and resource management (MS); physical therapy (DPT); physician assistant studies (MS); public health (MPH). *Application deadline:* For fall admission, 3/1 priority date for domestic students, 5/1 priority date for international students; for spring admission, 10/1 priority date for domestic students, 9/1 priority date for international students. Applications are processed on a rolling basis. *Application fee:* $25 ($30 for international students). Electronic applications accepted. *Application Contact:* Brandi Weber-Mortimer, Director of Graduate Admissions, 724-738-2051, Fax: 724-738-2146, E-mail: graduate.admissions@sru.edu. *Interim Dean,* Dr. Jerry Chmielewski, 724-738-2489, Fax: 724-738-2881, E-mail: jerry.chmielewski@sru.edu.

College of Liberal Arts Students: 13 full-time (10 women), 65 part-time (34 women); includes 10 minority (4 Black or African American, non-Hispanic/Latino; 1 Asian, non-Hispanic/Latino; 1 Hispanic/Latino; 1 Native Hawaiian or other Pacific Islander, non-Hispanic/Latino; 3 Two or more races, non-Hispanic/Latino). Average age 30. 83 applicants, 75% accepted, 43 enrolled. *Faculty:* 15 full-time (10 women). Expenses: Contact institution. *Financial support:* In 2016–17, 10 students received support. Career-related internships or fieldwork, Federal Work-Study, institutionally sponsored loans, scholarships/grants, tuition waivers (partial), and unspecified assistantships available. Support available to part-time students. Financial award application deadline: 5/1; financial award applicants required to submit FAFSA. In 2016, 19 master's awarded. *Program availability:* Part-time, evening/weekend, online only, 100% online. Offers criminal justice (MA); English (MA); history (MA); liberal arts (MA, MMT); music therapy (MMT); teaching English to speakers of other languages (MA). *Application deadline:* For fall admission, 3/1 priority date for domestic students, 5/1 priority date for international students; for spring admission, 10/1 priority date for domestic students, 9/1 priority date for international students. Applications are processed on a rolling basis. *Application fee:* $25 ($30 for international students). Electronic applications accepted. *Application Contact:* Brandi Weber-Mortimer, Director of Graduate Admissions, 724-738-2051, Fax: 724-738-2146, E-mail: graduate.admissions@sru.edu. *Interim Dean,* Dr. Jennifer Keller-Birkes, 724-738-2773, Fax: 724-738-2146, E-mail: jennifer.keller@sru.edu.

SMITH COLLEGE, Northampton, MA 01063

General Information Independent, coed; undergraduate: women only; graduate: coed, comprehensive institution. *Enrollment:* 2,896 graduate, professional, and undergraduate students; 309 full-time matriculated graduate/professional students (262 women), 87 part-time matriculated graduate/professional students (70 women). *Enrollment by degree level:* 310 master's, 64 doctoral, 22 other advanced degrees. *Graduate faculty:* 270 full-time (149 women), 24 part-time/adjunct (13 women). *Tuition:* Full-time $34,560; part-time $1440 per credit. Tuition and fees vary according to course load and program. *Graduate housing:* Room and/or apartments available on a first-come, first-served basis to single students; on-campus housing not available to married students. Typical cost: $7740 per year ($15,470 including board). Housing application deadline: 5/1. *Student services:* Campus employment opportunities, campus safety program, career counseling, child daycare facilities, exercise/wellness program, international student services, low-cost health insurance, multicultural affairs office, services for students with disabilities, teacher training, writing training. *Library facilities:* Neilson Library.

Computer facilities: Computer purchase and lease plans are available. A campuswide network can be accessed from student residence rooms and from off campus. Online class registration is available.
Website: http://www.smith.edu/

General Application Contact: Danielle Ramdath, Director of Graduate Programs, 413-585-3050, Fax: 413-585-3054, E-mail: dramdath@smith.edu.

GRADUATE UNITS

Graduate and Special Programs Students: 54 full-time (48 women), 9 part-time (7 women); includes 13 minority (4 Black or African American, non-Hispanic/Latino; 4 Asian, non-Hispanic/Latino; 4 Hispanic/Latino; 1 Two or more races, non-Hispanic/Latino), 2 international. Average age 27. 156 applicants, 42% accepted, 52 enrolled. *Faculty:* 270 full-time (148 women), 23 part-time/adjunct (13 women). Expenses: Contact institution. *Financial support:* In 2016–17, 62 students received support, including 7 fellowships with full tuition reimbursements available, 7 research assistantships with full tuition reimbursements available (averaging $13,820 per year), 17 teaching assistantships with full tuition reimbursements available (averaging $13,850 per year); scholarships/grants also available. Support available to part-time students. Financial award application deadline: 1/15; financial award applicants required to submit CSS PROFILE or FAFSA. In 2016, 49 master's, 12 other advanced degrees awarded. *Program availability:* Part-time. Offers biological sciences (MS); dance (MFA); elementary education (MAT); exercise and sport studies (MS); middle school education (MAT); secondary education (MAT); secondary teaching (MAT); theatre (MFA); women in mathematics (Postbaccalaureate Certificate). *Application deadline:* For fall admission, 4/1 for domestic students, 1/15 for international students; for spring admission, 12/1 for domestic students. *Application fee:* $60. *Application Contact:* Ruth Morgan, Program

Assistant, 413-585-3050, Fax: 413-585-3054, E-mail: gradstdy@smith.edu. *Director,* Danielle Ramdath, 413-585-3050, Fax: 413-585-3054, E-mail: dramdath@smith.edu.
School for Social Work Students: 260 full-time (222 women), 45 part-time (35 women); includes 82 minority (24 Black or African American, non-Hispanic/Latino; 4 American Indian or Alaska Native, non-Hispanic/Latino; 18 Asian, non-Hispanic/Latino; 22 Hispanic/Latino; 1 Native Hawaiian or other Pacific Islander, non-Hispanic/Latino; 13 Two or more races, non-Hispanic/Latino), 9 international. Average age 33. 490 applicants, 53% accepted, 147 enrolled. *Faculty:* 14 full-time (11 women), 98 part-time/adjunct (79 women). Expenses: Contact institution. *Financial support:* In 2016–17, 246 students received support. Career-related internships or fieldwork and scholarships/grants available. Financial award application deadline: 3/1; financial award applicants required to submit FAFSA. In 2016, 118 master's, 13 doctorates awarded. Offers clinical social work (MSW, PhD). *Application deadline:* For fall admission, 2/21 for domestic students, 2/15 for international students. Applications are processed on a rolling basis. *Application fee:* $60. Electronic applications accepted. *Application Contact:* Irene Rodriguez Martin, Associate Dean, Graduate Enrollment and Student Services, 413-585-7960, Fax: 413-585-7994, E-mail: imartin@smith.edu. *Dean/Professor,* Dr. Marianne Yoshioka, 413-585-7977, E-mail: myoshioka@smith.edu.

SOFIA UNIVERSITY, Palo Alto, CA 94303

General Information Independent, coed, graduate-only institution. *Graduate housing:* On-campus housing not available.

GRADUATE UNITS

Hybrid: Face-to-Face/Online Programs *Program availability:* Online learning. Offers transpersonal psychology (MA, PhD). Electronic applications accepted.
Residential Programs *Program availability:* Part-time, evening/weekend. Offers clinical psychology (Psy D); computer science (MS); counseling psychology (MA); transpersonal psychology (MA, PhD). Electronic applications accepted.

SOKA UNIVERSITY OF AMERICA, Aliso Viejo, CA 92656

General Information Independent, coed, comprehensive institution. *Graduate housing:* Room and/or apartments available to single students; on-campus housing not available to married students.

GRADUATE UNITS

Graduate School *Program availability:* Evening/weekend. Offers educational leadership and societal change (MA).

SONOMA STATE UNIVERSITY, Rohnert Park, CA 94928-3609

General Information State-supported, coed, comprehensive institution. *Enrollment:* 9,323 graduate, professional, and undergraduate students; 391 full-time matriculated graduate/professional students (304 women), 326 part-time matriculated graduate/professional students (228 women). *Enrollment by degree level:* 472 master's, 242 other advanced degrees. *Graduate faculty:* 57 full-time (27 women), 33 part-time/adjunct (25 women). *Tuition,* state resident: full-time $6738; part-time $3906 per unit. *Required fees:* $1916; $1916 per year. Tuition and fees vary according to course load, degree level and program. *Graduate housing:* Room and/or apartments available on a first-come, first-served basis to single students; on-campus housing not available to married students. Typical cost: $8760 per year ($12,560 including board). Room and board charges vary according to board plan and housing facility selected. Housing application deadline: 1/1. *Student services:* Campus employment opportunities, career counseling, child daycare facilities, exercise/wellness program, free psychological counseling, international student services, multicultural affairs office, services for students with disabilities. *Library facilities:* Jean and Charles Schultz Information Center plus 1 other. *Collection:* Books: 790,148 (physical), 168,724 (digital/electronic); Serial titles: 44,834 (physical). Students can reserve study rooms. *Research affiliation:* Biomimetica (bioacoustics, metabolic flux modeling), Gallo Family Vineyards (science), Kenwood Vineyards (science), Natural Industries, Inc. (Sudden Oak Death research), Clean Filtration Technologies (environmental microbiology).

Computer facilities: A campuswide network can be accessed from student residence rooms and from off campus. Online class registration is available.
Website: http://www.sonoma.edu/

General Application Contact: David Hartranft, Analyst, Academic Programs, 707-664-2237, Fax: 707-664-4060, E-mail: david.hartranft@sonoma.edu.

GRADUATE UNITS

Department of English Expenses: Contact institution. *Financial support:* Fellowships, teaching assistantships, career-related internships or fieldwork, and Federal Work-Study available. Financial award application deadline: 3/2; financial award applicants required to submit FAFSA. *Program availability:* Part-time, evening/weekend. Offers American literature (MA); creative writing (MA); English literature (MA); world literature (MA). *Application deadline:* For fall admission, 11/30 priority date for domestic students. *Application fee:* $55. *Application Contact:* Dr. Anne Goldman, Chair of Graduate Studies, 707-664-2651, Fax: 707-664-6040, E-mail: goldmana@sonoma.edu. *Chair,* Brantley L. Bryant, 707-664-2164, E-mail: brantley.bryant@sonoma.edu.

School of Business and Economics Expenses: Contact institution. *Financial support:* Career-related internships or fieldwork, Federal Work-Study, institutionally sponsored loans, and scholarships/grants available. Support available to part-time students. Financial award application deadline: 3/2; financial award applicants required to submit FAFSA. *Program availability:* Part-time, evening/weekend. Offers business administration (MBA); executive business administration (MBA); wine business (MBA). *Application deadline:* For fall admission, 1/31 priority date for domestic students; for spring admission, 8/31 for domestic students. Applications are processed on a rolling basis. *Application fee:* $55. *Application Contact:* John Stayton, Executive Director, Graduate and Executive Programs, 707-664-3954, E-mail: john.stayton@sonoma.edu. *Dean,* Dr. William Silver, 707-664-2377.

School of Education Expenses: Contact institution. *Financial support:* Fellowships, research assistantships, career-related internships or fieldwork, and Federal Work-Study available. Support available to part-time students. Financial award application deadline: 3/2; financial award applicants required to submit FAFSA. *Program availability:* Part-time, evening/weekend. Offers administrative services (Credential); curriculum, teaching, and learning (MA); early childhood education (MA); education specialist (Credential); educational leadership (MA); multiple subject (Credential); reading and literacy (MA, Credential); single subject (Credential); special education (MA). *Application fee:* $55. *Application Contact:* Dr. Jennifer Mahdavi, Coordinator of Graduate Studies, 707-664-3311, E-mail: jennifer.mahdavi@sonoma.edu. *Dean,* Dr. Carlos Ayala, 707-664-4412, E-mail: carlos.ayala@sonoma.edu.

School of Science and Technology Expenses: Contact institution. *Financial support:* Fellowships, research assistantships, teaching assistantships, career-related internships or fieldwork, Federal Work-Study, and tuition waivers (full) available. Support available to part-time students. Financial award application deadline: 3/2; financial award applicants required to submit FAFSA. *Program availability:* Part-time. Offers adapted physical education (MA); biochemistry (MA); ecology (MS); environmental biology (MS); evolutionary biology (MS); family nurse practitioner (MSN); functional morphology (MS); interdisciplinary (MA); interdisciplinary pre-occupational therapy (MA); lifetime physical activity (MA); molecular and cell biology (MS); organismal biology (MS); physical education (MA); pre-physical therapy (MA); science and technology (MA, MS, MSN). *Application deadline:* For fall admission, 11/30 for domestic students. *Application fee:* $55. *Application Contact:* Dr. Farid Farahmand, Coordinator of Graduate Studies, 707-664-3491, E-mail: farahman@sonoma.edu. *Dean,* Lynn Stauffer, 707-664-2171, E-mail: lynn.stauffer@sonoma.edu.

School of Social Sciences Expenses: Contact institution. *Financial support:* Fellowships, research assistantships, teaching assistantships, career-related internships or fieldwork, and Federal Work-Study available. Support available to part-time students. Financial award application deadline: 3/2. *Program availability:* Part-time, evening/weekend. Offers administration of nonprofit agencies (Certificate); clinical mental health counseling (MA); cultural resources management (MA); history (MA); public administration (MPA); school counseling (MA); social sciences (MA, MPA, Certificate). *Application deadline:* For fall admission, 11/30 for domestic students. *Application fee:* $55. *Application Contact:* Elaine Sundberg, Associate Vice President, Academic Programs and Graduate Studies, 707-664-2215, Fax: 707-664-4060, E-mail: elaine.sundberg@sonoma.edu. *Dean,* John Wingard, 707-664-2112, E-mail: wingard@sonoma.edu.

SOTHEBY'S INSTITUTE OF ART–LONDON, WC1B 3EE London, United Kingdom

General Information Private, coed, graduate-only institution. *Enrollment by degree level:* 181 master's. *Graduate faculty:* 41 full-time (25 women). *Tuition:* Full-time 24,900 British pounds. Tuition and fees vary according to class time, program and student level. *Graduate housing:* On-campus housing not available. *Student services:* Campus safety program, career counseling, international student services, writing training. *Library facilities:* Sotheby's Institute of Art library plus 1 other. *Collection:* Books: 20,000 (physical). *Research affiliation:* University of Manchester.

Computer facilities: Online class registration is available.
Website: http://www.sothebysinstitute.com/london/index.html

General Application Contact: Jessica Bearne, Admissions Manager, 44 20 7462 3250, E-mail: j.bearne@sothebysinstitute.com.

GRADUATE UNITS

Graduate Programs Students: 181 full-time (159 women). *Faculty:* 41 full-time (25 women). Expenses: Contact institution. Offers art business (MA); contemporary art (MA); fine and decorative art and design (MA); modern and contemporary Asian art (MA). *Application deadline:* Applications are processed on a rolling basis. Electronic applications accepted. *Application Contact:* Jessica Bearne, Admissions Manager, 44 20 7462 3250, E-mail: j.bearne@sothebysinstitute.com.

SOTHEBY'S INSTITUTE OF ART–NEW YORK, New York, NY 10021

General Information Proprietary, coed, graduate-only institution. *Graduate housing:* On-campus housing not available.

GRADUATE UNITS

Graduate Programs Offers art business (MA); contemporary art (MA); fine and decorative art and design (MA). Electronic applications accepted.

SOUTH BAYLO UNIVERSITY, Anaheim, CA 92801-1701

General Information Independent, coed, graduate-only institution. *Graduate housing:* On-campus housing not available. *Research affiliation:* University of California Irvine College of Medicine (complimentary and alternative medicine), National Nutritional Foods Association (herbs and nutritional supplements), Henan College of Traditional Chinese Medicine (herbology and acupuncture), Kaiser Permanente (patient care: acupuncture and Oriental medicine), University of Illinois at Chicago (testing of herbal formulations).

GRADUATE UNITS

Program in Oriental Medicine and Acupuncture *Program availability:* Evening/weekend. Offers Oriental medicine and acupuncture (MS). Electronic applications accepted.

SOUTH CAROLINA STATE UNIVERSITY, Orangeburg, SC 29117-0001

General Information State-supported, coed, comprehensive institution. *Enrollment:* 2,905 graduate, professional, and undergraduate students; 211 full-time matriculated graduate/professional students (164 women), 157 part-time matriculated graduate/professional students (122 women). *Enrollment by degree level:* 278 master's, 55 doctoral, 35 other advanced degrees. *Graduate faculty:* 46 full-time (25 women), 15 part-time/adjunct (8 women). Tuition, state resident: full-time $8938; part-time $579 per credit hour. Tuition, nonresident: full-time $19,018; part-time $1139 per credit hour. *Required fees:* $1482; $82 per credit hour. *Graduate housing:* Room and/or apartments available on a first-come, first-served basis to single students; on-campus housing not available to married students. Typical cost: $8000 per year. *Student services:* Campus employment opportunities, career counseling, exercise/wellness program, free psychological counseling, international student services, low-cost health insurance, multicultural affairs office, services for students with disabilities, teacher training, writing training. *Library facilities:* Miller F. Whittaker Library. *Collection:* Books: 317,233 (physical), 195,578 (digital/electronic); Serial titles: 18,334 (digital/electronic); Databases: 114. Weekly public service hours: 74; students can reserve study rooms.

Computer facilities: 600 computers available on campus for general student use. A campuswide network can be accessed from student residence rooms. Online class registration is available.
Website: http://www.scsu.edu/

General Application Contact: Dr. Frederick Evans, Dean, College of Graduate and Professional Studies, 803-536-7097, Fax: 803-536-8812, E-mail: fevans6@scsu.edu.

GRADUATE UNITS

College of Graduate and Professional Studies Students: 211 full-time (164 women), 157 part-time (122 women); includes 320 minority (315 Black or African American, non-Hispanic/Latino; 1 American Indian or Alaska Native, non-Hispanic/Latino; 1 Asian, non-Hispanic/Latino; 2 Hispanic/Latino; 1 Two or more races, non-Hispanic/Latino), 1 international. Average age 33. 216 applicants, 81% accepted, 144 enrolled. Expenses: Contact institution. *Financial support:* Fellowships, career-related internships or fieldwork, Federal Work-Study, scholarships/grants, and unspecified assistantships available. Financial award application deadline: 6/1. In 2016, 124 master's, 16 doctorates, 10 other advanced degrees awarded. *Program availability:* Part-time, evening/weekend. Offers counselor education (M Ed); early childhood education (MAT); education (M Ed); educational leadership and administration (Ed D, Ed S); elementary education (M Ed, MAT); English (MAT); general science/biology (MAT); individual and family development (MS); mathematics (MAT); nutritional sciences (MS); rehabilitation counseling (MA); secondary education (M Ed); special education (M Ed); speech pathology and audiology (MA); transportation (MS). *Application deadline:* For fall admission, 6/15 for domestic and international students; for spring admission, 11/1 for domestic and international students. *Application fee:* $25. Electronic applications accepted. *Application Contact:* Curtis Foskey, Coordinator of Graduate Admission, 803-536-8419, Fax: 803-536-8812, E-mail: cfoskey@scsu.edu. *Dean, College of Graduate and Professional Studies,* Dr. Frederick Evans, 803-536-7097, Fax: 803-536-8812, E-mail: fevans6@scsu.edu.

School of Business Students: 19 full-time (11 women), 10 part-time (5 women); includes 27 minority (all Black or African American, non-Hispanic/Latino). Average age 27. 17 applicants, 94% accepted, 15 enrolled. *Faculty:* 7 full-time (3 women). Expenses: Contact institution. *Financial support:* Fellowships, research assistantships, career-related internships or fieldwork, Federal Work-Study, scholarships/grants, and unspecified assistantships available. Financial award application deadline: 6/1. In 2016, 6 master's awarded. *Program availability:* Part-time, evening/weekend. Offers agribusiness (MBA); entrepreneurship (MBA); general business administration (MBA); healthcare management (MBA). *Application deadline:* For fall admission, 6/15 for domestic and international students; for spring admission, 11/1 for domestic and international students. *Application fee:* $25. Electronic applications accepted. *Application Contact:* Ellen R. Ricoma, MBA Program Director, 803-533-3777, Fax: 803-516-4651, E-mail: ericoma1@scsu.edu. *Chair,* Dr. Matthew Guah, 803-516-4834, Fax: 803-536-8078, E-mail: mguah@scsu.edu.

SOUTH COLLEGE, Knoxville, TN 37917

General Information Proprietary, coed, primarily women, comprehensive institution.

GRADUATE UNITS

Program in Pharmacy Offers pharmacy (Pharm D).

Program in Physician Assistant Studies Offers physician assistant studies (MHS).

SOUTH DAKOTA SCHOOL OF MINES AND TECHNOLOGY, Rapid City, SD 57701-3995

General Information State-supported, coed, university. *Graduate housing:* Room and/or apartments available on a first-come, first-served basis to single students; on-campus housing not available to married students. *Research affiliation:* Raven Industries (composite and thin films), Black Hills Power (NDA-Lightning (experimental and data collection)), CalxAqua (filtration media), RESPEC, Inc. (mining and waste storage), HF Webster (cold spray applications), Nanofiber Sperations (cutting edge separation media composed of functionalized nanofibers).

GRADUATE UNITS

Graduate Division *Program availability:* Part-time. Offers atmospheric and environmental sciences (MS, PhD); biomedical engineering (MS, PhD); chemical and biological engineering (PhD); chemical engineering (MS); civil and environmental engineering (MS, PhD); computational sciences and robotics (MS); construction engineering management (MS); electrical engineering (MS); engineering management (MS); geology and geological engineering (MS, PhD); materials engineering and science (MS, PhD); mechanical engineering (MS, PhD); mining engineering (MS); nanoscience and nanoengineering (PhD); paleontology (MS); physics (MS, PhD). Electronic applications accepted.

College of Engineering *Program availability:* Part-time, online learning. Offers engineering (MS, PhD). Electronic applications accepted.

College of Science and Letters *Program availability:* Part-time. Offers science and letters (MS, PhD).

SOUTH DAKOTA STATE UNIVERSITY, Brookings, SD 57007

General Information State-supported, coed, university. CGS member. *Graduate housing:* Rooms and/or apartments available to single and married students.

GRADUATE UNITS

Graduate School *Program availability:* Part-time, evening/weekend, online learning.

College of Agriculture and Biological Sciences *Program availability:* Part-time. Offers agricultural and biosystems engineering (MS, PhD); agriculture and biological sciences (MS, PhD); agronomy (PhD); animal science (MS, PhD); animal sciences (MS, PhD); biological sciences (MS, PhD); economics (MS); plant science (MS); sociology (MS, PhD); wildlife and fisheries sciences (MS, PhD).

College of Arts and Science *Program availability:* Part-time. Offers arts and science (MA, MS, PhD); chemistry (MS, PhD); communication studies and journalism (MS); English (MA); geography (MS); industrial/organizational psychology (MS).

College of Education and Human Sciences Offers agricultural education (MS); athletic training (MS); counseling and human resource development (M Ed, MS); curriculum and instruction (M Ed); dietetics (MS); education and human sciences (M Ed, MFCS, MS, PhD); educational administration (M Ed); family financial planning (MS); human sciences (MS); merchandising (MS); nutrition and exercise sciences (MS, PhD); sport and recreation studies (MS).

College of Engineering *Program availability:* Part-time. Offers agricultural, biosystems and mechanical engineering (PhD); biological sciences (MS, PhD); computational science and statistics (PhD); electrical engineering (PhD); engineering (MS); geospatial science and engineering (PhD); industrial management (MS); mathematics (MS); statistics (MS).

College of Nursing *Program availability:* Part-time, evening/weekend, online learning. Offers nursing (MS, PhD).

College of Pharmacy Offers biological science (MS); pharmaceutical sciences (PhD); pharmacy (MS, PhD, Pharm D).

SOUTHEASTERN BAPTIST THEOLOGICAL SEMINARY, Wake Forest, NC 27588-1889

General Information Independent-religious, coed, comprehensive institution. *Graduate housing:* Rooms and/or apartments available on a first-come, first-served basis to single and married students.

GRADUATE UNITS

Graduate and Professional Programs Offers advanced biblical studies (M Div); Christian education (M Div, MACE); Christian ethics (PhD); Christian ministry (M Div); Christian planting (M Div); church music (MACM); counseling (MACO); evangelism (PhD); language (M Div); ministry (D Min); New Testament (PhD); Old Testament (PhD); philosophy (PhD); theology (Th M, PhD); women's studies (M Div).

SOUTHEASTERN LOUISIANA UNIVERSITY, Hammond, LA 70402

General Information State-supported, coed, comprehensive institution. *Enrollment:* 14,499 graduate, professional, and undergraduate students; 382 full-time matriculated graduate/professional students (252 women), 532 part-time matriculated graduate/professional students (418 women). *Enrollment by degree level:* 699 master's, 109 doctoral, 106 other advanced degrees. *Graduate faculty:* 139 full-time (70 women), 21 part-time/adjunct (12 women). Tuition, state resident: full-time $6540; part-time $465 per credit hour. Tuition, nonresident: full-time $19,017; part-time $1158 per credit hour. *Required fees:* $1829. *Graduate housing:* Room and/or apartments available on a first-come, first-served basis to single students; on-campus housing not available to married students. Typical cost: $4800 per year ($7510 including board). Room and board charges vary according to board plan and housing facility selected. Housing application deadline: 6/15. *Student services:* Campus employment opportunities, campus safety program, career counseling, exercise/wellness program, free psychological counseling, international student services, low-cost health insurance, multicultural affairs office, services for students with disabilities, teacher training, writing training. *Library facilities:* Linus A. Sims Memorial Library plus 1 other. *Collection:* Books: 1.5 million (physical), 233,457 (digital/electronic); Serial titles: 1,167 (physical), 362 (digital/electronic). Students can reserve study rooms. *Research affiliation:* Bradken Manufacturing (steel), Petroleum Research Fund (chemistry), Gaylord Chemical Company (chemical manufacturing), Ochsner Medical Center (medicine), Lake Ponchartrain Basin Foundation (water quality and wetland ecology).

Computer facilities: 1,031 computers available on campus for general student use. A campuswide network can be accessed from student residence rooms and from off campus. Online class registration, campus Webmail, student newspaper, transcripts, bookstore are available.
Website: http://www.southeastern.edu/

General Application Contact: Amanda Harper, Graduate Admissions Analyst, 985-549-5620, Fax: 985-549-5882, E-mail: admissions@southeastern.edu.

GRADUATE UNITS

College of Arts, Humanities and Social Sciences Students: 73 full-time (42 women), 81 part-time (42 women); includes 27 minority (12 Black or African American, non-Hispanic/Latino; 3 Asian, non-Hispanic/Latino; 6 Hispanic/Latino; 6 Two or more races, non-Hispanic/Latino), 10 international. Average age 28. 99 applicants, 71% accepted, 40 enrolled. *Faculty:* 50 full-time (18 women), 7 part-time/adjunct (2 women). Expenses: Contact institution. *Financial support:* In 2016–17, 92 students received support, including 30 research assistantships (averaging $9,580 per year), 18 teaching assistantships (averaging $9,117 per year); career-related internships or fieldwork, institutionally sponsored loans, scholarships/grants, tuition waivers (full), and unspecified assistantships also available. Support available to part-time students. Financial award application deadline: 5/1; financial award applicants required to submit FAFSA. In 2016, 68 master's awarded. *Program availability:* Part-time. Offers applied sociology (MS); arts, humanities and social sciences (M Mus, MA, MS); choral conducting (M Mus); creative writing (MA); history (MA); industrial/organizational (MA); instrumental conducting (M Mus); language and theory (MA); music performance (M Mus); music theory (M Mus); organizational communication (MA); professional writing (MA); publishing studies (MA). *Application deadline:* For fall admission, 7/15 priority date for domestic students, 6/1 priority date for international students; for spring admission, 12/1 priority date for domestic students, 10/1 priority date for international students. Applications are processed on a rolling basis. *Application fee:* $20 ($30 for international students). Electronic applications accepted. *Application Contact:* Amanda Harper, Graduate Admissions Analyst, 985-549-5620, Fax: 985-549-5632, E-mail: admissions@southeastern.edu. *Dean,* Dr. Karen Fontenot, 985-549-2101, Fax: 985-549-5014, E-mail: kfontenot@southeastern.edu.

College of Business Students: 69 full-time (32 women), 10 part-time (4 women); includes 14 minority (3 Black or African American, non-Hispanic/Latino; 8 Hispanic/Latino; 3 Two or more races, non-Hispanic/Latino), 11 international. Average age 25. 81 applicants, 57% accepted, 26 enrolled. *Faculty:* 13 full-time (1 woman). Expenses: Contact institution. *Financial support:* In 2016–17, 18 students received support. Research assistantships, career-related internships or fieldwork, Federal Work-Study, institutionally sponsored loans, scholarships/grants, and unspecified assistantships available. Support available to part-time students. Financial award application deadline: 5/1; financial award applicants required to submit FAFSA. In 2016, 31 master's awarded. Offers business (MBA). *Application deadline:* For fall admission, 7/15 priority date for domestic students, 6/1 priority date for international students; for spring admission, 12/1 priority date for domestic students, 10/1 priority date for international students. Applications are processed on a rolling basis. *Application fee:* $20 ($30 for international students). Electronic applications accepted. *Application Contact:* Amanda Harper, Graduate Admissions Analyst, 985-549-5620, Fax: 985-549-5882, E-mail: admissions@southeastern.edu. *Interim Dean,* Dr. Antoinette Phillips, 985-549-2258, Fax: 985-549-5038, E-mail: business@southeastern.edu.

College of Education Students: 10 full-time (all women), 162 part-time (136 women); includes 58 minority (51 Black or African American, non-Hispanic/Latino; 5 Hispanic/Latino; 2 Two or more races, non-Hispanic/Latino), 1 international. Average age 37. 94 applicants, 65% accepted, 28 enrolled. *Faculty:* 22 full-time (19 women), 3 part-time/adjunct (1 woman). Expenses: Contact institution. *Financial support:* In 2016–17, 21 students received support. Research assistantships, teaching assistantships, career-related internships or fieldwork, Federal Work-Study, institutionally sponsored loans, scholarships/grants, and unspecified assistantships available. Support available to part-time students. Financial award application deadline: 5/1; financial award applicants required to submit FAFSA. In 2016, 103 master's, 2 doctorates awarded. *Program availability:* Part-time. Offers curriculum and instruction (M Ed); education (M Ed, MAT, Ed D); educational leadership (M Ed, Ed D); elementary education (MAT); special education (M Ed); special education: early interventionist (MAT). *Application deadline:* For fall admission, 7/15 priority date for domestic students, 6/1 priority date for international students; for spring admission, 12/1 priority date for domestic students, 10/1 priority date for international students. Applications are processed on a rolling basis. *Application fee:* $20 ($30 for international students). Electronic applications accepted. *Application Contact:* Amanda Harper, Graduate Admissions Analyst, 985-549-5620, Fax: 985-549-5632, E-mail: admissions@southeastern.edu. *Interim Dean,* Dr. Shirley Jacob, 985-549-2217, Fax: 985-549-2070, E-mail: shirly.jacob@southeastern.edu.

College of Nursing and Health Sciences Students: 163 full-time (132 women), 188 part-time (168 women); includes 81 minority (39 Black or African American, non-Hispanic/Latino; 1 American Indian or Alaska Native, non-Hispanic/Latino; 1 Asian, non-Hispanic/Latino; 24 Hispanic/Latino; 1 Native Hawaiian or other Pacific Islander, non-Hispanic/Latino; 15 Two or more races, non-Hispanic/Latino), 2 international. Average age 31. 292 applicants, 60% accepted, 60 enrolled. *Faculty:* 36 full-time (29 women), 11 part-time/adjunct (9 women). Expenses: Contact institution. *Financial support:* In 2016–

17, 28 students received support, including 8 research assistantships (averaging $9,413 per year), 4 teaching assistantships (averaging $9,275 per year); career-related internships or fieldwork, Federal Work-Study, institutionally sponsored loans, scholarships/grants, and unspecified assistantships also available. Support available to part-time students. Financial award application deadline: 5/1; financial award applicants required to submit FAFSA. In 2016, 113 master's, 4 doctorates awarded. *Program availability:* Part-time. Offers communication sciences and disorders (MS); counseling (MS); health and kinesiology (MS); nursing and health sciences (MS, MSN, DNP). *Application deadline:* For fall admission, 7/15 priority date for domestic students, 6/1 priority date for international students; for spring admission, 12/1 priority date for domestic students, 10/1 priority date for international students. Applications are processed on a rolling basis. *Application fee:* $20 ($30 for international students). Electronic applications accepted. *Application Contact:* Amanda Harper, Graduate Admissions Analyst, 985-549-5620, Fax: 985-549-5632, E-mail: admissions@southeastern.edu. *Dean,* Dr. Ann Carruth, 985-549-3772, Fax: 985-549-5179, E-mail: acarruth@southeastern.edu.

School of Nursing Students: 41 full-time (35 women), 131 part-time (115 women); includes 34 minority (18 Black or African American, non-Hispanic/Latino; 1 Asian, non-Hispanic/Latino; 13 Hispanic/Latino; 2 Two or more races, non-Hispanic/Latino). Average age 35. 42 applicants, 60% accepted, 17 enrolled. *Faculty:* 14 full-time (12 women), 5 part-time/adjunct (4 women). Expenses: Contact institution. *Financial support:* In 2016–17, 48 students received support. Federal Work-Study, institutionally sponsored loans, scholarships/grants, traineeships, tuition waivers (full), and unspecified assistantships available. Support available to part-time students. Financial award application deadline: 5/1; financial award applicants required to submit FAFSA. In 2016, 50 master's, 4 doctorates awarded. *Program availability:* Part-time. Offers family nurse practitioner (MSN); nursing education (MSN); nursing practice (DNP); psychiatric/mental health nurse practitioner (MSN). *Application deadline:* For fall admission, 7/15 priority date for domestic students, 6/1 priority date for international students; for spring admission, 12/1 priority date for domestic students, 10/1 priority date for international students. Applications are processed on a rolling basis. *Application fee:* $20 ($30 for international students). Electronic applications accepted. *Application Contact:* Sandra Meyers, Graduate Admissions Analyst, 985-549-5620, Fax: 985-549-5632, E-mail: admissions@southeastern.edu. *Department Head, School of Nursing,* Dr. Eileen Creel, 985-549-2156, Fax: 985-549-2869, E-mail: eileen.creel@southeastern.edu.

College of Science and Technology Students: 36 full-time (20 women), 8 part-time (3 women); includes 9 minority (1 Black or African American, non-Hispanic/Latino; 1 Asian, non-Hispanic/Latino; 7 Hispanic/Latino), 11 international. Average age 26. 47 applicants, 51% accepted, 17 enrolled. *Faculty:* 20 full-time (3 women). Expenses: Contact institution. *Financial support:* In 2016–17, 31 students received support, including 4 fellowships (averaging $10,800 per year), 9 research assistantships (averaging $9,978 per year), 10 teaching assistantships (averaging $9,722 per year); career-related internships or fieldwork, Federal Work-Study, institutionally sponsored loans, and unspecified assistantships also available. Support available to part-time students. Financial award application deadline: 5/1; financial award applicants required to submit FAFSA. In 2016, 20 master's awarded. *Program availability:* Part-time. Offers biology (MS); integrated science and technology (MS); science and technology (MS). *Application deadline:* For fall admission, 7/15 priority date for domestic students, 6/1 priority date for international students; for spring admission, 12/1 priority date for domestic students, 10/1 priority date for international students. Applications are processed on a rolling basis. *Application fee:* $20 ($30 for international students). Electronic applications accepted. *Application Contact:* Amanda Harper, Graduate Admissions Analyst, 985-549-5620, Fax: 985-549-5632, E-mail: admissions@southeastern.edu. *Dean,* Dr. Daniel McCarthy, 985-549-2055, Fax: 985-549-3396, E-mail: dmccarthy@southeastern.edu.

SOUTHEASTERN OKLAHOMA STATE UNIVERSITY, Durant, OK 74701-0609

General Information State-supported, coed, comprehensive institution. *Graduate housing:* Rooms and/or apartments available on a first-come, first-served basis to single and married students. Housing application deadline: 6/15. *Research affiliation:* U.S. Department of the Interior (biological sciences), U.S. Department of Agriculture (USDA) (biological sciences), National Science Foundation (chemistry, computer science, physical sciences), U.S. Fish and Wildlife Service (biological sciences), National Institutes of Health (biological sciences, chemistry, computer science, physical sciences).

GRADUATE UNITS

Department of Aviation Science *Program availability:* Part-time, evening/weekend. Offers aerospace administration and logistics (MS). Electronic applications accepted.

John Massey School of Business *Program availability:* Part-time, evening/weekend. Offers business (MBA). Electronic applications accepted.

School of Arts and Sciences *Program availability:* Part-time, evening/weekend. Offers biology (MT); computer information systems (MT); occupational safety and health (MT). Electronic applications accepted.

School of Behavioral Sciences *Program availability:* Part-time, evening/weekend. Offers clinical mental health counseling (MS). Electronic applications accepted.

School of Education *Program availability:* Part-time, evening/weekend. Offers math specialist (M Ed); reading specialist (M Ed); school administration (M Ed); school counseling (M Ed). Electronic applications accepted.

SOUTHEASTERN UNIVERSITY, Lakeland, FL 33801-6099

General Information Independent-religious, coed, comprehensive institution. *Enrollment:* 5,804 graduate, professional, and undergraduate students; 313 full-time matriculated graduate/professional students (198 women), 428 part-time matriculated graduate/professional students (273 women). *Enrollment by degree level:* 633 master's, 108 doctoral. *Graduate faculty:* 36 full-time (13 women), 7 part-time/adjunct (3 women). *Tuition:* Full-time $9450; part-time $6300 per credit. *Required fees:* $500; $250 per semester. One-time fee: $150. Tuition and fees vary according to degree level, campus/location and program. *Graduate housing:* On-campus housing not available. *Student services:* Campus employment opportunities, campus safety program, career counseling, exercise/wellness program, free psychological counseling, international student services, low-cost health insurance, services for students with disabilities, writing training. *Library facilities:* Steelman Library. *Collection:* Books: 81,194 (physical), 169,763 (digital/electronic).

Computer facilities: 156 computers available on campus for general student use. A campuswide network can be accessed from student residence rooms and from off campus. Online class registration, network programs are available.
Website: http://www.seu.edu/

GRADUATE UNITS

Barnett College of Ministry and Theology Expenses: Contact institution. *Program availability:* Evening/weekend, online learning. Offers ministerial leadership (MA, D Min); theological studies (MA); theology (M Div). *Dean,* 863-667-5000.

College of Behavioral and Social Sciences Expenses: Contact institution. *Program availability:* Evening/weekend. Offers human services (MA); international community development (MA); marriage and family counseling (MS); professional counseling (MS); school counseling (MS); social work (MSW). *Dean,* Erica H. Sirrine, 863-667-5341, E-mail: ehsirrine@seu.edu.

College of Education Expenses: Contact institution. Offers curriculum and instruction (Ed D); educational leadership (M Ed); elementary education (M Ed); exceptional student education (M Ed); exceptional student education/educational therapy (M Ed); organizational leadership (Ed D); reading education (M Ed); teaching English to speakers of other languages (M Ed). *Dean,* Amy N. Bratten, 863-667-5238, E-mail: anbratten@seu.edu.

Jannetides College of Business and Entrepreneurial Leadership Expenses: Contact institution. *Program availability:* Evening/weekend, online learning. Offers executive leadership (MBA); missional leadership (MBA); sport management (MBA). Electronic applications accepted. *Dean,* Lyle L. Bowlin, 863-667-5118, E-mail: llbowlin@seu.edu.

SOUTHEAST MISSOURI STATE UNIVERSITY, Cape Girardeau, MO 63701-4799

General Information State-supported, coed, comprehensive institution. CGS member. *Enrollment:* 11,978 graduate, professional, and undergraduate students; 442 full-time matriculated graduate/professional students (254 women), 784 part-time matriculated graduate/professional students (495 women). *Enrollment by degree level:* 1,120 master's, 17 doctoral, 89 other advanced degrees. *Graduate faculty:* 223 full-time (109 women), 42 part-time/adjunct (29 women). Tuition, state resident: full-time $3130; part-time $260.80 per credit hour. Tuition, nonresident: full-time $5842; part-time $486.80 per credit hour. *Required fees:* $33.70 per credit hour. *Graduate housing:* Room and/or apartments available on a first-come, first-served basis to single students; on-campus housing not available to married students. Typical cost: $5728 per year ($8508 including board). Housing application deadline: 12/1. *Student services:* Campus employment opportunities, campus safety program, career counseling, child daycare facilities, exercise/wellness program, free psychological counseling, international student services, multicultural affairs office, services for students with disabilities, teacher training, writing training. *Library facilities:* Kent Library. *Collection:* Books: 488,369 (physical), 180,596 (digital/electronic); Serial titles: 11,646 (physical), 66,947 (digital/electronic); Databases: 135. Weekly public service hours: 92.

Computer facilities: 1,550 computers available on campus for general student use. A campuswide network can be accessed from student residence rooms. Online class registration is available. Website: http://www.semo.edu/

General Application Contact: Dr. Allen Gathman, Interim Dean, School of Graduate Studies, 573-651-2062, Fax: 573-651-2001, E-mail: graduateschool@semo.edu.

GRADUATE UNITS

School of Graduate Studies Students: 448 full-time (258 women), 840 part-time (547 women); includes 96 minority (61 Black or African American, non-Hispanic/Latino; 4 American Indian or Alaska Native, non-Hispanic/Latino; 12 Asian, non-Hispanic/Latino; 19 Hispanic/Latino), 309 international. Average age 31. 840 applicants, 67% accepted, 445 enrolled. *Faculty:* 223 full-time (109 women), 42 part-time/adjunct (29 women). Expenses: Contact institution. *Financial support:* In 2016–17, 357 students received support, including 102 teaching assistantships with full tuition reimbursements available; career-related internships or fieldwork, Federal Work-Study, scholarships/grants, traineeships, tuition waivers (full), and unspecified assistantships also available. Financial award application deadline: 6/30; financial award applicants required to submit FAFSA. In 2016, 383 master's, 54 other advanced degrees awarded. *Program availability:* Part-time, evening/weekend, 100% online, blended/hybrid learning. Offers biology (MNS); career counseling (MA); chemistry (MNS); communication disorders (MA); counseling (MA, Ed S); criminal justice (MS); educational administration (MA, Ed D, Ed S); educational leadership (Ed D); elementary education (MA); environmental science (MS); exceptional child education (MA); health, human performance and recreation (MS); heritage interpretation (Certificate); higher education administration (MA); historic preservation (Certificate); history (MA); human environmental studies (MA); mathematics (MNS); mental health counseling (MA); middle and secondary education (MA); nursing (MSN); political science, philosophy and religion (MPA); polytechnic studies (MS); public history (MA); school counseling (MA); secondary administration (MA); teacher leadership (MA, Ed S); teaching English to speakers of other languages (MA). *Application deadline:* For fall admission, 8/1 for domestic students, 6/1 for international students; for spring admission, 11/21 for domestic students, 10/1 for international students; for summer admission, 5/15 for domestic students. Applications are processed on a rolling basis. *Application fee:* $30 ($40 for international students). Electronic applications accepted. *Application Contact:* Alisa Aleen McFerron, Assistant Director of Admissions for Operations, 573-651-5937, E-mail: amcferron@semo.edu. *Interim Dean of the School of Graduate Studies,* Dr. Allen Gathman, 573-651-2062, Fax: 573-651-2001, E-mail: graduateschool@semo.edu.

Harrison College of Business Students: 72 full-time (39 women), 112 part-time (41 women); includes 20 minority (10 Black or African American, non-Hispanic/Latino; 6 Asian, non-Hispanic/Latino; 4 Hispanic/Latino), 64 international. Average age 29. 106 applicants, 70% accepted, 55 enrolled. *Faculty:* 27 full-time (7 women), 1 (woman) part-time/adjunct. Expenses: Contact institution. *Financial support:* In 2016–17, 61 students received support. Career-related internships or fieldwork, Federal Work-Study, scholarships/grants, traineeships, tuition waivers (full), and unspecified assistantships available. Financial award application deadline: 6/30; financial award applicants required to submit FAFSA. In 2016, 65 master's awarded. *Program availability:* Part-time, evening/weekend, 100% online. Offers accounting (MBA); entrepreneurship (MBA); financial management (MBA); sport management (MBA). *Application deadline:* For fall admission, 8/1 for domestic students, 6/1 for international students; for spring admission, 11/21 for domestic students, 10/1 for international students; for summer admission, 5/15 for domestic students. Applications are processed on a rolling basis. *Application fee:* $30 ($40 for international students). Electronic applications accepted. *Application Contact:* Gail Amick, Admissions Specialist, 573-651-2590, Fax: 573-651-5936, E-mail: gamick@semo.edu. *Director, Graduate Business Studies,* Dr. James L. Caldwell, 573-651-2851, Fax: 573-651-5032, E-mail: jcaldwell@semo.edu.

SOUTHERN ADVENTIST UNIVERSITY, Collegedale, TN 37315-0370

General Information Independent-religious, coed, comprehensive institution. *Graduate housing:* Rooms and/or apartments available on a first-come, first-served basis to single and married students. Housing application deadline: 7/1.

GRADUATE UNITS

School of Business and Management *Program availability:* Part-time, evening/weekend, online learning. Offers accounting (MBA); church administration (MSA); church and nonprofit leadership (MBA); financial management (MFM); healthcare administration (MBA); management (MBA); marketing management (MBA); outdoor education (MSA). Electronic applications accepted.

School of Education and Psychology *Program availability:* Part-time, evening/weekend. Offers clinical mental health counseling (MS); inclusive education (MS Ed); instructional leadership (MS Ed); literacy education (MS Ed); outdoor teacher education (MS Ed); school counseling (MS). Electronic applications accepted.

School of Nursing *Program availability:* Part-time. Offers acute care nurse practitioner (MSN); adult nurse practitioner (MSN); family nurse practitioner (MSN); nurse educator (MSN). Electronic applications accepted.

School of Religion *Program availability:* Part-time. Offers Biblical and theological studies (MA); church leadership and management (M Min); church ministry and homiletics (M Min); evangelism and world mission (M Min); religious studies (MA).

School of Social Work *Program availability:* Online learning. Offers social work (MSW).

SOUTHERN ARKANSAS UNIVERSITY–MAGNOLIA, Magnolia, AR 71753

General Information State-supported, coed, comprehensive institution. *Enrollment:* 4,771 graduate, professional, and undergraduate students; 604 full-time matriculated graduate/professional students (143 women), 835 part-time matriculated graduate/professional students (315 women). *Enrollment by degree level:* 1,439 master's. *Graduate faculty:* 38 full-time (19 women), 33 part-time/adjunct (14 women). Tuition, state resident: full-time $2511; part-time $279 per credit hour. Tuition, nonresident: full-time $3726; part-time $414 per credit hour. *Required fees:* $307 per semester. Tuition and fees vary according to course load and program. *Graduate housing:* Rooms and/or apartments available on a first-come, first-served basis to single and married students. Typical cost: $2885 per year ($3285 including board) for single students; $5727 per year ($6127 including board) for married students. Room and board charges vary according to board plan and housing facility selected. Housing application deadline: 8/1. *Student services:* Campus employment opportunities, campus safety program, career counseling, exercise/wellness program, free psychological counseling, international student services, low-cost health insurance, multicultural affairs office, services for students with disabilities, writing training. *Library facilities:* Magale Library. *Collection:* Books: 176,437 (physical), 7,779 (digital/electronic); Serial titles: 301 (physical), 80 (digital/electronic); Databases: 155. Weekly public service hours: 87.

Computer facilities: 199 computers available on campus for general student use. A campuswide network can be accessed from student residence rooms and from off campus. Online class registration is available. Website: http://www.saumag.edu/

General Application Contact: Talia Burton, Administrative Assistant, School of Graduate Studies, 870-235-4150, Fax: 870-235-5227, E-mail: taliaburton@saumag.edu.

GRADUATE UNITS

School of Graduate Studies Students: 605 full-time (143 women), 879 part-time (352 women); includes 130 minority (113 Black or African American, non-Hispanic/Latino; 7 American Indian or Alaska Native, non-Hispanic/Latino; 2 Asian, non-Hispanic/Latino; 2 Hispanic/Latino; 6 Two or more races, non-Hispanic/Latino), 1,048 international. Average age 28. 904 applicants, 81% accepted, 262 enrolled. *Faculty:* 36 full-time (19 women), 33 part-time/adjunct (14 women). Expenses: Contact institution. *Financial support:* Career-related internships or fieldwork, Federal Work-Study, scholarships/grants, tuition waivers (full), and unspecified assistantships available. Financial award applicants required to submit FAFSA. In 2016, 278 master's awarded. *Program availability:* Part-time, 100% online, blended/hybrid learning. Offers agriculture (MS); business administration (MBA); clinical and mental health counseling (MS); computer and information sciences (MS); gifted and talented (M Ed); higher, adult and lifelong education (M Ed); kinesiology (M Ed); library media and information specialist (M Ed); public administration (MPA); school counseling K-12 (M Ed); student affairs and college counseling (M Ed); teaching (MAT). *Application deadline:* For fall admission, 7/20 for domestic students, 7/10 for international students; for spring admission, 12/1 for domestic students, 11/15 for international students; for summer admission, 4/1 for domestic students, 5/1 for international students. Applications are processed on a rolling basis. *Application fee:* $25 ($50 for international students). Electronic applications accepted. *Application Contact:* Shrijana Malakar, Admissions Specialist, 870-235-4150, Fax: 870-235-5227, E-mail: smalakar@saumag.edu. *Dean, School of Graduate Studies,* Dr. Kim Bloss, 870-235-4150, Fax: 870-235-5227, E-mail: kkbloss@saumag.edu.

THE SOUTHERN BAPTIST THEOLOGICAL SEMINARY, Louisville, KY 40280-0004

General Information Independent-religious, coed, comprehensive institution. *Graduate housing:* Rooms and/or apartments available on a first-come, first-served basis to single and married students.

GRADUATE UNITS

Billy Graham School of Missions, Evangelism and Ministry *Program availability:* Part-time, evening/weekend, online learning. Offers ministry (D Min); missiology (MA, D Miss); missions and evangelism (M Div, Th M, PhD); theological studies (MA).

School of Theology *Program availability:* Part-time, evening/weekend, online learning. Offers applied theology (D Min); biblical and theological studies (M Div); biblical counseling (M Div, MA, D Min); biblical spirituality (D Min); Christian ministry (M Div); expository preaching (D Min); pastoral studies (M Div); theological studies (MA); theology (Th M, PhD); worldview and apologetics (M Div).

SOUTHERN CALIFORNIA INSTITUTE OF ARCHITECTURE, Los Angeles, CA 90013

General Information Independent, coed, comprehensive institution. *Graduate housing:* On-campus housing not available.

GRADUATE UNITS

Graduate Program in Architecture Offers architecture (M Arch). Electronic applications accepted.

SOUTHERN CALIFORNIA SEMINARY, El Cajon, CA 92019

General Information Independent-religious, coed, comprehensive institution. *Graduate housing:* Rooms and/or apartments available on a first-come, first-served basis to single and married students.

GRADUATE UNITS

Graduate and Professional Programs *Program availability:* Part-time, evening/weekend, online learning. Offers Biblical studies (MABS); counseling psychology (MACP); marriage and family therapy (MAMFT); psychology (Psy D); religious studies (MRS); theology (M Div). Electronic applications accepted.

SOUTHERN CALIFORNIA UNIVERSITY OF HEALTH SCIENCES, Whittier, CA 90609-1166

General Information Independent, coed, graduate-only institution. *Graduate housing:* On-campus housing not available. *Research affiliation:* Samueli Institute (alternative health care), Anton B. Burg Foundation (alternative health care).

GRADUATE UNITS

College of Eastern Medicine *Program availability:* Part-time, evening/weekend. Offers Eastern medicine (MAOM, DAOM). Electronic applications accepted.

Los Angeles College of Chiropractic Offers chiropractic (DC). Electronic applications accepted.

SOUTHERN COLLEGE OF OPTOMETRY, Memphis, TN 38104-2222

General Information Independent, coed, graduate-only institution. *Graduate housing:* On-campus housing not available.

GRADUATE UNITS

Professional Program Offers optometry (OD).

SOUTHERN CONNECTICUT STATE UNIVERSITY, New Haven, CT 06515-1355

General Information State-supported, coed, comprehensive institution. CGS member. *Enrollment:* 10,320 graduate, professional, and undergraduate students; 893 full-time matriculated graduate/professional students (688 women), 1,464 part-time matriculated graduate/professional students (1,046 women). *Enrollment by degree level:* 2,082 master's, 89 doctoral, 186 other advanced degrees. *Graduate faculty:* 190 full-time (100 women), 64 part-time/adjunct (23 women). Tuition, state resident: full-time $6497; part-time $519 per credit hour. Tuition, nonresident: full-time $18,102; part-time $535 per credit hour. *Required fees:* $4722; $55 per semester. Tuition and fees vary according to program. *Graduate housing:* Room and/or apartments available on a first-come, first-served basis to single students; on-campus housing not available to married students. Typical cost: $6594 per year ($11,870 including board). Room and board charges vary according to board plan and housing facility selected. *Student services:* Campus employment opportunities, campus safety program, career counseling, exercise/wellness program, free psychological counseling, international student services, low-cost health insurance, multicultural affairs office, services for students with disabilities, teacher training, writing training. *Library facilities:* Hilton C. Buley Library. Collection: Books: 478,191 (physical), 135,134 (digital/electronic); Serial titles: 14,528 (physical), 158 (digital/electronic); Databases: 203. Students can reserve study rooms.

Computer facilities: 1,000 computers available on campus for general student use. A campuswide network can be accessed from student residence rooms and from off campus. Online class registration is available.
Website: http://www.southernct.edu/

General Application Contact: Lisa Galvin, Director of Graduate Admissions, 203-392-5250, Fax: 203-392-5235, E-mail: gradinfo@southernct.edu.

GRADUATE UNITS

School of Graduate Studies Students: 893 full-time (688 women), 1,464 part-time (1,046 women); includes 462 minority (225 Black or African American, non-Hispanic/Latino; 3 American Indian or Alaska Native, non-Hispanic/Latino; 44 Asian, non-Hispanic/Latino; 153 Hispanic/Latino; 1 Native Hawaiian or other Pacific Islander, non-Hispanic/Latino; 36 Two or more races, non-Hispanic/Latino), 30 international. Average age 33. 2,140 applicants, 49% accepted, 676 enrolled. *Faculty:* 190 full-time (100 women), 64 part-time/adjunct (23 women). Expenses: Contact institution. *Financial support:* Fellowships, research assistantships, teaching assistantships, career-related internships or fieldwork, Federal Work-Study, scholarships/grants, and unspecified assistantships available. Support available to part-time students. Financial award application deadline: 4/15; financial award applicants required to submit FAFSA. In 2016, 624 master's, 21 doctorates, 213 other advanced degrees awarded. *Program availability:* Part-time, evening/weekend, online learning. *Application deadline:* Applications are processed on a rolling basis. *Application fee:* $50. Electronic applications accepted. *Application Contact:* Lisa Galvin, Director of Graduate Admissions, 203-392-5240, Fax: 203-392-5235, E-mail: galvinl1@southernct.edu. *Dean,* Dr. Christine Broadbridge, 203-392-5236, Fax: 203-392-5235, E-mail: broadbridgc1@southernct.edu.

School of Arts and Sciences Students: 146 full-time (78 women), 213 part-time (132 women); includes 81 minority (30 Black or African American, non-Hispanic/Latino; 10 Asian, non-Hispanic/Latino; 33 Hispanic/Latino; 8 Two or more races, non-Hispanic/Latino), 7 international. Average age 32. 334 applicants, 49% accepted, 118 enrolled. *Faculty:* 78 full-time (36 women), 5 part-time/adjunct (1 woman). Expenses: Contact institution. *Financial support:* Teaching assistantships and career-related internships or fieldwork available. In 2016, 136 master's awarded. Offers art education (MS); arts and sciences (MA, MFA, MS, Diploma); biology (MS); chemistry (MS); computer science (MS; English (MA, MS); environmental education (MS); history (MA, MS); mathematics (MS); multicultural-bilingual education/teaching English to speakers of other languages (MS); political science (MS); psychology (MA); romance languages (MA); science education (MS, Diploma); sociology (MS); women's studies (MA). *Application deadline:* Applications are processed on a rolling basis. *Application fee:* $50. Electronic applications accepted. *Application Contact:* Lisa Galvin, Director of Graduate Admissions, 203-392-5240, Fax: 203-392-5235, E-mail: galvinl1@southernct.edu. *Dean,* Steven Breese, 203-392-5468, Fax: 203-392-6807, E-mail: breese@southernct.edu.

School of Business Students: 92 full-time (46 women), 82 part-time (45 women); includes 63 minority (35 Black or African American, non-Hispanic/Latino; 7 Asian, non-Hispanic/Latino; 17 Hispanic/Latino; 4 Two or more races, non-Hispanic/Latino), 8 international. Average age 31. 102 applicants, 66% accepted, 49 enrolled. *Faculty:* 17 full-time (2 women), 5 part-time/adjunct (1 woman). Expenses: Contact institution. *Financial support:* Career-related internships or fieldwork, scholarships/grants, and unspecified assistantships available. Financial award application deadline: 4/15; financial award applicants required to submit FAFSA. In 2016, 54 master's awarded. *Program availability:* Part-time, evening/weekend. Offers business (MBA); business

administration (MBA). *Application deadline:* For fall admission, 7/1 priority date for domestic students. Applications are processed on a rolling basis. *Application fee:* $50. Electronic applications accepted. *Application Contact:* Lisa Galvin, Director of Graduate Admissions, 203-392-5240, Fax: 203-392-5235, E-mail: galvinl1@southernct.edu. *Dean,* Dr. Samuel Andoh, 203-392-5616, Fax: 203-392-5674, E-mail: andohs1@southernct.edu.

School of Education Students: 190 full-time (159 women), 440 part-time (336 women); includes 83 minority (45 Black or African American, non-Hispanic/Latino; 1 American Indian or Alaska Native, non-Hispanic/Latino; 5 Asian, non-Hispanic/Latino; 27 Hispanic/Latino; 5 Two or more races, non-Hispanic/Latino), 4 international. Average age 32. 644 applicants, 48% accepted, 245 enrolled. *Faculty:* 40 full-time (27 women), 22 part-time/adjunct (17 women). Expenses: Contact institution. *Financial support:* Career-related internships or fieldwork, scholarships/grants, and unspecified assistantships available. Financial award application deadline: 4/15; financial award applicants required to submit FAFSA. In 2016, 232 master's, 15 doctorates, 203 other advanced degrees awarded. *Program availability:* Part-time. Offers classroom teacher specialist (Diploma); community counseling (MS); counseling (Diploma); education (MLS, MS, MS Ed, Ed D, Diploma); educational coach (Diploma); educational leadership (Ed D, Diploma); elementary education (MS); information studies (Diploma); library science (MLS); reading (MS, Diploma); research, statistics, and measurement (MS); school counseling (MS); school psychology (MS, Diploma); special education (MS Ed). *Application fee:* $50. Electronic applications accepted. *Application Contact:* Lisa Galvin, Director of Graduate Admissions, 203-392-5240, Fax: 203-392-5235, E-mail: galvinl1@southernct.edu. *Dean,* Dr. Stephen Hegedus, 203-392-5900, E-mail: hegeduss1@southernct.edu.

School of Health and Human Services Students: 426 full-time (378 women), 244 part-time (185 women); includes 137 minority (72 Black or African American, non-Hispanic/Latino; 12 Asian, non-Hispanic/Latino; 44 Hispanic/Latino; 9 Two or more races, non-Hispanic/Latino), 10 international. Average age 30. 1,045 applicants, 48% accepted, 264 enrolled. *Faculty:* 52 full-time (33 women), 31 part-time/adjunct (22 women). Expenses: Contact institution. *Financial support:* Career-related internships or fieldwork, scholarships/grants, and unspecified assistantships available. Financial award application deadline: 4/15; financial award applicants required to submit FAFSA. In 2016, 202 master's awarded. *Program availability:* Part-time, evening/weekend. Offers family nurse practitioner (MSN); health and human services (MPH, MS, MSN, MSW, Ed D); human performance (MS); nursing (Ed D); nursing education (MSN); physical education (MS); public health (MPH); recreation and leisure studies (MS); school health education (MS); social work (MSW); speech pathology (MS). *Application fee:* $50. Electronic applications accepted. *Application Contact:* Lisa Galvin, Director of Graduate Admissions, 203-392-5240, Fax: 203-392-5235, E-mail: galvinl1@southernct.edu. *Dean,* Dr. Sandra Bulmer, 203-392-7015, Fax: 203-302-8067, E-mail: bulmers1@southernct.edu.

SOUTHERN EVANGELICAL SEMINARY, Matthews, NC 28105

General Information Independent-religious, coed, primarily men, graduate-only institution. *Graduate housing:* On-campus housing not available.

GRADUATE UNITS

Graduate Programs *Program availability:* Part-time, evening/weekend, online learning. Offers apologetics (MA, D Min, Certificate); Christian education (MA); church ministry (MA, Certificate); divinity (Certificate); Islamic studies (MA, Certificate); Jewish studies (MA); philosophy (MA); philosophy of religion (PhD); religion (MA); theology (M Div); youth ministry (MA).

SOUTHERN ILLINOIS UNIVERSITY CARBONDALE, Carbondale, IL 62901-4701

General Information State-supported, coed, university. CGS member. *Enrollment:* 15,987 graduate, professional, and undergraduate students; 1,729 full-time matriculated graduate/professional students (901 women), 1,371 part-time matriculated graduate/professional students (669 women). *Enrollment by degree level:* 2,175 master's, 925 doctoral. *Graduate faculty:* 803 full-time (209 women), 26 part-time/adjunct (15 women). *Graduate housing:* Rooms and/or apartments available on a first-come, first-served basis to single and married students. Typical cost: $7680 per year ($12,010 including board) for single students; $8412 per year for married students. *Student services:* Campus employment opportunities, campus safety program, career counseling, child daycare facilities, exercise/wellness program, free psychological counseling, grant writing training, international student services, low-cost health insurance, multicultural affairs office, services for students with disabilities, teacher training, writing training. *Library facilities:* Morris Library plus 1 other. Collection: Books: 310,152 (physical), 307,707 (digital/electronic); Serial titles: 309 (physical), 49,681 (digital/electronic); Databases: 171. Weekly public service hours: 100; students can reserve study rooms. *Research affiliation:* NASA-Ames Research Center, Argonne National Laboratory.

Computer facilities: Computer purchase and lease plans are available. 1,900 computers available on campus for general student use. A campuswide network can be accessed from student residence rooms and from off campus. Online class registration is available.
Website: http://www.siu.edu/

General Application Contact: Susan Babbit, Admissions Supervisor, 618-453-4557, Fax: 618-453-4562, E-mail: susan@siu.edu.

GRADUATE UNITS

Graduate School *Program availability:* Part-time. Offers molecular, cellular and systemic physiology (MS, PhD); molecular, cellular, and systemic physiology (PhD); pharmacology (MS, PhD); physician assistant studies (MSPA).

College of Agriculture *Program availability:* Part-time. Offers agribusiness economics (MS); agriculture (MS); animal science (MS); food and nutrition (MS); forestry (MS); plant, soil, and general agriculture (MS).

College of Applied Science Offers applied science (M Arch, MS); architecture (M Arch); fire service and homeland security (MS); medical dosimetry (MS). Electronic applications accepted.

College of Business and Administration *Program availability:* Part-time. Offers accountancy (M Acc, PhD); business administration (MBA, PhD); business and administration (M Acc, MBA, PhD). Electronic applications accepted.

College of Education and Human Services *Program availability:* Part-time. Offers behavior analysis and therapy (MS); communication disorders and sciences (MS); community health education (MPH); curriculum and instruction (MS Ed, PhD); education (MS Ed); education and human services (MPH, MS, MS Ed, MSW, PhD); educational administration (MS Ed, PhD); educational psychology (MS Ed, PhD); health education (MS Ed, PhD); higher education (MS Ed); kinesiology (MS Ed);

recreation (MS Ed); social work (MSW); special education (MS Ed, PhD); workforce education and development (MS Ed, PhD). Electronic applications accepted.

College of Engineering Offers biomedical engineering (ME, MS); civil and environmental engineering (ME); civil engineering (MS); electrical and computer engineering (MS, PhD); engineering (ME, MS, PhD); engineering science (PhD); engineering sciences (PhD); mechanical engineering (MS); mining engineering (MS); quality engineering and management (MS).

College of Liberal Arts *Program availability:* Part-time. Offers anthropology (MA, PhD); clinical psychology (PhD); communication studies (MA, MS, PhD); composition (MA, PhD); counseling psychology (PhD); creative writing (MFA); criminology and criminal justice (MA, PhD); drawing (MFA); economics (MA, MS, PhD); experimental psychology (MA, MS); fiber/weaving (MFA); foreign languages and literatures (MA); geography (MS, PhD); glass (MFA); history (MA, PhD); liberal arts (MA, MFA, MM, MPA, MS, PhD); linguistics (MA); metalsmithing/blacksmithing (MFA); music (MM); painting (MFA); philosophy (MA, PhD); political science (MA, PhD); public administration (MPA); sociology (MA, PhD); speech/theater (PhD); teaching English to speakers of other languages (MA); theater (MFA).

College of Mass Communication and Media Arts *Program availability:* Part-time. Offers mass communication and media arts (MA, MFA, MS, PhD); media theory and research (MA); professional media and media management studies (MS).

College of Science *Program availability:* Part-time. Offers biological sciences (MS); chemistry and biochemistry (MS, PhD); computer science (MS, PhD); environmental resources and policy (PhD); geology (MS); geosciences (PhD); mathematics (MA, MS, PhD); molecular biology, microbiology, and biochemistry (MS, PhD); physics (MS, PhD); plant biology (MS, PhD); science (MA, MS, PhD); zoology (MS, PhD).

School of Law *Program availability:* Part-time. Offers general law (LL M, MLS); health law and policy (LL M, MLS); law (JD); legal studies (MLS). Electronic applications accepted.

SOUTHERN ILLINOIS UNIVERSITY EDWARDSVILLE, Edwardsville, IL 62026-0001

General Information State-supported, coed, comprehensive institution. CGS member. *Graduate housing:* Rooms and/or apartments available on a first-come, first-served basis to single and married students. Housing application deadline: 5/1. *Research affiliation:* Long Island Veterinary Clinic (electrical engineering), SSM DePaul Health Center (nursing), Nurturenergy (mechanical engineering), Tulsa Dental Products (dental medicine), Mallinckrodt (pharmacy), Schlumberger (mechanical engineering).

GRADUATE UNITS

Graduate School *Program availability:* Part-time, evening/weekend, blended/hybrid learning. Offers cultural heritage and resources management (MA, MS); diversity training (MA, MS); healthcare informatics (MS); organizational design thinking (MS); sustainability (MS). Electronic applications accepted.

College of Arts and Sciences *Program availability:* Part-time, evening/weekend, online learning. Offers art studio (MFA); art therapy counseling (MA); arts and sciences (MA, MFA, MM, MPA, MS, MSW, PSM, Postbaccalaureate Certificate); biology (MA, MS); chemistry (MS); computational and applied mathematics (MS); corporate and organizational communication (MA); creative writing (MA); environmental science management (PSM); environmental sciences (MS); geography (MS); health communication (MA); history (MA); interpersonal communication (MA); literature (MA, Postbaccalaureate Certificate); mass communications (MS); media literacy (Postbaccalaureate Certificate); museum studies (Postbaccalaureate Certificate); music (MM); music education (MM); music performance (MM); piano pedagogy (Postbaccalaureate Certificate); postsecondary mathematics education (MS); public administration (MPA); public relations (MA); pure mathematics (MS); school social work (MSW); social work (MSW); sociology (MS); statistics and operations research (MS); teaching English as a second language (MA, Postbaccalaureate Certificate); teaching of writing (MA, Postbaccalaureate Certificate); vocal pedagogy (Postbaccalaureate Certificate). Electronic applications accepted.

School of Business *Program availability:* Part-time, evening/weekend. Offers accountancy (MSA); business (MA, MBA, MMR, MS, MSA); business analytics (MBA); computer management and information systems (MS); economics and finance (MA, MS); management information systems (MBA); marketing research (MMR); project management (MBA); taxation (MSA). Electronic applications accepted.

School of Education, Health, and Human Behavior *Program availability:* Part-time, evening/weekend. Offers clinical child and school psychology (MS); clinical psychology (MA); college student personnel administration (MS Ed); curriculum and instruction (MS Ed); education, health, and human behavior (MA, MS, MS Ed, Ed D, Ed S, Post-Master's Certificate, Postbaccalaureate Certificate, SD); educational administration (MS Ed, Ed S); educational leadership (MS Ed, Ed D, Ed S, Postbaccalaureate Certificate); exercise and sport psychology (MS); exercise physiology (MS); industrial-organizational psychology (MA); instructional technology (MS Ed); learning, culture, and society (MS Ed); literacy education (MS Ed); literacy specialist (Post-Master's Certificate); physical education and coaching pedagogy (MS Ed); school psychology (SD); special education (MS Ed, Post-Master's Certificate); speech-language pathology (MS); Web-based learning (Postbaccalaureate Certificate). Electronic applications accepted.

School of Engineering *Program availability:* Part-time, evening/weekend. Offers computer science (MS); electrical engineering (MS); engineering (MS); environmental engineering (MS); geotechnical engineering (MS); industrial engineering (MS); mechanical engineering (MS); structural engineering (MS); transportation engineering (MS). Electronic applications accepted.

School of Nursing *Program availability:* Part-time, evening/weekend. Offers family nurse practitioner (MS, Post-Master's Certificate); health care and nursing administration (MS, Post-Master's Certificate); nurse anesthesia (DNP); nurse educator (MS, Post-Master's Certificate); nursing (MS, DNP, Post-Master's Certificate). Electronic applications accepted.

School of Dental Medicine Offers dental medicine (DMD). Electronic applications accepted.

School of Pharmacy Offers pharmacy education (Pharm D); pharmacy pediatrics (Pharm D). Electronic applications accepted.

SOUTHERN METHODIST UNIVERSITY, Dallas, TX 75275

General Information Independent-religious, coed, university. CGS member. *Graduate housing:* Rooms and/or apartments available on a first-come, first-served basis to single and married students. Housing application deadline: 5/31.

GRADUATE UNITS

Annette Caldwell Simmons School of Education and Human Development *Program availability:* Part-time, evening/weekend. Offers bilingual/ESL education (MBE);

counseling (MS); dispute resolution (MA); education (M Ed, PhD); education and human development (M Ed, MA, MBE, MLS, MS, PhD, Certificate); gifted education (MBE); liberal studies (MLS); reading and writing (M Ed); special education (M Ed); sport management (MS).

Bobby B. Lyle School of Engineering *Program availability:* Part-time, evening/weekend, online learning. Offers air pollution control and atmospheric sciences (PhD); applied science (MS); civil engineering (MS); computer engineering (MS, PhD); computer science (MS, PhD); datacenter systems engineering (MS); electrical engineering (MSEE, PhD); engineering (MA, MS, MS Cp E, MSEE, MSEM, MSIEM, MSME, DE, PhD); engineering management (MSEM, DE); environmental engineering (MS); environmental science (MS); information engineering and management (MSIEM); manufacturing systems management (MS); mechanical engineering (MSME, PhD); operations research (MS, PhD); packaging of electronic and optical devices (MS); security engineering (MS); software engineering (MS, DE); structural engineering (PhD); sustainability and development (MA); systems engineering (MS, PhD); telecommunications (MS); water and wastewater engineering (PhD).

Cox School of Business *Program availability:* Part-time, evening/weekend. Offers accounting (MSA); business (Exec MBA); business administration (EMBA, MBA); entrepreneurship (MS); finance (MBA, MSF); financial statement analysis (PMBA); general business (MBA); information technology and operations management (MBA); management (MSM); marketing (MBA); real estate (MBA); strategy (MBA); strategy and entrepreneurship (MBA). Electronic applications accepted.

Dedman College of Humanities and Sciences *Program availability:* Part-time, evening/weekend. Offers anthropology (PhD); applied economics (MA); applied economics and predictive analytics (MS); applied geophysics (MS); chemistry (MS, PhD); classical/medieval history (MA); clinical psychology (PhD); computational and applied mathematics (MS, PhD); earth sciences (MS, PhD); economics (PhD); English (MA, PhD); European history (MA); Hebrew Bible/Old Testament (PhD); history (PhD); history of the Christian tradition (PhD); humanities and sciences (MA, MS, PhD); Ibero-American history (MA); law and economics (MA); materials science and engineering (MS, PhD); medical anthropology (MA); medieval studies (MA); molecular and cellular biology (MA, MS, PhD); New Testament (PhD); physics (MS, PhD); religion and culture (PhD); religious ethics (PhD); religious studies (MA); statistical science (MS, PhD); systematics theology (PhD); United States history (MA). Electronic applications accepted.

Dedman School of Law *Program availability:* Part-time, evening/weekend. Offers law (JD, SJD); law (for foreign law school graduates) (LL M); law (general) (LL M); taxation (LL M). Electronic applications accepted.

Meadows School of the Arts *Program availability:* Evening/weekend. Offers arts (MA, MFA, MM, MM, MSM, PhD, Diploma). Electronic applications accepted.

Division of Art Offers studio art (MFA).

Division of Art History *Program availability:* Part-time, evening/weekend. Offers art history (MA); rhetorics of art, space and culture (PhD).

Division of Arts Management and Arts Entrepreneurship Offers international arts management (MM). MM offered jointly with Bocconi University Graduate School of Management in Milan and HEC Montreal. Electronic applications accepted.

Division of Music *Program availability:* Part-time. Offers composition (MM); conducting (MM); music education (MM); music history and literature (MM); performance (MM); piano performance and pedagogy (MM); theory pedagogy (MM). Electronic applications accepted.

Division of Theatre Offers acting (MFA); design (MFA). Electronic applications accepted.

Temerlin Advertising Institute Offers advertising (MA). Electronic applications accepted.

Perkins School of Theology *Program availability:* Part-time. Offers theology (CMM, M Div, MSM, MTS, D Min).

SOUTHERN NAZARENE UNIVERSITY, Bethany, OK 73008

General Information Independent-religious, coed, comprehensive institution. *Graduate housing:* Rooms and/or apartments available on a first-come, first-served basis to single and married students. Housing application deadline: 8/1.

GRADUATE UNITS

College of Professional and Graduate Studies *Program availability:* Part-time, evening/weekend. Offers counseling psychology (MA, MSCP); marital and family therapy (MA). Electronic applications accepted.

School of Business *Program availability:* Part-time, evening/weekend, online learning. Offers business administration (MBA); health care management (MBA); management (MS Mgt). Electronic applications accepted.

School of Kinesiology Offers sports management and administration (MA).

School of Nursing *Program availability:* Part-time, evening/weekend. Offers education (MS); nursing leadership (MS).

SOUTHERN NEW HAMPSHIRE UNIVERSITY, Manchester, NH 03106-1045

General Information Independent, coed, university. *Graduate housing:* Room and/or apartments available on a first-come, first-served basis to single students; on-campus housing not available to married students.

GRADUATE UNITS

Program in Nursing *Program availability:* Online learning. Offers clinical nurse leader (MSN); nursing (MSN); nursing education (Post Master's Certificate); nursing educator (MSN); patient safety and quality (MSN, Post Master's Certificate).

School of Arts and Sciences *Program availability:* Part-time, evening/weekend. Offers community mental health (Graduate Certificate); community mental health and mental health counseling (MS); fiction and nonfiction (MFA); teaching English as a foreign language (MS). Electronic applications accepted.

School of Business *Program availability:* Part-time, evening/weekend, online learning. Offers accounting (MBA, MS, Graduate Certificate); accounting finance (MS); accounting/auditing (MS); accounting/forensic accounting (MS); accounting/taxation (MS); athletic administration (MBA, Graduate Certificate); business administration (IMBA, MBA, Certificate, Graduate Certificate); corporate social responsibility (MBA); entrepreneurship (MBA); finance (MBA, MS, Graduate Certificate); finance/corporate finance (MS); finance/investments and securities (MS); forensic accounting (MBA); healthcare informatics (MBA); healthcare management (MBA); human resource management (Graduate Certificate); information technology (MS, Graduate Certificate); information technology management (MBA); international business (Graduate Certificate); international business and information technology (Graduate Certificate); international finance (Graduate Certificate); international sport management (Graduate Certificate); justice studies (MBA); leadership of nonprofit organizations (Graduate

Certificate); management (MS); marketing (MBA, MS, Graduate Certificate); operations and project management (MS); operations and supply chain management (MBA, Graduate Certificate); organizational leadership (MS); project management (MBA, Graduate Certificate); Six Sigma (MBA); Six Sigma quality (Graduate Certificate); social media marketing (MBA); sport management (MBA, MS, Graduate Certificate); sustainability and environmental compliance (MBA); workplace conflict management (MBA). Electronic applications accepted.

School of Education *Program availability:* Part-time, evening/weekend, online learning. Offers business education (M Ed); child development (M Ed); curriculum and instruction (M Ed); education (M Ed); educational leadership (M Ed, Ed D); educational studies (M Ed); elementary education (M Ed); English (MAT); English for speakers of other languages (M Ed); reading and writing specialist (M Ed); school business administration (Certificate); secondary education (M Ed); special education (M Ed); technology integration specialist (M Ed). Electronic applications accepted.

SOUTHERN OREGON UNIVERSITY, Ashland, OR 97520

General Information State-supported, coed, comprehensive institution. *Enrollment:* 5,916 graduate, professional, and undergraduate students; 235 full-time matriculated graduate/professional students (161 women), 125 part-time matriculated graduate/professional students (87 women). *Enrollment by degree level:* 360 master's. *Graduate faculty:* 212 full-time (92 women), 104 part-time/adjunct (67 women). Tuition, state resident: full-time $10,719; part-time $397 per credit. Tuition, nonresident: full-time $13,419; part-time $497 per credit. *Required fees:* $548. *Graduate housing:* Rooms and/or apartments available on a first-come, first-served basis to single and married students. Housing application deadline: 8/1. *Student services:* Campus employment opportunities, campus safety program, career counseling, child daycare facilities, exercise/wellness program, free psychological counseling, international student services, low-cost health insurance, multicultural affairs office, services for students with disabilities, teacher training, writing training. *Library facilities:* Lenn and Dixie Hannon Library. *Collection:* Books: 340,015 (physical), 135,298 (digital/electronic); Databases: 80. Students can reserve study rooms. *Research affiliation:* U.S. Forest Service (biology, ecology studies), U.S. Fish and Wildlife Service (forensics), Oregon Shakespeare Festival (theatre arts), Crater Lake National Park (scientific studies), Bureau of Land Management (ecological studies), Bear Creek Corporation (environmental studies).

Computer facilities: Computer purchase and lease plans are available. 750 computers available on campus for general student use. A campuswide network can be accessed from student residence rooms and from off campus. Online class registration, online account information including bill payment, online employee records for student workers are available.

Website: http://www.sou.edu/

General Application Contact: Kelly Moutsatson, Director of Admissions, 541-552-6411, Fax: 541-552-8403, E-mail: admissions@sou.edu.

GRADUATE UNITS

Graduate Studies Students: 235 full-time (161 women), 125 part-time (87 women); includes 52 minority (1 Black or African American, non-Hispanic/Latino; 6 American Indian or Alaska Native, non-Hispanic/Latino; 6 Asian, non-Hispanic/Latino; 23 Hispanic/Latino; 16 Two or more races, non-Hispanic/Latino), 22 international. Average age 34. 230 applicants, 64% accepted, 105 enrolled. *Faculty:* 150 full-time (64 women), 85 part-time/adjunct (52 women). Expenses: Contact institution. *Financial support:* In 2016–17, 15 students received support, including 15 research assistantships with partial tuition reimbursements available; career-related internships or fieldwork, Federal Work-Study, institutionally sponsored loans, scholarships/grants, and unspecified assistantships also available. Support available to part-time students. In 2016, 225 master's awarded. *Program availability:* Part-time, evening/weekend, online learning. Offers applied computer science (PSM); environmental education (MS); French language teaching (MA); interdisciplinary studies (MIS); performance (MM); psychology (MHC); Spanish language teaching (MA). *Application deadline:* For fall admission, 7/31 priority date for domestic and international students; for winter admission, 11/15 priority date for domestic and international students; for spring admission, 1/7 priority date for domestic and international students. Applications are processed on a rolling basis. *Application fee:* $60. Electronic applications accepted. *Application Contact:* Kelly Moutsatson, Director of Admissions, 541-552-6411, Fax: 541-552-8403, E-mail: admissions@sou.edu. *Dean of Graduate Studies,* Dr. Jody Waters, 541-552-6121, E-mail: watersj@sou.edu.

Ashland Center for Theatre Studies Students: 45 full-time (30 women), 3 part-time (2 women); includes 6 minority (2 Hispanic/Latino; 4 Two or more races, non-Hispanic/Latino), 2 international. Average age 40. 23 applicants, 87% accepted, 16 enrolled. *Faculty:* 5 full-time (2 women), 1 part-time/adjunct (0 women). Expenses: Contact institution. *Financial support:* Career-related internships or fieldwork, institutionally sponsored loans, scholarships/grants, and unspecified assistantships available. In 2016, 20 master's awarded. *Program availability:* Part-time. Offers theatre studies (MTS). *Application deadline:* For fall admission, 7/31 priority date for domestic and international students; for winter admission, 11/15 priority date for domestic and international students; for spring admission, 1/7 priority date for domestic and international students. Applications are processed on a rolling basis. *Application fee:* $60. Electronic applications accepted. *Application Contact:* Kelly Moutsatson, Director of Admissions, 541-552-6411, Fax: 541-552-8403, E-mail: admissions@sou.edu. *Graduate Program Coordinator,* Dr. Eric Levin, 541-552-6364, E-mail: levine@sou.edu.

School of Business Students: 28 full-time (13 women), 30 part-time (10 women); includes 13 minority (1 Black or African American, non-Hispanic/Latino; 2 Asian, non-Hispanic/Latino; 7 Hispanic/Latino; 3 Two or more races, non-Hispanic/Latino), 19 international. Average age 33. 65 applicants, 49% accepted, 25 enrolled. *Faculty:* 18 full-time (6 women), 8 part-time/adjunct (5 women). Expenses: Contact institution. *Financial support:* In 2016–17, 1 student received support, including 1 research assistantship with partial tuition reimbursement available; career-related internships or fieldwork, institutionally sponsored loans, scholarships/grants, and unspecified assistantships also available. In 2016, 16 master's awarded. *Program availability:* Part-time, evening/weekend, online learning. Offers accounting (Postbaccalaureate Certificate); business administration (MBA); international management (MIM). *Application deadline:* For fall admission, 7/31 priority date for domestic and international students; for winter admission, 11/15 priority date for domestic students, 11/14 priority date for international students; for spring admission, 1/7 priority date for domestic and international students. Applications are processed on a rolling basis. *Application fee:* $60. Electronic applications accepted. *Application Contact:* Kelly Moutsatson, Director of Admissions, 541-552-6411, Fax: 541-552-8403, E-mail: admissions@sou.edu. *Graduate Program Coordinator,* Dr. Mark Siders, 541-552-6709, E-mail: sidersm@sou.edu.

School of Education Students: 116 full-time (82 women), 86 part-time (68 women); includes 22 minority (1 American Indian or Alaska Native, non-Hispanic/Latino; 4

Asian, non-Hispanic/Latino; 8 Hispanic/Latino; 9 Two or more races, non-Hispanic/Latino). Average age 34. 81 applicants, 80% accepted, 49 enrolled. *Faculty:* 15 full-time (10 women), 27 part-time/adjunct (21 women). Expenses: Contact institution. *Financial support:* In 2016–17, 2 students received support. Career-related internships or fieldwork, institutionally sponsored loans, scholarships/grants, and unspecified assistantships available. In 2016, 107 master's awarded. *Program availability:* Online learning. Offers elementary education (MA Ed, MS Ed); secondary education (MA Ed, MS Ed); teaching (MAT). *Application deadline:* For fall admission, 7/31 priority date for domestic and international students; for winter admission, 11/15 priority date for domestic and international students; for spring admission, 1/7 priority date for domestic and international students. Applications are processed on a rolling basis. *Application fee:* $60. Electronic applications accepted. *Application Contact:* Kelly Moutsatson, Director of Admissions, 541-552-6411, Fax: 541-552-8403, E-mail: admissions@sou.edu. *Graduate Program Coordinator,* Dr. Gerry McCain, 541-552-6934, E-mail: mccaing@sou.edu.

SOUTHERN UNIVERSITY AND AGRICULTURAL AND MECHANICAL COLLEGE, Baton Rouge, LA 70813

General Information State-supported, coed, university. CGS member. *Graduate housing:* Room and/or apartments available on a first-come, first-served basis to single students; on-campus housing not available to married students. Housing application deadline: 6/30. *Research affiliation:* Michigan State University (language screening of African-Americans), University of Georgia (substance abuse prevention), The University of Alabama (diabetes), NASA (drinking water remote sensing, mechanical engineering), Livingston Observatory (gravitational waves, cosmic gravity waves, black waves).

GRADUATE UNITS

College of Business Offers business (MBA).

College of Nursing and Allied Health Offers nursing and allied health (MS, MSN, DNP, PhD); speech-language pathology (MS); therapeutic recreation (MS).

School of Nursing *Program availability:* Part-time. Offers educator/administrator (PhD); family health nursing (MSN); family nurse practitioner (Post Master's Certificate); geriatric nurse practitioner/gerontology (PhD); nursing (DNP).

Graduate School *Program availability:* Part-time. Offers science/mathematics education (PhD); special education (M Ed, PhD).

College of Agricultural, Family and Consumer Sciences Offers urban forestry (MS).

College of Arts and Humanities Offers arts and humanities (MA); mass communication (MA); social sciences (MA).

College of Education Offers administration and supervision (M Ed); counselor education (MA); education (M Ed, MA, MS, PhD); educational leadership (M Ed); elementary education (M Ed); media (M Ed); mental health counseling (MA); secondary education (M Ed).

College of Engineering Offers engineering (ME).

College of Sciences *Program availability:* Part-time. Offers analytical chemistry (MS); biochemistry (MS); biology (MS); environmental sciences (MS); information systems (MS); inorganic chemistry (MS); mathematics (MS); micro/minicomputer architecture (MS); operating systems (MS); organic chemistry (MS); physical chemistry (MS); physics (MS); rehabilitation counseling (MS); sciences (MA, MS).

Nelson Mandela School of Public Policy and Urban Affairs Offers criminal justice (MS); public administration (MPA); public policy (PhD); public policy and urban affairs (MA, MPA, MS, PhD); social sciences (MA).

Southern University Law Center *Program availability:* Part-time, evening/weekend. Offers law (JD). Electronic applications accepted.

SOUTHERN UNIVERSITY AT NEW ORLEANS, New Orleans, LA 70126-1009

General Information State-supported, coed, primarily women, comprehensive institution. *Graduate housing:* Room and/or apartments available on a first-come, first-served basis to single students; on-campus housing not available to married students.

GRADUATE UNITS

School of Graduate Studies *Program availability:* Part-time, evening/weekend. Offers criminal justice (MA); management information systems (MS); museum studies (MA); social work (MSW).

SOUTHERN UTAH UNIVERSITY, Cedar City, UT 84720-2498

General Information State-supported, coed, comprehensive institution. *Enrollment:* 9,299 graduate, professional, and undergraduate students; 165 full-time matriculated graduate/professional students (67 women), 697 part-time matriculated graduate/professional students (422 women). *Enrollment by degree level:* 862 master's. *Graduate faculty:* 48 full-time (13 women), 41 part-time/adjunct (13 women). Tuition and fees vary according to program. *Graduate housing:* Room and/or apartments available on a first-come, first-served basis to single students; on-campus housing not available to married students. Typical cost: $3167 per year ($7067 including board). Room and board charges vary according to board plan and housing facility selected. *Student services:* Campus employment opportunities, campus safety program, career counseling, exercise/wellness program, free psychological counseling, international student services, low-cost health insurance, multicultural affairs office, services for students with disabilities, teacher training. *Library facilities:* Gerald R Sherratt Library. *Collection:* Books: 239,788 (physical), 420,411 (digital/electronic); Databases: 218. Students can reserve study rooms.

Computer facilities: A campuswide network can be accessed from student residence rooms and from off campus. Online class registration is available.
Website: http://www.suu.edu/

General Application Contact: Dr. Mark C. Atkinson, Dean of Graduate and Continuing Studies, 435-865-8099, E-mail: onlineadmissions@suu.edu.

GRADUATE UNITS

Master of Accountancy/MBA Dual Degree Program Students: 1 full-time (0 women). Average age 29. 3 applicants, 100% accepted, 1 enrolled. Expenses: Contact institution. *Financial support:* Unspecified assistantships available. *Program availability:* Part-time, 100% online. *Application deadline:* For fall admission, 3/1 for domestic and international students; for spring admission, 10/1 for domestic and international students; for summer admission, 3/1 for domestic and international students. Applications are processed on a rolling basis. *Application fee:* $60 ($65 for international students). Electronic applications accepted. *Application Contact:* Patricia Palmer, Academic Advisor and Graduate Program Coordinator, 435-865-8167, Fax: 435-586-5493, E-mail: patriciapalmer@suu.edu.

Program in Accounting Students: 46 full-time (15 women), 36 part-time (13 women); includes 4 minority (1 Black or African American, non-Hispanic/Latino; 1 Asian, non-Hispanic/Latino; 1 Hispanic/Latino; 1 Two or more races, non-Hispanic/Latino). Average

age 27. 46 applicants, 74% accepted, 28 enrolled. *Faculty:* 5 full-time (0 women). Expenses: Contact institution. *Financial support:* Unspecified assistantships available. In 2016, 61 master's awarded. *Program availability:* Part-time, online learning. Offers accounting (M Acc). *Application deadline:* For fall admission, 3/1 for domestic and international students; for spring admission, 10/1 for domestic and international students; for summer admission, 3/1 for domestic and international students. Applications are processed on a rolling basis. *Application fee:* $60 ($65 for international students). Electronic applications accepted. *Application Contact:* Patricia Palmer, Academic Advisor and Graduate Program Coordinator, 435-865-8167, Fax: 435-586-5493, E-mail: patriciapalmer@suu.edu. *Chair, Accounting Department,* Dr. Robin Boneck, 435-586-7773, Fax: 435-586-5493, E-mail: boneck@suu.edu.

Program in Arts Administration Students: 10 full-time (6 women), 27 part-time (22 women); includes 8 minority (2 Asian, non-Hispanic/Latino; 5 Hispanic/Latino; 1 Native Hawaiian or other Pacific Islander, non-Hispanic/Latino), 1 international. Average age 31. 47 applicants, 77% accepted, 32 enrolled. *Faculty:* 1 (woman) full-time, 4 part-time/adjunct (1 woman). Expenses: Contact institution. *Financial support:* Tuition waivers and unspecified assistantships available. In 2016, 10 master's awarded. *Program availability:* Part-time, online learning. Offers arts administration (MA, MFA). *Application deadline:* For fall admission, 2/15 for domestic and international students. Applications are processed on a rolling basis. *Application fee:* $60 ($65 for international students). Electronic applications accepted. *Program Director/Assistant Professor,* Rachel Bishop, 435-586-7873, Fax: 435-865-8657, E-mail: bishopr@suu.edu.

Program in Business Administration Students: 18 full-time (5 women), 37 part-time (11 women); includes 4 minority (2 Black or African American, non-Hispanic/Latino; 2 Hispanic/Latino). Average age 33. 63 applicants, 40% accepted, 13 enrolled. *Faculty:* 8 full-time (0 women). Expenses: Contact institution. *Financial support:* Unspecified assistantships available. In 2016, 13 master's awarded. *Program availability:* Part-time, evening/weekend, 100% online. Offers business administration (MBA). *Application deadline:* For fall admission, 3/1 for domestic and international students; for spring admission, 10/1 for domestic and international students; for summer admission, 3/1 for domestic and international students. Applications are processed on a rolling basis. *Application fee:* $60 ($65 for international students). Electronic applications accepted. *Application Contact:* Patricia Palmer, Academic Advisor and Graduate Program Coordinator, 435-865-8167, Fax: 435-586-5493, E-mail: patriciapalmer@suu.edu. *Department Chair/MBA Program Director,* Dr. Kim Craft, 435-865-5414, Fax: 435-586-5493, E-mail: craft@suu.edu.

Program in Communication Students: 15 full-time (11 women), 42 part-time (24 women); includes 7 minority (1 Black or African American, non-Hispanic/Latino; 1 Asian, non-Hispanic/Latino; 4 Hispanic/Latino; 1 Native Hawaiian or other Pacific Islander, non-Hispanic/Latino). Average age 30. 32 applicants, 63% accepted, 17 enrolled. *Faculty:* 7 full-time (1 woman). Expenses: Contact institution. *Financial support:* Teaching assistantships with tuition reimbursements and unspecified assistantships available. Financial award application deadline: 3/15. In 2016, 17 master's awarded. *Program availability:* Part-time, online learning. Offers communication (MA). *Application deadline:* For fall admission, 6/15 for domestic and international students; for spring admission, 10/15 for domestic and international students. Applications are processed on a rolling basis. *Application fee:* $60 ($65 for international students). Electronic applications accepted. *Application Contact:* Dr. Matthew Barton, Graduate Coordinator, 435-586-7970, Fax: 435-865-8352, E-mail: bartonm@suu.edu. *Department Chair,* Dr. Arthur Challis, 435-586-7861, Fax: 435-865-8352, E-mail: challis@suu.edu.

Program in Cyber Security and Information Assurance Students: 4 full-time (1 woman), 18 part-time (1 woman); includes 3 minority (1 Asian, non-Hispanic/Latino; 1 Hispanic/Latino; 1 Native Hawaiian or other Pacific Islander, non-Hispanic/Latino). Average age 36. 17 applicants, 71% accepted, 9 enrolled. *Faculty:* 2 full-time (1 woman), 1 part-time/adjunct (0 women). Expenses: Contact institution. *Program availability:* Part-time, online only. Offers cyber security and information assurance (MS). *Application fee:* $60 ($65 for international students). Electronic applications accepted. *Application Contact:* Mary Gillins, Administrative Assistant, 435-586-5405, Fax: 435-865-8444, E-mail: marygillins@suu.edu. *Department Chair/Graduate Director,* Dr. Rob Robertson, 435-865-8560, Fax: 435-865-8444, E-mail: robertson@suu.edu.

Program in Education Students: 5 full-time (all women), 431 part-time (313 women); includes 25 minority (4 Black or African American, non-Hispanic/Latino; 2 American Indian or Alaska Native, non-Hispanic/Latino; 8 Asian, non-Hispanic/Latino; 8 Hispanic/Latino; 3 Native Hawaiian or other Pacific Islander, non-Hispanic/Latino). Average age 39. 85 applicants, 92% accepted, 64 enrolled. *Faculty:* 12 full-time (6 women), 28 part-time/adjunct (10 women). Expenses: Contact institution. *Financial support:* Tuition waivers (partial) available. In 2016, 119 master's awarded. *Program availability:* Part-time, 100% online. Offers education (M Ed, Certificate). *Application deadline:* For fall admission, 7/15 for domestic and international students; for spring admission, 11/15 for domestic and international students; for summer admission, 4/15 for domestic and international students. Applications are processed on a rolling basis. *Application fee:* $60 ($65 for international students). Electronic applications accepted. *Application Contact:* Tamara Lovell, Program Specialist, 435-865-8759, Fax: 435-865-8485, E-mail: tamaralovell@suu.edu. *Department Chair,* Dr. Bart Reynolds, 435-865-8125, Fax: 435-865-8485, E-mail: reynolds@suu.edu.

Program in Music Students: 13 full-time (4 women), 8 part-time (2 women); includes 1 minority (Hispanic/Latino). Average age 30. 15 applicants, 100% accepted, 14 enrolled. *Faculty:* 2 full-time (1 woman), 3 part-time/adjunct (0 women). Expenses: Contact institution. *Program availability:* Part-time, 100% online. Offers music education (MM Ed); music technology (MM). *Application fee:* $60 ($65 for international students). *Department Chair,* Dr. Keith Bradshaw, 435-586-7891, E-mail: bradshaw@suu.edu.

Program in Public Administration Students: 38 full-time (14 women), 61 part-time (27 women); includes 11 minority (2 Black or African American, non-Hispanic/Latino; 1 American Indian or Alaska Native, non-Hispanic/Latino; 3 Asian, non-Hispanic/Latino; 3 Hispanic/Latino; 2 Native Hawaiian or other Pacific Islander, non-Hispanic/Latino), 2 international. Average age 34. 53 applicants, 66% accepted, 35 enrolled. *Faculty:* 8 full-time (2 women), 1 part-time/adjunct (0 women). Expenses: Contact institution. *Financial support:* Tuition waivers (full and partial) and unspecified assistantships available. Financial award application deadline: 5/31. In 2016, 39 master's awarded. *Program availability:* Part-time, evening/weekend, 100% online. Offers public administration (MPA). *Application deadline:* For fall admission, 7/15 for domestic and international students; for spring admission, 11/15 for domestic and international students; for summer admission, 4/15 for domestic and international students. Applications are processed on a rolling basis. *Application fee:* $60 ($65 for international students). Electronic applications accepted. *MPA Program Director,* Dr. Angela Pool-Funai, 435-865-8153, Fax: 435-586-1925, E-mail: angelapoolfunai@suu.edu.

Program in Sports Conditioning Students: 15 full-time (6 women), 37 part-time (9 women); includes 5 minority (3 Black or African American, non-Hispanic/Latino; 1 American Indian or Alaska Native, non-Hispanic/Latino; 1 Hispanic/Latino). Average age 28. 26 applicants, 77% accepted, 18 enrolled. *Faculty:* 7 full-time (3 women). Expenses:

Contact institution. In 2016, 9 master's awarded. *Program availability:* Part-time, online only, three intensive summer courses/clinical workshops on campus for 1-2 weeks. Offers sports conditioning (MS). *Application deadline:* For fall admission, 7/15 for domestic and international students; for spring admission, 10/15 for domestic and international students; for summer admission, 2/15 for domestic and international students. Applications are processed on a rolling basis. *Application fee:* $60 ($65 for international students). Electronic applications accepted. *Application Contact:* Joan Anderson, Administrative Assistant, 435-586-7816, Fax: 435-865-8057, E-mail: stephanie-smith@leavitt.com. *Department Chair,* Dr. Camille Thomas, 435-586-7815, Fax: 435-865-8057, E-mail: camillethomas1@suu.edu.

SOUTHERN WESLEYAN UNIVERSITY, Central, SC 29630-1020

General Information Independent-religious, coed, comprehensive institution. *Graduate housing:* On-campus housing not available.

GRADUATE UNITS

Program in Business Administration *Program availability:* Evening/weekend. Offers business administration (MBA).

Program in Christian Ministries *Program availability:* Part-time, evening/weekend. Offers Christian ministries (M Min).

Program in Education *Program availability:* Evening/weekend. Offers education (M Ed). Program also offered at Greenville, S. C. site.

Program in Management *Program availability:* Evening/weekend. Offers management (MSM).

SOUTH FLORIDA BIBLE COLLEGE AND THEOLOGICAL SEMINARY, Deerfield Beach, FL 33441

General Information Proprietary, coed, comprehensive institution.

GRADUATE UNITS

Graduate Programs Offers biblical studies (MA); theology (M Div).

SOUTH TEXAS COLLEGE OF LAW HOUSTON, Houston, TX 77002-7000

General Information Independent, coed, graduate-only institution.

GRADUATE UNITS

Professional Program *Program availability:* Part-time, evening/weekend. Offers law (JD). Electronic applications accepted.

SOUTH UNIVERSITY, Montgomery, AL 36116-1120

General Information Proprietary, coed, comprehensive institution.

GRADUATE UNITS

Program in Business Administration Offers business administration (MBA).

Program in Clinical Mental Health Counseling Offers clinical mental health counseling (MA).

Program in Criminal Justice Offers criminal justice (MS).

Program in Healthcare Administration Offers healthcare administration (MBA).

Program in Information Systems and Technology Offers information systems and technology (MS).

Program in Nursing Offers nursing (MSN).

Program in Public Administration Offers public administration (MPA).

SOUTH UNIVERSITY, Royal Palm Beach, FL 33411

General Information Proprietary, coed, comprehensive institution.

GRADUATE UNITS

Program in Business Administration Offers business administration (MBA); healthcare administration (MBA).

Program in Clinical Mental Health Counseling Offers clinical mental health counseling (MA).

Program in Criminal Justice Offers criminal justice (MS).

Program in Information Systems and Technology Offers information systems and technology (MS).

Program in Nursing Offers family nurse practitioner (MS).

Program in Occupational Therapy Offers occupational therapy (OTD).

Program in Public Administration Offers public administration (MPA).

SOUTH UNIVERSITY, Tampa, FL 33614

General Information Proprietary, coed, comprehensive institution.

GRADUATE UNITS

Program in Business Administration Offers business administration (MBA).

Program in Criminal Justice Offers criminal justice (MS).

Program in Healthcare Administration Offers healthcare administration (MBA).

Program in Information Systems and Technology Offers information systems and technology (MS).

Program in Nursing Offers adult health nurse practitioner (MS); family nurse practitioner (MS); nurse educator (MS).

Program in Physician Assistant Studies Offers physician assistant studies (MS).

SOUTH UNIVERSITY, Savannah, GA 31406

General Information Proprietary, coed, comprehensive institution.

GRADUATE UNITS

Graduate Programs

College of Arts and Sciences Offers arts and sciences (MA, MS); clinical mental health counseling (MA); criminal justice (MS).

College of Business Offers corrections (MBA); entrepreneurship and small business (MBA); healthcare administration (MBA); hospitality management (MBA); leadership (MS); public administration (MPA); sustainability (MBA).

College of Health Professions Offers anesthesiologist assistant (MM Sc); health professions (MM Sc, MS); physician assistant studies (MS).

College of Nursing Offers nurse educator (MS).

Doctor of Ministry Program Offers ministry (D Min).

School of Pharmacy

SOUTH UNIVERSITY, Novi, MI 48377

General Information Proprietary, coed, comprehensive institution.

GRADUATE UNITS

Program in Business Administration Offers business administration (MBA).

Program in Clinical Mental Health Counseling Offers clinical mental health counseling (MA).
Program in Leadership Offers leadership (MS).
Program in Ministry Offers ministry (D Min).
Program in Nursing Offers nursing (MSN).

SOUTH UNIVERSITY, High Point, NC 27265
General Information Proprietary, coed, comprehensive institution.
GRADUATE UNITS
Program in Business Administration Offers business administration (MBA).
Program in Clinical Mental Health Counseling Offers clinical mental health counseling (MA).

SOUTH UNIVERSITY, Cleveland, OH 44128
General Information Proprietary, coed, comprehensive institution.
GRADUATE UNITS
Program in Business Administration Offers business administration (MBA).
Program in Clinical Mental Health Counseling Offers clinical mental health counseling (MA).

SOUTH UNIVERSITY, Columbia, SC 29203
General Information Proprietary, coed, comprehensive institution.
GRADUATE UNITS
Program in Business Administration Offers business administration (MBA).
Program in Clinical Mental Health Counseling Offers clinical mental health counseling (MA).
Program in Criminal Justice Offers criminal justice (MS).
Program in Healthcare Administration Offers healthcare administration (MBA).
Program in Leadership Offers leadership (MS).
Program in Nursing Offers nursing (MSN).
Program in Pharmacy Offers pharmacy (Pharm D).

SOUTH UNIVERSITY, Round Rock, TX 78681
General Information Proprietary, coed, comprehensive institution.
GRADUATE UNITS
Program in Business Administration Offers business administration (MBA).
Program in Clinical Mental Health Counseling Offers clinical mental health counseling (MA).
Program in Information Systems and Technology Offers information systems and technology (MS).

SOUTH UNIVERSITY, Glen Allen, VA 23060
General Information Proprietary, coed, comprehensive institution.
GRADUATE UNITS
Program in Business Administration Offers business administration (MBA).
Program in Clinical Mental Health Counseling Offers clinical mental health counseling (MA).
Program in Nursing Offers nursing (MSN).

SOUTH UNIVERSITY, Virginia Beach, VA 23452
General Information Proprietary, coed, comprehensive institution.
GRADUATE UNITS
Program in Business Administration Offers business administration (MBA).
Program in Clinical Mental Health Counseling Offers clinical mental health counseling (MA).
Program in Information Systems and Technology Offers information systems and technology (MS).
Program in Leadership Offers leadership (MS).
Program in Nursing Offers family nurse practitioner (MSN).

SOUTHWEST ACUPUNCTURE COLLEGE, Santa Fe, NM 87505
General Information Private, coed, primarily women, graduate-only institution. *Enrollment by degree level:* 290 master's. *Graduate faculty:* 63 full-time (35 women). *Tuition:* Full-time $17,000. *Graduate housing:* On-campus housing not available. *Student services:* Campus employment opportunities, services for students with disabilities. *Library facilities:* Southwest Acupuncture College Library.
Computer facilities: 14 computers available on campus for general student use. Online class registration is available.
Website: http://www.acupuncturecollege.edu/
General Application Contact: Academic Dean, 505-888-8898, E-mail: admin@acupuncturecollege.edu.
GRADUATE UNITS
Program in Oriental Medicine, Boulder Campus Expenses: Contact institution. *Financial support:* Scholarships/grants available. Financial award applicants required to submit FAFSA. *Program availability:* Part-time. Offers Oriental medicine (MS). *Application deadline:* For fall admission, 8/30 priority date for domestic students; for winter admission, 12/15 priority date for domestic students; for spring admission, 12/15 priority date for domestic students. Applications are processed on a rolling basis. *Application fee:* $50. *Application Contact:* Corine Danchik, Academic Dean, 303-581-9955, Fax: 303-581-9944, E-mail: boulder@acupuncturecollege.edu. *Campus Director,* Heather Lang, 303-581-9955, Fax: 303-581-9944, E-mail: boulder@acupuncturecollege.edu.
Program in Oriental Medicine, Santa Fe Campus Expenses: Contact institution. *Financial support:* Scholarships/grants available. Financial award applicants required to submit FAFSA. *Program availability:* Part-time. Offers Oriental medicine (MS). *Application deadline:* Applications are processed on a rolling basis. *Application fee:* $50. Electronic applications accepted. *Application Contact:* Susan Chaney, Academic Dean, 505-438-8884, Fax: 505-438-8883. *Campus Director,* Paul Rossignol, 505-438-8884, Fax: 505-438-8883.

SOUTHWEST BAPTIST UNIVERSITY, Bolivar, MO 65613-2597
General Information Independent-religious, coed, comprehensive institution. *Graduate housing:* Room and/or apartments available on a first-come, first-served basis to single students; on-campus housing not available to married students.

GRADUATE UNITS
Program in Business *Program availability:* Part-time, online learning. Offers business administration (MBA); health administration (MBA).
Program in Education *Program availability:* Part-time. Offers education (MS); educational administration (MS, Ed S).
Program in Physical Therapy Offers physical therapy (DPT).

SOUTHWEST COLLEGE OF NATUROPATHIC MEDICINE AND HEALTH SCIENCES, Tempe, AZ 85282
General Information Independent, coed, graduate-only institution. *Enrollment by degree level:* 376 doctoral. *Graduate faculty:* 18 full-time (10 women), 30 part-time/adjunct (19 women). *Tuition:* Full-time $33,660; part-time $330 per credit. *Required fees:* $1754. One-time fee: $860 full-time. Tuition and fees vary according to course load, program and student level. *Graduate housing:* On-campus housing not available. *Student services:* Campus employment opportunities, career counseling, exercise/wellness program, international student services, services for students with disabilities. *Library facilities:* SCNM Library plus 1 other. *Collection:* Books: 5,000 (physical), 270 (digital/electronic); Serial titles: 36 (physical), 85 (digital/electronic); Databases: 15. Weekly public service hours: 95; students can reserve study rooms. *Research affiliation:* Gaia Herbs, Arizona State University, Biodesign Institute (immune modulation, virology, genomics, herbal medicine), Emory University, Aviratek, LLC (antimicrobial botanicals).
Computer facilities: 16 computers available on campus for general student use. A campuswide network can be accessed from off campus. Online class registration is available.
Website: http://www.scnm.edu/
General Application Contact: Eve Adams, Director of Admissions, 480-858-9100 Ext. 213, Fax: 480-222-9413, E-mail: e.adams@scnm.edu.
GRADUATE UNITS
Doctor of Naturopathic Medicine Program Students: 343 full-time (258 women), 33 part-time (8 women); includes 130 minority (33 Black or African American, non-Hispanic/Latino; 26 Asian, non-Hispanic/Latino; 60 Hispanic/Latino; 11 Two or more races, non-Hispanic/Latino), 22 international. Average age 30. 199 applicants, 80% accepted, 100 enrolled. *Faculty:* 18 full-time (10 women), 29 part-time/adjunct (18 women). Expenses: Contact institution. *Financial support:* In 2016–17, 169 students received support. Federal Work-Study and scholarships/grants available. Financial award application deadline: 5/1; financial award applicants required to submit FAFSA. In 2016, 96 doctorates awarded. Offers naturopathic medicine (ND). *Application deadline:* For fall admission, 3/1 priority date for domestic and international students; for spring admission, 12/1 priority date for domestic and international students. Applications are processed on a rolling basis. *Application fee:* $115. Electronic applications accepted. *Application Contact:* Eve Adams, Director of Admissions, 480-858-9100 Ext. 213, Fax: 480-222-9413, E-mail: e.adams@scnm.edu. *Dean of Academic Affairs,* Dr. Garrett Thompson, 480-858-9100 Ext. 207, E-mail: g.thompson@scnm.edu.

SOUTHWESTERN ADVENTIST UNIVERSITY, Keene, TX 76059
General Information Independent-religious, coed, comprehensive institution. *Graduate housing:* Rooms and/or apartments available on a first-come, first-served basis to single and married students. Housing application deadline: 8/31.
GRADUATE UNITS
Business Administration Department *Program availability:* Part-time, evening/weekend. Offers accounting (MBA); finance (MBA); management/leadership (MBA).
Education Department *Program availability:* Part-time, evening/weekend. Offers curriculum and instruction with reading emphasis (M Ed); educational leadership (M Ed).

SOUTHWESTERN ASSEMBLIES OF GOD UNIVERSITY, Waxahachie, TX 75165-5735
General Information Independent-religious, coed, comprehensive institution. *Graduate housing:* Room and/or apartments guaranteed to single students.
GRADUATE UNITS
Thomas F. Harrison School of Graduate Studies *Program availability:* Part-time, evening/weekend, online learning. Offers Bible and theology (MS); Biblical studies (M Div); Christian school administration (MS); counseling (M Div); counseling psychology (clinical) (MCP); cross cultural missions (M Div); curriculum development (MS); early education administration (M Ed); history (MA); human services counseling (MS); middle and secondary education (M Ed); practical theology (M Div); theological studies (M Div). Electronic applications accepted.

SOUTHWESTERN BAPTIST THEOLOGICAL SEMINARY, Fort Worth, TX 76122-0000
General Information Independent-religious, coed, primarily men, graduate-only institution. *Graduate housing:* Rooms and/or apartments available on a first-come, first-served basis to single and married students. *Research affiliation:* Campus Crusade for Christ/Jesus Film Project (evangelical missions), DAWN: Discipling A Whole Nation (evangelical missions).
GRADUATE UNITS
Jack D. Terry School of Church and Family Ministries *Program availability:* Part-time, evening/weekend. Offers church and family ministries (MA, MACE, MACSE, DEM, PhD). Electronic applications accepted.
Roy Fish School of Evangelism and Missions Offers cross-cultural missions (MTS); evangelism (M Div); evangelism and missions (D Min); international church planting (M Div); Islamic studies (M Div, MA Islamic); missiology (MA Miss); missions (M Div); North American church planting (M Div); North American evangelism and international missions (D Min); theology (Th M); world Christian studies (PhD).
School of Church Music *Program availability:* Part-time. Offers church music (MACM, MAWSHP, MM, DMA, PhD). Electronic applications accepted.
School of Preaching Offers preaching (Th M, D Min, PhD, Certificate).
School of Theology *Program availability:* Part-time, evening/weekend. Offers ministry (D Min); theology (PhD). Electronic applications accepted.

SOUTHWESTERN CHRISTIAN UNIVERSITY, Bethany, OK 73008-0340
General Information Independent-religious, coed, comprehensive institution.
GRADUATE UNITS
Program in Ministry *Program availability:* Part-time. Offers church planting (M Min); church revitalization and renewal (M Min); intercultural studies (M Min); leadership

(M Min); life coaching (M Min); pastoral ministries (M Min); work place ministries (M Min). Electronic applications accepted.

SOUTHWESTERN COLLEGE, Winfield, KS 67156-2499

General Information Independent-religious, coed, comprehensive institution. *Enrollment:* 1,467 graduate, professional, and undergraduate students; 49 full-time matriculated graduate/professional students (25 women), 194 part-time matriculated graduate/professional students (109 women). *Enrollment by degree level:* 183 master's, 57 doctoral, 3 other advanced degrees. *Graduate faculty:* 10 full-time (7 women), 27 part-time/adjunct (16 women). *Tuition:* Full-time $8730; part-time $485 per credit hour. *Required fees:* $150. Tuition and fees vary according to degree level, campus/location and program. *Graduate housing:* Rooms and/or apartments available on a first-come, first-served basis to single and married students. Typical cost: $3350 per year ($7250 including board) for single students. Room and board charges vary according to board plan, campus/location and housing facility selected. *Student services:* Campus employment opportunities, campus safety program, career counseling, exercise/wellness program, free psychological counseling, international student services, services for students with disabilities, teacher training, writing training. *Library facilities:* Harold and Mary Ellen Deets Library. *Collection:* Books: 47,687 (physical), 478,000 (digital/electronic); Serial titles: 12 (physical), 19 (digital/electronic); Databases: 78. Weekly public service hours: 91; students can reserve study rooms.

Computer facilities: Computer purchase and lease plans are available. 50 computers available on campus for general student use. A campuswide network can be accessed from student residence rooms and from off campus. Online class registration is available.
Website: http://www.sckans.edu/

General Application Contact: Dean Clark, Executive Vice President, 620-229-6364, Fax: 620-229-6344, E-mail: dean.clark@sckans.edu.

GRADUATE UNITS

Education Programs Students: 27 full-time (18 women), 102 part-time (77 women); includes 17 minority (8 Black or African American, non-Hispanic/Latino; 1 American Indian or Alaska Native, non-Hispanic/Latino; 1 Asian, non-Hispanic/Latino; 6 Hispanic/Latino; 1 Native Hawaiian or other Pacific Islander, non-Hispanic/Latino), 32 international. Average age 38. 36 applicants, 64% accepted, 16 enrolled. *Faculty:* 7 full-time (5 women), 15 part-time/adjunct (12 women). Expenses: Contact institution. *Financial support:* In 2016–17, 8 students received support. Scholarships/grants available. Financial award applicants required to submit FAFSA. In 2016, 71 master's, 10 doctorates awarded. *Program availability:* Part-time, evening/weekend, 100% online, blended/hybrid learning. Offers curriculum and instruction (M Ed); early childhood education (M Ed); educational leadership (Ed D); special education (M Ed); teaching (MA). *Application deadline:* Applications are processed on a rolling basis. *Application fee:* $40. Electronic applications accepted. *Application Contact:* Dennis Russell, Director of Admissions and Student Services, 888-684-5335 Ext. 3372, Fax: 888-684-5218, E-mail: dennis.russell@sckans.edu. *Director of Education Operations,* Dana Thomson, 800-846-1543 Ext. 6253, Fax: 620-229-6253, E-mail: dana.thomson@sckans.edu.

Fifth-Year Graduate Programs Students: 22 full-time (7 women), 11 part-time (6 women); includes 10 minority (5 Black or African American, non-Hispanic/Latino; 2 American Indian or Alaska Native, non-Hispanic/Latino; 2 Hispanic/Latino; 1 Two or more races, non-Hispanic/Latino), 12 international. Average age 24. 33 applicants, 100% accepted, 24 enrolled. *Faculty:* 3 full-time (2 women), 1 part-time/adjunct (0 women). Expenses: Contact institution. *Financial support:* In 2016–17, 14 students received support, including 1 fellowship (averaging $23,940 per year); scholarships/grants and unspecified assistantships also available. Financial award applicants required to submit FAFSA. In 2016, 17 master's awarded. *Program availability:* Part-time. Offers management (MBA). *Application deadline:* For fall admission, 8/28 for domestic students; for spring admission, 1/23 for domestic students. Applications are processed on a rolling basis. *Application fee:* $25. Electronic applications accepted. *Application Contact:* Dean Clark, Executive Vice President, 800-846-1543 Ext. 6364, Fax: 620-229-6344, E-mail: dean.clark@sckans.edu. *Professor/Division Chair,* Dr. Kurt Keiser, 620-229-6361, E-mail: kurt.keiser@sckans.edu.

Professional Studies Programs Students: 81 part-time (26 women); includes 24 minority (10 Black or African American, non-Hispanic/Latino; 4 American Indian or Alaska Native, non-Hispanic/Latino; 1 Asian, non-Hispanic/Latino; 9 Hispanic/Latino). Average age 37. 61 applicants, 75% accepted, 18 enrolled. *Faculty:* 1 full-time (0 women), 12 part-time/adjunct (4 women). Expenses: Contact institution. *Financial support:* In 2016–17, 9 students received support. Unspecified assistantships and employee tuition benefits available. Financial award applicants required to submit FAFSA. In 2016, 61 master's awarded. *Program availability:* Part-time, evening/weekend, online only, 100% online. Offers business administration (MBA); leadership (MS); management (MS); security administration (MS); specialized ministries (MA). *Application deadline:* Applications are processed on a rolling basis. *Application fee:* $40. Electronic applications accepted. *Director of Admissions and Student Services,* Dennis Russell, 888-684-5335 Ext. 3372, Fax: 316-688-5218, E-mail: dennis.russell@sckans.edu.

SOUTHWESTERN COLLEGE, Santa Fe, NM 87502-4788

General Information Independent, coed, primarily women, graduate-only institution. *Graduate housing:* On-campus housing not available.

GRADUATE UNITS

Program in Art Therapy/Counseling *Program availability:* Part-time, evening/weekend. Offers art therapy/counseling (MA).

Program in Counseling *Program availability:* Part-time, evening/weekend. Offers counseling (MA).

Program in Grief, Loss and Trauma Counseling *Program availability:* Part-time, evening/weekend, online learning. Offers grief, loss and trauma counseling (MA, Certificate).

Program in Integral Somatic Psychology Offers integral somatic psychology (Certificate).

Program in Psychodrama and Action Methods Offers psychodrama and action methods (Certificate).

Program in Transformational Ecopsychology Offers transformational ecopsychology (Certificate).

SOUTHWESTERN LAW SCHOOL, Los Angeles, CA 90010

General Information Independent, coed, graduate-only institution. *Enrollment by degree level:* 977 doctoral. *Graduate faculty:* 60 full-time (30 women), 85 part-time/adjunct (33 women). *Tuition:* Full-time $50,090; part-time $33,470 per year. *Required fees:* $200; $200 per year. Tuition and fees vary according to degree level.

Graduate housing: Rooms and/or apartments available on a first-come, first-served basis to single and married students. Typical cost: $17,265 per year for single students; $17,265 per year for married students. Room charges vary according to housing facility selected. *Student services:* Campus employment opportunities, campus safety program, career counseling, exercise/wellness program, free psychological counseling, international student services, low-cost health insurance, multicultural affairs office, services for students with disabilities, writing training. *Library facilities:* Leigh H. Taylor Law Library. *Collection:* Books: 81,552 (physical), 44,027 (digital/electronic); Serial titles: 5,555 (physical), 5,831 (digital/electronic); Databases: 137. Weekly public service hours: 108; students can reserve study rooms.

Computer facilities: 107 computers available on campus for general student use. A campuswide network can be accessed from student residence rooms. Online class registration is available.
Website: http://www.swlaw.edu/

General Application Contact: Lisa Gear, Assistant Dean of Admissions, 213-738-6834, Fax: 213-383-1688, E-mail: admissions@swlaw.edu.

GRADUATE UNITS

Graduate and Professional Programs Students: 659 full-time (393 women), 318 part-time (173 women); includes 418 minority (64 Black or African American, non-Hispanic/Latino; 1 American Indian or Alaska Native, non-Hispanic/Latino; 86 Asian, non-Hispanic/Latino; 202 Hispanic/Latino; 5 Native Hawaiian or other Pacific Islander, non-Hispanic/Latino; 60 Two or more races, non-Hispanic/Latino), 16 international. Average age 27. 1,806 applicants, 52% accepted, 278 enrolled. *Faculty:* 60 full-time (30 women), 85 part-time/adjunct (33 women). Expenses: Contact institution. *Financial support:* Federal Work-Study, institutionally sponsored loans, and scholarships/grants available. Support available to part-time students. Financial award application deadline: 4/1; financial award applicants required to submit FAFSA. *Program availability:* Part-time, evening/weekend. Offers individualized studies (LL M); law (JD). *Application deadline:* For fall admission, 3/1 priority date for domestic students, 4/1 priority date for international students. Applications are processed on a rolling basis. *Application fee:* $60. Electronic applications accepted. *Application Contact:* Lisa Gear, Assistant Dean of Admissions, 213-738-6834, Fax: 213-383-1688, E-mail: admissions@swlaw.edu. *Dean,* Susan Westerberg Prager, 213-738-6710, Fax: 213-383-1688.

SOUTHWESTERN OKLAHOMA STATE UNIVERSITY, Weatherford, OK 73096-3098

General Information State-supported, coed, comprehensive institution. *Graduate housing:* Rooms and/or apartments available on a first-come, first-served basis to single and married students. Housing application deadline: 8/19. *Research affiliation:* Gulf Coast Research Laboratory.

GRADUATE UNITS

College of Arts and Sciences *Program availability:* Part-time. Offers art education (M Ed); arts and sciences (M Ed, MM); English (M Ed); mathematics (M Ed); music education (MM); natural sciences (M Ed); performance (MM); social sciences (M Ed).

College of Pharmacy Offers pharmacy (Pharm D).

College of Professional and Graduate Studies *Program availability:* Part-time, evening/weekend, online learning.

School of Behavioral Sciences and Education *Program availability:* Part-time, evening/weekend, online learning. Offers community counseling (M Ed); early childhood education (M Ed); educational administration (M Ed); elementary education (M Ed); health sciences and microbiology (M Ed); kinesiology (M Ed); parks and recreation management (M Ed); school counseling (MS); school psychology (MS); school psychometry (M Ed); secondary education (M Ed); special education (M Ed).

School of Business and Technology *Program availability:* Part-time, evening/weekend, online learning. Offers business and technology (MBA). MBA distance learning degree program offered to Oklahoma residents only.

SOUTHWEST MINNESOTA STATE UNIVERSITY, Marshall, MN 56258

General Information State-supported, coed, comprehensive institution. *Graduate housing:* Room and/or apartments available to single students; on-campus housing not available to married students.

GRADUATE UNITS

Department of Business and Public Affairs *Program availability:* Part-time, evening/weekend, online learning. Offers leadership (MBA); management (MBA); marketing (MBA). Electronic applications accepted.

Department of Education *Program availability:* Part-time, evening/weekend, online learning. Offers ESL (MS); math (MS); reading (MS); special education (MS); teaching, learning and leadership (MS).

SOUTHWEST UNIVERSITY, Kenner, LA 70062

General Information Proprietary, coed, comprehensive institution.

GRADUATE UNITS

MBA Program Offers business administration (MBA); management (MBA); organizational management (MBA).

Program in Criminal Justice Offers criminal justice (MS).

Program in Management Offers management (MA).

Program in Organizational Management Offers organizational management (MA).

SOUTHWEST UNIVERSITY OF VISUAL ARTS, Tucson, AZ 85716-2505

General Information Proprietary, coed, comprehensive institution.

GRADUATE UNITS

MFA Programs Offers motion arts (MFA); painting and drawing (MFA); photography (MFA).

SPALDING UNIVERSITY, Louisville, KY 40203-2188

General Information Independent-religious, coed, comprehensive institution. CGS member. *Enrollment:* 2,322 graduate, professional, and undergraduate students; 723 full-time matriculated graduate/professional students (584 women), 283 part-time matriculated graduate/professional students (221 women). *Enrollment by degree level:* 818 master's, 181 doctoral, 7 other advanced degrees. *Graduate faculty:* 143 full-time (95 women), 70 part-time/adjunct (46 women). *Tuition:* Full-time $15,300. *Graduate housing:* Room and/or apartments available on a first-come, first-served basis to single students; on-campus housing not available to married students. Typical cost: $4800 per year ($7600 including board). Room and board charges vary according to board plan and housing facility selected. *Student services:* Campus employment opportunities, campus safety program, career counseling, exercise/wellness program, free psychological counseling, international student services, services for students with disabilities, writing training. *Library facilities:* Spalding Library. *Collection:* Books: 70,000 (physical), 425,638 (digital/electronic); Serial titles: 102 (physical), 100,000 (digital/electronic); Databases: 70. Students can reserve study rooms.

Computer facilities: 259 computers available on campus for general student use. A campuswide network can be accessed from student residence rooms and from off campus. Online class registration is available.
Website: http://www.spalding.edu/

General Application Contact: Patricia Goodman, Director, Graduate Admissions, 502-873-4178, E-mail: pgoodman@spalding.edu.

GRADUATE UNITS

Graduate Studies Students: 723 full-time (584 women), 283 part-time (221 women); includes 225 minority (169 Black or African American, non-Hispanic/Latino; 2 American Indian or Alaska Native, non-Hispanic/Latino; 13 Asian, non-Hispanic/Latino; 16 Hispanic/Latino; 4 Native Hawaiian or other Pacific Islander, non-Hispanic/Latino; 21 Two or more races, non-Hispanic/Latino), 2 international. Average age 35. 512 applicants, 54% accepted, 244 enrolled. *Faculty:* 143 full-time (95 women), 70 part-time/adjunct (46 women). Expenses: Contact institution. *Financial support:* In 2016–17, 70 research assistantships (averaging $5,853 per year) were awarded; career-related internships or fieldwork, Federal Work-Study, scholarships/grants, and unspecified assistantships also available. Support available to part-time students. Financial award applicants required to submit FAFSA. In 2016, 241 master's, 33 doctorates awarded. *Program availability:* Part-time, evening/weekend. *Application deadline:* Applications are processed on a rolling basis. *Application fee:* $30. *Application Contact:* Admissions Office, 502-585-7111, E-mail: admissions@spalding.edu. Provost, Dr. Joann Berryman, 502-873-4405, E-mail: jberryman@spalding.edu.

College of Education Students: 123 full-time (92 women), 57 part-time (42 women); includes 67 minority (58 Black or African American, non-Hispanic/Latino; 1 Asian, non-Hispanic/Latino; 5 Hispanic/Latino; 3 Two or more races, non-Hispanic/Latino). Average age 38. 86 applicants, 59% accepted, 51 enrolled. *Faculty:* 24 full-time (17 women), 12 part-time/adjunct (4 women). Expenses: Contact institution. *Financial support:* In 2016–17, 125 students received support. Tuition waivers and unspecified assistantships available. Financial award applicants required to submit FAFSA. In 2016, 49 master's, 8 doctorates awarded. *Program availability:* Part-time, evening/weekend. Offers art teacher education (MAT); business teacher education (MAT); education (M Ed, MA, MAT, Ed D); elementary school education (MAT); executive (Ed D); foreign language (MAT); high school education (MAT); middle school education (MAT); scholar-practitioner (Ed D); secondary education (MAT); special education (learning and behavioral disorders) (MAT); student guidance counselor (M Ed); teacher leader (M Ed). *Application deadline:* Applications are processed on a rolling basis. *Application fee:* $30. Electronic applications accepted. *Application Contact:* Valerie Anderson, Administrative Assistant, 502-873-4260, E-mail: vanderson@spalding.edu. Associate Dean, Dr. Chris Walsh, 502-873-4272, E-mail: cwalsh@spalding.edu.

College of Social Sciences and Humanities Students: 144 full-time (107 women), 64 part-time (39 women); includes 48 minority (34 Black or African American, non-Hispanic/Latino; 2 American Indian or Alaska Native, non-Hispanic/Latino; 5 Asian, non-Hispanic/Latino; 1 Hispanic/Latino; 1 Native Hawaiian or other Pacific Islander, non-Hispanic/Latino; 5 Two or more races, non-Hispanic/Latino), 1 international. Average age 42. 83 applicants, 82% accepted, 67 enrolled. *Faculty:* 14 full-time (6 women), 4 part-time/adjunct (all women). Expenses: Contact institution. *Financial support:* In 2016–17, 2 research assistantships (averaging $10,148 per year) were awarded; career-related internships or fieldwork, Federal Work-Study, scholarships/grants, and unspecified assistantships also available. Financial award applicants required to submit FAFSA. In 2016, 103 master's awarded. *Program availability:* Part-time, evening/weekend, online learning. Offers business and communication (MS); social sciences and humanities (MFA, MS); writing (MFA). *Application fee:* $30. *Application Contact:* Gloria Johansen, Administrative Assistant, 502-873-4262, E-mail: gjohansen@spalding.edu. Chair, Dr. Melissa Chastain, 502-873-4251, E-mail: mchastain@spalding.edu.

Kosair College of Health and Natural Sciences Students: 378 full-time (317 women), 117 part-time (104 women); includes 73 minority (46 Black or African American, non-Hispanic/Latino; 6 Asian, non-Hispanic/Latino; 8 Hispanic/Latino; 2 Native Hawaiian or other Pacific Islander, non-Hispanic/Latino; 11 Two or more races, non-Hispanic/Latino), 1 international. Average age 30. 226 applicants, 50% accepted, 86 enrolled. *Faculty:* 62 full-time (42 women), 29 part-time/adjunct (25 women). Expenses: Contact institution. *Financial support:* In 2016–17, 66 research assistantships (averaging $13,380 per year) were awarded; career-related internships or fieldwork, scholarships/grants, and unspecified assistantships also available. Support available to part-time students. Financial award applicants required to submit FAFSA. In 2016, 121 master's, 25 doctorates awarded. *Program availability:* Part-time, evening/weekend. Offers adult nurse practitioner (MSN); athletic training (MS); clinical psychology (MA, Psy D); family nurse practitioner (MSN); health and natural sciences (MA, MS, MSN, MSW, DNP, Psy D, Post-Master's Certificate); leadership in nursing and healthcare (MSN); nurse educator (Post-Master's Certificate); nurse practitioner (Post-Master's Certificate); occupational therapy (MS); pediatric nurse practitioner (MSN); social work (MSW). *Application deadline:* For winter admission, 2/1 for domestic students. *Application fee:* $30. *Application Contact:* Cynthia James, Administrative Assistant, 502-873-4290, E-mail: cjames@spalding.edu.

SPERTUS INSTITUTE FOR JEWISH LEARNING AND LEADERSHIP, Chicago, IL 60605-1901

General Information Independent, coed, graduate-only institution. *Graduate housing:* On-campus housing not available.

GRADUATE UNITS

Program in Jewish Studies *Program availability:* Part-time, evening/weekend, online learning. Offers Jewish studies (MAJPS, MAJS, DJS, DSJS).

SPRING ARBOR UNIVERSITY, Spring Arbor, MI 49283-9799

General Information Independent-religious, coed, comprehensive institution. *Graduate housing:* Rooms and/or apartments available on a first-come, first-served basis to single and married students. Housing application deadline: 5/1.

GRADUATE UNITS

Gainey School of Business *Program availability:* Part-time, evening/weekend, online learning. Offers business (MBA).

School of Arts and Sciences *Program availability:* Part-time, online learning. Offers communication (MA); spiritual formation and leadership (MA).

School of Education *Program availability:* Part-time, evening/weekend, online learning. Offers education (MAE); reading (MAR); special education (MSE). Electronic applications accepted.

School of Human Services *Program availability:* Part-time, evening/weekend, online learning. Offers counseling (MAC); family studies (MAFS); nursing (MSN). Electronic applications accepted.

★ **SPRINGFIELD COLLEGE, Springfield, MA 01109-3797**
General Information Independent, coed, comprehensive institution. *Enrollment:* 839 full-time matriculated graduate/professional students (592 women), 192 part-time matriculated graduate/professional students (139 women). *Enrollment by degree level:* 886 master's, 145 doctoral. *Graduate faculty:* 211 full-time (110 women). *Tuition:* Full-time $29,640; part-time $988 per credit. *Required fees:* $195. *Graduate housing:* Rooms and/or apartments available on a first-come, first-served basis to single and married students. *Student services:* Campus employment opportunities, campus safety program, career counseling, child daycare facilities, exercise/wellness program, free psychological counseling, international student services, low-cost health insurance, multicultural affairs office, services for students with disabilities, teacher training, writing training. *Library facilities:* Babson Library.

Computer facilities: Computer purchase and lease plans are available. A campuswide network can be accessed from student residence rooms and from off campus.
Website: http://www.springfield.edu/

General Application Contact: Anne Griffin, Director of Graduate Admissions, 413-748-3225, Fax: 413-748-3694, E-mail: agriffin2@springfieldcollege.edu.

GRADUATE UNITS

Graduate Programs *Program availability:* Part-time, evening/weekend. Offers adapted physical education (MS); advanced-level coaching (M Ed); alcohol and substance abuse services (M Ed); art therapy (M Ed, MS, CAGS); athletic administration (MS); athletic counseling (MS, CAGS); athletic training (MS); business administration (MBA); clinical mental health counseling (M Ed, CAGS); counseling psychology (Psy D); educational studies (M Ed); exercise physiology (MS); health promotion and disease prevention (MS); human services (MS); industrial and organizational psychology (M Ed, CAGS); occupational therapy (MS); physical therapy (DPT); physician assistant (MS); psychiatric rehabilitation and substance abuse counseling (M Ed); recreation management (M Ed); school guidance counseling (M Ed, CAGS); secondary education (M Ed); special education (M Ed); sport and exercise psychology (MS); sport management (M Ed, MS); student personnel administration in higher education (M Ed). Electronic applications accepted.

School of Social Work *Program availability:* Part-time, evening/weekend. Offers advanced practice with children and adolescents (Post-Master's Certificate); social work (MSW). Electronic applications accepted.

See Display on next page and Close-Up on page 899.

SPRING HILL COLLEGE, Mobile, AL 36608-1791

General Information Independent-religious, coed, comprehensive institution. *Enrollment:* 1,491 graduate, professional, and undergraduate students; 6 full-time matriculated graduate/professional students (4 women), 89 part-time matriculated graduate/professional students (41 women). *Enrollment by degree level:* 77 master's, 18 other advanced degrees. *Graduate faculty:* 19 full-time (6 women), 4 part-time/adjunct (3 women). *Tuition:* Full-time $8200; part-time $490 per credit hour. Tuition and fees vary according to program. *Graduate housing:* On-campus housing not available. *Student services:* Campus safety program, career counseling, exercise/wellness program, writing training. *Library facilities:* Marnie and John Burke Memorial Library plus 1 other.

Computer facilities: A campuswide network can be accessed from student residence rooms and from off campus. Online class registration is available.
Website: http://www.shc.edu/

General Application Contact: Robert Stewart, Vice President of Enrollment, 251-380-3030, Fax: 251-460-2186, E-mail: rstewart@shc.edu.

GRADUATE UNITS

Graduate Programs Students: 6 full-time (4 women), 89 part-time (41 women); includes 15 minority (8 Black or African American, non-Hispanic/Latino; 1 American Indian or Alaska Native, non-Hispanic/Latino; 2 Asian, non-Hispanic/Latino; 4 Hispanic/Latino), 5 international. Average age 39. *Faculty:* 19 full-time (6 women), 4 part-time/adjunct (3 women). Expenses: Contact institution. *Financial support:* Applicants required to submit FAFSA. In 2016, 29 master's, 16 other advanced degrees awarded. *Program availability:* Part-time, evening/weekend. Offers business administration (MBA); clinical nurse leader (MSN, Post-Master's Certificate); early childhood education (MAT, MS Ed); educational theory (MS Ed); elementary education (MAT, MS Ed); faith companioning (Postbaccalaureate Certificate); fine arts (MLA); history and social science (MLA); leadership and ethics (MLA, Postbaccalaureate Certificate); literature (MLA); pastoral ministry (Postbaccalaureate Certificate); pastoral studies (MPS); secondary education (MAT, MS Ed); spiritual direction (Postbaccalaureate Certificate); studio art (Postbaccalaureate Certificate); theological studies (MTS); theology (MA). *Application deadline:* For fall admission, 8/1 priority date for domestic and international students; for spring admission, 12/1 priority date for domestic and international students. Applications are processed on a rolling basis. *Application fee:* $25 ($35 for international students). Electronic applications accepted. *Vice President of Enrollment*, Robert Stewart, 251-380-3030, Fax: 251-460-2186, E-mail: rstewart@shc.edu.

STANBRIDGE UNIVERSITY, Irvine, CA 92612

General Information Proprietary, coed, comprehensive institution.

GRADUATE UNITS

Program in Nursing *Program availability:* Online learning. Offers nursing (MSN).

Program in Occupational Therapy Offers occupational therapy (MS).

STANFORD UNIVERSITY, Stanford, CA 94305-2004

General Information Independent, coed, university. CGS member. *Enrollment:* 16,914 graduate, professional, and undergraduate students; 9,017 full-time matriculated graduate/professional students (3,507 women), 287 part-time matriculated graduate/professional students (80 women). *Enrollment by degree level:* 3,514 master's, 5,780 doctoral. *Graduate faculty:* 2,180 full-time (610 women). *Tuition:* Full-time $47,331. *Required fees:* $609. *Graduate housing:* Rooms and/or apartments guaranteed to single and married students. Typical cost: $15,412 per year for single students; $22,061 per year for married students. Room charges vary according to housing facility selected. Housing application deadline: 5/8. *Student services:* Campus employment opportunities, campus safety program, career counseling, child daycare facilities, exercise/wellness program, free psychological counseling, international student services, low-cost health insurance, multicultural affairs office, services for students with disabilities, teacher training. *Library facilities:* Green Library plus 20 others. *Collection:* Books: 9.5 million (physical), 1.5 million (digital/electronic); Serial titles: 77,000 (physical). Study areas open 24 hours, 5–7 days a week; students can reserve study rooms.

Computer facilities: Computer purchase and lease plans are available. 1,000 computers available on campus for general student use. A campuswide network can be accessed from student residence rooms and from off campus. Online class registration is available.

Website: http://www.stanford.edu/

General Application Contact: Graduate Admissions, 866-432-7472, Fax: 650-723-8371, E-mail: gradadmissions@stanford.edu.

GRADUATE UNITS

Graduate School of Business Offers business (MBA, PhD). Electronic applications accepted.

Graduate School of Education Offers curriculum and teacher education (MA); education (MA, MAE, PhD); elementary education (MAE); international comparative education (MA, PhD); learning, design, and technology (MA); policy, organization, and leadership studies (MA); secondary education (MAE). Electronic applications accepted.

Law School Offers corporate governance and practice (LL M); environmental law and policy (LL M); international economic law, business and policy (LL M); international legal studies (JSM); law (JD, JSD); law, science and technology (LL M); legal studies (MLS). Electronic applications accepted.

School of Earth, Energy and Environmental Sciences Offers earth system science (MS, PhD); earth, energy and environmental sciences (MS, PhD, Eng); energy resources engineering (MS, PhD, Eng); geological sciences (MS, PhD, Eng); geophysics (MS, PhD); petroleum engineering (MS, PhD). Electronic applications accepted.

School of Engineering Offers aeronautics and astronautics (MS, PhD, Eng); atmosphere and energy (MS, PhD); biomechanical engineering (MSE); chemical engineering (MS, PhD); computer science (MS, PhD); construction (MS); design impact (MSE); electrical engineering (MS, PhD); engineering (MS, MSE, PhD, Engr); environmental engineering and science (MS, PhD, Eng); environmental fluid mechanics and hydrology (PhD); geomechanics (MS); management science and engineering (MS, PhD); materials science and engineering (MS, PhD, Engr); mechanical engineering (MS, PhD, Engr); product design (MS); structural engineering (MS). Electronic applications accepted.

Institute for Computational and Mathematical Engineering Offers computational and mathematical engineering (MS, PhD). Electronic applications accepted.

School of Humanities and Sciences Offers anthropology (MA); applied and engineering physics (MS); applied physics (PhD); archaeology (PhD); art history (PhD); art practice (MFA); biology (MS, PhD); biophysics (PhD); chemistry (PhD); Chinese (MA, PhD); classics (MA, PhD); communication (MA, PhD); comparative literature (PhD); composition (DMA); computer-based music theory and acoustics (PhD); culture and society (PhD); data science (MS); design (MFA); documentary film and video (MFA); ecology and environment (PhD); economics (PhD); English (MA, PhD); financial mathematics (MS); French (MA, PhD); French and Italian (PhD); German studies (MA, PhD); history (MA, PhD); humanities and sciences (MA, MFA, MS, DMA, PhD); Italian (MA, PhD); Japanese (MA, PhD); linguistics (MA, PhD); mathematics (PhD); modern thought and literature (PhD); music, science, and technology (MA); musicology (PhD); philosophy (MA, PhD); physics (PhD); political science (MA, PhD); psychology (PhD); religious studies (PhD); Slavic languages and literatures (PhD); sociology (PhD);

Spanish (MA, PhD); statistics (PhD); theater and performance studies (PhD). Electronic applications accepted.

Center for East Asian Studies Offers East Asian studies (MA). Electronic applications accepted.

Center for Russian, East European and Eurasian Studies Offers Russian, East European and Eurasian studies (MA). Electronic applications accepted.

School of Medicine Offers bioengineering (MS, PhD); medicine (MS, MD, PhD). Electronic applications accepted.

Graduate Programs in Medicine Offers biochemistry (PhD); biostatistics (PhD); chemical and systems biology (PhD); developmental biology (MS, PhD); epidemiology and clinical research (MS, PhD); genetics (PhD); health policy (MS, PhD); medicine (MS, PhD); microbiology and immunology (PhD); molecular and cellular physiology (PhD); structural biology (PhD). Electronic applications accepted.

Stanford Center for Biomedical Informatics Research Offers biomedical informatics research (MS, PhD). Electronic applications accepted.

STARR KING SCHOOL FOR THE MINISTRY, Berkeley, CA 94709-1209

General Information Independent-religious, coed, graduate-only institution. *Graduate housing:* On-campus housing not available.

GRADUATE UNITS

Professional Program Offers theology (M Div).

STATE UNIVERSITY OF NEW YORK AT FREDONIA, Fredonia, NY 14063-1136

General Information State-supported, coed, comprehensive institution. *Enrollment:* 4,612 graduate, professional, and undergraduate students; 143 full-time matriculated graduate/professional students (115 women), 77 part-time matriculated graduate/professional students (50 women). *Enrollment by degree level:* 200 master's, 20 other advanced degrees. *Graduate faculty:* 54 full-time (31 women), 14 part-time/adjunct (11 women). Tuition, state resident: full-time $10,370; part-time $453 per credit. Tuition, nonresident: full-time $20,190; part-time $925 per credit. *Required fees:* $1619; $67.30 per credit hour. $403.80 per semester. *Graduate housing:* Room and/or apartments available on a first-come, first-served basis to single students; on-campus housing not available to married students. Typical cost: $8900 per year. Room charges vary according to board plan and housing facility selected. Housing application deadline: 8/24. *Student services:* Campus employment opportunities, campus safety program, career counseling, child daycare facilities, exercise/wellness program, free psychological counseling, grant writing training, international student services, low-cost health insurance, multicultural affairs office, services for students with disabilities, teacher training, writing training. *Library facilities:* Daniel A. Reed Library. *Collection:* Books: 18 million (physical); Serial titles: 48,000 (physical). Weekly public service hours: 68; students can reserve study rooms.

Computer facilities: Computer purchase and lease plans are available. 500 computers available on campus for general student use. A campuswide network can be accessed from student residence rooms and from off campus. Online class registration is available.

Website: http://www.fredonia.edu/

General Application Contact: Wendy S. Dunst, Interim Graduate Recruitment and Admissions Associate, 716-673-3808, Fax: 716-673-3712, E-mail: wendy.dunst@fredonia.edu.

GRADUATE UNITS

College of Education Students: 39 full-time (32 women), 54 part-time (33 women); includes 8 minority (1 Black or African American, non-Hispanic/Latino; 4 Asian, non-Hispanic/Latino; 2 Hispanic/Latino; 1 Two or more races, non-Hispanic/Latino). Average age 29. 60 applicants, 97% accepted, 39 enrolled. *Faculty:* 21 full-time (17 women), 11 part-time/adjunct (9 women). Expenses: Contact institution. *Financial support:* In 2016–17, 4 teaching assistantships with full and partial tuition reimbursements (averaging $7,075 per year) were awarded. Financial award application deadline: 3/15; financial award applicants required to submit FAFSA. In 2016, 56 master's awarded. *Program availability:* Part-time. Offers curriculum and instruction (MS Ed); literacy education (MS Ed); TESOL (MS Ed). *Application deadline:* For fall admission, 4/1 priority date for domestic and international students; for spring admission, 11/1 priority date for domestic students, 11/1 for international students. Applications are processed on a rolling basis. *Application fee:* $75. Electronic applications accepted. *Application Contact:* Wendy S. Dunst, Interim Graduate Recruitment and Admissions Associate, 716-673-3808, Fax: 716-673-3712, E-mail: wendy.dunst@fredonia.edu. *Dean*, Dr. Christine Givner, 716-673-3311, E-mail: christine.givner@fredonia.edu.

College of Liberal Arts and Sciences Students: 73 full-time (62 women), 9 part-time (6 women); includes 7 minority (1 Black or African American, non-Hispanic/Latino; 1 Asian, non-Hispanic/Latino; 2 Hispanic/Latino; 1 Native Hawaiian or other Pacific Islander, non-Hispanic/Latino; 2 Two or more races, non-Hispanic/Latino). Average age 24. 200 applicants, 25% accepted, 43 enrolled. *Faculty:* 58 full-time (28 women), 24 part-time/adjunct (16 women). Expenses: Contact institution. *Financial support:* In 2016–17, 5 students received support, including 14 teaching assistantships with full and partial tuition reimbursements available (averaging $5,957 per year); tuition waivers (full and partial) and unspecified assistantships also available. In 2016, 41 master's awarded. *Program availability:* Part-time, evening/weekend. Offers biology (MS); interdisciplinary studies (MS); speech pathology (MS). *Application deadline:* For fall admission, 4/1 priority date for domestic and international students; for spring admission, 11/1 priority date for domestic students, 11/1 for international students. Applications are processed on a rolling basis. *Application fee:* $75. Electronic applications accepted. *Application Contact:* Wendy S. Dunst, Interim Graduate Recruitment and Admissions Associate, 716-673-3808, Fax: 716-673-3712, E-mail: wendy.dunst@fredonia.edu. *Dean*, Dr. John L. Kijinski, 716-673-3173, E-mail: kijinski@fredonia.edu.

School of Music Students: 31 full-time (21 women), 14 part-time (11 women); includes 4 minority (2 Asian, non-Hispanic/Latino; 1 Hispanic/Latino; 1 Two or more races, non-Hispanic/Latino), 12 international. Average age 25. 46 applicants, 72% accepted, 14 enrolled. *Faculty:* 44 full-time (17 women), 58 part-time/adjunct (31 women). Expenses: Contact institution. *Financial support:* In 2016–17, 14 students received support, including 4 fellowships (averaging $7,314 per year). Financial award application deadline: 3/15; financial award applicants required to submit FAFSA. In 2016, 16 master's awarded. *Program availability:* Part-time. Offers music education (MM); music performance (MM); music theory/composition (MM); music therapy (MM). *Application deadline:* For fall admission, 4/1 priority date for domestic and international students; for spring admission, 11/1 priority date for domestic students, 11/1 for international students. Applications are processed on a rolling basis. *Application fee:* $75. Electronic applications accepted. *Application Contact:* Dr. Barry Kilpatrick, Admissions Coordinator, School of Music, 716-673-4635, E-mail: barry.kilpatrick@fredonia.edu. *Director, School of Music*, Dr. Melvin Unger, 716-673-3151, E-mail: melvin.unger@fredonia.edu.

STATE UNIVERSITY OF NEW YORK AT NEW PALTZ, New Paltz, NY 12561

General Information State-supported, coed, comprehensive institution. *Enrollment:* 7,628 graduate, professional, and undergraduate students; 431 full-time matriculated graduate/professional students (270 women), 404 part-time matriculated graduate/professional students (287 women). *Enrollment by degree level:* 835 master's. *Graduate housing:* On-campus housing not available. *Student services:* Campus employment opportunities, campus safety program, career counseling, child daycare facilities, free psychological counseling, international student services, low-cost health insurance, services for students with disabilities, teacher training. *Library facilities:* Sojourner Truth Library. *Collection:* Books: 447,549 (physical), 125,825 (digital/electronic); Serial titles: 240 (physical), 83,500 (digital/electronic); Databases: 95. Weekly public service hours: 103; students can reserve study rooms.

Computer facilities: 800 computers available on campus for general student use. A campuswide network can be accessed from student residence rooms and from off campus. Online class registration is available. Website: http://www.newpaltz.edu/

General Application Contact: Vika Shock, Director of Graduate Admissions, 845-257-3285, Fax: 845-257-3284, E-mail: gradschool@newpaltz.edu.

GRADUATE UNITS

Graduate School Students: 431 full-time (270 women), 404 part-time (287 women); includes 131 minority (25 Black or African American, non-Hispanic/Latino; 1 American Indian or Alaska Native, non-Hispanic/Latino; 17 Asian, non-Hispanic/Latino; 75 Hispanic/Latino; 13 Two or more races, non-Hispanic/Latino), 140 international. 884 applicants, 52% accepted, 233 enrolled. Expenses: Contact institution. *Financial support:* In 2016–17, 15 fellowships with partial tuition reimbursements (averaging $1,360 per year), 30 research assistantships with partial tuition reimbursements (averaging $5,000 per year), 40 teaching assistantships with partial tuition reimbursements (averaging $5,000 per year) were awarded; career-related internships or fieldwork, scholarships/grants, traineeships, health care benefits, and unspecified assistantships also available. Financial award application deadline: 8/1; financial award applicants required to submit FAFSA. In 2016, 430 master's, 29 other advanced degrees awarded. *Program availability:* Part-time, evening/weekend. *Application deadline:* For fall admission, 5/15 for domestic and international students; for spring admission, 11/15 for domestic and international students. *Application fee:* $50. Electronic applications accepted. *Application Contact:* Vika Shock, Director of Graduate Admissions, 845-257-3285, Fax: 845-257-3284, E-mail: shockv@newpaltz.edu. *Associate Provost for Academic Affairs/Dean*, Dr. Laurel M. Garrick Duhaney, 845-257-3947, Fax: 845-257-3284, E-mail: duhaneyl@newpaltz.edu.

School of Business Students: 57 full-time (27 women), 23 part-time (13 women); includes 23 minority (3 Black or African American, non-Hispanic/Latino; 7 Asian, non-Hispanic/Latino; 10 Hispanic/Latino; 3 Two or more races, non-Hispanic/Latino), 12 international. 57 applicants, 72% accepted, 27 enrolled. Expenses: Contact institution. *Financial support:* In 2016–17, 6 research assistantships with partial tuition reimbursements (averaging $5,000 per year), 1 teaching assistantship with partial tuition reimbursement (averaging $5,000 per year) were awarded;

scholarships/grants, traineeships, and unspecified assistantships also available. Financial award application deadline: 8/1. In 2016, 55 master's awarded. *Program availability:* Part-time, evening/weekend. Offers business administration (MBA); public accountancy (MBA). *Application deadline:* Applications are processed on a rolling basis. *Application fee:* $50. Electronic applications accepted. *Application Contact:* Aaron Hines, Director of MBA Program, 845-257-2968, E-mail: mba@newpaltz.edu. *Dean*, Dr. Kristin Backhaus, 845-257-2930, E-mail: mba@newpaltz.edu.

School of Education Students: 131 full-time (95 women), 269 part-time (217 women); includes 77 minority (14 Black or African American, non-Hispanic/Latino; 1 American Indian or Alaska Native, non-Hispanic/Latino; 6 Asian, non-Hispanic/Latino; 50 Hispanic/Latino; 6 Two or more races, non-Hispanic/Latino). 132 applicants, 79% accepted, 73 enrolled. Expenses: Contact institution. *Financial support:* Scholarships/grants available. Financial award application deadline: 8/1. In 2016, 177 master's, 29 other advanced degrees awarded. *Program availability:* Part-time, evening/weekend. Offers adolescence education: biology (MAT, MS Ed); adolescence education: chemistry (MAT, MS Ed); adolescence education: earth science (MAT, MS Ed); adolescence education: English (MAT, MS Ed); adolescence education: French (MAT, MS Ed); adolescence education: social studies (MAT, MS Ed); adolescence education: Spanish (MAT, MS Ed); adolescence special education (7-12) (MS Ed); adolescence special education and literacy (MS Ed); childhood education 1-6 (MS Ed, MST); childhood special education (1-6) (MS Ed); childhood special education and literacy (MS Ed); early childhood special education (B-2) (MS Ed); education (MAT, MPS, MS Ed, MST, AC, CAS); educational leadership (MS Ed); humanistic/multicultural education (MPS, AC); literacy education 5-12 (MS Ed); literacy education and childhood special education (MS Ed); literacy education B-6 (MS Ed); multicultural education (AC); school building leader (CAS); school district business leader (CAS); school district leader (CAS); second language education (MS Ed, AC); special education (MS Ed); teaching English language learners (AC). *Application deadline:* For fall admission, 3/1 for domestic and international students; for spring admission, 10/1 for domestic and international students. *Application fee:* $50. Electronic applications accepted. *Application Contact:* Vika Shock, Director of Graduate Admissions, 845-257-3285, Fax: 845-257-3284, E-mail: gradschool@newpaltz.edu. *Dean*, Dr. Michael Rosenberg, 845-257-2800, E-mail: schoolofed@newpaltz.edu.

School of Fine and Performing Arts Students: 53 full-time (41 women), 19 part-time (17 women); includes 5 minority (1 Black or African American, non-Hispanic/Latino; 1 Asian, non-Hispanic/Latino; 2 Hispanic/Latino; 1 Two or more races, non-Hispanic/Latino), 13 international. 16 applicants, 81% accepted, 9 enrolled. Expenses: Contact institution. *Financial support:* In 2016–17, 8 research assistantships with partial tuition reimbursements (averaging $5,000 per year), 7 teaching assistantships with partial tuition reimbursements (averaging $5,000 per year) were awarded; scholarships/grants also available. Financial award application deadline: 8/1. In 2016, 27 master's awarded. *Program availability:* Part-time, evening/weekend. Offers ceramics (MFA); fine and performing arts (MFA, MS, MS Ed); metal (MFA); music therapy (MS); painting/drawing (MFA); printmaking (MFA); sculpture (MFA); visual arts education (MS Ed). *Application deadline:* For fall admission, 2/15 priority date for domestic students, 2/15 for international students. Applications are processed on a rolling basis. *Application fee:* $50. Electronic applications accepted. *Application Contact:* Vika Shock, Director of Graduate Admissions, 845-257-3286, Fax: 845-257-3284, E-mail: gradschool@newpaltz.edu. *Dean*, Prof. Jeni Mokren, 845-257-3860, E-mail: mokrenj@newpaltz.edu.

School of Liberal Arts and Sciences Students: 102 full-time (82 women), 50 part-time (30 women); includes 20 minority (3 Black or African American, non-Hispanic/Latino; 2 Asian, non-Hispanic/Latino; 12 Hispanic/Latino; 3 Two or more races, non-Hispanic/Latino), 1 international. 282 applicants, 34% accepted, 65 enrolled. Expenses: Contact institution. *Financial support:* In 2016–17, 1 research assistantship with partial tuition reimbursement (averaging $5,000 per year), 28 teaching assistantships with partial tuition reimbursements (averaging $5,000 per year) were awarded. Financial award application deadline: 8/1. In 2016, 52 master's awarded. *Program availability:* Part-time, evening/weekend. Offers communication disorders (MS); English (MA); liberal arts and sciences (MA, MS, AC); mental health counseling (MS, AC); psychology (MA); school counseling (MS). *Application deadline:* For fall admission, 2/1 for domestic and international students; for spring admission, 11/15 for domestic and international students. Applications are processed on a rolling basis. *Application fee:* $50. Electronic applications accepted. *Application Contact:* Vika Shock, Director of Graduate Admissions, 845-257-3286, E-mail: gradschool@newpaltz.edu. *Dean*, Dr. Laura Barrett, 845-257-3520, E-mail: barrett@newpaltz.edu.

School of Science and Engineering Students: 88 full-time (24 women), 49 part-time (13 women); includes 6 minority (4 Black or African American, non-Hispanic/Latino; 2 Asian, non-Hispanic/Latino), 114 international. 278 applicants, 54% accepted, 26 enrolled. Expenses: Contact institution. *Financial support:* In 2016–17, 15 fellowships with partial tuition reimbursements (averaging $1,360 per year), 4 teaching assistantships with partial tuition reimbursements (averaging $5,000 per year) were awarded. Financial award application deadline: 8/1. In 2016, 120 master's awarded. *Program availability:* Part-time, evening/weekend. Offers computer science (MS); electrical engineering (MS); science and engineering (MS). *Application deadline:* For fall admission, 5/15 for domestic and international students; for spring admission, 11/15 for domestic and international students. Applications are processed on a rolling basis. *Application fee:* $50. Electronic applications accepted. *Application Contact:* Vika Shock, Director of Graduate Admission, 845-257-3286, E-mail: gradschool@newpaltz.edu. *Dean*, Dr. Daniel Freedman, 845-257-3728, E-mail: freedmad@newpaltz.edu.

STATE UNIVERSITY OF NEW YORK AT OSWEGO, Oswego, NY 13126

General Information State-supported, coed, comprehensive institution. CGS member. *Graduate housing:* Room and/or apartments available on a first-come, first-served basis to single students; on-campus housing not available to married students. Housing application deadline: 4/1. *Research affiliation:* Intel Corporation (research and education), IBM (research and education), Alcan (research and education), MACTEC (research and education), Entergy (research and education).

GRADUATE UNITS

Graduate Studies *Program availability:* Part-time. Offers art (MA); graphic design and digital media (MA).

College of Liberal Arts and Sciences *Program availability:* Part-time. Offers chemistry (MS); English (MA); history (MA); human computer interaction (MA); liberal arts and sciences (MA, MS).

School of Business *Program availability:* Part-time, evening/weekend. Offers business (MBA).

School of Communication, Media and the Arts Offers strategic communication (MA).

School of Education *Program availability:* Part-time. Offers adolescence education (MST); agriculture (MS Ed); art education (MAT); business and marketing (MS Ed); childhood education (MST); curriculum and instruction (MS Ed); education (MAT, MS, MS Ed, MST, CAS); educational administration (CAS); family and consumer sciences (MS Ed); health careers (MS Ed); literacy education (MS Ed); mental health counseling (MS); school building leadership (CAS); special education (MS Ed); technical education (MS Ed); technology (MS Ed); trade education (MS Ed).

STATE UNIVERSITY OF NEW YORK AT PLATTSBURGH, Plattsburgh, NY 12901-2681

General Information State-supported, coed, comprehensive institution. *Graduate housing:* Room and/or apartments available on a first-come, first-served basis to single students; on-campus housing not available to married students. Housing application deadline: 5/1. *Research affiliation:* New York State Sea Grant (environmental science), Miner Agricultural Research Institute (environmental science).

GRADUATE UNITS

School of Arts and Sciences *Program availability:* Part-time. Offers arts and sciences (MA, MS, PSM, CAS); natural science (MS, PSM); school psychology (MA, CAS).

School of Education, Health, and Human Services *Program availability:* Part-time. Offers adolescence education (MST); biology 7-12 (MST); birth to grade 2 (MS Ed); birth to grade 6 (MS Ed); birth-grade 6 (MS Ed); chemistry 7-12 (MST); childhood education (grades 1-6) (MST); clinical mental health counseling (MS, Advanced Certificate); early childhood birth-grade 6 (Advanced Certificate); earth science 7-12 (MST); education, health, and human services (MA, MS, MS Ed, MST, Advanced Certificate, CAS); educational leadership (CAS); English 7-12 (MST); French 7-12 (MST); grades 1 to 6 (MS Ed); grades 5-12 (MS Ed); grades 7 to 12 (MS Ed); mathematics 7-12 (MST); physics 7-12 (MST); school counselor (MS Ed, CAS); social studies 7-12 (MST); Spanish 7-12 (MST); speech-language pathology (MA); student affairs counseling (MS); teacher education: teaching and learning (MS Ed).

STATE UNIVERSITY OF NEW YORK COLLEGE AT CORTLAND, Cortland, NY 13045

General Information State-supported, coed, comprehensive institution. *Graduate housing:* Room and/or apartments available on a first-come, first-served basis to single students; on-campus housing not available to married students.

GRADUATE UNITS

Graduate Studies *Program availability:* Part-time, evening/weekend. Electronic applications accepted.

School of Arts and Sciences *Program availability:* Part-time, evening/weekend. Offers arts and sciences (MA, MAT, MS Ed); biology (MAT); chemistry (MAT); English (MA); history (MA); mathematics (MAT); mathematics and physics (MS Ed); physics (MAT, MS Ed); second language education (MS Ed).

School of Education *Program availability:* Part-time, evening/weekend. Offers childhood education (MST); education (MS Ed, MST, CAS); literacy education (MS Ed); school building leader (CAS); school building leader and school district leader (CAS); school district business leader (CAS); school district leader (CAS); teaching students with disabilities (MS Ed).

School of Professional Studies *Program availability:* Part-time, evening/weekend. Offers adapted physical education (MS Ed); coaching pedagogy (MS Ed); communication sciences and disorders (MS); community health (MS); health education (MST); international sport management (MS); outdoor education (MS, MS Ed); physical education leadership (MS Ed); recreation management (MS, MS Ed); sport management (MS); therapeutic recreation (MS, MS Ed).

STATE UNIVERSITY OF NEW YORK COLLEGE AT GENESEO, Geneseo, NY 14454-1401

General Information State-supported, coed, comprehensive institution. *Enrollment:* 5,521 graduate, professional, and undergraduate students; 33 full-time matriculated graduate/professional students (23 women), 46 part-time matriculated graduate/professional students (36 women). *Enrollment by degree level:* 79 master's. *Graduate faculty:* 13 full-time (7 women), 2 part-time/adjunct (both women). Tuition, state resident: full-time $10,870; part-time $453 per credit. Tuition, nonresident: full-time $22,210; part-time $925 per credit. *Required fees:* $865; $35.85 per credit hour. *Graduate housing:* Room and/or apartments available on a first-come, first-served basis to single students; on-campus housing not available to married students. Typical cost: $8650 per year ($12,872 including board). Room and board charges vary according to board plan and housing facility selected. Housing application deadline: 5/1. *Student services:* Campus employment opportunities, campus safety program, career counseling, exercise/wellness program, free psychological counseling, grant writing training, international student services, low-cost health insurance, multicultural affairs office, services for students with disabilities, teacher training. *Library facilities:* Milne Library plus 1 other. *Collection:* Books: 335,648 (physical), 147,389 (digital/electronic); Serial titles: 1,420 (physical), 224,286 (digital/electronic); Databases: 420. Weekly public service hours: 109; students can reserve study rooms. *Research affiliation:* Rochester City School District/School #19 (education), Avon School District (education), The Community Place of Greater Rochester (reading literacy), Central Library of Rochester (education), The Genesee Valley Educational Partnership (education), Greater Rochester Summer Learning Association (education).

Computer facilities: 351 computers available on campus for general student use. A campuswide network can be accessed from student residence rooms and from off campus. Online class registration is available. Website: http://www.geneseo.edu/

General Application Contact: Michael R. George, Graduate Enrollment Coordinator, 585-245-5148, Fax: 585-245-5550, E-mail: georgem@geneseo.edu.

GRADUATE UNITS

Graduate Studies Students: 33 full-time (23 women), 46 part-time (36 women); includes 8 minority (3 Black or African American, non-Hispanic/Latino; 1 American Indian or Alaska Native, non-Hispanic/Latino; 2 Asian, non-Hispanic/Latino; 2 Hispanic/Latino). Average age 24. 57 applicants, 63% accepted, 28 enrolled. *Faculty:* 13 full-time (7 women), 2 part-time/adjunct (both women). Expenses: Contact institution. *Financial support:* Research assistantships with full tuition reimbursements, career-related internships or fieldwork, scholarships/grants, health care benefits, tuition waivers (full), and unspecified assistantships available. Support available to part-time students. Financial award application deadline: 4/1; financial award applicants required to submit FAFSA. *Program availability:* Part-time, evening/weekend. *Application deadline:* For fall admission, 4/1 priority date for domestic students; for spring admission, 11/1 priority date for domestic students. *Application fee:* $50. *Application Contact:* Michael R. George, Graduate Enrollment Coordinator, 585-245-5148, E-mail: georgem@

geneseo.edu. *Assistant Provost for Curriculum and Assessment,* Dr. Savitri V. Iyer, 585-245-5531, Fax: 585-245-5032, E-mail: iyer@geneseo.edu.

School of Business Students: 17 full-time (8 women). Average age 22. 29 applicants, 76% accepted, 17 enrolled. *Faculty:* 5 full-time (2 women). Expenses: Contact institution. *Financial support:* Research assistantships with full tuition reimbursements available. Financial award application deadline: 4/1; financial award applicants required to submit FAFSA. In 2016, 15 master's awarded. Offers accounting (MS). *Application deadline:* For fall admission, 6/1 priority date for domestic students. Applications are processed on a rolling basis. *Application fee:* $50. Electronic applications accepted. *Application Contact:* Michael R. George, Graduate Enrollment Coordinator, 585-245-5148, Fax: 585-245-5550, E-mail: georgem@geneseo.edu. *Dean of the School of Business,* Dr. Denise Rotondo, 585-245-5367, Fax: 585-245-5467, E-mail: rotondo@geneseo.edu.

School of Education Students: 16 full-time (15 women), 46 part-time (36 women); includes 8 minority (3 Black or African American, non-Hispanic/Latino; 1 American Indian or Alaska Native, non-Hispanic/Latino; 2 Asian, non-Hispanic/Latino; 2 Hispanic/Latino). Average age 26. 28 applicants, 50% accepted, 11 enrolled. *Faculty:* 8 full-time (5 women), 2 part-time/adjunct (both women). Expenses: Contact institution. *Financial support:* In 2016–17, 9 students received support, including 9 research assistantships with full tuition reimbursements available (averaging $8,823 per year); fellowships, career-related internships or fieldwork, scholarships/grants, health care benefits, tuition waivers (full), and unspecified assistantships also available. Support available to part-time students. Financial award application deadline: 4/1; financial award applicants required to submit FAFSA. In 2016, 40 master's awarded. *Program availability:* Part-time. Offers childhood multicultural education (MS Ed); early childhood education (MS Ed); education (MS Ed); English 7-12 (MS Ed); math 7-12 (MS Ed); reading and literacy (MS Ed); Spanish 7-12 (MS Ed). *Application deadline:* For fall admission, 4/1 priority date for domestic students; for spring admission, 11/1 for domestic students. Applications are processed on a rolling basis. *Application fee:* $50. Electronic applications accepted. *Application Contact:* Michael R. George, Graduate Enrollment Coordinator, 585-245-5148, Fax: 585-245-5550, E-mail: georgem@geneseo.edu. *Dean of School of Education,* Dr. Anjoo Sikka, 585-245-5151, Fax: 585-245-5220, E-mail: sikka@geneseo.edu.

STATE UNIVERSITY OF NEW YORK COLLEGE AT OLD WESTBURY, Old Westbury, NY 11568-0210

General Information State-supported, coed, comprehensive institution. *Enrollment:* 4,461 graduate, professional, and undergraduate students; 125 full-time matriculated graduate/professional students (70 women), 94 part-time matriculated graduate/professional students (42 women). *Enrollment by degree level:* 187 master's, 5 other advanced degrees. *Graduate faculty:* 39 full-time (17 women), 11 part-time/adjunct (7 women). Tuition, state resident: full-time $10,870; part-time $453 per credit. Tuition, nonresident: full-time $22,210; part-time $925 per credit. *Required fees:* $24.35 per credit. $76 per semester. Tuition and fees vary according to course load. *Graduate housing:* Room and/or apartments available on a first-come, first-served basis to single students; on-campus housing not available to married students. Typical cost: $7240 per year ($10,870 including board). Room and board charges vary according to board plan. *Student services:* Campus safety program, career counseling, child daycare facilities, exercise/wellness program, free psychological counseling, international student services, services for students with disabilities, teacher training, writing training. *Library facilities:* SUNY College at Old Westbury Library plus 1 other. *Collection:* Books: 156,872 (physical), 144,263 (digital/electronic); Databases: 138. Weekly public service hours: 99.

Computer facilities: 480 computers available on campus for general student use. A campuswide network can be accessed from student residence rooms and from off campus. Online class registration, financial aid, billing information are available. Website: http://www.oldwestbury.edu/

General Application Contact: Philip D'Angelo, Graduate Admissions Office, 516-876-3073, E-mail: enroll@oldwestbury.edu.

GRADUATE UNITS

Program in Liberal Studies Students: 5 full-time (1 woman), 4 part-time (3 women); includes 4 minority (1 Black or African American, non-Hispanic/Latino; 1 Asian, non-Hispanic/Latino; 2 Hispanic/Latino). Average age 38. 10 applicants, 80% accepted, 5 enrolled. *Faculty:* 2 full-time (both women). Expenses: Contact institution. *Financial support:* Applicants required to submit FAFSA. In 2016, 1 master's awarded. *Program availability:* Part-time, evening/weekend. Offers liberal studies (MA). *Application deadline:* Applications are processed on a rolling basis. *Application fee:* $50. Electronic applications accepted. *Application Contact:* Philip D'Angelo, Graduate Admissions Office, 516-876-3073, E-mail: enroll@oldwestbury.edu. *Associate Professor, American Studies,* Dr. Amanda Frisken, 516-876-4853, E-mail: friskena@oldwestbury.edu.

Program in Mental Health Counseling Students: 34 full-time (29 women); includes 11 minority (4 Black or African American, non-Hispanic/Latino; 2 Asian, non-Hispanic/Latino; 5 Hispanic/Latino). Average age 29. 39 applicants, 64% accepted, 21 enrolled. *Faculty:* 3 full-time (0 women), 2 part-time/adjunct (both women). Expenses: Contact institution. In 2016, 14 master's awarded. Offers mental health counseling (MS). *Application fee:* $50. *Application Contact:* Philip D'Angelo, Graduate Admissions Office, 516-876-3073, E-mail: enroll@oldwestbury.edu.

School of Business Students: 30 full-time (13 women), 47 part-time (15 women); includes 19 minority (3 Black or African American, non-Hispanic/Latino; 11 Asian, non-Hispanic/Latino; 5 Hispanic/Latino). Average age 31. 35 applicants, 91% accepted, 25 enrolled. *Faculty:* 10 full-time (2 women), 1 part-time/adjunct (0 women). Expenses: Contact institution. *Financial support:* Applicants required to submit FAFSA. In 2016, 25 master's awarded. *Program availability:* Part-time, evening/weekend. Offers accounting (MS); taxation (MS). *Application deadline:* For fall admission, 6/15 priority date for domestic students; for spring admission, 11/15 priority date for domestic students. Applications are processed on a rolling basis. *Application fee:* $50. Electronic applications accepted. *Application Contact:* Philip D'Angelo, Graduate Admissions Office, 516-876-3073, E-mail: enroll@oldwestbury.edu. *Director of Graduate Business Programs,* Rita Buttermilch, 516-876-3900, E-mail: langec@oldwestbury.edu.

School of Education Students: 46 full-time (19 women), 26 part-time (17 women); includes 20 minority (1 Black or African American, non-Hispanic/Latino; 4 Asian, non-Hispanic/Latino; 15 Hispanic/Latino). Average age 30. 35 applicants, 77% accepted, 23 enrolled. *Faculty:* 17 full-time (9 women), 5 part-time/adjunct (2 women). Expenses: Contact institution. *Financial support:* Applicants required to submit FAFSA. In 2016, 25 master's awarded. *Program availability:* Part-time, evening/weekend. Offers biology (MAT, MS); chemistry (MAT, MS); English language arts (MAT, MS); math (MAT, MS); social studies (MAT, MS); Spanish (MAT, MS). *Application fee:* $50. *Application Contact:* Philip D'Angelo, Graduate Admissions Office, 516-876-3073, E-mail: enroll@

oldwestbury.edu. *Dean, School of Education*, Dr. Nancy Brown, 516-876-3275, E-mail: brownn@oldwestbury.edu.

STATE UNIVERSITY OF NEW YORK COLLEGE AT ONEONTA, Oneonta, NY 13820-4015

General Information State-supported, coed, comprehensive institution. *Enrollment:* 101 full-time matriculated graduate/professional students (76 women), 185 part-time matriculated graduate/professional students (152 women). *Enrollment by degree level:* 286 master's, 19 other advanced degrees. *Graduate housing:* Room and/or apartments available on a first-come, first-served basis to single students; on-campus housing not available to married students. Housing application deadline: 5/1. *Student services:* Campus employment opportunities, campus safety program, career counseling, child daycare facilities, exercise/wellness program, free psychological counseling, grant writing training, international student services, low-cost health insurance, multicultural affairs office, services for students with disabilities, teacher training, writing training. *Library facilities:* Milne Library. *Research affiliation:* New York State Historical Association (museum studies (history and science)).

Computer facilities: Computer purchase and lease plans are available. 700 computers available on campus for general student use. A campuswide network can be accessed from student residence rooms and from off campus. Online class registration, digital video/audio editing suites, presentation rehearsal room using lecture capture software, large format printing, network file storage space are available.
Website: http://www.oneonta.edu/

General Application Contact: Patrick J. Mente, Graduate Office, 607-436-2523, Fax: 607-436-3084, E-mail: gradstudies@oneonta.edu.

GRADUATE UNITS

Graduate Programs Expenses: Contact institution. *Financial support:* Fellowships, teaching assistantships, Federal Work-Study, and scholarships/grants available. Financial award applicants required to submit FAFSA. *Program availability:* Part-time, evening/weekend, online learning. Offers biology (MS); history museum studies (MA); lake management (MS); nutrition and dietetics (MS); science museum studies (MA). *Application deadline:* Applications are processed on a rolling basis. *Application fee:* $50. *Director of Graduate Studies*, Patrick J. Mente, 607-436-2523, Fax: 607-436-3084, E-mail: gradstudies@oneonta.edu.

Division of Education Expenses: Contact institution. *Program availability:* Part-time, evening/weekend. Offers childhood education (MS Ed); educational psychology, counseling and special education (MS Ed, CAS); elementary education and reading (MS Ed); literacy education (MS Ed); school counselor K-12 (MS Ed, CAS); special education (MS Ed). *Application deadline:* For fall admission, 3/25 priority date for domestic students; for spring admission, 10/1 priority date for domestic students. Applications are processed on a rolling basis. *Application fee:* $50. *Application Contact:* Patrick J. Mente, Director of Graduate Studies, 607-436-2523, Fax: 607-436-3084, E-mail: gradstudies@oneonta.edu. *Dean*, Dr. Jan Bowers, 607-436-2541, Fax: 607-436-2554.

STATE UNIVERSITY OF NEW YORK COLLEGE AT POTSDAM, Potsdam, NY 13676

General Information State-supported, coed, comprehensive institution. *Graduate housing:* Room and/or apartments available on a first-come, first-served basis to single students; on-campus housing not available to married students.

GRADUATE UNITS

Crane School of Music *Program availability:* Part-time. Offers music education (MM); music performance (MM). Electronic applications accepted.

School of Arts and Sciences *Program availability:* Part-time, evening/weekend. Offers arts and sciences (MA); English and communication (MA); mathematics (MA). Electronic applications accepted.

School of Education and Professional Studies *Program availability:* Online learning. Offers adolescence (grades 7-12) (MS Ed); childhood (grades 1-6) (MS Ed); childhood education (MST); community health (MS); curriculum and instruction (MS Ed); early childhood (birth-grade 2) (MS Ed); education and professional studies (MS Ed, MST); educational technology specialist (MS Ed); English education (MST); literacy educator (MS Ed); literacy specialist (MS Ed); mathematics education (MST); organizational performance, leadership and technology (MS Ed); science education (MST); social studies education (MST). Electronic applications accepted.

STATE UNIVERSITY OF NEW YORK COLLEGE OF ENVIRONMENTAL SCIENCE AND FORESTRY, Syracuse, NY 13210-2779

General Information State-supported, coed, university. CGS member. *Enrollment:* 2,716 graduate, professional, and undergraduate students; 352 full-time matriculated graduate/professional students (192 women), 81 part-time matriculated graduate/professional students (41 women). *Enrollment by degree level:* 268 master's, 165 doctoral. *Graduate faculty:* 119 full-time (34 women), 43 part-time/adjunct (13 women). Tuition, state resident: full-time $10,870; part-time $453 per credit. Tuition, nonresident: full-time $22,210; part-time $925 per credit. *Required fees:* $1075; $89.22 per credit. *Graduate housing:* On-campus housing not available. *Student services:* Campus employment opportunities, campus safety program, career counseling, exercise/wellness program, free psychological counseling, grant writing training, international student services, low-cost health insurance, multicultural affairs office, writing training. *Library facilities:* F. Franklin Moon Library plus 1 other. *Collection:* Books: 137,535 (physical), 348,596 (digital/electronic); Serial titles: 1,741 (physical), 241,084 (digital/electronic); Databases: 171. Weekly public service hours: 97. *Research affiliation:* U.S. Department of Agriculture (USDA) (forest and natural resources management), NASA (remote sensing and GIS), New York State Department of Agriculture & Markets (green infrastructure and food systems), New York State Department of Environmental Conservation (environmental conservation and wildlife management), Honeywell (brownfields remediation), U.S. Department of Commerce (Great Lakes water).

Computer facilities: Computer purchase and lease plans are available. 350 computers available on campus for general student use. A campuswide network can be accessed from student residence rooms and from off campus. Online class registration is available.
Website: http://www.esf.edu/

General Application Contact: Scott Shannon, Dean, Instruction and Graduate Studies, 315-470-6599, Fax: 315-470-6978, E-mail: esfgrad@esf.edu.

GRADUATE UNITS

Department of Chemistry Students: 33 full-time (14 women), 4 part-time (3 women); includes 2 minority (1 Black or African American, non-Hispanic/Latino; 1 Asian, non-Hispanic/Latino), 11 international. Average age 26. 51 applicants, 43% accepted, 3 enrolled. *Faculty:* 17 full-time (2 women), 1 part-time/adjunct (0 women). Expenses: Contact institution. *Financial support:* In 2016–17, 24 students received support. Application deadline: 6/30; applicants required to submit FAFSA. In 2016, 2 master's, 1 doctorate awarded. Offers biochemistry (MPS, MS, PhD); environmental chemistry (MPS, MS, PhD); organic chemistry of natural products (MPS, MS, PhD); polymer chemistry (MPS, MS, PhD). *Application deadline:* For fall admission, 2/1 priority date for domestic and international students; for spring admission, 11/1 priority date for domestic and international students. Applications are processed on a rolling basis. *Application fee:* $60. Electronic applications accepted. *Application Contact:* Scott Shannon, Associate Provost for Instruction/Dean of the Graduate School, 315-470-6599, Fax: 315-470-6978, E-mail: sshannon@esf.edu. *Chair*, Prof. Ivan Gitsov, 315-470-6851, Fax: 315-470-6856, E-mail: igivanov@syr.edu.

Department of Environmental and Forest Biology Students: 105 full-time (56 women), 27 part-time (17 women); includes 8 minority (1 Black or African American, non-Hispanic/Latino; 3 American Indian or Alaska Native, non-Hispanic/Latino; 1 Asian, non-Hispanic/Latino; 2 Hispanic/Latino; 1 Two or more races, non-Hispanic/Latino), 11 international. Average age 30. 100 applicants, 44% accepted, 16 enrolled. *Faculty:* 31 full-time (11 women), 1 part-time/adjunct (0 women). Expenses: Contact institution. *Financial support:* In 2016–17, 44 students received support. Application deadline: 6/30; applicants required to submit FAFSA. In 2016, 12 master's, 6 doctorates awarded. Offers applied ecology (MPS); chemical ecology (MPS, MS, PhD); conservation biology (MPS, MS, PhD); ecology (MPS, MS, PhD); entomology (MPS, MS, PhD); environmental interpretation (MPS, MS, PhD); environmental physiology (MPS, MS, PhD); fish and wildlife biology and management (MPS, MS, PhD); forest pathology and mycology (MPS, MS, PhD); plant biotechnology (MPS); plant science and biotechnology (MPS, MS, PhD). *Application deadline:* For fall admission, 2/1 priority date for domestic and international students; for spring admission, 11/1 priority date for domestic and international students. Applications are processed on a rolling basis. *Application fee:* $60. *Application Contact:* Scott Shannon, Associate Provost for Instruction/Dean of the Graduate School, 315-470-6599, E-mail: esfgrad@esf.edu. *Chair*, Dr. Donald J. Leopold, 315-470-6760, Fax: 315-470-6934, E-mail: djleopold@esf.edu.

Department of Environmental Resources Engineering Students: 34 full-time (13 women), 13 part-time (2 women); includes 3 minority (1 Black or African American, non-Hispanic/Latino; 1 Asian, non-Hispanic/Latino; 1 Hispanic/Latino), 21 international. Average age 28. 44 applicants, 48% accepted, 10 enrolled. *Faculty:* 8 full-time (1 woman), 9 part-time/adjunct (3 women). Expenses: Contact institution. *Financial support:* In 2016–17, 7 students received support. Application deadline: 6/30; applicants required to submit FAFSA. In 2016, 8 master's, 1 doctorate awarded. *Program availability:* Part-time. Offers ecological engineering (MPS, MS, PhD); environmental management (MPS); environmental resources engineering (MPS, MS, PhD); geospatial information science and engineering (MPS, MS, PhD); water resources engineering (MPS, MS, PhD). *Application deadline:* For fall admission, 1/15 priority date for domestic and international students; for spring admission, 11/1 priority date for domestic and international students. Applications are processed on a rolling basis. *Application fee:* $60. *Application Contact:* Scott Shannon, Associate Provost for Instruction/Dean of the Graduate School, 315-470-6599, Fax: 315-470-6978, E-mail: esfgrad@esf.edu. *Chair*, Dr. Theodore Endreny, 315-470-6565, Fax: 315-470-6958, E-mail: te@esf.edu.

Department of Environmental Studies Students: 15 full-time (10 women), 3 part-time (2 women); includes 1 minority (Black or African American, non-Hispanic/Latino), 1 international. Average age 26. 10 applicants, 90% accepted, 4 enrolled. *Faculty:* 10 full-time (7 women), 7 part-time/adjunct (5 women). Expenses: Contact institution. *Financial support:* In 2016–17, 3 students received support. Application deadline: 6/30; applicants required to submit FAFSA. In 2016, 2 master's awarded. Offers environmental communication (MPS, MS); environmental policy (MPS, MS). *Application fee:* $60. *Application Contact:* Scott Shannon, Associate Provost for Instruction/Dean of the Graduate School, 315-470-6599, Fax: 315-470-6978, E-mail: esfgrad@esf.edu. *Chair*, Bennette Whitmore, 315-470-6636, E-mail: bwhitmor@esf.edu.

Department of Forest and Natural Resources Management Students: 37 full-time (23 women), 8 part-time (1 woman); includes 5 minority (2 American Indian or Alaska Native, non-Hispanic/Latino; 1 Asian, non-Hispanic/Latino; 1 Hispanic/Latino; 1 Two or more races, non-Hispanic/Latino), 10 international. Average age 29. 28 applicants, 79% accepted, 8 enrolled. *Faculty:* 34 full-time (9 women), 7 part-time/adjunct (0 women). Expenses: Contact institution. *Financial support:* In 2016–17, 18 students received support. Application deadline: 6/30; applicants required to submit FAFSA. In 2016, 9 master's, 3 doctorates awarded. Offers ecology and ecosystems (MPS, MS, PhD); economics, governance and human dimensions (MPS, MS, PhD); forest and natural resources management (MPS, MS, PhD); monitoring, analysis and modeling (MPS, MS, PhD). *Application deadline:* For fall admission, 2/1 priority date for domestic and international students; for spring admission, 11/1 priority date for domestic and international students. Applications are processed on a rolling basis. *Application fee:* $60. *Application Contact:* Scott Shannon, Associate Provost for Instruction/Dean of the Graduate School, 315-470-6599, Fax: 315-470-6978, E-mail: esfgrad@esf.edu. *Chair*, Dr. David Newman, 315-470-6534, Fax: 315-470-6535.

Department of Landscape Architecture Students: 31 full-time (17 women), 3 part-time (2 women); includes 4 minority (2 Black or African American, non-Hispanic/Latino; 1 Asian, non-Hispanic/Latino; 1 Hispanic/Latino), 6 international. Average age 26. 53 applicants, 72% accepted, 12 enrolled. *Faculty:* 11 full-time (4 women), 9 part-time/adjunct (3 women). Expenses: Contact institution. *Financial support:* In 2016–17, 16 students received support. Application deadline: 6/30; applicants required to submit FAFSA. In 2016, 9 master's awarded. Offers community design and planning (MLA, MS); cultural landscape studies and conservation (MLA, MS); landscape and urban ecology (MLA, MS). *Application deadline:* For fall admission, 2/1 priority date for domestic and international students; for spring admission, 11/1 priority date for domestic and international students. Applications are processed on a rolling basis. *Application fee:* $60. *Application Contact:* Scott Shannon, Associate Provost for Instruction/Dean of the Graduate School, 315-470-6599, Fax: 315-470-6978, E-mail: esfgrad@esf.edu. *Chair*, Dr. Douglas Johnston, 315-470-6544, Fax: 315-470-6540, E-mail: dmjohnst@esf.edu.

Department of Paper and Bioprocess Engineering Students: 28 full-time (14 women), 3 part-time (2 women); includes 1 minority (Asian, non-Hispanic/Latino), 19 international. Average age 29. 19 applicants, 89% accepted, 6 enrolled. *Faculty:* 13 full-time (2 women), 4 part-time/adjunct (0 women). Expenses: Contact institution. *Financial support:* In 2016–17, 14 students received support. Application deadline: 6/30; applicants required to submit FAFSA. In 2016, 6 master's, 1 doctorate, 4 other advanced degrees awarded. Offers biomaterials engineering (MS, PhD); bioprocess engineering (MPS, MS, PhD); bioprocessing (Advanced Certificate); paper science and engineering (MPS, MS, PhD); sustainable engineering management (MPS). *Application deadline:* For fall admission, 2/1 priority date for domestic and international students; for spring admission, 11/1 priority date for domestic and international students. Applications are processed on a rolling basis. *Application fee:* $60. *Application Contact:* Scott Shannon,

Associate Provost and Dean, Instruction and Graduate Studies, 315-470-6599, Fax: 315-470-6978, E-mail: esfgrad@esf.edu. *Chair*, Dr. Gary M. Scott, 315-470-6501, Fax: 315-470-6945, E-mail: gscott@esf.edu.

Department of Sustainable Construction Management and Engineering Students: 8 full-time (5 women), 4 part-time (1 woman); includes 1 minority (Hispanic/Latino), 5 international. Average age 29. 5 applicants, 80% accepted, 1 enrolled. Expenses: Contact institution. *Financial support:* In 2016–17, 2 students received support. Application deadline: 6/30; applicants required to submit FAFSA. In 2016, 1 master's awarded. Offers construction management (MPS, MS, PhD); sustainable construction (MPS, MS, PhD); wood science (MPS, MS, PhD). *Application deadline:* For fall admission, 2/1 priority date for domestic and international students; for spring admission, 11/1 priority date for domestic and international students. Applications are processed on a rolling basis. *Application fee:* $60. *Application Contact:* Scott Shannon, Associate Provost for Instruction/Dean of the Graduate School, 315-470-6599, Fax: 315-470-6879, E-mail: esfgrad@esf.edu. *Chair*, Dr. Susan E. Anagnost, 315-470-6880, Fax: 315-470-6879, E-mail: seanagno@esf.edu.

Program in Environmental Science Students: 59 full-time (39 women), 16 part-time (10 women); includes 6 minority (1 Black or African American, non-Hispanic/Latino; 1 Asian, non-Hispanic/Latino; 3 Hispanic/Latino; 1 Two or more races, non-Hispanic/Latino), 25 international. Average age 30. 70 applicants, 59% accepted, 20 enrolled. *Faculty:* 1 full-time (0 women), 1 (woman) part-time/adjunct. Expenses: Contact institution. *Financial support:* In 2016–17, 32 students received support. Application deadline: 6/30; applicants required to submit FAFSA. In 2016, 13 master's, 8 doctorates awarded. *Program availability:* Part-time. Offers biophysical and ecological economics (MPS); coupled natural and human systems (MPS); ecosystem restoration (MPS); environmental and community land planning (MPS, MS); environmental and natural resources policy (PhD); environmental communication and participatory processes (PhD); environmental monitoring and modeling (MPS); water and wetland resource studies (MPS, MS). *Application deadline:* For fall admission, 2/1 priority date for domestic and international students; for spring admission, 11/1 priority date for domestic and international students. Applications are processed on a rolling basis. *Application fee:* $60. *Application Contact:* Scott Shannon, Associate Provost for Instruction/Dean of the Graduate School, 315-470-6599, Fax: 315-470-6978, E-mail: esfgrad@esf.edu. *Coordinator*, Dr. Ruth Yanai, 315-470-6955, Fax: 315-470-6700, E-mail: rdyanai@esf.edu.

STATE UNIVERSITY OF NEW YORK COLLEGE OF OPTOMETRY, New York, NY 10036

General Information State-supported, coed, graduate-only institution. *Graduate housing:* On-campus housing not available. *Research affiliation:* Schnurmacher Institute for Vision Research (vision science).

GRADUATE UNITS

Graduate Programs *Program availability:* Part-time. Offers vision science (PhD).
Professional Program Offers optometry (OD). Electronic applications accepted.

STATE UNIVERSITY OF NEW YORK COLLEGE OF TECHNOLOGY AT DELHI, Delhi, NY 13753

General Information State-supported, coed, comprehensive institution.

GRADUATE UNITS

Program in Nursing Education Offers nursing education (MS).

STATE UNIVERSITY OF NEW YORK DOWNSTATE MEDICAL CENTER, Brooklyn, NY 11203-2098

General Information State-supported, coed, upper-level institution. *Graduate housing:* Rooms and/or apartments available on a first-come, first-served basis to single and married students. Housing application deadline: 5/29. *Research affiliation:* Brooklyn Veterans Administration Medical Center, Polytechnic Institute of New York University (biomedical engineering).

GRADUATE UNITS

College of Medicine Offers medicine (MPH, MD); urban and immigrant health (MPH).
College of Nursing *Program availability:* Part-time, evening/weekend. Offers clinical nurse specialist (MS, Post Master's Certificate); nurse anesthesia (MS); nurse midwifery (MS, Post Master's Certificate); nurse practitioner (MS, Post Master's Certificate); nursing (MS).
School of Graduate Studies Offers bioimaging and neuroengineering (PhD); biomedical engineering (MS); molecular and cellular biology (PhD); neural and behavioral science (PhD); occupational therapy (MS).

STATE UNIVERSITY OF NEW YORK EMPIRE STATE COLLEGE, Saratoga Springs, NY 12866-4391

General Information State-supported, coed, comprehensive institution. *Graduate housing:* On-campus housing not available.

GRADUATE UNITS

School for Graduate Studies *Program availability:* Part-time, evening/weekend, online learning. Offers adult learning (MA); community and economic development (MA); global leadership (MBA); labor and policy studies (MA); learning and emerging technologies (MA); liberal studies (MA); management (MBA); nursing education (MSN); social policy (MA); teaching (MAT); teaching and learning (M Ed). Electronic applications accepted.

STATE UNIVERSITY OF NEW YORK MARITIME COLLEGE, Throggs Neck, NY 10465-4198

General Information State-supported, coed, comprehensive institution. *Graduate housing:* Room and/or apartments available to single students; on-campus housing not available to married students. *Research affiliation:* Port Authority of New York and New Jersey (transportation), Transportation Infrastructure Research Consortium, Transportation Research Board (maritime transportation).

GRADUATE UNITS

Program in International Transportation Management *Program availability:* Part-time, evening/weekend. Offers international transportation management (MS).

STATE UNIVERSITY OF NEW YORK POLYTECHNIC INSTITUTE, Utica, NY 13502

General Information State-supported, coed, comprehensive institution. *Graduate housing:* Room and/or apartments available on a first-come, first-served basis to single students; on-campus housing not available to married students. Housing application deadline: 6/15. *Research affiliation:* Assured Information Security, Inc. (cyber security), Masconic Research Laboratory (heart research), New West Technologies (mechanical

engineering), Air Force Research Laboratory (computer science/systems and signal processing).

GRADUATE UNITS

Colleges of Nanoscale Science and Engineering Offers nanoscale engineering (MS, PhD); nanoscale science (MS, PhD).
Program in Accountancy *Program availability:* Part-time, online learning. Offers accountancy (MS). Electronic applications accepted.
Program in Business Administration in Technology Management *Program availability:* Part-time, online learning. Offers accounting and finance (MBA); business management (MBA); health services management (MBA); human resource management (MBA); marketing management (MBA). Electronic applications accepted.
Program in Computer and Information Science *Program availability:* Part-time, evening/weekend. Offers computer and information science (MS). Electronic applications accepted.
Program in Family Nurse Practitioner *Program availability:* Part-time, online learning. Offers family nurse practitioner (MS, CAS). Electronic applications accepted.
Program in Information Design and Technology *Program availability:* Part-time, online learning. Offers information design and technology (MS). Electronic applications accepted.
Program in Network and Computer Security *Program availability:* Part-time. Offers network and computer security (MS). Electronic applications accepted.
Program in Nursing Education *Program availability:* Part-time, online learning. Offers nursing education (MS, CAS). Electronic applications accepted.
Program in Telecommunications *Program availability:* Part-time, evening/weekend. Offers telecommunications (MS). Electronic applications accepted.

STATE UNIVERSITY OF NEW YORK UPSTATE MEDICAL UNIVERSITY, Syracuse, NY 13210

General Information State-supported, coed, upper-level institution. CGS member. *Graduate housing:* Rooms and/or apartments available on a first-come, first-served basis to single and married students. Housing application deadline: 8/1.

GRADUATE UNITS

College of Graduate Studies Offers anatomy (MS, PhD); biochemistry (MS); biochemistry and molecular biology (PhD); microbiology (MS); microbiology and immunology (PhD); neuroscience (PhD); pharmacology (PhD); physiology (MS, PhD). Electronic applications accepted.
College of Medicine Offers medicine (MD). Electronic applications accepted.
College of Nursing *Program availability:* Part-time, online learning. Offers nurse practitioner (Post Master's Certificate); nursing (MS). Electronic applications accepted.
Department of Physical Therapy *Program availability:* Part-time, evening/weekend, online learning. Offers physical therapy (DPT). Electronic applications accepted.
Program in Medical Technology Offers medical technology (MS).

STEPHEN F. AUSTIN STATE UNIVERSITY, Nacogdoches, TX 75962

General Information State-supported, coed, comprehensive institution. *Graduate housing:* Rooms and/or apartments available on a first-come, first-served basis to single students and available to married students. Housing application deadline: 6/1. *Research affiliation:* University Health Center at Tyler (biotechnology, environmental science).

GRADUATE UNITS

Graduate School *Program availability:* Part-time, evening/weekend, online learning. Electronic applications accepted.
College of Applied Arts and Science *Program availability:* Part-time. Offers applied arts and science (MA, MIS, MSW); communication (MA); interdisciplinary studies (MIS); mass communication (MA); social work (MSW).
College of Business *Program availability:* Part-time, evening/weekend. Offers business (MBA, MPAC, MS); computer science (MS); management and marketing (MBA); professional accountancy (MPAC).
College of Education *Program availability:* Part-time, evening/weekend. Offers athletic training (MS); counseling (MA); early childhood education (M Ed); education (M Ed, MA, MS, Ed D); educational leadership (Ed D); elementary education (M Ed); human sciences (MS); kinesiology (M Ed); school psychology (MA); secondary education (M Ed); special education (M Ed); speech pathology (MS).
College of Fine Arts *Program availability:* Part-time. Offers art (MA); design (MFA); drawing (MFA); fine arts (MA, MFA, MM); music (MA, MM); painting (MFA); sculpture (MFA).
College of Forestry and Agriculture Offers agriculture (MS); forestry (MF, MS, PhD); forestry and agriculture (MF, MS, PhD).
College of Liberal Arts *Program availability:* Part-time, evening/weekend. Offers English (MA); history (MA); liberal arts (MA, MPA); psychology (MA); public administration (MPA).
College of Sciences and Mathematics *Program availability:* Part-time. Offers biology (MS); biotechnology (MS); chemistry (MS); environmental science (MS); geology (MS, MSNS); mathematics (MS); mathematics education (MS); physics (MS); sciences and mathematics (MS, MSNS); statistics (MS).

STEPHENS COLLEGE, Columbia, MO 65215-0002

General Information Independent, Undergraduate: women only; graduate: coed, comprehensive institution. *Enrollment:* 891 graduate, professional, and undergraduate students; 118 full-time matriculated graduate/professional students (102 women), 107 part-time matriculated graduate/professional students (96 women). *Enrollment by degree level:* 224 master's, 1 other advanced degree. *Graduate faculty:* 14 full-time (9 women), 30 part-time/adjunct (19 women). *Tuition:* Full-time $3564; part-time $396 per credit hour. *Required fees:* $45 per credit hour. *Graduate housing:* On-campus housing not available. *Student services:* Campus employment opportunities, career counseling, teacher training. *Library facilities:* Hugh Stephens Library.

Computer facilities: 130 computers available on campus for general student use. A campuswide network can be accessed from student residence rooms and from off campus. Online class registration is available.
Website: http://www.stephens.edu/

General Application Contact: Lindsey Boudinot, Director of Graduate, Online and Certificate Programs, 800-388-7579, E-mail: online@stephens.edu.

GRADUATE UNITS

Division of Graduate and Continuing Studies Students: 117 full-time (101 women), 107 part-time (96 women); includes 25 minority (2 Black or African American, non-Hispanic/Latino; 2 American Indian or Alaska Native, non-Hispanic/Latino; 1 Asian, non-

Hispanic/Latino; 2 Hispanic/Latino; 1 Native Hawaiian or other Pacific Islander, non-Hispanic/Latino; 17 Two or more races, non-Hispanic/Latino), 1 international. Average age 35. 226 applicants, 43% accepted, 87 enrolled. *Faculty:* 14 full-time (9 women), 30 part-time/adjunct (19 women). Expenses: Contact institution. *Financial support:* In 2016–17, 5 fellowships with full tuition reimbursements (averaging $7,673 per year) were awarded; unspecified assistantships also available. Financial award applicants required to submit FAFSA. In 2016, 44 master's awarded. *Program availability:* Part-time, evening/weekend, online learning. Offers counseling (M Ed); health information administration (Postbaccalaureate Certificate); physician assistant studies (MPAS); TV and screenwriting (MFA). *Application deadline:* For fall admission, 8/15 priority date for domestic and international students; for winter admission, 1/9 priority date for domestic and international students; for spring admission, 6/5 priority date for domestic and international students. Applications are processed on a rolling basis. *Application fee:* $50. Electronic applications accepted. *Application Contact:* Lindsey Boudinot, Director of Graduate and Online Admissions, 800-388-7579, E-mail: online@stephens.edu. *Vice President of Strategic Enrollment Management,* Dr. Brian Sajko, 800-388-7579, Fax: 573-876-7237, E-mail: online@stephens.edu.

STETSON UNIVERSITY, DeLand, FL 32723

General Information Independent, coed, comprehensive institution. *Enrollment:* 1,074 full-time matriculated graduate/professional students (611 women), 162 part-time matriculated graduate/professional students (90 women). *Enrollment by degree level:* 357 master's, 879 doctoral. *Graduate faculty:* 74 full-time (36 women), 78 part-time/adjunct (30 women). *Graduate housing:* Rooms and/or apartments available to single and married students. *Student services:* Campus employment opportunities, campus safety program, career counseling, free psychological counseling, international student services, multicultural affairs office, services for students with disabilities, teacher training. *Library facilities:* DuPont-Ball Library plus 1 other. *Collection:* Books: 454,022 (physical), 1.6 million (digital/electronic); Serial titles: 311 (physical), 114,491 (digital/electronic); Databases: 130. Weekly public service hours: 99; students can reserve study rooms. *Research affiliation:* New Teacher Center (teacher education), Teacher Prep Inspection-Us, LLC (teacher preparation), Erin Deady, PA (environmental policy and legal affairs).

Computer facilities: 500 computers available on campus for general student use. A campuswide network can be accessed from student residence rooms and from off campus. Online class registration is available.
Website: http://www.stetson.edu/

General Application Contact: Jamie Vanderlip, Senior Associate Director of Admissions, 386-822-7100, Fax: 386-822-7112, E-mail: gradadmissions@stetson.edu.

GRADUATE UNITS

College of Arts and Sciences Students: 206 full-time (173 women), 17 part-time (13 women); includes 59 minority (20 Black or African American, non-Hispanic/Latino; 1 Asian, non-Hispanic/Latino; 32 Hispanic/Latino; 6 Two or more races, non-Hispanic/Latino), 3 international. Average age 32. 157 applicants, 81% accepted, 106 enrolled. *Faculty:* 12 full-time (8 women), 12 part-time/adjunct (9 women). Expenses: Contact institution. *Financial support:* In 2016–17, 120 students received support. Career-related internships or fieldwork, Federal Work-Study, scholarships/grants, unspecified assistantships, and tuition waivers for staff and dependents available. Support available to part-time students. In 2016, 47 master's awarded. *Program availability:* Part-time, evening/weekend. Offers arts and sciences (M Ed, MFA, MS); English (MFA). *Application deadline:* For fall admission, 8/1 priority date for domestic students; for spring admission, 1/1 priority date for domestic students; for summer admission, 5/1 priority date for domestic students. Applications are processed on a rolling basis. *Application fee:* $50. Electronic applications accepted. *Application Contact:* Jamie Vanderlip, Senior Associate Director of Admissions, 386-822-7100, Fax: 386-822-7112, E-mail: jlvander@stetson.edu. *Dean,* Dr. Karen Ryan, 386-822-7515.

Division of Education Students: 190 full-time (160 women), 17 part-time (13 women); includes 56 minority (20 Black or African American, non-Hispanic/Latino; 1 Asian, non-Hispanic/Latino; 30 Hispanic/Latino; 5 Two or more races, non-Hispanic/Latino), 3 international. Average age 32. 145 applicants, 81% accepted, 98 enrolled. *Faculty:* 12 full-time (8 women), 8 part-time/adjunct (7 women). Expenses: Contact institution. *Financial support:* In 2016–17, 119 students received support. Career-related internships or fieldwork, Federal Work-Study, institutionally sponsored loans, scholarships/grants, unspecified assistantships, and tuition waivers for staff and dependents available. Support available to part-time students. In 2016, 47 master's awarded. *Program availability:* Part-time, evening/weekend. Offers counselor education (MS); educating for social justice (M Ed); educational leadership (M Ed); marriage, couple and family counseling (MS); mental health counseling (MS); school counseling (MS); teacher education (M Ed). *Application deadline:* For fall admission, 8/1 priority date for domestic students; for spring admission, 1/1 priority date for domestic students; for summer admission, 5/1 priority date for domestic students. Applications are processed on a rolling basis. *Application fee:* $50. Electronic applications accepted. *Application Contact:* Jamie Vanderlip, Senior Associate Director of Graduate Admissions, 386-822-7100, Fax: 386-822-7112, E-mail: jlvander@stetson.edu. *Dean,* Dr. Karen Ryan, 386-822-7515.

College of Law Students: 769 full-time (390 women), 110 part-time (51 women); includes 234 minority (53 Black or African American, non-Hispanic/Latino; 3 American Indian or Alaska Native, non-Hispanic/Latino; 23 Asian, non-Hispanic/Latino; 128 Hispanic/Latino; 27 Two or more races, non-Hispanic/Latino), 30 international. Average age 28. 1,812 applicants, 51% accepted, 271 enrolled. *Faculty:* 46 full-time (26 women), 61 part-time/adjunct (21 women). Expenses: Contact institution. *Financial support:* In 2016–17, 510 students received support, including 86 research assistantships (averaging $911 per year), 42 teaching assistantships (averaging $933 per year); career-related internships or fieldwork, Federal Work-Study, and scholarships/grants also available. Support available to part-time students. Financial award application deadline: 8/15; financial award applicants required to submit FAFSA. In 2016, 31 master's, 345 doctorates awarded. *Program availability:* Part-time, evening/weekend, 100% online. Offers advocacy (LL M); elder law (LL M); international law (LL M); law (JD). *Application deadline:* For fall admission, 5/15 for domestic and international students. Applications are processed on a rolling basis. *Application fee:* $55. Electronic applications accepted. *Application Contact:* Darren Kettles, Director of Admissions, 727-562-7802, Fax: 727-343-0136, E-mail: lawadmit@law.stetson.edu. *Dean/Professor of Law,* Christopher M. Pietruszkiewicz, 727-562-7809, Fax: 727-562-6428, E-mail: cmp@law.stetson.edu.

School of Business Administration Students: 99 full-time (48 women), 35 part-time (26 women); includes 26 minority (8 Black or African American, non-Hispanic/Latino; 3 Asian, non-Hispanic/Latino; 14 Hispanic/Latino; 1 Two or more races, non-Hispanic/Latino), 12 international. Average age 31. 126 applicants, 64% accepted, 56 enrolled. *Faculty:* 17 full-time (3 women), 5 part-time/adjunct (0 women). Expenses: Contact institution. *Financial support:* In 2016–17, 40 students received support. Career-related internships or fieldwork, Federal Work-Study, institutionally sponsored loans,

unspecified assistantships, and tuition waivers for staff and dependents available. Support available to part-time students. In 2016, 93 master's awarded. *Program availability:* Part-time, evening/weekend. Offers accounting (M Acc); business administration (EMBA, M Acc, MBA). *Application deadline:* For fall admission, 8/1 for domestic students; for spring admission, 1/1 for domestic students; for summer admission, 5/1 for domestic students. Applications are processed on a rolling basis. *Application fee:* $50. Electronic applications accepted. *Application Contact:* Jamie Vanderlip, Senior Associate Director of Admissions, 386-822-7100, Fax: 386-822-7112, E-mail: jlvander@stetson.edu. *Dean, School of Business Administration,* Dr. Neal P. Mero, 386-822-7405.

STEVENS-HENAGER COLLEGE, Salt Lake City, UT 84123

General Information Independent, coed, comprehensive institution.

STEVENS INSTITUTE OF TECHNOLOGY, Hoboken, NJ 07030

General Information Independent, coed, university. CGS member. *Enrollment:* 6,617 graduate, professional, and undergraduate students; 2,928 full-time matriculated graduate/professional students (686 women), 1,073 part-time matriculated graduate/professional students (293 women). *Enrollment by degree level:* 2,928 master's, 369 doctoral, 74 other advanced degrees. *Graduate faculty:* 297 full-time (73 women), 159 part-time/adjunct (36 women). *Tuition:* Full-time $33,328; part-time $1501 per credit. *Required fees:* $1186; $566 per credit. $283 per semester. *Graduate housing:* Room and/or apartments available on a first-come, first-served basis to single students; on-campus housing not available to married students. Typical cost: $13,500 (including board). Room and board charges vary according to board plan, campus/location and housing facility selected. Housing application deadline: 6/1. *Student services:* Campus employment opportunities, campus safety program, career counseling, exercise/wellness program, free psychological counseling, grant writing training, international student services, low-cost health insurance, multicultural affairs office, services for students with disabilities, teacher training, writing training. *Library facilities:* Samuel C. Williams Library. *Collection:* Books: 66,492 (physical), 210,243 (digital/electronic); Serial titles: 898 (physical), 35,353 (digital/electronic); Databases: 71. Students can reserve study rooms. *Research affiliation:* U.S. Department of Homeland Security (secure maritime systems), U.S. Department of Defense (systems engineering), National Science Foundation (nanotechnology and multi-scale systems), AT&T (intelligent networked systems), National Science Foundation (secure systems and information assurance).

Computer facilities: 500 computers available on campus for general student use. A campuswide network can be accessed from student residence rooms and from off campus. Online class registration, online account information, debit dining program, laundry status are available.
Website: http://www.stevens.edu/

General Application Contact: 888-783-8367, Fax: 888-555-1306, E-mail: graduate@stevens.edu.

GRADUATE UNITS

Graduate School Students: 2,298 full-time (686 women), 1,073 part-time (294 women); includes 309 minority (75 Black or African American, non-Hispanic/Latino; 6 American Indian or Alaska Native, non-Hispanic/Latino; 205 Asian, non-Hispanic/Latino; 23 Hispanic/Latino), 2,098 international. Average age 28. 7,688 applicants, 57% accepted, 1217 enrolled. *Faculty:* 297 full-time (73 women), 159 part-time/adjunct (36 women). Expenses: Contact institution. *Financial support:* Fellowships, research assistantships, teaching assistantships, career-related internships or fieldwork, Federal Work-Study, scholarships/grants, and unspecified assistantships available. Financial award application deadline: 2/15; financial award applicants required to submit FAFSA. In 2016, 1,542 master's, 51 doctorates, 565 other advanced degrees awarded. *Program availability:* Part-time, evening/weekend, online learning. *Application deadline:* For fall admission, 6/1 for domestic students, 4/15 for international students; for spring admission, 11/30 for domestic students, 11/1 for international students. Applications are processed on a rolling basis. *Application fee:* $65. Electronic applications accepted. *Application Contact:* 888-783-8367, Fax: 888-511-1306, E-mail: graduate@stevens.edu. *Interim Director of Graduate Admissions and Enrollment,* Paul Easterling, 201-216-3670, Fax: 555-511-1306, E-mail: paul.easterling@stevens.edu.

Charles V. Schaefer Jr. School of Engineering and Science Students: 1,301 full-time (352 women), 331 part-time (76 women); includes 119 minority (28 Black or African American, non-Hispanic/Latino; 1 American Indian or Alaska Native, non-Hispanic/Latino; 72 Asian, non-Hispanic/Latino; 9 Hispanic/Latino; 9 Two or more races, non-Hispanic/Latino), 1,180 international. Average age 26. 4,438 applicants, 54% accepted, 589 enrolled. *Faculty:* 173 full-time (36 women), 80 part-time/adjunct (8 women). Expenses: Contact institution. *Financial support:* Fellowships, research assistantships, teaching assistantships, career-related internships or fieldwork, Federal Work-Study, scholarships/grants, and unspecified assistantships available. Financial award application deadline: 2/15; financial award applicants required to submit FAFSA. In 2016, 804 master's, 38 doctorates, 196 other advanced degrees awarded. *Program availability:* Part-time, evening/weekend, online learning. Offers additive manufacturing (Certificate); advanced manufacturing (Certificate); air pollution technology (Certificate); analytical chemistry (Certificate); applied mathematics (MS); applied optics (Certificate); applied statistics (Certificate); armament engineering (M Eng); atmospheric and environmental science and engineering (Certificate); autonomous robotics (Certificate); bioinformatics (Certificate); biomedical chemistry (Certificate); biomedical engineering (M Eng, PhD); chemical biology (MS, PhD, Certificate); chemical engineering (M Eng, PhD, Engr); chemical physiology (Certificate); chemistry (MS, PhD); civil engineering (M Eng, PhD, Certificate, Engr); computational fluid mechanics and heat transfer (Certificate); computer and electrical engineering (M Eng); computer engineering (M Eng, PhD, Certificate); computer graphics (Certificate); computer science (MS, PhD); computer systems (M Eng, Certificate); construction management (MS, Certificate); cybersecurity (MS); data communications and networks (M Eng); database management systems (Certificate); design and production management (Certificate); digital systems design (M Eng); distributed systems (Certificate); electrical engineering (M Eng, PhD, Certificate); elements of computer science (Certificate); engineered software systems (M Eng); engineering and science (M Eng, MS, PhD, Certificate, Engr); enterprise and cloud computing (MS); enterprise computing (Certificate); enterprise security and information assurance (Certificate); environmental engineering (M Eng, PhD, Certificate); environmental hydrology (Certificate); environmental processes (M Eng); geotechnical/geoenvironmental engineering (M Eng, Engr); health informatics (Certificate); hydraulics (Certificate); hydrologic modeling (M Eng); image processing and multimedia (M Eng); information system security (M Eng); information systems (M Eng); inland and coastal environmental hydrodynamics (M Eng); integrated product development (M Eng); manufacturing technologies (M Eng); maritime systems (MS); materials science and

Stevens Institute of Technology

engineering (M Eng, PhD); mathematics (MS, PhD); mechanical engineering (M Eng, PhD); media and broadcast engineering (MS); medical devices (Certificate); microdevices and microsystems (Certificate); microelectronics (Certificate); microelectronics and photonics (M Eng, MS, PhD); modeling of environmental systems (M Eng); multi-hazard engineering (Certificate); multimedia experience and management (Certificate); nanotechnology (PhD); networked information systems (MS, Certificate); networks and systems administration (Certificate); nuclear power engineering (Certificate); ocean engineering (M Eng, PhD); ordnance engineering (Certificate); pharmaceutical manufacturing (M Eng, MS, Certificate); photonics (Certificate); physics (M Eng, MS, PhD); polymer chemistry (Certificate); power generation (Certificate); product architecture and engineering (M Eng); robotics and control (Certificate); service oriented computing (Certificate); ship hydrodynamics (Certificate); soil and groundwater pollution control (M Eng); stochastic systems (MS, Certificate); stochastic systems and optimization (MS); stormwater management (M Eng); structural analysis and design (Certificate); structural engineering (M Eng, Certificate, Engr); surface water hydrology (Certificate); systems reliability and design (M Eng); transportation engineering (M Eng); vibration and noise control (Certificate); water resources engineering (M Eng, Certificate). *Application deadline:* For fall admission, 6/1 for domestic students, 4/15 for international students; for spring admission, 11/30 for domestic students, 11/1 for international students. Applications are processed on a rolling basis. *Application fee:* $65. Electronic applications accepted. *Application Contact:* Graduate Admissions, 888-783-8367, Fax: 888-555-1306, E-mail: graduate@stevens.edu. *Interim Dean,* Dr. Keith G. Sheppard, 201-216-5263, E-mail: keith.sheppard@stevens.edu.

College of Arts and Letters 2 applicants, 100% accepted. *Faculty:* 37 full-time (17 women), 11 part-time/adjunct (7 women). Expenses: Contact institution. *Financial support:* Fellowships, research assistantships, teaching assistantships, career-related internships or fieldwork, Federal Work-Study, scholarships/grants, and unspecified assistantships available. Financial award application deadline: 2/15; financial award applicants required to submit FAFSA. In 2016, 2 master's awarded. *Program availability:* Part-time, evening/weekend. Offers arts and letters (MA, Graduate Certificate); policy and innovation (MA, Graduate Certificate). *Application deadline:* For fall admission, 6/1 for domestic students, 4/15 for international students; for spring admission, 11/30 for domestic students, 11/1 for international students. Applications are processed on a rolling basis. *Application fee:* $65. Electronic applications accepted. *Application Contact:* Graduate Admission, 888-783-8367, Fax: 888-511-1306, E-mail: graduate@stevens.edu. *Dean,* Dr. Kelland Thomas.

School of Business Students: 612 full-time (220 women), 444 part-time (157 women); includes 138 minority (31 Black or African American, non-Hispanic/Latino; 5 American Indian or Alaska Native, non-Hispanic/Latino; 93 Asian, non-Hispanic/Latino; 9 Hispanic/Latino), 588 international. Average age 30. 2,203 applicants, 59% accepted, 391 enrolled. *Faculty:* 44 full-time (9 women), 31 part-time/adjunct (11 women). Expenses: Contact institution. *Financial support:* Fellowships, research assistantships, teaching assistantships, career-related internships or fieldwork, Federal Work-Study, scholarships/grants, and unspecified assistantships available. Financial award application deadline: 2/15; financial award applicants required to submit FAFSA. In 2016, 392 master's, 2 doctorates, 101 other advanced degrees awarded. *Program availability:* Part-time, evening/weekend, online learning. Offers business (EMBA, EMTM, MBA, MS, PhD, Certificate); business administration (EMBA); business intelligence and analytics (MS, Certificate); computer science (MS); e-commerce (MS); engineering management (MBA); enterprise systems (MS); entrepreneurial information technology (MS); finance (MBA); general management (MS); global innovation management (MS); human resource management (MS); information architecture (MS); information management (MS, PhD, Certificate); information security (MS); information systems (MBA); information technology in financial services industry (MS); information technology in the pharmaceutical industry (MS); information technology outsourcing management (MS); innovation and entrepreneurship (MBA); management of wireless networks (MS); marketing (MBA); network and communication management and services (MS); online security, technology and business (MS); pharmaceutical management (MBA); professional communications (Certificate); project management (MBA, MS, Certificate); software engineering (MS); technical management (MS); technology commercialization (MS); technology management (EMBA, MBA, MS, PhD); technology management for experienced professionals (MS, Certificate); telecommunications (MS); telecommunications management (MBA, PhD, Certificate). *Application deadline:* For fall admission, 6/1 for domestic students, 4/15 for international students; for spring admission, 11/30 for domestic students, 11/1 for international students. Applications are processed on a rolling basis. *Application fee:* $65. Electronic applications accepted. *Application Contact:* Graduate Admissions, 888-793-8367, Fax: 888-511-1306, E-mail: graduate@stevens.edu. *Dean,* Dr. Gregory Prastacos, 201-216-8366, E-mail: gprastac@stevens.edu.

School of Systems and Enterprises Students: 385 full-time (114 women), 297 part-time (60 women); includes 61 minority (16 Black or African American, non-Hispanic/Latino; 40 Asian, non-Hispanic/Latino; 5 Hispanic/Latino), 330 international. Average age 29. 1,036 applicants, 66% accepted, 236 enrolled. *Faculty:* 40 full-time (10 women), 22 part-time/adjunct (3 women). Expenses: Contact institution. *Financial support:* Fellowships, research assistantships, teaching assistantships, career-related internships or fieldwork, Federal Work-Study, scholarships/grants, and unspecified assistantships available. Financial award application deadline: 2/15; financial award applicants required to submit FAFSA. In 2016, 344 master's, 11 doctorates, 268 other advanced degrees awarded. *Program availability:* Part-time, evening/weekend. Offers engineering management (M Eng, PhD, Certificate); enterprise systems (Certificate); financial engineering (MS, PhD, Certificate); socio-technical systems (MS, PhD); software engineering (MS, Certificate); space systems engineering (M Eng, Certificate); systems and enterprises (M Eng, MS, PhD, Certificate); systems and supportability engineering (Certificate); systems design and operational effectiveness (Certificate); systems engineering (M Eng, PhD); systems engineering and architecting (Certificate); systems engineering management (Certificate); systems engineering of embedded/cyber-physical systems (Certificate); systems engineering security (Certificate). *Application deadline:* For fall admission, 6/1 for domestic students, 4/15 for international students; for spring admission, 11/30 for domestic students, 11/1 for international students. Applications are processed on a rolling basis. *Application fee:* $65. Electronic applications accepted. *Application Contact:* Graduate Admissions, 888-783-8367, Fax: 888-511-1306, E-mail: graduate@stevens.edu. *Dean,* Dr. Dinesh Verma, 201-216-8645, Fax: 201-216-5541, E-mail: dinesh.verma@stevens.edu.

STEVENSON UNIVERSITY, Stevenson, MD 21153

General Information Independent, coed, comprehensive institution. *Enrollment:* 4,122 graduate, professional, and undergraduate students; 86 full-time matriculated graduate/professional students (60 women), 512 part-time matriculated graduate/professional students (383 women). *Enrollment by degree level:* 598 master's. *Graduate faculty:* 9 full-time (7 women), 51 part-time/adjunct (27 women). *Tuition:* Full-time 12,060; part-time $670 per credit. Tuition and fees vary according to program. *Graduate housing:* On-campus housing not available. *Student services:* Campus employment opportunities, campus safety program, career counseling, exercise/wellness program, multicultural affairs office, services for students with disabilities. *Library facilities:* Stevenson University Learning Resource Center-Greenspring Campus plus 1 other. *Collection:* Books: 80,717 (physical), 324,297 (digital/electronic); Serial titles: 518 (physical), 35,771 (digital/electronic); Databases: 91. Students can reserve study rooms.

Computer facilities: Computer purchase and lease plans are available. 300 computers available on campus for general student use. A campuswide network can be accessed from student residence rooms and from off campus. Online class registration is available.
Website: http://www.stevenson.edu/

General Application Contact: Angela Reynolds, Director, Recruitment and Admissions, 443-352-4414, Fax: 443-352-4440, E-mail: amreynolds@stevenson.edu.

GRADUATE UNITS

Master of Arts in Teaching Program Students: 17 part-time (10 women); includes 3 minority (2 Black or African American, non-Hispanic/Latino; 1 Asian, non-Hispanic/Latino). Average age 29. 13 applicants, 85% accepted, 10 enrolled. *Faculty:* 3 part-time/adjunct (all women). Expenses: Contact institution. *Financial support:* Unspecified assistantships available. Financial award applicants required to submit FAFSA. In 2016, 8 master's awarded. *Program availability:* Part-time, blended/hybrid learning. Offers secondary biology (MAT); secondary chemistry (MAT); secondary mathematics (MAT). *Application deadline:* Applications are processed on a rolling basis. Electronic applications accepted. *Application Contact:* Amanda Courter, Senior Enrollment Counselor, 443-352-4243, Fax: 443-352-4440, E-mail: acourter@stevenson.edu. *Associate Dean of Teacher Education,* Anne P. Davis.

Program in Business and Technology Management Students: 17 full-time (7 women), 118 part-time (62 women); includes 66 minority (58 Black or African American, non-Hispanic/Latino; 1 American Indian or Alaska Native, non-Hispanic/Latino; 4 Asian, non-Hispanic/Latino; 3 Hispanic/Latino). Average age 32. 52 applicants, 73% accepted, 24 enrolled. *Faculty:* 1 full-time (0 women), 13 part-time/adjunct (3 women). Expenses: Contact institution. *Financial support:* Unspecified assistantships available. Financial award applicants required to submit FAFSA. In 2016, 55 master's awarded. *Program availability:* Part-time, online only, 100% online. Offers emerging technology (MS); innovative leadership (MS). *Application deadline:* Applications are processed on a rolling basis. *Application fee:* $0. Electronic applications accepted. *Application Contact:* Tonia Cristino, Assistant Director, Recruitment and Admissions, 443-352-4058, Fax: 443-394-0538, E-mail: tcristino@stevenson.edu. *Coordinator,* Steven Engorn, 443-352-4220, Fax: 443-394-0538, E-mail: sengorn@stevenson.edu.

Program in Communication Studies Students: 10 full-time (6 women), 22 part-time (15 women); includes 13 minority (9 Black or African American, non-Hispanic/Latino; 1 Asian, non-Hispanic/Latino; 3 Hispanic/Latino). Average age 27. 27 applicants, 85% accepted, 13 enrolled. *Faculty:* 6 part-time/adjunct (4 women). Expenses: Contact institution. *Financial support:* Unspecified assistantships available. Financial award applicants required to submit FAFSA. *Program availability:* Part-time, online only, 100% online, blended/hybrid learning. Offers communication studies (MS). *Application deadline:* Applications are processed on a rolling basis. Electronic applications accepted. *Application Contact:* Amanda Courter, Senior Enrollment Counselor, 443-352-4243, Fax: 443-352-4440, E-mail: acourter@stevenson.edu. *Associate Dean, Communications Studies,* Dr. Nadene Vevea, 443-394-9498, E-mail: nvevea@stevenson.edu.

Program in Cyber Forensics Students: 4 full-time (1 woman), 30 part-time (14 women); includes 13 minority (11 Black or African American, non-Hispanic/Latino; 1 Asian, non-Hispanic/Latino; 1 Hispanic/Latino). Average age 38. 14 applicants, 50% accepted, 7 enrolled. *Faculty:* 6 part-time/adjunct (0 women). Expenses: Contact institution. *Financial support:* Unspecified assistantships available. Financial award applicants required to submit FAFSA. In 2016, 13 master's awarded. *Program availability:* Part-time, 100% online. Offers cyber forensics (MS). *Application deadline:* Applications are processed on a rolling basis. Electronic applications accepted. *Application Contact:* William Wellein, Enrollment Counselor, 443-352-5843, Fax: 443-394-0538, E-mail: wwellein@stevenson.edu. *Program Coordinator,* Thomas Byrd, E-mail: tbyrd6@stevenson.edu.

Program in Forensic Science Students: 31 full-time (26 women), 20 part-time (16 women); includes 26 minority (20 Black or African American, non-Hispanic/Latino; 1 American Indian or Alaska Native, non-Hispanic/Latino; 1 Asian, non-Hispanic/Latino; 4 Hispanic/Latino). Average age 26. 29 applicants, 90% accepted, 21 enrolled. *Faculty:* 4 full-time (3 women), 6 part-time/adjunct (3 women). Expenses: Contact institution. *Financial support:* Unspecified assistantships available. Financial award applicants required to submit FAFSA. In 2016, 16 master's awarded. *Program availability:* Part-time. Offers biology (MS); chemistry (MS); crime scene investigation (MS). Program offered in partnership with Maryland State Police Forensic Sciences Division. *Application deadline:* Applications are processed on a rolling basis. *Application fee:* $0. Electronic applications accepted. *Application Contact:* William Wellein, Enrollment Counselor, 443-352-5843, Fax: 443-394-0538, E-mail: wwellein@stevenson.edu. *Coordinator,* John Tobin, PhD, 443-352-4142, Fax: 443-394-0538, E-mail: jtobin@stevenson.edu.

Program in Forensic Studies Students: 21 full-time (17 women), 103 part-time (73 women); includes 59 minority (52 Black or African American, non-Hispanic/Latino; 1 American Indian or Alaska Native, non-Hispanic/Latino; 2 Asian, non-Hispanic/Latino; 4 Hispanic/Latino). Average age 29. 85 applicants, 74% accepted, 43 enrolled. *Faculty:* 3 full-time (all women), 12 part-time/adjunct (2 women). Expenses: Contact institution. *Financial support:* Unspecified assistantships available. Financial award applicants required to submit FAFSA. In 2016, 54 master's awarded. *Program availability:* Part-time, blended/hybrid learning. Offers computer forensics (MS); criminalistics (MS); forensic accounting (MS); forensic legal professional (MS); interdisciplinary track (MS); investigations (MS). *Application deadline:* Applications are processed on a rolling basis. *Application fee:* $0. Electronic applications accepted. *Application Contact:* William Wellein, Enrollment Counselor, 443-352-5843, Fax: 443-394-0538, E-mail: wwellein@stevenson.edu. *Associate Dean,* Thomas Coogan, JD, 443-352-4075, Fax: 443-394-0538, E-mail: tcoogan@stevenson.edu.

Program in Healthcare Management Students: 3 full-time (all women), 22 part-time (20 women); includes 10 minority (8 Black or African American, non-Hispanic/Latino; 1 Asian, non-Hispanic/Latino; 1 Hispanic/Latino). Average age 32. 26 applicants, 54% accepted, 8 enrolled. *Faculty:* 1 (woman) full-time, 9 part-time/adjunct (6 women). Expenses: Contact institution. *Financial support:* Unspecified assistantships available. Financial award applicants required to submit FAFSA. In 2016, 17 master's awarded.

Program availability: Part-time, online only, 100% online. Offers project management (MS); quality management and patient safety (MS). *Application deadline:* Applications are processed on a rolling basis. Electronic applications accepted. *Application Contact:* Amanda Courter, Enrollment Counselor, 443-352-4243, Fax: 443-394-0538, E-mail: acourter@stevenson.edu. *Coordinator,* Sharon Buchbinder, PhD, 443-394-9290, Fax: 443-394-0538, E-mail: sbuchbinder@stevenson.edu.

Program in Nursing Students: 180 part-time (173 women); includes 56 minority (45 Black or African American, non-Hispanic/Latino; 7 Asian, non-Hispanic/Latino; 4 Hispanic/Latino). Average age 41. 70 applicants, 77% accepted, 43 enrolled. *Faculty:* 3 full-time (all women), 12 part-time/adjunct (all women). Expenses: Contact institution. *Financial support:* Unspecified assistantships available. Financial award applicants required to submit FAFSA. In 2016, 64 master's awarded. *Program availability:* Part-time, blended/hybrid learning. Offers nursing education (MS); nursing leadership/management (MS); population-based care coordination (MS). *Application deadline:* Applications are processed on a rolling basis. *Application fee:* $0. Electronic applications accepted. *Application Contact:* Amanda Courter, Enrollment Counselor, 443-352-4243, Fax: 443-394-0538, E-mail: acourter@stevenson.edu. *Associate Dean,* Judith Feustle, PhD, 443-352-4292, Fax: 443-394-0538, E-mail: jfeustle@stevenson.edu.

STOCKTON UNIVERSITY, Galloway, NJ 08205-9441

General Information State-supported, coed, comprehensive institution. CGS member. *Enrollment:* 8,728 graduate, professional, and undergraduate students; 363 full-time matriculated graduate/professional students (283 women), 466 part-time matriculated graduate/professional students (361 women). *Enrollment by degree level:* 698 master's, 131 doctoral. *Graduate faculty:* 63 full-time (43 women), 33 part-time/adjunct (20 women). Tuition, state resident: full-time $16,632; part-time $594 per credit. Tuition, nonresident: full-time $25,592; part-time $914 per credit. *Required fees:* $5012; $179 per credit. $100. Tuition and fees vary according to degree level. *Graduate housing:* Room and/or apartments available on a first-come, first-served basis to single students; on-campus housing not available to married students. Typical cost: $10,528 per year ($14,151 including board). Room and board charges vary according to board plan and housing facility selected. Housing application deadline: 6/1. *Student services:* Campus employment opportunities, campus safety program, career counseling, child daycare facilities, exercise/wellness program, free psychological counseling, grant writing training, international student services, low-cost health insurance, services for students with disabilities, teacher training, writing training. *Library facilities:* Richard E. Bjork Library. *Collection:* 222,477 (physical), 142,000 (digital/electronic); Serial titles: 127 (physical), 132,055 (digital/electronic); Databases: 176. Weekly public service hours: 91. *Research affiliation:* Jewish Foundation (Holocaust studies), Wetlands Institute (marine biology), Aviation Research and Technology Park (aviation research), Nature Conservancy of New Jersey (environmental studies), Association of State Colleges (civic engagement).

Computer facilities: 1,255 computers available on campus for general student use. A campuswide network can be accessed from student residence rooms and from off campus. Online class registration is available.
Website: http://www.stockton.edu/

General Application Contact: Tara Williams, Assistant Director of Graduate Enrollment Management, 609-626-3640, E-mail: gradschool@stockton.edu.

GRADUATE UNITS

Office of Graduate Studies Students: 363 full-time (283 women), 466 part-time (361 women); includes 169 minority (55 Black or African American, non-Hispanic/Latino; 2 American Indian or Alaska Native, non-Hispanic/Latino; 29 Asian, non-Hispanic/Latino; 67 Hispanic/Latino; 1 Native Hawaiian or other Pacific Islander, non-Hispanic/Latino; 15 Two or more races, non-Hispanic/Latino), 3 international. Average age 32. 1,454 applicants, 33% accepted, 332 enrolled. *Faculty:* 63 full-time (43 women), 33 part-time/adjunct (20 women). Expenses: Contact institution. *Financial support:* Fellowships, research assistantships, career-related internships or fieldwork, Federal Work-Study, scholarships/grants, and unspecified assistantships available. Support available to part-time students. Financial award application deadline: 3/1; financial award applicants required to submit FAFSA. In 2016, 259 master's, 32 doctorates awarded. *Program availability:* Part-time, evening/weekend, 100% online, blended/hybrid learning. Offers American studies (MA, Certificate); business administration (MBA); communication disorders (MS); computational science (MS); criminal justice (MA); education (MA); environmental science (PSM); Holocaust and genocide studies (MA); instructional technology (MA); nursing (MSN); occupational therapy (MSOT); organizational leadership (Ed D); physical therapy (DPT); social work (MSW). *Application deadline:* For fall admission, 7/1 for domestic and international students. Applications are processed on a rolling basis. *Application fee:* $50. Electronic applications accepted. *Application Contact:* Tara Williams, Assistant Director of Graduate Enrollment, 609-626-3640, Fax: 609-626-6050, E-mail: gradschool@stockton.edu. *Director of Graduate Enrollment Management,* AmyBeth Glass, 609-652-4298, E-mail: graduatestudies@stockton.edu.

STONY BROOK UNIVERSITY, STATE UNIVERSITY OF NEW YORK, Stony Brook, NY 11794

General Information State-supported, coed, university. CGS member. *Enrollment:* 25,734 graduate, professional, and undergraduate students; 5,363 full-time matriculated graduate/professional students (2,698 women), 2,668 part-time matriculated graduate/professional students (1,866 women). *Enrollment by degree level:* 4,252 master's, 3,235 doctoral, 544 other advanced degrees. *Graduate faculty:* 1,826 full-time (705 women), 748 part-time/adjunct (386 women). Tuition, state resident: full-time $10,870; part-time $453 per credit hour. Tuition, nonresident: full-time $22,210; part-time $925 per credit hour. *Graduate housing:* Rooms and/or apartments available to single and married students. Housing application deadline: 5/1. *Student services:* Campus employment opportunities, campus safety program, career counseling, child daycare facilities, exercise/wellness program, free psychological counseling, grant writing training, international student services, multicultural affairs office, services for students with disabilities, teacher training, writing training. *Library facilities:* Frank Melville, Jr. Memorial Library plus 7 others. *Collection:* Books: 901,520 (physical), 347,609 (digital/electronic); Serial titles: 1,283 (physical), 161,834 (digital/electronic); Databases: 661. Weekly public service hours: 128; study areas open 24 hours, 5–7 days a week; students can reserve study rooms. *Research affiliation:* Mount Sinai Health System, Veterans Affairs Medical Center, Nassau University Medical Center, Winthrop University Hospital, Cold Spring Harbor Laboratory, Brookhaven National Laboratory.

Computer facilities: Computer purchase and lease plans are available. 1,670 computers available on campus for general student use. A campuswide network can be accessed from student residence rooms and from off campus. Online class registration is available.
Website: http://www.stonybrook.edu/

General Application Contact: Melissa Jordan, Assistant Dean for Records and Admission, 631-632-9712, Fax: 631-632-7243, E-mail: gradadmissions@stonybrook.edu.

GRADUATE UNITS

Graduate School Students: 3,431 full-time (1,459 women), 685 part-time (296 women); includes 678 minority (114 Black or African American, non-Hispanic/Latino; 4 American Indian or Alaska Native, non-Hispanic/Latino; 317 Asian, non-Hispanic/Latino; 189 Hispanic/Latino; 2 Native Hawaiian or other Pacific Islander, non-Hispanic/Latino; 52 Two or more races, non-Hispanic/Latino), 1,938 international. 8,542 applicants, 36% accepted, 1078 enrolled. *Faculty:* 919 full-time (305 women), 348 part-time/adjunct (169 women). Expenses: Contact institution. *Financial support:* In 2016–17, 96 fellowships, 472 research assistantships, 821 teaching assistantships were awarded; career-related internships or fieldwork, Federal Work-Study, institutionally sponsored loans, scholarships/grants, traineeships, health care benefits, tuition waivers (full), and unspecified assistantships also available. In 2016, 1,027 master's, 349 doctorates, 29 other advanced degrees awarded. *Program availability:* Part-time, evening/weekend. *Application deadline:* For fall admission, 1/15 for domestic and international students; for spring admission, 10/1 for domestic and international students. *Application fee:* $100. Electronic applications accepted. *Application Contact:* Melissa Jordan, Assistant Dean for Records and Admission, 631-632-7243, E-mail: gradadmissions@stonybrook.edu. *Dean,* Dr. Charles Taber, 631-632-7035, Fax: 631-632-7243, E-mail: charles.taber@sunysb.edu.

College of Arts and Sciences Students: 1,580 full-time (757 women), 162 part-time (94 women); includes 295 minority (47 Black or African American, non-Hispanic/Latino; 3 American Indian or Alaska Native, non-Hispanic/Latino; 106 Asian, non-Hispanic/Latino; 103 Hispanic/Latino; 36 Two or more races, non-Hispanic/Latino), 642 international. 3,333 applicants, 33% accepted, 387 enrolled. *Faculty:* 537 full-time (201 women), 164 part-time/adjunct (86 women). Expenses: Contact institution. *Financial support:* In 2016–17, 59 fellowships, 230 research assistantships, 585 teaching assistantships were awarded; career-related internships or fieldwork, Federal Work-Study, scholarships/grants, traineeships, health care benefits, and unspecified assistantships also available. Financial award applicants required to submit FAFSA. In 2016, 241 master's, 224 doctorates, 19 other advanced degrees awarded. *Program availability:* Part-time, evening/weekend. Offers Africana studies (MA, Certificate); anthropological sciences (PhD); anthropology (MA, PhD); applied ecology (MA); art history and criticism (MA, PhD); arts and sciences (MA, MAPP, MAT, MFA, MM, MS, DMA, PhD, Advanced Certificate, Certificate, Graduate Certificate); astronomy (PhD); biochemistry and cell biology (MS); biochemistry and molecular biology (PhD); biochemistry and structural biology (PhD); biological sciences (MA); chemistry (MS, PhD); clinical psychology (PhD); cognitive psychology (PhD); comparative literature (MA, PhD); contemporary Asian and Asian American studies (MA); cultural studies (PhD, Certificate); dramaturgy (MFA); earth science (MAT); ecology and evolution (PhD); economics (MA, PhD); English (MA, PhD); English education (MAT); French (MA); genetics (PhD); geosciences (MS, PhD); Hispanic languages and literature (MA, PhD); history (MA, PhD); immunology and pathology (PhD); integrative neuroscience (PhD); Italian (MA); linguistics (MA, PhD); mathematics (MA, MAT, PhD); modern research instrumentation (MS); molecular and cellular biology (MA, PhD); music history/theory (MA, PhD); music performance (MM, DMA); neuroscience (MS, PhD); philosophy (MA, PhD, Advanced Certificate); physics (MA, MAT, MS, PhD); physics education (MAT); political science (MA, PhD); psychology (MA); public policy (MAPP); public policy and urban development (MA); Romance languages (MA); social and health psychology (PhD); sociology (MA, PhD); STEM education (PhD); studio art (MFA); teaching English to speakers of other languages (MA); teaching writing (Graduate Certificate); theatre arts (MA); women's, gender, and sexuality studies (Certificate). *Application deadline:* For fall admission, 1/15 for domestic students; for spring admission, 10/1 for domestic students. *Application fee:* $100. Electronic applications accepted. *Application Contact:* Melissa Jordan, Assistant Dean for Records and Admission, 631-632-9712, Fax: 631-632-7243, E-mail: melissa.jordan@stonybrook.edu. *Dean,* Dr. Sacha Kopp, 631-632-6976, Fax: 631-632-6900, E-mail: sacha.kopp@stonybrook.edu.

College of Business Students: 217 full-time (117 women), 143 part-time (65 women); includes 85 minority (19 Black or African American, non-Hispanic/Latino; 44 Asian, non-Hispanic/Latino; 18 Hispanic/Latino; 1 Native Hawaiian or other Pacific Islander, non-Hispanic/Latino; 3 Two or more races, non-Hispanic/Latino), 94 international. Average age 29. 383 applicants, 57% accepted, 109 enrolled. *Faculty:* 37 full-time (12 women), 12 part-time/adjunct (4 women). Expenses: Contact institution. *Financial support:* Research assistantships and teaching assistantships available. In 2016, 119 master's awarded. Offers accounting (MBA); business (MBA, MS, AGC, Certificate); business administration (MBA); finance (MS, AGC); health care management (MBA); innovation, human resources, management, or operations management (MBA); marketing (MBA). *Application deadline:* For fall admission, 5/15 for domestic students, 3/15 priority date for international students; for spring admission, 11/15 for domestic students, 10/15 for international students. *Application fee:* $100. *Application Contact:* Erica Robey, Graduate Coordinator, 631-632-7722, Fax: 631-632-8181, E-mail: erica.robey@stonybrook.edu. *Dean,* Dr. Manuel London, 631-632-7159, E-mail: manuel.london@stonybrook.edu.

College of Engineering and Applied Sciences Students: 1,226 full-time (356 women), 279 part-time (72 women); includes 154 minority (17 Black or African American, non-Hispanic/Latino; 100 Asian, non-Hispanic/Latino; 31 Hispanic/Latino; 6 Two or more races, non-Hispanic/Latino), 1,140 international. Average age 26. 4,273 applicants, 37% accepted, 459 enrolled. *Faculty:* 181 full-time (35 women), 55 part-time/adjunct (15 women). Expenses: Contact institution. *Financial support:* In 2016–17, 8 fellowships, 167 research assistantships, 201 teaching assistantships were awarded; career-related internships or fieldwork also available. In 2016, 540 master's, 92 doctorates awarded. *Program availability:* Part-time, evening/weekend. Offers applied mathematics and statistics (MS, PhD, Advanced Certificate); biomedical engineering (MS, PhD, Certificate); biomedical informatics (MS, PhD, AGC); civil engineering (MS, PhD, Graduate Certificate); computer engineering (MS, PhD); computer science (MS, PhD); educational technology (MS); electrical engineering (MS, PhD); energy and environmental systems (MS, Advanced Certificate); engineering and applied sciences (MS, PhD, AGC, Advanced Certificate, Certificate, Graduate Certificate); global operations management (MS); information systems (Certificate); information systems engineering (MS); materials science and engineering (MS, PhD); mechanical engineering (MS, PhD); medical physics (MS, PhD); software engineering (Certificate); technology, policy, and innovation (PhD). *Application deadline:* For fall admission, 1/15 for domestic students; for spring admission, 10/1 for domestic students. *Application fee:* $100. *Application Contact:* Melissa Jordan, Assistant Dean for Records and Admission, 631-632-9712, Fax: 631-632-7243, E-mail: gradadmissions@stonybrook.edu. *Dean,* Dr. Fotis Sotiropoulos, 631-632-8380, Fax: 631-632-8205, E-mail: fotis.sotiropoulos@stonybrook.edu.

School of Marine and Atmospheric Sciences Students: 128 full-time (76 women), 16 part-time (7 women); includes 22 minority (1 American Indian or Alaska Native, non-Hispanic/Latino; 6 Asian, non-Hispanic/Latino; 11 Hispanic/Latino; 4 Two or more races, non-Hispanic/Latino), 33 international. Average age 27. 161 applicants, 46% accepted, 38 enrolled. *Faculty:* 55 full-time (15 women), 10 part-time/adjunct (4 women). Expenses: Contact institution. *Financial support:* In 2016–17, 10 fellowships, 50 research assistantships, 32 teaching assistantships were awarded; career-related internships or fieldwork and tuition waivers (full) also available. In 2016, 28 master's, 11 doctorates, 10 other advanced degrees awarded. Offers atmospheric sciences (MS, PhD); geospatial sciences (Graduate Certificate); marine and atmospheric sciences (MA, MS, PhD, Graduate Certificate); marine conservation and policy (MA); marine sciences (MS, PhD). *Application deadline:* For fall admission, 1/15 for domestic students; for spring admission, 10/1 for domestic students. *Application fee:* $100. *Application Contact:* Ginny Clancy, Educational Programs Coordinator, 631-632-8681, Fax: 631-632-8200. *Interim Dean*, Dr. Larry Swanson, 631-632-8700, Fax: 631-632-8820, E-mail: larry.swanson@stonybrook.edu.

School of Journalism Students: 3 full-time (2 women), 3 part-time (2 women); includes 1 minority (Hispanic/Latino), 1 international. Average age 29. *Faculty:* 9 full-time (2 women), 22 part-time/adjunct (7 women). Expenses: Contact institution. *Financial support:* In 2016–17, 1 teaching assistantship was awarded. In 2016, 4 master's awarded. Offers health communication (Certificate); journalism (MS). *Application deadline:* For fall admission, 4/30 for domestic students; for spring admission, 10/1 for domestic students. *Application fee:* $100. *Application Contact:* Maureen Robinson, Coordinator, 631-632-7403, Fax: 631-632-7550, E-mail: maureen.robinson@stonybrook.edu. *Dean*, Prof. Howard Schneider, 631-632-7403, E-mail: howard.schneider@stonybrook.edu.

School of Professional Development Students: 197 full-time (125 women), 965 part-time (674 women); includes 222 minority (79 Black or African American, non-Hispanic/Latino; 2 American Indian or Alaska Native, non-Hispanic/Latino; 35 Asian, non-Hispanic/Latino; 87 Hispanic/Latino; 1 Native Hawaiian or other Pacific Islander, non-Hispanic/Latino; 18 Two or more races, non-Hispanic/Latino), 5 international. Average age 33. 462 applicants, 87% accepted, 317 enrolled. *Faculty:* 4 full-time (3 women), 77 part-time/adjunct (34 women). Expenses: Contact institution. *Financial support:* Fellowships, research assistantships, teaching assistantships, and career-related internships or fieldwork available. Support available to part-time students. In 2016, 348 master's, 159 other advanced degrees awarded. *Program availability:* Part-time, evening/weekend, online learning. Offers biology (MAT); chemistry (MAT); coaching (Graduate Certificate); earth science (MAT); educational computing (Graduate Certificate); educational leadership (Advanced Certificate); English (MAT); environmental management (MPS, Graduate Certificate); French (MAT); German (MAT); higher education administration (MA, Certificate); human resource management (MS, Graduate Certificate); industrial management (Graduate Certificate); information systems management (Graduate Certificate); Italian (MAT); liberal studies (MA); mathematics (MAT); operations research (Graduate Certificate); physics (MAT); school district business leadership (Advanced Certificate); social studies (MAT); Spanish (MAT). *Application deadline:* For fall admission, 1/15 for domestic students, 6/1 for international students; for spring admission, 10/1 for domestic and international students. Applications are processed on a rolling basis. *Application fee:* $100. *Application Contact:* Melissa Jordan, Assistant Dean, 631-632-7751, E-mail: melissa.jordan@stonybrook.edu. *Dean*, Dr. Ken Lindblom, 631-632-7049, Fax: 631-632-9046, E-mail: kenneth.lindblom@stonybrook.edu.

Stony Brook Medicine Students: 1,964 full-time (1,237 women), 1,036 part-time (905 women); includes 1,057 minority (284 Black or African American, non-Hispanic/Latino; 7 American Indian or Alaska Native, non-Hispanic/Latino; 468 Asian, non-Hispanic/Latino; 257 Hispanic/Latino; 3 Native Hawaiian or other Pacific Islander, non-Hispanic/Latino; 38 Two or more races, non-Hispanic/Latino), 55 international. 10,864 applicants, 18% accepted, 1190 enrolled. Expenses: Contact institution. *Financial support:* In 2016–17, 24 fellowships, 34 research assistantships, 8 teaching assistantships were awarded. In 2016, 587 master's, 294 doctorates, 67 other advanced degrees awarded. Offers medicine (MHA, MPH, MS, MSW, DDS, DNP, DPT, MD, PhD, Advanced Certificate, Certificate). *Application deadline:* For fall admission, 1/15 for domestic students; for spring admission, 10/1 for domestic students. *Application fee:* $100. *Application Contact:* Melissa Jordan, Assistant Dean for Records and Admission, 631-632-9712, Fax: 631-632-7243, E-mail: gradadmissions@stonybrook.edu. *Dean*, Dr. Kenneth Kaushansky, 631-444-8234, E-mail: kenneth.kaushansky@stonybrook.edu.

School of Dental Medicine Students: 200 full-time (106 women), 1 (woman) part-time; includes 58 minority (4 Black or African American, non-Hispanic/Latino; 40 Asian, non-Hispanic/Latino; 11 Hispanic/Latino; 3 Two or more races, non-Hispanic/Latino), 5 international. Average age 26. 1,471 applicants, 8% accepted, 53 enrolled. *Faculty:* 34 full-time (15 women), 78 part-time/adjunct (20 women). Expenses: Contact institution. *Financial support:* Fellowships, research assistantships, teaching assistantships, and Federal Work-Study available. In 2016, 40 doctorates, 9 other advanced degrees awarded. Offers dental medicine (DDS); endodontics (Certificate); oral biology and pathology (MS, PhD); orthodontics (Certificate); periodontics (Certificate). *Application deadline:* For fall admission, 1/15 for domestic students; for spring admission, 10/1 for domestic students. *Application fee:* $100. *Application Contact:* Patricia Berry, Director of Admissions, 631-632-8871, Fax: 631-632-7130, E-mail: patricia.berry@stonybrook.edu. *Dean*, Dr. Mary R. Truhlar, 631-632-6985, Fax: 631-632-6621, E-mail: mary.truhlar@stonybrookmedicine.edu.

School of Health Technology and Management Students: 573 full-time (381 women), 68 part-time (52 women); includes 186 minority (32 Black or African American, non-Hispanic/Latino; 1 American Indian or Alaska Native, non-Hispanic/Latino; 94 Asian, non-Hispanic/Latino; 50 Hispanic/Latino; 2 Native Hawaiian or other Pacific Islander, non-Hispanic/Latino; 7 Two or more races, non-Hispanic/Latino), 12 international. Average age 28. 2,672 applicants, 15% accepted, 258 enrolled. *Faculty:* 62 full-time (41 women), 64 part-time/adjunct (44 women). Expenses: Contact institution. *Financial support:* In 2016–17, 1 research assistantship was awarded; fellowships, teaching assistantships, career-related internships or fieldwork, Federal Work-Study, and institutionally sponsored loans also available. Financial award application deadline: 3/15. In 2016, 133 master's, 91 doctorates, 28 other advanced degrees awarded. Offers applied health informatics (MS); disability studies (Certificate); health administration (MHA); health and rehabilitation sciences (PhD); health care management (Advanced Certificate); health care policy and management (MS); occupational therapy (MS); physical therapy (DPT); physician assistant (MS). *Application deadline:* For fall admission, 1/15 for domestic students; for spring admission, 10/1 for domestic students. *Application fee:* $100. *Application Contact:* Dr. Richard W. Johnson, Associate Dean for Graduate Studies, 631-444-3251, Fax: 631-444-7621, E-mail: richard.johnson@stonybrook.edu. *Dean*, Dr. Craig A. Lehmann, 631-444-2253, Fax: 631-444-7621, E-mail: craig.lehmann@stonybrook.edu.

School of Medicine Students: 701 full-time (337 women), 89 part-time (74 women); includes 324 minority (49 Black or African American, non-Hispanic/Latino; 213 Asian, non-Hispanic/Latino; 51 Hispanic/Latino; 11 Two or more races, non-Hispanic/Latino), 33 international. 5,292 applicants, 10% accepted, 189 enrolled. *Faculty:* 795 full-time (322 women), 107 part-time/adjunct (63 women). Expenses: Contact institution. *Financial support:* In 2016–17, 20 fellowships, 23 research assistantships, 2 teaching assistantships were awarded; career-related internships or fieldwork, Federal Work-Study, and tuition waivers (full) also available. In 2016, 66 master's, 141 doctorates, 2 other advanced degrees awarded. Offers anatomical sciences (PhD); community health (MPH); evaluation sciences (MPH); family violence (MPH); health communication (Certificate); health economics (MPH); medicine (MPH, MS, MD, PhD, Advanced Certificate, Certificate); molecular and cellular pharmacology (MS, PhD); molecular genetics and microbiology (PhD); nutrition (MS, Advanced Certificate); physiology and biophysics (PhD); population health (MPH); population health and clinical outcomes research (PhD); substance abuse (MPH). *Application deadline:* For fall admission, 1/15 for domestic students; for spring admission, 10/1 for domestic students. *Application fee:* $100. *Application Contact:* Dr. Jack Fuhrer, Associate Dean of Admissions, 631-444-2113, Fax: 631-444-6032, E-mail: somadmissions@stonybrook.edu. *Dean*, Dr. Kenneth Kaushansky, 631-444-2121, Fax: 631-632-6621, E-mail: kenneth.kaushansky@stonybrook.edu.

School of Nursing Students: 36 full-time (35 women), 859 part-time (764 women); includes 327 minority (121 Black or African American, non-Hispanic/Latino; 5 American Indian or Alaska Native, non-Hispanic/Latino; 109 Asian, non-Hispanic/Latino; 83 Hispanic/Latino; 9 Two or more races, non-Hispanic/Latino), 4 international. Average age 37. 715 applicants, 60% accepted, 360 enrolled. *Faculty:* 36 full-time (33 women), 44 part-time/adjunct (40 women). Expenses: Contact institution. *Financial support:* Fellowships, research assistantships, teaching assistantships, career-related internships or fieldwork, Federal Work-Study, institutionally sponsored loans, and traineeships available. Financial award application deadline: 3/15. In 2016, 227 master's, 28 doctorates, 22 other advanced degrees awarded. *Program availability:* Blended/hybrid learning. Offers adult health nurse practitioner (Certificate); adult health/primary care nursing (MS, DNP); child health nurse practitioner (Certificate); child health nursing (MS, DNP); family nurse practitioner (MS, DNP, Certificate); neonatal nurse practitioner (Certificate); neonatal nursing (MS, DNP); nurse midwifery (MS, DNP, Certificate); nursing (MS, DNP, Certificate); nursing education (MS, Certificate); nursing leadership (MS, Certificate); nursing practice (DNP); perinatal women's health nursing (MS, DNP, Certificate); psychiatric-mental health nurse practitioner (MS, DNP, Certificate). *Application deadline:* For fall admission, 3/3 for domestic students. *Application fee:* $100. Electronic applications accepted. *Application Contact:* Karen Allard, Admissions Coordinator, 631-444-6628, Fax: 631-444-3136, E-mail: karen.allard@stonybrook.edu. *Dean*, Dr. Lee Anne Xippolitos, 631-444-1041, Fax: 631-444-6621, E-mail: lee.xippolitos@stonybrook.edu.

School of Social Welfare Students: 454 full-time (378 women), 19 part-time (14 women); includes 162 minority (78 Black or African American, non-Hispanic/Latino; 1 American Indian or Alaska Native, non-Hispanic/Latino; 12 Asian, non-Hispanic/Latino; 62 Hispanic/Latino; 1 Native Hawaiian or other Pacific Islander, non-Hispanic/Latino; 8 Two or more races, non-Hispanic/Latino), 1 international. Average age 29. 525 applicants, 77% accepted, 270 enrolled. *Faculty:* 18 full-time (12 women), 44 part-time/adjunct (32 women). Expenses: Contact institution. *Financial support:* Fellowships, research assistantships, teaching assistantships, career-related internships or fieldwork, Federal Work-Study, and institutionally sponsored loans available. Financial award applicants required to submit FAFSA. In 2016, 165 master's, 3 doctorates awarded. *Program availability:* Part-time. Offers social welfare (PhD); social work (MSW). *Application deadline:* For fall admission, 1/15 for domestic students; for spring admission, 10/1 for domestic students. *Application fee:* $100. *Application Contact:* Mamie Gladden, Staff Assistant, 631-444-3142, Fax: 631-444-7565, E-mail: mamie.gladden@stonybrook.edu. *Dean and Assistant Vice President for Social Determinants of Health*, Dr. Jacqueline B. Mondros, 631-444-2139, E-mail: jacqueline.mondros@stonybrook.edu.

Stony Brook Southampton Students: 48 full-time (28 women), 64 part-time (47 women); includes 11 minority (1 Black or African American, non-Hispanic/Latino; 3 Asian, non-Hispanic/Latino; 7 Hispanic/Latino), 3 international. Average age 36. 82 applicants, 63% accepted, 19 enrolled. *Faculty:* 5 full-time (3 women), 36 part-time/adjunct (19 women). Expenses: Contact institution. *Financial support:* In 2016–17, 7 teaching assistantships were awarded. In 2016, 30 master's awarded. Offers fiction (MFA); film (MFA); poetry (MFA); scientific writing (MFA); scriptwriting (MFA). *Application deadline:* For fall admission, 1/15 for domestic students; for spring admission, 10/1 for domestic students. *Application fee:* $100. *Application Contact:* Adrienne Unger, Coordinator, 631-632-5030, E-mail: adrienne.unger@stonybrook.edu. *Associate Provost*, Dr. Robert Reeves, 631-632-5030, Fax: 631-632-2576, E-mail: robert.reeves@stonybrook.edu.

STRATFORD UNIVERSITY, Baltimore, MD 21202

General Information Proprietary, coed, comprehensive institution.

GRADUATE UNITS

Program in International Hospitality Management *Program availability:* Part-time, evening/weekend, online learning. Offers international hospitality management (MS).

STRATFORD UNIVERSITY, Falls Church, VA 22043

General Information Proprietary, coed, comprehensive institution. *Enrollment:* 809 graduate, professional, and undergraduate students; 505 full-time matriculated graduate/professional students (186 women), 172 part-time matriculated graduate/professional students (88 women). *Enrollment by degree level:* 677 master's. *Tuition:* Full-time $4455; part-time $2227.50 per course. One-time fee: $100. *Graduate housing:* On-campus housing not available. *Student services:* Campus employment opportunities, career counseling, exercise/wellness program, international student services, multicultural affairs office, services for students with disabilities, writing training. *Library facilities:* Learning Resource Center.

Computer facilities: A campuswide network can be accessed from off campus. Online class registration is available.
Website: http://www.stratford.edu/

General Application Contact: Admissions, 800-444-0804, E-mail: fcadmissions@stratford.edu.

GRADUATE UNITS

School of Graduate Studies Students: 505 full-time (186 women), 172 part-time (88 women); includes 532 minority (165 Black or African American, non-Hispanic/Latino; 18 American Indian or Alaska Native, non-Hispanic/Latino; 324 Asian, non-Hispanic/Latino; 13 Hispanic/Latino; 10 Native Hawaiian or other Pacific Islander, non-Hispanic/Latino; 2 Two or more races, non-Hispanic/Latino). Average age 27. Expenses: Contact institution. *Financial support:* Federal Work-Study and scholarships/grants available. Financial award applicants required to submit FAFSA. In 2016, 520 master's awarded. *Program availability:* Part-time, evening/weekend, 100% online, blended/hybrid learning. Offers accounting (MS); business administration (IMBA, MBA); cyber security (MS); cyber security leadership and policy (MS); digital forensics (MS); enterprise business management (MS); entrepreneurial management (MS); healthcare administration (MS); information systems (MS); international hospitality management (MS); networking and telecommunications (MS); software engineering (MS). *Application deadline:* Applications are processed on a rolling basis. *Application fee:* $50. Electronic applications accepted. *Application Contact:* Admissions, 800-444-0804, E-mail: fcadmissions@stratford.edu. *President,* Dr. Richard R. Shurtz, 703-539-6890, Fax: 703-539-6960.

STRAYER UNIVERSITY, Washington, DC 20005-2603

General Information Proprietary, coed, comprehensive institution. *Graduate housing:* On-campus housing not available.

GRADUATE UNITS

Graduate Studies *Program availability:* Part-time, evening/weekend, online learning. Offers accounting (MS); acquisition (MBA); business administration (MBA); communications technology (MS); educational management (M Ed); finance (MBA); health services administration (MHSA); hospitality and tourism management (MBA); human resource management (MBA); information systems (MS); management (MBA); management information systems (MS); marketing (MBA); professional accounting (MS); public administration (MPA); supply chain management (MBA); technology in education (M Ed). Programs also offered at campus locations in Birmingham, AL; Chamblee, GA; Cobb County, GA; Morrow, GA; White Marsh, MD; Charleston, SC; Columbia, SC; Greensboro, NC; Greenville, SC; Lexington, KY; Louisville, KY; Nashville, TN; North Raleigh, NC; Washington, DC. Electronic applications accepted.

SUFFOLK UNIVERSITY, Boston, MA 02108-2770

General Information Independent, coed, comprehensive institution. *Enrollment:* 7,560 graduate, professional, and undergraduate students; 1,116 full-time matriculated graduate/professional students (649 women), 1,075 part-time matriculated graduate/professional students (629 women). *Enrollment by degree level:* 1,064 master's, 1,102 doctoral, 25 other advanced degrees. *Graduate faculty:* 148 full-time (66 women), 100 part-time/adjunct (41 women). *Tuition:* Full-time $41,490; part-time $1383 per credit hour. *Required fees:* $52; $52 per credit hour. Part-time tuition and fees vary according to course load and program. *Graduate housing:* On-campus housing not available. *Student services:* Campus employment opportunities, campus safety program, career counseling, exercise/wellness program, free psychological counseling, grant writing training, international student services, low-cost health insurance, multicultural affairs office, services for students with disabilities, writing training. *Library facilities:* Mildred Sawyer Library plus 3 others. *Collection:* Books: 159,014 (physical), 212,904 (digital/electronic); Serial titles: 302 (physical), 35,386 (digital/electronic); Databases: 1,904. Weekly public service hours: 16; students can reserve study rooms.

Computer facilities: Computer purchase and lease plans are available. 539 computers available on campus for general student use. A campuswide network can be accessed from student residence rooms and from off campus. Online class registration is available.

Website: http://www.suffolk.edu/

General Application Contact: John Bresnahan, Director of Graduate Admissions, 617-573-8302, Fax: 617-305-1733, E-mail: grad.admission@suffolk.edu.

GRADUATE UNITS

College of Arts and Sciences Students: 161 full-time (127 women), 141 part-time (117 women); includes 75 minority (21 Black or African American, non-Hispanic/Latino; 16 Asian, non-Hispanic/Latino; 33 Hispanic/Latino; 5 Two or more races, non-Hispanic/Latino), 45 international. Average age 28. 604 applicants, 46% accepted, 133 enrolled. *Faculty:* 43 full-time (21 women), 32 part-time/adjunct (19 women). Expenses: Contact institution. *Financial support:* In 2016–17, 201 students received support, including 185 fellowships (averaging $8,677 per year); career-related internships or fieldwork, Federal Work-Study, institutionally sponsored loans, scholarships/grants, and unspecified assistantships also available. Support available to part-time students. Financial award application deadline: 4/1; financial award applicants required to submit FAFSA. In 2016, 130 master's, 14 doctorates, 22 other advanced degrees awarded. *Program availability:* Part-time, evening/weekend. Offers administration of higher education (M Ed, CAGS); arts and sciences (M Ed, MA, MAC, MS, MSCJS, MSPS, PhD, CAGS, Certificate, Graduate Certificate); clinical psychology (PhD); college admission counseling (Certificate); communication studies (MAC); ethics and public policy (MS); integrated marketing communication (MAC); international relations (MSPS); mental health counseling (MS); political science (MSPS); professional politics (MSPS, CAGS); public relations and advertising (MAC); school counseling (MS, CAGS); sociology (MSCJS). *Application deadline:* For fall admission, 3/15 priority date for domestic and international students; for spring admission, 10/15 priority date for domestic students, 10/1 priority date for international students. Applications are processed on a rolling basis. *Application fee:* $50. Electronic applications accepted. *Application Contact:* Mara Marzocchi, Associate Director of Graduate Admissions, 617-573-8302, Fax: 617-305-1733, E-mail: grad.admission@suffolk.edu. *Dean,* Maria Toyada, 617-573-8265, Fax: 617-573-8513, E-mail: mtoyada@suffolk.edu.

Law School Students: 647 full-time (357 women), 380 part-time (197 women); includes 219 minority (61 Black or African American, non-Hispanic/Latino; 1 American Indian or Alaska Native, non-Hispanic/Latino; 50 Asian, non-Hispanic/Latino; 82 Hispanic/Latino; 25 Two or more races, non-Hispanic/Latino), 42 international. Average age 27. 1,924 applicants, 64% accepted, 355 enrolled. *Faculty:* 58 full-time (26 women), 47 part-time/adjunct (17 women). Expenses: Contact institution. *Financial support:* In 2016–17, 572 students received support, including 1 fellowship (averaging $31,390 per year); career-related internships or fieldwork, Federal Work-Study, institutionally sponsored loans, and scholarships/grants also available. Support available to part-time students. Financial award application deadline: 3/1; financial award applicants required to submit FAFSA. In 2016, 21 master's, 416 doctorates awarded. *Program availability:* Part-time, evening/weekend. Offers business law and financial services (JD); civil litigation (JD); global law and technology (LL M); health and biomedical law (JD); intellectual property law (JD); international law (JD). *Application deadline:* For fall admission, 4/1 for domestic and international students. Applications are processed on a rolling basis. *Application fee:* $60. Electronic applications accepted. *Application Contact:* Matthew Gavin, Assistant Dean for Admissions and Financial Aid, 617-573-8144, Fax: 617-994-6838, E-mail: lawadm@suffolk.edu. *Dean,* Andrew Perlman, 617-573-8144, Fax: 617-994-6838, E-mail: lawadmin@suffolk.edu.

New England School of Art and Design Students: 37 full-time (30 women), 25 part-time (23 women); includes 11 minority (1 Black or African American, non-Hispanic/Latino; 7 Asian, non-Hispanic/Latino; 3 Hispanic/Latino), 19 international. Average age 29. 63 applicants, 73% accepted, 20 enrolled. *Faculty:* 12 full-time (8

women), 20 part-time/adjunct (12 women). Expenses: Contact institution. *Financial support:* In 2016–17, 44 students received support, including 40 fellowships (averaging $6,900 per year); career-related internships or fieldwork, Federal Work-Study, institutionally sponsored loans, scholarships/grants, and unspecified assistantships also available. Financial award application deadline: 4/1; financial award applicants required to submit FAFSA. In 2016, 29 master's awarded. *Program availability:* Part-time, evening/weekend. Offers graphic design (MA); interior architecture (MA). *Application deadline:* For fall admission, 3/15 priority date for domestic and international students; for spring admission, 10/15 priority date for domestic and international students. Applications are processed on a rolling basis. *Application fee:* $50. Electronic applications accepted. *Application Contact:* Mara Marzocchi, Associate Director of Graduate Admissions, 617-573-8302, Fax: 617-305-1733, E-mail: grad.admission@suffolk.edu. *Department Chair,* Audrey Goldstein, 617-997-4290, E-mail: agoldstein@suffolk.edu.

Sawyer Business School Students: 308 full-time (165 women), 554 part-time (315 women); includes 201 minority (74 Black or African American, non-Hispanic/Latino; 54 Asian, non-Hispanic/Latino; 67 Hispanic/Latino; 6 Two or more races, non-Hispanic/Latino), 146 international. Average age 30. 909 applicants, 76% accepted, 307 enrolled. *Faculty:* 43 full-time (16 women), 23 part-time/adjunct (7 women). Expenses: Contact institution. *Financial support:* In 2016–17, 488 students received support, including 442 fellowships (averaging $9,085 per year); career-related internships or fieldwork, Federal Work-Study, institutionally sponsored loans, scholarships/grants, and unspecified assistantships also available. Support available to part-time students. Financial award application deadline: 4/1; financial award applicants required to submit FAFSA. In 2016, 398 master's, 2 other advanced degrees awarded. *Program availability:* Part-time, evening/weekend, 100% online, blended/hybrid learning. Offers accounting (MBA, MSA, Graduate Certificate); business (EMBA, GMBA, MBA, MBAH, MHA, MPA, MSA, MSF, MSFSB, MST, Graduate Certificate); community health (MPA); entrepreneurship (MBA); executive business administration (EMBA); finance (MSF, MSFSB); global business administration (GMBA); health (MBAH); health administration (MBA); healthcare administration (MHA); information systems, performance management, and big data analytics (MPA); international business (MBA); marketing (MBA); nonprofit management (MBA, MPA); organizational behavior (MBA); state and local government (MPA); strategic management (MBA); supply chain management (MBA); taxation (MBA, MST). *Application deadline:* For fall admission, 3/15 priority date for domestic and international students; for spring admission, 10/15 for domestic students, 3/15 priority date for international students. Applications are processed on a rolling basis. *Application fee:* $50. Electronic applications accepted. *Application Contact:* Mara Marzocchi, Associate Director of Graduate Admissions, 617-573-8302, Fax: 617-305-1733, E-mail: grad.admission@suffolk.edu. *Dean,* William J. O'Neill, JD, 617-573-2665, Fax: 617-573-8704, E-mail: woneill@suffolk.edu.

SULLIVAN UNIVERSITY, Louisville, KY 40205

General Information Proprietary, coed, comprehensive institution. *Graduate housing:* On-campus housing not available.

GRADUATE UNITS

College of Pharmacy Offers pharmacy (Pharm D).

School of Business *Program availability:* Part-time, online learning. Offers business (EMBA, MBA, MPM, MSCM, MSCS, MSHRL, MSM, MSMIT, PhD, Pharm D).

SUL ROSS STATE UNIVERSITY, Alpine, TX 79832

General Information State-supported, coed, comprehensive institution. *Graduate housing:* Rooms and/or apartments available on a first-come, first-served basis to single and married students. *Research affiliation:* Chihuahuan Desert Research Institute (biology, geology), Big Bend National Park (biology, geology).

GRADUATE UNITS

College of Arts and Sciences *Program availability:* Part-time, evening/weekend. Offers art history (MA); arts and sciences (MA, MS); biology (MS); English (MA); geology (MS); history (MA); political science (MA); psychology (MA); studio art (MA).

College of Professional Studies *Program availability:* Part-time, evening/weekend. Offers business administration (EMBA, MBA); counseling (M Ed); criminal justice (MS); educational diagnostics (M Ed, Certificate); homeland security (MS); master reading teacher (Certificate); physical education (M Ed); reading specialist (M Ed, Certificate); school administration (M Ed); Texas reading specialist (M Ed). Two-year Executive MBA program in cooperation with La Universidad de Chihuahua, Mexico (UACH).

Division of Agricultural and Natural Resource Science *Program availability:* Part-time. Offers agricultural and natural resource science (M Ag, MS); animal science (M Ag, MS); range and wildlife management (M Ag, MS).

Rio Grande College of Sul Ross State University *Program availability:* Part-time, evening/weekend, online learning. Offers business administration (MBA); teacher education (M Ed).

SUM BIBLE COLLEGE & THEOLOGICAL SEMINARY, Oakland, CA 94603

General Information Independent-religious, coed, comprehensive institution.

GRADUATE UNITS

Graduate Programs Offers biblical studies (MA); Christian leadership (MA); theology (M Div).

SWEDISH INSTITUTE, COLLEGE OF HEALTH SCIENCES, New York, NY 10001-6700

General Information Proprietary, coed, comprehensive institution. *Graduate housing:* On-campus housing not available.

GRADUATE UNITS

Graduate Program *Program availability:* Part-time, evening/weekend.

SWEET BRIAR COLLEGE, Sweet Briar, VA 24595

General Information Independent, women only, comprehensive institution. *Graduate housing:* Room and/or apartments available on a first-come, first-served basis to single students; on-campus housing not available to married students.

GRADUATE UNITS

Department of Education *Program availability:* Part-time. Offers education (M Ed, MAT). Electronic applications accepted.

SYRACUSE UNIVERSITY, Syracuse, NY 13244

General Information Independent, coed, university. CGS member. *Enrollment:* 21,970 graduate, professional, and undergraduate students; 4,536 full-time matriculated graduate/professional students (2,284 women), 2,043 part-time matriculated graduate/professional students (964 women). *Enrollment by degree level:* 4,552 master's, 1,895 doctoral, 132 other advanced degrees. *Graduate faculty:* 1,110 full-time (443 women), 600 part-time/adjunct (279 women). *Tuition:* Full-time $25,974; part-time $1443 per credit hour. *Required fees:* $802; $50 per course. Tuition and fees vary according to course load and program. *Graduate housing:* On-campus housing not available. *Student services:* Campus employment opportunities, campus safety program, career counseling, child daycare facilities, exercise/wellness program, free psychological counseling, grant writing training, international student services, low-cost health insurance, multicultural affairs office, services for students with disabilities, teacher training, writing training. *Library facilities:* E. S. Bird Library plus 3 others. *Collection:* Books: 3.5 million (physical), 348,958 (digital/electronic); Serial titles: 35,735 (physical), 143,341 (digital/electronic); Databases: 1,154. Weekly public service hours: 146; study areas open 24 hours, 5–7 days a week; students can reserve study rooms. *Research affiliation:* South Side Innovation Center (business incubator and entrepreneurship development), IBM Green Data Center (advanced infrastructure and smarter computing technologies), Institute for Manufacturing Enterprises (promoting learning in manufacturing enterprises through teaching, application, integration, discovery, and service), Syracuse Research Corporation (defense, environmental and intelligence systems), Center of Excellence (environmental and energy systems innovation), Say Yes to Education, Inc. (academic support and funding to high school students).

Computer facilities: Computer purchase and lease plans are available. 3,500 computers available on campus for general student use. A campuswide network can be accessed from student residence rooms and from off campus. Online class registration, web conferencing, learning management system, blogging service, personal Websites, "View My Advising Report" digital asset management system, office software, online video training are available.
Website: http://www.syr.edu/

General Application Contact: 315-443-4492, Fax: 315-443-3423, E-mail: grad@syr.edu.

GRADUATE UNITS

College of Arts and Sciences Students: 752 full-time (428 women), 54 part-time (32 women); includes 123 minority (21 Black or African American, non-Hispanic/Latino; 3 American Indian or Alaska Native, non-Hispanic/Latino; 25 Asian, non-Hispanic/Latino; 56 Hispanic/Latino; 1 Native Hawaiian or other Pacific Islander, non-Hispanic/Latino; 17 Two or more races, non-Hispanic/Latino), 206 international. Average age 27. 2,341 applicants, 24% accepted, 268 enrolled. *Faculty:* 344 full-time (138 women), 131 part-time/adjunct (79 women). Expenses: Contact institution. *Financial support:* Fellowships with full tuition reimbursements, research assistantships with tuition reimbursements, teaching assistantships with tuition reimbursements, career-related internships or fieldwork, Federal Work-Study, scholarships/grants, health care benefits, tuition waivers, and unspecified assistantships available. Support available to part-time students. Financial award application deadline: 1/1. In 2016, 169 master's, 52 doctorates, 59 other advanced degrees awarded. *Program availability:* Part-time. Offers applied statistics (MS); art history (MA); arts and sciences (MA, MFA, MS, Au D, PhD, CAS); audiology (Au D, PhD); biology (MS, PhD); chemistry (MS, PhD); clinical psychology (PhD); cognition, brain, and behavior (PhD); college science teaching (PhD); composition and cultural rhetoric (PhD); computational linguistics (MS); creative writing (MFA); earth sciences (MA, MS, PhD); English (MA, PhD); forensic science (MS, CAS); French and Francophone studies (MA); language teaching: TESOL/TLOTE (CAS); linguistic studies (MA); mathematics (PhD); mathematics education (MS); neuroscience (PhD); Pan-African studies (MA); philosophy (MA, PhD); physics (MS, PhD); religion (MA, PhD); school psychology (PhD); social psychology (PhD); Spanish literature and culture (MA); speech-language pathology (MS). *Application fee:* $75. *Application Contact:* Cassidy Perreault, Administrative Specialist, 315-443-2875, E-mail: clperrea@syr.edu. *Dean,* Dr. Karin Ruhlandt, 315-443-4070, E-mail: kruhland@syr.edu.

College of Engineering and Computer Science Students: 883 full-time (211 women), 207 part-time (40 women); includes 62 minority (17 Black or African American, non-Hispanic/Latino; 32 Asian, non-Hispanic/Latino; 10 Hispanic/Latino; 3 Two or more races, non-Hispanic/Latino), 838 international. Average age 26. 3,045 applicants, 39% accepted, 392 enrolled. *Faculty:* 94 full-time (20 women), 20 part-time/adjunct (2 women). Expenses: Contact institution. *Financial support:* Fellowships with full tuition reimbursements, research assistantships with tuition reimbursements, teaching assistantships with tuition reimbursements, scholarships/grants, and tuition waivers (partial) available. Financial award application deadline: 1/1; financial award applicants required to submit FAFSA. In 2016, 453 master's, 24 doctorates, 2 other advanced degrees awarded. *Program availability:* Part-time, evening/weekend. Offers bioengineering (MS, PhD); chemical engineering (MS, PhD); civil engineering (MS, PhD); computer and information science and engineering (PhD); computer engineering (MS); computer science (MS); cybersecurity (MS, CAS); electrical and computer engineering (PhD); electrical engineering (MS); energy systems engineering (MS); engineering and computer science (MS, PhD, CAS); engineering management (MS); environmental engineering (MS); environmental engineering science (MS); environmental health (CAS); mechanical and aerospace engineering (MS, PhD); microwave engineering (CAS); sustainable enterprise (CAS). *Application deadline:* For fall admission, 7/1 priority date for domestic students, 6/1 priority date for international students; for spring admission, 11/15 priority date for domestic students, 10/15 priority date for international students. Applications are processed on a rolling basis. *Application fee:* $75. Electronic applications accepted. *Application Contact:* Kathleen Joyce, Assistant Dean, 314-443-2219, E-mail: topgrads@syr.edu. *Dean, College of Engineering and Computer Science,* Dr. Teresa Dahlberg, 315-443-2545, E-mail: dahlbery@syr.edu.

College of Law Students: 566 full-time (271 women), 6 part-time (2 women); includes 109 minority (27 Black or African American, non-Hispanic/Latino; 2 American Indian or Alaska Native, non-Hispanic/Latino; 22 Asian, non-Hispanic/Latino; 44 Hispanic/Latino; 14 Two or more races, non-Hispanic/Latino), 60 international. Average age 25. 2,148 applicants, 49% accepted, 260 enrolled. *Faculty:* 43 full-time (15 women), 21 part-time/adjunct (9 women). Expenses: Contact institution. *Financial support:* In 2016–17, 487 students received support. Fellowships, research assistantships, career-related internships or fieldwork, Federal Work-Study, institutionally sponsored loans, scholarships/grants, and tuition waivers (partial) available. Support available to part-time students. Financial award application deadline: 2/15. In 2016, 38 master's, 165 doctorates awarded. *Program availability:* Part-time. Offers American law (LL M); law (LL M, JD). *Application deadline:* For fall admission, 4/1 priority date for domestic and international students. Applications are processed on a rolling basis. *Application fee:* $70. Electronic applications accepted. *Application Contact:* Nolana McKinstry, Associate Director of Admissions, 315-443-1962, Fax: 315-443-9568, E-mail: admissions@law.syr.edu. *Dean and Professor of Law,* Craig M. Boise, 315-443-9580, E-mail: cmboise@law.syr.edu.

College of Visual and Performing Arts Students: 194 full-time (122 women), 8 part-time (6 women); includes 28 minority (5 Black or African American, non-Hispanic/Latino;

4 Asian, non-Hispanic/Latino; 4 Hispanic/Latino; 15 Two or more races, non-Hispanic/Latino), 72 international. Average age 26. 444 applicants, 39% accepted, 94 enrolled. *Faculty:* 129 full-time (52 women), 127 part-time/adjunct (53 women). Expenses: Contact institution. *Financial support:* Fellowships with full tuition reimbursements, teaching assistantships with tuition reimbursements, institutionally sponsored loans, and unspecified assistantships available. Financial award application deadline: 1/1; financial award applicants required to submit FAFSA. In 2016, 63 master's awarded. Offers art photography (MFA); art video (MFA); audio arts (MA); communication and rhetorical studies (MA); composition (MM); conducting (MM); film (MFA); illustration (MFA); museum studies (MA); music and performance (MM); studio arts (MFA); visual and performing arts (M Mu, M Mus, MA, MFA, MM, MS); voice pedagogy (MM). *Application deadline:* For fall admission, 2/1 priority date for domestic and international students; for spring admission, 3/1 priority date for domestic students. *Application fee:* $75. Electronic applications accepted. *Application Contact:* Therese West, Information Contact, 315-443-0137, E-mail: admissg@syr.edu. *Dean, College of Visual and Performing Arts,* Dr. Michael S. Tick, 315-443-8070, E-mail: mtick1@syr.edu.

David B. Falk College of Sport and Human Dynamics Students: 222 full-time (180 women), 105 part-time (79 women); includes 69 minority (35 Black or African American, non-Hispanic/Latino; 2 American Indian or Alaska Native, non-Hispanic/Latino; 5 Asian, non-Hispanic/Latino; 16 Hispanic/Latino; 1 Native Hawaiian or other Pacific Islander, non-Hispanic/Latino; 10 Two or more races, non-Hispanic/Latino), 30 international. Average age 29. 474 applicants, 74% accepted, 172 enrolled. *Faculty:* 71 full-time (42 women), 25 part-time/adjunct (18 women). Expenses: Contact institution. *Financial support:* Fellowships with full tuition reimbursements, research assistantships with tuition reimbursements, teaching assistantships with tuition reimbursements, and tuition waivers available. Financial award application deadline: 1/1; financial award applicants required to submit FAFSA. In 2016, 147 master's, 27 other advanced degrees awarded. *Program availability:* Part-time, evening/weekend. Offers addiction studies (MA, CAS); child and family studies (MA, MS, PhD); food studies (MS, CAS); global health (MS); marriage and family therapy (MA, PhD); nutrition science (MA, MS, PhD); social work (MSW); sport and human dynamics (MA, MS, MSW, PhD, CAS); sport venue and event management (MS); trauma-informed practice (CAS). *Application deadline:* For fall admission, 2/15 priority date for domestic and international students; for spring admission, 11/15 priority date for domestic students, 11/15 for international students; for summer admission, 3/15 priority date for domestic students, 3/15 for international students. Applications are processed on a rolling basis. *Application fee:* $75. Electronic applications accepted. *Application Contact:* Felicia Otero, Director of College Admissions, 315-443-5555, Fax: 315-443-2562, E-mail: falk@syr.edu. *Dean,* Dr. Diane Lyden Murphy, 315-443-5582, Fax: 315-443-2562.

Martin J. Whitman School of Management Students: 307 full-time (143 women), 890 part-time (299 women); includes 356 minority (142 Black or African American, non-Hispanic/Latino; 3 American Indian or Alaska Native, non-Hispanic/Latino; 82 Asian, non-Hispanic/Latino; 99 Hispanic/Latino; 3 Native Hawaiian or other Pacific Islander, non-Hispanic/Latino; 27 Two or more races, non-Hispanic/Latino), 209 international. Average age 33. 1,579 applicants, 49% accepted, 308 enrolled. *Faculty:* 73 full-time (24 women), 53 part-time/adjunct (18 women). Expenses: Contact institution. *Financial support:* In 2016–17, 45 students received support. Fellowships with full tuition reimbursements available, research assistantships with tuition reimbursements available, teaching assistantships with tuition reimbursements available, career-related internships or fieldwork, and scholarships/grants available. Financial award application deadline: 2/15. In 2016, 294 master's, 3 doctorates awarded. *Program availability:* Part-time, 100% online. Offers accounting (MBA); business analytics (MS); entrepreneurship (MBA); finance (PhD); management (MBA, MS, PhD); management information systems (PhD); marketing management (MBA); professional accounting (MS); real estate (MBA); supply chain management (MS). *Application deadline:* For fall admission, 11/30 for domestic and international students; for winter admission, 1/1 for domestic and international students; for spring admission, 2/15 for domestic and international students; for summer admission, 4/19 for domestic students. *Application fee:* $75. Electronic applications accepted. *Application Contact:* Shri Ramakrishnan, Assistant Director, Graduate Recruitment, 315-443-3497, Fax: 315-443-9517, E-mail: sramak01@syr.edu. *Associate Dean for Master's Programs,* Don Harter, 315-443-3502, Fax: 315-443-9517, E-mail: dharter@syr.edu.

Maxwell School of Citizenship and Public Affairs Students: 496 full-time (250 women), 93 part-time (51 women); includes 81 minority (21 Black or African American, non-Hispanic/Latino; 1 American Indian or Alaska Native, non-Hispanic/Latino; 23 Asian, non-Hispanic/Latino; 29 Hispanic/Latino; 7 Two or more races, non-Hispanic/Latino), 198 international. Average age 31. 1,270 applicants, 49% accepted, 293 enrolled. *Faculty:* 152 full-time (62 women), 28 part-time/adjunct (8 women). Expenses: Contact institution. *Financial support:* Fellowships with full tuition reimbursements, research assistantships with tuition reimbursements, and teaching assistantships with tuition reimbursements available. Financial award application deadline: 1/1. In 2016, 296 master's, 28 doctorates, 137 other advanced degrees awarded. *Program availability:* Part-time, online learning. Offers anthropology (MA, PhD); citizenship and public affairs (EMIR, EMPA, MA, MPA, MPH, MS Sc, PhD, CAS); conflict resolution (CAS); economics (MA, PhD); economics and international relationsgeography (MA, PhD); health services management and policy (CAS); history (MA, PhD); international relations (EMIR, MA); leadership of international and non-governmental organizations (CAS); political science (MA, PhD); public administration (EMPA, MPA, PhD); public administration and international relationspublic diplomacypublic health (MPH); public infrastructure management and leadership (CAS); social sciences (MA, PhD); sociology (MA, PhD). *Application deadline:* For fall admission, 2/1 priority date for domestic and international students. Applications are processed on a rolling basis. *Application fee:* $75. Electronic applications accepted. *Application Contact:* Christine Omolino, Director, Admission and Financial Aid, 315-443-4000, E-mail: comolino@maxwell.syr.edu. *Dean,* Dr. David Van Slyke, 315-443-3461, E-mail: vanslyke@maxwell.syr.edu.

School of Architecture Students: 101 full-time (43 women), 1 part-time (0 women); includes 8 minority (1 Black or African American, non-Hispanic/Latino; 2 Asian, non-Hispanic/Latino; 4 Hispanic/Latino; 1 Two or more races, non-Hispanic/Latino), 79 international. Average age 26. 251 applicants, 58% accepted, 42 enrolled. *Faculty:* 38 full-time (14 women), 11 part-time/adjunct (1 woman). Expenses: Contact institution. *Financial support:* Fellowships with full tuition reimbursements, research assistantships with tuition reimbursements, and teaching assistantships with tuition reimbursements available. Financial award application deadline: 1/1. In 2016, 43 master's awarded. Offers architecture (M Arch, MS). *Application deadline:* For fall admission, 2/1 priority date for domestic and international students. *Application fee:* $75. Electronic applications accepted. *Application Contact:* Vittoria Buccina, Director, Graduate and Undergraduate Recruitment, 315-443-5074, E-mail: vabuccin@syr.edu. *Dean, School of Architecture,* Michael Speaks, 315-443-0790, E-mail: maspeaks@syr.edu.

School of Education Students: 342 full-time (246 women), 216 part-time (143 women); includes 134 minority (62 Black or African American, non-Hispanic/Latino; 8 American Indian or Alaska Native, non-Hispanic/Latino; 15 Asian, non-Hispanic/Latino; 36 Hispanic/Latino; 1 Native Hawaiian or other Pacific Islander, non-Hispanic/Latino; 12 Two or more races, non-Hispanic/Latino), 77 international. Average age 33. 486 applicants, 61% accepted, 137 enrolled. *Faculty:* 50 full-time (28 women), 50 part-time/adjunct (35 women). Expenses: Contact institution. *Financial support:* Fellowships with full tuition reimbursements, research assistantships with tuition reimbursements, teaching assistantships with tuition reimbursements, career-related internships or fieldwork, institutionally sponsored loans, scholarships/grants, health care benefits, tuition waivers (partial), and unspecified assistantships available. Financial award application deadline: 1/15; financial award applicants required to submit FAFSA. In 2016, 161 master's, 31 doctorates, 34 other advanced degrees awarded. *Program availability:* Part-time. Offers art education (MS); biology (MS); chemistry (MS, PhD); clinical mental health counseling (MS); counseling and counselor education (PhD); cultural foundations of education (MS, PhD, CAS); disability studies (CAS); early childhood special education (MS); education (M Mus, MM, MS, Ed D, PhD, CAS); educational leadership (MS, Ed D, CAS); educational technology (CAS); English education preparation (grades 7-12) (MS); exercise science (MS); higher education (MS, PhD); inclusive special education (grades 1-6) (MS); inclusive special education (grades 7-12) (MS); inclusive special education: severe/multiple disabilities (MS); instructional design foundations (CAS); instructional design, development, and evaluation (MS, PhD, CAS); instructional technology (MS); literacy education (PhD); literacy education (birth - grade 12) (MS); mathematics education (MS, PhD); music education (MM, MS); school counseling (MS, CAS); school district business leadership (CAS); social studies education preparation (grades 7-12) (MS); special education (PhD); student affairs counseling (MS); teaching and curriculum (MS, PhD); teaching English language learners (Pre-K-12) (MS). *Application deadline:* Applications are processed on a rolling basis. *Application fee:* $75. Electronic applications accepted. *Application Contact:* Speranza Migliore, Graduate Recruiter, School of Education, 315-443-2505, E-mail: gradrcrt@syr.edu. *Dean,* Dr. Joanna Masingila, 315-443-4751, E-mail: jomasing@syr.edu.

School of Information Studies Students: 430 full-time (213 women), 215 part-time (114 women); includes 71 minority (34 Black or African American, non-Hispanic/Latino; 11 Asian, non-Hispanic/Latino; 14 Hispanic/Latino; 12 Two or more races, non-Hispanic/Latino), 334 international. Average age 29. 1,379 applicants, 44% accepted, 280 enrolled. *Faculty:* 38 full-time (15 women), 45 part-time/adjunct (15 women). Expenses: Contact institution. *Financial support:* Fellowships with full tuition reimbursements, research assistantships with tuition reimbursements, teaching assistantships with tuition reimbursements, and scholarships/grants available. Financial award application deadline: 1/1. In 2016, 295 master's, 6 doctorates, 188 other advanced degrees awarded. *Program availability:* Part-time, evening/weekend, online learning. Offers applied data science (MS); data science (CAS); e-government management and leadership (CAS); enterprise data systems (MS); information management (MS); information science and technology (PhD); information security management (CAS); information studies (MS, PhD, CAS); library and information science (MS); library and information science: school media (MS); school media (CAS). *Application deadline:* For fall admission, 1/1 priority date for domestic students, 2/1 priority date for international students; for spring admission, 10/15 priority date for domestic and international students. Applications are processed on a rolling basis. *Application fee:* $75. Electronic applications accepted. *Application Contact:* Susan Corieri, Director of Enrollment Management, 315-443-2575, E-mail: ist@syr.edu. *Dean/Professor,* Dr. Elizabeth D. Liddy, 315-443-2736, E-mail: liddy@syr.edu.

S. I. Newhouse School of Public Communications Students: 234 full-time (170 women), 243 part-time (193 women); includes 159 minority (82 Black or African American, non-Hispanic/Latino; 3 American Indian or Alaska Native, non-Hispanic/Latino; 14 Asian, non-Hispanic/Latino; 41 Hispanic/Latino; 1 Native Hawaiian or other Pacific Islander, non-Hispanic/Latino; 14 Two or more races, non-Hispanic/Latino), 115 international. Average age 28. 805 applicants, 65% accepted, 240 enrolled. *Faculty:* 73 full-time (29 women), 63 part-time/adjunct (32 women). Expenses: Contact institution. *Financial support:* Fellowships with full tuition reimbursements, research assistantships with partial tuition reimbursements, scholarships/grants, and instructional associate positions with partial tuition reimbursements available. Financial award application deadline: 2/1. In 2016, 213 master's, 3 doctorates awarded. *Program availability:* Online learning. Offers advertising (MA); arts journalism (MA); broadcast and digital journalism (MS); communications management (MS); computational journalism (MS); documentary film and history (MA); magazine, newspaper and online journalism (MA); mass communications (PhD); media studies (MA); new media management (MS); photography (MS); public communications (MA, MS, PhD); public diplomacy public relations (MS); television, radio, and film (MA). *Application deadline:* For fall admission, 1/15 priority date for domestic and international students; for summer admission, 1/15 priority date for domestic and international students. *Application fee:* $45. Electronic applications accepted. *Application Contact:* Martha Coria, Graduate Records Office, 315-443-4039, Fax: 315-443-1834, E-mail: pcgrad@syr.edu. *Dean,* Lorraine Branham, 315-443-3372, E-mail: lbranham@syr.edu.

TABOR COLLEGE, Hillsboro, KS 67063
General Information Independent-religious, coed, comprehensive institution.

GRADUATE UNITS

Graduate Program Offers accounting (MBA). Program offered at the Wichita campus only.

TAFT UNIVERSITY SYSTEM, Denver, CO 80246
General Information Proprietary, coed, graduate-only institution.

GRADUATE UNITS

The Boyer Graduate School of Education Offers education (M Ed).
Taft Law School Offers American jurisprudence (LL M); law (JD); taxation (LL M).
W. Edwards Deming School of Business Offers taxation (MS).

TALMUDICAL ACADEMY OF NEW JERSEY, Adelphia, NJ 07710
General Information Independent-religious, men only, comprehensive institution.

GRADUATE UNITS

Graduate Program

TALMUDIC UNIVERSITY, Miami Beach, FL 33140
General Information Independent-religious, men only, comprehensive institution. *Graduate housing:* Rooms and/or apartments available on a first-come, first-served basis to single and married students.

GRADUATE UNITS

Program in Talmudic Law Offers Talmudic law (MRE).

TARLETON STATE UNIVERSITY, Stephenville, TX 76402
General Information State-supported, coed, comprehensive institution. *Enrollment:* 13,052 graduate, professional, and undergraduate students; 298 full-time matriculated graduate/professional students (178 women), 1,291 part-time matriculated graduate/professional students (834 women). *Enrollment by degree level:* 1,452 master's, 137 doctoral. *Graduate faculty:* 126 full-time (54 women), 52 part-time/adjunct (25 women). Tuition, state resident: full-time $1836; part-time $204 per credit hour. Tuition, nonresident: full-time $5508; part-time $612 per credit hour. *Required fees:* $2437 per credit hour. *Graduate housing:* Rooms and/or apartments available on a first-come, first-served basis to single and married students. Typical cost: $3870 per year ($7620 including board) for single students. Room and board charges vary according to board plan and housing facility selected. Housing application deadline: 8/1. *Student services:* Campus employment opportunities, campus safety program, career counseling, child daycare facilities, exercise/wellness program, free psychological counseling, grant writing training, international student services, low-cost health insurance, multicultural affairs office, services for students with disabilities, teacher training, writing training. *Library facilities:* Dick Smith Library plus 1 other. *Collection:* Students can reserve study rooms.

Computer facilities: 1,200 computers available on campus for general student use. A campuswide network can be accessed from student residence rooms and from off campus. Online class registration is available.
Website: http://www.tarleton.edu/

General Application Contact: Wendy Weiss, Graduate Admissions Coordinator, 254-968-9104, Fax: 254-968-9670, E-mail: weiss@tarleton.edu.

GRADUATE UNITS

College of Graduate Studies Students: 298 full-time (178 women), 1,291 part-time (834 women); includes 458 minority (178 Black or African American, non-Hispanic/Latino; 6 American Indian or Alaska Native, non-Hispanic/Latino; 20 Asian, non-Hispanic/Latino; 209 Hispanic/Latino; 45 Two or more races, non-Hispanic/Latino), 22 international. Average age 36. 662 applicants, 92% accepted, 451 enrolled. *Faculty:* 126 full-time (54 women), 52 part-time/adjunct (25 women). Expenses: Contact institution. *Financial support:* Research assistantships, teaching assistantships, career-related internships or fieldwork, Federal Work-Study, institutionally sponsored loans, scholarships/grants, and tuition waivers (partial) available. Support available to part-time students. Financial award application deadline: 5/1; financial award applicants required to submit FAFSA. In 2016, 463 master's, 15 doctorates awarded. *Program availability:* Part-time, evening/weekend, 100% online, blended/hybrid learning. *Application deadline:* For fall admission, 8/15 priority date for domestic students; for spring admission, 1/7 for domestic students. *Application fee:* $45 ($130 for international students). Electronic applications accepted. *Application Contact:* Wendy Weiss, Graduate Admissions Coordinator, 254-968-9104, Fax: 254-968-9670, E-mail: weiss@tarleton.edu. *Dean,* Dr. Barry Lambert, 254-968-9463, Fax: 254-968-9670, E-mail: blambert@tarleton.edu.

College of Agricultural and Environmental Sciences Students: 48 full-time (33 women), 51 part-time (35 women); includes 16 minority (1 Black or African American, non-Hispanic/Latino; 8 Hispanic/Latino; 7 Two or more races, non-Hispanic/Latino). Average age 27. 39 applicants, 95% accepted, 29 enrolled. *Faculty:* 17 full-time (4 women), 12 part-time/adjunct (2 women). Expenses: Contact institution. *Financial support:* Research assistantships, teaching assistantships, career-related internships or fieldwork, Federal Work-Study, and institutionally sponsored loans available. Support available to part-time students. Financial award application deadline: 5/1; financial award applicants required to submit FAFSA. In 2016, 41 master's awarded. *Program availability:* Part-time, evening/weekend, online learning. Offers agricultural and consumer resources (MS); agricultural and environmental sciences (MS); agricultural and natural resource management (MS). *Application deadline:* For fall admission, 8/15 priority date for domestic students; for spring admission, 1/7 for domestic students. Applications are processed on a rolling basis. *Application fee:* $45 ($130 for international students). Electronic applications accepted. *Application Contact:* Wendy Weiss, Information Contact, 254-968-9104, Fax: 254-968-9670, E-mail: gradoffice@tarleton.edu. *Dean,* Dr. Steve Damron, 254-968-9227, Fax: 254-968-9655, E-mail: sdamron@tarleton.edu.

College of Business Administration Students: 109 full-time (68 women), 350 part-time (204 women); includes 129 minority (39 Black or African American, non-Hispanic/Latino; 1 American Indian or Alaska Native, non-Hispanic/Latino; 10 Asian, non-Hispanic/Latino; 60 Hispanic/Latino; 19 Two or more races, non-Hispanic/Latino), 4 international. Average age 33. 184 applicants, 89% accepted, 126 enrolled. *Faculty:* 26 full-time (3 women), 7 part-time/adjunct (2 women). Expenses: Contact institution. *Financial support:* Research assistantships, teaching assistantships, career-related internships or fieldwork, Federal Work-Study, and institutionally sponsored loans available. Support available to part-time students. Financial award application deadline: 5/1; financial award applicants required to submit FAFSA. In 2016, 158 master's awarded. *Program availability:* Part-time, evening/weekend, online learning. Offers accounting (M Acc); business administration (M Acc, MBA, MS); human resources management (MS); information systems (MS). *Application deadline:* For fall admission, 8/15 priority date for domestic students; for spring admission, 1/7 for domestic students. Applications are processed on a rolling basis. *Application fee:* $45 ($130 for international students). Electronic applications accepted. *Application Contact:* Jodie Dearing, Graduate Program Manager, 254-968-9055, E-mail: jdearing@tarleton.edu. *Dean,* Dr. Steve Steed, 254-968-9645, E-mail: ssteed@tarleton.edu.

College of Education Students: 67 full-time (40 women), 502 part-time (376 women); includes 158 minority (73 Black or African American, non-Hispanic/Latino; 5 American Indian or Alaska Native, non-Hispanic/Latino; 2 Asian, non-Hispanic/Latino; 68 Hispanic/Latino; 10 Two or more races, non-Hispanic/Latino), 3 international. Average age 36. 135 applicants, 96% accepted, 80 enrolled. *Faculty:* 35 full-time (21 women), 22 part-time/adjunct (16 women). Expenses: Contact institution. *Financial support:* Research assistantships, teaching assistantships with partial tuition reimbursements, career-related internships or fieldwork, Federal Work-Study, institutionally sponsored loans, and tuition waivers (partial) available. Support available to part-time students. Financial award application deadline: 5/1; financial award applicants required to submit FAFSA. In 2016, 146 master's, 15 doctorates awarded. *Program availability:* Part-time, evening/weekend, online learning. Offers applied psychology (MS); athletic training (MS); education (M Ed, MS, Ed D, Certificate); educational administration (M Ed); educational diagnostician (M Ed); educational leadership (Ed D, Certificate); elementary education (M Ed); instructional design and technology (M Ed); instructional leadership (M Ed); kinesiology (MS); professional reading specialist (M Ed); secondary education (M Ed); special education (M Ed); technology applications (M Ed); technology director (M Ed). *Application deadline:* For fall admission, 8/15 priority date for domestic students; for spring admission, 1/7 for domestic students. Applications are processed on a rolling basis. *Application fee:* $45 ($130 for international students). Electronic applications accepted. *Application Contact:* Wendy Weiss, Information Contact, 254-968-9104, Fax: 254-968-9670, E-mail: weiss@tarleton.edu. *Dean,* Dr. Jordan Barkley, 254-968-9088, Fax: 254-968-9525, E-mail: jbarkley@tarleton.edu.

College of Health Sciences and Human Services Expenses: Contact institution. Offers health sciences and human services (MS, MSN, MSW); medical laboratory sciences (MS); nursing administration (MSN); nursing education (MSN); social work (MSW). *Application Contact:* Wendy Weiss, Graduate Admissions Coordinator, 254-968-9104, Fax: 254-968-9670, E-mail: weiss@tarleton.edu. *Dean,* Dr. Vimala Pillari, 254-968-1692.

College of Liberal and Fine Arts Students: 28 full-time (17 women), 236 part-time (127 women); includes 97 minority (45 Black or African American, non-Hispanic/Latino; 4 Asian, non-Hispanic/Latino; 44 Hispanic/Latino; 4 Two or more races, non-Hispanic/Latino), 5 international. Average age 35. 141 applicants, 94% accepted, 101 enrolled. *Faculty:* 18 full-time (9 women), 6 part-time/adjunct (3 women). Expenses: Contact institution. *Financial support:* Research assistantships and teaching assistantships available. Financial award application deadline: 5/1; financial award applicants required to submit FAFSA. In 2016, 81 master's awarded. *Program availability:* Part-time, evening/weekend. Offers communication studies (MA); criminal justice (MCJ); English (MA); history (MA); liberal and fine arts (MA, MCJ, MM, MMA); music education (MM); public administration (MPA). *Application deadline:* For fall admission, 8/15 priority date for domestic students; for spring admission, 1/7 for domestic students. Applications are processed on a rolling basis. *Application fee:* $45 ($130 for international students). Electronic applications accepted. *Application Contact:* Wendy Weiss, Information Contact, 254-968-9104, Fax: 254-968-9670, E-mail: weiss@tarleton.edu. *Interim Dean,* Kelli Styron, 254-968-9141, Fax: 254-968-9784, E-mail: styron@tarleton.edu.

College of Science and Technology Students: 41 full-time (17 women), 83 part-time (40 women); includes 31 minority (13 Black or African American, non-Hispanic/Latino; 2 Asian, non-Hispanic/Latino; 16 Hispanic/Latino), 8 international. Average age 32. 74 applicants, 86% accepted, 51 enrolled. *Faculty:* 30 full-time (17 women), 4 part-time/adjunct (2 women). Expenses: Contact institution. *Financial support:* Research assistantships, teaching assistantships, career-related internships or fieldwork, Federal Work-Study, and tuition waivers (partial) available. Support available to part-time students. Financial award application deadline: 5/1; financial award applicants required to submit FAFSA. In 2016, 37 master's awarded. *Program availability:* Part-time, evening/weekend, online learning. Offers biology (MS); environmental science (MS); mathematics (MS); quality and engineering management (MS); science and technology (MS). *Application deadline:* For fall admission, 8/15 priority date for domestic students; for spring admission, 1/7 for domestic students. Applications are processed on a rolling basis. *Application fee:* $45 ($130 for international students). Electronic applications accepted. *Application Contact:* Wendy Weiss, Information Contact, 254-968-9104, Fax: 254-968-9670, E-mail: weiss@tarleton.edu. *Dean,* Dr. James Pierce, 254-968-9781, Fax: 254-968-0549, E-mail: jrpierce@tarleton.edu.

TAYLOR COLLEGE AND SEMINARY, Edmonton, AB T6J 4T3, Canada

General Information Independent-religious, coed, comprehensive institution. *Graduate housing:* Room and/or apartments available on a first-come, first-served basis to single students; on-campus housing not available to married students. Housing application deadline: 8/1.

GRADUATE UNITS

Graduate and Professional Programs *Program availability:* Part-time, online learning. Offers Christian studies (Diploma); intercultural studies (MA, Diploma); theology (M Div, MTS).

TAYLOR UNIVERSITY, Upland, IN 46989-1001

General Information Independent-religious, coed, comprehensive institution. *Graduate housing:* On-campus housing not available.

GRADUATE UNITS

Master of Arts in Higher Education and Student Development Program *Program availability:* Part-time. Offers higher education and student development (MA).

Master of Business Administration Program *Program availability:* Part-time. Offers emerging business strategies (MBA); global leadership (MBA).

TEACHERS COLLEGE, COLUMBIA UNIVERSITY, New York, NY 10027-6696

General Information Independent, coed, graduate-only institution. *Enrollment by degree level:* 3,599 master's, 1,293 doctoral. *Graduate faculty:* 170. *Tuition:* Full-time $36,288; part-time $1512 per credit. *Required fees:* $438 per semester. One-time fee: $510 full-time. Full-time tuition and fees vary according to course load. *Graduate housing:* Rooms and/or apartments available on a first-come, first-served basis to single and married students. Housing application deadline: 12/1. *Student services:* Campus employment opportunities, campus safety program, career counseling, exercise/wellness program, free psychological counseling, grant writing training, international student services, low-cost health insurance, multicultural affairs office, services for students with disabilities, teacher training, writing training. *Library facilities:* Gottesman Libraries. *Collection:* Books: 845,365 (physical), 191,963 (digital/electronic); Serial titles: 47,206 (digital/electronic); Databases: 228. Weekly public service hours: 100; students can reserve study rooms.

Computer facilities: A campuswide network can be accessed from student residence rooms and from off campus. Online class registration is available. Website: http://www.tc.columbia.edu/

General Application Contact: David Estrella, Director of Admissions, 212-678-3305, E-mail: dpe2103@tc.columbia.edu.

GRADUATE UNITS

Department of Arts and Humanities Students: 429 full-time (329 women), 467 part-time (332 women); includes 268 minority (62 Black or African American, non-Hispanic/Latino; 1 American Indian or Alaska Native, non-Hispanic/Latino; 108 Asian, non-Hispanic/Latino; 76 Hispanic/Latino; 21 Two or more races, non-Hispanic/Latino), 212 international. 1,068 applicants, 53% accepted, 272 enrolled. Expenses: Contact institution. *Financial support:* Fellowships, research assistantships, teaching assistantships, career-related internships or fieldwork, Federal Work-Study, institutionally sponsored loans, tuition waivers (full and partial), and unspecified assistantships available. Support available to part-time students. *Program availability:* Part-time, evening/weekend. Offers applied linguistics (MA, Ed D); art and art education (Ed M, MA, Ed D, Ed DCT); arts administration (MA); bilingual and bicultural education (MA); global competence (Certificate); history and education (Ed D, PhD); music and music education (Ed DCT); philosophy and education (MA, Ed D, PhD); social studies education (Ed M, PhD); teaching English to speakers of other languages (Ed M); teaching of English and English education (Ed M, MA, Ed D, PhD); teaching of social studies (MA); TESOL (MA, Ed D). *Application Contact:* David Estrella, Director of Admissions, 212-678-3305, Fax: 212-678-4171, E-mail: estrella@tc.columbia.edu. *Department Chair,* Prof. William Gaudelli, 212-678-3150, E-mail: wg74@columbia.edu.

Department of Biobehavioral Sciences Students: 162 full-time (133 women), 158 part-time (116 women); includes 119 minority (20 Black or African American, non-Hispanic/Latino; 38 Asian, non-Hispanic/Latino; 54 Hispanic/Latino; 7 Two or more races, non-Hispanic/Latino), 28 international. 821 applicants, 33% accepted, 125 enrolled. Expenses: Contact institution. *Financial support:* Fellowships, teaching assistantships, career-related internships or fieldwork, Federal Work-Study, institutionally sponsored loans, traineeships, and tuition waivers (full and partial) available. Support available to part-time students. *Program availability:* Part-time, evening/weekend. Offers applied exercise physiology (Ed M, MA, Ed D); communication sciences and disorders (MS, Ed D, PhD); kinesiology (PhD); motor learning and control (Ed M, MA); motor learning/movement science (Ed D); neuroscience and education (MS); physical education (MA, Ed D). *Application Contact:* David Estrella, Director of Admissions, 212-678-3305, E-mail: estrella@tc.columbia.edu. *Chair,* Prof. Carol Garber, 212-678-3891, E-mail: garber@tc.columbia.edu.

Department of Counseling and Clinical Psychology Students: 434 full-time (366 women), 232 part-time (184 women); includes 247 minority (62 Black or African American, non-Hispanic/Latino; 1 American Indian or Alaska Native, non-Hispanic/Latino; 80 Asian, non-Hispanic/Latino; 84 Hispanic/Latino; 20 Two or more races, non-Hispanic/Latino), 134 international. 1,470 applicants, 39% accepted, 253 enrolled. Expenses: Contact institution. *Program availability:* Part-time. Offers clinical psychology (PhD); counseling psychology (Ed M, Ed D, PhD); mental health counseling (ME); psychological counseling (ME, ND); psychology in education (MA, ND); school counselor (ME). *Application Contact:* David Estrella, Director of Admission, 212-678-3305, E-mail: estrella@tc.columbia.edu. *Head,* Prof. Marie Miville, 212-678-3343, Fax: 212-678-3275, E-mail: miville@tc.columbia.edu.

Department of Curriculum and Teaching Students: 236 full-time (219 women), 198 part-time (176 women); includes 160 minority (53 Black or African American, non-Hispanic/Latino; 1 American Indian or Alaska Native, non-Hispanic/Latino; 43 Asian, non-Hispanic/Latino; 41 Hispanic/Latino; 22 Two or more races, non-Hispanic/Latino), 38 international. 399 applicants, 66% accepted, 104 enrolled. Expenses: Contact institution. *Program availability:* Part-time, evening/weekend. Offers curriculum and teaching (Ed M, MA, Ed D); curriculum and teaching: elementary education (MA); curriculum and teaching: secondary education (MA); early childhood education (MA, Ed D); early childhood education: special education (MA); elementary education-gifted extension (MA); elementary inclusive education (MA); gifted education (MA); literacy specialist (MA); secondary inclusive education (MA); special inclusive elementary education (MA). *Application Contact:* David Estrella, Director of Admission, 212-678-3305, Fax: 212-678-4171, E-mail: estrella@tc.columbia.edu. *Chair,* Prof. Nancy Lesko, 212-678-3264, E-mail: lesko@tc.columbia.edu.

Department of Education Policy and Social Analysis Students: 148 full-time (110 women), 107 part-time (85 women); includes 95 minority (40 Black or African American, non-Hispanic/Latino; 23 Asian, non-Hispanic/Latino; 26 Hispanic/Latino; 6 Two or more races, non-Hispanic/Latino), 74 international. 516 applicants, 54% accepted, 98 enrolled. Expenses: Contact institution. Offers economics and education (Ed M, MA, PhD); education policy (Ed M, MA, Ed D, PhD); politics and education (Ed M, MA, Ed D, PhD); sociology and education (Ed M, MA, Ed D, PhD). *Application Contact:* David Estrella, Director of Admissions, 212-678-3305, E-mail: estrella@tc.columbia.edu. *Chair,* Dr. Jeffrey Henig, 212-678-8313, Fax: 212-678-3589, E-mail: henig@tc.columbia.edu.

Department of Health and Behavior Studies Students: 282 full-time (262 women), 262 part-time (222 women); includes 180 minority (54 Black or African American, non-Hispanic/Latino; 1 American Indian or Alaska Native, non-Hispanic/Latino; 56 Asian, non-Hispanic/Latino; 56 Hispanic/Latino; 1 Native Hawaiian or other Pacific Islander, non-Hispanic/Latino; 12 Two or more races, non-Hispanic/Latino), 55 international. 503 applicants, 57% accepted, 146 enrolled. Expenses: Contact institution. *Program availability:* Part-time, evening/weekend. Offers applied behavior analysis (MA, PhD); applied educational psychology: school psychology (Ed M, PhD); behavioral nutrition (PhD); community health education (MS); community nutrition education (Ed M); education of deaf and hard of hearing (MA, PhD); health education (MA, Ed D); hearing impairment (Ed D); intellectual disability/autism (MA, Ed D, PhD); nursing education (Ed D, Advanced Certificate); nutrition and education (MS); nutrition and exercise physiology (MS); nutrition and public health (MS); nutrition education (Ed D); physical disabilities (Ed D); reading specialist (MA); severe or multiple disabilities (MA); special education (Ed M, MA, Ed D); teaching of sign language (MA). *Application Contact:* David Estrella, Director of Admission, 212-678-3305, E-mail: estrella@tc.columbia.edu. *Chair,* Prof. Stephen T. Peverly, 212-678-3964, Fax: 212-678-8259, E-mail: stp4@columbia.edu.

Department of Human Development Students: 217 full-time (168 women), 131 part-time (93 women); includes 83 minority (30 Black or African American, non-Hispanic/Latino; 31 Asian, non-Hispanic/Latino; 18 Hispanic/Latino; 4 Two or more races, non-Hispanic/Latino), 182 international. 450 applicants, 69% accepted, 132 enrolled. Expenses: Contact institution. *Program availability:* Part-time. Offers applied statistics (MS); cognitive studies in education (MA, Ed D, PhD); developmental psychology (MA, Ed D, PhD); educational psychology-human cognition and learning (Ed M, MA, Ed D, PhD); learning analytics (MS); measurement and evaluation (ME, Ed D, PhD); measurement, evaluation, and statistics (MA, MS, Ed D, PhD). *Application Contact:* David Estrella, Director of Admission, 212-678-3305, E-mail: estrella@tc.columbia.edu. *Chair,* Prof. Matthew S. Johnson, 212-678-3882, Fax: 212-678-3837, E-mail: johnson@tc.columbia.edu.

Department of International and Transcultural Studies Students: 151 full-time (128 women), 119 part-time (95 women); includes 83 minority (17 Black or African American, non-Hispanic/Latino; 32 Asian, non-Hispanic/Latino; 23 Hispanic/Latino; 11 Two or more races, non-Hispanic/Latino), 97 international. 422 applicants, 67% accepted, 138 enrolled. Expenses: Contact institution. *Program availability:* Part-time. Offers anthropology and education (MA, Ed D, PhD); applied anthropology (PhD); comparative and international education (MA, Ed D, PhD); international educational development (Ed M, MA, Ed D, PhD). *Application Contact:* David Estrella, Director of Admission, 212-678-3305, E-mail: estrella@tc.columbia.edu. *Chair,* Prof. Herve Varenne, 212-678-3190, E-mail: varenne@tc.columbia.edu.

Department of Mathematics, Science and Technology Students: 195 full-time (133 women), 222 part-time (139 women); includes 152 minority (44 Black or African American, non-Hispanic/Latino; 66 Asian, non-Hispanic/Latino; 32 Hispanic/Latino; 10 Two or more races, non-Hispanic/Latino), 106 international. 368 applicants, 65% accepted, 123 enrolled. Expenses: Contact institution. *Program availability:* Part-time, evening/weekend, online learning. Offers biology 7-12 (MA); chemistry 7-12 (MA);

communication and education (MA, Ed D); computing in education (MA); earth science 7-12 (MA); instructional technology and media (Ed M, MA, Ed D); mathematics education (Ed M, MA, Ed D, Ed DCT, PhD); physics 7-12 (MA); science and dental education (MA); science education (Ed M, MS, Ed DCT, PhD); supervisor/teacher of science education (MA); technology specialist (MA). *Application Contact:* David Estrella, Director of Admission, 212-678-3305, E-mail: estrella@tc.columbia.edu. *Chair,* Dr. O. Roger Anderson, 212-678-3405, Fax: 212-678-8129, E-mail: ora@ldeo.columbia.edu.

Department of Organization and Leadership Students: 310 full-time (214 women), 390 part-time (250 women); includes 276 minority (116 Black or African American, non-Hispanic/Latino; 3 American Indian or Alaska Native, non-Hispanic/Latino; 61 Asian, non-Hispanic/Latino; 79 Hispanic/Latino; 17 Two or more races, non-Hispanic/Latino), 93 international. 624 applicants, 57% accepted, 172 enrolled. Expenses: Contact institution. *Program availability:* Part-time, evening/weekend. Offers adult education guided intensive study (Ed D); adult learning and leadership (Ed M, MA, Ed D); educational leadership (Ed D); higher and postsecondary education (MA, Ed D); leadership, policy and politics (Ed D); nurse executive (MA, Ed D); private school leadership (Ed M, MA); public school building leadership (Ed M, MA); social and organizational psychology (MA); urban education leaders (Ed D). *Application Contact:* David Estrella, Director of Admission, 212-678-3305, E-mail: estrella@tc.columbia.edu. *Chair,* Prof. Anna Neumann, 212-678-3272, Fax: 212-678-3036, E-mail: neumann@tc.columbia.edu.

Interdisciplinary Programs Students: 16 full-time (11 women), 21 part-time (13 women); includes 11 minority (6 Black or African American, non-Hispanic/Latino; 3 Asian, non-Hispanic/Latino; 1 Hispanic/Latino; 1 Two or more races, non-Hispanic/Latino), 12 international. 27 applicants, 85% accepted, 15 enrolled. Expenses: Contact institution. *Program availability:* Part-time. Offers interdisciplinary studies (Ed M, MA, ME, Ed D). *Application Contact:* David Estrella, Director of Admissions, 212-678-3305, E-mail: estrella@tc.columbia.edu.

TÉLÉ-UNIVERSITÉ, Québec, QC G1K 9H5, Canada
General Information Province-supported, coed, comprehensive institution. *Graduate housing:* On-campus housing not available.

GRADUATE UNITS
Graduate Programs *Program availability:* Part-time. Offers computer science (PhD); corporate finance (MS); distance learning (MS).

TELSHE YESHIVA–CHICAGO, Chicago, IL 60625-5598
General Information Independent-religious, men only, comprehensive institution.

GRADUATE UNITS
Graduate Program

★ TEMPLE UNIVERSITY, Philadelphia, PA 19122-6096
General Information State-related, coed, university. CGS member. *Enrollment:* 39,308 graduate, professional, and undergraduate students; 4,580 full-time matriculated graduate/professional students (2,695 women), 1,638 part-time matriculated graduate/professional students (1,096 women). *Enrollment by degree level:* 2,434 master's, 3,160 doctoral, 144 other advanced degrees. *Graduate faculty:* 943 full-time (421 women), 590 part-time/adjunct (317 women). *Graduate housing:* Rooms and/or apartments available on a first-come, first-served basis to single and married students. Housing application deadline: 5/1. *Student services:* Campus employment opportunities, campus safety program, career counseling, exercise/wellness program, free psychological counseling, grant writing training, international student services, low-cost health insurance, multicultural affairs office, services for students with disabilities, teacher training, writing training. *Library facilities:* Paley Library plus 6 others. *Collection:* Books: 3.8 million (physical), 1.2 million (digital/electronic); Serial titles: 1,080 (physical), 51,077 (digital/electronic); Databases: 1,939. Students can reserve study rooms.

Computer facilities: Computer purchase and lease plans are available. 8,324 computers available on campus for general student use. A campuswide network can be accessed from student residence rooms and from off campus. Online class registration, student accounts, Web hosting are available. Website: http://www.temple.edu/

General Application Contact: Coordinator of Outreach, 215-204-1380, Fax: 215-204-8781, E-mail: grad@temple.edu.

GRADUATE UNITS
Beasley School of Law Students: 534 full-time (282 women), 153 part-time (66 women); includes 191 minority (59 Black or African American, non-Hispanic/Latino; 2 American Indian or Alaska Native, non-Hispanic/Latino; 60 Asian, non-Hispanic/Latino; 62 Hispanic/Latino; 8 Two or more races, non-Hispanic/Latino), 9 international. Average age 26. 2,046 applicants, 42% accepted, 218 enrolled. *Faculty:* 64 full-time (30 women), 102 part-time/adjunct (37 women). Expenses: Contact institution. *Financial support:* In 2016–17, 469 students received support, including research assistantships (averaging $5,500 per year), teaching assistantships (averaging $5,500 per year); fellowships, Federal Work-Study, scholarships/grants, tuition waivers (full and partial), and unspecified assistantships also available. Support available to part-time students. Financial award application deadline: 3/1; financial award applicants required to submit FAFSA. In 2016, 202 doctorates awarded. *Program availability:* Part-time, evening/weekend. Offers law (JD); legal education (SJD); taxation (LL M); transnational law (LL M); trial advocacy (LL M). *Application deadline:* For fall admission, 3/1 for domestic and international students. Applications are processed on a rolling basis. *Application fee:* $60. Electronic applications accepted. *Application Contact:* Johanne L. Johnston, Assistant Dean for Admissions and Financial Aid, 800-560-1428, Fax: 215-204-9319, E-mail: lawadmis@temple.edu. *Dean,* Gregory N. Mandel, 215-204-7863, Fax: 215-204-1185, E-mail: law@temple.edu.

Center for the Performing and Cinematic Arts Students: 313 full-time (195 women), 42 part-time (26 women); includes 63 minority (24 Black or African American, non-Hispanic/Latino; 13 Asian, non-Hispanic/Latino; 16 Hispanic/Latino; 10 Two or more races, non-Hispanic/Latino), 116 international. 528 applicants, 61% accepted, 133 enrolled. *Faculty:* 77 full-time (36 women), 93 part-time/adjunct (44 women). Expenses: Contact institution. *Financial support:* Fellowships, research assistantships, teaching assistantships, Federal Work-Study, scholarships/grants, health care benefits, and unspecified assistantships available. In 2016, 139 master's, 15 doctorates awarded. Offers performing and cinematic arts (Ed M, MA, MFA, MM, MMT, DMA, PhD). *Application fee:* $60. Electronic applications accepted. *Application Contact:* Dr. Robert Stroker, Dean/Vice Provost for the Arts, 215-777-9196, E-mail: robert.stroker@temple.edu. *Dean/Vice Provost for the Arts,* Dr. Robert Stroker, 215-777-9196, E-mail: robert.stroker@temple.edu.

Boyer College of Music and Dance Students: 244 full-time (157 women), 41 part-time (25 women); includes 46 minority (14 Black or African American, non-Hispanic/Latino;

12 Asian, non-Hispanic/Latino; 13 Hispanic/Latino; 7 Two or more races, non-Hispanic/Latino), 100 international. 426 applicants, 66% accepted, 109 enrolled. *Faculty:* 45 full-time (22 women), 55 part-time/adjunct (28 women). Expenses: Contact institution. *Financial support:* Fellowships with tuition reimbursements, research assistantships with tuition reimbursements, teaching assistantships with tuition reimbursements, career-related internships or fieldwork, Federal Work-Study, scholarships/grants, health care benefits, and unspecified assistantships available. Financial award application deadline: 3/1; financial award applicants required to submit FAFSA. In 2016, 61 master's, 11 doctorates awarded. *Program availability:* Part-time, online learning. Offers choral conducting (MM); collaborative piano/chamber music (MM); collaborative piano/opera coaching (MM); composition (MM, PhD); dance (MA, MFA, PhD); instrumental conducting (MM); music and dance (MA, MFA, MM, MMT, DMA, PhD); music education (MM, PhD); music history (MM); music performance (MM, DMA); music studies (PhD); music theory (MM, PhD); music therapy (MMT, PhD); musicology (MM, PhD); opera (MM); piano pedagogy (MM); string pedagogy (MM). *Application deadline:* For fall admission, 12/15 for international students; for spring admission, 8/1 for international students. Applications are processed on a rolling basis. *Application fee:* $60. Electronic applications accepted. *Application Contact:* James Short, Director of Undergraduate and Graduate Admissions, 215-204-8598, Fax: 215-204-4957, E-mail: jshort@temple.edu. *Dean,* Dr. Robert Stroker, 215-204-8301, Fax: 215-204-4957, E-mail: rstroker@temple.edu.

School of Theater, Film and Media Arts Students: 69 full-time (38 women), 1 (woman) part-time; includes 17 minority (10 Black or African American, non-Hispanic/Latino; 1 Asian, non-Hispanic/Latino; 3 Hispanic/Latino; 3 Two or more races, non-Hispanic/Latino), 16 international. 102 applicants, 41% accepted, 24 enrolled. *Faculty:* 32 full-time (14 women), 38 part-time/adjunct (16 women). Expenses: Contact institution. *Financial support:* Application deadline: 3/1; applicants required to submit FAFSA. In 2016, 6 master's awarded. Offers acting (MFA); design (MFA); directing (MFA); film and media arts (MA, MFA); musical theater collaboration (MFA); musical theater studies (MA); playwriting (MFA); theater, film and media arts (MA, MFA). *Application fee:* $60. Electronic applications accepted. *Application Contact:* Leah Dempsey, Assistant Director for Administration, 215-204-3859, E-mail: leahdempsey@temple.edu. *Dean/Vice Provost for the Arts,* Dr. Robert Stroker, 215-204-8598, E-mail: robert.stroker@temple.edu.

College of Education Students: 490 full-time (354 women), 496 part-time (326 women); includes 261 minority (162 Black or African American, non-Hispanic/Latino; 2 American Indian or Alaska Native, non-Hispanic/Latino; 38 Asian, non-Hispanic/Latino; 38 Hispanic/Latino; 21 Two or more races, non-Hispanic/Latino), 43 international. 822 applicants, 59% accepted, 281 enrolled. *Faculty:* 56 full-time (31 women), 101 part-time/adjunct (67 women). Expenses: Contact institution. *Financial support:* Research assistantships with full tuition reimbursements, teaching assistantships with full tuition reimbursements, career-related internships or fieldwork, Federal Work-Study, scholarships/grants, health care benefits, and unspecified assistantships available. Financial award application deadline: 1/15; financial award applicants required to submit FAFSA. In 2016, 220 master's, 63 doctorates, 63 other advanced degrees awarded. *Program availability:* Part-time, evening/weekend. Offers applied behavior analysis (MS Ed); career and technical education (Ed M); counseling psychology (Ed M); education (Ed M, MS Ed, Ed D, PhD, Ed S); educational leadership (Ed M, Ed D); educational psychology (Ed M); middle grades education (Ed M); school psychology (PhD, Ed S); secondary education (Ed M); teaching English to speakers of other languages (MS Ed); urban education (Ed M). *Application deadline:* For fall admission, 4/1 for domestic students; 1/1 for international students; for spring admission, 10/1 for domestic students, 7/3 for international students. Applications are processed on a rolling basis. *Application fee:* $60. Electronic applications accepted. *Application Contact:* Elizabeth Jung, Enrollment Management, 215-204-5634, E-mail: educate@temple.edu. *Dean,* Dr. Gregory Anderson, 215-204-8017, Fax: 215-204-5622, E-mail: coedean@temple.edu.

College of Engineering Students: 138 full-time (42 women), 68 part-time (11 women); includes 38 minority (12 Black or African American, non-Hispanic/Latino; 14 Asian, non-Hispanic/Latino; 10 Hispanic/Latino; 2 Two or more races, non-Hispanic/Latino), 87 international. 305 applicants, 56% accepted, 76 enrolled. *Faculty:* 67 full-time (13 women), 11 part-time/adjunct (1 woman). Expenses: Contact institution. *Financial support:* In 2016–17, 71 students received support, including 6 fellowships with full tuition reimbursements available, 22 research assistantships with full tuition reimbursements available, 40 teaching assistantships with full tuition reimbursements available; Federal Work-Study, institutionally sponsored loans, scholarships/grants, health care benefits, and unspecified assistantships also available. Financial award application deadline: 3/1; financial award applicants required to submit FAFSA. In 2016, 43 master's, 11 doctorates, 17 other advanced degrees awarded. *Program availability:* Part-time, evening/weekend, 100% online, blended/hybrid learning. Offers bioengineering (PhD); civil engineering (MSCE, PhD); electrical and computer engineering (PhD); electrical engineering (MSEE, PhD); engineering (MS, MS Env E, MSCE, MSEE, MSME, PhD, Certificate, Graduate Certificate); engineering management (MS, Certificate); environmental engineering (MS Env E, PhD); mechanical engineering (MSME); storm water management (Graduate Certificate). *Application deadline:* For fall admission, 3/1 priority date for domestic and international students; for spring admission, 11/1 priority date for domestic students, 8/1 priority date for international students. Applications are processed on a rolling basis. *Application fee:* $60. Electronic applications accepted. *Application Contact:* Leslie Levin, Director, Admissions and Graduate Student Services, 215-204-7800, Fax: 215-204-6936, E-mail: gradengr@temple.edu. *Dean,* Dr. Keya Sadeghipour, 215-204-5285.

College of Liberal Arts Students: 626 full-time (345 women), 94 part-time (47 women); includes 155 minority (73 Black or African American, non-Hispanic/Latino; 1 American Indian or Alaska Native, non-Hispanic/Latino; 24 Asian, non-Hispanic/Latino; 44 Hispanic/Latino; 13 Two or more races, non-Hispanic/Latino), 83 international. 1,127 applicants, 32% accepted, 169 enrolled. *Faculty:* 296 full-time (132 women), 110 part-time/adjunct (59 women). Expenses: Contact institution. *Financial support:* Fellowships, research assistantships, teaching assistantships, career-related internships or fieldwork, Federal Work-Study, institutionally sponsored loans, scholarships/grants, and tuition waivers (full and partial) available. Support available to part-time students. Financial award application deadline: 1/15; financial award applicants required to submit FAFSA. In 2016, 87 master's, 69 doctorates, 6 other advanced degrees awarded. *Program availability:* Part-time. Offers African American studies (MA, PhD); anthropology (PhD); creative writing (MFA); criminal justice (MA, PhD); economics (MA, PhD); English (MA, PhD); geographic information systems (PSM, Graduate Certificate); geography and urban studies (MA, PhD); history (MA, PhD); liberal arts (MA, MFA, MS, PSM, PhD, Graduate Certificate); philosophy (MA, PhD); political science (MA, PhD); psychology (MA, MS, PhD); religion (MA, PhD); sociology (MA, PhD); Spanish (MA, PhD). *Application deadline:* For fall admission, 12/15 for international students; for spring admission, 8/1 for international students. *Application fee:* $60. Electronic applications accepted. *Application Contact:* Dr. Shawn Schurr, Vice Dean, 215-204-7743, E-mail: schurr@temple.edu. *Dean,* Richard Deeg, 215-204-7747, Fax: 215-204-5022, E-mail: rdeeg@temple.edu.

College of Public Health Students: 694 full-time (579 women), 435 part-time (330 women); includes 356 minority (180 Black or African American, non-Hispanic/Latino; 64 Asian, non-Hispanic/Latino; 79 Hispanic/Latino; 1 Native Hawaiian or other Pacific Islander, non-Hispanic/Latino; 32 Two or more races, non-Hispanic/Latino), 28 international. 1,248 applicants, 45% accepted, 241 enrolled. *Faculty:* 132 full-time (87 women), 33 part-time/adjunct (23 women). Expenses: Contact institution. *Financial support:* Fellowships, research assistantships, teaching assistantships with full tuition reimbursements, career-related internships or fieldwork, Federal Work-Study, institutionally sponsored loans, traineeships, and tuition waivers (partial) available. Support available to part-time students. Financial award application deadline: 1/15. In 2016, 380 master's, 121 doctorates awarded. *Program availability:* Part-time, evening/weekend, online learning. Offers adult-gerontology primary care (DNP); applied biostatistics (MPH); athletic training (MSAT, DAT); communication sciences and disorders (PhD); environmental health (MPH); epidemiology (MPH, MS, PhD); family-individual across the lifespan (DNP); health informatics (MS); health policy (PhD); health policy and management (MPH); kinesiology (MS, PhD); neuromotor science (MS, PhD); nursing (DNP); occupational therapy (MOT, DOT); physical therapy (DPT, TDPT); public health (MA, MOT, MPH, MS, MSAT, MSW, DAT, DNP, DOT, DPT, PhD, TDPT); social and behavioral sciences (MPH, PhD); speech-language-hearing (MA); therapeutic recreation (MS). *Application fee:* $60. *Application Contact:* Dr. Laura Siminoff, Dean, 215-707-8624, Fax: 215-707-7819, E-mail: laura.siminoff@temple.edu. *Dean,* Dr. Laura Siminoff, 215-707-8624, Fax: 215-707-7819, E-mail: laura.siminoff@temple.edu.

School of Social Work Students: 258 full-time (224 women), 167 part-time (139 women); includes 178 minority (119 Black or African American, non-Hispanic/Latino; 9 Asian, non-Hispanic/Latino; 35 Hispanic/Latino; 15 Two or more races, non-Hispanic/Latino), 3 international. 362 applicants, 63% accepted, 100 enrolled. *Faculty:* 28 full-time (15 women), 10 part-time/adjunct (8 women). Expenses: Contact institution. *Financial support:* Research assistantships with tuition reimbursements, career-related internships or fieldwork, Federal Work-Study, scholarships/grants, traineeships, tuition waivers (partial), unspecified assistantships, and field assistantships available. Support available to part-time students. Financial award application deadline: 1/1. In 2016, 221 master's awarded. *Program availability:* Part-time, evening/weekend. Offers social work (MSW). *Application deadline:* For fall admission, 3/15 priority date for domestic students, 2/15 for international students; for spring admission, 11/1 priority date for domestic students, 10/15 for international students; for summer admission, 3/15 for domestic students, 2/15 for international students. Applications are processed on a rolling basis. *Application fee:* $60. Electronic applications accepted. *Application Contact:* Cheryl A. Hyde, Associate Professor/MSW Program Director, 215-204-7112, E-mail: chyde@temple.edu. *Chairperson,* Bernie Newman, 215-204-1205, Fax: 215-204-9606, E-mail: bernie.newman@temple.edu.

College of Science and Technology Students: 398 full-time (137 women), 49 part-time (18 women); includes 57 minority (11 Black or African American, non-Hispanic/Latino; 27 Asian, non-Hispanic/Latino; 12 Hispanic/Latino; 7 Two or more races, non-Hispanic/Latino), 212 international. 584 applicants, 38% accepted, 113 enrolled. *Faculty:* 175 full-time (39 women), 8 part-time/adjunct (2 women). Expenses: Contact institution. *Financial support:* Fellowships, research assistantships, teaching assistantships, career-related internships or fieldwork, Federal Work-Study, institutionally sponsored loans, scholarships/grants, tuition waivers (full and partial), and laboratory assistantships available. Financial award application deadline: 1/15; financial award applicants required to submit FAFSA. In 2016, 53 master's, 42 doctorates awarded. *Program availability:* Part-time, evening/weekend. Offers applied mathematics (MS); biology (MS, PMS, PhD); biotechnology (MS); chemistry (MA, PhD); computational data science (MS); computer and information sciences (PhD); computer science (MS); cyber defense and information assurance (PSM); geology (MS); geosciences (PhD); information science and technology (MS); mathematics (MS, PhD); physics (MS, PhD); science and technology (MA, MS, PMS, PhD). *Application deadline:* For fall admission, 1/5 for domestic students, 12/15 for international students; for spring admission, 9/15 for domestic students, 8/1 for international students. Applications are processed on a rolling basis. *Application fee:* $60. Electronic applications accepted. *Application Contact:* Tara Schumacher, Coordinator of Outreach, 215-204-1380, Fax: 215-204-8781, E-mail: tara.schumacher@temple.edu. *Associate Director of Graduate Studies,* Eileen Weinberg, 215-204-2150, E-mail: eileen.weinberg@temple.edu.

Fox School of Business *Program availability:* Part-time, evening/weekend, online learning. Offers accountancy (MS); accounting (MBA, PhD); actuarial science (MS); business (EMBA, IMBA, MBA, MHM, MS, PhD); business management (MBA); entrepreneurship (PhD); finance (MS, PhD); financial engineering (MS); financial management (MBA); healthcare and life sciences innovation (MBA); human resource management (MBA, MS); innovation management and entrepreneurship (MS); international business (IMBA, PhD); IT management (MBA); management information systems (PhD); marketing (MS, PhD); marketing management (MBA); pharmaceutical management (MBA); risk management and insurance (PhD); statistics (MS, PhD); strategic management (EMBA, MBA, PhD); tourism and sport (PhD). Electronic applications accepted.

Klein College of Media and Communication Students: 87 full-time (57 women), 56 part-time (37 women); includes 29 minority (15 Black or African American, non-Hispanic/Latino; 1 American Indian or Alaska Native, non-Hispanic/Latino; 5 Asian, non-Hispanic/Latino; 5 Hispanic/Latino; 3 Two or more races, non-Hispanic/Latino), 38 international. 178 applicants, 42% accepted, 32 enrolled. *Faculty:* 67 full-time (35 women), 75 part-time/adjunct (39 women). Expenses: Contact institution. *Financial support:* Fellowships, teaching assistantships with partial tuition reimbursements, career-related internships or fieldwork, Federal Work-Study, institutionally sponsored loans, tuition waivers (full and partial), and unspecified assistantships available. Financial award application deadline: 1/15; financial award applicants required to submit FAFSA. In 2016, 20 master's, 8 doctorates awarded. *Program availability:* Part-time, evening/weekend. Offers communication management (MS); globalization and development communication (MS); journalism (MJ); media and communication (MA, MJ, MS, PhD); media studies and production (MA). *Application deadline:* For fall admission, 12/15 for international students. *Application fee:* $60. Electronic applications accepted. *Application Contact:* Nicole McKenna, Director, Office of Research and Graduate Studies, 215-204-1497, Fax: 215-204-0310, E-mail: nmckenna@temple.edu. *Dean,* David Boardman, 215-204-8422, Fax: 215-204-4811, E-mail: dboardman@temple.edu.

Kornberg School of Dentistry Offers advanced education in general dentistry (Certificate); dentistry (MS, DMD, Certificate); endodontics (Certificate); oral biology (MS); orthodontics (Certificate); periodontology (Certificate). Electronic applications accepted.

Lewis Katz School of Medicine Students: 1,049 full-time (506 women), 17 part-time (14 women); includes 382 minority (57 Black or African American, non-Hispanic/Latino; 204 Asian, non-Hispanic/Latino; 90 Hispanic/Latino; 2 Native Hawaiian or other Pacific Islander, non-Hispanic/Latino; 29 Two or more races, non-Hispanic/Latino), 26 international. 162 applicants, 36% accepted, 41 enrolled. *Faculty:* 20 full-time (7 women). Expenses: Contact institution. *Financial support:* Fellowships with full tuition reimbursements, research assistantships with full tuition reimbursements, scholarships/grants, and health care benefits available. Financial award application deadline: 2/15; financial award applicants required to submit FAFSA. In 2016, 17 master's, 215 doctorates awarded. Offers biomedical sciences (MS); medicine (MS, MD, PhD). *Application deadline:* For fall admission, 2/15 for domestic and international students. *Application fee:* $60. Electronic applications accepted. *Application Contact:* Jacob Ufberg, Associate Dean of Admissions, 215-707-5308, E-mail: tusmgrad@temple.edu. *Dean,* Larry R. Kaiser, 215-707-8773, Fax: 215-707-5072, E-mail: sks@temple.edu.

School of Pharmacy Students: 624 full-time (345 women), 347 part-time (240 women); includes 347 minority (51 Black or African American, non-Hispanic/Latino; 170 Asian, non-Hispanic/Latino; 22 Hispanic/Latino; 104 Two or more races, non-Hispanic/Latino), 96 international. 138 applicants, 64% accepted, 68 enrolled. *Faculty:* 33 full-time (15 women), 36 part-time/adjunct (13 women). Expenses: Contact institution. *Financial support:* Fellowships with tuition reimbursements, research assistantships with tuition reimbursements, teaching assistantships with tuition reimbursements, career-related internships or fieldwork, Federal Work-Study, and institutionally sponsored loans available. Financial award application deadline: 1/15; financial award applicants required to submit FAFSA. In 2016, 88 master's, 153 doctorates awarded. *Program availability:* Part-time, evening/weekend, online learning. Offers medicinal chemistry (MS, PhD); pharmaceutics (MS, PhD); pharmacodynamics (MS, PhD); pharmacy (MS, PhD, Pharm D); regulatory affairs and quality assurance (MS). *Application deadline:* For fall admission, 2/1 priority date for domestic and international students. *Application fee:* $60. Electronic applications accepted. *Application Contact:* Dr. Peter H. Doukas, Dean, 215-707-4990, Fax: 215-707-5620, E-mail: peter.doukas@temple.edu. *Dean,* Dr. Peter H. Doukas, 215-707-4990, Fax: 215-707-5620, E-mail: peter.doukas@temple.edu.

School of Podiatric Medicine Offers podiatric medicine (DPM). DPM/PhD offered jointly with Drexel University, University of Pennsylvania.

School of Sport, Tourism and Hospitality Management Students: 95 full-time (47 women), 32 part-time (16 women); includes 37 minority (27 Black or African American, non-Hispanic/Latino; 6 Hispanic/Latino; 4 Two or more races, non-Hispanic/Latino), 22 international. 152 applicants, 70% accepted, 66 enrolled. *Faculty:* 21 full-time (7 women), 10 part-time/adjunct (3 women). Expenses: Contact institution. *Financial support:* Fellowships with full tuition reimbursements, research assistantships with full tuition reimbursements, and teaching assistantships with full tuition reimbursements available. Financial award application deadline: 3/1; financial award applicants required to submit FAFSA. In 2016, 31 master's awarded. *Program availability:* Part-time, evening/weekend. Offers sport business (MS); tourism and hospitality management (MTHM); tourism and sport (PhD); travel and tourism (MS). *Application deadline:* For fall admission, 3/1 priority date for domestic students, 1/15 priority date for international students; for spring admission, 8/15 priority date for domestic students, 6/30 priority date for international students. Applications are processed on a rolling basis. *Application fee:* $60. Electronic applications accepted. *Application Contact:* James Alton, Manager of Graduate Student Services, 215-204-7140, Fax: 215-204-8705, E-mail: jim.alton@temple.edu. *Dean,* Dr. M. Moshe Porat, 215-204-1836, Fax: 215-204-8705, E-mail: porat@temple.edu.

Tyler School of Art Students: 192 full-time (125 women), 38 part-time (26 women); includes 40 minority (10 Black or African American, non-Hispanic/Latino; 9 Asian, non-Hispanic/Latino; 15 Hispanic/Latino; 6 Two or more races, non-Hispanic/Latino), 24 international. 561 applicants, 29% accepted, 79 enrolled. *Faculty:* 63 full-time (31 women), 122 part-time/adjunct (66 women). Expenses: Contact institution. *Financial support:* Fellowships with full tuition reimbursements, research assistantships with full tuition reimbursements, teaching assistantships with full tuition reimbursements, career-related internships or fieldwork, Federal Work-Study, and institutionally sponsored loans available. Support available to part-time students. Financial award application deadline: 1/15; financial award applicants required to submit FAFSA. In 2016, 59 master's, 4 doctorates, 1 other advanced degree awarded. *Program availability:* Part-time, evening/weekend. Offers architecture (M Arch); art (Ed M, M Arch, MA, MFA, ML Arch, MS, PhD, Graduate Certificate); art education (Ed M); art history (MA, PhD); ceramics (MFA); city and regional planning (MS); fibers and material studies (MFA); glass (MFA); graphic and interactive design (MFA); landscape architecture (ML Arch); metals/jewelry/CAD-CAM (MFA); painting (MFA); photography (MFA); printmaking (MFA); sculpture (MFA); sustainable community planning (Graduate Certificate); transportation planning (Graduate Certificate). *Application deadline:* Applications are processed on a rolling basis. *Application fee:* $60. Electronic applications accepted. *Application Contact:* Tamryn McDermott, Director of Admissions, 215-777-9090, E-mail: tylerart@temple.edu. *Dean,* Susan E. Cahan, 215-777-9000, E-mail: tyler@temple.edu.

See Display on next page and Close-Up on page 901.

TENNESSEE STATE UNIVERSITY, Nashville, TN 37209-1561

General Information State-supported, coed, comprehensive institution. CGS member. *Graduate housing:* Rooms and/or apartments available on a first-come, first-served basis to single and married students. Housing application deadline: 8/1.

GRADUATE UNITS

The School of Graduate Studies and Research

College of Agriculture, Human and Natural Sciences *Program availability:* Part-time, evening/weekend. Offers agricultural sciences (MS); biological sciences (MS, PhD); biotechnology (PhD); chemistry (MS).

College of Business *Program availability:* Part-time, evening/weekend, online learning. Offers business (MBA). Electronic applications accepted.

College of Education *Program availability:* Part-time, evening/weekend. Offers counseling psychology (MS); curriculum and instruction (M Ed, Ed D); education (M Ed, MA Ed, MS, Ed D, PhD, Ed S); elementary education (M Ed); special education (M Ed).

College of Engineering *Program availability:* Part-time, evening/weekend. Offers biomedical engineering (ME); civil engineering (ME); computer and information systems engineering (MS, PhD); electrical engineering (ME); environmental engineering (ME); manufacturing engineering (ME); mathematical sciences (MS); mechanical engineering (ME).

College of Health Sciences *Program availability:* Part-time, evening/weekend. Offers exercise science (MA Ed); family nurse practitioner (MSN, Certificate); health sciences (MA Ed, MOT, MPH, MS, MSN, DPT, Certificate); holistic nurse practitioner

(MSN); holistic nursing (Certificate); nursing education (MSN, Certificate); occupational therapy (MOT); physical therapy (DPT); public health (MPH); speech and hearing science (MS); sports administration (MA Ed). Electronic applications accepted.

College of Liberal Arts *Program availability:* Part-time, evening/weekend. Offers criminal justice (MCJ); liberal arts (MCJ). Electronic applications accepted.

College of Public Service *Program availability:* Part-time, evening/weekend. Offers human resource management (MPS); public administration (MPA, PhD); social work (MSW); strategic leadership (MPS); training and development (MPS).

TENNESSEE TECHNOLOGICAL UNIVERSITY, Cookeville, TN 38505

General Information State-supported, coed, university. CGS member. *Enrollment:* 317 full-time matriculated graduate/professional students (171 women), 725 part-time matriculated graduate/professional students (376 women). *Enrollment by degree level:* 838 master's, 135 doctoral, 69 other advanced degrees. *Graduate faculty:* 341 full-time (62 women). Tuition, state resident: full-time $9375; part-time $534 per credit hour. Tuition, nonresident: full-time $22,443; part-time $1260 per credit hour. *Graduate housing:* Rooms and/or apartments available on a first-come, first-served basis to single and married students. Housing application deadline: 6/1. *Student services:* Campus employment opportunities, campus safety program, career counseling, child daycare facilities, exercise/wellness program, free psychological counseling, international student services, low-cost health insurance, multicultural affairs office, services for students with disabilities, teacher training. *Library facilities:* Angelo and Jennette Volpe Library and Media Center. *Research affiliation:* Center for Excellence in Teacher Evaluation, Appalachian Center for Crafts, Center of Excellence in Water Resources, Center of Excellence in Manufacturing Resources, Center of Excellence in Energy Systems Research.

Computer facilities: 227 computers available on campus for general student use. A campuswide network can be accessed from student residence rooms. Online class registration, 590 additional computers are available for student use in individual departmental labs are available.
Website: http://www.tntech.edu/

General Application Contact: Shelia K. Kendrick, Coordinator of Graduate Studies, 931-372-3808, Fax: 931-372-3497, E-mail: skendrick@tntech.edu.

GRADUATE UNITS

College of Graduate Studies Students: 317 full-time (171 women), 725 part-time (376 women); includes 90 minority (38 Black or African American, non-Hispanic/Latino; 1 American Indian or Alaska Native, non-Hispanic/Latino; 10 Asian, non-Hispanic/Latino; 16 Hispanic/Latino; 2 Native Hawaiian or other Pacific Islander, non-Hispanic/Latino; 23 Two or more races, non-Hispanic/Latino), 145 international. 1,035 applicants, 51% accepted, 267 enrolled. *Faculty:* 341 full-time (62 women). Expenses: Contact institution. *Financial support:* In 2016–17, 277 students received support, including 50 fellowships (averaging $8,000 per year), 114 research assistantships (averaging $6,973 per year), 158 teaching assistantships (averaging $6,213 per year); career-related internships or fieldwork and Federal Work-Study also available. Support available to part-time students. Financial award application deadline: 4/1; financial award applicants required to submit FAFSA. In 2016, 300 master's, 12 doctorates, 29 other advanced degrees awarded. *Program availability:* Part-time, evening/weekend, online learning. *Application deadline:* For fall admission, 7/1 for domestic students, 5/1 for international students; for spring admission, 12/1 for domestic students, 10/1 for international students; for summer admission, 5/1 for domestic students, 2/1 for international students. Applications are processed on a rolling basis. *Application fee:* $35 ($40 for international students). Electronic applications accepted. *Application Contact:* Shelia K. Kendrick, Coordinator of Graduate Studies, 931-372-3808, Fax: 931-372-3497, E-mail: skendrick@tntech.edu. *Senior Associate Provost and Dean of Graduate Studies*, Dr. Mark A. Stephens, 931-372-3233, Fax: 931-372-3497, E-mail: mstephens@tntech.edu.

College of Arts and Sciences Students: 21 full-time (14 women), 33 part-time (17 women); includes 4 minority (2 Hispanic/Latino; 2 Two or more races, non-Hispanic/Latino), 8 international. Average age 27. 65 applicants, 40% accepted, 15 enrolled. *Faculty:* 78 full-time (15 women). Expenses: Contact institution. *Financial support:* In 2016–17, 10 research assistantships (averaging $7,600 per year), 36 teaching assistantships (averaging $6,630 per year) were awarded; fellowships and career-related internships or fieldwork also available. Support available to part-time students. Financial award application deadline: 4/1. In 2016, 20 master's awarded. *Program availability:* Part-time. Offers arts and sciences (MA, MS); chemistry (MS); English (MA); fish, game, and wildlife management (MS); mathematics (MS). *Application deadline:* For fall admission, 8/1 for domestic students, 5/1 for international students; for spring admission, 12/1 for domestic students, 10/1 for international students; for summer admission, 5/1 for domestic students, 2/1 for international students. Applications are processed on a rolling basis. *Application fee:* $35 ($40 for international students). Electronic applications accepted. *Application Contact:* Shelia K. Kendrick, Coordinator of Graduate Studies, 931-372-3808, Fax: 931-372-3497, E-mail: skendrick@tntech.edu. *Dean*, Dr. Paul Semmes, 931-372-3118, Fax: 931-372-6142, E-mail: psemmes@tntech.edu.

College of Business Students: 45 full-time (22 women), 167 part-time (51 women); includes 18 minority (5 Black or African American, non-Hispanic/Latino; 4 Asian, non-Hispanic/Latino; 4 Hispanic/Latino; 5 Two or more races, non-Hispanic/Latino), 14 international. Average age 25. 173 applicants, 54% accepted, 52 enrolled. *Faculty:* 28 full-time (5 women). Expenses: Contact institution. *Financial support:* In 2016–17, 5 fellowships (averaging $10,000 per year), 1 teaching assistantship (averaging $5,200 per year) were awarded; research assistantships also available. Support available to part-time students. Financial award application deadline: 4/1. In 2016, 78 master's awarded. *Program availability:* Part-time, evening/weekend, online learning. Offers accounting (MBA); finance (MBA); human resource management (MBA); international business (MBA); management information systems (MBA). *Application deadline:* For fall admission, 8/1 for domestic students, 5/1 for international students; for spring admission, 12/1 for domestic students, 10/1 for international students; for summer admission, 5/1 for domestic students, 2/1 for international students. Applications are processed on a rolling basis. *Application fee:* $35 ($40 for international students). Electronic applications accepted. *Application Contact:* Shelia K. Kendrick, Coordinator of Graduate Studies, 931-372-3808, Fax: 931-372-3497, E-mail: skendrick@tntech.edu. *Director*, Kate Nicewicz, 931-372-3600, Fax: 931-372-6249, E-mail: knicewicz@tntech.edu.

College of Education Students: 121 full-time (84 women), 244 part-time (178 women); includes 40 minority (21 Black or African American, non-Hispanic/Latino; 1 American Indian or Alaska Native, non-Hispanic/Latino; 1 Asian, non-Hispanic/Latino; 7 Hispanic/Latino; 10 Two or more races, non-Hispanic/Latino), 7 international. Average age 27. 226 applicants, 61% accepted, 104 enrolled. *Faculty:* 58 full-time (16 women).

Expenses: Contact institution. *Financial support:* In 2016–17, 42 fellowships (averaging $8,000 per year), 12 research assistantships (averaging $8,566 per year), 24 teaching assistantships (averaging $4,483 per year) were awarded; career-related internships or fieldwork also available. Support available to part-time students. Financial award application deadline: 4/1. In 2016, 114 master's, 5 doctorates, 27 other advanced degrees awarded. *Program availability:* Part-time, evening/weekend. Offers adapted physical education (MA); advanced studies in teaching and learning (M Ed); applied behavior analysis (PhD); counseling and psychology (MA, Ed S); curriculum (MA, Ed S); early childhood education (MA, Ed S); education (M Ed, MA, PhD, Ed S); educational technology (MA, Ed S); elementary education (MA, Ed S); elementary/middle school physical education (MA); exceptional learning (PhD); instructional leadership (MA, Ed S); library science (MA, Ed S); lifetime wellness (MA); literacy (PhD); music (MA); program planning and evaluation (MA); reading (MA, Ed S); secondary education (Ed S); special education (MA, Ed S); sport management (MA); STEM education (MA, PhD, Ed S). *Application deadline:* For fall admission, 8/1 for domestic students, 5/1 for international students; for spring admission, 12/1 for domestic students, 10/1 for international students; for summer admission, 5/1 for domestic students, 2/1 for international students. Applications are processed on a rolling basis. *Application fee:* $35 ($40 for international students). Electronic applications accepted. *Application Contact:* Shelia K. Kendrick, Coordinator of Graduate Studies, 931-372-3808, Fax: 931-372-3497, E-mail: skendrick@tntech.edu. *Dean,* Dr. Jennifer Shank, 931-372-3124, Fax: 931-372-6319, E-mail: jshank@tntech.edu.

College of Engineering Students: 82 full-time (20 women), 127 part-time (25 women); includes 12 minority (4 Black or African American, non-Hispanic/Latino; 3 Asian, non-Hispanic/Latino; 1 Hispanic/Latino; 1 Native Hawaiian or other Pacific Islander, non-Hispanic/Latino; 3 Two or more races, non-Hispanic/Latino), 110 international. Average age 28. 489 applicants, 45% accepted, 53 enrolled. *Faculty:* 76 full-time (2 women). Expenses: Contact institution. *Financial support:* In 2016–17, 3 fellowships (averaging $8,000 per year), 99 research assistantships (averaging $9,293 per year), 80 teaching assistantships (averaging $8,000 per year) were awarded; career-related internships or fieldwork also available. Support available to part-time students. Financial award application deadline: 4/1. In 2016, 37 master's, 12 doctorates awarded. *Program availability:* Part-time. Offers chemical engineering (MS); civil and environmental engineering (MS); computer software and scientific applications (MS); electrical and computer engineering (MS); engineering (MS, PhD); Internet-based computing (MS); mechanical engineering (MS). *Application deadline:* For fall admission, 8/1 for domestic students, 5/1 for international students; for spring admission, 12/1 for domestic students, 10/1 for international students. Applications are processed on a rolling basis. *Application fee:* $35 ($40 for international students). Electronic applications accepted. *Application Contact:* Shelia K. Kendrick, Coordinator of Graduate Studies, 931-372-3808, Fax: 931-372-3497, E-mail: skendrick@tntech.edu. *Dean,* Dr. Joseph Rencis, 931-372-3172, Fax: 931-372-6172, E-mail: jjrencis@tntech.edu.

College of Interdisciplinary Studies Students: 26 full-time (12 women), 72 part-time (37 women); includes 12 minority (7 Black or African American, non-Hispanic/Latino; 1 Asian, non-Hispanic/Latino; 1 Hispanic/Latino; 1 Native Hawaiian or other Pacific Islander, non-Hispanic/Latino; 2 Two or more races, non-Hispanic/Latino), 6 international. 55 applicants, 56% accepted, 20 enrolled. Expenses: Contact institution. *Financial support:* In 2016–17, 3 research assistantships (averaging $1,541 per year), 7 teaching assistantships (averaging $1,541 per year) were awarded. In 2016, 12 master's awarded. *Program availability:* Part-time. Offers biology (PhD); chemistry (PhD); environmental informatics (PSM); environmental studies (PSM, PhD); human resources leadership (MPS); interdisciplinary studies (MPS, PSM, PhD); strategic leadership (MPS); training and development (MPS). *Application deadline:* For fall admission, 7/1 for domestic students, 5/1 for international students; for spring admission, 11/1 for domestic students, 10/1 for international students; for summer admission, 5/1 for domestic students, 2/1 for international students. Applications are processed on a rolling basis. *Application fee:* $35 ($40 for international students). Electronic applications accepted. *Application Contact:* Shelia K. Kendrick, Coordinator of Graduate Studies, 931-372-3808, Fax: 931-372-3497, E-mail: skendrick@tntech.edu. *Dean,* Dr. Mike Gotcher, 931-372-6238, E-mail: mgotcher@tntech.edu.

Whitson-Hester School of Nursing Students: 22 full-time (19 women), 82 part-time (68 women); includes 4 minority (1 Black or African American, non-Hispanic/Latino; 1 Asian, non-Hispanic/Latino; 1 Hispanic/Latino; 1 Two or more races, non-Hispanic/Latino). 45 applicants, 64% accepted, 17 enrolled. Expenses: Contact institution. *Financial support:* In 2016–17, 5 teaching assistantships (averaging $6,000 per year) were awarded. Financial award application deadline: 4/1. In 2016, 39 master's awarded. *Program availability:* Part-time, evening/weekend, online learning. Offers family nurse practitioner (MSN); informatics (MSN); nursing administration (MSN); nursing education (MSN). *Application deadline:* For fall admission, 7/1 for domestic students, 5/1 for international students; for spring admission, 11/1 for domestic students, 10/1 for international students; for summer admission, 5/1 for domestic students, 2/1 for international students. Applications are processed on a rolling basis. *Application fee:* $35 ($40 for international students). Electronic applications accepted. *Application Contact:* Shelia K. Kendrick, Coordinator of Graduate Studies, 931-372-3808, Fax: 931-372-3497, E-mail: skendrick@tntech.edu. *Dean,* Dr. Huey-Ming Tzeng, 931-372-3547, Fax: 931-372-6244, E-mail: htzeng@tntech.edu.

TENNESSEE WESLEYAN UNIVERSITY, Athens, TN 37303

General Information Independent-religious, coed, comprehensive institution. *Enrollment:* 1,037 graduate, professional, and undergraduate students; 4 full-time matriculated graduate/professional students (2 women), 18 part-time matriculated graduate/professional students (11 women). *Enrollment by degree level:* 22 master's. *Graduate faculty:* 8 full-time (4 women), 3 part-time/adjunct (2 women). *Tuition:* Full-time $9000; part-time $500 per hour. *Graduate housing:* Room and/or apartments available on a first-come, first-served basis to single students; on-campus housing not available to married students. Typical cost: $7540 (including board). Room and board charges vary according to housing facility selected. Housing application deadline: 8/5. *Student services:* Career counseling, international student services. *Library facilities:* Merner-Pfeiffer Library plus 1 other. *Collection:* Books: 52,369 (physical), 156,820 (digital/electronic); Serial titles: 82 (physical); Databases: 76. Weekly public service hours: 69.

Computer facilities: 205 computers available on campus for general student use. A campuswide network can be accessed from student residence rooms. Online class registration is available.
Website: http://www.tnwesleyan.edu/

General Application Contact: Mark Bucco, Adult and Graduate Admissions Counselor, 423-252-1114, Fax: 423-745-9335, E-mail: mbucco@tnwesleyan.edu.

GRADUATE UNITS

Graduate Programs Students: 4 full-time (2 women), 18 part-time (11 women). *Faculty:* 8 full-time (4 women), 3 part-time/adjunct (2 women). Expenses: Contact institution. *Program availability:* Evening/weekend. Offers accounting (MBA); management (MBA). *Application Contact:* Mark Bucco, Adult and Graduate Admissions Counselor, 423-252-1114, Fax: 423-745-9335, E-mail: mbucco@tnwesleyan.edu.

TEXAS A&M INTERNATIONAL UNIVERSITY, Laredo, TX 78041-1900

General Information State-supported, coed, comprehensive institution. CGS member. *Graduate housing:* Rooms and/or apartments available on a first-come, first-served basis to single and married students.

GRADUATE UNITS

Office of Graduate Studies and Research *Program availability:* Part-time.

A.R. Sanchez, Jr. School of Business *Program availability:* Part-time, evening/weekend. Offers accounting (MP Acc); business (MBA, MP Acc, MSIS, PhD); information systems (MSIS); international banking and finance (MBA); international business management (MBA, PhD).

College of Arts and Sciences *Program availability:* Part-time, online learning. Offers arts and sciences (MA, MACP, MPA, MS, PhD); biology (MS); counseling psychology (MACP); criminal justice (MS); English (MA); Hispanic studies (PhD); history and political thought (MA); language, literature and translation (MA); mathematics (MS); political science (MA); psychology (MS); public administration (MPA).

College of Education *Program availability:* Part-time, evening/weekend. Offers curriculum and pedagogy (MS); education (MS, Ed S); educational administration (MS Ed); generic special education (MS Ed); school counseling (MS).

College of Nursing and Health Sciences Offers family nurse practitioner (MSN).

TEXAS A&M UNIVERSITY, College Station, TX 77843

General Information State-supported, coed, university. CGS member. *Enrollment:* 65,302 graduate, professional, and undergraduate students; 11,808 full-time matriculated graduate/professional students (5,127 women), 2,833 part-time matriculated graduate/professional students (1,401 women). *Enrollment by degree level:* 6,839 master's, 7,707 doctoral, 95 other advanced degrees. Tuition, state resident: full-time $5783; part-time $2891 per semester hour. Tuition, nonresident: full-time $15,953; part-time $7976 per semester hour. *Required fees:* $2927; $1463 per semester hour. $731 per semester. Tuition and fees vary according to course load and program. *Graduate housing:* Rooms and/or apartments available on a first-come, first-served basis to single and married students. Typical cost: $10,368 (including board) for single students; $10,368 (including board) for married students. Room and board charges vary according to housing facility selected. *Student services:* Campus employment opportunities, campus safety program, career counseling, child daycare facilities, exercise/wellness program, free psychological counseling, grant writing training, international student services, low-cost health insurance, multicultural affairs office, services for students with disabilities, teacher training, writing training. *Library facilities:* Sterling C. Evans Library plus 6 others. *Collection:* Books: 3.8 million (physical), 1.8 million (digital/electronic); Serial titles: 7,647 (physical), 121,167 (digital/electronic); Databases: 1,712. Weekly public service hours: 144; study areas open 24 hours, 5–7 days a week; students can reserve study rooms. *Research affiliation:* U.S. Department of Agriculture (USDA) (agriculture), National Science Foundation (geosciences), Joint Oceanographic Institutions, Inc. (geosciences), Texas Department of Transportation (transportation).

Computer facilities: 2,666 computers available on campus for general student use. A campuswide network can be accessed from student residence rooms and from off campus. Online class registration is available.
Website: http://www.tamu.edu/

General Application Contact: Graduate Admissions, 979-458-0427, E-mail: admissions@tamu.edu.

GRADUATE UNITS

Bush School of Government and Public Service Students: 324 full-time (165 women), 26 part-time (10 women); includes 89 minority (19 Black or African American, non-Hispanic/Latino; 4 Asian, non-Hispanic/Latino; 58 Hispanic/Latino; 1 Native Hawaiian or other Pacific Islander, non-Hispanic/Latino; 7 Two or more races, non-Hispanic/Latino), 44 international. Average age 27. 261 applicants, 96% accepted, 165 enrolled. *Faculty:* 68. Expenses: Contact institution. *Financial support:* In 2016–17, 413 students received support, including 16 fellowships with tuition reimbursements available (averaging $18,236 per year), 61 research assistantships with tuition reimbursements available (averaging $5,904 per year), 1 teaching assistantship (averaging $4,025 per year); career-related internships or fieldwork, institutionally sponsored loans, scholarships/grants, traineeships, health care benefits, tuition waivers (full and partial), and unspecified assistantships also available. Support available to part-time students. Financial award application deadline: 3/15; financial award applicants required to submit FAFSA. In 2016, 164 master's awarded. Offers homeland security (Certificate); international affairs (MIA, Certificate); national security affairs (Certificate); non-profit management (Certificate); public service and administration (MPSA). *Application deadline:* For fall admission, 1/15 for domestic and international students. *Application fee:* $50 ($90 for international students). Electronic applications accepted. *Application Contact:* Kathryn Meyer, Director of Recruitment and Admissions, 979-458-4767, Fax: 979-845-4155, E-mail: bushschooladmissions@tamu.edu. *Dean,* Dr. Mark Welsh, 979-862-8007, E-mail: mwelsh@tamu.edu.

College of Agriculture and Life Sciences Students: 1,014 full-time (497 women), 308 part-time (164 women); includes 229 minority (32 Black or African American, non-Hispanic/Latino; 2 American Indian or Alaska Native, non-Hispanic/Latino; 37 Asian, non-Hispanic/Latino; 141 Hispanic/Latino; 1 Native Hawaiian or other Pacific Islander, non-Hispanic/Latino; 16 Two or more races, non-Hispanic/Latino), 418 international. Average age 29. 555 applicants, 56% accepted, 225 enrolled. *Faculty:* 356. Expenses: Contact institution. *Financial support:* In 2016–17, 1,064 students received support, including 159 fellowships with tuition reimbursements available (averaging $11,549 per year), 513 research assistantships with tuition reimbursements available (averaging $5,883 per year), 318 teaching assistantships with tuition reimbursements available (averaging $8,855 per year); career-related internships or fieldwork, institutionally sponsored loans, scholarships/grants, traineeships, health care benefits, tuition waivers (full and partial), and unspecified assistantships also available. Support available to part-time students. Financial award application deadline: 3/15; financial award applicants required to submit FAFSA. In 2016, 247 master's, 98 doctorates awarded. *Program availability:* Part-time, blended/hybrid learning. Offers agricultural development (M Agr); agricultural economics (M Agr, MS, PhD); agricultural education (Ed D); agricultural leadership, education and communication (M Ed, MS, Ed D, PhD); agricultural systems management (M Agr, MS); agriculture and life sciences (M Agr, M Ed, M Engr, MEIM,

MNRD, MRRD, MS, MWSc, Ed D, PhD); agronomy (MS, PhD); animal breeding (MS, PhD); animal science (M Agr, MS, PhD); biochemistry (MS, PhD); biological and agricultural engineering (M Engr, MS, PhD); ecosystem science and management (M Agr, MNRD, MS, PhD); entomology (MS, PhD); equine industry management (MEIM); food science and technology (M Agr); forestry (MS, PhD); horticulture (M Agr, MS, PhD); nutrition (MS, PhD); physiology of reproduction (MS, PhD); plant pathology (MS, PhD); poultry science (M Agr, MS, PhD); recreation and resources development (MRRD); recreation, park, and tourism sciences (MS, PhD); soil science (MS, PhD); wildlife and fisheries sciences (MS, PhD); wildlife science (MWSc). *Application deadline:* For fall admission, 7/21 priority date for domestic students, 6/1 priority date for international students; for spring admission, 12/1 priority date for domestic students, 10/1 priority date for international students. Applications are processed on a rolling basis. *Application fee:* $50 ($90 for international students). Electronic applications accepted. *Application Contact:* Graduate Admissions, 979-845-1044, E-mail: graduate-admissions@tamu.edu. *Vice Chancellor and Dean for Agriculture and Life Sciences,* Dr. Mark A. Hussey, 979-845-4747, Fax: 979-845-9938, E-mail: mhussey@tamu.edu.

College of Architecture Students: 415 full-time (213 women), 55 part-time (17 women); includes 68 minority (6 Black or African American, non-Hispanic/Latino; 20 Asian, non-Hispanic/Latino; 40 Hispanic/Latino; 1 Native Hawaiian or other Pacific Islander, non-Hispanic/Latino; 1 Two or more races, non-Hispanic/Latino), 238 international. Average age 28. 584 applicants, 57% accepted, 150 enrolled. *Faculty:* 100. Expenses: Contact institution. *Financial support:* In 2016–17, 340 students received support, including 12 fellowships with tuition reimbursements available (averaging $4,524 per year), 97 research assistantships with tuition reimbursements available (averaging $3,712 per year), 118 teaching assistantships with tuition reimbursements available (averaging $5,292 per year); career-related internships or fieldwork, institutionally sponsored loans, scholarships/grants, traineeships, health care benefits, tuition waivers (full and partial), and unspecified assistantships also available. Support available to part-time students. Financial award application deadline: 3/15; financial award applicants required to submit FAFSA. In 2016, 177 master's, 15 doctorates awarded. Offers architecture (M Arch, MS, PhD); construction management (MS); land and property development (MLPD); landscape architecture (MLA); urban and regional planning (MUP); urban and regional science (PhD); visualization (MFA, MS). *Application deadline:* For fall admission, 1/15 priority date for domestic and international students. Applications are processed on a rolling basis. *Application fee:* $50 ($90 for international students). Electronic applications accepted. *Application Contact:* Graduate Admissions, 979-458-0427, E-mail: admissions@tamu.edu. *Dean,* Dr. Jorge Vanegas, 979-845-1223, Fax: 979-845-4491, E-mail: jvanegas@tamu.edu.

College of Dentistry Students: 496 full-time (248 women), 40 part-time (16 women); includes 277 minority (52 Black or African American, non-Hispanic/Latino; 2 American Indian or Alaska Native, non-Hispanic/Latino; 108 Asian, non-Hispanic/Latino; 108 Hispanic/Latino; 1 Native Hawaiian or other Pacific Islander, non-Hispanic/Latino; 6 Two or more races, non-Hispanic/Latino), 20 international. Average age 27. 12 applicants, 33% accepted, 2 enrolled. *Faculty:* 259. Expenses: Contact institution. *Financial support:* In 2016–17, 285 students received support, including 31 research assistantships with tuition reimbursements available (averaging $4,250 per year), 46 teaching assistantships with tuition reimbursements available (averaging $10,559 per year); career-related internships or fieldwork, institutionally sponsored loans, scholarships/grants, traineeships, health care benefits, tuition waivers (full and partial), and unspecified assistantships also available. Support available to part-time students. Financial award applicants required to submit FAFSA. In 2016, 13 master's, 105 other advanced degrees awarded. Offers advanced education in general dentistry (Certificate); biomedical sciences (MS); dental hygiene (MS); dental public health (Certificate); endodontics (Certificate); maxillofacial surgery (Certificate); oral and maxillofacial pathology (Certificate); oral and maxillofacial radiology (Certificate); oral and maxillofacial surgery (Certificate); oral biology (MS, PhD); orthodontics (Certificate); pediatric dentistry (Certificate); periodontics (Certificate); prosthodontics (Certificate). *Application fee:* $35. Electronic applications accepted. *Application Contact:* Dr. Jack L. Long, Associate Dean for Student Affairs, 214-828-8232, Fax: 214-874-4572, E-mail: jlong@bcd.tamhsc.edu. *Dean,* Dr. Lawrence E. Wolinsky, 214-828-8300, E-mail: wolinsky@bcd.tamhsc.edu.

College of Education and Human Development Students: 680 full-time (486 women), 955 part-time (691 women); includes 529 minority (169 Black or African American, non-Hispanic/Latino; 1 American Indian or Alaska Native, non-Hispanic/Latino; 53 Asian, non-Hispanic/Latino; 276 Hispanic/Latino; 3 Native Hawaiian or other Pacific Islander, non-Hispanic/Latino; 27 Two or more races, non-Hispanic/Latino), 170 international. Average age 33. 634 applicants, 66% accepted, 287 enrolled. *Faculty:* 179. Expenses: Contact institution. *Financial support:* In 2016–17, 785 students received support, including 18 fellowships with tuition reimbursements available (averaging $11,766 per year), 231 research assistantships with tuition reimbursements available (averaging $5,798 per year), 137 teaching assistantships with tuition reimbursements available (averaging $9,224 per year); career-related internships or fieldwork, institutionally sponsored loans, scholarships/grants, traineeships, health care benefits, tuition waivers (full and partial), and unspecified assistantships also available. Support available to part-time students. Financial award application deadline: 3/15; financial award applicants required to submit FAFSA. In 2016, 413 master's, 104 doctorates awarded. *Program availability:* Part-time, evening/weekend, blended/hybrid learning. Offers athletic training (MS); bilingual education (M Ed, MS); counseling psychology (PhD); curriculum and instruction (M Ed, MS, Ed D, PhD); education and human development (M Ed, MS, Ed D, PhD); educational administration (M Ed, MS, Ed D, PhD); educational human resource development (MS, PhD); educational psychology (M Ed, MS, PhD); educational technology (M Ed); health education (M Ed, MS, Ed D, PhD); kinesiology (MS, PhD); school psychology (PhD); special education (M Ed, MS); sports management (MS). *Application deadline:* Applications are processed on a rolling basis. *Application fee:* $50 ($90 for international students). Electronic applications accepted. *Application Contact:* Dr. George Cunningham, Professor and Associate Dean for Academic Affairs, 979-845-5311, E-mail: gbcunningham@tamu.edu. *Professor and Dean,* Dr. Joyce Alexander, 979-862-6649, E-mail: joycemalexander@tamu.edu.

College of Engineering Students: 2,987 full-time (638 women), 587 part-time (112 women); includes 442 minority (62 Black or African American, non-Hispanic/Latino; 4 American Indian or Alaska Native, non-Hispanic/Latino; 139 Asian, non-Hispanic/Latino; 195 Hispanic/Latino; 2 Native Hawaiian or other Pacific Islander, non-Hispanic/Latino; 40 Two or more races, non-Hispanic/Latino), 2,278 international. Average age 28. 9,256 applicants, 23% accepted, 1011 enrolled. *Faculty:* 475. Expenses: Contact institution. *Financial support:* In 2016–17, 2,564 students received support, including 286 fellowships with tuition reimbursements available (averaging $10,608 per year), 1,326 research assistantships with tuition reimbursements available (averaging $6,134 per year), 541 teaching assistantships with tuition reimbursements available (averaging $8,228 per year); career-related internships or fieldwork, institutionally sponsored loans, scholarships/grants, traineeships, health care benefits, tuition waivers (full and partial),

and unspecified assistantships also available. Support available to part-time students. Financial award applicants required to submit FAFSA. In 2016, 884 master's, 245 doctorates awarded. *Program availability:* Part-time, online learning. Offers aerospace engineering (M Eng, MS, PhD); biomedical engineering (M Eng, MS, PhD); chemical engineering (M Eng, MS, PhD); civil engineering (M Eng, MS, PhD); computer engineering (M Eng, MS, PhD); computer science (MCS, MS, PhD); electrical engineering (M Eng, MS, PhD); engineering (M Eng, MCS, METM, MID, MS, PhD); engineering systems management (MS); health physics (MS); industrial distribution (MID); industrial engineering (M Eng, MS, PhD); materials science and engineering (M Eng, MS, PhD); mechanical engineering (M Eng, MS, PhD); nuclear engineering (M Eng, MS, PhD); petroleum engineering (M Eng, MS, PhD); technical management (METM). *Application fee:* $50 ($90 for international students). Electronic applications accepted. *Application Contact:* Dr. John C. Criscione, Assistant Dean for Graduate Programs, 979-845-5428, E-mail: jccriscione@tamu.edu. *Dean and Vice Chancellor,* Dr. M. Katherine Banks, 979-845-1306, E-mail: k-banks@tamu.edu.

College of Geosciences Students: 293 full-time (122 women), 59 part-time (27 women); includes 44 minority (4 Black or African American, non-Hispanic/Latino; 8 Asian, non-Hispanic/Latino; 28 Hispanic/Latino; 4 Two or more races, non-Hispanic/Latino), 126 international. Average age 28. 488 applicants, 23% accepted, 64 enrolled. *Faculty:* 100. Expenses: Contact institution. *Financial support:* In 2016–17, 291 students received support, including 62 fellowships with tuition reimbursements available (averaging $6,411 per year), 131 research assistantships with tuition reimbursements available (averaging $6,430 per year), 117 teaching assistantships with tuition reimbursements available (averaging $9,816 per year); career-related internships or fieldwork, institutionally sponsored loans, traineeships, health care benefits, tuition waivers (full and partial), and unspecified assistantships also available. Support available to part-time students. Financial award application deadline: 3/15; financial award applicants required to submit FAFSA. In 2016, 52 master's, 21 doctorates awarded. *Program availability:* Part-time. Offers atmospheric sciences (MS, PhD); geography (MS, PhD); geology (MS, PhD); geophysics (MS, PhD); geosciences (MGsc, MS, PhD); oceanography (MS, PhD). *Application deadline:* For fall admission, 1/1 priority date for domestic students; for spring admission, 8/15 for domestic students. Applications are processed on a rolling basis. *Application fee:* $50 ($90 for international students). Electronic applications accepted. *Application Contact:* Dr. Eric A. Riggs, Associate Professor and Associate Dean, 979-845-3651, E-mail: emriggs@geos.tamu.edu. *Dean,* Dr. Kate C. Miller, 979-845-3651, E-mail: dean@geosciences.tamu.edu.

College of Liberal Arts Students: 670 full-time (348 women), 153 part-time (82 women); includes 166 minority (32 Black or African American, non-Hispanic/Latino; 2 American Indian or Alaska Native, non-Hispanic/Latino; 17 Asian, non-Hispanic/Latino; 105 Hispanic/Latino; 10 Two or more races, non-Hispanic/Latino), 306 international. Average age 30. 1,140 applicants, 35% accepted, 205 enrolled. *Faculty:* 362. Expenses: Contact institution. *Financial support:* In 2016–17, 618 students received support, including 77 fellowships with tuition reimbursements available (averaging $14,712 per year), 140 research assistantships with tuition reimbursements available (averaging $5,499 per year), 366 teaching assistantships with tuition reimbursements available (averaging $10,328 per year); career-related internships or fieldwork, institutionally sponsored loans, scholarships/grants, traineeships, health care benefits, tuition waivers (full and partial), unspecified assistantships, and assistant lecturer positions also available. Support available to part-time students. Financial award application deadline: 3/15; financial award applicants required to submit FAFSA. In 2016, 128 master's, 78 doctorates awarded. *Program availability:* Part-time. Offers anthropology (MA, PhD); clinical psychology (PhD); communication (MA, PhD); economics (MS, PhD); English (MA, PhD); Hispanic studies (MA, PhD); history (MA, PhD); industrial/organizational psychology (PhD); liberal arts (MA, MS, PhD); maritime archaeology and conservation (MS); modern languages (MA); performance studies (MS); philosophy (MA, PhD); political science (MA, PhD); psychology (MS, PhD); sociology (MS, PhD). *Application fee:* $50 ($90 for international students). Electronic applications accepted. *Application Contact:* Dr. Patricia A. Hurley, Associate Dean for Faculty and Graduate Programs, 979-845-8541, Fax: 979-845-5164, E-mail: pat-hurley@tamu.edu. *Dean,* Dr. Pamela R. Matthews, 979-862-6797, Fax: 979-845-5164, E-mail: p-matthews@tamu.edu.

College of Medicine Students: 891 full-time (426 women), 15 part-time (13 women); includes 424 minority (33 Black or African American, non-Hispanic/Latino; 2 American Indian or Alaska Native, non-Hispanic/Latino; 280 Asian, non-Hispanic/Latino; 95 Hispanic/Latino; 2 Native Hawaiian or other Pacific Islander, non-Hispanic/Latino; 12 Two or more races, non-Hispanic/Latino), 63 international. Average age 27. 304 applicants, 82% accepted, 222 enrolled. *Faculty:* 123. Expenses: Contact institution. *Financial support:* In 2016–17, 408 students received support, including 1 fellowship with tuition reimbursement available (averaging $6,562 per year), 124 research assistantships with tuition reimbursements available (averaging $8,728 per year); career-related internships or fieldwork, institutionally sponsored loans, scholarships/grants, traineeships, health care benefits, tuition waivers (full and partial), and unspecified assistantships also available. Support available to part-time students. Financial award applicants required to submit FAFSA. In 2016, 12 master's, 6 doctorates awarded. Offers education for healthcare professionals (MS); medical sciences (PhD); medicine (MD). *Application deadline:* For fall admission, 9/30 for domestic students. *Application fee:* $200. Electronic applications accepted. *Application Contact:* Filomeno G. Maldonado, Associate Dean of Admissions, 979-436-0231, Fax: 979-436-0097, E-mail: fgmaldonado@medicine.tamhsc.edu. *Interim Senior Vice President and Chief Operating Officer,* Dr. Paul E. Ogden, MD, 979-436-0202, Fax: 979-436-0092, E-mail: ogden@medicine.tamhsc.edu.

College of Nursing Students: 14 full-time (13 women), 39 part-time (33 women); includes 10 minority (1 Black or African American, non-Hispanic/Latino; 9 Hispanic/Latino). Average age 36. *Faculty:* 13. Expenses: Contact institution. *Financial support:* In 2016–17, 17 students received support, including 1 fellowship (averaging $4,345 per year); career-related internships or fieldwork, institutionally sponsored loans, scholarships/grants, traineeships, health care benefits, tuition waivers (full and partial), and unspecified assistantships also available. Support available to part-time students. Financial award applicants required to submit FAFSA. In 2016, 19 master's awarded. Offers family nurse practitioner (MSN); nursing education (MSN). *Application Contact:* Jennifer Frank, Program Coordinator for Recruitment and Admission, 979-436-0110, E-mail: conadmissions@tamhsc.edu. *Founding Dean,* Dr. Sharon A. Wilkerson, 979-436-0111, Fax: 979-436-0098, E-mail: wilkerson@tamhsc.edu.

College of Science Students: 876 full-time (246 women), 400 part-time (127 women); includes 213 minority (27 Black or African American, non-Hispanic/Latino; 1 American Indian or Alaska Native, non-Hispanic/Latino; 87 Asian, non-Hispanic/Latino; 79 Hispanic/Latino; 19 Two or more races, non-Hispanic/Latino), 500 international. Average age 30. 873 applicants, 53% accepted, 272 enrolled. *Faculty:* 267. Expenses: Contact institution. *Financial support:* In 2016–17, 768 students received support, including 108 fellowships with tuition reimbursements available (averaging $11,309 per year), 350 research assistantships with tuition reimbursements available (averaging $6,289 per year), 412 teaching assistantships with tuition reimbursements available (averaging $11,275 per year); career-related internships or fieldwork, institutionally sponsored loans, scholarships/grants, traineeships, health care benefits, tuition waivers (full and partial), and unspecified assistantships also available. Support available to part-time students. Financial award applicants required to submit FAFSA. In 2016, 137 master's, 144 doctorates awarded. *Program availability:* Part-time. Offers analytics (MS); applied physics (PhD); astronomy (MS, PhD); biology (MS, PhD); chemistry (MS, PhD); mathematics (MS, PhD); microbiology (MS, PhD); physics (MS, PhD); science (MS, PhD); statistics (MS, PhD). *Application fee:* $50 ($90 for international students). *Application Contact:* Mark Zoran, Associate Dean for Graduate Studies, 979-458-8001, Fax: 979-845-6077, E-mail: zoran@science.tamu.edu. *Dean,* Dr. Meigan Aronson, 979-845-8817, Fax: 979-845-6077, E-mail: maronson@science.tamu.edu.

College of Veterinary Medicine and Biomedical Sciences Students: 806 full-time (598 women), 54 part-time (36 women); includes 208 minority (26 Black or African American, non-Hispanic/Latino; 53 Asian, non-Hispanic/Latino; 111 Hispanic/Latino; 18 Two or more races, non-Hispanic/Latino), 59 international. Average age 26. 317 applicants, 79% accepted, 218 enrolled. *Faculty:* 167. Expenses: Contact institution. *Financial support:* In 2016–17, 747 students received support, including 25 fellowships with tuition reimbursements available (averaging $13,449 per year), 114 research assistantships with tuition reimbursements available (averaging $6,825 per year), 19 teaching assistantships with tuition reimbursements available (averaging $10,011 per year); career-related internships or fieldwork, institutionally sponsored loans, scholarships/grants, traineeships, health care benefits, tuition waivers (full and partial), unspecified assistantships, and clinical associateships also available. Support available to part-time students. Financial award application deadline: 3/15; financial award applicants required to submit FAFSA. In 2016, 86 master's, 17 doctorates awarded. *Program availability:* Part-time. Offers veterinary medicine and biomedical sciences (MS, DVM, PhD). *Application deadline:* For fall admission, 6/1 for domestic students, 3/1 for international students; for spring admission, 11/1 for domestic students, 8/1 for international students; for summer admission, 3/1 for domestic students, 12/1 for international students. *Application fee:* $50 ($90 for international students). *Application Contact:* Graduate Admissions, 979-845-1044, E-mail: admissions@tamu.edu. *Dean,* Dr. Eleanor M. Green, 979-845-5053, Fax: 979-845-5088, E-mail: emgreen@tamu.edu.

Galveston Campus Students: 134 full-time (67 women), 34 part-time (9 women); includes 30 minority (3 Black or African American, non-Hispanic/Latino; 6 Asian, non-Hispanic/Latino; 15 Hispanic/Latino; 6 Two or more races, non-Hispanic/Latino), 12 international. Average age 29. 68 applicants, 87% accepted, 3 enrolled. Expenses: Contact institution. *Financial support:* In 2016–17, 121 students received support, including 1 fellowship with tuition reimbursement available (averaging $22,500 per year), 24 research assistantships with tuition reimbursements available (averaging $5,584 per year), 63 teaching assistantships with tuition reimbursements available (averaging $11,349 per year). In 2016, 35 master's, 4 doctorates awarded. Offers marine biology (MS, PhD); marine resources management (MMRM); maritime administration and logistics (MMAL). *Application Contact:* Nicole Kinslow, Director of Graduate Studies, 409-740-4937, Fax: 409-740-4754, E-mail: kinslown@tamug.edu.

Irma Lerma Rangel College of Pharmacy Students: 406 full-time (215 women), 1 (woman) part-time; includes 334 minority (27 Black or African American, non-Hispanic/Latino; 161 Asian, non-Hispanic/Latino; 136 Hispanic/Latino; 1 Native Hawaiian or other Pacific Islander, non-Hispanic/Latino; 9 Two or more races, non-Hispanic/Latino), 2 international. Average age 27. *Faculty:* 46. Expenses: Contact institution. *Financial support:* In 2016–17, 148 students received support. Career-related internships or fieldwork, institutionally sponsored loans, scholarships/grants, traineeships, health care benefits, tuition waivers (full and partial), and unspecified assistantships available. Support available to part-time students. Financial award applicants required to submit FAFSA. Offers pharmacy (Pharm D). *Application deadline:* For fall admission, 11/1 for domestic students. *Application fee:* $100. Electronic applications accepted. *Application Contact:* Maria de Leon, Director of Admission, 361-221-0642, E-mail: mdeleon@tamhsc.edu. *Dean,* Dr. Indra K. Reddy, 361-593-4273, Fax: 361-593-4929, E-mail: ireddy@pharmacy.tamhsc.edu.

Mays Business School Students: 1,159 full-time (458 women), 33 part-time (10 women); includes 205 minority (27 Black or African American, non-Hispanic/Latino; 1 American Indian or Alaska Native, non-Hispanic/Latino; 69 Asian, non-Hispanic/Latino; 93 Hispanic/Latino; 15 Two or more races, non-Hispanic/Latino), 323 international. Average age 27. 2,010 applicants, 35% accepted, 412 enrolled. *Faculty:* 139. Expenses: Contact institution. *Financial support:* In 2016–17, 908 students received support, including 30 fellowships with tuition reimbursements available (averaging $6,770 per year), 133 research assistantships with tuition reimbursements available (averaging $4,903 per year), 106 teaching assistantships with tuition reimbursements available (averaging $4,436 per year); career-related internships or fieldwork, institutionally sponsored loans, scholarships/grants, traineeships, health care benefits, tuition waivers, and unspecified assistantships also available. Support available to part-time students. Financial award application deadline: 3/15; financial award applicants required to submit FAFSA. In 2016, 708 master's awarded. Offers accounting (MS); business (MBA, MFM, MRE, MS); entrepreneurial leadership (MS); finance (MS); financial management (MFM); human resource management (MS); land economics and real estate (MRE); management (MS); management information systems (MS); marketing (MS). *Application deadline:* Applications are processed on a rolling basis. *Application fee:* $50 ($90 for international students). Electronic applications accepted. *Application Contact:* Director, MBA Program, 979-845-4714, Fax: 979-862-2393, E-mail: msprogram@mays.tamu.edu. *Dean,* Dr. Eli Jones, 979-845-4711, Fax: 979-845-6639, E-mail: elijones@tamu.edu.

School of Law Students: 466 full-time (234 women), 17 part-time (6 women); includes 115 minority (29 Black or African American, non-Hispanic/Latino; 2 American Indian or Alaska Native, non-Hispanic/Latino; 12 Asian, non-Hispanic/Latino; 65 Hispanic/Latino; 7 Two or more races, non-Hispanic/Latino), 6 international. Average age 28. 1,893 applicants, 24% accepted, 133 enrolled. *Faculty:* 88. Expenses: Contact institution. *Financial support:* In 2016–17, 359 students received support, including 4 fellowships with tuition reimbursements available (averaging $13,649 per year); career-related internships or fieldwork, institutionally sponsored loans, scholarships/grants, traineeships, health care benefits, and tuition waivers (full and partial) also available. Support available to part-time students. Financial award applicants required to submit FAFSA. Offers law (JM, LL M, M Jur, JD). *Application deadline:* For fall admission, 7/1 for domestic students. Applications are processed on a rolling basis. *Application fee:* $55. *Application Contact:* Law School Admissions, 817-212-4040, E-mail: law-admissions@law.tamu.edu. *Dean,* Dr. Andrew P. Morriss, 817-212-4139, Fax: 817-212-4139, E-mail: amorriss@law.tamu.edu.

School of Public Health Students: 313 full-time (189 women), 71 part-time (41 women); includes 152 minority (42 Black or African American, non-Hispanic/Latino; 64 Hispanic/Latino; 5 Two or more races, non-Hispanic/Latino), 70 international. Average age 29. 179 applicants, 96% accepted, 148 enrolled. *Faculty:* 52. Expenses: Contact institution. *Financial support:* In 2016–17, 225 students received support, including 3 fellowships with tuition reimbursements available (averaging $19,819 per year), 73 research assistantships with tuition reimbursements available (averaging $5,913 per year), 13 teaching assistantships with tuition reimbursements available (averaging $11,317 per year); career-related internships or fieldwork, institutionally sponsored loans, scholarships/grants, traineeships, health care benefits, tuition waivers (full and partial), and unspecified assistantships also available. Support available to part-time students. Financial award applicants required to submit FAFSA. In 2016, 160 master's, 12 doctorates awarded. *Program availability:* Part-time, blended/hybrid learning. Offers health administration (MHA); health policy and management (MPH); health promotion and community health sciences (MPH); health services research (PhD). *Application fee:* $120. Electronic applications accepted. *Application Contact:* Erin E. Schneider, Associate Director of Admissions and Recruitment, 979-436-9380, E-mail: eschneider@sph.tamhsc.edu. *Dean,* Dr. Jay Maddock, 979-436-9322, Fax: 979-458-1878, E-mail: maddock@tamhsc.edu.

TEXAS A&M UNIVERSITY–CENTRAL TEXAS, Killeen, TX 76549

General Information State-supported, coed, upper-level institution. CGS member.

GRADUATE UNITS
Graduate Studies and Research

TEXAS A&M UNIVERSITY–COMMERCE, Commerce, TX 75429-3011

General Information State-supported, coed, university. CGS member. *Enrollment:* 12,385 graduate, professional, and undergraduate students; 1,343 full-time matriculated graduate/professional students (745 women), 3,437 part-time matriculated graduate/professional students (2,205 women). *Enrollment by degree level:* 4,042 master's, 619 doctoral, 119 other advanced degrees. *Graduate faculty:* 241 full-time (101 women), 62 part-time/adjunct (29 women). Tuition, state resident: full-time $3630. Tuition, nonresident: full-time $10,974. *Required fees:* $2146. Tuition and fees vary according to course load, degree level and program. *Graduate housing:* Rooms and/or apartments available on a first-come, first-served basis to single and married students. Typical cost: $8326 (including board) for single students; $8326 (including board) for married students. Room and board charges vary according to board plan and housing facility selected. *Student services:* Campus employment opportunities, campus safety program, career counseling, child daycare facilities, exercise/wellness program, free psychological counseling, international student services, multicultural affairs office, services for students with disabilities, teacher training, writing training. *Library facilities:* Gee Library.

Computer facilities: A campuswide network can be accessed from student residence rooms and from off campus. Online class registration is available.
Website: http://www.tamuc.edu/

General Application Contact: Kimberly Stringer, Graduate Liaison, 903-468-3066, E-mail: kimberly.stringer@tamuc.edu.

GRADUATE UNITS

College of Business Students: 463 full-time (232 women), 1,109 part-time (539 women); includes 653 minority (280 Black or African American, non-Hispanic/Latino; 7 American Indian or Alaska Native, non-Hispanic/Latino; 131 Asian, non-Hispanic/Latino; 202 Hispanic/Latino; 1 Native Hawaiian or other Pacific Islander, non-Hispanic/Latino; 32 Two or more races, non-Hispanic/Latino), 211 international. Average age 33. 1,021 applicants, 59% accepted, 424 enrolled. *Faculty:* 48 full-time (17 women), 8 part-time/adjunct (2 women). Expenses: Contact institution. *Financial support:* In 2016–17, 90 students received support, including 20 research assistantships with partial tuition reimbursements available (averaging $8,000 per year); Federal Work-Study, institutionally sponsored loans, scholarships/grants, health care benefits, and unspecified assistantships also available. Financial award application deadline: 5/1; financial award applicants required to submit FAFSA. In 2016, 617 master's awarded. *Program availability:* Part-time, evening/weekend, 100% online, blended/hybrid learning. Offers accounting (MSA); business administration (MBA); business analytics (MS); finance (MSF); management (MS); marketing (MS). *Application deadline:* For fall admission, 5/15 priority date for international students; for spring admission, 10/1 priority date for international students; for summer admission, 2/1 priority date for international students. Applications are processed on a rolling basis. *Application fee:* $50 ($75 for international students). Electronic applications accepted. *Application Contact:* Shanna Hoskison, Director, Graduate Advising, 903-886-5190, E-mail: shanna.hoskison@tamuc.edu. *Dean of College of Business,* Dr. Shanan G. Gibson, 903-886-5191, Fax: 903-886-5650, E-mail: shanan.gibson@tamuc.edu.

College of Education and Human Services Students: 341 full-time (276 women), 1,495 part-time (1,156 women); includes 762 minority (429 Black or African American, non-Hispanic/Latino; 4 American Indian or Alaska Native, non-Hispanic/Latino; 27 Asian, non-Hispanic/Latino; 247 Hispanic/Latino; 1 Native Hawaiian or other Pacific Islander, non-Hispanic/Latino; 54 Two or more races, non-Hispanic/Latino), 18 international. Average age 37. 1,070 applicants, 54% accepted, 452 enrolled. *Faculty:* 88 full-time (52 women), 31 part-time/adjunct (24 women). Expenses: Contact institution. *Financial support:* In 2016–17, 301 students received support, including 39 research assistantships with partial tuition reimbursements available (averaging $9,000 per year), 17 teaching assistantships with partial tuition reimbursements available (averaging $9,000 per year); career-related internships or fieldwork, Federal Work-Study, institutionally sponsored loans, scholarships/grants, health care benefits, and unspecified assistantships also available. Financial award application deadline: 5/1; financial award applicants required to submit FAFSA. In 2016, 579 master's, 31 doctorates awarded. *Program availability:* Part-time, 100% online, blended/hybrid learning. Offers counseling (MS); curriculum and instruction (M Ed, MS); early childhood education (M Ed, MS); educational administration (M Ed, Ed D); educational psychology (PhD); educational technology leadership (MS); educational technology library science (MS); health, kinesiology and sports studies (MS); higher education (MS, Ed D); organization, learning, and technology (MS); psychology (MS); reading (M Ed, MS); school psychology (SSP); secondary education (M Ed, MS); social work (MSW); special education (M Ed); supervision, curriculum and instruction-elementary education (Ed D). *Application deadline:* For fall admission, 6/1 priority date for international students; for spring admission, 10/15 priority date for international students; for summer admission, 3/15 priority date for international students. Applications are processed on a rolling basis. *Application fee:* $50. Electronic applications accepted. *Application Contact:* Jennifer Faunce, Graduate Recruiter, 903-886-5030, Fax: 903-886-5905, E-mail: jennifer.faunce@tamuc.edu. *Dean,* Dr. Timothy Letzring, 903-886-5181, Fax: 903-886-5905, E-mail: tim.letzring@tamuc.edu.

College of Humanities, Social Sciences and Arts Students: 87 full-time (55 women), 528 part-time (362 women); includes 198 minority (86 Black or African American, non-

Hispanic/Latino; 2 American Indian or Alaska Native, non-Hispanic/Latino; 8 Asian, non-Hispanic/Latino; 84 Hispanic/Latino; 18 Two or more races, non-Hispanic/Latino; 27 international. Average age 37. 333 applicants, 56% accepted, 149 enrolled. *Faculty:* 53 full-time (26 women), 7 part-time/adjunct (2 women). Expenses: Contact institution. *Financial support:* In 2016–17, 255 students received support, including 9 research assistantships with partial tuition reimbursements available (averaging $9,000 per year), 68 teaching assistantships with partial tuition reimbursements available (averaging $9,000 per year); Federal Work-Study, institutionally sponsored loans, scholarships/grants, health care benefits, and unspecified assistantships also available. Financial award application deadline: 5/1; financial award applicants required to submit FAFSA. In 2016, 66 master's, 8 doctorates awarded. *Program availability:* Part-time. Offers applied criminology (MS); applied linguistics (MA, MS); art (MA, MFA); Christianity in history (Graduate Certificate); computational linguistics (Graduate Certificate); creative writing (Graduate Certificate); English (MA, MS, PhD); film studies (Graduate Certificate); history (MA, MS); music (MM); political science (MA, MS); public history (Graduate Certificate); sociology (MS); Spanish (MA); studies in children's and adolescent literature and culture (Graduate Certificate); teaching English to speakers of other languages (Graduate Certificate); theater (MA, MS). *Application deadline:* Applications are processed on a rolling basis. *Application fee:* $50. Electronic applications accepted. *Application Contact:* Shelby Miller, Graduate Recruiter, 903-468-8123, Fax: 903-886-5774, E-mail: shelby.miller@tamuc.edu. *Dean,* Dr. Salvatore Attardo, 903-886-5166, Fax: 903-886-5774, E-mail: salvatore.attardo@tamuc.edu.

College of Science and Engineering Students: 427 full-time (166 women), 276 part-time (130 women); includes 80 minority (26 Black or African American, non-Hispanic/Latino; 1 American Indian or Alaska Native, non-Hispanic/Latino; 14 Asian, non-Hispanic/Latino; 32 Hispanic/Latino; 7 Two or more races, non-Hispanic/Latino), 452 international. Average age 28. 1,103 applicants, 53% accepted, 282 enrolled. *Faculty:* 44 full-time (4 women), 15 part-time/adjunct (0 women). Expenses: Contact institution. *Financial support:* In 2016–17, 211 students received support, including 11 research assistantships with partial tuition reimbursements available (averaging $8,000 per year), 41 teaching assistantships with partial tuition reimbursements available (averaging $8,000 per year); scholarships/grants, health care benefits, and unspecified assistantships also available. Financial award application deadline: 5/1; financial award applicants required to submit FAFSA. In 2016, 303 master's awarded. *Program availability:* Part-time, 100% online, blended/hybrid learning. Offers biological science (MS); chemistry (MS); computational linguistics (Graduate Certificate); computational science (MS); computer science (MS); environmental science (Graduate Certificate); mathematics (MS); physics (MS); technology management (MS). *Application deadline:* For fall admission, 6/1 priority date for international students; for spring admission, 10/15 priority date for international students; for summer admission, 3/15 priority date for international students. Applications are processed on a rolling basis. *Application fee:* $50 ($75 for international students). Electronic applications accepted. *Application Contact:* Shaine L. Marsden, Graduate Recruiter, 903-886-5775, E-mail: shaine.marsden@tamuc.edu. *Dean,* Dr. Brent L. Donham, 903-886-5390, Fax: 903-886-5199, E-mail: brent.donham@tamuc.edu.

School of Agriculture Students: 25 full-time (16 women), 29 part-time (18 women); includes 12 minority (4 Black or African American, non-Hispanic/Latino; 5 Hispanic/Latino; 3 Two or more races, non-Hispanic/Latino), 4 international. Average age 26. 22 applicants, 50% accepted, 9 enrolled. *Faculty:* 5 full-time (0 women), 1 (woman) part-time/adjunct. Expenses: Contact institution. *Financial support:* In 2016–17, 34 students received support, including 6 research assistantships with partial tuition reimbursements available (averaging $8,000 per year), 6 teaching assistantships with partial tuition reimbursements available (averaging $8,000 per year); career-related internships or fieldwork, Federal Work-Study, institutionally sponsored loans, scholarships/grants, health care benefits, and unspecified assistantships also available. Financial award application deadline: 5/1; financial award applicants required to submit FAFSA. In 2016, 16 master's awarded. *Program availability:* Part-time, evening/weekend, 100% online, blended/hybrid learning. Offers agricultural sciences (MS). *Application deadline:* For fall admission, 6/1 priority date for international students; for spring admission, 10/15 priority date for international students; for summer admission, 10/15 priority date for international students. Applications are processed on a rolling basis. *Application fee:* $50. Electronic applications accepted. *Application Contact:* Shaine L. Marsden, Graduate Recruiter, 903-886-5775, E-mail: shaine.marsden@tamuc.edu. *Director,* Dr. Randy Harp, 903-886-5351, Fax: 903-886-5990, E-mail: randy.harp@tamuc.edu.

TEXAS A&M UNIVERSITY–CORPUS CHRISTI, Corpus Christi, TX 78412-5503

General Information State-supported, coed, university. CGS member. *Enrollment:* 12,202 graduate, professional, and undergraduate students; 573 full-time matriculated graduate/professional students (360 women), 1,389 part-time matriculated graduate/professional students (946 women). *Enrollment by degree level:* 1,694 master's, 216 doctoral, 52 other advanced degrees. *Graduate faculty:* 268 full-time (112 women), 124 part-time/adjunct (58 women). *Graduate housing:* Room and/or apartments available on a first-come, first-served basis to single students; on-campus housing not available to married students. Housing application deadline: 5/1. *Student services:* Campus employment opportunities, campus safety program, career counseling, exercise/wellness program, free psychological counseling, grant writing training, international student services, low-cost health insurance, multicultural affairs office, services for students with disabilities, teacher training, writing training. *Library facilities:* Mary and Jeff Bell Library. *Collection:* Books: 342,196 (physical), 163,385 (digital/electronic); Serial titles: 1,691 (physical), 64,357 (digital/electronic); Databases: 276. Weekly public service hours: 106; students can reserve study rooms.

Computer facilities: 1,236 computers available on campus for general student use. A campuswide network can be accessed from student residence rooms and from off campus. Online class registration is available. Website: http://www.tamucc.edu/

General Application Contact: Graduate Admissions Coordinator, 361-825-2177, Fax: 361-825-2755, E-mail: gradweb@tamucc.edu.

GRADUATE UNITS

College of Graduate Studies Students: 573 full-time (360 women), 1,389 part-time (946 women); includes 880 minority (111 Black or African American, non-Hispanic/Latino; 5 American Indian or Alaska Native, non-Hispanic/Latino; 84 Asian, non-Hispanic/Latino; 654 Hispanic/Latino; 1 Native Hawaiian or other Pacific Islander, non-Hispanic/Latino; 25 Two or more races, non-Hispanic/Latino), 229 international. Average age 33. 1,510 applicants, 50% accepted, 606 enrolled. *Faculty:* 268 full-time (112 women), 124 part-time/adjunct (58 women). Expenses: Contact institution. *Financial support:* Research assistantships, teaching assistantships, career-related internships or fieldwork, institutionally sponsored loans, scholarships/grants, health care benefits, and unspecified assistantships available. Support available to part-time students. Financial award application deadline: 3/15; financial award applicants required to submit FAFSA. In 2016, 564 master's, 26 doctorates awarded. *Program availability:* Part-time, evening/weekend, 100% online, blended/hybrid learning. *Application deadline:* For fall admission, 7/15 priority date for domestic students, 5/1 priority date for international students; for spring admission, 11/15 priority date for domestic students, 9/1 priority date for international students. Applications are processed on a rolling basis. *Application fee:* $50 ($70 for international students). Electronic applications accepted. *Application Contact:* Sandra Kureska, Director, Graduate Studies, 361-825-3883, Fax: 361-825-2755, E-mail: gradweb@tamucc.edu. *Dean, College of Graduate Studies,* Dr. JoAnn Canales, 361-825-3847, Fax: 361-825-2755, E-mail: joann.canales@tamucc.edu.

College of Business Students: 132 full-time (71 women), 495 part-time (232 women); includes 261 minority (49 Black or African American, non-Hispanic/Latino; 44 Asian, non-Hispanic/Latino; 160 Hispanic/Latino; 8 Two or more races, non-Hispanic/Latino), 111 international. Average age 32. 444 applicants, 55% accepted, 192 enrolled. *Faculty:* 31 full-time (11 women), 2 part-time/adjunct (0 women). Expenses: Contact institution. *Financial support:* Research assistantships, teaching assistantships, career-related internships or fieldwork, Federal Work-Study, institutionally sponsored loans, scholarships/grants, health care benefits, and unspecified assistantships available. Support available to part-time students. Financial award application deadline: 3/15; financial award applicants required to submit FAFSA. In 2016, 205 master's awarded. *Program availability:* Part-time, evening/weekend, 100% online, blended/hybrid learning. Offers accounting (M Acc); business (MBA); finance (MBA); health care administration (MBA); international business (MBA). *Application deadline:* For fall admission, 7/15 priority date for domestic students, 5/1 priority date for international students; for spring admission, 11/15 priority date for domestic students, 9/1 priority date for international students; for summer admission, 4/15 priority date for domestic students, 2/1 priority date for international students. Applications are processed on a rolling basis. *Application fee:* $50 ($70 for international students). Electronic applications accepted. *Application Contact:* Sharon Polansky, Director, Master's Program, 361-825-3448, Fax: 361-825-2755, E-mail: gradweb@tamucc.edu. *Dean,* Dr. John Gamble, 361-825-6045, Fax: 361-825-2725, E-mail: john.gamble@tamucc.edu.

College of Education Students: 158 full-time (130 women), 344 part-time (281 women); includes 288 minority (28 Black or African American, non-Hispanic/Latino; 2 American Indian or Alaska Native, non-Hispanic/Latino; 8 Asian, non-Hispanic/Latino; 246 Hispanic/Latino; 4 Two or more races, non-Hispanic/Latino), 22 international. Average age 35. 273 applicants, 60% accepted, 142 enrolled. *Faculty:* 50 full-time (29 women), 29 part-time/adjunct (18 women). Expenses: Contact institution. *Financial support:* Research assistantships, teaching assistantships, career-related internships or fieldwork, Federal Work-Study, institutionally sponsored loans, scholarships/grants, health care benefits, and unspecified assistantships available. Support available to part-time students. Financial award application deadline: 3/15; financial award applicants required to submit FAFSA. In 2016, 67 master's, 13 doctorates awarded. *Program availability:* Part-time, evening/weekend, online learning. Offers counseling (MS); counselor education (PhD); curriculum and instruction (MS, PhD); early childhood education (MS); educational administration (MS); educational leadership (Ed D); elementary education (MS); instructional design and educational technology (MS); kinesiology (MS); reading (MS); secondary education (MS); special education (MS). *Application deadline:* For fall admission, 7/15 priority date for domestic students, 5/1 priority date for international students; for spring admission, 11/15 priority date for domestic students, 9/1 priority date for international students. Applications are processed on a rolling basis. *Application fee:* $50 ($70 for international students). Electronic applications accepted. *Application Contact:* Graduate Admissions Coordinator, 361-825-2177, Fax: 361-825-2755, E-mail: gradweb@tamucc.edu. *Dean,* Dr. Arthur Hernandez, 361-825-2660, E-mail: art.hernandez@tamucc.edu.

College of Liberal Arts Students: 81 full-time (49 women), 102 part-time (71 women); includes 90 minority (8 Black or African American, non-Hispanic/Latino; 2 Asian, non-Hispanic/Latino; 76 Hispanic/Latino; 4 Two or more races, non-Hispanic/Latino), 13 international. Average age 32. 134 applicants, 56% accepted, 57 enrolled. *Faculty:* 76 full-time (39 women), 9 part-time/adjunct (4 women). Expenses: Contact institution. *Financial support:* Research assistantships, teaching assistantships, career-related internships or fieldwork, Federal Work-Study, institutionally sponsored loans, scholarships/grants, health care benefits, and unspecified assistantships available. Support available to part-time students. Financial award application deadline: 3/15; financial award applicants required to submit FAFSA. In 2016, 48 master's awarded. *Program availability:* Part-time, evening/weekend. Offers clinical psychology (MA); communication (MA); English (MA); general psychology (MA); history (MA); psychology (MA); public administration (MPA); studio art (MFA). *Application deadline:* For fall admission, 7/15 priority date for domestic students, 5/1 priority date for international students; for spring admission, 11/15 priority date for domestic students, 9/1 priority date for international students. Applications are processed on a rolling basis. *Application fee:* $50 ($70 for international students). Electronic applications accepted. *Application Contact:* Graduate Admissions Coordinator, 361-825-2177, Fax: 361-825-2755, E-mail: gradweb@tamucc.edu. *Interim Dean,* Dr. Mark Hartlaub, 361-825-2659, Fax: 361-825-5844, E-mail: mark.hartlaub@tamucc.edu.

College of Nursing and Health Sciences Students: 6 full-time (all women), 379 part-time (322 women); includes 196 minority (22 Black or African American, non-Hispanic/Latino; 1 American Indian or Alaska Native, non-Hispanic/Latino; 23 Asian, non-Hispanic/Latino; 143 Hispanic/Latino; 1 Native Hawaiian or other Pacific Islander, non-Hispanic/Latino; 6 Two or more races, non-Hispanic/Latino), 1 international. Average age 37. 336 applicants, 41% accepted, 128 enrolled. *Faculty:* 17 full-time (16 women), 21 part-time/adjunct (15 women). Expenses: Contact institution. *Financial support:* Research assistantships, teaching assistantships, career-related internships or fieldwork, Federal Work-Study, institutionally sponsored loans, scholarships/grants, health care benefits, and unspecified assistantships available. Support available to part-time students. Financial award application deadline: 3/15; financial award applicants required to submit FAFSA. In 2016, 107 master's awarded. *Program availability:* Part-time, evening/weekend, online only, 100% online. Offers family nurse practitioner (MSN); leadership in nursing systems (MSN); nurse educator (MSN). *Application deadline:* For fall admission, 4/15 priority date for domestic and international students; for spring admission, 1/7 for domestic and international students; for summer admission, 5/27 for domestic and international students. Applications are processed on a rolling basis. *Application fee:* $50 ($70 for international students). Electronic applications accepted. *Application Contact:* Graduate Admissions Coordinator, 361-825-2177, Fax: 361-825-2755, E-mail: gradweb@tamucc.edu. *Dean,* Dr. Mary Jane Hamilton, 361-825-2469, E-mail: mary.hamilton@tamucc.edu.

College of Science and Engineering Students: 196 full-time (104 women), 69 part-time (40 women); includes 45 minority (4 Black or African American, non-Hispanic/Latino; 2 American Indian or Alaska Native, non-Hispanic/Latino; 7 Asian, non-Hispanic/Latino; 29 Hispanic/Latino; 3 Two or more races, non-Hispanic/Latino), 82 international. Average age 29. 323 applicants, 39% accepted, 87 enrolled. *Faculty:* 94 full-time (17 women), 63 part-time/adjunct (21 women). Expenses: Contact institution. *Financial support:* Research assistantships, teaching assistantships, career-related internships or fieldwork, Federal Work-Study, institutionally sponsored loans, scholarships/grants, health care benefits, and unspecified assistantships available. Support available to part-time students. Financial award application deadline: 3/15; financial award applicants required to submit FAFSA. In 2016, 87 master's, 1 doctorate awarded. *Program availability:* Part-time, evening/weekend. Offers biology (MS); coastal and marine system science (MS, PhD); computer science (MS); environmental science (MS); fisheries and mariculture (MS); geospatial computing science (PhD); geospatial surveying engineering (MS); marine biology (PhD); mathematics (MS). *Application deadline:* For fall admission, 7/15 priority date for domestic students, 5/1 priority date for international students; for spring admission, 11/15 priority date for domestic students, 9/1 priority date for international students. Applications are processed on a rolling basis. *Application fee:* $50 ($70 for international students). Electronic applications accepted. *Application Contact:* Graduate Admissions Coordinator, 361-825-2177, Fax: 361-825-2755, E-mail: gradweb@tamucc.edu. *Dean,* Dr. Frank Pezold, 361-825-2349, E-mail: frank.pezold@tamucc.edu.

TEXAS A&M UNIVERSITY–KINGSVILLE, Kingsville, TX 78363

General Information State-supported, coed, university. *Graduate housing:* Room and/or apartments available on a first-come, first-served basis to single students; on-campus housing not available to married students. Housing application deadline: 8/1. *Research affiliation:* American Chemical Society (chemistry: the use of terminally-functionalized atactic-polypropylene oligomers as supports for catalysis), Texas Citrus Producers Board (agriculture: citrus center grapefruit research), ExxonMobil, East Wildlife Foundation (agriculture: bird populations, deer research), The Brown Foundation (agriculture: invasive grass research), Wildlife Pharmaceuticals, Inc. (agriculture: deer).

GRADUATE UNITS

College of Graduate Studies *Program availability:* Part-time, online learning. Electronic applications accepted.

College of Arts and Sciences Offers arts and sciences (MA, MM, MS); biology (MS); chemistry (MS); communication sciences and disorders (MS); criminology (MS); cultural studies (MA); elementary music (MM); English (MA, MS); Hispanic culture (PhD); instrumental (MM); instrumental performance (MM); mathematics (MS); music (MM); music education (MM); psychology (MA, MS); sociology (MA, MS); Spanish (MA); statistical analytics, computing and modeling (MS); vocal (MM); vocal performance (MM). Electronic applications accepted.

College of Business Administration *Program availability:* Online only, 100% online, blended/hybrid learning. Offers business administration (MBA). Electronic applications accepted.

College of Education and Human Performance *Program availability:* 100% online, blended/hybrid learning. Offers adult education (M Ed); bilingual education (M Ed, Ed D); counseling and guidance (MA, MS); early childhood education (M Ed); education and human performance (M Ed, MA, MS, Ed D, Certificate); educational administration (MA, MS); educational leadership (PhD); health and kinesiology (MA, MS); instructional technology (MS); reading specialization (MS); secondary education (MS); special education (M Ed). Electronic applications accepted.

Dick and Mary Lewis Kleberg College of Agriculture, Natural Resources and Human Sciences Offers agribusiness (MS); agricultural science (MS); agriculture, natural resources and human sciences (MS, PhD); animal science (MS); horticulture (PhD); human sciences (MS); plant and soil science (MS); ranch management (MS); range and wildlife management (MS); wildlife science (PhD). Electronic applications accepted.

Frank H. Dotterweich College of Engineering Offers chemical engineering (ME, MS); civil engineering (ME, MS); computer science (MS); electrical engineering (ME, MS); engineering (ME, MS, PhD); environmental engineering (ME, MS, PhD); industrial engineering (ME, MS); industrial management (MS); mechanical engineering (ME, MS); natural gas engineering (ME, MS); sustainable energy systems engineering (PhD). Electronic applications accepted.

TEXAS A&M UNIVERSITY–SAN ANTONIO, San Antonio, TX 78224

General Information State-supported, coed, comprehensive institution.

GRADUATE UNITS

Department of Curriculum and Kinesiology *Program availability:* Part-time, evening/weekend. Offers bilingual education (MA); early childhood education (M Ed); kinesiology (MS); reading (MS); special education (M Ed). Electronic applications accepted.

Department of Leadership and Counseling *Program availability:* Part-time, evening/weekend. Offers counseling and guidance (MA); educational leadership (MA). Electronic applications accepted.

School of Arts and Sciences *Program availability:* Part-time, evening/weekend. Offers English (MA). Electronic applications accepted.

School of Business *Program availability:* Part-time, evening/weekend. Offers business administration (MBA); enterprise resource planning systems (MBA); finance (MBA); healthcare management (MBA); human resources management (MBA); information assurance and security (MBA); international business (MBA); professional accounting (MPA); project management (MBA); supply chain management (MBA). Electronic applications accepted.

TEXAS A&M UNIVERSITY–TEXARKANA, Texarkana, TX 75505-5518

General Information State-supported, coed, upper-level institution. *Graduate housing:* On-campus housing not available.

GRADUATE UNITS

Graduate Studies and Research *Program availability:* Part-time, evening/weekend. Electronic applications accepted.

College of Business *Program availability:* Part-time, evening/weekend. Offers accounting (MSA); business administration (MBA, MS). Electronic applications accepted.

College of Education and Liberal Arts *Program availability:* Part-time, evening/weekend. Offers adult education (MS); curriculum and instruction (M Ed); education (MS); educational administration (M Ed); English (MA); instructional

technology (MS); interdisciplinary studies (MA, MS); special education (MS). Electronic applications accepted.

College of Health and Behavioral Sciences *Program availability:* Part-time, evening/weekend. Offers counseling psychology (MS). Electronic applications accepted.

TEXAS CHIROPRACTIC COLLEGE, Pasadena, TX 77505-1699

General Information Independent, coed, graduate-only institution. *Graduate housing:* On-campus housing not available.

GRADUATE UNITS

Professional Program Offers chiropractic (DC).

TEXAS CHRISTIAN UNIVERSITY, Fort Worth, TX 76129-0002

General Information Independent-religious, coed, university. CGS member. *Enrollment:* 10,394 graduate, professional, and undergraduate students; 1,360 full-time matriculated graduate/professional students (758 women), 126 part-time matriculated graduate/professional students (71 women). *Enrollment by degree level:* 957 master's, 508 doctoral, 21 other advanced degrees. *Graduate faculty:* 373 full-time (154 women), 76 part-time/adjunct (29 women). *Tuition:* Full-time $26,640; part-time $1480 per credit hour. *Required fees:* $48. Tuition and fees vary according to program. *Graduate housing:* Rooms and/or apartments available on a first-come, first-served basis to single and married students. Typical cost: $9200 per year for single students; $10,000 per year for married students. Room charges vary according to housing facility selected. Housing application deadline: 5/1. *Student services:* Campus employment opportunities, campus safety program, career counseling, exercise/wellness program, free psychological counseling, international student services, low-cost health insurance, multicultural affairs office, services for students with disabilities, teacher training, writing training. *Library facilities:* Mary Couts Burnett Library. *Collection:* Books: 1.4 million (physical), 903,006 (digital/electronic); Serial titles: 10,139 (physical), 120,085 (digital/electronic); Databases: 475. Study areas open 24 hours, 5–7 days a week; students can reserve study rooms. *Research affiliation:* Lockheed Martin Corporation (business), Botanical Research Institute of Texas, Inc. (biology, environmental science, ranch management), The University of Texas Southwestern Medical School (health sciences), NextEra (environmental science, wind energy), University of North Texas Health Science Center at Fort Worth (physics, biology), Bell Helicopter (engineering).

Computer facilities: 1,400 computers available on campus for general student use. A campuswide network can be accessed from student residence rooms and from off campus. Online class registration is available. Website: http://www.tcu.edu/

General Application Contact: Anita Unger, Admissions, TCU Graduate Studies Office, 817-257-7515, Fax: 817-257-7484, E-mail: frogmail@tcu.edu.

GRADUATE UNITS

AddRan College of Liberal Arts Students: 136 full-time (82 women); includes 31 minority (8 Black or African American, non-Hispanic/Latino; 18 Hispanic/Latino; 1 Native Hawaiian or other Pacific Islander, non-Hispanic/Latino; 4 Two or more races, non-Hispanic/Latino), 2 international. Average age 32. 74 applicants, 51% accepted, 33 enrolled. *Faculty:* 59 full-time (24 women), 1 (woman) part-time/adjunct. Expenses: Contact institution. *Financial support:* In 2016–17, 114 students received support. Fellowships, research assistantships, teaching assistantships, Federal Work-Study, scholarships/grants, tuition waivers, and unspecified assistantships available. In 2016, 23 master's, 10 doctorates awarded. Offers criminal justice and criminology (MS); English (MA, PhD); Latin America (MA, PhD); liberal arts (MA, MS, PhD); rhetoric and composition (PhD); United States (MA, PhD). *Application deadline:* Applications are processed on a rolling basis. *Application fee:* $60. Electronic applications accepted. *Application Contact:* Admissions, TCU Graduate Studies Office, 817-257-7515, Fax: 817-257-7484, E-mail: frogmail@tcu.edu. *Associate Dean,* Dr. Don M. Coerver, 817-257-6290, Fax: 817-257-7709, E-mail: d.coerver@tcu.edu.

Bob Schieffer College of Communication Students: 28 full-time (23 women), 1 part-time (0 women); includes 6 minority (1 Black or African American, non-Hispanic/Latino; 2 Asian, non-Hispanic/Latino; 1 Hispanic/Latino; 2 Two or more races, non-Hispanic/Latino), 1 international. Average age 26. 35 applicants, 46% accepted, 9 enrolled. *Faculty:* 26 full-time (12 women). Expenses: Contact institution. *Financial support:* In 2016–17, 25 students received support, including 18 teaching assistantships with full tuition reimbursements available (averaging $10,000 per year); research assistantships, health care benefits, tuition waivers (full and partial), and unspecified assistantships also available. Financial award application deadline: 2/15. In 2016, 11 master's awarded. *Program availability:* Part-time. Offers communication studies (MS); strategic communication (MS). *Application deadline:* For fall admission, 2/15 for domestic and international students; for spring admission, 10/15 for domestic and international students. *Application fee:* $60. Electronic applications accepted. *Application Contact:* Alicia E. Craff, Academic Program Specialist, 817-257-5917, Fax: 817-257-5921, E-mail: a.e.craff@tcu.edu. *Associate Dean,* Dr. Daxton Stewart, 817-257-5911, Fax: 817-257-5921, E-mail: d.stewart@tcu.edu.

College of Education Students: 189 full-time (151 women), 31 part-time (18 women); includes 72 minority (18 Black or African American, non-Hispanic/Latino; 7 Asian, non-Hispanic/Latino; 42 Hispanic/Latino; 1 Native Hawaiian or other Pacific Islander, non-Hispanic/Latino; 4 Two or more races, non-Hispanic/Latino), 8 international. Average age 32. 141 applicants, 72% accepted, 79 enrolled. *Faculty:* 29 full-time (21 women), 8 part-time/adjunct (5 women). Expenses: Contact institution. *Financial support:* In 2016–17, 164 students received support, including 14 research assistantships with full tuition reimbursements available (averaging $18,166 per year), 38 teaching assistantships with full tuition reimbursements available (averaging $15,875 per year); career-related internships or fieldwork, scholarships/grants, health care benefits, and unspecified assistantships also available. Support to part-time students. Financial award application deadline: 2/1; financial award applicants required to submit FAFSA. In 2016, 54 master's, 5 doctorates awarded. *Program availability:* Part-time, evening/weekend. Offers counseling (M Ed); counseling and counselor education (PhD); curriculum and instruction (M Ed); curriculum studies (PhD); education (M Ed, Ed D, PhD, Certificate); educational leadership (M Ed, Ed D); higher educational leadership (Ed D); science education (PhD); special education (M Ed). *Application deadline:* For fall admission, 2/1 for domestic and international students; for spring admission, 11/16 for domestic and international students; for summer admission, 2/1 for domestic and international students. *Application fee:* $60. Electronic applications accepted. *Application Contact:* Lori Kimball, Administrative Program Specialist, 817-257-7661, Fax: 817-257-7466, E-mail: l.kimball@tcu.edu. *Associate Dean,* Dr. Jan Lacina, 817-257-6786, Fax: 817-257-7466, E-mail: j.lacina@tcu.edu.

College of Fine Arts Students: 68 full-time (37 women), 6 part-time (3 women); includes 8 minority (2 Asian, non-Hispanic/Latino; 4 Hispanic/Latino; 2 Two or more races, non-Hispanic/Latino), 17 international. Average age 27. 111 applicants, 41%

accepted, 33 enrolled. *Faculty:* 51 full-time (11 women), 15 part-time/adjunct (6 women). Expenses: Contact institution. *Financial support:* In 2016–17, 66 students received support, including 88 teaching assistantships with full tuition reimbursements available (averaging $34,120 per year); career-related internships or fieldwork, scholarships/grants, health care benefits, tuition waivers (full and partial), and unspecified assistantships also available. Financial award application deadline: 4/15. In 2016, 29 master's, 2 doctorates awarded. Offers fine arts (M Mus, MA, MFA, MM Ed, DMA, Artist Diploma). *Application deadline:* For fall admission, 2/1 for domestic and international students; for spring admission, 10/1 for domestic and international students. Applications are processed on a rolling basis. *Application fee:* $60. Electronic applications accepted. *Application Contact:* Donna Smolik, TCU College of Fine Arts Graduate Office, 817-257-7603, Fax: 817-257-5672, E-mail: cfagradinfo@tcu.edu. *Associate Dean, College of Fine Arts,* Dr. H. Joseph Butler, 817-257-7603, Fax: 817-257-5672, E-mail: cfagradinfo@tcu.edu.

School of Art Students: 17 full-time (16 women), 1 (woman) part-time; includes 2 minority (both Hispanic/Latino), 2 international. Average age 30. 24 applicants, 46% accepted, 9 enrolled. *Faculty:* 12 full-time (5 women), 3 part-time/adjunct (2 women). Expenses: Contact institution. *Financial support:* In 2016–17, 18 students received support, including 17 teaching assistantships (averaging $10,000 per year); institutionally sponsored loans, scholarships/grants, health care benefits, tuition waivers (full and partial), and unspecified assistantships also available. Financial award application deadline: 4/15. In 2016, 7 master's awarded. Offers art history (MA); studio art (MFA). *Application deadline:* For fall admission, 2/1 for domestic and international students. *Application fee:* $60. Electronic applications accepted. *Application Contact:* Donna Smolik, TCU College of Fine Arts Graduate Office, 817-257-7603, Fax: 817-257-5672, E-mail: cfagradinfo@tcu.edu. *Director,* Dr. Sally Packard, 817-257-7643, E-mail: s.packard@tcu.edu.

School of Music Students: 51 full-time (21 women), 6 part-time (3 women); includes 6 minority (2 Asian, non-Hispanic/Latino; 2 Hispanic/Latino; 2 Two or more races, non-Hispanic/Latino), 15 international. Average age 27. 87 applicants, 40% accepted, 24 enrolled. *Faculty:* 38 full-time (6 women), 12 part-time/adjunct (4 women). Expenses: Contact institution. *Financial support:* In 2016–17, 54 students received support, including 54 research assistantships with full tuition reimbursements available (averaging $9,000 per year); career-related internships or fieldwork, institutionally sponsored loans, scholarships/grants, tuition waivers (full and partial), and unspecified assistantships also available. Financial award application deadline: 12/1; financial award applicants required to submit CSS PROFILE or FAFSA. In 2016, 22 master's, 2 doctorates awarded. Offers composition (DMA); conducting (M Mus, DMA); music (M Mus, MM Ed, DMA); music education (MM Ed); music theory (M Mus); musicology (M Mus); percussion (Artist Diploma); performance (M Mus, DMA); piano pedagogy (M Mus, DMA); voice pedagogy (M Mus); winds (Artist Diploma). *Application deadline:* For fall admission, 12/1 for domestic and international students; for spring admission, 9/1 for domestic and international students. *Application fee:* $60. Electronic applications accepted. *Application Contact:* Dr. Joseph Butler, Associate Dean, College of Fine Arts, 817-257-6629, E-mail: j.butler@tcu.edu. *Director,* Dr. Richard C. Gipson, 817-257-7602.

College of Science and Engineering Students: 131 full-time (63 women), 6 part-time (1 woman); includes 23 minority (2 Black or African American, non-Hispanic/Latino; 1 American Indian or Alaska Native, non-Hispanic/Latino; 3 Asian, non-Hispanic/Latino; 11 Hispanic/Latino; 6 Two or more races, non-Hispanic/Latino), 23 international. Average age 27. 180 applicants, 54% accepted, 47 enrolled. *Faculty:* 86 full-time (25 women), 4 part-time/adjunct (2 women). Expenses: Contact institution. *Financial support:* Tuition waivers and unspecified assistantships available. Financial award application deadline: 2/1. In 2016, 34 master's, 10 doctorates awarded. *Program availability:* Part-time. Offers applied mathematics (MS); biology (MA, MS); chemistry and biochemistry (MA, MS, PhD); developmental trauma (MS); experimental psychology (PhD); mathematics (MAT, PhD); physics (MA, MS, PhD); pure mathematics (MS); science and engineering (MA, MAT, MEM, MS, PhD). *Application deadline:* For fall admission, 2/1 for domestic and international students; for spring admission, 9/1 for domestic and international students. *Application fee:* $60. Electronic applications accepted. *Associate Dean for Administration and Graduate Programs,* Dr. Magnus Rittby, 817-257-7729, Fax: 817-257-7736, E-mail: m.rittby@tcu.edu.

School of Geology, Energy and the Environment Students: 37 full-time (12 women), 2 part-time (1 woman); includes 5 minority (1 Black or African American, non-Hispanic/Latino; 1 American Indian or Alaska Native, non-Hispanic/Latino; 2 Hispanic/Latino; 1 Two or more races, non-Hispanic/Latino), 2 international. Average age 26. 61 applicants, 54% accepted, 17 enrolled. *Faculty:* 13 full-time (4 women), 1 part-time/adjunct (0 women). Expenses: Contact institution. *Financial support:* In 2016–17, 15 teaching assistantships with full tuition reimbursements (averaging $16,000 per year) were awarded; unspecified assistantships also available. Financial award application deadline: 2/1. In 2016, 18 master's awarded. *Program availability:* Part-time. Offers environmental science (MA, MEM, MS); geology (MS). *Application deadline:* For fall admission, 2/1 for domestic and international students; for spring admission, 9/1 for domestic and international students. *Application fee:* $60. Electronic applications accepted. *Graduate Advisor,* Dr. Helge Alsleben, 817-257-7270, Fax: 817-257-7789, E-mail: h.alsleben@tcu.edu.

Harris College of Nursing and Health Sciences Students: 385 full-time (263 women), 27 part-time (25 women); includes 95 minority (15 Black or African American, non-Hispanic/Latino; 3 American Indian or Alaska Native, non-Hispanic/Latino; 22 Asian, non-Hispanic/Latino; 43 Hispanic/Latino; 2 Native Hawaiian or other Pacific Islander, non-Hispanic/Latino; 10 Two or more races, non-Hispanic/Latino), 7 international. Average age 33. 602 applicants, 39% accepted, 173 enrolled. *Faculty:* 54 full-time (40 women), 13 part-time/adjunct (7 women). Expenses: Contact institution. *Financial support:* Applicants required to submit FAFSA. In 2016, 53 master's, 69 doctorates awarded. *Program availability:* Online learning. Offers advanced generalist (MSW); advanced practice registered nurse (DNP); clinical nurse leader (MSN, Certificate); clinical nurse specialist (MSN); clinical nurse specialist - adult/gerontology nursing (DNP); clinical nurse specialist - pediatrics (DNP); family nurse practitioner (DNP); kinesiology (MS); nursing administration (DNP); nursing and health sciences (MS, MSN, MSW, DNP, DNP-A, Certificate); nursing education (MSN). *Application fee:* $60. Electronic applications accepted. *Dean,* Dr. Susan Weeks, 817-257-6749, E-mail: s.weeks@tcu.edu.

Davies School of Communication Sciences and Disorders Students: 40 full-time (37 women); includes 10 minority (1 Asian, non-Hispanic/Latino; 9 Hispanic/Latino; 1 Two or more races, non-Hispanic/Latino), 2 international. Average age 24. 256 applicants, 19% accepted, 20 enrolled. *Faculty:* 8 full-time (7 women). Expenses: Contact institution. *Financial support:* In 2016–17, 40 students received support, including 40 research assistantships (averaging $35,000 per year); tuition waivers (partial) and unspecified assistantships also available. Financial award application deadline: 1/15; financial award applicants required to submit FAFSA. In 2016, 19 master's awarded.

Offers speech-language pathology (MS). *Application deadline:* For fall admission, 1/15 for domestic and international students. *Application fee:* $60. Electronic applications accepted. *Application Contact:* Janet Schwartz, Administrative Assistant, 817-257-7620, E-mail: janet.schwartz@tcu.edu. *Director,* Dr. Christopher Watts, 817-257-7620, E-mail: c.watts@tcu.edu.

School of Nurse Anesthesia Students: 185 full-time (95 women); includes 31 minority (1 Black or African American, non-Hispanic/Latino; 2 American Indian or Alaska Native, non-Hispanic/Latino; 9 Asian, non-Hispanic/Latino; 14 Hispanic/Latino; 1 Native Hawaiian or other Pacific Islander, non-Hispanic/Latino; 4 Two or more races, non-Hispanic/Latino). Average age 31. 194 applicants, 37% accepted, 66 enrolled. *Faculty:* 11 full-time (5 women), 3 part-time/adjunct (1 woman). Expenses: Contact institution. *Financial support:* In 2016–17, 3 students received support. Scholarships/grants available. Financial award application deadline: 7/1; financial award applicants required to submit FAFSA. In 2016, 51 doctorates awarded. Offers nurse anesthesia (DNP-A). *Application deadline:* For fall and spring admission, 7/1 for domestic and international students. Applications are processed on a rolling basis. *Application fee:* $60. Electronic applications accepted. *Application Contact:* Stephanie Morton Dwight, Administrative Assistant, 817-257-7887, Fax: 817-257-5472, E-mail: s.m.dwight@tcu.edu. *Director,* Dr. Kay K. Sanders, 817-257-7887, Fax: 817-257-5472, E-mail: k.sanders@tcu.edu.

Master of Liberal Arts Program Students: 77 full-time (40 women), 31 part-time (17 women); includes 27 minority (13 Black or African American, non-Hispanic/Latino; 1 Asian, non-Hispanic/Latino; 11 Hispanic/Latino; 1 Native Hawaiian or other Pacific Islander, non-Hispanic/Latino; 1 Two or more races, non-Hispanic/Latino), 4 international. Average age 32. 61 applicants, 98% accepted, 43 enrolled. *Faculty:* 12 part-time/adjunct (1 woman). Expenses: Contact institution. *Financial support:* In 2016–17, 50 students received support. Scholarships/grants, unspecified assistantships, and employee tuition benefits available. Financial award applicants required to submit FAFSA. In 2016, 35 master's awarded. *Program availability:* Part-time, evening/weekend, 100% online. Offers liberal arts (MLA). *Application deadline:* For fall admission, 8/15 for domestic students, 6/1 for international students; for spring admission, 1/15 for domestic students, 11/1 for international students. Applications are processed on a rolling basis. *Application fee:* $60. Electronic applications accepted. *Application Contact:* Anita Unger, Graduate Program Coordinator, 817-257-7515, Fax: 817-257-7484, E-mail: a.unger@tcu.edu. *Associate Provost/Dean of University Programs,* Dr. Bonnie Melhart, 817-257-7104, Fax: 817-257-7484, E-mail: b.melhart@tcu.edu.

Neeley School of Business Students: 344 full-time (97 women), 24 part-time (7 women); includes 54 minority (11 Black or African American, non-Hispanic/Latino; 5 American Indian or Alaska Native, non-Hispanic/Latino; 12 Asian, non-Hispanic/Latino; 26 Hispanic/Latino), 37 international. Average age 30. 430 applicants, 70% accepted, 204 enrolled. *Faculty:* 60 full-time (17 women), 17 part-time/adjunct (4 women). Expenses: Contact institution. *Financial support:* Career-related internships or fieldwork, scholarships/grants, and unspecified assistantships available. Financial award application deadline: 4/1; financial award applicants required to submit FAFSA. In 2016, 220 master's awarded. *Program availability:* Part-time, evening/weekend. Offers accounting (MBA); audit (M Ac); business (M Ac, MBA); business administration (MBA); finance (MBA); marketing (MBA); supply and value chain management (MBA); taxation (M Ac); valuation and reporting (M Ac). *Application deadline:* For fall admission, 3/1 for domestic and international students; for winter admission, 1/15 for domestic and international students; for spring admission, 11/1 for domestic and international students; for summer admission, 1/15 for domestic and international students. Applications are processed on a rolling basis. *Application fee:* $100. Electronic applications accepted. *Application Contact:* Graduate Programs Admissions Office, 817-257-7531, E-mail: mbainfo@tcu.edu. *Dean,* Dr. Homer Erekson, 817-257-7511, E-mail: neeleynews@tcu.edu.

TEXAS HEALTH AND SCIENCE UNIVERSITY, Austin, TX 78704

General Information Private, coed, graduate-only institution. *Graduate housing:* On-campus housing not available.

GRADUATE UNITS

Graduate Programs Offers acupuncture and Oriental medicine (MS, DAOM); business administration (MBA); healthcare management (MBA). Electronic applications accepted.

TEXAS LUTHERAN UNIVERSITY, Seguin, TX 78155-5999

General Information Independent-religious, coed, comprehensive institution.

GRADUATE UNITS

Program in Accounting Offers accounting (M Acy).

TEXAS SOUTHERN UNIVERSITY, Houston, TX 77004-4584

General Information State-supported, coed, university. CGS member. *Graduate housing:* Room and/or apartments available on a first-come, first-served basis to single students; on-campus housing not available to married students. Housing application deadline: 7/15. *Research affiliation:* Environmental Research and Technology Transfer Center (chemistry and environmental toxicology), Institute for International and Immigration Law/Center on Legal Pedagogy (law), Innovative Transportation Research Institute (transportation planning and management), NASA University Research Biotechnology & Environmental Health (biology), Economic Development Center/JP Chase Center for Financial Education (business), Gerald B. Smith Center for Entrepreneurship and Executive Development (business, urban planning and environmental policy).

GRADUATE UNITS

College of Education *Program availability:* Part-time, evening/weekend. Offers bilingual education (M Ed); counseling (M Ed); counselor education (Ed D); curriculum and instruction (Ed D); education (M Ed, MS, Ed D); educational administration (M Ed, Ed D); health education (MS); human performance (MS); secondary education (M Ed). Electronic applications accepted.

College of Liberal Arts and Behavioral Sciences *Program availability:* Part-time, evening/weekend. Offers English (MA); fine arts (MA); history (MA); human services and consumer sciences (MS); liberal arts and behavioral sciences (MA, MS); music (MA); psychology (MA); sociology (MA). Electronic applications accepted.

College of Pharmacy and Health Sciences *Program availability:* Online learning. Offers health care administration (MS); pharmaceutical sciences (MS, PhD); pharmacy and health sciences (MS, PhD, Pharm D); pharmacy practice (Pharm D). Electronic applications accepted.

Jesse H. Jones School of Business *Program availability:* Part-time, evening/weekend. Offers business (MBA, MS); business administration (MBA); management information systems (MS). Electronic applications accepted.

School of Public Affairs *Program availability:* Part-time. Offers administration of justice (MS, PhD); public administration (MPA); public affairs (MPA, MS, PhD); urban planning and environmental policy (MS, PhD). Electronic applications accepted.

School of Science and Technology *Program availability:* Part-time, evening/weekend. Offers biology (MS); chemistry (MS); computer science (MS); environmental toxicology (MS, PhD); industrial technology (MS); mathematics (MS); science and technology (MS, PhD); transportation, planning and management (MS). Electronic applications accepted.

Tavis Smiley School of Communication *Program availability:* Part-time. Offers communication (MA). Electronic applications accepted.

Thurgood Marshall School of Law Offers law (JD). Electronic applications accepted.

TEXAS STATE UNIVERSITY, San Marcos, TX 78666

General Information State-supported, coed, university. CGS member. *Enrollment:* 38,808 graduate, professional, and undergraduate students; 2,381 full-time matriculated graduate/professional students (1,542 women), 1,620 part-time matriculated graduate/professional students (1,056 women). *Enrollment by degree level:* 3,515 master's, 363 doctoral, 123 other advanced degrees. *Graduate faculty:* 721 full-time (349 women), 140 part-time/adjunct (76 women). Tuition, state resident: full-time $7670; part-time $320 per credit hour. Tuition, nonresident: full-time $17,630; part-time $735 per credit hour. *Required fees:* $2032; $693 per semester. Full-time tuition and fees vary according to course load. *Graduate housing:* Room and/or apartments available on a first-come, first-served basis to single students; on-campus housing not available to married students. Typical cost: $5390 per year ($8100 including board). Room and board charges vary according to board plan and housing facility selected. Housing application deadline: 7/1. *Student services:* Campus employment opportunities, campus safety program, career counseling, exercise/wellness program, free psychological counseling, international student services, low-cost health insurance, multicultural affairs office, services for students with disabilities, teacher training, writing training. *Library facilities:* Alkek Library plus 1 other. *Collection:* Books: 1.5 million (physical), 664,569 (digital/electronic); Serial titles: 32,501 (physical), 129,479 (digital/electronic); Databases: 503. Students can reserve study rooms. *Research affiliation:* MicroPower Global Corporation (chip prototype development), Quantum Materials Corporation (material physics), Magellan Pipeline and Bridge (environmental conservation), National Fish and Wildlife Foundation (environmental conservation), The Ewing Halsell Foundation (education: improving STEM learning), NEC Coorporation of America (high-speed data analysis).

Computer facilities: Computer purchase and lease plans are available. 3,233 computers available on campus for general student use. A campuswide network can be accessed from student residence rooms and from off campus. Online class registration is available.
Website: http://www.txstate.edu/

General Application Contact: Dr. Andrea Golato, Dean of Graduate School, 512-245-2581, Fax: 512-245-8365, E-mail: gradcollege@txstate.edu.

GRADUATE UNITS

The Graduate College Students: 2,381 full-time (1,542 women), 1,620 part-time (1,056 women); includes 1,476 minority (303 Black or African American, non-Hispanic/Latino; 12 American Indian or Alaska Native, non-Hispanic/Latino; 103 Asian, non-Hispanic/Latino; 958 Hispanic/Latino; 1 Native Hawaiian or other Pacific Islander, non-Hispanic/Latino; 99 Two or more races, non-Hispanic/Latino), 338 international. Average age 31. 4,009 applicants, 51% accepted, 1169 enrolled. *Faculty:* 721 full-time (349 women), 140 part-time/adjunct (76 women). Expenses: Contact institution. *Financial support:* In 2016–17, 2,313 students received support, including 216 research assistantships (averaging $17,220 per year), 711 teaching assistantships (averaging $15,910 per year); fellowships, career-related internships or fieldwork, Federal Work-Study, institutionally sponsored loans, scholarships/grants, unspecified assistantships, and laboratory instructorships, stipends also available. Support available to part-time students. Financial award application deadline: 4/1; financial award applicants required to submit FAFSA. In 2016, 1,356 master's, 44 doctorates, 37 other advanced degrees awarded. *Program availability:* Part-time, evening/weekend, blended/hybrid learning. *Application deadline:* For fall admission, 6/15 for domestic students, 6/1 for international students; for spring admission, 10/15 for domestic students, 10/1 for international students. Applications are processed on a rolling basis. *Application fee:* $40 ($90 for international students). Electronic applications accepted. *Dean,* Dr. Andrea Golato, 512-245-2581, Fax: 512-245-8365, E-mail: gradcollege@txstate.edu.

College of Applied Arts Students: 295 full-time (235 women), 274 part-time (217 women); includes 272 minority (75 Black or African American, non-Hispanic/Latino; 3 American Indian or Alaska Native, non-Hispanic/Latino; 8 Asian, non-Hispanic/Latino; 168 Hispanic/Latino; 18 Two or more races, non-Hispanic/Latino), 10 international. Average age 32. 660 applicants, 52% accepted, 202 enrolled. *Faculty:* 69 full-time (42 women), 24 part-time/adjunct (19 women). Expenses: Contact institution. *Financial support:* In 2016–17, 357 students received support, including 42 research assistantships (averaging $14,510 per year), 34 teaching assistantships (averaging $18,060 per year); career-related internships or fieldwork, Federal Work-Study, institutionally sponsored loans, and scholarships/grants also available. Support available to part-time students. Financial award application deadline: 4/1; financial award applicants required to submit FAFSA. In 2016, 206 master's, 5 doctorates awarded. *Program availability:* Part-time, evening/weekend, blended/hybrid learning. Offers agricultural education (M Ed); applied arts (M Ed, MAIS, MS, MSCJ, MSIS, MSW, PhD); criminal justice (MSCJ, PhD); family and child studies (MS); human nutrition (MS); management of technical education (M Ed); merchandising and consumer studies (MS); occupational education (MAIS, MSIS); social work (MSW). *Application deadline:* For fall admission, 2/15 priority date for domestic and international students; for spring admission, 10/15 priority date for domestic students, 10/1 for international students. Applications are processed on a rolling basis. *Application fee:* $40 ($90 for international students). Electronic applications accepted. *Application Contact:* Dr. Andrea Golato, Dean of Graduate School, 512-245-2581, Fax: 512-245-8365, E-mail: gradcollege@txstate.edu. *Dean,* Dr. T. Jaime Chahin, 512-245-3333, Fax: 512-245-3338, E-mail: tc03@txstate.edu.

College of Education Students: 569 full-time (440 women), 573 part-time (423 women); includes 464 minority (84 Black or African American, non-Hispanic/Latino; 1 American Indian or Alaska Native, non-Hispanic/Latino; 29 Asian, non-Hispanic/Latino; 320 Hispanic/Latino; 30 Two or more races, non-Hispanic/Latino), 26 international. Average age 32. 764 applicants, 64% accepted, 304 enrolled. *Faculty:* 123 full-time (79 women), 51 part-time/adjunct (37 women). Expenses: Contact institution. *Financial support:* In 2016–17, 624 students received support, including 64 research assistantships (averaging $18,495 per year), 73 teaching assistantships (averaging $15,290 per year); fellowships, career-related internships or fieldwork, Federal Work-Study, institutionally sponsored loans, and scholarships/grants also available. Support available to part-time students. Financial award application

deadline: 3/1; financial award applicants required to submit FAFSA. In 2016, 384 master's, 19 doctorates awarded. *Program availability:* Part-time, evening/weekend. Offers adult education (MA); adult, professional and community education (PhD); athletic training (MS); community counseling (MA); developmental education (MA, PhD); education (M Ed, MA, MS, MSRLS, Ed D, PhD, SSP); educational leadership (M Ed); educational technology (M Ed); elementary education (M Ed, MA); elementary education - bilingual/bicultural (M Ed, MA); health education (M Ed); instructional leadership (MA); marital, couple and family counseling (MA); physical education (M Ed); reading education (M Ed); recreation management (MSRLS); school counseling (MA); school improvement (PhD); school psychology (SSP); secondary education (M Ed, MA); special education (M Ed); student affairs in higher education (M Ed). *Application deadline:* For fall admission, 1/15 priority date for domestic and international students; for spring admission, 10/1 priority date for domestic and international students. Applications are processed on a rolling basis. *Application fee:* $40 ($90 for international students). Electronic applications accepted. *Application Contact:* Dr. Andrea Golato, Dean of Graduate School, 512-245-2581, Fax: 512-245-8365, E-mail: gradcollege@txstate.edu. *Dean,* Dr. Stan Carpenter, 512-245-2150, Fax: 512-245-3158, E-mail: sc33@txstate.edu.

College of Fine Arts and Communication Students: 172 full-time (107 women), 69 part-time (44 women); includes 84 minority (15 Black or African American, non-Hispanic/Latino; 1 American Indian or Alaska Native, non-Hispanic/Latino; 1 Asian, non-Hispanic/Latino; 60 Hispanic/Latino; 7 Two or more races, non-Hispanic/Latino), 20 international. Average age 30. 201 applicants, 62% accepted, 84 enrolled. *Faculty:* 94 full-time (51 women), 14 part-time/adjunct (4 women). Expenses: Contact institution. *Financial support:* In 2016–17, 168 students received support, including 109 teaching assistantships (averaging $12,251 per year); research assistantships, career-related internships or fieldwork, Federal Work-Study, institutionally sponsored loans, scholarships/grants, and unspecified assistantships also available. Support available to part-time students. Financial award application deadline: 3/1; financial award applicants required to submit FAFSA. In 2016, 64 master's awarded. *Program availability:* Part-time, evening/weekend. Offers communication design (MFA); communication studies (MA); design (MFA); directing (MFA); dramatic writing (MFA); fine arts and communication (MA, MFA, MM); mass communication (MA); music (MM); music education (MM); theatre history, dramatic criticism and dramaturgy (MA). *Application deadline:* For fall admission, 6/15 priority date for domestic students, 6/1 for international students; for spring admission, 10/15 priority date for domestic students, 10/1 for international students. Applications are processed on a rolling basis. *Application fee:* $40 ($90 for international students). Electronic applications accepted. *Application Contact:* Dr. Andrea Golato, Dean of Graduate School, 512-245-2581, Fax: 512-245-8365, E-mail: gradcollege@txstate.edu. *Dean of the College of Fine Arts and Communication,* Dr. John Fleming, 512-245-2308, Fax: 512-245-8386, E-mail: jf18@txstate.edu.

College of Health Professions Students: 331 full-time (250 women), 33 part-time (26 women); includes 148 minority (40 Black or African American, non-Hispanic/Latino; 3 American Indian or Alaska Native, non-Hispanic/Latino; 11 Asian, non-Hispanic/Latino; 86 Hispanic/Latino; 8 Two or more races, non-Hispanic/Latino), 24 international. Average age 29. 652 applicants, 29% accepted, 110 enrolled. *Faculty:* 50 full-time (36 women), 13 part-time/adjunct (5 women). Expenses: Contact institution. *Financial support:* In 2016–17, 227 students received support, including 4 research assistantships (averaging $8,518 per year), 38 teaching assistantships (averaging $10,358 per year); fellowships, career-related internships or fieldwork, Federal Work-Study, institutionally sponsored loans, scholarships/grants, unspecified assistantships, and stipends also available. Support available to part-time students. Financial award application deadline: 3/1; financial award applicants required to submit FAFSA. In 2016, 87 master's awarded. *Program availability:* Part-time, evening/weekend. Offers communication disorders (MA, MSCD); family nurse practitioner (MSN); health information management (MHIIM); health professions (MA, MHA, MHIIM, MSCD, MSN, DPT); healthcare administration (MHA); physical therapy (DPT). *Application deadline:* For fall admission, 1/15 priority date for domestic and international students; for spring admission, 10/1 for domestic and international students. Applications are processed on a rolling basis. *Application fee:* $40 ($90 for international students). Electronic applications accepted. *Application Contact:* Dr. Andrea Golato, Dean of Graduate School, 512-245-2581, Fax: 512-245-8365, E-mail: gradcollege@txstate.edu. *Dean,* Dr. Ruth Welborn, 512-245-3300, Fax: 512-245-3791, E-mail: mw01@txstate.edu.

College of Liberal Arts Students: 465 full-time (271 women), 332 part-time (186 women); includes 288 minority (49 Black or African American, non-Hispanic/Latino; 22 Asian, non-Hispanic/Latino; 197 Hispanic/Latino; 20 Two or more races, non-Hispanic/Latino), 39 international. Average age 31. 720 applicants, 58% accepted, 229 enrolled. *Faculty:* 194 full-time (82 women), 22 part-time/adjunct (9 women). Expenses: Contact institution. *Financial support:* In 2016–17, 502 students received support, including 25 research assistantships (averaging $14,876 per year), 229 teaching assistantships (averaging $16,082 per year); fellowships, career-related internships or fieldwork, Federal Work-Study, institutionally sponsored loans, scholarships/grants, and unspecified assistantships also available. Support available to part-time students. Financial award application deadline: 3/1; financial award applicants required to submit FAFSA. In 2016, 262 master's, 5 doctorates awarded. *Program availability:* Part-time, evening/weekend. Offers anthropology (MA); applied philosophy and ethics (MA); applied sociology (MS); creative writing (MFA); dementia and aging studies (MS); geographic education (PhD); geographic information science (PhD); geography (MAG, MS, PhD); history (M Ed, MA); international relations (MPA); international studies (MA); legal and judicial administration (MPA); legal studies (MA); liberal arts (M Ed, MA, MAG, MFA, MPA, MS, PhD); literature (MA); political science (MA); psychological research (MA); rhetoric and composition (MA); sociology (MA); Spanish (MA); sustainability (MA, MS); technical communication (MA). *Application deadline:* For fall admission, 6/15 priority date for domestic students, 6/1 for international students; for spring admission, 10/15 priority date for domestic students, 10/1 for international students. Applications are processed on a rolling basis. *Application fee:* $40 ($90 for international students). Electronic applications accepted. *Application Contact:* Dr. Andrea Golato, Dean of Graduate School, 512-245-2581, Fax: 512-245-8365, E-mail: gradcollege@txstate.edu. *Dean,* Dr. Michael Hennessy, 512-245-2317, Fax: 512-245-8291, E-mail: liberalarts@txstate.edu.

College of Science and Engineering Students: 359 full-time (149 women), 137 part-time (61 women); includes 100 minority (19 Black or African American, non-Hispanic/Latino; 2 American Indian or Alaska Native, non-Hispanic/Latino; 16 Asian, non-Hispanic/Latino; 58 Hispanic/Latino; 5 Two or more races, non-Hispanic/Latino), 192 international. Average age 29. 719 applicants, 48% accepted, 140 enrolled. *Faculty:* 138 full-time (41 women), 11 part-time/adjunct (2 women). Expenses: Contact institution. *Financial support:* In 2016–17, 248 students received support, including 79 research assistantships (averaging $18,893 per year), 203 teaching assistantships (averaging $18,841 per year); career-related internships or fieldwork, Federal Work-Study, institutionally sponsored loans, scholarships/grants, health care benefits, unspecified assistantships, and laboratory instructorships also available. Support available to part-time students. Financial award application deadline: 3/1; financial award applicants required to submit FAFSA. In 2016, 159 master's, 15 doctorates awarded. *Program availability:* Part-time, evening/weekend. Offers applied mathematics (MS); aquatic resources (MS, PhD); biochemistry (MS); biology (MA, MS); chemistry (MA, MS); computer science (MA, MS, PhD); electrical engineering (MS); industrial engineering (MS); manufacturing engineering (MS); material physics (MS); materials science, engineering, and commercialization (PhD); mathematics (M Ed, MS); mathematics education (PhD); middle school mathematics teaching (M Ed); physics (MS); population and conservation biology (MS); science and engineering (M Ed, MA, MS, MSIS, PhD); software engineering (MS); technology management (MS); wildlife ecology (MS). *Application deadline:* For fall admission, 1/15 priority date for domestic and international students; for spring admission, 10/15 for domestic students, 10/1 for international students. Applications are processed on a rolling basis. *Application fee:* $40 ($90 for international students). Electronic applications accepted. *Application Contact:* Dr. Andrea Golato, Dean of Graduate School, 512-245-2581, Fax: 512-245-8365, E-mail: gradcollege@txstate.edu. *Dean,* Dr. Christine Hailey, 512-245-2119, Fax: 512-245-8095, E-mail: ceh138@txstate.edu.

Emmett and Miriam McCoy College of Business Administration Students: 190 full-time (90 women), 202 part-time (99 women); includes 118 minority (21 Black or African American, non-Hispanic/Latino; 1 American Indian or Alaska Native, non-Hispanic/Latino; 16 Asian, non-Hispanic/Latino; 69 Hispanic/Latino; 11 Two or more races, non-Hispanic/Latino), 27 international. Average age 30. 342 applicants, 49% accepted, 100 enrolled. *Faculty:* 53 full-time (18 women), 5 part-time/adjunct (0 women). Expenses: Contact institution. *Financial support:* In 2016–17, 193 students received support, including 2 research assistantships (averaging $14,000 per year), 25 teaching assistantships (averaging $13,719 per year); Federal Work-Study, institutionally sponsored loans, scholarships/grants, health care benefits, and unspecified assistantships also available. Support available to part-time students. Financial award application deadline: 3/1; financial award applicants required to submit FAFSA. In 2016, 176 master's awarded. *Program availability:* Part-time. Offers accounting (M Acy); accounting and information technology (MS); business administration (M Acy, MBA, MS); human resource management (MS). *Application deadline:* For fall admission, 6/1 for domestic and international students; for spring admission, 10/1 for domestic and international students. Applications are processed on a rolling basis. *Application fee:* $40 ($90 for international students). Electronic applications accepted. *Application Contact:* Dr. Andrea Golato, Dean of Graduate School, 512-245-2581, Fax: 512-245-8365, E-mail: gradcollege@txstate.edu. *Dean of the College of Business Administration,* Dr. Denise Smart, 512-245-2311, Fax: 512-245-8375, E-mail: ds37@txstate.edu.

TEXAS TECH UNIVERSITY, Lubbock, TX 79409

General Information State-supported, coed, university. CGS member. *Enrollment:* 36,551 graduate, professional, and undergraduate students; 4,140 full-time matriculated graduate/professional students (1,930 women), 2,132 part-time matriculated graduate/professional students (1,247 women). *Enrollment by degree level:* 3,232 master's, 3,040 doctoral. *Graduate faculty:* 1,454 full-time (571 women), 193 part-time/adjunct (95 women). Tuition, state resident: full-time $7200; part-time $300 per credit hour. Tuition, nonresident: full-time $16,992; part-time $708 per credit hour. *Required fees:* $2428; $50.50 per credit hour. $608 per semester. Tuition and fees vary according to program. *Graduate housing:* Room and/or apartments available on a first-come, first-served basis to single students; on-campus housing not available to married students. Typical cost: $4510 per year ($8505 including board). Room and board charges vary according to board plan and housing facility selected. Housing application deadline: 5/1. *Student services:* Campus employment opportunities, campus safety program, career counseling, exercise/wellness program, free psychological counseling, grant writing training, international student services, low-cost health insurance, multicultural affairs office, services for students with disabilities, teacher training, writing training. *Library facilities:* Texas Tech Library plus 3 others. *Collection:* Books: 2.9 million (physical), 157,061 (digital/electronic); Serial titles: 3,340 (physical), 155,013 (digital/electronic); Databases: 399. Weekly public service hours: 146; study areas open 24 hours, 5–7 days a week; students can reserve study rooms. *Research affiliation:* U.S. Department of Education (DOE) (student achievement and preparation for global competitiveness), U.S. Department of Health and Human Services (advances in medicine, public health, and social sciences), U.S. Department of Defense (pulsed power and nanotechnology for defense applications), U.S. Department of Agriculture (USDA) (food safety, development and production in agriculture), U.S. Department of Energy (research and development in wind energy), Bill and Melinda Gates Foundation (education through innovation).

Computer facilities: Computer purchase and lease plans are available. 2,728 computers available on campus for general student use. A campuswide network can be accessed from student residence rooms and from off campus. Online class registration, online degree plans, accounts, transcripts, financial aid, course and instructor evaluations are available.
Website: http://www.ttu.edu/

General Application Contact: Shelby Cearley, Director of Graduate and International Admissions, 806-742-2787, Fax: 806-742-4038, E-mail: graduate.admissions@ttu.edu.

GRADUATE UNITS

Graduate School Students: 3,616 full-time (1,697 women), 2,131 part-time (1,246 women); includes 1,274 minority (267 Black or African American, non-Hispanic/Latino; 15 American Indian or Alaska Native, non-Hispanic/Latino; 90 Asian, non-Hispanic/Latino; 761 Hispanic/Latino; 2 Native Hawaiian or other Pacific Islander, non-Hispanic/Latino; 139 Two or more races, non-Hispanic/Latino), 1,544 international. Average age 31. 6,181 applicants, 44% accepted, 1620 enrolled. *Faculty:* 1,417 full-time (560 women), 191 part-time/adjunct (94 women). Expenses: Contact institution. *Financial support:* In 2016–17, 4,036 students received support, including 3,539 fellowships (averaging $3,288 per year), 1,152 research assistantships (averaging $12,792 per year), 1,651 teaching assistantships (averaging $13,526 per year); career-related internships or fieldwork, Federal Work-Study, scholarships/grants, traineeships, health care benefits, and unspecified assistantships also available. Support available to part-time students. Financial award application deadline: 4/15; financial award applicants required to submit FAFSA. In 2016, 1,639 master's, 330 doctorates awarded. *Program availability:* Part-time, evening/weekend, online learning. Offers arid land studies (MS); biotechnology (MS); interdisciplinary studies (MA, MS); museum science (MA); wind science and engineering (PhD). *Application deadline:* For fall admission, 6/1 priority date for domestic students, 1/15 priority date for international students; for spring admission, 9/1 priority date for domestic students, 6/15 priority date for international students. Applications are processed on a rolling basis. *Application fee:* $75. Electronic

applications accepted. *Application Contact:* Shelby L. Cearley, Director of Graduate Admissions, 806-742-2787, Fax: 806-742-4038, E-mail: graduate.admissions@ttu.edu. *Vice Provost for Graduate and Postdoctoral Affairs/Dean of the Graduate School,* Dr. Mark Sheridan, 806-834-5537, Fax: 806-742-1746, E-mail: info.gradschool@ttu.edu.

College of Agricultural Sciences and Natural Resources Students: 287 full-time (150 women), 131 part-time (64 women); includes 48 minority (3 Black or African American, non-Hispanic/Latino; 3 Asian, non-Hispanic/Latino; 31 Hispanic/Latino; 11 Two or more races, non-Hispanic/Latino), 105 international. Average age 30. 258 applicants, 53% accepted, 92 enrolled. *Faculty:* 117 full-time (38 women), 16 part-time/adjunct (4 women). Expenses: Contact institution. *Financial support:* In 2016–17, 337 students received support, including 273 fellowships (averaging $3,385 per year), 245 research assistantships (averaging $13,700 per year), 27 teaching assistantships (averaging $10,907 per year); scholarships/grants, health care benefits, and unspecified assistantships also available. Support available to part-time students. Financial award application deadline: 12/1; financial award applicants required to submit FAFSA. In 2016, 88 master's, 26 doctorates awarded. *Program availability:* Part-time, 100% online, blended/hybrid learning. Offers agribusiness (MAB); agricultural and applied economics (MS, PhD); agricultural communications (MS); agricultural communications and education (PhD); agricultural education (MS, Ed D); agricultural sciences and natural resources (MAB, MLA, MS, Ed D, PhD); animal science (MS); food science (MS); horticulture science (MS); landscape architecture (MLA); plant and soil science (MS, PhD); wildlife, aquatic, and wildlands science and management (MS, PhD). *Application deadline:* For fall admission, 6/1 priority date for domestic students, 1/15 priority date for international students; for spring admission, 9/1 priority date for domestic students, 6/15 priority date for international students. Applications are processed on a rolling basis. *Application fee:* $75. Electronic applications accepted. *Application Contact:* Dr. Michael Ballou, Associate Dean for Research, 806-834-6513, Fax: 806-742-2836, E-mail: michael.ballou@ttu.edu. *Professor and Interim Dean,* Dr. Steve D. Fraze, 806-834-7115, Fax: 806-742-2836, E-mail: steven.fraze@ttu.edu.

College of Architecture Students: 84 full-time (26 women), 20 part-time (5 women); includes 45 minority (3 Black or African American, non-Hispanic/Latino; 38 Hispanic/Latino; 4 Two or more races, non-Hispanic/Latino), 22 international. Average age 26. 71 applicants, 58% accepted, 19 enrolled. *Faculty:* 33 full-time (8 women), 16 part-time/adjunct (5 women). Expenses: Contact institution. *Financial support:* In 2016–17, 83 students received support, including 83 fellowships (averaging $4,422 per year); research assistantships, teaching assistantships, career-related internships or fieldwork, Federal Work-Study, institutionally sponsored loans, scholarships/grants, traineeships, health care benefits, and unspecified assistantships also available. Support available to part-time students. Financial award application deadline: 2/1; financial award applicants required to submit FAFSA. In 2016, 38 master's, 2 doctorates awarded. *Program availability:* Part-time. Offers architecture (M Arch, MS); land-use planning, management, and design (PhD). *Application deadline:* For fall admission, 6/1 priority date for domestic students, 1/15 priority date for international students; for spring admission, 9/1 priority date for domestic students, 6/15 priority date for international students. Applications are processed on a rolling basis. *Application fee:* $75. Electronic applications accepted. *Application Contact:* Jeff Rammage, Graduate Advisor, 806-742-3169, Fax: 806-742-1400, E-mail: joffrey.rammage@ttu.edu. *Dean,* Prof. James Williamson, 806-742-3136, Fax: 806-742-1400, E-mail: james.p.williamson@ttu.edu.

College of Arts and Sciences Students: 1,069 full-time (527 women), 251 part-time (129 women); includes 218 minority (37 Black or African American, non-Hispanic/Latino; 5 American Indian or Alaska Native, non-Hispanic/Latino; 24 Asian, non-Hispanic/Latino; 125 Hispanic/Latino; 1 Native Hawaiian or other Pacific Islander, non-Hispanic/Latino; 26 Two or more races, non-Hispanic/Latino), 440 international. Average age 29. 1,451 applicants, 36% accepted, 315 enrolled. *Faculty:* 504 full-time (190 women), 60 part-time/adjunct (27 women). Expenses: Contact institution. *Financial support:* In 2016–17, 1,148 students received support, including 918 fellowships (averaging $2,523 per year), 295 research assistantships (averaging $10,167 per year), 914 teaching assistantships (averaging $13,733 per year); career-related internships or fieldwork, Federal Work-Study, institutionally sponsored loans, scholarships/grants, traineeships, health care benefits, and unspecified assistantships also available. Support available to part-time students. Financial award application deadline: 2/1; financial award applicants required to submit FAFSA. In 2016, 242 master's, 90 doctorates awarded. *Program availability:* Part-time, evening/weekend, 100% online, blended/hybrid learning. Offers anthropology (MA); applied linguistics (MA); arts and sciences (MA, MPA, MS, MSW, PSM, PhD); atmospheric science (MS); biology (MS, PhD); chemical biology (MS); chemistry (MS, PhD); classics (MA); clinical psychology (PhD); counseling psychology (MA, PhD); economics (MA, PhD); English (MA, PhD); environmental sustainability and natural resource management (PSM); environmental toxicology (MS, PhD); forensic sciences (MS); general experimental psychology (MA, PhD); geography (MS); geosciences (MS, PhD); German (MA); history (MA, PhD); kinesiology (MS); languages and cultures (MA); mathematics (MA, MS, PhD); microbiology (MS); philosophy (MA); physics (MS, PhD); political science (MA, PhD); psychology (MA); public administration (MPA); Romance languages (MA); social work (MSW); sociology (MA); Spanish (PhD); sport management (MS); statistics (MS); technical communication (MA); technical communication and rhetoric (PhD); zoology (MS). *Application deadline:* For fall admission, 6/1 priority date for domestic students, 1/15 priority date for international students; for spring admission, 9/1 priority date for domestic students, 6/15 priority date for international students. Applications are processed on a rolling basis. *Application fee:* $75. Electronic applications accepted. *Application Contact:* Dr. Jorge Iber, Associate Dean, 806-742-3833, Fax: 806-742-3893, E-mail: jorge.iber@ttu.edu. *Dean,* Dr. W. Brent Lindquist, 806-742-3831, Fax: 806-742-3893, E-mail: brent.lindquist@ttu.edu.

College of Education Students: 365 full-time (270 women), 893 part-time (673 women); includes 417 minority (117 Black or African American, non-Hispanic/Latino; 6 American Indian or Alaska Native, non-Hispanic/Latino; 15 Asian, non-Hispanic/Latino; 247 Hispanic/Latino; 32 Two or more races, non-Hispanic/Latino), 92 international. Average age 36. 840 applicants, 56% accepted, 363 enrolled. *Faculty:* 83 full-time (46 women), 4 part-time/adjunct (3 women). Expenses: Contact institution. *Financial support:* In 2016–17, 511 students received support, including 494 fellowships (averaging $3,521 per year), 108 research assistantships (averaging $11,570 per year), 10 teaching assistantships (averaging $9,227 per year); career-related internships or fieldwork, Federal Work-Study, institutionally sponsored loans, scholarships/grants, traineeships, health care benefits, and unspecified assistantships also available. Support available to part-time students. Financial award application deadline: 2/15; financial award applicants required to submit FAFSA. In 2016, 191 master's, 75 doctorates awarded. *Program availability:* Part-time, evening/weekend. Offers bilingual education (M Ed); counselor education (M Ed, PhD); curriculum and instruction (M Ed); distance education (M Ed); education (M Ed, MS, Ed D, PhD); educational leadership (M Ed, Ed D, PhD); educational psychology (M Ed, PhD); elementary education (M Ed); higher education (M Ed, Ed D); higher education research (PhD); instructional technology (M Ed, Ed D); language/literacy education (M Ed); multidisciplinary science (MS); secondary education (M Ed); special education (M Ed, Ed D, PhD). *Application deadline:* For fall admission, 6/1 priority date for domestic students, 1/15 priority date for international students; for spring admission, 9/1 priority date for domestic students, 6/15 priority date for international students. Applications are processed on a rolling basis. *Application fee:* $75. Electronic applications accepted. *Application Contact:* Brianna Sanchez, Coordinator, 806-834-2353, Fax: 806-742-2179, E-mail: brianna.sanchez@ttu.edu. *Dean,* Dr. Scott Ridley, 806-834-1431, Fax: 806-742-2179, E-mail: scott.ridley@ttu.edu.

College of Human Sciences Students: 294 full-time (173 women), 118 part-time (82 women); includes 86 minority (14 Black or African American, non-Hispanic/Latino; 1 American Indian or Alaska Native, non-Hispanic/Latino; 3 Asian, non-Hispanic/Latino; 55 Hispanic/Latino; 13 Two or more races, non-Hispanic/Latino), 108 international. Average age 30. 364 applicants, 53% accepted, 122 enrolled. *Faculty:* 109 full-time (71 women), 23 part-time/adjunct (19 women). Expenses: Contact institution. *Financial support:* In 2016–17, 342 students received support, including 323 fellowships (averaging $4,316 per year), 90 research assistantships (averaging $9,852 per year), 128 teaching assistantships (averaging $11,940 per year); institutionally sponsored loans, scholarships/grants, and unspecified assistantships also available. Financial award application deadline: 2/1; financial award applicants required to submit FAFSA. In 2016, 96 master's, 37 doctorates awarded. *Program availability:* Part-time, 100% online, blended/hybrid learning. Offers environmental design (MS); family and consumer sciences education (MS, PhD); hospitality administration (PhD); hospitality and retail management (MS); human development and family studies (MS, PhD); human sciences (MS, PhD); interior and environmental design (PhD); marriage and family therapy (MS, PhD); nutrition and dietetics (MS); nutritional sciences (MS, PhD); personal financial planning (MS, PhD). *Application deadline:* For fall admission, 6/1 priority date for domestic students, 1/15 priority date for international students; for spring admission, 9/1 priority date for domestic students, 6/15 priority date for international students. Applications are processed on a rolling basis. *Application fee:* $75. Electronic applications accepted. *Application Contact:* Prof. Mitzi Lauderdale, Associate Dean for Students, 806-834-0529, Fax: 806-742-1849, E-mail: mitzi.lauderdale@ttu.edu. *Dean,* Dr. Linda C. Hoover, 806-742-3031, Fax: 806-742-3042, E-mail: linda.hoover@ttu.edu.

College of Media and Communication Students: 83 full-time (53 women), 103 part-time (73 women); includes 55 minority (12 Black or African American, non-Hispanic/Latino; 2 Asian, non-Hispanic/Latino; 36 Hispanic/Latino; 5 Two or more races, non-Hispanic/Latino), 13 international. Average age 29. 158 applicants, 56% accepted, 68 enrolled. *Faculty:* 56 full-time (21 women), 13 part-time/adjunct (7 women). Expenses: Contact institution. *Financial support:* In 2016–17, 128 students received support, including 89 fellowships (averaging $3,859 per year), 32 research assistantships (averaging $8,757 per year), 80 teaching assistantships (averaging $8,592 per year); career-related internships or fieldwork, scholarships/grants, and unspecified assistantships also available. Support available to part-time students. Financial award application deadline: 4/15; financial award applicants required to submit FAFSA. In 2016, 58 master's, 7 doctorates awarded. *Program availability:* Part-time, evening/weekend, 100% online. Offers communication studies (MA); mass communications (MA, PhD); media and communication (MA); strategic communication and innovation (MA). *Application deadline:* For fall admission, 6/1 priority date for domestic students, 1/15 priority date for international students; for spring admission, 9/1 priority date for domestic students, 6/15 priority date for international students. Applications are processed on a rolling basis. *Application fee:* $75. Electronic applications accepted. *Application Contact:* Shannon Samson, Coordinator of Graduate School Recruitment, 806-834-5201, Fax: 806-742-1746, E-mail: gradschool@ttu.edu. *Graduate Director,* Dr. Coy Callison, 806-834-5344, E-mail: coy.callison@ttu.edu.

Edward E. Whitacre Jr. College of Engineering Students: 663 full-time (162 women), 233 part-time (41 women); includes 102 minority (19 Black or African American, non-Hispanic/Latino; 1 American Indian or Alaska Native, non-Hispanic/Latino; 19 Asian, non-Hispanic/Latino; 54 Hispanic/Latino; 9 Two or more races, non-Hispanic/Latino), 587 international. Average age 29. 1,837 applicants, 34% accepted, 241 enrolled. *Faculty:* 176 full-time (30 women), 16 part-time/adjunct (1 woman). Expenses: Contact institution. *Financial support:* In 2016–17, 654 students received support, including 574 fellowships (averaging $3,309 per year), 343 research assistantships (averaging $16,212 per year), 209 teaching assistantships (averaging $17,931 per year); health care benefits also available. Financial award application deadline: 4/15; financial award applicants required to submit FAFSA. In 2016, 259 master's, 51 doctorates awarded. *Program availability:* Part-time, evening/weekend, 100% online, blended/hybrid learning. Offers bioengineering (MS); chemical engineering (MS Ch E, PhD); civil engineering (MSCE, PhD); computer science (MS, PhD); electrical engineering (MSEE, PhD); engineering (M Engr, MENVEGR, MS, MS Ch E, MSCE, MSEE, MSIE, MSME, MSPE, MSSEM, PhD); environmental engineering (MENVEGR); industrial engineering (MSIE, PhD); mechanical engineering (MSME, PhD); petroleum engineering (MSPE, PhD); software engineering (MS); systems and engineering management (MSSEM, PhD). *Application deadline:* For fall admission, 6/1 priority date for domestic students, 1/15 priority date for international students; for spring admission, 9/1 priority date for domestic students, 6/15 priority date for international students. Applications are processed on a rolling basis. *Application fee:* $75. Electronic applications accepted. *Application Contact:* Dr. Brandon Weeks, Associate Dean of Research and Graduate Programs, Edward E. Whitacre Jr. College of Engineering, 806-834-7450, Fax: 806-742-3493, E-mail: brandon.weeks@ttu.edu. *Dean, Edward E. Whitacre Jr. College of Engineering,* Dr. Albert Sacco, Jr., 806-742-3451, Fax: 806-742-3493, E-mail: al.sacco-jr@ttu.edu.

J.T. and Margaret Talkington College of Visual and Performing Arts Students: 218 full-time (114 women), 97 part-time (63 women); includes 51 minority (8 Black or African American, non-Hispanic/Latino; 2 Asian, non-Hispanic/Latino; 32 Hispanic/Latino; 9 Two or more races, non-Hispanic/Latino), 59 international. Average age 33. 212 applicants, 54% accepted, 78 enrolled. *Faculty:* 112 full-time (45 women), 18 part-time/adjunct (13 women). Expenses: Contact institution. *Financial support:* In 2016–17, 308 students received support, including 281 fellowships (averaging $2,940 per year), 7 research assistantships (averaging $7,169 per year), 205 teaching assistantships (averaging $10,117 per year); Federal Work-Study, institutionally sponsored loans, scholarships/grants, health care benefits, tuition waivers (partial), and unspecified assistantships also available. Financial award application deadline: 2/1; financial award applicants required to submit FAFSA. In 2016, 62 master's, 28 doctorates awarded. *Program availability:* Part-time. Offers art (MFA); art education (MAE); art history (MA); fine arts (PhD); music (MM, DMA); music education (MM Ed);

theatre arts (MA, MFA); visual and performing arts (MA, MAE, MFA, MM, MM Ed, DMA, PhD). *Application deadline:* For fall admission, 6/1 priority date for domestic students, 1/15 priority date for international students; for spring admission, 9/1 priority date for domestic students, 6/15 priority date for international students. Applications are processed on a rolling basis. *Application fee:* $75. Electronic applications accepted. *Application Contact:* Shannon Samson, Coordinator of Graduate School Recruitment, 806-834-5201, Fax: 806-742-1746, E-mail: gradschool@ttu.edu. *Dean,* Dr. Noel Zahler, 806-742-0700, Fax: 806-742-0695, E-mail: noel.zahler@ttu.edu.

Rawls College of Business Administration Students: 741 full-time (275 women); includes 198 minority (38 Black or African American, non-Hispanic/Latino; 1 American Indian or Alaska Native, non-Hispanic/Latino; 24 Asian, non-Hispanic/Latino; 116 Hispanic/Latino; 1 Native Hawaiian or other Pacific Islander, non-Hispanic/Latino; 18 Two or more races, non-Hispanic/Latino), 95 international. Average age 28. 905 applicants, 48% accepted, 251 enrolled. *Faculty:* 74 full-time (13 women). Expenses: Contact institution. *Financial support:* In 2016–17, 157 students received support, including 25 research assistantships (averaging $22,725 per year), 27 teaching assistantships (averaging $22,725 per year); fellowships, career-related internships or fieldwork, Federal Work-Study, scholarships/grants, health care benefits, and unspecified assistantships also available. Financial award application deadline: 3/1; financial award applicants required to submit FAFSA. In 2016, 545 master's, 13 doctorates awarded. *Program availability:* Evening/weekend. Offers accounting (MSA, PhD); business statistics (MS, PhD); data science (MS); finance (PhD); general business (MBA); healthcare management (MS); information systems and operations management (PhD); management (PhD); marketing (PhD); STEM (MBA). *Application deadline:* For fall admission, 7/1 priority date for domestic students, 1/15 for international students; for spring admission, 12/1 priority date for domestic students, 6/15 for international students; for summer admission, 5/1 for domestic students. Applications are processed on a rolling basis. *Application fee:* $60. Electronic applications accepted. *Application Contact:* Chathry Keaton, Applications Manager, Graduate and Professional Programs, 806-742-3184, Fax: 806-742-3958, E-mail: rawlsgrad@ttu.edu. *Dean,* Dr. Margaret Williams, 806-742-3188, Fax: 806-742-1092, E-mail: margaret.l.williams@ttu.edu.

School of Law Students: 524 full-time (233 women), 1 (woman) part-time; includes 131 minority (9 Black or African American, non-Hispanic/Latino; 16 Asian, non-Hispanic/Latino; 83 Hispanic/Latino; 23 Two or more races, non-Hispanic/Latino), 18 international. Average age 26. 1,236 applicants, 52% accepted, 167 enrolled. *Faculty:* 37 full-time (11 women), 2 part-time/adjunct (1 woman). Expenses: Contact institution. *Financial support:* In 2016–17, 402 students received support, including 31 research assistantships, 31 teaching assistantships; Federal Work-Study, tuition waivers, and tutorships also available. Financial award application deadline: 5/1; financial award applicants required to submit FAFSA. In 2016, 9 master's, 182 doctorates awarded. Offers law (JD); United States legal studies (LL M). *Application deadline:* For fall admission, 3/1 priority date for domestic and international students. Applications are processed on a rolling basis. *Application fee:* $50. Electronic applications accepted. *Application Contact:* Wendy A. Humphrey, Associate Dean for Admissions and Financial Aid, 806-834-4446, E-mail: admissions.law@ttu.edu. *Interim Dean and Professor,* Richard Rosen, 806-834-7585, Fax: 806-742-4014, E-mail: richard.rosen@ttu.edu.

TEXAS TECH UNIVERSITY HEALTH SCIENCES CENTER, Lubbock, TX 79430

General Information State-supported, coed, graduate-only institution. *Graduate housing:* On-campus housing not available.

GRADUATE UNITS

Graduate School of Biomedical Sciences Offers biomedical sciences (MS, PhD); biotechnology (MS); pharmaceutical sciences (MS, PhD). Electronic applications accepted.

School of Health Professions Students: 624 full-time (466 women), 352 part-time (225 women); includes 332 minority (56 Black or African American, non-Hispanic/Latino; 2 American Indian or Alaska Native, non-Hispanic/Latino; 82 Asian, non-Hispanic/Latino; 172 Hispanic/Latino; 5 Native Hawaiian or other Pacific Islander, non-Hispanic/Latino; 15 Two or more races, non-Hispanic/Latino). Average age 30. 2,981 applicants, 16% accepted, 477 enrolled. *Faculty:* 73 full-time (41 women), 9 part-time/adjunct (6 women). Expenses: Contact institution. *Financial support:* Research assistantships, teaching assistantships, career-related internships or fieldwork, institutionally sponsored loans, scholarships/grants, and unspecified assistantships available. Financial award application deadline: 9/1; financial award applicants required to submit FAFSA. In 2016, 275 master's, 101 doctorates awarded. *Program availability:* 100% online, blended/hybrid learning. Offers athletic training (MAT); health professions (MAT, MOT, MPAS, MRC, MS, Au D, DPT, PhD, Sc D, TDPT); healthcare administration (MS); molecular pathology (MS); occupational therapy (MOT); physical therapy (DPT, Sc D, TDPT); physician assistant studies (MPAS); rehabilitation counseling (MRC); rehabilitation sciences (PhD); speech, language and hearing sciences (MS, Au D, PhD). *Application deadline:* Applications are processed on a rolling basis. *Application fee:* $40. Electronic applications accepted. *Application Contact:* Lindsay Johnson, Associate Dean for Admissions and Student Affairs, 806-743-3220, Fax: 806-743-2994, E-mail: lindsay.johnson@ttuhsc.edu. *Associate Dean for Admissions and Student Affairs,* Lindsay R. Johnson, 806-743-3220, Fax: 806-743-2994, E-mail: lindsay.johnson@ttuhsc.edu.

School of Medicine Offers medicine (MD). Open only to residents of Texas, eastern New Mexico, and southwestern Oklahoma; MD/PhD offered jointly with Texas Tech University; JD/MD with School of Law. Electronic applications accepted.

School of Nursing *Program availability:* Part-time, online learning. Offers acute care nurse practitioner (MSN, Certificate); administration (MSN); advanced practice (DNP); education (MSN); executive leadership (DNP); family nurse practitioner (MSN, Certificate); geriatric nurse practitioner (MSN, Certificate); pediatric nurse practitioner (MSN, Certificate).

TEXAS WESLEYAN UNIVERSITY, Fort Worth, TX 76105

General Information Independent-religious, coed, comprehensive institution. *Enrollment:* 2,619 graduate, professional, and undergraduate students; 438 full-time matriculated graduate/professional students (238 women), 275 part-time matriculated graduate/professional students (232 women). *Enrollment by degree level:* 578 master's, 135 doctoral. *Graduate faculty:* 42 full-time (23 women), 15 part-time/adjunct (12 women). Tuition and fees vary according to course level, course load, degree level and program. *Graduate housing:* Room and/or apartments available on a first-come, first-served basis to single students; on-campus housing not available to married students. Typical cost: $5646 per year ($9630 including board). Housing application deadline: 8/12. *Student services:* Campus employment opportunities, campus safety program, career counseling, exercise/wellness program, free psychological counseling, international student services, low-cost health insurance, multicultural affairs office, services for students with disabilities, teacher training, writing training. *Library facilities:* Eunice and James L. West Library plus 1 other. *Collection:* Books: 185,461 (physical), 171,492 (digital/electronic); Serial titles: 1,500 (physical), 150,836 (digital/electronic); Databases: 104. Weekly public service hours: 101.

Computer facilities: 507 computers available on campus for general student use. A campuswide network can be accessed from student residence rooms and from off campus. Online class registration is available.
Website: http://www.txwes.edu/

General Application Contact: Amy Orcutt, Interim Director of Graduate Admissions, 817-531-4930, Fax: 817-531-4261, E-mail: arorcutt@txwes.edu.

GRADUATE UNITS

Graduate Programs Students: 438 full-time (238 women), 236 part-time (202 women); includes 250 minority (83 Black or African American, non-Hispanic/Latino; 6 American Indian or Alaska Native, non-Hispanic/Latino; 30 Asian, non-Hispanic/Latino; 105 Hispanic/Latino; 2 Native Hawaiian or other Pacific Islander, non-Hispanic/Latino; 24 Two or more races, non-Hispanic/Latino), 36 international. Average age 33. 657 applicants, 49% accepted, 265 enrolled. *Faculty:* 35 full-time (15 women), 15 part-time/adjunct (9 women). Expenses: Contact institution. *Financial support:* In 2016–17, 8 students received support. Fellowships with tuition reimbursements available, career-related internships or fieldwork, Federal Work-Study, institutionally sponsored loans, scholarships/grants, and tuition waivers (full and partial) available. Support available to part-time students. Financial award application deadline: 3/15; financial award applicants required to submit FAFSA. In 2016, 179 master's, 36 doctorates awarded. *Program availability:* Part-time, evening/weekend, 100% online. Offers business administration (MBA); education (M Ed, Ed D); marriage and family therapy (MSMFT, PhD); nurse anesthesia (MHS, MSNA, DNAP); professional counseling (MA); school counseling (MS). *Application deadline:* Applications are processed on a rolling basis. *Application fee:* $64. Electronic applications accepted. *Application Contact:* Amy Orcutt, Interim Director of Graduate Admissions, 817-531-4288, E-mail: arorcutt@txwes.edu. *Provost,* Dr. Allen Henderson, 817-531-4405, Fax: 817-531-4499, E-mail: ahenderson@txwes.edu.

TEXAS WOMAN'S UNIVERSITY, Denton, TX 76201

General Information State-supported, coed, primarily women, university. CGS member. *Enrollment:* 15,655 graduate, professional, and undergraduate students; 2,035 full-time matriculated graduate/professional students (1,749 women), 3,212 part-time matriculated graduate/professional students (2,848 women). *Enrollment by degree level:* 3,956 master's, 1,069 doctoral, 133 other advanced degrees. *Graduate faculty:* 335 full-time (240 women), 143 part-time/adjunct (111 women). *International tuition:* $23,046 full-time. Tuition, state resident: full-time $9046; part-time $251 per credit hour. Tuition, nonresident: full-time $22,922; part-time $614 per credit hour. *Required fees:* $2690; $1285 per credit hour. One-time fee: $50. Tuition and fees vary according to course level, course load, program and reciprocity agreements. *Graduate housing:* Rooms and/or apartments available on a first-come, first-served basis to single and married students. Typical cost: $3720 per year ($7578 including board) for single students; $3720 per year ($7578 including board) for married students. Room and board charges vary according to board plan and housing facility selected. Housing application deadline: 2/18. *Student services:* Campus employment opportunities, campus safety program, career counseling, exercise/wellness program, free psychological counseling, grant writing training, international student services, low-cost health insurance, multicultural affairs office, services for students with disabilities, teacher training, writing training. *Library facilities:* Blagg-Huey Library. *Collection:* Books: 523,507 (physical), 336,902 (digital/electronic); Databases: 223. Weekly public service hours: 116; students can reserve study rooms.

Computer facilities: Computer purchase and lease plans are available. 1,000 computers available on campus for general student use. A campuswide network can be accessed from student residence rooms and from off campus. Online class registration is available.
Website: http://www.twu.edu/

General Application Contact: Dr. Samuel Wheeler, Assistant Director of Admissions, 940-898-3188, Fax: 940-898-3081, E-mail: wheelersr@twu.edu.

GRADUATE UNITS

Graduate School Students: 2,028 full-time (1,744 women), 3,130 part-time (2,775 women); includes 2,336 minority (901 Black or African American, non-Hispanic/Latino; 22 American Indian or Alaska Native, non-Hispanic/Latino; 519 Asian, non-Hispanic/Latino; 755 Hispanic/Latino; 8 Native Hawaiian or other Pacific Islander, non-Hispanic/Latino; 131 Two or more races, non-Hispanic/Latino), 183 international. Average age 33. 2,764 applicants, 58% accepted, 1188 enrolled. *Faculty:* 335 full-time (240 women), 143 part-time/adjunct (111 women). Expenses: Contact institution. *Financial support:* In 2016–17, 1,521 students received support, including 276 research assistantships (averaging $11,930 per year), 123 teaching assistantships (averaging $11,970 per year); career-related internships or fieldwork, Federal Work-Study, institutionally sponsored loans, scholarships/grants, traineeships, health care benefits, tuition waivers, and unspecified assistantships also available. Support available to part-time students. Financial award application deadline: 3/1; financial award applicants required to submit FAFSA. In 2016, 1,380 master's, 213 doctorates awarded. *Program availability:* Part-time, evening/weekend, 100% online, blended/hybrid learning. *Application deadline:* For fall admission, 3/1 priority date for domestic and international students; for spring admission, 7/1 priority date for domestic students, 5/1 priority date for international students. Applications are processed on a rolling basis. *Application fee:* $50 ($75 for international students). Electronic applications accepted. *Application Contact:* Dr. Samuel Wheeler, Assistant Director of Admissions, 940-898-3188, Fax: 940-898-3081, E-mail: wheelersr@twu.edu. *Interim Dean of Graduate School,* Dr. Holly Hansen-Thomas, 940-898-3415, Fax: 940-898-3412, E-mail: gradschool@twu.edu.

College of Arts and Sciences Students: 616 full-time (508 women), 800 part-time (648 women); includes 786 minority (398 Black or African American, non-Hispanic/Latino; 5 American Indian or Alaska Native, non-Hispanic/Latino; 142 Asian, non-Hispanic/Latino; 197 Hispanic/Latino; 4 Native Hawaiian or other Pacific Islander, non-Hispanic/Latino; 40 Two or more races, non-Hispanic/Latino), 86 international. Average age 34. *Faculty:* 115 full-time (65 women), 23 part-time/adjunct (10 women). Expenses: Contact institution. *Financial support:* In 2016–17, 438 students received support. Research assistantships, teaching assistantships, career-related internships or fieldwork, Federal Work-Study, institutionally sponsored loans, scholarships/grants, traineeships, health care benefits, and unspecified assistantships available. Support available to part-time students. Financial award application deadline: 3/1; financial award applicants required to submit FAFSA. In 2016, 512 master's, 37 doctorates awarded. *Program availability:* Part-time, evening/weekend, online learning. Offers art (MA, MFA); arts (MA, MFA, PhD); arts and sciences (MA, MFA, MS, PhD, SSP); biology (MS); chemistry (MS); counseling psychology (MA, PhD); dance (MA, MFA,

PhD); English (MA); government (MA); history (MA); informatics (MS); instrumental pedagogy (MA); instrumental performance (MA); mathematics (MS); mathematics teaching (MS); molecular biology (PhD); multicultural women's and gender studies (MA, PhD); music (MA); music education (MA); piano performance (MA); rhetoric (PhD); school psychology (PhD, SSP); sociology (MA, PhD); vocal pedagogy (MA); vocal performance (MA). *Application deadline:* For fall admission, 7/1 priority date for domestic students, 3/1 for international students; for spring admission, 12/1 priority date for domestic students, 7/1 for international students. Applications are processed on a rolling basis. *Application fee:* $50 ($75 for international students). Electronic applications accepted. *Application Contact:* Dr. Samuel Wheeler, Assistant Director of Admissions, 940-898-3188, Fax: 940-898-3081, E-mail: wheelersr@twu.edu. *Dean,* Dr. Abigail Tilton, 940-898-3326, Fax: 940-898-3366, E-mail: cas@twu.edu.

College of Health Sciences Students: 1,111 full-time (950 women), 521 part-time (442 women); includes 587 minority (143 Black or African American, non-Hispanic/Latino; 5 American Indian or Alaska Native, non-Hispanic/Latino; 150 Asian, non-Hispanic/Latino; 249 Hispanic/Latino; 1 Native Hawaiian or other Pacific Islander, non-Hispanic/Latino; 39 Two or more races, non-Hispanic/Latino), 62 international. Average age 29. 1,629 applicants, 28% accepted, 332 enrolled. *Faculty:* 96 full-time (72 women), 28 part-time/adjunct (24 women). Expenses: Contact institution. *Financial support:* In 2016–17, 747 students received support, including 59 research assistantships (averaging $11,499 per year), 15 teaching assistantships (averaging $11,499 per year); career-related internships or fieldwork, Federal Work-Study, institutionally sponsored loans, scholarships/grants, traineeships, health care benefits, and unspecified assistantships also available. Support available to part-time students. Financial award application deadline: 3/1; financial award applicants required to submit FAFSA. In 2016, 397 master's, 20 doctorates awarded. *Program availability:* Part-time, evening/weekend, online learning. Offers adapted physical activity (MS, PhD); biomechanics (MS, PhD); coaching (MS); deaf education (MS); exercise physiology (MS, PhD); food science and flavor chemistry (MS); health care administration (MHA); health sciences (MA, MHA, MOT, MS, DPT, OTD, PhD); health studies (MS, PhD); nutrition (MS, PhD); occupational therapy (MA, MOT, OTD, PhD); physical therapy (DPT, PhD); speech-language pathology (MS); sport management (MS, PhD). *Application deadline:* For fall admission, 7/1 priority date for domestic students, 3/1 for international students; for spring admission, 12/1 priority date for domestic students, 7/1 for international students. Applications are processed on a rolling basis. *Application fee:* $50 ($75 for international students). Electronic applications accepted. *Application Contact:* Dr. Samuel Wheeler, Assistant Director of Admissions, 940-898-3188, Fax: 940-898-3081, E-mail: wheelersr@twu.edu. *Dean,* Dr. Christopher T. Ray, 940-898-2852, Fax: 940-898-2853, E-mail: chrisray@twu.edu.

College of Nursing Students: 24 full-time (22 women), 904 part-time (840 women); includes 527 minority (204 Black or African American, non-Hispanic/Latino; 5 American Indian or Alaska Native, non-Hispanic/Latino; 200 Asian, non-Hispanic/Latino; 90 Hispanic/Latino; 3 Native Hawaiian or other Pacific Islander, non-Hispanic/Latino; 25 Two or more races, non-Hispanic/Latino), 21 international. Average age 36. 430 applicants, 65% accepted, 193 enrolled. *Faculty:* 55 full-time (51 women), 42 part-time/adjunct (35 women). Expenses: Contact institution. *Financial support:* In 2016–17, 149 students received support, including 10 research assistantships (averaging $5,600 per year), 1 teaching assistantship (averaging $5,600 per year); career-related internships or fieldwork, Federal Work-Study, institutionally sponsored loans, scholarships/grants, traineeships, health care benefits, and unspecified assistantships also available. Support available to part-time students. Financial award application deadline: 3/1; financial award applicants required to submit FAFSA. In 2016, 237 master's, 10 doctorates awarded. *Program availability:* Part-time, online learning. Offers acute care nurse practitioner (MS); adult health clinical nurse specialist (MS); adult health nurse practitioner (MS); child health clinical nurse specialist (MS); clinical nurse leader (MS); family nurse practitioner (MS); health systems management (MS); nursing education (MS); nursing practice (DNP); nursing science (PhD); pediatric nurse practitioner (MS); women's health clinical nurse specialist (MS); women's health nurse practitioner (MS). *Application deadline:* For fall admission, 5/1 priority date for domestic students, 3/1 for international students; for spring admission, 9/15 priority date for domestic students, 7/1 for international students. Applications are processed on a rolling basis. *Application fee:* $50 ($75 for international students). Electronic applications accepted. *Application Contact:* Dr. Samuel Wheeler, Assistant Director of Admissions, 940-898-3188, Fax: 940-898-3081, E-mail: wheelersr@twu.edu. *Dean,* Dr. Anita G. Hufft, 940-898-2401, Fax: 940-898-2437, E-mail: nursing@twu.edu.

College of Professional Education Students: 277 full-time (264 women), 885 part-time (825 women); includes 436 minority (156 Black or African American, non-Hispanic/Latino; 7 American Indian or Alaska Native, non-Hispanic/Latino; 27 Asian, non-Hispanic/Latino; 219 Hispanic/Latino; 27 Two or more races, non-Hispanic/Latino), 14 international. Average age 35. 429 applicants, 61% accepted, 206 enrolled. *Faculty:* 62 full-time (48 women), 50 part-time/adjunct (41 women). Expenses: Contact institution. *Financial support:* In 2016–17, 332 students received support, including 40 research assistantships (averaging $12,164 per year), 8 teaching assistantships (averaging $12,164 per year); career-related internships or fieldwork, Federal Work-Study, institutionally sponsored loans, scholarships/grants, traineeships, health care benefits, and unspecified assistantships also available. Support available to part-time students. Financial award application deadline: 3/1; financial award applicants required to submit FAFSA. In 2016, 376 master's, 13 doctorates awarded. *Program availability:* Part-time, evening/weekend. Offers child development (MS); counseling and development (MS); early childhood development and education (PhD); early childhood education (M Ed); educational administration (M Ed, MA); family studies (MS, PhD); family therapy (MS, PhD); library science (MA, MLS, PhD); professional education (M Ed, MA, MAT, MLS, MS, PhD); reading education (M Ed, MA, PhD); special education (M Ed, MA, PhD); teaching (MAT); teaching, learning, and curriculum (M Ed, MA). *Application deadline:* For fall admission, 7/1 priority date for domestic students, 3/1 for international students; for spring admission, 12/1 priority date for domestic students, 7/1 for international students. Applications are processed on a rolling basis. *Application fee:* $50 ($75 for international students). Electronic applications accepted. *Application Contact:* Dr. Samuel Wheeler, Assistant Director of Admissions, 940-898-3188, Fax: 940-898-3081, E-mail: wheelersr@twu.edu. *Interim Dean,* Dr. Jerry Whitworth, 940-898-2202, Fax: 940-898-2209, E-mail: cope@twu.edu.

School of Management Students: 432 full-time (357 women), 442 part-time (356 women); includes 598 minority (341 Black or African American, non-Hispanic/Latino; 2 American Indian or Alaska Native, non-Hispanic/Latino; 111 Asian, non-Hispanic/Latino; 121 Hispanic/Latino; 3 Native Hawaiian or other Pacific Islander, non-Hispanic/Latino; 20 Two or more races, non-Hispanic/Latino), 46 international. Average age 35. Expenses: Contact institution. *Financial support:* Research assistantships, career-related internships or fieldwork, Federal Work-Study, institutionally sponsored loans, scholarships/grants, traineeships, health care benefits, and unspecified assistantships available. Support available to part-time students. Financial award application deadline: 3/1; financial award applicants required to submit FAFSA. In 2016, 604 master's awarded. *Program availability:* Part-time. Offers accounting (MBA); business administration (MBA); health systems management (MHSM). *Application deadline:* For fall admission, 8/1 priority date for domestic students, 3/1 for international students; for spring admission, 12/1 priority date for domestic students, 7/1 for international students. Applications are processed on a rolling basis. *Application fee:* $50 ($75 for international students). Electronic applications accepted. *Application Contact:* Dr. Samuel Wheeler, Assistant Director of Admissions, 940-898-3188, Fax: 940-898-3081, E-mail: wheelersr@twu.edu. *Director,* Dr. Margaret A. Young, 940-898-2105, Fax: 940-898-2120, E-mail: myoung13@twu.edu.

THEOLOGICAL UNIVERSITY OF THE CARIBBEAN, Saint Just, PR 00978-0901

General Information Independent-religious, coed, comprehensive institution.

GRADUATE UNITS

Graduate Programs Offers childhood and adolescent education (MA); counseling and pastoral care (MA); ministry (D Min); missions (MA).

THOMAS COLLEGE, Waterville, ME 04901-5097

General Information Independent, coed, comprehensive institution. *Graduate housing:* On-campus housing not available.

GRADUATE UNITS

Graduate School *Program availability:* Part-time, evening/weekend. Offers business (MBA); computer technology education (MS); education (MS); human resource management (MBA). Electronic applications accepted.

THOMAS JEFFERSON SCHOOL OF LAW, San Diego, CA 92110-2905

General Information Independent, coed, graduate-only institution. *Graduate housing:* Rooms and/or apartments available on a first-come, first-served basis to single and married students. Housing application deadline: 5/1.

GRADUATE UNITS

Graduate and Professional Programs *Program availability:* Part-time, evening/weekend. Offers law (JD). JD/MBA offered in partnership with San Diego State University. Electronic applications accepted.

THOMAS JEFFERSON UNIVERSITY, Philadelphia, PA 19107

General Information Independent, coed, university. CGS member. *Graduate housing:* Rooms and/or apartments available to single and married students. *Research affiliation:* Christiana Care Health Services (biomedical research), Lankenau Institute for Medical Research (biomedical research), A.I. du Pont for Children Nemours (biomedical research), University of Delaware (biomedical research).

GRADUATE UNITS

Jefferson College of Biomedical Sciences Students: 123 full-time (66 women), 128 part-time (78 women); includes 64 minority (22 Black or African American, non-Hispanic/Latino; 27 Asian, non-Hispanic/Latino; 9 Hispanic/Latino; 6 Two or more races, non-Hispanic/Latino), 28 international. 164 applicants, 78% accepted, 72 enrolled. *Faculty:* 190 full-time (53 women), 37 part-time/adjunct (15 women). Expenses: Contact institution. *Financial support:* Fellowships, Federal Work-Study, institutionally sponsored loans, scholarships/grants, and traineeships available. Support available to part-time students. Financial award application deadline: 5/1; financial award applicants required to submit FAFSA. In 2016, 30 master's, 19 doctorates, 6 other advanced degrees awarded. *Program availability:* Part-time, evening/weekend. Offers biochemistry and molecular pharmacology (PhD); biomedical sciences (MS, PhD, Certificate); cell and developmental biology (MS); cell biology and regenerative medicine (PhD); clinical research (MS); clinical research and trials: implementation (Certificate); clinical research: operations (Certificate); forensic toxicology (MS); genetics, genomics and cancer biology (PhD); human clinical investigation: theory (Certificate); human genetics and genetic counseling (MS); immunology and microbial pathogenesis (PhD); infectious disease control (Certificate); microbiology (MS); neuroscience (PhD); patient-centered research (Certificate); pharmacology (MS). *Application deadline:* Applications are processed on a rolling basis. *Application fee:* $50. Electronic applications accepted. *Application Contact:* Marc E. Stearns, Director of Admissions, 215-503-0155, Fax: 215-503-3433, E-mail: jgsbs-info@jefferson.edu. *Dean,* Dr. Gerald B. Grunwald, 215-503-4191, Fax: 215-503-6690, E-mail: gerald.grunwald@jefferson.edu.

Jefferson College of Health Professions Students: 500 full-time (384 women), 58 part-time (54 women); includes 68 minority (22 Black or African American, non-Hispanic/Latino; 36 Asian, non-Hispanic/Latino; 2 Hispanic/Latino; 8 Two or more races, non-Hispanic/Latino), 20 international. Expenses: Contact institution. *Financial support:* In 2016–17, 278 students received support. Teaching assistantships, Federal Work-Study, institutionally sponsored loans, scholarships/grants, and unspecified assistantships available. Financial award application deadline: 4/1; financial award applicants required to submit FAFSA. Offers biotechnology (MS); couple and family therapy (MFT); cytotechnology (MS); health professions (MFT, MS, DPT, OTD); medical laboratory science (MS); occupational therapy (MS, OTD); physical therapy (DPT); physician assistant studies (MS); radiologic and imaging sciences (MS). *Application deadline:* Applications are processed on a rolling basis. Electronic applications accepted. *Application Contact:* Donald Sharples, Director of Graduate Admissions, 215-503-1044, E-mail: donald.sharples@jefferson.edu. *Interim Dean,* Dr. Debra S. Zelnick, 215-503-8707.

Jefferson College of Nursing Students: 83 full-time (55 women), 475 part-time (421 women); includes 123 minority (43 Black or African American, non-Hispanic/Latino; 73 Asian, non-Hispanic/Latino; 1 Hispanic/Latino; 6 Two or more races, non-Hispanic/Latino), 1 international. Average age 32. 258 applicants, 66% accepted, 123 enrolled. *Faculty:* 16 full-time (all women), 39 part-time/adjunct (all women). Expenses: Contact institution. *Financial support:* In 2016–17, 26 students received support. Scholarships/grants available. Financial award application deadline: 4/1; financial award applicants required to submit FAFSA. In 2016, 226 master's, 9 doctorates awarded. *Program availability:* Part-time, online only, 100% online, blended/hybrid learning. Offers nursing (MS, DNP). *Application deadline:* For fall admission, 6/1 for domestic students; for spring admission, 10/15 for domestic students; for summer admission, 2/15 for domestic students. Applications are processed on a rolling basis. *Application fee:* $60. Electronic applications accepted. *Application Contact:* Tina Heuges, Associate Director of Admissions, 215-503-1754, Fax: 215-503-7241, E-mail: tina.heuges@jefferson.edu. *Associate Dean, Graduate Programs,* Dr. Ksenia Zukowsky, 215-503-9426, E-mail: ksenia.zukowsky@jefferson.edu.

Jefferson College of Pharmacy Students: 272 full-time (173 women), 6 part-time (4 women); includes 91 minority (17 Black or African American, non-Hispanic/Latino; 71 Asian, non-Hispanic/Latino; 1 Hispanic/Latino; 2 Two or more races, non-Hispanic/Latino), 10 international. Average age 25. 541 applicants, 31% accepted, 65 enrolled. *Faculty:* 26 full-time (17 women), 15 part-time/adjunct (4 women). Expenses: Contact institution. *Financial support:* In 2016–17, 144 students received support. Federal Work-Study and scholarships/grants available. Financial award application deadline: 4/1; financial award applicants required to submit FAFSA. In 2016, 55 doctorates awarded. Offers pharmacy (Pharm D). *Application deadline:* For fall admission, 3/1 for domestic and international students. Applications are processed on a rolling basis. *Application fee:* $205. Electronic applications accepted. *Application Contact:* Dr. Mary Hess, Associate Dean, Student Affairs, 215-503-9000, E-mail: jcpapplication@jefferson.edu. *Dean,* Dr. Rebecca S. Finley, 215-503-9000, E-mail: jcpapplication@jefferson.edu.

Jefferson School of Population Health *Program availability:* Part-time, evening/weekend, online learning. Offers applied health economics and outcomes research (MS, PhD, Certificate); behavioral health science (PhD); health policy (MS, PhD, Certificate); healthcare quality and safety (MS, PhD, Certificate); population health (Certificate); public health (MPH, Certificate). Electronic applications accepted.

Sidney Kimmel Medical College Students: 1,070 full-time (533 women); includes 339 minority (24 Black or African American, non-Hispanic/Latino; 5 American Indian or Alaska Native, non-Hispanic/Latino; 237 Asian, non-Hispanic/Latino; 73 Hispanic/Latino), 37 international. Average age 23. 10,726 applicants, 42% accepted, 266 enrolled. *Faculty:* 1,215 full-time (447 women), 80 part-time/adjunct (39 women). Expenses: Contact institution. *Financial support:* In 2016–17, 514 students received support. Federal Work-Study, institutionally sponsored loans, and scholarships/grants available. Financial award application deadline: 3/1; financial award applicants required to submit FAFSA. In 2016, 281 doctorates awarded. Offers medicine (MD). *Application deadline:* For fall admission, 11/15 for domestic and international students. Applications are processed on a rolling basis. *Application fee:* $80. Electronic applications accepted. *Application Contact:* Dr. Clara Callahan, Dean for Students and Admissions, 215-955-4077, Fax: 215-955-5151, E-mail: clara.callahan@jefferson.edu. *Dean,* Dr. Mark Tykowcinski, 215-955-6980, Fax: 215-923-6939, E-mail: mark.tykowcinski@jefferson.edu.

THOMAS MORE COLLEGE, Crestview Hills, KY 41017-3495

General Information Independent-religious, coed, comprehensive institution. *Graduate housing:* On-campus housing not available.

GRADUATE UNITS

Program in Business Administration *Program availability:* Evening/weekend, 100% online. Offers business administration (MBA). Electronic applications accepted.

Program in Teacher Leader *Program availability:* Part-time, evening/weekend. Offers teacher leader (M Ed). Electronic applications accepted.

Program in Teaching *Program availability:* Part-time. Offers teaching (MAT). Electronic applications accepted.

THOMAS UNIVERSITY, Thomasville, GA 31792-7499

General Information Independent, coed, comprehensive institution. *Graduate housing:* Room and/or apartments available on a first-come, first-served basis to single students; on-campus housing not available to married students. Housing application deadline: 8/1.

GRADUATE UNITS

Department of Business Administration *Program availability:* Part-time. Offers business administration (MBA). Electronic applications accepted.

Department of Education *Program availability:* Part-time. Offers education (M Ed). Electronic applications accepted.

Department of Human Services *Program availability:* Part-time. Offers community counseling (MSCC); rehabilitation counseling (MRC). Electronic applications accepted.

Department of Nursing *Program availability:* Part-time. Offers nursing (MSN). Electronic applications accepted.

THOMPSON RIVERS UNIVERSITY, Kamloops, BC V2C 0C8, Canada

General Information Province-supported, coed, comprehensive institution. CGS member.

GRADUATE UNITS

Program in Business Administration *Program availability:* Part-time. Offers business administration (MBA).

Program in Education *Program availability:* Part-time. Offers education (M Ed).

Program in Environmental Science Offers environmental science (MS).

Program in Social Work Offers social work (MSW).

TIFFIN UNIVERSITY, Tiffin, OH 44883-2161

General Information Independent, coed, comprehensive institution. *Enrollment:* 3,350 graduate, professional, and undergraduate students; 123 full-time matriculated graduate/professional students (92 women), 929 part-time matriculated graduate/professional students (521 women). *Enrollment by degree level:* 1,048 master's, 4 other advanced degrees. *Graduate faculty:* 85 full-time (40 women), 64 part-time/adjunct (25 women). *Tuition:* Full-time $21,000; part-time $700 per credit hour. *Required fees:* $150. Tuition and fees vary according to program. *Graduate housing:* Room and/or apartments available on a first-come, first-served basis to single students; on-campus housing not available to married students. Typical cost: $9900 (including board). Room and board charges vary according to board plan, campus/location and housing facility selected. Housing application deadline: 8/1. *Student services:* Campus employment opportunities, campus safety program, career counseling, exercise/wellness program, free psychological counseling, international student services, low-cost health insurance, multicultural affairs office, services for students with disabilities. *Library facilities:* Pfeiffer Library plus 1 other. *Collection:* Books: 40,849 (physical), 125,971 (digital/electronic); Serial titles: 120 (physical), 25,420 (digital/electronic); Databases: 187. Weekly public service hours: 73.

Computer facilities: Computer purchase and lease plans are available. 280 computers available on campus for general student use. A campuswide network can be accessed from student residence rooms and from off campus. Online class registration is available.
Website: http://www.tiffin.edu/

General Application Contact: Nikki Hintze, Director of Graduate Admissions and Student Services, 800-968-6446 Ext. 3445, Fax: 419-443-5002, E-mail: hintzenm@tiffin.edu.

GRADUATE UNITS

Program in Business Administration Students: 10 full-time (4 women), 497 part-time (240 women); includes 91 minority (67 Black or African American, non-Hispanic/Latino; 1 American Indian or Alaska Native, non-Hispanic/Latino; 5 Asian, non-Hispanic/Latino; 15 Hispanic/Latino; 3 Two or more races, non-Hispanic/Latino), 102 international. Average age 31. 214 applicants, 86% accepted, 146 enrolled. Expenses: Contact institution. *Financial support:* Unspecified assistantships available. Support available to part-time students. Financial award application deadline: 7/31; financial award applicants required to submit FAFSA. In 2016, 183 master's awarded. *Program availability:* Part-time, evening/weekend, online learning. Offers finance (MBA); general management (MBA); healthcare administration (MBA); human resource management (MBA); international business (MBA); leadership (MBA); marketing (MBA); non-profit management (MBA); sports management (MBA). *Application deadline:* For fall admission, 8/15 for domestic students, 8/1 for international students; for spring admission, 1/9 for domestic students, 12/1 for international students. Applications are processed on a rolling basis. *Application fee:* $50. Electronic applications accepted. *Application Contact:* Nikki Hintze, Director of Graduate and Distance Education Academic Advising, 800-968-6446 Ext. 3596, Fax: 419-443-5002, E-mail: hintzenm@tiffin.edu. *Dean of Graduate Studies,* Dr. Bonnie Tiell, 419-448-3261, Fax: 419-443-5002, E-mail: btiell@tiffin.edu.

Program in Criminal Justice Students: 83 full-time (61 women), 191 part-time (109 women); includes 85 minority (71 Black or African American, non-Hispanic/Latino; 6 Hispanic/Latino; 1 Native Hawaiian or other Pacific Islander, non-Hispanic/Latino; 7 Two or more races, non-Hispanic/Latino), 6 international. Average age 31. Expenses: Contact institution. *Financial support:* Available to part-time students. Application deadline: 7/31; applicants required to submit FAFSA. In 2016, 59 master's awarded. *Program availability:* Part-time, evening/weekend, 100% online, blended/hybrid learning. Offers criminal justice (MS). *Application deadline:* For fall admission, 9/3 for domestic students, 8/1 for international students; for spring admission, 1/9 priority date for domestic students, 12/1 for international students. Applications are processed on a rolling basis. *Application fee:* $50. Electronic applications accepted. *Application Contact:* Nikki Hintze, Director of Graduate and Distance Education Academic Advising, 800-968-6446 Ext. 3596, Fax: 419-443-5002, E-mail: cashenk@tiffin.edu. *Dean of Criminal Justice and Security Studies,* Dr. Kevin Cashen, 419-448-3322, Fax: 419-443-5002, E-mail: cashenk@tiffin.edu.

Program in Education Students: 99 part-time (75 women); includes 26 minority (20 Black or African American, non-Hispanic/Latino; 1 Asian, non-Hispanic/Latino; 4 Hispanic/Latino; 1 Two or more races, non-Hispanic/Latino). Average age 32. 31 applicants, 90% accepted, 24 enrolled. Expenses: Contact institution. *Financial support:* Unspecified assistantships available. In 2016, 45 master's awarded. *Program availability:* Part-time, evening/weekend, online only, 100% online, blended/hybrid learning. Offers educational technology management (M Ed); higher education administration (M Ed). *Application deadline:* Applications are processed on a rolling basis. Electronic applications accepted. *Application Contact:* Nikki Hintze, Director of Graduate Admissions and Student Services, 800-968-6446 Ext. 3445, Fax: 419-443-5002, E-mail: hintzenm@tiffin.edu.

Program in Humanities Students: 17 full-time (15 women), 116 part-time (75 women); includes 25 minority (15 Black or African American, non-Hispanic/Latino; 2 Asian, non-Hispanic/Latino; 6 Hispanic/Latino; 2 Two or more races, non-Hispanic/Latino). Average age 36. 84 applicants, 80% accepted, 43 enrolled. Expenses: Contact institution. *Financial support:* Unspecified assistantships available. Financial award applicants required to submit FAFSA. In 2016, 42 master's awarded. *Program availability:* Part-time, evening/weekend, online only, 100% online, blended/hybrid learning. Offers art and visual media (MH); communication (MH); creative writing (MH); English (MH); film studies (MH); humanities (MH); individualized studies (MH). *Application deadline:* For fall admission, 9/1 for domestic students; for spring admission, 1/9 for domestic students. Applications are processed on a rolling basis. *Application fee:* $50. Electronic applications accepted. *Application Contact:* Nikki Hintze, Director of Graduate and Distance Education Academic Advising, 800-968-6446 Ext. 3596, Fax: 419-443-5002, E-mail: hintzenm@tiffin.edu. *Program Chair,* Dr. Jason Slone, 419-448-5851, Fax: 419-443-5002, E-mail: slonedj@tiffin.edu.

Program in Psychology Students: 13 full-time (12 women), 21 part-time (17 women); includes 10 minority (8 Black or African American, non-Hispanic/Latino; 2 Hispanic/Latino). Average age 30. 34 applicants, 82% accepted, 20 enrolled. Expenses: Contact institution. In 2016, 1 master's awarded. *Program availability:* Part-time, evening/weekend, online only, 100% online. Offers psychology (MS). *Application deadline:* Applications are processed on a rolling basis. Electronic applications accepted. *Application Contact:* Nikki Hintze, Director of Graduate Admissions and Student Services, 800-968-6446 Ext. 3445, Fax: 419-443-5002, E-mail: hintzenm@tiffin.edu.

TORONTO SCHOOL OF THEOLOGY, Toronto, ON M5S 2C3, Canada

General Information Independent-religious, coed, graduate-only institution.

GRADUATE UNITS

Graduate Programs *Program availability:* Online learning. Offers theology (M Div, MA, MAMS, MPS, MRE, MSM, MTS, Th M, D Min, PhD, Th D). Electronic applications accepted.

TOURO COLLEGE, New York, NY 10010

General Information Independent, coed, comprehensive institution. *Enrollment:* 1,760 full-time matriculated graduate/professional students (1,296 women), 2,271 part-time matriculated graduate/professional students (1,831 women). *Enrollment by degree level:* 3,989 master's, 42 doctoral. *Graduate faculty:* 94 full-time, 157 part-time/adjunct. *Student services:* Career counseling, free psychological counseling, low-cost health insurance. *Library facilities:* Touro College Library plus 14 others.

Computer facilities: A campuswide network can be accessed from off campus. Online class registration is available.
Website: http://www.touro.edu/

General Application Contact: Dr. Benjamin Enoma, Director, Graduate Admissions, 212-463-0400.

GRADUATE UNITS

Graduate School of Education Students: 578 full-time (483 women), 1,932 part-time (1,626 women); includes 749 minority (318 Black or African American, non-Hispanic/Latino; 5 American Indian or Alaska Native, non-Hispanic/Latino; 108 Asian, non-Hispanic/Latino; 288 Hispanic/Latino; 2 Native Hawaiian or other Pacific Islander, non-Hispanic/Latino; 28 Two or more races, non-Hispanic/Latino), 17 international. Average age 32. 1,422 applicants, 50% accepted, 675 enrolled. *Faculty:* 52 full-time (34 women), 199 part-time/adjunct (136 women). Expenses: Contact institution. *Financial*

---

support: Federal Work-Study available. Financial award applicants required to submit FAFSA. In 2016, 6 master's awarded. *Program availability:* Part-time, evening/weekend, online learning. Offers education and special education (MS); education biology (MS); instructional technology (MS); mathematics education (MS); school leadership (MS); teaching English to speakers of other languages (MS); teaching literacy (MS). *Application deadline:* For fall admission, 8/26 for domestic students, 7/15 for international students; for spring admission, 12/31 for domestic students, 12/15 for international students. Applications are processed on a rolling basis. *Application fee:* $50. *Application Contact:* Luna Feliciano, Admissions, 212-463-0400. *Dean,* Dr. Arnold Spinner, 212-463-0400 Ext. 5561, Fax: 212-462-4889, E-mail: aspinner@touro.edu.

Graduate School of Jewish Studies Students: 5 full-time (2 women), 29 part-time (16 women), 1 international. Average age 38. *Faculty:* 4 full-time (2 women), 5 part-time/adjunct (2 women). Expenses: Contact institution. *Financial support:* Tuition waivers (full and partial) available. Support available to part-time students. *Program availability:* Part-time. Offers Jewish studies (MA). *Application fee:* $50. *Application Contact:* Karen Rubin, Executive Assistant to the Dean, 212-463-0400 Ext. 5581, E-mail: karen.rubin@touro.edu. *Dean,* Dr. Michael Shmidman, 212-213-2230.

Graduate School of Social Work Students: 226 full-time (194 women), 85 part-time (66 women); includes 165 minority (100 Black or African American, non-Hispanic/Latino; 6 Asian, non-Hispanic/Latino; 56 Hispanic/Latino; 3 Two or more races, non-Hispanic/Latino), 4 international. Average age 34. *Faculty:* 9 full-time (6 women), 54 part-time/adjunct (32 women). Expenses: Contact institution. Offers social work (MSW). *Application Contact:* Peter Stewart, Director of Recruitment, Admissions and Enrollment Management, 212-463-0400 Ext. 5630, Fax: 212-627-3693, E-mail: peter.stewart@touro.edu. *Dean,* Dr. Steven Huberman, 212-463-0400 Ext. 5269, E-mail: msw@touro.edu.

Graduate School of Technology Students: 100 full-time (37 women), 122 part-time (59 women); includes 78 minority (31 Black or African American, non-Hispanic/Latino; 1 American Indian or Alaska Native, non-Hispanic/Latino; 25 Asian, non-Hispanic/Latino; 18 Hispanic/Latino; 3 Two or more races, non-Hispanic/Latino), 83 international. Average age 34. *Faculty:* 18 part-time/adjunct (6 women). Expenses: Contact institution. Offers information systems (MS); instructional technology (MS); Web and multimedia design (MA). *Application Contact:* Jack Romano, Program Director, 212-463-0400 Ext. 5462. *Dean of the Graduate School of Technology,* Dr. Issac Herskowitz, 202-463-0400 Ext. 5231, E-mail: issac.herskowitz@touro.edu.

Jacob D. Fuchsberg Law Center Students: 445 full-time (245 women), 22 part-time (15 women); includes 166 minority (47 Black or African American, non-Hispanic/Latino; 2 American Indian or Alaska Native, non-Hispanic/Latino; 41 Asian, non-Hispanic/Latino; 72 Hispanic/Latino; 4 Two or more races, non-Hispanic/Latino), 9 international. Average age 30. *Faculty:* 35 full-time (17 women), 30 part-time/adjunct (7 women). Expenses: Contact institution. *Financial support:* Fellowships, career-related internships or fieldwork, and Federal Work-Study available. Support available to part-time students. Financial award application deadline: 5/1. *Program availability:* Part-time, evening/weekend. Offers general law (LL M); law (JD); U.S. legal studies (LL M). JD/MBA and JD/MPA offered with Long Island University-LIU Post; JD/MSW offered with Stony Brook University, State University of New York. *Application deadline:* Applications are processed on a rolling basis. *Application fee:* $60. *Application Contact:* Dr. Susan Thompson, Office of Admissions, 631-761-7010, E-mail: admissions@tourolaw.edu. *Dean,* Dr. Harry Ballan, 631-761-7100.

School of Health Sciences Students: 628 full-time (470 women), 113 part-time (73 women); includes 143 minority (31 Black or African American, non-Hispanic/Latino; 1 American Indian or Alaska Native, non-Hispanic/Latino; 61 Asian, non-Hispanic/Latino; 42 Hispanic/Latino; 1 Native Hawaiian or other Pacific Islander, non-Hispanic/Latino; 7 Two or more races, non-Hispanic/Latino), 63 international. Average age 28. *Faculty:* 81 full-time (55 women), 77 part-time/adjunct (46 women). Expenses: Contact institution. *Financial support:* Fellowships available. Offers industrial-organizational psychology (MS); mental health counseling (MS); occupational therapy (MS); physical therapy (DPT); physician assistant (MS); speech-language pathology (MS). *Application Contact:* Brian J. Diele, Director of Student Administrative Services, 631-665-1600 Ext. 6311, E-mail: brian.diele@touro.edu. *Dean, School of Health Sciences,* Dr. Louis Primavera, 516-673-3200, E-mail: louis.primavera@touro.edu.

TOURO UNIVERSITY CALIFORNIA, Vallejo, CA 94592

General Information Independent, coed, graduate-only institution. *Graduate housing:* On-campus housing not available. *Research affiliation:* University of California San Francisco (cancer, HIV/AIDS), Genetech (cancer), National Institutes of Health (diabetes, cardiac arrest in teens).

GRADUATE UNITS

Graduate Programs *Program availability:* Part-time, evening/weekend. Offers education (MA); medical health sciences (MS); osteopathic medicine (DO); pharmacy (Pharm D); public health (MPH). Electronic applications accepted.

TOWSON UNIVERSITY, Towson, MD 21252-0001

General Information State-supported, coed, university. CGS member. *Enrollment:* 22,343 graduate, professional, and undergraduate students; 1,080 full-time matriculated graduate/professional students (773 women), 2,005 part-time matriculated graduate/professional students (1,470 women). *Enrollment by degree level:* 2,699 master's, 155 doctoral, 231 other advanced degrees. *Graduate faculty:* 303 full-time (158 women), 120 part-time/adjunct (79 women). Tuition, state resident: full-time $7580; part-time $379 per unit. Tuition, nonresident: full-time $15,700; part-time $785 per unit. *Required fees:* $2480. *Graduate housing:* On-campus housing not available. *Student services:* Campus employment opportunities, campus safety program, career counseling, child daycare facilities, exercise/wellness program, free psychological counseling, international student services, low-cost health insurance, multicultural affairs office, services for students with disabilities, teacher training, writing training. *Library facilities:* Cook Library. *Collection:* Books: 400,658 (physical), 264,958 (digital/electronic); Serial titles: 525 (physical), 48,289 (digital/electronic); Databases: 192. Weekly public service hours: 109; study areas open 24 hours, 5–7 days a week; students can reserve study rooms. *Research affiliation:* Exelon Generation Company (biology), Prometheus Computing (computer science), Mutch Associates (chemistry), Intelligent Fusion (computer science), Plant Sensory Systems (computer science), RTR Technologies (computer science).

Computer facilities: 2,500 computers available on campus for general student use. A campuswide network can be accessed from student residence rooms and from off campus. Online class registration is available.
Website: http://www.towson.edu/

General Application Contact: Coverley Beidleman, Assistant Director of Graduate Admissions, 410-704-2113, Fax: 410-704-3030, E-mail: grads@towson.edu.

Towson University

GRADUATE UNITS

Baltimore Hebrew Institute Students: 6 full-time (5 women), 11 part-time (6 women); includes 2 minority (1 Black or African American, non-Hispanic/Latino; 1 Hispanic/Latino), 1 international. Expenses: Contact institution. Offers Jewish communal service (MAJCS, Postbaccalaureate Certificate); Jewish education (Postbaccalaureate Certificate); Jewish studies (MAJS). *Application deadline:* Applications are processed on a rolling basis. *Application fee:* $45. Electronic applications accepted. *Application Contact:* Coverley Beidleman, Assistant Director of Graduate Admissions, 410-704-2113, Fax: 410-704-3030, E-mail: grads@towson.edu. *Director,* Jill Max, 410-704-7120, E-mail: jmax@towson.edu.

Program in Accounting and Business Advisory Services Students: 27 full-time (12 women), 14 part-time (6 women); includes 12 minority (4 Black or African American, non-Hispanic/Latino; 8 Asian, non-Hispanic/Latino), 10 international. Expenses: Contact institution. *Program availability:* Part-time, evening/weekend. Offers accounting and business advisory services (MS). Program offered jointly with University of Baltimore. *Application deadline:* Applications are processed on a rolling basis. *Application fee:* $45. Electronic applications accepted. *Application Contact:* University Admissions, 410-704-2113, Fax: 410-704-3030, E-mail: grads@towson.edu. *Graduate Program Director,* Dr. Martin Freedman, 410-704-4143, E-mail: mfreedman@towson.edu.

Program in Action Research for School Improvement Expenses: Contact institution. Offers action research for school improvement (Postbaccalaureate Certificate). *Application deadline:* Applications are processed on a rolling basis. *Application fee:* $45. Electronic applications accepted. *Application Contact:* Coverley Beidleman, Assistant Director of Graduate Admissions, 410-704-2113, Fax: 410-704-3030, E-mail: grads@towson.edu. *Director,* Carla Finkelstein, 410-704-2974, E-mail: cfinkelstein@towson.edu.

Program in Applied and Industrial Mathematics Students: 14 full-time (9 women), 12 part-time (6 women); includes 5 minority (1 Black or African American, non-Hispanic/Latino; 1 Asian, non-Hispanic/Latino; 2 Hispanic/Latino; 1 Two or more races, non-Hispanic/Latino), 7 international. Expenses: Contact institution. *Financial support:* Application deadline: 4/1; applicants required to submit FAFSA. *Program availability:* Part-time, evening/weekend. Offers applied and industrial mathematics (MS). *Application deadline:* Applications are processed on a rolling basis. *Application fee:* $45. Electronic applications accepted. *Application Contact:* Coverley Beidleman, Assistant Director of Graduate Admissions, 410-704-2113, Fax: 410-704-3030, E-mail: grads@towson.edu. *Graduate Program Director,* Dr. Tatyana Sorokina, 410-704-3308, E-mail: tsorokina@towson.edu.

Program in Applied Information Technology Students: 135 full-time (50 women), 154 part-time (50 women); includes 119 minority (81 Black or African American, non-Hispanic/Latino; 26 Asian, non-Hispanic/Latino; 4 Hispanic/Latino; 8 Two or more races, non-Hispanic/Latino), 82 international. Expenses: Contact institution. Offers applied information technology (MS, D Sc); database management systems (Postbaccalaureate Certificate); information security and assurance (Postbaccalaureate Certificate); information systems management (Postbaccalaureate Certificate); Internet applications development (Postbaccalaureate Certificate); networking technologies (Postbaccalaureate Certificate); software engineering (Postbaccalaureate Certificate). *Application deadline:* Applications are processed on a rolling basis. *Application fee:* $45. Electronic applications accepted. *Application Contact:* Coverley Beidleman, Assistant Director of Graduate Admissions, 410-704-2113, Fax: 410-704-3030, E-mail: grads@towson.edu. *Graduate Program Director,* Dr. Jinjuan Feng, 410-704-3463, E-mail: ait@towson.edu.

Program in Applied Physics Students: 6 full-time (0 women), 7 part-time (1 woman); includes 1 minority (Black or African American, non-Hispanic/Latino), 1 international. Expenses: Contact institution. Offers applied physics (MS). *Application deadline:* Applications are processed on a rolling basis. *Application fee:* $45. Electronic applications accepted. *Application Contact:* Coverley Beidleman, Assistant Director of Graduate Admissions, 410-704-2113, Fax: 410-704-3030, E-mail: grads@towson.edu. *Graduate Program Director,* Dr. Raj Kolagani, 410-704-3134, E-mail: rkolagani@towson.edu.

Program in Art Education Students: 20 part-time (16 women); includes 6 minority (2 Black or African American, non-Hispanic/Latino; 1 Asian, non-Hispanic/Latino; 1 Hispanic/Latino; 2 Two or more races, non-Hispanic/Latino). Expenses: Contact institution. *Financial support:* Application deadline: 4/1. *Program availability:* Part-time, evening/weekend. Offers art education (M Ed). *Application deadline:* Applications are processed on a rolling basis. *Application fee:* $45. Electronic applications accepted. *Application Contact:* Coverley Beidleman, Assistant Director of Graduate Admissions, 410-704-2113, Fax: 410-704-3030, E-mail: grads@towson.edu. *Graduate Program Director,* Dr. Ray Martens, 410-704-3819, E-mail: rmartens@towson.edu.

Program in Arts Integration Students: 29 part-time (28 women). Expenses: Contact institution. Offers arts integration (Postbaccalaureate Certificate). Program offered jointly with Johns Hopkins University, University of Maryland, College Park and University of Maryland, Baltimore County. *Application deadline:* Applications are processed on a rolling basis. *Application fee:* $45. Electronic applications accepted. *Application Contact:* Coverley Beidleman, Assistant Director of Graduate Admissions, 410-704-2113, Fax: 410-704-3030, E-mail: grads@towson.edu. *Program Director,* Prof. Susan Rotkovitz, 410-704-3658, E-mail: srotkovitz@towson.edu.

Program in Audiology Students: 47 full-time (45 women), 2 part-time (both women); includes 4 minority (all Black or African American, non-Hispanic/Latino), 1 international. Expenses: Contact institution. *Financial support:* Application deadline: 4/1. Offers audiology (Au D). *Application deadline:* For fall admission, 2/1 for domestic students. *Application fee:* $45. Electronic applications accepted. *Application Contact:* Coverley Beidleman, Assistant Director of Graduate Admissions, 410-704-2113, Fax: 410-704-3030, E-mail: grads@towson.edu. *Graduate Program Director,* Dr. Jennifer Smart, 410-704-5903, E-mail: audiology@towson.edu.

Program in Autism Studies Students: 8 full-time (all women), 48 part-time (41 women); includes 6 minority (4 Black or African American, non-Hispanic/Latino; 2 Hispanic/Latino). Expenses: Contact institution. Offers autism studies (Postbaccalaureate Certificate). *Application deadline:* Applications are processed on a rolling basis. *Application fee:* $45. Electronic applications accepted. *Application Contact:* Coverley Beidleman, Assistant Director of Graduate Admissions, 410-704-2113, Fax: 410-704-3030, E-mail: grads@towson.edu. *Graduate Program Director,* Dr. Connie Anderson, 410-704-4640, E-mail: connieanderson@towson.edu.

Program in Biology Students: 16 full-time (10 women), 21 part-time (13 women); includes 9 minority (5 Black or African American, non-Hispanic/Latino; 2 Asian, non-Hispanic/Latino; 1 Hispanic/Latino; 1 Two or more races, non-Hispanic/Latino), 3 international. Expenses: Contact institution. *Financial support:* Application deadline: 4/1. *Program availability:* Part-time, evening/weekend. Offers biology (MS). *Application fee:* $45. Electronic applications accepted. *Application Contact:* Coverley Beidleman, Assistant Director of Graduate Admissions, 410-704-2113, Fax: 410-704-3030, E-mail:

grads@towson.edu. *Graduate Program Co-Director,* Dr. Peko Tsuji, 410-704-4117, E-mail: ptsuji@towson.edu.

Program in Child Life, Administration and Family Collaboration Students: 13 full-time (12 women), 11 part-time (all women); includes 4 minority (1 Black or African American, non-Hispanic/Latino; 2 Asian, non-Hispanic/Latino; 1 Hispanic/Latino). Expenses: Contact institution. Offers child life, administration and family collaboration (MS). *Application fee:* $45. Electronic applications accepted. *Application Contact:* Coverley Beidleman, Assistant Director of Graduate Admissions, 410-704-2113, Fax: 410-704-3030, E-mail: grads@towson.edu. *Graduate Program Director,* Prof. Lisa Martinelli Beasley, 410-704-3766, E-mail: lmartinelli@towson.edu.

Program in Clinician to Administrator Transition Students: 3 full-time (all women), 19 part-time (17 women); includes 5 minority (4 Black or African American, non-Hispanic/Latino; 1 Asian, non-Hispanic/Latino). Expenses: Contact institution. *Financial support:* Application deadline: 4/1. Offers clinician to administrator transition (MS, Postbaccalaureate Certificate). *Application deadline:* Applications are processed on a rolling basis. *Application fee:* $45. Electronic applications accepted. *Application Contact:* Coverley Beidleman, Assistant Director of Graduate Admissions, 410-704-2113, Fax: 410-704-3030, E-mail: grads@towson.edu. *Graduate Program Director,* Dr. Marcie Weinstein, 410-704-4049, E-mail: mweinstein@towson.edu.

Program in Communications Management Students: 3 full-time (2 women), 18 part-time (14 women); includes 6 minority (all Black or African American, non-Hispanic/Latino). Expenses: Contact institution. *Financial support:* Application deadline: 4/1. Offers communications management (MS). *Application deadline:* For fall admission, 1/15 for domestic students. *Application fee:* $45. Electronic applications accepted. *Application Contact:* Coverley Beidleman, Assistant Director of Graduate Admissions, 410-704-2113, Fax: 410-704-3030, E-mail: grads@towson.edu. *Graduate Program Director,* Dr. Beth Haller, 410-704-2442, E-mail: bhaller@towson.edu.

Program in Computer Science Students: 46 full-time (14 women), 91 part-time (25 women); includes 38 minority (12 Black or African American, non-Hispanic/Latino; 21 Asian, non-Hispanic/Latino; 2 Hispanic/Latino; 3 Two or more races, non-Hispanic/Latino), 29 international. Expenses: Contact institution. *Financial support:* Application deadline: 4/1. *Program availability:* Part-time, evening/weekend. Offers computer science (MS). *Application deadline:* Applications are processed on a rolling basis. *Application fee:* $45. Electronic applications accepted. *Application Contact:* Coverley Beidleman, Assistant Director of Graduate Admissions, 410-704-2113, Fax: 410-704-3030, E-mail: grads@towson.edu. *Graduate Program Director,* Dr. Yanggon Kim, 410-704-3782, E-mail: ykim@towson.edu.

Program in Early Childhood Education Students: 3 full-time (2 women), 107 part-time (all women); includes 15 minority (7 Black or African American, non-Hispanic/Latino; 2 Asian, non-Hispanic/Latino; 5 Hispanic/Latino; 1 Native Hawaiian or other Pacific Islander, non-Hispanic/Latino), 1 international. Expenses: Contact institution. *Financial support:* Application deadline: 4/1. *Program availability:* Part-time, evening/weekend. Offers early childhood education (M Ed, CAS). *Application deadline:* Applications are processed on a rolling basis. *Application fee:* $45. Electronic applications accepted. *Application Contact:* Coverley Beidleman, Assistant Director of Graduate Admissions, 410-704-2113, Fax: 410-704-3030, E-mail: grads@towson.edu. *Graduate Program Director,* Dr. Janese Daniels, 410-704-4832, E-mail: ecedgrad@towson.edu.

Program in e-Business and Technology Management Students: 2 full-time (1 woman), 22 part-time (8 women); includes 7 minority (3 Black or African American, non-Hispanic/Latino; 1 Asian, non-Hispanic/Latino; 3 Two or more races, non-Hispanic/Latino), 2 international. Expenses: Contact institution. Offers project, program and portfolio management (Postbaccalaureate Certificate); supply chain management (MS, Postbaccalaureate Certificate). *Application deadline:* Applications are processed on a rolling basis. *Application fee:* $45. Electronic applications accepted. *Application Contact:* Coverley Beidleman, Assistant Director of Graduate Admissions, 410-704-2113, Fax: 410-704-3030, E-mail: grads@towson.edu. *Director,* Dr. Tobin Porterfield, 410-704-3265, E-mail: tporterfield@towson.edu.

Program in Elementary Education Students: 5 part-time (4 women); includes 2 minority (both Black or African American, non-Hispanic/Latino). Expenses: Contact institution. *Financial support:* Application deadline: 4/1. *Program availability:* Part-time, evening/weekend. Offers elementary education (M Ed). *Application fee:* $45. Electronic applications accepted. *Application Contact:* Coverley Beidleman, Assistant Director of Graduate Admissions, 410-704-2113, Fax: 410-704-3030, E-mail: grads@towson.edu. *Graduate Program Director,* Dr. Todd Kenreich, 410-704-4956, E-mail: scedmed@towson.edu.

Program in Environmental Science Students: 5 full-time (2 women), 27 part-time (17 women); includes 3 minority (1 Black or African American, non-Hispanic/Latino; 1 Asian, non-Hispanic/Latino; 1 Hispanic/Latino). Expenses: Contact institution. *Financial support:* Application deadline: 4/1. *Program availability:* Part-time, evening/weekend. Offers environmental science (MS, Postbaccalaureate Certificate). *Application deadline:* Applications are processed on a rolling basis. *Application fee:* $45. Electronic applications accepted. *Application Contact:* Coverley Beidleman, Assistant Director of Graduate Admissions, 410-704-2113, Fax: 410-704-3030, E-mail: grads@towson.edu. *Graduate Program Director,* Dr. David Ownby, 410-704-2946, E-mail: downby@towson.edu.

Program in Family-Professional Collaboration Students: 15 full-time (14 women), 13 part-time (all women); includes 6 minority (3 Black or African American, non-Hispanic/Latino; 2 Asian, non-Hispanic/Latino; 1 Hispanic/Latino). Expenses: Contact institution. Offers family-professional collaboration (Postbaccalaureate Certificate). *Application deadline:* Applications are processed on a rolling basis. *Application fee:* $45. Electronic applications accepted. *Application Contact:* Coverley Beidleman, Assistant Director of Graduate Admissions, 410-704-2113, Fax: 410-704-3030, E-mail: grads@towson.edu. *Graduate Program Director,* Dr. Catherine Breneman, 410-704-4871, E-mail: cbreneman@towson.edu.

Program in Forensic Science Students: 42 full-time (35 women), 9 part-time (8 women); includes 16 minority (8 Black or African American, non-Hispanic/Latino; 3 Asian, non-Hispanic/Latino; 1 Hispanic/Latino; 4 Two or more races, non-Hispanic/Latino), 3 international. Expenses: Contact institution. Offers forensic science (MS). *Application deadline:* Applications are processed on a rolling basis. *Application fee:* $45. Electronic applications accepted. *Application Contact:* Coverley Beidleman, Assistant Director of Graduate Admissions, 410-704-2113, Fax: 410-704-3030, E-mail: grads@towson.edu. *Graduate Program Director,* Mark Profili, 410-704-2668, E-mail: mprofili@towson.edu.

Program in Geography and Environmental Planning Students: 7 full-time (2 women), 12 part-time (4 women); includes 3 minority (2 Black or African American, non-Hispanic/Latino; 1 Two or more races, non-Hispanic/Latino), 1 international. Expenses: Contact institution. *Financial support:* Application deadline: 4/1. *Program availability:* Part-time, evening/weekend. Offers geography and environmental planning (MA). *Application deadline:* Applications are processed on a rolling basis. *Application fee:* $45.

Electronic applications accepted. *Application Contact:* Coverley Beidleman, Assistant Director of Graduate Admissions, 410-704-2113, Fax: 410-704-3030, E-mail: grads@towson.edu. *Graduate Program Director,* Dr. Charles Schmitz, 410-704-2966, E-mail: cschmitz@towson.edu.

Program in Health Science Students: 21 full-time (17 women), 50 part-time (44 women); includes 35 minority (28 Black or African American, non-Hispanic/Latino; 4 Asian, non-Hispanic/Latino; 3 Hispanic/Latino), 2 international. Expenses: Contact institution. *Financial support:* Application deadline: 4/1. *Program availability:* Part-time, evening/weekend. Offers health science (MS). *Application deadline:* Applications are processed on a rolling basis. *Application fee:* $45. Electronic applications accepted. *Application Contact:* Coverley Beidleman, Assistant Director of Graduate Admissions, 410-704-2113, Fax: 410-704-3030, E-mail: grads@towson.edu. *Graduate Program Director,* Dr. Niya Werts, 410-704-2378, E-mail: nwerts@towson.edu.

Program in Human Resource Development Students: 13 full-time (all women), 248 part-time (192 women); includes 59 minority (36 Black or African American, non-Hispanic/Latino; 1 American Indian or Alaska Native, non-Hispanic/Latino; 7 Asian, non-Hispanic/Latino; 7 Hispanic/Latino; 8 Two or more races, non-Hispanic/Latino). Expenses: Contact institution. *Financial support:* Application deadline: 4/1. *Program availability:* Part-time, evening/weekend. Offers education leadership (MS); general (MS). *Application deadline:* Applications are processed on a rolling basis. *Application fee:* $45. Electronic applications accepted. *Application Contact:* Coverley Beidleman, Assistant Director of Graduate Admissions, 410-704-2113, Fax: 410-704-3030, E-mail: grads@towson.edu. *Graduate Program Director,* Dr. Abby Mello, 410-704-3364, E-mail: amello@towson.edu.

Program in Instructional Technology Students: 26 full-time (20 women), 214 part-time (186 women); includes 26 minority (17 Black or African American, non-Hispanic/Latino; 2 Asian, non-Hispanic/Latino; 5 Hispanic/Latino; 2 Two or more races, non-Hispanic/Latino), 3 international. Expenses: Contact institution. *Financial support:* Application deadline: 4/1. *Program availability:* Part-time, evening/weekend. Offers instructional design and training (MS). *Application deadline:* For fall admission, 8/1 for domestic students, 7/15 for international students. *Application fee:* $45. Electronic applications accepted. *Application Contact:* Coverley Beidleman, Assistant Director of Graduate Admissions, 410-704-2113, Fax: 410-704-3030, E-mail: grads@towson.edu. *Graduate Program Director,* Dr. Gilda Martinez-Alba, 410-704-2576, E-mail: gmartinez@towson.edu.

Program in Integrated Homeland Security Management Students: 5 full-time (3 women), 27 part-time (15 women); includes 15 minority (12 Black or African American, non-Hispanic/Latino; 1 Asian, non-Hispanic/Latino; 1 Hispanic/Latino; 1 Two or more races, non-Hispanic/Latino). Expenses: Contact institution. *Financial support:* Application deadline: 4/1. *Program availability:* Part-time, evening/weekend. Offers integrated homeland security management (MS); security assessment and management (Postbaccalaureate Certificate). *Application deadline:* Applications are processed on a rolling basis. *Application fee:* $45. Electronic applications accepted. *Application Contact:* Coverley Beidleman, Assistant Director of Graduate Admissions, 410-704-2113, Fax: 410-704-3030, E-mail: grads@towson.edu. *Graduate Program Director,* Dr. Joseph Clark, 410-704-4490, E-mail: jrclark@towson.edu.

Program in Integrated STEM Instructional Leadership Students: 14 part-time (12 women); includes 1 minority (Two or more races, non-Hispanic/Latino). Expenses: Contact institution. Offers integrated STEM instructional leadership (Postbaccalaureate Certificate). Electronic applications accepted. *Application Contact:* Coverley Beidleman, Assistant Director of Graduate Admissions, 410-704-2113, Fax: 410-704-3030, E-mail: grads@towson.edu. *Director,* Dr. Pam Lottero-Perdue, 410-704-4598, E-mail: plotteroperdue@towson.edu.

Program in Interactive Media Design Students: 9 part-time (4 women); includes 1 minority (Black or African American, non-Hispanic/Latino). Expenses: Contact institution. *Program availability:* Online learning. Offers interactive media design (Postbaccalaureate Certificate). *Application deadline:* Applications are processed on a rolling basis. *Application fee:* $45. Electronic applications accepted. *Application Contact:* Coverley Beidleman, Assistant Director of Graduate Admissions, 410-704-2113, Fax: 410-704-3030, E-mail: grads@towson.edu. *Graduate Program Director,* Prof. Bridget Sullivan, 410-704-2802, E-mail: bsullivan@towson.edu.

Program in Interdisciplinary Arts Infusion Students: 20 part-time (19 women); includes 6 minority (5 Black or African American, non-Hispanic/Latino; 1 Hispanic/Latino). Expenses: Contact institution. Offers interdisciplinary arts infusion (MA). *Application deadline:* For fall admission, 4/22 priority date for domestic students. *Application Contact:* Coverley Beidleman, Assistant Director of Graduate Admissions, 410-704-2113, Fax: 410-704-3030, E-mail: grads@towson.edu. *Director,* Dr. Kate Collins, 410-704-5614, E-mail: maiai@towson.edu.

Program in Marketing Intelligence Students: 11 full-time (7 women), 18 part-time (12 women); includes 9 minority (5 Black or African American, non-Hispanic/Latino; 2 Asian, non-Hispanic/Latino; 1 Hispanic/Latino; 1 Two or more races, non-Hispanic/Latino), 9 international. Expenses: Contact institution. Offers marketing intelligence (MS). *Application Contact:* Coverley Beidleman, Assistant Director of Graduate Admissions, 410-704-2113, Fax: 410-704-3030, E-mail: grads@towson.edu. *Director,* Dr. Philippe Duverger, 410-704-3538, E-mail: pduverger@towson.edu.

Program in Mathematics Education Students: 1 (woman) full-time, 34 part-time (27 women); includes 4 minority (1 Black or African American, non-Hispanic/Latino; 2 Asian, non-Hispanic/Latino; 1 Two or more races, non-Hispanic/Latino). Expenses: Contact institution. *Financial support:* Application deadline: 4/1. *Program availability:* Part-time, evening/weekend. Offers mathematics education (MS). *Application deadline:* Applications are processed on a rolling basis. *Application fee:* $45. Electronic applications accepted. *Application Contact:* Coverley Beidleman, Assistant Director of Graduate Admissions, 410-704-2113, Fax: 410-704-3030, E-mail: grads@towson.edu. *Graduate Program Director,* Dr. Maureen Yarnevich, 410-704-2988, E-mail: myarnevich@towson.edu.

Program in Music Education Students: 6 full-time (2 women), 17 part-time (13 women); includes 2 minority (both Hispanic/Latino). Expenses: Contact institution. *Financial support:* Application deadline: 4/1. *Program availability:* Part-time, evening/weekend. Offers music education (MS, Postbaccalaureate Certificate). *Application deadline:* Applications are processed on a rolling basis. *Application fee:* $45. Electronic applications accepted. *Application Contact:* Coverley Beidleman, Assistant Director of Graduate Admissions, 410-704-2113, Fax: 410-704-3030, E-mail: grads@towson.edu. *Graduate Program Director,* Dr. Melissa McCabe, 410-704-5175, E-mail: mmccabe@towson.edu.

Program in Music Performance and Composition Students: 11 full-time (7 women), 7 part-time (4 women); includes 8 minority (4 Black or African American, non-Hispanic/Latino; 1 Asian, non-Hispanic/Latino; 1 Hispanic/Latino; 2 Two or more races, non-Hispanic/Latino), 1 international. Expenses: Contact institution. *Financial support:* Application deadline: 4/1. *Program availability:* Part-time, evening/weekend. Offers

music performance and composition (MM). *Application deadline:* Applications are processed on a rolling basis. *Application fee:* $45. Electronic applications accepted. *Application Contact:* Coverley Beidleman, Assistant Director of Graduate Admissions, 410-704-2113, Fax: 410-704-3030, E-mail: grads@towson.edu. *Graduate Program Director,* Dr. Terry Ewell, 410-704-2824, E-mail: tewell@towson.edu.

Program in Nursing Students: 12 full-time (10 women), 31 part-time (27 women); includes 18 minority (15 Black or African American, non-Hispanic/Latino; 2 Asian, non-Hispanic/Latino; 1 Hispanic/Latino), 1 international. Expenses: Contact institution. *Financial support:* Application deadline: 4/1. *Program availability:* Part-time. Offers nursing education (Postbaccalaureate Certificate). *Application deadline:* Applications are processed on a rolling basis. *Application fee:* $45. Electronic applications accepted. *Application Contact:* Coverley Beidleman, Assistant Director of Graduate Admissions, 410-704-2113, Fax: 410-704-3030, E-mail: grads@towson.edu. *Graduate Program Director,* Dr. Nikki Austin, 410-704-2067, E-mail: eaustin@towson.edu.

Program in Occupational Science Students: 4 full-time (all women), 7 part-time (3 women); includes 4 minority (1 Black or African American, non-Hispanic/Latino; 1 Asian, non-Hispanic/Latino; 2 Two or more races, non-Hispanic/Latino), 1 international. Expenses: Contact institution. *Financial support:* Application deadline: 4/1. *Program availability:* Part-time, evening/weekend. Offers occupational science (Sc D). *Application deadline:* For fall admission, 8/15 for domestic and international students; for winter admission, 11/15 for domestic and international students; for spring admission, 1/15 for domestic and international students. Applications are processed on a rolling basis. *Application fee:* $45. Electronic applications accepted. *Application Contact:* Coverley Beidleman, Assistant Director of Graduate Admissions, 410-704-2113, Fax: 410-704-3030, E-mail: grads@towson.edu. *Graduate Program Director,* Dr. Beth Merryman, 410-704-3499, E-mail: bmerryman@towson.edu.

Program in Occupational Therapy Students: 150 full-time (145 women); includes 24 minority (10 Black or African American, non-Hispanic/Latino; 9 Asian, non-Hispanic/Latino; 3 Hispanic/Latino; 2 Two or more races, non-Hispanic/Latino). Expenses: Contact institution. *Financial support:* Application deadline: 4/1. Offers occupational therapy (MS). *Application deadline:* For spring admission, 8/1 for domestic students. Applications are processed on a rolling basis. *Application fee:* $45. Electronic applications accepted. *Application Contact:* Coverley Beidleman, Assistant Director of Graduate Admissions, 410-704-2113, Fax: 410-704-3030, E-mail: grads@towson.edu. *Graduate Program Director,* Dr. Sonia Lawson, 410-704-2762, E-mail: slawson@towson.edu.

Program in Organizational Change Students: 86 part-time (68 women); includes 26 minority (21 Black or African American, non-Hispanic/Latino; 2 Asian, non-Hispanic/Latino; 2 Hispanic/Latino; 1 Two or more races, non-Hispanic/Latino). Expenses: Contact institution. Offers organizational change (CAS). *Application deadline:* Applications are processed on a rolling basis. *Application fee:* $45. Electronic applications accepted. *Application Contact:* Coverley Beidleman, Assistant Director of Graduate Admissions, 410-704-2113, Fax: 410-704-3030, E-mail: grads@towson.edu. *Graduate Program Director,* Carla Finkelstein, 410-704-2974, E-mail: cfinkelstein@towson.edu.

Program in Physician Assistant Studies Students: 86 full-time (65 women); includes 30 minority (10 Black or African American, non-Hispanic/Latino; 11 Asian, non-Hispanic/Latino; 6 Hispanic/Latino; 3 Two or more races, non-Hispanic/Latino), 1 international. Expenses: Contact institution. *Financial support:* Application deadline: 4/1. Offers physician assistant studies (MS). *Application deadline:* Applications are processed on a rolling basis. *Application fee:* $45. Electronic applications accepted. *Application Contact:* Coverley Beidleman, Assistant Director of Graduate Admissions, 410-704-2113, Fax: 410-704-3030, E-mail: grads@towson.edu. *Graduate Program Director,* Robert Solomon, 443-840-2854, E-mail: rsolomon@ccbmd.edu.

Program in Professional Studies Students: 10 full-time (6 women), 13 part-time (11 women); includes 5 minority (4 Black or African American, non-Hispanic/Latino; 1 Two or more races, non-Hispanic/Latino). Expenses: Contact institution. *Financial support:* Application deadline: 4/1. *Program availability:* Part-time, evening/weekend. Offers art history (MA); individualized plan (MA). *Application deadline:* Applications are processed on a rolling basis. *Application fee:* $45. Electronic applications accepted. *Application Contact:* Coverley Beidleman, Assistant Director of Graduate Admissions, 410-704-2113, Fax: 410-704-3030, E-mail: grads@towson.edu. *Graduate Program Director,* Dr. James Smith, 410-704-4620, E-mail: jmsmith@towson.edu.

Program in Professional Writing Students: 18 full-time (10 women), 49 part-time (41 women); includes 17 minority (11 Black or African American, non-Hispanic/Latino; 1 Asian, non-Hispanic/Latino; 3 Hispanic/Latino; 2 Two or more races, non-Hispanic/Latino). Expenses: Contact institution. *Financial support:* Application deadline: 4/1. *Program availability:* Part-time, evening/weekend. Offers professional writing (MS). *Application deadline:* For fall admission, 3/1 for domestic students; for spring admission, 10/1 for domestic students. Applications are processed on a rolling basis. *Application fee:* $45. Electronic applications accepted. *Application Contact:* Coverley Beidleman, Assistant Director of Graduate Admissions, 410-704-2113, Fax: 410-704-3030, E-mail: grads@towson.edu. *Graduate Program Director,* Prof. Goeffrey Becker, 410-704-5196, E-mail: gbecker@towson.edu.

Program in Psychology Students: 104 full-time (72 women), 27 part-time (23 women); includes 34 minority (12 Black or African American, non-Hispanic/Latino; 7 Asian, non-Hispanic/Latino; 10 Hispanic/Latino; 5 Two or more races, non-Hispanic/Latino). Expenses: Contact institution. *Financial support:* Application deadline: 4/1. *Program availability:* Part-time, evening/weekend. Offers clinical psychology (MA); counseling psychology (MA); experimental psychology (MA); school psychology (MA). *Application deadline:* For fall admission, 2/1 for domestic and international students. *Application fee:* $45. Electronic applications accepted. *Application Contact:* Coverley Beidleman, Assistant Director of Graduate Admissions, 410-704-2113, Fax: 410-704-3030, E-mail: grads@towson.edu. *Graduate Program Director,* Dr. Geoffrey Munro, 410-704-2634, E-mail: psyc@towson.edu.

Program in Reading Students: 1 (woman) full-time, 159 part-time (149 women); includes 14 minority (7 Black or African American, non-Hispanic/Latino; 3 Hispanic/Latino; 4 Two or more races, non-Hispanic/Latino). Expenses: Contact institution. *Financial support:* Application deadline: 4/1. *Program availability:* Part-time, evening/weekend. Offers reading (M Ed); reading education (CAS). *Application deadline:* Applications are processed on a rolling basis. *Application fee:* $45. Electronic applications accepted. *Application Contact:* Coverley Beidleman, Assistant Director of Graduate Admissions, 410-704-2113, Fax: 410-704-3030, E-mail: grads@towson.edu. *Graduate Program Director,* Dr. Gilda Martinez-Alba, 410-704-2480, E-mail: gmartinez@towson.edu.

Program in Secondary Education Students: 1 (woman) full-time, 5 part-time (4 women); includes 1 minority (Black or African American, non-Hispanic/Latino). Expenses: Contact institution. *Financial support:* Application deadline: 4/1. *Program availability:* Part-time, evening/weekend. Offers secondary education (M Ed). *Application deadline:* Applications are processed on a rolling basis. *Application fee:* $45. Electronic applications accepted. *Application Contact:* Coverley Beidleman, Assistant Director of Graduate Admissions, 410-704-2113, Fax: 410-704-3030, E-mail: grads@towson.edu. *Graduate Program Director,* Dr. Todd Kenreich, 410-704-4956, E-mail: scedmed@towson.edu.

Program in Social Science Students: 7 full-time (4 women), 9 part-time (7 women); includes 8 minority (5 Black or African American, non-Hispanic/Latino; 1 Hispanic/Latino; 2 Two or more races, non-Hispanic/Latino). Expenses: Contact institution. *Financial support:* Application deadline: 4/1. *Program availability:* Part-time, evening/weekend. Offers social science (MS). *Application deadline:* For fall admission, 10/15 for domestic and international students; for spring admission, 4/15 for domestic and international students. Applications are processed on a rolling basis. *Application fee:* $45. Electronic applications accepted. *Application Contact:* Coverley Beidleman, Assistant Director of Graduate Admissions, 410-704-2113, Fax: 410-704-3030, E-mail: grads@towson.edu. *Graduate Program Director,* Dr. Paul McCartney, 410-704-5218, E-mail: pmccartney@towson.edu.

Program in Special Education Students: 2 full-time (both women), 133 part-time (121 women); includes 19 minority (7 Black or African American, non-Hispanic/Latino; 1 American Indian or Alaska Native, non-Hispanic/Latino; 1 Asian, non-Hispanic/Latino; 8 Hispanic/Latino; 2 Two or more races, non-Hispanic/Latino). Expenses: Contact institution. *Program availability:* Part-time, evening/weekend. Offers special education (M Ed). *Application deadline:* For fall admission, 2/15 for domestic and international students; for spring admission, 10/15 for domestic and international students. Applications are processed on a rolling basis. *Application fee:* $45. Electronic applications accepted. *Application Contact:* Coverley Beidleman, Assistant Director of Graduate Admissions, 410-704-2113, Fax: 410-704-3030, E-mail: grads@towson.edu. *Graduate Program Director,* Dr. Andrea Parrish, 410-704-3835, E-mail: aparrish@towson.edu.

Program in Speech-Language Pathology Students: 95 full-time (all women), 1 (woman) part-time; includes 5 minority (2 Black or African American, non-Hispanic/Latino; 3 Two or more races, non-Hispanic/Latino). Expenses: Contact institution. *Financial support:* Application deadline: 4/1. Offers speech-language pathology (MS). *Application deadline:* For fall admission, 1/15 for domestic students. Applications are processed on a rolling basis. *Application fee:* $45. Electronic applications accepted. *Application Contact:* Coverley Beidleman, Assistant Director of Graduate Admissions, 410-704-2113, Fax: 410-704-3030, E-mail: grads@towson.edu. *Graduate Program Director,* Dr. Karen Fallon, 410-704-2437, E-mail: slpgradprogram@towson.edu.

Program in Studio Arts Students: 12 full-time (5 women), 7 part-time (4 women); includes 6 minority (2 Black or African American, non-Hispanic/Latino; 1 Asian, non-Hispanic/Latino; 1 Hispanic/Latino; 2 Two or more races, non-Hispanic/Latino), 1 international. Expenses: Contact institution. *Financial support:* Application deadline: 4/1. Offers studio arts (MFA). *Application deadline:* For fall admission, 2/1 for domestic students; for spring admission, 11/1 for domestic students. *Application fee:* $45. Electronic applications accepted. *Application Contact:* Coverley Beidleman, Assistant Director of Graduate Admissions, 410-704-2113, Fax: 410-704-3030, E-mail: grads@towson.edu. *Graduate Program Director,* Prof. Tonia Matthews, 410-704-2803, E-mail: tmatthews@towson.edu.

Program in Teaching Students: 93 full-time (67 women), 75 part-time (53 women); includes 25 minority (10 Black or African American, non-Hispanic/Latino; 1 American Indian or Alaska Native, non-Hispanic/Latino; 8 Asian, non-Hispanic/Latino; 3 Hispanic/Latino; 3 Two or more races, non-Hispanic/Latino), 2 international. Expenses: Contact institution. *Financial support:* Application deadline: 4/1. Offers teaching (MAT). *Application deadline:* For fall admission, 6/15 for domestic and international students; for spring admission, 10/15 for domestic and international students. Applications are processed on a rolling basis. *Application fee:* $45. Electronic applications accepted. *Application Contact:* Coverley Beidleman, Assistant Director of Graduate Admissions, 410-704-2113, Fax: 410-704-3030, E-mail: grads@towson.edu. *Graduate Program Director,* Dr. Marie Heath, 410-704-4935, E-mail: mheath@towson.edu.

Program in Theatre Students: 6 full-time (5 women), 1 international. Expenses: Contact institution. *Financial support:* Application deadline: 4/1. Offers theatre (MFA). *Application deadline:* For fall admission, 3/1 for domestic students. *Application fee:* $45. Electronic applications accepted. *Application Contact:* Coverley Beidleman, Assistant Director of Graduate Admissions, 410-704-2113, Fax: 410-704-3030, E-mail: grads@towson.edu. *Graduate Program Director,* Prof. Naoko Maeshiba, 410-704-2791, E-mail: nmaeshiba@towson.edu.

Program in Women's Studies Students: 6 full-time (5 women), 5 part-time (all women); includes 2 minority (both Black or African American, non-Hispanic/Latino), 3 international. Expenses: Contact institution. *Financial support:* Application deadline: 4/1. Offers women's studies (MS, Postbaccalaureate Certificate). *Application deadline:* Applications are processed on a rolling basis. *Application fee:* $45. Electronic applications accepted. *Application Contact:* Coverley Beidleman, Assistant Director of Graduate Admissions, 410-704-2113, Fax: 410-704-3030, E-mail: grads@towson.edu. *Graduate Program Director,* Dr. Esther Wangari, 410-704-2580, E-mail: ewangari@towson.edu.

TOYOTA TECHNOLOGICAL INSTITUTE AT CHICAGO, Chicago, IL 60637

General Information Proprietary, coed, graduate-only institution.

GRADUATE UNITS

Program in Computer Science Offers computer science (PhD).

TRENT UNIVERSITY, Peterborough, ON K9J 7B8, Canada

General Information Province-supported, coed, university. *Graduate housing:* Room and/or apartments available to single students; on-campus housing not available to married students. Housing application deadline: 7/10. *Research affiliation:* Watershed Science Centre (watershed studies), Ontario Power Generation, Inc. (acid rain deposition), Enbridge Consumers Gas (ozone depletion), Forensics Laboratory (DNA testing).

GRADUATE UNITS

Graduate Studies *Program availability:* Part-time. Offers anthropology (MA); applications of modeling in the natural and social sciences (MA); biology (M Sc, PhD); chemistry (M Sc); computer studies (M Sc); cultural studies (PhD); environmental and resource studies (M Sc, PhD); geography (M Sc, PhD); indigenous studies (PhD); materials science (M Sc); physics (M Sc).

The Frost Centre for Canadian Studies and Indigenous Studies *Program availability:* Part-time. Offers Canadian studies (PhD); Canadian studies and indigenous studies (MA).

TREVECCA NAZARENE UNIVERSITY, Nashville, TN 37210-2877

General Information Independent-religious, coed, comprehensive institution. *Enrollment:* 3,221 graduate, professional, and undergraduate students; 756 full-time matriculated graduate/professional students (527 women), 358 part-time matriculated graduate/professional students (258 women). *Enrollment by degree level:* 768 master's, 328 doctoral, 18 other advanced degrees. *Graduate faculty:* 36 full-time (15 women), 62 part-time/adjunct (29 women). *Tuition:* Full-time $9737. Tuition and fees vary according to degree level and program. *Graduate housing:* Rooms and/or apartments available to single and married students. Housing application deadline: 6/15. *Student services:* Services for students with disabilities, teacher training. *Library facilities:* Waggoner Library. *Collection:* Books: 87,390 (physical), 48,974 (digital/electronic); Serial titles: 431 (physical); Databases: 3,346. Weekly public service hours: 95; students can reserve study rooms.

Computer facilities: 200 computers available on campus for general student use. A campuswide network can be accessed from student residence rooms and from off campus. Online class registration is available.
Website: http://www.trevecca.edu/

General Application Contact: School of Graduate and Continuing Studies, 844-TNU-GRAD, E-mail: sgcsadmissions@trevecca.edu.

GRADUATE UNITS

Graduate Business Programs Students: 168 full-time (108 women), 24 part-time (13 women); includes 98 minority (81 Black or African American, non-Hispanic/Latino; 6 Asian, non-Hispanic/Latino; 8 Hispanic/Latino; 1 Native Hawaiian or other Pacific Islander, non-Hispanic/Latino; 2 Two or more races, non-Hispanic/Latino), 3 international. Average age 32. *Faculty:* 8 full-time (1 woman), 8 part-time/adjunct (3 women). Expenses: Contact institution. *Financial support:* Applicants required to submit FAFSA. In 2016, 44 master's awarded. *Program availability:* Evening/weekend, online learning. Offers business administration (MBA); management (MSM). *Application deadline:* Applications are processed on a rolling basis. *Application fee:* $0. Electronic applications accepted. *Application Contact:* 615-248-1529, E-mail: sgcsadmissions@trevecca.edu. *Director of Graduate and Professional Programs for School of Business,* Dr. Rick Mann, 615-248-1529, E-mail: management@trevecca.edu.

Graduate Counseling Program Students: 135 full-time (94 women), 76 part-time (63 women); includes 49 minority (40 Black or African American, non-Hispanic/Latino; 1 American Indian or Alaska Native, non-Hispanic/Latino; 2 Hispanic/Latino; 6 Two or more races, non-Hispanic/Latino). Average age 34. *Faculty:* 5 full-time (1 woman), 10 part-time/adjunct (6 women). Expenses: Contact institution. *Financial support:* Applicants required to submit FAFSA. In 2016, 55 master's, 5 doctorates awarded. *Program availability:* Part-time, evening/weekend. Offers clinical counseling: teaching and supervision (PhD); clinical mental health counseling (MA); marriage and family counseling/therapy (MMFC/T). *Application deadline:* Applications are processed on a rolling basis. *Application fee:* $0. Electronic applications accepted. *Application Contact:* 615-248-1384, Fax: 615-248-1662, E-mail: admissions_gradcouns@trevecca.edu. *Director,* Dr. Peter Wilson, 615-248-1384, Fax: 615-248-1662, E-mail: admissions_gradcouns@trevecca.edu.

Graduate Education Program Students: 80 full-time (64 women), 16 part-time (13 women); includes 19 minority (17 Black or African American, non-Hispanic/Latino; 2 Hispanic/Latino). Average age 35. *Faculty:* 5 full-time (3 women), 18 part-time/adjunct (12 women). Expenses: Contact institution. *Financial support:* Applicants required to submit FAFSA. In 2016, 68 master's, 7 other advanced degrees awarded. *Program availability:* Part-time, evening/weekend, online learning. Offers accountability and instructional leadership (Ed S); curriculum and instruction for Christian school educators (M Ed); curriculum and instruction K-12 (M Ed); educational leadership (M Ed); English second language (M Ed); library and information science (MLI Sc); special education: visual impairments (M Ed); teaching (MAT). *Application deadline:* Applications are processed on a rolling basis. Electronic applications accepted. *Application Contact:* 844-TNU-GRAD, E-mail: sgcsadmissions@trevecca.edu. *Dean, School of Education/Director of Graduate Education Programs,* Dr. Suzie Harris, 615-248-1201, Fax: 615-248-1597, E-mail: admissions_ged@trevecca.edu.

Graduate Instructional Design and Technology Program Students: 10 full-time (9 women); includes 1 minority (Black or African American, non-Hispanic/Latino). Average age 40. *Faculty:* 1 (woman) full-time, 1 (woman) part-time/adjunct. Expenses: Contact institution. *Financial support:* Applicants required to submit FAFSA. *Program availability:* Online only. Offers instructional design and technology (MS). *Application deadline:* Applications are processed on a rolling basis. *Application fee:* $0. Electronic applications accepted. *Application Contact:* 844-TNU-GRAD, E-mail: sgcsadmissions@trevecca.edu.

Graduate Leadership Programs Students: 209 full-time (150 women), 220 part-time (159 women); includes 240 minority (209 Black or African American, non-Hispanic/Latino; 1 American Indian or Alaska Native, non-Hispanic/Latino; 2 Asian, non-Hispanic/Latino; 16 Hispanic/Latino; 12 Two or more races, non-Hispanic/Latino), 1 international. Average age 39. *Faculty:* 10 full-time (4 women), 19 part-time/adjunct (6 women). Expenses: Contact institution. *Financial support:* Applicants required to submit FAFSA. In 2016, 32 master's, 43 doctorates awarded. *Program availability:* Online learning. Offers leadership and professional practice (Ed D); organizational leadership (MOL). *Application deadline:* Applications are processed on a rolling basis. *Application fee:* $0. Electronic applications accepted. *Application Contact:* 844-TNU-GRAD, E-mail: sgcsadmissions@trevecca.edu. *Associate Vice President for Academic Services/Director of Master of Organizational Leadership,* Dr. Tom Middendorf, 615-248-1529, E-mail: sgcsadmissions@trevecca.edu.

Graduate Physician Assistant Program Students: 91 full-time (70 women); includes 3 minority (2 Asian, non-Hispanic/Latino; 1 Hispanic/Latino). Average age 25. *Faculty:* 5 full-time (all women), 2 part-time/adjunct (both women). Expenses: Contact institution. *Financial support:* Applicants required to submit FAFSA. In 2016, 50 master's awarded. Offers physician assistant (MS). *Application deadline:* For fall admission, 10/1 for domestic students. *Application Contact:* 615-248-1225, E-mail: admissions_pa@trevecca.edu. *Director,* Bret Reeves, 615-248-1504, E-mail: admissions_pa@trevecca.edu.

Graduate Religion Programs Students: 63 full-time (32 women), 22 part-time (10 women); includes 32 minority (24 Black or African American, non-Hispanic/Latino; 1 Asian, non-Hispanic/Latino; 6 Hispanic/Latino; 1 Two or more races, non-Hispanic/Latino), 1 international. Average age 41. *Faculty:* 6 full-time (1 woman), 6 part-time/adjunct (0 women). Expenses: Contact institution. *Financial support:* Applicants required to submit FAFSA. In 2016, 9 master's awarded. *Program availability:* Part-time, online learning. Offers biblical and theological studies (MA); Christian ministry (MA); pastoral counseling (MA). *Application deadline:* Applications are processed on a rolling basis. *Application fee:* $0. Electronic applications accepted. *Application Contact:* 844-

TNU-GRAD, E-mail: sgcsadmissions@trevecca.edu. *Dean, School of Theology and Christian Ministry/Director, Graduate Religion Program,* Dr. Tim Green, 615-248-1378, Fax: 615-248-7417.

TRIDENT UNIVERSITY INTERNATIONAL, Cypress, CA 90630

General Information Independent, coed, university.

GRADUATE UNITS

College of Business Administration *Program availability:* Part-time, evening/weekend, online learning. Offers business administration (MBA, PhD); conflict and negotiation management (MBA); criminal justice administration (MBA); entrepreneurship (MBA); finance (MBA); general management (MBA); government accounting (MBA); human resource management (MBA); information security and digital assurance management (MBA); information technology management (MBA); international business (MBA); logistics management (MBA); marketing (MBA); project management (MBA); public management (MBA); quality management (MBA); strategic leadership (MBA). Electronic applications accepted.

College of Education *Program availability:* Part-time, evening/weekend, online learning. Offers adult education (MA Ed); aviation education (MA Ed); children's literacy development (MA Ed); e-learning (MA Ed); e-learning leadership (MA Ed, PhD); early childhood education (MA Ed); education (MA Ed, PhD); educational leadership (MA Ed); enrollment management (MA Ed); higher education (MA Ed); higher education leadership (PhD); K-12 leadership (PhD); teaching and instruction (MA Ed); training and development (MA Ed). Electronic applications accepted.

College of Health Sciences *Program availability:* Part-time, evening/weekend, online learning. Offers clinical research administration (MS, Certificate); emergency and disaster management (MS, Certificate); environmental health science (Certificate); health care administration (PhD); health care management (MS); health education (MS, Certificate); health informatics (Certificate); health sciences (MS, PhD, Certificate); international health (MS); international health: educator or researcher option (PhD); international health: practitioner option (PhD); law and expert witness studies (MS, Certificate); public health (MS); quality assurance (Certificate). Electronic applications accepted.

College of Information Systems *Program availability:* Part-time, evening/weekend, online learning. Offers business intelligence (Certificate); information technology management (MS). Electronic applications accepted.

TRINE UNIVERSITY, Angola, IN 46703-1764

General Information Independent, coed, comprehensive institution. *Enrollment:* 3,730 graduate, professional, and undergraduate students; 40 full-time matriculated graduate/professional students (23 women), 1 part-time matriculated graduate/professional student. *Enrollment by degree level:* 358 master's. *Tuition:* Full-time $13,320. *Required fees:* $460. Tuition and fees vary according to degree level, campus/location, program and student level. *Graduate housing:* Room and/or apartments available on a first-come, first-served basis to single students; on-campus housing not available to married students. Typical cost: $6100 per year ($10,350 including board). Room and board charges vary according to board plan and housing facility selected. Housing application deadline: 3/1. *Student services:* Campus employment opportunities, career counseling, exercise/wellness program, free psychological counseling, teacher training, writing training. *Library facilities:* Sponsel Library plus 1 other. *Collection:* Books: 23,523 (physical), 225,584 (digital/electronic); Serial titles: 19 (physical), 21,141 (digital/electronic); Databases: 87.

Computer facilities: Computer purchase and lease plans are available. 400 computers available on campus for general student use. A campuswide network can be accessed from student residence rooms. Online class registration, online campus billing accounts, course management system are available.
Website: http://www.trine.edu/

General Application Contact: Scott Goplin, Vice President for Enrollment Management, 260-665-4149, E-mail: goplins@trine.edu.

GRADUATE UNITS

Program in Criminal Justice Expenses: Contact institution. *Financial support:* Application deadline: 3/1; applicants required to submit FAFSA. *Program availability:* Part-time, evening/weekend. Offers emergency management (MS); forensic psychology (MS); law (MS); public administration (MS). *Dean, College of Graduate and Professional Studies/Associate Professor,* Craig Laker, 260-665-4862, E-mail: lakerc@trine.edu.

Program in Physical Therapy Expenses: Contact institution. Offers physical therapy (DPT). *Application Contact:* Scott Goplin, Vice President for Enrollment Management, 260-665-4149, E-mail: goplins@trine.edu.

Program in Physician Assistant Studies Expenses: Contact institution. Offers physician assistant studies (MPAS). *Application Contact:* Scott Goplin, Vice President for Enrollment Management, 260-665-4149, E-mail: goplins@trine.edu. *Director,* Dr. Dawn M. LaBarbera, 260-702-8023, E-mail: labarberad@trine.edu.

TRINITY BAPTIST COLLEGE, Jacksonville, FL 32221

General Information Independent-religious, coed, comprehensive institution. *Graduate housing:* On-campus housing not available.

GRADUATE UNITS

Graduate Programs *Program availability:* Online learning. Offers educational leadership (M Ed); special education (M Ed).

TRINITY BIBLE COLLEGE AND GRADUATE SCHOOL, Ellendale, ND 58436

General Information Independent-religious, coed, comprehensive institution.

GRADUATE UNITS

Graduate School Offers global theology (MA); missional leadership (MA).

TRINITY CHRISTIAN COLLEGE, Palos Heights, IL 60463-0929

General Information Independent-religious, coed, comprehensive institution.

GRADUATE UNITS

Program in Counseling Psychology *Program availability:* Evening/weekend, online learning. Offers counseling psychology (MA).

Program in Special Education *Program availability:* Evening/weekend. Offers special education (MA). Electronic applications accepted.

TRINITY COLLEGE, Toronto, ON M5S 1H8, Canada

General Information Independent-religious, coed, graduate-only institution. *Graduate housing:* Room and/or apartments available on a first-come, first-served basis to single students; on-campus housing not available to married students. Housing application deadline: 7/15.

GRADUATE UNITS

Faculty of Divinity *Program availability:* Part-time. Offers ministry (Diploma); ministry for church musicians (Diploma); theology (M Div, MA, MTS, Th M, D Min, PhD, Th D, Diploma, L Th).

TRINITY COLLEGE, Hartford, CT 06106-3100

General Information Independent, coed, comprehensive institution. *Graduate housing:* On-campus housing not available.

GRADUATE UNITS

Graduate Programs *Program availability:* Part-time, evening/weekend. Offers American culture studies (MA); health care policy (MA); literary studies (MA); museums and communities (MA); public policy studies (MA); writing, rhetoric, and media arts (MA). Electronic applications accepted.

TRINITY INTERNATIONAL UNIVERSITY, Deerfield, IL 60015-1284

General Information Independent-religious, coed, university. *Enrollment:* 766 full-time matriculated graduate/professional students (267 women), 856 part-time matriculated graduate/professional students (276 women). *Enrollment by degree level:* 1,151 master's, 447 doctoral, 24 other advanced degrees. *Graduate faculty:* 49 full-time (7 women), 124 part-time/adjunct (34 women). *Tuition:* Full-time $19,898. *Required fees:* $200. *Graduate housing:* Rooms and/or apartments available on a first-come, first-served basis to single and married students. *Student services:* Campus employment opportunities, campus safety program, career counseling, child daycare facilities, exercise/wellness program, international student services, low-cost health insurance, multicultural affairs office, services for students with disabilities. *Library facilities:* Rolfing Memorial Library.

Computer facilities: 130 computers available on campus for general student use. A campuswide network can be accessed from student residence rooms and from off campus. Online class registration is available.
Website: http://www.tiu.edu/

General Application Contact: Blaise Brankatelli, Director of Graduate Admissions, 800-345-8337, Fax: 847-317-8097, E-mail: gradadmissions@tiu.edu.

GRADUATE UNITS

Trinity Evangelical Divinity School Students: 578 full-time (141 women), 711 part-time (202 women). Expenses: Contact institution. *Financial support:* Fellowships with partial tuition reimbursements, teaching assistantships with partial tuition reimbursements, career-related internships or fieldwork, Federal Work-Study, scholarships/grants, and tuition waivers (partial) available. Financial award application deadline: 4/1; financial award applicants required to submit FAFSA. *Program availability:* Part-time, online learning. Offers academic ministry (M Div); Biblical and Near Eastern archaeology and languages (MA); chaplaincy and ministry care (MA); Christian studies (Certificate); church and parachurch ministry (M Div); church history (MA, Th M); counseling (Th M); educational ministries (MA); educational ministry (Th M); educational studies (PhD); intercultural studies (MA, PhD); leadership and management (D Min); mental health counseling (MA); military chaplaincy (D Min); ministry (MA); missions (Th M); missions and evangelism (D Min); New Testament (MA, Th M); Old Testament (Th M); Old Testament and Semitic languages (MA); pastoral ministry and care (D Min); pastoral theology (Th M); preaching and teaching (D Min); spiritual formation and education (D Min); systematic theology (MA, Th M); theological studies (MA, PhD); urban ministry (MA). *Application deadline:* For fall admission, 7/15 priority date for domestic and international students. Applications are processed on a rolling basis. *Application fee:* $25. Electronic applications accepted. *Application Contact:* Ron Campbell, Director of Admissions, 800-345-8337, Fax: 847-317-8097, E-mail: rcampbel@tiu.edu. *Academic Dean,* Dr. Tite Tienou, 847-317-8086, Fax: 847-317-8014, E-mail: ttienou@teds.edu.

Trinity Graduate School Expenses: Contact institution. *Financial support:* Career-related internships or fieldwork, Federal Work-Study, institutionally sponsored loans, and tuition waivers (partial) available. Support available to part-time students. Financial award application deadline: 4/1; financial award applicants required to submit FAFSA. *Program availability:* Part-time, evening/weekend, online learning. Offers athletic training (MA); bioethics (MA); counseling psychology (MA); diverse learning (M Ed); leadership (MA); teaching (MA). *Application deadline:* For fall admission, 8/1 priority date for domestic students, 5/1 for international students; for spring admission, 12/1 priority date for domestic students, 12/1 for international students. Applications are processed on a rolling basis. *Application fee:* $25. Electronic applications accepted. *Application Contact:* Blaise Brankatelli, Director of Graduate Admissions, 847-317-8000, Fax: 847-317-8097, E-mail: gradadmissions@tiu.edu. *Dean,* Dr. Thomas Cornman, 847-317-7001, Fax: 847-317-4786.

Trinity Law School Expenses: Contact institution. *Financial support:* Scholarships/grants available. Financial award application deadline: 8/15; financial award applicants required to submit FAFSA. *Program availability:* Part-time, evening/weekend. Offers bioethics (MLS); church and ministry management (MLS); general legal studies (MLS); human resources management (MLS); human rights (MLS); law (JD); nonprofit organizations (MLS). *Application deadline:* For fall admission, 5/1 priority date for domestic and international students; for spring admission, 12/1 priority date for domestic and international students. Applications are processed on a rolling basis. *Application fee:* $35. *Application Contact:* Doug Eaton, Director of Admissions, 714-796-7103, Fax: 714-796-7190, E-mail: deaton@tiu.edu. *Academic Dean,* Kevin P. Holsclaw, 714-836-7160, Fax: 714-796-7190, E-mail: kholscla@tiu.edu.

TRINITY INTERNATIONAL UNIVERSITY FLORIDA, Davie, FL 33324

General Information Independent-religious, coed, graduate-only institution. *Graduate housing:* On-campus housing not available.

GRADUATE UNITS

Divinity School Offers Christian studies (MA, Certificate).

Graduate School Offers counseling psychology (MA).

TRINITY LUTHERAN SEMINARY, Columbus, OH 43209-2334

General Information Independent-religious, coed, graduate-only institution. *Graduate housing:* Rooms and/or apartments available on a first-come, first-served basis to single and married students. Housing application deadline: 5/15.

GRADUATE UNITS

Graduate and Professional Programs *Program availability:* Part-time. Offers African American studies (MTS); Biblical studies (MTS, STM); Christian education (MA); Christian spirituality (STM); church in the world (MTS); church music (MA); divinity (M Div); general theological studies (MTS); mission and evangelism (STM); pastoral leadership and practice (STM); youth and family ministry (MA). Electronic applications accepted.

TRINITY SCHOOL FOR MINISTRY, Ambridge, PA 15003-2397

General Information Independent-religious, coed, graduate-only institution. *Graduate housing:* On-campus housing not available.

GRADUATE UNITS

Graduate Programs *Program availability:* Part-time. Offers Anglican studies (Diploma); basic Christian studies (Diploma); divinity (M Div); ministry (D Min); mission and evangelism (MAME, Diploma); religion (MAR); youth ministry (Diploma).

TRINITY UNIVERSITY, San Antonio, TX 78212-7200

General Information Independent-religious, coed, comprehensive institution. *Enrollment:* 2,502 graduate, professional, and undergraduate students; 118 full-time matriculated graduate/professional students (62 women), 50 part-time matriculated graduate/professional students (31 women). *Enrollment by degree level:* 168 master's. *Tuition:* Full-time $38,974. *Required fees:* $586. *Graduate housing:* On-campus housing not available. *Student services:* Campus employment opportunities, campus safety program, career counseling, exercise/wellness program, free psychological counseling, grant writing training, international student services, services for students with disabilities, teacher training, writing training. *Library facilities:* Elizabeth Huth Coates Library plus 1 other. *Collection:* Books: 819,196 (physical); Serial titles: 2,176 (physical), 95,000 (digital/electronic); Databases: 304. Weekly public service hours: 96.

Computer facilities: Computer purchase and lease plans are available. 500 computers available on campus for general student use. A campuswide network can be accessed from student residence rooms and from off campus. Online class registration is available.

Website: http://www.trinity.edu/

General Application Contact: Office of the Registrar, 210-999-7201, Fax: 210-999-7202, E-mail: roffice@trinity.edu.

GRADUATE UNITS

Department of Education *Program availability:* Part-time, evening/weekend. Offers school leadership (M Ed); school psychology (MA); teaching (MAT).

Department of Health Care Administration *Program availability:* Part-time, online learning. Offers health care administration (MS). Electronic applications accepted.

School of Business Offers accounting (MS). Electronic applications accepted.

TRINITY WASHINGTON UNIVERSITY, Washington, DC 20017-1094

General Information Independent-religious, women only, comprehensive institution. *Graduate housing:* Room and/or apartments available on a first-come, first-served basis to single students; on-campus housing not available to married students.

GRADUATE UNITS

School of Business and Graduate Studies *Program availability:* Part-time, evening/weekend. Offers business administration (MBA); communication (MA); international security studies (MA); organizational management (MSA).

School of Education *Program availability:* Part-time, evening/weekend. Offers clinical mental health counseling (MA); early childhood education (MAT); educating for change (M Ed); educational administration (MSA); elementary education (MAT); reading (M Ed); school counseling (MA); secondary education (MAT); special education (MAT).

TRINITY WESTERN UNIVERSITY, Langley, BC V2Y 1Y1, Canada

General Information Independent-religious, coed, comprehensive institution. *Graduate housing:* On-campus housing not available.

GRADUATE UNITS

ACTS Seminaries *Program availability:* Part-time. Offers Christian studies (MA); cross cultural ministry (MA); theology (M Div, M Th, MAMFT, MLE, MTS, D Min).

School of Graduate Studies Offers biblical studies (MA); business (MA, Certificate); Christian ministry (MA); counseling psychology (MA); education (MA, Certificate); general humanities (MAIH); healthcare (MA, Certificate); international business (MBA); linguistics (MA); management of the growing enterprise (MBA); non-profit (MA, Certificate); non-profit and charitable organization management (MBA); specialized (MAIH); teaching English to speakers of other languages (TESOL) (MA).

School of Nursing Offers nursing (MSN).

TRI-STATE BIBLE COLLEGE, South Point, OH 45680-8402

General Information Independent-religious, coed, comprehensive institution.

GRADUATE UNITS

Graduate Program Offers Biblical studies (MA). Electronic applications accepted.

TRI-STATE COLLEGE OF ACUPUNCTURE, New York, NY 10011

General Information Independent, coed, graduate-only institution. *Enrollment by degree level:* 112 master's. *Graduate faculty:* 5 full-time (2 women), 32 part-time/adjunct (24 women). *Tuition:* Full-time $23,600; part-time $11,800 per semester. *Required fees:* $480; $480 per year. *Graduate housing:* On-campus housing not available. *Student services:* Campus safety program, career counseling, low-cost health insurance, teacher training.

Computer facilities: 5 computers available on campus for general student use. A campuswide network can be accessed.

Website: http://www.tsca.edu/

General Application Contact: Sandra Turner, Admissions Office, 212-242-5499, Fax: 212-242-2920, E-mail: sandra.turner@tsca.edu.

GRADUATE UNITS

Graduate Programs Students: 95 full-time (65 women), 17 part-time (11 women); includes 16 minority (1 Black or African American, non-Hispanic/Latino; 13 Asian, non-Hispanic/Latino; 2 Hispanic/Latino). *Faculty:* 5 full-time (2 women), 32 part-time/adjunct (24 women). *Expenses:* Contact institution. *Financial support:* Application deadline: 7/15; applicants required to submit FAFSA. *Program availability:* Evening/weekend. Offers acupuncture (MS); Chinese herbology (Certificate); Oriental medicine (MS). *Application deadline:* For fall admission, 6/15 priority date for domestic students. Applications are processed on a rolling basis. *Application fee:* $50. Electronic applications accepted. *Application Contact:* Sandra Turner, Admissions Office, 212-242-5499, Fax: 212-242-2920, E-mail: sandra.turner@tsca.edu.

TROY UNIVERSITY, Troy, AL 36082

General Information State-supported, coed, comprehensive institution. *Enrollment:* 17,903 graduate, professional, and undergraduate students; 956 full-time matriculated graduate/professional students (614 women), 2,097 part-time matriculated graduate/professional students (1,332 women). *Enrollment by degree level:* 3,053 master's. *Graduate faculty:* 229 full-time (99 women), 94 part-time/adjunct (53 women). *Tuition, state resident:* full-time $7146; part-time $397 per credit hour. *Tuition,*

nonresident: full-time $14,292; part-time $794 per credit hour. *Required fees:* $802; $50 per semester. Tuition and fees vary according to campus/location and program. *Graduate housing:* Rooms and/or apartments available on a first-come, first-served basis to single students and available to married students. Typical cost: $5815 (including board) for single students. Housing application deadline: 7/31. *Student services:* Campus employment opportunities, campus safety program, career counseling, child daycare facilities, exercise/wellness program, free psychological counseling, grant writing training, international student services, low-cost health insurance, services for students with disabilities, teacher training, writing training. *Library facilities:* Lurleen B. Wallace Library (Troy Campus) plus 2 others. *Collection:* Books: 624,347 (physical), 120,402 (digital/electronic); Serial titles: 37,650 (physical), 22,415 (digital/electronic); Databases: 192. *Research affiliation:* Systemics Research Fund (protozoan symbionts), Birmingham Audubon Society (Alabama flora and fauna).

Computer facilities: 1,435 computers available on campus for general student use. A campuswide network can be accessed from student residence rooms and from off campus. Online class registration is available.

Website: http://www.troy.edu/

General Application Contact: Jessica A Kimbro, Director of Graduate Admissions, 334-670-3178, Fax: 334-670-3733, E-mail: jacord@troy.edu.

GRADUATE UNITS

Graduate School Students: 956 full-time (614 women), 2,097 part-time (1,332 women); includes 1,127 minority (896 Black or African American, non-Hispanic/Latino; 14 American Indian or Alaska Native, non-Hispanic/Latino; 60 Asian, non-Hispanic/Latino; 76 Hispanic/Latino; 9 Native Hawaiian or other Pacific Islander, non-Hispanic/Latino; 72 Two or more races, non-Hispanic/Latino). Average age 31. 2,650 applicants, 88% accepted, 495 enrolled. *Faculty:* 229 full-time (99 women), 94 part-time/adjunct (53 women). Expenses: Contact institution. *Financial support:* Fellowships, career-related internships or fieldwork, and scholarships/grants available. Support available to part-time students. Financial award application deadline: 5/1; financial award applicants required to submit FAFSA. In 2016, 1,179 master's, 13 doctorates, 25 other advanced degrees awarded. *Program availability:* Part-time, evening/weekend, 100% online, blended/hybrid learning. *Application deadline:* Applications are processed on a rolling basis. *Application fee:* $50. Electronic applications accepted. *Application Contact:* Jessica A. Kimbro, Director of Graduate Admissions, 334-670-3178, E-mail: jacord@troy.edu. *Associate Provost/Dean,* Dr. Mary Anne C. Templeton, 334-670-3189, Fax: 334-670-3912, E-mail: mtempleton@troy.edu.

College of Arts and Sciences Students: 269 full-time (99 women), 736 part-time (368 women); includes 280 minority (203 Black or African American, non-Hispanic/Latino; 6 American Indian or Alaska Native, non-Hispanic/Latino; 23 Asian, non-Hispanic/Latino; 28 Hispanic/Latino; 7 Native Hawaiian or other Pacific Islander, non-Hispanic/Latino; 13 Two or more races, non-Hispanic/Latino). Average age 30. 1,133 applicants, 80% accepted, 54 enrolled. *Faculty:* 68 full-time (21 women), 25 part-time/adjunct (7 women). Expenses: Contact institution. *Financial support:* Fellowships, career-related internships or fieldwork, and scholarships/grants available. Support available to part-time students. Financial award applicants required to submit FAFSA. In 2016, 371 master's awarded. *Program availability:* Part-time, evening/weekend. Offers American history (MA); arts and sciences (MA, MPA, MS, MS Sc, Certificate); biomedical sciences (MS, Certificate); computer science (MS); criminal justice (MS); environmental and biological sciences (MS); European history (MA); government contracting (MPA); international relations (MS); social science (MS Sc). *Application deadline:* Applications are processed on a rolling basis. *Application fee:* $50. Electronic applications accepted. *Application Contact:* Jessica A. Kimbro, Director of Graduate Admissions, 334-670-3178, E-mail: jacord@troy.edu. *Dean,* Dr. Steven Taylor, 334-670-3673, Fax: 334-670-3399, E-mail: rinehart@troy.edu.

College of Business Students: 190 full-time (113 women), 628 part-time (392 women); includes 296 minority (239 Black or African American, non-Hispanic/Latino; 3 American Indian or Alaska Native, non-Hispanic/Latino; 18 Asian, non-Hispanic/Latino; 17 Two or more races, non-Hispanic/Latino). Average age 33. 653 applicants, 94% accepted, 143 enrolled. *Faculty:* 42 full-time (13 women), 3 part-time/adjunct (0 women). Expenses: Contact institution. *Financial support:* In 2016–17, 5 research assistantships were awarded; career-related internships or fieldwork and scholarships/grants also available. Support available to part-time students. Financial award applicants required to submit FAFSA. In 2016, 261 master's awarded. *Program availability:* Part-time, evening/weekend, 100% online, blended/hybrid learning. Offers accountancy (M Acc); accounting (EMBA, MBA); business (EMBA, M Acc, MA, MBA, MBAi, MS, MSM, MTX, Certificate); criminal justice (MBA); economics (MA); finance (MBA); general management (EMBA, MBA); healthcare management (EMBA); human resources management (MS); information systems (EMBA, MBA); international economic development (MBA); management (MS, MSM); taxation (MTX, Certificate). *Application deadline:* Applications are processed on a rolling basis. *Application fee:* $50. Electronic applications accepted. *Application Contact:* Jessica A. Kimbro, Director of Graduate Admissions, 334-670-3178, Fax: 334-670-3733, E-mail: bcamp@troy.edu. *Dean,* Dr. Judson Edwards, 334-670-3989, Fax: 334-670-3708, E-mail: jcedwards@troy.edu.

College of Communication and Fine Arts Students: 35 full-time (24 women), 58 part-time (42 women); includes 68 minority (30 Black or African American, non-Hispanic/Latino; 2 Hispanic/Latino; 1 Native Hawaiian or other Pacific Islander, non-Hispanic/Latino; 35 Two or more races, non-Hispanic/Latino). Average age 29. 52 applicants, 100% accepted, 24 enrolled. *Faculty:* 6 full-time (3 women). Expenses: Contact institution. *Financial support:* Fellowships, career-related internships or fieldwork, and scholarships/grants available. Support available to part-time students. Financial award applicants required to submit FAFSA. In 2016, 58 master's awarded. *Program availability:* Part-time, evening/weekend. Offers strategic communication (MS). *Application deadline:* For fall admission, 6/1 for international students; for spring admission, 10/15 for international students. Applications are processed on a rolling basis. *Application fee:* $50. Electronic applications accepted. *Application Contact:* Jessica A. Kimbro, Director of Graduate Admissions, 334-670-3178, E-mail: jacord@troy.edu. *Dean,* Dr. Larry Blocher, 334-670-3869, Fax: 334-670-3547, E-mail: lblocher@troy.edu.

College of Education Students: 165 full-time (136 women), 372 part-time (298 women); includes 252 minority (221 Black or African American, non-Hispanic/Latino; 3 American Indian or Alaska Native, non-Hispanic/Latino; 2 Asian, non-Hispanic/Latino; 11 Hispanic/Latino; 15 Two or more races, non-Hispanic/Latino). Average age 34. 491 applicants, 198% accepted, 136 enrolled. *Faculty:* 89 full-time (43 women), 46 part-time/adjunct (30 women). Expenses: Contact institution. *Financial support:* Fellowships, career-related internships or fieldwork, and scholarships/grants available. Support available to part-time students. Financial award applicants required to submit FAFSA. In 2016, 474 master's, 11 other advanced degrees awarded. *Program availability:* Part-time, evening/weekend. Offers adult education (MS); community counseling (MS); early childhood education (MS, Ed S); education (MS, MS Ed, Ed S); educational administration/leadership (MS, Ed S); K–6 elementary and collaborative education (MS, Ed S); postsecondary education (MS Ed); school counseling (MS, Ed S); second language instruction (MS); secondary education (MS); teacher education-multiple levels (MS). *Application deadline:* For fall admission, 1/1 for domestic students, 6/1 for international students; for spring admission, 10/15 for international students. Applications are processed on a rolling basis. *Application fee:* $50. Electronic applications accepted. *Application Contact:* Jessica A. Kimbro, Director of Graduate Admissions, 334-670-3178, E-mail: jacord@troy.edu. *Dean,* Dr. Royce Dasinger, 334-670-3365, Fax: 334-670-3474, E-mail: rdasinger@troy.edu.

College of Health and Human Services Students: 300 full-time (243 women), 300 part-time (231 women); includes 222 minority (160 Black or African American, non-Hispanic/Latino; 2 American Indian or Alaska Native, non-Hispanic/Latino; 17 Asian, non-Hispanic/Latino; 11 Hispanic/Latino; 1 Native Hawaiian or other Pacific Islander, non-Hispanic/Latino; 31 Two or more races, non-Hispanic/Latino). Average age 31. 321 applicants, 92% accepted, 135 enrolled. *Faculty:* 44 full-time (28 women), 22 part-time/adjunct (18 women). Expenses: Contact institution. *Financial support:* Tuition waivers and unspecified assistantships available. Support available to part-time students. Financial award application deadline: 4/5; financial award applicants required to submit FAFSA. In 2016, 167 master's, 17 doctorates awarded. *Program availability:* Part-time, evening/weekend. Offers adult health (MSN); family nurse practitioner (DNP); health and human services (MS, MS Sc, MSN, MSW, DNP, PMC); maternal infant (MSN); nursing informatics specialist (MSN); social work (MSW); sport and fitness management (MS). *Application deadline:* Applications are processed on a rolling basis. *Application fee:* $50. Electronic applications accepted. *Application Contact:* Jessica A. Kimbro, Director of Graduate Admissions, 334-670-3178, E-mail: jacord@troy.edu. *Interim Dean,* Dr. Denise Green, 334-670-3712, Fax: 334-670-3743, E-mail: mdtillman@troy.edu.

TRUETT MCCONNELL UNIVERSITY, Cleveland, GA 30528

General Information Independent-religious, coed, comprehensive institution. *Enrollment:* 2,187 graduate, professional, and undergraduate students; 18 full-time matriculated graduate/professional students (1 woman), 17 part-time matriculated graduate/professional students (7 women). *Enrollment by degree level:* 35 master's. *Tuition:* Full-time $2925; part-time $325 per semester hour. *Required fees:* $660 per semester hour. Tuition and fees vary according to course load. *Graduate housing:* Rooms and/or apartments available on a first-come, first-served basis to single and married students. Typical cost: $2450 per year ($4310 including board) for single students; $4800 per year for married students. Room and board charges vary according to housing facility selected. Housing application deadline: 7/1. *Student services:* Career counseling, services for students with disabilities. *Library facilities:* Cofer Library.

Computer facilities: 40 computers available on campus for general student use. A campuswide network can be accessed from student residence rooms. Online class registration is available.
Website: http://www.truett.edu/

General Application Contact: Jim Dunnington, Coordinator of Online and Graduate Admissions, 706-865-2134 Ext. 2131, E-mail: jdunnington@truett.edu.

GRADUATE UNITS

Balthasar Hubmaier School of Theology and Missions Expenses: Contact institution. *Financial support:* Application deadline: 8/1; applicants required to submit FAFSA. In 2016, 1 master's awarded. *Program availability:* Part-time, 100% online. Offers theology (MA). *Application deadline:* Applications are processed on a rolling basis. Electronic applications accepted. *Application Contact:* Morgan Graffagnino, Administrative Assistant, 706-865-2134 Ext. 3002, E-mail: mgraffagnino@truett.edu. *Dean,* Dr. Jason Graffagnino, 706-865-2134 Ext. 3002, E-mail: jgraffagnino@truett.edu.

TRUMAN STATE UNIVERSITY, Kirksville, MO 63501-4221

General Information State-supported, coed, comprehensive institution. CGS member. *Enrollment:* 6,379 graduate, professional, and undergraduate students; 282 full-time matriculated graduate/professional students (208 women), 77 part-time matriculated graduate/professional students (62 women). *Enrollment by degree level:* 359 master's. *Graduate faculty:* 89 full-time (35 women). Tuition, state resident: full-time $6300; part-time $350 per credit hour. Tuition, nonresident: full-time $10,818; part-time $601 per credit hour. Tuition and fees vary according to course load and program. *Graduate housing:* Rooms and/or apartments available on a first-come, first-served basis to single and married students. Typical cost: $8480 (including board) for single students; $8480 (including board) for married students. Room and board charges vary according to board plan and campus/location. Housing application deadline: 5/1. *Student services:* Campus employment opportunities, campus safety program, career counseling, grant writing training, international student services, low-cost health insurance, multicultural affairs office, services for students with disabilities, writing training. *Library facilities:* Pickler Memorial Library. *Collection:* Books: 495,359 (physical), 325,994 (digital/electronic); Serial titles: 601 (physical), 2,584 (digital/electronic); Databases: 107. Students can reserve study rooms. *Research affiliation:* Gulf Coast Research Laboratory (marine science), Kirksville College of Osteopathic Medicine (biology).

Computer facilities: 1,056 computers available on campus for general student use. A campuswide network can be accessed from student residence rooms and from off campus. Online class registration is available.
Website: http://www.truman.edu/

General Application Contact: Stephanie Rudolph, Graduate Office Administrative Assistant, 660-785-4109, Fax: 660-785-7460, E-mail: gradinfo@truman.edu.

GRADUATE UNITS

Graduate School Students: 282 full-time (208 women), 77 part-time (62 women); includes 27 minority (3 Black or African American, non-Hispanic/Latino; 12 Asian, non-Hispanic/Latino; 7 Hispanic/Latino; 5 Two or more races, non-Hispanic/Latino). Average age 23. 129 applicants, 82% accepted, 106 enrolled. *Faculty:* 94 full-time (39 women). Expenses: Contact institution. *Financial support:* In 2016–17, 30 fellowships (averaging $500 per year), 18 research assistantships with full and partial tuition reimbursements (averaging $6,000 per year), 24 teaching assistantships with full and partial tuition reimbursements (averaging $8,000 per year) were awarded; career-related internships or fieldwork, Federal Work-Study, institutionally sponsored loans, scholarships/grants, and unspecified assistantships also available. Financial award application deadline: 5/1; financial award applicants required to submit FAFSA. In 2016, 137 master's awarded. *Application deadline:* For fall admission, 6/1 priority date for domestic and international students; for spring admission, 11/1 priority date for domestic and international students. Applications are processed on a rolling basis. *Application fee:* $40 ($0 for international students). Electronic applications accepted. *Application Contact:* Stephanie Rudolph,

Graduate Office Administrative Assistant, 660-785-4109, E-mail: gradinfo@truman.edu. *Dean of Graduate Studies,* Dr. Maria Di Stefano, 660-785-4109, Fax: 660-785-7460, E-mail: mdistefa@truman.edu.

School of Arts and Letters Students: 224 full-time (171 women); includes 16 minority (4 Asian, non-Hispanic/Latino; 7 Hispanic/Latino; 5 Two or more races, non-Hispanic/Latino). Average age 23. 45 applicants, 51% accepted, 17 enrolled. *Faculty:* 44 full-time (19 women). Expenses: Contact institution. *Financial support:* In 2016–17, research assistantships with tuition reimbursements (averaging $8,000 per year), teaching assistantships with tuition reimbursements (averaging $8,000 per year) were awarded; career-related internships or fieldwork and Federal Work-Study also available. Financial award application deadline: 5/1; financial award applicants required to submit FAFSA. In 2016, 10 master's awarded. Offers arts and letters (MA, MS); biology (MS); English (MA); music (MA). *Application deadline:* For fall admission, 6/1 priority date for domestic and international students; for spring admission, 11/1 priority date for domestic students, 11/1 for international students. Applications are processed on a rolling basis. *Application fee:* $40. Electronic applications accepted. *Application Contact:* Stephanie Rudolph, Graduate Office Administrative Assistant, 660-785-4109, E-mail: gradinfo@truman.edu. *Dean,* Dr. Jim O'Donnell, 660-785-7777, Fax: 660-785-7109.

School of Business Students: 30 full-time (16 women), 2 part-time (1 woman). Expenses: Contact institution. *Financial support:* Research assistantships with tuition reimbursements, teaching assistantships with tuition reimbursements, career-related internships or fieldwork, and Federal Work-Study available. Financial award application deadline: 5/1; financial award applicants required to submit FAFSA. Offers accounting (M Ac); business (M Ac). *Application deadline:* For fall admission, 6/1 for domestic and international students; for spring admission, 11/1 for domestic and international students; for summer admission, 4/1 for domestic and international students. Applications are processed on a rolling basis. *Application fee:* $40. Electronic applications accepted. *Application Contact:* Stephanie Rudolph, Graduate Office Secretary, 660-785-4109, Fax: 660-785-7460, E-mail: sdunn@truman.edu. *Dean,* Dr. Renee Wachter, 660-785-4346, Fax: 660-785-7471, E-mail: rwachter@truman.edu.

School of Health Sciences and Education Students: 225 full-time (187 women), 14 part-time (12 women); includes 9 minority (2 Asian, non-Hispanic/Latino; 3 Hispanic/Latino; 4 Two or more races, non-Hispanic/Latino). Average age 23. Expenses: Contact institution. *Financial support:* Fellowships, career-related internships or fieldwork, and Federal Work-Study available. Financial award application deadline: 5/1; financial award applicants required to submit FAFSA. Offers communication disorders (MA); education (MAE); health sciences and education (MA, MAE). *Application deadline:* For fall admission, 6/15 priority date for domestic and international students; for spring admission, 11/1 for domestic students, 11/1 priority date for international students. Applications are processed on a rolling basis. *Application fee:* $40. Electronic applications accepted. *Application Contact:* Stephanie Rudolph, Graduate Office Secretary, 660-785-4109, Fax: 660-785-7460, E-mail: sdunn@truman.edu. *Dean,* Dr. Janet Gooch, 660-785-4248, Fax: 660-785-4393, E-mail: jquinzer@truman.edu.

★ TUFTS UNIVERSITY, Medford, MA 02155

General Information Independent, coed, university. CGS member. *Enrollment:* 11,489 graduate, professional, and undergraduate students; 5,094 full-time matriculated graduate/professional students (3,024 women), 641 part-time matriculated graduate/professional students (411 women). *Enrollment by degree level:* 2,442 master's, 2,996 doctoral, 297 other advanced degrees. *Graduate faculty:* 999 full-time (449 women), 542 part-time/adjunct (272 women). *Tuition:* Full-time $49,892; part-time $1248 per credit hour. *Required fees:* $844. Full-time tuition and fees vary according to degree level, program and student level. Part-time tuition and fees vary according to course load. *Graduate housing:* Room and/or apartments available on a first-come, first-served basis to single students; on-campus housing not available to married students. Housing application deadline: 4/15. *Student services:* Campus employment opportunities, campus safety program, career counseling, child daycare facilities, exercise/wellness program, free psychological counseling, international student services, low-cost health insurance, multicultural affairs office, services for students with disabilities, teacher training, writing training. *Library facilities:* Tisch Library plus 3 others. *Collection:* Books: 1.3 million (physical), 432,877 (digital/electronic); Serial titles: 1,012 (physical); Databases: 83,216. Weekly public service hours: 110; students can reserve study rooms. *Research affiliation:* Maine Medical Center (medicine), The Stockholm Environmental Institute (environmental science and policy), Caritas St. Elizabeth's Medical Center (medicine), Tufts Medical Center (medicine), Lahey Clinic Medical Center (medicine), Baystate Medical Center (medicine).

Computer facilities: Computer purchase and lease plans are available. 1,039 computers available on campus for general student use. A campuswide network can be accessed from student residence rooms and from off campus. Online class registration, Cloud storage for all students, staff, and faculty are available.
Website: http://www.tufts.edu/

General Application Contact: Information Contact, 617-628-5000.

GRADUATE UNITS

Cummings School of Veterinary Medicine Offers animals and public policy (MS); biomedical sciences (PhD); conservation medicine (MS); veterinary medicine (DVM). Electronic applications accepted.

The Fletcher School of Law and Diplomacy *Program availability:* Online learning. Offers law and diplomacy (LL M, MA, MALD, MIB, PhD). Electronic applications accepted.

The Gerald J. and Dorothy R. Friedman School of Nutrition Science and Policy *Program availability:* Part-time. Offers agriculture, food and environment (MS, PhD); biochemical and molecular nutrition (PhD); dietetic internship (MS); food policy and applied nutrition (MS, PhD); humanitarian assistance (MAHA); nutrition (MS, PhD); nutrition communication (MS); nutritional epidemiology (MS, PhD). Electronic applications accepted.

Graduate School of Arts and Sciences Students: 921 full-time (624 women), 48 part-time (35 women); includes 185 minority (42 Black or African American, non-Hispanic/Latino; 68 Asian, non-Hispanic/Latino; 49 Hispanic/Latino; 26 Two or more races, non-Hispanic/Latino), 187 international. Average age 28. 2,125 applicants, 41% accepted, 366 enrolled. Expenses: Contact institution. *Financial support:* In 2016–17, 860 students received support. Fellowships, research assistantships, teaching assistantships, Federal Work-Study, scholarships/grants, health care benefits, tuition waivers (full and partial), and unspecified assistantships available. Support available to part-time students. Financial award application deadline: 1/15. In 2016, 271 master's, 33 doctorates, 14 other advanced degrees awarded. *Program availability:* Part-time. Offers art education (MAT); art history (MA); art history and museum studies (MA); arts and sciences (MA, MAT, MPP, MS, OTD, PhD, Certificate, Ed S); astrophysics (MS, PhD); bioengineering (Certificate); biology (MS, PhD); biotechnology (Certificate); biotechnology engineering (Certificate); chemical physics (PhD); chemistry (MS, PhD); chemistry/biotechnology (PhD); child study and human development (MA, PhD); classical archaeology (MA); classics (MA); classics with teaching licensure (MA); cognitive science (PhD); community development (MA); community environmental studies (Certificate); composition (MA); computer science (Certificate); computer science minor (Certificate); drama (MA, PhD); early childhood education (MAT); economics (MS); education (MA, MAT, MS, PhD); educational studies (MA); elementary education (MAT); English (MA, PhD); environmental management (Certificate); environmental policy (MA); epidemiology (Certificate); ethnomusicology (MA); French (MA); German (MA); German with teaching licensure (MA); health and human welfare (MA); history (MA, PhD); history and museum studies (MA); housing policy (MA); human-computer interaction (Certificate); interdisciplinary studies (PhD); international environment/development policy (MA); management of community organizations (Certificate); manufacturing engineering (Certificate); mathematics (MS, PhD); microwave and wireless engineering (Certificate); middle and secondary education (MAT); museum education (MA); museum studies (Certificate); music theory (MA); occupational therapy (Certificate); philosophy (MA); physics (MS, PhD); physics education (PhD); program evaluation (Certificate); psychology (MS, PhD); public policy (MPP); school psychology (MA, Ed S); secondary education (MA); soft materials robotics (PhD); STEM education (MS, PhD). *Application deadline:* For fall admission, 1/15 for domestic and international students. Applications are processed on a rolling basis. *Application fee:* $85. Electronic applications accepted. *Application Contact:* Office of Graduate Admissions, 617-627-3395, E-mail: gradadmissions@tufts.edu. *Dean,* Dr. Robert Cook.

Sackler School of Graduate Biomedical Sciences Students: 228 full-time (140 women), 3 part-time (1 woman); includes 55 minority (10 Black or African American, non-Hispanic/Latino; 29 Asian, non-Hispanic/Latino; 8 Hispanic/Latino; 8 Two or more races, non-Hispanic/Latino), 41 international. Average age 33. 566 applicants, 21% accepted, 52 enrolled. *Faculty:* 200 full-time (60 women). Expenses: Contact institution. *Financial support:* In 2016–17, 183 students received support, including 183 research assistantships with full tuition reimbursements available (averaging $33,000 per year); traineeships also available. Financial award application deadline: 12/1. In 2016, 23 master's, 33 doctorates awarded. Offers biomedical sciences (MS, PhD, Certificate); cancer biology (PhD); clinical and translational science (MS, PhD, Certificate); developmental and regenerative biology (PhD); genetics (PhD); immunology (PhD); mammalian genetics (PhD); medically-oriented research in graduate education (PhD); molecular and cellular medicine (PhD); molecular microbiology (PhD); neuroscience (PhD); structural and chemical biology (PhD). *Application deadline:* For fall admission, 12/1 priority date for domestic and international students. *Application fee:* $90. Electronic applications accepted. *Application Contact:* Dr. Elizabeth Storrs, Registrar/Director of Enrollment Services, 617-636-6767, Fax: 617-636-0375, E-mail: sackler-school@tufts.edu. *Dean,* Dr. Naomi Rosenberg, 617-636-6767, Fax: 617-636-0375, E-mail: naomi.rosenberg@tufts.edu.

School of Dental Medicine Offers dental medicine (MS, DMD, Certificate); dentistry (Certificate). DMD/MPH offered with School of Medicine.

School of Engineering *Program availability:* Part-time. Offers bioengineering (ME, MS); bioinformatics (MS); biomedical engineering (PhD); biotechnology engineering (PhD); chemical and biological engineering (ME, MS, PhD); civil engineering (ME, MS, PhD);

cognitive science (PhD); computer science (MS, PhD); electrical engineering (MS, PhD); engineering (ME, MS, MSEM, PhD); environmental engineering (ME, MS, PhD); human factors (MS); mechanical engineering (ME, MS, PhD). Electronic applications accepted.

The Gordon Institute *Program availability:* Part-time. Offers engineering management (MSEM); innovation and management (MS). Electronic applications accepted.

School of Medicine Offers biomedical sciences (MS); health communication (MS, Certificate); medicine (MPH, MS, Dr PH, MD, Certificate); pain research, education and policy (MS, Certificate); physician assistant (MS); public health (MPH, Dr PH).

School of the Museum of Fine Arts Offers art education (MAT); studio art (MFA, Postbaccalaureate Certificate). Electronic applications accepted.

See Display below and Close-Up on page 903.

TULANE UNIVERSITY, New Orleans, LA 70118-5669

General Information Independent, coed, university. CGS member. *Enrollment:* 11,034 graduate, professional, and undergraduate students; 4,278 full-time matriculated graduate/professional students (2,310 women), 851 part-time matriculated graduate/professional students (455 women). *Enrollment by degree level:* 2,267 master's, 2,706 doctoral, 156 other advanced degrees. *Graduate faculty:* 59 full-time (29 women), 34 part-time/adjunct (20 women). *Tuition:* Full-time $50,920; part-time $2829 per credit hour. *Required fees:* $2040; $44.50 per credit hour. $580 per term. Tuition and fees vary according to course load, degree level and program. *Graduate housing:* Rooms and/or apartments available on a first-come, first-served basis to single and married students. Typical cost: $9660 per year for single students; $19,200 per year for married students. Room charges vary according to board plan, campus/location and housing facility selected. *Student services:* Campus employment opportunities, campus safety program, career counseling, child daycare facilities, exercise/wellness program, free psychological counseling, grant writing training, international student services, low-cost health insurance, multicultural affairs office, services for students with disabilities, teacher training, writing training. *Library facilities:* Howard Tilton Memorial Library plus 8 others. *Collection:* Books: 4.6 million (physical); Serial titles: 107,639 (physical). *Research affiliation:* AbbVie (hepatitis and diabetes), Boehringer Ingelheim (heart disease, lung disease, stroke, diabetes), Genentech (antiviral treatment and pulmonary disease), New Orleans BioInnovation Center (NOBIC) (business consulting and start-up support, including educational events), Louisiana Cancer Research Consortium (treatment and prevention of cancer), American Heart Association (clinical research in cardiovascular diseases).

Computer facilities: 556 computers available on campus for general student use. A campuswide network can be accessed from student residence rooms and from off campus. Online class registration is available. Website: http://www.tulane.edu/

General Application Contact: Jennifer O'Brien, Program Manager, 504-247-1213, Fax: 504-865-6723, E-mail: ogps@tulane.edu.

GRADUATE UNITS

A. B. Freeman School of Business Students: 488 full-time (240 women), 414 part-time (198 women); includes 81 minority (31 Black or African American, non-Hispanic/Latino; 1 American Indian or Alaska Native, non-Hispanic/Latino; 17 Asian, non-Hispanic/Latino; 29 Hispanic/Latino; 3 Two or more races, non-Hispanic/Latino), 575 international. Average age 27. 2,038 applicants, 71% accepted, 511 enrolled. *Faculty:* 46 full-time (11 women), 36 part-time/adjunct (3 women). Expenses: Contact institution.

Financial support: In 2016–17, 153 students received support. Fellowships with tuition reimbursements available, research assistantships, teaching assistantships, career-related internships or fieldwork, Federal Work-Study, tuition waivers (full and partial), and unspecified assistantships available. Support available to part-time students. Financial award application deadline: 4/15; financial award applicants required to submit FAFSA. In 2016, 694 master's, 9 doctorates awarded. *Program availability:* Part-time, evening/weekend. Offers accounting (M Acct); analytics (MBA); banking and financial services (M Fin); energy (M Fin, MBA); entrepreneurship (MBA); finance (MBA, PhD); international business (MBA); international management (MBA); strategic management and leadership (MBA). *Application deadline:* For fall admission, 11/1 priority date for domestic and international students; for winter admission, 1/6 for domestic and international students; for spring admission, 3/1 priority date for domestic and international students; for summer admission, 5/5 for domestic students. Applications are processed on a rolling basis. *Application fee:* $125. Electronic applications accepted. *Application Contact:* Melissa Booth, Director of Graduate Admissions and Financial Aid, 800-223-5402, E-mail: freeman.admissions@tulane.edu. *Dean,* Ira Solomon, PhD, 504-865-5407, Fax: 504-865-5491, E-mail: businessdean@tulane.edu.

Program in Liberal Arts *Program availability:* Part-time. Offers liberal arts (MLA).

School of Architecture *Program availability:* Part-time. Offers architecture (M Arch, M Arch II, MPS, MSRED).

School of Law Offers American business law (LL M); international development (MS, PhD); law (JD, SJD). Electronic applications accepted.

The Payson Center for International Development *Program availability:* Part-time. Offers international development (MS, PhD); law and development (LL M). Electronic applications accepted.

School of Liberal Arts *Program availability:* Part-time. Offers anthropology (PhD); classical studies (MA); design and technical production (MFA); economics (MA, PhD); English (MA); French (MA, PhD); history (MA, PhD); history of art (MA); liberal arts (MA, MFA, PhD); music (MA, MFA); philosophy (MA, PhD); political science (PhD); Portuguese (MA); sociology (MA); Spanish and Portuguese (PhD); studio art (MFA). Electronic applications accepted.

Roger Thayer Stone Center for Latin American Studies Offers Latin American studies (MA, PhD). Electronic applications accepted.

School of Medicine Offers medicine (MS, MD, PhD).

Graduate Programs in Biomedical Sciences Offers biochemistry and molecular biology (MS); biomedical sciences (MS, PhD); human genetics (MS); microbiology and immunology (MS); molecular and cellular biology (PhD); neuroscience (MS, PhD); pharmacology (MS); physiology (MS); structural and cellular biology (MS, PhD).

School of Public Health and Tropical Medicine *Program availability:* Part-time, evening/weekend, online learning. Offers biostatistics and bioinformatics (MS, MSPH, PhD); clinical tropical medicine and travelers health (Diploma); community health sciences (MPH); epidemiology (MPH, MS, Dr PH, PhD); global community health and behavioral sciences (Dr PH, PhD); global environmental health sciences (MPH, MSPH, PhD); global health management and policy (MHA, MPH, PhD, Sc D); parasitology (PhD); public health (MSPH); public health and tropical medicine (MPHTM). MS and PhD offered through the Graduate School. Electronic applications accepted.

School of Science and Engineering *Program availability:* Part-time. Offers biomedical engineering (MS, PhD); cell and molecular biology (MS, PhD); chemical and biomolecular engineering (MS, PhD); chemistry (MS, PhD); ecology and evolutionary biology (MS, PhD); interdisciplinary studies (PhD); mathematics (MS, PhD); neuroscience (MS, PhD); physics (PhD); psychology (MS, PhD); science and engineering (MS, PhD). MS and PhD offered through the Graduate School. Electronic applications accepted.

School of Social Work *Program availability:* Part-time. Offers city, culture and community (PhD); disaster resilience leadership (MS); social work (MSW, DSW). Electronic applications accepted.

TUSCULUM COLLEGE, Greeneville, TN 37743-9997

General Information Independent-religious, coed, comprehensive institution. *Tuition:* Full-time $7497; part-time $357 per credit hour. *Graduate housing:* On-campus housing not available. *Student services:* Career counseling, child daycare facilities. *Library facilities:* Thomas J. Garland Library plus 2 others. *Collection:* Books: 47,855 (physical), 432,852 (digital/electronic); Databases: 152. Students can reserve study rooms.

Computer facilities: 200 computers available on campus for general student use. A campuswide network can be accessed from student residence rooms and from off campus. Online class registration is available.
Website: http://www.tusculum.edu/

General Application Contact: Lindsey Seal, Director of Enrollment, 423-636-7300 Ext. 5006, E-mail: lseal@tusculum.edu.

GRADUATE UNITS

Graduate and Professional Studies Expenses: Contact institution. *Program availability:* Evening/weekend. Offers general management (MBA); healthcare administration (MBA); human resources (MBA); mathematics education (MA Ed); nonprofit management (MBA); special education (MA Ed); teaching (MAT). *Application deadline:* Applications are processed on a rolling basis. *Application fee:* $0. *Application Contact:* Lindsey Seal, Director of Enrollment, 423-636-7300 Ext. 5006, E-mail: lseal@tusculum.edu. *Vice President of Academic Affairs,* Dr. Jason Pierce, 423-636-7300 Ext. 5305, Fax: 423-638-7166, E-mail: jpierce@tusculum.edu.

TUSKEGEE UNIVERSITY, Tuskegee, AL 36088

General Information Independent, coed, comprehensive institution. *Graduate housing:* Rooms and/or apartments available to single students and available on a first-come, first-served basis to married students. Housing application deadline: 5/1. *Research affiliation:* Boeing (engineering), Chevron (engineering), 3M Corporation (engineering), U.S. Department of Education (DOE) (agriculture), U.S. Department of Defense (agriculture).

GRADUATE UNITS

Graduate Programs *Program availability:* Part-time. Offers integrative biosciences (PhD).

Andrew F. Brimmer College of Business and Information Science Offers information systems and security management (MS).

College of Agriculture, Environment and Nutrition Sciences Offers agricultural and resource economics (MS); agriculture, environment and nutrition sciences (MS); animal and poultry breeding (MS); animal and poultry nutrition (MS); animal and poultry physiology (MS); animal and poultry sciences (MS); environmental sciences (MS); food and nutritional sciences (MS); plant and soil sciences (MS).

College of Arts and Sciences Offers arts and sciences (MS); biology (MS); chemistry (MS).

College of Engineering Offers electrical engineering (MSEE); engineering (MSEE, MSME, PhD); materials science and engineering (PhD); mechanical engineering (MSME).

College of Veterinary Medicine, Nursing and Allied Health Offers occupational therapy (MS); veterinary medicine (MS, DVM); veterinary medicine, nursing and allied health (MS, DVM).

TYNDALE UNIVERSITY COLLEGE & SEMINARY, Toronto, ON M2M 3S4, Canada

General Information Independent-religious, coed, comprehensive institution. *Graduate housing:* Room and/or apartments available on a first-come, first-served basis to single students; on-campus housing not available to married students.

GRADUATE UNITS

Graduate Programs *Program availability:* Part-time, online learning. Offers Biblical studies (M Div); Christian foundations (MTS); Christian studies (Diploma); counseling (M Div); educational ministry (M Div); missions (M Div, Diploma); pastoral and Chinese ministry (M Div); pastoral ministry (M Div); Pentecostal studies (MTS); spiritual formation (M Div, Diploma); theological studies (M Div); theology (Th M); worship and liturgy (M Div, MTS); youth and family ministry (M Div). Electronic applications accepted.

UNIFICATION THEOLOGICAL SEMINARY, Barrytown, NY 12507

General Information Independent-religious, coed, graduate-only institution. *Enrollment by degree level:* 73 master's, 27 doctoral. *Graduate faculty:* 6 full-time (1 woman), 10 part-time/adjunct (2 women). *Tuition:* Full-time $11,760; part-time $490 per credit. *Required fees:* $320; $250 per credit. $125 per semester. Tuition and fees vary according to degree level. *Graduate housing:* Rooms and/or apartments available on a first-come, first-served basis to single and married students. Typical cost: $5400 per year for single students; $9600 per year for married students. Room charges vary according to housing facility selected. *Student services:* Campus employment opportunities, career counseling, free psychological counseling, international student services, writing training. *Library facilities:* Seminary Library plus 1 other. *Collection:* Books: 58,613 (physical), 71,216 (digital/electronic); Databases: 26. Weekly public service hours: 45.

Computer facilities: 10 computers available on campus for general student use. A campuswide network can be accessed from student residence rooms. Online class registration is available.
Website: http://www.uts.edu/

General Application Contact: Henry Christopher, Director of Admissions, 212-563-6647 Ext. 205, Fax: 212-563-6431, E-mail: h.christopher@uts.edu.

GRADUATE UNITS

Graduate Program, Main Campus Students: 27 full-time (8 women); includes 15 minority (11 Black or African American, non-Hispanic/Latino; 2 Asian, non-Hispanic/Latino; 1 Hispanic/Latino; 1 Two or more races, non-Hispanic/Latino), 6 international. Average age 50. *Faculty:* 3 full-time (1 woman), 3 part-time/adjunct (0 women). Expenses: Contact institution. *Financial support:* In 2016–17, 2 students received support. Scholarships/grants available. Financial award application deadline: 6/15; financial award applicants required to submit FAFSA. In 2016, 12 master's, 5 doctorates awarded. *Program availability:* Part-time, evening/weekend. Offers divinity (M Div); ministry (D Min); religious education (MRE); religious studies (MA). *Application deadline:* For fall admission, 3/15 priority date for domestic and international students; for spring admission, 9/15 priority date for domestic and international students. Applications are processed on a rolling basis. *Application fee:* $30. Electronic applications accepted. *Application Contact:* Henry Christopher, Director of Admissions, 212-563-6647 Ext. 105, Fax: 845-752-3014, E-mail: h.christopher@uts.edu. *Vice-President for Academic Affairs,* Dr. Kathy Winings, 845-752-3000 Ext. 228, Fax: 845-752-3014, E-mail: academics@uts.edu.

Graduate Program, Maryland Satellite Center Students: 25 part-time (14 women); all minorities (all Black or African American, non-Hispanic/Latino). Average age 41. *Faculty:* 1 full-time, 1 (woman) part-time/adjunct. Expenses: Contact institution. *Financial support:* In 2016–17, 25 students received support. Scholarships/grants available. Financial award application deadline: 6/15; financial award applicants required to submit FAFSA. *Program availability:* Part-time, evening/weekend. Offers theology (M Div, MA, MRE). *Application deadline:* For fall admission, 3/15 priority date for domestic and international students; for spring admission, 9/15 priority date for domestic and international students. Applications are processed on a rolling basis. *Application fee:* $30. Electronic applications accepted. *Application Contact:* Henry Christopher, Director of Admissions and Financial Aid, 212-563-6647 Ext. 105, E-mail: admissions@uts.edu. *Director,* John Paul James, 240-384-7860.

New York Extension Center Students: 25 full-time (9 women), 23 part-time (6 women); includes 24 minority (8 Black or African American, non-Hispanic/Latino; 9 Asian, non-Hispanic/Latino; 3 Hispanic/Latino; 4 Two or more races, non-Hispanic/Latino), 14 international. Average age 43. *Faculty:* 4 full-time (0 women), 7 part-time/adjunct (1 woman). Expenses: Contact institution. *Financial support:* In 2016–17, 48 students received support. Career-related internships or fieldwork, scholarships/grants, tuition waivers (partial), and on-campus employment (for international students) available. Support available to part-time students. Financial award application deadline: 6/15; financial award applicants required to submit FAFSA. *Program availability:* Part-time, evening/weekend. Offers divinity (M Div); religious education (MRE); religious studies (MA). *Application deadline:* For fall admission, 8/15 for domestic students, 3/15 priority date for international students; for spring admission, 1/15 for domestic students, 9/15 priority date for international students. Applications are processed on a rolling basis. *Application fee:* $30. Electronic applications accepted. *Application Contact:* Joy Theriot, Recruiter, 212-563-6647 Ext. 110, Fax: 212-563-6431, E-mail: j.theriot@uts.edu. *Vice-President for Academic Affairs,* Dr. Kathy Winings, 212-563-6647 Ext. 101, Fax: 212-563-6431, E-mail: academics@uts.edu.

UNIFORMED SERVICES UNIVERSITY OF THE HEALTH SCIENCES, Bethesda, MD 20814-4799

General Information Federally supported, coed, graduate-only institution. *Enrollment by degree level:* 44 master's, 780 doctoral. *Graduate faculty:* 372 full-time (119 women), 4,044 part-time/adjunct (908 women). *Graduate housing:* On-campus housing not available. *Student services:* Campus safety program, career counseling, child daycare facilities, exercise/wellness program, free psychological counseling, grant writing training, low-cost health insurance, multicultural affairs office, teacher training, writing training. *Library facilities:* James A. Zimble Learning Resource Center. *Collection:* Study areas open 24 hours, 5–7 days a week; students can reserve study rooms. *Research affiliation:* National Library of Medicine, National Institutes of Health, Walter Reed Army Institute of Research, Armed Forces Institute of Pathology, U.S. Armed Forces Radiobiology Research Institute.

Computer facilities: 100 computers available on campus for general student use. A campuswide network can be accessed. Online class registration is available. Website: http://www.usuhs.edu/

General Application Contact: Tina Finley, Program Administrative Specialist, 301-295-9474, Fax: 301-295-6772, E-mail: netina.finley@usuhs.edu.

GRADUATE UNITS

Daniel K. Inouye Graduate School of Nursing Students: 151 full-time (89 women); includes 41 minority (17 Black or African American, non-Hispanic/Latino; 2 American Indian or Alaska Native, non-Hispanic/Latino; 9 Asian, non-Hispanic/Latino; 13 Hispanic/Latino). Average age 34. 88 applicants, 76% accepted, 67 enrolled. *Faculty:* 42 full-time (25 women), 2 part-time/adjunct (1 woman). Expenses: Contact institution. In 2016, 1 master's, 52 doctorates awarded. Offers adult-gerontology clinical nurse specialist (MSN, DNP); family nurse practitioner (DNP); nurse anesthesia (DNP); nursing science (PhD); psychiatric mental health nurse practitioner (DNP); women's health nurse practitioner (DNP). *Application deadline:* For winter admission, 2/15 for domestic students; for summer admission, 8/15 for domestic students. *Application fee:* $0. Electronic applications accepted. *Application Contact:* Terry Lynn Malavakis, Registrar, 301-295-1055, Fax: 301-295-1707, E-mail: terry.malavakis@usuhs.edu. *Associate Dean for Academic Affairs,* Dr. Diane C. Seibert, 301-295-1080, Fax: 301-295-1707, E-mail: diane.seibert@usuhs.edu.

F. Edward Hebert School of Medicine Offers medicine (MPH, MS, MSPH, MTMH, Dr PH, MD, PhD).

Graduate Programs in the Biomedical Sciences and Public Health Offers clinical psychology (PhD); emerging infectious diseases (PhD); environmental health sciences (PhD); healthcare administration and policy (MS); medical and clinical psychology (PhD); medical psychology (PhD); medical zoology (PhD); medicine (MS, PhD); molecular and cell biology (MS, PhD); neuroscience (PhD); preventive medicine and biometrics (MPH, MS, MSPH, MTMH, Dr PH, PhD); public health (MPH, MSPH, Dr PH); tropical medicine and hygiene (MTMH). Electronic applications accepted.

UNION COLLEGE, Barbourville, KY 40906-1499

General Information Independent-religious, coed, comprehensive institution. *Graduate housing:* Rooms and/or apartments available to single and married students.

GRADUATE UNITS

Graduate Programs *Program availability:* Part-time, evening/weekend. Offers clinical psychology (MA); counseling psychology (MA); elementary education (MA); health (MA Ed); health and physical education (MA); middle grades (MA); music education (MA); principalship (MA); reading specialist (MA); school psychology (MA); secondary education (MA); special education (MA).

UNION COLLEGE, Lincoln, NE 68506-4300

General Information Independent-religious, coed, comprehensive institution. *Graduate housing:* Rooms and/or apartments available on a first-come, first-served basis to single and married students.

GRADUATE UNITS

Physician Assistant Program Offers physician assistant (MPAS). Electronic applications accepted.

UNION INSTITUTE & UNIVERSITY, Cincinnati, OH 45206-1925

General Information Independent, coed, university. *Enrollment:* 1,133 graduate, professional, and undergraduate students; 313 full-time matriculated graduate/professional students (228 women), 134 part-time matriculated graduate/professional students (101 women). *Enrollment by degree level:* 172 master's, 179 doctoral, 11 other advanced degrees. *Graduate faculty:* 26 full-time (14 women), 31 part-time/adjunct (20 women). *Tuition:* Full-time $13,080; part-time $6540 per credit. *Required fees:* $176; $176 per credit. $88 per semester. Tuition and fees vary according to degree level and program. *Student services:* Campus employment opportunities, career counseling, international student services, low-cost health insurance, services for students with disabilities, writing training. *Library facilities:* Union Institute & University Library. *Collection:* Books: 3 million (digital/electronic); Serial titles: 77,317 (digital/electronic); Databases: 171. Weekly public service hours: 50.

Computer facilities: Computer purchase and lease plans are available. 65 computers available on campus for general student use. A campuswide network can be accessed from off campus. Online class registration, CampusWeb: access to basic information are available. Website: http://www.myunion.edu/

General Application Contact: Admissions Office, 513-861-6400, E-mail: admissions@myunion.edu.

GRADUATE UNITS

Master of Arts Program Students: 9 full-time (7 women), 70 part-time (56 women); includes 33 minority (22 Black or African American, non-Hispanic/Latino; 1 American Indian or Alaska Native, non-Hispanic/Latino; 6 Hispanic/Latino; 4 Two or more races, non-Hispanic/Latino). Average age 40. *Faculty:* 2 full-time (both women), 9 part-time/adjunct (7 women). Expenses: Contact institution. *Financial support:* Career-related internships or fieldwork and tuition waivers available. Financial award applicants required to submit FAFSA. In 2016, 45 master's awarded. *Program availability:* Part-time, online only, 100% online. Offers creativity studies (MA); health and wellness (MA); history and culture (MA); leadership, public policy, and social issues (MA); literature and writing (MA). *Application deadline:* For spring admission, 3/13 for domestic students. Applications are processed on a rolling basis. *Application fee:* $50. Electronic applications accepted. *Application Contact:* Director of Admissions, 800-861-6400. *Director,* Elden Golden, 513-487-1153, E-mail: elden.golden@myunion.edu.

Master of Arts Program in Clinical Mental Health Counseling Students: 34 full-time (29 women), 29 part-time (20 women); includes 11 minority (7 Black or African American, non-Hispanic/Latino; 1 Asian, non-Hispanic/Latino; 2 Hispanic/Latino; 1 Two or more races, non-Hispanic/Latino). Average age 40. *Faculty:* 4 full-time (2 women), 6 part-time/adjunct (4 women). Expenses: Contact institution. *Financial support:* Federal Work-Study available. Financial award applicants required to submit FAFSA. In 2016, 12 master's awarded. *Program availability:* Online only, blended/hybrid learning. Offers clinical mental health counseling (MA). *Application deadline:* Applications are processed on a rolling basis. *Application fee:* $50. Electronic applications accepted. *Application Contact:* Director of Admissions, 888-828-8575. *Dean,* Dr. Bill Lax, 802-254-0152, E-mail: bill.lax@myunion.edu.

Master of Science Program in Organizational Leadership Students: 49 full-time (21 women), 5 part-time (2 women); includes 33 minority (18 Black or African American, non-Hispanic/Latino; 2 American Indian or Alaska Native, non-Hispanic/Latino; 1 Asian, non-Hispanic/Latino; 7 Hispanic/Latino; 2 Native Hawaiian or other Pacific Islander, non-

Hispanic/Latino; 3 Two or more races, non-Hispanic/Latino). Average age 40. *Faculty:* 6 part-time/adjunct (2 women). Expenses: Contact institution. *Financial support:* Federal Work-Study available. In 2016, 14 master's awarded. *Program availability:* Part-time, online only, 100% online. Offers organizational leadership (MS). *Application deadline:* Applications are processed on a rolling basis. *Application fee:* $50. Electronic applications accepted. *Application Contact:* Admissions Office, 513-861-6400, E-mail: admissions@myunion.edu. *Director,* Nadine Wheat, E-mail: nadine.wheat@myunion.edu.

PhD Program in Interdisciplinary Studies Students: 122 full-time (76 women), 19 part-time (14 women); includes 76 minority (58 Black or African American, non-Hispanic/Latino; 4 American Indian or Alaska Native, non-Hispanic/Latino; 2 Asian, non-Hispanic/Latino; 8 Hispanic/Latino; 3 Native Hawaiian or other Pacific Islander, non-Hispanic/Latino; 1 Two or more races, non-Hispanic/Latino). Average age 46. *Faculty:* 9 full-time (5 women), 16 part-time/adjunct (7 women). Expenses: Contact institution. *Financial support:* Federal Work-Study and scholarships/grants available. Financial award application deadline: 5/1; financial award applicants required to submit FAFSA. In 2016, 22 doctorates awarded. *Program availability:* Part-time, online only, blended/hybrid learning. Offers education studies (PhD). Program requires participation in brief on-campus residencies twice each year (January and July). *Application deadline:* Applications are processed on a rolling basis. *Application fee:* $50. Electronic applications accepted. *Application Contact:* Admissions Counselor, 800-486-3116. *Dean,* Dr. Michael Raffanti, 513-861-6400, E-mail: michael.raffanti@myunion.edu.

UNION PRESBYTERIAN SEMINARY, Richmond, VA 23227-4597

General Information Independent-religious, coed, graduate-only institution. *Graduate housing:* Rooms and/or apartments available on a first-come, first-served basis to single and married students. Housing application deadline: 6/30.

GRADUATE UNITS

Graduate and Professional Programs *Program availability:* Part-time, evening/weekend, online learning. Electronic applications accepted.

UNION THEOLOGICAL SEMINARY IN THE CITY OF NEW YORK, New York, NY 10027-5710

General Information Independent-religious, coed, graduate-only institution. *Graduate housing:* Rooms and/or apartments available on a first-come, first-served basis to single and married students. Housing application deadline: 5/15.

GRADUATE UNITS

Graduate and Professional Programs *Program availability:* Part-time. Offers theology (M Div, MA, STM, Ed D, PhD). Ed D offered jointly with Teachers College, Columbia University; M Div/MSSW with Columbia University.

UNION UNIVERSITY, Jackson, TN 38305-3697

General Information Independent-religious, coed, comprehensive institution. *Enrollment:* 3,339 graduate, professional, and undergraduate students; 598 full-time matriculated graduate/professional students (389 women), 322 part-time matriculated graduate/professional students (209 women). *Enrollment by degree level:* 774 master's, 85 doctoral, 61 other advanced degrees. *Graduate faculty:* 19 full-time (13 women), 45 part-time/adjunct (27 women). *Tuition:* Full-time $10,300. *Required fees:* $20. *Graduate housing:* Rooms and/or apartments available on a first-come, first-served basis to single and married students. Housing application deadline: 8/1. *Student services:* Career counseling, exercise/wellness program, free psychological counseling, international student services, services for students with disabilities, teacher training. *Library facilities:* The Logos Library plus 1 other. *Collection:* Books: 133,129 (physical), 265,144 (digital/electronic); Serial titles: 1,272 (physical), 42,526 (digital/electronic); Databases: 123. Weekly public service hours: 94; students can reserve study rooms.

Computer facilities: A campuswide network can be accessed from student residence rooms and from off campus. Online class registration is available. Website: http://www.uu.edu/

General Application Contact: Christopher R. Brown, Director of Recruitment and Enrollment, 731-661-5947, E-mail: cbrown@uu.edu.

GRADUATE UNITS

Institute for International and Intercultural Studies *Program availability:* Part-time, evening/weekend. Offers international and intercultural studies (MAIS). Electronic applications accepted.

McAfee School of Business Administration *Program availability:* Evening/weekend, online learning. Offers accountancy (M Acc). Program also available at Germantown campus. Electronic applications accepted.

School of Education *Program availability:* Part-time, evening/weekend, online learning. Offers education (M Ed, MA Ed); education administration generalist (Ed S); educational leadership (Ed D); educational supervision (Ed S); higher education (Ed D). M Ed also available at Germantown campus. Electronic applications accepted.

School of Nursing Offers executive leadership (DNP); nurse anesthesia (DNP); nurse practitioner (DNP); nursing education (MSN, PMC). Electronic applications accepted.

School of Pharmacy Offers pharmacy (Pharm D).

School of Social Work Offers social work (MSW).

School of Theology and Missions *Program availability:* Part-time, evening/weekend, online learning. Offers Christian studies (MCS); expository preaching (D Min). Electronic applications accepted.

UNITED STATES ARMY COMMAND AND GENERAL STAFF COLLEGE, Fort Leavenworth, KS 66027-2301

General Information Federally supported, coed, primarily men, graduate-only institution. *Graduate housing:* Rooms and/or apartments available to single and married students.

GRADUATE UNITS

Graduate Program Offers military art and science (MMAS). Only career military officers are selected to attend United States Army Command and General Staff College; Graduate Program is voluntary for first-year students, but mandatory for second-year students.

UNITED STATES INTERNATIONAL UNIVERSITY–AFRICA, Nairobi 00800, Kenya

General Information Independent, coed, comprehensive institution. *Graduate housing:* Room and/or apartments available on a first-come, first-served basis to single students; on-campus housing not available to married students. Housing application deadline: 7/31.

GRADUATE UNITS

School of Arts and Sciences *Program availability:* Part-time, evening/weekend. Offers counseling psychology (MA); international relations (MA).

School of Business Administration *Program availability:* Part-time, evening/weekend. Offers business administration (GEMBA); entrepreneurship (MBA); finance (MBA); human resource management (MBA); information technology management (MBA); integrated studies (MBA); international business administration (MBA); management and organizational development (MS); marketing (MBA); organizational development (EMS); strategic management (MBA).

UNITED STATES MERCHANT MARINE ACADEMY, Kings Point, NY 11024-1699

General Information Federally supported, coed, comprehensive institution.

GRADUATE UNITS

Graduate Program Offers marine engineering (MS).

UNITED STATES SPORTS ACADEMY, Daphne, AL 36526-7055

General Information Independent, coed, upper-level institution. *Graduate housing:* On-campus housing not available.

GRADUATE UNITS

Graduate Programs *Program availability:* Part-time, online learning. Offers sport management (MSS, Ed D); sport studies (MSS); sports coaching (MSS); sports fitness and health (MSS); sports medicine (MSS). Electronic applications accepted.

UNITED STATES UNIVERSITY, San Diego, CA 92108

General Information Proprietary, coed, comprehensive institution.

GRADUATE UNITS

Family Nurse Practitioner Program Offers family nurse practitioner (MSN).

UNITED TALMUDICAL SEMINARY, Brooklyn, NY 11211

General Information Independent-religious, men only, comprehensive institution.

GRADUATE UNITS

Graduate Programs

UNITED THEOLOGICAL SEMINARY, Dayton, OH 45426

General Information Independent-religious, coed, graduate-only institution. *Tuition:* Full-time $13,630; part-time $6815 per semester. Tuition and fees vary according to program. *Student services:* Campus employment opportunities, international student services, writing training. *Library facilities:* O'Brien Library.

Computer facilities: 12 computers available on campus for general student use. Website: http://www.united.edu/

General Application Contact: Kathleen Boston, Admissions Associate, 937-529-2225 Ext. 4237, Fax: 866-359-9350, E-mail: utsadmis@united.edu.

GRADUATE UNITS

Graduate and Professional Programs Expenses: Contact institution. *Financial support:* Career-related internships or fieldwork, Federal Work-Study, and scholarships/grants available. Financial award application deadline: 4/1; financial award applicants required to submit CSS PROFILE or FAFSA. *Program availability:* Part-time, evening/weekend, online learning. Offers Christian ministries (MA); ministry (M Div, D Min); theological studies (MTS). *Application deadline:* For fall admission, 8/1 for domestic students, 1/15 for international students; for spring admission, 1/1 for domestic students. Applications are processed on a rolling basis. *Application fee:* $60. Electronic applications accepted. *Application Contact:* Kathleen Boston, Admissions Associate, 937-529-2225 Ext. 4237, E-mail: utsadmis@united.edu. *Academic Dean/Vice President for Academic Affairs,* Dr. David Watson, 937-529-2257, E-mail: dwatson@united.edu.

UNITED THEOLOGICAL SEMINARY OF THE TWIN CITIES, New Brighton, MN 55112-2598

General Information Independent-religious, coed, graduate-only institution. *Graduate housing:* Rooms and/or apartments available on a first-come, first-served basis to single and married students.

GRADUATE UNITS

Graduate Programs *Program availability:* Part-time, evening/weekend. Offers advanced theological studies (Diploma); justice and peace studies (M Div, MA); leadership toward racial justice (M Div, MA, Certificate); Methodist studies (M Div, MA, Certificate); ministry (D Min); ministry renewal and professional development (Certificate); pastoral care and counseling (M Div, MA, MARL); religion and theology (MA); theological and religious studies (Certificate); theology and the arts (M Div, MA); urban ministry (M Div, MA, MARL); women's studies: religion, theology and ministry (M Div, MA).

UNITY COLLEGE, Unity, ME 04988

General Information Independent, coed, comprehensive institution.

GRADUATE UNITS

Program in Professional Science *Program availability:* Online learning. Offers sustainability science (MS); sustainable natural resource management (MS).

UNIVERSIDAD ADVENTISTA DE LAS ANTILLAS, Mayagüez, PR 00681-0118

General Information Independent-religious, coed, comprehensive institution. *Graduate housing:* Rooms and/or apartments available on a first-come, first-served basis to single and married students.

GRADUATE UNITS

EGECED Department Offers curriculum and instruction (M Ed); medical surgical nursing (MN); school administration and supervision (M Ed). Electronic applications accepted.

UNIVERSIDAD CENTRAL DEL CARIBE, Bayamón, PR 00960-6032

General Information Independent, coed, comprehensive institution. *Graduate housing:* On-campus housing not available.

GRADUATE UNITS

Program in Substance Abuse Counseling Offers substance abuse counseling (MHS).

School of Medicine Offers anatomy and cell biology (MA, MS); biochemistry (MS); biomedical sciences (MA); cellular and molecular biology (PhD); medicine (MA, MS, MD, PhD); microbiology and immunology (MA, MS); pharmacology (MS); physiology (MS).

UNIVERSIDAD DE LAS AMERICAS, A.C., 06700 Mexico City, Mexico

General Information Independent, coed, comprehensive institution.

GRADUATE UNITS

Program in Business Administration Offers finance (MBA); marketing research (MBA); production and quality (MBA).

Program in Education Offers education (M Ed).

Program in International Organizations and Institutions Offers international organizations and institutions (MA).

Program in Psychology Offers family therapy (MA).

UNIVERSIDAD DE LAS AMÉRICAS PUEBLA, Puebla CP 72810, Mexico

General Information Independent, coed, university. CGS member. *Graduate housing:* On-campus housing not available. *Research affiliation:* Empacadora San Marcos S. A. de C. U. (food service), Volkswagen de Mexico S. A. de C. U. (mechanical engineering), Institute Mexicano del Tecnologa del agua (electronic engineering), Frugosa S. A. de C. U. (chemical engineering).

GRADUATE UNITS

Division of Graduate Studies *Program availability:* Part-time, evening/weekend.

School of Business and Economics *Program availability:* Part-time, evening/weekend. Offers business administration (MBA); finance (M Adm).

School of Engineering *Program availability:* Part-time, evening/weekend. Offers chemical engineering (MS); computer science (PhD); construction management (M Adm); electronic engineering (MS); engineering (M Adm, MS, PhD); food sciences (MS); food technology (MS); industrial engineering (MS); manufacturing administration (MS); production management (M Adm).

School of Humanities *Program availability:* Part-time, evening/weekend. Offers humanities (MA); information design (MA); linguistics (MA); literature (MA).

School of Sciences *Program availability:* Part-time, evening/weekend. Offers biotechnology (MS); clinical analysis (biomedicine) (MA); sciences (MS).

School of Social Sciences *Program availability:* Part-time, evening/weekend. Offers American studies (MA); anthropology (MA); archaeology (MA); economics (MA); education (MA); finance (M Adm); psychology (MA); social sciences (M Adm, MA).

UNIVERSIDAD DEL ESTE, Carolina, PR 00984

General Information Independent, coed, comprehensive institution.

GRADUATE UNITS

Graduate School Offers accounting (MBA); adult education (M Ed); agribusiness (MBA); criminal justice and criminology (MA); curriculum and instruction - early education (M Ed); curriculum and instruction - elementary (M Ed); curriculum and instruction - English (M Ed); curriculum and instruction - Spanish (M Ed); human resources (MBA); information security management (MBA); information technology and Web business development (MBA); management (MBA); public policy (MPA); social work (MA); special education (M Ed); strategic leadership (MBA).

UNIVERSIDAD DEL TURABO, Gurabo, PR 00778-3030

General Information Independent, coed, university. CGS member. *Enrollment:* 978 full-time matriculated graduate/professional students (665 women), 1,020 part-time matriculated graduate/professional students (650 women). *Enrollment by degree level:* 1,509 master's, 446 doctoral, 43 other advanced degrees. *Graduate faculty:* 154 full-time (76 women), 777 part-time/adjunct (406 women). *Graduate housing:* On-campus housing not available. *Student services:* Campus employment opportunities, career counseling, child daycare facilities, free psychological counseling, services for students with disabilities, teacher training.

Computer facilities: A campuswide network can be accessed from off campus. Website: http://www.suagm.edu/ut/

General Application Contact: Carmen J. Rivera, Director of Admissions and Financial Aid, 787-743-7979 Ext. 4352, E-mail: ut_crivera@suagm.edu.

GRADUATE UNITS

Graduate Programs Students: 978 full-time (665 women), 1,020 part-time (650 women); all minorities (all Hispanic/Latino). Average age 34. 1,820 applicants, 50% accepted, 704 enrolled. Expenses: Contact institution. *Financial support:* Research assistantships, teaching assistantships, Federal Work-Study, institutionally sponsored loans, and unspecified assistantships available. Support available to part-time students. Financial award applicants required to submit FAFSA. In 2016, 459 master's, 70 doctorates, 5 other advanced degrees awarded. *Program availability:* Part-time, evening/weekend, 100% online, blended/hybrid learning. Offers athletic therapeutic (MPHE); coaching (MPHE); counseling (M Ed); curriculum and instruction and appropriate environment (D Ed); curriculum and teaching (M Ed); education (M Ed, MPHE, D Ed); educational administration (M Ed); educational leadership (D Ed); environmental analysis (MSE); environmental management (MSE); environmental science (D Sc); library service and information technology (M Ed); special education (M Ed); teaching at primary level (M Ed); teaching English as a second language (M Ed); teaching of fine arts (M Ed); wellness (MPHE). *Application deadline:* Applications are processed on a rolling basis. *Application fee:* $25. Electronic applications accepted. *Application Contact:* Diriee Rodríguez, Director of Admissions, 787-743-7979 Ext. 4453. *Dean,* Sharon Cantrell Mendez, 787-743-7979.

School of Business and Entrepreneurship Students: 234 full-time (135 women), 284 part-time (153 women); all minorities (all Hispanic/Latino). Average age 34. 494 applicants, 41% accepted, 187 enrolled. Expenses: Contact institution. *Financial support:* Institutionally sponsored loans available. Financial award applicants required to submit FAFSA. In 2016, 108 master's, 9 doctorates awarded. *Program availability:* Part-time, evening/weekend. Offers accounting (MBA); business and entrepreneurship (MBA, DBA); human resources (MBA); logistics and materials management (MBA); management (MBA, DBA); management of information systems (DBA); marketing (MBA); project management (MBA); quality management (MBA). *Application deadline:* For fall admission, 8/5 for domestic students. Applications are processed on a rolling basis. Electronic applications accepted. *Application Contact:* Diriee Rodríguez, Admissions Director, 787-743-7979 Ext. 4453, E-mail: admisiones-ut@suagm.edu. *Dean,* Juan Sosa, 787-743-7979 Ext. 4118, E-mail: negocios_ut@suagm.edu.

School of Engineering Students: 14 full-time (0 women), 46 part-time (7 women); all minorities (all Hispanic/Latino). Average age 34. 74 applicants, 41% accepted, 20 enrolled. Expenses: Contact institution. *Financial support:* Institutionally sponsored loans available. Financial award applicants required to submit FAFSA. In 2016, 13 master's awarded. Offers computer engineering (M Eng); electrical engineering

(M Eng); mechanical engineering (M Eng); telecommunications and network systems administration (M Eng). *Application deadline:* Applications are processed on a rolling basis. *Application fee:* $25. Electronic applications accepted. *Application Contact:* Diriee Rodríguez, Admissions Director, 787-743-7979 Ext. 4453, E-mail: admisiones-ut@suagm.edu. *Dean,* Héctor Rodríguez, 787-743-7979 Ext. 4144.

School of Health Sciences Students: 152 full-time (122 women), 26 part-time (17 women); all minorities (all Hispanic/Latino). Average age 31. 322 applicants, 48% accepted, 78 enrolled. Expenses: Contact institution. *Financial support:* Institutionally sponsored loans available. Financial award applicants required to submit FAFSA. In 2016, 58 master's, 28 doctorates awarded. Offers family nurse practitioner (MSN, Certificate); family nurse practitioner - adult nursing (MSN, Certificate); health sciences (MS, MSN, ND, Certificate); naturopathy (ND); speech and language pathology (MS). *Application deadline:* Applications are processed on a rolling basis. Electronic applications accepted. *Application Contact:* Diriee Rodríguez, Admissions Director, 787-743-7979 Ext. 4453, E-mail: admisiones-ut@suagm.edu. *Dean,* Nydia Bou, 787-743-7979 Ext. 4029.

School of Social Sciences and Humanities Students: 315 full-time (227 women), 219 part-time (166 women); all minorities (all Hispanic/Latino). Average age 31. 415 applicants, 52% accepted, 167 enrolled. Expenses: Contact institution. *Financial support:* Institutionally sponsored loans available. Financial award applicants required to submit FAFSA. In 2016, 129 master's, 10 doctorates, 2 Certificates awarded. Offers arts administration (MPA); conflict and mediation studies (MPA); counseling psychology (M Psych, Psy D, Certificate); criminal justice studies (MPA); forensic psychology (Certificate); forensic science (MPA); human services administration (MPA); psychology (M Psych); social sciences and humanities (M Psych, MPA, Psy D, Certificate). *Application deadline:* Applications are processed on a rolling basis. Electronic applications accepted. *Application Contact:* Diriee Rodríguez, Admissions Director, 787-743-7979 Ext. 4453, E-mail: admisiones-ut@suagm.edu. *Dean,* María del Carmen Santos, 787-743-7979 Ext. 4232.

UNIVERSIDAD DE MONTERREY, 66238 San Pedro Garza Garcia, NL, Mexico

General Information Independent-religious, coed, comprehensive institution.

GRADUATE UNITS

Graduate Programs

UNIVERSIDAD METROPOLITANA, San Juan, PR 00928-1150

General Information Independent, coed, comprehensive institution. *Graduate housing:* On-campus housing not available. *Research affiliation:* Berkeley National Laboratories (bioremediation), University Corporation for Atmospheric Research (computer science, atmospheric science), University of Colorado Boulder (computer science, biology), University of Puerto Rico (physics, chemistry), University of Utah (computational chemistry), Howard University (computational chemistry).

GRADUATE UNITS

School of Business Administration *Program availability:* Part-time, evening/weekend. Offers accounting (MBA); finance (MBA); human resources management (MBA); international business (MBA); management (MBA); management information systems (MBA); marketing (MBA). Electronic applications accepted.

School of Education *Program availability:* Part-time, evening/weekend. Offers administration and supervision (M Ed); curriculum and teaching (M Ed); education (M Ed, Ed D); educational administration and supervision (M Ed); managing recreation and sports services (M Ed); pedagogy (PhD); pre-school centers administration (M Ed); special education (M Ed); teaching of adult physical education (M Ed); teaching of elementary physical education (M Ed); teaching of physical education (M Ed); teaching of secondary physical education (M Ed). Electronic applications accepted.

School of Environmental Affairs *Program availability:* Part-time. Offers environmental management (MSEM); environmental planning (MP); environmental studies (MAES). Electronic applications accepted.

School of Health Sciences Offers case management (Certificate); health sciences (MSN, Certificate); nursing (MSN); oncology nursing (Certificate).

School of Social Sciences, Humanities and Communications Offers counseling psychology (MA).

UNIVERSITÉ DE MONCTON, Moncton, NB E1A 3E9, Canada

General Information Province-supported, coed, comprehensive institution. *Graduate housing:* Rooms and/or apartments available on a first-come, first-served basis to single and married students.

GRADUATE UNITS

Faculty of Administration Students: 38 full-time (15 women), 18 international. Average age 28. 125 applicants, 41% accepted, 17 enrolled. *Faculty:* 25 full-time (10 women), 16 part-time/adjunct (5 women). Expenses: Contact institution. *Financial support:* In 2016–17, 7 fellowships (averaging $2,500 per year) were awarded; teaching assistantships and institutionally sponsored loans also available. Support available to part-time students. Financial award application deadline: 5/30. In 2016, 20 master's awarded. *Program availability:* Part-time, evening/weekend, online learning. Offers administration (MBA). *Application deadline:* For fall admission, 6/1 for domestic students, 2/1 for international students; for winter admission, 11/15 for domestic students, 9/1 for international students; for spring admission, 3/31 for domestic students, 1/1 for international students; for summer admission, 3/31 for domestic students, 1/1 for international students. Applications are processed on a rolling basis. *Application fee:* $60. Electronic applications accepted. *Application Contact:* Natalie Allain, Admission Counselor, 506-858-4273, Fax: 506-858-4093, E-mail: natalie.allain@umoncton.ca. *Director,* Dr. Nha Nguyen, 506-858-4231, Fax: 506-858-4093, E-mail: nha.nguyen@umoncton.ca.

Faculty of Arts and Social Sciences *Program availability:* Part-time. Offers arts and social sciences (MA, MPA, MSW, PhD); economics (MA); French studies (MA, PhD); history (MA); public administration (MPA). Electronic applications accepted.

School of Social Work Offers social work (MSW).

Faculty of Education *Program availability:* Part-time. Offers education (M Ed, MA Ed).

Graduate Studies in Education *Program availability:* Part-time. Offers educational psychology (M Ed, MA Ed); guidance (M Ed, MA Ed); school administration (M Ed, MA Ed); teaching (M Ed, MA Ed).

Faculty of Engineering Offers civil engineering (M Sc A); electrical engineering (M Sc A); industrial engineering (M Sc A); mechanical engineering (M Sc A).

Faculty of Sciences *Program availability:* Part-time. Offers biochemistry (M Sc); biology (M Sc); chemistry (M Sc); information technology (M Sc, Certificate, Diploma); mathematics (M Sc); physics and astronomy (M Sc); sciences (M Sc, Certificate, Diploma). Electronic applications accepted.

School of Food Science, Nutrition and Family Studies *Program availability:* Part-time. Offers foods/nutrition (M Sc). Electronic applications accepted.

UNIVERSITÉ DE MONTRÉAL, Montréal, QC H3C 3J7, Canada

General Information Province-supported, coed, university. *Graduate housing:* Room and/or apartments available on a first-come, first-served basis to single students; on-campus housing not available to married students. Housing application deadline: 2/1. *Research affiliation:* Centre Hospitalier Universitaire Mere-Enfant de l'Hopital Sainte-Justine, Centre de Recherche de L'Hopital Sacre-Coeur, Institut de Recherches Cliniques de Montreal, Institut de Cardiologie de Montreal, Institut Universitaire de geriatric de Montreal.

GRADUATE UNITS

Department of Kinesiology Offers kinesiology (M Sc, DESS); physical activity (M Sc, PhD). Electronic applications accepted.

Faculty of Arts and Sciences *Program availability:* Part-time. Offers anthropology (M Sc, PhD); applied human sciences (PhD); art history (MA, PhD); arts and sciences (M Sc, MA, MIS, PhD, DESS); biological sciences (M Sc, PhD); chemistry (M Sc, PhD); classical studies (MA); communication (PhD); communication sciences (M Sc); comparative literature (MA); computer systems (M Sc, PhD); demography (M Sc, PhD); economics (M Sc, PhD); electronic commerce (M Sc); English studies (MA, PhD); environment and durable development (DESS); film studies (MA, PhD); French literature (MA, PhD); geography (M Sc, PhD, DESS); German literature (PhD); German studies (MA); Hispanic literature (PhD); Hispanic studies (MA); history (MA, PhD); international studies (M Sc, DESS); linguistics (MA, PhD); literature (PhD); mathematical and computational finance (M Sc, DESS); mathematics (M Sc, PhD); museology (MA); philosophy (MA, PhD); physics (M Sc, PhD); political science (M Sc, PhD); psychology (M Sc, PhD); societies, public policies and health (DESS); sociology (M Sc, PhD); statistics (M Sc, PhD); translation (MA, PhD, DESS). Electronic applications accepted.

School of Criminology Offers criminology (M Sc, PhD). Electronic applications accepted.

School of Industrial Relations *Program availability:* Part-time. Offers industrial relations (M Sc, PhD, DESS). Electronic applications accepted.

School of Library and Information Sciences Offers information sciences (MIS, PhD). Electronic applications accepted.

School of Psychoeducation *Program availability:* Part-time. Offers psychoeducation (M Sc, PhD). Electronic applications accepted.

School of Social Service *Program availability:* Part-time. Offers social administration (DESS); social work (M Sc, PhD). M Sc and PhD offered jointly with McGill University. Electronic applications accepted.

Faculty of Dental Medicine Offers dental medicine (M Sc, Certificate); multidisciplinary residency (Certificate); oral and dental sciences (M Sc); orthodontics (M Sc); pediatric dentistry (M Sc); prosthodontics rehabilitation (M Sc); stomatology residency (Certificate). Electronic applications accepted.

Faculty of Education *Program availability:* Part-time, evening/weekend. Offers administration and foundations of education (M Ed, MA, PhD, DESS); didactics (M Ed, MA, PhD, DESS); education (M Ed, MA, PhD, DESS); psychopedagogy and andragogy (M Ed, MA, PhD, DESS). Electronic applications accepted.

Faculty of Environmental Design and Planning Offers environmental design and planning (M Sc A, PhD); environmental planning and design projects (DESS); game design (DESS); urban management for developing countries (DESS); urban planning (M Urb). DESS programs offered jointly with HEC Montreal and École Polytechnique de Montréal. Electronic applications accepted.

Faculty of Law *Program availability:* Part-time. Offers business law (DESS); common law (North America) (JD); international law (DESS); law (LL M, LL D, DDN, DESS, LL B); tax law (LL M). Electronic applications accepted.

Faculty of Medicine Offers biochemistry (M Sc, PhD, DEPD); bioethics (MA, DESS); bioinformatics (M Sc, PhD); biomedical sciences (M Sc, PhD); clinical biochemistry (DEPD); community health (M Sc, DESS); echography transoephagian perioperatoryenvironment, health and disaster management (DESS); environmental and occupational health (M Sc); genetic counseling (DESS); health administration (M Sc, DESS); health sciencesinsurance medicine and expertise (English) (DESS); insurance medicine and expertise in health sciences (DESS); medical genetics (DESS); medicine (M Sc, M Sc A, MA, PMS, DES, MD, PhD, DEPD, DESS); microbiology and immunology (M Sc, PhD); mobility and posture (DESS); molecular biology (M Sc, PhD); neurological sciences (M Sc, PhD); nutrition (M Sc, PhD, DESS); occupational therapy (DESS); pathology and cellular biology (M Sc, PhD); pharmacology (M Sc, PhD); physiology (M Sc, PhD); public health (PhD); toxicology and risk analysis (DESS). Electronic applications accepted.

Institute of Biomedical Engineering Offers biomedical engineering (M Sc A, PhD, DESS). M Sc A and PhD programs offered jointly with École Polytechnique de Montréal. Electronic applications accepted.

School of Speech Therapy and Audiology Offers audiology (PMS); speech therapy (PMS, DESS). Electronic applications accepted.

Faculty of Music Offers composition (M Mus, D Mus); interpretation (M Mus, D Mus, DESS); music (MA, PhD); orchestral repertoire (DESS). Electronic applications accepted.

Faculty of Nursing *Program availability:* Part-time. Offers nursing (M Sc, PhD, Certificate, DESS). PhD offered jointly with McGill University. Electronic applications accepted.

Faculty of Pharmacy *Program availability:* Part-time. Offers drugs development (DESS); pharmaceutical care (DESS); pharmaceutical practice (M Sc); pharmaceutical sciences (M Sc, PhD); pharmacist-supervisor teacher (DESS). Electronic applications accepted.

Faculty of Theology and Sciences of Religions Offers health, spirituality and bioethics (DESS); practical theology (MA, PhD); religious sciences (MA, PhD); theology (MA, D Th, PhD, L Th); theology-Biblical studies (PhD). Electronic applications accepted.

Faculty of Veterinary Medicine Offers veterinary medicine (M Sc, DES, PhD); veterinary sciences (M Sc, PhD); virology and immunology (PhD). Electronic applications accepted.

School of Optometry *Program availability:* Part-time. Offers optometry (M Sc, OD, DESS); vision sciences (M Sc); visual impairment intervention-orientation and mobility (DESS); visual impairment intervention-readaptation (DESS). Electronic applications accepted.

UNIVERSITÉ DE SAINT-BONIFACE, Saint-Boniface, MB R2H 0H7, Canada

General Information Independent-religious, coed, comprehensive institution.

GRADUATE UNITS
Department of Education Offers education (M Ed).
Program in Canadian Studies Offers Canadian studies (MA).

UNIVERSITÉ DE SHERBROOKE, Sherbrooke, QC J1K 2R1, Canada
General Information Independent, coed, university. *Graduate housing:* Room and/or apartments available to single students; on-campus housing not available to married students. Housing application deadline: 6/1. *Research affiliation:* Societe de Microelectronique Industrielle.
GRADUATE UNITS
Faculty of Administration *Program availability:* Part-time, evening/weekend. Offers accounting (M Sc); administration (EMBA, M Adm, M Sc, M Tax, MBA, DBA, PhD, Diploma); business administration (EMBA, MBA, DBA); e-commerce (M Sc); economic development (PhD); economics (M Sc); executive business administration (EMBA); finance (M Sc); general management (MBA); governance, audit and security of information technology (M Adm); international business (M Sc); management and governance of cooperatives and mutuals (M Adm); management information systems (M Sc); marketing (M Sc); marketing communications (M Adm); organizational change and intervention (M Sc); public management (M Adm); taxation (M Tax, Diploma).
Faculty of Education *Program availability:* Part-time, evening/weekend. Offers education (M Ed, MA, Diploma); elementary education (M Ed, Diploma); postsecondary education training (M Ed, Diploma); school administration (M Ed); sciences of education (MA); special education (M Ed, Diploma).
Faculty of Engineering *Program availability:* Part-time. Offers chemical engineering (M Sc A, PhD); civil engineering (M Sc A, PhD); electrical engineering (M Sc A, PhD); engineering (M Eng, M Env, M Sc A, PhD, Diploma); engineering management (M Eng, Diploma); environment (M Env); mechanical engineering (M Sc A, PhD). Electronic applications accepted.
Faculty of Law *Program availability:* Part-time, evening/weekend. Offers alternative dispute resolution (LL M, Diploma); business law (Diploma); common law (JD); criminal and penal law (Diploma); health law (LL M, Diploma); international law (LL M); law (LL D); legal management (Diploma); notarial law (Diploma); transnational law (Diploma). Electronic applications accepted.
Faculty of Letters and Human Sciences *Program availability:* Part-time. Offers comparative Canadian literature (MA, PhD); economics (MA); French literature (MA, PhD); geography and remote sensing (M Sc, PhD); gerontology (MA); history (MA); letters and human sciences (M Psych, M Sc, MA, MSS, PhD, Diploma); linguistics (MA); philosophy (MA); social service (MSS); theatre (MA).
Institute of Management and Development of Cooperatives Offers management and development of cooperatives (MA, Diploma).
Faculty of Medicine and Health Sciences *Program availability:* Part-time. Offers medicine (MD); medicine and health sciences (M Sc, MD, PhD). Electronic applications accepted.
Graduate Programs in Medicine *Program availability:* Part-time. Offers biochemistry (M Sc, PhD); cell biology (M Sc, PhD); clinical sciences (M Sc, PhD); immunology (M Sc, PhD); medicine (M Sc, PhD); microbiology (M Sc, PhD); pharmacology (M Sc, PhD); physiology and biophysics (M Sc, PhD); radiobiology (M Sc, PhD). Electronic applications accepted.
Faculty of Physical Education and Sports *Program availability:* Part-time. Offers kinanthropology (M Sc); physical activity (Diploma); physical education (M Sc, Diploma).
Faculty of Sciences Offers biology (M Sc, PhD, Diploma); chemistry (M Sc, PhD, Diploma); informatics (M Sc, PhD); mathematics (M Sc, PhD); physics (M Sc, PhD); sciences (M Sc, PhD, Diploma).
Centre de Formation en Technologies de L'information Offers information technologies (M Sc, Diploma). Electronic applications accepted.
Centre Universitaire de Formation en Environnement *Program availability:* Online learning. Offers environment (M Sc, Diploma). Electronic applications accepted.
Faculty of Theology and Religious Studies *Program availability:* Part-time, evening/weekend, online learning. Offers applied ethics (Diploma); human science of religions (MA); intercultural training (Diploma); philosophy (MA, PhD); spiritual anthropology (Diploma); theology (MA, PhD, Diploma).

UNIVERSITÉ DU QUÉBEC À CHICOUTIMI, Chicoutimi, QC G7H 2B1, Canada
General Information Province-supported, coed, university. CGS member. *Graduate housing:* Room and/or apartments available to single students; on-campus housing not available to married students.
GRADUATE UNITS
Graduate Programs *Program availability:* Part-time. Offers didactics of French-mother tongue (Diploma); earth sciences (M Sc A); education (M Ed, MA, PhD); engineering (M Sc A, PhD); ethics (Diploma); fine arts (MA); genetics (MA); linguistics (MA); literary studies (MA); mineral resources (PhD); project management (M Sc); regional studies (MA); renewable resources (M Sc); small and medium-sized organization management (M Sc); theology (pastoral studies) (MA, PhD).

UNIVERSITÉ DU QUÉBEC À MONTRÉAL, Montréal, QC H3C 3P8, Canada
General Information Province-supported, coed, university. CGS member. *Graduate housing:* Room and/or apartments available to single students; on-campus housing not available to married students. *Research affiliation:* Labopharm, Inc. (pharmacology), Hydro-Quebec (environmental sciences), Bell (computer sciences), Microcreatif (computer sciences), University Corporation for Atmospheric Research.
GRADUATE UNITS
Graduate Programs *Program availability:* Part-time. Offers accounting (M Sc, MPA, Diploma); actuarial sciences (Diploma); art history (PhD); art studies (MA); atmospheric sciences (M Sc); biology (M Sc, PhD); business administration (PhD); business administration (research) (MBA); chemistry (M Sc, PhD); communications (MA, PhD); dance (MA); death (Diploma); Earth and atmospheric sciences (PhD); Earth science (M Sc); earth sciences (M Sc); economics (M Sc, PhD); education (M Ed, MA, PhD); education of the environmental sciences (Diploma); environmental sciences (M Sc, PhD, Certificate); ergonomics in occupational health and safety (Diploma); finance (Diploma); fine arts (MA); geographical information systems (Diploma); geography (M Sc); history (MA, PhD); human movement studies (M Sc); linguistics (MA, PhD); literary studies (MA, PhD); management consultant (Diploma); management information systems (M Sc, M Sc A); mathematics (M Sc, PhD); meteorology (PhD, Diploma); mineral resources (PhD); museology (MA); non-renewable resources (DESS); philosophy (MA, PhD); political science (MA, PhD); project management (MGP, Diploma); psychology (D Ps,

PhD); religious sciences (MA, PhD); semiology (PhD); sexology (MA); social and labor law (Certificate); social intervention (MA); sociology (MA, PhD); study and practices of the arts (PhD); technology and management (MA); urban studies (MA, PhD).

UNIVERSITÉ DU QUÉBEC À RIMOUSKI, Rimouski, QC G5L 3A1, Canada
General Information Province-supported, coed, comprehensive institution. CGS member. *Graduate housing:* Rooms and/or apartments available on a first-come, first-served basis to single and married students. *Research affiliation:* Institut des Sciences de la Mer de Rimouski (ISMER) (marine sciences), CRDT (territory development), Centre d'Etudes Nordiques (Nordicity), Quebec Ocean (oceans), Centre Recherche en Forestere (forestry).
GRADUATE UNITS
Graduate Programs *Program availability:* Part-time. Offers biology (PhD); business administration (MBA); education (M Ed, MA, PhD, Diploma); engineering (M Sc A); ethics (MA, Diploma); literary studies (MA, PhD); management of marine resources (M Sc, Diploma); management of people in working situation (M Sc, Diploma); nursing studies (M Sc, Diploma); oceanography (M Sc, PhD); project management (M Sc, Diploma); psychosocial studies (MA); regional development (MA, PhD, Diploma); wildlife resources management (M Sc, Diploma).

UNIVERSITÉ DU QUÉBEC À TROIS-RIVIÈRES, Trois-Rivières, QC G9A 5H7, Canada
General Information Province-supported, coed, university. CGS member. *Graduate housing:* Room and/or apartments available to single students; on-campus housing not available to married students. Housing application deadline: 2/1.
GRADUATE UNITS
Graduate Programs *Program availability:* Part-time. Offers accounting science (MBA); biophysics and cellular biology (M Sc, PhD); business administration (MBA, DBA); chemistry (M Sc); chiropractic (DC); education (M Ed, PhD); educational administration (DESS); electrical engineering (M Sc A, PhD); environmental sciences (M Sc, PhD); finance (DESS); industrial engineering (M Sc, DESS); labor relations (DESS); leisure, culture and tourism sciences (MA, DESS); literary studies (MA); mathematics and computer science (M Sc); matter and energy (MS, PhD); nursing sciences (M Sc, DESS); philosophy (MA, PhD); physical education (M Sc); psychoeducation (M Ed, PhD); psychology (PhD, Certificate); social communication (MA, DESS).

UNIVERSITÉ DU QUÉBEC, ÉCOLE DE TECHNOLOGIE SUPÉRIEURE, Montréal, QC H3C 1K3, Canada
General Information Province-supported, coed, primarily men, comprehensive institution. CGS member. *Graduate housing:* Rooms and/or apartments available on a first-come, first-served basis to single and married students.
GRADUATE UNITS
Graduate Programs *Program availability:* Online learning. Offers engineering (M Eng, PhD, Diploma).

UNIVERSITÉ DU QUÉBEC, ÉCOLE NATIONALE D'ADMINISTRATION PUBLIQUE, Quebec, QC G1K 9E5, Canada
General Information Province-supported, coed, graduate-only institution. CGS member. *Graduate housing:* On-campus housing not available.
GRADUATE UNITS
Graduate Programs in Public Administration *Program availability:* Part-time. Offers international administration (MAP, Diploma); public administration (MAGU, MAP, PhD, Diploma); urban analysis and management (MAGU).

UNIVERSITÉ DU QUÉBEC EN ABITIBI-TÉMISCAMINGUE, Rouyn-Noranda, QC J9X 5E4, Canada
General Information Province-supported, coed, comprehensive institution. CGS member. *Graduate housing:* Room and/or apartments available on a first-come, first-served basis to single students; on-campus housing not available to married students. Housing application deadline: 3/1.
GRADUATE UNITS
Graduate Programs *Program availability:* Part-time. Offers biology (MS); business administration (MBA); education (M Ed, MA, PhD, DESS); engineering (ME); environmental sciences (PhD); mineral engineering (ME); mining engineering (DESS); organization management (M Sc); project management (M Sc, DESS); social work (MSW); sustainable forest ecosystem management (MS).

UNIVERSITÉ DU QUÉBEC EN OUTAOUAIS, Gatineau, QC J8X 3X7, Canada
General Information Province-supported, coed, university. CGS member. *Graduate housing:* Rooms and/or apartments available on a first-come, first-served basis to single and married students.
GRADUATE UNITS
Graduate Programs *Program availability:* Part-time, evening/weekend. Offers accounting (MA, DESS, Diploma); computer science (M Sc, PhD, DESS); education (M Ed, MA, PhD, DESS, Diploma); executive certified management accounting (MA, MBA, DESS); financial services (MBA, DESS, Diploma); industrial relations (M Sc, MA, PhD, Diploma); nursing (M Sc, DESS, Diploma); project management (M Sc, MA, DESS, Diploma); psychoeducation (M Ed, MA); regional development (MA); second and foreign language teaching (Diploma); social work (MA). Electronic applications accepted.

UNIVERSITÉ DU QUÉBEC, INSTITUT NATIONAL DE LA RECHERCHE SCIENTIFIQUE, Québec, QC G1K 9A9, Canada
General Information Province-supported, coed, graduate-only institution. CGS member. *Enrollment by degree level:* 222 master's, 411 doctoral, 2 other advanced degrees. *Graduate faculty:* 149 full-time. *Graduate housing:* On-campus housing not available. *Student services:* Exercise/wellness program, free psychological counseling, international student services, low-cost health insurance, services for students with disabilities. *Library facilities:* Service de documentation et d'information specialisees (SDIS) plus 3 others. *Research affiliation:* Axis Photonique, Tecosol Inc., Bio-K Plus International Inc.
Computer facilities: 500 computers available on campus for general student use. Online class registration is available.
Website: http://www.inrs.ca/
General Application Contact: Sylvie Richard, Registrar, 418-654-2518, Fax: 418-654-3858, E-mail: sylvie.richard@inrs.ca.

Université du Québec, Institut National de la Recherche Scientifique

GRADUATE UNITS

Graduate Programs Students: 585 full-time (267 women), 50 part-time (27 women), 370 international. Average age 31. 134 applicants, 86% accepted, 88 enrolled. *Faculty:* 149 full-time. Expenses: Contact institution. *Financial support:* In 2016–17, fellowships (averaging $16,500 per year) were awarded; research assistantships and scholarships/grants also available. In 2016, 65 master's, 60 doctorates awarded. *Program availability:* Part-time. *Application deadline:* For fall admission, 3/30 for domestic and international students; for winter admission, 11/1 for domestic and international students; for spring admission, 3/1 for domestic and international students. *Application fee:* $45. Electronic applications accepted. *Application Contact:* Sylvie Richard, Registrar, 418-654-2518, Fax: 418-654-3858, E-mail: sylvie.richard@adm.inrs.ca. *Vice Rector, Research and Academic Affairs,* Yves Begin, 418-654-2575, E-mail: yves.begin@ete.inrs.ca.

Centre for Energie Materiaux Telecommunications Students: 185 full-time (47 women), 10 part-time (2 women), 154 international. Average age 31. 27 applicants, 78% accepted, 13 enrolled. *Faculty:* 36 full-time. Expenses: Contact institution. *Financial support:* In 2016–17, fellowships (averaging $16,500 per year) were awarded; research assistantships and scholarships/grants also available. In 2016, 13 master's, 23 doctorates awarded. *Program availability:* Part-time. Offers energy and materials science (M Sc, PhD); telecommunications (M Sc, PhD). *Application deadline:* For fall admission, 3/30 for domestic and international students; for winter admission, 11/1 for domestic and international students; for spring admission, 3/1 for domestic and international students. *Application fee:* $45. Electronic applications accepted. *Application Contact:* Sylvie Richard, Registrar, 418-654-2518, Fax: 418-654-3858, E-mail: sylvie.richard@adm.inrs.ca. *Director,* Federico Rosei, 450-228-6905, E-mail: rosei@emt.inrs.ca.

Centre for Urbanisation Culture Societe Students: 79 full-time (43 women), 14 part-time (10 women), 13 international. Average age 32. 40 applicants, 88% accepted, 20 enrolled. *Faculty:* 34 full-time. Expenses: Contact institution. *Financial support:* In 2016–17, fellowships (averaging $16,500 per year) were awarded; research assistantships also available. In 2016, 17 master's, 5 doctorates awarded. *Program availability:* Part-time. Offers demography (M Sc, PhD); research practices and public action (MA, DESS); urban studies (M Sc, PhD). *Application deadline:* For fall admission, 3/30 for domestic and international students; for winter admission, 11/1 for domestic and international students; for spring admission, 3/1 for domestic and international students. *Application fee:* $45. Electronic applications accepted. *Application Contact:* Sylvie Richard, Registrar, 418-654-2518, Fax: 418-654-3858, E-mail: sylvie.richard@adm.inrs.ca. *Director,* Claire Poitras, 514-499-4002, E-mail: claire.poitras@ucs.inrs.ca.

INRS - Institut Armand-Frappier Students: 147 full-time (86 women), 12 part-time (7 women), 83 international. Average age 30. 28 applicants, 93% accepted, 26 enrolled. *Faculty:* 44 full-time. Expenses: Contact institution. *Financial support:* In 2016–17, fellowships (averaging $16,500 per year) were awarded; research assistantships also available. In 2016, 16 master's, 14 doctorates awarded. *Program availability:* Part-time. Offers applied microbiology (M Sc); biology (PhD); experimental health sciences (M Sc); virology and immunology (M Sc, PhD). *Application deadline:* For fall admission, 3/30 for domestic and international students; for winter admission, 11/1 for domestic and international students; for spring admission, 3/1 for domestic and international students. *Application fee:* $45 Canadian dollars. Electronic applications accepted. *Application Contact:* Sylvie Richard, Registrar, 418-654-2518, Fax: 418-654-3858, E-mail: sylvie.richard@adm.inrs.ca. *Director,* Pierre Talbot, 450-687-5010, Fax: 450-686-5501, E-mail: pierre.talbot@iaf.inrs.ca.

Research Center–Water Earth Environment Students: 174 full-time (91 women), 14 part-time (8 women), 120 international. Average age 30. 39 applicants, 85% accepted, 29 enrolled. *Faculty:* 35 full-time. Expenses: Contact institution. *Financial support:* In 2016–17, fellowships (averaging $16,500 per year) were awarded; research assistantships also available. In 2016, 19 master's, 18 doctorates awarded. *Program availability:* Part-time. Offers earth sciences (M Sc, PhD); earth sciences - environmental technologies (M Sc); water sciences (M Sc, PhD). *Application deadline:* For fall admission, 3/30 for domestic and international students; for winter admission, 11/1 for domestic and international students; for spring admission, 3/1 for domestic and international students. *Application fee:* $45. Electronic applications accepted. *Application Contact:* Sylvie Richard, Registrar, 418-654-2518, Fax: 418-654-3858, E-mail: sylvie.richard@adm.inrs.ca. *Director,* Jean-Francois Blais, 418-654-3674, Fax: 418-654-2600, E-mail: jean-francois.blais@ete.inrs.ca.

UNIVERSITÉ LAVAL, Québec, QC G1K 7P4, Canada

General Information Independent, coed, university. *Graduate housing:* Room and/or apartments available on a first-come, first-served basis to single students; on-campus housing not available to married students. *Research affiliation:* Centre Hospitalier Universitaire de Quebec (biomedical research), Institut National d'optique (optics and photonics), Centre de Developpement de la Geomatique (applied geomatics), Institut Maurice-Lamontagne (oceanography), Forintek Canada (forestry and wood processing), Societe des pades de Sciences Naturelles du Quebec (biology).

GRADUATE UNITS

Faculty of Administrative Sciences *Program availability:* Part-time, online learning. Offers accounting (MBA); administrative sciences (M Sc, MBA, PhD, Diploma); administrative studies (M Sc, PhD); agri-food management (MBA); electronic business (MBA, Diploma); factory management and logistics (MBA); finance (MBA); financial engineering (M Sc); firm management (MBA); geomatic management (MBA); information technology management (MBA); international management (MBA); management (MBA); management accounting (MBA, Diploma); marketing (MBA); modeling and organizational decision (MBA); occupational health and safety management (MBA); organizations management and development (Diploma); pharmacy management (MBA); public accountancy (MBA, Diploma); social and environmental responsibility (MBA); technological entrepreneurship (Diploma). Electronic applications accepted.

Faculty of Agricultural and Food Sciences *Program availability:* Part-time. Offers agri-food engineering (M Sc); agricultural and food sciences (M Sc, PhD, Diploma); agricultural economics (M Sc); agricultural microbiology (M Sc); agro-food microbiology (PhD); animal sciences (M Sc, PhD); consumer sciences (Diploma); environmental technology (M Sc); food sciences and technology (M Sc, PhD); integrated rural development (Diploma); nutrition (M Sc, PhD); plant biology (M Sc, PhD); soils and environment science (M Sc, PhD). Electronic applications accepted.

Faculty of Architecture, Planning and Visual Arts Offers architecture, planning and visual arts (M Arch, M Sc, MA, MATDR, PhD); planning and regional development (MATDR, PhD). Electronic applications accepted.

School of Architecture *Program availability:* Part-time. Offers architecture (M Arch, M Sc). Electronic applications accepted.

School of Visual Arts Offers graphic design and multimedia (MA); visual arts (MA). Electronic applications accepted.

Faculty of Dentistry Offers buccal and maxillofacial surgery (DESS); dentistry (M Sc, DMD, DESS); gerodontology (DESS); multidisciplinary dentistry (DESS); periodontics (DESS). Electronic applications accepted.

Faculty of Education *Program availability:* Part-time. Offers didactics (MA, PhD); education (MA, PhD, Diploma); educational administration and evaluation (MA, PhD); educational pedagogy (Diploma); educational practice (Diploma); educational psychology (MA, PhD); orientation sciences (MA, PhD); pedagogy management and development (Diploma); school adaptation (Diploma); teaching technology (MA, PhD). Electronic applications accepted.

Faculty of Forestry, Geography and Geomatics Offers agroforestry (M Sc); forestry sciences (M Sc, PhD); forestry, geography and geomatics (M Sc, M Sc Geogr, PhD); geographical sciences (M Sc Geogr, PhD); geography (M Sc Geogr, PhD); geomatics sciences (M Sc, PhD); wood sciences (M Sc, PhD). Electronic applications accepted.

Faculty of Law *Program availability:* Part-time. Offers environment, sustainable development and food safety (LL M); international and transnational law (LL M, Diploma); law (LL M, LL D, Diploma); law of business (LL M, Diploma); notarial law (Diploma). Electronic applications accepted.

Faculty of Letters *Program availability:* Part-time. Offers ancient civilization (MA, PhD); archaeology (MA, PhD); art history (MA, PhD); English literatures (MA, PhD); ethnology of French-speaking people in North America (MA, PhD); history (MA, PhD, Diploma); international journalism (Diploma); letters (MA, PhD, Diploma); linguistics (MA, PhD); literary studies (MA, PhD); literature and arts of the screen and stage (PhD); literature and arts of the screen and stage (MA); museology (Diploma); public communication (MA, PhD); public relations (Diploma); Spanish literature (MA, PhD); terminology and translation (MA, Diploma). Electronic applications accepted.

Faculty of Medicine *Program availability:* Part-time. Offers accident prevention and occupational health and safety management (Diploma); anatomy–pathology (DESS); anesthesiology (DESS); cardiology (DESS); care of older people (Diploma); cellular and molecular biology (M Sc, PhD); clinical research (DESS); community health (M Sc, PhD); dermatology (DESS); diagnostic radiology (DESS); emergency medicine (Diploma); epidemiology (M Sc, PhD); experimental medicine (M Sc, PhD); family medicine (DESS); general surgery (DESS); geriatrics (DESS); hematology (DESS); internal medicine (DESS); kinesiology (M Sc, PhD); maternal and fetal medicine (Diploma); medical biochemistry (DESS); medical microbiology and infectious diseases (DESS); medical oncology (DESS); medicine (M Sc, MD, PhD, DESS, Diploma); microbiology-immunology (M Sc, PhD); nephrology (DESS); neurobiology (M Sc, PhD); neurology (DESS); neurosurgery (DESS); obstetrics and gynecology (DESS); ophthalmology (DESS); orthopedic surgery (DESS); oto-rhino-laryngology (DESS); palliative medicine (Diploma); pediatrics (DESS); physiology-endocrinology (M Sc, PhD); plastic surgery (DESS); psychiatry (DESS); pulmonary medicine (DESS); radiology–oncology (DESS); speech therapy (M Sc); thoracic surgery (DESS); urology (DESS). Electronic applications accepted.

Faculty of Music Offers composition (M Mus); instrumental didactics (M Mus); interpretation (M Mus); music (M Mus, PhD); music education (M Mus, PhD); musicology (MA, PhD). Electronic applications accepted.

Faculty of Nursing Offers nursing (M Sc, PhD, DESS, Diploma). Electronic applications accepted.

Faculty of Pharmacy *Program availability:* Part-time. Offers community pharmacy (DESS); hospital pharmacy (M Sc); pharmacy (M Sc, PhD, DESS). Electronic applications accepted.

Faculty of Philosophy Offers philosophy (MA, PhD). Electronic applications accepted.

Faculty of Sciences and Engineering *Program availability:* Part-time. Offers aerospace engineering (M Sc); biochemistry (M Sc, PhD); biology (M Sc, PhD); chemical engineering (M Sc, PhD); chemistry (M Sc, PhD); civil engineering (M Sc, PhD); computer science (M Sc, PhD); earth sciences (M Sc, PhD); electrical engineering (M Sc, PhD); environmental technologies (M Sc); environmental technology (M Sc); geology (M Sc, PhD); industrial engineering (Diploma); mathematics (M Sc, PhD); mechanical engineering (M Sc, PhD); metallurgical engineering (M Sc, PhD); microbiology (M Sc, PhD); mining engineering (M Sc, PhD); oceanography (M Sc, PhD); physics (M Sc, PhD); sciences and engineering (M Sc, PhD, Diploma); software engineering (Diploma); statistics (M Sc); urban infrastructure engineering (Diploma). Electronic applications accepted.

Faculty of Social Sciences *Program availability:* Part-time. Offers anthropology (MA, PhD); economics (MA, PhD); feminist studies (Diploma); industrial relations (MA, PhD); policy analysis (MA); political science (MA, PhD); social sciences (M Serv Soc, MA, PhD, Psy D, Diploma); sociology (MA, PhD). Electronic applications accepted.

School of Psychology Offers clinical psychology (PhD); community psychology (PhD); psychology (PhD, Psy D). Electronic applications accepted.

School of Social Work Offers social work (M Serv Soc, PhD). Electronic applications accepted.

Faculty of Theology and Religious Sciences Offers applied ethics (DESS); human sciences of religion (MA, PhD); practical theology (D Th P); theology (MA, PhD); theology and religious sciences (MA, D Th P, PhD, DESS). Electronic applications accepted.

Québec Institute for Advanced International Studies Offers advanced international studies (MA, PhD); international relations (MA, PhD). Electronic applications accepted.

UNIVERSITÉ SAINTE-ANNE, Church Point, NS B0W 1M0, Canada

General Information Province-supported, coed, comprehensive institution.

GRADUATE UNITS

Program in Education *Program availability:* Part-time. Offers education (M Ed).

UNIVERSITY AT ALBANY, STATE UNIVERSITY OF NEW YORK, Albany, NY 12222-0001

General Information State-supported, coed, university. CGS member. *Enrollment:* 17,178 graduate, professional, and undergraduate students; 2,082 full-time matriculated graduate/professional students (1,244 women), 1,923 part-time matriculated graduate/professional students (1,192 women). *Enrollment by degree level:* 2,391 master's, 1,463 doctoral, 168 other advanced degrees. *Graduate faculty:* 365 full-time (135 women), 152 part-time/adjunct (82 women). *International tuition:* $21,550 full-time. Tuition, state resident: full-time $10,870; part-time $453 per credit hour. Tuition, nonresident: full-time $22,210; part-time $925 per credit hour. *Required fees:* $1864; $96 per credit hour. *Graduate housing:* Rooms and/or apartments available on a first-come, first-served basis to single and married students. Typical cost: $13,464 (including board) for single students; $13,464 (including board) for married students. Housing application deadline: 9/1. *Student services:* Campus employment opportunities, campus safety program, career counseling, child daycare facilities, exercise/wellness program, free psychological counseling, grant writing training, international student services, low-cost health insurance, multicultural affairs office, services for students with disabilities, teacher training, writing training. *Library facilities:* University Library plus 2 others. *Collection:* Books: 2.3 million (physical), 342,263 (digital/electronic); Serial titles: 97,614 (digital/electronic). Weekly public service hours: 113; students can reserve study rooms. *Research affiliation:* Naval Research Laboratories (organizational structures (public administration)), General Electric Corporate Research and Development Center (nanoscale science and engineering), IBM-Watson Research Laboratories (artificial intelligence, computer science), Whiteface Mountain Observatory (earth and atmospheric sciences), Woods Hole Oceanographic Institution, Wadsworth Laboratories, New York State Department of Health (biomedical sciences, epidemiology, environmental health).

Computer facilities: Computer purchase and lease plans are available. 500 computers available on campus for general student use. A campuswide network can be accessed from student residence rooms and from off campus. Online class registration is available.
Website: http://www.albany.edu/
General Application Contact: Michael DeRensis, Director, Graduate Admissions, 518-442-3980, Fax: 518-442-3922, E-mail: graduate@albany.edu.

GRADUATE UNITS

College of Arts and Sciences Students: 584 full-time (291 women), 568 part-time (317 women); includes 209 minority (48 Black or African American, non-Hispanic/Latino; 3 American Indian or Alaska Native, non-Hispanic/Latino; 50 Asian, non-Hispanic/Latino; 84 Hispanic/Latino; 1 Native Hawaiian or other Pacific Islander, non-Hispanic/Latino; 23 Two or more races, non-Hispanic/Latino), 258 international. 1,381 applicants, 43% accepted, 285 enrolled. *Faculty:* 205 full-time (65 women), 19 part-time/adjunct (7 women). Expenses: Contact institution. *Financial support:* Fellowships, research assistantships, teaching assistantships, career-related internships or fieldwork, Federal Work-Study, institutionally sponsored loans, traineeships, and unspecified assistantships available. Financial award applicants required to submit FAFSA. In 2016, 202 master's, 79 doctorates, 13 other advanced degrees awarded. *Program availability:* Part-time, evening/weekend, 100% online, blended/hybrid learning. Offers African studies (MA); Afro-American studies (MA); anthropology (MA, PhD); art (MA, MFA); arts and sciences (MA, MALS, MFA, MRP, MS, PhD, Certificate); atmospheric science (MS, PhD); behavioral neuroscience (PhD); chemistry (MS, PhD); clinical psychology (PhD); cognitive psychology (PhD); communication (MA); demography (Certificate); economic forecasting (MA); economics (MA, PhD); English (MA, PhD); forensic biology (MS); geographic information science (Certificate); geography (MA); history (MA, PhD); industrial/organizational psychology (MA, PhD); Latin American, Caribbean, and U.S. Latino studies (MA, PhD, Certificate); liberal studies (MALS); mathematics (MA, PhD); philosophy (MA, PhD); physics (MS, PhD); public history (Certificate); regional planning (MRP); social-personality psychology (PhD); sociology (MA, PhD); sociology and communication (PhD); Spanish (MA, PhD); urban policy (Certificate); women's, gender and sexuality studies (MA). *Application deadline:* Applications are processed on a rolling basis. *Application fee:* $75. Electronic applications accepted. *Application Contact:* Michael DeRensis, Director, Graduate Admissions, 518-442-3980, Fax: 518-442-3922, E-mail: graduate@albany.edu. *Dean,* Edelgard Wulfert, 518-442-4654, Fax: 518-442-4651.

College of Emergency Preparedness, Homeland Security and Cybersecurity Students: 8 part-time (5 women). 13 applicants, 100% accepted, 5 enrolled. *Faculty:* 3 part-time/adjunct (0 women). Expenses: Contact institution. In 2016, 5 Certificates awarded. Offers cybersecurity (Certificate); emergency preparedness (Certificate); homeland security (Certificate). *Application Contact:* Michael DeRensis, Director, Graduate Admissions, 518-442-3980, Fax: 518-442-3922, E-mail: graduate@albany.edu. *Dean,* Dr. Robert Griffin, 518-442-5258.

College of Engineering and Applied Sciences Students: 177 full-time (64 women), 155 part-time (69 women); includes 35 minority (8 Black or African American, non-Hispanic/Latino; 11 Asian, non-Hispanic/Latino; 11 Hispanic/Latino; 2 Two or more races, non-Hispanic/Latino), 186 international. Average age 27. 563 applicants, 60% accepted, 116 enrolled. *Faculty:* 45 full-time (17 women), 36 part-time/adjunct (9 women). Expenses: Contact institution. *Financial support:* Fellowships and Federal Work-Study available. Financial award application deadline: 4/1. In 2016, 131 master's, 8 doctorates awarded. *Program availability:* Part-time. Offers computer science (MS, PhD); engineering and applied sciences (MS, PhD, CAS); informatics (PhD); information science (MS); library and information science (CAS). *Application deadline:* For fall admission, 3/1 for domestic students. Applications are processed on a rolling basis. *Application fee:* $75. Electronic applications accepted. *Dean,* Kim L. Boyer, 518-956-8240, Fax: 518-442-5367, E-mail: ceasinfo@albany.edu.

Nelson A. Rockefeller College of Public Affairs and Policy Students: 133 full-time (73 women), 119 part-time (56 women); includes 44 minority (12 Black or African American, non-Hispanic/Latino; 9 Asian, non-Hispanic/Latino; 20 Hispanic/Latino; 3 Two or more races, non-Hispanic/Latino), 47 international. Average age 33. 293 applicants, 69% accepted, 103 enrolled. *Faculty:* 49 full-time (17 women), 23 part-time/adjunct (10 women). Expenses: Contact institution. *Financial support:* Fellowships, research assistantships, teaching assistantships, career-related internships or fieldwork, Federal Work-Study, and institutionally sponsored loans available. Financial award application deadline: 2/1. In 2016, 56 master's, 15 doctorates, 19 other advanced degrees awarded. *Program availability:* Part-time. Offers financial management and public economics (MPA); financial market regulation (MPA); health policy (MPA); healthcare management (MPA); homeland security (MPA); human resources management (MPA); information strategy and management (MPA); local government management (MPA); nonprofit management (MPA); nonprofit management and leadership (Certificate); organizational behavior and theory (MPA, PhD); planning and policy analysis (CAS); policy analysis (MPA); political science (MA, PhD); politics and administration (PhD); public affairs and policy (MA, MPA, PhD, CAS, Certificate); public finance (PhD); public management (PhD); public policy (PhD); public sector management (Certificate); women and public policy (Certificate). *Application deadline:* For fall admission, 2/1 priority date for domestic students, 5/1 for international students. Applications are processed on a rolling basis. *Application fee:* $75. Electronic applications accepted. *Dean,* David L. Rousseau, 518-442-5244, E-mail: drousseau@albany.edu.

School of Business Students: 270 full-time (116 women), 200 part-time (81 women); includes 100 minority (21 Black or African American, non-Hispanic/Latino; 1 American Indian or Alaska Native, non-Hispanic/Latino; 47 Asian, non-Hispanic/Latino; 22 Hispanic/Latino; 9 Two or more races, non-Hispanic/Latino), 49 international. 489 applicants, 70% accepted, 260 enrolled. *Faculty:* 21 full-time (5 women), 20 part-time/adjunct (7 women). Expenses: Contact institution. *Financial support:* Fellowships, research assistantships, career-related internships or fieldwork, and Federal Work-Study available. In 2016, 225 master's awarded. *Program availability:* Part-time,

evening/weekend. Offers accounting (MS); business (MBA, MS); business administration (MBA); cyber security (MBA); entrepreneurship (MBA); finance (MBA); forensic accounting (MS); human resource information systems (MBA); information technology management (MBA); marketing (MBA); professional accounting (MS); tax practice (MS); taxation (MS). *Application deadline:* For fall admission, 3/1 for domestic students, 5/1 for international students. Applications are processed on a rolling basis. *Application fee:* $75. Electronic applications accepted. *Application Contact:* Michael DeRensis, Director, Graduate Admissions, 518-442-3980, Fax: 518-442-3922, E-mail: graduate@albany.edu. *Dean,* Donald S. Siegel, 518-956-8370, E-mail: dsiegel@albany.edu.

School of Criminal Justice Students: 73 full-time (48 women), 37 part-time (22 women); includes 45 minority (19 Black or African American, non-Hispanic/Latino; 1 Asian, non-Hispanic/Latino; 22 Hispanic/Latino; 3 Two or more races, non-Hispanic/Latino), 8 international. 114 applicants, 64% accepted, 25 enrolled. *Faculty:* 10 full-time (4 women), 6 part-time/adjunct (5 women). Expenses: Contact institution. *Financial support:* Fellowships, research assistantships, teaching assistantships, career-related internships or fieldwork, Federal Work-Study, and institutionally sponsored loans available. Financial award application deadline: 4/1. In 2016, 32 master's, 5 doctorates awarded. *Program availability:* Part-time. Offers criminal justice (MA, PhD). *Application deadline:* For fall admission, 7/1 for domestic students, 5/1 for international students. Applications are processed on a rolling basis. *Application fee:* $75. Electronic applications accepted. *Application Contact:* Jane Champagne, Director, Graduate Admissions, 518-442-3980, Fax: 518-442-3922, E-mail: graduate@albany.edu. *Dean,* William Alex Pridemore, 518-442-5210, E-mail: pridemore@albany.edu.

School of Education Students: 327 full-time (247 women), 577 part-time (439 women); includes 125 minority (44 Black or African American, non-Hispanic/Latino; 1 American Indian or Alaska Native, non-Hispanic/Latino; 23 Asian, non-Hispanic/Latino; 45 Hispanic/Latino; 12 Two or more races, non-Hispanic/Latino), 66 international. Average age 31. 457 applicants, 63% accepted, 325 enrolled. *Faculty:* 38 full-time (20 women), 46 part-time/adjunct (36 women). Expenses: Contact institution. *Financial support:* Fellowships, career-related internships or fieldwork, and Federal Work-Study available. In 2016, 283 master's, 35 doctorates, 36 other advanced degrees awarded. *Program availability:* Part-time, evening/weekend, 100% online, blended/hybrid learning. Offers curriculum and instruction (PhD, CAS); curriculum development and instructional technology (MS); education (MS, PhD, Psy D, CAS); educational policy and leadership (MS, PhD); educational psychology (PhD); educational psychology and methodology (MS); educational research (CAS); general education studies (MS); higher education (MS); international education management (CAS); literacy teaching and learning (MS, PhD, CAS); school psychology (Psy D, CAS). *Application fee:* $75. Electronic applications accepted. *Dean,* Robert Bangert-Drowns, 518-442-4988, E-mail: rbangert-drowns@albany.edu.

Division of Counseling Psychology Expenses: Contact institution. *Financial support:* Career-related internships or fieldwork available. *Program availability:* Evening/weekend. Offers counseling psychology (PhD); mental health counseling (MS). *Application deadline:* For fall admission, 2/15 for domestic and international students. *Application fee:* $75. Electronic applications accepted. *Director,* Micki Friedlander, 518-442-5049, E-mail: mfriedlander@albany.edu.

Division of Special Education Expenses: Contact institution. *Financial support:* Fellowships and career-related internships or fieldwork available. Offers special education (MS). *Application deadline:* For fall admission, 3/1 for domestic students, 5/1 for international students. Applications are processed on a rolling basis. *Application fee:* $75. Electronic applications accepted. *Program Director,* Bruce Saddler, 516-442-5062, E-mail: bsaddler@albany.edu.

School of Public Health Students: 199 full-time (160 women), 291 part-time (211 women); includes 135 minority (57 Black or African American, non-Hispanic/Latino; 1 American Indian or Alaska Native, non-Hispanic/Latino; 37 Asian, non-Hispanic/Latino; 28 Hispanic/Latino; 12 Two or more races, non-Hispanic/Latino), 59 international. 515 applicants, 69% accepted, 181 enrolled. *Faculty:* 38 full-time (15 women), 20 part-time/adjunct (12 women). Expenses: Contact institution. *Financial support:* Fellowships and research assistantships available. In 2016, 94 master's, 16 doctorates, 36 other advanced degrees awarded. *Program availability:* Part-time, evening/weekend, 100% online, blended/hybrid learning. Offers biomedical sciences (MS, PhD); environmental and occupational health (MS, PhD); environmental chemistry (MS, PhD); epidemiology and biostatistics (MS, PhD); health policy, management, and behavior (MPH, MS, Dr PH, PhD); public health (MPH, MS, Dr PH, PhD, Certificate); toxicology (MS, PhD). *Application deadline:* For fall admission, 1/1 for domestic students. Applications are processed on a rolling basis. *Application fee:* $75. Electronic applications accepted. *Application Contact:* Michael DeRensis, Director, Graduate Admissions, 518-442-3980, Fax: 518-442-3922, E-mail: graduate@albany.edu. *Dean,* Dr. Philip Nasca, 518-485-5500.

School of Social Welfare Students: 283 full-time (242 women), 146 part-time (120 women); includes 111 minority (53 Black or African American, non-Hispanic/Latino; 1 American Indian or Alaska Native, non-Hispanic/Latino; 11 Asian, non-Hispanic/Latino; 36 Hispanic/Latino; 10 Two or more races, non-Hispanic/Latino), 15 international. 405 applicants, 66% accepted, 190 enrolled. *Faculty:* 18 full-time (8 women), 27 part-time/adjunct (22 women). Expenses: Contact institution. *Financial support:* Fellowships, career-related internships or fieldwork, and Federal Work-Study available. Financial award application deadline: 2/15. In 2016, 173 master's, 9 doctorates awarded. *Program availability:* Part-time, evening/weekend. Offers social welfare (MSW, PhD). *Application deadline:* For fall admission, 2/15 for domestic and international students. *Application fee:* $75. Electronic applications accepted. *Dean,* Katharine Briar-Lawson, 518-442-5324.

UNIVERSITY AT BUFFALO, THE STATE UNIVERSITY OF NEW YORK, Buffalo, NY 14260
General Information State-supported, coed, university. CGS member. *Enrollment:* 30,183 graduate, professional, and undergraduate students; 7,966 full-time matriculated graduate/professional students (3,782 women), 1,871 part-time matriculated graduate/professional students (1,061 women). *Enrollment by degree level:* 4,878 master's, 4,780 doctoral, 179 other advanced degrees. *Graduate faculty:* 1,622 full-time (573 women), 215 part-time/adjunct (76 women). *Graduate housing:* Rooms and/or apartments available on a first-come, first-served basis to single students and available to married students. Housing application deadline: 5/1. *Student services:* Campus employment opportunities, campus safety program, career counseling, child daycare facilities, exercise/wellness program, free psychological counseling, international student services, low-cost health insurance, multicultural affairs office, services for students with disabilities, teacher training, writing training. *Library facilities:* Lockwood Memorial Library plus 11 others. *Collection:* Books: 3.4 million (physical), 766,305 (digital/electronic); Serial titles: 3,828 (physical), 158,728 (digital/electronic); Databases: 376. Weekly public service hours: 168; study areas open 24 hours, 5–7 days a week;

students can reserve study rooms. *Research affiliation:* Hauptman-Woodward Medical Research Institute, Roswell Park Cancer Institute, Veterans Administration Medical Center, Calspan-University of Buffalo Research Center, Roswell Park Cancer Institute.

Computer facilities: 3,061 computers available on campus for general student use. A campuswide network can be accessed from student residence rooms and from off campus. Online class registration is available. **Website:** http://www.buffalo.edu/

General Application Contact: Christopher S. Connor, Director of Graduate Enrollment Management Services, 716-645-3482, Fax: 716-645-6998, E-mail: cconnor@buffalo.edu.

GRADUATE UNITS

Graduate School Students: 6,247 full-time (3,187 women), 3,249 part-time (1,606 women); includes 1,461 minority (375 Black or African American, non-Hispanic/Latino; 29 American Indian or Alaska Native, non-Hispanic/Latino; 634 Asian, non-Hispanic/Latino; 294 Hispanic/Latino; 129 Two or more races, non-Hispanic/Latino), 2,987 international. 24,303 applicants, 34% accepted, 3613 enrolled. *Faculty:* 1,645 full-time (603 women), 190 part-time/adjunct (68 women). Expenses: Contact institution. *Financial support:* In 2016–17, 2,451 students received support. Fellowships with tuition reimbursements available, research assistantships with tuition reimbursements available, teaching assistantships with tuition reimbursements available, career-related internships or fieldwork, Federal Work-Study, institutionally sponsored loans, scholarships/grants, traineeships, tuition waivers (full and partial), unspecified assistantships, and stipends available. Support available to part-time students. Financial award applicants required to submit FAFSA. In 2016, 2,220 master's, 490 doctorates, 730 other advanced degrees awarded. *Program availability:* Part-time, evening/weekend, 100% online. *Application deadline:* Applications are processed on a rolling basis. *Application fee:* $75. Electronic applications accepted. *Application Contact:* Lisa C. Coia, Assistant Director, 716-645-3482, Fax: 716-645-6998, E-mail: grad@buffalo.edu. *Vice Provost for Graduate Education/Dean of the Graduate School,* Dr. Graham Hammill, 716-645-2939, Fax: 716-645-6142, E-mail: grad@buffalo.edu.

College of Arts and Sciences *Program availability:* Part-time. Offers American studies (MA, PhD); anthropology (MA, PhD); arts and sciences (MA, MAH, MFA, MM, MS, Au D, PhD, Advanced Certificate, Certificate); arts management (MA); audiology (Au D); biological sciences (MA, MS, PhD); Canadian studies (MA, Advanced Certificate); Caribbean and Latin/o American studies (MA); chemistry (MA, PhD); classics (MA, PhD); communication (MA, PhD); communicative disorders and sciences (MA, PhD); comparative literature (MA, PhD); computational science (Advanced Certificate); contemporary performance (Advanced Certificate); critical museum studies (MA); earth systems science (MA, MS); economic geography and business geographics (MS); economics (MA, MS, PhD); English (MA, PhD); environmental modeling and analysis (MA); evolution, ecology and behavior (MS, PhD, Certificate); film and media study (MAH); financial economics (Certificate); French (MA, PhD); geographic information science (MA, MS); geography (MA, PhD); geology (MA, MS, PhD); global gender studies (MA, PhD); health geography (MS); health services (Certificate); historical musicology and music theory (PhD); history (MA, PhD, Advanced Certificate); humanities (MA); information and Internet economics (Certificate); interdisciplinary computational linguistics (MS); international economics (Certificate); international trade (MA); Latin (MA); law and regulation (Certificate); linguistics (MA, PhD); mathematics (MA, PhD); media arts production (MFA); media study (PhD); medicinal chemistry (MS, PhD); music composition (MA, PhD); music history (MA); music performance (MM); music theory (MA); natural sciences (MS); new media design (Certificate); philosophy (MA, PhD); physics (MS, PhD); political science (MA, PhD); psychology (MA, PhD); public history (MA); social media (MAH); social sciences (MS); sociology (MA, PhD); Spanish (MA, PhD); studio art (MFA); theatre and performance (MA, PhD); urban and regional analysis (MA); urban and regional economics (Certificate); visual studies (MA, PhD). Electronic applications accepted.

Graduate Programs in Cancer Research and Biomedical Sciences at Roswell Park Cancer Institute Students: 106 full-time (60 women); includes 15 minority (6 Black or African American, non-Hispanic/Latino; 3 Asian, non-Hispanic/Latino; 4 Hispanic/Latino; 1 Native Hawaiian or other Pacific Islander, non-Hispanic/Latino; 1 Two or more races, non-Hispanic/Latino), 31 international. 147 applicants, 32% accepted, 25 enrolled. *Faculty:* 118 full-time (35 women). Expenses: Contact institution. *Financial support:* In 2016–17, 91 students received support, including 91 research assistantships with full tuition reimbursements available (averaging $27,000 per year); scholarships/grants, health care benefits, and unspecified assistantships also available. Financial award application deadline: 1/5. In 2016, 15 master's, 11 doctorates awarded. Offers cancer pathology and prevention (PhD); cellular and molecular biology (PhD); immunology (PhD); interdisciplinary natural sciences (MS); molecular and cellular biophysics and biochemistry (PhD); molecular pharmacology and cancer therapeutics (PhD). *Application deadline:* For fall admission, 1/5 priority date for domestic and international students. *Application fee:* $75. Electronic applications accepted. *Application Contact:* Dr. Norman J. Karin, Associate Dean, 716-845-2339, Fax: 716-845-8178, E-mail: norman.karin@roswellpark.edu. *Associate Dean,* Dr. Norman J. Karin, 716-845-2339, Fax: 716-845-8178, E-mail: norman.karin@roswellpark.edu.

Graduate School of Education Students: 470 full-time (362 women), 718 part-time (517 women); includes 116 minority (76 Black or African American, non-Hispanic/Latino; 7 American Indian or Alaska Native, non-Hispanic/Latino; 26 Asian, non-Hispanic/Latino; 7 Hispanic/Latino), 113 international. Average age 33. 894 applicants, 74% accepted, 417 enrolled. *Faculty:* 80 full-time (47 women), 136 part-time/adjunct (106 women). Expenses: Contact institution. *Financial support:* In 2016–17, 96 fellowships (averaging $5,091 per year), 110 research assistantships with tuition reimbursements (averaging $10,240 per year) were awarded; teaching assistantships, Federal Work-Study, institutionally sponsored loans, scholarships/grants, tuition waivers (full and partial), and unspecified assistantships also available. Support available to part-time students. Financial award applicants required to submit FAFSA. In 2016, 339 master's, 45 doctorates, 101 other advanced degrees awarded. *Program availability:* Part-time, 100% online. Offers applied statistical analysis (Advanced Certificate); biology education (Ed M, Certificate); chemistry education (Ed M, Certificate); childhood education (Ed M); childhood education with bilingual extension (Ed M); college teaching (Advanced Certificate); counseling/school psychology (PhD); counselor education (PhD); curriculum, instruction and the science of learning (PhD); early childhood education (Ed M); early childhood education with bilingual extension (Ed M); earth science education (Ed M, Certificate); economics and education policy analysis (MA); education (Ed M, MA, MS, Ed D, PhD, Advanced Certificate, Certificate); education and technology (Ed M); education studies (Ed M); educational administration (Ed M, Ed D, PhD); educational culture, policy and society (PhD); educational psychology (MA, PhD); educational technology and new literacies (Certificate); educational technology and new literacies

(Advanced Certificate); elementary education (Ed D); English education (Ed M, Certificate); English education studies (Ed M); English for speakers of other languages (Ed M); foreign and second language education (PhD); French education (Ed M, Certificate); German education (Ed M, Certificate); gifted education (Certificate); higher education administration (Ed M, PhD); information and library science (MS); Latin education (Ed M, Certificate); library and information studies (Certificate); literacy education studies (Ed M); literacy specialist (Ed M); literacy teaching and learning (Certificate); mathematics education (Ed M, Certificate); mental health counseling (MS, Certificate); mindful counseling for wellness and engagement (Advanced Certificate); music education (Ed M, Certificate); music education studies (Ed M); music learning theory (Advanced Certificate); online education (Advanced Certificate); physics education (Ed M, Certificate); rehabilitation counseling (MS, Advanced Certificate); school building leadership (Certificate); school business and human resource administration (Certificate); school counseling (Ed M, Certificate); school district business leadership (Certificate); school district leadership (Certificate); school librarianship (MS); science and the public (Ed M); social studies education (Ed M, Certificate); Spanish education (Ed M, Certificate); special education (PhD); teaching English to speakers of other languages (Ed M). *Application deadline:* Applications are processed on a rolling basis. *Application fee:* $50. Electronic applications accepted. *Application Contact:* Dr. Radhika Suresh, Assistant Dean for Enrollment Management, 716-645-2110, Fax: 716-645-7937, E-mail: gse-info@buffalo.edu. *Dean,* Dr. Jaekyung Lee, 716-645-6640, Fax: 716-645-2479, E-mail: gse-info@buffalo.edu.

Jacobs School of Medicine and Biomedical Sciences Offers anatomical sciences (MA, PhD); bio-informatics (PhD); biochemistry (MA, PhD); biomedical informatics (MS); biomedical ontology (PhD); biomedical sciences (MS, PhD); biophysics (MS, PhD); biotechnology (MS); clinical informatics (PhD); genetics, genomics and bioinformatics (MS, PhD); medical physics (MS, PhD); medicine (MD); medicine and biomedical sciences (MA, MS, MD, PhD); microbiology and immunology (MS, PhD); neuroscience (MS, PhD); pathology (MA, PhD); pharmacology (MS, PhD); physiology (MA, PhD); structural biology (MS, PhD). Electronic applications accepted.

School of Architecture and Planning Students: 212 full-time (85 women), 27 part-time (12 women); includes 48 minority (23 Black or African American, non-Hispanic/Latino; 6 Asian, non-Hispanic/Latino; 13 Hispanic/Latino; 6 Two or more races, non-Hispanic/Latino), 51 international. Average age 26. 483 applicants, 29% accepted, 99 enrolled. *Faculty:* 46 full-time (17 women), 21 part-time/adjunct (6 women). Expenses: Contact institution. *Financial support:* In 2016–17, 8 fellowships with full tuition reimbursements (averaging $21,440 per year), 7 research assistantships with partial tuition reimbursements (averaging $21,951 per year), 58 teaching assistantships with partial tuition reimbursements (averaging $8,021 per year) were awarded; career-related internships or fieldwork, Federal Work-Study, institutionally sponsored loans, scholarships/grants, health care benefits, tuition waivers (partial), and unspecified assistantships also available. Support available to part-time students. Financial award application deadline: 3/1; financial award applicants required to submit FAFSA. In 2016, 97 master's awarded. *Program availability:* Part-time. Offers architecture (M Arch); architecture and planning (M Arch, MS Arch, MUP, PhD, Certificate); ecological practices (MS Arch); historic preservation (Certificate); historic preservation and urban design (MS Arch); inclusive design (MS Arch); real estate development (MS Arch); situated technology (MS Arch); urban and regional planning (PhD). *Application fee:* $75. Electronic applications accepted. *Application Contact:* Shannon Phillips, Assistant Dean for Graduate Education, 716-829-5900, Fax: 716-829-3256, E-mail: smp2@buffalo.edu. *Dean,* Robert G. Shibley, 716-829-3485 Ext. 121, Fax: 716-829-2297, E-mail: rshibley@buffalo.edu.

School of Dental Medicine Offers biomaterials (MS); dental medicine (MS, DDS, PhD, Certificate); oral biology (PhD); oral sciences (MS); orthodontics (MS, Certificate). Electronic applications accepted.

School of Engineering and Applied Sciences *Program availability:* Part-time, evening/weekend, online learning. Offers aerospace engineering (MS, PhD); biomedical engineering (MS, PhD); chemical and biological engineering (ME, MS, PhD); civil engineering (ME, MS, PhD); computer science and engineering (MS, PhD); electrical engineering (ME, MS, PhD); engineering and applied sciences (ME, MS, PhD, Certificate); engineering science (MS); industrial and systems engineering (ME, MS, PhD); information assurance (Certificate); mechanical engineering (MS, PhD). Electronic applications accepted.

School of Law Students: 455 full-time (228 women), 4 part-time (3 women); includes 79 minority (20 Black or African American, non-Hispanic/Latino; 15 Asian, non-Hispanic/Latino; 30 Hispanic/Latino; 14 Two or more races, non-Hispanic/Latino), 19 international. Average age 26. 1,202 applicants, 48% accepted, 151 enrolled. *Faculty:* 42 full-time (23 women), 53 part-time/adjunct (21 women). Expenses: Contact institution. *Financial support:* In 2016–17, 325 students received support. Federal Work-Study, institutionally sponsored loans, scholarships/grants, tuition waivers (full and partial), and unspecified assistantships available. Financial award application deadline: 3/1; financial award applicants required to submit FAFSA. In 2016, 189 doctorates awarded. Offers criminal law (LL M); general law (LL M); law (JD). *Application deadline:* For fall admission, 3/1 priority date for domestic and international students. Applications are processed on a rolling basis. *Application fee:* $85. Electronic applications accepted. *Application Contact:* Lindsay J. Gladney, Vice Dean for Admissions, 716-645-2907, Fax: 716-645-6676, E-mail: law-admissions@buffalo.edu. *Interim Dean,* James A. Gardner, 716-645-2052, Fax: 716-645-2064, E-mail: jgard@buffalo.edu.

School of Management Students: 683 full-time (277 women), 196 part-time (63 women); includes 76 minority (23 Black or African American, non-Hispanic/Latino; 1 American Indian or Alaska Native, non-Hispanic/Latino; 48 Asian, non-Hispanic/Latino; 3 Hispanic/Latino; 1 Two or more races, non-Hispanic/Latino), 371 international. Average age 31. 2,451 applicants, 42% accepted, 484 enrolled. *Faculty:* 80 full-time (26 women), 36 part-time/adjunct (6 women). Expenses: Contact institution. *Financial support:* Fellowships with full and partial tuition reimbursements, research assistantships with full and partial tuition reimbursements, teaching assistantships with full and partial tuition reimbursements, career-related internships or fieldwork, Federal Work-Study, institutionally sponsored loans, scholarships/grants, health care benefits, and unspecified assistantships available. Financial award application deadline: 2/15. In 2016, 515 master's, 10 doctorates awarded. *Program availability:* Part-time, evening/weekend. Offers accounting (MS); analytics (MBA); business administration (PMBA); consulting (MBA); finance (MBA, MS); healthcare (MBA); information assurance (MBA); information systems (MBA); international management (MBA); management (EMBA, PhD); management information systems (MS); marketing (MBA); supply chain and operations (MBA); supply chains and operations management (MS). *Application deadline:* For fall admission, 10/15 priority date for domestic and international students; for winter admission, 2/1 priority date for domestic and international students; for spring admission, 4/15 for domestic students;

for summer admission, 5/15 for domestic students. *Application fee:* $100. Electronic applications accepted. *Application Contact:* Meghan Felser, Associate Director of Admissions and Recruiting, 716-645-3204, Fax: 716-645-2341, E-mail: mpwood@buffalo.edu. *Assistant Dean and Director of Graduate Programs,* Erin K. O'Brien, 716-645-3204, Fax: 716-645-2341, E-mail: ekobrien@buffalo.edu.

School of Nursing Students: 73 full-time (43 women), 129 part-time (115 women); includes 40 minority (16 Black or African American, non-Hispanic/Latino; 1 American Indian or Alaska Native, non-Hispanic/Latino; 21 Asian, non-Hispanic/Latino; 2 Hispanic/Latino), 4 international. Average age 34. 168 applicants, 45% accepted, 60 enrolled. *Faculty:* 41 full-time (36 women), 15 part-time/adjunct (all women). Expenses: Contact institution. *Financial support:* In 2016–17, 80 students received support, including 2 fellowships with tuition reimbursements available (averaging $17,000 per year), 4 research assistantships with tuition reimbursements available (averaging $10,600 per year), 7 teaching assistantships with tuition reimbursements available (averaging $10,600 per year); scholarships/grants, traineeships, health care benefits, and unspecified assistantships also available. Financial award application deadline: 2/1; financial award applicants required to submit FAFSA. In 2016, 2 master's, 31 doctorates awarded. *Program availability:* Part-time, 100% online. Offers adult gerontology nurse practitioner (DNP); family nurse practitioner (DNP); health care systems and leadership (MS); nurse anesthetist (DNP); nursing (PhD); nursing education (Certificate); psychiatric/mental health nurse practitioner (DNP). *Application deadline:* For fall admission, 7/1 for domestic students, 2/1 for international students; for spring admission, 12/1 for domestic students, 10/1 for international students; for summer admission, 4/1 for domestic students. Applications are processed on a rolling basis. *Application fee:* $75. Electronic applications accepted. *Application Contact:* Jennifer H. VanLaeken, Director of Graduate Student Services, 716-829-3311, Fax: 716-829-2067, E-mail: jhv2@buffalo.edu. *Dean and Professor,* Dr. Marsha L. Lewis, 716-829-2533, Fax: 716-829-2566, E-mail: ubnursingdean@buffalo.edu.

School of Pharmacy and Pharmaceutical Sciences Students: 621 full-time (353 women), 11 part-time (5 women); includes 240 minority (31 Black or African American, non-Hispanic/Latino; 204 Asian, non-Hispanic/Latino; 5 Hispanic/Latino), 51 international. Average age 24. 938 applicants, 23% accepted, 153 enrolled. *Faculty:* 36 full-time (11 women), 9 part-time/adjunct (5 women). Expenses: Contact institution. *Financial support:* In 2016–17, 345 students received support, including 41 research assistantships with full tuition reimbursements available (averaging $23,994 per year); scholarships/grants also available. Financial award application deadline: 3/1; financial award applicants required to submit FAFSA. In 2016, 11 master's, 113 doctorates awarded. Offers pharmaceutical sciences (MS, PhD); pharmacy (Pharm D); pharmacy and pharmaceutical sciences (MS, PhD, Pharm D). *Application deadline:* For fall admission, 2/1 priority date for domestic and international students. Applications are processed on a rolling basis. *Application fee:* $50. Electronic applications accepted. *Application Contact:* Dr. Jennifer M. Rosenberg, Associate Dean, 716-645-2825 Ext. 1, Fax: 716-829-6568, E-mail: prepharm@buffalo.edu. *Dean,* Dr. James M. O'Donnell, 716-645-2823, Fax: 716-829-6568.

School of Public Health and Health Professions *Program availability:* Part-time. Offers assistive and rehabilitation technology (Certificate); biostatistics (MA, MPH, PhD); community health and health behavior (MPH, PhD); epidemiology (MS, PhD); exercise science (MS, PhD); nutrition (MS, Advanced Certificate); occupational therapy (MS); physical therapy (DPT); public health (MPH); public health and health professions (MA, MPH, MS, DPT, Advanced Certificate, Certificate); rehabilitation science (PhD). Electronic applications accepted.

School of Social Work Students: 309 full-time (270 women), 227 part-time (182 women); includes 83 minority (62 Black or African American, non-Hispanic/Latino; 21 Asian, non-Hispanic/Latino). Average age 28. 413 applicants, 70% accepted, 197 enrolled. *Faculty:* 29 full-time (23 women), 58 part-time/adjunct (48 women). Expenses: Contact institution. *Financial support:* In 2016–17, 6 fellowships with full tuition reimbursements (averaging $12,400 per year), 3 research assistantships with full tuition reimbursements (averaging $16,000 per year), 6 teaching assistantships with full tuition reimbursements (averaging $5,000 per year) were awarded; Federal Work-Study, scholarships/grants, health care benefits, tuition waivers (full and partial), unspecified assistantships, and instructorships and research grants (for PhD students) also available. Financial award application deadline: 4/30; financial award applicants required to submit FAFSA. In 2016, 205 master's, 2 doctorates awarded. *Program availability:* Part-time, 100% online, blended/hybrid learning. Offers social welfare (PhD); social work (MSW). *Application deadline:* For fall admission, 3/1 priority date for domestic and international students; for spring admission, 9/15 for domestic and international students; for summer admission, 2/1 for domestic and international students. *Application fee:* $75. Electronic applications accepted. *Application Contact:* Maria Carey, Admissions Processor, 716-645-3381, Fax: 716-645-3456, E-mail: sw-info@buffalo.edu. *Dean,* Dr. Nancy J. Smyth, 716-645-3381, Fax: 716-645-3883, E-mail: sw-dean@buffalo.edu.

UNIVERSITY OF ADVANCING TECHNOLOGY, Tempe, AZ 85283-1042

General Information Proprietary, coed, primarily men, comprehensive institution. *Graduate housing:* Room and/or apartments available on a first-come, first-served basis to single students; on-campus housing not available to married students.

GRADUATE UNITS

Master of Science Program in Technology Offers advancing computer science (MS); emerging technologies (MS); game production and management (MS); information assurance (MS); technology leadership (MS). Electronic applications accepted.

THE UNIVERSITY OF AKRON, Akron, OH 44325

General Information State-supported, coed, university. CGS member. *Enrollment:* 21,099 graduate, professional, and undergraduate students; 2,040 full-time matriculated graduate/professional students (1,006 women), 1,207 part-time matriculated graduate/professional students (786 women). *Enrollment by degree level:* 2,213 master's, 914 doctoral, 120 other advanced degrees. *Graduate faculty:* 449 full-time (158 women), 436 part-time/adjunct (246 women). Tuition, state resident: full-time $8618; part-time $359 per credit hour. Tuition, nonresident: full-time $17,149; part-time $715 per credit hour. *Required fees:* $1652. *Graduate housing:* Room and/or apartments available on a first-come, first-served basis to single students; on-campus housing not available to married students. Typical cost: $7020 per year ($10,684 including board). Housing application deadline: 3/1. *Student services:* Campus employment opportunities, campus safety program, career counseling, exercise/wellness program, free psychological counseling, international student services, low-cost health insurance, multicultural affairs office, services for students with disabilities. *Library facilities:* Bierce Library plus 2 others. *Collection:* Books: 1.3 million (physical), 449,783 (digital/electronic); Serial titles: 28,058 (physical), 80,870 (digital/electronic); Databases: 389. Study areas open 24 hours, 5–7 days a week; students can reserve study rooms.

Computer facilities: Computer purchase and lease plans are available. 3,150 computers available on campus for general student use. A campuswide network can be accessed from student residence rooms and from off campus. Online class registration, library laptops for student checkout are available. Website: http://www.uakron.edu/

General Application Contact: Lauri Thorpe, Associate Dean, Enrollment, 330-972-6367, Fax: 330-972-6475, E-mail: lauri@uakron.edu.

GRADUATE UNITS

Graduate School Students: 2,033 full-time (1,003 women), 1,094 part-time (698 women); includes 394 minority (190 Black or African American, non-Hispanic/Latino; 4 American Indian or Alaska Native, non-Hispanic/Latino; 74 Asian, non-Hispanic/Latino; 67 Hispanic/Latino; 59 Two or more races, non-Hispanic/Latino), 924 international. Average age 29. 2,483 applicants, 61% accepted, 786 enrolled. *Faculty:* 429 full-time (135 women), 426 part-time/adjunct (231 women). Expenses: Contact institution. *Financial support:* In 2016–17, 38 fellowships with full tuition reimbursements, 500 research assistantships with full tuition reimbursements, 758 teaching assistantships with full tuition reimbursements were awarded; unspecified assistantships and administrative assistantships also available. Financial award application deadline: 12/1; financial award applicants required to submit FAFSA. In 2016, 1,121 master's, 140 doctorates awarded. *Program availability:* Part-time, evening/weekend. *Application deadline:* For fall admission, 12/1 priority date for domestic and international students. Applications are processed on a rolling basis. *Application fee:* $45 ($70 for international students). Electronic applications accepted. *Application Contact:* Charles Beneke, Associate Dean, Academics, 330-972-2565, Fax: 330-972-6475, E-mail: beneke@uakron.edu. *Executive Dean,* Dr. Chand Midha, 330-972-7664, Fax: 330-972-6475, E-mail: cmidha@uakron.edu.

Buchtel College of Arts and Sciences Students: 520 full-time (257 women), 256 part-time (180 women); includes 115 minority (53 Black or African American, non-Hispanic/Latino; 21 Asian, non-Hispanic/Latino; 24 Hispanic/Latino; 17 Two or more races, non-Hispanic/Latino), 158 international. Average age 30. 774 applicants, 56% accepted, 302 enrolled. *Faculty:* 196 full-time (62 women), 126 part-time/adjunct (55 women). Expenses: Contact institution. *Financial support:* In 2016–17, 2 fellowships with full tuition reimbursements, 48 research assistantships with full tuition reimbursements, 279 teaching assistantships with full and partial tuition reimbursements were awarded; career-related internships or fieldwork, Federal Work-Study, institutionally sponsored loans, scholarships/grants, and unspecified assistantships also available. Support available to part-time students. Financial award application deadline: 12/1; financial award applicants required to submit FAFSA. In 2016, 272 master's, 29 doctorates awarded. *Program availability:* Part-time, evening/weekend. Offers accompanying (MM); adult development and aging (PhD); applied mathematics (MS); applied politics (MAP); arts administration (MA); arts and sciences (MA, MAP, MFA, MM, MPA, MS, PhD); biology (MS); chemistry (MS, PhD); child and family development (MA); clothing, textiles and interiors (MA); communication (MA); composition (MA, MM); computer science (MS); counseling psychology (MA, PhD); creative writing (MFA); earth science (MS); engineering geology (MS); environmental geology (MS); geology (MS); history (MA, PhD); industrial/organizational psychology (MA, PhD); integrated bioscience (PhD); literature (MA); mathematics (MS); music education (MM); music technology (MM); performance (MM); physics (MS); political science (MA, MAP); psychology (MA); public administration (MPA); public administration and urban studies (MPA); sociology (MA, PhD); Spanish (MA); statistics (MS); theatre arts (MA); theory (MM). *Application deadline:* For fall admission, 1/15 for domestic and international students. Applications are processed on a rolling basis. *Application fee:* $45 ($70 for international students). Electronic applications accepted. *Interim Dean,* Dr. John Green, 330-972-7857, E-mail: green@uakron.edu.

College of Business Administration Students: 219 full-time (93 women), 167 part-time (68 women); includes 39 minority (11 Black or African American, non-Hispanic/Latino; 16 Asian, non-Hispanic/Latino; 7 Hispanic/Latino; 5 Two or more races, non-Hispanic/Latino), 122 international. Average age 29. 705 applicants, 52% accepted, 207 enrolled. *Faculty:* 53 full-time (14 women), 48 part-time/adjunct (12 women). Expenses: Contact institution. *Financial support:* In 2016–17, 2 research assistantships with full tuition reimbursements, 12 teaching assistantships with full and partial tuition reimbursements were awarded; Federal Work-Study and instructional support assistantships, administrative assistantships also available. In 2016, 216 master's awarded. *Program availability:* Part-time, evening/weekend. Offers accounting (MSA); business administration (MA, MBA, MS, MSA, MSM, MT); economics (MA); finance (MBA); healthcare management (MBA); information systems management (MSM); international business (MBA); management (MBA, MSM); marketing (MBA); supply chain management (MBA); taxation (MT). *Application deadline:* For fall admission, 7/15 for domestic and international students; for spring admission, 11/15 for domestic and international students; for summer admission, 4/15 for domestic students, 3/15 for international students. Electronic applications accepted. *Application Contact:* Dr. William Hauser, Director of Graduate Business Programs, 330-972-7043, Fax: 330-972-6588, E-mail: whauser@uakron.edu. *Dean,* Dr. Ravi Krovi, 330-972-7442, E-mail: cbadean@uakron.edu.

College of Education Students: 84 full-time (51 women), 192 part-time (149 women); includes 41 minority (27 Black or African American, non-Hispanic/Latino; 1 American Indian or Alaska Native, non-Hispanic/Latino; 2 Asian, non-Hispanic/Latino; 3 Hispanic/Latino; 8 Two or more races, non-Hispanic/Latino), 22 international. Average age 33. 98 applicants, 79% accepted, 71 enrolled. *Faculty:* 25 full-time (18 women), 60 part-time/adjunct (41 women). Expenses: Contact institution. *Financial support:* In 2016–17, 6 teaching assistantships with full tuition reimbursements were awarded; instructional support assistantships, administrative assistantships also available. In 2016, 163 master's awarded. *Program availability:* Part-time. Offers adolescent to young adult education (MS); art education (MS); assessment and evaluation (MA, Certificate); chemistry (MS); chemistry and physics (MS); curriculum and instruction (MS); drama/theatre (MS); earth science (MS); earth science and chemistry (MS); earth science and physics (MS); education (MA, MS); elementary education - literacy (MA); higher education administration (MA, MS); instructional technology (MA); integrated language arts (MS); integrated mathematics (MS); integrated social studies (MS); life science (MS); life science and chemistry (MS); life science and earth science (MS); life science and physics (MS); P-12 multi-age education (MS); physics (MS); principalship (MA, MS); special education (MA). *Application deadline:* Applications are processed on a rolling basis. *Application fee:* $45 ($70 for international students). Electronic applications accepted. *Application Contact:* Kelly Chaff, College Program Specialist, 330-972-7028, E-mail: klchaff@uakron.edu. *Interim Dean,* Dr. Susan Clark, 330-972-7780, E-mail: sclark1@uakron.edu.

College of Engineering Students: 359 full-time (89 women), 75 part-time (14 women); includes 15 minority (7 Asian, non-Hispanic/Latino; 5 Hispanic/Latino; 3 Two or more races, non-Hispanic/Latino), 322 international. Average age 30. 387 applicants, 71% accepted, 99 enrolled. *Faculty:* 89 full-time (15 women), 25 part-time/adjunct (1 woman). Expenses: Contact institution. *Financial support:* In 2016–17, 1 fellowship with full tuition reimbursement, 150 research assistantships with full tuition reimbursements, 32 teaching assistantships with full tuition reimbursements were awarded; career-related internships or fieldwork, Federal Work-Study, and instructional support assistantships also available. In 2016, 74 master's, 46 doctorates awarded. *Program availability:* Part-time, evening/weekend. Offers biomedical engineering (MS); chemical and biomolecular engineering (MS, PhD); civil engineering (MS); engineering (PhD); mechanical engineering (MS). *Application deadline:* Applications are processed on a rolling basis. *Application fee:* $45 ($70 for international students). Electronic applications accepted. *Application Contact:* Dr. Craig Menzemer, Associate Dean for Graduate Studies and Administration, 330-972-5536, E-mail: ccmenze@uakron.edu. *Interim Dean,* Dr. Donald Visco, 330-972-6978, E-mail: dviscoj@uakron.edu.

College of Health Professions Students: 531 full-time (411 women), 487 part-time (366 women); includes 181 minority (100 Black or African American, non-Hispanic/Latino; 3 American Indian or Alaska Native, non-Hispanic/Latino; 24 Asian, non-Hispanic/Latino; 29 Hispanic/Latino; 25 Two or more races, non-Hispanic/Latino), 21 international. Average age 30. 853 applicants, 48% accepted, 296 enrolled. *Faculty:* 38 full-time (22 women), 161 part-time/adjunct (122 women). Expenses: Contact institution. *Financial support:* In 2016–17, 28 fellowships with full and partial tuition reimbursements, 40 research assistantships with full and partial tuition reimbursements, 46 teaching assistantships with full and partial tuition reimbursements were awarded. In 2016, 338 master's, 23 doctorates awarded. Offers audiology (Au D); classroom guidance for teachers (MA, MS); clinical mental health counseling (MA); counseling psychology (PhD); counselor education and supervision (PhD); exercise physiology/adult fitness (MS); health professions (MA, MPH, MS, MSN, MSW, Au D, DNP, PhD); marriage and family counseling/therapy (MA, MS); nursing (MSN, PhD); nursing practice (DNP); public health (MPH); school counseling (MA, MS); social work (MSW); speech-language pathology (MA); speech-language pathology and audiology (MA, Au D); sport science/coaching (MA, MS). *Application deadline:* For fall admission, 1/1 for domestic and international students. Applications are processed on a rolling basis. *Application fee:* $45 ($70 for international students). Electronic applications accepted. *Associate Dean,* 330-972-5515.

College of Polymer Science and Polymer Engineering Students: 327 full-time (105 women), 30 part-time (9 women); includes 19 minority (6 Black or African American, non-Hispanic/Latino; 1 American Indian or Alaska Native, non-Hispanic/Latino; 6 Asian, non-Hispanic/Latino; 4 Hispanic/Latino; 2 Two or more races, non-Hispanic/Latino), 283 international. Average age 25. 257 applicants, 57% accepted, 111 enrolled. *Faculty:* 28 full-time (4 women), 6 part-time/adjunct (0 women). Expenses: Contact institution. *Financial support:* In 2016–17, 4 fellowships with full tuition reimbursements, 214 research assistantships with full and partial tuition reimbursements were awarded. In 2016, 53 master's, 32 doctorates awarded. *Program availability:* Part-time, evening/weekend. Offers polymer engineering (MS, PhD); polymer science (MS, PhD). *Application deadline:* For fall admission, 12/1 priority date for domestic and international students. *Application fee:* $45 ($70 for international students). Electronic applications accepted. *Application Contact:* Kevin Cavicchi, Associate Dean of Academic Affairs, 330-972-8368, E-mail: kac58@uakron.edu. *Dean,* Dr. Eric Amis, 330-972-7500, E-mail: amis@uakron.edu.

School of Law Students: 270 full-time (115 women), 114 part-time (65 women); includes 61 minority (23 Black or African American, non-Hispanic/Latino; 14 Asian, non-Hispanic/Latino; 15 Hispanic/Latino; 9 Two or more races, non-Hispanic/Latino), 5 international. Average age 28. 885 applicants, 51% accepted, 159 enrolled. *Faculty:* 38 full-time (16 women), 16 part-time/adjunct (2 women). Expenses: Contact institution. *Financial support:* In 2016–17, 264 students received support. Career-related internships or fieldwork, scholarships/grants, and tuition waivers (full and partial) available. Support available to part-time students. Financial award applicants required to submit FAFSA. In 2016, 6 master's, 125 doctorates awarded. *Program availability:* Part-time, evening/weekend. Offers law (LL M, JD). *Application deadline:* For fall admission, 3/1 priority date for domestic and international students. Applications are processed on a rolling basis. *Application fee:* $45 ($70 for international students). Electronic applications accepted. *Application Contact:* Lauri S. File, Assistant Dean of Admission and Financial Aid, 330-972-7331, Fax: 330-258-2343, E-mail: lfile@uakron.edu. *Dean,* Martin H. Belsky, 330-972-6359, Fax: 330-258-2343, E-mail: belsky@uakron.edu.

THE UNIVERSITY OF ALABAMA, Tuscaloosa, AL 35487

General Information State-supported, coed, university. CGS member. *Enrollment:* 37,663 graduate, professional, and undergraduate students; 3,195 full-time matriculated graduate/professional students (1,727 women), 1,719 part-time matriculated graduate/professional students (1,132 women). *Enrollment by degree level:* 2,826 master's, 2,014 doctoral, 74 other advanced degrees. *Graduate faculty:* 983 full-time (394 women), 59 part-time/adjunct (21 women). Tuition, state resident: full-time $10,470. Tuition, nonresident: full-time $26,950. *Graduate housing:* On-campus housing not available. *Student services:* Campus employment opportunities, campus safety program, career counseling, child daycare facilities, exercise/wellness program, free psychological counseling, grant writing training, international student services, low-cost health insurance, multicultural affairs office, services for students with disabilities, teacher training, writing training. *Library facilities:* Amelia Gayle Gorgas Library plus 8 others. *Collection:* Books: 3.3 million (physical), 1.5 million (digital/electronic); Serial titles: 727 (physical), 127,820 (digital/electronic); Databases: 905. Weekly public service hours: 146; study areas open 24 hours, 5–7 days a week; students can reserve study rooms. *Research affiliation:* Mercedes-Benz (automotive engineering), Alabama Power (utilities), TDK Corp. (materials science), Nucor Steel (materials science), Boeing (aerospace, manufacturing), Lockheed Martin Corporation (business analytics).

Computer facilities: 2,500 computers available on campus for general student use. A campuswide network can be accessed from student residence rooms and from off campus. Online class registration is available.
Website: http://www.ua.edu/

General Application Contact: Patrick D. Fuller, Senior Graduate Admissions Counselor, 205-348-5923, Fax: 205-348-0400, E-mail: patrick.d.fuller@ua.edu.

GRADUATE UNITS

Graduate School Students: 3,195 full-time (1,727 women), 1,719 part-time (1,132 women); includes 1,005 minority (645 Black or African American, non-Hispanic/Latino; 24 American Indian or Alaska Native, non-Hispanic/Latino; 73 Asian, non-Hispanic/Latino; 167 Hispanic/Latino; 7 Native Hawaiian or other Pacific Islander, non-Hispanic/Latino; 89 Two or more races, non-Hispanic/Latino), 541 international. Average age 31. 6,883 applicants, 40% accepted, 1698 enrolled. *Faculty:* 943 full-time (378 women), 21 part-time/adjunct (11 women). Expenses: Contact institution. *Financial support:* Fellowships with tuition reimbursements, research assistantships with tuition reimbursements, teaching assistantships with tuition reimbursements, career-related internships or fieldwork, Federal Work-Study, institutionally sponsored loans, scholarships/grants, traineeships, health care benefits, tuition waivers (full and partial), and unspecified assistantships available. Support available to part-time students. Financial award application deadline: 2/15; financial award applicants required to submit FAFSA. In 2016, 1,656 master's, 431 doctorates, 45 other advanced degrees awarded. *Program availability:* Part-time, evening/weekend, online learning. *Application deadline:* For fall admission, 7/1 priority date for domestic students, 3/15 for international students; for spring admission, 11/1 priority date for domestic students, 7/1 for international students. Applications are processed on a rolling basis. *Application fee:* $50 ($60 for international students). Electronic applications accepted. *Application Contact:* Lesley Campbell, Director of Graduate Recruitment, 205-348-0051, Fax: 205-348-0400, E-mail: lesley.campbell@ua.edu. *Dean,* Dr. Susan Carvalho, 205-348-5921, Fax: 205-348-0400, E-mail: scarvalho@ua.edu.

Capstone College of Nursing Students: 146 full-time (126 women), 178 part-time (153 women); includes 109 minority (73 Black or African American, non-Hispanic/Latino; 3 American Indian or Alaska Native, non-Hispanic/Latino; 9 Asian, non-Hispanic/Latino; 17 Hispanic/Latino; 2 Native Hawaiian or other Pacific Islander, non-Hispanic/Latino; 5 Two or more races, non-Hispanic/Latino), 1 international. Average age 42. 395 applicants, 50% accepted, 147 enrolled. *Faculty:* 27 full-time (23 women), 1 part-time/adjunct (0 women). Expenses: Contact institution. *Financial support:* Scholarships/grants available. Financial award application deadline: 6/15; financial award applicants required to submit FAFSA. In 2016, 42 master's, 54 doctorates awarded. *Program availability:* Part-time, online learning. Offers nursing (MSN, DNP). *Application deadline:* For fall admission, 4/1 priority date for domestic students. Applications are processed on a rolling basis. *Application fee:* $50 ($60 for international students). Electronic applications accepted. *Application Contact:* Vickie L. Samuel, Graduate Recruitment and Retention Liaison, 205-348-8163, Fax: 205-348-5559, E-mail: vsamuel@ua.edu. *Dean,* Dr. Suzanne Prevost, 205-348-1040, Fax: 205-348-5559, E-mail: sprevost@ua.edu.

College of Arts and Sciences Students: 881 full-time (454 women), 105 part-time (52 women); includes 146 minority (70 Black or African American, non-Hispanic/Latino; 3 American Indian or Alaska Native, non-Hispanic/Latino; 13 Asian, non-Hispanic/Latino; 45 Hispanic/Latino; 15 Two or more races, non-Hispanic/Latino), 187 international. Average age 28. 1,725 applicants, 28% accepted, 258 enrolled. *Faculty:* 416 full-time (166 women), 9 part-time/adjunct (4 women). Expenses: Contact institution. *Financial support:* Career-related internships or fieldwork, Federal Work-Study, institutionally sponsored loans, scholarships/grants, and unspecified assistantships available. Support available to part-time students. Financial award applicants required to submit FAFSA. In 2016, 258 master's, 93 doctorates awarded. *Program availability:* Part-time, online learning. Offers acting (MFA); American studies (MA); anthropology (MA, PhD); applied mathematics (PhD); arranging (MM); art history (MA); arts and sciences (MA, MATESOL, MFA, MM, MPA, MS, DMA, PhD); biological sciences (MS, PhD); chemistry (MS, PhD); choral conducting (MM, DMA); church music (MM); clinical psychology (PhD); composition (MM, DMA); composition and rhetoric (PhD); costume design (MFA); creative writing (MFA); criminal justice (MS); directing (MFA); earth system science (MS, PhD); environment and natural resources (MS, PhD); environment and society (MS, PhD); experimental psychology (PhD); French (MA, PhD); French and Spanish (PhD); geographic information science (MS, PhD); geological sciences (MS, PhD); German (MA); history (MA, PhD); literature (MA, PhD); mathematics (MA, PhD); music education (MA, PhD); musicology (MM); performance (MM, DMA); physics and astronomy (MS, PhD); political science (MA, PhD); public administration (MPA); pure mathematics (PhD); rhetoric and composition (MA); Romance languages (MA, PhD); scene design/technical production (MFA); Spanish (MA, PhD); speech language pathology (MS); stage management (MFA); studio art (MA, MFA); teaching English as a second language (MATESOL); theatre (MFA); theatre management/administration (MFA); theory (MM); wind conducting (MM, DMA); women's studies (MA). *Application fee:* $50 ($60 for international students). Electronic applications accepted. *Application Contact:* Patrick D. Fuller, Senior Graduate Admissions Counselor, 205-348-5923, Fax: 205-348-0400, E-mail: patrick.d.fuller@ua.edu. *Dean,* Dr. Robert F. Olin, 205-348-7007, Fax: 205-348-0272, E-mail: olin@as.ua.edu.

College of Communication and Information Sciences Students: 131 full-time (83 women), 194 part-time (150 women); includes 49 minority (24 Black or African American, non-Hispanic/Latino; 1 American Indian or Alaska Native, non-Hispanic/Latino; 3 Asian, non-Hispanic/Latino; 12 Hispanic/Latino; 9 Two or more races, non-Hispanic/Latino), 31 international. Average age 32. 277 applicants, 61% accepted, 132 enrolled. *Faculty:* 61 full-time (28 women), 1 (woman) part-time/adjunct. Expenses: Contact institution. *Financial support:* Fellowships with tuition reimbursements, research assistantships with tuition reimbursements, teaching assistantships with tuition reimbursements, institutionally sponsored loans, health care benefits, and unspecified assistantships available. Financial award application deadline: 2/15. In 2016, 139 master's, 8 doctorates awarded. Offers advertising and public relations (MA); book arts (MFA); communication and information sciences (MA, MFA, MLIS, PhD); communication studies (MA); journalism and creative media (MA); library and information studies (MLIS, PhD). *Application deadline:* For fall admission, 2/15 priority date for domestic and international students; for winter admission, 11/1 priority date for international students; for spring admission, 11/1 priority date for domestic students. Applications are processed on a rolling basis. *Application fee:* $50 ($60 for international students). Electronic applications accepted. *Application Contact:* Marylou Cox, Information Contact, 205-348-8593, Fax: 205-348-6774, E-mail: mcox@ua.edu. *Dean,* Dr. Mark Nelson, 205-348-4787, E-mail: mnelson@ua.edu.

College of Education Students: 362 full-time (254 women), 523 part-time (374 women); includes 239 minority (172 Black or African American, non-Hispanic/Latino; 6 American Indian or Alaska Native, non-Hispanic/Latino; 10 Asian, non-Hispanic/Latino; 28 Hispanic/Latino; 2 Native Hawaiian or other Pacific Islander, non-Hispanic/Latino; 21 Two or more races, non-Hispanic/Latino), 38 international. Average age 36. 465 applicants, 61% accepted, 214 enrolled. *Faculty:* 109 full-time (57 women), 3 part-time/adjunct (all women). Expenses: Contact institution. *Financial support:* In 2016–17, 65 research assistantships with tuition reimbursements, 25 teaching assistantships with tuition reimbursements were awarded; career-related internships or fieldwork, Federal Work-Study, institutionally sponsored loans, scholarships/grants, and unspecified assistantships also available. Financial award applicants required to submit FAFSA. In 2016, 205 master's, 69 doctorates, 45 other advanced degrees awarded. *Program availability:* Part-time, online learning. Offers alternative sport pedagogy (MA); choral music education (MA); collaborative special education (M Ed, Ed S); early intervention (M Ed, Ed S); education (M Ed, MA, Ed D, PhD, Ed S); educational administration (Ed D, PhD); educational leadership (MA, Ed S); educational studies in psychology, research methodology and counseling (MA, Ed D, PhD, Ed S); elementary education (MA, Ed D, PhD, Ed S); exercise science

(PhD); gifted and talented education (M Ed, Ed S); higher education administration (MA, Ed D, PhD); instructional leadership (Ed D, PhD); instrumental music education (MA); multiple abilities (M Ed); music education (Ed D, PhD, Ed S); secondary education (MA, Ed D, PhD, Ed S); special education (Ed D, PhD). *Application deadline:* For fall admission, 7/1 for domestic and international students; for spring admission, 11/15 for domestic students, 11/17 for international students. Applications are processed on a rolling basis. *Application fee:* $50 ($60 for international students). *Application Contact:* Dr. Kathy S. Wetzel, Assistant Dean for Student Services, 205-348-1154, Fax: 205-348-0080, E-mail: kwetzel@bamaed.ua.edu. *Dean,* Dr. Peter Hlebowitsh, E-mail: peter.hleb@ua.edu.

College of Engineering Students: 235 full-time (51 women), 43 part-time (4 women); includes 15 minority (9 Black or African American, non-Hispanic/Latino; 2 Asian, non-Hispanic/Latino; 3 Hispanic/Latino; 1 Two or more races, non-Hispanic/Latino), 152 international. Average age 27. 355 applicants, 45% accepted, 71 enrolled. *Faculty:* 123 full-time (15 women). Expenses: Contact institution. *Financial support:* In 2016–17, 188 students received support, including 23 fellowships with full tuition reimbursements available (averaging $16,022 per year), 85 research assistantships with full tuition reimbursements available (averaging $16,022 per year), 73 teaching assistantships with full tuition reimbursements available (averaging $16,022 per year); career-related internships or fieldwork, Federal Work-Study, and institutionally sponsored loans also available. Financial award application deadline: 2/15. In 2016, 82 master's, 22 doctorates awarded. *Program availability:* Part-time, online learning. Offers aerospace engineering (MSAEM); chemical and biological engineering (MS Ch E, PhD); civil engineering (MSCE, PhD); computer science (MS, PhD); electrical engineering (MS, PhD); engineering (MS, MS Ch E, MS Met E, MSAEM, MSCE, PhD); engineering science and mechanics (PhD); environmental engineering (MS); materials science (PhD); mechanical engineering (MS, PhD); metallurgical and materials engineering (MS Met E, PhD). *Application deadline:* For fall admission, 7/1 for domestic students, 4/15 for international students; for spring admission, 11/15 for domestic students, 9/1 for international students. Applications are processed on a rolling basis. *Application fee:* $50 ($60 for international students). Electronic applications accepted. *Application Contact:* Dr. David A. Francko, Dean, 205-348-8280, Fax: 205-348-0400, E-mail: dfrancko@ua.edu. *Dean,* Dr. Charles Karr, 205-348-6405, Fax: 205-348-8573.

College of Human Environmental Sciences Students: 213 full-time (138 women), 392 part-time (278 women); includes 142 minority (105 Black or African American, non-Hispanic/Latino; 3 American Indian or Alaska Native, non-Hispanic/Latino; 4 Asian, non-Hispanic/Latino; 17 Hispanic/Latino; 2 Native Hawaiian or other Pacific Islander, non-Hispanic/Latino; 11 Two or more races, non-Hispanic/Latino), 5 international. Average age 33. 147 applicants, 82% accepted, 112 enrolled. *Faculty:* 52 full-time (36 women), 3 part-time/adjunct (2 women). Expenses: Contact institution. *Financial support:* In 2016–17, 2 research assistantships with full tuition reimbursements (averaging $9,000 per year) were awarded; fellowships with tuition reimbursements, teaching assistantships with full tuition reimbursements, career-related internships or fieldwork, Federal Work-Study, institutionally sponsored loans, and scholarships/grants also available. In 2016, 90 master's awarded. *Program availability:* Part-time, evening/weekend, online learning. Offers apparel and textiles (MSHES); consumer sciences (MS); health education and promotion (PhD); health studies (MA); human development and family studies (MSHES); human environmental sciences (MA, MS, MSHES, PhD); human nutrition and hospitality management (MSHES); interactive technology (MS); marriage and family therapy (MSHES); parent and family life education (MSHES); quality management (MS); restaurant and meeting management (MS); rural community health (MS); sport management (MS). *Application deadline:* For fall admission, 7/6 for domestic students. Applications are processed on a rolling basis. *Application fee:* $50 ($60 for international students). Electronic applications accepted. *Application Contact:* Patrick D. Fuller, Admissions Officer, 205-348-5923, Fax: 205-348-0400, E-mail: patrick.d.fuller@ua.edu. *Dean,* Dr. Milla D. Boschung, 205-348-6250, Fax: 205-348-1786, E-mail: mboschun@ches.ua.edu.

Manderson Graduate School of Business Students: 485 full-time (179 women), 123 part-time (44 women); includes 80 minority (44 Black or African American, non-Hispanic/Latino; 2 American Indian or Alaska Native, non-Hispanic/Latino; 13 Asian, non-Hispanic/Latino; 10 Hispanic/Latino; 1 Native Hawaiian or other Pacific Islander, non-Hispanic/Latino; 10 Two or more races, non-Hispanic/Latino), 83 international. Average age 27. 999 applicants, 51% accepted, 281 enrolled. *Faculty:* 116 full-time (25 women), 3 part-time/adjunct (0 women). Expenses: Contact institution. *Financial support:* In 2016–17, 64 research assistantships with tuition reimbursements (averaging $14,500 per year), 69 teaching assistantships with tuition reimbursements (averaging $16,500 per year) were awarded; fellowships with tuition reimbursements, career-related internships or fieldwork, Federal Work-Study, institutionally sponsored loans, and scholarships/grants also available. Support available to part-time students. Financial award application deadline: 2/5. In 2016, 400 master's, 21 doctorates awarded. *Program availability:* Part-time, evening/weekend, online learning. Offers accounting (M Acc, PhD); applied statistics (MS, PhD); business (EMBA, M Acc, MA, MBA, MS, MTA, PhD); economics (MA, PhD); finance (MS, PhD); general commerce and business (EMBA, MBA); management (MA, MS, PhD); marketing (MS, PhD); operations management (MS, PhD); tax accounting (MTA). *Application deadline:* For fall admission, 4/15 priority date for domestic and international students. Applications are processed on a rolling basis. *Application fee:* $60 ($75 for international students). Electronic applications accepted. *Application Contact:* Patricia Wilson, Director of MBA Recruiting and Admissions, 205-348-9122, Fax: 205-348-4504, E-mail: pewilson@cba.ua.edu. *Associate Dean,* Dr. J. Brian Gray, 205-348-8912, Fax: 205-348-4504, E-mail: bgray@cba.ua.edu.

School of Social Work Students: 292 full-time (260 women), 43 part-time (37 women); includes 120 minority (97 Black or African American, non-Hispanic/Latino; 1 American Indian or Alaska Native, non-Hispanic/Latino; 3 Asian, non-Hispanic/Latino; 10 Hispanic/Latino; 9 Two or more races, non-Hispanic/Latino), 8 international. Average age 30. 492 applicants, 43% accepted, 142 enrolled. *Faculty:* 29 full-time (22 women), 1 (woman) part-time/adjunct. Expenses: Contact institution. *Financial support:* In 2016–17, 113 students received support, including 6 research assistantships with full tuition reimbursements available (averaging $12,744 per year), 5 teaching assistantships with full tuition reimbursements available (averaging $12,744 per year); career-related internships or fieldwork, scholarships/grants, traineeships, health care benefits, and unspecified assistantships also available. Financial award application deadline: 2/1; financial award applicants required to submit FAFSA. In 2016, 207 master's, 9 doctorates awarded. *Program availability:* Part-time, blended/hybrid learning. Offers social work (MSW, PhD). *Application deadline:* For fall admission, 2/1 priority date for domestic and international students; for spring admission, 9/1 priority date for domestic and international students; for summer admission, 2/1 priority date for domestic and international students. *Application fee:* $50 ($60 for international

students). Electronic applications accepted. *Application Contact:* Amanda Moore, Coordinator of Student Services, 205-348-5272, Fax: 205-348-9419, E-mail: almoore2@ua.edu. *Professor and Dean,* Dr. Vikki L. Vandiver, 205-348-3924, Fax: 205-348-9419, E-mail: vlvandiver@sw.ua.edu.

Interdisciplinary Programs Students: 6 full-time (4 women), 8 part-time (5 women); includes 2 minority (both Black or African American, non-Hispanic/Latino). Average age 41. 2 applicants, 100% accepted, 2 enrolled. Expenses: Contact institution. In 2016, 2 doctorates awarded. *Program availability:* Part-time, evening/weekend. Offers interdisciplinary studies (PhD). *Application deadline:* For fall admission, 5/1 for international students; for winter admission, 9/15 for international students. Applications are processed on a rolling basis. Electronic applications accepted. *Application Contact:* Patrick D. Fuller, Senior Graduate Admissions Counselor, 205-348-5923, Fax: 205-348-0400, E-mail: patrick.d.fuller@ua.edu. *Assistant Dean of the Graduate School,* Dr. Andrew Mark Goodliffe, 205-348-8283, Fax: 205-348-0400, E-mail: amg@ua.edu.

School of Law Students: 417 full-time (185 women), 74 part-time (27 women); includes 98 minority (51 Black or African American, non-Hispanic/Latino; 5 American Indian or Alaska Native, non-Hispanic/Latino; 14 Asian, non-Hispanic/Latino; 20 Hispanic/Latino; 8 Two or more races, non-Hispanic/Latino), 7 international. Average age 27. 1,634 applicants, 21% accepted, 172 enrolled. *Faculty:* 40 full-time (16 women), 38 part-time/adjunct (10 women). Expenses: Contact institution. *Financial support:* Applicants required to submit FAFSA. In 2016, 60 master's, 144 doctorates awarded. Offers business transactions (LL M); comparative law (LL M, JSD); law (JD, JSD); taxation (LL M). *Application deadline:* Applications are processed on a rolling basis. *Application fee:* $40. Electronic applications accepted. *Application Contact:* Martha Griffith, Assistant Director for Admissions, 205-348-7945, Fax: 205-348-3917, E-mail: mgriffith@law.ua.edu. *Associate Dean for Admissions,* Claude R. Arrington, 205-348-6557, Fax: 205-348-3077, E-mail: carrington@law.ua.edu.

THE UNIVERSITY OF ALABAMA AT BIRMINGHAM, Birmingham, AL 35294

General Information State-supported, coed, university. CGS member. *Enrollment:* 19,535 graduate, professional, and undergraduate students; 3,638 full-time matriculated graduate/professional students (2,176 women), 3,236 part-time matriculated graduate/professional students (2,280 women). *Enrollment by degree level:* 4,211 master's, 2,456 doctoral, 207 other advanced degrees. *Graduate faculty:* 1,791 full-time (649 women), 142 part-time/adjunct (60 women). Full-time tuition and fees vary according to course load and program. *Graduate housing:* Room and/or apartments available on a first-come, first-served basis to single students; on-campus housing not available to married students. Typical cost: $6020 per year ($9970 including board). Room and board charges vary according to board plan. Housing application deadline: 5/1. *Student services:* Campus employment opportunities, campus safety program, career counseling, exercise/wellness program, free psychological counseling, grant writing training, international student services, low-cost health insurance, multicultural affairs office, services for students with disabilities, teacher training, writing training. *Library facilities:* Mervyn Sterne Library plus 2 others. *Collection:* Books: 1.3 million (physical). Students can reserve study rooms. *Research affiliation:* Southern Research Institute (cancer therapeutics, biodefense).

Computer facilities: A campuswide network can be accessed from student residence rooms and from off campus. Online class registration, transcript requests are available. Website: http://www.uab.edu/

General Application Contact: Holly Hebard, Director of Graduate School Operations, 205-934-8227, Fax: 205-934-8413, E-mail: gradschool@uab.edu.

GRADUATE UNITS

Collat School of Business *Program availability:* Part-time, online learning. Offers accounting (M Acct); business (M Acct, MBA, MS); business administration (MBA); management information systems (MS). MD/MBA program offered in partnership with the School of Medicine. Electronic applications accepted.

College of Arts and Sciences *Program availability:* Part-time, evening/weekend, online learning. Offers anthropology (MA); applied mathematics (PhD); art history (MA); arts and sciences (MA, MPA, MS, MSCJ, MSFS, PhD); behavioral neuroscience (PhD); biology (MS, PhD); chemistry (MS, PhD); communication management (MA); computer and information sciences (MS, PhD); computer forensics and security management (MS); creative writing (MA); criminal justice (MSCJ); forensic science (MSFS); history (MA); lifespan developmental psychology (PhD); literature (MA); mathematics (MS); medical sociology (PhD); medical/clinical psychology (PhD); physics (MS, PhD); psychology (MA); public administration (MPA); rhetoric and composition (MA). Electronic applications accepted.

Graduate Programs in Joint Health Sciences Offers basic medical sciences (MSBMS); biochemistry, structural and stem cell biology (PhD); cancer biology (PhD); cell, molecular, and developmental biology (PhD); genetics, genomics and bioinformatics (PhD); health sciences (MSBMS, PhD); microbiology (PhD); neurobiology (PhD); pathobiology and molecular medicine (PhD); pharmacology and toxicology (PhD). Electronic applications accepted.

School of Dentistry Offers dentistry (MS, DMD).

School of Education *Program availability:* Part-time, evening/weekend, online learning. Offers arts education (MA Ed); community health and human services (MA Ed); counseling (MA); curriculum education (Ed S); early childhood education (MA Ed, PhD); education (MA, MA Ed, Ed D, PhD, Ed S); educational leadership (MA Ed, Ed D, Ed S); elementary education (MA Ed); English as a second language (MA Ed, Ed S); high school education (MA Ed); reading (MA Ed); special education (MA Ed). Electronic applications accepted.

School of Engineering Students: 131 full-time (25 women), 341 part-time (63 women); includes 132 minority (92 Black or African American, non-Hispanic/Latino; 1 American Indian or Alaska Native, non-Hispanic/Latino; 13 Asian, non-Hispanic/Latino; 13 Hispanic/Latino; 13 Two or more races, non-Hispanic/Latino), 93 international. Average age 33. 278 applicants, 82% accepted, 136 enrolled. *Faculty:* 78 full-time (14 women), 19 part-time/adjunct (3 women). Expenses: Contact institution. *Financial support:* Fellowships with full tuition reimbursements, research assistantships with full tuition reimbursements, career-related internships or fieldwork, Federal Work-Study, and institutionally sponsored loans available. Support available to part-time students. In 2016, 150 master's, 19 doctorates awarded. *Program availability:* Part-time, evening/weekend, 100% online, blended/hybrid learning. Offers advanced safety engineering and management (M Eng); biomedical engineering (MSBME, PhD); computational engineering (PhD); computer engineering (PhD); construction engineering management (M Eng); electrical engineering (MSEE); engineering (M Eng, MS Mt E, MSBME, MSCE, MSEE, MSME, PhD); materials engineering (MS Mt E, PhD); mechanical engineering (MSME); structural engineering (M Eng); sustainable smart cities (M Eng). *Application deadline:* For fall admission, 7/1 for domestic and international students; for spring admission, 11/1 for domestic and international students; for summer admission, 4/1 for domestic and international students. Applications are processed on a rolling basis. *Application fee*: $50 ($60 for international students). Electronic applications accepted. *Application Contact*: Holly Hebard, Director of Graduate School Operations, 205-934-8227, Fax: 205-934-8413, E-mail: gradschool@uab.edu. *Dean*, Dr. J. Iwan Alexander, 205-975-5890, Fax: 205-934-8437, E-mail: ialex@uab.edu.

School of Health Professions *Program availability*: Part-time, online learning. Offers administration/health services (D Sc, PhD); biotechnology (MS); clinical laboratory science (MS); genetic counseling (MS); health administration (MSHA); health informatics (MSHI); health professions (MS, MSHA, MSHI, MSPAS, D Sc, DPT, PhD, Certificate); low vision rehabilitation (Certificate); nutrition sciences (MS, PhD); occupational therapy (MS); physical therapy (DPT); physician assistant studies (MSPAS); rehabilitation science (PhD). Electronic applications accepted.

School of Medicine Offers medicine (MD). Electronic applications accepted.

School of Nursing Students: 228 full-time (165 women), 1,393 part-time (1,234 women); includes 398 minority (267 Black or African American, non-Hispanic/Latino; 4 American Indian or Alaska Native, non-Hispanic/Latino; 52 Asian, non-Hispanic/Latino; 41 Hispanic/Latino; 34 Two or more races, non-Hispanic/Latino), 3 international. Average age 33. 1,027 applicants, 55% accepted, 421 enrolled. *Faculty*: 86 full-time (79 women), 42 part-time/adjunct (35 women). Expenses: Contact institution. *Financial support*: In 2016–17, 23 fellowships (averaging $34,685 per year), 12 research assistantships (averaging $9,042 per year), 2 teaching assistantships (averaging $22,000 per year) were awarded; scholarships/grants, traineeships, health care benefits, and unspecified assistantships also available. Support available to part-time students. In 2016, 557 master's, 19 doctorates awarded. *Program availability*: Part-time, online only, blended/hybrid learning. Offers clinical nurse leader (MSN); nurse anesthesia (DNP); nurse practitioner (MSN, DNP); nursing (MSN, DNP, PhD); nursing health systems administration (MSN); nursing informatics (MSN). *Application deadline*: For fall admission, 2/24 for domestic students; for summer admission, 10/15 for domestic students. *Application fee*: $50. Electronic applications accepted. *Application Contact*: John Updegraff, Director of Student Affairs, 205-975-3370, Fax: 205-934-5490, E-mail: jupde22@uab.edu. *Dean*, Dr. Doreen C. Harper, 205-934-5360, Fax: 205-934-1894, E-mail: dcharper@uab.edu.

School of Optometry Offers optometry (MS, OD, PhD); sensory impairment (PhD); vision science (MS, PhD). Electronic applications accepted.

School of Public Health *Program availability*: Part-time. Offers applied epidemiology and pharmacoepidemiology (MSPH); biostatistics (MPH, MS, MSPH, PhD); clinical and translational science (MSPH); environmental health (MPH); environmental health and toxicology (MSPH); environmental health sciences research (PhD); epidemiology (MPH); general theory and practice (MPH); health behavior (MPH); health care organization (MPH); health education and promotion (MPH); health policy quantitative policy analysis (MPH); industrial hygiene (MPH, MSPH, PhD); maternal and child health policy (Dr PH); maternal and child health policy and leadership (MPH); occupational health and safety (MPH); outcomes research (MSPH, Dr PH); public health (MPH, MS, MSPH, Dr PH, PhD); public health management (Dr PH); public health preparedness management (MPH). Electronic applications accepted.

THE UNIVERSITY OF ALABAMA IN HUNTSVILLE, Huntsville, AL 35899

General Information State-supported, coed, university. CGS member. *Enrollment*: 8,468 graduate, professional, and undergraduate students; 756 full-time matriculated graduate/professional students (337 women), 1,122 part-time matriculated graduate/professional students (542 women). *Enrollment by degree level*: 1,447 master's, 403 doctoral, 28 other advanced degrees. *Graduate faculty*: 260 full-time (82 women), 44 part-time/adjunct (17 women). Tuition, state resident: full-time $9834; part-time $600 per credit hour. Tuition, nonresident: full-time $21,830; part-time $1325 per credit hour. *Graduate housing*: Rooms and/or apartments available on a first-come, first-served basis to single and married students. Housing application deadline: 6/1. *Student services*: Campus employment opportunities, campus safety program, career counseling, child daycare facilities, exercise/wellness program, free psychological counseling, grant writing training, international student services, low-cost health insurance, multicultural affairs office, services for students with disabilities, teacher training, writing training. *Library facilities*: Louis Salmon Library. *Collection*: Books: 239,503 (physical), 387,481 (digital/electronic); Serial titles: 3,441 (physical), 42,868 (digital/electronic); Databases: 133. *Research affiliation*: Oak Ridge, Lawrence Livermore and Savannah River National Labs - Y12National Security Complex (neutron science, energy technologies, high-performance computing, systems biology, materials science at the nanoscale, national security), Cummings Research Park/Boeing/ADTRAN/SAIC/Teledyne Brown Engineering/Lockheed Martin/Dynetics, Inc. (computer science, aerospace engineering, information systems, space systems, defense systems, informatics), National Oceanic and Atmospheric Administration (NOAA) (climate modeling, weather and air quality research, oceans, satellites), Hudson Alpha Institute for Biotechnology (medical research, biotechnology, genomic research, molecular biology), U.S. Department of Defense/U.S. Army Aviation and Missile Command (missile research, development and engineering and manufacturing technology), NASA/Marshall Space Flight Center/Goddard Space Flight Center (space science, earth science, information technology, materials science, optical science).

Computer facilities: 1,227 computers available on campus for general student use. A campuswide network can be accessed from student residence rooms and from off campus. Online class registration is available. Website: http://www.uah.edu/

General Application Contact: Kim Gray, Admissions Coordinator, Graduate Studies, 256-824-6198, Fax: 256-824-6002, E-mail: deangrad@uah.edu.

GRADUATE UNITS

School of Graduate Studies Students: 756 full-time (337 women), 1,122 part-time (542 women); includes 289 minority (152 Black or African American, non-Hispanic/Latino; 19 American Indian or Alaska Native, non-Hispanic/Latino; 52 Asian, non-Hispanic/Latino; 50 Hispanic/Latino; 16 Two or more races, non-Hispanic/Latino), 314 international. Average age 32. 1,750 applicants, 72% accepted, 659 enrolled. *Faculty*: 260 full-time (82 women), 44 part-time/adjunct (17 women). Expenses: Contact institution. *Financial support*: Fellowships, research assistantships, teaching assistantships, career-related internships or fieldwork, Federal Work-Study, institutionally sponsored loans, scholarships/grants, traineeships, health care benefits, tuition waivers (full and partial), and unspecified assistantships available. Support available to part-time students. Financial award application deadline: 4/1; financial award applicants required to submit FAFSA. In 2016, 485 master's, 51 doctorates awarded. *Program availability*: Part-time, evening/weekend, 100% online, blended/hybrid learning. *Application deadline*: For fall admission, 7/16 priority date for domestic students, 4/1 priority date for international students; for spring admission, 11/30 priority date for domestic students, 9/1 priority date

for international students. Applications are processed on a rolling basis. *Application fee*: $50. Electronic applications accepted. *Application Contact*: Kim Gray, Graduate Studies Admissions Coordinator, 256-824-6002, Fax: 256-824-6405, E-mail: deangrad@uah.edu. *Dean of Graduate Studies*, Dr. David Berkowitz, 256-824-6002, Fax: 256-824-6405, E-mail: deangrad@uah.edu.

College of Arts, Humanities, and Social Sciences *Program availability*: Part-time, evening/weekend. Offers arts, humanities, and social sciences (MA, Certificate); education (MA); English (MA); history (MA); industrial/organizational psychology (MA); psychology (MA); public affairs (MA); technical writing (Certificate); TESOL (Certificate). Electronic applications accepted.

College of Business Administration *Program availability*: Part-time, evening/weekend. Offers accounting (M Acc); business administration (M Acc, MBA, MS, MSIS, MSM, MSMS, Certificate); business analytics (MSMS); cybersecurity (MS, Certificate); enterprise resource planning (Certificate); federal contracting and procurement management (Certificate); human resource management (MSM); information systems (MSIS); management (MBA); supply chain and logistics management (MS); supply chain management (Certificate); technology and innovation management (Certificate). Electronic applications accepted.

College of Education Offers autism spectrum disorders (M Ed, Graduate Certificate); biology (MAT); chemistry (MAT); differentiated instruction in elementary education (M Ed); English language arts (MAT); English speakers of other languages (M Ed, MAT); history (MAT); mathematics (MAT); physics (MAT); reading education (M Ed); secondary education (M Ed).

College of Engineering *Program availability*: Part-time, evening/weekend, online learning. Offers aerospace systems engineering (MS, PhD); biotechnology science and engineering (PhD); chemical and materials engineering (MSE); civil and environmental engineering (PhD); civil engineering (MSE); computer engineering (MSE, PhD); electrical engineering (MSE, PhD); engineering (MS, MSE, MSOR, MSSE, PhD); engineering management (MSE, PhD); industrial engineering (MSE, PhD); materials science (PhD); mechanical engineering (MSE, PhD); operations research (MSOR); optical science and engineering (PhD); software engineering (MSSE); systems engineering (MSE, PhD). Electronic applications accepted.

College of Nursing *Program availability*: Part-time, evening/weekend, online learning. Offers family nurse practitioner (Certificate); nursing (MSN, DNP); nursing education (Certificate). DNP offered jointly with The University of Alabama at Birmingham. Electronic applications accepted.

College of Science *Program availability*: Part-time, evening/weekend. Offers applied mathematics (PhD); atmospheric science (MS, PhD); biology (MS); biotechnology science and engineering (PhD); chemistry (MS); computer science (MS, PhD); cybersecurity (MS); earth system science (MS); education (MA, MS); materials science (MS, PhD); mathematics (MA, MS); modeling and simulation (MS, PhD, Certificate); optics and photonics technology (MS); physics (MS, PhD); science (MA, MS, MSSE, PhD, Certificate); software engineering (MSSE, Certificate); space science (MS, PhD). Electronic applications accepted.

UNIVERSITY OF ALASKA ANCHORAGE, Anchorage, AK 99508

General Information State-supported, coed, comprehensive institution. *Graduate housing*: Rooms and/or apartments available on a first-come, first-served basis to single and married students. Housing application deadline: 7/1. *Research affiliation*: Conoco Phillips (energy), Habitat for Humanity (project management), BP Alaska (energy), Municipality of Anchorage (government), Providence Hospital (health care).

GRADUATE UNITS

College of Arts and Sciences *Program availability*: Part-time. Offers anthropology (MA); arts and sciences (MA, MFA, MS, PhD); biological sciences (MS); clinical psychology (MS); clinical-community psychology with rural-indigenous emphasis (PhD); creative writing and literary arts (MFA); English (MA); interdisciplinary studies (MA, MS).

College of Business and Public Policy *Program availability*: Part-time, evening/weekend. Offers business administration (MBA); business and public policy (MBA, MPA, MS, Certificate); global supply chain management (MS); public administration (MPA); supply chain management (Certificate).

College of Education *Program availability*: Part-time. Offers counseling and guidance (M Ed); early childhood special education (M Ed); education (M Ed, Certificate); educational leadership (M Ed); master teacher (M Ed); principal licensure (Certificate); special education (M Ed, Certificate); superintendent (Certificate); teaching (MAT).

College of Health *Program availability*: Part-time, evening/weekend. Offers health (MPH, MS, MSW, Certificate); public health practice (MPH).

School of Nursing *Program availability*: Part-time, evening/weekend. Offers nursing (MS).

School of Social Work *Program availability*: Part-time, evening/weekend, online learning. Offers clinical social work practice (Certificate); social work (MSW); social work management (Certificate). Electronic applications accepted.

School of Engineering *Program availability*: Part-time, evening/weekend. Offers applied environmental science and technology (M AEST, MS); arctic engineering (MS); civil engineering (MCE, MS); coastal, ocean, and port engineering (Certificate); engineering (M AEST, MCE, MS, Certificate); engineering management (MS); project management (MS); science management (MS).

UNIVERSITY OF ALASKA FAIRBANKS, Fairbanks, AK 99775-7520

General Information State-supported, coed, university. CGS member. *Enrollment*: 8,360 graduate, professional, and undergraduate students; 507 full-time matriculated graduate/professional students (265 women), 530 part-time matriculated graduate/professional students (331 women). *Enrollment by degree level*: 664 master's, 313 doctoral, 60 other advanced degrees. *Graduate faculty*: 295 full-time (119 women), 13 part-time/adjunct (4 women). Tuition, state resident: full-time $7992; part-time $444 per credit. Tuition, nonresident: full-time $16,326; part-time $907 per credit. *Required fees*: $39 per credit. Tuition: $322 per semester. Tuition and fees vary according to course level, course load, campus/location, program and reciprocity agreements. *Graduate housing*: Rooms and/or apartments available on a first-come, first-served basis to single and married students. Typical cost: $4700 per year ($9090 including board) for single students; $8865 per year ($13,255 including board) for married students. Room and board charges vary according to board plan, campus/location and housing facility selected. Housing application deadline: 8/1. *Student services*: Campus employment opportunities, campus safety program, career counseling, exercise/wellness program, free psychological counseling, grant writing training, international student services, low-cost health insurance, multicultural affairs office, services for students with disabilities, teacher training, writing training. *Library facilities*: Rasmuson Library plus 2 others. *Collection*: Weekly public service hours: 87; students can reserve study rooms. *Research affiliation*: Institute of Northern Forestry, Alaska Cooperative Fishery and Wildlife Research Unit.

Computer facilities: 125 computers available on campus for general student use. A campuswide network can be accessed from student residence rooms and from off campus. Online class registration, university portal are available.
Website: http://www.uaf.edu/

General Application Contact: Mary Kreta, Director of Admissions, 907-474-7500, E-mail: admissions@uaf.edu.

GRADUATE UNITS

College of Engineering and Mines Students: 63 full-time (15 women), 42 part-time (9 women); includes 12 minority (3 Black or African American, non-Hispanic/Latino; 2 American Indian or Alaska Native, non-Hispanic/Latino; 2 Asian, non-Hispanic/Latino; 2 Hispanic/Latino; 3 Two or more races, non-Hispanic/Latino), 38 international. Average age 30. 118 applicants, 33% accepted, 20 enrolled. *Faculty:* 43 full-time (7 women), 3 part-time/adjunct (0 women). Expenses: Contact institution. *Financial support:* In 2016–17, 26 research assistantships with full tuition reimbursements (averaging $9,040 per year), 34 teaching assistantships with full tuition reimbursements (averaging $6,596 per year) were awarded; fellowships with full tuition reimbursements, career-related internships or fieldwork, Federal Work-Study, scholarships/grants, health care benefits, and unspecified assistantships also available. Support available to part-time students. Financial award application deadline: 7/1; financial award applicants required to submit FAFSA. In 2016, 31 master's, 7 doctorates, 1 other advanced degree awarded. *Program availability:* Part-time. Offers civil engineering (MS); computer science (MS); design and construction management (Graduate Certificate); electrical engineering (MEE, MS); engineering (PhD); engineering and mines (MCE, MEE, MS, PhD, Graduate Certificate); environmental engineering (PhD); geological engineering (MS); mechanical engineering (MS); mineral preparation engineering (MS); mining engineering (MS); petroleum engineering (MS). *Application deadline:* For fall admission, 6/1 for domestic students, 3/1 for international students; for spring admission, 10/15 for domestic students, 9/1 for international students. Applications are processed on a rolling basis. *Application fee:* $60. Electronic applications accepted. *Application Contact:* Mary Kreta, Director of Admissions, 907-474-7500, Fax: 907-474-7097, E-mail: admissions@uaf.edu. *Dean,* Dr. Douglas J. Goering, 907-474-7730, Fax: 907-474-6994, E-mail: fycem@uaf.edu.

College of Fisheries and Ocean Sciences Students: 60 full-time (34 women), 49 part-time (33 women); includes 7 minority (1 Black or African American, non-Hispanic/Latino; 1 American Indian or Alaska Native, non-Hispanic/Latino; 1 Asian, non-Hispanic/Latino; 3 Hispanic/Latino; 1 Two or more races, non-Hispanic/Latino), 9 international. Average age 31. 55 applicants, 31% accepted, 17 enrolled. *Faculty:* 52 full-time (21 women), 3 part-time/adjunct (1 woman). Expenses: Contact institution. *Financial support:* In 2016–17, 38 research assistantships with full tuition reimbursements (averaging $12,124 per year), 7 teaching assistantships with full tuition reimbursements (averaging $10,957 per year) were awarded; fellowships with full tuition reimbursements, career-related internships or fieldwork, Federal Work-Study, scholarships/grants, health care benefits, and unspecified assistantships also available. Support available to part-time students. Financial award application deadline: 2/15; financial award applicants required to submit FAFSA. In 2016, 15 master's, 12 doctorates awarded. *Program availability:* Part-time. Offers fisheries (MS, PhD); fisheries and ocean sciences (MS, PhD); marine biology (MS, PhD); oceanography (MS, PhD). *Application deadline:* For fall admission, 5/1 for domestic students, 4/1 for international students; for spring admission, 9/15 for domestic students, 8/15 for international students. Applications are processed on a rolling basis. *Application fee:* $60. Electronic applications accepted. *Application Contact:* Mary Kreta, Director of Admissions, 907-474-7500, Fax: 907-474-7097, E-mail: admissions@ alaska.edu. *Dean,* Dr. Michael Castellini, 907-474-7824, Fax: 907-474-7204, E-mail: info@sfos.uaf.edu.

College of Liberal Arts Students: 82 full-time (55 women), 124 part-time (84 women); includes 46 minority (5 Black or African American, non-Hispanic/Latino; 17 American Indian or Alaska Native, non-Hispanic/Latino; 3 Asian, non-Hispanic/Latino; 8 Hispanic/Latino; 2 Native Hawaiian or other Pacific Islander, non-Hispanic/Latino; 11 Two or more races, non-Hispanic/Latino), 14 international. Average age 36. 106 applicants, 49% accepted, 37 enrolled. *Faculty:* 64 full-time (29 women). Expenses: Contact institution. *Financial support:* In 2016–17, 5 research assistantships with tuition reimbursements (averaging $12,475 per year), 64 teaching assistantships with tuition reimbursements (averaging $5,652 per year) were awarded; fellowships with tuition reimbursements, career-related internships or fieldwork, Federal Work-Study, scholarships/grants, health care benefits, and unspecified assistantships also available. Support available to part-time students. Financial award application deadline: 7/1; financial award applicants required to submit FAFSA. In 2016, 47 master's, 3 doctorates awarded. *Program availability:* Part-time, 100% online, blended/hybrid learning. Offers anthropology (MA, PhD); applied linguistics (MA); Arctic policy (MA); art (MFA); ceramics (MFA); clinical-community psychology (PhD); computer art (MFA); creative writing (MFA); cross-cultural studies (MA); drawing (MFA); environmental politics and policy (MA); justice (MA); liberal arts (MA, MFA, MM, PhD); literature (MA); music (MM); Northern history (MA); painting (MFA); photography (MFA); printmaking (MFA); professional communication (MA); sculpture (MFA). *Application deadline:* For fall admission, 6/1 for domestic students, 3/1 for international students; for spring admission, 10/15 for domestic students, 9/1 for international students. Applications are processed on a rolling basis. *Application fee:* $60. Electronic applications accepted. *Application Contact:* Mary Kreta, Director of Admissions, 907-474-7500, Fax: 907-474-7097, E-mail: admissions@uaf.edu. *Dean,* Todd Sherman, 907-474-7231, Fax: 907-474-5817, E-mail: uaf-cla@uaf.edu.

College of Natural Sciences and Mathematics Students: 182 full-time (89 women), 58 part-time (31 women); includes 22 minority (3 American Indian or Alaska Native, non-Hispanic/Latino; 9 Asian, non-Hispanic/Latino; 3 Hispanic/Latino; 7 Two or more races, non-Hispanic/Latino), 46 international. Average age 31. 224 applicants, 19% accepted, 38 enrolled. *Faculty:* 80 full-time (31 women), 2 part-time/adjunct (0 women). Expenses: Contact institution. *Financial support:* In 2016–17, 87 research assistantships with full tuition reimbursements (averaging $16,954 per year), 66 teaching assistantships with full tuition reimbursements (averaging $13,635 per year) were awarded; fellowships with full tuition reimbursements, career-related internships or fieldwork, Federal Work-Study, scholarships/grants, health care benefits, and unspecified assistantships also available. Support available to part-time students. Financial award application deadline: 7/1; financial award applicants required to submit FAFSA. In 2016, 43 master's, 18 doctorates, 4 other advanced degrees awarded. *Program availability:* Part-time. Offers atmospheric science (MS, PhD); biochemistry and neuroscience (PhD); biology and wildlife (MS, PhD, Graduate Certificate); chemistry (MA, MS); computational physics (MS); environmental chemistry (PhD); geophysics (MS); mathematics (PhD); natural sciences and mathematics (MA, MS, PhD, Graduate Certificate); physics (MS, PhD); space physics (MS); statistics (MS, Graduate Certificate). *Application deadline:* For fall admission, 6/1 for domestic students, 3/1 for international students; for spring admission, 10/15 for domestic students, 9/1 for international students. Applications are processed on a rolling basis. *Application fee:* $60. Electronic applications accepted. *Application Contact:* Mary Kreta, Director of Admissions, 907-474-7500, Fax: 907-474-7097, E-mail:

admissions@uaf.edu. *Dean,* Dr. Paul Layer, 907-474-7608, Fax: 907-474-5101, E-mail: fycnsm@uaf.edu.

College of Rural and Community Development Students: 5 full-time (3 women), 15 part-time (10 women); includes 10 minority (8 American Indian or Alaska Native, non-Hispanic/Latino; 2 Two or more races, non-Hispanic/Latino), 1 international. Average age 38. 11 applicants, 64% accepted, 6 enrolled. *Faculty:* 8 full-time (all women). Expenses: Contact institution. *Financial support:* In 2016–17, 1 teaching assistantship with full tuition reimbursement (averaging $5,034 per year) was awarded; fellowships with full tuition reimbursements, research assistantships with full tuition reimbursements, Federal Work-Study, scholarships/grants, and health care benefits also available. Support available to part-time students. Financial award application deadline: 2/15; financial award applicants required to submit FAFSA. In 2016, 7 master's awarded. *Program availability:* Part-time, 100% online, blended/hybrid learning. Offers rural and community development (MA); rural development (MA). *Application deadline:* For fall admission, 6/1 for domestic students, 3/1 for international students; for spring admission, 10/15 for domestic students, 9/1 for international students. Applications are processed on a rolling basis. *Application fee:* $60. Electronic applications accepted. *Application Contact:* Mary Kreta, Director of Admissions, 907-474-7500, Fax: 907-474-7097, E-mail: admissions@uaf.edu. *Vice Chancellor for the College of Rural and Community Development,* Evon Peter, 907-474-7143, Fax: 907-474-5824, E-mail: uaf-crcd-vice-chancellor@alaska.edu.

Graduate School for Interdisciplinary Studies Students: 6 full-time (all women), 21 part-time (17 women); includes 11 minority (7 American Indian or Alaska Native, non-Hispanic/Latino; 1 Hispanic/Latino; 1 Native Hawaiian or other Pacific Islander, non-Hispanic/Latino; 2 Two or more races, non-Hispanic/Latino), 1 international. Average age 49. 30 applicants, 3% accepted, 1 enrolled. *Faculty:* 4 full-time (all women). Expenses: Contact institution. *Financial support:* In 2016–17, 1 research assistantship with full tuition reimbursement (averaging $1,416 per year), 1 teaching assistantship with full tuition reimbursement (averaging $4,798 per year) were awarded; fellowships with full tuition reimbursements, career-related internships or fieldwork, Federal Work-Study, scholarships/grants, health care benefits, and unspecified assistantships also available. Support available to part-time students. Financial award application deadline: 2/15; financial award applicants required to submit FAFSA. In 2016, 2 master's, 3 doctorates awarded. *Program availability:* Part-time. Offers indigenous studies (PhD); interdisciplinary studies (MA, MS, PhD). *Application deadline:* For fall admission, 3/1 for domestic and international students; for spring admission, 10/1 for domestic students, 9/1 for international students. Applications are processed on a rolling basis. *Application fee:* $60. Electronic applications accepted. *Application Contact:* Mary Kreta, Director of Admissions, 907-474-7500, Fax: 907-474-7097, E-mail: admissions@uaf.edu. *Dean,* John Eichelberger, 907-474-7716, Fax: 907-474-1984, E-mail: fyinds@uaf.edu.

School of Education Students: 46 full-time (31 women), 127 part-time (105 women); includes 22 minority (8 American Indian or Alaska Native, non-Hispanic/Latino; 5 Hispanic/Latino; 9 Two or more races, non-Hispanic/Latino), 3 international. Average age 37. 74 applicants, 58% accepted, 39 enrolled. *Faculty:* 16 full-time (11 women), 2 part-time/adjunct (1 woman). Expenses: Contact institution. *Financial support:* In 2016–17, 1 research assistantship with full tuition reimbursement (averaging $5,251 per year), 1 teaching assistantship with full tuition reimbursement (averaging $4,247 per year) were awarded; fellowships with full tuition reimbursements, career-related internships or fieldwork, Federal Work-Study, scholarships/grants, health care benefits, and unspecified assistantships also available. Support available to part-time students. Financial award application deadline: 6/1; financial award applicants required to submit FAFSA. In 2016, 41 master's, 21 other advanced degrees awarded. *Program availability:* 100% online, blended/hybrid learning. Offers community counseling (M Ed); education (M Ed, Graduate Certificate); special education (M Ed). *Application deadline:* For fall admission, 2/15 for domestic and international students; for spring admission, 10/1 for domestic students, 8/1 for international students. *Application fee:* $60. Electronic applications accepted. *Application Contact:* Mary Kreta, Director of Admissions, 907-474-7500, Fax: 907-474-7097, E-mail: admissions@uaf.edu. *Interim Dean,* Steve Atwater, 907-474-7341, Fax: 907-474-5451, E-mail: uaf-soe-school@alaska.edu.

School of Management Students: 46 full-time (20 women), 75 part-time (33 women); includes 28 minority (4 Black or African American, non-Hispanic/Latino; 7 American Indian or Alaska Native, non-Hispanic/Latino; 4 Asian, non-Hispanic/Latino; 8 Hispanic/Latino; 1 Native Hawaiian or other Pacific Islander, non-Hispanic/Latino; 4 Two or more races, non-Hispanic/Latino), 7 international. Average age 32. 89 applicants, 64% accepted, 43 enrolled. *Faculty:* 17 full-time (5 women). Expenses: Contact institution. *Financial support:* In 2016–17, 15 teaching assistantships with full tuition reimbursements (averaging $13,113 per year) were awarded; fellowships with full tuition reimbursements, research assistantships with full tuition reimbursements, career-related internships or fieldwork, Federal Work-Study, scholarships/grants, health care benefits, and unspecified assistantships also available. Support available to part-time students. Financial award application deadline: 7/1; financial award applicants required to submit FAFSA. In 2016, 35 master's awarded. *Program availability:* Part-time, 100% online, blended/hybrid learning. Offers capital markets (MBA); general management (MBA); management (MBA, MS, MSDM); resource and applied economics (MS); security and disaster management (MSDM). *Application deadline:* For fall admission, 3/1 priority date for domestic students, 2/15 for international students; for spring admission, 9/1 priority date for domestic students, 9/1 for international students. Applications are processed on a rolling basis. *Application fee:* $60. Electronic applications accepted. *Application Contact:* Mary Kreta, Director of Admissions, 907-474-7500, Fax: 907-474-7097, E-mail: admissions@uaf.edu. *Dean,* Dr. Mark Herrmann, 907-474-7461, Fax: 907-474-5219, E-mail: uaf-som@alaska.edu.

School of Natural Resources and Extension Students: 16 full-time (12 women), 19 part-time (9 women); includes 2 minority (1 Hispanic/Latino; 1 Two or more races, non-Hispanic/Latino), 1 international. Average age 37. 20 applicants, 45% accepted, 5 enrolled. *Faculty:* 12 full-time (3 women), 3 part-time/adjunct (2 women). Expenses: Contact institution. *Financial support:* In 2016–17, 5 research assistantships with full tuition reimbursements (averaging $16,539 per year), 6 teaching assistantships with full tuition reimbursements (averaging $5,874 per year) were awarded; fellowships with full tuition reimbursements, career-related internships or fieldwork, Federal Work-Study, scholarships/grants, health care benefits, and unspecified assistantships also available. Support available to part-time students. Financial award application deadline: 2/15; financial award applicants required to submit FAFSA. In 2016, 6 master's, 4 doctorates awarded. *Program availability:* Part-time. Offers natural resources and sustainability (PhD); natural resources management (MS). *Application deadline:* For fall admission, 6/1 for domestic students, 3/1 for international students; for spring admission, 10/15 for domestic students, 9/1 for international students. Applications are processed on a rolling basis. *Application fee:* $60. Electronic applications accepted. *Application Contact:* Mary Kreta, Director of Admissions, 907-474-7500, Fax: 907-474-7097, E-mail: admissions@ uaf.edu. *Dean,* Stephen Sparrow, 907-474-9450, Fax: 907-474-6268, E-mail: fysnras@ uaf.edu.

UNIVERSITY OF ALASKA SOUTHEAST, Juneau, AK 99801

General Information State-supported, coed, comprehensive institution. *Enrollment:* 90 full-time matriculated graduate/professional students (59 women), 223 part-time matriculated graduate/professional students (179 women). *Enrollment by degree level:* 313 master's. Tuition, state resident: part-time $466 per credit. Tuition, nonresident: part-time $979 per credit. *Required fees:* $19 per credit. Part-time tuition and fees vary according to course level, campus/location and reciprocity agreements. *Graduate housing:* Rooms and/or apartments available on a first-come, first-served basis to single and married students. Housing application deadline: 5/1. *Student services:* Campus employment opportunities, campus safety program, career counseling, exercise/wellness program, free psychological counseling, grant writing training, international student services, low-cost health insurance, multicultural affairs office, services for students with disabilities, teacher training, writing training. *Library facilities:* Egan Memorial Library. *Research affiliation:* National Park Service (environmental resources, cultural studies), North Pacific Research Board (marine biology, oceanography), U.S. Department of Education (DOE) (teaching, early childhood education), Natural Science Foundation (marine biology), U.S. Department of Agriculture (USDA) (forest service), Alaska Department of Education (teaching).

Computer facilities: A campuswide network can be accessed from student residence rooms and from off campus. Online class registration is available.
Website: http://www.uas.alaska.edu/

General Application Contact: Susan A. Stuck, Administrative Assistant, 866-465-6424, Fax: 866-465-5159, E-mail: jnsas@uas.alaska.edu.

GRADUATE UNITS

Graduate Programs Students: 90 full-time (59 women), 223 part-time (179 women); includes 37 minority (4 Black or African American, non-Hispanic/Latino; 21 American Indian or Alaska Native, non-Hispanic/Latino; 7 Asian, non-Hispanic/Latino; 5 Hispanic/Latino), 11 international. Average age 34. Expenses: Contact institution. *Financial support:* Federal Work-Study, scholarships/grants, and tuition waivers (full and partial) available. Support available to part-time students. Financial award applicants required to submit FAFSA. In 2016, 134 degrees awarded. *Program availability:* Part-time, evening/weekend, online learning. Offers educational leadership (M Ed); elementary education (MAT); learning design and technology (M Ed); mathematics education (M Ed); public administration (MPA); reading specialist (M Ed); secondary education (MAT); special education (M Ed, MAT). *Application deadline:* For fall admission, 4/1 priority date for domestic and international students; for spring admission, 11/1 priority date for domestic and international students. Applications are processed on a rolling basis. *Application fee:* $60. Electronic applications accepted. *Application Contact:* Susan A. Stuck, Administrative Assistant, 866-465-6424, Fax: 866-465-5159, E-mail: jnsas@uas.alaska.edu. *Provost,* Dr. Karen Carey, 907-796-6486, Fax: 907-796-6040, E-mail: provost@uas.alaska.edu.

UNIVERSITY OF ALBERTA, Edmonton, AB T6G 2E1, Canada

General Information Province-supported, coed, university. CGS member. *Graduate housing:* Rooms and/or apartments available on a first-come, first-served basis to single and married students.

GRADUATE UNITS

Faculty of Extension Offers communications and technology (MA).

Faculty of Graduate Studies and Research *Program availability:* Part-time, evening/weekend. Offers accounting (PhD); adult education (M Ed, Ed D, PhD); agricultural economics (M Ag, M Sc, PhD); agricultural, food and nutritional science (M Ag, M Eng, M Sc, PhD); agroforestry (M Ag, M Sc, MF); ancient history (PhD); anthropology (MA, PhD); applied linguistics (Germanic, Romance, Slavic) (MA); applied mathematics (M Sc, PhD); applied music (M Mus); astrophysics (M Sc, PhD); biostatistics (M Sc); business administration (Exec MBA, MBA); chemical engineering (M Eng, M Sc, PhD); chemistry (M Sc, PhD); Chinese literature (MA); choral conducting (M Mus); classical archaeology (MA, PhD); classical literature (PhD); classics (MA); communications (M Eng, M Sc, PhD); communications and technology (MACT); composition (M Mus); computer engineering (M Eng, M Sc, PhD); computing science (M Sc, PhD); condensed matter (M Sc, PhD); conservation biology (M Sc, PhD); construction engineering and management (M Eng, M Sc, PhD); counseling psychology (M Ed, PhD); criminal justice (MA); demography (MA, PhD); design (MFA); directing (MFA); drama (MA); drawing (MFA); earth and atmospheric sciences (M Sc, MA, PhD); East Asian interdisciplinary studies (MA); economics (MA, PhD); economics and finance (MA); educational administration and leadership (M Ed, Ed D, PhD, Postgraduate Diploma); educational psychology (M Ed, PhD); electromagnetics (M Eng, M Sc, PhD); elementary education (M Ed, Ed D, PhD); engineering management (M Eng); English (MA, PhD); environmental and natural resource economics (PhD); environmental biology and ecology (M Sc, PhD); environmental engineering (M Eng, M Sc, PhD); environmental science (M Sc, PhD); experimental linguistics (M Sc, PhD); family ecology and practice (M Sc, PhD); finance (PhD); First Nations education (M Ed, Ed D, PhD); forest biology and management (M Sc, PhD); forest economics (M Ag, M Sc, PhD); French language, literatures and linguistics (PhD); French language, literatures, and linguistics (MA); geoenvironmental engineering (M Eng, M Sc, PhD); geophysics (M Sc, PhD); geotechnical engineering (M Eng, M Sc, PhD); Germanic languages, literatures and linguistics (PhD); Germanic languages, literatures, and linguistics (MA); history (MA, PhD); history of art, design, and visual culture (MA); human resources/industrial relations (PhD); industrial design (M Des); instructional technology (M Ed); international business (MBA); Italian studies (MA); Japanese literature (MA); land reclamation and remediation (M Sc, PhD); leisure and sport management (MBA); management science (PhD); marketing (PhD); materials engineering (M Eng, M Sc, PhD); mathematical finance (M Sc, PhD); mathematical physics (M Sc, PhD); mathematics (M Sc, PhD); mechanical engineering (M Eng, M Sc, PhD); medical physics (M Sc, PhD); microbiology and biotechnology (M Sc, PhD); mining engineering (M Eng, M Sc, PhD); molecular biology and genetics (M Sc, PhD); music (PhD); nanotechnology and microdevices (M Eng, M Sc, PhD); natural resources and energy (MBA); occupational therapy (M Sc, PhD); organ and choral conductors (D Mus); organizational analysis (PhD); painting (MFA); petroleum engineering (M Eng, M Sc, PhD); pharmacology (M Sc, PhD); pharmacy and pharmaceutical sciences (M Sc, PhD); philosophy (MA, PhD); physical education (M Sc); physical therapy (M Sc, PhD); physiology and cell biology (M Sc, PhD); piano (D Mus); plant biology (M Sc, PhD); political science (MA, PhD); power/power electronics (M Eng, M Sc, PhD); printmaking (MFA); process control (M Eng, M Sc, PhD); protected areas and wildlands management (M Sc, PhD); psychology (M Sc, MA, PhD); recreation and physical education (MA, PhD); rural sociology (M Ag, M Sc); school counseling (M Ed); school psychology (M Ed, PhD); sculpture (MFA); secondary education (M Ed, Ed D, PhD); Slavic languages and literatures (Russian, Ukrainian) (MA, PhD); Slavic linguistics (Russian, Ukrainian) (MA, PhD); sociology (MA, PhD); soil science (M Ag, M Sc, PhD); Spanish and Latin American studies (MA, PhD); special education (M Ed, PhD); special education-

deafness studies (M Ed); speech pathology and audiology (PhD); speech-language pathology (M Sc); statistics (M Sc, PhD, Postgraduate Diploma); structural engineering (M Eng, M Sc, PhD); subatomic physics (M Sc, PhD); systematics and evolution (M Sc, PhD); systems (M Eng, M Sc, PhD); teaching English as a second language (M Ed); technology commercialization (MBA); textiles and clothing (M Sc, MA, PhD); theoretical, cultural and international studies in education (M Ed, Ed D, PhD); Ukrainian folklore (MA, PhD); visual communication design (M Des); water and land resources (M Ag, M Sc, PhD); water resources (M Eng, M Sc, PhD); welding (M Eng); wildlife ecology and management (M Sc, PhD). Electronic applications accepted.

Faculté Saint Jean *Program availability:* Part-time, evening/weekend, online learning. Offers education (M Ed).

Faculty of Nursing *Program availability:* Part-time. Offers nursing (MN, PhD).

Faculty of Rehabilitation Medicine Offers rehabilitation medicine (PhD). Electronic applications accepted.

School of Library and Information Studies Offers library and information studies (MLIS). Electronic applications accepted.

Faculty of Law *Program availability:* Part-time. Offers law (LL M, PhD). Electronic applications accepted.

Faculty of Medicine and Dentistry Offers dental hygiene (Diploma); dentistry (DDS); medicine and dentistry (M Sc, DDS, MD, PhD, Diploma); orthodontics (M Sc, PhD); TMD/orofacial pain (M Sc). Electronic applications accepted.

Graduate Programs in Medicine *Program availability:* Part-time. Offers biochemistry (M Sc, PhD); biomedical engineering (M Sc); cell and molecular biology (M Sc, PhD); medical genetics (M Sc, PhD); medical microbiology and immunology (M Sc, PhD); medical sciences (M Sc, PhD); medicine (M Sc, MD, PhD); neuroscience (M Sc, PhD); obstetrics and gynecology (MD); oncology (M Sc, PhD); ophthalmology (M Sc, PhD); pediatrics (M Sc, PhD); physiology (M Sc, PhD); psychiatry (M Sc, PhD); radiology and diagnostic imaging (M Sc); surgery (M Sc, PhD).

School of Public Health Offers clinical epidemiology (M Sc, MPH); environmental and occupational health (MPH); environmental health sciences (M Sc); epidemiology (M Sc); global health (M Sc, MPH); health policy and management (MPH); health policy research (M Sc); health technology assessment (MPH); occupational health (M Sc); population health (M Sc, MPH); public health (M Sc, MPH, PhD, Postgraduate Diploma); public health leadership (MPH); public health sciences (PhD); quantitative methods (MPH).

Centre for Health Promotion Studies *Program availability:* Part-time, online learning. Offers health promotion (M Sc, Postgraduate Diploma).

UNIVERSITY OF ANTELOPE VALLEY, Lancaster, CA 93534

General Information Proprietary, coed, comprehensive institution.

GRADUATE UNITS

Program in Business Management Offers business management (MS).

Program in Criminal Justice Offers criminal justice (MS).

THE UNIVERSITY OF ARIZONA, Tucson, AZ 85721

General Information State-supported, coed, university. CGS member. *Graduate housing:* Rooms and/or apartments available on a first-come, first-served basis to single students and available to married students. Housing application deadline: 5/1. *Research affiliation:* Smithsonian Astrophysical Observatory (astronomy), Research Corporation (astronomy), National Center for Atmospheric Research (atmospheric physics), Kitt Peak National Observatory (astronomy), Argonne National Laboratory (physics).

GRADUATE UNITS

College of Agriculture and Life Sciences *Program availability:* Part-time. Offers agricultural and biosystems engineering (MS, PhD); agricultural and resource economics (MS); agricultural education (MAE, MS, Graduate Certificate); agriculture and life sciences (MAE, MHE Ed, MS, PhD, Graduate Certificate); animal sciences (MS, PhD); arid lands resource sciences (PhD); nutritional sciences (MS, PhD); soil, water and environmental science (MS, PhD, Graduate Certificate). Electronic applications accepted.

School of Animal and Comparative Biomedical Sciences Offers animal and comparative biomedical sciences (MS, PhD). Electronic applications accepted.

School of Family and Consumer Sciences *Program availability:* Part-time. Offers family and consumer sciences (PhD). Electronic applications accepted.

School of Natural Resources and the Environment Offers ecology and management of rangelands (MS, PhD); natural resources (MS); water, society, and policy (MS); watershed management (MS, PhD). Electronic applications accepted.

School of Plant Sciences *Program availability:* Part-time. Offers plant pathology (MS, PhD); plant sciences (MS, PhD). Electronic applications accepted.

College of Architecture, Planning, and Landscape Architecture *Program availability:* Part-time. Offers architecture, planning, and landscape architecture (M Ar, M Arch, ML Arch, MRED, MS, PhD, Graduate Certificate); landscape architecture (ML Arch); planning (MS). Electronic applications accepted.

School of Architecture Offers architecture (M Arch, MS). Electronic applications accepted.

College of Education *Program availability:* Part-time, online learning. Offers counseling and mental health (MA); cross-categorical special education (MA); deaf and hard of hearing (MA); education (M Ed, MA, MS, Ed D, PhD, Certificate, Ed S); educational leadership (M Ed, Ed D, Ed S); educational psychology (MA, PhD); educational research methodology (Certificate); family studies and human development (M Ed); higher education (MA, PhD); language, reading and culture (MA, Ed D, PhD, Ed S); learning disabilities (MA); motivating learning environments (Certificate); reading instruction (Graduate Certificate); rehabilitation counseling (MA, PhD); school counseling (MA); school psychology (PhD, Ed S); severe and multiple disabilities (MA); special education (MA, PhD); teaching and teacher education (M Ed, MA, PhD); visual impairment (MA). Electronic applications accepted.

College of Engineering *Program availability:* Part-time, online learning. Offers aerospace engineering (MS, PhD); chemical engineering (MS, PhD); civil engineering and engineering mechanics (MS, PhD); electrical and computer engineering (MS, PhD); engineering (ME, MS, PhD, Certificate); engineering management (Graduate Certificate); environmental engineering (MS, PhD); industrial engineering (MS); materials science and engineering (MS, PhD); mechanical engineering (MS, PhD); mining and geological engineering (MS, PhD); mining engineering (Certificate); systems and industrial engineering (MS, PhD); systems engineering (MS, PhD, Graduate Certificate). Electronic applications accepted.

College of Fine Arts *Program availability:* Part-time. Offers fine arts (MA, MFA, MM, PhD, Graduate Certificate). Electronic applications accepted.

School of Art *Program availability:* Part-time. Offers art (MA, MFA, PhD); art education (MA); art history (MA); art history and education (PhD); history and theory of art (PhD). Electronic applications accepted.

School of Dance Offers dance (MFA). Electronic applications accepted.

School of Music *Program availability:* Part-time. Offers composition (MM, DMA); conducting (MM, DMA); ethnomusicology (MM); music (MM, PhD); music education (MM, PhD); music theory (MM, PhD); musical arts (DMA); musicology (MM); performance (MM, DMA). Electronic applications accepted.

School of Theatre, Film and Television Offers theatre, film and television (MFA). Electronic applications accepted.

College of Humanities *Program availability:* Part-time. Offers classics (MA); creative writing (MFA); East Asian studies (MA, PhD); English (MA, PhD); English language/linguistics (MA, PhD); ESL (MA); French (MA); German (MA); humanities (MA, MFA, PhD); rhetoric, composition and the teaching of English (MA, PhD); Russian (MA); Spanish (MA, PhD); teaching English as a second language (Graduate Certificate); transcultural German (PhD). Electronic applications accepted.

College of Medicine *Program availability:* Part-time. Offers cellular and molecular medicine (MS, PhD); immunobiology (PhD); medical sciences (MS, PhD); medicine (MS, MD, PhD, Graduate Certificate). MD program open only to state residents.

College of Nursing *Program availability:* Part-time, online learning. Offers health care informatics (Certificate); nurse practitioner (MS); nursing (DNP, PhD). Electronic applications accepted.

College of Optical Sciences *Program availability:* Part-time. Offers optical sciences (MS, PhD, Graduate Certificate). Electronic applications accepted.

College of Pharmacy Offers medical pharmacology (MS, PhD); medicinal and natural products chemistry (MS, PhD); perfusion science (MS); pharmaceutical economics (MS, PhD); pharmaceutics and pharmacokinetics (MS, PhD); pharmacy (MS, PhD, Pharm D).

College of Science *Program availability:* Part-time. Offers applied biosciences (PSM); astronomy (PhD); atmospheric sciences (MS, PhD); biochemistry (PhD); biochemistry and molecular and cellular biology (PhD); chemistry (MA, MS, PhD); computer science (MS, PhD); ecology and evolutionary biology (MS, PhD); geosciences (MS, PSM, PhD); hydrology (PhD); mathematics (MA, MS, PhD); medical physics (PSM); physics (PhD); planetary sciences (MS, PhD); psychology (MA, PhD); science (MS, PSM, PhD, Certificate, Graduate Certificate); secondary mathematics education (MA); speech, language, and hearing sciences (MS, PhD, Certificate). Electronic applications accepted.

College of Social and Behavioral Sciences *Program availability:* Part-time, evening/weekend. Offers communication (MA, PhD); gender and women's studies (MA, PhD, Certificate); history (MA, PhD, Graduate Certificate); human language technology (MS); linguistics and anthropology (PhD); Native American linguistics (MA); philosophy (MA, PhD); political science (MA, PhD); public administration (MPA); public administration and policy (PhD); social and behavioral sciences (MA, MPA, MS, PhD, Certificate, Graduate Certificate); sociology (MA, PhD). Electronic applications accepted.

Center for Latin American Studies *Program availability:* Part-time. Offers Latin American studies (MA). Electronic applications accepted.

School of Anthropology *Program availability:* Part-time. Offers anthropology (MA, MS, PhD, Graduate Certificate). Electronic applications accepted.

School of Geography and Development *Program availability:* Part-time. Offers geographic information systems technology (MA); geography (PhD). Electronic applications accepted.

School of Information Resources and Library Science *Program availability:* Part-time. Offers information resources and library science (MA, PhD). Electronic applications accepted.

School of Journalism *Program availability:* Part-time. Offers international journalism studies (MA); professional journalism (MA). Electronic applications accepted.

School of Middle Eastern and North African Studies *Program availability:* Part-time, evening/weekend. Offers Middle Eastern and North African studies (MA, PhD, Graduate Certificate). Electronic applications accepted.

Eller College of Management *Program availability:* Evening/weekend. Offers accounting (M Ac, MS); business administration (MBA); economics (MA); finance (MS); management (M Ac, MA, MBA, MS, PhD, Graduate Certificate); management and organization (MS, PhD); management information systems (MS, Graduate Certificate); marketing (MBA, MS, PhD). Electronic applications accepted.

Graduate Interdisciplinary Programs *Program availability:* Part-time. Offers American Indian studies (MA, PhD); applied mathematics (MS, PMS, PhD); biomedical engineering (MS, PhD); cancer biology (PhD); entomology (MA); entomology and insect science (MS, PhD); genetics (MS, PhD); mathematical sciences (PMS); neuroscience (PhD); physiological sciences (MS, PhD); second language acquisition and teaching (PhD); statistics (MS, PhD).

James E. Rogers College of Law Offers indigenous peoples law and policy (LL M); international trade and business law (LL M); law (JD). Electronic applications accepted.

Mel and Enid Zuckerman College of Public Health Offers biostatistics (MS, PhD); epidemiology (MS, PhD); public health (MPH, MS, MSPH, Dr PH, PhD, Graduate Certificate). Electronic applications accepted.

UNIVERSITY OF ARKANSAS, Fayetteville, AR 72701

General Information State-supported, coed, university. CGS member. *Enrollment:* 27,194 graduate, professional, and undergraduate students. *Graduate housing:* Room and/or apartments available on a first-come, first-served basis to single students; on-campus housing not available to married students. *Student services:* Campus employment opportunities, campus safety program, career counseling, exercise/wellness program, free psychological counseling, international student services, low-cost health insurance, multicultural affairs office, services for students with disabilities, teacher training, writing training. *Library facilities:* David W. Mullins Library plus 4 others. *Collection:* Books: 1.9 million (physical), 570,318 (digital/electronic); Serial titles: 3,154 (physical), 63,090 (digital/electronic); Databases: 318. Weekly public service hours: 109; students can reserve study rooms. *Research affiliation:* Southern Regional Education Board, Southeastern Universities Research Association, Southern Regional Education Board Uncommon Facilities Program, Oak Ridge Associated Universities, Science Coalition, National Minority Graduate Feeder Project.

Computer facilities: Computer purchase and lease plans are available. 675 computers available on campus for general student use. A campuswide network can be accessed from student residence rooms and from off campus. Online class registration is available.
Website: http://www.uark.edu/

General Application Contact: The Graduate School, 479-575-4401, Fax: 479-575-5908, E-mail: gradinfo@uark.edu.

GRADUATE UNITS

Graduate School Expenses: Contact institution. *Financial support:* In 2016–17, 761 research assistantships, 484 teaching assistantships with full tuition reimbursements were awarded; fellowships with tuition reimbursements, career-related internships or fieldwork, Federal Work-Study, institutionally sponsored loans, scholarships/grants, traineeships, and unspecified assistantships also available. Support available to part-time students. Financial award application deadline: 4/1; financial award applicants required to submit FAFSA. In 2016, 1,182 master's, 178 doctorates, 7 other advanced degrees awarded. *Program availability:* Part-time, online learning. Offers cell and molecular biology (MS, PhD); comparative literature and cultural studies (MA, PhD); environmental dynamics (PhD); microelectronics and photonics (MS, PhD); public policy (PhD); space and planetary sciences (MS, PhD). *Application deadline:* Applications are processed on a rolling basis. *Application fee:* $40 ($50 for international students). Electronic applications accepted. *Application Contact:* Graduate Admissions, 479-575-6246, Fax: 479-575-5908, E-mail: gradinfo@uark.edu. *Dean,* Dr. Kim L. Needy, 479-575-4401, Fax: 479-575-5908, E-mail: gradinfo@uark.edu.

College of Education and Health Professions Expenses: Contact institution. *Financial support:* In 2016–17, 110 research assistantships, 15 teaching assistantships were awarded; fellowships with tuition reimbursements, career-related internships or fieldwork, and Federal Work-Study also available. Support available to part-time students. Financial award application deadline: 4/1; financial award applicants required to submit FAFSA. In 2016, 399 master's, 43 doctorates awarded. Offers adult and lifelong learning (M Ed, Ed D); athletic training (MAT); childhood education (MAT); communication disorders (MS); community health promotion (MS, PhD); counseling (MS, PhD, Ed S); curriculum and instruction (M Ed, PhD, Ed S); education and health professions (M Ed, MAT, MAT, MS, MSN, Ed D, PhD, Ed S); education policy (PhD); educational leadership (M Ed, Ed D, Ed S); educational statistics and research methods (MS, PhD); educational technology (M Ed); health science (MS, PhD); higher education (M Ed, Ed D, Ed S); human resource and workforce development education (M Ed, Ed D); kinesiology (MS, PhD); middle-level education (MAT); nursing (MSN); physical education (M Ed, MAT); recreation and sports management (M Ed, Ed D); rehabilitation (M Ed, PhD); secondary education (M Ed, MAT, Ed S); special education (M Ed, MAT); vocational education (MAT). *Application deadline:* For fall admission, 4/1 for international students; for spring admission, 10/1 for international students. Applications are processed on a rolling basis. *Application fee:* $40 ($50 for international students). Electronic applications accepted. *Application Contact:* Graduate Admissions, 479-575-6246, Fax: 479-575-5908, E-mail: gradinfo@uark.edu. *Dean,* Dr. Michael T. Miller, 479-575-3208, Fax: 479-575-3119, E-mail: mtmille@uark.edu.

College of Engineering Expenses: Contact institution. *Financial support:* In 2016–17, 198 research assistantships, 21 teaching assistantships were awarded; fellowships with tuition reimbursements, career-related internships or fieldwork, and Federal Work-Study also available. Support available to part-time students. Financial award application deadline: 4/1; financial award applicants required to submit FAFSA. In 2016, 296 master's, 22 doctorates awarded. Offers biological and agricultural engineering (MSE, PhD); biological engineering (MSBE); biomedical engineering (MSBME); chemical engineering (MS Ch E, MSE, PhD); civil engineering (MSCE, MSE, PhD); computer engineering (MS Cmp E, MSE, PhD); computer science (MS, PhD); electrical engineering (MSEE, PhD); engineering (MS, MS Cmp E, MS Ch E, MS En E, MS Tc E, MSBE, MSBME, MSCE, MSE, MSEE, MSIE, MSME, MSOR, MSTE); environmental engineering (MS En E, MSE); industrial engineering (MSE, MSIE, PhD); mechanical engineering (MSE, MSME, PhD); operations management (MS); operations research (MSE, MSOR); telecommunications engineering (MS Tc E); transportation engineering (MSE, MSTE). *Application deadline:* For fall admission, 4/1 for international students; for spring admission, 10/1 for international students. Applications are processed on a rolling basis. *Application fee:* $40 ($50 for international students). Electronic applications accepted. *Application Contact:* Dr. Norman Dennis, Associate Dean, 479-575-3052, E-mail: ndennis@uark.edu. *Dean,* Dr. John English, 479-575-4153, Fax: 479-575-4346.

Dale Bumpers College of Agricultural, Food and Life Sciences 164 applicants, 59% accepted. Expenses: Contact institution. *Financial support:* In 2016–17, 167 research assistantships, 7 teaching assistantships were awarded; fellowships with tuition reimbursements, career-related internships or fieldwork, Federal Work-Study, scholarships/grants, and unspecified assistantships also available. Support available to part-time students. Financial award application deadline: 4/1; financial award applicants required to submit FAFSA. In 2016, 97 master's, 24 doctorates awarded. Offers agricultural and extension education (MS); agricultural economics (MS); agricultural, food and life sciences (MS, PhD); agronomy (MS, PhD); animal science (MS, PhD); entomology (MS, PhD); food safety (MS); food science (MS, PhD); horticulture (MS); human environmental sciences (MS); plant pathology (MS); plant science (PhD); poultry science (MS, PhD). *Application deadline:* For fall admission, 4/1 for international students; for spring admission, 10/1 for international students. Applications are processed on a rolling basis. *Application fee:* $40 ($50 for international students). Electronic applications accepted. *Application Contact:* Graduate Admissions, 479-575-6246, Fax: 479-575-5908, E-mail: gradinfo@uark.edu. *Dean,* Dr. Lona Robertson, 479-575-2034, Fax: 479-575-7273, E-mail: ljrobert@uark.edu.

J. William Fulbright College of Arts and Sciences Expenses: Contact institution. *Financial support:* In 2016–17, 143 research assistantships, 373 teaching assistantships with full tuition reimbursements were awarded; fellowships, career-related internships or fieldwork, Federal Work-Study, institutionally sponsored loans, and traineeships also available. Support available to part-time students. Financial award application deadline: 4/1; financial award applicants required to submit FAFSA. In 2016, 206 master's, 47 doctorates awarded. Offers anthropology (MA, PhD); applied physics (MS); art (MFA); arts and sciences (MA, MFA, MM, MPA, MS, MSW, PhD); biological sciences (MA, MS, PhD); chemistry (MS, PhD); communication (MA); creative writing (MFA); English (MA, PhD); French (MA); geography (MA); geology (MS); German (MA); history (MA, PhD); journalism (MA); mathematics (MS, PhD); music (MM); philosophy (MA, PhD); physics (MS, PhD); physics education (MA); political science (MA, MPA); psychology (MA, PhD); public administration (MPA); secondary mathematics (MA); social work (MSW); sociology (MA); Spanish (MA); statistics (MS); theatre (MA, MFA). *Application deadline:* For fall admission, 4/1 for international students; for spring admission, 10/1 for international students. Applications are processed on a rolling basis. *Application fee:* $40 ($50 for international students). Electronic applications accepted. *Application Contact:* Dr. Steven Beaupre, Associate Dean, 479-575-7561, E-mail: sbeaupre@uark.edu. *Dean,* Dr. Todd Shields, 479-575-4801, Fax: 479-575-2642, E-mail: tshield@uark.edu.

Sam M. Walton College of Business Administration Expenses: Contact institution. *Financial support:* In 2016–17, 64 research assistantships, 17 teaching assistantships were awarded; fellowships, career-related internships or fieldwork, and Federal Work-

Study also available. Support available to part-time students. Financial award application deadline: 4/1; financial award applicants required to submit FAFSA. In 2016, 185 master's, 8 doctorates awarded. Offers accounting (M Acc); business administration (M Acc, MA, MBA, MIS, PhD); economics (MA, PhD); information systems (MIS). *Application fee:* $40 ($50 for international students). *Application Contact:* Rebel Smith, Assistant Director of Marketing and Recruiting, 479-575-6123, E-mail: gsb@walton.uark.edu. *Dean,* Dr. Matt Waller, 479-575-5949, E-mail: mwaller@walton.uark.edu.

School of Law Expenses: Contact institution. *Financial support:* In 2016–17, fellowships with full tuition reimbursements (averaging $6,000 per year), 8 research assistantships (averaging $2,500 per year) were awarded; teaching assistantships, career-related internships or fieldwork, Federal Work-Study, and scholarships/grants also available. Support available to part-time students. Financial award application deadline: 4/1; financial award applicants required to submit FAFSA. In 2016, 104 doctorates awarded. Offers agricultural law (LL M); law (JD). *Application deadline:* For fall admission, 4/1 for domestic students. Applications are processed on a rolling basis. *Application fee:* $0. *Dean,* Stacy L. Leeds, 479-575-5601, Fax: 479-575-3320, E-mail: sleeds@uark.edu.

UNIVERSITY OF ARKANSAS AT LITTLE ROCK, Little Rock, AR 72204-1099

General Information State-supported, coed, university. CGS member. *Graduate housing:* Room and/or apartments available on a first-come, first-served basis to single students; on-campus housing not available to married students. Housing application deadline: 9/1.

GRADUATE UNITS

Graduate School *Program availability:* Part-time, evening/weekend, online learning. Electronic applications accepted.

Clinton School of Public Service Offers public service (MPS, Graduate Certificate).

College of Arts, Letters, and Sciences *Program availability:* Part-time, evening/weekend. Offers applied statistics (Graduate Certificate); art education (MA); art history (MA); arts, letters, and sciences (MA, MS, Graduate Certificate); biology (MS); chemistry (MA, MS); mathematical sciences (MS); philosophy and interdisciplinary studies (MA); public history (MA); second languages (MA); studio art (MA).

College of Business *Program availability:* Part-time, evening/weekend. Offers business administration (MBA); business information systems (MS, Graduate Certificate); management (Graduate Certificate).

College of Education and Health Professions *Program availability:* Part-time, evening/weekend. Offers administration (MA); adult education (M Ed); clinical social work (MSW); college student affairs (MA); counselor education (M Ed); curriculum and instruction (M Ed); education and health professions (M Ed, MA, MS, MSW, Ed D, Ed S, Graduate Certificate); educational administration and supervision (M Ed, Ed D, Ed S); exercise science (MS); gerontology (Graduate Certificate); gifted and talented education (M Ed, Graduate Certificate); health education and promotion (MS); health professions teaching and learning (MA); higher education (MA, Ed D); learning systems technology education (M Ed); management and community practice (MSW); middle childhood education (M Ed); reading education (M Ed, PhD, Ed S); rehabilitation counseling (MA, Graduate Certificate); rehabilitation for the blind: orientation and mobility (MA); secondary education (M Ed); social work (MSW, Graduate Certificate); special education (M Ed); sport management (MS); two-year college teaching (MA).

College of Social Sciences and Communication *Program availability:* Part-time, evening/weekend. Offers applied communication studies (MA); applied psychology (MAP); conflict mediation (Graduate Certificate); criminal justice (MA, MS, PhD); mass communication (MA); nonprofit management (Graduate Certificate); professional and technical writing (MA); public administration (MPA); social sciences and communication (MA, MAP, MPA, MS, PhD, Graduate Certificate).

George W. Donaghey College of Engineering and Information Technology *Program availability:* Part-time, evening/weekend. Offers applied science (MS, PhD); bioinformatics (MS, PhD); computer science (MS, PhD); construction management (MS); engineering and information technology (MS, PhD, Graduate Certificate); geospatial technology (Graduate Certificate); information quality (MS, PhD, Graduate Certificate); systems engineering (MS, PhD, Graduate Certificate); technology innovation (Graduate Certificate).

William H. Bowen School of Law *Program availability:* Part-time, evening/weekend. Offers law (JD). Electronic applications accepted.

UNIVERSITY OF ARKANSAS AT MONTICELLO, Monticello, AR 71656

General Information State-supported, coed, comprehensive institution. *Graduate housing:* Rooms and/or apartments guaranteed to single students and available on a first-come, first-served basis to married students. Housing application deadline: 8/15.

GRADUATE UNITS

School of Education *Program availability:* Part-time, evening/weekend, online learning. Offers education (M Ed, MAT); educational leadership (M Ed). Electronic applications accepted.

School of Forest Resources *Program availability:* Part-time. Offers forest resources (MS). Electronic applications accepted.

UNIVERSITY OF ARKANSAS AT PINE BLUFF, Pine Bluff, AR 71601-2799

General Information State-supported, coed, comprehensive institution. *Enrollment:* 3 full-time matriculated graduate/professional students (2 women), 69 part-time matriculated graduate/professional students (46 women). *Enrollment by degree level:* 98 master's, 2 doctoral. *Graduate faculty:* 27 full-time (10 women), 2 part-time/adjunct (both women). Tuition, state resident: full-time $4776. Tuition, nonresident: full-time $10,824. *Required fees:* $1612. Tuition and fees vary according to course load. *Graduate housing:* Room and/or apartments available on a first-come, first-served basis to single students; on-campus housing not available to married students. Typical cost: $6200 per year ($9572 including board). Room and board charges vary according to board plan and housing facility selected. Housing application deadline: 8/1. *Student services:* Campus safety program, career counseling, child daycare facilities, exercise/wellness program, free psychological counseling, international student services, teacher training. *Library facilities:* John Brown Watson Memorial Library plus 4 others.

Computer facilities: 175 computers available on campus for general student use. A campuswide network can be accessed from student residence rooms and from off campus. Online class registration is available.
Website: http://www.uapb.edu/

General Application Contact: Dr. George Herts, Dean, 870-575-8057, E-mail: hertsg@uapb.edu.

GRADUATE UNITS

Division of Graduate Studies and Continuing Education Expenses: Contact institution. Offers addiction studies (MS). *Application deadline:* For fall admission, 7/15 for domestic students; for spring admission, 12/1 for domestic students; for summer admission, 4/15 for domestic students. *Application fee:* $45. *Application Contact:* Dr. Jerry Ingram, Interim Chair, 870-575-8168, E-mail: ingramj@uapb.edu. *Interim Dean,* Dr. George Herts.

School of Agriculture, Fisheries and Human Sciences Expenses: Contact institution. Offers agricultural regulations (MS); aquaculture and fisheries (MS, PhD). *Interim Dean,* Dr. Edmund Buckner, 870-575-8529, E-mail: bucknere@uapb.edu.

School of Education Expenses: Contact institution. *Financial support:* Research assistantships with full and partial tuition reimbursements, teaching assistantships with full and partial tuition reimbursements, institutionally sponsored loans, and scholarships/grants available. Support available to part-time students. *Program availability:* Part-time, evening/weekend. Offers elementary education (M Ed); secondary education (M Ed); teaching (MAT). *Application fee:* $25. *Dean,* Dr. George Herts, 870-575-8000, E-mail: johnson_c@uapb.edu.

UNIVERSITY OF ARKANSAS FOR MEDICAL SCIENCES, Little Rock, AR 72205-7199

General Information State-supported, coed, university. *Graduate housing:* Rooms and/or apartments available on a first-come, first-served basis to single and married students. Housing application deadline: 7/15. *Research affiliation:* National Center for Toxicological Research, Veterans Administration Hospital, Oak Ridge Associated Universities, Arkansas Children's Hospital.

GRADUATE UNITS

College of Health Professions *Program availability:* Part-time, online learning. Offers audiology (Au D); communication sciences and disorders (MS, PhD); genetic counseling (MS); nuclear medicine advanced associate (MIS); physician assistant studies (MPAS); radiologist assistant (MIS). PhD offered through consortium with University of Arkansas at Little Rock and University of Central Arkansas. Electronic applications accepted.

College of Medicine Offers medicine (MD). Electronic applications accepted.

College of Nursing *Program availability:* Part-time. Offers nursing (PhD).

College of Pharmacy Offers pharmacy (MS, Pharm D). Electronic applications accepted.

College of Public Health *Program availability:* Part-time. Offers biostatistics (MPH); environmental and occupational health (MPH, Certificate); epidemiology (MPH, PhD); health behavior and health education (MPH); health policy and management (MPH); health promotion and prevention research (PhD); health services administration (MHSA); health systems research (PhD); public health (Certificate); public health leadership (Dr PH). Electronic applications accepted.

Graduate School *Program availability:* Part-time. Offers biochemistry and molecular biology (MS, PhD); bioinformatics (MS, PhD); cellular physiology and molecular biophysics (MS, PhD); clinical nutrition (MS); interdisciplinary biomedical sciences (MS, PhD, Certificate); interdisciplinary toxicology (MS); microbiology and immunology (PhD); neurobiology and developmental sciences (PhD); pharmacology (PhD). Bioinformatics programs hosted jointly with the University of Arkansas at Little Rock. Electronic applications accepted.

UNIVERSITY OF ARKANSAS–FORT SMITH, Fort Smith, AR 72913-3649

General Information State and locally supported, coed.

GRADUATE UNITS

Program in Healthcare Administration *Program availability:* Online learning. Offers healthcare administration (MS).

UNIVERSITY OF BALTIMORE, Baltimore, MD 21201-5779

General Information State-supported, coed, comprehensive institution. *Graduate housing:* On-campus housing not available.

GRADUATE UNITS

Graduate School *Program availability:* Part-time, evening/weekend, online learning. Electronic applications accepted.

College of Public Affairs Offers criminal justice (MS); health systems management (MS); human services administration (MS); negotiations and conflict management (MS); public administration (MPA, DPA); public affairs (MPA, MS, DPA).

Merrick School of Business *Program availability:* Part-time, evening/weekend, online learning. Offers accounting and business advisory services (MS); accounting fundamentals (Graduate Certificate); business (MBA, MS, Graduate Certificate); business/finance (MS); forensic accounting (Graduate Certificate); global leadership (MS); innovation management and technology commercialization (MS); taxation (MS). Electronic applications accepted.

Yale Gordon College of Arts and Sciences *Program availability:* Part-time, evening/weekend. Offers arts and sciences (MA, MFA, MS, DS); counseling psychology (MS); creative writing and publishing arts (MFA); information and interaction design (DS); integrated design (MFA); interaction design and information architecture (MS); legal and ethical studies (MA); publications design (MA). Electronic applications accepted.

Joint University of Baltimore/Towson University (UB/Towson) MBA Program *Program availability:* Part-time, evening/weekend, online learning. Offers business administration (MBA). MBA/MSN, MBA/Pharm D offered jointly with University of Maryland, Baltimore.

School of Law Students: 464 full-time (233 women), 297 part-time (140 women); includes 243 minority (142 Black or African American, non-Hispanic/Latino; 35 Asian, non-Hispanic/Latino; 38 Hispanic/Latino; 28 Two or more races, non-Hispanic/Latino), 20 international. Average age 27. 1,090 applicants, 58% accepted, 208 enrolled. *Faculty:* 53 full-time (25 women), 61 part-time/adjunct (18 women). Expenses: Contact institution. *Financial support:* In 2016–17, 344 students received support. Research assistantships, teaching assistantships, career-related internships or fieldwork, Federal Work-Study, and scholarships/grants available. Support available to part-time students. Financial award application deadline: 4/1; financial award applicants required to submit FAFSA. In 2016, 279 doctorates awarded. *Program availability:* Part-time, evening/weekend. Offers business law (JD); criminal practice (JD); estate planning (JD); family law (JD); intellectual property (JD); international law (JD); law (JD); law of the United States (LL M); litigation and advocacy (JD); public service (JD); real estate practice (JD); taxation (LL M). JD/MS offered jointly with Division of Criminology, Criminal Justice, and Social Policy; JD/PhD with University of Maryland, Baltimore.

Application deadline: For fall admission, 7/30 for domestic students, 4/1 priority date for international students. Applications are processed on a rolling basis. *Application fee:* $60. Electronic applications accepted. *Application Contact:* Jeffrey L. Zavrotny, Assistant Dean for Admissions, 410-837-5809, Fax: 410-837-4188, E-mail: jzavrotny@ubalt.edu. *Dean,* Ronald Weich, 410-837-4458.

UNIVERSITY OF BRIDGEPORT, Bridgeport, CT 06604

General Information Independent, coed, comprehensive institution. CGS member. *Graduate housing:* Rooms and/or apartments guaranteed to single students and available on a first-come, first-served basis to married students. Housing application deadline: 8/15. *Research affiliation:* Connecticut Medicine Research Consortia, Marine Biology Station, Burndy Library.

GRADUATE UNITS

Acupuncture Institute *Program availability:* Part-time. Offers acupuncture (MS). Electronic applications accepted.

College of Chiropractic Offers chiropractic (DC). Electronic applications accepted.

College of Naturopathic Medicine Offers naturopathic medicine (ND). Electronic applications accepted.

College of Public and International Affairs *Program availability:* Part-time, evening/weekend. Offers East Asian and Pacific Rim studies (MA); global development and peace (MA); global media and communication studies (MA).

Fones School of Dental Hygiene *Program availability:* Part-time, evening/weekend, online learning. Offers dental hygiene (MS).

Nutrition Institute *Program availability:* Part-time, evening/weekend, online learning. Offers human nutrition (MS). Electronic applications accepted.

Physician Assistant Institute Offers physician assistant (MS).

School of Arts and Sciences *Program availability:* Part-time, evening/weekend. Offers arts and sciences (MS); clinical mental health counseling (MS); college student personnel (MS); community counseling (MS); human resource development (MS); human service (MS). Electronic applications accepted.

School of Business *Program availability:* Part-time, evening/weekend. Offers accounting (MBA); finance (MBA); general business (MBA); global financial services (MBA); human resource management (MBA); information systems and knowledge management (MBA); international business (MBA); management (MBA); marketing (MBA); operations management (MBA); small business and entrepreneurship (MBA); specialized business (MBA). Electronic applications accepted.

School of Education *Program availability:* Part-time, evening/weekend. Offers education (MS, Ed D, Diploma); educational management (Ed D, Diploma); elementary education (MS, Diploma); intermediate administrator or supervisor (Diploma); leadership (Ed D); middle school education (MS); music education (MS); remedial reading and language arts (Diploma); secondary education (MS, Diploma). Electronic applications accepted.

School of Engineering *Program availability:* Part-time, evening/weekend, online learning. Offers biomedical engineering (MS); computer engineering (MS); computer science (MS); computer science and engineering (PhD); electrical engineering (MS); engineering (MS, PhD); mechanical engineering (MS); technology management (MS, PhD). Electronic applications accepted.

Shintaro Akatsu School of Design *Program availability:* Part-time, evening/weekend. Offers design management (MPS). Electronic applications accepted.

THE UNIVERSITY OF BRITISH COLUMBIA, Vancouver, BC V6T 1Z1, Canada

General Information Province-supported, coed, university. CGS member. *Enrollment:* 9,737 full-time matriculated graduate/professional students. *Enrollment by degree level:* 6,169 master's, 3,568 doctoral. *Graduate faculty:* 2,282 full-time. *International tuition:* $8271 Canadian dollars full-time. Tuition, province resident: full-time $4708 Canadian dollars. Tuition, Canadian resident: full-time $4708 Canadian dollars. *Required fees:* $884 Canadian dollars. Tuition and fees vary according to program. *Graduate housing:* Rooms and/or apartments available on a first-come, first-served basis to single and married students. Housing application deadline: 3/1. *Student services:* Campus employment opportunities, campus safety program, career counseling, child daycare facilities, exercise/wellness program, free psychological counseling, grant writing training, international student services, low-cost health insurance, multicultural affairs office, services for students with disabilities, teacher training, writing training. *Library facilities:* UBC Library plus 9 others. *Research affiliation:* British Columbia Research (chemical and biological science technology), Forintek Canada (forest technology), National Research Council of Canada Institute of Machinery Research (machinery research), Pulp and Paper Research Institute of Canada, Pacific Environment Institute, Pacific Biological Station (fisheries and oceanography).

Computer facilities: A campuswide network can be accessed from student residence rooms and from off campus. Online class registration is available. Website: http://www.ubc.ca/

General Application Contact: Graduate Inquiries, 604-822-2848, Fax: 604-822-5802, E-mail: graduate.apply@ubc.ca.

GRADUATE UNITS

Faculty of Applied Science Expenses: Contact institution. *Financial support:* Fellowships, research assistantships, teaching assistantships, career-related internships or fieldwork, Federal Work-Study, institutionally sponsored loans, scholarships/grants, health care benefits, tuition waivers (partial), unspecified assistantships, and tuition waivers (for all PhD students) available. Financial award application deadline: 9/30. In 2016, 308 master's, 36 doctorates awarded. *Program availability:* Part-time. Offers applied science (M Arch, M Eng, M Sc, M Sc P, MA Sc, MAP, MASA, MASLA, MCRP, MLA, MN, MSN, MUD, PhD); chemical and biological engineering (M Eng, M Sc, MA Sc, PhD); civil engineering (M Eng, MA Sc, PhD); electrical and computer engineering (M Eng, MA Sc, PhD); materials engineering (M Sc, MA Sc, PhD); mechanical engineering (M Eng, MA Sc, PhD); mining engineering (M Eng, MA Sc, PhD). *Application fee:* $102 Canadian dollars ($165 Canadian dollars for international students). Electronic applications accepted. *Dean, Faculty of Applied Science,* Dr. Marc Parlange, E-mail: dean@apsc.ubc.ca.

School of Architecture and Landscape Architecture Expenses: Contact institution. *Financial support:* Fellowships, research assistantships, teaching assistantships, Federal Work-Study, institutionally sponsored loans, scholarships/grants, and tuition waivers (partial) available. Offers advanced studies in landscape architecture (MASLA); architecture (M Arch, MASA); landscape architecture (MASLA, MLA, MUD); urban design (MUD). *Application fee:* $100 Canadian dollars ($162 Canadian dollars for international students). Electronic applications accepted. *Application Contact:* Jaynus O'Donnell, Graduate Program Staff, 604-822-2779, E-mail: jodonnell@sala.ubc.ca.

School of Community and Regional Planning Expenses: Contact institution. *Financial support:* Fellowships with partial tuition reimbursements, research assistantships, teaching assistantships, career-related internships or fieldwork, Federal Work-Study, institutionally sponsored loans, scholarships/grants, tuition waivers (full and partial), and research travel bursaries available. Offers community and regional planning (M Sc P, MAP, MCRP, PhD). *Application fee:* $100 Canadian dollars ($162 Canadian dollars for international students). Electronic applications accepted. *Application Contact:* Laura Keith, Graduate Program Staff, 604-822-4422, Fax: 604-822-3787, E-mail: grad.scarp@ubc.ca.

School of Nursing Expenses: Contact institution. *Financial support:* Fellowships, research assistantships, and teaching assistantships available. *Program availability:* Part-time. Offers nurse practitioner (MN); nursing (MSN, PhD). *Application fee:* $100 ($162 for international students). Electronic applications accepted. *Application Contact:* Rana Hakami, Graduate Program Staff, 604-822-7497, Fax: 604-822-7466, E-mail: rana.hakami@nursing.ubc.ca.

Faculty of Arts Expenses: Contact institution. Offers ancient culture, religion, and ethnicity (MA); anthropology (MA, PhD); art history (MA, PhD); arts (M Mus, M Sc, MA, MAS, MFA, MJ, MLIS, MSW, DMA, PhD, CAS, Diploma); Asian studies (MA, PhD); behavioral neuroscience (MA, PhD); classical and Near eastern archaeology (MA); classics (MA, PhD); clinical psychology (MA, PhD); cognitive science (MA, PhD); creative writing (MFA); creative writing and theatre (MFA); critical and curatorial studies (MA); developmental psychology (MA, PhD); English (MA, PhD); film (MA, MFA); film production (MFA); film production and creative writing (MFA); film studies (MA); French (MA, PhD); geography (M Sc, MA, PhD); Germanic studies (MA, PhD); health psychology (MA, PhD); Hispanic studies (MA, PhD); history (MA, PhD); linguistics (MA, PhD); philosophy (MA, PhD); political science (MA, PhD); quantitative methods (MA, PhD); religious studies (MA, PhD); social/personality psychology (MA, PhD); sociology (MA, PhD); theatre (MA, MFA, PhD); theatre design (MFA); theatre directing (MFA); visual art (MFA). *Application fee:* $102 ($165 for international students). Electronic applications accepted. *Acting Dean,* Dr. Kathryn Harrison, 604-822-3751, E-mail: sec.dean@ubc.ca.

Institute for Gender, Race, Sexuality, and Social Justice Expenses: Contact institution. Offers gender, race, sexuality, and social justice (MA, PhD). *Application fee:* $100 ($162 for international students). *Application Contact:* Wynn Archibald, Graduate Program Staff, 604-822-9171, Fax: 604-822-9169, E-mail: wynn.archibald@ubc.ca.

School of Journalism Expenses: Contact institution. *Financial support:* Fellowships, research assistantships, and teaching assistantships available. Offers journalism (MJ). *Application fee:* $100 Canadian dollars ($162 Canadian dollars for international students). Electronic applications accepted. *Application Contact:* Andrea Yan, Graduate Program Staff, 604-822-6688, Fax: 604-822-6707, E-mail: jrnl.journal@ubc.ca.

School of Library, Archival and Information Studies Expenses: Contact institution. *Financial support:* Fellowships, research assistantships, teaching assistantships, Federal Work-Study, institutionally sponsored loans, scholarships/grants, health care benefits, tuition waivers (partial), and unspecified assistantships available. *Program availability:* Part-time. Offers archival studies (MAS); children's literature (MA); library and information studies (MLIS); library, archival and information studies (PhD). *Application fee:* $102 Canadian dollars ($165 Canadian dollars for international students). Electronic applications accepted. *Application Contact:* Alynne Pols, Program Assistant, 604-822-3459, E-mail: ischool.program@ubc.ca. *Acting Director,* Prof. Luanne Freund, 604-822-0825, Fax: 604-822-6006, E-mail: luanne.freund@ubc.ca.

School of Music Expenses: Contact institution. *Financial support:* Fellowships, research assistantships, teaching assistantships, institutionally sponsored loans, scholarships/grants, tuition waivers (partial), and unspecified assistantships available. *Program availability:* Part-time. Offers music (M Mus, MA, DMA, PhD). *Application deadline:* Applications are processed on a rolling basis. *Application fee:* $100 Canadian dollars ($162 Canadian dollars for international students). Electronic applications accepted. *Application Contact:* Robert Ablenas, Manager, Academic Advising, 604-822-5502, Fax: 604-822-4884, E-mail: music.advisor@ubc.ca.

School of Social Work Expenses: Contact institution. *Financial support:* Fellowships, research assistantships, teaching assistantships, career-related internships or fieldwork, Federal Work-Study, institutionally sponsored loans, scholarships/grants, and unspecified assistantships available. Financial award application deadline: 4/1. Offers social work (MSW, PhD). *Application fee:* $100 Canadian dollars ($162 Canadian dollars for international students). Electronic applications accepted. *Application Contact:* Christine Graham, Program Advisor, 604-822-4119, Fax: 604-822-8656, E-mail: sowk.advisor@ubc.ca.

Vancouver School of Economics Expenses: Contact institution. *Financial support:* Fellowships, research assistantships, teaching assistantships, and tuition waivers (partial) available. Offers economics (MA, PhD). *Application fee:* $100 Canadian dollars ($162 Canadian dollars for international students). Electronic applications accepted. *Application Contact:* Maureen Chin, Graduate Admissions, 604-822-4616, Fax: 604-822-5915, E-mail: econ.grad@ubc.ca.

Faculty of Dentistry Expenses: Contact institution. *Financial support:* Fellowships with partial tuition reimbursements, research assistantships with partial tuition reimbursements, teaching assistantships with partial tuition reimbursements, career-related internships or fieldwork, Federal Work-Study, scholarships/grants, tuition waivers (full and partial), and unspecified assistantships available. *Program availability:* Part-time. Offers craniofacial science (M Sc, PhD); dentistry (M Sc, DMD, PhD). *Application deadline:* Applications are processed on a rolling basis. *Application fee:* $102 Canadian dollars ($281 Canadian dollars for international students). Electronic applications accepted. *Application Contact:* Viki Koulouris, Graduate Program Staff, 604-822-4486, Fax: 604-822-8279, E-mail: vkoulouris@dentistry.ubc.ca. *Dean,* Dr. Charles Shuler, 604-822-5773, Fax: 604-822-4532, E-mail: cshuler@dentistry.ubc.ca.

Faculty of Education Expenses: Contact institution. *Financial support:* In 2016–17, 200 students received support. Fellowships with full and partial tuition reimbursements available, research assistantships with full and partial tuition reimbursements available, teaching assistantships with full and partial tuition reimbursements available, career-related internships or fieldwork, Federal Work-Study, institutionally sponsored loans, scholarships/grants, and unspecified assistantships available. *Program availability:* Part-time, evening/weekend, online learning. Offers adult learning and education (M Ed); adult learning and global change (M Ed); art education (M Ed, MA); counseling psychology (M Ed, MA, PhD); curriculum and leadership (M Ed); curriculum studies (M Ed, MA, PhD); education (M Ed, M Kin, M Sc, MA, MET, MHPCTL, Ed D, PhD, Diploma); educational administration and leadership (M Ed); educational leadership and policy (Ed D); educational studies (M Ed, MA, PhD); guidance studies (Diploma); higher education (M Ed); home economics education (M Ed, MA); human development, learning and culture (M Ed, MA, PhD); literacy education (M Ed, MA, PhD); mathematics education (M Ed, MA); measurement, evaluation, and research methodology (M Ed, MA, PhD); media and technology studies education (M Ed, MA); modern languages education (M Ed, MA); music education (M Ed, MA); physical education (M Ed, MA); school psychology (M Ed, MA, PhD); science education (M Ed, MA); social studies education (M Ed, MA); society, culture and politics in education (M Ed); special education (M Ed, MA, PhD, Diploma); teaching English as a second language (M Ed, MA, PhD). *Application fee:* $102 Canadian dollars ($165 Canadian dollars for international students). Electronic applications accepted. *Dean,* Dr. Blye Frank, 604-822-2221, Fax: 604-822-8971.

School of Kinesiology Expenses: Contact institution. *Financial support:* Fellowships, research assistantships, teaching assistantships, career-related internships or fieldwork, Federal Work-Study, institutionally sponsored loans, scholarships/grants, and tuition waivers (full and partial) available. Financial award application deadline: 3/1. *Program availability:* Part-time. Offers high performance coaching and technical leadership (MHPCTL); kinesiology (M Kin, M Sc, MA, PhD). *Application deadline:* Applications are processed on a rolling basis. *Application fee:* $100 Canadian dollars ($162 Canadian dollars for international students). Electronic applications accepted. *Application Contact:* Gayle Kosh, Manager, Graduate Programs, 604-827-4454, Fax: 604-822-8645, E-mail: forestry.grad@ubc.ca.

Faculty of Forestry Expenses: Contact institution. *Financial support:* Fellowships, research assistantships, teaching assistantships, career-related internships or fieldwork, scholarships/grants, health care benefits, and unspecified assistantships available. Offers forestry (M Sc, MA Sc, MF, MGEM, MIF, MSFM, PhD); geomatics for environmental management (MGEM); international forestry (MIF); sustainable forest management (MSFM). *Application deadline:* Applications are processed on a rolling basis. *Application fee:* $102 Canadian dollars ($165 Canadian dollars for international students). Electronic applications accepted. *Application Contact:* Helen Luk, Graduate Program Staff, 604-822-4641, Fax: 604-822-6842, E-mail: kin.gradsec@ubc.ca.

Faculty of Land and Food Systems *Program availability:* Part-time. Offers applied animal biology (M Sc, PhD); food science (M Sc, MFS, PhD); human nutrition (M Sc, PhD); land and food systems (M Sc, MFRE, MFS, MLWS, PhD); plant science (M Sc, PhD); soil science (M Sc, PhD). Electronic applications accepted.

Faculty of Medicine Expenses: Contact institution. *Financial support:* Fellowships, research assistantships, teaching assistantships, career-related internships or fieldwork, Federal Work-Study, and institutionally sponsored loans available. Support available to part-time students. *Program availability:* Part-time. Offers biochemistry and molecular biology (M Sc, PhD); bioinformatics (M Sc, PhD); cell and developmental biology (M Sc, PhD); experimental medicine (M Sc, PhD); genetic counselling (M Sc); genome science and technology (M Sc, PhD); medical genetics (M Sc, PhD); medicine (M Sc, MH Sc, MHA, MOT, MPH, MPT, MRSc, MD, PhD); neuroscience (M Sc, PhD); occupational therapy (MOT); pathology (M Sc, PhD); pharmacology (M Sc, PhD); reproductive and developmental sciences (M Sc, PhD); surgery (M Sc). Open only to Canadian residents. *Application fee:* $102 ($165 for international students). *Dean,* Dr. Dermot Kelleher, 604-822-2421, Fax: 604-822-6061, E-mail: fomdn.reception@ubc.ca.

School of Audiology and Speech Sciences Expenses: Contact institution. *Financial support:* Fellowships, research assistantships, teaching assistantships, career-related internships or fieldwork, Federal Work-Study, institutionally sponsored loans, scholarships/grants, and unspecified assistantships available. Offers audiology and speech sciences (M Sc, PhD). *Application deadline:* Applications are processed on a rolling basis. *Application fee:* $100 Canadian dollars ($162 Canadian dollars for international students). Electronic applications accepted. *Application Contact:* Sue Bryant, Graduate Program Staff, 604-827-5920, Fax: 604-822-6569, E-mail: inquiry@audiospeech.ubc.ca.

School of Population and Public Health Expenses: Contact institution. *Financial support:* Research assistantships, teaching assistantships, career-related internships or fieldwork, scholarships/grants, traineeships, and unspecified assistantships available. *Program availability:* Online learning. Offers health administration (MHA); health sciences (MH Sc); occupational and environmental hygiene (M Sc); population and public health (M Sc, MPH, PhD). *Application fee:* $102 ($162 for international students). Electronic applications accepted. *Application Contact:* Winona Kent, Graduate Program Staff, 604-822-9437, E-mail: info@spph.ubc.ca. *Interim Co-Director,* Carolyn Gotay, 604-822-2772, Fax: 604-822-4994, E-mail: carolyn.gotay@ubc.ca.

School of Rehabilitation Sciences Expenses: Contact institution. *Financial support:* Fellowships with partial tuition reimbursements, research assistantships, teaching assistantships, Federal Work-Study, institutionally sponsored loans, scholarships/grants, and tuition waivers (full and partial) available. Offers rehabilitation sciences (M Sc, MRSc, PhD). *Application fee:* $100 Canadian dollars ($162 Canadian dollars for international students). Electronic applications accepted. *Application Contact:* Michael Jenner, Graduate Program Staff, 604-827-7044, Fax: 604-822-7324, E-mail: rehab.gradprogram@ubc.ca.

Faculty of Pharmaceutical Sciences Expenses: Contact institution. *Financial support:* Fellowships, research assistantships, teaching assistantships, career-related internships or fieldwork, institutionally sponsored loans, scholarships/grants, traineeships, and unspecified assistantships available. Offers pharmaceutical sciences (M Sc, PhD, Pharm D). *Application fee:* $102 Canadian dollars ($165 Canadian dollars for international students). Electronic applications accepted. *Application Contact:* Shirley Wong, Manager, Graduate and Postdoctoral Programs, 604-827-0188, Fax: 604-822-3035, E-mail: phar.gradask@ubc.ca. *Dean,* Dr. Michael Coughtrie, 604-827-2178, Fax: 604-822-3035, E-mail: michael.coughtrie@ubc.ca.

Faculty of Science Expenses: Contact institution. *Financial support:* Fellowships, research assistantships, teaching assistantships, career-related internships or fieldwork, Federal Work-Study, institutionally sponsored loans, and tuition waivers (partial) available. *Program availability:* Part-time. Offers astronomy (M Sc, PhD); atmospheric science (M Sc, PhD); botany (M Sc, PhD); chemistry (M Sc, PhD); computer science (M Sc, PhD); data science (MDS); geological engineering (M Eng, MA Sc, PhD); geological sciences (M Sc, PhD); geophysics (M Sc, PhD); mathematics (M Sc, PhD); microbiology and immunology (M Sc, PhD); oceanography (M Sc, PhD); physics (M Sc, PhD); science (M Eng, M Sc, MA, MA Sc, MDS, PhD); statistics (M Sc, PhD); zoology (M Sc, PhD). *Application fee:* $102 ($165 for international students). Electronic applications accepted. *Application Contact:* Shahbano Bhatti, Student Information Support, 604-827-4045, E-mail: bhatti@science.ubc.ca. *Dean,* Dr. Simon Peacock, 604-822-3336, Fax: 604-822-5558, E-mail: scidean@science.ubc.ca.

Institute for Resources, Environment and Sustainability Expenses: Contact institution. *Financial support:* Fellowships with partial tuition reimbursements, research assistantships, teaching assistantships, institutionally sponsored loans, scholarships/grants, and unspecified assistantships available. Offers resources, environment and sustainability (M Sc, MA, PhD). *Application fee:* $100 Canadian dollars ($162 Canadian dollars for international students). Electronic applications

accepted. *Application Contact:* Lisa Johannesen, Graduate Program Staff, 604-822-9034, Fax: 604-822-9250, E-mail: admissions@ires.ubc.ca.

Institute of Asian Research Expenses: Contact institution. *Financial support:* Fellowships with tuition reimbursements, research assistantships, career-related internships or fieldwork, institutionally sponsored loans, scholarships/grants, and tuition waivers (partial) available. Offers Asia Pacific policy studies (MAAPPS); public policy and global affairs (MPPGA). *Application fee:* $100 ($162 for international students). Electronic applications accepted. *Application Contact:* Kerry Ross, Graduate Program Staff, 604-822-4571, E-mail: mppga.program@ubc.ca.

Peter A. Allard School of Law Expenses: Contact institution. *Financial support:* Fellowships, research assistantships, teaching assistantships, Federal Work-Study, scholarships/grants, and unspecified assistantships available. Financial award application deadline: 9/1. *Program availability:* Part-time. Offers common law (LL M CL); law (LL M, PhD); taxation (LL M). *Application deadline:* Applications are processed on a rolling basis. *Application fee:* $100 ($162 for international students). Electronic applications accepted. *Application Contact:* Joanne Chung, Graduate Administrator, 604-822-6449, Fax: 604-822-4781, E-mail: graduates@law.ubc.ca.

Sauder School of Business Expenses: Contact institution. *Financial support:* Fellowships with full tuition reimbursements, research assistantships with full tuition reimbursements, teaching assistantships with full tuition reimbursements, career-related internships or fieldwork, Federal Work-Study, institutionally sponsored loans, scholarships/grants, and tuition waivers (full and partial) available. *Program availability:* Part-time, evening/weekend. Offers accounting (PhD); business (IMBA, M Sc, MBA, MM, MSBA, PhD); business administration (IMBA, MBA, PhD); business analytics (MSBA); finance (PhD); management information systems (PhD); management science (PhD); marketing (PhD); organizational behavior (PhD); strategy and business economics (PhD); transportation and logistics (PhD); urban land economics (PhD). *Application deadline:* Applications are processed on a rolling basis. *Application fee:* $102 ($165 for international students). Electronic applications accepted. *Application Contact:* Elaine Cho, Administrator, PhD and M Sc Programs, 604-822-8366, Fax: 604-822-8755, E-mail: phd.program@sauder.ubc.ca.

UNIVERSITY OF CALGARY, Calgary, AB T2N 1N4, Canada

General Information Province-supported, coed, university. CGS member. *Graduate housing:* Rooms and/or apartments available on a first-come, first-served basis to single and married students. Housing application deadline: 3/31. *Research affiliation:* Alta Telecommunications Research Centre, Alberta Sulphur Research, Calgary Society for Students with Learning Difficulties, Canadian Institute of Resources Law, Canadian Music Centre, Canadian Energy Research Institute.

GRADUATE UNITS

Cumming School of Medicine *Program availability:* Part-time. Offers biochemistry and molecular biology (M Sc, PhD); biomedical technology (MBT); cancer biology (M Sc, PhD); cardiovascular and respiratory sciences (M Sc, PhD); community health sciences (M Sc, PhD); critical care medicine (M Sc, PhD); gastrointestinal sciences (M Sc, PhD); joint injury and arthritis (M Sc, PhD); medicine (M Sc, MBT, MCM, MD, PhD); microbiology, immunology and infectious diseases (M Sc, PhD); molecular and medical genetics (M Sc, PhD); mountain medicine and high altitude physiology (M Sc, PhD); neuroscience (M Sc, PhD); pathologists' assistant (M Sc, PhD). Electronic applications accepted.

Faculty of Graduate Studies Students: 5,672 full-time (3,040 women), 382 part-time (189 women). Average age 33. Expenses: Contact institution. *Financial support:* Fellowships with partial tuition reimbursements, research assistantships with partial tuition reimbursements, teaching assistantships with partial tuition reimbursements, career-related internships or fieldwork, institutionally sponsored loans, scholarships/grants, tuition waivers (full and partial), and unspecified assistantships available. Financial award application deadline: 2/1. In 2016, 1,328 master's, 335 doctorates, 167 other advanced degrees awarded. *Program availability:* Part-time, evening/weekend, blended/hybrid learning. Offers interdisciplinary research (M Sc, MA, PhD); resources and the environment (M Sc, MA, PhD). *Application fee:* $125 ($145 for international students). Electronic applications accepted. *Application Contact:* Safia Nathoo, Manager, Admissions and Records, 403-220-4454, Fax: 403-289-7635, E-mail: graduate@ucalgary.ca. *Vice Provost/Dean,* Dr. Lisa Young, 403-220-5116.

Centre for Military and Strategic Studies *Program availability:* Part-time. Offers military and strategic studies (MSS, PhD). PhD offered in special cases only.

Faculty of Arts *Program availability:* Part-time, evening/weekend. Offers anthropology (MA, PhD); archaeology (MA); art (MA, MFA); arts (MA, PhD); clinical psychology (M Sc, PhD); communication and culture (MA, MCS, PhD); design and technical theatre (MFA); directing (MFA); economics (MA, PhD); English (MA, PhD); French (MA, PhD); geography (MA, MGIS, PhD); German (MA); Greek and Roman studies (MA, PhD); history (MA, PhD); linguistics (MA, PhD); music (M Mus, MA, PhD); philosophy (MA, PhD); playwriting (MFA); political science (MA, PhD); psychology (M Sc, PhD); religious studies (MA, PhD); sociology (MA, PhD); Spanish (MA, PhD); theatre studies (PhD). Electronic applications accepted.

Faculty of Environmental Design Offers architecture (M Arch); environmental design (M Env Des, PhD); planning (M Plan).

Faculty of Kinesiology Offers kinesiology (M Kin, M Sc, PhD). Electronic applications accepted.

Faculty of Law Offers law (LL M, JD, Postbaccalaureate Certificate); natural resources, energy and environmental law (LL M, Postbaccalaureate Certificate).

Faculty of Nursing *Program availability:* Part-time. Offers nursing (MN, PhD, PMD). Electronic applications accepted.

Faculty of Science *Program availability:* Part-time. Offers analytical chemistry (M Sc, PhD); applied chemistry (M Sc, PhD); biological sciences (M Sc, PhD); computer science (M Sc, PhD); geology (M Sc, PhD); geophysics (M Sc, PhD); hydrology (M Sc, PhD); inorganic chemistry (M Sc, PhD); mathematics and statistics (M Sc, PhD); organic chemistry (M Sc, PhD); physical chemistry (M Sc, PhD); physics and astronomy (M Sc, PhD); polymer chemistry (M Sc, PhD); science (M Sc, PhD); software engineering (M Sc); theoretical chemistry (M Sc, PhD).

Faculty of Social Work Offers social work (MSW, PhD, Postgraduate Diploma). Electronic applications accepted.

Haskayne School of Business *Program availability:* Part-time, evening/weekend. Offers business (EMBA, GEMBA, MBA, PhD); business administration (EMBA, MBA); management (MBA, PhD).

Schulich School of Engineering *Program availability:* Part-time, evening/weekend. Offers avalanche mechanics (M Sc, PhD); biomedical engineering (M Sc, PhD); chemical engineering (M Eng, M Sc, PhD); civil engineering (M Eng, M Sc, PhD); electrical and computer engineering (M Eng, M Sc, PhD); energy and environment engineering (M Eng, M Sc, PhD); energy and environmental systems (M Eng, M Sc, PhD); engineering (M Eng, M Sc, MPM, PhD); environmental engineering (M Eng,

M Sc, PhD); geomatics engineering (M Eng, M Sc, PhD); geotechnical engineering (M Eng, M Sc, PhD); materials science (M Eng, M Sc, PhD); mechanical and manufacturing engineering (M Eng, M Sc, PhD); petroleum engineering (M Eng, M Sc, PhD); project management (M Eng, M Sc, PhD); reservoir characterization (M Eng, M Sc); structures and solid mechanics (M Eng, M Sc, PhD); transportation engineering (M Eng, M Sc, PhD); water resources (M Eng, M Sc, PhD). Electronic applications accepted.

Werklund School of Education *Program availability:* Part-time, evening/weekend, online learning. Offers adult learning (M Ed, MA, Ed D, PhD); counseling psychology (M Sc, MC, PhD); curriculum and learning (M Ed, MA, Ed D, PhD); education (M Ed, M Sc, MA, MC, Ed D, PhD); educational leadership (M Ed, MA, Ed D, PhD); languages and diversity (M Ed, MA, Ed D, PhD); learning sciences (M Ed, MA, Ed D, PhD); school and applied child psychology (M Ed, M Sc, PhD). Electronic applications accepted.

UNIVERSITY OF CALIFORNIA, BERKELEY, Berkeley, CA 94720-1500

General Information State-supported, coed, university. CGS member. *Enrollment:* 10,105 full-time matriculated graduate/professional students (4,804 women), 946 part-time matriculated graduate/professional students (266 women). *Graduate faculty:* 1,500. *Graduate housing:* Rooms and/or apartments available to single and married students. *Student services:* Campus employment opportunities, campus safety program, career counseling, child daycare facilities, exercise/wellness program, free psychological counseling, grant writing training, international student services, low-cost health insurance, multicultural affairs office, services for students with disabilities, teacher training, writing training. *Library facilities:* Doe Library.

Computer facilities: A campuswide network can be accessed from student residence rooms and from off campus. Online class registration is available. Website: http://www.berkeley.edu/

General Application Contact: Information Contact, 510-642-7405.

GRADUATE UNITS

Graduate Division Students: 8,281 full-time (3,900 women), 19 part-time (2 women); includes 2,341 minority (298 Black or African American, non-Hispanic/Latino; 57 American Indian or Alaska Native, non-Hispanic/Latino; 1,308 Asian, non-Hispanic/Latino; 674 Hispanic/Latino; 4 Native Hawaiian or other Pacific Islander, non-Hispanic/Latino), 2,023 international. Average age 26. 27,806 applicants, 2510 enrolled. Expenses: Contact institution. *Financial support:* Fellowships, research assistantships, teaching assistantships, career-related internships or fieldwork, Federal Work-Study, institutionally sponsored loans, traineeships, health care benefits, tuition waivers (full and partial), and unspecified assistantships available. Support available to part-time students. Financial award applicants required to submit FAFSA. In 2016, 1,575 master's, 785 doctorates awarded. *Program availability:* Part-time, blended/hybrid learning. Offers bioengineering (PhD); comparative biochemistry (PhD); East Asian studies (MA); global studies (MA); neuroscience (PhD); Northeast Asian studies (MA); South Asian studies (MA); Southeast Asian studies (MA); vision science (MS, PhD). *Application fee:* $105 ($125 for international students). *Application Contact:* 510-642-7405, E-mail: gradadm@berkeley.edu. *Graduate Dean,* Prof. Fiona M. Doyle, 510-642-5473.

College of Chemistry Students: 520 full-time (197 women); includes 103 minority (7 Black or African American, non-Hispanic/Latino; 4 American Indian or Alaska Native, non-Hispanic/Latino; 68 Asian, non-Hispanic/Latino; 24 Hispanic/Latino), 140 international. Average age 26. 1,350 applicants, 123 enrolled. *Faculty:* 51 full-time, 3 part-time/adjunct. Expenses: Contact institution. *Financial support:* Fellowships with tuition reimbursements, research assistantships with tuition reimbursements, teaching assistantships with tuition reimbursements, institutionally sponsored loans, and unspecified assistantships available. Financial award applicants required to submit FAFSA. In 2016, 41 master's, 78 doctorates awarded. Offers chemical engineering (PhD); chemistry (MS, PhD); product development (MS). *Application deadline:* For fall admission, 12/1 for domestic students. *Application fee:* $105 ($125 for international students). Electronic applications accepted. *Application Contact:* 510-642-7405. *Dean,* Dr. Douglas Clark, 510-642-5060, E-mail: cocdean@berkeley.edu.

College of Engineering Students: 1,970 full-time (597 women), 19 part-time (2 women); includes 458 minority (43 Black or African American, non-Hispanic/Latino; 1 American Indian or Alaska Native, non-Hispanic/Latino; 311 Asian, non-Hispanic/Latino; 102 Hispanic/Latino; 1 Native Hawaiian or other Pacific Islander, non-Hispanic/Latino), 866 international. Average age 27. 8,893 applicants, 771 enrolled. Expenses: Contact institution. *Financial support:* Applicants required to submit FAFSA. In 2016, 548 master's, 204 doctorates awarded. *Program availability:* Part-time, 100% online, blended/hybrid learning. Offers applied science and technology (PhD); bioengineering (M Eng, MTM); computer science (MS, PhD); decision analytics (M Eng); electrical engineering (M Eng, MS, PhD); engineering (M Eng, MS, MTM, PhD); engineering and project management (M Eng, MS, PhD); engineering science (M Eng, MS, PhD); environmental engineering (M Eng, MS, PhD); geoengineering (M Eng, MS, PhD); industrial engineering and operations research (M Eng, MS, PhD); mechanical engineering (M Eng, MS, PhD); nuclear engineering (M Eng, MS, PhD); structural engineering, mechanics and materials (M Eng, MS, PhD); transportation engineering (M Eng, MS, PhD). *Application fee:* $105 ($125 for international students). Electronic applications accepted. *Application Contact:* 510-642-7594, E-mail: ess@berkeley.edu. *Dean,* Dr. Shankar Sastry, 510-642-5771, E-mail: engineeringdean@berkeley.edu.

College of Environmental Design Students: 400 full-time (215 women); includes 91 minority (14 Black or African American, non-Hispanic/Latino; 1 American Indian or Alaska Native, non-Hispanic/Latino; 31 Asian, non-Hispanic/Latino; 45 Hispanic/Latino), 143 international. Average age 30. 1,875 applicants, 150 enrolled. Expenses: Contact institution. *Financial support:* Fellowships, research assistantships, teaching assistantships, career-related internships or fieldwork, Federal Work-Study, institutionally sponsored loans, health care benefits, and tuition waivers (partial) available. Financial award applicants required to submit FAFSA. In 2016, 126 master's, 21 doctorates awarded. Offers architecture (M Arch); building science (MS, PhD); building structures, construction and materials (MS, PhD); city and regional planning (MCP, PhD); design theories, methods, and practices (MS, PhD); environmental design (M Arch, MA, MCP, MLA, MS, MUD, PhD); environmental design in developing countries (MS, PhD); history of architecture and urbanism (MS, PhD); landscape architecture (MLA); landscape architecture and environmental planning (PhD); social and cultural processes in architecture and urbanism (MS, PhD); urban design (MUD). *Application fee:* $105 ($125 for international students). Electronic applications accepted. *Application Contact:* 510-642-7405. *Dean,* Prof. Jennifer Wolch, 510-642-0831, Fax: 510-642-7560.

College of Letters and Science Students: 2,620 full-time (1,144 women); includes 662 minority (102 Black or African American, non-Hispanic/Latino; 26 American Indian or Alaska Native, non-Hispanic/Latino; 315 Asian, non-Hispanic/Latino; 219 Hispanic/Latino), 489 international. Average age 30. 9,095 applicants, 434 enrolled. Expenses: Contact institution. *Financial support:* Fellowships, research assistantships, teaching assistantships, career-related internships or fieldwork, Federal Work-Study, institutionally sponsored loans, health care benefits, tuition waivers (full and partial), and unspecified assistantships available. Financial award applicants required to submit FAFSA. In 2016, 208 master's, 329 doctorates awarded. Offers African American studies (PhD); ancient history and Mediterranean archaeology (MA, PhD); anthropology (MA, PhD); applied mathematics (PhD); art practice (MFA); astrophysics (PhD); biophysics (PhD); Buddhist studies (PhD); Chinese language (PhD); classical archaeology (MA, PhD); classics (MA, PhD); comparative literature (PhD); composition (PhD); Czech (PhD); demography (PhD); economics (PhD); endocrinology (MA, PhD); English (PhD); ethnic studies (PhD); ethnomusicology (PhD); film and media (PhD); folklore (MA); French (PhD); geography (PhD); geology (MA, MS, PhD); geophysics (MA, MS, PhD); German (PhD); Greek (MA); Hindi (MA, PhD); Hispanic languages and literatures (PhD); history (PhD); history of art (PhD); Indonesian (MA, PhD); integrative biology (PhD); Italian (PhD); Italian studies (PhD); Japanese language (PhD); Latin (MA); letters and science (MA, MFA, MS, PhD); linguistics (PhD); logic and the methodology of science (PhD); mathematics (MA, PhD); medical anthropology (PhD); molecular and cell biology (PhD); musicology (PhD); Near Eastern studies (MA, PhD); performance studies (PhD); philosophy (PhD); physics (PhD); Polish (PhD); political science (PhD); psychology (PhD); rhetoric (PhD); Russian (PhD); Sanskrit (MA, PhD); Scandinavian languages and literatures (PhD); Serbo-Croatian (PhD); sociology (PhD); sociology and demography (MA, PhD); Spanish (PhD); statistics (MA, PhD); Tamil (MA, PhD). *Application fee:* $105 ($125 for international students). Electronic applications accepted. *Application Contact:* 510-642-7405. *Executive Dean,* Dr. Carla Hesse, 510-642-3331, E-mail: lsdo@berkeley.edu.

College of Natural Resources Students: 465 full-time (249 women); includes 109 minority (14 Black or African American, non-Hispanic/Latino; 5 American Indian or Alaska Native, non-Hispanic/Latino; 52 Asian, non-Hispanic/Latino; 37 Hispanic/Latino; 1 Native Hawaiian or other Pacific Islander, non-Hispanic/Latino), 83 international. Average age 30. 1,079 applicants, 101 enrolled. Expenses: Contact institution. *Financial support:* Fellowships, research assistantships, teaching assistantships, Federal Work-Study, institutionally sponsored loans, tuition waivers (full and partial), and unspecified assistantships available. Financial award applicants required to submit FAFSA. In 2016, 64 master's, 70 doctorates awarded. Offers agricultural and resource economics (PhD); development practice (MDP); energy and resources (MA, MS, PhD); environmental science, policy, and management (MS, PhD); forestry (MF); metabolic biology (MS, PhD); microbiology (PhD); molecular toxicology (PhD); natural resources (MA, MDP, MF, MS, PhD); plant biology (PhD); range management (MS). *Application fee:* $105 ($125 for international students). *Application Contact:* 510-642-7405. *Dean,* Prof. J. Keith Gilless, 510-642-7171, E-mail: cnrmain@nature.berkeley.edu.

Graduate School of Journalism Students: 105 full-time (69 women); includes 32 minority (9 Black or African American, non-Hispanic/Latino; 4 American Indian or Alaska Native, non-Hispanic/Latino; 9 Asian, non-Hispanic/Latino; 10 Hispanic/Latino), 14 international. Average age 29. 315 applicants, 53 enrolled. Expenses: Contact institution. *Financial support:* Fellowships, research assistantships, career-related internships or fieldwork, Federal Work-Study, institutionally sponsored loans, scholarships/grants, tuition waivers (full and partial), and unspecified assistantships available. Financial award applicants required to submit FAFSA. In 2016, 68 master's awarded. Offers journalism (MJ). *Application deadline:* For fall admission, 12/1 for domestic students. *Application fee:* $105 ($125 for international students). Electronic applications accepted. *Application Contact:* Information Contact, 510-642-7928, E-mail: applysoj@journalism.berkeley.edu. *Dean,* Edward Wasserman, 510-642-3383.

Graduate School of Public Policy Students: 224 full-time (131 women); includes 68 minority (13 Black or African American, non-Hispanic/Latino; 2 American Indian or Alaska Native, non-Hispanic/Latino; 32 Asian, non-Hispanic/Latino; 20 Hispanic/Latino; 1 Native Hawaiian or other Pacific Islander, non-Hispanic/Latino), 36 international. Average age 29. 754 applicants, 119 enrolled. Expenses: Contact institution. *Financial support:* Fellowships, research assistantships, teaching assistantships, institutionally sponsored loans, health care benefits, and unspecified assistantships available. In 2016, 89 master's awarded. Offers public affairs (MPA); public policy (MPA, MPP, PhD). *Application deadline:* For fall admission, 12/1 for domestic students. *Application fee:* $105 ($125 for international students). Electronic applications accepted. *Application Contact:* 510-642-4670, Fax: 510-643-9657, E-mail: gsppadm@berkeley.edu. *Dean,* Prof. Henry Brady, 510-642-4670, E-mail: gsppadm@berkeley.edu.

Haas School of Business Students: 649 full-time (241 women), 865 part-time (254 women); includes 604 minority (47 Black or African American, non-Hispanic/Latino; 1 American Indian or Alaska Native, non-Hispanic/Latino; 477 Asian, non-Hispanic/Latino; 46 Hispanic/Latino; 33 Two or more races, non-Hispanic/Latino), 242 international. *Faculty:* 85 full-time (18 women), 164 part-time/adjunct (34 women). Expenses: Contact institution. *Financial support:* Application deadline: 3/1. *Program availability:* Part-time, evening/weekend. Offers accounting (PhD); business (EMBA, MBA, MFE, PhD); business administration (EMBA, MBA, PhD); business and public policy (PhD); finance (PhD); financial engineering (MFE); management of organizations (PhD); marketing (PhD); real estate (PhD). *Dean,* Richard K. Lyons, 510-643-2027, Fax: 510-642-9128, E-mail: lyons@haas.berkeley.edu.

School of Education Students: 323 full-time (239 women); includes 137 minority (31 Black or African American, non-Hispanic/Latino; 2 American Indian or Alaska Native, non-Hispanic/Latino; 46 Asian, non-Hispanic/Latino; 58 Hispanic/Latino), 34 international. Average age 34. 676 applicants, 91 enrolled. Expenses: Contact institution. *Financial support:* Fellowships, research assistantships, teaching assistantships, career-related internships or fieldwork, institutionally sponsored loans, health care benefits, and unspecified assistantships available. In 2016, 105 master's, 38 doctorates awarded. Offers development in mathematics and science (MA); education (MA, PhD); education in mathematics, science, and technology (MA, PhD); human development and education (MA, PhD); leadership education (MA); science and mathematics education (PhD); special education (PhD); teacher education (MA). *Application deadline:* For fall admission, 12/16 for domestic students. *Application fee:* $105 ($125 for international students). Electronic applications accepted. *Application Contact:* 510-642-5345, E-mail: gse_info@berkeley.edu. *Dean,* Prof. Prudence L. Carter, 510-642-3726, E-mail: gsedean@berkeley.edu.

School of Information Students: 448 full-time (141 women); includes 117 minority (2 Black or African American, non-Hispanic/Latino; 1 American Indian or Alaska Native, non-Hispanic/Latino; 99 Asian, non-Hispanic/Latino; 15 Hispanic/Latino), 133 international. Average age 31. 1,434 applicants, 227 enrolled. Expenses: Contact institution. *Financial support:* Fellowships, research assistantships, teaching assistantships, institutionally sponsored loans, health care benefits, and unspecified assistantships available. In 2016, 146 master's, 1 doctorate awarded. Offers information (MIDS, MIMS, PhD); information and data science (MIDS); information management and systems (MIMS, PhD). *Application deadline:* For fall admission, 12/1 for domestic students. *Application fee:* $105 ($125 for international students). Electronic applications accepted. *Application Contact:* 510-642-1464, Fax: 510-642-5814, E-mail: admissions@ischool.berkeley.edu. *Dean,* Prof. AnnaLee Saxenian, 510-642-1464, E-mail: admissions@ischool.berkeley.edu.

School of Public Health Students: 673 full-time (488 women); includes 265 minority (40 Black or African American, non-Hispanic/Latino; 5 American Indian or Alaska Native, non-Hispanic/Latino; 137 Asian, non-Hispanic/Latino; 82 Hispanic/Latino; 1 Native Hawaiian or other Pacific Islander, non-Hispanic/Latino), 61 international. Average age 30. 1,592 applicants, 259 enrolled. Expenses: Contact institution. *Financial support:* Fellowships, research assistantships, teaching assistantships, career-related internships or fieldwork, institutionally sponsored loans, scholarships/grants, traineeships, health care benefits, and unspecified assistantships available. Financial award applicants required to submit FAFSA. In 2016, 242 master's, 37 doctorates awarded. *Program availability:* Blended/hybrid learning. Offers biostatistics (MA, PhD); environmental health sciences (MS, PhD); epidemiology (MS, PhD); health policy (PhD); infectious diseases (PhD); infectious diseases and immunity (PhD); public health (MA, MPH, MS, Dr PH, PhD). *Application deadline:* For fall admission, 12/1 for domestic students. *Application fee:* $105 ($125 for international students). Electronic applications accepted. *Dean,* Prof. Stefano M. Bertozzi, 510-664-7771, Fax: 510-643-5056, E-mail: ph_dean@berkeley.edu.

School of Social Welfare Students: 209 full-time (173 women); includes 94 minority (16 Black or African American, non-Hispanic/Latino; 5 American Indian or Alaska Native, non-Hispanic/Latino; 29 Asian, non-Hispanic/Latino; 44 Hispanic/Latino), 3 international. Average age 31. 390 applicants, 87 enrolled. Expenses: Contact institution. *Financial support:* Fellowships, research assistantships with partial tuition reimbursements, teaching assistantships with partial tuition reimbursements, career-related internships or fieldwork, Federal Work-Study, scholarships/grants, traineeships, health care benefits, and unspecified assistantships available. Financial award applicants required to submit FAFSA. In 2016, 94 master's, 4 doctorates awarded. Offers social welfare (MSW, PhD). *Application deadline:* For fall admission, 12/1 for domestic students. *Application fee:* $105 ($125 for international students). Electronic applications accepted. *Application Contact:* 510-642-9042, E-mail: socwelf@berkeley.edu. *Dean,* Prof. Lorraine Midanik, 510-642-4341, E-mail: swdean@berkeley.edu.

School of Law Students: 1,185 full-time (671 women); includes 390 minority (66 Black or African American, non-Hispanic/Latino; 9 American Indian or Alaska Native, non-Hispanic/Latino; 192 Asian, non-Hispanic/Latino; 123 Hispanic/Latino), 229 international. Average age 25. 7,316 applicants, 547 enrolled. *Faculty:* 70 full-time (27 women), 52 part-time/adjunct (17 women). Expenses: Contact institution. *Financial support:* In 2016–17, 718 students received support, including 44 fellowships with partial tuition reimbursements available (averaging $13,541 per year), 162 research assistantships with partial tuition reimbursements available (averaging $4,393 per year), 23 teaching assistantships (averaging $10,440 per year); career-related internships or fieldwork, Federal Work-Study, institutionally sponsored loans, scholarships/grants, health care benefits, tuition waivers (partial), and unspecified assistantships also available. Financial award application deadline: 3/2; financial award applicants required to submit FAFSA. In 2016, 194 master's, 350 doctorates awarded. Offers jurisprudence and social policy (PhD); law (LL M, JD, JSD). *Application deadline:* For fall admission, 2/1 for domestic students. Applications are processed on a rolling basis. *Application fee:* $75. *Application Contact:* Edward Tom, Director of Admissions, 510-642-2273, Fax: 510-643-6222, E-mail: admissions@law.berkeley.edu. *Dean,* Prof. Melissa Murray, 510-642-6483.

School of Optometry Students: 265 full-time (214 women); includes 185 minority (5 Black or African American, non-Hispanic/Latino; 1 American Indian or Alaska Native, non-Hispanic/Latino; 162 Asian, non-Hispanic/Latino; 17 Hispanic/Latino), 14 international. Average age 23. 266 applicants, 71 enrolled. *Faculty:* 21 full-time, 86 part-time/adjunct. Expenses: Contact institution. *Financial support:* In 2016–17, 54 students received support. Career-related internships or fieldwork, Federal Work-Study, institutionally sponsored loans, scholarships/grants, health care benefits, unspecified assistantships, and departmental awards available. Financial award application deadline: 3/2; financial award applicants required to submit FAFSA. In 2016, 54 doctorates awarded. Offers optometry (OD, Certificate). *Application deadline:* For fall admission, 12/1 for domestic and international students. *Application fee:* $105 ($125 for international students). Electronic applications accepted. *Dean,* Dr. John Flanagan, 510-642-3414, Fax: 510-642-7806, E-mail: optometry-admissions@berkeley.edu.

UC Berkeley Extension *Program availability:* Part-time, evening/weekend, online learning. Offers accounting (Certificate); alcohol and drug abuse studies (Certificate); business administration (Certificate); clinical research conduct and management (Certificate); college admissions and career planning (Certificate); construction management (Certificate); finance (Certificate); global business management (Certificate); human resource management (Certificate); HVAC (Certificate); information systems and management (Postbaccalaureate Certificate); integrated circuit design and techniques (online) (Certificate); interior design and interior architecture (Certificate); landscape architecture (Certificate); leadership in sustainability and environmental management (Professional Certificate); management (Certificate); marketing (Certificate); project management (Certificate); solar energy and green building (Professional Certificate); sustainable design (Professional Certificate); teaching English as a second language (Certificate); UNIX/LINUX system administration (Certificate); visual arts (Postbaccalaureate Certificate); writing (Postbaccalaureate Certificate).

UNIVERSITY OF CALIFORNIA, DAVIS, Davis, CA 95616

General Information State-supported, coed, university. CGS member. *Graduate housing:* Rooms and/or apartments available to single and married students. Housing application deadline: 4/1.

GRADUATE UNITS

College of Engineering *Program availability:* Part-time. Offers aeronautical engineering (M Engr, MS, D Engr, PhD, Certificate); applied science (MS, PhD); biological systems engineering (M Engr, MS, D Engr, PhD); biomedical engineering (MS, PhD); chemical engineering (MS, PhD); civil and environmental engineering (M Engr, MS, D Engr, PhD, Certificate); computer science (MS, PhD); electrical and computer engineering (MS, PhD); engineering (M Engr, MS, D Engr, PhD, Certificate); materials science and engineering (MS, PhD); mechanical engineering (M Engr, MS, D Engr, PhD, Certificate); transportation, technology and policy (MS, PhD). Electronic applications accepted.

Graduate School of Management Students: 155 full-time (65 women), 352 part-time (138 women); includes 197 minority (7 Black or African American, non-Hispanic/Latino;

120 Asian, non-Hispanic/Latino; 42 Hispanic/Latino; 4 Native Hawaiian or other Pacific Islander, non-Hispanic/Latino; 24 Two or more races, non-Hispanic/Latino), 79 international. Average age 29. 1,060 applicants, 24% accepted, 214 enrolled. *Faculty:* 30 full-time (10 women), 43 part-time/adjunct (7 women). Expenses: Contact institution. *Financial support:* In 2016–17, 147 students received support. Fellowships, teaching assistantships with partial tuition reimbursements available, career-related internships or fieldwork, institutionally sponsored loans, scholarships/grants, health care benefits, tuition waivers (partial), and unspecified assistantships available. Support available to part-time students. Financial award application deadline: 3/2; financial award applicants required to submit FAFSA. In 2016, 230 master's awarded. *Program availability:* Part-time, evening/weekend. Offers business administration (MBA); management (MBA, MP Ac); professional accountancy (MP Ac). *Application deadline:* For fall admission, 11/2 priority date for domestic and international students. *Application fee:* $125. Electronic applications accepted. *Application Contact:* Kathy Gleed, Senior Director of Admissions, 530-752-7658, Fax: 530-754-9355, E-mail: admissions@gsm.ucdavis.edu. *Senior Assistant Dean of Student Affairs,* James Stevens, 530-752-7658, Fax: 530-754-9355, E-mail: admissions@gsm.ucdavis.edu.

Graduate Studies Offers acting (MFA); agricultural and environmental chemistry (MS, PhD); agricultural and resource economics (MS, PhD); animal behavior (PhD); animal biology (MAM, MS, PhD); anthropology (MA, PhD); applied linguistics (MA, PhD); applied mathematics (MS, PhD); art (MFA); art history (MA); atmospheric sciences (MS, PhD); avian sciences (MS); biochemistry and molecular biology (MS, PhD); biophysics (MS, PhD); biostatistics (MS, PhD); cell and developmental biology (MS, PhD); chemistry (MS, PhD); child development (MS); clinical research (MAS); communication (MA); community development (MS); comparative literature (PhD); comparative pathology (MS, PhD); composition (MA, PhD); conducting (MA, PhD); creative writing (MA); cultural studies (MA, PhD); dramatic art (PhD); ecology (MS, PhD); economics (MA, PhD); education (MA, Ed D); English (MA, PhD); entomology (MS, PhD); epidemiology (MS, PhD); exercise science (MS); food science (MS, PhD); forensic science (MS); French (PhD); genetics (MS, PhD); geography (MA, PhD); geology (MS, PhD); German (MA, PhD); health informatics (MS); history (MA, PhD); horticulture and agronomy (MS); human development (PhD); hydrologic sciences (MS, PhD); immunology (MS, PhD); instructional studies (MS); integrated pest management (MS); international agricultural development (MS); linguistics (MA); mathematics (MA, MAT, PhD); microbiology (MS, PhD); molecular, cellular and integrative physiology (MS, PhD); musicology (MA, PhD); Native American studies (MA, PhD); neuroscience (PhD); nutrition (MS, PhD); pharmacology/toxicology (MS, PhD); philosophy (MA, PhD); physics (MS, PhD); plant biology (MS, PhD); plant pathology (MS, PhD); political science (MA, PhD); population biology (PhD); psychological studies (PhD); psychology (PhD); sociocultural studies (PhD); sociology (MA, PhD); soils and biogeochemistry (MS, PhD); Spanish (MA, PhD); statistics (MS, PhD); textile arts and costume design (MFA); textiles (MS); viticulture and enology (MS, PhD). Electronic applications accepted.

School of Law Students: 505 full-time (270 women); includes 210 minority (7 Black or African American, non-Hispanic/Latino; 1 American Indian or Alaska Native, non-Hispanic/Latino; 87 Asian, non-Hispanic/Latino; 76 Hispanic/Latino; 1 Native Hawaiian or other Pacific Islander, non-Hispanic/Latino; 38 Two or more races, non-Hispanic/Latino), 22 international. Average age 24. 2,852 applicants, 33% accepted, 156 enrolled. *Faculty:* 54 full-time (28 women), 27 part-time/adjunct (7 women). Expenses: Contact institution. *Financial support:* In 2016–17, 431 students received support, including 35 research assistantships, 27 teaching assistantships with partial tuition reimbursements available; Federal Work-Study, institutionally sponsored loans, scholarships/grants, and health care benefits also available. Financial award application deadline: 3/2; financial award applicants required to submit FAFSA. In 2016, 138 doctorates awarded. Offers law (LL M, JD). *Application deadline:* For fall admission, 3/15 priority date for domestic students, 3/15 for international students. Applications are processed on a rolling basis. *Application fee:* $0. Electronic applications accepted. *Application Contact:* Kristen Mercado, JD, Director, Admissions, 530-752-6477, Fax: 530-754-8371, E-mail: admissions@law.ucdavis.edu. *Dean,* Kevin R. Johnson, 530-752-0243, Fax: 530-752-7279, E-mail: krjohnson@ucdavis.edu.

School of Medicine Offers medicine (MD). Electronic applications accepted.

School of Veterinary Medicine Offers preventive veterinary medicine (MPVM); veterinary medicine (MPVM, DVM, Certificate).

UNIVERSITY OF CALIFORNIA, HASTINGS COLLEGE OF THE LAW, San Francisco, CA 94102-4978

General Information State-supported, coed, graduate-only institution. *Enrollment by degree level:* 74 master's, 933 doctoral. *Graduate housing:* Rooms and/or apartments available on a first-come, first-served basis to single and married students. *Student services:* Campus employment opportunities, campus safety program, career counseling, exercise/wellness program, free psychological counseling, international student services, low-cost health insurance, services for students with disabilities, writing training. *Library facilities:* UC Hastings Law Library. *Collection:* Books: 111,102 (physical), 230,048 (digital/electronic); Serial titles: 4,435 (physical), 21,861 (digital/electronic); Databases: 107. Weekly public service hours: 102; students can reserve study rooms.

Computer facilities: A campuswide network can be accessed from student residence rooms. Online class registration is available. Website: http://www.uchastings.edu/

General Application Contact: Bryan Zerbe, Admissions Office, 415-565-4623, Fax: 415-565-4863, E-mail: admiss@uchastings.edu.

GRADUATE UNITS

Graduate Programs Students: 977 full-time (550 women), 30 part-time (25 women); includes 382 minority (36 Black or African American, non-Hispanic/Latino; 14 American Indian or Alaska Native, non-Hispanic/Latino; 159 Asian, non-Hispanic/Latino; 159 Hispanic/Latino; 3 Native Hawaiian or other Pacific Islander, non-Hispanic/Latino; 11 Two or more races, non-Hispanic/Latino), 76 international. Average age 24. 3,416 applicants, 47% accepted, 348 enrolled. Expenses: Contact institution. *Financial support:* Fellowships, research assistantships, teaching assistantships, career-related internships or fieldwork, Federal Work-Study, institutionally sponsored loans, scholarships/grants, traineeships, health care benefits, and unspecified assistantships available. Support available to part-time students. Financial award application deadline: 3/1; financial award applicants required to submit FAFSA. In 2016, 31 master's, 301 doctorates awarded. Offers law (LL M, MA, MSL, JD). MSL and MS offered jointly with University of California, San Francisco. *Application deadline:* For fall admission, 3/1 for domestic students, 5/1 for international students. Applications are processed on a rolling basis. *Application fee:* $75. Electronic applications accepted. *Application Contact:* Admissions Office, 415-565-4623, Fax: 415-565-4863, E-mail: admiss@uchastings.edu. *Admissions Office,* Bryan Zerbe, 415-565-4623, Fax: 415-581-8946, E-mail: admiss@uchastings.edu.

UNIVERSITY OF CALIFORNIA, IRVINE, Irvine, CA 92697

General Information State-supported, coed, university. CGS member. *Graduate housing:* Rooms and/or apartments available on a first-come, first-served basis to single and married students. *Student services:* Campus employment opportunities, campus safety program, career counseling, child daycare facilities, exercise/wellness program, free psychological counseling, grant writing training, international student services, low-cost health insurance, multicultural affairs office, services for students with disabilities, teacher training, writing training. *Library facilities:* Langson Library plus 4 others. *Collection:* Books: 2 million (physical), 1.2 million (digital/electronic); Serial titles: 4,826 (physical), 145,231 (digital/electronic); Databases: 1,274. Study areas open 24 hours, 5–7 days a week; students can reserve study rooms.

Computer facilities: 1,500 computers available on campus for general student use. A campuswide network can be accessed from student residence rooms and from off campus. Online class registration is available.
Website: http://www.uci.edu/

General Application Contact: Sheree McPeak, Student Affairs Officer, Graduate Division, 949-824-4611, Fax: 949-824-9096, E-mail: ymcpeak@uci.edu.

GRADUATE UNITS

Claire Trevor School of the Arts Students: 131 full-time (76 women), 4 part-time (2 women); includes 50 minority (5 Black or African American, non-Hispanic/Latino; 10 Asian, non-Hispanic/Latino; 22 Hispanic/Latino; 13 Two or more races, non-Hispanic/Latino), 5 international. Average age 31. 404 applicants, 15% accepted, 48 enrolled. Expenses: Contact institution. *Financial support:* Fellowships, teaching assistantships, institutionally sponsored loans, traineeships, health care benefits, and unspecified assistantships available. Financial award application deadline: 3/1; financial award applicants required to submit FAFSA. In 2016, 56 master's, 2 doctorates awarded. Offers accompanying (MFA); acting (MFA); art (MFA); arts (MFA, PhD); choral conducting (MFA); composition and technology (MFA); dance (MFA); design and stage management (MFA); directing (MFA); drama (MFA); drama and theatre (PhD); guitar/lute performance (MFA); instrumental performance (MFA); jazz instrumental/composition (MFA); piano performance (MFA); vocal performance (MFA). *Application deadline:* For fall admission, 1/15 for domestic and international students. Applications are processed on a rolling basis. *Application fee:* $105 ($125 for international students). Electronic applications accepted. *Application Contact:* Prof. Vincent Olivieri, Associate Dean, 949-824-5684, Fax: 949-824-2450, E-mail: olivieri@uci.edu. *Dean,* Dr. Stephen Barker, 949-824-8792, Fax: 949-824-2450, E-mail: barker@uci.edu.

Donald Bren School of Information and Computer Sciences Students: 456 full-time (147 women), 29 part-time (6 women); includes 52 minority (3 Black or African American, non-Hispanic/Latino; 1 American Indian or Alaska Native, non-Hispanic/Latino; 35 Asian, non-Hispanic/Latino; 6 Hispanic/Latino; 7 Two or more races, non-Hispanic/Latino), 346 international. Average age 27. 4,116 applicants, 11% accepted, 191 enrolled. Expenses: Contact institution. *Financial support:* Fellowships, research assistantships with full tuition reimbursements, teaching assistantships, institutionally sponsored loans, traineeships, health care benefits, and unspecified assistantships available. Financial award applicants required to submit FAFSA. In 2016, 147 master's, 37 doctorates awarded. Offers computer science (MS, PhD); informatics (MS, PhD); information and computer science (MS, PhD); networked systems (MS, PhD); statistics (MS, PhD). *Application deadline:* For fall admission, 12/15 for domestic and international students. *Application fee:* $105 ($125 for international students). Electronic applications accepted. *Application Contact:* Kris Bolcer, Director of Student Affairs, 949-824-5156, Fax: 949-824-4163, E-mail: kbolcer@uci.edu. *Dean,* Marios C. Papaefthymiou, 949-824-7427, E-mail: marios@uci.edu.

Francisco J. Ayala School of Biological Sciences Students: 272 full-time (147 women), 4 part-time (1 woman); includes 100 minority (3 Black or African American, non-Hispanic/Latino; 2 American Indian or Alaska Native, non-Hispanic/Latino; 46 Asian, non-Hispanic/Latino; 41 Hispanic/Latino; 1 Native Hawaiian or other Pacific Islander, non-Hispanic/Latino; 7 Two or more races, non-Hispanic/Latino), 39 international. Average age 26. 909 applicants, 19% accepted, 76 enrolled. Expenses: Contact institution. *Financial support:* Fellowships with full tuition reimbursements, research assistantships with full tuition reimbursements, teaching assistantships with full tuition reimbursements, career-related internships or fieldwork, institutionally sponsored loans, scholarships/grants, traineeships, health care benefits, and unspecified assistantships available. Financial award application deadline: 3/1; financial award applicants required to submit FAFSA. In 2016, 51 master's, 30 doctorates awarded. Offers biological science (MS); biological sciences (MS, PhD); biological sciences and educational media design (MS); biotechnology (MS); biotechnology management (MS); interdisciplinary cellular and molecular biosciences (PhD); mathematical, computational and systems biology (PhD); neuroscience (PhD). *Application deadline:* For fall admission, 12/15 for domestic and international students. Applications are processed on a rolling basis. *Application fee:* $105 ($125 for international students). Electronic applications accepted. *Application Contact:* Prof. R. Michael Mulligan, Associate Dean, 949-824-8433, Fax: 949-824-4709, E-mail: rmmullig@uci.edu. *Dean,* Prof. Frank Laferla, 949-824-5315, Fax: 949-824-3035, E-mail: laferla@uci.edu.

Henry Samueli School of Engineering Students: 905 full-time (287 women), 55 part-time (16 women); includes 155 minority (8 Black or African American, non-Hispanic/Latino; 1 American Indian or Alaska Native, non-Hispanic/Latino; 106 Asian, non-Hispanic/Latino; 30 Hispanic/Latino; 10 Two or more races, non-Hispanic/Latino), 618 international. Average age 26. 4,165 applicants, 26% accepted, 312 enrolled. Expenses: Contact institution. *Financial support:* Fellowships with tuition reimbursements, research assistantships with tuition reimbursements, teaching assistantships with tuition reimbursements, institutionally sponsored loans, traineeships, health care benefits, and unspecified assistantships available. Financial award application deadline: 3/1; financial award applicants required to submit FAFSA. In 2016, 336 master's, 63 doctorates awarded. *Program availability:* Part-time. Offers biomedical engineering (MS, PhD); chemical and biochemical engineering (MS, PhD); civil and environmental engineering (MS, PhD); electrical engineering and computer science (MS, PhD); engineering (MS, PhD); engineering management (MS); materials science and engineering (MS, PhD); mechanical and aerospace engineering (MS, PhD); networked systems (MS, PhD). *Application deadline:* For fall admission, 1/15 priority date for domestic students, 1/15 for international students. Applications are processed on a rolling basis. *Application fee:* $105 ($125 for international students). Electronic applications accepted. *Application Contact:* Jean Bennett, Director of Graduate Student Affairs, 949-824-6475, Fax: 949-824-8200, E-mail: jean.bennett@uci.edu. *Dean,* Gregory N. Washington, 949-824-4333, Fax: 949-824-8200, E-mail: engineering@uci.edu.

Institute of Transportation Studies Students: 15 full-time (9 women); includes 4 minority (all Asian, non-Hispanic/Latino), 10 international. Average age 29. 29 applicants, 55% accepted, 4 enrolled. Expenses: Contact institution. *Financial support:* Fellowships, research assistantships with full tuition reimbursements, teaching assistantships, institutionally sponsored loans, traineeships, health care benefits, and unspecified assistantships available. Financial award application deadline: 3/1. Offers transportation studies (MA, PhD). *Application deadline:* For fall admission, 1/15 for domestic and international students. *Application fee:* $105 ($125 for international students). *Application Contact:* Anne Marie DeFeo, Administrative Manager, 949-824-6564, E-mail: amdefeo@uci.edu. *Director,* Stephen G. Ritchie, 949-824-4214, E-mail: sritchie@uci.edu.

The Paul Merage School of Business Students: 528 full-time (228 women), 256 part-time (97 women); includes 285 minority (11 Black or African American, non-Hispanic/Latino; 21 American Indian or Alaska Native, non-Hispanic/Latino; 241 Asian, non-Hispanic/Latino; 10 Hispanic/Latino; 2 Native Hawaiian or other Pacific Islander, non-Hispanic/Latino), 260 international. Average age 33. 1,973 applicants, 32% accepted, 361 enrolled. Expenses: Contact institution. *Financial support:* Career-related internships or fieldwork, Federal Work-Study, institutionally sponsored loans, scholarships/grants, traineeships, health care benefits, and unspecified assistantships available. Support available to part-time students. Financial award application deadline: 3/1; financial award applicants required to submit FAFSA. In 2016, 407 master's, 6 doctorates awarded. *Program availability:* Part-time, evening/weekend. Offers business (EMBA, MBA, MPA, PhD); business administration (EMBA, MBA); health care administration (MBA); management (PhD); professional accountancy (MPA). *Application deadline:* For fall admission, 1/2 priority date for domestic and international students. Applications are processed on a rolling basis. *Application fee:* $105 ($125 for international students). Electronic applications accepted. *Dean,* Eric Spangenberg, 949-824-8470, E-mail: ers@uci.edu.

Programs in Health Sciences Students: 93 full-time (73 women), 24 part-time (19 women); includes 71 minority (2 Black or African American, non-Hispanic/Latino; 40 Asian, non-Hispanic/Latino; 16 Hispanic/Latino; 13 Two or more races, non-Hispanic/Latino), 11 international. Average age 30. 338 applicants, 38% accepted, 51 enrolled. Expenses: Contact institution. In 2016, 38 master's awarded. Offers health sciences (MPH, MSN, PhD); medicinal chemistry and pharmacology (PhD); nursing science (MSN); public health (MPH). *Application fee:* $105 ($125 for international students). *Application Contact:* Sheree McPeak, Graduate Division, 949-824-4611, Fax: 949-824-9096, E-mail: ogsfront@uci.edu.

School of Education Students: 189 full-time (139 women), 1 part-time (0 women); includes 101 minority (44 Asian, non-Hispanic/Latino; 40 Hispanic/Latino; 1 Native Hawaiian or other Pacific Islander, non-Hispanic/Latino; 16 Two or more races, non-Hispanic/Latino), 16 international. Average age 27. 456 applicants, 54% accepted, 131 enrolled. Expenses: Contact institution. *Financial support:* Fellowships, research assistantships with full tuition reimbursements, institutionally sponsored loans, traineeships, health care benefits, and unspecified assistantships available. Financial award application deadline: 3/1; financial award applicants required to submit FAFSA. In 2016, 139 master's, 16 doctorates awarded. *Program availability:* Part-time, evening/weekend. Offers educational administration (Ed D); educational administration and leadership (Ed D); elementary and secondary education (MAT). *Application deadline:* For fall admission, 1/2 priority date for domestic students, 1/2 for international students. *Application fee:* $105 ($125 for international students). Electronic applications accepted. *Application Contact:* Denise Earley, Assistant Director of Student Affairs, 949-824-4022, E-mail: denise.earley@uci.edu. *Dean,* Richard Arum, 949-824-2534, E-mail: richard.arum@uci.edu.

School of Humanities Students: 272 full-time (141 women), 3 part-time (2 women); includes 96 minority (6 Black or African American, non-Hispanic/Latino; 21 Asian, non-Hispanic/Latino; 42 Hispanic/Latino; 27 Two or more races, non-Hispanic/Latino), 27 international. Average age 32. 930 applicants, 12% accepted, 52 enrolled. Expenses: Contact institution. *Financial support:* Fellowships with tuition reimbursements, research assistantships with full tuition reimbursements, teaching assistantships with tuition reimbursements, institutionally sponsored loans, traineeships, health care benefits, and unspecified assistantships available. Financial award application deadline: 3/1; financial award applicants required to submit FAFSA. In 2016, 63 master's, 42 doctorates awarded. Offers Chinese (MA, PhD); classics (MA, PhD); comparative literature (MA, PhD); creative writing (MFA); culture and theory (PhD); East Asian languages and literatures (MA, PhD); English (MA, PhD); English and American literature (PhD); French (MA, PhD); German (MA, PhD); history (MA, PhD); humanities (MA, MAT, MFA, PhD); Japanese (MA, PhD); philosophy (MA, PhD); Spanish (MA, MAT, PhD); visual studies (MA, PhD); writing (MFA). *Application deadline:* For fall admission, 1/15 for domestic and international students. Applications are processed on a rolling basis. *Application fee:* $105 ($125 for international students). Electronic applications accepted. *Application Contact:* Amy Fujitani, Director of Graduate Student Affairs, 949-824-4303, Fax: 949-824-1360, E-mail: amy.fujitani@uci.edu. *Dean,* Georges Van Den Abbeele, 949-824-5133, E-mail: gvandena@uci.edu.

School of Law Expenses: Contact institution. Offers law (JD). *Application deadline:* For fall admission, 3/1 for domestic students. *Application fee:* $0. Electronic applications accepted. *Dean,* Erwin Chemerinsky, 949-824-7722, E-mail: echemerinsky@law.uci.edu.

School of Medicine Students: 568 full-time (302 women), 47 part-time (24 women); includes 109 minority (10 Black or African American, non-Hispanic/Latino; 1 American Indian or Alaska Native, non-Hispanic/Latino; 56 Asian, non-Hispanic/Latino; 38 Hispanic/Latino; 4 Two or more races, non-Hispanic/Latino), 30 international. Average age 28. 277 applicants, 25% accepted, 40 enrolled. Expenses: Contact institution. *Financial support:* Fellowships, research assistantships with full tuition reimbursements, teaching assistantships, career-related internships or fieldwork, institutionally sponsored loans, traineeships, health care benefits, and unspecified assistantships available. Financial award application deadline: 3/1; financial award applicants required to submit FAFSA. In 2016, 28 master's, 131 doctorates awarded. Offers biological sciences (MS, PhD); biomedical and translational science (MS); environmental health sciences (MS); environmental toxicology (PhD); epidemiology (MS, PhD); experimental pathology (PhD); exposure sciences and risk assessment (PhD); genetic counseling (MS); medicine (MS, MD, PhD); pharmacological sciences (PhD). *Application deadline:* For fall admission, 1/15 for domestic and international students. *Application fee:* $105 ($125 for international students). Electronic applications accepted. *Application Contact:* Leora Fellus, Graduate Studies Director, 949-824-1028, E-mail: lfellus@uci.edu. *Interim Dean,* Dr. Michael Stamos, 949-824-1046, E-mail: mstamos@uci.edu.

School of Physical Sciences Students: 507 full-time (152 women), 4 part-time (0 women); includes 136 minority (3 Black or African American, non-Hispanic/Latino; 2 American Indian or Alaska Native, non-Hispanic/Latino; 72 Asian, non-Hispanic/Latino; 37 Hispanic/Latino; 1 Native Hawaiian or other Pacific Islander, non-Hispanic/Latino; 21 Two or more races, non-Hispanic/Latino), 110 international. Average age 27. 996 applicants, 33% accepted, 109 enrolled. Expenses: Contact institution. *Financial support:* Fellowships, research assistantships with full tuition reimbursements, teaching assistantships, career-related internships or fieldwork, institutionally sponsored loans, traineeships, health care benefits, and unspecified assistantships available. Financial award application deadline: 3/1; financial award applicants required to submit FAFSA. In 2016, 69 master's, 90 doctorates awarded. Offers chemical and materials physics (MS, PhD); chemistry (MS, PhD); earth system science (MS, PhD); mathematics (MS, PhD); physical sciences (MS, PhD); physics (MS, PhD). *Application deadline:* For fall admission, 1/15 priority basis for domestic and international students. Applications are processed on a rolling basis. *Application fee:* $105 ($125 for international students). Electronic applications accepted. *Application Contact:* Prof. Roger McWilliams, Associate Dean, 949-824-6228, Fax: 949-824-2174, E-mail: mcw@uci.edu. *Dean,* Kenneth C. Janda, 949-824-6022, Fax: 949-824-2261, E-mail: kcjanda@uci.edu.

School of Social Ecology Students: 309 full-time (195 women), 58 part-time (34 women); includes 154 minority (14 Black or African American, non-Hispanic/Latino; 2 American Indian or Alaska Native, non-Hispanic/Latino; 45 Asian, non-Hispanic/Latino; 70 Hispanic/Latino; 23 Two or more races, non-Hispanic/Latino), 59 international. Average age 29. 729 applicants, 41% accepted, 128 enrolled. Expenses: Contact institution. *Financial support:* Fellowships, research assistantships with full tuition reimbursements, teaching assistantships, institutionally sponsored loans, traineeships, health care benefits, and unspecified assistantships available. Financial award application deadline: 3/1; financial award applicants required to submit FAFSA. In 2016, 119 master's, 22 doctorates awarded. Offers criminology, law and society (MAS, PhD); environmental analysis and design (PhD); epidemiology and public health (PhD); planning, policy and design (PhD); psychology and social behavior (PhD); social ecology (PhD); urban and regional planning (MURP). *Application deadline:* For fall admission, 1/15 priority date for domestic students, 1/15 for international students. Applications are processed on a rolling basis. *Application fee:* $105 ($125 for international students). Electronic applications accepted. *Application Contact:* Jennifer Craig, Director of Graduate Student Services, 949-824-5918, E-mail: craigj@uci.edu. *Dean,* Nancy Guerra, 949-824-5466, Fax: 949-824-1845, E-mail: nguerra1@uci.edu.

School of Social Sciences Students: 386 full-time (176 women), 10 part-time (8 women); includes 126 minority (9 Black or African American, non-Hispanic/Latino; 2 American Indian or Alaska Native, non-Hispanic/Latino; 45 Asian, non-Hispanic/Latino; 48 Hispanic/Latino; 22 Two or more races, non-Hispanic/Latino), 64 international. Average age 29. 754 applicants, 28% accepted, 101 enrolled. Expenses: Contact institution. *Financial support:* Fellowships, research assistantships with full tuition reimbursements, teaching assistantships, institutionally sponsored loans, traineeships, health care benefits, and unspecified assistantships available. Financial award application deadline: 3/1; financial award applicants required to submit FAFSA. In 2016, 61 master's, 62 doctorates awarded. Offers anthropology (MA, PhD); demographic and social analysis (MA); economics (MA, PhD); philosophy (PhD); political psychology (PhD); political sciences (PhD); psychology (PhD); public choice (MA, PhD); social networks (PhD); social science (PhD); social sciences (MA, PhD); sociology and social relations (PhD); transportation economics (MA, PhD). *Application deadline:* For fall admission, 1/15 priority date for domestic students, 1/15 for international students. Applications are processed on a rolling basis. *Application fee:* $105 ($125 for international students). Electronic applications accepted. *Application Contact:* John Sommerhauser, Director of Graduate Affairs, 949-824-4074, E-mail: john.sommerhauser@uci.edu. *Dean,* William M. Maurer, 949-824-6802, E-mail: wmmaurer@uci.edu.

Institute for Mathematical Behavioral Sciences Students: 9 full-time (4 women); includes 5 minority (2 Asian, non-Hispanic/Latino; 1 Hispanic/Latino; 2 Two or more races, non-Hispanic/Latino), 1 international. Average age 32. 9 applicants, 33% accepted, 2 enrolled. Expenses: Contact institution. *Financial support:* Fellowships, research assistantships with full tuition reimbursements, teaching assistantships, institutionally sponsored loans, traineeships, health care benefits, and unspecified assistantships available. Financial award application deadline: 3/1; financial award applicants required to submit FAFSA. In 2016, 5 master's, 2 doctorates awarded. Offers games, decisions, and dynamical systems (PhD); mathematical behavioral sciences (MA). *Application deadline:* For fall admission, 1/15 priority date for domestic students, 1/15 for international students. Applications are processed on a rolling basis. *Application fee:* $105 ($125 for international students). Electronic applications accepted. *Application Contact:* John Sommerhauser, Director of Graduate Affairs, 949-824-4074, E-mail: john.sommerhauser@uci.edu. *Graduate Program Director,* Louis Narens, 949-824-5360, E-mail: lnarens@uci.edu.

UNIVERSITY OF CALIFORNIA, LOS ANGELES, Los Angeles, CA 90095

General Information State-supported, coed, university. CGS member. *Graduate housing:* Rooms and/or apartments available on a first-come, first-served basis to single and married students.

GRADUATE UNITS

David Geffen School of Medicine Offers biological chemistry (MS, PhD); biomathematics (MS, PhD); biomedical physics (MS, PhD); cellular and molecular pathology (MS, PhD); clinical research (MS); experimental pathology (MS, PhD); human genetics (MS, PhD); medicine (MS, MD, PhD); microbiology, immunology and molecular genetics (MS, PhD); molecular and medical pharmacology (MS, PhD); neurobiology (MS, PhD); neuroscience (PhD); physiology (PhD). Electronic applications accepted.

Graduate Division Electronic applications accepted.

College of Letters and Science Offers Afro-American studies (MA); American Indian studies (MA); anthropology (MA, PhD); applied linguistics (PhD); applied linguistics and teaching English as a second language (MA); archaeology (MA, PhD); art history (MA, PhD); Asian languages and cultures (MA, PhD); Asian-American studies (MA); astronomy (MAT, MS, PhD); atmospheric and oceanic sciences (MS, PhD); biochemistry and molecular biology (MS, PhD); bioinformatics (MS, PhD); biological chemistry (PhD); cellular and molecular pathology (PhD); chemistry (MS, PhD); classics (MA, PhD); comparative literature (MA, PhD); conservation of archaeological and ethnographic materials (MA); ecology and evolutionary biology (MA, PhD); economics (MA, PhD); English (MA, PhD); French and Francophone studies (MA, PhD); gender studies (MA, PhD); geochemistry (MS, PhD); geography (MA, PhD); geology (MS, PhD); geophysics and space physics (MS, PhD); Germanic languages (MA, PhD); Greek (MA); Hispanic languages and literature (PhD); history (MA, PhD); human genetics (PhD); Indo-European studies (PhD); Italian (MA, PhD); Latin (MA); letters and science (MA, MAT, MS, PhD, Certificate); linguistics (MA, PhD); mathematics (MA, MAT, PhD); microbiology, immunology, and molecular genetics (PhD); molecular biology (PhD); molecular toxicology (PhD); molecular, cell and developmental biology (MA, PhD); molecular, cellular and integrative physiology (PhD); musicology (MA, PhD); Near Eastern languages and cultures (MA, PhD); neurobiology (PhD); oral biology (PhD); philosophy (MA, PhD); physics (MS, PhD); physiological science (MS); physiology (PhD); political science (MA, PhD); Portuguese (MA); psychology (MA, PhD); Scandinavian (MA); Slavic languages and literatures (MA, PhD); sociology (MA, PhD); Spanish (MA); statistics (MS, PhD); teaching English as a second language (Certificate). Electronic applications accepted.

Graduate School of Education and Information Studies Program availability: Part-time, evening/weekend. Offers archival studies (MLIS); education (M Ed, MA, Ed D, PhD); education and information studies (M Ed, MA, MLIS, Ed D, PhD, Certificate); educational leadership (Ed D); informatics (MLIS); information studies (PhD); library and information science (Certificate); library studies (MLIS); moving image archive studies (MA); rare books, print and visual culture (MLIS); special education (PhD). Electronic applications accepted.

Henry Samueli School of Engineering and Applied Science Students: 2,187 full-time (503 women); includes 517 minority (14 Black or African American, non-Hispanic/Latino; 4 American Indian or Alaska Native, non-Hispanic/Latino; 358 Asian, non-Hispanic/Latino; 101 Hispanic/Latino; 1 Native Hawaiian or other Pacific Islander, non-Hispanic/Latino; 39 Two or more races, non-Hispanic/Latino), 1,217 international. 7,218 applicants, 27% accepted, 760 enrolled. *Faculty:* 172 full-time (23 women), 24 part-time/adjunct (1 woman). Expenses: Contact institution. *Financial support:* In 2016–17, 740 fellowships, 1,387 research assistantships, 747 teaching assistantships were awarded; career-related internships or fieldwork, Federal Work-Study, institutionally sponsored loans, and tuition waivers (full and partial) also available. Financial award application deadline: 3/2; financial award applicants required to submit FAFSA. In 2016, 639 master's, 163 doctorates awarded. *Program availability:* Evening/weekend, blended/hybrid learning. Offers aerospace engineering (MS, PhD); bioengineering (MS, PhD); chemical and biomolecular engineering (MS, PhD); civil and environmental engineering (MS, PhD); computer science (MS, PhD); electrical engineering (MS, PhD); engineering (MS); engineering and applied science (MS, PhD); manufacturing engineering (MS); materials science and engineering (MS, PhD); mechanical and aerospace engineering (MS, PhD); mechanical engineering (MS, PhD). *Application deadline:* For fall admission, 12/1 for domestic and international students. *Application fee:* $105 ($125 for international students). Electronic applications accepted. *Application Contact:* Jan LaBuda, Director, Office of Academic and Student Affairs, 310-825-2514, Fax: 310-825-2473, E-mail: jan@seas.ucla.edu. *Associate Dean, Academic and Student Affairs,* Dr. Richard D. Wesel, 310-825-2942, E-mail: wesel@ee.ucla.edu.

Institute of the Environment and Sustainability Offers environmental science and engineering (D Env).

International Institute Offers African studies (MA); East Asian studies (MA); Islamic studies (MA, PhD); Latin American studies (MA). Electronic applications accepted.

School of Nursing Offers nursing (MSN, PhD). Electronic applications accepted.

School of Public Affairs Offers public affairs (MA, MPP, MSW, PhD); public policy (MPP); social welfare (MSW, PhD); urban planning (MA, PhD). Electronic applications accepted.

School of Public Health Offers biostatistics (MPH, MS, Dr PH, PhD); environmental health sciences (MS, PhD); environmental science and engineering (D Env); epidemiology (MPH, MS, Dr PH, PhD); health services (MPH, MS, Dr PH, PhD); molecular toxicology (PhD); public health (MPH, MS, D Env, Dr PH, PhD). Electronic applications accepted.

School of the Arts and Architecture Offers architecture and urban design (M Arch, MA, PhD); art (MFA); arts and architecture (M Arch, MA, MFA, MM, DMA, PhD); composition (MA, PhD); culture and performance (MA, PhD); dance (MFA); design media arts (MFA); ethnomusicology (MA, PhD); performance (MM, DMA). Electronic applications accepted.

School of Theater, Film and Television Offers animation (MFA); cinema and media studies (MA, PhD); cinematography (MFA); film and television (MA, MFA, PhD); moving image archive studies (MA); production (MFA); screenwriting (MFA); theater (MA, MFA); theater and performance studies (MA); theater, film and television (MA, MFA, PhD). Electronic applications accepted.

UCLA Anderson School of Management Students: 865 full-time (263 women), 1,201 part-time (337 women); includes 710 minority (48 Black or African American, non-Hispanic/Latino; 1 American Indian or Alaska Native, non-Hispanic/Latino; 505 Asian, non-Hispanic/Latino; 88 Hispanic/Latino; 4 Native Hawaiian or other Pacific Islander, non-Hispanic/Latino; 64 Two or more races, non-Hispanic/Latino), 451 international. Average age 31. 5,643 applicants, 26% accepted, 881 enrolled. *Faculty:* 90 full-time (20 women), 98 part-time/adjunct (19 women). Expenses: Contact institution. *Financial support:* In 2016–17, 633 students received support, including 455 fellowships (averaging $30,253 per year); research assistantships with partial tuition reimbursements available, teaching assistantships with partial tuition reimbursements available, career-related internships or fieldwork, institutionally sponsored loans, and scholarships/grants also available. Support available to part-time students. In 2016, 807 master's, 7 doctorates awarded. *Program availability:* Part-time, evening/weekend. Offers accounting (PhD); behavioral decision making (PhD); business administration (EMBA, MBA); decisions, operations, and technology management (PhD); finance (PhD); financial engineering (MFE); global economics and management (PhD); management and organizations (PhD); marketing (PhD); strategy and policy (PhD). *Application deadline:* For fall admission, 10/6 priority date for domestic and international students; for winter admission, 1/5 for domestic and international students; for spring admission, 4/12 for domestic and international students. Applications are processed on a rolling basis. *Application fee:* $200. Electronic applications accepted. *Application Contact:* Alex Lawrence, Assistant Dean and Director of MBA Admissions, 310-825-6944, Fax: 310-825-8582, E-mail: mba.admissions@anderson.ucla.edu. *Dean/Chair in Management,* Dr. Judy D. Olian, 310-825-7982, Fax: 310-206-2073, E-mail: judy.olian@anderson.ucla.edu.

School of Dentistry Offers dentistry (MS, DDS, PhD, Certificate); oral biology (MS, PhD). Electronic applications accepted.

School of Law Offers law (LL M, JD, SJD). Electronic applications accepted.

UNIVERSITY OF CALIFORNIA, MERCED, Merced, CA 95343

General Information State-supported, coed, university. CGS member. *Enrollment:* 515 full-time matriculated graduate/professional students (229 women), 6 part-time matriculated graduate/professional students (3 women). *Enrollment by degree level:* 49 master's, 472 doctoral. *Graduate faculty:* 202 full-time (73 women), 3 part-time/adjunct (all women). Tuition, state resident: full-time $11,220; part-time $5610 per semester. Tuition, nonresident: full-time $26,322; part-time $13,161 per semester. *Required fees:* $1657; $1657 per year. *Graduate housing:* On-campus housing not available. *Student services:* Campus employment opportunities, campus safety program, career counseling, child daycare facilities, exercise/wellness program, free psychological counseling, grant writing training, international student services, low-cost health insurance, multicultural affairs office, services for students with disabilities, teacher training, writing training. *Library facilities:* Kolligian Library. *Collection:* Students can reserve study rooms. *Research affiliation:* NASA (nanotechnology and engineering), National Science Foundation (STEM), National Institutes of Health (health and behavioral sciences), DARPA (STEM), Department of Defense (physics and engineering), Keck (bioengineering and nanotechnology).

Computer facilities: 230 computers available on campus for general student use. A campuswide network can be accessed from student residence rooms and from off campus. Online class registration, student calendar, 10Gb online cloud storage, free office software are available.
Website: http://www.ucmerced.edu/

General Application Contact: Tsu Ya, Director of Admissions and Academic Services, 209-228-4521, Fax: 209-228-6906, E-mail: tya@ucmerced.edu.

GRADUATE UNITS

Graduate Division Students: 515 full-time (229 women), 6 part-time (3 women); includes 165 minority (11 Black or African American, non-Hispanic/Latino; 48 Asian, non-Hispanic/Latino; 82 Hispanic/Latino; 3 Native Hawaiian or other Pacific Islander, non-Hispanic/Latino; 21 Two or more races, non-Hispanic/Latino), 164 international. Average age 29. 609 applicants, 48% accepted, 138 enrolled. *Faculty:* 202 full-time (73 women), 3 part-time/adjunct (all women). Expenses: Contact institution. *Financial support:* In 2016–17, 487 students received support, including 35 fellowships with full tuition reimbursements available (averaging $19,700 per year), 88 research assistantships with full tuition reimbursements available (averaging $19,320 per year), 365 teaching assistantships with full tuition reimbursements available (averaging $19,801 per year); scholarships/grants, traineeships, and health care benefits also available. Financial award application deadline: 1/15. In 2016, 33 master's, 30 doctorates awarded. *Application deadline:* For fall admission, 1/15 for domestic and international students. *Application fee:* $90 ($110 for international students). Electronic applications accepted. *Application Contact:* Tsu Ya, Director of Admissions and Academic Services, 209-228-4521, Fax: 209-228-6906, E-mail: tya@ucmerced.edu. *Dean,* Dr. Marjorie S. Zatz, 209-228-2408, E-mail: mzatz@ucmerced.edu.

School of Engineering Students: 170 full-time (52 women), 2 part-time (0 women); includes 34 minority (2 Black or African American, non-Hispanic/Latino; 11 Asian, non-Hispanic/Latino; 14 Hispanic/Latino; 2 Native Hawaiian or other Pacific Islander, non-Hispanic/Latino; 5 Two or more races, non-Hispanic/Latino), 99 international. Average age 28. 307 applicants, 35% accepted, 46 enrolled. *Faculty:* 44 full-time (7 women). Expenses: Contact institution. *Financial support:* In 2016–17, 150 students received support, including 16 fellowships with full tuition reimbursements available (averaging $19,088 per year), 45 research assistantships with full tuition reimbursements available (averaging $18,389 per year), 89 teaching assistantships with full tuition reimbursements available (averaging $19,249 per year); scholarships/grants, traineeships, and health care benefits also available. Financial award application deadline: 1/15. In 2016, 15 master's, 12 doctorates awarded. Offers biological engineering and small scale technologies (MS, PhD); electrical engineering and computer science (MS, PhD); environmental systems (MS, PhD); mechanical engineering (MS); mechanical engineering and applied mechanics (PhD). *Application deadline:* For fall admission, 1/15 priority date for domestic and international students. Applications are processed on a rolling basis. *Application fee:* $90 ($110 for international students). Electronic applications accepted. *Application Contact:* Tsu Ya, Director of Admissions and Academic Services, 209-228-4521, Fax: 209-228-6906, E-mail: tya@ucmerced.edu. *Dean,* Dr. Mark Matsumoto, Fax: 209-228-4047, E-mail: mmatsumoto@ucmerced.edu.

School of Natural Sciences Students: 173 full-time (65 women), 1 (woman) part-time; includes 62 minority (5 Black or African American, non-Hispanic/Latino; 22 Asian, non-Hispanic/Latino; 25 Hispanic/Latino; 1 Native Hawaiian or other Pacific Islander, non-Hispanic/Latino; 9 Two or more races, non-Hispanic/Latino), 40 international. Average age 28. 212 applicants, 52% accepted, 48 enrolled. *Faculty:* 65 full-time (25 women). Expenses: Contact institution. *Financial support:* In 2016–17, 170 students received support, including 6 fellowships with full tuition reimbursements available (averaging $20,331 per year), 31 research assistantships with full tuition reimbursements available (averaging $20,542 per year), 133 teaching assistantships with full tuition reimbursements available (averaging $19,627 per year); scholarships/grants, traineeships, and health care benefits also available. Financial award application deadline: 1/15. In 2016, 10 master's, 14 doctorates awarded. Offers applied mathematics (MS, PhD); chemistry and chemical biology (MS, PhD); physics (MS, PhD); quantitative and systems biology (MS, PhD). *Application deadline:* For fall admission, 1/15 for domestic and international students. *Application fee:* $90 ($110 for international students). Electronic applications accepted. *Application Contact:* Tsu Ya, Director of Graduate Admissions and Academic Services, 209-228-4521, Fax: 209-228-6906, E-mail: tya@ucmerced.edu. *Dean,* Dr. Juan C. Meza, 209-228-4487, Fax: 209-228-4060, E-mail: jcmeza@ucmerced.edu.

School of Social Sciences, Humanities and Arts Students: 172 full-time (112 women), 3 part-time (2 women); includes 69 minority (4 Black or African American, non-Hispanic/Latino; 15 Asian, non-Hispanic/Latino; 43 Hispanic/Latino; 7 Two or more races, non-Hispanic/Latino), 25 international. Average age 31. 195 applicants, 50% accepted, 52 enrolled. *Faculty:* 93 full-time (41 women), 3 part-time/adjunct (all women). Expenses: Contact institution. *Financial support:* In 2016–17, 167 students received support, including 12 fellowships with full tuition reimbursements available (averaging $20,247 per year), 12 research assistantships with full tuition reimbursements available (averaging $18,842 per year), 121 teaching assistantships with full tuition reimbursements available (averaging $19,655 per year); scholarships/grants, traineeships, and health care benefits also available. Financial award application deadline: 1/15. In 2016, 13 master's, 11 doctorates awarded. Offers cognitive and information sciences (PhD); interdisciplinary humanities (MA, PhD); psychological sciences (MA, PhD); social sciences (MA, PhD); sociology (MA, PhD). *Application deadline:* For fall admission, 1/15 for domestic and international students. *Application fee:* $90 ($110 for international students). Electronic applications accepted. *Application Contact:* Tsu Ya, Director of Admissions and Academic Services, 209-228-4521, Fax: 209-228-6906, E-mail: tya@ucmerced.edu. *Dean,* Dr. Jill Robbins, E-mail: jillrobbins@ucmerced.edu.

UNIVERSITY OF CALIFORNIA, RIVERSIDE, Riverside, CA 92521-0102

General Information State-supported, coed, university. CGS member. *Enrollment:* 22,921 graduate, professional, and undergraduate students; 3,084 full-time matriculated graduate/professional students (1,376 women), 14 part-time matriculated graduate/professional students (5 women). *Enrollment by degree level:* 909 master's, 2,008 doctoral, 181 other advanced degrees. *Graduate faculty:* 689 full-time (221 women). Tuition, area resident: full-time $16,666. Tuition, nonresident: full-time $31,768. *Required fees:* $11,055.54 per quarter. $3685.18 per quarter. Tuition and fees vary according to campus/location and program. *Graduate housing:* Rooms and/or apartments available on a first-come, first-served basis to single and married students.

Housing application deadline: 6/1. *Student services:* Campus employment opportunities, campus safety program, career counseling, child daycare facilities, exercise/wellness program, free psychological counseling, grant writing training, international student services, low-cost health insurance, multicultural affairs office, services for students with disabilities, teacher training, writing training. *Library facilities:* Tomas Rivera Library plus 4 others. *Research affiliation:* Los Alamos National Laboratory (botany and plant sciences, chemistry, earth sciences, physics), Brookhaven National Laboratory (chemistry, physics), U.S. Salinity Laboratory (environmental sciences, biochemistry), J. Paul Getty Museum (art history), Lawrence Livermore National Laboratory (anthropology), Fermi National Accelerator Laboratory (physics).

Computer facilities: Computer purchase and lease plans are available. 556 computers available on campus for general student use. A campuswide network can be accessed from student residence rooms and from off campus. Online class registration, online viewing of financial information are available.
Website: http://www.ucr.edu/

GRADUATE UNITS

Graduate Division *Program availability:* Part-time, evening/weekend. Offers anthropology (MA, MS, PhD); archival management (MA); art history (MA, PhD); biochemistry and molecular biology (MS, PhD); bioengineering (MS, PhD); biomedical sciences (PhD); cell, molecular, and developmental biology (MS, PhD); chemical and environmental engineering (MS, PhD); chemistry (MS, PhD); classics (PhD); comparative literature (MA, PhD); composition (PhD); computer engineering (MS); computer science (MS, PhD); creative writing and writing for the performing arts (MFA); cultural politics and production (PhD); economics (MA, PhD); electrical engineering (MS, PhD); English (PhD); entomology (MS, PhD); environmental sciences (MS, PhD); environmental toxicology (MS, PhD); ethnomusicology (MA); evolution, ecology and organismal biology (MS, PhD); experimental choreography (MFA); genetics, genomics, and bioinformatics (PhD); geological sciences (MS, PhD); history (PhD); materials science and engineering (MS); mathematics (MS, PhD); mechanical engineering (MS, PhD); microbiology (MS, PhD); neuroscience (PhD); philosophy (MA, PhD); physics (MS, PhD); plant biology (MS, PhD); plant pathology (MS, PhD); political science (MA, PhD); psychology (PhD); religious studies (MA, PhD); sociology (MA, PhD); Southeast Asian studies (MA); Spanish (MA, PhD); statistics (MS); visual arts (MFA). Electronic applications accepted.

The A. Gary Anderson Graduate School of Management *Program availability:* Part-time, evening/weekend. Offers business administration (MBA, PhD). Electronic applications accepted.

Graduate School of Education Offers autism (M Ed); diversity and equity (M Ed); education specialist (Credential); education, society, and culture (MA, PhD); educational psychology (MA, PhD); general education (M Ed); higher education administration and policy (M Ed, PhD); multiple subject (Credential); reading (M Ed); school psychology (PhD); single subject (Credential); special education (M Ed, MA, PhD); TESOL (M Ed). Electronic applications accepted.

School of Public Policy Offers global health (MS); public policy (MPP, PhD). MD/MPP offered in partnership with School of Medicine.

UNIVERSITY OF CALIFORNIA, SAN DIEGO, La Jolla, CA 92093

General Information State-supported, coed, university. CGS member. *Enrollment:* 34,979 graduate, professional, and undergraduate students; 5,465 full-time matriculated graduate/professional students (1,996 women), 630 part-time matriculated graduate/professional students (244 women). *Enrollment by degree level:* 2,878 master's, 3,217 doctoral. Tuition, state resident: full-time $11,220. Tuition, nonresident: full-time $26,322. *Required fees:* $1864. *Graduate housing:* Rooms and/or apartments available on a first-come, first-served basis to single and married students. *Student services:* Campus employment opportunities, campus safety program, career counseling, child daycare facilities, exercise/wellness program, free psychological counseling, grant writing training, international student services, low-cost health insurance, multicultural affairs office, services for students with disabilities, teacher training, writing training. *Library facilities:* Geisel Library plus 1 other. *Collection:* Books: 3.5 million (physical), 958,000 (digital/electronic). Study areas open 24 hours, 5–7 days a week; students can reserve study rooms. *Research affiliation:* Sanford Burnham Institute, National Oceanic and Atmospheric Administration (NOAA) Fisheries, Veterans Administration Medical Center, Scripps Research Institute, La Jolla Institute for Allergy and Immunology, Salk Institute for Biological Studies.

Computer facilities: A campuswide network can be accessed from student residence rooms and from off campus. Online class registration is available.
Website: http://www.ucsd.edu/

General Application Contact: Graduate Admissions Office, 858-534-3554, E-mail: gradadmissions@ucsd.edu.

GRADUATE UNITS

Graduate Division Students: 5,465 full-time (1,996 women), 630 part-time (244 women); includes 1,403 minority (129 Black or African American, non-Hispanic/Latino; 29 American Indian or Alaska Native, non-Hispanic/Latino; 824 Asian, non-Hispanic/Latino; 414 Hispanic/Latino; 7 Native Hawaiian or other Pacific Islander, non-Hispanic/Latino), 2,682 international. 20,925 applicants, 26% accepted, 2158 enrolled. Expenses: Contact institution. *Financial support:* Fellowships with tuition reimbursements, research assistantships with tuition reimbursements, teaching assistantships with partial tuition reimbursements, career-related internships or fieldwork, institutionally sponsored loans, scholarships/grants, traineeships, health care benefits, and unspecified assistantships available. Support available to part-time students. Financial award applicants required to submit FAFSA. In 2016, 1,342 master's, 541 doctorates awarded. Offers acting (MFA); aerospace engineering (MS, PhD); anthropology (PhD); applied mathematics (MA); applied mechanics (MS, PhD); applied ocean science (MS, PhD); applied physics (MS, PhD); architecture-based enterprise systems engineering (MAS); art history, theory and criticism (PhD); bioengineering (M Eng, MS, PhD); bioinformatics and systems biology (PhD); biophysics (PhD); chemical engineering (MS, PhD); chemistry (MS, PhD); climate science and policy (MAS); clinical psychology (PhD); cognitive science (PhD); communication (PhD); communication of science (PhD); communication theory and systems (MS, PhD); computational neuroscience (PhD); computational science (PhD); computational science, mathematics and engineering (MS); computer engineering (MS, PhD); computer science (MS, PhD); contemporary dance and performance (MFA); contemporary music performance (DMA); data science and engineering (MAS); design (MFA); directing (MFA); drama and theatre (PhD); earth sciences (MS, PhD); economics (PhD); education (M Ed, PhD); educational leadership (Ed D); electronic circuits and systems (MS, PhD); engineering physics (MS, PhD); engineering sciences (PhD); epidemiology (PhD); ethnic studies (PhD); geophysics (PhD); global health (PhD); health behavior (PhD); health policy and law (MAS); history (MA, PhD); history of science (PhD); intelligent systems, robotics and control (MS, PhD); Judaic studies (MA);

language and communicative disorders (PhD); Latin American studies (MA); linguistics (PhD); literature (PhD); marine biodiversity and conservation (MAS); marine biology (MS, PhD); materials science and engineering (MS, PhD); mathematics (MA, PhD); mathematics and science education (PhD); mechanical engineering (MS, PhD); medical device engineering (MAS); medical devices and systems (MS, PhD); multi-scale biology (PhD); music (MA, PhD); nanoengineering (MS, PhD); nanoscale devices and systems (MS, PhD); oceanography (MS, PhD); philosophy (PhD); philosophy of science (PhD); photonics (MS, PhD); physics (MS, PhD); playwriting (MFA); political science (PhD); political science and international affairs (PhD); psychology (PhD); quantitative biology (PhD); signal and image processing (MS, PhD); sociology (PhD); sociology of science (PhD); stage management (MFA); statistics (MS, PhD); structural engineering (MS, PhD); structural health monitoring, prognosis, and validated simulations (MS); teaching and learning (MA, Ed D); visual arts (MFA); wireless embedded systems (MAS); writing (MFA). *Application fee:* $105 ($125 for international students). Electronic applications accepted. *Application Contact:* Graduate Admissions, 858-534-3554, E-mail: gradadmissions@ucsd.edu. *Dean,* Dr. Kit Pogliano, 858-534-6655, E-mail: graduatedean@ucsd.edu.

Division of Biological Sciences Students: 300 full-time (168 women), 4 part-time (1 woman). 718 applicants, 24% accepted, 100 enrolled. Expenses: Contact institution. *Financial support:* Fellowships, research assistantships, teaching assistantships, scholarships/grants, traineeships, and unspecified assistantships available. Financial award applicants required to submit FAFSA. In 2016, 29 doctorates awarded. Offers anthropogeny (PhD); bioinformatics (PhD); biology (PhD); interdisciplinary environmental research (PhD); multi-scale biology (PhD); quantitative biology (PhD). PhD in biology offered jointly with San Diego State University. *Application deadline:* For fall admission, 11/29 for domestic students. *Application fee:* $105 ($125 for international students). Electronic applications accepted. *Application Contact:* Brandon Keith, Graduate Admissions/Program Coordinator, 858-534-8983, E-mail: biogradprog@ucsd.edu. Chair, Jens Lykke-Andersen, 858-822-3659.

Rady School of Management Students: 433 full-time (183 women), 89 part-time (35 women). 2,021 applicants, 32% accepted, 313 enrolled. *Faculty:* 28 full-time (5 women), 5 part-time/adjunct (1 woman). Expenses: Contact institution. *Financial support:* Fellowships, teaching assistantships, and scholarships/grants available. Financial award applicants required to submit FAFSA. In 2016, 152 master's, 5 doctorates awarded. *Program availability:* Part-time, evening/weekend. Offers business administration (MBA); business analytics (MS); finance (MF); management (PhD). *Application deadline:* Applications are processed on a rolling basis. *Application fee:* $200. Electronic applications accepted. *Application Contact:* Jay Bryant, Director of Graduate Recruitment and Admissions, 858-534-0864, E-mail: radygradadmissions@ucsd.edu. *Dean,* Robert Sullivan, 858-822-0830, E-mail: rssullivan@ucsd.edu.

School of Global Policy and Strategy Students: 390 full-time, 6 part-time. Average age 26. 590 applicants, 165 enrolled. *Faculty:* 33 full-time (9 women), 20 part-time/adjunct (4 women). Expenses: Contact institution. *Financial support:* In 2016–17, 140 students received support, including 60 fellowships with full and partial tuition reimbursements available (averaging $50,000 per year), 15 research assistantships with full tuition reimbursements available (averaging $20,000 per year), 20 teaching assistantships with full tuition reimbursements available (averaging $20,000 per year); career-related internships or fieldwork, scholarships/grants, and unspecified assistantships also available. Financial award application deadline: 1/15. In 2016, 160 master's, 3 doctorates awarded. *Program availability:* Part-time. Offers American policy in global context (MPP); business, government and regulation (MPP); Chinese economic and political affairs (MCEPA); energy and environmental policy (MPP); health policy (MPP); international affairs (MAS, MIA); international development and nonprofit management (MIA); international economics (MIA); international environmental policy (MIA); international management (MIA); international politics (MIA); political science and international affairs (PhD); program design and evaluation (MPP); public policy (MPP); security policy (MPP). *Application deadline:* For fall admission, 1/15 for domestic and international students. Applications are processed on a rolling basis. *Application fee:* $102 ($125 for international students). Electronic applications accepted. *Application Contact:* Admissions Representative, 858-534-5914, Fax: 858-534-5914, E-mail: gps-apply@uscd.edu. *Director of Enrollment,* Sonja Steinbrech, 858-534-7162, E-mail: ssteinbrech@ucsd.edu.

School of Medicine Students: 509. Expenses: Contact institution. Offers anthropogeny (PhD); audiology (Au D); bioinformatics (PhD); biomedical science (PhD); biostatistics (PhD); clinical research (MAS); leadership of healthcare organizations (MAS); medicine (MAS, Au D, MD, PhD); multi-scale biology (PhD); neurosciences (PhD). *Application Contact:* 858-534-3880, E-mail: somadmissions@ucsd.edu. *Associate Dean for Admissions,* Dr. Carolyn J. Kelly, MD.

Skaggs School of Pharmacy and Pharmaceutical Sciences Students: 248. Expenses: Contact institution. Offers pharmacy and pharmaceutical sciences (Pharm D). *Application Contact:* 858-822-4900, Fax: 858-822-5591, E-mail: sppsadmissions@ucsd.edu. *Dean,* Dr. James McKerrow.

UNIVERSITY OF CALIFORNIA, SAN FRANCISCO, San Francisco, CA 94143

General Information State-supported, coed, graduate-only institution. CGS member. *Graduate housing:* Rooms and/or apartments available to single and married students.

GRADUATE UNITS

Graduate Division *Program availability:* Part-time. Offers biochemistry and molecular biology (PhD); bioengineering (PhD); biomedical imaging (MS); biomedical sciences (PhD); cell biology (PhD); developmental biology (PhD); genetics (PhD); health policy and law (MS); history of health sciences (MA, PhD); medical anthropology (PhD); neuroscience (PhD); oral and craniofacial sciences (MS, PhD); physical therapy (DPT, DPTSc).

School of Nursing Offers nursing (MS, PhD); sociology (MS, PhD).

School of Dentistry Offers dentistry (DDS).

School of Medicine Students: 633 full-time (328 women); includes 370 minority (46 Black or African American, non-Hispanic/Latino; 1 American Indian or Alaska Native, non-Hispanic/Latino; 163 Asian, non-Hispanic/Latino; 103 Hispanic/Latino; 11 Native Hawaiian or other Pacific Islander, non-Hispanic/Latino; 46 Two or more races, non-Hispanic/Latino). Average age 24. 8,204 applicants, 149 enrolled. *Faculty:* 2,200 full-time (978 women), 386 part-time/adjunct (209 women). Expenses: Contact institution. *Financial support:* In 2016–17, 550 students received support. Federal Work-Study, institutionally sponsored loans, scholarships/grants, and tuition waivers (partial) available. Financial award application deadline: 2/1; financial award applicants required to submit FAFSA. In 2016, 177 doctorates awarded. Offers medicine (MD, PhD). *Application deadline:* For fall admission, 10/15 for domestic students. *Application fee:* $80 ($100 for international students). Electronic applications accepted. Application

Contact: Hallen Chung, Director of Admissions, 415-476-8090, Fax: 415-476-5490, E-mail: hallen.chung@ucsf.edu. *Dean,* Dr. Talmadge E. King, Jr., 415-476-2342, Fax: 415-476-0689.

School of Pharmacy Offers bioinformatics (PhD); biophysics (PhD); chemistry and chemical biology (PhD); pharmaceutical sciences and pharmacogenomics (PhD); pharmacy (MS, PhD, Pharm D). Electronic applications accepted.

UNIVERSITY OF CALIFORNIA, SANTA BARBARA, Santa Barbara, CA 93106-2014

General Information State-supported, coed, university. CGS member. *Graduate housing:* Rooms and/or apartments guaranteed to single students and available on a first-come, first-served basis to married students. Housing application deadline: 6/1. *Research affiliation:* California NanoSystems Institute, The Institute for Social, Behavioral and Economic Research, National Center for Ecological Analysis and Synthesis, The Institute for Collaborative Biotechnologies, Institute for Polymers and Organic Solids, Mitsubishi Chemical Center for Advanced Materials.

GRADUATE UNITS

Graduate Division Electronic applications accepted.

College of Engineering Offers bioengineering (PhD); chemical engineering (MS, PhD); communications, control and signal processing (MS, PhD); computer engineering (MS, PhD); computer science (MS, PhD); electronics and photonics (MS, PhD); engineering (MS, MTM, PhD); materials (MS, PhD); mechanical engineering (MS); technology management (MTM). Electronic applications accepted.

College of Letters and Sciences Offers ancient history (PhD); ancient Mediterranean studies (PhD); applied linguistics (PhD); applied mathematics (MA); art (MFA); art history (PhD); astrophysics (PhD); biochemistry and molecular biology (PhD); bioengineering (PhD); brass (MM); chemistry (MA, MS, PhD); classics (MA, PhD); cognitive science (PhD); communication (PhD); comparative literature (PhD); composition (MA, PhD); conducting (MM, DMA); dynamical neuroscience (PhD); earth science (MS, PhD); East Asian languages and cultural studies (MA); East Asian literatures (PhD); ecology, evolution, and marine biology (MA, PhD); economics (MA); English (PhD); ethnomusicology (MA, PhD); European medieval studies (PhD); feminist studies (MA, PhD); film and media studies (PhD); financial mathematics and statistics (PhD); French (PhD); geography (MA, PhD); global culture, ideology, and religion (MA, PhD); global government, human rights, and civil society (MA, PhD); global studies (PhD); Hispanic languages and literatures (PhD); Hispanic linguistics (MA); humanities and fine arts (MA, MFA, MM, MS, DMA, PhD); interdisciplinary emphasis: Black studies (PhD); interdisciplinary emphasis: environment and society (PhD); interdisciplinary emphasis: feminist studies (PhD); interdisciplinary emphasis: global studies (PhD); interdisciplinary emphasis: language, interaction and social organization (PhD); interdisciplinary emphasis: quantitative methods in the social sciences (PhD); interdisciplinary emphasis: technology and society (PhD); keyboard (MM, DMA); language, interaction and social organization (PhD); Latin American and Iberian studies (MA); letters and sciences (MA, MFA, MM, MS, DMA, PhD); linguistics (PhD); literature and theory (MA); Luso-Brazilian literature (MA); marine science (MS, PhD); mathematical economics (PhD); mathematics (MA, PhD); mathematics, life, and physical sciences (MA, MS, PhD); media arts and technology (MS, PhD); molecular, cellular, and developmental biology (MA, PhD); musicology (MA, PhD); philosophy (PhD); physics (PhD); piano accompanying (MM); political economy, sustainable development, and the environment (MA, PhD); political science (PhD); psychology (PhD); public finance (PhD); public historical studies (PhD); quantitative methods in the social sciences (MA, PhD); religious studies (MA, PhD); social sciences (MA, PhD); society and technology (PhD); sociocultural anthropology (PhD); sociology (PhD); Spanish or Spanish-American literature (MA); statistics (MA); statistics and applied probability (PhD); strings (MM, DMA); technology and society (PhD); theater studies (MA, PhD); theory (MA, PhD); translation studies (PhD); transportation (PhD); voice (MM, DMA); women's studies (PhD); woodwinds (MM). Electronic applications accepted.

Donald Bren School of Environmental Science and Management Offers economics and environmental science (PhD); environmental science and management (MESM, PhD); technology and society (PhD). Electronic applications accepted.

Gevirtz Graduate School of Education Offers counseling, clinical and school psychology (MA, PhD, Credential); education (MA, PhD); teacher education (M Ed, Credential). Electronic applications accepted.

UNIVERSITY OF CALIFORNIA, SANTA CRUZ, Santa Cruz, CA 95064

General Information State-supported, coed, university. CGS member. *Graduate housing:* Rooms and/or apartments available on a first-come, first-served basis to single and married students. Housing application deadline: 5/20. *Research affiliation:* Center for Biomimetic MicroElectronic Systems (science and engineering), Center for Information Technology Research in the Interest of Society (science and engineering), Institute for Regenerative Medicine (science and engineering), Center for Adaptive Optics (science and engineering), Center for Biomolecular Science and Engineering (science and engineering), Institute for Quantitative Biology (science and engineering).

GRADUATE UNITS

Division of Graduate Studies Electronic applications accepted.

Division of Humanities Offers history (MA, PhD); history of consciousness (PhD); humanities (MA, PhD); linguistics (MA, PhD); literature (MA, PhD); philosophy (MA, PhD). Electronic applications accepted.

Division of Physical and Biological Sciences Offers astronomy and astrophysics (PhD); chemistry and biochemistry (MS, PhD); earth and planetary sciences (MS, PhD); ecology and evolutionary biology (MA, PhD); environmental toxicology (MS, PhD); mathematics (MA, PhD); molecular, cellular, and developmental biology (MA, PhD); ocean sciences (MS, PhD); physical and biological sciences (MA, MS, PhD, Certificate); physics (MS, PhD); science communication (Certificate). Electronic applications accepted.

Division of Social Sciences Offers applied economics and finance (MS); cultural anthropology (PhD); education (MA, PhD); environmental studies (PhD); international economics (PhD); politics (PhD); psychology (PhD); social documentation (MA); social sciences (MA, MS, PhD); sociology (PhD). Electronic applications accepted.

Division of the Arts Offers arts (MA, MFA, DMA, PhD, Certificate); digital arts and new media (MFA); ethnomusicology (MA); film and digital media (PhD); music (PhD); music composition (MA, DMA); music composition (DMA); performance practice (MA); theater arts (Certificate); visual studies (PhD). Electronic applications accepted.

Jack Baskin School of Engineering Students: 537 full-time (134 women), 53 part-time (11 women); includes 87 minority (6 Black or African American, non-Hispanic/Latino; 3 American Indian or Alaska Native, non-Hispanic/Latino; 45 Asian, non-Hispanic/Latino; 25 Hispanic/Latino; 8 Native Hawaiian or other Pacific Islander, non-Hispanic/Latino),

318 international. 1,804 applicants, 40% accepted, 248 enrolled. Expenses: Contact institution. *Financial support:* Fellowships, research assistantships, teaching assistantships, institutionally sponsored loans, traineeships, health care benefits, and tuition waivers available. Financial award applicants required to submit FAFSA. In 2016, 116 master's, 35 doctorates awarded. *Program availability:* Part-time. Offers biomolecular engineering and bioinformatics (MS, PhD); computer engineering (MS, PhD); computer science (MS, PhD); electrical engineering (MS, PhD); engineering (MS, PhD); scientific computing and applied mathematics (MS); statistics and applied mathematics (MS, PhD); technology management (PhD). *Application fee:* $105 ($125 for international students). Electronic applications accepted. *Application Contact:* BSOE Graduate Advising Office, 831-459-3531, E-mail: bsoe-ga@rt.ucsc.edu. *Associate Dean of Graduate Studies*, Dr. Abel Rodriguez, E-mail: abel@soe.ucsc.edu.

UNIVERSITY OF CENTRAL ARKANSAS, Conway, AR 72035-0001

General Information State-supported, coed, university. CGS member. *Graduate housing:* Rooms and/or apartments available on a first-come, first-served basis to single and married students. Housing application deadline: 7/1. *Research affiliation:* 3M Corporation, State Farm Foundation (insurance), Arkansas Game and Fish Commission, Acxiom (math, computers), Arkansas Educational Television Network.

GRADUATE UNITS

Graduate School *Program availability:* Part-time, evening/weekend, online learning. Offers leadership studies (PhD).

College of Business Administration *Program availability:* Part-time, evening/weekend. Offers accounting (M Acc); business administration (M Acc, MBA).

College of Education *Program availability:* Part-time, evening/weekend, online learning. Offers collaborative instructional specialist (ages 0-8) (MSE); collaborative instructional specialist (grades 4-12) (MSE); college student personnel (MS); district-level administration (PMC); education (MAT, MS, MSE, Ed S, Graduate Certificate, PMC); educational leadership - district level (Ed S); gifted and talented education (Graduate Certificate); instructional facilitator (Graduate Certificate); instructional technology (MS); library media and information technology (MS); reading education (MSE); school counseling (MS); school leadership (MS); school-based leadership adult education program administration (PMC); school-based leadership building administration (PMC); school-based leadership curriculum administration (PMC); school-based leadership gifted and talented program administration (PMC); school-based leadership special education program administration (PMC); special education (MSE, Graduate Certificate); special education instructional specialist grades 4-12 (Graduate Certificate); special education instructional specialist P-4 (Graduate Certificate); teaching (MAT); teaching and learning (MSE). Electronic applications accepted.

College of Fine Arts and Communication *Program availability:* Part-time. Offers choral conducting (MM); creative writing (MFA); digital filmmaking (MFA); fine arts and communication (MFA, MM, PC); instrumental conducting (MM); music (PC); music education (MM); music theory (MM); performance (MM). Electronic applications accepted.

College of Health and Behavioral Sciences *Program availability:* Part-time, evening/weekend, online learning. Offers adult nurse practitioner (PMC); clinical nurse leader (PMC); clinical nurse specialist (MSN); communication sciences and disorders (PhD); community counseling (MS); counseling psychology (MS); family and consumer sciences (MS); family nurse practitioner (PMC); health and behavioral sciences (MS, MSN, DPT, PhD, PMC); health education (MS); kinesiology (MS); nurse educator (PMC); nurse practitioner (MSN); occupational therapy (MS); physical therapy (DPT, PhD); school psychology (MS, PhD, PMC); speech-language pathology (MS). Electronic applications accepted.

College of Liberal Arts *Program availability:* Part-time. Offers community and economic development (MS); English (MA); foreign languages (MA); geographic and information systems (MGIS, Graduate Certificate); geographic information systems (MGIS, Certificate); history (MA); liberal arts (MA, MGIS, MS, Certificate, Graduate Certificate). Electronic applications accepted.

College of Natural Sciences and Math *Program availability:* Part-time. Offers applied computing (MS); applied mathematics (MS); biological science (MS); math education (MA); natural sciences and math (MA, MS). Electronic applications accepted.

UNIVERSITY OF CENTRAL FLORIDA, Orlando, FL 32816

General Information State-supported, coed, university. CGS member. *Enrollment:* 64,321 graduate, professional, and undergraduate students; 3,943 full-time matriculated graduate/professional students (2,091 women), 3,783 part-time matriculated graduate/professional students (2,360 women). *Graduate faculty:* 1,578 full-time (675 women), 628 part-time/adjunct (335 women). Tuition, state resident: part-time $288.16 per credit hour. Tuition, nonresident: part-time $1071.31 per credit hour. *Graduate housing:* Room and/or apartments available on a first-come, first-served basis to single students; on-campus housing not available to married students. Housing application deadline: 3/1. *Student services:* Campus employment opportunities, campus safety program, career counseling, child daycare facilities, exercise/wellness program, free psychological counseling, grant writing training, international student services, low-cost health insurance, multicultural affairs office, services for students with disabilities, teacher training, writing training. *Library facilities:* University Library plus 1 other. *Collection:* Books: 1.5 million (physical), 156,190 (digital/electronic); Serial titles: 838 (physical), 52,337 (digital/electronic); Databases: 365. Weekly public service hours: 106; students can reserve study rooms.

Computer facilities: Computer purchase and lease plans are available. 4,154 computers available on campus for general student use. A campuswide network can be accessed from student residence rooms and from off campus. Online class registration is available.

Website: http://www.ucf.edu/

General Application Contact: Assistant Director, Graduate Admissions, 407-823-2766, Fax: 407-823-6442, E-mail: gradadmissions@ucf.edu.

GRADUATE UNITS

College of Arts and Humanities Students: 264 full-time (129 women), 231 part-time (131 women); includes 115 minority (22 Black or African American, non-Hispanic/Latino; 11 Asian, non-Hispanic/Latino; 72 Hispanic/Latino; 10 Two or more races, non-Hispanic/Latino), 37 international. Average age 31. 484 applicants, 64% accepted, 209 enrolled. *Faculty:* 312 full-time (152 women), 103 part-time/adjunct (54 women). Expenses: Contact institution. *Financial support:* In 2016–17, 115 students received support, including 39 fellowships with partial tuition reimbursements available (averaging $5,928 per year), 26 research assistantships with partial tuition reimbursements available (averaging $7,925 per year), 82 teaching assistantships with partial tuition reimbursements available (averaging $8,884 per year); career-related internships or fieldwork, Federal Work-Study, institutionally sponsored loans, scholarships/grants, health care benefits, tuition waivers (partial), and unspecified assistantships also available. Financial award application deadline: 3/1; financial award applicants required to submit FAFSA. In 2016, 155 master's, 7 doctorates, 38 other advanced degrees awarded. *Program availability:* Part-time, evening/weekend. Offers arts and humanities (MA, MFA, MS, PhD, Certificate); creative writing (MFA); English (MA, Certificate); ESOL endorsement K-12 (Certificate); history (MA); Spanish (MA); teaching English as a foreign language (Certificate); teaching English to speakers of other languages (MA, Certificate); texts and technology (PhD). *Application fee:* $30. Electronic applications accepted. *Application Contact:* Assistant Director, Graduate Admissions, 407-823-2766, Fax: 407-823-6442, E-mail: gradadmissions@ucf.edu. *Dean*, Dr. Jose Fernandez, 407-823-2573, E-mail: jose.fernandez@ucf.edu.

Florida Interactive Entertainment Academy Students: 70 full-time (17 women), 53 part-time (15 women); includes 36 minority (8 Black or African American, non-Hispanic/Latino; 5 Asian, non-Hispanic/Latino; 17 Hispanic/Latino; 6 Two or more races, non-Hispanic/Latino), 17 international. Average age 26. 138 applicants, 64% accepted, 70 enrolled. *Faculty:* 9 full-time (0 women), 3 part-time/adjunct (1 woman). Expenses: Contact institution. *Financial support:* Application deadline: 3/1; applicants required to submit FAFSA. In 2016, 63 master's awarded. Offers interactive entertainment (MS). *Application deadline:* For fall admission, 7/15 for domestic students. *Application fee:* $30. Electronic applications accepted. *Application Contact:* Assistant Director, Graduate Admissions, 407-823-2766, Fax: 407-823-6442, E-mail: gradadmissions@ucf.edu. *Executive Director*, Ben Noel, 407-235-3580, Fax: 407-317-7094, E-mail: bnoel@fiea.ucf.edu.

School of Performing Arts Students: 34 full-time (20 women), 18 part-time (10 women); includes 7 minority (5 Hispanic/Latino; 2 Two or more races, non-Hispanic/Latino), 5 international. Average age 31. 55 applicants, 51% accepted, 20 enrolled. *Faculty:* 53 full-time (20 women), 13 part-time/adjunct (6 women). Expenses: Contact institution. *Financial support:* In 2016–17, 28 students received support, including 6 fellowships with partial tuition reimbursements available (averaging $7,167 per year), 6 research assistantships with partial tuition reimbursements available (averaging $9,088 per year), 20 teaching assistantships with partial tuition reimbursements available (averaging $8,267 per year); career-related internships or fieldwork, Federal Work-Study, institutionally sponsored loans, tuition waivers (partial), and unspecified assistantships also available. Financial award application deadline: 3/1; financial award applicants required to submit FAFSA. In 2016, 18 master's awarded. *Program availability:* Part-time. Offers music (MA); theatre (MA, MFA). *Application deadline:* For fall admission, 7/15 for domestic students; for spring admission, 12/1 for domestic students. *Application fee:* $30. Electronic applications accepted. *Application Contact:* Assistant Director, Graduate Admissions, 407-823-2766, Fax: 407-823-6442, E-mail: gradadmissions@ucf.edu. *Interim Director*, Dr. Steven Chicurel-Stein, 407-823-2519, Fax: 407-823-3378, E-mail: steven.chicurel@ucf.edu.

School of Visual Arts and Design Students: 26 full-time (12 women), 13 part-time (3 women); includes 7 minority (3 Black or African American, non-Hispanic/Latino; 1 Asian, non-Hispanic/Latino; 3 Hispanic/Latino), 2 international. Average age 31. 49 applicants, 57% accepted, 19 enrolled. *Faculty:* 57 full-time (23 women), 15 part-time/adjunct (4 women). Expenses: Contact institution. *Financial support:* In 2016–17, 15 students received support, including 4 fellowships with partial tuition reimbursements available (averaging $10,000 per year), 2 research assistantships with partial tuition reimbursements available (averaging $3,214 per year), 13 teaching assistantships with partial tuition reimbursements available (averaging $7,570 per year); scholarships/grants and unspecified assistantships also available. Financial award application deadline: 3/1; financial award applicants required to submit FAFSA. In 2016, 7 master's awarded. *Program availability:* Part-time. Offers digital media (MA); emerging media (MFA). *Application deadline:* For fall admission, 7/1 for domestic students. *Application fee:* $30. Electronic applications accepted. *Application Contact:* Assistant Director, Graduate Admissions, 407-823-2766, Fax: 407-823-6442, E-mail: gradadmissions@ucf.edu. *Interim Director*, Dr. Rudy McDaniel, 407-823-3145, E-mail: rudy@ucf.edu.

College of Business Administration Students: 268 full-time (114 women), 614 part-time (285 women); includes 313 minority (68 Black or African American, non-Hispanic/Latino; 2 American Indian or Alaska Native, non-Hispanic/Latino; 62 Asian, non-Hispanic/Latino; 164 Hispanic/Latino; 17 Two or more races, non-Hispanic/Latino), 43 international. Average age 31. 808 applicants, 46% accepted, 297 enrolled. *Faculty:* 125 full-time (33 women), 21 part-time/adjunct (6 women). Expenses: Contact institution. *Financial support:* In 2016–17, 117 students received support, including 24 fellowships with partial tuition reimbursements available (averaging $4,811 per year), 42 research assistantships with partial tuition reimbursements available (averaging $8,319 per year), 64 teaching assistantships with partial tuition reimbursements available (averaging $13,403 per year); career-related internships or fieldwork, Federal Work-Study, institutionally sponsored loans, health care benefits, and tuition waivers (partial) also available. Financial award application deadline: 3/1; financial award applicants required to submit FAFSA. In 2016, 335 master's, 7 doctorates, 13 other advanced degrees awarded. *Program availability:* Part-time, evening/weekend. Offers business administration (MBA, MSA, MSBM, MSM, MSRE, MST, PhD, Graduate Certificate); entrepreneurship (Graduate Certificate); management (MSM); sport business management (MSBM); technology ventures (Graduate Certificate). *Application fee:* $30. Electronic applications accepted. *Application Contact:* Assistant Director, Graduate Admissions, 407-823-2776, Fax: 407-823-6442, E-mail: gradadmissions@ucf.edu. *Dean*, Dr. Paul Jarley, 407-823-5133, E-mail: pjarley@bus.ucf.edu.

Dr. P. Phillips School of Real Estate Students: 21 part-time (8 women); includes 10 minority (1 Black or African American, non-Hispanic/Latino; 4 Asian, non-Hispanic/Latino; 5 Hispanic/Latino). Average age 37. Expenses: Contact institution. *Financial support:* Application deadline: 3/1; applicants required to submit FAFSA. *Program availability:* Part-time. Offers real estate (MSRE). *Application deadline:* For fall admission, 7/1 for domestic students. *Application fee:* $30. Electronic applications accepted. *Application Contact:* Assistant Director, Graduate Admissions, 407-823-2776, Fax: 407-823-6442, E-mail: gradadmissions@ucf.edu. *Chair and Director*, Dr. Ajai Singh, 407-823-5756, Fax: 407-823-6676, E-mail: ajai.singh@ucf.edu.

Kenneth G. Dixon School of Accounting Students: 79 full-time (34 women), 83 part-time (42 women); includes 44 minority (17 Asian, non-Hispanic/Latino; 20 Hispanic/Latino; 7 Two or more races, non-Hispanic/Latino), 5 international. Average age 27. 109 applicants, 55% accepted, 47 enrolled. *Faculty:* 24 full-time (11 women), 3 part-time/adjunct (2 women). Expenses: Contact institution. *Financial support:* In 2016–17, 23 students received support, including 1 research assistantship with partial tuition reimbursement available (averaging $9,416 per year), 22 teaching assistantships with partial tuition reimbursements available (averaging $9,542 per year); fellowships, career-related internships or fieldwork, Federal Work-Study, institutionally sponsored loans, tuition waivers (partial), and unspecified assistantships also available. Financial award application deadline: 3/1; financial

University of Central Florida

award applicants required to submit FAFSA. In 2016, 68 master's awarded. *Program availability:* Part-time, evening/weekend. Offers accounting (MSA). *Application deadline:* For fall admission, 7/15 for domestic students; for spring admission, 12/1 for domestic students. *Application fee:* $30. Electronic applications accepted. *Application Contact:* Assistant Director, Graduate Admissions, 407-823-2776, Fax: 407-823-6442, E-mail: gradadmissions@ucf.edu. *Director,* Dr. Sean Robb, 407-823-2876, Fax: 407-823-3881, E-mail: srobb@ucf.edu.

College of Education and Human Performance Students: 639 full-time (485 women), 953 part-time (759 women); includes 524 minority (202 Black or African American, non-Hispanic/Latino; 3 American Indian or Alaska Native, non-Hispanic/Latino; 37 Asian, non-Hispanic/Latino; 256 Hispanic/Latino; 26 Two or more races, non-Hispanic/Latino), 38 international. Average age 32. 1,195 applicants, 58% accepted, 448 enrolled. *Faculty:* 137 full-time (91 women), 126 part-time/adjunct (91 women). Expenses: Contact institution. *Financial support:* In 2016–17, 140 students received support, including 48 fellowships with partial tuition reimbursements available (averaging $5,611 per year), 97 research assistantships with partial tuition reimbursements available (averaging $7,815 per year), 57 teaching assistantships with partial tuition reimbursements available (averaging $9,488 per year); career-related internships or fieldwork, Federal Work-Study, institutionally sponsored loans, health care benefits, tuition waivers (partial), and unspecified assistantships also available. Financial award application deadline: 3/1; financial award applicants required to submit FAFSA. In 2016, 431 master's, 81 doctorates, 176 other advanced degrees awarded. *Program availability:* Part-time, evening/weekend. Offers applied exercise physiology (MS); autism spectrum disorders (Certificate); career and technical education (MA); career counseling (Certificate); communication sciences and disorders (PhD); community college education (Certificate); counselor education (M Ed, MA, Certificate, Ed S); curriculum and instruction (Ed D); e-learning professional development (Certificate); early childhood development and education (MS); early childhood education (PhD); education and human performance (M Ed, MA, MAT, MS, Ed D, PhD, Certificate, Ed S); educational leadership (MA, Ed D, Ed S); elementary education (PhD); exceptional education (PhD); exceptional student education (M Ed, MA, Certificate); exceptional student education K-12 (MA); exercise physiology (PhD); higher education (PhD); instructional design and technology (MA, Certificate); instructional design for simulations (Certificate); instructional technology (PhD); instructional/educational technology (Certificate); intervention specialist (Certificate); marriage, couple, and family therapy (MA, Certificate); mathematics education (PhD); methodology, measurement and analysis (PhD); play therapy (Certificate); pre-kindergarten disabilities (Certificate); reading education (PhD); school psychology (Ed S); science education (PhD); severe or profound disabilities (Certificate); social science education (PhD); special education (Certificate); sport and exercise science (MS); TESOL (PhD). *Application fee:* $30. Electronic applications accepted. *Application Contact:* Assistant Director, Graduate Admissions, 407-823-2766, Fax: 407-823-6442, E-mail: gradadmissions@ucf.edu. *Dean,* Dr. Pamela S. Carroll, 407-823-1463, E-mail: pamela.carroll@ucf.edu.

School of Teaching, Learning, and Leadership Students: 75 full-time (64 women), 304 part-time (257 women); includes 125 minority (46 Black or African American, non-Hispanic/Latino; 2 American Indian or Alaska Native, non-Hispanic/Latino; 11 Asian, non-Hispanic/Latino; 59 Hispanic/Latino; 7 Two or more races, non-Hispanic/Latino), 4 international. Average age 32. 229 applicants, 76% accepted, 102 enrolled. *Faculty:* 72 full-time (53 women), 55 part-time/adjunct (42 women). Expenses: Contact institution. *Financial support:* In 2016–17, 2 students received support, including 2 research assistantships with partial tuition reimbursements available (averaging $9,463 per year); teaching assistantships, career-related internships or fieldwork, Federal Work-Study, institutionally sponsored loans, tuition waivers (partial), and unspecified assistantships also available. Financial award application deadline: 3/1; financial award applicants required to submit FAFSA. In 2016, 151 master's, 34 other advanced degrees awarded. *Program availability:* Part-time, evening/weekend. Offers applied learning and instruction (MA); art education (M Ed, MAT); educational and instructional technology (MA); educational leadership (Ed S); elementary education (M Ed, MA); English language (MAT); English language arts education (M Ed); K-8 mathematics and science education (M Ed, Certificate); mathematics education (MAT); middle school mathematics (MAT); middle school science (MAT); reading education (M Ed); science education (M Ed, MAT); social science education (M Ed, MAT); teacher education (MAT); teacher leadership (M Ed); teaching excellence (Certificate). *Application deadline:* For fall admission, 7/15 for domestic students; for spring admission, 12/15 for domestic students. *Application fee:* $30. Electronic applications accepted. *Application Contact:* Assistant Director, Graduate Admissions, 407-823-2766, Fax: 407-823-6442, E-mail: gradadmissions@ucf.edu. *Co-Director,* Dr. Michael Hynes, 407-823-6076, E-mail: michael.hynes@ucf.edu.

College of Engineering and Computer Science Students: 901 full-time (187 women), 548 part-time (134 women); includes 351 minority (62 Black or African American, non-Hispanic/Latino; 75 Asian, non-Hispanic/Latino; 191 Hispanic/Latino; 23 Two or more races, non-Hispanic/Latino), 623 international. Average age 30. 1,668 applicants, 67% accepted, 459 enrolled. *Faculty:* 175 full-time (27 women), 54 part-time/adjunct (2 women). Expenses: Contact institution. *Financial support:* In 2016–17, 512 students received support, including 127 fellowships with partial tuition reimbursements available (averaging $12,948 per year), 338 research assistantships with partial tuition reimbursements available (averaging $11,586 per year), 190 teaching assistantships with partial tuition reimbursements available (averaging $10,822 per year); career-related internships or fieldwork, Federal Work-Study, institutionally sponsored loans, tuition waivers (partial), and unspecified assistantships also available. Financial award application deadline: 3/1; financial award applicants required to submit FAFSA. In 2016, 388 master's, 89 doctorates, 22 other advanced degrees awarded. *Program availability:* Part-time, evening/weekend. Offers aerospace engineering (MSAE); civil engineering (MS, MSCE, PhD, Certificate); computer engineering (MS Cp E, PhD); computer science (MS, PhD); digital forensics (MS); electrical engineering (MSEE, PhD); engineering and computer science (MS, MS Cp E, MS Env E, MSAE, MSCE, MSEE, MSIE, MSME, MSMSE, PhD, Certificate); environmental engineering (MS, MS Env E, PhD); industrial engineering and management systems (MSIE, PhD, Certificate); materials science and engineering (MSMSE, PhD); mechanical engineering (MSME, PhD). *Application deadline:* For fall admission, 7/15 for domestic students; for spring admission, 12/1 for domestic students. *Application fee:* $30. Electronic applications accepted. *Application Contact:* Assistant Director, Graduate Admissions, 407-823-2766, Fax: 407-823-6442, E-mail: gradadmissions@ucf.edu. *Dean,* Dr. Michael Georgiopoulos, 407-823-2156, E-mail: michaelg@ucf.edu.

College of Graduate Studies Students: 79 full-time (37 women), 60 part-time (25 women); includes 46 minority (17 Black or African American, non-Hispanic/Latino; 7 Asian, non-Hispanic/Latino; 20 Hispanic/Latino; 2 Two or more races, non-Hispanic/Latino), 18 international. Average age 31. 200 applicants, 53% accepted, 76 enrolled. *Faculty:* 2 full-time (1 woman), 1 (woman) part-time/adjunct. Expenses:

Contact institution. *Financial support:* In 2016–17, 54 students received support, including 21 fellowships with partial tuition reimbursements available (averaging $15,162 per year), 54 research assistantships with partial tuition reimbursements available (averaging $8,483 per year), 13 teaching assistantships with partial tuition reimbursements available (averaging $12,754 per year). Financial award application deadline: 3/1; financial award applicants required to submit FAFSA. In 2016, 11 master's, 1 other advanced degree awarded. Offers geographic information systems (Certificate); interdisciplinary studies (MA, MS); modeling and simulation (MS, PhD, Certificate); nanotechnology (MS, PSM). *Application deadline:* For fall admission, 7/15 for domestic students; for spring admission, 12/1 for domestic students. *Application fee:* $30. Electronic applications accepted. *Application Contact:* Assistant Director, Graduate Admissions, 407-823-2766, Fax: 407-823-6442, E-mail: gradadmissions@ucf.edu. *Vice President for Research/Dean, College of Graduate Studies,* Dr. Elizabeth Klonoff, 407-823-6432, Fax: 407-823-6442, E-mail: elizabeth.klonoff@ucf.edu.

College of Health and Public Affairs Students: 827 full-time (645 women), 786 part-time (588 women); includes 696 minority (307 Black or African American, non-Hispanic/Latino; 5 American Indian or Alaska Native, non-Hispanic/Latino; 76 Asian, non-Hispanic/Latino; 272 Hispanic/Latino; 3 Native Hawaiian or other Pacific Islander, non-Hispanic/Latino; 33 Two or more races, non-Hispanic/Latino), 26 international. Average age 30. 1,284 applicants, 59% accepted, 484 enrolled. *Faculty:* 183 full-time (103 women), 125 part-time/adjunct (71 women). Expenses: Contact institution. *Financial support:* In 2016–17, 74 students received support, including 26 fellowships with partial tuition reimbursements available (averaging $7,179 per year), 45 research assistantships with partial tuition reimbursements available (averaging $8,187 per year), 25 teaching assistantships with partial tuition reimbursements available (averaging $8,242 per year); career-related internships or fieldwork, Federal Work-Study, institutionally sponsored loans, traineeships, tuition waivers (partial), and unspecified assistantships also available. Financial award application deadline: 3/1; financial award applicants required to submit FAFSA. In 2016, 534 master's, 45 doctorates, 76 other advanced degrees awarded. *Program availability:* Part-time, evening/weekend. Offers communication sciences and disorders (MA); corrections leadership (Certificate); criminal justice (MS, PhD); health and public affairs (MA, MNM, MPA, MRA, MS, MSW, DPT, PhD, Certificate); health care informatics (MS); health information administration (Certificate); health services administration (MS); juvenile justice leadership (Certificate); medical speech-language pathology (Certificate); physical therapy (DPT); police leadership (Certificate); public affairs (PhD); research administration (MRA, Certificate). *Application fee:* $30. Electronic applications accepted. *Application Contact:* Assistant Director, Graduate Admissions, 407-823-2766, Fax: 407-823-6442, E-mail: gradadmissions@ucf.edu. *Dean,* Dr. Michael Frumkin, 407-823-6424, E-mail: michael.frumkin@ucf.edu.

School of Public Administration Students: 87 full-time (60 women), 257 part-time (190 women); includes 157 minority (83 Black or African American, non-Hispanic/Latino; 1 American Indian or Alaska Native, non-Hispanic/Latino; 9 Asian, non-Hispanic/Latino; 62 Hispanic/Latino; 2 Two or more races, non-Hispanic/Latino), 7 international. Average age 32. 192 applicants, 79% accepted, 108 enrolled. *Faculty:* 24 full-time (11 women), 11 part-time/adjunct (6 women). Expenses: Contact institution. *Financial support:* In 2016–17, 9 students received support, including 1 fellowship with partial tuition reimbursement available (averaging $4,000 per year), 9 research assistantships with partial tuition reimbursements available (averaging $6,704 per year); career-related internships or fieldwork, Federal Work-Study, institutionally sponsored loans, tuition waivers (partial), and unspecified assistantships also available. Financial award application deadline: 3/1; financial award applicants required to submit FAFSA. In 2016, 118 master's, 36 other advanced degrees awarded. *Program availability:* Part-time, evening/weekend. Offers emergency management and homeland security (Certificate); fundraising (Certificate); non-profit management (MNM, Certificate); urban and regional planning (MS). *Application deadline:* For fall admission, 6/15 for domestic students; for spring admission, 11/1 for domestic students. *Application fee:* $30. Electronic applications accepted. *Application Contact:* Assistant Director, Graduate Admissions, 407-823-2766, Fax: 407-823-6442, E-mail: gradadmissions@ucf.edu. *Director,* Dr. Naim Kapucu, 407-823-3693, Fax: 407-823-5651, E-mail: naim.kapucu@ucf.edu.

School of Social Work Students: 171 full-time (155 women), 160 part-time (141 women); includes 148 minority (70 Black or African American, non-Hispanic/Latino; 4 Asian, non-Hispanic/Latino; 61 Hispanic/Latino; 2 Native Hawaiian or other Pacific Islander, non-Hispanic/Latino; 11 Two or more races, non-Hispanic/Latino), 1 international. Average age 30. 289 applicants, 60% accepted, 119 enrolled. *Faculty:* 28 full-time (24 women), 23 part-time/adjunct (15 women). Expenses: Contact institution. *Financial support:* In 2016–17, 3 students received support, including 1 fellowship with partial tuition reimbursement available (averaging $1,000 per year), 2 research assistantships with partial tuition reimbursements available (averaging $4,536 per year); career-related internships or fieldwork, institutionally sponsored loans, and unspecified assistantships also available. Financial award application deadline: 3/1; financial award applicants required to submit FAFSA. In 2016, 127 master's, 15 other advanced degrees awarded. *Program availability:* Part-time, evening/weekend. Offers military social work (Certificate); social work (MSW). *Application deadline:* For fall admission, 4/1 for domestic students. *Application fee:* $30. Electronic applications accepted. *Application Contact:* Assistant Director, Graduate Admissions, 407-823-2766, Fax: 407-823-6442, E-mail: gradadmissions@ucf.edu. *Director,* Dr. Bonnie Yegidis, 407-823-2114, E-mail: bonnie.yegidis@ucf.edu.

College of Medicine Expenses: Contact institution. *Financial support:* Fellowships, research assistantships, and teaching assistantships available. Offers medicine (MS, MD, PhD). *Application Contact:* Assistant Director, Graduate Admissions, 407-823-2766, Fax: 407-823-6442, E-mail: gradadmissions@ucf.edu. *Vice President for Medical Affairs/Dean,* Dr. Deborah C. German, 407-266-1000, E-mail: deborah.german@ucf.edu.

Burnett School of Biomedical Sciences Students: 86 full-time (49 women), 12 part-time (8 women); includes 32 minority (11 Black or African American, non-Hispanic/Latino; 5 Asian, non-Hispanic/Latino; 15 Hispanic/Latino; 1 Two or more races, non-Hispanic/Latino), 23 international. Average age 27. 123 applicants, 60% accepted, 46 enrolled. *Faculty:* 67 full-time (28 women), 7 part-time/adjunct (3 women). Expenses: Contact institution. *Financial support:* In 2016–17, 49 students received support, including 8 fellowships with partial tuition reimbursements available (averaging $5,411 per year), 41 research assistantships with partial tuition reimbursements available (averaging $6,925 per year), 36 teaching assistantships with partial tuition reimbursements available (averaging $8,129 per year). Financial award application deadline: 3/1; financial award applicants required to submit FAFSA. In 2016, 21 master's, 9 doctorates awarded. Offers biomedical sciences (MS, PhD); biotechnology (MS). *Application deadline:* For fall admission, 1/15 for domestic students. *Application fee:* $30. Electronic applications accepted. *Application Contact:*

Assistant Director, Graduate Admissions, 407-823-2766, Fax: 407-823-6442, E-mail: gradadmissions@ucf.edu. *Director*, Dr. Griffith Parks, 407-226-1000, E-mail: griffith.parks@ucf.edu.

College of Nursing Students: 52 full-time (46 women), 290 part-time (256 women); includes 92 minority (27 Black or African American, non-Hispanic/Latino; 3 American Indian or Alaska Native, non-Hispanic/Latino; 13 Asian, non-Hispanic/Latino; 44 Hispanic/Latino; 1 Native Hawaiian or other Pacific Islander, non-Hispanic/Latino; 4 Two or more races, non-Hispanic/Latino), 1 international. Average age 37. 273 applicants, 51% accepted, 111 enrolled. *Faculty:* 58 full-time (50 women), 63 part-time/adjunct (61 women). Expenses: Contact institution. *Financial support:* In 2016–17, 24 students received support, including 23 fellowships with partial tuition reimbursements available (averaging $10,156 per year), 1 research assistantship with partial tuition reimbursement available (averaging $12,096 per year); career-related internships or fieldwork, Federal Work-Study, institutionally sponsored loans, traineeships, and unspecified assistantships also available. Financial award application deadline: 3/1; financial award applicants required to submit FAFSA. In 2016, 100 master's, 24 doctorates, 2 other advanced degrees awarded. *Program availability:* Part-time, evening/weekend. Offers nursing (MSN, DNP, PhD, Post-Master's Certificate). *Application deadline:* For fall admission, 2/15 for domestic students; for spring admission, 9/15 for domestic students. *Application fee:* $30. Electronic applications accepted. *Application Contact:* Assistant Director, Graduate Admissions, 407-823-2766, Fax: 407-823-6442, E-mail: gradadmissions@ucf.edu. *Dean*, Dr. Mary Lou Sole, 407-823-5496, Fax: 407-823-5675, E-mail: mary.sole@ucf.edu.

College of Optics and Photonics Students: 107 full-time (17 women), 8 part-time (0 women); includes 10 minority (4 Asian, non-Hispanic/Latino; 5 Hispanic/Latino; 1 Two or more races, non-Hispanic/Latino), 74 international. Average age 27. 194 applicants, 39% accepted, 35 enrolled. *Faculty:* 40 full-time (5 women), 8 part-time/adjunct (1 woman). Expenses: Contact institution. *Financial support:* In 2016–17, 96 students received support, including 31 fellowships with partial tuition reimbursements available (averaging $18,839 per year), 72 research assistantships with partial tuition reimbursements available (averaging $15,627 per year), 11 teaching assistantships with partial tuition reimbursements available (averaging $12,023 per year); career-related internships or fieldwork, Federal Work-Study, institutionally sponsored loans, tuition waivers (partial), and unspecified assistantships also available. Financial award application deadline: 3/1; financial award applicants required to submit FAFSA. In 2016, 24 master's, 17 doctorates awarded. *Program availability:* Part-time, evening/weekend. Offers optics and photonics (MS, PhD). *Application deadline:* For fall admission, 7/15 for domestic students; for spring admission, 12/1 for domestic students. *Application fee:* $30. Electronic applications accepted. *Application Contact:* Assistant Director, Graduate Admissions, 407-823-2766, Fax: 407-823-6442, E-mail: gradadmissions@ucf.edu. *Dean and Director*, Dr. Bahaa E. Saleh, 407-823-6817, E-mail: besaleh@creol.ucf.edu.

College of Sciences Students: 660 full-time (345 women), 159 part-time (88 women); includes 197 minority (40 Black or African American, non-Hispanic/Latino; 3 American Indian or Alaska Native, non-Hispanic/Latino; 44 Asian, non-Hispanic/Latino; 92 Hispanic/Latino; 18 Two or more races, non-Hispanic/Latino), 161 international. Average age 29. 1,169 applicants, 40% accepted, 266 enrolled. *Faculty:* 360 full-time (127 women), 59 part-time/adjunct (24 women). Expenses: Contact institution. *Financial support:* In 2016–17, 509 students received support, including 127 fellowships with partial tuition reimbursements available (averaging $8,668 per year), 147 research assistantships with partial tuition reimbursements available (averaging $12,200 per year), 382 teaching assistantships with partial tuition reimbursements available (averaging $11,425 per year); health care benefits also available. Financial award application deadline: 3/1; financial award applicants required to submit FAFSA. In 2016, 204 master's, 57 doctorates, 23 other advanced degrees awarded. Offers anthropology (MA); applied experimental and human factors psychology (MA, PhD); applied sociology (MA); biology (MS); chemistry (MS, PhD); clinical psychology (MA, PhD); computer forensics (Certificate); conservation biology (PhD, Certificate); data mining (MS); industrial/organizational psychology (MS, PhD); intelligence and national security (Certificate); mathematical science (MS, Certificate); mathematics (PhD); Maya studies (Certificate); physics (MS, PhD); political science (MA); SAS data mining (Certificate); sciences (MA, MS, PhD, Certificate); security studies (PhD); sociology (PhD); statistical computing (MS). *Application fee:* $30. Electronic applications accepted. *Application Contact:* Assistant Director, Graduate Admissions, 407-823-2766, Fax: 407-823-6442, E-mail: gradadmissions@ucf.edu. *Dean*, Dr. Michael Johnson, 407-823-1911, E-mail: michael.johnson@ucf.edu.

Nicholson School of Communication Students: 34 full-time (24 women), 21 part-time (16 women); includes 19 minority (7 Black or African American, non-Hispanic/Latino; 10 Hispanic/Latino; 2 Two or more races, non-Hispanic/Latino), 11 international. Average age 27. 41 applicants, 83% accepted, 29 enrolled. *Faculty:* 46 full-time (21 women), 17 part-time/adjunct (11 women). Expenses: Contact institution. *Financial support:* In 2016–17, 20 students received support, including 1 fellowship with partial tuition reimbursement available (averaging $4,000 per year), 5 research assistantships with partial tuition reimbursements available (averaging $6,742 per year), 15 teaching assistantships with partial tuition reimbursements available (averaging $9,141 per year); career-related internships or fieldwork, Federal Work-Study, institutionally sponsored loans, tuition waivers (partial), and unspecified assistantships also available. Financial award application deadline: 3/1; financial award applicants required to submit FAFSA. In 2016, 26 master's, 12 other advanced degrees awarded. *Program availability:* Part-time, evening/weekend. Offers communication (MA); corporate communication (Certificate). *Application deadline:* For fall admission, 6/1 for domestic students; for spring admission, 11/1 for domestic students. *Application fee:* $30. Electronic applications accepted. *Application Contact:* Assistant Director, Graduate Admissions, 407-823-2766, Fax: 407-823-6442, E-mail: gradadmissions@ucf.edu. *Acting Director*, Dr. Arlen Chase, 407-823-2316, E-mail: arlen.chase@ucf.edu.

Rosen College of Hospitality Management Students: 60 full-time (37 women), 122 part-time (86 women); includes 47 minority (21 Black or African American, non-Hispanic/Latino; 1 American Indian or Alaska Native, non-Hispanic/Latino; 3 Asian, non-Hispanic/Latino; 17 Hispanic/Latino; 5 Two or more races, non-Hispanic/Latino), 20 international. Average age 30. 180 applicants, 62% accepted, 73 enrolled. *Faculty:* 63 full-time (28 women), 38 part-time/adjunct (11 women). Expenses: Contact institution. *Financial support:* In 2016–17, 16 students received support, including 2 fellowships with partial tuition reimbursements available (averaging $4,500 per year), 16 teaching assistantships with partial tuition reimbursements available (averaging $13,994 per year); research assistantships also available. Financial award application deadline: 3/1; financial award applicants required to submit FAFSA. In 2016, 15 master's, 2 doctorates, 2 other advanced degrees awarded. *Program availability:* Part-time. Offers destination marketing and management (Certificate); event management (Certificate); hospitality and tourism management (MS); hospitality management (PhD). *Application deadline:* For fall admission, 7/15 for domestic students; for spring admission, 12/1 for domestic

students. *Application fee:* $30. Electronic applications accepted. *Application Contact:* Assistant Director, Graduate Admissions, 407-823-2766, Fax: 407-823-6442, E-mail: gradadmissions@ucf.edu. *Dean*, Dr. Abraham C. Pizam, 407-903-8010, E-mail: abraham.pizam@ucf.edu.

UNIVERSITY OF CENTRAL MISSOURI, Warrensburg, MO 64093

General Information State-supported, coed, comprehensive institution. CGS member. *Graduate housing:* Rooms and/or apartments available on a first-come, first-served basis to single and married students. Housing application deadline: 8/1.

GRADUATE UNITS

The Graduate School *Program availability:* Part-time, 100% online, blended/hybrid learning. Offers accountancy (MA); accounting (MBA); applied mathematics (MS); aviation safety (MS); biology (MS); business administration (MBA); career and technical education leadership (MS); college student personnel administration (MS); communication (MA); computer science (MS); counseling (MS); criminal justice (MS); educational leadership (Ed D); educational technology (MS); elementary and early childhood education (MSE); English (MA); environmental studies (MA); finance (MBA); history (MA); human services/educational technology (Ed S); human services/learning resources (Ed S); human services/professional counseling (Ed S); industrial hygiene (MS); industrial management (MS); information systems (MBA); information technology (MS); kinesiology (MS); library science and information services (MS); literacy education (MSE); marketing (MBA); mathematics (MS); music (MS); occupational safety management (MS); psychology (MS); rural family nursing (MS); school administration (MSE); social gerontology (MS); sociology (MS); special education (MSE); speech language pathology (MS); superintendency (Ed S); teaching (MAT); teaching English as a second language (MA); technology (MS); technology management (PhD); theatre (MA). Electronic applications accepted.

UNIVERSITY OF CENTRAL OKLAHOMA, Edmond, OK 73034-5209

General Information State-supported, coed, comprehensive institution. CGS member. *Graduate housing:* Rooms and/or apartments available on a first-come, first-served basis to single and married students. Housing application deadline: 7/1. *Research affiliation:* National Science Foundation, U.S. Department of Education (DOE), U.S. Department of Veteran Affairs, Oklahoma Department of Human Services, Oklahoma Idea Network of Biomedical Research Excellence, Oklahoma Small Business Administration.

GRADUATE UNITS

The Jackson College of Graduate Studies *Program availability:* Part-time, evening/weekend. Electronic applications accepted.

College of Business *Program availability:* Part-time. Offers accounting (MBA); management (MBA). Electronic applications accepted.

College of Education and Professional Studies *Program availability:* Part-time. Offers adult and higher education (M Ed); athletic training (MS); bilingual education/teaching English as a second language (M Ed); counseling psychology (MA); early childhood education (M Ed); education and professional studies (M Ed, MA, MS); educational leadership (M Ed); elementary education (M Ed); experimental psychology (MA); family and child studies (MS); forensic psychology (MA); general psychology (MA); library media education (M Ed); nutrition-food management (MS); reading (M Ed); school counseling (MS); school psychology (MA); secondary education (M Ed); special education (M Ed); speech-language pathology (MS); wellness management (MS). Electronic applications accepted.

College of Fine Arts and Design *Program availability:* Part-time, evening/weekend, online learning. Offers design (MFA); fine arts and design (MFA, MM); jazz (MM); music (MM). Electronic applications accepted.

College of Liberal Arts *Program availability:* Part-time. Offers creative writing (MA, MFA); crime and intelligence analysis (MA); criminal justice management and administration (MA); gerontology (MA); history (MA); international affairs (MA); liberal arts (MA, MFA, MPA); museum studies (MA); political science (MA); public administration (MPA); sociology (MA); traditional studies (MA). Electronic applications accepted.

College of Mathematics and Science *Program availability:* Part-time. Offers applied mathematical sciences (MS); biology (MS); biomedical engineering (MS); electrical engineering (MS); mathematics and science (MS); mechanical systems (MS); nursing (MS); physics (MS). Electronic applications accepted.

Forensic Science Institute Offers biology/chemistry (MS); forensic science (MS). Electronic applications accepted.

UNIVERSITY OF CHARLESTON, Charleston, WV 25304-1099

General Information Independent, coed, comprehensive institution. *Enrollment:* 2,425 graduate, professional, and undergraduate students; 631 full-time matriculated graduate/professional students (293 women), 33 part-time matriculated graduate/professional students (10 women). *Enrollment by degree level:* 285 master's, 379 doctoral. *Graduate faculty:* 40 full-time (28 women), 20 part-time/adjunct (3 women). *Tuition:* Full-time $20,602; part-time $425 per credit. *Required fees:* $200. Tuition and fees vary according to course load, campus/location, program and student level. *Graduate housing:* Rooms and/or apartments available on a first-come, first-served basis to single and married students. Typical cost: $4250 per year for single students; $4500 per year for married students. Room charges vary according to board plan, campus/location and housing facility selected. *Student services:* Campus employment opportunities, campus safety program, career counseling, free psychological counseling, international student services, low-cost health insurance, services for students with disabilities. *Library facilities:* Schoenbaum Library plus 1 other. *Collection:* Books: 189,000 (physical), 210,000 (digital/electronic); Databases: 56. Students can reserve study rooms. *Research affiliation:* Walmart (pharmacy).

Computer facilities: 200 computers available on campus for general student use. A campuswide network can be accessed from student residence rooms and from off campus. Online class registration is available.
Website: http://www.ucwv.edu/

General Application Contact: Sandy Dolin, Application Coordinator, 800-357-4752, Fax: 304-357-4750, E-mail: admissions@ucwv.edu.

GRADUATE UNITS

Doctor of Executive Leadership Program Students: 86 full-time (30 women), 15 part-time (6 women); includes 17 minority (13 Black or African American, non-Hispanic/Latino; 1 American Indian or Alaska Native, non-Hispanic/Latino; 1 Asian, non-Hispanic/Latino; 2 Hispanic/Latino). Average age 46. Expenses: Contact institution. *Financial support:* Unspecified assistantships available. In 2016, 2 doctorates awarded. Offers leadership (DEL). *Application deadline:* Applications are processed on a rolling basis. Electronic applications accepted. *Application Contact:* David Cooper,

Applications Coordinator, 304-352-0013, E-mail: davidcooper@ucwv.edu. *Program Director*, Dr. Ruth Wylie, E-mail: ruthwylie@ucwv.edu.

Master of Business Administration Program Students: 51 full-time (20 women); includes 6 minority (5 Black or African American, non-Hispanic/Latino; 1 Two or more races, non-Hispanic/Latino), 5 international. Average age 31. Expenses: Contact institution. *Financial support:* Scholarships/grants and unspecified assistantships available. Financial award application deadline: 3/1; financial award applicants required to submit FAFSA. In 2016, 36 master's awarded. *Program availability:* Part-time, evening/weekend. Offers business administration (MBA). *Application deadline:* Applications are processed on a rolling basis. *Application fee:* $50. Electronic applications accepted. *Application Contact:* Bobby Redd, Admissions Representative, 304-860-5621, E-mail: bobbyredd@ucwv.edu. *Program Director*, Rick Ferris, 304-720-6680, E-mail: mba@ucwv.edu.

Master of Forensic Accounting Program Students: 23 full-time (16 women); includes 4 minority (2 Black or African American, non-Hispanic/Latino; 1 Hispanic/Latino; 1 Native Hawaiian or other Pacific Islander, non-Hispanic/Latino), 1 international. Average age 36. Expenses: Contact institution. *Financial support:* Applicants required to submit FAFSA. *Program availability:* Part-time, blended/hybrid learning. Offers forensic accounting (EMFA). *Application deadline:* Applications are processed on a rolling basis. *Application fee:* $50. Electronic applications accepted. *Application Contact:* Bobby Redd, Admissions Representative, 304-860-5621, E-mail: bobbyredd@ucwv.edu. *Program Director*, Christina Chard, 304-352-0033, E-mail: christinachard@ucwv.edu.

Master of Science in Strategic Leadership Program Students: 136 full-time (35 women), 18 part-time (4 women); includes 25 minority (18 Black or African American, non-Hispanic/Latino; 4 Hispanic/Latino; 1 Native Hawaiian or other Pacific Islander, non-Hispanic/Latino; 2 Two or more races, non-Hispanic/Latino), 1 international. Average age 38. Expenses: Contact institution. In 2016, 36 master's awarded. Offers strategic leadership (MS). *Application deadline:* Applications are processed on a rolling basis. Electronic applications accepted. *Application Contact:* David Cooper, Admissions Representative, 304-352-0013, E-mail: davidcooper@ucwv.edu. *Associate Dean of Leadership*, Dr. John Barnette, 304-720-6688, E-mail: johnbarnette@ucwv.edu.

Physician Assistant Program Students: 57 full-time (42 women); includes 1 minority (Two or more races, non-Hispanic/Latino). Average age 26. Expenses: Contact institution. *Financial support:* Career-related internships or fieldwork available. In 2016, 20 master's awarded. Offers physician assistant (MPAS). *Application deadline:* Applications are processed on a rolling basis. Electronic applications accepted. *Application Contact:* Pam Carden, Admissions Coordinator, 304-357-4968, E-mail: pamcarden@ucwv.edu. *Program Director*, Jennifer Pack, 304-357-4790, E-mail: jenniferpack@ucwv.edu.

School of Pharmacy Students: 277 full-time (149 women); includes 107 minority (49 Black or African American, non-Hispanic/Latino; 1 American Indian or Alaska Native, non-Hispanic/Latino; 39 Asian, non-Hispanic/Latino; 13 Hispanic/Latino; 1 Native Hawaiian or other Pacific Islander, non-Hispanic/Latino; 4 Two or more races, non-Hispanic/Latino), 10 international. Average age 27. Expenses: Contact institution. *Financial support:* Career-related internships or fieldwork and scholarships/grants available. Financial award applicants required to submit FAFSA. Offers pharmacy (Pharm D). *Application deadline:* Applications are processed on a rolling basis. Electronic applications accepted. *Application Contact:* Stacie Geise, Director of Recruitment and Admissions, 304-357-4889, Fax: 304-357-4868, E-mail: staciegeise@ucwv.edu. *Dean*, Dr. Michelle Easton, 304-357-4889, Fax: 304-357-4868, E-mail: michelleeaston@ucwv.edu.

UNIVERSITY OF CHICAGO, Chicago, IL 60637-1513

General Information Independent, coed, university. CGS member. *Enrollment:* 13,322 graduate, professional, and undergraduate students; 6,858 full-time matriculated graduate/professional students (2,925 women), 2,077 part-time matriculated graduate/professional students (509 women). *Enrollment by degree level:* 5,841 master's, 3,094 doctoral. *Graduate faculty:* 2,215 full-time (752 women), 519 part-time/adjunct (187 women). *Graduate housing:* Rooms and/or apartments available on a first-come, first-served basis to single and married students. *Student services:* Campus employment opportunities, campus safety program, career counseling, exercise/wellness program, free psychological counseling, grant writing training, international student services, low-cost health insurance, multicultural affairs office, services for students with disabilities, teacher training, writing training. *Library facilities:* Joseph Regenstein Library plus 5 others. *Collection:* Books: 9.6 million (physical), 1.4 million (digital/electronic); Databases: 1,337. *Research affiliation:* National Opinion Research Center (social science), Fermilab (high-energy physics), Argonne National Laboratory (energy, materials), Marine Biological Laboratory (molecular biology), Fermilab (high-energy physics), Argonne National Laboratory (energy, materials).

Computer facilities: Computer purchase and lease plans are available. 300 computers available on campus for general student use. A campuswide network can be accessed from student residence rooms and from off campus. Online class registration is available.

Website: http://www.uchicago.edu/

General Application Contact: Program Coordinator, Graduate Enrollment and Initiatives, 773-702-3760, Fax: 773-702-4199, E-mail: gradadmissions@uchicago.edu.

GRADUATE UNITS

Booth School of Business Students: 1,416 full-time (510 women), 1,627 part-time (395 women). *Faculty:* 158 full-time (22 women), 16 part-time/adjunct (3 women). Expenses: Contact institution. *Financial support:* Fellowships and scholarships/grants available. Financial award applicants required to submit FAFSA. In 2016, 1,349 master's, 25 doctorates awarded. *Program availability:* Part-time, evening/weekend. Offers accounting (MBA); analytic finance (MBA); analytic management (MBA); business (MBA, PhD, Certificate); business administration (MBA, Certificate); econometrics and statistics (MBA); economics (MBA); entrepreneurship (MBA); executive business administration (MBA); finance (MBA); general management (MBA); health administration and policy (Certificate); international business (MBA); managerial and organizational behavior (MBA); marketing analytics (MBA); marketing management (MBA); operations management (MBA); strategic management (MBA). Electronic applications accepted. *Application Contact:* Admissions, 773-702-7369, E-mail: admissions@chicagobooth.edu. *Interim Dean*, Douglas J. Skinner, 773-702-1680, E-mail: dskinner@chicagobooth.edu.

Divinity School Students: 305 full-time (119 women), 11 part-time (5 women); includes 41 minority (17 Black or African American, non-Hispanic/Latino; 16 Asian, non-Hispanic/Latino; 4 Hispanic/Latino; 4 Two or more races, non-Hispanic/Latino), 44 international. 381 applicants, 51% accepted, 93 enrolled. *Faculty:* 30 full-time (7 women), 3 part-time/adjunct (0 women). Expenses: Contact institution. *Financial support:* In 2016–17, 305 students received support, including 21 fellowships with tuition reimbursements available (averaging $24,000 per year); career-related internships or fieldwork, Federal Work-Study, institutionally sponsored loans, scholarships/grants, health care benefits, and tuition waivers (full and partial) also available. Support available to part-time students. Financial award application deadline: 12/15; financial award applicants required to submit FAFSA. In 2016, 59 master's, 12 doctorates awarded. *Program availability:* Part-time. Offers anthropology and sociology of religions (PhD); Bible (PhD); divinity (M Div, MA, PhD); history of Christianity (PhD); history of Judaism (PhD); history of religions (PhD); Islamic studies (PhD); ministry (M Div); philosophy of religions (PhD); religion (MA, PhD); religion, literature, and visual culture (PhD); religions in America (PhD); religious ethics (PhD); religious studies (MA); theology (PhD). *Application deadline:* For fall admission, 12/15 for domestic and international students. *Application fee:* $75. Electronic applications accepted. *Application Contact:* John W. Howell, Coordinator for Recruiting and Admissions, 773-702-8249, Fax: 773-834-4581, E-mail: divinityadmissions@uchicago.edu. *Dean/Associate Professor of Religion and Literature*, Dr. Richard A. Rosengarten, 773-702-8200.

Division of the Biological Sciences Students: 415 full-time (187 women), 24 part-time (13 women); includes 99 minority (17 Black or African American, non-Hispanic/Latino; 44 Asian, non-Hispanic/Latino; 32 Hispanic/Latino; 1 Native Hawaiian or other Pacific Islander, non-Hispanic/Latino; 5 Two or more races, non-Hispanic/Latino), 77 international. 1,161 applicants, 21% accepted, 99 enrolled. *Faculty:* 195 full-time (59 women), 7 part-time/adjunct (0 women). Expenses: Contact institution. *Financial support:* Fellowships, research assistantships with full tuition reimbursements, institutionally sponsored loans, scholarships/grants, traineeships, and health care benefits available. Financial award applicants required to submit FAFSA. In 2016, 29 master's, 65 doctorates awarded. Offers biochemistry and molecular biology (PhD); biological sciences (MS, PhD); cancer biology (PhD); cell and molecular biology (PhD); computational neuroscience (PhD); development, regeneration, and stem cell biology (PhD); ecology and evolution (PhD); evolutionary biology (PhD); genetics, genomics and systems biology (PhD); human genetics (PhD); immunology (PhD); integrative biology (PhD); medical physics (PhD); microbiology (PhD); molecular metabolism and nutrition (PhD); neurobiology (PhD); public health sciences (MS, PhD). *Application deadline:* For fall admission, 12/1 for domestic and international students. *Application fee:* $90. Electronic applications accepted. *Application Contact:* E-mail: bsd.ogpa@lists.uchicago.edu. *Dean and Executive Vice President for Medical Affairs*, Kenneth Polonsky, MD.

Division of the Humanities Students: 793 full-time (389 women), 8 part-time (4 women); includes 110 minority (20 Black or African American, non-Hispanic/Latino; 4 American Indian or Alaska Native, non-Hispanic/Latino; 28 Asian, non-Hispanic/Latino; 40 Hispanic/Latino; 18 Two or more races, non-Hispanic/Latino), 205 international. 2,122 applicants, 24% accepted, 420 enrolled. *Faculty:* 243 full-time (101 women), 47 part-time/adjunct (19 women). Expenses: Contact institution. *Financial support:* Fellowships, teaching assistantships, career-related internships or fieldwork, Federal Work-Study, institutionally sponsored loans, scholarships/grants, health care benefits, and tuition waivers (full and partial) available. Financial award application deadline: 12/15; financial award applicants required to submit FAFSA. In 2016, 145 master's, 66 doctorates awarded. Offers ancient Greek and Roman philosophy (PhD); ancient Mediterranean world (PhD); ancient philosophy (PhD); anthropology and linguistics (PhD); art history (MA); cinema and media studies (PhD); classic languages (MA); classical languages and literatures (PhD); comparative literature (PhD); composition (MA); creative writing (MA); cultural policy studies (MA); digital humanities (MA); East Asian languages and civilizations (PhD); English language and literature (PhD); ethnomusicology (PhD); French and Francophone studies (PhD); gender and sexuality studies (MA); Germanic studies (PhD); Hispanic and Luso-Brazilian studies (PhD); humanities (MA, MFA, PhD); Italian studies (PhD); linguistics (MA, PhD); music (MA); music history and theory (PhD); near Eastern languages and civilizations (MA); Near Eastern languages and civilizations (PhD); philosophy (MA, PhD); poetics (MA); race, politics and culture (MA); Renaissance and early modern studies (PhD); Romance languages and literatures (MA); Slavic languages and literatures (MA); South Asian languages and civilizations (MA, PhD); theater and performance studies (MA); transformations in the classical tradition (PhD); visual arts (MFA). *Application deadline:* For fall admission, 12/15 for domestic and international students. *Application fee:* $90. Electronic applications accepted. *Application Contact:* Michael Beetley, Assistant Dean of Students, 773-702-1552, Fax: 773-834-9148, E-mail: humanitiesadmissions@uchicago.edu. *Dean of Students*, Martina Munsters, 770-702-3636, E-mail: mmunster@uchicago.edu.

Division of the Physical Sciences Students: 841 full-time (198 women), 119 part-time (21 women); includes 95 minority (9 Black or African American, non-Hispanic/Latino; 60 Asian, non-Hispanic/Latino; 19 Hispanic/Latino; 7 Two or more races, non-Hispanic/Latino), 502 international. 5,379 applicants, 24% accepted, 338 enrolled. *Faculty:* 263 full-time (42 women), 60 part-time/adjunct (8 women). Expenses: Contact institution. *Financial support:* Fellowships, research assistantships, teaching assistantships, career-related internships or fieldwork, Federal Work-Study, institutionally sponsored loans, scholarships/grants, traineeships, health care benefits, and unspecified assistantships available. Support available to part-time students. Financial award applicants required to submit FAFSA. In 2016, 275 master's, 80 doctorates awarded. Offers astronomy and astrophysics (PhD); atmospheric sciences (PhD); biophysical sciences (PhD); chemistry (PhD); computer science (MS, PhD); earth sciences (PhD); financial mathematics (MS); mathematics (PhD); paleobiology (PhD); physical sciences (MS, PhD); physics (PhD); planetary and space sciences (PhD); statistics (MS, PhD). Electronic applications accepted. *Application Contact:* Emily Easton, Associate Dean of Students, 773-702-9708, E-mail: psd-admissions@lists.uchicago.edu. *Dean*, Edward Kolb, 773-702-7950.

Division of the Social Sciences Students: 1,140 full-time (505 women), 2 part-time (1 woman); includes 221 minority (58 Black or African American, non-Hispanic/Latino; 10 American Indian or Alaska Native, non-Hispanic/Latino; 47 Asian, non-Hispanic/Latino; 66 Hispanic/Latino; 40 Two or more races, non-Hispanic/Latino), 395 international. 2,843 applicants, 38% accepted, 315 enrolled. *Faculty:* 190 full-time (63 women), 14 part-time/adjunct (1 woman). Expenses: Contact institution. *Financial support:* In 2016–17, 275 students received support, including 99 fellowships with full tuition reimbursements available (averaging $23,000 per year); career-related internships or fieldwork, Federal Work-Study, institutionally sponsored loans, scholarships/grants, and health care benefits also available. Financial award application deadline: 12/15. In 2016, 321 master's, 119 doctorates awarded. Offers archaeology (PhD); comparative human development (PhD); computational social science (MA); conceptual and historical studies of science (PhD); economics (PhD); history (PhD); international relations (MA); political science (PhD); psychology (PhD); social sciences (MA, PhD); social thought (PhD); sociocultural and linguistic anthropology (PhD); sociology (PhD). *Application deadline:* For fall admission, 12/15 for domestic and international students. *Application fee:* $90. Electronic applications accepted. *Application Contact:* Office of the Dean of Students, 773-702-8415, E-mail: admissions@ssd.uchicago.edu. *Dean*, Prof. David Nirenberg.

Center for Latin American Studies Students: 6 full-time (4 women); includes 1 minority (Hispanic/Latino). Average age 25. 16 applicants, 50% accepted, 3 enrolled. Expenses: Contact institution. *Financial support:* In 2016–17, 6 students received support. Federal Work-Study, institutionally sponsored loans, and scholarships/grants available. Financial award application deadline: 1/5. In 2016, 3 master's awarded. Offers Latin American studies (MA). *Application deadline:* For fall admission, 1/5 priority date for domestic and international students. *Application fee:* $90. Electronic applications accepted. *Application Contact:* Office of the Dean of Students, 773-702-8415, E-mail: admissions@ssd.uchicago.edu. *Director,* Prof. Brodwyn Fischer, 773-834-4608, Fax: 773-702-7550, E-mail: clas@uchicago.edu.

Center for Middle Eastern Studies Students: 23 full-time (15 women); includes 2 minority (1 Asian, non-Hispanic/Latino; 1 Hispanic/Latino), 7 international. 35 applicants, 86% accepted. Expenses: Contact institution. *Financial support:* In 2016–17, 8 students received support. Federal Work-Study, institutionally sponsored loans, and scholarships/grants available. Financial award application deadline: 1/5. In 2016, 11 master's awarded. Offers Middle Eastern studies (MA). *Application deadline:* For fall admission, 1/5 for domestic and international students. *Application fee:* $90. Electronic applications accepted. *Application Contact:* Office of the Dean of Students, 773-702-8415, E-mail: admissions@ssd.uchicago.edu. *Director,* Prof. Hakan Karateke, 773-702-5375, E-mail: karateke@uchicago.edu.

Graham School of Continuing Liberal and Professional Studies Students: 54 full-time (32 women), 199 part-time (80 women); includes 81 minority (30 Black or African American, non-Hispanic/Latino; 32 Asian, non-Hispanic/Latino; 18 Hispanic/Latino; 1 Two or more races, non-Hispanic/Latino), 14 international. 236 applicants, 84% accepted, 118 enrolled. Expenses: Contact institution. *Financial support:* Applicants required to submit FAFSA. *Program availability:* Part-time, evening/weekend. Offers analytics (M Sc); liberal arts (MLA); threat and response management (M Sc); urban teacher education (MAT). *Application deadline:* Applications are processed on a rolling basis. *Application fee:* $75. Electronic applications accepted. *Application Contact:* 773-702-1722, E-mail: grahamschool@uchicago.edu.

Harris School of Public Policy Students: 339 full-time (167 women), 11 part-time (6 women); includes 57 minority (15 Black or African American, non-Hispanic/Latino; 24 Asian, non-Hispanic/Latino; 15 Hispanic/Latino; 3 Two or more races, non-Hispanic/Latino), 166 international. 1,094 applicants, 46% accepted, 158 enrolled. *Faculty:* 28 full-time (7 women), 6 part-time/adjunct (0 women). Expenses: Contact institution. *Financial support:* In 2016–17, 149 fellowships with full and partial tuition reimbursements (averaging $11,000 per year) were awarded; career-related internships or fieldwork, Federal Work-Study, institutionally sponsored loans, and scholarships/grants also available. Support available to part-time students. Financial award application deadline: 1/10; financial award applicants required to submit FAFSA. In 2016, 135 master's, 6 doctorates awarded. Offers computational analysis and public policy (MS); environmental science and policy (MS); public policy (AM, MPP, MS, PhD); public policy studies (AM). *Application deadline:* For fall admission, 1/10 priority date for domestic and international students. *Application fee:* $75. Electronic applications accepted. *Application Contact:* Allison Bevan, Director of Admissions, 773-702-8401, E-mail: harrisadmissions@uchicago.edu. *Dean,* Katherine Baicker, 773-702-8400.

Institute for Molecular Engineering Students: 73 full-time (22 women); includes 11 minority (5 Asian, non-Hispanic/Latino; 2 Hispanic/Latino; 4 Two or more races, non-Hispanic/Latino), 32 international. 242 applicants, 29% accepted, 25 enrolled. *Faculty:* 21 full-time (4 women). Expenses: Contact institution. *Financial support:* In 2016–17, 36 students received support, including 7 fellowships (averaging $4,000 per year), 45 research assistantships with full tuition reimbursements available (averaging $31,362 per year); career-related internships or fieldwork, scholarships/grants, traineeships, health care benefits, and unspecified assistantships also available. In 2016, 1 master's, 7 doctorates awarded. Offers molecular engineering (MA, PhD). *Application deadline:* For fall admission, 1/5 for domestic and international students. *Application fee:* $0. Electronic applications accepted. *Application Contact:* Dr. Novia Pagone, Associate Dean of Students, 773-834-1437, E-mail: ime@uchicago.edu. *Senior Associate Dean,* Dr. Sharon Feng.

The Law School Offers law (LL M, MCL, DCL, JD, JSD). Electronic applications accepted.

Pritzker School of Medicine Students: 389 full-time (184 women); includes 153 minority (32 Black or African American, non-Hispanic/Latino; 1 American Indian or Alaska Native, non-Hispanic/Latino; 73 Asian, non-Hispanic/Latino; 31 Hispanic/Latino; 16 Two or more races, non-Hispanic/Latino), 4 international. 5,803 applicants, 4% accepted, 90 enrolled. *Faculty:* 880 full-time (351 women), 229 part-time/adjunct (101 women). Expenses: Contact institution. *Financial support:* In 2016–17, 354 students received support. Career-related internships or fieldwork, Federal Work-Study, institutionally sponsored loans, and scholarships/grants available. Financial award application deadline: 4/1; financial award applicants required to submit FAFSA. In 2016, 102 doctorates awarded. Offers medicine (MD). *Application deadline:* For fall admission, 10/15 for domestic and international students. Applications are processed on a rolling basis. *Application fee:* $85. Electronic applications accepted. *Application Contact:* Dr. Keme Carter, Assistant Dean for Admissions, 773-702-1937, Fax: 773-834-5412, E-mail: pritzkeradmissions@bsd.uchicago.edu.

School of Social Service Administration Students: 451 full-time (373 women), 20 part-time (16 women); includes 143 minority (50 Black or African American, non-Hispanic/Latino; 5 American Indian or Alaska Native, non-Hispanic/Latino; 37 Asian, non-Hispanic/Latino; 46 Hispanic/Latino; 1 Native Hawaiian or other Pacific Islander, non-Hispanic/Latino; 4 Two or more races, non-Hispanic/Latino), 29 international. 716 applicants, 57% accepted, 197 enrolled. *Faculty:* 34 full-time (21 women), 21 part-time/adjunct (13 women). Expenses: Contact institution. *Financial support:* In 2016–17, 415 students received support. Fellowships, research assistantships, teaching assistantships, Federal Work-Study, institutionally sponsored loans, scholarships/grants, and health care benefits available. Financial award application deadline: 4/1; financial award applicants required to submit FAFSA. In 2016, 197 master's, 11 doctorates awarded. *Program availability:* Part-time, evening/weekend. Offers social service administration (AM, MA, PhD). AM/M Div offered jointly with the Divinity School, MBA/AM offered jointly with Booth School of Business, MPP/AM offered jointly with Harris School of Public Policy. *Application deadline:* For fall admission, 12/15 priority date for domestic and international students. *Application fee:* $75. Electronic applications accepted. *Application Contact:* Laura Chavez Hardy, Director of Admissions, 773-702-1250, Fax: 773-834-4751, E-mail: admissions@ssa.uchicago.edu. *Interim Dean,* Deborah Gorman-Smith, 773-702-1250.

UNIVERSITY OF CINCINNATI, Cincinnati, OH 45221

General Information State-supported, coed, university. CGS member. *Enrollment:* 36,637 graduate, professional, and undergraduate students; 5,406 full-time matriculated graduate/professional students (2,810 women), 5,371 part-time matriculated graduate/professional students (3,629 women). *Enrollment by degree level:* 6,308

master's, 3,370 doctoral, 669 other advanced degrees. *Graduate faculty:* 1,350 full-time (526 women), 410 part-time/adjunct (227 women). *International tuition:* $24,832 full-time. *Tuition, area resident:* Full-time $12,790; part-time $389 per credit hour. Tuition, state resident: full-time $13,290; part-time $419 per credit hour. Tuition, nonresident: full-time $24,532; part-time $976 per credit hour. *Required fees:* $3958; $140 per credit hour. Tuition and fees vary according to course load, degree level, program and reciprocity agreements. *Graduate housing:* Rooms and/or apartments available on a first-come, first-served basis to single and married students. Typical cost: $10,500 per year ($17,600 including board) for single students. Room and board charges vary according to board plan, campus/location and housing facility selected. *Student services:* Campus employment opportunities, campus safety program, career counseling, child daycare facilities, exercise/wellness program, free psychological counseling, grant writing training, international student services, low-cost health insurance, multicultural affairs office, services for students with disabilities, teacher training. *Library facilities:* Walter C. Langsam Library plus 13 others. *Collection:* Books: 3 million (physical), 1.5 million (digital/electronic); Serial titles: 1,608 (physical), 154,043 (digital/electronic). Weekly public service hours: 107; study areas open 24 hours, 5–7 days a week; students can reserve study rooms. *Research affiliation:* Cincinnati Children's Hospital Medical Center, Cincinnati Department of Veterans Affairs Medical Center, Shriners Hospitals for Children-Cincinnati.

Computer facilities: 406 computers available on campus for general student use. A campuswide network can be accessed from student residence rooms and from off campus. Online class registration is available.
Website: http://www.uc.edu/

General Application Contact: Dr. Marshall Montrose, Vice Provost and Dean, The Graduate School, 513-556-4336, E-mail: marshall.montrose@uc.edu.

GRADUATE UNITS

College of Law Students: 286 full-time (130 women), 3 part-time (all women); includes 51 minority (23 Black or African American, non-Hispanic/Latino; 1 American Indian or Alaska Native, non-Hispanic/Latino; 8 Asian, non-Hispanic/Latino; 17 Hispanic/Latino; 2 Two or more races, non-Hispanic/Latino), 5 international. Average age 25. 829 applicants, 52% accepted, 126 enrolled. *Faculty:* 31 full-time (15 women), 58 part-time/adjunct (21 women). Expenses: Contact institution. *Financial support:* In 2016–17, 235 students received support. Fellowships, research assistantships, career-related internships or fieldwork, Federal Work-Study, scholarships/grants, tuition waivers (full and partial), and unspecified assistantships available. Financial award application deadline: 3/15; financial award applicants required to submit FAFSA. In 2016, 8 master's, 109 doctorates awarded. Offers law (LL M, JD). *Application deadline:* For fall admission, 3/15 priority date for domestic and international students. Applications are processed on a rolling basis. *Application fee:* $35. Electronic applications accepted. *Application Contact:* Al Watson, Senior Assistant Dean and Director of Admissions, 513-556-0077, Fax: 513-556-2391, E-mail: alfred.watson@uc.edu. *Interim Dean,* Verna L. Williams, 513-556-0080, Fax: 513-556-2391, E-mail: verna.williams@uc.edu.

Graduate School *Program availability:* Part-time, evening/weekend, online learning. Offers neuroscience (PhD). Electronic applications accepted.

Carl H. Lindner College of Business Students: 452 full-time (183 women), 711 part-time (314 women); includes 161 minority (62 Black or African American, non-Hispanic/Latino; 2 American Indian or Alaska Native, non-Hispanic/Latino; 55 Asian, non-Hispanic/Latino; 25 Hispanic/Latino; 2 Native Hawaiian or other Pacific Islander, non-Hispanic/Latino; 15 Two or more races, non-Hispanic/Latino), 403 international. Average age 30. 2,268 applicants, 28% accepted, 511 enrolled. *Faculty:* 93 full-time (27 women), 36 part-time/adjunct (6 women). Expenses: Contact institution. *Financial support:* In 2016–17, 242 students received support, including 25 research assistantships with tuition reimbursements available (averaging $23,250 per year), 25 teaching assistantships with tuition reimbursements available (averaging $3,000 per year); scholarships/grants, tuition waivers (full and partial), and unspecified assistantships also available. Financial award application deadline: 3/15; financial award applicants required to submit FAFSA. In 2016, 554 master's, 4 doctorates awarded. *Program availability:* Part-time, evening/weekend, 100% online, blended/hybrid learning. Offers accounting (MS, PhD); applied economics (MA); business (MA, MBA, MS, PhD); business administration (MBA); business analytics (MS); economics (PhD); finance (MS, PhD); information systems (MS, PhD); management (PhD); marketing (MS, PhD); operations and business analytics (PhD); taxation (MS). *Application deadline:* For fall admission, 8/1 priority date for domestic students, 3/15 for international students; for winter admission, 12/15 for domestic students, 9/15 for international students; for spring admission, 12/15 for domestic students, 9/15 for international students; for summer admission, 4/15 for domestic and international students. Applications are processed on a rolling basis. *Application fee:* $65 ($70 for international students). Electronic applications accepted. *Application Contact:* Dona Clary, Director, Graduate Programs, 513-556-3546, Fax: 513-558-7006, E-mail: dona.clary@uc.edu. *Dean,* Dr. David Szymanski, 513-556-7001, Fax: 513-556-4891, E-mail: david.szymanski@uc.edu.

College-Conservatory of Music Offers arts administration (MA); choral conducting (MM, DMA); composition (MM, DMA); directing (MFA); keyboard studies (MM, DMA, AD); music (MA, MFA, MM, DMA, PhD, AD); music education (MM); music history (MM); music theory (MM, PhD); musicology (PhD); orchestral conducting (MM, DMA); performance (MM, DMA, AD); theater design and production (MFA); voice and opera (MM, DMA); wind conducting (MM, DMA). Electronic applications accepted.

College of Allied Health Sciences *Program availability:* Part-time. Offers allied health sciences (MA, MS, MSW, Au D, DPT, PhD); communication sciences and disorders (MA, Au D, PhD); health informatics (MHI); medical genetics (MS); nutritional sciences (MS); physical therapy (DPT); social work (MSW).

College of Design, Architecture, Art, and Planning *Program availability:* Part-time. Offers architecture (M Arch); art history (MA); community planning (MCP); design, architecture, art, and planning (M Arch, M Des, MA, MCP, MFA, PhD); fashion design (M Des); fine arts (MFA); graphic design (M Des); industrial design (M Des); interaction design (M Des); product development (M Des); regional development planning (PhD); visual arts education (MA). Electronic applications accepted.

College of Education, Criminal Justice, and Human Services *Program availability:* Part-time, online learning. Offers counselor education (Ed D); criminal justice (MS, PhD); curriculum and instruction (M Ed, Ed D); deaf studies (Certificate); early childhood education (M Ed); education (M Ed, Ed D, PhD, Ed S); education, criminal justice, and human services (M Ed, MA, MS, Ed D, PhD, CAGS, Certificate, Ed S); educational leadership (M Ed, Ed S); educational studies (M Ed, PhD); exercise and fitness (MS); health education (PhD); human services (M Ed, MA, MPH, MS, Ed D, PhD, Ed S, Graduate Certificate); mental health (MS); middle childhood education (M Ed); postsecondary literacy instruction (Certificate); public and community health (MS); public health (MPH); reading/literacy (M Ed, Ed D); school counseling (M Ed); school psychology (PhD, Ed S); secondary education (M Ed); special education

(M Ed, Ed D); sport administration (MS); substance abuse prevention (Graduate Certificate); teaching English as a second language (Ed D, Certificate); teaching science (MS); urban educational leadership (Ed D). Electronic applications accepted.

College of Engineering and Applied Science Program availability: Part-time, evening/weekend. Offers aerospace engineering and engineering mechanics (MS, PhD); biomechanics (PhD); chemical engineering (MS, PhD); civil engineering (MS, PhD); computer engineering (MS); computer science (MS); computer science and engineering (PhD); electrical engineering (MS, PhD); engineering and applied science (MS, PhD); environmental engineering (MS, PhD); environmental sciences (MS, PhD); industrial engineering (PhD); materials science and engineering (MS, PhD); mechanical engineering (MS, PhD); medical imaging (PhD); nuclear engineering (PhD); tissue engineering (PhD).

College of Medicine Offers biomedical informatics (PhD, Graduate Certificate); biomedical research (MS); biomedical sciences (MS, PhD, Graduate Certificate); cancer and cell biology (PhD); cell biophysics (PhD); environmental and industrial hygiene (MS, PhD); environmental and occupational medicine (MS); environmental genetics and molecular toxicology (MS, PhD); epidemiology and biostatistics (MS, PhD); immunobiology (PhD); immunology (MS, PhD); medical physics (MS); medicine (MS, MD, PhD, Graduate Certificate); molecular and developmental biology (PhD); molecular genetics, biochemistry and microbiology (MS, PhD); occupational safety and ergonomics (MS, PhD); pathology (PhD); pharmacology (PhD); systems biology and physiology (PhD). Electronic applications accepted.

College of Nursing Program availability: Part-time, online learning. Offers clinical nurse specialist (MSN); nurse anesthesia (MSN); nurse midwifery (MSN); nurse practitioner (MSN); nursing (MSN). Electronic applications accepted.

McMicken College of Arts and Sciences Program availability: Part-time, evening/weekend. Offers analytical chemistry (MS, PhD); anthropology (MA); applied mathematics (MS, PhD); arts and sciences (MA, MALER, MAT, MS, PhD, Certificate); biochemistry (MS, PhD); biological sciences (MS, PhD); classics (MA, PhD); clinical psychology (PhD); communication (MA); English and comparative literature (MA, MAT, PhD); experimental psychology (PhD); French (MA, PhD); geography (MA, PhD); geology (MS, PhD); German studies (MA, PhD); history (MA, PhD); inorganic chemistry (MS, PhD); interdisciplinary studies (PhD); labor and employment relations (MALER); mathematics education (MAT); organic chemistry (MS, PhD); organizational leadership (MALER); philosophy (MA, PhD); physical chemistry (MS, PhD); physics (MS, PhD); political science (MA, PhD); polymer chemistry (MS, PhD); pure mathematics (MS, PhD); Romance languages and literatures (PhD); sensors (PhD); sociology (MA, PhD); Spanish (MA, PhD); statistics (MS, PhD); women's, gender, and sexuality studies (MA, Certificate).

James L. Winkle College of Pharmacy Program availability: Part-time. Offers pharmacy (MS, PhD, Pharm D).

Division of Pharmaceutical Sciences Offers pharmaceutical sciences (MS, PhD).

Division of Pharmacy Practice Offers pharmacy practice (Pharm D).

UNIVERSITY OF COLORADO BOULDER, Boulder, CO 80309

General Information State-supported, coed, university. CGS member. *Enrollment:* 33,771 graduate, professional, and undergraduate students; 5,293 full-time matriculated graduate/professional students (2,188 women), 551 part-time matriculated graduate/professional students (281 women). *Graduate faculty:* 1,197 full-time (395 women). *Graduate housing:* Rooms and/or apartments available to single and married students. *Student services:* Campus employment opportunities, campus safety program, career counseling, child daycare facilities, free psychological counseling, international student services, low-cost health insurance. *Library facilities:* Norlin Library plus 5 others. *Collection:* Books: 664,601 (physical), 984,952 (digital/electronic); Databases: 594. Students can reserve study rooms. *Research affiliation:* National Institute of Standards and Technology (NIST), National Oceanic and Atmospheric Administration (NOAA), U.S. West Advanced Technologies, NASA, National Center for Atmospheric Research.

Computer facilities: Computer purchase and lease plans are available. 1,804 computers available on campus for general student use. A campuswide network can be accessed from student residence rooms and from off campus. Online class registration, training, tutorials, workshops, seminars, standard and academic software, student government voting are available. Website: http://www.colorado.edu/

GRADUATE UNITS

Graduate School Students: 4,267 full-time (1,741 women), 533 part-time (274 women); includes 648 minority (57 Black or African American, non-Hispanic/Latino; 11 American Indian or Alaska Native, non-Hispanic/Latino; 153 Asian, non-Hispanic/Latino; 298 Hispanic/Latino; 4 Native Hawaiian or other Pacific Islander, non-Hispanic/Latino; 125 Two or more races, non-Hispanic/Latino), 1,079 international. Average age 29. 10,965 applicants, 31% accepted, 1216 enrolled. *Faculty:* 1,098 full-time (368 women). Expenses: Contact institution. *Financial support:* In 2016–17, 9,613 students received support, including 2,549 fellowships (averaging $6,916 per year), 1,274 research assistantships with full and partial tuition reimbursements available (averaging $35,741 per year), 1,527 teaching assistantships with full and partial tuition reimbursements available (averaging $33,370 per year); institutionally sponsored loans, scholarships/grants, health care benefits, and unspecified assistantships also available. Financial award applicants required to submit FAFSA. In 2016, 865 master's, 409 doctorates awarded. Offers museum and field studies (MS). *Application fee:* $60 ($80 for international students). Electronic applications accepted. *Application Contact:* E-mail: gradinfo@colorado.edu.

College of Arts and Sciences Students: 2,080 full-time (995 women), 68 part-time (36 women); includes 290 minority (20 Black or African American, non-Hispanic/Latino; 5 American Indian or Alaska Native, non-Hispanic/Latino; 62 Asian, non-Hispanic/Latino; 134 Hispanic/Latino; 1 Native Hawaiian or other Pacific Islander, non-Hispanic/Latino; 68 Two or more races, non-Hispanic/Latino), 278 international. Average age 28. 6,065 applicants, 22% accepted, 490 enrolled. *Faculty:* 737 full-time (263 women). Expenses: Contact institution. *Financial support:* In 2016–17, 5,122 students received support, including 1,141 fellowships (averaging $7,049 per year), 603 research assistantships with full and partial tuition reimbursements available (averaging $34,894 per year), 1,094 teaching assistantships with full and partial tuition reimbursements available (averaging $34,884 per year); institutionally sponsored loans, scholarships/grants, health care benefits, and unspecified assistantships also available. Financial award applicants required to submit FAFSA. In 2016, 290 master's, 212 doctorates awarded. Offers anthropology (MA); applied mathematics (MS, PhD); art history (MA); arts and sciences (MA, MFA, MS, Au D, PhD); Asian languages and civilizations (MA, PhD); astrophysics (MS, PhD); atmospheric and oceanic sciences (MS, PhD); cellular structure and function (MA, PhD); ceramics (MFA); chemistry and biochemistry (MS, PhD); classics (MA, PhD);

comparative literature (MA, PhD); dance (MFA); developmental biology (PhD); economics (MA, PhD); environmental studies (MS, PhD); ethnic studies (PhD); French and Italian (MA, PhD); geography (MA, PhD); geology (MS, PhD); geophysics (PhD); Germanic and Slavic languages and literatures (MA); Hispanic linguistics (MA); history (MA, PhD); integrative physiology (MS, PhD); linguistics (MA, PhD); literature (MA, PhD); mathematical physics (PhD); mathematics (MA, MS, PhD); medieval and early modern Hispanic literatures (PhD); molecular biology (PhD); peninsular and Latin American literature (MA); philosophy (MA, PhD); photography and media arts (MFA); planetary science (PhD); political science (MA, PhD); population biology (MA); printmaking (MFA); psychology and neuroscience (MA, PhD); religious studies (MA); sculpture (MFA); sociology (PhD); speech, language and hearing sciences (MA, Au D, PhD); theatre (MA, PhD). *Application fee:* $60 ($80 for international students). Electronic applications accepted.

College of Engineering and Applied Science Students: 1,729 full-time (475 women), 233 part-time (53 women); includes 214 minority (19 Black or African American, non-Hispanic/Latino; 4 American Indian or Alaska Native, non-Hispanic/Latino; 73 Asian, non-Hispanic/Latino; 74 Hispanic/Latino; 1 Native Hawaiian or other Pacific Islander, non-Hispanic/Latino; 43 Two or more races, non-Hispanic/Latino), 765 international. Average age 28. 3,826 applicants, 40% accepted, 546 enrolled. *Faculty:* 208 full-time (38 women). Expenses: Contact institution. *Financial support:* In 2016–17, 3,133 students received support, including 941 fellowships (averaging $8,707 per year), 537 research assistantships with full and partial tuition reimbursements available (averaging $38,013 per year), 197 teaching assistantships with full and partial tuition reimbursements available (averaging $35,143 per year); institutionally sponsored loans, scholarships/grants, health care benefits, and unspecified assistantships also available. Financial award applicants required to submit FAFSA. In 2016, 410 master's, 139 doctorates awarded. Offers aerospace engineering sciences (MS, PhD); chemical and biological engineering (ME, MS, PhD); civil, environmental, and architectural engineering (MS, PhD); computer science (ME, MS, PhD); electrical, computer and energy engineering (ME, MS, PhD); engineering and applied science (ME, MS, PhD); engineering management (ME); mechanical engineering (ME, MS, PhD); technology, learning, and society (MS, PhD); telecommunications (MS). *Application fee:* $60 ($80 for international students). Electronic applications accepted.

College of Media, Communication and Information Students: 136 full-time (81 women), 8 part-time (5 women); includes 14 minority (1 Black or African American, non-Hispanic/Latino; 4 Asian, non-Hispanic/Latino; 9 Hispanic/Latino), 11 international. Average age 30. 226 applicants, 50% accepted, 63 enrolled. *Faculty:* 55 full-time (26 women). Expenses: Contact institution. *Financial support:* In 2016–17, 366 students received support, including 99 fellowships (averaging $3,721 per year), 52 research assistantships with full and partial tuition reimbursements available (averaging $27,137 per year), 82 teaching assistantships with full and partial tuition reimbursements available (averaging $30,022 per year); institutionally sponsored loans, scholarships/grants, health care benefits, and unspecified assistantships also available. Financial award application deadline: 3/1; financial award applicants required to submit FAFSA. In 2016, 25 master's, 12 doctorates awarded. Offers communication (MA, PhD); information science (PhD); interdisciplinary documentary media practices (MFA); intermedia art, writing and performance (PhD); journalism (MA); media research and practice (PhD); media studies (PhD); media, communication and information (MA, MFA, PhD); strategic communication design (MA). *Application deadline:* For fall admission, 2/1 for domestic students, 12/1 for international students. Applications are processed on a rolling basis. *Application fee:* $60 ($80 for international students). Electronic applications accepted. *Application Contact:* E-mail: cmcigrad@colorado.edu.

College of Music Students: 163 full-time (77 women), 43 part-time (25 women); includes 26 minority (4 Black or African American, non-Hispanic/Latino; 7 Asian, non-Hispanic/Latino; 9 Hispanic/Latino; 6 Two or more races, non-Hispanic/Latino), 18 international. Average age 30. 458 applicants, 38% accepted, 51 enrolled. *Faculty:* 62 full-time (19 women). Expenses: Contact institution. *Financial support:* In 2016–17, 496 students received support, including 234 fellowships (averaging $2,277 per year), 1 research assistantship with full and partial tuition reimbursement available (averaging $6,020 per year), 108 teaching assistantships with full and partial tuition reimbursements available (averaging $22,460 per year); institutionally sponsored loans, scholarships/grants, health care benefits, and unspecified assistantships also available. Financial award application deadline: 3/1; financial award applicants required to submit FAFSA. In 2016, 39 master's, 27 doctorates awarded. Offers composition (M Mus, D Mus A); conducting (M Mus); instrumental conducting and literature (D Mus A); literature and performance of choral music (D Mus A); music education (M Mus Ed, PhD); music theory (M Mus); performance (M Mus, D Mus A); performance and pedagogy (M Mus, D Mus A). *Application deadline:* For fall admission, 12/1 for domestic and international students; for spring admission, 10/1 for domestic and international students. Applications are processed on a rolling basis. *Application fee:* $60 ($80 for international students). Electronic applications accepted. *Application Contact:* E-mail: gradmusc@colorado.edu.

School of Education Students: 144 full-time (99 women), 181 part-time (155 women); includes 102 minority (13 Black or African American, non-Hispanic/Latino; 1 American Indian or Alaska Native, non-Hispanic/Latino; 7 Asian, non-Hispanic/Latino; 72 Hispanic/Latino; 2 Native Hawaiian or other Pacific Islander, non-Hispanic/Latino; 7 Two or more races, non-Hispanic/Latino), 6 international. Average age 33. 345 applicants, 53% accepted, 58 enrolled. *Faculty:* 34 full-time (20 women). Expenses: Contact institution. *Financial support:* In 2016–17, 438 students received support, including 115 fellowships (averaging $3,501 per year), 78 research assistantships with full and partial tuition reimbursements available (averaging $33,196 per year), 33 teaching assistantships with full and partial tuition reimbursements available (averaging $20,617 per year); institutionally sponsored loans, scholarships/grants, health care benefits, and unspecified assistantships also available. Financial award applicants required to submit FAFSA. In 2016, 93 master's, 19 doctorates awarded. Offers curriculum and instruction (MA, PhD); education (MA, PhD); educational and psychological studies (MA, PhD); educational equity and cultural diversity (PhD); educational foundations, policy, and practice (MA, PhD); multicultural education (MA); research and evaluation methodology (PhD). *Application deadline:* For fall admission, 2/1 for domestic students, 12/1 for international students; for spring admission, 9/1 for domestic and international students. *Application fee:* $60 ($80 for international students). Electronic applications accepted.

Leeds School of Business Students: 497 full-time (185 women), 9 part-time (4 women); includes 69 minority (4 Black or African American, non-Hispanic/Latino; 27 Asian, non-Hispanic/Latino; 25 Hispanic/Latino; 13 Two or more races, non-Hispanic/Latino), 77 international. Average age 28. 753 applicants, 60% accepted, 158 enrolled. *Faculty:* 58 full-time (11 women). Expenses: Contact institution. *Financial support:* In 2016–17, 449 students received support, including 284 fellowships (averaging $5,193 per year), 30 research assistantships with full and partial tuition reimbursements available (averaging $44,449 per year), 11 teaching assistantships with full and partial tuition reimbursements available (averaging $33,080 per year); institutionally sponsored loans, scholarships/grants, health care benefits, and unspecified assistantships also available. Financial award applicants required to submit FAFSA. In 2016, 219 master's, 7 doctorates awarded. Offers business (MBA, MS, PhD); business administration (MBA, MS, PhD). *Application deadline:* For fall admission, 3/1 for domestic and international students. Applications are processed on a rolling basis. *Application fee:* $60 ($80 for international students). Electronic applications accepted.

School of Law Students: 529 full-time (262 women), 9 part-time (3 women); includes 100 minority (10 Black or African American, non-Hispanic/Latino; 14 American Indian or Alaska Native, non-Hispanic/Latino; 25 Asian, non-Hispanic/Latino; 48 Hispanic/Latino; 3 Two or more races, non-Hispanic/Latino), 6 international. Average age 27. 1,118 applicants, 100% accepted, 178 enrolled. *Faculty:* 41 full-time (16 women). Expenses: Contact institution. *Financial support:* In 2016–17, 1,078 students received support, including 817 fellowships (averaging $7,178 per year); institutionally sponsored loans, scholarships/grants, health care benefits, and unspecified assistantships also available. Financial award applicants required to submit FAFSA. In 2016, 184 doctorates awarded. Offers law (JD). *Application deadline:* For fall admission, 2/15 for domestic students. Applications are processed on a rolling basis. *Application fee:* $60 ($80 for international students). Electronic applications accepted. *Application Contact:* E-mail: lawadmin@colorado.edu.

UNIVERSITY OF COLORADO COLORADO SPRINGS, Colorado Springs, CO 80918

General Information State-supported, coed, university. CGS member. *Enrollment:* 12,258 graduate, professional, and undergraduate students; 392 full-time matriculated graduate/professional students (228 women), 1,304 part-time matriculated graduate/professional students (699 women). *Enrollment by degree level:* 1,427 master's, 224 doctoral, 45 other advanced degrees. *Graduate faculty:* 399 full-time (206 women), 362 part-time/adjunct (196 women). Tuition, state resident: full-time $9983. Tuition, nonresident: full-time $20,153. Tuition and fees vary according to course load, degree level, program and reciprocity agreements. *Graduate housing:* Room and/or apartments available on a first-come, first-served basis to single students; on-campus housing not available to married students. Typical cost: $8600 per year ($9800 including board). Room and board charges vary according to board plan and housing facility selected. *Student services:* Campus employment opportunities, campus safety program, career counseling, child daycare facilities, exercise/wellness program, free psychological counseling, grant writing training, international student services, low-cost health insurance, multicultural affairs office, services for students with disabilities, teacher training, writing training. *Library facilities:* Kraemer Family Library. *Collection:* Students can reserve study rooms. *Research affiliation:* Caring for Colorado Foundation (psychology), The Coleman Institute for Cognitive Disabilities (age-related cognitive decline), Western Regional Radon Training Center (radon mitigation), National Geographic Society Education Foundation (geography and environmental studies), Robert Bosch Security Technologies (physics), Global Circuit Innovations (electrical and computer engineering).

Computer facilities: Computer purchase and lease plans are available. A campuswide network can be accessed from student residence rooms and from off campus. Online class registration, student portal, learning management system are available. Website: http://www.uccs.edu/

General Application Contact: KrisAnn McBroom, Graduate School Administrator, 719-255-3417, Fax: 719-255-3045, E-mail: gradinfo@uccs.edu.

GRADUATE UNITS

College of Business Students: 67 full-time (27 women), 241 part-time (112 women); includes 59 minority (8 Black or African American, non-Hispanic/Latino; 14 Asian, non-Hispanic/Latino; 20 Hispanic/Latino; 17 Two or more races, non-Hispanic/Latino), 13 international. Average age 34. 107 applicants, 66% accepted, 50 enrolled. *Faculty:* 24 full-time (9 women), 14 part-time/adjunct (3 women). Expenses: Contact institution. *Financial support:* In 2016–17, 37 students received support. Career-related internships or fieldwork, Federal Work-Study, and scholarships/grants available. Support available to part-time students. Financial award application deadline: 3/1; financial award applicants required to submit FAFSA. In 2016, 98 master's awarded. *Program availability:* Part-time, evening/weekend, 100% online, blended/hybrid learning. Offers business (MBA, MSA). *Application deadline:* For fall admission, 6/1 for domestic and international students; for spring admission, 11/1 for domestic and international students; for summer admission, 4/1 for domestic and international students. Applications are processed on a rolling basis. *Application fee:* $60 ($100 for international students). Electronic applications accepted. *Application Contact:* Whitney Porter, Assistant Director of Graduate Programs, 719-255-3408, E-mail: cobgrad@uccs.edu. *Interim Dean,* Dr. Cathy Claiborne, 719-255-3113, Fax: 719-255-3100, E-mail: cclaibor@uccs.edu.

College of Education Students: 136 full-time (94 women), 264 part-time (177 women); includes 99 minority (17 Black or African American, non-Hispanic/Latino; 1 American Indian or Alaska Native, non-Hispanic/Latino; 8 Asian, non-Hispanic/Latino; 55 Hispanic/Latino; 18 Two or more races, non-Hispanic/Latino), 9 international. Average age 35. 152 applicants, 89% accepted, 88 enrolled. *Faculty:* 26 full-time (18 women), 33 part-time/adjunct (21 women). Expenses: Contact institution. *Financial support:* In 2016–17, 108 students received support. Career-related internships or fieldwork, Federal Work-Study, scholarships/grants, and unspecified assistantships available. Support available to part-time students. Financial award application deadline: 3/1; financial award applicants required to submit FAFSA. In 2016, 161 master's, 11 doctorates awarded. *Program availability:* Part-time, evening/weekend, 100% online, blended/hybrid learning. Offers counseling and human services (MA); curriculum and instruction (MA); educational leadership (MA); educational leadership, research and policy (PhD); special education (MA); teaching English to speakers of other languages (MA). *Application deadline:* For fall admission, 2/1 priority date for domestic students, 2/1 for international students; for spring admission, 10/15 for domestic students, 10/1 for international students. Applications are processed on a rolling basis. *Application fee:* $60 ($100 for international students). Electronic applications accepted. *Application Contact:* The College of Education Student Resource Office, 719-255-4996, E-mail: education@uccs.edu. *Dean,* Dr. Valerie Martin Conley, 719-255-4133, E-mail: vmconley@uccs.edu.

College of Engineering and Applied Science Students: 42 full-time (8 women), 263 part-time (53 women); includes 57 minority (6 Black or African American, non-Hispanic/Latino; 15 Asian, non-Hispanic/Latino; 23 Hispanic/Latino; 13 Two or more races, non-Hispanic/Latino), 96 international. Average age 33. 181 applicants, 68% accepted, 64 enrolled. *Faculty:* 33 full-time (7 women), 20 part-time/adjunct (6 women). Expenses: Contact institution. *Financial support:* In 2016–17, 45 students received support. Career-related internships or fieldwork, Federal Work-Study, and scholarships/grants available. Support available to part-time students. Financial award application deadline: 3/1; financial award applicants required to submit FAFSA. In 2016,

70 master's, 8 doctorates awarded. *Program availability:* Part-time, evening/weekend. Offers computer science (MS); electrical engineering (MS); energy engineering (ME); engineering and applied science (ME, ME, PhD); engineering management (ME); information assurance (ME); mechanical engineering (MS); software engineering (ME); space operations (ME); systems engineering (ME). *Application deadline:* For fall admission, 6/1 for domestic students, 4/1 for international students; for spring admission, 11/1 for domestic students, 10/1 for international students. Applications are processed on a rolling basis. *Application fee:* $60 ($100 for international students). *Application Contact:* Ali Langfels, Office of Student Support, 719-255-3544, E-mail: alangfel@uccs.edu. *Dean,* Dr. Ramaswami Dandapani, 719-255-3543, Fax: 719-255-3542, E-mail: rdan@cas.uccs.edu.

College of Letters, Arts and Sciences Students: 59 full-time (38 women), 194 part-time (100 women); includes 44 minority (6 Black or African American, non-Hispanic/Latino; 1 American Indian or Alaska Native, non-Hispanic/Latino; 6 Asian, non-Hispanic/Latino; 22 Hispanic/Latino; 9 Two or more races, non-Hispanic/Latino), 6 international. Average age 33. 414 applicants, 30% accepted, 75 enrolled. *Faculty:* 88 full-time (35 women), 17 part-time/adjunct (12 women). Expenses: Contact institution. *Financial support:* In 2016–17, 127 students received support. Career-related internships or fieldwork, Federal Work-Study, scholarships/grants, and unspecified assistantships available. Support available to part-time students. Financial award application deadline: 3/1; financial award applicants required to submit FAFSA. In 2016, 59 master's, 3 doctorates awarded. *Program availability:* Part-time, evening/weekend, blended/hybrid learning. Offers applied mathematics (MS); communication (MA); geography and environmental studies (MA); history (MA); interdisciplinary sciences (M Sc); letters, arts and sciences (M Sc, MA, MS, PhD); mathematics (PhD); physics (PhD); psychology (MA, PhD); sociology (MA). *Application deadline:* Applications are processed on a rolling basis. *Application fee:* $60 ($100 for international students). Electronic applications accepted. *Application Contact:* Sarah Elsey, Graduate Recruitment and Retention Specialist, 719-255-3072, E-mail: gradinfo@uccs.edu. *Dean of the Graduate School,* Dr. Kelli Klebe, 719-255-3779, Fax: 719-255-3045, E-mail: kklebe@uccs.edu.

Helen and Arthur E. Johnson Beth-El College of Nursing and Health Sciences Students: 12 full-time (all women), 186 part-time (168 women); includes 44 minority (5 Black or African American, non-Hispanic/Latino; 1 American Indian or Alaska Native, non-Hispanic/Latino; 9 Asian, non-Hispanic/Latino; 23 Hispanic/Latino; 6 Two or more races, non-Hispanic/Latino). Average age 38. 83 applicants, 57% accepted, 27 enrolled. *Faculty:* 15 full-time (14 women), 2 part-time/adjunct (both women). Expenses: Contact institution. *Financial support:* In 2016–17, 41 students received support. Research assistantships, career-related internships or fieldwork, Federal Work-Study, and scholarships/grants available. Support available to part-time students. Financial award application deadline: 3/1; financial award applicants required to submit FAFSA. In 2016, 35 master's, 5 doctorates awarded. *Program availability:* Part-time, 100% online, blended/hybrid learning. Offers nursing practice (DNP); primary care nurse practitioner (MSN). *Application deadline:* For fall admission, 3/15 priority date for domestic students, 3/15 for international students; for spring admission, 8/15 for domestic and international students; for summer admission, 2/3 for domestic and international students. Applications are processed on a rolling basis. *Application fee:* $60 ($100 for international students). Electronic applications accepted. *Application Contact:* Diane Busch, Program Assistant II, 719-255-4424, Fax: 719-255-4416, E-mail: dbusch@uccs.edu. *Nursing Department Chair,* Dr. Deborah Pollard, 719-255-3577, Fax: 719-255-4416, E-mail: dpollard@uccs.edu.

School of Public Affairs Students: 22 full-time (12 women), 142 part-time (79 women); includes 44 minority (6 Black or African American, non-Hispanic/Latino; 1 American Indian or Alaska Native, non-Hispanic/Latino; 4 Asian, non-Hispanic/Latino; 25 Hispanic/Latino; 8 Two or more races, non-Hispanic/Latino). Average age 35. 62 applicants, 94% accepted, 44 enrolled. *Faculty:* 11 full-time (4 women), 5 part-time/adjunct (3 women). Expenses: Contact institution. *Financial support:* In 2016–17, 36 students received support. Career-related internships or fieldwork, scholarships/grants, and tuition waivers available. Support available to part-time students. Financial award application deadline: 3/1; financial award applicants required to submit FAFSA. In 2016, 32 master's awarded. *Program availability:* Part-time, evening/weekend, 100% online, blended/hybrid learning. Offers criminal justice (MCJ); public administration (MPA). *Application deadline:* Applications are processed on a rolling basis. *Application fee:* $60 ($100 for international students). Electronic applications accepted. *Application Contact:* Crista Hill, Outreach Student Services Specialist, 719-255-4993, Fax: 719-255-4183, E-mail: chill12@uccs.edu. *Dean,* Dr. George Reed, 719-255-4109, E-mail: george.reed@uccs.edu.

UNIVERSITY OF COLORADO DENVER, Denver, CO 80217-3364

General Information State-supported, coed, university. CGS member. *Enrollment:* 23,960 graduate, professional, and undergraduate students; 6,693 full-time matriculated graduate/professional students (4,018 women), 1,636 part-time matriculated graduate/professional students (1,017 women). *Enrollment by degree level:* 5,184 master's, 3,044 doctoral, 101 other advanced degrees. *Graduate faculty:* 3,462 full-time (1,849 women), 877 part-time/adjunct (459 women). Tuition, state resident: full-time $11,006; part-time $474 per credit. Tuition, nonresident: full-time $28,212; part-time $1264 per credit hour. *Required fees:* $256 per semester. One-time fee: $94.32. Tuition and fees vary according to campus/location and program. *Graduate housing:* Room and/or apartments available on a first-come, first-served basis to single students; on-campus housing not available to married students. Typical cost: $9190 per year ($11,358 including board). Room and board charges vary according to board plan. *Student services:* Campus employment opportunities, campus safety program, career counseling, child daycare facilities, exercise/wellness program, free psychological counseling, international student services, low-cost health insurance, services for students with disabilities, teacher training, writing training. *Library facilities:* Auraria Library plus 1 other. *Collection:* Books: 632,468 (physical), 716,415 (digital/electronic); Serial titles: 6,521 (physical), 89,954 (digital/electronic); Databases: 298. Weekly public service hours: 85; students can reserve study rooms. *Research affiliation:* The Children's Hospital (pediatrics), National Jewish Health (pediatrics, immunology, respiratory disease), Denver Health (trauma, primary care, under-served populations).

Computer facilities: 750 computers available on campus for general student use. A campuswide network can be accessed from student residence rooms and from off campus. Online class registration is available. Website: http://www.ucdenver.edu/

General Application Contact: Graduate School Admissions, 303-556-2704, E-mail: admissions@ucdenver.edu.

GRADUATE UNITS

Business School Students: 993 full-time (394 women), 292 part-time (112 women); includes 203 minority (28 Black or African American, non-Hispanic/Latino; 6 American Indian or Alaska Native, non-Hispanic/Latino; 76 Asian, non-Hispanic/Latino; 76

Hispanic/Latino; 17 Two or more races, non-Hispanic/Latino), 195 international. Average age 33. 914 applicants, 63% accepted, 333 enrolled. *Faculty:* 59 full-time (18 women), 54 part-time/adjunct (14 women). Expenses: Contact institution. *Financial support:* In 2016–17, 314 students received support. Fellowships, research assistantships, teaching assistantships, Federal Work-Study, institutionally sponsored loans, scholarships/grants, and traineeships available. Financial award application deadline: 4/1; financial award applicants required to submit FAFSA. In 2016, 516 master's awarded. *Program availability:* Part-time, evening/weekend, online learning. Offers accounting and information systems audit and control (MS); accounting and information systems audit control (MS); auditing and forensic accounting (MS); bioinnovation and entrepreneurship (MBA); brand management and marketing communication (MS); business (MBA, MS, MSIB, PhD); business intelligence (MBA); business intelligence systems (MS); business strategy (MBA, MS); business to business marketing (MBA); business to consumer marketing (MBA); change and innovation (MS); change management (MBA); computer science and information systems (PhD); controllership and financial leadership (MS); corporate financial management (MS); decision sciences (MS); digital health entrepreneurship (MS); economics (MS); enterprise risk management (MS); enterprise technology management (MBA, MS); entrepreneurship (MBA); entrepreneurship and innovation (MS); finance (MS); financial analysis and management (MS); financial and commodities risk management (MS); geographic information systems (MS); global energy management (MS); global management (MS); global marketing (MS); health administration (MS); health information technology (MS); high-tech and entrepreneurial marketing (MS); human resources management (MBA); international business (MBA); investment management (MBA); leadership (MS); managing for sustainability (MBA, MS); managing human resources (MS); marketing for sustainability (MS); marketing research (MS); risk management and insurance (MS); sports and entertainment management (MBA, MS); sports and entertainment marketing (MS); taxation (MS); technology innovation and entrepreneurship (MS); Web and mobile computing (MS). *Application deadline:* For fall admission, 4/15 priority date for domestic students, 3/15 priority date for international students; for spring admission, 10/15 priority date for domestic students, 9/15 priority date for international students; for summer admission, 2/15 priority date for domestic students, 1/15 priority date for international students. Applications are processed on a rolling basis. *Application fee:* $50 ($75 for international students). Electronic applications accepted. *Application Contact:* 303-315-8200, E-mail: bschool.admissions@ucdenver.edu. *Dean and Professor of Finance,* Dr. Rohan Christie-David, 303-315-8000, E-mail: rohan.christie-david@ucdenver.edu.

College of Architecture and Planning Students: 357 full-time (188 women), 24 part-time (12 women); includes 63 minority (7 Black or African American, non-Hispanic/Latino; 7 Asian, non-Hispanic/Latino; 37 Hispanic/Latino; 12 Two or more races, non-Hispanic/Latino), 38 international. Average age 30. 490 applicants, 42% accepted, 132 enrolled. *Faculty:* 32 full-time (11 women), 27 part-time/adjunct (8 women). Expenses: Contact institution. *Financial support:* In 2016–17, 120 students received support. Fellowships with tuition reimbursements available, research assistantships, teaching assistantships, Federal Work-Study, institutionally sponsored loans, scholarships/grants, and traineeships available. Financial award application deadline: 4/1; financial award applicants required to submit FAFSA. In 2016, 164 master's, 3 doctorates awarded. *Program availability:* Part-time. Offers architecture (M Arch); architecture and planning (M Arch, MLA, MS, MUD, MURP, PhD); economic and community development planning (MURP); historic preservation (MS); history of architecture, landscape and urbanism (PhD); land use and environmental planning (MURP); landscape architecture (MLA); sustainable and healthy environments (PhD); urban design (MUD); urban place making (MURP). *Application deadline:* For fall admission, 2/1 for domestic students, 1/1 for international students; for spring admission, 10/1 for domestic students. Applications are processed on a rolling basis. *Application fee:* $50 ($75 for international students). Electronic applications accepted. *Application Contact:* Rachael Kuroiwa, Manager of Admissions and Outreach, 303-315-2325, E-mail: rachael.kuroiwa@ucdenver.edu. *Dean,* Dr. Mark Gelernter, 303-315-1000, E-mail: mark.gelernter@ucdenver.edu.

College of Arts and Media Students: 27 full-time (9 women), 5 part-time (2 women); includes 9 minority (2 Black or African American, non-Hispanic/Latino; 1 Asian, non-Hispanic/Latino; 4 Hispanic/Latino; 2 Two or more races, non-Hispanic/Latino), 2 international. Average age 31. 26 applicants, 92% accepted, 16 enrolled. *Faculty:* 34 full-time (12 women), 1 (woman) part-time/adjunct. Expenses: Contact institution. *Financial support:* In 2016–17, 4 students received support. Federal Work-Study, institutionally sponsored loans, scholarships/grants, traineeships, and unspecified assistantships available. Financial award application deadline: 4/1; financial award applicants required to submit FAFSA. In 2016, 13 master's awarded. *Program availability:* Part-time, evening/weekend. Offers recording arts (MS). *Application deadline:* For fall admission, 4/1 for domestic students, 3/1 for international students. *Application fee:* $50 ($75 for international students). Electronic applications accepted. *Application Contact:* Lisa Funderburg, Program Assistant, 303-352-3833, E-mail: lisa.funderburg@ucdenver.edu. *Dean, College of Arts and Media,* Laurence D. Kaptain, 303-556-2279, E-mail: laurence.kaptain@ucdenver.edu.

College of Engineering and Applied Science Students: 321 full-time (94 women), 138 part-time (31 women); includes 66 minority (10 Black or African American, non-Hispanic/Latino; 1 American Indian or Alaska Native, non-Hispanic/Latino; 23 Asian, non-Hispanic/Latino; 22 Hispanic/Latino; 1 Native Hawaiian or other Pacific Islander, non-Hispanic/Latino; 9 Two or more races, non-Hispanic/Latino), 189 international. Average age 30. 708 applicants, 55% accepted, 98 enrolled. *Faculty:* 73 full-time (16 women), 27 part-time/adjunct (4 women). Expenses: Contact institution. *Financial support:* In 2016–17, 237 students received support. Fellowships, research assistantships, teaching assistantships, Federal Work-Study, institutionally sponsored loans, scholarships/grants, and traineeships available. Financial award application deadline: 4/1; financial award applicants required to submit FAFSA. In 2016, 145 master's, 8 doctorates awarded. *Program availability:* Part-time, evening/weekend. Offers basic research (MS, PhD); biomedical device design (MS); civil engineering (M Eng, EASPh D); civil engineering systems (PhD); computer science (MS); computer science and engineering (EASPh D); computer science and information systems (PhD); electrical engineering (M Eng); engineering and applied science (M Eng, MS, EASPh D, PhD); entrepreneurship (MS, PhD); environmental and sustainability engineering (MS, PhD); geographic information systems (MS); geotechnical engineering (MS, PhD); hydrology and hydraulics (MS, PhD); mechanical engineering (M Eng, MS); mechanics (MS); structural engineering (MS, PhD); thermal sciences (MS); translational bioengineering (PhD); transportation engineering (MS, PhD). *Application fee:* $50 ($75 for international students). Electronic applications accepted. *Application Contact:* Graduate School Admissions, 303-556-2704, E-mail: admissions@ucdenver.edu. *Dean,* Dr. Mark Ingber, 303-556-2870, Fax: 303-556-2511, E-mail: marc.ingber@ucdenver.edu.

College of Liberal Arts and Sciences Students: 370 full-time (216 women), 198 part-time (112 women); includes 124 minority (20 Black or African American, non-

Hispanic/Latino; 6 American Indian or Alaska Native, non-Hispanic/Latino; 19 Asian, non-Hispanic/Latino; 59 Hispanic/Latino; 20 Two or more races, non-Hispanic/Latino), 30 international. Average age 32. 618 applicants, 46% accepted, 137 enrolled. *Faculty:* 211 full-time (85 women), 26 part-time/adjunct (10 women). Expenses: Contact institution. *Financial support:* In 2016–17, 178 students received support. Fellowships, research assistantships, teaching assistantships, Federal Work-Study, institutionally sponsored loans, scholarships/grants, and traineeships available. Financial award application deadline: 4/1; financial award applicants required to submit FAFSA. In 2016, 175 master's, 11 doctorates awarded. *Program availability:* Part-time, evening/weekend. Offers animal behavior (MS); applied linguistics (MA); applied mathematics (MS, PhD); applied science (MIS); archaeological studies (MA); biological anthropology (MA); biology (MS); cell and developmental biology (MS); chemistry (MS); clinical health (PhD); communication (MA); community health science (MSS); computer science (MIS); ecology (MS); economics (MA); environmental sciences (MA); European history (MA); evolutionary biology (MS); genetics (MS); global history (MA); health and behavioral sciences (PhD); humanities (MH); integrative and systems biology (PhD); international studies (MSS); liberal arts and sciences (MA, MH, MIS, MS, MSS, PhD); literature (MA); mathematics (MS); medical anthropology (MA); microbiology (MS); molecular biology (MS); neurobiology (MS); philosophy and theory (MH); plant systematics (MS); political science (MA); psychology (MA); public history (MA); rhetoric and teaching of writing (MA); social justice (MSS); society and the environment (MSS); sociology (MA); Spanish (MA); sustainable development and political ecology (MA); U.S. history (MA); visual studies (MH); women's and gender studies (MSS). *Application fee:* $50 ($75 for international students). Electronic applications accepted. *Application Contact:* College of Liberal Arts and Sciences, 303-556-2555, E-mail: clas@ucdenver.edu. *Dean,* Pamela Jansma, 303-556-2557, E-mail: pamela.jansma@ucdenver.edu.

College of Nursing Students: 408 full-time (376 women), 118 part-time (98 women); includes 91 minority (20 Black or African American, non-Hispanic/Latino; 2 American Indian or Alaska Native, non-Hispanic/Latino; 19 Asian, non-Hispanic/Latino; 36 Hispanic/Latino; 14 Two or more races, non-Hispanic/Latino), 3 international. Average age 39. 340 applicants, 42% accepted, 112 enrolled. *Faculty:* 118 full-time (110 women), 91 part-time/adjunct (83 women). Expenses: Contact institution. *Financial support:* In 2016–17, 244 students received support. Fellowships, research assistantships, teaching assistantships, Federal Work-Study, institutionally sponsored loans, scholarships/grants, traineeships, and unspecified assistantships available. Support available to part-time students. Financial award application deadline: 4/1; financial award applicants required to submit FAFSA. In 2016, 138 master's, 23 doctorates awarded. *Program availability:* Part-time, evening/weekend, online learning. Offers adult clinical nurse specialist (MS); adult nurse practitioner (MS); family nurse practitioner (MS); family psychiatric mental health nurse practitioner (MS); health care informatics (MS); nurse-midwifery (MS); nursing (DNP, PhD); nursing leadership and health care systems (MS); pediatric nurse practitioner (MS); women's health (MS). *Application deadline:* For fall admission, 2/15 for domestic students, 1/15 for international students; for spring admission, 7/1 for domestic students, 6/1 for international students. *Application fee:* $50 ($75 for international students). Electronic applications accepted. *Application Contact:* Judy Campbell, Graduate Programs Coordinator, 303-724-8503, E-mail: judy.campbell@ucdenver.edu. *Dean,* Dr. Sarah Thompson, 303-724-1679, E-mail: sarah.a.thompson@ucdenver.edu.

Colorado School of Public Health Students: 483 full-time (394 women), 100 part-time (79 women); includes 135 minority (21 Black or African American, non-Hispanic/Latino; 4 American Indian or Alaska Native, non-Hispanic/Latino; 35 Asian, non-Hispanic/Latino; 56 Hispanic/Latino; 1 Native Hawaiian or other Pacific Islander, non-Hispanic/Latino; 18 Two or more races, non-Hispanic/Latino), 19 international. Average age 31. 1,005 applicants, 65% accepted, 205 enrolled. *Faculty:* 95 full-time (69 women), 29 part-time/adjunct (20 women). Expenses: Contact institution. *Financial support:* In 2016–17, 404 students received support. Fellowships, research assistantships, teaching assistantships, Federal Work-Study, institutionally sponsored loans, scholarships/grants, traineeships, and unspecified assistantships available. Financial award application deadline: 4/1. In 2016, 194 master's, 4 doctorates awarded. *Program availability:* Part-time. Offers biostatistics and informatics (MS, PhD); community and behavioral health (MPH, Dr PH); environmental and occupational health (MPH); epidemiology (MS, PhD); health services research (MS, PhD); health systems, management and policy (MPH); public health (MPH, MS, Dr PH, PhD). *Application deadline:* For fall admission, 1/15 for domestic and international students. *Application fee:* $50 ($75 for international students). Electronic applications accepted. *Application Contact:* Office of Student Affairs, 303-724-4613, Fax: 303-724-4620, E-mail: admissions.csph@ucdenver.edu. *Interim Dean,* Dr. Elaine Morrato, 303-724-4450, E-mail: elaine.morrato@ucdenver.edu.

School of Dental Medicine Students: 447 full-time (227 women), 1 part-time (0 women); includes 136 minority (8 Black or African American, non-Hispanic/Latino; 2 American Indian or Alaska Native, non-Hispanic/Latino; 72 Asian, non-Hispanic/Latino; 43 Hispanic/Latino; 1 Native Hawaiian or other Pacific Islander, non-Hispanic/Latino; 10 Two or more races, non-Hispanic/Latino), 11 international. Average age 29. 2,000 applicants, 7% accepted, 95 enrolled. *Faculty:* 99 full-time (43 women), 51 part-time/adjunct (15 women). Expenses: Contact institution. *Financial support:* In 2016–17, 214 students received support. Fellowships, research assistantships, teaching assistantships, Federal Work-Study, institutionally sponsored loans, scholarships/grants, and traineeships available. Financial award application deadline: 4/1; financial award applicants required to submit FAFSA. In 2016, 28 master's, 117 doctorates awarded. Offers dental surgery (DDS); orthodontics (MS); periodontics (MS). *Application deadline:* For fall admission, 12/31 for domestic students, 12/15 for international students. *Application fee:* $50 ($75 for international students). Electronic applications accepted. *Application Contact:* Graduate Student Admissions, 303-724-7122, Fax: 303-724-7109, E-mail: ddsadmissioninquiries@ucdenver.edu. *Dean,* Dr. Denise K. Kassebaum, 303-724-7100, Fax: 303-724-7109, E-mail: denise.kassebaum@ucdenver.edu.

School of Education and Human Development Students: 867 full-time (691 women), 447 part-time (369 women); includes 251 minority (47 Black or African American, non-Hispanic/Latino; 4 American Indian or Alaska Native, non-Hispanic/Latino; 26 Asian, non-Hispanic/Latino; 145 Hispanic/Latino; 2 Native Hawaiian or other Pacific Islander, non-Hispanic/Latino; 27 Two or more races, non-Hispanic/Latino), 20 international. Average age 34. 519 applicants, 59% accepted, 215 enrolled. *Faculty:* 72 full-time (44 women), 82 part-time/adjunct (63 women). Expenses: Contact institution. *Financial support:* In 2016–17, 272 students received support. Fellowships, research assistantships, teaching assistantships, Federal Work-Study, institutionally sponsored loans, scholarships/grants, and traineeships available. Financial award application deadline: 4/1; financial award applicants required to submit FAFSA. In 2016, 479 master's, 23 doctorates, 18 other advanced degrees awarded. *Program availability:* Part-time, evening/weekend, online learning. Offers administrative leadership and policy studies (MA, Ed S); counseling (MA); e-learning design and implementation (MA); early childhood education (MA); education and human development (MA, MS Ed, Ed D, PhD, Psy D, Ed S); educational psychology (MA); educational studies and research (PhD); elementary linguistically diverse education (MA); elementary math and science education (MA); elementary math education (MA); elementary reading and writing (MA); elementary science education (MA); executive leadership (Ed D); instructional design and adult learning (MA); instructional leadership (Ed D); K-12 teaching (MA); mathematics education (MS Ed); school counseling (MA); school psychology (Psy D, Ed S); secondary English education (MA); secondary linguistically diverse education (MA); secondary math education (MA); secondary reading and writing (MA); secondary science education (MA); special education (MA). *Application fee:* $50 ($75 for international students). Electronic applications accepted. *Application Contact:* Student Services Center, 303-315-6300, Fax: 303-315-6311, E-mail: education@ucdenver.edu. *Dean*, Rebecca Kantor, 303-315-6343, E-mail: rebecca.kantor@ucdenver.edu.

School of Medicine Students: 1,488 full-time (847 women), 41 part-time (27 women); includes 295 minority (29 Black or African American, non-Hispanic/Latino; 4 American Indian or Alaska Native, non-Hispanic/Latino; 110 Asian, non-Hispanic/Latino; 110 Hispanic/Latino; 1 Native Hawaiian or other Pacific Islander, non-Hispanic/Latino; 41 Two or more races, non-Hispanic/Latino), 24 international. Average age 29. 1,186 applicants, 27% accepted, 310 enrolled. *Faculty:* 3,092 full-time (1,742 women), 574 part-time/adjunct (318 women). Expenses: Contact institution. *Financial support:* In 2016, 94 master's, 256 doctorates awarded. Fellowships, research assistantships, teaching assistantships, career-related internships or fieldwork, Federal Work-Study, institutionally sponsored loans, scholarships/grants, traineeships, and unspecified assistantships available. Financial award application deadline: 3/15; financial award applicants required to submit FAFSA. In 2016, 94 master's, 256 doctorates awarded. Offers anesthesiology (MS); biochemistry (PhD); biochemistry and molecular genetics (PhD); bioinformatics (PhD); biomedical sciences (MS, PhD); biomolecular structure (PhD); biophysics and genetics (MS, PhD); cancer biology (PhD); cell biology, stem cells, and developmental biology (PhD); child health associate (MPAS); clinical investigation (PhD); clinical sciences (MS); computational bioscience (PhD); health information technology (PhD); health services research (PhD); human medical genetics and genomics (PhD); immunology (PhD); medicine (MPAS, MS, DPT, MD, PhD); microbiology (PhD); microbiology and immunology (PhD); modern human anatomy (MS); molecular biology (PhD); neuroscience (PhD); pharmacology (PhD); physical therapy (DPT); physiology (PhD); rehabilitation science (PhD). *Application fee:* $50 ($75 for international students). Electronic applications accepted. *Application Contact:* W. Vidal Dickerson, Director of Student Life, 303-724-6407, E-mail: somadmin@ucdenver.edu. *Dean*, Dr. John Reilly, Jr., 303-724-0882, E-mail: john.reillyjr@ucdenver.edu.

School of Public Affairs Students: 264 full-time (161 women), 152 part-time (94 women); includes 65 minority (16 Black or African American, non-Hispanic/Latino; 1 American Indian or Alaska Native, non-Hispanic/Latino; 11 Asian, non-Hispanic/Latino; 27 Hispanic/Latino; 2 Native Hawaiian or other Pacific Islander, non-Hispanic/Latino; 8 Two or more races, non-Hispanic/Latino), 27 international. Average age 34. 253 applicants, 71% accepted, 98 enrolled. *Faculty:* 23 full-time (13 women), 15 part-time/adjunct (6 women). Expenses: Contact institution. *Financial support:* In 2016–17, 97 students received support, including 3 fellowships with full tuition reimbursements available (averaging $15,000 per year); research assistantships, teaching assistantships, Federal Work-Study, institutionally sponsored loans, scholarships/grants, traineeships, and unspecified assistantships also available. Support available to part-time students. Financial award application deadline: 4/1; financial award applicants required to submit FAFSA. In 2016, 184 master's, 8 doctorates awarded. *Program availability:* Part-time, evening/weekend, online learning. Offers criminal justice (MCJ); public administration (MPA); public affairs (PhD). *Application deadline:* For fall admission, 2/1 priority date for domestic students, 1/15 priority date for international students; for spring admission, 10/15 priority date for domestic students. *Application fee:* $50 ($75 for international students). Electronic applications accepted. *Application Contact:* Antoinette Sandoval, Student Service Specialist, 303-315-2487, Fax: 303-315-2229, E-mail: antoinette.sandoval@ucdenver.edu. *Dean*, Paul Teske, 303-315-2805, Fax: 303-315-2229, E-mail: paul.teske@ucdenver.edu.

Skaggs School of Pharmacy and Pharmaceutical Sciences Students: 668 full-time (421 women), 120 part-time (81 women); includes 311 minority (48 Black or African American, non-Hispanic/Latino; 5 American Indian or Alaska Native, non-Hispanic/Latino; 183 Asian, non-Hispanic/Latino; 61 Hispanic/Latino; 1 Native Hawaiian or other Pacific Islander, non-Hispanic/Latino; 13 Two or more races, non-Hispanic/Latino), 31 international. Average age 29. 295 applicants, 70% accepted, 186 enrolled. *Faculty:* 110 full-time (54 women), 35 part-time/adjunct (19 women). Expenses: Contact institution. *Financial support:* In 2016–17, 593 students received support. Fellowships, research assistantships, teaching assistantships, Federal Work-Study, institutionally sponsored loans, scholarships/grants, traineeships, and unspecified assistantships available. Financial award application deadline: 3/15; financial award applicants required to submit FAFSA. In 2016, 225 doctorates awarded. *Program availability:* Online learning. Offers clinical pharmaceutical sciences (PhD); pharmaceutical biotechnology (PhD); pharmaceutical outcomes research (PhD); pharmacy (Pharm D); pharmacy and pharmaceutical sciences (PhD, Pharm D); toxicology (PhD). *Application deadline:* For fall admission, 12/1 for domestic students, 11/1 for international students. *Application fee:* $150. Electronic applications accepted. *Application Contact:* Jackie Milowski, Department of Pharmaceutical Sciences Administrative Assistant, 303-724-7263, E-mail: jackie.milowski@ucdenver.edu. *Dean*, Dr. Ralph Altiere, 303-724-2631, E-mail: ralph.altiere@ucdenver.edu.

UNIVERSITY OF CONNECTICUT, Storrs, CT 06269

General Information State-supported, coed, university. CGS member. *Graduate housing:* Rooms and/or apartments available on a first-come, first-served basis to single and married students. Housing application deadline: 4/1. *Research affiliation:* U.S. Navy–Submarine Medical Research Laboratory, Haskins Laboratories.

GRADUATE UNITS

Graduate School *Program availability:* Part-time, evening/weekend, online learning. Electronic applications accepted.

College of Agriculture, Health and Natural Resources Offers agricultural and resource economics (MS, PhD); agriculture, health and natural resources (MS, PhD); animal science (MS, PhD); exercise science (MS, PhD); natural resources management and engineering (MS, PhD); nutritional sciences (MS, PhD); pathobiology (MS, PhD); physical therapy (DPT); plant and soil sciences (MS, PhD); sport management (MS). Electronic applications accepted.

College of Liberal Arts and Sciences Offers anthropology (MA, PhD); applied financial mathematics (MS); applied genomics (PSM); audiology (Au D, PhD); behavioral neuroscience (PhD); biopsychology (PhD); botany (MS, PhD); cell and developmental biology (MS, PhD); chemistry (MS, PhD); clinical psychology (MA, PhD); cognition and instruction (PhD); communication processes (MA); comparative physiology (MS, PhD); developmental psychology (MA, PhD); ecological psychology (PhD); economics (MA, PhD); English (MA, PhD); European studies (MA); experimental psychology (PhD); general psychology (MA, PhD); genetics and genomics (MS, PhD);

geography (MA, PhD); geological sciences (MS, PhD); history (MA, PhD); human development and family studies (MA, PhD); industrial/organizational psychology (PhD); international studies (MA); Italian history and culture (MA); Judaic studies (MA); language and cognition (PhD); Latino and Latin American studies (MA); liberal arts and sciences (MA, MPA, MS, Au D, PhD, Certificate, Graduate Certificate); linguistics (MA, PhD); medieval studies (MA, PhD); microbial systems analysis (PSM); microbiology (MS, PhD); neuroscience (PhD); philosophy (MA, PhD); physics (MS, PhD); political science (MA, PhD); public administration (MPA, Graduate Certificate); quantitative research methods (Graduate Certificate); social psychology (MA, PhD); sociology (MA, PhD); speech-language pathology (MA, Au D, PhD); statistics (MS, PhD); structural biology, biochemistry and biophysics (MS, PhD); survey research (MA, Graduate Certificate). Electronic applications accepted.

eCampus *Program availability:* Online learning. Offers continuing studies (MS, Certificate); human resource management (MS); occupational safety and health management (Certificate).

Neag School of Education Offers adult learning (MA, PhD); agriculture (MA); agriculture education (PhD); bilingual and bicultural education (MA, PhD); cognition and instruction (MA, PhD); cognition, instruction, and learning technology (MA, PhD); counseling psychology (PhD); education (MA, PhD); educational administration (MA); elementary education (MA, PhD); English education (MA, PhD); gifted and talented education (Graduate Certificate); higher education and student affairs (MA); history and social sciences education (MA, PhD); mathematics education (MA, PhD); music education (MA); reading education (MA, PhD); school counseling (MA); science education (MA, PhD); secondary education (MA, PhD); world languages education (MA, PhD). Electronic applications accepted.

School of Business Offers accounting (MS); business administration (MBA, PhD); finance (PhD); health care management and insurance studies (MBA); management (PhD); management consulting (MBA); marketing (PhD); marketing intelligence (MBA). Electronic applications accepted.

School of Engineering Offers biomedical engineering (MS, PhD); chemical engineering (MS, PhD); civil engineering (MS, PhD); computer science (MS, PhD); electrical engineering (MS, PhD); engineering (M Eng, MS, PhD); environmental engineering (MS, PhD); materials science and engineering (MS, PhD); mechanical engineering (MS, PhD); metallurgy and materials engineering (M Eng). Electronic applications accepted.

School of Fine Arts Offers acting (MA, MFA); conducting (M Mus, DMA); design (MA, MFA); fine arts (M Mus, MA, MFA, DMA, PhD); historical musicology (MA); music theory (MA); music theory and history (PhD); performance (M Mus, DMA); puppetry (MA, MFA); technical direction (MA, MFA). Electronic applications accepted.

School of Nursing Offers nursing (MS, DNP, PhD, Post-Master's Certificate). Electronic applications accepted.

School of Pharmacy Offers medicinal chemistry (MS, PhD); pharmaceutics (MS, PhD); pharmacology (MS, PhD); pharmacology and toxicology (MS, PhD); pharmacy (MS, PhD, Pharm D); toxicology (MS, PhD). Electronic applications accepted.

School of Social Work Offers social work (MSW, PhD). Electronic applications accepted.

Institute of Materials Science Offers materials science (MS, PhD); polymer science and engineering (MS, PhD).

School of Law *Program availability:* Part-time. Offers law (JD). Electronic applications accepted.

UNIVERSITY OF CONNECTICUT HEALTH CENTER, Farmington, CT 06030

General Information State-supported, coed, graduate-only institution. *Graduate housing:* On-campus housing not available.

GRADUATE UNITS

Graduate School *Program availability:* Part-time, evening/weekend. Offers biomedical sciences (PhD); biomedical sciences - integrated (PhD); cell analysis and modeling (PhD); cell biology (PhD); clinical and translational research (MS); genetics and developmental biology (PhD); immunology (PhD); molecular biology and biochemistry (PhD); neuroscience (PhD); public health (MPH); skeletal biology and regeneration (PhD).

School of Dental Medicine Offers dental medicine (MDS, DMD, Certificate); dental science (MDS). Electronic applications accepted.

School of Medicine Offers medicine (MD). Electronic applications accepted.

UNIVERSITY OF DALLAS, Irving, TX 75062-4736

General Information Independent-religious, coed, university. *Graduate housing:* Room and/or apartments available on a first-come, first-served basis to single students; on-campus housing not available to married students. Housing application deadline: 6/1.

GRADUATE UNITS

Braniff Graduate School of Liberal Arts *Program availability:* Part-time. Offers American studies (MAS); art (MA, MFA); classics (MA, MC); English (MA); humanities (M Hum, MA); liberal arts (M Hum, M Pol, M Psych, M Th, MA, MAS, MC, MCSL, MEL, MFA, MPM, MRE, MTS, PhD); philosophy (MA); politics (M Pol, MA); psychology (M Psych, MA); theology (M Th, MA).

Institute of Philosophic Studies Offers literature (PhD); philosophy (PhD); politics (PhD).

Institute for Religious and Pastoral Studies *Program availability:* Part-time, evening/weekend, online learning. Offers religious and pastoral studies (MCSL, MPM, MRE, MTS).

Satish and Yasmin Gupta College of Business *Program availability:* Part-time, evening/weekend, online learning. Offers accounting (MBA, MS); business administration (DBA); business analytics (MS); business management (MBA); corporate finance (MBA); cybersecurity (MS); finance (MS); financial services (MBA); global business (MBA, MS); health services management (MBA); human resource management (MBA); information and technology management (MS); information assurance (MBA); information technology (MBA); information technology service management (MBA); marketing management (MBA); organization development (MBA); project management (MBA); sports and entertainment management (MBA); strategic leadership (MBA); supply chain management (MBA). Electronic applications accepted.

UNIVERSITY OF DAYTON, Dayton, OH 45469

General Information Independent-religious, coed, university. CGS member. *Enrollment:* 10,803 graduate, professional, and undergraduate students; 1,637 full-time matriculated graduate/professional students (822 women), 513 part-time matriculated graduate/professional students (287 women). *Enrollment by degree level:* 1,581 master's, 634 doctoral, 35 other advanced degrees. Tuition and fees vary according to degree level and program. *Graduate housing:* Room and/or apartments available on a first-come, first-served basis to single students; on-campus housing not available to married students. *Student services:* Campus employment opportunities, campus safety program, career counseling, child daycare facilities, exercise/wellness program, free psychological counseling, international student services, multicultural affairs office, services for students with disabilities, writing training. *Library facilities:* Roesch Library plus 3 others. *Collection:* Books: 671,817 (physical), 1.3 million (digital/electronic); Databases: 301. Weekly public service hours: 131; students can reserve study rooms. *Research affiliation:* California Institute of Technology (materials development), Dayton Area Graduate Studies Institute (materials testing), Kern Family Foundation (curriculum development), Ohio Aerospace Institute (engine analysis), Riverside Research Institute (radar and materials research), Southwest Research Institute (engineering services).

Computer facilities: Computer purchase and lease plans are available. 7,675 computers available on campus for general student use. A campuswide network can be accessed from student residence rooms and from off campus. Online class registration, applications, admission/enrollment status, virtual orientation, online digital resources, online courses, assistive technology, learning management system, multimedia labs, payment, cyber cafes, centrally-licensed, downloadable software and training are available.
Website: http://www.udayton.edu/

General Application Contact: Graduate Admissions, 937-229-4411, E-mail: graduateadmission@udayton.edu.

GRADUATE UNITS

Department of Biology Students: 17 full-time (10 women); includes 2 minority (both Asian, non-Hispanic/Latino), 7 international. Average age 26. 63 applicants, 8% accepted, 5 enrolled. *Faculty:* 16 full-time (6 women). Expenses: Contact institution. *Financial support:* In 2016–17, 3 research assistantships with full tuition reimbursements (averaging $18,760 per year), 15 teaching assistantships with full tuition reimbursements (averaging $18,760 per year) were awarded; institutionally sponsored loans, health care benefits, and unspecified assistantships also available. Financial award application deadline: 1/31; financial award applicants required to submit FAFSA. In 2016, 3 master's, 5 doctorates awarded. *Application deadline:* For fall admission, 1/31 priority date for domestic and international students. Applications are processed on a rolling basis. *Application fee:* $25. Electronic applications accepted. *Application Contact:* Dr. Amit Singh, Director, Biology Graduate Programs, 937-229-2894, Fax: 937-229-2021, E-mail: asingh1@udayton.edu. *Chair,* Dr. Mark G. Nielsen, 937-229-2521, Fax: 937-229-2021, E-mail: mnielsen1@udayton.edu.

Department of Chemical Engineering Students: 26 full-time (8 women), 6 part-time (1 woman); includes 1 minority (Black or African American, non-Hispanic/Latino), 24 international. Average age 26. 92 applicants, 22% accepted. *Faculty:* 9 full-time (2 women), 2 part-time/adjunct (0 women). Expenses: Contact institution. *Financial support:* In 2016–17, 2 research assistantships with full tuition reimbursements (averaging $15,000 per year) were awarded; teaching assistantships, institutionally sponsored loans, and health care benefits also available. Financial award application deadline: 3/1; financial award applicants required to submit FAFSA. In 2016, 33 master's awarded. *Program availability:* Part-time, evening/weekend. Offers bioengineering (MS); chemical engineering (MS Ch E). *Application deadline:* Applications are processed on a rolling basis. *Application fee:* $0 ($50 for international students). Electronic applications accepted. *Application Contact:* Dr. Kevin Myers, Graduate Program Director, 937-229-2627, E-mail: kmyers1@udayton.edu. *Chair,* Dr. Charles Browning, 937-229-2627, E-mail: cbrowning1@udayton.edu.

Department of Chemistry Students: 4 full-time (3 women), 2 part-time (1 woman); includes 1 minority (Asian, non-Hispanic/Latino), 1 international. Average age 32. 56 applicants, 14% accepted. *Faculty:* 10 full-time (2 women). Expenses: Contact institution. *Financial support:* In 2016–17, 3 students received support, including 4 teaching assistantships with full tuition reimbursements available (averaging $13,600 per year); research assistantships, institutionally sponsored loans, and health care benefits also available. Financial award application deadline: 5/15; financial award applicants required to submit FAFSA. In 2016, 1 master's awarded. Offers chemistry (MS). *Application deadline:* For fall admission, 5/1 priority date for domestic and international students; for winter admission, 7/1 priority date for international students; for spring admission, 11/1 priority date for international students. *Application fee:* $0 ($50 for international students). Electronic applications accepted. *Application Contact:* Dr. Kevin Church, Graduate Program Director, 937-229-2659, E-mail: kchurch1@udayton.edu. *Chair,* Dr. David Johnson, 937-229-2631, E-mail: djohnson1@udayton.edu.

Department of Civil and Environmental Engineering and Engineering Mechanics Students: 40 full-time (8 women), 2 part-time (0 women); includes 1 minority (Asian, non-Hispanic/Latino), 30 international. Average age 26. 137 applicants, 17% accepted. *Faculty:* 9 full-time (2 women), 3 part-time/adjunct (1 woman). Expenses: Contact institution. *Financial support:* Research assistantships, institutionally sponsored loans, scholarships/grants, and department-funded awards (averaging $2448 per year) available. Financial award application deadline: 3/1; financial award applicants required to submit FAFSA. In 2016, 14 master's awarded. *Program availability:* Part-time, evening/weekend. Offers engineering mechanics (MSEM); environmental engineering (MSCE); geotechnical engineering (MSCE); structural engineering (MSCE); transportation engineering (MSCE); water resources engineering (MSCE). *Application deadline:* For fall admission, 8/1 priority date for domestic students, 5/1 priority date for international students; for spring admission, 11/1 priority date for international students. Applications are processed on a rolling basis. *Application fee:* $0 ($50 for international students). Electronic applications accepted. *Application Contact:* 937-229-4462, E-mail: graduateadmission@udayton.edu. *Chair,* Dr. Donald V. Chase, 937-229-3847, Fax: 937-229-3491, E-mail: dchase1@udayton.edu.

Department of Communication Students: 15 full-time (13 women), 3 part-time (2 women); includes 1 minority (Black or African American, non-Hispanic/Latino), 3 international. Average age 33. 58 applicants, 33% accepted, 10 enrolled. *Faculty:* 11 full-time (5 women). Expenses: Contact institution. *Financial support:* In 2016–17, 7 students received support, including 1 research assistantship with full tuition reimbursement available (averaging $10,914 per year), 8 teaching assistantships with full tuition reimbursements available (averaging $10,914 per year); institutionally sponsored loans, health care benefits, and unspecified assistantships also available. Financial award application deadline: 3/9; financial award applicants required to submit FAFSA. In 2016, 22 master's awarded. *Program availability:* Part-time, evening/weekend. Offers communication (MA); interdisciplinary communication (MA). *Application deadline:* Applications are processed on a rolling basis. *Application fee:* $0 ($50 for international students). Electronic applications accepted. *Application Contact:* Dr. JeeHee Han, Graduate Program Director, 937-229-2486, E-mail: jhan01@udayton.edu. *Chair,* Dr. Jon A. Hess, 937-229-2028, E-mail: jhess1@udayton.edu.

Department of Computer Science Students: 130 full-time (62 women), 19 part-time (5 women); includes 2 minority (1 Asian, non-Hispanic/Latino; 1 Hispanic/Latino), 139

international. Average age 24. 279 applicants, 36% accepted. *Faculty:* 9 full-time (1 woman). Expenses: Contact institution. *Financial support:* In 2016–17, 9 teaching assistantships with full tuition reimbursements (averaging $11,025 per year) were awarded; research assistantships, institutionally sponsored loans, health care benefits, and unspecified assistantships also available. Financial award application deadline: 5/1; financial award applicants required to submit FAFSA. In 2016, 16 master's awarded. *Program availability:* Part-time. Offers computer science (MCS). *Application deadline:* Applications are processed on a rolling basis. *Application fee:* $0 ($50 for international students). Electronic applications accepted. *Application Contact:* 937-229-4462, E-mail: graduateadmission@udayton.edu. *Chair,* Dr. Mehdi Zarghtam, 937-229-3831, E-mail: mzargham1@udayton.edu.

Department of Counselor Education and Human Services Students: 198 full-time (155 women), 95 part-time (75 women); includes 15 minority (8 Black or African American, non-Hispanic/Latino; 2 Asian, non-Hispanic/Latino; 2 Hispanic/Latino; 3 Two or more races, non-Hispanic/Latino), 3 international. Average age 36. 426 applicants, 28% accepted. *Faculty:* 10 full-time (6 women), 24 part-time/adjunct (15 women). Expenses: Contact institution. *Financial support:* In 2016–17, 7 research assistantships with partial tuition reimbursements (averaging $8,038 per year), 4 teaching assistantships with partial tuition reimbursements (averaging $9,390 per year) were awarded; career-related internships or fieldwork, institutionally sponsored loans, health care benefits, and unspecified assistantships also available. Financial award application deadline: 1/9; financial award applicants required to submit FAFSA. In 2016, 115 master's, 9 Ed Ss awarded. *Program availability:* Part-time, evening/weekend. Offers clinical mental health counseling (MS Ed); college student personnel (MS Ed); higher education administration (MS Ed); human services (MS Ed); school counseling (MS Ed); school psychology (MS Ed, Ed S). *Application deadline:* For fall admission, 3/10 priority date for domestic and international students; for spring admission, 9/10 priority date for domestic and international students; for summer admission, 12/1 priority date for domestic and international students. *Application fee:* $0 ($50 for international students). Electronic applications accepted. *Application Contact:* Kathleen Brown, Administrative Assistant, 937-229-3644, Fax: 937-229-1055, E-mail: kbrown1@udayton.edu. *Chair,* Dr. Alan Demmitt, 937-229-3644, Fax: 937-229-1055, E-mail: ademmitt1@udayton.edu.

Department of Educational Administration Students: 49 full-time (30 women), 66 part-time (45 women); includes 7 minority (4 Black or African American, non-Hispanic/Latino; 1 Hispanic/Latino; 2 Two or more races, non-Hispanic/Latino), 13 international. Average age 34. 121 applicants, 47% accepted. *Faculty:* 6 full-time (3 women), 21 part-time/adjunct (9 women). Expenses: Contact institution. *Financial support:* In 2016–17, 5 research assistantships with partial tuition reimbursements (averaging $8,038 per year) were awarded; career-related internships or fieldwork and institutionally sponsored loans also available. Financial award application deadline: 3/15; financial award applicants required to submit FAFSA. In 2016, 87 master's, 3 Ed Ss awarded. *Program availability:* Part-time, blended/hybrid learning. Offers Catholic school leadership (MS Ed); educational administration (Ed S); educational leadership (MS Ed); leadership for educational systems (MS Ed). *Application deadline:* For fall admission, 5/1 priority date for domestic and international students; for spring admission, 11/1 priority date for domestic and international students. *Application fee:* $0 ($50 for international students). Electronic applications accepted. *Application Contact:* Janice Keivel, Administrative Associate, 937-229-3738, Fax: 937-229-1055, E-mail: jkeivel1@udayton.edu. *Chair,* Dr. David D. Dolph, 937-229-3105, Fax: 937-229-1055, E-mail: ddolph1@udayton.edu.

Department of Electrical and Computer Engineering Students: 145 full-time (30 women), 14 part-time (4 women); includes 10 minority (2 Black or African American, non-Hispanic/Latino; 6 Asian, non-Hispanic/Latino; 2 Two or more races, non-Hispanic/Latino), 100 international. Average age 28. 82 applicants, 22% accepted. *Faculty:* 17 full-time (0 women), 16 part-time/adjunct (2 women). Expenses: Contact institution. *Financial support:* In 2016–17, 17 research assistantships with full tuition reimbursements (averaging $12,500 per year), 30 teaching assistantships with full tuition reimbursements (averaging $10,000 per year) were awarded; institutionally sponsored loans, health care benefits, and unspecified assistantships also available. Financial award application deadline: 3/1; financial award applicants required to submit FAFSA. In 2016, 88 master's, 8 doctorates awarded. *Program availability:* Part-time. Offers computer engineering (MS); electrical engineering (MSEE, PhD). *Application deadline:* For fall admission, 8/1 for domestic students; 5/1 priority date for international students; for spring admission, 11/1 priority date for international students. Applications are processed on a rolling basis. *Application fee:* $0 ($50 for international students). Electronic applications accepted. *Application Contact:* E-mail: graduateadmission@udayton.edu. *Chair,* Dr. Guru Subramanyam, 937-229-3188, Fax: 937-229-4529, E-mail: gsubramanyam1@udayton.edu.

Department of Electro-Optics and Photonics Students: 44 full-time (9 women), 8 part-time (1 woman); includes 4 minority (3 Black or African American, non-Hispanic/Latino; 1 Asian, non-Hispanic/Latino), 25 international. Average age 30. 41 applicants, 22% accepted. *Faculty:* 5 full-time (0 women). Expenses: Contact institution. *Financial support:* In 2016–17, 19 research assistantships with full tuition reimbursements (averaging $21,000 per year), 7 teaching assistantships with full tuition reimbursements (averaging $21,000 per year) were awarded; institutionally sponsored loans, health care benefits, and unspecified assistantships also available. Financial award application deadline: 3/1; financial award applicants required to submit FAFSA. In 2016, 14 master's, 4 doctorates awarded. *Program availability:* Part-time. Offers electro-optics and photonics (MSEO, PhD). *Application deadline:* Applications are processed on a rolling basis. *Application fee:* $0 ($50 for international students). Electronic applications accepted. *Application Contact:* Meghan L. Brophy, Administrative Assistant, 937-229-2797, Fax: 937-229-2097, E-mail: graduateadmission@udayton.edu. *Director,* Dr. Partha P. Banerjee, 937-229-2797, Fax: 937-229-2099, E-mail: pbanerjee1@udayton.edu.

Department of Engineering Management and Systems Students: 40 full-time (8 women), 23 part-time (7 women); includes 8 minority (4 Black or African American, non-Hispanic/Latino; 1 Asian, non-Hispanic/Latino; 1 Hispanic/Latino; 2 Two or more races, non-Hispanic/Latino), 18 international. Average age 31. 205 applicants, 16% accepted. *Faculty:* 4 full-time (1 woman), 9 part-time/adjunct (1 woman). Expenses: Contact institution. *Financial support:* Application deadline: 3/1; applicants required to submit FAFSA. In 2016, 27 master's awarded. *Program availability:* Part-time, evening/weekend, blended/hybrid learning. Offers engineering management (MSEM); management science (MSMS). *Application deadline:* Applications are processed on a rolling basis. *Application fee:* $0 ($50 for international students). Electronic applications accepted. *Application Contact:* 937-229-4462, E-mail: graduateadmission@udayton.edu. *Chair,* Dr. Edward Mykytka, 937-229-2238, E-mail: emykytka1@udayton.edu.

Department of English Students: 15 full-time (10 women), 2 part-time (1 woman); includes 1 minority (Black or African American, non-Hispanic/Latino), 7 international. Average age 27. 55 applicants, 29% accepted. *Faculty:* 22 full-time (11 women).

Expenses: Contact institution. *Financial support:* In 2016–17, 9 teaching assistantships with full tuition reimbursements (averaging $11,000 per year) were awarded; institutionally sponsored loans and health care benefits also available. Financial award application deadline: 12/15; financial award applicants required to submit FAFSA. In 2016, 8 master's awarded. *Program availability:* Part-time. Offers literary and cultural studies (MA); teaching English to speakers of other languages (TESOL) (MA); writing and rhetoric (MA). *Application deadline:* For fall admission, 6/15 priority date for domestic and international students; for spring admission, 12/15 priority date for domestic and international students. Applications are processed on a rolling basis. *Application fee:* $0 ($50 for international students). Electronic applications accepted. *Application Contact:* Dr. Tereza Szeghi, Director of Graduate Studies, 937-229-3443, E-mail: tszeghi1@udayton.edu. Chair, Dr. Andrew Slade, 937-229-3434, Fax: 937-229-3563, E-mail: aslade1@udayton.edu.

Department of Health and Sport Science Students: 12 full-time (3 women), 1 (woman) part-time; includes 5 minority (3 Black or African American, non-Hispanic/Latino; 1 Asian, non-Hispanic/Latino; 1 Two or more races, non-Hispanic/Latino), 2 international. Average age 23. 37 applicants, 30% accepted. *Faculty:* 7 full-time (3 women). Expenses: Contact institution. *Financial support:* In 2016–17, 2 research assistantships with partial tuition reimbursements (averaging $9,390 per year), 2 teaching assistantships with partial tuition reimbursements (averaging $9,390 per year) were awarded; career-related internships or fieldwork, institutionally sponsored loans, health care benefits, and unspecified assistantships also available. Financial award application deadline: 3/1; financial award applicants required to submit FAFSA. In 2016, 5 master's awarded. Offers exercise science (MS Ed). *Application deadline:* Applications are processed on a rolling basis. *Application fee:* $0 ($50 for international students). Electronic applications accepted. *Application Contact:* Laura Greger, Administrative Assistant, 937-229-4225, E-mail: lgreger1@udayton.edu. Chair, Dr. Lloyd Laubach, 937-229-4240, Fax: 937-229-4244, E-mail: llaubach1@udayton.edu.

Department of Materials Engineering Students: 50 full-time (16 women), 13 part-time (3 women); includes 8 minority (3 Black or African American, non-Hispanic/Latino; 3 Asian, non-Hispanic/Latino; 2 Hispanic/Latino), 18 international. Average age 29. 67 applicants, 37% accepted. *Faculty:* 4 full-time (0 women), 9 part-time/adjunct (0 women). Expenses: Contact institution. *Financial support:* In 2016–17, 6 research assistantships with full tuition reimbursements (averaging $13,500 per year) were awarded; Federal Work-Study, institutionally sponsored loans, health care benefits, and unspecified assistantships also available. Support available to part-time students. Financial award application deadline: 3/1; financial award applicants required to submit FAFSA. In 2016, 33 master's, 6 doctorates awarded. *Program availability:* Part-time, evening/weekend, blended/hybrid learning. Offers materials engineering (MS Mat E, DE, PhD). *Application deadline:* For fall admission, 8/1 priority date for domestic students, 5/1 priority date for international students; for spring admission, 11/1 priority date for international students. Applications are processed on a rolling basis. *Application fee:* $0 ($50 for international students). Electronic applications accepted. *Chair/Interim Graduate Program Director*, Dr. Charles Browning, 937-229-2679, E-mail: cbrowning1@udayton.edu.

Department of Mathematics Students: 31 full-time (13 women), 5 part-time (2 women); includes 3 minority (2 Black or African American, non-Hispanic/Latino; 1 Hispanic/Latino), 27 international. Average age 26. 112 applicants, 20% accepted. *Faculty:* 19 full-time (7 women). Expenses: Contact institution. *Financial support:* In 2016–17, 6 students received support, including 6 teaching assistantships with full tuition reimbursements available (averaging $14,750 per year); institutionally sponsored loans and health care benefits also available. Financial award application deadline: 3/1; financial award applicants required to submit FAFSA. In 2016, 26 master's awarded. *Program availability:* Part-time, evening/weekend. Offers applied mathematics (MAS); financial mathematics (MFM); mathematics education (MME). *Application deadline:* Applications are processed on a rolling basis. *Application fee:* $0 ($50 for international students). Electronic applications accepted. *Application Contact:* Dr. Paul W. Eloe, Graduate Program Director/Professor, 937-229-2016, E-mail: peloe1@udayton.edu. Chair, Dr. Joe D. Mashburn, 937-229-2511, Fax: 937-229-2566, E-mail: jmashburn1@udayton.edu.

Department of Mechanical and Aerospace Engineering Students: 143 full-time (19 women), 31 part-time (7 women); includes 14 minority (1 Black or African American, non-Hispanic/Latino; 5 Asian, non-Hispanic/Latino; 4 Hispanic/Latino; 4 Two or more races, non-Hispanic/Latino), 94 international. Average age 28. 432 applicants, 15% accepted. *Faculty:* 17 full-time (3 women), 9 part-time/adjunct (1 woman). Expenses: Contact institution. *Financial support:* In 2016–17, 19 research assistantships with full tuition reimbursements (averaging $13,000 per year), 2 teaching assistantships with full tuition reimbursements (averaging $9,150 per year) were awarded; institutionally sponsored loans and health care benefits also available. Support available to part-time students. Financial award application deadline: 3/1; financial award applicants required to submit FAFSA. In 2016, 66 master's awarded. *Program availability:* Part-time, blended/hybrid learning. Offers aerospace engineering (MSAE, DE, PhD); mechanical engineering (MSME, DE, PhD); renewable and clean energy (MS). *Application deadline:* Applications are processed on a rolling basis. *Application fee:* $0 ($50 for international students). Electronic applications accepted. *Application Contact:* Dr. Vinod Jain, Graduate Program Director, 937-229-2992, Fax: 937-229-4766, E-mail: vjain1@udayton.edu. Chair, Dr. Kelly Kissock, 937-229-2999, Fax: 937-229-4766, E-mail: jkissock1@udayton.edu.

Department of Physical Therapy Students: 111 full-time (71 women); includes 8 minority (1 Asian, non-Hispanic/Latino; 2 Hispanic/Latino; 5 Two or more races, non-Hispanic/Latino), 1 international. Average age 24. 77 applicants, 64% accepted. *Faculty:* 8 full-time (3 women), 23 part-time/adjunct (15 women). Expenses: Contact institution. *Financial support:* In 2016–17, 6 research assistantships with partial tuition reimbursements (averaging $13,691 per year) were awarded; institutionally sponsored loans and unspecified assistantships also available. Financial award application deadline: 3/1; financial award applicants required to submit FAFSA. In 2016, 34 doctorates awarded. Offers physical therapy (DPT). *Application deadline:* For fall admission, 10/1 priority date for domestic and international students. *Application fee:* $50 for international students. Electronic applications accepted. *Application Contact:* Trista Cathcart, Admissions Coordinator, 937-229-5611, Fax: 937-229-5601, E-mail: tcathcart1@udayton.edu. *Chair/Associate Professor*, Dr. Philip A. Anloague, 937-229-5600, Fax: 937-229-5601, E-mail: panalogue1@udayton.edu.

Department of Physician Assistant Education Students: 103 full-time (74 women), 1 (woman) part-time; includes 12 minority (1 Black or African American, non-Hispanic/Latino; 4 Asian, non-Hispanic/Latino; 5 Hispanic/Latino; 2 Two or more races, non-Hispanic/Latino). Average age 27. 942 applicants, 4% accepted, 40 enrolled. *Faculty:* 6 full-time (all women), 2 part-time/adjunct (both women). Expenses: Contact institution. *Financial support:* Career-related internships or fieldwork and institutionally sponsored loans available. Financial award application deadline: 3/1; financial award applicants required to submit FAFSA. In 2016, 30 master's awarded. Offers physician assistant practice (MPAP). *Application deadline:* For fall admission, 11/1 priority date for

domestic and international students. Electronic applications accepted. *Application Contact:* Amy Kidwell, 937-229-2900, E-mail: akidwell1@udayton.edu. *Founding Chair/Director*, Susan Wulff, 937-229-3377, E-mail: swulff1@udayton.edu.

Department of Religious Studies Students: 48 full-time (17 women), 8 part-time (4 women); includes 6 minority (1 Black or African American, non-Hispanic/Latino; 3 Asian, non-Hispanic/Latino; 2 Hispanic/Latino), 1 international. Average age 33. 62 applicants, 48% accepted. *Faculty:* 19 full-time (7 women), 6 part-time/adjunct (2 women). Expenses: Contact institution. *Financial support:* In 2016–17, 36 students received support, including 4 fellowships with full tuition reimbursements available (averaging $17,600 per year), 7 research assistantships with full tuition reimbursements available (averaging $11,000 per year), 16 teaching assistantships with full tuition reimbursements available (averaging $17,952 per year); scholarships/grants, health care benefits, and unspecified assistantships also available. Support available to part-time students. Financial award application deadline: 2/2; financial award applicants required to submit FAFSA. In 2016, 15 master's, 5 doctorates awarded. *Program availability:* Part-time. Offers pastoral ministry (MA); theological studies (MA); theology (PhD). *Application deadline:* For fall admission, 2/2 priority date for domestic and international students. Applications are processed on a rolling basis. *Application fee:* $0 ($50 for international students). Electronic applications accepted. *Application Contact:* Amy Doorley, Graduate Program Coordinator, 937-229-4321, Fax: 937-229-4330, E-mail: adoorley1@udayton.edu. Chair, Dr. Daniel Thompson, 937-229-4321, Fax: 937-229-4330.

Department of Teacher Education Students: 52 full-time (47 women), 89 part-time (76 women); includes 6 minority (2 Black or African American, non-Hispanic/Latino; 2 Hispanic/Latino; 2 Two or more races, non-Hispanic/Latino), 24 international. Average age 31. 106 applicants, 28% accepted. *Faculty:* 23 full-time (18 women), 49 part-time/adjunct (42 women). Expenses: Contact institution. *Financial support:* Institutionally sponsored loans available. Financial award application deadline: 3/1; financial award applicants required to submit FAFSA. In 2016, 69 master's awarded. *Program availability:* Part-time, evening/weekend, blended/hybrid learning. Offers early childhood leadership and advocacy (MS Ed); interdisciplinary education studies (MS Ed); leadership in educational systems (MS Ed); literacy (MS Ed); mathematics education (MS Ed); music education (MS Ed); teacher as leader (MS Ed); teacher education (MS Ed); technology-enhanced learning (MS Ed); trans-disciplinary early childhood education (MS Ed). *Application deadline:* Applications are processed on a rolling basis. *Application fee:* $0 ($50 for international students). Electronic applications accepted. *Application Contact:* Gina Seiter, Graduate Program Advisor, 937-229-3103, E-mail: gseiter1@udayton.edu. Chair, Dr. Connie L. Bowman, 937-229-3305, E-mail: cbowman1@udayton.edu.

Master of Public Administration Program Students: 19 full-time (12 women), 8 part-time (5 women); includes 3 minority (1 Black or African American, non-Hispanic/Latino; 2 Two or more races, non-Hispanic/Latino), 1 international. Average age 31. 39 applicants, 21% accepted. *Faculty:* 6 full-time (2 women), 4 part-time/adjunct (2 women). Expenses: Contact institution. *Financial support:* In 2016–17, 5 research assistantships with full tuition reimbursements (averaging $11,700 per year) were awarded; health care benefits and unspecified assistantships also available. Financial award application deadline: 3/1; financial award applicants required to submit FAFSA. In 2016, 7 master's awarded. *Program availability:* Part-time, evening/weekend. Offers public administration (MPA). *Application deadline:* Applications are processed on a rolling basis. *Application fee:* $0 ($50 for international students). Electronic applications accepted. *Application Contact:* Dr. Michelle Pautz, Director, MPA Program, 937-229-3651, Fax: 937-229-1400, E-mail: graduateadmission@udayton.edu. *Director, MPA Program*, Dr. Michelle Pautz, 937-229-3651, Fax: 937-229-1400, E-mail: mpautz1@udayton.edu.

PhD Program in Educational Leadership Students: 50 full-time (26 women); includes 6 minority (4 Black or African American, non-Hispanic/Latino; 1 Hispanic/Latino; 1 Two or more races, non-Hispanic/Latino), 2 international. Average age 41. 59 applicants, 17% accepted. *Faculty:* 5 full-time (3 women), 1 part-time/adjunct (0 women). Expenses: Contact institution. *Financial support:* In 2016–17, 1 fellowship (averaging $2,400 per year) was awarded; institutionally sponsored loans also available. Financial award application deadline: 3/1; financial award applicants required to submit FAFSA. In 2016, 6 doctorates awarded. *Program availability:* Part-time, blended/hybrid learning. Offers educational leadership (PhD); higher education administration (PhD); PreK-12 school administration (PhD). *Application deadline:* Applications are processed on a rolling basis. *Application fee:* $0 ($50 for international students). Electronic applications accepted. *Application Contact:* Elizabeth Pearn, Administrative Assistant, 937-229-4003, Fax: 937-229-4729, E-mail: epearn1@udayton.edu. *Director*, Dr. Charles J. Russo, 937-229-3722, Fax: 937-229-4824, E-mail: crusso1@udayton.edu.

Program in Clinical Psychology Students: 11 full-time (8 women). Average age 23. 84 applicants, 7% accepted. *Faculty:* 6 full-time (2 women). Expenses: Contact institution. *Financial support:* In 2016–17, 5 research assistantships with full tuition reimbursements (averaging $11,500 per year) were awarded; teaching assistantships, institutionally sponsored loans, traineeships, and health care benefits also available. Financial award application deadline: 3/1; financial award applicants required to submit FAFSA. In 2016, 7 master's awarded. Offers clinical psychology (MA). *Application deadline:* For fall admission, 2/15 priority date for domestic and international students. *Application fee:* $0 ($50 for international students). Electronic applications accepted. *Application Contact:* 937-229-4411, E-mail: graduateadmission@udayton.edu. *Director*, Dr. Catherine L. Zois, 937-229-2164, Fax: 937-229-3900, E-mail: czois1@udayton.edu.

Program in General Psychology Students: 5 full-time (3 women), 2 part-time (both women); includes 3 minority (2 Black or African American, non-Hispanic/Latino; 1 Hispanic/Latino). Average age 25. 62 applicants, 8% accepted. *Faculty:* 12 full-time (5 women). Expenses: Contact institution. *Financial support:* In 2016–17, 5 students received support, including 5 research assistantships with full tuition reimbursements available (averaging $12,000 per year); teaching assistantships, institutionally sponsored loans, traineeships, and health care benefits also available. Financial award application deadline: 3/1; financial award applicants required to submit FAFSA. In 2016, 4 master's awarded. Offers general psychology (MA). *Application deadline:* For fall admission, 3/1 priority date for domestic and international students. *Application fee:* $0 ($50 for international students). Electronic applications accepted. *Application Contact:* 937-229-4411, E-mail: graduateadmission@udayton.edu. *Graduate Program Director*, Dr. R. Matthew Montoya, 937-229-2656, Fax: 937-229-3900, E-mail: mmontoya1@udayton.edu.

School of Business Administration Students: 94 full-time (35 women), 85 part-time (38 women); includes 14 minority (5 Black or African American, non-Hispanic/Latino; 4 Asian, non-Hispanic/Latino; 5 Hispanic/Latino), 26 international. Average age 30. 269 applicants, 31% accepted. *Faculty:* 23 full-time (5 women), 18 part-time/adjunct (9 women). Expenses: Contact institution. *Financial support:* In 2016–17, 7 research assistantships with partial tuition reimbursements (averaging $8,535 per year), 2 teaching assistantships with partial tuition reimbursements (averaging $8,535 per year) were awarded; institutionally sponsored loans, health care benefits, and unspecified assistantships also available. Financial award application deadline: 3/1; financial award applicants required to submit FAFSA. In 2016, 93 master's awarded. *Program availability:* Part-time, evening/weekend, blended/hybrid learning. Offers accounting (MBA); cyber security (MBA); finance (MBA); marketing (MBA). *Application deadline:* Applications are processed on a rolling basis. *Application fee:* $0 ($50 for international students). Electronic applications accepted. *Application Contact:* Mandy Bingaman, MBA Program Manager, 937-229-3733, Fax: 937-229-3882, E-mail: mbingaman1@udayton.edu. *Director, MBA Program,* Scott MacDonald, 937-229-3733, Fax: 937-229-3882, E-mail: smacdonald1@udayton.edu.

School of Law Students: 263 full-time (128 women), 16 part-time (5 women); includes 48 minority (24 Black or African American, non-Hispanic/Latino; 1 American Indian or Alaska Native, non-Hispanic/Latino; 4 Asian, non-Hispanic/Latino; 19 Hispanic/Latino), 13 international. Average age 27. 545 applicants, 21% accepted. *Faculty:* 24 full-time (12 women), 25 part-time/adjunct (10 women). Expenses: Contact institution. *Financial support:* In 2016–17, 12 research assistantships (averaging $400 per year) were awarded; fellowships; teaching assistantships, Federal Work-Study, and scholarships/grants also available. Financial award application deadline: 3/1; financial award applicants required to submit FAFSA. In 2016, 9 master's, 93 doctorates awarded. Offers intellectual property and technology (LL M, MSL); law (JD). *Application deadline:* For fall admission, 8/1 priority date for domestic students; for summer admission, 4/15 for domestic students. Applications are processed on a rolling basis. *Application fee:* $0. Electronic applications accepted. *Application Contact:* Claire Schrader, Assistant Dean/Executive Director of Enrollment Management and Marketing, 937-229-3555, Fax: 937-229-4194, E-mail: lawinfo@udayton.edu. *Dean,* Andrew Strauss, 937-229-3795, Fax: 937-229-2469, E-mail: astrauss1@udayton.edu.

UNIVERSITY OF DELAWARE, Newark, DE 19716

General Information State-related, coed, university. CGS member. *Graduate housing:* Rooms and/or apartments available to single and married students. Housing application deadline: 3/15. *Research affiliation:* Hagley Museum, Winterthur Museum, Longwood Gardens, Bartol Research Foundation.

GRADUATE UNITS

Alfred Lerner College of Business and Economics *Program availability:* Part-time, evening/weekend. Offers accounting (MS); business administration (MBA); business and economics (MA, MBA, MS, PhD); economic education (PhD); economics (MA, MS, PhD); economics for entrepreneurship and educators (MA); finance (MS); financial service analytics (PhD); hospitality information management (MS); information systems and technology management (MS). Electronic applications accepted.

Center for Energy and Environmental Policy Offers energy and environmental policy (MA, MEEP, PhD); urban affairs and public policy (PhD). Electronic applications accepted.

College of Agriculture and Natural Resources *Program availability:* Part-time. Offers agricultural and resource economics (MS); agricultural education (MA); agriculture and natural resources (MA, MS, PhD); animal sciences (MS, PhD); bioresources engineering (MS); entomology and applied ecology (MS, PhD); food sciences (MS); operations research (MS); plant and soil sciences (MS, PhD); public horticulture (MS); statistics (MS). Electronic applications accepted.

College of Arts and Sciences *Program availability:* Part-time, evening/weekend. Offers acting (MFA); American material culture (MA); applied mathematics (MS, PhD); art (MA, MFA); art conservation (MS); art history (MA, PhD); arts and sciences (MA, MALS, MFA, MM, MS, DPT, PhD); behavioral neuroscience (PhD); biochemistry (MA, MS, PhD); biomechanics and movement science (MS, PhD); biotechnology (MS); cancer biology (MS, PhD); cell and extracellular matrix biology (MS, PhD); cell and systems physiology (MS, PhD); chemistry (MA, MS, PhD); clinical psychology (PhD); cognitive psychology (PhD); communication (MA); composition (MM); criminology (MA, PhD); developmental biology (MS, PhD); ecology and evolution (MS, PhD); English and American literature (MA, PhD); fashion and apparel studies (MS); foreign languages and literatures (MA); foreign languages pedagogy (MA); history (MA, PhD); history of technology and industrialization (MA, PhD); liberal studies (MALS); linguistics (PhD); linguistics and cognitive science (MA); mathematics (MS, PhD); microbiology (MS, PhD); molecular biology and genetics (MS, PhD); music education (MM); performance (MM); physics and astronomy (MS, PhD); political science and international relations (MA, PhD); preservation studies (PhD); social psychology (PhD); sociology (MA, PhD); stage management (MFA); technical Chinese translation (MA); technical production (MFA). Electronic applications accepted.

School of Public Policy and Administration *Program availability:* Part-time, evening/weekend. Offers disaster science and management (MS, PhD); governance planning and management (PhD); historic preservation (MA); public administration (MPA); public policy and administration (MA, MPA, PhD); social and urban policy (PhD); technology, environment and society (PhD); urban affairs and public policy (MA). Electronic applications accepted.

College of Earth, Ocean, and Environment Offers geography (MA, MS, PhD); geological sciences (MA, PhD); geology (MS, PhD); marine science and policy (MMP, MS, PhD); ocean engineering (MS, PhD). Electronic applications accepted.

School of Marine Science and Policy Offers marine policy (MMP); marine studies (MS, PhD); oceanography (PhD).

College of Education and Human Development *Program availability:* Part-time, evening/weekend. Offers education and human development (M Ed, MA, MEEP, MI, MPA, MS, Ed D, PhD, Ed S); human development and family studies (MS, PhD). Electronic applications accepted.

School of Education *Program availability:* Part-time, evening/weekend. Offers education (PhD); educational leadership (Ed D); higher education (M Ed); instruction (MI); reading (M Ed); school leadership (M Ed); school psychology (MA, Ed S); teaching English as a second language (TESL) (MA). Electronic applications accepted.

College of Engineering *Program availability:* Part-time, evening/weekend, online learning. Offers chemical engineering (M Ch E, PhD); computer and information sciences (MS, PhD); electrical and computer engineering (MSECE, PhD); engineering (M Ch E, MAS, MCE, MEM, MMSE, MS, MSECE, MSME, PhD); environmental engineering (MAS, MCE, PhD); geotechnical engineering (MAS, MCE, PhD); materials science and engineering (MMSE, PhD); mechanical engineering (MEM, MSME, PhD); ocean engineering (MAS, MCE, PhD); structural engineering (MAS, MCE, PhD); transportation engineering (MAS, MCE, PhD); water resource engineering (MAS, MCE, PhD). Electronic applications accepted.

College of Health Sciences *Program availability:* Part-time, evening/weekend, online learning. Offers adult nurse practitioner (MSN, PMC); cardiopulmonary clinical nurse specialist (MSN, PMC); cardiopulmonary clinical nurse specialist/adult nurse practitioner (MSN, PMC); family nurse practitioner (MSN, PMC); gerontology clinical nurse specialist (MSN, PMC); gerontology clinical nurse specialist geriatric nurse practitioner (PMC); gerontology clinical nurse specialist/geriatric nurse practitioner (MSN); health promotion

(MS); health sciences (MS, MSN, DPT, PMC); health services administration (MSN, PMC); human nutrition (MS); kinesiology and applied physiology (MS, PhD); nursing of children clinical nurse specialist (MSN, PMC); nursing of children clinical nurse specialist/pediatric nurse practitioner (MSN, PMC); oncology/immune deficiency clinical nurse specialist (MSN, PMC); oncology/immune deficiency clinical nurse specialist/adult nurse practitioner (MSN, PMC); perinatal/women's health clinical nurse specialist (MSN, PMC); perinatal/women's health clinical nurse specialist/women's health nurse practitioner (MSN, PMC); physical therapy (DPT); psychiatric nursing clinical nurse specialist (MSN, PMC); speech-language pathology (MA). Electronic applications accepted.

UNIVERSITY OF DENVER, Denver, CO 80208

General Information Independent, coed, university. CGS member. *Enrollment:* 11,614 graduate, professional, and undergraduate students; 3,094 full-time matriculated graduate/professional students (1,944 women), 2,626 part-time matriculated graduate/professional students (1,514 women). *Enrollment by degree level:* 3,784 master's, 1,529 doctoral, 407 other advanced degrees. *Graduate faculty:* 722 full-time (320 women), 560 part-time/adjunct (315 women). Tuition and fees vary according to course load, campus/location and program. *Graduate housing:* Rooms and/or apartments available on a first-come, first-served basis to single and married students. Housing application deadline: 5/1. *Student services:* Campus employment opportunities, campus safety program, career counseling, exercise/wellness program, free psychological counseling, international student services, low-cost health insurance, multicultural affairs office, services for students with disabilities, teacher training, writing training. *Library facilities:* Anderson Academic Commons plus 1 other. *Collection:* Books: 1.7 million (physical), 2.3 million (digital/electronic); Serial titles: 553,655 (physical), 127,847 (digital/electronic); Databases: 1,273. Weekly public service hours: 145; study areas open 24 hours, 5–7 days a week; students can reserve study rooms. *Research affiliation:* National Center for Atmospheric Research (infrared measurements).

Computer facilities: Computer purchase and lease plans are available. 150 computers available on campus for general student use. A campuswide network can be accessed from student residence rooms and from off campus. Online class registration is available.
Website: http://www.du.edu/

General Application Contact: Office of Graduate Studies, 303-871-2706, E-mail: gradinfo@du.edu.

GRADUATE UNITS

Daniel Felix Ritchie School of Engineering and Computer Science Students: 22 full-time (4 women), 111 part-time (31 women); includes 19 minority (2 Black or African American, non-Hispanic/Latino; 7 Asian, non-Hispanic/Latino; 8 Hispanic/Latino; 2 Two or more races, non-Hispanic/Latino), 65 international. Average age 29. 198 applicants, 64% accepted, 43 enrolled. *Faculty:* 38 full-time (4 women), 9 part-time/adjunct (4 women). Expenses: Contact institution. *Financial support:* In 2016–17, 78 students received support, including 14 research assistantships with tuition reimbursements available (averaging $12,410 per year), 14 teaching assistantships with tuition reimbursements available (averaging $14,494 per year); Federal Work-Study, institutionally sponsored loans, scholarships/grants, health care benefits, and unspecified assistantships also available. Financial award application deadline: 2/15; financial award applicants required to submit FAFSA. In 2016, 68 master's, 16 doctorates awarded. Offers bioengineering (MS); computer engineering (MS); computer science (MS, PhD); cybersecurity (MS); electrical and computer engineering (PhD); electrical engineering (MS); engineering (MS, PhD); engineering and computer science (MS, PhD); materials science (MS, PhD); mechanical engineering (MS, PhD); mechatronic systems engineering (MS, PhD). *Application deadline:* Applications are processed on a rolling basis. *Application fee:* $65. Electronic applications accepted. *Application Contact:* Information Contact, 303-871-3787, E-mail: ritchieschool@du.edu. *Dean,* Dr. JB Holston, 303-871-3733, Fax: 303-871-2716, E-mail: jb.holston@du.edu.

Daniels College of Business Students: 417 full-time (176 women), 314 part-time (134 women); includes 127 minority (22 Black or African American, non-Hispanic/Latino; 33 Asian, non-Hispanic/Latino; 53 Hispanic/Latino; 19 Two or more races, non-Hispanic/Latino), 147 international. Average age 30. 1,266 applicants, 60% accepted, 341 enrolled. *Faculty:* 104 full-time (36 women), 48 part-time/adjunct (12 women). Expenses: Contact institution. *Financial support:* In 2016–17, 525 students received support, including 34 teaching assistantships with tuition reimbursements available (averaging $1,864 per year); career-related internships or fieldwork, Federal Work-Study, institutionally sponsored loans, scholarships/grants, and unspecified assistantships also available. Support available to part-time students. Financial award application deadline: 2/15; financial award applicants required to submit FAFSA. In 2016, 501 master's awarded. *Program availability:* Part-time, evening/weekend. Offers business (M Acc, MBA, MS); business administration (MBA); business analytics (MBA, MS); general business administration (MBA); management (MBA, MS); marketing (MBA, MS). *Application deadline:* For fall admission, 11/15 priority date for domestic and international students; for spring admission, 10/1 priority date for domestic and international students. Applications are processed on a rolling basis. *Application fee:* $100. Electronic applications accepted. *Application Contact:* Information Contact, 303-871-3416, Fax: 303-871-4466, E-mail: daniels@du.edu. *Dean,* Dr. Brent Chrite, 303-871-4324, Fax: 303-871-2156, E-mail: brent.chrite@du.edu.

Franklin L. Burns School of Real Estate and Construction Management Students: 19 full-time (1 woman), 68 part-time (19 women); includes 19 minority (2 Black or African American, non-Hispanic/Latino; 4 Asian, non-Hispanic/Latino; 7 Hispanic/Latino; 6 Two or more races, non-Hispanic/Latino), 3 international. Average age 35. 62 applicants, 90% accepted, 39 enrolled. *Faculty:* 7 full-time (1 woman), 7 part-time/adjunct (1 woman). Expenses: Contact institution. *Financial support:* In 2016–17, 54 students received support, including 2 teaching assistantships with tuition reimbursements available (averaging $1,492 per year); Federal Work-Study, institutionally sponsored loans, scholarships/grants, and unspecified assistantships also available. Support available to part-time students. Financial award application deadline: 2/15; financial award applicants required to submit FAFSA. In 2016, 30 master's awarded. *Program availability:* Part-time, evening/weekend. Offers real estate and the built environment (MBA, MS). *Application deadline:* For fall admission, 11/15 priority date for domestic and international students; for spring admission, 10/1 priority date for domestic and international students. Applications are processed on a rolling basis. *Application fee:* $100. Electronic applications accepted. *Associate Professor and Director,* Dr. Barbara Jackson, 303-871-3470, Fax: 303-871-2971, E-mail: barbara.jackson@du.edu.

Reiman School of Finance Students: 45 full-time (19 women), 28 part-time (6 women); includes 7 minority (1 Black or African American, non-Hispanic/Latino; 1 Asian, non-Hispanic/Latino; 4 Hispanic/Latino; 1 Two or more races, non-Hispanic/Latino), 38 international. Average age 25. 324 applicants, 48% accepted, 31 enrolled. *Faculty:* 18 full-time (4 women), 3 part-time/adjunct (0 women). Expenses: Contact institution.

Financial support: In 2016–17, 58 students received support, including 3 teaching assistantships with tuition reimbursements available (averaging $2,236 per year); career-related internships or fieldwork, Federal Work-Study, institutionally sponsored loans, scholarships/grants, tuition waivers, and unspecified assistantships also available. Support available to part-time students. Financial award application deadline: 2/15; financial award applicants required to submit FAFSA. In 2016, 51 master's awarded. *Program availability:* Part-time, evening/weekend. Offers applied quantitative finance (MS); finance (MBA). *Application deadline:* For fall admission, 11/15 priority date for domestic and international students; for spring admission, 10/1 priority date for domestic and international students. Applications are processed on a rolling basis. *Application fee:* $100. Electronic applications accepted. *Interim Director,* Dr. Mac Clouse, 303-871-3322, E-mail: mclouse@du.edu.

School of Accountancy Students: 34 full-time (18 women), 49 part-time (31 women); includes 13 minority (5 Asian, non-Hispanic/Latino; 8 Hispanic/Latino), 41 international. Average age 26. 258 applicants, 61% accepted, 44 enrolled. *Faculty:* 19 full-time (8 women), 7 part-time/adjunct (1 woman). Expenses: Contact institution. **Financial support:** In 2016–17, 70 students received support, including 3 teaching assistantships with tuition reimbursements available (averaging $1,242 per year); career-related internships or fieldwork, Federal Work-Study, institutionally sponsored loans, scholarships/grants, and unspecified assistantships also available. Support available to part-time students. Financial award application deadline: 2/15; financial award applicants required to submit FAFSA. In 2016, 123 master's awarded. *Program availability:* Part-time, evening/weekend. Offers accounting (M Acc, MBA). *Application deadline:* For fall admission, 11/15 priority date for domestic and international students; for spring admission, 10/1 priority date for domestic and international students. Applications are processed on a rolling basis. *Application fee:* $100. Electronic applications accepted. *Professor/Director, School of Accountancy,* Dr. Sharon Lassar, 303-871-2032, Fax: 303-871-2016, E-mail: slassar@du.edu.

Division of Arts, Humanities and Social Sciences Students: 123 full-time (77 women), 168 part-time (103 women); includes 58 minority (9 Black or African American, non-Hispanic/Latino; 2 American Indian or Alaska Native, non-Hispanic/Latino; 8 Asian, non-Hispanic/Latino; 29 Hispanic/Latino; 10 Two or more races, non-Hispanic/Latino), 33 international. Average age 29. 843 applicants, 35% accepted, 131 enrolled. *Faculty:* 132 full-time (61 women), 33 part-time/adjunct (16 women). Expenses: Contact institution. *Financial support:* In 2016–17, 251 students received support, including 5 research assistantships with tuition reimbursements available (averaging $16,000 per year), 84 teaching assistantships with tuition reimbursements available (averaging $12,312 per year); career-related internships or fieldwork, Federal Work-Study, institutionally sponsored loans, scholarships/grants, and unspecified assistantships also available. Support available to part-time students. Financial award application deadline: 2/15; financial award applicants required to submit FAFSA. In 2016, 83 master's, 20 doctorates, 2 other advanced degrees awarded. *Program availability:* Part-time. Offers affect/social psychology (PhD); archaeology (MA); arts, humanities and social sciences (MA, MFA, MM, MPP, MS, PhD, Certificate); clinical child psychology (PhD); cognitive psychology (PhD); creative writing (PhD); critical theory and religion (MA); cultural anthropology (MA); culture and communication (MA, PhD); developmental psychology (PhD); economics (MA); emergent digital practices (MA, MFA); international and intercultural communication (MA); interpersonal and family communication (MA, PhD); literary studies (MA, PhD); lived religions (MA); media and globalization (MA); museum and heritage studies (MA); philosophy of religion (MA); religion and international studies (MA); rhetoric and communication ethics (MA, PhD); sacred texts (MA). *Application deadline:* Applications are processed on a rolling basis. *Application fee:* $65. Electronic applications accepted. *Application Contact:* Information Contact, 360-871-4449, Fax: 303-871-4436, E-mail: ahss@du.edu. *Dean,* Dr. Danny McIntosh, 303-871-4449, Fax: 303-871-4436, E-mail: daniel.mcintosh@du.edu.

Lamont School of Music Students: 30 full-time (9 women), 71 part-time (35 women); includes 16 minority (2 Black or African American, non-Hispanic/Latino; 1 American Indian or Alaska Native, non-Hispanic/Latino; 2 Asian, non-Hispanic/Latino; 7 Hispanic/Latino; 4 Two or more races, non-Hispanic/Latino), 16 international. Average age 27. 150 applicants, 81% accepted, 58 enrolled. *Faculty:* 32 full-time (9 women), 33 part-time/adjunct (15 women). Expenses: Contact institution. *Financial support:* In 2016–17, 89 students received support, including 25 teaching assistantships with tuition reimbursements available (averaging $6,933 per year); career-related internships or fieldwork, Federal Work-Study, institutionally sponsored loans, scholarships/grants, tuition waivers, and unspecified assistantships also available. Support available to part-time students. Financial award application deadline: 2/15; financial award applicants required to submit FAFSA. In 2016, 24 master's, 2 other advanced degrees awarded. *Program availability:* Part-time. Offers composition (MM); composition - jazz emphasis (MM); conducting (MM, Certificate); jazz studies (Certificate); music theory (MA); musicology (MA); orchestral studies (Certificate); pedagogy (MM); performance (MM, Certificate); performance - jazz emphasis (MM); Suzuki teaching (Certificate). *Application deadline:* For fall admission, 1/15 priority date for domestic and international students. Applications are processed on a rolling basis. *Application fee:* $65. Electronic applications accepted. *Application Contact:* Stephen Campbell, Director of Admission, 303-871-6973, Fax: 303-871-3118, E-mail: stephen.l.campbell@du.edu. *Professor and Director,* Dr. Nancy Cochran, 303-871-6986, Fax: 303-871-3118, E-mail: nancy.cochran@du.edu.

School of Art and Art History Students: 3 full-time (all women), 12 part-time (all women). Average age 25. 29 applicants, 83% accepted, 6 enrolled. *Faculty:* 16 full-time (10 women), 8 part-time/adjunct (7 women). Expenses: Contact institution. *Financial support:* In 2016–17, 14 students received support, including 4 teaching assistantships with tuition reimbursements available (averaging $7,500 per year); research assistantships with tuition reimbursements available, career-related internships or fieldwork, Federal Work-Study, institutionally sponsored loans, scholarships/grants, and unspecified assistantships also available. Support available to part-time students. Financial award application deadline: 2/15; financial award applicants required to submit FAFSA. In 2016, 5 master's awarded. *Program availability:* Part-time. Offers art history (MA); museum studies (MA). *Application deadline:* For fall admission, 1/31 priority date for domestic and international students. Applications are processed on a rolling basis. *Application fee:* $65. Electronic applications accepted. *Application Contact:* Dr. Annette Stott, Acting Graduate Art History Advisor, 303-871-3278, Fax: 303-871-4112, E-mail: astott@du.edu. *Associate Professor and Director,* Dr. Catherine Chauvin, 303-871-2367, Fax: 303-871-4112, E-mail: catherine.chauvin@du.edu.

Division of Natural Sciences and Mathematics Students: 16 full-time (8 women), 124 part-time (60 women); includes 27 minority (3 Black or African American, non-Hispanic/Latino; 4 Asian, non-Hispanic/Latino; 15 Hispanic/Latino; 5 Two or more races, non-Hispanic/Latino), 21 international. Average age 29. 254 applicants, 53% accepted, 64 enrolled. *Faculty:* 86 full-time (28 women), 19 part-time/adjunct (8 women). Expenses: Contact institution. *Financial support:* In 2016–17, 133 students received

support, including 10 research assistantships with tuition reimbursements available (averaging $17,333 per year), 44 teaching assistantships with tuition reimbursements available (averaging $18,523 per year); career-related internships or fieldwork, institutionally sponsored loans, scholarships/grants, and unspecified assistantships also available. Support available to part-time students. Financial award application deadline: 2/15; financial award applicants required to submit FAFSA. In 2016, 50 master's, 18 doctorates awarded. *Program availability:* Part-time, evening/weekend. Offers biology, ecology and evolution (MS, PhD); biomedical sciences (PSM); cell and molecular biology (MS, PhD); mathematics (MA, MS, PhD); natural sciences and mathematics (MA, MS, PSM, PhD); physics (MS, PhD). *Application deadline:* Applications are processed on a rolling basis. *Application fee:* $65. Electronic applications accepted. *Application Contact:* Kirsten Norwood, Executive Assistant to the Dean, 303-871-2693, Fax: 303-871-3223, E-mail: kirsten.norwood@du.edu. *Dean,* Dr. Andrei Kutateladze, 303-871-2995, Fax: 303-871-3223, E-mail: andrei.kutateladze@du.edu.

Graduate School of Professional Psychology Students: 230 full-time (187 women), 72 part-time (46 women); includes 69 minority (16 Black or African American, non-Hispanic/Latino; 1 American Indian or Alaska Native, non-Hispanic/Latino; 9 Asian, non-Hispanic/Latino; 29 Hispanic/Latino; 1 Native Hawaiian or other Pacific Islander, non-Hispanic/Latino; 13 Two or more races, non-Hispanic/Latino), 14 international. Average age 27. 800 applicants, 30% accepted, 129 enrolled. *Faculty:* 23 full-time (13 women), 25 part-time/adjunct (14 women). Expenses: Contact institution. *Financial support:* In 2016–17, 124 students received support, including 15 teaching assistantships with tuition reimbursements available (averaging $2,708 per year); career-related internships or fieldwork, Federal Work-Study, institutionally sponsored loans, scholarships/grants, unspecified assistantships, and clinical assistantships also available. Support available to part-time students. Financial award application deadline: 2/15; financial award applicants required to submit FAFSA. In 2016, 80 master's, 38 doctorates awarded. Offers clinical psychology (Psy D); forensic psychology (MA); international disaster psychology (MA); sport and performance psychology (MA); sport coaching (MA). *Application deadline:* For fall admission, 1/5 for domestic and international students. *Application fee:* $65. Electronic applications accepted. *Application Contact:* Admissions Counselor, 303-871-3736, Fax: 303-871-4220, E-mail: gsppinfo@du.edu. *Dean,* Dr. Shelly Smith-Acuna, 303-871-3880, Fax: 303-871-4220, E-mail: shelly.smith-acuna@du.edu.

Graduate School of Social Work Students: 483 full-time (428 women), 13 part-time (11 women); includes 110 minority (16 Black or African American, non-Hispanic/Latino; 5 American Indian or Alaska Native, non-Hispanic/Latino; 9 Asian, non-Hispanic/Latino; 56 Hispanic/Latino; 24 Two or more races, non-Hispanic/Latino), 2 international. Average age 28. 868 applicants, 78% accepted, 277 enrolled. *Faculty:* 40 full-time (27 women), 103 part-time/adjunct (88 women). Expenses: Contact institution. *Financial support:* In 2016–17, 462 students received support, including 8 teaching assistantships with tuition reimbursements available (averaging $12,559 per year); Federal Work-Study, scholarships/grants, and unspecified assistantships also available. Support available to part-time students. Financial award application deadline: 2/15; financial award applicants required to submit FAFSA. In 2016, 265 master's, 6 doctorates, 70 other advanced degrees awarded. *Program availability:* Part-time, evening/weekend. Offers animal-assisted social work (Certificate); couples and family therapy (Certificate); social work (MSW, PhD); social work with Latinos/as (Certificate). *Application deadline:* For fall admission, 1/15 priority date for domestic and international students. Applications are processed on a rolling basis. *Application fee:* $65. Electronic applications accepted. *Application Contact:* Colin Schneider, Director of Enrollment Management, 303-871-3634, Fax: 303-871-2845, E-mail: gssw-admission@du.edu. *Dean,* Dr. Amanda Moore McBride, 303-871-2203, Fax: 303-871-2845.

Josef Korbel School of International Studies Students: 368 full-time (204 women), 26 part-time (10 women); includes 82 minority (15 Black or African American, non-Hispanic/Latino; 2 American Indian or Alaska Native, non-Hispanic/Latino; 11 Asian, non-Hispanic/Latino; 43 Hispanic/Latino; 11 Two or more races, non-Hispanic/Latino), 38 international. Average age 27. 764 applicants, 82% accepted, 138 enrolled. *Faculty:* 46 full-time (16 women), 28 part-time/adjunct (8 women). Expenses: Contact institution. *Financial support:* In 2016–17, 244 students received support, including 1 research assistantship with tuition reimbursement available (averaging $7,250 per year), 5 teaching assistantships with tuition reimbursements available (averaging $2,842 per year); career-related internships or fieldwork, Federal Work-Study, institutionally sponsored loans, scholarships/grants, and unspecified assistantships also available. Support available to part-time students. Financial award application deadline: 2/15; financial award applicants required to submit FAFSA. In 2016, 197 master's, 10 doctorates, 28 other advanced degrees awarded. *Program availability:* Part-time. Offers conflict resolution (MA); global business and corporate social responsibility (Certificate); global finance, trade and economic integration (MA); global health affairs (Certificate); homeland security (Certificate); humanitarian assistance (Certificate); international administration (MA); international development (MA); international human rights (MA); international security (MA); international studies (MA, PhD); public policy studies (MPP); religion and international affairs (Certificate). *Application deadline:* For fall admission, 1/15 priority date for domestic and international students; for winter admission, 11/1 for domestic and international students. Applications are processed on a rolling basis. *Application fee:* $65. Electronic applications accepted. *Application Contact:* Admissions Contact, E-mail: korbeladm@du.edu. *Dean,* Dr. Christopher R. Hill, 303-871-2359, Fax: 303-871-2456, E-mail: christopher.r.hill@du.edu.

Institute for Public Policy Studies Students: 16 full-time (8 women), 3 part-time (1 woman); includes 2 minority (both Hispanic/Latino), 1 international. Average age 26. 21 applicants, 81% accepted, 4 enrolled. *Faculty:* 10 full-time (5 women), 4 part-time/adjunct (2 women). Expenses: Contact institution. *Financial support:* In 2016–17, 17 students received support, including 2 teaching assistantships with tuition reimbursements available (averaging $3,750 per year); Federal Work-Study, scholarships/grants, and unspecified assistantships also available. Financial award application deadline: 2/15; financial award applicants required to submit FAFSA. In 2016, 9 master's awarded. Offers public policy studies (MPP). *Application deadline:* For fall admission, 7/1 priority date for domestic and international students; for winter admission, 11/15 priority date for domestic and international students. Applications are processed on a rolling basis. *Application fee:* $65. Electronic applications accepted. *Co-Director,* Dr. Richard Caldwell, 303-871-2468, Fax: 303-871-3066, E-mail: richard.caldwell@du.edu.

Morgridge College of Education Students: 498 full-time (392 women), 362 part-time (282 women); includes 223 minority (63 Black or African American, non-Hispanic/Latino; 6 American Indian or Alaska Native, non-Hispanic/Latino; 20 Asian, non-Hispanic/Latino; 102 Hispanic/Latino; 1 Native Hawaiian or other Pacific Islander, non-Hispanic/Latino; 31 Two or more races, non-Hispanic/Latino), 40 international. Average age 32. 1,027 applicants, 69% accepted, 386 enrolled. *Faculty:* 39 full-time (29 women), 60 part-time/adjunct (42 women). Expenses: Contact institution. *Financial support:* In 2016–17, 697 students received support, including 37 research assistantships with tuition reimbursements available (averaging $11,209 per year), 66 teaching assistantships with tuition reimbursements available (averaging $3,742 per year); career-related internships or fieldwork, Federal Work-Study, institutionally sponsored loans, scholarships/grants, and unspecified assistantships also available. Support available to part-time students. Financial award application deadline: 2/15; financial award applicants required to submit FAFSA. In 2016, 252 master's, 36 doctorates, 141 other advanced degrees awarded. *Program availability:* Part-time, evening/weekend, online learning. Offers child, family and school psychology (MA, PhD, Ed S); counseling psychology (MA, PhD); curriculum and instruction (MA, Ed D, PhD); curriculum instruction and teaching (Certificate); early childhood special education (MA, Certificate); educational leadership and policy studies (MA, Ed D, PhD, Certificate); higher education (Ed D, PhD); library and information science (MLIS); research methods and statistics (MA, PhD). *Application deadline:* Applications are processed on a rolling basis. *Application fee:* $65. Electronic applications accepted. *Application Contact:* Jodi Dye, Director of Admissions, 303-871-2510, Fax: 303-871-4456, E-mail: jodi.dye@du.edu. *Dean,* Dr. Karen Riley, 303-871-3665, Fax: 303-871-4456, E-mail: karen.riley@du.edu.

Sturm College of Law Students: 847 full-time (436 women), 132 part-time (79 women); includes 200 minority (26 Black or African American, non-Hispanic/Latino; 5 American Indian or Alaska Native, non-Hispanic/Latino; 25 Asian, non-Hispanic/Latino; 109 Hispanic/Latino; 35 Two or more races, non-Hispanic/Latino), 69 international. Average age 29. 2,471 applicants, 57% accepted, 364 enrolled. *Faculty:* 86 full-time (42 women), 70 part-time/adjunct (31 women). Expenses: Contact institution. *Financial support:* In 2016–17, 537 students received support, including 7 teaching assistantships with tuition reimbursements available (averaging $7,748 per year); career-related internships or fieldwork, Federal Work-Study, institutionally sponsored loans, scholarships/grants, unspecified assistantships, and tutorships also available. Support available to part-time students. Financial award application deadline: 2/15; financial award applicants required to submit FAFSA. In 2016, 119 master's, 267 doctorates, 83 Certificates awarded. *Program availability:* Part-time, evening/weekend. Offers environmental and natural resources law and policy (LL M, MLS); law (LL M, MLS, MRLS, MSLA, MT, JD, Certificate); legal administration (MSLA, Certificate); natural resources law and policy (Certificate); tax (LL M, MT). *Application deadline:* Applications are processed on a rolling basis. *Application fee:* $65. Electronic applications accepted. *Application Contact:* Yvonne Cherena-Pacheco, Associate Director of Admissions, 303-871-6192, Fax: 303-871-6992, E-mail: admissions@law.du.edu. *Dean,* Dr. Bruce Smith, 303-871-6103, Fax: 303-871-6992.

University College Students: 59 full-time (22 women), 1,285 part-time (750 women); includes 316 minority (111 Black or African American, non-Hispanic/Latino; 8 American Indian or Alaska Native, non-Hispanic/Latino; 39 Asian, non-Hispanic/Latino; 123 Hispanic/Latino; 3 Native Hawaiian or other Pacific Islander, non-Hispanic/Latino; 32 Two or more races, non-Hispanic/Latino), 85 international. Average age 35. 703 applicants, 89% accepted, 390 enrolled. *Faculty:* 118 part-time/adjunct (62 women). Expenses: Contact institution. *Financial support:* In 2016–17, 27 students received support, including 1 teaching assistantship (averaging $1,489 per year). Financial award applicants required to submit FAFSA. In 2016, 428 master's, 138 other advanced degrees awarded. *Program availability:* Part-time, evening/weekend, online learning. Offers arts and culture (MA, Certificate); communication management (MS, Certificate); environmental policy and management (MS); geographic information systems (MS); global affairs (MA, Certificate); healthcare leadership (MS); information communications and technology (MS); leadership and organizations (MS); professional creative writing (MA, Certificate); security management (MS, Certificate); strategic human resources (Certificate). *Application deadline:* For fall admission, 6/21 priority date for domestic students, 5/1 priority date for international students; for winter admission, 9/14 priority date for domestic students, 9/19 priority date for international students; for spring admission, 1/11 priority date for domestic students, 12/12 priority date for international students; for summer admission, 3/29 priority date for domestic students, 3/6 priority date for international students. Applications are processed on a rolling basis. *Application fee:* $75. Electronic applications accepted. *Application Contact:* Information Contact, 303-871-2291, E-mail: ucoladm@du.edu. *Dean,* Dr. Michael McGuire, 303-871-3518, Fax: 303-871-3303, E-mail: mmcguire@du.edu.

UNIVERSITY OF DETROIT MERCY, Detroit, MI 48221

General Information Independent-religious, coed, university. *Graduate housing:* Room and/or apartments available on a first-come, first-served basis to single students; on-campus housing not available to married students.

GRADUATE UNITS

College of Business Administration *Program availability:* Part-time, evening/weekend, 100% online, blended/hybrid learning. Offers business administration (MBA); business fundamentals (Certificate); business turnaround management (Certificate); ethical leadership and change management (Certificate); finance (Certificate); forensic accounting (Certificate). Electronic applications accepted.

College of Engineering and Science *Program availability:* Part-time, evening/weekend. Offers chemistry (MS); civil and environmental engineering (DE); electrical and computer engineering (ME); electrical engineering (DE); engineering management (M Eng Mgt); environmental engineering (MEE); mechanical engineering (MME, DE); product development (MS); software engineering (MSSE); teaching of mathematics (MATM). Electronic applications accepted.

College of Health Professions Offers clinical nurse leader (MSN); family nurse practitioner (MSN); health services administration (MHSA); health systems management (MSN); nurse anesthesia (MS); nursing (DNP); nursing education (MSN, Certificate); nursing leadership and financial management (Certificate); outcomes performance management (Certificate); physician assistant (MS).

College of Liberal Arts and Education *Program availability:* Part-time, evening/weekend. Offers addiction counseling (MA); addiction studies (Certificate); clinical mental health counseling (MA); clinical psychology (MA, PhD); computer and information systems (MS); criminal justice (MA); curriculum and instruction (MA); economics (MA); educational administration (MA); financial economics (MA); industrial/organizational psychology (MA); information assurance (MS); intelligence analysis (MA); liberal studies (MALS); religious studies (MA); school counseling (MA, Certificate); school psychology (Spec); security administration (MS); special education: emotionally impaired/behaviorally disordered (MA); special education: learning disabilities (MA).

School of Architecture Offers architecture (M Arch); community development (MA).

School of Dentistry Offers dentistry (MS, DDS, Certificate).

School of Law *Program availability:* Part-time. Offers law (JD).

UNIVERSITY OF DUBUQUE, Dubuque, IA 52001-5099

General Information Independent-religious, coed, comprehensive institution. *Graduate housing:* Rooms and/or apartments available on a first-come, first-served basis to single students and available to married students.

GRADUATE UNITS

Program in Business Administration *Program availability:* Part-time, evening/weekend. Offers business administration (MBA). Electronic applications accepted.

Program in Communication *Program availability:* Part-time, evening/weekend. Offers information technologies communication (MAC); leadership and management (MAC); strategic and corporate communication (MAC). Electronic applications accepted.

University of Dubuque Theological Seminary Students: 92 full-time (52 women); includes 8 minority (7 Black or African American, non-Hispanic/Latino; 1 Asian, non-Hispanic/Latino). Average age 38. 72 applicants, 76% accepted, 38 enrolled. *Faculty:* 10 full-time (4 women), 11 part-time/adjunct (5 women). Expenses: Contact institution. *Financial support:* In 2016–17, 69 students received support. Career-related internships or fieldwork, Federal Work-Study, institutionally sponsored loans, scholarships/grants, and tuition waivers (full and partial) available. Support available to part-time students. Financial award application deadline: 6/1; financial award applicants required to submit FAFSA. In 2016, 20 master's, 7 doctorates awarded. *Program availability:* Part-time, 100% online, blended/hybrid learning. Offers theology (M Div, D Min). *Application deadline:* For fall admission, 4/15 priority date for domestic students, 12/1 priority date for international students; for spring admission, 11/1 priority date for domestic students. Applications are processed on a rolling basis. *Application fee:* $30. Electronic applications accepted. *Application Contact:* Kimberly S. Burnett-Hackbarth, Director, Seminary Admissions, 563-589-3405, Fax: 563-589-3490, E-mail: khackbarth@dbq.edu. *Associate Dean,* Dr. Annette Huizenga, 563-589-3858, Fax: 563-589-3110, E-mail: ahuizenga@dbq.edu.

UNIVERSITY OF EAST-WEST MEDICINE, Sunnyvale, CA 94085-3922

General Information Proprietary, coed, graduate-only institution. *Enrollment by degree level:* 300 master's, 40 doctoral. *Graduate faculty:* 5 full-time (1 woman), 52 part-time/adjunct (12 women). *Tuition:* Full-time $8100. *Required fees:* $429. Full-time tuition and fees vary according to degree level. *Graduate housing:* On-campus housing not available. *Student services:* Campus safety program, career counseling, international student services, low-cost health insurance, teacher training. *Library facilities:* Library. *Collection:* Books: 900 (physical); Databases: 3.

Computer facilities: 10 computers available on campus for general student use. A campuswide network can be accessed. X available.
Website: http://www.uewm.edu/

General Application Contact: Sharon Yang Zhou, Director of Admissions, 408-733-1878, E-mail: sharon@uewm.edu.

GRADUATE UNITS

Graduate Programs Students: 5 full-time (1 woman), 35 part-time (5 women). *Faculty:* 5 full-time (1 woman), 52 part-time/adjunct (12 women). Expenses: Contact institution. Offers acupuncture and Oriental medicine (DAOM); Tai Chi (MS); traditional Chinese medicine (MSTCM). *Application Contact:* Sharon Yang Zhou, Director of Admissions, 408-733-1878, E-mail: sharon@uewm.edu.

UNIVERSITY OF EVANSVILLE, Evansville, IN 47722

General Information Independent-religious, coed, comprehensive institution. *Enrollment:* 2,514 graduate, professional, and undergraduate students; 161 full-time matriculated graduate/professional students (119 women), 5 part-time matriculated graduate/professional students (all women). *Enrollment by degree level:* 54 master's, 112 doctoral. *Tuition:* Full-time $32,900; part-time $920 per hour. *Required fees:* $1066; $140 per semester. *Graduate housing:* Room and/or apartments available to single students; on-campus housing not available to married students. *Student services:* Career counseling, free psychological counseling, international student services, multicultural affairs office, services for students with disabilities. *Library facilities:* University of Evansville Libraries. *Collection:* Books: 236,405 (physical), 48,641 (digital/electronic); Serial titles: 55,604 (digital/electronic); Databases: 115. Weekly public service hours: 97; students can reserve study rooms. *Research affiliation:* The New American Colleges and Universities (higher education administration), Independent Colleges of Indiana (higher education administration), Council of Independent Colleges (higher education administration), Military Family Research Institute (higher education administration).

Computer facilities: 223 computers available on campus for general student use. A campuswide network can be accessed from student residence rooms and from off campus. Online class registration is available.
Website: http://www.evansville.edu/

General Application Contact: Lindsay Roberts, Director of Adult Education, 812-488-2981, Fax: 812-488-2432, E-mail: cae@evansville.edu.

GRADUATE UNITS

Center for Adult Education Expenses: Contact institution. *Financial support:* Unspecified assistantships available. Financial award application deadline: 6/1; financial award applicants required to submit FAFSA. *Program availability:* Part-time, evening/weekend. Offers public service administration (MS). *Application deadline:* For fall admission, 7/15 for domestic students; for spring admission, 11/30 for domestic students. *Application fee:* $35. *Director,* Lindsay Roberts, 812-488-3101, Fax: 812-488-2432, E-mail: cae@evansville.edu.

College of Education and Health Sciences Expenses: Contact institution. *Financial support:* Scholarships/grants and unspecified assistantships available. Financial award application deadline: 4/1; financial award applicants required to submit FAFSA. Offers education and health sciences (MPH, MS, MSAT, DPT); physical therapy (DPT). *Dean,* Mary Kessler, 812-488-2579, Fax: 812-488-1146, E-mail: mk43@evansville.edu.

School of Health Sciences Expenses: Contact institution. *Financial support:* Unspecified assistantships available. Financial award application deadline: 6/1; financial award applicants required to submit FAFSA. *Program availability:* Part-time, evening/weekend. Offers athletic training (MSAT); health policy (MPH); health services administration (MS). *Application deadline:* For fall admission, 7/1 for domestic and international students; for spring admission, 10/1 for domestic students. *Application fee:* $35. *Chair,* Dr. William Stroube, 812-488-2870, Fax: 812-488-2087, E-mail: bs52@evansville.edu.

THE UNIVERSITY OF FINDLAY, Findlay, OH 45840-3653

General Information Independent-religious, coed, comprehensive institution. *Enrollment:* 5,078 graduate, professional, and undergraduate students; 751 full-time matriculated graduate/professional students (452 women), 573 part-time matriculated graduate/professional students (323 women). *Enrollment by degree level:* 958 master's, 366 doctoral. *Graduate faculty:* 114 full-time (63 women), 44 part-time/adjunct (18 women). *Graduate housing:* Room and/or apartments available on a first-come, first-served basis to single students; on-campus housing not available to married students. *Student services:* Campus employment opportunities, campus safety program, career counseling, exercise/wellness program, free psychological counseling, grant writing training, international student services, low-cost health insurance, multicultural affairs office, services for students with disabilities, teacher training, writing training. *Library facilities:* Shafer Library plus 4 others. *Collection:* Books: 98,669 (physical), 285,706 (digital/electronic); Serial titles: 361 (physical), 72,953 (digital/electronic); Databases: 173. Weekly public service hours: 94; study areas open 24 hours, 5–7 days a week. *Research affiliation:* The Ohio State University Research Foundation (biology), Rollin M. Gerstacker Foundation (environmental research), U.S. Department of Agriculture (USDA) (wildlife research), U.S. Department of Education (DOE) (technology innovation, bilingual teaching research), U.S. Department of Health and Human Services (terrorism preparedness).

Computer facilities: Computer purchase and lease plans are available. 151 computers available on campus for general student use. A campuswide network can be accessed from student residence rooms and from off campus. Online class registration is available.
Website: http://www.findlay.edu/

General Application Contact: Madeline Fauser Brennan, Graduate Admissions Counselor, 419-434-4636, Fax: 419-434-4898, E-mail: fauserbrennan@findlay.edu.

GRADUATE UNITS

Office of Graduate Admissions Students: 751 full-time (452 women), 573 part-time (323 women); includes 164 minority (82 Black or African American, non-Hispanic/Latino; 1 American Indian or Alaska Native, non-Hispanic/Latino; 27 Asian, non-Hispanic/Latino; 37 Hispanic/Latino; 17 Two or more races, non-Hispanic/Latino), 280 international. Average age 28. 661 applicants, 52% accepted, 288 enrolled. *Faculty:* 114 full-time (63 women), 44 part-time/adjunct (18 women). Expenses: Contact institution. *Financial support:* In 2016–17, 139 students received support, including 15 research assistantships with partial tuition reimbursements available (averaging $7,200 per year), 25 teaching assistantships with partial tuition reimbursements available (averaging $7,200 per year); Federal Work-Study, institutionally sponsored loans, and unspecified assistantships also available. Financial award application deadline: 4/1; financial award applicants required to submit FAFSA. In 2016, 366 master's, 137 doctorates awarded. *Program availability:* Part-time, evening/weekend, 100% online, blended/hybrid learning. Offers applied security and analytics (MSAS); athletic training (MAT); business (MBA); education (MA Ed, Ed D); environmental, safety and health management (MSEM); health informatics (MS); occupational therapy (MOT); pharmacy (Pharm D); physical therapy (DPT); physician assistant (MPA); rhetoric and writing (MA); teaching English to speakers of other languages (TESOL) and bilingual education (MA). *Application deadline:* For fall admission, 6/15 for international students; for spring admission, 12/1 for international students; for summer admission, 4/1 for international students. Applications are processed on a rolling basis. Electronic applications accepted.
Application Contact: Madeline Fauser Brennan, Graduate Admissions Counselor, 419-434-4636, Fax: 419-434-4898, E-mail: fauserbrennan@findlay.edu. *Director of Admissions,* Christopher M. Harris, 419-434-4347, E-mail: harrisc1@findlay.edu.

UNIVERSITY OF FLORIDA, Gainesville, FL 32611

General Information State-supported, coed, university. CGS member. *Graduate housing:* Rooms and/or apartments available on a first-come, first-served basis to single and married students. *Research affiliation:* Los Alamos National Laboratory (high magnetic field research), National Center for Automated Information Research (law and business data), Oracle Corporation (database management), IBM (information infrastructure), Association of Universities for Research in Astronomy (Gemini multinational telescope).

GRADUATE UNITS

College of Dentistry Offers dentistry (MS, DMD, PhD, Certificate); endodontics (MS, Certificate); foreign trained dentistry (Certificate); oral biology (PhD); orthodontics (MS, Certificate); periodontology (MS, Certificate); prosthodontics (MS, Certificate).

College of Medicine Offers biochemistry and molecular biology (PhD); biomedical sciences (MS, PhD); clinical investigation (MS); epidemiology (MS); genetics (PhD); immunology and microbiology (MS); medicine (MPAS, MPH, MS, MD, PhD); molecular cell biology (PhD); molecular genetics and microbiology (MS); neuroscience (PhD); physician assistant (MPAS); physiology and pharmacology (MS); public health (MPH). Electronic applications accepted.

College of Veterinary Medicine *Program availability:* Part-time. Offers forensic toxicology (Certificate); veterinary medical sciences (MS, PhD); veterinary medicine (MS, DVM, PhD, Certificate).

Graduate School *Program availability:* Part-time, evening/weekend, online learning. Electronic applications accepted.

College of Agricultural and Life Sciences *Program availability:* Part-time. Offers agribusiness (MS); agricultural and life sciences (MAB, MFAS, MFRC, MS, DPM, PhD, Certificate); agricultural education and communication (MS, PhD); agroecology (MS); agronomy (MS, PhD); animal molecular and cellular biology (MS, PhD); animal sciences (MS, PhD); community studies (MS); environmental education and communications (Certificate); environmental horticulture (MS, PhD); family and youth development (MS); family, youth and community sciences (MS); fisheries and aquatic sciences (MFAS, MS, PhD); food and resource economics (MAB, MS, PhD); food science (PhD); food science and human nutrition (MS); forest resources and conservation (MFRC, MS, PhD); geographic information systems (MS); horticultural sciences (MS, PhD); hydrologic sciences (MS, PhD); microbiology and cell science (MS, PhD); nonprofit organization development (MS); nutritional sciences (MS, PhD); plant medicine (DPM); plant molecular and cellular biology (MS, PhD); plant pathology (MS, PhD); soil and water science (MS, PhD); toxicology (MS, PhD); tropical conservation and development (MAB, MS, DPM, PhD); wildlife ecology and conservation (MS, PhD). Electronic applications accepted.

College of Design, Construction and Planning *Program availability:* Part-time, online learning. Offers architecture (M Arch, MSAS); construction management (MSCM, PhD); design, construction and planning (M Arch, MAURP, MFES, MICM, MID, MLA, MSAS, MSCM, MURP, PhD); fire and emergency services (MFES); geographic information systems (MAURP, MLA, PhD); historic preservation (M Arch, MAURP, MID, MLA, MSAS, MSCM, PhD); interior design (MID, PhD); international construction (MICM); landscape architecture (MLA, PhD); sustainable architecture (M Arch, MSAS); sustainable construction (MSCM); sustainable design (M Arch, MAURP, MID,

MLA, MSAS, MSCM); tropical conservation and development (MAURP); urban and regional planning (MAURP, MURP, PhD); wetland sciences (MAURP, MLA). Electronic applications accepted.

College of Education *Program availability:* Part-time, evening/weekend, online learning. Offers counseling and counselor education (Ed D, PhD); curriculum and instruction (M Ed, MAE, Ed D, PhD, Ed S); early childhood education (M Ed, MAE); education (M Ed, MAE, Ed D, PhD, Ed S); educational leadership (M Ed, MAE, Ed D, PhD, Ed S); elementary education (M Ed, MAE); English education (M Ed, MAE); higher education administration (Ed D, PhD); marriage and family counseling (M Ed, MAE, Ed D, PhD, Ed S); mathematics education (M Ed, MAE); mental health counseling (M Ed, MAE, Ed D, PhD, Ed S); reading education (M Ed, MAE); research and evaluation methodology (M Ed, MAE, Ed D, PhD); school counseling and guidance (M Ed, MAE, Ed D, PhD, Ed S); school psychology (M Ed, MAE, Ed D, PhD, Ed S); science education (M Ed, MAE); social studies education (M Ed, MAE); special education (M Ed, MAE, Ed D, PhD, Ed S); student personnel in higher education (M Ed, MAE). Electronic applications accepted.

College of Health and Human Performance *Program availability:* Part-time. Offers applied physiology and kinesiology (MS); athletic training/sports medicine (MS); biobehavioral science (MS); clinical exercise physiology (MS); exercise physiology (MS); health and human performance (PhD); health communication (Graduate Certificate); health education and behavior (MS); human performance (MS); recreation, parks and tourism (MS); sport management (MS). Electronic applications accepted.

College of Journalism and Communications *Program availability:* Part-time, online learning. Offers advertising (M Adv); international/intercultural communication (MAMC); journalism (MAMC); mass communication (MAMC, PhD); public relations (MAMC); science/health communication (MAMC); telecommunication (MAMC). Electronic applications accepted.

College of Liberal Arts and Sciences *Program availability:* Part-time. Offers anthropology (MA, MAT, PhD); applications of geographic technologies (MA, MS); astronomy (MS, MST, PhD); botany (MS, MST, PhD); chemistry (MS, MST, PhD); classical studies (MA, PhD); clinical and translational science (PhD); counseling psychology (PhD); creative writing (MFA); criminology, law, and society (MA, PhD); educational policy (PhD); English (MA, PhD); French and Francophone studies (MA, PhD); gender and development (Graduate Certificate); geographic information systems (MA, MS, PhD); geography (MA, MS, PhD); geology (MS, MST, PhD); German (MA, PhD); historic preservation (MA, PhD); history (MA, PhD); hydrologic sciences (MS, PhD); imaging science and technology (PhD); international development policy and administration (MA, Certificate); international relations (MA, MAT); Jewish studies (MA); Latin (MA, MAT, ML); Latin American studies (MA, Certificate); liberal arts and sciences (M Ag, M Stat, MA, MAT, MDP, MFA, ML, MS, MS Stat, MST, MWS, PhD, Certificate, Graduate Certificate); linguistics (MA, PhD); mathematics (MAT, MS, MST, PhD); philosophy (MA, PhD); physics (MS, MST, PhD); political campaigning (MA, Certificate); political science (MA, PhD); psychology (MA, MS, PhD); public affairs (MA, Certificate); quantitative finance (PhD); religion (MA, PhD); sociology (MA, PhD); Spanish (MA, MAT, PhD); statistics (M Stat, MS Stat, PhD); sustainable development practice (MDP); teaching English as a second language (Certificate); tropical conservation and development (MA, MS, MST, PhD); wetland sciences (MA, MS, MST, PhD); women's and gender studies (MA, PhD); women's studies (MA, Graduate Certificate); zoology (MS, MST, PhD). Electronic applications accepted.

College of Nursing *Program availability:* Part-time. Offers clinical and translational science (PhD); clinical nursing (DNP); nursing (MSN); nursing sciences (PhD). Electronic applications accepted.

College of Pharmacy *Program availability:* Part-time, evening/weekend, online learning. Offers clinical and translational sciences (PhD); clinical pharmaceutical sciences (PhD); clinical pharmacy (MSP); clinical toxicology (MSP, Certificate); drug chemistry (Certificate); environmental forensics (Certificate); forensic death investigation (Certificate); forensic DNA and serology (MSP, Certificate); forensic drug chemistry (MSP); forensic science (MSP); forensic toxicology (Certificate); medicinal chemistry (MSP, PhD); pharmaceutical chemistry (MSP); pharmaceutical outcomes and policy (MSP, PhD); pharmaceutical sciences (MSP, PhD); pharmacodynamics (MSP, PhD); pharmacy (MSP, PhD). Electronic applications accepted.

College of Public Health and Health Professions *Program availability:* Part-time. Offers audiology (Au D); biostatistics (MS, PhD); clinical and translational science (PhD); communication sciences and disorders (MA, PhD); environmental health (MPH, PhD); epidemiology (MPH, MS, PhD); health administration (MHA); health management and policy (MPH); health services research (PhD); occupational therapy (MHS, MOT); one health (MHS, PhD); physical therapy (DPT); psychology (MS); public health (MPH, PhD, Certificate); public health and health professions (MA, MHA, MHS, MHS, MOT, MPH, MS, Au D, DPT, PhD, Certificate); public health practice (MPH); rehabilitation science (PhD); social and behavioral sciences (MPH). Electronic applications accepted.

College of The Arts *Program availability:* Online learning. Offers art (MA); art education (MA); art history (MA, PhD); arts (MA, MFA, MM, PhD, Graduate Certificate); choral conducting (MM); composition (MM, PhD); electronic music (MM); ethnomusicology (MM); instrumental conducting (MM); museology (MA); music (MM, PhD); music education (MM, PhD); music history and literature (MM, PhD); music theory (MM); performance (MM); sacred music (MM); theatre (MFA). Electronic applications accepted.

Herbert Wertheim College of Engineering *Program availability:* Part-time, online learning. Offers aerospace engineering (ME, MS, PhD); agricultural and biological engineering (ME, MS, PhD); biological systems modeling (Certificate); biomedical engineering (ME, MS, PhD, Certificate); chemical engineering (ME, MS, PhD, Engr); civil engineering (ME, MS, PhD); clinical and translational science (PhD); coastal and oceanographic engineering (ME, MS, PhD); computer engineering (ME, MS, PhD); computer science (MS); digital arts and sciences (MS); electrical and computer engineering (ME, MS, PhD); engineering (ME, MS, PhD, Certificate, Engr); environmental engineering sciences (ME, MS, PhD, Engr); geographic information systems (ME, MS, PhD); hydrologic sciences (ME, MS, PhD); imaging science and technology (PhD); industrial and systems engineering (ME, MS, PhD, Engr); material science and engineering (MS); materials science and engineering (ME, PhD); mechanical engineering (ME, MS, PhD); medical physics (MS, PhD); nuclear engineering (ME, PhD); nuclear engineering (MS); nuclear engineering sciences (ME, MS, PhD); quantitative finance (PhD); structural engineering (ME, MS); wetland sciences (ME, MS, PhD). Electronic applications accepted.

School of Natural Resources and Environment Offers interdisciplinary ecology (MS, PhD). Electronic applications accepted.

Warrington College of Business Administration *Program availability:* Part-time, evening/weekend, online learning. Offers accounting (M Acc, PhD); business administration (M Acc, MA, MBA, MS, PhD, Certificate); competitive strategy (MBA); economics (MA, PhD); entrepreneurship (MS); finance (MBA, MS, PhD); financial services (Certificate); global management (MBA); Graham-Buffett security analysis (MBA); health care risk management (MS); human resource management (MBA); information systems and operations management (MBA, PhD); insurance (PhD); international business (MA); international studies (MBA); management (MBA, MS, PhD); marketing (MA, MS, PhD); quantitative finance (PhD); real estate (MBA, MS); real estate and urban analysis (PhD); supply chain management (Certificate). Electronic applications accepted.

Levin College of Law Offers comparative law (LL M); environmental and land use law (LL M); international taxation (LL M); law (JD); taxation (LL M, SJD). Electronic applications accepted.

UNIVERSITY OF FORT LAUDERDALE, Lauderhill, FL 33313
General Information Independent-religious, coed, comprehensive institution.
GRADUATE UNITS
Graduate Program Offers ministry (MS).

UNIVERSITY OF GEORGIA, Athens, GA 30602
General Information State-supported, coed, comprehensive institution. CGS member. *Graduate housing:* Rooms and/or apartments available on a first-come, first-served basis to single and married students. *Student services:* Campus employment opportunities, campus safety program, career counseling, child daycare facilities, exercise/wellness program, free psychological counseling, grant writing training, international student services, low-cost health insurance, multicultural affairs office, services for students with disabilities, teacher training, writing training. *Library facilities:* Ilah Dunlap Little Memorial Library plus 4 others. *Collection:* Books: 5.2 million (digital/electronic). Students can reserve study rooms. *Research affiliation:* Skidaway Institute of Oceanography, Southeast Water Laboratory, Russell Research Laboratory, Organization for Tropical Studies.

Computer facilities: A campuswide network can be accessed from student residence rooms and from off campus. Online class registration is available.
Website: http://www.uga.edu/

General Application Contact: Dr. Melissa Barry, Assistant Dean of The Graduate School, 706-425-2934, Fax: 706-425-3093, E-mail: mjb14@uga.edu.

GRADUATE UNITS
Biomedical and Health Sciences Institute Expenses: Contact institution. *Financial support:* Unspecified assistantships available. Financial award application deadline: 12/31. Offers neuroscience (PhD). *Application Contact:* James D. Launderdale, Graduate Coordinator, 706-542-5922, E-mail: neurophd@uga.edu. *Director,* Dr. Harry Dailey, 706-542-5922, Fax: 706-542-5285, E-mail: hdailey@uga.edu.

College of Agricultural and Environmental Sciences Expenses: Contact institution. *Financial support:* Fellowships, research assistantships, teaching assistantships, career-related internships or fieldwork, and unspecified assistantships available. Offers agricultural and environmental sciences (MAE, MS, PhD); agricultural economics (MAE, MS, PhD); animal and dairy science (PhD); animal nutrition (PhD); animal science (MS); crop and soil sciences (MS, PhD); entomology (MS, PhD); environmental economics (MS); food science (MS, PhD); horticulture (MS); plant pathology (MS, PhD); poultry science (MS, PhD). *Application deadline:* For fall admission, 7/1 priority date for domestic students; for spring admission, 11/15 for domestic students. *Application fee:* $50. Electronic applications accepted. *Application Contact:* Krista Haynes, Director of Enrolled Student Services, 706-425-1789, Fax: 706-425-3094, E-mail: gradoff@uga.edu. *Dean,* Dr. J. Scott Angle, 706-542-3924, Fax: 706-542-0803, E-mail: caesdean@uga.edu.

Institute of Plant Breeding, Genetics and Genomics Expenses: Contact institution. *Financial support:* Tuition waivers and unspecified assistantships available. Offers plant breeding, genetics and genomics (MS, PhD). *Application Contact:* Scott A. Jackson, Graduate Coordinator, 706-542-5607, E-mail: pbgg@uga.edu. *Director,* Dr. John H. Dayton, 706-542-5607, Fax: 706-583-8120, E-mail: pbgg@uga.edu.

College of Education Expenses: Contact institution. *Financial support:* Fellowships, research assistantships, teaching assistantships, and unspecified assistantships available. Offers adult education (Ed D, Ed S); college student affairs administration (M Ed, PhD); communication science and disorders (M Ed, MA, PhD, Ed S); education (M Ed, MA, MA Ed, MAT, MS, Ed D, PhD, Ed S); educational psychology (Ed S); English education (M Ed); higher education (M Ed, Ed D, PhD); kinesiology (MS, PhD); language and literacy education (PhD); learning, design, and technology (M Ed, PhD, Ed S); lifelong education, administration and policy (PhD); mathematics education (M Ed, PhD, Ed S); professional school counseling (Ed S); special education (Ed D); workforce education (MAT, Ed D). *Application deadline:* For fall admission, 7/1 priority date for domestic students; for spring admission, 11/15 for domestic students. *Application fee:* $50. Electronic applications accepted. *Interim Dean,* Dr. Arthur M. Horne, 706-542-6446, Fax: 706-542-0360, E-mail: ahorne@uga.edu.

College of Engineering Expenses: Contact institution. Offers engineering (MS). *Application Contact:* Lawrence Hornak, Graduate Coordinator, 706-542-2462, E-mail: lahornak@uga.edu. *Dean,* Dr. E. Dale Threadgill, 706-542-1653.

College of Environment and Design Expenses: Contact institution. Offers environmental planning and design (MEPD); historic preservation (MHP); landscape architecture (MLA). *Application deadline:* For fall admission, 7/1 priority date for domestic students; for spring admission, 11/15 for domestic students. *Application fee:* $50. *Application Contact:* Umit Yilmaz, Graduate Coordinator, 706-542-4720, E-mail: yilmaz@uga.edu. *Acting Dean,* Daniels J. Nadenicek, 706-542-1100, Fax: 706-542-4485, E-mail: dnadeni@uga.edu.

College of Family and Consumer Sciences Expenses: Contact institution. *Financial support:* Fellowships, research assistantships, teaching assistantships, and unspecified assistantships available. Offers child and family development (MS); family and consumer sciences (MS, PhD); foods and nutrition (MS, PhD); historical and cultural aspects of dress and textiles (MS); interior environments (MS); international merchandising (PhD); merchandising and international trade (MS); polymer, fiber and textile science (MS); polymer, fiber, and textile sciences (PhD). *Application deadline:* For fall admission, 7/1 priority date for domestic students; for spring admission, 11/15 for domestic students. *Application fee:* $50. Electronic applications accepted.

College of Pharmacy Expenses: Contact institution. *Financial support:* Fellowships, research assistantships, teaching assistantships, career-related internships or fieldwork, Federal Work-Study, institutionally sponsored loans, tuition waivers, and unspecified assistantships available. Support available to part-time students. Financial award application deadline: 2/15. Offers clinical and experimental therapeutics (PhD); pharmaceutical and biomedical sciences (MS, PhD); pharmacy (MS, PhD, Pharm D,

Certificate); pharmacy care administration (PhD). *Application deadline:* For fall admission, 7/1 priority date for domestic students; for spring admission, 11/15 for domestic students. *Application fee:* $50. Electronic applications accepted. *Application Contact:* Dr. Melissa Barry, Assistant Dean of The Graduate School, 706-425-2934, Fax: 706-425-3093, E-mail: mjb14@uga.edu. *Dean,* Dr. Svein Oie, 706-542-1914, Fax: 706-542-5269, E-mail: soie@rx.uga.edu.

College of Public Health Expenses: Contact institution. Offers environmental health science (MPH, MS, PhD); health promotion and behavior (MA, MPH, Dr PH, PhD); public health (MA, MPH, MS, Dr PH, PhD, Certificate). *Application deadline:* For fall admission, 7/1 for domestic students; for spring admission, 11/15 for domestic students. *Application fee:* $50.

Institute of Gerontology Expenses: Contact institution. Offers gerontology (Certificate). *Application Contact:* Mary Ann Johnson, Graduate Coordinator, 706-542-4286, E-mail: noahnet@geron.uga.edu.

College of Veterinary Medicine Expenses: Contact institution. *Financial support:* Fellowships, research assistantships, teaching assistantships, Federal Work-Study, scholarships/grants, and unspecified assistantships available. Financial award applicants required to submit FAFSA. Offers infectious diseases (PhD); pharmacology (MS, PhD); veterinary medicine (MS, DVM, PhD); veterinary pathology (MS, PhD). *Application deadline:* For fall admission, 7/1 priority date for domestic students; for spring admission, 11/15 for domestic students. *Application fee:* $50. Electronic applications accepted. *Application Contact:* Malik McKinley, Director of Graduate Admissions, 706-542-5727, E-mail: dvmadmit@uga.edu. *Dean,* Dr. Lisa K. Nolan, 706-542-3461, Fax: 706-542-8254.

Eugene P. Odum School of Ecology Expenses: Contact institution. *Financial support:* Fellowships, research assistantships, teaching assistantships, and unspecified assistantships available. Offers conservation ecology and sustainable development (MS); ecology (PhD). *Application deadline:* For fall admission, 7/1 priority date for domestic students; for spring admission, 11/15 for domestic students. *Application fee:* $50. Electronic applications accepted. *Application Contact:* Ford Ballantyne, Graduate Coordinator, 706-542-3404, E-mail: fb4@uga.edu. *Dean,* Dr. John L. Gittleman, 706-542-2968, Fax: 706-542-4819, E-mail: ecohead@uga.edu.

Franklin College of Arts and Sciences Expenses: Contact institution. *Financial support:* Fellowships, research assistantships, teaching assistantships, Federal Work-Study, institutionally sponsored loans, and unspecified assistantships available. Offers analytical chemistry (MS, PhD); anthropology (MA, PhD); applied mathematical science (MAMS); arts and sciences (MA, MAMS, -MAT, MFA, MM, MM Ed, MS, DMA, PhD, Certificate); biochemistry and molecular biology (MS, PhD); cellular biology (MS, PhD); classical languages (MA); comparative literature (MA, PhD); computer science (MS, PhD); English (MA, MAT, PhD); French (PhD); genetics (MS, PhD); geography (MA, MS, PhD); geology (MS, PhD); German (MA); Greek (MA); history (MA, PhD); Italian (MA, PhD); Latin (MA); linguistics (MA, PhD); marine sciences (MS, PhD); mathematics (MA, PhD); microbiology (MS, PhD); philosophy (MA, PhD); physics (MS, PhD); plant biology (MS, PhD); Portuguese (MA, PhD); psychology (PhD); religion (MA); romance linguistics (MA); sociology (MA, PhD); Spanish (PhD); statistics (MA, PhD); theatre (MFA, PhD). *Application deadline:* For fall admission, 7/1 priority date for domestic students; for spring admission, 11/15 for domestic students. *Application fee:* $50. Electronic applications accepted. *Dean,* Alan Dorsey, 706-542-3400, E-mail: atdorsey@uga.edu.

Artificial Intelligence Center Expenses: Contact institution. *Financial support:* Unspecified assistantships available. Offers artificial intelligence (MS). *Application deadline:* For fall admission, 7/1 priority date for domestic students; for spring admission, 11/15 for domestic students. *Application fee:* $50. Electronic applications accepted. *Application Contact:* Adam Goodle, Graduate Coordinator, 706-542-3444, E-mail: goodie@uga.edu. *Director,* Dr. Walter Don Potter, 706-542-0361, E-mail: potter@uga.edu.

Hugh Hodgson School of Music Expenses: Contact institution. *Financial support:* Fellowships, research assistantships, teaching assistantships, and unspecified assistantships available. Offers composition (MM, DMA); conducting (MM, DMA); music (PhD); music education (MM Ed, Ed D); musicology (MA); performance (MM, DMA). Ed D offered jointly with College of Education. *Application deadline:* For fall admission, 7/1 priority date for domestic students; for spring admission, 11/15 for domestic students. *Application fee:* $50. Electronic applications accepted. *Application Contact:* Peter Jutras, Graduate Coordinator, 206-542-2765, E-mail: pjutras@uga.edu. *Director,* Dr. Dale Monson, 706-542-2776, Fax: 706-542-2773, E-mail: dmonson@uga.edu.

Institute for Women's Studies Expenses: Contact institution. Offers women's studies (Certificate). *Application Contact:* Dr. Patricia L. Richards, Assistant Director, 706-542-3235, Fax: 706-542-0049, E-mail: plr333@uga.edu. *Director,* Dr. Juanita Johnson-Bailey, 706-542-2846, E-mail: jjb@uga.edu.

Lamar Dodd School of Art Expenses: Contact institution. *Financial support:* Fellowships, research assistantships, teaching assistantships, and unspecified assistantships available. Offers art (MFA, PhD); art history (MA). *Application deadline:* For fall admission, 7/1 priority date for domestic students; for spring admission, 11/15 for domestic students. *Application fee:* $50. Electronic applications accepted. *Application Contact:* Isabelle Wallace, Graduate Coordinator, 706-542-1624, E-mail: iwallace@uga.edu. *Director,* Prof. Georgia Strange, 706-542-1600, Fax: 706-542-0226, E-mail: strange@uga.edu.

Grady College of Journalism and Mass Communication Expenses: Contact institution. *Financial support:* Research assistantships, teaching assistantships, tuition waivers (full), and unspecified assistantships available. Offers journalism and mass communication (MA); mass communication (PhD). *Application deadline:* For spring admission, 2/15 for domestic students. *Application fee:* $50. Electronic applications accepted. *Application Contact:* Dr. Jeffrey K. Springston, Associate Dean, 706-542-7833, Fax: 706-542-2183, E-mail: jspring@grady.uga.edu. *Dean,* Dr. E. Culpepper Clark, 706-542-1704, Fax: 706-542-2183, E-mail: cully@uga.edu.

Institute of Bioinformatics Expenses: Contact institution. Offers bioinformatics (MS, PhD). *Application Contact:* Jonathan Arnold, Graduate Coordinator, 706-542-7783, E-mail: arnold@uga.edu. *Director,* Dr. Jessica Kissinger, 706-542-6562, E-mail: jkissing@uga.edu.

School of Forestry and Natural Resources Expenses: Contact institution. *Financial support:* Fellowships, research assistantships, teaching assistantships, and unspecified assistantships available. Offers forestry and natural resources (MFR, MS, PhD). *Application deadline:* For fall admission, 7/1 priority date for domestic students; for spring admission, 11/15 for domestic students. *Application fee:* $50. Electronic applications accepted. *Application Contact:* Robert Bringolf, 706-542-1183, E-mail: graduatecoordinator@warnell.uga.edu. *Professor,* Michael L. Clutter, 706-542-4741, Fax: 706-542-8356, E-mail: mclutter@warnell.uga.edu.

School of Law Expenses: Contact institution. *Financial support:* Fellowships, research assistantships, teaching assistantships, Federal Work-Study, institutionally sponsored loans, tuition waivers (partial), and unspecified assistantships available. Financial award application deadline: 1/31. Offers law (LL M, MSL, JD). *Application deadline:* For fall admission, 7/1 priority date for domestic students; for spring admission, 11/15 for domestic students. *Application fee:* $50. Electronic applications accepted. *Application Contact:* Laura Tate Kagel, Graduate Coordinator, 706-542-7875, E-mail: lkagel@uga.edu. *Dean,* Rebecca H. White, 706-542-7140, Fax: 706-542-5283, E-mail: rhwhite@uga.edu.

School of Public and International Affairs Expenses: Contact institution. *Financial support:* Fellowships, research assistantships, teaching assistantships, and unspecified assistantships available. Offers international affairs (MA, MIP, PhD); political science (MA, PhD); public administration (MPA, PhD); public and international affairs (MA, MIP, MPA, PhD). *Application deadline:* For fall admission, 7/1 priority date for domestic students; for spring admission, 11/15 for domestic students. *Application fee:* $50. Electronic applications accepted. *Application Contact:* Dr. Jeffrey K. Berejikian, Director of Graduate Admissions, 706-425-1789, E-mail: gradoff@uga.edu. *Dean,* Dr. Matthew R. Auer, 706-542-2149.

School of Social Work Expenses: Contact institution. *Financial support:* Fellowships, research assistantships, teaching assistantships, career-related internships or fieldwork, Federal Work-Study, scholarships/grants, tuition waivers (full and partial), and unspecified assistantships available. Support available to part-time students. Financial award application deadline: 2/10; financial award applicants required to submit FAFSA. *Program availability:* Part-time, evening/weekend. Offers social work (MA, MSW, PhD, Certificate). *Application deadline:* For fall admission, 7/1 priority date for domestic students, 7/1 for international students; for spring admission, 11/15 for domestic and international students. Applications are processed on a rolling basis. *Application fee:* $50. Electronic applications accepted. *Application Contact:* Shari Miller, Graduate Coordinator, 706-542-2328, E-mail: semiller@uga.edu. *Dean,* Dr. Maurice C. Daniels, 706-542-5424, Fax: 706-542-3282, E-mail: daniels@uga.edu.

Terry College of Business Expenses: Contact institution. *Financial support:* Fellowships, research assistantships, teaching assistantships, and unspecified assistantships available. Offers business (Exec MBA, M Acc, MA, MBA, MMR, PhD); business administration (Exec MBA, MBA); economics (MA, PhD). *Application deadline:* For fall admission, 7/1 priority date for domestic students; for spring admission, 11/15 for domestic students. *Application fee:* $50. Electronic applications accepted. *Application Contact:* Dr. Rich Daniels, Interim Associate Dean, 404-842-4862, E-mail: rdaniels@terry.uga.edu. *Dean,* Ben Ayers, 706-542-8100, E-mail: busdean@uga.edu.

J.M. Tull School of Accounting Expenses: Contact institution. *Financial support:* Fellowships, research assistantships, teaching assistantships, and unspecified assistantships available. Offers accounting (M Acc). *Application deadline:* For fall admission, 7/1 priority date for domestic students; for spring admission, 11/15 for domestic students. *Application fee:* $50. Electronic applications accepted. *Application Contact:* Jennifer Chapman, Graduate Coordinator, 706-542-3601, E-mail: jennchap@uga.edu.

UNIVERSITY OF GREAT FALLS, Great Falls, MT 59405

General Information Independent-religious, coed, comprehensive institution. *Enrollment:* 952 graduate, professional, and undergraduate students; 22 full-time matriculated graduate/professional students (16 women), 49 part-time matriculated graduate/professional students (36 women). *Enrollment by degree level:* 71 master's. *Graduate faculty:* 6 full-time (4 women), 21 part-time/adjunct (13 women). *Tuition:* Full-time $14,256; part-time $9504 per semester. *Graduate housing:* On-campus housing not available. *Student services:* Teacher training, writing training. *Library facilities:* University of Great Falls Library.

Computer facilities: A campuswide network can be accessed from student residence rooms and from off campus. Online class registration is available. Website: http://www.ugf.edu/

General Application Contact: Denise Ostberg, Graduate Admission Counselor, 406-868-1933, Fax: 406-791-5209, E-mail: denise.ostberg@ugf.edu.

GRADUATE UNITS

Graduate Studies Expenses: Contact institution. *Financial support:* Career-related internships or fieldwork and institutionally sponsored loans available. Support available to part-time students. Financial award application deadline: 6/1; financial award applicants required to submit FAFSA. *Program availability:* Part-time, online learning. Offers counseling (MSC); criminal justice (MSM); human development (MSM); management (MSM). *Application deadline:* For fall admission, 8/15 priority date for domestic students, 6/15 priority date for international students; for spring admission, 12/15 priority date for domestic students, 10/15 priority date for international students. Applications are processed on a rolling basis. *Application fee:* $50. Electronic applications accepted. *Application Contact:* Melanie Houge, Director of Admissions, 406-791-5210, Fax: 406-791-5209, E-mail: melanie.houge@ugf.edu. *Associate Dean for Graduate Studies,* Dr. Katrina Stark, 406-791-5332, Fax: 406-791-5990, E-mail: katrina.stark@ugf.edu.

UNIVERSITY OF GUAM, Mangilao, GU 96923

General Information Territory-supported, coed, comprehensive institution. *Graduate housing:* Room and/or apartments available on a first-come, first-served basis to single students; on-campus housing not available to married students. Housing application deadline: 5/1. *Research affiliation:* Bernice Pauahi Bishop Museum (science, cultural preservation), Pilar Project, Inc. (salvage of artifacts, archaeology), Cancer Research Center of Hawaii (cancer research).

GRADUATE UNITS

Office of Graduate Studies *Program availability:* Part-time.

College of Liberal Arts and Social Sciences *Program availability:* Part-time. Offers ceramics (MA); English (MA); graphics (MA); liberal arts and social sciences (MA); Micronesian studies (MA); painting (MA).

College of Natural and Applied Sciences Offers environmental science (MS); natural and applied sciences (MS, MSW); social work (MSW); tropical marine biology (MS).

School of Business and Public Administration *Program availability:* Part-time. Offers business administration (PMBA); business and public administration (MPA, PMBA); public administration (MPA).

School of Education *Program availability:* Part-time. Offers administration and supervision (M Ed); counseling (MA); education (M Ed, MA); language and literacy (M Ed); secondary education (M Ed); special education (M Ed); teaching English to speakers of other languages (M Ed).

UNIVERSITY OF GUELPH, Guelph, ON N1G 2W1, Canada

General Information Province-supported, coed, university. *Graduate housing:* Rooms and/or apartments available to single and married students. Housing application deadline: 5/28.

GRADUATE UNITS

Graduate Studies *Program availability:* Part-time, evening/weekend, online learning. Offers biophysics (M Sc, PhD). Electronic applications accepted.

Collaborative International Development Studies *Program availability:* Part-time. Offers international development studies (M Eng, M Sc, MA, MBA, PhD).

College of Arts *Program availability:* Part-time. Offers arts (MA, MFA, PhD); drama (MA); English (MA); European studies (MA); French studies (MA); history (MA, PhD); literary studies/theatre studies in English (PhD); philosophy (MA, PhD); studio art (MFA).

College of Biological Science *Program availability:* Part-time. Offers biochemistry (M Sc, PhD); biological science (M Sc, PhD); biophysics (M Sc, PhD); botany (M Sc, PhD); microbiology (M Sc, PhD); molecular biology and genetics (M Sc, PhD); nutritional sciences (M Sc, PhD); zoology (M Sc, PhD). Electronic applications accepted.

College of Management and Economics Offers economics (MA, PhD); food and agribusiness management (MBA); hospitality and tourism management (MBA); leadership (M Sc); management and economics (M Sc, MA, MBA, PhD); marketing and consumer studies (M Sc).

College of Physical and Engineering Science *Program availability:* Part-time. Offers applied computer science (M Sc); applied mathematics (PhD); applied statistics (PhD); biological engineering (M Eng, M Sc, MA Sc, PhD); chemistry and biochemistry (M Sc, PhD); computer science (PhD); engineering systems and computing (M Eng, M Sc, MA Sc, PhD); environmental engineering (M Eng, M Sc, MA Sc, PhD); mathematics and statistics (M Sc); physical and engineering science (M Eng, M Sc, MA Sc, PhD); physics (M Sc, PhD); water resources engineering (M Eng, M Sc, MA Sc, PhD).

College of Social and Applied Human Sciences *Program availability:* Part-time. Offers anthropology (MA); applied nutrition (MAN); applied social psychology (MA, PhD); clinical psychology: applied development emphasis (PhD); clinical psychology: applied developmental emphasis (MA); comparative politics (MA); crime and criminal justice policy (MA); criminology and criminal justice policy (MA); family relations and human development (M Sc, MA, PhD); geography (M Sc, MA, PhD); industrial/organizational psychology (MA, PhD); international development (MA); neuroscience and applied cognitive science (MA, PhD); political science (MA); public policy and public administration (MA); social and applied human sciences (M Sc, MA, MAN, PhD); sociology (MA, PhD); the Americas (Canada emphasis) (MA).

Ontario Agricultural College *Program availability:* Part-time, online learning. Offers agricultural economics (M Sc, PhD); agriculture (M Sc, MLA, PhD, Diploma); animal and poultry science (M Sc, PhD); aquaculture (M Sc); atmospheric science (M Sc, PhD); capacity development and extension (M Sc); entomology (M Sc, PhD); environmental and agricultural earth sciences (M Sc, PhD); environmental microbiology and biotechnology (M Sc, PhD); environmental toxicology (M Sc, PhD); food safety and quality assurance (M Sc); food science (M Sc, PhD); international rural planning and development (M Sc); land resources management (M Sc, PhD); landscape architecture (MLA); plant agriculture (M Sc, PhD); plant and forest systems (M Sc, PhD); plant pathology (M Sc, PhD); rural planning and development (M Sc); rural planning and development in Canada (M Sc); rural studies (PhD); soil science (M Sc, PhD).

Ontario Veterinary College Offers toxicology (M Sc, PhD); veterinary medicine (M Sc, DV Sc, PhD, Diploma).

Graduate Programs in Veterinary Sciences Offers anatomic pathology (DV Sc, Diploma); anesthesiology (M Sc, DV Sc); cardiology (DV Sc, Diploma); clinical pathology (Diploma); clinical studies (Diploma); comparative pathology (M Sc, PhD); dermatology (M Sc); diagnostic imaging (M Sc, DV Sc); emergency/critical care (M Sc, DV Sc, Diploma); epidemiology (M Sc, DV Sc, PhD); health management (DV Sc); immunology (M Sc, PhD); laboratory animal science (DV Sc); medicine (M Sc, DV Sc); morphology (M Sc, DV Sc, PhD); neurology (M Sc, DV Sc); neuroscience (M Sc, DV Sc, PhD); ophthalmology (M Sc, DV Sc); pathology (M Sc, PhD, Diploma); pharmacology (M Sc, DV Sc, PhD); physiology (M Sc, DV Sc, PhD); population medicine and health management (M Sc); surgery (M Sc, DV Sc); swine health management (M Sc); theriogenology (M Sc, DV Sc); toxicology (M Sc, DV Sc, PhD); veterinary infectious diseases (M Sc, PhD); veterinary sciences (M Sc, PhD, Diploma); zoo animal/wildlife medicine (DV Sc).

UNIVERSITY OF HARTFORD, West Hartford, CT 06117-1599

General Information Independent, coed, comprehensive institution. CGS member. *Graduate housing:* On-campus housing not available.

GRADUATE UNITS

Barney School of Business *Program availability:* Part-time, evening/weekend. Offers business (MBA, MSAT, Certificate); business administration (MBA); professional accounting (Certificate); taxation (MSAT). Electronic applications accepted.

College of Arts and Sciences *Program availability:* Part-time, evening/weekend. Offers arts and sciences (MA, MS, Psy D); biology (MS); clinical practices (MA, Psy D); communication (MA); general experimental psychology (MA); neuroscience (MS); organizational behavior (MS); psychology (MA); school psychology (MS). Electronic applications accepted.

College of Education, Nursing, and Health Professions *Program availability:* Part-time, evening/weekend. Offers administration and supervision (CAGS); community/public health nursing (MSN); counseling (M Ed, MS, Sixth Year Certificate); early childhood education (M Ed); education, nursing, and health professions (M Ed, MS, MSN, MSPT, DPT, Ed D, CAGS, Sixth Year Certificate); educational leadership (Ed D, CAGS); educational technology (M Ed); elementary education (M Ed); nursing education (MSN); nursing management (MSN); physical therapy (MSPT, DPT). Electronic applications accepted.

College of Engineering, Technology and Architecture *Program availability:* Part-time, evening/weekend. Offers architecture (M Arch); engineering (M Eng); engineering, technology and architecture (M Arch, M Eng). Electronic applications accepted.

Hartford Art School *Program availability:* Part-time. Offers art (MFA). Electronic applications accepted.

The Hartt School *Program availability:* Part-time. Offers choral conducting (MM Ed); composition (MM, DMA, Artist Diploma, Diploma); conducting (MM, DMA, Artist Diploma, Diploma); early childhood education (MM Ed); instrumental conducting (MM Ed); Kodály (MM Ed); music (CAGS); music education (DMA, PhD); music history (MM); music theory (MM); pedagogy (MM Ed); performance (MM, MM Ed, DMA, Artist Diploma, Diploma); research (MM Ed); technology (MM Ed). Electronic applications accepted.

UNIVERSITY OF HAWAII AT HILO, Hilo, HI 96720-4091

General Information State-supported, coed, comprehensive institution. *Graduate housing:* Rooms and/or apartments available on a first-come, first-served basis to single and married students.

GRADUATE UNITS

Program in Clinical Psychopharmacology Offers clinical psychopharmacology (MS). Electronic applications accepted.

Program in Counseling Psychology Offers counseling psychology (MA).

Program in Education *Program availability:* Part-time, evening/weekend. Offers education (M Ed). Electronic applications accepted.

Program in Hawaiian and Indigenous Language and Culture Revitalization Offers Hawaiian and indigenous language and culture revitalization (PhD). Electronic applications accepted.

Program in Hawaiian Language and Literature Offers Hawaiian language and literature (MA). Electronic applications accepted.

Program in Indigenous Language and Culture Education Offers indigenous language and culture education (MA). Electronic applications accepted.

Program in Nursing Practice Offers nursing practice (DNP). Electronic applications accepted.

Program in Pharmaceutical Sciences Offers pharmaceutical sciences (PhD). Electronic applications accepted.

Program in Pharmacy Offers pharmacy (Pharm D). Electronic applications accepted.

Program in Teaching Offers teaching (MA). Electronic applications accepted.

Program in Tropical Conservation Biology and Environmental Science Offers tropical conservation biology and environmental science (MS). Electronic applications accepted.

UNIVERSITY OF HOLY CROSS, New Orleans, LA 70131-7399

General Information Independent-religious, coed, comprehensive institution. *Graduate housing:* On-campus housing not available.

GRADUATE UNITS

Program in Education and Counseling *Program availability:* Part-time, evening/weekend. Offers administration and supervision (M Ed); curriculum and instruction (M Ed); marriage and family counseling (MA); school counseling (M Ed, MA).

UNIVERSITY OF HOUSTON, Houston, TX 77204

General Information State-supported, coed, university. CGS member. *Graduate housing:* Rooms and/or apartments available on a first-come, first-served basis to single and married students. *Research affiliation:* Keck Consortium.

GRADUATE UNITS

Bauer College of Business *Program availability:* Part-time, evening/weekend. Offers accountancy (MS Accy); accountancy and taxation (PhD); business (MBA, MS, MS Accy, PhD); decision and information sciences (PhD); finance (MS); management (PhD); marketing (PhD). Electronic applications accepted.

College of Architecture Offers architecture (MS); architecture studies (MA); space architecture (MS). Electronic applications accepted.

College of Education *Program availability:* Part-time. Offers administration and supervision (M Ed, Ed D); administration and supervision - higher education (M Ed); counseling (M Ed); counseling psychology (PhD); curriculum and instruction (M Ed, Ed D); education (M Ed, Ed D, PhD); educational psychology (M Ed); higher education (M Ed); historical, social, and cultural foundations of education (M Ed); professional leadership (Ed D); school psychology (PhD); school psychology and individual differences (PhD); special education (M Ed). Electronic applications accepted.

College of Liberal Arts and Social Sciences *Program availability:* Part-time, online learning. Offers anthropology (MA); applied economics (MA); applied English linguistics (MA); clinical psychology (PhD); communication sciences and disorders (MA); creative writing (MFA); creative writing and literature (MA, PhD); developmental psychology (PhD); economics (MA, PhD); English (MA, PhD); exercise science (MS); history (MA, PhD); human nutrition (MS); human space exploration sciences (MS); industrial/organizational psychology (PhD); kinesiology (PhD); liberal arts and social sciences (M Ed, MA, MFA, MM, MS, DMA, PhD); philosophy (MA); physical education (M Ed); political science (MA, PhD); psychology (MA); public administration (MA); social psychology (PhD); sociology (MA); Spanish (MA, PhD); world cultures and literatures (MA). Electronic applications accepted.

Hobby School of Public Affairs *Program availability:* Part-time. Offers public policy (MPP).

Jack J. Valenti School of Communication *Program availability:* Part-time. Offers health communication (MA); mass communication studies (MA); public relations studies (MA); speech communication (MA). Electronic applications accepted.

Moores School of Music *Program availability:* Part-time. Offers accompanying and chamber music (MM); applied music (MM); composition (MM); music education (DMA); music theory (MM); performance (DMA). Electronic applications accepted.

School of Art Offers art history (MA); interdisciplinary practice and emerging forms (MFA); painting (MFA); studio art (MFA). Electronic applications accepted.

School of Theatre and Dance *Program availability:* Part-time. Offers theatre (MA, MFA). Electronic applications accepted.

College of Natural Sciences and Mathematics *Program availability:* Part-time, online learning. Offers applied mathematics (MS); atmospheric science (PhD); biochemistry (MA, PhD); biology (MA); chemistry (MA, PhD); computer science (MA, PhD); geology (MA, PhD); geophysics (PhD); mathematics (MA, PhD); natural sciences and mathematics (MA, MS, PhD); physics (MA, PhD). Electronic applications accepted.

College of Optometry *Program availability:* Part-time. Offers optometry (MS, OD, PhD); physiological optics (MS, PhD). Electronic applications accepted.

College of Pharmacy *Program availability:* Part-time. Offers pharmaceutics (MSPHR, PhD); pharmacology (MSPHR, PhD); pharmacy (Pharm D); pharmacy administration (MSPHR, PhD). Electronic applications accepted.

College of Technology *Program availability:* Part-time. Offers construction management (MS); engineering technology (MS); future studies in commerce (MS); human resources development (MS); information security (MS); network communications (M Tech); supply chain and logistics technology (MS); technology (M Tech, MS); technology project management (MS). Electronic applications accepted.

Conrad N. Hilton College of Hotel and Restaurant Management *Program availability:* Part-time. Offers hospitality management (MS).

Cullen College of Engineering *Program availability:* Part-time. Offers biomedical engineering (PhD); chemical engineering (MCHE, PhD); civil engineering (MCE, PhD); electrical engineering (MEE, MSEE, PhD); engineering (M Pet E, MCE, MCHE, MEE, MIE, MME, MSEE, MSME, PhD); industrial engineering (MIE, PhD); mechanical engineering (MME, MSME, PhD); petroleum engineering (M Pet E).

Graduate College of Social Work *Program availability:* Part-time. Offers social work (MSW, PhD).

Law Center *Program availability:* Part-time, evening/weekend. Offers energy, environment, and natural resources (LL M); health law (LL M); intellectual property and information law (LL M); international law (LL M); law (LL M, JD); tax law (LL M). Electronic applications accepted.

School of Nursing Offers family nurse practitioner (MSN); nursing administration (MSN); nursing education (MSN). Electronic applications accepted.

UNIVERSITY OF HOUSTON–CLEAR LAKE, Houston, TX 77058-1002

General Information State-supported, coed, comprehensive institution. CGS member. *Graduate housing:* Rooms and/or apartments available on a first-come, first-served basis to single students and available to married students. *Research affiliation:* Baylor College of Medicine (life sciences), NASA–Johnson Space Center (computer science, computer engineering), Schlumberger (ergonomic software).

GRADUATE UNITS

School of Business *Program availability:* Part-time, evening/weekend. Offers accounting (MS); business (MA, MBA, MHA, MS); business administration (MBA); environmental management (MS); finance (MS); healthcare administration (MHA); human resource management (MS); management information systems (MS); professional accounting (MS). Electronic applications accepted.

School of Education *Program availability:* Part-time, evening/weekend. Offers counseling (MS); curriculum and instruction (MS); early childhood education (MS); education (MS, Ed D); educational leadership (Ed D); educational management (MS); instructional technology (MS); multicultural studies (MS); reading (MS); school library and information science (MS). Electronic applications accepted.

School of Human Sciences and Humanities *Program availability:* Part-time, evening/weekend. Offers behavioral sciences (MA); clinical psychology (MA); criminology (MA); cross cultural studies (MA); family therapy (MA); fitness and human performance (MA); history (MA); human sciences and humanities (MA); humanities (MA); literature (MA); school psychology (MA).

School of Science and Computer Engineering *Program availability:* Part-time, evening/weekend. Offers biological sciences (MS); biotechnology (MS); chemistry (MS); computer engineering (MS); computer information systems (MS); computer science (MS); environmental science (MS); mathematical sciences (MS); physics (MS); science and computer engineering (MS); software engineering (MS); statistics (MS); system engineering (MS).

UNIVERSITY OF HOUSTON–DOWNTOWN, Houston, TX 77002

General Information State-supported, coed, comprehensive institution. *Enrollment:* 14,251 graduate, professional, and undergraduate students; 93 full-time matriculated graduate/professional students (55 women), 1,293 part-time matriculated graduate/professional students (735 women). *Enrollment by degree level:* 1,386 master's. *Graduate faculty:* 67 full-time (27 women), 7 part-time/adjunct (2 women). Tuition, state resident: full-time $7704; part-time $428 per credit hour. Tuition, nonresident: full-time $14,148; part-time $786 per credit hour. *Required fees:* $1166; $970 per credit hour. Tuition and fees vary according to program. *Graduate housing:* On-campus housing not available. *Student services:* Campus employment opportunities, campus safety program, career counseling, child daycare facilities, exercise/wellness program, free psychological counseling, international student services, low-cost health insurance, services for students with disabilities, teacher training. *Library facilities:* W. I. Dykes Library.

Computer facilities: A campuswide network can be accessed from off campus. Online class registration is available.
Website: http://www.uhd.edu/

General Application Contact: Ceshia Love, Director of Graduate and International Admissions, 713-221-8093, Fax: 713-221-8658, E-mail: gradadmissions@uhd.edu.

GRADUATE UNITS

College of Humanities and Social Sciences Students: 29 full-time (20 women), 105 part-time (76 women); includes 88 minority (54 Black or African American, non-Hispanic/Latino; 2 American Indian or Alaska Native, non-Hispanic/Latino; 2 Asian, non-Hispanic/Latino; 30 Hispanic/Latino). Average age 36. 68 applicants, 87% accepted, 53 enrolled. *Faculty:* 12 full-time (6 women), 2 part-time/adjunct (0 women). Expenses: Contact institution. *Financial support:* Federal Work-Study and scholarships/grants available. Financial award application deadline: 4/1; financial award applicants required to submit FAFSA. In 2016, 14 master's awarded. *Program availability:* Part-time, evening/weekend, 100% online. Offers humanities and social sciences (MA, MS); non-profit management (MA); rhetoric and composition (MA); technical communication (MS). *Application fee:* $35 ($60 for international students). Electronic applications accepted. *Application Contact:* Ceshia Love, Director of Graduate and International Admissions, 713-221-8093, Fax: 713-223-7408, E-mail: gradadmissions@uhd.edu. *Dean,* Dr. DoVeanna Fulton, 713-221-8009, Fax: 713-223-7465, E-mail: fultond@uhd.edu.

College of Public Service Students: 22 full-time (13 women), 97 part-time (77 women); includes 88 minority (42 Black or African American, non-Hispanic/Latino; 8 Asian, non-Hispanic/Latino; 38 Hispanic/Latino). Average age 34. 67 applicants, 81% accepted, 45 enrolled. *Faculty:* 15 full-time (8 women), 2 part-time/adjunct (1 woman). Expenses: Contact institution. *Financial support:* Federal Work-Study and scholarships/grants available. Financial award application deadline: 4/1; financial award applicants required to submit FAFSA. In 2016, 37 master's awarded. *Program availability:* Part-time, evening/weekend, 100% online. Offers criminal justice and social work (MS); curriculum and instruction (MAT); elementary and secondary education (MAT); public service (MAT, MS). *Application fee:* $35 ($60 for international students). Electronic applications accepted. *Application Contact:* Ceshia Love, Director of Graduate and International Admissions, 713-221-8093, Fax: 713-223-7408, E-mail: gradadmissions@uhd.edu. *Interim Dean,* Dr. Leigh Van Horn, 713-221-8991, Fax: 713-226-5274, E-mail: vanhornl@uhd.edu.

College of Sciences and Technology Students: 35 full-time (19 women), 31 part-time (11 women); includes 36 minority (9 Black or African American, non-Hispanic/Latino; 13 Asian, non-Hispanic/Latino; 14 Hispanic/Latino), 15 international. Average age 33. 62 applicants, 81% accepted, 38 enrolled. *Faculty:* 5 full-time (2 women), 1 part-time/adjunct (0 women). Expenses: Contact institution. *Financial support:* Federal Work-Study and scholarships/grants available. Financial award application deadline: 4/1; financial award applicants required to submit FAFSA. *Program availability:* Part-time, evening/weekend. Offers data analytics (MS). *Application deadline:* For fall admission, 7/15 for domestic and international students. *Application fee:* $35 ($60 for international students). Electronic applications accepted. *Application Contact:* Ceshia Love, Director of Graduate and International Admissions, 713-221-8093, Fax: 713-221-8658, E-mail: gradadmissions@uhd.edu. *Dean,* Dr. J. Akif Uzman, 713-221-8019, E-mail: st_dean@uhd.edu.

Davies College of Business Students: 7 full-time (3 women), 1,060 part-time (571 women); includes 788 minority (369 Black or African American, non-Hispanic/Latino; 2 American Indian or Alaska Native, non-Hispanic/Latino; 136 Asian, non-Hispanic/Latino; 281 Hispanic/Latino), 32 international. Average age 33. 586 applicants, 85% accepted, 409 enrolled. *Faculty:* 35 full-time (13 women), 2 part-time/adjunct (0 women). Expenses: Contact institution. *Financial support:* Federal Work-Study and scholarships/grants available. Financial award application deadline: 4/1; financial award applicants required to submit FAFSA. In 2016, 193 master's awarded. *Program availability:* Part-time, evening/weekend, 100% online. Offers business (MBA, MSM); finance (MBA); human resource management (MBA); investment management (MBA); leadership (MBA); sales management and business development (MBA); security management (MSM); supply chain management (MBA). *Application deadline:* For fall admission, 7/15 for domestic and international students. *Application fee:* $35 ($60 for international students). Electronic applications accepted. *Application Contact:* Ceshia Love, Director of Graduate and International Admissions, 713-221-8093, Fax: 713-223-7408, E-mail: gradadmissions@uhd.edu. *Dean, Davies College of Business,* Dr. D. Michael Fields, 713-221-8179, Fax: 713-221-8675, E-mail: fieldsd@uhd.edu.

UNIVERSITY OF HOUSTON–VICTORIA, Victoria, TX 77901-4450

General Information State-supported, coed, upper-level institution. *Graduate housing:* On-campus housing not available.

GRADUATE UNITS

School of Arts and Sciences *Program availability:* Part-time, evening/weekend, online learning. Offers arts and sciences (MA, MAIS, MFA, MS); biological sciences (MS); biomedical sciences (MS); computer information systems (MS); computer science (MS); counseling psychology (MA); creative writing (MFA); forensic psychology (MA); forensic science (MS); interdisciplinary studies (MAIS); publishing (MS); school psychology (MA). Electronic applications accepted.

School of Business Administration *Program availability:* Part-time, evening/weekend, online learning. Offers accounting (MBA); economic development and entrepreneurship (MS); finance (GMBA, MBA); general business (MBA); international business (MBA); management (GMBA, MBA); marketing (MBA). Electronic applications accepted.

School of Education, Health Professions and Human Development *Program availability:* Part-time, evening/weekend, online learning. Offers administration and supervision (M Ed); adult and higher education (M Ed); counselor education (M Ed); curriculum and instruction (M Ed); educational technology (M Ed); special education (M Ed). Electronic applications accepted.

UNIVERSITY OF IDAHO, Moscow, ID 83844-2282

General Information State-supported, coed, university. CGS member. *Enrollment:* 11,780 graduate, professional, and undergraduate students; 1,221 full-time matriculated graduate/professional students (548 women), 719 part-time matriculated graduate/professional students (310 women). *Enrollment by degree level:* 1,166 master's, 747 doctoral, 52 other advanced degrees. *Graduate faculty:* 441 full-time (143 women), 48 part-time/adjunct (21 women). Tuition, state resident: full-time $6460; part-time $414 per credit hour. Tuition, nonresident: full-time $21,268; part-time $1237 per credit hour. *Required fees:* $2070; $60 per credit hour. Full-time tuition and fees vary according to course load and reciprocity agreements. *Graduate housing:* Rooms and/or apartments available on a first-come, first-served basis to single and married students. Typical cost: $8354 (including board) for single students. Room and board charges vary according to board plan and housing facility selected. *Student services:* Campus employment opportunities, campus safety program, career counseling, exercise/wellness program, free psychological counseling, grant writing training, international student services, low-cost health insurance, multicultural affairs office, services for students with disabilities, writing training. *Library facilities:* University of Idaho Library plus 1 other. *Collection:* Books: 1.4 million (physical), 552,875 (digital/electronic); Serial titles: 43,777 (physical), 78,174 (digital/electronic). *Research affiliation:* Battelle Energy Alliance LLC (energy research), Columbia River Inter-Tribal Fish Commission (fish research), Idaho Power Company (architecture), J. A. and Kathryn Albertson Foundation, Inc. (education), Micron Foundation (computer science), M. J. Murdock Charitable Trust (equipment support).

Computer facilities: Computer purchase and lease plans are available. 510 computers available on campus for general student use. A campuswide network can be accessed from student residence rooms and from off campus. Online class registration is available.
Website: http://www.uidaho.edu/

General Application Contact: Sean Scoggin, Graduate Recruitment Coordinator, 208-885-4723, Fax: 208-885-4406, E-mail: graduateadmissions@uidaho.edu.

GRADUATE UNITS

College of Graduate Studies Students: 933 full-time (424 women), 716 part-time (309 women); includes 198 minority (19 Black or African American, non-Hispanic/Latino; 24 American Indian or Alaska Native, non-Hispanic/Latino; 28 Asian, non-Hispanic/Latino; 86 Hispanic/Latino; 41 Two or more races, non-Hispanic/Latino), 219 international. Average age 33. 1,971 applicants, 37% accepted, 471 enrolled. *Faculty:* 441 full-time (143 women), 48 part-time/adjunct (21 women). Expenses: Contact institution. *Financial support:* Fellowships, research assistantships, teaching assistantships, career-related internships or fieldwork, Federal Work-Study, institutionally sponsored loans, scholarships/grants, and tuition waivers (full and partial) available. Support available to part-time students. Financial award applicants required to submit FAFSA. In 2016, 511 master's, 69 doctorates, 34 other advanced degrees awarded. *Program availability:* Online learning. Offers interdisciplinary studies (MA, MS). *Application deadline:* For fall admission, 8/1 for domestic students; for spring admission, 12/15 for domestic students. Applications are processed on a rolling basis. *Application fee:* $60 ($70 for international students). Electronic applications accepted. *Application Contact:* Rance Larsen, Director of Graduate Admissions, 208-885-2809, E-mail: graduateadmissions@uidaho.edu. *Dean of the College of Graduate Studies,* Dr. Jerry McMurtry, 208-885-6243, Fax: 208-885-6198, E-mail: uigrad@uidaho.edu.

College of Agricultural and Life Sciences Students: 100 full-time (56 women), 48 part-time (21 women). Average age 31. *Faculty:* 75 full-time, 1 part-time/adjunct. Expenses: Contact institution. *Financial support:* Research assistantships, teaching assistantships, career-related internships or fieldwork, and Federal Work-Study available. Support available to part-time students. Financial award application deadline: 2/15; financial award applicants required to submit FAFSA. In 2016, 34 master's, 9 doctorates awarded. Offers agricultural and life sciences (MS, PhD); animal physiology (PhD); animal science (MS); applied economics (MS); engineering and science (PhD); engineering and science (MS); entomology (MS, PhD); family and

consumer sciences (MS); food science (MS, PhD); law, management and policy (MS, PhD); plant science (MS, PhD); science and management (MS, PhD); soil and land resources (MS, PhD). *Application deadline:* For fall admission, 8/1 for domestic students; for spring admission, 12/15 for domestic students. Applications are processed on a rolling basis. *Application fee:* $60 ($70 for international students). Electronic applications accepted. *Application Contact:* Sean Scoggin, Graduate Recruitment Coordinator, 208-885-4723, Fax: 208-885-6198, E-mail: gadms@uidaho.edu. *Dean,* Dr. Michael Parrella, 208-885-6681, E-mail: ag@uidaho.edu.

College of Art and Architecture Students: 67 full-time, 9 part-time. Average age 28. *Faculty:* 14 full-time, 2 part-time/adjunct (0 women). Expenses: Contact institution. *Financial support:* Applicants required to submit FAFSA. In 2016, 42 master's awarded. Offers architecture (M Arch); art (MFA); bioregional planning and community design (MS); integrated architecture and design (MS); landscape architecture (MLA). *Application deadline:* For fall admission, 8/1 for domestic students; for spring admission, 12/15 for domestic students. Applications are processed on a rolling basis. *Application fee:* $60. Electronic applications accepted. *Application Contact:* Sean Scoggin, Graduate Recruitment Coordinator, 208-885-4001, Fax: 208-885-4406, E-mail: gradadmissions@uidaho.edu. *Interim Dean,* Dr. Shauna Corry, 208-885-4409, E-mail: caa@uidaho.edu.

College of Business and Economics Students: 49 full-time (21 women), 5 part-time (all women). Average age 35. *Faculty:* 12 full-time, 1 part-time/adjunct. Expenses: Contact institution. *Financial support:* Research assistantships, teaching assistantships, Federal Work-Study, and scholarships/grants available. Support available to part-time students. Financial award applicants required to submit FAFSA. In 2016, 39 master's awarded. Offers accountancy (M Acct); business and economics (M Acct, MBA); general management (MBA). *Application deadline:* For fall admission, 8/1 for domestic students; for spring admission, 12/15 for domestic students. Applications are processed on a rolling basis. *Application fee:* $60. Electronic applications accepted. *Application Contact:* Sean Scoggin, Graduate Recruitment Coordinator, 208-885-4001, Fax: 208-885-4406, E-mail: graduateadmissions@uidaho.edu. *Dean,* Dr. Marc Chopin, 208-885-6725, E-mail: cbe@uidaho.edu.

College of Education Students: 162 full-time (103 women), 258 part-time (154 women). Average age 37. *Faculty:* 52 full-time (26 women), 14 part-time/adjunct (9 women). Expenses: Contact institution. *Financial support:* Teaching assistantships and Federal Work-Study available. Support available to part-time students. Financial award applicants required to submit FAFSA. In 2016, 116 master's, 13 doctorates, 27 other advanced degrees awarded. Offers adult/organizational learning and leadership (MS, Ed S); athletic training (MSAT, DAT); career and technology education (M Ed); curriculum and instruction (M Ed, Ed S); education (M Ed, MS, MSAT, DAT, Ed D, PhD, Ed S); educational leadership (M Ed, Ed S); movement and leisure sciences (MS); physical education (M Ed); rehabilitation counseling and human services (M Ed, MS); school counseling (M Ed, MS); special education (M Ed). *Application deadline:* For fall admission, 8/1 for domestic students; for spring admission, 12/15 for domestic students. Applications are processed on a rolling basis. *Application fee:* $60. Electronic applications accepted. *Application Contact:* Sean Scoggin, Graduate Recruitment Coordinator, 208-885-4001, Fax: 208-885-4406, E-mail: graduateadmissions@uidaho.edu. *Dean,* Dr. Alison Carr-Chellman, 208-885-6772, E-mail: coe@uidaho.edu.

College of Engineering Students: 132 full-time (21 women), 202 part-time (36 women). Average age 34. *Faculty:* 71 full-time, 9 part-time/adjunct. Expenses: Contact institution. *Financial support:* Fellowships, research assistantships, teaching assistantships, career-related internships or fieldwork, and Federal Work-Study available. Support available to part-time students. Financial award applicants required to submit FAFSA. In 2016, 92 master's, 13 doctorates awarded. Offers biological engineering (M Engr, MS, PhD); chemical engineering (M Engr, MS, PhD); civil engineering (M Engr, MS, PhD); computer engineering (M Engr, MS); computer science (MS, PhD); electrical engineering (M Engr, MS, PhD); engineering (M Engr, MS, PhD); engineering management (M Engr); geological engineering (MS); materials science and engineering (MS, PhD); mechanical engineering (M Engr, MS, PhD); metallurgical engineering (MS); nuclear engineering (M Engr, MS, PhD); technology management (MS). *Application deadline:* For fall admission, 8/1 for domestic students; for spring admission, 12/15 for domestic students. Applications are processed on a rolling basis. *Application fee:* $60. Electronic applications accepted. *Application Contact:* Sean Scoggin, Graduate Recruitment Coordinator, 208-885-4001, Fax: 208-885-4406, E-mail: graduateadmissions@uidaho.edu. *Dean,* Dr. Larry Stauffer, 208-885-6470, E-mail: deanengr@uidaho.edu.

College of Letters, Arts and Social Sciences Students: 138 full-time (65 women), 47 part-time (29 women). Average age 32. *Faculty:* 76 full-time, 3 part-time/adjunct. Expenses: Contact institution. *Financial support:* Fellowships, research assistantships, teaching assistantships, and Federal Work-Study available. Support available to part-time students. Financial award applicants required to submit FAFSA. In 2016, 79 master's, 1 doctorate awarded. Offers anthropology (MA); creative writing (MFA); English (MA, MAT); experimental psychology (PhD); history (MA, PhD); letters, arts and social sciences (M Mus, MA, MAT, MFA, MPA, MS, PhD); music (M Mus, MA); political science (MA, PhD); psychology (MS); public administration (MPA); teaching English as a second language (MA); theatre arts (MFA). *Application deadline:* For fall admission, 8/1 for domestic students; for spring admission, 12/15 for domestic students. Applications are processed on a rolling basis. *Application fee:* $60. Electronic applications accepted. *Application Contact:* Sean Scoggin, Graduate Recruitment Coordinator, 208-885-4001, Fax: 208-885-4406, E-mail: graduateadmissions@uidaho.edu. *Dean,* Dr. Andrew Kersten, 208-885-6426, E-mail: class@uidaho.edu.

College of Natural Resources Students: 153 full-time (85 women), 117 part-time (50 women). Average age 32. *Faculty:* 61 full-time, 3 part-time/adjunct. Expenses: Contact institution. *Financial support:* Fellowships, research assistantships, teaching assistantships, and Federal Work-Study available. Support available to part-time students. Financial award applicants required to submit FAFSA. In 2016, 67 master's, 16 doctorates awarded. Offers environmental science (MS, PhD); natural resources (MNR, MS, PSM, PhD). *Application deadline:* For fall admission, 8/1 for domestic students; for spring admission, 12/15 for domestic students. Applications are processed on a rolling basis. *Application fee:* $60. Electronic applications accepted. *Application Contact:* Sean Scoggin, Graduate Recruitment Coordinator, 208-885-4723, Fax: 208-885-4406, E-mail: graduateadmissions@uidaho.edu. *Dean,* Dr. Kurt Scott Pregitzer, 208-885-8981, Fax: 208-885-5534, E-mail: cnr@uidaho.edu.

College of Science Students: 134 full-time (47 women), 30 part-time (13 women). Average age 31. *Faculty:* 76 full-time, 1 part-time/adjunct. Expenses: Contact institution. *Financial support:* Applicants required to submit FAFSA. In 2016, 41 master's, 17 doctorates awarded. Offers bioinformatics and computational biology (MS, PhD); biology (MS, PhD); chemistry (MS, PhD); geography (MS, PhD); geology (MS, PhD); mathematics (MAT, MS, PhD); microbiology, molecular biology and biochemistry (PhD); physics (MS, PhD); science (MAT, MS, PhD); statistical science (MS). *Application deadline:* Applications are processed on a rolling basis. *Application fee:* $60. Electronic applications accepted. *Application Contact:* Sean Scoggin, Graduate Recruitment Coordinator, 208-885-4001, Fax: 208-885-4406, E-mail: graduateadmissions@uidaho.edu. *Interim Dean,* Dr. Mark Nielson, 208-885-6195, E-mail: science@uidaho.edu.

College of Law Average age 28. *Faculty:* 32 full-time, 11 part-time/adjunct. Expenses: Contact institution. *Financial support:* Career-related internships or fieldwork, Federal Work-Study, and institutionally sponsored loans available. Financial award applicants required to submit FAFSA. Offers business law and entrepreneurship (JD); law (JD); litigation and alternative dispute resolution (JD); Native American law (JD); natural resources and environmental law (JD). *Application deadline:* For fall admission, 3/15 priority date for domestic students. Applications are processed on a rolling basis. *Application fee:* $50 ($60 for international students). Electronic applications accepted. *Application Contact:* Carole Wells, Director of Admissions, 208-885-2300, Fax: 208-885-2252, E-mail: lawadmit@uidaho.edu. *Dean,* Mark Adams, 208-885-4977, E-mail: uilaw@uidaho.edu.

UNIVERSITY OF ILLINOIS AT CHICAGO, Chicago, IL 60607-7128

General Information State-supported, coed, university. CGS member. *Graduate housing:* Room and/or apartments available on a first-come, first-served basis to single students; on-campus housing not available to married students. Housing application deadline: 3/1. *Research affiliation:* Chicago Manufacturing Technology Extension Center (manufacturing research and development, industrial research), Eastern Cooperative Oncology Group (clinical cancer research), Argonne National Laboratory (battery performance), National Surgical Adjuvant Breast and Bowel Project (prevention of breast cancer).

GRADUATE UNITS

College of Applied Health Sciences *Program availability:* Part-time. Offers applied health sciences (MS, DPT, OTD, PhD, CAS, Certificate); biomedical visualization (MS); disability and human development (MS, PhD); health informatics (MS, CAS); health information management (Certificate); kinesiology (MS, PhD); nutrition (MS, PhD); occupational therapy (MS, OTD); physical therapy (MS, DPT). Electronic applications accepted.

College of Architecture, Design and the Arts *Program availability:* Part-time, evening/weekend. Offers architecture, design and the arts (M Arch, M Des, MA, MFA, MS, MS Arch, PhD). Electronic applications accepted.

School of Architecture Offers architecture (M Arch, MA, MS, MS Arch). Electronic applications accepted.

School of Art and Art History *Program availability:* Part-time, evening/weekend. Offers art history (MA); electronic visualization (MFA); museum and exhibition studies (MA); new media arts (MFA). Electronic applications accepted.

School of Design Offers graphic design (M Des); industrial design (M Des). Electronic applications accepted.

College of Dentistry Offers dentistry (MS, DDS, DMD, PhD); oral sciences (MS, PhD). Electronic applications accepted.

College of Education *Program availability:* Part-time, evening/weekend. Offers curriculum studies (PhD); early childhood education (M Ed); education (M Ed, Ed D, PhD); educational psychology (PhD); elementary education (M Ed); measurement, evaluation, statistics, and assessment (M Ed); policy studies (M Ed); policy studies in urban education (PhD); secondary education (M Ed); special education (M Ed, PhD); urban education leadership (Ed D); youth development (M Ed). Electronic applications accepted.

College of Engineering *Program availability:* Part-time, evening/weekend. Offers bioengineering (MS, PhD); chemical engineering (MS, PhD); civil and materials engineering (MS, PhD); computer science (MS, PhD); electrical and computer engineering (MS, PhD); energy engineering (MEE); engineering (M Eng, MEE, MS, PhD); fluids engineering (MS, PhD); industrial engineering (MS, PhD); industrial engineering and operations research (PhD); mechanical analysis and design (MS, PhD); mechanical engineering (MS, PhD); thermomechanical and power engineering (MS, PhD). Electronic applications accepted.

College of Liberal Arts and Sciences *Program availability:* Part-time, evening/weekend. Offers anthropology (MA, PhD); biological sciences (MS, PhD); chemistry (MS, PhD); communication (MA, PhD); criminology, law, and justice (MA, PhD); earth and environmental sciences (MS, PhD); economics (MA, PhD); English (MA, PhD); environmental and urban geography (MA); history (MA, MAT, PhD); Latin American and Latino studies (MA); liberal arts and sciences (MA, MAT, MS, MST, DA, PhD); mathematics (DA); philosophy (MA, PhD); physics (MS, PhD); political science (MA, PhD); probability and statistics (PhD); psychology (MA, PhD); secondary school mathematics (MST); sociology (MA, PhD); statistics (MS). Electronic applications accepted.

School of Literatures, Cultural Studies and Linguistics *Program availability:* Part-time. Offers French and Francophone studies (MA); Germanic studies (MA, PhD); Hispanic and Italian studies (MAT, PhD); Hispanic linguistics (PhD); linguistics (MA); Slavic and Baltic languages and literatures (MA); Slavic and Baltic languages and literatures (PhD); Slavic studies (MA, PhD). Electronic applications accepted.

College of Medicine *Program availability:* Part-time. Offers anatomy and cell biology (MS); biochemistry and molecular genetics (PhD); medical education (MHPE); medicine (MHPE, MS, MD, PhD); microbiology and immunology (PhD); pharmacology (PhD); physiology and biophysics (MS, PhD); surgery (MS).

College of Nursing *Program availability:* Part-time. Offers acute care clinical nurse specialist (MS); administrative nursing leadership (Certificate); adult nurse practitioner (MS); adult/geriatric nurse practitioner (MS); advanced community health nurse specialist (MS); family nurse practitioner (MS); geriatric clinical nurse specialist (MS); geriatric nurse practitioner (MS); nurse midwifery (MS); nursing (MS, DNP, PhD, Certificate); nursing practice (DNP); nursing science (PhD); occupational health/advanced community health nurse specialist (MS); occupational health/family nurse practitioner (MS); pediatric nurse practitioner (MS); perinatal clinical nurse specialist (MS); school/advanced community health nurse specialist (MS); school/family nurse practitioner (MS); women's health nurse practitioner (MS). Electronic applications accepted.

College of Pharmacy Offers biopharmaceutical sciences (MS, PhD); forensic science (MS); medicinal chemistry (MS); pharmacognosy (MS, PhD); pharmacy (MS, PhD, Pharm D); pharmacy administration (MS, PhD).

College of Urban Planning and Public Affairs *Program availability:* Part-time, evening/weekend. Offers public administration (MPA, PhD); urban planning and policy (MUPP, PhD); urban planning and public affairs (MPA, MUPP, PhD). Electronic applications accepted.

Jane Addams College of Social Work *Program availability:* Part-time. Offers social work (MSW, PhD, Certificate). Electronic applications accepted.

Liautaud Graduate School of Business *Program availability:* Part-time, evening/weekend. Offers accounting (MS); business (MA, MBA, MS, PhD); business administration (MBA, PhD); finance (MS); management information systems (PhD); real estate (MA). Electronic applications accepted.

Program in Learning Sciences Offers learning sciences (PhD).

Program in Neuroscience Offers cellular and systems neuroscience and cell biology (PhD); neuroscience (MS).

School of Public Health *Program availability:* Part-time. Offers public health (MHA, MPH, MS, Dr PH, PhD). Electronic applications accepted.

Division of Community Health Sciences *Program availability:* Part-time. Offers community health sciences (MPH, MS, Dr PH, PhD). Electronic applications accepted.

Division of Environmental and Occupational Health Sciences *Program availability:* Part-time. Offers environmental and occupational health sciences (MPH, MS, Dr PH, PhD). Electronic applications accepted.

Division of Health Policy and Administration *Program availability:* Part-time. Offers clinical and translational science (MS); health policy (PhD); health services research (PhD); healthcare administration (MHA); public health policy management (MPH). Electronic applications accepted.

Epidemiology and Biostatistics Division *Program availability:* Part-time. Offers biostatistics (MPH, MS, PhD); epidemiology (MPH, MS, PhD). Electronic applications accepted.

UNIVERSITY OF ILLINOIS AT SPRINGFIELD, Springfield, IL 62703-5407

General Information State-supported, coed, comprehensive institution. CGS member. *Enrollment:* 5,428 graduate, professional, and undergraduate students; 1,109 full-time matriculated graduate/professional students (466 women), 1,203 part-time matriculated graduate/professional students (558 women). *Enrollment by degree level:* 2,246 master's, 21 doctoral, 45 other advanced degrees. *Graduate faculty:* 112 full-time (49 women), 42 part-time/adjunct (19 women). Tuition, state resident: part-time $329 per credit hour. Tuition, nonresident: part-time $675 per credit hour. *Graduate housing:* Rooms and/or apartments available on a first-come, first-served basis to single and married students. Housing application deadline: 5/1. *Student services:* Campus employment opportunities, campus safety program, career counseling, child daycare facilities, exercise/wellness program, free psychological counseling, international student services, low-cost health insurance, multicultural affairs office, services for students with disabilities, teacher training, writing training. *Library facilities:* Norris L Brookens Library plus 1 other. *Collection:* Books: 467,511 (physical), 171,279 (digital/electronic); Serial titles: 10,567 (physical), 14,463 (digital/electronic); Databases: 135. Weekly public service hours: 90; students can reserve study rooms. *Research affiliation:* Council of Public Liberal Arts Colleges (COPLAC), Interuniversity Consortium for Political and Social Research, Council of Undergraduate Research, The Nature Conservancy, Illinois Flood Plan Restoration, Public Responsibility in Medicine and Research (PRIM&R).

Computer facilities: 550 computers available on campus for general student use. A campuswide network can be accessed from student residence rooms and from off campus. Online class registration is available.
Website: http://www.uis.edu/

General Application Contact: Dr. Cecelia Cornell, Associate Vice Chancellor for Graduate Education, 888-977-4847, Fax: 217-206-7230, E-mail: ccorn1@uis.edu.

GRADUATE UNITS

Graduate Programs Students: 1,109 full-time (466 women), 1,203 part-time (558 women); includes 368 minority (182 Black or African American, non-Hispanic/Latino; 3 American Indian or Alaska Native, non-Hispanic/Latino; 84 Asian, non-Hispanic/Latino; 70 Hispanic/Latino; 1 Native Hawaiian or other Pacific Islander, non-Hispanic/Latino; 28 Two or more races, non-Hispanic/Latino), 935 international. Average age 30. 2,738 applicants, 46% accepted, 591 enrolled. *Faculty:* 112 full-time (49 women), 42 part-time/adjunct (19 women). Expenses: Contact institution. *Financial support:* In 2016–17, 1 fellowship with full tuition reimbursement (averaging $9,900 per year), 9 research assistantships with full tuition reimbursements (averaging $9,991 per year), 7 teaching assistantships with full tuition reimbursements (averaging $10,059 per year) were awarded; career-related internships or fieldwork, Federal Work-Study, scholarships/grants, health care benefits, and unspecified assistantships also available. Support available to part-time students. Financial award application deadline: 11/15; financial award applicants required to submit FAFSA. In 2016, 1,032 master's, 41 other advanced degrees awarded. *Program availability:* Part-time, evening/weekend, 100% online, blended/hybrid learning. *Application deadline:* Applications are processed on a rolling basis. *Application fee:* $60 ($75 for international students). Electronic applications accepted. *Associate Vice Chancellor for Graduate Education,* Dr. Cecelia Cornell, 217-206-7230, Fax: 217-206-7623, E-mail: ccorn1@uis.edu.

College of Business and Management Students: 385 full-time (161 women), 233 part-time (89 women); includes 78 minority (27 Black or African American, non-Hispanic/Latino; 1 American Indian or Alaska Native, non-Hispanic/Latino; 30 Asian, non-Hispanic/Latino; 15 Hispanic/Latino; 5 Two or more races, non-Hispanic/Latino), 334 international. Average age 29. 966 applicants, 38% accepted, 135 enrolled. *Faculty:* 23 full-time (4 women), 12 part-time/adjunct (4 women). Expenses: Contact institution. *Financial support:* In 2016–17, fellowships with full tuition reimbursements (averaging $9,900 per year), research assistantships with full tuition reimbursements (averaging $9,991 per year), teaching assistantships with full tuition reimbursements (averaging $10,059 per year) were awarded; career-related internships or fieldwork, Federal Work-Study, scholarships/grants, health care benefits, and unspecified assistantships also available. Support available to part-time students. Financial award application deadline: 11/15; financial award applicants required to submit FAFSA. In 2016, 289 master's awarded. *Program availability:* Part-time, evening/weekend, 100% online, blended/hybrid learning. Offers accountancy (MA); business administration (MBA); business and management (MA, MBA, MS); management information systems (MS). *Application deadline:* Applications are processed on a rolling basis. *Application fee:* $60 ($75 for international students). Electronic applications accepted. *Application Contact:* Dr. Cecelia Cornell, Associate Vice Chancellor for Graduate Education, 217-206-7230, E-mail: ccorn1@uis.edu. *Dean,* Dr. Ronald McNeil, 217-206-6534, Fax: 217-206-7541, E-mail: rmcne1@uis.edu.

College of Education and Human Services Students: 72 full-time (62 women), 211 part-time (148 women); includes 58 minority (44 Black or African American, non-Hispanic/Latino; 1 American Indian or Alaska Native, non-Hispanic/Latino; 10 Hispanic/Latino; 3 Two or more races, non-Hispanic/Latino), 3 international. Average age 34. 141 applicants, 52% accepted, 56 enrolled. *Faculty:* 15 full-time (10 women),

12 part-time/adjunct (9 women). Expenses: Contact institution. *Financial support:* In 2016–17, fellowships with full tuition reimbursements (averaging $9,900 per year), research assistantships with full tuition reimbursements (averaging $9,991 per year), teaching assistantships with full tuition reimbursements (averaging $10,059 per year) were awarded; career-related internships or fieldwork, Federal Work-Study, scholarships/grants, health care benefits, and unspecified assistantships also available. Support available to part-time students. Financial award application deadline: 11/15; financial award applicants required to submit FAFSA. In 2016, 81 master's, 7 other advanced degrees awarded. *Program availability:* Part-time, evening/weekend, 100% online, blended/hybrid learning. Offers alcohol and substance abuse (Graduate Certificate); alcoholism and substance abuse (MA); chief school business official (CAS); child and family services (MA); education and human services (MA, CAS, Certificate, Graduate Certificate); educational leadership (MA); educational technology (Graduate Certificate); English as a second language (Graduate Certificate); gerontology (MA); higher education online pedagogy (Graduate Certificate); human development counseling (MA); leadership and learning (Graduate Certificate); legal aspects of education (Graduate Certificate); social services administration (MA); superintendent (CAS); teacher leadership (MA). *Application deadline:* Applications are processed on a rolling basis. *Application fee:* $60 ($75 for international students). Electronic applications accepted. *Application Contact:* Dr. Cecelia Cornell, Associate Vice Chancellor for Graduate Education, 217-206-7230, E-mail: ccorn1@uis.edu. *Dean,* Dr. Hanfu Mi, 217-206-6784, Fax: 217-206-6775, E-mail: hmi2@uis.edu.

College of Liberal Arts and Sciences Students: 508 full-time (154 women), 409 part-time (120 women); includes 97 minority (39 Black or African American, non-Hispanic/Latino; 1 American Indian or Alaska Native, non-Hispanic/Latino; 33 Asian, non-Hispanic/Latino; 17 Hispanic/Latino; 7 Two or more races, non-Hispanic/Latino), 570 international. Average age 28. 1,185 applicants, 51% accepted, 254 enrolled. Faculty: 40 full-time (18 women), 8 part-time/adjunct (1 woman). Expenses: Contact institution. *Financial support:* In 2016–17, fellowships with full tuition reimbursements (averaging $9,900 per year), research assistantships with full tuition reimbursements (averaging $9,991 per year) teaching assistantships with full tuition reimbursements (averaging $10,059 per year) were awarded; career-related internships or fieldwork, Federal Work-Study, scholarships/grants, health care benefits, and unspecified assistantships also available. Support available to part-time students. Financial award application deadline: 11/15; financial award applicants required to submit FAFSA. In 2016, 481 master's, 1 other advanced degree awarded. *Program availability:* Part-time, evening/weekend, 100% online, blended/hybrid learning. Offers biology (MA); communication (MA); computer science (MS); data analytics (MS); English (MA); history (MA); liberal and integrative studies (MA); liberal arts and sciences (MA, MS, Graduate Certificate); teaching English (Graduate Certificate). *Application deadline:* Applications are processed on a rolling basis. *Application fee:* $60 ($75 for international students). Electronic applications accepted. *Application Contact:* Dr. Cecelia Cornell, Associate Vice Chancellor for Graduate Education, 217-206-7230, E-mail: ccorn1@uis.edu. *Interim Dean,* Dr. Lucia Vazquez, 217-206-6512, Fax: 217-206-6217, E-mail: lvazq1@uis.edu.

College of Public Affairs and Administration Students: 144 full-time (89 women), 350 part-time (201 women); includes 135 minority (72 Black or African American, non-Hispanic/Latino; 21 Asian, non-Hispanic/Latino; 28 Hispanic/Latino; 1 Native Hawaiian or other Pacific Islander, non-Hispanic/Latino; 13 Two or more races, non-Hispanic/Latino), 28 international. Average age 34. 446 applicants, 49% accepted, 146 enrolled. Faculty: 34 full-time (17 women), 10 part-time/adjunct (5 women). Expenses: Contact institution. *Financial support:* In 2016–17, fellowships with full tuition reimbursements (averaging $9,900 per year), research assistantships with full tuition reimbursements (averaging $9,991 per year), teaching assistantships with full tuition reimbursements (averaging $10,059 per year) were awarded; career-related internships or fieldwork, Federal Work-Study, scholarships/grants, health care benefits, and unspecified assistantships also available. Support available to part-time students. Financial award application deadline: 11/15; financial award applicants required to submit FAFSA. In 2016, 181 master's, 1 doctorate, 32 other advanced degrees awarded. *Program availability:* Part-time, evening/weekend, 100% online, blended/hybrid learning. Offers community health education (Graduate Certificate); emergency preparedness and homeland security (Graduate Certificate); environmental health (Graduate Certificate); environmental risk assessment (Graduate Certificate); environmental science (MS); environmental studies (MA); epidemiology (Graduate Certificate); legal studies (MA); management of nonprofit organizations (Graduate Certificate); political science (MA); public administration (MPA, DPA); public affairs and administration (MA, MPA, MPH, MS, DPA, Graduate Certificate); public affairs reporting (MA); public health (MPH). *Application deadline:* Applications are processed on a rolling basis. *Application fee:* $60 ($75 for international students). Electronic applications accepted. *Application Contact:* Dr. Cecelia Cornell, Associate Vice Chancellor for Graduate Education, 217-206-7230, E-mail: ccorn1@uis.edu. *Interim Dean,* Dr. Hanfu Mi, 217-206-6523, Fax: 217-206-7807, E-mail: cpaa@uis.edu.

UNIVERSITY OF ILLINOIS AT URBANA–CHAMPAIGN, Champaign, IL 61820

General Information State-supported, coed, university. CGS member. *Graduate housing:* Rooms and/or apartments available to single and married students. *Research affiliation:* Midwest Universities Research Association, Sandia National Laboratories, National Center for Atmospheric Research.

GRADUATE UNITS

College of Law Offers law (LL M, MCL, JD, JSD).

College of Veterinary Medicine Offers comparative biosciences (MS, PhD); pathobiology (MS, PhD); veterinary clinical medicine (MS, PhD); veterinary medical science (DVM); veterinary medicine (MS, DVM, PhD).

Graduate College

College of Agricultural, Consumer and Environmental Sciences Offers agricultural and applied economics (MS, PhD); agricultural and biological engineering (MS, PhD); agricultural education (MS); agricultural production (MS); agricultural, consumer and environmental sciences (MS, PSM, MA); animal sciences (MS, PhD); bioenergy (PSM); bioinformatics: animal sciences (MS); bioinformatics: crop sciences (MS); crop sciences (MS, PhD); food science (MS); food science and human nutrition (MS, PhD); human and community development (MS, PhD); human nutrition (MS); natural resources and environmental science (MS, PhD); nutritional sciences (MS, PhD); technical systems management (MS, PSM).

College of Applied Health Sciences Offers applied health sciences (MA, MPH, MS, MSPH, Au D, PhD); audiology (Au D); community health (MS, MSPH, PhD);

kinesiology (MS, PhD); public health (MPH); recreation, sport and tourism (MS, PhD); rehabilitation (MS); speech and hearing science (MA, PhD).

College of Business Program availability: Online learning. Offers accountancy (MAS, MS, PhD); business (MAS, MBA, MS, PhD); business administration (MS, PhD); finance (MS, PhD); taxation (MS); technology management (MS).

College of Education Program availability: Part-time, online learning. Offers curriculum and instruction (Ed M, MA, MS, Ed D, PhD, CAS); early childhood education (Ed M); education (Ed M, MA, MS, Ed D, PhD, CAS); educational organization and leadership (Ed M, MS, Ed D, PhD, CAS); educational policy studies (Ed M, MA, PhD); educational psychology (Ed M, MA, MS, PhD, CAS); elementary education (Ed M); human resource education (Ed M, MS, Ed D, PhD, CAS); secondary education (Ed M); special education (Ed M, MS, Ed D, PhD, CAS).

College of Engineering Program availability: Part-time, evening/weekend, online learning. Offers aerospace engineering (MS, PhD); bioengineering (MS, PhD); bioinformatics (MS); civil engineering (MS, PhD); computer science (MCS, MS, PhD); electrical and computer engineering (MS, PhD); energy systems (M Eng); engineering (M Eng, MCS, MS, PhD); environmental engineering in civil engineering (MS, PhD); financial engineering (MS); industrial engineering (MS, PhD); materials science and engineering (M Eng, MS, PhD); mechanical engineering (MS, PhD); nuclear, plasma, and radiological engineering (MS, PhD); physics (MS, PhD); systems and entrepreneurial engineering (MS, PhD); teaching of physics (MS); theoretical and applied mechanics (MS, PhD).

College of Fine and Applied Arts Offers architectural studies (MS); architecture (M Arch, PhD); art and design (MFA); art education (Ed M, MA, PhD); art history (MA, PhD); crafts (MFA); dance (MFA); fine and applied arts (Ed M, M Arch, M Mus, MA, MFA, MLA, MME, MS, MUP, AD, DMA, PhD); graphic design (MFA); industrial design (MFA); landscape architecture (MLA, PhD); metals (MFA); music (M Mus, AD, DMA); music education (MME, PhD); musicology (PhD); painting (MFA); photography (MFA); regional planning (PhD); sculpture (MFA); theatre (MA, MFA, PhD); urban planning (MUP).

College of Liberal Arts and Sciences Program availability: Online learning. Offers African studies (MA); analytics (MS); animal biology (ecology, ethology and evolution) (MS, PhD); anthropology (MA, PhD); applied mathematics (MS); applied mathematics: actuarial science (MS); applied statistics (MS); astrochemistry (PhD); astronomy (MS, PhD); atmospheric sciences (MS, PhD); biochemistry (MS, PhD); bioinformatics: chemical and biomolecular engineering (MS); biophysics and computational biology (MS, PhD); cell and developmental biology (PhD); chemical engineering (MS, PhD); chemical physics (PhD); chemical sciences (MA, MS, PhD); chemistry (MA, MS, PhD); classical philology (PhD); classics (MA); communication (MA, PhD); comparative literature (MA, PhD); creative writing (MFA); earth, society and environment (MA, MS, PhD); East Asian languages and cultures (PhD); East Asian studies (MA); ecology, evolution and conservation biology (MS, PhD); economics (MS, PhD); English (MA, PhD); entomology (MS, PhD); European Union studies (MA); French (MA, PhD); geography and geographic information science (MA, MS, PhD); geology (MS, PhD); German (MA, PhD); history (MA, PhD); integrative biology (MS, MST, PSM, PhD); Italian (MA, PhD); Latin American studies (MA); liberal arts and sciences (MA, MFA, MS, MST, PSM, PhD); linguistics (MA, PhD); literatures, cultures and linguistics (MA, MS, PhD); mathematics (MS, PhD); microbiology (MS, PhD); molecular and cellular biology (MS, PhD); molecular and integrative physiology (MS, PhD); neuroscience (PhD); philosophy (MA, PhD); plant biology (MS, PhD); plant biotechnology (PSM); policy economics (MS); political science (MA, PhD); Portuguese (MA, PhD); psychology (MA, MS, PhD); religious studies (MA); romance linguistics (PhD); Russian, East European, and Eurasian studies (MA); second language acquisition and teacher education (PhD); Slavic languages and literatures (MA, PhD); sociology (MA, PhD); south Asian and Middle Eastern studies (MA); Spanish (MA, PhD); statistics (MS); teaching of chemistry (MS); teaching of earth sciences (MS); teaching of English as a second language (MA); teaching of Latin (MA); teaching of mathematics (MS); translation and interpreting (MA).

College of Media Offers advertising (MS); communications and media (PhD); journalism (MS); media (MS, PhD).

School of Information Sciences Program availability: Part-time, online learning. Offers bioinformatics (MS); digital libraries (CAS); information management (MS); library and information science (MS, PhD, CAS).

School of Labor and Employment Relations Offers human resources and industrial relations (MHRIR, PhD).

School of Social Work Offers advocacy, leadership, and social change (MSW); children, youth and family services (MSW); health care (MSW); mental health (MSW); school social work (MSW); social work (PhD).

Illinois Informatics Institute Offers informatics (PhD).

UNIVERSITY OF INDIANAPOLIS, Indianapolis, IN 46227-3697

General Information Independent-religious, coed, comprehensive institution. CGS member. *Graduate housing:* Rooms and/or apartments available on a first-come, first-served basis to single and married students.

GRADUATE UNITS

Graduate Programs *Program availability:* Part-time, evening/weekend, online learning.

Center for Aging and Community *Program availability:* Part-time, evening/weekend, online learning. Offers gerontology (MS, Certificate).

College of Arts and Sciences *Program availability:* Part-time, evening/weekend. Offers anthropology (MS); applied sociology (MA); art (MA); arts and sciences (MA, MS); English (MA); history (MA); human biology (MS); international relations (MA).

College of Health Sciences Offers health sciences (MHS, MOT, MPH, MS, DHS, DPT, OTD); occupational therapy (MOT, DHS, OTD); physical therapy (MHS, DHS, DPT); public health (MPH); sport management (MS).

School of Business *Program availability:* Part-time, evening/weekend. Offers business (EMBA, MBA, Graduate Certificate).

School of Education *Program availability:* Part-time, evening/weekend. Offers art education (MAT); biology (MAT); chemistry (MAT); curriculum and instruction (MA); earth sciences (MAT); education (MA, MAT); educational leadership (MA); elementary education (MA); English (MAT); French (MAT); math (MAT); physical education (MAT); physics (MAT); secondary education (MA); social studies (MAT); Spanish (MAT).

School of Nursing Offers advanced practice nursing (DNP); family nurse practitioner (MSN); gerontological nurse practitioner (MSN); neonatal nurse practitioner (MSN); nurse-midwifery (MSN); nursing (MSN); nursing and health systems leadership (MSN); nursing education (MSN); women's health nurse practitioner (MSN). Electronic applications accepted.

School of Psychological Sciences Offers clinical psychology (Psy D); clinical psychology/mental health counseling (MA).

THE UNIVERSITY OF IOWA, Iowa City, IA 52242-1316

General Information State-supported, coed, university. CGS member. *Graduate housing:* Rooms and/or apartments available on a first-come, first-served basis to single and married students.

GRADUATE UNITS

College of Dentistry Offers dental public health (MS); dentistry (MS, DDS, PhD, Certificate); endodontics (MS, Certificate); operative dentistry (MS, Certificate); oral and maxillofacial surgery (MS, PhD, Certificate); oral pathology, radiology and medicine (MS, PhD, Certificate); oral science (MS); orthodontics (MS, Certificate); pediatric dentistry (Certificate); periodontics (MS, Certificate); preventive and community dentistry (MS); prosthodontics (MS, Certificate).

College of Law Students: 439 full-time (188 women), 4 part-time (3 women); includes 88 minority (16 Black or African American, non-Hispanic/Latino; 2 American Indian or Alaska Native, non-Hispanic/Latino; 19 Asian, non-Hispanic/Latino; 36 Hispanic/Latino; 15 Two or more races, non-Hispanic/Latino), 28 international. Average age 25. 1,406 applicants, 44% accepted, 154 enrolled. *Faculty:* 37 full-time (13 women), 14 part-time/adjunct (4 women). Expenses: Contact institution. *Financial support:* In 2016–17, 340 students received support, including 338 fellowships with partial tuition reimbursements available (averaging $19,195 per year), 109 research assistantships with partial tuition reimbursements available (averaging $2,175 per year), career-related internships or fieldwork, Federal Work-Study, scholarships/grants, and health care benefits also available. Financial award applicants required to submit FAFSA. In 2016, 4 master's, 100 doctorates awarded. Offers law (LL M, MSL, JD, SJD). *Application deadline:* For fall admission, 5/1 priority date for domestic and international students. Applications are processed on a rolling basis. *Application fee:* $0. Electronic applications accepted. *Application Contact:* Collins Byrd, Assistant Dean of Enrollment Management, 319-335-9095, Fax: 319-335-9646, E-mail: law-admissions@uiowa.edu. *Dean,* Gail Agrawal, 319-335-9034, Fax: 319-335-9019, E-mail: gail-agrawal@uiowa.edu.

College of Pharmacy Offers clinical pharmaceutical sciences (PhD); medicinal and natural products chemistry (PhD); pharmaceutics (PhD); pharmaceutical socioeconomics (PhD); pharmaceutics (MS); pharmacy (Pharm D). Electronic applications accepted.

Graduate College *Program availability:* Part-time, evening/weekend, online learning. Offers applied mathematical and computational sciences (PhD); bioinformatics (MS, PhD); bioinformatics and computational biology (Certificate); genetics (PhD); geoinformatics (MS, PhD, Certificate); health informatics (MS, PhD, Certificate); human toxicology (MS, PhD); immunology (PhD); information science (MS, PhD, Certificate); molecular and cellular biology (PhD); neuroscience (PhD); translational biomedicine (MS, PhD); urban and regional planning (MA, MS). Electronic applications accepted.

College of Education Offers art education (MA); counseling psychology (PhD); counselor education and supervision (PhD); couple and family therapy (PhD); developmental reading (MA); education (MA, MAT, MM, PhD); educational leadership (MA, PhD, Ed S); educational measurement and statistics (MA, PhD); educational psychology (MA, PhD); elementary education (MA); English education (MA, MAT); foreign and second language education (MAT); foreign language education (MA); foreign language/ESL education (PhD); higher education and student affairs (MA, PhD); language, literacy and culture (PhD); mathematics education (MA, MAT, PhD); music education (MM, PhD); rehabilitation and mental health counseling (MA); rehabilitation counselor education (PhD); school counseling (MA); school psychology (PhD, Ed S); schools, culture, and society (MA, PhD); science education (MA); secondary education (MA); social studies (MA, PhD); special education (MA, PhD). Electronic applications accepted.

College of Engineering Students: 238 full-time (57 women), 62 part-time (14 women); includes 24 minority (4 Black or African American, non-Hispanic/Latino; 8 Asian, non-Hispanic/Latino; 5 Hispanic/Latino; 7 Two or more races, non-Hispanic/Latino), 143 international. Average age 27. 628 applicants, 18% accepted, 62 enrolled. *Faculty:* 93 full-time (12 women), 17 part-time/adjunct (3 women). Expenses: Contact institution. *Financial support:* In 2016–17, 295 students received support, including 23 fellowships with full and partial tuition reimbursements available (averaging $25,500 per year), 217 research assistantships with full and partial tuition reimbursements available (averaging $22,981 per year), 55 teaching assistantships with full and partial tuition reimbursements available (averaging $18,809 per year); career-related internships or fieldwork, Federal Work-Study, scholarships/grants, traineeships, health care benefits, and unspecified assistantships also available. Financial award application deadline: 1/15; financial award applicants required to submit FAFSA. In 2016, 52 master's, 38 doctorates awarded. Offers biomedical engineering (MS, PhD); chemical and biochemical engineering (MS, PhD); civil and environmental engineering (MS, PhD); electrical and computer engineering (MS, PhD); energy systems (MS, PhD); engineering (MS, PhD); engineering design (MS, PhD); engineering design and manufacturing (MS, PhD); fluid dynamics (MS, PhD); healthcare systems (MS, PhD); human factors (MS, PhD); information and engineering management (MS, PhD); materials and manufacturing (MS, PhD); operations research (MS, PhD); wind energy (MS, PhD). *Application deadline:* For fall admission, 1/15 priority date for domestic and international students; for spring admission, 8/1 priority date for domestic and international students; for summer admission, 1/1 for domestic and international students. Applications are processed on a rolling basis. *Application fee:* $60 ($100 for international students). Electronic applications accepted. *Application Contact:* Dr. Brent Gage, Associate Vice President for Enrollment Management, 319-335-1525, Fax: 319-335-1535, E-mail: gradmail@uiowa.edu. *Dean,* Dr. Alec Scranton, 319-335-5766, Fax: 319-335-6086, E-mail: alec-scranton@uiowa.edu.

College of Liberal Arts and Sciences *Program availability:* Part-time, online learning. Offers actuarial science (MS); American studies (MA, PhD); anthropology (MA, PhD); art history (MA, PhD); astronomy (MS); athletic training (MS); biology (MS, PhD); cell and developmental biology (MS, PhD); chemistry (PhD); Chinese (MA); classics (MA, PhD); clinical exercise physiology (MS); communication sciences and disorders (MA, Au D, PhD); computer science (MCS, PhD); dance (MFA); earth and environmental science (MS, PhD); English (PhD); evolution (MS, PhD); film and video production (MFA); film studies (MA, PhD); French (MA, PhD); gender, women's and sexuality studies (Certificate); genetics (MS, PhD); geographical and sustainability sciences (MA, PhD, Certificate); Greek (MA); health and human physiology (PhD); Hindi (MA); history (MA, PhD); interpersonal communication and relationships (MA, PhD); journalism and media communication (MA); Latin (MA); leisure studies (MA, PhD); liberal arts and sciences (MA, MCS, MFA, MS, MSW, Au D, DMA, PhD, Certificate); linguistics (MA, PhD); literary studies (MA); mass communication (PhD); mathematics (MS, PhD); media studies (MA, PhD); music (MA, MFA, DMA, PhD); neurobiology (MS, PhD); nonfiction writing (MFA); philosophy (MA, PhD); physics (MS, PhD); political science (PhD); psychology (MA, PhD); religious studies (PhD); rhetoric and public advocacy (MA, PhD); Sanskrit (MA); second language acquisition (PhD); social

work (MSW, PhD); sociology (MA, PhD); South Asian studies (MA); Spanish (MA, PhD); Spanish creative writing (MFA); statistics (MS, PhD); strategic communication (MA); studio art (MA, MFA); theatre arts (MFA). Electronic applications accepted.

College of Nursing Offers nursing (MSN, DNP, PhD). Electronic applications accepted.

College of Public Health Offers agricultural safety and health (MS, PhD); biostatistics (MS, PhD, Certificate); clinical investigation (MS); community and behavioral health (MPH, MS, PhD); epidemiology (MPH, MS, PhD); ergonomics (MPH); health management and policy (MHA, PhD); industrial hygiene (MS, PhD); occupational and environmental health (MPH, MS, PhD, Certificate); public health (MHA, MPH, MS, PhD, Certificate); quantitative methods (MPH). Electronic applications accepted.

School of Library and Information Science Offers library and information science (MA, PhD). Electronic applications accepted.

Henry B. Tippie College of Business *Faculty:* 133 full-time (34 women), 70 part-time/adjunct (18 women). Expenses: Contact institution. *Financial support:* Applicants required to submit FAFSA. In 2016, 412 master's, 15 doctorates awarded. Offers accounting (M Ac, PhD); business (EMBA, M Ac, MBA, MS, PhD); business administration (EMBA, MBA); business analytics (MS); economics (PhD); finance (PhD); management and organizations (PhD); management sciences (PhD); marketing (PhD). *Application deadline:* Applications are processed on a rolling basis. Electronic applications accepted. *Dean,* Prof. Sarah Fisher Gardial, 319-335-0862, Fax: 319-335-0860, E-mail: sarah-gardial@uiowa.edu.

Roy J. and Lucille A. Carver College of Medicine *Program availability:* Part-time. Offers medicine (MA, MPAS, MS, DPT, MD, PhD). Electronic applications accepted.

Graduate Programs in Medicine *Program availability:* Part-time. Offers anatomy and cell biology (PhD); biochemistry (MS, PhD); free radical and radiation biology (MS); general microbiology and microbial physiology (MS, PhD); immunology (MS, PhD); medicine (MA, MPAS, MS, DPT, PhD); microbial genetics (MS, PhD); molecular physiology and biophysics (MS, PhD); pathogenic bacteriology (MS, PhD); pathology (MS); pharmacology (MS, PhD); physical rehabilitation science (MA, PhD); physical therapy (DPT); physician assistant studies and services (MPAS); virology (MS, PhD). Electronic applications accepted.

UNIVERSITY OF JAMESTOWN, Jamestown, ND 58405

General Information Independent-religious, coed, comprehensive institution.

GRADUATE UNITS

Program in Education Offers curriculum and instruction (M Ed).

Program in Physical Therapy Offers physical therapy (DPT).

THE UNIVERSITY OF KANSAS, Lawrence, KS 66045

General Information State-supported, coed, university. CGS member. *Enrollment:* 27,565 graduate, professional, and undergraduate students; 5,714 full-time matriculated graduate/professional students (3,100 women), 2,373 part-time matriculated graduate/professional students (1,523 women). *Enrollment by degree level:* 3,558 master's, 4,321 doctoral, 208 other advanced degrees. *Graduate housing:* Rooms and/or apartments available on a first-come, first-served basis to single and married students. Housing application deadline: 3/1. *Student services:* Campus employment opportunities, campus safety program, career counseling, child daycare facilities, exercise/wellness program, free psychological counseling, grant writing training, international student services, low-cost health insurance, multicultural affairs office, services for students with disabilities, teacher training, writing training. *Library facilities:* Watson Library plus 11 others. *Collection:* Books: 4.7 million (physical), 988,900 (digital/electronic). Weekly public service hours: 168; study areas open 24 hours, 5–7 days a week; students can reserve study rooms.

Computer facilities: 1,500 computers available on campus for general student use. A campuswide network can be accessed from student residence rooms and from off campus. Online class registration, online payments are available.
Website: http://www.ku.edu/

General Application Contact: Graduate Studies, 785-864-8040, Fax: 785-864-7209, E-mail: graduate@ku.edu.

GRADUATE UNITS

Graduate Studies Students: 3,452 full-time (1,843 women), 1,878 part-time (1,142 women); includes 722 minority (213 Black or African American, non-Hispanic/Latino; 55 American Indian or Alaska Native, non-Hispanic/Latino; 128 Asian, non-Hispanic/Latino; 147 Hispanic/Latino; 1 Native Hawaiian or other Pacific Islander, non-Hispanic/Latino; 178 Two or more races, non-Hispanic/Latino), 1,009 international. Average age 30. 5,818 applicants, 52% accepted, 1798 enrolled. Expenses: Contact institution. *Financial support:* Fellowships, research assistantships, teaching assistantships, career-related internships or fieldwork, Federal Work-Study, institutionally sponsored loans, scholarships/grants, traineeships, and unspecified assistantships available. Support available to part-time students. Financial award application deadline: 4/15; financial award applicants required to submit FAFSA. In 2016, 1,482 master's, 336 doctorates, 363 other advanced degrees awarded. *Program availability:* Part-time, evening/weekend, online learning. *Application fee:* $65 ($85 for international students). Electronic applications accepted. *Application Contact:* Abby Ehling, Assistant Dean, 785-864-8040, Fax: 785-864-7209, E-mail: graduate@ku.edu. *Dean of Graduate Studies,* Michael Roberts, 785-864-8040, E-mail: mroberts@ku.edu.

College of Liberal Arts and Sciences Students: 1,488 full-time (793 women), 214 part-time (117 women); includes 198 minority (51 Black or African American, non-Hispanic/Latino; 23 American Indian or Alaska Native, non-Hispanic/Latino; 32 Asian, non-Hispanic/Latino; 44 Hispanic/Latino; 48 Two or more races, non-Hispanic/Latino), 386 international. Average age 30. 2,345 applicants, 36% accepted, 431 enrolled. Expenses: Contact institution. *Financial support:* Fellowships, research assistantships with partial tuition reimbursements, teaching assistantships with tuition reimbursements, career-related internships or fieldwork, Federal Work-Study, institutionally sponsored loans, scholarships/grants, traineeships, and unspecified assistantships available. Support available to part-time students. Financial award applicants required to submit FAFSA. In 2016, 299 master's, 146 doctorates, 18 other advanced degrees awarded. *Program availability:* Part-time, evening/weekend, online learning. Offers African and African-American studies (MA); African studies (Graduate Certificate); American studies (MA, PhD); anthropology (MA, PhD); applied behavioral science (MA); applied mathematics (Graduate Certificate); art history (MA, PhD); atmospheric science (MS); audiology (PhD); behavioral psychology (PhD); biochemistry and biophysics (PhD); botany (MA, PhD); Brazilian studies (Graduate Certificate); Central American and Mexican studies (Graduate Certificate); ceramics (MFA); chemistry (MS, PhD); child language (MA, PhD); city and county management (Graduate Certificate); classics (MA, PhD); clinical psychology (PhD); cognitive and brain sciences (MA, PhD); communication studies (MA, PhD); community health and development (Graduate Certificate); computational biology (PhD); creative writing (MFA); developmental psychology (MA, PhD); drawing and painting (MFA); East Asian languages and cultures (MA, Graduate Certificate); ecology and evolutionary biology (MA, PhD); economics (MA, PhD); English (MA, PhD); entomology (MA, PhD); expanded media (MFA); film and media studies (MA, PhD); foreign area officer (MA); French (MA, PhD); geographic information science (Graduate Certificate); geography (MA, PhD); geology (MS, PhD); German (MA, PhD); gerontology (PhD); global and international studies (MA); history (MA, PhD); indigenous studies (MA, Graduate Certificate); Latin American and Caribbean studies (Graduate Certificate); Latin American studies (MA); liberal arts and sciences (MA, MFA, MPA, MS, PhD, Graduate Certificate); linguistics (MA, PhD); mathematics (MA, PhD); metalsmithing/jewelry (MFA); microbiology (PhD); molecular, cellular, and developmental biology (PhD); museum studies (MA, Graduate Certificate); performance management (Graduate Certificate); philosophy (MA, PhD); physics and astronomy (MS, PhD); political science (MA, PhD); printmaking (MFA); professional workplace communication (Graduate Certificate); public administration (MPA, PhD); quantitative psychology (PhD); religious studies (MA, Graduate Certificate); Russian, East European and Eurasian studies (MA, Graduate Certificate); sculpture (MFA); Slavic languages and literatures (MA, PhD); social psychology (MA, PhD); sociology (PhD); Spanish (MA, PhD); speech-language pathology (MA, PhD); textiles/fibers (MFA); theatre (MA, PhD); theatre design (MFA); visual art education (MA). *Application fee:* $65 ($85 for international students). Electronic applications accepted. *Application Contact:* Kristine Latta, Director of the College Office of Graduate Affairs, 785-864-1784, E-mail: klatta@ku.edu. *Dean, College of Liberal Arts and Sciences,* Carl W. Lejuez, 785-864-3661, E-mail: clejuez@ku.edu.

School of Architecture, Design, and Planning Students: 142 full-time (67 women), 36 part-time (20 women); includes 24 minority (7 Black or African American, non-Hispanic/Latino; 7 Asian, non-Hispanic/Latino; 6 Hispanic/Latino; 4 Two or more races, non-Hispanic/Latino), 51 international. Average age 27. 168 applicants, 74% accepted, 36 enrolled. Expenses: Contact institution. *Financial support:* Fellowships, research assistantships, teaching assistantships, career-related internships or fieldwork, scholarships/grants, health care benefits, and unspecified assistantships available. Financial award application deadline: 1/15; financial award applicants required to submit FAFSA. In 2016, 116 master's, 2 doctorates, 10 other advanced degrees awarded. *Program availability:* Part-time. Offers architectural acoustics (Certificate); architecture (M Arch, PhD); architecture, design, and planning (M Arch, MA, MUP, PhD, Certificate, Graduate Certificate); design management (MA); health and wellness (Certificate); historic preservation (Certificate); interaction design (MA); urban design (Certificate); urban planning (MUP). *Application deadline:* For fall admission, 1/15 priority date for domestic and international students; for summer admission, 1/15 priority date for domestic and international students. *Application fee:* $65 ($85 for international students). Electronic applications accepted. *Application Contact:* Gera Elliott, Admissions Coordinator, 785-864-3167, E-mail: archku@ku.edu. *Dean,* Mahesh Daas, 785-864-3114, E-mail: mahesh@ku.edu.

School of Business Students: 281 full-time (89 women), 384 part-time (155 women); includes 102 minority (22 Black or African American, non-Hispanic/Latino; 8 American Indian or Alaska Native, non-Hispanic/Latino; 19 Asian, non-Hispanic/Latino; 28 Hispanic/Latino; 25 Two or more races, non-Hispanic/Latino), 56 international. Average age 30. 644 applicants, 70% accepted, 361 enrolled. Expenses: Contact institution. *Financial support:* Fellowships, research assistantships, teaching assistantships, career-related internships or fieldwork, Federal Work-Study, and unspecified assistantships available. Financial award application deadline: 1/15; financial award applicants required to submit FAFSA. In 2016, 256 master's, 9 doctorates awarded. *Program availability:* Part-time, evening/weekend. Offers accounting (M Acc); business (M Acc, MBA, MS, PhD); business and organizational leadership (MS); decision sciences and supply chain management (PhD); finance (MBA, PhD); human resources management (MBA, PhD); information systems (MBA); international business (MBA); management (MBA); marketing (MBA, PhD); organizational behavior (PhD); strategic management (MBA, PhD); supply chain management and logistics (MS). *Application deadline:* For fall admission, 1/15 priority date for domestic and international students. *Application fee:* $65 ($85 for international students). Electronic applications accepted. *Application Contact:* Patricia McCaffrey, MBA Coordinator, 785-864-9692, E-mail: pmccaffr@ku.edu. *Dean,* Dr. James P. Guthrie, 785-864-7546, E-mail: jguthrie@ku.edu.

School of Education Students: 546 full-time (364 women), 821 part-time (662 women); includes 207 minority (75 Black or African American, non-Hispanic/Latino; 14 American Indian or Alaska Native, non-Hispanic/Latino; 26 Asian, non-Hispanic/Latino; 35 Hispanic/Latino; 57 Two or more races, non-Hispanic/Latino), 107 international. Average age 33. 948 applicants, 72% accepted, 490 enrolled. Expenses: Contact institution. *Financial support:* Fellowships, research assistantships, teaching assistantships, career-related internships or fieldwork, scholarships/grants, and unspecified assistantships available. Financial award application deadline: 2/1. In 2016, 214 master's, 55 doctorates, 40 other advanced degrees awarded. *Program availability:* Part-time, online learning. Offers autism spectrum disorder (MS Ed, Certificate); counseling psychology (MS, PhD); curriculum and instruction (MA, MS Ed, PhD); early childhood unified (MS Ed); education (MA, MS, MS Ed, MSE, Ed D, PhD, Certificate, Ed S); education leadership and policy (MSE, PhD); educational administration (MSE, Ed D, PhD); educational psychology and research (MS Ed, PhD); educational technology (MS Ed, PhD); exercise science (MS Ed); health and physical education (MS Ed, PhD); high incidence disabilities (MS Ed); higher education administration (MS Ed, Ed D, PhD); leadership in special and inclusive education (Certificate); low incidence disabilities (MS Ed); policy studies (PhD); school psychology (PhD, Ed S); secondary special education and transition (MS Ed); social and cultural studies in education (MSE, PhD); special education (PhD); sport management (MS Ed). *Application fee:* $65 ($85 for international students). Electronic applications accepted. *Application Contact:* Kim Huggett, Graduate Student Services Manager, 785-864-4510, E-mail: khuggett@ku.edu. *Dean,* Dr. Rick J. Ginsberg, 785-864-3726, E-mail: ginsberg@ku.edu.

School of Engineering Students: 398 full-time (99 women), 241 part-time (52 women); includes 59 minority (15 Black or African American, non-Hispanic/Latino; 1 American Indian or Alaska Native, non-Hispanic/Latino; 24 Asian, non-Hispanic/Latino; 8 Hispanic/Latino; 11 Two or more races, non-Hispanic/Latino), 305 international. Average age 29. 847 applicants, 44% accepted, 131 enrolled. Expenses: Contact institution. *Financial support:* Fellowships, research assistantships, teaching assistantships, career-related internships or fieldwork, Federal Work-Study, scholarships/grants, and unspecified assistantships available. In 2016, 155 master's, 31 doctorates awarded. *Program availability:* Part-time, evening/weekend, online learning. Offers aerospace engineering (ME, MS, DE, PhD); architectural engineering (MS); bioengineering (MS, PhD); chemical and petroleum engineering (PhD); chemical engineering (MS); civil engineering (MCE, MS, PhD); computer engineering (MS); computer science (MS, PhD); construction management (MCM); electrical engineering (MS, PhD); engineering (MCE, MCM, ME, MS, DE, PhD, Certificate);

engineering management (MS, Certificate); environmental engineering (MS, PhD); environmental science (MS, PhD); information technology (MS); mechanical engineering (MS, PhD); petroleum engineering (MS); petroleum management (Certificate); project management (ME, MS). *Application fee:* $65 ($85 for international students). Electronic applications accepted. *Application Contact:* Amy Wierman, Assistant to the Dean, 785-864-2930, E-mail: awierman@ku.edu. *Dean,* Dr. Michael S. Branicky, 785-864-2930, E-mail: msb@ku.edu.

School of Music Students: 172 full-time (90 women), 34 part-time (21 women); includes 17 minority (3 Black or African American, non-Hispanic/Latino; 6 Asian, non-Hispanic/Latino; 2 Hispanic/Latino; 6 Two or more races, non-Hispanic/Latino), 53 international. Average age 29. 228 applicants, 57% accepted, 62 enrolled. Expenses: Contact institution. *Financial support:* Fellowships, research assistantships, teaching assistantships, scholarships/grants, and unspecified assistantships available. In 2016, 44 master's, 30 doctorates awarded. Offers music (MM, MME, DMA, PhD); music education (MME, PhD); music therapy (MME, PhD). *Application fee:* $65 ($85 for international students). Electronic applications accepted. *Application Contact:* Jane Gnojek, Graduate Services Coordinator, 785-864-2862, E-mail: jgnojek@ku.edu. *Dean,* Dr. Robert Walzel, 785-864-3421, E-mail: robert.walzel@ku.edu.

School of Pharmacy Students: 101 full-time (54 women), 24 part-time (11 women); includes 11 minority (1 Black or African American, non-Hispanic/Latino; 4 Asian, non-Hispanic/Latino; 4 Hispanic/Latino; 2 Two or more races, non-Hispanic/Latino), 45 international. Average age 28. 194 applicants, 22% accepted, 30 enrolled. Expenses: Contact institution. *Financial support:* Fellowships, research assistantships, teaching assistantships, career-related internships or fieldwork, scholarships/grants, traineeships, and unspecified assistantships available. In 2016, 20 master's, 11 doctorates awarded. Offers distance learning (MS, PhD); medicinal chemistry (MS, PhD); neurosciences (MS, PhD); pharmaceutical chemistry (MS, PhD); pharmacology and toxicology (MS, PhD); pharmacy (MS, PhD). *Application fee:* $65 ($85 for international students). Electronic applications accepted. *Application Contact:* Gina King, Senior Administrative Associate, 785-864-3592, E-mail: ginaking@ku.edu. *Dean,* Kenneth L. Audus, 785-864-3591, E-mail: audus@ku.edu.

School of Social Welfare Students: 328 full-time (283 women), 73 part-time (63 women); includes 89 minority (33 Black or African American, non-Hispanic/Latino; 8 American Indian or Alaska Native, non-Hispanic/Latino; 8 Asian, non-Hispanic/Latino; 20 Hispanic/Latino; 20 Two or more races, non-Hispanic/Latino), 4 international. Average age 31. 370 applicants, 88% accepted, 212 enrolled. Expenses: Contact institution. *Financial support:* Fellowships, research assistantships, teaching assistantships, Federal Work-Study, scholarships/grants, and tuition waivers (partial) available. Support available to part-time students. Financial award application deadline: 1/17; financial award applicants required to submit FAFSA. In 2016, 171 master's, 7 doctorates awarded. *Program availability:* Part-time, online learning. Offers social work (MSW, PhD). *Application deadline:* For fall admission, 1/17 for domestic and international students. *Application fee:* $65 ($85 for international students). Electronic applications accepted. *Application Contact:* Becky Hofer, Director of Graduate Admissions, 785-864-8956, E-mail: bhofer@ku.edu. *Interim Dean,* Steve Kapp, 785-864-2269, E-mail: stevek@ku.edu.

William Allen White School of Journalism and Mass Communications Students: 29 full-time (21 women), 55 part-time (43 women); includes 17 minority (6 Black or African American, non-Hispanic/Latino; 1 American Indian or Alaska Native, non-Hispanic/Latino; 2 Asian, non-Hispanic/Latino; 1 Hispanic/Latino; 1 Native Hawaiian or other Pacific Islander, non-Hispanic/Latino; 6 Two or more races, non-Hispanic/Latino), 7 international. Average age 33. 74 applicants, 81% accepted, 46 enrolled. Expenses: Contact institution. *Financial support:* Fellowships, research assistantships, teaching assistantships, career-related internships or fieldwork, scholarships/grants, and unspecified assistantships available. Support available to part-time students. Financial award application deadline: 2/1; financial award applicants required to submit FAFSA. In 2016, 16 master's, 1 doctorate awarded. *Program availability:* Part-time. Offers journalism (MS); journalism and mass communications (PhD). *Application deadline:* For fall admission, 1/1 priority date for domestic and international students; for spring admission, 11/1 for domestic and international students. *Application fee:* $65 ($85 for international students). Electronic applications accepted. *Application Contact:* Jammie A. Johnson, Graduate Advisor/Administrative Assistant, 785-864-7649, E-mail: jamjohn@ku.edu. *Dean,* Ann Brill, 785-864-4755, E-mail: abrill@ku.edu.

School of Law Students: 351 full-time (146 women), 19 part-time (1 woman); includes 52 minority (11 Black or African American, non-Hispanic/Latino; 4 American Indian or Alaska Native, non-Hispanic/Latino; 8 Asian, non-Hispanic/Latino; 22 Hispanic/Latino; 7 Two or more races, non-Hispanic/Latino), 22 International. Average age 25. 644 applicants, 57% accepted, 107 enrolled. *Faculty:* 32 full-time (17 women), 22 part-time/adjunct (10 women). Expenses: Contact institution. *Financial support:* In 2016–17, 8 fellowships (averaging $1,350 per year), 62 research assistantships (averaging $1,358 per year), 8 teaching assistantships (averaging $2,000 per year) were awarded; career-related internships or fieldwork, Federal Work-Study, institutionally sponsored loans, and scholarships/grants also available. Financial award application deadline: 2/15; financial award applicants required to submit FAFSA. In 2016, 109 doctorates awarded. Offers law (JD). *Application deadline:* For fall admission, 5/1 for domestic and international students. Applications are processed on a rolling basis. *Application fee:* $55. Electronic applications accepted. *Application Contact:* Steven Freedman, Assistant Dean for Admissions, 866-220-3654, E-mail: admitlaw@ku.edu. *Dean,* Stephen W. Mazza, 785-864-4550, Fax: 785-864-5054.

University of Kansas Medical Center Students: 1,553 full-time (881 women), 471 part-time (376 women); includes 378 minority (61 Black or African American, non-Hispanic/Latino; 13 American Indian or Alaska Native, non-Hispanic/Latino; 109 Asian, non-Hispanic/Latino; 93 Hispanic/Latino; 102 Two or more races, non-Hispanic/Latino), 102 international. Average age 28. *Faculty:* 1,477. Expenses: Contact institution. In 2016, 191 master's, 327 doctorates, 37 other advanced degrees awarded. Offers health informatics (MS, Post Master's Certificate). *Executive Vice Chancellor,* Dr. Doug Girod, 913-588-1440, E-mail: dgirod@kumc.edu.

School of Health Professions Students: 445 full-time (322 women), 65 part-time (53 women); includes 58 minority (10 Black or African American, non-Hispanic/Latino; 4 American Indian or Alaska Native, non-Hispanic/Latino; 11 Asian, non-Hispanic/Latino; 16 Hispanic/Latino; 17 Two or more races, non-Hispanic/Latino), 24 international. Average age 27. *Faculty:* 100. Expenses: Contact institution. In 2016, 47 master's, 84 doctorates, 28 other advanced degrees awarded. Offers audiology (Au D, PhD); dietetic internship (Graduate Certificate); dietetics and integrative medicine (Graduate Certificate); dietetics and nutrition (MS); health professions (MOT, MS, Au D, DNAP, DPT, OTD, SLPD, Graduate Certificate); medical nutrition science (PhD); molecular biotechnology (MS); nurse anesthesia education (DNAP); occupational therapy (MOT, OTD); physical therapy (DPT); rehabilitation science

(PhD); speech-language pathology (SLPD); therapeutic science (PhD). *Dean*, Dr. Abiodun Akinwuntan, 913-588-5235, Fax: 913-588-5254, E-mail: aakinwuntan@kumc.edu.

School of Medicine Students: 1,060 full-time (516 women), 129 part-time (74 women); includes 270 minority (36 Black or African American, non-Hispanic/Latino; 6 American Indian or Alaska Native, non-Hispanic/Latino; 89 Asian, non-Hispanic/Latino; 67 Hispanic/Latino; 72 Two or more races, non-Hispanic/Latino), 74 international. Average age 27. *Faculty:* 1,324. Expenses: Contact institution. In 2016, 54 master's, 218 doctorates, 205 other advanced degrees awarded. Offers anatomy and cell biology (MS, PhD); applied statistics and analytics (MS); biochemistry and molecular biology (PhD); biomedical sciences (PhD); biostatistics (MS, PhD, Graduate Certificate); cancer biology (MS, PhD); clinical research (MS); epidemiology (MPH); health policy and management (PhD); health services administration (MHSA); medicine (MHSA, MPH, MS, MD, PhD, Graduate Certificate); microbiology, molecular genetics and immunology (MS, PhD); molecular and integrative physiology (PhD); neuroscience (PhD); pathology and laboratory medicine (MS, PhD); pharmacology (PhD); public health management (MPH); social and behavioral health (MPH); statistical applications (Graduate Certificate); toxicology (PhD). *Executive Dean*, Dr. Robert Simari, 913-588-7201, E-mail: rsimari@kumc.edu.

School of Nursing Students: 41 full-time (40 women), 270 part-time (244 women); includes 47 minority (15 Black or African American, non-Hispanic/Latino; 2 American Indian or Alaska Native, non-Hispanic/Latino; 9 Asian, non-Hispanic/Latino; 10 Hispanic/Latino; 11 Two or more races, non-Hispanic/Latino), 1 international. Average age 37. 95 applicants, 97% accepted, 67 enrolled. *Faculty:* 53. Expenses: Contact institution. *Financial support:* In 2016–17, 50 students received support, including 5 research assistantships with tuition reimbursements available (averaging $20,000 per year), 30 teaching assistantships with tuition reimbursements available (averaging $20,000 per year); scholarships/grants and traineeships also available. Financial award application deadline: 3/1; financial award applicants required to submit FAFSA. In 2016, 87 master's, 25 doctorates, 9 other advanced degrees awarded. *Program availability:* Part-time, 100% online, blended/hybrid learning. Offers adult/gerontological clinical nurse specialist (PMC); adult/gerontological nurse practitioner (PMC); health care informatics (PMC); health professions educator (PMC); nurse midwife (PMC); nursing (MS, DNP, PhD); organizational leadership (PMC); psychiatric/mental health nurse practitioner (PMC); public health nursing (PMC). *Application deadline:* For fall admission, 4/1 for domestic and international students; for spring admission, 9/1 for domestic and international students. *Application fee:* $60. Electronic applications accepted. *Application Contact:* Dr. Pamela K. Barnes, Associate Dean, Student Affairs, 913-588-1619, Fax: 913-588-1615, E-mail: pbarnes2@kumc.edu. *Dean*, Dr. Sally Maliski, 913-588-1601, Fax: 913-588-1660, E-mail: smaliski@kumc.edu.

UNIVERSITY OF KENTUCKY, Lexington, KY 40506-0032

General Information State-supported, coed, university. CGS member. *Graduate housing:* Rooms and/or apartments available to single and married students. *Research affiliation:* Continuous Electron Beam Accelerator Facility (high-energy physics), Battelle–Pacific Northwest National Laboratory (environmental sciences), Oak Ridge National Laboratory (nuclear physics), National Institute of Occupational Health and Safety (environmental health), National Drug Addiction Center (drug abuse and prevention).

GRADUATE UNITS

College of Dentistry Students: 265 full-time (133 women); includes 73 minority (15 Black or African American, non-Hispanic/Latino; 1 American Indian or Alaska Native, non-Hispanic/Latino; 27 Asian, non-Hispanic/Latino; 13 Hispanic/Latino; 17 Two or more races, non-Hispanic/Latino), 3 international. Average age 27. 1,913 applicants, 6% accepted, 65 enrolled. *Faculty:* 64 full-time (19 women), 51 part-time/adjunct (20 women). Expenses: Contact institution. *Financial support:* In 2016–17, 173 students received support. Fellowships, research assistantships, teaching assistantships, career-related internships or fieldwork, Federal Work-Study, institutionally sponsored loans, and scholarships/grants available. Support available to part-time students. Financial award application deadline: 4/15; financial award applicants required to submit FAFSA. In 2016, 52 doctorates awarded. Offers dentistry (DMD). *Application deadline:* For fall admission, 12/1 priority date for domestic students. Applications are processed on a rolling basis. *Application fee:* $75. Electronic applications accepted. *Application Contact:* Miranda Scurlock, Student Affairs Officer, 859-323-6071, Fax: 859-257-5550, E-mail: miranda.scurlock@uky.edu. *Dean*, Dr. Stephanos Kyrkanides, 859-323-1884, Fax: 859-323-1042, E-mail: stephanos@uky.edu.

College of Law Offers law (JD). Electronic applications accepted.

College of Medicine Students: 547 full-time (233 women); includes 104 minority (32 Black or African American, non-Hispanic/Latino; 1 American Indian or Alaska Native, non-Hispanic/Latino; 62 Asian, non-Hispanic/Latino; 9 Hispanic/Latino), 21 international. Average age 24. Expenses: Contact institution. *Financial support:* Institutionally sponsored loans available. Financial award applicants required to submit FAFSA. Offers medicine (MD). *Application deadline:* For fall admission, 11/1 for domestic students. Applications are processed on a rolling basis. *Application fee:* $50. Electronic applications accepted. *Application Contact:* Kimberly Scott, Assistant Director of Admissions, 859-323-6161, E-mail: kymedap@uky.edu. *Associate Dean for Admissions*, Dr. Carol L. Elam, 859-323-6161.

Graduate School *Program availability:* Part-time, evening/weekend. Offers dentistry (MS); pharmaceutical sciences (MS, PhD); pharmacy (Pharm D). Electronic applications accepted.

College of Agriculture, Food and Environment *Program availability:* Part-time. Offers agricultural economics (MS, PhD); agriculture, food and environment (MS, MSFOR, PhD); animal and food sciences (MS, PhD); biosystems and agricultural engineering (MS, PhD); entomology (MS, PhD); family studies, human development, and resource management (MS, PhD); forestry (MSFOR); hospitality and dietetics administration (MS); integrated plant and soil sciences (MS, PhD); plant pathology (MS, PhD); veterinary science (MS, PhD). Electronic applications accepted.

College of Arts and Sciences *Program availability:* Part-time. Offers anthropology (MA, PhD); applied mathematics (MS); arts and sciences (MA, MS, PhD); biology (MS, PhD); chemistry (MS, PhD); English (MA, PhD); geography (MA, PhD); geology (MS, PhD); German (MA); Hispanic studies (MA, PhD); history (MA, PhD); mathematics (MA, MS, PhD); modern and classical languages and literatures (MA); philosophy (MA, PhD); physics and astronomy (MS, PhD); political science (MA, PhD); psychology (MA, PhD); sociology (MA, MS, PhD); statistics (MS, PhD); teaching world languages (MA). Electronic applications accepted.

College of Communication and Information *Program availability:* Part-time. Offers communication (MA, PhD); communication and information (MA, MSLS, PhD); library and information science (MA, MSLS). Electronic applications accepted.

College of Design Offers architecture (M Arch); design (M Arch, MAIDM, MHP, MSIDM); historic preservation (MHP); interior design (MA). Electronic applications accepted.

College of Education *Program availability:* Part-time, evening/weekend. Offers biomechanics (MS); counseling psychology (MS, PhD, Ed S); curriculum and instruction (Ed D, PhD); early childhood (MS Ed); education (M Ed, MA Ed, MRC, MS, MS Ed, Ed D, PhD, Ed S); educational leadership (M Ed, Ed D, PhD, Ed S); educational policy studies and evaluation (Ed D); educational psychology (MS, PhD); educational sciences (PhD); elementary education (MA Ed); exercise physiology (MS, PhD); exercise science (PhD); family resource and youth services (M Ed, Ed S); health promotion (MS, Ed D); higher education (MS Ed, PhD); instructional system design (MS Ed); literacy (MA Ed); middle school education (MA Ed, MS Ed); physical education training (Ed D); principalship (Ed D, Ed S); rehabilitation counseling (MRC, PhD); school psychology (PhD, Ed S); school technology leadership (M Ed, PhD, Ed S); secondary education (MA Ed, MS Ed); social and philosophical studies (MS Ed); special education (MS Ed, PhD); sport leadership (MS); teacher leadership (M Ed, Ed S); teaching and coaching (MS). Electronic applications accepted.

College of Engineering *Program availability:* Part-time. Offers biomedical engineering (MSBE, PBME, PhD); chemical engineering (MS, PhD); civil engineering (MSCE, PhD); computer science (MS, PhD); electrical engineering (MSEE, PhD); engineering (M Eng, MCE, MME, MS, MS Ch E, MS Min, MSCE, MSEE, MSEM, MSMAE, MSME, MSMSE, PhD); manufacturing systems engineering (MSMSE); materials science and engineering (MS, PhD); mechanical engineering (MSME, PhD); mining engineering (MME, MS Min, PhD). Electronic applications accepted.

College of Fine Arts *Program availability:* Part-time, evening/weekend. Offers art education (MA); art history (MA); art studio (MFA); arts administration (MA); composition (MM, DMA); conducting (MM, DMA); fine arts (MA, MFA, MM, DMA, PhD); music education (MM, PhD); music theory (MA, PhD); music therapy (MM); musicology (MA, PhD); performance (MM, DMA); sacred music (MM). Electronic applications accepted.

College of Health Sciences *Program availability:* Part-time. Offers athletic training (MS); communication disorders (MS); health administration (MHA); health sciences (MHA, MS, MSCD, MSHP, MSNS, MSPAS, MSPT, MSRMP, DS, PhD); nutritional sciences (MSNS, PhD); physical therapy (DPT); physician assistant studies (MSPAS); rehabilitation sciences (PhD). Electronic applications accepted.

College of Nursing Offers nursing (DNP, PhD). Electronic applications accepted.

College of Public Health Offers clinical research design (MS); epidemiology and biostatistics (PhD); gerontology (PhD, Graduate Certificate); public health (MPH, Dr PH, PhD). Electronic applications accepted.

College of Social Work Offers social work (MSW, PhD). Electronic applications accepted.

Gatton College of Business and Economics *Program availability:* Part-time, evening/weekend. Offers accounting (MSACC); business administration (MBA, PhD); business and economics (MBA, MS, MSACC, PhD); economics (MS, PhD). Electronic applications accepted.

Graduate School Programs from the College of Medicine Offers anatomy and neurobiology (PhD); medical science (MS); medicine (MS, PhD); microbiology and immunology (PhD); molecular and biomedical pharmacology (PhD); molecular and cellular biochemistry (PhD); physiology (PhD); radiation sciences (MSRMP); toxicology (MS, PhD). Electronic applications accepted.

Martin School of Public Policy and Administration Students: 74 full-time (26 women), 15 part-time (7 women); includes 7 minority (3 Black or African American, non-Hispanic/Latino; 4 Asian, non-Hispanic/Latino), 27 international. Average age 30. 98 applicants, 63% accepted, 33 enrolled. *Faculty:* 10 full-time (2 women), 3 part-time/adjunct (1 woman). Expenses: Contact institution. *Financial support:* In 2016–17, 22 students received support, including 4 fellowships with full tuition reimbursements available (averaging $10,000 per year), 13 research assistantships with full tuition reimbursements available (averaging $12,500 per year); career-related internships or fieldwork, scholarships/grants, health care benefits, and unspecified assistantships also available. Financial award application deadline: 2/1. In 2016, 22 master's, 4 doctorates awarded. *Program availability:* Part-time, evening/weekend, 100% online. Offers public administration (MPA); public financial management (MPFM, Graduate Certificate); public policy (MPP); public policy and administration (PhD). *Application deadline:* For fall admission, 7/15 priority date for domestic students, 3/15 priority date for international students; for spring admission, 12/15 priority date for domestic students, 8/15 priority date for international students. Applications are processed on a rolling basis. *Application fee:* $65 ($75 for international students). Electronic applications accepted. *Application Contact:* Jackie McCuddy, Student Affairs Officer, 859-257-5594, Fax: 859-323-1937, E-mail: jackie.mccuddy@uky.edu. *Director of the Martin School*, Dr. Ron W. Zimmer, 859-323-5413, Fax: 859-323-1937, E-mail: ron.zimmer@uky.edu.

Patterson School of Diplomacy and International Commerce Offers diplomacy and international commerce (MA). Electronic applications accepted.

UNIVERSITY OF KING'S COLLEGE, Halifax, NS B3H 2A1, Canada

General Information Province-supported, coed, comprehensive institution. *Graduate housing:* Room and/or apartments available on a first-come, first-served basis to single students; on-campus housing not available to married students. Housing application deadline: 4/1.

GRADUATE UNITS

Graduate and Advanced Programs Offers creative nonfiction (MFA); journalism (MJ).

UNIVERSITY OF LA VERNE, La Verne, CA 91750-4443

General Information Independent, coed, university. *Enrollment:* 4,873 graduate, professional, and undergraduate students; 1,588 full-time matriculated graduate/professional students (1,027 women), 1,519 part-time matriculated graduate/professional students (1,029 women). *Enrollment by degree level:* 1,955 master's, 536 doctoral, 316 other advanced degrees. *Graduate faculty:* 152 full-time (82 women), 237 part-time/adjunct (121 women). *Tuition:* Part-time $795 per credit hour. Tuition and fees vary according to campus/location and program. *Graduate housing:* Room and/or apartments available on a first-come, first-served basis to single students; on-campus housing not available to married students. *Student services:* Campus employment opportunities, campus safety program, career counseling, exercise/wellness program, free psychological counseling, international student services, low-cost health insurance, multicultural affairs office, services for students with disabilities, teacher training, writing training. *Library facilities:* Wilson Library. *Collection:* Students can reserve study rooms. *Research affiliation:* San Antonio Community Hospital, Riverside Community Hospital, Presbyterian Intercommunity Hospital,

Huntington Memorial Hospital (health services management), Southern California Healthcare Systems, Methodist Hospital of Southern California.

Computer facilities: A campuswide network can be accessed from student residence rooms and from off campus. Online class registration, MyLaVerne (online) are available. Website: http://www.laverne.edu/

General Application Contact: Graduate Admission Office, 877-GO-TO-ULV, Fax: 909-392-2761, E-mail: gradadmission@laverne.edu.

GRADUATE UNITS

College of Arts and Sciences Students: 72 full-time (63 women), 65 part-time (57 women); includes 74 minority (7 Black or African American, non-Hispanic/Latino; 5 Asian, non-Hispanic/Latino; 60 Hispanic/Latino; 2 Two or more races, non-Hispanic/Latino), 1 international. Average age 29. Expenses: Contact institution. *Financial support:* Career-related internships or fieldwork, institutionally sponsored loans, scholarships/grants, and unspecified assistantships available. Financial award application deadline: 3/2; financial award applicants required to submit FAFSA. *Program availability:* Part-time. Offers arts and sciences (MS, Psy D); clinical psychology (Psy D); marriage and family therapy (MS). *Application deadline:* Applications are processed on a rolling basis. *Application Contact:* Christy Ranells, Associate Director of Graduate Admissions, 909-448-4644, Fax: 909-971-2295, E-mail: cranells@laverne.edu. *Dean, College of Arts and Sciences,* Dr. Lawrence Potter, 909-448-4188, E-mail: lpotter@laverne.edu.

College of Business and Public Management Students: 625 full-time (338 women), 291 part-time (165 women); includes 275 minority (26 Black or African American, non-Hispanic/Latino; 2 American Indian or Alaska Native, non-Hispanic/Latino; 32 Asian, non-Hispanic/Latino; 211 Hispanic/Latino; 2 Native Hawaiian or other Pacific Islander, non-Hispanic/Latino; 2 Two or more races, non-Hispanic/Latino), 466 international. Average age 30. Expenses: Contact institution. *Financial support:* Career-related internships or fieldwork, institutionally sponsored loans, and scholarships/grants available. Financial award application deadline: 3/2; financial award applicants required to submit FAFSA. *Program availability:* Part-time, evening/weekend, online learning. Offers accounting (MS); business and public management (MBA, MBA-EP, MHA, MPA, MS, DPA, Certificate); finance (MS); financial management (MHA); geriatric care management (MS); gerontology (Certificate); gerontology administration (MS); health services management (MBA, MS); human resource management (Certificate); information technology (MBA, MBA-EP); international business (MBA, MBA-EP); leadership and management (MS); management and leadership (MBA, MBA-EP, MHA); marketing (MBA, MBA-EP); marketing and business development (MHA); nonprofit (MPA); nonprofit management (Certificate); organizational leadership (Certificate); public administration (MPA, DPA); supply chain management (MBA, MBA-EP); urban management and affairs (MPA). *Application deadline:* Applications are processed on a rolling basis. *Application fee:* $50. Electronic applications accepted. *Application Contact:* Rina Lazarian-Chehab, Senior Associate Director of Graduate Admissions, 909-448-4317, Fax: 909-971-2295, E-mail: rlazarian@laverne.edu. *Dean, College of Business and Public Management,* Dr. Abe Helou, 909-448-4455, E-mail: ihelou@laverne.edu.

College of Law *Program availability:* Part-time, evening/weekend. Offers law (JD). Electronic applications accepted.

LaFetra College of Education Students: 301 full-time (238 women), 569 part-time (439 women); includes 477 minority (46 Black or African American, non-Hispanic/Latino; 2 American Indian or Alaska Native, non-Hispanic/Latino; 30 Asian, non-Hispanic/Latino; 388 Hispanic/Latino; 11 Two or more races, non-Hispanic/Latino), 10 international. Average age 34. Expenses: Contact institution. *Financial support:* Federal Work-Study, institutionally sponsored loans, and scholarships/grants available. Financial award application deadline: 3/2; financial award applicants required to submit FAFSA. *Program availability:* Part-time, evening/weekend, 100% online, blended/hybrid learning. Offers advanced teaching skills (M Ed); child development (MS); child life (MS); education (M Ed); educational counseling (MS); educational leadership (M Ed); mild/moderate education specialist (Credential); multiple subject (Credential); organizational leadership (Ed D); pupil personnel services (Credential); reading (M Ed, Certificate); reading and language arts specialist (Credential); school psychology (MS); single subject (Credential); special education studies (MS); special emphasis (M Ed); teaching (Credential). *Application deadline:* Applications are processed on a rolling basis. *Application fee:* $50. *Application Contact:* Christy Ranells, Associate Director of Graduate Admission, 909-448-4644, Fax: 909-971-2295, E-mail: cranells@laverne.edu. *Dean of LaFetra College of Education,* Dr. Kimberly White-Smith, 909-448-4583, E-mail: kwhite-smith@laverne.edu.

Regional and Online Campuses *Program availability:* Part-time, evening/weekend. Offers administration services (preliminary) (Credential); business administration (MBA, MBA-EP); business administration for experienced professionals (MBA, MBA-EP, MS); education (special emphasis) (M Ed); education specialist: mild/moderate (Credential); educational counseling (MS); educational leadership (M Ed); English (Certificate); health administration (MHA); leadership and management (MS); mild/moderate education specialist (Credential); multiple subject (elementary) (Credential); multiple subject teaching (Credential); organizational leadership (Ed D); preliminary administrative services (Credential); pupil personnel services (Credential); pupil personnel services: school counseling (Credential); single subject (secondary) (Credential); single subject teaching (Credential); special education (MS); special education studies (MS); special emphasis (M Ed).

UNIVERSITY OF LETHBRIDGE, Lethbridge, AB T1K 3M4, Canada

General Information Province-supported, coed, university. CGS member. *Graduate housing:* Rooms and/or apartments available on a first-come, first-served basis to single and married students. Housing application deadline: 4/1. *Research affiliation:* Plains Midstream Canada ULC, Pacific Forestry Institution.

GRADUATE UNITS

School of Graduate Studies *Program availability:* Part-time, evening/weekend. Offers addictions counseling (M Sc); agricultural biotechnology (M Sc); agricultural studies (M Sc, MA); anthropology (MA); archaeology (M Sc, MA); art (MA, MFA); biochemistry (M Sc); biological sciences (M Sc); biomolecular science (PhD); biosystems and biodiversity (PhD); Canadian studies (MA); chemistry (M Sc); computer science (M Sc); computer science and geographical information science (M Sc); counseling (MC); counseling psychology (M Ed); dramatic arts (MA); earth, space, and physical science (PhD); economics (MA); education (MA, PhD); educational leadership (M Ed); English (MA); environmental science (M Sc); evolution and behavior (PhD); exercise science (M Sc); French (MA); French/German (MA); French/Spanish (MA); general education (M Ed); geography (M Sc, MA); German (MA); health sciences (M Sc); individualized multidisciplinary (M Sc, MA); kinesiology (M Sc, MA); management (M Sc); mathematics (M Sc); music (M Mus, MA); Native American studies (MA); neuroscience (M Sc, PhD); new media (MA, MFA); nursing (M Sc, MN); philosophy (MA); physics (M Sc); political science (MA); psychology (M Sc, MA); religious studies (MA); sociology (MA); theatre and dramatic arts (MFA); theoretical and computational science (PhD); urban and regional studies (MA); women and gender studies (MA). Electronic applications accepted.

UNIVERSITY OF LOUISIANA AT LAFAYETTE, Lafayette, LA 70504

General Information State-supported, coed, university. CGS member. *Graduate housing:* Rooms and/or apartments available on a first-come, first-served basis to single and married students. *Research affiliation:* National Wetlands Research Center (biology, wetlands restoration), Louisiana Universities Marine Consortium (marine biology), U.S. Fish and Wildlife Service (ecology), Army Corps of Engineers (wetlands), U.S. Geological Survey (USGS), U.S. Department of Agriculture (USDA).

GRADUATE UNITS

BI Moody III College of Business Administration MBA Program *Program availability:* Part-time, evening/weekend. Offers business administration (MBA).

College of Education *Program availability:* Part-time. Offers education (M Ed, Ed D). Electronic applications accepted.

Graduate Studies and Research in Education Offers administration and supervision (M Ed); curriculum and instruction (M Ed); education of the gifted (M Ed); educational leadership (M Ed, Ed D).

College of Engineering *Program availability:* Part-time, evening/weekend. Offers chemical engineering (MSE); civil engineering (MSE); computer engineering (MS, PhD); engineering (MS, MSE, MSET, MSTC, PhD); engineering and technology management (MSET); mechanical engineering (MSE); petroleum engineering (MSE); telecommunications (MSTC). Electronic applications accepted.

Center for Advanced Computer Studies *Program availability:* Part-time. Offers computer engineering (MS, PhD); computer science (MS, PhD). Electronic applications accepted.

College of Liberal Arts *Program availability:* Part-time. Offers British and American literature (MA); communicative disorders (MS, PhD); creative writing (PhD); Francophone studies (PhD); French (MA); history (MA); liberal arts (MA, MS, PhD); literature (PhD); mass communications (MS); psychology (MS); rehabilitation counseling (MS); rhetoric (PhD). Electronic applications accepted.

College of Nursing and Allied Health Professions Offers family nurse practitioner (MSN); nursing education (MSN). Program offered jointly with Southern Louisiana University, McNeese State University, Southern University and Agricultural and Mechanical College. Electronic applications accepted.

College of Sciences *Program availability:* Part-time. Offers biology (MS); environmental and evolutionary biology (PhD); geology (MS); mathematics (MS, PhD); physics (MS); sciences (MS, PhD). Electronic applications accepted.

Institute of Cognitive Science Offers cognitive science (PhD). Electronic applications accepted.

College of the Arts Offers arts (M Arch, MM). Electronic applications accepted.

School of Architecture Offers architecture (M Arch). Electronic applications accepted.

School of Music Offers conducting (MM); pedagogy (MM); vocal and instrumental performance (MM). Electronic applications accepted.

Department of Counselor Education Offers counselor education (MS). Electronic applications accepted.

UNIVERSITY OF LOUISIANA AT MONROE, Monroe, LA 71209-0001

General Information State-supported, coed, university. Enrollment: 8,645 graduate, professional, and undergraduate students; 802 full-time matriculated graduate/professional students (517 women), 458 part-time matriculated graduate/professional students (330 women). Enrollment by degree level: 647 master's, 544 doctoral, 57 other advanced degrees. Graduate faculty: 119 full-time (66 women), 28 part-time/adjunct (19 women). Tuition, state resident: full-time $6489. Tuition, nonresident: full-time $18,589. *Required fees:* $8984. Tuition and fees vary according to course level, course load, degree level and program. *Graduate housing:* Room and/or apartments available on a first-come, first-served basis to single students; on-campus housing not available to married students. Typical cost: $7688 (including board). Room and board charges vary according to board plan and housing facility selected. Housing application deadline: 5/1. *Student services:* Campus employment opportunities, career counseling, child daycare facilities, exercise/wellness program, free psychological counseling, international student services, services for students with disabilities. *Library facilities:* University Library. Collection: Books: 419,336 (physical), 225,998 (digital/electronic); Serial titles: 9,950 (physical); Databases: 47. Students can reserve study rooms. *Research affiliation:* Juvenile Diabetes Research Foundation (pharmacology), Philip Morris, Inc. (medicinal chemistry), Harvard Hughes Medical Institute (biology), Xenoport, Inc. (pharmaceutics), U.S. Army Corps of Engineers (toxicology, environmental science), National Center for Toxicological Research (toxicology).

Computer facilities: Computer purchase and lease plans are available. A campuswide network can be accessed from student residence rooms and from off campus. Online class registration is available. Website: http://www.ulm.edu/

General Application Contact: Dr. Leonard Clark, Director of Graduate Studies, 318-342-1036, Fax: 318-342-1042, E-mail: gradadmissions@ulm.edu.

GRADUATE UNITS

Graduate School Students: 802 full-time (517 women), 458 part-time (330 women); includes 332 minority (210 Black or African American, non-Hispanic/Latino; 4 American Indian or Alaska Native, non-Hispanic/Latino; 58 Asian, non-Hispanic/Latino; 31 Hispanic/Latino; 29 Two or more races, non-Hispanic/Latino), 80 international. Average age 29. 872 applicants, 39% accepted, 267 enrolled. *Faculty:* 91 full-time (49 women), 17 part-time/adjunct (10 women). Expenses: Contact institution. *Financial support:* In 2016–17, 200 teaching assistantships with full tuition reimbursements were awarded; research assistantships, career-related internships or fieldwork, Federal Work-Study, institutionally sponsored loans, tuition waivers (full and partial), and unspecified assistantships also available. Support available to part-time students. Financial award application deadline: 4/1; financial award applicants required to submit FAFSA. In 2016, 270 master's, 123 doctorates awarded. *Program availability:* Part-time, evening/weekend, online learning. *Application deadline:* For fall admission, 3/1 priority date for domestic and international students; for winter admission, 4/1 priority date for domestic students, 4/1 for international students; for spring admission, 8/1 priority date for domestic and international students. Applications are processed on a rolling basis. *Application fee:* $20 ($30 for international students). Electronic applications accepted. *Director,* Dr. Leonard Clark, 318-342-1036, Fax: 318-342-1042, E-mail: leclark@ulm.edu.

College of Arts, Education, and Sciences Students: 63 full-time (42 women), 141 part-time (110 women); includes 65 minority (50 Black or African American, non-Hispanic/Latino; 1 American Indian or Alaska Native, non-Hispanic/Latino; 2 Asian, non-Hispanic/Latino; 7 Hispanic/Latino; 5 Two or more races, non-Hispanic/Latino), 10 international. Average age 34. 51 applicants, 84% accepted, 43 enrolled. *Faculty:* 26 full-time (14 women), 7 part-time/adjunct (4 women). Expenses: Contact institution. *Financial support:* Research assistantships with full tuition reimbursements, teaching assistantships with full tuition reimbursements, career-related internships or fieldwork, Federal Work-Study, institutionally sponsored loans, and unspecified assistantships available. Support available to part-time students. Financial award application deadline: 4/1; financial award applicants required to submit FAFSA. In 2016, 60 master's, 5 doctorates awarded. *Program availability:* Part-time, evening/weekend. Offers art education (M Ed); arts, education, and sciences (M Ed, MA, MAT, MS, Ed D); biology (MS); biology education (M Ed); chemistry education (M Ed); communication (MA); curriculum and instruction (M Ed, Ed D); early childhood education (M Ed); earth science education (M Ed); educational leadership (M Ed); elementary education (MAT); elementary education (1-5) (M Ed); English (MA); English as a second language (M Ed); English education (M Ed); family and consumer education (M Ed); French education (M Ed); history (MA); history education (M Ed); math education (M Ed); middle school education (M Ed); music education (M Ed); reading education (K-12) (M Ed); secondary education (MAT); Spanish education (M Ed); special education (MAT); special education - academically gifted (M Ed); special education - early intervention (M Ed); special education - educational diagnostician (M Ed); special education - mild/moderate disabilities (M Ed); speech education (M Ed). *Application deadline:* For fall admission, 8/24 priority date for domestic students, 3/1 priority date for international students; for winter admission, 12/14 priority date for domestic students, 4/1 priority date for international students; for spring admission, 1/19 priority date for domestic students, 8/1 priority date for international students. Applications are processed on a rolling basis. *Application fee:* $20 ($30 for international students). Electronic applications accepted. *Application Contact:* Michael Camille, Associate Dean, 318-342-1243, Fax: 318-342-1755, E-mail: camille@ulm.edu. *Dean,* Dr. Sandi M. Lemoine, 318-342-1238, Fax: 318-342-1755, E-mail: slemoine@ulm.edu.

College of Business and Social Sciences Students: 51 full-time (28 women), 62 part-time (41 women); includes 54 minority (43 Black or African American, non-Hispanic/Latino; 2 American Indian or Alaska Native, non-Hispanic/Latino; 2 Asian, non-Hispanic/Latino; 4 Hispanic/Latino; 3 Two or more races, non-Hispanic/Latino), 16 international. Average age 28. 471 applicants, 40% accepted, 40 enrolled. *Faculty:* 17 full-time (6 women), 1 part-time/adjunct (0 women). Expenses: Contact institution. *Financial support:* Research assistantships, career-related internships or fieldwork, Federal Work-Study, and unspecified assistantships available. Financial award application deadline: 4/1; financial award applicants required to submit FAFSA. In 2016, 33 master's awarded. *Program availability:* Part-time, evening/weekend, online learning. Offers business administration (MBA); business and social sciences (MA, MBA, MPA, MS); criminal justice (MA); forensic psychology (MS); general psychology (MS); psychometrics (MS); public administration (MPA). *Application deadline:* For fall admission, 8/24 for domestic students, 7/1 for international students; for winter admission, 12/14 for domestic students; for spring admission, 1/19 for domestic students, 11/1 for international students. Applications are processed on a rolling basis. *Application fee:* $20 ($30 for international students). Electronic applications accepted. *Dean,* Dr. Ronald Berry, 318-342-1103, E-mail: rberry@ulm.edu.

College of Health and Pharmaceutical Sciences Students: 218 full-time (154 women), 88 part-time (69 women); includes 55 minority (37 Black or African American, non-Hispanic/Latino; 6 Asian, non-Hispanic/Latino; 6 Hispanic/Latino; 6 Two or more races, non-Hispanic/Latino), 44 international. Average age 30. *Faculty:* 41 full-time (25 women), 8 part-time/adjunct (5 women). Expenses: Contact institution. *Financial support:* Research assistantships, career-related internships or fieldwork, Federal Work-Study, and unspecified assistantships available. Financial award application deadline: 4/1; financial award applicants required to submit FAFSA. In 2016, 98 master's, 20 doctorates awarded. Offers aging studies (MA); applied exercise science (MS); clinical exercise physiology (MS); clinical mental health counseling (MS); gerontology (CGS); health and pharmaceutical sciences (MA, MOT, MS, PhD, CGS); marriage and family therapy (MA, PhD); occupational therapy (MOT); pharmacy (PhD); program administration (MA); school counseling (MS); speech-language pathology (MS); sports, fitness and recreation management (MS); toxicology (PhD). *Application deadline:* For fall admission, 8/24 priority date for domestic students, 7/1 for international students; for winter admission, 12/14 priority date for domestic students; for spring admission, 1/19 for domestic students, 11/1 for international students. Applications are processed on a rolling basis. *Application fee:* $20 ($30 for international students). Electronic applications accepted. *Dean,* Dr. Benny L. Blaylock, 318-342-1603, E-mail: blaylock@ulm.edu.

UNIVERSITY OF LOUISVILLE, Louisville, KY 40292-0001

General Information State-supported, coed, university. CGS member. *Enrollment:* 21,579 graduate, professional, and undergraduate students; 4,102 full-time matriculated graduate/professional students (2,058 women), 1,467 part-time matriculated graduate/professional students (786 women). *Enrollment by degree level:* 2,893 master's, 2,530 doctoral, 146 other advanced degrees. *Graduate faculty:* 1,786 full-time (733 women), 653 part-time/adjunct (348 women). Tuition, state resident: full-time $12,246; part-time $681 per credit hour. Tuition, nonresident: full-time $25,486; part-time $1417 per credit hour. *Required fees:* $196. Tuition and fees vary according to program and reciprocity agreements. *Graduate housing:* Rooms and/or apartments available on a first-come, first-served basis to single and married students. Typical cost: $5030 per year ($8130 including board) for single students. Room and board charges vary according to board plan and housing facility selected. *Student services:* Campus employment opportunities, campus safety program, career counseling, child daycare facilities, exercise/wellness program, free psychological counseling, grant writing training, international student services, low-cost health insurance, multicultural affairs office, services for students with disabilities, teacher training, writing training. *Library facilities:* William F. Ekstrom Library plus 6 others. *Collection:* Books: 2.2 million (physical), 156,972 (digital/electronic); Serial titles: 2,181 (physical), 51,544 (digital/electronic); Databases: 343. Weekly public service hours: 97; study areas open 24 hours, 5–7 days a week; students can reserve study rooms. *Research affiliation:* Ford Motor Company, General Electric Company (GE), Oak Ridge National Laboratory, Argonne National Laboratory.

Computer facilities: Computer purchase and lease plans are available. 400 computers available on campus for general student use. A campuswide network can be accessed from student residence rooms and from off campus. Online class registration is available.

Website: http://www.louisville.edu/

General Application Contact: Libby Leggett, Executive Director, Graduate Admissions and Recruitment, 502-852-3108, E-mail: gradadm@louisville.edu.

GRADUATE UNITS

Graduate School Students: 4,102 full-time (2,058 women), 1,467 part-time (786 women); includes 1,099 minority (493 Black or African American, non-Hispanic/Latino; 5 American Indian or Alaska Native, non-Hispanic/Latino; 244 Asian, non-Hispanic/Latino; 192 Hispanic/Latino; 4 Native Hawaiian or other Pacific Islander, non-Hispanic/Latino; 161 Two or more races, non-Hispanic/Latino), 472 international. Average age 30. 7,515 applicants, 31% accepted, 1613 enrolled. *Faculty:* 1,786 full-time (733 women), 653 part-time/adjunct (348 women). Expenses: Contact institution. *Financial support:* Fellowships with full tuition reimbursements, research assistantships with full tuition reimbursements, teaching assistantships with tuition reimbursements, career-related internships or fieldwork, Federal Work-Study, institutionally sponsored loans, scholarships/grants, traineeships, health care benefits, tuition waivers (full), and unspecified assistantships available. Support available to part-time students. Financial award applicants required to submit FAFSA. In 2016, 828 master's, 438 doctorates, 77 other advanced degrees awarded. *Program availability:* Part-time. *Application deadline:* For fall admission, 12/1 priority date for domestic and international students; for winter admission, 11/1 for domestic students, 6/1 for international students; for spring admission, 11/1 for domestic students, 6/1 for international students; for summer admission, 4/1 for domestic students, 1/1 for international students. Applications are processed on a rolling basis. *Application fee:* $65. Electronic applications accepted. *Application Contact:* Dr. Paul DeMarco, Associate Dean, 502-852-6490, E-mail: gradadm@louisville.edu. *Dean and Vice Provost for Graduate Affairs,* Dr. Beth A. Boehm, 502-852-6495, Fax: 502-852-2365, E-mail: beth.boehm@louisville.edu.

College of Arts and Sciences Students: 545 full-time (288 women), 271 part-time (143 women); includes 146 minority (78 Black or African American, non-Hispanic/Latino; 15 Asian, non-Hispanic/Latino; 24 Hispanic/Latino; 29 Two or more races, non-Hispanic/Latino), 93 international. Average age 32. 625 applicants, 52% accepted, 192 enrolled. *Faculty:* 407 full-time (172 women), 175 part-time/adjunct (105 women). Expenses: Contact institution. *Financial support:* In 2016–17, 10 research assistantships with full tuition reimbursements (averaging $18,000 per year), 240 teaching assistantships with full tuition reimbursements (averaging $18,000 per year) were awarded; scholarships/grants, health care benefits, and unspecified assistantships also available. In 2016, 125 master's, 16 doctorates, 43 other advanced degrees awarded. *Program availability:* Part-time, 100% online. Offers African and Diaspora studies (MA); African-American studies (MA); analytical chemistry (MS, PhD); anthropology (MA); applied and industrial mathematics (PhD); applied geography (MS); applied sociology (PhD); art history (MA, PhD); arts and sciences (MA, MFA, MPA, MS, MUP, PhD, Certificate); biochemistry (MS, PhD); biology (MS); chemical physics (PhD); civic leadership (MA); clinical psychology (PhD); communication (MA); criminal justice (MS, PhD); culture, criticism, and contemporary thought (PhD); curatorial studies (MA); design (MFA); digital politics (MA); English (MA); English rhetoric and composition (PhD); environmental biology (PhD); experimental psychology (PhD); French (MA); history (MA); humanities (MA, PhD); inorganic chemistry (MS, PhD); linguistics (MA); mathematics (MA); organic chemistry (MS, PhD); performance (MFA); physical chemistry (MS, PhD); physics (MS, PhD); political science (MA); public administration (MPA); public arts and letters (PhD); public history (Certificate); sociology (MA); Spanish (MA); studio art (MFA); traditional humanities (MA); translation and interpretation (Certificate); urban and public affairs (MA); urban planning (MUP); women's and gender studies (MA, Certificate). *Application deadline:* Applications are processed on a rolling basis. *Application fee:* $60. Electronic applications accepted. *Application Contact:* Dr. Janet Woodruff-Borden, Associate Dean for Graduate Education, 502-852-8966, Fax: 502-852-6888, E-mail: j.woodruff-borden@louisville.edu. *Dean,* Dr. Kimberly Kempf-Leonard, 502-852-6490, Fax: 502-852-6888, E-mail: kleonard@louisville.edu.

College of Business Students: 281 full-time (100 women), 36 part-time (13 women); includes 44 minority (15 Black or African American, non-Hispanic/Latino; 1 American Indian or Alaska Native, non-Hispanic/Latino; 13 Asian, non-Hispanic/Latino; 10 Hispanic/Latino; 5 Two or more races, non-Hispanic/Latino), 27 international. Average age 30. 342 applicants, 61% accepted, 177 enrolled. *Faculty:* 78 full-time (25 women), 19 part-time/adjunct (2 women). Expenses: Contact institution. *Financial support:* Fellowships with full tuition reimbursements, research assistantships with full tuition reimbursements, teaching assistantships with full tuition reimbursements, scholarships/grants, health care benefits, and unspecified assistantships available. Financial award application deadline: 3/15; financial award applicants required to submit FAFSA. In 2016, 52 master's awarded. *Program availability:* Part-time. Offers accountancy (MAC); business (MAC, MBA, PhD); entrepreneurship (PhD); global business (MBA); health sector management (MBA). *Application deadline:* For fall admission, 3/31 for domestic students, 5/1 priority date for international students; for spring admission, 12/1 for domestic students, 11/1 priority date for international students; for summer admission, 4/1 priority date for international students. Applications are processed on a rolling basis. *Application fee:* $60. *Application Contact:* Susan E. Hildebrand, Program Director, 502-852-7257, Fax: 502-852-4901, E-mail: s.hildebrand@louisville.edu. *Dean,* Dr. Todd Mooradian, 502-852-6443, Fax: 502-852-7557, E-mail: todd.mooradian@louisville.edu.

College of Education and Human Development Students: 582 full-time (267 women), 625 part-time (414 women); includes 306 minority (185 Black or African American, non-Hispanic/Latino; 2 American Indian or Alaska Native, non-Hispanic/Latino; 25 Asian, non-Hispanic/Latino; 57 Hispanic/Latino; 3 Native Hawaiian or other Pacific Islander, non-Hispanic/Latino; 34 Two or more races, non-Hispanic/Latino), 14 international. Average age 33. 627 applicants, 67% accepted, 282 enrolled. *Faculty:* 100 full-time (66 women), 115 part-time/adjunct (72 women). Expenses: Contact institution. *Financial support:* In 2016–17, 3 fellowships with full tuition reimbursements (averaging $20,694 per year), 31 research assistantships with full tuition reimbursements (averaging $20,694 per year), 7 teaching assistantships with full tuition reimbursements (averaging $20,694 per year) were awarded; Federal Work-Study, scholarships/grants, health care benefits, and unspecified assistantships also available. Financial award application deadline: 3/1; financial award applicants required to submit FAFSA. In 2016, 180 master's, 8 doctorates, 17 other advanced degrees awarded. *Program availability:* Part-time, evening/weekend, 100% online, blended/hybrid learning. Offers art education (MAT); autism and applied behavior analysis (Certificate); community health education (M Ed); counseling and personnel services (M Ed, PhD); curriculum and instruction (PhD); early elementary education (MAT); education and human development (M Ed, MA, MAT, MS, Ed D, PhD, Certificate, Ed S); educational leadership and organizational development (Ed D, PhD); exercise physiology (MS); health and physical education (MAT); health professions education (Certificate); higher education (MA); higher education administration (MA); human resources and organization development (MS); instructional technology (M Ed); interdisciplinary early childhood education (MAT);

middle school education (MAT); music education (MAT); P-12 educational administration (Ed S); secondary education (MAT); special education (MAT); sport administration (MS); teacher leadership (M Ed). *Application deadline:* For fall admission, 6/1 priority date for domestic students; for spring admission, 10/1 priority date for domestic students; for summer admission, 3/1 priority date for domestic students. *Application fee:* $60. *Application Contact:* Betty Hampton, Director, Graduate Student Services, 502-852-0411, Fax: 502-852-1465, E-mail: betty.hampton@louisville.edu. *Dean, College of Education and Human Development,* Dr. Elisabeth A. Larson, 502-852-6411, Fax: 502-852-1464, E-mail: ann.larson@louisville.edu.

Raymond A. Kent School of Social Work Students: 384 full-time (324 women), 81 part-time (65 women); includes 116 minority (65 Black or African American, non-Hispanic/Latino; 7 Asian, non-Hispanic/Latino; 18 Hispanic/Latino; 1 Native Hawaiian or other Pacific Islander, non-Hispanic/Latino; 25 Two or more races, non-Hispanic/Latino), 7 international. Average age 31. 419 applicants, 63% accepted, 184 enrolled. *Faculty:* 29 full-time (19 women), 51 part-time/adjunct (42 women). Expenses: Contact institution. *Financial support:* In 2016–17, 12 research assistantships with full tuition reimbursements (averaging $21,500 per year) were awarded; health care benefits and unspecified assistantships also available. Financial award application deadline: 5/15; financial award applicants required to submit FAFSA. In 2016, 191 master's, 2 doctorates awarded. *Program availability:* Part-time, evening/weekend, 100% online, blended/hybrid learning. Offers marriage and family therapy (PMC); social work (MSSW, PhD). *Application deadline:* For fall admission, 5/30 for domestic and international students; for spring admission, 9/30 for domestic and international students; for summer admission, 2/28 for domestic and international students. Applications are processed on a rolling basis. *Application fee:* $60. Electronic applications accepted. *Application Contact:* Misty Kupka, Program Manager for Admissions and Recruitment, 502-852-0414, Fax: 502-852-0422, E-mail: misty.kupka@louisville.edu. *Dean,* Dr. David Jenkins, 502-852-3944, Fax: 502-852-0422, E-mail: dajenk03@exchange.louisville.edu.

School of Music Students: 54 full-time (20 women), 5 part-time (3 women); includes 5 minority (2 Black or African American, non-Hispanic/Latino; 1 Hispanic/Latino; 2 Two or more races, non-Hispanic/Latino), 7 international. Average age 25. 62 applicants, 66% accepted, 25 enrolled. *Faculty:* 36 full-time (10 women), 39 part-time/adjunct (18 women). Expenses: Contact institution. *Financial support:* In 2016–17, 1 fellowship with full tuition reimbursement (averaging $12,000 per year), 12 teaching assistantships with full tuition reimbursements (averaging $12,000 per year) were awarded; Federal Work-Study, scholarships/grants, health care benefits, and unspecified assistantships also available. Financial award application deadline: 3/1. In 2016, 31 master's awarded. *Program availability:* Part-time. Offers composition (MM); electronic composition (MM); music education (MME); music history and literature (MM); music performance (MM); music theory (MM). *Application fee:* $60. Electronic applications accepted. *Application Contact:* Laura Angermeier, Admissions Counselor/Senior Advising Counselor, 502-852-1623, Fax: 502-852-0520, E-mail: leange01@louisville.edu. *Dean,* Dr. Christopher P. Doane, 502-852-6907, Fax: 502-852-0520, E-mail: c0doan01@louisville.edu.

School of Nursing Students: 135 full-time (120 women), 27 part-time (25 women); includes 26 minority (13 Black or African American, non-Hispanic/Latino; 5 Asian, non-Hispanic/Latino; 3 Hispanic/Latino; 5 Two or more races, non-Hispanic/Latino), 4 international. Average age 33. 77 applicants, 78% accepted, 51 enrolled. *Faculty:* 51 full-time (46 women), 37 part-time/adjunct (34 women). Expenses: Contact institution. *Financial support:* In 2016–17, 8 research assistantships with full tuition reimbursements (averaging $20,000 per year), 4 teaching assistantships with full tuition reimbursements (averaging $15,000 per year) were awarded; fellowships with full tuition reimbursements, scholarships/grants, and unspecified assistantships also available. Financial award application deadline: 10/1; financial award applicants required to submit FAFSA. In 2016, 43 master's, 2 doctorates awarded. *Program availability:* Part-time. Offers adult gerontology nurse practitioner (MSN, DNP); education and administration (MSN); family nurse practitioner (MSN, DNP); neonatal nurse practitioner (MSN, DNP); nursing research (PhD); psychiatric/mental health nurse practitioner (MSN, DNP); women's health nurse practitioner (MSN). *Application deadline:* For fall admission, 1/15 priority date for domestic students, 1/15 for international students; for summer admission, 10/15 priority date for domestic students. *Application fee:* $60. Electronic applications accepted. *Application Contact:* Trish Hart, Assistant Dean for Student Affairs, 502-852-5825, Fax: 502-852-8783, E-mail: trish.hart@louisville.edu. *Dean and Professor,* Dr. Marcia J. Hern, 502-852-8300, Fax: 502-852-8783, E-mail: m.hern@louisville.edu.

School of Public Health and Information Sciences Students: 115 full-time (77 women), 62 part-time (45 women); includes 50 minority (25 Black or African American, non-Hispanic/Latino; 15 Asian, non-Hispanic/Latino; 6 Hispanic/Latino; 4 Two or more races, non-Hispanic/Latino), 31 international. Average age 31. 169 applicants, 67% accepted, 67 enrolled. *Faculty:* 40 full-time (15 women), 8 part-time/adjunct (4 women). Expenses: Contact institution. *Financial support:* In 2016–17, 3 fellowships with full tuition reimbursements (averaging $20,000 per year), 8 research assistantships with full tuition reimbursements (averaging $20,000 per year), 2 teaching assistantships with full tuition reimbursements (averaging $20,000 per year) were awarded; career-related internships or fieldwork, Federal Work-Study, scholarships/grants, health care benefits, and unspecified assistantships also available. Support available to part-time students. Financial award application deadline: 5/1; financial award applicants required to submit FAFSA. In 2016, 38 master's, 8 doctorates awarded. *Program availability:* Part-time, evening/weekend. Offers biostatistics (MPH, MS, PhD); decision science (MS); epidemiology (MPH, MS); health policy (MPH); population health management (MPH); public health and information sciences (MPH, MS, PhD); public health sciences (PhD). *Application deadline:* For fall admission, 7/1 for domestic students, 3/1 for international students; for spring admission, 11/1 for domestic students, 10/1 for international students; for summer admission, 4/1 for domestic students, 3/1 for international students. Applications are processed on a rolling basis. *Application fee:* $60. Electronic applications accepted. *Application Contact:* Vicki Lewis, Administrative Assistant, 502-852-1798, Fax: 502-852-3294, E-mail: vicki.lewis@louisville.edu. *Associate Dean for Academic Affairs,* Dr. Craig Elliot Blakely, 502-852-3297, Fax: 502-852-3291, E-mail: craig.blakely@louisville.edu.

J. B. Speed School of Engineering Students: 327 full-time (74 women), 302 part-time (49 women); includes 81 minority (22 Black or African American, non-Hispanic/Latino; 1 American Indian or Alaska Native, non-Hispanic/Latino; 22 Asian, non-Hispanic/Latino; 23 Hispanic/Latino; 13 Two or more races, non-Hispanic/Latino), 217 international. Average age 29. 367 applicants, 39% accepted, 98 enrolled. *Faculty:* 103 full-time (21 women), 14 part-time/adjunct (4 women). Expenses: Contact institution. *Financial support:* In 2016–17, 12 students received support. Fellowships with full tuition reimbursements available, research assistantships with full tuition reimbursements

available, teaching assistantships with full tuition reimbursements available, scholarships/grants, health care benefits, and tuition waivers (full) available. Financial award application deadline: 2/1. In 2016, 130 master's, 9 doctorates, 2 other advanced degrees awarded. *Program availability:* Online learning. Offers bioengineering (M Eng); chemical engineering (M Eng, MS, PhD); civil engineering (M Eng, MS, PhD); computer engineering and computer science (M Eng, MS, PhD); data mining (Certificate); electrical and computer engineering (M Eng, MS, PhD); engineering (M Eng, MS, PhD, Certificate, Graduate Certificate); engineering management (M Eng); industrial engineering (M Eng, MS, PhD); logistics and distribution (Certificate); mechanical engineering (M Eng, MS, PhD); network and information security (Certificate). *Application deadline:* For fall admission, 6/1 for domestic students, 6/1 priority date for international students; for spring admission, 11/1 for domestic students, 11/1 priority date for international students; for summer admission, 3/1 for domestic students, 4/1 priority date for international students. *Application fee:* $60. Electronic applications accepted. *Application Contact:* Dr. Michael Harris, Director of Academic Programs, J. B. Speed School of Engineering, 502-852-6278, Fax: 502-852-7294, E-mail: mharris@louisville.edu. *Dean,* Dr. John S. Usher, 502-852-6281, Fax: 502-852-7033, E-mail: john.usher@louisville.edu.

Louis D. Brandeis School of Law *Program availability:* Part-time. Offers law (JD). Electronic applications accepted.

School of Dentistry Students: 516 full-time (225 women), 18 part-time (10 women); includes 113 minority (21 Black or African American, non-Hispanic/Latino; 56 Asian, non-Hispanic/Latino; 22 Hispanic/Latino; 14 Two or more races, non-Hispanic/Latino), 25 international. Average age 26. 185 applicants, 95% accepted, 142 enrolled. *Faculty:* 80 full-time (28 women), 77 part-time/adjunct (20 women). Expenses: Contact institution. *Financial support:* In 2016–17, 1 research assistantship with full tuition reimbursement (averaging $20,000 per year) was awarded. Financial award application deadline: 3/15; financial award applicants required to submit FAFSA. In 2016, 7 master's, 113 doctorates awarded. *Program availability:* Part-time. Offers dentistry (DMD); oral biology (MS). *Application deadline:* For fall admission, 1/1 for domestic and international students. Applications are processed on a rolling basis. *Application fee:* $60. Electronic applications accepted. *Application Contact:* Robin Benningfield, Admissions Counselor, 502-852-5081, Fax: 502-852-1210, E-mail: dmdadms@louisville.edu. *Dean,* Dr. T Gerry Bradley, 502-852-5295, E-mail: t0brad03@exchange.louisville.edu.

School of Interdisciplinary and Graduate Studies Students: 24 full-time (16 women), 8 part-time (4 women); includes 4 minority (1 Asian, non-Hispanic/Latino; 1 Hispanic/Latino; 2 Two or more races, non-Hispanic/Latino), 7 international. Average age 31. 35 applicants, 51% accepted, 12 enrolled. Expenses: Contact institution. *Financial support:* In 2016–17, 120 fellowships with full tuition reimbursements (averaging $20,000 per year) were awarded. Financial award application deadline: 1/15. *Program availability:* Part-time. Offers interdisciplinary (MA, MS, PhD). *Application deadline:* For fall admission, 12/1 priority date for domestic and international students; for winter admission, 11/1 for domestic students, 6/1 for international students; for spring admission, 11/1 for domestic students, 6/1 for international students; for summer admission, 4/1 for domestic students, 1/1 for international students. Applications are processed on a rolling basis. *Application fee:* $65. Electronic applications accepted. *Application Contact:* Dr. Paul DeMarco, Associate Dean, 502-852-6490, E-mail: gradadm@louisville.edu. *Dean and Vice Provost for Graduate Affairs,* Dr. Beth A. Boehm, 502-852-6495, E-mail: beth.boehm@louisville.edu.

School of Medicine Students: 888 full-time (447 women), 30 part-time (15 women); includes 182 minority (56 Black or African American, non-Hispanic/Latino; 80 Asian, non-Hispanic/Latino; 19 Hispanic/Latino; 27 Two or more races, non-Hispanic/Latino), 43 international. Average age 26. 4,225 applicants, 10% accepted, 271 enrolled. *Faculty:* 793 full-time (293 women), 110 part-time/adjunct (47 women). Expenses: Contact institution. *Financial support:* In 2016–17, 165 students received support, including 55 fellowships with full tuition reimbursements available (averaging $23,500 per year), 110 research assistantships with full tuition reimbursements available (averaging $24,000 per year); institutionally sponsored loans, scholarships/grants, traineeships, and unspecified assistantships also available. In 2016, 28 master's, 169 doctorates awarded. Offers anatomical sciences and neurobiology (MS, PhD); audiology (Au D); biochemistry and molecular biology (MS, PhD); medicine (MS, Au D, MD, PhD); microbiology and immunology (MS, PhD); pharmacology and toxicology (MS, PhD); physiology and biophysics (MS, PhD); speech-language pathology (MS). *Application deadline:* For fall admission, 10/28 for domestic students, 10/15 for international students. Applications are processed on a rolling basis. *Application fee:* $60. Electronic applications accepted. *Application Contact:* Judy C. Hollkamp, Program Coordinator, 502-852-3805, E-mail: jcholl01@louisville.edu. *Dean,* Dr. Toni M. Ganzel, 502-852-1499, Fax: 502-852-1484, E-mail: toni.ganzel@louisville.edu.

UNIVERSITY OF MAINE, Orono, ME 04469

General Information State-supported, coed, university. CGS member. *Enrollment:* 11,219 graduate, professional, and undergraduate students; 1,169 full-time matriculated graduate/professional students (637 women), 395 part-time matriculated graduate/professional students (291 women). *Enrollment by degree level:* 1,011 master's, 434 doctoral, 119 other advanced degrees. *Graduate faculty:* 637 full-time (221 women), 198 part-time/adjunct (87 women). Tuition, state resident: full-time $7524; part-time $2508 per credit. Tuition, nonresident: full-time $24,498; part-time $8166 per credit. *Required fees:* $1148; $571 per credit. *Graduate housing:* Rooms and/or apartments available on a first-come, first-served basis to single and married students. Typical cost: $7612 (including board) for single students; $9396 (including board) for married students. Housing application deadline: 8/1. *Student services:* Campus employment opportunities, campus safety program, career counseling, child daycare facilities, exercise/wellness program, free psychological counseling, grant writing training, international student services, low-cost health insurance, multicultural affairs office, services for students with disabilities, teacher training, writing training. *Library facilities:* Fogler Library. *Collection:* Books: 1.2 million (physical), 850,047 (digital/electronic); Serial titles: 420 (physical), 117,230 (digital/electronic); Databases: 379. Weekly public service hours: 103; students can reserve study rooms. *Research affiliation:* Jackson Laboratory (medical genetics), Bigelow Laboratories for Ocean Sciences (marine science), Mount Desert Island Biological Laboratory (marine molecular biology), Sensor Research Development Corporation (electrical sensors), Maine Medical Center Research Institute (clinical medicine), Maine Institute for Human Genetics (medical genetics).

Computer facilities: Computer purchase and lease plans are available. 600 computers available on campus for general student use. A campuswide network can be accessed from student residence rooms and from off campus. Online class registration, online housing and financial aid information are available.
Website: http://www.umaine.edu/

University of Maine

General Application Contact: Scott G. Delcourt, Assistant Vice President for Graduate Studies and Senior Associate Dean, 207-581-3291, Fax: 207-581-3232, E-mail: graduate@maine.edu.

GRADUATE UNITS

Graduate School Students: 1,169 full-time (637 women), 395 part-time (291 women); includes 89 minority (11 Black or African American, non-Hispanic/Latino; 34 American Indian or Alaska Native, non-Hispanic/Latino; 13 Asian, non-Hispanic/Latino; 26 Hispanic/Latino; 2 Native Hawaiian or other Pacific Islander, non-Hispanic/Latino; 3 Two or more races, non-Hispanic/Latino), 218 international. Average age 33. 1,520 applicants, 59% accepted, 549 enrolled. *Faculty:* 637 full-time (221 women), 198 part-time/adjunct (87 women). Expenses: Contact institution. *Financial support:* In 2016–17, 700 students received support, including 30 fellowships with full tuition reimbursements available (averaging $20,200 per year), 277 research assistantships with full tuition reimbursements available (averaging $16,800 per year), 263 teaching assistantships with full tuition reimbursements available (averaging $14,100 per year); career-related internships or fieldwork, Federal Work-Study, institutionally sponsored loans, scholarships/grants, tuition waivers (full and partial), and unspecified assistantships also available. Support available to part-time students. Financial award application deadline: 3/1; financial award applicants required to submit FAFSA. In 2016, 361 master's, 60 doctorates, 59 other advanced degrees awarded. *Program availability:* Part-time, evening/weekend, online learning. Offers interdisciplinary studies (MA, PhD); intermedia (MFA). *Application deadline:* For fall admission, 1/15 priority date for domestic and international students; for spring admission, 11/15 priority date for domestic and international students. Applications are processed on a rolling basis. *Application fee:* $65. Electronic applications accepted. *Assistant Vice President for Graduate Studies/Senior Associate Dean,* Scott G. Delcourt, 207-581-3291, Fax: 207-581-3232, E-mail: graduate@maine.edu.

Climate Change Institute Students: 10 full-time (9 women), 2 part-time (1 woman). Average age 26. 17 applicants, 53% accepted, 5 enrolled. *Faculty:* 41 full-time (11 women). Expenses: Contact institution. *Financial support:* In 2016–17, 8 students received support, including 5 research assistantships with full tuition reimbursements available (averaging $15,200 per year); unspecified assistantships also available. Financial award application deadline: 3/1. In 2016, 4 master's awarded. *Program availability:* Part-time. Offers climate change (MS, CGS). *Application deadline:* For fall admission, 11/1 priority date for domestic and international students; for spring admission, 2/1 priority date for domestic and international students. Applications are processed on a rolling basis. *Application fee:* $65. Electronic applications accepted. *Application Contact:* Dr. Karl Kreutz, Graduate Coordinator, 207-581-3011, E-mail: karl.kreutz@maine.edu. *Director,* Dr. Paul Mayewski, 207-581-3019, Fax: 207-581-1203, E-mail: paul.mayewski@maine.edu.

College of Education and Human Development Students: 150 full-time (118 women), 269 part-time (225 women); includes 24 minority (3 Black or African American, non-Hispanic/Latino; 10 American Indian or Alaska Native, non-Hispanic/Latino; 7 Hispanic/Latino; 1 Native Hawaiian or other Pacific Islander, non-Hispanic/Latino; 3 Two or more races, non-Hispanic/Latino), 7 international. Average age 37. 235 applicants, 94% accepted, 168 enrolled. *Faculty:* 36 full-time (21 women), 40 part-time/adjunct (30 women). Expenses: Contact institution. *Financial support:* In 2016–17, 51 students received support, including 19 teaching assistantships with full tuition reimbursements available (averaging $14,600 per year); fellowships, career-related internships or fieldwork, Federal Work-Study, institutionally sponsored loans, scholarships/grants, and unspecified assistantships also available. Support available to part-time students. Financial award application deadline: 3/1. In 2016, 85 master's, 4 doctorates, 58 other advanced degrees awarded. *Program availability:* Part-time, evening/weekend. Offers classroom technology integrationist (CGS); counselor education (M Ed, MA, MS, CAS); early childhood teacher (CGS); education (PhD); education and human development (M Ed, MA, MAT, MS, Ed D, PhD, CAS, CGS); education data specialist (CGS); educational leadership (M Ed, CAS); educational technology coordinator (CGS); elementary education (M Ed, CAS); higher education (CAS); human development (MS); individualized education (M Ed); kinesiology and physical education (M Ed, MS); literacy education (CAS); response to intervention for behavior (CGS); science education (M Ed, MS); secondary education (M Ed, CAS); social studies education (M Ed); special education (M Ed, CAS); STEM education (PhD). *Application deadline:* For fall admission, 1/15 priority date for domestic students. Applications are processed on a rolling basis. *Application fee:* $65. Electronic applications accepted. *Application Contact:* Scott G. Delcourt, Senior Associate Dean of the Graduate School, 207-581-3291, Fax: 207-581-3232, E-mail: graduate@maine.edu. *Dean,* Dr. Timothy Reagan, 207-581-2441, Fax: 207-581-2423.

College of Engineering Students: 96 full-time (21 women), 43 part-time (7 women); includes 10 minority (1 Black or African American, non-Hispanic/Latino; 1 American Indian or Alaska Native, non-Hispanic/Latino; 4 Asian, non-Hispanic/Latino; 2 Hispanic/Latino; 2 Two or more races, non-Hispanic/Latino), 60 international. Average age 31. 118 applicants, 69% accepted, 28 enrolled. *Faculty:* 47 full-time (8 women), 9 part-time/adjunct (1 woman). Expenses: Contact institution. *Financial support:* In 2016–17, 67 students received support, including 3 fellowships (averaging $25,100 per year), 30 research assistantships (averaging $14,600 per year), 22 teaching assistantships (averaging $14,600 per year); Federal Work-Study, institutionally sponsored loans, scholarships/grants, tuition waivers (full and partial), and unspecified assistantships also available. Financial award application deadline: 3/1. In 2016, 19 master's, 12 doctorates awarded. *Program availability:* Part-time. Offers chemical engineering (MS, PhD); civil and environmental engineering (MS, PSM, PhD); computer engineering (MS); electrical engineering (MS, PhD); engineering (ME, MS, PSM, PhD); mechanical engineering (MS, PSM, PhD). *Application deadline:* For fall admission, 2/1 priority date for domestic students. Applications are processed on a rolling basis. *Application fee:* $65. Electronic applications accepted. *Application Contact:* Scott G. Delcourt, Assistant Vice President for Graduate Studies and Senior Associate Dean, 207-581-3291, Fax: 207-581-3232, E-mail: graduate@maine.edu. *Dean,* Dr. Dana Humphrey, 207-581-2217, Fax: 207-581-2220, E-mail: dana.humphrey@umit.maine.edu.

College of Liberal Arts and Sciences Students: 235 full-time (95 women), 69 part-time (32 women); includes 26 minority (3 Black or African American, non-Hispanic/Latino; 4 American Indian or Alaska Native, non-Hispanic/Latino; 4 Asian, non-Hispanic/Latino; 7 Hispanic/Latino; 8 Two or more races, non-Hispanic/Latino), 58 international. Average age 30. 335 applicants, 49% accepted, 87 enrolled. *Faculty:* 140 full-time (41 women), 40 part-time/adjunct (18 women). Expenses: Contact institution. *Financial support:* In 2016–17, 223 students received support, including 18 fellowships (averaging $17,000 per year), 34 research assistantships (averaging $14,600 per year), 142 teaching assistantships (averaging $14,600 per year); career-related internships or fieldwork, Federal Work-Study, institutionally sponsored loans, scholarships/grants, and tuition waivers (full and partial) also available. Support

available to part-time students. Financial award application deadline: 3/1. In 2016, 71 master's, 14 doctorates, 2 other advanced degrees awarded. *Program availability:* Part-time, evening/weekend. Offers anthropology and environmental policy (PhD); chemistry (MS, PhD); communication and journalism (MA, PhD); computing and information science (MS, PhD, CGS); English (MA); French (MA, MAT); global policy (MA); history (MA, PhD); liberal arts and sciences (MA, MAT, ME, MM, MS, MST, PhD, CGS); mathematics (MA); performing arts (MM); physics and astronomy (ME, MS, PhD); psychological sciences (PhD); Spanish (MAT). *Application deadline:* For fall admission, 2/1 priority date for domestic students. Applications are processed on a rolling basis. *Application fee:* $65. Electronic applications accepted. *Application Contact:* Scott G. Delcourt, Assistant Vice President for Graduate Studies and Senior Associate Dean, 207-581-3291, Fax: 207-581-3232, E-mail: graduate@maine.edu. *Dean,* Dr. Emily Haddad, 207-581-1954, Fax: 207-581-1947, E-mail: emily.haddad@maine.edu.

College of Natural Sciences, Forestry, and Agriculture Students: 419 full-time (277 women), 92 part-time (58 women); includes 32 minority (3 Black or African American, non-Hispanic/Latino; 10 American Indian or Alaska Native, non-Hispanic/Latino; 6 Asian, non-Hispanic/Latino; 8 Hispanic/Latino; 5 Two or more races, non-Hispanic/Latino), 75 international. Average age 30. 707 applicants, 44% accepted, 187 enrolled. *Faculty:* 191 full-time (83 women), 104 part-time/adjunct (34 women). Expenses: Contact institution. *Financial support:* In 2016–17, 293 students received support, including 7 fellowships (averaging $23,400 per year), 177 research assistantships (averaging $16,300 per year), 66 teaching assistantships (averaging $14,600 per year); career-related internships or fieldwork, Federal Work-Study, institutionally sponsored loans, scholarships/grants, health care benefits, tuition waivers (full and partial), and unspecified assistantships also available. Support available to part-time students. Financial award application deadline: 3/1. In 2016, 129 master's, 27 doctorates, 9 other advanced degrees awarded. *Program availability:* Part-time, evening/weekend. Offers biological sciences (PhD); botany and plant pathology (MS); communication sciences and disorders (MA); earth and climate sciences (MS, PhD); economics (MA); entomology (MS); financial economics (MA); forest resources (MF, MS, PhD); horticulture (MS); individualized (MS); marine sciences (MS, PSM, PhD); microbiology (PhD); natural sciences, forestry, and agriculture (MA, MF, MPS, MS, MSW, MWC, PSM, PhD, CAS, CGS); nursing education (CGS); resource economics and policy (MS); rural health family nurse practitioner (MS, CAS); social work (MSW, CGS); wildlife ecology (PhD); zoology (MS, PhD). *Application deadline:* For fall admission, 2/1 priority date for domestic students. Applications are processed on a rolling basis. *Application fee:* $65. Electronic applications accepted. *Application Contact:* Scott G. Delcourt, Assistant Vice President for Graduate Studies and Senior Associate Dean, 207-581-3291, Fax: 207-581-3232, E-mail: graduate@maine.edu. *Interim Dean,* Dr. Fred Servello, 207-581-3206, Fax: 207-581-3207.

Graduate School of Biomedical Science and Engineering Students: 28 full-time (17 women), 16 part-time (9 women); includes 1 minority (Two or more races, non-Hispanic/Latino), 13 international. Average age 30. 51 applicants, 20% accepted, 8 enrolled. *Faculty:* 149 full-time (47 women). Expenses: Contact institution. *Financial support:* In 2016–17, 33 students received support, including 2 fellowships with full tuition reimbursements available (averaging $21,500 per year), 28 research assistantships with full tuition reimbursements available (averaging $22,500 per year), 3 teaching assistantships (averaging $9,300 per year). Financial award application deadline: 3/1. In 2016, 8 doctorates awarded. Offers bioinformatics (PSM); biomedical engineering (PhD); biomedical science (PhD). *Application deadline:* For fall admission, 1/1 priority date for domestic and international students. *Application fee:* $65. *Application Contact:* Scott G. Delcourt, Assistant Vice President for Graduate Studies and Senior Associate Dean, 207-581-3291, Fax: 207-581-3232, E-mail: graduate@maine.edu. *Director,* Dr. David Neivandt, 207-581-2803.

The Maine Business School Students: 42 full-time (15 women), 38 part-time (20 women); includes 8 minority (1 Black or African American, non-Hispanic/Latino; 3 American Indian or Alaska Native, non-Hispanic/Latino; 2 Asian, non-Hispanic/Latino; 2 Two or more races, non-Hispanic/Latino), 6 international. Average age 29. 72 applicants, 90% accepted, 45 enrolled. *Faculty:* 24 full-time (6 women), 1 (woman) part-time/adjunct. Expenses: Contact institution. *Financial support:* In 2016–17, 11 students received support, including 3 teaching assistantships (averaging $14,600 per year); career-related internships or fieldwork, Federal Work-Study, institutionally sponsored loans, scholarships/grants, tuition waivers (full and partial), and unspecified assistantships also available. Financial award application deadline: 3/1. In 2016, 22 master's, 4 other advanced degrees awarded. *Program availability:* Part-time, evening/weekend, online learning. Offers business (MBA, CGS). *Application deadline:* For fall admission, 2/1 priority date for domestic students, 5/1 priority date for international students; for spring admission, 11/1 priority date for domestic students, 9/1 priority date for international students; for summer admission, 4/1 priority date for domestic students, 2/1 priority date for international students. Applications are processed on a rolling basis. *Application fee:* $65. Electronic applications accepted. *Application Contact:* Scott G. Delcourt, Assistant Vice President for Graduate Studies and Senior Associate Dean, 207-581-3291, Fax: 207-581-3232, E-mail: graduate@maine.edu. *Manager of MBA Programs, Executive Education and Internships,* Richard Borgman, 207-581-1870, Fax: 207-581-1930, E-mail: borgman@maine.edu.

University of Maine School of Law Students: 219 full-time (109 women), 15 part-time (9 women); includes 21 minority (7 Black or African American, non-Hispanic/Latino; 4 American Indian or Alaska Native, non-Hispanic/Latino; 4 Asian, non-Hispanic/Latino; 6 Hispanic/Latino), 2 international. Average age 27. 486 applicants, 66% accepted, 76 enrolled. *Faculty:* 19 full-time (8 women), 21 part-time/adjunct (14 women). Expenses: Contact institution. *Financial support:* In 2016–17, 168 students received support, including 28 fellowships (averaging $3,300 per year), 6 research assistantships (averaging $2,000 per year); teaching assistantships, Federal Work-Study, and scholarships/grants also available. Financial award application deadline: 2/15; financial award applicants required to submit FAFSA. In 2016, 82 doctorates awarded. *Program availability:* Part-time. Offers law (JD). JD/MBA offered in conjunction with the University of Southern Maine; JD/MPH and JD/MPPM offered with the Muskie School of Public Service. *Application deadline:* For fall admission, 4/15 for domestic and international students. Applications are processed on a rolling basis. *Application fee:* $0. Electronic applications accepted. *Application Contact:* Caroline Wilshusen, Director of Admissions, 207-780-4341, Fax: 207-780-4239, E-mail: lawadmissions@maine.edu. *Dean,* Danielle Conway, 207-780-4344, Fax: 207-780-4239.

UNIVERSITY OF MAINE AT FARMINGTON, Farmington, ME 04938

General Information State-supported, coed, comprehensive institution. *Enrollment:* 2,000 graduate, professional, and undergraduate students; 73 full-time matriculated graduate/professional students (62 women). *Enrollment by degree level:* 73 master's. *Graduate faculty:* 6 full-time (5 women), 7 part-time/adjunct (5 women). *Student* *services:* Exercise/wellness program, low-cost health insurance, services for students with disabilities. *Library facilities:* Mantor Library plus 1 other. *Collection:* Books: 59,750 (physical), 249,038 (digital/electronic); Serial titles: 184 (physical), 76,545 (digital/electronic); Databases: 135. Weekly public service hours: 88; students can reserve study rooms.

Computer facilities: Computer purchase and lease plans are available. 220 computers available on campus for general student use. A campuswide network can be accessed from student residence rooms and from off campus. Online class registration is available.
Website: http://www.umf.maine.edu/

General Application Contact: Valerie Soucie, Administrative Specialist, 207-778-7502, Fax: 207-778-8134, E-mail: gradstudies@maine.edu.

GRADUATE UNITS

Graduate Programs in Education Students: 90 part-time (76 women). Average age 36. 30 applicants, 100% accepted, 29 enrolled. *Faculty:* 7 full-time (6 women), 6 part-time/adjunct (3 women). *Expenses:* Contact institution. *Financial support:* Applicants required to submit FAFSA. In 2016, 14 master's awarded. *Program availability:* Part-time-only, evening/weekend, 100% online, blended/hybrid learning. Offers early childhood education (MS Ed); educational leadership (MS Ed); instructional technology (M Ed). M Ed offered in collaboration with University of Maine and University of Southern Maine. *Application deadline:* For fall admission, 8/10 for domestic students; for spring admission, 1/5 for domestic students; for summer admission, 4/10 for domestic students. Applications are processed on a rolling basis. *Application fee:* $60. Electronic applications accepted. *Application Contact:* Valerie Soucie, Administrative Specialist, 207-778-7502, Fax: 207-778-8134, E-mail: gradstudies@maine.edu. *Director of Graduate Programs in Education*, Dr. Johanna Prince, 207-778-7066, E-mail: gradstudies@maine.edu.

UNIVERSITY OF MANAGEMENT AND TECHNOLOGY, Arlington, VA 22209-1609

General Information Proprietary, coed, comprehensive institution. *Enrollment:* 1,293 graduate, professional, and undergraduate students; 238 full-time matriculated graduate/professional students (64 women), 65 part-time matriculated graduate/professional students (26 women). *Graduate faculty:* 50 full-time (8 women). *Graduate housing:* On-campus housing not available. *Student services:* Career counseling, international student services. *Collection:* Books: 9,149 (physical), 35 (digital/electronic).

Computer facilities: A campuswide network can be accessed from off campus. Online class registration is available.
Website: http://www.umtweb.edu/

General Application Contact: Kenny Hickey, Admissions, 703-516-0035, Fax: 703-516-0985, E-mail: admissions@umtweb.edu.

GRADUATE UNITS

Program in Business Administration *Program availability:* Part-time, evening/weekend, online learning. Offers general management (MBA, DBA); project management (MBA). Electronic applications accepted.

Program in Computer Science *Program availability:* Part-time, evening/weekend, online learning. Offers computer science (MS); information technology (AC); project management (AC); software engineering (MS). Electronic applications accepted.

Program in Criminal Justice *Program availability:* Part-time, evening/weekend, online learning. Offers homeland security (MS).

Program in Engineering Management Offers engineering management (MS).

Program in Health Administration Offers health administration (MHA).

Program in Homeland Security Offers homeland security (MS).

Program in Information Technology Offers information technology (MS, Advanced Certificate).

Program in Management *Program availability:* Part-time, evening/weekend, online learning. Offers acquisition management (MS, AC); criminal justice administration (MS); general management (MS); project management (MS, AC). Electronic applications accepted.

Program in Public Administration Offers public administration (MPA, Advanced Certificate).

THE UNIVERSITY OF MANCHESTER, Manchester M13 9PL, United Kingdom

General Information Public, coed, comprehensive institution.

GRADUATE UNITS

Alliance Manchester Business School Offers accounting and finance (M Sc); business (M Ent); business analysis and strategic management (M Sc); business analytics: operational research and risk analysis (M Sc); business psychology (M Sc); corporate communications and reputation management (M Sc); finance (M Sc); finance and business economics (M Sc); human resource management and industrial relations (M Sc); innovation management and entrepreneurship (M Sc); international business and management (M Sc); international human resource management and comparative industrial relations (M Sc); management (M Sc); marketing (M Sc); operations, project and supply chain management (M Sc); organizational psychology (M Sc); quantitative finance (M Sc). Electronic applications accepted.

Faculty of Life Sciences Offers adaptive organismal biology (M Phil, PhD); animal biology (M Phil, PhD); biochemistry (M Phil, PhD); bioinformatics (M Phil, PhD); biomolecular sciences (M Phil, PhD); biotechnology (M Phil, PhD); cell biology (M Phil, PhD); cell matrix research (M Phil, PhD); channels and transporters (M Phil, PhD); developmental biology (M Phil, PhD); Egyptology (M Phil, PhD); environmental biology (M Phil, PhD); evolutionary biology (M Phil, PhD); gene expression (M Phil, PhD); genetics (M Phil, PhD); history of science, technology and medicine (M Phil, PhD); immunology (M Phil, PhD); integrative neurobiology and behavior (M Phil, PhD); membrane trafficking (M Phil, PhD); microbiology (M Phil, PhD); molecular and cellular neuroscience (M Phil, PhD); molecular biology (M Phil, PhD); molecular cancer studies (M Phil, PhD); neuroscience (M Phil, PhD); ophthalmology (M Phil, PhD); optometry (M Phil, PhD); organelle function (M Phil, PhD); pharmacology (M Phil, PhD); physiology (M Phil, PhD); plant sciences (M Phil, PhD); stem cell research (M Phil, PhD); structural biology (M Phil, PhD); systems neuroscience (M Phil, PhD); toxicology (M Phil, PhD).

School of Arts, Histories and Cultures Offers anthropology, media and performance (PhD); applied theatre professional (PhD); archaeology (PhD); art history and visual studies (PhD); arts management and cultural policy (PhD); classics and ancient history (PhD); composition (PhD); creative writing (PhD); drama (PhD); economic and social history (PhD); electroacoustic composition (PhD); English and American studies (PhD);

history (PhD); humanitarianism and conflict response (PhD); museology (PhD); music (PhD); musicology (PhD); religions and theology (PhD).

School of Chemical Engineering and Analytical Science Offers biocatalysis (M Phil, PhD); chemical engineering (M Phil, PhD); chemical engineering and analytical science (M Phil, D Eng, PhD); colloids, crystals, interfaces and materials (M Phil, PhD); environment and sustainable technology (M Phil, PhD); instrumentation (M Phil, PhD); multi-scale modeling (M Phil, PhD); process integration (M Phil, PhD); systems biology (M Phil, PhD).

School of Chemistry Offers biological chemistry (PhD); chemistry (M Ent, M Phil, M Sc, D Ent, PhD); inorganic chemistry (PhD); materials chemistry (PhD); nanoscience (PhD); nuclear fission (PhD); organic chemistry (PhD); physical chemistry (PhD); theoretical chemistry (PhD).

School of Computer Science Offers computer science (M Phil, PhD).

School of Dentistry Offers basic dental sciences (cancer studies) (M Phil, PhD); basic dental sciences (molecular genetics) (M Phil, PhD); basic dental sciences (stem cell biology) (M Phil, PhD); biomaterials sciences and dental technology (M Phil, PhD); dental public health/community dentistry (M Phil, PhD); dental science (clinical) (M Phil, PhD); endodontology (M Phil, PhD); fixed and removable prosthodontics (M Phil, PhD); operative dentistry (M Phil, PhD); oral and maxillofacial surgery (M Phil, PhD); oral radiology (M Phil, PhD); orthodontics (M Phil, PhD); restorative dentistry (M Phil, PhD).

School of Earth, Atmospheric and Environmental Sciences Offers atmospheric sciences (M Phil, M Sc, PhD); basin studies and petroleum geosciences (M Phil, M Sc, PhD); earth, atmospheric and environmental sciences (M Phil, M Sc, PhD); environmental geochemistry and cosmochemistry (M Phil, M Sc, PhD); isotope geochemistry and cosmochemistry (M Phil, M Sc, PhD); paleontology (M Phil, M Sc, PhD); physics and chemistry of minerals and fluids (M Phil, M Sc, PhD); structural and petrological geosciences (M Phil, M Sc, PhD).

School of Education Offers counseling (D Couns); counseling psychology (D Couns); education (M Phil, Ed D, PhD); educational and child psychology (Ed D); educational psychology (Ed D).

School of Electrical and Electronic Engineering Offers electrical and electronic engineering (M Phil, PhD).

School of Environment and Development Offers architecture (M Phil, PhD); development policy and management (M Phil, PhD); human geography (M Phil, PhD); physical geography (M Phil, PhD); planning and landscape (M Phil, PhD).

School of Languages, Linguistics and Cultures Offers Arab world studies (PhD); Chinese studies (M Phil, PhD); East Asian studies (M Phil, PhD); English language (PhD); French studies (M Phil, PhD); German studies (M Phil, PhD); interpreting studies (PhD); Italian studies (M Phil, PhD); Japanese studies (M Phil, PhD); Latin American cultural studies (M Phil, PhD); linguistics (M Phil, PhD); Middle Eastern studies (M Phil, PhD); Polish studies (M Phil, PhD); Portuguese studies (M Phil, PhD); Russian studies (M Phil, PhD); Spanish studies (M Phil, PhD); translation and intercultural studies (M Phil, PhD).

School of Law Offers bioethics and medical jurisprudence (PhD); criminology (M Phil, PhD); law (M Phil, PhD).

School of Materials Offers advanced aerospace materials engineering (M Sc); advanced metallic systems (PhD); biomedical materials (M Phil, M Sc, PhD); ceramics and glass (M Phil, M Sc, PhD); composite materials (M Phil, M Sc, PhD); corrosion and protection (M Phil, M Sc, PhD); materials (M Phil, M Sc, PhD); metallic materials (M Phil, M Sc, PhD); nanostructural materials (M Phil, M Sc, PhD); paper science (M Phil, M Sc, PhD); polymer science and engineering (M Phil, M Sc, PhD); technical textiles (M Sc); textile design, fashion and management (M Phil, M Sc, PhD); textile science and technology (M Phil, M Sc, PhD); textiles (M Phil, PhD); textiles and fashion (M Ent).

School of Mathematics Offers actuarial science (PhD); applied mathematics (M Phil, PhD); applied numerical computing (M Phil, PhD); financial mathematics (M Phil, PhD); mathematical logic (M Phil); probability (M Phil, PhD); pure mathematics (M Phil, PhD); statistics (M Phil, PhD).

School of Mechanical, Aerospace and Civil Engineering Offers advanced manufacturing technology (M Ent); aerospace engineering (M Phil, M Sc, PhD); civil engineering (M Phil, M Sc, PhD); environmental engineering (M Phil, PhD); management of projects (M Phil, M Sc, PhD); mechanical engineering (M Phil, M Sc, PhD); mechanical engineering design (M Ent); nuclear engineering (M Phil, D Eng, PhD).

School of Medicine Offers medicine (M Phil, PhD).

School of Nursing, Midwifery and Social Work Offers nursing (M Phil, PhD); social work (M Phil, PhD).

School of Pharmacy and Pharmaceutical Sciences Offers pharmacy and pharmaceutical sciences (M Phil, PhD).

School of Physics and Astronomy Offers astronomy and astrophysics (M Sc, PhD); biological physics (M Sc, PhD); condensed matter physics (M Sc, PhD); nonlinear and liquid crystals physics (M Sc, PhD); nuclear physics (M Sc, PhD); particle physics (M Sc, PhD); photon physics (M Sc, PhD); physics (M Sc, PhD); theoretical physics (M Sc, PhD).

School of Psychological Sciences Offers audiology (M Phil, PhD); clinical psychology (M Phil, PhD, Psy D); psychology (M Phil, PhD).

School of Social Sciences Offers ethnographic documentary (M Phil); interdisciplinary study of culture (PhD); philosophy (PhD); politics (PhD); social anthropology (PhD); social anthropology with visual media (PhD); social change (PhD); social statistics (PhD); sociology (PhD); visual anthropology (M Phil).

UNIVERSITY OF MANITOBA, Winnipeg, MB R3T 2N2, Canada

General Information Province-supported, coed, university. CGS member. *Graduate housing:* Rooms and/or apartments available to single and married students. *Research affiliation:* Canada Department of Agriculture Research Station, Freshwater Institute, Atomic Energy of Canada, Manitoba Department of Mines, Resources, and Environmental Management, Northern Scientific Training Program (Northern studies), Taiga Biological Research Trust.

GRADUATE UNITS

Faculty of Dentistry Offers dental diagnostic and surgical sciences (M Dent); dentistry (M Dent, M Sc, DMD); oral and maxillofacial surgery (M Dent); oral biology (M Sc, PhD); orthodontics (M Sc); periodontology (M Dent); preventive dental science (M Sc); restorative dentistry (M Dent).

Faculty of Graduate Studies *Program availability:* Part-time.

Asper School of Business Offers business (M Sc, MBA, PhD).

Clayton H. Riddell Faculty of Environment, Earth, and Resources Offers environment (M Env); environment and geography (M Sc); environment, earth, and resources (M Env, M Sc, MA, MNRM, PhD); geography (MA, PhD); geology (M Sc,

PhD); geophysics (M Sc, PhD); natural resources and environmental management (PhD); natural resources management (MNRM).

College Universitaire de Saint Boniface Offers Canadian studies (MA); education (M Ed).

Faculty of Agricultural and Food Sciences Offers agribusiness (M Sc, PhD); agricultural and food sciences (M Sc, PhD); agronomy and plant protection (M Sc, PhD); animal science (M Sc, PhD); entomology (M Sc, PhD); food and nutritional sciences (PhD); food science (M Sc); foods and nutrition (M Sc); horticulture (M Sc, PhD); plant breeding and genetics (M Sc, PhD); plant physiology-biochemistry (M Sc, PhD); soil science (M Sc, PhD).

Faculty of Architecture Offers architecture (M Arch, M Land Arch, MCP, MID); city planning (MCP); interior design (MID); landscape architecture (M Land Arch).

Faculty of Arts Offers anthropology (MA, PhD); archival studies (MA); arts (MA, MPA, PhD); classics (MA); clinical psychology (PhD); economics (MA, PhD); English (MA, PhD); French (MA, PhD); German language and literature (MA); history (MA, PhD); Icelandic language and literature (MA); linguistics (MA, PhD); native studies (MA); philosophy (MA); political studies (MA); psychology (MA, PhD); public administration (MPA); religion (MA, PhD); school psychology (MA); Slavic languages and literatures (MA); sociology (MA, PhD).

Faculty of Education Offers adult and post-secondary education (M Ed); education (M Ed, PhD); educational administration (M Ed); guidance and counseling (M Ed); inclusive special education (M Ed); language and literacy (M Ed); second language education (M Ed); social foundations of education (M Ed); studies in curriculum, teaching and learning (M Ed).

Faculty of Engineering Offers biosystems engineering (M Eng, M Sc, PhD); civil engineering (M Eng, M Sc, PhD); electrical and computer engineering (M Eng, M Sc, PhD); engineering (M Eng, M Sc, PhD); mechanical and manufacturing engineering (M Eng, M Sc, PhD).

Faculty of Human Ecology Offers family social sciences (M Sc); human ecology (M Sc); human nutritional sciences (M Sc); textile sciences (M Sc).

Faculty of Kinesiology and Recreation Management Offers kinesiology and recreation (M Sc, MA).

Faculty of Law Offers law (LL M). Electronic applications accepted.

Faculty of Nursing Offers cancer nursing (MN); nursing (MN).

Faculty of Pharmacy Offers pharmacy (M Sc, PhD).

Faculty of Science Offers botany (M Sc, PhD); chemistry (M Sc, PhD); computer science (M Sc, PhD); ecology (M Sc, PhD); mathematical, computational and statistical sciences (MMCSS); mathematics (M Sc, PhD); microbiology (M Sc, PhD); physics and astronomy (M Sc, PhD); science (M Sc, MMCSS, PhD); statistics (M Sc, PhD); zoology (M Sc, PhD).

Faculty of Social Work Offers social work (MSW, PhD).

Interdisciplinary Programs Offers disability studies (M Sc, MA); individual interdisciplinary studies (M Sc, MA, PhD); interdisciplinary studies (M Sc, MA, PhD).

Marcel A. Desautels Faculty of Music Offers music (M Mus).

School of Medical Rehabilitation Offers applied health sciences (PhD); occupational therapy (MOT); physical therapy (MPT); rehabilitation (M Sc).

Faculty of Medicine *Program availability:* Part-time. Offers medicine (M Sc, PhD). Electronic applications accepted.

Graduate Programs in Medicine *Program availability:* Part-time. Offers biochemistry and medical genetics (M Sc, PhD); community health sciences (M Sc, MPH, PhD, G Dip); human anatomy and cell science (M Sc, PhD); immunology (M Sc, PhD); medical microbiology (M Sc, PhD); medicine (M Sc, MPH, PhD, G Dip); pathology (M Sc); pediatrics and child health (M Sc); pharmacology and therapeutics (M Sc, PhD); physiology (M Sc, PhD); psychiatry (M Sc); rehabilitation (M Sc); surgery (M Sc).

UNIVERSITY OF MARY, Bismarck, ND 58504-9652

General Information Independent-religious, coed, comprehensive institution. *Graduate housing:* Room and/or apartments available on a first-come, first-served basis to single students; on-campus housing not available to married students. Housing application deadline: 7/15.

GRADUATE UNITS

Gary Tharaldson School of Business *Program availability:* Part-time, evening/weekend. Offers business administration (MBA); energy management (MBA, MS); executive (MBA, MS); health care (MBA, MS); human resource management (MBA); project management (MBA, MPM); virtuous leadership (MBA, MPM, MS). Electronic applications accepted.

Liffrig Family School of Education and Behavioral Sciences Offers curriculum, instruction and assessment (M Ed); education (Ed D); education and behavioral sciences (M Ed, Ed D); elementary administration (M Ed); reading (M Ed); secondary administration (M Ed); special education strategist (M Ed).

School of Health Sciences Offers bioethics (MS); clinical exercise physiology (MS); health sciences (MS, MSN, MSOT, DNP, DPT); kinesiology (MS); occupational therapy (MSOT); physical therapy (DPT); respiratory therapy (MS); sports and physical education administration (MS). Electronic applications accepted.

Division of Nursing *Program availability:* Part-time, evening/weekend, online learning. Offers family nurse practitioner (DNP); nurse administrator (MSN); nursing educator (MSN). Electronic applications accepted.

UNIVERSITY OF MARY HARDIN-BAYLOR, Belton, TX 76513

General Information Independent-religious, coed, comprehensive institution. *Enrollment:* 3,906 graduate, professional, and undergraduate students; 436 full-time matriculated graduate/professional students (230 women), 190 part-time matriculated graduate/professional students (108 women). *Enrollment by degree level:* 460 master's, 165 doctoral, 1 other advanced degree. *Graduate faculty:* 58 full-time (32 women), 28 part-time/adjunct (14 women). *Tuition:* Full-time $14,940; part-time $830 per credit hour. *Required fees:* $1350; $75 per credit hour. $50 per term. Tuition and fees vary according to course load and degree level. *Graduate housing:* On-campus housing not available. *Student services:* Campus employment opportunities, career counseling, exercise/wellness program, free psychological counseling, international student services, multicultural affairs office, services for students with disabilities, teacher training. *Library facilities:* Townsend Memorial Library. *Collection:* Books: 188,001 (physical), 27,676 (digital/electronic); Serial titles: 720 (physical), 140,549 (digital/electronic); Databases: 128. Weekly public service hours: 99; students can reserve study rooms.

Computer facilities: Computer purchase and lease plans are available. 275 computers available on campus for general student use. A campuswide network can be accessed from student residence rooms and from off campus. Online class registration is available.
Website: http://www.umhb.edu/

General Application Contact: Melissa Williams, Director of Graduate Student Services and Engagement, 254-295-4020, Fax: 254-295-5038, E-mail: mwilliams@umhb.edu.

GRADUATE UNITS

Graduate Studies in Business Administration Students: 21 full-time (12 women), 44 part-time (14 women); includes 23 minority (12 Black or African American, non-Hispanic/Latino; 1 Asian, non-Hispanic/Latino; 10 Hispanic/Latino), 11 international. Average age 29. 96 applicants, 70% accepted, 21 enrolled. *Faculty:* 11 full-time (5 women), 6 part-time/adjunct (2 women). *Expenses:* Contact institution. *Financial support:* In 2016–17, 33 students received support. Federal Work-Study, unspecified assistantships, and scholarships for some active duty military personnel available. Financial award applicants required to submit FAFSA. In 2016, 22 master's awarded. *Program availability:* Part-time, evening/weekend. Offers accounting (MBA); information systems management (MBA); international business (MBA); management (MBA). *Application deadline:* For fall admission, 6/1 for domestic students, 4/30 priority date for international students; for spring admission, 11/1 for domestic students, 9/30 priority date for international students. Applications are processed on a rolling basis. *Application fee:* $35 ($135 for international students). Electronic applications accepted. *Application Contact:* Sharon Aguilera, Assistant Director, Graduate Admissions, 254-295-4835, Fax: 254-295-5038, E-mail: saguilera@umhb.edu. *Assistant Professor/Director, Graduate Programs in McLane College of Business,* Dr. Kirk Fischer, 254-295-4655, E-mail: kfischer@umhb.edu.

Graduate Studies in Counseling Students: 49 full-time (39 women), 22 part-time (16 women); includes 30 minority (17 Black or African American, non-Hispanic/Latino; 12 Hispanic/Latino; 1 Two or more races, non-Hispanic/Latino). Average age 32. 51 applicants, 71% accepted, 23 enrolled. *Faculty:* 13 full-time (8 women), 8 part-time/adjunct (3 women). *Expenses:* Contact institution. *Financial support:* In 2016–17, 41 students received support. Federal Work-Study, unspecified assistantships, and scholarships for some active duty military personnel available. Support available to part-time students. Financial award applicants required to submit FAFSA. In 2016, 25 master's awarded. *Program availability:* Part-time, evening/weekend. Offers clinical and mental health counseling (MA); marriage, family and child counseling (MA); non-clinical professional studies (MA). *Application deadline:* For fall admission, 6/1 for domestic students, 4/30 priority date for international students; for spring admission, 11/1 for domestic students, 9/30 priority date for international students. Applications are processed on a rolling basis. *Application fee:* $35 ($135 for international students). Electronic applications accepted. *Application Contact:* Sharon Aguilera, Assistant Director, Graduate Admissions, 254-295-4835, Fax: 254-295-5038, E-mail: saguilera@umhb.edu. *Director, Graduate Counseling,* Dr. Dan Williamson, 254-295-5018, E-mail: dwilliamson@umhb.edu.

Graduate Studies in Education Students: 55 full-time (40 women), 79 part-time (60 women); includes 50 minority (29 Black or African American, non-Hispanic/Latino; 1 Asian, non-Hispanic/Latino; 18 Hispanic/Latino; 2 Two or more races, non-Hispanic/Latino), 3 international. Average age 38. 20 applicants, 95% accepted, 19 enrolled. *Faculty:* 15 full-time (11 women), 9 part-time/adjunct (5 women). *Expenses:* Contact institution. *Financial support:* In 2016–17, 99 students received support. Federal Work-Study and scholarships for some active duty military personnel available. Support available to part-time students. Financial award application deadline: 6/1; financial award applicants required to submit FAFSA. In 2016, 23 master's, 19 doctorates awarded. *Program availability:* Part-time, evening/weekend. Offers curriculum and instruction (M Ed); educational administration (M Ed, Ed D). *Application deadline:* For fall admission, 6/1 for domestic students, 4/30 priority date for international students; for spring admission, 11/1 for domestic students, 9/30 priority date for international students. Applications are processed on a rolling basis. *Application fee:* $35 ($135 for international students). Electronic applications accepted. *Application Contact:* Sharon Aguilera, Assistant Director, Graduate Admissions, 254-295-4835, Fax: 254-295-5038, E-mail: saguilera@umhb.edu. *Director, Graduate Programs in Education,* Dr. Craig Hammonds, 254-295-4189, E-mail: rhammonds@umhb.edu.

Graduate Studies in Exercise Science Students: 9 full-time (2 women), 29 part-time (12 women); includes 21 minority (8 Black or African American, non-Hispanic/Latino; 1 Asian, non-Hispanic/Latino; 12 Hispanic/Latino). Average age 27. 19 applicants, 84% accepted, 13 enrolled. *Faculty:* 6 full-time (1 woman). *Expenses:* Contact institution. *Financial support:* In 2016–17, 31 students received support. Federal Work-Study, unspecified assistantships, and scholarships for some active duty military personnel available. Support available to part-time students. Financial award application deadline: 6/1; financial award applicants required to submit FAFSA. In 2016, 18 master's awarded. *Program availability:* Part-time, evening/weekend, 100% online. Offers exercise physiology (MS Ed); sport administration (MS Ed). *Application deadline:* For fall admission, 6/1 for domestic students, 4/30 priority date for international students; for spring admission, 11/1 for domestic students, 9/30 priority date for international students. Applications are processed on a rolling basis. *Application fee:* $35 ($135 for international students). Electronic applications accepted. *Application Contact:* Sharon Aguilera, Assistant Director, Graduate Admissions, 254-295-4835, Fax: 254-295-5038, E-mail: saguilera@umhb.edu. *Director, MS Ed in Exercise Physiology Program,* Dr. Lem Taylor, 254-295-4895, E-mail: ltaylor@umhb.edu.

Graduate Studies in Information Systems Students: 183 full-time (47 women), 14 part-time (4 women); includes 2 minority (both Hispanic/Latino), 190 international. Average age 24. 623 applicants, 80% accepted, 35 enrolled. *Faculty:* 7 full-time (1 woman), 1 (woman) part-time/adjunct. *Expenses:* Contact institution. *Financial support:* In 2016–17, 143 students received support. Federal Work-Study, unspecified assistantships, and scholarships for some active duty military personnel available. Support available to part-time students. Financial award applicants required to submit FAFSA. In 2016, 174 master's awarded. *Program availability:* Part-time, evening/weekend. Offers information systems (MS). *Application deadline:* For fall admission, 6/1 for domestic students, 4/30 priority date for international students; for spring admission, 11/1 for domestic students, 9/30 priority date for international students. Applications are processed on a rolling basis. *Application fee:* $35 ($135 for international students). Electronic applications accepted. *Application Contact:* Sharon Aguilera, Assistant Director, Graduate Admissions, 254-295-4835, Fax: 254-295-5038, E-mail: saguilera@umhb.edu. *Associate Dean, Graduate Programs in McLane College of Business,* Dr. Kirk Fischer, 254-295-4655, E-mail: kfischer@umhb.edu.

Graduate Studies in Nursing Students: 43 full-time (37 women), 2 part-time (both women); includes 14 minority (6 Black or African American, non-Hispanic/Latino; 5 Hispanic/Latino; 3 Two or more races, non-Hispanic/Latino), 1 international. Average age 36. 49 applicants, 61% accepted, 26 enrolled. *Faculty:* 6 full-time (all women), 4 part-time/adjunct (3 women). *Expenses:* Contact institution. *Financial support:* In 2016–17, 36 students received support. Federal Work-Study, unspecified assistantships, and scholarships for some active duty military personnel available. Support available to part-time students. Financial award applicants required to submit FAFSA. In 2016, 24 master's, 2 other advanced degrees awarded. *Program availability:* Part-time, evening/weekend. Offers family nurse practitioner (MSN, Post-Master's Certificate); nurse educator (Post-Master's Certificate); nurse practice (DNP); nursing education (MSN). *Application deadline:* For fall admission, 6/1 for domestic students, 4/30 priority date for international students; for spring admission, 11/1 for domestic students, 9/30 priority date for international students. Applications are processed on a rolling basis. *Application fee:* $35 ($135 for international students). Electronic applications accepted. *Application Contact:* Sharon Aguilera, Assistant Director, Graduate Admissions, 254-295-4835, Fax: 254-295-5038, E-mail: saguilera@umhb.edu. *Dean, College of Nursing/Program Director,* Dr. Sharon Souter, 254-295-4662, E-mail: ssouter@umhb.edu.

Graduate Studies in Physical Therapy Students: 76 full-time (53 women); includes 18 minority (5 Black or African American, non-Hispanic/Latino; 2 Asian, non-Hispanic/Latino; 11 Hispanic/Latino). Average age 26. 109 applicants, 56% accepted, 40 enrolled. *Faculty:* 7 full-time (5 women), 5 part-time/adjunct (2 women). Expenses: Contact institution. *Financial support:* In 2016–17, 73 students received support. Federal Work-Study, unspecified assistantships, and scholarships for some active duty military personnel available. Financial award applicants required to submit FAFSA. Offers physical therapy (DPT). *Application deadline:* For fall admission, 6/1 for domestic students, 4/30 priority date for international students; for spring admission, 11/1 for domestic students, 9/30 priority date for international students. Applications are processed on a rolling basis. *Application fee:* $35 ($135 for international students). Electronic applications accepted. *Application Contact:* Sharon Aguilera, Assistant Director, Graduate Admissions, 254-295-4835, Fax: 254-295-5038, E-mail: saguilera@umhb.edu. *Director,* Dr. Barbara Gresham, 254-295-4921, E-mail: bgresham@umhb.edu.

UNIVERSITY OF MARYLAND, BALTIMORE, Baltimore, MD 21201

General Information State-supported, coed, graduate-only institution. CGS member. Enrollment by degree level: 1,957 master's, 3,444 doctoral, 95 other advanced degrees. *Graduate faculty:* 1,820 full-time (844 women), 923 part-time/adjunct (611 women). Tuition and fees vary according to program. *Graduate housing:* Rooms and/or apartments available on a first-come, first-served basis to single and married students. *Student services:* Campus employment opportunities, campus safety program, career counseling, exercise/wellness program, free psychological counseling, grant writing training, international student services, low-cost health insurance, services for students with disabilities, writing training. *Library facilities:* Health Sciences and Human Services Library plus 1 other. *Collection:* Books: 363,204 (physical), 13,000 (digital/electronic); Serial titles: 4,970 (digital/electronic); Databases: 116. Students can reserve study rooms. *Research affiliation:* University of Maryland Medical System (medical research), University of Maryland Biotechnology Institute (biology), University of Maryland BioPark (biology).

Computer facilities: A campuswide network can be accessed from student residence rooms and from off campus. Online class registration is available.
Website: http://www.umaryland.edu/

General Application Contact: Keith T. Brooks, Director, Graduate Enrollment Affairs, 410-706-7131, Fax: 410-706-3473, E-mail: kbrooks@umaryland.edu.

GRADUATE UNITS

Francis King Carey School of Law Students: 530 full-time (275 women), 204 part-time (112 women); includes 263 minority (114 Black or African American, non-Hispanic/Latino; 2 American Indian or Alaska Native, non-Hispanic/Latino; 68 Asian, non-Hispanic/Latino; 53 Hispanic/Latino; 26 Two or more races, non-Hispanic/Latino), 41 international. Average age 27. 1,911 applicants, 55% accepted, 280 enrolled. *Faculty:* 54 full-time (29 women), 52 part-time/adjunct (17 women). Expenses: Contact institution. *Financial support:* In 2016–17, 529 students received support, including 28 fellowships (averaging $4,000 per year), 90 research assistantships (averaging $1,500 per year); Federal Work-Study, institutionally sponsored loans, and scholarships/grants also available. Support available to part-time students. Financial award application deadline: 3/1; financial award applicants required to submit FAFSA. In 2016, 19 master's, 215 doctorates awarded. *Program availability:* Part-time, evening/weekend, 100% online. Offers law (LL M, JD). *Application deadline:* For fall admission, 4/1 priority date for domestic and international students. Applications are processed on a rolling basis. *Application fee:* $70. Electronic applications accepted. *Application Contact:* Susan Krinsky, Associate Dean for Student Affairs and Communications, 410-706-3492, Fax: 410-706-1793, E-mail: admissions@law.umaryland.edu. *Dean/Professor,* Donald B. Tobin, 410-706-7214, Fax: 410-706-4045, E-mail: dtobin@law.umaryland.edu.

Graduate School Students: 686 full-time (495 women), 598 part-time (462 women); includes 460 minority (214 Black or African American, non-Hispanic/Latino; 1 American Indian or Alaska Native, non-Hispanic/Latino; 150 Asian, non-Hispanic/Latino; 59 Hispanic/Latino; 2 Native Hawaiian or other Pacific Islander, non-Hispanic/Latino; 34 Two or more races, non-Hispanic/Latino), 146 international. Average age 32. 1,462 applicants, 38% accepted, 331 enrolled. Expenses: Contact institution. *Financial support:* Fellowships with full and partial tuition reimbursements, research assistantships with full tuition reimbursements, teaching assistantships with full tuition reimbursements, Federal Work-Study, institutionally sponsored loans, scholarships/grants, health care benefits, and unspecified assistantships available. Support available to part-time students. Financial award application deadline: 3/1; financial award applicants required to submit FAFSA. In 2016, 286 master's, 63 doctorates, 8 other advanced degrees awarded. *Program availability:* Part-time, evening/weekend, online learning. Offers biochemistry (MS, PhD); biochemistry and molecular biology (MS, PhD); biomedical sciences (MS, PhD); cancer biology (PhD); cell and molecular physiology (PhD); cellular and molecular biomedical science (MS); clinical research (Postbaccalaureate Certificate); epidemiology (MS, PhD); gerontology (PhD); human genetics and genomic medicine (PhD); marine-estuarine-environmental sciences (MS, PhD); medical and research technology (MS); molecular medicine (PhD); molecular microbiology and immunology (PhD); molecular toxicology and pharmacology (PhD); neuroscience (PhD); oral pathology (PhD); pharmaceutical health service research (MS, PhD); pharmaceutical sciences (PhD); pharmacometrics (MS); pharmacy administration (PhD); physical rehabilitation science (PhD); regulatory science (MS); research ethics (Certificate); thanatology (Certificate); toxicology (MS, PhD). *Application deadline:* For fall admission, 4/15 priority date for domestic students, 1/15 priority date for international students. Applications are processed on a rolling basis. *Application fee:* $75. Electronic applications accepted. *Application Contact:* Keith T. Brooks, Assistant Dean, 410-706-7131, Fax: 410-706-3473, E-mail: kbrooks@umaryland.edu. *Chief Academic and Research Officer/Dean of the Graduate School,* Dr. Bruce E. Jarrell, 410-706-2304, Fax: 410-706-0500, E-mail: bjarrell@som.umaryland.edu.

School of Nursing Students: 460 full-time (406 women), 463 part-time (418 women); includes 383 minority (226 Black or African American, non-Hispanic/Latino; 94 Asian, non-Hispanic/Latino; 40 Hispanic/Latino; 2 Native Hawaiian or other Pacific Islander,

non-Hispanic/Latino; 21 Two or more races, non-Hispanic/Latino), 18 international. Average age 34. 939 applicants, 44% accepted, 307 enrolled. Expenses: Contact institution. *Financial support:* Fellowships, research assistantships, and teaching assistantships available. Financial award application deadline: 2/15; financial award applicants required to submit FAFSA. In 2016, 243 master's, 29 doctorates, 19 other advanced degrees awarded. *Program availability:* Part-time. Offers clinical nurse leader (MS); community health nursing (MS); maternal-child nursing (MS); nurse anesthesia (MS); nurse-midwifery education (MS); nursing (MS, DNP, PhD, Postbaccalaureate Certificate); nursing administration (MS); nursing education (MS); nursing health policy (MS); primary care nursing (MS); psychiatric nursing (MS). MS/MBA offered jointly with University of Baltimore. *Application deadline:* For fall admission, 3/1 for domestic students, 1/15 for international students. *Application fee:* $50. Electronic applications accepted. *Application Contact:* Keith T. Brooks, Assistant Dean, 410-706-7131, Fax: 410-706-3473, E-mail: kbrooks@umaryland.edu. *Professor/Director of Master's Program,* Dr. Jane Kapustin, 410-706-3890.

School of Social Work Offers social work (MSW, PhD). MSW/MA offered jointly with Baltimore Hebrew University; MBA/MSW with University of Maryland, College Park; MSW/MPH with The Johns Hopkins University. Electronic applications accepted.

Professional and Advanced Education Programs in Dentistry Students: 592 full-time (313 women); includes 245 minority (60 Black or African American, non-Hispanic/Latino; 119 Asian, non-Hispanic/Latino; 42 Hispanic/Latino; 1 Native Hawaiian or other Pacific Islander, non-Hispanic/Latino; 23 Two or more races, non-Hispanic/Latino), 32 international. Average age 26. 729 applicants, 81% accepted, 136 enrolled. Expenses: Contact institution. *Financial support:* Career-related internships or fieldwork, Federal Work-Study, scholarships/grants, and traineeships available. Financial award application deadline: 3/1; financial award applicants required to submit FAFSA. In 2016, 124 doctorates, 23 Certificates awarded. Offers advanced general dentistry (Certificate); dentistry (DDS); endodontics (Certificate); oral-maxillofacial surgery (Certificate); orthodontics (Certificate); pediatric dentistry (Certificate); periodontics (Certificate); prosthodontics (Certificate). *Application deadline:* Applications are processed on a rolling basis. *Application fee:* $85. Electronic applications accepted. *Application Contact:* Dr. Judith A. Porter, Assistant Dean for Admissions and Recruitment, 410-706-7472, Fax: 410-706-0945, E-mail: ddsadmissions@umaryland.edu. *Dean,* Dr. Mark A. Reynolds, 410-706-7461.

Professional Program in Pharmacy Offers pharmacy (Pharm D). Electronic applications accepted.

School of Medicine Students: 1,147 full-time (708 women), 80 part-time (44 women); includes 417 minority (90 Black or African American, non-Hispanic/Latino; 2 American Indian or Alaska Native, non-Hispanic/Latino; 233 Asian, non-Hispanic/Latino; 64 Hispanic/Latino; 28 Two or more races, non-Hispanic/Latino), 61 international. Average age 26. 5,758 applicants, 14% accepted, 365 enrolled. Expenses: Contact institution. *Financial support:* In 2016–17, research assistantships with partial tuition reimbursements (averaging $25,000 per year) were awarded; fellowships, Federal Work-Study, scholarships/grants, health care benefits, and unspecified assistantships also available. Financial award application deadline: 3/1; financial award applicants required to submit FAFSA. In 2016, 71 master's, 258 doctorates awarded. *Program availability:* Part-time. Offers biostatistics (MS); clinical research (MS); epidemiology and preventive medicine (MPH, MS, PhD); genetic counseling (MGC); gerontology (PhD); human genetics and genomic medicine (MS, PhD); medicine (MGC, MPH, MS, DPT, MD, PhD); molecular epidemiology (MS, PhD); pathologists' assistant (MS); physical rehabilitation science (PhD); physical therapy and rehabilitation science (DPT); toxicology (MS, PhD). Electronic applications accepted. *Application Contact:* 410-706-7478, Fax: 410-706-0467, E-mail: admissions@som.umaryland.edu. *Dean and Vice President for Medical Affairs,* Dr. E. Albert Reece, 410-706-7410, Fax: 410-706-0235, E-mail: deanmed@som.umaryland.edu.

UNIVERSITY OF MARYLAND, BALTIMORE COUNTY, Baltimore, MD 21250

General Information State-supported, coed, university. CGS member. Enrollment: 13,640 graduate, professional, and undergraduate students; 1,167 full-time matriculated graduate/professional students (548 women), 1,250 part-time matriculated graduate/professional students (599 women). Enrollment by degree level: 1,590 master's, 694 doctoral, 57 other advanced degrees. *Graduate faculty:* 503 full-time, 195 part-time/adjunct. Tuition, state resident: full-time $13,294. Tuition, nonresident: full-time $20,286. *Graduate housing:* Room and/or apartments available on a first-come, first-served basis to single students; on-campus housing not available to married students. Housing application deadline: 6/1. *Student services:* Campus employment opportunities, campus safety program, career counseling, child daycare facilities, exercise/wellness program, free psychological counseling, grant writing training, international student services, low-cost health insurance, multicultural affairs office, services for students with disabilities, teacher training, writing training. *Library facilities:* Albin O. Kuhn Library and Gallery. *Collection:* Books: 727,421 (physical), 171,487 (digital/electronic); Serial titles: 27,505 (physical), 14,296 (digital/electronic); Databases: 388. Weekly public service hours: 94; study areas open 24 hours, 5–7 days a week; students can reserve study rooms. *Research affiliation:* Sciences Applications International Corporation (information systems and technology), Halliburton Energy Services, IBM (computers and information technology), BouMatic (dairy industry), Pfizer, Inc. (pharmaceuticals), Fujitsu Laboratories of America (information technology and communications).

Computer facilities: Computer purchase and lease plans are available. 1,065 computers available on campus for general student use. A campuswide network can be accessed from student residence rooms and from off campus. Online class registration, billing, housing, parking, degree audit and advising are available.
Website: http://www.umbc.edu/

General Application Contact: Kathryn Nee, Coordinator of Domestic Admissions, 410-455-2944, E-mail: nee@umbc.edu.

GRADUATE UNITS

The Graduate School Students: 1,167 full-time (548 women), 1,250 part-time (599 women); includes 636 minority (279 Black or African American, non-Hispanic/Latino; 4 American Indian or Alaska Native, non-Hispanic/Latino; 202 Asian, non-Hispanic/Latino; 100 Hispanic/Latino; 4 Native Hawaiian or other Pacific Islander, non-Hispanic/Latino; 47 Two or more races, non-Hispanic/Latino), 571 international. Average age 32. 2,592 applicants, 51% accepted, 634 enrolled. *Faculty:* 503 full-time, 195 part-time/adjunct. Expenses: Contact institution. *Financial support:* In 2016–17, 602 students received support, including 27 fellowships with tuition reimbursements available (averaging $18,909 per year), 274 research assistantships with tuition reimbursements available (averaging $18,909 per year), 301 teaching assistantships with tuition reimbursements available (averaging $18,909 per year); career-related internships or fieldwork, Federal Work-Study, scholarships/grants, traineeships, health care benefits, and unspecified assistantships also available. Financial award applicants required to submit FAFSA.

Offers engineering management (MS, Postbaccalaureate Certificate); marine-estuarine-environmental sciences (MS, PhD); systems engineering (MS, Postbaccalaureate Certificate). *Application deadline:* For fall admission, 1/1 for international students; for spring admission, 5/1 for international students. Applications are processed on a rolling basis. *Application fee:* $50. Electronic applications accepted.

College of Arts, Humanities and Social Sciences Students: 380 full-time (260 women), 592 part-time (399 women); includes 267 minority (122 Black or African American, non-Hispanic/Latino; 1 American Indian or Alaska Native, non-Hispanic/Latino; 68 Asian, non-Hispanic/Latino; 49 Hispanic/Latino; 3 Native Hawaiian or other Pacific Islander, non-Hispanic/Latino; 24 Two or more races, non-Hispanic/Latino), 52 international. Average age 33. 764 applicants, 57% accepted, 243 enrolled. *Faculty:* 289 full-time, 116 part-time/adjunct. Expenses: Contact institution. *Financial support:* In 2016–17, 202 students received support, including 11 fellowships (averaging $19,000 per year), 97 research assistantships (averaging $19,000 per year), 94 teaching assistantships (averaging $19,000 per year); career-related internships or fieldwork, scholarships/grants, health care benefits, and unspecified assistantships also available. Financial award applicants required to submit FAFSA. In 2016, 263 master's, 24 doctorates, 113 other advanced degrees awarded. *Program availability:* Part-time, evening/weekend, online learning. Offers administration, planning, and policy (MS); aging policy issues (MS); American contemporary music (Postbaccalaureate Certificate); applied behavioral analysis (MA); applied developmental psychology (PhD); applied sociology (MA); arts, humanities and social science (MA, MAE, MAE, MAT, MFA, MPP, MPS, MS, PhD, Certificate, Graduate Certificate, Postbaccalaureate Certificate); distance education (Graduate Certificate); early childhood education (MAT); economic policy analysis (MA); education (MAE, MAE, MS); elementary education (MAT); emergency health services (MS); emergency management (Postbaccalaureate Certificate); English: texts, technologies, and literature (MA); epidemiology of aging (PhD); geographic information systems (MPS, Certificate); geography and environmental systems (MPS, MS, PhD, Certificate); historical studies (MA); human services psychology (MA, PhD); industrial/organizational psychology (MPS); instructional systems development (MA, Graduate Certificate); instructional technology (Graduate Certificate); intercultural communication (MA); intermedia and digital arts (MFA); K-8 mathematics instructional leadership (MAE); K-8 science education (MAE); K-8 STEM education (MAE); language, literacy, and culture (PhD); non-profit sector (Postbaccalaureate Certificate); preventive medicine and epidemiology (MS); public policy (MPP, PhD); secondary mathematics education (MAE); secondary science education (MAE); secondary STEM education (MAE); social, cultural, and behavioral sciences (PhD); teaching (MAT); teaching English to speakers of other languages (MA, Postbaccalaureate Certificate). *Application deadline:* For fall admission, 1/1 for international students; for spring admission, 5/1 for international students. Applications are processed on a rolling basis. *Application fee:* $50. Electronic applications accepted. *Application Contact:* Kathryn Nee, Coordinator of Domestic Admissions, 410-455-2944, E-mail: nee@umbc.edu. *Dean,* Dr. Scot E. Casper, 410-455-2385, Fax: 410-455-1095, E-mail: casper@umbc.edu.

College of Engineering and Information Technology Students: 576 full-time (191 women), 604 part-time (175 women); includes 302 minority (130 Black or African American, non-Hispanic/Latino; 3 American Indian or Alaska Native, non-Hispanic/Latino; 106 Asian, non-Hispanic/Latino; 44 Hispanic/Latino; 1 Native Hawaiian or other Pacific Islander, non-Hispanic/Latino; 18 Two or more races, non-Hispanic/Latino), 451 international. Average age 31. 1,435 applicants, 51% accepted, 314 enrolled. *Faculty:* 103 full-time (32 women), 37 part-time/adjunct (7 women). Expenses: Contact institution. *Financial support:* In 2016–17, 9 fellowships with full tuition reimbursements (averaging $21,750 per year), 127 research assistantships with full tuition reimbursements (averaging $19,250 per year), 101 teaching assistantships with full tuition reimbursements (averaging $16,750 per year) were awarded; career-related internships or fieldwork, Federal Work-Study, scholarships/grants, health care benefits, tuition waivers (partial), and unspecified assistantships also available. Support available to part-time students. Financial award application deadline: 6/30; financial award applicants required to submit FAFSA. In 2016, 343 master's, 27 doctorates, 45 other advanced degrees awarded. *Program availability:* Part-time. Offers biochemical regulatory engineering (Postbaccalaureate Certificate); chemical and biochemical engineering (MS, PhD); computational thermal fluid dynamics (Postbaccalaureate Certificate); computer engineering (MS, PhD); computer science (MS, PhD); cybersecurity (MPS, Postbaccalaureate Certificate); cybersecurity strategy and policy (Postbaccalaureate Certificate); electrical engineering (MS, PhD); engineering and information technology (MPS, MS, PhD, Postbaccalaureate Certificate); environmental engineering (MS, PhD); health information technology (MPS); human-centered computing (MS, PhD); information systems (MPS, MS, PhD); mechanical engineering (MS, PhD); mechatronics (Postbaccalaureate Certificate). *Application deadline:* For fall admission, 6/1 for domestic students, 1/1 for international students; for spring admission, 11/1 for domestic students, 6/1 for international students. Applications are processed on a rolling basis. *Application fee:* $70. Electronic applications accepted. *Application Contact:* Graduate School, 410-455-2537, E-mail: umbcgrad@umbc.edu. *Dean and Professor,* Dr. Julia M. Ross, 410-455-3270, Fax: 410-455-3559, E-mail: jross@umbc.edu.

College of Natural and Mathematical Sciences Students: 196 full-time (87 women), 51 part-time (23 women); includes 61 minority (21 Black or African American, non-Hispanic/Latino; 28 Asian, non-Hispanic/Latino; 7 Hispanic/Latino; 5 Two or more races, non-Hispanic/Latino), 67 international. Average age 29. 378 applicants, 39% accepted, 67 enrolled. *Faculty:* 111 full-time, 17 part-time/adjunct. Expenses: Contact institution. *Financial support:* In 2016–17, 163 students received support, including 7 fellowships (averaging $18,909 per year), 50 research assistantships with tuition reimbursements available (averaging $18,909 per year), 106 teaching assistantships with full tuition reimbursements available (averaging $18,909 per year). In 2016, 44 master's, 31 doctorates, 2 other advanced degrees awarded. *Program availability:* Part-time. Offers applied mathematics (MS, PhD); applied molecular biology (MS); atmospheric physics (MS, PhD); biochemistry (PhD); biological sciences (MS, PhD); biostatistics (PhD); biotechnology (MPS); biotechnology (Graduate Certificate); biotechnology management (Graduate Certificate); chemistry (MS, PhD); chemistry and biochemistry (Postbaccalaureate Certificate); environmental statistics (MS); molecular and cell biology (PhD); natural and mathematical sciences (MPS, MS, PhD, Graduate Certificate, Postbaccalaureate Certificate); neuroscience and cognitive sciences (PhD); physics (MS, PhD); statistics (MS, PhD). *Application deadline:* Applications are processed on a rolling basis. *Application fee:* $50. Electronic applications accepted. *Application Contact:* Kathryn Nee, Coordinator of Domestic Admissions, 410-455-2944, E-mail: nee@umbc.edu. *Interim Dean,* Dr. William R. LaCourse, 410-455-5827, Fax: 410-455-5831, E-mail: lacourse@umbc.edu.

Erickson School of Aging Studies Students: 18 full-time (11 women); includes 9 minority (8 Black or African American, non-Hispanic/Latino; 1 Hispanic/Latino). Average age 30. 23 applicants, 91% accepted, 18 enrolled. *Faculty:* 4 full-time (1 woman), 7 part-time/adjunct (1 woman). Expenses: Contact institution. *Financial support:* In 2016–17, 15 students received support, including 1 teaching assistantship with full tuition reimbursement available (averaging $21,600 per year). Financial award applicants required to submit FAFSA. In 2016, 13 master's awarded. *Program availability:* Part-time. Offers management of aging services (MA). *Application deadline:* Applications are processed on a rolling basis. *Application fee:* $50. Electronic applications accepted. *Application Contact:* Michelle Howell, Administrative Assistant, 443-543-5607, E-mail: mhowell@umbc.edu. *Graduate Program Director,* Bill Holman, 443-543-5603, E-mail: holman1@umbc.edu.

UNIVERSITY OF MARYLAND, COLLEGE PARK, College Park, MD 20742

General Information State-supported, coed, university. CGS member. *Graduate housing:* On-campus housing not available. *Research affiliation:* Battelle–Pacific Northwest National Laboratory, Canon U.S. Life Sciences, Inc. (technology development and analysis), Bill and Melinda Gates Foundation (international aid and outreach), Lockheed Martin Corporation (science and technology), BAE Systems (science and technology).

GRADUATE UNITS

Academic Affairs *Program availability:* Part-time, evening/weekend, online learning. Offers history, library, and information services. Electronic applications accepted.

A. James Clark School of Engineering *Program availability:* Part-time, evening/weekend, online learning. Offers advanced engineering education (M Eng); aerospace engineering (M Eng, MS, PhD); bioengineering (MS, PhD); chemical engineering (M Eng, MS, PhD); civil and environmental engineering (M Eng, MS, PhD); electrical and computer engineering (M Eng, MS, PhD); electrical engineering (MS, PhD); electronic packaging and reliability (MS); engineering (M Eng, ME, MS, PhD, Certificate); engineering and public policy (MS); fire protection engineering (M Eng, MS); manufacturing and design (MS, PhD); materials science and engineering (MS, PhD); mechanics and materials (MS, PhD); nuclear engineering (ME, MS, PhD); reliability engineering (M Eng, MS, PhD); systems engineering (M Eng, MS); telecommunications (MS); thermal and fluid sciences (MS, PhD).

College of Agriculture and Natural Resources *Program availability:* Part-time, evening/weekend. Offers agriculture and natural resources (MS, DVM, PhD); agriculture economics (MS, PhD); animal sciences (MS, PhD); environmental science and technology (MS, PhD); food science (MS, PhD); landscape architecture (MLA); natural resource sciences (MS, PhD); nutrition (MS, PhD); plant science (MS, PhD); resource economics (MS, PhD); veterinary medical sciences (MS, PhD); veterinary medicine (MS, DVM, PhD). Electronic applications accepted.

College of Arts and Humanities *Program availability:* Part-time, evening/weekend. Offers American studies (MA, PhD); art (MFA); art history (MA, PhD); arts and humanities (M Ed, MA, MFA, MM, DMA, Ed D, PhD); classics (MA); communication (MA, PhD); comparative literature (MA, PhD); creative writing (MA, MFA, PhD); dance (MFA); English language and literature (MA, PhD); ethnomusicology (MA); French language and literature (MA, PhD); Germanic language and literature (MA, PhD); history (MA, PhD); Jewish studies (MA); languages, literatures, and cultures (MA, PhD); linguistics (MA, PhD); modern French studies (PhD); music (M Ed, MA, MM, DMA, Ed D, PhD); performance (MFA); philosophy (MA, PhD); second language instruction (PhD); second language learning (PhD); second language measurement and assessment (PhD); second language use (PhD); Spanish language and literatures (MA, PhD); theatre (MA, MFA, PhD); theatre and performance studies (MA, PhD); theatre design (MFA); women's studies (MA, PhD). Electronic applications accepted.

College of Behavioral and Social Sciences *Program availability:* Part-time, evening/weekend. Offers American politics (PhD); applied anthropology (MAA); audiology (MA, PhD); behavioral and social sciences (MA, MAA, MS, Au D, PhD); clinical psychology (PhD); comparative politics (PhD); criminology and criminal justice (MA, PhD); developmental psychology (PhD); economics (MA, PhD); experimental psychology (PhD); geography (MA, PhD); hearing and speech sciences (Au D); industrial psychology (MA, MS, PhD); international relations (PhD); language pathology (MA, PhD); neuroscience (PhD); neurosciences and cognitive sciences (PhD); political economy (PhD); political theory (PhD); social psychology (PhD); sociology (MA, PhD); speech (MA, PhD); survey methodology (MS, PhD). Electronic applications accepted.

College of Computer, Mathematical and Natural Sciences *Program availability:* Part-time, evening/weekend, online learning. Offers analytical chemistry (MS, PhD); applied mathematics (MS, PhD); astronomy (MS, PhD); atmospheric and oceanic science (MS, PMS, PhD); behavior, ecology, and systematics (PhD); behavior, ecology, evolution, and systematics (MS, PhD); biochemistry (MS, PhD); biological sciences (PhD); biology (MS, PhD); biophysics (PhD); cell biology and molecular genetics (MS, PhD); chemical physics (MS, PhD); chemistry (MS, PhD); computational biology, bioinformatics, and genomics (PhD); computer science (MS, PhD); computer, mathematical and natural sciences (MA, MLS, MS, PMS, PhD); entomology (MS, PhD); geology (MS, PhD); inorganic chemistry (MS, PhD); life sciences (MLS); marine-estuarine-environmental sciences (MS, PhD); mathematical statistics (MA, PhD); mathematics (MA, PhD); molecular and cellular biology (PhD); organic chemistry (MS, PhD); physical chemistry (MS, PhD); physics (MS, PhD); physiological systems (PhD); plant biology (MS, PhD); sustainable development and conservation biology (MS).

College of Education *Program availability:* Part-time, evening/weekend, online learning. Offers college student personnel (M Ed, MA); college student personnel administration (PhD); community counseling (CAGS); community/career counseling (M Ed, MA); counseling and personnel services (M Ed, MA, PhD); counseling psychology (PhD); counselor education (PhD); curriculum and educational communications (M Ed, MA, Ed D, PhD, AGSC); education (M Ed, MA, Ed D, PhD, AGSC, CAGS); human development and quantitative methodology (MA, Ed D, PhD); reading (M Ed, MA, PhD, CAGS); rehabilitation counseling (M Ed, MA, AGSC); school counseling (M Ed, MA); school psychology (M Ed, MA, PhD); secondary education (M Ed, MA, Ed D, PhD, CAGS); social foundations of education (M Ed, MA, Ed D, PhD, CAGS); teaching English to speakers of other languages (M Ed). Electronic applications accepted.

College of Information Studies *Program availability:* Part-time, evening/weekend. Offers information studies (MIM, MLS, PhD). Electronic applications accepted.

Phillip Merrill College of Journalism *Program availability:* Part-time, evening/weekend. Offers broadcast journalism (MA); journalism (MA); journalism and media studies (PhD); online news (MA); public affairs reporting (MA). Electronic applications accepted.

Robert H. Smith School of Business *Program availability:* Part-time, evening/weekend, online learning. Offers business (EMBA, MBA, MS, PhD); business administration (MBA); business and management (MS, PhD); executive business administration (EMBA). Electronic applications accepted.

School of Architecture, Planning and Preservation *Program availability:* Part-time, evening/weekend. Offers architecture (M Arch); architecture, planning and preservation (M Arch, MCP, MHP, MRED, PhD, Certificate); historic preservation (MHP, Certificate); real estate development (MRED); urban and regional planning/design (PhD); urban studies and planning (MCP). Electronic applications accepted.

School of Public Health *Program availability:* Part-time, evening/weekend. Offers biostatistics (MPH); community health education (MPH); environmental health sciences (MPH); epidemiology (MPH, PhD); family studies (PhD); health services administration (MHA, PhD); kinesiology (MA, PhD); marriage and family therapy (MS); maternal and child health (PhD); public health (MA, MHA, MPH, MS, PhD); public/community health (PhD). Electronic applications accepted.

School of Public Policy *Program availability:* Part-time, evening/weekend, online learning. Offers policy studies (PhD); public management (MPM); public policy (MPM, MPP, PhD). Electronic applications accepted.

UNIVERSITY OF MARYLAND EASTERN SHORE, Princess Anne, MD 21853-1299

General Information State-supported, coed, university. CGS member. *Graduate housing:* On-campus housing not available.

GRADUATE UNITS

Graduate Programs *Program availability:* Part-time, evening/weekend. Offers applied computer science (MS); career and technology education (M Ed); chemistry (MS); criminal justice (MS); education leadership (Ed D); food and agricultural sciences (MS); food science and technology (PhD); guidance and counseling (M Ed); marine-estuarine-environmental sciences (MS, PhD); organizational leadership (PhD); physical therapy (DPT); quantitative fisheries and resource economics (PMS); rehabilitation counseling (MS); special education (M Ed); teaching (MAT); toxicology (MS, PhD). Electronic applications accepted.

School of Pharmacy Offers pharmaceutical sciences (MS, PhD); pharmacy (Pharm D).

UNIVERSITY OF MARYLAND UNIVERSITY COLLEGE, Adelphi, MD 20783

General Information State-supported, coed, comprehensive institution. *Enrollment:* 57,529 graduate, professional, and undergraduate students; 2,419 full-time matriculated graduate/professional students (1,215 women), 10,531 part-time matriculated graduate/professional students (5,756 women). *Enrollment by degree level:* 12,230 master's, 141 doctoral, 579 other advanced degrees. *Graduate faculty:* 200 full-time (85 women), 3,237 part-time/adjunct (1,478 women). Tuition, state resident: part-time $458 per credit. Tuition, nonresident: part-time $659 per credit. *Graduate housing:* On-campus housing not available. *Student services:* Campus employment opportunities, career counseling, international student services, services for students with disabilities, writing training. *Library facilities:* Information and Library Services plus 1 other. *Collection:* Books: 1,234 (physical), 110,012 (digital/electronic).

Computer facilities: Computer purchase and lease plans are available. 448 computers available on campus for general student use. A campuswide network can be accessed from off campus. Online class registration is available. Website: http://www.umuc.edu/

General Application Contact: Coordinator, Graduate Admissions, 800-888-UMUC, Fax: 240-684-2151, E-mail: newgrad@umuc.edu.

GRADUATE UNITS

The Graduate School Students: 2,419 full-time (1,215 women), 10,531 part-time (5,756 women); includes 7,631 minority (5,408 Black or African American, non-Hispanic/Latino; 45 American Indian or Alaska Native, non-Hispanic/Latino; 807 Asian, non-Hispanic/Latino; 907 Hispanic/Latino; 31 Native Hawaiian or other Pacific Islander, non-Hispanic/Latino; 433 Two or more races, non-Hispanic/Latino; 241 international. Average age 34. 4,522 applicants, 100% accepted, 2790 enrolled. *Faculty:* 200 full-time (85 women), 3,237 part-time/adjunct (1,478 women). Expenses: Contact institution. *Financial support:* Federal Work-Study and scholarships/grants available. Support available to part-time students. Financial award application deadline: 6/1; financial award applicants required to submit FAFSA. In 2016, 3,594 master's, 49 doctorates, 657 other advanced degrees awarded. *Program availability:* Part-time, evening/weekend, online learning. Offers accounting and financial management (MS); biotechnology (MS, Certificate); business administration (MBA); cybersecurity management and policy (MS, Certificate); cybersecurity technology (MS, Certificate); data analytics (MS, Certificate); digital forensics and cyber investigation (MS); distance education and e-learning (MDE); environmental management (MS); health care administration (MS); health informatics administration (MS); information technology (MS); learning design and technology (MS); management (MS, DM, Certificate); management and technology (MAT, MBA, MDE, MS, DM, Certificate); teaching (MAT). *Application deadline:* Applications are processed on a rolling basis. *Application fee:* $50. Electronic applications accepted. *Application Contact:* Coordinator, Graduate Admissions, 800-888-8682, Fax: 240-684-2151, E-mail: newgrad@umuc.edu.

UNIVERSITY OF MARY WASHINGTON, Fredericksburg, VA 22401-5358

General Information State-supported, coed, comprehensive institution. *Enrollment:* 4,726 graduate, professional, and undergraduate students; 133 full-time matriculated graduate/professional students (103 women), 236 part-time matriculated graduate/professional students (161 women). *Enrollment by degree level:* 369 master's. *Graduate faculty:* 23 full-time (12 women), 21 part-time/adjunct (14 women). Tuition, state resident: full-time $6588; part-time $531 per credit hour. Tuition, nonresident: full-time $15,462; part-time $1024 per credit hour. Tuition and fees vary according to course load and program. *Graduate housing:* Room and/or apartments available on a first-come, first-served basis to single students; on-campus housing not available to married students. *Student services:* Campus employment opportunities, career counseling, free psychological counseling, international student services, multicultural affairs office, services for students with disabilities, teacher training, writing training. *Library facilities:* Simpson Library plus 2 others. *Collection:* Books: 338,183 (physical), 201,723

(digital/electronic); Serial titles: 3,272 (physical), 77,774 (digital/electronic); Databases: 208. Weekly public service hours: 90; students can reserve study rooms.

Computer facilities: Computer purchase and lease plans are available. 579 computers available on campus for general student use. A campuswide network can be accessed from student residence rooms and from off campus. Online class registration, student Web hosting are available. Website: http://www.umw.edu/

General Application Contact: Christy Pack, Director of Graduate Admissions, 540-286-8038, Fax: 540-286-8085, E-mail: dclark@umw.edu.

GRADUATE UNITS

College of Business 112 applicants, 52% accepted, 49 enrolled. *Faculty:* 12 full-time (3 women), 1 part-time/adjunct (0 women). Expenses: Contact institution. *Financial support:* In 2016–17, 8 students received support. Available to part-time students. Application deadline: 3/15; applicants required to submit FAFSA. *Program availability:* Part-time-only, evening/weekend. Offers business (MBA). *Application deadline:* For fall admission, 6/1 priority date for domestic students, 6/1 for international students; for spring admission, 10/1 for domestic and international students. Applications are processed on a rolling basis. *Application fee:* $50. Electronic applications accepted. *Application Contact:* Christy Pack, Director of Graduate Admissions, 540-286-8086, Fax: 540-286-8085, E-mail: dpack@umw.edu. *Dean,* Dr. Lynne D. Richardson, 540-654-2470, Fax: 540-654-2430, E-mail: lynne.richardson@umw.edu.

College of Education Students: 102 full-time (90 women), 106 part-time (89 women); includes 34 minority (11 Black or African American, non-Hispanic/Latino; 2 Asian, non-Hispanic/Latino; 12 Hispanic/Latino; 9 Two or more races, non-Hispanic/Latino). Average age 29. 231 applicants, 59% accepted, 79 enrolled. *Faculty:* 12 full-time (9 women), 18 part-time/adjunct (12 women). Expenses: Contact institution. *Financial support:* In 2016–17, 29 students received support, including 3 fellowships with partial tuition reimbursements available (averaging $9,000 per year); research assistantships, teaching assistantships, and scholarships/grants also available. Financial award application deadline: 4/25; financial award applicants required to submit FAFSA. In 2016, 107 master's awarded. *Program availability:* Part-time, evening/weekend. Offers education (M Ed); elementary education (MS). *Application deadline:* For fall admission, 4/15 for domestic and international students; for spring admission, 9/15 for domestic and international students. Applications are processed on a rolling basis. *Application fee:* $50. Electronic applications accepted. *Application Contact:* Deanna C. Pack, Director of Graduate Admissions, 540-286-8030, Fax: 540-286-8085, E-mail: dpack@umw.edu. *Dean,* Dr. Marie Sheckels, 540-654-1334.

UNIVERSITY OF MASSACHUSETTS AMHERST, Amherst, MA 01003

General Information State-supported, coed, university. CGS member. *Graduate housing:* Rooms and/or apartments available on a first-come, first-served basis to single and married students. Housing application deadline: 6/15.

GRADUATE UNITS

Graduate School *Program availability:* Part-time, evening/weekend. Electronic applications accepted.

College of Education *Program availability:* Part-time, online learning. Offers bilingual, English as a second language, and multicultural education (M Ed, Ed S); child study and early education (M Ed); children, families and schools (Ed D, Ed S); early childhood and elementary teacher education (M Ed); education (M Ed, Ed D, PhD, Ed S); educational leadership (M Ed); educational policy and leadership (Ed D); higher education (M Ed); international education (M Ed); language, literacy and culture (Ed D); learning, media and technology (M Ed, Ed S); mathematics, science, and learning technologies (Ed D); reading and writing (M Ed); research, educational measurement and psychometrics (Ed D); school counselor education (M Ed, Ed S); school psychology (M Ed, PhD, Ed S); science education (Ed D, Ed S); secondary teacher education (M Ed); social justice education (M Ed, Ed D, Ed S); special education (M Ed, Ed D, Ed S); teacher education and school improvement (Ed D, Ed S). Electronic applications accepted.

College of Engineering *Program availability:* Part-time. Offers chemical engineering (MSChE, PhD); civil engineering (MSCE, PhD); electrical and computer engineering (MSECE, PhD); engineering (MS, MS Env E, MSCE, MSChE, MSECE, MSEM, MSIE, MSME, PhD); environmental and water resources engineering (MSCE); geotechnical engineering (MSCE); industrial engineering and operations research (MS, PhD); mechanical engineering (MSME, PhD); structural engineering and mechanics (MSCE); transportation engineering (MSCE). Electronic applications accepted.

College of Humanities and Fine Arts *Program availability:* Part-time. Offers Afro-American studies (MA, PhD); American studies (PhD); architecture (M Arch); art (MA, MFA); Asian languages and literatures (MA); Chinese (MA); collaborative piano (MM); comparative literature (MA, PhD); composition (MM); composition and rhetoric (PhD); conducting (MM); costume design (MFA); creative writing (MFA); design (MS); design in historic preservation (MS); directing (MFA); dramaturgy (MFA); English and American literature (MA, PhD); French (MAT); French and Francophone studies (MA, MAT); German and Scandinavian studies (MA, PhD); Hispanic literatures, cultures and linguistics (MA, PhD); history (MA, PhD); history of art and architecture (MA); humanities and fine arts (M Arch, MA, MAT, MFA, MM, MS, PhD); Italian studies (MAT); Japanese (MA); jazz composition/arranging (MM); Latin and classical humanities (MAT); lighting design (MFA); linguistics (MA, PhD); music education (MM, PhD); music history (MM); music theory (MM); performance (MM); philosophy (MA, PhD); scenic design (MFA); Spanish and Portuguese studies (MA, MAT, PhD); teaching Spanish (MAT). Electronic applications accepted.

College of Natural Sciences *Program availability:* Part-time. Offers animal biotechnology and biomedical sciences (MS); applied mathematics (MS); astronomy (MS, PhD); biochemistry and molecular biology (MS, PhD); building systems (MS, PhD); chemistry (MS, PhD); clinical psychology (MS, PhD); cognitive psychology (MS, PhD); computer science (MS, PhD); developmental science (MS, PhD); environmental policy and human dimensions (MS, PhD); food science (MS, PhD); forest resources (MS, PhD); geography (MS); geosciences (MS, PhD); mathematics (MS, PhD); microbiology (MS, PhD); natural sciences (MS, PhD); physics (MS, PhD); polymer science and engineering (MS, PhD); psychology of peace and violence (MS, PhD); social psychology (MS, PhD); statistics (MS, PhD); sustainability science (MS); water, wetlands and watersheds (MS, PhD); wildlife and fisheries conservation (MS, PhD). Electronic applications accepted.

College of Nursing *Program availability:* Part-time, online learning. Offers adult gerontology primary care nurse practitioner (DNP); clinical nurse leader (MS); family nurse practitioner (DNP); nursing (PhD); public health nurse leader (DNP). Electronic applications accepted.

College of Social and Behavioral Sciences *Program availability:* Part-time. Offers anthropology (MA, PhD); communication (MA, PhD); economics (MA, PhD); labor studies (MS); landscape architecture (MLA); political science (MA, PhD); public policy and administration (MPP, MPPA); regional planning (MRP, PhD); resource economics (MS, PhD); social and behavioral sciences (MA, MLA, MPP, MPPA, MRP, MS, PhD); sociology (MA, PhD); union leadership and administration (MS). Electronic applications accepted.

Interdisciplinary Programs *Program availability:* Part-time. Offers animal behavior and learning (PhD); biochemistry and metabolism (MS, PhD); biological chemistry and molecular biophysics (PhD); biomedicine (PhD); cell biology and physiology (MS, PhD); cellular and developmental biology (PhD); environmental, ecological and integrative biology (MS, PhD); genetics and evolution (MS, PhD); interdisciplinary studies (MS, PhD); marine science and technology (MS, PhD); molecular and cellular neuroscience (PhD); neural and behavioral development (PhD); neuroendocrinology (PhD); neuroscience and behavior (MS); organismic and evolutionary biology (MS, PhD); sensorimotor, cognitive, and computational neuroscience (PhD). Electronic applications accepted.

Isenberg School of Management *Program availability:* Part-time, evening/weekend, online learning. Offers accounting (MSA); business administration (MBA); entrepreneurship (MBA); finance (MBA, PhD); healthcare administration (MBA); hospitality and tourism management (PhD); management (MBA, MS, MSA, PhD); management science (PhD); marketing (MBA, PhD); organization studies (PhD); sport management (PhD); strategic management (PhD). Electronic applications accepted.

School of Public Health and Health Sciences *Program availability:* Part-time, evening/weekend, online learning. Offers audiology (Au D, PhD); biostatistics (MPH, MS, PhD); clinical audiology (PhD); community health education (MPH, MS, PhD); community nutrition (MS); environmental health sciences (MPH, MS, PhD); epidemiology (MPH, MS, PhD); health policy and management (MPH, MS, PhD); kinesiology (MS, PhD); nutrition (MS); nutrition science (MS); public health and health sciences (MA, MPH, MS, Au D, PhD); public health practice (MPH); speech-language pathology (MA, PhD). Electronic applications accepted.

UNIVERSITY OF MASSACHUSETTS BOSTON, Boston, MA 02125-3393

General Information State-supported, coed, university. CGS member. *Enrollment:* 16,847 graduate, professional, and undergraduate students; 1,389 full-time matriculated graduate/professional students (905 women), 2,060 part-time matriculated graduate/professional students (1,432 women). *Enrollment by degree level:* 2,348 master's, 716 doctoral, 385 other advanced degrees. *Graduate faculty:* 714 full-time (362 women), 529 part-time/adjunct (319 women). Tuition, state resident: full-time $16,863. Tuition, nonresident: full-time $32,913. *Required fees:* $177. *Graduate housing:* On-campus housing not available. *Student services:* Campus employment opportunities, campus safety program, career counseling, child daycare facilities, exercise/wellness program, free psychological counseling, international student services, low-cost health insurance, multicultural affairs office, services for students with disabilities, teacher training, writing training. *Library facilities:* Joseph P. Healey Library. *Collection:* Books: 459,163 (physical), 547,086 (digital/electronic); Databases: 124. *Research affiliation:* New England Aquarium (environmental sciences), Dana Farber/Harvard Cancer Center (biomedical sciences), John F. Kennedy Presidential Library (history).

Computer facilities: 350 computers available on campus for general student use. A campuswide network can be accessed from off campus. Online class registration is available.
Website: http://www.umb.edu/

General Application Contact: Peggy Roldan Patel, Graduate Admissions Coordinator, 617-287-6400, Fax: 617-287-6236, E-mail: gadm@umb.edu.

GRADUATE UNITS

College of Advancing and Professional Studies Students: 20 full-time (16 women), 107 part-time (74 women). Expenses: Contact institution. *Program availability:* Online learning. Offers critical and creative thinking (MA, Certificate); instructional design (M Ed, Certificate). *Application Contact:* Peggy Roldan Patel, Graduate Admissions Coordinator, 617-287-6400, Fax: 617-287-6236, E-mail: bos.gadm@dpc.umassp.edu. *Dean,* Dr. Philip DiSalvio, 617-287-5700, Fax: 617-287-5699, E-mail: kristine.alster@umb.edu.

College of Education and Human Development Students: 341 full-time (275 women), 494 part-time (364 women). Expenses: Contact institution. *Financial support:* Research assistantships with full tuition reimbursements, teaching assistantships with full tuition reimbursements, career-related internships or fieldwork, Federal Work-Study, and unspecified assistantships available. Support available to part-time students. Financial award application deadline: 3/1; financial award applicants required to submit FAFSA. *Program availability:* Part-time, evening/weekend. Offers counseling and school psychology (PhD); early childhood education and care (PhD); education (M Ed, Ed D, PhD); education and human development (M Ed, MS, Ed D, PhD); family therapy (MS); higher education (Ed D, PhD); leadership in education (M Ed, CAGS); mental health counseling (MS); school counseling (M Ed); school psychology (M Ed); special education (M Ed); urban education, leadership, and policy studies (Ed D, PhD). *Application deadline:* For fall admission, 3/1 for domestic students. *Application Contact:* Peggy Roldan Patel, Graduate Admissions Coordinator, 617-287-6400, Fax: 617-287-6236, E-mail: bos.gadm@dpc.umassp.edu. *Interim Dean,* Dr. Peter Langer, 617-287-7600.

College of Liberal Arts Students: 208 full-time (161 women), 357 part-time (230 women). Expenses: Contact institution. *Financial support:* Research assistantships with full tuition reimbursements, teaching assistantships with full tuition reimbursements, career-related internships or fieldwork, Federal Work-Study, and unspecified assistantships available. Support available to part-time students. Financial award application deadline: 3/1; financial award applicants required to submit FAFSA. *Program availability:* Part-time, evening/weekend. Offers American studies (MA); applied economics (MA); applied linguistics (PhD); applied sociology (MA); archival methods (MA); clinical psychology (PhD); creative writing (MFA); developmental and brain sciences (MA); English (MA); historical archaeology (MA); Latin and classical humanities (MA, MFA, MS, PhD); liberal arts (MA, MFA, MS, PhD); sociology (PhD); transnational, cultural, and community studies (MS). *Application deadline:* For fall admission, 3/1 for domestic students; for spring admission, 1/1 for domestic students. *Application Contact:* Peggy Roldan Patel, Graduate Admissions Coordinator, 617-287-6400, Fax: 617-287-6236, E-mail: bos.gadm@dpc.umassp.edu.

College of Management Students: 291 full-time (141 women), 264 part-time (120 women). Expenses: Contact institution. *Financial support:* Research assistantships with full tuition reimbursements, teaching assistantships with full tuition reimbursements, career-related internships or fieldwork, Federal Work-Study, and unspecified assistantships available. Support available to part-time students. Financial award application deadline: 3/1; financial award applicants required to submit FAFSA. *Program availability:* Part-time, evening/weekend. Offers accounting (MS); business administration (MBA); finance (MS); information technology (MS); international management (MS); management (MBA, MS). *Application deadline:* For fall admission, 3/1 for domestic students; for spring admission, 11/1 for domestic students. *Application Contact:* Peggy Roldan Patel, Graduate Admissions Coordinator, 617-287-6400, Fax: 617-287-6236, E-mail: bos.gadm@dpc.umassp.edu. *Dean,* Dr. Philip Quaglieri, 617-287-7700, E-mail: philip.quaglieri@umb.edu.

College of Nursing and Health Sciences Students: 104 full-time (89 women), 259 part-time (237 women). Expenses: Contact institution. *Financial support:* Research assistantships with full tuition reimbursements, teaching assistantships with full tuition reimbursements, career-related internships or fieldwork, Federal Work-Study, and unspecified assistantships available. Support available to part-time students. Financial award application deadline: 3/1; financial award applicants required to submit FAFSA. *Program availability:* Part-time, evening/weekend. Offers exercise and health sciences (MS, PhD); nursing (MS, DNP, PhD); nursing practice (DNP). *Application deadline:* For fall admission, 3/1 for domestic students; for spring admission, 11/1 for domestic students. *Application Contact:* Peggy Roldan Patel, Graduate Admissions Coordinator, 617-287-6400, Fax: 617-287-6236, E-mail: bos.gadm@dpc.umassp.edu. *Dean,* Dr. Greer Glazer, 617-287-7500.

College of Public and Community Service Students: 3 part-time (all women). Expenses: Contact institution. *Financial support:* Research assistantships with full tuition reimbursements, teaching assistantships with full tuition reimbursements, career-related internships or fieldwork, Federal Work-Study, and unspecified assistantships available. Support available to part-time students. Financial award application deadline: 3/1; financial award applicants required to submit FAFSA. *Program availability:* Part-time, evening/weekend. Offers human services (MS); public and community service (MS). *Application deadline:* For fall admission, 3/1 for domestic students. Applications are processed on a rolling basis. *Application Contact:* Peggy Roldan Patel, Graduate Admissions Coordinator, 617-287-6400, Fax: 617-287-6236, E-mail: bos.gadm@dpc.umassp.edu. *Dean,* Adenrele Awotona, 617-287-7231, Fax: 617-287-5699.

College of Science and Mathematics Students: 209 full-time (75 women), 91 part-time (40 women). Expenses: Contact institution. *Financial support:* Research assistantships with full tuition reimbursements, teaching assistantships with full tuition reimbursements, career-related internships or fieldwork, Federal Work-Study, institutionally sponsored loans, and unspecified assistantships available. Support available to part-time students. Financial award application deadline: 3/1; financial award applicants required to submit FAFSA. *Program availability:* Part-time, evening/weekend. Offers applied physics (MS); biology (MS, PhD); biomedical engineering and biotechnology (PhD); biotechnology and biomedical sciences (MS); chemistry (MS, PhD); computer science (MS, PhD); environmental sciences (MS, PhD); marine science and technology (MS, PhD); science and mathematics (MS, PhD); urban planning and community development (MS). *Application deadline:* For fall admission, 3/1 for domestic students; for spring admission, 11/1 for domestic students. Applications are processed on a rolling basis. *Application Contact:* Peggy Roldan Patel, Graduate Admissions Coordinator, 617-287-6236, E-mail: bos.gadm@dpc.umassp.edu. *Interim Dean,* Dr. William Hagar, 617-287-5777.

Graduate School of Global Inclusion and Social Development Students: 45 full-time (35 women), 212 part-time (176 women). Expenses: Contact institution. Offers global inclusion and social development (M Ed, MA, MS, PhD); rehabilitation counseling (MS); vision studies (M Ed). *Application Contact:* Peggy Roldan Patel, Graduate Admissions Coordinator, 617-287-6400, Fax: 617-287-6236, E-mail: bos.gadm@dpc.umassp.edu. *Associate Provost,* Dr. Kristy Alster, 617-287-5700, Fax: 617-287-5699, E-mail: kristine.alster@umb.edu.

John W. McCormack Graduate School of Policy and Global Studies Students: 124 full-time (90 women), 245 part-time (171 women). Expenses: Contact institution. *Financial support:* Research assistantships with full tuition reimbursements, teaching assistantships with full tuition reimbursements, career-related internships or fieldwork, Federal Work-Study, and unspecified assistantships available. Support available to part-time students. Financial award application deadline: 3/1; financial award applicants required to submit FAFSA. *Program availability:* Part-time, evening/weekend. Offers conflict resolution (MA, Certificate); gerontology (PhD); global comparative public administration (MPA); global governance and human security (MA); policy and global studies (MA, MPA, MS, PhD, Certificate); public administration (MPA); public policy (MS, PhD). *Application Contact:* Peggy Roldan Patel, Graduate Admissions Coordinator, 617-287-6400, Fax: 617-287-6236, E-mail: bos.gadm@dpc.umassp.edu. *Dean,* Dr. Stephen Crosby, 617-287-5550, E-mail: stephen.crosby@umb.edu.

UNIVERSITY OF MASSACHUSETTS DARTMOUTH, North Dartmouth, MA 02747-2300

General Information State-supported, coed, university. *Enrollment:* 8,647 graduate, professional, and undergraduate students; 683 full-time matriculated graduate/professional students (311 women), 834 part-time matriculated graduate/professional students (493 women). *Enrollment by degree level:* 972 master's, 462 doctoral, 83 other advanced degrees. *Graduate faculty:* 302 full-time (134 women), 137 part-time/adjunct (86 women). Tuition, state resident: full-time $14,994; part-time $624.75 per credit. Tuition, nonresident: full-time $27,068; part-time $1127.83 per credit. *Required fees:* $405; $25.88 per credit. Tuition and fees vary according to course load and reciprocity agreements. *Graduate housing:* Room and/or apartments available on a first-come, first-served basis to single students; on-campus housing not available to married students. Typical cost: $8897 per year ($13,416 including board). Room and board charges vary according to board plan and housing facility selected. Housing application deadline: 3/14. *Student services:* Campus employment opportunities, campus safety program, career counseling, exercise/wellness program, free psychological counseling, grant writing training, international student services, low-cost health insurance, multicultural affairs office, services for students with disabilities, teacher training, writing training. *Library facilities:* Claire T. Carney Library plus 1 other. *Collection:* Books: 239,929 (physical), 84,639 (digital/electronic); Serial titles: 1,436 (physical), 87,444 (digital/electronic); Databases: 133. Students can reserve study rooms. *Research affiliation:* Massachusetts Department of Transportation (civil engineering), National Oceanic and Atmospheric Administration (NOAA) (marine sciences and technology), Environmental Protection Agency (public policy), National Institutes of Health (biomedical engineering and biotechnology), National Science Foundation (STEM education and teacher development), L'Oreal USA (chemistry).

Computer facilities: Computer purchase and lease plans are available. 368 computers available on campus for general student use. A campuswide network can be accessed from student residence rooms and from off campus. Online class registration is available.
Website: http://www.umassd.edu/

General Application Contact: Steven Briggs, Director of Marketing and Recruitment for Graduate Studies, 508-999-8604, Fax: 508-999-8183, E-mail: graduate@umassd.edu.

GRADUATE UNITS

Graduate School Students: 683 full-time (311 women), 834 part-time (493 women); includes 238 minority (64 Black or African American, non-Hispanic/Latino; 2 American Indian or Alaska Native, non-Hispanic/Latino; 54 Asian, non-Hispanic/Latino; 79 Hispanic/Latino; 1 Native Hawaiian or other Pacific Islander, non-Hispanic/Latino; 38 Two or more races, non-Hispanic/Latino), 367 international. Average age 31. 1,958 applicants, 67% accepted, 533 enrolled. *Faculty:* 302 full-time (134 women), 137 part-time/adjunct (86 women). Expenses: Contact institution. *Financial support:* In 2016–17, 63 fellowships (averaging $13,987 per year), 70 research assistantships (averaging $15,279 per year), 64 teaching assistantships (averaging $12,320 per year) were awarded; institutionally sponsored loans, scholarships/grants, and unspecified assistantships also available. Support available to part-time students. Financial award application deadline: 3/1; financial award applicants required to submit FAFSA. In 2016, 413 master's, 93 doctorates, 37 other advanced degrees awarded. *Program availability:* Part-time, 100% online, blended/hybrid learning. Offers adult gerontology primary care (MS, DNP); adult health clinical nurse specialist (DNP); adult health/advance practice (MS); adult nurse practitioner (Post-Master's Certificate); community health nurse specialist (DNP); community health/advance practice (MS); data science (MS); global public health (MS); nursing (PhD); nursing and healthcare education (MS); psychiatric and mental health nurse practitioner (DNP). *Application deadline:* For fall admission, 8/1 for domestic students, 6/1 priority date for international students; for spring admission, 11/15 for domestic students, 10/15 priority date for international students. *Application fee:* $60. Electronic applications accepted. *Application Contact:* Steven Briggs, Director of Marketing and Recruitment for Graduate Studies, 508-999-8604, Fax: 508-999-8183, E-mail: graduate@umassd.edu. *Director of Graduate Studies and Admissions,* Scott Webster, 508-999-8202, Fax: 508-999-8183, E-mail: graduate@umassd.edu.

Charlton College of Business Students: 169 full-time (72 women), 215 part-time (125 women); includes 63 minority (13 Black or African American, non-Hispanic/Latino; 1 American Indian or Alaska Native, non-Hispanic/Latino; 24 Asian, non-Hispanic/Latino; 18 Hispanic/Latino; 7 Two or more races, non-Hispanic/Latino), 122 international. Average age 32. 312 applicants, 80% accepted, 171 enrolled. *Faculty:* 41 full-time (15 women), 20 part-time/adjunct (9 women). Expenses: Contact institution. *Financial support:* In 2016–17, 2 research assistantships (averaging $2,667 per year) were awarded; institutionally sponsored loans, scholarships/grants, and unspecified assistantships also available. Support available to part-time students. Financial award application deadline: 3/1; financial award applicants required to submit FAFSA. In 2016, 143 master's, 13 other advanced degrees awarded. *Program availability:* Part-time, 100% online, blended/hybrid learning. Offers accounting (MS, Postbaccalaureate Certificate); accounting and finance (MS, Postbaccalaureate Certificate); business administration (MBA, Graduate Certificate, Postbaccalaureate Certificate); business analytics (Postbaccalaureate Certificate); business foundations (Graduate Certificate); decision and information sciences (MS); finance (Postbaccalaureate Certificate); healthcare management (MS); international business (Graduate Certificate); management (Postbaccalaureate Certificate); marketing (Postbaccalaureate Certificate); organizational leadership (Graduate Certificate); supply chain management and information systems (Postbaccalaureate Certificate); technology management (MS). *Application fee:* $60. Electronic applications accepted. *Application Contact:* Steven Briggs, Director of Recruitment and Marketing for Graduate Studies, 508-999-8604, Fax: 508-999-8183, E-mail: graduate@umassd.edu. *Assistant Dean of Graduate Studies,* Melissa Pacheco, 508-999-8543, Fax: 508-999-8646, E-mail: mpacheco@umassd.edu.

College of Arts and Sciences Students: 126 full-time (82 women), 282 part-time (183 women); includes 77 minority (19 Black or African American, non-Hispanic/Latino; 1 American Indian or Alaska Native, non-Hispanic/Latino; 9 Asian, non-Hispanic/Latino; 31 Hispanic/Latino; 17 Two or more races, non-Hispanic/Latino), 29 international. Average age 33. 314 applicants, 72% accepted, 140 enrolled. *Faculty:* 114 full-time (56 women), 39 part-time/adjunct (23 women). Expenses: Contact institution. *Financial support:* In 2016–17, 24 fellowships (averaging $17,333 per year), 13 research assistantships (averaging $13,557 per year), 28 teaching assistantships (averaging $13,161 per year) were awarded; institutionally sponsored loans, scholarships/grants, unspecified assistantships, and instructional assistantships, doctoral support, Fulbright scholarships also available. Support available to part-time students. Financial award application deadline: 3/1; financial award applicants required to submit FAFSA. In 2016, 126 master's, 12 doctorates, 19 other advanced degrees awarded. *Program availability:* Part-time, 100% online. Offers applied behavioral analysis (MA, Post-Master's Certificate); arts and sciences (MA, MAT, MPP, MS, Ed D, PhD, Graduate Certificate, Post-Master's Certificate, Postbaccalaureate Certificate); autism studies (Graduate Certificate); biology (MS); chemistry (MS, PhD); clinical psychology (MA); education ESL preK-12 (Postbaccalaureate Certificate); educational leadership (Ed D, PhD); educational leadership and policy studies (Ed D, PhD); educational policy (Graduate Certificate); environmental policy (Graduate Certificate); Luso-Afro Brazilian studies and theory (PhD); marine biology (MS); mathematics education (PhD); middle school education (MAT); Portuguese (MA); professional writing (MA, Postbaccalaureate Certificate); public management (Graduate Certificate); public policy (MPP); research psychology (MA); secondary school education (Postbaccalaureate Certificate); STEM education and teacher development (MAT, PhD, Postbaccalaureate Certificate); teaching secondary school education (MAT). *Application fee:* $60. Electronic applications accepted. *Application Contact:* Steven Briggs, Director of Recruitment and Marketing for Graduate Studies, 508-999-8604, Fax: 508-999-8183, E-mail: graduate@umassd.edu. *Associate Dean, College of Arts and Sciences,* Amy Shapiro, 508-910-9101, E-mail: ashapiro@umassd.edu.

College of Engineering Students: 197 full-time (52 women), 114 part-time (21 women); includes 21 minority (5 Black or African American, non-Hispanic/Latino; 7 Asian, non-Hispanic/Latino; 5 Hispanic/Latino; 4 Two or more races, non-Hispanic/Latino), 189 international. Average age 27. 372 applicants, 67% accepted, 98 enrolled. *Faculty:* 54 full-time (9 women), 5 part-time/adjunct (0 women). Expenses: Contact institution. *Financial support:* In 2016–17, 25 fellowships (averaging $16,520 per year), 31 research assistantships (averaging $14,696 per year), 34 teaching assistantships (averaging $12,059 per year) were awarded; institutionally sponsored loans, scholarships/grants, unspecified assistantships, and instructional assistantships, doctoral support also available. Support available to part-time students. Financial award application deadline: 3/1; financial award applicants required to submit FAFSA. In 2016, 105 master's, 9 doctorates, 3 other advanced degrees awarded. *Program availability:* Part-time, 100% online, blended/hybrid learning. Offers acoustics (Postbaccalaureate Certificate); applied mechanics and materials (PhD); bioengineering (PhD); biology (PhD); biomedical engineering/biotechnology (MS, PhD); chemistry (PhD); civil engineering (MS, PhD); communications

(Postbaccalaureate Certificate); computational science and engineering (PhD); computer and information science (PhD); computer engineering (MS, PhD); computer networks and distributed systems (Postbaccalaureate Certificate); computer science (MS, Postbaccalaureate Certificate); computer science and information systems (PhD); computing infrastructure (Postbaccalaureate Certificate); digital security signal processing (Postbaccalaureate Certificate); electrical and computer engineering (PhD); electrical engineering (MS, PhD); engineering (MS, PhD, Postbaccalaureate Certificate); engineering and applied science (PhD); industrial and systems engineering (MS, PhD); mathematics (PhD); mechanical engineering (MS, PhD); medical laboratory science (MS); physics (MS); software development and design (Postbaccalaureate Certificate). *Application fee:* $60. Electronic applications accepted. *Application Contact:* Steven Briggs, Director of Marketing and Recruitment for Graduate Studies, 508-999-8604, Fax: 508-999-8183, E-mail: graduate@umassd.edu. *Associate Dean, College of Engineering,* Ramprasad Balasubramanian, 508-910-6919, Fax: 508-999-9144, E-mail: rbala@umassd.edu.

College of Visual and Performing Arts Students: 32 full-time (22 women), 30 part-time (22 women); includes 4 minority (1 Black or African American, non-Hispanic/Latino; 2 Hispanic/Latino; 1 Two or more races, non-Hispanic/Latino), 8 international. Average age 35. 80 applicants, 56% accepted, 19 enrolled. *Faculty:* 33 full-time (16 women), 10 part-time/adjunct (4 women). Expenses: Contact institution. *Financial support:* In 2016–17, 13 fellowships (averaging $3,554 per year), 1 teaching assistantship (averaging $2,000 per year) were awarded; institutionally sponsored loans, scholarships/grants, and studio assistantships, distinguished art fellowships also available. Support available to part-time students. Financial award application deadline: 3/1; financial award applicants required to submit FAFSA. In 2016, 17 master's, 2 other advanced degrees awarded. *Program availability:* Part-time. Offers art education (MAE); ceramics (MFA, Postbaccalaureate Certificate); digital media (MFA); digital multi-media (MFA); drawing (MFA, Postbaccalaureate Certificate); fibers (MFA, Postbaccalaureate Certificate); graphic design (MFA); illustration (MFA); jewelry/metals (MFA, Postbaccalaureate Certificate); painting (MFA, Postbaccalaureate Certificate); photography (MFA); printmaking (MFA, Postbaccalaureate Certificate); sculpture (MFA, Postbaccalaureate Certificate); typography (MFA); visual and performing arts (MAE, MFA, Postbaccalaureate Certificate); wood/furniture design (MFA, Postbaccalaureate Certificate). *Application fee:* $60. Electronic applications accepted. *Application Contact:* Steven Briggs, Director of Marketing and Recruitment for Graduate Studies, 508-999-8604, Fax: 508-999-8183, E-mail: graduate@umassd.edu. *Dean, College of Visual and Performing Arts,* David Klamen, 508-999-9286, E-mail: dklamen@umassd.edu.

School for Marine Science and Technology Students: 26 full-time (17 women), 24 part-time (10 women); includes 5 minority (1 Asian, non-Hispanic/Latino; 1 Hispanic/Latino; 3 Two or more races, non-Hispanic/Latino), 10 international. Average age 31. 26 applicants, 73% accepted, 11 enrolled. *Faculty:* 13 full-time (1 woman), 1 part-time/adjunct (0 women). Expenses: Contact institution. *Financial support:* In 2016–17, 24 research assistantships (averaging $18,018 per year), 1 teaching assistantship (averaging $8,000 per year) were awarded; institutionally sponsored loans, scholarships/grants, and dissertation writing support also available. Support available to part-time students. Financial award application deadline: 3/1; financial award applicants required to submit FAFSA. In 2016, 4 master's, 2 doctorates awarded. *Program availability:* Part-time. Offers coastal and ocean administration, science and technology (PSM); coastal systems science (MS, PhD); integrated coastal management (MS, PhD); living marine resources science and management (MS, PhD); marine and atmospheric system modeling and analysis (MS, PhD); marine biogeochemical cycles and environmental change (MS, PhD); marine observation technologies (MS, PhD); ocean and human health (MS, PhD). *Application deadline:* For fall admission, 2/15 priority date for domestic students, 1/15 priority date for international students; for spring admission, 11/15 priority date for domestic students, 10/15 priority date for international students. *Application fee:* $60. Electronic applications accepted. *Application Contact:* Steven Briggs, Director of Marketing and Recruitment for Graduate Studies, 508-999-8604, Fax: 508-999-8183, E-mail: graduate@umassd.edu. *Graduate Program Director, Marine Science,* Pingguo He, 508-910-6323, E-mail: phe@umassd.edu.

University of Massachusetts School of Law –Dartmouth Students: 124 full-time (65 women), 61 part-time (36 women); includes 49 minority (16 Black or African American, non-Hispanic/Latino; 9 Asian, non-Hispanic/Latino; 18 Hispanic/Latino; 1 Native Hawaiian or other Pacific Islander, non-Hispanic/Latino; 5 Two or more races, non-Hispanic/Latino), 1 international. Average age 30. 800 applicants, 60% accepted, 66 enrolled. *Faculty:* 17 full-time (8 women), 11 part-time/adjunct (2 women). Expenses: Contact institution. *Financial support:* Fellowships, institutionally sponsored loans, and scholarships/grants available. Support available to part-time students. Financial award application deadline: 3/1; financial award applicants required to submit FAFSA. In 2016, 53 doctorates awarded. *Program availability:* Part-time, evening/weekend. Offers law (JD). *Application deadline:* For fall admission, 6/30 priority date for domestic students, 5/30 priority date for international students. *Application fee:* $50. Electronic applications accepted. *Application Contact:* Nancy Fitzsimmons-Hebert, Assistant Director of Marketing and Recruitment, 508-985-1110, Fax: 508-985-1175, E-mail: lawadmissions@umassd.edu. *Assistant Dean, University of Massachusetts School of Law - Dartmouth,* Daniel Fitzpatrick, 508-985-1110, Fax: 508-985-1175, E-mail: lawadmissions@umassd.edu.

UNIVERSITY OF MASSACHUSETTS LOWELL, Lowell, MA 01854

General Information State-supported, coed, university. CGS member. *Graduate housing:* Rooms and/or apartments available on a first-come, first-served basis to single students and available to married students. Housing application deadline: 4/1.

GRADUATE UNITS

College of Fine Arts, Humanities and Social Sciences Offers community social psychology (MA); fine arts, humanities and social sciences (MA, MM, PhD); music education (MM); peace and conflict studies (MA); regional economic and social development (MA, Graduate Certificate).

School of Criminology and Justice Studies *Program availability:* Part-time, evening/weekend. Offers criminal justice (MA). Electronic applications accepted.

College of Health Sciences *Program availability:* Part-time. Offers cleaner production and pollution prevention (Sc D); clinical laboratory sciences (MS); health sciences (MS, DNP, DPT, PhD); physical therapy (DPT).

School of Nursing Offers adult/gerontological nursing (MS); family health nursing (MS); nursing (DNP, PhD).

College of Sciences *Program availability:* Part-time, evening/weekend. Offers analytical chemistry (PhD); biochemistry (PhD); biological sciences (MS); chemistry (MS, PhD); computer science (MS, PhD); environmental studies (PhD); green chemistry (PhD); inorganic chemistry (PhD); mathematical sciences (Ed D); organic chemistry (PhD);

physics (MS, PhD); polymer science (MS); radiological sciences and protection (MS, PSM); sciences (MA, MM, MS, Ed D, PhD).

Francis College of Engineering *Program availability:* Part-time, evening/weekend. Offers chemical engineering (MS Eng, PhD); computer engineering (MS Eng, PhD); electrical engineering (MS Eng, PhD); energy engineering (MS Eng, PhD); engineering (MS, MS Eng, PhD); environmental studies (PhD); mechanical engineering (MS Eng, PhD); plastics engineering (MS Eng, PhD).

Graduate School of Education *Program availability:* Part-time, evening/weekend, online learning. Offers curriculum and instruction (M Ed). Electronic applications accepted.

Manning School of Business *Program availability:* Part-time, evening/weekend. Offers business administration (MBA, PhD); healthcare innovation and entrepreneurship (MS).

UNIVERSITY OF MASSACHUSETTS MEDICAL SCHOOL, Worcester, MA 01655-0115

General Information State-supported, coed, graduate-only institution. CGS member. *Enrollment by degree level:* 67 master's, 995 doctoral. *Graduate faculty:* 1,373 full-time (556 women), 336 part-time/adjunct (213 women). *Graduate housing:* On-campus housing not available. *Student services:* Campus employment opportunities, campus safety program, career counseling, child daycare facilities, exercise/wellness program, free psychological counseling, grant writing training, international student services, low-cost health insurance, multicultural affairs office, services for students with disabilities, teacher training, writing training. *Library facilities:* Lamar Soutter Library. *Collection:* Books: 178,673 (physical), 49,974 (digital/electronic); Serial titles: 10 (physical), 5,187 (digital/electronic); Databases: 372. Weekly public service hours: 84; study areas open 24 hours, 5–7 days a week. *Research affiliation:* Abbott Bioresearch Center (biomedical research and training), Charles River Laboratories (pre-clinical biomedical research).

Computer facilities: 107 computers available on campus for general student use. A campuswide network can be accessed from student residence rooms and from off campus. Online class registration is available.
Website: http://www.umassmed.edu/

General Application Contact: Karen Lawton, Director of Admissions, 508-856-2323, Fax: 508-856-3629, E-mail: admissions@umassmed.edu.

GRADUATE UNITS

Graduate School of Biomedical Sciences Students: 341 full-time (176 women); includes 57 minority (12 Black or African American, non-Hispanic/Latino; 1 American Indian or Alaska Native, non-Hispanic/Latino; 31 Asian, non-Hispanic/Latino; 13 Hispanic/Latino), 129 international. Average age 29. 617 applicants, 29% accepted, 51 enrolled. *Faculty:* 1,354 full-time (540 women), 311 part-time/adjunct (192 women). Expenses: Contact institution. *Financial support:* In 2016–17, 7 fellowships (averaging $34,000 per year), 391 research assistantships with full tuition reimbursements (averaging $31,000 per year) were awarded; scholarships/grants also available. Support available to part-time students. Financial award application deadline: 5/15. In 2016, 4 master's, 55 doctorates awarded. Offers biomedical sciences (PhD); biomedical sciences (millennium program) (PhD); clinical and population health research (PhD); clinical investigation (MS). *Application deadline:* For fall admission, 12/15 for domestic and international students; for spring admission, 5/15 for domestic students. *Application fee:* $80. Electronic applications accepted. *Application Contact:* Dr. Kendall Knight, Assistant Vice Provost for Admissions, 508-856-5628, Fax: 508-856-3659, E-mail: kendall.knight@umassmed.edu. *Dean,* Dr. Anthony Carruthers, 508-856-4135, E-mail: anthony.carruthers@umassmed.edu.

Graduate School of Nursing Students: 151 full-time (128 women), 27 part-time (26 women); includes 30 minority (17 Black or African American, non-Hispanic/Latino; 9 Asian, non-Hispanic/Latino; 4 Hispanic/Latino), 1 international. Average age 34. 145 applicants, 72% accepted, 60 enrolled. *Faculty:* 19 full-time (16 women), 25 part-time/adjunct (21 women). Expenses: Contact institution. *Financial support:* In 2016–17, 6 students received support. Scholarships/grants available. Support available to part-time students. Financial award application deadline: 5/15; financial award applicants required to submit FAFSA. In 2016, 48 master's, 10 doctorates, 2 other advanced degrees awarded. Offers adult gerontological acute care nurse practitioner (DNP, Post Master's Certificate); adult gerontological primary care nurse practitioner (DNP, Post Master's Certificate); family nursing practitioner (DNP); nurse administrator (DNP); nurse educator (MS, Post Master's Certificate); nursing (PhD); nursing practitioner (DNP); population health (MS). *Application deadline:* For fall admission, 12/1 priority date for domestic students. Applications are processed on a rolling basis. *Application fee:* $60. Electronic applications accepted. *Application Contact:* Diane Brescia, Admissions Coordinator, 508-856-3488, Fax: 508-856-5851, E-mail: diane.brescia@umassmed.edu. *Dean,* Dr. Joan Vitello-Cicciu, 508-856-5081, Fax: 508-856-6552, E-mail: joan.vitello@umassmed.edu.

School of Medicine Students: 543 full-time (295 women); includes 166 minority (30 Black or African American, non-Hispanic/Latino; 2 American Indian or Alaska Native, non-Hispanic/Latino; 120 Asian, non-Hispanic/Latino; 14 Hispanic/Latino), 1 international. Average age 26. 3,513 applicants, 8% accepted, 150 enrolled. *Faculty:* 1,354 full-time (540 women), 311 part-time/adjunct (192 women). Expenses: Contact institution. *Financial support:* In 2016–17, 485 students received support, including 13 fellowships with full tuition reimbursements available (averaging $31,000 per year), 39 research assistantships with full tuition reimbursements available (averaging $35,000 per year); institutionally sponsored loans, scholarships/grants, and tuition waivers (partial) also available. Support available to part-time students. Financial award application deadline: 3/31; financial award applicants required to submit FAFSA. In 2016, 119 doctorates awarded. Offers medicine (MD). *Application deadline:* For fall admission, 12/1 for domestic students. Applications are processed on a rolling basis. *Application fee:* $100. Electronic applications accepted. *Application Contact:* Dr. Mariann M. Manno, Associate Dean for Admissions, 508-856-2323, Fax: 508-856-3629, E-mail: admissions@umassmed.edu. *Dean/Provost/Executive Deputy Chancellor,* Dr. Terence R. Flotte, 508-856-8000, E-mail: terry.flotte@umassmed.edu.

UNIVERSITY OF MEMPHIS, Memphis, TN 38152

General Information State-supported, coed, university. CGS member. *Enrollment:* 1,978 full-time matriculated graduate/professional students (1,121 women), 1,964 part-time matriculated graduate/professional students (1,211 women). *Graduate faculty:* 516 full-time (195 women), 104 part-time/adjunct (56 women). Tuition, state resident: full-time $10,463; part-time $9483 per year. Tuition, nonresident: full-time $19,247; part-time $17,291 per year. *Required fees:* $821.50 per semester. Tuition and fees vary according to course load and program. *Graduate housing:* Rooms and/or apartments available on a first-come, first-served basis to single and married students. Typical cost: $6700 per year ($9000 including board) for single students; $7500 per year for married students. Room and board charges vary according to board plan, campus/location and housing facility selected. *Student services:* Campus employment opportunities, campus safety

program, career counseling, child daycare facilities, exercise/wellness program, free psychological counseling, grant writing training, international student services, low-cost health insurance, multicultural affairs office, services for students with disabilities, teacher training, writing training. *Library facilities:* McWherter Library plus 4 others. *Collection:* Books: 2.3 million (physical), 113,204 (digital/electronic); Serial titles: 288 (physical), 1,098 (digital/electronic); Databases: 739. Weekly public service hours: 83; students can reserve study rooms. *Research affiliation:* Memphis Biotech Foundation, Campbell Clinic Orthopaedics, Federal Express, Oak Ridge National Laboratory, St. Jude Children's Research Hospital, Gulf Coast Research Laboratory.

Computer facilities: 1,600 computers available on campus for general student use. A campuswide network can be accessed from student residence rooms and from off campus. Online class registration is available.
Website: http://www.memphis.edu/

General Application Contact: Dr. Jasbir Dhaliwal, Dean of the Graduate School, 901-678-4653, Fax: 901-678-0378, E-mail: graduateschool@memphis.edu.

GRADUATE UNITS

Cecil C. Humphreys School of Law Students: 308 full-time (135 women), 17 part-time (12 women); includes 80 minority (52 Black or African American, non-Hispanic/Latino; 4 American Indian or Alaska Native, non-Hispanic/Latino; 8 Asian, non-Hispanic/Latino; 16 Hispanic/Latino). Average age 25. 583 applicants, 55% accepted, 106 enrolled. *Faculty:* 25 full-time (11 women), 23 part-time/adjunct (7 women). Expenses: Contact institution. *Financial support:* In 2016–17, 138 students received support, including 26 fellowships (averaging $12,118 per year), 20 research assistantships (averaging $5,000 per year); teaching assistantships, career-related internships or fieldwork, Federal Work-Study, scholarships/grants, and tuition waivers (partial) also available. Support available to part-time students. Financial award application deadline: 5/1; financial award applicants required to submit FAFSA. In 2016, 1 doctorate awarded. *Program availability:* Part-time. Offers law (JD). *Application deadline:* For fall admission, 3/15 priority date for domestic and international students. Applications are processed on a rolling basis. *Application fee:* $0 ($40 for international students). Electronic applications accepted. *Application Contact:* Dr. Sue Ann McClellan, Assistant Dean for Law Admissions, Recruiting and Scholarships, 901-678-5403, Fax: 901-678-0741, E-mail: smcclell@memphis.edu. *Dean,* Peter V. Letsou, 901-678-2421, Fax: 901-678-5210, E-mail: pvletsou@memphis.edu.

Graduate School Students: 1,967 full-time (1,109 women), 1,979 part-time (1,193 women); includes 1,293 minority (911 Black or African American, non-Hispanic/Latino; 6 American Indian or Alaska Native, non-Hispanic/Latino; 154 Asian, non-Hispanic/Latino; 119 Hispanic/Latino; 2 Native Hawaiian or other Pacific Islander, non-Hispanic/Latino; 101 Two or more races, non-Hispanic/Latino), 456 international. Average age 32. 2,964 applicants, 60% accepted, 560 enrolled. *Faculty:* 533 full-time (189 women), 103 part-time/adjunct (51 women). Expenses: Contact institution. *Financial support:* In 2016–17, 2,179 students received support, including 4 research assistantships with full tuition reimbursements available (averaging $23,318 per year); fellowships with full tuition reimbursements available, teaching assistantships with full tuition reimbursements available, career-related internships or fieldwork, Federal Work-Study, institutionally sponsored loans, scholarships/grants, and unspecified assistantships also available. Support available to part-time students. Financial award application deadline: 2/1; financial award applicants required to submit FAFSA. In 2016, 1,062 master's, 130 doctorates, 112 other advanced degrees awarded. *Program availability:* Part-time, evening/weekend, 100% online, blended/hybrid learning. *Application deadline:* For fall admission, 7/1 for domestic students; 5/1 for international students; for spring admission, 12/1 for domestic students, 9/15 for international students. Applications are processed on a rolling basis. *Application fee:* $35 ($60 for international students). Electronic applications accepted. *Application Contact:* Lemmie Griggs, Supervisor of Graduate Admissions, 901-678-5580, Fax: 901-678-0378, E-mail: lgriggs@memphis.edu. *Interim Vice Provost for Graduate Studies,* Dr. Jasbir Dhaliwal, 901-678-4653, Fax: 901-678-0378, E-mail: gradsch@memphis.edu.

College of Arts and Sciences Students: 632 full-time (348 women), 345 part-time (196 women); includes 295 minority (203 Black or African American, non-Hispanic/Latino; 26 Asian, non-Hispanic/Latino; 45 Hispanic/Latino; 21 Two or more races, non-Hispanic/Latino), 176 international. Average age 31. 843 applicants, 56% accepted, 293 enrolled. *Faculty:* 206 full-time (76 women), 37 part-time/adjunct (20 women). Expenses: Contact institution. *Financial support:* In 2016–17, 467 students received support, including 3 research assistantships with full tuition reimbursements available (averaging $20,334 per year), 9 teaching assistantships with full tuition reimbursements available (averaging $19,194 per year); fellowships with full tuition reimbursements available, career-related internships or fieldwork, Federal Work-Study, institutionally sponsored loans, scholarships/grants, tuition waivers (full and partial), and unspecified assistantships also available. Financial award application deadline: 2/1; financial award applicants required to submit FAFSA. In 2016, 354 master's, 59 doctorates, 73 other advanced degrees awarded. *Program availability:* Part-time, evening/weekend. Offers adults and families (MSW); African-American literature (Graduate Certificate); analytical chemistry (MS, PhD); ancient Egyptian history (MA, PhD); applied linguistics (PhD); applied mathematics (MS); applied statistics (PhD); arts and sciences (MA, MCRP, MFA, MPA, MS, MSW, PhD, Ed S, Graduate Certificate); bioinformatics (MS); biology (MS, PhD); children, youth, and families (MSW); city and regional planning (MCRP); clinical psychology (PhD); composition studies (PhD); computational chemistry (MS, PhD); computational physics (MS); computer science (MS, PhD); creative writing (MFA); criminology and criminal justice (MA); earth sciences (MA, MS, PhD); English as a second language (MA); experimental psychology (PhD); general physics (MS); general psychology (MS); geographic information systems (Graduate Certificate); inorganic chemistry (MS, PhD); linguistics (MA); literary and cultural studies (PhD); literature (MA); local government management (Graduate Certificate); material science (MS); mathematics (MS, PhD); medical anthropology (MA); museum studies (Graduate Certificate); organic chemistry (MS, PhD); philanthropy and nonprofit leadership (Graduate Certificate); philosophy (MA, PhD); physical chemistry (MS, PhD); political science (MA); professional writing (MA, PhD); romance languages (MA); school psychology (MA, PhD, Ed S); sociology (MA); statistics (MS); teaching English as a second/foreign language (Graduate Certificate); teaching of mathematics (MS); women's and gender studies (Graduate Certificate). *Application deadline:* Applications are processed on a rolling basis. *Application fee:* $35 ($60 for international students). Electronic applications accepted. *Associate Dean for Graduate Studies,* Dr. Henry A. Kurtz, 901-678-3067, Fax: 901-678-4831, E-mail: hkurtz@memphis.edu.

College of Communication and Fine Arts Students: 123 full-time (77 women), 104 part-time (57 women); includes 68 minority (31 Black or African American, non-Hispanic/Latino; 8 Asian, non-Hispanic/Latino; 16 Hispanic/Latino; 13 Two or more races, non-Hispanic/Latino), 20 international. Average age 34. 179 applicants, 73% accepted, 77 enrolled. *Faculty:* 87 full-time (28 women), 10 part-time/adjunct (4 women). Expenses: Contact institution. *Financial support:* In 2016–17, 182 students received support, including 54 research assistantships with full tuition reimbursements available, 44 teaching assistantships with full tuition reimbursements available; career-related internships or fieldwork, Federal Work-Study, institutionally sponsored loans, scholarships/grants, and unspecified assistantships also available. Financial award application deadline: 2/1; financial award applicants required to submit FAFSA. In 2016, 92 master's, 19 doctorates, 23 other advanced degrees awarded. *Program availability:* Part-time, online learning. Offers architecture (M Arch); art history (MA); ceramics (MFA); communication (MA); communication and fine arts (M Arch, M Mu, MA, MFA, DMA, PhD, Graduate Certificate); communication arts (PhD); composition (M Mu, DMA); conducting (M Mu, DMA); entrepreneurial journalism (Graduate Certificate); film and video production (MA); graphic design (MFA); jazz and studio music (M Mu); journalism and strategic media (MA); museum studies (Graduate Certificate); music education (M Mu, PhD); music theory (DCC); musicology (PhD); Orff-Schulwerk (M Mu); painting (MFA); pedagogy (M Mu); performance (M Mu, DMA); printmaking/photography (MFA); sculpture (MFA); theatre (MFA). *Application deadline:* Applications are processed on a rolling basis. Application fee: $35 ($60 for international students). Electronic applications accepted. *Application Contact:* Dr. Janet Page, Interim Director of Graduate Studies, 901-678-2350, Fax: 901-678-5118, E-mail: jpage2@memphis.edu. *Interim Dean*, Dr. Moira Logan, 901-678-5085, Fax: 901-678-5118, E-mail: mlogan1@memphis.edu.

College of Education Students: 212 full-time (164 women), 575 part-time (423 women); includes 324 minority (266 Black or African American, non-Hispanic/Latino; 1 American Indian or Alaska Native, non-Hispanic/Latino; 11 Asian, non-Hispanic/Latino; 23 Hispanic/Latino; 1 Native Hawaiian or other Pacific Islander, non-Hispanic/Latino; 22 Two or more races, non-Hispanic/Latino), 13 international. Average age 38. 377 applicants, 79% accepted, 223 enrolled. *Faculty:* 58 full-time (36 women), 32 part-time/adjunct (21 women). Expenses: Contact institution. *Financial support:* In 2016–17, 921 students received support, including 18 research assistantships with full tuition reimbursements available, 14 teaching assistantships with full tuition reimbursements available; career-related internships or fieldwork, Federal Work-Study, scholarships/grants, tuition waivers (partial), and unspecified assistantships also available. Financial award application deadline: 2/1; financial award applicants required to submit FAFSA. In 2016, 187 master's, 43 doctorates, 55 other advanced degrees awarded. *Program availability:* Part-time, evening/weekend, 100% online, blended/hybrid learning. Offers adult education (Ed D); advanced studies in teaching and learning (M Ed); applied behavior analysis (Graduate Certificate); autism studies (Graduate Certificate); community college teaching and leadership (Graduate Certificate); community education (Ed D); counseling (MS, Ed D); counseling psychology (PhD); early childhood education (MAT, MS, Ed D); education (M Ed, MAT, MS, Ed D, PhD, Graduate Certificate); educational leadership (Ed D); educational psychology and research (MS, PhD); elementary education (MAT); higher education (Ed D); instruction and curriculum (MS, Ed D); instruction design and technology (MS, Ed D); instructional design and technology (Graduate Certificate); leadership (MS); literacy, leadership, and coaching (Graduate Certificate); policy studies (Ed D); reading (MS, Ed D); school administration and supervision (MS); school library information specialist (Graduate Certificate); secondary education (MAT); special education (MAT, MS, Ed D); STEM teacher leadership (Graduate Certificate); student personnel (MS); urban education (Graduate Certificate). *Application deadline:* Applications are processed on a rolling basis. Application fee: $35 ($60 for international students). Electronic applications accepted. *Application Contact:* Dr. Suzanne Lease, Interim Assistant Dean of Education for Graduate Programs, 901-678-2352, Fax: 901-678-4476, E-mail: slease@memphis.edu. *Dean*, Dr. Kandi Hill-Clarke, 901-678-5495, Fax: 901-678-4778, E-mail: k.hill-clarke@memphis.edu.

Fogelman College of Business and Economics Students: 208 full-time (86 women), 382 part-time (132 women); includes 183 minority (92 Black or African American, non-Hispanic/Latino; 1 American Indian or Alaska Native, non-Hispanic/Latino; 53 Asian, non-Hispanic/Latino; 17 Hispanic/Latino; 1 Native Hawaiian or other Pacific Islander, non-Hispanic/Latino; 19 Two or more races, non-Hispanic/Latino), 106 international. 380 applicants, 66% accepted, 81 enrolled. *Faculty:* 51 full-time (9 women), 4 part-time/adjunct (0 women). Expenses: Contact institution. *Financial support:* In 2016–17, 199 students received support, including 1 research assistantship with full tuition reimbursement available (averaging $6,000 per year); fellowships, teaching assistantships with full tuition reimbursements available, career-related internships or fieldwork, Federal Work-Study, scholarships/grants, and unspecified assistantships also available. Financial award application deadline: 2/1; financial award applicants required to submit FAFSA. In 2016, 318 master's, 9 doctorates, 50 other advanced degrees awarded. *Program availability:* Part-time, evening/weekend, online learning. Offers accountancy (MS); accounting (MBA, MS, PhD); business administration (IMBA, MBA, MS, PhD); business information and technology (MS, PhD, Graduate Certificate); economics (MA, PhD); executive business administration (MBA); finance (PhD); management (PhD); marketing (MS); marketing and supply chain management (PhD); real estate development (MS). *Application deadline:* For fall admission, 7/1 for domestic students, 5/1 for international students; for winter admission, 9/15 for international students; for spring admission, 12/1 for domestic students. Application fee: $35 ($60 for international students). Electronic applications accepted. *Application Contact:* Dr. Lloyd Brooks, Associate Dean for Academic Affairs, 901-678-4620, Fax: 901-678-3759, E-mail: lbrooks@memphis.edu. *Dean*, Dr. Rajiv Grover, 901-678-3633, Fax: 901-678-4705, E-mail: rgrover@memphis.edu.

Herff College of Engineering Students: 88 full-time (29 women), 86 part-time (20 women); includes 33 minority (17 Black or African American, non-Hispanic/Latino; 1 American Indian or Alaska Native, non-Hispanic/Latino; 8 Asian, non-Hispanic/Latino; 3 Hispanic/Latino; 4 Two or more races, non-Hispanic/Latino), 93 international. Average age 32. 183 applicants, 67% accepted, 36 enrolled. *Faculty:* 41 full-time (4 women), 2 part-time/adjunct (0 women). Expenses: Contact institution. *Financial support:* In 2016–17, 29 students received support, including 12 research assistantships with full tuition reimbursements available (averaging $21,092 per year), 1 teaching assistantship with full tuition reimbursement available (averaging $5,504 per year); fellowships with full tuition reimbursements available, career-related internships or fieldwork, Federal Work-Study, scholarships/grants, tuition waivers (full and partial), and unspecified assistantships also available. Financial award application deadline: 2/1; financial award applicants required to submit FAFSA. In 2016, 30 master's, 18 doctorates, 11 other advanced degrees awarded. *Program availability:* Part-time. Offers applied lean leadership (Graduate Certificate); biomedical engineering (MS, PhD); civil engineering (PhD); computer engineering (MS, PhD); electrical engineering (MS, PhD); engineering (MS, PhD, Graduate Certificate); engineering seismology (MS); engineering technology (MS); environmental engineering (MS); freight transportation (Graduate Certificate); geotechnical engineering (MS); imaging and signal processing (Graduate Certificate);

power systems (MS); structural engineering (MS); transportation engineering (MS); water resources engineering (MS). *Application deadline:* For fall admission, 8/1 for domestic students, 5/1 for international students; for spring admission, 12/1 for domestic students, 9/15 for international students; for summer admission, 5/1 for domestic students. Application fee: $35 ($60 for international students). Electronic applications accepted. *Application Contact:* Dr. Warren Haggard, Associate Dean for Research and Graduate Studies, 901-678-4346, Fax: 901-678-5030, E-mail: whaggrd1@memphis.edu. *Dean*, Dr. Richard Joseph Sweigard, 901-678-4306, Fax: 901-678-4180, E-mail: rjswgard@memphis.edu.

Kemmons Wilson School of Hospitality and Resort Management Students: 15 full-time (1 woman), 10 part-time (4 women); includes 9 minority (8 Black or African American, non-Hispanic/Latino; 1 Hispanic/Latino), 1 international. Average age 26. 26 applicants, 92% accepted, 21 enrolled. *Faculty:* 3 full-time (0 women), 2 part-time/adjunct (0 women). Expenses: Contact institution. *Financial support:* In 2016–17, 10 research assistantships (averaging $7,200 per year) were awarded; career-related internships or fieldwork, Federal Work-Study, scholarships/grants, and unspecified assistantships also available. Support available to part-time students. Financial award application deadline: 2/1. *Program availability:* Part-time. Offers hospitality management specialist (Graduate Certificate); sports commerce (MS). *Application deadline:* For fall admission, 7/1 for domestic students, 5/1 for international students; for spring admission, 12/1 for domestic students, 9/1 for international students; for summer admission, 5/1 for domestic students, 2/1 for international students. Application fee: $35 ($60 for international students). Electronic applications accepted. *Application Contact:* Dr. Timothy Ryan, Coordinator of Graduate Studies, 901-678-5003, E-mail: tdryan@memphis.edu. *Director*, Dr. Radesh Palakurthi, 901-678-3430, E-mail: rplkrthi@memphis.edu.

School of Communication Sciences and Disorders Students: 88 full-time (85 women), 14 part-time (11 women); includes 10 minority (1 Black or African American, non-Hispanic/Latino; 5 Asian, non-Hispanic/Latino; 2 Hispanic/Latino; 2 Two or more races, non-Hispanic/Latino), 6 international. Average age 28. 442 applicants, 26% accepted, 40 enrolled. *Faculty:* 11 full-time (7 women), 3 part-time/adjunct (all women). Expenses: Contact institution. *Financial support:* In 2016–17, 25 research assistantships with full tuition reimbursements (averaging $8,560 per year) were awarded; Federal Work-Study, scholarships/grants, and unspecified assistantships also available. Financial award application deadline: 2/1; financial award applicants required to submit FAFSA. In 2016, 16 master's, 10 doctorates awarded. *Program availability:* Part-time. Offers audiology (Au D); communication sciences and disorders (PhD); speech-language pathology (MA). *Application deadline:* For fall admission, 2/1 priority date for domestic students. Applications are processed on a rolling basis. Application fee: $35 ($60 for international students). Electronic applications accepted. *Application Contact:* Dr. Lisa Mendel, Interim Associate Dean, 901-678-5800, E-mail: lmendel@memphis.edu. *Interim Dean*, Dr. Linda Jarmulowicz, 901-678-5800, Fax: 901-525-1282, E-mail: ljrmlwcz@memphis.edu.

School of Health Studies Students: 73 full-time (58 women), 39 part-time (24 women); includes 31 minority (22 Black or African American, non-Hispanic/Latino; 1 American Indian or Alaska Native, non-Hispanic/Latino; 6 Asian, non-Hispanic/Latino; 2 Hispanic/Latino), 4 international. Average age 27. 62 applicants, 89% accepted, 45 enrolled. *Faculty:* 19 full-time (10 women), 2 part-time/adjunct (both women). Expenses: Contact institution. *Financial support:* In 2016–17, 20 research assistantships (averaging $11,360 per year), 8 teaching assistantships (averaging $10,062 per year) were awarded; career-related internships or fieldwork, Federal Work-Study, scholarships/grants, and unspecified assistantships also available. Financial award application deadline: 2/1; financial award applicants required to submit FAFSA. In 2016, 42 master's awarded. *Program availability:* 100% online. Offers faith and health (Graduate Certificate); health studies (MS); nutrition (MS). *Application deadline:* For fall admission, 4/15 priority date for domestic students; for spring admission, 10/15 priority date for domestic students; for summer admission, 4/15 priority date for domestic students. Application fee: $35 ($60 for international students). *Application Contact:* Dr. Lawrence Weiss, Director of Graduate Programs, 901-678-5037, E-mail: lweiss@memphis.edu. *Director*, Dr. Richard J. Bloomer, 901-678-4316, Fax: 901-678-3591, E-mail: rbloomer@memphis.edu.

School of Public Health Students: 116 full-time (74 women), 60 part-time (46 women); includes 84 minority (54 Black or African American, non-Hispanic/Latino; 18 Asian, non-Hispanic/Latino; 8 Hispanic/Latino; 4 Two or more races, non-Hispanic/Latino), 19 international. Average age 31. 121 applicants, 92% accepted, 76 enrolled. *Faculty:* 20 full-time (7 women), 6 part-time/adjunct (2 women). Expenses: Contact institution. *Financial support:* In 2016–17, 46 students received support, including 11 research assistantships with full tuition reimbursements available (averaging $13,000 per year); Federal Work-Study, scholarships/grants, and unspecified assistantships also available. Financial award application deadline: 2/1; financial award applicants required to submit FAFSA. In 2016, 72 master's, 3 doctorates awarded. *Program availability:* Part-time, evening/weekend. Offers biostatistics (MPH); environmental health (MPH); epidemiology (MPH, PhD); health systems and policy (PhD); health systems management (MPH); public health (MHA); social and behavioral sciences (MPH, PhD). *Application deadline:* For fall admission, 4/1 for domestic students; for spring admission, 11/1 for domestic students. Application fee: $35 ($60 for international students). Electronic applications accepted. *Application Contact:* Dr. Marian Levy, Assistant Dean, 901-678-4514, Fax: 901-678-5023, E-mail: sph-admin@memphis.edu. *Dean*, Dr. Lisa M. Klesges, 901-678-4501, E-mail: lmklsges@memphis.edu.

University College Students: 25 full-time (14 women), 98 part-time (71 women); includes 85 minority (76 Black or African American, non-Hispanic/Latino; 1 Asian, non-Hispanic/Latino; 5 Hispanic/Latino; 3 Two or more races, non-Hispanic/Latino), 2 international. Average age 38. 59 applicants, 73% accepted, 29 enrolled. *Faculty:* 3 full-time (1 woman), 2 part-time/adjunct (0 women). Expenses: Contact institution. *Financial support:* In 2016–17, 123 students received support, including 2 research assistantships with full tuition reimbursements available (averaging $17,000 per year), 3 teaching assistantships with tuition reimbursements available (averaging $11,334 per year); Federal Work-Study, scholarships/grants, and unspecified assistantships also available. Financial award application deadline: 2/3; financial award applicants required to submit FAFSA. In 2016, 53 master's, 4 other advanced degrees awarded. *Program availability:* Part-time, evening/weekend. Offers human resources (MPS); liberal studies (MALS, Graduate Certificate); strategic leadership (MPS, Graduate Certificate); training and development (MPS). *Application deadline:* For fall admission, 7/1 for domestic students, 5/1 for international students; for spring admission, 11/1 for domestic students, 9/15 for international students. Applications are processed on a rolling basis. Application fee: $35 ($60 for international students). Electronic applications accepted. *Application Contact:* Dr. Colin Chapell, Graduate Coordinator, 901-678-4171, Fax: 901-678-2971, E-mail: cbshpell@memphis.edu. *Dean*, Dr. Dan Lattimore, 901-678-2991, E-mail: dlattimr@memphis.edu.

Loewenberg College of Nursing Students: 44 full-time (39 women), 247 part-time (224 women); includes 107 minority (93 Black or African American, non-Hispanic/Latino; 1 American Indian or Alaska Native, non-Hispanic/Latino; 7 Asian, non-Hispanic/Latino; 3 Hispanic/Latino; 3 Two or more races, non-Hispanic/Latino). Average age 35. 218 applicants, 43% accepted, 67 enrolled. *Faculty:* 17 full-time (all women), 4 part-time/adjunct (all women). Expenses: Contact institution. *Financial support:* In 2016–17, 147 students received support. Federal Work-Study and scholarships/grants available. Financial award application deadline: 2/1; financial award applicants required to submit FAFSA. In 2016, 87 master's, 5 other advanced degrees awarded. *Program availability:* Part-time, evening/weekend, online learning. Offers advanced practice nursing (Graduate Certificate); executive leadership (MSN); family nurse practitioner (MSN); nursing administration (MSN, Graduate Certificate); nursing education (MSN, Graduate Certificate). *Application deadline:* For fall admission, 2/15 for domestic and international students; for spring admission, 10/1 for domestic and international students. *Application fee:* $35 ($60 for international students). *Application Contact:* Dr. Shirleatha Lee, Associate Dean for Academic Programs, 901-678-2036, Fax: 901-678-5023, E-mail: sntaylr1@memphis.edu. *Dean,* Dr. Lin Zhan, 901-678-2003, Fax: 901-678-4907, E-mail: lzhan@memphis.edu.

UNIVERSITY OF MIAMI, Coral Gables, FL 33124

General Information Independent, coed, university. CGS member. *Graduate housing:* On-campus housing not available. *Research affiliation:* Howard Hughes Medical Institute (biology), The Buoniconti Fund: Miami Project to Cure Paralysis (paralysis research), Organization for Tropical Studies, National Center for Atmospheric Research (atmospheric science).

GRADUATE UNITS

Graduate School *Program availability:* Part-time, evening/weekend, online learning. Offers international administration (MAIA). Electronic applications accepted.

College of Arts and Sciences *Program availability:* Part-time, evening/weekend. Offers adult clinical (PhD); art history (MA); arts and sciences (MA, MAIA, MALS, MFA, MPA, MS, PhD); behavioral neuroscience (PhD); biology (MS, PhD); ceramics/glass (MFA); chemistry (MS); child clinical (PhD); computer science (MS, PhD); creative writing (MFA); developmental psychology (PhD); English (MA, PhD); genetics and evolution (MS, PhD); geography (MA); graphic design/multimedia (MFA); health clinical (PhD); history (MA, PhD); inorganic chemistry (PhD); international studies (MA, PhD); Latin American studies (MA); liberal studies (MALS); mathematical finance (MS); mathematics (MA, MS, PhD); organic chemistry (PhD); painting (MFA); philosophy (MA, PhD); photography/digital imaging (MFA); physical chemistry (PhD); physics (MS, PhD); political science (MPA); printmaking (MFA); psychology (MS); romance studies (PhD); sculpture (MFA); sociology (MA, PhD). Electronic applications accepted.

College of Engineering *Program availability:* Part-time, evening/weekend. Offers architectural engineering (MSAE); biomedical engineering (MSBE, PhD); civil engineering (MSCE, PhD); electrical and computer engineering (MSECE, PhD); engineering (MS, MSAE, MSBE, MSCE, MSECE, MSIE, MSME, MSOES, PhD); environmental health and safety (MS); ergonomics (PhD); industrial engineering (MSIE, PhD); management of technology (MS); mechanical and aerospace engineering (MSME, PhD); occupational ergonomics and safety (MS, MSOES). Electronic applications accepted.

Frost School of Music Offers accompanying and chamber music (MM, DMA); choral conducting (MM, DMA); composition (MM, DMA); electronic music (MM); instrumental conducting (MM, DMA); instrumental performance (MM, DMA, AD); jazz composition (DMA); jazz pedagogy (MM); jazz performance (MM, DMA); keyboard performance and pedagogy (MM, DMA); media writing and production (MM); multiple woodwinds (MM, DMA); music (MM, MS, DMA, PhD, AD, Spec M); music business and entertainment industries (MM); music education (MM, PhD, Spec M); music engineering (MS); music theory (MM); music therapy (MM); musicology (MM); piano performance (MM, DMA, AD); studio jazz writing (MM); vocal pedagogy (DMA); vocal performance (MM, DMA, AD). Electronic applications accepted.

Miller School of Medicine Offers biochemistry and molecular biology (PhD); cancer biology (PhD); epidemiology (PhD); medicine (MPH, MSPH, DPT, MD, PhD); microbiology and immunology (PhD); molecular and cellular pharmacology (PhD); molecular cell and developmental biology (PhD); neuroscience (PhD); physical therapy (DPT, PhD); physiology and biophysics (PhD); public health (MPH, MSPH). Electronic applications accepted.

Rosenstiel School of Marine and Atmospheric Science *Program availability:* Part-time. Offers applied marine physics (MS, PhD); marine affairs and policy (MA, MS); marine and atmospheric chemistry (MS, PhD); marine and atmospheric science (MA, MS, PhD); marine biology and fisheries (MA, MS, PhD); marine geology and geophysics (MS, PhD); meteorology (MS, PhD); physical oceanography (MS, PhD). Electronic applications accepted.

School of Architecture Offers architecture (M Arch); suburb and town design (M Arch). Electronic applications accepted.

School of Business Administration *Program availability:* Part-time, evening/weekend. Offers business administration (MA, MBA, MP Acc, MS, MS Tax, MSPM, PhD). Electronic applications accepted.

School of Communication *Program availability:* Part-time. Offers communication (PhD); communication studies (MA); film studies (MA, PhD); motion pictures (MFA); print journalism (MA); public relations (MA); Spanish language journalism (MA); television broadcast journalism (MA). Electronic applications accepted.

School of Education and Human Development Students: 404 full-time (209 women), 86 part-time (61 women); includes 241 minority (81 Black or African American, non-Hispanic/Latino; 2 American Indian or Alaska Native, non-Hispanic/Latino; 1 Asian, non-Hispanic/Latino; 129 Hispanic/Latino; 2 Native Hawaiian or other Pacific Islander, non-Hispanic/Latino; 16 Two or more races, non-Hispanic/Latino), 34 international. Average age 30. 613 applicants, 44% accepted, 152 enrolled. *Faculty:* 72 full-time (37 women), 51 part-time/adjunct (31 women). Expenses: Contact institution. *Financial support:* Fellowships, research assistantships, teaching assistantships, career-related internships or fieldwork, institutionally sponsored loans, scholarships/grants, health care benefits, tuition waivers (full and partial), and unspecified assistantships available. Support available to part-time students. Financial award application deadline: 3/1; financial award applicants required to submit FAFSA. In 2016, 100 master's, 19 doctorates, 3 other advanced degrees awarded. *Program availability:* 100% online. Offers athletic training (MS Ed); community and social change (MS Ed); community well-being (PhD); counseling (MS Ed, Certificate); counseling and research (MS Ed); counseling psychology (PhD); early childhood special education (MS Ed, Ed S); education and human development (MS Ed, Ed D, PhD, Certificate, Ed S); education and social change (MS Ed); enrollment management (MS Ed, Certificate); exercise physiology (MS Ed, PhD); higher education administration (MS Ed, Ed D, Certificate); higher education leadership (Ed D); language and literacy learning in multilingual settings (PhD); Latino mental health (Certificate); marriage and family therapy (MS Ed); mental health counseling (MS Ed); nutrition for health and human performance (MS Ed); research, measurement, and evaluation (MS Ed, PhD); science, technology, engineering and mathematics (PhD); special education (PhD); sport administration (MS Ed); sports medicine (MS Ed); strength and conditioning (MS Ed); student life and development (MS Ed, Certificate); teaching and learning (PhD); women's health (Certificate). *Application deadline:* For fall admission, 10/1 for international students. *Application fee:* $65. Electronic applications accepted. *Application Contact:* Lois Heffernan, Graduate Admissions Coordinator, 305-284-2167, Fax: 305-284-9395, E-mail: lheffernan@miami.edu. *Senior Associate Dean,* Dr. Walter Secada, 305-284-2102, Fax: 305-284-9395, E-mail: wsecada@miami.edu.

School of Nursing and Health Studies *Program availability:* Part-time. Offers acute care (MSN); nursing (PhD); primary care (MSN). Electronic applications accepted.

University of Miami School of Law Students: 995 full-time (464 women), 74 part-time (33 women); includes 457 minority (69 Black or African American, non-Hispanic/Latino; 3 American Indian or Alaska Native, non-Hispanic/Latino; 31 Asian, non-Hispanic/Latino; 323 Hispanic/Latino; 1 Native Hawaiian or other Pacific Islander, non-Hispanic/Latino; 30 Two or more races, non-Hispanic/Latino), 82 international. 2,443 applicants, 55% accepted, 300 enrolled. *Faculty:* 78 full-time (35 women), 98 part-time/adjunct (22 women). Expenses: Contact institution. *Financial support:* Fellowships, research assistantships, career-related internships or fieldwork, Federal Work-Study, institutionally sponsored loans, scholarships/grants, and unspecified assistantships available. Financial award application deadline: 3/1; financial award applicants required to submit FAFSA. *Program availability:* Part-time. Offers entertainment, arts, and sports law (LL M); estate planning (LL M); international arbitration (LL M); international law (LL M); law (JD); maritime law (LL M); real estate/property development (LL M); taxation (LL M); taxation of cross-border investment (LL M). *Application deadline:* For fall admission, 7/31 for domestic and international students. Applications are processed on a rolling basis. *Application fee:* $60. Electronic applications accepted. *Application Contact:* Therese Lambert, Director of Student Recruitment, 305-284-6746, Fax: 305-284-3084, E-mail: tlambert@law.miami.edu. *Associate Dean of Admissions and Enrollment Management,* Michael Goodnight, 305-284-2527, Fax: 305-284-3084, E-mail: mgoodnig@law.miami.edu.

UNIVERSITY OF MICHIGAN, Ann Arbor, MI 48109

General Information State-supported, coed, university. CGS member. *Enrollment:* 44,718 graduate, professional, and undergraduate students; 14,120 full-time matriculated graduate/professional students (6,730 women), 1,264 part-time matriculated graduate/professional students (466 women). *Enrollment by degree level:* 7,599 master's, 7,785 doctoral, 50 other advanced degrees. *Graduate faculty:* 4,585 full-time (1,818 women), 1,220 part-time/adjunct (681 women). Tuition, state resident: full-time $21,466; part-time $1152 per credit hour. Tuition, nonresident: full-time $43,346; part-time $2367 per credit hour. Part-time tuition and fees vary according to course load, degree level and program. *Graduate housing:* Rooms and/or apartments available on a first-come, first-served basis to single and married students. Typical cost: $6350 per year for single students; $12,170 per year for married students. Room charges vary according to housing facility selected. *Student services:* Campus employment opportunities, campus safety program, career counseling, child daycare facilities, exercise/wellness program, free psychological counseling, grant writing training, international student services, low-cost health insurance, multicultural affairs office, services for students with disabilities, teacher training, writing training. *Library facilities:* Shapiro Undergraduate Library plus 9 others. *Collection:* Books: 9 million (physical), 3.3 million (digital/electronic); Serial titles: 464,460 (physical), 163,830 (digital/electronic); Databases: 10,078. Weekly public service hours: 168; study areas open 24 hours, 5–7 days a week; students can reserve study rooms.

Computer facilities: Computer purchase and lease plans are available. 3,940 computers available on campus for general student use. A campuswide network can be accessed from student residence rooms and from off campus. Online class registration, file storage, personal Web pages, printing are available. Website: http://www.umich.edu/

General Application Contact: Admissions Office, 734-764-8129, Fax: 734-647-7740, E-mail: rackadmis@umich.edu.

GRADUATE UNITS

College of Engineering Students: 3,248 full-time (794 women), 322 part-time (62 women). 10,718 applicants, 27% accepted, 1198 enrolled. *Faculty:* 409 full-time (82 women). Expenses: Contact institution. *Financial support:* Fellowships, research assistantships, teaching assistantships, career-related internships or fieldwork, Federal Work-Study, institutionally sponsored loans, scholarships/grants, traineeships, health care benefits, tuition waivers (full and partial), and unspecified assistantships available. Support available to part-time students. Financial award applicants required to submit FAFSA. In 2016, 1,088 master's, 255 doctorates awarded. *Program availability:* Part-time, 100% online. Offers aerospace engineering (M Eng, MS, MSE, PhD); applied climate (M Eng); atmospheric, oceanic and space sciences (MS, PhD); automotive engineering (M Eng); biomedical engineering (MS, MSE, PhD); chemical engineering (MSE, PhD, Ch E); civil engineering (MSE, PhD, CE); computer science and engineering (MS, MSE, PhD); construction engineering and management (M Eng, MSE); design science (MS, PhD); electrical and computer engineering (MS, MSE, PhD); energy systems engineering (M Eng, MS); engineering (M Eng, MS, MSE, D Eng, PhD, CE, Certificate, Ch E, Mar Eng, Nav Arch, Nuc E); environmental engineering (MSE, PhD); geoscience and remote sensing (PhD); global automotive and manufacturing engineering (M Eng); industrial and operations engineering (MS, MSE, PhD); manufacturing engineering (M Eng, D Eng); materials science and engineering (MS, PhD); mechanical engineering (MSE, PhD); naval architecture and marine engineering (MS, MSE, PhD, Mar Eng, Nav Arch); nuclear engineering (Nuc E); nuclear engineering and radiological sciences (MSE, PhD); nuclear science (MS, PhD); pharmaceutical engineering (M Eng); robotics (MS, PhD); robotics and autonomous vehicles (M Eng); space and planetary sciences (PhD); space engineering (M Eng); structural engineering (M Eng); systems engineering and design (M Eng). *Application deadline:* Applications are processed on a rolling basis. Electronic applications accepted. *Application Contact:* Kim Elliott, Director of Graduate Education, 734-647-7077, Fax: 734-647-7045, E-mail: elliottk@umich.edu. *Dean of Engineering,* Prof. Alec D. Gallimore, 734-647-7008, Fax: 734-647-7009, E-mail: rasta@umich.edu.

College of Pharmacy Students: 329 full-time (218 women), 2 part-time (1 woman); includes 111 minority (7 Black or African American, non-Hispanic/Latino; 92 Asian, non-Hispanic/Latino; 5 Hispanic/Latino; 7 Two or more races, non-Hispanic/Latino), 13 international. Average age 25. 412 applicants, 33% accepted, 85 enrolled. *Faculty:* 22 full-time (6 women), 7 part-time/adjunct (0 women). Expenses: Contact institution. Offers clinical pharmacy (PhD); medicinal chemistry (PhD); pharmaceutical sciences (PhD); pharmacy (PhD, Pharm D). *Application deadline:* For fall admission, 1/5 for domestic and international students. Applications are processed on a rolling basis. *Application fee:* $150. Electronic applications accepted. *Application Contact:* Admissions Office, 734-764-8129, Fax: 734-647-7740, E-mail: rackadmis@umich.edu. *Dean,* James T. Dalton, 734-764-7144, Fax: 734-763-2022, E-mail: cop.deansoffice@med.umich.edu.

Gerald R. Ford School of Public Policy Students: 262 full-time (133 women); includes 72 minority (24 Black or African American, non-Hispanic/Latino; 1 American Indian or Alaska Native, non-Hispanic/Latino; 21 Asian, non-Hispanic/Latino; 17 Hispanic/Latino; 9 Two or more races, non-Hispanic/Latino), 56 international. Average age 28. 631 applicants, 65% accepted, 114 enrolled. *Faculty:* 36 full-time (13 women), 37 part-time/adjunct (16 women). Expenses: Contact institution. *Financial support:* In 2016–17, 205 students received support, including 181 fellowships with tuition reimbursements available, 27 teaching assistantships with tuition reimbursements available; research assistantships, career-related internships or fieldwork, traineeships, health care benefits, and unspecified assistantships also available. Financial award application deadline: 1/15; financial award applicants required to submit FAFSA. In 2016, 103 master's, 7 doctorates awarded. Offers public policy (MPA, MPP, PhD). *Application deadline:* For fall admission, 1/15 priority date for domestic students, 1/15 for international students. *Application fee:* $75 ($90 for international students). Electronic applications accepted. *Application Contact:* Beth Soboleski, Director, Admissions and Recruiting, 734-764-0453, Fax: 734-647-7486, E-mail: fspp-admissions@umich.edu. *Dean,* Dr. Susan M. Collins, 734-764-3490.

Law School Students: 933 full-time (438 women); includes 205 minority (35 Black or African American, non-Hispanic/Latino; 8 American Indian or Alaska Native, non-Hispanic/Latino; 78 Asian, non-Hispanic/Latino; 42 Hispanic/Latino; 42 Two or more races, non-Hispanic/Latino), 59 international. 5,076 applicants, 24% accepted, 305 enrolled. *Faculty:* 107 full-time (36 women), 36 part-time/adjunct (8 women). Expenses: Contact institution. *Financial support:* In 2016–17, 779 students received support. Career-related internships or fieldwork, Federal Work-Study, institutionally sponsored loans, and scholarships/grants available. Financial award applicants required to submit FAFSA. In 2016, 36 master's, 328 doctorates awarded. Offers comparative law (MCL); international tax (LL M); law (LL M, JD, SJD). *Application deadline:* For fall admission, 2/15 for domestic students. Applications are processed on a rolling basis. *Application fee:* $75. Electronic applications accepted. *Application Contact:* Sarah C. Zearfoss, Assistant Dean and Director of Admissions, 734-764-0537, Fax: 734-647-3218, E-mail: law.jd.admissions@umich.edu. *Dean,* Mark D. West, 734-764-1358.

Medical School Students: 719 full-time (381 women); includes 196 minority (43 Black or African American, non-Hispanic/Latino; 3 American Indian or Alaska Native, non-Hispanic/Latino; 131 Asian, non-Hispanic/Latino; 19 Hispanic/Latino). Average age 27. 6,926 applicants, 6% accepted, 170 enrolled. *Faculty:* 2,390 full-time (889 women), 1,307 part-time/adjunct (685 women). Expenses: Contact institution. *Financial support:* In 2016–17, 426 students received support. Institutionally sponsored loans and scholarships/grants available. Financial award application deadline: 9/30; financial award applicants required to submit FAFSA. In 2016, 164 doctorates awarded. Offers medicine (MD). *Application deadline:* For fall admission, 9/30 for domestic students. Applications are processed on a rolling basis. Electronic applications accepted. *Application Contact:* Carol Teener, Director of Admissions, 734-764-6317, Fax: 734-936-3510, E-mail: cteener@umich.edu. *Dean,* Dr. Marschall S. Runge, MD, 734-764-8175, E-mail: mrunge@umich.edu.

Rackham Graduate School Students: 7,733 full-time (3,303 women), 678 part-time (266 women); includes 1,480 minority (280 Black or African American, non-Hispanic/Latino; 18 American Indian or Alaska Native, non-Hispanic/Latino; 528 Asian, non-Hispanic/Latino; 470 Hispanic/Latino; 4 Native Hawaiian or other Pacific Islander, non-Hispanic/Latino; 180 Two or more races, non-Hispanic/Latino), 3,454 international. Average age 26. 27,101 applicants, 26% accepted, 2673 enrolled. Expenses: Contact institution. *Financial support:* Fellowships with full and partial tuition reimbursements, research assistantships with full and partial tuition reimbursements, teaching assistantships with full and partial tuition reimbursements, career-related internships or fieldwork, Federal Work-Study, scholarships/grants, traineeships, health care benefits, and unspecified assistantships available. Support available to part-time students. In 2016, 2,105 master's, 833 doctorates awarded. Offers cancer chemical biology (MS); chemical biology (PhD); data science (MS, PhD); education and psychology (PhD); English and education (PhD); social and psychological (MS, PhD); statistical (MS, PhD); survey methodology (Certificate). *Application deadline:* Applications are processed on a rolling basis. *Application fee:* $75 ($90 for international students). Electronic applications accepted. *Application Contact:* Admissions Office, 734-764-8129, E-mail: rackadmis@umich.edu. *Dean/Vice Provost for Academic Affairs,* Dr. Carol A. Fierke, 734-764-4400.

College of Literature, Science, and the Arts Offers American culture (AM, PhD); analytical (PhD); ancient Near Eastern studies (AM, PhD); anthropological archaeology (PhD); anthropology and history (PhD); applied and interdisciplinary mathematics (AM, MS, PhD); applied economics (AM); applied physics (PhD); applied statistics (MS); Arabic for professional purposes (AM); Arabic language and literature (AM, PhD); Armenian studies (AM, PhD); Asian languages and cultures (PhD); astronomy and astrophysics (PhD); biological anthropology (PhD); biophysics (PhD); biopsychology (PhD); chemical biology (PhD); Chinese studies (MA, Graduate Certificate); Christianity in late antiquity (AM, PhD); classical art and archaeology (MA, PhD); classical studies (PhD); clinical science (PhD); cognition and cognitive neuroscience (PhD); communication studies (PhD); comparative literature (PhD); creative writing (MFA); developmental psychology (PhD); earth and environmental sciences (MS, PhD); ecology and evolutionary biology (MS, PhD); economics (AM, PhD); Egyptology (AM, PhD); English and education (PhD); English and women's studies (PhD); English language and literature (PhD); French (PhD); German (AM, PhD); German studies (Certificate); Greek and Roman history (PhD, Certificate); Hebrew Bible and ancient Israel (AM, PhD); Hebrew literature (AM, PhD); history (PhD); history and women's studies (PhD); history of art (PhD); inorganic (PhD); Islamic studies (AM, PhD); Italian (PhD); Japanese studies (AM); Jewish cultural studies (AM, PhD); Jewish mysticism (AM, PhD); Judaic studies (MA, Graduate Certificate); LGBTQ studies (Certificate); linguistic anthropology (PhD); linguistics (PhD); literature, science, and the arts (AM, MA, MAT, MFA, MS, PhD, Certificate, Graduate Certificate); materials (PhD); mathematics (AM, MS, PhD); Middle Eastern and North African studies (AM); molecular, cellular, and developmental biology (MS, PhD); organic (PhD); Persian and Iranian studies (AM, PhD); personality and social contexts (PhD); philosophy (AM, PhD); physical (PhD); physics (PhD); political science (PhD); political science and public policy (PhD); psychology and women's studies (PhD); public policy and economics (PhD); public policy and sociology (PhD); Rabbinic literature (AM, PhD); Russian, East European, and Eurasian studies (AM, Certificate); screen arts and cultures (PhD, Certificate); Second Temple Judaism (AM, PhD); Slavic languages and literatures (AM, PhD); social psychology (PhD); social work and economics (PhD); social work and political science (PhD); social work and sociology (PhD); sociocultural anthropology (PhD); sociology (PhD); South Asian

studies (MA, Certificate); Southeast Asian studies (MA, Graduate Certificate); Spanish (PhD); statistics (AM, PhD); teaching Arabic as a foreign language (AM); teaching Latin (MAT); Turkish studies (AM, PhD); women's studies (Certificate). Electronic applications accepted.

Penny W. Stamps School of Art and Design Students: 19 (13 women); includes 2 minority (1 Black or African American, non-Hispanic/Latino; 1 Asian, non-Hispanic/Latino). 146 applicants, 8% accepted, 10 enrolled. *Faculty:* 37. Expenses: Contact institution. *Financial support:* In 2016–17, 19 students received support. Fellowships with tuition reimbursements available, research assistantships with tuition reimbursements available, teaching assistantships with tuition reimbursements available, Federal Work-Study, scholarships/grants, health care benefits, tuition waivers (full and partial), and unspecified assistantships available. Support available to part-time students. Financial award application deadline: 1/1. In 2016, 6 master's awarded. Offers art and design (MFA); integrative design (M Des). *Application deadline:* For fall admission, 1/1 for domestic and international students. *Application fee:* $75 ($90 for international students). Electronic applications accepted. *Application Contact:* Meghan Jellema, Graduate Programs Coordinator, 734-763-5247, E-mail: stamps-graduate@umich.edu. *Dean,* Gunalan Nadarajan, 734-763-4093, E-mail: artdes-dean@umich.edu.

Program in Biomedical Sciences (PIBS) Offers bioinformatics (MS, PhD); biological chemistry (MS, PhD); biomedical sciences (MS, PhD); cancer biology (PhD); cell and developmental biology (PhD); cellular and molecular biology (PhD); genetic counseling (MS); human genetics (MS, PhD); immunology (PhD); microbiology and immunology (MS, PhD); molecular and cellular pathology (PhD); molecular and integrative physiology (MS, PhD); neuroscience (PhD); pharmacology (MS, PhD). Electronic applications accepted.

School of Information Students: 453 full-time (270 women), 32 part-time (20 women); includes 99 minority (16 Black or African American, non-Hispanic/Latino; 49 Asian, non-Hispanic/Latino; 21 Hispanic/Latino; 13 Two or more races, non-Hispanic/Latino), 212 international. Average age 27. 829 applicants, 53% accepted, 199 enrolled. Expenses: Contact institution. *Financial support:* In 2016–17, 122 students received support, including 2 fellowships (averaging $28,200 per year), 33 research assistantships (averaging $28,200 per year), 41 teaching assistantships (averaging $28,200 per year); scholarships/grants and tuition waivers (full and partial) also available. In 2016, 179 master's, 7 doctorates awarded. *Program availability:* Part-time. Offers health informatics (MHI); information (MSI, PhD). *Application deadline:* Applications are processed on a rolling basis. *Application fee:* $75 ($90 for international students). Electronic applications accepted. *Application Contact:* School of Information Admissions, 734-763-2285, Fax: 734-615-3587, E-mail: umsi.admissions@umich.edu. *Dean, School of Information,* Dr. Thomas A. Finholt, 734-647-3576.

School of Kinesiology Students: 87 full-time (32 women); includes 39 minority (5 Black or African American, non-Hispanic/Latino; 1 American Indian or Alaska Native, non-Hispanic/Latino; 23 Asian, non-Hispanic/Latino; 6 Hispanic/Latino; 4 Two or more races, non-Hispanic/Latino). 229 applicants, 45% accepted, 49 enrolled. *Faculty:* 31 full-time (16 women). Expenses: Contact institution. *Financial support:* In 2016–17, 3 fellowships, 18 research assistantships, 12 teaching assistantships were awarded; Federal Work-Study, scholarships/grants, traineeships, health care benefits, and unspecified assistantships also available. Financial award application deadline: 1/15. In 2016, 30 master's, 6 doctorates awarded. Offers movement science (MS, PhD); sport management (MS, PhD). *Application deadline:* For fall admission, 1/15 priority date for domestic students, 1/15 for international students. Applications are processed on a rolling basis. *Application fee:* $75 ($90 for international students). Electronic applications accepted. *Application Contact:* Charlene F. Ruloff, Graduate Program Coordinator, 734-764-1343, Fax: 734-647-2808, E-mail: cruloff@umich.edu. *Associate Dean for Graduate Programs and Faculty Affairs,* Dr. Ketra L. Armstrong, 734-647-3027, Fax: 734-647-2808, E-mail: ketra@umich.edu.

School of Music, Theatre, and Dance Students: 99 full-time (46 women); includes 38 minority (6 Black or African American, non-Hispanic/Latino; 24 Asian, non-Hispanic/Latino; 8 Hispanic/Latino). Average age 27. 400 applicants, 11% accepted, 35 enrolled. *Faculty:* 117 full-time (40 women). Expenses: Contact institution. *Financial support:* In 2016–17, 120 students received support, including 20 fellowships (averaging $42,000 per year), 100 teaching assistantships (averaging $42,000 per year); career-related internships or fieldwork, Federal Work-Study, institutionally sponsored loans, scholarships/grants, health care benefits, and unspecified assistantships also available. Financial award application deadline: 2/1; financial award applicants required to submit FAFSA. In 2016, 4 master's, 32 doctorates awarded. Offers composition (MA, MM, A Mus D); composition and theory (PhD); conducting (MM, A Mus D); media arts (MA); modern dance performance and choreography (MFA); music education (MM, PhD, Spec M); music theory (PhD); music, theatre, and dance (MA, MFA, MM, A Mus D, PhD, Spec M); musicology (MA, PhD); performance (MM, A Mus D, Spec M). *Application deadline:* For fall admission, 12/1 for domestic and international students; for winter admission, 9/15 for domestic and international students. Applications are processed on a rolling basis. *Application fee:* $75 ($90 for international students). Electronic applications accepted. *Application Contact:* Laura Hoffman, Assistant Dean for Enrollment Management and Student Services, 734-764-0593, Fax: 734-763-5097, E-mail: lauras@umich.edu. *Dean,* Aaron Dworkin, 734-764-0584, Fax: 734-763-5097, E-mail: aaronpau@umich.edu.

School of Nursing Expenses: Contact institution. *Program availability:* Part-time, online learning. Offers acute care pediatric nurse practitioner (MS); nursing (DNP, PhD, Post Master's Certificate). *Application Contact:* E-mail: sn-osams@umich.edu. *Dean,* Dr. Patricia D. Hurn, 734-764-7185, Fax: 734-764-7186.

Ross School of Business *Program availability:* Part-time, evening/weekend. Offers accounting (M Acc); business (MBA); business administration (PhD); supply chain management (MSCM). Electronic applications accepted.

School for Environment and Sustainability Students: 374 full-time (229 women); includes 52 minority (4 Black or African American, non-Hispanic/Latino; 15 Asian, non-Hispanic/Latino; 20 Hispanic/Latino; 1 Native Hawaiian or other Pacific Islander, non-Hispanic/Latino; 12 Two or more races, non-Hispanic/Latino), 97 international. Average age 26. 487 applicants. *Faculty:* 37 full-time (14 women), 44 part-time/adjunct (12 women). Expenses: Contact institution. *Financial support:* Fellowships, research assistantships, teaching assistantships, career-related internships or fieldwork, Federal Work-Study, scholarships/grants, and health care benefits available. Financial award application deadline: 1/6; financial award applicants required to submit FAFSA. In 2016, 129 master's, 9 doctorates awarded. Offers behavior, education and communication (MS); conservation ecology (MS); environmental informatics (MS); environmental justice (MS, Certificate); environmental policy and planning (MS); industrial ecology (Certificate); landscape architecture (MLA); natural resources and environment (MS, PhD); spatial analysis (Certificate); sustainability (Certificate); sustainable systems (MS). *Application deadline:* For fall admission, 4/30 for domestic and international students. *Application fee:* $75 ($90 for international students). Electronic applications accepted. *Application Contact:* Sara O'Brien, Director of Academic Programs, 734-764-6453, Fax: 734-936-2195, E-mail: seas-admissions@umich.edu. *Interim Dean,* Dr. Daniel Brown, 734-763-5803, E-mail: danbrown@umich.edu.

School of Dentistry Students: 560 full-time (264 women); includes 133 minority (17 Black or African American, non-Hispanic/Latino; 87 Asian, non-Hispanic/Latino; 18 Hispanic/Latino; 11 Two or more races, non-Hispanic/Latino; 79 international. 2,699 applicants, 8% accepted, 142 enrolled. Expenses: Contact institution. In 2016, 39 master's, 113 doctorates awarded. Offers dental hygiene (MS); dentistry (MS, DDS, PhD); endodontics (MS); oral health sciences (PhD); orthodontics (MS); pediatric dentistry (MS); periodontics (MS); prosthodontics (MS); restorative dentistry (MS). *Application deadline:* Applications are processed on a rolling basis. *Application fee:* $75 ($90 for international students). Electronic applications accepted. *Application Contact:* Patricia Katcher, Admissions Associate Director, 734-763-3316, Fax: 734-764-1922, E-mail: ddsadmissions@umich.edu. *Dean,* Dr. Laurie McCauley, 734-763-3311, E-mail: mccauley@umich.edu.

School of Education Offers education (MA, MS, PhD). Electronic applications accepted.

School of Public Health Students: 918 full-time (637 women), 12 part-time (5 women); includes 214 minority (51 Black or African American, non-Hispanic/Latino; 3 American Indian or Alaska Native, non-Hispanic/Latino; 95 Asian, non-Hispanic/Latino; 42 Hispanic/Latino; 23 Two or more races, non-Hispanic/Latino; 198 international. Average age 27. 2,225 applicants, 58% accepted, 540 enrolled. *Faculty:* 136 full-time (64 women), 163 part-time/adjunct (84 women). Expenses: Contact institution. *Financial support:* Fellowships, research assistantships with tuition reimbursements, teaching assistantships with tuition reimbursements, career-related internships or fieldwork, Federal Work-Study, institutionally sponsored loans, scholarships/grants, traineeships, health care benefits, and unspecified assistantships available. In 2016, 327 master's, 30 doctorates awarded. *Program availability:* Evening/weekend. Offers biostatistics (MPH, MS, PhD); clinical research design and statistical analysis (MS); dietetics (MPH); environmental health policy and promotion (MPH); environmental health sciences (MS, PhD); environmental quality, sustainability and health (MPH); epidemiological science (PhD); general epidemiology (MPH); global health epidemiology (MPH); health behavior and health education (MPH, PhD); health management and policy (MHSA, MPH); health services organization and policy (PhD); hospital and molecular epidemiology (MPH); industrial hygiene (MPH, MS); nutritional sciences (MPH, MS, PhD); occupational and environmental epidemiology (MPH); public health (MHSA, MPH, MS, PhD); toxicology (MPH, MS, PhD). MS and PhD offered through the Rackham Graduate School. *Application deadline:* For fall admission, 12/15 priority date for domestic students, 1/15 for international students. *Application fee:* $75. Electronic applications accepted. *Application Contact:* Charles Dill, Admissions Coordinator, 734-764-5425, Fax: 734-763-5455, E-mail: sph.inquiries@umich.edu. *Dean,* Martin Philbert, 734-763-4523, Fax: 734-763-5455, E-mail: philbert@umich.edu.

School of Social Work Students: 709 full-time (607 women); includes 214 minority (82 Black or African American, non-Hispanic/Latino; 1 American Indian or Alaska Native, non-Hispanic/Latino; 27 Asian, non-Hispanic/Latino; 74 Hispanic/Latino; 2 Native Hawaiian or other Pacific Islander, non-Hispanic/Latino; 28 Two or more races, non-Hispanic/Latino; 30 international. Average age 24. 1,396 applicants, 65% accepted, 397 enrolled. *Faculty:* 50 full-time (29 women), 62 part-time/adjunct (48 women). Expenses: Contact institution. *Financial support:* In 2016–17, 560 students received support. Career-related internships or fieldwork, Federal Work-Study, scholarships/grants, traineeships, and unspecified assistantships available. Financial award application deadline: 3/15; financial award applicants required to submit FAFSA. In 2016, 350 master's awarded. Offers social work (MSW, PhD); social work and anthropology (PhD); social work and economics (PhD); social work and political science (PhD); social work and psychology (PhD); social work and sociology (PhD). PhD offered through the Rackham Graduate School. *Application deadline:* For fall admission, 3/1 priority date for domestic students, 2/1 priority date for international students. Applications are processed on a rolling basis. *Application fee:* $75. Electronic applications accepted. *Application Contact:* Timothy Colenback, Assistant Dean for Student Services, 734-936-0961, Fax: 734-936-1961, E-mail: timot@umich.edu. *Dean,* Lynn Videka, 734-764-5347, Fax: 734-615-5403, E-mail: lvideka@umich.edu.

Taubman College of Architecture and Urban Planning *Faculty:* 108. Expenses: Contact institution. Offers architecture (M Arch); architecture and urban planning (M Arch, MS, MUD, PhD, Graduate Certificate); design and health (MS); digital technologies (MS); material systems (MS); urban and regional planning (PhD, Graduate Certificate); urban design (MUD). Electronic applications accepted. *Application Contact:* Lisa Hauser, Assistant Director for Admissions and Recruiting, 734-763-1275, E-mail: taubmancollegestudentservices@umich.edu.

UNIVERSITY OF MICHIGAN–DEARBORN, Dearborn, MI 48128

General Information State-supported, coed, comprehensive institution. *Enrollment:* 9,131 graduate, professional, and undergraduate students; 564 full-time matriculated graduate/professional students (176 women), 1,399 part-time matriculated graduate/professional students (460 women). *Enrollment by degree level:* 1,900 master's, 53 doctoral, 10 other advanced degrees. *Graduate faculty:* 300 full-time (122 women), 238 part-time/adjunct (99 women). Tuition, state resident: full-time $13,118; part-time $2280 per term. Tuition, nonresident: full-time $21,816; part-time $3771 per term. *Required fees:* $866; $658 per unit. $329 per term. Tuition and fees vary according to program. *Student services:* Campus employment opportunities, campus safety program, career counseling, child daycare facilities, exercise/wellness program, free psychological counseling, grant writing training, international student services, low-cost health insurance, multicultural affairs office, services for students with disabilities, teacher training, writing training. *Library facilities:* Mardigian Library. *Collection:* Books: 308,824 (physical), 569,242 (digital/electronic); Serial titles: 390 (physical), 80,875 (digital/electronic). Weekly public service hours: 48; students can reserve study rooms. *Research affiliation:* Henry W. Patton Center for Engineering Education and Practice, Center for Lightweighting Automotive Materials and Processing, Center for Electric Drive Transportation, DTE Power Electronics and Electric Drives Lab, Cybersecurity Center (CCERO).

Computer facilities: Computer purchase and lease plans are available. 975 computers available on campus for general student use. A campuswide network can be accessed from off campus. Online class registration, tuition and application payments accepted online are available.
Website: http://www.umdearborn.edu/

General Application Contact: Office of Graduate Studies, 313-583-6321, E-mail: umd-graduatestudies@umich.edu.

GRADUATE UNITS

College of Arts, Sciences, and Letters Students: 35 full-time (27 women), 82 part-time (52 women); includes 36 minority (18 Black or African American, non-Hispanic/Latino; 6 Asian, non-Hispanic/Latino; 8 Hispanic/Latino; 4 Two or more races, non-Hispanic/Latino), 5 international. Average age 34. 101 applicants, 52% accepted, 22 enrolled. *Faculty:* 59 full-time (28 women), 11 part-time/adjunct (5 women). Expenses: Contact institution. *Financial support:* In 2016–17, 38 students received support. Scholarships/grants and non-resident tuition scholarships available. Financial award application deadline: 3/1; financial award applicants required to submit FAFSA. In 2016, 45 master's awarded. *Program availability:* Part-time, evening/weekend. Offers applied and computational mathematics (MS); arts, sciences, and letters (MPA, MS); clinical health psychology (MS); criminology and criminal justice (MS); environmental science (MS); health psychology (MS); public administration (MPA). *Application deadline:* For fall admission, 8/1 priority date for domestic students, 5/1 priority date for international students; for winter admission, 12/1 priority date for domestic students, 9/1 priority date for international students; for spring admission, 4/1 priority date for domestic students, 1/1 priority date for international students. Applications are processed on a rolling basis. *Application fee:* $60. Electronic applications accepted. *Application Contact:* Carol Ligienza, Coordinator, CASL Graduate Programs, 313-593-1183, Fax: 313-583-6700, E-mail: caslgrad@umich.edu. *Dean,* Dr. Martin Hershock, 313-593-5490, Fax: 313-593-5552, E-mail: mhershoc@umich.edu.

College of Business Students: 110 full-time (54 women), 285 part-time (91 women); includes 59 minority (15 Black or African American, non-Hispanic/Latino; 29 Asian, non-Hispanic/Latino; 9 Hispanic/Latino; 6 Two or more races, non-Hispanic/Latino), 109 international. Average age 30. 515 applicants, 53% accepted, 124 enrolled. *Faculty:* 33 full-time (14 women), 10 part-time/adjunct (5 women). Expenses: Contact institution. *Financial support:* In 2016–17, 125 students received support. Scholarships/grants and non-resident tuition scholarships available. Financial award application deadline: 3/1; financial award applicants required to submit FAFSA. In 2016, 161 master's awarded. *Program availability:* Part-time, evening/weekend, 100% online. Offers accounting (MS); business (MBA, MS); business administration (MBA); business analytics (MS); finance (MS); information systems (MS); supply chain management (MS). *Application deadline:* For fall admission, 8/1 priority date for domestic students, 5/1 priority date for international students; for winter admission, 12/1 priority date for domestic students, 9/1 priority date for international students; for spring admission, 4/1 priority date for domestic students, 1/1 priority date for international students. Applications are processed on a rolling basis. *Application fee:* $60. Electronic applications accepted. *Application Contact:* Joan Doherty, Academic Advisor/Counselor, 313-593-5460, Fax: 313-271-9838, E-mail: umd-gradbusiness@umich.edu. *Dean,* Dr. Raju Balakrishnan, 313-593-5460, Fax: 313-271-9835, E-mail: umd-cob-dean@umich.edu.

College of Education, Health, and Human Services Students: 26 full-time (20 women), 204 part-time (163 women); includes 46 minority (26 Black or African American, non-Hispanic/Latino; 6 Asian, non-Hispanic/Latino; 8 Hispanic/Latino; 6 Two or more races, non-Hispanic/Latino), 2 international. Average age 34. 107 applicants, 80% accepted, 60 enrolled. *Faculty:* 17 full-time (12 women), 37 part-time/adjunct (20 women). Expenses: Contact institution. *Financial support:* In 2016–17, 39 students received support. Career-related internships or fieldwork and scholarships/grants available. Financial award application deadline: 3/1; financial award applicants required to submit FAFSA. In 2016, 100 master's, 3 doctorates, 2 other advanced degrees awarded. *Program availability:* Part-time, evening/weekend, 100% online. Offers community based education (MA); curriculum and practice (Ed D, Ed S); early childhood education (MA); education (MA, Ed D, Ed S); education, health, and human services (M Ed, MA, MAT, MS, Ed D, Certificate, Ed S); educational leadership (Ed D, Ed S); educational technology (MA); health information technology (MS); metropolitan education (Ed D, Ed S); program evaluation and assessment (MA); science education (MS); special education (M Ed); teaching (MAT). *Application deadline:* For fall admission, 8/1 priority date for domestic students, 5/1 priority date for international students; for winter admission, 12/1 priority date for domestic students, 9/1 priority date for international students; for spring admission, 4/1 priority date for domestic students, 1/1 priority date for international students. Applications are processed on a rolling basis. *Application fee:* $60. Electronic applications accepted. *Application Contact:* Dr. Stein Brunvand, Director, Master's Programs, 313-583-6415, E-mail: sbrunvan@umich.edu. *Dean,* Dr. Janine Janosky, 313-593-5435, E-mail: jjanosky@umich.edu.

College of Engineering and Computer Science Students: 393 full-time (75 women), 828 part-time (154 women); includes 170 minority (39 Black or African American, non-Hispanic/Latino; 2 American Indian or Alaska Native, non-Hispanic/Latino; 73 Asian, non-Hispanic/Latino; 35 Hispanic/Latino; 1 Native Hawaiian or other Pacific Islander, non-Hispanic/Latino; 20 Two or more races, non-Hispanic/Latino), 580 international. Average age 27. 1,517 applicants, 53% accepted, 444 enrolled. *Faculty:* 73 full-time (10 women), 34 part-time/adjunct (3 women). Expenses: Contact institution. *Financial support:* Research assistantships, teaching assistantships, career-related internships or fieldwork, scholarships/grants, health care benefits, and non-residential student scholarships available. Financial award application deadline: 3/1; financial award applicants required to submit FAFSA. In 2016, 365 master's, 2 doctorates awarded. *Program availability:* Part-time, evening/weekend, 100% online. Offers automotive systems engineering (MSE, PhD); bioengineering (MSE); computer and information science (MS, PhD); computer engineering (MSE); data management (PhD); data science (PhD); electrical and computer engineering (PhD); electrical engineering (MSE); energy systems engineering (MSE); engineering and computer science (MS, MSE, PhD); engineering management (MS); industrial and systems engineering (MSE, PhD); information systems and technology (MS); information systems engineering (PhD); manufacturing systems engineering (MSE); mechanical engineering (MSE); mechanical sciences and engineering (PhD); program and project management (MS); software engineering (MS); systems and security (PhD). *Application deadline:* For fall admission, 8/1 priority date for domestic students, 5/1 priority date for international students; for winter admission, 12/1 priority date for domestic students, 9/1 priority date for international students; for spring admission, 4/1 priority date for domestic students, 1/1 priority date for international students. Applications are processed on a rolling basis. *Application fee:* $60. Electronic applications accepted. *Application Contact:* Office of Graduate Studies Staff, 313-583-6321, E-mail: umd-graduatestudies@umich.edu. *Dean,* Dr. Anthony England, 313-593-5290, Fax: 313-593-9967, E-mail: england@umich.edu.

UNIVERSITY OF MICHIGAN–FLINT, Flint, MI 48502-1950

General Information State-supported, coed, comprehensive institution. CGS member. *Enrollment:* 8,044 graduate, professional, and undergraduate students; 544 full-time matriculated graduate/professional students (361 women), 915 part-time matriculated graduate/professional students (556 women). *Enrollment by degree level:* 917 master's, 517 doctoral, 25 other advanced degrees. *Graduate faculty:* 316 full-time (164 women), 254 part-time/adjunct (168 women). *Graduate housing:* Room and/or apartments available on a first-come, first-served basis to single students; on-campus housing not available to married students. Typical cost: $7320 per year ($10,320 including board). Room and board charges vary according to board plan and housing facility selected. *Student services:* Campus employment opportunities, campus safety program, career counseling, child daycare facilities, exercise/wellness program, free psychological counseling, international student services, services for students with disabilities, teacher training, writing training. *Library facilities:* Frances Willson Thompson Library plus 1 other. *Collection:* Books: 262,791 (physical), 746,088 (digital/electronic); Serial titles: 1,862 (physical), 146,663 (digital/electronic); Databases: 1,227. Weekly public service hours: 96; students can reserve study rooms.

Computer facilities: Computer purchase and lease plans are available. 517 computers available on campus for general student use. A campuswide network can be accessed from student residence rooms and from off campus. Online class registration is available.

Website: http://www.umflint.edu/

General Application Contact: Bradley T. Maki, Director of Graduate Admissions, 810-762-3171, Fax: 810-766-6789, E-mail: bmaki@umflint.edu.

GRADUATE UNITS

College of Arts and Sciences Students: 52 full-time (26 women), 181 part-time (91 women); includes 41 minority (20 Black or African American, non-Hispanic/Latino; 3 Asian, non-Hispanic/Latino; 10 Hispanic/Latino; 1 Native Hawaiian or other Pacific Islander, non-Hispanic/Latino; 7 Two or more races, non-Hispanic/Latino), 86 international. Average age 32. 792 applicants, 34% accepted, 67 enrolled. *Faculty:* 121 full-time (52 women), 34 part-time/adjunct (19 women). Expenses: Contact institution. *Financial support:* Federal Work-Study, scholarships/grants, and unspecified assistantships available. Support available to part-time students. Financial award application deadline: 3/1; financial award applicants required to submit FAFSA. In 2016, 203 master's awarded. *Program availability:* Part-time. Offers applied communication (MA); arts and sciences (MA, MS, MSE); biology (MS); computer science (MS); gender studies (MA); global studies (MA); information systems (MS); literature (MA); mathematics (MA); mechanical engineering (MSE); U.S. history and politics (MA); writing and rhetoric (MA). *Application deadline:* For fall admission, 8/1 for domestic students, 5/1 for international students; for winter admission, 11/15 for domestic students, 9/1 for international students; for spring admission, 3/15 for domestic students, 1/1 for international students; for summer admission, 5/15 for domestic students. Applications are processed on a rolling basis. *Application fee:* $55. Electronic applications accepted. *Application Contact:* Bradley T. Maki, Director of Graduate Admissions, 810-762-3171, Fax: 810-766-6789, E-mail: bmaki@umflint.edu. *Dean,* Dr. Susan Gano-Phillips, 810-762-3234, Fax: 810-762-3006, E-mail: sganop@umflint.edu.

Graduate Programs Students: 21 full-time (16 women), 122 part-time (70 women); includes 53 minority (39 Black or African American, non-Hispanic/Latino; 2 American Indian or Alaska Native, non-Hispanic/Latino; 2 Asian, non-Hispanic/Latino; 3 Hispanic/Latino; 1 Native Hawaiian or other Pacific Islander, non-Hispanic/Latino; 6 Two or more races, non-Hispanic/Latino), 5 international. Average age 37. 84 applicants, 76% accepted, 50 enrolled. *Faculty:* 11 full-time (8 women), 8 part-time/adjunct (6 women). Expenses: Contact institution. *Financial support:* Federal Work-Study, scholarships/grants, and unspecified assistantships available. Support available to part-time students. Financial award application deadline: 3/1; financial award applicants required to submit FAFSA. In 2016, 64 master's awarded. *Program availability:* Part-time, evening/weekend, 100% online. Offers administration of non-profit agencies (MPA); criminal justice administration (MPA); educational administration (MPA); general public administration (MPA); healthcare administration (MPA); liberal studies (MA, MLS); museum and visual arts (MA). *Application deadline:* For fall admission, 8/1 for domestic students, 5/1 for international students; for winter admission, 11/15 for domestic students, 9/1 for international students; for spring admission, 3/15 for domestic students, 1/1 for international students; for summer admission, 5/15 for domestic students. Applications are processed on a rolling basis. *Application fee:* $55. Electronic applications accepted. *Application Contact:* Bradley T. Maki, Director of Graduate Admissions, 810-762-3171, Fax: 810-766-6789, E-mail: bmaki@umflint.edu. *Dean of Graduate Programs,* Dr. Vahid Lotfi, 810-762-3171, Fax: 810-766-6789, E-mail: vahid@umflint.edu.

School of Education and Human Services Students: 31 full-time (18 women), 200 part-time (145 women); includes 61 minority (48 Black or African American, non-Hispanic/Latino; 1 Asian, non-Hispanic/Latino; 6 Hispanic/Latino; 1 Native Hawaiian or other Pacific Islander, non-Hispanic/Latino; 5 Two or more races, non-Hispanic/Latino), 2 international. Average age 39. 124 applicants, 86% accepted, 75 enrolled. *Faculty:* 14 full-time (9 women), 30 part-time/adjunct (17 women). Expenses: Contact institution. *Financial support:* Federal Work-Study, scholarships/grants, and unspecified assistantships available. Support available to part-time students. Financial award application deadline: 3/1; financial award applicants required to submit FAFSA. In 2016, 77 master's, 1 doctorate awarded. *Program availability:* Part-time, 100% online, mixed mode format. Offers curriculum and instruction (Ed S); early childhood education (MA); education (Ed D); education and human services (MA, Ed D, Ed S); educational leadership (Ed S); educational technology (MA); literacy education (MA); secondary education with certification (MA). *Application deadline:* For fall admission, 7/1 for domestic students, 4/1 for international students; for winter admission, 11/15 for domestic students, 9/1 for international students; for spring admission, 3/15 for domestic students, 1/1 for international students. Applications are processed on a rolling basis. *Application fee:* $55. Electronic applications accepted. *Application Contact:* Bradley T. Maki, Director of Graduate Admissions, 810-762-3171, Fax: 810-766-6789, E-mail: bmaki@umflint.edu. *Dean,* Dr. Bob Barnett, 810-766-6878, Fax: 810-766-6891, E-mail: rbarnett@umflint.edu.

School of Health Professions and Studies Students: 245 full-time (140 women), 135 part-time (104 women); includes 70 minority (20 Black or African American, non-Hispanic/Latino; 4 American Indian or Alaska Native, non-Hispanic/Latino; 29 Asian, non-Hispanic/Latino; 7 Hispanic/Latino; 10 Two or more races, non-Hispanic/Latino), 27 international. Average age 30. 661 applicants, 33% accepted, 116 enrolled. *Faculty:* 30 full-time (22 women), 48 part-time/adjunct (25 women). Expenses: Contact institution. *Financial support:* Federal Work-Study, scholarships/grants, and unspecified assistantships available. Support available to part-time students. Financial award application deadline: 3/1; financial award applicants required to submit FAFSA. In 2016, 30 master's, 84 doctorates, 3 other advanced degrees awarded. *Program availability:* Part-time, 100% online. Offers anesthesia (MS, DrAP); geriatrics (DPT, PhD, Certificate); health administration (MPH); health education (MS); health professions and studies (MPH, MS, DPT, DrAP, PhD, Certificate); neurology (DPT, PhD, Certificate); orthopedics (DPT, PhD, Certificate); pediatrics (DPT, PhD, Certificate); physical therapy (DPT). *Application deadline:* For fall admission, 8/1 for domestic students, 5/1 for international students; for winter admission, 11/15 for domestic students, 9/1 for international students; for spring admission, 3/15 for domestic students, 1/1 for international students. Applications are processed on a rolling basis. *Application fee:* $55. Electronic applications accepted. *Application Contact:* Bradley T. Maki, Director of Graduate

Admissions, 810-762-3171, Fax: 810-766-6789, E-mail: bmaki@umflint.edu. *Dean,* Dr. Donna Fry, 810-237-6503, Fax: 810-237-6532, E-mail: donnafry@umflint.edu.

School of Management Students: 29 full-time (13 women), 171 part-time (58 women); includes 45 minority (21 Black or African American, non-Hispanic/Latino; 2 American Indian or Alaska Native, non-Hispanic/Latino; 12 Asian, non-Hispanic/Latino; 6 Hispanic/Latino; 1 Native Hawaiian or other Pacific Islander, non-Hispanic/Latino; 3 Two or more races, non-Hispanic/Latino), 23 international. Average age 33. 198 applicants, 51% accepted, 49 enrolled. *Faculty:* 33 full-time (9 women), 6 part-time/adjunct (1 woman). Expenses: Contact institution. *Financial support:* Federal Work-Study, scholarships/grants, and unspecified assistantships available. Support available to part-time students. Financial award application deadline: 3/1; financial award applicants required to submit FAFSA. In 2016, 86 master's, 3 other advanced degrees awarded. *Program availability:* Part-time, evening/weekend, mixed mode format. Offers accounting (MBA, MSA, Post-Master's Certificate); business (Graduate Certificate); business administration (MBA, Post-Master's Certificate); computer information systems (MBA); finance (MBA, Post-Master's Certificate); general business (Graduate Certificate); general business administration (MBA); health care management (MBA); international business (MBA, Post-Master's Certificate); lean manufacturing (MBA); marketing (MBA, Post-Master's Certificate); organizational leadership (MBA, Post-Master's Certificate). *Application deadline:* For fall admission, 8/1 for domestic students, 5/1 for international students; for winter admission, 11/15 for domestic students, 9/1 for international students; for spring admission, 3/15 for domestic students; for summer admission, 5/15 for domestic students. Applications are processed on a rolling basis. *Application fee:* $55. Electronic applications accepted. *Application Contact:* Bradley T. Maki, Director of Graduate Admissions, 810-762-3171, Fax: 810-766-6789, E-mail: bmaki@umflint.edu. *Dean, School of Management,* Dr. Scott Johnson, 810-762-6579, Fax: 810-237-6685, E-mail: scotjohn@umflint.edu.

School of Nursing Students: 166 full-time (148 women), 106 part-time (89 women); includes 68 minority (33 Black or African American, non-Hispanic/Latino; 2 American Indian or Alaska Native, non-Hispanic/Latino; 14 Asian, non-Hispanic/Latino; 8 Hispanic/Latino; 11 Two or more races, non-Hispanic/Latino), 2 international. Average age 37. 106 applicants, 84% accepted, 62 enrolled. *Faculty:* 31 full-time (29 women), 82 part-time/adjunct (75 women). Expenses: Contact institution. *Financial support:* Federal Work-Study, scholarships/grants, and unspecified assistantships available. Support available to part-time students. Financial award application deadline: 3/1; financial award applicants required to submit FAFSA. In 2016, 34 doctorates, 5 other advanced degrees awarded. *Program availability:* Part-time, evening/weekend, 100% online. Offers adult-gerontology acute care (DNP); adult-gerontology primary care (DNP); family nurse practitioner (DNP); nursing (MSN); psychiatric mental health (DNP); psychiatric mental health nurse practitioner (Certificate). *Application deadline:* For fall admission, 7/1 for domestic students, 4/1 for international students; for winter admission, 11/1 for domestic students, 9/1 for international students; for spring admission, 3/15 for domestic students, 1/1 for international students. Applications are processed on a rolling basis. *Application fee:* $55. Electronic applications accepted. *Application Contact:* Bradley T. Maki, Director of Graduate Admissions, 810-762-3171, Fax: 810-766-6789, E-mail: bmaki@umflint.edu. *Director,* Dr. Constance J. Creech, 810-762-3420, Fax: 810-766-6851, E-mail: ccreech@umflint.edu.

UNIVERSITY OF MINNESOTA, DULUTH, Duluth, MN 55812-2496

General Information State-supported, coed, comprehensive institution. *Graduate housing:* Room and/or apartments available to single students; on-campus housing not available to married students. Housing application deadline: 3/1. *Research affiliation:* Environmental Protection Agency Environmental Research Laboratory (aquatic biology), Minnesota Geological Survey, Northeastern Minnesota National Historical Center (local history), U.S. Forest Service, Northcentral Forest Experiment Station.

GRADUATE UNITS

Graduate School *Program availability:* Part-time, evening/weekend, online learning. Offers toxicology (MS, PhD).

College of Education and Human Service Professions *Program availability:* Part-time, evening/weekend, online learning. Offers communication sciences and disorders (MA); education (M Ed, Ed D); education and human service professions (M Ed, MA, MSW, Ed D); social work (MSW).

College of Liberal Arts *Program availability:* Part-time. Offers criminology (MA); English (MA); liberal arts (MA, MLS); liberal studies (MLS).

Labovitz School of Business and Economics *Program availability:* Part-time, evening/weekend. Offers business administration (MBA); business and economics (MBA).

School of Fine Arts *Program availability:* Part-time. Offers fine arts (MFA, MM); graphic design (MFA); music education (MM); performance (MM).

Swenson College of Science and Engineering *Program availability:* Part-time, evening/weekend, online learning. Offers applied and computational mathematics (MS); chemistry and biochemistry (MS); computer science (MS); electrical and computer engineering (MSECE); engineering management (MSEM); environmental health and safety (MEHS); geological sciences (MS, PhD); integrated biosciences (MS, PhD); physics (MS); science and engineering (MEHS, MS, MSECE, MSEM, PhD).

Medical School *Program availability:* Part-time. Offers biochemistry, molecular biology and biophysics (MS); biology and biophysics (PhD); medicine (MS, MD, PhD); microbiology, immunology and molecular pathobiology (MS, PhD); pharmacology (MS, PhD); physiology (MS, PhD); social, administrative, and clinical pharmacy (MS, PhD); toxicology (MS, PhD).

UNIVERSITY OF MINNESOTA ROCHESTER, Rochester, MN 55904

General Information State-supported, coed, comprehensive institution.

GRADUATE UNITS

Graduate Programs

UNIVERSITY OF MINNESOTA, TWIN CITIES CAMPUS, Minneapolis, MN 55455-0213

General Information State-supported, coed, university. CGS member. *Graduate housing:* Rooms and/or apartments available on a first-come, first-served basis to single and married students. Housing application deadline: 5/1.

GRADUATE UNITS

Carlson School of Management Students: 556 full-time (248 women), 1,142 part-time (393 women); includes 175 minority (32 Black or African American, non-Hispanic/Latino; 5 American Indian or Alaska Native, non-Hispanic/Latino; 79 Asian, non-Hispanic/Latino; 32 Hispanic/Latino; 1 Native Hawaiian or other Pacific Islander, non-Hispanic/Latino; 26 Two or more races, non-Hispanic/Latino), 329 international. Average age 27. *Faculty:* 139 full-time (39 women), 49 part-time/adjunct (10 women). Expenses:

University of Minnesota, Twin Cities Campus

Contact institution. *Financial support:* Fellowships with full and partial tuition reimbursements, research assistantships with full tuition reimbursements, teaching assistantships with full and partial tuition reimbursements, career-related internships or fieldwork, Federal Work-Study, institutionally sponsored loans, scholarships/grants, health care benefits, tuition waivers (full and partial), and unspecified assistantships available. Support available to part-time students. Financial award application deadline: 4/1; financial award applicants required to submit FAFSA. In 2016, 609 master's, 10 doctorates awarded. *Program availability:* Part-time, evening/weekend. Offers accountancy (M Acc); accounting (PhD); business analytics (MS); business taxation (MBT); finance (MBA, PhD); human resources and industrial relations (MA); information and decision sciences (PhD); information technology (MBA); management (EMBA, M Acc, MA, MBA, MBT, MS, PhD); marketing (MBA, PhD); medical industry orientation (MBA); strategic management and entrepreneurship (MBA); supply chain and operations (MBA, PhD); work and organizations (PhD). Electronic applications accepted. *Application Contact:* Graduate School Admissions, 612-625-3014, Fax: 612-625-6002, E-mail: gsquest@umn.edu. *Associate Dean of Faculty and Research,* Prof. Alok Gupta, 612-626-0276, Fax: 612-624-6374, E-mail: gupta037@umn.edu.

College of Pharmacy *Program availability:* Part-time. Offers experimental and clinical pharmacology (MS, PhD); medicinal chemistry (MS, PhD); pharmaceutics (PhD); pharmacy (MS, PhD, Pharm D); social and administrative pharmacy (MS, PhD).

College of Science and Engineering *Program availability:* Part-time, evening/weekend, online learning. Offers aerospace engineering and mechanics (MS, PhD); biomedical engineering (MS, PhD); chemical engineering (M Ch E, MS Ch E, PhD); chemical physics (MS, PhD); chemistry (MS, PhD); civil engineering (MCE, MS, PhD); computer science (MCS, MS, PhD); data science (MS); earth sciences (MS, PhD); electrical and computer engineering (MSEE, PhD); geological engineering (M Geo E, MS); history of science, technology and medicine (MA, PhD); industrial and systems engineering (MS, PhD); materials science and engineering (M Mat SE, MS Mat SE, PhD); mechanical engineering (MSME, PhD); science and engineering (M Ch E, M Geo E, M Mat SE, MA, MCE, MCS, MFM, MS, MS Ch E, MS Mat SE, MSEE, MSME, MSMOT, MSSE, MSST, PhD, Certificate); scientific computation (MS, PhD); software engineering (MSSE); stream restoration science and engineering (Certificate). Electronic applications accepted.

School of Mathematics *Program availability:* Part-time. Offers mathematics (MS, PhD); quantitative finance (Certificate). Electronic applications accepted.

School of Physics and Astronomy *Program availability:* Part-time. Offers astrophysics (MS, PhD); physics (MS, PhD).

Technological Leadership Institute *Program availability:* Evening/weekend. Offers management of technology (MSMOT); medical device innovation (MS); security technologies (MSST). Electronic applications accepted.

College of Veterinary Medicine *Program availability:* Part-time. Offers comparative and molecular bioscience (MS, PhD); veterinary medicine (MS, PhD). Electronic applications accepted.

Graduate School *Program availability:* Part-time, evening/weekend, online learning. Offers biophysical sciences and medical physics (MS, PhD); genetic counseling (MS); health informatics (MHI, MS, PhD); history of science, technology and medicine (MA, PhD); integrative biology and physiology (PhD); microbial engineering (MS); microbiology, immunology and cancer biology (PhD); molecular, cellular, developmental biology and genetics (PhD); neuroscience (MS, PhD); stem cell biology (MS). Electronic applications accepted.

College of Biological Sciences *Program availability:* Part-time. Offers biochemistry, molecular biology and biophysics (PhD); biological science (MBS); biological sciences (MBS, MS, PhD); ecology, evolution, and behavior (MS, PhD); plant biological sciences (MS, PhD). Electronic applications accepted.

College of Design Offers apparel (MA, MS, PhD); architecture (M Arch); design (M Arch, MA, MFA, MLA, MS, PhD, Postbaccalaureate Certificate); design communication (MA, MS, PhD); housing studies (MA, MS, PhD, Postbaccalaureate Certificate); interactive design (MFA); interior design (MA, MS, PhD); landscape architecture (MLA, MS); sustainable design (MS). Electronic applications accepted.

College of Education and Human Development Students: 1,469 full-time (1,059 women), 768 part-time (527 women); includes 482 minority (137 Black or African American, non-Hispanic/Latino; 17 American Indian or Alaska Native, non-Hispanic/Latino; 119 Asian, non-Hispanic/Latino; 131 Hispanic/Latino; 1 Native Hawaiian or other Pacific Islander, non-Hispanic/Latino; 77 Two or more races, non-Hispanic/Latino), 179 international. Average age 32. 2,091 applicants, 53% accepted, 1005 enrolled. *Faculty:* 178 full-time (95 women). Expenses: Contact institution. *Financial support:* In 2016–17, 157 fellowships, 300 research assistantships with full tuition reimbursements (averaging $11,689 per year), 214 teaching assistantships with full tuition reimbursements (averaging $11,785 per year) were awarded; scholarships/grants and tuition waivers (partial) also available. Financial award applicants required to submit FAFSA. In 2016, 1,159 master's, 155 doctorates, 74 other advanced degrees awarded. *Program availability:* Part-time. Offers adult education (M Ed, Certificate); adult literacy (Certificate); applied child and adolescent development (MA); art education (M Ed, MA, PhD); autism spectrum disorder (Certificate); child psychology (PhD); comparative and international development education (MA, PhD); counseling and student personnel psychology (MA); curriculum and instruction (M Ed, MA, PhD, Certificate); disability policy and services (Certificate); early childhood education (M Ed); early childhood special education (M Ed); education and human development (M Ed, MA, MS, MSW, Ed D, PhD, Certificate, Ed S); education policy and leadership (M Ed, MA, Ed D, PhD); educational policy and leadership (MA, Ed D, PhD); elementary education (MA, PhD); English education (PhD); evaluation studies (MA, PhD); family education (M Ed); higher education (MA, Ed D, PhD); human resource development (M Ed, MA, Ed D, PhD, Certificate); kinesiology (MS, PhD); language and immersion education (Certificate); leadership in education (M Ed); learning technologies (MA, PhD); literacy education (MA, PhD); marriage and family therapy (MA, PhD); multicultural college teaching and learning (MA); PK-12 administrative licensure (Certificate); prevention science (MA); private college leadership (Certificate); professional development (Certificate); program evaluation (Certificate); psychological foundations of education (MA, PhD); quantitative methods in education (MA, PhD); school psychology (MA, PhD, Ed S); second language education (MA, PhD); social studies education (MA, PhD); social work (MSW, PhD); special education (M Ed, MA, PhD); sport and exercise science (M Ed); sport management (M Ed, MA); STEM education (MA, PhD); talent development and gifted education (Certificate); teaching (M Ed); teaching English to speakers of other languages (MA); technical education (Certificate); technology enhanced learning (Certificate); undergraduate multicultural teaching and learning (Certificate); work and human resource education (M Ed); youth development leadership (M Ed). *Application fee:* $75 ($95 for international students). *Application Contact:* Dr. Brianne Keeney, Director of Graduate Education

Initiatives, 612-626-9145, E-mail: keen0113@umn.edu. *Dean,* Dr. Jean K. Quam, 612-626-9252, Fax: 612-626-7496, E-mail: jquam@umn.edu.

College of Food, Agricultural and Natural Resource Sciences *Program availability:* Part-time. Offers animal sciences (MS, PhD); applied economics (MS, PhD); applied plant sciences (MS, PhD); assessment, monitoring, and geospatial analysis (MS, PhD); bioproducts and biosystems science, engineering and management (MS, PhD); conservation biology (MS, PhD); economics, policy, management, and society (MS, PhD); entomology (MS, PhD); food science (MS, PhD); food, agricultural and natural resource sciences (MS, PhD); forest hydrology and watershed management (MS, PhD); forest products (MS, PhD); forests: biology, ecology, conservation, and management (MS, PhD); land and atmospheric science (MS, PhD); natural resources science and management (MS, PhD); nutrition (MS, PhD); paper science and engineering (MS, PhD); plant pathology (MS, PhD); recreation resources, tourism, and environmental education (MS, PhD); water resources science (MS, PhD); wildlife ecology and management (MS, PhD). Electronic applications accepted.

College of Liberal Arts *Program availability:* Part-time, evening/weekend. Offers American studies (PhD); ancient and medieval art and archaeology (MA, PhD); anthropology (MA, PhD); art (MFA); art history (MA, PhD); Asian literatures, cultures, and media (PhD); audiology (Au D); biological psychopathology (PhD); classics (MA, PhD); clinical psychology (PhD); cognitive and biological psychology (PhD); communication studies (MA, PhD); comparative literature (PhD); comparative studies in discourse and society (PhD); counseling psychology (PhD); design technology (MFA); economics (MA, PhD); English (MA, PhD); English as a second language (MA); feminist studies (PhD); French (MA, PhD); geographic information science (MGIS); geography, environment and society (MA, PhD); Germanic studies (MA, PhD); Greek (MA, PhD); Hispanic and Lusophone literatures, cultures and linguistics (PhD); Hispanic linguistics (MA); Hispanic literature (MA); history (MA, PhD); industrial/organizational psychology (PhD); Latin (MA, PhD); liberal arts (MA, MFA, MGIS, MM, MS, Au D, DMA, PhD); linguistics (MA, PhD); Lusophone literature (MA); mass communication (MA, PhD); music (MA, MM, DMA, PhD); personality, individual differences, and behavior genetics (PhD); philosophy (MA, PhD); political science (PhD); quantitative/psychometric methods (PhD); religions in antiquity (MA); school psychology (PhD); social psychology (PhD); sociology (MA, PhD); speech-language pathology (MA); speech-language-hearing sciences (PhD); statistics (MS, PhD); strategic communication (professional program) (MA); theatre arts (MA, PhD). Electronic applications accepted.

Hubert H. Humphrey School of Public Affairs *Program availability:* Part-time, evening/weekend. Offers development practice (MDP); management and governance (PhD); public affairs (MDP, MPA, MPP, MS, MURP, PhD); public policy (PhD); science, technology, and environmental policy (PhD); urban and regional planning (MURP); urban planning (PhD). Electronic applications accepted.

School of Nursing Students: 167 full-time (152 women), 183 part-time (166 women); includes 28 minority (9 Black or African American, non-Hispanic/Latino; 3 American Indian or Alaska Native, non-Hispanic/Latino; 8 Asian, non-Hispanic/Latino; 8 Hispanic/Latino). Average age 37. 220 applicants, 76% accepted. *Faculty:* 58 full-time (56 women), 22 part-time/adjunct (20 women). Expenses: Contact institution. *Financial support:* Fellowships, research assistantships, teaching assistantships, career-related internships or fieldwork, and traineeships available. Financial award applicants required to submit FAFSA. In 2016, 87 master's, 7 doctorates awarded. *Program availability:* Part-time, online learning. Offers adult/gerontological clinical nurse specialist (DNP); adult/gerontological primary care nurse practitioner (DNP); family nurse practitioner (DNP); health innovation and leadership (DNP); integrative health and healing (DNP); nurse anesthesia (DNP); nurse midwifery (DNP); nursing (MN, PhD); nursing informatics (DNP); pediatric clinical nurse specialist (DNP); primary care certified pediatric nurse practitioner (DNP); psychiatric/mental health nurse practitioner (DNP); women's health nurse practitioner (DNP). *Application fee:* $55 ($75 for international students). *Application Contact:* Information Contact, 612-624-4454, Fax: 612-624-3174, E-mail: nurseoss@umn.edu. *Dean,* Dr. Connie Delaney, 612-624-5959, Fax: 612-626-2359.

Law School Students: 721 full-time (307 women), 12 part-time (8 women); includes 102 minority (14 Black or African American, non-Hispanic/Latino; 3 American Indian or Alaska Native, non-Hispanic/Latino; 43 Asian, non-Hispanic/Latino; 12 Hispanic/Latino; 30 Two or more races, non-Hispanic/Latino), 55 international. Average age 25. 1,960 applicants, 45% accepted, 176 enrolled. *Faculty:* 54 full-time (22 women), 102 part-time/adjunct (31 women). Expenses: Contact institution. *Financial support:* In 2016–17, 514 students received support. Fellowships, research assistantships, career-related internships or fieldwork, Federal Work-Study, institutionally sponsored loans, and scholarships/grants available. Financial award application deadline: 7/15; financial award applicants required to submit FAFSA. In 2016, 73 master's, 246 doctorates awarded. Offers law (LL M, MS, JD, SJD). *Application deadline:* For fall admission, 5/2 for domestic students. Applications are processed on a rolling basis. *Application fee:* $60. Electronic applications accepted. *Application Contact:* Robin Ingli, Director of Admissions, 612-625-3487, Fax: 612-625-2011, E-mail: jdadmissions@umn.edu. *Dean,* Garry Jenkins, 612-625-4841.

Medical School *Program availability:* Part-time, evening/weekend. Offers medicine (MA, MS, DPT, MD, PhD); pharmacology (MS, PhD).

School of Dentistry Offers dentistry (MS, DDS, PhD, Certificate); endodontics (MS, Certificate); oral biology (MS, PhD); oral health services for older adults (geriatrics) (MS, Certificate); orthodontics (MS); pediatric dentistry (MS); periodontology (MS); prosthodontics (MS); temporomandibular joint disorders (MS).

School of Public Health *Program availability:* Part-time, online learning. Offers biostatistics (MPH, MS, PhD); clinical research (MS); community health education (MPH); core concepts (Certificate); epidemiology (MPH, PhD); food safety and biosecurity (Certificate); health services research, policy, and administration (MS, PhD); healthcare administration (MHA); maternal and child health (MPH); occupational health and safety (Certificate); preparedness, response and recovery (Certificate); public health (MHA, MPH, MS, PhD, Certificate); public health administration and policy (MPH); public health nutrition (MPH); public health practice (MPH). Electronic applications accepted.

Division of Environmental Health Sciences *Program availability:* Part-time. Offers environmental and occupational epidemiology (MPH, MS, PhD); environmental chemistry (MS, PhD); environmental health policy (MPH, MS, PhD); environmental infectious diseases (MPH, MS, PhD); environmental toxicology (MPH, MS, PhD); exposure sciences (MS); general environmental health (MPH, MS); global environmental health (MPH, MS, PhD); industrial hygiene (MPH, MS, PhD); occupational health nursing (MPH, MS, PhD); occupational medicine (MPH). Electronic applications accepted.

UNIVERSITY OF MISSISSIPPI, University, MS 38677

General Information State-supported, coed, university. CGS member. *Enrollment:* 2,025 full-time matriculated graduate/professional students (1,099 women), 718 part-time matriculated graduate/professional students (412 women). *Graduate faculty:* 878 full-time (386 women), 217 part-time/adjunct (118 women). *Graduate housing:* Rooms and/or apartments available to single and married students. *Student services:* Campus employment opportunities, campus safety program, career counseling, exercise/wellness program, free psychological counseling, international student services, low-cost health insurance, multicultural affairs office, services for students with disabilities, teacher training, writing training. *Library facilities:* J. D. Williams Library plus 1 other. *Collection:* Books: 3.3 million (physical), 814,143 (digital/electronic); Serial titles: 39,667 (physical), 135,210 (digital/electronic); Databases: 389. Weekly public service hours: 109. *Research affiliation:* Mississippi Geographic Alliance, Mississippi Research Consortium, Mississippi - Alabama Sea Grant Consortium, Oak Ridge Associated Universities, Southeastern Universities Research Association, Mississippi Space Grant Consortium.

Computer facilities: 75 computers available on campus for general student use. A campuswide network can be accessed from student residence rooms and from off campus. Online class registration is available.
Website: http://www.olemiss.edu/

General Application Contact: Dr. Christy M. Wyandt, Associate Dean of Graduate School, 662-915-7474, Fax: 662-915-7577, E-mail: cwyandt@olemiss.edu.

GRADUATE UNITS

Graduate School Students: 2,025 full-time (1,099 women), 718 part-time (412 women); includes 567 minority (382 Black or African American, non-Hispanic/Latino; 4 American Indian or Alaska Native, non-Hispanic/Latino; 67 Asian, non-Hispanic/Latino; 65 Hispanic/Latino; 1 Native Hawaiian or other Pacific Islander, non-Hispanic/Latino; 48 Two or more races, non-Hispanic/Latino), 321 international. Average age 26. Expenses: Contact institution. *Financial support:* Fellowships, research assistantships, teaching assistantships, career-related internships or fieldwork, Federal Work-Study, institutionally sponsored loans, scholarships/grants, tuition waivers (full), and unspecified assistantships available. Financial award application deadline: 3/1; financial award applicants required to submit FAFSA. *Program availability:* Part-time. *Application deadline:* For fall admission, 4/1 for domestic students; for spring admission, 10/1 for domestic students. Applications are processed on a rolling basis. *Application fee:* $50. Electronic applications accepted. *Application Contact:* Dr. Christy M. Wyandt, Associate Dean, 662-915-7474, Fax: 662-915-7577, E-mail: cwyandt@olemiss.edu. *Dean,* Dr. Johns Z. Kiss, 662-915-7474, Fax: 662-915-7577, E-mail: gschool@olemiss.edu.

College of Liberal Arts Students: 415 full-time (210 women), 57 part-time (20 women); includes 70 minority (35 Black or African American, non-Hispanic/Latino; 13 Asian, non-Hispanic/Latino; 14 Hispanic/Latino; 8 Two or more races, non-Hispanic/Latino), 102 international. Average age 27. *Faculty:* 472 full-time (263 women), 75 part-time/adjunct (35 women). Expenses: Contact institution. *Financial support:* Fellowships, research assistantships, teaching assistantships, career-related internships or fieldwork, Federal Work-Study, institutionally sponsored loans, scholarships/grants, and unspecified assistantships available. Financial award application deadline: 3/1; financial award applicants required to submit FAFSA. *Program availability:* Part-time. Offers anthropology (MA); biology (MS, PhD); chemistry (MS, PhD); economics (MA, PhD); English (MA, PhD); experimental psychology (PhD); history (MA, PhD); mathematics (MS, PhD); modern languages (MA); music (MM); philosophy (MA); physics (MA, MS, PhD); political science (MA, PhD); studio art (MFA). *Application deadline:* For fall admission, 4/1 for domestic students; for spring admission, 10/1 for domestic students. Applications are processed on a rolling basis. *Application fee:* $40. Electronic applications accepted. *Application Contact:* Dr. Christy M. Wyandt, Associate Dean of Graduate School, 662-915-7474, Fax: 662-915-7577, E-mail: cwyandt@olemiss.edu. *Dean,* Dr. Lee Michael Cohen, 662-915-7177, Fax: 662-915-5792, E-mail: libarts@olemiss.edu.

Meek School of Journalism and New Media Students: 47 full-time (21 women), 15 part-time (4 women); includes 16 minority (10 Black or African American, non-Hispanic/Latino; 1 Asian, non-Hispanic/Latino; 2 Hispanic/Latino; 1 Native Hawaiian or other Pacific Islander, non-Hispanic/Latino; 2 Two or more races, non-Hispanic/Latino), 6 international. Average age 24. *Faculty:* 28 full-time (14 women), 21 part-time/adjunct (13 women). Expenses: Contact institution. In 2016, 11 master's awarded. Offers journalism (MA). *Application fee:* $40. *Application Contact:* Dr. Christy M. Wyandt, Associate Dean, 662-915-7474, Fax: 662-915-7577, E-mail: cwyandt@olemiss.edu. *Dean,* Dr. Will Norton, Jr., 662-915-7146, Fax: 662-915-7765, E-mail: meekschool@olemiss.edu.

School of Accountancy Students: 143 full-time (64 women), 7 part-time (4 women); includes 12 minority (7 Black or African American, non-Hispanic/Latino; 1 American Indian or Alaska Native, non-Hispanic/Latino; 1 Asian, non-Hispanic/Latino; 1 Hispanic/Latino; 2 Two or more races, non-Hispanic/Latino), 6 international. Average age 22. *Faculty:* 17 full-time (12 women), 4 part-time/adjunct (3 women). Expenses: Contact institution. *Financial support:* Scholarships/grants available. Financial award application deadline: 3/1; financial award applicants required to submit FAFSA. Offers accountancy (M Acc); taxation accounting (M Tax). *Application deadline:* For fall admission, 4/1 for domestic students; for spring admission, 10/1 for domestic students. Applications are processed on a rolling basis. *Application fee:* $40. *Application Contact:* Dr. Christy M. Wyandt, Associate Dean, 662-915-7474, Fax: 662-915-7577, E-mail: cwyandt@olemiss.edu. *Dean, School of Accountancy,* Dr. W. Mark Wilder, 662-915-7468, Fax: 662-915-7483, E-mail: umaccy@olemiss.edu.

School of Applied Sciences Students: 176 full-time (137 women), 36 part-time (21 women); includes 45 minority (40 Black or African American, non-Hispanic/Latino; 4 Hispanic/Latino; 1 Two or more races, non-Hispanic/Latino), 9 international. Average age 24. *Faculty:* 68 full-time (29 women), 29 part-time/adjunct (17 women). Expenses: Contact institution. *Financial support:* Scholarships/grants available. Financial award application deadline: 3/1; financial award applicants required to submit FAFSA. Offers communicative disorders (MS); exercise science (MS); food and nutrition services (MS); health and kinesiology (PhD); health promotion (MS); park and recreation management (MA); social work (MSW). *Application deadline:* For fall admission, 4/1 for domestic students; for spring admission, 10/1 for domestic students. Applications are processed on a rolling basis. *Application fee:* $40. Electronic applications accepted. *Application Contact:* Dr. Christy M. Wyandt, Associate Dean of Graduate School, 662-915-7474, Fax: 662-915-7577, E-mail: cwyandt@olemiss.edu. *Dean,* Dr. Velmer Stanley Burton, 662-915-1081, Fax: 662-915-5717, E-mail: applsci@olemiss.edu.

School of Business Administration Students: 78 full-time (25 women), 111 part-time (20 women); includes 18 minority (3 Black or African American, non-Hispanic/Latino; 5 Asian, non-Hispanic/Latino; 6 Hispanic/Latino; 4 Two or more races, non-Hispanic/Latino), 19 international. Average age 28. *Faculty:* 56 full-time (40 women), 9 part-time/adjunct (4 women). Expenses: Contact institution. *Financial support:* Fellowships, career-related internships or fieldwork, scholarships/grants, tuition waivers (full), and unspecified assistantships available. Financial award application

deadline: 3/1; financial award applicants required to submit FAFSA. In 2016, 83 master's, 6 doctorates awarded. Offers business administration (PhD); systems management (MS). *Application deadline:* For fall admission, 2/1 for domestic students; for spring admission, 10/1 for domestic students. Applications are processed on a rolling basis. *Application fee:* $40. Electronic applications accepted. *Application Contact:* Dr. Christy M. Wyandt, Associate Dean, 662-915-7474, Fax: 662-915-7577, E-mail: cwyandt@olemiss.edu. *Dean,* Dr. Ken Cyree, 662-915-5820, Fax: 662-915-5821, E-mail: info@bus.olemiss.edu.

School of Education Students: 203 full-time (158 women), 404 part-time (299 women); includes 219 minority (185 Black or African American, non-Hispanic/Latino; 6 Asian, non-Hispanic/Latino; 21 Hispanic/Latino; 7 Two or more races, non-Hispanic/Latino), 9 international. Average age 31. *Faculty:* 58 full-time (22 women), 35 part-time/adjunct (27 women). Expenses: Contact institution. *Financial support:* Scholarships/grants available. Financial award application deadline: 3/1; financial award applicants required to submit FAFSA. In 2016, 176 master's, 20 doctorates, 37 other advanced degrees awarded. Offers education (M Ed, MA, Ed D, PhD, Ed S, Specialist). *Application deadline:* For fall admission, 4/1 for domestic students; for spring admission, 10/1 for domestic students. Applications are processed on a rolling basis. *Application fee:* $40. Electronic applications accepted. *Application Contact:* Dr. Christy M. Wyandt, Associate Dean, 662-915-7474, Fax: 662-915-7577, E-mail: cwyandt@olemiss.edu. *Dean,* Dr. David Rock, 662-915-7063, Fax: 662-915-7249, E-mail: soe@olemiss.edu.

School of Engineering Students: 116 full-time (27 women), 22 part-time (1 woman); includes 14 minority (5 Black or African American, non-Hispanic/Latino; 6 Asian, non-Hispanic/Latino; 2 Hispanic/Latino; 1 Two or more races, non-Hispanic/Latino), 71 international. Average age 27. *Faculty:* 61 full-time (50 women), 6 part-time/adjunct (3 women). Expenses: Contact institution. *Financial support:* Scholarships/grants available. Financial award application deadline: 3/1; financial award applicants required to submit FAFSA. In 2016, 28 master's, 12 doctorates awarded. Offers engineering (MS, PhD). *Application deadline:* For fall admission, 4/1 for domestic students; for spring admission, 10/1 for domestic students. Applications are processed on a rolling basis. *Application fee:* $40. Electronic applications accepted. *Application Contact:* Dr. Christy M. Wyandt, Associate Dean, 662-915-7474, Fax: 662-915-7577, E-mail: cwyandt@olemiss.edu. *Dean,* Dr. Alexander Cheng, 662-915-7407, Fax: 662-915-1287, E-mail: engineer@olemiss.edu.

School of Pharmacy Students: 430 full-time (264 women), 14 part-time (5 women); includes 68 minority (28 Black or African American, non-Hispanic/Latino; 2 American Indian or Alaska Native, non-Hispanic/Latino; 29 Asian, non-Hispanic/Latino; 2 Hispanic/Latino; 1 Native Hawaiian or other Pacific Islander, non-Hispanic/Latino; 6 Two or more races, non-Hispanic/Latino), 87 international. *Faculty:* 66 full-time (29 women), 18 part-time/adjunct (7 women). Expenses: Contact institution. *Financial support:* Fellowships, research assistantships, teaching assistantships, career-related internships or fieldwork, Federal Work-Study, institutionally sponsored loans, scholarships/grants, tuition waivers (full), and unspecified assistantships available. Financial award application deadline: 3/1; financial award applicants required to submit FAFSA. In 2016, 22 master's, 49 doctorates awarded. *Program availability:* Part-time. Offers pharmacy (MS, PhD, Pharm D). *Application deadline:* For fall admission, 4/1 for domestic students; for spring admission, 10/1 for domestic students. Applications are processed on a rolling basis. *Application fee:* $40. Electronic applications accepted. *Dean,* Dr. David D. Allen, II, 662-915-7265, Fax: 662-915-5118, E-mail: sopdean@olemiss.edu.

School of Law Students: 364 full-time (161 women), 3 part-time (1 woman); includes 83 minority (53 Black or African American, non-Hispanic/Latino; 1 American Indian or Alaska Native, non-Hispanic/Latino; 2 Asian, non-Hispanic/Latino; 12 Hispanic/Latino; 15 Two or more races, non-Hispanic/Latino), 1 international. Average age 24. *Faculty:* 32 full-time (19 women), 8 part-time/adjunct (6 women). Expenses: Contact institution. *Financial support:* Fellowships, research assistantships, teaching assistantships, career-related internships or fieldwork, Federal Work-Study, institutionally sponsored loans, and scholarships/grants available. Support available to part-time students. Financial award application deadline: 3/1; financial award applicants required to submit FAFSA. In 2016, 179 doctorates awarded. Offers law (LL M, JD). *Application deadline:* For fall admission, 4/1 for domestic students. *Application fee:* $40. *Application Contact:* Macey Edmondson, Assistant Dean for Admissions and Scholarships, 662-915-6819, Fax: 662-915-7577, E-mail: clee@olemiss.edu. *Dean,* Dr. Deborah Bell, 662-915-6900, Fax: 662-915-6895, E-mail: lawadmin@olemiss.edu.

UNIVERSITY OF MISSISSIPPI MEDICAL CENTER, Jackson, MS 39216-4505

General Information State-supported, coed, upper-level institution. *Graduate housing:* On-campus housing not available. *Research affiliation:* NASA-Stennis Space Center (imaging technology), Catfish Genetics Research Unit (immunology), Oak Ridge National Laboratory (physiology, biomedical engineering), Gulf Coast Research Laboratory (microbiology).

GRADUATE UNITS

School of Dentistry Offers craniofacial and dental research (MS, PhD); dentistry (MS, DMD, PhD).

School of Graduate Studies in the Health Sciences *Program availability:* Part-time. Offers biochemistry (PhD); biomedical materials science (MS, PhD); biomedical sciences (MS); clinical anatomy (MS, PhD); health sciences (MS, PhD); microbiology (PhD); neuroscience (PhD); pathology (PhD); pharmacology and toxicology (PhD); physiology and biophysics (PhD).

School of Health Related Professions *Program availability:* Part-time. Offers health related professions (MOT, MPT); occupational therapy (MOT); physical therapy (MPT).

School of Medicine *Program availability:* Part-time. Offers medicine (MD). Electronic applications accepted.

School of Nursing *Program availability:* Part-time, evening/weekend, online learning. Offers nursing (MSN, DNP, PhD). Electronic applications accepted.

UNIVERSITY OF MISSOURI, Columbia, MO 65211

General Information State-supported, coed, university. CGS member. *Enrollment:* 4,769 full-time matriculated graduate/professional students (2,631 women), 2,599 part-time matriculated graduate/professional students (1,582 women). *Enrollment by degree level:* 3,084 master's, 3,788 doctoral, 252 other advanced degrees. *Graduate faculty:* 1,627 full-time (633 women), 122 part-time/adjunct (44 women). Tuition, state resident: full-time $6347; part-time $352.60 per credit hour. Tuition, nonresident: full-time $17,379; part-time $965.50 per credit hour. *Required fees:* $1035. Tuition and fees vary according to course load, campus/location and program. *Graduate housing:* Rooms and/or apartments available on a first-come, first-served basis to single and married students. Typical cost: $8160 per year for single students; $9060 per year for married students. *Student services:* Campus employment opportunities, campus safety program, career

University of Missouri

counseling, child daycare facilities, exercise/wellness program, free psychological counseling, grant writing training, international student services, low-cost health insurance, multicultural affairs office, services for students with disabilities, teacher training, writing training. *Library facilities:* Ellis Library plus 10 others. *Collection:* Books: 4.7 million (physical), 1.4 million (digital/electronic). Students can reserve study rooms.

Computer facilities: Computer purchase and lease plans are available. 1,242 computers available on campus for general student use. A campuswide network can be accessed from student residence rooms and from off campus. Online class registration is available.
Website: http://www.missouri.edu/

General Application Contact: Terrence Grus, Director of Graduate Admissions and Student Services, 573-882-6311, E-mail: gradadmin@missouri.edu.

GRADUATE UNITS

College of Veterinary Medicine Students: 474 full-time (379 women), 38 part-time (27 women); includes 25 minority (4 Black or African American, non-Hispanic/Latino; 3 Asian, non-Hispanic/Latino; 16 Hispanic/Latino; 2 Two or more races, non-Hispanic/Latino), 5 international. Average age 25. *Faculty:* 115 full-time (45 women), 12 part-time/adjunct (3 women). Expenses: Contact institution. *Financial support:* Fellowships, research assistantships, teaching assistantships, career-related internships or fieldwork, institutionally sponsored loans, scholarships/grants, traineeships, health care benefits, tuition waivers (full and partial), and unspecified assistantships available. Support available to part-time students. Financial award applicants required to submit FAFSA. Offers veterinary medicine (MS, DVM, PhD). *Application deadline:* For fall admission, 1/5 for domestic and international students; for spring admission, 9/15 for domestic and international students; for summer admission, 1/5 for domestic and international students. *Application fee:* $65 ($90 for international students). Electronic applications accepted.

Graduate Programs in Veterinary Medicine Offers biomedical sciences (MS, PhD); comparative medicine (MS); pathobiology (MS, PhD); veterinary medicine (MS, PhD); veterinary medicine and surgery (MS). Electronic applications accepted.

Office of Research and Graduate Studies *Program availability:* Part-time, evening/weekend. Offers dispute resolution (LL M, Certificate, Graduate Certificate); genetics (PhD); global public health (Graduate Certificate); health administration (MHA); health informatics (MS, Certificate); health promotion and policy (MPH); neuroscience (MS, PhD, Graduate Certificate); public health (Graduate Certificate); veterinary public health (MPH).

College of Agriculture, Food and Natural Resources Students: 230 full-time (108 women), 75 part-time (47 women); includes 16 minority (5 Black or African American, non-Hispanic/Latino; 3 Asian, non-Hispanic/Latino; 4 Hispanic/Latino; 4 Two or more races, non-Hispanic/Latino), 117 international. Average age 29. *Faculty:* 172 full-time (43 women), 3 part-time/adjunct (0 women). Expenses: Contact institution. *Financial support:* Fellowships with tuition reimbursements, research assistantships with tuition reimbursements, teaching assistantships with tuition reimbursements, institutionally sponsored loans, scholarships/grants, traineeships, health care benefits, and unspecified assistantships available. Support available to part-time students. *Program availability:* Part-time. Offers agricultural economics (MS, PhD); agricultural education (MS, PhD); agriculture, food and natural resources (MS, PhD, Certificate, Graduate Certificate); agroforestry (MS, Certificate); animal sciences (MS, PhD); biochemistry (MS, PhD); conservation biology (Certificate, Graduate Certificate); crop, soil and pest management (MS, PhD); entomology (MS, PhD); fisheries and wildlife sciences (MS, PhD); food science (MS, PhD); forestry (MS, PhD); geographical information science (Certificate); horticulture (MS, PhD); human dimensions of natural resources (MS, PhD); parks, recreation and tourism (MS); plant biology and genetics (MS, PhD); plant stress biology (MS, PhD); rural sociology (MS, PhD); society and ecosystems (Certificate); soil, environmental and atmospheric sciences (MS, PhD); water resources (MS, PhD). *Application deadline:* Applications are processed on a rolling basis. *Application fee:* $75 ($90 for international students). Electronic applications accepted.

College of Arts and Science *Faculty:* 513 full-time (184 women), 29 part-time/adjunct (16 women). Expenses: Contact institution. *Financial support:* Fellowships with tuition reimbursements, research assistantships with tuition reimbursements, teaching assistantships with tuition reimbursements, career-related internships or fieldwork, institutionally sponsored loans, scholarships/grants, health care benefits, tuition waivers (full and partial), and unspecified assistantships available. Support available to part-time students. *Program availability:* Part-time. Offers analytical chemistry (MS, PhD); anthropology (MA, PhD); applied mathematics (MS); art (MFA); art history and archaeology (MA, PhD); arts and science (MA, MFA, MM, MS, MST, PhD, Graduate Certificate); classical languages (MA, PhD); classical studies (MA, PhD); communication (MA, PhD); economics (MA, PhD); English (MA, PhD); evolutionary biology and ecology (MA, PhD); French (MA, PhD); geographic information science (Graduate Certificate); geography (MA); geological sciences (MS, PhD); German and Russian studies (MA); history (MA, PhD); literature (MA); mathematics (MA, MST, PhD); music (MA, MM); philosophy (PhD); physics and astronomy (MS, PhD); political science (MA, PhD); psychological sciences (MA, MS, PhD); religious studies (MA); sociology (PhD); Spanish (MA, PhD); statistics (MA, PhD); teaching (MA); theatre (MA, PhD). *Application deadline:* Applications are processed on a rolling basis. *Application fee:* $75 ($90 for international students). Electronic applications accepted.

College of Education Students: 640 full-time (430 women), 727 part-time (471 women); includes 157 minority (70 Black or African American, non-Hispanic/Latino; 2 American Indian or Alaska Native, non-Hispanic/Latino; 14 Asian, non-Hispanic/Latino; 44 Hispanic/Latino; 1 Native Hawaiian or other Pacific Islander, non-Hispanic/Latino; 26 Two or more races, non-Hispanic/Latino), 72 international. Average age 34. *Faculty:* 100 full-time (62 women), 4 part-time/adjunct (1 woman). Expenses: Contact institution. *Financial support:* Fellowships, research assistantships, teaching assistantships, institutionally sponsored loans, scholarships/grants, traineeships, health care benefits, and unspecified assistantships available. Support available to part-time students. *Program availability:* Part-time, evening/weekend. Offers administration and supervision of special education (PhD); agricultural education (M Ed, PhD, Ed S); art education (M Ed, PhD, Ed S); behavior disorders (M Ed, PhD); business and office education (M Ed, PhD, Ed S); counseling psychology (M Ed, MA, PhD, Ed S); curriculum development of exceptional students (M Ed, PhD); early childhood education (M Ed, PhD, Ed S); early childhood special education (M Ed, PhD); education (M Ed, MA, Ed D, PhD, Certificate, Ed S); education administration (M Ed, MA, Ed D, PhD, Ed S); educational psychology (M Ed, MA, PhD, Ed S); educational technology (M Ed, Ed S); elementary education (M Ed, PhD, Ed S); English education (M Ed, PhD, Ed S); foreign language education (M Ed, PhD, Ed S); general special education (M Ed, MA, PhD); health education and promotion (M Ed, PhD); higher and adult education (M Ed, MA, Ed D, PhD, Ed S); information science and learning technology (PhD, Certificate); learning and

instruction (M Ed); learning disabilities (M Ed, PhD); library science (MA); marketing education (M Ed, PhD, Ed S); mathematics education (M Ed, PhD, Ed S); mental retardation (M Ed, PhD); music education (M Ed, PhD, Ed S); reading education (M Ed, PhD, Ed S); school psychology (M Ed, MA, PhD, Ed S); science education (M Ed, PhD, Ed S); social studies education (M Ed, PhD, Ed S); vocational education (M Ed, PhD, Ed S). *Application deadline:* Applications are processed on a rolling basis. *Application fee:* $75 ($90 for international students).

College of Engineering Students: 280 full-time (65 women), 307 part-time (65 women); includes 21 minority (6 Black or African American, non-Hispanic/Latino; 5 Asian, non-Hispanic/Latino; 7 Hispanic/Latino; 3 Two or more races, non-Hispanic/Latino), 465 international. Average age 28. *Faculty:* 122 full-time (18 women), 9 part-time/adjunct (3 women). Expenses: Contact institution. *Financial support:* Fellowships, research assistantships, teaching assistantships, institutionally sponsored loans, scholarships/grants, traineeships, health care benefits, and unspecified assistantships available. Support available to part-time students. *Program availability:* Part-time. Offers agricultural engineering (MS); biological engineering (MS, PhD); chemical engineering (MS, PhD); civil engineering (MS, PhD); computer science (MS, PhD); electrical and computer engineering (MS, PhD); engineering (ME, MS, PhD, Certificate); environmental and regulatory compliance (MS, PhD); environmental engineering (MS, PhD); geotechnical engineering (MS, PhD); industrial and manufacturing systems engineering (ME, MS, PhD); mechanical and aerospace engineering (MS, PhD); nuclear engineering (Certificate); structural engineering (MS, PhD); transportation and highway engineering (MS); water resources (MS, PhD). *Application deadline:* Applications are processed on a rolling basis. *Application fee:* $75 ($90 for international students).

College of Human Environmental Sciences Students: 83 full-time (57 women), 87 part-time (64 women); includes 22 minority (8 Black or African American, non-Hispanic/Latino; 4 Asian, non-Hispanic/Latino; 7 Hispanic/Latino; 3 Two or more races, non-Hispanic/Latino), 33 international. Average age 33. *Faculty:* 63 full-time (41 women). Expenses: Contact institution. *Financial support:* Fellowships with tuition reimbursements, research assistantships with tuition reimbursements, teaching assistantships with tuition reimbursements, institutionally sponsored loans, scholarships/grants, traineeships, health care benefits, and unspecified assistantships available. Support available to part-time students. *Program availability:* Part-time. Offers architectural studies (M Arch, PhD); exercise physiology (MS); human development and family studies (MA, MS, PhD); human environmental sciences (MA, MS, PhD, Certificate, Graduate Certificate); nutrition sciences (MS); personal financial planning (MS, PhD, Certificate, Graduate Certificate); textile and apparel management (MS, PhD). *Application deadline:* Applications are processed on a rolling basis. *Application fee:* $75 ($90 for international students).

Harry S Truman School of Public Affairs Students: 76 full-time (37 women), 168 part-time (88 women); includes 36 minority (21 Black or African American, non-Hispanic/Latino; 1 American Indian or Alaska Native, non-Hispanic/Latino; 2 Asian, non-Hispanic/Latino; 6 Hispanic/Latino; 6 Two or more races, non-Hispanic/Latino), 24 international. Average age 34. *Faculty:* 10 full-time (7 women), 2 part-time/adjunct (0 women). Expenses: Contact institution. *Financial support:* Fellowships, research assistantships, teaching assistantships, institutionally sponsored loans, scholarships/grants, traineeships, health care benefits, and unspecified assistantships available. Support available to part-time students. Offers grantsmanship (Graduate Certificate); nonprofit management (Graduate Certificate); organizational change (Graduate Certificate); public affairs (MPA, PhD); public management (Graduate Certificate); science and public policy (Graduate Certificate). *Application deadline:* For fall admission, 2/1 priority date for domestic and international students. Applications are processed on a rolling basis. *Application fee:* $75 ($90 for international students). Electronic applications accepted.

Informatics Institute Students: 25 full-time (10 women), 20 part-time (6 women). Expenses: Contact institution. *Financial support:* Scholarships/grants, health care benefits, and unspecified assistantships available. Support available to part-time students. Offers informatics (PhD). *Application deadline:* For fall admission, 1/15 priority date for domestic and international students. Applications are processed on a rolling basis. *Application fee:* $75 ($90 for international students). Electronic applications accepted.

Robert J. Trulaske, Sr. College of Business Students: 355 full-time (134 women), 16 part-time (7 women); includes 34 minority (12 Black or African American, non-Hispanic/Latino; 7 Asian, non-Hispanic/Latino; 7 Hispanic/Latino; 8 Two or more races, non-Hispanic/Latino), 67 international. Average age 26. *Faculty:* 66 full-time (22 women), 1 (woman) part-time/adjunct. Expenses: Contact institution. *Financial support:* Fellowships, research assistantships, teaching assistantships, and institutionally sponsored loans available. *Program availability:* Part-time. Offers accountancy (M Acc, PhD); business (M Acc, MBA, PhD, Certificate); business administration (MBA); executive business administration (MBA); finance (PhD); management (PhD); marketing (PhD); taxation (Certificate). *Application deadline:* Applications are processed on a rolling basis. *Application fee:* $75 ($90 for international students).

School of Journalism Students: 134 full-time (97 women), 76 part-time (50 women); includes 29 minority (6 Black or African American, non-Hispanic/Latino; 5 Asian, non-Hispanic/Latino; 12 Hispanic/Latino; 6 Two or more races, non-Hispanic/Latino), 50 international. Average age 29. *Faculty:* 72 full-time (34 women), 3 part-time/adjunct (0 women). Expenses: Contact institution. *Financial support:* Fellowships with tuition reimbursements, research assistantships with tuition reimbursements, teaching assistantships with tuition reimbursements, career-related internships or fieldwork, institutionally sponsored loans, scholarships/grants, health care benefits, and unspecified assistantships available. Support available to part-time students. *Program availability:* Part-time. Offers health communications (MA); journalism (PhD). *Application deadline:* For fall admission, 12/15 priority date for domestic and international students; for winter admission, 9/1 priority date for domestic and international students. Applications are processed on a rolling basis. *Application fee:* $75 ($90 for international students). Electronic applications accepted.

School of Social Work Students: 84 full-time (77 women), 138 part-time (127 women); includes 21 minority (11 Black or African American, non-Hispanic/Latino; 6 Hispanic/Latino; 4 Two or more races, non-Hispanic/Latino), 2 international. Average age 29. *Faculty:* 15 full-time (10 women). Expenses: Contact institution. *Financial support:* Fellowships with tuition reimbursements, research assistantships with tuition reimbursements, teaching assistantships with tuition reimbursements, institutionally sponsored loans, scholarships/grants, health care benefits, and unspecified assistantships available. Support available to part-time students. *Program availability:* Part-time. Offers gerontological social work (Certificate); military social work (Certificate); social work (MSW, PhD). *Application deadline:* For fall admission, 1/15 priority date for domestic and international students. Applications are processed on a rolling basis. *Application fee:* $75 ($90 for international students). Electronic applications accepted.

Sinclair School of Nursing Students: 70 full-time (65 women), 218 part-time (205 women); includes 36 minority (14 Black or African American, non-Hispanic/Latino; 3 American Indian or Alaska Native, non-Hispanic/Latino; 3 Asian, non-Hispanic/Latino; 7 Hispanic/Latino; 9 Two or more races, non-Hispanic/Latino), 10 international. Average age 37. *Faculty:* 32 full-time (30 women), 1 (woman) part-time/adjunct. Expenses: Contact institution. *Financial support:* Fellowships, research assistantships, teaching assistantships, career-related internships or fieldwork, institutionally sponsored loans, scholarships/grants, traineeships, health care benefits, tuition waivers (full), and unspecified assistantships available. Support available to part-time students. *Program availability:* Part-time. Offers adult-gerontology clinical nurse specialist (DNP, Certificate); family nurse practitioner (DNP); family psychiatric and mental health nurse practitioner (DNP); nursing (MS, PhD); nursing leadership and innovations in health care (DNP); pediatric clinical nurse specialist (DNP, Certificate); pediatric nurse practitioner (DNP). *Application deadline:* For fall admission, 2/1 priority date for domestic and international students. Applications are processed on a rolling basis. *Application fee:* $75 ($90 for international students). Electronic applications accepted.

School of Health Professions Students: 286 full-time (216 women); includes 23 minority (5 Black or African American, non-Hispanic/Latino; 2 American Indian or Alaska Native, non-Hispanic/Latino; 1 Asian, non-Hispanic/Latino; 7 Hispanic/Latino; 8 Two or more races, non-Hispanic/Latino). Average age 24. *Faculty:* 85 full-time (56 women), 8 part-time/adjunct (6 women). Expenses: Contact institution. *Financial support:* Fellowships, research assistantships, teaching assistantships, and institutionally sponsored loans available. Offers communication science and disorders (MHS, PhD); diagnostic medical ultrasound (MHS); health professions (MHS, MOT, DPT, PhD); occupational therapy (MOT); physical therapy (DPT). *Application deadline:* For fall admission, 3/1 priority date for domestic students. Applications are processed on a rolling basis. *Application fee:* $75 ($90 for international students).

School of Law Students: 304 full-time (123 women), 15 part-time (10 women); includes 54 minority (35 Black or African American, non-Hispanic/Latino; 5 Asian, non-Hispanic/Latino; 5 Hispanic/Latino; 1 Native Hawaiian or other Pacific Islander, non-Hispanic/Latino; 8 Two or more races, non-Hispanic/Latino), 6 international. Average age 26. *Faculty:* 34 full-time (14 women), 5 part-time/adjunct (2 women). Expenses: Contact institution. *Financial support:* Fellowships, Federal Work-Study, and institutionally sponsored loans available. Financial award application deadline: 3/1; financial award applicants required to submit FAFSA. Offers dispute resolution (LL M); law (JD). *Application deadline:* For fall admission, 3/1 priority date for domestic students. Applications are processed on a rolling basis.

School of Medicine Students: 544 full-time (262 women), 37 part-time (25 women); includes 54 minority (20 Black or African American, non-Hispanic/Latino; 1 American Indian or Alaska Native, non-Hispanic/Latino; 15 Asian, non-Hispanic/Latino; 16 Hispanic/Latino; 2 Two or more races, non-Hispanic/Latino), 33 international. Average age 27. Expenses: Contact institution. *Financial support:* Fellowships, research assistantships, teaching assistantships, career-related internships or fieldwork, institutionally sponsored loans, and scholarships/grants available. Support available to part-time students. Financial award applicants required to submit FAFSA. *Program availability:* Part-time. Offers family and community medicine (MS); health administration (MS); medical pharmacology and physiology (MS, PhD); medicine (MS, MD, PhD, Graduate Certificate); molecular microbiology and immunology (PhD); pathology and anatomical sciences (MS). *Application deadline:* Applications are processed on a rolling basis.

UNIVERSITY OF MISSOURI–KANSAS CITY, Kansas City, MO 64110-2499

General Information State-supported, coed, university. CGS member. *Enrollment:* 16,944 graduate, professional, and undergraduate students; 3,235 full-time matriculated graduate/professional students (1,606 women), 1,870 part-time matriculated graduate/professional students (1,054 women). *Enrollment by degree level:* 2,471 master's, 2,591 doctoral, 43 other advanced degrees. *Graduate faculty:* 745 full-time (355 women), 462 part-time/adjunct (213 women). *Graduate housing:* Room and/or apartments available on a first-come, first-served basis to single students; on-campus housing not available to married students. *Student services:* Campus employment opportunities, campus safety program, career counseling, child daycare facilities, exercise/wellness program, free psychological counseling, international student services, multicultural affairs office, services for students with disabilities, teacher training, writing training. *Library facilities:* Miller-Nichols Library plus 3 others. *Collection:* Students can reserve study rooms. *Research affiliation:* Children's Mercy Hospital (health sciences), Truman Medical Center (health sciences), Veterans Administration Hospital (health sciences), Midwest Research Institute (health sciences), St. Luke's Hospital (health sciences).

Computer facilities: Computer purchase and lease plans are available. 400 computers available on campus for general student use. A campuswide network can be accessed from student residence rooms and from off campus. Online class registration is available.
Website: http://www.umkc.edu/

General Application Contact: Tamara Byland, Director of Admissions, 816-235-1111, Fax: 816-235-5544, E-mail: admit@umkc.edu.

GRADUATE UNITS

College of Arts and Sciences Students: 265 full-time (172 women), 273 part-time (161 women); includes 114 minority (60 Black or African American, non-Hispanic/Latino; 6 American Indian or Alaska Native, non-Hispanic/Latino; 5 Asian, non-Hispanic/Latino; 35 Hispanic/Latino; 8 Two or more races, non-Hispanic/Latino), 40 international. Average age 31. 528 applicants, 42% accepted, 193 enrolled. *Faculty:* 220 full-time (100 women), 160 part-time/adjunct (76 women). Expenses: Contact institution. *Financial support:* In 2016–17, 34 research assistantships with tuition reimbursements (averaging $13,240 per year), 140 teaching assistantships with tuition reimbursements (averaging $12,708 per year) were awarded; career-related internships or fieldwork, Federal Work-Study, institutionally sponsored loans, scholarships/grants, and tuition waivers (full and partial) also available. Support available to part-time students. Financial award application deadline: 3/1; financial award applicants required to submit FAFSA. In 2016, 211 master's, 3 doctorates awarded. *Program availability:* Part-time, evening/weekend. Offers analytical chemistry (PhD); art and art history (MA, PhD); arts and sciences (MA, MFA, MS, MSW, PhD); community psychology (PhD); criminal justice and criminology (MS); economics (MA, PhD); English (MA, PhD); geosciences (MS); history (MA, PhD); inorganic chemistry (PhD); mathematics and statistics (MA, MS, PhD); organic chemistry (PhD); physical chemistry (PhD); physics (MS, PhD); political science (MA); polymer chemistry (MS, PhD); romance languages and literatures (MA); sociology (MA);

theatre (MA, MFA). *Application deadline:* Applications are processed on a rolling basis. *Application fee:* $45 ($50 for international students). Electronic applications accepted. *Application Contact:* Tamara Byland, Director of Admissions, 816-235-1111, Fax: 816-235-5544, E-mail: admit@umkc.edu. *Dean,* Dr. Wayne Vaught, 816-235-5421, Fax: 816-235-1308.

School of Social Work Students: 109 full-time (94 women), 42 part-time (33 women); includes 38 minority (23 Black or African American, non-Hispanic/Latino; 2 American Indian or Alaska Native, non-Hispanic/Latino; 1 Asian, non-Hispanic/Latino; 6 Hispanic/Latino; 6 Two or more races, non-Hispanic/Latino), 1 international. Average age 32. 127 applicants, 68% accepted, 71 enrolled. *Faculty:* 8 full-time (6 women), 19 part-time/adjunct (12 women). Expenses: Contact institution. *Financial support:* In 2016–17, 4 teaching assistantships (averaging $11,760 per year) were awarded; research assistantships with partial tuition reimbursements, career-related internships or fieldwork, and institutionally sponsored loans also available. Financial award application deadline: 3/1; financial award applicants required to submit FAFSA. In 2016, 59 master's awarded. *Program availability:* Part-time, evening/weekend. Offers social work (MSW). *Application deadline:* For fall admission, 4/30 for domestic and international students; for spring admission, 12/1 for domestic and international students. Applications are processed on a rolling basis. *Application fee:* $45 ($50 for international students). *Application Contact:* Tamara Byland, Director of Admissions, 816-235-1111, Fax: 816-235-5544, E-mail: admit@umkc.edu. *Department Chair,* Dr. Bob Prue, 816-235-6308, E-mail: pruer@umkc.edu.

Conservatory of Music and Dance Students: 165 full-time (67 women), 64 part-time (34 women); includes 21 minority (4 Black or African American, non-Hispanic/Latino; 7 Asian, non-Hispanic/Latino; 7 Hispanic/Latino; 3 Two or more races, non-Hispanic/Latino), 49 international. Average age 28. 368 applicants, 49% accepted, 88 enrolled. *Faculty:* 55 full-time (24 women), 39 part-time/adjunct (12 women). Expenses: Contact institution. *Financial support:* In 2016–17, 32 teaching assistantships with partial tuition reimbursements (averaging $8,238 per year) were awarded; career-related internships or fieldwork, Federal Work-Study, institutionally sponsored loans, scholarships/grants, tuition waivers (partial), and unspecified assistantships also available. Support available to part-time students. Financial award application deadline: 3/1; financial award applicants required to submit FAFSA. In 2016, 49 master's, 26 doctorates awarded. *Program availability:* Part-time. Offers composition (MM, DMA); conducting (MM, DMA); music (MA); music education (MME, PhD); music history and literature (MM); music theory (MM); music therapy (MA); performance (MM, DMA). PhD (interdisciplinary) offered through the School of Graduate Studies. *Application deadline:* For fall admission, 1/15 priority date for domestic students, 1/15 for international students. *Application fee:* $45 ($50 for international students). *Application Contact:* William Everett, Associate Dean for Graduate Studies, 816-235-2857, Fax: 816-235-5264, E-mail: everettw@umkc.edu. *Dean,* Peter Witte, 816-235-2731, Fax: 816-235-5265, E-mail: wittep@umkc.edu.

Henry W. Bloch School of Management Students: 204 full-time (97 women), 308 part-time (151 women); includes 70 minority (29 Black or African American, non-Hispanic/Latino; 1 American Indian or Alaska Native, non-Hispanic/Latino; 17 Asian, non-Hispanic/Latino; 18 Hispanic/Latino; 5 Two or more races, non-Hispanic/Latino), 82 international. Average age 30. 389 applicants, 49% accepted, 190 enrolled. *Faculty:* 60 full-time (19 women), 40 part-time/adjunct (11 women). Expenses: Contact institution. *Financial support:* In 2016–17, 31 research assistantships with partial tuition reimbursements (averaging $10,597 per year), 10 teaching assistantships with partial tuition reimbursements (averaging $14,592 per year) were awarded; career-related internships or fieldwork, Federal Work-Study, institutionally sponsored loans, scholarships/grants, tuition waivers (full and partial), and unspecified assistantships also available. Support available to part-time students. Financial award application deadline: 3/1; financial award applicants required to submit FAFSA. In 2016, 248 master's, 2 doctorates awarded. *Program availability:* Part-time, evening/weekend. Offers accounting (MS); finance (MS); public affairs (MPA, PhD). PhD (interdisciplinary) offered through the School of Graduate Studies. *Application deadline:* For fall admission, 5/1 priority date for domestic and international students; for spring admission, 10/1 priority date for domestic and international students. Applications are processed on a rolling basis. *Application fee:* $45 ($50 for international students). Electronic applications accepted. *Application Contact:* 816-235-1111, E-mail: admit@umkc.edu. *Dean,* Dr. David Donnelly, 816-235-1333, Fax: 816-235-2206, E-mail: donnellyd@umkc.edu.

School of Biological Sciences Students: 8 full-time (3 women), 8 part-time (4 women); includes 5 minority (2 Asian, non-Hispanic/Latino; 2 Hispanic/Latino; 1 Two or more races, non-Hispanic/Latino). Average age 25. 57 applicants, 23% accepted, 8 enrolled. *Faculty:* 31 full-time (9 women), 2 part-time/adjunct (1 woman). Expenses: Contact institution. *Financial support:* In 2016–17, 12 research assistantships with full tuition reimbursements (averaging $24,750 per year), 16 teaching assistantships with full tuition reimbursements (averaging $15,123 per year) were awarded; Federal Work-Study, institutionally sponsored loans, scholarships/grants, tuition waivers (full and partial), and unspecified assistantships available. Support available to part-time students. Financial award application deadline: 3/1; financial award applicants required to submit FAFSA. In 2016, 12 master's awarded. *Program availability:* Part-time, evening/weekend. Offers biology (MA); cell biology and biophysics (PhD); cellular and molecular biology (MS); molecular biology and biochemistry (PhD). PhD (interdisciplinary) offered through the School of Graduate Studies. *Application deadline:* For fall admission, 2/15 priority date for domestic and international students. Applications are processed on a rolling basis. *Application fee:* $45 ($50 for international students). *Application Contact:* Information Contact, 816-235-1330, Fax: 816-235-5158, E-mail: sbsgradrecruit@umkc.edu. *Dean,* Dr. Theodore White, 816-235-2538, Fax: 816-235-5158, E-mail: whitetc@umkc.edu.

School of Computing and Engineering Students: 473 full-time (155 women), 207 part-time (42 women); includes 24 minority (10 Black or African American, non-Hispanic/Latino; 10 Asian, non-Hispanic/Latino; 4 Hispanic/Latino), 581 international. Average age 25. 1,143 applicants, 44% accepted, 227 enrolled. *Faculty:* 45 full-time (6 women), 26 part-time/adjunct (4 women). Expenses: Contact institution. *Financial support:* In 2016–17, 37 research assistantships with partial tuition reimbursements (averaging $15,679 per year), 47 teaching assistantships with partial tuition reimbursements (averaging $16,830 per year) were awarded; career-related internships or fieldwork, Federal Work-Study, scholarships/grants, tuition waivers (partial), and unspecified assistantships also available. Support available to part-time students. Financial award application deadline: 3/1; financial award applicants required to submit FAFSA. In 2016, 446 master's, 2 other advanced degrees awarded. *Program availability:* Part-time. Offers civil engineering (MS); computer and electrical engineering (PhD); computer science (MS); computer science and informatics (PhD); computing (PhD); electrical engineering (MS); engineering (PhD); engineering and construction management (Graduate Certificate); mechanical engineering (MS); telecommunications and computer networking (PhD). PhD (interdisciplinary) offered through the School of Graduate Studies. *Application deadline:* For fall admission, 1/15 priority date for domestic students, 1/15 for international students. Applications are processed on a rolling basis. *Application fee:* $45 ($50 for international students). *Application Contact:* 816-235-2399, Fax: 816-235-5159. *Dean,* Dr. Kevin Z. Truman, 816-235-2399, Fax: 816-235-5159.

School of Dentistry Students: 439 full-time (190 women), 39 part-time (22 women); includes 102 minority (9 Black or African American, non-Hispanic/Latino; 2 American Indian or Alaska Native, non-Hispanic/Latino; 51 Asian, non-Hispanic/Latino; 28 Hispanic/Latino; 12 Two or more races, non-Hispanic/Latino), 8 international. Average age 27. 843 applicants, 16% accepted, 127 enrolled. *Faculty:* 88 full-time (42 women), 57 part-time/adjunct (18 women). Expenses: Contact institution. *Financial support:* Research assistantships, career-related internships or fieldwork, Federal Work-Study, institutionally sponsored loans, and tuition waivers (full and partial) available. Support available to part-time students. Financial award application deadline: 3/1; financial award applicants required to submit FAFSA. In 2016, 6 master's, 105 doctorates, 17 other advanced degrees awarded. Offers advanced education in dentistry (Graduate Dental Certificate); dental hygiene education (MS); endodontics (Graduate Dental Certificate); oral and maxillofacial surgery (Graduate Dental Certificate); oral biology (MS, PhD); orthodontics and dentofacial orthopedics (Graduate Dental Certificate); periodontics (Graduate Dental Certificate). PhD (interdisciplinary) offered through the School of Graduate Studies. *Application deadline:* For fall admission, 2/1 for domestic and international students. *Application fee:* $45 ($50 for international students). *Application Contact:* Richard Bigham, Assistant Dean for Student Programs, 816-235-2082, E-mail: bighamr@umkc.edu. *Dean,* Dr. Marsha Pyle, 816-235-2010, E-mail: pylem@umkc.edu.

School of Education Students: 136 full-time (103 women), 275 part-time (194 women); includes 110 minority (71 Black or African American, non-Hispanic/Latino; 3 American Indian or Alaska Native, non-Hispanic/Latino; 8 Asian, non-Hispanic/Latino; 22 Hispanic/Latino; 6 Two or more races, non-Hispanic/Latino), 20 international. Average age 32. 324 applicants, 45% accepted, 108 enrolled. *Faculty:* 33 full-time (26 women), 51 part-time/adjunct (39 women). Expenses: Contact institution. *Financial support:* In 2016–17, 12 research assistantships with partial tuition reimbursements (averaging $12,476 per year) were awarded; career-related internships or fieldwork, Federal Work-Study, institutionally sponsored loans, and tuition waivers (full and partial) also available. Support available to part-time students. Financial award application deadline: 3/1; financial award applicants required to submit FAFSA. In 2016, 152 master's, 13 doctorates, 50 other advanced degrees awarded. *Program availability:* Part-time, evening/weekend. Offers administration (Ed D); counseling and guidance (MA, Ed S); counseling psychology (PhD); curriculum and instruction (MA, Ed S); education (PhD); educational administration (MA, Ed S); reading education (MA); special education (MA). PhD in education offered through the School of Graduate Studies. *Application deadline:* For fall admission, 4/1 priority date for domestic and international students; for spring admission, 11/1 priority date for domestic and international students. Applications are processed on a rolling basis. *Application fee:* $45 ($50 for international students). *Dean,* Justin Perry, 816-235-5663, Fax: 816-235-5270, E-mail: education@umkc.edu.

School of Graduate Studies Students: 74 full-time (23 women), 314 part-time (120 women); includes 52 minority (24 Black or African American, non-Hispanic/Latino; 1 American Indian or Alaska Native, non-Hispanic/Latino; 10 Asian, non-Hispanic/Latino; 14 Hispanic/Latino; 3 Two or more races, non-Hispanic/Latino), 155 international. Average age 35. 252 applicants, 33% accepted, 73 enrolled. Expenses: Contact institution. *Financial support:* Career-related internships or fieldwork, Federal Work-Study, tuition waivers (partial), and unspecified assistantships available. Support available to part-time students. Financial award application deadline: 3/1; financial award applicants required to submit FAFSA. In 2016, 48 doctorates awarded. Offers interdisciplinary studies (PhD). *Application deadline:* For fall admission, 1/15 priority date for domestic and international students. Applications are processed on a rolling basis. *Application fee:* $45 ($50 for international students). Electronic applications accepted. *Application Contact:* Quincy Bennett Johnson, Coordinator of Admissions and Recruitment, Interdisciplinary PhD Program, 816-235-1559, Fax: 816-235-1310, E-mail: bennettq@umkc.edu. *Dean,* Dr. Denis M. Medeiros, 816-235-1301, Fax: 816-235-1310, E-mail: medeirosd@umkc.edu.

School of Law Students: 403 full-time (171 women), 43 part-time (25 women); includes 72 minority (22 Black or African American, non-Hispanic/Latino; 1 American Indian or Alaska Native, non-Hispanic/Latino; 7 Asian, non-Hispanic/Latino; 36 Hispanic/Latino; 6 Two or more races, non-Hispanic/Latino), 24 international. Average age 27. 588 applicants, 25% accepted, 154 enrolled. *Faculty:* 36 full-time (17 women), 9 part-time/adjunct (2 women). Expenses: Contact institution. *Financial support:* In 2016–17, 21 teaching assistantships with partial tuition reimbursements (averaging $2,350 per year) were awarded; career-related internships or fieldwork, Federal Work-Study, institutionally sponsored loans, scholarships/grants, and tuition waivers (full and partial) also available. Support available to part-time students. Financial award application deadline: 3/1; financial award applicants required to submit FAFSA. In 2016, 25 master's, 159 doctorates awarded. *Program availability:* Part-time. Offers law (LL M, JD). *Application deadline:* For fall admission, 3/1 priority date for domestic and international students. Applications are processed on a rolling basis. *Application fee:* $50. Electronic applications accepted. *Application Contact:* Lydia Dagenais, Director of Law School Admissions, 816-235-1677, Fax: 816-235-5276, E-mail: dagenaisl@umkc.edu. *Acting Dean,* Barbara Glesner Fines, 816-235-2380, Fax: 816-235-5276, E-mail: glesnerb@umkc.edu.

School of Medicine Students: 519 full-time (273 women), 35 part-time (22 women); includes 259 minority (34 Black or African American, non-Hispanic/Latino; 2 American Indian or Alaska Native, non-Hispanic/Latino; 159 Asian, non-Hispanic/Latino; 19 Hispanic/Latino; 1 Native Hawaiian or other Pacific Islander, non-Hispanic/Latino; 44 Two or more races, non-Hispanic/Latino), 8 international. Average age 24. 1,065 applicants, 12% accepted, 121 enrolled. *Faculty:* 47 full-time (18 women), 29 part-time/adjunct (12 women). Expenses: Contact institution. *Financial support:* In 2016–17, 4 fellowships (averaging $35,935 per year), 2 research assistantships (averaging $12,684 per year) were awarded; career-related internships or fieldwork, Federal Work-Study, institutionally sponsored loans, scholarships/grants, and tuition waivers (partial) also available. Financial award application deadline: 3/1; financial award applicants required to submit FAFSA. In 2016, 37 master's, 94 doctorates awarded. Offers health professions education (MS). *Application deadline:* For fall admission, 11/15 for domestic and international students. *Application fee:* $50. *Dean,* Dr. Steven L. Kanter, MD, 816-235-1803, E-mail: kantersl@umkc.edu.

School of Nursing and Health Studies Students: 91 full-time (75 women), 304 part-time (279 women); includes 67 minority (30 Black or African American, non-Hispanic/Latino; 20 Asian, non-Hispanic/Latino; 12 Hispanic/Latino; 5 Two or more races, non-Hispanic/Latino). Average age 35. 166 applicants, 42% accepted, 70 enrolled. *Faculty:* 92 full-time (84 women), 98 part-time/adjunct (90 women). Expenses: Contact institution. *Financial support:* Fellowships, research assistantships, teaching assistantships with partial tuition reimbursements, career-related internships or fieldwork, Federal Work-Study, institutionally sponsored loans, and tuition waivers (full

and partial) available. Support available to part-time students. Financial award application deadline: 3/1; financial award applicants required to submit FAFSA. In 2016, 27 master's, 28 doctorates awarded. *Program availability:* Part-time, online learning. Offers adult clinical nurse specialist (MSN); adult clinical nursing practice (DNP); clinical nursing practice (DNP); neonatal nurse practitioner (MSN); nurse educator (MSN); nurse executive (MSN); nursing practice (DNP); pediatric clinical nursing practice (DNP); pediatric nurse practitioner (MSN). *Application deadline:* For fall admission, 2/1 priority date for domestic and international students; for spring admission, 9/1 priority date for domestic and international students. *Application fee:* $45 ($50 for international students). *Dean,* Dr. Ann Cary, 816-235-1723, Fax: 816-235-1701, E-mail: caryah@umkc.edu.

School of Pharmacy Students: 458 full-time (277 women); includes 104 minority (33 Black or African American, non-Hispanic/Latino; 49 Asian, non-Hispanic/Latino; 9 Hispanic/Latino; 13 Two or more races, non-Hispanic/Latino), 6 international. Average age 25. 374 applicants, 33% accepted, 123 enrolled. *Faculty:* 52 full-time (30 women), 7 part-time/adjunct (1 woman). Expenses: Contact institution. *Financial support:* In 2016–17, 3 fellowships (averaging $40,000 per year), 9 research assistantships with tuition reimbursements (averaging $16,744 per year), 28 teaching assistantships with full tuition reimbursements (averaging $15,604 per year) were awarded; career-related internships or fieldwork, Federal Work-Study, institutionally sponsored loans, tuition waivers (full and partial), and unspecified assistantships also available. Financial award application deadline: 3/1; financial award applicants required to submit FAFSA. In 2016, 122 doctorates awarded. *Program availability:* Online learning. Offers pharmacy (PhD, Pharm D). PhD offered through School of Graduate Studies. *Application deadline:* For fall admission, 3/1 for domestic and international students. Applications are processed on a rolling basis. *Application fee:* $45 ($50 for international students). Electronic applications accepted. *Application Contact:* Shelly M. Janasz, Director, Student Services, 816-235-2400, Fax: 816-235-5190, E-mail: janaszs@umkc.edu. *Dean,* Dr. Russell B. Melchert, 816-235-1609, Fax: 816-235-5190, E-mail: melchertr@umkc.edu.

UNIVERSITY OF MISSOURI–ST. LOUIS, St. Louis, MO 63121

General Information State-supported, coed, university. CGS member. *Enrollment:* 17,014 graduate, professional, and undergraduate students; 873 full-time matriculated graduate/professional students (562 women), 1,919 part-time matriculated graduate/professional students (1,290 women). *Enrollment by degree level:* 1,978 master's, 617 doctoral, 197 other advanced degrees. *Graduate faculty:* 371 full-time (171 women), 174 part-time/adjunct (94 women). *Graduate housing:* Rooms and/or apartments available on a first-come, first-served basis to single and married students. Housing application deadline: 7/1. *Student services:* Campus employment opportunities, campus safety program, career counseling, child daycare facilities, exercise/wellness program, free psychological counseling, grant writing training, international student services, low-cost health insurance, multicultural affairs office, services for students with disabilities, teacher training. *Library facilities:* Thomas Jefferson Library plus 1 other. *Collection:* Books: 1.3 million (physical), 206,207 (digital/electronic); Serial titles: 1,041 (physical), 1,232 (digital/electronic); Databases: 205. Weekly public service hours: 82; students can reserve study rooms. *Research affiliation:* Express Scripts (business), St. Louis Zoo (biology), Missouri Botanical Garden (biology), Donald Danforth Plant Science Center (biology).

Computer facilities: Computer purchase and lease plans are available. 1,280 computers available on campus for general student use. A campuswide network can be accessed from student residence rooms and from off campus. Online class registration is available.
Website: http://www.umsl.edu/

General Application Contact: Graduate Admissions, 314-516-5458, Fax: 314-516-6996, E-mail: gradadm@umsl.edu.

GRADUATE UNITS

College of Arts and Sciences Students: 366 full-time (203 women), 289 part-time (139 women); includes 88 minority (36 Black or African American, non-Hispanic/Latino; 1 American Indian or Alaska Native, non-Hispanic/Latino; 21 Asian, non-Hispanic/Latino; 19 Hispanic/Latino; 1 Native Hawaiian or other Pacific Islander, non-Hispanic/Latino; 10 Two or more races, non-Hispanic/Latino), 134 international. 728 applicants, 43% accepted, 158 enrolled. *Faculty:* 215 full-time (83 women), 56 part-time/adjunct (19 women). Expenses: Contact institution. *Financial support:* Research assistantships with tuition reimbursements, teaching assistantships with tuition reimbursements, career-related internships or fieldwork, Federal Work-Study, health care benefits, and unspecified assistantships available. Support available to part-time students. Financial award applicants required to submit FAFSA. *Program availability:* Part-time, evening/weekend. Offers American politics (MA); applied physics (MS); arts and sciences (MA, MFA, MME, MS, PhD, Certificate); astrophysics (MS); behavioral neuroscience (MA, PhD); biochemistry and biotechnology (MS); biology (MS, PhD, Certificate); chemistry (MS, PhD); clinical psychology (PhD); clinical psychology respecialization (Certificate); communication (MA); comparative politics (MA); computer science (MS); creative writing (MFA); criminology and criminal justice (MA, PhD); economics (MA); English (MA); gerontology (MS, Certificate); history (MA); industrial/organizational psychology (MA, PhD); international politics (MA); mathematical and computational sciences (PhD); mathematics (MA); museum studies (MA, Certificate); philosophy (MA); physics (PhD); political process and behavior (MA); political science (PhD); public administration and public policy (MA); public history and cultural heritage (Certificate); trauma studies (Certificate); urban and regional politics (MA). *Application deadline:* For fall admission, 7/1 for domestic and international students; for spring admission, 12/1 for domestic and international students. *Application fee:* $50 ($40 for international students). Electronic applications accepted. *Application Contact:* Graduate Admissions, 314-516-5458, Fax: 314-516-6996, E-mail: gradadm@umsl.edu. *Dean,* Dr. Ronald Yasbin, 314-516-5501, E-mail: yasbinr@usml.edu.

School of Fine and Performing Arts *Faculty:* 17 full-time (7 women), 5 part-time/adjunct (3 women). Expenses: Contact institution. *Financial support:* Teaching assistantships available. Offers fine and performing arts (MME); music education (MME). *Application deadline:* For fall admission, 7/1 priority date for domestic and international students; for spring admission, 12/1 priority date for domestic and international students. Applications are processed on a rolling basis. *Application fee:* $50 ($40 for international students). Electronic applications accepted. *Application Contact:* 314-516-5458, Fax: 314-516-6996, E-mail: gradadm@umsl.edu. *Dean,* Barbara Harbach, 314-516-5911, Fax: 314-516-5910.

College of Business Administration Students: 181 full-time (88 women), 355 part-time (154 women); includes 83 minority (30 Black or African American, non-Hispanic/Latino; 36 Asian, non-Hispanic/Latino; 12 Hispanic/Latino; 2 Native Hawaiian or other Pacific Islander, non-Hispanic/Latino; 3 Two or more races, non-Hispanic/Latino), 100 international. Average age 31. 245 applicants, 83% accepted, 139 enrolled. *Faculty:* 49 full-time (19 women), 21 part-time/adjunct (6 women). Expenses: Contact institution. *Financial support:* Research assistantships with tuition reimbursements, teaching assistantships with tuition reimbursements, career-related internships or fieldwork, Federal Work-Study, and institutionally sponsored loans available. Support available to part-time students. Financial award application deadline: 4/1; financial award applicants required to submit FAFSA. *Program availability:* Part-time, evening/weekend. Offers accounting (MBA); business administration (M Acc, MBA, MS, PhD, Certificate); business intelligence (Certificate); cybersecurity (Certificate); digital and social media marketing (Certificate); finance (MBA); human resources management (Certificate); information systems (MBA); international business (MBA); logistics and supply chain management (MBA, PhD, Certificate); management (MBA); marketing (MBA); marketing management (Certificate); operations management (MBA). *Application deadline:* For fall admission, 7/1 priority date for domestic and international students; for spring admission, 12/1 priority date for domestic and international students. Applications are processed on a rolling basis. *Application fee:* $50 ($40 for international students). Electronic applications accepted. *Application Contact:* 314-516-5458, Fax: 314-516-6996, E-mail: gradadm@umsl.edu. *Dean,* Charles E. Hoffman, 314-516-5885, Fax: 314-516-6420.

College of Education Students: 198 full-time (161 women), 981 part-time (744 women); includes 331 minority (253 Black or African American, non-Hispanic/Latino; 3 American Indian or Alaska Native, non-Hispanic/Latino; 21 Asian, non-Hispanic/Latino; 41 Hispanic/Latino; 1 Native Hawaiian or other Pacific Islander, non-Hispanic/Latino; 12 Two or more races, non-Hispanic/Latino), 13 international. 469 applicants, 86% accepted, 281 enrolled. *Faculty:* 62 full-time (39 women), 76 part-time/adjunct (55 women). Expenses: Contact institution. *Financial support:* Research assistantships with tuition reimbursements and teaching assistantships with tuition reimbursements available. Financial award application deadline: 4/1; financial award applicants required to submit FAFSA. *Program availability:* Part-time, evening/weekend. Offers adult and higher education (M Ed); clinical mental health counseling (M Ed); counseling (PhD); education (M Ed, Ed D, PhD, Certificate, Ed S); educational leadership and policy studies (PhD); educational psychology (M Ed, PhD); elementary education (M Ed); elementary school counseling (M Ed); leadership in educational practice (Ed D); program evaluation (Certificate); school psychology (Ed S); secondary education (M Ed); secondary school counseling (M Ed); special education (M Ed); teaching-learning processes (PhD). *Application deadline:* For fall admission, 7/1 priority date for domestic and international students; for spring admission, 12/1 priority date for domestic and international students. Applications are processed on a rolling basis. *Application fee:* $50 ($40 for international students). Electronic applications accepted. *Application Contact:* 314-516-5458, Fax: 314-516-6996, E-mail: gradadm@umsl.edu. *Interim Dean,* Ann Taylor, 314-516-5106, Fax: 314-516-5227, E-mail: taylorann@umsl.edu.

College of Nursing Students: 38 full-time (37 women), 176 part-time (166 women); includes 39 minority (25 Black or African American, non-Hispanic/Latino; 9 Asian, non-Hispanic/Latino; 3 Hispanic/Latino; 2 Two or more races, non-Hispanic/Latino), 2 international. 84 applicants, 90% accepted, 60 enrolled. *Faculty:* 20 full-time (17 women), 6 part-time/adjunct (all women). Expenses: Contact institution. *Financial support:* Research assistantships with tuition reimbursements available. Financial award application deadline: 4/1; financial award applicants required to submit FAFSA. *Program availability:* Part-time. Offers adult/geriatric nurse practitioner (Post Master's Certificate); family nurse practitioner (Post Master's Certificate); nursing (DNP, PhD); pediatric acute care nurse practitioner (Post Master's Certificate); pediatric nurse practitioner (Post Master's Certificate); psychiatric-mental health nurse practitioner (Post Master's Certificate); women's health nurse practitioner (Post Master's Certificate). *Application deadline:* For fall admission, 2/15 for domestic and international students. *Application fee:* $50 ($40 for international students). Electronic applications accepted. *Application Contact:* 314-516-5458, Fax: 314-516-6996, E-mail: gradadm@umsl.edu. *Dean,* Sue Dean-Baar, 314-516-6066.

College of Optometry Students: 168 full-time (101 women); includes 26 minority (5 Black or African American, non-Hispanic/Latino; 1 American Indian or Alaska Native, non-Hispanic/Latino; 18 Asian, non-Hispanic/Latino; 2 Hispanic/Latino), 1 international. Average age 23. 403 applicants, 26% accepted, 45 enrolled. *Faculty:* 3 full-time (0 women), 2 part-time/adjunct (0 women). Expenses: Contact institution. *Financial support:* In 2016–17, 131 students received support, including 35 research assistantships (averaging $1,200 per year); fellowships with full tuition reimbursements available, Federal Work-Study, institutionally sponsored loans, and scholarships/grants also available. Financial award applicants required to submit FAFSA. Offers optometry (OD). *Application deadline:* For fall admission, 2/15 for domestic and international students. Applications are processed on a rolling basis. *Application fee:* $50. Electronic applications accepted. *Application Contact:* Nick Palisch, Director, Student Services, 314-516-6263, Fax: 314-516-6708, E-mail: optstuaff@umsl.edu. *Dean,* Dr. Larry J. Davis, 314-516-5606, Fax: 314-516-6708, E-mail: optometry@umsl.edu.

Graduate School Students: 10 full-time (5 women), 53 part-time (33 women); includes 20 minority (18 Black or African American, non-Hispanic/Latino; 2 Asian, non-Hispanic/Latino). 37 applicants, 86% accepted, 22 enrolled. *Faculty:* 2 full-time (both women), 6 part-time/adjunct (2 women). Expenses: Contact institution. *Financial support:* Research assistantships with full tuition reimbursements available. Financial award application deadline: 4/1; financial award applicants required to submit FAFSA. *Program availability:* Part-time, evening/weekend. Offers local government management (MPPA, Certificate); nonprofit management and leadership (MPPA, Certificate); policy and program evaluation (MPPA, Certificate). *Application deadline:* For fall admission, 7/1 priority date for domestic and international students; for spring admission, 12/1 priority date for domestic and international students. Applications are processed on a rolling basis. *Application fee:* $50 ($40 for international students). Electronic applications accepted. *Application Contact:* Graduate Admissions, 314-516-5458, Fax: 314-516-6996, E-mail: gradadm@umsl.edu. *Vice Provost for Graduate Studies and Research,* Christopher Spilling, 314-516-5437, Fax: 314-516-7015, E-mail: graduate@umsl.edu.

School of Social Work Students: 80 full-time (68 women), 65 part-time (54 women); includes 35 minority (29 Black or African American, non-Hispanic/Latino; 1 Asian, non-Hispanic/Latino; 3 Hispanic/Latino; 1 Native Hawaiian or other Pacific Islander, non-Hispanic/Latino; 1 Two or more races, non-Hispanic/Latino), 1 international. 101 applicants, 52% accepted, 33 enrolled. *Faculty:* 11 full-time (9 women), 2 part-time/adjunct (both women). Expenses: Contact institution. *Financial support:* Research assistantships with tuition reimbursements, teaching assistantships with tuition reimbursements, and scholarships/grants available. Financial award applicants required to submit FAFSA. *Program availability:* Part-time. Offers social work (MSW). *Application deadline:* For fall admission, 3/1 for domestic and international students; for spring admission, 10/15 for domestic and international students. *Application fee:* $50 ($40 for international students). Electronic applications accepted. *Application Contact:* 314-516-5458, Fax: 314-516-6996, E-mail: gradadm@umsl.edu. *Dean,* Sharon Johnson, 314-516-6385, Fax: 314-516-5816, E-mail: socialwork@umsl.edu.

UNIVERSITY OF MOBILE, Mobile, AL 36613

General Information Independent-religious, coed, comprehensive institution. *Graduate housing:* Room and/or apartments available on a first-come, first-served basis to single students; on-campus housing not available to married students. Housing application deadline: 8/15.

GRADUATE UNITS

Graduate Studies *Program availability:* Part-time, evening/weekend. Offers business administration (MBA); education (MA); marriage and family counseling (MA); nursing (MSN). Electronic applications accepted.

UNIVERSITY OF MONTANA, Missoula, MT 59812-0002

General Information State-supported, coed, university. CGS member. *Graduate housing:* Rooms and/or apartments available on a first-come, first-served basis to single and married students. *Research affiliation:* Arthur Carhart National Wilderness Training Center (environmental research), Nature Center at Ft. Missoula Museum (environmental research), Rocky Mountain National Laboratories (medical research), Community Hospital Medical Center (medical research), Aldo Leopold Wilderness Institute (forestry).

GRADUATE UNITS

Graduate School *Program availability:* Part-time. Offers individualized interdisciplinary studies (PhD); interdisciplinary studies (MIS).

College of Forestry and Conservation Offers fish and wildlife biology (PhD); forest and conservation sciences (PhD); forestry (MS); recreation management (MS); resource conservation (MS); systems ecology (MS, PhD); wildlife biology (MS).

College of Health Professions and Biomedical Sciences Offers biomedical and pharmaceutical sciences (MS, PhD); biomedical sciences (PhD); health professions and biomedical sciences (MPH, MS, MSW, DPT, PhD, Pharm D, CPH); medicinal chemistry (MS, PhD); molecular and cellular toxicology (MS, PhD); neuroscience (PhD); pharmaceutical sciences (MS); pharmacy (Pharm D); physical therapy (DPT); public health (MPH, CPH); social work (MSW).

College of Humanities and Sciences *Program availability:* Part-time. Offers anthropology (MA, PhD); applied anthropology (PhD); applied medical anthropology (MA); cellular and developmental biology (PhD); cellular, molecular and microbial biology (PhD); chemistry (MS, PhD); clinical psychology (PhD); communication studies (MA); community and environmental planning (MA); computer science (MS); creative writing (MFA); criminology (MA); cultural heritage (MA, PhD); economics (MA); environmental studies (MS); experimental psychology (PhD); fiction (MFA); forensic anthropology (MA); French (MA); geography (MA, MS); geosciences (MS, PhD); German (MA); history (MA, PhD); humanities and sciences (MA, MFA, MPA, MS, PhD, Ed S); inequality and social justice (MA); linguistic anthropology (MA); linguistics (MA); literature (MA); mathematics (MA, PhD); mathematics education (MA); microbial evolution and ecology (PhD); microbiology and immunology (PhD); molecular biology and biochemistry (PhD); non-fiction (MFA); organismal biology and ecology (MS, PhD); philosophy (MA); poetry (MFA); political science (MA); public administration (MPA); rural and environmental change (MA); school psychology (MA, PhD, Ed S); sociology (MA); Spanish (MA); systems ecology (MS, PhD); teaching (MA).

College of Visual and Performing Arts Offers design/technology (MFA); digital filmmaking (MFA); fine arts (MA); integrated arts and education (MA); integrated digital media (MFA); performance (MM); photography (MFA); theatre (MA); visual and performing arts (MA, MFA, MM).

Phyllis J. Washington College of Education and Human Sciences *Program availability:* Part-time. Offers clinical mental health counseling (MA); community health (MS); counseling and supervision (Ed D); counselor education (Ed S); curriculum and instruction (M Ed, Ed D); early childhood education (M Ed); education (MA); education and human sciences (M Ed, MA, MS, Ed D, Ed S); educational leadership (M Ed, Ed D, Ed S); exercise science (MS); health and human performance generalist (MS); intercultural youth and family development (MA); school counseling (MA); speech-language pathology (MS, Postbaccalaureate Certificate); teaching and learning (PhD).

School of Business Administration *Program availability:* Part-time, evening/weekend, online learning. Offers accounting (M Acct); business administration (M Acct, MBA).

School of Journalism Offers journalism (MA). Electronic applications accepted.

School of Law Offers law (JD).

UNIVERSITY OF MONTEVALLO, Montevallo, AL 35115

General Information State-supported, coed, comprehensive institution. *Enrollment:* 2,800 graduate, professional, and undergraduate students; 155 full-time matriculated graduate/professional students (125 women), 219 part-time matriculated graduate/professional students (157 women). *Enrollment by degree level:* 334 master's, 40 other advanced degrees. Tuition, state resident: full-time $9936. Tuition, nonresident: full-time $20,592. *Required fees:* $640. *Graduate housing:* Room and/or apartments guaranteed to single students; on-campus housing not available to married students. Typical cost: $4762 per year ($7462 including board). *Student services:* Campus employment opportunities, campus safety program, career counseling, free psychological counseling, international student services, low-cost health insurance, services for students with disabilities, writing training. *Library facilities:* Carmichael Library. *Collection:* Students can reserve study rooms.

Computer facilities: 340 computers available on campus for general student use. A campuswide network can be accessed from student residence rooms and from off campus. Online class registration is available. Website: http://www.montevallo.edu/

General Application Contact: Kevin Thornthwaite, Director, Graduate Admissions and Records, 205-665-6350, E-mail: graduate@montevallo.edu.

GRADUATE UNITS

College of Arts and Sciences Students: 53 full-time (52 women), 14 part-time (13 women); includes 4 minority (2 Black or African American, non-Hispanic/Latino; 2 Hispanic/Latino). Expenses: Contact institution. *Financial support:* Federal Work-Study, scholarships/grants, and unspecified assistantships available. In 2016, 28 master's awarded. *Program availability:* Part-time, evening/weekend. Offers arts and sciences (MA, MS); communication science and disorders (MS); English (MA). *Application deadline:* For fall admission, 7/15 for domestic students; for spring admission, 11/15 for domestic students. *Application fee:* $25. *Application Contact:* Kevin Thornthwaite, Director, Graduate Admissions and Records, 205-665-6350, E-mail: graduate@montevallo.edu. *Dean,* Dr. Mary Beth Armstrong, 205-665-6508.

College of Education Students: 86 full-time (65 women), 186 part-time (135 women); includes 55 minority (45 Black or African American, non-Hispanic/Latino; 1 Asian, non-Hispanic/Latino; 6 Hispanic/Latino; 3 Two or more races, non-Hispanic/Latino).

Expenses: Contact institution. *Financial support:* Federal Work-Study, scholarships/grants, and unspecified assistantships available. In 2016, 120 master's, 17 Ed Ss awarded. *Program availability:* Part-time, evening/weekend. Offers counseling (M Ed); education (M Ed, Ed S); educational administration (M Ed, Ed S); elementary education (M Ed); secondary/high school education (M Ed). *Application deadline:* For fall admission, 7/15 for domestic students; for spring admission, 11/15 for domestic students. *Application fee:* $25. *Application Contact:* Kevin Thornthwaite, Director, Graduate Admissions and Records, 205-665-6350, E-mail: graduate@montevallo.edu. *Dean,* Dr. Anna E. McEwan, 205-665-6360, E-mail: mcewanae@montevallo.edu.

Stephens College of Business Students: 16 full-time (8 women), 19 part-time (9 women); includes 7 minority (4 Black or African American, non-Hispanic/Latino; 2 Hispanic/Latino; 1 Two or more races, non-Hispanic/Latino), 7 international. Expenses: Contact institution. In 2016, 12 master's awarded. *Program availability:* Part-time, evening/weekend. Offers business (MBA). *Application deadline:* For fall admission, 7/15 for domestic students; for spring admission, 11/15 for domestic students. *Application fee:* $25. *Application Contact:* Kevin Thornthwaite, Director, Graduate Admissions and Records, 205-665-6350, E-mail: graduate@montevallo.edu. *Dean,* Dr. Stephen H. Craft, 205-665-6540.

UNIVERSITY OF MOUNT OLIVE, Mount Olive, NC 28365
General Information Independent-religious, coed, comprehensive institution.

GRADUATE UNITS
Graduate Programs *Program availability:* Online learning.

UNIVERSITY OF MOUNT UNION, Alliance, OH 44601-3993
General Information Independent-religious, coed, comprehensive institution. *Enrollment:* 2,281 graduate, professional, and undergraduate students; 141 full-time matriculated graduate/professional students (92 women). *Enrollment by degree level:* 113 master's, 28 doctoral. *Graduate faculty:* 11 full-time (7 women), 2 part-time/adjunct (1 woman). Tuition and fees vary according to degree level and program. *Graduate housing:* Rooms and/or apartments available on a first-come, first-served basis to single and married students. Typical cost: $5100 per year for single students; $5100 per year for married students. *Student services:* Campus safety program, career counseling, exercise/wellness program, international student services, low-cost health insurance, multicultural affairs office, services for students with disabilities, writing training. *Library facilities:* University of Mount Union Library plus 1 other. *Collection:* Study areas open 24 hours, 5–7 days a week; students can reserve study rooms.

Computer facilities: Computer purchase and lease plans are available. 265 computers available on campus for general student use. A campuswide network can be accessed from student residence rooms and from off campus. Online class registration is available.
Website: http://www.mountunion.edu/

General Application Contact: Jess Canavan, Director of Admissions, 330-823-2579, E-mail: canavajl@mountunion.edu.

GRADUATE UNITS
Program in Educational Leadership Students: 37 full-time (23 women), 2 part-time (1 woman); includes 1 minority (Hispanic/Latino). 61 applicants, 39% accepted, 18 enrolled. *Faculty:* 1 (woman) full-time. Expenses: Contact institution. *Financial support:* Applicants required to submit FAFSA. In 2016, 13 master's awarded. *Program availability:* Part-time, online only, blended/hybrid learning. Offers educational leadership (MA). *Application deadline:* For fall admission, 8/15 for domestic and international students. Applications are processed on a rolling basis. *Application fee:* $30. Electronic applications accepted. *Application Contact:* Jess Canavan, Director of Admissions, 330-823-2579, E-mail: canavajl@mountunion.edu. *Director,* Dr. Mandy Capel, 800-992-6682, E-mail: capelml@mountunion.edu.

Program in Physician Assistant Studies Students: 74 full-time (54 women); includes 7 minority (2 Asian, non-Hispanic/Latino; 2 Hispanic/Latino; 3 Two or more races, non-Hispanic/Latino). Average age 25. 273 applicants, 18% accepted, 40 enrolled. *Faculty:* 4 full-time (3 women), 2 part-time/adjunct (1 woman). Expenses: Contact institution. *Financial support:* Applicants required to submit FAFSA. In 2016, 30 master's awarded. Offers physician assistant studies (MS). *Application deadline:* Applications are processed on a rolling basis. Electronic applications accepted. *Application Contact:* Jess Canavan, Director of Admissions, 330-823-2579, E-mail: canavajl@mountunion.edu. *Director,* Betsey Ekey, 800-992-6682, E-mail: ekeybd@mountunion.edu.

UNIVERSITY OF NEBRASKA AT KEARNEY, Kearney, NE 68849-0001
General Information State-supported, coed, comprehensive institution. CGS member. *Enrollment:* 6,788 graduate, professional, and undergraduate students; 179 full-time matriculated graduate/professional students (141 women), 1,088 part-time matriculated graduate/professional students (722 women). *Enrollment by degree level:* 1,206 master's, 61 other advanced degrees. *Graduate faculty:* 232 full-time (94 women). Tuition, state resident: full-time $4064; part-time $225.75 per credit hour. Tuition, nonresident: full-time $8915; part-time $495.25 per credit hour. *Required fees:* $772; $23 per credit hour. Part-time tuition and fees vary according to course load, campus/location, program and reciprocity agreements. *Graduate housing:* Room and/or apartments available on a first-come, first-served basis to single students; on-campus housing not available to married students. Typical cost: $6288 per year. Room charges vary according to board plan and housing facility selected. Housing application deadline: 6/15. *Student services:* Campus employment opportunities, campus safety program, career counseling, child daycare facilities, exercise/wellness program, free psychological counseling, grant writing training, international student services, low-cost health insurance, multicultural affairs office, services for students with disabilities, teacher training, writing training. *Library facilities:* Calvin T. Ryan Library.

Computer facilities: 600 computers available on campus for general student use. A campuswide network can be accessed from student residence rooms and from off campus. Online class registration, online degree audit, online personal information update, online bill viewing and payment, online financial aid awards and acceptance are available.
Website: http://www.unk.edu/

General Application Contact: Linda Johnson, Director, Graduate Admissions and Programs, 800-717-7881, Fax: 308-865-8837, E-mail: gradstudies@unk.edu.

GRADUATE UNITS
College of Business and Technology Students: 11 full-time (5 women), 30 part-time (14 women), 8 international. Average age 39. 13 applicants, 100% accepted, 10 enrolled. *Faculty:* 32 full-time (13 women). Expenses: Contact institution. *Financial support:* In 2016–17, 2 research assistantships with full tuition reimbursements (averaging $10,500 per year), 2 teaching assistantships with full tuition reimbursements

(averaging $10,500 per year) were awarded; career-related internships or fieldwork, scholarships/grants, health care benefits, and unspecified assistantships also available. Support available to part-time students. Financial award application deadline: 2/28; financial award applicants required to submit FAFSA. In 2016, 6 master's awarded. *Program availability:* Part-time, evening/weekend. Offers accounting (MBA); business and technology (MBA); generalist (MBA); human resources (MBA); human services (MBA); marketing (MBA). *Application deadline:* For fall admission, 6/15 for domestic and international students; for spring admission, 10/15 for domestic and international students; for summer admission, 3/15 for domestic and international students. *Application fee:* $45. Electronic applications accepted. *Application Contact:* Linda Johnson, Director, Graduate Admissions and Programs, 800-717-7881, Fax: 308-865-8837, E-mail: gradstudies@unk.edu. *Graduate Program Chair,* Dr. Sri Seshadri, 308-865-8190, Fax: 308-865-8114, E-mail: seshadris@unk.edu.

College of Education Students: 129 full-time (106 women), 569 part-time (397 women); includes 52 minority (7 Black or African American, non-Hispanic/Latino; 3 Asian, non-Hispanic/Latino; 33 Hispanic/Latino; 1 Native Hawaiian or other Pacific Islander, non-Hispanic/Latino; 8 Two or more races, non-Hispanic/Latino), 5 international. Average age 31. 223 applicants, 91% accepted, 138 enrolled. *Faculty:* 50 full-time (26 women). Expenses: Contact institution. *Financial support:* Research assistantships with full tuition reimbursements, teaching assistantships with full tuition reimbursements, career-related internships or fieldwork, scholarships/grants, health care benefits, and unspecified assistantships available. Support available to part-time students. Financial award application deadline: 2/28; financial award applicants required to submit FAFSA. In 2016, 236 master's, 20 Ed Ss awarded. *Program availability:* Part-time, evening/weekend, 100% online. Offers clinical mental health counseling (MS Ed); curriculum and instruction (MA Ed); curriculum supervisor of academic area (MA Ed); education (MA Ed, MS Ed, Ed S); general physical education (MA Ed); instructional technology (MS Ed); physical education exercise science (MA Ed); physical education master teacher (MA Ed); reading PK-12 (MA Ed); school counseling (MS Ed); school principalship 7-12 (MA Ed); school principalship PK-8 (MA Ed); school psychology (Ed S); school superintendent (Ed S); special education (MA Ed); speech/language pathology (MS Ed); student affairs (MS Ed); supervisor of special education (MA Ed). *Application deadline:* For fall admission, 6/15 for domestic and international students; for spring admission, 10/15 for domestic and international students; for summer admission, 3/15 for domestic and international students. *Application fee:* $45. Electronic applications accepted. *Application Contact:* Linda Johnson, Director, Graduate Admissions and Programs, 800-717-7881, Fax: 308-865-8837, E-mail: johnsonli@unk.edu. *Dean,* Dr. Sheryl Feinstein, 308-865-8502.

College of Fine Arts and Humanities Students: 5 full-time (4 women), 136 part-time (107 women); includes 17 minority (2 Black or African American, non-Hispanic/Latino; 12 Hispanic/Latino; 3 Two or more races, non-Hispanic/Latino), 1 international. Average age 35. 38 applicants, 95% accepted, 19 enrolled. *Faculty:* 41 full-time (19 women). Expenses: Contact institution. *Financial support:* In 2016–17, 1 research assistantship with full tuition reimbursement (averaging $10,500 per year), 2 teaching assistantships with full tuition reimbursements (averaging $10,500 per year) were awarded; career-related internships or fieldwork, scholarships/grants, health care benefits, and unspecified assistantships also available. Support available to part-time students. Financial award application deadline: 2/28; financial award applicants required to submit FAFSA. In 2016, 38 master's awarded. *Program availability:* Part-time, evening/weekend, 100% online. Offers art education (MA Ed); creative writing (MA); fine arts and humanities (MA, MA Ed); literature (MA); music education (MA Ed); Spanish education (MA Ed); writing (MA). *Application deadline:* For fall admission, 6/15 for domestic and international students; for spring admission, 10/15 for domestic and international students; for summer admission, 2/15 for domestic students, 3/15 for international students. *Application fee:* $45. Electronic applications accepted. *Application Contact:* Linda Johnson, Director, Graduate Admissions and Programs, 800-717-7881, Fax: 308-865-8837, E-mail: gradstudies@unk.edu. *Dean,* Dr. William Jurma, 308-865-8521, E-mail: jurmaw@unk.edu.

College of Natural and Social Sciences Students: 34 full-time (26 women), 353 part-time (204 women); includes 55 minority (12 Black or African American, non-Hispanic/Latino; 3 American Indian or Alaska Native, non-Hispanic/Latino; 6 Asian, non-Hispanic/Latino; 20 Hispanic/Latino; 1 Native Hawaiian or other Pacific Islander, non-Hispanic/Latino; 12 Two or more races, non-Hispanic/Latino), 3 international. Average age 36. 111 applicants, 86% accepted, 66 enrolled. *Faculty:* 31 full-time (10 women). Expenses: Contact institution. *Financial support:* In 2016–17, 4 research assistantships with full tuition reimbursements (averaging $10,500 per year), 11 teaching assistantships with full tuition reimbursements (averaging $10,500 per year) were awarded; career-related internships or fieldwork, scholarships/grants, health care benefits, and unspecified assistantships also available. Support available to part-time students. Financial award application deadline: 3/1; financial award applicants required to submit FAFSA. In 2016, 114 master's awarded. *Program availability:* Part-time, evening/weekend, online learning. Offers biology (MS); history (MA); natural and social sciences (MA, MA Ed, MS); science/math education (MA Ed). *Application deadline:* For fall admission, 6/15 for domestic and international students; for spring admission, 10/15 for domestic and international students; for summer admission, 3/15 for domestic and international students. *Application fee:* $45. Electronic applications accepted. *Application Contact:* Linda Johnson, Graduate Studies and Research Director, 800-717-7881, E-mail: gradstudies@unk.edu. *Interim Dean,* Dr. Peter Longo, 308-865-8039, Fax: 308-865-8880, E-mail: longop@unk.edu.

UNIVERSITY OF NEBRASKA AT OMAHA, Omaha, NE 68182
General Information State-supported, coed, university. CGS member. *Enrollment:* 947 full-time matriculated graduate/professional students (530 women), 1,791 part-time matriculated graduate/professional students (1,115 women). *Enrollment by degree level:* 2,489 master's, 190 doctoral, 59 other advanced degrees. *Graduate faculty:* 268 full-time (125 women). *Graduate housing:* Room and/or apartments available on a first-come, first-served basis to single students; on-campus housing not available to married students. *Student services:* Campus employment opportunities, campus safety program, career counseling, child daycare facilities, exercise/wellness program, free psychological counseling, grant writing training, international student services, low-cost health insurance, multicultural affairs office, services for students with disabilities, teacher training, writing training. *Library facilities:* Criss Library.

Computer facilities: Computer purchase and lease plans are available. 2,450 computers available on campus for general student use. A campuswide network can be accessed from student residence rooms and from off campus. Online class registration is available.
Website: http://www.unomaha.edu/

General Application Contact: Jerilyn Kamm, Director of Graduate Admissions and Academic Services, 402-554-2341, Fax: 402-554-3143, E-mail: graduate@unomaha.edu.

GRADUATE UNITS

Graduate Studies Students: 947 full-time (530 women), 1,791 part-time (1,115 women); includes 360 minority (100 Black or African American, non-Hispanic/Latino; 4 American Indian or Alaska Native, non-Hispanic/Latino; 56 Asian, non-Hispanic/Latino; 124 Hispanic/Latino; 2 Native Hawaiian or other Pacific Islander, non-Hispanic/Latino; 74 Two or more races, non-Hispanic/Latino), 383 international. Average age 31. 2,186 applicants, 57% accepted, 862 enrolled. *Faculty:* 268 full-time (125 women). Expenses: Contact institution. *Financial support:* In 2016–17, 341 students received support. Fellowships with tuition reimbursements available, research assistantships with tuition reimbursements available, teaching assistantships with tuition reimbursements available, career-related internships or fieldwork, Federal Work-Study, institutionally sponsored loans, health care benefits, tuition waivers (partial), and unspecified assistantships available. Support available to part-time students. Financial award application deadline: 3/1; financial award applicants required to submit FAFSA. In 2016, 888 master's, 33 doctorates, 89 other advanced degrees awarded. *Program availability:* Part-time, evening/weekend, online learning. *Application deadline:* Applications are processed on a rolling basis. *Application fee:* $45. Electronic applications accepted. *Dean of Graduate Studies,* Dr. Deborah Smith-Howell, 402-554-2341, E-mail: graduate@unomaha.edu.

College of Arts and Sciences Students: 143 full-time (91 women), 308 part-time (161 women); includes 54 minority (17 Black or African American, non-Hispanic/Latino; 1 American Indian or Alaska Native, non-Hispanic/Latino; 7 Asian, non-Hispanic/Latino; 20 Hispanic/Latino; 1 Native Hawaiian or other Pacific Islander, non-Hispanic/Latino; 8 Two or more races, non-Hispanic/Latino), 23 international. Average age 31. 383 applicants, 50% accepted, 142 enrolled. *Faculty:* 97 full-time (40 women). Expenses: Contact institution. *Financial support:* In 2016–17, 124 students received support. Fellowships with tuition reimbursements available, research assistantships with tuition reimbursements available, teaching assistantships with tuition reimbursements available, career-related internships or fieldwork, Federal Work-Study, institutionally sponsored loans, scholarships/grants, health care benefits, tuition waivers (partial), and unspecified assistantships available. Support available to part-time students. Financial award application deadline: 3/1; financial award applicants required to submit FAFSA. In 2016, 136 master's, 6 doctorates, 25 other advanced degrees awarded. *Program availability:* Part-time, evening/weekend, online learning. Offers advanced writing (Certificate); American government (Certificate); applied behavior analysis (Certificate); arts and sciences (MA, MAT, MS, PhD, Certificate, Ed S); biology (MS); business for biosciences (Certificate); critical and creative thinking (MA); English (MA); geographic information science (Certificate); geography (MA); global information operations (Certificate); history (MA); human resources and training (Certificate); industrial/organizational psychology (MS); intelligence and national security (Certificate); language teaching (MA); mathematics (MA, MAT, MS); political science (MS); psychology (MA, PhD); school psychology (MS, Ed S); sociology (MA); teaching English to speakers of other languages (Certificate); technical communication (Certificate). *Application deadline:* Applications are processed on a rolling basis. *Application fee:* $45. Electronic applications accepted. *Dean,* Dr. David Boocker, 402-554-2341, E-mail: graduate@unomaha.edu.

College of Business Administration Students: 119 full-time (40 women), 245 part-time (95 women); includes 51 minority (10 Black or African American, non-Hispanic/Latino; 1 American Indian or Alaska Native, non-Hispanic/Latino; 16 Asian, non-Hispanic/Latino; 14 Hispanic/Latino; 10 Two or more races, non-Hispanic/Latino), 50 international. Average age 30. 241 applicants, 49% accepted, 97 enrolled. *Faculty:* 31 full-time (13 women). Expenses: Contact institution. *Financial support:* In 2016–17, 23 students received support. Fellowships, research assistantships with tuition reimbursements available, teaching assistantships with tuition reimbursements available, career-related internships or fieldwork, Federal Work-Study, scholarships/grants, health care benefits, tuition waivers (partial), and unspecified assistantships available. Support available to part-time students. Financial award application deadline: 3/1; financial award applicants required to submit FAFSA. In 2016, 168 master's, 5 other advanced degrees awarded. *Program availability:* Part-time, evening/weekend. Offers accounting (M Acc); business administration (MBA); business for biosciences (Certificate); economics (MA, MS); executive business administration (EMBA); human resources and training (Certificate). *Application deadline:* Applications are processed on a rolling basis. *Application fee:* $45. Electronic applications accepted. *Dean,* Dr. Louis Pol, 402-554-2341, E-mail: graduate@unomaha.edu.

College of Communication, Fine Arts and Media Students: 40 full-time (24 women), 52 part-time (30 women); includes 13 minority (2 Black or African American, non-Hispanic/Latino; 2 Asian, non-Hispanic/Latino; 5 Hispanic/Latino; 4 Two or more races, non-Hispanic/Latino), 5 international. Average age 32. 62 applicants, 58% accepted, 23 enrolled. *Faculty:* 29 full-time (13 women). Expenses: Contact institution. *Financial support:* In 2016–17, 21 students received support. Fellowships, research assistantships with tuition reimbursements available, teaching assistantships with tuition reimbursements available, career-related internships or fieldwork, Federal Work-Study, institutionally sponsored loans, traineeships, tuition waivers (full), and unspecified assistantships available. Support available to part-time students. Financial award application deadline: 3/1; financial award applicants required to submit FAFSA. In 2016, 33 master's, 5 other advanced degrees awarded. *Program availability:* Part-time, evening/weekend. Offers arts (MA); communication (MA); communication, fine arts and media (MA, MFA, MM, Certificate); human resources and training (Certificate); music (MM); technical communication (Certificate); writing (MFA). *Application deadline:* Applications are processed on a rolling basis. *Application fee:* $45. Electronic applications accepted. *Dean,* Dr. Gail Baker, 402-554-2341, E-mail: graduate@unomaha.edu.

College of Education Students: 201 full-time (127 women), 600 part-time (497 women); includes 89 minority (27 Black or African American, non-Hispanic/Latino; 16 Asian, non-Hispanic/Latino; 28 Hispanic/Latino; 18 Two or more races, non-Hispanic/Latino), 26 international. Average age 32. 343 applicants, 59% accepted, 162 enrolled. *Faculty:* 33 full-time (25 women). Expenses: Contact institution. *Financial support:* In 2016–17, 68 students received support. Fellowships, research assistantships with tuition reimbursements available, teaching assistantships with tuition reimbursements available, career-related internships or fieldwork, Federal Work-Study, institutionally sponsored loans, scholarships/grants, health care benefits, tuition waivers (full), and unspecified assistantships available. Support available to part-time students. Financial award application deadline: 3/1; financial award applicants required to submit FAFSA. In 2016, 245 master's, 14 doctorates, 1 other advanced degree awarded. *Program availability:* Part-time, evening/weekend. Offers athletic training (MA); counseling (MA, MS); education (MA, MS, Ed D, PhD, Certificate, Ed S); educational administration and supervision (Ed D); educational leadership (MS, Ed S); elementary education (MS); exercise science (PhD); health, physical education, and recreation (MA, MS); instruction in urban schools

(Certificate); secondary education (MS, Certificate); special education (MS); speech-language pathology (MS). *Application deadline:* Applications are processed on a rolling basis. *Application fee:* $45. Electronic applications accepted. *Dean,* Dr. Nancy Edick, 402-554-2341, E-mail: graduate@unomaha.edu.

College of Information Science and Technology Students: 239 full-time (81 women), 180 part-time (49 women); includes 42 minority (14 Black or African American, non-Hispanic/Latino; 12 Asian, non-Hispanic/Latino; 9 Hispanic/Latino; 7 Two or more races, non-Hispanic/Latino), 261 international. Average age 29. 538 applicants, 52% accepted, 118 enrolled. *Faculty:* 29 full-time (8 women). Expenses: Contact institution. *Financial support:* In 2016–17, 52 students received support. Fellowships, research assistantships with tuition reimbursements available, teaching assistantships with tuition reimbursements available, career-related internships or fieldwork, Federal Work-Study, institutionally sponsored loans, scholarships/grants, health care benefits, tuition waivers (full), and unspecified assistantships available. Financial award application deadline: 3/1; financial award applicants required to submit FAFSA. In 2016, 156 master's, 8 doctorates, 54 other advanced degrees awarded. *Program availability:* Part-time, evening/weekend. Offers artificial intelligence (Certificate); biomedical informatics (MS, PhD); communication networks (Certificate); computer science (MA, MS); computer science education (MS, Certificate); data analytics (Certificate); information assurance (MS, Certificate); information science and technology (MA, MIT, MS, PhD, Certificate); information technology (MIT, PhD); management information systems (MS); project management (Certificate); software engineering (Certificate); system and architecture (Certificate); systems analysis and design (Certificate). *Application deadline:* Applications are processed on a rolling basis. *Application fee:* $45. Electronic applications accepted. *Dean,* Dr. Hesham Ali, 402-554-2341, E-mail: graduate@unomaha.edu.

College of Public Affairs and Community Service Students: 239 full-time (197 women), 423 part-time (292 women); includes 121 minority (30 Black or African American, non-Hispanic/Latino; 2 American Indian or Alaska Native, non-Hispanic/Latino; 5 Asian, non-Hispanic/Latino; 53 Hispanic/Latino; 1 Native Hawaiian or other Pacific Islander, non-Hispanic/Latino; 30 Two or more races, non-Hispanic/Latino), 22 international. Average age 32. 463 applicants, 66% accepted, 248 enrolled. *Faculty:* 41 full-time (24 women). Expenses: Contact institution. *Financial support:* In 2016–17, 59 students received support. Fellowships, research assistantships with tuition reimbursements available, teaching assistantships with tuition reimbursements available, career-related internships or fieldwork, Federal Work-Study, institutionally sponsored loans, scholarships/grants, health care benefits, tuition waivers (partial), and unspecified assistantships available. Support available to part-time students. Financial award application deadline: 3/1; financial award applicants required to submit FAFSA. In 2016, 150 master's, 5 doctorates, 8 other advanced degrees awarded. *Program availability:* Part-time, evening/weekend, online learning. Offers criminology and criminal justice (MA, MS, PhD); gerontology (PhD, Certificate); managing juvenile and adult populations (Certificate); public administration (MPA, PhD); public affairs and community service (MA, MPA, MS, MSW, PhD, Certificate); public management (Certificate); social opportunity (MA); social work (MSW); urban studies (MS). *Application deadline:* Applications are processed on a rolling basis. *Application fee:* $45. Electronic applications accepted. *Dean,* Dr. John Bartle, 402-554-2341, E-mail: graduate@unomaha.edu.

UNIVERSITY OF NEBRASKA–LINCOLN, Lincoln, NE 68588

General Information State-supported, coed, university. CGS member. *Graduate housing:* Rooms and/or apartments available on a first-come, first-served basis to single and married students. Housing application deadline: 7/1. *Research affiliation:* U.S. Department of Agriculture (USDA), U.S. Department of Defense, NASA, National Science Foundation, National Institutes of Health, U.S. Meat Animal Research Center.

GRADUATE UNITS

College of Law Offers law (JD); legal studies (MLS); space and telecommunications law (LL M). Electronic applications accepted.

Graduate College *Program availability:* Part-time, evening/weekend, online learning. Offers environmental health, occupational health and toxicology (MS, PhD); survey research and methodology (MS, PhD). Electronic applications accepted.

College of Agricultural Sciences and Natural Resources Offers agribusiness (MBA); agricultural economics (MS, PhD); agricultural sciences and natural resources (M Ag, MA, MBA, MS, PhD); agronomy (MS, PhD); animal science (MS, PhD); biochemistry (MS, PhD); community development (M Ag); entomology (MS, PhD); food science and technology (MS, PhD); geography (PhD); horticulture (MS, PhD); leadership development (MS); leadership education (MS); mechanized systems management (MS); natural resources (MS, PhD); nutrition (MS, PhD); statistics (MS, PhD); teaching and extension education (MS); veterinary science (MS). Electronic applications accepted.

College of Architecture Offers architecture (M Arch, MS, PhD); community and regional planning (MCRP); interior design (MS). Electronic applications accepted.

College of Arts and Sciences Offers analytical chemistry (PhD); anthropology (MA); arts and sciences (M Sc T, MA, MAT, MS, PhD, Graduate Certificate); astronomy (MS, PhD); biochemistry (PhD); bioinformatics (MS, PhD); biological sciences (MA, MS, PhD); biopsychology (PhD); chemistry (MS); classics and religious studies (MA); clinical psychology (PhD); cognitive psychology (PhD); composition and rhetoric (MA, PhD); computer engineering (MS, PhD); computer science (MS, PhD); creative writing (MA, PhD); developmental psychology (PhD); French (MA, PhD); geography (MA, PhD); geosciences (MS, PhD); German (MA, PhD); history (MA, PhD); information technology (PhD); inorganic chemistry (PhD); instructional communication (MA, PhD); interpersonal communication (MA, PhD); literature studies (MA, PhD); marketing, communication studies, and advertising (MA, PhD); materials chemistry (PhD); mathematics (MA, MAT, MS, PhD); mathematics and computer science (PhD); organic chemistry (PhD); organizational communication (MA, PhD); philosophy (MA, PhD); physical chemistry (PhD); physics (MS, PhD); political science (MA, PhD); professional archaeology (MA); psychology (MA); public policy analysis (Graduate Certificate); rhetoric and culture (MA, PhD); social/personality psychology (PhD); sociology (MA, PhD); Spanish (MA, PhD). Electronic applications accepted.

College of Business Administration *Program availability:* Part-time, evening/weekend. Offers accountancy (MPA, PhD); actuarial science (MS); business (MA, MBA, PhD); business administration (MA, MBA, MPA, MS, PhD); economics (MA, PhD); finance (MA, PhD); management (MA, PhD); marketing (MA, PhD). Electronic applications accepted.

College of Education and Human Sciences Offers administration, curriculum and instruction (Ed D, PhD); adult and continuing education (MA); audiology and hearing science (Au D); audiology research (PhD); child development/early childhood education (MS, PhD); child, youth and family studies (MS); clinical audiology (Au D); cognition, learning and development (MA); community nutrition and health promotion (MS); counseling psychology (MA); education and human sciences (M Ed, MA, MS,

MST, Au D, Ed D, PhD, Certificate, Ed S); educational administration (M Ed, MA, Ed D, Certificate); educational psychology (MA, Ed S); educational studies (Ed D, PhD); family and consumer sciences education (MS, PhD); family financial planning (MS); family science (MS, PhD); gerontology (PhD); human sciences (PhD); marriage and family therapy (MS); medical family therapy (PhD); merchandising (MS); nutrition (MS, PhD); nutrition and exercise (MS); nutrition and health sciences (MS, PhD); psychological studies in education (PhD); quantitative, qualitative, and psychometric methods (MA); school psychology (MA, Ed S); special education (M Ed, MA, Ed S); speech-language pathology and audiology (MS, Au D); teaching, learning and teacher education (M Ed, MA, MST, Ed D, PhD); textile history/quilt studies (MA); textile science (MS); textile-apparel (MA); textiles, clothing and design (MA, MS); vocational and adult education (M Ed, MA); youth development (MS). Electronic applications accepted.

College of Engineering Offers agricultural and biological systems engineering (MS, PhD); architectural engineering (M Eng, MAE, MS, PhD); biological engineering (PhD); biomedical engineering (PhD); chemical and biomolecular engineering (MS, PhD); civil engineering (MS, PhD); electrical engineering (MS, PhD); engineering (M Eng, MAE, MEE, MS, PhD); engineering management (M Eng); engineering mechanics (MS, PhD); environmental engineering (MS, PhD); industrial and management systems engineering (MS, PhD); manufacturing systems engineering (MS); materials engineering (PhD); mechanical engineering (MS); mechanical engineering and applied mechanics (PhD); mechanized systems management (MS). Electronic applications accepted.

College of Fine and Performing Arts Offers acting (MFA); art history (MA); composition (MM, DMA); conducting (MM, DMA); costume (MFA); directing (MFA); fine and performing arts (MA, MFA, MM, DMA, PhD); music education (MM, PhD); music history (MM); music theory (MM); performance (MM, DMA); piano pedagogy (MM); stage design (MFA); studio art (MFA); woodwind specialties (MM). Electronic applications accepted.

College of Journalism and Mass Communications Program availability: Online learning. Offers marketing, communication and advertising (MA); professional journalism (MA). Electronic applications accepted.

UNIVERSITY OF NEBRASKA MEDICAL CENTER, Omaha, NE 68198

General Information State-supported, coed, upper-level institution. CGS member. *Enrollment:* 2,039 full-time matriculated graduate/professional students (1,207 women), 427 part-time matriculated graduate/professional students (342 women). *Enrollment by degree level:* 715 master's, 1,589 doctoral, 116 other advanced degrees. *Graduate faculty:* 1,104 full-time (453 women), 200 part-time/adjunct (114 women). Tuition, state resident: full-time $7911; part-time $3955 per credit hour. Tuition, nonresident: full-time $22,950; part-time $11,475 per credit hour. *Required fees:* $589. *Student services:* Campus safety program, child daycare facilities, exercise/wellness program, free psychological counseling, international student services, low-cost health insurance, multicultural affairs office, services for students with disabilities. *Library facilities:* McGoogan Library of Medicine. *Research affiliation:* UNeMed Corporation (biotechnology).

Computer facilities: 120 computers available on campus for general student use. A campuswide network can be accessed from off campus. Online class registration is available.

Website: http://www.unmc.edu/

GRADUATE UNITS

College of Dentistry Offers dentistry (MS, DDS, PhD, Certificate). Electronic applications accepted.

College of Medicine Students: 506 full-time (207 women); includes 83 minority (11 Black or African American, non-Hispanic/Latino; 1 American Indian or Alaska Native, non-Hispanic/Latino; 46 Asian, non-Hispanic/Latino; 25 Hispanic/Latino). Average age 24. 1,973 applicants, 8% accepted, 126 enrolled. *Faculty:* 735 full-time, 153 part-time/adjunct. Expenses: Contact institution. *Financial support:* In 2016–17, 161 students received support. Career-related internships or fieldwork, Federal Work-Study, institutionally sponsored loans, and tuition waivers (full and partial) available. Financial award application deadline: 4/1; financial award applicants required to submit FAFSA. In 2016, 121 doctorates awarded. Offers medicine (MD, Certificate). *Application deadline:* For fall admission, 11/1 for domestic students. Applications are processed on a rolling basis. *Application fee:* $70. Electronic applications accepted. *Application Contact:* Lindsay J. Meyer, Admissions and Recruitment Coordinator, 402-559-2259, Fax: 402-559-6840, E-mail: comadmissions@unmc.edu. *Dean,* Dr. Bradley E. Britigan, 402-559-4283, Fax: 402-559-4148, E-mail: bradley.britigan@unmc.edu.

College of Pharmacy Offers pharmacy (Pharm D). Electronic applications accepted.

College of Public Health *Program availability:* Part-time, online learning. Offers public health (MPH). Electronic applications accepted.

Department of Biochemistry and Molecular Biology Students: 39 full-time (21 women); includes 4 minority (3 Asian, non-Hispanic/Latino; 1 Two or more races, non-Hispanic/Latino), 22 international. Average age 28. 13 applicants, 23% accepted, 3 enrolled. *Faculty:* 27 full-time (7 women). Expenses: Contact institution. *Financial support:* In 2016–17, 13 students received support, including 4 fellowships with full tuition reimbursements available (averaging $23,100 per year), 7 research assistantships with full tuition reimbursements available (averaging $23,100 per year); scholarships/grants, health care benefits, and unspecified assistantships also available. Financial award application deadline: 2/15; financial award applicants required to submit FAFSA. Offers biochemistry and molecular biology (MS). *Application deadline:* For fall admission, 6/1 for domestic students, 4/1 for international students; for spring admission, 8/1 for domestic and international students; for summer admission, 1/1 for domestic and international students. *Application fee:* $45. Electronic applications accepted. *Application Contact:* Karen Hankins, Office Associate, 402-559-4417, E-mail: karen.hankins@unmc.edu. *Chairman, Graduate Committee,* Dr. Paul Sorgen, 402-559-7557, Fax: 402-559-6650, E-mail: psorgen@unmc.edu.

Department of Biostatistics Students: 6 full-time (1 woman), 2 part-time (1 woman); includes 1 minority (Asian, non-Hispanic/Latino), 3 international. Average age 28. *Faculty:* 8 full-time (5 women). Expenses: Contact institution. *Financial support:* In 2016–17, 6 research assistantships with full tuition reimbursements (averaging $23,000 per year), 6 teaching assistantships with full tuition reimbursements (averaging $23,000 per year) were awarded; health care benefits and unspecified assistantships also available. Financial award application deadline: 4/1. *Program availability:* Part-time. Offers biostatistics (PhD). *Application deadline:* For fall admission, 6/1 for domestic students, 4/1 for international students. *Application fee:* $125. Electronic applications accepted. *Application Contact:* Dr. Gleb Haynatzki, Graduate Program Director/Professor, 402-559-3294, E-mail: ghaynatzki@unmc.edu. *Professor and Chair,* Dr. Jane Meza, 402-559-6825, E-mail: jmeza@unmc.edu.

Department of Epidemiology Students: 17 full-time (14 women), 3 part-time (0 women); includes 4 minority (all Asian, non-Hispanic/Latino), 10 international. Average age 31. 21 applicants, 24% accepted, 5 enrolled. *Faculty:* 11 full-time (5 women), 5 part-time/adjunct (2 women). Expenses: Contact institution. *Financial support:* In 2016–17, 1 teaching assistantship with full tuition reimbursement (averaging $23,100 per year) was awarded; research assistantships with full tuition reimbursements, scholarships/grants, and unspecified assistantships also available. Financial award applicants required to submit FAFSA. *Program availability:* Part-time. Offers epidemiology (PhD). *Application deadline:* For fall admission, 6/1 for domestic students, 3/1 for international students. *Application fee:* $45. Electronic applications accepted. *Application Contact:* KM Islam, Director of Graduate Program, 402-559-8283, E-mail: kmislam@unmc.edu. *Chair,* Dr. Deborah Levy, 402-552-9879, E-mail: deborah.levy@unmc.edu.

Department of Genetics, Cell Biology and Anatomy Students: 41 full-time (17 women); includes 7 minority (3 Black or African American, non-Hispanic/Latino; 1 American Indian or Alaska Native, non-Hispanic/Latino; 2 Asian, non-Hispanic/Latino; 1 Hispanic/Latino), 9 international. Average age 25. 99 applicants, 24% accepted, 22 enrolled. *Faculty:* 23 full-time (6 women), 1 (woman) part-time/adjunct. Expenses: Contact institution. *Financial support:* In 2016–17, 25 students received support, including 5 fellowships with full tuition reimbursements available (averaging $26,500 per year), 20 research assistantships with full tuition reimbursements available (averaging $26,500 per year); scholarships/grants, health care benefits, tuition waivers (full), unspecified assistantships, and stipends (for all PhD students) also available. Support available to part-time students. Financial award application deadline: 6/1; financial award applicants required to submit FAFSA. In 2016, 14 master's, 7 doctorates awarded. Offers genetics, cell biology and anatomy (PhD); medical anatomy (MS); molecular genetics and cell biology (MS). *Application deadline:* For fall admission, 6/1 priority date for domestic students, 4/1 priority date for international students; for summer admission, 4/1 for domestic students, 1/1 for international students. Applications are processed on a rolling basis. *Application fee:* $60. Electronic applications accepted. *Application Contact:* Megan Brown, Instructional Technologist/Education Program Coordinator, 402-559-8328, Fax: 402-559-3400, E-mail: mebrown@unmc.edu. *Graduate Committee Chair,* Dr. Karen Gould, 402-559-2456, E-mail: kagould@unmc.edu.

Department of Health Promotion, Social and Behavioral Health Students: 11 full-time (6 women), 2 part-time (both women); includes 2 minority (1 Black or African American, non-Hispanic/Latino; 1 Asian, non-Hispanic/Latino), 2 international. Average age 35. 12 applicants, 33% accepted, 4 enrolled. *Faculty:* 13 full-time (9 women), 1 (woman) part-time/adjunct. Expenses: Contact institution. *Financial support:* In 2016–17, research assistantships with full tuition reimbursements (averaging $23,100 per year) were awarded; scholarships/grants also available. Support available to part-time students. Financial award application deadline: 2/15; financial award applicants required to submit FAFSA. In 2016, 2 doctorates awarded. *Program availability:* Part-time. Offers health promotion and disease prevention research (PhD). *Application deadline:* For fall admission, 4/1 for domestic and international students. *Application fee:* $45. Electronic applications accepted. *Application Contact:* Kate Kusnerik, Coordinator, 402-559-4325, E-mail: kate.kusnerik@unmc.edu. *Graduate Program Director,* Dr. Ghada Soliman, 402-559-5157, E-mail: ghada.soliman@unmc.edu.

Department of Health Services Research and Administration Students: 13 full-time (10 women), 3 part-time (2 women); includes 1 minority (Two or more races, non-Hispanic/Latino), 10 international. Average age 31. 11 applicants, 36% accepted, 4 enrolled. *Faculty:* 9 full-time (4 women), 1 part-time/adjunct (0 women). Expenses: Contact institution. *Financial support:* In 2016–17, 5 students received support, including 1 research assistantship with full tuition reimbursement available (averaging $23,100 per year); scholarships/grants and unspecified assistantships also available. Financial award application deadline: 2/15; financial award applicants required to submit FAFSA. In 2016, 5 doctorates awarded. Offers health services research, administration, and policy (PhD). *Application deadline:* For fall admission, 6/1 for domestic students, 4/1 for international students. *Application fee:* $45. Electronic applications accepted. *Application Contact:* Denise Howard, Coordinator, 402-559-5260, E-mail: denise.howard@unmc.edu. *Associate Professor,* Dr. Fernando Wilson, 402-552-6948, E-mail: fernando.wilson@unmc.edu.

Department of Pathology and Microbiology Students: 37 full-time (22 women), 2 part-time (both women); includes 3 minority (1 Black or African American, non-Hispanic/Latino; 2 Asian, non-Hispanic/Latino), 21 international. Average age 28. 20 applicants, 50% accepted, 5 enrolled. *Faculty:* 72 full-time (23 women). Expenses: Contact institution. *Financial support:* In 2016–17, 7 students received support, including 2 fellowships with full tuition reimbursements available (averaging $23,400 per year), 3 research assistantships with full tuition reimbursements available (averaging $23,400 per year); scholarships/grants also available. Support available to part-time students. Financial award application deadline: 3/1; financial award applicants required to submit FAFSA. In 2016, 10 doctorates awarded. *Program availability:* Part-time. Offers pathology and microbiology (MS, PhD). *Application deadline:* For fall admission, 3/1 for domestic and international students; for spring admission, 10/1 for domestic and international students; for summer admission, 3/1 for domestic and international students. Applications are processed on a rolling basis. *Application fee:* $60. Electronic applications accepted. *Application Contact:* Tuire Cechin, Office Associate, 402-559-4042, Fax: 402-559-5900, E-mail: tcechin@unmc.edu. *Chair, Graduate Committee,* Dr. Rakesh K. Singh, 402-559-9949, Fax: 402-559-5900, E-mail: rsingh@unmc.edu.

Department of Pharmaceutical Sciences Students: 55 full-time (22 women), 48 international. Average age 27. 51 applicants, 39% accepted, 17 enrolled. *Faculty:* 20 full-time (3 women), 1 part-time/adjunct (0 women). Expenses: Contact institution. *Financial support:* In 2016–17, 2 fellowships with full tuition reimbursements (averaging $23,100 per year), 10 research assistantships with full tuition reimbursements (averaging $23,000 per year), teaching assistantships with full tuition reimbursements (averaging $23,000 per year) were awarded; scholarships/grants also available. Support available to part-time students. Financial award application deadline: 3/1; financial award applicants required to submit FAFSA. In 2016, 4 doctorates awarded. Offers pharmaceutical sciences (MS, PhD). *Application deadline:* For fall admission, 4/1 priority date for domestic and international students; for spring admission, 10/1 for domestic students, 8/1 for international students. Applications are processed on a rolling basis. *Application fee:* $45. Electronic applications accepted. *Application Contact:* Brianna Simmons, Office Associate, 402-559-5320, E-mail: briannasimmons@unmc.edu. *Chair, Pharmaceutical Sciences Graduate Program Committee,* Dr. Ram Mahato, 402-559-5422, E-mail: ram.mahato@unmc.edu.

Department of Pharmacology and Experimental Neuroscience Students: 28 full-time (9 women); includes 1 minority (Black or African American, non-Hispanic/Latino), 10 international. 8 applicants, 25% accepted, 2 enrolled. *Faculty:* 26 full-time (8 women), 2 part-time/adjunct (0 women). Expenses: Contact institution. *Financial support:* Fellowships, research assistantships, scholarships/grants, health care benefits, and unspecified assistantships available. Financial award application deadline: 2/15. In 2016, 10 doctorates awarded. Offers pharmacology and experimental neuroscience (PhD).

Application deadline: For fall admission, 4/1 for domestic and international students. Applications are processed on a rolling basis. *Application fee:* $45. Electronic applications accepted. *Application Contact:* Reed Felderman, Office Administrator, 402-559-4044, Fax: 402-559-7495, E-mail: reed.felderman@unmc.edu. *Chair, Graduate Studies*, Dr. Keshore Bidasee, 402-559-9018, Fax: 402-559-7495, E-mail: kbidasee@unmc.edu.

Environmental Health, Occupational Health and Toxicology Graduate Program Students: 7 full-time (3 women), 1 (woman) part-time; includes 4 minority (1 Black or African American, non-Hispanic/Latino; 3 Asian, non-Hispanic/Latino). Average age 32. 12 applicants, 100% accepted, 10 enrolled. *Faculty:* 6 full-time (2 women), 1 part-time/adjunct (0 women). Expenses: Contact institution. *Financial support:* In 2016–17, fellowships with full tuition reimbursements (averaging $23,100 per year), 1 research assistantship with full tuition reimbursement (averaging $23,100 per year) was awarded; teaching assistantships and scholarships/grants also available. Financial award application deadline: 2/15; financial award applicants required to submit FAFSA. In 2016, 2 doctorates awarded. Offers environmental health, occupational health and toxicology (PhD). *Application deadline:* For fall admission, 6/1 for domestic students, 4/1 for international students; for spring admission, 10/1 for domestic students, 8/1 for international students; for summer admission, 1/1 for domestic and international students. Applications are processed on a rolling basis. *Application fee:* $60. Electronic applications accepted. *Application Contact:* Sherry Cherek, Coordinator, 402-559-8924, Fax: 402-559-4961, E-mail: scherek@unmc.edu. *Associate Professor*, Dr. Chandran Achutan, 402-559-8599, Fax: 402-559-4961, E-mail: cachutan@unmc.edu.

Interdisciplinary Graduate Program in Biomedical Sciences Students: 18 full-time (12 women); includes 3 minority (1 Black or African American, non-Hispanic/Latino; 2 Asian, non-Hispanic/Latino), 4 international. Average age 23. 129 applicants, 40% accepted, 39 enrolled. Expenses: Contact institution. *Financial support:* In 2016–17, 18 students received support. Tuition waivers (full) available. Financial award application deadline: 6/1. Offers biochemistry and molecular biology (PhD); cancer research (PhD); immunology, pathology and infectious disease (PhD); integrative physiology and molecular medicine (PhD); molecular genetics and cell biology (PhD); neuroscience (PhD). *Application deadline:* For fall admission, 6/1 for domestic students, 4/1 for international students; for summer admission, 3/1 for domestic students, 1/1 for international students. Applications are processed on a rolling basis. *Application fee:* $60. Electronic applications accepted. *IGPBS Program Coordinator*, Kimberly Rothgeb, 402-559-3362, Fax: 402-559-5368, E-mail: krothgeb@unmc.edu.

Medical Sciences Interdepartmental Area Students: 44 full-time (27 women), 57 part-time (38 women); includes 13 minority (1 Black or African American, non-Hispanic/Latino; 11 Asian, non-Hispanic/Latino; 1 Hispanic/Latino), 20 international. Average age 32. 82 applicants, 59% accepted, 32 enrolled. *Faculty:* 170 full-time, 20 part-time/adjunct. Expenses: Contact institution. *Financial support:* In 2016–17, 85 students received support, including 1 fellowship with full tuition reimbursement available (averaging $23,400 per year), 37 research assistantships with full tuition reimbursements available (averaging $23,400 per year), 2 teaching assistantships with full tuition reimbursements available (averaging $23,400 per year); scholarships/grants and health care benefits also available. Support available to part-time students. Financial award application deadline: 2/15; financial award applicants required to submit FAFSA. In 2016, 16 master's, 9 doctorates awarded. *Program availability:* Part-time. Offers applied behavior analysis (PhD); clinical translational research (MS, PhD); cytotechnology (MS); family medicine (MS, PhD); genetics, cell biology and anatomy (MS, PhD); internal medicine (MS); medical nutrition (MS, PhD); obstetrics and gynecology (MS, PhD); ophthalmology and visual sciences (MS, PhD); oral biology (MS, PhD); orthopedic surgery (MS, PhD); pathology and microbiology (MS, PhD); pediatrics (MS, PhD); pharmacology and experimental neuroscience (MS). *Application deadline:* For fall admission, 6/1 for domestic students, 4/1 for international students; for spring admission, 10/1 for domestic students, 9/1 for international students. Applications are processed on a rolling basis. *Application fee:* $60. Electronic applications accepted. *Application Contact:* Rhonda Sheibal-Carver, Interdisciplinary Programs Coordinator, 402-559-5141, E-mail: rhonda.sheibalcarver@unmc.edu. *Graduate Committee Chair*, Dr. Laura Bilek, 402-559-6923, E-mail: lbilek@unmc.edu.

PhD in Nursing Program Students: 17 full-time (15 women), 6 part-time (all women); includes 3 minority (1 Black or African American, non-Hispanic/Latino; 1 Hispanic/Latino; 1 Two or more races, non-Hispanic/Latino), 1 international. Average age 40. 6 applicants, 100% accepted, 6 enrolled. *Faculty:* 57 full-time (56 women), 6 part-time/adjunct (all women). Expenses: Contact institution. *Financial support:* In 2016–17, 15 students received support. Scholarships/grants and unspecified assistantships available. Financial award application deadline: 2/1; financial award applicants required to submit FAFSA. In 2016, 10 doctorates awarded. *Program availability:* Part-time, online learning. Offers nursing (PhD). *Application deadline:* For spring admission, 1/15 for domestic and international students. *Application fee:* $65. Electronic applications accepted. *Application Contact:* Rolee Kelly, Director, Student Services, 402-559-6639, E-mail: rolee.kelly@unmc.edu. *Professor*, Dr. Kathleen Hanna, 402-559-5468, E-mail: kathy.hanna@unmc.edu.

Program in Biomedical Informatics Students: 4 full-time (2 women), 6 part-time (2 women), 3 international. Average age 32. 3 applicants, 67% accepted, 2 enrolled. *Faculty:* 29 full-time (7 women). Expenses: Contact institution. *Financial support:* In 2016–17, 8 students received support, including 1 fellowship with full tuition reimbursement available (averaging $23,400 per year), 4 research assistantships with full tuition reimbursements available (averaging $23,400 per year); scholarships/grants also available. Support available to part-time students. Financial award application deadline: 2/15; financial award applicants required to submit FAFSA. In 2016, 1 doctorate awarded. *Program availability:* Part-time. Offers biomedical informatics (MS, PhD). *Application deadline:* For fall admission, 6/1 for domestic students, 4/1 for international students; for spring admission, 10/1 for domestic students, 9/1 for international students; for summer admission, 3/1 for domestic students, 1/1 for international students. Applications are processed on a rolling basis. *Application fee:* $60. Electronic applications accepted. *Application Contact:* Rhonda Sheibal-Carver, Academic Program Coordinator, 402-559-5141, E-mail: rhonda.sheibalcarver@unmc.edu. *Director*, Dr. Jim McClay, 402-559-3587, E-mail: jmcclay@unmc.edu.

Program in Emergency Preparedness Students: 2 full-time (both women), 4 part-time (2 women); includes 1 minority (Black or African American, non-Hispanic/Latino). Average age 28. 5 applicants, 60% accepted, 3 enrolled. Expenses: Contact institution. *Financial support:* Scholarships/grants available. Support available to part-time students. Financial award application deadline: 2/15; financial award applicants required to submit FAFSA. *Program availability:* Part-time, 100% online, blended/hybrid learning. Offers emergency preparedness (MS). *Application deadline:* For fall admission, 6/1 for domestic students, 4/1 for international students; for spring admission, 10/1 for domestic students, 8/1 for international students. *Application fee:* $45. Electronic applications accepted. *Application Contact:* Jessica Tschirren, Coordinator, 402-561-7586, Fax: 402-561-7599, E-mail: jtschirren@unmc.edu. *Associate Director, Center for Emergency Preparedness*, Dr. Sharon Medcalf, 402-552-2529, E-mail: smedcalf@unmc.edu.

School of Allied Health Professions Offers allied health professions (MPAS, MPS, DPT, Certificate); cytotechnology (Certificate); dietetic internship (Certificate); distance education perfusion education (MPS); perfusion science (MPS).

Division of Physical Therapy Education Offers physical therapy education (DPT).

Division of Physician Assistant Education Offers physician assistant education (MPAS). Electronic applications accepted.

UNIVERSITY OF NEVADA, LAS VEGAS, Las Vegas, NV 89154

General Information State-supported, coed, university. CGS member. *Enrollment:* 29,702 graduate, professional, and undergraduate students; 2,222 full-time matriculated graduate/professional students (1,320 women), 1,379 part-time matriculated graduate/professional students (829 women). *Enrollment by degree level:* 2,496 master's, 997 doctoral, 108 other advanced degrees. *Graduate faculty:* 497 full-time (172 women), 156 part-time/adjunct (87 women). Tuition, state resident: full-time $9364. Tuition, nonresident: full-time $23,274. *Required fees:* $2355. One-time fee: $291 part-time. Tuition and fees vary according to course load, program and reciprocity agreements. *Graduate housing:* Room and/or apartments available on a first-come, first-served basis to single students; on-campus housing not available to married students. Typical cost: $6400 per year ($8700 including board). Room and board charges vary according to board plan and housing facility selected. Housing application deadline: 6/1. *Student services:* Campus employment opportunities, campus safety program, career counseling, child daycare facilities, exercise/wellness program, free psychological counseling, grant writing training, international student services, low-cost health insurance, multicultural affairs office, services for students with disabilities, teacher training, writing training. *Library facilities:* Lied Library. *Collection:* Books: 939,652 (physical), 1.3 million (digital/electronic); Serial titles: 20,453 (physical), 59,248 (digital/electronic); Databases: 320. Weekly public service hours: 101; students can reserve study rooms. *Research affiliation:* Switch, Tesla Motors, NV Energy, Lockheed Martin Corporation, The Desert Research Institute.

Computer facilities: 2,100 computers available on campus for general student use. A campuswide network can be accessed from student residence rooms and from off campus. Online class registration is available. Website: http://www.unlv.edu/

General Application Contact: Sebern Coleman, Graduate Recruitment and CRM Specialist, 702-895-3423, Fax: 702-895-4180, E-mail: sebern.coleman@unlv.edu.

GRADUATE UNITS

Graduate College Students: 2,222 full-time (1,320 women), 1,379 part-time (829 women); includes 1,233 minority (251 Black or African American, non-Hispanic/Latino; 15 American Indian or Alaska Native, non-Hispanic/Latino; 250 Asian, non-Hispanic/Latino; 481 Hispanic/Latino; 23 Native Hawaiian or other Pacific Islander, non-Hispanic/Latino; 213 Two or more races, non-Hispanic/Latino), 364 international. Average age 33. 2,518 applicants, 57% accepted, 997 enrolled. *Faculty:* 497 full-time (172 women), 156 part-time/adjunct (87 women). Expenses: Contact institution. *Financial support:* In 2016–17, 12 fellowships with partial tuition reimbursements (averaging $18,333 per year), 315 research assistantships with partial tuition reimbursements (averaging $13,759 per year), 698 teaching assistantships with partial tuition reimbursements (averaging $13,092 per year) were awarded; institutionally sponsored loans, scholarships/grants, health care benefits, and unspecified assistantships also available. Financial award application deadline: 3/15. In 2016, 1,031 master's, 166 doctorates, 38 other advanced degrees awarded. *Program availability:* Part-time. *Application deadline:* For fall admission, 8/1 for domestic students, 5/1 for international students; for spring admission, 11/1 for domestic students, 10/1 for international students. *Application fee:* $60 ($95 for international students). Electronic applications accepted. *Dean*, Dr. Kathryn Korgan, 702-895-0446, Fax: 702-895-4180, E-mail: kate.korgan@unlv.edu.

College of Education Students: 623 full-time (476 women), 480 part-time (338 women); includes 429 minority (119 Black or African American, non-Hispanic/Latino; 6 American Indian or Alaska Native, non-Hispanic/Latino; 49 Asian, non-Hispanic/Latino; 179 Hispanic/Latino; 7 Native Hawaiian or other Pacific Islander, non-Hispanic/Latino; 69 Two or more races, non-Hispanic/Latino), 46 international. Average age 35. 555 applicants, 74% accepted, 333 enrolled. *Faculty:* 63 full-time (34 women), 43 part-time/adjunct (31 women). Expenses: Contact institution. *Financial support:* In 2016–17, 44 research assistantships with partial tuition reimbursements (averaging $14,535 per year), 76 teaching assistantships with partial tuition reimbursements (averaging $15,479 per year) were awarded; institutionally sponsored loans, scholarships/grants, health care benefits, and unspecified assistantships also available. Financial award application deadline: 3/15. In 2016, 356 master's, 31 doctorates, 9 other advanced degrees awarded. *Program availability:* Part-time, evening/weekend. Offers addiction studies (Advanced Certificate); chief diversity officer in higher education (Certificate); college sport leadership (Certificate); counselor education (M Ed, MS); curriculum and instruction (M Ed, MS, Ed D, PhD, Ed S); early childhood education (M Ed); early childhood special education (Certificate); education (M Ed, MS, Ed D, PhD, Advanced Certificate, Certificate, Ed S); educational psychology (M Ed, MS, PhD, Ed S); elementary teaching (Certificate); English language learning (M Ed); higher education (M Ed, PhD, Certificate); mental health counseling (Advanced Certificate); online teaching and training (Certificate); psychology/learning and technology (PhD); secondary teaching (Certificate); social justice studies (Certificate); special education (M Ed, PhD); teaching and learning (PhD); workforce development/educational leadership (PhD). *Application fee:* $60 ($95 for international students). Electronic applications accepted. *Dean*, Dr. Kim Metcalf, 702-895-3375, Fax: 702-895-4068, E-mail: kim.metcalf@unlv.edu.

College of Fine Arts Students: 148 full-time (70 women), 44 part-time (28 women); includes 66 minority (16 Black or African American, non-Hispanic/Latino; 10 Asian, non-Hispanic/Latino; 34 Hispanic/Latino; 2 Native Hawaiian or other Pacific Islander, non-Hispanic/Latino; 4 Two or more races, non-Hispanic/Latino), 22 international. Average age 32. 167 applicants, 61% accepted, 69 enrolled. *Faculty:* 54 full-time (14 women), 27 part-time/adjunct (8 women). Expenses: Contact institution. *Financial support:* In 2016–17, 17 research assistantships with partial tuition reimbursements (averaging $13,824 per year), 86 teaching assistantships with partial tuition reimbursements (averaging $13,422 per year) were awarded; institutionally sponsored loans, scholarships/grants, health care benefits, and unspecified assistantships also available. Financial award application deadline: 3/15. In 2016, 64 master's, 12 doctorates awarded. *Program availability:* Part-time. Offers architecture (M Arch); art (MFA); film/writing for dramatic media (MFA); fine arts (M Arch, MA, MFA, MHID, MM, DMA, Certificate); healthcare interior design (MHID); hospitality design (Certificate); K-12 music (Certificate); music (MM); musical arts (DMA); theatre

(MA, MFA); writing for dramatic media (Certificate). *Application fee:* $60 ($95 for international students). Electronic applications accepted. *Dean/Professor,* Dr. Nancy J. Uscher, 702-895-4210, Fax: 702-895-4194, E-mail: nancy.uscher@unlv.edu.

College of Liberal Arts Students: 230 full-time (127 women), 106 part-time (59 women); includes 76 minority (7 Black or African American, non-Hispanic/Latino; 1 American Indian or Alaska Native, non-Hispanic/Latino; 12 Asian, non-Hispanic/Latino; 39 Hispanic/Latino; 2 Native Hawaiian or other Pacific Islander, non-Hispanic/Latino; 15 Two or more races, non-Hispanic/Latino), 14 international. Average age 33. 388 applicants, 29% accepted, 77 enrolled. *Faculty:* 94 full-time (40 women), 5 part-time/adjunct (3 women). Expenses: Contact institution. *Financial support:* In 2016–17, 7 fellowships with partial tuition reimbursements (averaging $18,571 per year), 57 research assistantships with partial tuition reimbursements (averaging $15,629 per year), 152 teaching assistantships with partial tuition reimbursements (averaging $15,141 per year) were awarded; institutionally sponsored loans, scholarships/grants, health care benefits, and unspecified assistantships also available. Financial award application deadline: 3/15. In 2016, 52 master's, 20 doctorates awarded. *Program availability:* Part-time. Offers anthropology (MA, PhD); creative writing (MFA); English (MA, PhD); Hispanic studies (MA); history (MA, PhD); liberal arts (MA, MFA, PhD, Certificate); political science (MA, PhD); psychology (MA, PhD, Certificate); sociology (MA, PhD). *Application fee:* $60 ($95 for international students). Electronic applications accepted. *Dean,* Dr. Chris Heavey, 702-895-3401, Fax: 702-895-4097, E-mail: chris.heavey@unlv.edu.

College of Sciences Students: 183 full-time (65 women), 62 part-time (27 women); includes 56 minority (5 Black or African American, non-Hispanic/Latino; 18 Asian, non-Hispanic/Latino; 22 Hispanic/Latino; 11 Two or more races, non-Hispanic/Latino), 46 international. Average age 31. 166 applicants, 46% accepted, 51 enrolled. *Faculty:* 79 full-time (12 women), 3 part-time/adjunct (1 woman). Expenses: Contact institution. *Financial support:* In 2016–17, 3 fellowships with partial tuition reimbursements (averaging $18,333 per year), 54 research assistantships with partial tuition reimbursements (averaging $18,692 per year), 134 teaching assistantships with partial tuition reimbursements (averaging $18,899 per year) were awarded; institutionally sponsored loans, scholarships/grants, health care benefits, and unspecified assistantships also available. Financial award application deadline: 3/15. In 2016, 28 master's, 15 doctorates awarded. *Program availability:* Part-time. Offers astronomy (MS, PhD); biochemistry (MS); biological sciences (MS, PhD); chemistry (MS, PhD); geoscience (MS, PhD); mathematical sciences (MS, PhD); physics (MS, PhD); radio chemistry (PhD); science (MA); sciences (MA, MS, PhD); water resources management (MS). *Application fee:* $60 ($95 for international students). Electronic applications accepted. *Dean,* Dr. Stanley D. Smith, 702-895-3487, Fax: 702-895-4159, E-mail: stan.smith@unlv.edu.

Greenspun College of Urban Affairs Students: 339 full-time (263 women), 190 part-time (130 women); includes 238 minority (65 Black or African American, non-Hispanic/Latino; 2 American Indian or Alaska Native, non-Hispanic/Latino; 22 Asian, non-Hispanic/Latino; 106 Hispanic/Latino; 7 Native Hawaiian or other Pacific Islander, non-Hispanic/Latino; 36 Two or more races, non-Hispanic/Latino), 21 international. Average age 33. 391 applicants, 62% accepted, 177 enrolled. *Faculty:* 45 full-time (26 women), 32 part-time/adjunct (17 women). Expenses: Contact institution. *Financial support:* In 2016–17, 32 research assistantships with partial tuition reimbursements (averaging $11,708 per year), 72 teaching assistantships with partial tuition reimbursements (averaging $12,903 per year) were awarded; institutionally sponsored loans, scholarships/grants, health care benefits, and unspecified assistantships also available. Financial award application deadline: 3/15. In 2016, 203 master's, 9 doctorates, 21 other advanced degrees awarded. *Program availability:* Part-time. Offers communication studies (MA); criminal justice (MA); criminology and criminal justice (PhD); crisis and emergency management (MS); journalism and media studies (MA); marriage and family therapy (MS); non-profit management (Certificate); public administration (MPA); public affairs (PhD); public management (Certificate); social work (MSW); urban affairs (MA, MPA, MS, MSW, PhD, Certificate); urban leadership (MA). *Application fee:* $60 ($95 for international students). Electronic applications accepted. *Dean,* Dr. Robert Ulmer, 702-895-0628, E-mail: robert.ulmer@unlv.edu.

Howard R. Hughes College of Engineering Students: 150 full-time (40 women), 95 part-time (19 women); includes 54 minority (3 Black or African American, non-Hispanic/Latino; 1 American Indian or Alaska Native, non-Hispanic/Latino; 16 Hispanic/Latino; 12 Two or more races, non-Hispanic/Latino), 108 international. Average age 30. 233 applicants, 59% accepted, 53 enrolled. *Faculty:* 57 full-time (8 women), 6 part-time/adjunct (1 woman). Expenses: Contact institution. *Financial support:* In 2016–17, 2 fellowships with partial tuition reimbursements (averaging $17,500 per year), 49 research assistantships with partial tuition reimbursements (averaging $15,855 per year), 101 teaching assistantships with partial tuition reimbursements (averaging $13,753 per year) were awarded; institutionally sponsored loans, scholarships/grants, health care benefits, and unspecified assistantships also available. Financial award application deadline: 3/15. In 2016, 48 master's, 16 doctorates, 6 other advanced degrees awarded. *Program availability:* Part-time. Offers aerospace engineering (MS); biomedical engineering (MS); civil and environmental engineering (PhD); computer science (MS, PhD); construction management (MS); electrical and computer engineering (MS, PhD); engineering (MS, PhD, Certificate); materials and nuclear engineering (MS); mechanical engineering (MS, PhD); nuclear criticality safety (Certificate); nuclear safeguards and security (Certificate); solar and renewable energy (Certificate); transportation (MS). *Application fee:* $60 ($95 for international students). Electronic applications accepted. *Dean,* Dr. Rama Venkat, 702-895-3699, Fax: 702-895-4059, E-mail: rama.venkat@unlv.edu.

Lee Business School Students: 221 full-time (93 women), 177 part-time (71 women); includes 141 minority (15 Black or African American, non-Hispanic/Latino; 54 Asian, non-Hispanic/Latino; 44 Hispanic/Latino; 3 Native Hawaiian or other Pacific Islander, non-Hispanic/Latino; 25 Two or more races, non-Hispanic/Latino), 56 international. Average age 32. 215 applicants, 69% accepted, 98 enrolled. *Faculty:* 34 full-time (5 women), 10 part-time/adjunct (4 women). Expenses: Contact institution. *Financial support:* In 2016–17, 26 research assistantships with partial tuition reimbursements (averaging $10,202 per year), 20 teaching assistantships with partial tuition reimbursements (averaging $10,750 per year) were awarded; institutionally sponsored loans, scholarships/grants, health care benefits, and unspecified assistantships also available. Financial award application deadline: 3/15. In 2016, 176 master's, 2 other advanced degrees awarded. *Program availability:* Part-time. Offers accounting (MS, Advanced Certificate, Certificate); business (Exec MBA, MA, MBA, MS, Advanced Certificate, Certificate); business administration (Exec MBA, MBA, Certificate); data analytics (Certificate); data analytics and applied economics (MS); economics (MA); management information systems (MS, Certificate); new venture management (Certificate). *Application fee:* $60 ($95 for international students).

Electronic applications accepted. *Dean,* Dr. Brent Hathaway, 702-895-3362, Fax: 702-895-4090, E-mail: brent.hathaway@unlv.edu.

School of Allied Health Sciences Students: 157 full-time (68 women), 17 part-time (7 women); includes 44 minority (2 Black or African American, non-Hispanic/Latino; 1 American Indian or Alaska Native, non-Hispanic/Latino; 17 Asian, non-Hispanic/Latino; 11 Hispanic/Latino; 1 Native Hawaiian or other Pacific Islander, non-Hispanic/Latino; 12 Two or more races, non-Hispanic/Latino), 9 international. Average age 28. 78 applicants, 60% accepted, 30 enrolled. *Faculty:* 21 full-time (8 women), 11 part-time/adjunct (6 women). Expenses: Contact institution. *Financial support:* In 2016–17, 20 research assistantships with partial tuition reimbursements (averaging $16,232 per year), 24 teaching assistantships with partial tuition reimbursements (averaging $13,583 per year) were awarded; institutionally sponsored loans, scholarships/grants, health care benefits, and unspecified assistantships also available. Financial award application deadline: 3/15. In 2016, 14 master's, 34 doctorates awarded. *Program availability:* Part-time. Offers allied health sciences (MS, DMP, DPT, PhD, Advanced Certificate); exercise physiology (MS); health physics and diagnostic sciences (MS, DMP, PhD, Advanced Certificate); kinesiology (PhD); nutrition sciences (MS); physical therapy (DPT). *Application fee:* $60 ($95 for international students). Electronic applications accepted. *Dean,* Dr. Ronald T. Brown, 702-895-3693, Fax: 702-895-1356, E-mail: ronald.brown@unlv.edu.

School of Community Health Sciences Students: 66 full-time (44 women), 70 part-time (52 women); includes 58 minority (14 Black or African American, non-Hispanic/Latino; 2 American Indian or Alaska Native, non-Hispanic/Latino; 14 Asian, non-Hispanic/Latino; 16 Hispanic/Latino; 1 Native Hawaiian or other Pacific Islander, non-Hispanic/Latino; 11 Two or more races, non-Hispanic/Latino), 14 international. Average age 32. 73 applicants, 75% accepted, 36 enrolled. *Faculty:* 22 full-time (9 women), 5 part-time/adjunct (3 women). Expenses: Contact institution. *Financial support:* In 2016–17, 12 research assistantships with partial tuition reimbursements (averaging $12,288 per year), 6 teaching assistantships with partial tuition reimbursements (averaging $12,000 per year) were awarded; institutionally sponsored loans, scholarships/grants, health care benefits, and unspecified assistantships also available. Financial award application deadline: 3/15. In 2016, 27 master's, 7 doctorates awarded. *Program availability:* Part-time. Offers community health sciences (Exec MHA, MHA, MPH, PhD, Certificate); health care administration and policy (Exec MHA, MHA); infection prevention (Certificate); public health (MPH, PhD, Certificate). *Application fee:* $60 ($95 for international students). Electronic applications accepted. *Dean,* Dr. Shawn Gerstenberger, 702-895-1565, Fax: 702-895-5184, E-mail: shawn.gerstenberger@unlv.edu.

School of Nursing Students: 55 full-time (51 women), 70 part-time (63 women); includes 37 minority (1 Black or African American, non-Hispanic/Latino; 16 Asian, non-Hispanic/Latino; 10 Hispanic/Latino; 10 Two or more races, non-Hispanic/Latino), 5 international. Average age 37. 155 applicants, 41% accepted, 47 enrolled. *Faculty:* 12 full-time (11 women), 12 part-time/adjunct (all women). Expenses: Contact institution. *Financial support:* In 2016–17, 1 research assistantship with partial tuition reimbursement (averaging $20,250 per year), 3 teaching assistantships with partial tuition reimbursements (averaging $16,208 per year) were awarded; institutionally sponsored loans, scholarships/grants, health care benefits, and unspecified assistantships also available. Financial award application deadline: 3/15. In 2016, 23 master's, 15 doctorates awarded. *Program availability:* Part-time, 100% online, blended/hybrid learning. Offers biobehavioral nursing (Advanced Certificate); family nurse practitioner (Advanced Certificate); nursing (MS, DNP, PhD); nursing education (Advanced Certificate). *Application deadline:* For fall admission, 2/1 for domestic students. *Application fee:* $60 ($95 for international students). Electronic applications accepted. *Dean,* Dr. Carolyn Yucha, 702-895-3906, Fax: 702-895-4807, E-mail: carolyn.yucha@unlv.edu.

William F. Harrah College of Hotel Administration Students: 33 full-time (15 women), 68 part-time (35 women); includes 30 minority (4 Black or African American, non-Hispanic/Latino; 2 American Indian or Alaska Native, non-Hispanic/Latino; 12 Asian, non-Hispanic/Latino; 4 Hispanic/Latino; 8 Two or more races, non-Hispanic/Latino), 20 international. Average age 34. 92 applicants, 45% accepted, 21 enrolled. *Faculty:* 16 full-time (5 women), 2 part-time/adjunct (1 woman). Expenses: Contact institution. *Financial support:* In 2016–17, 4 research assistantships with partial tuition reimbursements (averaging $15,890 per year), 24 teaching assistantships with partial tuition reimbursements (averaging $12,500 per year) were awarded; institutionally sponsored loans, scholarships/grants, health care benefits, and unspecified assistantships also available. Financial award application deadline: 3/15. In 2016, 36 master's, 7 doctorates awarded. *Program availability:* Part-time, evening/weekend, 100% online, blended/hybrid learning. Offers hotel administration (MHA, MS, PhD). *Application deadline:* For fall admission, 8/1 for domestic students, 5/1 for international students; for spring admission, 11/15 for domestic students, 10/1 for international students. *Application fee:* $60 ($95 for international students). Electronic applications accepted. *Dean,* Dr. Stowe Shoemaker, 702-895-3308, Fax: 702-895-4109, E-mail: stowe.shoemaker@unlv.edu.

School of Dental Medicine Students: 83 full-time (34 women); includes 49 minority (1 Black or African American, non-Hispanic/Latino; 1 American Indian or Alaska Native, non-Hispanic/Latino; 41 Asian, non-Hispanic/Latino; 5 Hispanic/Latino; 1 Native Hawaiian or other Pacific Islander, non-Hispanic/Latino). Average age 26. 1,961 applicants, 9% accepted, 83 enrolled. *Faculty:* 62 full-time (22 women), 37 part-time/adjunct (8 women). Expenses: Contact institution. *Financial support:* In 2016–17, 28 students received support. Federal Work-Study, institutionally sponsored loans, scholarships/grants, health care benefits, and unspecified assistantships available. Support available to part-time students. Financial award applicants required to submit FAFSA. *Program availability:* Part-time, evening/weekend, online learning. Offers dental medicine (DMD); oral biology (MS). *Application deadline:* For winter admission, 1/30 for domestic students. Applications are processed on a rolling basis. *Application fee:* $75 ($100 for international students). Electronic applications accepted. *Application Contact:* Victoria Arthur, Administrative Assistant, 702-774-2524, Fax: 702-774-2521, E-mail: victoria.arthur@unlv.edu. *Assistant Dean of Admissions and Student Affairs,* Dr. Christine Ancajas, 702-774-2522, Fax: 702-774-2521, E-mail: christine.ancajas@unlv.edu.

William S. Boyd School of Law Students: 294 full-time (137 women), 102 part-time (47 women); includes 135 minority (24 Black or African American, non-Hispanic/Latino; 3 American Indian or Alaska Native, non-Hispanic/Latino; 18 Asian, non-Hispanic/Latino; 69 Hispanic/Latino; 1 Native Hawaiian or other Pacific Islander, non-Hispanic/Latino; 20 Two or more races, non-Hispanic/Latino), 9 international. Average age 30. 669 applicants, 35% accepted, 116 enrolled. *Faculty:* 39 full-time (25 women), 22 part-time/adjunct (5 women). Expenses: Contact institution. *Financial support:* In 2016–17, 249 students received support, including 13 fellowships (averaging $12,950 per year), 61 research assistantships (averaging $1,000 per year); career-related internships or fieldwork and scholarships/grants also available. Support available to part-time students.

Financial award application deadline: 6/1; financial award applicants required to submit FAFSA. In 2016, 9 master's, 116 doctorates awarded. *Program availability:* Part-time, evening/weekend. Offers gaming law and regulation (LL M); law (JD). *Application deadline:* For fall admission, 6/1 for domestic and international students. Applications are processed on a rolling basis. *Application fee:* $50. Electronic applications accepted. *Application Contact:* Christina Prendergast, Admission and Records Assistant, 702-895-2424, Fax: 702-895-2414, E-mail: christina.prendergast@unlv.edu. *Dean,* Daniel W. Hamilton, 702-895-3671, Fax: 702-895-1095, E-mail: christine.smith@unlv.edu.

UNIVERSITY OF NEVADA, RENO, Reno, NV 89557

General Information State-supported, coed, university. CGS member. *Graduate housing:* Rooms and/or apartments available on a first-come, first-served basis to single and married students. Housing application deadline: 5/16. *Research affiliation:* National Institutes of Health (nursing), Desert Research Institute (natural resource sciences, environmental sciences).

GRADUATE UNITS

Graduate School *Program availability:* Part-time, evening/weekend, online learning. Offers atmospheric sciences (MS, PhD); Basque studies (PhD); biomedical engineering (MS, PhD); cell and molecular biology (MS, PhD); cellular and molecular pharmacology and physiology (PhD); chemical physics (PhD); ecology, evolution, and conservation biology (PhD); environmental sciences and health (MS, PhD); hydrogeology (MS, PhD); hydrology (MS, PhD); social psychology (PhD). Electronic applications accepted.

College of Agriculture, Biotechnology and Natural Resources Offers agriculture, biotechnology and natural resources (MS, PhD); animal science (MS); biochemistry (MS, PhD); biotechnology (MS); natural resources and environmental sciences (MS); nutrition (MS); resource economics (MS, PhD). Electronic applications accepted.

College of Business Administration *Program availability:* Part-time, online learning. Offers accounting and information systems (M Acc); business administration (M Acc, MA, MBA, MS); economics (MA, MS); finance (MS); information systems (MS). Electronic applications accepted.

College of Education Offers counseling and educational psychology (M Ed, MA, MS, Ed D, PhD, Ed S); curriculum and instruction (PhD); curriculum, teaching and learning (Ed D, PhD); education (M Ed, MA, MS, Ed D, PhD, Ed S); educational leadership (M Ed, MA, MS, Ed D, PhD, Ed S); educational specialties (M Ed, MS, Ed D, PhD); elementary education (M Ed, MA, MS); human studies and family studies (MS); literacy studies (M Ed, MA, Ed D, PhD); secondary education (M Ed, MA, MS); special education (M Ed, MA, MS, Ed D, PhD); special education and disability studies (PhD); teaching English to speakers of other languages (MA). Electronic applications accepted.

College of Engineering Offers chemical engineering (MS, PhD); civil and environmental engineering (MS, PhD); computer science and engineering (MS, PhD); electrical engineering (MS, PhD); engineering (MS, PhD); materials science and engineering (MS, PhD); mechanical engineering (MS, PhD). Electronic applications accepted.

College of Liberal Arts *Program availability:* Part-time, evening/weekend, online learning. Offers anthropology (MA, PhD); behavior analysis (MA, PhD); clinical psychology (MA, PhD); cognitive brain science (MA, PhD); criminal justice (MA); English (MA, MATE, PhD); fine arts (MFA); French (MA); German (MA); history (MA, PhD); judicial studies (MJS, PhD); justice management (MJM); liberal arts (MA, MATE, MFA, MJM, MJS, MM, MPA, PhD); music (MA, MM); philosophy (MA); political science (MA, PhD); public administration (MPA); public administration and policy (MPA); social research and justice studies (MA, MJM, MJS, PhD); sociology (MA); Spanish (MA); speech communications (MA). Electronic applications accepted.

College of Science Offers biology (MS); chemistry (MS, PhD); earth sciences and engineering (MS, PhD); geochemistry (MS, PhD); geography (MS, PhD); geological engineering (MS, PhD); geology (MS, PhD); geophysics (MS, PhD); land use planning (MS); mathematics (MS); mining engineering (MS); physics (MS, PhD); science (MATM, MS, PhD); teaching mathematics (MATM). Electronic applications accepted.

Division of Health Sciences Offers health sciences (MPH, MS, MSN, MSW, DNP, PhD); nursing (MSN, DNP); public health (MPH, PhD); social work (MSW); speech pathology (PhD); speech pathology and audiology (MS). Electronic applications accepted.

Donald W. Reynolds School of Journalism Offers journalism (MA). Electronic applications accepted.

School of Medicine Offers medicine (MD).

UNIVERSITY OF NEW BRUNSWICK FREDERICTON, Fredericton, NB E3B 5A3, Canada

General Information Province-supported, coed, university. *Graduate housing:* Rooms and/or apartments available on a first-come, first-served basis to single and married students. Housing application deadline: 5/31. *Research affiliation:* Petroleum Research Atlantic Canada (petroleum), Atlantic Associate for Research in the Mathematical Sciences (mathematical sciences), Atlantic Hydrogen, Inc. (hydrogen), Pulp and Paper Research Institute of Canada (pulp and paper), National Research Council Institute for Information Technology (information technology), Huntsman Marine Science Centre (marine sciences).

GRADUATE UNITS

School of Graduate Studies *Program availability:* Part-time, evening/weekend, online learning. Offers applied health services (MAHSR); citizen engagement/dispute resolution (M Phil); community development (M Phil); interdisciplinary studies (M IDST, PhD); international development (M Phil); leadership (M Phil); sustainability/environmental issues (M Phil); worldviews (PhD).

Faculty of Arts *Program availability:* Part-time. Offers anthropology (MA); applied economics and finance (M Sc); arts (M Sc, MA, PhD); classics (MA); economics (MA); English (MA, PhD); history (MA, PhD); political science (MA); psychology (MA, PhD); sociology (MA, PhD). Electronic applications accepted.

Faculty of Business Administration *Program availability:* Part-time. Offers business administration (MBA); engineering management (MBA); entrepreneurship (MBA); sports and recreation management (MBA). Electronic applications accepted.

Faculty of Computer Science *Program availability:* Part-time. Offers computer science (M Sc CS, PhD). Electronic applications accepted.

Faculty of Education *Program availability:* Part-time, online learning. Offers education (M Ed, PhD). Electronic applications accepted.

Faculty of Engineering *Program availability:* Part-time. Offers applied mechanics (M Eng, M Sc E, PhD); chemical engineering (M Eng, M Sc E, PhD); construction engineering and management (M Eng, M Sc E, PhD); electrical and computer engineering (M Eng, M Sc E, PhD); engineering (M Eng, M Sc E, PhD, Certificate); environmental engineering (M Eng, M Sc E, PhD); environmental studies (M Eng);

geodesy and geomatics engineering (M Eng, M Sc E, PhD); geotechnical engineering (M Eng, M Sc E, PhD); groundwater/hydrology (M Eng, M Sc E, PhD); materials (M Eng, M Sc E, PhD); mechanical engineering (M Eng, M Sc E, PhD); pavements (M Eng, M Sc E, PhD); structures (M Eng, M Sc E, PhD); transportation (M Eng, M Sc E, PhD). Electronic applications accepted.

Faculty of Forestry and Environmental Management *Program availability:* Part-time. Offers ecological foundations of forest management (PhD); environmental management (MEM); forest engineering (M Sc FE, MFE); forest products marketing (MBA); forest resources (M Sc F, MF, PhD). Electronic applications accepted.

Faculty of Kinesiology *Program availability:* Part-time. Offers exercise and sport science (M Sc); sport and recreation management (MBA); sport and recreation studies (MA). Electronic applications accepted.

Faculty of Nursing *Program availability:* Part-time, online learning. Offers nurse educator (MN); nurse practitioner (MN); nursing (MN). Electronic applications accepted.

Faculty of Science *Program availability:* Part-time. Offers biology (M Sc, PhD); chemistry (M Sc, PhD); earth sciences (M Sc); mathematics and statistics (M Sc, PhD); physics (M Sc, PhD); science (M Sc, PhD). Electronic applications accepted.

UNIVERSITY OF NEW BRUNSWICK SAINT JOHN, Saint John, NB E2L 4L5, Canada

General Information Province-supported, coed, comprehensive institution. *Graduate housing:* Rooms and/or apartments available on a first-come, first-served basis to single and married students. Housing application deadline: 3/31. *Research affiliation:* Cook Aquaculture (aquaculture), Horizon Health (health research), Dalhousie Medicine New Brunswick (cancer and general health), Fisheries and Oceans Canada (biology/ecology), New Brunswick Community College (health research).

GRADUATE UNITS

Department of Biology *Program availability:* Part-time. Offers biology (M Sc, PhD). Electronic applications accepted.

Department of Psychology *Program availability:* Part-time. Offers clinical psychology (PhD); experimental psychology (MA, PhD). Electronic applications accepted.

Faculty of Business *Program availability:* Part-time. Offers administration (MBA); electronic commerce (MBA); international business (MBA); natural resource management (MBA). Electronic applications accepted.

UNIVERSITY OF NEW ENGLAND, Biddeford, ME 04005-9526

General Information Independent, coed, comprehensive institution. Enrollment: 8,276 graduate, professional, and undergraduate students; 3,337 full-time matriculated graduate/professional students (2,298 women), 651 part-time matriculated graduate/professional students (520 women). Enrollment by degree level: 2,065 master's, 1,759 doctoral, 164 other advanced degrees. *Graduate faculty:* 147 full-time (81 women), 209 part-time/adjunct (129 women). Tuition and fees vary according to degree level, program and student level. *Graduate housing:* On-campus housing not available. *Student services:* Campus employment opportunities, campus safety program, career counseling, exercise/wellness program, free psychological counseling, international student services, low-cost health insurance, multicultural affairs office, services for students with disabilities, teacher training, writing training. *Library facilities:* Jack S. Ketchum Library plus 1 other. Collection: Books: 135,000 (physical), 660,000 (digital/electronic); Serial titles: 95,000 (digital/electronic); Databases: 200. Weekly public service hours: 146; study areas open 24 hours, 5–7 days a week; students can reserve study rooms.

Computer facilities: Computer purchase and lease plans are available. 91 computers available on campus for general student use. A campuswide network can be accessed from student residence rooms and from off campus. Online class registration is available.

Website: http://www.une.edu/

General Application Contact: Scott Steinberg, Dean of University Admission, 207-221-4225, Fax: 207-523-1925, E-mail: ssteinberg@une.edu.

GRADUATE UNITS

College of Arts and Sciences Students: 15 full-time (10 women), 4 part-time (2 women); includes 1 minority (Asian, non-Hispanic/Latino). Average age 25. 32 applicants, 22% accepted, 6 enrolled. *Faculty:* 35 full-time (21 women), 4 part-time/adjunct (2 women). Expenses: Contact institution. *Financial support:* Fellowships, research assistantships, teaching assistantships, career-related internships or fieldwork, scholarships/grants, traineeships, and unspecified assistantships available. Financial award application deadline: 5/1; financial award applicants required to submit FAFSA. In 2016, 15 master's awarded. *Program availability:* Part-time. Offers biological science (MS); marine science (MS). *Application deadline:* Applications are processed on a rolling basis. Electronic applications accepted. *Application Contact:* Scott Steinberg, Dean of University Admissions, 207-221-4225, Fax: 207-523-1925, E-mail: ssteinberg@une.edu. *Dean, College of Arts and Sciences,* Dr. Jeanne A.K. Hey, 207-602-2371, Fax: 207-602-5973, E-mail: jhey@une.edu.

College of Dental Medicine Students: 252 full-time (127 women); includes 42 minority (4 Black or African American, non-Hispanic/Latino; 33 Asian, non-Hispanic/Latino; 1 Hispanic/Latino; 4 Two or more races, non-Hispanic/Latino), 9 international. Average age 27. 1,850 applicants, 10% accepted, 64 enrolled. *Faculty:* 20 full-time (10 women), 24 part-time/adjunct (5 women). Expenses: Contact institution. *Financial support:* Application deadline: 5/1; applicants required to submit FAFSA. Offers dental medicine (DMD). *Application deadline:* For fall admission, 11/1 for domestic and international students. Electronic applications accepted. *Application Contact:* Scott Steinberg, Dean of University Admissions, 207-221-4225, Fax: 207-523-1925, E-mail: ssteinberg@une.edu. *Dean, College of Dental Medicine,* Dr. Jon Ryder, 207-221-4707, Fax: 207-523-1915, E-mail: jryder2@une.edu.

College of Graduate and Professional Studies Students: 891 full-time (667 women), 359 part-time (261 women); includes 309 minority (215 Black or African American, non-Hispanic/Latino; 2 American Indian or Alaska Native, non-Hispanic/Latino; 63 Asian, non-Hispanic/Latino; 2 Native Hawaiian or other Pacific Islander, non-Hispanic/Latino; 9 Two or more races, non-Hispanic/Latino). Average age 36. 777 applicants, 50% accepted, 316 enrolled. *Faculty:* 67 part-time/adjunct (46 women). Expenses: Contact institution. *Financial support:* Application deadline: 5/1; applicants required to submit FAFSA. In 2016, 292 master's, 34 doctorates, 130 other advanced degrees awarded. *Program availability:* Part-time, evening/weekend, online only, 100% online. Offers applied nutrition (MS); career and technical education (MS Ed); curriculum and instruction (MS Ed); education (CAGS, Post-Master's Certificate); education leadership (Ed D); educational leadership (MS Ed); generalist (MS Ed); health informatics (MS, Graduate Certificate); inclusion education (MS Ed); literacy K-12 (MS Ed); medical education leadership (MMEL); public health (Graduate Certificate);

reading specialist (MS Ed); social work (MSW). *Application deadline:* Applications are processed on a rolling basis. Electronic applications accepted. *Associate Provost for Online Worldwide Learning/Dean of the College of Graduate and Professional Studies,* Dr. Martha Wilson, 207-221-4985, E-mail: mwilson13@une.edu.

College of Osteopathic Medicine Students: 694 full-time (339 women); includes 110 minority (3 Black or African American, non-Hispanic/Latino; 2 American Indian or Alaska Native, non-Hispanic/Latino; 90 Asian, non-Hispanic/Latino; 5 Hispanic/Latino; 10 Two or more races, non-Hispanic/Latino), 27 international. Average age 27. 4,346 applicants, 9% accepted, 178 enrolled. *Faculty:* 34 full-time (14 women), 31 part-time/adjunct (12 women). Expenses: Contact institution. *Financial support:* Application deadline: 5/1; applicants required to submit FAFSA. In 2016, 118 doctorates awarded. *Program availability:* Part-time. Offers osteopathic medicine (DO). *Application deadline:* For fall admission, 3/1 for domestic students. *Application Contact:* Scott Steinberg, Dean of University Admission, 207-221-4225, Fax: 207-523-1925, E-mail: ssteinberg@une.edu. *Dean, College of Osteopathic Medicine,* Dr. Jane Carreiro, 207-602-2898, E-mail: deanunecom@une.edu.

College of Pharmacy Students: 369 full-time (219 women); includes 136 minority (42 Black or African American, non-Hispanic/Latino; 3 American Indian or Alaska Native, non-Hispanic/Latino; 68 Asian, non-Hispanic/Latino; 14 Hispanic/Latino; 1 Native Hawaiian or other Pacific Islander, non-Hispanic/Latino; 8 Two or more races, non-Hispanic/Latino), 4 international. Average age 26. 447 applicants, 42% accepted, 68 enrolled. *Faculty:* 24 full-time (9 women), 3 part-time/adjunct (1 woman). Expenses: Contact institution. *Financial support:* Application deadline: 5/1; applicants required to submit FAFSA. In 2016, 88 doctorates awarded. Offers pharmacy (Pharm D). *Application deadline:* For fall admission, 3/1 for domestic students. Applications are processed on a rolling basis. Electronic applications accepted. *Application Contact:* Scott Steinberg, Dean of University Admission, 207-221-4225, Fax: 207-523-1925, E-mail: ssteinberg@une.edu. *Dean, College of Pharmacy,* Dr. Gayle A. Brazeau, 207-221-4500, Fax: 207-523-1927, E-mail: gbrazeau@une.edu.

Westbrook College of Health Professions Students: 1,116 full-time (936 women), 288 part-time (257 women); includes 261 minority (168 Black or African American, non-Hispanic/Latino; 6 American Indian or Alaska Native, non-Hispanic/Latino; 41 Asian, non-Hispanic/Latino; 20 Hispanic/Latino; 9 Native Hawaiian or other Pacific Islander, non-Hispanic/Latino; 17 Two or more races, non-Hispanic/Latino), 2 international. Average age 32. 3,327 applicants, 22% accepted, 453 enrolled. *Faculty:* 42 full-time (31 women), 81 part-time/adjunct (63 women). Expenses: Contact institution. *Financial support:* Application deadline: 5/1; applicants required to submit FAFSA. In 2016, 472 master's, 71 doctorates awarded. *Program availability:* Part-time, online learning. Offers nurse anesthesia (MSNA); occupational therapy (MS); physical therapy (DPT); physician assistant (MS); social work (MSW). *Application deadline:* Applications are processed on a rolling basis. Electronic applications accepted. *Application Contact:* Scott Steinberg, Dean of University Admission, 207-221-4225, Fax: 207-523-1925, E-mail: ssteinberg@une.edu. *Dean, Westbrook College of Health Professions,* Dr. Elizabeth Francis-Connolly, 207-221-4523, E-mail: efrancisconnolly@une.edu.

UNIVERSITY OF NEW HAVEN, West Haven, CT 06516

General Information Independent, coed, comprehensive institution. CGS member. *Enrollment:* 6,835 graduate, professional, and undergraduate students; 1,181 full-time matriculated graduate/professional students (568 women), 634 part-time matriculated graduate/professional students (264 women). *Enrollment by degree level:* 1,764 master's, 33 doctoral, 18 other advanced degrees. *Graduate faculty:* 112 full-time (36 women), 87 part-time/adjunct (19 women). *Tuition:* Full-time $15,660; part-time $870 per credit hour. *Required fees:* $200; $85 per term. Tuition and fees vary according to program. *Graduate housing:* Room and/or apartments available on a first-come, first-served basis to single students; on-campus housing not available to married students. *Student services:* Campus employment opportunities, campus safety program, career counseling, free psychological counseling, international student services, low-cost health insurance, multicultural affairs office, services for students with disabilities, writing training. *Library facilities:* Marvin K. Peterson Library.

Computer facilities: Computer purchase and lease plans are available. A campuswide network can be accessed from student residence rooms. Online class registration, computer repair services are available.
Website: http://www.newhaven.edu/

General Application Contact: Michelle Mason, Director of Graduate Enrollment, 203-932-7440, E-mail: gradinfo@newhaven.edu.

GRADUATE UNITS

Graduate School Students: 1,181 full-time (568 women), 634 part-time (264 women); includes 335 minority (175 Black or African American, non-Hispanic/Latino; 5 American Indian or Alaska Native, non-Hispanic/Latino; 57 Asian, non-Hispanic/Latino; 64 Hispanic/Latino; 1 Native Hawaiian or other Pacific Islander, non-Hispanic/Latino; 33 Two or more races, non-Hispanic/Latino), 629 international. Average age 28. 2,986 applicants, 65% accepted, 618 enrolled. *Faculty:* 112 full-time (36 women), 87 part-time/adjunct (19 women). Expenses: Contact institution. *Financial support:* Research assistantships with partial tuition reimbursements, teaching assistantships with partial tuition reimbursements, career-related internships or fieldwork, Federal Work-Study, scholarships/grants, and unspecified assistantships available. Support available to part-time students. Financial award applicants required to submit FAFSA. In 2016, 932 master's, 2 doctorates, 125 other advanced degrees awarded. *Program availability:* Part-time, evening/weekend, 100% online, blended/hybrid learning. *Application deadline:* Applications are processed on a rolling basis. *Application fee:* $50. Electronic applications accepted. *Application Contact:* Michelle Mason, Director of Graduate Admissions, 203-932-7440, E-mail: gradinfo@newhaven.edu.

College of Arts and Sciences Students: 182 full-time (133 women), 56 part-time (37 women); includes 49 minority (23 Black or African American, non-Hispanic/Latino; 2 American Indian or Alaska Native, non-Hispanic/Latino; 10 Asian, non-Hispanic/Latino; 7 Hispanic/Latino; 7 Two or more races, non-Hispanic/Latino), 23 international. Average age 26. 272 applicants, 85% accepted, 101 enrolled. *Faculty:* 23 full-time (14 women), 13 part-time/adjunct (5 women). Expenses: Contact institution. *Financial support:* Research assistantships with partial tuition reimbursements, teaching assistantships with partial tuition reimbursements, career-related internships or fieldwork, Federal Work-Study, scholarships/grants, and unspecified assistantships available. Support available to part-time students. Financial award application deadline: 5/1; financial award applicants required to submit FAFSA. In 2016, 209 master's, 21 other advanced degrees awarded. *Program availability:* Part-time, evening/weekend. Offers applications of psychology (Graduate Certificate); arts and sciences (MA, MS, Graduate Certificate); cellular and molecular biology (MS, Graduate Certificate); community clinical services (MA); community psychology (MA); conflict management (MA); environmental ecology (MS); environmental education (MS); environmental geoscience (MS); environmental health and management (MS); environmental science (MS); forensic psychology (MA);

geographical information systems (MS, Graduate Certificate); human nutrition (MS); industrial organizational psychology (MA); industrial-human resources psychology (MA); nutritional genomics (MS, Graduate Certificate); organizational development and consultation (MA); program development (MA); psychology of conflict management (Graduate Certificate). *Application deadline:* Applications are processed on a rolling basis. *Application fee:* $50. Electronic applications accepted. *Application Contact:* Michelle Mason, Director of Graduate Admissions, 203-932-7440, E-mail: gradinfo@newhaven.edu. *Dean of the College of Arts and Sciences,* Dr. Lourdes Álvarez, 203-932-7256, Fax: 203-931-6080, E-mail: lalvarez@newhaven.edu.

College of Business Students: 247 full-time (130 women), 170 part-time (90 women); includes 107 minority (63 Black or African American, non-Hispanic/Latino; 17 Asian, non-Hispanic/Latino; 18 Hispanic/Latino; 9 Two or more races, non-Hispanic/Latino), 103 international. Average age 30. 337 applicants, 83% accepted, 151 enrolled. *Faculty:* 23 full-time (7 women), 15 part-time/adjunct (5 women). Expenses: Contact institution. *Financial support:* Research assistantships with partial tuition reimbursements, teaching assistantships with partial tuition reimbursements, career-related internships or fieldwork, Federal Work-Study, scholarships/grants, and unspecified assistantships available. Support available to part-time students. Financial award application deadline: 5/1; financial award applicants required to submit FAFSA. In 2016, 213 master's, 38 other advanced degrees awarded. *Program availability:* Part-time, evening/weekend. Offers accounting (MBA); business (EMBA, MBA, MS, Graduate Certificate); business administration (EMBA, MBA, Graduate Certificate); business intelligence (MBA); business management (Graduate Certificate); business policy and strategic leadership (MBA); collegiate athletic administration (MS); facility management (MS); finance (MBA); global marketing (MBA); health care administration (MS); health care management (Graduate Certificate); health care marketing (MS); health policy and finance (MS); human resource management in health care (MS); human resources management (MBA, Graduate Certificate); long-term care (MS); long-term health care (Graduate Certificate); managed care (MS); medical group management (MS); sport analytics (MS); sport management (MBA, Graduate Certificate); taxation (MS), Graduate Certificate). *Application deadline:* Applications are processed on a rolling basis. *Application fee:* $50. Electronic applications accepted. *Application Contact:* Michelle Mason, Director of Graduate Enrollment, 203-932-7067, E-mail: mmason@newhaven.edu. *Dean,* Dr. Brian Kench, 203-932-7115, E-mail: bkench@newhaven.edu.

Henry C. Lee College of Criminal Justice and Forensic Sciences Students: 304 full-time (179 women), 241 part-time (105 women); includes 146 minority (77 Black or African American, non-Hispanic/Latino; 1 American Indian or Alaska Native, non-Hispanic/Latino; 15 Asian, non-Hispanic/Latino; 37 Hispanic/Latino; 1 Native Hawaiian or other Pacific Islander, non-Hispanic/Latino; 15 Two or more races, non-Hispanic/Latino), 51 international. Average age 30. 395 applicants, 88% accepted, 205 enrolled. *Faculty:* 32 full-time (10 women), 32 part-time/adjunct (7 women). Expenses: Contact institution. *Financial support:* Research assistantships with partial tuition reimbursements, teaching assistantships with partial tuition reimbursements, career-related internships or fieldwork, Federal Work-Study, scholarships/grants, and unspecified assistantships available. Support available to part-time students. Financial award applicants required to submit FAFSA. In 2016, 177 master's, 2 doctorates, 42 other advanced degrees awarded. *Program availability:* Part-time, evening/weekend, online learning. Offers advanced investigation (MS); city management (MPA); community-clinical services (MPA); crime analysis (MS); criminal investigations (MS); criminal justice (MS, PhD); criminal justice and forensic sciences (MPA, MS, PhD, Graduate Certificate); criminal justice management (MS, Graduate Certificate); criminalistics (MS); emergency management (MS, Graduate Certificate); financial crimes investigations (MS); fire administration (MS); fire science (MS); fire science administration (MS); fire/arson investigation (MS, Graduate Certificate); forensic computer investigation (MS, Graduate Certificate); forensic computer investigations (MS); forensic psychology (MS, Graduate Certificate); forensic science (MS); forensic science/fire science (Graduate Certificate); forensic technology (MS); health care management (MPA); information protection and security (MS, Graduate Certificate); long-term health care (MPA); national security (MS, Graduate Certificate); national security administration (Graduate Certificate); personnel and labor relations (MPA); public administration (MPA, Graduate Certificate); public safety management (MS, Graduate Certificate); victim advocacy and services management (Graduate Certificate); victimology (MS). *Application deadline:* Applications are processed on a rolling basis. *Application fee:* $50. Electronic applications accepted. *Application Contact:* Michelle Mason, Director of Graduate Enrollment, 203-932-7067, E-mail: mmason@newhaven.edu. *Dean,* Dr. Mario Gaboury, 203-932-7253, E-mail: mgaboury@newhaven.edu.

Tagliatela College of Engineering Students: 448 full-time (126 women), 167 part-time (32 women); includes 33 minority (12 Black or African American, non-Hispanic/Latino; 2 American Indian or Alaska Native, non-Hispanic/Latino; 15 Asian, non-Hispanic/Latino; 2 Hispanic/Latino; 2 Two or more races, non-Hispanic/Latino), 452 international. Average age 26. 1,982 applicants, 54% accepted, 161 enrolled. Expenses: Contact institution. *Financial support:* Research assistantships with partial tuition reimbursements, teaching assistantships with partial tuition reimbursements, career-related internships or fieldwork, Federal Work-Study, scholarships/grants, and unspecified assistantships available. Support available to part-time students. Financial award applicants required to submit FAFSA. In 2016, 333 master's, 24 other advanced degrees awarded. *Program availability:* Part-time, evening/weekend. Offers biomedical engineering (MS); computer programming (Graduate Certificate); computer science (MS); control systems (MS); cyber systems (MS); data science (MS); digital signal processing and communication (MS); electrical and computer engineering (MS); electrical engineering (MS); engineering (MS, MSIE, Graduate Certificate); engineering and operations management (MS); engineering management (MS); environmental engineering (MS); industrial and hazardous waste (MS); industrial engineering (MSIE); Lean Six Sigma (Graduate Certificate); mechanical engineering (MS); network systems (MS); quality engineering (Graduate Certificate); software development (MS); water and wastewater treatment (MS); water resources (MS). *Application deadline:* Applications are processed on a rolling basis. *Application fee:* $50. Electronic applications accepted. *Application Contact:* Michelle Mason, Director of Graduate Enrollment, 203-932-7440, E-mail: mmason@newhaven.edu. *Dean,* Dr. Ronald Harichandran, 203-932-7167, E-mail: rharichandran@newhaven.edu.

UNIVERSITY OF NEW MEXICO, Albuquerque, NM 87131-2039

General Information State-supported, coed, university. CGS member. *Enrollment:* 2,173 full-time matriculated graduate/professional students (1,141 women), 2,045 part-time matriculated graduate/professional students (1,153 women). *Enrollment by degree level:* 2,312 master's, 1,798 doctoral, 108 other advanced degrees. *Graduate faculty:* 794 full-time (365 women), 78 part-time/adjunct (39 women). *Graduate housing:* Rooms and/or apartments available on a first-come, first-served basis to single and married students. Typical cost: $5590 per year for single students; $6390 per year for married students. Room charges vary according to board plan, campus/location and housing facility selected. Housing application deadline: 7/16. *Student services:* Campus employment opportunities, campus safety program, career counseling, child daycare facilities, exercise/wellness program, free psychological counseling, grant writing training, international student services, low-cost health insurance, multicultural affairs office, services for students with disabilities, teacher training, writing training. *Library facilities:* College of University Libraries and Learning Sciences plus 7 others. *Collection:* Students can reserve study rooms. *Research affiliation:* Phillips Laboratory, Oak Ridge National Laboratory, Sandia National Laboratories, New Mexico Consortium, Los Alamos National Laboratory, Lovelace Respiratory Research Institute.

Computer facilities: Computer purchase and lease plans are available. 990 computers available on campus for general student use. A campuswide network can be accessed from student residence rooms and from off campus. Online class registration is available.

Website: http://www.unm.edu/

General Application Contact: Deborah Kieltyka, Associate Director, Admissions, 505-277-3140, Fax: 505-277-6686, E-mail: deborahk@unm.edu.

GRADUATE UNITS

Anderson School of Management Students: 277 full-time (118 women), 357 part-time (182 women); includes 284 minority (10 Black or African American, non-Hispanic/Latino; 20 American Indian or Alaska Native, non-Hispanic/Latino; 23 Asian, non-Hispanic/Latino; 206 Hispanic/Latino; 25 Two or more races, non-Hispanic/Latino), 61 international. Average age 31. 338 applicants, 56% accepted, 176 enrolled. *Faculty:* 64 full-time (24 women), 23 part-time/adjunct (11 women). Expenses: Contact institution. *Financial support:* In 2016–17, 101 students received support, including 30 fellowships (averaging $13,838 per year), 52 research assistantships with partial tuition reimbursements available (averaging $8,655 per year); career-related internships or fieldwork, Federal Work-Study, scholarships/grants, and unspecified assistantships also available. Support available to part-time students. Financial award application deadline: 6/1; financial award applicants required to submit FAFSA. In 2016, 246 master's awarded. *Program availability:* Part-time, evening/weekend. Offers accounting (MBA); advanced accounting (M Acct); entrepreneurship (MBA); finance (MBA); information assurance (M Acct, MBA); information systems and assurance (MS); international management (MBA); international management in Latin America (MBA); management (EMBA, M Acct, MBA, MS); management information systems (MBA); management of technology (MBA); marketing management (MBA); operations management (MBA); organizational behavior and human resources management (MBA); professional accounting (M Acct); strategic management and policy (MBA); tax accounting (M Acct). *Application deadline:* For fall admission, 4/1 priority date for domestic and international students; for spring admission, 10/1 priority date for domestic and international students. Applications are processed on a rolling basis. *Application fee:* $50. Electronic applications accepted. *Application Contact:* Lisa Beauchene, Student Recruitment Specialist, 505-277-6471, E-mail: andersonadvising@unm.edu. *Acting Dean,* Dr. Shawn Berman, 505-277-1792, E-mail: sberman@unm.edu.

Graduate Studies Students: 2,173 full-time (1,141 women), 2,045 part-time (1,153 women); includes 1,467 minority (83 Black or African American, non-Hispanic/Latino; 177 American Indian or Alaska Native, non-Hispanic/Latino; 102 Asian, non-Hispanic/Latino; 993 Hispanic/Latino; 4 Native Hawaiian or other Pacific Islander, non-Hispanic/Latino; 108 Two or more races, non-Hispanic/Latino), 707 international. Average age 34. 3,699 applicants, 39% accepted, 1058 enrolled. *Faculty:* 794 full-time (365 women), 78 part-time/adjunct (39 women). Expenses: Contact institution. *Financial support:* Fellowships, research assistantships, teaching assistantships, career-related internships or fieldwork, Federal Work-Study, institutionally sponsored loans, scholarships/grants, health care benefits, tuition waivers (full and partial), and project assistantships, residencies available. Support available to part-time students. Financial award application deadline: 3/1; financial award applicants required to submit FAFSA. In 2016, 975 master's, 257 doctorates, 57 other advanced degrees awarded. *Program availability:* Part-time, evening/weekend, online only, 100% online, blended/hybrid learning. Offers hydroscience (MWR); policy management (MWR). *Application fee:* $50. Electronic applications accepted. *Application Contact:* Deborah Kieltyka, Associate Director, Admissions, 505-277-3140, Fax: 505-277-6686, E-mail: deborahk@unm.edu. *Dean,* Dr. Julie A. Coonrod, 505-277-2711, Fax: 505-277-7405, E-mail: jcoonrod@unm.edu.

College of Arts and Sciences Students: 698 full-time (357 women), 564 part-time (276 women); includes 330 minority (13 Black or African American, non-Hispanic/Latino; 25 American Indian or Alaska Native, non-Hispanic/Latino; 28 Asian, non-Hispanic/Latino; 222 Hispanic/Latino; 1 Native Hawaiian or other Pacific Islander, non-Hispanic/Latino; 41 Two or more races, non-Hispanic/Latino), 264 international. Average age 32. 1,496 applicants, 29% accepted, 286 enrolled. *Faculty:* 321 full-time (136 women), 8 part-time/adjunct (3 women). Expenses: Contact institution. *Financial support:* Scholarships/grants, health care benefits, tuition waivers (full and partial), and unspecified assistantships available. Financial award application deadline: 3/1; financial award applicants required to submit FAFSA. In 2016, 225 master's, 114 doctorates awarded. *Program availability:* Part-time. Offers American studies (MA, PhD); archaeology (MA, MS, PhD); arts and sciences (MA, MFA, MS, PhD); behavioral neuroscience (PhD); biology (MS, PhD); chemistry (MS, PhD); clinical psychology (PhD); cognitive neuroimaging (PhD); communication (MA, PhD); comparative literature and cultural studies (MA); creative writing (MFA); developmental psychology (PhD); earth and planetary sciences (MS, PhD); econometrics (MA); economic theory (MA); English (MA, PhD); environmental/natural resource economics (MA, PhD); ethnology (MA, MS, PhD); evolution (PhD); evolutionary anthropology (PhD); French (MA); French studies (PhD); geography and environmental studies (MS); German studies (MA); health psychology (PhD); history (MA, PhD); imaging science (MS, PhD); international/development and sustainability economics (MA, PhD); Latin American studies (MA, PhD); linguistics (MA, PhD); mathematics (MS, PhD); optical science and engineering (MS, PhD); philosophy (MA, PhD); photonics (MS, PhD); physics (MS, PhD); political science (MA, PhD); Portuguese (MA); public archaeology (MA, MS, PhD); public economics (MA, PhD); quantitative methodology (MS); sociology (MA, PhD); Spanish (MA); Spanish and Portuguese (PhD); speech-language pathology (MS); statistics (MS, PhD). *Application fee:* $50. Electronic applications accepted. *Application Contact:* Vicki Hall, Academic Administrator III, 505-277-6131, Fax: 505-277-0351, E-mail: vhall@unm.edu. *Dean,* Dr. Brenda J. Claiborne, 505-277-6131, Fax: 505-277-0351, E-mail: brendac@unm.edu.

College of Education Students: 389 full-time (253 women), 603 part-time (457 women); includes 463 minority (34 Black or African American, non-Hispanic/Latino; 68 American Indian or Alaska Native, non-Hispanic/Latino; 21 Asian, non-Hispanic/Latino; 316 Hispanic/Latino; 24 Two or more races, non-Hispanic/Latino), 81

international. Average age 37. 427 applicants, 64% accepted, 224 enrolled. *Faculty:* 110 full-time (70 women), 16 part-time/adjunct (12 women). Expenses: Contact institution. *Financial support:* Career-related internships or fieldwork, Federal Work-Study, scholarships/grants, health care benefits, and unspecified assistantships available. Support available to part-time students. Financial award application deadline: 3/1; financial award applicants required to submit FAFSA. In 2016, 288 master's, 33 doctorates, 39 other advanced degrees awarded. *Program availability:* Part-time, evening/weekend. Offers American Indian education (MA); art education (MA); bilingual education (MA, PhD); community health education (MS); counseling (MA); counselor education (PhD); curriculum and instruction (PhD); education (MA, MS, Ed D, PhD, Ed S, Graduate Certificate); educational leadership (MA, Ed D, Ed S); educational linguistics (PhD); educational psychology (MA, PhD); educational thought and sociocultural studies (MA, PhD); exercise science (PhD); family life education (MA); family relations (MA); family studies (PhD); human development in families (MA); intensive social, language and behavioral needs (Graduate Certificate); learning and behavioral exceptionalities (MA); literacy/language arts (MA, PhD); math, science, and educational technology (MA); mental retardation and severe disabilities (MA); multicultural teacher and childhood education (Ed D, PhD); nutrition (MS); social studies (MA); special education (Ed D, PhD, Ed S); sports administration (PhD); TESOL (MA, PhD). *Application deadline:* For fall admission, 3/1 for international students; for spring admission, 8/1 for international students. *Application fee:* $50. Electronic applications accepted. *Application Contact:* Academic Graduate Coordinator, 505-277-3190, E-mail: coeac@unm.edu. *Dean,* Dr. Richard Howell, 505-277-2231, Fax: 505-277-8427, E-mail: rhowell@unm.edu.

College of Fine Arts Students: 96 full-time (56 women), 86 part-time (56 women); includes 44 minority (2 Black or African American, non-Hispanic/Latino; 6 American Indian or Alaska Native, non-Hispanic/Latino; 3 Asian, non-Hispanic/Latino; 26 Hispanic/Latino; 7 Two or more races, non-Hispanic/Latino), 24 international. Average age 32. 199 applicants, 50% accepted, 59 enrolled. *Faculty:* 67 full-time (35 women), 12 part-time/adjunct (9 women). Expenses: Contact institution. *Financial support:* Unspecified assistantships available. Financial award application deadline: 3/1; financial award applicants required to submit FAFSA. In 2016, 41 master's awarded. *Program availability:* Part-time. Offers art history (MA); art of the Americas (MA); collaborative piano (M Mu); conducting (M Mu); dance (MFA); dance history (MA); dramatic writing (MFA); fine arts (M Mu, MA, MFA, PhD); history of architecture (PhD); history of graphic arts (PhD); history of photography (PhD); modern Latin American art (PhD); music education (M Mu); music history and literature (M Mu); Native American art (PhD); performance (M Mu); Pre-Columbian art and architecture (PhD); Spanish colonial art (PhD); studio art (MFA); theatre education and outreach (MA); theory and composition (M Mu). *Application fee:* $50. *Application Contact:* Deanna Sanchez-Mulcahy, Associate Director, Admissions, 505-277-4817, Fax: 505-277-0708, E-mail: dmulcahy@unm.edu. *Dean,* Dr. Jim Linnell, 505-277-2112, Fax: 505-277-0708, E-mail: jlinnell@unm.edu.

College of Pharmacy *Program availability:* Part-time. Offers pharmaceutical sciences (MS, PhD); pharmacy (MS, PhD, Pharm D). Electronic applications accepted.

College of University Libraries and Learning Sciences Students: 26 full-time (15 women), 76 part-time (51 women); includes 42 minority (1 Black or African American, non-Hispanic/Latino; 4 American Indian or Alaska Native, non-Hispanic/Latino; 5 Asian, non-Hispanic/Latino; 29 Hispanic/Latino; 3 Two or more races, non-Hispanic/Latino), 6 international. Average age 45. 30 applicants, 80% accepted, 21 enrolled. *Faculty:* 12 full-time (9 women). Expenses: Contact institution. *Financial support:* Fellowships, research assistantships, teaching assistantships with tuition reimbursements, and career-related internships or fieldwork available. Financial award application deadline: 3/1; financial award applicants required to submit FAFSA. In 2016, 19 master's, 4 doctorates awarded. *Program availability:* Part-time, evening/weekend, online learning. Offers organization, information and learning sciences (MA, PhD, Ed S). *Application deadline:* For fall admission, 3/15 for domestic and international students; for spring admission, 10/15 for domestic and international students. *Application fee:* $50. Electronic applications accepted. *Application Contact:* Linda Wood, Program Coordinator, 505-277-4131, Fax: 505-277-1427, E-mail: woodl@unm.edu. *Program Director,* Dr. Charlotte Gunawardens, 505-277-5046, Fax: 505-277-1427, E-mail: lani@unm.edu.

Health Sciences Center Students: 267 full-time (181 women), 109 part-time (75 women); includes 164 minority (6 Black or African American, non-Hispanic/Latino; 12 American Indian or Alaska Native, non-Hispanic/Latino; 14 Asian, non-Hispanic/Latino; 123 Hispanic/Latino; 2 Native Hawaiian or other Pacific Islander, non-Hispanic/Latino; 7 Two or more races, non-Hispanic/Latino), 25 international. Average age 30. 218 applicants, 47% accepted, 94 enrolled. *Faculty:* 92 full-time (51 women), 6 part-time/adjunct (3 women). Expenses: Contact institution. Offers biochemistry and molecular biology (MS, PhD); cell biology and physiology (MS, PhD); clinical and translational science (Certificate); community health (MPH); dental hygiene (MS); education (MS); epidemiology (MPH); health sciences (MOT, MPH, MPT, MS, MSN, DNP, DPT, MD, PhD, Pharm D, Certificate); health systems, services and policy (MPH); laboratory management (MS); molecular genetics and microbiology (MS, PhD); neuroscience (MS, PhD); nursing (MSN, DNP, PhD); occupational therapy (MOT); pathology (MS, PhD); physical therapy (DPT); physician assistant studies (MS); research and development (MS); toxicology (MS, PhD). *Application Contact:* Deborah Kieltyka, Associate Director, Admissions, 505-277-3140, Fax: 505-277-6686, E-mail: deborahk@unm.edu. *Interim Vice President,* Dr. R. Philip Eaton.

School of Architecture and Planning Students: 146 full-time (66 women), 32 part-time (17 women); includes 72 minority (3 Black or African American, non-Hispanic/Latino; 18 American Indian or Alaska Native, non-Hispanic/Latino; 1 Asian, non-Hispanic/Latino; 46 Hispanic/Latino; 4 Two or more races, non-Hispanic/Latino), 32 international. Average age 32. 151 applicants, 52% accepted, 58 enrolled. *Faculty:* 31 full-time (13 women), 14 part-time/adjunct (3 women). Expenses: Contact institution. *Financial support:* Application deadline: 3/1; applicants required to submit FAFSA. In 2016, 73 master's, 11 other advanced degrees awarded. Offers architecture (M Arch); architecture and planning (M Arch, MCRP, MLA, Graduate Certificate); community and regional planning (MCRP); historic preservation and regionalism (Graduate Certificate); landscape architecture (MLA). *Application deadline:* For fall admission, 2/1 for domestic and international students. *Application fee:* $50. Electronic applications accepted. *Application Contact:* Elizabeth M. Rowe, Senior Academic Adviser, 505-277-1303, Fax: 505-277-0076, E-mail: erowe@unm.edu. *Dean,* Geraldine Forbes Isais, 505-277-2053, E-mail: gforbes@unm.edu.

School of Engineering Students: 363 full-time (71 women), 375 part-time (75 women); includes 154 minority (7 Black or African American, non-Hispanic/Latino; 3 American Indian or Alaska Native, non-Hispanic/Latino; 19 Asian, non-Hispanic/Latino; 111 Hispanic/Latino; 14 Two or more races, non-Hispanic/Latino), 257 international. Average age 30. 798 applicants, 27% accepted, 171 enrolled. *Faculty:* 113 full-time (20 women), 14 part-time/adjunct (5 women). Expenses: Contact institution. *Financial* *support:* Federal Work-Study, scholarships/grants, health care benefits, and unspecified assistantships available. Financial award application deadline: 3/1; financial award applicants required to submit FAFSA. In 2016, 142 master's, 53 doctorates awarded. *Program availability:* Part-time. Offers biomedical engineering (MS, PhD); chemical engineering (MS, PhD); civil engineering (M Eng, MSCE); computer engineering (MS, PhD); computer science (MS, PhD); construction management (MCM); electrical and computer engineering (MS, PhD); engineering (M Eng, MCM, MEME, MS, MSCE, PhD); manufacturing engineering (MEME); mechanical engineering (MS, PhD); nanoscience and microsystems engineering (MS, PhD); nuclear engineering (MS, PhD). *Application deadline:* For fall admission, 1/15 priority date for domestic and international students; for spring admission, 7/14 priority date for domestic and international students. Applications are processed on a rolling basis. *Application fee:* $50. Electronic applications accepted. *Application Contact:* Deborah Kieltyka, Associate Director, Admissions, 505-277-3140, Fax: 505-277-6686, E-mail: deborahk@unm.edu. *Dean,* Christos Christodoulou, 505-277-5522, Fax: 505-277-5521, E-mail: christos@unm.edu.

School of Public Administration Students: 76 full-time (50 women), 113 part-time (81 women); includes 110 minority (8 Black or African American, non-Hispanic/Latino; 25 American Indian or Alaska Native, non-Hispanic/Latino; 3 Asian, non-Hispanic/Latino; 71 Hispanic/Latino; 3 Two or more races, non-Hispanic/Latino), 12 international. Average age 37. 81 applicants, 64% accepted, 47 enrolled. *Faculty:* 14 full-time (6 women), 4 part-time/adjunct (1 woman). Expenses: Contact institution. *Financial support:* Fellowships with partial tuition reimbursements, research assistantships with partial tuition reimbursements, career-related internships or fieldwork, scholarships/grants, health care benefits, and unspecified assistantships available. Financial award application deadline: 3/31; financial award applicants required to submit FAFSA. In 2016, 95 master's awarded. *Program availability:* Part-time, evening/weekend, online learning. Offers health administration (MHA); public administration (MHA, MPA). *Application deadline:* For fall admission, 4/1 for domestic students, 3/1 for international students; for spring admission, 10/1 for domestic students, 8/1 for international students. *Application fee:* $50. Electronic applications accepted. *Application Contact:* Gene V. Henley, Associate Director and Graduate Academic Advisor, 505-277-9196, Fax: 505-277-2529, E-mail: spadvise@unm.edu. *Director,* Dr. Uday Desai, 505-277-1092, Fax: 505-277-2529, E-mail: ucdesai@unm.edu.

School of Law Offers law (JD). Electronic applications accepted.

School of Medicine Offers medicine (MOT, MPH, MS, DPT, MD, PhD, Certificate); university science teaching (Certificate). Electronic applications accepted.

UNIVERSITY OF NEW ORLEANS, New Orleans, LA 70148

General Information State-supported, coed, university. *Graduate housing:* Rooms and/or apartments available on a first-come, first-served basis to single and married students. *Research affiliation:* John C. Stennis Space Center (acoustics, computer science), Northrop Grumman Corporation (engineering), TJ Watson Research Center—IBM (chemistry), Paratek Microwave, Inc. (nanotechnology), Applied Research Lab-Penn State University (engineering), Lockheed Martin Corporation (materials).

GRADUATE UNITS

Graduate School *Program availability:* Part-time, evening/weekend. Electronic applications accepted.

College of Business Administration *Program availability:* Part-time, evening/weekend. Offers accounting (MS); business administration (MBA, MS, PhD); economics and finance (MS); financial economics (PhD); health care management (MS); hospitality and tourism management (MS); taxation (MS). Electronic applications accepted.

College of Education and Human Development *Program availability:* Part-time, online learning. Offers counselor education (M Ed, PhD); curriculum and instruction (M Ed, PhD); education and human development (M Ed, MAT, PhD); educational leadership (M Ed, PhD); special education and habilitative services (M Ed). Electronic applications accepted.

College of Engineering *Program availability:* Part-time. Offers engineering (MS, PhD); engineering and applied sciences (PhD); engineering management (MS); mechanical engineering (MS). Electronic applications accepted.

College of Liberal Arts *Program availability:* Part-time, evening/weekend. Offers arts administration (MA); design (MFA); English (MA); film production (MFA); fine arts (MFA); foreign languages (MA); geography (MA); history (MA); liberal arts (MA, MFA, MM, MPA, MS, MURP, PhD); music (MM); political science (MA, PhD); public administration (MPA); sociology (MA); theatre performance (MFA); transportation (MS); urban and regional planning (MURP); urban studies (MS, PhD). Electronic applications accepted.

College of Sciences *Program availability:* Part-time, evening/weekend. Offers biological sciences (MS, PhD); chemistry (MS, PhD); computer science (MS); earth and environmental sciences (MS); mathematics (MS); physics (MS, PhD); psychology (MS, PhD); sciences (MS, PhD). Electronic applications accepted.

UNIVERSITY OF NORTH ALABAMA, Florence, AL 35632-0001

General Information State-supported, coed, comprehensive institution. *Enrollment:* 7,492 graduate, professional, and undergraduate students; 351 full-time matriculated graduate/professional students (194 women), 776 part-time matriculated graduate/professional students (472 women). *Enrollment by degree level:* 1 master's, 78 other advanced degrees. *Graduate faculty:* 101 full-time (44 women), 16 part-time/adjunct (6 women). Tuition, state resident: full-time $2799; part-time $1866 per semester. Tuition, nonresident: full-time $5598; part-time $3732 per semester. *Required fees:* $915; $642 per semester. Tuition and fees vary according to course load. *Graduate housing:* Rooms and/or apartments available on a first-come, first-served basis to single and married students. Typical cost: $5757 per year for single students; $8280 per year for married students. Room charges vary according to board plan and housing facility selected. *Student services:* Campus employment opportunities, campus safety program, career counseling, exercise/wellness program, free psychological counseling, grant writing training, international student services, multicultural affairs office, services for students with disabilities, writing training. *Library facilities:* Collier Library plus 3 others. *Collection:* Books: 224,081 (physical), 421,886 (digital/electronic); Serial titles: 4,086 (physical), 54,780 (digital/electronic); Databases: 150. Weekly public service hours: 98; students can reserve study rooms.

Computer facilities: 925 computers available on campus for general student use. A campuswide network can be accessed. Online class registration is available. Website: http://www.una.edu/

General Application Contact: Hillary N. Coats, Graduate Admissions Coordinator, 256-765-4447, E-mail: hcoats@una.edu.

GRADUATE UNITS

Anderson College of Nursing Students: 46 full-time (44 women), 50 part-time (44 women); includes 19 minority (18 Black or African American, non-Hispanic/Latino; 1 Hispanic/Latino). Average age 38. 39 applicants, 87% accepted, 29 enrolled. *Faculty:* 5 full-time (all women). Expenses: Contact institution. *Financial support:* In 2016–17, 3 students received support. Scholarships/grants available. Financial award application deadline: 2/1; financial award applicants required to submit FAFSA. In 2016, 29 master's awarded. *Program availability:* 100% online, blended/hybrid learning. Offers nursing (MSN). *Application deadline:* Applications are processed on a rolling basis. *Application fee:* $50 ($100 for international students). Electronic applications accepted. *Application Contact:* Hillary N. Coats, Graduate Admissions Coordinator, 256-465-4447, E-mail: graduate@una.edu. *Dean,* Dr. Vicky G. Pierce, 256-765-6301, E-mail: vgpierce@una.edu.

College of Arts and Sciences Students: 40 full-time (19 women), 100 part-time (62 women); includes 18 minority (13 Black or African American, non-Hispanic/Latino; 3 Asian, non-Hispanic/Latino; 1 Hispanic/Latino; 1 Two or more races, non-Hispanic/Latino), 15 international. Average age 32. 74 applicants, 78% accepted, 48 enrolled. *Faculty:* 32 full-time (16 women), 5 part-time/adjunct (2 women). Expenses: Contact institution. *Financial support:* In 2016–17, 31 students received support. Career-related internships or fieldwork, scholarships/grants, and unspecified assistantships available. Financial award application deadline: 2/1; financial award applicants required to submit FAFSA. In 2016, 30 master's awarded. *Program availability:* Part-time, 100% online. Offers arts and sciences (MA, MPS, MS, MSCJ); criminal justice (MSCJ); English (MA); family studies (MS); geospatial science (MS); history (MA); professional studies (MPS); public history (MA). *Application deadline:* Applications are processed on a rolling basis. *Application fee:* $50 ($100 for international students). Electronic applications accepted. *Application Contact:* Hillary N. Coats, Graduate Admissions Coordinator, 256-765-4447, E-mail: graduate@una.edu. *Dean,* Dr. Carmen L. Burkhalter, 256-765-4288, Fax: 256-765-4778, E-mail: cburkhalter@una.edu.

College of Business Students: 180 full-time (77 women), 411 part-time (199 women); includes 208 minority (84 Black or African American, non-Hispanic/Latino; 4 American Indian or Alaska Native, non-Hispanic/Latino; 106 Asian, non-Hispanic/Latino; 6 Hispanic/Latino; 8 Two or more races, non-Hispanic/Latino), 37 international. Average age 34. 263 applicants, 84% accepted, 173 enrolled. *Faculty:* 24 full-time (2 women), 6 part-time/adjunct (3 women). Expenses: Contact institution. *Financial support:* In 2016–17, 114 students received support. Scholarships/grants available. Financial award application deadline: 2/1; financial award applicants required to submit FAFSA. In 2016, 156 master's awarded. *Program availability:* Part-time, 100% online, blended/hybrid learning. Offers business administration (MBA). *Application deadline:* Applications are processed on a rolling basis. *Application fee:* $50 ($100 for international students). Electronic applications accepted. *Application Contact:* Hillary N. Coats, Graduate Admissions Coordinator, 256-765-4447, E-mail: graduate@una.edu. *Dean,* Dr. Gregory A. Carnes, 256-765-4261, Fax: 256-765-4170, E-mail: gacarnes@una.edu.

College of Education Students: 85 full-time (54 women), 215 part-time (167 women); includes 37 minority (20 Black or African American, non-Hispanic/Latino; 6 American Indian or Alaska Native, non-Hispanic/Latino; 6 Hispanic/Latino; 5 Two or more races, non-Hispanic/Latino), 3 international. Average age 33. 118 applicants, 72% accepted, 69 enrolled. *Faculty:* 40 full-time (21 women), 4 part-time/adjunct (0 women). Expenses: Contact institution. *Financial support:* In 2016–17, 33 students received support. Scholarships/grants and unspecified assistantships available. Financial award application deadline: 2/1; financial award applicants required to submit FAFSA. In 2016, 109 master's, 25 other advanced degrees awarded. *Program availability:* Part-time, 100% online, blended/hybrid learning. Offers clinical mental health counseling (MA); collaborative teacher special education (MA Ed); counseling (MA Ed); education (MA, MA Ed, MS, Ed S); education leadership (MA Ed); elementary education (MA Ed, Ed S); health and human performance (MS); instructional leadership (MA Ed); secondary education (MA Ed); special education (MA Ed); teacher education multiple levels (MA Ed). *Application deadline:* Applications are processed on a rolling basis. *Application fee:* $50 ($100 for international students). Electronic applications accepted. *Application Contact:* Hillary N. Coats, Graduate Admissions Coordinator, 256-765-4447, E-mail: graduate@una.edu. *Dean,* Dr. Donna Lefort, 256-765-4252, Fax: 256-765-4664, E-mail: dpjacobs@una.edu.

UNIVERSITY OF NORTH CAROLINA AT ASHEVILLE, Asheville, NC 28804-3299

General Information State-supported, coed, comprehensive institution. *Enrollment:* 3,830 graduate, professional, and undergraduate students; 2 full-time matriculated graduate/professional students (1 woman), 19 part-time matriculated graduate/professional students (10 women). *Enrollment by degree level:* 21 master's. *Graduate faculty:* 5 full-time (1 woman), 4 part-time/adjunct (0 women). Tuition, state resident: full-time $4818. Tuition, nonresident: full-time $20,820. *Required fees:* $2936. Part-time tuition and fees vary according to course load. *Graduate housing:* Room and/or apartments available on a first-come, first-served basis to single students; on-campus housing not available to married students. Typical cost: $4890 per year ($8746 including board). Room and board charges vary according to board plan and housing facility selected. Housing application deadline: 5/1. *Student services:* Campus employment opportunities, career counseling, exercise/wellness program, international student services, low-cost health insurance, multicultural affairs office, services for students with disabilities, writing training. *Library facilities:* D. Hiden Ramsey Library. *Collection:* Books: 282,040 (physical), 539,250 (digital/electronic); Serial titles: 187 (physical), 48,748 (digital/electronic); Databases: 138. Students can reserve study rooms.

Computer facilities: Computer purchase and lease plans are available. 477 computers available on campus for general student use. A campuswide network can be accessed from student residence rooms and from off campus. Online class registration is available. Website: http://www.unca.edu/

General Application Contact: Jordan Dolfi, Program Associate, Graduate Studies, 828-250-2399.

GRADUATE UNITS

Master of Liberal Arts and Sciences Program Students: 2 full-time (1 woman), 19 part-time (9 women); includes 2 minority (1 Black or African American, non-Hispanic/Latino; 1 Asian, non-Hispanic/Latino). Average age 43. 18 applicants, 83% accepted, 8 enrolled. *Faculty:* 5 full-time (1 woman), 4 part-time/adjunct (0 women). Expenses: Contact institution. *Financial support:* Health care benefits available. Financial award application deadline: 5/1; financial award applicants required to submit FAFSA. In 2016, 19 master's awarded. *Program availability:* Part-time, evening/weekend. Offers climate change and society (Graduate Certificate); environmental and cultural sustainability (Graduate Certificate). *Application deadline:*

For fall admission, 4/15 for domestic students; for spring admission, 11/15 for domestic students. Applications are processed on a rolling basis. *Application fee:* $75. Electronic applications accepted. *Application Contact:* Jordan Dolfi, Program Associate, Master of Liberal Arts and Sciences Program and the Asheville Graduate Center, 828-251-6099, E-mail: jdolfi@unca.edu. *Director, Master of Liberal Arts and Sciences Program and the Asheville Graduate Center,* Gerard Voos, 828-232-5040, E-mail: gvoos@unca.edu.

THE UNIVERSITY OF NORTH CAROLINA AT CHAPEL HILL, Chapel Hill, NC 27599

General Information State-supported, coed, university. CGS member. *Enrollment:* 29,469 graduate, professional, and undergraduate students; 9,234 full-time matriculated graduate/professional students (5,058 women), 1,175 part-time matriculated graduate/professional students (586 women). *Enrollment by degree level:* 4,568 master's, 5,835 doctoral, 6 other advanced degrees. *Graduate faculty:* 3,558 full-time (1,665 women), 289 part-time/adjunct (171 women). *Graduate housing:* Rooms and/or apartments available on a first-come, first-served basis to single and married students. *Student services:* Campus employment opportunities, campus safety program, career counseling, child daycare facilities, exercise/wellness program, free psychological counseling, grant writing training, international student services, low-cost health insurance, multicultural affairs office, services for students with disabilities, teacher training, writing training. *Library facilities:* Davis Library plus 12 others. *Collection:* Books: 7.6 million (physical), 1.6 million (digital/electronic); Serial titles: 161,097 (digital/electronic); Databases: 1,282. Weekly public service hours: 109; study areas open 24 hours, 5–7 days a week; students can reserve study rooms. *Research affiliation:* Research Triangle Institute, Centers for Disease Control (CDC), Triangle Universities Nuclear Laboratory.

Computer facilities: Computer purchase and lease plans are available. 867 computers available on campus for general student use. A campuswide network can be accessed from student residence rooms and from off campus. Online class registration is available.
Website: http://www.unc.edu/

GRADUATE UNITS

Eshelman School of Pharmacy Students: 108 full-time (54 women); includes 33 minority (5 Black or African American, non-Hispanic/Latino; 3 American Indian or Alaska Native, non-Hispanic/Latino; 11 Asian, non-Hispanic/Latino; 5 Hispanic/Latino; 1 Native Hawaiian or other Pacific Islander, non-Hispanic/Latino; 8 Two or more races, non-Hispanic/Latino), 14 international. Average age 26. 268 applicants, 9% accepted, 25 enrolled. *Faculty:* 118 full-time (51 women), 378 part-time/adjunct (200 women). Expenses: Contact institution. *Financial support:* In 2016–17, 18 fellowships with full tuition reimbursements (averaging $30,000 per year), 56 research assistantships with full tuition reimbursements (averaging $30,000 per year) were awarded; career-related internships or fieldwork, Federal Work-Study, institutionally sponsored loans, scholarships/grants, traineeships, health care benefits, tuition waivers (full), and unspecified assistantships also available. Financial award application deadline: 12/13. In 2016, 8 master's, 16 doctorates awarded. Offers pharmaceutical sciences (PhD); pharmaceutical sciences - health system pharmacy administration (MS); pharmacy (Pharm D). *Application deadline:* For fall admission, 12/13 for domestic students, 12/13 priority date for international students. Applications are processed on a rolling basis. *Application fee:* $85. Electronic applications accepted. *Application Contact:* Mimi Lewis, Assistant Director of Recruitment and Admissions, 919-962-0097, Fax: 919-966-9428, E-mail: mimi_lewis@unc.edu. *Dean,* Dr. Robert A. Blouin, 919-966-1122, Fax: 919-966-6919, E-mail: bob_blouin@unc.edu.

Graduate School Students: 5,112 full-time (3,194 women), 661 part-time (403 women); includes 1,477 minority (397 Black or African American, non-Hispanic/Latino; 15 American Indian or Alaska Native, non-Hispanic/Latino; 300 Asian, non-Hispanic/Latino; 310 Hispanic/Latino; 5 Native Hawaiian or other Pacific Islander, non-Hispanic/Latino; 450 Two or more races, non-Hispanic/Latino), 799 international. Average age 30. 12,730 applicants, 27% accepted, 1671 enrolled. *Faculty:* 1,880 full-time (849 women), 112 part-time/adjunct (57 women). Expenses: Contact institution. *Financial support:* Fellowships with full and partial tuition reimbursements, research assistantships with full and partial tuition reimbursements, teaching assistantships with full and partial tuition reimbursements, career-related internships or fieldwork, Federal Work-Study, institutionally sponsored loans, scholarships/grants, traineeships, health care benefits, and unspecified assistantships available. Support available to part-time students. Financial award applicants required to submit FAFSA. In 2016, 1,305 master's, 548 doctorates awarded. *Program availability:* Online learning. *Application deadline:* For fall admission, 12/12 priority date for domestic and international students. Applications are processed on a rolling basis. *Application fee:* $85. Electronic applications accepted. *Application Contact:* Director of Admissions and Enrolled Students. *Dean.*

College of Arts and Sciences *Program availability:* Part-time. Offers acting (MFA); anthropology (MA, PhD); art history (MA, PhD); arts and sciences (MA, MCRP, MFA, MPA, MRP, MS, MSRA, PhD, Certificate); athletic training (MA); behavioral neuroscience psychology (PhD); botany (MA, MS, PhD); cell biology, development, and physiology (MA, MS, PhD); cell motility and cytoskeleton (PhD); chemistry (MA, MS, PhD); city and regional planning (MCRP); classical archaeology (MA, PhD); classics (MA, PhD); clinical psychology (PhD); cognitive psychology (PhD); communication studies (MA, PhD); computer science (MS, PhD); costume production (MFA); developmental psychology (PhD); ecology (MA, MS, PhD); ecology and behavior (MA, MS, PhD); economics (MS, PhD); English (MA, PhD); exercise physiology (MA); folklore (MA); French (MA, PhD); genetics and molecular biology (MA, MS, PhD); geography (MA, PhD); geological sciences (MS, PhD); German studies (PhD); global studies (MA); history (MA, PhD); Italian (MA, PhD); Latin American studies (Certificate); linguistics (MA); marine sciences (MS, PhD); mathematics (MA, MS, PhD); morphology, systematics, and evolution (MA, MS, PhD); music (MA, PhD); operations research (MS, PhD); philosophy (MA, PhD); physics (MS, PhD); planning (PhD); political science (MA, PhD); Portuguese (MA, PhD); public policy (PhD); public policy analysis (PhD); quantitative psychology (PhD); religious studies (MA, PhD); Romance languages (MA, PhD); Romance philology (MA, PhD); social psychology (MA, PhD); sociology (MA, PhD); Spanish (MA, PhD); sport administration (MA); statistics (MS, PhD); studio art (MFA); technical production (MFA); trans-Atlantic studies (MA). Electronic applications accepted.

Gillings School of Global Public Health Students: 748 full-time (534 women), 556 part-time (387 women); includes 416 minority (118 Black or African American, non-Hispanic/Latino; 2 American Indian or Alaska Native, non-Hispanic/Latino; 122 Asian, non-Hispanic/Latino; 87 Hispanic/Latino; 87 Two or more races, non-Hispanic/Latino), 164 international. Average age 31. 1,985 applicants, 41% accepted, 375 enrolled. *Faculty:* 358 full-time (182 women), 420 part-time/adjunct (217 women). Expenses: Contact institution. *Financial support:* Fellowships, research assistantships, teaching assistantships, career-related internships or fieldwork, Federal Work-Study, scholarships/grants, traineeships, health care benefits, and unspecified assistantships

available. Financial award application deadline: 12/10; financial award applicants required to submit FAFSA. In 2016, 399 master's, 112 doctorates awarded. *Program availability:* Part-time, 100% online, blended/hybrid learning. Offers biostatistics (MPH, MS, Dr PH, PhD); clinical research (MSCR); environmental engineering (MPH, MS, MSEE, MSPH); environmental health sciences (MPH, MS, MSPH, PhD); epidemiology (MPH, PhD); global public health (MHA, MPH, MS, MSCR, MSEE, MSPH, Dr PH, PhD); health behavior (MPH, PhD); health care and prevention (MPH); health policy and management (MHA, MPH, MSPH, Dr PH, PhD); leadership (MPH); maternal and child health (MPH, MSPH, Dr PH, PhD); nutrition (MPH, PhD); nutrition with registered dietitian component (MPH); nutritional biochemistry (MS); occupational health nursing (MPH); veterinary epidemiology (MPH). *Application deadline:* For fall admission, 1/10 for domestic and international students. Applications are processed on a rolling basis. *Application fee:* $85. Electronic applications accepted. *Application Contact:* Johnston King, Enrollment Management Coordinator, 919-962-6314, Fax: 919-966-6352, E-mail: sph-osa@unc.edu. *Dean,* Dr. Barbara K. Rimer, 919-966-3245, Fax: 919-966-7678.

School of Education *Program availability:* Part-time. Offers culture, curriculum and change (MA, PhD); early childhood intervention and family support (M Ed); early childhood, intervention and literacy (MA, PhD); education (M Ed, MA, MAT, MSA, Ed D, PhD); education for experienced teachers (K-12) (M Ed); educational leadership (Ed D); educational psychology, measurement and evaluation (MA, PhD); English (Grades 9-12) (MAT); English as a second language (MAT); French (Grades K-12) (MAT); German (Grades K-12) (MAT); Japanese (Grades K-12) (MAT); Latin (Grades 9-12) (MAT); mathematics (Grades 9-12) (MAT); music (Grades K-12) (MAT); school administration (MSA); school counseling (M Ed); school psychology (M Ed, MA, PhD); science (Grades 9-12) (MAT); social studies (Grades 9-12) (MAT); Spanish (Grades K-12) (MAT). Electronic applications accepted.

School of Government Offers government (MPA). Electronic applications accepted.

School of Information and Library Science Students: 190 full-time (140 women), 26 part-time (15 women); includes 35 minority (7 Black or African American, non-Hispanic/Latino; 7 Asian, non-Hispanic/Latino; 6 Hispanic/Latino; 15 Two or more races, non-Hispanic/Latino), 36 international. Average age 28. 258 applicants, 68% accepted, 83 enrolled. *Faculty:* 26 full-time (11 women), 46 part-time/adjunct (23 women). Expenses: Contact institution. *Financial support:* In 2016–17, 59 fellowships with full tuition reimbursements (averaging $2,565 per year), 46 research assistantships with full tuition reimbursements (averaging $25,120 per year), 15 teaching assistantships with full tuition reimbursements (averaging $11,628 per year) were awarded; career-related internships or fieldwork, Federal Work-Study, scholarships/grants, health care benefits, and unspecified assistantships also available. Financial award application deadline: 12/13. In 2016, 69 master's, 4 doctorates awarded. *Program availability:* Part-time. Offers data curation (PMC); information and library science (PhD); information science (MSIS); library science (MSLS). *Application deadline:* For fall admission, 12/13 priority date for domestic and international students; for spring admission, 10/11 for domestic and international students. Applications are processed on a rolling basis. *Application fee:* $85. Electronic applications accepted. *Application Contact:* Lara Bailey, Student Services Coordinator, 919-962-7601, Fax: 919-962-8071, E-mail: bailey@email.unc.edu. *Dean,* Dr. Gary Marchionini, 919-962-8363, Fax: 919-962-8071, E-mail: gary@ils.unc.edu.

School of Media and Journalism Students: 68 full-time (51 women), 59 part-time (42 women); includes 35 minority (10 Black or African American, non-Hispanic/Latino; 4 Asian, non-Hispanic/Latino; 4 Hispanic/Latino; 1 Native Hawaiian or other Pacific Islander, non-Hispanic/Latino; 16 Two or more races, non-Hispanic/Latino), 8 international. Average age 33. 179 applicants, 28% accepted, 42 enrolled. *Faculty:* 47 full-time (21 women), 4 part-time/adjunct (2 women). Expenses: Contact institution. *Financial support:* In 2016–17, 55 students received support, including 47 fellowships with full tuition reimbursements available (averaging $17,319 per year), 3 research assistantships with full tuition reimbursements available (averaging $14,000 per year); scholarships/grants and health care benefits also available. Financial award application deadline: 12/5; financial award applicants required to submit FAFSA. In 2016, 11 master's, 10 doctorates awarded. *Program availability:* Part-time, online learning. Offers mass communication (MA, PhD); technology and communication (MA, Certificate). MA/JD and JD/PhD offered jointly with School of Law. *Application fee:* $85. Electronic applications accepted. *Application Contact:* Casey Hart, Marketing and Instructional Design Coordinator, 919-843-9471, Fax: 919-962-0620, E-mail: mjgrad@unc.edu. *Dean,* Susan King, 919-962-1204, Fax: 919-962-0620, E-mail: susanking@unc.edu.

School of Social Work *Program availability:* Part-time. Offers social work (MSW, PhD). Electronic applications accepted.

Kenan-Flagler Business School *Program availability:* Evening/weekend, online learning. Offers accounting (MAC); business (MAC, MBA, PhD); business administration (MBA, PhD); finance (PhD); marketing (PhD); operations management (PhD); organizational behavior (PhD); strategy (PhD). Electronic applications accepted.

School of Dentistry Offers dental hygiene (MS); dentistry (MS, DDS, PhD); endodontics (MS); epidemiology (MS); operative dentistry (MS); oral and maxillofacial pathology (MS); oral and maxillofacial radiology (MS); oral biology (PhD); orthodontics (MS); pediatric dentistry (MS); periodontology (MS); prosthodontics (MS). Electronic applications accepted.

School of Medicine Offers allied health sciences (MPT, MS, Au D, DPT, PhD); audiology (Au D); biochemistry and biophysics (MS, PhD); bioinformatics and computational biology (PhD); biomedical engineering (MS, PhD); cell and developmental biology (PhD); cell and molecular physiology (PhD); clinical rehabilitation and mental health counseling (MS); experimental pathology (PhD); genetics and molecular biology (PhD); human movement science (PhD); immunology (MS, PhD); medicine (MPT, MS, Au D, DPT, MD, PhD); microbiology (MS, PhD); microbiology and immunology (MS, PhD); neurobiology (PhD); occupational science (MS, PhD); occupational therapy (MS); pathology and laboratory medicine (PhD); pharmacology (PhD); physical therapy (DPT); physical therapy - off campus (DPT); physical therapy - on campus (DPT); rehabilitation counseling and psychology (MS); speech and hearing sciences (MS, Au D, PhD); toxicology (MS, PhD). Electronic applications accepted.

School of Nursing *Program availability:* Part-time. Offers advanced practice registered nurse (DNP); health care systems (DNP); nursing (MSN, PhD, PMC). Electronic applications accepted.

THE UNIVERSITY OF NORTH CAROLINA AT CHARLOTTE, Charlotte, NC 28223-0001

General Information State-supported, coed, university. CGS member. *Enrollment:* 28,721 graduate, professional, and undergraduate students; 2,491 full-time matriculated graduate/professional students (1,278 women), 2,826 part-time matriculated graduate/professional students (1,712 women). *Enrollment by degree level:* 3,348 master's, 905 doctoral, 1,064 other advanced degrees. *Graduate faculty:* 844 full-time (347 women), 78 part-time/adjunct (44 women). Tuition, state resident: full-time $4252. Tuition, nonresident: full-time $17,423. *Required fees:* $3026. Tuition and fees vary according to course load and program. *Graduate housing:* Room and/or apartments available on a first-come, first-served basis to single students; on-campus housing not available to married students. Typical cost: $5910 per year ($10,540 including board). Room and board charges vary according to board plan and housing facility selected. Housing application deadline: 6/1. *Student services:* Campus employment opportunities, campus safety program, career counseling, exercise/wellness program, free psychological counseling, international student services, low-cost health insurance, multicultural affairs office, services for students with disabilities, teacher training, writing training. *Library facilities:* J. Murrey Atkins Library plus 1 other. *Collection:* Books: 1.5 million (physical), 527,672 (digital/electronic); Serial titles: 29,969 (physical), 83,784 (digital/electronic); Databases: 672. Study areas open 24 hours, 5–7 days a week; students can reserve study rooms. *Research affiliation:* McGraw Hill Education (special education and child development), SAS Institute (computer science), SURVICE Engineering Company (physics, optical sciences), Health Resources and Services Administration (public health sciences), National Science Foundation (bioinformatics, genomics), HDR Engineering, Inc. of the Carolinas (civil and environmental engineering).

Computer facilities: 1,600 computers available on campus for general student use. A campuswide network can be accessed from student residence rooms and from off campus. Online class registration is available.
Website: http://www.uncc.edu/

General Application Contact: Kathy B. Giddings, Director of Graduate Admissions, 704-687-5503, Fax: 704-687-1668, E-mail: gradadm@uncc.edu.

GRADUATE UNITS

Belk College of Business Students: 250 full-time (112 women), 388 part-time (113 women); includes 107 minority (34 Black or African American, non-Hispanic/Latino; 31 Asian, non-Hispanic/Latino; 28 Hispanic/Latino; 14 Two or more races, non-Hispanic/Latino), 187 international. Average age 29. 566 applicants, 76% accepted, 251 enrolled. *Faculty:* 81 full-time (26 women), 6 part-time/adjunct (0 women). Expenses: Contact institution. *Financial support:* In 2016–17, 74 students received support, including 13 research assistantships (averaging $17,569 per year), 61 teaching assistantships (averaging $9,885 per year); career-related internships or fieldwork, institutionally sponsored loans, scholarships/grants, unspecified assistantships, and administrative assistantships also available. Support available to part-time students. Financial award application deadline: 3/1; financial award applicants required to submit FAFSA. In 2016, 265 master's, 3 doctorates, 2 other advanced degrees awarded. *Program availability:* Part-time, evening/weekend. Offers applied econometrics (Graduate Certificate); business (M Acct, MBA, MS, DBA, PhD, Graduate Certificate, Post-Master's Certificate, Postbaccalaureate Certificate); business administration (MBA, DBA, PhD); business foundations (Graduate Certificate); economics (MS); management (Post-Master's Certificate); mathematical finance (MS); real estate (MS, Graduate Certificate). *Application deadline:* Applications are processed on a rolling basis. *Application fee:* $75. Electronic applications accepted. *Application Contact:* Kathy B. Giddings, Director of Graduate Admissions, 704-687-5503, Fax: 704-687-1668, E-mail: gradadm@uncc.edu. *Dean,* Dr. Steven Ott, 704-687-7577, Fax: 704-687-1393, E-mail: cob-dean@uncc.edu.

Turner School of Accountancy Students: 68 full-time (40 women), 38 part-time (19 women); includes 14 minority (4 Black or African American, non-Hispanic/Latino; 4 Asian, non-Hispanic/Latino; 3 Hispanic/Latino; 3 Two or more races, non-Hispanic/Latino), 10 international. Average age 27. 138 applicants, 79% accepted, 76 enrolled. *Faculty:* 10 full-time (4 women), 1 part-time/adjunct (0 women). Expenses: Contact institution. *Financial support:* Career-related internships or fieldwork, institutionally sponsored loans, scholarships/grants, and unspecified assistantships available. Support available to part-time students. Financial award application deadline: 3/1; financial award applicants required to submit FAFSA. In 2016, 73 master's awarded. *Program availability:* Part-time, evening/weekend. Offers accountancy (M Acct). *Application deadline:* For fall admission, 3/1 priority date for domestic and international students; for spring admission, 10/1 priority date for domestic and international students; for summer admission, 4/1 priority date for domestic and international students. Applications are processed on a rolling basis. *Application fee:* $75. Electronic applications accepted. *Application Contact:* Kathy B. Giddings, Director of Graduate Admissions, 704-687-5503, Fax: 704-687-1668, E-mail: gradadm@uncc.edu. *Chair,* Dr. Hughlene Burton, 704-687-7701, Fax: 704-687-1382, E-mail: haburton@uncc.edu.

Cato College of Education Students: 286 full-time (228 women), 1,174 part-time (923 women); includes 422 minority (313 Black or African American, non-Hispanic/Latino; 1 American Indian or Alaska Native, non-Hispanic/Latino; 25 Asian, non-Hispanic/Latino; 62 Hispanic/Latino; 21 Two or more races, non-Hispanic/Latino), 23 international. Average age 33. 886 applicants, 85% accepted, 593 enrolled. *Faculty:* 109 full-time (66 women), 28 part-time/adjunct (20 women). Expenses: Contact institution. *Financial support:* In 2016–17, 51 students received support, including 1 fellowship (averaging $32,786 per year), 38 research assistantships (averaging $13,450 per year), 10 teaching assistantships (averaging $8,448 per year); career-related internships or fieldwork, institutionally sponsored loans, scholarships/grants, unspecified assistantships, and administrative assistantships also available. Support available to part-time students. Financial award application deadline: 3/1; financial award applicants required to submit FAFSA. In 2016, 212 master's, 26 doctorates, 266 other advanced degrees awarded. *Program availability:* Part-time, evening/weekend, 100% online, blended/hybrid learning. Offers academically or intellectually gifted (Graduate Certificate); art education (Graduate Certificate); autism spectrum disorders (Graduate Certificate); child and family development: birth through kindergarten (Graduate Certificate); child and family development: early childhood education (MAT); child and family studies: early education (M Ed); counseling (MA); counselor education and supervision (PhD); curriculum and instruction (PhD); education (M Ed, MA, MAT, MSA, Ed D, PhD, Graduate Certificate, Post-Master's Certificate, Postbaccalaureate Certificate); education research, measurement, and evaluation (PhD); educational leadership (Ed D); elementary education (M Ed, MAT, Graduate Certificate); elementary mathematics education (Graduate Certificate); foreign language education (MAT); instructional systems technology (M Ed, Graduate Certificate); middle grades and secondary education (M Ed); middle grades education (MAT); play therapy (Postbaccalaureate Certificate); quantitative analysis (Graduate Certificate); reading education (M Ed); school administration (MSA, Post-Master's Certificate); school counseling (Post-Master's Certificate); secondary education (MAT); special education (M Ed, MAT, PhD, Graduate Certificate); substance abuse counseling (Postbaccalaureate Certificate); teaching (Graduate Certificate); teaching English as a second language (M Ed, MAT, Graduate Certificate); theatre education (Graduate Certificate); university and college teaching (Graduate Certificate). *Application:* Applications are processed on a rolling

basis. *Application fee:* $75. Electronic applications accepted. *Application Contact:* Kathy B. Giddings, Director of Graduate Admissions, 704-687-5503, Fax: 704-687-1668, E-mail: gradadm@uncc.edu. *Dean,* Dr. Ellen McIntyre, 704-687-8722, E-mail: ellen.mcintyre@uncc.edu.

College of Arts and Architecture Students: 100 full-time (57 women), 2 part-time (1 woman); includes 21 minority (9 Black or African American, non-Hispanic/Latino; 1 Asian, non-Hispanic/Latino; 8 Hispanic/Latino; 3 Two or more races, non-Hispanic/Latino), 23 international. Average age 25. 164 applicants, 74% accepted, 47 enrolled. *Faculty:* 48 full-time (18 women). Expenses: Contact institution. *Financial support:* In 2016–17, 39 students received support, including 27 research assistantships (averaging $7,685 per year), 12 teaching assistantships (averaging $3,388 per year); career-related internships or fieldwork, institutionally sponsored loans, scholarships/grants, and unspecified assistantships also available. Support available to part-time students. Financial award application deadline: 3/1; financial award applicants required to submit FAFSA. In 2016, 31 master's, 2 other advanced degrees awarded. *Program availability:* Part-time. Offers arts and architecture (M Arch I, M Arch II, MUD, Graduate Certificate); vocal pedagogy (Graduate Certificate). *Application deadline:* Applications are processed on a rolling basis. *Application fee:* $75. Electronic applications accepted. *Application Contact:* Kathy B. Giddings, Director of Graduate Admissions, 704-687-5503, Fax: 704-687-1668, E-mail: gradadm@uncc.edu. *Dean,* Kenneth A. Lambla, 704-687-0090, E-mail: kalambla@uncc.edu.

School of Architecture Students: 100 full-time (57 women), 2 part-time (1 woman); includes 21 minority (9 Black or African American, non-Hispanic/Latino; 1 Asian, non-Hispanic/Latino; 8 Hispanic/Latino; 3 Two or more races, non-Hispanic/Latino), 23 international. Average age 25. 164 applicants, 74% accepted, 47 enrolled. *Faculty:* 21 full-time (7 women). Expenses: Contact institution. *Financial support:* In 2016–17, 33 students received support, including 25 research assistantships (averaging $7,500 per year), 8 teaching assistantships (averaging $3,112 per year); institutionally sponsored loans, scholarships/grants, and unspecified assistantships also available. Financial award application deadline: 3/1; financial award applicants required to submit FAFSA. In 2016, 31 master's awarded. Offers architecture (M Arch I, M Arch II); urban design (MUD). *Application deadline:* For fall admission, 1/15 priority date for domestic and international students. Applications are processed on a rolling basis. *Application fee:* $75. Electronic applications accepted. *Application Contact:* Kathy B. Giddings, Director of Graduate Admissions, 704-687-5503, Fax: 704-687-1668, E-mail: gradadm@uncc.edu. *Dean,* Kenneth A. Lambla, 704-687-0090, E-mail: kalambla@uncc.edu.

College of Computing and Informatics Students: 499 full-time (170 women), 219 part-time (85 women); includes 58 minority (23 Black or African American, non-Hispanic/Latino; 16 Asian, non-Hispanic/Latino; 11 Hispanic/Latino; 1 Native Hawaiian or other Pacific Islander, non-Hispanic/Latino; 7 Two or more races, non-Hispanic/Latino), 565 international. Average age 26. 2,254 applicants, 38% accepted, 268 enrolled. *Faculty:* 59 full-time (20 women), 9 part-time/adjunct (1 woman). Expenses: Contact institution. *Financial support:* In 2016–17, 183 students received support, including 10 fellowships (averaging $41,745 per year), 64 research assistantships (averaging $10,454 per year), 107 teaching assistantships (averaging $8,532 per year); career-related internships or fieldwork, institutionally sponsored loans, scholarships/grants, unspecified assistantships, and administrative assistantships also available. Support available to part-time students. Financial award application deadline: 3/1; financial award applicants required to submit FAFSA. In 2016, 380 master's, 16 doctorates, 19 other advanced degrees awarded. *Program availability:* Part-time, evening/weekend. Offers advanced databases and knowledge discovery (Graduate Certificate); bioinformatics (PSM); bioinformatics and computational biology (PhD); bioinformatics applications (Graduate Certificate); bioinformatics technology (Graduate Certificate); computer science (MS); computing and informatics (MS, PSM, PhD, Graduate Certificate); computing and information systems (PhD); game design and development (Graduate Certificate); information security and privacy (Graduate Certificate); information technology (MS); management of information technology (Graduate Certificate); network security (Graduate Certificate); secure software development (Graduate Certificate). *Application deadline:* Applications are processed on a rolling basis. *Application fee:* $75. Electronic applications accepted. *Application Contact:* Kathy B. Giddings, Director of Graduate Admissions, 704-687-5503, Fax: 704-687-1668, E-mail: gradadm@uncc.edu. *Interim Dean,* Dr. William J. Tolone, 704-687-8664, E-mail: wjtolone@uncc.edu.

College of Health and Human Services Students: 391 full-time (316 women), 170 part-time (142 women); includes 164 minority (115 Black or African American, non-Hispanic/Latino; 3 American Indian or Alaska Native, non-Hispanic/Latino; 16 Asian, non-Hispanic/Latino; 21 Hispanic/Latino; 9 Two or more races, non-Hispanic/Latino), 17 international. Average age 30. 698 applicants, 55% accepted, 260 enrolled. *Faculty:* 79 full-time (53 women), 19 part-time/adjunct (16 women). Expenses: Contact institution. *Financial support:* In 2016–17, 100 students received support, including 59 research assistantships (averaging $5,900 per year), 40 teaching assistantships (averaging $9,267 per year); career-related internships or fieldwork, institutionally sponsored loans, scholarships/grants, traineeships, unspecified assistantships, and administrative assistantships also available. Support available to part-time students. Financial award application deadline: 3/1; financial award applicants required to submit FAFSA. In 2016, 213 master's, 10 doctorates, 11 other advanced degrees awarded. *Program availability:* Part-time, evening/weekend, 100% online, blended/hybrid learning. Offers community health (Certificate); health administration (MHA); health and human services (MHA, MPH, MS, MSN, MSW, DNP, PhD, Certificate, Graduate Certificate, Post-Master's Certificate); health services research (PhD); kinesiology (MS); public health (MPH); public health core concepts (Graduate Certificate); public health sciences (PhD); respiratory care (MS). *Application deadline:* Applications are processed on a rolling basis. *Application fee:* $75. Electronic applications accepted. *Application Contact:* Kathy B. Giddings, Director of Graduate Admissions, 704-687-5503, Fax: 704-687-1668, E-mail: gradadm@uncc.edu. *Dean,* Dr. Nancy Fey-Yensan, 704-687-7917, E-mail: fey-yensan@uncc.edu.

School of Nursing Students: 112 full-time (82 women), 121 part-time (109 women); includes 53 minority (43 Black or African American, non-Hispanic/Latino; 1 American Indian or Alaska Native, non-Hispanic/Latino; 4 Asian, non-Hispanic/Latino; 3 Hispanic/Latino; 2 Two or more races, non-Hispanic/Latino). Average age 34. 295 applicants, 39% accepted, 90 enrolled. *Faculty:* 24 full-time (22 women), 4 part-time/adjunct (3 women). Expenses: Contact institution. *Financial support:* In 2016–17, 10 students received support, including 8 research assistantships (averaging $3,508 per year), 2 teaching assistantships (averaging $3,450 per year); career-related internships or fieldwork, institutionally sponsored loans, scholarships/grants, traineeships, and unspecified assistantships also available. Support available to part-time students. Financial award application deadline: 3/1; financial award applicants required to submit FAFSA. In 2016, 79 master's, 5 doctorates, 8 other advanced degrees awarded. *Program availability:* Part-time, blended/hybrid learning. Offers adult-gerontology acute care nurse practitioner (Post-Master's Certificate); advanced clinical nursing (MSN); family nurse practitioner across the lifespan (Post-Master's Certificate); nurse anesthesia (MSN); nurse anesthesia across the lifespan (Post-Master's Certificate); nursing (DNP); nursing administration (Graduate Certificate); nursing education (Graduate Certificate); systems/population nursing (MSN). *Application deadline:* For fall admission, 1/10 for domestic and international students; for spring admission, 9/10 for domestic and international students; for summer admission, 4/1 for domestic and international students. Applications are processed on a rolling basis. *Application fee:* $75. Electronic applications accepted. *Application Contact:* Kathy B. Giddings, Director of Graduate Admissions, 704-687-5503, Fax: 704-687-1668, E-mail: gradadm@uncc.edu. *Associate Dean,* Dr. Dee Baldwin, 704-687-7952, Fax: 704-687-6017, E-mail: dbaldwi5@uncc.edu.

School of Social Work Students: 148 full-time (136 women), 1 (woman) part-time; includes 43 minority (29 Black or African American, non-Hispanic/Latino; 3 Asian, non-Hispanic/Latino; 8 Hispanic/Latino; 3 Two or more races, non-Hispanic/Latino). Average age 28. 200 applicants, 70% accepted, 98 enrolled. *Faculty:* 16 full-time (12 women), 10 part-time/adjunct (9 women). Expenses: Contact institution. *Financial support:* In 2016–17, 16 students received support, including 15 research assistantships (averaging $3,720 per year), 1 teaching assistantship (averaging $2,400 per year); career-related internships or fieldwork, Federal Work-Study, institutionally sponsored loans, scholarships/grants, and unspecified assistantships also available. Support available to part-time students. Financial award application deadline: 3/1; financial award applicants required to submit FAFSA. In 2016, 79 master's awarded. *Program availability:* Part-time. Offers social work (MSW). *Application deadline:* For fall admission, 2/1 for domestic and international students. Applications are processed on a rolling basis. *Application fee:* $75. Electronic applications accepted. *Application Contact:* Kathy B. Giddings, Director of Graduate Admissions, 704-687-5503, Fax: 704-687-1668, E-mail: gradadm@uncc.edu. *Associate Professor and MSW Program Director,* Dr. Robert Herman-Smith, 704-687-7180, Fax: 704-687-1658, E-mail: bherman@uncc.edu.

College of Liberal Arts and Sciences Students: 433 full-time (259 women), 367 part-time (232 women); includes 166 minority (67 Black or African American, non-Hispanic/Latino; 2 American Indian or Alaska Native, non-Hispanic/Latino; 19 Asian, non-Hispanic/Latino; 57 Hispanic/Latino; 21 Two or more races, non-Hispanic/Latino), 127 international. Average age 29. 918 applicants, 48% accepted, 253 enrolled. *Faculty:* 342 full-time (147 women), 12 part-time/adjunct (4 women). Expenses: Contact institution. *Financial support:* In 2016–17, 373 students received support, including 16 fellowships (averaging $31,958 per year), 106 research assistantships (averaging $10,228 per year), 248 teaching assistantships (averaging $10,940 per year); career-related internships or fieldwork, institutionally sponsored loans, scholarships/grants, and administrative assistantships also available. Support available to part-time students. Financial award application deadline: 3/1; financial award applicants required to submit FAFSA. In 2016, 190 master's, 34 doctorates, 29 other advanced degrees awarded. *Program availability:* Part-time, evening/weekend. Offers Africana studies (Graduate Certificate); anthropology (MA); applied linguistics (Graduate Certificate); applied mathematics (PhD); applied physics (MS); biological sciences (MS); chemistry (MS); cognitive science (Graduate Certificate); communication studies (MA); criminal justice and criminology (MS); earth sciences (MS); emergency management (Graduate Certificate); English (MA); ethics and applied philosophy (MA, Graduate Certificate); gender, sexuality, and women's studies (Graduate Certificate); geography (MA); geography and urban regional analysis (PhD); gerontology (MA, Graduate Certificate); health psychology (PhD); history (MA); industrial/organizational psychology (MA); languages and culture studies: translating (MA); Latin American studies (MA); liberal arts and sciences (MA, MPA, MS, PhD, Graduate Certificate); liberal studies (MA); mathematics (MS); nanoscale science (PhD); non-profit management (Graduate Certificate); optical science and engineering (MS, PhD); organizational science (PhD); psychology (MA); public administration (MPA); public budgeting and finance (Graduate Certificate); public policy (PhD); religious studies (MA); sociology (MA); technical and professional writing (Graduate Certificate); translating (Graduate Certificate); urban management and policy (Graduate Certificate). *Application deadline:* Applications are processed on a rolling basis. *Application fee:* $75. Electronic applications accepted. *Application Contact:* Kathy B. Giddings, Director of Graduate Admissions, 704-687-5503, Fax: 704-687-1668, E-mail: gradadm@uncc.edu. *Dean,* Dr. Nancy A. Gutierrez, 704-687-0081, E-mail: ngutierr@uncc.edu.

The Graduate School Students: 64 full-time (32 women), 93 part-time (45 women); includes 48 minority (22 Black or African American, non-Hispanic/Latino; 16 Asian, non-Hispanic/Latino; 5 Hispanic/Latino; 1 Native Hawaiian or other Pacific Islander, non-Hispanic/Latino; 4 Two or more races, non-Hispanic/Latino), 57 international. Average age 32. 402 applicants, 36% accepted, 70 enrolled. *Faculty:* 2 full-time (1 woman), 2 part-time/adjunct (both women). Expenses: Contact institution. *Financial support:* In 2016–17, 36 students received support, including 19 research assistantships (averaging $13,567 per year), 3 teaching assistantships (averaging $14,000 per year); career-related internships or fieldwork, institutionally sponsored loans, scholarships/grants, traineeships, unspecified assistantships, and administrative assistantships also available. Support available to part-time students. Financial award application deadline: 3/1; financial award applicants required to submit FAFSA. In 2016, 46 master's, 23 other advanced degrees awarded. *Program availability:* Part-time, evening/weekend. Offers data science and business analytics (MS, PSM, Graduate Certificate); health informatics (PSM). *Application deadline:* Applications are processed on a rolling basis. *Application fee:* $75. Electronic applications accepted. *Application Contact:* Kathy B. Giddings, Director of Graduate Admissions, 704-687-5503, Fax: 704-687-1668, E-mail: gradadm@uncc.edu. *Dean and Associate Provost,* Dr. Thomas L. Reynolds, 704-687-7248, E-mail: gradadm@uncc.edu.

William States Lee College of Engineering Students: 446 full-time (93 women), 192 part-time (39 women); includes 45 minority (20 Black or African American, non-Hispanic/Latino; 9 Asian, non-Hispanic/Latino; 15 Hispanic/Latino; 1 Two or more races, non-Hispanic/Latino), 420 international. Average age 27. 1,373 applicants, 57% accepted, 193 enrolled. *Faculty:* 122 full-time (15 women), 2 part-time/adjunct (1 woman). Expenses: Contact institution. *Financial support:* In 2016–17, 239 students received support, including 5 fellowships (averaging $34,552 per year), 129 research assistantships (averaging $9,419 per year), 105 teaching assistantships (averaging $5,996 per year); career-related internships or fieldwork, institutionally sponsored loans, scholarships/grants, and unspecified assistantships also available. Support available to part-time students. Financial award application deadline: 3/1; financial award applicants required to submit FAFSA. In 2016, 235 master's, 26 doctorates, 5 other advanced degrees awarded. *Program availability:* Part-time, evening/weekend, blended/hybrid learning. Offers applied energy (Graduate Certificate); applied energy and electromechanical systems (PhD); civil engineering (MSCE); construction and facilities management (MS); electrical engineering (MSEE, PhD); energy analytics (Graduate Certificate); engineering (MS, MSCE, MSE, MSEE, MSEM, MSME, PhD, Graduate

Certificate); engineering management (MSEM); fire protection and administration (MS); infrastructure and environmental systems (PhD); Lean Six Sigma (Graduate Certificate); logistics and supply chains (Graduate Certificate); mechanical engineering (MSME, PhD); systems analytics (Graduate Certificate). *Application deadline:* Applications are processed on a rolling basis. *Application fee:* $75. Electronic applications accepted. *Application Contact:* Kathy B. Giddings, Director of Graduate Admissions, 704-687-5503, Fax: 704-687-1668, E-mail: gradadm@uncc.edu. *Dean,* Dr. Robert E. Johnson, 704-687-8242, E-mail: robejohn@uncc.edu.

THE UNIVERSITY OF NORTH CAROLINA AT GREENSBORO, Greensboro, NC 27412-5001

General Information State-supported, coed, university. CGS member. *Graduate housing:* Room and/or apartments available to single students; on-campus housing not available to married students. Housing application deadline: 5/15. *Research affiliation:* Moses Cone Memorial Hospital, North Carolina Zoological Park, North Carolina Baptist Hospital.

GRADUATE UNITS

Graduate School *Program availability:* Part-time, evening/weekend, online learning. Offers liberal studies (MALS). Electronic applications accepted.

Bryan School of Business and Economics *Program availability:* Part-time. Offers accounting (MS); applied economics (MA); business administration (MBA, PMC, Postbaccalaureate Certificate); business and economics (MA, MBA, MS, PhD, Certificate, PMC, Postbaccalaureate Certificate); consumer, apparel, and retail studies (MS, PhD); economics (MA, PhD); financial analysis (PMC); financial economics (MA); information systems (PhD); information technology (Certificate); information technology and management (MS); supply chain management (Certificate). Electronic applications accepted.

College of Arts and Sciences *Program availability:* Part-time. Offers advanced Spanish language and Hispanic cultural studies (Certificate); American literature (PhD); applied geography (MA); arts and sciences (M Ed, MA, MFA, MPA, MS, PhD, Certificate); biochemistry (MS); biology (MS); chemistry (MS); clinical psychology (MA, PhD); cognitive psychology (MA, PhD); communication studies (MA); computer science (MS); creative writing (MFA); criminology (MA); developmental psychology (MA, PhD); English (M Ed, MA, PhD, Certificate); English literature (PhD); film and video production (MFA); French (MA); geographic information science (Certificate); geography (PhD); historic preservation (Certificate); history (MA); interior architecture (MS); Latin (M Ed); mathematics (MA, PhD); museum studies (Certificate); nonprofit management (Certificate); public affairs (MPA); rhetoric and composition (PhD); social psychology (MA, PhD); sociology (MA); Spanish (MA, Certificate); studio arts (MFA); U.S. history (PhD); urban and economic development (Certificate); women's and gender studies (MA, Certificate). Electronic applications accepted.

School of Education *Program availability:* Part-time, evening/weekend. Offers advanced school counseling (PMC); college teaching and adult learning (Certificate); counseling and counselor education (PhD); counseling and educational development (MS); couple and family counseling (PMC); cross-categorical special education (M Ed); curriculum and instruction (M Ed); curriculum and teaching (PhD); education (M Ed, MLIS, MS, MSA, Ed D, PhD, Certificate, Ed S, PMC); educational leadership (Ed D, Ed S); educational research, measurement and evaluation (PhD); English as a second language (Certificate); higher education (M Ed, PhD); interdisciplinary studies in special education (M Ed); leadership early care and education (Certificate); library and information studies (MLIS); school administration (MSA); school counseling (PMC); special education (M Ed, PhD); supervision (M Ed); teacher education and development (PhD). Electronic applications accepted.

School of Health and Human Sciences Offers athletic training (MSAT); community health education (MPH, Dr PH); community recreation management (MS); genetic counseling (MS); gerontology (MS, Certificate); health and human sciences (M Ed, MA, MFA, MPH, MS, Dr PH, Ed D, PhD); human development and family studies (M Ed, MS, PhD); kinesiology (MS, Ed D, PhD); nutrition (MS, PhD); peace and conflict studies (MA, Certificate); social work (MSW); speech language pathology (PhD); speech pathology and audiology (MA); therapeutic recreation (MS). Electronic applications accepted.

School of Music, Theatre and Dance Offers acting (MFA); composition (MM); dance (MA, MFA); design (MFA); directing (MFA); education (MM); music education (PhD); performance (MM, DMA); theater education (M Ed); theater for youth (MFA); theatre (M Ed, MFA); theory (MM). Electronic applications accepted.

School of Nursing Offers adult clinical nurse specialist (MSN, PMC); adult/gerontological nurse practitioner (MSN, PMC); nurse anesthesia (MSN, PMC); nursing (PhD); nursing administration (MSN); nursing education (MSN). Electronic applications accepted.

THE UNIVERSITY OF NORTH CAROLINA AT PEMBROKE, Pembroke, NC 28372-1510

General Information State-supported, coed, comprehensive institution. CGS member. *Graduate housing:* Room and/or apartments available to single students; on-campus housing not available to married students. Housing application deadline: 4/15.

GRADUATE UNITS

The Graduate School Students: 155 full-time (113 women), 599 part-time (423 women); includes 247 minority (121 Black or African American, non-Hispanic/Latino; 107 American Indian or Alaska Native, non-Hispanic/Latino; 5 Asian, non-Hispanic/Latino; 14 Hispanic/Latino). *Faculty:* 157 full-time, 38 part-time/adjunct. Expenses: Contact institution. *Financial support:* In 2016–17, 40 research assistantships with partial tuition reimbursements (averaging $8,000 per year) were awarded; career-related internships or fieldwork, scholarships/grants, and unspecified assistantships also available. Support available to part-time students. Financial award application deadline: 4/15; financial award applicants required to submit FAFSA. In 2016, 226 master's awarded. *Program availability:* Part-time, evening/weekend, 100% online, blended/hybrid learning. Offers art education (MA, MAT); clinical nurse leader (MSN); English education (MA, MAT); mathematics education (MA); nurse educator (MSN); public administration (MPA); rural case manager (MSN); science education (MA, MAT); social studies education (MA, MAT); social work (MSW). *Application deadline:* For fall admission, 3/15 priority date for domestic and international students; for spring admission, 10/15 priority date for domestic and international students. Applications are processed on a rolling basis. *Application fee:* $45 ($60 for international students). Electronic applications accepted. *Application Contact:* Gary Locklear, Executive Assistant, 910-521-6271, Fax: 910-521-6751, E-mail: grad@uncp.edu. *Dean,* Dr. Irene P. Aiken, 910-521-6271, Fax: 910-521-6751, E-mail: grad@uncp.edu.

School of Business *Program availability:* Part-time, evening/weekend. Offers business (MBA).

School of Education *Program availability:* Part-time, evening/weekend. Offers clinical mental health counseling (MA Ed); counseling (MA Ed); elementary education (MA Ed); health and human performance (MA); physical education (MA); professional school counseling (MA Ed); reading education (MA Ed); school administration (MSA).

UNIVERSITY OF NORTH CAROLINA SCHOOL OF THE ARTS, Winston-Salem, NC 27127-2738

General Information State-supported, coed, comprehensive institution. *Enrollment:* 1,040 graduate, professional, and undergraduate students; 130 full-time matriculated graduate/professional students (69 women), 3 part-time matriculated graduate/professional students (2 women). *Enrollment by degree level:* 133 master's. *Graduate faculty:* 68. Tuition, state resident: full-time $7996; part-time $444 per credit hour. Tuition, nonresident: full-time $21,403; part-time $1189 per credit hour. *Required fees:* $2769; $153.83 per credit hour. *Graduate housing:* Room and/or apartments available on a first-come, first-served basis to single students. Housing application deadline: 5/1. *Student services:* Campus employment opportunities, campus safety program, career counseling, exercise/wellness program, free psychological counseling, grant writing training, international student services, low-cost health insurance, services for students with disabilities, writing training. *Library facilities:* UNCSA Library. *Collection:* Books: 125,840 (physical), 44,708 (digital/electronic); Serial titles: 422 (physical), 17,788 (digital/electronic); Databases: 150. Weekly public service hours: 90; students can reserve study rooms.

Computer facilities: Computer purchase and lease plans are available. 86 computers available on campus for general student use. A campuswide network can be accessed from student residence rooms and from off campus. Online class registration is available.

Website: http://www.uncsa.edu/

General Application Contact: Sheeler Lawson, Director of Admissions, 336-770-3290, Fax: 336-770-3370, E-mail: admissions@uncsa.edu.

GRADUATE UNITS

School of Design and Production Students: 49 full-time (33 women), 1 (woman) part-time; includes 7 minority (2 Black or African American, non-Hispanic/Latino; 4 Hispanic/Latino; 1 Two or more races, non-Hispanic/Latino), 3 international. Average age 27. 37 applicants, 62% accepted, 18 enrolled. *Faculty:* 21 full-time (6 women), 4 part-time/adjunct (1 woman). Expenses: Contact institution. *Financial support:* Career-related internships or fieldwork, Federal Work-Study, and unspecified assistantships available. Support available to part-time students. Financial award application deadline: 3/15; financial award applicants required to submit FAFSA. Offers costume design (MFA); costume technology (MFA); scene design (MFA); scenic art (MFA); sound design (MFA); stage automation (MFA); stage properties (MFA); technical direction (MFA); wig and makeup design (MFA). *Application deadline:* For fall admission, 4/1 priority date for domestic students. Applications are processed on a rolling basis. *Application fee:* $95 ($100 for international students). Electronic applications accepted. *Application Contact:* Sheeler Lawson, Director of Admissions, 336-770-3290, Fax: 336-770-3370, E-mail: admissions@uncsa.edu. *Dean*, Michael J. Kelley, 336-770-1307, Fax: 336-770-3213, E-mail: kelleym@uncsa.edu.

School of Filmmaking Expenses: Contact institution. *Financial support:* Fellowships, research assistantships, career-related internships or fieldwork, and Federal Work-Study available. Support available to part-time students. Financial award application deadline: 3/15; financial award applicants required to submit FAFSA. Offers creative producing (MFA); film music composition (MFA); screenwriting (MFA). *Application deadline:* For fall admission, 4/1 priority date for domestic students. Applications are processed on a rolling basis. *Application fee:* $95 ($100 for international students). Electronic applications accepted. *Application Contact:* Sheeler Lawson, Director of Admissions, 336-770-3290, Fax: 336-770-3370, E-mail: admissions@uncsa.edu. *Dean*, Susan Ruskin, 336-770-1334, Fax: 336-770-1339, E-mail: ruskins@uncsa.edu.

School of Music Expenses: Contact institution. *Financial support:* Fellowships with partial tuition reimbursements, teaching assistantships with partial tuition reimbursements, career-related internships or fieldwork, and Federal Work-Study available. Financial award application deadline: 3/15; financial award applicants required to submit FAFSA. Offers music (Artist Certificate); music performance (MM); vocal performance (MM). *Application deadline:* For fall admission, 4/1 priority date for domestic students. Applications are processed on a rolling basis. *Application fee:* $95 ($100 for international students). Electronic applications accepted. *Application Contact:* Sheeler Lawson, Director of Admissions, 336-770-3290, Fax: 336-770-3370, E-mail: admissions@uncsa.edu. *Dean*, Brian Cole, 336-770-3251, Fax: 336-770-3248, E-mail: coleb@uncsa.edu.

THE UNIVERSITY OF NORTH CAROLINA WILMINGTON, Wilmington, NC 28403-3297

General Information State-supported, coed, comprehensive institution. CGS member. *Enrollment:* 15,740 graduate, professional, and undergraduate students; 754 full-time matriculated graduate/professional students (508 women), 985 part-time matriculated graduate/professional students (703 women). *Enrollment by degree level:* 1,586 master's, 131 doctoral, 22 other advanced degrees. *Graduate faculty:* 471 full-time (225 women), 11 part-time/adjunct (6 women). Tuition, state resident: full-time $4448. Tuition, nonresident: full-time $16,667. *Required fees:* $2595. Tuition and fees vary according to program. *Graduate housing:* Room and/or apartments available on a first-come, first-served basis to single students; on-campus housing not available to married students. Typical cost: $5879 per year ($9489 including board). Room and board charges vary according to board plan and housing facility selected. Housing application deadline: 4/30. *Student services:* Campus employment opportunities, campus safety program, career counseling, exercise/wellness program, free psychological counseling, international student services, low-cost health insurance, multicultural affairs office, services for students with disabilities. *Library facilities:* William Madison Randall Library. *Collection:* Books: 932,549 (physical), 79,711 (digital/electronic); Serial titles: 5,256 (physical), 44,165 (digital/electronic); Databases: 215. Weekly public service hours: 97; study areas open 24 hours, 5–7 days a week; students can reserve study rooms. *Research affiliation:* Seatox Research Inc. (biotechnology research and development), CMS Technology (seafood technology and safety), A-1 Biochem Labs (pharmaceuticals development), O.TM Biotech (environmental testing), OCIS Biotechnology (pharmaceuticals development).

Computer facilities: Computer purchase and lease plans are available. 1,361 computers available on campus for general student use. A campuswide network can be accessed from student residence rooms and from off campus. Online class registration is available.

Website: http://www.uncw.edu/

General Application Contact: Dr. Ron Vetter, Dean, Graduate School, 910-962-7303, Fax: 910-962-3787, E-mail: vetterr@uncw.edu.

GRADUATE UNITS

Cameron School of Business Students: 131 full-time (62 women), 45 part-time (18 women); includes 25 minority (9 Black or African American, non-Hispanic/Latino; 1 American Indian or Alaska Native, non-Hispanic/Latino; 5 Asian, non-Hispanic/Latino; 6 Hispanic/Latino; 4 Two or more races, non-Hispanic/Latino), 17 international. Average age 29. 182 applicants, 80% accepted, 114 enrolled. *Faculty:* 55 full-time (18 women). Expenses: Contact institution. *Financial support:* Teaching assistantships, scholarships/grants, and unspecified assistantships available. Financial award application deadline: 3/15; financial award applicants required to submit FAFSA. In 2016, 96 master's awarded. *Program availability:* Part-time. Offers accountancy (MSA); business administration (MBA); international business administration (MBA). *Application deadline:* Applications are processed on a rolling basis. *Application fee:* $60. Electronic applications accepted. *Application Contact:* Candace Wilhelm, Graduate Programs Coordinator, 910-962-3903, Fax: 910-962-2184, E-mail: wilhelmc@uncw.edu. *Dean*, Dr. Robert Burrus, 910-962-3226, Fax: 910-962-3815, E-mail: burrusr@uncw.edu.

Center for Marine Science Students: 8 full-time (3 women), 16 part-time (7 women); includes 2 minority (1 Hispanic/Latino; 1 Two or more races, non-Hispanic/Latino). Average age 27. 16 applicants, 56% accepted, 9 enrolled. *Faculty:* 51 full-time (13 women). Expenses: Contact institution. *Financial support:* Scholarships/grants and unspecified assistantships available. Financial award application deadline: 3/15; financial award applicants required to submit FAFSA. In 2016, 14 master's awarded. *Program availability:* Part-time. Offers marine science (MS). *Application deadline:* For fall admission, 6/15 for domestic students; for spring admission, 11/15 for domestic students. Applications are processed on a rolling basis. *Application fee:* $60. Electronic applications accepted. *Director*, Dr. Stephen Skrabal, 910-962-7160, E-mail: skrabals@uncw.edu.

College of Arts and Sciences Students: 279 full-time (177 women), 374 part-time (223 women); includes 95 minority (38 Black or African American, non-Hispanic/Latino; 2 American Indian or Alaska Native, non-Hispanic/Latino; 12 Asian, non-Hispanic/Latino; 33 Hispanic/Latino; 10 Two or more races, non-Hispanic/Latino), 10 international. Average age 30. 667 applicants, 51% accepted, 216 enrolled. *Faculty:* 245 full-time (103 women), 5 part-time/adjunct (3 women). Expenses: Contact institution. *Financial support:* Research assistantships, teaching assistantships, Federal Work-Study, scholarships/grants, unspecified assistantships, and tuition remission available. Support available to part-time students. Financial award application deadline: 3/15; financial award applicants required to submit FAFSA. In 2016, 210 master's, 2 doctorates awarded. *Program availability:* Part-time. Offers arts and sciences (MA, MFA, MPA, MS, PhD); biology (MS); chemistry (MS); coastal and ocean policy (MS); conflict management and resolution (MA); creative writing (MFA); English (MA); environmental studies (MS); geoscience (MS); history (MA); liberal studies (MA); marine biology (MS, PhD); mathematics (MS); psychology (MA); public administration (MPA); sociology and criminology (MA); Spanish (MA). *Application deadline:* Applications are processed on a rolling basis. *Application fee:* $60. Electronic applications accepted. *Application Contact:* Dr. Ron Vetter, Dean, Graduate School and Research, 910-962-3224, Fax: 910-962-3787, E-mail: vetterr@uncw.edu. *Dean, College of Arts and Sciences*, Dr. Aswani Volety, 910-962-3111, Fax: 910-962-3114, E-mail: voletya@uncw.edu.

Interdisciplinary Program in Computer Science and Information Systems Students: 13 full-time (3 women), 10 part-time (2 women); includes 3 minority (1 Black or African American, non-Hispanic/Latino; 1 Asian, non-Hispanic/Latino; 1 Hispanic/Latino), 6 international. Average age 28. 22 applicants, 73% accepted, 10 enrolled. *Faculty:* 11 full-time (3 women). Expenses: Contact institution. *Financial support:* Scholarships/grants and unspecified assistantships available. Financial award application deadline: 3/15; financial award applicants required to submit FAFSA. In 2016, 10 master's awarded. *Program availability:* Part-time. Offers computer science and information systems (MS). *Application deadline:* For fall admission, 6/1 for domestic students; for spring admission, 11/1 for domestic students. Applications are processed on a rolling basis. *Application fee:* $60. Electronic applications accepted. *Application Contact:* Candace Wilhelm, Graduate Coordinator, 910-962-3903, Fax: 910-962-7457, E-mail: wilhelmc@uncw.edu. *Program Coordinator*, Dr. Clayton Ferner, 910-962-7552, E-mail: cferner@uncw.edu.

School of Health and Applied Human Sciences Students: 6 full-time (all women), 2 part-time (both women); includes 1 minority (Black or African American, non-Hispanic/Latino). Average age 33. 6 applicants, 100% accepted, 6 enrolled. *Faculty:* 13 full-time (7 women). Expenses: Contact institution. *Financial support:* Scholarships/grants and unspecified assistantships available. Financial award application deadline: 3/15; financial award applicants required to submit FAFSA. In 2016, 1 master's awarded. *Program availability:* Part-time, online learning. Offers applied gerontology (MS); gerontology (Postbaccalaureate Certificate). *Application deadline:* For fall admission, 6/15 for domestic students; for spring admission, 11/15 for domestic students; for summer admission, 3/15 for domestic students. Applications are processed on a rolling basis. *Application fee:* $60. Electronic applications accepted. *Application Contact:* Dr. Anne Glass, Program Coordinator, 910-962-7816, E-mail: glassa@uncw.edu. *Director*, Dr. Chris Lantz, 910-962-2364, Fax: 910-962-7073, E-mail: lantzc@uncw.edu.

School of Nursing Students: 64 full-time (55 women), 143 part-time (123 women); includes 38 minority (24 Black or African American, non-Hispanic/Latino; 4 American Indian or Alaska Native, non-Hispanic/Latino; 2 Asian, non-Hispanic/Latino; 4 Hispanic/Latino; 4 Two or more races, non-Hispanic/Latino). Average age 35. 230 applicants, 53% accepted, 91 enrolled. *Faculty:* 37 full-time (33 women). Expenses: Contact institution. *Financial support:* Scholarships/grants available. Financial award application deadline: 3/15; financial award applicants required to submit FAFSA. In 2016, 34 master's awarded. *Program availability:* Part-time, 100% online. Offers clinical research and product development (MS); family nurse practitioner (Post-Master's Certificate); nurse educator (Post-Master's Certificate); nursing (MSN); nursing practice (DNP). *Application deadline:* For fall admission, 3/1 for domestic students. Applications are processed on a rolling basis. *Application fee:* $60. Electronic applications accepted. *Application Contact:* Dr. Jim Lyon, Graduate Coordinator, 910-962-2936, E-mail: lyonj@uncw.edu. *Director*, Dr. Laurie Badzek, 910-962-7410, Fax: 910-962-3723, E-mail: badzekl@uncw.edu.

School of Social Work Students: 75 full-time (68 women), 29 part-time (27 women); includes 20 minority (4 Black or African American, non-Hispanic/Latino; 1 Asian, non-Hispanic/Latino; 13 Hispanic/Latino; 2 Two or more races, non-Hispanic/Latino). Average age 31. 110 applicants, 53% accepted, 44 enrolled. *Faculty:* 14 full-time (9 women). Expenses: Contact institution. *Financial support:* Teaching assistantships, scholarships/grants, and out-of-state tuition remission available. Financial award application deadline: 3/15; financial award applicants required to submit FAFSA. In 2016, 20 master's awarded. *Program availability:* Part-time. Offers social work (MSW). *Application deadline:* For fall admission, 2/1 for domestic students. Applications are processed on a rolling basis. *Application fee:* $60. Electronic applications accepted. *Application Contact:* Dr. Peter Nguyen, Graduate Coordinator, 910-962-7642, Fax: 910-

962-7283, E-mail: nguyenp@uncw.edu. *Director*, Dr. Stacey Kolomer, 910-962-2853, Fax: 910-962-7283, E-mail: kolomers@uncw.edu.

Watson College of Education Students: 180 full-time (135 women), 364 part-time (299 women); includes 144 minority (104 Black or African American, non-Hispanic/Latino; 7 American Indian or Alaska Native, non-Hispanic/Latino; 3 Asian, non-Hispanic/Latino; 18 Hispanic/Latino; 1 Native Hawaiian or other Pacific Islander, non-Hispanic/Latino; 11 Two or more races, non-Hispanic/Latino), 6 international. Average age 34. 311 applicants, 78% accepted, 181 enrolled. *Faculty:* 68 full-time (44 women), 5 part-time/adjunct (3 women). Expenses: Contact institution. *Financial support:* Scholarships/grants and unspecified assistantships available. Support available to part-time students. Financial award application deadline: 3/15; financial award applicants required to submit FAFSA. In 2016, 151 master's, 19 doctorates awarded. *Program availability:* Part-time. Offers academically or intellectually gifted (M Ed); curriculum, instruction and supervision (M Ed); education (M Ed, MAT, MS, MSA, Ed D); educational leadership and administration (Ed D); educational leadership, policy, and advocacy (M Ed); elementary education (M Ed, MAT); English as a second language (M Ed, MAT); higher education (M Ed); instructional technology (MS); language and literacy (M Ed); middle grades education (M Ed, MAT); physical education and health (M Ed, MAT); school administration (MSA); secondary education (M Ed, MAT); Spanish (MAT); Spanish education (MASS). *Application deadline:* For fall admission, 5/15 for domestic students; for spring admission, 10/15 for domestic students. Applications are processed on a rolling basis. *Application fee:* $60. Electronic applications accepted. *Application Contact:* Dr. Ron Vetter, Dean, Graduate School, 910-962-3224, Fax: 910-962-3787, E-mail: vetter@uncw.edu. *Dean,* Dr. Van Dempsey, 910-962-3354, Fax: 910-962-4081, E-mail: dempseyv@uncw.edu.

UNIVERSITY OF NORTH DAKOTA, Grand Forks, ND 58202

General Information State-supported, coed, university. CGS member. *Enrollment:* 14,648 graduate, professional, and undergraduate students; 1,219 full-time matriculated graduate/professional students (755 women), 1,653 part-time matriculated graduate/professional students (1,076 women). *Enrollment by degree level:* 1,973 master's, 656 doctoral, 85 other advanced degrees. *Graduate housing:* Rooms and/or apartments guaranteed to single students and available on a first-come, first-served basis to married students. *Student services:* Campus employment opportunities, campus safety program, career counseling, child daycare facilities, exercise/wellness program, free psychological counseling, grant writing training, international student services, multicultural affairs office, services for students with disabilities, teacher training, writing training. *Library facilities:* Chester Fritz Library plus 2 others. *Collection:* Books: 571,458 (physical), 146,797 (digital/electronic); Serial titles: 26,062 (physical), 62,508 (digital/electronic); Databases: 90. Weekly public service hours: 99. *Research affiliation:* U.S. Department of Agriculture (USDA), Human Nutrition Research Center, Neuropsychiatric Research Institute (neurosciences), Environmental Energy Research Center.

Computer facilities: Computer purchase and lease plans are available. 1,000 computers available on campus for general student use. A campuswide network can be accessed from student residence rooms and from off campus. Online class registration is available.
Website: http://www.und.edu/

General Application Contact: Laura Look, Director of Admissions, 701-777-3299, Fax: 701-777-3619, E-mail: admissions@gradschool.und.edu.

GRADUATE UNITS

Graduate School Expenses: Contact institution. *Financial support:* Fellowships with full and partial tuition reimbursements, research assistantships with full and partial tuition reimbursements, teaching assistantships with full and partial tuition reimbursements, career-related internships or fieldwork, Federal Work-Study, institutionally sponsored loans, scholarships/grants, traineeships, health care benefits, tuition waivers (full and partial), and unspecified assistantships available. Support available to part-time students. Financial award application deadline: 3/15; financial award applicants required to submit FAFSA. *Program availability:* Part-time, evening/weekend, online learning. Offers clinical translation science (MS, PhD); medicine (MOT, MPAS, MS, DPT, PhD); occupational therapy (MOT); physical therapy (DPT); physician assistant (MPAS). *Application deadline:* For fall admission, 8/1 priority date for domestic and international students; for spring admission, 12/1 priority date for domestic and international students. Applications are processed on a rolling basis. *Application fee:* $35. Electronic applications accepted. *Application Contact:* Evan Nelson, Director of Graduate Admissions and Recruitment, 701-777-2945, Fax: 701-777-3619, E-mail: evan.nelson@gradschool.und.edu. *Dean,* Dr. Joseph N. Benoit, 701-777-2786, Fax: 701-777-3619, E-mail: joseph.benoit@und.edu.

College of Arts and Sciences Expenses: Contact institution. *Financial support:* Fellowships with full and partial tuition reimbursements, research assistantships with full tuition reimbursements, teaching assistantships with full tuition reimbursements, career-related internships or fieldwork, Federal Work-Study, institutionally sponsored loans, scholarships/grants, health care benefits, tuition waivers (full and partial), and unspecified assistantships available. Support available to part-time students. Financial award application deadline: 3/15; financial award applicants required to submit FAFSA. *Program availability:* Part-time, online learning. Offers arts and sciences (M Ed, MA, MFA, MM, MS, DA, PhD); biology (MS); chemistry (MS, PhD); clinical psychology (PhD); communication and public discourse (PhD); criminal justice (PhD); English (MA, PhD); fisheries/wildlife (PhD); forensic psychology (MA, MS); genetics (PhD); geography and geographic information science (MA, MS); history (M Ed, MA, DA, PhD); linguistics (MA); mathematics (M Ed, MS); music (MM); music education (PhD); physics and astrophysics (MA, MS, PhD); sociology (MA); speech-language pathology (MS); visual arts (MFA); zoology (PhD). *Application deadline:* For fall admission, 8/1 for domestic and international students; for spring admission, 12/15 for domestic and international students. *Application fee:* $35. Electronic applications accepted. *Application Contact:* Evan Nelson, Director of Admissions and Recruitment, 701-777-2945, Fax: 701-777-3619, E-mail: evan.nelson@gradschool.und.edu. *Dean,* Dr. Kathleen Tiemann, 701-777-2749, Fax: 701-777-4397, E-mail: kathleen.tiemann@as.und.edu.

College of Business and Public Administration Expenses: Contact institution. *Financial support:* Fellowships with full and partial tuition reimbursements, research assistantships with full tuition reimbursements, teaching assistantships with full tuition reimbursements, Federal Work-Study, institutionally sponsored loans, scholarships/grants, health care benefits, tuition waivers (full and partial), and unspecified assistantships available. Support available to part-time students. Financial award application deadline: 3/15; financial award applicants required to submit FAFSA. *Program availability:* Part-time, evening/weekend, online learning. Offers applied economics (MSAE); business administration (MBA); business and public administration (MBA, MPA, MSAE, MSIT); public administration (MPA). *Application deadline:* For fall admission, 8/1 priority date for domestic and

international students; for spring admission, 12/1 priority date for domestic and international students. Applications are processed on a rolling basis. *Application fee:* $35. Electronic applications accepted. *Application Contact:* Evan Nelson, Director of Graduate Admissions and Recruitment, 701-777-2945, Fax: 701-777-3619, E-mail: evan.nelson@gradschool.und.edu. *Dean,* Dr. Dennis J. Elbert, 701-777-2135, Fax: 701-777-5099, E-mail: dennis.elbert@mail.und.nodak.edu.

College of Education and Human Development Expenses: Contact institution. *Financial support:* Fellowships with full and partial tuition reimbursements, research assistantships with full and partial tuition reimbursements, teaching assistantships with full and partial tuition reimbursements, career-related internships or fieldwork, Federal Work-Study, institutionally sponsored loans, scholarships/grants, tuition waivers (full and partial), and unspecified assistantships available. Support available to part-time students. Financial award application deadline: 3/15; financial award applicants required to submit FAFSA. *Program availability:* Part-time, evening/weekend, online learning. Offers counseling (MA); counseling psychology (PhD); early childhood education (MS); education and human development (M Ed, MA, MS, MSW, Ed D, PhD, Ed S); education/general studies (MS); educational leadership (M Ed, Ed D, PhD, Ed S); elementary education (M Ed, MS); instructional design and technology (M Ed, MS); kinesiology (MS); reading education (M Ed, MS); special education (M Ed, MS). *Application deadline:* Applications are processed on a rolling basis. *Application fee:* $35. Electronic applications accepted. *Application Contact:* Evan Nelson, Director of Admissions and Recruitment, 701-777-2945, Fax: 701-777-3619, E-mail: evan.nelson@gradschool.und.edu. *Dean,* Dr. Dan R. Rice, 701-777-4255, Fax: 701-777-4393, E-mail: dan.rice@mail.und.nodak.edu.

College of Nursing and Professional Disciplines Expenses: Contact institution. *Financial support:* Fellowships with full and partial tuition reimbursements, research assistantships with full and partial tuition reimbursements, teaching assistantships with full and partial tuition reimbursements, Federal Work-Study, institutionally sponsored loans, scholarships/grants, traineeships, health care benefits, and tuition waivers (full and partial) available. Support available to part-time students. Financial award application deadline: 3/15; financial award applicants required to submit FAFSA. *Program availability:* Part-time, evening/weekend, online learning. Offers adult-gerontological nurse practitioner (MS); advanced public health nurse (MS); family nurse practitioner (MS); nurse anesthesia (MS); nurse educator (MS); nursing (PhD, Post-Master's Certificate); nursing and professional disciplines (MS, MSW, DNP, PhD, Post-Master's Certificate); nursing practice (DNP); psychiatric and mental health nurse practitioner (MS); social work (MSW). *Application deadline:* For fall admission, 1/15 for domestic and international students. *Application fee:* $35. Electronic applications accepted. *Application Contact:* Matt Anderson, Admissions Specialist, 701-777-2947, Fax: 701-777-3619, E-mail: matthew.anderson@gradschool.und.edu. *Associate Dean of Graduate Studies,* Dr. Darla Adams, 701-777-4509, Fax: 701-777-4096, E-mail: darla.adams@email.und.edu.

John D. Odegard School of Aerospace Sciences Expenses: Contact institution. *Financial support:* In 2016-17, 49 students received support. Fellowships with full and partial tuition reimbursements available, research assistantships with full and partial tuition reimbursements available, teaching assistantships with full and partial tuition reimbursements available, career-related internships or fieldwork, Federal Work-Study, institutionally sponsored loans, scholarships/grants, health care benefits, tuition waivers (full and partial), and unspecified assistantships available. Support available to part-time students. Financial award application deadline: 3/15; financial award applicants required to submit FAFSA. *Program availability:* Part-time, evening/weekend, online learning. Offers aerospace sciences (MEM, MS, PhD); atmospheric sciences (MS, PhD); aviation (MS); computer science (MS); earth system science and policy (MEM, MS, PhD); space studies (MS). *Application deadline:* For fall and spring admission, 8/1 priority date for domestic and international students. Applications are processed on a rolling basis. *Application fee:* $35. Electronic applications accepted. *Application Contact:* Matt Anderson, Admissions Specialist, 701-777-2947, Fax: 701-777-3619, E-mail: matthew.anderson@gradschool.und.edu. *Dean,* Bruce A. Smith, 701-777-2791, Fax: 701-777-3016, E-mail: bsmith@aero.und.nodak.edu.

School of Engineering and Mines Expenses: Contact institution. *Financial support:* Fellowships with full and partial tuition reimbursements, research assistantships with full and partial tuition reimbursements, teaching assistantships with full and partial tuition reimbursements, career-related internships or fieldwork, Federal Work-Study, institutionally sponsored loans, scholarships/grants, health care benefits, tuition waivers (full and partial), and unspecified assistantships available. Support available to part-time students. Financial award application deadline: 3/15; financial award applicants required to submit FAFSA. *Program availability:* Part-time. Offers chemical engineering (M Engr, MS, PhD); civil engineering (M Engr); electrical engineering (M Engr, MS, PhD); engineering (PhD); engineering and mines (M Engr, MA, MS, PhD); environmental engineering (M Engr, MS, PhD); geological engineering (MS, PhD); geology (MA, MS, PhD); mechanical engineering (M Engr, MS, PhD). *Application deadline:* For fall admission, 8/1 priority date for domestic and international students; for spring admission, 12/1 priority date for domestic and international students. Applications are processed on a rolling basis. *Application fee:* $35. Electronic applications accepted. *Application Contact:* Evan Nelson, Director of Graduate Admissions and Recruitment, 701-777-2945, Fax: 701-777-3619, E-mail: evan.nelson@gradschool.und.edu. *Dean,* Dr. Hesham El-Rewini, 701-777-3411, Fax: 701-777-4838, E-mail: rewini@mail.und.edu.

School of Medicine and Health Sciences Expenses: Contact institution. *Financial support:* Fellowships, research assistantships, teaching assistantships, Federal Work-Study, institutionally sponsored loans, and tuition waivers (full and partial) available. Support available to part-time students. Financial award applicants required to submit FAFSA. *Program availability:* Online learning. Offers medicine and health sciences (MPH); public health (MPH).

UNIVERSITY OF NORTHERN BRITISH COLUMBIA, Prince George, BC V2N 4Z9, Canada

General Information Province-supported, coed, university. *Graduate housing:* Room and/or apartments available on a first-come, first-served basis to single students; on-campus housing not available to married students. Housing application deadline: 2/15. *Research affiliation:* Houston Forest Products (forestry–wood debris management), TRC Cedar Ltd. (forestry–cyanolicen growth rate study), Remote Law Online Systems Corporation (computer science), Canadian Natural Oils Ltd. (chemistry–oil fractionation), Stella Jones, Inc. (forestry–Douglas fir cores), Insurance Corporation of British Columbia (moose involved in highway traffic accidents).

GRADUATE UNITS

Office of Graduate Studies *Program availability:* Part-time, evening/weekend, online learning.

UNIVERSITY OF NORTHERN COLORADO, Greeley, CO 80639

General Information State-supported, coed, university. CGS member. *Graduate housing:* Rooms and/or apartments available on a first-come, first-served basis to single and married students. Housing application deadline: 5/30. *Student services:* Campus employment opportunities, campus safety program, career counseling, exercise/wellness program, free psychological counseling, international student services, low-cost health insurance, multicultural affairs office, services for students with disabilities, teacher training. *Library facilities:* James A. Michener Library plus 2 others. *Collection:* Books: 1.3 million (physical), 170,533 (digital/electronic); Serial titles: 19,826 (physical), 65,044 (digital/electronic); Databases: 199. Weekly public service hours: 97; students can reserve study rooms.

Computer facilities: Computer purchase and lease plans are available. 1,723 computers available on campus for general student use. A campuswide network can be accessed from student residence rooms and from off campus. Online class registration is available.
Website: http://www.unco.edu/

General Application Contact: Linda Sisson, Graduate Student Admissions Coordinator, 970-351-1807, Fax: 970-351-2371, E-mail: linda.sisson@unco.edu.

GRADUATE UNITS

Graduate School Expenses: Contact institution. *Financial support:* Fellowships, research assistantships, teaching assistantships, career-related internships or fieldwork, Federal Work-Study, institutionally sponsored loans, scholarships/grants, traineeships, tuition waivers (partial), and unspecified assistantships available. Support available to part-time students. Financial award application deadline: 3/1; financial award applicants required to submit FAFSA. *Program availability:* Part-time, evening/weekend, online learning. *Application deadline:* Applications are processed on a rolling basis. *Application fee:* $50 ($60 for international students). Electronic applications accepted. *Application Contact:* Linda Sisson, Graduate Student Admission Coordinator, 970-351-1807, Fax: 970-351-2371, E-mail: linda.sisson@unco.edu. *Assistant Vice President, Research and Extended Studies/Dean,* Dr. Robbyn Wacker, 970-351-2817, Fax: 970-351-2371.

College of Education and Behavioral Sciences Expenses: Contact institution. *Financial support:* Fellowships, research assistantships, teaching assistantships, and unspecified assistantships available. Financial award application deadline: 3/1; financial award applicants required to submit FAFSA. *Program availability:* Part-time, online learning. Offers applied statistics and research methods (MS, PhD); clinical counseling (MA); counseling psychology (PhD); counselor education and supervision (PhD); curriculum studies (MAT); deaf/hard of hearing (MA); early childhood special education (MA); education and behavioral sciences (MA, MAT, MS, Ed D, PhD, Ed S); educational leadership (MA, Ed S); educational leadership and policy studies (MA, Ed D, Ed S); educational psychology (MA, PhD); educational studies (Ed D); elementary education (MAT); English education (MAT); gifted and talented (MA); higher education and student affairs leadership (PhD); literacy (MA); multilingual education (MA); school counseling (MA); school psychology (Ed S); special education (MA, PhD); teaching diverse learners (MA); visual impairment (MA). *Application deadline:* Applications are processed on a rolling basis. *Application fee:* $50 ($60 for international students). *Application Contact:* Linda Sisson, Graduate Student Admission Coordinator, 970-351-1807, Fax: 970-351-2371, E-mail: linda.sisson@unco.edu. *Dean,* Dr. Eugene P. Sheehan, 970-351-2817, Fax: 970-351-2312, E-mail: coeinfo@unco.edu.

College of Humanities and Social Sciences Expenses: Contact institution. *Financial support:* Fellowships, research assistantships, teaching assistantships, and unspecified assistantships available. Financial award application deadline: 3/1; financial award applicants required to submit FAFSA. *Program availability:* Part-time. Offers communication (MA); criminal justice (MA); English (MA); history (MA); humanities and social sciences (MA); sociology (MA). *Application deadline:* Applications are processed on a rolling basis. *Application fee:* $50 ($60 for international students). Electronic applications accepted. *Application Contact:* Linda Sisson, Graduate Student Admission Coordinator, 970-351-1807, Fax: 970-351-2371, E-mail: linda.sisson@unco.edu. *Dean,* Dr. David Caldwell, 970-351-2707, Fax: 970-351-1571.

College of Natural and Health Sciences Expenses: Contact institution. *Financial support:* Fellowships, research assistantships, teaching assistantships, and unspecified assistantships available. Financial award application deadline: 3/1; financial award applicants required to submit FAFSA. Offers adult-gerontology acute care nurse practitioner (MSN, DNP); audiology (Au D); biological sciences (MS); biology education (PhD); biomedical sciences (MBS); chemical education (MS, PhD); chemistry (MS); community health education (MPH); earth sciences (MA); educational mathematics (PhD); exercise science (MS, PhD); family nurse practitioner (MSN, DNP); gerontology (MA); global health and community health education (MPH); healthy aging and community health education (MPH); human sciences (MA, MPH, Au D, PhD); mathematical teaching (MA); mathematics (MA); natural and health sciences (MA, MAT, MBS, MPH, MS, MSN, Au D, DNP, PhD); nursing education (PhD); nursing practice (DNP); physical education and physical activity leadership (MAT); rehabilitation counseling (MA); rehabilitation sciences (PhD); speech-language pathology (MA); sport administration (MS, PhD); sport pedagogy (MS, PhD); sports coaching (MA). *Application deadline:* Applications are processed on a rolling basis. *Application fee:* $50 ($60 for international students). Electronic applications accepted. *Application Contact:* Linda Sisson, Graduate Student Admission Coordinator, 970-351-1807, Fax: 970-351-2371, E-mail: linda.sisson@unco.edu. *Dean,* Dr. Denise A. Battles, 970-351-2877, Fax: 970-351-2176.

College of Performing and Visual Arts Expenses: Contact institution. *Financial support:* Fellowships, research assistantships, teaching assistantships, and unspecified assistantships available. Financial award application deadline: 3/1; financial award applicants required to submit FAFSA. *Program availability:* Part-time. Offers art education (MA); art history (MA); collaborative piano (MM); composition (DA); conducting (MM, DA); instrumental performance (MM); jazz studies (MM, DA); music education (MM, DA); music history and literature (MM, DA); music theory and composition (MM); performance (DA); performing and visual arts (MA, MM, DA); studio art (MA); vocal performance (MM). *Application deadline:* Applications are processed on a rolling basis. *Application fee:* $50 ($60 for international students). Electronic applications accepted. *Application Contact:* Linda Sisson, Graduate Student Admission Coordinator, 970-351-1807, Fax: 970-351-2371, E-mail: linda.sisson@unco.edu. *Dean,* Dr. Andrew J. Svedlow, 970-351-2515, Fax: 970-351-2699.

Monfort College of Business Expenses: Contact institution. Offers accounting (MA); general business management (MBA); healthcare administration (MBA); human resources management (MBA). *Application Contact:* Linda Sisson, Graduate Student Admission Coordinator, 970-351-1807, Fax: 970-351-2371, E-mail: linda.sisson@unco.edu. *Dean,* Donald Gudmundson, 970-351-2411, E-mail: don.gudmundson@unco.edu.

UNIVERSITY OF NORTHERN IOWA, Cedar Falls, IA 50614

General Information State-supported, coed, comprehensive institution. CGS member. *Graduate housing:* Rooms and/or apartments available on a first-come, first-served basis to single and married students.

GRADUATE UNITS

Graduate College *Program availability:* Part-time, evening/weekend. Offers philanthropy and nonprofit development (MA); women's and gender studies (MA). Electronic applications accepted.

College of Business Administration *Program availability:* Part-time, evening/weekend. Offers accounting (M Acc); business administration (M Acc, MBA).

College of Education *Program availability:* Part-time, evening/weekend. Offers allied health, recreation, and community services (Ed D); athletic training (MS); career/vocational programming and transition (MAE); community health education (MA); consultant (MAE); curriculum and instruction (Ed D); early childhood education (MAE); education (MA, MAE, MS, Ed D, Ed S); educational leadership (Ed D); educational psychology: context and techniques of assessment (MAE); educational psychology: context and techniques of assessment (MAE); educational psychology: professional development for teachers (MAE); elementary education (MAE); field specialization (MAE); health education (MA); health promotion/fitness management (MA); instructional technology (MA); kinesiology (MA); leisure, youth and human services (MA); literacy education (MAE); performance and training technology (MA); physical education (MA); postsecondary education: student affairs (MA); principalship (MAE); school health education (MA); school library endorsement (MA); school library studies (MA); school psychology (Ed S); special education (MAE); teaching/coaching (MA). Electronic applications accepted.

College of Humanities, Arts and Sciences *Program availability:* Part-time, evening/weekend. Offers art education (MA); biology (MS); communication studies (MA); community college teaching (MA); composition (MM); conducting (MM); creative writing (MA); earth science education (MA); English (MA); humanities, arts and sciences (MA, MM, MS, PSM, DIT); industrial mathematics (PSM); industrial technology (DIT); jazz pedagogy (MM); literature (MA); mathematics (MA); mathematics for the middle grades (MA); music (MA, MM); music education (MM); music history (MM); percussion (MM); performance (MM); physics education (MA); piano performance and pedagogy (MM); piano/organ (MM); science education (MA); secondary teaching (MA); Spanish (MA); Spanish teaching (MA); speech-language pathology (MA); strings (MM); teaching English in secondary schools (MA); teaching English to speakers of other languages (MA); technology (MS, DIT); TESOL/Spanish (MA); voice (MM); woodwind (MM). Electronic applications accepted.

College of Social and Behavioral Sciences *Program availability:* Part-time, evening/weekend. Offers counseling (MA); geography (MA); history (MA); mental health counseling (MA); psychology (MA); public history (MA); public policy (MPP); school counseling (MA); social and behavioral sciences (MA, MPP, MSW); social science (MA); social work (MSW). Electronic applications accepted.

UNIVERSITY OF NORTH FLORIDA, Jacksonville, FL 32224

General Information State-supported, coed, comprehensive institution. CGS member. *Enrollment:* 15,762 graduate, professional, and undergraduate students; 844 full-time matriculated graduate/professional students (556 women), 1,040 part-time matriculated graduate/professional students (654 women). *Enrollment by degree level:* 1,431 master's, 453 doctoral. *Graduate faculty:* 406 full-time (193 women), 33 part-time/adjunct (23 women). Tuition and fees vary according to course load, campus/location and program. *Graduate housing:* Room and/or apartments available on a first-come, first-served basis to single students; on-campus housing not available to married students. Housing application deadline: 6/1. *Student services:* Campus employment opportunities, campus safety program, career counseling, child daycare facilities, exercise/wellness program, free psychological counseling, international student services, low-cost health insurance, multicultural affairs office, services for students with disabilities, teacher training, writing training. *Library facilities:* Thomas G. Carpenter Library. *Collection:* Books: 860,144 (physical), 269,885 (digital/electronic); Serial titles: 16,185 (physical), 44,772 (digital/electronic); Databases: 271. Weekly public service hours: 137; students can reserve study rooms.

Computer facilities: Computer purchase and lease plans are available. 700 computers available on campus for general student use. A campuswide network can be accessed from student residence rooms and from off campus. Online class registration, reduced prices for students on certain business and design software are available.
Website: http://www.unf.edu/

General Application Contact: Dr. Amanda Pascale, Director, The Graduate School, 904-620-1360, Fax: 904-620-1362, E-mail: graduateschool@unf.edu.

GRADUATE UNITS

Brooks College of Health Students: 415 full-time (308 women), 204 part-time (163 women); includes 192 minority (72 Black or African American, non-Hispanic/Latino; 3 American Indian or Alaska Native, non-Hispanic/Latino; 38 Asian, non-Hispanic/Latino; 54 Hispanic/Latino; 2 Native Hawaiian or other Pacific Islander, non-Hispanic/Latino; 23 Two or more races, non-Hispanic/Latino), 10 international. Average age 33. 335 applicants, 48% accepted, 119 enrolled. Faculty: 65 full-time (48 women), 11 part-time/adjunct (8 women). Expenses: Contact institution. *Financial support:* In 2016–17, 73 students received support, including 29 research assistantships (averaging $2,415 per year), 2 teaching assistantships (averaging $4,000 per year); career-related internships or fieldwork, Federal Work-Study, scholarships/grants, and tuition waivers (partial) also available. Support available to part-time students. Financial award application deadline: 4/1; financial award applicants required to submit FAFSA. In 2016, 160 master's, 36 doctorates awarded. *Program availability:* Part-time, evening/weekend. Offers aging services (Certificate); clinical and applied movement sciences (MSH, DPT); community health (MPH); health (MHA, MPH, MS, MSH, MSN, DNP, DPT, Certificate); nutrition and dietetics (MSH). *Application deadline:* For fall admission, 7/1 priority date for domestic students, 5/1 for international students; for spring admission, 11/1 priority date for domestic students, 10/1 for international students. *Application fee:* $30. Electronic applications accepted. *Application Contact:* Miwa Nguyen, Director of Advising, 904-620-2810, Fax: 904-620-1030, E-mail: cohadvis@unf.edu. *Dean,* Dr. Pamela Chally, 904-620-2810, Fax: 904-620-1030, E-mail: pchally@unf.edu.

School of Nursing Students: 148 full-time (124 women), 132 part-time (102 women); includes 97 minority (40 Black or African American, non-Hispanic/Latino; 2 American Indian or Alaska Native, non-Hispanic/Latino; 21 Asian, non-Hispanic/Latino; 26 Hispanic/Latino; 2 Native Hawaiian or other Pacific Islander, non-Hispanic/Latino; 6 Two or more races, non-Hispanic/Latino), 3 international. Average age 38. 160

applicants, 79% accepted, 89 enrolled. *Faculty:* 25 full-time (20 women), 1 (woman) part-time/adjunct. *Expenses:* Contact institution. *Financial support:* In 2016–17, 32 students received support, including 1 teaching assistantship (averaging $6,000 per year). Financial award application deadline: 4/1; financial award applicants required to submit FAFSA. In 2016, 44 master's, 10 doctorates awarded. *Program availability:* Part-time. Offers family nurse practitioner (Certificate); nurse anesthetist (MSN). *Application deadline:* For fall admission, 4/1 for domestic students, 5/1 for international students. *Application fee:* $30. Electronic applications accepted. *Application Contact:* Beth Dibble, Assistant Director of Admissions for Nursing and Physical Therapy, 904-620-2684, Fax: 904-620-1832, E-mail: nursingadmissions@unf.edu. *Chair,* Dr. Li Loriz, 904-620-1053, E-mail: lloriz@unf.edu.

Coggin College of Business Students: 144 full-time (68 women), 255 part-time (125 women); includes 98 minority (35 Black or African American, non-Hispanic/Latino; 1 American Indian or Alaska Native, non-Hispanic/Latino; 25 Asian, non-Hispanic/Latino; 24 Hispanic/Latino; 2 Native Hawaiian or other Pacific Islander, non-Hispanic/Latino; 11 Two or more races, non-Hispanic/Latino), 42 international. Average age 29. 340 applicants, 57% accepted, 150 enrolled. *Faculty:* 50 full-time (13 women), 3 part-time/adjunct (1 woman). *Expenses:* Contact institution. *Financial support:* In 2016–17, 36 students received support, including 1 research assistantship (averaging $2,501 per year); career-related internships or fieldwork, Federal Work-Study, scholarships/grants, and tuition waivers (partial) also available. Financial award application deadline: 4/1; financial award applicants required to submit FAFSA. In 2016, 136 master's awarded. *Program availability:* Part-time, evening/weekend. Offers accountancy (M Acc); accounting (MBA); business (M Acc, MBA); construction management (MBA); e-commerce (MBA); economics (MBA); finance (MBA); human resource management (MBA); international business (MBA); logistics (MBA); management applications (MBA). *Application deadline:* For fall admission, 8/1 priority date for domestic students, 5/1 for international students; for spring admission, 12/1 priority date for domestic students, 10/1 for international students. *Application fee:* $30. Electronic applications accepted. *Application Contact:* Paul Schreier, Interim Director of Student Services, 904-620-2575, Fax: 904-620-2832, E-mail: coggin.students@unf.edu. *Dean,* Dr. Mark Dawkins, 904-620-5280, Fax: 904-620-2594, E-mail: mark.dawkins@unf.edu.

College of Arts and Sciences Students: 142 full-time (74 women), 160 part-time (98 women); includes 63 minority (32 Black or African American, non-Hispanic/Latino; 4 Asian, non-Hispanic/Latino; 21 Hispanic/Latino; 6 Two or more races, non-Hispanic/Latino), 9 international. Average age 30. 289 applicants, 54% accepted, 101 enrolled. *Faculty:* 201 full-time (94 women), 7 part-time/adjunct (5 women). *Expenses:* Contact institution. *Financial support:* In 2016–17, 74 students received support, including 3 research assistantships (averaging $5,340 per year), 15 teaching assistantships (averaging $4,192 per year); career-related internships or fieldwork, Federal Work-Study, scholarships/grants, and tuition waivers (partial) also available. Support available to part-time students. Financial award application deadline: 4/1; financial award applicants required to submit FAFSA. In 2016, 105 master's awarded. *Program availability:* Part-time, evening/weekend. Offers applied ethics (Graduate Certificate); arts and sciences (MA, MAC, MPA, MS, Graduate Certificate); biology (MA, MS); counseling psychology (MAC); criminal justice (MS); English (MA); European history (MA); general psychology (MA); mathematical sciences (MS); nonprofit management (Graduate Certificate); practical philosophy and applied ethics (MA); public administration (MPA); statistics (MS); U.S. history (MA). *Application deadline:* For fall admission, 7/1 priority date for domestic students, 5/1 for international students; for spring admission, 11/1 priority date for domestic students, 10/1 for international students. *Application fee:* $30. Electronic applications accepted. *Application Contact:* Dr. Amanda Pascale, Director, The Graduate School, 904-620-1360, Fax: 904-620-1362, E-mail: graduateschool@unf.edu. *Interim Dean,* Dr. Daniel Moon, 904-620-2560, Fax: 904-620-2929, E-mail: dmoon@unf.edu.

College of Computing, Engineering, and Construction Students: 28 full-time (9 women), 81 part-time (20 women); includes 24 minority (2 Black or African American, non-Hispanic/Latino; 11 Asian, non-Hispanic/Latino; 6 Hispanic/Latino; 5 Two or more races, non-Hispanic/Latino), 33 international. Average age 29. 105 applicants, 44% accepted, 24 enrolled. *Faculty:* 38 full-time (5 women), 1 part-time/adjunct (0 women). *Expenses:* Contact institution. *Financial support:* In 2016–17, 33 students received support, including 15 research assistantships (averaging $3,601 per year), 8 teaching assistantships (averaging $2,740 per year); Federal Work-Study, scholarships/grants, tuition waivers (partial), and unspecified assistantships also available. Support available to part-time students. Financial award application deadline: 4/1; financial award applicants required to submit FAFSA. In 2016, 17 master's awarded. *Program availability:* Part-time. Offers computing, engineering, and construction (MS, MSCE, MSEE, MSME). *Application deadline:* For fall admission, 7/1 priority date for domestic students, 5/1 for international students; for spring admission, 11/1 priority date for domestic students, 10/1 for international students. *Application fee:* $30. Electronic applications accepted. *Application Contact:* Dr. Amanda Pascale, Director, The Graduate School, 904-620-1360, Fax: 904-620-1362, E-mail: graduateschool@unf.edu. *Dean,* Dr. Mark Tumeo, 904-620-1350, E-mail: m.tumeo@unf.edu.

School of Computing Students: 13 full-time (5 women), 47 part-time (14 women); includes 14 minority (2 Black or African American, non-Hispanic/Latino; 9 Asian, non-Hispanic/Latino; 1 Hispanic/Latino; 2 Two or more races, non-Hispanic/Latino), 20 international. Average age 30. 62 applicants, 31% accepted, 7 enrolled. *Faculty:* 12 full-time (2 women), 1 part-time/adjunct (0 women). *Expenses:* Contact institution. *Financial support:* In 2016–17, 4 research assistantships (averaging $2,332 per year) were awarded; teaching assistantships, Federal Work-Study, scholarships/grants, and unspecified assistantships also available. Financial award application deadline: 4/1; financial award applicants required to submit FAFSA. In 2016, 3 master's awarded. *Program availability:* Part-time. Offers computer science (MS); information systems (MS); software engineering (MS). *Application deadline:* For fall admission, 8/1 priority date for domestic students, 5/1 for international students; for spring admission, 12/1 priority date for domestic students, 10/1 for international students; for summer admission, 3/15 priority date for domestic students, 2/1 for international students. *Application fee:* $30. Electronic applications accepted. *Application Contact:* Dr. Amanda Pascale, Director, The Graduate School, 904-620-1360, Fax: 904-620-1362, E-mail: graduateschool@unf.edu. *Director/Professor,* Dr. Sherif Elfayoumy, 904-620-2985, E-mail: selfayou@unf.edu.

School of Engineering Students: 15 full-time (4 women), 34 part-time (6 women); includes 10 minority (2 Asian, non-Hispanic/Latino; 5 Hispanic/Latino; 3 Two or more races, non-Hispanic/Latino), 13 international. Average age 28. 43 applicants, 63% accepted, 17 enrolled. *Faculty:* 19 full-time (1 woman). *Expenses:* Contact institution. *Financial support:* In 2016–17, 30 students received support, including 11 research assistantships (averaging $3,925 per year), 8 teaching assistantships (averaging $2,552 per year); Federal Work-Study, scholarships/grants, tuition waivers, and unspecified assistantships also available. Financial award application deadline: 4/1; financial award applicants required to submit FAFSA. In 2016, 14 master's awarded.

Program availability: Part-time. Offers engineering (MSCE, MSEE, MSME). *Application deadline:* For fall admission, 8/1 priority date for domestic students, 5/1 for international students; for spring admission, 12/1 priority date for domestic students, 10/1 for international students; for summer admission, 3/15 priority date for domestic students, 2/1 for international students. *Application fee:* $30. *Application Contact:* Dr. Amanda Pascale, Director, The Graduate School, 904-320-1360, Fax: 904-620-1362, E-mail: graduateschool@unf.edu. *Director,* Dr. Murat Tiryakioglu, 904-620-1393, E-mail: m.tiryakioglu@unf.edu.

College of Education and Human Services Students: 115 full-time (97 women), 340 part-time (248 women); includes 136 minority (84 Black or African American, non-Hispanic/Latino; 1 American Indian or Alaska Native, non-Hispanic/Latino; 10 Asian, non-Hispanic/Latino; 24 Hispanic/Latino; 1 Native Hawaiian or other Pacific Islander, non-Hispanic/Latino; 16 Two or more races, non-Hispanic/Latino), 20 international. Average age 34. 197 applicants, 53% accepted, 74 enrolled. *Faculty:* 53 full-time (33 women), 11 part-time/adjunct (9 women). *Expenses:* Contact institution. *Financial support:* In 2016–17, 58 students received support, including 1 research assistantship (averaging $3,241 per year), 1 teaching assistantship (averaging $5,378 per year); career-related internships or fieldwork, Federal Work-Study, scholarships/grants, and tuition waivers (partial) also available. Support available to part-time students. Financial award application deadline: 4/1; financial award applicants required to submit FAFSA. In 2016, 174 master's, 7 doctorates awarded. *Program availability:* Part-time, evening/weekend. Offers adult learning (M Ed); American Sign Language (MS); American Sign Language/English interpreting (M Ed); applied behavior analysis (M Ed); autism (M Ed); counselor education (M Ed); deaf education (M Ed); disability services (M Ed); education and human services (M Ed, MS, Ed D); educational leadership (M Ed, Ed D); exceptional student education (M Ed); literacy (M Ed); professional education (M Ed); TESOL (M Ed). *Application deadline:* For fall admission, 7/1 priority date for domestic students, 5/1 for international students; for spring admission, 11/1 priority date for domestic students, 10/1 for international students. *Application fee:* $30. Electronic applications accepted. *Application Contact:* Dr. John Kemppainen, Director, Office of Student Services, 904-620-2530, Fax: 904-620-1135, E-mail: jkemppai@unf.edu. *Dean,* Dr. Diane Yendol-Hoppey, 904-620-2520, E-mail: diane.yendol-hoppey@unf.edu.

UNIVERSITY OF NORTH GEORGIA, Dahlonega, GA 30597

General Information State-supported, coed, comprehensive institution. *Enrollment:* 18,219 graduate, professional, and undergraduate students; 150 full-time matriculated graduate/professional students (110 women), 365 part-time matriculated graduate/professional students (240 women). *Enrollment by degree level:* 404 master's, 88 doctoral, 23 other advanced degrees. *Graduate faculty:* 79 full-time (41 women), 7 part-time/adjunct (5 women). *Tuition,* state resident: full-time $2025; part-time $225 per credit hour. *Tuition,* nonresident: full-time $8082; part-time $898 per credit hour. *Required fees:* $938; $620.50 per credit hour. Tuition and fees vary according to degree level and program. *Graduate housing:* Room and/or apartments available on a first-come, first-served basis to single students; on-campus housing not available to married students. Typical cost: $1798 per year ($3958 including board). Room and board charges vary according to board plan and housing facility selected. Housing application deadline: 2/1. *Student services:* Campus employment opportunities, campus safety program, career counseling, exercise/wellness program, free psychological counseling, international student services, low-cost health insurance, multicultural affairs office, services for students with disabilities, teacher training, writing training. *Library facilities:* Library Technology Center plus 4 others. *Collection:* Books: 270,623 (physical), 291,155 (digital/electronic); Serial titles: 115,466 (physical); Databases: 240. Students can reserve study rooms. *Research affiliation:* Northeast Georgia Medical Center, Morehouse School of Medicine, St. Joseph's Hospital, Mettler Electronic Corporation.

Computer facilities: 2,443 computers available on campus for general student use. A campuswide network can be accessed from student residence rooms and from off campus. Online class registration is available.
Website: http://www.ung.edu

General Application Contact: Melinda Maxwell, Director of Graduate Admissions, 706-864-1543, E-mail: melinda.maxwell@ung.edu.

GRADUATE UNITS

College of Education Students: 11 full-time (8 women), 146 part-time (107 women); includes 19 minority (10 Black or African American, non-Hispanic/Latino; 2 Asian, non-Hispanic/Latino; 6 Hispanic/Latino; 1 Two or more races, non-Hispanic/Latino). Average age 28. 77 applicants, 83% accepted, 47 enrolled. *Faculty:* 16 full-time (12 women), 3 part-time/adjunct (all women). *Expenses:* Contact institution. *Financial support:* Teaching assistantships, career-related internships or fieldwork, scholarships/grants, and unspecified assistantships available. Financial award application deadline: 5/1; financial award applicants required to submit CSS PROFILE or FAFSA. In 2016, 79 master's awarded. *Program availability:* Part-time, evening/weekend, online learning. Offers early childhood education (M Ed); middle grades education (M Ed, MAT); physical education (MS); school leadership (Ed S); secondary education (M Ed). *Application deadline:* For fall admission, 8/1 priority date for domestic students, 7/1 priority date for international students; for spring admission, 12/1 priority date for domestic students, 11/1 priority date for international students. Applications are processed on a rolling basis. *Application fee:* $40. Electronic applications accepted. *Application Contact:* Regina Boling, Teacher Education Graduate Admissions, 706-864-1533, E-mail: regina.boling@ung.edu. *Dean, College of Education,* Dr. Susan Ayers, 706-864-1998, E-mail: susan.ayres@ung.edu.

Department of Clinical Mental Health Counseling Students: 25 full-time (21 women), 23 part-time (17 women); includes 9 minority (3 Black or African American, non-Hispanic/Latino; 1 Asian, non-Hispanic/Latino; 4 Hispanic/Latino; 1 Two or more races, non-Hispanic/Latino). Average age 29. 53 applicants, 43% accepted, 22 enrolled. *Faculty:* 3 full-time (1 woman). *Expenses:* Contact institution. *Financial support:* Fellowships, research assistantships, teaching assistantships, and career-related internships or fieldwork available. Financial award application deadline: 3/17; financial award applicants required to submit FAFSA. In 2016, 8 master's awarded. *Program availability:* Part-time. Offers clinical mental health counseling (MS). *Application deadline:* For fall admission, 3/1 for domestic students. *Application fee:* $40. Electronic applications accepted. *Application Contact:* Melinda Maxwell, Director of Graduate Admissions, 706-864-1543, E-mail: melinda.maxwell@ung.edu. *Department Head,* Dr. P. Clay Rowell, 706-867-2791, E-mail: clay.rowell@ung.edu.

Department of Criminal Justice Students: 5 full-time (all women), 23 part-time (12 women); includes 8 minority (5 Black or African American, non-Hispanic/Latino; 1 Hispanic/Latino; 2 Two or more races, non-Hispanic/Latino). Average age 31. 18 applicants, 67% accepted, 9 enrolled. *Faculty:* 4 full-time (3 women). *Expenses:* Contact institution. *Financial support:* Fellowships and research assistantships available. Financial award application deadline: 3/17; financial award applicants required to submit FAFSA. In 2016, 12 master's awarded. *Program availability:* Part-time, evening/weekend, online only, 100% online. Offers criminal justice (MS). *Application* *deadline:* For fall admission, 8/10 for domestic students; for spring admission, 12/10 for domestic students; for summer admission, 5/10 for domestic students. *Application fee:* $40. Electronic applications accepted. *Application Contact:* Melinda Maxwell, Director of Graduate Admissions, 706-864-1543, E-mail: melinda.maxwell@ung.edu. *Interim Department Head,* Dr. Brent Paterline, 706-864-1914, E-mail: brent.paterline@ung.edu.

Department of History, Anthropology and Philosophy Students: 4 full-time (0 women), 11 part-time (5 women); includes 1 minority (Two or more races, non-Hispanic/Latino). Average age 32. 12 applicants, 92% accepted, 11 enrolled. *Faculty:* 11 full-time (4 women), 1 part-time/adjunct (0 women). Expenses: Contact institution. *Financial support:* Unspecified assistantships available. Financial award application deadline: 3/17; financial award applicants required to submit FAFSA. In 2016, 2 master's awarded. *Program availability:* Part-time, evening/weekend. Offers history (MA). *Application deadline:* For fall admission, 4/15 priority date for domestic students, 7/1 priority date for international students. Applications are processed on a rolling basis. *Application fee:* $40. Electronic applications accepted. *Application Contact:* Melinda Maxwell, Director of Graduate Admissions, 706-864-1543, E-mail: melinda.maxwell@ung.edu. *Department Head,* Dr. Jeff Pardue, 678-717-3867.

Department of Nursing Students: 56 part-time (49 women); includes 10 minority (7 Black or African American, non-Hispanic/Latino; 1 Asian, non-Hispanic/Latino; 1 Hispanic/Latino; 1 Two or more races, non-Hispanic/Latino). Average age 37. 5 applicants. *Faculty:* 5 full-time (all women), 2 part-time/adjunct (both women). Expenses: Contact institution. *Financial support:* Career-related internships or fieldwork and unspecified assistantships available. Financial award application deadline: 5/1; financial award applicants required to submit CSS PROFILE or FAFSA. In 2016, 24 master's awarded. *Program availability:* Part-time. Offers family nurse practitioner (MS, Post-Master's Certificate). *Application deadline:* For fall admission, 7/1 priority date for domestic students, 6/1 for international students. *Application fee:* $40. Electronic applications accepted. *Application Contact:* Melinda Maxwell, Director of Graduate Admissions, 706-864-1543, E-mail: melinda.maxwell@ung.edu. *Department Head,* Dr. Kim Hudson-Gallogly, 706-864-1934, E-mail: kim.hudson-gallogly@ung.edu.

Department of Physical Therapy Students: 88 full-time (61 women); includes 8 minority (4 Black or African American, non-Hispanic/Latino; 2 Hispanic/Latino; 2 Two or more races, non-Hispanic/Latino). Average age 25. *Faculty:* 6 full-time (all women), 2 part-time/adjunct (both women). Expenses: Contact institution. *Financial support:* Unspecified assistantships available. Financial award application deadline: 5/1; financial award applicants required to submit CSS PROFILE or FAFSA. In 2016, 30 doctorates awarded. Offers physical therapy (DPT). *Application deadline:* For fall admission, 10/3 for domestic students. Applications are processed on a rolling basis. *Application fee:* $50. Electronic applications accepted. *Application Contact:* Melinda Maxwell, Director of Graduate Admissions, 706-864-1543, E-mail: melinda.maxwell@ung.edu. *Department Head,* Dr. Mary Ellen Oesterle, 706-867-4589, E-mail: maryellen.oesterle@ung.edu.

Mike Cottrell College of Business Students: 56 part-time (25 women); includes 11 minority (3 Black or African American, non-Hispanic/Latino; 6 Asian, non-Hispanic/Latino; 2 Hispanic/Latino). Average age 35. 69 applicants, 83% accepted, 43 enrolled. *Faculty:* 5 full-time (3 women), 1 part-time/adjunct (0 women). Expenses: Contact institution. *Financial support:* Unspecified assistantships available. Financial award application deadline: 3/17; financial award applicants required to submit CSS PROFILE or FAFSA. In 2016, 11 master's awarded. *Program availability:* Part-time, evening/weekend. Offers business (MBA). *Application deadline:* For fall admission, 4/1 priority date for domestic and international students. *Application fee:* $40. Electronic applications accepted. *Application Contact:* Melinda Maxwell, Director of Graduate Admissions, 706-864-1543, E-mail: melinda.maxwell@ung.edu. *Dean,* Dr. Donna Mayo, 706-864-1620, E-mail: donna.mayo@ung.edu.

Program in International Affairs Students: 8 full-time (7 women), 31 part-time (13 women); includes 8 minority (6 Black or African American, non-Hispanic/Latino; 1 Asian, non-Hispanic/Latino; 1 Two or more races, non-Hispanic/Latino). Average age 32. 29 applicants, 76% accepted, 11 enrolled. *Faculty:* 9 full-time (1 woman). Expenses: Contact institution. *Financial support:* Career-related internships or fieldwork, scholarships/grants, and unspecified assistantships available. Financial award application deadline: 3/17; financial award applicants required to submit CSS PROFILE or FAFSA. In 2016, 11 master's awarded. *Program availability:* Part-time, evening/weekend, 100% online. Offers international affairs (MAIA). *Application deadline:* For fall admission, 8/1 priority date for domestic students; for spring admission, 12/1 priority date for domestic students; for summer admission, 5/1 priority date for domestic students. Applications are processed on a rolling basis. *Application fee:* $40. Electronic applications accepted. *Application Contact:* Melinda Maxwell, Director of Graduate Admissions, 706-864-1543, E-mail: melinda.maxwell@ung.edu. *Department Head,* Dr. Cristian Harris, 706-867-3251, E-mail: cristian.harris@ung.edu.

Program in Public Administration Students: 9 full-time (8 women), 1 (woman) part-time; includes 1 minority (Hispanic/Latino). Average age 29. 8 applicants, 50% accepted, 3 enrolled. *Faculty:* 9 full-time (1 woman). Expenses: Contact institution. *Financial support:* Research assistantships and teaching assistantships available. Financial award application deadline: 3/17; financial award applicants required to submit FAFSA. In 2016, 10 master's awarded. *Program availability:* Part-time, online only, 100% online. Offers public administration (MPA). *Application deadline:* For fall admission, 8/10 for domestic students; for spring admission, 12/10 for domestic students; for summer admission, 5/10 for domestic students. *Application fee:* $40. Electronic applications accepted. *Application Contact:* Melinda Maxwell, Director of Graduate Admissions, 706-864-1543, E-mail: melinda.maxwell@ung.edu. *Program Coordinator,* Dr. Luisa Diaz-Kope, 706-864-1699, E-mail: luisa.diazkope@ung.edu.

UNIVERSITY OF NORTH TEXAS, Denton, TX 76203

General Information State-supported, coed, university. CGS member. *Graduate housing:* Rooms and/or apartments available on a first-come, first-served basis to single and married students. Housing application deadline: 9/1. *Research affiliation:* Delta and Pine Land Company (natural science), Semiconductor Research Corporation (materials science), Tech America (technology transfer), National Business Incubation Association (entrepreneurship), International Economic Development Council (economic growth).

GRADUATE UNITS

Robert B. Toulouse School of Graduate Studies *Program availability:* Part-time, evening/weekend, online learning. Offers accounting (MS); applied anthropology (MA, MS); applied behavior analysis (Certificate); applied geography (MA); applied technology and performance improvement (M Ed, MS); art education (MA); art history (MA); art museum education (Certificate); arts leadership (Certificate); audiology (Au D); behavior analysis (MS); behavioral science (PhD); biochemistry and molecular biology (MS); biology (MA, MS); biomedical engineering (MS); business analysis (MS); chemistry (MS); clinical health psychology (PhD); communication studies (MA, MS); computer engineering (MS); computer science (MS); counseling (M Ed, MS); creative writing (MA); criminal justice (MS); curriculum and instruction (M Ed); decision sciences (MBA); design (MA, MFA); early childhood studies (MS); economics (MS); educational leadership (M Ed, Ed D); educational psychology (MS, PhD); electrical engineering (MS); emergency management (MPA); engineering technology (MS); English (MA); English as a second language (MA); environmental science (MS); finance (MBA, MS); financial management (MPA); French (MA); health services management (MBA); higher education (M Ed, Ed D); history (MA, MS); hospitality management (MS); human resources management (MPA); information science (MS); information systems (PhD); information technologies (MBA); interdisciplinary studies (MA, MS); international studies (MA); international sustainable tourism (MS); jazz studies (MM); journalism (MA, MJ, Graduate Certificate); kinesiology (MS); linguistics (MA); local government management (MPA); logistics (PhD); logistics and supply chain management (MBA); long-term care, senior housing, and aging services (MA); management (PhD); marketing (MBA); mathematics (MA, MS); mechanical and energy engineering (MS, PhD); music (MA); music composition (PhD); music education (MM Ed, PhD); nonprofit management (MPA); operations and supply chain management (MBA); performance (MM, DMA); philosophy (MA); political science (MA); professional and technical communication (MA); radio, television and film (MA, MFA); rehabilitation counseling (Certificate); sociology (MA); Spanish (MA); special education (M Ed); speech-language pathology (MA); strategic management (MBA); studio art (MFA); teaching (M Ed). Electronic applications accepted.

UNIVERSITY OF NORTH TEXAS AT DALLAS, Dallas, TX 75241

General Information State-supported, coed, comprehensive institution.

GRADUATE UNITS

Graduate School

UNIVERSITY OF NORTH TEXAS HEALTH SCIENCE CENTER AT FORT WORTH, Fort Worth, TX 76107-2699

General Information State-supported, coed, graduate-only institution. CGS member. *Graduate housing:* On-campus housing not available. *Student services:* Campus employment opportunities, campus safety program, career counseling, exercise/wellness program, free psychological counseling, grant writing training, international student services, low-cost health insurance, multicultural affairs office, services for students with disabilities. *Library facilities:* Gibson D. Lewis Health Science Library. *Research affiliation:* Myogen, Inc. (cardiac research), My-tech, Inc. (cardiovascular research), Novopharm, Inc. (gene control), Ethnobotanical Product Investigation Consortium (natural plant products), Genelink (familial DNA depository), Botanical Research Institutions of Texas.
Website: http://www.hsc.unt.edu/

General Application Contact: Information Contact, 817-735-2000.

GRADUATE UNITS

Graduate School of Biomedical Sciences Expenses: Contact institution. *Financial support:* Fellowships, research assistantships, teaching assistantships, career-related internships or fieldwork, Federal Work-Study, institutionally sponsored loans, scholarships/grants, and traineeships available. Support available to part-time students. Financial award application deadline: 4/1; financial award applicants required to submit FAFSA. Offers biochemistry and cancer biology (MS, PhD); biotechnology (MS); cell biology, immunology and microbiology (MS, PhD); clinical research management (MS); forensic genetics (MS); genetics (MS, PhD); integrative physiology (MS, PhD); medical sciences (MS); pharmaceutical sciences and pharmacotherapy (MS, PhD); pharmacology and neuroscience (MS, PhD); structural anatomy and rehabilitation sciences (MS, PhD). *Application deadline:* For fall admission, 5/1 for domestic students. *Application fee:* $25 ($50 for international students). *Application Contact:* Carla Lee, Director of Graduate Admissions and Services, 817-735-2560, Fax: 817-735-0243, E-mail: gsbs@hsc.unt.edu. *Dean,* Dr. Thomas Yorio, 817-735-2560, Fax: 817-735-0243, E-mail: yoriot@hsc.unt.edu.

School of Health Professions Expenses: Contact institution. *Financial support:* Fellowships, research assistantships, teaching assistantships, career-related internships or fieldwork, Federal Work-Study, institutionally sponsored loans, scholarships/grants, and tuition waivers available. Financial award application deadline: 4/1; financial award applicants required to submit FAFSA. Offers physical therapy (DPT); physician assistant studies (MPAS). *Application deadline:* For winter admission, 11/15 for domestic students. *Application fee:* $50. *Application Contact:* Jane Anderson, Director of Admissions, 817-735-2204, Fax: 817-735-2225. *Interim Dean,* Dr. Nicoleta Bugnariu, 817-735-2301, Fax: 817-735-2529.

School of Public Health Students: 134 full-time (89 women), 92 part-time (63 women); includes 94 minority (39 Black or African American, non-Hispanic/Latino; 3 American Indian or Alaska Native, non-Hispanic/Latino; 20 Asian, non-Hispanic/Latino; 32 Hispanic/Latino), 39 international. Average age 33. 302 applicants, 59% accepted, 51 enrolled. *Faculty:* 26 full-time (6 women). Expenses: Contact institution. *Financial support:* In 2016–17, 9 research assistantships with partial tuition reimbursements (averaging $16,000 per year), 2 teaching assistantships (averaging $8,100 per year) were awarded; fellowships, Federal Work-Study, institutionally sponsored loans, and scholarships/grants also available. Support available to part-time students. Financial award application deadline: 4/1; financial award applicants required to submit FAFSA. In 2016, 61 master's, 6 doctorates awarded. *Program availability:* Part-time, evening/weekend, 100% online. Offers biostatistics (MS); epidemiology (MPH, MS, PhD); food security and public health (Graduate Certificate); GIS in public health (Graduate Certificate); global health (Graduate Certificate); global health for medical professionals (Graduate Certificate); health administration (MHA); health behavior research (MS, PhD); maternal and child health (MPH); public health (Graduate Certificate); public health practice (MPH). *Application deadline:* For fall admission, 7/1 for domestic students. Applications are processed on a rolling basis. *Application fee:* $25 ($50 for international students). Electronic applications accepted. *Application Contact:* Julie Herrmann, Recruitment and Outreach Coordinator, 817-735-2401. *Director of Admissions,* Beth Hargrove, 817-735-2401, E-mail: sph@unthsc.edu.

Texas College of Osteopathic Medicine Expenses: Contact institution. *Financial support:* Research assistantships, teaching assistantships with tuition reimbursements, career-related internships or fieldwork, Federal Work-Study, institutionally sponsored loans, scholarships/grants, and tuition waivers (full) available. Financial award applicants required to submit FAFSA. Offers osteopathic medicine (DO). Electronic applications accepted. *Application Contact:* Jane Anderson, Director of Admissions, 817-735-2204, Fax: 817-735-2225. *Dean,* Dr. Marc B. Hahn, 817-735-2416, Fax: 817-735-2486.

UNIVERSITY OF NORTHWESTERN–ST. PAUL, St. Paul, MN 55113-1598

General Information Independent-religious, coed, comprehensive institution. *Graduate housing:* On-campus housing not available. *Student services:* Campus employment opportunities, campus safety program, career counseling, international student services, multicultural affairs office, services for students with disabilities, writing training. *Library facilities:* Berntsen Library.

Computer facilities: Computer purchase and lease plans are available. 200 computers available on campus for general student use. A campuswide network can be accessed from student residence rooms and from off campus. Online class registration, network file space, personal web site, integrated student portal, b/w and color printing, virtual labs are available.
Website: http://www.unwsp.edu/

General Application Contact: Tami Treder, Graduate Admission Counselor, 651-628-3351, E-mail: tjtreder@unwsp.edu.

GRADUATE UNITS

Master of Arts in Education Program Expenses: Contact institution. *Program availability:* Part-time, evening/weekend, online learning. Offers education (MA Ed). *Application deadline:* Applications are processed on a rolling basis. Electronic applications accepted. *Application Contact:* College of Adult and Graduate Studies Admissions, 651-631-5200, E-mail: gradstudies@unwsp.edu.

Master of Arts in Human Services Program Expenses: Contact institution. *Program availability:* Part-time, evening/weekend, online learning. Offers human services (MAHS). *Application deadline:* Applications are processed on a rolling basis. Electronic applications accepted. *Application Contact:* College of Adult and Graduate Studies Admissions, 651-631-5200, E-mail: gradstudies@unwsp.edu.

Master of Arts in Theological Studies Program Expenses: Contact institution. *Program availability:* Part-time, evening/weekend, online learning. Offers theological studies (MATS). *Application deadline:* Applications are processed on a rolling basis. Electronic applications accepted. *Application Contact:* College of Adult and Graduate Studies Admissions, 651-631-5200, E-mail: gradstudies@unwsp.edu.

Master of Business Administration Program Expenses: Contact institution. *Program availability:* Part-time, evening/weekend, online learning. Offers business administration (MBA). *Application deadline:* Applications are processed on a rolling basis. Electronic applications accepted. *Application Contact:* College of Adult and Graduate Studies Admissions, 651-631-5200, E-mail: gradstudies@unwsp.edu.

Master of Divinity Program Expenses: Contact institution. *Program availability:* Part-time, evening/weekend, online learning. Offers theology and Christian ministry (M Div). *Application deadline:* Applications are processed on a rolling basis. Electronic applications accepted. *Application Contact:* College of Adult and Graduate Studies Admissions, 651-631-5200, E-mail: gradstudies@unwsp.edu.

Master of Organizational Leadership Program Expenses: Contact institution. *Program availability:* Part-time, evening/weekend, online learning. Offers organizational leadership (MOL). *Application deadline:* Applications are processed on a rolling basis. Electronic applications accepted. *Application Contact:* College of Adult and Graduate Studies Admissions, 651-631-5200, E-mail: gradstudies@unwsp.edu.

UNIVERSITY OF NOTRE DAME, Notre Dame, IN 46556

General Information Independent-religious, coed, university. CGS member. *Graduate housing:* Rooms and/or apartments available on a first-come, first-served basis to single and married students. Housing application deadline: 5/1. *Research affiliation:* Space Telescope Science Institute, Brookhaven National Laboratory, Fermi National Accelerator Laboratory, Argonne National Laboratory.

GRADUATE UNITS

Graduate School *Program availability:* Part-time. Electronic applications accepted.

College of Arts and Letters *Program availability:* Part-time. Offers art history (MA); arts and letters (M Div, M Ed, MA, MFA, MMS, MSM, MTS, PhD); cognitive psychology (PhD); counseling psychology (PhD); creative writing (MFA); design (MFA); developmental psychology (PhD); early Christian studies (MA); economics and econometrics (MA, PhD); educational initiatives (M Ed, MA); English (MA, PhD); French and Francophone studies (MA); history (MA, PhD); history and philosophy of science (MA, PhD); humanities (M Div, MA, MFA, MMS, MSM, MTS, PhD); Iberian and Latin American studies (MA); international peace studies (MA, PhD); Italian studies (MA); literature (PhD); medieval studies (MMS, PhD); philosophy (PhD); political science (PhD); quantitative psychology (PhD); Romance literatures (MA); social science (M Ed, MA, PhD); sociology (PhD); studio art (MFA); theology (M Div, MA, MSM, MTS, PhD); theology and science (PhD). Electronic applications accepted.

College of Engineering Offers aerospace and mechanical engineering (M Eng, PhD); aerospace engineering (MS Aero E); bioengineering (MS Bio E); chemical and biomolecular engineering (MS Ch E); civil engineering (MSCE); civil engineering and geological sciences (PhD); computer science and engineering (MSCSE, PhD); electrical engineering (MSEE, PhD); engineering (M Eng, MEME, MS, MS Aero E, MS Bio E, MS Ch E, MS Env E, MSCE, MSCSE, MSEE, MSME, PhD); environmental engineering (MS Env E); geological sciences (MS); mechanical engineering (MEME, MSME). Electronic applications accepted.

College of Science Offers algebra (PhD); algebraic geometry (PhD); applied and computational mathematics and statistics (PhD); applied mathematics (MSAM); applied statistics (MS); aquatic ecology, evolution and environmental biology (MS, PhD); biochemistry (MS, PhD); cellular and molecular biology (MS, PhD); complex analysis (PhD); computational finance (MS); differential geometry (PhD); genetics (MS, PhD); inorganic chemistry (MS, PhD); logic (PhD); organic chemistry (MS, PhD); partial differential equations (PhD); physical chemistry (MS, PhD); physics (MS, PhD); physiology (MS, PhD); science (MS, MSAM, PhD); topology (PhD); vector biology and parasitology (MS, PhD). Electronic applications accepted.

Keough School of Global Affairs Offers global affairs (MGA); international peace studies (MGA); sustainable development (MGA).

School of Architecture Offers architectural design and urbanism (M ADU); architecture (M Arch). Electronic applications accepted.

Law School Students: 645 full-time (291 women), 1 part-time (0 women); includes 158 minority (28 Black or African American, non-Hispanic/Latino; 3 American Indian or Alaska Native, non-Hispanic/Latino; 44 Asian, non-Hispanic/Latino; 60 Hispanic/Latino; 23 Two or more races, non-Hispanic/Latino), 51 international. 2,797 applicants, 32% accepted, 223 enrolled. *Faculty:* 56 full-time (17 women), 60 part-time/adjunct (24 women). Expenses: Contact institution. *Financial support:* In 2016–17, 503 students received support, including 503 fellowships with tuition reimbursements available (averaging $28,332 per year); research assistantships, teaching assistantships, career-related internships or fieldwork, Federal Work-Study, institutionally sponsored loans, scholarships/grants, health care benefits, unspecified assistantships, and university dormitory rector assistantships also available. Financial award application deadline: 2/28; financial award applicants required to submit FAFSA. In 2016, 26 master's, 173 doctorates awarded. Offers human rights (LL M, JSD); international and comparative law (LL M); law (JD). *Application deadline:* For fall admission, 3/15 for domestic and international students. Applications are processed on a rolling basis. *Application fee:* $75. Electronic applications accepted. *Application Contact:* Jacob Baska, Director of

Admissions, 574-631-6626, Fax: 574-631-5474, E-mail: lawadmit@nd.edu. *Dean*, Nell Jessup Newton, 574-631-6789, Fax: 574-631-8400, E-mail: nell.newton@nd.edu.

Mendoza College of Business Students: 611 full-time (170 women), 157 part-time (52 women); includes 134 minority (36 Black or African American, non-Hispanic/Latino; 3 American Indian or Alaska Native, non-Hispanic/Latino; 21 Asian, non-Hispanic/Latino; 62 Hispanic/Latino; 2 Native Hawaiian or other Pacific Islander, non-Hispanic/Latino; 10 Two or more races, non-Hispanic/Latino), 115 international. Average age 30. *Faculty:* 46 full-time (8 women), 37 part-time/adjunct (7 women). Expenses: Contact institution. *Financial support:* In 2016–17, 454 students received support, including 454 fellowships; career-related internships or fieldwork, Federal Work-Study, institutionally sponsored loans, scholarships/grants, health care benefits, and unspecified assistantships also available. Financial award applicants required to submit FAFSA. In 2016, 535 master's awarded. Offers assurance and advisory services (MSA); business (MBA, MNA, MSA, MSBA, MSF, MSM); business analytics (MSBA); business leadership (MBA); consulting (MBA); corporate finance (MBA); executive business administration (MBA); finance (MSF); innovation and entrepreneurship (MBA); investments (MBA); management (MSM); marketing (MBA); nonprofit administration (MNA); tax services (MSA). *Application deadline:* Applications are processed on a rolling basis. Electronic applications accepted. *Dean*, Dr. Roger D. Huang, 574-631-1691, Fax: 574-631-4825, E-mail: roger.huang.31@nd.edu.

UNIVERSITY OF OKLAHOMA, Norman, OK 73019-0390

General Information State-supported, coed, university. CGS member. *Enrollment:* 27,918 graduate, professional, and undergraduate students; 3,040 full-time matriculated graduate/professional students (1,507 women), 3,196 part-time matriculated graduate/professional students (1,633 women). *Enrollment by degree level:* 4,166 master's, 2,045 doctoral, 25 other advanced degrees. *Graduate faculty:* 1,240 full-time (424 women), 61 part-time/adjunct (29 women). *Tuition,* state resident: full-time $4886; part-time $203.60 per credit hour. Tuition, nonresident: full-time $18,989; part-time $791.20 per credit hour. *Required fees:* $3283; $126.25 per credit hour. $126.50 per semester. *Graduate housing:* Rooms and or apartments available on a first-come, first-served basis to single and married students. Typical cost: $6768 per year ($11,036 including board) for single students; $6768 per year for married students. Room and board charges vary according to board plan, campus/location and housing facility selected. *Student services:* Campus employment opportunities, campus safety program, career counseling, child daycare facilities, exercise/wellness program, free psychological counseling, grant writing training, international student services, low-cost health insurance, multicultural affairs office, services for students with disabilities, teacher training, writing training. *Library facilities:* Bizzell Memorial Library plus 5 others. *Collection:* Books: 5.7 million (physical), 1.3 million (digital/electronic); Serial titles: 116,374 (physical), 71,040 (digital/electronic); Databases: 310. Students can reserve study rooms. *Research affiliation:* National Oceanic and Atmospheric Administration (NOAA)/National Severe Storms Laboratory (weather), Nanowave Technologies, Inc. (radar), Department of the Interior South Central Region Climate Science Center (climate science), Weathernews International (weather), Sandia National Laboratories (national security), U.S. Department of Transportation Southern Plains Transportation Center (transportation infrastructure).

Computer facilities: Computer purchase and lease plans are available. 4,500 computers available on campus for general student use. A campuswide network can be accessed from student residence rooms and from off campus. Online class registration is available.
Website: http://www.ou.edu/

General Application Contact: Dr. Randall S. Hewes, Interim Dean, 405-325-6765, Fax: 405-325-5346, E-mail: gradinfo@ou.edu.

GRADUATE UNITS

College of Architecture Students: 95 full-time (52 women), 21 part-time (10 women); includes 24 minority (3 Black or African American, non-Hispanic/Latino; 4 American Indian or Alaska Native, non-Hispanic/Latino; 3 Asian, non-Hispanic/Latino; 6 Hispanic/Latino; 8 Two or more races, non-Hispanic/Latino), 39 international. Average age 30. 114 applicants, 51% accepted, 41 enrolled. *Faculty:* 38 full-time (16 women), 1 part-time/adjunct (0 women). Expenses: Contact institution. *Financial support:* In 2016–17, 95 students received support, including 2 fellowships (averaging $3,750 per year), 39 research assistantships with partial tuition reimbursements available (averaging $11,549 per year), 3 teaching assistantships with partial tuition reimbursements available (averaging $12,957 per year); scholarships/grants and unspecified assistantships also available. Financial award application deadline: 6/1; financial award applicants required to submit FAFSA. In 2016, 30 master's awarded. *Program availability:* Part-time, evening/weekend. Offers architecture (M Arch, MCM, MLA, MRCP, MS, PhD, Graduate Certificate). *Application deadline:* For fall admission, 6/1 for international students. *Application fee:* $50 ($100 for international students). Electronic applications accepted. *Application Contact:* Dr. Charlie Warnken, Associate Dean for Instructional Services, 405-325-2444, Fax: 405-325-7558, E-mail: cwarnken@ou.edu. *Dean*, Hans Butzer, 405-325-2444, Fax: 405-325-7558, E-mail: butzer@ou.edu.

Division of Architecture Students: 35 full-time (19 women), 9 part-time (4 women); includes 6 minority (1 Black or African American, non-Hispanic/Latino; 1 American Indian or Alaska Native, non-Hispanic/Latino; 1 Asian, non-Hispanic/Latino; 3 Two or more races, non-Hispanic/Latino), 17 international. Average age 31. 47 applicants, 47% accepted, 16 enrolled. *Faculty:* 38 full-time (16 women), 1 part-time/adjunct (0 women). Expenses: Contact institution. *Financial support:* In 2016–17, 25 students received support, including 10 research assistantships with partial tuition reimbursements available (averaging $10,372 per year), 2 teaching assistantships with partial tuition reimbursements available (averaging $12,686 per year); career-related internships or fieldwork, scholarships/grants, health care benefits, tuition waivers, and unspecified assistantships also available. Financial award application deadline: 6/1; financial award applicants required to submit FAFSA. In 2016, 14 master's awarded. *Program availability:* Part-time. Offers architecture (MS, PhD); data and digital representation (M Arch); design entrepreneurship and real estate (M Arch); resilient planning, design, and construction (M Arch). *Application deadline:* For spring admission, 5/1 for domestic students, 3/1 for international students. Applications are processed on a rolling basis. *Application fee:* $50 ($100 for international students). Electronic applications accepted. *Application Contact:* Marjorie Callahan, Graduate Liaison, Fax: 405-325-7588, E-mail: mcallahan@ou.edu. *Director*, Dr. Stephanie Pilat, 405-325-9352, Fax: 405-325-7588, E-mail: architecture.director@ou.edu.

Division of Interior Design Students: 6 full-time (5 women); includes 2 minority (both American Indian or Alaska Native, non-Hispanic/Latino), 2 international. Average age 34. 11 applicants, 55% accepted, 4 enrolled. Expenses: Contact institution. *Financial support:* In 2016–17, 3 students received support, including 3 research assistantships with partial tuition reimbursements available (averaging $10,372 per year); teaching assistantships with full and partial tuition reimbursements available, career-related internships or fieldwork, scholarships/grants, tuition waivers, and unspecified assistantships also available. Financial award application deadline: 6/1; financial award applicants required to submit FAFSA. In 2016, 1 master's awarded. *Program availability:* Part-time. Offers interior design (MS); planning, design and construction (PhD); professional applications of interior design (Graduate Certificate). *Application deadline:* Applications are processed on a rolling basis. *Application fee:* $50 ($100 for international students). Electronic applications accepted. *Application Contact:* Dr. Suchismita Bhattacharjee, Assistant Professor and Graduate Liaison, 405-325-2548, Fax: 405-325-7558, E-mail: suchi@ou.edu. *Academic Director and Associate Professor,* Mia Kile, 405-325-1051, Fax: 405-325-7558, E-mail: mkile@ou.edu.

Division of Landscape Architecture Students: 19 full-time (13 women), 1 part-time (0 women); includes 4 minority (2 Asian, non-Hispanic/Latino; 2 Two or more races, non-Hispanic/Latino), 8 international. Average age 28. 22 applicants, 45% accepted, 8 enrolled. Expenses: Contact institution. *Financial support:* In 2016–17, 19 students received support, including 11 research assistantships with full and partial tuition reimbursements available (averaging $13,671 per year); scholarships/grants and unspecified assistantships also available. Financial award application deadline: 6/1; financial award applicants required to submit FAFSA. In 2016, 2 master's awarded. Offers landscape architectural studies (MLA); landscape architecture (MLA). *Application deadline:* For fall admission, 2/15 priority date for domestic and international students. Applications are processed on a rolling basis. *Application fee:* $50 ($100 for international students). Electronic applications accepted. *Associate Dean and Director,* Leehu Loon, 405-325-1519, Fax: 405-325-7558, E-mail: lloon@ou.edu.

Division of Regional and City Planning Students: 20 full-time (13 women), 4 part-time (3 women); includes 6 minority (2 Black or African American, non-Hispanic/Latino; 1 American Indian or Alaska Native, non-Hispanic/Latino; 1 Hispanic/Latino; 2 Two or more races, non-Hispanic/Latino), 3 international. Average age 28. 12 applicants, 67% accepted, 5 enrolled. Expenses: Contact institution. *Financial support:* In 2016–17, 26 students received support, including 2 fellowships (averaging $3,750 per year), 3 research assistantships with tuition reimbursements available (averaging $11,915 per year); teaching assistantships, career-related internships or fieldwork, Federal Work-Study, scholarships/grants, health care benefits, tuition waivers, and unspecified assistantships also available. Financial award application deadline: 6/1; financial award applicants required to submit FAFSA. In 2016, 13 master's awarded. *Program availability:* Part-time. Offers community and economic development (MRCP); physical planning (MRCP). *Application deadline:* For fall admission, 4/1 priority date for international students. Applications are processed on a rolling basis. *Application fee:* $50 ($100 for international students). Electronic applications accepted. *Director,* Dr. Charles Warnken, 405-325-2444, Fax: 405-325-7558, E-mail: cwarnken@ou.edu.

Haskell and Irene Lemon Division of Construction Science Students: 16 full-time (3 women), 7 part-time (3 women); includes 6 minority (5 Hispanic/Latino; 1 Two or more races, non-Hispanic/Latino), 9 international. Average age 30. 22 applicants, 55% accepted, 8 enrolled. Expenses: Contact institution. *Financial support:* In 2016–17, 22 students received support, including 8 research assistantships with full and partial tuition reimbursements available (averaging $10,372 per year), 1 teaching assistantship with full and partial tuition reimbursement available (averaging $13,500 per year); fellowships with full and partial tuition reimbursements available, career-related internships or fieldwork, and scholarships/grants also available. Financial award application deadline: 6/1; financial award applicants required to submit FAFSA. *Program availability:* Part-time, evening/weekend. Offers construction science (MCM); planning, design, and construction (PhD). *Application fee:* $50 ($100 for international students). Electronic applications accepted. *Application Contact:* Anthony Perrenoud, Graduate Liaison, 405-325-2674, E-mail: perrenoud@ou.edu. *Interim Director,* Lisa Holliday, 405-325-9464, E-mail: lisaholliday@ou.edu.

College of Arts and Sciences Students: 1,131 full-time (673 women), 1,132 part-time (707 women); includes 727 minority (259 Black or African American, non-Hispanic/Latino; 97 American Indian or Alaska Native, non-Hispanic/Latino; 59 Asian, non-Hispanic/Latino; 184 Hispanic/Latino; 4 Native Hawaiian or other Pacific Islander, non-Hispanic/Latino; 124 Two or more races, non-Hispanic/Latino), 222 international. Average age 32. 1,201 applicants, 54% accepted, 497 enrolled. *Faculty:* 531 full-time (207 women), 24 part-time/adjunct (18 women). Expenses: Contact institution. *Financial support:* In 2016–17, 1,198 students received support, including 42 fellowships with full tuition reimbursements available (averaging $3,240 per year), 190 research assistantships with tuition reimbursements available (averaging $14,800 per year), 588 teaching assistantships with tuition reimbursements available (averaging $15,198 per year); career-related internships or fieldwork, Federal Work-Study, institutionally sponsored loans, scholarships/grants, traineeships, health care benefits, and unspecified assistantships also available. Support available to part-time students. Financial award application deadline: 6/1; financial award applicants required to submit FAFSA. In 2016, 633 master's, 83 doctorates, 120 other advanced degrees awarded. *Program availability:* Part-time, evening/weekend, online learning. Offers anthropology (MA, PhD); applied economics (MA); applied linguistic anthropology (MA); archaeology (PhD); arts and sciences (MA, MHR, MLIS, MPA, MS, MSW, PhD, Graduate Certificate); biochemistry (MS, PhD); cellular and behavioral neurobiology (PhD); chemistry (MS, PhD); clinical mental health (MHR); communication (MA); communication technology (PhD); composition and rhetoric (MA, PhD); ecology and evolutionary biology (PhD); economics (PhD); engineering physics (MS); exercise physiology (MS, PhD); French (MA, PhD); general (MPA); German (MA); health and exercise science (MS); health and human biology (PhD); health communication (PhD); health promotion (MS, PhD); helping skills in human relations (Graduate Certificate); history (MA, PhD); history of science, technology and medicine (MA, PhD); human relations (MHR); human resource diversity and development (Graduate Certificate); human resource management (MA, Graduate Certificate); human resources (MHR); individualized intensive study (MPA); industrial organizational psychology (MS, PhD); intercultural/international communication (PhD); interpersonal communication/social influence (PhD); licensed professional counselor (MHR); literary and cultural studies (MA, PhD); managerial economics (MA); mathematics (MA, MS, PhD); microbiology (MS, PhD); Native American studies (MA); nonprofit management (MPA); organizational communication (PhD); organizational dynamics (MA, Graduate Certificate); philosophy (MA, PhD); physics (MS, PhD); plant biology (MS, PhD); political science (MA, MPA, PhD); political/mass communication (PhD); project management (MA, Graduate Certificate); psychology (MS, PhD); public administration (MPA); socio-cultural and linguistics (PhD); socio-cultural anthropology (MA); sociology (MA, PhD); Spanish (MA, PhD); women's and gender studies (Graduate Certificate). *Application fee:* $50 ($100 for international students). Electronic applications accepted. *Dean,* Kelly Damphousse, 405-325-2077, Fax: 405-325-7709, E-mail: kdamp@ou.edu.

Anne and Henry Zarrow School of Social Work Students: 210 full-time (178 women), 190 part-time (157 women); includes 166 minority (64 Black or African American, non-Hispanic/Latino; 34 American Indian or Alaska Native, non-Hispanic/Latino; 3 Asian, non-Hispanic/Latino; 25 Hispanic/Latino; 1 Native Hawaiian or other Pacific Islander, non-Hispanic/Latino; 39 Two or more races, non-Hispanic/Latino), 1 international. Average age 32. 214 applicants, 90% accepted, 152 enrolled. *Faculty:* 24 full-time (17 women), 12 part-time/adjunct (11 women). Expenses: Contact institution. *Financial support:* In 2016–17, 119 students received support, including 20 research assistantships with partial tuition reimbursements available (averaging $10,491 per year); career-related internships or fieldwork, scholarships/grants, and unspecified assistantships also available. Support available to part-time students. Financial award application deadline: 6/1; financial award applicants required to submit FAFSA. In 2016, 134 master's awarded. *Program availability:* Part-time, evening/weekend. Offers direct practice (MSW). *Application deadline:* For fall admission, 2/1 priority date for domestic and international students; for summer admission, 2/1 priority date for domestic and international students. *Application fee:* $50 ($100 for international students). Electronic applications accepted. *Application Contact:* Amy Ann Arnold, Admissions and Enrollment Coordinator, 918-660-3385, Fax: 918-660-3383, E-mail: aarnold@ou.edu. *Director,* Dr. Julie Miller-Cribbs, 918-660-3378, Fax: 918-660-3383, E-mail: jmcribbs@ou.edu.

School of Library and Information Studies Students: 49 full-time (43 women), 97 part-time (76 women); includes 30 minority (3 Black or African American, non-Hispanic/Latino; 5 American Indian or Alaska Native, non-Hispanic/Latino; 2 Asian, non-Hispanic/Latino; 8 Hispanic/Latino; 1 Native Hawaiian or other Pacific Islander, non-Hispanic/Latino; 11 Two or more races, non-Hispanic/Latino), 1 international. Average age 32. 40 applicants, 85% accepted, 27 enrolled. *Faculty:* 11 full-time (8 women). Expenses: Contact institution. *Financial support:* In 2016–17, 81 students received support, including 4 research assistantships with full tuition reimbursements available (averaging $12,801 per year), 5 teaching assistantships (averaging $10,579 per year); scholarships/grants, health care benefits, and unspecified assistantships also available. Financial award application deadline: 6/1; financial award applicants required to submit FAFSA. In 2016, 45 master's awarded. *Program availability:* Part-time, evening/weekend, online learning. Offers library and information studies (MLIS). *Application deadline:* Applications are processed on a rolling basis. *Application fee:* $50 ($100 for international students). Electronic applications accepted. *Application Contact:* Sarah Connelly, Admissions and Student Services Coordinator, 405-325-3921, Fax: 405-325-7648, E-mail: sarahee@ou.edu. *Interim Director,* Dr. Susan Burke, 405-325-3921, Fax: 405-325-7648, E-mail: sburke@ou.edu.

College of Atmospheric and Geographic Sciences Students: 58 full-time (32 women), 52 part-time (11 women); includes 9 minority (1 American Indian or Alaska Native, non-Hispanic/Latino; 1 Asian, non-Hispanic/Latino; 4 Hispanic/Latino; 3 Two or more races, non-Hispanic/Latino), 16 international. Average age 27. 76 applicants, 25% accepted, 18 enrolled. *Faculty:* 64 full-time (15 women). Expenses: Contact institution. *Financial support:* In 2016–17, 112 students received support, including 5 fellowships with full tuition reimbursements available (averaging $4,200 per year), 106 research assistantships with full tuition reimbursements available (averaging $18,972 per year), 30 teaching assistantships with full tuition reimbursements available (averaging $18,027 per year); career-related internships or fieldwork, Federal Work-Study, institutionally sponsored loans, scholarships/grants, traineeships, health care benefits, and unspecified assistantships also available. Financial award application deadline: 6/1; financial award applicants required to submit FAFSA. In 2016, 15 master's, 13 doctorates awarded. *Program availability:* Part-time. Offers atmospheric and geographic sciences (MA, MS, PhD); environmental sustainability (MS); geography (MA, MS, PhD). *Application deadline:* For fall admission, 1/15 for domestic and international students; for spring admission, 10/1 for domestic and international students. *Application fee:* $50 ($100 for international students). Electronic applications accepted. *Application Contact:* Mary Anne Hempe, Assistant Dean for Student Services, 405-325-3095, Fax: 405-325-3148, E-mail: mahempe@ou.edu. *Dean,* Dr. Berrien Moore, 405-325-3095, Fax: 405-325-1180, E-mail: berrien@ou.edu.

School of Meteorology Students: 36 full-time (14 women), 42 part-time (8 women); includes 5 minority (1 Asian, non-Hispanic/Latino; 2 Hispanic/Latino; 2 Two or more races, non-Hispanic/Latino), 12 international. Average age 26. 60 applicants, 23% accepted, 14 enrolled. *Faculty:* 41 full-time (8 women). Expenses: Contact institution. *Financial support:* In 2016–17, 76 students received support, including 3 fellowships with full tuition reimbursements available (averaging $4,667 per year), 51 research assistantships with full tuition reimbursements available (averaging $19,483 per year), 19 teaching assistantships with full tuition reimbursements available (averaging $20,386 per year); health care benefits, tuition waivers (full and partial), and unspecified assistantships also available. Support available to part-time students. Financial award application deadline: 6/1; financial award applicants required to submit FAFSA. In 2016, 7 master's, 7 doctorates awarded. Offers meteorology (MS, PhD). *Application deadline:* For fall admission, 1/15 for domestic students, 2/1 for international students; for spring admission, 10/1 for domestic and international students. Applications are processed on a rolling basis. *Application fee:* $50 ($100 for international students). Electronic applications accepted. *Application Contact:* Christie Upchurch, Academic Coordinator, Graduate Program, 405-325-6571, Fax: 405-325-7689, E-mail: cupchurch@ou.edu. *Director,* Dr. David Parsons, 405-325-6561, Fax: 405-325-7689, E-mail: dparsons@ou.edu.

College of International Studies Students: 48 full-time (21 women), 231 part-time (53 women); includes 85 minority (21 Black or African American, non-Hispanic/Latino; 2 American Indian or Alaska Native, non-Hispanic/Latino; 13 Asian, non-Hispanic/Latino; 33 Hispanic/Latino; 3 Native Hawaiian or other Pacific Islander, non-Hispanic/Latino; 13 Two or more races, non-Hispanic/Latino), 4 international. Average age 32. 60 applicants, 88% accepted, 36 enrolled. *Faculty:* 18 full-time (6 women), 1 part-time/adjunct (0 women). Expenses: Contact institution. *Financial support:* In 2016–17, 27 students received support, including 7 research assistantships with full tuition reimbursements available (averaging $13,500 per year), 3 teaching assistantships with full tuition reimbursements available (averaging $13,500 per year); fellowships with full tuition reimbursements available, career-related internships or fieldwork, scholarships/grants, health care benefits, and unspecified assistantships also available. Financial award application deadline: 6/1; financial award applicants required to submit FAFSA. In 2016, 68 master's awarded. *Program availability:* Part-time, online courses with an 8-10 day study abroad. Offers economics and development (MAIS); global affairs (MA). *Application deadline:* For fall admission, 2/15 for domestic and international students. *Application fee:* $50 ($100 for international students). Electronic applications accepted. *Application Contact:* Katie Watkins, Academic Advisor, 405-325-2337, Fax: 405-325-7738, E-mail: kwatkins@ou.edu. *Professor/Associate Dean for Academic Affairs,* Dr. Mitchell Smith, 405-325-1584, Fax: 405-325-7738, E-mail: mps@ou.edu.

College of Law Students: 544 full-time (239 women), 58 part-time (30 women); includes 169 minority (22 Black or African American, non-Hispanic/Latino; 59 American Indian or Alaska Native, non-Hispanic/Latino; 16 Asian, non-Hispanic/Latino; 24 Hispanic/Latino; 48 Two or more races, non-Hispanic/Latino), 3 international. Average age 28. 853 applicants, 50% accepted, 176 enrolled. *Faculty:* 38 full-time (18 women), 14 part-time/adjunct (5 women). Expenses: Contact institution. *Financial support:* In 2016–17,

401 students received support. Career-related internships or fieldwork, Federal Work-Study, scholarships/grants, and tuition waivers (full and partial) available. Financial award application deadline: 6/1; financial award applicants required to submit FAFSA. In 2016, 25 master's, 143 doctorates awarded. *Program availability:* Part-time, 100% online. Offers law (LL M, JD). *Application deadline:* For fall admission, 3/15 for domestic and international students. Applications are processed on a rolling basis. *Application fee:* $50. Electronic applications accepted. *Application Contact:* Vicki Ferguson, Admissions Coordinator, 405-325-4728, Fax: 405-325-0502, E-mail: admissions@law.ou.edu. *Dean,* Joseph Harroz, Jr., 405-325-4884, Fax: 405-325-7712, E-mail: jharroz@ou.edu.

College of Liberal Studies Students: 74 full-time (48 women), 598 part-time (289 women); includes 175 minority (45 Black or African American, non-Hispanic/Latino; 39 American Indian or Alaska Native, non-Hispanic/Latino; 8 Asian, non-Hispanic/Latino; 46 Hispanic/Latino; 1 Native Hawaiian or other Pacific Islander, non-Hispanic/Latino; 36 Two or more races, non-Hispanic/Latino), 2 international. Average age 35. 191 applicants, 95% accepted, 120 enrolled. *Faculty:* 13 full-time (7 women), 1 part-time/adjunct (0 women). Expenses: Contact institution. *Financial support:* In 2016–17, 124 students received support. Career-related internships or fieldwork, institutionally sponsored loans, scholarships/grants, health care benefits, and tuition waivers available. Support available to part-time students. Financial award application deadline: 6/1; financial award applicants required to submit FAFSA. In 2016, 192 master's, 6 other advanced degrees awarded. *Program availability:* Part-time, online only, 100% online, blended/hybrid learning. Offers administrative leadership (Graduate Certificate); corrections management (Graduate Certificate); criminal justice (MS); government and military leadership (MA); human and health services administration (MA); liberal studies (MPS); organizational leadership (MA); restorative justice administration (Graduate Certificate); volunteer and non-profit leadership (MA). *Application deadline:* For fall admission, 7/1 for domestic and international students; for winter admission, 12/1 for domestic and international students; for spring admission, 5/1 for domestic and international students. Applications are processed on a rolling basis. *Application fee:* $50 ($100 for international students). Electronic applications accepted. *Application Contact:* Michelle Shults, Academic Advisement Services Coordinator, 405-325-2928, Fax: 405-325-7132, E-mail: mshults@ou.edu. *Associate Provost for Continuing Education/Interim Dean, College of Liberal Studies,* Dr. Martha L. Banz, 405-325-1061, Fax: 405-325-7132, E-mail: mlbanz@ou.edu.

Gallogly College of Engineering Students: 341 full-time (89 women), 197 part-time (47 women); includes 70 minority (17 Black or African American, non-Hispanic/Latino; 3 American Indian or Alaska Native, non-Hispanic/Latino; 19 Asian, non-Hispanic/Latino; 17 Hispanic/Latino; 14 Two or more races, non-Hispanic/Latino), 317 international. Average age 29. 662 applicants, 32% accepted, 130 enrolled. *Faculty:* 159 full-time (22 women), 2 part-time/adjunct (0 women). Expenses: Contact institution. *Financial support:* In 2016–17, 385 students received support, including 5 fellowships with full tuition reimbursements available (averaging $3,820 per year), 184 research assistantships with partial tuition reimbursements available (averaging $15,320 per year), 102 teaching assistantships with partial tuition reimbursements available (averaging $12,839 per year); career-related internships or fieldwork, scholarships/grants, health care benefits, tuition waivers (partial), and unspecified assistantships also available. Financial award application deadline: 6/1; financial award applicants required to submit FAFSA. In 2016, 105 master's, 42 doctorates awarded. *Program availability:* Part-time. Offers data science and analytics (MS); engineering (M Env Sc, MS, PhD); engineering physics (MS, PhD); general engineering (MS, PhD). *Application deadline:* For fall admission, 1/15 for domestic and international students; for spring admission, 1/1 for domestic students, 5/15 for international students. *Application fee:* $50 ($100 for international students). Electronic applications accepted. *Application Contact:* Dr. John Antonio, Senior Associate Dean, 405-325-4397, Fax: 405-325-7508, E-mail: antonio@ou.edu. *Dean,* Dr. Thomas Landers, 405-325-2621, Fax: 405-325-7508, E-mail: landers@ou.edu.

School of Aerospace and Mechanical Engineering Students: 30 full-time (5 women), 18 part-time (3 women); includes 4 minority (1 Black or African American, non-Hispanic/Latino; 1 Hispanic/Latino; 2 Two or more races, non-Hispanic/Latino), 30 international. Average age 29. 44 applicants, 43% accepted, 11 enrolled. *Faculty:* 25 full-time (2 women). Expenses: Contact institution. *Financial support:* In 2016–17, 42 students received support, including 17 research assistantships with full tuition reimbursements available (averaging $13,751 per year), 29 teaching assistantships with full tuition reimbursements available (averaging $12,759 per year); fellowships and scholarships/grants also available. Financial award application deadline: 6/1; financial award applicants required to submit FAFSA. In 2016, 8 master's, 2 doctorates awarded. *Program availability:* Part-time. Offers aerospace engineering (MS, PhD); mechanical engineering (MS, PhD). *Application deadline:* For fall admission, 1/15 for domestic and international students; for spring admission, 9/1 for domestic and international students. *Application fee:* $50 ($100 for international students). Electronic applications accepted. *Application Contact:* Kate O'Brien-Hamoush, Student Services Coordinator, 405-325-5013, Fax: 405-325-1088, E-mail: kobrien@ou.edu. *Director,* Dr. M. Cengiz Altan, 405-325-5011, Fax: 405-325-1088, E-mail: altan@ou.edu.

School of Biomedical Engineering Students: 16 full-time (7 women), 2 part-time (1 woman); includes 4 minority (1 Black or African American, non-Hispanic/Latino; 1 Asian, non-Hispanic/Latino; 2 Two or more races, non-Hispanic/Latino), 7 international. Average age 27. 22 applicants, 27% accepted, 5 enrolled. *Faculty:* 17 full-time (2 women). Expenses: Contact institution. *Financial support:* In 2016–17, 18 students received support, including 13 research assistantships with tuition reimbursements available (averaging $14,586 per year), 3 teaching assistantships with partial tuition reimbursements available (averaging $12,975 per year); fellowships with full tuition reimbursements available, scholarships/grants, health care benefits, and unspecified assistantships also available. Financial award application deadline: 6/1; financial award applicants required to submit FAFSA. In 2016, 1 master's awarded. *Program availability:* Part-time. Offers biomedical engineering (MS, PhD). *Application deadline:* For fall admission, 1/15 priority date for domestic and international students; for spring admission, 9/15 priority date for domestic and international students. *Application fee:* $50 ($100 for international students). Electronic applications accepted. *Application Contact:* Shayla Palmer, Student Programs Coordinator, 405-325-3947, E-mail: chrishaylapalmer@ou.edu. *Director,* Dr. Michael Detamore, 405-325-2144, E-mail: detamore@ou.edu.

School of Chemical, Biological and Materials Engineering Students: 23 full-time (5 women), 8 part-time (5 women); includes 2 minority (1 Black or African American, non-Hispanic/Latino; 1 American Indian or Alaska Native, non-Hispanic/Latino), 20 international. Average age 26. 83 applicants, 11% accepted, 9 enrolled. *Faculty:* 12 full-time (1 woman). Expenses: Contact institution. *Financial support:* In 2016–17, 31 students received support, including 29 research assistantships with full tuition reimbursements available (averaging $17,305 per year), 2 teaching assistantships

(averaging $1,870 per year). Financial award application deadline: 6/1; financial award applicants required to submit FAFSA. In 2016, 6 master's, 9 doctorates awarded. *Program availability:* Part-time. Offers chemical engineering (MS, PhD). *Application deadline:* Applications are processed on a rolling basis. *Application fee:* $50 ($100 for international students). Electronic applications accepted. *Application Contact:* Donna King, Graduate Program Staff Assistant, 405-325-5812, Fax: 405-325-5813, E-mail: donnaking@ou.edu. *Director,* Dr. Brian Grady, 405-325-5814, Fax: 405-325-5813, E-mail: cbme@ou.edu.

School of Civil Engineering and Environmental Science Students: 44 full-time (19 women), 16 part-time (5 women); includes 9 minority (2 Black or African American, non-Hispanic/Latino; 2 Hispanic/Latino; 5 Two or more races, non-Hispanic/Latino), 28 international. Average age 28. 62 applicants, 31% accepted, 12 enrolled. *Faculty:* 28 full-time (6 women). Expenses: Contact institution. *Financial support:* In 2016–17, 56 students received support, including 1 fellowship with full tuition reimbursement available (averaging $5,000 per year), 39 research assistantships with full tuition reimbursements available (averaging $16,282 per year), 14 teaching assistantships with full tuition reimbursements available (averaging $14,809 per year); scholarships/grants also available. Financial award application deadline: 6/1; financial award applicants required to submit FAFSA. In 2016, 5 master's, 8 doctorates awarded. *Program availability:* Part-time. Offers civil engineering (MS, PhD); environmental engineering (MS, PhD); environmental science (M Env Sc, PhD). *Application deadline:* For fall admission, 1/15 for domestic and international students; for spring admission, 8/15 for domestic and international students. *Application fee:* $50 ($100 for international students). Electronic applications accepted. *Application Contact:* Susan Williams, Graduate Programs Assistant, 405-325-2344, Fax: 405-325-4217, E-mail: srwilliams@ou.edu. *Director,* Dr. Randall Kolar, 405-325-4267, Fax: 405-325-4217, E-mail: kolar@ou.edu.

School of Computer Science Students: 56 full-time (14 women), 12 part-time (3 women); includes 1 minority (Black or African American, non-Hispanic/Latino), 61 international. Average age 26. 123 applicants, 32% accepted, 22 enrolled. *Faculty:* 17 full-time (3 women). Expenses: Contact institution. *Financial support:* In 2016–17, 52 students received support, including 18 research assistantships with full tuition reimbursements available (averaging $15,167 per year), 23 teaching assistantships with full tuition reimbursements available (averaging $12,679 per year); fellowships with full tuition reimbursements available, career-related internships or fieldwork, scholarships/grants, and unspecified assistantships also available. Financial award application deadline: 6/1; financial award applicants required to submit FAFSA. In 2016, 33 master's, 4 doctorates awarded. *Program availability:* Part-time. Offers computer science (MS, PhD). *Application deadline:* For fall admission, 4/1 for domestic students, 3/1 for international students; for spring admission, 10/1 for domestic students, 9/1 for international students. Applications are processed on a rolling basis. *Application fee:* $50 ($100 for international students). Electronic applications accepted. *Application Contact:* Virginie Perez Woods, Academic Programs Coordinator, 405-325-0145, Fax: 405-325-4044, E-mail: vpw@cs.ou.edu. *Director,* Dr. Sridhar Radhakrishnan, 405-325-4042, Fax: 405-325-4044, E-mail: sridhar@ou.edu.

School of Electrical and Computer Engineering Students: 86 full-time (16 women), 57 part-time (12 women); includes 14 minority (2 Black or African American, non-Hispanic/Latino; 1 American Indian or Alaska Native, non-Hispanic/Latino; 5 Asian, non-Hispanic/Latino; 1 Two or more races, non-Hispanic/Latino), 94 international. Average age 28. 136 applicants, 36% accepted, 24 enrolled. *Faculty:* 41 full-time (3 women), 2 part-time/adjunct (0 women). Expenses: Contact institution. *Financial support:* In 2016–17, 117 students received support, including 1 fellowship (averaging $2,500 per year), 52 research assistantships with full and partial tuition reimbursements available (averaging $15,014 per year), 18 teaching assistantships with full and partial tuition reimbursements available (averaging $11,536 per year); career-related internships or fieldwork, scholarships/grants, and health care benefits also available. Financial award application deadline: 6/1; financial award applicants required to submit FAFSA. In 2016, 27 master's, 15 doctorates awarded. *Program availability:* Part-time. Offers electrical and computer engineering (MS, PhD); telecommunications engineering (MS). *Application deadline:* For fall admission, 4/1 for domestic students, 3/1 for international students; for spring admission, 11/1 for domestic students, 10/1 for international students. Applications are processed on a rolling basis. *Application fee:* $50 ($100 for international students). Electronic applications accepted. *Application Contact:* Lisa Wilkins, Graduate Program Assistant III, 405-325-4285, Fax: 405-325-7066, E-mail: lawilkins@ou.edu. *Director,* Dr. J.R. Cruz, 405-325-8131, Fax: 405-325-7066, E-mail: jcruz@ou.edu.

School of Industrial and Systems Engineering Students: 49 full-time (13 women), 21 part-time (8 women); includes 9 minority (3 Black or African American, non-Hispanic/Latino; 2 Asian, non-Hispanic/Latino; 1 Hispanic/Latino; 3 Two or more races, non-Hispanic/Latino), 51 international. Average age 27. 131 applicants, 24% accepted, 15 enrolled. *Faculty:* 16 full-time (3 women). Expenses: Contact institution. *Financial support:* In 2016–17, 30 students received support, including 11 research assistantships with full tuition reimbursements available (averaging $12,961 per year), 11 teaching assistantships with full tuition reimbursements available (averaging $11,160 per year); Federal Work-Study, institutionally sponsored loans, scholarships/grants, and health care benefits also available. Financial award application deadline: 6/1; financial award applicants required to submit FAFSA. In 2016, 19 master's, 4 doctorates awarded. Offers data science and analytics (MS); industrial and systems engineering (MS, PhD). *Application deadline:* For fall admission, 6/1 priority date for domestic students, 4/1 for international students; for spring admission, 10/15 priority date for domestic students, 9/1 for international students. Applications are processed on a rolling basis. *Application fee:* $50 ($100 for international students). Electronic applications accepted. *Application Contact:* Dr. Janet Allen, Chair/Graduate Liaison, 405-550-3969, Fax: 405-325-7555, E-mail: janet.allen@ou.edu. *Professor/Interim Director,* Dr. Shivakumar Raman, 405-819-3710, Fax: 405-325-7555, E-mail: raman@ou.edu.

Gaylord College of Journalism and Mass Communication Students: 37 full-time (19 women), 19 part-time (8 women); includes 9 minority (3 Black or African American, non-Hispanic/Latino; 1 American Indian or Alaska Native, non-Hispanic/Latino; 1 Asian, non-Hispanic/Latino; 2 Hispanic/Latino; 2 Two or more races, non-Hispanic/Latino), 18 international. Average age 32. 26 applicants, 58% accepted, 14 enrolled. *Faculty:* 35 full-time (14 women), 2 part-time/adjunct (0 women). Expenses: Contact institution. *Financial support:* In 2016–17, 41 students received support, including 1 fellowship (averaging $2,000 per year), 4 research assistantships with full tuition reimbursements available (averaging $16,260 per year), 22 teaching assistantships with full tuition reimbursements available (averaging $15,120 per year); career-related internships or fieldwork, scholarships/grants, health care benefits, unspecified assistantships, and research and research travel awards also available. Financial award application deadline: 6/1; financial award applicants required to submit FAFSA. In 2016, 14 master's, 2 doctorates awarded. *Program availability:* Part-time. Offers journalism and mass communication (MA, MPW, PhD, Graduate Certificate); professional writing (MPW). *Application deadline:* For fall admission, 2/1 priority date for domestic and international students; for spring admission, 10/1 priority date for domestic students, 9/1 priority date for international students; for summer admission, 2/1 priority date for domestic students. Applications are processed on a rolling basis. *Application fee:* $50 ($100 for international students). Electronic applications accepted. *Application Contact:* Larry Laneer, Graduate Advisor, 405-325-2722, Fax: 405-325-7565, E-mail: llaneer@ou.edu. *Director of Graduate Studies/Professor of Strategic Communication*, Dr. Katerina Tsetsura, 405-325-2722, Fax: 405-325-7565, E-mail: tsetsura@ou.edu.

Graduate College Students: 13 full-time (5 women), 128 part-time (44 women); includes 35 minority (8 Black or African American, non-Hispanic/Latino; 3 American Indian or Alaska Native, non-Hispanic/Latino; 8 Asian, non-Hispanic/Latino; 12 Hispanic/Latino; 4 Two or more races, non-Hispanic/Latino), 4 international. Average age 37. 28 applicants, 50% accepted, 1 enrolled. *Faculty:* 49 full-time (20 women), 1 (woman) part-time/adjunct. Expenses: Contact institution. *Financial support:* In 2016–17, 11 students received support, including 5 research assistantships with partial tuition reimbursements available (averaging $13,050 per year); teaching assistantships, career-related internships or fieldwork, Federal Work-Study, institutionally sponsored loans, scholarships/grants, health care benefits, and unspecified assistantships also available. Support available to part-time students. Financial award application deadline: 6/1; financial award applicants required to submit FAFSA. In 2016, 89 master's, 7 doctorates awarded. *Program availability:* Part-time, evening/weekend, blended/hybrid learning. Offers interdisciplinary studies (MA, MS, PhD). *Application deadline:* For fall admission, 4/1 for international students; for spring admission, 9/1 for international students; for summer admission, 2/1 for international students. Applications are processed on a rolling basis. *Application fee:* $50 ($100 for international students). Electronic applications accepted. *Application Contact:* Amy Shaw, Director, Office of Graduate Admissions, 405-325-6765, Fax: 405-325-5345, E-mail: ashaw@ou.edu. *Interim Dean and Professor*, Dr. Randall S. Hewes, 405-325-3811, Fax: 405-325-5343, E-mail: hewes@ou.edu.

Jeannine Rainbolt College of Education Students: 293 full-time (201 women), 478 part-time (351 women); includes 230 minority (75 Black or African American, non-Hispanic/Latino; 42 American Indian or Alaska Native, non-Hispanic/Latino; 10 Asian, non-Hispanic/Latino; 47 Hispanic/Latino; 2 Native Hawaiian or other Pacific Islander, non-Hispanic/Latino; 54 Two or more races, non-Hispanic/Latino), 39 international. Average age 34. 348 applicants, 61% accepted, 158 enrolled. *Faculty:* 77 full-time (46 women), 7 part-time/adjunct (4 women). Expenses: Contact institution. *Financial support:* In 2016–17, 481 students received support, including 51 research assistantships with partial tuition reimbursements available (averaging $13,519 per year), 15 teaching assistantships with partial tuition reimbursements available (averaging $12,960 per year); fellowships with full tuition reimbursements available, career-related internships or fieldwork, Federal Work-Study, scholarships/grants, health care benefits, and unspecified assistantships also available. Support available to part-time students. Financial award application deadline: 6/1; financial award applicants required to submit FAFSA. In 2016, 202 master's, 37 doctorates, 12 other advanced degrees awarded. *Program availability:* Part-time, evening/weekend. Offers 21st century teaching and learning (M Ed); adult and higher education (M Ed, PhD); applied behavior analysis (M Ed); college teaching (Graduate Certificate); counseling psychology (PhD); education (M Ed, Ed D, PhD, Graduate Certificate); educational administration, curriculum and supervision (M Ed, Ed D, PhD); educational psychology (M Ed); educational studies (M Ed, PhD); higher education and community support (PhD); higher education professor (PhD); instructional design and technology (M Ed); instructional leadership and academic curriculum (M Ed, PhD); instructional psychology and technology (M Ed, PhD); integrating technology in teaching (M Ed); professional counseling (M Ed); school instructional leaders (PhD); secondary transition (M Ed); special education (M Ed, PhD). *Application deadline:* For fall admission, 6/1 for domestic students, 3/1 for international students; for spring admission, 11/1 for domestic students, 9/1 for international students. *Application fee:* $50 ($100 for international students). Electronic applications accepted. *Application Contact:* Dr. Sherry Cox, Assistant Dean, 405-325-2238, Fax: 405-325-7620, E-mail: scox@ou.edu. *Dean*, Dr. Gregg Garn, 405-325-1082, Fax: 405-325-7390, E-mail: garn@ou.edu.

Mewbourne College of Earth and Energy Students: 148 full-time (34 women), 88 part-time (23 women); includes 18 minority (2 Black or African American, non-Hispanic/Latino; 1 American Indian or Alaska Native, non-Hispanic/Latino; 5 Asian, non-Hispanic/Latino; 5 Hispanic/Latino; 5 Two or more races, non-Hispanic/Latino), 157 international. Average age 28. 418 applicants, 14% accepted, 50 enrolled. *Faculty:* 51 full-time (5 women), 1 part-time/adjunct (0 women). Expenses: Contact institution. *Financial support:* In 2016–17, 181 students received support, including 114 research assistantships with partial tuition reimbursements available (averaging $15,900 per year), 55 teaching assistantships with partial tuition reimbursements available (averaging $15,258 per year); scholarships/grants and unspecified assistantships also available. Financial award application deadline: 6/1; financial award applicants required to submit FAFSA. In 2016, 60 master's, 10 doctorates awarded. *Program availability:* Part-time, evening/weekend. Offers earth and energy (MS, PhD, Graduate Certificate). *Application fee:* $50 ($100 for international students). Electronic applications accepted. *Dean*, Dr. J. Mike Stice, 405-325-3821, Fax: 405-325-3180, E-mail: mstice@ou.edu.

ConocoPhillips School of Geology and Geophysics Students: 67 full-time (21 women), 35 part-time (12 women); includes 11 minority (1 American Indian or Alaska Native, non-Hispanic/Latino; 2 Asian, non-Hispanic/Latino; 4 Hispanic/Latino; 4 Two or more races, non-Hispanic/Latino), 52 international. Average age 27. 202 applicants, 15% accepted, 26 enrolled. *Faculty:* 30 full-time (4 women). Expenses: Contact institution. *Financial support:* In 2016–17, 81 students received support, including 39 research assistantships with partial tuition reimbursements available (averaging $18,836 per year), 24 teaching assistantships with partial tuition reimbursements available (averaging $17,528 per year); career-related internships or fieldwork, scholarships/grants, and unspecified assistantships also available. Financial award application deadline: 6/1; financial award applicants required to submit FAFSA. In 2016, 33 master's, 4 doctorates awarded. *Program availability:* Part-time. Offers geology (MS, PhD); geophysics (MS, PhD). *Application deadline:* For fall admission, 1/10 priority date for domestic and international students; for spring admission, 9/1 for domestic and international students. *Application fee:* $50 ($100 for international students). Electronic applications accepted. *Application Contact:* Rebecca Fay, Coordinator of Academic Student Services, 405-325-3253, Fax: 405-325-3140, E-mail: rfay@ou.edu. *Director*, Dr. R. Douglas Elmore, 405-325-3253, Fax: 405-325-3140, E-mail: delmore@ou.edu.

Mewbourne School of Petroleum and Geological Engineering Students: 83 full-time (13 women), 53 part-time (11 women); includes 7 minority (2 Black or African American, non-Hispanic/Latino; 3 Asian, non-Hispanic/Latino; 1 Hispanic/Latino; 1 Two or more races, non-Hispanic/Latino), 107 international. Average age 29. 221 applicants, 14% accepted, 25 enrolled. *Faculty:* 21 full-time (1 woman), 1 part-time/adjunct (0 women). Expenses: Contact institution. *Financial support:* In 2016–17, 100 students received support, including 64 research assistantships with partial tuition reimbursements available (averaging $13,780 per year), 31 teaching assistantships with partial tuition reimbursements available (averaging $13,500 per year); scholarships/grants also available. Financial award application deadline: 6/1; financial award applicants required to submit FAFSA. In 2016, 38 master's, 6 doctorates awarded. *Program availability:* Part-time, evening/weekend. Offers geological engineering (MS, PhD); natural gas engineering and management (MS, Graduate Certificate); natural gas technology (Graduate Certificate); petroleum engineering (MS, PhD). *Application deadline:* For fall admission, 3/1 for domestic and international students; for spring admission, 9/1 for domestic and international students. *Application fee:* $50 ($100 for international students). Electronic applications accepted. *Application Contact:* Sheriee Parnell, Graduate Student Coordinator, 405-325-2921, E-mail: sheriee@ou.edu. *Director/Chair*, Dr. Chandra Rai, 405-325-2921, E-mail: crai@ou.edu.

Price College of Business Students: 162 full-time (45 women), 157 part-time (33 women); includes 47 minority (6 Black or African American, non-Hispanic/Latino; 8 American Indian or Alaska Native, non-Hispanic/Latino; 11 Asian, non-Hispanic/Latino; 13 Hispanic/Latino; 9 Two or more races, non-Hispanic/Latino), 49 international. Average age 30. 318 applicants, 29% accepted, 79 enrolled. *Faculty:* 69 full-time (18 women), 4 part-time/adjunct (0 women). Expenses: Contact institution. *Financial support:* In 2016–17, 156 students received support, including 9 fellowships with full tuition reimbursements available (averaging $3,056 per year), 38 research assistantships with partial tuition reimbursements available (averaging $12,301 per year), 30 teaching assistantships with partial tuition reimbursements available (averaging $14,507 per year); career-related internships or fieldwork, scholarships/grants, health care benefits, and unspecified assistantships also available. Support available to part-time students. Financial award application deadline: 6/1; financial award applicants required to submit FAFSA. In 2016, 152 master's, 5 doctorates, 8 other advanced degrees awarded. *Program availability:* Part-time, evening/weekend. Offers accounting (M Acc, PhD); business administration (EMBA, MBA, PMBA, Professional MBA, PhD); business entrepreneurship (Graduate Certificate); entrepreneurship and economic development (PhD); finance (PhD); management and international business (PhD); management information systems (MS, Graduate Certificate); management of information systems (PhD); marketing/supply chain (PhD). *Application deadline:* For fall admission, 2/1 for domestic and international students; for spring admission, 11/15 for domestic students, 8/1 for international students. *Application fee:* $50 ($100 for international students). Electronic applications accepted. *Application Contact:* Amber Hasbrook, Academic Counselor, 405-325-5815, Fax: 405-325-7753, E-mail: ahasbrook@ou.edu. *Dean*, Daniel Pullin, JD, 405-325-0100, Fax: 405-325-3421, E-mail: dpullin@ou.edu.

Division of Management Information Systems Students: 38 full-time (13 women), 15 part-time (2 women); includes 7 minority (1 American Indian or Alaska Native, non-Hispanic/Latino; 1 Asian, non-Hispanic/Latino; 2 Hispanic/Latino; 3 Two or more races, non-Hispanic/Latino), 17 international. Average age 28. 30 applicants, 33% accepted, 9 enrolled. *Faculty:* 11 full-time (6 women). Expenses: Contact institution. *Financial support:* In 2016–17, 37 students received support, including 6 research assistantships with full tuition reimbursements available (averaging $10,373 per year), 4 teaching assistantships with full tuition reimbursements available (averaging $13,368 per year); career-related internships or fieldwork, scholarships/grants, and unspecified assistantships also available. Support available to part-time students. Financial award application deadline: 6/1; financial award applicants required to submit FAFSA. In 2016, 14 master's, 1 other advanced degree awarded. *Program availability:* Part-time, evening/weekend. Offers management information systems (MS, Graduate Certificate). *Application deadline:* For fall admission, 6/15 for domestic students, 3/1 for international students; for spring admission, 10/1 for domestic students, 8/1 for international students. Applications are processed on a rolling basis. *Application fee:* $50 ($100 for international students). Electronic applications accepted. *Application Contact:* Jennifer Aragon, Academic Advisor, 405-325-2074, Fax: 405-325-7118, E-mail: jhardman@ou.edu. *Chair/Director of MIS Division*, Radhika Santhanam, 405-325-0791, E-mail: radhika@ou.edu.

John T. Steed School of Accounting Students: 25 full-time (11 women), 3 part-time (2 women); includes 7 minority (1 Black or African American, non-Hispanic/Latino; 1 American Indian or Alaska Native, non-Hispanic/Latino; 3 Asian, non-Hispanic/Latino; 2 Two or more races, non-Hispanic/Latino), 6 international. Average age 27. 27 applicants, 41% accepted, 11 enrolled. *Faculty:* 12 full-time (4 women). Expenses: Contact institution. *Financial support:* In 2016–17, 12 students received support, including 4 research assistantships with partial tuition reimbursements available (averaging $16,364 per year), 10 teaching assistantships with partial tuition reimbursements available (averaging $11,896 per year); career-related internships or fieldwork, scholarships/grants, and unspecified assistantships also available. Support available to part-time students. Financial award application deadline: 6/1; financial award applicants required to submit FAFSA. In 2016, 11 master's awarded. *Program availability:* Part-time, 100% online. Offers accounting (M Acc). *Application deadline:* For fall admission, 6/15 for domestic students, 3/1 for international students; for spring admission, 11/15 for domestic students, 8/1 for international students; for summer admission, 3/15 for domestic students, 1/1 for international students. Applications are processed on a rolling basis. *Application fee:* $50 ($100 for international students). Electronic applications accepted. *Application Contact:* Jennifer Aragon, Academic Advisor, 405-325-2074, Fax: 405-325-7118, E-mail: jhardman@ou.edu. *Director/Chair*, Ervin Black, 405-325-2401, Fax: 405-325-7348, E-mail: ervblack@ou.edu.

Weitzenhoffer Family College of Fine Arts Students: 140 full-time (69 women), 83 part-time (46 women); includes 43 minority (5 Black or African American, non-Hispanic/Latino; 6 American Indian or Alaska Native, non-Hispanic/Latino; 8 Asian, non-Hispanic/Latino; 13 Hispanic/Latino; 11 Two or more races, non-Hispanic/Latino), 28 international. Average age 30. 196 applicants, 44% accepted, 67 enrolled. *Faculty:* 98 full-time (30 women), 3 part-time/adjunct (1 woman). Expenses: Contact institution. *Financial support:* In 2016–17, 155 students received support, including 4 fellowships with full and partial tuition reimbursements available (averaging $5,750 per year), 32 research assistantships with full tuition reimbursements available (averaging $10,551 per year), 86 teaching assistantships with full tuition reimbursements available (averaging $10,629 per year); career-related internships or fieldwork, Federal Work-Study, institutionally sponsored loans, scholarships/grants, health care benefits, tuition waivers (full and partial), and unspecified assistantships also available. Support available to part-time students. Financial award application deadline: 6/1; financial award applicants required to submit FAFSA. In 2016, 45 master's, 13 doctorates awarded. Offers fine arts (M Mus, M Mus Ed, MA, MFA, DMA, PhD, Graduate Certificate). *Application fee:* $50 ($100 for international students). Electronic applications accepted.

Application Contact: Teri Lodes, Assistant to the Dean, 405-325-7375, Fax: 405-325-1667, E-mail: talodes@ou.edu. *Dean*, Dr. Mary Margaret Holt, 405-325-7370, Fax: 405-325-1667, E-mail: marymholt@ou.edu.

Helmerich School of Drama Students: 1 full-time (0 women), 1 (woman) part-time; includes 1 minority (American Indian or Alaska Native, non-Hispanic/Latino). Average age 26. *Faculty:* 7 full-time (3 women), 1 part-time/adjunct (0 women). Expenses: Contact institution. *Financial support:* In 2016–17, 3 teaching assistantships with full tuition reimbursements (averaging $12,818 per year) were awarded; Federal Work-Study, health care benefits, tuition waivers, and unspecified assistantships also available. Financial award application deadline: 6/1; financial award applicants required to submit FAFSA. Offers drama (MA). *Application deadline:* For fall admission, 3/15 for domestic students; for spring admission, 11/1 for domestic and international students. *Application fee:* $50 ($100 for international students). Electronic applications accepted. *Application Contact:* Dr. Kae Koger, Graduate Liaison, E-mail: akoger@ou.edu. *Director, School of Drama,* Dr. Tom Huston Orr, 405-325-4021, Fax: 405-325-0400, E-mail: thorr@ou.edu.

School of Dance Students: 5 full-time (all women), 1 (woman) part-time; includes 1 minority (Two or more races, non-Hispanic/Latino), 1 international. Average age 41.5 applicants, 80% accepted, 4 enrolled. *Faculty:* 5 full-time (2 women). Expenses: Contact institution. *Financial support:* In 2016–17, 4 students received support, including 1 fellowship with full tuition reimbursement available (averaging $8,000 per year), 4 teaching assistantships (averaging $12,091 per year); health care benefits and unspecified assistantships also available. Financial award application deadline: 6/1; financial award applicants required to submit FAFSA. In 2016, 3 master's awarded. Offers ballet (MFA); modern dance (MFA). *Application deadline:* For fall admission, 4/15 for domestic students, 3/1 for international students. Applications are processed on a rolling basis. *Application fee:* $50 ($100 for international students). Electronic applications accepted. *Application Contact:* Jeremy Lindberg, Associate Professor, 405-325-0567 Ext. 15, Fax: 405-325-7024, E-mail: jlindberg@ou.edu. *Dean/Professor/Director,* Dr. Mary Margaret Holt, 405-325-4051, Fax: 405-325-7024, E-mail: marymholt@ou.edu.

School of Music Students: 113 full-time (49 women), 68 part-time (32 women); includes 32 minority (5 Black or African American, non-Hispanic/Latino; 4 American Indian or Alaska Native, non-Hispanic/Latino; 7 Asian, non-Hispanic/Latino; 11 Hispanic/Latino; 5 Two or more races, non-Hispanic/Latino), 26 international. Average age 29. 161 applicants, 43% accepted, 50 enrolled. *Faculty:* 61 full-time (17 women), 1 part-time/adjunct (0 women). Expenses: Contact institution. *Financial support:* In 2016–17, 121 students received support, including 3 fellowships with full tuition reimbursements available (averaging $5,000 per year), 31 research assistantships with full tuition reimbursements available (averaging $10,557 per year), 64 teaching assistantships with full tuition reimbursements available (averaging $10,494 per year); health care benefits and unspecified assistantships also available. Financial award application deadline: 6/1; financial award applicants required to submit FAFSA. In 2016, 35 master's, 13 doctorates awarded. Offers choral conducting (M Mus); composition (M Mus, DMA); conducting (M Mus Ed, DMA); general music education (M Mus Ed); instrumental (M Mus Ed); instrumental conducting (M Mus); music education (DMA); music performance (Graduate Certificate); music theory (M Mus); musicology (M Mus); organ (M Mus, DMA); piano (M Mus, DMA); piano pedagogy (M Mus Ed); voice (M Mus, DMA); wind/percussion/string instruments (M Mus, DMA). *Application deadline:* For fall admission, 2/1 for domestic and international students; for spring admission, 10/1 for domestic students, 9/1 for international students; for summer admission, 2/1 for domestic and international students. Applications are processed on a rolling basis. *Application fee:* $50 ($100 for international students). Electronic applications accepted. *Application Contact:* Jan Russell, Graduate Admissions and Recruiting Advisor, 405-325-7574, E-mail: jrussell@ou.edu. *Interim Director,* Dr. Roland Barrett, 405-325-2081, Fax: 405-325-7574, E-mail: rebarrett@ou.edu.

School of Visual Arts Students: 21 full-time (15 women), 13 part-time (12 women); includes 9 minority (1 American Indian or Alaska Native, non-Hispanic/Latino; 1 Asian, non-Hispanic/Latino; 2 Hispanic/Latino; 5 Two or more races, non-Hispanic/Latino), 1 international. Average age 32. 30 applicants, 47% accepted, 13 enrolled. *Faculty:* 24 full-time (8 women), 1 (woman) part-time/adjunct. Expenses: Contact institution. *Financial support:* In 2016–17, 20 students received support, including 1 research assistantship with full tuition reimbursement available (averaging $10,377 per year), 15 teaching assistantships with full tuition reimbursements available (averaging $10,377 per year); fellowships with full tuition reimbursements available, career-related internships or fieldwork, Federal Work-Study, institutionally sponsored loans, scholarships/grants, health care benefits, tuition waivers (full and partial), and unspecified assistantships also available. Support available to part-time students. Financial award application deadline: 6/1; financial award applicants required to submit FAFSA. In 2016, 7 master's awarded. Offers art (MFA); art history (MA, PhD); art of the American West (PhD); art, technology and culture (MFA); ceramics (MFA); Native American art history (PhD); painting (MFA); printmaking (MFA); sculpture (MFA); visual communication (MFA). *Application deadline:* For fall admission, 2/1 for domestic and international students. Electronic applications accepted. *Application fee:* $50 ($100 for international students). *Application Contact:* Jason Cytacki, Graduate Coordinator, E-mail: jason.cytacki@ou.edu. *Director,* Dr. Bette Talvacchia, 405-325-2691, Fax: 405-325-1668, E-mail: bette.talvacchia-1@ou.edu.

UNIVERSITY OF OKLAHOMA HEALTH SCIENCES CENTER, Oklahoma City, OK 73190

General Information State-supported, coed, upper-level institution. CGS member. *Graduate housing:* Rooms and/or apartments available on a first-come, first-served basis to single and married students. *Research affiliation:* Oklahoma Medical Research Foundation, Dean A. McGee Eye Institute (ophthalmology), Oklahoma Children's Memorial Hospital (pediatrics), Veterans Administration Medical Center (clinical and applied medicine), University of Oklahoma Medical Center, Peggy and Charles Stephenson Oklahoma Cancer Center (cancer research).

GRADUATE UNITS

College of Dentistry Offers dentistry (MS, DDS, Certificate); general dentistry (Certificate); orthodontics (MS); periodontics (MS). Electronic applications accepted.

College of Medicine Offers biochemistry (MS, PhD); biochemistry and molecular biology (MS, PhD); biological psychology (MS, PhD); cell biology (MS, PhD); genetic counseling (MS); immunology (MS, PhD); medical radiation physics (MS, PhD); medical sciences (MS); medicine (MHS, MS, MD, PhD); microbiology (MS, PhD); microbiology and immunology (MS, PhD); molecular biology (MS, PhD); neuroscience (MS, PhD); pathology (PhD); physician associate (MHS); physiology (MS, PhD); psychiatry and behavioral sciences (MS, PhD); radiological sciences (MS, PhD). Electronic applications accepted.

College of Pharmacy Offers pharmacy (MS, PhD, Pharm D).

Graduate College *Program availability:* Part-time, evening/weekend.

College of Allied Health *Program availability:* Part-time. Offers allied health (MOT, MPT, MS, Au D, PhD, Certificate); allied health sciences (PhD); audiology (MS, Au D, PhD); communication sciences and disorders (Certificate); education of the deaf (MS); nutritional sciences (MS); occupational therapy (MOT); physical therapy (MPT); rehabilitation sciences (MS); speech-language pathology (MS, PhD).

College of Nursing *Program availability:* Part-time. Offers nursing (MS). MS/MBA offered jointly with Oklahoma State University and University of Oklahoma.

College of Public Health *Program availability:* Part-time. Offers biostatistics (MPH, MS, Dr PH, PhD); epidemiology (MPH, MS, Dr PH, PhD); general public health (MPH, Dr PH); health administration and policy (MHA, MPH, MS, Dr PH, PhD); health promotion sciences (MPH, MS, Dr PH, PhD); occupational and environmental health (MPH, MS, Dr PH, PhD); preparedness and terrorism (MPH); public health (MHA, MPH, MS, Dr PH, PhD).

UNIVERSITY OF OREGON, Eugene, OR 97403

General Information State-supported, coed, university. CGS member. *Graduate housing:* Rooms and/or apartments available to single and married students. *Research affiliation:* Oregon Research Institute, Battelle–Pacific Northwest National Laboratory, National Renewable Energy Laboratory (NREL), Stanford Linear Accelerator Center, Naval Research Laboratories.

GRADUATE UNITS

Graduate School *Program availability:* Part-time, evening/weekend. Offers applied information management (MS).

Charles H. Lundquist College of Business *Program availability:* Part-time, evening/weekend. Offers accounting (M Actg, PhD); business (M Actg, MA, MBA, MS, PhD); decision sciences (MA, MS); finance (PhD); management (PhD); management: general business (MBA); marketing (PhD); sports product management (MS).

College of Arts and Sciences *Program availability:* Part-time, evening/weekend. Offers anthropology (MA, MS, PhD); arts and sciences (MA, MFA, MS, PhD); Asian studies (MA); biochemistry (MA, MS, PhD); chemistry (MA, MS, PhD); Chinese (MA, PhD); classical civilization (MA); classics (MA); clinical psychology (PhD); cognitive psychology (MA, MS, PhD); comparative literature (MA, PhD); computer and information science (MA, MS, PhD); creative writing (MFA); developmental psychology (MA, MS, PhD); ecology and evolution (MA, MS, PhD); economics (MA, MS, PhD); English (MA, PhD); environmental science, studies, and policy (PhD); environmental studies (MA, MS); French (MA); geography (MA, MS, PhD); geological sciences (MA, MS, PhD); Germanic languages and literatures (MA, PhD); Greek (MA); history (MA, PhD); human physiology (MS, PhD); independent study: folklore (MA, MS); international studies (MA); Italian (MA); Japanese (MA, PhD); Latin (MA); linguistics (MA, PhD); marine biology (MA, MS, PhD); mathematics (MA, MS, PhD); molecular, cellular and genetic biology (PhD); neuroscience and development (PhD); philosophy (MA, PhD); physics (MA, MS, PhD); physiological psychology (MA, MS, PhD); political science (MA, MS, PhD); psychology (MA, MS, PhD); Romance languages (MA, PhD); Russian and East European Studies (MA); social/personality psychology (MA, MS, PhD); sociology (MA, MS, PhD); Spanish (MA); theater arts (MA, MFA, MS, PhD).

College of Education *Program availability:* Part-time. Offers education (M Ed, MA, MS, D Ed, PhD).

School of Architecture and Allied Arts *Program availability:* Part-time, evening/weekend. Offers architecture (M Arch); architecture and allied arts (M Arch, MA, MCRP, MFA, MI Arch, MLA, MPA, MS, PhD); art (MFA); art history (MA, PhD); arts management (MA, MS); community and regional planning (MCRP); historic preservation (MS); interior architecture (MI Arch); landscape architecture (MLA); media management (MA, MS); public policy and management (MA, MPA, MS).

School of Journalism and Communication *Program availability:* Part-time. Offers journalism (MA, MS); media studies (MA, MS, PhD); multimedia journalism (MA, MS); strategic communication (MA, MS).

School of Music *Program availability:* Part-time. Offers composition (M Mus, DMA, PhD); conducting (M Mus); dance (MA, MS); jazz studies (M Mus); music (M Mus, MA, MS, DMA, PhD); music education (M Mus, DMA, PhD); music history (PhD); music theory (PhD); performance (M Mus, DMA); piano pedagogy (M Mus).

School of Law Offers law (MA, MS, JD).

UNIVERSITY OF OTTAWA, Ottawa, ON K1N 6N5, Canada

General Information Province-supported, coed, university. *Graduate housing:* Rooms and/or apartments available on a first-come, first-served basis to single and married students. Housing application deadline: 3/15. *Research affiliation:* IBM (performance analytics software, supercomputing), General Electric Company (GE) (hardware, imaging, medical devices), Rio Tinto Alcan (aluminum and aluminum products), Pratt and Whitney Canada (turbine engines, advanced materials, aerospace), Wright Medical Technology Canada (orthopedic medical devices), Air Products and Chemicals Inc. (industrial gases (hydrogen), performance materials, equipment and technology).

GRADUATE UNITS

Faculty of Graduate and Postdoctoral Studies *Program availability:* Part-time, evening/weekend. Offers biomedical engineering (MA Sc); e-business technologies (M Sc, MEBT); globalization and international development (MA); population health (PhD); systems science (M Sc, M Sys Sc, Certificate). MCL, MRE, MP Th offered jointly with Saint Paul University. Electronic applications accepted.

Faculty of Arts *Program availability:* Part-time, evening/weekend. Offers arts (M Geog, M Mus, M Sc, MA, PhD, Certificate); classical studies (MA); communication (MA); directing for theatre (MA); economics (PhD); English (MA, PhD); geography (M Geog, M Sc, MA, PhD); history (PhD); interpreting (MA); lettres Franfcaises (MA, PhD); linguistics (MA, PhD); music (M Mus, MA); orchestral studies (Certificate); philosophy (PhD); piano pedagogy research (Certificate); political science (PhD); psychology (PhD); religious studies (PhD); Spanish (MA, PhD); Spanish translation (MA); translation (MA); translation studies (PhD). Electronic applications accepted.

Faculty of Education *Program availability:* Online learning. Offers education (M Ed, MA Ed, PhD, Certificate). Electronic applications accepted.

Faculty of Engineering Offers chemical and biological engineering (M Eng, MA Sc, PhD); civil engineering (M Eng, MA Sc, PhD); computer science (MCS, PhD); electrical and computer engineering (M Eng, MA Sc, PhD); engineering (M Eng, MA Sc, MCS, PhD, Certificate); engineering management (M Eng); information technology (Certificate); mechanical and aerospace engineering (M Eng, MA Sc, PhD); project management (Certificate). Electronic applications accepted.

Faculty of Health Sciences *Program availability:* Part-time, evening/weekend. Offers audiology (M Sc); health sciences (M Sc, MA, PhD, Certificate); human kinetics (MA);

nurse practitioner (Certificate); nursing (M Sc, PhD); nursing/primary health care (M Sc); orthophony (M Sc). Electronic applications accepted.

Faculty of Law *Program availability:* Part-time, evening/weekend. Offers law (LL M, LL D). Electronic applications accepted.

Faculty of Medicine Offers biochemistry (M Sc, PhD); cellular and molecular medicine (M Sc, PhD); epidemiology (M Sc); medicine (M Sc, MD, PhD); microbiology and immunology (M Sc, PhD). Electronic applications accepted.

Faculty of Science *Program availability:* Part-time, evening/weekend. Offers biology (M Sc, PhD); chemistry (M Sc, PhD); earth sciences (M Sc, PhD); mathematics and statistics (M Sc, PhD); physics (M Sc, PhD); science (M Sc, PhD). Electronic applications accepted.

Faculty of Social Sciences *Program availability:* Part-time, evening/weekend. Offers criminology (MA, MCA); economics (MA, PhD); education (MA); English (MA); history (MA); human kinetics (MA); law (LL M); lettres Franlfcaises (MA); nursing (M Sc); pastoral studies (MA); political science (MA); political studies (MA, PhD); psychology (PhD); religious studies (MA); social sciences (LL M, M Sc, MA, MCA, MSS, PhD); social work (MSS); sociology (MA); sociology and anthropology (MA). Electronic applications accepted.

Telfer School of Management *Program availability:* Part-time, evening/weekend. Offers business administration (MBA); executive business administration (EMBA); health administration (MHA); management (EMBA, MBA, MHA). Electronic applications accepted.

UNIVERSITY OF PENNSYLVANIA, Philadelphia, PA 19104

General Information Independent, coed, university. CGS member. *Enrollment:* 21,826 graduate, professional, and undergraduate students; 10,847 full-time matriculated graduate/professional students (5,664 women), 1,959 part-time matriculated graduate/professional students (1,301 women). *Enrollment by degree level:* 6,625 master's, 5,813 doctoral, 368 other advanced degrees. *Graduate faculty:* 2,568 full-time (834 women), 2,300 part-time/adjunct (906 women). *Tuition:* Full-time $31,068; part-time $5762 per course. *Required fees:* $3200; $336 per course. Full-time tuition and fees vary according to degree level, program and student level. Part-time tuition and fees vary according to course load, degree level and program. *Graduate housing:* Rooms and/or apartments available on a first-come, first-served basis to single and married students. *Student services:* Campus employment opportunities, campus safety program, career counseling, child daycare facilities, exercise/wellness program, free psychological counseling, international student services, low-cost health insurance, multicultural affairs office, services for students with disabilities, writing training. *Library facilities:* Van Pelt Library plus 14 others. *Collection:* Books: 6.4 million (physical); Serial titles: 188,604 (physical). Study areas open 24 hours, 5–7 days a week; students can reserve study rooms. *Research affiliation:* Children's Hospital of Philadelphia, The Wistar Institute (anatomy and biology), BioAdvance, Regional Nanotechnology Center.

Computer facilities: Computer purchase and lease plans are available. A campuswide network can be accessed from student residence rooms and from off campus. Online class registration, billing information, financial aid application, status, academic records, student services are available.
Website: http://www.upenn.edu/

GRADUATE UNITS

Annenberg School for Communication Students: 80 full-time (43 women), 1 part-time (0 women); includes 9 minority (2 Black or African American, non-Hispanic/Latino; 3 Asian, non-Hispanic/Latino; 3 Hispanic/Latino; 1 Two or more races, non-Hispanic/Latino), 28 international. Average age 30. 257 applicants, 7% accepted, 11 enrolled. *Faculty:* 20 full-time (9 women), 5 part-time/adjunct (1 woman). Expenses: Contact institution. *Financial support:* In 2016–17, 80 students received support. In 2016, 6 doctorates awarded. Offers communication (PhD). *Application Contact:* Joanne Murray, 215-573-6349, Fax: 215-898-2024, E-mail: joanne.murray@asc.upenn.edu.

Graduate School of Education Students: 1,039 full-time (739 women), 365 part-time (266 women); includes 468 minority (199 Black or African American, non-Hispanic/Latino; 110 Asian, non-Hispanic/Latino; 109 Hispanic/Latino; 1 Native Hawaiian or other Pacific Islander, non-Hispanic/Latino; 49 Two or more races, non-Hispanic/Latino), 324 international. Average age 31. 3,103 applicants, 50% accepted, 850 enrolled. *Faculty:* 70 full-time (28 women), 44 part-time/adjunct (23 women). Expenses: Contact institution. In 2016, 559 master's, 77 doctorates awarded. *Program availability:* Part-time, evening/weekend, online learning. Offers education (M Phil, MS, MS Ed, Ed D, PhD, Certificate); educational leadership (Ed D); learning leadership (Ed D); medical education (MS Ed, Certificate); teaching (MS Ed); urban teaching (MS Ed). *Application fee:* $75. Electronic applications accepted.

Division of Educational Linguistics Students: 157 full-time (140 women), 28 part-time (17 women); includes 16 minority (1 Black or African American, non-Hispanic/Latino; 8 Asian, non-Hispanic/Latino; 5 Hispanic/Latino; 2 Two or more races, non-Hispanic/Latino), 136 international. Average age 25. 554 applicants, 34% accepted, 98 enrolled. Expenses: Contact institution. *Financial support:* In 2016–17, 55 students received support. Fellowships, research assistantships, teaching assistantships, Federal Work-Study, scholarships/grants, health care benefits, and unspecified assistantships available. In 2016, 91 master's, 6 doctorates awarded. *Program availability:* Part-time. Offers educational linguistics (MS Ed, PhD); intercultural communication (MS Ed); teaching English to speakers of other languages (MS Ed). *Application deadline:* For fall admission, 12/8 priority date for domestic and international students. Applications are processed on a rolling basis. *Application fee:* $75. Electronic applications accepted. *Program Manager,* Kristina Lewis, 215-898-5212, E-mail: klewi@upenn.edu.

Division of Education Policy Students: 38 full-time (27 women), 6 part-time (4 women); includes 15 minority (7 Black or African American, non-Hispanic/Latino; 3 Asian, non-Hispanic/Latino; 4 Hispanic/Latino; 1 Two or more races, non-Hispanic/Latino), 11 international. Average age 28. 250 applicants, 50% accepted, 34 enrolled. Expenses: Contact institution. *Financial support:* In 2016–17, 13 students received support. Fellowships, research assistantships, teaching assistantships, Federal Work-Study, scholarships/grants, and health care benefits available. In 2016, 16 master's, 2 doctorates awarded. *Program availability:* Part-time. Offers education policy (MS Ed, PhD). *Application deadline:* For fall admission, 12/8 priority date for domestic and international students. Applications are processed on a rolling basis. *Application fee:* $75. Electronic applications accepted. *Program Manager,* Krista Featherstone, 215-573-8075, E-mail: kfeat@upenn.edu.

Division of Higher Education Students: 97 full-time (59 women), 54 part-time (43 women); includes 61 minority (32 Black or African American, non-Hispanic/Latino; 8 Asian, non-Hispanic/Latino; 17 Hispanic/Latino; 4 Two or more races, non-Hispanic/Latino), 2 international. Average age 35. 401 applicants, 46% accepted, 90 enrolled. Expenses: Contact institution. *Financial support:* In 2016–17, 24 students received support. Fellowships, research assistantships, teaching assistantships,

Federal Work-Study, scholarships/grants, health care benefits, and unspecified assistantships available. In 2016, 45 master's, 29 doctorates awarded. *Program availability:* Part-time. Offers higher education (MS Ed, Ed D, PhD); higher education management (Ed D). *Application deadline:* For fall admission, 12/8 priority date for domestic and international students. *Application fee:* $75. Electronic applications accepted. *Program Manager,* Dr. Ross Aikins, 215-898-8398, E-mail: raikins@upenn.edu.

Division of Human Development and Quantitative Methods Students: 236 full-time (185 women), 18 part-time (17 women); includes 58 minority (21 Black or African American, non-Hispanic/Latino; 16 Asian, non-Hispanic/Latino; 13 Hispanic/Latino; 1 Native Hawaiian or other Pacific Islander, non-Hispanic/Latino; 7 Two or more races, non-Hispanic/Latino), 103 international. Average age 27. 622 applicants, 52% accepted, 192 enrolled. Expenses: Contact institution. *Financial support:* In 2016–17, 95 students received support. Fellowships, research assistantships, teaching assistantships, career-related internships or fieldwork, Federal Work-Study, scholarships/grants, health care benefits, and unspecified assistantships available. In 2016, 134 master's, 1 doctorate awarded. *Program availability:* Part-time-only, evening/weekend. Offers counseling and mental health services (M Phil, MS Ed); human development (MS Ed, PhD); quantitative methods (M Phil, MS, PhD); school and mental health counseling (MS Ed); statistics, measurement, assessment, and research technology (MS). *Application deadline:* For fall admission, 12/8 priority date for domestic and international students. Applications are processed on a rolling basis. *Application fee:* $75. Electronic applications accepted. *Application Contact:* 215-898-6415, Fax: 215-746-6884, E-mail: admissions@gse.upenn.edu. *Program Manager,* Dr. Elizabeth Mackenzie, 215-898-4176, E-mail: emackenz@upenn.edu.

Division of Literacy, Culture, and International Education Students: 132 full-time (100 women), 45 part-time (35 women); includes 74 minority (32 Black or African American, non-Hispanic/Latino; 17 Asian, non-Hispanic/Latino; 16 Hispanic/Latino; 9 Two or more races, non-Hispanic/Latino), 32 international. Average age 30. 462 applicants, 47% accepted, 95 enrolled. Expenses: Contact institution. *Financial support:* In 2016–17, 44 students received support. Fellowships, research assistantships, teaching assistantships, Federal Work-Study, scholarships/grants, and health care benefits available. In 2016, 54 master's, 11 doctorates awarded. *Program availability:* Part-time. Offers education, culture and society (MS Ed, PhD); international educational development (MS Ed); language and literacy (MS Ed); reading/writing/literacy (MS Ed, Ed D, PhD). *Application deadline:* For fall admission, 12/8 priority date for domestic and international students. Applications are processed on a rolling basis. *Application fee:* $75. Electronic applications accepted. *Program Manager,* Dr. Alex Posecznick, 215-573-3947, E-mail: alpos@upenn.edu.

Division of Teaching, Learning, and Leadership Students: 190 full-time (121 women), 48 part-time (39 women); includes 80 minority (27 Black or African American, non-Hispanic/Latino; 26 Asian, non-Hispanic/Latino; 18 Hispanic/Latino; 9 Two or more races, non-Hispanic/Latino), 25 international. Average age 32. 546 applicants, 56% accepted, 174 enrolled. Expenses: Contact institution. *Financial support:* In 2016–17, 13 students received support. Fellowships, research assistantships, teaching assistantships, Federal Work-Study, scholarships/grants, health care benefits, and unspecified assistantships available. In 2016, 122 master's, 3 doctorates awarded. *Program availability:* Part-time. Offers education entrepreneurship (MS Ed); educational leadership (MS Ed, Ed D, PhD); elementary education (MS Ed); learning sciences and technologies (MS Ed); school leadership (MS Ed); secondary education (MS Ed); teacher education (MS Ed); teaching and learning (MS Ed); teaching, learning, and leadership (MS Ed); teaching, learning, and teacher education (Ed D, PhD). *Application deadline:* For fall admission, 12/8 priority date for domestic and international students. Applications are processed on a rolling basis. *Application fee:* $75. Electronic applications accepted. *Application Contact:* Mercury Meulman, Administrative Coordinator, 215-898-4176, E-mail: mercury@upenn.edu. *Program Manager,* Dr. Veronica Aplenc, 215-898-2566, E-mail: vaplenc@upenn.edu.

Law School Students: 749 full-time (346 women); includes 216 minority (51 Black or African American, non-Hispanic/Latino; 2 American Indian or Alaska Native, non-Hispanic/Latino; 95 Asian, non-Hispanic/Latino; 46 Hispanic/Latino; 22 Two or more races, non-Hispanic/Latino), 42 international. Average age 27. 5,593 applicants, 17% accepted, 242 enrolled. *Faculty:* 75 full-time (26 women), 75 part-time/adjunct (24 women). Expenses: Contact institution. *Financial support:* In 2016–17, 366 students received support, including 1 fellowship (averaging $3,500 per year), 119 research assistantships (averaging $3,255 per year), 11 teaching assistantships (averaging $2,782 per year); career-related internships or fieldwork, Federal Work-Study, institutionally sponsored loans, and scholarships/grants also available. Financial award application deadline: 3/1; financial award applicants required to submit FAFSA. In 2016, 117 master's, 258 doctorates awarded. Offers law (LL CM, LL M, ML, JD, SJD). JD/LL M offered jointly with Hong Kong University. *Application deadline:* For fall admission, 3/1 for domestic students, 12/15 for international students. Applications are processed on a rolling basis. *Application fee:* $80. Electronic applications accepted. *Application Contact:* Renee Post, Associate Dean of Admissions and Financial Aid, 215-898-7400, Fax: 215-898-9606, E-mail: contactadmissions@law.upenn.edu. *Dean,* Theodore W. Ruger, 215-898-7463, Fax: 215-573-2025.

Perelman School of Medicine Students: 1,806 full-time (949 women), 96 part-time (75 women); includes 767 minority (108 Black or African American, non-Hispanic/Latino; 3 American Indian or Alaska Native, non-Hispanic/Latino; 363 Asian, non-Hispanic/Latino; 204 Hispanic/Latino; 89 Two or more races, non-Hispanic/Latino), 124 international. 7,609 applicants, 11% accepted, 435 enrolled. *Faculty:* 3,068 full-time (1,240 women), 1,199 part-time/adjunct (530 women). Expenses: Contact institution. *Financial support:* Applicants required to submit FAFSA. In 2016, 144 master's, 117 doctorates awarded. *Program availability:* Part-time. Offers environmental health (MPH); generalist (MPH); global health (MPH); health policy research (MS); medical ethics and health policy (MBE, MSME); medicine (MBE, MPH, MRA, MS, MSCE, MSME, MTR, MD, PhD); regulatory affairs (MRA); translational research (MTR). *Application Contact:* Gaye Sheffler, Director, Admissions, 215-898-8000, E-mail: sheffler@mail.med.upenn.edu. *Senior Vice Dean for Education,* Dr. Gail Morrison, 215-898-8034, E-mail: morrisog@mail.med.upenn.edu.

Biomedical Graduate Studies Students: 814 full-time (453 women), 27 part-time (22 women); includes 282 minority (32 Black or African American, non-Hispanic/Latino; 3 American Indian or Alaska Native, non-Hispanic/Latino; 132 Asian, non-Hispanic/Latino; 78 Hispanic/Latino; 37 Two or more races, non-Hispanic/Latino), 97 international. 1,445 applicants, 25% accepted, 182 enrolled. *Faculty:* 1,050. Expenses: Contact institution. *Financial support:* In 2016–17, 635 students received support. In 2016, 57 master's, 117 doctorates awarded. Offers biochemistry and molecular biophysics (PhD); biomedical studies (MS, PhD); biostatistics (MS, PhD); cancer biology (PhD); cell biology, physiology, and metabolism (PhD); developmental stem cell regenerative biology (PhD); epidemiology (PhD); gene therapy and vaccines (PhD); genetics and gene regulation (PhD); genomics and computational biology

(PhD); immunology (PhD); microbiology, virology, and parasitology (PhD); neuroscience (PhD); pharmacology (PhD). *Application deadline:* For fall admission, 12/1 priority date for domestic students, 12/1 for international students. Applications are processed on a rolling basis. *Application fee:* $80. Electronic applications accepted. *Application Contact:* Aislinn Wallace, Admissions Coordinator, 215-746-6349, E-mail: aislinnw@mail.med.upenn.edu. *Director,* Dr. Michael Nusbaum, 215-898-1585, E-mail: nusbaum@mail.med.upenn.edu.

Center for Clinical Epidemiology Students: 93 full-time (58 women), 3 part-time (2 women); includes 31 minority (9 Black or African American, non-Hispanic/Latino; 15 Asian, non-Hispanic/Latino; 7 Hispanic/Latino). Average age 35. 42 applicants, 93% accepted, 31 enrolled. *Faculty:* 97 full-time (47 women), 10 part-time/adjunct (27 women). Expenses: Contact institution. *Financial support:* In 2016–17, 50 students received support, including 50 fellowships with tuition reimbursements available (averaging $45,500 per year). Financial award application deadline: 12/1. In 2016, 37 master's awarded. *Program availability:* Part-time. Offers clinical epidemiology (MSCE). *Application deadline:* For fall admission, 12/1 priority date for domestic students, 12/1 for international students. *Application fee:* $0. *Application Contact:* Jennifer Kuklinski, Program Coordinator, 215-573-2382, E-mail: jkuklins@mail.med.upenn.edu. *Director,* Dr. Harold I. Feldman, 215-573-0901, E-mail: hfeldman@mail.med.upenn.edu.

School of Arts and Sciences Students: 1,592 full-time (757 women), 450 part-time (256 women); includes 333 minority (84 Black or African American, non-Hispanic/Latino; 2 American Indian or Alaska Native, non-Hispanic/Latino; 102 Asian, non-Hispanic/Latino; 91 Hispanic/Latino; 54 Two or more races, non-Hispanic/Latino), 645 international. Average age 30. 6,611 applicants, 18% accepted, 595 enrolled. *Faculty:* 477 full-time (153 women), 14 part-time/adjunct (4 women). Expenses: Contact institution. In 2016, 482 master's, 204 doctorates, 33 other advanced degrees awarded. *Program availability:* Part-time, evening/weekend. Offers Africana studies (MA, PhD); ancient history (AM, PhD); anthropology (AM, MS, PhD); applied mathematics and computational science (PhD); art and archaeology of the Mediterranean world (AM, PhD); arts and sciences (AM, MA, MBA, MES, MGA, MLA, MPA, MS, PhD, Certificate); biology (PhD); chemistry (MS, PhD); classical studies (AM, PhD); comparative literature (AM, PhD); criminology (MA, MS, PhD); demography (AM, PhD); earth and environmental science (MS, PhD); East Asian languages and civilizations (AM, PhD); economics (AM, PhD); English (AM, PhD); French (AM, PhD); Germanic languages (AM, PhD); history (AM, PhD); history and sociology of science (AM, PhD); history of art (AM, PhD); international studies (AM); Italian (AM, PhD); linguistics (AM, PhD); literary theory (AM, PhD); mathematics (AM, PhD); medical physics (MS); music (AM, PhD); Near Eastern languages and civilizations (AM, PhD); philosophy (AM, PhD); physics (PhD); political science (AM, PhD); psychology (PhD); religious studies (PhD); sociology (AM, PhD); South Asian regional studies (AM, PhD); Spanish (AM, PhD).

College of Liberal and Professional Studies Students: 143 full-time (75 women), 337 part-time (189 women); includes 90 minority (28 Black or African American, non-Hispanic/Latino; 2 American Indian or Alaska Native, non-Hispanic/Latino; 22 Asian, non-Hispanic/Latino; 26 Hispanic/Latino; 12 Two or more races, non-Hispanic/Latino), 66 international. Average age 35. 618 applicants, 51% accepted, 231 enrolled. Expenses: Contact institution. In 2016, 161 master's awarded. Offers applied geosciences (MSAG); applied positive psychology (MAP); chemical sciences (MCS); environmental studies (MES); individualized study (MLA); liberal arts (M Phil); medical physics (MMP); organization dynamics (M Phil). *Vice Dean, Professional and Liberal Education,* Nora Lewis, 215-898-7326, E-mail: nlewis@sas.upenn.edu.

Fels Institute of Government Students: 49 full-time (29 women), 65 part-time (35 women); includes 28 minority (13 Black or African American, non-Hispanic/Latino; 6 Asian, non-Hispanic/Latino; 6 Hispanic/Latino; 3 Two or more races, non-Hispanic/Latino), 18 international. Average age 30. 371 applicants, 39% accepted, 71 enrolled. Expenses: Contact institution. *Financial support:* Application deadline: 1/1. In 2016, 52 master's, 17 other advanced degrees awarded. *Program availability:* Part-time, evening/weekend. Offers economic development and growth (Certificate); government administration (MGA); nonprofit administration (Certificate); organization dynamics (MS); politics (Certificate); public administration (MPA); public finance (Certificate).

Joseph H. Lauder Institute of Management and International Studies Offers international studies (MA); management and international studies (MBA). Applications must be made concurrently and separately to the Wharton MBA program. Electronic applications accepted.

School of Dental Medicine Offers dental medicine (DMD).

School of Design Students: 686 full-time (401 women), 13 part-time (8 women); includes 98 minority (15 Black or African American, non-Hispanic/Latino; 36 Asian, non-Hispanic/Latino; 34 Hispanic/Latino; 1 Native Hawaiian or other Pacific Islander, non-Hispanic/Latino; 12 Two or more races, non-Hispanic/Latino), 385 international. Average age 26. 1,732 applicants, 49% accepted, 340 enrolled. *Faculty:* 38 full-time (15 women), 18 part-time/adjunct (4 women). Expenses: Contact institution. *Financial support:* In 2016–17, 29 students received support. In 2016, 259 master's, 9 doctorates, 50 other advanced degrees awarded. *Program availability:* Part-time. Offers architecture (M Arch, PhD); city and regional planning (PhD); city planning (MCP); design (M Arch, MCP, MEBD, MFA, MLA, MS, MUSA, PhD, Advanced Certificate, Certificate); ecological architecture (Certificate); emerging design and research (Certificate); environmental building design (MEBD); fine arts (MFA); GIS and spatial analysis (Certificate); historic preservation (MS, Certificate); land preservation (Certificate); landscape architecture (MLA); landscape studies (Certificate); time-based and interactive media (Certificate); urban design (Certificate); urban redevelopment (Certificate); urban spatial analytics (MUSA).

School of Engineering and Applied Science Students: 1,109 full-time (333 women), 301 part-time (102 women); includes 180 minority (13 Black or African American, non-Hispanic/Latino; 116 Asian, non-Hispanic/Latino; 38 Hispanic/Latino; 13 Two or more races, non-Hispanic/Latino), 880 international. Average age 25. 6,263 applicants, 23% accepted, 817 enrolled. *Faculty:* 115 full-time (18 women), 26 part-time/adjunct (3 women). Expenses: Contact institution. In 2016, 581 master's, 78 doctorates awarded. *Program availability:* Part-time. Offers bioengineering (MSE, PhD); biotechnology (MBT); chemical and biomolecular engineering (MSE, PhD); computer and information science (MSE, PhD); computer and information technology (MCIT); computer graphics and game technology (MSE); electrical and systems engineering (MSE, PhD); embedded systems (MSE); engineering and applied science (MBT, MCIT, MIPD, MSE, PhD); integrated product design (MIPD, MSE); materials science and engineering (MSE, PhD); mechanical engineering and applied mechanics (MSE, PhD); nanotechnology (MSE); robotics (MSE); scientific computing (MSE). *Application deadline:* For fall admission, 3/15 priority date for domestic and international students. *Application fee:* $80. Electronic applications accepted. *Application Contact:* William Fenton, Assistant Director of Graduate Admissions, 215-898-4542, Fax: 215-573-5577, E-mail: gradstudies@seas.upenn.edu.

School of Nursing Students: 244 full-time (222 women), 439 part-time (393 women); includes 198 minority (51 Black or African American, non-Hispanic/Latino; 2 American Indian or Alaska Native, non-Hispanic/Latino; 84 Asian, non-Hispanic/Latino; 41 Hispanic/Latino; 20 Two or more races, non-Hispanic/Latino), 13 international. Average age 32. 759 applicants, 60% accepted, 405 enrolled. *Faculty:* 55 full-time (48 women), 34 part-time/adjunct (32 women). Expenses: Contact institution. In 2016, 294 master's, 13 doctorates awarded. *Program availability:* Part-time, online learning. Offers adult and special populations (MSN); adult gerontology clinical nurse specialist (MSN); adult-gerontology acute care nurse practitioner (MSN); adult-gerontology primary care nurse practitioner (MSN); child and family (MSN); family nurse practitioner (MSN, Certificate); geropsychiatrics (MSN); health leadership (MSN); neonatal clinical nurse specialist (MSN); neonatal nurse practitioner (MSN); nurse anesthesia (MSN); nurse midwifery (MSN); nursing (MSN, PhD, Certificate); nursing and health care administration (MSN, PhD); pediatric acute care nurse practitioner (MSN); pediatric clinical nurse specialist (MSN); pediatric primary care nurse practitioner (MSN); women's health/gender related nurse practitioner (MSN). *Application Contact:* Sylvia English, Enrollment Management Coordinator, 215-898-8439, Fax: 215-573-8439, E-mail: sylviaj@nursing.upenn.edu. *Assistant Dean for Admissions and Academic Affairs,* Dr. Christina Costanzo Clark, 215-898-4271, Fax: 215-573-8439, E-mail: costanzo@nursing.upenn.edu.

School of Social Policy and Practice Students: 400 full-time (326 women), 51 part-time (43 women); includes 131 minority (57 Black or African American, non-Hispanic/Latino; 23 Asian, non-Hispanic/Latino; 11 Hispanic/Latino; 40 Two or more races, non-Hispanic/Latino), 42 international. Average age 27. 883 applicants, 260 enrolled. *Faculty:* 27 full-time (14 women), 51 part-time/adjunct (39 women). Expenses: Contact institution. *Financial support:* In 2016–17, 291 students received support, including 24 fellowships (averaging $24,378 per year); career-related internships or fieldwork, Federal Work-Study, institutionally sponsored loans, scholarships/grants, tuition waivers (partial), and unspecified assistantships also available. Support available to part-time students. Financial award applicants required to submit FAFSA. In 2016, 249 master's, 13 doctorates awarded. *Program availability:* Part-time, blended/hybrid learning. Offers social policy and practice (MNPL, MSSP, MSW, DSW, PhD); social welfare (PhD); social work (MNPL, MSSP, MSW, DSW). *Application deadline:* For fall admission, 2/1 priority date for domestic and international students. Applications are processed on a rolling basis. *Application fee:* $65. Electronic applications accepted. *Application Contact:* Dr. Mary C. Mazzola, Associate Dean, Enrollment Management, 215-898-5550, Fax: 215-573-2099, E-mail: rmazzola@sp2.upenn.edu. *Dean,* John L. Jackson, Jr., 215-898-5541, Fax: 215-573-2099, E-mail: jjackson@sp2.upenn.edu.

School of Veterinary Medicine Students: 481 full-time (394 women), 10 part-time (8 women); includes 59 minority (6 Black or African American, non-Hispanic/Latino; 27 Asian, non-Hispanic/Latino; 21 Hispanic/Latino; 5 Two or more races, non-Hispanic/Latino), 3 international. Average age 26. 1,093 applicants, 11% accepted, 113 enrolled. *Faculty:* 107 full-time (57 women), 32 part-time/adjunct (13 women). Expenses: Contact institution. In 2016, 119 doctorates awarded. Offers veterinary medicine (VMD).

Wharton School *Program availability:* Evening/weekend. Offers accounting (PhD); applied economics (PhD); business (MBA, PhD); business administration (MBA); business and public policy (MBA, PhD); ethics and legal studies (PhD); finance (PhD); health care management (MBA, PhD); health care management and economics (PhD); insurance and risk management (MBA, PhD); legal studies and business ethics (MBA, PhD); management (PhD); marketing (PhD); operations and information management (PhD); real estate (MBA, PhD); statistics (MBA, PhD). Electronic applications accepted.

The Wharton MBA Program for Executives *Program availability:* Evening/weekend. Offers executive business administration (MBA).

UNIVERSITY OF PHILOSOPHICAL RESEARCH, Los Angeles, CA 90027

General Information Proprietary, coed, graduate-only institution.

GRADUATE UNITS

Master's in Consciousness Studies Program Offers consciousness studies (MA). Electronic applications accepted.

Master's in Transformational Psychology Program Offers transformational psychology (MA). Electronic applications accepted.

UNIVERSITY OF PHOENIX–ATLANTA CAMPUS, Sandy Springs, GA 30350-4147

General Information Proprietary, coed, comprehensive institution. *Graduate housing:* On-campus housing not available.

GRADUATE UNITS

College of Information Systems and Technology *Program availability:* Evening/weekend. Offers information systems (MIS); technology management (MBA). Electronic applications accepted.

College of Nursing *Program availability:* Evening/weekend, online learning. Offers health administration (MHA); nursing (MSN); nursing/health care education (MSN). Electronic applications accepted.

School of Business *Program availability:* Evening/weekend, online learning. Offers accounting (MBA); business administration (MBA); global management (MBA); human resources management (MBA, MM); management (MM); marketing (MBA); public administration (MM).

UNIVERSITY OF PHOENIX–AUGUSTA CAMPUS, Augusta, GA 30909-4583

General Information Proprietary, coed, comprehensive institution.

GRADUATE UNITS

College of Criminal Justice and Security Offers administration of justice and security (MS).

College of Information Systems and Technology Offers information systems (MIS); technology management (MBA).

College of Nursing *Program availability:* Online learning. Offers health administration (MHA); nursing (MSN); nursing/health care education (MSN).

School of Business *Program availability:* Online learning. Offers accounting (MBA); business administration (MBA); business and management (MBA, MM); global management (MBA, MM); human resources management (MBA, MM); management (MM); marketing (MBA); public administration (MBA, MM).

UNIVERSITY OF PHOENIX–BAY AREA CAMPUS, San Jose, CA 95134-1805

General Information Proprietary, coed, comprehensive institution. *Graduate housing:* On-campus housing not available.

GRADUATE UNITS

College of Criminal Justice and Security Offers administration of justice and security (MS).

College of Education *Program availability:* Evening/weekend, online learning. Offers administration and supervision (MA Ed); adult education and training (MA Ed); early childhood education (MA Ed); education (Ed S); educational leadership (Ed D); elementary teacher education (MA Ed); higher education administration (PhD); secondary teacher education (MA Ed); special education (MA Ed); teacher leadership (MA Ed). Electronic applications accepted.

College of Information Systems and Technology *Program availability:* Evening/weekend. Offers information systems (MIS); organizational leadership/information systems and technology (DM). Electronic applications accepted.

College of Nursing *Program availability:* Evening/weekend, online learning. Offers education (MHA); gerontology (MHA); health administration (MHA, DHA); informatics (MHA, MSN); nursing (MSN, PhD); nursing/health care education (MSN). Electronic applications accepted.

College of Social Sciences *Program availability:* Evening/weekend. Offers marriage, family, and child therapy (MSC).

School of Business *Program availability:* Evening/weekend, online learning. Offers accountancy (MS); accounting (MBA); business administration (MBA, DBA); energy management (MBA); global management (MBA); health care management (MBA); human resource management (MBA); human resources management (MM); management (MM); marketing (MBA); organizational leadership (DM); project management (MBA); public administration (MPA); technology management (MBA). Electronic applications accepted.

UNIVERSITY OF PHOENIX–CENTRAL FLORIDA CAMPUS, Orlando, FL 32819

General Information Proprietary, coed, comprehensive institution. *Graduate housing:* On-campus housing not available.

UNIVERSITY OF PHOENIX–CENTRAL VALLEY CAMPUS, Fresno, CA 93720-1552

General Information Proprietary, coed, comprehensive institution.

GRADUATE UNITS

College of Education Offers curriculum and instruction (MA Ed); curriculum and instruction-computer education (MA Ed); elementary teacher education (MA Ed); secondary teacher education (MA Ed).

College of Human Services Offers marriage, family and child therapy (MSC).

College of Information Systems and Technology Offers information systems (MIS); technology management (MBA).

College of Nursing Offers education (MHA); gerontology (MHA); health administration (MHA); nursing (MSN).

School of Business Offers accounting (MBA); business administration (MBA); global management (MBA); human resources management (MBA, MM); management (MM); marketing (MBA); public administration (MBA, MM).

UNIVERSITY OF PHOENIX–CHARLOTTE CAMPUS, Charlotte, NC 28273-3409

General Information Proprietary, coed, comprehensive institution. *Graduate housing:* On-campus housing not available.

GRADUATE UNITS

College of Information Systems and Technology *Program availability:* Evening/weekend. Offers information systems (MIS); information systems management (MISM); technology management (MBA). Electronic applications accepted.

College of Nursing *Program availability:* Evening/weekend. Offers education (MHA); gerontology (MHA); health administration (MHA); informatics (MHA, MSN); nursing (MSN); nursing/health care education (MSN). Electronic applications accepted.

School of Business *Program availability:* Evening/weekend. Offers accounting (MBA); business administration (MBA); global management (MBA). Electronic applications accepted.

UNIVERSITY OF PHOENIX–COLORADO CAMPUS, Lone Tree, CO 80124-5453

General Information Proprietary, coed, comprehensive institution. *Graduate housing:* On-campus housing not available.

GRADUATE UNITS

College of Education *Program availability:* Evening/weekend. Offers administration and supervision (MAEd); curriculum instruction (MAEd); elementary teacher education (MAEd); school counseling (MSC); secondary teacher education (MAEd). Electronic applications accepted.

College of Information Systems and Technology *Program availability:* Evening/weekend, online learning. Offers e-business (MBA); management (MIS); technology management (MBA). Electronic applications accepted.

College of Nursing *Program availability:* Evening/weekend, online learning. Offers health administration (MHA); nursing (MSN). Electronic applications accepted.

School of Business *Program availability:* Evening/weekend, online learning. Offers accountancy (MSA); accounting (MBA); business administration (MBA); e-business (MBA); global management (MBA); human resources management (MBA, MM); management (MM); marketing (MBA); public administration (MBA, MM). Electronic applications accepted.

UNIVERSITY OF PHOENIX–COLORADO SPRINGS DOWNTOWN CAMPUS, Colorado Springs, CO 80903

General Information Proprietary, coed, comprehensive institution. *Graduate housing:* On-campus housing not available.

GRADUATE UNITS

College of Education *Program availability:* Evening/weekend. Offers administration and supervision (MA Ed); curriculum and instruction (MA Ed); elementary teacher education (MA Ed); principal licensure certification (Certificate); school counseling (MSC); secondary teacher education (MA Ed). Electronic applications accepted.

College of Information Systems and Technology *Program availability:* Evening/weekend. Offers technology management (MBA). Electronic applications accepted.

College of Nursing *Program availability:* Evening/weekend. Offers education (MHA); gerontology (MHA); health administration (MHA); nursing (MSN). Electronic applications accepted.

School of Business *Program availability:* Evening/weekend. Offers accounting (MBA); business administration (MBA); global management (MBA); human resources management (MBA, MM); management (MM); marketing (MBA); public administration (MM). Electronic applications accepted.

UNIVERSITY OF PHOENIX–COLUMBUS GEORGIA CAMPUS, Columbus, GA 31909

General Information Proprietary, coed, comprehensive institution. *Graduate housing:* On-campus housing not available.

GRADUATE UNITS

College of Information Systems and Technology *Program availability:* Evening/weekend, online learning. Offers e-business (MBA); information systems (MIS); technology management (MBA). Electronic applications accepted.

College of Nursing *Program availability:* Online learning. Offers health administration (MHA); nursing (MSN). Electronic applications accepted.

School of Business *Program availability:* Evening/weekend. Offers accounting (MBA); business administration (MBA); global management (MBA); human resources management (MBA, MM); management (MM); marketing (MBA); public administration (MBA). Electronic applications accepted.

UNIVERSITY OF PHOENIX–DALLAS CAMPUS, Dallas, TX 75251

General Information Proprietary, coed, comprehensive institution. *Graduate housing:* On-campus housing not available.

GRADUATE UNITS

College of Criminal Justice and Security *Program availability:* Online learning. Offers administration of justice and security (MS). Electronic applications accepted.

College of Education Offers curriculum and instruction (MA Ed).

College of Information Systems and Technology *Program availability:* Evening/weekend. Offers e-business (MBA); information systems (MIS); technology management (MBA). Electronic applications accepted.

School of Business *Program availability:* Evening/weekend, online learning. Offers accounting (MBA); business administration (MBA); global management (MBA); human resources management (MBA, MM); management (MM); marketing (MBA); public administration (MBA, MM). Electronic applications accepted.

UNIVERSITY OF PHOENIX–HAWAII CAMPUS, Honolulu, HI 96813-3800

General Information Proprietary, coed, comprehensive institution. *Graduate housing:* On-campus housing not available.

GRADUATE UNITS

College of Education *Program availability:* Evening/weekend. Offers administration and supervision (MA Ed); curriculum and instruction (MA Ed); elementary education (MA Ed); secondary education (MA Ed); special education (MA Ed); teacher education for elementary licensure (MA Ed). Electronic applications accepted.

College of Information Systems and Technology *Program availability:* Evening/weekend. Offers information systems (MIS); technology management (MBA). Electronic applications accepted.

College of Nursing *Program availability:* Evening/weekend. Offers education (MHA); family nurse practitioner (MSN); gerontology (MHA); health administration (MHA); nursing (MSN); nursing/health care education (MSN). Electronic applications accepted.

School of Business *Program availability:* Evening/weekend. Offers accounting (MBA); business administration (MBA); global management (MBA); human resources management (MBA, MM); management (MM); marketing (MBA); public administration (MBA, MM). Electronic applications accepted.

UNIVERSITY OF PHOENIX–HOUSTON CAMPUS, Houston, TX 77079-2004

General Information Proprietary, coed, comprehensive institution. *Graduate housing:* On-campus housing not available.

GRADUATE UNITS

College of Education Offers curriculum and instruction (MA Ed).

College of Information Systems and Technology *Program availability:* Evening/weekend, online learning. Offers e-business (MBA); information systems (MIS); technology management (MBA). Electronic applications accepted.

College of Nursing *Program availability:* Online learning. Offers health administration (MHA). Electronic applications accepted.

School of Business *Program availability:* Evening/weekend, online learning. Offers accounting (MBA); business administration (MBA); global management (MBA); human resources management (MBA, MM); management (MM); marketing (MBA); public administration (MBA, MM). Electronic applications accepted.

UNIVERSITY OF PHOENIX–JERSEY CITY CAMPUS, Jersey City, NJ 07310

General Information Proprietary, coed, comprehensive institution.

GRADUATE UNITS

College of Criminal Justice and Security *Program availability:* Online learning. Offers administration of justice and security (MS).

College of Information Systems and Technology *Program availability:* Online learning. Offers information systems (MIS); technology management (MBA).

College of Social Services *Program availability:* Online learning. Offers psychology (MS).

School of Business Offers accounting (MBA); business administration (MBA); global management (MBA); human resources management (MBA, MM); management (MM); marketing (MBA); public administration (MBA, MM).

UNIVERSITY OF PHOENIX–LAS VEGAS CAMPUS, Las Vegas, NV 89135

General Information Proprietary, coed, comprehensive institution. *Graduate housing:* On-campus housing not available.

GRADUATE UNITS

College of Education *Program availability:* Evening/weekend. Offers administration and supervision (MA Ed); curriculum and instruction (MA Ed); school counseling (MSC); teacher education-elementary licensure (MA Ed). Electronic applications accepted.

College of Human Services *Program availability:* Online learning. Offers marriage, family, and child therapy (MSC); mental health counseling (MSC); school counseling (MSC). Electronic applications accepted.

College of Information Systems and Technology *Program availability:* Evening/weekend. Offers information systems (MIS); technology management (MBA). Electronic applications accepted.

School of Business *Program availability:* Evening/weekend, online learning. Offers accounting (MBA); business administration (MBA); global management (MBA); human resources management (MBA, MM); management (MM); marketing (MBA); public administration (MM). Electronic applications accepted.

UNIVERSITY OF PHOENIX–NEW MEXICO CAMPUS, Albuquerque, NM 87113-1570

General Information Proprietary, coed, comprehensive institution. *Graduate housing:* On-campus housing not available.

GRADUATE UNITS

College of Education *Program availability:* Evening/weekend. Offers administration and supervision (MAEd); curriculum and instruction (MAEd); elementary teacher education (MAEd); school counseling (MSC); secondary teacher education (MAEd). Electronic applications accepted.

College of Information Systems and Technology *Program availability:* Evening/weekend. Offers e-business (MBA); information systems (MS); technology management (MBA). Electronic applications accepted.

College of Nursing *Program availability:* Evening/weekend. Offers health administration (MHA); health care education (MSN); nursing (MSN). Electronic applications accepted.

School of Business *Program availability:* Evening/weekend. Offers accounting (MBA); business administration (MBA); global management (MBA); human resources management (MBA, MM); management (MM); marketing (MBA). Electronic applications accepted.

UNIVERSITY OF PHOENIX–NORTH FLORIDA CAMPUS, Jacksonville, FL 32216-0959

General Information Proprietary, coed, comprehensive institution. *Graduate housing:* On-campus housing not available.

GRADUATE UNITS

College of Education *Program availability:* Evening/weekend. Offers administration and supervision (MA Ed); curriculum and instruction (MA Ed); early childhood education (MA Ed); elementary teacher education (MA Ed); secondary teacher education (MA Ed). Electronic applications accepted.

College of Information Systems and Technology *Program availability:* Evening/weekend. Offers information systems (MIS); management (MIS). Electronic applications accepted.

College of Nursing *Program availability:* Evening/weekend. Offers health administration (MHA); health care education (MSN); nursing (MSN). Electronic applications accepted.

School of Business *Program availability:* Evening/weekend. Offers accounting (MBA); business administration (MBA); global management (MBA); human resources management (MBA, MM); management (MM); marketing (MBA); public administration (MBA, MM). Electronic applications accepted.

UNIVERSITY OF PHOENIX–ONLINE CAMPUS, Phoenix, AZ 85034-7209

General Information Proprietary, coed, comprehensive institution. *Graduate housing:* On-campus housing not available.

GRADUATE UNITS

College of Education *Program availability:* Evening/weekend, online learning. Offers administration and supervision (MAEd, Certificate); adult education and training (MAEd); curriculum and instruction (MAEd); early childhood education (MAEd); educational studies (MAEd); elementary teacher education (MAEd); principal licensure (Certificate); secondary teacher education (MAEd); special education (MAEd, Certificate); teacher education (MAEd); teacher education middle level mathematics (MAEd); teacher education middle level science (MAEd); teacher education secondary mathematics (MAEd); teacher education secondary science (MAEd); teacher leadership (MAEd); teachers of English learners (Certificate); transition to teaching (Certificate). Electronic applications accepted.

College of Health Sciences and Nursing *Program availability:* Evening/weekend, online learning. Offers family nurse practitioner (Certificate); health care (Certificate); health care education (Certificate); health care informatics (Certificate); informatics (MSN); nursing (MSN); nursing and health care education (MSN). Electronic applications accepted.

College of Information Systems and Technology *Program availability:* Evening/weekend, online learning. Offers information systems and technology (MIS). Electronic applications accepted.

College of Justice and Security *Program availability:* Evening/weekend, online learning. Offers administration of justice and security (MS); public administration (MPA). Electronic applications accepted.

College of Social Science *Program availability:* Evening/weekend, online learning. Offers mediation (Certificate); psychology (MS). Electronic applications accepted.

School of Advanced Studies *Program availability:* Evening/weekend, online learning. Offers business administration (DBA); education (Ed S); educational leadership (Ed D); health administration (DHA); higher education administration (PhD); industrial/organizational psychology (PhD); nursing (PhD); organizational leadership (DM). Electronic applications accepted.

School of Business *Program availability:* Evening/weekend, online learning. Offers accountancy (MS); accounting (MBA, Certificate); business administration (MBA); energy management (MBA); global management (MBA); health care management (MBA); human resource management (MBA, Certificate); human resources management (MM); management (MM); marketing (MBA, Certificate); project management (MBA, Certificate); public administration (MBA, MM); technology management (MBA). Electronic applications accepted.

UNIVERSITY OF PHOENIX–PHOENIX CAMPUS, Tempe, AZ 85282-2371

General Information Proprietary, coed, comprehensive institution. CGS member. *Graduate housing:* On-campus housing not available.

GRADUATE UNITS

College of Criminal Justice and Security *Program availability:* Evening/weekend, online learning. Offers administration of justice and security (MS); global and homeland security (MS); law enforcement organizations (MS); public administration (MPA). Electronic applications accepted.

College of Education *Program availability:* Evening/weekend, online learning. Offers administration and supervision (MA Ed); adult education and training (MA Ed); curriculum and instruction reading (MA Ed); early childhood education (MA Ed); education studies (MA Ed); elementary teacher education (MA Ed); secondary teacher education (MA Ed); special education (MA Ed); teacher leadership (MA Ed). Electronic applications accepted.

College of Health Sciences and Nursing *Program availability:* Evening/weekend, online learning. Offers family nurse practitioner (MSN, Certificate); gerontology health care (Certificate); health care education (MSN, Certificate); health care informatics (Certificate); informatics (MSN); nursing (MSN). Electronic applications accepted.

College of Social Sciences *Program availability:* Evening/weekend, online learning. Offers counseling (MS); psychology (MS). Electronic applications accepted.

School of Business *Program availability:* Evening/weekend, online learning. Offers accounting (MBA, MS, Certificate); business administration (MBA); energy management (MBA); global management (MBA); health care management (MBA); human resource management (MBA, Certificate); management (MM); marketing (MBA); project management (MBA); technology management (MBA). Electronic applications accepted.

UNIVERSITY OF PHOENIX–SACRAMENTO VALLEY CAMPUS, Sacramento, CA 95833-4334

General Information Proprietary, coed, comprehensive institution. *Graduate housing:* On-campus housing not available.

GRADUATE UNITS

College of Education *Program availability:* Evening/weekend. Offers adult education (MA Ed); curriculum instruction (MA Ed); elementary teacher education (MA Ed); secondary teacher education (MA Ed); teacher education (Certificate). Electronic applications accepted.

College of Information Systems and Technology *Program availability:* Evening/weekend. Offers management (MIS); technology management (MBA). Electronic applications accepted.

College of Nursing *Program availability:* Evening/weekend. Offers family nurse practitioner (MSN); health administration (MHA); health care education (MSN); nursing (MSN). Electronic applications accepted.

School of Business *Program availability:* Evening/weekend. Offers accounting (MBA); business administration (MBA); global management (MBA); human resources management (MBA, MM); management (MM); marketing (MBA); public administration (MBA, MM). Electronic applications accepted.

UNIVERSITY OF PHOENIX–SAN ANTONIO CAMPUS, San Antonio, TX 78230

General Information Proprietary, coed, comprehensive institution.

GRADUATE UNITS

College of Criminal Justice and Security Offers administration of justice and security (MS).

College of Education Offers curriculum and instruction (MA Ed).

College of Information Systems and Technology Offers information systems (MIS); technology management (MBA).

College of Nursing Offers health administration (MHA).

School of Business Offers accounting (MBA); business administration (MBA); e-business (MBA); global management (MBA); human resources management (MBA, MM); management (MM); marketing (MBA); public administration (MBA, MM).

UNIVERSITY OF PHOENIX–SAN DIEGO CAMPUS, San Diego, CA 92123

General Information Proprietary, coed, comprehensive institution. *Graduate housing:* On-campus housing not available.

GRADUATE UNITS

College of Education *Program availability:* Evening/weekend. Offers curriculum and instruction (MA Ed); elementary teacher education (MA Ed); secondary teacher education (MA Ed). Electronic applications accepted.

College of Information Systems and Technology *Program availability:* Evening/weekend. Offers management (MIS); technology management (MBA). Electronic applications accepted.

College of Nursing *Program availability:* Evening/weekend. Offers health care education (MSN); nursing (MSN). Electronic applications accepted.

School of Business *Program availability:* Evening/weekend. Offers accounting (MBA); business administration (MBA); global management (MBA); human resources management (MBA, MM); management (MM); marketing (MBA). Electronic applications accepted.

UNIVERSITY OF PHOENIX–SOUTHERN ARIZONA CAMPUS, Tucson, AZ 85711

General Information Proprietary, coed, comprehensive institution. *Graduate housing:* On-campus housing not available.

GRADUATE UNITS

College of Education *Program availability:* Evening/weekend. Offers administration and supervision (MA Ed); adult education and training (MA Ed); curriculum instruction (MA Ed); educational counseling (MA Ed); elementary teacher education (MA Ed); school counseling (MSC); secondary teacher education (MA Ed); special education (MA Ed, Certificate). Electronic applications accepted.

College of Information Systems and Technology *Program availability:* Evening/weekend. Offers information systems (MIS); technology management (MBA). Electronic applications accepted.

College of Social Sciences *Program availability:* Evening/weekend. Offers psychology (MS). Electronic applications accepted.

School of Business *Program availability:* Evening/weekend. Offers accountancy (MS); accounting (MBA); business administration (MBA); global management (MBA); human resources management (MBA); management (MM); marketing (MBA). Electronic applications accepted.

UNIVERSITY OF PHOENIX–SOUTHERN CALIFORNIA CAMPUS, Costa Mesa, CA 92626

General Information Proprietary, coed, comprehensive institution. *Graduate housing:* On-campus housing not available.

University of Phoenix–Southern California Campus

GRADUATE UNITS

College of Criminal Justice and Security *Program availability:* Evening/weekend, online learning. Offers administration of justice and security (MS); public administration (MPA). Electronic applications accepted.

College of Education *Program availability:* Evening/weekend, online learning. Offers administration and supervision (MA Ed, Certificate); adult education and training (MA Ed); educational studies (MA Ed); elementary teacher education (MA Ed); secondary teacher education (MA Ed); teacher leadership (MA Ed); teachers of English learners (Certificate). Electronic applications accepted.

College of Health Sciences and Nursing *Program availability:* Evening/weekend, online learning. Offers family nurse practitioner (MSN, Certificate); health care (Certificate); informatics (MSN); nursing (MSN); nursing/health care education (MSN, Certificate). Electronic applications accepted.

College of Social Sciences *Program availability:* Evening/weekend, online learning. Offers counseling (MS); psychology (MS). Electronic applications accepted.

School of Business *Program availability:* Evening/weekend, online learning. Offers accounting (MBA); business administration (MBA); energy management (MBA); global management (MBA); health care management (MBA); human resource management (MBA); management (MM); marketing (MBA); project management (MBA); technology management (MBA). Electronic applications accepted.

UNIVERSITY OF PHOENIX–SOUTH FLORIDA CAMPUS, Miramar, FL 33027-4145

General Information Proprietary, coed, comprehensive institution. *Graduate housing:* On-campus housing not available.

GRADUATE UNITS

College of Education *Program availability:* Evening/weekend. Offers administration and supervision (MA Ed); curriculum and instruction (MA Ed); early childhood education (MA Ed); elementary teacher education (MA Ed); secondary teacher education (MA Ed). Electronic applications accepted.

College of Information Systems and Technology *Program availability:* Evening/weekend. Offers management (MIS); technology management (MBA). Electronic applications accepted.

College of Nursing *Program availability:* Evening/weekend. Offers health administration (MHA); health care education (MSN); nursing (MSN). Electronic applications accepted.

School of Business *Program availability:* Evening/weekend. Offers accounting (MBA); business administration (MBA); global management (MBA); human resource management (MBA); human resources management (MM); management (MM); marketing (MBA); public administration (MBA, MM). Electronic applications accepted.

UNIVERSITY OF PHOENIX–UTAH CAMPUS, Salt Lake City, UT 84123-4642

General Information Proprietary, coed, comprehensive institution. *Graduate housing:* On-campus housing not available.

GRADUATE UNITS

College of Education *Program availability:* Evening/weekend. Offers administration and supervision (MA Ed); curriculum and instruction (MA Ed); elementary teacher education (MA Ed); school counseling (MSC); secondary teacher education (MA Ed); special education (MA Ed). Electronic applications accepted.

College of Information Systems and Technology *Program availability:* Evening/weekend. Offers information systems and technology (MIS). Electronic applications accepted.

College of Nursing *Program availability:* Evening/weekend. Offers health care education (MSN); nursing (MSN). Electronic applications accepted.

School of Business *Program availability:* Evening/weekend. Offers accounting (MBA); business administration (MBA); global management (MBA); human resource management (MBA, MM); management (MM); marketing (MBA); technology management (MBA). Electronic applications accepted.

UNIVERSITY OF PHOENIX–WASHINGTON D.C. CAMPUS, Washington, DC 20001

General Information Proprietary, coed, comprehensive institution.

GRADUATE UNITS

College of Criminal Justice and Security Offers administration of justice and security (MS).

College of Education Offers administration and supervision (MA Ed); adult education and training (MA Ed); computer education (MA Ed); curriculum and instruction (MA Ed, Ed D); early childhood education (MA Ed); education (Ed S); educational leadership (Ed D); educational technology (Ed D); elementary teacher education (MA Ed); English and language arts education (MA Ed); English as a second language (MA Ed); higher education administration (PhD); mathematics education (MA Ed); secondary teacher education (MA Ed); special education (MA Ed); teacher leadership (MA Ed).

College of Information Systems and Technology Offers information systems (MIS); organizational leadership/information systems and technology (DM).

College of Nursing Offers education (MHA); gerontology (MHA); health administration (MHA, DHA); informatics (MHA, MSN); nursing (MSN, PhD); nursing/health care education (MSN).

College of Social Sciences Offers industrial/organizational psychology (PhD); psychology (MS).

School of Business Offers accountancy (MS); business administration (MBA, DBA); human resources management (MM); management (MM); organizational leadership (DM); public administration (MPA).

UNIVERSITY OF PHOENIX–WESTERN WASHINGTON CAMPUS, Tukwila, WA 98188

General Information Proprietary, coed, comprehensive institution. *Graduate housing:* On-campus housing not available.

GRADUATE UNITS

College of Criminal Justice and Security *Program availability:* Evening/weekend. Offers administration of justice and security (MS). Electronic applications accepted.

School of Business *Program availability:* Evening/weekend. Offers business (MBA). Electronic applications accepted.

UNIVERSITY OF PIKEVILLE, Pikeville, KY 41501

General Information Independent-religious, coed, comprehensive institution. *Enrollment:* 2,366 graduate, professional, and undergraduate students; 707 full-time matriculated graduate/professional students (343 women), 1 part-time matriculated graduate/professional student. *Enrollment by degree level:* 116 master's, 591 doctoral. *Graduate faculty:* 45 full-time (16 women), 16 part-time/adjunct (9 women). *Graduate housing:* Room and/or apartments available on a first-come, first-served basis to single students; on-campus housing not available to married students. Housing application deadline: 5/1. *Student services:* Campus employment opportunities, campus safety program, career counseling, exercise/wellness program, free psychological counseling, international student services, low-cost health insurance, services for students with disabilities. *Library facilities:* Allara Library plus 2 others. *Collection:* Books: 73,924 (physical), 214,499 (digital/electronic); Serial titles: 1,437 (physical), 88,386 (digital/electronic); Databases: 73. Weekly public service hours: 105; students can reserve study rooms.

Computer facilities: 308 computers available on campus for general student use. A campuswide network can be accessed from student residence rooms and from off campus.
Website: http://www.upike.edu/

General Application Contact: John Yancey, Director of Admissions, 606-218-5251, Fax: 606-218-5255, E-mail: johnyancey@upike.edu.

GRADUATE UNITS

Coleman College of Business Students: 44 full-time (23 women), 1 part-time (0 women); includes 4 minority (all Black or African American, non-Hispanic/Latino), 6 international. Average age 28. *Faculty:* 4 part-time/adjunct (0 women). Expenses: Contact institution. *Financial support:* Tuition waivers (full) and university employee grants available. Financial award application deadline: 2/15; financial award applicants required to submit FAFSA. In 2016, 17 master's awarded. *Program availability:* Part-time, evening/weekend. Offers business (MBA). *Application deadline:* For fall admission, 8/15 for domestic students, 7/1 for international students. Applications are processed on a rolling basis. *Application fee:* $50. *Application Contact:* Cathy Maynard, Secretary, Business and Economics, 606-218-5040, Fax: 606-218-5031, E-mail: cathymaynard@upike.edu. *Dean,* Dr. Howard V. Roberts, 606-218-5019, Fax: 606-218-5031, E-mail: howardroberts@upike.edu.

Kentucky College of Optometry Students: 65 full-time (38 women); includes 8 minority (2 Black or African American, non-Hispanic/Latino; 1 American Indian or Alaska Native, non-Hispanic/Latino; 1 Asian, non-Hispanic/Latino; 4 Hispanic/Latino). Average age 24. 412 applicants, 27% accepted, 65 enrolled. *Faculty:* 25 full-time (9 women). Expenses: Contact institution. *Financial support:* Fellowships available. Financial award application deadline: 7/1; financial award applicants required to submit FAFSA. Offers optometry (OD). *Application deadline:* For fall admission, 4/15 for domestic students. *Application Contact:* Casey Price, Coordinator of Admissions, 606-218-5517, E-mail: caseyprice@upike.edu. *Dean,* Dr. Andrew Buzzelli, 606-218-5510, E-mail: andrewbuzzelli@upike.edu.

Kentucky College of Osteopathic Medicine Students: 526 full-time (221 women); includes 54 minority (7 Black or African American, non-Hispanic/Latino; 2 American Indian or Alaska Native, non-Hispanic/Latino; 20 Asian, non-Hispanic/Latino; 24 Hispanic/Latino; 1 Native Hawaiian or other Pacific Islander, non-Hispanic/Latino), 1 international. Average age 26. 3,710 applicants, 10% accepted, 135 enrolled. *Faculty:* 25 full-time (9 women), 37 part-time/adjunct (14 women). Expenses: Contact institution. *Financial support:* In 2016–17, 4 students received support, including 4 fellowships with full tuition reimbursements available (averaging $42,975 per year); scholarships/grants also available. Financial award application deadline: 8/1; financial award applicants required to submit FAFSA. In 2016, 116 doctorates awarded. Offers osteopathic medicine (DO). *Application deadline:* For fall admission, 5/1 for domestic students. Applications are processed on a rolling basis. *Application fee:* $75. *Application Contact:* Dr. Linda Dunatov, Associate Dean for Student Affairs, 606-218-5408, Fax: 606-218-5442, E-mail: lindadunatov@upike.edu. *Dean,* Dr. Boyd Buser, 606-218-5410, Fax: 606-218-8442, E-mail: boydbuser@upike.edu.

Patton College of Education Students: 71 full-time (61 women); includes 1 minority (Black or African American, non-Hispanic/Latino). Average age 35. *Faculty:* 12 part-time/adjunct (9 women). Expenses: Contact institution. *Financial support:* Application deadline: 2/1; applicants required to submit FAFSA. *Program availability:* Part-time, evening/weekend. Offers teacher leader (MA). *Application deadline:* For fall admission, 8/15 for domestic students. Applications are processed on a rolling basis. *Application fee:* $50. *Application Contact:* Fairy Coleman, Administrative Assistant, 606-218-5314, E-mail: fairycoleman@upike.edu. *Interim Dean,* Coletta Parsley, 606-218-5318, E-mail: colettaparsley@upike.edu.

UNIVERSITY OF PITTSBURGH, Pittsburgh, PA 15260

General Information State-related, coed, university. CGS member. *Enrollment:* 28,664 graduate, professional, and undergraduate students; 7,418 full-time matriculated graduate, professional, and undergraduate students; 7,418 full-time matriculated graduate/professional students (4,066 women), 1,950 part-time matriculated graduate/professional students (1,117 women). *Enrollment by degree level:* 4,343 master's, 4,846 doctoral, 179 other advanced degrees. *Graduate faculty:* 4,207 full-time (1,730 women), 770 part-time/adjunct (365 women). Tuition and fees vary according to program. *Student services:* Campus employment opportunities, campus safety program, career counseling, exercise/wellness program, free psychological counseling, international student services, low-cost health insurance, services for students with disabilities, writing training. *Library facilities:* Hillman Library plus 16 others. *Collection:* Books: 5.9 million (physical), 1.5 million (digital/electronic); Serial titles: 110,789 (physical), 223,301 (digital/electronic); Databases: 570. Weekly public service hours: 145; study areas open 24 hours, 5–7 days a week; students can reserve study rooms. *Research affiliation:* National Institutes of Health, National Science Foundation, General Electric Company (GE), Shire, Phillips.

Computer facilities: Computer purchase and lease plans are available. 1,200 computers available on campus for general student use. A campuswide network can be accessed from student residence rooms and from off campus. Online class registration, online class listings, online tuition payment are available.
Website: http://www.pitt.edu/

General Application Contact: Information Contact, 412-624-4141, E-mail: graduate@pitt.edu.

GRADUATE UNITS

Dietrich School of Arts and Sciences Expenses: Contact institution. *Financial support:* Fellowships with full tuition reimbursements, research assistantships with full tuition reimbursements, teaching assistantships with full tuition reimbursements, career-related internships or fieldwork, Federal Work-Study, institutionally sponsored loans, scholarships/grants, traineeships, health care benefits, tuition waivers (full and partial), and unspecified assistantships available. Support available to part-time students. Financial award applicants required to submit FAFSA. *Program availability:* Part-time. Offers anthropology (MA, PhD); applied mathematics (MA, MS); applied statistics (MA, MS); arts and sciences (MA, MFA, MS, Pro-MS, PhD, Certificate, Doctoral Certificate, Master's Certificate); biological science (PhD); chemistry (MS, PhD); Chinese (MA);

clinical psychology (PhD); communication (MA, PhD); composition and theory (PhD); computer science (PhD); cultural studies (Certificate); ecology and evolution (PhD); economics (PhD); English (MA, PhD); ethnomusicology (PhD); film studies (MA, PhD, Certificate); French (MA, PhD); gender, sexuality, and women's studies (Doctoral Certificate, Master's Certificate); geographical information systems and remote sensing (Pro-MS); geology and environmental science (MS, PhD); geology and environmental sciences (PhD); Hispanic languages and literatures (MA, PhD); Hispanic linguistics (MA); history (MA, PhD); history and philosophy of science (PhD); history of art and architecture (MA, PhD); intelligent systems (MS); Italian (MA); Japanese (MA); jazz studies (PhD); mathematics (MA, MS, PhD); medieval and Renaissance studies (Certificate); molecular, cellular, and developmental biology (PhD); music (MA); musicology (PhD); philosophy (PhD); physics and astronomy (PhD); political science (MA, PhD); psychology (PhD); Russian literature and culture (MA, PhD); sociology (MA, PhD); statistics (MA, MS, PhD); teaching English to speakers of other languages (Certificate); TESOL (PhD); theatre arts (MA, MFA, PhD); writing (MFA). *Application deadline:* Applications are processed on a rolling basis. *Application fee:* $50. Electronic applications accepted. *Application Contact:* Katelyn White, Student Services Assistant, 412-624-6094, Fax: 412-624-6855, E-mail: kmw127@pitt.edu. *Associate Dean, Graduate Studies and Research,* Dr. Holger Hoock, 412-624-6094, Fax: 412-624-6855.

Center for Bioethics and Health Law Students: 4 part-time (all women). Average age 29. 7 applicants, 57% accepted, 3 enrolled. *Faculty:* 10 full-time (3 women), 1 part-time/adjunct (0 women). Expenses: Contact institution. *Financial support:* Scholarships/grants and tuition waivers (partial) available. Financial award application deadline: 3/1. In 2016, 4 master's awarded. *Program availability:* Part-time. Offers bioethics (MA). *Application deadline:* For fall admission, 3/1 priority date for domestic and international students. Applications are processed on a rolling basis. *Application fee:* $50. Electronic applications accepted. *Application Contact:* Beth Ann Pischke, Administrator, 412-648-7007, Fax: 412-648-2649, E-mail: pischke@pitt.edu. *Director,* Lisa S. Parker, 412-648-7007, Fax: 412-648-2649, E-mail: lisap@pitt.edu.

Center for Neuroscience Students: 70 full-time (39 women); includes 13 minority (1 American Indian or Alaska Native, non-Hispanic/Latino; 8 Asian, non-Hispanic/Latino; 3 Hispanic/Latino; 1 Two or more races, non-Hispanic/Latino), 5 international. Average age 25. 183 applicants, 22% accepted, 15 enrolled. *Faculty:* 110 full-time (34 women). Expenses: Contact institution. *Financial support:* In 2016–17, 62 students received support, including 38 fellowships with full tuition reimbursements available (averaging $28,500 per year), 21 research assistantships with full tuition reimbursements available (averaging $28,500 per year), 3 teaching assistantships with full tuition reimbursements available (averaging $28,500 per year); traineeships, health care benefits, tuition waivers (full), and one-time educational enrichment ($2,000) also available. Financial award application deadline: 12/1. In 2016, 14 degrees awarded. Offers neurobiology (PhD); neuroscience (PhD). Program held jointly with School of Medicine. *Application deadline:* For fall admission, 12/1 for domestic and international students. *Application fee:* $50. Electronic applications accepted. *Application Contact:* Lisa M. Summe, Graduate Program Administrator, 412-383-7582, Fax: 412-624-9198, E-mail: lms232@pitt.edu. *Co-Director,* Dr. Alan F. Sved, 412-624-6996, Fax: 412-624-9198, E-mail: sved@pitt.edu.

Graduate School of Public and International Affairs Students: 284 full-time (156 women), 147 part-time (95 women); includes 59 minority (25 Black or African American, non-Hispanic/Latino; 10 Asian, non-Hispanic/Latino; 15 Hispanic/Latino; 9 Two or more races, non-Hispanic/Latino), 118 international. Average age 32. 626 applicants, 78% accepted, 178 enrolled. *Faculty:* 34 full-time (12 women), 17 part-time/adjunct (5 women). Expenses: Contact institution. *Financial support:* Fellowships, research assistantships, scholarships/grants, unspecified assistantships, and student employment available. Support available to part-time students. Financial award application deadline: 2/1. *Program availability:* Part-time, evening/weekend. Offers energy and environment (MID, MPA); governance and international public management (MID, MPA); human security (MID, MPIA); international affairs (PhD); international development (PhD); international political economy (MPIA); nongovernmental organizations and civil society (MID); policy research and analysis (MPA); public administration (PhD); public and international affairs (MID, MPA, MPIA, MPPM, PhD); public and nonprofit management (MPA); public policy (PhD); public policy and management (MPPM); security and intelligence studies (MPIA); urban affairs and planning (MID, MPA). *Application deadline:* For fall admission, 2/1 for domestic students, 1/15 for international students; for spring admission, 11/1 for domestic students, 8/1 for international students. *Application fee:* $50. Electronic applications accepted. *Application Contact:* Dr. Michael T. Rizzi, Director of Student Services, 412-648-7643, Fax: 412-648-7641, E-mail: rizzim@pitt.edu. *Dean and Professor,* Dr. John T.S. Keeler, 412-648-7600, Fax: 412-648-2605, E-mail: keeler@pitt.edu.

Graduate School of Public Health Students: 426 full-time (289 women), 195 part-time (144 women); includes 108 minority (28 Black or African American, non-Hispanic/Latino; 52 Asian, non-Hispanic/Latino; 28 Hispanic/Latino), 130 international. Average age 28. 1,715 applicants, 48% accepted, 215 enrolled. *Faculty:* 158 full-time (74 women), 254 part-time/adjunct (112 women). Expenses: Contact institution. *Financial support:* In 2016–17, 131 students received support, including 8 fellowships (averaging $9,838 per year), 118 research assistantships (averaging $20,360 per year), 5 teaching assistantships (averaging $16,339 per year); career-related internships or fieldwork, scholarships/grants, traineeships, health care benefits, and unspecified assistantships also available. Financial award applicants required to submit FAFSA. In 2016, 169 master's, 34 doctorates awarded. *Program availability:* Part-time. Offers applied research and leadership in behavioral and community health sciences (Dr PH); applied social and behavioral concepts in public health (MPH); biostatistics (MPH, MS, PhD); community-based participatory research and practice (Certificate); decision sciences (MS); environmental and occupational health (MPH, MS, Dr PH, PhD); epidemiology (MPH, MS, PhD); evaluation of public health promotion and health education programs (Certificate); genetic counseling (MS); health equity (Certificate); health policy and economics (MS); health policy and management (MHA, MPH, PhD); human genetics (MS, PhD); infectious disease management, intervention, and community practice (MPH); infectious disease pathogenesis, eradication, and laboratory practice (MPH); infectious diseases and microbiology (MS, PhD); LGBT health and wellness (Certificate); maternal and child health (MPH); public health (MHA, MPH, MS, Dr PH, PhD, Certificate); public health genetics (MS); theory and research methods (Dr PH). *Application deadline:* For fall admission, 1/15 for domestic and international students; for spring admission, 10/15 for domestic students, 8/1 for international students; for summer admission, 3/15 for domestic students, 12/1 for international students. Applications are processed on a rolling basis. *Application fee:* $120. Electronic applications accepted. *Application Contact:* Karrie A. Lukin, Admissions Manager, 412-624-3003, Fax: 412-624-3755, E-mail: presutti@pitt.edu. *Dean,* Dr. Donald S. Burke, 412-624-3001, Fax: 412-624-3013, E-mail: bradym1@pitt.edu.

Katz Graduate School of Business Students: 423 full-time (201 women), 414 part-time (131 women); includes 94 minority (32 Black or African American, non-Hispanic/Latino;

36 Asian, non-Hispanic/Latino; 15 Hispanic/Latino; 11 Two or more races, non-Hispanic/Latino), 292 international. Average age 30. 2,038 applicants, 37% accepted, 342 enrolled. *Faculty:* 88 full-time (27 women), 42 part-time/adjunct (15 women). Expenses: Contact institution. *Financial support:* Research assistantships with full tuition reimbursements, teaching assistantships with full tuition reimbursements, Federal Work-Study, scholarships/grants, health care benefits, and unspecified assistantships available. Financial award application deadline: 6/1; financial award applicants required to submit FAFSA. In 2016, 571 master's, 5 doctorates awarded. *Program availability:* Part-time, evening/weekend, blended/hybrid learning. Offers accounting (MS); business (EMBA, MBA, MS, PhD, Certificate); business administration (EMBA, MBA, PhD); business analytics and operations (PhD); customer insights (MS); finance (MS); information systems (MBA); information systems and technology management (PhD); international business administration (Certificate); management information systems (MS); marketing (MBA, PhD); operations (MBA); organizational behavior and human resources (MBA, PhD); public and international affairs-strategic management (PhD); strategy, environment and organizations (MBA); supply chain management (MS). *Application deadline:* For fall admission, 4/1 priority date for domestic students, 2/1 priority date for international students. *Application fee:* $50. Electronic applications accepted. *Application Contact:* Thomas Keller, Director of MBA Admissions, 412-648-1700, Fax: 412-648-1659, E-mail: mba@katz.pitt.edu. *Dean,* Dr. Arjang A. Assad, 412-648-1556, Fax: 412-648-1552, E-mail: aassad@katz.pitt.edu.

School of Dental Medicine Expenses: Contact institution. *Financial support:* Scholarships/grants and stipends available. Financial award application deadline: 4/30; financial award applicants required to submit FAFSA. Offers craniofacial tissue regeneration (PhD); dental anesthesia (Certificate); dental medicine (MDS, MS, DMD, PhD, Advanced Certificate, Certificate); endodontics (Certificate); general dentistry (Certificate); general practice residency (Certificate); oral and maxillofacial pathology (Advanced Certificate, Certificate); oral and maxillofacial surgery (Certificate); oral biology (MS, PhD); orthodontics (MDS, Certificate); orthodontics and dentofacial orthopedics (MDS, Certificate); pediatric craniofacial maxillofacial surgery (Certificate); pediatric dentistry (Certificate); periodontics (MDS, Certificate); periodontics and preventive dentistry (MDS, Certificate); prosthodontics (MDS, Certificate). *Application deadline:* For fall admission, 11/1 for domestic and international students. Applications are processed on a rolling basis. *Application fee:* $50 ($75 for international students). Electronic applications accepted. *Application Contact:* Katherine Adomitis, Student Services and Admissions Assistant, 412-648-8422, Fax: 412-648-9571, E-mail: kaa77@pitt.edu. *Dean,* Dr. Thomas W. Braun, 412-648-1938, Fax: 412-648-8219, E-mail: twb3@pitt.edu.

School of Education *Program availability:* Part-time, evening/weekend, online learning. Offers applied behavior analysis (M Ed); applied developmental psychology (M Ed, MS, PhD); developmental movement (MS); early childhood education (M Ed); early intervention (M Ed, PhD); education (M Ed, MA, MAT, MS, Ed D, PhD); elementary education (M Ed, MAT); elementary education (MAT); English and communications education (M Ed, MAT); exercise physiology (MS, PhD); foreign language education (M Ed, MAT); general special education (M Ed, Ed D); higher education management (M Ed, Ed D, PhD); language, literacy and culture education (Ed D, PhD); learning sciences and policy (PhD); mathematics education (M Ed, MAT, Ed D, PhD); reading education (PhD); research methodology (M Ed, MA, PhD); school leadership (M Ed, Ed D, PhD); science education (M Ed, MAT, Ed D, PhD); secondary education (M Ed, MAT, Ed D, PhD); social and comparative analysis in education (M Ed, MA, Ed D, PhD); social studies education (M Ed, MAT); special education (M Ed, PhD); special education (Ed D); special education teacher preparation (M Ed); STEM education (Ed D); vision studies (M Ed, PhD). Electronic applications accepted.

School of Health and Rehabilitation Sciences Students: 711 full-time (518 women), 52 part-time (41 women); includes 50 minority (11 Black or African American, non-Hispanic/Latino; 1 American Indian or Alaska Native, non-Hispanic/Latino; 18 Asian, non-Hispanic/Latino; 6 Two or more races, non-Hispanic/Latino), 92 international. Average age 27. 3,032 applicants, 25% accepted, 325 enrolled. *Faculty:* 131 full-time (81 women), 25 part-time/adjunct (14 women). Expenses: Contact institution. *Financial support:* Fellowships with full tuition reimbursements, research assistantships with tuition reimbursements, teaching assistantships with full tuition reimbursements, career-related internships or fieldwork, Federal Work-Study, scholarships/grants, traineeships, and unspecified assistantships available. Financial award applicants required to submit FAFSA. *Program availability:* Part-time, evening/weekend. Offers communication science and disorders (MA, MS, Au D, CScD, PhD); health and rehabilitation sciences (MS); nutrition and dietetics (MS); occupational therapy (MOT, OTD); physical therapy (DPT); physician assistant studies (MS); prosthetics and orthotics (MS); rehabilitation science (PhD). *Application deadline:* For fall admission, 3/1 for international students; for spring admission, 9/1 for international students; for summer admission, 2/1 for international students. Applications are processed on a rolling basis. *Application fee:* $0. Electronic applications accepted. *Application Contact:* Jessica Maguire, Director of Admissions, 412-383-6557, Fax: 412-383-6535, E-mail: maguire@pitt.edu. *Dean,* Dr. Anthony Delitto, 412-383-6560, Fax: 412-383-6535, E-mail: delitto@pitt.edu.

School of Information Sciences Students: 343 full-time (152 women), 118 part-time (69 women); includes 20 minority (4 Black or African American, non-Hispanic/Latino; 6 Asian, non-Hispanic/Latino; 7 Hispanic/Latino; 3 Two or more races, non-Hispanic/Latino), 302 international. Average age 29. 956 applicants, 73% accepted, 197 enrolled. *Faculty:* 29 full-time (8 women), 20 part-time/adjunct (7 women). Expenses: Contact institution. *Financial support:* Fellowships with full and partial tuition reimbursements, research assistantships with full and partial tuition reimbursements, teaching assistantships with full and partial tuition reimbursements, career-related internships or fieldwork, scholarships/grants, traineeships, health care benefits, and unspecified assistantships available. Support available to part-time students. Financial award application deadline: 1/15; financial award applicants required to submit FAFSA. In 2016, 220 master's, 10 doctorates awarded. *Program availability:* Part-time, evening/weekend, 100% online. Offers big data (Post-Master's Certificate, Postbaccalaureate Certificate); information science (MSIS, PhD); information science and technology (Certificate); information sciences (MLIS, MSIS, MST, PhD, Certificate, Post-Master's Certificate, Postbaccalaureate Certificate); library and information science (MLIS, PhD); security assured information systems (Post-Master's Certificate, Postbaccalaureate Certificate); telecommunications and networking (MST, Certificate). *Application deadline:* For fall admission, 1/15 priority date for domestic and international students; for winter admission, 9/15 priority date for domestic students, 6/15 priority date for international students; for spring admission, 9/15 priority date for domestic students, 6/15 priority date for international students; for summer admission, 1/15 priority date for domestic students, 12/15 priority date for international students. Applications are processed on a rolling basis. *Application fee:* $50. Electronic applications accepted. *Application Contact:* Shabana Reza, Enrollment Manager, 412-624-3988, Fax: 412-624-

5231, E-mail: sreza@sis.pitt.edu. *Dean and Professor*, Dr. Ronald L. Larsen, 412-624-5139, Fax: 412-624-5231, E-mail: rlarsen@sis.pitt.edu.

School of Law Students: 450 full-time (215 women), 1 part-time (0 women); includes 77 minority (30 Black or African American, non-Hispanic/Latino; 1 American Indian or Alaska Native, non-Hispanic/Latino; 17 Asian, non-Hispanic/Latino; 21 Hispanic/Latino; 8 Two or more races, non-Hispanic/Latino), 12 international. Average age 24. 1,341 applicants, 36% accepted, 140 enrolled. *Faculty:* 48 full-time (21 women), 104 part-time/adjunct (34 women). Expenses: Contact institution. *Financial support:* In 2016–17, 297 students received support. Scholarships/grants available. Financial award application deadline: 3/1; financial award applicants required to submit FAFSA. *Program availability:* Part-time, online learning. Offers American law (LL M); business law (MSL); Constitutional law (MSL); criminal law and justice (MSL); disability law (MSL); disability legal studies (Certificate); education law (MSL); elder and estate planning law (MSL); employment and labor law (MSL); energy law (MSL); environmental and real estate law (MSL); family law (MSL); health law (MSL); intellectual property and technology law (MSL); international and human rights law (MSL); jurisprudence (MSL); law (LL M, MSL, JD, SJD, Certificate); personal injury and civil litigation (MSL); regulatory law (MSL); self-designed (MSL); sports and entertainment law (MSL). *Application deadline:* For fall admission, 4/1 for domestic and international students. Applications are processed on a rolling basis. *Application fee:* $65. Electronic applications accepted. *Application Contact:* Charmaine McCall, Assistant Dean for Admissions and Financial Aid, 412-648-1414, Fax: 412-648-1318, E-mail: admitlaw@pitt.edu. *Dean*, William M. Carter, Jr., 412-648-1401, Fax: 412-648-2647, E-mail: william.carter@law.pitt.edu.

School of Medicine Students: 861 full-time (411 women), 81 part-time (55 women); includes 325 minority (58 Black or African American, non-Hispanic/Latino; 2 American Indian or Alaska Native, non-Hispanic/Latino; 185 Asian, non-Hispanic/Latino; 52 Hispanic/Latino; 28 Two or more races, non-Hispanic/Latino), 80 international. Average age 28. 6,794 applicants, 9% accepted, 258 enrolled. *Faculty:* 3,230 full-time (1,118 women), 94 part-time/adjunct (54 women). Expenses: Contact institution. *Financial support:* In 2016–17, 601 students received support. Fellowships with full tuition reimbursements available, research assistantships with full tuition reimbursements available, teaching assistantships with full tuition reimbursements available, institutionally sponsored loans, scholarships/grants, traineeships, and employee benefits available. Financial award application deadline: 4/15; financial award applicants required to submit FAFSA. In 2016, 32 master's, 189 doctorates, 5 other advanced degrees awarded. *Program availability:* Part-time, evening/weekend, blended/hybrid learning. Offers biomedical informatics (MS, PhD, Certificate); cell biology and molecular physiology (PhD); cellular and molecular pathology (PhD); clinical and translational science (PhD); clinical research (MS, Certificate); computational biology (PhD); immunology (PhD); integrative systems biology (PhD); interdisciplinary biomedical sciences (PhD); medical education (MS, Certificate); medicine (MS, MD, PhD, Certificate); molecular biophysics and structural biology (PhD); molecular genetics and developmental biology (PhD); molecular pharmacology (PhD); molecular virology and microbiology (PhD). *Application deadline:* For fall admission, 10/15 for domestic and international students. *Application fee:* $85. Electronic applications accepted. *Vice Dean*, Dr. Ann Thompson, 412-648-9000, E-mail: upsom@medschool.pitt.edu.

School of Nursing Students: 208 full-time (165 women), 179 part-time (147 women); includes 32 minority (12 Black or African American, non-Hispanic/Latino; 1 American Indian or Alaska Native, non-Hispanic/Latino; 17 Asian, non-Hispanic/Latino; 2 Hispanic/Latino), 15 international. Average age 31. 328 applicants, 37% accepted, 101 enrolled. *Faculty:* 57 full-time (48 women), 8 part-time/adjunct (7 women). Expenses: Contact institution. *Financial support:* In 2016–17, 31 students received support, including 13 fellowships with tuition reimbursements available (averaging $14,592 per year), 8 research assistantships with tuition reimbursements available (averaging $10,369 per year), 10 teaching assistantships with tuition reimbursements available (averaging $9,851 per year); scholarships/grants, traineeships, health care benefits, and unspecified assistantships also available. Support available to part-time students. Financial award applicants required to submit FAFSA. In 2016, 61 master's, 58 doctorates awarded. *Program availability:* Part-time. Offers adult-gerontology (DNP); adult-gerontology acute care (DNP); adult-gerontology primary care (DNP); clinical nurse leader (MSN); family (individual across the lifespan) (DNP); health systems executive leadership (DNP); neonatal (MSN, DNP); nurse anesthesia (DNP); nurse-midwife (DNP); nursing (MSN, DNP, PhD); nursing informatics (MSN); pediatric primary care (DNP); psychiatric mental health (DNP). *Application deadline:* For fall admission, 5/1 priority date for domestic students, 2/15 priority date for international students. *Application fee:* $50. Electronic applications accepted. *Application Contact:* Laurie Lapsley, Graduate Administrator, 412-624-9670, Fax: 412-624-2409, E-mail: lapsleyl@pitt.edu. *Dean*, Dr. Jacqueline Dunbar-Jacob, 412-624-7838, Fax: 412-624-2401, E-mail: dunbar@pitt.edu.

School of Pharmacy Students: 520 full-time (343 women), 3 part-time (1 woman); includes 117 minority (14 Black or African American, non-Hispanic/Latino; 1 American Indian or Alaska Native, non-Hispanic/Latino; 88 Asian, non-Hispanic/Latino; 5 Hispanic/Latino; 9 Two or more races, non-Hispanic/Latino), 55 international. Average age 27. *Faculty:* 129 full-time (56 women), 9 part-time/adjunct (2 women). Expenses: Contact institution. *Financial support:* Fellowships with full tuition reimbursements, research assistantships with full tuition reimbursements, teaching assistantships with full tuition reimbursements, Federal Work-Study, institutionally sponsored loans, scholarships/grants, health care benefits, tuition waivers (full), and unspecified assistantships available. Financial award application deadline: 10/1. *Program availability:* Part-time. Offers pharmaceutical sciences (MS, PhD); pharmacy (MS, PhD, Pharm D); pharmacy business administration (MS). *Application deadline:* For fall admission, 12/1 for domestic students; for winter admission, 1/5 for domestic students. Applications are processed on a rolling basis. Electronic applications accepted. *Application Contact:* Marcia L. Borrelli, Director of Student Services, 412-383-9000, Fax: 412-383-9996, E-mail: borrelli@pitt.edu. *Dean*, Dr. Patricia D. Kroboth, 412-624-2400, Fax: 412-648-1086, E-mail: pkroboth@pitt.edu.

School of Social Work Students: 431 full-time (367 women), 57 part-time (48 women); includes 120 minority (61 Black or African American, non-Hispanic/Latino; 1 American Indian or Alaska Native, non-Hispanic/Latino; 21 Asian, non-Hispanic/Latino; 24 Hispanic/Latino; 13 Two or more races, non-Hispanic/Latino). Average age 28. 597 applicants, 79% accepted, 202 enrolled. *Faculty:* 24 full-time (14 women), 40 part-time/adjunct (26 women). Expenses: Contact institution. *Financial support:* In 2016–17, 40 fellowships (averaging $10,000 per year), 11 teaching assistantships with full tuition reimbursements (averaging $17,910 per year) were awarded; research assistantships with full tuition reimbursements, career-related internships or fieldwork, institutionally sponsored loans, scholarships/grants, traineeships, tuition waivers (full), and unspecified assistantships also available. Financial award application deadline: 3/31; financial award applicants required to submit FAFSA. In 2016, 261 master's, 6 doctorates awarded. *Program availability:* Part-time. Offers social work (MSW, PhD, Certificate). *Application deadline:* For fall admission, 12/31 priority date for domestic and international students.

Applications are processed on a rolling basis. *Application fee:* $40 ($50 for international students). Electronic applications accepted. *Application Contact:* Philip Mack, Director of Admissions, 412-624-6346, Fax: 412-624-6323, E-mail: psm8@pitt.edu. *Dean*, Dr. Larry E. Davis, 412-624-6304, Fax: 412-624-6323, E-mail: ledavis@pitt.edu.

Swanson School of Engineering Students: 722 full-time (200 women), 223 part-time (51 women); includes 106 minority (26 Black or African American, non-Hispanic/Latino; 1 American Indian or Alaska Native, non-Hispanic/Latino; 39 Asian, non-Hispanic/Latino; 23 Hispanic/Latino; 1 Native Hawaiian or other Pacific Islander, non-Hispanic/Latino; 16 Two or more races, non-Hispanic/Latino), 490 international. 2,867 applicants, 37% accepted, 287 enrolled. *Faculty:* 132 full-time (19 women), 102 part-time/adjunct (12 women). Expenses: Contact institution. *Financial support:* In 2016–17, 82 fellowships with full tuition reimbursements (averaging $30,720 per year), 229 research assistantships with full tuition reimbursements (averaging $27,396 per year), 137 teaching assistantships with full tuition reimbursements (averaging $26,328 per year) were awarded; scholarships/grants, traineeships, and tuition waivers (full) also available. Financial award application deadline: 3/1. In 2016, 244 master's, 78 doctorates awarded. *Program availability:* Part-time, 100% online. Offers bioengineering (MSBENG, PhD); chemical engineering (MS Ch E, PhD); civil and environmental engineering (MSCEE, PhD); computer engineering (MS, PhD); electrical and computer engineering (MS, PhD); engineering (MS, MS Ch E, MSBENG, MSCEE, MSIE, MSME, MSNE, MSPE, PhD); industrial engineering (MSIE, PhD); mechanical engineering and materials science (MSME, MSNE, PhD); petroleum engineering (MSPE). *Application deadline:* For fall admission, 3/1 priority date for domestic and international students; for spring admission, 7/1 priority date for domestic and international students. Applications are processed on a rolling basis. *Application fee:* $50. Electronic applications accepted. *Application Contact:* Rama Bazaz, Director, 412-624-9800, Fax: 412-624-9808, E-mail: ssoeadm@pitt.edu. *Dean*, Dr. Gerald D. Holder, 412-624-9809, Fax: 412-624-0412, E-mail: holder@engr.pitt.edu.

University Center for International Studies Students: 175 full-time (105 women), 14 part-time (10 women); includes 78 minority (5 Black or African American, non-Hispanic/Latino; 30 Asian, non-Hispanic/Latino; 42 Hispanic/Latino; 1 Two or more races, non-Hispanic/Latino). Average age 29. Expenses: Contact institution. *Financial support:* In 2016–17, 22 fellowships with full tuition reimbursements (averaging $17,878 per year) were awarded; scholarships/grants, traineeships, health care benefits, tuition waivers, and unspecified assistantships also available. *Program availability:* Part-time, evening/weekend, online learning. Offers African studies (Certificate); Asian studies (Certificate); European Union studies (Certificate); global studies (Certificate); Latin American studies (Certificate); Russian and East European studies (Certificate); West European studies (Certificate). *Director*, Dr. Ariel Armony, 412-648-7374, Fax: 412-624-4672, E-mail: armony@pitt.edu.

UNIVERSITY OF PORTLAND, Portland, OR 97203-5798

General Information Independent-religious, coed, comprehensive institution. *Graduate housing:* On-campus housing not available. *Research affiliation:* Portland Area Nursing Consortium, Kaiser Center Health Resources.

GRADUATE UNITS

Department of Communication Studies *Program availability:* Part-time, evening/weekend. Offers communication (MA); management communication (MS).

Department of Performing and Fine Arts *Program availability:* Part-time, evening/weekend. Offers directing (MFA).

Department of Theology *Program availability:* Part-time. Offers pastoral ministry (MA).

Dr. Robert B. Pamplin, Jr. School of Business *Program availability:* Part-time, evening/weekend. Offers entrepreneurship (MBA); finance (MBA, MS); health care management (MBA); marketing (MBA); nonprofit management (EMBA); operations and technology management (MBA, MS); sustainability (MBA).

School of Education *Program availability:* Part-time, evening/weekend. Offers education (MA, MAT); educational leadership (M Ed); English for speakers of other languages (M Ed); initial administrator licensure (M Ed); neuroeducation (M Ed, Ed D); organizational leadership and development (Ed D); reading (M Ed); school leadership and development (Ed D); special education (M Ed). M Ed also available through the Graduate Outreach Program for teachers residing in the Oregon and Washington state areas.

School of Engineering *Program availability:* Part-time, evening/weekend. Offers biomedical engineering (MBME); civil engineering (ME); computer science (ME); electrical engineering (ME); mechanical engineering (ME).

School of Nursing *Program availability:* Part-time, evening/weekend, online learning. Offers clinical nurse leader (MS); family nurse practitioner (DNP); nurse educator (MS).

UNIVERSITY OF PRINCE EDWARD ISLAND, Charlottetown, PE C1A 4P3, Canada

General Information Province-supported, coed, comprehensive institution. *Graduate housing:* Room and/or apartments available on a first-come, first-served basis to single students; on-campus housing not available to married students. *Student services:* Campus employment opportunities, campus safety program, career counseling, child daycare facilities, exercise/wellness program, free psychological counseling, grant writing training, international student services, low-cost health insurance, multicultural affairs office, services for students with disabilities, teacher training, writing training. *Library facilities:* Robertson Library. *Research affiliation:* National Research Council of Canada Institute for Nutrisciences and Health, PEI Food Technology Centre, Agriculture Canada Research Station, Diagnostic Chemicals, Ltd., Canadian Food Inspection Agency, AquaHealth.

Computer facilities: 240 computers available on campus for general student use. A campuswide network can be accessed from student residence rooms and from off campus. Online class registration, email forwarding, course management system presence for each course registered are available.
Website: http://home.upei.ca/

General Application Contact: Registrar's Office, 902-566-0439, Fax: 902-566-0795, E-mail: registrar@upei.ca.

GRADUATE UNITS

Atlantic Veterinary College Expenses: Contact institution. *Financial support:* Fellowships, research assistantships, and career-related internships or fieldwork available. *Program availability:* Part-time. Offers anatomy (M Sc, PhD); bacteriology (M Sc, PhD); clinical pharmacology (M Sc, PhD); clinical sciences (M Sc, PhD); epidemiology (M Sc, PhD); fish health (M Sc, PhD); food animal nutrition (M Sc, PhD); immunology (M Sc, PhD); microanatomy (M Sc, PhD); parasitology (M Sc, PhD); pathology (M Sc, PhD); pharmacology (M Sc, PhD); physiology (M Sc, PhD); toxicology (M Sc, PhD); veterinary medicine (M Sc, M Vet Sc, DVM, PhD); veterinary science (M Vet Sc); virology (M Sc, PhD). *Application deadline:* Applications are processed on a rolling basis. *Application Contact:* Jack MacDougall, Admissions Coordinator, 902-566-

0608, Fax: 902-566-0795, E-mail: registrar@upei.ca. *Dean*, Dr. Greg Keefe, 902-566-0825, E-mail: gkeefe@upei.ca.

Faculty of Arts Expenses: Contact institution. *Program availability:* Part-time. Offers island studies (MA). *Application deadline:* For fall admission, 2/1 priority date for domestic and international students. Applications are processed on a rolling basis. *Application fee:* $75 ($100 for international students). *Application Contact:* Jane McKay, Administrative Assistant, 902-566-0307. *Dean*, Dr. Nebojsa Kujundzic, 902-566-0310, Fax: 902-566-0304.

Faculty of Education Expenses: Contact institution. *Program availability:* Part-time. Offers educational studies (PhD); leadership in learning (M Ed). *Application deadline:* For fall admission, 1/15 for domestic and international students. *Application fee:* $75 ($100 for international students). *Application Contact:* Dr. Ronald J. MacDonald, Dean, 902-566-0349, Fax: 902-566-0416. *Dean*, Dr. Ronald J. MacDonald, 902-566-0349, Fax: 902-566-0416.

Faculty of Science Expenses: Contact institution. Offers environmental sciences (M Sc, PhD); human biology (M Sc); molecular and macromolecular sciences (M Sc, PhD); sustainable design engineering (M Sc). *Application deadline:* For fall admission, 12/15 priority date for domestic and international students. Applications are processed on a rolling basis. *Application fee:* $75 ($100 for international students). *Application Contact:* Jack MacDougall, Admissions Coordinator, 902-566-0608, Fax: 902-566-0795, E-mail: registrar@upei.ca. *Dean*, Dr. Debbie MacLellan, 902-566-0320, Fax: 902-628-4303.

UNIVERSITY OF PUERTO RICO, MAYAGÜEZ CAMPUS, Mayagüez, PR 00681-9000

General Information Commonwealth-supported, coed, university. *Enrollment:* 929 full-time matriculated graduate/professional students (424 women), 104 part-time matriculated graduate/professional students (49 women). *Enrollment by degree level:* 861 master's, 172 doctoral. *Graduate faculty:* 316 full-time (101 women), 1 part-time/adjunct (0 women). *International tuition:* $7166 full-time. *Tuition, area resident:* Full-time $2466. *Required fees:* $210. Tuition and fees vary according to course level, campus/location, program and student level. *Graduate housing:* On-campus housing not available. *Student services:* Campus employment opportunities, campus safety program, career counseling, child daycare facilities, free psychological counseling, grant writing training, international student services, low-cost health insurance, services for students with disabilities, teacher training, writing training. *Library facilities:* General Library plus 1 other. *Research affiliation:* U.S. Department of Education (DOE) (STEM education), National Endowment for the Humanities, Tropical Agriculture Research Station (agriculture), Corporation for the Development and Administration of Marine Resources of Puerto Rico (marine science), National Science Foundation.

Computer facilities: A campuswide network can be accessed from off campus. Online class registration is available. Website: http://www.uprm.edu/

General Application Contact: Dr. Carlos E. Quiñones-Padovani, Graduate Studies Director, 787-265-3809, Fax: 787-265-5489, E-mail: director.eg.aa@uprm.edu.

GRADUATE UNITS

Graduate Studies Students: 929 full-time (424 women), 104 part-time (49 women); includes 837 minority (9 Asian, non-Hispanic/Latino; 828 Hispanic/Latino), 194 international. Average age 25. 388 applicants, 67% accepted, 173 enrolled. *Faculty:* 316 full-time (101 women), 1 part-time/adjunct (0 women). Expenses: Contact institution. *Financial support:* In 2016–17, 2,010 students received support, including 985 research assistantships with tuition reimbursements available (averaging $3,594 per year), 1,025 teaching assistantships with tuition reimbursements available (averaging $1,856 per year); scholarships/grants and unspecified assistantships also available. In 2016, 166 master's, 10 doctorates awarded. *Program availability:* Part-time, evening/weekend. *Application deadline:* For fall admission, 2/15 for domestic and international students; for spring admission, 9/15 for domestic and international students. Applications are processed on a rolling basis. *Application fee:* $25. Electronic applications accepted. *Application Contact:* Madeline I. Cabán, Administrative Secretary V, 787-265-3809, Fax: 787-265-5489, E-mail: madeline.caban@uprm.edu. *Director and Associate Dean of Academic Affairs*, Carlos E. Quiñones-Padovani, PhD, 787-265-3809 Ext. 5726, Fax: 787-265-5489, E-mail: director.eg.aa@uprm.edu.

College of Agricultural Sciences Students: 161 full-time (90 women), 30 part-time (13 women); includes 188 minority (all Hispanic/Latino), 3 international. Average age 25. 74 applicants, 58% accepted, 27 enrolled. *Faculty:* 70 full-time (24 women), 3 part-time/adjunct (1 woman). Expenses: Contact institution. *Financial support:* In 2016–17, 165 students received support, including 84 research assistantships with tuition reimbursements available (averaging $5,931 per year), 131 teaching assistantships with tuition reimbursements available (averaging $4,669 per year); fellowships with full tuition reimbursements available, career-related internships or fieldwork, Federal Work-Study, institutionally sponsored loans, scholarships/grants, traineeships, and unspecified assistantships also available. In 2016, 30 degrees awarded. *Program availability:* Part-time. Offers agricultural economics and rural sociology (MS); agricultural education (MS); agricultural extension (MS); agricultural sciences (MS); agronomy (MS); animal science (MS); crop protection (MS); food science and technology (MS); horticulture (MS); soils (MS). *Application deadline:* For fall admission, 2/15 for domestic and international students; for spring admission, 9/15 for domestic and international students. Applications are processed on a rolling basis. *Application fee:* $25. *Application Contact:* Dr. Francisco M. Monroig, Associate Dean, 787-832-4040 Ext. 3108, E-mail: franciscom.monroig@upr.edu. *Director/Dean*, Dr. Raúl Macchiavelli, 787-832-4040 Ext. 2184, Fax: 787-832-4220, E-mail: raul.macchiavelli@upr.edu.

College of Arts and Sciences Students: 370 full-time (192 women), 20 part-time (10 women); includes 310 minority (all Hispanic/Latino), 56 international. Average age 25. 128 applicants, 59% accepted, 64 enrolled. *Faculty:* 203 full-time (66 women), 10 part-time/adjunct (5 women). Expenses: Contact institution. *Financial support:* Fellowships with full tuition reimbursements, research assistantships with tuition reimbursements, teaching assistantships with tuition reimbursements, career-related internships or fieldwork, Federal Work-Study, institutionally sponsored loans, scholarships/grants, traineeships, and unspecified assistantships available. *Program availability:* Part-time. Offers applied chemistry (MS, PhD); applied mathematics (MS); arts and sciences (MA, MS, PhD); biology (MS); English education (MA); geology (MS); Hispanic studies (MA); kinesiology (MA); marine sciences (MS, PhD); physics (MS); pre-college math education (MS); pure mathematics (MS); scientific computing (MS); statistics (MS). *Application deadline:* For fall admission, 2/15 for domestic and international students; for spring admission, 9/15 for domestic and international students. Applications are processed on a rolling basis. *Application fee:* $25. *Application Contact:* Nancy I. Damiani Gonzalez, Executive Secretary, 787-832-4040 Ext. 3828, Fax: 787-265-1225, E-mail: nancyi.damiani@upr.edu. *Interim Dean*,

Fernando Gilbes Santaella, 787-832-4040 Ext. 3828, Fax: 787-265-1225, E-mail: decano.arci@uprm.edu.

College of Business Administration Students: 37 full-time (24 women), 27 part-time (18 women); includes 60 minority (all Hispanic/Latino). Average age 25. 22 applicants, 68% accepted, 12 enrolled. *Faculty:* 24 full-time (10 women). Expenses: Contact institution. *Financial support:* In 2016–17, 6 students received support, including 5 research assistantships with full and partial tuition reimbursements available (averaging $4,489 per year), 4 teaching assistantships with full and partial tuition reimbursements available (averaging $4,605 per year); unspecified assistantships also available. In 2016, 6 master's awarded. *Program availability:* Part-time, evening/weekend. Offers business administration (MBA); finance (MBA); human resources (MBA); industrial management (MBA). *Application deadline:* For fall admission, 2/15 for domestic and international students; for spring admission, 9/15 for domestic and international students. Applications are processed on a rolling basis. *Application fee:* $25. Electronic applications accepted. *Application Contact:* Judith Valentín, Administrative Secretary, 787-265-3887, Fax: 787-832-5320, E-mail: grad.adem@uprm.edu. *Department Head*, Roberto L. Seijo, PhD, 787-832-4040 Ext. 3887, Fax: 787-832-5320, E-mail: roberto.seijo@upr.edu.

College of Engineering Students: 33 full-time (10 women), 7 part-time (3 women); includes 32 minority (all Hispanic/Latino), 8 international. Average age 25. 10 applicants, 80% accepted, 3 enrolled. *Faculty:* 36 full-time (13 women), 7 part-time/adjunct (3 women). Expenses: Contact institution. *Financial support:* In 2016–17, 9 students received support, including 6 research assistantships with full and partial tuition reimbursements available (averaging $4,087 per year), 4 teaching assistantships with full and partial tuition reimbursements available (averaging $4,020 per year); unspecified assistantships also available. *Program availability:* Part-time. Offers chemical engineering (ME, MS, PhD); civil engineering (ME, MS, PhD); computer engineering (ME, MS); computer science and engineering (PhD); computing and information sciences and engineering (PhD); electrical engineering (ME, MS); engineering (ME, MS, PhD); industrial engineering (ME, MS); mechanical engineering (ME, MS, PhD). *Application deadline:* For fall admission, 2/15 for domestic and international students; for spring admission, 9/15 for domestic and international students. Applications are processed on a rolling basis. *Application fee:* $25. Electronic applications accepted. *Application Contact:* Lucía Mercado, Administrative Secretary V, 787-832-4040 Ext. 2398, E-mail: lucia.mercado@upr.edu. *Dean*, Dr. Agustin Rullan, 787-832-4040 Ext. 3822, E-mail: decano.ingenieria@upr.edu.

UNIVERSITY OF PUERTO RICO, MEDICAL SCIENCES CAMPUS, San Juan, PR 00936-5067

General Information Commonwealth-supported, coed, primarily women, university. *Graduate housing:* On-campus housing not available.

GRADUATE UNITS

Graduate School of Public Health *Program availability:* Part-time. Offers biostatistics (MPH); demography (MS); developmental disabilities-early intervention (Certificate); environmental health (MS, Dr PH); epidemiology (MPH, MS); evaluative research of health systems (MS); gerontology (MPH, Certificate); health services administration (MHSA, MS); industrial hygiene (MS); maternal and child health (MPH); nurse midwifery (MPH, Certificate); nutrition (MS); public health (MHSA, MPH, MPHE, MS, Dr PH, Certificate); public health education (MPHE); school health promotion (Certificate).

School of Dental Medicine Offers dental medicine (DMD, Certificate); dentistry (DMD, Certificate); general dentistry (Certificate); oral and maxillofacial surgery (Certificate); orthodontics (Certificate); pediatric dentistry (Certificate); prosthodontics (Certificate). Electronic applications accepted.

School of Health Professions Offers audiology (Au D); clinical laboratory science (MS); clinical research (MS, Graduate Certificate); cytotechnology (Certificate); dietetics (Certificate); health information administration (MS); health professions (MS, Au D, Certificate); medical technology (Certificate); occupational therapy (MS); physical therapy (MS); speech-language pathology (MS). Electronic applications accepted.

School of Medicine Offers medicine (MS, MD, PhD). Electronic applications accepted.

Biomedical Sciences Graduate Program Offers anatomy (MS, PhD); biochemistry (MS, PhD); biomedical sciences (MS, PhD); microbiology and medical zoology (MS, PhD); pharmacology and toxicology (MS, PhD); physiology (MS, PhD). Electronic applications accepted.

School of Nursing Offers adult and elderly nursing (MSN); child and adolescent nursing (MSN); critical care nursing (MSN); family and community nursing (MSN); family nurse practitioner (MSN); maternity nursing (MSN); mental health and psychiatric nursing (MSN). Electronic applications accepted.

School of Pharmacy *Program availability:* Part-time, evening/weekend. Offers industrial pharmacy (MS); pharmaceutical sciences (MS); pharmacy (Pharm D). Electronic applications accepted.

UNIVERSITY OF PUERTO RICO, RÍO PIEDRAS CAMPUS, San Juan, PR 00931-3300

General Information Commonwealth-supported, coed, university. CGS member. *Graduate housing:* Room and/or apartments available to single students; on-campus housing not available to married students. Housing application deadline: 6/15. *Research affiliation:* U.S. Department of Education (DOE) (social sciences, general studies, physics, biology), U.S. Department of Health and Human Services (social sciences, biology), National Science Foundation (ecology, biology), Ocean Conservancy (ecology, biology), Ford International (ecology).

GRADUATE UNITS

College of Business Administration *Program availability:* Part-time. Offers accounting (MBA); finance (MBA, PhD); general business (MBA); human resources management (MBA); international trade and business (MBA, PhD); marketing (MBA); operations management (MBA); quantitative methods (MBA).

College of Education *Program availability:* Part-time. Offers biology education (M Ed); chemistry education (M Ed); curriculum and teaching (Ed D); early child education (M Ed); education (M Ed, MS, Ed D); educational research and evaluation (M Ed); exercise sciences (MS); family ecology and nutrition (M Ed); guidance and counseling (M Ed, Ed D); history education (M Ed); mathematics education (M Ed); physics education (M Ed); school administration and supervision (M Ed, Ed D); Spanish education (M Ed); special and differentiated education (M Ed); teaching English as a second language (M Ed).

College of Humanities *Program availability:* Part-time. Offers Caribbean history (PhD); Caribbean linguistics (PhD); Caribbean literature (PhD); comparative literature (MA); English (MA); Hispanic linguistics (PhD); Hispanic studies (MA); history (MA); humanities (MA, PhD, Certificate); Latin American literature (PhD); linguistics (MA);

philosophy (MA); Puerto Rican history (PhD); Puerto Rican literature (PhD); Spanish literature (PhD); translation (MA, Certificate).

College of Natural Sciences *Program availability:* Part-time. Offers chemical physics (PhD); chemistry (MS, PhD); ecology/systematics (MS, PhD); environmental sciences (MS, PhD); evolution/genetics (MS, PhD); mathematics (MS, PhD); molecular/cellular biology (MS, PhD); natural sciences (MS, PhD); neuroscience (MS, PhD); physics (MS, PhD).

College of Social Sciences *Program availability:* Part-time. Offers clinical psychology (MA); economics (MA); industrial organizational psychology (MA); investigative academic psychology (MA); psychology (PhD); social sciences (MA, MPA, MRC, MSW, PhD); social-community psychology (MA); sociology (MA).

Graduate School of Rehabilitation Counseling *Program availability:* Part-time. Offers rehabilitation counseling (MRC).

Graduate School of Social Work *Program availability:* Part-time. Offers social work (MSW, PhD).

School of Public Administration *Program availability:* Part-time. Offers public administration (MPA).

Graduate School of Information Sciences and Technologies *Program availability:* Part-time. Offers administration of academic libraries (PMC); administration of public libraries (PMC); administration of special libraries (PMC); consultant in information services (PMC); documents and files administration (Post-Graduate Certificate); electronic information resources analyst (Post-Graduate Certificate); information science (MIS); librarianship and information services (MLS); school librarian (Post-Graduate Certificate); school librarian distance education mode (Post-Graduate Certificate); specialist in legal information (PMC).

Graduate School of Planning *Program availability:* Part-time. Offers economic planning systems (MP); environmental planning (MP); social policy and planning (MP); urban and territorial planning (MP).

School of Architecture *Program availability:* Part-time. Offers architecture (M Arch).

School of Communication *Program availability:* Part-time. Offers communication (MA); communication theory and research (MA); journalism (MA).

School of Law *Program availability:* Part-time, evening/weekend. Offers law (LL M, JD).

UNIVERSITY OF PUGET SOUND, Tacoma, WA 98416

General Information Independent, coed, comprehensive institution. *Enrollment:* 2,791 graduate, professional, and undergraduate students; 215 full-time matriculated graduate/professional students (167 women), 62 part-time matriculated graduate/professional students (56 women). *Enrollment by degree level:* 163 master's, 114 doctoral. *Graduate faculty:* 26 full-time (18 women), 22 part-time/adjunct (18 women). *Graduate housing:* On-campus housing not available. *Student services:* Campus employment opportunities, campus safety program, career counseling, exercise/wellness program, free psychological counseling, international student services, low-cost health insurance, multicultural affairs office, services for students with disabilities, teacher training, writing training. *Library facilities:* Collins Memorial Library.

Computer facilities: A campuswide network can be accessed from student residence rooms and from off campus. Online class registration, financial aid, admission, student employment are available.
Website: http://www.pugetsound.edu/

General Application Contact: Shannon Carr, Director of Admission, 253-879-3211, Fax: 253-879-3993, E-mail: admission@pugetsound.edu.

GRADUATE UNITS

School of Education Students: 26 full-time (20 women), 29 part-time (27 women); includes 11 minority (1 American Indian or Alaska Native, non-Hispanic/Latino; 3 Asian, non-Hispanic/Latino; 2 Hispanic/Latino; 5 Two or more races, non-Hispanic/Latino). Average age 29. 93 applicants, 66% accepted, 44 enrolled. *Faculty:* 8 full-time (5 women), 2 part-time/adjunct (both women). Expenses: Contact institution. *Financial support:* In 2016–17, 24 students received support. Scholarships/grants available. Financial award application deadline: 3/31; financial award applicants required to submit FAFSA. In 2016, 42 master's awarded. *Program availability:* Part-time. Offers education (M Ed, MAT); elementary education (MAT); mental health counseling (M Ed); school counseling (M Ed); secondary education (MAT). *Application deadline:* For fall admission, 3/1 priority date for domestic and international students. Applications are processed on a rolling basis. *Application fee:* $60. Electronic applications accepted. *Application Contact:* Karen Stump, Certification Officer/Admission Coordinator, 253-879-3382, Fax: 253-879-3926, E-mail: kstump@pugetsound.edu. *Dean,* Amy Ryken, 253-879-2810, Fax: 253-879-3926, E-mail: aryken@pugetsound.edu.

School of Occupational Therapy Students: 77 full-time (72 women), 31 part-time (28 women); includes 24 minority (1 Black or African American, non-Hispanic/Latino; 8 Asian, non-Hispanic/Latino; 4 Hispanic/Latino; 11 Two or more races, non-Hispanic/Latino). Average age 28. 360 applicants, 23% accepted, 32 enrolled. *Faculty:* 10 full-time (8 women), 9 part-time/adjunct (all women). Expenses: Contact institution. *Financial support:* In 2016–17, 29 students received support, including 18 fellowships (averaging $13,489 per year); scholarships/grants also available. Financial award application deadline: 3/31; financial award applicants required to submit FAFSA. In 2016, 31 master's awarded. Offers occupational therapy (MSOT, Dr OT). *Application deadline:* For fall admission, 12/1 priority date for domestic and international students. *Application fee:* $50. Electronic applications accepted. *Application Contact:* Valerie Walston, Program Coordinator, 253-879-3517, Fax: 253-879-3518, E-mail: vwalston@pugetsound.edu. *Professor and Department Chair,* Yvonne Swinth, 253-879-3514, Fax: 253-879-3518, E-mail: ot@pugetsound.edu.

School of Physical Therapy Students: 112 full-time (75 women), 2 part-time (1 woman); includes 20 minority (8 Asian, non-Hispanic/Latino; 6 Hispanic/Latino; 6 Two or more races, non-Hispanic/Latino), 1 international. Average age 27. 530 applicants, 17% accepted, 37 enrolled. *Faculty:* 8 full-time (5 women), 11 part-time/adjunct (7 women). Expenses: Contact institution. *Financial support:* In 2016–17, 27 students received support, including 20 fellowships (averaging $13,961 per year); scholarships/grants also available. Financial award application deadline: 3/31; financial award applicants required to submit FAFSA. In 2016, 35 doctorates awarded. Offers physical therapy (DPT). *Application deadline:* For fall admission, 11/1 priority date for domestic and international students. *Application fee:* $50. Electronic applications accepted. *Application Contact:* Holly Roberts, Clinical Associate Professor, 253-879-3531, Fax: 253-879-3518, E-mail: hjroberts@pugetsound.edu. *Director,* Dr. Robert Boyles, 253-879-3633, Fax: 253-879-2933, E-mail: bboyles@pugetsound.edu.

UNIVERSITY OF REDLANDS, Redlands, CA 92373-0999

General Information Independent, coed, comprehensive institution. *Graduate housing:* Rooms and/or apartments available on a first-come, first-served basis to single students and available to married students. Housing application deadline: 8/19. *Research affiliation:* Environmental Systems Research Institute (geographic information systems).

GRADUATE UNITS

College of Arts and Sciences Offers arts and sciences (MM, MS); communicative disorders (MS); geographic information systems (MS). Electronic applications accepted.

School of Music *Program availability:* Part-time. Offers music (MM).

School of Business *Program availability:* Evening/weekend. Offers business (MBA); information technology (MS); management (MA).

School of Education *Program availability:* Part-time, evening/weekend. Offers education (MA, Ed D, Certificate).

UNIVERSITY OF REGINA, Regina, SK S4S 0A2, Canada

General Information Province-supported, coed, university. CGS member. *Enrollment:* 14,849 graduate, professional, and undergraduate students; 959 full-time matriculated graduate/professional students (486 women), 693 part-time matriculated graduate/professional students (465 women). *Enrollment by degree level:* 1,248 master's, 258 doctoral, 51 other advanced degrees. *Graduate faculty:* 456 full-time (182 women), 204 part-time/adjunct (67 women). *Graduate housing:* Room and/or apartments available on a first-come, first-served basis to single students; on-campus housing not available to married students. *Student services:* Campus employment opportunities, campus safety program, career counseling, child daycare facilities, exercise/wellness program, international student services, multicultural affairs office, services for students with disabilities, writing training. *Library facilities:* Dr. John Archer Library plus 5 others. *Collection:* Books: 839,614 (physical), 330,732 (digital/electronic); Serial titles: 163,120 (physical), 131,946 (digital/electronic); Databases: 535. Weekly public service hours: 105; students can reserve study rooms. *Research affiliation:* TR Labs (telecommunications), Regional Centre of Expertise on Education for Sustainable Development in Saskatchewan (sustainable development), Petroleum Technology Research Center (green energy technologies), Saskatchewan Population Health and Evaluation Research Unit (health research), Canadian Plains Research Centre (CPRC) (climate change adaptation), Prairie Adaptation Research Collaborative (climate change and adaptation options).

Computer facilities: 412 computers available on campus for general student use. A campuswide network can be accessed from student residence rooms and from off campus. Online class registration is available.
Website: http://www.uregina.ca/

General Application Contact: Dr. Karen Meagher, Associate Dean, Faculty of Graduate Studies and Research, 306-585-5186, Fax: 306-337-2444, E-mail: grad.studies@uregina.ca.

GRADUATE UNITS

Faculty of Graduate Studies and Research Students: 959 full-time (486 women), 693 part-time (465 women). 1,590 applicants, 27% accepted. *Faculty:* 456 full-time (182 women), 204 part-time/adjunct (67 women). Expenses: Contact institution. *Financial support:* In 2016–17, 208 fellowships (averaging $5,774 per year), 419 teaching assistantships (averaging $1,294 per year) were awarded; career-related internships or fieldwork, institutionally sponsored loans, and scholarships/grants also available. Financial award application deadline: 6/15. In 2016, 388 master's, 36 doctorates, 34 other advanced degrees awarded. *Program availability:* Part-time, evening/weekend. *Application deadline:* For fall admission, 3/15 for domestic and international students; for winter admission, 8/15 for domestic and international students; for spring admission, 9/15 for domestic and international students. Applications are processed on a rolling basis. *Application fee:* $100. Electronic applications accepted. *Application Contact:* Dr. Karen Meagher, Associate Dean, 306-585-5186, Fax: 306-337-2444, E-mail: grad.assocdean1@uregina.ca. *Dean,* Dr. Thomas Bredohl, 306-585-5185, Fax: 306-337-2444, E-mail: grad.dean@uregina.ca.

Faculty of Arts Students: 126 full-time (80 women), 38 part-time (21 women). 187 applicants, 25% accepted. *Faculty:* 141 full-time (54 women), 49 part-time/adjunct (11 women). Expenses: Contact institution. *Financial support:* In 2016–17, 16 fellowships (averaging $9,186 per year), 41 teaching assistantships (averaging $2,844 per year) were awarded; career-related internships or fieldwork and scholarships/grants also available. Financial award application deadline: 6/15. In 2016, 43 master's, 7 doctorates awarded. *Program availability:* Part-time. Offers anthropology (MA); applied economics and policy analysis (MA); arts (M Sc, MA, MJ, PhD); Canadian plains studies (MA, PhD); clinical psychology (MA, PhD); creative writing (MA); English (MA, PhD); experimental and applied psychology (MA, PhD); French (MA); geography (M Sc, MA, PhD); gerontology (M Sc, MA); history (MA); journalism (MJ); justice studies (MA); linguistics (MA); philosophy (MA); police studies (MA); religious studies (MA); social and political thought (MA); social studies (MA); sociology (MA); women's and gender studies (MA). *Application deadline:* For fall admission, 2/15 for domestic and international students; for winter admission, 9/15 for domestic and international students. Applications are processed on a rolling basis. *Application fee:* $100. Electronic applications accepted. *Application Contact:* Dr. Nilgun Onder, Associate Dean, Research and Graduate Studies, 306-585-4336, Fax: 306-585-5368, E-mail: arts.assocdean-rg@uregina.ca. *Dean,* Dr. Richard Kleer, 306-585-4895, Fax: 306-585-5368, E-mail: arts.dean@uregina.ca.

Faculty of Education Students: 96 full-time (72 women), 204 part-time (147 women). 110 applicants, 30% accepted. *Faculty:* 50 full-time (32 women), 26 part-time/adjunct (4 women). Expenses: Contact institution. *Financial support:* In 2016–17, 24 fellowships (averaging $5,042 per year), 18 teaching assistantships (averaging $2,562 per year) were awarded; career-related internships or fieldwork and scholarships/grants also available. Financial award application deadline: 6/15. In 2016, 84 master's, 2 doctorates, 1 other advanced degree awarded. *Program availability:* Part-time. Offers adult education (MA Ed); curriculum and instruction (M Ed); education (M Ed, MA Ed, MHRD, PhD, Master's Certificate); educational administration (M Ed); educational psychology (M Ed); human resource development (MHRD). *Application deadline:* For fall admission, 2/15 for domestic and international students; for winter admission, 10/15 for domestic and international students; for spring admission, 2/15 for domestic and international students. *Application fee:* $100. Electronic applications accepted. *Application Contact:* Tania Gates, Graduate Program Coordinator, 306-585-4506, Fax: 306-585-5387, E-mail: edgrad@uregina.ca. *Associate Dean, Research and Graduate Programs in Education,* Dr. Ken Montgomery, 306-585-5031, Fax: 306-585-5387, E-mail: ken.montgomery@uregina.ca.

Faculty of Engineering and Applied Science Students: 266 full-time (69 women), 29 part-time (6 women). 500 applicants, 13% accepted. *Faculty:* 43 full-time (4 women), 21 part-time/adjunct (5 women). Expenses: Contact institution. *Financial support:* In 2016–17, 60 fellowships (averaging $5,317 per year), 61 teaching assistantships (averaging $2,990 per year) were awarded; career-related internships or fieldwork and scholarships/grants also available. Financial award application deadline: 6/15. In 2016, 78 master's, 16 doctorates awarded. *Program availability:* Part-time. Offers electronic systems engineering (M Eng, MA Sc, PhD); engineering and applied science (M Eng, MA Sc, PhD); environmental systems engineering (M Eng, MA Sc, PhD); industrial systems engineering (M Eng, MA Sc, PhD); petroleum systems engineering (M Eng, MA Sc, PhD); process systems engineering (M Eng, MA Sc); software systems engineering (M Eng, MA Sc). *Application deadline:* For fall admission, 3/31 for domestic and international students; for winter admission, 7/31 for domestic and international students; for spring admission, 11/30 for domestic and international students. *Application fee:* $100. Electronic applications accepted. *Application Contact:* Dr. Amr Henni, Associate Dean, Graduate Studies and Research, 306-585-4960, Fax: 306-585-4855, E-mail: amr.henni@uregina.ca. *Dean,* Dr. Esam Hussein, 306-585-4160, Fax: 306-585-4556, E-mail: esam.hussein@uregina.ca.

Faculty of Kinesiology and Health Studies Students: 28 full-time (14 women), 7 part-time (5 women). 15 applicants, 47% accepted. *Faculty:* 17 full-time (8 women), 26 part-time/adjunct (14 women). Expenses: Contact institution. *Financial support:* In 2016–17, 8 fellowships (averaging $6,750 per year), 7 teaching assistantships (averaging $2,518 per year) were awarded; scholarships/grants also available. Financial award application deadline: 6/15. In 2016, 3 master's, 1 doctorate awarded. *Offers* kinesiology and health studies (M Sc, PhD). *Application deadline:* Applications are processed on a rolling basis. *Application fee:* $100. Electronic applications accepted. *Application Contact:* Dr. Darren Candow, Associate Dean, Graduate Studies and Research, 306-585-4906, Fax: 306-585-4854, E-mail: darren.candow@uregina.ca. *Dean,* Dr. Harold Riemer, 306-585-4535, Fax: 306-585-4854, E-mail: khs.dean@uregina.ca.

Faculty of Media, Art, and Performance Students: 18 full-time (9 women), 3 part-time (2 women). 23 applicants, 43% accepted. *Faculty:* 31 full-time (18 women), 4 part-time/adjunct (1 woman). Expenses: Contact institution. *Financial support:* In 2016–17, 10 fellowships (averaging $7,200 per year), 10 teaching assistantships (averaging $2,513 per year) were awarded; scholarships/grants also available. Financial award application deadline: 6/15. In 2016, 5 master's awarded. *Program availability:* Part-time. *Offers* ceramics (MFA); composition (MMus); conducting (MMus); drawing (MFA); interdisciplinary studies (MA, MFA); intermedia (MFA); media production (MFA); media studies (MA); media, art, and performance (MA, MFA, MMus); music theory (MA); musicology (MA); painting (MFA); performance (MMus); sculpture (MFA). *Application deadline:* For fall admission, 1/15 for domestic and international students. *Application fee:* $100. Electronic applications accepted. *Application Contact:* Dr. Kathleen Irwin, Associate Dean, Graduate and Research, 306-585-5519, Fax: 306-585-5544, E-mail: kathleen.irwin@uregina.ca. *Dean,* Dr. Rae Staseson, 306-585-5510, Fax: 306-585-5544, E-mail: map.dean@uregina.ca.

Faculty of Nursing Students: 20 full-time (all women), 27 part-time (25 women). 46 applicants, 52% accepted. *Faculty:* 18 full-time (14 women), 5 part-time/adjunct (1 woman). Expenses: Contact institution. *Financial support:* In 2016–17, 3 fellowships (averaging $6,000 per year) were awarded; teaching assistantships and scholarships/grants also available. Financial award application deadline: 6/15. In 2016, 6 master's awarded. *Offers* nursing (MN). *Application deadline:* For fall admission, 1/15 for domestic and international students. *Application fee:* $100. Electronic applications accepted. *Application Contact:* Tracy Martin, Graduate Program Assistant, 306-337-2113, Fax: 306-337-8493, E-mail: tracy.martin@uregina.ca. *Associate Dean, Graduate Programs and Research,* Dr. Glenn Donnelly, 306-337-8544, Fax: 306-337-8493, E-mail: glenn.donnelly@uregina.ca.

Faculty of Science Students: 174 full-time (67 women), 32 part-time (12 women). 258 applicants, 16% accepted. *Faculty:* 82 full-time (18 women), 44 part-time/adjunct (19 women). Expenses: Contact institution. *Financial support:* In 2016–17, 42 fellowships (averaging $6,333 per year), 46 teaching assistantships (averaging $2,581 per year) were awarded; career-related internships or fieldwork and scholarships/grants also available. Financial award application deadline: 6/15. In 2016, 55 master's, 10 doctorates awarded. *Program availability:* Part-time. *Offers* analytical/environmental chemistry (M Sc, PhD); biology (M Sc, PhD); biophysics of biological interfaces (M Sc, PhD); computer science (M Sc, PhD); enzymology/chemical biology (M Sc, PhD); geology (M Sc, PhD); inorganic/organometallic chemistry (M Sc, PhD); mathematics (M Sc, PhD); physics (M Sc, PhD); science (M Sc, PhD); signal transduction and mechanisms of cancer cell regulation (M Sc, PhD); statistics (M Sc, PhD); supramolecular organic photochemistry and photophysics (M Sc, PhD); synthetic organic chemistry (M Sc, PhD); theoretical/computational chemistry (M Sc, PhD). *Application deadline:* Applications are processed on a rolling basis. *Application fee:* $100. Electronic applications accepted. *Application Contact:* Dr. Cory Butz, Associate Dean for Research, 306-585-4201, Fax: 306-585-4291, E-mail: cory.butz@uregina.ca. *Dean,* Dr. Douglas Farenick, 306-337-2110, Fax: 306-585-4291, E-mail: douglas.farenick@uregina.ca.

Faculty of Social Work Students: 35 full-time (34 women), 65 part-time (54 women). 72 applicants, 54% accepted. *Faculty:* 22 full-time (15 women), 5 part-time/adjunct (3 women). Expenses: Contact institution. *Financial support:* In 2016–17, 6 fellowships (averaging $6,000 per year), 3 teaching assistantships (averaging $2,501 per year) were awarded; career-related internships or fieldwork and scholarships/grants also available. Financial award application deadline: 6/15. In 2016, 15 master's awarded. *Program availability:* Part-time. *Offers* indigenous social work (MISW); social work (MSW, PhD). PhD offered as a special case program. *Application deadline:* For fall admission, 1/31 for domestic and international students. *Application fee:* $100. Electronic applications accepted. *Application Contact:* Dr. Nuelle Novik, Graduate Program Coordinator, 306-585-4573, Fax: 306-585-4872, E-mail: nuelle.novik@uregina.ca. *Dean,* Dr. Judy White, 306-585-4037, Fax: 306-585-5691, E-mail: sw.dean@uregina.ca.

Johnson-Shoyama Graduate School of Public Policy Students: 88 full-time (56 women), 159 part-time (103 women). 202 applicants, 43% accepted. *Faculty:* 9 full-time (4 women), 15 part-time/adjunct (4 women). Expenses: Contact institution. *Financial support:* In 2016–17, 17 fellowships (averaging $6,059 per year), 19 teaching assistantships (averaging $2,507 per year) were awarded; career-related internships or fieldwork and scholarships/grants also available. Financial award application deadline: 6/15. In 2016, 43 master's, 20 other advanced degrees awarded. *Program availability:* Part-time. *Offers* economic analysis for public policy (Master's Certificate); health administration (MHA); health systems management (Master's Certificate); public management (MPA, Master's Certificate); public policy (MPA, MPP, PhD); public policy analysis (Master's Certificate). *Application deadline:* For fall admission, 2/1 for domestic and international students. *Application fee:* $100. Electronic applications accepted. *Application Contact:* Constance Heshka-Argue, Manager, Main Campus, 306-585-5462, Fax: 306-585-5461, E-mail: connie.heska-argue@uregina.ca. *Executive Director, Main Campus,* Dr. Kathleen McNutt, 306-585-4759, Fax: 306-585-5461, E-mail: kathy.mcnutt@uregina.ca.

Kenneth Levene Graduate School of Business Students: 83 full-time (47 women), 76 part-time (54 women). 175 applicants, 41% accepted. *Faculty:* 43 full-time (15 women), 7 part-time/adjunct (5 women). Expenses: Contact institution. *Financial*

support: In 2016–17, 8 fellowships (averaging $6,000 per year), 7 teaching assistantships (averaging $2,501 per year) were awarded; career-related internships or fieldwork and scholarships/grants also available. Financial award application deadline: 6/15. In 2016, 57 master's, 13 other advanced degrees awarded. *Program availability:* Part-time, evening/weekend. *Offers* business (EMBA, M Admin, MBA, MHRM, Master's Certificate, PGD); business foundations (PGD); engineering management (MBA); executive business administration (EMBA); human resources management (MHRM, Master's Certificate); international business (MBA); leadership (M Admin); organizational leadership (Master's Certificate); project management (Master's Certificate); public safety management (MBA). *Application deadline:* Applications are processed on a rolling basis. *Application fee:* $100. Electronic applications accepted. *Application Contact:* Dr. Gina Grandy, Associate Dean, Research and Graduate Programs/Director of Kenneth Levene Graduate School, 306-585-5647, Fax: 306-585-5361, E-mail: gina.grandy@uregina.ca. *Dean,* Dr. Andrew Gaudes, 306-585-4435, Fax: 306-585-4805, E-mail: andrew.gaudes@uregina.ca.

UNIVERSITY OF RHODE ISLAND, Kingston, RI 02881

General Information State-supported, coed, university. CGS member. *Enrollment:* 17,834 graduate, professional, and undergraduate students; 1,894 full-time matriculated graduate/professional students (1,169 women), 980 full-time matriculated graduate/professional students (584 women). *Enrollment by degree level:* 1,336 master's, 1,413 doctoral, 125 other advanced degrees. *Graduate faculty:* 635 full-time (304 women), 15 part-time/adjunct (11 women). Tuition, state resident: full-time $11,796; part-time $655 per credit. Tuition, nonresident: full-time $24,206; part-time $1345 per credit. Required fees: $1546; $44 per credit. One-time fee: $155 full-time; $35 part-time. *Graduate housing:* Rooms and/or apartments available on a first-come, first-served basis to single and married students. Housing application deadline: 5/1. *Student services:* Campus employment opportunities, campus safety program, career counseling, free psychological counseling, international student services, low-cost health insurance, multicultural affairs office, services for students with disabilities. *Library facilities:* Robert L. Carothers Library and Learning Commons plus 3 others. *Research affiliation:* Sustainable Coastal Communities and Ecosystems (SUCCESS)-Leader with Associates, Rhode Island Network for Molecular Toxicology, Rhode Island Teacher Education Renewal (RITER), U.S. Department of Agriculture (USDA) (food stamp nutrition education).

Computer facilities: Computer purchase and lease plans are available. 2,500 computers available on campus for general student use. A campuswide network can be accessed from student residence rooms and from off campus. Online class registration is available.
Website: http://www.uri.edu/

General Application Contact: Shandra Pelagio, Graduate Admission, 401-874-2873, E-mail: shandra@uri.edu.

GRADUATE UNITS

Graduate School Students: 1,894 full-time (1,169 women), 980 part-time (584 women); includes 380 minority (95 Black or African American, non-Hispanic/Latino; 15 American Indian or Alaska Native, non-Hispanic/Latino; 150 Asian, non-Hispanic/Latino; 84 Hispanic/Latino; 3 Native Hawaiian or other Pacific Islander, non-Hispanic/Latino; 33 Two or more races, non-Hispanic/Latino; 292 international. *Faculty:* 635 full-time (304 women), 15 part-time/adjunct (11 women). Expenses: Contact institution. *Financial support:* In 2016–17, 130 research assistantships with tuition reimbursements (averaging $12,035 per year), 311 teaching assistantships with tuition reimbursements (averaging $14,411 per year) were awarded; unspecified assistantships also available. Financial award applicants required to submit FAFSA. In 2016, 529 master's, 252 doctorates, 70 other advanced degrees awarded. *Program availability:* Part-time, evening/weekend, 100% online, blended/hybrid learning. *Application fee:* $65. Electronic applications accepted. *Application Contact:* Shandra Pelagio, Graduate Admissions, 401-874-2873, E-mail: shandra@uri.edu. *Dean of the Graduate School,* Dr. Nasser H. Zawia, 401-874-5909, Fax: 401-874-5787, E-mail: nzawia@uri.edu.

Alan Shawn Feinstein College of Education and Professional Studies Offers education (PhD); education and professional studies (MA, MM, MS, PhD); reading (MA); special education (MA).

College of Arts and Sciences Students: 256 full-time (133 women), 272 part-time (135 women); includes 70 minority (28 Black or African American, non-Hispanic/Latino; 4 American Indian or Alaska Native, non-Hispanic/Latino; 16 Asian, non-Hispanic/Latino; 18 Hispanic/Latino; 2 Native Hawaiian or other Pacific Islander, non-Hispanic/Latino; 2 Two or more races, non-Hispanic/Latino; 53 international. *Faculty:* 197 full-time (91 women), 2 part-time/adjunct (both women). Expenses: Contact institution. *Financial support:* In 2016–17, 9 research assistantships with tuition reimbursements (averaging $10,517 per year), 130 teaching assistantships with tuition reimbursements (averaging $16,583 per year) were awarded; unspecified assistantships also available. Financial award applicants required to submit FAFSA. In 2016, 90 master's, 18 doctorates, 14 other advanced degrees awarded. *Program availability:* Part-time, evening/weekend. *Offers* American and British literature and culture (PhD); applied mathematical sciences (MS, PhD); archaeology and anthropology (MA); arts and sciences (MA, MLIS, MM, MPA, MS, PSM, PhD, Graduate Certificate); chemistry (MS, PhD); communication studies (MA); computer science (MS, PhD); creative writing (PhD); digital forensics (Graduate Certificate); English (MA); film (PhD); gender and women's studies (Graduate Certificate); gender studies (PhD); history (MA); libraries, leadership and transforming communities (MLIS); mathematics (MS, PhD); music education (MM); music performance (MM); organization of digital media (MLIS); physics (MS, PhD); political science (MA); public policy and administration (MPA); school library media (MLIS); Spanish (MA); statistics (MS). *Application fee:* $65. Electronic applications accepted. *Application Contact:* Graduate Admissions, 401-874-2872, E-mail: gradadm@etal.uri.edu. *Dean,* Dr. Winifed E. Brownell, 401-874-4101, Fax: 401-874-2892, E-mail: winnie@uri.edu.

College of Business Administration Students: 94 full-time (45 women), 166 part-time (84 women); includes 37 minority (6 Black or African American, non-Hispanic/Latino; 1 American Indian or Alaska Native, non-Hispanic/Latino; 22 Asian, non-Hispanic/Latino; 3 Hispanic/Latino; 5 Two or more races, non-Hispanic/Latino; 18 international. *Faculty:* 57 full-time (24 women). Expenses: Contact institution. *Financial support:* In 2016–17, 17 teaching assistantships with tuition reimbursements (averaging $15,347 per year) were awarded; research assistantships also available. Financial award applicants required to submit FAFSA. In 2016, 124 master's, 4 doctorates awarded. *Program availability:* Part-time, evening/weekend. *Offers* accounting (MS); business administration (PhD); finance (MBA, MS); general business (MBA); health care management (MBA); management (MBA); marketing (MBA); oceanography (MBA); strategic innovation (MBA); supply chain management (MBA). *Application deadline:* For fall admission, 2/1 for domestic and international students. *Application fee:* $65. Electronic applications accepted. *Application Contact:* Lisa Lancellotta, Coordinator, MBA Programs, 401-

874-4241, Fax: 401-874-4312, E-mail: mba@uri.edu. *Dean*, Dr. Maling Ebrahimpour, 401-874-4348, Fax: 401-874-4312, E-mail: mebrahimpour@uri.edu.

College of Engineering Students: 125 full-time (29 women), 76 part-time (13 women); includes 29 minority (2 Black or African American, non-Hispanic/Latino; 1 American Indian or Alaska Native, non-Hispanic/Latino; 7 Asian, non-Hispanic/Latino; 10 Hispanic/Latino; 2 Two or more races, non-Hispanic/Latino), 78 international. *Faculty:* 72 full-time (14 women). Expenses: Contact institution. *Financial support:* In 2016–17, 25 research assistantships with tuition reimbursements (averaging $9,604 per year), 17 teaching assistantships with tuition reimbursements (averaging $10,217 per year) were awarded. Financial award applicants required to submit FAFSA. In 2016, 50 master's, 18 doctorates, 1 other advanced degree awarded. *Program availability:* Part-time. Offers acoustics (MS, PhD); acoustics and underwater acoustics (MS, PhD); biomedical engineering (MS, PhD); chemical engineering (MS, PhD); circuits and devices (MS); communication theory (MS, PhD); computer architectures and digital systems (MS, PhD); computer networks (MS, PhD); digital signal processing (MS); embedded systems and computer applications (MS, PhD); engineering (MS, PhD, Graduate Certificate, Postbaccalaureate Certificate); environmental engineering (MS, PhD); fault-tolerant computing (MS, PhD); geotechnical engineering (MS, PhD); industrial and systems engineering (MS, PhD); materials and optics (MS, PhD); structural engineering (MS, PhD); systems theory (MS, PhD); transportation engineering (MS, PhD). *Application fee:* $65. Electronic applications accepted. *Application Contact:* Graduate Admission, 401-874-2872, E-mail: gradadm@etal.uri.edu. *Dean*, Dr. Raymond Wright, 401-874-2186, Fax: 401-782-1066, E-mail: dean@egr.uri.edu.

College of Health Sciences Students: 280 full-time (214 women), 119 part-time (93 women); includes 54 minority (21 Black or African American, non-Hispanic/Latino; 2 American Indian or Alaska Native, non-Hispanic/Latino; 17 Asian, non-Hispanic/Latino; 10 Hispanic/Latino; 4 Two or more races, non-Hispanic/Latino), 7 international. *Faculty:* 82 full-time (53 women), 3 part-time/adjunct (2 women). Expenses: Contact institution. *Financial support:* In 2016–17, 11 research assistantships with tuition reimbursements (averaging $14,238 per year), 46 teaching assistantships with tuition reimbursements (averaging $11,618 per year) were awarded. Financial award applicants required to submit FAFSA. In 2016, 86 master's, 45 doctorates awarded. *Program availability:* Part-time, evening/weekend, 100% online, blended/hybrid learning. Offers behavioral science (PhD); clinical psychology (PhD); college student personnel (MS); cultural studies of sport and physical culture (MS); dietetic internship (MS); exercise science (MS); health sciences (MA, MM, MS, DPT, PhD); human development and family studies (MS); marriage and family therapy (MS); nutrition (MS, PhD); physical therapy (DPT); psychosocial/behavioral aspects of physical activity (MS); school psychology (MS, PhD); speech-language pathology (MS). *Application fee:* $65. Electronic applications accepted. *Application Contact:* Graduate Admission, 401-874-2872, E-mail: gradadm@etal.uri.edu. *Dean*, Dr. Gary Liguori, 401-874-9330, E-mail: gliguori@uri.edu.

College of Nursing Students: 47 full-time (43 women), 78 part-time (72 women); includes 16 minority (11 Black or African American, non-Hispanic/Latino; 3 Asian, non-Hispanic/Latino; 1 Hispanic/Latino; 1 Two or more races, non-Hispanic/Latino), 2 international. *Faculty:* 26 full-time (25 women), 3 part-time/adjunct (all women). Expenses: Contact institution. *Financial support:* In 2016–17, 2 research assistantships with tuition reimbursements (averaging $17,828 per year), 6 teaching assistantships with tuition reimbursements (averaging $14,831 per year) were awarded. Financial award application deadline: 2/15; financial award applicants required to submit FAFSA. In 2016, 53 master's, 12 doctorates awarded. *Program availability:* Part-time. Offers acute care nurse practitioner (MS); adult-gerontological nurse practitioner/clinical nurse specialist (MS); family nurse practitioner (MS); nursing (PhD); nursing education (MS); nursing practice (DNP). *Application deadline:* For fall admission, 2/15 for domestic students, 2/1 for international students; for spring admission, 10/15 for domestic students, 7/15 for international students. *Application fee:* $65. Electronic applications accepted. *Application Contact:* Graduate Admission, 401-874-2872, E-mail: gradadm@etal.uri.edu. *Dean*, Dr. Barbara Wolfe, 401-874-5324, E-mail: bwolfe@uri.edu.

College of Pharmacy Students: 764 full-time (498 women), 12 part-time (6 women); includes 124 minority (11 Black or African American, non-Hispanic/Latino; 64 Asian, non-Hispanic/Latino; 32 Hispanic/Latino; 17 Two or more races, non-Hispanic/Latino), 58 international. *Faculty:* 53 full-time (35 women). Expenses: Contact institution. *Financial support:* In 2016–17, 2 research assistantships with tuition reimbursements (averaging $17,828 per year), 16 teaching assistantships with tuition reimbursements (averaging $17,597 per year) were awarded. Financial award applicants required to submit FAFSA. In 2016, 6 master's, 126 doctorates awarded. *Program availability:* Part-time. Offers medicinal chemistry and pharmacognosy (MS, PhD); pharmaceutics and pharmacokinetics (MS, PhD); pharmacoepidemiology and pharmacoeconomics (MS, PhD); pharmacology and toxicology (MS, PhD); pharmacy (MS, PhD, Pharm D); pharmacy practice (Pharm D). *Application fee:* $65. Electronic applications accepted. *Application Contact:* Graduate Admission, 401-874-8272, E-mail: gradadm@etal.uri.edu. *Dean/Professor*, Dr. E. Paul Larrat, 401-874-5003, Fax: 401-874-2181, E-mail: larrat@uri.edu.

College of the Environment and Life Sciences Students: 211 full-time (128 women), 66 part-time (44 women); includes 22 minority (5 Black or African American, non-Hispanic/Latino; 12 Asian, non-Hispanic/Latino; 3 Hispanic/Latino; 1 Native Hawaiian or other Pacific Islander, non-Hispanic/Latino; 1 Two or more races, non-Hispanic/Latino), 54 international. *Faculty:* 94 full-time (35 women), 2 part-time/adjunct (1 woman). Expenses: Contact institution. *Financial support:* In 2016–17, 52 research assistantships with tuition reimbursements (averaging $13,958 per year), 61 teaching assistantships with tuition reimbursements (averaging $13,668 per year) were awarded. Financial award applicants required to submit FAFSA. In 2016, 77 master's, 16 doctorates awarded. *Program availability:* Part-time. Offers animal health and disease (MS); animal science (MS); aquaculture (MS); aquatic pathology (MS); biochemistry (MS, PhD); biological sciences (MS); clinical laboratory sciences (MS); environment and life sciences (MA, MESM, MMA, MS, PhD); environmental and natural resource economics (MESM, MS, PhD); environmental science and management (MESM); environmental sciences (MS, PhD); fisheries (MS); marine affairs (MA, MESM, MMA, PhD); microbiology (MS, PhD); molecular genetics (MS, PhD); natural resources science (MESM, MS, PhD). *Application fee:* $65. Electronic applications accepted. *Application Contact:* Graduate Admission, 401-874-2872, E-mail: gradadm@etal.uri.edu. *Dean*, Dr. John Kirby, 401-874-2957, Fax: 401-874-4017, E-mail: jdkirby@uri.edu.

Graduate School of Oceanography Students: 49 full-time (26 women), 14 part-time (5 women); includes 2 minority (both Asian, non-Hispanic/Latino), 9 international. *Faculty:* 28 full-time (10 women), 1 part-time/adjunct (0 women). Expenses: Contact institution. *Financial support:* In 2016–17, 24 research assistantships with tuition reimbursements (averaging $11,564 per year), 12 teaching assistantships with tuition

reimbursements (averaging $13,882 per year) were awarded. Financial award application deadline: 1/15; financial award applicants required to submit FAFSA. In 2016, 12 master's, 6 doctorates awarded. *Program availability:* Part-time. Offers biological oceanography (MS, PhD); coastal ocean management (MO); general oceanography (MO); marine and atmospheric chemistry (PhD); marine fisheries management (MO); marine geology and geophysics (PhD); physical oceanography (PhD). *Application deadline:* For fall admission, 1/15 for domestic and international students; for spring admission, 11/15 for domestic students, 7/15 for international students. *Application fee:* $65. Electronic applications accepted. *Application Contact:* Graduate Admission, 401-874-8272, E-mail: gradadm@etal.uri.edu. *Dean*, Dr. Bruce Corliss, 401-874-6222, Fax: 401-874-6931, E-mail: bruce.corliss@gso.uri.edu.

Schmidt Labor Research Center Students: 3 full-time (2 women), 30 part-time (24 women); includes 6 minority (4 Black or African American, non-Hispanic/Latino; 1 American Indian or Alaska Native, non-Hispanic/Latino; 1 Hispanic/Latino). *Faculty:* 1 full-time (0 women), 3 part-time/adjunct (2 women). Expenses: Contact institution. *Financial support:* In 2016–17, 2 teaching assistantships with tuition reimbursements (averaging $17,184 per year) were awarded; institutionally sponsored loans also available. Financial award application deadline: 2/1; financial award applicants required to submit FAFSA. In 2016, 5 master's awarded. *Program availability:* Part-time, evening/weekend. Offers human resources (MS, Graduate Certificate); labor relations (MS, Graduate Certificate). *Application deadline:* For fall admission, 7/15 for domestic students; for spring admission, 11/15 for domestic students, 7/15 for international students; for summer admission, 4/15 for domestic students. *Application fee:* $65. Electronic applications accepted. *Application Contact:* Graduate Admission, 401-874-2872, E-mail: gradadm@etal.uri.edu. *Acting Director*, Dr. Aimee Phelps, 401-874-4693, E-mail: aimee@uri.edu.

UNIVERSITY OF RICHMOND, University of Richmond, VA 23173

General Information Independent, coed, comprehensive institution. *Graduate housing:* On-campus housing not available.

GRADUATE UNITS

Robins School of Business *Program availability:* Part-time, evening/weekend. Offers business (MBA). Electronic applications accepted.

School of Law Offers law (JD). JD/MSW, JD/MHA, JD/MPA offered jointly with Virginia Commonwealth University; JD/MURP with Virginia Commonwealth University; JD/MA with Department of History; JD/MS with Department of Biology. Electronic applications accepted.

UNIVERSITY OF RIO GRANDE, Rio Grande, OH 45674

General Information Independent, coed, comprehensive institution. *Graduate housing:* Room and/or apartments available on a first-come, first-served basis to single students; on-campus housing not available to married students. *Student services:* Campus employment opportunities, campus safety program, career counseling, child daycare facilities, free psychological counseling, grant writing training, international student services, low-cost health insurance, multicultural affairs office, services for students with disabilities, teacher training. *Library facilities:* Jeanette Albiez Davis Library.

Computer facilities: 300 computers available on campus for general student use. A campuswide network can be accessed from student residence rooms and from off campus. Online class registration is available.
Website: http://www.rio.edu/

General Application Contact: Bethany Davies, Admissions Secretary, 740-245-7206, Fax: 740-245-7175, E-mail: bethanyd@rio.edu.

GRADUATE UNITS

Graduate School Expenses: Contact institution. *Financial support:* Career-related internships or fieldwork available. Support available to part-time students. Financial award application deadline: 7/1; financial award applicants required to submit FAFSA. *Program availability:* Part-time. Offers athletic coaching leadership (M Ed); educational leadership (M Ed); integrated arts (M Ed); intervention specialist in early childhood (M Ed); intervention specialist in mild/moderate (M Ed). *Application deadline:* Applications are processed on a rolling basis. *Application fee:* $20. *Application Contact:* Nancy Downs, Secretary, 740-245-7328, Fax: 740-245-7175, E-mail: ndowns@rio.edu. *Director*, Dr. Greg Miller, 740-245-7030, E-mail: gmiller@rio.edu.

UNIVERSITY OF ROCHESTER, Rochester, NY 14627

General Information Independent, coed, university. CGS member. *Enrollment:* 11,168 graduate, professional, and undergraduate students; 3,399 full-time matriculated graduate/professional students (1,583 women), 1,141 part-time matriculated graduate/professional students (697 women). *Enrollment by degree level:* 2,177 master's, 2,206 doctoral, 157 other advanced degrees. *Tuition:* Full-time $47,450; part-time $1482 per credit hour. *Required fees:* $528. Tuition and fees vary according to program. *Graduate housing:* Rooms and/or apartments available on a first-come, first-served basis to single and married students. *Student services:* Campus employment opportunities, campus safety program, career counseling, exercise/wellness program, free psychological counseling, grant writing training, international student services, low-cost health insurance, multicultural affairs office, services for students with disabilities, teacher training. *Library facilities:* Rush Rhees Library plus 7 others. *Collection:* Study areas open 24 hours, 5–7 days a week; students can reserve study rooms. *Research affiliation:* General Motors (chemical engineering, mechanical engineering, biomedical engineering), American Heart and Lung Associations (biochemistry/biophysics, cardiovascular research, environmental toxicology, oral biology, pulmonary medicine, pathology, pharmacology and physiology), Bausch & Lomb (optics, ophthalmology), Fermilab, Jet Propulsion Laboratory, and Lawrence Livermore National Laboratory (physics and astronomy, laser energetics), Johnson & Johnson (biology, neurosurgery, ophthalmology, psychiatry), IBM (computer science, electrical engineering, computer engineering).

Computer facilities: Computer purchase and lease plans are available. 700 computers available on campus for general student use. A campuswide network can be accessed from student residence rooms and from off campus. Online class registration is available.
Website: http://www.rochester.edu/

General Application Contact: Dr. Margaret H. Kearney, RN, Vice Provost and University Dean of Graduate Studies, 585-275-3540, E-mail: margaret.kearney@rochester.edu.

GRADUATE UNITS

Eastman School of Music *Program availability:* Part-time. Offers conducting (MM, DMA); ethnomusicology (MA); jazz studies/contemporary media (MM); music composition (MA, MM, DMA, PhD); music education (MA, MM, DMA, PhD); music theory (PhD); music theory pedagogy (MA); musicology (PhD); performance and literature (MM, DMA); piano accompanying and chamber music (MM, DMA).

Hajim School of Engineering and Applied Sciences Students: 596 full-time (144 women), 23 part-time (7 women); includes 53 minority (9 Black or African American, non-Hispanic/Latino; 1 American Indian or Alaska Native, non-Hispanic/Latino; 18 Asian, non-Hispanic/Latino; 16 Hispanic/Latino; 9 Two or more races, non-Hispanic/Latino), 382 international. Average age 25. 2,605 applicants, 39% accepted, 259 enrolled. *Faculty:* 92 full-time (13 women). Expenses: Contact institution. In 2016, 210 master's, 46 doctorates awarded. *Program availability:* Part-time. Offers alternative energy (MS); biomedical engineering (MS); chemical engineering (MS, PhD); computer science (MS, PhD); electrical and computer engineering (MS); energy and the environment (MS); engineering and applied sciences (MS, PhD); materials science (MS, PhD); mechanical engineering (MS, PhD); optics (MS). *Application deadline:* For fall admission, 1/1 for domestic and international students. *Application fee:* $60. Electronic applications accepted. *Application Contact:* Dr. Margaret Kearney, Dean of Graduate Studies, 585-275-3540, E-mail: margaret.kearney@rochester.edu. *Dean,* Dr. Wendi Heinzelman, 585-273-3958.

Institute of Optics Students: 127 full-time (32 women), 5 part-time (1 woman); includes 13 minority (6 Asian, non-Hispanic/Latino; 4 Hispanic/Latino; 3 Two or more races, non-Hispanic/Latino), 63 international. Average age 25. 287 applicants, 47% accepted, 47 enrolled. *Faculty:* 17 full-time (1 woman). Expenses: Contact institution. *Financial support:* In 2016–17, 140 students received support, including 33 fellowships with full tuition reimbursements available (averaging $32,000 per year), 62 research assistantships with full tuition reimbursements available (averaging $30,000 per year), 60 teaching assistantships (averaging $2,300 per year); career-related internships or fieldwork, traineeships, tuition waivers (partial), and unspecified assistantships also available. Financial award application deadline: 1/15. In 2016, 24 master's, 9 doctorates awarded. Offers optics (MS, PhD). *Application deadline:* For fall admission, 2/1 for domestic students. *Application fee:* $60. Electronic applications accepted. *Application Contact:* Kari Brick, Graduate Program Coordinator, 585-275-7720, E-mail: kari.brick@rochester.edu. *Director of the Institute of Optics,* Xi-Cheng Zhang, 585-275-0333.

Margaret Warner Graduate School of Education and Human Development *Program availability:* Part-time, evening/weekend. Offers counseling (Ed D); education and human development (MS, Ed D); educational administration (Ed D); educational policy (MS); educational policy and theory (PhD); higher education (MS, PhD); higher education student affairs (MS); human development (MS); human development in educational context (PhD); school and community counseling (MS); school counseling (MS); school leadership (MS); teaching and curriculum (MS); teaching, curriculum, and change (PhD).

School of Arts and Sciences Students: 634 full-time (268 women), 5 part-time (1 woman); includes 70 minority (6 Black or African American, non-Hispanic/Latino; 1 American Indian or Alaska Native, non-Hispanic/Latino; 17 Asian, non-Hispanic/Latino; 33 Hispanic/Latino; 13 Two or more races, non-Hispanic/Latino), 210 international. Average age 27. 2,009 applicants, 22% accepted, 145 enrolled. *Faculty:* 229 full-time (58 women). Expenses: Contact institution. In 2016, 115 master's, 91 doctorates awarded. *Program availability:* Part-time. Offers American history (MA, PhD); arts and sciences (MA, MS, PhD, Graduate Certificate); biology (MS, PhD); brain and cognitive sciences (PhD); chemistry (PhD); clinical psychology (PhD); computational linguistics (MS); developmental psychology (PhD); economics (PhD); English (MA, PhD); European history (MA, PhD); geological sciences (MS, PhD); global history (MA, PhD); language documentation (MA); linguistics (MA); literary translation studies (MA, Graduate Certificate); mathematics (PhD); philosophy (PhD); photographic preservation and collections management (MA); physics and astronomy (MA, MS, PhD); political science (PhD); social-personality psychology (PhD); visual and cultural studies (PhD). *Application fee:* $60. Electronic applications accepted. *Application Contact:* Gretchen Briscoe, Recruiting and Marketing Manager, 585-275-5029, E-mail: graduate.admissions@rochester.edu. *Dean of the School of Arts and Sciences,* Gloria Culver, 585-273-5000.

Goergen Institute for Data Science Students: 28 full-time (7 women), 1 part-time (0 women); includes 2 minority (1 Black or African American, non-Hispanic/Latino; 1 Hispanic/Latino), 20 international. Average age 24. 144 applicants, 50% accepted, 29 enrolled. Expenses: Contact institution. *Financial support:* In 2016–17, 33 students received support. Tuition waivers (partial) available. Financial award application deadline: 1/15. In 2016, 20 master's awarded. Offers data science (MS). *Application deadline:* For fall admission, 1/1 for domestic and international students. *Application fee:* $60. Electronic applications accepted. *Application Contact:* Michele Foster, Graduate Coordinator, 585-275-4054, E-mail: michele.foster@rochester.edu. *Director,* Henry Kautz, 585-520-1200, E-mail: kautz@cs.rochester.edu.

School of Medicine and Dentistry *Program availability:* Part-time. Offers medicine (MD); medicine and dentistry (MA, MPH, MS, MD, Certificate). Electronic applications accepted.

Graduate Programs in Medicine and Dentistry *Program availability:* Part-time. Offers biochemistry (PhD); biochemistry and molecular biology (PhD); biophysics (PhD); biophysics, structural and computational biology (PhD); clinical investigation (MS); clinical translational research (MS); dental science (MS); epidemiology (PhD); genetics, genomics and development (PhD); health services research and policy (PhD); marriage and family therapy (MS); medical microbiology (MS, PhD); medical statistics (MS); medicine and dentistry (MA, MPH, MS, PhD); microbiology and immunology (MS, PhD); neurobiology and anatomy (MS); neuroscience (PhD); pathology (PhD); pharmacology (MS, PhD); physiology (MS, PhD); public health (MPH, MS); statistics (MA, PhD); toxicology (MS, PhD); translational biomedical science (PhD). Electronic applications accepted.

School of Nursing Students: 18 full-time (17 women), 240 part-time (199 women); includes 39 minority (18 Black or African American, non-Hispanic/Latino; 4 American Indian or Alaska Native, non-Hispanic/Latino; 6 Asian, non-Hispanic/Latino; 8 Hispanic/Latino; 1 Native Hawaiian or other Pacific Islander, non-Hispanic/Latino; 2 Two or more races, non-Hispanic/Latino), 4 international. Average age 35. 143 applicants, 71% accepted, 87 enrolled. *Faculty:* 61 full-time (50 women), 73 part-time/adjunct (63 women). Expenses: Contact institution. *Financial support:* In 2016–17, 48 students received support, including 2 fellowships with full and partial tuition reimbursements available (averaging $30,000 per year); scholarships/grants, traineeships, health care benefits, tuition waivers (full and partial), and unspecified assistantships also available. Support available to part-time students. Financial award application deadline: 6/30. In 2016, 42 master's, 11 doctorates awarded. *Program availability:* Part-time, blended/hybrid learning. Offers adult gerontological acute care nurse practitioner (MS); adult gerontological primary care nurse practitioner (MS); clinical nurse leader (MS); family nurse practitioner (MS); family psychiatric mental health nurse practitioner (MS); health care organization management and leadership (MS); health practice research (PhD); nursing (DNP); nursing education (MS); pediatric nurse practitioner (MS); pediatric nurse practitioner/neonatal nurse practitioner (MS). *Application deadline:* For fall admission, 4/1 for domestic and international students; for spring admission, 9/1 for

domestic and international students; for summer admission, 1/2 for domestic and international students. *Application fee:* $50. Electronic applications accepted. *Application Contact:* Elaine Andolina, Director of Admissions, 585-275-2375, Fax: 585-756-8299, E-mail: elaine_andolina@urmc.rochester.edu. *Dean,* Dr. Kathy H. Rideout, 585-273-8902, Fax: 585-273-1268, E-mail: kathy_rideout@urmc.rochester.edu.

Simon Business School Students: 464 full-time (166 women), 395 part-time (88 women); includes 107 minority (38 Black or African American, non-Hispanic/Latino; 40 Asian, non-Hispanic/Latino; 23 Hispanic/Latino; 6 Two or more races, non-Hispanic/Latino), 481 international. 5,045 applicants, 27% accepted, 516 enrolled. *Faculty:* 66 full-time (13 women), 22 part-time/adjunct (2 women). Expenses: Contact institution. *Financial support:* In 2016–17, 585 students received support. Fellowships, research assistantships, teaching assistantships, institutionally sponsored loans, scholarships/grants, tuition waivers (full and partial), and unspecified assistantships available. In 2016, 470 master's, 6 doctorates awarded. *Program availability:* Part-time, evening/weekend. Offers accountancy (MS); accounting (PhD); business (MBA, MS, PhD); business administration (MBA, PhD); business analytics (MS); business systems consulting (MBA); competitive and organizational strategy (MBA); computer information systems (PhD); computers and information systems (MBA); corporate accounting (MBA); entrepreneurship (MBA); finance (MS); health sciences management (MBA); marketing (MBA, PhD); marketing analytics (MS); operations management (MBA, PhD); public accounting (MBA). *Application deadline:* For fall admission, 10/15 for domestic and international students; for winter admission, 1/5 for domestic and international students; for spring admission, 3/15 for domestic and international students; for summer admission, 5/15 for domestic and international students. Applications are processed on a rolling basis. *Application fee:* $150. Electronic applications accepted. *Application Contact:* Rebekah S. Lewin, Assistant Dean for Admissions and Financial Aid, 585-275-3533, E-mail: admissions@simon.rochester.edu. *Dean,* Andrew Ainslie, 585-275-3316, E-mail: andrew.ainslie@simon.rochester.edu.

UNIVERSITY OF ST. AUGUSTINE FOR HEALTH SCIENCES, San Marcos, CA 92069

General Information Proprietary, coed, graduate-only institution. *Graduate housing:* On-campus housing not available.

GRADUATE UNITS

Graduate Programs *Program availability:* Part-time, evening/weekend, online learning. Offers athletic training (MHS); executive leadership (MHS); health administration (MHA); health science (DH Sc); health sciences education (Ed D); informatics (MHS); nurse educator (MSN); nurse executive (MSN); nurse informatics (MSN); nursing (MSN, DNP); occupational therapy (TOTD); physical therapy (DPT); teaching and learning (MHS).

UNIVERSITY OF ST. FRANCIS, Joliet, IL 60435-6169

General Information Independent-religious, coed, comprehensive institution. *Enrollment:* 2,578 graduate, professional, and undergraduate students; 400 full-time matriculated graduate/professional students (293 women), 1,051 part-time matriculated graduate/professional students (829 women). *Enrollment by degree level:* 1,231 master's, 158 doctoral, 62 other advanced degrees. *Graduate faculty:* 38 full-time (28 women), 97 part-time/adjunct (69 women). *Tuition:* Part-time $739 per credit hour. *Required fees:* $125 per semester. Part-time tuition and fees vary according to degree level and program. *Graduate housing:* Room and/or apartments available on a first-come, first-served basis to single students; on-campus housing not available to married students. Typical cost: $9672 per year. Room charges vary according to board plan. Housing application deadline: 8/1. *Student services:* Campus employment opportunities, campus safety program, career counseling, free psychological counseling, international student services, multicultural affairs office, services for students with disabilities, teacher training, writing training. *Library facilities:* Brown Library. *Collection:* Books: 113,077 (physical), 4,118 (digital/electronic); Serial titles: 605 (physical), 113 (digital/electronic); Databases: 76. Weekly public service hours: 74; students can reserve study rooms.

Computer facilities: 560 computers available on campus for general student use. A campuswide network can be accessed from student residence rooms and from off campus. Online class registration, billing/payment are available.
Website: http://www.stfrancis.edu/

General Application Contact: Sandra Sloka, Director of Admissions for Graduate and Degree Completion Programs, 800-735-7500, Fax: 815-740-3431, E-mail: ssloka@stfrancis.edu.

GRADUATE UNITS

College of Arts and Sciences Students: 114 full-time (92 women), 26 part-time (24 women); includes 49 minority (17 Black or African American, non-Hispanic/Latino; 1 American Indian or Alaska Native, non-Hispanic/Latino; 7 Asian, non-Hispanic/Latino; 20 Hispanic/Latino; 1 Native Hawaiian or other Pacific Islander, non-Hispanic/Latino; 3 Two or more races, non-Hispanic/Latino), 1 international. Average age 29. 101 applicants, 38% accepted, 24 enrolled. *Faculty:* 9 full-time (7 women). Expenses: Contact institution. *Financial support:* In 2016–17, 15 students received support. Career-related internships or fieldwork, scholarships/grants, and unspecified assistantships available. Support available to part-time students. Financial award applicants required to submit FAFSA. In 2016, 58 master's awarded. Offers forensic social work (Post-Master's Certificate); physician assistant practice (MS); social work (MSW). *Application deadline:* Applications are processed on a rolling basis. *Application fee:* $30. Electronic applications accepted. *Application Contact:* Sandra Sloka, Director of Admissions for Graduate and Degree Completion Programs, 800-735-7500, Fax: 815-740-3431, E-mail: ssloka@stfrancis.edu. *Dean,* Dr. Robert Kase, 815-740-3367, Fax: 815-740-6366.

College of Business and Health Administration Students: 167 full-time (93 women), 256 part-time (177 women); includes 107 minority (56 Black or African American, non-Hispanic/Latino; 12 Asian, non-Hispanic/Latino; 34 Hispanic/Latino; 1 Native Hawaiian or other Pacific Islander, non-Hispanic/Latino; 4 Two or more races, non-Hispanic/Latino), 18 international. Average age 39. 290 applicants, 49% accepted, 112 enrolled. *Faculty:* 12 full-time (1 woman), 21 part-time/adjunct (13 women). Expenses: Contact institution. *Financial support:* In 2016–17, 116 students received support. Scholarships/grants and unspecified assistantships available. Support available to part-time students. Financial award applicants required to submit FAFSA. In 2016, 252 master's, 6 other advanced degrees awarded. *Program availability:* Part-time, evening/weekend, 100% online, blended/hybrid learning. Offers business and health administration (MBA, MS, MSM, Certificate). *Application deadline:* Applications are processed on a rolling basis. *Application fee:* $30. Electronic applications accepted. *Application Contact:* Sandra Sloka, Director of Admissions for Graduate and Degree Completion Programs, 800-735-7500, Fax: 815-740-3431, E-mail: ssloka@stfrancis.edu. *Dean,* Dr. Orlando Griego, 815-740-3395, Fax: 815-740-3537, E-mail: ogriego@stfrancis.edu.

University of St. Francis

School of Business Students: 78 full-time (28 women), 110 part-time (62 women); includes 41 minority (22 Black or African American, non-Hispanic/Latino; 3 Asian, non-Hispanic/Latino; 15 Hispanic/Latino; 1 Two or more races, non-Hispanic/Latino), 8 international. Average age 36. 171 applicants, 44% accepted, 58 enrolled. *Faculty:* 6 full-time (3 women), 12 part-time/adjunct (6 women). Expenses: Contact institution. *Financial support:* In 2016–17, 51 students received support. Career-related internships or fieldwork, scholarships/grants, tuition waivers (partial), and unspecified assistantships available. Support available to part-time students. Financial award applicants required to submit FAFSA. In 2016, 62 master's, 3 other advanced degrees awarded. *Program availability:* Part-time, evening/weekend, 100% online, blended/hybrid learning. Offers accounting (MBA, Certificate); business analytics (MBA, Certificate); finance (MBA, Certificate); health administration (MBA); human resource management (MBA); logistics (Certificate); management (MBA, MSM); training and development (MBA); transportation and logistics (MBA). *Application deadline:* Applications are processed on a rolling basis. *Application fee:* $30. Electronic applications accepted. *Application Contact:* Sandra Sloka, Director of Admissions for Graduate and Degree Completion Programs, 800-735-7500, Fax: 815-740-3431, E-mail: ssloka@stfrancis.edu. *Dean,* Dr. Orlando Griego, 815-740-3395, Fax: 815-740-3537, E-mail: ogriego@stfrancis.edu.

School of Health Administration Students: 83 full-time (61 women), 97 part-time (78 women); includes 46 minority (21 Black or African American, non-Hispanic/Latino; 8 Asian, non-Hispanic/Latino; 14 Hispanic/Latino; 3 Two or more races, non-Hispanic/Latino), 10 international. Average age 41. 83 applicants, 60% accepted, 41 enrolled. *Faculty:* 5 full-time (3 women), 7 part-time/adjunct (5 women). Expenses: Contact institution. *Financial support:* In 2016–17, 57 students received support. Tuition waivers (partial) and unspecified assistantships available. Support available to part-time students. Financial award applicants required to submit FAFSA. In 2016, 130 master's awarded. *Program availability:* Part-time, evening/weekend, 100% online. Offers health administration (MS). *Application deadline:* Applications are processed on a rolling basis. *Application fee:* $30. Electronic applications accepted. *Application Contact:* Sandra Sloka, Director of Admissions for Graduate and Degree Completion Programs, 800-735-7500, Fax: 815-740-3431, E-mail: ssloka@stfrancis.edu. *Dean,* Dr. Orlando Griego, 815-740-3395, Fax: 815-740-3537, E-mail: ogriego@stfrancis.edu.

School of Professional Studies Students: 6 full-time (4 women), 49 part-time (37 women); includes 20 minority (13 Black or African American, non-Hispanic/Latino; 1 Asian, non-Hispanic/Latino; 5 Hispanic/Latino; 1 Native Hawaiian or other Pacific Islander, non-Hispanic/Latino). Average age 42. 36 applicants, 47% accepted, 13 enrolled. *Faculty:* 1 (woman) full-time, 2 part-time/adjunct (both women). Expenses: Contact institution. *Financial support:* In 2016–17, 8 students received support. Tuition waivers (partial) and unspecified assistantships available. Support available to part-time students. Financial award applicants required to submit FAFSA. In 2016, 26 master's, 3 other advanced degrees awarded. *Program availability:* Part-time, evening/weekend, 100% online. Offers e-learning (Certificate); management of training and development (Certificate); training and development (MS); training specialist (Certificate). *Application deadline:* Applications are processed on a rolling basis. *Application fee:* $30. Electronic applications accepted. *Application Contact:* Sandra Sloka, Director of Admissions for Graduate and Degree Completion Programs, 800-735-7500, Fax: 815-740-3431, E-mail: ssloka@stfrancis.edu. *Dean,* Dr. Orlando Griego, 815-740-3395, Fax: 815-740-3537, E-mail: ogriego@stfrancis.edu.

College of Education Students: 34 full-time (26 women), 420 part-time (318 women); includes 92 minority (51 Black or African American, non-Hispanic/Latino; 5 Asian, non-Hispanic/Latino; 31 Hispanic/Latino; 5 Two or more races, non-Hispanic/Latino), 4 international. Average age 36. 242 applicants, 48% accepted, 96 enrolled. *Faculty:* 11 full-time (8 women), 60 part-time/adjunct (42 women). Expenses: Contact institution. *Financial support:* In 2016–17, 48 students received support. Career-related internships or fieldwork and unspecified assistantships available. Support available to part-time students. Financial award applicants required to submit FAFSA. In 2016, 229 master's, 44 doctorates, 10 other advanced degrees awarded. *Program availability:* Part-time, evening/weekend, 100% online, blended/hybrid learning. Offers educational leadership (MS, Ed D); elementary education (M Ed); reading (MS); secondary education (M Ed); special education (M Ed); teaching and learning (MS); TESOL (Certificate). *Application deadline:* Applications are processed on a rolling basis. *Application fee:* $30. Electronic applications accepted. *Application Contact:* Sandra Sloka, Director of Admissions for Graduate and Degree Completion Programs, 800-735-7500, Fax: 815-740-3431, E-mail: ssloka@stfrancis.edu. *Dean,* Dr. John Gambro, 815-740-3829, Fax: 815-740-2264, E-mail: jgambro@stfrancis.edu.

Leach College of Nursing Students: 85 full-time (82 women), 349 part-time (310 women); includes 149 minority (68 Black or African American, non-Hispanic/Latino; 1 American Indian or Alaska Native, non-Hispanic/Latino; 25 Asian, non-Hispanic/Latino; 40 Hispanic/Latino; 3 Native Hawaiian or other Pacific Islander, non-Hispanic/Latino; 12 Two or more races, non-Hispanic/Latino). Average age 41. 331 applicants, 41% accepted, 105 enrolled. *Faculty:* 6 full-time (all women), 16 part-time/adjunct (14 women). Expenses: Contact institution. *Financial support:* In 2016–17, 118 students received support. Career-related internships or fieldwork and scholarships/grants available. Support available to part-time students. Financial award applicants required to submit FAFSA. In 2016, 104 master's, 11 doctorates, 14 other advanced degrees awarded. *Program availability:* Part-time, evening/weekend, 100% online. Offers family nurse practitioner (MSN, Post-Master's Certificate); family psychology/mental health nurse practitioner (MSN, Post-Master's Certificate); nursing administration (MSN); nursing education (MSN); nursing practice (DNP); teaching in nursing (Certificate). *Application deadline:* Applications are processed on a rolling basis. *Application fee:* $30. Electronic applications accepted. *Application Contact:* Sandra Sloka, Director of Admissions for Graduate and Degree Completion Programs, 800-735-7500, Fax: 815-740-3431, E-mail: ssloka@stfrancis.edu. *Dean,* Dr. Carol Wilson, 815-740-3840, Fax: 815-740-4243, E-mail: cwilson@stfrancis.edu.

UNIVERSITY OF SAINT FRANCIS, Fort Wayne, IN 46808-3994

General Information Independent-religious, coed, comprehensive institution. *Enrollment:* 2,212 graduate, professional, and undergraduate students; 192 full-time matriculated graduate/professional students (140 women), 210 part-time matriculated graduate/professional students (129 women). *Enrollment by degree level:* 390 master's, 2 other advanced degrees. *Graduate faculty:* 26 full-time (14 women), 33 part-time/adjunct (20 women). *Tuition:* Full-time $16,290; part-time $905 per credit hour. *Required fees:* $25 per credit hour. $140 per semester. Tuition and fees vary according to campus/location and program. *Graduate housing:* Room and/or apartments available on a first-come, first-served basis to single students; on-campus housing not available to married students. Typical cost: $10,114 (including board). Room and board charges vary according to board plan and housing facility selected. Housing application deadline: 8/23. *Student services:* Campus employment opportunities, campus safety program,

career counseling, exercise/wellness program, multicultural affairs office, services for students with disabilities. *Library facilities:* Lee and Jim Vann Library. *Collection:* Books: 71,000 (physical), 152,000 (digital/electronic); Serial titles: 805 (physical), 42,445 (digital/electronic); Databases: 112. Weekly public service hours: 86; study areas open 24 hours, 5–7 days a week; students can reserve study rooms.

Computer facilities: Computer purchase and lease plans are available. 435 computers available on campus for general student use. A campuswide network can be accessed from student residence rooms and from off campus. Online class registration is available.
Website: http://www.sf.edu/

General Application Contact: Kyle Richardson, Enrollment Service Specialist, 260-399-7700 Ext. 6310, E-mail: krichardson@sf.edu.

GRADUATE UNITS

Graduate School Students: 192 full-time (140 women), 200 part-time (124 women); includes 57 minority (32 Black or African American, non-Hispanic/Latino; 4 Asian, non-Hispanic/Latino; 16 Hispanic/Latino; 1 Native Hawaiian or other Pacific Islander, non-Hispanic/Latino; 4 Two or more races, non-Hispanic/Latino), 2 international. Average age 32. 147 applicants, 99% accepted, 106 enrolled. *Faculty:* 26 full-time (14 women), 33 part-time/adjunct (20 women). Expenses: Contact institution. *Financial support:* In 2016–17, 46 students received support. Federal Work-Study, scholarships/grants, and unspecified assistantships available. Financial award application deadline: 3/10; financial award applicants required to submit FAFSA. In 2016, 183 master's, 2 other advanced degrees awarded. *Program availability:* Part-time, evening/weekend, 100% online, blended/hybrid learning. Offers clinical mental health counseling (MS, Post Master's Certificate); education (MAT); family nurse practitioner (MSN, Post Master's Certificate); nurse anesthesia (DNP); physician assistant studies (MS); psychology (MS); school counseling (MS Ed); secondary education (MAT); special education (MS Ed); studio art (MA). *Application deadline:* Applications are processed on a rolling basis. *Application fee:* $0. Electronic applications accepted. *Application Contact:* Kyle Richardson, Enrollment Services Specialist, 260-399-7700 Ext. 6310, E-mail: krichardson@sf.edu. *Associate Vice President of Academic Affairs,* Joseph M Friona, 260-399-7700 Ext. 8400, E-mail: jfriona@sf.edu.

Keith Busse School of Business and Entrepreneurial Leadership Students: 77 full-time (51 women), 102 part-time (45 women); includes 40 minority (22 Black or African American, non-Hispanic/Latino; 3 Asian, non-Hispanic/Latino; 12 Hispanic/Latino; 1 Native Hawaiian or other Pacific Islander, non-Hispanic/Latino; 2 Two or more races, non-Hispanic/Latino). Average age 33. 71 applicants, 100% accepted, 46 enrolled. *Faculty:* 6 full-time (3 women), 13 part-time/adjunct (4 women). Expenses: Contact institution. *Financial support:* Application deadline: 3/10; applicants required to submit FAFSA. In 2016, 107 master's awarded. *Program availability:* Part-time, evening/weekend, online only, 100% online. Offers business administration (MBA); environmental health (MEH); healthcare administration (MHA); organizational leadership (MOL). *Application deadline:* Applications are processed on a rolling basis. *Application fee:* $0. Electronic applications accepted. *Application Contact:* Kyle Richardson, Enrollment Services Specialist, 260-399-7700 Ext. 6310, E-mail: krichardson@sf.edu. *Director of Virtual Campus Business Programs,* Dr. Karen Palumbo, 260-399-7700 Ext. 8312, Fax: 260-399-8174, E-mail: kpalumbo@sf.edu.

UNIVERSITY OF SAINT JOSEPH, West Hartford, CT 06117-2700

General Information Independent-religious, coed, primarily women, comprehensive institution. *Enrollment:* 2,467 graduate, professional, and undergraduate students; 541 full-time matriculated graduate/professional students (435 women), 1,032 part-time matriculated graduate/professional students (852 women). *Enrollment by degree level:* 1,223 master's, 269 doctoral, 50 other advanced degrees. *Graduate faculty:* 68 full-time (47 women), 8 part-time/adjunct (7 women). *Tuition:* Full-time $14,580; part-time $729 per credit hour. *Required fees:* $920; $46 per credit hour. Tuition and fees vary according to course load, degree level and program. *Graduate housing:* Room and/or apartments available on a first-come, first-served basis to single students; on-campus housing not available to married students. Typical cost: $6250 per year ($11,095 including board). Room and board charges vary according to board plan and housing facility selected. Housing application deadline: 6/1. *Student services:* Campus employment opportunities, campus safety program, career counseling, exercise/wellness program, free psychological counseling, multicultural affairs office, services for students with disabilities, teacher training, writing training. *Library facilities:* Pope Pius XII Library.

Computer facilities: 72 computers available on campus for general student use. A campuswide network can be accessed from student residence rooms and from off campus. Online class registration is available.
Website: http://www.usj.edu/

General Application Contact: Admissions Office, 860-231-5261, E-mail: graduate@usj.edu.

GRADUATE UNITS

Department of Biology *Program availability:* Part-time, online learning. Offers biology (MS). Electronic applications accepted.

Department of Business Administration *Program availability:* Part-time, evening/weekend. Offers management (MS). Electronic applications accepted.

Department of Chemistry *Program availability:* Part-time, evening/weekend, online learning. Offers biochemistry (MS); chemistry (MS). Electronic applications accepted.

Department of Counseling and Applied Behavioral Studies *Program availability:* Part-time, evening/weekend. Offers applied behavioral analysis (Graduate Certificate); clinical mental health counseling (MA); school counseling (MA). Electronic applications accepted.

Department of Education *Program availability:* Part-time, evening/weekend. Offers curriculum and instruction (MA); educational technology (MA); literacy internship (MA); multiple intelligences (MA); reading/language (MA); TESOL (MA). Electronic applications accepted.

Department of Nursing *Program availability:* Part-time, evening/weekend. Offers family nurse practitioner (MS); family psychiatric/mental health nurse practitioner (MS); nurse educator (MS); nursing practice (DNP). Electronic applications accepted.

Department of Nutrition and Dietetics *Program availability:* Part-time, evening/weekend, online learning. Offers nutrition (MS). Electronic applications accepted.

Department of Special Education *Program availability:* Part-time, evening/weekend. Offers autism and applied behavior analysis (MS); special education (MA). Electronic applications accepted.

Program in Gerontology *Program availability:* Part-time, evening/weekend. Offers gerontology (Certificate). Electronic applications accepted.

Program in Marriage and Family Therapy *Program availability:* Part-time, evening/weekend. Offers marriage and family therapy (MA). Electronic applications accepted.

School of Pharmacy Offers pharmacy (Pharm D). Electronic applications accepted.

UNIVERSITY OF SAINT MARY, Leavenworth, KS 66048-5082

General Information Independent-religious, coed, comprehensive institution. *Enrollment:* 1,409 graduate, professional, and undergraduate students; 462 full-time matriculated graduate/professional students (284 women), 110 part-time matriculated graduate/professional students (81 women). *Enrollment by degree level:* 452 master's, 120 doctoral. *Tuition:* Full-time $22,140; part-time $615 per credit hour. Tuition and fees vary according to campus/location and program. *Graduate housing:* Room and/or apartments available on a first-come, first-served basis to single students; on-campus housing not available to married students. *Student services:* Career counseling, free psychological counseling. *Library facilities:* De Paul Library plus 1 other. *Collection:* Books: 105,000 (physical), 103,000 (digital/electronic); Serial titles: 10 (physical), 12,000 (digital/electronic); Databases: 59. Weekly public service hours: 68; students can reserve study rooms.

Computer facilities: 30 computers available on campus for general student use. A campuswide network can be accessed from student residence rooms and from off campus. Online class registration is available.
Website: http://www.stmary.edu/

General Application Contact: Dr. Ron Logan, Graduate Dean, 913-345-8288, Fax: 913-345-2802, E-mail: loganr@stmary.edu.

GRADUATE UNITS

Graduate Programs Students: 465 full-time (278 women), 88 part-time (61 women); includes 118 minority (43 Black or African American, non-Hispanic/Latino; 4 American Indian or Alaska Native, non-Hispanic/Latino; 19 Asian, non-Hispanic/Latino; 43 Hispanic/Latino; 1 Native Hawaiian or other Pacific Islander, non-Hispanic/Latino; 8 Two or more races, non-Hispanic/Latino), 10 international. Average age 34. Expenses: Contact institution. *Financial support:* Unspecified assistantships available. Financial award applicants required to submit FAFSA. *Program availability:* Part-time, evening/weekend, online learning. Offers counseling psychology (MA); education (MA); elementary education (MA); enterprise risk management (MBA); finance (MBA); general management (MBA); health care management (MBA); human resource management (MBA); marketing and advertising management (MBA); nurse administrator (MSN); nurse educator (MSN); physical therapy (DPT); psychology (MA); special education (MA); teaching (MAT). *Application deadline:* Applications are processed on a rolling basis. *Application fee:* $25. Electronic applications accepted. *Application Contact:* Dr. Ron Logan, Graduate Dean, 913-758-4338, E-mail: loganr@stmary.edu.

UNIVERSITY OF SAINT MARY OF THE LAKE–MUNDELEIN SEMINARY, Mundelein, IL 60060

General Information Independent-religious, men only, graduate-only institution. *Enrollment by degree level:* 221 master's, 19 doctoral, 26 other advanced degrees. *Graduate faculty:* 60 full-time (6 women), 21 part-time/adjunct (9 women). *Tuition:* Full-time $25,366. *Required fees:* $300. Full-time tuition and fees vary according to program. *Graduate housing:* Room and/or apartments guaranteed to single students; on-campus housing not available to married students. Typical cost: $10,714 (including board). Room and board charges vary according to campus/location. Housing application deadline: 8/1. *Student services:* Campus employment opportunities, campus safety program, international student services, low-cost health insurance, multicultural affairs office. *Library facilities:* Feehan Memorial Library and McEssy Theological Resource Center. *Collection:* Books: 181,691 (physical), 605 (digital/electronic); Serial titles: 381 (physical), 116 (digital/electronic); Databases: 18. Weekly public service hours: 84.

Computer facilities: 20 computers available on campus for general student use. A campuswide network can be accessed from student residence rooms and from off campus.
Website: http://www.usml.edu/

General Application Contact: Very Rev. John Kartje, Rector-President, 847-566-6401, Fax: 847-932-3305, E-mail: mulz@usml.edu.

GRADUATE UNITS

Graduate and Professional Programs Students: 266 full-time (8 women); includes 10 minority (2 Black or African American, non-Hispanic/Latino; 3 Asian, non-Hispanic/Latino; 5 Hispanic/Latino), 78 international. 99 applicants, 81% accepted, 80 enrolled. *Faculty:* 60 full-time (6 women), 21 part-time/adjunct (9 women). Expenses: Contact institution. *Financial support:* Career-related internships or fieldwork available. In 2016, 34 master's awarded. Offers liturgical studies (MA); ministry (D Min); pastoral studies (MA); theology (M Div). *Application deadline:* For fall admission, 8/1 for domestic and international students. Applications are processed on a rolling basis. *Application fee:* $0. Electronic applications accepted. *Application Contact:* Very Rev. John Kartje, Rector-President, 847-566-6401, Fax: 847-932-3305. *Dean of the Graduate School,* Very Rev. Thomas A. Baima, 847-566-6401.

UNIVERSITY OF ST. MICHAEL'S COLLEGE, Toronto, ON M5S 1J4, Canada

General Information Independent-religious, coed, graduate-only institution. *Graduate housing:* Rooms and/or apartments available on a first-come, first-served basis to single and married students. Housing application deadline: 8/15.

GRADUATE UNITS

Faculty of Theology *Program availability:* Part-time. Offers Catholic leadership (MA); eastern Christian studies (Diploma); religious education (Diploma); theological studies (Diploma); theology (M Div, MA, MRE, MTS, D Min, PhD, Th D); theology and Jewish studies (MA). Th D offered jointly with University of Toronto. Electronic applications accepted.

UNIVERSITY OF ST. THOMAS, St. Paul, MN 55105-1096

General Information Independent-religious, coed, university. *Enrollment:* 9,983 graduate, professional, and undergraduate students; 1,235 full-time matriculated graduate/professional students (682 women), 2,637 part-time matriculated graduate/professional students (1,422 women). *Enrollment by degree level:* 2,801 master's, 582 doctoral, 452 other advanced degrees. *Graduate faculty:* 173 full-time (64 women), 264 part-time/adjunct (121 women). *Tuition:* Full-time $19,354; part-time $1320 per credit. *One-time fee:* $214. Tuition and fees vary according to course load, degree level, program and reciprocity agreements. *Graduate housing:* Room and/or apartments available on a first-come, first-served basis to single students; on-campus housing not available to married students. Typical cost: $4460 per year ($6213 including board). Room and board charges vary according to board plan and housing facility selected. Housing application deadline: 5/1. *Student services:* Campus employment opportunities, campus safety program, career counseling, child daycare facilities, exercise/wellness program, free psychological counseling, international student services, low-cost health insurance, multicultural affairs office, services for students with disabilities. *Library facilities:* O'Shaughnessy-Frey Library plus 7 others. *Collection:* Books: 502,033 (physical), 251,462 (digital/electronic); Serial titles: 16,463 (physical), 118,059 (digital/electronic); Databases: 406. Students can reserve study rooms.

Computer facilities: A campuswide network can be accessed from student residence rooms and from off campus. Online class registration is available.
Website: http://www.stthomas.edu/

General Application Contact: E-mail: admissions@stthomas.edu.

GRADUATE UNITS

Graduate Studies Expenses: Contact institution. *Program availability:* Part-time, evening/weekend, online learning. *Executive Vice President and Provost,* Dr. Richard G. Plumb, 651-962-6720, Fax: 651-962-6702, E-mail: plum0019@stthomas.edu.

College of Arts and Sciences Expenses: Contact institution. *Financial support:* Fellowships, research assistantships, teaching assistantships, career-related internships or fieldwork, institutionally sponsored loans, and scholarships/grants available. Support available to part-time students. Financial award application deadline: 4/1; financial award applicants required to submit FAFSA. *Program availability:* Part-time, evening/weekend. Offers art history (MA); arts and sciences (MA, Ed D); Catholic studies (MA); choral (MA); English (MA); instrumental (MA); Kodaly (MA); leadership in music education (Ed D); Orff Schulwerk (MA); piano pedagogy (MA). *Application deadline:* For fall admission, 4/1 for domestic students, 5/1 priority date for international students; for spring admission, 11/1 for domestic students, 10/1 priority date for international students. *Application fee:* $50. *Dean,* Dr. Terence Langan, 651-962-6001, Fax: 651-962-6004, E-mail: t9langan@stthomas.edu.

College of Education, Leadership and Counseling Expenses: Contact institution. *Financial support:* Research assistantships, career-related internships or fieldwork, institutionally sponsored loans, scholarships/grants, and unspecified assistantships available. Support available to part-time students. Financial award application deadline: 8/1; financial award applicants required to submit FAFSA. *Program availability:* Part-time, evening/weekend, 100% online, blended/hybrid learning. Offers counseling psychology (MA, Psy D); education leadership and administration (MA); education, leadership and counseling (MA, Ed D, Psy D, Certificate, Ed S); educational leadership and learning (Ed D); executive coaching (Certificate); K-12 administration (Ed S); leadership in student affairs (MA); organization development and change (MA, Ed D); public safety and law enforcement leadership (MA); special education (MA, Certificate, Ed S); teacher education (MA). *Application deadline:* For fall admission, 7/15 priority date for domestic students, 7/15 for international students; for spring admission, 12/9 priority date for domestic students, 12/9 for international students; for summer admission, 4/3 for domestic and international students. Applications are processed on a rolling basis. Electronic applications accepted. *Dean,* Dr. Joseph L. Kreitzer, 651-962-6032, Fax: 651-962-4169, E-mail: jlkreitzer@stthomas.edu.

Opus College of Business Expenses: Contact institution. Offers accountancy (MS); business (MBA, MS); business administration (MBA); executive business administration (MBA); health care business administration (MBA); health care communication (MBA). *Application Contact:* Tiffany Cork, Director of Recruiting and Admissions, 651-962-8801, Fax: 651-962-4129, E-mail: ustmba@stthomas.edu. *Dean,* Dr. Stefanie Lenway, 651-962-4200, Fax: 651-962-4129, E-mail: ocbdean@stthomas.edu.

The Saint Paul Seminary School of Divinity Expenses: Contact institution. *Financial support:* Fellowships, research assistantships, institutionally sponsored loans, and scholarships/grants available. Support available to part-time students. Financial award application deadline: 4/1; financial award applicants required to submit FAFSA. *Program availability:* Part-time, evening/weekend. Offers pastoral ministry (MAPM); religious education (MARE); theology (MA). *Application deadline:* For fall admission, 6/1 priority date for domestic students. Applications are processed on a rolling basis. *Application fee:* $40. Electronic applications accepted. *Application Contact:* Rev. Peter Williams, Vice Rector for Formation, 651-962-5775, Fax: 651-962-5790, E-mail: will2750@stthomas.edu. *Rector/Vice President,* Rev. Msgr. Aloysius R. Callaghan, 651-962-5052, Fax: 651-962-5790, E-mail: arcallaghan@stthomas.edu.

School of Engineering Expenses: Contact institution. *Financial support:* Fellowships, research assistantships, institutionally sponsored loans, and scholarships/grants available. Support available to part-time students. Financial award application deadline: 4/1; financial award applicants required to submit FAFSA. Offers data science (MS); electrical engineering (MS); information technology (MS); manufacturing engineering (MS); manufacturing systems (Certificate); mechanical engineering (MS); medical device development (Certificate); regulatory science (MS); software engineering (MS); software management (MS); systems engineering (MS); technology leadership (Certificate); technology management (MS). *Application deadline:* For fall admission, 8/1 priority date for domestic students; for spring admission, 1/1 priority date for domestic students. Applications are processed on a rolling basis. *Application fee:* $50. Electronic applications accepted. *Application Contact:* Tina M. Hansen, Graduate Program Manager, 651-962-5755, Fax: 651-962-6419, E-mail: tina.hansen@stthomas.edu. *Dean,* Don Weinkauf, 651-962-5760, Fax: 651-962-6419, E-mail: dhweinkauf@stthomas.edu.

School of Law Expenses: Contact institution. *Financial support:* Scholarships/grants available. Financial award application deadline: 7/1; financial award applicants required to submit FAFSA. Offers law (JD); organizational ethics and compliance (LL M, MSL); U.S. law (LL M). *Application deadline:* For fall admission, 7/1 priority date for domestic and international students. Applications are processed on a rolling basis. *Application fee:* $0. Electronic applications accepted. *Application Contact:* Cari Haaland, Assistant Dean for Admissions, 651-962-4872, Fax: 651-962-4876, E-mail: lawschool@stthomas.edu. *Dean,* Robert K. Vischer, 651-962-4838, Fax: 651-962-4881, E-mail: rkvischer@stthomas.edu.

School of Social Work Expenses: Contact institution. *Financial support:* Fellowships, research assistantships, career-related internships or fieldwork, Federal Work-Study, institutionally sponsored loans, scholarships/grants, and unspecified assistantships available. Support available to part-time students. Financial award application deadline: 7/1; financial award applicants required to submit FAFSA. *Program availability:* Part-time, evening/weekend, blended/hybrid learning. Offers social work (MSW). Programs offered in collaboration with St. Catherine University. *Application deadline:* For fall admission, 1/10 for domestic students. *Application fee:* $35. Electronic applications accepted. *Application Contact:* Mary Palin, Graduate Admissions Counselor, 651-690-6185, Fax: 651-690-6549, E-mail: mbpalin@stkate.edu. *Dean and Professor,* Dr. Barbara W. Shank, 651-962-5801, Fax: 651-962-5819, E-mail: bwshank@stthomas.edu.

UNIVERSITY OF ST. THOMAS, Houston, TX 77006-4696

General Information Independent-religious, coed, comprehensive institution. *Enrollment:* 3,312 graduate, professional, and undergraduate students; 315 full-time matriculated graduate/professional students (140 women), 1,267 part-time matriculated graduate/professional students (973 women). *Enrollment by degree level:* 1,522 master's, 25 doctoral, 35 other advanced degrees. *Graduate faculty:* 113 full-time (49 women), 61 part-time/adjunct (30 women). *Tuition:* Full-time $20,934; part-time $1163 per credit hour. *Required fees:* $81 per semester. One-time fee: $100. Part-time tuition and fees vary according to course level, course load, campus/location and program. *Graduate housing:* Room and/or apartments available on a first-come, first-served basis to single students; on-campus housing not available to married students. *Student services:* Campus employment opportunities, campus safety program, career counseling, free psychological counseling, international student services, services for students with disabilities. *Library facilities:* Doherty Library. *Collection:* 262,422 (physical), 2,491 (digital/electronic); Serial titles: 78,316 (physical), 78,316 (digital/electronic); Databases: 265. Weekly public service hours: 100.

Computer facilities: Computer purchase and lease plans are available. 390 computers available on campus for general student use. A campuswide network can be accessed from student residence rooms. Online class registration is available.
Website: http://www.stthom.edu/

General Application Contact: Dr. Ravi Srinivas, Associate Vice President for Academic Affairs, 713-525-3804, Fax: 713-525-6924, E-mail: srinivas@stthom.edu.

GRADUATE UNITS

Cameron School of Business Students: 178 full-time (86 women), 222 part-time (127 women); includes 182 minority (38 Black or African American, non-Hispanic/Latino; 36 Asian, non-Hispanic/Latino; 104 Hispanic/Latino; 4 Two or more races, non-Hispanic/Latino), 115 international. Average age 31. 144 applicants, 97% accepted, 72 enrolled. *Faculty:* 26 full-time (8 women), 7 part-time/adjunct (2 women). Expenses: Contact institution. *Financial support:* In 2016–17, 56 students received support, including research assistantships with partial tuition reimbursements available (averaging $3,000 per year); Federal Work-Study, scholarships/grants, unspecified assistantships, and state work-study, institutional employment also available. Support available to part-time students. Financial award application deadline: 4/15; financial award applicants required to submit FAFSA. In 2016, 164 master's awarded. *Program availability:* Part-time, evening/weekend. Offers business (MBA, MCTM, MIB, MSA, MSF). *Application deadline:* For fall admission, 7/15 for domestic and international students; for winter admission, 7/15 for domestic and international students; for spring admission, 11/15 for domestic students, 10/15 for international students. Applications are processed on a rolling basis. *Application fee:* $35. Electronic applications accepted. *Application Contact:* Fran Wilson Mayes, Academic Coordinator, 713-525-2110, Fax: 713-525-2110, E-mail: cameron@stthom.edu. *Dean,* Dr. Beena George, 713-525-2100, Fax: 713-525-2110, E-mail: cameron@stthom.edu.

Center for Faith and Culture Students: 1 full-time (0 women), 15 part-time (9 women); includes 8 minority (4 Black or African American, non-Hispanic/Latino; 2 Asian, non-Hispanic/Latino; 2 Hispanic/Latino). Average age 44. 2 applicants, 100% accepted. *Faculty:* 2 full-time (0 women), 1 part-time/adjunct (0 women). Expenses: Contact institution. *Financial support:* In 2016–17, 11 students received support. Federal Work-Study, scholarships/grants, and state work-study, institutional employment available. Support available to part-time students. Financial award application deadline: 4/15; financial award applicants required to submit FAFSA. In 2016, 3 master's awarded. *Program availability:* Part-time. Offers faith and culture (MA). *Application deadline:* For fall admission, 7/1 for domestic students, 6/1 for international students; for spring admission, 11/1 for domestic students, 10/1 for international students. Applications are processed on a rolling basis. *Application fee:* $35. Electronic applications accepted. *Application Contact:* Dr. Adam Martinez, Program Director, 713-942-5066, E-mail: cfc@stthom.edu. *Director,* Fr. Donald S. Nesti, 713-942-5066, E-mail: cfc@stthom.edu.

Center for Thomistic Studies Students: 8 full-time (3 women), 26 part-time (3 women); includes 5 minority (1 Asian, non-Hispanic/Latino; 4 Hispanic/Latino; 2 international. Average age 34. 6 applicants, 100% accepted, 5 enrolled. *Faculty:* 6 full-time (1 woman). Expenses: Contact institution. *Financial support:* In 2016–17, 18 students received support. Fellowships with tuition reimbursements available, teaching assistantships, Federal Work-Study, scholarships/grants, unspecified assistantships, and state work-study, institutional employment available. Support available to part-time students. Financial award application deadline: 2/1; financial award applicants required to submit FAFSA. *Program availability:* Part-time. Offers philosophy (MA, PhD). *Application deadline:* For fall admission, 2/1 priority date for domestic and international students. Applications are processed on a rolling basis. *Application fee:* $35. Electronic applications accepted. *Application Contact:* Valerie Hall, Administrative Assistant II, 713-525-3591, Fax: 713-942-3464, E-mail: hallvl@stthom.edu. *Director,* Dr. Thomas Osborne, 713-942-3483, Fax: 713-942-3464, E-mail: osborntm@stthom.edu.

Program in Liberal Arts Students: 9 full-time (7 women), 50 part-time (41 women); includes 31 minority (10 Black or African American, non-Hispanic/Latino; 2 Asian, non-Hispanic/Latino; 19 Hispanic/Latino). Average age 38. 18 applicants, 100% accepted, 11 enrolled. *Faculty:* 24 full-time (9 women), 13 part-time/adjunct (7 women). Expenses: Contact institution. *Financial support:* In 2016–17, 15 students received support. Federal Work-Study, scholarships/grants, and state work-study, institutional employment available. Support available to part-time students. Financial award application deadline: 4/15; financial award applicants required to submit FAFSA. In 2016, 35 master's awarded. *Program availability:* Part-time, evening/weekend. Offers liberal arts (MLA). *Application deadline:* Applications are processed on a rolling basis. *Application fee:* $35. Electronic applications accepted. *Application Contact:* Kate Henderson, Program Coordinator, 713-525-3556, Fax: 713-525-6924, E-mail: mla@stthom.edu. *Associate Vice President for Academic Affairs/Dean of Extended Programs/MLA Director,* Dr. Ravi Srinivas, 713-525-3804, Fax: 713-525-6924, E-mail: mla@stthom.edu.

School of Arts and Sciences Students: 9 full-time (6 women), 17 part-time (10 women); includes 16 minority (3 Black or African American, non-Hispanic/Latino; 1 Asian, non-Hispanic/Latino; 12 Hispanic/Latino). Average age 33. 14 applicants, 86% accepted, 9 enrolled. *Faculty:* 2 full-time (0 women), 4 part-time/adjunct (all women). Expenses: Contact institution. *Financial support:* In 2016–17, 23 students received support. Federal Work-Study, scholarships/grants, and state work-study, institutional employment available. Support available to part-time students. Financial award application deadline: 4/15; financial award applicants required to submit FAFSA. In 2016, 7 master's awarded. *Program availability:* Part-time. Offers public policy administration (MPPA); sacred music (MSM). *Application deadline:* For fall admission, 7/15 priority date for domestic and international students; for spring admission, 12/1 priority date for domestic and international students; for summer admission, 5/1 priority date for domestic and international students. Applications are processed on a rolling basis. *Application fee:* $35. Electronic applications accepted. *Application Contact:* Todd Boutte, Director of Graduate Admissions, 713-942-3403, E-mail: bouttet@stthom.edu.

Interim Dean, School of Arts and Sciences, Dr. John W. Starner, Jr., 713-525-3527, E-mail: starner@stthom.edu.

School of Education and Human Services Students: 65 full-time (61 women), 719 part-time (645 women); includes 515 minority (169 Black or African American, non-Hispanic/Latino; 25 Asian, non-Hispanic/Latino; 315 Hispanic/Latino; 2 Native Hawaiian or other Pacific Islander, non-Hispanic/Latino; 4 Two or more races, non-Hispanic/Latino), 24 international. Average age 36. 297 applicants, 92% accepted, 211 enrolled. *Faculty:* 44 full-time (29 women), 31 part-time/adjunct (17 women). Expenses: Contact institution. *Financial support:* In 2016–17, 52 students received support. Federal Work-Study, scholarships/grants, and state work-study, institutional employment available. Support available to part-time students. Financial award application deadline: 4/15; financial award applicants required to submit FAFSA. In 2016, 403 master's awarded. *Program availability:* Part-time, evening/weekend, online learning. Offers all level education (M Ed); bilingual/dual language (M Ed); Catholic school teaching (M Ed); Catholic/private school leadership (M Ed); counselor education (M Ed); curriculum and instruction (M Ed); education (Ed D); educational leadership (M Ed); elementary teaching (M Ed); English as a second language (M Ed); exceptionality/educational diagnostician (M Ed); exceptionality/special education (M Ed); generalist (M Ed); reading (M Ed); secondary teaching (M Ed); teaching (MAT). *Application deadline:* Applications are processed on a rolling basis. *Application fee:* $35. Electronic applications accepted. *Application Contact:* Rita Paredes, Administrative Assistant, 713-525-3442, Fax: 713-525-3871, E-mail: rparede@stthom.edu. *Dean,* Dr. Robert LeBlanc, 713-525-3540, Fax: 713-525-3871, E-mail: education@stthom.edu.

School of Theology Students: 89 full-time (1 woman), 70 part-time (24 women); includes 62 minority (5 Black or African American, non-Hispanic/Latino; 22 Asian, non-Hispanic/Latino; 33 Hispanic/Latino; 2 Two or more races, non-Hispanic/Latino), 20 international. Average age 37. 50 applicants, 100% accepted, 37 enrolled. *Faculty:* 8 full-time (2 women), 5 part-time/adjunct (0 women). Expenses: Contact institution. *Financial support:* In 2016–17, 4 students received support. Scholarships/grants available. Support available to part-time students. Financial award application deadline: 4/15; financial award applicants required to submit FAFSA. In 2016, 32 master's awarded. *Program availability:* Part-time. Offers divinity (M Div); pastoral studies (MAPS); theological studies (MA). *Application deadline:* Applications are processed on a rolling basis. *Application fee:* $10. Electronic applications accepted. *Application Contact:* Connie M. Henry, Office Manager, 713-686-4345 Ext. 231, Fax: 713-683-8673, E-mail: sms@stthom.edu. *Dean,* Dr. Sandra C. Magie, 713-686-4345 Ext. 242, Fax: 713-683-8673, E-mail: smagie@stthom.edu.

UNIVERSITY OF SAN DIEGO, San Diego, CA 92110-2492

General Information Independent-religious, coed, university. *Enrollment:* 8,508 graduate, professional, and undergraduate students; 1,435 full-time matriculated graduate/professional students (870 women), 1,189 part-time matriculated graduate/professional students (678 women). *Enrollment by degree level:* 1,708 master's, 915 doctoral, 1 other advanced degree. *Graduate faculty:* 163 full-time (70 women), 222 part-time/adjunct (171 women). *Graduate housing:* Rooms and/or apartments available on a first-come, first-served basis to single and married students. Housing application deadline: 5/1. *Student services:* Campus employment opportunities, career counseling, child daycare facilities, exercise/wellness program, free psychological counseling, international student services, low-cost health insurance, multicultural affairs office, services for students with disabilities, teacher training. *Library facilities:* Helen K. and James S. Copley Library plus 1 other. *Collection:* Books: 713,623 (physical), 817,563 (digital/electronic); Serial titles: 15,789 (physical), 975 (digital/electronic). Weekly public service hours: 116; students can reserve study rooms. *Research affiliation:* Leon R. Hubbard Hatchery (marine science), Southwest Fisheries Science Center (marine science), Hubbs Seaworld Research Institute (marine science), Tijuana River National Estuarine Research Reserve (marine science), Old Globe Theater (dramatic arts).

Computer facilities: Computer purchase and lease plans are available. 951 computers available on campus for general student use. A campuswide network can be accessed from student residence rooms and from off campus. Online class registration is available.
Website: http://www.sandiego.edu/

General Application Contact: Monica Mahon, Associate Director of Graduate Admissions, 619-260-4524, Fax: 619-260-4158, E-mail: grads@sandiego.edu.

GRADUATE UNITS

College of Arts and Sciences Students: 33 full-time (16 women), 33 part-time (19 women); includes 17 minority (4 Black or African American, non-Hispanic/Latino; 1 American Indian or Alaska Native, non-Hispanic/Latino; 3 Asian, non-Hispanic/Latino; 9 Hispanic/Latino), 6 international. Average age 29. *Faculty:* 17 full-time (8 women), 4 part-time/adjunct (1 woman). Expenses: Contact institution. *Financial support:* In 2016–17, 57 students received support. Fellowships, career-related internships or fieldwork, Federal Work-Study, institutionally sponsored loans, scholarships/grants, and unspecified assistantships available. Support available to part-time students. Financial award application deadline: 4/1; financial award applicants required to submit FAFSA. In 2016, 25 master's awarded. *Program availability:* Part-time, evening/weekend. Offers acting (MFA); arts and sciences (MA, MFA, MS); international relations (MA); marine science (MS). *Application deadline:* Applications are processed on a rolling basis. *Application fee:* $45. Electronic applications accepted. *Application Contact:* Monica Mahon, Associate Director of Graduate Admissions, 619-260-4524, Fax: 619-260-4158, E-mail: grads@sandiego.edu. *Dean,* Dr. Noelle Norton, 619-260-4545.

Division of Professional and Continuing Education Students: 200 part-time (44 women); includes 88 minority (10 Black or African American, non-Hispanic/Latino; 22 Asian, non-Hispanic/Latino; 54 Hispanic/Latino; 2 Two or more races, non-Hispanic/Latino). Average age 37. 120 applicants, 88% accepted, 83 enrolled. *Faculty:* 1 full-time (0 women). Expenses: Contact institution. *Financial support:* Application deadline: 4/1; applicants required to submit FAFSA. *Program availability:* Part-time-only, evening/weekend, 100% online. Offers cyber security operations and leadership (MS); law enforcement and public safety leadership, (MS). *Application deadline:* For fall admission, 8/2 for domestic students; for spring admission, 11/7 for domestic students; for summer admission, 4/11 for domestic students. Applications are processed on a rolling basis. *Application fee:* $45. Electronic applications accepted. *Application Contact:* Monica Mahon, Associate Director of Graduate Admissions, 619-260-4524, Fax: 619-260-4158, E-mail: grads@sandiego.edu. *Dean,* Dr. Jason Lemon, 619-260-4585, E-mail: continuinged@sandiego.edu.

Hahn School of Nursing and Health Science Students: 193 full-time (159 women), 178 part-time (149 women); includes 169 minority (25 Black or African American, non-Hispanic/Latino; 1 American Indian or Alaska Native, non-Hispanic/Latino; 72 Asian, non-Hispanic/Latino; 58 Hispanic/Latino; 3 Native Hawaiian or other Pacific Islander, non-Hispanic/Latino; 10 Two or more races, non-Hispanic/Latino), 13 international. Average age 35. *Faculty:* 24 full-time (19 women), 50 part-time/adjunct (44 women).

Expenses: Contact institution. *Financial support:* In 2016–17, 227 students received support. Scholarships/grants and traineeships available. Support available to part-time students. Financial award application deadline: 4/1; financial award applicants required to submit FAFSA. In 2016, 84 master's, 34 doctorates awarded. *Program availability:* Part-time, evening/weekend. Offers adult-gerontology clinical nurse specialist (MSN); adult-gerontology nurse practitioner/family nurse practitioner (MSN); executive nurse leader (MSN); family nurse practitioner (MSN); family/lifespan psychiatric-mental health nurse practitioner (MSN); healthcare informatics (MS, MSN); nursing (PhD); nursing practice (DNP). *Application deadline:* Applications are processed on a rolling basis. *Application fee:* $45. Electronic applications accepted. *Application Contact:* Monica Mahon, Associate Director of Graduate Admissions, 619-260-4524, Fax: 619-260-4158, E-mail: grads@sandiego.edu. *Dean,* Dr. Sally Hardin, 619-260-4550, Fax: 619-260-6814, E-mail: nursing@sandiego.edu.

Joan B. Kroc School of Peace Studies Students: 38 full-time (25 women), 8 part-time (7 women); includes 14 minority (2 Black or African American, non-Hispanic/Latino; 1 Asian, non-Hispanic/Latino; 10 Hispanic/Latino; 1 Two or more races, non-Hispanic/Latino), 8 international. Average age 33. *Faculty:* 5 full-time (2 women), 2 part-time/adjunct (0 women). Expenses: Contact institution. *Financial support:* In 2016–17, 31 students received support. Career-related internships or fieldwork, Federal Work-Study, institutionally sponsored loans, scholarships/grants, and unspecified assistantships available. Support available to part-time students. Financial award application deadline: 4/1; financial award applicants required to submit FAFSA. In 2016, 18 master's awarded. Offers peace and justice (MA); social innovation (MA). *Application deadline:* For fall admission, 1/15 for domestic and international students. *Application fee:* $45. Electronic applications accepted. *Application Contact:* Monica Mahon, Associate Director of Graduate Admissions, 619-260-4524, Fax: 619-260-4158, E-mail: grads@sandiego.edu. *Dean,* Dr. Patricia Marquez, 619-260-7919, E-mail: krocschool@sandiego.edu.

School of Business Students: 182 full-time (69 women), 201 part-time (73 women); includes 103 minority (17 Black or African American, non-Hispanic/Latino; 24 Asian, non-Hispanic/Latino; 51 Hispanic/Latino; 4 Native Hawaiian or other Pacific Islander, non-Hispanic/Latino; 7 Two or more races, non-Hispanic/Latino), 89 international. Average age 31. *Faculty:* 38 full-time (10 women), 21 part-time/adjunct (5 women). Expenses: Contact institution. *Financial support:* In 2016–17, 202 students received support. Career-related internships or fieldwork, Federal Work-Study, institutionally sponsored loans, and scholarships/grants available. Support available to part-time students. Financial award application deadline: 4/1; financial award applicants required to submit FAFSA. In 2016, 242 master's awarded. *Program availability:* Part-time, evening/weekend. Offers accountancy (MS); business (MBA, MS, MSF, Certificate); business administration (MBA); executive leadership (MS); finance (MSF); global leadership (MS); real estate (MS); supply chain management (MS, Certificate); taxation (MS). *Application fee:* $80. Electronic applications accepted. *Application Contact:* Monica Mahon, Associate Director of Graduate Admissions, 619-260-4524, Fax: 619-260-4158, E-mail: grads@sandiego.edu. *Dean,* Dr. Jaime Alonso Gómez, 619-260-4886, E-mail: sbadean@sandiego.edu.

School of Law Students: 644 full-time (320 women), 118 part-time (46 women); includes 250 minority (24 Black or African American, non-Hispanic/Latino; 11 American Indian or Alaska Native, non-Hispanic/Latino; 96 Asian, non-Hispanic/Latino; 106 Hispanic/Latino; 3 Native Hawaiian or other Pacific Islander, non-Hispanic/Latino; 10 Two or more races, non-Hispanic/Latino), 26 international. Average age 27. 3,106 applicants, 192 enrolled. *Faculty:* 46 full-time (14 women), 71 part-time/adjunct (21 women). Expenses: Contact institution. *Financial support:* In 2016–17, 567 students received support. Career-related internships or fieldwork, Federal Work-Study, institutionally sponsored loans, and scholarships/grants available. Support available to part-time students. Financial award application deadline: 3/1; financial award applicants required to submit FAFSA. In 2016, 65 master's, 216 doctorates awarded. *Program availability:* Part-time, evening/weekend. Offers business and corporate law (LL M); comparative law (LL M); general studies (LL M); international law (LL M); law (JD); taxation (LL M, Diploma). *Application deadline:* For fall admission, 2/1 priority date for domestic students. Applications are processed on a rolling basis. Electronic applications accepted. *Application Contact:* Jorge Garcia, Assistant Dean, JD Admissions, 619-260-4528, Fax: 619-260-2218, E-mail: jdinfo@sandiego.edu. *Dean,* Dr. Stephen C. Ferruolo, 619-260-4527, E-mail: lawdean@sandiego.edu.

School of Leadership and Education Sciences Students: 345 full-time (281 women), 448 part-time (340 women); includes 327 minority (42 Black or African American, non-Hispanic/Latino; 1 American Indian or Alaska Native, non-Hispanic/Latino; 51 Asian, non-Hispanic/Latino; 198 Hispanic/Latino; 3 Native Hawaiian or other Pacific Islander, non-Hispanic/Latino; 32 Two or more races, non-Hispanic/Latino), 43 international. Average age 31. *Faculty:* 31 full-time (17 women), 74 part-time/adjunct (46 women). Expenses: Contact institution. *Financial support:* In 2016–17, 383 students received support. Career-related internships or fieldwork, Federal Work-Study, institutionally sponsored loans, unspecified assistantships, and stipends available. Support available to part-time students. Financial award application deadline: 4/1; financial award applicants required to submit FAFSA. In 2016, 243 master's, 21 doctorates awarded. *Program availability:* Part-time, evening/weekend. Offers clinical mental health counseling (MA); higher education leadership (MA); inclusive learning (M Ed); leadership and education sciences (M Ed, MA, MAT, PhD, Certificate); leadership studies (MA, PhD, Certificate); literacy and digital learning (M Ed); marital and family therapy (MA); nonprofit leadership and management (MA); school leadership (M Ed); special education with deaf and hard of hearing (M Ed); STEAM (science, technology, engineering, arts, and mathematics) (M Ed); teaching (MAT); TESOL, literacy and culture (M Ed). *Application fee:* $45. *Application Contact:* Monica Mahon, Associate Director of Graduate Admissions, 619-260-4524, Fax: 619-260-4158, E-mail: grads@sandiego.edu. *Dean,* Dr. Nicholas Ladany, 619-260-4540, Fax: 619-260-6835, E-mail: nladany@sandiego.edu.

Shiley-Marcos School of Engineering Students: 3 part-time (0 women); includes 1 minority (Asian, non-Hispanic/Latino). 17 applicants, 82% accepted, 3 enrolled. *Faculty:* 1 full-time (0 women). Expenses: Contact institution. Offers cyber security engineering (MS). *Application deadline:* For fall admission, 8/2 for domestic students; for spring admission, 11/7 for domestic students; for summer admission, 4/11 for domestic students. *Application fee:* $45. *Application Contact:* Monica Mahon, Associate Director of Graduate Admissions, 619-260-4524, Fax: 619-260-4158, E-mail: grads@sandiego.edu. *Dean,* Dr. Chell Roberts, 619-260-4627, E-mail: croberts@sandiego.edu.

UNIVERSITY OF SAN FRANCISCO, San Francisco, CA 94117-1080

General Information Independent-religious, coed, university. *Enrollment:* 11,018 graduate, professional, and undergraduate students; 3,476 full-time matriculated graduate/professional students (2,295 women), 733 part-time matriculated graduate/professional students (513 women). *Enrollment by degree level:* 3,285 master's, 934 doctoral. *Graduate faculty:* 223 full-time (119 women), 285 part-time/adjunct (153 women). *Tuition:* Full-time $23,310; part-time $1295 per credit. Tuition and fees vary according to course load, degree level, campus/location and program. *Graduate housing:* Room and/or apartments available on a first-come, first-served basis to single students; on-campus housing not available to married students. Typical cost: $11,290 per year ($15,880 including board). Room and board charges vary according to board plan, campus/location and housing facility selected. Housing application deadline: 5/1. *Student services:* Campus employment opportunities, career counseling, exercise/wellness program, free psychological counseling, international student services, low-cost health insurance, multicultural affairs office, services for students with disabilities, teacher training, writing training. *Library facilities:* Gleeson Library|Geschke Center plus 1 other. *Collection:* Books: 723,469 (physical), 526,891 (digital/electronic); Serial titles: 4,808 (physical), 71,733 (digital/electronic); Databases: 255. Weekly public service hours: 142; study areas open 24 hours, 5–7 days a week; students can reserve study rooms. *Research affiliation:* NASA-Ames Research Center.

Computer facilities: Computer purchase and lease plans are available. 265 computers available on campus for general student use. A campuswide network can be accessed from student residence rooms and from off campus. Online class registration is available.
Website: http://www.usfca.edu/

General Application Contact: Information Contact, 415-422-4723, Fax: 415-422-2217, E-mail: graduate@usfca.edu.

GRADUATE UNITS

College of Arts and Sciences Students: 812 full-time (453 women), 97 part-time (57 women); includes 310 minority (48 Black or African American, non-Hispanic/Latino; 91 Asian, non-Hispanic/Latino; 122 Hispanic/Latino; 3 Native Hawaiian or other Pacific Islander, non-Hispanic/Latino; 46 Two or more races, non-Hispanic/Latino), 228 international. Average age 27. 2,078 applicants, 54% accepted, 457 enrolled. *Faculty:* 65 full-time (29 women), 50 part-time/adjunct (17 women). Expenses: Contact institution. *Financial support:* In 2016–17, 415 students received support. Fellowships, research assistantships, teaching assistantships, career-related internships or fieldwork, Federal Work-Study, institutionally sponsored loans, scholarships/grants, and tuition waivers (partial) available. Support available to part-time students. Financial award application deadline: 8/1; financial award applicants required to submit FAFSA. In 2016, 369 master's awarded. *Program availability:* Part-time, evening/weekend. Offers analytics (MS); arts and sciences (MA, MFA, MMS, MMS, MPA, MS, PSM); Asia Pacific studies (MA); biology (MS); biotechnology (PSM); chemistry (MS); computer science (MS); economics (MA, MS); energy systems management (MS); environmental management (MS); international and development economics (MA); international studies (MA); migration studies (MMS); museum studies (MA); professional communication (MA); public affairs (MPA); sport management (MA); urban and public affairs (MA); writing (MFA). *Application fee:* $55. Electronic applications accepted. *Application Contact:* Mark Landerghini, Information Contact, 415-422-5101, Fax: 415-422-5134, E-mail: asgraduate@usfca.edu. *Dean,* Dr. Marcelo Camperi, 415-422-6373.

School of Education Students: 794 full-time (616 women), 253 part-time (191 women); includes 522 minority (91 Black or African American, non-Hispanic/Latino; 140 Asian, non-Hispanic/Latino; 230 Hispanic/Latino; 9 Native Hawaiian or other Pacific Islander, non-Hispanic/Latino; 52 Two or more races, non-Hispanic/Latino), 75 international. Average age 32. 929 applicants, 83% accepted, 387 enrolled. *Faculty:* 39 full-time (26 women), 114 part-time/adjunct (70 women). Expenses: Contact institution. *Financial support:* In 2016–17, 155 students received support. Fellowships, research assistantships, and teaching assistantships available. Financial award application deadline: 3/2; financial award applicants required to submit FAFSA. In 2016, 364 master's, 36 doctorates awarded. *Program availability:* Part-time, evening/weekend. Offers Catholic school leadership (Ed D); counseling (MA); digital media and learning (MA); digital technologies for teaching and learning (MA); education (MA, Ed D); international and multicultural education (MA, Ed D); leadership studies (MA, Ed D); learning and instruction (MA, Ed D); special education (MA, Ed D); teaching (MA); teaching reading (MA); teaching urban education and social justice (MA). *Application deadline:* For fall admission, 5/1 priority date for domestic and international students; for spring admission, 10/1 priority date for domestic and international students. Applications are processed on a rolling basis. *Application fee:* $55 ($65 for international students). Electronic applications accepted. *Application Contact:* Peter Cole, Admission Coordinator, 415-422-5467, E-mail: schoolofeducation@usfca.edu. *Acting Dean,* Dr. Shabnam Koirala-Azad, 415-422-6525.

School of Law Students: 446 full-time (252 women), 160 part-time (84 women); includes 308 minority (42 Black or African American, non-Hispanic/Latino; 106 Asian, non-Hispanic/Latino; 127 Hispanic/Latino; 2 Native Hawaiian or other Pacific Islander, non-Hispanic/Latino; 31 Two or more races, non-Hispanic/Latino), 28 international. Average age 29. 2,047 applicants, 65% accepted, 215 enrolled. *Faculty:* 34 full-time (18 women), 35 part-time/adjunct (12 women). Expenses: Contact institution. *Financial support:* In 2016–17, 277 students received support. Career-related internships or fieldwork, Federal Work-Study, and institutionally sponsored loans available. Support available to part-time students. Financial award application deadline: 3/2; financial award applicants required to submit FAFSA. In 2016, 30 master's, 140 doctorates awarded. *Program availability:* Part-time, evening/weekend. Offers intellectual property and technology law (LL M); international transactions and comparative law (LL M); law (LL M, JD). *Application deadline:* For fall admission, 4/1 for domestic students. Applications are processed on a rolling basis. *Application fee:* $60. Electronic applications accepted. *Application Contact:* Alan P. Guerrero, Director of Admissions, 415-422-2975, E-mail: lawadmissions@usfca.edu. *Dean,* John Trasvina, 415-422-6304.

School of Management Students: 752 full-time (422 women), 27 part-time (18 women); includes 321 minority (59 Black or African American, non-Hispanic/Latino; 117 Asian, non-Hispanic/Latino; 119 Hispanic/Latino; 4 Native Hawaiian or other Pacific Islander, non-Hispanic/Latino; 23 Two or more races, non-Hispanic/Latino), 200 international. Average age 31. 987 applicants, 76% accepted, 389 enrolled. *Faculty:* 35 full-time (9 women), 24 part-time/adjunct (7 women). Expenses: Contact institution. *Financial support:* In 2016–17, 202 students received support. Scholarships/grants available. Support available to part-time students. Financial award application deadline: 3/2; financial award applicants required to submit FAFSA. In 2016, 367 master's awarded. *Program availability:* Part-time, evening/weekend, online learning. Offers entrepreneurship and innovation (MBA); executive business administration (MBA); finance (MBA); financial analysis (MSFA); global entrepreneurial management (MGEM); health services administration (MPA); information systems (MS); management (MBA, MGEM, MNA, MPA, MS, MSFA, MSOD, MSRM); marketing (MBA); nonprofit administration (MNA); organization development (MSOD); public administration (MPA). *Application fee:* $55. Electronic applications accepted. *Application Contact:* Elisabeth Merkel, 415-422-2221, Fax: 415-422-6315, E-mail: management@usfca.edu. *Dean,* Dr. Elizabeth Davis, 415-422-2221, E-mail: management@usfca.edu.

School of Nursing and Health Professions Students: 672 full-time (552 women), 196 part-time (163 women); includes 508 minority (84 Black or African American, non-Hispanic/Latino; 225 Asian, non-Hispanic/Latino; 143 Hispanic/Latino; 20 Native Hawaiian or other Pacific Islander, non-Hispanic/Latino; 36 Two or more races, non-Hispanic/Latino), 30 international. Average age 34. 799 applicants, 60% accepted, 275 enrolled. *Faculty:* 50 full-time (37 women), 62 part-time/adjunct (47 women). Expenses: Contact institution. *Financial support:* In 2016–17, 193 students received support. Institutionally sponsored loans available. Financial award application deadline: 3/2. In 2016, 237 master's, 51 doctorates awarded. *Program availability:* Part-time, 100% online, blended/hybrid learning. Offers behavioral health (MS); clinical psychology (Psy D); health informatics (MS); nursing and health professions (MPH, MS, MSBH, MSN, DNP, Psy D); nursing practice (DNP); public health (MPH). *Application deadline:* Applications are processed on a rolling basis. Electronic applications accepted. *Application Contact:* Ingrid McVanner, Information Contact, 415-422-2746, Fax: 415-422-2217. *Dean,* Dr. Margaret Baker, 415-422-6681, Fax: 415-422-6877, E-mail: nursing@usfca.edu.

UNIVERSITY OF SASKATCHEWAN, Saskatoon, SK S7N 5A2, Canada

General Information Province-supported, coed, university. *Graduate housing:* Rooms and/or apartments available on a first-come, first-served basis to single and married students. *Research affiliation:* Canada Agriculture (agriculture research), Saskatchewan Research Council, University Hospital (cancer research), Innovation Place, Vaccine and Infectious Disease Organization/InterVac Laboratory (vaccinology and immunotherapeutics), Canadian Light Source.

GRADUATE UNITS

College of Dentistry Offers dentistry (DMD). Electronic applications accepted.

College of Graduate Studies and Research *Program availability:* Part-time. Electronic applications accepted.

College of Agriculture *Program availability:* Part-time. Offers agricultural economics (M Ag, M Sc, MA, PhD, PGD); agriculture (M Ag, M Sc, MA, PhD, Diploma, PGD); animal and poultry science (M Ag, M Sc, PhD); applied microbiology and food science (M Ag, M Sc, PhD); plant sciences (M Sc, PhD); soil science (M Ag, M Sc, PhD, Diploma).

College of Arts and Science *Program availability:* Part-time. Offers archaeology (MA, PhD); art and art history (MFA); arts and science (M Math, M Mus, M Sc, MA, MFA, PhD, Diploma); biology (M Sc, PhD); chemistry (M Sc, PhD); computer science (M Sc, PhD); drama (MA); economics (MA, Diploma); English (MA, PhD); geography (M Sc, MA, PhD); geological sciences (M Sc, PhD, Diploma); history (MA, PhD); languages and linguistics (MA); mathematics and statistics (M Math, MA, PhD); music (M Mus, MA); native studies (MA, PhD); philosophy (MA); physics and engineering physics (M Sc, PhD); political studies (MA); psychology (MA, PhD); religion and culture (MA); sociology (MA, PhD); women's and gender studies (MA, PhD). Electronic applications accepted.

College of Education *Program availability:* Part-time. Offers curriculum studies (M Ed, PhD, Diploma); education (M Ed, MC Ed, PhD, Diploma); educational administration (M Ed, PhD, Diploma); educational foundations (M Ed, MC Ed, PhD, Diploma); educational psychology and special education (M Ed, PhD, Diploma). Electronic applications accepted.

College of Engineering *Program availability:* Part-time. Offers biological engineering (M Eng, M Sc, PhD); biomedical engineering (M Eng, M Sc, PhD); chemical engineering (M Eng, M Sc, PhD); civil and geological engineering (M Eng, M Sc, PhD); electrical engineering (M Eng, M Sc, PhD, PGD); engineering (M Eng, M Sc, PhD, PGD); mechanical engineering (M Eng, M Sc, PhD). Electronic applications accepted.

College of Kinesiology Offers kinesiology (M Sc, PhD).

College of Law *Program availability:* Part-time. Offers law (LL M, JD).

College of Nursing *Program availability:* Part-time. Offers nursing (MN).

College of Pharmacy and Nutrition Offers pharmacy and nutrition (M Sc, PhD).

Edwards School of Business *Program availability:* Part-time. Offers accounting (M Sc, MP Acc); agribusiness management (MBA); biotechnology management (MBA); business (M Sc, MBA, MP Acc); finance (M Sc); health services management (MBA); indigenous management (MBA); international business management (MBA); marketing (M Sc).

School of Environment and Sustainability Offers environment and sustainability (MES).

School of Public Policy Offers public policy (MIT, MPA, MPP, PhD).

Toxicology Centre Offers toxicology (M Sc, PhD, Diploma).

College of Medicine Offers anatomy and cell biology (M Sc, PhD); biochemistry (M Sc, PhD); community health and epidemiology (M Sc, PhD); medicine (M Sc, DPT, MD, PhD); microbiology and immunology (M Sc, PhD); obstetrics, gynecology and reproductive services (M Sc, PhD); pathology (M Sc, PhD); pharmacology (M Sc, PhD); physiology (M Sc, PhD); psychiatry (M Sc, PhD); surgery (M Sc).

Western College of Veterinary Medicine Offers large animal clinical sciences (M Sc, M Vet Sc, PhD); small animal clinical sciences (M Sc, M Vet Sc, PhD); veterinary anatomy (M Sc); veterinary anesthesiology, radiology and surgery (M Vet Sc); veterinary biomedical sciences (M Sc, M Vet Sc, PhD); veterinary internal medicine (M Vet Sc); veterinary medicine (M Sc, M Vet Sc, DVM, PhD); veterinary microbiology (M Sc, M Vet Sc, PhD); veterinary pathology (M Sc, M Vet Sc, PhD); veterinary physiological sciences (M Sc, PhD).

THE UNIVERSITY OF SCRANTON, Scranton, PA 18510

General Information Independent-religious, coed, comprehensive institution. CGS member. *Graduate housing:* Room and/or apartments available on a first-come, first-served basis to single students; on-campus housing not available to married students. *Research affiliation:* Allied Services (rehabilitation), Lackawanna River Corridor Association (environment), Universidad Iberoamericana (counseling and human services), Wyoming Valley Health Care System (nursing), Community Medical Center (health services), National Health Management Center (health care management).

GRADUATE UNITS

College of Arts and Sciences *Program availability:* Part-time, evening/weekend, 100% online. Offers arts and sciences (MA, MS); biochemistry (MS); chemistry (MS); clinical chemistry (MS); theology (MA). Electronic applications accepted.

Kania School of Management Offers accountancy (M Acc); accounting (MBA); finance (MBA); general business administration (MBA); health care management (MBA); international business (MBA); management (M Acc, MBA, MS); management information systems (MBA); marketing (MBA); operations management (MBA); software engineering (MS).

Panuska College of Professional Studies Offers clinical mental health counseling (MS); curriculum and instruction (MS); educational administration (MS); family nurse practitioner (MSN, PMC); health administration (MHA); human resources (MS); nurse anesthesia (MSN, PMC); nursing leadership (DNP); occupational therapy (MS); physical therapy (DPT); professional counseling (CAGS); reading education (MS); rehabilitation counseling (MS); school counseling (MS); secondary education (MS); special education (MS).

UNIVERSITY OF SIOUX FALLS, Sioux Falls, SD 57105-1699

General Information Independent-religious, coed, comprehensive institution. *Graduate housing:* Rooms and/or apartments available on a first-come, first-served basis to single and married students.

GRADUATE UNITS

Fredrikson School of Education *Program availability:* Part-time, evening/weekend. Offers educational administration (Ed S); leadership in reading (M Ed); leadership in schools (M Ed); leadership in technology (M Ed); teaching (M Ed). Admission in summer only.

Vucurevich School of Business *Program availability:* Part-time, evening/weekend. Offers entrepreneurial leadership (MBA); general management (MBA); health care management (MBA); marketing (MBA).

UNIVERSITY OF SOUTH AFRICA, Pretoria 0003, South Africa

General Information Private, coed, university.

GRADUATE UNITS

College of Agriculture and Environmental Sciences Offers agriculture (MS); consumer science (MCS); environmental management (MA, MS, PhD); environmental science (MA, MS, PhD); geography (MA, MS, PhD); horticulture (M Tech); human ecology (MHE); life sciences (MS); nature conservation (M Tech).

College of Economic and Management Sciences Offers accounting (D Admin, D Com); accounting science (DA); auditing (D Admin, D Com); business administration (M Tech); business economics (D Admin); business leadership (DBL); business management (D Admin, D Com); economic management analysis (M Tech); economics (D Admin, D Com, PhD); human resource development (M Tech); industrial psychology (D Admin, D Com, PhD); logistics (D Admin); marketing (M Tech); public administration (D Admin, D Com, DPA, PhD); public management (M Tech); quantitative management (D Admin, D Com); real estate (M Tech); statistics (D Admin, PhD); tourism management (D Admin, D Com); transport economics (D Admin, D Com).

College of Human Sciences Offers adult education (M Ed); African languages (MA, PhD); African politics (MA, PhD); Afrikaans (MA, PhD); ancient history (MA, PhD); ancient Near Eastern studies (MA, PhD); anthropology (MA, PhD); applied linguistics (MA); Arabic (MA, PhD); archaeology (MA); art history (MA); Biblical archaeology (MA); Biblical studies (M Th, D Th, PhD); Christian spirituality (M Th, D Th); church history (M Th, D Th); classical studies (MA, PhD); clinical psychology (MA); communication (MA, PhD); comparative education (M Ed, Ed D); consulting psychology (D Admin, D Com, PhD); curriculum studies (M Ed, Ed D); development studies (M Admin, MA, D Admin, PhD); didactics (M Ed, Ed D); education (M Tech); education management (M Ed, Ed D); educational psychology (M Ed); English (MA); environmental education (M Ed); French (MA, PhD); German (MA, PhD); Greek (MA); guidance and counseling (M Ed); health studies (MA, PhD); history (MA, PhD); history of education (Ed D); inclusive education (M Ed, Ed D); information and communications technology policy and regulation (MA); information science (MA, MIS, PhD); international politics (MA, PhD); Islamic studies (MA, PhD); Italian (MA, PhD); Judaica (MA, PhD); linguistics (MA, PhD); mathematical education (M Ed); mathematics education (MA); missiology (M Th, D Th); modern Hebrew (MA, PhD); musicology (MA, MMus, D Mus, PhD); natural science education (M Ed); New Testament (M Th, D Th); Old Testament (D Th); pastoral therapy (M Th, D Th); philosophy (MA); philosophy of education (M Ed, Ed D); politics (MA, PhD); Portuguese (MA, PhD); practical theology (M Th, D Th); psychology (MA, MS, PhD); psychology of education (M Ed, Ed D); public health (MA); religious studies (MA, D Th, PhD); Romance languages (MA); Russian (MA, PhD); Semitic languages (MA, PhD); social behavior studies in HIV/AIDS (MA); social science (mental health) (MA); social science in development studies (MA); social science in psychology (MA); social science in social work (MA); social science in sociology (MA); social work (MSW, DSW, PhD); socio-education (M Ed, Ed D); sociolinguistics (MA); sociology (MA, PhD); Spanish (MA, PhD); systematic theology (M Th, D Th); TESOL (teaching English to speakers of other languages) (MA); theological ethics (M Th, D Th); theory of literature (MA, PhD); urban ministries (D Th); urban ministry (M Th).

College of Law Offers correctional services management (M Tech); criminology (MA, PhD); law (LL M, LL D); penology (MA, PhD); police science (MA, PhD); policing (M Tech); security risk management (M Tech); social science in criminology (MA).

College of Science, Engineering and Technology Offers chemical engineering (M Tech); information technology (M Tech).

Graduate School of Business Leadership Offers business leadership (MBA, MBL, DBL).

Institute for Science and Technology Education Offers mathematics, science and technology education (M Sc, PhD).

UNIVERSITY OF SOUTH ALABAMA, Mobile, AL 36688-0002

General Information State-supported, coed, university. CGS member. *Enrollment:* 16,436 graduate, professional, and undergraduate students; 4,093 full-time matriculated graduate/professional students (3,130 women), 588 part-time matriculated graduate/professional students (454 women). *Enrollment by degree level:* 3,542 master's, 1,018 doctoral, 121 other advanced degrees. *Graduate faculty:* 311 full-time (154 women), 133 part-time/adjunct (115 women). Tuition, state resident: full-time $9768; part-time $407 per credit hour. Tuition, nonresident: full-time $19,536; part-time $814 per credit hour. *Graduate housing:* Room and/or apartments available on a first-come, first-served basis to single students; on-campus housing not available to married students. Typical cost: $3850 per year ($7340 including board). Room and board charges vary according to board plan and housing facility selected. Housing application deadline: 5/1. *Student services:* Campus employment opportunities, career counseling, exercise/wellness program, free psychological counseling, grant writing training, international student services, low-cost health insurance, multicultural affairs office, services for students with disabilities, writing training. *Library facilities:* Marx Library plus 5 others. *Collection:* Books: 703,077 (physical), 34,645 (digital/electronic); Serial titles: 4,077 (physical), 1.2 million (digital/electronic); Databases: 32. *Research affiliation:* Dauphin Island Marine Laboratory (marine sciences), Gynecologic Oncology Group (oncology), Eastern Cooperative Oncology Group (oncology), Radiation Therapy Oncology Group (oncology), Oak Ridge National Laboratory (physics), American College of Surgeons Oncology Group (oncology).

Computer facilities: A campuswide network can be accessed from student residence rooms and from off campus. Online class registration is available. Website: http://www.southalabama.edu/

General Application Contact: Dr. Julio F. Turrens, Interim Dean, Graduate School, 251-460-6310, Fax: 251-461-1513, E-mail: julioturrens@southalabama.edu.

GRADUATE UNITS

College of Arts and Sciences Students: 134 full-time (76 women), 53 part-time (32 women); includes 34 minority (18 Black or African American, non-Hispanic/Latino; 1 American Indian or Alaska Native, non-Hispanic/Latino; 2 Asian, non-Hispanic/Latino; 6 Hispanic/Latino; 1 Native Hawaiian or other Pacific Islander, non-Hispanic/Latino; 6 Two or more races, non-Hispanic/Latino), 3 international. Average age 29. 177 applicants, 50% accepted, 55 enrolled. *Faculty:* 87 full-time (25 women), 5 part-time/adjunct (4 women). Expenses: Contact institution. *Financial support:* Research assistantships, teaching assistantships, career-related internships or fieldwork, Federal Work-Study, institutionally sponsored loans, scholarships/grants, and unspecified assistantships available. Support available to part-time students. Financial award application deadline: 5/31; financial award applicants required to submit FAFSA. In 2016, 57 master's, 4 doctorates awarded. *Program availability:* Part-time, evening/weekend. Offers arts and sciences (MA, MFA, MM, MPA, MS, PhD); biological sciences (MS); collaborative keyboard (MM); communication (MA); creative technologies and practice (MFA); creative writing (MA); history (MA); literature (MA); marine conservation and resource management (MS); marine sciences (MS, PhD); mathematics (MS); music education (MM); performance (MM); psychology (MS); public administration (MPA); sociology (MA). *Application deadline:* For fall admission, 7/15 priority date for domestic students, 6/15 priority date for international students; for spring admission, 12/1 priority date for domestic students, 11/1 priority date for international students; for summer admission, 5/1 priority date for domestic students. Applications are processed on a rolling basis. *Application fee:* $35. Electronic applications accepted. *Application Contact:* Dr. Eric Loomis, Associate Dean, College of Arts and Sciences, 251-460-7811, Fax: 251-461-1744, E-mail: ejloomis@southalabama.edu. *Dean, College of Arts and Sciences,* Dr. Andrez Wierzbicki, 251-460-6280, Fax: 251-460-7928, E-mail: awierzbicki@southalabama.edu.

College of Education and Professional Studies Students: 359 full-time (254 women), 153 part-time (120 women); includes 147 minority (113 Black or African American, non-Hispanic/Latino; 4 American Indian or Alaska Native, non-Hispanic/Latino; 5 Asian, non-Hispanic/Latino; 16 Hispanic/Latino; 2 Native Hawaiian or other Pacific Islander, non-Hispanic/Latino; 7 Two or more races, non-Hispanic/Latino), 7 international. Average age 34. 277 applicants, 54% accepted, 130 enrolled. *Faculty:* 35 full-time (22 women), 12 part-time/adjunct (8 women). Expenses: Contact institution. *Financial support:* Fellowships, research assistantships, teaching assistantships, career-related internships or fieldwork, Federal Work-Study, institutionally sponsored loans, scholarships/grants, and unspecified assistantships available. Support available to part-time students. Financial award application deadline: 5/31; financial award applicants required to submit FAFSA. In 2016, 124 master's, 9 doctorates awarded. *Program availability:* Part-time, online learning. Offers art education (M Ed); clinical mental health counseling (MS); early childhood education (M Ed); education and professional studies (M Ed, MS, Ed D, PhD); educational leadership (M Ed, Ed D); educational media (M Ed, MS); elementary education (M Ed); exercise science (MS); health education (M Ed); instructional design and development (MS, PhD); physical education (M Ed); reading education (M Ed); school counseling (M Ed); science education (M Ed); secondary education (M Ed); special education (M Ed); sport management (MS). *Application deadline:* For fall admission, 7/15 priority date for domestic students, 6/15 priority date for international students; for spring admission, 11/1 priority date for domestic and international students; for summer admission, 4/15 priority date for domestic students. Applications are processed on a rolling basis. *Application fee:* $35. Electronic applications accepted. *Application Contact:* Dr. Susan Santoli, Director of Graduate Studies, 251-380-2738, Fax: 251-380-2758, E-mail: ssantoli@southalabama.edu. *Dean, College of Education,* Dr. Andrea M. Kent, 251-380-2738, Fax: 251-380-2748, E-mail: akent@southalabama.edu.

College of Engineering Students: 92 full-time (21 women), 17 part-time (2 women); includes 9 minority (5 Black or African American, non-Hispanic/Latino; 2 Asian, non-Hispanic/Latino; 1 Native Hawaiian or other Pacific Islander, non-Hispanic/Latino; 1 Two or more races, non-Hispanic/Latino), 58 international. Average age 26. 218 applicants, 50% accepted, 26 enrolled. *Faculty:* 28 full-time (2 women), 7 part-time/adjunct (0 women). Expenses: Contact institution. *Financial support:* Fellowships, research assistantships, teaching assistantships, career-related internships or fieldwork, Federal Work-Study, institutionally sponsored loans, scholarships/grants, and unspecified assistantships available. Support available to part-time students. Financial award application deadline: 5/31; financial award applicants required to submit FAFSA. In 2016, 114 master's awarded. *Program availability:* Part-time. Offers chemical engineering (MS Ch E); civil, coastal, and environmental engineering (MSCE); computer engineering (MSEE); electrical engineering (MSEE); engineering (MS Ch E, MSCE, MSEE, MSME, D Sc); mechanical engineering (MSME); systems engineering (D Sc). *Application deadline:* For fall admission, 7/1 priority date for domestic students, 6/1 priority date for international students; for spring admission, 12/1 priority date for domestic students, 11/1 priority date for international students; for summer admission, 5/1 priority date for domestic students, 4/1 priority date for international students. Applications are processed on a rolling basis. *Application fee:* $35. Electronic applications accepted. *Application Contact:* Brenda Poole, Academic Records Specialist, 251-460-6140, Fax: 251-460-6343, E-mail: engineering@southalabama.edu. *Dean, College of Engineering,* Dr. John Steadman, 251-460-6140, Fax: 251-460-6343, E-mail: engineering@southalabama.edu.

College of Medicine Students: 343 full-time (146 women), 1 part-time (0 women); includes 80 minority (36 Black or African American, non-Hispanic/Latino; 2 American Indian or Alaska Native, non-Hispanic/Latino; 35 Asian, non-Hispanic/Latino; 3 Hispanic/Latino; 4 Two or more races, non-Hispanic/Latino), 5 international. Average age 25. *Faculty:* 188 full-time (55 women), 27 part-time/adjunct (9 women). Expenses: Contact institution. *Financial support:* Fellowships, research assistantships, teaching assistantships, career-related internships or fieldwork, institutionally sponsored loans, scholarships/grants, and unspecified assistantships available. Support available to part-time students. Financial award application deadline: 5/31; financial award applicants required to submit FAFSA. In 2016, 82 doctorates awarded. Offers basic medical sciences (PhD); medicine (MD). *Application deadline:* For fall admission, 11/15 for domestic and international students. *Application fee:* $75. Electronic applications accepted. *Application Contact:* Mark Scott, Director, Medical Admissions, 251-460-7176, Fax: 251-460-6278, E-mail: mscott@southalabama.edu. *Vice President of Medical Affairs/Dean of the College of Medicine,* Dr. John Marymont, 251-341-3030, Fax: 251-341-3994, E-mail: jmarymont@southalabama.edu.

College of Nursing Students: 2,566 full-time (2,264 women), 326 part-time (287 women); includes 850 minority (543 Black or African American, non-Hispanic/Latino; 24 American Indian or Alaska Native, non-Hispanic/Latino; 133 Asian, non-Hispanic/Latino; 96 Hispanic/Latino; 8 Native Hawaiian or other Pacific Islander, non-Hispanic/Latino; 46 Two or more races, non-Hispanic/Latino), 7 international. Average age 35. 966 applicants, 81% accepted, 554 enrolled. *Faculty:* 71 full-time (67 women), 115 part-time/adjunct (105 women). Expenses: Contact institution. *Financial support:* Fellowships, research assistantships, teaching assistantships, career-related internships or fieldwork, Federal Work-Study, institutionally sponsored loans, scholarships/grants, and unspecified assistantships available. Support available to part-time students. Financial award application deadline: 5/31; financial award applicants required to submit FAFSA. In 2016, 579 master's, 135 doctorates, 82 other advanced degrees awarded. *Program availability:* Part-time, online learning. Offers nursing (MSN, DNP); nursing administration (Certificate); nursing education (Certificate); nursing practice (Certificate). *Application deadline:* For fall admission, 2/15 for domestic students; for spring admission, 7/15 priority date for domestic students; for summer admission, 1/15 priority date for domestic students. Applications are processed on a rolling basis. *Application fee:* $100. Electronic applications accepted. *Application Contact:* Brea Mosley, Academic Advisor, 251-445-9400, Fax: 251-445-9416, E-mail: bmosley@southalabama.edu. *Dean, College of Nursing,* Dr. Debra Davis, 251-445-9400, Fax: 251-445-9416, E-mail: ddavis@southalabama.edu.

Graduate School Students: 36 full-time (22 women), 7 part-time (5 women); includes 7 minority (5 Black or African American, non-Hispanic/Latino; 1 American Indian or Alaska Native, non-Hispanic/Latino; 1 Two or more races, non-Hispanic/Latino). Average age 27. 123 applicants, 15% accepted, 16 enrolled. *Faculty:* 8 full-time (4 women). Expenses: Contact institution. *Financial support:* Fellowships, research assistantships, teaching assistantships, career-related internships or fieldwork, Federal Work-Study, institutionally sponsored loans, scholarships/grants, and unspecified assistantships available. Support available to part-time students. Financial award application deadline: 5/31; financial award applicants required to submit FAFSA. In 2016, 9 master's, 5 doctorates awarded. *Program availability:* Part-time, evening/weekend. Offers clinical and counseling psychology (PhD); environmental toxicology (MS). *Application deadline:* For fall admission, 7/1 priority date for domestic students, 6/1 priority date for international students; for spring admission, 12/1 priority date for domestic students, 11/1 priority date for international students. Applications are processed on a rolling basis. *Application fee:* $35. Electronic applications accepted. *Application Contact:* Deanna Cobb, Graduate School Services Specialist, 251-460-6310, E-mail: dcobb@southalabama.edu. *Interim Dean of the Graduate School,* Dr. Julio Turrens, 251-460-6310, E-mail: jturrens@southalabama.edu.

Mitchell College of Business Students: 77 full-time (28 women), 10 part-time (2 women); includes 16 minority (9 Black or African American, non-Hispanic/Latino; 1 American Indian or Alaska Native, non-Hispanic/Latino; 3 Asian, non-Hispanic/Latino; 2 Hispanic/Latino; 1 Two or more races, non-Hispanic/Latino), 7 international. Average age 32. 109 applicants, 42% accepted, 33 enrolled. *Faculty:* 12 full-time (2 women). Expenses: Contact institution. *Financial support:* Fellowships, research assistantships, teaching assistantships, career-related internships or fieldwork, Federal Work-Study, institutionally sponsored loans, scholarships/grants, and unspecified assistantships available. Support available to part-time students. Financial award application deadline: 5/31; financial award applicants required to submit FAFSA. In 2016, 31 master's, 3 doctorates awarded. *Program availability:* Part-time, evening/weekend. Offers accounting (M Acc); business administration (MBA, DBA). *Application deadline:* For fall admission, 7/15 for domestic students, 6/15 for international students; for spring admission, 12/1 for domestic students, 11/1 for international students. *Application fee:* $35. Electronic applications accepted. *Application Contact:* Dr. Alex Sharland, Assistant Dean and Director of Graduate Studies, 251-460-6412, Fax: 251-460-6529, E-mail: mcobgraduate@southalabama.edu. *Dean, Business,* Dr. Bob Wood, 251-460-7167, Fax: 251-460-6529, E-mail: bgwood@southalabama.edu.

Pat Capps Covey College of Allied Health Professions Students: 365 full-time (284 women); includes 12 minority (8 Black or African American, non-Hispanic/Latino; 2 Asian, non-Hispanic/Latino; 2 Hispanic/Latino), 2 international. Average age 25. 610 applicants, 37% accepted, 90 enrolled. *Faculty:* 32 full-time (23 women), 3 part-time/adjunct (2 women). Expenses: Contact institution. *Financial support:* Fellowships, research assistantships, teaching assistantships, career-related internships or fieldwork, Federal Work-Study, institutionally sponsored loans, scholarships/grants, and unspecified assistantships available. Support available to part-time students. Financial award application deadline: 5/31; financial award applicants required to submit FAFSA. In 2016, 90 master's, 49 doctorates awarded. Offers allied health professions (MHS, MS, Au D, DPT, PhD); audiology (Au D); communication sciences and disorders (PhD); occupational therapy (MS); physical therapy (DPT); physician assistant studies (MHS); speech-language pathology (MS). *Application deadline:* For fall admission, 7/15 priority date for domestic students, 6/15 priority date for international students; for spring admission, 12/1 priority date for domestic students, 11/1 priority date for international students. Applications are processed on a rolling basis. *Application fee:* $35. Electronic applications accepted. *Application Contact:* Dr. Susan Gordon-Hickey, Associate Dean, College of Allied Health, 251-445-9250, Fax: 251-445-9259, E-mail: gordonhickey@southalabama.edu. *Dean, College of Allied Health,* Dr. Gregory Frazer, 251-445-9250, Fax: 251-445-9259, E-mail: gfrazer@southalabama.edu.

School of Computing Students: 121 full-time (35 women), 21 part-time (6 women); includes 10 minority (2 Black or African American, non-Hispanic/Latino; 4 Asian, non-Hispanic/Latino; 1 Hispanic/Latino; 1 Native Hawaiian or other Pacific Islander, non-Hispanic/Latino; 2 Two or more races, non-Hispanic/Latino), 87 international. Average age 27. 204 applicants, 53% accepted, 29 enrolled. *Faculty:* 18 full-time (3 women). Expenses: Contact institution. *Financial support:* Fellowships, research assistantships, teaching assistantships, Federal Work-Study, institutionally sponsored loans, scholarships/grants, and unspecified assistantships available. Support available to part-time students. Financial award application deadline: 5/31; financial award applicants required to submit FAFSA. In 2016, 67 master's awarded. *Program availability:* Part-time, evening/weekend. Offers computer science (MS); information systems (MS). *Application deadline:* For fall admission, 7/15 priority date for domestic students, 6/15 priority date for international students; for spring admission, 12/1 priority date for domestic students, 11/1 priority date for international students; for summer admission, 5/1 priority date for domestic students, 4/1 priority date for international students. Applications are processed on a rolling basis. *Application fee:* $35. Electronic applications accepted. *Application Contact:* Dr. Harold Pardue, Director of School of Computing Graduate Studies, 251-460-1600, Fax: 251-460-7274, E-mail: hpardue@southalabama.edu. *Dean, School of Computing,* Dr. Alec Yasinsac, 251-460-6390, Fax: 251-460-7274, E-mail: yasinsac@southalabama.edu.

UNIVERSITY OF SOUTH CAROLINA, Columbia, SC 29208

General Information State-supported, coed, university. CGS member. *Graduate housing:* Rooms and/or apartments available to single and married students. *Research affiliation:* E.I. du Pont de Nemours and Company (engineering, chemical engineering), Westinghouse/Savannah River Corporation (environmental restoration, hazardous waste remediation), Motorola Corporation–Energy Production Division (electrochemical engineering), Glaxo-Wellcome (pharmaceuticals), NCR Corporation (electrical and computer engineering).

GRADUATE UNITS

The Graduate School *Program availability:* Part-time, evening/weekend, online learning. Offers gerontology (Certificate). Electronic applications accepted.

Arnold School of Public Health *Program availability:* Part-time, online learning. Offers biostatistics (MPH, MSPH, Dr PH, PhD); communication sciences and disorders (MCD, MSP, PhD); environmental health science (MS); environmental quality (MPH, MS, MSPH, PhD); epidemiology (MPH, MSPH, Dr PH, PhD); exercise science (MS, DPT, PhD); general public health (MPH); hazardous materials management (MPH, MSPH, PhD); health education (MAT); health promotion, education, and behavior (MPH, MS, MSPH, Dr PH, PhD); health services policy and management (MHA, MPH, Dr PH, PhD); industrial hygiene (MPH, MSPH, PhD); physical activity and public health (MPH); public health (MAT, MCD, MHA, MPH, MS, MSP, MSPH, DPT, Dr PH, Certificate); school health education (Certificate). Electronic applications accepted.

College of Arts and Sciences *Program availability:* Part-time, evening/weekend. Offers anthropology (MA, PhD); applied statistics (CAS); archive management (MA); art education (IMA, MA, MAT); art history (MA); art studio (MA); arts and sciences (IMA, M Math, MA, MAT, MFA, MIS, MMA, MPA, MS, PSM, CAS, Certificate); biology (MS, PhD); biology education (IMA, MAT); chemistry and biochemistry (IMA, MAT, MS, PhD); clinical/community psychology (MA, PhD); comparative literature (MA, PhD); creative writing (MFA); criminology and criminal justice (MA, PhD); ecology, evolution and organismal biology (MS, PhD); English (MA, PhD); English education (MAT); experimental psychology (MA, PhD); foreign languages (MAT); French (MA); general psychology (MA); geography (MA, MS, PhD); geography education (IMA); geological sciences (MS, PhD); German (MA); historic preservation (MA); history (MA, PhD); industrial statistics (MIS); international studies (MA, PhD); linguistics (MA, PhD); marine science (MS, PhD); mathematics (MA, MS, PhD); mathematics education (M Math, MAT); media arts (MMA); molecular, cellular, and developmental biology (MS, PhD); museum administration (MA); museum management (Certificate); philosophy (MA, PhD); physics and astronomy (IMA, MAT, MS, PSM, PhD); political science (MA, MPA, PhD); public administration (MPA); public history (MA, Certificate); religious studies (MA); school psychology (PhD); sociology (MA, PhD); Spanish (MA); statistics (MS, PhD); studio art (MFA); teaching English to speakers of other languages (Certificate); theatre (MA, MAT, MFA); women's studies (Certificate). Electronic applications accepted.

College of Education *Program availability:* Part-time, evening/weekend, online learning. Offers art education (IMA, MAT); business education (IMA, MAT); counseling education (PhD, Ed S); curriculum and instruction (Ed D); early childhood education (M Ed, Ed D, PhD); education (IMA, M Ed, MAT, MS, MT, Ed D, Certificate, Ed S); educational administration (M Ed, PhD, Ed S); educational psychology, research (M Ed, PhD); educational technology (M Ed); elementary education (MAT, Ed D, PhD); English (MAT); foreign language (MAT); foundations in education (PhD); health education (MAT); higher education and student affairs (M Ed); higher education leadership (Certificate); language and literacy (M Ed, PhD); mathematics (MAT); physical education (IMA, MAT, MS, PhD); science (IMA, MAT); secondary (Ed D); secondary education (IMA, MAT, MT, Ed D, PhD); social studies (MAT); special education (M Ed, MAT, PhD); teaching (M Ed, Ed S); theatre and speech (MAT). Electronic applications accepted.

College of Engineering and Computing *Program availability:* Part-time, evening/weekend, online learning. Offers chemical engineering (ME, MS, PhD); civil engineering (ME, MS, PhD); computer science and engineering (ME, MS, PhD); electrical engineering (ME, MS, PhD); engineering and computing (ME, MS, PhD); mechanical engineering (ME, MS, PhD); nuclear engineering (ME, MS, PhD); software engineering (MS). Electronic applications accepted.

College of Hospitality, Retail, and Sport Management *Program availability:* Part-time, online learning. Offers hospitality, retail, and sport management (MIHTM, MR, MS); hotel, restaurant and tourism management (MIHTM); live sport and entertainment events (MS); public assembly facilities management (MS); retailing (MR). Electronic applications accepted.

College of Mass Communications and Information Studies Offers journalism and mass communications (MA, MMC, PhD); library and information science (MLIS, PhD, Certificate, Specialist); mass communications and information studies (MA, MLIS, MMC, PhD, Certificate, Specialist).

College of Nursing *Program availability:* Part-time, online learning. Offers acute care clinical specialist (MSN); acute care nurse practitioner (MSN, Certificate); adult nurse practitioner (MSN); advanced practice clinical nursing (MSN, Certificate); advanced practice nursing in primary care (MSN, Certificate); advanced practice nursing in psychiatric mental health (MSN, Certificate); clinical nursing (MSN); community mental health and psychiatric health nursing (MSN); community/public health clinical nurse specialist (MSN); family nurse practitioner (MSN); health nursing (MSN); nursing administration (MSN); nursing practice (DNP); nursing science (PhD); pediatric nurse practitioner (MSN); psychiatric/mental health nurse practitioner (MSN); psychiatric/mental health specialist (MSN); women's health nurse practitioner (MSN). Electronic applications accepted.

College of Social Work *Program availability:* Part-time. Offers social work (MSW, PhD). Electronic applications accepted.

Darla Moore School of Business *Program availability:* Part-time, evening/weekend, online learning. Offers accountancy (M Acc); business administration (MBA, PhD); business measurement and assurance (M Acc); economics (MA, PhD); human resources (MHR); international business administration (IMBA). Electronic applications accepted.

School of Music *Program availability:* Part-time. Offers composition (MM, DMA); conducting (MM, DMA); jazz studies (MM); music education (MM Ed, PhD); music history (MM); music performance (Certificate); music theory (MM); opera theater (MM); performance (MM, DMA); piano pedagogy (MM, DMA). Electronic applications accepted.

School of the Environment *Program availability:* Part-time, online learning. Offers earth and environmental resources management (MEERM); environment (MEERM). Electronic applications accepted.

School of Law Offers law (JD).

School of Medicine Offers biomedical science (MBS, PhD); genetic counseling (MS); medicine (MBS, MNA, MRC, MS, MD, PhD, Certificate); nurse anesthesia (MNA); psychiatric rehabilitation (Certificate); rehabilitation counseling (MRC, Certificate). Electronic applications accepted.

South Carolina College of Pharmacy *Program availability:* Part-time. Offers pharmaceutical sciences (MS, PhD); pharmacy (MS, PhD, Pharm D). Electronic applications accepted.

UNIVERSITY OF SOUTH CAROLINA AIKEN, Aiken, SC 29801

General Information State-supported, coed, comprehensive institution. *Enrollment:* 3,548 graduate, professional, and undergraduate students; 20 full-time matriculated graduate/professional students (16 women), 37 part-time matriculated graduate/professional students (23 women). *Enrollment by degree level:* 57 master's. *Graduate faculty:* 17 full-time (11 women). Tuition, state resident: full-time $12,798; part-time $533 per credit hour. Tuition, nonresident: full-time $27,408; part-time $1142 per credit hour. *Required fees:* $11 per credit hour. $25 per semester. Full-time tuition and fees vary according to course load. *Graduate housing:* Room and/or apartments available on a first-come, first-served basis to single students; on-campus housing not available to married students. Typical cost: $4880 per year ($7466 including board). Room and board charges vary according to board plan. Housing application deadline: 6/1. *Student services:* Campus employment opportunities, campus safety program, career counseling, child daycare facilities, exercise/wellness program, free psychological counseling, grant writing training, international student services, multicultural affairs office, services for students with disabilities, teacher training, writing training. *Library facilities:* Gregg-Graniteville Library. *Collection:* Books: 138,795 (physical), 349,394 (digital/electronic); Serial titles: 2,277 (physical), 104,068 (digital/electronic); Databases: 236. Weekly public service hours: 78; students can reserve study rooms. *Research affiliation:* VA Boston Healthcare System (Post Traumatic Stress Disorder), Dwight D. Eisenhower Army Medical Center (neuroscience), University of South Florida (psychology), Baruch College (psychology), Illinois Institute of Technology (psychology), University of Rochester (psychology).

Computer facilities: 550 computers available on campus for general student use. A campuswide network can be accessed from student residence rooms and from off campus. Online class registration is available.
Website: http://www.usca.edu/

General Application Contact: Dan Robb, Associate Vice Chancellor for Enrollment Management, 803-641-3487, Fax: 803-641-3727, E-mail: danr@usca.edu.

GRADUATE UNITS

Program in Applied Clinical Psychology Students: 19 full-time (16 women), 11 part-time (9 women); includes 5 minority (3 Black or African American, non-Hispanic/Latino; 1 Native Hawaiian or other Pacific Islander, non-Hispanic/Latino; 1 Two or more races, non-Hispanic/Latino). Average age 26. 53 applicants, 34% accepted, 12 enrolled. *Faculty:* 9 full-time (7 women). Expenses: Contact institution. *Financial support:* In 2016–17, 23 students received support, including 16 research assistantships with partial tuition reimbursements available (averaging $3,594 per year), 4 teaching assistantships with partial tuition reimbursements available (averaging $3,438 per year); career-related internships or fieldwork, Federal Work-Study, scholarships/grants, tuition waivers (partial), and unspecified assistantships also available. Financial award application deadline: 3/15; financial award applicants required to submit FAFSA. In 2016, 7 master's awarded. *Program availability:* Part-time. Offers applied clinical psychology (MS). *Application deadline:* For fall admission, 5/15 priority date for domestic and international students. Applications are processed on a rolling basis. *Application fee:* $45. Electronic applications accepted. *Application Contact:* Dan Robb, Associate Vice Chancellor for Enrollment Management, 803-641-3487, Fax: 803-641-3727, E-mail: danr@usca.edu. *Director,* Dr. Jane Stafford, 803-641-3358, Fax: 803-641-3720, E-mail: jstafford@usca.edu.

Program in Business Administration for STEM and Liberal Arts Students: 1 full-time (0 women), 22 part-time (12 women); includes 1 minority (Black or African American, non-Hispanic/Latino), 1 international. Average age 34. 11 applicants, 82% accepted, 7 enrolled. *Faculty:* 4 full-time (2 women). Expenses: Contact institution. *Financial support:* In 2016–17, 8 students received support. Scholarships/grants and tuition waivers (partial) available. Support available to part-time students. Financial award application deadline: 3/15; financial award applicants required to submit FAFSA. *Program availability:* Part-time-only, evening/weekend. Offers business administration (MBA). *Application deadline:* For fall admission, 8/1 for domestic and international students; for spring admission, 12/3 for domestic and international students. Applications are processed on a rolling basis. *Application fee:* $45. Electronic applications accepted. *Application Contact:* Dan Robb, Associate Vice Chancellor for Enrollment Management, 803-641-3487, Fax: 803-641-3727, E-mail: danr@usca.edu. *Dean for School of Business Administration,* Dr. Michael J. Fekula, 803-641-3340, E-mail: mickf@usca.edu.

Program in Educational Technology Students: 4 part-time (2 women); includes 1 minority (Black or African American, non-Hispanic/Latino). Average age 33. 3 applicants, 33% accepted, 1 enrolled. *Faculty:* 4 full-time (2 women). Expenses: Contact institution. *Financial support:* In 2016–17, 1 student received support. Fellowships with partial tuition reimbursements available, career-related internships or fieldwork, Federal Work-Study, scholarships/grants, tuition waivers (partial), and unspecified assistantships available. Support available to part-time students. Financial award application deadline: 3/15; financial award applicants required to submit FAFSA. In 2016, 4 master's awarded. *Program availability:* Part-time, evening/weekend, online only, 100% online. Offers educational technology (M Ed). Program offered with University of South Carolina in Columbia. *Application deadline:* Applications are processed on a rolling basis. *Application fee:* $45. Electronic applications accepted. *Application Contact:* Dan Robb, Associate Vice Chancellor for Enrollment Management, 803-641-3487, Fax: 803-641-3727, E-mail: danr@usca.edu. *Educational Technology Program Coordinator,* Dr. Erin Besser, 803-641-3712, E-mail: erinbe@usca.edu.

UNIVERSITY OF SOUTH CAROLINA UPSTATE, Spartanburg, SC 29303-4999

General Information State-supported, coed, comprehensive institution. *Graduate housing:* On-campus housing not available.

GRADUATE UNITS

Graduate Programs *Program availability:* Part-time, evening/weekend. Offers early childhood education (M Ed); elementary education (M Ed); informatics (MS); special education: visual impairment (M Ed).

THE UNIVERSITY OF SOUTH DAKOTA, Vermillion, SD 57069

General Information State-supported, coed, university. CGS member. *Graduate housing:* Rooms and/or apartments available on a first-come, first-served basis to single and married students. Housing application deadline: 5/1.

GRADUATE UNITS

Graduate School *Program availability:* Part-time, evening/weekend, 100% online, blended/hybrid learning. Offers interdisciplinary studies (MA). Electronic applications accepted.

Beacom School of Business *Program availability:* Part-time, evening/weekend, online learning. Offers business (MBA, MP Acc); business administration (MBA); business analytics (MBA); health services administration (MBA); professional accountancy (MP Acc). Electronic applications accepted.

College of Arts and Sciences *Program availability:* Part-time, online learning. Offers addiction studies (MSA); American political institutions (PhD); American politics and public policy (MA); arts and sciences (EMPA, MA, MNS, MPA, MS, MSA, Au D, PhD); audiology (Au D); biology (MA, MS, PhD); chemistry (MS, PhD); clinical psychology (MA, PhD); communication studies (MA); computer science (MS); criminal justice studies (MSA); English (MA, PhD); health services administration (MSA); history (MA); human factors (MA, PhD); human resources (MSA); interdisciplinary studies (MSA); long term care administration (MSA); mathematics (MA, MS); organizational leadership (MSA); physics (MS, PhD); political science (EMPA, MA); public administration (MPA, PhD); public policy (PhD); speech-language pathology (MA). Electronic applications accepted.

College of Fine Arts Offers art education (MFA); ceramics (MFA); collaborative piano (MM); conducting (MM); design/technology (MFA); directing (MFA); fine arts (MA, MFA, MM); graphic design (MFA); history of musical instruments (MM); music education (MM); music history (MM); music performance (MM); painting (MFA); photography (MFA); printmaking (MFA); sculpture (MFA); theatre (MA). Electronic applications accepted.

Sanford School of Medicine *Program availability:* Part-time. Offers cardiovascular research (MS, PhD); cellular and molecular biology (MS, PhD); medicine (MS, MD, PhD); molecular microbiology and immunology (MS, PhD); neuroscience (MS, PhD); physiology and pharmacology (MS, PhD).

School of Education *Program availability:* Part-time, evening/weekend, online learning. Offers counseling (MA, PhD, Ed S); curriculum and instruction (Ed D, Ed S); education (MA, MS, Ed D, PhD, Ed S); educational administration (MA, Ed D, Ed S); elementary education (MA); human development and educational psychology (MA, PhD, Ed S); kinesiology and sport management (MA); school psychology (PhD, Ed S); secondary education (MA); secondary education plus certification (MA); special education (MA); technology for education and training (MS). Electronic applications accepted.

School of Health Sciences *Program availability:* Part-time. Offers health sciences (MA, MPH, MS, MSW, DPT, OTD, PhD, TDPT, Graduate Certificate); occupational therapy (MS, OTD); physical therapy (DPT, TDPT); physician assistant studies (MS); post-professional occupational therapy (OTD); public health (MPH); social work (MSW).

School of Law *Program availability:* Part-time. Offers law (JD). Electronic applications accepted.

UNIVERSITY OF SOUTHERN CALIFORNIA, Los Angeles, CA 90089

General Information Independent, coed, university. CGS member. *Graduate housing:* Rooms and/or apartments available on a first-come, first-served basis to single and married students. *Research affiliation:* SETI Institute (astronomy/astrobiology), Rancho Los Amigos Medical Center (medicine), Children's Hospital Los Angeles (medicine), Doheny Eye Institute (medicine), House Ear Institute (medicine), Jet Propulsion Laboratory (engineering and technology).

GRADUATE UNITS

Graduate School Electronic applications accepted.

Annenberg School for Communication and Journalism Students: 158 part-time; includes 301 minority (94 Black or African American, non-Hispanic/Latino; 3 American Indian or Alaska Native, non-Hispanic/Latino; 67 Asian, non-Hispanic/Latino; 115 Hispanic/Latino; 1 Native Hawaiian or other Pacific Islander, non-Hispanic/Latino; 21 Two or more races, non-Hispanic/Latino), 175 international. Average age 27. 1,325 applicants, 40% accepted, 319 enrolled. *Faculty:* 98 full-time, 100 part-time/adjunct. *Expenses:* Contact institution. *Financial support:* In 2016–17, 28 fellowships with full tuition reimbursements (averaging $22,287 per year), 16 research assistantships with partial tuition reimbursements (averaging $15,000 per year), 6 teaching assistantships with full tuition reimbursements (averaging $22,287 per year) were awarded; career-related internships or fieldwork, Federal Work-Study, institutionally sponsored loans, scholarships/grants, health care benefits, tuition waivers (partial), and unspecified assistantships also available. Support available to part-time students. Financial award application deadline: 1/2; financial award applicants required to submit FAFSA. In 2016, 419 master's, 21 doctorates awarded. *Program availability:* Part-time, evening/weekend, online learning. Offers communication (MA, MCM, MPD, MS, PhD); communication and journalism (MA, MCM, MPD, MS, PhD); communication management (MCM); culture and community (PhD); digital social media (MS); global and transnational communication (PhD); groups, organizations and networks (PhD); health communication and social dynamics (PhD); information, political economy and entertainment (PhD); journalism (MA, MS); new media and technology (PhD); public diplomacy (MPD); rhetoric, politics and public media (PhD); specialized journalism (MA); specialized journalism (the arts) (MA); strategic public relations (MA). *Application deadline:* For fall admission, 12/1 priority date for domestic and international students; for summer admission, 1/1 priority date for domestic and international students. Applications are processed on a rolling basis. *Application fee:* $90. Electronic applications accepted. *Application Contact:* Allyson Hill, Associate Dean for Admissions, 213-821-0770, Fax: 213-740-1933, E-mail: ascadm@usc.edu. *Dean,* Dr. Ernest J. Wilson, III, 213-740-6180, Fax: 213-740-3772, E-mail: ascdean@usc.edu.

Dana and David Dornsife College of Letters, Arts and Sciences Offers American studies and ethnicity (PhD); applied mathematics (MA, MS, PhD); art history (MA, PhD); biology (MS); brain and cognitive science (PhD); chemistry (PhD); classical Chinese literature (MA, PhD); classical Japanese literature (MA, PhD); classics (MA, PhD); clinical science (PhD); comparative literature (PhD); comparative media and culture (PhD); computational biology and bioinformatics (PhD); computational molecular biology (MS); developmental psychology (PhD); earth sciences (MS, PhD); East Asian linguistics (PhD); East Asian studies (MA); economic development programming (MA, PhD); English (MA, PhD); geographic information science and technology (MS, Graduate Certificate); Hispanic linguistics (PhD); history (PhD); human behavior (MHB); integrative and evolutionary biology (PhD); letters, arts and sciences (MA, MHB, MMM, MPW, MS, PhD, Graduate Certificate); linguistics (MA, PhD); literature and creative writing (PhD); marine and environmental biology (MS); marine biology and biological oceanography (MS, PhD); mathematical finance (MS); mathematics (MA, PhD); modern Chinese literature (MA, PhD); modern Japanese literature (MA, PhD); modern Korean literature (MA, PhD); molecular and computational biology (PhD); molecular biology (PhD); neurobiology (PhD); neuroscience (MS, PhD); ocean sciences (MS, PhD); philosophy (MA, PhD); physical chemistry (PhD); physics (MA, MS, PhD); political science and international relations (PhD); professional writing (MPW); quantitative methods (PhD); Slavic languages and literatures (MA, PhD); Slavic linguistics (PhD); social psychology (PhD); sociology (PhD); Spanish and Latin American studies (PhD); statistics (MS); visual studies (Graduate Certificate). Electronic applications accepted.

Davis School of Gerontology *Program availability:* Part-time, online learning. Offers aging services management (MASM); biology of aging (PhD); gerontology (MA, MS, PhD, Graduate Certificate); long term care administration (MLTCA). PhD in biology of aging offered jointly with Buck Institute for Research on Aging. Electronic applications accepted.

Gould School of Law Offers comparative law for foreign attorneys (MCL); law (JD); law for foreign-educated attorneys (LL M).

Herman Ostrow School of Dentistry Offers biokinesiology (MS, PhD); craniofacial biology (MS, PhD, Graduate Certificate); dentistry (MA, MS, DDS, DPT, OTD, PhD, Graduate Certificate); occupational science (PhD); occupational therapy (MA, OTD); physical therapy (DPT). Electronic applications accepted.

Marshall School of Business Offers accounting (M Acc); business (M Acc, MBA, MBT, MBV, MMM, MS, PhD); business administration (MBA, MMM, MS, PhD); business taxation (MBT); entrepreneurship and innovation (MS). Electronic applications accepted.

Roski School of Fine Arts Offers art and curatorial practices in the public sphere (MA); fine arts (MA, MFA); new genres (MFA); painting/drawing (MFA); photography (MFA); sculpture (MFA). Electronic applications accepted.

Rossier School of Education Offers education (MAT, ME, MMFT, Ed D, PhD); educational counseling (ME); educational psychology (Ed D, PhD); higher education administration (Ed D); higher education administration and policy (PhD); K-12 leadership in urban school settings (Ed D); K-12 policy and practice (PhD); marriage, family and child counseling (MMFT); postsecondary administration and student affairs [PASA] (ME); school counseling (ME); teacher education in multicultural societies (Ed D); teaching (online) (MAT); teaching and teaching credential (MAT); teaching English to speakers of other languages (MAT). Electronic applications accepted.

School of Architecture Offers architecture (M Arch, MBS, MHP, MLA, PhD). Electronic applications accepted.

School of Cinematic Arts Offers animation and digital arts (MFA); cinema-television (MA); cinema-television (critical studies) (PhD); cinematic arts (MA, MFA, PhD); film and television production (MFA); interactive media (MFA); media arts and practice (PhD); motion picture producing (MFA); writing for screen and television (MFA). Electronic applications accepted.

School of Dramatic Arts Offers acting (MFA); dramatic writing (MFA). Electronic applications accepted.

School of Pharmacy Offers clinical and experimental therapeutics (PhD); clinical research design and management (Graduate Certificate); food safety (Graduate Certificate); healthcare decision analysis (MS); patient and product safety (Graduate Certificate); pharmaceutical economics and policy (MS, PhD); pharmacology and pharmaceutical sciences (MS, PhD); pharmacy (MS, DRSc, PhD, Pharm D, Graduate Certificate); preclinical drug development (Graduate Certificate); regulatory and clinical affairs (Graduate Certificate); regulatory science (MS, DRSc).

School of Policy, Planning, and Development Offers ambulatory care (Graduate Certificate); health administration (EMHA, MHA, Graduate Certificate); homeland security and public policy (Graduate Certificate); international public policy and management (MPPM); leadership (EML); long-term care (Graduate Certificate); nonprofit management and policy (Graduate Certificate); policy, planning, and development (EMHA, EML, M PI, MHA, MPA, MPP, MPPM, MRED, DPPD, PhD, Graduate Certificate); political management (Graduate Certificate); public administration (MPA); public management (Graduate Certificate); public policy (MPP, Graduate Certificate); public policy and management (PhD); real estate development (MRED); sustainable cities (Graduate Certificate); transportation systems (Graduate Certificate); urban planning (M PI); urban planning and development (PhD). Electronic applications accepted.

School of Social Work Offers community organization, planning and administration (MSW); families and children (MSW); health (MSW); mental health (MSW); military social work and veterans services (MSW); older adults (MSW); public child welfare (MSW); school settings (MSW); social work (MSW, PhD); systems of mental illness recovery (MSW); work and life (MSW). Electronic applications accepted.

Thornton School of Music *Program availability:* Part-time, evening/weekend. Offers brass performance (MM, DMA, Graduate Certificate); choral and sacred music (MM, DMA); classical guitar (MM, DMA, Graduate Certificate); composition (MM, DMA); early music (MA, DMA); harp performance (MM, DMA, Graduate Certificate); historical musicology (PhD); jazz studies (MM, DMA, Graduate Certificate); keyboard collaborative arts (MM, DMA, Graduate Certificate); music education (MM, DMA); organ performance (MM, DMA, Graduate Certificate); percussion performance (MM, DMA, Graduate Certificate); piano performance (MM, DMA, Graduate Certificate); scoring for motion pictures and television (Graduate Certificate); strings performance (MM, DMA, Graduate Certificate); studio jazz guitar (MM, DMA, Graduate Certificate); teaching music (MA); vocal arts (classical voice/opera) (MM, DMA, Graduate Certificate); woodwind performance (MM, DMA, Graduate Certificate). Electronic applications accepted.

Viterbi School of Engineering *Program availability:* Part-time, online learning. Offers aerospace and mechanical engineering: computational fluid and solid mechanics (MS); aerospace and mechanical engineering: dynamics and control (MS); aerospace engineering (MS, PhD, Engr); applied mechanics (MS); astronautical engineering (MS, PhD, Engr, Graduate Certificate); biomedical engineering (PhD); chemical engineering (MS, PhD, Engr); civil engineering (MS, PhD); computer engineering (MS, PhD); computer networks (MS); computer science (MS, PhD); computer security (MS); computer-aided engineering (ME, Graduate Certificate); construction management (MCM); digital supply chain management (MS); electric power (MS); electrical engineering (MS, PhD, Engr); engineering (MCM, ME, MS, PhD, Engr, Graduate Certificate); engineering management (MS); engineering technology commercialization (Graduate Certificate); engineering technology communication (Graduate Certificate); environmental engineering (MS, PhD); environmental quality management (ME); game development (MS); geoscience technologies (MS); green technologies (MS); health systems operations (Graduate Certificate); high performance computing and simulations (MS); human language technology (MS); industrial and systems engineering (MS, PhD, Engr); intelligent robotics (MS); manufacturing engineering (MS); materials engineering (MS); materials science (MS, PhD, Engr); mechanical engineering (MS, PhD, Engr); medical device and diagnostic engineering (MS); medical imaging and imaging informatics (MS); multimedia and creative technologies (MS); operations research engineering (MS); optimization and supply chain management (Graduate Certificate); petroleum engineering (MS, PhD, Engr); product development engineering (MS); safety systems and security (MS); smart oilfield technologies (MS, Graduate Certificate); software engineering (MS); structural design (ME); sustainable cities (Graduate Certificate); systems architecting and engineering (MS, Graduate Certificate); systems safety and security (Graduate Certificate); telecommunications (MS); transportation systems (MS, Graduate Certificate); VLSI design (MS); water and waste management (MS); wireless health technology (MS). Electronic applications accepted.

Keck School of Medicine Students: 1,384 full-time (756 women), 59 part-time (41 women); includes 745 minority (87 Black or African American, non-Hispanic/Latino; 3 American Indian or Alaska Native, non-Hispanic/Latino; 489 Asian, non-Hispanic/Latino; 127 Hispanic/Latino; 6 Native Hawaiian or other Pacific Islander, non-Hispanic/Latino; 33 Two or more races, non-Hispanic/Latino), 188 international. Average age 25. 9,500 applicants, 10% accepted, 451 enrolled. *Faculty:* 420 full-time (128 women), 20 part-time/adjunct (9 women). Expenses: Contact institution. *Financial support:* In 2016–17, 43 fellowships with tuition reimbursements (averaging $32,000 per year), 98 research assistantships with tuition reimbursements (averaging $32,000 per year), 29 teaching assistantships with tuition reimbursements (averaging $32,000 per year) were awarded; career-related internships or fieldwork, Federal Work-Study, institutionally sponsored loans, scholarships/grants, traineeships, and health care benefits also available. Support available to part-time students. Financial award applicants required to submit CSS PROFILE or FAFSA. In 2016, 256 master's, 186 doctorates awarded. Offers cancer biology and genomics (PhD); development, stem cell and regenerative medicine (PhD); medical biology (PhD); medicine (MPAP, MPH, MS, MD, PhD, Certificate); molecular structure and signaling (PhD). *Application deadline:* Applications are processed on a rolling basis. *Application fee:* $90. Electronic applications accepted. *Application Contact:* Marisela Zuniga, Department Business Administrator, 323-442-1607, Fax: 323-442-1199, E-mail: mzuniga@usc.edu. *Dean,* Dr. Rohit Varma, 323-442-1900.

Graduate Programs in Medicine Students: 621 full-time (401 women), 59 part-time (41 women); includes 314 minority (31 Black or African American, non-Hispanic/Latino; 2 American Indian or Alaska Native, non-Hispanic/Latino; 208 Asian, non-Hispanic/Latino; 58 Hispanic/Latino; 5 Native Hawaiian or other Pacific Islander, non-Hispanic/Latino; 10 Two or more races, non-Hispanic/Latino), 186 international. Average age 26. 1,243 applicants, 43% accepted, 265 enrolled. *Faculty:* 332 full-time (125 women), 8 part-time/adjunct (2 women). Expenses: Contact institution. *Financial support:* In 2016–17, 42 fellowships with tuition reimbursements (averaging $32,000 per year), 82 research assistantships with tuition reimbursements (averaging $32,000 per year), 28 teaching assistantships with tuition reimbursements (averaging $32,000 per year) were awarded; career-related internships or fieldwork, Federal Work-Study, institutionally sponsored loans, scholarships/grants, traineeships, and health care benefits also available. Support available to part-time students. Financial award application deadline: 5/4; financial award applicants required to submit CSS PROFILE or FAFSA. In 2016, 256 master's, 22 doctorates awarded. Offers applied biostatistics and epidemiology (MS); biochemistry and molecular biology (MS); biomedical and biological sciences (PhD); biostatistics (MS, PhD); biostatistics and epidemiology (MPH); biotechnology (MS); child and family health (MPH); environmental health (MPH); epidemiology (PhD); experimental and molecular pathology (MS); global health leadership (MPH); global medicine (MS, Certificate); health behavior research (PhD); health communication (MPH); health education and promotion (MPH); medicine (MPAP, MPH, MS, PhD, Certificate); molecular epidemiology (MS); molecular microbiology and immunology (MS); physiology and biophysics (MS); primary care physician assistant (MPAP); public health (MPH); public health policy (MPH); stem cell biology and regenerative medicine (MS). *Application deadline:* Applications are processed on a rolling basis. *Application fee:* $90. Electronic applications accepted. *Application Contact:* Marisela Zuniga, Administrative Coordinator, 323-442-1607, Fax: 323-442-1199, E-mail: mzuniga@usc.edu. *Associate Dean for Graduate Affairs,* Dr. Ite Laird-Offringa, 323-442-1607, Fax: 323-442-1199, E-mail: ilaird@usc.edu.

UNIVERSITY OF SOUTHERN INDIANA, Evansville, IN 47712-3590

General Information State-supported, coed, comprehensive institution. CGS member. *Enrollment:* 9,024 graduate, professional, and undergraduate students; 554 full-time matriculated graduate/professional students (379 women), 514 part-time matriculated graduate/professional students (413 women). *Enrollment by degree level:* 964 master's, 29 doctoral, 28 other advanced degrees. *Graduate faculty:* 123 full-time (60 women), 15 part-time/adjunct (8 women). Tuition, state resident: full-time $8497. Tuition, nonresident: full-time $16,691. *Required fees:* $500. *Graduate housing:* Room and/or apartments available on a first-come, first-served basis to single students; on-campus housing not available to married students. Typical cost: $9942 per year ($13,982 including board). Room and board charges vary according to board plan. Housing application deadline: 3/1. *Student services:* Campus employment opportunities, campus safety program, career counseling, child daycare facilities, exercise/wellness program, free psychological counseling, international student services, low-cost health insurance, multicultural affairs office, services for students with disabilities. *Library facilities:* David L. Rice Library. *Collection:* Books: 222,413 (physical), 215,058 (digital/electronic); Serial titles: 127 (physical), 52,315 (digital/electronic); Databases: 122. Weekly public service hours: 114; students can reserve study rooms.

Computer facilities: 1,165 computers available on campus for general student use. A campuswide network can be accessed from student residence rooms and from off campus. Online class registration is available. Website: http://www.usi.edu/

General Application Contact: Dr. Mayola Rowser, Director, Graduate Studies, 812-465-7015, Fax: 812-464-1956, E-mail: mrowser@usi.edu.

GRADUATE UNITS

Graduate Studies Students: 554 full-time (379 women), 514 part-time (413 women); includes 107 minority (61 Black or African American, non-Hispanic/Latino; 2 American Indian or Alaska Native, non-Hispanic/Latino; 10 Asian, non-Hispanic/Latino; 25 Hispanic/Latino; 9 Two or more races, non-Hispanic/Latino), 23 international. Average age 33. 1,064 applicants, 56% accepted, 465 enrolled. *Faculty:* 123 full-time (60 women), 15 part-time/adjunct (8 women). Expenses: Contact institution. *Financial support:* In 2016–17, 87 students received support. Federal Work-Study, tuition waivers (full and partial), and unspecified assistantships available. Financial award application deadline: 3/1; financial award applicants required to submit FAFSA. In 2016, 271 master's, 20 doctorates, 8 other advanced degrees awarded. *Program availability:* Part-time, evening/weekend. *Application deadline:* Applications are processed on a rolling basis. *Application fee:* $40. Electronic applications accepted. *Director,* Dr. Mayola Rowser, 812-465-7015, Fax: 812-464-1956, E-mail: mrowser@usi.edu.

College of Liberal Arts Students: 168 full-time (134 women), 29 part-time (21 women); includes 18 minority (9 Black or African American, non-Hispanic/Latino; 1 American Indian or Alaska Native, non-Hispanic/Latino; 1 Asian, non-Hispanic/Latino; 4 Hispanic/Latino; 3 Two or more races, non-Hispanic/Latino), 12 international. Average age 30. *Faculty:* 63 full-time (33 women), 7 part-time/adjunct (3 women). Expenses: Contact institution. *Financial support:* In 2016–17, 29 students received support. Federal Work-Study, scholarships/grants, tuition waivers (full and partial), and

unspecified assistantships available. Financial award application deadline: 3/1; financial award applicants required to submit FAFSA. In 2016, 60 master's awarded. *Program availability:* Part-time, evening/weekend. Offers communication (MA); English (MA); liberal studies (MA); nonprofit administration (MPA); public administration (MPA); public sector administration (MPA); second language acquisition, policy, and culture (MA); social work (MSW). *Application deadline:* Applications are processed on a rolling basis. *Application fee:* $40. Electronic applications accepted. *Application Contact:* Dr. Mayola Rowser, Director, Graduate Studies, 812-465-7015, E-mail: mrowser@usi.edu. *Dean,* Dr. James M. Beeby, 812-464-1853, E-mail: jmbeeby@usi.edu.

College of Nursing and Health Professions Students: 189 full-time (156 women), 368 part-time (328 women); includes 51 minority (26 Black or African American, non-Hispanic/Latino; 1 American Indian or Alaska Native, non-Hispanic/Latino; 6 Asian, non-Hispanic/Latino; 15 Hispanic/Latino; 3 Two or more races, non-Hispanic/Latino). Average age 35. *Faculty:* 16 full-time (12 women), 3 part-time/adjunct (all women). Expenses: Contact institution. *Financial support:* In 2016–17, 23 students received support. Federal Work-Study, scholarships/grants, tuition waivers (full and partial), and unspecified assistantships available. Financial award application deadline: 3/1; financial award applicants required to submit FAFSA. In 2016, 162 master's, 20 doctorates, 8 other advanced degrees awarded. *Program availability:* Part-time, blended/hybrid learning. Offers adult-gerontology acute care nurse practitioner (MSN, PMC); adult-gerontology clinical nurse specialist (MSN, PMC); adult-gerontology primary care nurse practitioner (MSN, PMC); advanced nursing practice (DNP); family nurse practitioner (MSN, PMC); health administration (MHA); health informatics (MHA); nursing and health professions (MHA, MSN, MSOT, DNP, PMC); nursing education (MSN, PMC); nursing management and leadership (MSN, PMC); occupational therapy (MSOT); organizational and systems leadership (DNP); psychiatric mental health nurse practitioner (MSN, PMC). *Application deadline:* For fall admission, 2/1 for domestic and international students. Applications are processed on a rolling basis. *Application fee:* $40. Electronic applications accepted. *Application Contact:* Dr. Mayola Rowser, Director, Graduate Studies, 812-465-7015, Fax: 812-464-1956, E-mail: mrowser@usi.edu. *Dean,* Dr. Ann White, 812-465-1151, E-mail: awhite@usi.edu.

Pott College of Science, Engineering, and Education Students: 42 full-time (14 women), 21 part-time (14 women); includes 5 minority (3 Black or African American, non-Hispanic/Latino; 1 Hispanic/Latino; 1 Two or more races, non-Hispanic/Latino), 5 international. Average age 30. *Faculty:* 22 full-time (11 women), 3 part-time/adjunct (2 women). Expenses: Contact institution. *Financial support:* In 2016–17, 14 students received support. Federal Work-Study, scholarships/grants, tuition waivers (full and partial), and unspecified assistantships available. Financial award application deadline: 3/1; financial award applicants required to submit FAFSA. In 2016, 21 master's awarded. *Program availability:* Part-time, evening/weekend. Offers elementary education (MSE); industrial management (MSIM); mathematics teaching (MSE); school administration and leadership (MSE); science, engineering, and education (MSE, MSIM, MSSM); secondary education (MSE); sport management (MSSM). *Application deadline:* For fall admission, 8/15 priority date for domestic students, 3/1 priority date for international students. Applications are processed on a rolling basis. *Application fee:* $40. Electronic applications accepted. *Application Contact:* Dr. Mayola Rowser, Director, Graduate Studies, 812-465-7015, Fax: 812-464-1956, E-mail: mrowser@usi.edu. *Dean,* Dr. Zane W. Mitchell, 812-465-7137, E-mail: zwmitchell@usi.edu.

Romain College of Business Students: 149 full-time (70 women), 64 part-time (29 women); includes 25 minority (17 Black or African American, non-Hispanic/Latino; 1 Asian, non-Hispanic/Latino; 5 Hispanic/Latino; 2 Two or more races, non-Hispanic/Latino), 5 international. Average age 32. *Faculty:* 22 full-time (4 women), 2 part-time/adjunct (0 women). Expenses: Contact institution. *Financial support:* In 2016–17, 8 students received support. Career-related internships or fieldwork, Federal Work-Study, scholarships/grants, tuition waivers (full and partial), and unspecified assistantships available. Financial award application deadline: 3/1; financial award applicants required to submit FAFSA. In 2016, 36 master's awarded. *Program availability:* Part-time, evening/weekend. Offers accounting (MBA); business (MBA); business administration (MBA); data analytics (MBA); engineering management (MBA); health administration (MBA); human resources (MBA). *Application deadline:* For fall admission, 8/1 for domestic students, 3/1 priority date for international students. Applications are processed on a rolling basis. *Application fee:* $40. Electronic applications accepted. *Application Contact:* Dr. Jack Smothers, MBA Director, 812-461-5248, Fax: 812-464-1956, E-mail: jesmothers@usi.edu. *Dean,* Dr. Mohammed F. Khayum, 812-465-1681, E-mail: mkhayum@usi.edu.

UNIVERSITY OF SOUTHERN MAINE, Portland, ME 04103

General Information State-supported, coed, comprehensive institution. CGS member. *Graduate housing:* Rooms and/or apartments available on a first-come, first-served basis to single and married students. Housing application deadline: 5/1.

GRADUATE UNITS

College of Arts, Humanities, and Social Sciences *Program availability:* Part-time, evening/weekend, online learning. Offers American and New England studies (MA, CGS); arts, humanities, and social sciences (MA, MFA, MM, CGS); creative writing (MFA). Electronic applications accepted.

School of Music Offers composition (MM); conducting (MM); jazz studies (MM); music education (MM); performance (MM).

College of Management and Human Service Offers management and human service (MBA, MCPD, MPH, MPPM, MS, MS Ed, MSW, Psy D, CAS, CGS).

Muskie School of Public Service *Program availability:* Part-time, evening/weekend, online learning. Offers community planning and development (MCPD, CGS); health policy and management (MPH, CGS); public policy and management (MPPM). Electronic applications accepted.

School of Business *Program availability:* Part-time, evening/weekend. Offers accounting (MBA); business administration (MBA); finance (MBA); health management and policy (MBA); sustainability (MBA). Electronic applications accepted.

School of Education and Human Development *Program availability:* Part-time, evening/weekend, online learning. Offers adult and higher education (MS); adult learning (CAS); applied behavior analysis (MS, CGS); applied literacy (MS Ed); assistant principal (CGS); clinical mental health counseling (MS); counseling (CAS); culturally responsive practices in education and human development (CGS); education and human development (MS, MS Ed, Psy D, CAS, CGS); educational leadership (MS Ed, CAS); English as a second language (MS Ed, CAS, CGS); gifted and talented education (CGS); literacy education (MS Ed, CAS, CGS); mental health rehabilitation technician/community (CGS); professional educator (MS Ed); professional teacher (MS Ed); rehabilitation counseling (MS); school counseling (MS);

school psychology (MS, Psy D); special education (MS); substance abuse counseling (CGS); teaching all students (CGS); teaching and learning (MS Ed); youth with moderate to severe disabilities (CGS). Electronic applications accepted.

School of Social Work *Program availability:* Part-time, evening/weekend. Offers social work (MSW). Electronic applications accepted.

College of Science, Technology, and Health *Program availability:* Part-time, evening/weekend. Offers applied medical sciences (MS); biology (MS); computer science (MS); science, technology, and health (MS, DNP, CAS, CGS, PMC); software systems (CGS); statistics (MS, CGS). Electronic applications accepted.

School of Nursing *Program availability:* Part-time. Offers adult-gerontology primary care nurse practitioner (MS, PMC); education (MS); family nurse practitioner (MS, PMC); family psychiatric/mental health nurse practitioner (MS); management (MS); nursing (CAS, CGS); psychiatric-mental health nurse practitioner (PMC). Electronic applications accepted.

Lewiston-Auburn College Offers creative leadership/global strategies (CGS); leadership studies (MA); occupational therapy (MOT).

UNIVERSITY OF SOUTHERN MISSISSIPPI, Hattiesburg, MS 39406-0001

General Information State-supported, coed, university. CGS member. *Enrollment:* 14,552 graduate, professional, and undergraduate students; 1,494 full-time matriculated graduate/professional students (899 women), 1,193 part-time matriculated graduate/professional students (813 women). *Enrollment by degree level:* 1,658 master's, 955 doctoral, 81 other advanced degrees. *Graduate faculty:* 680 full-time (323 women), 216 part-time/adjunct (127 women). *Tuition, area resident:* Full-time $15,708; part-time $437 per credit hour. *Graduate housing:* Room and/or apartments available on a first-come, first-served basis to single students; on-campus housing not available to married students. Housing application deadline: 6/15. *Student services:* Campus employment opportunities, campus safety program, career counseling, child daycare facilities, exercise/wellness program, free psychological counseling, grant writing training, international student services, low-cost health insurance, multicultural affairs office, services for students with disabilities, teacher training, writing training. *Library facilities:* Cook Memorial Library plus 4 others. *Collection:* Books: 1.4 million (physical), 331,932 (digital/electronic); Serial titles: 27,243 (physical), 118,798 (digital/electronic); Databases: 200. Weekly public service hours: 117; students can reserve study rooms. *Research affiliation:* Oak Ridge Associated Universities.

Computer facilities: Computer purchase and lease plans are available. 436 computers available on campus for general student use. A campuswide network can be accessed from student residence rooms and from off campus. Online class registration is available.
Website: http://www.usm.edu/

General Application Contact: Tracy Barnhill, Manager of Graduate Admissions, 601-266-5137, Fax: 601-266-5138, E-mail: graduateschool@usm.edu.

GRADUATE UNITS

Graduate School Expenses: Contact institution. *Financial support:* Fellowships with full and partial tuition reimbursements, research assistantships with full and partial tuition reimbursements, teaching assistantships with full and partial tuition reimbursements, career-related internships or fieldwork, Federal Work-Study, institutionally sponsored loans, scholarships/grants, traineeships, and unspecified assistantships available. Support available to part-time students. Financial award application deadline: 3/15; financial award applicants required to submit FAFSA. *Program availability:* Part-time, evening/weekend. *Application deadline:* For fall admission, 2/1 priority date for domestic and international students. Applications are processed on a rolling basis. *Application fee:* $60. Electronic applications accepted. *Application Contact:* Tracy Barnhill, Manager of Graduate Admissions, 601-266-5908, Fax: 601-266-5138, E-mail: tracy.barnhill@usm.edu. *Dean,* Dr. Karen S. Coats, 601-266-4262, Fax: 601-266-5138, E-mail: karen.coats@usm.edu.

College of Arts and Letters Expenses: Contact institution. *Financial support:* Fellowships, research assistantships with full tuition reimbursements, teaching assistantships with full tuition reimbursements, Federal Work-Study, institutionally sponsored loans, scholarships/grants, health care benefits, and unspecified assistantships available. Financial award application deadline: 3/15; financial award applicants required to submit FAFSA. *Program availability:* Part-time, evening/weekend, online learning. Offers anthropology (MA); arts and letters (MA, MATL, MFA, MM, MME, MS, DMA, PhD); communication studies (MA, PhD); conducting (MM, DMA); costume design (MFA); creative writing (MA, PhD); directing (MFA); English education (MA); French (MATL); history (MA, MS, PhD); history and literature (MM); international development (PhD); lighting and sound design (MFA); literature (MA, PhD); mass communication (MA, MS, PhD); music education (MME, PhD); performance (MFA, MM); performance and pedagogy (DMA); piano accompanying (MM); political science (MA); public relations (MA, MS); scenic design (MFA); Spanish (MATL); teaching English to speakers of other languages (TESOL) (MATL); theory (MM); woodwind performance and pedagogy (MM). *Application deadline:* For fall admission, 5/1 for domestic students, 3/1 for international students. Applications are processed on a rolling basis. *Application fee:* $60. Electronic applications accepted. *Application Contact:* Shonna Breland, Manager of Graduate Admissions, 601-266-4369, Fax: 601-266-5138, E-mail: shonna.breland@usm.edu. *Dean,* Dr. Maureen Ryan, 601-266-4316, Fax: 601-266-6541, E-mail: maureen.ryan@usm.edu.

College of Business Expenses: Contact institution. *Financial support:* Research assistantships with full tuition reimbursements, teaching assistantships with full tuition reimbursements, Federal Work-Study, institutionally sponsored loans, scholarships/grants, and health care benefits available. Support available to part-time students. Financial award application deadline: 3/15; financial award applicants required to submit FAFSA. *Program availability:* Part-time, evening/weekend. Offers accountancy (MPA); business (MBA, MPA, MS); business administration (MBA); economic development (MS); sport management (MS); sport security management (MBA). *Application deadline:* For fall admission, 7/15 priority date for domestic students, 3/1 for international students; for spring admission, 11/15 priority date for domestic students, 11/5 for international students. Applications are processed on a rolling basis. *Application fee:* $60. Electronic applications accepted. *Application Contact:* Amy Yeend, Assistant Dean, Academic and Career Services, 601-266-4663, Fax: 601-266-5814. *Dean,* Dr. Faye W. Gilbert, 601-266-4659, Fax: 601-266-5814, E-mail: faye.gilbert@usm.edu.

College of Education and Psychology Expenses: Contact institution. *Financial support:* Research assistantships with full tuition reimbursements, teaching assistantships with full tuition reimbursements, career-related internships or fieldwork, Federal Work-Study, institutionally sponsored loans, scholarships/grants, health care benefits, and unspecified assistantships available. Financial award application

deadline: 3/15; financial award applicants required to submit FAFSA. *Program availability:* Part-time. Offers applied behavior analysis (MS); archives and special collections (Graduate Certificate); child and family studies (MS); clinical psychology (PhD); counseling psychology (MS, PhD); education and psychology (M Ed, MA, MAT, MLIS, MS, Ed D, PhD, Ed S, Graduate Certificate); educational administration (M Ed, Ed D, PhD, Ed S); educational administration and supervision (M Ed); educational studies and research (MS); elementary education (M Ed, PhD); higher education (Ed D); higher education administration (PhD); higher education: student affairs (M Ed); instructional technology (MS); instructional technology and design (PhD); library and information science (MLIS); marriage and family therapy (MS); research, evaluation, statistics, assessment (PhD); school counseling (M Ed); school psychology (PhD); secondary education (MAT); special education (M Ed, PhD); youth services and literature (Graduate Certificate). *Application deadline:* For fall admission, 3/1 priority date for domestic students, 3/1 for international students; for spring admission, 11/1 priority date for domestic students, 11/1 for international students. Applications are processed on a rolling basis. *Application fee:* $60. Electronic applications accepted. *Application Contact:* Shonna Breland, Manager of Graduate Admissions, 601-266-6563, Fax: 601-266-5138. *Dean,* Dr. Trent Gould, 601-266-4224, Fax: 601-266-4175, E-mail: trent.gould@usm.edu.

College of Health Expenses: Contact institution. *Financial support:* Fellowships with full tuition reimbursements, research assistantships with full tuition reimbursements, teaching assistantships with full tuition reimbursements, career-related internships or fieldwork, Federal Work-Study, institutionally sponsored loans, scholarships/grants, health care benefits, and unspecified assistantships available. Financial award application deadline: 3/15; financial award applicants required to submit FAFSA. *Program availability:* Part-time, evening/weekend. Offers audiology (Au D); epidemiology and biostatistics (MPH); health (MA, MLS, MPH, MS, MSW, Au D, PhD); health education (MPH); health policy and administration (MPH); kinesiology (MS, PhD); medical laboratory science (MLS); nutrition (MS); social work (MSW); speech-language pathology (MA, MS); sport coaching education (MS). *Application deadline:* For fall admission, 3/1 for domestic and international students; for spring admission, 1/10 priority date for domestic and international students. Applications are processed on a rolling basis. *Application fee:* $60. Electronic applications accepted. *Application Contact:* Shonna Breland, Manager of Graduate Admissions, 601-266-6563, Fax: 601-266-5138. *Dean,* Dr. Trent Gould, 601-266-5253.

College of Nursing Expenses: Contact institution. *Financial support:* Research assistantships with full tuition reimbursements, teaching assistantships, Federal Work-Study, institutionally sponsored loans, scholarships/grants, traineeships, health care benefits, and unspecified assistantships available. Financial award application deadline: 3/15; financial award applicants required to submit FAFSA. *Program availability:* Part-time, evening/weekend. Offers family nurse practitioner (MSN, Graduate Certificate); family psychiatric mental health nurse practitioner (MSN, Graduate Certificate); nursing (DNP, PhD); psychiatric mental health nurse practitioner (Graduate Certificate). *Application deadline:* For fall admission, 3/15 priority date for domestic students, 5/1 for international students; for spring admission, 1/10 priority date for domestic and international students. Applications are processed on a rolling basis. *Application fee:* $60. Electronic applications accepted. *Application Contact:* Dr. Sandra Bishop, Graduate Coordinator, 601-266-5500, Fax: 601-266-5927. *Interim Dean,* Dr. Kathleen Masters, 601-266-6485, Fax: 601-266-5927, E-mail: kathleen.masters@usm.edu.

College of Science and Technology Expenses: Contact institution. *Financial support:* Fellowships with full tuition reimbursements, research assistantships with full tuition reimbursements, teaching assistantships with full tuition reimbursements, career-related internships or fieldwork, Federal Work-Study, institutionally sponsored loans, scholarships/grants, health care benefits, and unspecified assistantships available. Financial award application deadline: 3/15; financial award applicants required to submit FAFSA. *Program availability:* Part-time, evening/weekend. Offers chemistry and biochemistry (PhD); coastal sciences (MS, PhD); computational science (MS, PhD); computer science (MS); criminal justice (MA, MS, PhD); environmental biology (MS); forensic science (MS); geography (MS, PhD); geology (MS); hydrographic science (MS); inorganic chemistry (MS); logistics, trade and transportation (MS); marine biology (MS); marine science (MS, PhD); mathematics (MS); microbiology (MS, PhD); molecular biology (MS, PhD); organic chemistry (MS); physical chemistry (MS); physics (MS); polymer science and engineering (MS, PhD); professional geology (MS); science and mathematics education (MS, PhD); science and technology (MA, MS, PhD). *Application deadline:* For fall admission, 3/1 priority date for domestic students, 3/1 for international students; for spring admission, 1/10 priority date for domestic and international students. Applications are processed on a rolling basis. *Application fee:* $60. *Application Contact:* Shonna Breland, Manager of Graduate School Admissions, 601-266-6567, Fax: 601-266-5138. *Interim Dean,* Dr. Chris Winstead, 601-266-4883, Fax: 601-266-5829.

UNIVERSITY OF SOUTH FLORIDA, Tampa, FL 33620-9951

General Information State-supported, coed, university. CGS member. *Enrollment:* 42,861 graduate, professional, and undergraduate students; 6,532 full-time matriculated graduate/professional students (3,466 women), 3,732 part-time matriculated graduate/professional students (2,362 women). *Enrollment by degree level:* 6,471 master's, 3,744 doctoral, 49 other advanced degrees. *Graduate faculty:* 1,194 full-time (493 women), 50 part-time/adjunct (19 women). *Tuition, state resident:* full-time $7766; part-time $431.43 per credit hour. *Tuition, nonresident:* full-time $15,789; part-time $877.17 per credit hour. *Required fees:* $37 per term. *Graduate housing:* Room and/or apartments available on a first-come, first-served basis to single students; on-campus housing not available to married students. Typical cost: $7520 per year ($1180 including board). Room and board charges vary according to board plan and housing facility selected. Housing application deadline: 8/18. *Student services:* Campus employment opportunities, campus safety program, career counseling, exercise/wellness program, free psychological counseling, international student services, multicultural affairs office, services for students with disabilities, teacher training, writing training. *Library facilities:* Tampa Campus Library plus 5 others. *Collection:* Books: 1.8 million (physical), 652,513 (digital/electronic); Serial titles: 537 (physical), 58,975 (digital/electronic); Databases: 930. Weekly public service hours: 116; study areas open 24 hours, 5–7 days a week; students can reserve study rooms. *Research affiliation:* Moffitt Cancer Center (medicine (primarily oncology)), Jaeb Center for Health Research (medicine), Florida Orthopaedic Institute (medicine), VA Hospitals (James A Haley and Bay Pines) (medicine), Florida Institute of Oceanography (marine science), National Science Foundation ICORPS (engineering, marine science, physics).

Computer facilities: 825 computers available on campus for general student use. A campuswide network can be accessed from student residence rooms and from off campus. Online class registration is available.
Website: http://www.usf.edu/

University of South Florida

General Application Contact: Dr. Dwayne Smith, Senior Vice Provost and Dean, Office of Graduate Studies, 813-974-2846, Fax: 813-974-5762, E-mail: mdsmith3@usf.edu.

GRADUATE UNITS

College of Arts and Sciences Students: 1,207 full-time (662 women), 547 part-time (334 women); includes 363 minority (91 Black or African American, non-Hispanic/Latino; 3 American Indian or Alaska Native, non-Hispanic/Latino; 58 Asian, non-Hispanic/Latino; 170 Hispanic/Latino; 3 Native Hawaiian or other Pacific Islander, non-Hispanic/Latino; 38 Two or more races, non-Hispanic/Latino), 315 international. Average age 31. 2,063 applicants, 40% accepted, 455 enrolled. *Faculty:* 378 full-time (140 women), 1 (woman) part-time/adjunct. Expenses: Contact institution. *Financial support:* In 2016–17, 395 students received support, including 2 research assistantships with tuition reimbursements available (averaging $13,650 per year); career-related internships or fieldwork, Federal Work-Study, institutionally sponsored loans, scholarships/grants, tuition waivers (full and partial), and unspecified assistantships also available. Support available to part-time students. Financial award applicants required to submit FAFSA. In 2016, 329 master's, 102 doctorates awarded. *Program availability:* Part-time, evening/weekend, online learning. Offers applied anthropology (MA, PhD); applied physics (PhD); arts and sciences (MA, MFA, MPA, MS, MURP, PhD, Graduate Certificate); biology (MS); cancer biology (PhD); cell and molecular biology (PhD); chemistry (MA, MS, PhD); communication (MA, PhD); creative writing (MFA); economics (MA, PhD); English (MA, PhD); French (MA); government (PhD); history (MA, PhD); integrative biology (PhD); Latin American, Caribbean and Latino studies (MA); liberal arts (MA); linguistics (MA); linguistics and applied linguistics studies (PhD); linguistics: English as a second language (MA); mathematics (MA, PhD); medical anthropology (Graduate Certificate); microbiology (MS); philosophy (MA, PhD); physics (MS); political science (MA); psychology (PhD); public administration (MPA); religious studies (MA); sociology (MA, PhD); Spanish (MA); statistics (MA, PhD); women's and gender studies (MA). *Application fee:* $30. Electronic applications accepted. *Application Contact:* Susan Hall, Executive Assistant to the Dean, 813-974-0853, Fax: 813-974-5911, E-mail: hall@usf.edu. *Dean,* Dr. Eric Eisenberg, 813-974-2804, Fax: 813-974-5911, E-mail: eisenberg@usf.edu.

School of Geosciences Students: 88 full-time (42 women), 44 part-time (17 women); includes 16 minority (7 Black or African American, non-Hispanic/Latino; 5 Asian, non-Hispanic/Latino; 3 Hispanic/Latino; 1 Two or more races, non-Hispanic/Latino), 34 international. Average age 32. 133 applicants, 51% accepted, 34 enrolled. *Faculty:* 31 full-time (6 women). Expenses: Contact institution. *Financial support:* In 2016–17, 47 students received support, including 3 research assistantships (averaging $12,345 per year), 25 teaching assistantships with tuition reimbursements available (averaging $12,807 per year); unspecified assistantships also available. Financial award application deadline: 3/1. In 2016, 28 master's, 7 doctorates awarded. *Program availability:* Part-time, evening/weekend. Offers environmental science and policy (MS); geography (MA); geography and environmental science and policy (PhD); geology (MS, PhD); urban and regional planning (MURP). *Application deadline:* For fall admission, 2/15 for domestic and international students; for spring admission, 10/15 for domestic students, 9/15 for international students. *Application fee:* $30. Electronic applications accepted. *Application Contact:* Dr. Jennifer Collins, Associate Professor and Graduate Program Coordinator, 813-974-4242, Fax: 813-974-5911, E-mail: collinsjm@usf.edu. *Professor and Chair, Geography Division,* Dr. Jayajit Chakraborty, 813-974-8188, Fax: 813-974-5911, E-mail: jchakrab@usf.edu.

School of Information Students: 112 full-time (73 women), 163 part-time (127 women); includes 80 minority (28 Black or African American, non-Hispanic/Latino; 11 Asian, non-Hispanic/Latino; 32 Hispanic/Latino; 1 Native Hawaiian or other Pacific Islander, non-Hispanic/Latino; 8 Two or more races, non-Hispanic/Latino), 1 international. Average age 33. 167 applicants, 84% accepted, 90 enrolled. *Faculty:* 17 full-time (8 women). Expenses: Contact institution. *Financial support:* In 2016–17, 47 students received support. Unspecified assistantships available. Financial award application deadline: 6/30. In 2016, 61 master's awarded. *Program availability:* Part-time, evening/weekend, online learning. Offers intelligence studies (MS); library and information science (MA). *Application deadline:* For fall admission, 6/1 for domestic students, 2/15 for international students; for spring admission, 10/15 for domestic students, 9/15 for international students. Applications are processed on a rolling basis. *Application fee:* $30. Electronic applications accepted. *Application Contact:* Diane Austin, Assistant Director, 813-974-6364, Fax: 813-974-6840, E-mail: dianeaustin@usf.edu. *Director and Associate Professor,* Dr. Jim Andrews, 813-974-2108, Fax: 813-974-6840, E-mail: jimandrews@usf.edu.

School of Mass Communications Students: 27 full-time (23 women), 18 part-time (10 women); includes 5 minority (2 Black or African American, non-Hispanic/Latino; 2 Hispanic/Latino; 1 Native Hawaiian or other Pacific Islander, non-Hispanic/Latino), 25 international. Average age 27. 39 applicants, 82% accepted, 21 enrolled. *Faculty:* 11 full-time (6 women). Expenses: Contact institution. *Financial support:* In 2016–17, 5 students received support, including 9 teaching assistantships with tuition reimbursements available (averaging $10,513 per year); unspecified assistantships also available. Financial award application deadline: 2/28. In 2016, 16 master's awarded. *Program availability:* Part-time, evening/weekend. Offers mass communications (MA). *Application deadline:* For fall admission, 2/15 for domestic and international students. *Application fee:* $30. Electronic applications accepted. *Application Contact:* Dr. Michael Mitrook, Assistant Professor, 813-974-8890, Fax: 813-974-2592, E-mail: mmitrook@usf.edu. *Interim Director/Associate Professor,* Dr. Jim Andrews, 813-974-2108, Fax: 813-974-2592, E-mail: jimandrews@usf.edu.

College of Behavioral and Community Sciences Students: 575 full-time (499 women), 239 part-time (196 women); includes 259 minority (87 Black or African American, non-Hispanic/Latino; 2 American Indian or Alaska Native, non-Hispanic/Latino; 22 Asian, non-Hispanic/Latino; 126 Hispanic/Latino; 22 Two or more races, non-Hispanic/Latino), 18 international. Average age 28. 1,282 applicants, 35% accepted, 328 enrolled. *Faculty:* 93 full-time (59 women), 2 part-time/adjunct (1 woman). Expenses: Contact institution. *Financial support:* In 2016–17, 212 students received support. In 2016, 223 master's, 26 doctorates awarded. Offers applied behavior analysis (MA, MS, PhD); audiology (Au D); behavioral and community sciences (MA, MS, MSW, Au D, PhD, Graduate Certificate); child and adolescent behavioral health (MS); communication sciences and disorders (PhD); criminal justice administration (MA); criminology (MA, PhD); rehabilitation and mental health counseling (MA); speech-language pathology (MS). *Application Contact:* Dr. Francisco Vera, Assistant Director for Graduate Admissions, 813-974-2829, E-mail: fvera@usf.edu. *Dean,* Dr. Julianne Serovich, 813-974-1990, Fax: 813-974-2365, E-mail: jserovich@usf.edu.

School of Aging Studies Students: 27 full-time (21 women), 5 part-time (all women); includes 13 minority (4 Black or African American, non-Hispanic/Latino; 1 Asian, non-Hispanic/Latino; 6 Hispanic/Latino; 2 Two or more races, non-Hispanic/Latino), 1 international. Average age 29. 35 applicants, 31% accepted, 7 enrolled. *Faculty:* 9 full-time (4 women). Expenses: Contact institution. *Financial support:* In 2016–17, 9 students received support, including 2 research assistantships with tuition reimbursements available (averaging $15,690 per year), 13 teaching assistantships with tuition reimbursements available (averaging $13,503 per year). Financial award application deadline: 2/3. In 2016, 5 master's, 4 doctorates awarded. *Program availability:* Part-time, evening/weekend. Offers aging studies (PhD); gerontology (MA). *Application deadline:* For fall admission, 12/11 priority date for domestic and international students; for spring admission, 10/15 for domestic students, 9/15 for international students; for summer admission, 2/15 for domestic students, 1/15 for international students. *Application fee:* $30. Electronic applications accepted. *Application Contact:* Brent Small, Professor, 813-974-9746, Fax: 813-974-9754, E-mail: bsmall@usf.edu. *Director and Professor,* Dr. Cathy L. McEvoy, 813-974-1940, Fax: 813-974-9754, E-mail: cmcevoy@usf.edu.

School of Social Work Students: 166 full-time (147 women), 25 part-time (22 women); includes 71 minority (33 Black or African American, non-Hispanic/Latino; 1 American Indian or Alaska Native, non-Hispanic/Latino; 2 Asian, non-Hispanic/Latino; 32 Hispanic/Latino; 3 Two or more races, non-Hispanic/Latino), 1 international. Average age 30. 213 applicants, 62% accepted, 88 enrolled. *Faculty:* 11 full-time (10 women). Expenses: Contact institution. *Financial support:* In 2016–17, 50 students received support, including 1 research assistantship with tuition reimbursement available (averaging $9,001 per year); unspecified assistantships also available. Financial award application deadline: 3/15; financial award applicants required to submit FAFSA. In 2016, 62 master's awarded. *Program availability:* Part-time, evening/weekend. Offers social work (MSW, PhD). *Application deadline:* For fall admission, 2/15 priority date for domestic students, 2/15 for international students. Applications are processed on a rolling basis. *Application fee:* $30. Electronic applications accepted. *Application Contact:* Dr. Marion Becker, MSW Chair/Professor, 813-974-7188, Fax: 813-974-4675, E-mail: mbecker2@usf.edu. *PhD Program Chair/Assistant Professor,* Dr. Nan Sook Park, 813-974-4194, Fax: 813-974-4675, E-mail: nanpark@usf.edu.

College of Education Students: 449 full-time (309 women), 710 part-time (525 women); includes 335 minority (144 Black or African American, non-Hispanic/Latino; 2 American Indian or Alaska Native, non-Hispanic/Latino; 30 Asian, non-Hispanic/Latino; 140 Hispanic/Latino; 2 Native Hawaiian or other Pacific Islander, non-Hispanic/Latino; 17 Two or more races, non-Hispanic/Latino), 110 international. Average age 35. 716 applicants, 50% accepted, 265 enrolled. *Faculty:* 88 full-time (54 women). Expenses: Contact institution. *Financial support:* In 2016–17, 188 students received support, including 9 fellowships with full tuition reimbursements available (averaging $15,000 per year), 2 research assistantships with full tuition reimbursements available (averaging $15,000 per year); career-related internships or fieldwork, Federal Work-Study, institutionally sponsored loans, scholarships/grants, health care benefits, and unspecified assistantships also available. Support available to part-time students. Financial award applicants required to submit FAFSA. In 2016, 348 master's, 62 doctorates, 10 other advanced degrees awarded. *Program availability:* Part-time, evening/weekend, online learning. Offers adult education (MA, Ed D, PhD, Ed S); career and technical education (MA); career and workforce education (PhD); college student affairs (M Ed); counselor education (MA, PhD, Ed S); early childhood education (M Ed, MA, PhD); education (M Ed, MA, MAT, Ed D, PhD, Ed S); elementary education (MA, MAT, PhD); higher education/community college teaching (MA, Ed D, PhD); interdisciplinary (PhD, Ed S); reading/language arts (MA, PhD, Ed S); school psychology (PhD, Ed S); vocational education (Ed S). *Application deadline:* For fall admission, 2/15 for domestic students, 1/2 for international students; for spring admission, 10/15 for domestic students, 6/1 for international students. *Application fee:* $30. Electronic applications accepted. *Application Contact:* Dr. Diane Briscoe, Coordinator of Graduate Studies, 813-974-1804, Fax: 813-974-3391, E-mail: briscoe@usf.edu. *Dean,* Dr. Colleen S. Kennedy, 813-974-3400, Fax: 813-974-3826.

College of Engineering Students: 915 full-time (211 women), 312 part-time (62 women); includes 141 minority (33 Black or African American, non-Hispanic/Latino; 32 Asian, non-Hispanic/Latino; 68 Hispanic/Latino; 8 Two or more races, non-Hispanic/Latino), 846 international. Average age 27. 2,235 applicants, 47% accepted, 366 enrolled. *Faculty:* 122 full-time (19 women), 1 part-time/adjunct (0 women). Expenses: Contact institution. *Financial support:* In 2016–17, 179 students received support. Career-related internships or fieldwork, Federal Work-Study, scholarships/grants, health care benefits, and unspecified assistantships available. Financial award application deadline: 3/1. In 2016, 362 master's, 63 doctorates awarded. *Program availability:* Part-time, evening/weekend. Offers biomedical engineering (MSBE, PhD); chemical engineering (MSCH, PhD); civil engineering (MCE, MSCE, PhD); computer engineering (MSCP); computer science (MSCS); computer science and engineering (PhD); electrical engineering (MSEE, PhD); engineering (MCE, MEVE, MME, MSBE, MSCE, MSCH, MSCP, MSCS, MSEE, MSEM, MSEV, MSIE, MSIT, MSME, PhD, Graduate Certificate); engineering management (MSEM); environmental engineering (MEVE, MSEV, PhD); industrial engineering (MSIE, PhD); information technology (MSIT); mechanical engineering (MME, MSME, PhD). *Application deadline:* For fall admission, 2/15 for domestic students, 1/2 priority date for international students; for spring admission, 10/15 for domestic students, 6/1 priority date for international students. Applications are processed on a rolling basis. *Application fee:* $30. Electronic applications accepted. *Application Contact:* Dr. Sanjukta Bhanja, Associate Dean for Academic Affairs, 813-974-4755, Fax: 813-974-5094, E-mail: bhanja@usf.edu. *Dean,* Dr. Robert Bishop, 813-974-3864, Fax: 813-974-5094, E-mail: robertbishop@usf.edu.

College of Global Sustainability Students: 59 full-time (35 women), 51 part-time (29 women); includes 25 minority (3 Black or African American, non-Hispanic/Latino; 1 American Indian or Alaska Native, non-Hispanic/Latino; 2 Asian, non-Hispanic/Latino; 16 Hispanic/Latino; 3 Two or more races, non-Hispanic/Latino), 30 international. Average age 28. 134 applicants, 59% accepted, 55 enrolled. *Faculty:* 4 full-time (0 women). Expenses: Contact institution. *Financial support:* In 2016–17, 20 students received support. In 2016, 36 master's awarded. Offers energy, global, water and sustainable tourism (Graduate Certificate); global sustainability (MA). *Application deadline:* For fall admission, 6/1 for domestic students, 5/1 for international students; for spring admission, 10/15 for domestic students, 9/15 for international students. Electronic applications accepted. *Interim Dean,* Dr. Rafael Perez, 813-974-9694, E-mail: perez@usf.edu.

College of Graduate Studies Students: 63 full-time (20 women), 199 part-time (55 women); includes 99 minority (33 Black or African American, non-Hispanic/Latino; 1 American Indian or Alaska Native, non-Hispanic/Latino; 9 Asian, non-Hispanic/Latino; 42 Hispanic/Latino; 3 Native Hawaiian or other Pacific Islander, non-Hispanic/Latino; 11 Two or more races, non-Hispanic/Latino), 1 international. Average age 35. 104 applicants, 68% accepted, 49 enrolled. *Faculty:* 1 (woman) full-time. Expenses: Contact institution. *Financial support:* In 2016–17, 5 students received support. Teaching assistantships available. Financial award application deadline: 2/1; financial award applicants required to submit FAFSA. In 2016, 24 master's awarded. *Program availability:* Part-time, evening/weekend, online learning. Offers cybersecurity (MS). *Application deadline:* For fall admission, 2/15 for domestic and international students; for spring admission, 10/15 for domestic students, 9/15 for international students; for summer admission, 2/15 for domestic and international students. *Application fee:* $30. Electronic applications accepted. *Application Contact:* Paul Crawford, Associate Director for Graduate Admissions, 813-974-8800, E-mail: pjcrawford@usf.edu. *Dean,* Dr. Dwayne Smith, 813-974-7359, Fax: 813-974-5762, E-mail: mdsmith8@usf.edu.

College of Marine Science Students: 84 full-time (57 women), 22 part-time (10 women); includes 16 minority (2 Black or African American, non-Hispanic/Latino; 1 Asian, non-Hispanic/Latino; 8 Hispanic/Latino; 5 Two or more races, non-Hispanic/Latino), 13 international. Average age 29. 94 applicants, 30% accepted, 23 enrolled. *Faculty:* 26 full-time (6 women). Expenses: Contact institution. *Financial support:* In 2016–17, 48 students received support, including 45 research assistantships with partial tuition reimbursements available (averaging $14,199 per year), 10 teaching assistantships with partial tuition reimbursements available (averaging $14,196 per year); health care benefits and unspecified assistantships also available. Financial award application deadline: 1/15. In 2016, 12 master's, 4 doctorates awarded. *Program availability:* Part-time. Offers marine science (MS, PhD). *Application deadline:* For fall admission, 1/10 for domestic students, 1/2 for international students; for spring admission, 10/1 for domestic students, 6/1 for international students. Applications are processed on a rolling basis. *Application fee:* $30. Electronic applications accepted. *Application Contact:* Dr. David F. Naar, Associate Professor and Director of Academic Affairs, 727-553-1637, Fax: 727-553-1189, E-mail: naar@usf.edu. *Dean,* Dr. Jacqueline E. Dixon, 727-553-3369, Fax: 727-553-1189, E-mail: jdixon@usf.edu.

College of Nursing Students: 194 full-time (151 women), 624 part-time (546 women); includes 273 minority (89 Black or African American, non-Hispanic/Latino; 2 American Indian or Alaska Native, non-Hispanic/Latino; 51 Asian, non-Hispanic/Latino; 105 Hispanic/Latino; 2 Native Hawaiian or other Pacific Islander, non-Hispanic/Latino; 24 Two or more races, non-Hispanic/Latino), 9 international. Average age 33. 672 applicants, 48% accepted, 262 enrolled. *Faculty:* 45 full-time (38 women), 3 part-time/adjunct (2 women). Expenses: Contact institution. *Financial support:* In 2016–17, 129 students received support, including 7 research assistantships with tuition reimbursements available (averaging $18,935 per year), 29 teaching assistantships with tuition reimbursements available (averaging $30,814 per year); tuition waivers (partial) and unspecified assistantships also available. Financial award application deadline: 2/1; financial award applicants required to submit FAFSA. In 2016, 317 master's, 27 doctorates awarded. *Program availability:* Part-time. Offers advanced pain management (Graduate Certificate); nursing (MS, DNP); nursing education (Post Master's Certificate); nursing science (PhD). *Application deadline:* For fall admission, 12/15 for domestic and international students; for spring admission, 10/1 for domestic students, 9/15 for international students. *Application fee:* $30. Electronic applications accepted. *Application Contact:* Dr. Brian Graves, Assistant Professor/Assistant Dean, 813-974-8054, Fax: 813-974-5418, E-mail: bgraves1@health.usf.edu. *Dean, College of Nursing,* Dr. Victoria Rich, 813-974-8939, Fax: 813-974-5418, E-mail: victoriarich@health.usf.edu.

College of Pharmacy Students: 391 full-time (233 women), 1 (woman) part-time; includes 170 minority (29 Black or African American, non-Hispanic/Latino; 63 Asian, non-Hispanic/Latino; 62 Hispanic/Latino; 4 Native Hawaiian or other Pacific Islander, non-Hispanic/Latino; 12 Two or more races, non-Hispanic/Latino). Average age 26. 679 applicants, 29% accepted, 102 enrolled. *Faculty:* 41 full-time (28 women), 2 part-time/adjunct (0 women). Expenses: Contact institution. *Financial support:* In 2016–17, 131 students received support. In 2016, 53 doctorates awarded. Offers pharmaceutical nanotechnology (MS); pharmacy (Pharm D). *Application deadline:* For fall admission, 2/15 for domestic and international students; for spring admission, 10/15 for domestic students, 9/15 for international students; for summer admission, 2/15 for domestic and international students. Electronic applications accepted. *Application Contact:* Dr. Amy Schwartz, Associate Dean, 813-974-2251, E-mail: aschwar1@health.usf.edu. *Dean,* Dr. Kevin Sneed, 813-974-5699, E-mail: ksneed@health.usf.edu.

College of Public Health Students: 399 full-time (278 women), 399 part-time (298 women); includes 237 minority (122 Black or African American, non-Hispanic/Latino; 1 American Indian or Alaska Native, non-Hispanic/Latino; 48 Asian, non-Hispanic/Latino; 64 Hispanic/Latino), 94 international. Average age 33. 1,200 applicants, 54% accepted, 400 enrolled. *Faculty:* 60 full-time (27 women), 34 part-time/adjunct (13 women). Expenses: Contact institution. *Financial support:* In 2016–17, 46 students received support, including 18 fellowships with full tuition reimbursements available (averaging $32,033 per year), 135 research assistantships with full and partial tuition reimbursements available (averaging $19,597 per year), 66 teaching assistantships (averaging $19,296 per year); career-related internships or fieldwork, Federal Work-Study, institutionally sponsored loans, scholarships/grants, traineeships, and unspecified assistantships also available. Support available to part-time students. Financial award application deadline: 11/15; financial award applicants required to submit FAFSA. In 2016, 136 master's, 6 doctorates awarded. *Program availability:* Part-time, evening/weekend, 100% online, blended/hybrid learning. Offers community and family health (MPH, MSPH, Dr PH, PhD); environmental and occupational health (MPH, MSPH, PhD); epidemiology and biostatistics (MPH, MSPH, PhD); global health (MPH, MSPH, Dr PH, PhD); health policy and management (MHA, MPH, MSPH, PhD); public health (MHA, MPH, MSPH, Dr PH, PhD); public health practice (MPH). *Application deadline:* For fall admission, 5/1 for domestic and international students; for spring admission, 6/15 for domestic and international students; for summer admission, 11/15 for domestic and international students. Applications are processed on a rolling basis. *Application fee:* $30. Electronic applications accepted. *Application Contact:* Kamala Dontamsetti, Assistant Director of Graduate Admissions, 813-974-8874, Fax: 813-974-8121, E-mail: kamalad@health.usf.edu. *Dean,* Dr. Donna J. Petersen, 813-974-3623, Fax: 813-974-7390.

College of The Arts Students: 204 full-time (84 women), 34 part-time (16 women); includes 66 minority (12 Black or African American, non-Hispanic/Latino; 8 Asian, non-Hispanic/Latino; 38 Hispanic/Latino; 8 Two or more races, non-Hispanic/Latino), 41 international. Average age 27. 236 applicants, 44% accepted, 79 enrolled. *Faculty:* 60 full-time (23 women), 1 part-time/adjunct (0 women). Expenses: Contact institution. *Financial support:* In 2016–17, 129 students received support. Unspecified assistantships available. In 2016, 96 master's, 3 doctorates awarded. *Program availability:* Part-time, evening/weekend. Offers the arts (M Arch, MA, MFA, MM, MUCD, PhD). *Application deadline:* For fall admission, 1/15 for domestic and international students; for spring admission, 10/15 for domestic students, 9/15 for international students; for summer admission, 2/15 for domestic students, 1/15 for international students. *Application fee:* $30. Electronic applications accepted. *Application Contact:* Prof. Barton Lee, Senior Associate Dean, 813-974-2301, Fax: 813-974-2091, E-mail: blee@usf.edu. *Dean,* Dr. James S. Moy, 813-974-7380, Fax: 813-974-2091, E-mail: moy@usf.edu.

School of Architecture and Community Design Students: 103 full-time (40 women), 13 part-time (8 women); includes 41 minority (6 Black or African American, non-Hispanic/Latino; 6 Asian, non-Hispanic/Latino; 26 Hispanic/Latino; 3 Two or more

races, non-Hispanic/Latino), 17 international. Average age 25. 83 applicants, 43% accepted, 25 enrolled. *Faculty:* 10 full-time (1 woman). Expenses: Contact institution. *Financial support:* In 2016–17, 48 students received support, including 3 teaching assistantships with tuition reimbursements available (averaging $9,360 per year); Federal Work-Study, scholarships/grants, and unspecified assistantships also available. In 2016, 51 master's awarded. Offers architecture (M Arch); urban and community design (MUCD). *Application deadline:* For fall admission, 2/1 priority date for domestic students, 2/1 for international students. Applications are processed on a rolling basis. *Application fee:* $30. Electronic applications accepted. *Application Contact:* Mildred Abreu, Academic Advisor, 813-974-1216, Fax: 813-974-2557, E-mail: abreu@arch.usf.edu. *Director and Professor, School of Architecture and Community Design,* Dr. Robert MacLeod, 813-974-6015, Fax: 813-974-2557, E-mail: rmacleod@arch.usf.edu.

School of Art and Art History Students: 35 full-time (17 women), 2 part-time (both women); includes 10 minority (7 Hispanic/Latino; 3 Two or more races, non-Hispanic/Latino), 3 international. Average age 29. 60 applicants, 27% accepted, 16 enrolled. *Faculty:* 20 full-time (10 women). Expenses: Contact institution. *Financial support:* In 2016–17, 33 students received support, including 37 teaching assistantships with partial tuition reimbursements available (averaging $9,440 per year); scholarships/grants, health care benefits, and unspecified assistantships also available. Support available to part-time students. Financial award application deadline: 2/15; financial award applicants required to submit FAFSA. In 2016, 16 master's awarded. *Program availability:* Part-time. Offers art (MFA); art history (MA). *Application deadline:* For fall admission, 1/15 for domestic students, 2/1 for international students; for spring admission, 10/15 for domestic students, 9/15 for international students; for summer admission, 2/15 for domestic students, 1/15 for international students. *Application fee:* $30. Electronic applications accepted. *Application Contact:* Prof. Neil Bender, Associate Professor and Graduate Program Director, 813-974-2360, Fax: 813-974-9226, E-mail: nb2@usf.edu. *Director,* Prof. Wallace Wilson, 813-974-2360, Fax: 813-974-9226, E-mail: wwilson2@usf.edu.

School of Music Students: 66 full-time (27 women), 19 part-time (6 women); includes 15 minority (6 Black or African American, non-Hispanic/Latino; 2 Asian, non-Hispanic/Latino; 5 Hispanic/Latino; 2 Two or more races, non-Hispanic/Latino), 21 international. Average age 29. 93 applicants, 56% accepted, 38 enrolled. *Faculty:* 26 full-time (9 women), 1 part-time/adjunct (0 women). Expenses: Contact institution. *Financial support:* In 2016–17, 48 students received support, including 1 research assistantship with tuition reimbursement available (averaging $15,724 per year), 46 teaching assistantships with tuition reimbursements available (averaging $10,099 per year); unspecified assistantships also available. Financial award application deadline: 2/15. In 2016, 29 master's, 3 doctorates awarded. *Program availability:* Part-time, evening/weekend. Offers music (MM, PhD); music education (MA). *Application deadline:* For fall admission, 2/15 priority date for domestic students, 2/1 for international students; for spring admission, 10/15 for domestic students, 9/15 for international students; for summer admission, 2/15 for domestic students, 1/15 for international students. *Application fee:* $30. Electronic applications accepted. *Application Contact:* Dr. William Hayden, Associate Professor and Graduate Program Director, 813-974-1753, Fax: 813-974-8721, E-mail: wphayden@usf.edu. *Director,* Dr. Karen Bryan, 813-974-2311, Fax: 813-974-8721, E-mail: kmbryan@usf.edu.

Innovative Education Expenses: Contact institution. Offers adult, career and higher education (Graduate Certificate); Africana studies (Graduate Certificate); aging studies (Graduate Certificate); art research (Graduate Certificate); business foundations (Graduate Certificate); chemical and biomedical engineering (Graduate Certificate); child and family studies (Graduate Certificate); civil and industrial engineering (Graduate Certificate); community and family health (Graduate Certificate); criminology (Graduate Certificate); educational measurement and research (Graduate Certificate); English (Graduate Certificate); entrepreneurship (Graduate Certificate); environmental health (Graduate Certificate); epidemiology and biostatistics (Graduate Certificate); geography, environment and planning (Graduate Certificate); geology (Graduate Certificate); global health (Graduate Certificate); government and international affairs (Graduate Certificate); health policy and management (Graduate Certificate); hearing specialist: early intervention (Graduate Certificate); industrial and management systems engineering (Graduate Certificate); information studies (Graduate Certificate); information systems/decision sciences (Graduate Certificate); instructional technology (Graduate Certificate); internal medicine, bioethics and medical humanities (Graduate Certificate); Latin American and Caribbean studies (Graduate Certificate); mass communications (Graduate Certificate); mathematics and statistics (Graduate Certificate); medicine (Graduate Certificate); national and competitive intelligence (Graduate Certificate); psychological and social foundations (Graduate Certificate); public affairs (Graduate Certificate); public health (Graduate Certificate); public health practices (Graduate Certificate); rehabilitation and mental health counseling (Graduate Certificate); secondary education (Graduate Certificate); social work (Graduate Certificate); special education (Graduate Certificate); world languages (Graduate Certificate). *Application Contact:* Karen Tylinski, Metro Initiatives, 813-974-9943, Fax: 813-974-7061, E-mail: ktylinsk@usf.edu. *Interdisciplinary Programs Coordinator,* Kathy Barnes, 813-974-8031, Fax: 813-974-7061, E-mail: barnesk@usf.edu.

Morsani College of Medicine Students: 1,293 full-time (637 women), 333 part-time (214 women); includes 689 minority (144 Black or African American, non-Hispanic/Latino; 7 American Indian or Alaska Native, non-Hispanic/Latino; 317 Asian, non-Hispanic/Latino; 190 Hispanic/Latino; 1 Native Hawaiian or other Pacific Islander, non-Hispanic/Latino; 30 Two or more races, non-Hispanic/Latino), 65 international. Average age 26. 7,530 applicants, 11% accepted, 643 enrolled. *Faculty:* 196 full-time (75 women), 32 part-time/adjunct (13 women). Expenses: Contact institution. *Financial support:* In 2016–17, 676 students received support. In 2016, 376 master's, 333 doctorates awarded. *Program availability:* Part-time. Offers advanced athletic training (MS); athletic training (MS); bioinformatics and computational biology (MSBCB); biotechnology (MSB); health informatics (MSHI); medical sciences (MSMS, PhD); medicine (MS, MSB, MSBCB, MSHI, MSMS, DPT, MD, PhD). *Application deadline:* For fall admission, 2/1 for domestic and international students. *Application fee:* $30. Electronic applications accepted. *Application Contact:* Dr. Michael Barber, Associate Dean/Professor, 813-974-9702, Fax: 813-974-4990, E-mail: mbarber@health.usf.edu. *Dean,* Dr. Charles J. Lockwood, 813-974-0533, Fax: 813-974-4990, E-mail: cjlockwood@health.usf.edu.

School of Physical Therapy Students: 129 full-time (86 women), 42 part-time (29 women); includes 61 minority (9 Black or African American, non-Hispanic/Latino; 1 American Indian or Alaska Native, non-Hispanic/Latino; 35 Asian, non-Hispanic/Latino; 16 Hispanic/Latino). Average age 29. 56 applicants, 80% accepted, 45 enrolled. *Faculty:* 13 full-time (6 women). Expenses: Contact institution. *Financial support:* In 2016–17, 93 students received support. Teaching assistantships available. In 2016, 148 doctorates awarded. Offers physical therapy (DPT); rehabilitation sciences (PhD). *Application deadline:* For fall admission, 6/1 for domestic students,

1/1 for international students; for spring admission, 10/15 for domestic students, 9/15 for international students. *Application fee:* $30. Electronic applications accepted. *Application Contact:* Dr. Gina Maria Musolino, Associate Professor and Coordinator for Clinical Education, 813-974-2254, Fax: 813-974-8915, E-mail: gmusolin@health.usf.edu. *Director,* Dr. William S. Quillen, 813-974-9863, Fax: 813-974-8915, E-mail: wquillen@health.usf.edu.

Muma College of Business Students: 690 full-time (271 women), 306 part-time (110 women); includes 146 minority (30 Black or African American, non-Hispanic/Latino; 1 American Indian or Alaska Native, non-Hispanic/Latino; 41 Asian, non-Hispanic/Latino; 67 Hispanic/Latino; 7 Two or more races, non-Hispanic/Latino), 451 international. Average age 29. 2,089 applicants, 43% accepted, 386 enrolled. *Faculty:* 67 full-time (19 women), 1 part-time/adjunct (0 women). Expenses: Contact institution. *Financial support:* In 2016–17, 203 students received support. Career-related internships or fieldwork, scholarships/grants, health care benefits, and unspecified assistantships available. Financial award applicants required to submit FAFSA. In 2016, 555 master's, 8 doctorates awarded. *Program availability:* Part-time, evening/weekend. Offers business (M Acc, MS, MSM, MSRE, DBA, PhD); business administration (PhD); business analytics and information systems (MS); finance (MS); management (MS); marketing (MSM); real estate (MSRE). *Application deadline:* For fall admission, 1/2 for domestic and international students; for spring admission, 10/1 for domestic students, 9/15 for international students. *Application fee:* $30. Electronic applications accepted. *Application Contact:* Dr. Jacqueline Reck, Professor/Interim Associate Dean, 813-974-6721, Fax: 813-974-6528, E-mail: jreck@usf.edu. *Dean,* Dr. Moez Limayem, 813-974-4281, Fax: 813-974-3030, E-mail: mlimayem@usf.edu.

Center for Entrepreneurship Students: 66 full-time (32 women), 32 part-time (12 women); includes 20 minority (3 Black or African American, non-Hispanic/Latino; 4 Asian, non-Hispanic/Latino; 11 Hispanic/Latino; 2 Two or more races, non-Hispanic/Latino), 46 international. Average age 29. 84 applicants, 64% accepted, 43 enrolled. *Faculty:* 4 full-time (2 women). Expenses: Contact institution. In 2016, 41 master's awarded. *Program availability:* Part-time, evening/weekend. Offers entrepreneurship and applied technologies (MS). *Application deadline:* For fall admission, 6/1 for domestic students, 2/1 for international students; for spring admission, 10/15 for domestic students, 7/1 for international students. Applications are processed on a rolling basis. *Application fee:* $30. Electronic applications accepted. *Application Contact:* Dr. Tapas Das, Assistant Director/Professor, 813-974-5585, Fax: 813-974-5953, E-mail: das@usf.edu. *Director, Center for Entrepreneurship,* Dr. Michael W. Fountain, 813-974-7825, Fax: 813-974-6175, E-mail: fountain@usf.edu.

Lynn Pippenger School of Accountancy Students: 67 full-time (36 women), 34 part-time (16 women); includes 22 minority (2 Black or African American, non-Hispanic/Latino; 3 Asian, non-Hispanic/Latino; 15 Hispanic/Latino; 2 Two or more races, non-Hispanic/Latino), 9 international. Average age 26. 89 applicants, 56% accepted, 41 enrolled. *Faculty:* 10 full-time (4 women). Expenses: Contact institution. *Financial support:* In 2016–17, 41 students received support, including 18 teaching assistantships with tuition reimbursements available (averaging $12,273 per year); scholarships/grants, health care benefits, and unspecified assistantships also available. Financial award applicants required to submit FAFSA. In 2016, 67 master's, 2 doctorates awarded. *Program availability:* Part-time, evening/weekend. Offers accountancy (M Acc); business administration (PhD). *Application deadline:* For fall admission, 1/2 for domestic and international students; for spring admission, 10/1 for domestic students, 9/15 for international students; for summer admission, 2/15 for domestic students, 1/15 for international students. *Application fee:* $30. Electronic applications accepted. *Application Contact:* Christy Ward, Advisor and Graduation Specialist, 813-974-4290, Fax: 813-974-2797, E-mail: cward@usf.edu. *Interim Director, School of Accountancy,* Dr. Uday Murthy, 813-974-6516, Fax: 813-974-6528, E-mail: umurthy@usf.edu.

UNIVERSITY OF SOUTH FLORIDA, ST. PETERSBURG, St. Petersburg, FL 33701

General Information State-supported, coed, comprehensive institution. *Graduate housing:* Rooms and/or apartments available on a first-come, first-served basis to single and married students.

GRADUATE UNITS

College of Arts and Sciences *Program availability:* Part-time, online learning. Offers digital journalism and design (MA); environmental science and policy (MA, MS); Florida studies (MLA); journalism and media studies (MA); liberal studies (MLA); psychology (MA). Electronic applications accepted.

College of Education *Program availability:* Part-time. Offers educational leadership development (M Ed); elementary education (MA); English education (MA); middle grades STEM education (MS); reading education (MA). Electronic applications accepted.

Kate Tiedemann College of Business *Program availability:* Part-time. Offers business (MBA). Electronic applications accepted.

UNIVERSITY OF SOUTH FLORIDA SARASOTA-MANATEE, Sarasota, FL 34243

General Information State-supported, coed, comprehensive institution. *Enrollment:* 2,077 graduate, professional, and undergraduate students; 57 full-time matriculated graduate/professional students (35 women), 121 part-time matriculated graduate/professional students (74 women). *Enrollment by degree level:* 178 master's. *Graduate faculty:* 29 full-time (18 women), 5 part-time/adjunct (all women). Tuition, state resident: full-time $8350; part-time $348 per credit hour. Tuition, nonresident: full-time $19,047; part-time $793 per credit hour. *Required fees:* $1689; $70 per credit hour. Tuition and fees vary according to program. *Student services:* Campus employment opportunities, campus safety program, career counseling, exercise/wellness program, free psychological counseling, international student services, low-cost health insurance, services for students with disabilities, teacher training, writing training. *Library facilities:* USF Libraries. Collection: 1,266 (physical), 652,513 (digital/electronic); Serial titles: 139 (physical), 58,975 (digital/electronic); Databases: 930. Weekly public service hours: 96; students can reserve study rooms.

Computer facilities: Computer purchase and lease plans are available. 46 computers available for general student use. A campuswide network can be accessed from off campus. Online class registration is available.
Website: http://www.usfsm.edu/

General Application Contact: Andy Telatovich, Director, Admissions, 941-359-4330, E-mail: atelatovich@sar.usf.edu.

GRADUATE UNITS

College of Business Students: 32 full-time (14 women), 56 part-time (26 women); includes 27 minority (6 Black or African American, non-Hispanic/Latino; 1 American

Indian or Alaska Native, non-Hispanic/Latino; 10 Asian, non-Hispanic/Latino; 10 Hispanic/Latino). Average age 33. 79 applicants, 47% accepted, 30 enrolled. *Faculty:* 10 full-time (1 woman). Expenses: Contact institution. *Financial support:* In 2016–17, 6 students received support. Federal Work-Study, scholarships/grants, health care benefits, and unspecified assistantships available. Support available to part-time students. Financial award application deadline: 3/1; financial award applicants required to submit FAFSA. In 2016, 15 master's awarded. *Program availability:* Part-time, evening/weekend. Offers business (MBA). *Application deadline:* For fall admission, 3/1 priority date for domestic students, 3/1 for international students; for spring admission, 10/1 priority date for domestic students, 10/1 for international students. Applications are processed on a rolling basis. *Application fee:* $30. Electronic applications accepted. *Application Contact:* Andy Telatovich, Director, Admissions, 941-359-4330, E-mail: atelatovich@sar.usf.edu. *Dean,* Dr. James M. Curran, 941-359-4605, Fax: 941-359-4367, E-mail: jmcurran@sar.usf.edu.

College of Hospitality and Technology Leadership Students: 14 full-time (10 women), 9 part-time (6 women); includes 6 minority (1 Black or African American, non-Hispanic/Latino; 5 Asian, non-Hispanic/Latino), 1 international. Average age 32. 27 applicants, 22% accepted, 4 enrolled. *Faculty:* 6 full-time (2 women). Expenses: Contact institution. *Financial support:* In 2016–17, 1 student received support, including 7 research assistantships with tuition reimbursements available (averaging $7,904 per year); teaching assistantships with tuition reimbursements available, career-related internships or fieldwork, institutionally sponsored loans, health care benefits, and unspecified assistantships also available. Support available to part-time students. Financial award application deadline: 3/1; financial award applicants required to submit FAFSA. In 2016, 10 master's awarded. *Program availability:* Part-time. Offers hospitality management (MS). *Application deadline:* For fall admission, 3/1 priority date for domestic students, 3/1 for international students; for spring admission, 10/1 priority date for domestic students, 10/1 for international students. Applications are processed on a rolling basis. *Application fee:* $30. Electronic applications accepted. *Application Contact:* Andy Telatovich, Director, Admissions, 941-359-4330, E-mail: atelatovich@sar.usf.edu. *Dean,* Dr. Pat Moreo, 941-359-4327, E-mail: pmoreo@sar.usf.edu.

College of Liberal Arts and Social Sciences Students: 11 full-time (all women), 55 part-time (41 women); includes 18 minority (5 Black or African American, non-Hispanic/Latino; 1 American Indian or Alaska Native, non-Hispanic/Latino; 2 Asian, non-Hispanic/Latino; 10 Hispanic/Latino). Average age 36. 40 applicants, 43% accepted, 17 enrolled. *Faculty:* 11 full-time (9 women), 7 part-time/adjunct (5 women). Expenses: Contact institution. *Financial support:* In 2016–17, 9 students received support. Career-related internships or fieldwork, institutionally sponsored loans, scholarships/grants, health care benefits, and unspecified assistantships available. Support available to part-time students. Financial award application deadline: 3/1; financial award applicants required to submit FAFSA. In 2016, 28 master's awarded. *Program availability:* Part-time, 100% online, blended/hybrid learning. Offers criminal justice (MA); education (MA); educational leadership (M Ed); elementary education (MAT); English education (MA); social work (MSW). *Application deadline:* For fall admission, 3/1 priority date for domestic students, 3/1 for international students; for spring admission, 10/1 priority date for domestic students, 10/1 for international students. Applications are processed on a rolling basis. *Application fee:* $30. Electronic applications accepted. *Application Contact:* Brandon Avery, Assistant Director, Admissions, 941-359-4331, E-mail: bavery@sar.usf.edu. *Dean,* Dr. Jane Rose, 941-359-4469, Fax: 941-359-4778, E-mail: jane.rose@sar.usf.edu.

★ THE UNIVERSITY OF TAMPA, Tampa, FL 33606-1490

General Information Independent, coed, comprehensive institution. *Enrollment:* 8,235 graduate, professional, and undergraduate students; 323 full-time matriculated graduate/professional students (131 women), 516 part-time matriculated graduate/professional students (321 women). *Enrollment by degree level:* 839 master's. *Graduate faculty:* 57 full-time (29 women), 19 part-time/adjunct (13 women). *Tuition:* Full-time $7236; part-time $603 per credit. *Required fees:* $80; $40 per term. Tuition and fees vary according to program. *Graduate housing:* Rooms and/or apartments available on a first-come, first-served basis to single and married students. Typical cost: $4208 per year for single students; $4208 per year for married students. Room charges vary according to board plan and housing facility selected. Housing application deadline: 5/1. *Student services:* Campus employment opportunities, campus safety program, career counseling, international student services, services for students with disabilities. *Library facilities:* Macdonald Kelce Library. Collection: Books: 195,067 (physical), 145,016 (digital/electronic); Serial titles: 1,214 (physical), 190,560 (digital/electronic); Databases: 214. Weekly public service hours: 100; students can reserve study rooms. *Research affiliation:* Tampa General Hospital (nursing).

Computer facilities: Computer purchase and lease plans are available. 802 computers available on campus for general student use. A campuswide network can be accessed from student residence rooms and from off campus. Online class registration is available.
Website: http://www.ut.edu/

General Application Contact: Dr. Joshua Stagner, Director of Graduate and Continuing Studies, 813-257-3016, Fax: 813-258-7451, E-mail: jstagner@ut.edu.

GRADUATE UNITS

Program in Creative Writing Students: 56 full-time (34 women); includes 13 minority (3 Black or African American, non-Hispanic/Latino; 1 Asian, non-Hispanic/Latino; 7 Hispanic/Latino; 2 Two or more races, non-Hispanic/Latino). Average age 39. 51 applicants, 55% accepted, 14 enrolled. *Faculty:* 3 full-time (1 woman), 11 part-time/adjunct (3 women). Expenses: Contact institution. *Financial support:* In 2016–17, 11 students received support. Career-related internships or fieldwork, scholarships/grants, and unspecified assistantships available. Financial award applicants required to submit FAFSA. In 2016, 30 master's awarded. *Program availability:* Part-time. Offers creative writing (MFA). *Application deadline:* Applications are processed on a rolling basis. *Application fee:* $40. Electronic applications accepted. *Application Contact:* Chanelle Cox, Staff Assistant, Graduate and Continuing Studies, 813-253-6249, E-mail: ccox@ut.edu. *Director,* Dr. Erica Dawson, 813-257-6311, E-mail: edawson@ut.edu.

Program in Exercise and Nutrition Science Students: 46 full-time (20 women), 3 part-time (1 woman); includes 8 minority (4 Black or African American, non-Hispanic/Latino; 1 Asian, non-Hispanic/Latino; 3 Two or more races, non-Hispanic/Latino), 2 international. Average age 25. 207 applicants, 52% accepted, 33 enrolled. *Faculty:* 4 full-time (2 women), 1 (woman) part-time/adjunct. Expenses: Contact institution. *Financial support:* In 2016–17, 1 student received support. Career-related internships or fieldwork, scholarships/grants, and unspecified assistantships available. Financial award applicants required to submit FAFSA. In 2016, 48 master's awarded. *Program availability:* Part-time, evening/weekend. Offers exercise and nutrition science (MS). *Application deadline:* Applications are processed on a rolling basis. *Application fee:* $40. Electronic applications accepted. *Application Contact:* Chanelle Cox, Staff Assistant,

Admissions for Graduate and Continuing Studies, 813-253-6249, E-mail: ccox@ut.edu. *Associate Professor, Health Sciences and Human Performance,* Dr. Ronda C. Sturgill, 813-257-3445, E-mail: rsturgill@ut.edu.

Program in Nursing Students: 4 full-time (all women), 166 part-time (148 women); includes 24 minority (10 Black or African American, non-Hispanic/Latino; 8 Asian, non-Hispanic/Latino; 6 Two or more races, non-Hispanic/Latino), 1 international. Average age 33. 132 applicants, 64% accepted, 51 enrolled. *Faculty:* 8 full-time (7 women), 6 part-time/adjunct (all women). Expenses: Contact institution. *Financial support:* In 2016–17, 9 students received support. Career-related internships or fieldwork, scholarships/grants, and unspecified assistantships available. Financial award applicants required to submit FAFSA. In 2016, 52 master's awarded. *Program availability:* Part-time, evening/weekend. Offers adult nursing practitioner (MSN); family nursing practitioner (MSN); nursing (MS). *Application deadline:* Applications are processed on a rolling basis. *Application fee:* $40. Electronic applications accepted. *Application Contact:* Chanelle Cox, Staff Assistant, Admissions for Graduate and Continuing Studies, 813-253-6249, E-mail: ccox@ut.edu. *Director,* Michele Wolf, 813-257-3179, E-mail: mwolf@ut.edu.

Programs in Education Students: 44 full-time (38 women), 18 part-time (14 women); includes 2 minority (both Black or African American, non-Hispanic/Latino), 7 international. Average age 31. 126 applicants, 40% accepted, 29 enrolled. *Faculty:* 2 full-time (1 woman), 3 part-time/adjunct (all women). Expenses: Contact institution. *Financial support:* In 2016–17, 20 students received support. Career-related internships or fieldwork, scholarships/grants, and unspecified assistantships available. Financial award applicants required to submit FAFSA. In 2016, 23 master's awarded. *Program availability:* Part-time, evening/weekend. Offers curriculum and instruction (M Ed); instructional design and technology (MS). *Application deadline:* Applications are processed on a rolling basis. *Application fee:* $40. Electronic applications accepted. *Application Contact:* Chanelle Cox, Staff Assistant, Admissions for Graduate and Continuing Studies, 813-253-6249, E-mail: ccox@ut.edu. *Chair,* Dr. Antony Erben, 813-257-3414, E-mail: terben@ut.edu.

Sykes College of Business Students: 438 full-time (176 women), 126 part-time (57 women); includes 37 minority (22 Black or African American, non-Hispanic/Latino; 11 Asian, non-Hispanic/Latino; 4 Two or more races, non-Hispanic/Latino), 203 international. Average age 28. 1,305 applicants, 39% accepted, 192 enrolled. *Faculty:* 43 full-time (19 women), 9 part-time/adjunct (3 women). Expenses: Contact institution. *Financial support:* In 2016–17, 116 students received support. Career-related internships or fieldwork, scholarships/grants, and unspecified assistantships available. Financial award applicants required to submit FAFSA. In 2016, 266 master's awarded. *Program availability:* Part-time, evening/weekend. Offers accounting (MS); entrepreneurship (MBA); finance (MBA, MS); information systems management (MBA); innovation management (MBA); international business (MBA); marketing (MBA, MS); nonprofit management (MBA). *Application deadline:* Applications are processed on a rolling basis. *Application fee:* $40. Electronic applications accepted. *Application Contact:* Chanelle Cox, Staff Assistant, Admissions for Graduate and Continuing Studies, 813-253-6249, E-mail: ccox@ut.edu. *Associate Dean,* Dr. Natasha F. Veltri, 813-253-6289, E-mail: nveltri@ut.edu.

See Display below and Close-Up on page 905.

THE UNIVERSITY OF TENNESSEE, Knoxville, TN 37996

General Information State-supported, coed, university. CGS member. *Graduate housing:* Room and/or apartments available on a first-come, first-served basis to single students; on-campus housing not available to married students. Housing application deadline: 2/1. *Research affiliation:* Intel Corporation (computational science), Boeing (mechanical and aerospace engineering), Eastman Chemical (chemical engineering, chemistry), Mars, Inc. (materials science and engineering, polymer science, food science), DuPont (biofuels), Goodyear (chemical engineering; materials science and engineering; polymer science).

GRADUATE UNITS

College of Law Students: 333 full-time (145 women); includes 57 minority (26 Black or African American, non-Hispanic/Latino; 1 American Indian or Alaska Native, non-Hispanic/Latino; 5 Asian, non-Hispanic/Latino; 9 Hispanic/Latino; 16 Two or more races, non-Hispanic/Latino), 1 international. Average age 24. 1,003 applicants, 36% accepted, 113 enrolled. *Faculty:* 43 full-time (23 women), 63 part-time/adjunct (25 women). Expenses: Contact institution. *Financial support:* In 2016–17, 248 students received support, including 12 research assistantships with full tuition reimbursements available (averaging $23,763 per year); career-related internships or fieldwork, Federal Work-Study, institutionally sponsored loans, scholarships/grants, and unspecified assistantships also available. Support available to part-time students. Financial award application deadline: 3/1; financial award applicants required to submit FAFSA. In 2016, 158 doctorates awarded. Offers business transactions (JD); law (JD); trial advocacy and dispute resolution (JD). *Application deadline:* For fall admission, 3/1 priority date for domestic and international students. Applications are processed on a rolling basis. *Application fee:* $15. Electronic applications accepted. *Application Contact:* Janet S. Hatcher, Associate Director of Admissions and Financial Aid, 865-974-4131, Fax: 865-974-1572, E-mail: hatcher@utk.edu. *Associate Director of Admissions and Financial Aid,* Janet S. Hatcher, 865-974-4131, Fax: 865-974-1572, E-mail: lawadmit@utk.edu.

Graduate School *Program availability:* Part-time, evening/weekend, online learning. Offers aviation systems (MS); comparative and experimental medicine (MS, PhD). Electronic applications accepted.

College of Agricultural Sciences and Natural Resources Program availability: Part-time, online learning. Offers agricultural education (MS); agricultural extension education (MS); agricultural sciences and natural resources (MS, PhD); animal anatomy (PhD); biosystems engineering (MS, PhD); biosystems engineering technology (MS); breeding (MS, PhD); entomology (MS, PhD); floriculture (MS); food science and technology (MS, PhD); forestry (MS); integrated pest management and bioactive natural products (PhD); landscape design (MS); management (MS, PhD); nutrition (MS, PhD); physiology (MS, PhD); plant pathology (MS, PhD); public horticulture (MS); turfgrass (MS); wildlife and fisheries science (MS); woody ornamentals (MS). Electronic applications accepted.

College of Architecture and Design Offers architecture (professional) (M Arch); architecture (research) (M Arch); architecture and design (M Arch, MA, MLA, MS); landscape architecture (MLA); landscape architecture (research) (MA, MS). Electronic applications accepted.

College of Arts and Sciences Program availability: Part-time, evening/weekend. Offers accompanying (MM); American history (PhD); analytical chemistry (MS, PhD); applied linguistics (PhD); applied mathematics (MS); archaeology (MA, PhD); arts and sciences (M Math, MA, MFA, MM, MPA, MS, PhD); audiology (MA); behavior (MS, PhD); biochemistry, cellular and molecular biology (MS, PhD); biological anthropology (MA, PhD); ceramics (MFA); chemical physics (PhD); choral conducting (MM); clinical psychology (PhD); composition (MM); computer science (MS, PhD); costume design (MFA); criminology (MA, PhD); cultural anthropology (MA, PhD); drawing (MFA); ecology (MS, PhD); energy, environment, and resource policy (MA, PhD); English (MA, PhD); environmental chemistry (MS, PhD); European history (PhD); evolutionary biology (MS, PhD); experimental psychology (MA, PhD); French (MA, PhD); genome science and technology (PhD); geography (MS, PhD); geology (MS, PhD); German (MA); graphic design (MFA); hearing science (PhD); history (MA); inorganic chemistry (MS, PhD); instrumental conducting (MM); inter-area studies (MFA); Italian (MA); jazz (MM); lighting design (MFA); mathematical ecology (PhD); mathematics (M Math, MS, PhD); media arts (MFA); medical ethics (MA, PhD); microbiology (MS, PhD); modern foreign languages (PhD); music education (MM); music theory (MM); musicology (MM); organic chemistry (MS, PhD); painting (MFA); performance (MFA, MM); philosophy (MA, PhD); physical chemistry (MS, PhD); physics (MS, PhD); piano pedagogy and literature (MM); plant physiology and genetics (MS, PhD); political economy (MA, MPA); political science (MA, MPA, PhD); polymer chemistry (PhD); Portuguese (PhD); printmaking (MFA); psychology (MA); public administration (MPA); religious studies (PhD); Russian (PhD); scene design (MFA); sculpture (MFA); Spanish (MA); speech and hearing science (PhD); speech and language pathology (PhD); speech and language science (PhD); speech pathology (MA); theatre technology (MFA); theoretical chemistry (PhD); watercolor (MFA); zoo-archaeology (MA, PhD). Electronic applications accepted.

College of Business Administration Program availability: Part-time, online learning. Offers accounting (M Acc, PhD); business administration (M Acc, MA, MBA, MS, PhD); economics (PhD); finance (MBA, PhD); industrial and organizational psychology (PhD); industrial statistics (MS); logistics and transportation (MBA, PhD); management (PhD); management science (MS, PhD); marketing (MBA, PhD); operations management (MBA); professional business administration (MBA); statistics (MS, PhD); systems (M Acc); taxation (M Acc); teacher licensure (MS); training and development (MS). Electronic applications accepted.

College of Communication and Information Program availability: Part-time, evening/weekend, online learning. Offers advertising (MS, PhD); broadcasting (MS, PhD); communications (MS, PhD); information sciences (MS, PhD); journalism (MS, PhD); public relations (MS, PhD); speech communication (MS, PhD). Electronic applications accepted.

College of Education, Health and Human Sciences Program availability: Part-time, evening/weekend, online learning. Offers adult education (MS); applied educational psychology (MS); art education (MS); biomechanics/sports medicine (MS, PhD); child and family studies (MS, PhD); collaborative learning (Ed D); college student personnel (MS); community health (PhD); community health education (MPH); consumer services management (MS); counseling education (PhD); cultural studies in education (PhD); curriculum (MS, Ed S); curriculum, educational research and evaluation (Ed D, PhD); early childhood education (MS, PhD); early childhood special education (MS); education of deaf and hard of hearing (MS); education, health and human sciences (MPH, MS, Ed D, PhD, Ed S); educational administration and policy studies (Ed D, PhD); educational administration and supervision (MS, Ed S); educational psychology (Ed D, PhD); elementary education (MS, Ed S); elementary teaching (MS); English education (MS, Ed S); exercise physiology (MS, PhD); exercise science (MS, PhD); foreign language/ESL education (MS, Ed S); gerontology (MPH); health planning/administration (MPH); health promotion and health education (MS); hospitality management (MS); hotel, restaurant, and tourism management (MS); instructional technology (MS, Ed D, PhD, Ed S); literacy, language and ESL education (PhD); literacy, language education, and ESL education (Ed D); mathematics education (MS, Ed S); mental health counseling (MS); modified and comprehensive special education (MS); nutrition (MS); nutrition science (PhD); reading education (MS, Ed S); recreation and leisure studies (MS); rehabilitation counseling (MS); retail and consumer sciences (MS); retailing and consumer sciences (PhD); safety (MS); school counseling (MS, Ed S); school psychology (PhD, Ed S); science education (MS, Ed S); secondary teaching (MS); social foundations (MS); social science education (MS, Ed S); socio-cultural foundations of sports and education (PhD); special education (Ed S); sport management (MS); sport studies (MS, PhD); teacher education (Ed D, PhD); textile science (MS, PhD); therapeutic recreation (MS); tourism (MS). Electronic applications accepted.

College of Nursing Program availability: Part-time. Offers nursing (MSN, PhD). Electronic applications accepted.

College of Social Work Program availability: Part-time, online learning. Offers clinical practice and leadership (DSW); evidenced-based interpersonal practice (MSSW); management leadership and community practice (MSSW); social work (MSSW, DSW, PhD). Electronic applications accepted.

College of Veterinary Medicine Offers veterinary medicine (DVM).

Tickle College of Engineering Students: 867 full-time (197 women), 236 part-time (36 women); includes 103 minority (23 Black or African American, non-Hispanic/Latino; 2 American Indian or Alaska Native, non-Hispanic/Latino; 33 Asian, non-Hispanic/Latino; 33 Hispanic/Latino; 12 Two or more races, non-Hispanic/Latino), 413 international. Average age 30. 1,346 applicants, 35% accepted, 263 enrolled. *Faculty:* 233 full-time (35 women), 57 part-time/adjunct (7 women). Expenses: Contact institution. *Financial support:* In 2016–17, 705 students received support, including 106 fellowships with full tuition reimbursements available (averaging $27,735 per year), 383 research assistantships with full tuition reimbursements available (averaging $23,278 per year), 198 teaching assistantships with full tuition reimbursements available (averaging $20,212 per year); career-related internships or fieldwork, Federal Work-Study, institutionally sponsored loans, health care benefits, and unspecified assistantships also available. Financial award application deadline: 2/1; financial award applicants required to submit FAFSA. In 2016, 177 master's, 89 doctorates awarded. *Program availability:* Part-time, online learning. Offers aerospace engineering (MS, PhD); biomedical engineering (MS, PhD); chemical engineering (MS, PhD); civil engineering (MS, PhD); computer engineering (MS, PhD); computer science (MS, PhD); electrical engineering (MS, PhD); energy science and engineering (PhD); engineering (MS, PhD); engineering management (MS); engineering science (MS, PhD); environmental engineering (MS); industrial engineering (MS, PhD); materials science and engineering (MS, PhD); mechanical engineering (MS, PhD); nuclear engineering (MS, PhD); polymer engineering (MS, PhD); reliability and maintainability engineering (MS). *Application deadline:* For fall admission, 2/1 priority date for domestic and international students; for spring admission, 6/15 for domestic and international students. Applications are processed on a rolling basis. *Application fee:* $35. Electronic applications accepted. *Application Contact:* Dr. Masood Parang, Associate Dean of Student Affairs, 865-974-2454, Fax: 865-974-9871, E-mail: mparang@utk.edu. *Dean,* Dr. Wayne T. Davis, 865-974-5321, Fax: 865-974-8890, E-mail: wtdavis@utk.edu.

The University of Tennessee Space Institute Program availability: Part-time, blended/hybrid learning. Offers aerospace engineering (MS, PhD); biomedical engineering (MS, PhD); engineering science (MS, PhD); industrial and systems engineering/engineering management (MS, PhD); mechanical engineering (MS, PhD); physics (MS, PhD). Electronic applications accepted.

THE UNIVERSITY OF TENNESSEE AT CHATTANOOGA, Chattanooga, TN 37403-2598

General Information State-supported, coed, comprehensive institution. CGS member. *Enrollment:* 11,533 graduate, professional, and undergraduate students; 621 full-time matriculated graduate/professional students (378 women), 744 part-time matriculated graduate/professional students (414 women). *Enrollment by degree level:* 995 master's, 305 doctoral, 65 other advanced degrees. *Graduate faculty:* 196 full-time (79 women), 14 part-time/adjunct (8 women). Tuition, state resident: full-time $8100; part-time $450 per credit hour. Tuition, nonresident: full-time $24,218; part-time $1345 per credit hour. *Required fees:* $1776; $264 per credit hour. *Graduate housing:* Room and/or apartments available on a first-come, first-served basis to single students; on-campus housing not available to married students. Typical cost: $5226 per year ($8678 including board). Room and board charges vary according to board plan and housing facility selected. Housing application deadline: 6/1. *Student services:* Campus employment opportunities, campus safety program, career counseling, exercise/wellness program, free psychological counseling, grant writing training, international student services, low-cost health insurance, multicultural affairs office, services for students with disabilities, teacher training, writing training. *Library facilities:* UTC Library plus 1 other. *Collection:* Books: 799,387 (physical); Databases: 154. Study areas open 24 hours, 5–7 days a week; students can reserve study rooms. *Research affiliation:* Law Enforcement Innovation Center (criminal justice), Highland Biological Field Station (biology and environmental science), Tennessee Valley Authority (engineering), Gulf Coast Research Laboratory (biology and environmental science), Tennessee Coalition against Domestic and Sexual Violence (criminal justice).

Computer facilities: A campuswide network can be accessed from student residence rooms and from off campus. Online class registration is available.
Website: http://www.utc.edu/

General Application Contact: Dr. Joanne Romagni, Dean of the Graduate School, 423-425-4478, Fax: 423-425-5223, E-mail: joanne-romagni@utc.edu.

GRADUATE UNITS

Department of Health and Human Performance Students: 43 full-time (32 women); includes 7 minority (2 Black or African American, non-Hispanic/Latino; 3 Hispanic/Latino; 2 Two or more races, non-Hispanic/Latino). Average age 23. 25 applicants, 92% accepted, 21 enrolled. *Faculty:* 4 full-time (1 woman). Expenses: Contact institution. *Financial support:* In 2016–17, 5 research assistantships with tuition reimbursements, 4 teaching assistantships with tuition reimbursements were awarded; career-related internships or fieldwork, scholarships/grants, and unspecified assistantships also available. Support available to part-time students. Financial award application deadline: 7/1; financial award applicants required to submit FAFSA. In 2016, 21 master's awarded. Offers athletic training (MSAT); health and human performance (MS). *Application deadline:* For fall admission, 6/15 priority date for domestic students, 7/1 for international students; for spring admission, 11/1 priority date for domestic students, 11/1 for international students. Applications are processed on a rolling basis. *Application fee:* $35 ($40 for international students). Electronic applications accepted. *Application Contact:* Dr. Joanne Romagni, Dean of the Graduate School, 423-425-4478, Fax: 423-425-5223, E-mail: joanne-romagni@utc.edu. *Interim Department Head,* Dr. Marisa Colston, 423-425-4743, E-mail: marisa-colston@utc.edu.

Department of Occupational Therapy Students: 56 full-time (51 women); includes 6 minority (2 Hispanic/Latino; 4 Two or more races, non-Hispanic/Latino). Average age 24. 32 applicants, 94% accepted, 21 enrolled. *Faculty:* 6 full-time (5 women). Expenses: Contact institution. *Financial support:* Fellowships, research assistantships, career-related internships or fieldwork, scholarships/grants, and unspecified assistantships available. Support available to part-time students. Financial award application deadline: 7/1; financial award applicants required to submit FAFSA. Offers occupational therapy (OTD). *Application deadline:* For fall admission, 6/15 priority date for domestic students, 7/1 for international students; for spring admission, 11/1 priority date for domestic students, 11/1 for international students. Applications are processed on a rolling basis. *Application fee:* $35 ($40 for international students). Electronic applications accepted. *Application Contact:* Dr. Joanne Romagni, Dean of the Graduate School, 423-425-4478, Fax: 423-425-5223, E-mail: joanne-romagni@utc.edu. *Program Director,* Susan McDonald, 423-425-5759, E-mail: susan-mcdonald@utc.edu.

Department of Political Science and Public Service Students: 8 full-time (2 women), 14 part-time (11 women); includes 6 minority (4 Black or African American, non-Hispanic/Latino; 1 Asian, non-Hispanic/Latino; 1 Two or more races, non-Hispanic/Latino). Average age 31. 14 applicants, 86% accepted, 7 enrolled. *Faculty:* 5 full-time (2 women). Expenses: Contact institution. *Financial support:* In 2016–17, 2 research assistantships were awarded; career-related internships or fieldwork, scholarships/grants, and unspecified assistantships also available. Support available to part-time students. Financial award application deadline: 7/1; financial award applicants required to submit FAFSA. In 2016, 11 master's awarded. *Program availability:* Part-time, evening/weekend. Offers local government management (MPA); non profit management (MPA); public administration (MPA); public administration and non-profit management (Postbaccalaureate Certificate). *Application deadline:* For fall admission, 6/15 priority date for domestic students, 7/1 for international students; for spring admission, 11/1 priority date for domestic students, 11/1 for international students. Applications are processed on a rolling basis. *Application fee:* $35 ($40 for international students). Electronic applications accepted. *Application Contact:* Dr. Joanne Romagni, Dean of the Graduate School, 423-425-4478, Fax: 423-425-5223, E-mail: joanne-romagni@utc.edu. *Department Head,* Dr. Michelle D. Deardorff, 423-425-4231, Fax: 423-425-2373, E-mail: michelle-deardorff@utc.edu.

Engineering Management and Technology Program Students: 14 full-time (3 women), 49 part-time (11 women); includes 17 minority (10 Black or African American, non-Hispanic/Latino; 2 Asian, non-Hispanic/Latino; 3 Hispanic/Latino; 2 Two or more races, non-Hispanic/Latino), 8 international. Average age 33. 29 applicants, 93% accepted, 15 enrolled. *Faculty:* 6 full-time (1 woman). Expenses: Contact institution. *Financial support:* In 2016–17, 4 research assistantships were awarded; teaching assistantships, career-related internships or fieldwork, scholarships/grants, and unspecified assistantships also available. Support available to part-time students. Financial award application deadline: 7/1; financial award applicants required to submit FAFSA. In 2016, 36 master's, 7 other advanced degrees awarded. *Program availability:* 100% online, blended/hybrid learning. Offers construction management (Graduate Certificate); engineering management (Graduate Certificate); fundamentals of engineering management (Graduate Certificate); leadership and ethics (Graduate Certificate); logistics and supply chain management (Graduate Certificate); power systems management (Graduate

Certificate); project and technology management (Graduate Certificate); quality management (Graduate Certificate). *Application deadline:* For fall admission, 6/15 priority date for domestic students, 7/1 for international students; for spring admission, 11/1 priority date for domestic students, 11/1 for international students. Applications are processed on a rolling basis. *Application fee:* $35 ($40 for international students). Electronic applications accepted. *Application Contact:* Dr. Joanne Romagni, Dean of the Graduate School, 423-425-4478, Fax: 423-425-5223, E-mail: joanne-romagni@utc.edu. *Department Head,* Dr. Neslihan Alp, 423-425-4032, Fax: 423-425-5818, E-mail: neslihan-alp@utc.edu.

Program in Accountancy Students: 12 full-time (7 women), 14 part-time (6 women); includes 7 minority (1 Black or African American, non-Hispanic/Latino; 2 Asian, non-Hispanic/Latino; 1 Hispanic/Latino; 3 Two or more races, non-Hispanic/Latino). Average age 26. 24 applicants, 67% accepted, 13 enrolled. *Faculty:* 4 full-time (2 women). Expenses: Contact institution. *Financial support:* In 2016–17, 2 research assistantships were awarded; teaching assistantships, career-related internships or fieldwork, scholarships/grants, and unspecified assistantships also available. Support available to part-time students. Financial award application deadline: 7/1; financial award applicants required to submit FAFSA. In 2016, 13 master's awarded. *Program availability:* Part-time, evening/weekend. Offers accountancy (M Acc). *Application deadline:* For fall admission, 6/15 priority date for domestic students, 7/1 for international students; for spring admission, 11/1 priority date for domestic students, 11/1 for international students. Applications are processed on a rolling basis. *Application fee:* $35 ($40 for international students). Electronic applications accepted. *Application Contact:* Dr. Joanne Romagni, Dean of the Graduate School, 413-425-4478, Fax: 423-425-5223, E-mail: randy-walker@utc.edu. *Department Head,* Dr. Dan Hollingsworth, 423-425-4664, Fax: 423-425-5255, E-mail: dan-hollingsworth@utc.edu.

Program in Business Administration Students: 49 full-time (22 women), 108 part-time (50 women); includes 22 minority (8 Black or African American, non-Hispanic/Latino; 3 Asian, non-Hispanic/Latino; 3 Hispanic/Latino; 8 Two or more races, non-Hispanic/Latino), 6 international. Average age 29. 151 applicants, 90% accepted, 92 enrolled. *Faculty:* 17 full-time (7 women), 1 part-time/adjunct (0 women). Expenses: Contact institution. *Financial support:* In 2016–17, 11 research assistantships were awarded; teaching assistantships, career-related internships or fieldwork, scholarships/grants, health care benefits, tuition waivers (partial), and unspecified assistantships also available. Support available to part-time students. Financial award application deadline: 7/1. In 2016, 102 master's awarded. *Program availability:* Part-time, evening/weekend. Offers business administration (EMBA, MBA, PMBA). *Application deadline:* For fall admission, 6/15 priority date for domestic students, 7/1 for international students; for spring admission, 11/1 priority date for domestic students, 11/1 for international students. Applications are processed on a rolling basis. *Application fee:* $35 ($40 for international students). Electronic applications accepted. *Application Contact:* Dr. Joanne Romagni, Dean of the Graduate School, 423-425-4478, Fax: 423-425-5223, E-mail: joanne-romagni@utc.edu. *Director of Graduate Programs,* Elizabeth Bell, 423-425-2326, Fax: 423-425-5255, E-mail: elizabeth-bell@utc.edu.

Program in Computational Science Students: 5 full-time (0 women), 15 part-time (4 women); includes 3 minority (2 Black or African American, non-Hispanic/Latino; 1 Asian, non-Hispanic/Latino), 8 international. Average age 33. 10 applicants, 90% accepted, 6 enrolled. *Faculty:* 4 full-time (0 women). Expenses: Contact institution. *Financial support:* In 2016–17, 13 research assistantships were awarded; career-related internships or fieldwork, scholarships/grants, and unspecified assistantships also available. Support available to part-time students. Financial award application deadline: 7/1. In 2016, 5 doctorates awarded. Offers computational science (PhD). *Application deadline:* For fall admission, 6/15 priority date for domestic students, 7/1 for international students; for spring admission, 11/1 priority date for domestic students, 11/1 for international students. Applications are processed on a rolling basis. *Application fee:* $35 ($40 for international students). Electronic applications accepted. *Application Contact:* Dr. Joanne Romagni, Dean of the Graduate School, 423-425-4478, Fax: 423-425-5223, E-mail: joanne-romagni@utc.edu. *Interim Department Head,* Dr. Reinhold Mann, 423-425-5493, Fax: 423-425-5311, E-mail: reinhold-c-mann@utc.edu.

Program in Computer Science Students: 21 full-time (8 women), 28 part-time (9 women); includes 15 minority (4 Black or African American, non-Hispanic/Latino; 1 American Indian or Alaska Native, non-Hispanic/Latino; 4 Asian, non-Hispanic/Latino; 2 Hispanic/Latino; 4 Two or more races, non-Hispanic/Latino), 10 international. Average age 30. 41 applicants, 83% accepted, 15 enrolled. *Faculty:* 10 full-time (4 women). Expenses: Contact institution. *Financial support:* In 2016–17, 6 research assistantships, 1 teaching assistantship were awarded; career-related internships or fieldwork, scholarships/grants, health care benefits, and unspecified assistantships also available. Support available to part-time students. Financial award application deadline: 7/1; financial award applicants required to submit FAFSA. In 2016, 12 master's awarded. *Program availability:* Part-time. Offers computer science (MS). *Application deadline:* For fall admission, 6/15 priority date for domestic students, 7/1 for international students; for spring admission, 11/1 priority date for domestic students, 11/1 for international students. Applications are processed on a rolling basis. *Application fee:* $35 ($40 for international students). Electronic applications accepted. *Application Contact:* Dr. Joanne Romagni, Dean of the Graduate School, 423-425-4478, Fax: 423-425-5223, E-mail: joanne-romagni@utc.edu. *Department Head,* Dr. Joseph Kizza, 423-425-4043, Fax: 423-425-5442, E-mail: joseph-kizza@utc.edu.

Program in Criminal Justice Students: 17 full-time (11 women), 18 part-time (9 women); includes 19 minority (13 Black or African American, non-Hispanic/Latino; 3 Hispanic/Latino; 3 Two or more races, non-Hispanic/Latino). Average age 28. 20 applicants, 100% accepted, 13 enrolled. *Faculty:* 8 full-time (6 women), 1 part-time/adjunct (0 women). Expenses: Contact institution. *Financial support:* In 2016–17, 6 research assistantships were awarded; teaching assistantships, career-related internships or fieldwork, scholarships/grants, and unspecified assistantships also available. Support available to part-time students. Financial award application deadline: 7/1; financial award applicants required to submit FAFSA. In 2016, 7 master's awarded. *Program availability:* Part-time. Offers criminal justice (MSCJ). *Application deadline:* For fall admission, 6/15 priority date for domestic students, 7/1 for international students; for spring admission, 11/1 priority date for domestic students, 11/1 for international students. Applications are processed on a rolling basis. *Application fee:* $35 ($40 for international students). Electronic applications accepted. *Application Contact:* Dr. Joanne Romagni, Dean of the Graduate School, 423-425-4478, Fax: 423-425-5223, E-mail: joanne-romagni@utc.edu. *Graduate Coordinator,* Dr. Tammy Garland, 423-425-5245, Fax: 423-425-2228, E-mail: tammy-garland@utc.edu.

Program in Engineering Students: 21 full-time (5 women), 26 part-time (7 women); includes 11 minority (4 Black or African American, non-Hispanic/Latino; 5 Asian, non-Hispanic/Latino; 1 Hispanic/Latino; 1 Two or more races, non-Hispanic/Latino), 18 international. Average age 28. 30 applicants, 83% accepted, 14 enrolled. *Faculty:* 21 full-time (2 women), 2 part-time/adjunct (1 woman). Expenses: Contact institution. *Financial support:* In 2016–17, 6 research assistantships, 5 teaching assistantships were awarded; career-related internships or fieldwork, scholarships/grants, health care benefits, and unspecified assistantships also available. Support available to part-time students. Financial award application deadline: 7/1. In 2016, 25 master's awarded. *Program availability:* Part-time. Offers automotive systems (MS Engr); chemical engineering (MS Engr); civil engineering (MS Engr); computational engineering (MS Engr); electrical engineering (MS Engr); industrial engineering (MS Engr); mechanical engineering (MS Engr). *Application deadline:* For fall admission, 6/15 priority date for domestic students, 7/1 for international students; for spring admission, 11/1 priority date for domestic students, 11/1 for international students. Applications are processed on a rolling basis. *Application fee:* $35 ($40 for international students). Electronic applications accepted. *Application Contact:* Dr. Joanne Romagni, Dean of the Graduate School, 423-425-4478, Fax: 423-425-5223, E-mail: joanne-romagni@utc.edu. *Dean,* Dr. Daniel Pack, 423-425-2256, Fax: 423-425-5311, E-mail: daniel-pack@utc.edu.

Program in English Students: 16 full-time (11 women), 21 part-time (16 women); includes 3 minority (1 Asian, non-Hispanic/Latino; 1 Hispanic/Latino; 1 Two or more races, non-Hispanic/Latino). Average age 28. 20 applicants, 100% accepted, 17 enrolled. *Faculty:* 22 full-time (11 women), 1 (woman) part-time/adjunct. Expenses: Contact institution. *Financial support:* In 2016–17, 4 teaching assistantships were awarded; research assistantships, career-related internships or fieldwork, scholarships/grants, health care benefits, and unspecified assistantships also available. Support available to part-time students. Financial award application deadline: 7/1; financial award applicants required to submit FAFSA. In 2016, 8 master's awarded. *Program availability:* Part-time. Offers creative writing (MA); literary study (MA); rhetoric and writing (MA). *Application deadline:* For fall admission, 6/15 priority date for domestic students, 7/1 for international students; for spring admission, 11/1 priority date for domestic students, 11/1 for international students. Applications are processed on a rolling basis. *Application fee:* $35 ($40 for international students). Electronic applications accepted. *Application Contact:* Dr. Joanne Romagni, Dean of the Graduate School, 423-425-4478, Fax: 423-425-5223, E-mail: joanne-romagni@utc.edu. *Department Head,* Dr. Christopher Stuart, 423-425-2140, Fax: 423-425-2282, E-mail: chris-stuart@utc.edu.

Program in Environmental Science Students: 14 full-time (7 women), 18 part-time (11 women); includes 6 minority (2 Black or African American, non-Hispanic/Latino; 1 Asian, non-Hispanic/Latino; 1 Hispanic/Latino; 2 Two or more races, non-Hispanic/Latino), 1 international. Average age 27. 11 applicants, 73% accepted, 7 enrolled. *Faculty:* 21 full-time (4 women), 1 part-time/adjunct (0 women). Expenses: Contact institution. *Financial support:* In 2016–17, 5 research assistantships, 9 teaching assistantships were awarded; career-related internships or fieldwork, scholarships/grants, and unspecified assistantships also available. Support available to part-time students. Financial award application deadline: 7/1; financial award applicants required to submit FAFSA. In 2016, 5 master's awarded. *Program availability:* Part-time. Offers environmental science (MS). *Application deadline:* For fall admission, 6/15 priority date for domestic students, 7/1 for international students; for spring admission, 11/1 priority date for domestic students, 11/1 for international students. Applications are processed on a rolling basis. *Application fee:* $35 ($40 for international students). Electronic applications accepted. *Application Contact:* Dr. Joanne Romagni, Dean of the Graduate School, 423-425-4478, Fax: 423-425-5223, E-mail: joanne-romagni@utc.edu. *Department Head,* Dr. John Tucker, 423-425-4341, Fax: 423-425-2285, E-mail: john-tucker@utc.edu.

Program in Mathematics Students: 15 full-time (9 women), 6 part-time (1 woman); includes 5 minority (1 Asian, non-Hispanic/Latino; 1 Native Hawaiian or other Pacific Islander, non-Hispanic/Latino; 3 Two or more races, non-Hispanic/Latino), 1 international. Average age 27. 16 applicants, 81% accepted, 8 enrolled. *Faculty:* 17 full-time (1 woman). Expenses: Contact institution. *Financial support:* In 2016–17, 1 research assistantship, 11 teaching assistantships were awarded. Financial award application deadline: 7/1; financial award applicants required to submit FAFSA. In 2016, 4 master's awarded. *Program availability:* Part-time. Offers applied mathematics (MS); applied statistics (MS); mathematics education (MS); pre-professional mathematics (MS). *Application deadline:* For fall admission, 7/1 for domestic students, 7/1 for international students; for spring admission, 11/1 for domestic and international students. Applications are processed on a rolling basis. *Application fee:* $35 ($40 for international students). Electronic applications accepted. *Application Contact:* Dr. Joanne Romagni, Dean of the Graduate School, 423-425-4478, Fax: 423-425-5223, E-mail: joanne-romagni@utc.edu. *Graduate Program Coordinator,* Dr. Francesco Barioli, 423-425-2198, E-mail: francesco-barioli@utc.edu.

Program in Music Students: 5 part-time (3 women); includes 1 minority (Black or African American, non-Hispanic/Latino). Average age 29. 1 applicant, 100% accepted. *Faculty:* 5 full-time (3 women). Expenses: Contact institution. *Financial support:* Research assistantships, Federal Work-Study, scholarships/grants, and unspecified assistantships available. Financial award application deadline: 7/1; financial award applicants required to submit FAFSA. In 2016, 7 master's awarded. Offers music education (MM); performance (MM). *Application deadline:* For fall admission, 6/15 priority date for domestic students, 7/1 for international students; for spring admission, 11/1 priority date for domestic students, 11/1 for international students. Applications are processed on a rolling basis. *Application fee:* $35 ($40 for international students). Electronic applications accepted. *Application Contact:* Dr. Joanne Romagni, Dean of the Graduate School, 423-425-4478, Fax: 423-425-5223, E-mail: joanne-romagni@utc.edu. *Department Head,* Dr. Lee Harris, 423-425-4601, Fax: 423-425-4603, E-mail: lee-harris@utc.edu.

Program in Physical Therapy Students: 105 full-time (67 women); includes 18 minority (1 Black or African American, non-Hispanic/Latino; 2 Hispanic/Latino; 15 Two or more races, non-Hispanic/Latino). Average age 24. 65 applicants, 75% accepted, 35 enrolled. *Faculty:* 8 full-time (7 women), 2 part-time/adjunct (both women). Expenses: Contact institution. *Financial support:* In 2016–17, 9 research assistantships were awarded; teaching assistantships, career-related internships or fieldwork, scholarships/grants, and unspecified assistantships also available. Support available to part-time students. Financial award application deadline: 7/1; financial award applicants required to submit FAFSA. In 2016, 30 doctorates awarded. Offers physical therapy (DPT). *Application deadline:* For fall admission, 6/15 priority date for domestic students, 7/1 for international students; for spring admission, 11/1 priority date for domestic students, 11/1 for international students. Applications are processed on a rolling basis. *Application fee:* $35 ($40 for international students). Electronic applications accepted. *Application Contact:* Dr. Joanne Romagni, Dean of the Graduate School, 423-425-4478, Fax: 423-425-5223, E-mail: joanne-romagni@utc.edu. *Interim Department Head,* Dr. Debbie Ingram, 423-425-4767, Fax: 423-425-2380, E-mail: debbie-ingram@utc.edu.

Program in Psychology Students: 41 full-time (25 women), 7 part-time (3 women); includes 5 minority (2 Black or African American, non-Hispanic/Latino; 1 Hispanic/Latino; 2 Two or more races, non-Hispanic/Latino). Average age 26. 99 applicants, 29% accepted, 25 enrolled. *Faculty:* 13 full-time (6 women), 1 part-time/adjunct (0 women). Expenses: Contact institution. *Financial support:* In 2016–17,

23 research assistantships, 1 teaching assistantship were awarded; career-related internships or fieldwork, scholarships/grants, and unspecified assistantships also available. Support available to part-time students. Financial award application deadline: 7/1; financial award applicants required to submit FAFSA. In 2016, 21 master's awarded. *Program availability:* Part-time. Offers industrial/organizational psychology (MS); research psychology (MS). *Application deadline:* For fall admission, 6/15 priority date for domestic students, 7/1 for international students; for spring admission, 11/1 priority date for domestic students, 11/1 for international students. Applications are processed on a rolling basis. *Application fee:* $35 ($40 for international students). Electronic applications accepted. *Application Contact:* Dr. Joanne Romagni, Dean of the Graduate School, 423-425-4478, Fax: 423-425-5223, E-mail: joanne-romagni@utc.edu. *Department Head,* Dr. Brian O'Leary, 423-425-4283, Fax: 423-425-4284, E-mail: brian-o'leary@utc.edu.

School of Education Students: 50 full-time (32 women), 157 part-time (107 women); includes 42 minority (28 Black or African American, non-Hispanic/Latino; 4 Asian, non-Hispanic/Latino; 2 Hispanic/Latino; 8 Two or more races, non-Hispanic/Latino), 1 international. Average age 36. 169 applicants, 76% accepted, 49 enrolled. *Faculty:* 13 full-time (8 women), 2 part-time/adjunct (both women). Expenses: Contact institution. *Financial support:* In 2016–17, 18 research assistantships, 5 teaching assistantships were awarded; career-related internships or fieldwork, institutionally sponsored loans, scholarships/grants, and unspecified assistantships also available. Support available to part-time students. Financial award application deadline: 7/1; financial award applicants required to submit FAFSA. In 2016, 77 master's, 5 other advanced degrees awarded. *Program availability:* Part-time. Offers counseling (M Ed); education (M Ed, Post-Master's Certificate); educational specialist (Ed S); learning and leadership (Ed D). *Application deadline:* For fall admission, 6/15 for domestic students, 7/1 for international students; for spring admission, 11/1 for domestic and international students. Applications are processed on a rolling basis. *Application fee:* $35 ($40 for international students). Electronic applications accepted. *Application Contact:* Dr. Joanne Romagni, Dean of the Graduate School, Fax: 423-425-5223, E-mail: joanne-romagni@utc.edu. *Director,* Dr. Renee Murley, 423-425-4684, Fax: 423-425-5380, E-mail: renee-murley@utc.edu.

School of Nursing Students: 61 full-time (32 women), 49 part-time (42 women); includes 15 minority (6 Black or African American, non-Hispanic/Latino; 2 Asian, non-Hispanic/Latino; 3 Hispanic/Latino; 4 Two or more races, non-Hispanic/Latino). Average age 35. 48 applicants, 98% accepted, 38 enrolled. *Faculty:* 12 full-time (9 women), 3 part-time/adjunct (2 women). Expenses: Contact institution. *Financial support:* In 2016–17, 1 teaching assistantship was awarded; career-related internships or fieldwork and scholarships/grants also available. Support available to part-time students. Financial award application deadline: 7/1; financial award applicants required to submit FAFSA. In 2016, 36 master's, 5 doctorates, 1 other advanced degree awarded. Offers administration (MSN); certified nurse anesthetist (Post-Master's Certificate); education (MSN); family nurse practitioner (MSN, Post-Master's Certificate); health care informatics (Post-Master's Certificate); nurse anesthesia (MSN); nurse education (Post-Master's Certificate); nursing (DNP). *Application deadline:* For fall admission, 6/15 priority date for domestic students, 7/1 for international students; for spring admission, 11/1 priority date for domestic students, 11/1 for international students. Applications are processed on a rolling basis. *Application fee:* $35 ($40 for international students). Electronic applications accepted. *Application Contact:* Dr. Joanne Romagni, Dean of the Graduate School, 423-425-4478, Fax: 423-425-5223, E-mail: joanne-romagni@utc.edu. *Director,* Dr. Chris Smith, 423-425-1741, Fax: 423-425-4668, E-mail: chris-smith@utc.edu.

THE UNIVERSITY OF TENNESSEE AT MARTIN, Martin, TN 38238

General Information State-supported, coed, comprehensive institution. *Enrollment:* 6,705 graduate, professional, and undergraduate students; 60 full-time matriculated graduate/professional students (38 women), 366 part-time matriculated graduate/professional students (237 women). *Enrollment by degree level:* 426 master's. *Graduate faculty:* 133. Tuition, state resident: full-time $8254; part-time $459 per credit hour. Tuition, nonresident: full-time $22,198; part-time $1234 per credit hour. *Required fees:* $79 per credit hour. Part-time tuition and fees vary according to course load and campus/location. *Graduate housing:* Rooms and/or apartments available on a first-come, first-served basis to single and married students. Typical cost: $2780 per year ($5896 including board) for single students; $5460 per year for married students. Room and board charges vary according to board plan and housing facility selected. Housing application deadline: 3/1. *Student services:* Campus employment opportunities, campus safety program, career counseling, child daycare facilities, exercise/wellness program, free psychological counseling, international student services, low-cost health insurance, multicultural affairs office, services for students with disabilities, teacher training, writing training. *Library facilities:* Paul Meek Library. *Collection:* Books: 345,939 (physical), 156,902 (digital/electronic); Serial titles: 156 (physical), 99,944 (digital/electronic); Databases: 79. Weekly public service hours: 92; study areas open 24 hours, 5–7 days a week. *Research affiliation:* U.S. Department of Education (DOE) (academic extensions), National Writing Project (humanities), U.S. Department of Health and Human Services (infant health), U.S. Department of Justice (criminal justice), The University of Tennessee Research Foundation (science and technology), Oak Ridge National Laboratory (science, technology, engineering, and math (STEM)).

Computer facilities: 1,119 computers available on campus for general student use. A campuswide network can be accessed from student residence rooms and from off campus. Online class registration, online fee payments, degree progress, financial aid data, housing applications, transcripts are available.
Website: http://www.utm.edu/

General Application Contact: Jolene L. Cunningham, Student Services Specialist, 731-881-7012, Fax: 731-881-7499, E-mail: jcunningham@utm.edu.

GRADUATE UNITS

Graduate Programs Students: 426 (275 women); includes 56 minority (39 Black or African American, non-Hispanic/Latino; 3 Asian, non-Hispanic/Latino; 10 Hispanic/Latino; 4 Two or more races, non-Hispanic/Latino), 5 international. Average age 32. 297 applicants, 64% accepted, 114 enrolled. *Faculty:* 133. Expenses: Contact institution. *Financial support:* In 2016–17, 32 students received support, including 9 research assistantships with full tuition reimbursements available (averaging $7,512 per year), 21 teaching assistantships with full tuition reimbursements available (averaging $7,313 per year); scholarships/grants and unspecified assistantships also available. Financial award application deadline: 2/1; financial award applicants required to submit FAFSA. In 2016, 100 master's awarded. *Program availability:* Part-time, 100% online, blended/hybrid learning. *Application deadline:* For fall admission, 7/27 priority date for domestic and international students; for spring admission, 12/17 priority date for domestic and international students; for summer admission, 5/10 priority date for domestic and international students. Applications are processed on a rolling basis. *Application fee:* $30 ($130 for international students). Electronic applications accepted.

Application Contact: Jolene L. Cunningham, Student Services Specialist, 731-881-7012, Fax: 731-881-7499, E-mail: jcunningham@utm.edu. *Associate Vice Chancellor and Dean of Graduate Studies,* Dr. Victoria S. Seng, 731-881-7012, Fax: 731-881-7499, E-mail: vseng@utm.edu.

College of Agriculture and Applied Sciences Students: 10 full-time (6 women), 66 part-time (42 women); includes 10 minority (9 Black or African American, non-Hispanic/Latino; 1 Two or more races, non-Hispanic/Latino). Average age 30. 65 applicants, 72% accepted, 20 enrolled. *Faculty:* 25. Expenses: Contact institution. *Financial support:* In 2016–17, 7 students received support, including 2 research assistantships with full tuition reimbursements available (averaging $8,042 per year), 5 teaching assistantships (averaging $7,830 per year); scholarships/grants and unspecified assistantships also available. Financial award application deadline: 2/1; financial award applicants required to submit FAFSA. In 2016, 15 master's awarded. *Program availability:* Part-time, 100% online, blended/hybrid learning. Offers agricultural and natural resources management (MSANR); agriculture and applied sciences (MSANR, MSFCS); dietetics (MSFCS); general family and consumer sciences (MSFCS). *Application deadline:* For fall admission, 7/27 priority date for domestic and international students; for spring admission, 12/17 priority date for domestic and international students; for summer admission, 5/10 priority date for domestic and international students. Applications are processed on a rolling basis. *Application fee:* $30 ($130 for international students). Electronic applications accepted. *Application Contact:* Jolene L. Cunningham, Student Services Specialist, 731-881-7012, Fax: 731-881-7499, E-mail: jcunningham@utm.edu. *Dean,* Dr. Todd Winters, 731-881-7250, E-mail: winters@utm.edu.

College of Business and Global Affairs Students: 15 full-time (6 women), 79 part-time (28 women); includes 13 minority (6 Black or African American, non-Hispanic/Latino; 2 Asian, non-Hispanic/Latino; 4 Hispanic/Latino; 1 Two or more races, non-Hispanic/Latino). Average age 33. 62 applicants, 40% accepted, 20 enrolled. *Faculty:* 31. Expenses: Contact institution. *Financial support:* In 2016–17, 10 students received support, including 5 research assistantships with full tuition reimbursements available (averaging $7,540 per year), 5 teaching assistantships with full tuition reimbursements available (averaging $7,560 per year); scholarships/grants and unspecified assistantships also available. Financial award application deadline: 2/1; financial award applicants required to submit FAFSA. In 2016, 34 master's awarded. *Program availability:* Part-time, 100% online, blended/hybrid learning. Offers agricultural business (MBA); business (MBA); financial services (MBA); general business (MBA). *Application deadline:* For fall admission, 7/27 priority date for domestic and international students; for spring admission, 12/17 priority date for domestic and international students; for summer admission, 5/10 priority date for domestic and international students. Applications are processed on a rolling basis. *Application fee:* $30 ($130 for international students). Electronic applications accepted. *Application Contact:* Jolene L. Cunningham, Student Services Specialist, 731-881-7012, Fax: 731-881-7499, E-mail: jcunningham@utm.edu. *Dean,* Dr. Ross Dickens, 731-881-7227, Fax: 731-881-7241, E-mail: rdicken2@utm.edu.

College of Education, Health and Behavioral Sciences Students: 35 full-time (26 women), 210 part-time (160 women); includes 34 minority (24 Black or African American, non-Hispanic/Latino; 1 Asian, non-Hispanic/Latino; 7 Hispanic/Latino; 2 Two or more races, non-Hispanic/Latino). Average age 33. 168 applicants, 70% accepted, 73 enrolled. *Faculty:* 45. Expenses: Contact institution. *Financial support:* In 2016–17, 13 students received support, including 2 research assistantships with full tuition reimbursements available (averaging $6,912 per year), 10 teaching assistantships with full tuition reimbursements available (averaging $6,909 per year); scholarships/grants and unspecified assistantships also available. Financial award application deadline: 2/1; financial award applicants required to submit FAFSA. In 2016, 51 master's awarded. *Program availability:* Part-time, online only, 100% online. Offers addictions counseling (MS Ed); community counseling (MS Ed); curriculum and instruction (MS Ed); education, health and behavioral sciences (MS Ed); educational leadership (MS Ed); initial licensure (MS Ed); initial licensure K-12 (MS Ed); interdisciplinary (MS Ed); school counseling (MS Ed); student affairs and college counseling (MS Ed). *Application deadline:* For fall admission, 7/27 priority date for domestic and international students; for spring admission, 12/17 priority date for domestic and international students; for summer admission, 5/10 priority date for domestic and international students. Applications are processed on a rolling basis. *Application fee:* $30 ($130 for international students). Electronic applications accepted. *Application Contact:* Jolene L. Cunningham, Student Services Specialist, 731-881-7012, Fax: 731-881-7499, E-mail: jcunningham@utm.edu. *Dean,* Cynthia West, 731-881-7127, Fax: 731-881-7975, E-mail: cwest@utm.edu.

College of Humanities and Fine Arts Students: 11 full-time (7 women). Average age 28. 2 applicants, 50% accepted, 1 enrolled. *Faculty:* 20 full-time (7 women). Expenses: Contact institution. *Financial support:* In 2016–17, 2 students received support, including 1 teaching assistantship (averaging $7,540 per year); research assistantships, scholarships/grants, and unspecified assistantships also available. Financial award application deadline: 2/1; financial award applicants required to submit FAFSA. *Program availability:* Part-time, blended/hybrid learning. Offers strategic communication (MASC). *Application deadline:* For fall admission, 7/27 priority date for domestic and international students; for spring admission, 12/15 priority date for domestic and international students; for summer admission, 5/10 priority date for domestic and international students. Applications are processed on a rolling basis. *Application fee:* $30 ($130 for international students). Electronic applications accepted. *Application Contact:* Jolene L. Cunningham, Student Services Specialist, 731-881-7012, Fax: 731-881-7499, E-mail: jcunningham@utm.edu. *Dean,* Dr. Lynn Alexander, 731-881-7490, Fax: 731-881-7276, E-mail: lalexand@utm.edu.

THE UNIVERSITY OF TENNESSEE HEALTH SCIENCE CENTER, Memphis, TN 38163-0002

General Information State-supported, coed, upper-level institution. CGS member. *Graduate housing:* On-campus housing not available. *Student services:* Campus employment opportunities, campus safety program, career counseling, child daycare facilities, exercise/wellness program, free psychological counseling, grant writing training, international student services, low-cost health insurance, multicultural affairs office, services for students with disabilities, writing training. *Library facilities:* Health Science Library plus 2 others. *Research affiliation:* Saint Jude's Children's Research Hospital, Veterans Administration Medical Center, University of Memphis, LeBonheur Children's Medical Center.

Computer facilities: 100 computers available on campus for general student use. A campuswide network can be accessed from student residence rooms and from off campus.
Website: http://www.uthsc.edu/

General Application Contact: Ann Salina, Director for Admissions, 901-448-1603, E-mail: asalina@uthsc.edu.

GRADUATE UNITS

College of Dentistry Offers dentistry (DDS). Electronic applications accepted.

College of Graduate Health Sciences Students: 258 full-time (130 women); includes 87 minority (14 Black or African American, non-Hispanic/Latino; 68 Asian, non-Hispanic/Latino; 5 Hispanic/Latino). Average age 28. 673 applicants, 17% accepted, 102 enrolled. *Faculty*: 528 full-time (176 women). Expenses: Contact institution. *Financial support*: In 2016–17, 150 students received support, including 150 research assistantships (averaging $25,000 per year); fellowships, Federal Work-Study, institutionally sponsored loans, scholarships/grants, health care benefits, and tuition waivers (full and partial) also available. Support available to part-time students. Financial award application deadline: 2/25. In 2016, 23 master's, 30 doctorates awarded. Offers biomedical engineering (MS, PhD); biomedical sciences (PhD); dental sciences (MDS); epidemiology (MS); health outcomes and policy research (PhD); laboratory research and management (MS); nursing science (PhD); pharmaceutical sciences (PhD); pharmacology (MS); speech and hearing science (PhD). MS and PhD programs in biomedical engineering offered jointly with University of Memphis. *Application deadline*: Applications are processed on a rolling basis. *Application fee*: $0. Electronic applications accepted. *Application Contact*: Dr. Isaac O. Donkor, Associate Dean for Student Affairs, 901-448-5538, E-mail: idonkor@uthsc.edu. *Dean*, Dr. Donald B. Thomason, 901-448-5538, E-mail: dthomaso@uthsc.edu.

College of Health Professions *Program availability*: Part-time, evening/weekend, online learning. Offers audiology (MS, Au D); clinical laboratory science (MSCLS); cytopathology practice (MCP); health informatics and information management (MHIIM); occupational therapy (MOT); physical therapy (DPT, ScDPT); physician assistant (MMS); speech-language pathology (MS). Electronic applications accepted.

College of Medicine Offers medicine (MD). Electronic applications accepted.

College of Nursing Students: 250 full-time (206 women), 22 part-time (21 women); includes 91 minority (76 Black or African American, non-Hispanic/Latino; 6 Asian, non-Hispanic/Latino; 6 Hispanic/Latino; 3 Two or more races, non-Hispanic/Latino), 2 international. Average age 32. 210 applicants, 52% accepted, 88 enrolled. *Faculty*: 54 full-time (50 women), 3 part-time/adjunct (1 woman). Expenses: Contact institution. *Financial support*: In 2016–17, 107 students received support, including 3 research assistantships (averaging $75,000 per year); Federal Work-Study, institutionally sponsored loans, scholarships/grants, and traineeships also available. Financial award application deadline: 3/15; financial award applicants required to submit FAFSA. *Program availability*: Part-time, blended/hybrid learning. Offers adult-gerontology acute care nurse practitioner (Certificate); advanced practice nursing (DNP). *Application deadline*: For fall admission, 1/15 for domestic students; for winter admission, 9/1 for domestic students; for summer admission, 9/15 for domestic students. *Application fee*: $65. Electronic applications accepted. *Application Contact*: Jamie Overton, Director, Student Affairs, 901-448-6139, Fax: 901-448-4121, E-mail: joverton@uthsc.edu. *Dean*, Dr. Wendy Likes, 901-448-6135, Fax: 901-448-4121, E-mail: wlikes@uthsc.edu.

College of Pharmacy Offers pharmacy (MS, PhD, Pharm D). Electronic applications accepted.

THE UNIVERSITY OF TENNESSEE–OAK RIDGE NATIONAL LABORATORY, Oak Ridge, TN 37830-8026

General Information State-supported, coed, graduate-only institution. *Research affiliation*: Oak Ridge National Laboratory.

GRADUATE UNITS

Graduate Program in Genome Science and Technology Offers life sciences (MS, PhD). Electronic applications accepted.

THE UNIVERSITY OF TEXAS AT ARLINGTON, Arlington, TX 76019

General Information State-supported, coed, university. CGS member. *Graduate housing*: Rooms and/or apartments available on a first-come, first-served basis to single and married students. *Student services*: Campus employment opportunities, campus safety program, career counseling, child daycare facilities, exercise/wellness program, free psychological counseling, international student services, multicultural affairs office, services for students with disabilities, teacher training, writing training. *Library facilities*: Central Library plus 2 others. *Research affiliation*: Texas Health Resources (medical technologies), Center for Innovation (technology development and commercialization), Facebook (energy efficient electronic systems), U.S. Department of Energy (bioengineering), National Science Foundation (materials science and engineering), Texas Instruments (medical technologies).

Computer facilities: 500 computers available on campus for general student use. A campuswide network can be accessed from student residence rooms. Online class registration is available.
Website: http://www.uta.edu/

General Application Contact: Raymond L. Jackson, Associate Dean of Graduate Studies, 817-272-5164, Fax: 817-272-2625, E-mail: graduate.school@uta.edu.

GRADUATE UNITS

Graduate School Expenses: Contact institution. *Financial support*: Fellowships, research assistantships, teaching assistantships, career-related internships or fieldwork, Federal Work-Study, institutionally sponsored loans, scholarships/grants, traineeships, and tuition waivers (partial) available. Financial award application deadline: 6/1; financial award applicants required to submit FAFSA. *Program availability*: Part-time, evening/weekend, online learning. *Application deadline*: For fall admission, 6/15 for domestic students. Applications are processed on a rolling basis. *Application fee*: $35 ($50 for international students). *Application Contact*: Dr. Phil Cohen, Dean of Graduate Studies, 817-272-3186, Fax: 817-272-2625, E-mail: graduate.school@uta.edu. *Dean of Graduate Studies*, Dr. Phil Cohen, 817-272-3186, Fax: 817-272-2625, E-mail: graduate.school@uta.edu.

College of Architecture, Planning and Public Affairs Expenses: Contact institution. *Financial support*: Fellowships with full tuition reimbursements, research assistantships, teaching assistantships with full tuition reimbursements, career-related internships or fieldwork, and Federal Work-Study available. Financial award application deadline: 6/1; financial award applicants required to submit FAFSA. *Program availability*: Part-time, evening/weekend, online learning. Offers architecture (M Arch); architecture, planning and public affairs (M Arch, MLA, MPA, MPP, PhD); landscape architecture (MLA); public administration (MPA); public and urban administration (PhD); public policy (MPP); urban planning and public policy (PhD). *Application deadline*: For fall admission, 6/1 for domestic students, 4/1 for international students; for spring admission, 10/15 for domestic students, 9/15 for international students. Applications are processed on a rolling basis. *Application fee*: $35 ($50 for international students). Electronic applications accepted. *Application Contact*: Tangie Fields, Academic Advisor, 817-272-3340, Fax: 817-272-3415, E-mail: nfields@uta.edu. *Dean*, Dr. Barbara Becker, 817-272-3071, Fax: 817-272-3255, E-mail: bbecker@uta.edu.

College of Business Expenses: Contact institution. *Financial support*: Fellowships, research assistantships, teaching assistantships, career-related internships or fieldwork, Federal Work-Study, institutionally sponsored loans, and scholarships/grants available. Financial award application deadline: 6/1; financial award applicants required to submit FAFSA. *Program availability*: Part-time, evening/weekend, online learning. Offers accounting (MP Acc, MS, PhD); business (MA, MBA, MP Acc, MS, MSHRM, PhD); economics (MA); finance (PhD); health care administration (MS); human resources (MSHRM); information systems (MS, PhD); marketing (MBA); marketing research (MS); quantitative finance (MS); real estate (MS); taxation (MS). *Application deadline*: For fall admission, 6/1 for domestic students, 4/1 for international students; for spring admission, 10/15 for domestic students, 9/15 for international students. Applications are processed on a rolling basis. *Application fee*: $40 ($70 for international students). Electronic applications accepted. *Application Contact*: Rebecca Neilson, Director of Graduate Business Services, 817-272-3649, Fax: 817-272-5799, E-mail: rneilson@uta.edu. *Interim Dean*, Dr. David Gray, 817-272-2881, Fax: 817-272-2073, E-mail: gray@uta.edu.

College of Education Expenses: Contact institution. Offers curriculum and instruction (M Ed); education (M Ed, M Ed T, PhD); educational leadership (PhD); higher education (M Ed); principal certification (M Ed); teaching (with certification) (M Ed T). *Application Contact*: Dr. Phil Cohen, Dean of Graduate Studies, 817-272-3186, Fax: 817-272-2625, E-mail: graduate.school@uta.edu. *Dean of Graduate Studies*, Dr. Phil Cohen, 817-272-3186, Fax: 817-272-2625, E-mail: graduate.school@uta.edu.

College of Engineering Expenses: Contact institution. *Financial support*: Fellowships, research assistantships, teaching assistantships, career-related internships or fieldwork, Federal Work-Study, institutionally sponsored loans, scholarships/grants, and tuition waivers (partial) available. Financial award application deadline: 6/1; financial award applicants required to submit FAFSA. *Program availability*: Part-time, evening/weekend, online learning. Offers aerospace engineering (M Engr, MS, PhD); bioengineering (MS, PhD); civil engineering (M Engr, MS, PhD); computer engineering (MS, PhD); computer science (MS, PhD); construction management (MCM); electrical engineering (M Engr, MS, PhD); engineering (M Engr, MCM, MS, PhD); engineering management (MS); industrial engineering (MS, PhD); logistics (MS); materials science and engineering (M Engr, MS, PhD); mechanical engineering (M Engr, MS, PhD); software engineering (MS); systems engineering (MS). *Application deadline*: For fall admission, 6/6 for domestic students, 4/4 for international students; for spring admission, 10/15 for domestic students, 9/5 for international students. Applications are processed on a rolling basis. *Application fee*: $35 ($50 for international students). *Application Contact*: Dr. Lynn L. Peterson, Associate Dean for Academic Affairs, 817-272-2571, Fax: 817-272-2548, E-mail: peterson@uta.edu. *Dean*, Dr. Jean-Pierre Bardet, 817-272-2571, Fax: 817-272-5110, E-mail: bardet@uta.edu.

College of Liberal Arts Expenses: Contact institution. *Financial support*: Fellowships with full tuition reimbursements, research assistantships, teaching assistantships, career-related internships or fieldwork, Federal Work-Study, institutionally sponsored loans, and scholarships/grants available. Financial award application deadline: 3/1; financial award applicants required to submit FAFSA. *Program availability*: Part-time, evening/weekend. Offers anthropology (MA); communication (MA); criminology and criminal justice (MA); education (MM); English (MA); film and video (MFA); French (MA); glass (MFA); history (MA); intermedia (MFA); liberal arts (MA, MFA, MM, PhD); linguistics (MA, PhD); literature (PhD); performance (MM); political science (MA); sociology (MA); Spanish (MA); teaching English to speakers of other languages (MA); transatlantic history (PhD); visual communication (MFA). *Application deadline*: For fall admission, 6/15 for domestic students. Applications are processed on a rolling basis. *Application fee*: $35 ($50 for international students). *Application Contact*: Dr. Kimberly Van Noort, Associate Dean, 817-272-3291, E-mail: vannoort@uta.edu. *Dean*, Dr. Beth S. Wright, 817-272-3291, Fax: 817-272-3255, E-mail: bwright@uta.edu.

College of Nursing and Health Innovation Expenses: Contact institution. *Financial support*: Fellowships with partial tuition reimbursements, research assistantships, teaching assistantships, career-related internships or fieldwork, scholarships/grants, and traineeships available. Financial award application deadline: 6/1; financial award applicants required to submit FAFSA. *Program availability*: Part-time, evening/weekend, online learning. Offers athletic training (MS); exercise science (MS); kinesiology (PhD); nurse practitioner (MSN); nursing (PhD); nursing administration (MSN); nursing education (MSN); nursing practice (DNP). *Application deadline*: For fall admission, 2/1 for domestic students, 4/1 for international students; for spring admission, 10/15 for domestic students, 9/5 for international students. Applications are processed on a rolling basis. *Application fee*: $40 ($70 for international students). *Application Contact*: Dr. Anne R. Bavier, Dean. *Dean*, Dr. Anne R. Bavier.

College of Science Expenses: Contact institution. *Financial support*: Fellowships, research assistantships with partial tuition reimbursements, teaching assistantships with partial tuition reimbursements, career-related internships or fieldwork, Federal Work-Study, institutionally sponsored loans, scholarships/grants, tuition waivers (partial), and unspecified assistantships available. Financial award application deadline: 6/1; financial award applicants required to submit FAFSA. *Program availability*: Part-time, evening/weekend. Offers applied math (MS); biology (MS); chemistry (MS, PhD); earth and environmental sciences (MS, PhD); experimental health psychology (PhD); experimental psychology (MS, PhD); health/neuroscience psychology (MS, PhD); industrial and organizational psychology (MS); mathematics (PhD); mathematics education (MA); physics (MS); physics and applied physics (PhD); quantitative biology (PhD); science (MA, MS, PhD). *Application deadline*: For fall admission, 6/1 for domestic students, 4/1 for international students; for spring admission, 10/15 for domestic students, 9/15 for international students. Applications are processed on a rolling basis. *Application fee*: $35 ($50 for international students). *Application Contact*: Dr. Morteza Khaledi, Dean, 817-272-3491, E-mail: morteza.khaledi@uta.edu. *Dean*, Dr. Morteza Khaledi, 817-272-3491, E-mail: morteza.khaledi@uta.edu.

School of Social Work Expenses: Contact institution. *Financial support*: Fellowships with full tuition reimbursements, research assistantships, teaching assistantships, career-related internships or fieldwork, Federal Work-Study, institutionally sponsored loans, scholarships/grants, and unspecified assistantships available. Support available to part-time students. Financial award application deadline: 6/1. *Program availability*: Part-time, evening/weekend, online learning. Offers social work (MSW, PhD). *Application deadline*: For fall admission, 6/5 for domestic students; for winter admission, 10/15 for domestic students. Applications are processed on a rolling basis. *Application fee*: $35 ($50 for international students). Electronic applications accepted. *Application Contact*: Darlene Santee, Director of Admissions, 817-272-3613, Fax: 817-272-5229. *Dean*, Dr. Scott D. Ryan, 817-272-1491, Fax: 817-272-5229, E-mail: sdryan@uta.edu.

THE UNIVERSITY OF TEXAS AT AUSTIN, Austin, TX 78712-1111

General Information State-supported, coed, university. CGS member. *Graduate housing:* Rooms and/or apartments available to single students and available on a first-come, first-served basis to married students.

GRADUATE UNITS

Graduate School *Program availability:* Part-time, evening/weekend. Offers computational science, engineering, and mathematics (MS, PhD). Electronic applications accepted.

Cockrell School of Engineering Program availability: Part-time, evening/weekend. Offers aerospace engineering (MSE, PhD); architectural engineering (MSE); biomedical engineering (MS, PhD); chemical engineering (MSE, PhD); civil engineering (MS, PhD); electrical and computer engineering (MS, PhD); energy and earth resources (MA); engineering (MA, MS, MSE, PhD); engineering mechanics (MS, PhD); environmental and water resources engineering (MS, PhD); materials science and engineering (MS, PhD); mechanical engineering (MS, PhD); operations research and industrial engineering (MS, PhD); petroleum engineering (MS, PhD). Electronic applications accepted.

College of Communication Program availability: Part-time. Offers advertising (MA, PhD); audiology (Au D); communication (MA, MFA, Au D, PhD); communication sciences and disorders (PhD); communication studies (MA, PhD); film and media production (MFA); journalism (MA, PhD); media studies (MA, PhD); screenwriting (MFA); speech language pathology (MA). Electronic applications accepted.

College of Education Program availability: Part-time. Offers academic educational psychology (M Ed, MA); autism and developmental disabilities (Ed D, PhD); autism and developmental disability (M Ed, MA); behavioral health (PhD); bilingual/bicultural education (M Ed, MA, PhD); counseling psychology (PhD); counselor education (M Ed); cultural studies in education (M Ed, MA, PhD); early childhood education (M Ed, MA, PhD); early childhood special education (M Ed, MA, Ed D, PhD); education (M Ed, MA, MS, Ed D, PhD); educational administration (M Ed, Ed D, PhD); exercise and sport psychology (M Ed, MA); exercise science (M Ed, MS, PhD); health education (M Ed, MS, Ed D, PhD); human development, culture and learning sciences (PhD); language and literacy studies (M Ed, PhD); learning disabilities (Ed D, PhD); learning disabilities/behavior disorders (M Ed, MA); learning technologies (M Ed, MA, PhD); multicultural special education (M Ed, MA, Ed D, PhD); physical education (M Ed, MA, PhD); program evaluation (M Ed, MA, PhD); quantitative methods (M Ed, MA, PhD); rehabilitation counselor (M Ed); rehabilitation counselor education (Ed D, PhD); school psychology (MA, PhD); special education administration (Ed D, PhD). Electronic applications accepted.

College of Fine Arts Program availability: Part-time. Offers acting (MFA); art education (MA); art history (MA, PhD); band and wind conducting (M Music, DMA); brass/woodwind/percussion (MM); chamber music (MM); choral conducting (MM, DMA); collaborative piano (MM, DMA); composition (MM, DMA); dance (MFA); design (MFA); directing (MFA); drama and theatre for youth (MFA); ethnomusicology (MM, PhD); fine arts (M Music, MA, MFA, MM, DMA, PhD); literature and pedagogy (MM); music and human learning (MM, PhD); music and human learning (DMA); musicology (MM, PhD); opera performance (MM, DMA); orchestral conducting (MM, DMA); organ (MM); organ performance (MM, DMA); performance (MM); performance (DMA); performance as public practice (MA, MFA, DMA); piano (DMA); piano literature and pedagogy (MM); piano performance (MM, DMA); playwriting (MFA); string performance (MM, DMA); studio art (MFA); theatre technology (MFA); theatrical design (MFA); theory (MM, PhD); vocal performance (MM, DMA); voice (DMA); voice performance pedagogy (DMA); woodwind, brass, percussion performance (MM). Electronic applications accepted.

College of Liberal Arts Program availability: Part-time. Offers African Diaspora studies (MA, PhD); American studies (MA, PhD); applied linguistics/pedagogy (PhD); archaeology (MA, PhD); Asian cultures and languages (MA, PhD); Asian studies (MA); behavioral neuroscience (PhD); classics (MA, PhD); clinical psychology (PhD); cognitive systems (PhD); comparative literature (MA, PhD); creative writing (MFA); cultural forms (MA, PhD); cultural politics of Afro-Latin and indigenous peoples (MA); development studies (MA); developmental psychology (PhD); economics (MA, MS Econ, PhD); English (MA, PhD); environmental studies (MA); French linguistics (MA, PhD); French studies (MA, PhD); geography and the environment (MA, PhD); Germanic studies (MA, PhD); government (MA, PhD); Hispanic linguistics (MA, PhD); Hispanic literature (MA, PhD); history (MA, PhD); human dimensions of organizations (MA); human rights (MA); Ibero-romance philology and linguistics (PhD); individual differences and evolutionary psychology (PhD); Italian studies (MA, PhD); Latin American and international law (LL M); liberal arts (LL M, MA, MFA, MS Econ, PhD); linguistic anthropology (MA, PhD); linguistics (MA, PhD); literature and culture (PhD); Luso-Brazilian literature (MA, PhD); Mexican American studies (MA); Middle Eastern languages and cultures (MA, PhD); Middle Eastern studies (MA); perceptual systems (PhD); philosophy (PhD); physical anthropology (MA, PhD); Romance linguistics (PhD); Russian, East European, and Eurasian studies (MA); Slavic languages (MA); Slavic linguistics (PhD); social anthropology (MA, PhD); social psychology (PhD); sociology (MA, PhD). Electronic applications accepted.

College of Natural Sciences Program availability: Part-time. Offers analytical chemistry (PhD); astronomy (PhD); biochemistry (PhD); computer sciences (MSCS, PhD); ecology, evolution and behavior (PhD); human development and family sciences (MA, PhD); inorganic chemistry (PhD); marine science (MS, PhD); mathematics (MA, PhD); microbiology (PhD); natural sciences (MA, MS, MSCS, PhD); nutrition (MA); nutritional sciences (MA, PhD); organic chemistry (PhD); physical chemistry (PhD); physics (MA, MS, PhD); plant biology (MA, PhD); statistics (MS, PhD); textile and apparel technology (MS). Electronic applications accepted.

College of Pharmacy Offers health outcomes and pharmacy practice (PhD); health outcomes and pharmacy practice (MS); medicinal chemistry (PhD); pharmaceutics (PhD); pharmacology and toxicology (PhD); pharmacotherapy (MS, PhD); pharmacy (MS, PhD, Pharm D); translational science (PhD). Electronic applications accepted.

Institute for Cellular and Molecular Biology Offers cellular and molecular biology (PhD).

The Institute for Neuroscience Offers neuroscience (PhD). Electronic applications accepted.

Jackson School of Geosciences Program availability: Part-time. Offers geosciences (MA, MS, PhD). Electronic applications accepted.

Lyndon B. Johnson School of Public Affairs Program availability: Part-time. Offers global policy studies (MGPS); public affairs (MP Aff); public leadership (EMPL); public policy (PhD). Electronic applications accepted.

McCombs School of Business Offers accounting (MPA, PhD); business (MBA, MPA, MS, MSF, PhD); business administration (MBA); executive business administration (MBA); finance (MSF, PhD); information management (MBA); information systems (PhD); management (PhD); marketing (MBA, MS, PhD); risk analysis and decision making (PhD); risk management (MBA); supply chain and operations management (MBA, PhD); technology commercialization (MS). Electronic applications accepted.

Michener Center for Writers Offers fiction (MFA); playwriting (MFA); poetry (MFA); screenwriting (MFA). Electronic applications accepted.

School of Architecture Offers architectural history (MA, PhD); architecture (M Arch, M Arch I, M Arch II, MA, MID, MLA, MS, MSAS, MSCRP, MSSD, MSUD, PhD); community and regional planning (MSCRP, PhD); historic preservation (M Arch, MS, MSCRP); interior design (MID); landscape architecture (MLA); sustainable design (M Arch I, M Arch II, MSSD); urban design (M Arch, MSUD). Electronic applications accepted.

School of Information Program availability: Part-time. Offers identity management and security (MSIMS); information (PhD); information studies (MSIS). MSIMS program offered in conjunction with the Center for Identity. Electronic applications accepted.

School of Nursing Program availability: Part-time. Offers adult - gerontology clinical nurse specialist (MSN); child health (MSN); family nurse practitioner (MSN); family psychiatric/mental health nurse practitioner (MSN); holistic adult health (MSN); maternity (MSN); nursing (MSN); nursing administration and healthcare systems management (MSN); nursing practice (DNP); pediatric nurse practitioner (MSN); public health nursing (MSN). Electronic applications accepted.

School of Social Work Program availability: Part-time. Offers social work (MSSW, PhD).

School of Law Students: 951 full-time (426 women); includes 280 minority (50 Black or African American, non-Hispanic/Latino; 3 American Indian or Alaska Native, non-Hispanic/Latino; 56 Asian, non-Hispanic/Latino; 126 Hispanic/Latino; 1 Native Hawaiian or other Pacific Islander, non-Hispanic/Latino; 44 Two or more races, non-Hispanic/Latino), 21 international. Average age 24. 4,424 applicants, 27% accepted, 295 enrolled. *Faculty:* 90 full-time (34 women), 115 part-time/adjunct (33 women). *Expenses:* Contact institution. *Financial support:* In 2016–17, 871 students received support, including 4 fellowships (averaging $55,000 per year), 175 research assistantships (averaging $4,000 per year), 30 teaching assistantships with partial tuition reimbursements available (averaging $3,000 per year); career-related internships or fieldwork, scholarships/grants, and tuition waivers (full) also available. Financial award application deadline: 12/1; financial award applicants required to submit FAFSA. In 2016, 34 master's, 361 doctorates awarded. Offers law (LL M, JD). *Application deadline:* For fall admission, 11/1 for domestic students; for spring admission, 3/1 for domestic students. *Application fee:* $70. Electronic applications accepted. *Application Contact:* School of Law Admissions, 512-232-1200, Fax: 512-471-2765, E-mail: admissions@law.utexas.edu. *Dean,* Ward Farnsworth, 512-232-1120, Fax: 512-471-6987, E-mail: wfarnsworth@law.utexas.edu.

THE UNIVERSITY OF TEXAS AT DALLAS, Richardson, TX 75080

General Information State-supported, coed, university. CGS member. *Enrollment:* 26,793 graduate, professional, and undergraduate students; 6,452 full-time matriculated graduate/professional students (2,740 women), 2,810 part-time matriculated graduate/professional students (1,233 women). *Enrollment by degree level:* 7,908 master's, 1,354 doctoral. *Graduate faculty:* 562 full-time (122 women), 131 part-time/adjunct (47 women). *Tuition,* state resident: full-time $12,418; part-time $690 per semester hour. *Tuition,* nonresident: full-time $24,150; part-time $1342 per semester hour. Tuition and fees vary according to course load. *Graduate housing:* Rooms and/or apartments available on a first-come, first-served basis to single and married students. Typical cost: $10,668 (including board) for single students; $10,668 (including board) for married students. Room and board charges vary according to board plan and housing facility selected. Housing application deadline: 5/31. *Student services:* Campus employment opportunities, campus safety program, career counseling, child daycare facilities, exercise/wellness program, free psychological counseling, grant writing training, international student services, low-cost health insurance, multicultural affairs office, services for students with disabilities, teacher training, writing training. *Library facilities:* Eugene McDermott Library plus 1 other. *Collection:* Books: 593,907 (physical), 1.6 million (digital/electronic); Serial titles: 93,747 (physical), 171,102 (digital/electronic); Databases: 517. Weekly public service hours: 152; study areas open 24 hours, 5–7 days a week; students can reserve study rooms.

Computer facilities: Computer purchase and lease plans are available. 170 computers available on campus for general student use. A campuswide network can be accessed from student residence rooms and from off campus. Online class registration is available.

Website: http://www.utdallas.edu/

General Application Contact: Dr. Marion Underwood, Dean of Graduate Studies, 972-883-2234, Fax: 972-883-4308, E-mail: undrwd@utdallas.edu.

GRADUATE UNITS

Erik Jonson School of Engineering and Computer Science Students: 1,902 full-time (542 women), 570 part-time (142 women); includes 171 minority (17 Black or African American, non-Hispanic/Latino; 2 American Indian or Alaska Native, non-Hispanic/Latino; 90 Asian, non-Hispanic/Latino; 48 Hispanic/Latino; 14 Two or more races, non-Hispanic/Latino), 2,053 international. Average age 27. 7,329 applicants, 34% accepted, 850 enrolled. *Faculty:* 154 full-time (18 women), 17 part-time/adjunct (4 women). *Expenses:* Contact institution. *Financial support:* In 2016–17, 738 students received support, including 37 fellowships (averaging $3,024 per year), 338 research assistantships with partial tuition reimbursements available (averaging $23,853 per year), 225 teaching assistantships with partial tuition reimbursements available (averaging $17,266 per year); career-related internships or fieldwork, Federal Work-Study, institutionally sponsored loans, scholarships/grants, and unspecified assistantships also available. Support available to part-time students. Financial award application deadline: 4/30; financial award applicants required to submit FAFSA. In 2016, 989 master's, 70 doctorates awarded. *Program availability:* Part-time, evening/weekend. Offers biomedical engineering (MS, PhD); computer engineering (MS, PhD); computer science (MS, PhD); electrical engineering (MSEE, PhD); engineering and computer science (MS, MSEE, MSME, MSTE, PhD); materials science and engineering (MS, PhD); mechanical engineering (MSME, PhD); software engineering (MS, PhD); systems engineering and management (MS); telecommunications engineering (MSTE, PhD). *Application deadline:* For fall admission, 7/15 for domestic students, 5/1 priority date for international students; for spring admission, 11/15 for domestic students, 9/1 priority date for international students. Applications are processed on a rolling basis. *Application fee:* $50 ($100 for international students). Electronic applications accepted. *Application Contact:* Leiane Davis, Administrative Associate, 972-883-6851, Fax: 972-883-2813, E-mail: leiane.davis@utdallas.edu. *Dean,* Dr. Mark W. Spong, 972-883-2974, Fax: 972-883-2813, E-mail: ecsdean@utdallas.edu.

Naveen Jindal School of Management Students: 3,051 full-time (1,320 women), 1,667 part-time (757 women); includes 805 minority (157 Black or African American, non-Hispanic/Latino; 4 American Indian or Alaska Native, non-Hispanic/Latino; 414 Asian, non-Hispanic/Latino; 152 Hispanic/Latino; 1 Native Hawaiian or other Pacific Islander, non-Hispanic/Latino; 77 Two or more races, non-Hispanic/Latino), 2,974 international. Average age 29. 6,998 applicants, 58% accepted, 1816 enrolled. *Faculty:* 105 full-time (19 women), 79 part-time/adjunct (23 women). Expenses: Contact institution. *Financial support:* In 2016–17, 1,138 students received support, including 1 fellowship (averaging $1,000 per year), 26 research assistantships with partial tuition reimbursements available (averaging $23,618 per year), 140 teaching assistantships with partial tuition reimbursements available (averaging $13,437 per year); career-related internships or fieldwork, Federal Work-Study, institutionally sponsored loans, scholarships/grants, and unspecified assistantships also available. Support available to part-time students. Financial award application deadline: 4/30; financial award applicants required to submit FAFSA. In 2016, 1,920 master's, 13 doctorates awarded. *Program availability:* Part-time, evening/weekend, online learning. Offers accounting (MBA); business administration (MBA); business analytics (MS); executive business administration (EMBA); finance (MS); global leadership (EMBA); healthcare management (MS); healthcare management for physicians (EMBA); information technology and management (MS); innovation and entrepreneurship (MS); international management studies (MS, PhD); management (EMBA, MBA, MS, PhD); management and administrative sciences (MS); management science (PhD); marketing (MS); professional sales (MS); project management (EMBA, MS); supply chain management (MS); systems engineering and management (MS). *Application deadline:* For fall admission, 7/15 for domestic students, 5/1 priority date for international students; for spring admission, 11/15 for domestic students, 9/1 priority date for international students. Applications are processed on a rolling basis. *Application fee:* $50 ($100 for international students). Electronic applications accepted. *Application Contact:* 972-883-2750, Fax: 972-883-6425, E-mail: jindal@utdallas.edu. *Dean,* Dr. Hasan Pirkul, 972-883-2705, Fax: 972-883-2799, E-mail: hpirkul@utdallas.edu.

School of Arts and Humanities Students: 129 full-time (78 women), 127 part-time (81 women); includes 63 minority (12 Black or African American, non-Hispanic/Latino; 4 American Indian or Alaska Native, non-Hispanic/Latino; 13 Asian, non-Hispanic/Latino; 23 Hispanic/Latino; 11 Two or more races, non-Hispanic/Latino), 27 international. Average age 41. 113 applicants, 58% accepted, 38 enrolled. *Faculty:* 46 full-time (15 women), 5 part-time/adjunct (1 woman). Expenses: Contact institution. *Financial support:* In 2016–17, 135 students received support, including 1 fellowship (averaging $2,000 per year), 12 research assistantships with partial tuition reimbursements available (averaging $23,948 per year), 69 teaching assistantships with partial tuition reimbursements available (averaging $15,001 per year); Federal Work-Study, institutionally sponsored loans, scholarships/grants, and unspecified assistantships also available. Support available to part-time students. Financial award application deadline: 4/30; financial award applicants required to submit FAFSA. In 2016, 39 master's, 16 doctorates awarded. *Program availability:* Part-time, evening/weekend. Offers history (MA); humanities (MA, PhD); Latin American studies (MA). *Application deadline:* For fall admission, 7/15 for domestic students, 5/1 priority date for international students; for spring admission, 11/15 for domestic students, 9/1 priority date for international students. Applications are processed on a rolling basis. *Application fee:* $50 ($100 for international students). Electronic applications accepted. *Application Contact:* Dr. John Gooch, Associate Dean of Graduate Studies, 972-883-2756, Fax: 972-883-2989, E-mail: john.gooch@utdallas.edu. *Dean,* Dr. Dennis M. Kratz, 972-883-2984, Fax: 972-883-2989, E-mail: dkratz@utdallas.edu.

School of Arts, Technology, and Emerging Communication Students: 73 full-time (34 women), 55 part-time (27 women); includes 38 minority (11 Black or African American, non-Hispanic/Latino; 9 Asian, non-Hispanic/Latino; 16 Hispanic/Latino; 2 Two or more races, non-Hispanic/Latino), 23 international. Average age 33. 127 applicants, 34% accepted, 29 enrolled. *Faculty:* 23 full-time (9 women), 3 part-time/adjunct (0 women). Expenses: Contact institution. *Financial support:* In 2016–17, 82 students received support, including 11 research assistantships with partial tuition reimbursements available (averaging $23,709 per year), 24 teaching assistantships with partial tuition reimbursements available (averaging $14,306 per year); career-related internships or fieldwork, Federal Work-Study, institutionally sponsored loans, scholarships/grants, and unspecified assistantships also available. Support available to part-time students. Financial award application deadline: 4/30; financial award applicants required to submit FAFSA. In 2016, 47 master's, 3 doctorates awarded. Offers arts and technology (MA, MFA, PhD); emerging media and communication (MA). *Application deadline:* For fall admission, 7/15 for domestic students, 5/1 priority date for international students; for spring admission, 11/15 for domestic students, 9/1 priority date for international students. Applications are processed on a rolling basis. *Application fee:* $50 ($100 for international students). Electronic applications accepted. *Application Contact:* Dr. Monica Evans, Associate Dean for Graduate Studies, 972-883-4332, E-mail: mevans@utdallas.edu. *Dean,* Dr. Anne Balsamo, 972-883-4376, E-mail: atecdean@utdallas.edu.

School of Behavioral and Brain Sciences Students: 529 full-time (434 women), 69 part-time (51 women); includes 164 minority (19 Black or African American, non-Hispanic/Latino; 1 American Indian or Alaska Native, non-Hispanic/Latino; 44 Asian, non-Hispanic/Latino; 80 Hispanic/Latino; 20 Two or more races, non-Hispanic/Latino), 68 international. Average age 27. 992 applicants, 23% accepted, 183 enrolled. *Faculty:* 54 full-time (26 women), 16 part-time/adjunct (all women). Expenses: Contact institution. *Financial support:* In 2016–17, 455 students received support, including 3 fellowships (averaging $2,667 per year), 38 research assistantships with partial tuition reimbursements available (averaging $27,878 per year), 83 teaching assistantships with partial tuition reimbursements available (averaging $17,379 per year); career-related internships or fieldwork, Federal Work-Study, institutionally sponsored loans, scholarships/grants, and unspecified assistantships also available. Support available to part-time students. Financial award application deadline: 4/30; financial award applicants required to submit FAFSA. In 2016, 232 master's, 17 doctorates awarded. *Program availability:* Part-time, evening/weekend. Offers applied cognition and neuroscience (MS); audiology (Au D); behavioral and brain sciences (MS, Au D, PhD); cognition and neuroscience (PhD); communication disorders (MS); communication science and disorders (PhD); early childhood disorders (MS); psychological sciences (MS, PhD). *Application deadline:* For fall admission, 7/15 for domestic students, 5/1 priority date for international students; for spring admission, 11/15 for domestic students, 9/1 priority date for international students. Applications are processed on a rolling basis. *Application fee:* $50 ($100 for international students). Electronic applications accepted. *Application Contact:* Dr. Robert D. Stillman, Associate Dean of Graduate Programs, 214-905-3106, Fax: 972-883-2491, E-mail: stillman@utdallas.edu. *Interim Dean,* Dr. James C. Bartlett, 972-883-2355, Fax: 972-883-2491, E-mail: jbartlet@utdallas.edu.

School of Economic, Political and Policy Sciences Students: 263 full-time (119 women), 200 part-time (116 women); includes 135 minority (53 Black or African American, non-Hispanic/Latino; 1 American Indian or Alaska Native, non-Hispanic/Latino; 21 Asian, non-Hispanic/Latino; 47 Hispanic/Latino; 13 Two or more races, non-Hispanic/Latino), 131 international. Average age 34. 431 applicants, 57%

accepted, 152 enrolled. *Faculty:* 64 full-time (16 women), 8 part-time/adjunct (2 women). Expenses: Contact institution. *Financial support:* In 2016–17, 218 students received support, including 5 fellowships (averaging $2,500 per year), 24 research assistantships with partial tuition reimbursements available (averaging $18,499 per year), 70 teaching assistantships with partial tuition reimbursements available (averaging $13,169 per year); career-related internships or fieldwork, Federal Work-Study, institutionally sponsored loans, scholarships/grants, and unspecified assistantships also available. Support available to part-time students. Financial award application deadline: 4/30; financial award applicants required to submit FAFSA. In 2016, 105 master's, 29 doctorates awarded. *Program availability:* Part-time, evening/weekend. Offers applied sociology (MS); Constitutional law (MA); criminology (MS, PhD); economic, political and policy sciences (MA, MPA, MPP, MS, PhD); economics (MS, PhD); geospatial information sciences (MS, PhD); international political economy (MS); justice administration and leadership (MS); legislative studies (MA); political science (MA, PhD); public affairs (MPA, PhD); public policy (MPP); public policy and political economy (PhD); social data analytics and research (MS). *Application deadline:* For fall admission, 7/15 for domestic students, 5/1 priority date for international students; for spring admission, 11/15 for domestic students, 9/1 priority date for international students. Applications are processed on a rolling basis. *Application fee:* $50 ($100 for international students). Electronic applications accepted. *Application Contact:* Dr. Alex Piquero, Associate Dean for Graduate Programs, 972-883-2482, Fax: 972-883-6297, E-mail: apiquero@utdallas.edu. *Dean,* Dr. Denis Dean, 972-883-6852, Fax: 972-883-6297, E-mail: denis.dean@utdallas.edu.

School of Interdisciplinary Studies Students: 10 full-time (6 women), 15 part-time (11 women); includes 12 minority (2 Black or African American, non-Hispanic/Latino; 1 Asian, non-Hispanic/Latino; 7 Hispanic/Latino; 2 Two or more races, non-Hispanic/Latino), 2 international. Average age 38. 48 applicants, 83% accepted, 9 enrolled. *Faculty:* 3 full-time (2 women). Expenses: Contact institution. *Financial support:* In 2016–17, 14 students received support. Research assistantships with partial tuition reimbursements available, teaching assistantships with partial tuition reimbursements available, career-related internships or fieldwork, Federal Work-Study, institutionally sponsored loans, and scholarships/grants available. Support available to part-time students. Financial award application deadline: 4/30; financial award applicants required to submit FAFSA. In 2016, 4 master's awarded. *Program availability:* Part-time, evening/weekend. Offers interdisciplinary studies (MA). *Application deadline:* For fall admission, 7/15 for domestic students, 5/1 priority date for international students; for spring admission, 11/15 for domestic students, 9/1 priority date for international students. Applications are processed on a rolling basis. *Application fee:* $50 ($100 for international students). Electronic applications accepted. *Application Contact:* Becky Wiser, 972-883-2354, Fax: 972-883-2440, E-mail: rwiser@utdallas.edu. *Dean,* Dr. George Fair, 972-883-2350, Fax: 972-883-2440, E-mail: gwfair@utdallas.edu.

School of Natural Sciences and Mathematics Students: 495 full-time (207 women), 107 part-time (48 women); includes 113 minority (22 Black or African American, non-Hispanic/Latino; 51 Asian, non-Hispanic/Latino; 31 Hispanic/Latino; 9 Two or more races, non-Hispanic/Latino), 323 international. Average age 30. 919 applicants, 31% accepted, 158 enrolled. *Faculty:* 113 full-time (17 women), 3 part-time/adjunct (1 woman). Expenses: Contact institution. *Financial support:* In 2016–17, 408 students received support, including 5 fellowships with partial tuition reimbursements available (averaging $2,670 per year), 100 research assistantships with partial tuition reimbursements available (averaging $23,638 per year), 239 teaching assistantships with partial tuition reimbursements available (averaging $17,142 per year); career-related internships or fieldwork, Federal Work-Study, institutionally sponsored loans, scholarships/grants, and unspecified assistantships also available. Support available to part-time students. Financial award application deadline: 4/30. In 2016, 128 master's, 35 doctorates awarded. *Program availability:* Part-time, evening/weekend. Offers actuarial science (MS); bioinformatics and computational biology (MS); biotechnology (MS); chemistry (MS, PhD); geochemistry (MS, PhD); geophysics (MS, PhD); geospatial information sciences (MS, PhD); hydrogeology (MS, PhD); mathematics (MS, PhD); mathematics education (MAT); molecular and cell biology (MS, PhD); natural sciences and mathematics (MAT, MS, PhD); physics (MS, PhD); science education (MAT); sedimentology, stratigraphy, and paleontology (MS, PhD); statistics (MS, PhD); structural geology and tectonics (MS, PhD). *Application deadline:* For fall admission, 7/15 for domestic students, 5/1 priority date for international students; for spring admission, 11/15 for domestic students, 9/1 priority date for international students. Applications are processed on a rolling basis. *Application fee:* $50 ($100 for international students). Electronic applications accepted. *Application Contact:* Dr. Juan E. Gonzalez, Associate Dean for Graduate Studies, 972-883-2526, Fax: 972-883-6371, E-mail: jgonzal@utdallas.edu. *Dean,* Dr. Bruce Novak, 972-883-2416, Fax: 972-883-6371, E-mail: bruce.novak@utdallas.edu.

THE UNIVERSITY OF TEXAS AT EL PASO, El Paso, TX 79968-0001

General Information State-supported, coed, university. CGS member. *Graduate housing:* Room and/or apartments available on a first-come, first-served basis to single students; on-campus housing not available to married students.

GRADUATE UNITS

Graduate School *Program availability:* Part-time, evening/weekend, online learning. Offers environmental science and engineering (PhD); materials science and engineering (PhD). Electronic applications accepted.

College of Business Administration *Program availability:* Part-time, evening/weekend, online learning. Offers accounting (M Acc); business administration (M Acc, MBA, MS, PhD, Certificate); economics (MS); international business (PhD). Electronic applications accepted.

College of Education *Program availability:* Part-time, evening/weekend, online learning. Offers education (M Ed, MA, Ed D, PhD); educational administration (M Ed); educational diagnostics (M Ed); educational leadership and administration (Ed D); guidance and counseling (M Ed); instruction (M Ed); reading education (M Ed); special education (M Ed); teaching, learning, and culture (PhD). Electronic applications accepted.

College of Engineering *Program availability:* Part-time, evening/weekend. Offers biomedical engineering (PhD); civil engineering (MEENE, MS, MSENE, PhD, Certificate); computer engineering (MS); computer science (MS, MSIT, PhD); construction management (MS, Certificate); education engineering (M Eng); electrical and computer engineering (MS, PhD); electrical engineering (MS); environmental engineering (MEENE, MSENE); environmental science and engineering (PhD); industrial engineering (MS, Certificate); information technology (MSIT); manufacturing engineering (MS); materials science and engineering (PhD); mechanical engineering (MS, PhD); metallurgical and materials engineering (MS, PhD); software engineering (M Eng); systems engineering (MS, Certificate). Electronic applications accepted.

College of Health Sciences *Program availability:* Part-time, evening/weekend, online learning. Offers health sciences (MOT, MPH, MRC, MS, MSN, MSW, DPT, PhD,

Graduate Certificate); interdisciplinary health sciences (PhD); kinesiology (MS); occupational therapy (MOT); physical therapy (DPT); public health sciences (MPH, Graduate Certificate); rehabilitation counseling (MRC); social work in the border region (MSW); speech-language pathology (MS). Electronic applications accepted.

College of Liberal Arts Program availability: Part-time, evening/weekend, online learning. Offers applied anthropology (Certificate); applied social sciences (Certificate); art education (MA); bilingual professional writing (Certificate); border history (MA); borderlands history (PhD); clinical psychology (MA); communication (MA); creative writing (MFA); creative writing of the Americas (MFA); English and American literature (MA); experimental psychology (MA); history (MA); interdisciplinary studies (MAIS); liberal arts (MA, MAIS, MAT, MFA, MM, PhD, Certificate); linguistics (MA); music education (MM); music performance (MM); philosophy (MA); political science (MA); psychology (PhD); rhetoric and composition (PhD); rhetoric and writing studies (MA); sociology (MA); Spanish (MA); studio art (MA); teaching English (MAT); teaching English to speakers of other languages (Certificate). Electronic applications accepted.

College of Science Program availability: Part-time, evening/weekend. Offers bioinformatics (MS); biological sciences (MS, PhD); chemistry (MS, PhD); computational science (MS, PMS, PhD); environmental science (MS); geological sciences (MS, PhD); geophysics (MS); mathematical sciences (MS); mathematics (teaching) (MAT); physics (MS); science (MAT, MS, PMS, PhD); statistics (MS); teaching science (MAT). Electronic applications accepted.

School of Nursing Program availability: Online learning. Offers family nurse practitioner (MSN); health care leadership and management (Certificate); interdisciplinary health sciences (PhD); nursing (DNP); nursing education (MSN, Certificate); nursing systems management (MSN). Electronic applications accepted.

THE UNIVERSITY OF TEXAS AT SAN ANTONIO, San Antonio, TX 78249-0617

General Information State-supported, coed, university. CGS member. *Enrollment:* 28,959 graduate, professional, and undergraduate students; 1,892 full-time matriculated graduate/professional students (973 women), 2,241 part-time matriculated graduate/professional students (1,323 women). *Enrollment by degree level:* 3,392 master's, 741 doctoral. *Graduate faculty:* 526 full-time (167 women), 95 part-time/adjunct (32 women). *Graduate housing:* Room and/or apartments available on a first-come, first-served basis to single students; on-campus housing not available to married students. *Student services:* Campus employment opportunities, campus safety program, career counseling, child daycare facilities, exercise/wellness program, free psychological counseling, grant writing training, international student services, low-cost health insurance, multicultural affairs office, services for students with disabilities, teacher training, writing training. *Library facilities:* John Peace Library plus 3 others. *Collection:* Students can reserve study rooms. *Research affiliation:* Air Force Research Laboratory (information assurance and security), Carnegie Mellon University/National Security Agency (computer security), National Science Foundation (virtual reality, computer architecture, real-time systems), Cancer Prevention and Research Institute of Texas (chemistry), Army Research Laboratory (computer science, management science and statistics, electrical engineering), CPS Energy (engineering).

Computer facilities: Computer purchase and lease plans are available. 510 computers available on campus for general student use. A campuswide network can be accessed from student residence rooms and from off campus. Online class registration is available.
Website: http://www.utsa.edu/

General Application Contact: Monica Rodriguez, Director of Graduate Admissions, 210-458-4331, Fax: 210-458-4332, E-mail: graduateadmissions@utsa.edu.

GRADUATE UNITS

College of Architecture Students: 70 full-time (37 women), 38 part-time (17 women); includes 67 minority (4 Black or African American, non-Hispanic/Latino; 6 Asian, non-Hispanic/Latino; 57 Hispanic/Latino), 14 international. Average age 34. 85 applicants, 67% accepted, 33 enrolled. *Faculty:* 21 full-time (6 women), 4 part-time/adjunct (0 women). Expenses: Contact institution. In 2016, 43 master's awarded. *Program availability:* Part-time. Offers architecture (M Arch, MS, MS Arch); urban and regional planning (MS). *Application deadline:* For fall admission, 7/1 for domestic students, 4/1 for international students; for spring admission, 11/1 for domestic students, 9/1 for international students. Applications are processed on a rolling basis. *Application fee:* $45 ($80 for international students). Electronic applications accepted. *Application Contact:* Monica Rodriguez, Director of Graduate Admissions, 210-458-4331, Fax: 210-458-3016, E-mail: graduatestudies@utsa.edu. *Dean,* Dr. John Murphy, 210-458-3162, Fax: 210-458-3091, E-mail: john.murphy@utsa.edu.

College of Business Students: 462 full-time (165 women), 306 part-time (94 women); includes 297 minority (28 Black or African American, non-Hispanic/Latino; 1 American Indian or Alaska Native, non-Hispanic/Latino; 49 Asian, non-Hispanic/Latino; 205 Hispanic/Latino; 1 Native Hawaiian or other Pacific Islander, non-Hispanic/Latino; 3 Two or more races, non-Hispanic/Latino), 110 international. Average age 31. 651 applicants, 67% accepted, 284 enrolled. *Faculty:* 71 full-time (13 women), 14 part-time/adjunct (3 women). Expenses: Contact institution. In 2016, 219 master's, 11 doctorates, 9 other advanced degrees awarded. *Program availability:* Part-time, evening/weekend. Offers accounting (M Acy, PhD); applied statistics (MS, PhD); business (M Acy, MA, MBA, MS, MSIT, PhD, Certificate); business economics (MBA); cyber security (MSIT); economics (MA); finance (MBA, MS, PhD); information technology (MS, PhD); management and organization studies (PhD); management of technology (MBA); management science (MBA); marketing (PhD); marketing management (MBA); technology entrepreneurship and management (Certificate); tourism destination development (MBA). *Application deadline:* For fall admission, 7/1 for domestic students, 4/1 for international students; for spring admission, 11/1 for domestic students, 9/1 for international students. Applications are processed on a rolling basis. *Application fee:* $45 ($80 for international students). Electronic applications accepted. *Application Contact:* Katherine Pope, Director, Graduate Student Services, 210-458-7316, Fax: 210-458-4641, E-mail: katherine.pope@utsa.edu. *Dean,* Dr. William Gerard Sanders, 210-458-4313, Fax: 210-458-4308, E-mail: gerry.sanders@utsa.edu.

College of Education and Human Development Students: 471 full-time (359 women), 954 part-time (742 women); includes 862 minority (104 Black or African American, non-Hispanic/Latino; 1 American Indian or Alaska Native, non-Hispanic/Latino; 29 Asian, non-Hispanic/Latino; 704 Hispanic/Latino; 1 Native Hawaiian or other Pacific Islander, non-Hispanic/Latino; 23 Two or more races, non-Hispanic/Latino), 23 international. Average age 33. 571 applicants, 78% accepted, 331 enrolled. *Faculty:* 102 full-time (57 women), 28 part-time/adjunct (15 women). Expenses: Contact institution. *Financial support:* Federal Work-Study, scholarships/grants, health care benefits, and unspecified assistantships available. Support available to part-time students. In 2016, 392 master's, 43 doctorates, 19 other advanced degrees awarded. *Program availability:* Part-time,

evening/weekend, online learning. Offers applied behavioral analysis (Certificate); bicultural and bilingual studies (MA); counselor education and supervision (PhD); culture, literacy, and language (PhD); digital learning design (Certificate); education (MA); education and human development (M Ed, MA, MS, Ed D, PhD, Certificate); educational leadership (Ed D); educational leadership and policy studies (M Ed); health and kinesiology (MS); interdisciplinary learning and teaching (PhD); language acquisition and bilingual psychoeducational assessment (Certificate); school counseling (M Ed); school psychology (MA); teaching English as a second language (MA). *Application deadline:* For fall admission, 7/1 for domestic students, 4/1 for international students; for spring admission, 11/1 for domestic students, 9/1 for international students. *Application fee:* $45 ($80 for international students). Electronic applications accepted. *Application Contact:* Monica Rodriguez, Director of Graduate Admissions, 210-458-4723, Fax: 210-458-4332, E-mail: monica.rodriguez@utsa.edu. *Dean,* Dr. Margo DelliCarpini, 210-458-4370, Fax: 210-458-4487, E-mail: margo.dellicarpini@utsa.edu.

College of Engineering Students: 262 full-time (66 women), 228 part-time (54 women); includes 134 minority (15 Black or African American, non-Hispanic/Latino; 28 Asian, non-Hispanic/Latino; 81 Hispanic/Latino; 2 Native Hawaiian or other Pacific Islander, non-Hispanic/Latino; 8 Two or more races, non-Hispanic/Latino), 231 international. Average age 29. 510 applicants, 66% accepted, 115 enrolled. *Faculty:* 66 full-time (7 women), 8 part-time/adjunct (0 women). Expenses: Contact institution. *Financial support:* In 2016–17, 120 students received support. Career-related internships or fieldwork, Federal Work-Study, institutionally sponsored loans, scholarships/grants, health care benefits, unspecified assistantships, and Valero Research Scholar awards available. Financial award application deadline: 9/15. In 2016, 182 master's, 24 doctorates awarded. *Program availability:* Part-time, evening/weekend. Offers advanced manufacturing and enterprise engineering (MS); advanced materials engineering (MS); biomedical engineering (MS, PhD); civil engineering (MCE, MSCE); computer engineering (MS); electrical engineering (MSEE, PhD); engineering (MCE, MS, MSCE, MSEE, PhD); environmental science and engineering (PhD); mechanical engineering (MS, PhD). *Application deadline:* For fall admission, 7/1 for domestic students, 4/1 for international students; for spring admission, 11/1 for domestic students, 9/1 for international students. *Application fee:* $45 ($80 for international students). *Application Contact:* Monica Rodriguez, Director of Graduate Admissions, 210-458-4331, Fax: 210-458-4332, E-mail: graduateadmissions@utsa.edu. *Dean of Engineering,* Dr. JoAnn Browning, 210-458-5515, E-mail: joann.browning@utsa.edu.

College of Liberal and Fine Arts Students: 153 full-time (100 women), 233 part-time (141 women); includes 177 minority (14 Black or African American, non-Hispanic/Latino; 5 Asian, non-Hispanic/Latino; 145 Hispanic/Latino; 2 Native Hawaiian or other Pacific Islander, non-Hispanic/Latino; 11 Two or more races, non-Hispanic/Latino), 12 international. Average age 31. 211 applicants, 66% accepted, 100 enrolled. *Faculty:* 124 full-time (52 women), 6 part-time/adjunct (3 women). Expenses: Contact institution. *Financial support:* In 2016–17, 92 students received support, including 21 fellowships with full tuition reimbursements available (averaging $23,810 per year), 24 research assistantships (averaging $8,105 per year), 47 teaching assistantships (averaging $9,078 per year); Federal Work-Study, scholarships/grants, and unspecified assistantships also available. Financial award applicants required to submit FAFSA. In 2016, 98 master's, 7 doctorates awarded. Offers anthropology (MA, PhD); art (MFA); art history (MA); communication (MA); English (MA, PhD); history (MA); liberal and fine arts (MA, MFA, MM, MS, PhD); music (MM); philosophy and classics (MA); political science (MA); psychology (MS, PhD); sociology (MS); Spanish (MA). *Application deadline:* For fall admission, 7/1 for domestic students, 4/1 for international students; for spring admission, 11/1 for domestic students, 9/1 for international students. *Application fee:* $45 ($80 for international students). Electronic applications accepted. *Application Contact:* Monica Rodriguez, Director of Graduate Admissions, 210-458-4331, Fax: 210-458-4332, E-mail: graduatestudies@utsa.edu. *Dean,* Dr. Daniel J. Gelo, 210-458-4359, Fax: 210-458-4347, E-mail: daniel.gelo@utsa.edu.

College of Public Policy Students: 160 full-time (111 women), 308 part-time (208 women); includes 312 minority (66 Black or African American, non-Hispanic/Latino; 2 American Indian or Alaska Native, non-Hispanic/Latino; 9 Asian, non-Hispanic/Latino; 225 Hispanic/Latino; 10 Two or more races, non-Hispanic/Latino), 15 international. Average age 33. 208 applicants, 80% accepted, 136 enrolled. *Faculty:* 29 full-time (15 women), 15 part-time/adjunct (8 women). Expenses: Contact institution. *Financial support:* In 2016–17, 12 fellowships with partial tuition reimbursements (averaging $22,500 per year), 27 research assistantships (averaging $8,445 per year), 4 teaching assistantships (averaging $8,418 per year) were awarded; scholarships/grants and unspecified assistantships also available. Financial award applicants required to submit FAFSA. In 2016, 117 master's, 7 doctorates awarded. *Program availability:* Part-time, evening/weekend. Offers applied demography (PhD); criminology (MS); public administration (MPA); public policy (MPA, MS, MSW, PhD); social work (MSW). *Application deadline:* For fall admission, 7/1 for domestic students, 4/1 for international students; for spring admission, 11/1 for domestic students, 9/1 for international students. *Application fee:* $45 ($80 for international students). *Application Contact:* Monica Rodriguez, Director of Graduate Admissions, 210-458-4331, Fax: 210-458-4332, E-mail: graduateadmissions@utsa.edu. *Dean,* Dr. Rogelio Saenz, 210-458-2715, E-mail: rogelio.saenz@utsa.edu.

College of Sciences Students: 314 full-time (135 women), 168 part-time (64 women); includes 166 minority (12 Black or African American, non-Hispanic/Latino; 1 American Indian or Alaska Native, non-Hispanic/Latino; 26 Asian, non-Hispanic/Latino; 115 Hispanic/Latino; 12 Two or more races, non-Hispanic/Latino), 141 international. Average age 29. 588 applicants, 53% accepted, 153 enrolled. *Faculty:* 109 full-time (17 women), 20 part-time/adjunct (3 women). Expenses: Contact institution. *Financial support:* Teaching assistantships available. Financial award applicants required to submit FAFSA. In 2016, 133 master's, 36 doctorates awarded. Offers applied mathematics (MS); biology (MS); biotechnology (MS); cell and molecular biology (PhD); chemistry (MS, PhD); computer science (MS, PhD); geological sciences (MS); mathematics (MS); mathematics education (PhD); neurobiology (PhD); physics (MS, PhD); sciences (MS, PhD). *Application deadline:* For fall admission, 7/1 for domestic students, 4/1 for international students; for spring admission, 11/1 for domestic students, 9/1 for international students. *Application fee:* $45 ($80 for international students). Electronic applications accepted. *Application Contact:* Monica Rodriguez, Director of Graduate Admissions, 210-458-4331, Fax: 210-458-4332, E-mail: graduateadmissions@utsa.edu. *Dean,* Dr. George Perry, 210-458-4450, Fax: 210-458-4445, E-mail: george.perry@utsa.edu.

Joint PhD Program in Translational Science Students: 6 part-time (3 women); includes 2 minority (both Hispanic/Latino), 2 international. Average age 33. Expenses: Contact institution. *Financial support:* In 2016–17, 1 student received support, including 3 research assistantships (averaging $26,000 per year), 3 teaching assistantships (averaging $34,000 per year); scholarships/grants and unspecified assistantships also available. *Program availability:* Part-time. Offers translational science (PhD). Program offered in partnership with The University of Texas Health Science Center at San

Antonio, The University of Texas at Austin, and The University of Texas Health Science Center at Houston. *Application deadline:* For fall admission, 11/1 for domestic and international students. *Application fee:* $45 ($80 for international students). Electronic applications accepted. *Application Contact:* Susan Stappenbeck, Senior Project Coordinator, 210-567-4304, Fax: 210-567-4301, E-mail: stappenbeck@uthscsa.edu. *Program Director,* Dr. Chris Frei, 210-567-8355, Fax: 210-564-4301, E-mail: freic@uthscsa.edu.

THE UNIVERSITY OF TEXAS AT TYLER, Tyler, TX 75799-0001

General Information State-supported, coed, comprehensive institution. *Graduate housing:* Rooms and/or apartments available on a first-come, first-served basis to single and married students. *Research affiliation:* Embassy of Arab Republic of Egypt Cultural and Education Bureau (electrical engineering), TransAtlantic Lines, Inc. (civil engineering), American Society of Civil Engineers (civil engineering), McGraw-Hill Company (civil engineering), Renaissance Society of America (art history), American Lung Association of the Central States (biology).

GRADUATE UNITS

Ben and Maytee Fisch College of Pharmacy Offers pharmacy (Pharm D).

College of Arts and Sciences *Program availability:* Part-time, evening/weekend, online learning. Offers art history (MA); arts and sciences (MA, MAIS, MAT, MFA, MPA, MS, MSIS); biology (MS); communication (MA); criminal justice (MS); English (MA); history (MA); interdisciplinary (MAIS); interdisciplinary studies (MAIS, MSIS); mathematics (MS, MSIS); political science (MA); public administration (MPA); sociology (MS); studio art (MFA). Electronic applications accepted.

College of Business and Technology *Program availability:* Part-time, evening/weekend, online learning. Offers accountancy (M Acc); business and technology (M Acc, MBA, MS, PhD); computer science (MS); cyber security (MBA); engineering management (MBA); general management (MBA); healthcare management (MBA); human resource development (MS, PhD); industrial management (MS); internal assurance and consulting (MBA); marketing (MBA); oil, gas and energy (MBA); organizational development (MBA); quality management (MBA). Electronic applications accepted.

College of Education and Psychology *Program availability:* Part-time, evening/weekend. Offers clinical psychology (MS); counseling psychology (MA); education and psychology (M Ed, MA, MS, MSIS); educational leadership (M Ed); interdisciplinary studies (MSIS); school counseling (MA).

School of Education *Program availability:* Part-time, evening/weekend. Offers early childhood education (M Ed, MA); reading (M Ed, MA); special education (M Ed, MA). Electronic applications accepted.

College of Engineering *Program availability:* Part-time. Offers electrical engineering (MS); engineering (MS, MSIS); environmental engineering (MS); industrial safety (MS); mechanical engineering (MS); structural engineering (MS); transportation engineering (MS); water resources engineering (MS). Electronic applications accepted.

College of Nursing and Health Sciences *Program availability:* Part-time, evening/weekend, online learning. Offers health and kinesiology (M Ed, MA); health sciences (MS); kinesiology (MS); nurse practitioner (MSN); nursing (PhD); nursing administration (MSN); nursing and health sciences (M Ed, MA, MS, MSN, PhD); nursing education (MSN). Electronic applications accepted.

THE UNIVERSITY OF TEXAS HEALTH SCIENCE CENTER AT HOUSTON, Houston, TX 77225-0036

General Information State-supported, coed, upper-level institution. CGS member. *Graduate housing:* On-campus housing not available.

GRADUATE UNITS

MD Anderson UTHealth Graduate School Offers biochemistry and cell biology (PhD); biomedical sciences (PhD); cancer biology (PhD); genetic counseling (MS); genetics and epigenetics (PhD); immunology (PhD); medical physics (MS, PhD); microbiology and infectious diseases (PhD); neuroscience (PhD); quantitative sciences (PhD); therapeutics and pharmacology (PhD). Electronic applications accepted.

School of Biomedical Informatics *Program availability:* Part-time, online learning. Offers biomedical informatics (MS, PhD, Certificate). Electronic applications accepted.

School of Nursing *Program availability:* Part-time. Offers nursing (MSN, DNP, PhD). Electronic applications accepted.

University of Texas Medical School at Houston Offers medicine (MD). Electronic applications accepted.

The University of Texas School of Dentistry at Houston Offers dentistry (MS, DDS). Electronic applications accepted.

The University of Texas School of Public Health *Program availability:* Part-time. Offers public health (MPH, MS, Dr PH, PhD, Certificate). Applications to dual degree programs are handled independently between the collaborating institutions. Electronic applications accepted.

THE UNIVERSITY OF TEXAS HEALTH SCIENCE CENTER AT SAN ANTONIO, San Antonio, TX 78229-3900

General Information State-supported, coed, upper-level institution. CGS member. *Research affiliation:* University Hospital, Southwest Research Institute, Southwest Foundation for Biomedical Research, Veterans Administration Hospital.

GRADUATE UNITS

Graduate School of Biomedical Sciences Offers biochemistry (MS, PhD); biomedical engineering (MS, PhD); biomedical sciences (MS, PhD); cellular and structural biology (MS, PhD); clinical investigation (MS); dental science (MS); integrated biomedical sciences (PhD); microbiology and immunology (MS, PhD); molecular medicine (MS, PhD); neuroscience (PhD); nursing science (PhD); radiological sciences (PhD); toxicology (MS); translational science (PhD).

School of Dentistry Students: 506 full-time (267 women), 36 part-time (15 women); includes 239 minority (18 Black or African American, non-Hispanic/Latino; 105 Asian, non-Hispanic/Latino; 102 Hispanic/Latino; 1 Native Hawaiian or other Pacific Islander, non-Hispanic/Latino; 13 Two or more races, non-Hispanic/Latino), 32 international. Average age 27. 1,485 applicants, 19% accepted, 185 enrolled. *Faculty:* 102 full-time (38 women), 94 part-time/adjunct (21 women). Expenses: Contact institution. *Financial support:* In 2016–17, 86 students received support, including 7 research assistantships (averaging $2,624 per year), 78 teaching assistantships (averaging $14,550 per year); Federal Work-Study and institutionally sponsored loans also available. Financial award application deadline: 3/1; financial award applicants required to submit FAFSA. In 2016, 22 master's, 99 doctorates, 44 other advanced degrees awarded. Offers dentistry (MS, DDS, Certificate). *Application deadline:* For fall admission, 10/1 for domestic students, 10/31 for international students. Applications are processed on a rolling basis. *Application fee:* $150. Electronic applications accepted. *Application Contact:* E-mail:

dsadmissions@uthscsa.edu. *Associate Dean for Student Affairs,* Dr. Adriana Segura, 210-567-3180, Fax: 210-567-4776, E-mail: seguraa@uthscsa.edu.

School of Health Professions Offers occupational therapy (MOT); physical therapy (DPT); physician assistant studies (MS).

School of Medicine Offers deaf education and hearing (MS); medicine (MD). Electronic applications accepted.

School of Nursing *Program availability:* Part-time. Offers administrative management (MSN); adult-gerontology acute care nurse practitioner (PGC); advanced practice leadership (DNP); clinical nurse leader (MSN); executive administrative management (DNP); family nurse practitioner (MSN, PGC); nursing (MSN, PhD); nursing education (MSN, PGC); pediatric nurse practitioner primary care (PGC); psychiatric mental health nurse practitioner (PGC); public health nurse leader (DNP).

THE UNIVERSITY OF TEXAS MD ANDERSON CANCER CENTER, Houston, TX 77030

General Information State-supported, coed, upper-level institution.

GRADUATE UNITS

School of Health Professions Offers diagnostic genetics (MS).

THE UNIVERSITY OF TEXAS MEDICAL BRANCH, Galveston, TX 77555

General Information State-supported, coed, comprehensive institution. CGS member. *Graduate housing:* Rooms and/or apartments available on a first-come, first-served basis to single and married students. *Research affiliation:* Shriners Hospitals (burns and wound healing).

GRADUATE UNITS

Graduate School of Biomedical Sciences Offers biochemistry (PhD); bioinformatics (PhD); biomedical sciences (MA, MMS, MPH, MS, PhD); biophysics (PhD); cell biology (PhD); clinical science (MS, PhD); computational biology (PhD); experimental pathology (PhD); human pathophysiology and translational medicine (MS, PhD); medical humanities (MA, PhD); medical science (MMS); microbiology and immunology (MS, PhD); molecular biophysics education (PhD); neuroscience (PhD); nursing (PhD); pharmacology (MS); pharmacology and toxicology (PhD); population health sciences (PhD); public health (MPH); rehabilitation sciences (PhD); structural biology (PhD). Electronic applications accepted.

School of Health Professions Offers health professions (MOT, MPAS, MPT, DPT); occupational therapy (MOT); physical therapy (MPT, DPT); physician assistant studies (MPAS). Electronic applications accepted.

School of Medicine Offers medicine (MD).

School of Nursing *Program availability:* Part-time, online learning. Offers nursing (MSN, PhD). Electronic applications accepted.

THE UNIVERSITY OF TEXAS OF THE PERMIAN BASIN, Odessa, TX 79762-0001

General Information State-supported, coed, comprehensive institution. *Graduate housing:* Rooms and/or apartments available on a first-come, first-served basis to single and married students. Housing application deadline: 6/15.

GRADUATE UNITS

Office of Graduate Studies *Program availability:* Part-time, evening/weekend.

College of Arts and Sciences *Program availability:* Part-time, evening/weekend. Offers applied research psychology (MA); arts and sciences (MA, MS); biology (MS); clinical psychology (MA); computer science (MS); criminal justice administration (MS); English (MA); geology (MS); history (MA); kinesiology (MS); political science (MPA); Spanish (MA).

School of Business *Program availability:* Part-time, evening/weekend. Offers accountancy (MPA); business (MBA, MPA); management (MBA).

School of Education Offers bilingual/English as a second language education (MA); counseling (MA); early childhood education (MA); education (MA); educational leadership (MA); professional education (MA); reading (MA); special education (MA).

THE UNIVERSITY OF TEXAS RIO GRANDE VALLEY, Edinburg, TX 78539

General Information State-supported, coed, comprehensive institution. CGS member. *Enrollment:* 27,560 graduate, professional, and undergraduate students; 1,028 full-time matriculated graduate/professional students (627 women), 2,099 part-time matriculated graduate/professional students (1,323 women). *Enrollment by degree level:* 2,832 master's, 295 doctoral. *Graduate faculty:* 361 full-time (133 women), 33 part-time/adjunct (15 women). Tuition and fees vary according to course load and program. *Graduate housing:* Rooms and/or apartments available on a first-come, first-served basis to single and married students. Housing application deadline: 7/1. *Student services:* Campus employment opportunities, campus safety program, career counseling, child daycare facilities, exercise/wellness program, free psychological counseling, grant writing training, international student services, low-cost health insurance, services for students with disabilities, teacher training, writing training. *Library facilities:* University Library. Collection: Students can reserve study rooms. *Research affiliation:* Robert Wood Johnson (health science), Lockheed Martin Corporation (manufacturing engineering), Texas Instruments (curriculum and instruction), Pfizer, Inc. (health disparities), Howard Hughes Medical Institute (medical science), Boeing (engineering).

Computer facilities: A campuswide network can be accessed from student residence rooms and from off campus. Online class registration is available. Website: http://www.utrgv.edu/

General Application Contact: Stephanie Ozuna, Graduate Student Recruiter, 956-665-3558, E-mail: stephanie.ozuna@utrgv.edu.

GRADUATE UNITS

College of Education and P-16 Integration *Program availability:* Part-time, evening/weekend. Offers bilingual education (M Ed); clinical mental health counseling (M Ed); curriculum and instruction (M Ed, Ed D); early childhood education (M Ed); early childhood special education (M Ed); education and P-16 integration (M Ed, MA, MS, Ed D, PhD); educational diagnostician (M Ed); educational leadership (M Ed, Ed D); educational technology (M Ed); reading and literacy (M Ed); school counseling (M Ed); school psychology (MA). Ed D offered jointly with The University of Texas at Austin.

College of Engineering and Computer Science *Program availability:* Part-time, evening/weekend. Offers computer science (MS); electrical engineering (MS); engineering and computer science (MS); engineering management (MS); information technology (MS); manufacturing engineering (MS); mechanical engineering (MS); systems engineering (MS).

College of Fine Arts Expenses: Contact institution. Offers creative writing (MFA); fine arts (M Mus, MAIS, MFA). *Application Contact:* Stephanie Ozuna, Graduate Student Recruiter, 956-665-3558, E-mail: stephanie.ozuna@utrgv.edu. *Interim Dean,* Dr. Dahlia Guerra.

School of Art Program availability: Part-time, evening/weekend, online learning. Offers art (MFA).

School of Music Program availability: Part-time. Offers ethnomusicology (M Mus); interdisciplinary studies (MAIS); music education (M Mus); performance (M Mus).

College of Health Affairs *Program availability:* Part-time, evening/weekend. Offers clinical laboratory sciences (MSHS); communication sciences and disorders (MS); exercise science (MS); health affairs (MPAS, MS, MSHS, MSN, MSSW, PhD); health care administration (MSHS); kinesiology (MS); nutrition (MSHS); occupational therapy (MS); physician assistant studies (MPAS); social work (MSSW).

School of Nursing Program availability: Part-time, evening/weekend. Offers adult health nursing (MSN); family nurse practitioner (MSN). Electronic applications accepted.

School of Rehabilitation Services and Counseling Program availability: Part-time, evening/weekend. Offers rehabilitation services and counseling (MS, PhD).

College of Liberal Arts *Program availability:* Part-time, evening/weekend. Offers communication (MA); communication training and consulting (Graduate Certificate); criminal justice (MS); English (MA, MAIS); English as a second language (MA); English: rhetoric, composition and literacy studies (MA); global security studies and leadership (MPA); history (MA, MAIS); interdisciplinary studies (MAIS, MSIS); liberal arts (M Mus, MA, MAIS, MFA, MS, MSIS, PhD, Graduate Certificate); psychology (MA); public administration (MPA); public policy and management (MPA); sociology and anthropology (MS); Spanish (MA); strategic communication and media relations (Graduate Certificate); theatre (MA).

College of Sciences *Program availability:* Part-time, evening/weekend. Offers biology (MS); chemistry (MS, MSIS); physics (MS); sciences (MS, MSIS). Electronic applications accepted.

School of Mathematical and Statistical Sciences Program availability: Part-time, evening/weekend, online learning. Offers mathematical sciences (MS); mathematics (MS). Electronic applications accepted.

Robert C. Vackar College of Business and Entrepreneurship *Program availability:* Part-time, evening/weekend. Offers accounting (M Acc, MS); business administration (MBA); business and entrepreneurship (M Acc, MBA, MS, PhD); finance (PhD); management (PhD); marketing (PhD).

School of Medicine *Program availability:* Part-time, evening/weekend, online learning. Offers medicine (MD).

THE UNIVERSITY OF TEXAS SOUTHWESTERN MEDICAL CENTER, Dallas, TX 75390

General Information State-supported, coed, graduate-only institution. *Graduate housing:* Rooms and/or apartments available on a first-come, first-served basis to single and married students.

GRADUATE UNITS

Southwestern Graduate School of Biomedical Sciences Offers biomedical sciences (MCS, MS, MSCS, PhD); clinical psychology (PhD); clinical science (MCS, MSCS); medical scientist training (PhD). Electronic applications accepted.

Division of Basic Science Offers biological chemistry (PhD); biomedical engineering (MS, PhD); cancer biology (PhD); cell regulation (PhD); genetics and development (PhD); immunology (PhD); integrative biology (PhD); molecular biophysics (PhD); molecular microbiology (PhD); neuroscience (PhD). Electronic applications accepted.

Southwestern Medical School Offers medicine (MD). Electronic applications accepted.

Southwestern School of Health Professions Offers clinical nutrition (MCN); health professions (MCN, MPAS, MPO, MRC, DPT); physical therapy (DPT); physician assistant studies (MPAS); prosthetics - orthotics (MPO); rehabilitation counseling psychology (MRC).

THE UNIVERSITY OF THE ARTS, Philadelphia, PA 19102-4944

General Information Independent, coed, comprehensive institution. *Graduate housing:* Room and/or apartments available to single students; on-campus housing not available to married students. Housing application deadline: 6/1. *Research affiliation:* The Franklin Institute (general science education), Philadelphia Museum of Art (arts and culture), School District of Philadelphia (education), Ben Franklin Technology Partners (high tech department and creative/cultural production in Philadelphia).

GRADUATE UNITS

College of Art, Media and Design *Program availability:* Part-time. Offers art education (MA); art, media and design (MA, MAT, MFA, MID); book arts/printmaking (MFA); industrial design (MID); museum communication (MA); museum education (MA); museum exhibition planning and design (MFA); studio art (MFA); visual arts (MAT). Electronic applications accepted.

College of Performing Arts *Program availability:* Part-time. Offers performing arts (MAT, MM).

School of Music Program availability: Part-time. Offers jazz studies (MM); music education (MAT, MM). Electronic applications accepted.

UNIVERSITY OF THE CUMBERLANDS, Williamsburg, KY 40769-1372

General Information Independent-religious, coed, university. *Graduate housing:* Room and/or apartments available on a first-come, first-served basis to single students; on-campus housing not available to married students.

GRADUATE UNITS

Graduate Programs in Education *Program availability:* Part-time, evening/weekend, online learning. Offers all grades (P-12) (M Ed); business and marketing (MA Ed, MAT); counselor education and supervision (Ed D); director of pupil personnel (Certificate); director of special education (Certificate); educational administration and supervision (Ed S); educational leadership (Ed D); elementary education (MA Ed, MAT); instructional leadership - principalship (MA Ed); instructional leadership - school principal (Certificate); middle school education (MA Ed, MAT); reading and writing (MA Ed); school counseling (MA Ed); school superintendent (Certificate); secondary education (MA Ed, MAT); special education (MAT); supervisor of instruction (Certificate); teacher leader (MA Ed). Electronic applications accepted.

Hutton School of Business *Program availability:* Part-time, online learning. Offers accounting (MBA); business (MBA). Electronic applications accepted.

Program in Christian Studies *Program availability:* Part-time, evening/weekend, online learning. Offers Christian studies (MA). Electronic applications accepted.

Program in Clinical Psychology *Program availability:* Part-time, evening/weekend, online learning. Offers clinical psychology (PhD).

Program in Physician Assistant Studies Offers physician assistant studies (MPAS). Electronic applications accepted.

Program in Professional Counseling *Program availability:* Part-time, evening/weekend, online learning. Offers professional counseling (MA). Program also offered in San Francisco. Electronic applications accepted.

UNIVERSITY OF THE DISTRICT OF COLUMBIA, Washington, DC 20008-1175

General Information District-supported, coed, comprehensive institution. CGS member.

GRADUATE UNITS

College of Agriculture, Urban Sustainability and Environmental Sciences Offers agriculture, urban sustainability and environmental sciences (M Arch, M Arch II, MS, PSM); architecture (M Arch, M Arch II); nutrition and dietetics (MS); water resources management (PSM).

College of Arts and Sciences *Program availability:* Part-time, evening/weekend. Offers adult education (Graduate Certificate); arts and sciences (MA, MAT, MS, Graduate Certificate); cancer biology, prevention and control (MS); counseling (MS); early childhood education (MA); elementary education (MAT); homeland security (MS); middle school mathematics (MAT); rehabilitation counseling (MA); secondary English language arts (MAT); secondary social studies (MAT); speech-language pathology (MS).

David A. Clarke School of Law *Program availability:* Part-time, evening/weekend. Offers clinical teaching and social justice (LL M); law (JD). Electronic applications accepted.

School of Business and Public Administration *Program availability:* Part-time, evening/weekend. Offers business administration (MBA); business and public administration (MBA, MPA); public administration (MPA).

School of Engineering and Applied Sciences Offers computer science (MS, MSCS); electrical engineering (MSEE); engineering and applied sciences (MSCS, MSEE).

UNIVERSITY OF THE FRASER VALLEY, Abbotsford, BC V2S 7M8, Canada

General Information Province-supported, coed, comprehensive institution. *Enrollment:* 8,518 graduate, professional, and undergraduate students; 36 full-time matriculated graduate/professional students (21 women), 2 part-time matriculated graduate/professional students (both women). *Enrollment by degree level:* 38 master's. *Graduate faculty:* 23 full-time (13 women). *Graduate housing:* Room and/or apartments available on a first-come, first-served basis to single students; on-campus housing not available to married students. Typical cost: $5769 Canadian dollars per year. Housing application deadline: 5/15. *Student services:* Campus employment opportunities, campus safety program, career counseling, exercise/wellness program, free psychological counseling, grant writing training, international student services, low-cost health insurance, services for students with disabilities, writing training. *Library facilities:* Peter Jones Library plus 3 others. *Collection:* Books: 180,000 (physical), 354,000 (digital/electronic). Students can reserve study rooms.

Computer facilities: Online class registration is available. Website: http://www.ufv.ca/

General Application Contact: Educational Advisors, 604-854-4528, Fax: 604-855-7614, E-mail: advising@ufv.ca.

GRADUATE UNITS

Graduate Studies Students: 47 full-time (26 women), 2 part-time (1 woman); includes 3 minority (all American Indian or Alaska Native, non-Hispanic/Latino). Average age 37. 79 applicants, 42% accepted, 32 enrolled. *Faculty:* 23 full-time (13 women). Expenses: Contact institution. *Financial support:* Research assistantships, scholarships/grants, health care benefits, and bursaries available. Financial award application deadline: 5/10. In 2016, 19 master's awarded. *Program availability:* Evening/weekend. Offers criminal justice (MA); social work (MSW). *Application deadline:* For fall admission, 1/31 priority date for domestic students, 4/1 priority date for international students; for winter admission, 9/30 priority date for domestic students, 10/1 priority date for international students; for spring admission, 12/31 priority date for domestic students, 2/1 priority date for international students. *Application fee:* $45 ($150 for international students). Electronic applications accepted. *Application Contact:* Educational Advisors, 604-854-4528, Fax: 604-855-7614, E-mail: advising@ufv.ca. *Associate Vice President for Research, Engagement and Graduate Studies,* Dr. Adrienne Chan, 604-504-4074, Fax: 778-880-0356, E-mail: adrienne.chan@ufv.ca.

UNIVERSITY OF THE INCARNATE WORD, San Antonio, TX 78209-6397

General Information Independent-religious, coed, comprehensive institution. *Enrollment:* 8,906 graduate, professional, and undergraduate students; 1,269 full-time matriculated graduate/professional students (783 women), 1,214 part-time matriculated graduate/professional students (664 women). *Enrollment by degree level:* 1,090 master's, 1,393 doctoral. *Graduate faculty:* 123 full-time (78 women), 134 part-time/adjunct (65 women). *Tuition:* Full-time $7965; part-time $885 per credit hour. *Required fees:* $40 per credit hour. Tuition and fees vary according to course load, degree level, campus/location, program and student level. *Graduate housing:* Room and/or apartments available on a first-come, first-served basis to single students; on-campus housing not available to married students. Typical cost: $6900 per year. Room charges vary according to board plan and housing facility selected. Housing application deadline: 5/1. *Student services:* Campus employment opportunities, campus safety program, career counseling, exercise/wellness program, free psychological counseling, grant writing training, international student services, low-cost health insurance, services for students with disabilities, teacher training, writing training. *Library facilities:* J. E. and M. E. Mabee Library plus 1 other. *Collection:* Books: 270,398 (physical), 31,458 (digital/electronic); Serial titles: 103 (physical), 224 (digital/electronic); Databases: 167. Weekly public service hours: 105.

Computer facilities: Computer purchase and lease plans are available. 185 computers available on campus for general student use. A campuswide network can be accessed from student residence rooms and from off campus. Online class registration is available.
Website: http://www.uiw.edu/

General Application Contact: Johnny Garcia, Assistant Director of Graduate Admissions, 210-805-3554, Fax: 210-829-3921, E-mail: jsgarcia@uiwtx.edu.

GRADUATE UNITS

Feik School of Pharmacy Students: 386 full-time (263 women), 12 part-time (10 women); includes 256 minority (20 Black or African American, non-Hispanic/Latino; 78

Asian, non-Hispanic/Latino; 146 Hispanic/Latino; 1 Native Hawaiian or other Pacific Islander, non-Hispanic/Latino; 11 Two or more races, non-Hispanic/Latino), 21 international. *Faculty:* 21 full-time (14 women), 2 part-time/adjunct (both women). Expenses: Contact institution. *Financial support:* Research assistantships, Federal Work-Study, scholarships/grants, and unspecified assistantships available. Financial award applicants required to submit FAFSA. In 2016, 86 doctorates awarded. Offers pharmacy (Pharm D). *Application deadline:* For fall admission, 12/1 for domestic and international students. *Application fee:* $50. Electronic applications accepted. *Application Contact:* Dr. Amy Diepenbrock, Assistant Dean, Student Affairs, 210-883-1060, Fax: 210-822-1521, E-mail: diepenbr@uiwtx.edu. *Dean,* Dr. David Maize, 210-883-1000, Fax: 210-822-1516, E-mail: maize@uiwtx.edu.

Rosenberg School of Optometry Students: 263 full-time (173 women), 1 part-time (0 women); includes 139 minority (8 Black or African American, non-Hispanic/Latino; 2 American Indian or Alaska Native, non-Hispanic/Latino; 75 Asian, non-Hispanic/Latino; 51 Hispanic/Latino; 1 Native Hawaiian or other Pacific Islander, non-Hispanic/Latino; 2 Two or more races, non-Hispanic/Latino), 6 international. *Faculty:* 15 full-time (5 women), 2 part-time/adjunct (both women). Expenses: Contact institution. *Financial support:* In 2016–17, 5 fellowships (averaging $4,000 per year) were awarded; Federal Work-Study and scholarships/grants also available. Financial award applicants required to submit FAFSA. In 2016, 66 doctorates awarded. Offers optometry (OD). *Application deadline:* For fall admission, 5/1 for domestic students. *Application fee:* $50. Electronic applications accepted. *Application Contact:* Kristine Benne, Assistant Dean of Student Affairs, 210-883-1190, Fax: 210-883-1191, E-mail: benne@uiwtx.edu. *Dean,* Dr. Timothy Wingert, 210-883-1195, Fax: 210-283-6890, E-mail: twingert@uiwtx.edu.

School of Graduate Studies and Research Students: 300 full-time (168 women), 460 part-time (297 women); includes 442 minority (71 Black or African American, non-Hispanic/Latino; 2 American Indian or Alaska Native, non-Hispanic/Latino; 18 Asian, non-Hispanic/Latino; 340 Hispanic/Latino; 1 Native Hawaiian or other Pacific Islander, non-Hispanic/Latino; 10 Two or more races, non-Hispanic/Latino), 114 international. *Faculty:* 81 full-time (51 women), 76 part-time/adjunct (36 women). Expenses: Contact institution. *Financial support:* In 2016–17, 25 research assistantships (averaging $3,600 per year) were awarded; Federal Work-Study, scholarships/grants, and tuition waivers (partial) also available. Financial award applicants required to submit FAFSA. In 2016, 256 master's, 12 doctorates awarded. *Program availability:* Part-time, evening/weekend. *Application deadline:* Applications are processed on a rolling basis. *Application fee:* $20. Electronic applications accepted. *Application Contact:* Johnny Garcia, Associate Director of Graduate Recruitment, 210-805-3554, Fax: 210-829-3921, E-mail: jsgarcia@uiwtx.edu. *Dean,* Dr. Osman Ozturgut, 210-805-5885, Fax: 210-805-3559, E-mail: ozturgut@uiwtx.edu.

College of Humanities, Arts, and Social Sciences Students: 2 part-time (0 women); includes 1 minority (Hispanic/Latino). *Faculty:* 3 full-time (all women), 1 part-time/adjunct (0 women). Expenses: Contact institution. *Financial support:* Research assistantships, scholarships/grants, tuition waivers, and unspecified assistantships available. Financial award applicants required to submit FAFSA. In 2016, 3 master's awarded. *Program availability:* Part-time, evening/weekend. Offers pastoral ministry (MA). *Application deadline:* Applications are processed on a rolling basis. *Application fee:* $20. Electronic applications accepted. *Application Contact:* Johnny Garcia, Graduate Admissions Counselor, 210-829-6005, Fax: 210-829-3921, E-mail: admis@uiwtx.edu. *Dean,* Dr. Kevin Vichcales, 210-829-2759, Fax: 210-829-3830, E-mail: vichcale@uiwtx.edu.

Dreeben School of Education Students: 28 full-time (18 women), 179 part-time (122 women); includes 123 minority (22 Black or African American, non-Hispanic/Latino; 3 Asian, non-Hispanic/Latino; 94 Hispanic/Latino; 4 Two or more races, non-Hispanic/Latino), 21 international. *Faculty:* 19 full-time (13 women), 14 part-time/adjunct (8 women). Expenses: Contact institution. *Financial support:* In 2016–17, 4 research assistantships were awarded; Federal Work-Study, scholarships/grants, tuition waivers (partial), and unspecified assistantships also available. Financial award applicants required to submit FAFSA. In 2016, 47 master's, 11 doctorates awarded. *Program availability:* Part-time, evening/weekend, online learning. Offers education (M Ed, MA, MAT, PhD). *Application deadline:* Applications are processed on a rolling basis. *Application fee:* $20. Electronic applications accepted. *Application Contact:* Johnny Garcia, Graduate Admissions Counselor, 210-805-3554, Fax: 210-829-3921, E-mail: admis@uiwtx.edu. *Dean,* Dr. Denise Staudt, 210-829-2761, Fax: 210-829-2765, E-mail: staudt@uiwtx.edu.

H-E-B School of Business and Administration Students: 190 full-time (100 women), 154 part-time (73 women); includes 186 minority (25 Black or African American, non-Hispanic/Latino; 7 Asian, non-Hispanic/Latino; 151 Hispanic/Latino; 1 Native Hawaiian or other Pacific Islander, non-Hispanic/Latino; 2 Two or more races, non-Hispanic/Latino), 74 international. *Faculty:* 25 full-time (13 women), 42 part-time/adjunct (14 women). Expenses: Contact institution. *Financial support:* In 2016–17, 4 research assistantships were awarded; Federal Work-Study, scholarships/grants, tuition waivers (partial), and unspecified assistantships also available. Financial award applicants required to submit FAFSA. In 2016, 165 master's, 1 doctorate awarded. *Program availability:* Part-time, evening/weekend, online learning. Offers business and administration (MAA, MBA, MHA, MS, DBA). *Application deadline:* Applications are processed on a rolling basis. *Application fee:* $20. Electronic applications accepted. *Application Contact:* Johnny Garcia, Assistant Director of Graduate Admissions, 210-805-3554, Fax: 210-829-3921, E-mail: jsgarcia@uiwtx.edu. *Dean,* Dr. Forrest Aven, 210-805-5884, Fax: 210-805-3564, E-mail: aven@uiwtx.edu.

School of Mathematics, Science, and Engineering Students: 23 full-time (18 women), 26 part-time (22 women); includes 26 minority (2 Black or African American, non-Hispanic/Latino; 1 American Indian or Alaska Native, non-Hispanic/Latino; 22 Hispanic/Latino; 1 Two or more races, non-Hispanic/Latino), 8 international. *Faculty:* 9 full-time (4 women), 4 part-time/adjunct (3 women). Expenses: Contact institution. *Financial support:* In 2016–17, 1 research assistantship (averaging $5,000 per year) was awarded; Federal Work-Study, scholarships/grants, tuition waivers (partial), and unspecified assistantships also available. Financial award applicants required to submit FAFSA. In 2016, 18 master's awarded. *Program availability:* Part-time, evening/weekend. Offers applied statistics (MS); biology (MA, MS); mathematics (MA); nutrition (MS). *Application deadline:* Applications are processed on a rolling basis. *Application fee:* $20. Electronic applications accepted. *Application Contact:* Johnny Garcia, Graduate Admissions Counselor, 210-805-3554, Fax: 210-829-3921, E-mail: admis@uiwtx.edu. *Dean,* Dr. Carlos A. Garcia, 210-829-2717, Fax: 210-829-3153, E-mail: cagarci9@uiwtx.edu.

School of Media and Design Students: 27 full-time (20 women), 6 part-time (5 women); includes 17 minority (1 Black or African American, non-Hispanic/Latino; 16 Hispanic/Latino), 5 international. *Faculty:* 8 full-time (4 women), 7 part-time/adjunct (4 women). Expenses: Contact institution. *Financial support:* Federal Work-Study, scholarships/grants, tuition waivers (partial), and unspecified assistantships available.

Financial award applicants required to submit FAFSA. In 2016, 14 master's awarded. *Program availability:* Part-time, evening/weekend. Offers communication arts (MA); fashion design (MA). *Application deadline:* Applications are processed on a rolling basis. *Application fee:* $20. Electronic applications accepted. *Application Contact:* Johnny Garcia, Graduate Admissions Counselor, 210-805-3554, Fax: 210-829-3921, E-mail: admis@uiwtx.edu. *Dean,* Dr. Sharon Welkey, 210-829-6091, Fax: 210-829-3196, E-mail: welkey@uiwtx.edu.

School of Nursing and Health Professions Students: 32 full-time (12 women), 93 part-time (75 women); includes 89 minority (21 Black or African American, non-Hispanic/Latino; 1 American Indian or Alaska Native, non-Hispanic/Latino; 8 Asian, non-Hispanic/Latino; 56 Hispanic/Latino; 3 Two or more races, non-Hispanic/Latino), 6 international. *Faculty:* 17 full-time (14 women), 8 part-time/adjunct (7 women). Expenses: Contact institution. *Financial support:* Research assistantships, Federal Work-Study, scholarships/grants, tuition waivers (partial), and unspecified assistantships available. Financial award applicants required to submit FAFSA. In 2016, 30 master's, 4 doctorates awarded. *Program availability:* Part-time, evening/weekend. Offers nursing and health professions (MS, MSN, DNP). *Application deadline:* Applications are processed on a rolling basis. *Application fee:* $20. Electronic applications accepted. *Application Contact:* Johnny Garcia, Graduate Admissions Counselor, 210-805-3554, Fax: 210-829-3921, E-mail: admis@uiwtx.edu. *Dean,* Dr. Mary Hoke, 210-829-3982, Fax: 210-829-3174, E-mail: mhoke@uiwtx.edu.

School of Osteopathic Medicine Students: 54 full-time (32 women), 1 (woman) part-time; includes 41 minority (7 Black or African American, non-Hispanic/Latino; 8 Asian, non-Hispanic/Latino; 25 Hispanic/Latino; 1 Two or more races, non-Hispanic/Latino). *Faculty:* 5 full-time (4 women), 3 part-time/adjunct (2 women). Expenses: Contact institution. *Financial support:* Research assistantships, career-related internships or fieldwork, scholarships/grants, and unspecified assistantships available. Financial award applicants required to submit FAFSA. Offers osteopathic medicine (MBS, DO). *Application deadline:* For fall admission, 9/1 for domestic students; for spring admission, 3/15 for domestic students. Applications are processed on a rolling basis. Electronic applications accepted. *Application Contact:* Alexandra R. Shipley, Admissions Recruiter, 210-283-6998, E-mail: ashipley@uiwtx.edu. *Dean,* Dr. Robyn Phillips-Madson, E-mail: rmadson@uiwtx.edu.

School of Physical Therapy Students: 105 full-time (59 women), 83 part-time (47 women); includes 59 minority (8 Black or African American, non-Hispanic/Latino; 1 Asian, non-Hispanic/Latino; 45 Hispanic/Latino; 5 Two or more races, non-Hispanic/Latino), 2 international. *Faculty:* 16 full-time (9 women), 18 part-time/adjunct (13 women). Expenses: Contact institution. *Financial support:* Scholarships/grants and unspecified assistantships available. Financial award applicants required to submit FAFSA. In 2016, 14 doctorates awarded. Offers physical therapy (DPT). *Application deadline:* For fall admission, 10/1 priority date for domestic students. *Application fee:* $50. *Application Contact:* Christina Immel, Director of Enrollment, 210-283-6918, E-mail: cimmel@uiwtx.edu. *Dean,* Dr. Caroline Goulet, 210-283-6924, E-mail: goulet@uiwtx.edu.

School of Professional Studies Students: 161 full-time (88 women), 657 part-time (309 women); includes 516 minority (107 Black or African American, non-Hispanic/Latino; 4 American Indian or Alaska Native, non-Hispanic/Latino; 25 Asian, non-Hispanic/Latino; 356 Hispanic/Latino; 8 Native Hawaiian or other Pacific Islander, non-Hispanic/Latino; 16 Two or more races, non-Hispanic/Latino), 2 international. *Faculty:* 34 part-time/adjunct (13 women). Expenses: Contact institution. *Financial support:* Scholarships/grants and unspecified assistantships available. Financial award applicants required to submit FAFSA. In 2016, 284 master's awarded. *Program availability:* Part-time, evening/weekend, 100% online, blended/hybrid learning. *Application deadline:* Applications are processed on a rolling basis. Electronic applications accepted. *Application Contact:* Julie Weber, Director of Marketing and Recruitment, 210-318-1876, Fax: 210-829-2756, E-mail: eapadmission@uiwtx.edu. *Vice President,* Dr. Cyndi Porter, 877-603-1130, E-mail: porter@uiwtx.edu.

UNIVERSITY OF THE PACIFIC, Stockton, CA 95211-0197

General Information Independent, coed, university. CGS member. *Enrollment:* 6,128 graduate, professional, and undergraduate students; 1,957 full-time matriculated graduate/professional students (1,138 women), 678 part-time matriculated graduate/professional students (424 women). *Enrollment by degree level:* 725 master's, 1,848 doctoral, 62 other advanced degrees. *Graduate faculty:* 266 full-time (116 women), 322 part-time/adjunct (156 women). *Graduate housing:* Rooms and/or apartments available on a first-come, first-served basis to single and married students. Housing application deadline: 7/1. *Student services:* Campus employment opportunities, campus safety program, career counseling, free psychological counseling, international student services, low-cost health insurance, multicultural affairs office, services for students with disabilities, teacher training. *Library facilities:* University of the Pacific Library plus 1 other. *Research affiliation:* Lawrence Hall of Science.

Computer facilities: A campuswide network can be accessed from student residence rooms and from off campus. Online class registration is available. Website: http://www.pacific.edu/

General Application Contact: Office of Graduate Admissions, 209-946-2011.

GRADUATE UNITS

Arthur A. Dugoni School of Dentistry Students: 517 full-time (218 women); includes 304 minority (4 Black or African American, non-Hispanic/Latino; 245 Asian, non-Hispanic/Latino; 34 Hispanic/Latino; 2 Native Hawaiian or other Pacific Islander, non-Hispanic/Latino; 19 Two or more races, non-Hispanic/Latino), 24 international. Average age 26. *Faculty:* 71 full-time (24 women), 199 part-time/adjunct (80 women). Expenses: Contact institution. *Financial support:* Institutionally sponsored loans, scholarships/grants, and stipends available. Support available to part-time students. Financial award application deadline: 3/2; financial award applicants required to submit FAFSA. In 2016, 8 master's, 156 doctorates awarded. Offers dentistry (MSD, DDS, Certificate). *Application deadline:* For fall admission, 9/15 priority date for international students. Applications are processed on a rolling basis. Electronic applications accepted. *Application Contact:* Dr. Craig S. Yarborough, 415-929-6430, E-mail: cyarborough@pacific.edu. *Dean,* Nader Nadershahi, 415-929-6425, E-mail: nnadershahi@pacific.edu.

College of the Pacific Students: 1 (woman) full-time, 102 part-time (69 women); includes 42 minority (3 Black or African American, non-Hispanic/Latino; 1 American Indian or Alaska Native, non-Hispanic/Latino; 18 Asian, non-Hispanic/Latino; 17 Hispanic/Latino; 3 Two or more races, non-Hispanic/Latino), 1 international. Average age 28. 120 applicants, 58% accepted, 50 enrolled. *Faculty:* 29 full-time (9 women), 4 part-time/adjunct (2 women). Expenses: Contact institution. *Financial support:* Teaching assistantships and institutionally sponsored loans available. Support available to part-time students. Financial award application deadline: 3/1; financial award applicants required to submit FAFSA. In 2016, 27 master's awarded. Offers biological sciences

(MS); communication (MA); food studies (MA); health, exercise and sport science (MA); psychology (MA). *Application fee:* $75. *Application Contact:* Information Contact, 209-946-2261. *Dean,* Dr. Rena Fraden, 209-946-2023.

Conservatory of Music Students: 10 full-time (7 women), 23 part-time (15 women); includes 8 minority (3 Asian, non-Hispanic/Latino; 4 Hispanic/Latino; 1 Two or more races, non-Hispanic/Latino), 4 international. Average age 33. 24 applicants, 129% accepted, 13 enrolled. Expenses: Contact institution. *Financial support:* Teaching assistantships and institutionally sponsored loans available. Support available to part-time students. Financial award application deadline: 3/1; financial award applicants required to submit FAFSA. In 2016, 4 master's awarded. Offers music education (MM); music therapy (MA). *Application deadline:* For fall admission, 3/1 priority date for domestic students; for spring admission, 10/1 priority date for domestic students. Applications are processed on a rolling basis. *Application fee:* $75. *Application Contact:* 209-946-2415, Fax: 209-946-2770. *Interim Dean,* Dr. Daniel Ebbers, 209-946-2415, E-mail: musicdean@pacific.edu.

Eberhardt School of Business Students: 24 full-time (12 women), 7 part-time (3 women); includes 14 minority (1 Black or African American, non-Hispanic/Latino; 7 Asian, non-Hispanic/Latino; 3 Hispanic/Latino; 3 Two or more races, non-Hispanic/Latino), 6 international. Average age 28. 66 applicants, 53% accepted, 10 enrolled. *Faculty:* 30 full-time (15 women), 2 part-time/adjunct (1 woman). Expenses: Contact institution. *Financial support:* Fellowships, research assistantships, Federal Work-Study, and institutionally sponsored loans available. Support available to part-time students. Financial award application deadline: 3/1; financial award applicants required to submit FAFSA. In 2016, 32 master's awarded. *Program availability:* Part-time. Offers business (M Acc, MBA). *Application deadline:* For fall admission, 7/31 priority date for domestic students; for spring admission, 11/30 for domestic students. Applications are processed on a rolling basis. *Application fee:* $75. *Application Contact:* 209-946-2239, E-mail: business@pacific.edu. *Interim Dean,* Dr. David Dauwalder, 209-946-7710, E-mail: ddauwalder@pacific.edu.

Gladys L. Benerd School of Education Students: 210 full-time (166 women), 234 part-time (178 women); includes 223 minority (49 Black or African American, non-Hispanic/Latino; 40 Asian, non-Hispanic/Latino; 107 Hispanic/Latino; 4 Native Hawaiian or other Pacific Islander, non-Hispanic/Latino; 23 Two or more races, non-Hispanic/Latino), 8 international. Average age 33. 182 applicants, 75% accepted, 106 enrolled. *Faculty:* 18 full-time (11 women), 37 part-time/adjunct (30 women). Expenses: Contact institution. *Financial support:* Teaching assistantships and institutionally sponsored loans available. Support available to part-time students. Financial award application deadline: 3/1; financial award applicants required to submit FAFSA. In 2016, 215 master's, 23 doctorates awarded. Offers curriculum and instruction (MA); education (M Ed, MA, Ed D, Ed S); educational administration (MA, Ed D); educational psychology (MA, Ed D); school psychology (Ed S); special education (MA). *Application deadline:* For fall admission, 3/1 priority date for domestic students; for spring admission, 10/15 for domestic students. Applications are processed on a rolling basis. *Application fee:* $75. *Application Contact:* Office of Graduate Admissions, 209-946-2344. *Dean,* Dr. Vanessa Sheared, 209-946-2683, E-mail: lwebster@pacific.edu.

McGeorge School of Law Students: 365 full-time (195 women), 188 part-time (105 women); includes 187 minority (24 Black or African American, non-Hispanic/Latino; 3 American Indian or Alaska Native, non-Hispanic/Latino; 43 Asian, non-Hispanic/Latino; 114 Hispanic/Latino; 1 Native Hawaiian or other Pacific Islander, non-Hispanic/Latino; 2 Two or more races, non-Hispanic/Latino), 1 international. Average age 28. *Faculty:* 38 full-time (17 women), 40 part-time/adjunct (11 women). Expenses: Contact institution. *Financial support:* Fellowships, research assistantships, teaching assistantships, career-related internships or fieldwork, Federal Work-Study, institutionally sponsored loans, and scholarships/grants available. Support available to part-time students. Financial award applicants required to submit FAFSA. In 2016, 56 master's, 158 doctorates awarded. *Program availability:* Part-time, evening/weekend. Offers advocacy (JD); international water resources law (JSD); public policy and law (LL M). *Application deadline:* For fall admission, 3/15 priority date for domestic students. Applications are processed on a rolling basis. *Application fee:* $50. Electronic applications accepted. *Application Contact:* 916-739-7105, Fax: 916-739-7301, E-mail: mcgeorge@pacific.edu. *Dean,* Francis Jay Mootz, III, 916-739-7151, E-mail: jmootz@pacific.edu.

School of Engineering and Computer Science Students: 23 full-time (7 women), 40 part-time (14 women); includes 32 minority (4 Black or African American, non-Hispanic/Latino; 16 Asian, non-Hispanic/Latino; 11 Hispanic/Latino; 1 Two or more races, non-Hispanic/Latino), 7 international. Average age 29. 83 applicants, 55% accepted, 31 enrolled. Expenses: Contact institution. *Financial support:* Teaching assistantships available. In 2016, 56 master's awarded. Offers engineering science (MS). *Application deadline:* For fall admission, 3/1 for domestic students; for spring admission, 10/1 for domestic students. Electronic applications accepted. *Application Contact:* Office of Graduate Admissions, 209-946-2011. *Dean,* Dr. Steve Howell, 209-946-3068, E-mail: showell@pacific.edu.

Thomas J. Long School of Pharmacy and Health Sciences Students: 807 full-time (532 women), 84 part-time (40 women); includes 620 minority (7 Black or African American, non-Hispanic/Latino; 1 American Indian or Alaska Native, non-Hispanic/Latino; 507 Asian, non-Hispanic/Latino; 58 Hispanic/Latino; 5 Native Hawaiian or other Pacific Islander, non-Hispanic/Latino; 42 Two or more races, non-Hispanic/Latino), 47 international. Average age 24. 2,106 applicants, 28% accepted, 307 enrolled. *Faculty:* 72 full-time (36 women), 40 part-time/adjunct (32 women). Expenses: Contact institution. *Financial support:* Teaching assistantships, career-related internships or fieldwork, Federal Work-Study, and institutionally sponsored loans available. Support available to part-time students. Financial award application deadline: 3/1; financial award applicants required to submit FAFSA. In 2016, 32 master's, 230 doctorates awarded. Offers pharmaceutical and chemical sciences (MS, PhD); pharmacy (Pharm D); pharmacy and health sciences (MS, DPT, PhD, Pharm D); physical therapy (MS, DPT); speech-language pathology (MS). *Application fee:* $75. *Application Contact:* 209-946-2211. *Dean,* Dr. Philip Oppenheimer, 209-946-2561.

UNIVERSITY OF THE POTOMAC, Washington, DC 20005

General Information Proprietary, coed, comprehensive institution.

GRADUATE UNITS

Program in Business Administration *Program availability:* Online learning. Offers business administration (MBA). Program also offered at Vienna, VA campus.

UNIVERSITY OF THE ROCKIES, Colorado Springs, CO 80903

General Information Independent, coed, graduate-only institution.

GRADUATE UNITS

Graduate Programs Offers psychology (MA, Psy D).

UNIVERSITY OF THE SACRED HEART, San Juan, PR 00914-0383

General Information Independent-religious, coed, comprehensive institution. *Graduate housing;* Room and/or apartments available on a first-come, first-served basis to single students; on-campus housing not available to married students. Housing application deadline: 5/31.

GRADUATE UNITS

Graduate Programs *Program availability:* Part-time, evening/weekend. Offers contemporary culture and media (MA); creative writing (MFA, Certificate); digital journalism (MA, Certificate); early childhood education (M Ed); editing for media (MA, Certificate); human resource management (MBA); human rights and anti-discriminatory processes (MASJ); information systems auditing (MS); information systems management (MBA); information technology (Certificate); information technology and multimedia (Certificate); instruction systems and education technology (M Ed); international marketing (MBA); management information systems (MBA); mediation and transformation of conflicts (MASJ); nonprofit organization administration (MBA); occupational health and safety (MS); occupational nursing (MSN); production and marketing of special events (Certificate); public relations (MA, Certificate); publicity (MA, Certificate); scriptwriting (MA, Certificate); taxation (MBA).

UNIVERSITY OF THE SCIENCES, Philadelphia, PA 19104-4495

General Information Independent, coed, university. CGS member. *Graduate housing:* On-campus housing not available. *Research affiliation:* Progenra (molecular biology), Encapsulation Systems (analytical chemistry), Johnson & Johnson (cell biology), Ortho-McNeil Pharmaceuticals, Inc. (pharmacy), Polymedix (computational chemistry).

GRADUATE UNITS

Doctor of Physical Therapy Program *Program availability:* Part-time, evening/weekend, online learning. Offers physical therapy (DPT).

Philadelphia College of Pharmacy Offers pharmacy (Pharm D).

Program in Bioinformatics *Program availability:* Part-time, evening/weekend. Offers bioinformatics (MS).

Program in Biomedical Writing *Program availability:* Part-time, evening/weekend, online learning. Offers biomedical writing (MS); medical marketing writing (Certificate); regulatory affairs writing (Certificate).

Program in Cell Biology and Biotechnology *Program availability:* Part-time, evening/weekend. Offers cell biology and biotechnology (MS).

Program in Chemistry, Biochemistry and Pharmacognosy *Program availability:* Part-time. Offers biochemistry (MS, PhD); chemistry (MS, PhD); pharmacognosy (MS, PhD).

Program in Health Policy *Program availability:* Part-time, evening/weekend, online learning. Offers health policy (MS, PhD).

Program in Health Psychology Offers health psychology (MS).

Program in Occupational Therapy *Program availability:* Online learning. Offers occupational therapy (MOT, Dr OT). Electronic applications accepted.

Program in Pharmaceutical and Healthcare Business *Program availability:* Part-time, evening/weekend, online learning. Offers pharmaceutical and healthcare business (MBA).

Program in Pharmaceutics *Program availability:* Part-time. Offers pharmaceutics (MS, PhD).

Program in Pharmacology and Toxicology Offers pharmacology (MS, PhD); toxicology (MS, PhD).

Program in Pharmacy Administration *Program availability:* Part-time. Offers pharmacy administration (MS).

Program in Physician Assistant Studies Offers physician assistant studies (MSPAS).

Program in Public Health *Program availability:* Part-time, evening/weekend, online learning. Offers public health (MPH).

UNIVERSITY OF THE SOUTHWEST, Hobbs, NM 88240-9129

General Information Independent-religious, coed, comprehensive institution. *Graduate housing:* On-campus housing not available.

GRADUATE UNITS

Graduate Programs *Program availability:* Part-time, evening/weekend, online learning. Offers business administration (MBA); curriculum and instruction (MSE); curriculum and instruction: bilingual (MSE); curriculum and instruction: TESOL (MSE); early childhood education (MSE); educational administration (MSE); mental health counseling (MSE); school counseling (MSE); special education (MSE); sports management (MBA). Electronic applications accepted.

UNIVERSITY OF THE VIRGIN ISLANDS, St. Thomas, VI 00802

General Information Territory-supported, coed, comprehensive institution. Tuition, territory resident: part-time $386 per credit hour. Tuition, nonresident: part-time $735 per credit hour. *Graduate housing:* On-campus housing not available. *Student services:* Campus employment opportunities, career counseling. *Library facilities:* Ralph M. Paiewonsky Library.

Computer facilities: 500 computers available on campus for general student use. A campuswide network can be accessed from student residence rooms. Online class registration is available.
Website: http://www.uvi.edu/

General Application Contact: Edward L. Alexander, Director of Admissions, 340-693-1224, Fax: 340-693-1167, E-mail: ealexan@uvi.edu.

GRADUATE UNITS

College of Liberal Arts and Social Sciences Students: 23 full-time (19 women), 13 part-time (9 women); includes 27 minority (24 Black or African American, non-Hispanic/Latino; 1 Asian, non-Hispanic/Latino; 1 Hispanic/Latino; 1 Two or more races, non-Hispanic/Latino), 6 international. Average age 34. 13 applicants, 85% accepted, 10 enrolled. *Faculty:* 7 full-time (5 women), 4 part-time/adjunct (0 women). Expenses: Contact institution. *Financial support:* Career-related internships or fieldwork and scholarships/grants available. Financial award application deadline: 4/15; financial award applicants required to submit FAFSA. In 2016, 4 master's awarded. *Program availability:* Part-time, evening/weekend. Offers liberal arts and social sciences (M Psych, MPA). *Application deadline:* For fall admission, 4/30 for domestic and international students; for spring admission, 10/30 for domestic and international students. *Application fee:* $30. Electronic applications accepted. *Application Contact:* Dr. Xuri M. Allen, Director of Admissions, 340-693-1224, Fax: 340-693-1167, E-mail: xallen@uvi.edu. *Dean,* Dr. Emily Allen-Williams, 340-693-1261, Fax: 340-693-1265, E-mail: emily.allenwilliams@uvi.edu.

College of Science and Mathematics Students: 12 full-time (10 women), 26 part-time (19 women); includes 7 minority (6 Black or African American, non-Hispanic/Latino; 1 Hispanic/Latino). Average age 27. 25 applicants, 80% accepted, 11 enrolled. *Faculty:* 5

full-time (4 women), 7 part-time/adjunct (2 women). Expenses: Contact institution. *Financial support:* Career-related internships or fieldwork and scholarships/grants available. Financial award application deadline: 4/15; financial award applicants required to submit FAFSA. In 2016, 6 master's awarded. *Program availability:* Part-time, online learning. Offers marine and environmental science (MS); mathematics for secondary teachers (MA). *Application deadline:* For fall admission, 4/30 for domestic and international students; for spring admission, 10/30 for domestic and international students. *Application fee:* $30. Electronic applications accepted. *Application Contact:* Dr. Xuri M. Allen, Director of Admissions, 340-693-1224; Fax: 340-693-1167, E-mail: xallen@uvi.edu. *Dean,* Dr. Sandra Romano, 340-693-1230, Fax: 340-693-1245, E-mail: sromano@uvi.edu.

School of Business Students: 32 full-time (20 women), 15 part-time (11 women); includes 31 minority (30 Black or African American, non-Hispanic/Latino; 1 Asian, non-Hispanic/Latino), 5 international. Average age 31. 39 applicants, 87% accepted, 29 enrolled. *Faculty:* 8 full-time (0 women). Expenses: Contact institution. *Financial support:* Application deadline: 4/15; applicants required to submit FAFSA. In 2016, 3 master's awarded. *Program availability:* Part-time, evening/weekend. Offers business (EMBA, MBA). *Application deadline:* For fall admission, 4/30 for domestic and international students; for spring admission, 10/30 for domestic and international students. Applications are processed on a rolling basis. *Application fee:* $30. Electronic applications accepted. *Application Contact:* Xuri M Allen, Director of Admissions, 340-693-1224, Fax: 340-693-1167, E-mail: xallen@uvi.edu. *Dean,* Dr. Stephen Reames, 340-693-1301, Fax: 340-693-1305, E-mail: stephen.reames@uvi.edu.

School of Education Students: 9 full-time (8 women), 107 part-time (89 women); includes 69 minority (67 Black or African American, non-Hispanic/Latino; 2 Hispanic/Latino), 17 international. Average age 43. 101 applicants, 80% accepted, 69 enrolled. *Faculty:* 8 full-time (2 women), 9 part-time/adjunct (4 women). Expenses: Contact institution. *Financial support:* Scholarships/grants available. Financial award application deadline: 4/15; financial award applicants required to submit FAFSA. In 2016, 9 master's awarded. *Program availability:* Part-time, evening/weekend. Offers creative leadership for innovation and change (PhD); educational leadership (MA); school counseling (MA); school psychology (Ed S). *Application deadline:* For fall admission, 4/30 for domestic and international students; for spring admission, 10/30 for domestic and international students. *Application fee:* $25. Electronic applications accepted. *Application Contact:* Dr. Xuri M. Allen, Director of Admissions, 340-693-1224, Fax: 340-693-1167, E-mail: xallen@uvi.edu. *Dean,* Dr. Linda Thomas, 340-693-1321, Fax: 340-693-1335, E-mail: lthomas2@uvi.edu.

UNIVERSITY OF THE WEST, Rosemead, CA 91770

General Information Independent, coed, comprehensive institution. *Enrollment:* 358 graduate, professional, and undergraduate students; 112 full-time matriculated graduate/professional students (63 women), 54 part-time matriculated graduate/professional students (19 women). *Enrollment by degree level:* 109 master's, 43 doctoral, 14 other advanced degrees. *Graduate faculty:* 12 full-time (2 women), 14 part-time/adjunct (4 women). *Tuition:* Full-time $9324; part-time $4662 per year. *Required fees:* $900; $640 per unit. $320 per semester. Tuition and fees vary according to program. *Graduate housing:* Rooms and/or apartments guaranteed to single students and available on a first-come, first-served basis to married students. Typical cost: $6884 (including board) for single students; $10,200 per year for married students. Room and board charges vary according to board plan. Housing application deadline: 9/22. *Student services:* Campus employment opportunities, campus safety program, career counseling, exercise/wellness program, free psychological counseling, international student services, low-cost health insurance, services for students with disabilities, teacher training, writing training. *Library facilities:* University of the West Library plus 1 other. *Collection:* Students can reserve study rooms.

Computer facilities: 501 computers available on campus for general student use. A campuswide network can be accessed from student residence rooms. Online class registration is available.
Website: http://www.uwest.edu/

General Application Contact: Rica Toribio, Director of Enrollment Services, 626-571-8811 Ext. 311, Fax: 626-571-1413, E-mail: ricat@uwest.edu.

GRADUATE UNITS

Department of Business Administration Students: 54 full-time (31 women), 14 part-time (3 women); includes 8 minority (4 Asian, non-Hispanic/Latino; 4 Hispanic/Latino), 59 international. Average age 29. *Faculty:* 3 full-time (1 woman), 6 part-time/adjunct (2 women). Expenses: Contact institution. *Financial support:* Career-related internships or fieldwork, Federal Work-Study, scholarships/grants, and tuition waivers (partial) available. Financial award applicants required to submit FAFSA. *Program availability:* Part-time, evening/weekend. Offers business administration (EMBA); computer information systems (MBA); finance (MBA); international business (MBA); nonprofit organization management (MBA). *Application deadline:* For fall admission, 6/15 for domestic and international students; for winter admission, 4/1 for domestic and international students; for spring admission, 11/15 for domestic and international students. Applications are processed on a rolling basis. *Application fee:* $50 ($100 for international students). *Application Contact:* Rica Toribio, Director of Enrollment Services, 626-571-8811 Ext. 311, Fax: 626-571-1413, E-mail: ricat@uwest.edu. *Chair,* Dr. Bill Y. Chen, 626-656-2125, Fax: 626-571-1413, E-mail: billchen@uwest.edu.

Department of Psychology Expenses: Contact institution. *Financial support:* Applicants required to submit FAFSA. *Program availability:* Part-time, evening/weekend. Offers Buddhist psychology (MA); multicultural counseling (MA). *Application deadline:* For fall admission, 3/15 for domestic and international students; for winter admission, 4/1 for domestic and international students; for spring admission, 11/15 for domestic and international students. Applications are processed on a rolling basis. *Application fee:* $50 ($100 for international students). *Application Contact:* Rica Toribio, Director of Enrollment Services, 626-571-8811 Ext. 311, Fax: 626-571-1413, E-mail: ricat@uwest.edu. *Chair,* Dr. Hiroshi Sasaki, 626-571-8811 Ext. 113, Fax: 626-571-1413, E-mail: hiroshis@uwest.edu.

Department of Religious Studies Expenses: Contact institution. *Financial support:* Fellowships, scholarships/grants, and tuition waivers (partial) available. *Program availability:* Part-time, evening/weekend. Offers religious studies (MA, PhD). *Application deadline:* For fall admission, 3/15 for domestic and international students; for spring admission, 11/15 for domestic and international students. Applications are processed on a rolling basis. *Application fee:* $50. *Application Contact:* Rica Toribio, Director of Enrollment Services, 626-571-8811 Ext. 311, Fax: 626-571-1413, E-mail: ricat@uwest.edu. *Chair,* Dr. Jane Iwamura, 626-571-8811 Ext. 342, Fax: 626-571-1413, E-mail: janei@uwest.edu.

Program in Buddhist Chaplaincy Expenses: Contact institution. Offers Buddhist chaplaincy (M Div). *Application deadline:* For fall admission, 3/15 for domestic and international students; for spring admission, 11/15 for domestic and international

students. Applications are processed on a rolling basis. *Application fee:* $50. *Application Contact:* Rica Toribio, Director of Enrollment Services, 626-571-8811 Ext. 311, Fax: 626-571-1413, E-mail: ricat@uwest.edu. *Coordinator,* Dr. Victor Gabriel, 626-571-8811 Ext. 359, E-mail: victorg@uwest.edu.

THE UNIVERSITY OF TOLEDO, Toledo, OH 43606-3390

General Information State-supported, coed, university. CGS member. *Graduate housing:* Room and/or apartments available to single students; on-campus housing not available to married students. *Research affiliation:* Merck & Company, Inc. (pharmaceutical research), Midwest Astronomical Data Reduction and Analysis Facility (astronomy), Edison Industrial Systems Center (systems integration, quality control, mathematical modeling), Ohio Aerospace Institute (aerospace research), National Renewable Energy Laboratory (NREL) (thin films, photovoltaics), NASA–Glen Research Center at Lewis Field (aerospace engineering).

GRADUATE UNITS

College of Graduate Studies *Program availability:* Part-time, evening/weekend, online learning. Electronic applications accepted.

College of Business and Innovation *Program availability:* Part-time, evening/weekend. Offers accounting (MBA, MSA); business administration-general (MBA); business and innovation (EMBA, MBA, MSA, DME, PhD, Certificate); finance (MBA); information operations and technology management (MBA, DME, PhD, Certificate); management (MBA); marketing and international business (MBA). Electronic applications accepted.

College of Communication and the Arts Offers communication (Certificate); communication and the arts (ME, MME, MMP, Certificate); music (Certificate); music performance (MMP). Electronic applications accepted.

College of Engineering *Program availability:* Part-time, evening/weekend, online learning. Offers bioengineering (MS, PhD); biomedical engineering (PhD); chemical engineering (MS, PhD); civil engineering (MS, PhD); computer science (MS, PhD); electrical engineering (MS, PhD); engineering (MS, PhD); general engineering (MS); industrial engineering (MS, PhD); mechanical engineering (MS, PhD). Electronic applications accepted.

College of Health and Human Services Offers exercise science (MSES, PhD); health and human services (MA, ME, MSES, DPT, OTD, PhD, Certificate, Ed S); health education (PhD); occupational therapy (OTD); physical therapy (DPT); recreation and leisure studies (MA); speech-language pathology (MA). Electronic applications accepted.

College of Languages, Literature and Social Sciences *Program availability:* Part-time. Offers applied econometric specialization (MA); clinical psychology (MA, PhD); economics (MA); English as a second language (MA); experimental psychology (MA, PhD); French (MA); geographic information science and applied geographics (Certificate); geography and planning (MA); German (MA); health care policy and administration (Certificate); history (MA, PhD); languages, literature and social sciences (MA, MLS, MPA, PhD, Certificate); liberal studies (MLS); management of non-profit organizations (Certificate); municipal administration (Certificate); philosophy (MA); political science (MA); public administration (MPA); sociology (MA); Spanish (MA); spatially-integrated social science (PhD); teaching of writing (Certificate); women's and gender studies (Certificate). Electronic applications accepted.

College of Medicine and Life Sciences *Program availability:* Part-time, evening/weekend. Offers bioinformatics and proteomics/genomics (MSBS); biomarkers and bioinformatics (Certificate); biomarkers and diagnostics (PSM); biostatistics and epidemiology (Certificate); cancer biology (MSBS, PhD); cardiovascular and metabolic diseases (MSBS, PhD); contemporary gerontological practice (Certificate); environmental and occupational health and safety (MPH); epidemiology (Certificate); global public health (Certificate); health promotion and education (MPH); human donation sciences (MSBS); industrial hygiene (MSOH); infection, immunity, and transplantation (MSBS, PhD); medical and health science teaching and learning (Certificate); medical physics (MSBS); medical sciences (MSBS); medicine and life sciences (MPH, ME, MSBS, MSOH, PhD, Certificate); neurosciences (MSBS, PhD); occupational health (Certificate); oral biology (MSBS); orthopedic surgery (MSBS); pathology (Certificate); pathology assistant (MSBS); physician assistant studies (MSBS); public health administration (MPH); public health and emergency response (Certificate); public health epidemiology (MPH); public health nutrition (MPH). Electronic applications accepted.

College of Natural Sciences and Mathematics *Program availability:* Part-time. Offers analytical chemistry (MS, PhD); applied mathematics (MS, PhD); biological chemistry (MS, PhD); biology (MS, PhD); geology (MS); inorganic chemistry (MS, PhD); natural sciences and mathematics (MS, PSM, PhD); organic chemistry (MS, PhD); photovoltaics (PSM); physical chemistry (MS, PhD); physics (MS, PhD); statistics (MS, PhD). Electronic applications accepted.

College of Nursing *Program availability:* Part-time, online learning. Offers clinical nurse leader (MSN); family nurse practitioner (MSN, Certificate); health promotions, outcomes, systems, and policy (MSN, DNP); nurse educator (MSN, Certificate); nursing (MSN, DNP, Certificate); pediatric nurse practitioner (MSN, Certificate). Electronic applications accepted.

College of Pharmacy and Pharmaceutical Sciences Offers administrative pharmacy (MSPS); experimental therapeutics (PhD); industrial pharmacy (MSPS); medicinal and biological chemistry (MS, PhD); pharmacology toxicology (MSPS); pharmacy and pharmaceutical sciences (MS, MSPS, PhD). Electronic applications accepted.

College of Social Justice and Human Service Offers child advocacy (Certificate); counselor education (MA, PhD); criminal justice (MA); elder law (Certificate); higher education (ME, PhD, Certificate); juvenile justice (Certificate); patient advocacy (Certificate); school psychology (MA, Ed S); social justice and human service (MA, ME, MSW, PhD, Certificate, Ed S); social work (MSW).

Judith Herb College of Education *Program availability:* Part-time, evening/weekend. Offers art education (ME); career and technical education (ME, Ed S); curriculum and instruction (ME, PhD, Ed S); early childhood education (ME, Ed S); education (MAE, ME, MES, MME, DE, PhD, Certificate, Ed S); education and anthropology (MAE); education and biology (MES); education and chemistry (MES); education and classics (MAE); education and economics (MAE); education and English (MAE); education and French (MAE); education and geology (MES); education and German (MAE); education and history (MAE); education and mathematics (MAE, MES); education and physics (MES); education and political science (MAE); education and sociology (MAE); education and Spanish (MAE); educational administration and supervision (ME, DE, Ed S); educational media (PhD); educational psychology (ME, PhD); educational research and measurement (ME, PhD); educational sociology (PhD); educational technology (ME); educational technology: virtual educator (Certificate); educational theory and social foundations (ME); elementary education (PhD); English as a second language (MAE); foundations of education (DE, PhD); gifted and talented education (PhD); history of education (PhD); middle childhood education (ME); philosophy of education (PhD); physical education (ME); secondary education (ME, PhD); special education (ME, PhD). Electronic applications accepted.

College of Law Students: 179 full-time (81 women), 62 part-time (37 women); includes 38 minority (22 Black or African American, non-Hispanic/Latino; 4 Asian, non-Hispanic/Latino; 9 Hispanic/Latino; 1 Native Hawaiian or other Pacific Islander, non-Hispanic/Latino; 2 Two or more races, non-Hispanic/Latino), 1 international. Average age 29. 428 applicants, 57% accepted, 85 enrolled. *Faculty:* 27 full-time (13 women), 12 part-time/adjunct (4 women). Expenses: Contact institution. *Financial support:* In 2016–17, 195 students received support, including 13 research assistantships (averaging $372 per year), 7 teaching assistantships; career-related internships or fieldwork, Federal Work-Study, and scholarships/grants also available. Support available to part-time students. Financial award application deadline: 8/1; financial award applicants required to submit FAFSA. In 2016, 3 master's, 88 doctorates awarded. *Program availability:* Part-time-only, evening/weekend, online only, 100% online. Offers compliance (Certificate); health care compliance (Certificate); higher education compliance (Certificate); law (MLW, JD). *Application deadline:* For fall admission, 8/1 priority date for domestic students, 7/31 for international students; for winter admission, 11/15 for domestic students; for summer admission, 4/15 priority date for domestic students. Applications are processed on a rolling basis. *Application fee:* $0. Electronic applications accepted. *Application Contact:* Jessica Mehl, Assistant Dean of Law Admissions, 419-530-4131, Fax: 419-530-4345, E-mail: law.admissions@utoledo.edu. *Dean,* D. Benjamin Barros, 419-530-2379, Fax: 419-530-4526, E-mail: ben.barros@utoledo.edu.

UNIVERSITY OF TORONTO, Toronto, ON M5S 1A1, Canada

General Information Province-supported, coed, university. CGS member. *Graduate housing:* Rooms and/or apartments available on a first-come, first-served basis to single students and available to married students. *Research affiliation:* Fields Institute for Research in Mathematical Sciences, Canadian Institute for Theoretical Astrophysics, Royal Ontario Museum, Pontifical Institute of Medieval Studies, Hospital for Sick Children, Center for Addiction and Mental Health.

GRADUATE UNITS

Faculty of Medicine Offers biochemistry (M Sc, PhD); genetic counseling (M Sc); immunology (M Sc, PhD); laboratory medicine and pathobiology (M Sc, PhD); management of innovation (MMI); medical biophysics (M Sc, PhD); medicine (M Sc, M Sc BMC, M Sc OT, M Sc PT, MH Sc, MD, PhD); molecular genetics (M Sc, PhD); nutritional sciences (M Sc, PhD); occupational therapy (M Sc OT); pharmacology (M Sc, PhD); physical therapy (M Sc PT); physiology (M Sc, PhD); rehabilitation science (M Sc, PhD); speech-language pathology (M Sc, MH Sc, PhD). Electronic applications accepted.

Institute of Health Policy, Management and Evaluation Offers health administration (MH Sc); health informatics (MHI); health policy, management and evaluation (PhD). Electronic applications accepted.

Institute of Medical Science Offers bioethics (MH Sc); biomedical communications (M Sc BMC); medical radiation science (MH Sc); medical science (PhD). Electronic applications accepted.

School of Graduate Studies *Program availability:* Part-time, evening/weekend. Offers biotechnology (MBiotech); environmental science (M Env Sc, PhD). Electronic applications accepted.

Advanced Design and Manufacturing Institute *Program availability:* Part-time. Offers design and manufacturing (M Eng). Program offered jointly with McMaster University, Queen's University, and The University of Western Ontario; available only to Canadian citizens and permanent residents of Canada. Electronic applications accepted.

Department of Nursing Science *Program availability:* Part-time. Offers nursing (MN, PhD). Electronic applications accepted.

Department of Public Health Sciences *Program availability:* Part-time. Offers biostatistics (M Sc, PhD); community health (M Sc); community nutrition (MPH); epidemiology (MPH, PhD); family and community medicine (MPH); occupational and environmental health (MPH); social and behavioral health science (PhD); social and behavioral health sciences (MPH). Electronic applications accepted.

Faculty of Applied Science and Engineering *Program availability:* Part-time. Offers aerospace studies (M Eng, MA Sc, PhD); applied science and engineering (M Eng, MA Sc, MH Sc, PhD); biomedical engineering (MA Sc, PhD); chemical engineering and applied chemistry (M Eng, MA Sc, PhD); civil engineering (M Eng, MA Sc, PhD); clinical engineering (MH Sc, PhD); electrical and computer engineering (M Eng, MA Sc, PhD); materials science and engineering (M Eng, MA Sc, PhD); mechanical and industrial engineering (M Eng, MA Sc, PhD).

Faculty of Arts and Science *Program availability:* Part-time. Offers anthropology (M Sc, MA, PhD); applied computing (M Sc AC); art history (MA, PhD); arts and science (M Sc, M Sc AC, M Sc Pl, MA, MA Sc, MFE, MIRHR, MMF, MUD, MUDS, MVS, PhD); astronomy and astrophysics (M Sc, PhD); cell and systems biology (M Sc, PhD); chemistry (M Sc, PhD); cinema studies (MA, PhD); classics (MA, PhD); comparative literature (MA, PhD); computer science (M Sc, PhD); creative writing (MA); criminology and sociolegal studies (MA, PhD); drama, theatre and performance studies (MA, PhD); earth sciences (M Sc, MA Sc, PhD); East Asian studies (MA, PhD); ecology and evolutionary biology (M Sc, PhD); economics (MA, PhD); English (MA, PhD); financial economics (MFE); French language and literature (MA, PhD); geography (M Sc, MA, PhD); German (MA, PhD); history (MA, PhD); history and philosophy of science and technology (MA, PhD); industrial relations and human resources (MIRHR, PhD); Italian studies (MA, PhD); linguistics (MA, PhD); mathematical finance (MMF); mathematics (M Sc, PhD); medieval studies (MA, PhD); Near and Middle Eastern civilizations (MA, PhD); philosophy (MA, PhD); physics (M Sc, PhD); planning (M Sc Pl, MUDS, PhD); political science (MA, PhD); psychology (MA, PhD); religion (MA, PhD); Slavic languages and literatures (MA, PhD); sociology (MA, PhD); Spanish and Portuguese (MA, PhD); statistical sciences (M Sc, PhD); urban design (MUD); women and gender studies (MA, PhD). Electronic applications accepted.

Faculty of Dentistry Offers dental public health (M Sc); dentistry (M Sc, DDS, PhD); endodontics (M Sc); oral and maxillofacial radiology (M Sc); oral and maxillofacial surgery (M Sc); oral medicine (M Sc); orthodontics and dentofacial orthopedics (M Sc); pediatric dentistry (M Sc); periodontology (M Sc). Electronic applications accepted.

Faculty of Forestry Offers forestry (M Sc F, MFC, PhD). Electronic applications accepted.

Faculty of Information *Program availability:* Part-time. Offers information (MI, PhD); museum studies (MM St). Electronic applications accepted.

Faculty of Kinesiology and Physical Education Offers kinesiology and physical education (M Sc, PhD). Electronic applications accepted.

Faculty of Law *Program availability:* Part-time. Offers law (LL M, MSL, JD, SJD). Electronic applications accepted.

Faculty of Music *Program availability:* Part-time. Offers composition (M Mus, DMA); ethnomusicology (MA, PhD); jazz (M Mus); music education (MA, PhD); musicology/theory (MA, PhD); opera (M Mus); performance (M Mus, DMA). Electronic applications accepted.

Faculty of Social Work *Program availability:* Part-time. Offers social work (MSW, PhD). Electronic applications accepted.

John H. Daniels Faculty of Architecture, Landscape, and Design Offers architecture, landscape, and design (M Arch, MLA, MUD, MVS). Electronic applications accepted.

Leslie Dan Faculty of Pharmacy *Program availability:* Part-time. Offers pharmacy (M Sc, PhD, Pharm D). Electronic applications accepted.

Munk School of Global Affairs Offers European, Russian and Eurasian studies (MA); global affairs (MGA). Electronic applications accepted.

Ontario Institute for Studies in Education *Program availability:* Part-time, evening/weekend. Offers education (M Ed, MA, MT, Ed D, PhD).

Rotman School of Management *Program availability:* Part-time, evening/weekend. Offers management (MBA, MF, PhD).

THE UNIVERSITY OF TULSA, Tulsa, OK 74104-3189

General Information Independent, coed, university. CGS member. *Enrollment:* 4,563 graduate, professional, and undergraduate students; 474 full-time matriculated graduate/professional students (195 women), 345 part-time matriculated graduate/professional students (114 women). *Enrollment by degree level:* 567 master's, 252 doctoral. *Graduate faculty:* 194 full-time (54 women), 11 part-time/adjunct (5 women). *Tuition:* Full-time $22,230; part-time $1235 per credit hour. *Required fees:* $990 per semester. Tuition and fees vary according to course load. *Graduate housing:* Rooms and/or apartments available on a first-come, first-served basis to single and married students. Typical cost: $6394 per year ($11,116 including board) for single students; $9394 per year ($14,116 including board) for married students. Room and board charges vary according to board plan, campus/location and housing facility selected. Housing application deadline: 2/1. *Student services:* Campus employment opportunities, campus safety program, career counseling, child daycare facilities, exercise/wellness program, free psychological counseling, grant writing training, international student services, low-cost health insurance, multicultural affairs office, services for students with disabilities, teacher training, writing training. *Library facilities:* McFarlin Library plus 1 other. *Collection:* Books: 1.2 million (physical), 460,240 (digital/electronic); Serial titles: 59,171 (digital/electronic); Databases: 289. Weekly public service hours: 94; study areas open 24 hours, 5–7 days a week; students can reserve study rooms. *Research affiliation:* Network of Excellence in Training (NEXT) (petrophysics), Chevron Texaco (petroleum engineering).

Computer facilities: Computer purchase and lease plans are available. 710 computers available on campus for general student use. A campuswide network can be accessed from student residence rooms and from off campus. Online class registration is available.

Website: http://www.utulsa.edu/

General Application Contact: Dr. Janet A. Haggerty, Vice Provost for Research/Dean of the Graduate School, 918-631-2336, Fax: 918-631-2156, E-mail: grad@utulsa.edu.

GRADUATE UNITS

College of Law Students: 233 full-time (103 women), 30 part-time (17 women); includes 70 minority (10 Black or African American, non-Hispanic/Latino; 16 American Indian or Alaska Native, non-Hispanic/Latino; 2 Asian, non-Hispanic/Latino; 12 Hispanic/Latino; 30 Two or more races, non-Hispanic/Latino), 5 international. Average age 27. 602 applicants, 40% accepted, 92 enrolled. *Faculty:* 23 full-time (13 women), 12 part-time/adjunct (4 women). Expenses: Contact institution. *Financial support:* In 2016–17, 255 students received support. Scholarships/grants available. Support available to part-time students. Financial award application deadline: 8/1; financial award applicants required to submit FAFSA. In 2016, 5 master's, 81 doctorates awarded. *Program availability:* Part-time, 100% online. Offers American Indian and indigenous law (LL M); American law for foreign lawyers (LL M); energy and natural resources law (LL M); energy law (MJ); health law (Certificate); Indian law (MJ); law (JD); Native American law (Certificate); natural resources, energy, and environmental law (Certificate). *Application deadline:* For fall admission, 7/31 priority date for domestic and international students; for spring admission, 12/5 priority date for domestic students, 12/5 for international students; for summer admission, 4/13 for domestic and international students. Applications are processed on a rolling basis. *Application fee:* $30. Electronic applications accepted. *Application Contact:* April M. Fox, Associate Dean of Admissions and Financial Aid, 918-631-2406, Fax: 918-631-3630, E-mail: april-fox@utulsa.edu. *Dean,* Prof. Lyn Suzanne Entzeroth, 918-631-2400, Fax: 918-631-3126, E-mail: lyn-entzeroth@utulsa.edu.

Graduate School Students: 474 full-time (195 women), 345 part-time (114 women); includes 112 minority (18 Black or African American, non-Hispanic/Latino; 28 American Indian or Alaska Native, non-Hispanic/Latino; 29 Asian, non-Hispanic/Latino; 25 Hispanic/Latino; 12 Two or more races, non-Hispanic/Latino), 218 international. Average age 30. 1,577 applicants, 33% accepted, 255 enrolled. *Faculty:* 194 full-time (54 women), 11 part-time/adjunct (5 women). Expenses: Contact institution. *Financial support:* In 2016–17, 400 students received support, including 116 fellowships with full tuition reimbursements available (averaging $9,235 per year), 189 research assistantships with full tuition reimbursements available (averaging $9,600 per year), 276 teaching assistantships with full tuition reimbursements available (averaging $11,267 per year); career-related internships or fieldwork, Federal Work-Study, institutionally sponsored loans, scholarships/grants, traineeships, health care benefits, tuition waivers (partial), and unspecified assistantships also available. Support available to part-time students. Financial award application deadline: 2/1; financial award applicants required to submit FAFSA. In 2016, 274 master's, 36 doctorates awarded. *Program availability:* Part-time, evening/weekend. Offers museum science and management (MA). *Application deadline:* Applications are processed on a rolling basis. *Application fee:* $55. Electronic applications accepted. *Application Contact:* Graduate School, 918-631-2336, Fax: 918-631-2156, E-mail: grad@utulsa.edu. *Vice Provost for Research/Dean of the Graduate School,* Dr. Janet A. Haggerty, 918-631-2336, Fax: 918-631-2156, E-mail: grad@utulsa.edu.

College of Engineering and Natural Sciences Students: 244 full-time (56 women), 96 part-time (26 women); includes 26 minority (3 Black or African American, non-Hispanic/Latino; 8 American Indian or Alaska Native, non-Hispanic/Latino; 3 Asian, non-Hispanic/Latino; 5 Hispanic/Latino; 1 Native Hawaiian or other Pacific Islander, non-Hispanic/Latino; 2 Two or more races, non-Hispanic/Latino), 184 international. Average age 28. 810 applicants, 27% accepted, 83 enrolled. *Faculty:* 102 full-time (11 women), 2 part-time/adjunct (1 woman). Expenses: Contact institution. *Financial support:* In 2016–17, 210 students received support, including 80 fellowships with full tuition reimbursements available (averaging $3,515 per year), 168 research assistantships with full tuition reimbursements available (averaging $11,945 per year), 95 teaching assistantships with full tuition reimbursements available (averaging $12,531 per year); career-related internships or fieldwork, Federal Work-Study, scholarships/grants, health care benefits, tuition waivers (full and partial), and unspecified assistantships also available. Support available to part-time students. Financial award application deadline: 2/1; financial award applicants required to submit FAFSA. In 2016, 95 master's, 20 doctorates awarded. *Program availability:* Part-time. Offers biochemistry (MS); biological science (MS, MTA, PhD); chemical engineering (ME, MSE, PhD); chemistry (MS, PhD); computer engineering (ME, MSE, PhD); computer science (MS, PhD); cyber security (MS); electrical engineering (ME, MSE); engineering and natural sciences (ME, MS, MSE, MTA, PhD); engineering physics (MS); geophysics (MS); geosciences (MS, PhD); mathematics (MS, MTA, PhD); mechanical engineering (ME, MSE, PhD); petroleum engineering (ME, MSE, PhD); physics (MS, PhD). *Application deadline:* Applications are processed on a rolling basis. *Application fee:* $55. Electronic applications accepted. *Application Contact:* Graduate School, 918-631-2336, Fax: 918-631-2156, E-mail: grad@utulsa.edu. *Dean,* Dr. James Sorem, 918-631-2288, E-mail: james-sorem@utulsa.edu.

Collins College of Business Students: 71 full-time (29 women), 162 part-time (36 women); includes 32 minority (7 Black or African American, non-Hispanic/Latino; 4 American Indian or Alaska Native, non-Hispanic/Latino; 7 Asian, non-Hispanic/Latino; 10 Hispanic/Latino; 4 Two or more races, non-Hispanic/Latino), 28 international. Average age 31. 281 applicants, 42% accepted, 56 enrolled. *Faculty:* 42 full-time (27 women), 2 part-time/adjunct (0 women). Expenses: Contact institution. *Financial support:* In 2016–17, 40 students received support, including 1 fellowship with tuition reimbursement available (averaging $10,500 per year), 1 research assistantship with full tuition reimbursement available (averaging $6,759 per year), 46 teaching assistantships with full tuition reimbursements available (averaging $9,451 per year); career-related internships or fieldwork, Federal Work-Study, institutionally sponsored loans, scholarships/grants, health care benefits, tuition waivers (full and partial), and unspecified assistantships also available. Support available to part-time students. Financial award application deadline: 2/1; financial award applicants required to submit FAFSA. In 2016, 107 master's awarded. *Program availability:* Part-time, evening/weekend, 100% online. Offers accounting (M Acc); business (M Acc, MBA, MEB, MS); business administration (MBA); corporate finance (MS); energy business (MEB); investments and portfolio management (MS); risk management (MS). *Application deadline:* Applications are processed on a rolling basis. *Application fee:* $55. Electronic applications accepted. *Application Contact:* Information Contact, 918-631-2242, E-mail: graduate-business@utulsa.edu. *Dean,* Dr. W. Gale Sullenburger, 918-631-2213, E-mail: gale-sullenberger@utulsa.edu.

Kendall College of Arts and Sciences Students: 143 full-time (90 women), 37 part-time (21 women); includes 40 minority (3 Black or African American, non-Hispanic/Latino; 6 American Indian or Alaska Native, non-Hispanic/Latino; 16 Asian, non-Hispanic/Latino; 11 Hispanic/Latino; 4 Two or more races, non-Hispanic/Latino), 5 international. Average age 29. 309 applicants, 28% accepted, 46 enrolled. *Faculty:* 65 full-time (30 women), 9 part-time/adjunct (5 women). Expenses: Contact institution. *Financial support:* In 2016–17, 118 students received support, including 32 fellowships with full tuition reimbursements available (averaging $9,582 per year), 18 research assistantships with full tuition reimbursements available (averaging $14,127 per year), 107 teaching assistantships with full tuition reimbursements available (averaging $13,106 per year); career-related internships or fieldwork, Federal Work-Study, scholarships/grants, traineeships, health care benefits, tuition waivers (full and partial), and unspecified assistantships also available. Support available to part-time students. Financial award application deadline: 2/1; financial award applicants required to submit FAFSA. In 2016, 54 master's, 16 doctorates awarded. *Program availability:* Part-time, evening/weekend. Offers anthropology (MA, PhD); art (MTA); arts and sciences (M Ed, MA, MFA, MS, MSMSE, MTA, PhD); biology (MTA); clinical psychology (MA, PhD); education (M Ed); educational studies (MA); elementary certification (M Ed); English (MTA); English language and literature (MA, PhD); history (MA, MTA); industrial/organizational psychology (MA, PhD); mathematics (MA, MTA); mathematics and science education (MSMSE); secondary certification (M Ed); teaching arts (MTA). *Application deadline:* Applications are processed on a rolling basis. *Application fee:* $55. Electronic applications accepted. *Application Contact:* Graduate School, 918-631-2336, Fax: 918-631-2156, E-mail: grad@utulsa.edu. *Dean,* Dr. Kalpana Misra, 918-631-2222, Fax: 918-631-3721, E-mail: kalpana-misra@utulsa.edu.

Oxley College of Health Sciences Students: 40 full-time (38 women), 3 part-time (2 women); includes 7 minority (1 Black or African American, non-Hispanic/Latino; 3 American Indian or Alaska Native, non-Hispanic/Latino; 1 Asian, non-Hispanic/Latino; 2 Hispanic/Latino), 2 international. Average age 25. 99 applicants, 41% accepted, 19 enrolled. Expenses: Contact institution. *Financial support:* In 2016–17, 26 students received support, including 3 fellowships with full tuition reimbursements available (averaging $13,346 per year), 23 teaching assistantships with full tuition reimbursements available (averaging $9,182 per year); career-related internships or fieldwork, Federal Work-Study, scholarships/grants, traineeships, health care benefits, tuition waivers (full and partial), and unspecified assistantships also available. Support available to part-time students. In 2016, 17 master's awarded. Offers adult-gerontology acute care nurse practitioner (DNP); communication sciences and disorders (MS); family nurse practitioner (DNP); health sciences (MAT, MS, DNP); kinesiology and rehabilitative sciences (MAT). *Application fee:* $55. Electronic applications accepted. *Application Contact:* Graduate School, 918-631-2336, Fax: 918-631-2156, E-mail: grad@utulsa.edu. *Interim Dean,* Robin Ploeger, 918-631-3170, E-mail: robin-ploeger@utulsa.edu.

UNIVERSITY OF UTAH, Salt Lake City, UT 84112-1107

General Information State-supported, coed, university. CGS member. *Enrollment:* 31,860 graduate, professional, and undergraduate students; 6,192 full-time matriculated graduate/professional students (2,872 women), 1,879 part-time matriculated graduate/professional students (812 women). *Enrollment by degree level:* 4,073 master's, 3,998 doctoral. *Graduate faculty:* 1,421 full-time (469 women), 1,887 part-time/adjunct (789 women). Tuition, state resident: full-time $7011; part-time $3918.24 per credit hour. Tuition, nonresident: full-time $22,154; part-time $11,665.42 per credit hour. *Graduate housing:* Rooms and/or apartments available on a first-come, first-served basis to single and married students. Typical cost: $4874 per year ($9406 including board) for single students. Room and board charges vary according to board plan and housing facility selected. Housing application deadline: 4/1. *Student services:* Campus employment opportunities, campus safety program, career counseling, child daycare facilities, exercise/wellness program, free psychological counseling, grant writing training, international student services, low-cost health insurance, multicultural affairs office, services for students with disabilities, teacher training, writing training.

Library facilities: J. Willard Marriott Library plus 3 others. *Collection:* Books: 3.2 million (physical), 460,000 (digital/electronic); Serial titles: 530 (physical), 11,500 (digital/electronic); Databases: 320. Weekly public service hours: 111; students can reserve study rooms. *Research affiliation:* Watson Laboratory (pharmaceutical research), Myriad Genetics (pharmaceutical research/manufacturing), Neuropsychiatric Institute (brain research, mental health and substance abuse treatment), ARUP Laboratories (medical research), John A. Moran Eye Center (vision treatment and research).

Computer facilities: 1,099 computers available on campus for general student use. A campuswide network can be accessed from student residence rooms and from off campus. Online class registration, online classes are available.
Website: http://www.utah.edu/

General Application Contact: 801-581-7283, Fax: 801-585-7864, E-mail: graduate@sa.utah.edu.

GRADUATE UNITS

Graduate School Students: 6,200 full-time (2,876 women), 1,879 part-time (812 women); includes 1,245 minority (80 Black or African American, non-Hispanic/Latino; 22 American Indian or Alaska Native, non-Hispanic/Latino; 371 Asian, non-Hispanic/Latino; 516 Hispanic/Latino; 12 Native Hawaiian or other Pacific Islander, non-Hispanic/Latino; 244 Two or more races, non-Hispanic/Latino), 1,289 international. Average age 30. 9,370 applicants, 38% accepted, 2511 enrolled. *Faculty:* 937 full-time (334 women), 783 part-time/adjunct (361 women). Expenses: Contact institution. *Financial support:* Fellowships with tuition reimbursements, research assistantships with tuition reimbursements, teaching assistantships with tuition reimbursements, career-related internships or fieldwork, Federal Work-Study, institutionally sponsored loans, scholarships/grants, traineeships, health care benefits, tuition waivers (full and partial), and unspecified assistantships available. Support available to part-time students. Financial award application deadline: 2/1; financial award applicants required to submit FAFSA. In 2016, 1,907 master's, 715 doctorates awarded. *Program availability:* Part-time, evening/weekend, online learning. Offers biostatistics (M Stat); biotechnology (PSM); computational science (PSM); econometrics (M Stat); educational psychology (M Stat); environmental science (PSM); mathematics (M Stat); science instrumentation (PSM); sociology (M Stat). *Application deadline:* For fall admission, 4/1 for domestic and international students; for spring admission, 11/1 for domestic and international students. *Application fee:* $55 ($65 for international students). Electronic applications accepted. *Application Contact:* Admissions Office, 801-581-7283, Fax: 801-585-7864, E-mail: graduate@sa.utah.edu. *Dean,* Dr. David Kieda, 801-581-6926, Fax: 801-585-7864, E-mail: dave.kieda@utah.edu.

College of Architecture and Planning Students: 103 full-time (30 women), 20 part-time (5 women); includes 17 minority (2 Black or African American, non-Hispanic/Latino; 1 American Indian or Alaska Native, non-Hispanic/Latino; 3 Asian, non-Hispanic/Latino; 8 Hispanic/Latino; 3 Two or more races, non-Hispanic/Latino), 16 international. Average age 30. 100 applicants, 91% accepted, 50 enrolled. *Faculty:* 18 full-time (9 women), 21 part-time/adjunct (6 women). Expenses: Contact institution. *Financial support:* Fellowships with tuition reimbursements, research assistantships with tuition reimbursements, teaching assistantships with partial tuition reimbursements, career-related internships or fieldwork, Federal Work-Study, institutionally sponsored loans, scholarships/grants, and unspecified assistantships available. Financial award application deadline: 1/1; financial award applicants required to submit FAFSA. In 2016, 48 master's, 3 doctorates awarded. *Program availability:* Part-time. Offers architectural studies (MS); architecture (M Arch); architecture and planning (M Arch, MCMP, MS, PhD); city and metropolitan planning (MCMP); metropolitan planning, policy and design (PhD). *Application deadline:* For fall admission, 1/1 for domestic students, 12/1 for international students. *Application fee:* $55 ($65 for international students). Electronic applications accepted. *Application Contact:* Saolo Utu, Recruitment and Admissions, 801-585-2361, Fax: 801-581-8217, E-mail: recruitment@arch.utah.edu. *Dean,* Dr. Keith Diaz Moore, 801-585-1766, Fax: 801-581-8217, E-mail: diazmoore@arch.utah.edu.

College of Education Students: 298 full-time (214 women), 309 part-time (213 women); includes 158 minority (16 Black or African American, non-Hispanic/Latino; 4 American Indian or Alaska Native, non-Hispanic/Latino; 17 Asian, non-Hispanic/Latino; 95 Hispanic/Latino; 1 Native Hawaiian or other Pacific Islander, non-Hispanic/Latino; 25 Two or more races, non-Hispanic/Latino), 10 international. Average age 33. 521 applicants, 46% accepted, 207 enrolled. *Faculty:* 52 full-time (32 women), 29 part-time/adjunct (24 women). Expenses: Contact institution. *Financial support:* Fellowships with tuition reimbursements, research assistantships with tuition reimbursements, teaching assistantships with tuition reimbursements, career-related internships or fieldwork, Federal Work-Study, institutionally sponsored loans, scholarships/grants, health care benefits, tuition waivers (full), and unspecified assistantships available. Support available to part-time students. Financial award application deadline: 2/1; financial award applicants required to submit FAFSA. In 2016, 125 master's, 25 doctorates awarded. Offers clinical mental health counseling (M Ed); counseling psychology (PhD); deaf and hard of hearing (M Ed); deaf/blind (M Ed, MS); early childhood deaf and hard of hearing (MS); early childhood special education (M Ed, MS, PhD); early childhood vision impairments (M Ed); education (M Ed, M Stat, MA, MS, Ed D, PhD, Ed S); education, culture, and society (M Ed, MA, MS, PhD); educational leadership and policy (Ed D, PhD); elementary education (M Ed); instructional design and educational technology (M Ed); instructional design and technology (MS); K-12 school administration (M Ed); K-12 teacher instructional leadership (M Ed); learning and cognition (MS, PhD); mild/moderate disabilities (M Ed, MS, PhD); reading and literacy (M Ed, PhD); school counseling (M Ed); school psychology (M Ed, PhD, Ed S); severe disabilities (M Ed, MS, PhD); statistics (M Stat); student affairs (M Ed); visual impairment (M Ed, MS). *Application deadline:* For fall admission, 2/15 for domestic and international students; for spring admission, 11/1 for domestic and international students. *Application fee:* $55 ($65 for international students). Electronic applications accepted. *Dean,* Maria E. Franquiz, 801-581-8221, E-mail: maria.franquiz@utah.edu.

College of Engineering Students: 948 full-time (219 women), 282 part-time (42 women); includes 111 minority (6 Black or African American, non-Hispanic/Latino; 55 Asian, non-Hispanic/Latino; 23 Hispanic/Latino; 1 Native Hawaiian or other Pacific Islander, non-Hispanic/Latino; 26 Two or more races, non-Hispanic/Latino), 560 international. Average age 28. 2,280 applicants, 42% accepted, 418 enrolled. *Faculty:* 146 full-time (22 women), 73 part-time/adjunct (10 women). Expenses: Contact institution. *Financial support:* Fellowships with full tuition reimbursements, research assistantships with tuition reimbursements, teaching assistantships with tuition reimbursements, career-related internships or fieldwork, Federal Work-Study, institutionally sponsored loans, scholarships/grants, traineeships, health care benefits, tuition waivers (full and partial), and unspecified assistantships available. Support available to part-time students. Financial award applicants required to submit FAFSA. In 2016, 288 master's, 80 doctorates awarded. *Program availability:* Part-time, evening/weekend. Offers bioengineering (MS, PhD); chemical engineering (MS, PhD); civil and environmental engineering (MS, PhD); computational engineering and science (MS); computer science (MS, PhD); computing (MS, PhD); electrical and computer engineering (MS, PhD); electrical engineering (ME); engineering (ME, MEAE, MS, PhD); game art (MEAE); game engineering (MEAE); game production (MEAE); materials science and engineering (MS, PhD); mechanical engineering (MS, PhD); nuclear engineering (MS, PhD); petroleum engineering (MS); technical art (MEAE). *Application fee:* $55 ($65 for international students). Electronic applications accepted. *Application Contact:* Megan Shannahan, Direct Admission and Graduate Coordinator, 801-581-8954, Fax: 801-581-8692, E-mail: megan.shannahan@utah.edu. *Dean,* Dr. Richard B. Brown, 801-585-7498, E-mail: brown@utah.edu.

College of Fine Arts Students: 119 full-time (70 women), 32 part-time (14 women); includes 21 minority (1 American Indian or Alaska Native, non-Hispanic/Latino; 6 Asian, non-Hispanic/Latino; 8 Hispanic/Latino; 6 Two or more races, non-Hispanic/Latino), 26 international. Average age 31. 222 applicants, 44% accepted, 52 enrolled. *Faculty:* 75 full-time (35 women), 132 part-time/adjunct (61 women). Expenses: Contact institution. *Financial support:* Fellowships with tuition reimbursements, research assistantships with tuition reimbursements, teaching assistantships with tuition reimbursements, career-related internships or fieldwork, Federal Work-Study, institutionally sponsored loans, scholarships/grants, health care benefits, tuition waivers (partial), and unspecified assistantships available. Financial award applicants required to submit FAFSA. In 2016, 37 master's, 13 doctorates awarded. Offers art history (MA); ceramics (MFA); choral conducting (M Mus, DMA); collaborative piano (M Mus); community-based art education (MFA); composition (M Mus, PhD); dance (MFA, Certificate); drawing (MFA); film and media arts (MFA); fine arts (M Mus, MA, MFA, DMA, PhD, Certificate); graphic design (MFA); instrumental conducting (M Mus, DMA); instrumental performance (M Mus, DMA); jazz studies (M Mus); music education (M Mus, PhD); music history and literature (M Mus); musicology (MA); organ performance (M Mus); painting (MFA); photography/digital imaging (MFA); piano performance (M Mus, DMA); piano performance and pedagogy (M Mus); printmaking (MFA); sculpture/intermedia (MFA); string performance and pedagogy (M Mus); theory (M Mus); vocal performance (DMA). *Application fee:* $55 ($65 for international students). *Application Contact:* Sarah Projansky, Associate Dean for Faculty and Academic Affairs, 801-581-6764, E-mail: sarah.projansky@utah.edu. *Dean and Associate Vice-President for the Arts,* Dr. Raymond Tymas Jones, 801-581-3887, Fax: 801-581-3066, E-mail: r.tymasjones@utah.edu.

College of Health Students: 578 full-time (399 women), 78 part-time (53 women); includes 83 minority (6 Black or African American, non-Hispanic/Latino; 2 American Indian or Alaska Native, non-Hispanic/Latino; 12 Asian, non-Hispanic/Latino; 39 Hispanic/Latino; 4 Native Hawaiian or other Pacific Islander, non-Hispanic/Latino; 20 Two or more races, non-Hispanic/Latino), 24 international. Average age 28. 1,167 applicants, 26% accepted, 211 enrolled. *Faculty:* 39 full-time (19 women), 72 part-time/adjunct (50 women). Expenses: Contact institution. *Financial support:* Fellowships with tuition reimbursements, research assistantships with tuition reimbursements, teaching assistantships with tuition reimbursements, career-related internships or fieldwork, Federal Work-Study, institutionally sponsored loans, scholarships/grants, traineeships, health care benefits, tuition waivers (partial), and unspecified assistantships available. Financial award applicants required to submit FAFSA. In 2016, 141 master's, 83 doctorates awarded. Offers audiology (Au D, PhD); health (M Phil, MA, MOT, MS, Au D, DPT, Ed D, OTD, PhD); health promotion and education (M Phil, MS, Ed D, PhD); kinesiology (MS, PhD); nutrition and integrative physiology (MS, PhD); occupational and recreational therapies (MOT, OTD); parks, recreation, and tourism (M Phil, MS, PhD); physical therapy (DPT); rehabilitation science (PhD); speech-language pathology (MA, MS, PhD). *Application fee:* $55 ($65 for international students). *Application Contact:* Dr. Shari Lindsey, Assistant Dean of Students, Academic Affairs, 801-585-5764, Fax: 801-581-5580, E-mail: shari.lindsey@health.utah.edu. *Dean,* Dr. David H. Perrin, 801-581-8537, Fax: 801-581-5580, E-mail: david.perrin@health.utah.edu.

College of Humanities Students: 166 full-time (100 women), 95 part-time (50 women); includes 46 minority (1 Black or African American, non-Hispanic/Latino; 1 American Indian or Alaska Native, non-Hispanic/Latino; 10 Asian, non-Hispanic/Latino; 22 Hispanic/Latino; 12 Two or more races, non-Hispanic/Latino), 22 international. Average age 34. 523 applicants, 24% accepted, 77 enrolled. *Faculty:* 7,538 full-time (67 women), 56 part-time/adjunct (21 women). Expenses: Contact institution. *Financial support:* In 2016–17, 144 students received support. Fellowships with full tuition reimbursements available, teaching assistantships with tuition reimbursements available, health care benefits, and unspecified assistantships available. Financial award application deadline: 2/1. In 2016, 63 master's, 33 doctorates awarded. Offers Arabic (MA, PhD); Asian studies (MA); communication (MA, MS, PhD); comparative literary and cultural studies (MA, PhD); English (MA, MFA, PhD); environmental humanities (MA, MS); French (MA); Hebrew (MA); history (MA, MS, PhD); humanities (MA, MALP, MFA, MS, PhD); Latin American studies (MA); linguistics (MA, PhD); Persian (MA, PhD); philosophy (MA, MS, PhD); political science (MA, PhD); Spanish (MA, MALP); world languages (MA). *Application deadline:* For fall admission, 4/1 for domestic and international students; for spring admission, 11/1 for domestic and international students. *Application fee:* $55 ($65 for international students). Electronic applications accepted. *Application Contact:* Dr. Stuart Culver, Associate Dean, 801-581-6214, E-mail: stuart.culver@utah.edu. *Dean,* Dr. Dianne Harris, 801-581-8816, E-mail: dianne.harris@utah.edu.

College of Mines and Earth Sciences Students: 140 full-time (43 women), 40 part-time (17 women); includes 17 minority (1 Black or African American, non-Hispanic/Latino; 1 American Indian or Alaska Native, non-Hispanic/Latino; 4 Asian, non-Hispanic/Latino; 9 Hispanic/Latino; 2 Two or more races, non-Hispanic/Latino), 57 international. Average age 28. 354 applicants, 23% accepted, 47 enrolled. *Faculty:* 47 full-time (7 women), 29 part-time/adjunct (5 women). Expenses: Contact institution. *Financial support:* Fellowships with full tuition reimbursements, research assistantships with full tuition reimbursements, teaching assistantships with full tuition reimbursements, career-related internships or fieldwork, institutionally sponsored loans, scholarships/grants, and unspecified assistantships available. Support available to part-time students. Financial award application deadline: 2/15; financial award applicants required to submit FAFSA. In 2016, 36 master's, 11 doctorates awarded. *Program availability:* Part-time. Offers atmospheric sciences (MS, PhD); environmental engineering (ME, MS, PhD); geological engineering (ME, MS, PhD); geology (MS, PhD); geophysics (MS, PhD); metallurgical engineering (ME, MS, PhD); mines and earth sciences (ME, MS, PhD); mining engineering (ME, MS, PhD). *Application deadline:* For fall admission, 4/1 for domestic and international students; for spring admission, 11/1 for domestic and international students. *Application fee:* $55 ($65 for international students). Electronic applications accepted. *Application Contact:* Anita Austin Tromp, Executive Assistant to the Dean, 801-581-8767, Fax:

801-581-5560, E-mail: anita.austin@utah.edu. *Dean,* Dr. Francis H. Brown, 801-581-8767, Fax: 801-581-5560, E-mail: frank.brown@utah.edu.

College of Nursing Students: 294 full-time (221 women), 54 part-time (44 women); includes 53 minority (10 Black or African American, non-Hispanic/Latino; 1 American Indian or Alaska Native, non-Hispanic/Latino; 16 Asian, non-Hispanic/Latino; 18 Hispanic/Latino; 1 Native Hawaiian or other Pacific Islander, non-Hispanic/Latino; 7 Two or more races, non-Hispanic/Latino), 9 international. Average age 36. 273 applicants, 58% accepted, 129 enrolled. *Faculty:* 25 full-time (24 women), 83 part-time/adjunct (72 women). Expenses: Contact institution. *Financial support:* In 2016–17, 77 students received support, including 77 fellowships with tuition reimbursements available, 4 research assistantships with tuition reimbursements available, 9 teaching assistantships with partial tuition reimbursements available; scholarships/grants, traineeships, health care benefits, and unspecified assistantships also available. Support available to part-time students. Financial award application deadline: 1/15; financial award applicants required to submit FAFSA. In 2016, 33 master's, 65 doctorates awarded. *Program availability:* Part-time, online learning. Offers gerontology (MS, Certificate); nursing (MS, DNP, PhD, Certificate). *Application deadline:* For fall admission, 1/15 for domestic and international students; for spring admission, 11/1 for domestic and international students. *Application fee:* $55 ($65 for international students). Electronic applications accepted. *Application Contact:* Carrie Radmall, Associate Director of Student Services, 801-581-8798, Fax: 801-585-9705, E-mail: carrie.radmall@nurs.utah.edu. *Dean,* Patricia Morton, PhD, 801-581-8262, Fax: 801-585-9705, E-mail: trish.morton@nurs.utah.edu.

College of Pharmacy Students: 265 full-time (132 women), 13 part-time (2 women); includes 82 minority (2 Black or African American, non-Hispanic/Latino; 58 Asian, non-Hispanic/Latino; 11 Hispanic/Latino; 11 Two or more races, non-Hispanic/Latino), 21 international. Average age 27. 198 applicants, 39% accepted, 59 enrolled. *Faculty:* 30 full-time (9 women), 42 part-time/adjunct (25 women). Expenses: Contact institution. *Financial support:* In 2016–17, fellowships with full tuition reimbursements (averaging $25,000 per year), research assistantships with full tuition reimbursements (averaging $25,000 per year), teaching assistantships (averaging $1,500 per year) were awarded; scholarships/grants, health care benefits, tuition waivers (full), and unspecified assistantships also available. In 2016, 3 master's, 66 doctorates awarded. Offers health system pharmacy administration (MS); medicinal chemistry (MS, PhD); outcomes research and health policy (PhD); pharmaceutics and pharmaceutical chemistry (PhD); pharmacology and toxicology (PhD); pharmacy (MS, PhD, Pharm D). *Application deadline:* For fall admission, 12/1 for domestic and international students. *Application fee:* $55 ($65 for international students). *Application Contact:* Dr. Madeline Marshall, Academic Advisor, 801-581-6731, Fax: 801-581-3716, E-mail: pharmd.admissions@pharm.utah.edu. *Interim Dean,* Dr. Kristen A. Keefe, 801-581-6731, Fax: 801-581-3716.

College of Science Students: 399 full-time (149 women), 136 part-time (45 women); includes 46 minority (3 Black or African American, non-Hispanic/Latino; 1 American Indian or Alaska Native, non-Hispanic/Latino; 17 Asian, non-Hispanic/Latino; 19 Hispanic/Latino; 6 Two or more races, non-Hispanic/Latino), 172 international. Average age 28. 772 applicants, 30% accepted, 97 enrolled. *Faculty:* 151 full-time (27 women), 88 part-time/adjunct (26 women). Expenses: Contact institution. *Financial support:* Fellowships with full tuition reimbursements, research assistantships with full tuition reimbursements, teaching assistantships with full tuition reimbursements, career-related internships or fieldwork, Federal Work-Study, institutionally sponsored loans, scholarships/grants, traineeships, health care benefits, tuition waivers (full), and unspecified assistantships available. Financial award application deadline: 2/15; financial award applicants required to submit FAFSA. In 2016, 61 master's, 45 doctorates awarded. *Program availability:* Part-time. Offers biology (MS, PhD); chemical physics (PhD); chemistry (MS, PhD); mathematics (MA, MS, PhD); mathematics teaching (MS); medical physics (MS, PhD); physics (MA, MS, PhD); physics teaching (PhD); science (M Stat, MA, MS, PhD); science teacher education (MS); statistics (M Stat). *Application deadline:* For fall admission, 4/1 for domestic and international students; for spring admission, 11/1 for domestic and international students. *Application fee:* $55 ($65 for international students). Electronic applications accepted. *Application Contact:* Lisa Batchelder, Administrative Program Coordinator, 801-581-3374, E-mail: office@science.utah.edu. *Dean,* Dr. Henry S. White, 801-581-6958, Fax: 801-585-3169, E-mail: white@chem.utah.edu.

College of Social and Behavioral Science Students: 264 full-time (152 women), 246 part-time (118 women); includes 78 minority (7 Black or African American, non-Hispanic/Latino; 1 American Indian or Alaska Native, non-Hispanic/Latino; 16 Asian, non-Hispanic/Latino; 38 Hispanic/Latino; 16 Two or more races, non-Hispanic/Latino), 56 international. Average age 32. 219 applicants, 40% accepted, 40 enrolled. *Faculty:* 133 full-time (53 women), 66 part-time/adjunct (23 women). Expenses: Contact institution. *Financial support:* Fellowships with tuition reimbursements, research assistantships with tuition reimbursements, teaching assistantships with tuition reimbursements, career-related internships or fieldwork, Federal Work-Study, scholarships/grants, health care benefits, and unspecified assistantships available. Financial award application deadline: 2/1; financial award applicants required to submit FAFSA. In 2016, 133 master's, 27 doctorates awarded. Offers American politics (MA, MS, PhD); anthropology (M Phil, MA, MS, PhD); clinical psychology (PhD); comparative politics (MA, MS, PhD); econometrics (M Stat); economics (M Phil, MA, MS, PhD); geographic information science (MS); geography (MS, PhD); human development and social policy (MS); international affairs and global enterprise (MS); international relations (MA, MS, PhD); political science (MA, MS, PhD); political theory (MA, MS, PhD); psychology (PhD); public administration (Exec MPA, MPA); public policy (MPP); social and behavioral science (Exec MPA, M Phil, M Stat, MA, MPA, MPP, MS, PhD); sociology (M Stat, MA, MS, PhD). *Application fee:* $55 ($65 for international students). *Application Contact:* Richard Foster, Interim Associate Dean, 801-581-8620, Fax: 801-585-5081, E-mail: rick.forster@csbs.utah.edu. *Interim Dean,* Cynthia Berg, 801-581-8620, Fax: 801-585-5081, E-mail: cynthia.berg@csbs.utah.edu.

College of Social Work Students: 304 full-time (232 women), 31 part-time (27 women); includes 82 minority (5 Black or African American, non-Hispanic/Latino; 4 American Indian or Alaska Native, non-Hispanic/Latino; 9 Asian, non-Hispanic/Latino; 43 Hispanic/Latino; 1 Native Hawaiian or other Pacific Islander, non-Hispanic/Latino; 20 Two or more races, non-Hispanic/Latino), 4 international. Average age 33. 254 applicants, 71% accepted, 135 enrolled. *Faculty:* 18 full-time (10 women), 38 part-time/adjunct (26 women). Expenses: Contact institution. *Financial support:* In 2016–17, 55 students received support, including 19 fellowships with tuition reimbursements available (averaging $8,505 per year), 14 research assistantships with tuition reimbursements available (averaging $14,250 per year), 8 teaching assistantships with partial tuition reimbursements available (averaging $3,250 per year); career-related internships or fieldwork, scholarships/grants, and unspecified assistantships also available. Financial award application deadline: 3/15; financial award applicants required to submit FAFSA. In 2016, 176 master's, 5 doctorates awarded. *Program availability:* Part-time, evening/weekend. Offers social work (MSW, PhD). *Application deadline:* For fall admission, 11/1 for domestic and international students. *Application fee:* $55 ($65 for international students). Electronic applications accepted. *Application Contact:* Dr. Mary Jane Taylor, Associate Dean, 801-581-6192, Fax: 801-585-3219, E-mail: hank.liese@socwk.utah.edu. *Interim Dean*, Dr. Hank Liese, 801-581-6192, Fax: 801-585-3219, E-mail: hank.liese@socwk.utah.edu.

David Eccles School of Business Students: 1,018 full-time (296 women), 323 part-time (77 women); includes 157 minority (3 Black or African American, non-Hispanic/Latino; 1 American Indian or Alaska Native, non-Hispanic/Latino; 41 Asian, non-Hispanic/Latino; 84 Hispanic/Latino; 2 Native Hawaiian or other Pacific Islander, non-Hispanic/Latino; 26 Two or more races, non-Hispanic/Latino), 227 international. Average age 30. 1,122 applicants, 74% accepted, 580 enrolled. *Faculty:* 64 full-time (22 women), 45 part-time/adjunct (10 women). Expenses: Contact institution. *Financial support:* Fellowships with partial tuition reimbursements, research assistantships with partial tuition reimbursements, teaching assistantships with tuition reimbursements, scholarships/grants, tuition waivers (full and partial), and unspecified assistantships available. Financial award applicants required to submit FAFSA. In 2016, 604 master's, 6 doctorates awarded. *Program availability:* Part-time, evening/weekend. Offers accounting (PhD); accounting information systems (M Acc); business (EMBA, M Acc, MBA, MHA, MRED, MS, MSF, PMBA, PhD, Graduate Certificate); business administration (EMBA, MBA, PMBA); finance (PhD); financial/audit (M Acc); healthcare administration (MHA); information systems (MS, PhD, Graduate Certificate); marketing (PhD); operations management (PhD); organizational behavior (PhD); real estate development (MRED); strategic management (PhD); tax (M Acc). *Application fee:* $55 ($65 for international students). Electronic applications accepted. *Application Contact:* Andrea Miller, Director of Graduate Admissions, 801-585-7366, E-mail: andrea.miller@business.utah.edu. *Dean*, Dr. Taylor Randall, 801-581-3074, E-mail: dean@business.utah.edu.

School of Dentistry Students: 95 full-time (30 women), 22 part-time (5 women); includes 21 minority (1 Black or African American, non-Hispanic/Latino; 3 Asian, non-Hispanic/Latino; 14 Hispanic/Latino; 3 Two or more races, non-Hispanic/Latino). Average age 26. 775 applicants, 6% accepted, 50 enrolled. *Faculty:* 3 full-time (2 women), 30 part-time/adjunct (4 women). Expenses: Contact institution. *Financial support:* In 2016–17, 7 students received support. Scholarships/grants available. Financial award application deadline: 4/1; financial award applicants required to submit FAFSA. Offers dentistry (DDS). *Application deadline:* For fall admission, 10/1 priority date for domestic students. *Application fee:* $75. Electronic applications accepted. *Application Contact:* Gary W. Lowder, DDS, Office of Admissions, 801-581-8951, Fax: 801-585-6485, E-mail: dental.admissions@hsc.utah.edu. *Dean*, Wyatt R. Hume, PhD, 801-587-1208, Fax: 801-585-6485, E-mail: wyatt.hume@hsc.utah.edu.

School of Medicine Offers biochemistry (MS, PhD); biostatistics (M Stat); experimental pathology (PhD); human genetics (MS, PhD); laboratory medicine and biomedical science (MS); medical informatics (MS, PhD, Certificate); medicine (M Phil, M Stat, MPAS, MPH, MS, MSPH, MD, PhD, Certificate); molecular biology (PhD); neurobiology and anatomy (PhD); neuroscience (PhD); oncological sciences (M Phil, MS, PhD); physician assistant (MPAS); physiology (PhD); public health (MPH, MSPH, PhD).

S. J. Quinney College of Law Students: 294 full-time (127 women), 12 part-time (4 women); includes 36 minority (2 Black or African American, non-Hispanic/Latino; 2 American Indian or Alaska Native, non-Hispanic/Latino; 10 Asian, non-Hispanic/Latino; 21 Hispanic/Latino; 1 Native Hawaiian or other Pacific Islander, non-Hispanic/Latino). Average age 28. 612 applicants, 49% accepted, 93 enrolled. *Faculty:* 32 full-time (13 women), 18 part-time/adjunct (7 women). Expenses: Contact institution. *Financial support:* In 2016–17, 174 students received support, including 165 fellowships with partial tuition reimbursements available (averaging $6,013 per year), 47 research assistantships with partial tuition reimbursements available (averaging $6,721 per year); career-related internships or fieldwork, Federal Work-Study, institutionally sponsored loans, scholarships/grants, and unspecified assistantships also available. Financial award application deadline: 4/7; financial award applicants required to submit FAFSA. In 2016, 124 doctorates awarded. Offers law (LL M, JD). *Application deadline:* For fall admission, 1/15 priority date for domestic students, 2/15 priority date for international students; for winter admission, 3/10 for domestic and international students. Applications are processed on a rolling basis. *Application fee:* $60. Electronic applications accepted. *Application Contact:* Susan Baca, Operations Manager for Admissions and Financial Aid, 801-581-7479, Fax: 801-581-6897, E-mail: susan.baca@law.utah.edu. *Associate Dean for Admissions and Financial Aid*, Reyes Aguilar, Jr., 801-581-6833, Fax: 801-581-6897, E-mail: reyes.aguilar@law.utah.edu.

UNIVERSITY OF VALLEY FORGE, Phoenixville, PA 19460

General Information Independent-religious, coed, comprehensive institution.

GRADUATE UNITS

Program in Christian Leadership Offers Christian leadership (MA).

Program in Music Technology *Program availability:* Online learning. Offers music technology (MM).

Program in Theology Offers theology (MA).

Program in Worship Studies Offers worship studies (MA).

UNIVERSITY OF VERMONT, Burlington, VT 05405

General Information State-supported, coed, university. CGS member. *Enrollment:* 13,105 graduate, professional, and undergraduate students; 1,485 full-time matriculated graduate/professional students (928 women). *Enrollment by degree level:* 864 master's, 621 doctoral, 23 other advanced degrees. Tuition, state resident: full-time $5814. Tuition, nonresident: full-time $14,670. *Graduate housing:* On-campus housing not available. *Student services:* Career counseling, free psychological counseling, low-cost health insurance. *Library facilities:* Bailey-Howe Library plus 2 others. *Collection:* Books: 3.3 million (physical), 351,994 (digital/electronic); Serial titles: 90,542 (physical). Weekly public service hours: 104; students can reserve study rooms. *Research affiliation:* Miner Institute (animal sciences).

Computer facilities: Computer purchase and lease plans are available. 850 computers available on campus for general student use. A campuswide network can be accessed from student residence rooms and from off campus. Online class registration, Web pages, online course support are available. Website: http://www.uvm.edu/

General Application Contact: Kimberly Hess, Director of Admissions and Enrollment Management, 802-656-2699, Fax: 802-656-0519, E-mail: graduate.admissions@uvm.edu.

GRADUATE UNITS

College of Medicine Offers medicine (MS, MD, PhD, Certificate).

Graduate Programs in Medicine Offers clinical and translational science (MS, PhD, Certificate); medicine (MS, PhD, Certificate); neuroscience (PhD); pathology and laboratory medicine (MS); pharmacology (MS, PhD). Electronic applications accepted.

Graduate College Students: 1,485 full-time (928 women); includes 86 minority (11 Black or African American, non-Hispanic/Latino; 2 American Indian or Alaska Native, non-Hispanic/Latino; 25 Asian, non-Hispanic/Latino; 36 Hispanic/Latino; 1 Native Hawaiian or other Pacific Islander, non-Hispanic/Latino; 11 Two or more races, non-Hispanic/Latino), 141 international. 1,997 applicants, 47% accepted, 396 enrolled. Expenses: Contact institution. *Financial support:* Fellowships, research assistantships, teaching assistantships, career-related internships or fieldwork, Federal Work-Study, traineeships, tuition waivers (full and partial), and analytical assistantships available. Support available to part-time students. In 2016, 243 master's, 69 doctorates awarded. *Program availability:* Part-time, online learning. Offers cellular, molecular and biomedical sciences (PhD). *Application deadline:* For fall admission, 4/1 priority date for domestic and international students; for spring admission, 11/15 priority date for domestic and international students. Applications are processed on a rolling basis. *Application fee:* $65. Electronic applications accepted. *Application Contact:* 802-656-2699, E-mail: graduate.admissions@uvm.edu.

College of Agriculture and Life Sciences Students: 116 full-time (77 women); includes 3 minority (1 Black or African American, non-Hispanic/Latino; 2 Asian, non-Hispanic/Latino), 13 international. Average age 25. 139 applicants, 60% accepted, 39 enrolled. Expenses: Contact institution. *Financial support:* Fellowships, research assistantships, teaching assistantships, career-related internships or fieldwork, Federal Work-Study, and tuition waivers (full and partial) available. Financial award application deadline: 3/1. In 2016, 19 master's, 8 doctorates awarded. *Program availability:* Part-time. Offers agriculture and life sciences (MPA, MS, MSD, PhD); animal sciences (MS); animal, nutrition and food sciences (PhD); community development and applied economics (MS); dietetics (MSD); field naturalist (MS); food systems (MS, MS); nutritional sciences (MS); plant and soil science (MS, PhD); plant biology (MS, PhD); public administration (MPA). *Application fee:* $65. Electronic applications accepted. *Application Contact:* Director of Graduate Admissions, 802-656-2699, Fax: 802-656-0519, E-mail: graduate.admissions@uvm.edu. *Dean*, Dr. Thomas C. Vogelmann, 802-656-0321.

College of Arts and Sciences *Program availability:* Part-time. Offers arts and sciences (MA, MS, MST, PhD); biology (MS, PhD); biology education (MST); chemistry (MS, PhD); clinical psychology (PhD); English (MA); geology (MS); German (MA); historic preservation (MS); history (MA); physics (MS); psychology (PhD). Electronic applications accepted.

College of Education and Social Services *Program availability:* Part-time. Offers counseling (MS); curriculum and instruction (MAT); education and social services (M Ed, MAT, MS, MSW, M Ed D, PhD); educational leadership (M Ed); educational leadership and policy studies (Ed D, PhD); higher education and student affairs administration (M Ed); interdisciplinary studies (M Ed); social work (MSW); special education (M Ed). Electronic applications accepted.

College of Engineering and Mathematics *Program availability:* Part-time. Offers bioengineering (PhD); biostatistics (MS); civil and environmental engineering (MS, PhD); computer science (MS, PhD); electrical engineering (MS, PhD); engineering and mathematics (MS, MST, PhD); materials science (MS, PhD); mathematics (MS, MST, PhD); mathematics education (MST); mechanical engineering (MS, PhD); statistics (MS). Electronic applications accepted.

College of Nursing and Health Sciences Offers communication sciences and disorders (MS); nursing (MS, DNP); nursing and health sciences (MS, DNP, DPT); physical therapy (DPT). Electronic applications accepted.

The Rubenstein School of Environment and Natural Resources *Program availability:* Part-time. Offers environment and natural resources (MS, PhD); natural resources (MS, PhD). Electronic applications accepted.

School of Business Administration *Program availability:* Part-time. Offers accounting (M Acc); business administration (M Acc, MBA). Electronic applications accepted.

UNIVERSITY OF VICTORIA, Victoria, BC V8W 2Y2, Canada

General Information Province-supported, coed, university. *Graduate housing:* Rooms and/or apartments available on a first-come, first-served basis to single and married students. Housing application deadline: 2/1. *Research affiliation:* Dominion Astrophysical Observatory, Bamfield Marine Research Station (marine biology), Tri-University Meson Facility, Canada/France/Hawaii Telescope Observatory, Institute of Ocean Sciences (geography, oceanography).

GRADUATE UNITS

Faculty of Graduate Studies *Program availability:* Part-time, online learning. Electronic applications accepted.

Faculty of Education Offers aboriginal communities counseling (M Ed); art education (M Ed, PhD); coaching studies (co-operative education) (M Ed); counseling (M Ed, MA); curriculum studies (M Ed, MA, PhD); early childhood education (M Ed, PhD); education (M Ed, M Sc, MA, PhD); educational psychology (M Ed, MA, PhD); educational studies (PhD); kinesiology (M Sc, MA); language and literacy (M Ed, MA, PhD); leadership studies (M Ed, MA); leisure service administration (MA); mathematics (M Ed, MA, PhD); music education (M Ed, MA, PhD); physical education (MA); science (M Ed, MA, PhD); social studies (M Ed, MA); social, cultural and foundational studies (MA, PhD); technology and environmental education (PhD).

Faculty of Engineering Offers computer science (M Sc, PhD); electrical and computer engineering (M Eng, MA Sc, PhD); engineering (M Eng, M Sc, MA Sc, PhD); mechanical engineering (M Eng, MA Sc, PhD).

Faculty of Fine Arts Offers composition (M Mus); design (MFA); digital multimedia (MFA); directing (MFA); drawing (MFA); fine arts (M Mus, MA, MFA, PhD); history in art (MA, PhD); musicology (MA, PhD); musicology with performance (MA); painting (MFA); performance (M Mus); photography (MFA); sculpture (MFA); theatre history (MA); video (MFA); writing (MFA).

Faculty of Human and Social Development Offers advanced nursing practice (advanced practice leadership option) (MN); advanced nursing practice (nurse educator option) (MN); advanced nursing practice (nurse practitioner option) (MN); child and youth care (MA, PhD); dispute resolution (MADR); health information science (M Sc); human and social development (M Sc, MA, MADR, MN, MPA, MSW, PhD); indigenous governance (MA); nursing (PhD); public administration (MPA, PhD); social work (MSW); studies in policy and practice (MA).

Faculty of Humanities Offers applied linguistics (MA); English (MA, PhD); German studies (MA); Greek and Roman studies (MA, PhD); Hispanic and Italian studies (MA); Hispanic studies (MA); history (MA, PhD); humanities (MA, PhD); linguistics (MA, PhD); literature (MA); Pacific and Asian studies (MA); philosophy (MA); teaching emphasis (MA).

Faculty of Science Offers astronomy and astrophysics (M Sc, PhD); biochemistry (M Sc, PhD); biology (M Sc, PhD); chemistry (M Sc, PhD); condensed matter physics (M Sc, PhD); earth and ocean sciences (M Sc, PhD); experimental particle physics (M Sc, PhD); mathematics and statistics (M Sc, MA, PhD); medical physics (M Sc, PhD); microbiology (M Sc, PhD); ocean physics (M Sc, PhD); science (M Sc, MA, PhD); theoretical physics (M Sc, PhD). Electronic applications accepted.

Faculty of Social Sciences Offers anthropology (MA); clinical psychology (PhD); clinical psychology (neuropsychology) (M Sc); cognition and brain science (M Sc, PhD); economics (MA, PhD); experimental neuropsychology (M Sc, PhD); geography (M Sc, MA, PhD); individualized study (M Sc, PhD); life span development psychology (PhD); life span developmental psychology (M Sc); political science (MA, PhD); social psychology (M Sc); social sciences (M Sc, MA, PhD); sociology (MA, PhD).

Peter B. Gustavson School of Business Program availability: Part-time. Offers business (MBA). Electronic applications accepted.

Faculty of Law Program availability: Part-time. Offers law (LL M, JD, PhD). Electronic applications accepted.

UNIVERSITY OF VIRGINIA, Charlottesville, VA 22903

General Information State-supported, coed, university. CGS member. *Enrollment:* 23,883 graduate, professional, and undergraduate students; 6,000 full-time matriculated graduate/professional students (2,787 women), 359 part-time matriculated graduate/professional students (232 women). *Enrollment by degree level:* 2,782 master's, 3,575 doctoral, 2 other advanced degrees. *Graduate faculty:* 2,231 full-time (796 women), 158 part-time/adjunct (101 women). Tuition, state resident: full-time $15,026; part-time $834 per credit hour. Tuition, nonresident: full-time $25,168; part-time $1378 per credit hour. *Required fees:* $2654. *Graduate housing:* Rooms and/or apartments available on a first-come, first-served basis to single and married students. Housing application deadline: 6/1. *Student services:* Campus employment opportunities, campus safety program, career counseling, child daycare facilities, exercise/wellness program, free psychological counseling, grant writing training, international student services, low-cost health insurance, multicultural affairs office, services for students with disabilities, teacher training, writing training. *Library facilities:* Alderman Library plus 14 others. *Collection:* Books: 4.7 million (physical), 521,356 (digital/electronic); Serial titles: 11,783 (physical), 188,351 (digital/electronic); Databases: 1,191. Weekly public service hours: 149; study areas open 24 hours, 5–7 days a week; students can reserve study rooms. *Research affiliation:* Oak Ridge National Laboratory (energy), National Institute of Aerospace, Jefferson National Accelerator Facility (nuclear physics), Federal Executive Institute (leadership development), National Radio Astronomy Observatory, The Judge Advocate General's School, U.S. Army (law).

Computer facilities: Computer purchase and lease plans are available. 250 computers available on campus for general student use. A campuswide network can be accessed from student residence rooms and from off campus. Online class registration, online course management tool are available.
Website: http://www.virginia.edu/

General Application Contact: 434-924-0311.

GRADUATE UNITS

College and Graduate School of Arts and Sciences Students: 1,177 full-time (542 women), 31 part-time (14 women); includes 114 minority (25 Black or African American, non-Hispanic/Latino; 1 American Indian or Alaska Native, non-Hispanic/Latino; 34 Asian, non-Hispanic/Latino; 32 Hispanic/Latino; 22 Two or more races, non-Hispanic/Latino), 354 international. Average age 27. 3,957 applicants, 21% accepted, 324 enrolled. *Faculty:* 648 full-time (239 women), 37 part-time/adjunct (19 women). Expenses: Contact institution. *Financial support:* Fellowships with partial tuition reimbursements, research assistantships, teaching assistantships with tuition reimbursements, career-related internships or fieldwork, Federal Work-Study, institutionally sponsored loans, traineeships, tuition waivers (full and partial), and unspecified assistantships available. Financial award applicants required to submit FAFSA. In 2016, 211 master's, 159 doctorates awarded. *Program availability:* Part-time. Offers anthropology (MA, PhD); art and architectural history (MA, PhD); arts and sciences (MA, MAPE, MFA, MS, PhD); astronomy (MS, PhD); biology (MA, MS, PhD); chemistry (MA, MS, PhD); classics (MA, PhD); creative writing (MFA); drama (MFA); East Asian studies (MA); economics (MA, PhD); English (MA, PhD); environmental sciences (MA, MS, PhD); foreign affairs (MA, PhD); French (MA, PhD); German (MA); government (MA, PhD); history (MA, PhD); linguistics (MA); math education (MA); mathematics (MA, MS, PhD); Middle Eastern and South Asian studies (MA); music (MA, PhD); philosophy (MA, PhD); physics (MA, MS, PhD); physics education (MAPE); psychology (MA, PhD); religion, politics and global society (MA); religious studies (MA, PhD); Slavic languages and literatures (MA, PhD); sociology (MA, PhD); Spanish (MA, PhD); statistics (MS, PhD). *Application deadline:* Applications are processed on a rolling basis. *Application fee:* $60. Electronic applications accepted. *Application Contact:* Dinko Pocanic, Associate Dean for the Graduate School of Arts and Sciences, 434-924-6738, Fax: 434-924-1317, E-mail: gsas.admission@virginia.edu. *Dean,* Ian Baucom, 434-924-4648, Fax: 434-924-1317, E-mail: 9bb4n@virginia.edu.

Curry School of Education Students: 766 full-time (601 women), 99 part-time (60 women); includes 176 minority (52 Black or African American, non-Hispanic/Latino; 49 Asian, non-Hispanic/Latino; 45 Hispanic/Latino; 30 Two or more races, non-Hispanic/Latino), 30 international. Average age 26. 1,140 applicants, 44% accepted, 301 enrolled. *Faculty:* 119 full-time (70 women), 8 part-time/adjunct (6 women). Expenses: Contact institution. *Financial support:* Fellowships, research assistantships, teaching assistantships, and Federal Work-Study available. Financial award application deadline: 1/5; financial award applicants required to submit FAFSA. In 2016, 379 master's, 40 doctorates, 43 other advanced degrees awarded. Offers administration and supervision (M Ed, Ed D, PhD, Ed S); applied developmental science (M Ed, PhD); clinical and school psychology (PhD); counselor education (M Ed, Ed D, PhD, Ed S); curriculum and instruction (M Ed, Ed D, PhD, Ed S); early childhood special education (MT); education (M Ed, MT, Ed D, PhD, Ed S); education evaluation (PhD); educational evaluation (M Ed); educational policy (PhD); educational psychology (M Ed, Ed D, PhD, Ed S); educational research (Ed D, PhD); elementary education (M Ed, MT, Ed D); English education (M Ed, MT, Ed D, PhD); foreign language education (M Ed, MT); gifted education (M Ed); higher education (M Ed, Ed D, PhD, Ed S); instructional technology (M Ed, PhD, Ed S); kinesiology (MT, PhD); math education (PhD); mathematics education (M Ed, Ed D); reading education (PhD); research statistics and evaluation (Ed D); research, statistics and evaluation (PhD); school psychology (Ed D, PhD); science education (Ed D, PhD); social studies education (M Ed, MT, PhD); special education (M Ed, Ed D, PhD, Ed S); speech communication disorders (M Ed); student affairs practice (M Ed); world languages education (MT). *Application deadline:* Applications are processed on a rolling basis. *Application fee:* $60. Electronic applications accepted. *Application Contact:* Eric Molnar, Assistant Director, Admissions and Enrollment Reporting, 434-243-2085, E-mail: eric.molnar@virginia.edu. *Dean,* Robert C. Pianta, 434-924-3334, E-mail: pianta@virginia.edu.

Darden School of Business Students: 905 full-time (312 women), 2 part-time (0 women); includes 172 minority (48 Black or African American, non-Hispanic/Latino; 2 American Indian or Alaska Native, non-Hispanic/Latino; 62 Asian, non-Hispanic/Latino; 43 Hispanic/Latino; 1 Native Hawaiian or other Pacific Islander, non-Hispanic/Latino; 16 Two or more races, non-Hispanic/Latino), 228 international. Average age 30. 2,747 applicants, 31% accepted, 467 enrolled. *Faculty:* 62 full-time (16 women), 3 part-time/adjunct (1 woman). Expenses: Contact institution. *Financial support:* Career-related internships or fieldwork available. Financial award applicants required to submit FAFSA. In 2016, 415 master's awarded. Offers business (MBA, PhD). *Application deadline:* For fall admission, 3/1 for domestic students, 3/2 for international students. Applications are processed on a rolling basis. *Application fee:* $200. Electronic applications accepted. *Application Contact:* Sara Neher, Assistant Dean of MBA Admissions, 434-924-3900, E-mail: darden@virginia.edu. *Dean,* Scott C. Beardsley, 434-924-7481, E-mail: dean@virginia.edu.

Data Science Institute Students: 49 full-time (16 women); includes 11 minority (2 Black or African American, non-Hispanic/Latino; 5 Asian, non-Hispanic/Latino; 2 Hispanic/Latino; 2 Two or more races, non-Hispanic/Latino), 10 international. Average age 25. 437 applicants, 23% accepted, 48 enrolled. Expenses: Contact institution. In 2016, 49 master's awarded. Offers data science (MS). *Application deadline:* Applications are processed on a rolling basis. *Application fee:* $85. *Application Contact:* Steven Boker, Program Director, 434-243-7275, E-mail: boker@virginia.edu. *Director,* Donald E. Brown, 434-982-2074, E-mail: deb@virginia.edu.

Frank Batten Sr. School of Leadership and Public Policy Students: 108 full-time (70 women); includes 21 minority (3 Black or African American, non-Hispanic/Latino; 5 Asian, non-Hispanic/Latino; 5 Hispanic/Latino; 8 Two or more races, non-Hispanic/Latino), 7 international. Average age 24. 200 applicants, 79% accepted, 73 enrolled. *Faculty:* 20 full-time (7 women), 3 part-time/adjunct (1 woman). Expenses: Contact institution. In 2016, 70 master's awarded. Offers leadership and public policy (MPP). *Application deadline:* For fall admission, 2/20 for domestic and international students. Applications are processed on a rolling basis. Electronic applications accepted. *Application Contact:* Patti Edson, Assistant Director of Admissions, 434-982-2583, Fax: 434-243-2318, E-mail: patti.edson@virginia.edu. *Dean,* Allan C. Stam, 434-924-0812, Fax: 434-243-2318, E-mail: stam@virginia.edu.

McIntire School of Commerce Students: 230 full-time (103 women); includes 46 minority (11 Black or African American, non-Hispanic/Latino; 20 Asian, non-Hispanic/Latino; 15 Hispanic/Latino), 35 international. Average age 23. 734 applicants, 49% accepted, 245 enrolled. *Faculty:* 69 full-time (23 women), 1 (woman) part-time/adjunct. Expenses: Contact institution. *Financial support:* In 2016–17, 65 students received support. Federal Work-Study, scholarships/grants, and unspecified assistantships available. Financial award application deadline: 2/1; financial award applicants required to submit FAFSA. In 2016, 240 master's awarded. Offers accounting (MS); business analytics (MSC); commerce (MS, MSC, Certificate); finance (MSC); global commerce (MS); global strategic management (MS); international management (Certificate); management of information technology (MS); marketing and management (MSC). *Application deadline:* Applications are processed on a rolling basis. *Application fee:* $75. Electronic applications accepted. *Application Contact:* Emma Candelier, Director of Graduate Recruiting, 434-243-4992, Fax: 434-924-4511, E-mail: ecandelier@virginia.edu. *Dean,* Carl Zeithaml, 877-349-2620, Fax: 434-924-7074, E-mail: mcintiregrad@virginia.edu.

School of Architecture Students: 220 full-time (120 women), 5 part-time (2 women); includes 25 minority (5 Black or African American, non-Hispanic/Latino; 10 Asian, non-Hispanic/Latino; 4 Hispanic/Latino; 6 Two or more races, non-Hispanic/Latino), 83 international. Average age 26. 779 applicants, 41% accepted, 123 enrolled. *Faculty:* 38 full-time (21 women), 3 part-time/adjunct (all women). Expenses: Contact institution. *Financial support:* Fellowships, career-related internships or fieldwork, Federal Work-Study, and institutionally sponsored loans available. Financial award applicants required to submit FAFSA. In 2016, 71 master's awarded. Offers architectural history (M Arch H, PhD); architecture (M Arch, M Arch H, M Land Arch, MUEP, PhD); landscape architecture (M Land Arch); the constructed environment (PhD); urban and environmental planning (MUEP). *Application deadline:* Applications are processed on a rolling basis. *Application fee:* $60. Electronic applications accepted. *Application Contact:* Kristine Nelson, Director of Graduate Admissions and Financial Aid, 434-924-6442, Fax: 434-982-2678, E-mail: arch-admissions@virginia.edu. *Dean,* Ila Berman, 434-924-7019, Fax: 434-982-2678, E-mail: ilb8r@virginia.edu.

School of Engineering and Applied Science Students: 694 full-time (195 women), 49 part-time (13 women); includes 82 minority (8 Black or African American, non-Hispanic/Latino; 46 Asian, non-Hispanic/Latino; 19 Hispanic/Latino; 9 Two or more races, non-Hispanic/Latino), 410 international. Average age 29. 1,816 applicants, 29% accepted, 239 enrolled. *Faculty:* 162 full-time (26 women), 4 part-time/adjunct (1 woman). Expenses: Contact institution. *Financial support:* Fellowships with full tuition reimbursements, research assistantships with full tuition reimbursements, teaching assistantships with full tuition reimbursements, and career-related internships or fieldwork available. Financial award application deadline: 1/15; financial award applicants required to submit FAFSA. In 2016, 136 master's, 57 doctorates awarded. *Program availability:* Part-time, online learning. Offers biomedical engineering (ME, MS, PhD); chemical engineering (ME, MS, PhD); civil and environmental engineering (ME, MS, PhD); computer engineering (ME, MS, PhD); computer science (MCS, MS, PhD); electrical engineering (ME, MS, PhD); engineering and applied science (MCS, ME, MEP, MMSE, MS, PhD); engineering physics (ME, MS, PhD); materials science (MMSE, MS, PhD); mechanical and aerospace engineering (ME, MS, PhD); systems and information engineering (ME, MS, PhD). *Application deadline:* For fall admission, 8/1 for domestic students, 4/1 for international students; for winter admission, 12/1 for domestic students, 8/1 for international students; for spring admission, 5/1 for domestic students, 1/1 for international students. Applications are processed on a rolling basis. Electronic applications accepted. *Application Contact:* Pamela M. Norris, Associate Dean for Research and Graduate Programs, 434-243-7683, Fax: 434-982-3044, E-mail: pamela@virginia.edu. *Dean,* Craig H. Benson, 434-924-3593, Fax: 434-924-3555, E-mail: engrdean@virginia.edu.

School of Law Students: 952 full-time (402 women); includes 190 minority (43 Black or African American, non-Hispanic/Latino; 69 Asian, non-Hispanic/Latino; 36 Hispanic/Latino; 1 Native Hawaiian or other Pacific Islander, non-Hispanic/Latino; 41 Two or more races, non-Hispanic/Latino), 61 international. Average age 25. 5,345 applicants, 21% accepted, 338 enrolled. *Faculty:* 83 full-time (22 women), 5 part-time/adjunct (2 women). Expenses: Contact institution. *Financial support:* Fellowships, career-related internships or fieldwork, Federal Work-Study, and institutionally sponsored loans available. Financial award applicants required to submit FAFSA. In 2016, 49 master's, 330 doctorates awarded. Offers law (LL M, JD, SJD). JD/MA in international relations offered jointly with The Johns Hopkins University. *Application deadline:* For fall admission, 3/1 priority date for domestic students, 3/2 for international students. Applications are processed on a rolling basis. *Application fee:* $75. Electronic applications accepted. *Application Contact:* Grace Applefeld Cleveland, Director of Admissions, 434-243-1456, Fax: 434-982-2128, E-mail: lawadmit@virginia.edu. *Dean,* Risa Goluboff, 434-924-7343, Fax: 434-982-2128, E-mail: goluboff@virginia.edu.

School of Medicine Students: 921 full-time (459 women), 16 part-time (8 women); includes 347 minority (79 Black or African American, non-Hispanic/Latino; 2 American Indian or Alaska Native, non-Hispanic/Latino; 129 Asian, non-Hispanic/Latino; 89 Hispanic/Latino; 2 Native Hawaiian or other Pacific Islander, non-Hispanic/Latino; 46 Two or more races, non-Hispanic/Latino), 49 international. Average age 26. 5,917 applicants, 10% accepted, 230 enrolled. *Faculty:* 1,050 full-time (358 women), 78 part-time/adjunct (52 women). Expenses: Contact institution. *Financial support:* Institutionally sponsored loans and scholarships/grants available. Financial award applicants required to submit FAFSA. In 2016, 50 master's, 172 doctorates awarded. Offers biochemistry (PhD); biological and physical sciences (MS); biophysics (PhD); cell biology (PhD); clinical investigation and patient-oriented research (MS); clinical research (MS); experimental pathology (PhD); informatics in medicine (MS); medicine (MPH, MS, MD, PhD); microbiology, immunology, and cancer biology (PhD); neuroscience (PhD); pharmacology (PhD); physiology (PhD); public health (MPH). *Application deadline:* Applications are processed on a rolling basis. *Application fee:* $80. Electronic applications accepted. *Application Contact:* Randolph J. Canterbury, Senior Associate Dean for Education, 434-243-2522, Fax: 434-982-2586, E-mail: rjc9s@virginia.edu. *Interim Dean,* David S. Wilkes, 434-924-4050, E-mail: dsw4n@virginia.edu.

School of Nursing Students: 167 full-time (138 women), 158 part-time (134 women); includes 75 minority (31 Black or African American, non-Hispanic/Latino; 2 American Indian or Alaska Native, non-Hispanic/Latino; 15 Asian, non-Hispanic/Latino; 15 Hispanic/Latino; 1 Native Hawaiian or other Pacific Islander, non-Hispanic/Latino; 11 Two or more races, non-Hispanic/Latino), 6 international. Average age 35. 179 applicants, 63% accepted, 88 enrolled. *Faculty:* 49 full-time (41 women), 17 part-time/adjunct (16 women). Expenses: Contact institution. *Financial support:* Fellowships, research assistantships, teaching assistantships, Federal Work-Study, and scholarships/grants available. Financial award applicants required to submit FAFSA. In 2016, 122 master's, 25 doctorates awarded. *Program availability:* Part-time. Offers acute and specialty care (MSN); acute care nurse practitioner (MSN); clinical nurse leadership (MSN); community-public health leadership (MSN); nursing (DNP, PhD); psychiatric mental health counseling (MSN). *Application deadline:* Applications are processed on a rolling basis. *Application fee:* $60. Electronic applications accepted. *Application Contact:* Teresa Carroll, Senior Assistant Dean for Academic and Student Services, 434-924-0141, Fax: 434-982-1809, E-mail: nur-osa@virginia.edu. *Dean,* Dorrie K. Fontaine, 434-924-0141, Fax: 434-982-1809, E-mail: dkf2u@virginia.edu.

UNIVERSITY OF WASHINGTON, Seattle, WA 98195

General Information State-supported, coed, university. CGS member. *Graduate housing:* Rooms and/or apartments available on a first-come, first-served basis to single and married students. Housing application deadline: 5/1. *Research affiliation:* Fred Hutchinson Cancer Research Center, Children's Hospital and Regional Medical Center (pediatric research).

GRADUATE UNITS

Graduate School *Program availability:* Part-time, evening/weekend, online learning. Offers biology for teachers (MS); global trade, transportation and logistics studies (Certificate); museology (MA); Near and Middle Eastern studies (PhD); quantitative ecology and resource management (MS, PhD). Electronic applications accepted.

College of Arts and Sciences *Program availability:* Part-time, evening/weekend. Offers acting (MFA); animal behavior (PhD); anthropology (MA, PhD); applied mathematics (MS, PhD); art (MFA); art history (MA, PhD); arts and sciences (MA, MAIS, MAT, MC, MFA, MM, MS, Au D, DMA, PhD); astronomy (MS, PhD); audiology (Au D); biology (PhD); Buddhist studies (MA, PhD); Central Asian studies (MAIS); chemistry (MS, PhD); child psychology (PhD); China studies (MAIS); Chinese language and literature (MA, PhD); choral conducting (MM, DMA); classics (MA, PhD); classics and philosophy (PhD); clinical psychology (PhD); cognition and perception (PhD); communication (MA, MC, PhD); comparative literature (MA, PhD); comparative religion (MAIS); computational linguistics (MS); costume design (MFA); creative writing (MFA); dance (MFA); design (MFA); developmental psychology (PhD); directing (MFA); dramatic theory (PhD); East European studies (MAIS); economics (PhD); English as a second language (MAT); English literature and language (MA, MAT, PhD); ethnomusicology (MA); French (MA, PhD); gender, women and sexuality studies (PhD); geography (MA, PhD); Germanics (MA, PhD); global studies (MAIS); Hispanic literary and cultural studies (MA); history (MA, PhD); industrial design (MFA); international studies (MAIS, PhD); Italian (MA); Japan studies (MAIS); Japanese language and literature (MA, PhD); Korea studies (MAIS); Korean language and literature (MA, PhD); lighting design (MFA); linguistics (MA, PhD); mathematics (MA, MS, PhD); Middle East studies (MAIS); music (MA, MM, DMA, PhD); music education (MA, PhD); music history (MA, PhD); Near Eastern languages and civilization (MA); numerical analysis (MS); optimization (MS); painting and drawing (MFA); philosophy (MA, PhD); photography (MFA); physics (MS, PhD); political science (MA, PhD); quantitative psychology (PhD); Romance linguistics (MA, PhD); Russian literature (MA, PhD); Russian studies (MAIS); Russian, East European and Central Asian studies (MAIS); Scandinavian studies (MA, PhD); scenic design (MFA); Slavic linguistics (MA, PhD); social psychology and personality (PhD); sociology (MA, PhD); South Asian language and literature (MA, PhD); South Asian studies (MAIS); Southeast Asian studies (MAIS); speech and hearing sciences (PhD); speech-language pathology (MS); statistics (MS, PhD); theatre and performance history (PhD); visual communication design (MFA). Electronic applications accepted.

College of Built Environments *Program availability:* Part-time, evening/weekend. Offers architecture (M Arch, MS); built environment (PhD); built environments (M Arch, MLA, MS, MSCM, MUP, PhD, Certificate); construction management (MSCM); design computing (Certificate); design firm leadership and management (Certificate); historic preservation (Certificate); landscape architecture (MLA); lighting (Certificate); urban design (Certificate); urban design and planning (PhD); urban planning (MUP). Electronic applications accepted.

College of Education *Program availability:* Part-time, evening/weekend. Offers curriculum and instruction (M Ed, Ed D, PhD); early childhood special education (M Ed); educational leadership and policy studies (M Ed, Ed D, PhD); educational psychology (M Ed, PhD); emotional and behavioral disabilities (M Ed); human development and cognition (M Ed); instructional leadership (M Ed); intercollegiate athletic leadership (M Ed); learning disabilities (M Ed); learning sciences (M Ed, PhD); low-incidence disabilities (M Ed); measurement, statistics and research design (M Ed); school psychology (M Ed); severe disabilities (M Ed); special education (M Ed, Ed D, PhD); teacher education (MIT). Electronic applications accepted.

College of Engineering Students: 1,581 full-time (481 women), 834 part-time (218 women); includes 510 minority (26 Black or African American, non-Hispanic/Latino; 1

American Indian or Alaska Native, non-Hispanic/Latino; 303 Asian, non-Hispanic/Latino; 114 Hispanic/Latino; 4 Native Hawaiian or other Pacific Islander, non-Hispanic/Latino; 62 Two or more races, non-Hispanic/Latino), 837 international. 7,119 applicants, 27% accepted, 850 enrolled. *Faculty:* 258 full-time (59 women). Expenses: Contact institution. *Financial support:* In 2016–17, 1,065 students received support, including 145 fellowships with full tuition reimbursements available, 660 research assistantships with full tuition reimbursements available, 259 teaching assistantships with full tuition reimbursements available; career-related internships or fieldwork, Federal Work-Study, institutionally sponsored loans, scholarships/grants, traineeships, health care benefits, tuition waivers (full), unspecified assistantships, and stipend supplements also available. Financial award application deadline: 2/28; financial award applicants required to submit FAFSA. In 2016, 562 master's, 131 doctorates awarded. *Program availability:* Part-time, online learning. Offers aeronautics and astronautics (MAE, MSAA, PhD); applied bioengineering (MAB); applied materials science and engineering (MS); bioengineering (MS, PhD); bioengineering and nanotechnology (PhD); chemical engineering (MS, PhD); chemical engineering and advanced data science (PhD); chemical engineering and nanotechnology (PhD); construction engineering (MSCE, PhD); electrical engineering (MS, PhD); electrical engineering and nanotechnology (PhD); engineering (MAB, MAE, MISE, MS, MSAA, MSCE, MSE, MSME, PhD, Certificate); environmental engineering (MSCE, PhD); geotechnical engineering (MSCE, PhD); human centered design and engineering (MS, PhD); hydrology and hydrodynamics (MSCE, PhD); industrial and systems engineering (MISE, MS, PhD); materials science and engineering (MS, PhD); mechanical engineering (MSE, MSME, PhD); pharmaceutical bioengineering (MS); structural engineering and mechanics (MSCE, PhD); transportation engineering (MSCE, PhD); user centered design (Certificate). *Application deadline:* For fall admission, 12/1 for domestic and international students. *Application fee:* $85. Electronic applications accepted. *Application Contact:* Scott Winter, Director, Academic Affairs, 206-685-4074, Fax: 206-685-0666, E-mail: swinter@uw.edu. *Dean of Engineering,* Dr. Michael B. Bragg, 206-543-0340, Fax: 206-685-0666, E-mail: mbragg@uw.edu.

College of the Environment Offers aquatic and fishery sciences (MS, PhD); atmospheric sciences (MS, PhD); biological oceanography (MS, PhD); bioresource science and engineering (MS, PhD); chemical oceanography (MS, PhD); environment (MEH, MFR, MMA, MS, PhD, Graduate Certificate); environmental horticulture (MEH); forest ecology (MS, PhD); forest management (MFR); forest soils (MS, PhD); geology (MS, PhD); geophysics (MS, PhD); marine and environmental affairs (MMA, Graduate Certificate); marine geology and geophysics (MS, PhD); physical oceanography (MS, PhD); restoration ecology (MS, PhD); restoration ecology and environmental horticulture (MS, PhD); social sciences (MS, PhD); sustainable resource management (MS, PhD); wildlife science (MS, PhD). Electronic applications accepted.

Evans School of Public Policy and Governance *Program availability:* Part-time, evening/weekend. Offers public administration (MPA); public policy and management (PhD). Electronic applications accepted.

Information School Students: 367 full-time (233 women), 237 part-time (170 women); includes 132 minority (20 Black or African American, non-Hispanic/Latino; 9 American Indian or Alaska Native, non-Hispanic/Latino; 59 Asian, non-Hispanic/Latino; 41 Hispanic/Latino; 3 Native Hawaiian or other Pacific Islander, non-Hispanic/Latino), 151 international. Average age 32. 1,208 applicants, 39% accepted, 254 enrolled. *Faculty:* 35 full-time (19 women), 22 part-time/adjunct (12 women). Expenses: Contact institution. *Financial support:* In 2016–17, 69 students received support, including 1 fellowship with full tuition reimbursement available (averaging $6,651 per year), 27 research assistantships with full tuition reimbursements available (averaging $19,418 per year), 27 teaching assistantships with full tuition reimbursements available (averaging $19,521 per year); Federal Work-Study, institutionally sponsored loans, scholarships/grants, health care benefits, tuition waivers (full and partial), and unspecified assistantships also available. Support available to part-time students. Financial award application deadline: 10/1; financial award applicants required to submit FAFSA. In 2016, 237 master's, 2 doctorates awarded. *Program availability:* Part-time, 100% online coursework with required attendance at on-campus orientation at start of program. Offers information management (MSIM); information science (PhD); library and information science (MLIS). *Application deadline:* For fall admission, 12/1 priority date for domestic and international students. *Application fee:* $85. Electronic applications accepted. *Application Contact:* Karl Brothers, Admissions Counselor, 206-616-5541, Fax: 206-616-3152, E-mail: kari683@uw.edu. *Dean,* Dr. Harry Bruce, 206-616-0985, E-mail: harryb@uw.edu.

Michael G. Foster School of Business *Program availability:* Part-time, evening/weekend. Offers auditing and assurance (MP Acc); business administration (MBA, PhD); entrepreneurship (MS); executive business administration (MBA); global executive business administration (MBA); information systems (MSIS); supply chain management (MSSCM); taxation (MP Acc); technology management (MBA). Electronic applications accepted.

School of Dentistry Offers dental surgery (DDS); dentistry (MS, MSD, DDS, PhD, Certificate); endodontics (MSD, Certificate); oral biology (MS, MSD, PhD); oral medicine (MSD); orthodontics (MSD, Certificate); pediatric dentistry (MSD, Certificate); periodontics (MSD, PhD, Certificate); prosthodontics (MSD, Certificate).

School of Law Offers Asian law (LL M, PhD); intellectual property law and policy (LL M); law (JD); law of sustainable international development (LL M); taxation (LL M).

School of Medicine *Program availability:* Part-time. Offers biochemistry (PhD); bioethics (MA); biological structure (PhD); biomedical and health informatics (MS, PhD); comparative medicine (MS); experimental and molecular pathology (PhD); genome sciences (PhD); immunology (PhD); laboratory medicine (MS); medicine (MA, MOT, MPO, MS, DPT, MD, PhD); microbiology (PhD); molecular and cellular biology (PhD); neurobiology and behavior (PhD); occupational therapy (MOT); pharmacology (PhD); physical therapy (DPT); physiology and biophysics (PhD); prosthetics and orthotics (MPO); rehabilitation science (PhD). Electronic applications accepted.

School of Nursing *Program availability:* Part-time. Offers nursing (MN, MS, DNP, PhD, Graduate Certificate).

School of Social Work *Program availability:* Evening/weekend, online learning. Offers social work (MSW, PhD).

School of Pharmacy Offers biomedical regulatory affairs (MS); medicinal chemistry (PhD); pharmaceutics (MS, PhD); pharmacy (MS, PhD).

UNIVERSITY OF WASHINGTON, BOTHELL, Bothell, WA 98011

General Information State-supported, coed, comprehensive institution. *Graduate housing:* Room and/or apartments available on a first-come, first-served basis to single students; on-campus housing not available to married students. Housing application deadline: 5/1. *Research affiliation:* Bill and Melinda Gates Foundation (improving health and reducing poverty in developing countries, providing opportunities to succeed in school and life in the U.S.), Carnegie Corporation of New York (doing real and permanent good in this world by creating ladders on which the aspiring can rise), American Institutes for Research (labor market success), Michael and Susan Dell Foundation (portfolio network scale-up project), William and Flora Hewlett Foundation (planning for the state education agency of the future), Walton Family Foundation (student-based allocation systems).

GRADUATE UNITS

Master of Arts in Cultural Studies Program *Program availability:* Evening/weekend. Offers cultural studies (MA). Electronic applications accepted.

Master of Arts in Policy Studies Program *Program availability:* Evening/weekend. Offers policy studies (MA). Electronic applications accepted.

Program in Computing and Software Systems *Program availability:* Part-time, evening/weekend. Offers computing and software systems (MS). Electronic applications accepted.

Program in Creative Writing and Poetics Offers creative writing and poetics (MFA).

Program in Education *Program availability:* Part-time, evening/weekend. Offers education (M Ed); leadership development for educators (M Ed); secondary/middle level endorsement (M Ed). Electronic applications accepted.

Program in Nursing *Program availability:* Part-time. Offers nursing (MN). Electronic applications accepted.

School of Business *Program availability:* Part-time, evening/weekend. Offers leadership (MBA); technology (MBA). Electronic applications accepted.

UNIVERSITY OF WASHINGTON, TACOMA, Tacoma, WA 98402-3100

General Information State-supported, coed, comprehensive institution. *Graduate housing:* Room and/or apartments available on a first-come, first-served basis to single students; on-campus housing not available to married students. Housing application deadline: 5/14. *Research affiliation:* City of Tacoma/Port of Tacoma (water quality and sustainability studies), South Sound Public and Private Schools (internships and educational research).

GRADUATE UNITS

Graduate Programs *Program availability:* Part-time, evening/weekend. Offers accounting (MBA); advanced integrative practice (MSW); business administration (MBA); certified financial analyst (MBA); communities, populations and health (MN); computing and software systems (MS); education (M Ed); educational administration (principal or program administrator certification) (M Ed); elementary education teacher certification (M Ed); elementary education/special education teacher certification (M Ed); interdisciplinary studies (MA); leadership in healthcare (MN); nurse educator (MN); secondary science or math teacher certification (M Ed); social work (MSW). Electronic applications accepted.

UNIVERSITY OF WATERLOO, Waterloo, ON N2L 3G1, Canada

General Information Province-supported, coed, university. CGS member. *Graduate housing:* Rooms and/or apartments available on a first-come, first-served basis to single and married students. *Research affiliation:* Waterloo Maple, Inc. (symbolic computation research), Bell Canada, GM Canada, IBM, COM DEV International (telecommunications), Nortel (telecommunications).

GRADUATE UNITS

Graduate Studies *Program availability:* Part-time, evening/weekend, online learning. Electronic applications accepted.

Faculty of Applied Health Sciences *Program availability:* Part-time. Offers applied health sciences (M Sc, MA, MHE, MHI, MPH, PhD); health evaluation (MHE); health informatics (MHI); health studies and gerontology (M Sc, PhD); kinesiology (M Sc, PhD); public health (MPH); recreation and leisure studies (MA, PhD). Electronic applications accepted.

Faculty of Arts *Program availability:* Part-time, evening/weekend. Offers accounting (M Acc, PhD); ancient Mediterranean cultures (MA); anthropology (MA); arts (M Acc, M Tax, MA, MA Sc, MFA, MPS, PhD); economics (MA, PhD); English language and literature (PhD); finance (M Acc); French (MA, PhD); German (MA, PhD); global governance (MA, PhD); history (MA, PhD); literary studies (MA); philosophy (MA, PhD); psychology (MA, MA Sc, PhD); public issues (MA); religious diversity in North America (PhD); rhetoric and communication design (MA); Russian (MA); sociology (MA, PhD); studio art (MFA); taxation (M Tax). Electronic applications accepted.

Faculty of Engineering *Program availability:* Part-time, evening/weekend, online learning. Offers applied operations research (MA Sc, MMS, PhD); architecture (M Arch); business, entrepreneurship and technology (MBET); chemical engineering (M Eng, MA Sc, PhD); civil and environmental engineering (M Eng, MA Sc, PhD); electrical and computer engineering (M Eng, MA Sc, PhD); engineering (M Arch, M Eng, MA Sc, MBET, MMS, PhD); information systems (MA Sc, MMS, PhD); management of technology (MA Sc, MMS, PhD); mechanical engineering (M Eng, MA Sc, PhD); mechanical engineering design and manufacturing (M Eng); systems design engineering (M Eng, MA Sc, PhD). Electronic applications accepted.

Faculty of Environment *Program availability:* Part-time. Offers environment (M Plan, MA, MAES, MES, PhD); environment, resources and sustainability (MES, PhD); geography and environmental management (MA, PhD); local economic development (MAES); planning (M Plan, MA, MAES, MES, PhD). Electronic applications accepted.

Faculty of Mathematics Offers actuarial science (M Math, MAS, PhD); applied mathematics (M Math, PhD); biostatistics (PhD); combinatorics and optimization (M Math, PhD); computer science (M Math, PhD); mathematics (M Math, MAS, MMT, PhD); pure mathematics (M Math, PhD); software engineering (M Math); statistics (M Math, PhD); statistics and computing (M Math); statistics-biostatistics (M Math); statistics-computing (M Math); statistics-finance (M Math). Electronic applications accepted.

Faculty of Science *Program availability:* Part-time. Offers biology (M Sc, PhD); chemistry and biochemistry (M Sc, PhD); earth and environmental sciences (M Sc, PhD); optometry (OD); physics (M Sc, PhD); science (M Sc, OD, PhD); vision science (M Sc, PhD). Electronic applications accepted.

THE UNIVERSITY OF WEST ALABAMA, Livingston, AL 35470

General Information State-supported, coed, comprehensive institution. *Enrollment:* 3,986 graduate, professional, and undergraduate students; 1,848 full-time matriculated graduate/professional students (1,521 women), 160 part-time matriculated graduate/professional students (108 women). *Enrollment by degree level:* 1,768 master's, 240 other advanced degrees. *Graduate faculty:* 53 full-time (29 women), 91 part-time/adjunct (58 women). Tuition, state resident: part-time $355 per credit hour. Tuition, nonresident: part-time $710 per credit hour. *Required fees:* $130 per semester.

Graduate housing: Room and/or apartments available on a first-come, first-served basis to single students; on-campus housing not available to married students. Typical cost: $4040 per year ($6640 including board). Room and board charges vary according to board plan and housing facility selected. Housing application deadline: 5/1. *Student services:* Campus employment opportunities, campus safety program, career counseling, exercise/wellness program, free psychological counseling, international student services, services for students with disabilities. *Library facilities:* Julia Tutwiler Library. *Collection:* Books: 166,174 (physical), 1,789 (digital/electronic); Serial titles: 36 (physical), 96,027 (digital/electronic); Databases: 177. Weekly public service hours: 94; students can reserve study rooms.

Computer facilities: 600 computers available on campus for general student use. A campuswide network can be accessed from student residence rooms. Online class registration is available.

Website: http://www.uwa.edu/

General Application Contact: Dr. B. J. Kimbrough, Dean of Graduate Studies, 205-652-3647, Fax: 205-652-3670, E-mail: bkimbrough@uwa.edu.

GRADUATE UNITS

School of Graduate Studies Students: 1,848 full-time (1,521 women), 160 part-time (108 women); includes 757 minority (699 Black or African American, non-Hispanic/Latino; 14 American Indian or Alaska Native, non-Hispanic/Latino; 5 Asian, non-Hispanic/Latino; 14 Hispanic/Latino; 1 Native Hawaiian or other Pacific Islander, non-Hispanic/Latino; 24 Two or more races, non-Hispanic/Latino), 56 international. Average age 34. 721 applicants, 87% accepted, 486 enrolled. *Faculty:* 53 full-time (29 women), 91 part-time/adjunct (58 women). Expenses: Contact institution. *Financial support:* In 2016–17, 22 teaching assistantships (averaging $7,344 per year) were awarded; Federal Work-Study, scholarships/grants, and unspecified assistantships also available. Support available to part-time students. Financial award application deadline: 3/1; financial award applicants required to submit FAFSA. In 2016, 533 master's, 124 other advanced degrees awarded. *Program availability:* Part-time, evening/weekend, 100% online. *Application deadline:* Applications are processed on a rolling basis. *Application fee:* $40. Electronic applications accepted. *Dean of Graduate Studies,* Dr. B. J. Kimbrough, 205-652-3647, Fax: 205-652-3670, E-mail: bkimbrough@uwa.edu.

College of Business Students: 70 (48 women); includes 39 minority (33 Black or African American, non-Hispanic/Latino; 1 American Indian or Alaska Native, non-Hispanic/Latino; 1 Asian, non-Hispanic/Latino; 3 Hispanic/Latino; 1 Two or more races, non-Hispanic/Latino). Average age 30. 42 applicants, 90% accepted, 31 enrolled. *Faculty:* 5 full-time (1 woman), 11 part-time/adjunct (8 women). Expenses: Contact institution. *Financial support:* Federal Work-Study and scholarships/grants available. Support available to part-time students. Financial award application deadline: 3/1; financial award applicants required to submit FAFSA. In 2016, 9 master's awarded. *Program availability:* Part-time, evening/weekend, 100% online. Offers finance (MBA); general business (MBA). *Application deadline:* Applications are processed on a rolling basis. *Application fee:* $40. Electronic applications accepted. *Dean,* Dr. Wayne Bedford, 205-652-3687, Fax: 205-652-3776, E-mail: dbedford@uwa.edu.

College of Education Students: 1,945 (1,593 women); includes 723 minority (667 Black or African American, non-Hispanic/Latino; 13 American Indian or Alaska Native, non-Hispanic/Latino; 6 Asian, non-Hispanic/Latino; 13 Hispanic/Latino; 1 Native Hawaiian or other Pacific Islander, non-Hispanic/Latino; 23 Two or more races, non-Hispanic/Latino). Average age 34. 670 applicants, 87% accepted, 450 enrolled. *Faculty:* 48 full-time (28 women), 80 part-time/adjunct (50 women). Expenses: Contact institution. *Financial support:* In 2016–17, 22 teaching assistantships (averaging $7,344 per year) were awarded; Federal Work-Study, scholarships/grants, and unspecified assistantships also available. Support available to part-time students. Financial award application deadline: 3/1; financial award applicants required to submit FAFSA. In 2016, 523 master's, 124 other advanced degrees awarded. *Program availability:* Part-time, evening/weekend, 100% online. Offers biology (MAT); collaborative special education 6-12 (Ed S); collaborative special education K-6 (Ed S); continuing education (MSCE); counseling and psychology (MSCE); early childhood development (M Ed); early childhood education (M Ed, Ed S); early childhood education P-3 (M Ed); education (M Ed, MAT, MSCE, Ed S); elementary education (M Ed, Ed S); elementary education K-6 (M Ed); English language arts (MAT); family counseling (MSCE); general (MSCE); guidance and counseling (MSCE); high school 6-12 (M Ed); history (MAT); instructional leadership (M Ed, Ed S); library media (M Ed, Ed S); mathematics (MAT); physical education (M Ed, MAT); school counseling (M Ed, Ed S); science (MAT); secondary education (M Ed, MAT); social science (MAT); special education (M Ed, Ed S); special education collaborative teacher 6-12 (M Ed); special education collaborative teacher K-6 (M Ed); student affairs in higher education (MSCE); teacher leader (Ed S). *Application deadline:* Applications are processed on a rolling basis. *Application fee:* $40. Electronic applications accepted. *Dean of Graduate Studies,* Dr. B. J. Kimbrough, 205-652-3647, Fax: 205-652-3706, E-mail: bkimbrough@uwa.edu.

College of Liberal Arts Students: 11 (9 women); includes 3 minority (all Black or African American, non-Hispanic/Latino). Average age 28. 9 applicants, 56% accepted, 5 enrolled. *Faculty:* 3 full-time (1 woman), 7 part-time/adjunct (4 women). Expenses: Contact institution. *Financial support:* Teaching assistantships, Federal Work-Study, scholarships/grants, and unspecified assistantships available. Support available to part-time students. Financial award application deadline: 3/1; financial award applicants required to submit FAFSA. In 2016, 1 master's awarded. *Program availability:* Part-time, evening/weekend, 100% online. Offers experimental psychology (MS). *Application deadline:* Applications are processed on a rolling basis. *Application fee:* $40. Electronic applications accepted. *Dean,* Dr. Mark Davis, 205-652-3570, Fax: 205-652-3717, E-mail: mdavis@uwa.edu.

College of Natural Sciences and Mathematics Students: 6 (2 women). Average age 26. *Faculty:* 8 full-time (3 women), 3 part-time/adjunct (1 woman). Expenses: Contact institution. *Financial support:* Teaching assistantships, Federal Work-Study, scholarships/grants, and unspecified assistantships available. Support available to part-time students. Financial award application deadline: 3/1; financial award applicants required to submit FAFSA. *Program availability:* Part-time, evening/weekend, 100% online. Offers conservation biology (MS). *Application deadline:* Applications are processed on a rolling basis. *Application fee:* $40. Electronic applications accepted. *Dean,* Dr. John McCall, 205-652-3412, E-mail: jmccall@uwa.edu.

THE UNIVERSITY OF WESTERN ONTARIO, London, ON N6A 5B8, Canada

General Information Province-supported, coed, university. CGS member. *Graduate housing:* Rooms and/or apartments available on a first-come, first-served basis to single and married students.

GRADUATE UNITS

Faculty of Graduate Studies *Program availability:* Part-time, evening/weekend, online learning. Electronic applications accepted.

Biosciences Division *Program availability:* Part-time, online learning. Offers anatomy and cell biology (M Sc, PhD); biochemistry (M Sc, PhD); biology (M Sc, PhD); biosciences (M Cl Sc, M Sc, MA, MPT, PhD, CAS); clinical anatomy (M Sc); clinical neurological sciences (M Sc, PhD); epidemiology and biostatistics (M Sc, PhD); family medicine (M Cl Sc); manipulative therapy (CAS); medical biophysics (M Sc, PhD); microbiology and immunology (M Sc, PhD); pathology (M Sc, PhD); physical therapy (MPT); physiology (M Sc, PhD); psychology (M Sc, PhD); wound healing (CAS).

Center for the Study of Theory and Criticism Offers theory and criticism (MA, PhD).

Don Wright Faculty of Music *Program availability:* Part-time. Offers music (M Mus, PhD); popular music and culture (MA).

Faculty of Arts and Humanities *Program availability:* Part-time. Offers arts and humanities (M Mus, MA, PhD); Canadian literature (MA); classical studies (MA); comparative literature (MA, PhD); English (PhD); English literature (MA); French studies (MA, PhD); Hispanic studies (MA, PhD); philosophy (MA, PhD).

Faculty of Information and Media Studies Offers journalism (MA); library and information science (MLIS, PhD); media studies (MA, PhD).

Health Sciences Division Offers audiology (M Cl Sc, M Sc); health sciences (M Cl Sc, M Sc, M Sc N, MA, MCTS, MN NP, PhD); kinesiology (M Sc, MA, PhD); nurse practitioner (MN NP); nursing (M Sc N, MN NP, PhD); occupational therapy (M Sc); speech-language pathology (M Cl Sc, M Sc).

Physical Sciences Division *Program availability:* Part-time. Offers applied mathematics (M Sc, PhD); astronomy (M Sc, PhD); chemical and biochemical engineering (M Sc, PhD); chemistry (M Sc, PhD); civil and environmental engineering (M Eng, ME Sc, PhD); computer science (M Sc, PhD); electrical and computer engineering (M Eng, ME Sc, PhD); environment and sustainability (MES); geology (M Sc, PhD); geology and environmental science (M Sc, PhD); geophysics (M Sc, PhD); geophysics and environmental science (M Sc, PhD); mathematics (M Sc, PhD); mechanical and materials engineering (M Eng, ME Sc, PhD); physical sciences (M Eng, M Sc, ME Sc, MES, PhD); physics (M Sc, PhD); statistical and actuarial sciences (M Sc, PhD); theoretical physics (PhD). Electronic applications accepted.

Social Sciences Division *Program availability:* Part-time, evening/weekend. Offers anthropology (MA, PhD); counseling psychology (M Ed); curriculum studies (M Ed); economics (MA, PhD); education (M Ed); educational policy studies (M Ed); educational psychology/special education (M Ed); geography (M Sc, MA, PhD); history (MA, PhD); political science (MA, MPA, PhD); social sciences (M Ed, M Sc, MA, MPA, PhD); sociology (MA, PhD).

Faculty of Law Offers law (LL M, MLS, JD, Diploma).

Richard Ivey School of Business Offers business (EMBA, PhD); corporate strategy and leadership elective (MBA); entrepreneurship elective (MBA); finance elective (MBA); health sector stream (MBA); international management elective (MBA); marketing elective (MBA). Electronic applications accepted.

Schulich School of Medicine and Dentistry Offers dentistry (M Cl D, DDS); medicine (MD); medicine and dentistry (M Cl D, M Cl Sc, M Sc, MA, DDS, MD, PhD); orthodontics (M Cl D).

UNIVERSITY OF WESTERN STATES, Portland, OR 97230-3099

General Information Independent, coed, graduate-only institution. *Graduate housing:* On-campus housing not available. *Research affiliation:* Oregon Center for Complimentary and Alternative Medicine in Craniofacial Disorders (complimentary and alternative medicine), Consortial Center for Chiropractic Research (Palmer College of Chiropractic) (chiropractic).

GRADUATE UNITS

Professional Program Offers chiropractic (DC).

UNIVERSITY OF WEST FLORIDA, Pensacola, FL 32514-5750

General Information State-supported, coed, comprehensive institution. CGS member. *Enrollment:* 506 full-time matriculated graduate/professional students (333 women), 1,273 part-time matriculated graduate/professional students (767 women). *Enrollment by degree level:* 1,536 master's, 183 doctoral, 60 other advanced degrees. *Graduate faculty:* 163 full-time (65 women), 44 part-time/adjunct (25 women). Tuition, state resident: full-time $5316. Tuition, nonresident: full-time $11,308. *Required fees:* $584. Tuition and fees vary according to course load and program. *Graduate housing:* Room and/or apartments available on a first-come, first-served basis to single students; on-campus housing not available to married students. *Student services:* Campus employment opportunities, campus safety program, career counseling, child daycare facilities, exercise/wellness program, free psychological counseling, international student services, low-cost health insurance, multicultural affairs office, services for students with disabilities, teacher training. *Library facilities:* John C. Pace Library plus 2 others. *Collection:* Books: 834,298 (physical), 163,625 (digital/electronic); Serial titles: 288 (physical), 80,370 (digital/electronic); Databases: 167. Weekly public service hours: 107. *Research affiliation:* Pensacola Bay Area Convention and Visitors Bureau (Pensacola tourism study), Software Engineering Research Consortium (Motorola, Northrup Grumman through Ball State University) (software engineering), University of Southern Mississippi Consortium on Coastal Estuarine Research (microbial biofilms and coastal estuarine research).

Computer facilities: Computer purchase and lease plans are available. 1,228 computers available on campus for general student use. A campuswide network can be accessed from student residence rooms and from off campus. Online class registration is available.

Website: http://www.uwf.edu/

General Application Contact: Mandi Lagergren, Assistant Director of Graduate Admissions, 850-473-7720, E-mail: gradadmissions@uwf.edu.

GRADUATE UNITS

College of Arts, Social Sciences, and Humanities Expenses: Contact institution. *Financial support:* Fellowships with partial tuition reimbursements, research assistantships with partial tuition reimbursements, teaching assistantships with partial tuition reimbursements, and unspecified assistantships available. Financial award application deadline: 4/15; financial award applicants required to submit FAFSA. *Program availability:* Part-time, evening/weekend. Offers arts, social sciences, and humanities (MA); creative writing (MA); early American studies (MA); literature (MA); political science (MA); public history (MA); strategic communication and leadership (MA); traditional history (MA). *Application deadline:* For fall admission, 6/1 for domestic and international students; for spring admission, 10/1 for domestic and international students. Applications are processed on a rolling basis. *Application fee:* $30. *Application

Contact: Terry McCray, Assistant Director of Graduate Admissions, 850-473-7718, Fax: 850-473-7714, E-mail: gradadmissions@uwf.edu. *Dean,* Dr. Jane Halonen, 850-474-2688.

Division of Anthropology and Archaeology Expenses: Contact institution. *Financial support:* Research assistantships with partial tuition reimbursements, teaching assistantships with partial tuition reimbursements, and unspecified assistantships available. Financial award application deadline: 4/15; financial award applicants required to submit FAFSA. Offers anthropology (MA); historical archaeology (MA). *Application deadline:* For fall admission, 6/1 for domestic and international students; for spring admission, 10/1 for domestic and international students. *Application fee:* $30. *Application Contact:* Terry McCray, Assistant Director of Graduate Admissions, 850-473-7718, Fax: 850-473-7714, E-mail: gradadmissions@uwf.edu. *Chair,* Dr. John Bratten, 850-474-2706, E-mail: jbratten@uwf.edu.

College of Business Expenses: Contact institution. *Financial support:* Fellowships, research assistantships with partial tuition reimbursements, and unspecified assistantships available. Financial award application deadline: 4/15; financial award applicants required to submit FAFSA. *Program availability:* Part-time, evening/weekend. Offers accounting (M Acc); business (M Acc, MBA); business administration (MBA). *Application deadline:* For fall admission, 6/30 for domestic students, 6/1 for international students; for spring admission, 10/1 for domestic and international students. Applications are processed on a rolling basis. *Application fee:* $30. *Application Contact:* Dr. W. Timothy O'Keefe, Associate Dean/Director, 850-474-2348. *Dean,* Dr. F. Edward Ranelli, 850-474-2348.

College of Education and Professional Studies Expenses: Contact institution. *Financial support:* Fellowships, research assistantships with partial tuition reimbursements, teaching assistantships with partial tuition reimbursements, and unspecified assistantships available. Financial award application deadline: 4/15; financial award applicants required to submit FAFSA. *Program availability:* Part-time, evening/weekend. Offers applied behavior analysis (MA); college student affairs administration (M Ed); criminal justice (MS); curriculum and assessment (Ed D); curriculum and instruction (M Ed, Ed S); education and professional studies (M Ed, MA, MS, MSA, MSW, Ed D, Ed S); educational leadership (M Ed); elementary education (M Ed); exceptional student education (MA); instructional design and technology (M Ed, Ed D); legal studies, public administration and sport management (MSA); middle level education (M Ed); network operations, performance and security (M Ed); reading education (M Ed); secondary education (M Ed); social work (MSW); special and alternative education (MA). *Application deadline:* For fall admission, 6/1 for domestic and international students; for spring admission, 10/1 for domestic and international students. Applications are processed on a rolling basis. *Application fee:* $30. *Application Contact:* Terry McCray, Assistant Director of Graduate Admissions, 850-473-7718, Fax: 850-473-7714, E-mail: gradadmissions@uwf.edu. *Interim Dean,* Dr. Pam Northrup, 850-474-2769, Fax: 850-474-3205.

Ed D Programs Expenses: Contact institution. *Program availability:* Part-time, evening/weekend. Offers administrative and leadership studies (Ed D); education (Ed D); instructional design and technology (Ed D); physical education and health (Ed D). *Application deadline:* For fall admission, 6/1 for domestic and international students; for spring admission, 10/1 for domestic students. Applications are processed on a rolling basis. *Application Contact:* Terry McCray, Assistant Director of Graduate Admissions, 850-473-7718, Fax: 850-473-7714, E-mail: gradadmissions@uwf.edu. *Interim Dean,* Dr. Pam Northrup, 850-474-2769, Fax: 850-474-3205.

Hal Marcus College of Science and Engineering Expenses: Contact institution. *Financial support:* Fellowships with partial tuition reimbursements, research assistantships with partial tuition reimbursements, teaching assistantships with partial tuition reimbursements, and unspecified assistantships available. Financial award application deadline: 4/15; financial award applicants required to submit FAFSA. *Program availability:* Part-time, evening/weekend. Offers biology (MS); computer science (MS); environmental science (MS); geographic information science administration (MS); information technology (MS); mathematical sciences (MS); science and engineering (MPH, MS, MSN, MST). *Application deadline:* For fall admission, 6/1 for domestic and international students; for spring admission, 10/1 for domestic and international students. Applications are processed on a rolling basis. *Application fee:* $30. *Application Contact:* Terry McCray, Assistant Director of Graduate Admissions, 850-473-7715, Fax: 850-473-7714, E-mail: gradadmissions@uwf.edu. *Dean,* Dr. Jane Halonen, 850-474-2688.

Usha Kundu, MD College of Health Expenses: Contact institution. *Financial support:* Fellowships with partial tuition reimbursements, research assistantships with partial tuition reimbursements, teaching assistantships with partial tuition reimbursements, and unspecified assistantships available. Financial award application deadline: 4/15; financial award applicants required to submit FAFSA. *Program availability:* Part-time. Offers applied experimental (MA); counseling (MA); health (MA, MHA, MPH, MS, MSN); health promotion (MS); health, leisure, and exercise science (MS); healthcare administration (MHA); industrial-organizational (MA); public health (MPH). *Application deadline:* For fall admission, 6/1 for domestic and international students; for spring admission, 10/1 for domestic and international students. Applications are processed on a rolling basis. *Application fee:* $30. *Application Contact:* Terry McCray, Assistant Director of Graduate Admissions, 850-473-7718, Fax: 850-473-7714, E-mail: gradadmissions@uwf.edu. *Interim Associate Dean,* Brandy Strahan, 850-474-2361.

School of Nursing Expenses: Contact institution. *Program availability:* Part-time, evening/weekend. Offers nursing (MSN). *Application deadline:* For fall admission, 5/1 for domestic students, 6/1 for international students; for spring admission, 10/1 for domestic students. Applications are processed on a rolling basis. *Application fee:* $30. *Application Contact:* Leslie Wyrosdick, Admissions Coordinator, 850-474-3197, E-mail: msnnursing@uwf.edu. *Admissions Coordinator,* Leslie Wyrosdick, 850-474-3197, E-mail: msnnursing@uwf.edu.

UNIVERSITY OF WEST GEORGIA, Carrollton, GA 30118

General Information State-supported, coed, comprehensive institution. CGS member. *Enrollment:* 13,308 graduate, professional, and undergraduate students; 587 full-time matriculated graduate/professional students (440 women), 1,396 part-time matriculated graduate/professional students (1,051 women). *Enrollment by degree level:* 1,351 master's, 174 doctoral, 458 other advanced degrees. *Graduate faculty:* 263 full-time (137 women). Tuition, state resident: full-time $5316; part-time $222 per semester hour. Tuition, nonresident: full-time $20,658; part-time $861 per semester hour. *Required fees:* $1962. Tuition and fees vary according to course load, degree level and program. *Graduate housing:* Rooms and/or apartments available on a first-come, first-served basis to single and married students. Housing application deadline: 6/1. *Student services:* Campus employment opportunities, campus safety program, career counseling, exercise/wellness program, free psychological counseling, international student services, multicultural affairs office, services for students with disabilities, teacher training, writing training. *Library facilities:* Irvine Sullivan Ingram Library plus 1 other. *Collection:* Weekly public service hours: 137; study areas open 24 hours, 5–7 days a week; students can reserve study rooms.

Computer facilities: 1,200 computers available on campus for general student use. A campuswide network can be accessed from student residence rooms and from off campus. Online class registration is available. Website: http://www.westga.edu/

General Application Contact: Dr. Toby Ziglar, Assistant Dean of the Graduate School, 678-839-1394, Fax: 678-839-1395, E-mail: graduate@westga.edu.

GRADUATE UNITS

College of Arts and Humanities Students: 23 full-time (16 women), 55 part-time (33 women); includes 18 minority (10 Black or African American, non-Hispanic/Latino; 1 American Indian or Alaska Native, non-Hispanic/Latino; 5 Hispanic/Latino; 2 Two or more races, non-Hispanic/Latino), 1 international. Average age 31. 24 applicants, 100% accepted, 23 enrolled. *Faculty:* 70 full-time (39 women). Expenses: Contact institution. *Financial support:* Fellowships, research assistantships, teaching assistantships, career-related internships or fieldwork, Federal Work-Study, institutionally sponsored loans, scholarships/grants, and unspecified assistantships available. Support available to part-time students. Financial award application deadline: 4/1; financial award applicants required to submit FAFSA. In 2016, 34 master's, 6 other advanced degrees awarded. *Program availability:* Part-time, evening/weekend, 100% online, blended/hybrid learning. Offers English (MA); history (MA); museum studies (Postbaccalaureate Certificate); music performance (M Mus); music teacher education (M Mus); public history (Postbaccalaureate Certificate). *Application deadline:* For fall admission, 8/1 for domestic students, 6/1 for international students; for spring admission, 11/15 for domestic students, 10/15 for international students; for summer admission, 5/15 for domestic students, 3/30 for international students. Applications are processed on a rolling basis. *Application fee:* $40. Electronic applications accepted. *Application Contact:* Dr. Toby Ziglar, Assistant Dean of the Graduate School, 678-839-1394, Fax: 678-839-1395, E-mail: graduate@westga.edu. *Dean of Arts and Humanities,* Dr. Pauline D. Gagnon, 678-839-5450, Fax: 678-839-5451, E-mail: pgagnon@westga.edu.

College of Education Students: 321 full-time (266 women), 1,007 part-time (813 women); includes 456 minority (389 Black or African American, non-Hispanic/Latino; 1 American Indian or Alaska Native, non-Hispanic/Latino; 13 Asian, non-Hispanic/Latino; 43 Hispanic/Latino; 10 Two or more races, non-Hispanic/Latino), 12 international. Average age 33. 541 applicants, 79% accepted, 305 enrolled. *Faculty:* 46 full-time (31 women). Expenses: Contact institution. *Financial support:* Fellowships, research assistantships, teaching assistantships, career-related internships or fieldwork, Federal Work-Study, institutionally sponsored loans, scholarships/grants, and unspecified assistantships available. Support available to part-time students. Financial award application deadline: 4/1; financial award applicants required to submit FAFSA. In 2016, 286 master's, 20 doctorates, 156 other advanced degrees awarded. *Program availability:* Part-time, evening/weekend, 100% online, blended/hybrid learning. Offers business education (M Ed); early childhood education (M Ed, Ed S); educational leadership (M Ed, Ed S); media (M Ed, Ed S); professional counseling (M Ed, Ed S); professional counseling and supervision (Ed D); reading instruction (M Ed); school improvement (Ed D); secondary education (M Ed); special education (M Ed, Ed S); speech language pathology (M Ed); teaching (MAT). *Application deadline:* For fall admission, 7/21 for domestic students, 6/1 for international students; for spring admission, 11/30 for domestic students, 10/15 for international students; for summer admission, 4/15 for domestic students, 3/30 for international students. Applications are processed on a rolling basis. *Application fee:* $40. Electronic applications accepted. *Application Contact:* Dr. Toby Ziglar, Assistant Dean of the Graduate School, 678-839-1394, Fax: 678-839-1395, E-mail: graduate@westga.edu. *Dean, College of Education,* Dr. Diane Hoff, 678-839-6570, Fax: 678-839-6098, E-mail: dhoff@westga.edu.

College of Science and Mathematics Students: 15 full-time (7 women), 61 part-time (26 women); includes 19 minority (14 Black or African American, non-Hispanic/Latino; 1 American Indian or Alaska Native, non-Hispanic/Latino; 3 Asian, non-Hispanic/Latino; 1 Two or more races, non-Hispanic/Latino), 6 international. Average age 33. 64 applicants, 86% accepted, 43 enrolled. *Faculty:* 49 full-time (17 women). Expenses: Contact institution. *Financial support:* Fellowships, research assistantships, teaching assistantships, career-related internships or fieldwork, Federal Work-Study, institutionally sponsored loans, scholarships/grants, and unspecified assistantships available. Support available to part-time students. Financial award application deadline: 4/1; financial award applicants required to submit FAFSA. In 2016, 21 master's, 4 other advanced degrees awarded. *Program availability:* Part-time, evening/weekend, 100% online, blended/hybrid learning. Offers biology (MS); computer science (MS); geographic information systems (Postbaccalaureate Certificate); mathematics (MS). *Application deadline:* For fall admission, 6/1 for domestic and international students; for spring admission, 11/15 for domestic students, 10/15 for international students; for summer admission, 4/1 for domestic students, 3/30 for international students. Applications are processed on a rolling basis. *Application fee:* $40. Electronic applications accepted. *Application Contact:* Dr. Toby Ziglar, Assistant Dean of the Graduate School, 678-839-1394, Fax: 678-839-1395, E-mail: graduate@westga.edu. *Dean of Science and Mathematics,* Dr. Lok C. Lew Yan Voon, 678-839-5190, Fax: 678-839-5191, E-mail: lokl@westga.edu.

College of Social Sciences Students: 107 full-time (67 women), 73 part-time (46 women); includes 47 minority (39 Black or African American, non-Hispanic/Latino; 4 Asian, non-Hispanic/Latino; 4 Hispanic/Latino), 10 international. Average age 31. 83 applicants, 88% accepted, 60 enrolled. *Faculty:* 45 full-time (21 women). Expenses: Contact institution. *Financial support:* Fellowships, research assistantships, teaching assistantships, career-related internships or fieldwork, Federal Work-Study, institutionally sponsored loans, scholarships/grants, and unspecified assistantships available. Support available to part-time students. Financial award application deadline: 4/1; financial award applicants required to submit FAFSA. In 2016, 56 master's, 7 doctorates, 5 other advanced degrees awarded. *Program availability:* Part-time, evening/weekend, 100% online, blended/hybrid learning. Offers criminology (MA); data analysis and evaluation methods (Postbaccalaureate Certificate); European Union studies (Postbaccalaureate Certificate); integrative health systems (Postbaccalaureate Certificate); nonprofit management and community development (Postbaccalaureate Certificate); psychology (MA, PhD); public administration (MPA); public management (Postbaccalaureate Certificate); sociology (MA). *Application deadline:* For fall admission, 7/15 for domestic students, 6/1 for international students; for spring admission, 11/30 for domestic students, 10/15 for international students; for summer admission, 5/15 for domestic students, 3/30 for international students. Applications are processed on a rolling basis. *Application fee:* $40. Electronic applications accepted. *Application Contact:* Dr. Toby Ziglar, Assistant Dean of the Graduate School, 678-839-1394, Fax: 678-839-1395, E-mail: graduate@westga.edu. *Dean of Social Sciences,* Dr. N. Jane McCandless, 678-839-5170, Fax: 678-839-5171, E-mail: jmccandl@westga.edu.

Richards College of Business Students: 56 full-time (24 women), 132 part-time (64 women); includes 61 minority (49 Black or African American, non-Hispanic/Latino; 1 American Indian or Alaska Native, non-Hispanic/Latino; 3 Asian, non-Hispanic/Latino; 7 Hispanic/Latino; 1 Two or more races, non-Hispanic/Latino), 12 international. Average age 29. 121 applicants, 94% accepted, 77 enrolled. *Faculty:* 38 full-time (14 women). Expenses: Contact institution. *Financial support:* Fellowships, research assistantships, teaching assistantships, career-related internships or fieldwork, Federal Work-Study, institutionally sponsored loans, scholarships/grants, and unspecified assistantships available. Support available to part-time students. Financial award application deadline: 4/1; financial award applicants required to submit FAFSA. In 2016, 123 master's awarded. *Program availability:* Part-time, evening/weekend, 100% online, blended/hybrid learning. Offers accounting (MP Acc); business administration (MBA). *Application deadline:* For fall admission, 7/15 for domestic students, 6/1 for international students; for spring admission, 11/15 for domestic students, 10/15 for international students; for summer admission, 5/15 for domestic students, 3/30 for international students. Applications are processed on a rolling basis. *Application fee:* $40. Electronic applications accepted. *Application Contact:* Dr. Toby Ziglar, Assistant Dean of the Graduate School, 678-839-1394, Fax: 678-839-1395, E-mail: graduate@westga.edu. *Dean of Richards College of Business,* Dr. Faye S. McIntyre, 678-839-6467, Fax: 678-839-5040, E-mail: fmcintyr@westga.edu.

Tanner Health System School of Nursing Students: 65 full-time (60 women), 75 part-time (71 women); includes 38 minority (34 Black or African American, non-Hispanic/Latino; 1 Asian, non-Hispanic/Latino; 3 Hispanic/Latino). Average age 39. 84 applicants, 99% accepted, 57 enrolled. *Faculty:* 15 full-time (all women). Expenses: Contact institution. *Financial support:* Fellowships, research assistantships, teaching assistantships, career-related internships or fieldwork, Federal Work-Study, institutionally sponsored loans, scholarships/grants, and unspecified assistantships available. Support available to part-time students. Financial award application deadline: 4/1; financial award applicants required to submit FAFSA. In 2016, 23 master's, 4 doctorates, 2 other advanced degrees awarded. *Program availability:* Part-time, evening/weekend, 100% online, blended/hybrid learning. Offers health systems leadership (Post-Master's Certificate); nursing (MSN); nursing education (Ed D, Post-Master's Certificate). *Application deadline:* For fall admission, 2/1 priority date for domestic and international students. Applications are processed on a rolling basis. *Application fee:* $40. Electronic applications accepted. *Application Contact:* Dr. Toby Ziglar, Assistant Dean of the Graduate School, 678-839-1390, Fax: 678-839-1395, E-mail: graduate@westga.edu. *Dean of the School of Nursing,* Dr. Jennifer Schuessler, 678-839-5640, Fax: 678-839-6553, E-mail: jschuess@westga.edu.

UNIVERSITY OF WINDSOR, Windsor, ON N9B 3P4, Canada

General Information Province-supported, coed, university. *Graduate housing:* Rooms and/or apartments available on a first-come, first-served basis to single and married students. Housing application deadline: 6/7. *Research affiliation:* Daimler/Chrysler Automotive Research and Development Centre.

GRADUATE UNITS

Faculty of Graduate Studies *Program availability:* Part-time, evening/weekend. Electronic applications accepted.

Faculty of Arts and Social Sciences *Program availability:* Part-time. Offers adult clinical (MA, PhD); applied social psychology (MA, PhD); arts and social sciences (MA, MFA, MSW, PhD); child clinical (MA, PhD); clinical neuropsychology (MA, PhD); communication and social justice (MA); criminology (MA); English: creative writing and language and literature (MA); English: language and literature (MA); history (MA); philosophy (MA); political science (MA); social work (MSW); sociology (MA); sociology-social justice (PhD); visual arts (MFA). Electronic applications accepted.

Faculty of Education *Program availability:* Part-time, evening/weekend. Offers education (M Ed); educational studies (PhD). Electronic applications accepted.

Faculty of Engineering *Program availability:* Part-time. Offers civil engineering (M Eng, MA Sc, PhD); electrical engineering (M Eng, MA Sc, PhD); engineering (M Eng, MA Sc, PhD); engineering materials (M Eng, MA Sc, PhD); environmental engineering (M Eng, MA Sc, PhD); industrial engineering (M Eng, MA Sc); manufacturing systems engineering (PhD); mechanical engineering (M Eng, MA Sc, PhD). Electronic applications accepted.

Faculty of Human Kinetics *Program availability:* Part-time. Offers human kinetics (MHK). Electronic applications accepted.

Faculty of Nursing Offers nursing (M Sc, MN). Electronic applications accepted.

Faculty of Science *Program availability:* Part-time. Offers biological sciences (M Sc, PhD); chemistry and biochemistry (M Sc, PhD); computer science (M Sc, PhD); earth sciences (M Sc, PhD); economics (MA); mathematics (M Sc); physics (M Sc, PhD); science (M Sc, MA, PhD); statistics (M Sc, PhD). Electronic applications accepted.

GLIER-Great Lakes Institute for Environmental Research Offers environmental science (M Sc, PhD). Electronic applications accepted.

Odette School of Business *Program availability:* Evening/weekend. Offers business (MBA, MM). Electronic applications accepted.

THE UNIVERSITY OF WINNIPEG, Winnipeg, MB R3B 2E9, Canada

General Information Province-supported, coed, comprehensive institution. *Graduate housing:* On-campus housing not available.

GRADUATE UNITS

Faculty of Theology *Program availability:* Part-time. Offers marriage and family therapy (MMFT, Certificate); sacred theology (STM); theology (M Div).

Graduate Studies *Program availability:* Part-time, evening/weekend. Offers history (MA); public administration (MPA); religious studies (MA).

UNIVERSITY OF WISCONSIN–EAU CLAIRE, Eau Claire, WI 54702-4004

General Information State-supported, coed, comprehensive institution. CGS member. *Graduate housing:* Room and/or apartments available on a first-come, first-served basis to single students; on-campus housing not available to married students. Housing application deadline: 5/1. *Research affiliation:* Geological Survey of Canada (geology), Chevron Phillips Chemical Company (chemistry), Excel Energy (geography), American Chemical Society Petroleum Research Fund (chemistry, geology), ASIANetwork (anthropology, biology, geography), Research Corporation (chemistry).

GRADUATE UNITS

College of Arts and Sciences Offers arts and sciences (MA, MSE, Ed S); literature and textual interpretation (MA); public history (MA); school psychology (MSE, Ed S); writing (MA). Electronic applications accepted.

College of Business Offers business (MBA); business administration (MBA). Electronic applications accepted.

College of Education and Human Sciences Offers communication sciences and disorders (MS); education and human sciences (ME-PD, MS, MSE, MST); professional development (ME-PD); reading (MST); special education (MSE). Electronic applications accepted.

College of Nursing and Health Sciences Offers adult-gerontological administration (DNP); adult-gerontological clinical nurse specialist (DNP); adult-gerontological education (MSN); adult-gerontological primary care nurse practitioner (DNP); family health administration (DNP); family health in education (MSN); family health nurse practitioner (DNP); nursing (MSN); nursing and health sciences (MSN, DNP); nursing practice (DNP). Electronic applications accepted.

UNIVERSITY OF WISCONSIN–GREEN BAY, Green Bay, WI 54311-7001

General Information State-supported, coed, comprehensive institution. *Enrollment:* 7,030 graduate, professional, and undergraduate students; 72 full-time matriculated graduate/professional students (50 women), 178 part-time matriculated graduate/professional students (102 women). *Enrollment by degree level:* 250 master's. *Graduate faculty:* 47 full-time (23 women), 5 part-time/adjunct (3 women). Tuition, state resident: full-time $7640; part-time $424 per credit hour. Tuition, nonresident: full-time $16,771; part-time $932 per credit hour. *Required fees:* $1580; $88 per credit hour. Tuition and fees vary according to program and reciprocity agreements. *Graduate housing:* Room and/or apartments available on a first-come, first-served basis to single students; on-campus housing not available to married students. Typical cost: $4380 per year ($7306 including board). Room and board charges vary according to housing facility selected. Housing application deadline: 5/1. *Student services:* Campus employment opportunities, campus safety program, career counseling, free psychological counseling, international student services, low-cost health insurance, multicultural affairs office, services for students with disabilities, teacher training. *Library facilities:* Cofrin Library. *Collection:* Books: 353,331 (physical); Serial titles: 7,592 (physical); Databases: 179. Weekly public service hours: 100; students can reserve study rooms. *Research affiliation:* Wisconsin Space Grant Consortium (space and aerospace science), UW Sea Grant Institute (Great Lakes and ocean sustainability and stewardship), UW System Applied Research Program (biogas generation), UW Extension Solid and Hazardous Waste Education Center (sustainable use of natural resources), Abbott Laboratories (anaerobic digestion systems).

Computer facilities: Computer purchase and lease plans are available. 550 computers available on campus for general student use. A campuswide network can be accessed from student residence rooms and from off campus. Online class registration, online degree progress, online financial records and bill paying are available. Website: http://www.uwgb.edu/

General Application Contact: Mary Valitchka, Coordinator of Graduate Programs, 920-465-2123, Fax: 920-465-2043, E-mail: valitchm@uwgb.edu.

GRADUATE UNITS

Graduate Studies Students: 58 full-time (41 women), 160 part-time (112 women); includes 33 minority (4 Black or African American, non-Hispanic/Latino; 7 American Indian or Alaska Native, non-Hispanic/Latino; 9 Asian, non-Hispanic/Latino; 5 Hispanic/Latino; 8 Two or more races, non-Hispanic/Latino), 5 international. Average age 33. 213 applicants, 89% accepted, 140 enrolled. *Faculty:* 31 full-time (14 women), 7 part-time/adjunct (4 women). Expenses: Contact institution. *Financial support:* In 2016–17, 21 students received support. Research assistantships, career-related internships or fieldwork, scholarships/grants, unspecified assistantships, and aid for veterans and their family members available. Support available to part-time students. Financial award application deadline: 7/15; financial award applicants required to submit FAFSA. In 2016, 59 master's awarded. *Program availability:* Part-time, evening/weekend, 100% online. Offers applied leadership for teaching and learning (MS Ed); environmental science and policy (MS); health and wellness management (MS); management (MS); nursing (MSN); social work (MSW); sustainable management (MS). *Application deadline:* For fall admission, 8/1 for domestic students; for spring admission, 11/1 for domestic students. Applications are processed on a rolling basis. *Application fee:* $56. Electronic applications accepted. *Application Contact:* Mary Valitchka, Graduate Studies Coordinator, 920-465-2123, Fax: 920-465-5043, E-mail: valitchm@uwgb.edu. *Director of Graduate Studies,* Dr. Matthew Dornbush, 920-465-2033, Fax: 920-465-2043, E-mail: dornbusm@uwgb.edu.

UNIVERSITY OF WISCONSIN–LA CROSSE, La Crosse, WI 54601-3742

General Information State-supported, coed, comprehensive institution. CGS member. *Enrollment:* 10,516 graduate, professional, and undergraduate students; 414 full-time matriculated graduate/professional students (285 women), 361 part-time matriculated graduate/professional students (246 women). *Enrollment by degree level:* 623 master's, 129 doctoral, 12 other advanced degrees. *Graduate faculty:* 98 full-time (39 women), 51 part-time/adjunct (35 women). *Graduate housing:* Room and/or apartments available on a first-come, first-served basis to single students; on-campus housing not available to married students. Housing application deadline: 5/1. *Student services:* Campus employment opportunities, campus safety program, career counseling, child daycare facilities, exercise/wellness program, free psychological counseling, grant writing training, international student services, low-cost health insurance, multicultural affairs office, services for students with disabilities, teacher training, writing training. *Library facilities:* Murphy Library plus 6 others. *Collection:* Weekly public service hours: 55; students can reserve study rooms.

Computer facilities: 200 computers available on campus for general student use. A campuswide network can be accessed from student residence rooms and from off campus. Online class registration is available. Website: http://www.uwlax.edu/

General Application Contact: Brandon Schaller, Senior Graduate Student Status Examiner, 608-785-8941, E-mail: admissions@uwlax.edu.

GRADUATE UNITS

College of Business Administration Students: 8 full-time (3 women), 19 part-time (7 women); includes 2 minority (1 Black or African American, non-Hispanic/Latino; 1 Asian, non-Hispanic/Latino), 6 international. Average age 30. 29 applicants, 90% accepted, 15 enrolled. *Faculty:* 10 full-time (3 women). Expenses: Contact institution. *Financial support:* Research assistantships with partial tuition reimbursements, Federal Work-Study, scholarships/grants, health care benefits, and tuition waivers (partial) available. Support available to part-time students. Financial award application deadline: 3/15; financial award applicants required to submit FAFSA. In 2016, 16 master's awarded. *Program availability:* Part-time, evening/weekend. Offers business administration (MBA). *Application deadline:* For fall admission, 6/15 priority date for domestic and international students; for spring admission, 11/15 priority date for domestic and international students. Applications are processed on a rolling basis. Electronic applications

accepted. *Application Contact:* Brandon Schaller, Senior Graduate Student Status Examiner, 608-785-8941, Fax: 608-785-6700, E-mail: bschaller@uwlax.edu. *Dean,* Dr. Laura Milner, 608-785-8090, Fax: 608-785-6700, E-mail: lmilner@uwlax.edu.

College of Liberal Studies Students: 65 full-time (51 women), 58 part-time (49 women); includes 14 minority (1 Black or African American, non-Hispanic/Latino; 3 Asian, non-Hispanic/Latino; 7 Hispanic/Latino; 3 Two or more races, non-Hispanic/Latino), 1 international. Average age 25. *Faculty:* 8 full-time (5 women), 6 part-time/adjunct (3 women). Expenses: Contact institution. *Financial support:* Research assistantships with partial tuition reimbursements, Federal Work-Study, scholarships/grants, health care benefits, and tuition waivers (partial) available. Support available to part-time students. Financial award applicants required to submit FAFSA. In 2016, 50 master's, 11 other advanced degrees awarded. Offers liberal studies (MS Ed, Ed D, Ed S); school psychology (MS Ed, Ed S); student affairs administration (MS Ed, Ed D). *Application fee:* $56. Electronic applications accepted. *Application Contact:* Brandon Schaller, Senior Graduate Student Status Examiner, 608-785-8941, E-mail: admissions@uwlax.edu. *Dean,* Dr. Julia Johnson, 608-785-8113, Fax: 608-785-8119, E-mail: jjohnson2@uwlax.edu.

College of Science and Health Students: 253 full-time (167 women), 158 part-time (86 women); includes 34 minority (3 Black or African American, non-Hispanic/Latino; 3 American Indian or Alaska Native, non-Hispanic/Latino; 15 Asian, non-Hispanic/Latino; 7 Hispanic/Latino; 6 Two or more races, non-Hispanic/Latino), 29 international. Average age 27. *Faculty:* 75 full-time (28 women), 20 part-time/adjunct (15 women). Expenses: Contact institution. *Financial support:* Research assistantships with tuition reimbursements, Federal Work-Study, scholarships/grants, health care benefits, and tuition waivers (partial) available. Support available to part-time students. Financial award applicants required to submit CSS PROFILE or FAFSA. In 2016, 177 master's, 44 doctorates awarded. Offers adapted physical education (MS); adventure education (MS); applied sport science (MS); aquatic sciences (MS); biology (MS); cellular and molecular biology (MS); clinical exercise physiology (MS); clinical microbiology (MS); community health education (MPH, MS); data science (MS); human performance (MS); medical dosimetry (MS); microbiology (MS); nurse anesthesia (MS); occupational therapy (MS); physical education teaching (MS); physical therapy (DPT); physician assistant studies (MS); physiology (MS); recreation management (MS); school health education (MS); science and health (MPH, MS, MSE, DPT); software engineering (MSE); strength and conditioning (MS); therapeutic recreation (MS). *Application fee:* $56. Electronic applications accepted. *Application Contact:* Brandon Schaller, Senior Graduate Student Status Examiner, 608-785-8941, E-mail: admissions@uwlax.edu. *Interim Dean,* Dr. Mark Sandheinrich, 608-785-8261, Fax: 608-785-8221, E-mail: msandheinrich@uwlax.edu.

School of Education Students: 85 part-time (74 women); includes 2 minority (1 Asian, non-Hispanic/Latino; 1 Hispanic/Latino). Average age 27. 32 applicants, 100% accepted, 23 enrolled. *Faculty:* 5 full-time (3 women), 25 part-time/adjunct (17 women). Expenses: Contact institution. *Financial support:* Research assistantships, Federal Work-Study, scholarships/grants, health care benefits, and tuition waivers (partial) available. Support available to part-time students. Financial award application deadline: 3/15; financial award applicants required to submit FAFSA. In 2016, 25 master's, 5 other advanced degrees awarded. *Program availability:* Part-time, evening/weekend. Offers English language arts elementary (Graduate Certificate); professional development (ME-PD); reading (MS Ed); special education (MS Ed). *Application deadline:* Applications are processed on a rolling basis. Electronic applications accepted. *Application Contact:* Brandon Schaller, Senior Graduate Student Status Examiner, 608-785-8941, E-mail: admissions@uwlax.edu. *Dean, School of Education,* Marcie Wycoff-Horn, 608-785-6786, E-mail: mwycoff-horn@uwlax.edu.

UNIVERSITY OF WISCONSIN–MADISON, Madison, WI 53706-1380

General Information State-supported, coed, university. CGS member. *Graduate housing:* Rooms and/or apartments available on a first-come, first-served basis to single and married students. *Research affiliation:* Morgridge Institute for Research (life sciences: biological sciences), WiCell Research Institute (life sciences: biological sciences), University of Wisconsin Hospitals and Clinics (life sciences: health and medical sciences), William S. Middleton Memorial Veterans Hospital (life sciences: health and medical sciences), Universities Research Association, Inc. (physical and earth sciences: physics and astronomy), U.S. Department of Agriculture (USDA), Dairy Forage Center (life sciences: agriculture).

GRADUATE UNITS

Graduate School *Program availability:* Part-time, evening/weekend, 100% online, blended/hybrid learning. Offers biophysics (PhD); cellular and molecular biology (PhD). Electronic applications accepted.

College of Agricultural and Life Sciences *Program availability:* Part-time. Offers agricultural and applied economics (MA, MS, PhD); agricultural and life sciences (MA, MPS, MS, PhD); agroecology (MS, PhD); agronomy (MS, PhD); animal sciences (MS, PhD); bacteriology (MS); biochemistry (PhD); biological systems engineering (MS, PhD); dairy science (MS, PhD); entomology (MS, PhD); food science (MS, PhD); forestry (MS, PhD); genetic counseling (MS); genetics (PhD); horticulture (MS, PhD); landscape architecture (MA, MS); life sciences communication (MPS, MS); mass communications (PhD); nutritional sciences (MS, PhD); plant breeding and plant genetics (MS, PhD); plant pathology (MS, PhD); soil science (MS, PhD); wildlife ecology (MS, PhD). Electronic applications accepted.

College of Engineering Students: 1,460 full-time (322 women), 361 part-time (83 women); includes 175 minority (22 Black or African American, non-Hispanic/Latino; 3 American Indian or Alaska Native, non-Hispanic/Latino; 62 Asian, non-Hispanic/Latino; 67 Hispanic/Latino; 2 Native Hawaiian or other Pacific Islander, non-Hispanic/Latino; 19 Two or more races, non-Hispanic/Latino), 913 international. Average age 27. 5,562 applicants, 20% accepted, 390 enrolled. *Faculty:* 212 full-time (41 women). Expenses: Contact institution. *Financial support:* In 2016–17, 1,215 students received support, including 68 fellowships with full tuition reimbursements available, 818 research assistantships with full tuition reimbursements available, 282 teaching assistantships with full tuition reimbursements available; career-related internships or fieldwork, Federal Work-Study, institutionally sponsored loans, scholarships/grants, health care benefits, and unspecified assistantships also available. Support available to part-time students. Financial award application deadline: 12/1; financial award applicants required to submit FAFSA. In 2016, 473 master's, 169 doctorates awarded. *Program availability:* Part-time, blended/hybrid learning. Offers biomedical engineering (MS, PhD); chemical engineering (PhD); civil and environmental engineering (MS, PhD); electrical engineering (MS, PhD); engineering (MS, PhD); engineering mechanics (MS, PhD); environmental chemistry and technology (MS, PhD); geological engineering (MS, PhD); industrial engineering (MS, PhD); machine learning and signal processing (MS); manufacturing systems engineering (MS); materials science and engineering (MS, PhD); mechanical engineering (MS, PhD); nuclear engineering and engineering physics (MS, PhD).

Application deadline: Applications are processed on a rolling basis. *Application fee:* $75 ($81 for international students). Electronic applications accepted. *Application Contact:* Information Contact, 608-262-2433, Fax: 608-265-9505, E-mail: gradadmiss@grad.wisc.edu. *Dean,* Dr. Ian M. Robertson, 608-262-3482, Fax: 608-262-6400, E-mail: engr-dean_engr@wisc.edu.

College of Letters and Science *Program availability:* Part-time, evening/weekend, online learning. Offers African history (MA, PhD); African languages and literature (MA, PhD); Afro-American studies (MA); applied English linguistics (MA); archaeology (PhD); area studies (MA); art history (PhD); astronomy (PhD); atmospheric and oceanic sciences (MS, PhD); biological anthropology (PhD); biology of brain and behavior (PhD); biometry (MS); botany (MS, PhD); cartography and geographic information systems (MS); Central Asian history (MA, PhD); chemistry (MS, PhD); Chinese literature (MA, PhD); Chinese thought (MA, PhD); choral (MM, DMA); civilizations and cultures (PhD); classics (MA, PhD); clinical psychology (PhD); cognitive neurosciences (PhD); communication science (MA, PhD); comparative literature (MA, PhD); comparative world history (MA, PhD); composition (MM, DMA); composition and rhetoric (PhD); computer sciences (MS, PhD); creative writing (MFA); cultural anthropology (PhD); curriculum and instruction (MS, PhD); developmental psychology (PhD); East Asian history (MA, PhD); economics (PhD); English language and linguistics (MA, PhD); ethnomusicology (MA, PhD); European history (MA, PhD); family and consumer journalism (PhD); film (MA, PhD); folklore (PhD); French (MA, PhD); French studies (MFS, Certificate); gender and women's history (MA, PhD); geographic information systems (Certificate); geography (MS, PhD); geology (MS, PhD); geophysics (MS, PhD); German (MA, PhD); Greek (MA); Hebrew and Semitic studies (MA, PhD); historical musicology (PhD); history of medicine (MA, PhD); history of science (MA, PhD); instrumental (MM, DMA); Italian (MA, PhD); Japanese linguistics (MA, PhD); Japanese literature (MA, PhD); journalism and mass communication (MA); languages and cultures of Asia (MA); languages and literatures (MA); Latin (MA); Latin American and Caribbean history (MA, PhD); Latin American, Caribbean and Iberian studies (MA); letters and science (MA, MFA, MFS, MIPA, MM, MPA, MS, MSW, DMA, PhD, Certificate); library and information studies (MA, PhD); linguistics (MA, PhD); literary studies (MA, PhD); literature (MA, PhD); mass communication (PhD); mathematics (PhD); media and cultural studies (MA, PhD); Middle Eastern history (MA, PhD); music (MA, MM, DMA, PhD); music education (MM); music history (MA); music performance (MM, DMA); music theory (MA, PhD); normal aspects of speech, language and hearing (MS, PhD); orchestral (MM, DMA); perception (PhD); philology (PhD); philosophy (MA, PhD); physics (MA, MS, PhD); political science (PhD); Portuguese (MA, PhD); psychology (PhD); public policy and administration (MIPA, MPA); religions of Asia (PhD); rhetoric (MA, PhD); rural sociology (MS); Slavic languages and literature (MA, PhD); social and personality psychology (PhD); social welfare (PhD); social work (MSW); sociology (MS, PhD); South Asian studies (MA, PhD); Southeast Asian history (MA, PhD); Southeast Asian studies (MA); Spanish (MA, PhD); speech-language pathology (MS, PhD); statistics (MS, PhD); theatre and drama (MA, MFA, PhD); United States history (MA, PhD); urban and regional planning (MS, PhD); zoology (MA, MS, PhD). Electronic applications accepted.

Gaylord Nelson Institute for Environmental Studies Students: 137 full-time, 15 part-time; includes 13 minority (3 Black or African American, non-Hispanic/Latino; 2 American Indian or Alaska Native, non-Hispanic/Latino; 3 Asian, non-Hispanic/Latino; 4 Hispanic/Latino; 1 Two or more races, non-Hispanic/Latino), 25 international. Average age 30. 209 applicants, 49% accepted, 53 enrolled. *Faculty:* 18 full-time (6 women), 51 part-time/adjunct (15 women). Expenses: Contact institution. *Financial support:* In 2016–17, 112 students received support, including 7 fellowships with full tuition reimbursements available (averaging $24,800 per year), 25 research assistantships with full tuition reimbursements available (averaging $22,081 per year), 44 teaching assistantships with full tuition reimbursements available (averaging $16,196 per year); career-related internships or fieldwork, scholarships/grants, traineeships, health care benefits, unspecified assistantships, and project assistantships also available. Financial award application deadline: 12/1. In 2016, 41 master's, 12 doctorates awarded. *Program availability:* Part-time. Offers environment and resources (MS, PhD); environmental conservation (MS); environmental studies (MS, PhD); water resources management (MS). *Application deadline:* For fall admission, 12/1 for domestic and international students; for spring admission, 10/15 for domestic and international students; for summer admission, 12/1 for domestic and international students. *Application fee:* $75 ($81 for international students). Electronic applications accepted. *Application Contact:* Jim Miller, Senior Student Services Coordinator, 608-263-4373, Fax: 608-262-2273, E-mail: jemiller@wisc.edu. *Associate Director for Research and Education,* Dr. Paul H. Zedler, 608-265-8018, Fax: 608-262-2273, E-mail: phzedler@wisc.edu.

School of Education Offers administration (Certificate); art (MA, MFA); art education (MA); counseling (MS); counseling psychology (MS, PhD); curriculum and instruction (MS, PhD); education (MA, MFA, MS, PhD, Certificate); education and mathematics (MA); educational policy (MS, PhD); educational policy studies (MA, PhD); educational psychology (MS, PhD); French education (MA); German education (MA); global higher education (MS); kinesiology (MS, PhD); music education (MS); occupational therapy (MS, PhD); rehabilitation psychology (MA, MS, PhD); science education (MS); Spanish education (MA, MS, PhD).

School of Human Ecology Offers consumer behavior and family economics (MS, PhD); design studies (MFA, MS, PhD); human development and family studies (MS, PhD). Electronic applications accepted.

Wisconsin School of Business *Program availability:* Part-time, evening/weekend. Offers accountancy (M Acc); accounting and information systems (PhD); actuarial science, risk management and insurance (PhD); applied security analysis (MBA); arts administration (MBA); brand and product management (MBA); business (M Acc, MBA, PhD); corporate finance and investment banking (MBA); finance, investment and banking (PhD); general management (MBA); information systems (PhD); management and human resources (PhD); marketing (PhD); marketing research (MBA); operations and technology management (MBA); operations management (PhD); real estate (MBA); real estate and urban land economics (PhD); risk management and insurance (MBA); strategic human resource management (MBA); supply chain management (MBA); taxation (M Acc). Electronic applications accepted.

Law School Students: 544 full-time (268 women), 26 part-time (17 women); includes 114 minority (32 Black or African American, non-Hispanic/Latino; 1 American Indian or Alaska Native, non-Hispanic/Latino; 13 Asian, non-Hispanic/Latino; 47 Hispanic/Latino; 21 Two or more races, non-Hispanic/Latino), 69 international. Average age 26. 1,406 applicants, 46% accepted, 149 enrolled. *Faculty:* 60 full-time (40 women), 44 part-time/adjunct (17 women). Expenses: Contact institution. *Financial support:* In 2016–17, 353 students received support. Fellowships, research assistantships, career-related internships or fieldwork, scholarships/grants, health care benefits, tuition waivers (full and partial), and unspecified assistantships available. Support available to part-time students. Financial award application deadline: 4/1; financial award applicants required to submit FAFSA. In 2016, 42 master's, 190 doctorates awarded. *Program availability:* Part-time, evening/weekend. Offers law (LL M, JD, SJD). *Application deadline:* For fall admission, 4/1 for domestic students, 3/1 for international students. Applications are processed on a rolling basis. *Application fee:* $60. Electronic applications accepted. *Application Contact:* Rebecca L. Scheller, Assistant Dean for Admissions and Financial Aid, 608-262-5914, Fax: 608-263-3190, E-mail: admissions@law.wisc.edu. *Dean,* Margaret Raymond, 608-262-0618, Fax: 608-262-5485.

School of Medicine and Public Health Expenses: Contact institution. Offers biochemistry (MS, PhD); biomedical data science (MS); cancer biology (PhD); cellular and molecular pathology (PhD); clinical investigation (MS, PhD); endocrinology-reproductive physiology (MS, PhD); epidemiology (MS, PhD); genetic counselor studies (MGCS); health physics (MS); medical physics (MS, PhD); medicine (MD); medicine and public health (MGCS, MPA, MPH, MS, DPT, MD, PhD); microbiology (PhD); molecular and cellular pharmacology (PhD); molecular and environmental toxicology (MS, PhD); neuroscience (PhD); physical therapy (DPT); physician assistant (MPA); physiology (PhD); population health (MS, PhD); public health (MPH). Electronic applications accepted. *Dean,* Dr. Robert N. Golden.

School of Nursing *Program availability:* Part-time. Offers adult/gerontology (DNP); nursing (PhD); pediatrics (DNP); psychiatric mental health (DNP). Electronic applications accepted.

School of Pharmacy Offers pharmaceutical sciences (PhD); pharmacy (MS, PhD, Pharm D); social and administrative sciences in pharmacy (MS, PhD). Electronic applications accepted.

School of Veterinary Medicine Offers veterinary medicine (MS, DVM, PhD).

UNIVERSITY OF WISCONSIN–MILWAUKEE, Milwaukee, WI 53201-0413

General Information State-supported, coed, university. CGS member. *Enrollment:* 26,011 graduate, professional, and undergraduate students; 2,680 full-time matriculated graduate/professional students (1,588 women), 1,772 part-time matriculated graduate/professional students (1,056 women). *Enrollment by degree level:* 2,877 master's, 1,416 doctoral, 159 other advanced degrees. *Graduate housing:* Rooms and/or apartments available on a first-come, first-served basis to single and married students. Typical cost: $6200 (including board) for single students. Housing application deadline: 5/1. *Student services:* Campus employment opportunities, campus safety program, career counseling, child daycare facilities, exercise/wellness program, free psychological counseling, grant writing training, international student services, low-cost health insurance, multicultural affairs office, services for students with disabilities, writing training. *Library facilities:* Golda Meir Library. *Collection:* Books: 2.5 million (physical), 178,268 (digital/electronic); Serial titles: 112,752 (physical). Students can reserve study rooms. *Research affiliation:* Rockwell Automation (informatics, sensors and devices, materials), Johnson Controls (environment, advanced automation), GE Healthcare (informatics, biomedical imaging), Veolia Water S. A. (water research), We Energies (environment, wind turbine technology).

Computer facilities: Computer purchase and lease plans are available. 500 computers available on campus for general student use. A campuswide network can be accessed from student residence rooms and from off campus. Online class registration is available.

Website: http://www.uwm.edu/

General Application Contact: General Information Contact, 414-229-6569, Fax: 414-229-6967, E-mail: gradschool@uwm.edu.

GRADUATE UNITS

Graduate School Students: 2,680 full-time (1,588 women), 1,772 part-time (1,056 women); includes 738 minority (241 Black or African American, non-Hispanic/Latino; 7 American Indian or Alaska Native, non-Hispanic/Latino; 162 Asian, non-Hispanic/Latino; 54 Hispanic/Latino; 2 Native Hawaiian or other Pacific Islander, non-Hispanic/Latino; 272 Two or more races, non-Hispanic/Latino), 702 international. Average age 32. 4,421 applicants, 51% accepted, 1319 enrolled. Expenses: Contact institution. *Financial support:* Fellowships with partial tuition reimbursements, research assistantships with full tuition reimbursements, teaching assistantships with full tuition reimbursements, career-related internships or fieldwork, Federal Work-Study, scholarships/grants, health care benefits, tuition waivers (partial), and unspecified assistantships available. Support available to part-time students. Financial award application deadline: 6/30; financial award applicants required to submit FAFSA. In 2016, 1,381 master's, 214 doctorates, 163 other advanced degrees awarded. *Program availability:* Part-time, evening/weekend. *Application deadline:* Applications are processed on a rolling basis. *Application fee:* $56 ($96 for international students). Electronic applications accepted. *Application Contact:* General Information Contact, 414-229-6569, Fax: 414-229-6967, E-mail: gradschool@uwm.edu. *Dean,* Marija Gajdardziska-Josifovska, 414-229-5220, E-mail: mgj@uwm.edu.

College of Engineering and Applied Science Students: 240 full-time (72 women), 189 part-time (43 women); includes 37 minority (5 Black or African American, non-Hispanic/Latino; 22 Asian, non-Hispanic/Latino; 3 Hispanic/Latino; 7 Two or more races, non-Hispanic/Latino), 285 international. Average age 30. 529 applicants, 54% accepted, 119 enrolled. Expenses: Contact institution. *Financial support:* Fellowships, research assistantships, teaching assistantships, career-related internships or fieldwork, Federal Work-Study, and unspecified assistantships available. Support available to part-time students. Financial award application deadline: 4/15. In 2016, 97 master's, 30 doctorates awarded. *Program availability:* Part-time. Offers biomedical engineering (MS); civil engineering (MS, PhD); computer science (PhD); electrical and computer engineering (MS); electrical engineering (PhD); engineering and applied science (MS, PhD); engineering mechanics (MS); health information systems (PhD); health services management and policy (PhD); industrial and management engineering (MS); industrial engineering (PhD); knowledge based systems (PhD); manufacturing engineering (MS); materials (PhD); materials engineering (MS); mechanical engineering (MS); medical imaging and instrumentation (PhD); public health informatics (PhD). *Application deadline:* For fall admission, 1/1 for domestic students; for spring admission, 9/1 for domestic students. Applications are processed on a rolling basis. *Application fee:* $56 ($96 for international students). Electronic applications accepted. *Application Contact:* Betty Warras, General Information Contact, 414-229-6169, Fax: 414-229-6958, E-mail: ceas-graduate@uwm.edu. *Dean,* Dr. Brett Peters, 414-229-4126, E-mail: ceas-deans-office@uwm.edu.

College of Health Sciences Students: 304 full-time (226 women), 39 part-time (28 women); includes 37 minority (5 Black or African American, non-Hispanic/Latino; 14 Asian, non-Hispanic/Latino; 2 Hispanic/Latino; 16 Two or more races, non-Hispanic/Latino), 22 international. Average age 28. 244 applicants, 50% accepted, 97 enrolled. Expenses: Contact institution. *Financial support:* Research assistantships, teaching assistantships, career-related internships or fieldwork, Federal Work-Study, and unspecified assistantships available. Support available to part-time students. Financial award application deadline: 3/30. In 2016, 77 master's, 29 doctorates, 9 other advanced degrees awarded. *Program availability:* Part-time. Offers assistive technology and accessible design (Graduate Certificate); assistive technology and design (MS); athletic training (MS); biomedical sciences (MS); communication sciences and disorders (MS); ergonomics (MS); health care informatics (MS); health sciences (MHA, MS, DPT, PhD, Graduate Certificate); healthcare administration (MHA); kinesiology (MS, PhD); physical therapy (DPT). *Application deadline:* For fall admission, 1/1 priority date for domestic students; for spring admission, 9/1 for domestic students. Applications are processed on a rolling basis. *Application fee:* $56 ($96 for international students). *Application Contact:* Office of Student Affairs, 414-229-2758, Fax: 414-229-3373, E-mail: chs-info@uwm.edu. *Dean,* Ron A. Cisler, PhD, 414-229-5663, E-mail: rac@uwm.edu.

College of Letters and Science Students: 701 full-time (357 women), 359 part-time (200 women); includes 118 minority (33 Black or African American, non-Hispanic/Latino; 2 American Indian or Alaska Native, non-Hispanic/Latino; 24 Asian, non-Hispanic/Latino; 9 Hispanic/Latino; 50 Two or more races, non-Hispanic/Latino), 217 international. Average age 32. 1,484 applicants, 38% accepted, 292 enrolled. Expenses: Contact institution. *Financial support:* Fellowships, research assistantships, teaching assistantships, career-related internships or fieldwork, Federal Work-Study, unspecified assistantships, and project assistantships available. Support available to part-time students. Financial award application deadline: 4/15. In 2016, 238 master's, 88 doctorates, 29 other advanced degrees awarded. *Program availability:* Part-time. Offers Africology (PhD); anthropology (MS, PhD); art history (MA); behavioral biology (MS, PhD); botany (MS, PhD); cellular and molecular biology (MS, PhD); chemistry (MS, PhD); classic Greek (MA); classics (MA); communication (MA, PhD); comparative literature (MA); conservation biology (MS, PhD); economics (MA, PhD); English (MA, PhD); evolution (MS, PhD); experimental psychology (MS, PhD); foreign language and literature (MA); French (MA); genetics (MS, PhD); geological sciences (MS, PhD); German (MA); global history (PhD); history (MA); human resources and labor relations (MHRLR); international human resources and labor relations (Certificate); international interests (MA, MS, PhD); Latin (MA); letters and science (MA, MAFLL, MHRLR, MLS, MPA, MS, MSP, PhD, Graduate Certificate); liberal studies (MLS); linguistics (MA, PhD); mathematics (MS, PhD); media studies (MA); mediation and negotiation (Certificate); microbiology (MS, PhD); modern studies (PhD); museum studies (Graduate Certificate); philosophy (MA); physical geography and environmental studies (MA, MS, PhD); physics (MS, PhD); physiology and morphology of plants and animals (MS, PhD); political science (MA, PhD); psychology (PhD); public administration (MPA); rhetorical leadership (Graduate Certificate); sociology (MA, PhD); Spanish (MA); Spanish and Portuguese (MA); teaching English to speakers of other languages, adult- and university-level (Graduate Certificate); terrestrial and aquatic ecology (MS, PhD); translation (MA, Graduate Certificate); urban development (MA, MS, PhD); urban history (PhD); women's and gender studies (MA, Graduate Certificate). *Application deadline:* For fall admission, 1/1 priority date for domestic students; for spring admission, 9/1 for domestic students. Applications are processed on a rolling basis. *Application fee:* $56 ($96 for international students). *Application Contact:* General Letters and Science Support, 414-229-7711, E-mail: let-sci@uwm.edu. *Acting Dean,* Dave Clark, 414-375-0457, E-mail: dclark@uwm.edu.

College of Nursing Students: 185 full-time (156 women), 132 part-time (124 women); includes 60 minority (18 Black or African American, non-Hispanic/Latino; 1 American Indian or Alaska Native, non-Hispanic/Latino; 16 Asian, non-Hispanic/Latino; 4 Hispanic/Latino; 21 Two or more races, non-Hispanic/Latino), 12 international. Average age 36. 168 applicants, 61% accepted, 80 enrolled. Expenses: Contact institution. *Financial support:* Fellowships, research assistantships, teaching assistantships, career-related internships or fieldwork, Federal Work-Study, health care benefits, unspecified assistantships, and project assistantships available. Support available to part-time students. Financial award application deadline: 4/15; financial award applicants required to submit FAFSA. In 2016, 22 master's, 39 doctorates, 2 other advanced degrees awarded. *Program availability:* Part-time. Offers nursing (MN, MS, MSP, DNP, PhD, Graduate Certificate). *Application deadline:* For fall admission, 1/1 priority date for domestic students; for spring admission, 9/1 for domestic students. Applications are processed on a rolling basis. *Application fee:* $56 ($96 for international students). Electronic applications accepted. *Application Contact:* Student Affairs Office, 414-229-5047, E-mail: uwmnurse@uwm.edu. *Interim Dean,* Dr. Kim Litwack, 414-229-4189, E-mail: litwack@uwm.edu.

Helen Bader School of Social Welfare Students: 252 full-time (205 women), 103 part-time (75 women); includes 91 minority (49 Black or African American, non-Hispanic/Latino; 1 American Indian or Alaska Native, non-Hispanic/Latino; 7 Asian, non-Hispanic/Latino; 2 Hispanic/Latino; 32 Two or more races, non-Hispanic/Latino), 3 international. Average age 30. 407 applicants, 59% accepted, 147 enrolled. Expenses: Contact institution. *Financial support:* Fellowships with full tuition reimbursements, research assistantships with full tuition reimbursements, teaching assistantships with full tuition reimbursements, career-related internships or fieldwork, Federal Work-Study, health care benefits, unspecified assistantships, and project assistantships available. Support available to part-time students. Financial award application deadline: 4/15; financial award applicants required to submit FAFSA. In 2016, 138 master's, 2 doctorates, 8 other advanced degrees awarded. *Program availability:* Part-time. Offers applied data analysis using SAS (Graduate Certificate); applied gerontology (Graduate Certificate); crime analytics (MS); criminal justice (MS); nonprofit management (Graduate Certificate); social welfare (PhD); social work (MSW, PhD). *Application deadline:* For fall admission, 1/1 priority date for domestic students; for spring admission, 9/1 for domestic students. Applications are processed on a rolling basis. *Application fee:* $56 ($96 for international students). Electronic applications accepted. *Application Contact:* Deb Padgett, Associate Professor, Social Work, 414-229-6452, E-mail: dpadgett@uwm.edu. *Dean and Professor,* Stan Stojkovic, PhD, 414-229-4400, E-mail: stojkovi@uwm.edu.

Joseph J. Zilber School of Public Health Students: 65 full-time (52 women), 24 part-time (17 women); includes 21 minority (6 Black or African American, non-Hispanic/Latino; 8 Asian, non-Hispanic/Latino; 1 Hispanic/Latino; 6 Two or more races, non-Hispanic/Latino), 10 international. Average age 30. 88 applicants, 73% accepted, 34 enrolled. Expenses: Contact institution. *Financial support:* Fellowships and scholarships/grants available. In 2016, 21 master's awarded. *Program availability:* Part-time. Offers biostatistics (MPH); community and behavioral health promotion (MPH); environmental health sciences (MPH); epidemiology (MPH); public health (MPH, PhD, Graduate Certificate); public health policy and administration (MPH); public health: biostatistics (PhD); public health: community and behavioral health promotion (PhD). *Application Contact:* Advisor, 414-227-3001, Fax: 414-227-3002, E-mail: applyph@uwm.edu. *Interim Dean,* Ronald Perez, 414-229-4587, E-mail: perez@uwm.edu.

Lubar School of Business Students: 304 full-time (120 women), 268 part-time (95 women); includes 107 minority (36 Black or African American, non-Hispanic/Latino; 1 American Indian or Alaska Native, non-Hispanic/Latino; 34 Asian, non-Hispanic/Latino; 10 Hispanic/Latino; 26 Two or more races, non-Hispanic/Latino), 79 international. Average age 32. 461 applicants, 62% accepted, 210 enrolled. Expenses: Contact institution. *Financial support:* Fellowships with full tuition reimbursements, research assistantships with full tuition reimbursements, teaching assistantships with full tuition reimbursements, career-related internships or fieldwork, Federal Work-Study, health care benefits, unspecified assistantships, and project assistantships available. Support available to part-time students. Financial award application deadline: 4/15; financial award applicants required to submit FAFSA. In 2016, 300 master's, 32 other advanced degrees awarded. *Program availability:* Part-time, evening/weekend. Offers business administration (MBA); business analytics (Graduate Certificate); enterprise resource planning (Graduate Certificate); executive business administration (EMBA); information technology management (MS); investment management (Graduate Certificate); management science (MS, Graduate Certificate); nonprofit management (Graduate Certificate); nonprofit management and leadership (MS); state and local taxation (Graduate Certificate). *Application deadline:* For fall admission, 1/1 priority date for domestic students; for spring admission, 9/1 for domestic students. Applications are processed on a rolling basis. *Application fee:* $56 ($96 for international students). Electronic applications accepted. *Application Contact:* Business Graduate Student Services, 414-229-5403, E-mail: mba-ms@uwm.edu. *Dean,* V. Kanti Prasad, 414-229-6256, E-mail: dean-prasad@uwm.edu.

Peck School of the Arts Students: 92 full-time (53 women), 18 part-time (12 women); includes 17 minority (3 Black or African American, non-Hispanic/Latino; 1 Asian, non-Hispanic/Latino; 3 Hispanic/Latino; 10 Two or more races, non-Hispanic/Latino), 20 international. Average age 30. 141 applicants, 28% accepted, 30 enrolled. Expenses: Contact institution. *Financial support:* Teaching assistantships, career-related internships or fieldwork, Federal Work-Study, health care benefits, unspecified assistantships, and project assistantships available. Support available to part-time students. Financial award application deadline: 4/15; financial award applicants required to submit FAFSA. In 2016, 34 master's awarded. *Program availability:* Part-time. Offers arts (MA, MFA, MM, MS, CAS, Graduate Certificate). *Application deadline:* For fall admission, 1/1 priority date for domestic students; for spring admission, 9/1 for domestic students. Applications are processed on a rolling basis. *Application fee:* $56 ($96 for international students). Electronic applications accepted. *Application Contact:* Arts Student Services, 414-229-4763, E-mail: uwmpsoa@uwm.edu. *Dean,* Scott Emmons, 414-229-4762, E-mail: semm@uwm.edu.

School of Architecture and Urban Planning Students: 128 full-time (56 women), 19 part-time (5 women); includes 21 minority (3 Black or African American, non-Hispanic/Latino; 1 American Indian or Alaska Native, non-Hispanic/Latino; 6 Asian, non-Hispanic/Latino; 3 Hispanic/Latino; 8 Two or more races, non-Hispanic/Latino), 22 international. Average age 30. 150 applicants, 62% accepted, 45 enrolled. Expenses: Contact institution. *Financial support:* Fellowships, research assistantships, teaching assistantships, career-related internships or fieldwork, Federal Work-Study, health care benefits, unspecified assistantships, and project assistantships available. Support available to part-time students. Financial award application deadline: 4/15; financial award applicants required to submit FAFSA. In 2016, 97 master's, 1 doctorate, 11 other advanced degrees awarded. *Program availability:* Part-time. Offers architecture (M Arch, MS Arch, PhD); architecture and urban planning (M Arch, MS Arch, MUP, PhD, Graduate Certificate); geographic information systems (Graduate Certificate); urban planning (MUP). *Application deadline:* For fall admission, 1/1 priority date for domestic students; for spring admission, 9/1 for domestic students. Applications are processed on a rolling basis. *Application fee:* $56 ($96 for international students). Electronic applications accepted. *Application Contact:* Student Advising Office, 414-229-4015, E-mail: sarup-grad@uwm.edu. *Dean,* Robert Greenstreet, 414-229-4016, E-mail: bobg@uwm.edu.

School of Education Students: 260 full-time (196 women), 348 part-time (255 women); includes 166 minority (67 Black or African American, non-Hispanic/Latino; 1 American Indian or Alaska Native, non-Hispanic/Latino; 18 Asian, non-Hispanic/Latino; 15 Hispanic/Latino; 1 Native Hawaiian or other Pacific Islander, non-Hispanic/Latino; 64 Two or more races, non-Hispanic/Latino), 14 international. Average age 34. 493 applicants, 55% accepted, 172 enrolled. Expenses: Contact institution. *Financial support:* Fellowships, teaching assistantships, career-related internships or fieldwork, Federal Work-Study, health care benefits, unspecified assistantships, and project assistantships available. Support available to part-time students. Financial award application deadline: 4/15; financial award applicants required to submit FAFSA. In 2016, 218 master's, 19 doctorates, 36 other advanced degrees awarded. *Program availability:* Part-time. Offers administrative leadership (MS, Graduate Certificate); autism spectrum disorders (Graduate Certificate); children's mental health for school professionals (Graduate Certificate); community counseling (MS); counseling psychology (PhD); cultural foundations of community engagement and education (MS); curriculum and instruction (MS); education (MS, PhD, CAS, Ed S, Graduate Certificate); educational policy (Graduate Certificate); educational statistics and measurement (MS, PhD); exceptional education (MS); learning and development (MS, PhD); multicultural knowledge of mental health practices (Graduate Certificate); school counseling (MS); school counseling (Graduate Certificate); school psychology (MS, PhD, Ed S); support services for online students in higher education (Graduate Certificate); teaching and learning in higher education (Graduate Certificate); transition for students with disabilities (Graduate Certificate); urban education (PhD). *Application deadline:* For fall admission, 1/1 priority date for domestic students; for spring admission, 9/1 for domestic students. Applications are processed on a rolling basis. *Application fee:* $56 ($96 for international students). Electronic applications accepted. *Application Contact:* Education Office of Student Services, 414-229-4721, E-mail: soeoss@uwm.edu. *Dean,* Alan Shoho, 414-229-4181, E-mail: shoho@uwm.edu.

School of Freshwater Sciences Students: 28 full-time (12 women), 17 part-time (5 women); includes 4 minority (all Two or more races, non-Hispanic/Latino), 2 international. Average age 30. 41 applicants, 44% accepted, 11 enrolled. Expenses: Contact institution. *Financial support:* Fellowships, research assistantships, teaching assistantships, and unspecified assistantships available. Financial award applicants required to submit FAFSA. In 2016, 23 master's, 1 doctorate awarded. Offers freshwater sciences (MS, PhD). *Application fee:* $56 ($96 for international students). *Application Contact:* Dr. Harvey Bootsma, Graduate Program Representative, 414-382-1717, E-mail: hbootsma@uwm.edu. *Dean,* J. Val Klump, 414-382-1715, E-mail: vklump@uwm.edu.

School of Information Studies Students: 119 full-time (82 women), 250 part-time (194 women); includes 55 minority (13 Black or African American, non-Hispanic/Latino; 12 Asian, non-Hispanic/Latino; 2 Hispanic/Latino; 1 Native Hawaiian or other Pacific Islander, non-Hispanic/Latino; 27 Two or more races, non-Hispanic/Latino), 15 international. Average age 35. 203 applicants, 75% accepted, 81 enrolled. Expenses: Contact institution. *Financial support:* In 2016–17, 4 teaching assistantships were awarded; fellowships, research assistantships, career-related internships or fieldwork, Federal Work-Study, health care benefits, unspecified assistantships, and project assistantships also available. Support available to part-time students. Financial award application deadline: 4/15; financial award applicants required to submit FAFSA. In 2016, 116 master's, 2 doctorates, 5 other advanced degrees awarded. *Program availability:* Part-time. Offers information studies (MLIS, MS, PhD, CAS). *Application deadline:* For fall admission, 1/1 priority date for domestic students; for spring admission, 9/1 for domestic students. Applications are processed on a rolling basis. *Application fee:* $56 ($96 for international students). Electronic applications accepted. *Application Contact:* Linda Barajas, Admissions Coordinator, 414-229-3316, E-mail: barajas@uwm.edu. *Dean/Professor*, Tomas A. Lipinski, 414-229-4707, E-mail: tlipinsk@uwm.edu.

UNIVERSITY OF WISCONSIN–OSHKOSH, Oshkosh, WI 54901

General Information State-supported, coed, comprehensive institution. *Graduate housing:* Room and/or apartments available on a first-come, first-served basis to single students; on-campus housing not available to married students.

GRADUATE UNITS

Graduate Studies *Program availability:* Part-time, evening/weekend. Offers social work (MSW). Electronic applications accepted.

College of Business *Program availability:* Part-time. Offers business (GMBA, MBA); business administration (MBA); global business administration (GMBA). Electronic applications accepted.

College of Education and Human Services *Program availability:* Part-time, evening/weekend. Offers counseling (MSE); cross-categorical (MSE); curriculum and instruction (MSE); early childhood: exceptional education needs (MSE); education and human services (MS, MSE); educational leadership (MS); non-licensure (MSE); reading education (MSE). Electronic applications accepted.

College of Letters and Science *Program availability:* Part-time, evening/weekend. Offers biology (MS); English (MA); experimental psychology (MS); general agency (MPA); health care (MPA); industrial/organizational psychology (MS); letters and science (MA, MPA, MS, MSW); mathematics education (MS). Electronic applications accepted.

College of Nursing *Program availability:* Part-time. Offers adult health and illness (MSN); family nurse practitioner (MSN). Electronic applications accepted.

UNIVERSITY OF WISCONSIN–PARKSIDE, Kenosha, WI 53141-2000

General Information State-supported, coed, comprehensive institution. *Graduate housing:* Room and/or apartments available on a first-come, first-served basis to single students; on-campus housing not available to married students.

GRADUATE UNITS

College of Natural and Health Sciences *Program availability:* Part-time. Offers applied molecular biology (MSBS); natural and health sciences (MSBS). Electronic applications accepted.

School of Business and Technology *Program availability:* Part-time, evening/weekend. Offers business administration (MBA); business and technology (MBA, MSCIS); computer and information systems (MSCIS). Electronic applications accepted.

UNIVERSITY OF WISCONSIN–PLATTEVILLE, Platteville, WI 53818-3099

General Information State-supported, coed, comprehensive institution. *Enrollment:* 8,693 graduate, professional, and undergraduate students; 65 full-time matriculated graduate/professional students (42 women), 786 part-time matriculated graduate/professional students (356 women). *Enrollment by degree level:* 851 master's. *Graduate housing:* On-campus housing not available. *Student services:* Campus employment opportunities, campus safety program, career counseling, child daycare facilities, exercise/wellness program, free psychological counseling, grant writing training, international student services, low-cost health insurance, multicultural affairs office, services for students with disabilities, teacher training, writing training. *Library facilities:* Karrmann Library plus 1 other. *Collection:* Books: 199,895 (physical), 61,518 (digital/electronic); Serial titles: 14,246 (physical), 264 (digital/electronic); Databases: 172. Weekly public service hours: 87.

Computer facilities: 228 computers available on campus for general student use. A campuswide network can be accessed from student residence rooms and from off campus. Online class registration is available. Website: http://www.uwplatt.edu/

General Application Contact: Dee Dunbar, School of Graduate Studies, 608-342-1322, Fax: 608-342-1389, E-mail: gradstudies@uwplatt.edu.

GRADUATE UNITS

School of Graduate Studies Students: 65 full-time (42 women), 786 part-time (356 women); includes 150 minority (77 Black or African American, non-Hispanic/Latino; 8 American Indian or Alaska Native, non-Hispanic/Latino; 25 Asian, non-Hispanic/Latino; 38 Hispanic/Latino; 2 Two or more races, non-Hispanic/Latino). 279 applicants, 80% accepted, 122 enrolled. Expenses: Contact institution. *Financial support:* Research assistantships with partial tuition reimbursements, career-related internships or fieldwork, Federal Work-Study, institutionally sponsored loans, scholarships/grants, and unspecified assistantships available. Support available to part-time students. Financial award applicants required to submit FAFSA. In 2016, 264 master's awarded. *Program availability:* Part-time, evening/weekend, online learning. *Application deadline:* For fall admission, 9/1 for domestic students, 7/1 for international students; for spring admission, 1/1 for domestic students, 11/15 for international students. Applications are processed on a rolling basis. *Application fee:* $56. Electronic applications accepted. *Application Contact:* Dee Dunbar, School of Graduate Studies, 608-342-1322, Fax: 608-342-1389, E-mail: gradstudies@uwplatt.edu. *Dean*, Dr. Chanaka Mendez, 608-342-1322, E-mail: gradstudies@uwplatt.edu.

College of Engineering, Mathematics and Science Students: 2 full-time (both women), 1 part-time (0 women); includes 1 minority (Asian, non-Hispanic/Latino). 10 applicants, 20% accepted. Expenses: Contact institution. *Financial support:* Research assistantships with partial tuition reimbursements available. In 2016, 1 master's awarded. *Program availability:* Part-time. Offers computer science (MS); engineering, mathematics and science (MS). *Application deadline:* For fall admission, 9/1 for domestic students, 7/1 for international students; for spring admission, 1/1 for domestic students, 11/15 for international students. *Application fee:* $56. *Application*

Contact: Dee Dunbar, School of Graduate Studies, 608-342-1322, Fax: 608-342-1389, E-mail: gradstudies@uwplatt.edu. *Dean*, Molly Gribb, 608-342-1561, Fax: 608-342-1566, E-mail: ems@uwplatt.edu.

College of Liberal Arts and Education Students: 42 full-time (30 women), 72 part-time (54 women); includes 20 minority (18 Black or African American, non-Hispanic/Latino; 1 American Indian or Alaska Native, non-Hispanic/Latino; 1 Hispanic/Latino). 37 applicants, 86% accepted, 25 enrolled. Expenses: Contact institution. *Financial support:* Research assistantships with partial tuition reimbursements, career-related internships or fieldwork, Federal Work-Study, institutionally sponsored loans, scholarships/grants, and unspecified assistantships available. Support available to part-time students. Financial award applicants required to submit FAFSA. In 2016, 75 master's awarded. *Program availability:* Part-time, evening/weekend. Offers adult education (MSE); counselor education (MSE); liberal arts and education (MSE). *Application deadline:* For fall admission, 9/1 for domestic students, 7/15 for international students; for spring admission, 1/1 for domestic students, 11/15 for international students. Applications are processed on a rolling basis. *Application fee:* $56. Electronic applications accepted. *Application Contact:* Dee Dunbar, School of Graduate Studies, 608-342-1322, Fax: 608-342-1389, E-mail: gradstudies@uwplatt.edu. *Interim Dean*, Melissa Gromley, 608-342-1151, E-mail: lae@uwplatt.edu.

Distance Learning Center Students: 18 full-time (6 women), 660 part-time (261 women); includes 128 minority (58 Black or African American, non-Hispanic/Latino; 7 American Indian or Alaska Native, non-Hispanic/Latino; 24 Asian, non-Hispanic/Latino; 39 Hispanic/Latino). 205 applicants, 73% accepted, 106 enrolled. Expenses: Contact institution. *Financial support:* Scholarships/grants available. Support available to part-time students. In 2016, 157 master's awarded. *Program availability:* Part-time, evening/weekend. Offers criminal justice (MS); engineering (MS); integrated supply chain management (MS); organizational change leadership (MS); project management (MS). *Application deadline:* For fall admission, 7/1 priority date for domestic students; for spring admission, 11/1 priority date for domestic students. Applications are processed on a rolling basis. *Application fee:* $56. Electronic applications accepted. *Application Contact:* 800-362-5460, E-mail: disted@uwplatt.edu. *Executive Director*, Dawn Drake, 800-362-5460, Fax: 608-342-1071, E-mail: disted@uwplatt.edu.

UNIVERSITY OF WISCONSIN–RIVER FALLS, River Falls, WI 54022

General Information State-supported, coed, comprehensive institution. *Graduate housing:* Room and/or apartments available on a first-come, first-served basis to single students; on-campus housing not available to married students.

GRADUATE UNITS

Outreach and Graduate Studies *Program availability:* Part-time. Electronic applications accepted.

College of Agriculture, Food, and Environmental Sciences *Program availability:* Part-time. Offers agricultural education (MS); agriculture, food, and environmental sciences (MS). Electronic applications accepted.

College of Arts and Science *Program availability:* Part-time. Offers arts and science (MA, MSE); fine arts (MSE); mathematics education (MSE); science education (MSE); social science education (MSE); teaching English to speakers of other languages (MA). Electronic applications accepted.

College of Business and Economics Offers business and economics (MBA, MM). Electronic applications accepted.

College of Education and Professional Studies *Program availability:* Part-time. Offers communicative disorders (MS); counseling (MSE); education and professional studies (MS, MSE, Ed S); elementary education (MSE); professional development shared inquiry communities (MSE); reading (MSE); school psychology (MSE, Ed S); secondary education-communicative disorders (MSE).

UNIVERSITY OF WISCONSIN–STEVENS POINT, Stevens Point, WI 54481-3897

General Information State-supported, coed, comprehensive institution. *Graduate housing:* Room and/or apartments available on a first-come, first-served basis to single students; on-campus housing not available to married students.

GRADUATE UNITS

College of Fine Arts and Communication *Program availability:* Part-time. Offers elementary/secondary (MM Ed); fine arts and communication (MA, MM Ed); studio pedagogy (MM Ed); Suzuki talent education (MM Ed).

Division of Communication *Program availability:* Part-time. Offers interpersonal communication (MA); media studies (MA); organizational communication (MA); public relations (MA).

College of Letters and Science Offers biology (MST); English (MST); history (MST); letters and science (MBA, MST).

Division of Business and Economics Offers business and economics (MBA). Program offered jointly with University of Wisconsin–Oshkosh.

College of Natural Resources *Program availability:* Part-time. Offers natural resources (MS).

College of Professional Studies *Program availability:* Part-time.

School of Communication Sciences and Disorders Offers audiology (Au D); speech and language pathology (MS).

School of Education *Program availability:* Part-time. Offers education—general/reading (MSE); education—general/special (MSE); educational administration (MSE); elementary education (MSE); guidance and counseling (MSE).

School of Health Promotion and Human Development *Program availability:* Part-time. Offers human and community resources (MS); nutritional sciences (MS).

UNIVERSITY OF WISCONSIN–STOUT, Menomonie, WI 54751

General Information State-supported, coed, comprehensive institution. *Graduate housing:* Room and/or apartments available on a first-come, first-served basis to single students; on-campus housing not available to married students.

GRADUATE UNITS

Graduate School *Program availability:* Part-time, online learning. Electronic applications accepted.

College of Arts, Humanities and Social Sciences Offers design (MFA); technical and professional communication (MS).

College of Education, Health and Human Sciences *Program availability:* Part-time, online learning. Offers applied psychology (MS); career and technical education (MS, Ed D, Ed S); clinical mental health counseling (MS); education (MS, MS Ed, Ed D, Ed S); education, health and human sciences (MS, Ed S); food and nutritional sciences (MS); marriage and family therapy (MS); school counseling (MS); school psychology (MS Ed, Ed S); vocational rehabilitation (MS). Electronic applications accepted.

College of Management Offers management (MS); operations management (MS); project management (MS); quality management (MS); risk control (MS); supply chain management (MS); sustainable management (MS); training and human resource development (MS).

College of Science, Technology, Engineering and Mathematics Program availability: Part-time, online learning. Offers conservation biology (PSM); construction management (MS); industrial and applied mathematics (PSM); information and communication technologies (MS); manufacturing engineering (MS); science, technology, engineering and mathematics (MS). Electronic applications accepted.

UNIVERSITY OF WISCONSIN–SUPERIOR, Superior, WI 54880-4500

General Information State-supported, coed, comprehensive institution. *Graduate housing:* Rooms and/or apartments available on a first-come, first-served basis to single students and available to married students. Housing application deadline: 7/1. *Research affiliation:* Great Lakes Indian Fish and Wildlife Commission, Wisconsin Department of Natural Resources (biology), Environmental Protection Agency (biology), The Mexican National Institute for Ecology (biology), The Mexican Marine National Park Service (biology), Coastal Zone Management Institute and Authority of Belize (biology), Fisheries Department, Government of Belize (biology).

GRADUATE UNITS

Graduate Division *Program availability:* Part-time, evening/weekend, online learning. Offers art education (MA); art history (MA); art therapy (MA); community counseling (MSE); educational administration (MSE, Ed S); emotional/behavior disabilities (MSE); human relations (MSE); instruction (MSE); learning disabilities (MSE); mass communication (MA); school counseling (MSE); special education (MSE); speech communication (MA); studio arts (MA); sustainable management (MS); teaching reading (MSE); theater (MA). Electronic applications accepted.

UNIVERSITY OF WISCONSIN–WHITEWATER, Whitewater, WI 53190-1790

General Information State-supported, coed, comprehensive institution. *Graduate housing:* Rooms and/or apartments available on a first-come, first-served basis to single students and available to married students. Housing application deadline: 9/1. *Research affiliation:* Generac Power Systems (manufacturing), American Ag-Tec International (international marketing), American Family Insurance (insurance), R.A. Smith and Associates (civil engineering), Sho-Deen (property management and development), Webco Industries, Inc. (lightning radioactive transfer).

GRADUATE UNITS

School of Graduate Studies *Program availability:* Part-time, evening/weekend, online learning. Electronic applications accepted.

College of Arts and Communications *Program availability:* Part-time, evening/weekend, online learning. Offers arts and communications (MS); corporate communication (MS); mass communication (MS). Electronic applications accepted.

College of Business and Economics *Program availability:* Part-time, evening/weekend, online learning. Offers accounting (MPA); business and economics (MBA, MPA, MS, MSE); business and marketing education (MS); finance (MBA); school business management (MSE). Electronic applications accepted.

College of Education and Professional Studies *Program availability:* Part-time, evening/weekend, online learning. Offers communication sciences and disorders (MS); cross categorical licensure (MSE); education and professional studies (MS, MSE, Postbaccalaureate Certificate); professional development (MSE); safety (MS); special education (Postbaccalaureate Certificate). Electronic applications accepted.

College of Letters and Sciences *Program availability:* Part-time, evening/weekend. Offers letters and sciences (MSE, Ed S); school psychology (MSE, Ed S). Electronic applications accepted.

UNIVERSITY OF WYOMING, Laramie, WY 82071

General Information State-supported, coed, university. CGS member. *Graduate housing:* Rooms and/or apartments available on a first-come, first-served basis to single and married students.

GRADUATE UNITS

College of Agriculture and Natural Resources *Program availability:* Part-time. Offers agricultural and applied economics (MS); agriculture and natural resources (MA, MS, PhD); agroecology (MS); agronomy (MS, PhD); animal sciences (MS, PhD); early childhood development (MS); entomology (MS, PhD); entomology/water resources (MS, PhD); family and consumer sciences (MS); food science and human nutrition (MS); molecular biology (MA, MS, PhD); pathobiology (MS); rangeland ecology and watershed management (MS, PhD); rangeland ecology and watershed management/water resources (MS, PhD); reproductive biology (MS, PhD); soil science (MS); soil science/water resources (PhD). Electronic applications accepted.

College of Arts and Sciences *Program availability:* Part-time. Offers American studies (MA); anthropology (MA, PhD); arts and sciences (MA, MAT, MFA, MM, MME, MP, MPA, MS, MST, PhD); botany (MS, PhD); botany/water resources (MS); chemistry (MS, PhD); communication (MA); community and regional planning and natural resources (MP); creative writing (MFA); English (MA); French (MA); geography (MA, MP, MST); geography/water resources (MA); geology (MS, PhD); geophysics (MS, PhD); German (MA); history (MA, MAT); international peace corps (MA); international studies (MA); mathematics (MA, MAT, MS, MST, PhD); mathematics/computer science (PhD); music education (MME); performance (MM); philosophy (MA); political science (MA, MPA); psychology (MA, MS, PhD); public administration (MPA); rural planning and natural resources (MP); sociology (MA); Spanish (MA); statistics (MS, PhD); zoology and physiology (MS, PhD). Electronic applications accepted.

College of Business *Program availability:* Part-time, evening/weekend, online learning. Offers accounting (MS); business (MBA, MS, PhD); business administration (MBA); economics (MS, PhD); economics and finance (MS); finance (MS).

College of Education *Program availability:* Online learning. Offers community mental health (MS); counselor education and supervision (PhD); curriculum and instruction (MA, Ed D, PhD); education (MA, MS, MST, Ed D, PhD, Certificate, Ed S); educational leadership (MA, Ed D, Certificate); instructional technology (MS, Ed D, PhD); school counseling (MS); special education (MA, PhD, Ed S); student affairs (MS). Electronic applications accepted.

Science and Mathematics Teaching Center Offers science and mathematics teaching (MS, MST). Electronic applications accepted.

College of Engineering and Applied Sciences *Program availability:* Part-time. Offers atmospheric science (MS, PhD); chemical engineering (MS, PhD); civil engineering (MS, PhD); computer science (MS, PhD); electrical engineering (MS, PhD); engineering and applied sciences (MS, PhD); environmental engineering (MS); mechanical engineering (MS, PhD); petroleum engineering (MS, PhD). Electronic applications accepted.

College of Health Sciences *Program availability:* Part-time, online learning. Offers health sciences (MS, MSW, Pharm D). Electronic applications accepted.

Division of Communication Disorders *Program availability:* Part-time, online learning. Offers speech-language pathology (MS). Electronic applications accepted.

Division of Kinesiology and Health *Program availability:* Part-time, online learning. Offers kinesiology and health (MS). Electronic applications accepted.

Division of Social Work Offers social work (MSW).

Fay W. Whitney School of Nursing *Program availability:* Part-time, online learning. Offers nursing (MS).

School of Pharmacy *Program availability:* Online learning. Offers health services administration (MS); pharmacy (Pharm D).

College of Law Offers law (JD). Electronic applications accepted.

Graduate Program in Molecular and Cellular Life Sciences Offers molecular and cellular life sciences (PhD).

Program in Ecology Offers ecology (MS, PhD).

UPPER IOWA UNIVERSITY, Fayette, IA 52142-1857

General Information Independent, coed, comprehensive institution. *Graduate housing:* Room and/or apartments available to single students.

GRADUATE UNITS

Master of Education Program Offers early childhood (M Ed); English as a second language (M Ed); higher education (M Ed); instructional strategist (M Ed); reading (M Ed); teacher leadership (M Ed).

Online Master's Programs *Program availability:* Part-time, online learning. Offers accounting (MBA); corporate financial management (MBA); emergency management and homeland security (MPA); general management (MBA); general studies (MPA); government administration (MPA); health and human services (MPA); human resources management (MBA); nonprofit organizational management (MPA); organizational development (MBA); public management (MPA); sport administration (MSA). MBA also available at Madison, WI campus. Electronic applications accepted.

URBANA UNIVERSITY, Urbana, OH 43078-2091

General Information Independent, coed, comprehensive institution. *Graduate housing:* Room and/or apartments available on a first-come, first-served basis to single students; on-campus housing not available to married students.

GRADUATE UNITS

College of Education and Sports Studies *Program availability:* Part-time, evening/weekend. Offers classroom education (M Ed).

College of Nursing and Allied Health Offers nursing (MSN).

College of Social and Behavioral Sciences Offers criminal justice administration (MA).

Division of Business Administration *Program availability:* Part-time, evening/weekend. Offers business administration (MBA).

URSHAN GRADUATE SCHOOL OF THEOLOGY, Florissant, MO 63031

General Information Independent-religious, coed, graduate-only institution.

GRADUATE UNITS

Graduate Programs *Program availability:* Online learning. Offers theology (M Div, MACM, MTS).

URSULINE COLLEGE, Pepper Pike, OH 44124-4398

General Information Independent-religious, coed, primarily women, comprehensive institution. *Tuition:* Full-time $19,692; part-time $9846 per semester. One-time fee: $100 full-time. Tuition and fees vary according to program. *Graduate housing:* Room and/or apartments available on a first-come, first-served basis to single students; on-campus housing not available to married students. Housing application deadline: 8/20. *Student services:* Campus employment opportunities, career counseling, exercise/wellness program, free psychological counseling, multicultural affairs office, services for students with disabilities, teacher training. *Library facilities:* Ralph M. Besse Library. *Collection:* Books: 134,397 (physical), 110,963 (digital/electronic); Serial titles: 880 (physical), 49,163 (digital/electronic); Databases: 161. Weekly public service hours: 91; students can reserve study rooms.

Computer facilities: 72 computers available on campus for general student use. A campuswide network can be accessed from student residence rooms. Online class registration is available.
Website: http://www.ursuline.edu/

General Application Contact: Melanie Steele, Director, Graduate Admission, 440-646-8119, Fax: 440-684-6138, E-mail: graduateadmissions@ursuline.edu.

GRADUATE UNITS

School of Graduate Studies Students: 56 full-time (55 women), 432 part-time (386 women); includes 121 minority (94 Black or African American, non-Hispanic/Latino; 2 American Indian or Alaska Native, non-Hispanic/Latino; 7 Asian, non-Hispanic/Latino; 8 Hispanic/Latino; 10 Two or more races, non-Hispanic/Latino), 6 international. Average age 36. 211 applicants, 99% accepted, 148 enrolled. Expenses: Contact institution. *Financial support:* In 2016–17, 51 students received support. Federal Work-Study and scholarships/grants available. Financial award application deadline: 3/1; financial award applicants required to submit FAFSA. In 2016, 160 master's, 1 doctorate awarded. *Program availability:* Part-time. Offers adolescent to young adult education (MA); adult-gerontology acute care nurse practitioner (MSN); adult-gerontology clinical nurse specialist (MSN); adult-gerontology nurse practitioner (MSN); counseling and art therapy (MA); early childhood education (MA); educational administration (MA); ethical and entrepreneurial leadership (MBA); family nurse practitioner (MSN); financial planning and accounting (MBA); health services management (MBA); historic preservation (MA); liberal studies (MALS); management (MBA); management and leadership (MBA); marketing and communications management (MBA); middle childhood education (MA); nursing (DNP); nursing education (MSN); palliative care (MSN); special education (MA); theological and pastoral studies (MA). *Application deadline:* For fall admission, 8/1 priority date for domestic students. Applications are processed on a rolling basis. *Application fee:* $25. Electronic applications accepted. *Application Contact:* Melanie

Stelle, Director, Graduate Admission, 440-646-8146, Fax: 440-684-6138, E-mail: graduateadmissions@ursuline.edu. *Dean,* Dr. James Connell, 440-646-8120, Fax: 440-684-6088, E-mail: jconnell@ursuline.edu.

UTAH STATE UNIVERSITY, Logan, UT 84322

General Information State-supported, coed, university. CGS member. *Graduate housing:* Rooms and/or apartments available on a first-come, first-served basis to single and married students. *Research affiliation:* Boeing Aerospace and Engineering (science and engineering), Duke Energy Corporation (engineering), Kennecott Copper Corporation (natural resources), Kraft Foods, Inc. (agriculture), National Endowment for Financial Education (education).

GRADUATE UNITS

School of Graduate Studies *Program availability:* Part-time, evening/weekend, online learning.

College of Agriculture Program availability: Part-time, online learning. Offers agricultural systems technology (MS); agriculture (MDA, MS, PhD); animal science (MS, PhD); biometeorology (MS, PhD); bioveterinary science (MS, PhD); dairy science (MS); dietetic administration (MDA); ecology (MS, PhD); family and consumer sciences education (MS); nutrition and food sciences (MS, PhD); plant science (MS, PhD); soil science (MS, PhD); toxicology (MS, PhD).

College of Business Program availability: Part-time, evening/weekend, online learning. Offers accountancy (M Acc); applied economics (MS); business (M Acc, MA, MBA, MS, Ed D, PhD); business administration (MBA); business education (MS); business information systems (MS); business information systems and education (Ed D); economics (MA, MS, PhD); education (PhD); human resource management (MS).

College of Engineering Program availability: Part-time, evening/weekend. Offers aerospace engineering (MS, PhD); biological and agricultural engineering (MS, PhD); civil and environmental engineering (ME, MS, PhD, CE); electrical engineering (ME, MS, PhD); engineering (ME, MS, PhD, CE); industrial technology (MS); irrigation engineering (MS, PhD); mechanical engineering (ME, MS, PhD). Electronic applications accepted.

College of Humanities, Arts and Social Sciences Program availability: Part-time, evening/weekend, online learning. Offers advanced technical practice (MFA); American studies (MA, MS); art (MA, MFA); bioregional planning (MS); design (MFA); English (MA, MS); folklore (MA, MS); history (MA, MS); humanities, arts and social sciences (MA, MFA, MLA, MS, MSLT, MSS, PhD); interior design (MS); journalism and communication (MA, MS); landscape architecture (MLA); political science (MA, MS); second language teaching (MSLT); sociology (MA, MS, MSS, PhD); theatre arts (MA, MFA); western American literature and culture (MA, MS).

College of Natural Resources Program availability: Part-time. Offers bioregional planning (MS); ecology (MS, PhD); fisheries biology (MS, PhD); forestry (MS, PhD); geography (MA, MS); human dimensions of ecosystem science and management (MS, PhD); natural resources (MA, MNR, MS, PhD); range science (MS, PhD); recreation resource management (MS, PhD); watershed science (MS, PhD); wildlife biology (MS, PhD).

College of Science Program availability: Part-time, evening/weekend. Offers biochemistry (MS, PhD); biology (MS, PhD); chemistry (MS, PhD); computer science (MCS, MS, PhD); ecology (MS, PhD); geology (MS); industrial mathematics (MS); mathematical sciences (PhD); mathematics (M Math, MS); physics (MS, PhD); science (M Math, MCS, MS, PhD); statistics (MS).

Emma Eccles Jones College of Education and Human Services Program availability: Part-time, evening/weekend, online learning. Offers audiology (Au D, Ed S); business information systems (Ed D, PhD); clinical/counseling/school psychology (PhD); communication disorders and deaf education (M Ed); communicative disorders and deaf education (MA, MS); curriculum and instruction (Ed D, PhD); disability disciplines (PhD); education and human services (M Ed, MA, MFHD, MRC, MS, Au D, Ed D, PhD, Ed S); elementary education (M Ed, MA, MS); family and human development (MFHD); family, consumer, and human development (MS, PhD); health, physical education and recreation (M Ed, MS); instructional technology and learning sciences (M Ed, MS, PhD, Ed S); rehabilitation counselor education (MRC); research and evaluation (PhD); research and evaluation methodology (PhD); school counseling (MS); school psychology (MS); secondary education (M Ed, MA, MS, Ed S).

UTAH VALLEY UNIVERSITY, Orem, UT 84058-5999

General Information State-supported, coed, comprehensive institution.

GRADUATE UNITS

MBA Program *Program availability:* Part-time, evening/weekend. Offers accounting (MBA); management (MBA). Electronic applications accepted.

Program in Cybersecurity Offers cybersecurity (Graduate Certificate).

Program in Education *Program availability:* Part-time. Offers educational technology (M Ed); elementary mathematics (M Ed); elementary STEM (M Ed); English as a second language (M Ed); reading (M Ed); teachers as leaders (M Ed). Electronic applications accepted.

Program in Nursing *Program availability:* Part-time, online learning. Offers nursing (MSN). Electronic applications accepted.

UTICA COLLEGE, Utica, NY 13502-4892

General Information Independent, coed, comprehensive institution. *Enrollment:* 5,119 graduate, professional, and undergraduate students; 217 full-time matriculated graduate/professional students (166 women), 1,336 part-time matriculated graduate/professional students (748 women). *Enrollment by degree level:* 1,026 master's, 494 doctoral, 33 other advanced degrees. *Graduate faculty:* 65 full-time (28 women). *Tuition:* Full-time $33,736; part-time $767 per credit hour. *Required fees:* $520; $70 per course. Tuition and fees vary according to course load, degree level, campus/location and program. *Graduate housing:* Room and/or apartments available on a first-come, first-served basis to single students; on-campus housing not available to married students. Housing application deadline: 3/1. *Student services:* Campus employment opportunities, campus safety program, career counseling, international student services, low-cost health insurance, services for students with disabilities. *Library facilities:* Frank E. Gannett Memorial Library. *Collection:* Books: 307,523 (physical); Serial titles: 267,023 (physical). Students can reserve study rooms.

Computer facilities: 430 computers available on campus for general student use. A campuswide network can be accessed from student residence rooms. Online class registration is available.
Website: http://www.utica.edu/

General Application Contact: John D. Rowe, Director of Graduate Admissions, 315-792-3824, Fax: 315-792-3003, E-mail: jrowe@utica.edu.

GRADUATE UNITS

Department of Physical Therapy Students: 83 full-time (53 women), 411 part-time (281 women); includes 282 minority (17 Black or African American, non-Hispanic/Latino; 251 Asian, non-Hispanic/Latino; 11 Hispanic/Latino; 3 Two or more races, non-Hispanic/Latino). Average age 36. 240 applicants, 98% accepted, 232 enrolled. *Faculty:* 10 full-time (4 women). Expenses: Contact institution. *Financial support:* Career-related internships or fieldwork, scholarships/grants, tuition waivers (partial), and unspecified assistantships available. Support available to part-time students. Financial award application deadline: 3/15; financial award applicants required to submit FAFSA. In 2016, 283 doctorates awarded. *Program availability:* Part-time, evening/weekend, online learning. Offers physical therapy (DPT, TDPT). *Application deadline:* Applications are processed on a rolling basis. *Application fee:* $50. Electronic applications accepted. *Application Contact:* John D. Rowe, Director of Graduate Admissions, 315-792-3824, Fax: 315-792-3003, E-mail: jrowe@utica.edu. *Director,* Dr. Ashraf Elazzazi, 315-792-3313, E-mail: aelazza@utica.edu.

Liberal Studies Program Students: 1 (woman) full-time, 16 part-time (10 women); includes 4 minority (2 Black or African American, non-Hispanic/Latino; 2 Hispanic/Latino). Average age 32. 11 applicants, 73% accepted, 8 enrolled. *Faculty:* 19 full-time (8 women). Expenses: Contact institution. *Financial support:* Career-related internships or fieldwork, scholarships/grants, tuition waivers (partial), and unspecified assistantships available. Support available to part-time students. Financial award application deadline: 3/15; financial award applicants required to submit FAFSA. In 2016, 5 master's awarded. *Program availability:* Part-time, evening/weekend, online only, 100% online. Offers liberal studies (MS). *Application deadline:* Applications are processed on a rolling basis. *Application fee:* $50. Electronic applications accepted. *Application Contact:* John D. Rowe, Director of Graduate Admissions, 315-792-3824, Fax: 315-792-3003, E-mail: jrowe@utica.edu. *Director, Liberal Studies,* Dr. Lawrence Aaronson, 315-792-3092, E-mail: laarons@utica.edu.

Program in Accountancy Students: 9 full-time (6 women), 13 part-time (9 women); includes 2 minority (both Hispanic/Latino). Average age 31. 16 applicants, 88% accepted, 11 enrolled. *Faculty:* 3 full-time (1 woman). Expenses: Contact institution. *Financial support:* Career-related internships or fieldwork, scholarships/grants, tuition waivers (partial), and unspecified assistantships available. Support available to part-time students. Financial award application deadline: 3/15; financial award applicants required to submit FAFSA. *Program availability:* Part-time, evening/weekend. Offers accountancy (MBA). *Application deadline:* Applications are processed on a rolling basis. *Application fee:* $50. Electronic applications accepted. *Application Contact:* John D. Rowe, Director of Graduate Admissions, 315-792-3824, Fax: 315-792-3003, E-mail: jrowe@utica.edu. *MBA Director,* Dr. Zhaodan Huang, 315-792-3247, E-mail: zhuang@utica.edu.

Program in Cybersecurity Students: 3 full-time (2 women), 374 part-time (106 women); includes 108 minority (50 Black or African American, non-Hispanic/Latino; 2 American Indian or Alaska Native, non-Hispanic/Latino; 18 Asian, non-Hispanic/Latino; 28 Hispanic/Latino; 10 Two or more races, non-Hispanic/Latino). Average age 35. 163 applicants, 98% accepted, 155 enrolled. *Faculty:* 5 full-time (0 women), 8 part-time/adjunct (0 women). Expenses: Contact institution. *Financial support:* Application deadline: 3/15; applicants required to submit FAFSA. In 2016, 133 master's awarded. *Program availability:* Part-time, evening/weekend, 100% online. Offers cybersecurity (MS). *Application deadline:* Applications are processed on a rolling basis. Electronic applications accepted. *Application Contact:* John D. Rowe, Director of Graduate Admissions, 315-792-3824, Fax: 315-792-3003, E-mail: jrowe@utica.edu. *Chair,* Joseph Giordano, 315-792-2521.

Program in Economic Crime and Fraud Management Students: 1 full-time (0 women), 96 part-time (53 women); includes 27 minority (19 Black or African American, non-Hispanic/Latino; 1 American Indian or Alaska Native, non-Hispanic/Latino; 2 Asian, non-Hispanic/Latino; 5 Hispanic/Latino). Average age 33. 42 applicants, 93% accepted, 37 enrolled. *Faculty:* 7 full-time (0 women). Expenses: Contact institution. *Financial support:* Career-related internships or fieldwork, scholarships/grants, tuition waivers (partial), and unspecified assistantships available. Support available to part-time students. Financial award application deadline: 3/15; financial award applicants required to submit FAFSA. In 2016, 54 master's awarded. *Program availability:* Part-time, evening/weekend, 100% online. Offers economic crime and fraud management (MS). *Application deadline:* Applications are processed on a rolling basis. *Application fee:* $50. Electronic applications accepted. *Application Contact:* John D. Rowe, Director of Graduate Admissions, 315-792-3824, Fax: 315-792-3003, E-mail: jrowe@utica.edu. *Director of Economic Crime Graduate Programs,* Dr. R. Bruce McBride, 315-792-3808, E-mail: rmcbride@utica.edu.

Program in Economic Crime Management Students: 1 (woman) full-time, 27 part-time (14 women); includes 10 minority (5 Black or African American, non-Hispanic/Latino; 1 Asian, non-Hispanic/Latino; 4 Hispanic/Latino). Average age 39. *Faculty:* 4 full-time (0 women). Expenses: Contact institution. *Financial support:* Career-related internships or fieldwork, scholarships/grants, tuition waivers (partial), and unspecified assistantships available. Support available to part-time students. Financial award application deadline: 3/15; financial award applicants required to submit FAFSA. In 2016, 19 master's awarded. *Program availability:* Part-time, evening/weekend, online learning. Offers economic crime management (MS). *Application deadline:* Applications are processed on a rolling basis. *Application fee:* $50. Electronic applications accepted. *Application Contact:* John D. Rowe, Director of Graduate Admissions, 315-792-3824, Fax: 315-792-3003, E-mail: jrowe@utica.edu. *Director of Economic Crime Graduate Programs,* Dr. R. Bruce McBride, 315-792-3808, E-mail: rmcbride@utica.edu.

Program in Health Care Administration Students: 8 full-time (all women), 165 part-time (140 women); includes 45 minority (21 Black or African American, non-Hispanic/Latino; 1 American Indian or Alaska Native, non-Hispanic/Latino; 11 Asian, non-Hispanic/Latino; 10 Hispanic/Latino; 2 Two or more races, non-Hispanic/Latino; 1 international. Average age 34. 67 applicants, 93% accepted, 60 enrolled. Expenses: Contact institution. *Financial support:* Application deadline: 3/15; applicants required to submit FAFSA. In 2016, 60 master's awarded. *Program availability:* Part-time, evening/weekend, online learning. Offers health care administration (MS). *Application deadline:* Applications are processed on a rolling basis. *Application fee:* $50. Electronic applications accepted. *Application Contact:* John D. Rowe, Director of Graduate Admissions, 315-792-3824, Fax: 315-792-3003, E-mail: jrowe@utica.edu. *Head,* Dr. Dana Hart, 315-792-3375, E-mail: dhart@utica.edu.

Program in Occupational Therapy Students: 90 full-time (80 women), 2 part-time (1 woman); includes 6 minority (1 Black or African American, non-Hispanic/Latino; 1 Asian, non-Hispanic/Latino; 3 Hispanic/Latino; 1 Two or more races, non-Hispanic/Latino). Average age 25. 62 applicants, 98% accepted, 58 enrolled. *Faculty:* 7 full-time (all women). Expenses: Contact institution. *Financial support:* Career-related internships or fieldwork, scholarships/grants, tuition waivers (partial), and unspecified assistantships available. Support available to part-time students. Financial award application deadline: 3/15; financial award applicants required to submit FAFSA. In 2016, 62 master's awarded. *Program availability:* Part-time, evening/weekend. Offers occupational therapy

(MS). *Application deadline:* Applications are processed on a rolling basis. *Application fee:* $50. Electronic applications accepted. *Application Contact:* John D. Rowe, Director of Graduate Admissions, 315-792-3824, Fax: 315-792-3003, E-mail: jrowe@utica.edu. *Director,* Cora Bruns, 315-792-3125, E-mail: cbruns@utica.edu.

Teacher Education Programs Students: 17 full-time (12 women), 30 part-time (21 women); includes 3 minority (1 Black or African American, non-Hispanic/Latino; 1 Hispanic/Latino; 1 Two or more races, non-Hispanic/Latino). Average age 27. 21 applicants, 76% accepted, 14 enrolled. *Faculty:* 10 full-time (7 women). Expenses: Contact institution. *Financial support:* Career-related internships or fieldwork, scholarships/grants, tuition waivers (partial), and unspecified assistantships available. Support available to part-time students. Financial award application deadline: 3/15; financial award applicants required to submit FAFSA. In 2016, 20 master's awarded. Offers teacher education (MS, MS Ed, CAS). *Application deadline:* Applications are processed on a rolling basis. *Application fee:* $50. Electronic applications accepted. *Application Contact:* John D. Rowe, Director of Graduate Admissions, 315-792-3824, Fax: 315-792-3003, E-mail: jrowe@utica.edu. *Director, Institute for Excellence in Education,* Dr. Patrice Hallock, 315-792-3162, E-mail: phallock@utica.edu.

VALDOSTA STATE UNIVERSITY, Valdosta, GA 31698

General Information State-supported, coed, university. CGS member. *Graduate housing:* Rooms and/or apartments available on a first-come, first-served basis to single and married students. Housing application deadline: 7/1.

GRADUATE UNITS

College of Nursing and Health Sciences *Program availability:* Part-time, online learning. Offers adult gerontology nurse practitioner (MSN); family nurse practitioner (MSN); family psychiatric mental health nurse practitioner (MSN). Electronic applications accepted.

Department of Communication Sciences and Disorders Offers communication disorders (M Ed); speech-language pathology (SLPD). Electronic applications accepted.

Department of Early Childhood and Special Education *Program availability:* Part-time, evening/weekend, blended/hybrid learning. Offers early childhood (M Ed); special education (M Ed, MAT, Ed S). Electronic applications accepted.

Department of English *Program availability:* Part-time, 100% online, blended/hybrid learning. Offers literature (MA); rhetoric and composition (MA); studies for language arts teachers (MA). Electronic applications accepted.

Department of Psychology, Counseling, and Family Therapy *Program availability:* Part-time, evening/weekend, 100% online, blended/hybrid learning. Offers school counseling (M Ed, Ed S). Electronic applications accepted.

Department of Social Work *Program availability:* Part-time, evening/weekend, online learning. Offers social work (MSW).

Master of Business Administration Program *Program availability:* Part-time, evening/weekend, 100% online, blended/hybrid learning. Offers business administration (MBA); healthcare administration (MBA). Program is a member of the Georgia WebMBA. Electronic applications accepted.

Program in Educational Leadership *Program availability:* 100% online, blended/hybrid learning. Offers educational leadership (M Ed). Electronic applications accepted.

Program in Library and Information Science *Program availability:* 100% online. Offers library and information science (MLIS).

VALLEY CITY STATE UNIVERSITY, Valley City, ND 58072

General Information State-supported, coed, comprehensive institution. *Enrollment:* 1,452 graduate, professional, and undergraduate students; 4 full-time matriculated graduate/professional students (3 women), 133 part-time matriculated graduate/professional students (92 women). *Enrollment by degree level:* 157 master's. *Graduate faculty:* 21 full-time (12 women), 15 part-time/adjunct (11 women). Tuition, state resident: full-time $7906; part-time $292.80 per credit. Tuition, nonresident: full-time $7906; part-time $292.80 per credit. *Required fees:* $2152; $79.70 per credit. $478.20 per semester. *Student services:* Career counseling, free psychological counseling, services for students with disabilities, writing training. *Library facilities:* Allen Memorial Library. *Collection:* Books: 77,407 (physical), 37,791 (digital/electronic); Serial titles: 1,202 (physical), 1,440 (digital/electronic); Databases: 91. Students can reserve study rooms.

Computer facilities: Computer purchase and lease plans are available. 995 computers available on campus for general student use. A campuswide network can be accessed from student residence rooms and from off campus. Online class registration is available. Website: http://www.vcsu.edu/

General Application Contact: Misty Lindgren, Administrative Assistant for Office of Graduate Studies and Research, 701-845-7303, Fax: 701-845-7190, E-mail: misty.lindgren@vcsu.edu.

GRADUATE UNITS

Online Master of Education Program Students: 4 full-time (3 women), 133 part-time (92 women); includes 9 minority (1 American Indian or Alaska Native, non-Hispanic/Latino; 4 Hispanic/Latino; 4 Two or more races, non-Hispanic/Latino), 1 international. Average age 34. 35 applicants, 91% accepted, 28 enrolled. *Faculty:* 21 full-time (12 women), 15 part-time/adjunct (11 women). Expenses: Contact institution. *Financial support:* In 2016–17, 23 students received support. Scholarships/grants, tuition waivers (full and partial), and unspecified assistantships available. Financial award application deadline: 6/14; financial award applicants required to submit FAFSA. In 2016, 45 master's awarded. *Program availability:* Part-time, evening/weekend, online only, 100% online. Offers elementary education (M Ed); English education (M Ed); library and information technologies (M Ed); teaching (MAT); teaching and technology (M Ed); teaching English language learners (M Ed); technology education (M Ed). *Application deadline:* For fall admission, 7/21 priority date for domestic and international students; for spring admission, 12/8 priority date for domestic and international students; for summer admission, 5/5 priority date for domestic and international students. Applications are processed on a rolling basis. *Application fee:* $35. Electronic applications accepted. *Application Contact:* Misty Lindgren, Graduate Studies, 701-845-7303, Fax: 701-845-7190, E-mail: misty.lindgren@vcsu.edu. *Dean,* Dr. Gary Thompson, 701-845-7197, E-mail: gary.thompson@vcsu.edu.

VALPARAISO UNIVERSITY, Valparaiso, IN 46383

General Information Independent-religious, coed, comprehensive institution. CGS member. *Enrollment:* 4,433 graduate, professional, and undergraduate students; 382 full-time matriculated graduate/professional students (187 women), 399 part-time matriculated graduate/professional students (200 women). *Enrollment by degree level:* 724 master's, 49 doctoral, 8 other advanced degrees. *Graduate faculty:* 39 full-time (18 women), 131 part-time/adjunct (65 women). *Tuition:* Full-time $11,070; part-time $615 per credit hour. *Required fees:* $116 per semester. Tuition and fees vary according to

course load, degree level and program. *Graduate housing:* On-campus housing not available. *Student services:* Campus employment opportunities, campus safety program, career counseling, exercise/wellness program, free psychological counseling, international student services, low-cost health insurance, multicultural affairs office, services for students with disabilities, teacher training, writing training. *Library facilities:* Christopher Center for Library and Information Resources plus 1 other. *Collection:* Books: 545,491 (physical); Serial titles: 2,588 (physical), 79,749 (digital/electronic). Weekly public service hours: 112.

Computer facilities: 500 computers available on campus for general student use. A campuswide network can be accessed from student residence rooms and from off campus. Online class registration, Web academic information, degree audit, online course evaluations are available.
Website: http://www.valpo.edu/

General Application Contact: Jessica Choquette, Assistant Director of Graduate Admissions, 219-464-5313, Fax: 219-464-5381, E-mail: graduate.school@valpo.edu.

GRADUATE UNITS

Graduate School and Continuing Education Students: 382 full-time (187 women), 399 part-time (200 women); includes 61 minority (28 Black or African American, non-Hispanic/Latino; 10 Asian, non-Hispanic/Latino; 15 Hispanic/Latino; 2 Native Hawaiian or other Pacific Islander, non-Hispanic/Latino; 6 Two or more races, non-Hispanic/Latino), 378 international. Average age 29. *Faculty:* 119 part-time/adjunct (59 women). Expenses: Contact institution. *Financial support:* Career-related internships or fieldwork, scholarships/grants, traineeships, health care benefits, and unspecified assistantships available. Support available to part-time students. Financial award applicants required to submit FAFSA. In 2016, 357 master's, 16 doctorates, 27 other advanced degrees awarded. *Program availability:* Part-time, evening/weekend, 100% online, blended/hybrid learning. Offers analytics and modeling (MS); arts and entertainment administration (MA); Chinese studies (MA); clinical mental health counseling (MA); computing (MS); cyber security (MS); digital media (MS, Certificate); English studies and communication (MA); health administration (MHA); health care administration (MS); history (MALS, Post-Master's Certificate); humane education (M Ed, MA, MALS, Graduate Certificate, Post-Master's Certificate); individualized liberal studies (MALS); initial licensure (M Ed); instructional leadership (M Ed); international commerce and policy (MS); international economics and finance (MS); liberal studies (MALS, Post-Master's Certificate); management (MS); school psychology (Ed S); secondary education (M Ed); security8441 (MS); sports administration (MS); sports media (MS, Certificate); TESOL (MA, Certificate); theology (MALS, Post-Master's Certificate); theology and ministry (MALS). *Application deadline:* Applications are processed on a rolling basis. *Application fee:* $30 ($50 for international students). Electronic applications accepted. *Application Contact:* Jessica Choquette, Assistant Director of Graduate Admissions and Recruitment, 219-464-5313 Ext. 6510, Fax: 219-464-5381, E-mail: jessica.choquette@valpo.edu. *Dean, Graduate School and Continuing Education,* Dr. Jennifer A. Ziegler, 219-464-5313, Fax: 219-464-5381, E-mail: jennifer.ziegler@valpo.edu.

College of Business Students: 7 full-time (5 women), 43 part-time (16 women); includes 5 minority (4 Black or African American, non-Hispanic/Latino; 1 Two or more races, non-Hispanic/Latino). Average age 31. Expenses: Contact institution. *Financial support:* Available to part-time students. Applicants required to submit FAFSA. *Program availability:* Part-time, evening/weekend, online learning. Offers business administration (MBA); business decision-making (Certificate); business intelligence (Certificate); engineering management (Certificate); finance (Certificate); general business (Certificate); leading the global enterprise (Certificate); management (Certificate). *Application deadline:* Applications are processed on a rolling basis. *Application fee:* $30 ($50 for international students). Electronic applications accepted. *Application Contact:* Cindy Scanlan, Director of Graduate Programs in Management, 219-465-7952, Fax: 219-464-5789, E-mail: cindy.scanlan@valpo.edu. *Dean,* Jim Brodzinski, 219-464-5035, E-mail: jim.brodzinski@valpo.edu.

College of Nursing and Health Professions Students: 56 full-time (47 women), 28 part-time (27 women); includes 9 minority (4 Black or African American, non-Hispanic/Latino; 1 Asian, non-Hispanic/Latino; 4 Hispanic/Latino), 19 international. Average age 33. Expenses: Contact institution. *Financial support:* Available to part-time students. Applicants required to submit FAFSA. *Program availability:* Part-time, evening/weekend, online learning. Offers nursing (DNP); nursing education (MSN, Certificate); physician assistant (MSPA); public health (MPH). *Application deadline:* Applications are processed on a rolling basis. *Application fee:* $30 ($50 for international students). Electronic applications accepted. *Application Contact:* Jessica Choquette, Graduate Admissions Specialist, 219-464-6510, Fax: 219-464-5381, E-mail: jessica.choquette@valpo.edu. *Dean,* Karen Allen, 219-464-5289, Fax: 219-464-5425.

Law School 928 applicants, 66% accepted, 130 enrolled. Expenses: Contact institution. *Financial support:* Fellowships, research assistantships, teaching assistantships, career-related internships or fieldwork, Federal Work-Study, institutionally sponsored loans, scholarships/grants, and tuition waivers (partial) available. Support available to part-time students. Financial award application deadline: 3/1; financial award applicants required to submit FAFSA. *Program availability:* Part-time. Offers law (LL M, JD). *Application deadline:* For fall admission, 7/15 priority date for domestic students. Applications are processed on a rolling basis. *Application fee:* $0. Electronic applications accepted. *Application Contact:* Kelly Anthony, Associate Director of Admissions, 219-465-7821, Fax: 219-465-7975, E-mail: law.admissions@valpo.edu. *Dean/Professor,* Andrea D. Lyon, 219-465-7834, Fax: 219-465-7872, E-mail: andrea.lyon@valpo.edu.

VAN ANDEL INSTITUTE GRADUATE SCHOOL, Grand Rapids, MI 49503

General Information Private, coed, graduate-only institution. *Enrollment by degree level:* 26 doctoral. *Graduate faculty:* 37 full-time (9 women). *Tuition:* Full-time $25,000; part-time $835 per credit. *Student services:* Career counseling, exercise/wellness program, free psychological counseling, grant writing training, international student services, low-cost health insurance, services for students with disabilities, teacher training, writing training. *Library facilities:* Van Andel Institute Library. *Collection:* Study areas open 24 hours, 5–7 days a week.

Computer facilities: 4 computers available on campus for general student use. A campuswide network can be accessed. Online class registration is available.
Website: http://www.vaei.vai.org/grad-school/

General Application Contact: Christy Mayo, Enrollment and Records Administrator, 616-234-5722, Fax: 616-234-5709, E-mail: christy.mayo@vai.org.

GRADUATE UNITS

PhD Program Students: 26 full-time (16 women); includes 6 minority (1 Black or African American, non-Hispanic/Latino; 4 Asian, non-Hispanic/Latino; 1 Hispanic/Latino). Average age 24. 41 applicants, 22% accepted, 6 enrolled. *Faculty:* 37 full-time (9 women). Expenses: Contact institution. *Financial support:* In 2016–17, 26 students received support, including 26 fellowships; health care benefits also available. In 2016, 2 doctorates awarded. Offers cell and molecular genetics (PhD). *Application deadline:* For fall admission, 12/1 for domestic and international students. Applications are processed on a rolling basis. *Application fee:* $0. Electronic applications accepted. *Application Contact:* Christy Mayo, Enrollment and Records Administrator, 616-234-5722, Fax: 616-234-5709, E-mail: christy.mayo@vai.org. *President and Dean,* Steve Triezeberg, 616-234-5708, Fax: 616-234-5709, E-mail: steve.triezenberg@vai.org.

VANCOUVER ISLAND UNIVERSITY, Nanaimo, BC V9R 5S5, Canada

General Information Province-supported, coed, comprehensive institution. *Graduate housing:* Room and/or apartments available on a first-come, first-served basis to single students; on-campus housing not available to married students. Housing application deadline: 3/5.

GRADUATE UNITS

Master of Business Administration Program *Program availability:* Part-time. Offers international business (MBA). Program offered jointly with University of Hertfordshire. Electronic applications accepted.

VANCOUVER SCHOOL OF THEOLOGY, Vancouver, BC V6T 1L4, Canada

General Information Independent-religious, coed, graduate-only institution. *Tuition:* Part-time $281 per credit hour. Part-time tuition and fees vary according to degree level, campus/location and program. *Graduate housing:* Rooms and/or apartments guaranteed to single students and available to married students. Housing application deadline: 4/7. *Student services:* Career counseling, free psychological counseling. *Library facilities:* H.R. MacMillan Library.

Computer facilities: 10 computers available on campus for general student use. Website: http://www.vst.edu/

General Application Contact: Anita Fast, Registrar, 604-822-9563, Fax: 604-822-9212, E-mail: afast@vst.edu.

GRADUATE UNITS

Graduate and Professional Programs Expenses: Contact institution. *Financial support:* Fellowships, research assistantships with partial tuition reimbursements, teaching assistantships with partial tuition reimbursements, career-related internships or fieldwork, scholarships/grants, and tuition waivers (partial) available. Support available to part-time students. Financial award application deadline: 3/30. *Program availability:* Part-time, online learning. Offers public and pastoral leadership (MA); public and pastoral leadership in spiritual care (MA); theological studies (MATS, Diploma); theology (M Div, Th M). *Application deadline:* Applications are processed on a rolling basis. *Application fee:* $75 Canadian dollars. Electronic applications accepted. *Application Contact:* Anita Fast, Registrar, 604-822-9563, Fax: 604-822-9212, E-mail: afast@vst.edu. *Principal,* Rev. Dr. Richard Topping, 604-822-9808, Fax: 604-822-9212.

VANDERBILT UNIVERSITY, Nashville, TN 37240-1001

General Information Independent, coed, university. CGS member. *Enrollment:* 12,587 graduate, professional, and undergraduate students; 5,049 full-time matriculated graduate/professional students (2,841 women), 699 part-time matriculated graduate/professional students (552 women). *Enrollment by degree level:* 2,589 master's, 3,123 doctoral, 36 other advanced degrees. *Graduate faculty:* 1,081 full-time (324 women), 14 part-time/adjunct (3 women). *Tuition:* Part-time $1854 per credit hour. *Graduate housing:* On-campus housing not available. *Student services:* Campus employment opportunities, campus safety program, career counseling, child daycare facilities, exercise/wellness program, free psychological counseling, grant writing training, international student services, low-cost health insurance, multicultural affairs office, services for students with disabilities, teacher training, writing training. *Library facilities:* Jean and Alexander Heard Library plus 7 others. *Collection:* Books: 3.1 million (physical), 1.7 million (digital/electronic); Databases: 3,700. *Research affiliation:* Medtronic, Incorporated (medical research), Celgene Corporation (biopharmaceuticals), Sandhill Scientific, Inc. (medical research), Westat, Inc. (research and evaluation), Amgen (medicine), Boston Scientific Corporation (health science and technology).

Computer facilities: A campuswide network can be accessed from student residence rooms and from off campus. Online class registration, productivity and educational software are available.
Website: http://www.vanderbilt.edu/

General Application Contact: Walter B. Bieschke, Program Coordinator for Graduate Admissions, 615-322-0236, Fax: 615-343-9936, E-mail: vandygrad@vanderbilt.edu.

GRADUATE UNITS

Center for Medicine, Health, and Society Students: 14 full-time (11 women), 1 (woman) part-time; includes 8 minority (3 Black or African American, non-Hispanic/Latino; 2 Asian, non-Hispanic/Latino; 2 Hispanic/Latino; 1 Two or more races, non-Hispanic/Latino). Average age 23. 17 applicants, 88% accepted, 13 enrolled. *Faculty:* 8 full-time (4 women). Expenses: Contact institution. *Financial support:* Federal Work-Study, scholarships/grants, and health care benefits available. Financial award application deadline: 1/15; financial award applicants required to submit CSS PROFILE or FAFSA. In 2016, 9 master's awarded. Offers medicine, health, and society (MA). *Application deadline:* For fall admission, 1/15 for domestic and international students. Electronic applications accepted. *Application Contact:* Dominique Behague, Acting Director/Director of Graduate Studies, 615-322-0919, Fax: 615-322-2731, E-mail: dominique.behague@vanderbilt.edu. *Director,* Dr. Jonathan Metzl, 615-343-2504, Fax: 615-343-8889, E-mail: jonathan.metzl@vanderbilt.edu.

Department of Anthropology Students: 27 full-time (20 women); includes 6 minority (all Hispanic/Latino), 9 international. Average age 33. 71 applicants, 8% accepted, 5 enrolled. *Faculty:* 13 full-time (4 women). Expenses: Contact institution. *Financial support:* Fellowships with tuition reimbursements, research assistantships with full tuition reimbursements, teaching assistantships with full tuition reimbursements, career-related internships or fieldwork, Federal Work-Study, institutionally sponsored loans, scholarships/grants, and health care benefits available. Financial award application deadline: 1/15; financial award applicants required to submit CSS PROFILE or FAFSA. In 2016, 3 master's, 2 doctorates awarded. Offers anthropology (MA, PhD). *Application deadline:* For fall admission, 1/15 for domestic and international students. *Application fee:* $0. Electronic applications accepted. *Application Contact:* John Janusek, Director of Graduate Studies, 615-343-6120, E-mail: john.w.janusek@vanderbilt.edu. *Chair,* Dr. Beth Conklin, 615-343-6120, Fax: 615-343-0230, E-mail: beth.a.conklin@vanderbilt.edu.

Department of Biological Sciences Students: 47 full-time (25 women); includes 9 minority (1 Black or African American, non-Hispanic/Latino; 4 Asian, non-Hispanic/Latino; 2 Hispanic/Latino; 2 Two or more races, non-Hispanic/Latino), 15 international. Average age 27. 81 applicants, 9% accepted, 3 enrolled. *Faculty:* 21 full-time (4 women). Expenses: Contact institution. *Financial support:* Fellowships with tuition reimbursements, research assistantships with full tuition reimbursements, teaching assistantships with full tuition reimbursements, Federal Work-Study, institutionally sponsored loans, scholarships/grants, traineeships, and health care benefits available. Financial award application deadline: 1/15; financial award applicants required to submit CSS PROFILE or FAFSA. In 2016, 6 doctorates awarded. Offers biological sciences (MS, PhD). *Application deadline:* For fall admission, 1/15 for domestic and international students. Electronic applications accepted. *Application Contact:* Donna Webb, Director of Graduate Studies, 615-322-2008. *Chair,* Dr. Douglas McMahon, 615-322-2008, Fax: 615-343-6707, E-mail: douglas.g.mcmahon@vanderbilt.edu.

Department of Biomedical Informatics Students: 20 full-time (11 women); includes 5 minority (2 Black or African American, non-Hispanic/Latino; 3 Asian, non-Hispanic/Latino), 1 international. Average age 30. 48 applicants, 4% accepted. *Faculty:* 26 full-time (7 women). Expenses: Contact institution. *Financial support:* Fellowships with tuition reimbursements, research assistantships with tuition reimbursements, teaching assistantships with tuition reimbursements, Federal Work-Study, institutionally sponsored loans, scholarships/grants, traineeships, and health care benefits available. Financial award application deadline: 1/15; financial award applicants required to submit CSS PROFILE or FAFSA. In 2016, 5 master's, 5 doctorates awarded. *Program availability:* Part-time. Offers biomedical informatics (MS, PhD). *Application deadline:* For fall admission, 1/15 for domestic and international students. Electronic applications accepted. *Application Contact:* Gretchen Jackson, Director of Graduate Studies, 615-936-1050, Fax: 615-936-1427, E-mail: rischelle.jenkins@vanderbilt.edu. *Chair,* Dr. Kevin Johnson, 615-936-1423, Fax: 615-936-1427, E-mail: kevin.johnson@vanderbilt.edu.

Department of Cancer Biology Students: 24 full-time (15 women); includes 11 minority (6 Black or African American, non-Hispanic/Latino; 4 Asian, non-Hispanic/Latino; 1 Hispanic/Latino), 1 international. Average age 28. *Faculty:* 10 full-time (5 women). Expenses: Contact institution. *Financial support:* Fellowships with tuition reimbursements, research assistantships with tuition reimbursements, Federal Work-Study, institutionally sponsored loans, scholarships/grants, traineeships, and health care benefits available. Financial award application deadline: 1/15; financial award applicants required to submit CSS PROFILE or FAFSA. In 2016, 12 doctorates awarded. Offers cancer biology (MS, PhD). *Application deadline:* For fall admission, 1/15 for domestic and international students. *Application fee:* $0. Electronic applications accepted. *Application Contact:* Jin Chen, Director of Graduate Studies, 615-322-0375, Fax: 615-936-2911, E-mail: jin.chen@vanderbilt.edu. *Acting Chair,* Dr. Hal Moses, 615-322-0375, Fax: 615-936-2911, E-mail: hal.moses@vanderbilt.edu.

Department of Chemistry Students: 117 full-time (53 women); includes 21 minority (8 Black or African American, non-Hispanic/Latino; 2 Asian, non-Hispanic/Latino; 9 Hispanic/Latino; 2 Two or more races, non-Hispanic/Latino), 7 international. Average age 25. 329 applicants, 25% accepted, 36 enrolled. *Faculty:* 20 full-time (4 women). Expenses: Contact institution. *Financial support:* Fellowships with tuition reimbursements, research assistantships with full tuition reimbursements, teaching assistantships with full tuition reimbursements, Federal Work-Study, institutionally sponsored loans, scholarships/grants, traineeships, and health care benefits available. Financial award application deadline: 1/15; financial award applicants required to submit CSS PROFILE or FAFSA. In 2016, 6 master's, 22 doctorates awarded. Offers analytical chemistry (MAT, MS, PhD); inorganic chemistry (MAT, MS, PhD); organic chemistry (MAT, MS, PhD); physical chemistry (MAT, MS, PhD); theoretical chemistry (MAT, MS). *Application deadline:* For fall admission, 1/15 for domestic and international students. *Application fee:* $0. Electronic applications accepted. *Application Contact:* Carmello Rizzo, Director of Graduate Studies, 615-322-2861, Fax: 615-322-4936, E-mail: c.rizzo@vanderbilt.edu. *Chair,* Dr. David Cliffel, 615-343-3937, Fax: 615-322-4936, E-mail: d.cliffel@vanderbilt.edu.

Department of Classical Studies *Faculty:* 3 full-time (2 women). Expenses: Contact institution. *Financial support:* Fellowships with tuition reimbursements, teaching assistantships with tuition reimbursements, Federal Work-Study, institutionally sponsored loans, scholarships/grants, and health care benefits available. Financial award application deadline: 1/15; financial award applicants required to submit CSS PROFILE or FAFSA. In 2016, 1 master's awarded. Offers classics (MA). *Application deadline:* For fall admission, 1/15 for domestic and international students. Electronic applications accepted. *Application Contact:* Walter B. Bieschke, Program Coordinator for Graduate Admissions, 615-322-0236, Fax: 615-343-9936, E-mail: vandygrad@vanderbilt.edu. *Director of Graduate Studies,* Dr. Barbara Tsakirgis, 615-322-2516, Fax: 615-343-7261, E-mail: barbara.tsakirgis@vanderbilt.edu.

Department of Earth and Environmental Sciences Students: 12 full-time (9 women), 1 part-time (0 women); includes 1 minority (Hispanic/Latino). Average age 24. 52 applicants, 15% accepted, 6 enrolled. *Faculty:* 10 full-time (2 women). Expenses: Contact institution. *Financial support:* Fellowships with tuition reimbursements, research assistantships with tuition reimbursements, teaching assistantships with full tuition reimbursements, career-related internships or fieldwork, Federal Work-Study, institutionally sponsored loans, and health care benefits available. Financial award application deadline: 1/15; financial award applicants required to submit CSS PROFILE or FAFSA. In 2016, 5 master's awarded. Offers earth and environmental sciences (MAT, MS). *Application deadline:* For fall admission, 1/15 for domestic and international students. *Application fee:* $0. Electronic applications accepted. *Application Contact:* Guil Gualda, Director of Graduate Studies, 615-322-2976, E-mail: g.gualda@vanderbilt.edu. *Chair,* Dr. Steven Goodbred, 615-322-2976, E-mail: g.gualda@vanderbilt.edu.

Department of Economics Students: 114 full-time (44 women); includes 11 minority (2 Black or African American, non-Hispanic/Latino; 2 Asian, non-Hispanic/Latino; 2 Hispanic/Latino; 5 Two or more races, non-Hispanic/Latino), 71 international. Average age 26. 621 applicants, 33% accepted, 46 enrolled. *Faculty:* 37 full-time (5 women). Expenses: Contact institution. *Financial support:* Fellowships with tuition reimbursements, teaching assistantships with tuition reimbursements, career-related internships or fieldwork, Federal Work-Study, institutionally sponsored loans, scholarships/grants, and health care benefits available. Financial award application deadline: 1/15; financial award applicants required to submit CSS PROFILE or FAFSA. In 2016, 39 master's, 7 doctorates awarded. Offers economic development (MA); economics (PhD). *Application deadline:* For fall admission, 1/15 for domestic and international students; for spring admission, 11/1 for domestic students. Applications are processed on a rolling basis. Electronic applications accepted. *Application Contact:* Jennifer Reinganum, Director of Graduate Studies, 615-322-2871, Fax: 615-343-8495, E-mail: jennifer.f.reinganum@vanderbilt.edu. *Chair,* Dr. Eric Bond, 615-322-2871, Fax: 615-343-8495, E-mail: k.saggi@vanderbilt.edu.

Department of English Students: 35 full-time (27 women); includes 13 minority (9 Black or African American, non-Hispanic/Latino; 2 Asian, non-Hispanic/Latino; 2

Hispanic/Latino), 3 international. Average age 28. 286 applicants, 6% accepted, 5 enrolled. *Faculty:* 32 full-time (22 women). Expenses: Contact institution. *Financial support:* Fellowships with tuition reimbursements, research assistantships with tuition reimbursements, teaching assistantships with full tuition reimbursements, Federal Work-Study, institutionally sponsored loans, scholarships/grants, and health care benefits available. Financial award application deadline: 1/15; financial award applicants required to submit CSS PROFILE or FAFSA. In 2016, 10 master's, 3 doctorates awarded. Offers English (MA, MAT, PhD). *Application deadline:* For fall admission, 1/15 for domestic and international students. Electronic applications accepted. *Application Contact:* Vera Kutzinski, Director of Graduate Studies, 615-322-2541, Fax: 615-343-8028, E-mail: vera.kutzinski@vanderbilt.edu. *Chair,* Dr. Dana Nelson, 615-322-2541, Fax: 615-343-8028, E-mail: dana.d.nelson@vanderbilt.edu.

Department of French and Italian Students: 13 full-time (10 women); includes 1 minority (Two or more races, non-Hispanic/Latino), 3 international. Average age 28. 10 applicants, 50% accepted, 5 enrolled. *Faculty:* 12 full-time (6 women). Expenses: Contact institution. *Financial support:* Fellowships with tuition reimbursements, teaching assistantships with tuition reimbursements, career-related internships or fieldwork, Federal Work-Study, institutionally sponsored loans, scholarships/grants, and health care benefits available. Financial award application deadline: 1/15; financial award applicants required to submit CSS PROFILE or FAFSA. Offers French (MA, MAT, PhD). *Application deadline:* For fall admission, 1/15 for domestic and international students. Electronic applications accepted. *Application Contact:* Paul Miller, Director of Graduate Studies, 615-322-6900, Fax: 615-343-6909, E-mail: paul.miller@vanderbilt.edu. *Chair,* Dr. Laura Schneider, 615-322-6900, Fax: 615-343-6909, E-mail: laura.c.schneider@vanderbilt.edu.

Department of Germanic and Slavic Languages Students: 24 full-time (16 women); includes 3 minority (1 Black or African American, non-Hispanic/Latino; 1 Hispanic/Latino; 1 Two or more races, non-Hispanic/Latino), 5 international. Average age 31. 8 applicants, 75% accepted, 4 enrolled. *Faculty:* 5 full-time (2 women). Expenses: Contact institution. *Financial support:* Fellowships with tuition reimbursements, teaching assistantships with tuition reimbursements, career-related internships or fieldwork, Federal Work-Study, institutionally sponsored loans, scholarships/grants, and health care benefits available. Financial award application deadline: 1/15; financial award applicants required to submit CSS PROFILE or FAFSA. In 2016, 4 doctorates awarded. Offers German (MA, MAT, PhD). *Application deadline:* For fall admission, 1/15 for domestic and international students. Electronic applications accepted. *Application Contact:* Christoph Zeller, Director of Graduate Studies, 615-875-9065, Fax: 615-343-7258, E-mail: christoph.zeller@vanderbilt.edu. *Chair,* Dr. Lutz Koepnick, 615-322-2611, Fax: 615-343-7258, E-mail: lutz.koepnick@vanderbilt.edu.

Department of History Students: 59 full-time (30 women), 1 (woman) part-time; includes 11 minority (2 Black or African American, non-Hispanic/Latino; 1 Asian, non-Hispanic/Latino; 5 Hispanic/Latino; 3 Two or more races, non-Hispanic/Latino), 13 international. Average age 29. 164 applicants, 15% accepted, 12 enrolled. *Faculty:* 40 full-time (11 women). Expenses: Contact institution. *Financial support:* Fellowships with full tuition reimbursements, teaching assistantships with full tuition reimbursements, Federal Work-Study, institutionally sponsored loans, scholarships/grants, and health care benefits available. Financial award application deadline: 1/15; financial award applicants required to submit CSS PROFILE or FAFSA. In 2016, 4 master's, 4 doctorates awarded. Offers history (MA, MAT, PhD). *Application deadline:* For fall admission, 1/15 for domestic and international students. *Application fee:* $0. Electronic applications accepted. *Application Contact:* Catherine Molineux, Director of Graduate Studies, 615-322-2575, Fax: 615-343-6002, E-mail: catherine.a.molineux@vanderbilt.edu. *Chair,* Dr. Joel Harrington, 615-322-2575, Fax: 615-343-6002, E-mail: joel.harrington@vanderbilt.edu.

Department of Mathematics Students: 37 full-time (6 women); includes 2 minority (1 Black or African American, non-Hispanic/Latino; 1 Asian, non-Hispanic/Latino), 22 international. Average age 25. 101 applicants, 28% accepted, 12 enrolled. *Faculty:* 31 full-time (2 women). Expenses: Contact institution. *Financial support:* Fellowships with tuition reimbursements, research assistantships with full tuition reimbursements, teaching assistantships with full tuition reimbursements, Federal Work-Study, institutionally sponsored loans, scholarships/grants, and health care benefits available. Financial award application deadline: 1/15; financial award applicants required to submit CSS PROFILE or FAFSA. In 2016, 3 master's, 7 doctorates awarded. Offers mathematics (MA, MAT, MS, PhD). *Application deadline:* For fall admission, 1/1 for domestic and international students. *Application fee:* $0. Electronic applications accepted. *Application Contact:* Denis Osin, Director of Graduate Studies, 615-322-6672, Fax: 315-343-0215, E-mail: denis.v.osin@vanderbilt.edu. *Chair,* Dr. Mike Neamtu, 615-322-6672, Fax: 615-343-0215, E-mail: mike.neamtu@vanderbilt.edu.

Department of Philosophy Students: 26 full-time (17 women); includes 9 minority (1 Black or African American, non-Hispanic/Latino; 2 Asian, non-Hispanic/Latino; 3 Hispanic/Latino; 3 Two or more races, non-Hispanic/Latino). Average age 29. 156 applicants, 4% accepted, 5 enrolled. *Faculty:* 15 full-time (4 women). Expenses: Contact institution. *Financial support:* Fellowships with full tuition reimbursements, teaching assistantships with full tuition reimbursements, Federal Work-Study, institutionally sponsored loans, scholarships/grants, and health care benefits available. Financial award application deadline: 1/15; financial award applicants required to submit CSS PROFILE or FAFSA. In 2016, 2 master's, 7 doctorates awarded. Offers philosophy (MA, PhD). *Application deadline:* For fall admission, 1/15 for domestic and international students. Electronic applications accepted. *Application Contact:* Julian Wuerth, Director of Graduate Studies, 615-322-2637, Fax: 615-343-7259, E-mail: julian.wuerth@vanderbilt.edu. *Chair,* Dr. Robert Talisse, 615-343-5349, Fax: 615-343-7259, E-mail: robert.talisse@vanderbilt.edu.

Department of Physics and Astronomy Students: 50 full-time (10 women), 1 part-time (0 women); includes 7 minority (3 Black or African American, non-Hispanic/Latino; 1 Asian, non-Hispanic/Latino; 1 Hispanic/Latino; 2 Two or more races, non-Hispanic/Latino), 17 international. Average age 27. 115 applicants, 21% accepted, 8 enrolled. *Faculty:* 26 full-time (4 women). Expenses: Contact institution. *Financial support:* Fellowships with tuition reimbursements, research assistantships with full tuition reimbursements, teaching assistantships with full tuition reimbursements, career-related internships or fieldwork, Federal Work-Study, and institutionally sponsored loans available. Financial award application deadline: 1/15; financial award applicants required to submit CSS PROFILE or FAFSA. In 2016, 4 master's, 16 doctorates awarded. Offers astronomy (MS); health physics (MA); physics (MAT, MS, PhD). *Application deadline:* For fall admission, 1/1 for domestic and international students. Electronic applications accepted. *Application Contact:* Julia Velkovska, Director of Graduate Studies, 615-322-2828, E-mail: julia.velkovska@vanderbilt.edu. *Chair,* Dr. Robert Sherrer, 615-322-2828, E-mail: robert.scherrer@vanderbilt.edu.

Department of Political Science Students: 32 full-time (12 women), 2 part-time (both women); includes 4 minority (1 Black or African American, non-Hispanic/Latino; 1 Asian, non-Hispanic/Latino; 1 Hispanic/Latino; 1 Two or more races, non-Hispanic/Latino), 10

international. Average age 28. 170 applicants, 13% accepted, 7 enrolled. *Faculty:* 26 full-time (11 women). Expenses: Contact institution. *Financial support:* Fellowships with full tuition reimbursements, research assistantships with full tuition reimbursements, teaching assistantships with full tuition reimbursements, Federal Work-Study, institutionally sponsored loans, scholarships/grants, and health care benefits available. Financial award application deadline: 1/15; financial award applicants required to submit CSS PROFILE or FAFSA. In 2016, 6 master's, 6 doctorates awarded. Offers political science (MA, MAT, PhD). *Application deadline:* For fall admission, 1/15 for domestic and international students. Electronic applications accepted. *Application Contact:* Jon Hiskey, Director of Graduate Studies, 615-322-6222, Fax: 615-343-6003, E-mail: j.hiskey@vanderbilt.edu. *Chair,* Dr. David Lewis, 615-322-6222, Fax: 615-343-6003, E-mail: david.lewis@vanderbilt.edu.

Department of Religion Students: 65 full-time (35 women); includes 17 minority (13 Black or African American, non-Hispanic/Latino; 1 Asian, non-Hispanic/Latino; 2 Hispanic/Latino; 1 Two or more races, non-Hispanic/Latino), 5 international. Average age 33. 152 applicants, 15% accepted, 9 enrolled. *Faculty:* 30 full-time (10 women). Expenses: Contact institution. *Financial support:* Fellowships with tuition reimbursements, teaching assistantships with tuition reimbursements, Federal Work-Study, institutionally sponsored loans, health care benefits, and tuition waivers (full and partial) available. Support available to part-time students. Financial award application deadline: 1/15; financial award applicants required to submit CSS PROFILE or FAFSA. In 2016, 2 master's, 13 doctorates awarded. Offers religion (MA, PhD). *Application deadline:* For fall admission, 12/15 for domestic and international students. Electronic applications accepted. *Application Contact:* Karen Eardley, Administrative Assistant, 615-343-3977, Fax: 615-343-9957, E-mail: karen.eardley@vanderbilt.edu. *Chair and Director of Graduate Studies,* Dr. James Byrd, Jr., 615-343-9977, Fax: 615-343-9957, E-mail: james.p.byrd@vanderbilt.edu.

Department of Sociology Students: 37 full-time (30 women); includes 13 minority (5 Black or African American, non-Hispanic/Latino; 4 Asian, non-Hispanic/Latino; 4 Hispanic/Latino), 4 international. Average age 28. 124 applicants, 6% accepted, 6 enrolled. *Faculty:* 15 full-time (5 women). Expenses: Contact institution. *Financial support:* Fellowships with full tuition reimbursements, research assistantships, teaching assistantships with full tuition reimbursements, Federal Work-Study, institutionally sponsored loans, scholarships/grants, and health care benefits available. Financial award application deadline: 1/15; financial award applicants required to submit CSS PROFILE or FAFSA. In 2016, 3 master's, 6 doctorates awarded. Offers sociology (MA, PhD). *Application deadline:* For fall admission, 1/15 for domestic and international students. Electronic applications accepted. *Application Contact:* Richard Pitt, Director of Graduate Studies, 615-322-7530, Fax: 615-322-7505, E-mail: r.pitt@vanderbilt.edu. *Chair,* Dr. Larry Isaac, 615-322-7626, Fax: 615-322-7505, E-mail: larry.isaac@vanderbilt.edu.

Department of Spanish and Portuguese Students: 25 full-time (11 women); includes 5 minority (all Hispanic/Latino), 11 international. Average age 31. 39 applicants, 31% accepted, 7 enrolled. *Faculty:* 13 full-time (6 women). Expenses: Contact institution. *Financial support:* Fellowships with tuition reimbursements, teaching assistantships with full tuition reimbursements, Federal Work-Study, institutionally sponsored loans, and health care benefits available. Financial award application deadline: 1/15; financial award applicants required to submit CSS PROFILE or FAFSA. In 2016, 2 master's, 3 doctorates awarded. Offers Portuguese (MA); Spanish (MA, MAT, PhD); Spanish and Portuguese (PhD). *Application deadline:* For fall admission, 1/15 for domestic and international students. Electronic applications accepted. *Application Contact:* Andres Zamora, Director of Graduate Studies, 615-322-6930, Fax: 615-343-7260, E-mail: andres.zamora@vanderbilt.edu. *Chair,* Dr. Benigno Trigo, 615-322-6930, Fax: 615-343-7260, E-mail: benigno.trigo@vanderbilt.edu.

Divinity School *Program availability:* Part-time. Offers divinity (M Div, MTS). Electronic applications accepted.

Peabody College Students: 544 full-time (458 women), 156 part-time (100 women); includes 115 minority (47 Black or African American, non-Hispanic/Latino; 19 Asian, non-Hispanic/Latino; 29 Hispanic/Latino; 1 Native Hawaiian or other Pacific Islander, non-Hispanic/Latino; 19 Two or more races, non-Hispanic/Latino), 94 international. Average age 26. 1,394 applicants, 59% accepted, 346 enrolled. *Faculty:* 165 full-time (107 women), 106 part-time/adjunct (68 women). Expenses: Contact institution. *Financial support:* In 2016–17, 418 students received support, including 4 fellowships with partial tuition reimbursements available, 138 research assistantships with partial tuition reimbursements available, 77 teaching assistantships with partial tuition reimbursements available; career-related internships or fieldwork, Federal Work-Study, institutionally sponsored loans, scholarships/grants, traineeships, tuition waivers (partial), and unspecified assistantships also available. Support available to part-time students. Financial award application deadline: 1/15; financial award applicants required to submit FAFSA. In 2016, 349 master's, 22 doctorates awarded. *Program availability:* Part-time. Offers child studies (M Ed); clinical psychological assessment (M Ed); community development and action (M Ed); education and human development (M Ed, MPP, Ed D); education policy (MPP); educational leadership and policy (Ed D); elementary education (M Ed); English language learners (M Ed); higher education (M Ed); higher education leadership and policy (Ed D); human development counseling (M Ed); independent school leadership (M Ed); international education policy and management (M Ed); leadership and organizational performance (M Ed); learning and design (M Ed); learning, diversity, and urban studies (M Ed); quantitative methods (M Ed); reading education (M Ed); secondary education (M Ed); special education (M Ed). *Application deadline:* For fall admission, 12/31 priority date for domestic and international students; for spring admission, 11/1 priority date for domestic and international students. Applications are processed on a rolling basis. *Application fee:* $0. Electronic applications accepted. *Application Contact:* Kimberly Brazil, Director of Graduate and Professional Admissions, 615-332-8410, Fax: 615-322-3474, E-mail: kim.brazil@vanderbilt.edu. *Dean,* Dr. Camilla P. Benbow, 615-322-8407, Fax: 615-322-8501, E-mail: camilla.benbow@vanderbilt.edu.

PhD Program in Special Education Students: 45 full-time (41 women); includes 7 minority (2 Asian, non-Hispanic/Latino; 2 Hispanic/Latino; 3 Two or more races, non-Hispanic/Latino), 1 international. Average age 31. 84 applicants, 20% accepted, 15 enrolled. *Faculty:* 21 full-time (13 women). Expenses: Contact institution. *Financial support:* Fellowships with full tuition reimbursements, research assistantships with full tuition reimbursements, teaching assistantships with full tuition reimbursements, Federal Work-Study, institutionally sponsored loans, traineeships, and health care benefits available. Financial award application deadline: 1/15; financial award applicants required to submit CSS PROFILE or FAFSA. In 2016, 8 doctorates awarded. Offers special education (PhD). *Application deadline:* For fall admission, 12/1 for domestic and international students. *Application fee:* $0. Electronic applications accepted. *Application Contact:* Dr. Robert Hodapp, Director of Graduate Studies, 615-322-8150, Fax: 615-343-1570, E-mail: robert.hodapp@vanderbilt.edu. *Chair,* Dr. Joseph Wehby, 615-322-8150, Fax: 615-343-1570, E-mail: joseph.wehby@vanderbilt.edu.

Program in Community Research and Action Students: 23 full-time (16 women); includes 8 minority (3 Black or African American, non-Hispanic/Latino; 1 Asian, non-Hispanic/Latino; 1 Hispanic/Latino; 3 Two or more races, non-Hispanic/Latino), 3 international. Average age 30. 95 applicants, 7% accepted, 4 enrolled. *Faculty:* 18 full-time (10 women). Expenses: Contact institution. *Financial support:* In 2016–17, 16 students received support. Fellowships with tuition reimbursements available, research assistantships with full tuition reimbursements available, teaching assistantships with full tuition reimbursements available, Federal Work-Study, scholarships/grants, health care benefits, tuition waivers, and unspecified assistantships available. Financial award application deadline: 1/15; financial award applicants required to submit FAFSA. In 2016, 8 doctorates awarded. Offers community research and action (PhD). *Application deadline:* For fall admission, 12/1 for domestic and international students. *Application fee:* $0. Electronic applications accepted. *Application Contact:* Sherrie Lane, Administrative Assistant, 615-322-8484, Fax: 615-322-1141, E-mail: sherrie.a.lane@vanderbilt.edu. *Director of Graduate Studies,* Dr. Douglas Perkins, 615-322-7213, Fax: 615-322-1769, E-mail: douglas.d.perkins@vanderbilt.edu.

Program in Creative Writing Students: 15 full-time (10 women); includes 5 minority (1 Black or African American, non-Hispanic/Latino; 1 Asian, non-Hispanic/Latino; 1 Hispanic/Latino; 2 Two or more races, non-Hispanic/Latino), 1 international. Average age 27. 519 applicants, 2% accepted, 7 enrolled. *Faculty:* 32 full-time (22 women). Expenses: Contact institution. *Financial support:* Fellowships with tuition reimbursements, teaching assistantships with tuition reimbursements, Federal Work-Study, institutionally sponsored loans, and health care benefits available. Financial award application deadline: 1/15; financial award applicants required to submit CSS PROFILE or FAFSA. In 2016, 6 master's awarded. Offers creative writing (MFA). *Application deadline:* For fall admission, 1/15 for domestic and international students. Electronic applications accepted. *Application Contact:* Katherine Daniels, Director of Graduate Studies, 615-322-2541, E-mail: kate.daniels@vanderbilt.edu. *Chair,* Dr. Dana Nelson, 615-322-2541, E-mail: dana.d.nelson@vanderbilt.edu.

Program in Human Genetics Students: 12 full-time (9 women), 1 international. Average age 26. *Faculty:* 27 full-time (7 women). Expenses: Contact institution. *Financial support:* Fellowships with tuition reimbursements, research assistantships with tuition reimbursements, Federal Work-Study, institutionally sponsored loans, traineeships, and health care benefits available. Financial award application deadline: 1/15; financial award applicants required to submit CSS PROFILE or FAFSA. In 2016, 4 doctorates awarded. Offers human genetics (PhD). *Application deadline:* For fall admission, 1/15 for domestic and international students. *Application fee:* $0. Electronic applications accepted. *Application Contact:* David Samuels, Director of Graduate Studies, 615-343-8555, E-mail: david.c.samuels@vanderbilt.edu. *Director,* Dr. Nancy Cox, 615-343-8555, Fax: 615-322-1453, E-mail: nancy.j.cox@vanderbilt.edu.

Program in Latin American Studies Students: 8 full-time (5 women); includes 1 minority (Hispanic/Latino), 1 international. Average age 26. 19 applicants, 37% accepted, 3 enrolled. *Faculty:* 63 full-time (22 women). Expenses: Contact institution. *Financial support:* Teaching assistantships with full tuition reimbursements, Federal Work-Study, institutionally sponsored loans, and health care benefits available. Financial award application deadline: 1/15; financial award applicants required to submit CSS PROFILE or FAFSA. In 2016, 5 master's awarded. Offers Latin American studies (MA). *Application deadline:* For fall admission, 1/15 for domestic and international students. *Application fee:* $0. Electronic applications accepted. *Application Contact:* Nicolette M. Kostiw, Assistant Director/Director of Graduate Studies, 615-322-2527, Fax: 615-343-6002, E-mail: nicolette.m.wilhide@vanderbilt.edu. *Director,* Dr. Edward Fischer, 615-322-2527, Fax: 615-343-6002, E-mail: edward.f.fischer@vanderbilt.edu.

Program in Leadership and Policy Studies Students: 38 full-time (16 women); includes 13 minority (3 Black or African American, non-Hispanic/Latino; 6 Asian, non-Hispanic/Latino; 3 Hispanic/Latino; 1 Two or more races, non-Hispanic/Latino), 2 international. Average age 31. 114 applicants, 11% accepted, 8 enrolled. *Faculty:* 23 full-time (9 women). Expenses: Contact institution. *Financial support:* Fellowships with full tuition reimbursements, research assistantships with full tuition reimbursements, teaching assistantships with full tuition reimbursements, Federal Work-Study, institutionally sponsored loans, scholarships/grants, traineeships, and health care benefits available. Financial award application deadline: 1/15; financial award applicants required to submit CSS PROFILE or FAFSA. In 2016, 4 degrees awarded. Offers higher education leadership and policy (PhD); K-12 educational leadership and policy (PhD). *Application deadline:* For fall admission, 12/1 for domestic and international students. *Application fee:* $0. Electronic applications accepted. *Application Contact:* Rosie Moody, Admissions and Education Coordinator, 615-322-8019, Fax: 615-343-7094, E-mail: rosie.moody@vanderbilt.edu. *Director of Graduate Studies,* Dr. Ron Zimmer, 615-322-0722, Fax: 615-343-7094, E-mail: ronald.w.zimmer@vanderbilt.edu.

Program in Learning, Teaching and Diversity Students: 44 full-time (33 women), 1 part-time (0 women); includes 11 minority (2 Black or African American, non-Hispanic/Latino; 4 Asian, non-Hispanic/Latino; 1 Hispanic/Latino; 4 Two or more races, non-Hispanic/Latino), 2 international. Average age 32. 144 applicants, 6% accepted, 9 enrolled. *Faculty:* 24 full-time (15 women). Expenses: Contact institution. *Financial support:* Fellowships with partial tuition reimbursements, research assistantships with full tuition reimbursements, teaching assistantships with full tuition reimbursements, Federal Work-Study, institutionally sponsored loans, scholarships/grants, traineeships, and health care benefits available. Financial award application deadline: 1/15; financial award applicants required to submit CSS PROFILE or FAFSA. In 2016, 4 degrees awarded. Offers learning, teaching and diversity (PhD). *Application deadline:* For fall admission, 12/1 for domestic and international students. *Application fee:* $0. Electronic applications accepted. *Application Contact:* Angela Saylor, Educational Coordinator, 615-322-8092, Fax: 615-322-8014, E-mail: angela.saylor@vanderbilt.edu. *Director of Graduate Studies,* Dr. Melissa Gresalfi, 615-322-8227, Fax: 615-322-8014, E-mail: melissa.gresalfi@vanderbilt.edu.

Program in Liberal Arts and Science Students: 1 (woman) full-time, 39 part-time (20 women); includes 10 minority (5 Black or African American, non-Hispanic/Latino; 1 American Indian or Alaska Native, non-Hispanic/Latino; 1 Asian, non-Hispanic/Latino; 3 Two or more races, non-Hispanic/Latino). Average age 42. 30 applicants, 57% accepted, 12 enrolled. Expenses: Contact institution. *Financial support:* Institutionally sponsored loans and tuition waivers (partial) available. In 2016, 12 master's awarded. *Program availability:* Part-time. Offers liberal arts and science (MLAS). *Application deadline:* For fall admission, 1/15 priority date for domestic students, 1/15 for international students; for spring admission, 11/15 for domestic and international students. Applications are processed on a rolling basis. *Application Contact:* Lisa Poynter, Coordinator, 615-343-3140, Fax: 615-343-8702, E-mail: lisa.poynter@vanderbilt.edu. *Associate Dean and Director of Graduate Studies,* Dr. Martin Rapisarda, 615-343-3140, Fax: 615-343-8702, E-mail: martin.rapisarda@vanderbilt.edu.

Program in Nursing Science Students: 24 full-time (20 women), 6 part-time (4 women); includes 7 minority (2 Black or African American, non-Hispanic/Latino; 2 Hispanic/Latino; 1 Native Hawaiian or other Pacific Islander, non-Hispanic/Latino; 2 Two or more races, non-Hispanic/Latino). Average age 37. 34 applicants, 18% accepted, 6 enrolled. *Faculty:* 20 full-time (15 women), 2 part-time/adjunct (1 woman). Expenses: Contact institution. *Financial support:* Fellowships with full tuition reimbursements, research assistantships with full tuition reimbursements, teaching assistantships with full tuition reimbursements, career-related internships or fieldwork, Federal Work-Study, institutionally sponsored loans, scholarships/grants, health care benefits, and tuition waivers (full and partial) available. Financial award application deadline: 1/15; financial award applicants required to submit CSS PROFILE or FAFSA. In 2016, 7 doctorates awarded. Offers nursing science (PhD). *Application deadline:* For fall admission, 1/15 for domestic and international students. Electronic applications accepted. *Application Contact:* Judy Vesterfelt, Program Manager, 615-322-7410, E-mail: judy.vesterfelt@vanderbilt.edu. *Director of Graduate Studies,* Sheila Ridner, 615-322-3800, Fax: 615-343-5898, E-mail: sheila.ridner@vanderbilt.edu.

Program in Psychological Sciences Students: 77 full-time (52 women), 1 (woman) part-time; includes 8 minority (3 Black or African American, non-Hispanic/Latino; 3 Asian, non-Hispanic/Latino; 2 Hispanic/Latino), 9 international. Average age 27. 583 applicants, 4% accepted, 12 enrolled. *Faculty:* 54 full-time (25 women), 1 (woman) part-time/adjunct. Expenses: Contact institution. *Financial support:* Fellowships with full tuition reimbursements, research assistantships with full tuition reimbursements, teaching assistantships with full tuition reimbursements, career-related internships or fieldwork, Federal Work-Study, institutionally sponsored loans, scholarships/grants, traineeships, and health care benefits available. Financial award application deadline: 1/15; financial award applicants required to submit CSS PROFILE or FAFSA. In 2016, 22 degrees awarded. Offers psychological sciences (PhD). *Application deadline:* For fall admission, 12/1 for domestic and international students. *Application fee:* $0. Electronic applications accepted. *Application Contact:* Dr. Rene Marois, Director of Graduate Studies for Psychological Studies in the College of Arts and Science, 615-322-1779, Fax: 615-343-5027, E-mail: r.marois@vanderbilt.edu. *Director of Graduate Studies for the Psychology of Human Development in Peabody College,* Dr. Daniel T. Levin, 615-322-1518, Fax: 615-343-9494, E-mail: daniel.t.levin@vanderbilt.edu.

School of Engineering *Program availability:* Part-time. Offers biomedical engineering (M Eng, MS, PhD); chemical and biomolecular engineering (M Eng, MS, PhD); civil engineering (M Eng, MS, PhD); computer science (M Eng, MS, PhD); electrical engineering (M Eng, MS, PhD); engineering (M Eng, MS, PhD); environmental engineering (M Eng, MS, PhD); environmental management (MS, PhD); materials science (M Eng, MS, PhD); mechanical engineering (M Eng, MS, PhD). MS and PhD offered through the Graduate School. Electronic applications accepted.

School of Medicine Expenses: Contact institution. *Financial support:* Institutionally sponsored loans and scholarships/grants available. Financial award application deadline: 3/1; financial award applicants required to submit FAFSA. Offers audiology (Au D, PhD); biochemistry (MS, PhD); cell and developmental biology (MS, PhD); chemical and physical biology (PhD); clinical investigation (MS); education of the deaf (MDE); medicine (MDE, MMP, MS, MSCI, Au D, DMP, MD, PhD); microbiology and immunology (MS, PhD); molecular physiology and biophysics (MS, PhD); pathology (PhD); pharmacology (PhD); speech-language pathology (MS, PhD). *Application deadline:* For fall admission, 11/15 for domestic and international students. *Application fee:* $50. *Dean, School of Medicine,* Dr. Jeffrey R. Balser, 615-936-3030, E-mail: jeffrey.balser@vanderbilt.edu.

Vanderbilt Law School Students: 572 full-time (292 women); includes 128 minority (60 Black or African American, non-Hispanic/Latino; 3 American Indian or Alaska Native, non-Hispanic/Latino; 25 Asian, non-Hispanic/Latino; 34 Hispanic/Latino; 6 Two or more races, non-Hispanic/Latino), 17 international. Average age 23. 4,380 applicants, 32% accepted, 204 enrolled. *Faculty:* 37 full-time (14 women), 51 part-time/adjunct (21 women). Expenses: Contact institution. *Financial support:* In 2016–17, 486 students received support. Career-related internships or fieldwork, Federal Work-Study, institutionally sponsored loans, scholarships/grants, and health care benefits available. Financial award application deadline: 2/15; financial award applicants required to submit FAFSA. In 2016, 35 master's, 195 doctorates awarded. Offers law (LL M, JD); law and economics (PhD). *Application deadline:* For fall admission, 4/1 for domestic and international students. Applications are processed on a rolling basis. *Application fee:* $50. Electronic applications accepted. *Application Contact:* Admissions Office, 615-322-6452, Fax: 615-322-1531, E-mail: admissions@law.vanderbilt.edu. *Assistant Dean of Admissions,* G. Todd Morton, 615-322-6452, Fax: 615-322-1531, E-mail: admissions@law.vanderbilt.edu.

Vanderbilt University Owen Graduate School of Management *Program availability:* Evening/weekend. Offers accountancy (M Acc); accounting (MBA); business administration (EMBA, MBA); finance (MS); general management (MBA); health care (MBA); human and organizational performance (MBA); management (EMBA, M Acc, M Mark, MBA, MM, MS); marketing (MBA); operations (MBA); strategy (MBA); valuation (M Acc).

Vanderbilt University School of Nursing Students: 501 full-time (435 women), 387 part-time (355 women); includes 153 minority (40 Black or African American, non-Hispanic/Latino; 1 American Indian or Alaska Native, non-Hispanic/Latino; 27 Asian, non-Hispanic/Latino; 48 Hispanic/Latino; 4 Native Hawaiian or other Pacific Islander, non-Hispanic/Latino; 33 Two or more races, non-Hispanic/Latino), 9 international. Average age 31. 1,210 applicants, 57% accepted, 473 enrolled. *Faculty:* 292 full-time (267 women), 321 part-time/adjunct (253 women). Expenses: Contact institution. *Financial support:* In 2016–17, 627 students received support. Scholarships/grants available. Financial award application deadline: 3/1; financial award applicants required to submit FAFSA. In 2016, 319 master's, 47 doctorates awarded. *Program availability:* Part-time, 100% online, blended/hybrid learning. Offers adult-gerontology acute care nurse practitioner (MSN); adult-gerontology primary care nurse practitioner (MSN); emergency nurse practitioner (MSN); family nurse practitioner (MSN); healthcare leadership (MSN); neonatal nurse practitioner (MSN); nurse midwifery (MSN); nurse midwifery/family nurse practitioner (MSN); nursing (Post-Master's Certificate); nursing informatics (MSN); nursing practice (DNP); nursing science (PhD); pediatric acute care nurse practitioner (MSN); pediatric primary care nurse practitioner (MSN); psychiatric-mental health nurse practitioner (MSN); women's health nurse practitioner (MSN); women's health nurse practitioner/adult gerontology primary care nurse practitioner (MSN). *Application deadline:* For fall admission, 11/1 priority date for domestic and international students. Applications are processed on a rolling basis. *Application fee:* $50. Electronic applications accepted. *Application Contact:* Patricia Peerman, Assistant Dean for Enrollment Management, 615-322-3800, Fax: 615-343-0333, E-mail: vusn-admissions@vanderbilt.edu. *Dean,* Dr. Linda Norman, 615-343-8876, Fax: 615-343-7711, E-mail: linda.norman@vanderbilt.edu.

VANDERCOOK COLLEGE OF MUSIC, Chicago, IL 60616-3731

General Information Independent, coed, comprehensive institution. *Graduate housing:* Rooms and/or apartments available on a first-come, first-served basis to single and married students. Housing application deadline: 6/1.

GRADUATE UNITS

Master of Music Education Program *Program availability:* Part-time. Offers music education (MM Ed).

VANGUARD UNIVERSITY OF SOUTHERN CALIFORNIA, Costa Mesa, CA 92626-9601

General Information Independent-religious, coed, comprehensive institution.

GRADUATE UNITS

Graduate Program in Clinical Psychology *Program availability:* Part-time, evening/weekend. Offers clinical psychology (MS). Electronic applications accepted.

Graduate Program in Nursing *Program availability:* Part-time, evening/weekend. Offers nursing (MS).

Graduate Programs in Education *Program availability:* Evening/weekend. Offers education (MA). Electronic applications accepted.

Graduate Programs in Religion *Program availability:* Part-time, evening/weekend. Offers leadership studies (MA); theological studies (MTS). Electronic applications accepted.

VAUGHN COLLEGE OF AERONAUTICS AND TECHNOLOGY, Flushing, NY 11369

General Information Independent, coed, primarily men, comprehensive institution.

GRADUATE UNITS

Graduate Programs Offers airport management (MS).

VERMONT COLLEGE OF FINE ARTS, Montpelier, VT 05602

General Information Independent, coed, graduate-only institution. *Enrollment by degree level:* 396 master's. *Graduate faculty:* 125 part-time/adjunct (67 women). *Tuition:* Full-time $24,038; part-time $797 per credit hour. *Required fees:* $1300; $1300 per credit hour. $650 per semester. Full-time tuition and fees vary according to program. *Graduate housing:* Room and/or apartments available on a first-come, first-served basis to single students; on-campus housing not available to married students. Typical cost: $2000 (including board). Room and board charges vary according to board plan. *Student services:* Campus safety program, international student services, services for students with disabilities. *Library facilities:* The Gary Library. *Collection:* Books: 60,000 (physical), 110,000 (digital/electronic); Serial titles: 250 (physical), 250 (digital/electronic); Databases: 10. Weekly public service hours: 40.

Computer facilities: 26 computers available on campus for general student use. A campuswide network can be accessed from student residence rooms. Website: http://www.vcfa.edu/

General Application Contact: David Markow, Director of Enrollment Management, 802-828-8535, E-mail: admissions@vcfa.edu.

GRADUATE UNITS

Graduate Studies in Art and Design Education Students: 19 full-time (14 women), 1 part-time (0 women); includes 6 minority (3 Black or African American, non-Hispanic/Latino; 1 American Indian or Alaska Native, non-Hispanic/Latino; 1 Native Hawaiian or other Pacific Islander, non-Hispanic/Latino; 1 Two or more races, non-Hispanic/Latino). Average age 32. *Faculty:* 4 full-time (3 women). Expenses: Contact institution. Offers art and design education (MA, MAT). *Application Contact:* David Markow, Director of Enrollment Management, 802-828-8535, E-mail: admissions@vcfa.edu. *Director,* Marni Leiken, E-mail: marni.leiken@vcfa.edu.

MFA in Film Program Students: 31 full-time (13 women); includes 5 minority (1 Black or African American, non-Hispanic/Latino; 1 American Indian or Alaska Native, non-Hispanic/Latino; 1 Hispanic/Latino; 1 Native Hawaiian or other Pacific Islander, non-Hispanic/Latino; 1 Two or more races, non-Hispanic/Latino), 1 international. Average age 39. *Faculty:* 7 part-time/adjunct (3 women). Expenses: Contact institution. *Financial support:* Application deadline: 6/15; applicants required to submit FAFSA. In 2016, 18 master's awarded. Offers film (MFA). *Application deadline:* For fall admission, 8/15 for domestic students; for spring admission, 2/15 for domestic students. Applications are processed on a rolling basis. *Application fee:* $75. Electronic applications accepted. *Application Contact:* Jennifer Skinder, Assistant Director of Admissions, 802-828-8829, E-mail: jennifer.skinder@vcfa.edu. *Director,* Stephen Pite, 802-828-8529, E-mail: stephen.pite@vcfa.edu.

MFA in Graphic Design Program Students: 41 full-time (21 women); includes 10 minority (3 Black or African American, non-Hispanic/Latino; 1 Asian, non-Hispanic/Latino; 6 Hispanic/Latino). Average age 37. 31 applicants, 74% accepted, 14 enrolled. *Faculty:* 10 part-time/adjunct (5 women). Expenses: Contact institution. *Financial support:* Scholarships/grants available. Financial award applicants required to submit FAFSA. In 2016, 15 master's awarded. Offers graphic design (MFA). *Application deadline:* For fall admission, 7/13 priority date for domestic and international students; for spring admission, 1/15 priority date for domestic and international students. Applications are processed on a rolling basis. *Application fee:* $75. Electronic applications accepted. *Application Contact:* Jennifer Renko, Program Director, 866-934-8232 Ext. 8896, E-mail: jennifer.renko@vcfa.edu. *Program Director,* Jennifer Renko, 866-934-8232 Ext. 8896, E-mail: jennifer.renko@vcfa.edu.

MFA in Music Composition Program Students: 35 full-time (4 women); includes 5 minority (2 Black or African American, non-Hispanic/Latino; 3 Hispanic/Latino), 3 international. Average age 43. 13 applicants, 77% accepted, 6 enrolled. *Faculty:* 10 part-time/adjunct (1 woman). Expenses: Contact institution. *Financial support:* Scholarships/grants available. Financial award applicants required to submit FAFSA. In 2016, 12 master's awarded. Offers music composition (MFA). *Application deadline:* For fall admission, 6/15 for domestic and international students; for spring admission, 12/15 for domestic and international students. Applications are processed on a rolling basis. *Application fee:* $75. *Application Contact:* Sarah Madru, Assistant Program Director, 802-828-8534, E-mail: sarah.madru@vcfa.edu. *Program Director,* Carol Beatty, 866-934-8232 Ext. 8610, E-mail: carol.beatty@vcfa.edu.

MFA in Visual Art Program Students: 41 full-time (30 women); includes 6 minority (1 Black or African American, non-Hispanic/Latino; 3 Hispanic/Latino; 1 Native Hawaiian or other Pacific Islander, non-Hispanic/Latino; 1 Two or more races, non-Hispanic/Latino), 3 international. Average age 44. 45 applicants, 58% accepted, 16 enrolled. *Faculty:* 12 part-time/adjunct (6 women). Expenses: Contact institution. *Financial support:* Scholarships/grants available. Financial award applicants required to submit FAFSA. In 2016, 24 master's awarded. Offers visual art (MFA). *Application deadline:* For fall admission, 2/15 priority date for domestic students, 2/15 for international students; for spring admission, 9/15 priority date for domestic students, 9/15 for international students. Applications are processed on a rolling basis. *Application fee:* $75. Electronic applications accepted. *Application Contact:* Thatiana Oliveria, Assistant Director of Admissions, 802-828-8636, E-mail: thatiana.oliveria@vcfa.edu. *Program Director,* Danielle Dahline, 802-828-8703, E-mail: danielle.dahline@vcfa.edu.

MFA in Writing and Publishing Program Students: 18 full-time (13 women); includes 2 minority (1 American Indian or Alaska Native, non-Hispanic/Latino; 1 Two or more races, non-Hispanic/Latino), 1 international. Average age 32. *Faculty:* 5 full-time (3 women). Expenses: Contact institution. *Financial support:* Fellowships and scholarships/grants available. Offers writing and publishing (MFA). *Application Contact:* David Markow, Director of Enrollment Management, 802-828-8535, E-mail: admissions@vcfa.edu. *Director,* Miciah Gault.

MFA in Writing for Children and Young Adults Program Students: 96 full-time (87 women); includes 12 minority (1 Black or African American, non-Hispanic/Latino; 2 Asian, non-Hispanic/Latino; 4 Hispanic/Latino; 5 Two or more races, non-Hispanic/Latino), 7 international. Average age 43. 47 applicants, 68% accepted, 28 enrolled. *Faculty:* 25 part-time/adjunct (18 women). Expenses: Contact institution. *Financial support:* Scholarships/grants available. Financial award applicants required to submit FAFSA. In 2016, 39 master's awarded. Offers writing for children and young adults (MFA). *Application deadline:* For fall admission, 3/1 for domestic and international students; for spring admission, 9/1 for domestic and international students. Applications are processed on a rolling basis. *Application fee:* $75. Electronic applications accepted. *Application Contact:* Jennifer Skinder, Assistant Director of Admissions, 802-828-8829, E-mail: jennifer.skinder@vcfa.edu. *Program Director,* Melissa Fisher, 802-828-8696, E-mail: melissa.fisher@vcfa.edu.

MFA in Writing Program Students: 114 full-time (86 women); includes 7 minority (2 Black or African American, non-Hispanic/Latino; 1 Asian, non-Hispanic/Latino; 2 Hispanic/Latino; 2 Two or more races, non-Hispanic/Latino), 4 international. Average age 42. 123 applicants, 63% accepted, 36 enrolled. *Faculty:* 36 part-time/adjunct (17 women). Expenses: Contact institution. *Financial support:* Scholarships/grants available. Financial award applicants required to submit FAFSA. In 2016, 66 master's awarded. Offers writing (MFA). *Application deadline:* For fall admission, 3/20 for domestic and international students; for spring admission, 8/15 for domestic and international students. *Application fee:* $75. *Application Contact:* Ann Cardinal, Director of Student Recruitment, 802-828-8589, E-mail: ann.cardinal@vcfa.edu. *Program Director,* Melissa Hammerle, 802-828-8840, E-mail: melissa.hammerle@vcfa.edu.

VERMONT LAW SCHOOL, South Royalton, VT 05068-0096

General Information Independent, coed, graduate-only institution. *Enrollment by degree level:* 383 doctoral. *Graduate faculty:* 48 full-time (26 women), 22 part-time/adjunct (7 women). *Tuition:* Full-time $47,998. *Graduate housing:* On-campus housing not available. *Student services:* Campus employment opportunities, campus safety program, career counseling, child daycare facilities, exercise/wellness program, free psychological counseling, low-cost health insurance, multicultural affairs office, writing training. *Library facilities:* Julien and Virginia Cornell Library. *Collection:* Books: 57,307 (physical), 221,546 (digital/electronic); Serial titles: 1,781 (physical), 72,871 (digital/electronic); Databases: 54. Weekly public service hours: 106; students can reserve study rooms.

Computer facilities: 54 computers available on campus for general student use. A campuswide network can be accessed from off campus. Website: http://www.vermontlaw.edu/

General Application Contact: John D. Miller, Jr., Vice President for Enrollment Management, Marketing and Communications, 802-831-1239, Fax: 802-831-1174, E-mail: admiss@vermontlaw.edu.

GRADUATE UNITS

Graduate and Professional Programs Students: 383 full-time (218 women); includes 95 minority (26 Black or African American, non-Hispanic/Latino; 10 American Indian or Alaska Native, non-Hispanic/Latino; 17 Asian, non-Hispanic/Latino; 27 Hispanic/Latino; 4 Native Hawaiian or other Pacific Islander, non-Hispanic/Latino; 11 Two or more races, non-Hispanic/Latino), 10 international. Average age 27. 647 applicants, 81% accepted, 139 enrolled. *Faculty:* 48 full-time (26 women), 22 part-time/adjunct (7 women). Expenses: Contact institution. *Financial support:* In 2016–17, 388 students received support, including 2 fellowships with full tuition reimbursements available (averaging $3,000 per year); career-related internships or fieldwork, Federal Work-Study, institutionally sponsored loans, scholarships/grants, and tuition waivers (partial) also available. Support available to part-time students. Financial award application deadline: 3/15; financial award applicants required to submit FAFSA. In 2016, 116 doctorates awarded. *Program availability:* Part-time. Offers law (LL M, MELP, MERL, MFALP, JD). *Application deadline:* For fall admission, 3/1 priority date for domestic students. Applications are processed on a rolling basis. *Application fee:* $60. Electronic applications accepted. *Application Contact:* John D. Miller, Jr., Vice President for Enrollment Management, Marketing and Communications, 802-831-1239, Fax: 802-831-1174, E-mail: admiss@vermontlaw.edu. *President and Dean,* Marc B. Mihaly, 802-831-1225, Fax: 802-831-1163, E-mail: kevans@vermontlaw.edu.

Master's Programs Expenses: Contact institution. *Financial support:* Fellowships with full tuition reimbursements, career-related internships or fieldwork, Federal Work-Study, institutionally sponsored loans, scholarships/grants, and tuition waivers (partial) available. Support available to part-time students. Financial award application deadline: 3/1; financial award applicants required to submit FAFSA. *Program availability:* Part-time, 100% online, blended/hybrid learning. Offers American legal studies (LL M); energy law (LL M); energy regulation and law (MERL); environmental law (LL M); environmental law and policy (MELP); food and agriculture law (LL M); food and agriculture law and policy (MFALP). *Application deadline:* For fall admission, 3/1 priority date for domestic students. Applications are processed on a rolling basis. *Application fee:* $60. *Application Contact:* John D. Miller, Jr., Vice President for Enrollment Management, Marketing and Communications, 802-831-1239, Fax: 802-831-1174, E-mail: admiss@vermontlaw.edu. *President and Dean,* Marc B. Mihaly, 802-831-1237, Fax: 802-763-2490.

VICTORIA UNIVERSITY, Toronto, ON M5S 1K7, Canada

General Information Independent-religious, coed, graduate-only institution. *Graduate housing:* Rooms and/or apartments available on a first-come, first-served basis to single and married students. Housing application deadline: 6/30.

GRADUATE UNITS

Emmanuel College Offers theology (M Div, MA, MPS, MRE, MSMus, MTS, Th M, D Min, PhD, Th D, Certificate, Diploma, L Th). M Div, MRE, Th M, Th D, M Div/MA, M Div/MRE, M Div/MPS offered jointly with University of Toronto; MA, PhD with University of St. Michael's College. Electronic applications accepted.

VILLANOVA UNIVERSITY, Villanova, PA 19085-1699

General Information Independent-religious, coed, comprehensive institution. CGS member. *Enrollment:* 10,842 graduate, professional, and undergraduate students; 2,649 full-time matriculated graduate/professional students (1,374 women), 1,231 part-time matriculated graduate/professional students (587 women). *Enrollment by degree level:* 3,068 master's, 759 doctoral, 53 other advanced degrees. *Graduate faculty:* 412.

Graduate housing: On-campus housing not available. *Student services:* Campus employment opportunities, campus safety program, career counseling, exercise/wellness program, free psychological counseling, international student services, multicultural affairs office, services for students with disabilities. *Library facilities:* Falvey Memorial Library plus 1 other. *Collection:* Study areas open 24 hours, 5–7 days a week; students can reserve study rooms.

Computer facilities: Computer purchase and lease plans are available. 700 computers available on campus for general student use. A campuswide network can be accessed from student residence rooms and from off campus. Online class registration, learning management system with anti-plagiarism software, testing software, online faculty hours, videoconferencing, electronic portfolios, data vaulting/backup service, software are available.

Website: http://www.villanova.edu/

GRADUATE UNITS

College of Engineering *Program availability:* Part-time, evening/weekend, online learning. Offers biochemical engineering (Certificate); chemical engineering (MSChE); civil engineering (MSCE); computer architectures (Certificate); computer engineering (MSCPE, Certificate); electric power systems (Certificate); electrical engineering (MSEE, Certificate); electro mechanical systems (Certificate); electro-mechanical systems (Certificate); engineering (MSCPE, MSChE, MSEE, MSME, MSWREE, PhD, Certificate); environmental protection in the chemical process industries (Certificate); high frequency systems (Certificate); intelligent control systems (Certificate); machinery dynamics (Certificate); mechanical engineering (MSME); nonlinear dynamics and control (Certificate); thermofluid systems (Certificate); urban water resources design (Certificate); water resources and environmental engineering (MSWREE, Certificate); wireless and digital communications (Certificate). Electronic applications accepted.

College of Nursing *Program availability:* Part-time, online learning. Offers adult nurse practitioner (MSN, Post Master's Certificate); family nurse practitioner (MSN, Post Master's Certificate); nurse anesthetist (MSN, Post Master's Certificate); nursing (PhD); nursing education (MSN, Post Master's Certificate); nursing practice (DNP); pediatric nurse practitioner (MSN, Post Master's Certificate). Electronic applications accepted.

Graduate School of Liberal Arts and Sciences Students: 845 full-time (513 women), 431 part-time (255 women); includes 251 minority (102 Black or African American, non-Hispanic/Latino; 4 American Indian or Alaska Native, non-Hispanic/Latino; 38 Asian, non-Hispanic/Latino; 80 Hispanic/Latino; 3 Native Hawaiian or other Pacific Islander, non-Hispanic/Latino; 24 Two or more races, non-Hispanic/Latino), 132 international. Average age 32. 673 applicants, 65% accepted, 344 enrolled. *Faculty:* 187. Expenses: Contact institution. *Financial support:* Research assistantships, teaching assistantships, career-related internships or fieldwork, scholarships/grants, and unspecified assistantships available. Financial award applicants required to submit FAFSA. In 2016, 560 master's, 10 doctorates, 60 other advanced degrees awarded. *Program availability:* Part-time, evening/weekend, 100% online. Offers applied statistics (MS); biology (MA, MS); chemistry (MS); city management (Certificate); clinical mental health counseling (MS); communication (MA); computer science (MS); education (MA); education plus teacher certification (MA); elementary school counseling (MS); English (MA); Greek/Latin (MA); Hispanic studies (MA); history (MA); human resource development (MS); liberal arts and sciences (MA, MPA, MS, PhD, Certificate); liberal studies (MA); mathematical sciences (MA, MS); nonprofit management (Certificate); philosophy (PhD); political science (MA); psychology (MA, MS); public administration (MPA, Certificate); secondary school counseling (MS); software engineering (MS); teacher leadership (MA); theatre (MA); theology (MA, PhD). *Application deadline:* For fall admission, 5/1 for international students; for spring admission, 10/15 for international students. Applications are processed on a rolling basis. *Application fee:* $50. Electronic applications accepted. *Dean,* Dr. Christine Palus, 610-519-7090, Fax: 610-519-7096.

School of Law *Program availability:* Part-time, evening/weekend. Offers law (LL M, JD); tax (LL M). Electronic applications accepted.

Villanova School of Business Students: 36 full-time (10 women), 1,008 part-time (379 women); includes 192 minority (61 Black or African American, non-Hispanic/Latino; 1 American Indian or Alaska Native, non-Hispanic/Latino; 75 Asian, non-Hispanic/Latino; 48 Hispanic/Latino; 7 Two or more races, non-Hispanic/Latino), 30 international. *Faculty:* 108 full-time (39 women), 29 part-time/adjunct (8 women). Expenses: Contact institution. *Financial support:* In 2016–17, 17 research assistantships with tuition reimbursements (averaging $13,100 per year) were awarded; institutionally sponsored loans and scholarships/grants also available. Support available to part-time students. Financial award application deadline: 6/30; financial award applicants required to submit FAFSA. *Program availability:* 100% online, blended/hybrid learning. Offers accountancy (MAC); analytics (MBA); business (EMBA, MAC, MBA, MSA, MSCM, MSF); business administration (MBA); church management (MSCM); cybersecurity (MBA); executive business administration (EMBA); finance (MSF); healthcare (MBA); international business (MBA); management information systems (MBA); marketing (MBA); real estate (MBA); strategic management (MBA); sustainability (MBA). *Application deadline:* For fall admission, 6/30 for domestic and international students; for winter admission, 11/15 for domestic and international students; for spring admission, 11/15 for domestic and international students; for summer admission, 3/31 for domestic and international students. Applications are processed on a rolling basis. *Application fee:* $65. Electronic applications accepted. *Application Contact:* Claire Bruno, Director of Recruitment and Enrollment Management, 610-519-4336, Fax: 610-519-6273, E-mail: claire.bruno@villanova.edu. *Associate Dean of Graduate and Executive Business Programs,* Michael L. Capella, 610-519-4336, Fax: 610-519-6273, E-mail: michael.l.capella@villanova.edu.

VIRGINIA BAPTIST COLLEGE, Fredericksburg, VA 22407

General Information Independent, coed, comprehensive institution.

GRADUATE UNITS

Graduate Programs Offers theology (MBS, MCE, MM).

VIRGINIA BEACH THEOLOGICAL SEMINARY, Virginia Beach, VA 23464

General Information Independent-religious, coed, graduate-only institution. *Enrollment by degree level:* 35 master's, 1 other advanced degree. *Graduate faculty:* 5 full-time (0 women), 2 part-time/adjunct (0 women). *Tuition:* Full-time $7920; part-time $330 per credit hour. *Required fees:* $265 per semester. *Graduate housing:* On-campus housing not available. *Library facilities:* Ernest D. Pickering Library. *Collection:* Books: 45,500 (physical); Serial titles: 300 (physical), 2,000 (digital/electronic); Databases: 3. Weekly public service hours: 12; study areas open 24 hours, 5–7 days a week.

Computer facilities: 2 computers available on campus for general student use. A campuswide network can be accessed. Online class registration is available.
Website: http://www.vbts.edu/

General Application Contact: Edward Estes, Director of Admissions, 757-479-3706, E-mail: eestes@vbts.edu.

GRADUATE UNITS

Graduate Programs Students: 7 full-time (0 women), 29 part-time (3 women). *Faculty:* 5 full-time (0 women), 2 part-time/adjunct (0 women). Expenses: Contact institution. *Financial support:* Scholarships/grants available. *Program availability:* Online learning. Offers Biblical studies (MBS, Th M); chaplaincy (MBS); ministry (M Div). Electronic applications accepted. *Application Contact:* Edward Estes, Director of Admissions, 757-479-3706, E-mail: eestes@vbts.edu.

VIRGINIA COLLEGE IN BIRMINGHAM, Birmingham, AL 35209

General Information Proprietary, coed, comprehensive institution.

GRADUATE UNITS

Program in Business Administration *Program availability:* Part-time, evening/weekend, online learning. Offers healthcare (MBA); management (MBA).

Virginia College Online *Program availability:* Part-time, evening/weekend, online learning. Offers business administration (MBA); criminal justice (MCJ); cybersecurity (MC).

VIRGINIA COMMONWEALTH UNIVERSITY, Richmond, VA 23284-9005

General Information State-supported, coed, university. CGS member. *Graduate housing:* Room and/or apartments available on a first-come, first-served basis to single students; on-campus housing not available to married students. *Student services:* Campus employment opportunities, campus safety program, career counseling, child daycare facilities, exercise/wellness program, free psychological counseling, grant writing training, international student services, low-cost health insurance, multicultural affairs office, services for students with disabilities, teacher training, writing training. *Library facilities:* Cabell Library and Thompkins McCaw Library plus 3 others. *Collection:* Books: 1.9 million (physical), 1 million (digital/electronic); Serial titles: 260,501 (physical), 116,369 (digital/electronic); Databases: 471. Weekly public service hours: 146; study areas open 24 hours, 5–7 days a week; students can reserve study rooms. *Research affiliation:* Virginia Biotechnology Research Park.

Computer facilities: Computer purchase and lease plans are available. 450 computers available on campus for general student use. A campuswide network can be accessed from student residence rooms and from off campus. Online class registration is available.
Website: http://www.vcu.edu/

GRADUATE UNITS

Graduate School Expenses: Contact institution. *Financial support:* Fellowships, research assistantships, teaching assistantships, career-related internships or fieldwork, Federal Work-Study, institutionally sponsored loans, scholarships/grants, and tuition waivers (full and partial) available. Support available to part-time students. Financial award applicants required to submit FAFSA. *Program availability:* Part-time, evening/weekend. Offers interdisciplinary studies (MIS). *Application fee:* $50. Electronic applications accepted. *Application Contact:* Dr. Sherry T. Sandkam, Associate Dean, 804-828-6916, Fax: 804-827-4546, E-mail: ssandkam@vcu.edu. *Dean, Graduate School,* Dr. F. Douglas Boudinot, 804-828-2233, Fax: 804-827-0724, E-mail: fdboudinot@vcu.edu.

College of Humanities and Sciences Expenses: Contact institution. *Financial support:* Fellowships, research assistantships, teaching assistantships, career-related internships or fieldwork, Federal Work-Study, institutionally sponsored loans, scholarships/grants, and tuition waivers (full and partial) available. Support available to part-time students. Financial award applicants required to submit FAFSA. *Program availability:* Part-time, evening/weekend. Offers analytical chemistry (MS, PhD); applied mathematics (MS); behavioral medicine (PhD); biology (MS); chemical physics (PhD); clinical child psychology (PhD); clinical psychology (PhD); counseling psychology (PhD); creative writing (MFA); criminal justice (MS, Postbaccalaureate Certificate); digital sociology (MS); dual genre (MFA); English (MA); fiction (MFA); financial management (MPA); forensic biology (MS); forensic chemistry/drugs and toxicology (MS); forensic chemistry/trace evidence (MS); forensic physical analysis (MS); geographic information systems (Certificate); government and public affairs (MA, MPA, MS, MURP, PhD, Certificate, Graduate Certificate, Postbaccalaureate Certificate); health and movement sciences (MS); health psychology (PhD); history (MA); homeland security and emergency preparedness (MA, Graduate Certificate); humanities and sciences (MA, MFA, MPA, MS, MURP, PhD, Certificate, Graduate Certificate, Postbaccalaureate Certificate); inorganic chemistry (MS, PhD); literature (MA); mass communications (MS, PhD); media, art, and text (PhD); medical physics (MS, PhD); multimedia journalism (MS); nanoscience and nanotechnology (PhD); nanosciences (PhD); nonprofit management (Graduate Certificate); organic chemistry (MS, PhD); physical chemistry (MS, PhD); physics and applied physics (MS); poetry (MFA); public policy and administration (PhD); rehabilitation and movement science (PhD); strategic public relations (MS); urban and regional planning (MURP). *Application fee:* $50. Electronic applications accepted. *Application Contact:* Dr. Sherry T. Sandkam, Associate Dean, 804-828-6916, Fax: 804-827-4546, E-mail: ssandkam@vcu.edu. *Interim Dean,* Dr. Fred M. Hawkridge, 804-828-1674, E-mail: fmhawkri@vcu.edu.

School of Allied Health Professions Expenses: Contact institution. *Financial support:* Fellowships, research assistantships, teaching assistantships, career-related internships or fieldwork, and tuition waivers (full and partial) available. *Program availability:* Part-time. Offers allied health professions (MHA, MS, MSHA, MSNA, MSOT, DNAP, DPT, OTD, PhD, CAS); clinical laboratory sciences (PhD); gerontology (MS, PhD); health administration (MHA, MSHA, PhD); health services organization and research (PhD); nurse anesthesia (PhD); occupational therapy (MSOT, OTD); patient counseling (MS); physical therapy (PhD); radiation sciences (PhD); rehabilitation counseling (MS); rehabilitation leadership (PhD). *Application fee:* $50. Electronic applications accepted. *Application Contact:* Monica L. White, Director of Student Services, 804-828-7247, Fax: 804-828-8656, E-mail: mlwhite1@vcu.edu. *Dean,* Dr. Cecil B. Drain, 804-828-7247.

School of Business Expenses: Contact institution. *Financial support:* Fellowships, research assistantships, teaching assistantships, Federal Work-Study, institutionally sponsored loans, and tuition waivers (full and partial) available. Support available to part-time students. Financial award application deadline: 3/15; financial award applicants required to submit FAFSA. *Program availability:* Part-time, evening/weekend. Offers accounting (M Acc); business (M Acc, MA, MBA, MS, PhD, Postbaccalaureate Certificate); business administration (MBA, PhD); economics (MA); information systems (MS); real estate and urban land development (Postbaccalaureate Certificate). *Application deadline:* Applications are processed on a rolling basis. *Application fee:* $50. Electronic applications accepted. *Application*

Contact: Jana P. McQuaid, Assistant Dean of Master's Programs, 804-828-4622, Fax: 804-828-7174, E-mail: jpmcquaid@vcu.edu. *Dean,* Ed Grier, 804-828-1595, Fax: 804-828-8884.

School of Education Expenses: Contact institution. *Financial support:* Fellowships, research assistantships, teaching assistantships, career-related internships or fieldwork, Federal Work-Study, institutionally sponsored loans, and tuition waivers (full and partial) available. Support available to part-time students. Financial award application deadline: 3/1; financial award applicants required to submit FAFSA. *Program availability:* Part-time. Offers adult literacy (M Ed); art education (PhD); college student development and counseling (M Ed); counselor education and supervision (PhD); curriculum, culture and change (PhD); early and elementary education (MT); early childhood (M Ed); education (M Ed, MT, Ed D, PhD, Certificate); educational leadership (M Ed); educational psychology (PhD); general education (M Ed); human resource development (M Ed); leadership (Ed D); reading (M Ed); reading specialist (Certificate); research and evaluation (PhD); school counseling (M Ed); severe disabilities (M Ed); special education and disability leadership (PhD); sport leadership (M Ed); teaching and learning with technology (M Ed); urban services leadership (PhD). *Application fee:* $50. Electronic applications accepted. *Application Contact:* Dr. Diane Simon, Associate Dean for Student Affairs, 804-828-3382, Fax: 804-828-1323, E-mail: dsimon@vcu.edu. *Dean,* Dr. Christine S. Walther-Thomas, 804-828-3382, E-mail: cswalthertho@vcu.edu.

School of Engineering Expenses: Contact institution. *Financial support:* Applicants required to submit FAFSA. Offers biomedical engineering (MS, PhD); computer science (MS); engineering (MS, PhD); mechanical and nuclear engineering (MS, PhD). *Application deadline:* For fall admission, 2/1 priority date for domestic students; for spring admission, 11/15 for domestic students. *Application fee:* $50. Electronic applications accepted. *Application Contact:* Mark D. Meadows, Director of Student Recruitment, 804-827-4005, E-mail: mdmeadows@vcu.edu. *Associate Dean for Graduate Affairs,* Dr. Rosalyn S. Hobson, 804-828-3925, E-mail: rhobson@vcu.edu.

School of Life Sciences Expenses: Contact institution. *Financial support:* Applicants required to submit FAFSA. Offers environmental studies (M Env Sc, MS); integrative life sciences (PhD); life sciences (M Env Sc, MS, PhD). *Application fee:* $50. Electronic applications accepted. *Application Contact:* Dr. Greg Garman, Director, Center for Environmental Studies, 804-828-1574, E-mail: ggarman@vcu.edu. *Vice Provost,* Dr. Thomas F. Huff, 804-827-5600.

School of Nursing Students: 144 full-time (133 women), 156 part-time (145 women); includes 55 minority (26 Black or African American, non-Hispanic/Latino; 18 Asian, non-Hispanic/Latino; 5 Hispanic/Latino; 6 Two or more races, non-Hispanic/Latino), 1 international. 165 applicants, 58% accepted, 73 enrolled. Expenses: Contact institution. *Financial support:* Fellowships, research assistantships, teaching assistantships, career-related internships or fieldwork, and institutionally sponsored loans available. Financial award applicants required to submit FAFSA. In 2016, 85 master's, 6 doctorates, 5 other advanced degrees awarded. *Program availability:* Part-time, evening/weekend, online learning. Offers adult health acute nursing (MS); adult health primary nursing (MS); biobehavioral clinical research (PhD); child health nursing (MS); clinical nurse leader (MS); family health nursing (MS); nurse educator (MS); nurse practitioner (MS); nursing (Certificate); nursing administration (MS); psychiatric-mental health nursing (MS); quality and safety in health care (DNP); women's health nursing (MS). *Application deadline:* For fall admission, 2/1 priority date for domestic students; for spring admission, 11/1 for domestic students. *Application fee:* $50. Electronic applications accepted. *Application Contact:* Susan Lipp, Assistant Dean, Enrollment and Student Services, 804-828-5171, Fax: 804-828-7743, E-mail: vcu_nurse@vcu.edu. *Dean,* Dr. Nancy F. Langston, 804-828-5174, Fax: 804-828-7743.

School of Social Work Expenses: Contact institution. *Financial support:* Fellowships, research assistantships, teaching assistantships, career-related internships or fieldwork, Federal Work-Study, institutionally sponsored loans, and tuition waivers (full and partial) available. Support available to part-time students. Financial award applicants required to submit FAFSA. Offers social work (MSW, PhD). *Application deadline:* For fall admission, 2/1 priority date for domestic students. *Application fee:* $50. Electronic applications accepted. *Application Contact:* Dr. Marcia P. Harrigan, Senior Associate Dean, Student and Academic Affairs, 804-828-0703, Fax: 804-828-0716, E-mail: mpharrig@vcu.edu. *Dean,* Dr. James E. Hinterlong, 804-828-1030, Fax: 804-828-0716, E-mail: jehinterlong@vcu.edu.

School of the Arts Expenses: Contact institution. *Financial support:* Fellowships, teaching assistantships, career-related internships or fieldwork, Federal Work-Study, institutionally sponsored loans, and tuition waivers (full and partial) available. Support available to part-time students. Financial award applicants required to submit FAFSA. *Program availability:* Part-time. Offers art education (MAE, PhD); art history (MA, PhD); ceramics (MFA); costume design (MFA); curatorial (PhD); design (MFA); fibers (MFA); furniture design (MFA); glassworking (MFA); historical studies (MA, PhD); jewelry/metalworking (MFA); kinetic imaging (MFA); museum studies (MA); music (MM); music education (MM); painting (MFA); pedagogy/literature (MA); pedagogy/performance (MFA); photography and film (MFA); printmaking (MFA); scene design/technical theatre (MFA); sculpture (MFA); theatre (MFA). *Application deadline:* For fall admission, 1/15 priority date for domestic students. *Application fee:* $50. Electronic applications accepted. *Application Contact:* Jack H. Risley, Associate Dean for Academic Affairs, 804-828-2787, Fax: 804-828-6469, E-mail: jhrisley@vcu.edu. *Dean,* Joseph H. Seipel, 804-828-2787, Fax: 804-828-6469, E-mail: arts@vcu.edu.

Medical College of Virginia-Professional Programs Expenses: Contact institution. *Financial support:* Fellowships, research assistantships, teaching assistantships, career-related internships or fieldwork, Federal Work-Study, institutionally sponsored loans, and tuition waivers (full and partial) available. *Program availability:* Part-time. Offers medicine (MPH, MS, MSD, DDS, MD, PhD, Pharm D, Certificate). *Application deadline:* Applications are processed on a rolling basis. *Application fee:* $50. Electronic applications accepted. *Application Contact:* Whitney A. Carswell, Recruitment Coordinator, Graduate School, 804-828-6916, Fax: 804-828-6949, E-mail: wcarswell@vcu.edu. *Vice President for Health Sciences,* Dr. Sheldin M. Retchin, 804-828-7235, Fax: 804-828-8002, E-mail: vphsweb@vcu.edu.

School of Dentistry Expenses: Contact institution. *Financial support:* Fellowships available. Offers dentistry (MS, DDS). *Application deadline:* For fall admission, 9/1 for domestic students. Electronic applications accepted. *Application Contact:* Dr. Garry L. Myers, Graduate Program Director, 804-628-2903, E-mail: gmyers3@vcu.edu. *Dean/Associate Vice President for Health Sciences,* Dr. David C. Sarrett, 804-828-7235, E-mail: bmarcus@vcu.edu.

School of Medicine Expenses: Contact institution. *Financial support:* Fellowships, research assistantships, teaching assistantships, career-related internships or fieldwork, Federal Work-Study, institutionally sponsored loans, and tuition waivers (full and partial) available. Offers anatomy and neurobiology (MS); biochemistry and molecular biology (MS, PhD); biostatistics (MS, PhD); genetic counseling (MS); healthcare policy and research (PhD); human genetics (PhD); medicine (MPH, MS, MD, PhD, Certificate); microbiology and immunology (MS, PhD); molecular biology and genetics (MS); neuroscience (PhD); pharmacology (Certificate); pharmacology and toxicology (MS, PhD); physical therapy (PhD); physiology (MS, PhD); social and behavioral sciences (PhD). *Application deadline:* Applications are processed on a rolling basis. Electronic applications accepted. *Application Contact:* Dr. Jan Chlebowski, Associate Dean for Graduate Education, 804-828-1023, E-mail: jfchlebo@vcu.edu. *Dean,* Dr. Jerome F. Strauss, III, 804-828-9788, Fax: 804-828-7628.

School of Pharmacy Expenses: Contact institution. *Financial support:* Fellowships, research assistantships, teaching assistantships, and institutionally sponsored loans available. Financial award application deadline: 3/1. *Program availability:* Part-time. Offers medicinal chemistry (MS); pharmaceutical sciences (PhD); pharmaceutics (MS); pharmacotherapy and pharmacy administration (MS); pharmacy (MS, PhD, Pharm D). *Application deadline:* For fall admission, 12/1 priority date for domestic students. Applications are processed on a rolling basis. *Application fee:* $50. Electronic applications accepted. *Application Contact:* Dr. Thomas P. Reinders, Associate Dean for Admissions and Student Services, 804-828-3000, Fax: 804-827-0002, E-mail: reinders@vcu.edu. *Dean,* Dr. Victor A. Yanchick, 804-828-3000, Fax: 804-828-1815, E-mail: pharmacy@vcu.edu.

Program in Pre-Medical Basic Health Sciences Expenses: Contact institution. Offers pre-medical basic health sciences (Postbaccalaureate Certificate). *Application deadline:* For fall admission, 6/1 for domestic students. *Application fee:* $50. Electronic applications accepted. *Application Contact:* Zack McDowell, Administrator, 804-828-9501, E-mail: premedcert@vcu.edu. *Director,* Dr. Louis J. De Felice, 804-828-9501, E-mail: premedcert@vcu.edu.

VIRGINIA INTERNATIONAL UNIVERSITY, Fairfax, VA 22030

General Information Proprietary, coed, comprehensive institution. *Research affiliation:* Apple Federal Credit Union (financial management).

GRADUATE UNITS

School of Business *Program availability:* Part-time, online learning. Offers accounting (MBA, MS); entrepreneurship (MBA); executive management (Graduate Certificate); global logistics (MBA); health care management (MBA); hospitality and tourism management (MBA); human resources management (MBA); international business management (MBA); international finance (MBA); marketing management (MBA); mass media and public relations (MBA); project management (MBA, MS). Electronic applications accepted.

School of Computer Information Systems *Program availability:* Part-time, online learning. Offers business intelligence (Graduate Certificate); business intelligence and data analytics (MIS); computer science (MS); cybersecurity (MIS); data management (MIS); enterprise project management (MIS); health informatics (MIS); information assurance (MIS); information systems (Graduate Certificate); information systems management (MS, Graduate Certificate); information technology (MIS); information technology audit and compliance (Graduate Certificate); knowledge management (MIS); software engineering (MS). Electronic applications accepted.

School of Education *Program availability:* Part-time, online learning. Offers applied linguistics (MS); education (M Ed); teaching English to speakers of other languages (MA). Electronic applications accepted.

School of Public and International Affairs Offers international relations (MS); public administration (MPA).

VIRGINIA POLYTECHNIC INSTITUTE AND STATE UNIVERSITY, Blacksburg, VA 24061

General Information State-supported, coed, university. CGS member. *Enrollment:* 33,170 graduate, professional, and undergraduate students; 5,097 full-time matriculated graduate/professional students (2,216 women), 2,282 part-time matriculated graduate/professional students (972 women). *Enrollment by degree level:* 3,870 master's, 3,509 doctoral. *Graduate faculty:* 1,777 full-time (593 women), 11 part-time/adjunct (6 women). Tuition, state resident: full-time $12,467; part-time $692.50 per credit hour. Tuition, nonresident: full-time $25,095; part-time $1394.25 per credit hour. *Required fees:* $2669; $491.50 per semester. Tuition and fees vary according to course load, campus/location and program. *Graduate housing:* Room and/or apartments available on a first-come, first-served basis to single students; on-campus housing not available to married students. Typical cost: $8862 per year ($12,700 including board). *Student services:* Campus employment opportunities, campus safety program, career counseling, exercise/wellness program, free psychological counseling, grant writing training, international student services, low-cost health insurance, multicultural affairs office, services for students with disabilities, teacher training, writing training. *Library facilities:* Newman Library plus 2 others. *Research affiliation:* Virginia Tech Carilion School of Medicine and Research Institute, Commonwealth Center for Advanced Manufacturing (CCAM), Wellcome Trust Centre for Neuroimaging (health research), Virginia Biosciences Health Research Corporation (health research), Transport Canada (transportation), Elanco Animal Health (agriculture).

Computer facilities: A campuswide network can be accessed from student residence rooms and from off campus. Online class registration is available.
Website: http://www.vt.edu/

GRADUATE UNITS

Graduate School Expenses: Contact institution. *Financial support:* Fellowships, research assistantships, and teaching assistantships available. *Application fee:* $65. *Vice President and Dean for Graduate Education,* Dr. Karen P. DePauw, 540-231-6691, E-mail: grads@vt.edu.

College of Agriculture and Life Sciences Students: 360 full-time (193 women), 150 part-time (89 women); includes 73 minority (30 Black or African American, non-Hispanic/Latino; 15 Asian, non-Hispanic/Latino; 15 Hispanic/Latino; 15 Two or more races, non-Hispanic/Latino), 113 international. Average age 29. 311 applicants, 45% accepted, 106 enrolled. *Faculty:* 235 full-time (69 women). Expenses: Contact institution. *Financial support:* In 2016–17, 258 research assistantships with full tuition reimbursements (averaging $20,636 per year), 107 teaching assistantships with full tuition reimbursements (averaging $20,004 per year) were awarded. Financial award application deadline: 3/1; financial award applicants required to submit FAFSA. In 2016, 111 master's, 50 doctorates awarded. Offers agricultural and applied economics (MS); agricultural and life sciences (MS); animal and poultry science (MS, PhD); crop and soil environmental sciences (MS, PhD); dairy science (MS); entomology (PhD); horticulture (MS, PhD); human nutrition, foods and exercise (MS, PhD); life sciences (MS, PhD); plant pathology, physiology and weed science (PhD). *Application deadline:* For fall admission, 8/1 for domestic students, 4/1 for international students; for spring admission, 1/1 for domestic students, 9/1 for international students. Applications are processed on a rolling basis. *Application fee:* $75. Electronic applications accepted. *Application Contact:* Crystal Tawney, Administrative Assistant, 540-231-4152, Fax: 540-231-4163, E-mail: cdtawney@vt.edu. *Dean,* Dr. Alan L. Grant, 540-231-4152, Fax: 540-231-4163, E-mail: algrant@vt.edu.

College of Architecture and Urban Studies Students: 371 full-time (185 women), 210 part-time (104 women); includes 118 minority (49 Black or African American, non-Hispanic/Latino; 1 American Indian or Alaska Native, non-Hispanic/Latino; 30 Asian, non-Hispanic/Latino; 32 Hispanic/Latino; 6 Two or more races, non-Hispanic/Latino), 137 international. Average age 31. 566 applicants, 55% accepted, 160 enrolled. *Faculty:* 136 full-time (53 women). Expenses: Contact institution. *Financial support:* In 2016–17, 11 research assistantships with full tuition reimbursements (averaging $19,474 per year), 45 teaching assistantships with full tuition reimbursements (averaging $16,014 per year) were awarded. Financial award application deadline: 3/1; financial award applicants required to submit FAFSA. In 2016, 137 master's, 24 doctorates awarded. Offers architecture (MS Arch); architecture and design research (PhD); building/construction science and management (MS); creative technologies (MFA); environmental design and planning (PhD); landscape architecture (MLA); planning, governance, and globalization (PhD); public administration (MPA); public administration/public affairs (PhD, Certificate); public and international affairs (MPIA); urban and regional planning (MURP). *Application deadline:* For fall admission, 8/1 for domestic students, 4/1 for international students; for spring admission, 1/1 for domestic students, 9/1 for international students. Applications are processed on a rolling basis. *Application fee:* $75. Electronic applications accepted. *Application Contact:* Christine Mattsson-Coon, Executive Assistant, 540-231-6416, Fax: 540-231-6332, E-mail: cmattsso@vt.edu. *Dean,* Dr. A. J. Davis, 540-231-6416, Fax: 540-231-6332, E-mail: davisa@vt.edu.

College of Engineering Students: 1,949 full-time (487 women), 393 part-time (69 women); includes 251 minority (56 Black or African American, non-Hispanic/Latino; 3 American Indian or Alaska Native, non-Hispanic/Latino; 87 Asian, non-Hispanic/Latino; 70 Hispanic/Latino; 35 Two or more races, non-Hispanic/Latino), 1,354 international. Average age 27. 4,903 applicants, 19% accepted, 569 enrolled. *Faculty:* 400 full-time (73 women), 3 part-time/adjunct (2 women). Expenses: Contact institution. *Financial support:* In 2016–17, 160 fellowships with full tuition reimbursements (averaging $7,387 per year), 872 research assistantships with full tuition reimbursements (averaging $22,329 per year), 313 teaching assistantships with full tuition reimbursements (averaging $18,714 per year) were awarded. Financial award application deadline: 3/1; financial award applicants required to submit FAFSA. In 2016, 364 master's, 200 doctorates awarded. Offers aerospace engineering (ME, MS, PhD); biological systems engineering (ME, MS, PhD); biomedical engineering (MS, PhD); chemical engineering (ME, MS, PhD); civil engineering (ME, MS, PhD); computer engineering (ME, MS, PhD); computer science (MS, PhD); electrical engineering (ME, PhD); engineering education (PhD); engineering mechanics (ME, MS, PhD); environmental engineering (MS); environmental science and engineering (MS); industrial and systems engineering (ME, MS, PhD); materials science and engineering (ME, MS, PhD); mechanical engineering (ME, MS, PhD); mining and minerals engineering (PhD); mining engineering (ME, MS); nuclear engineering (MS, PhD); ocean engineering (MS); systems engineering (ME, MS). *Application deadline:* For fall admission, 8/1 for domestic students, 4/1 for international students; for spring admission, 1/1 for domestic students, 9/1 for international students. Applications are processed on a rolling basis. *Application fee:* $75. Electronic applications accepted. *Application Contact:* Linda Perkins, Executive Assistant, 540-231-9752, Fax: 540-231-3031, E-mail: lperkins@vt.edu. *Dean,* Dr. Julia Ross, 540-231-9752, Fax: 540-231-3031, E-mail: deaneng@vt.edu.

College of Liberal Arts and Human Sciences Students: 657 full-time (446 women), 457 part-time (292 women); includes 213 minority (114 Black or African American, non-Hispanic/Latino; 3 American Indian or Alaska Native, non-Hispanic/Latino; 29 Asian, non-Hispanic/Latino; 44 Hispanic/Latino; 23 Two or more races, non-Hispanic/Latino), 93 international. Average age 33. 805 applicants, 55% accepted, 328 enrolled. *Faculty:* 408 full-time (204 women), 3 part-time/adjunct (2 women). Expenses: Contact institution. *Financial support:* In 2016–17, 21 research assistantships with full tuition reimbursements (averaging $19,817 per year), 237 teaching assistantships with full tuition reimbursements (averaging $15,497 per year) were awarded. Financial award application deadline: 3/1; financial award applicants required to submit FAFSA. In 2016, 270 master's, 91 doctorates awarded. Offers career and technical education (MS Ed, Ed D, PhD, Ed S); communication (MA); counselor education (MA Ed, Ed D, PhD, Ed S); creative writing (MFA); curriculum and instruction (MA Ed, Ed D, PhD, Ed S); educational leadership and policy studies (MA Ed, Ed D, PhD, Ed S); educational research and evaluation (PhD); English (MA); foreign languages, cultures, and literatures (MA); higher education (PhD); higher education and student affairs (MA Ed); history (MA); human development (MS, PhD); material culture and public humanities (MA); philosophy (MA); political science (MA); rhetoric and writing (PhD); science and technology studies (MS, PhD); social, political, ethical, and cultural thought (PhD); sociology (MS, PhD); theater arts (MFA). *Application deadline:* For fall admission, 8/1 for domestic students, 4/1 for international students; for spring admission, 1/1 for domestic students, 9/1 for international students. Applications are processed on a rolling basis. *Application fee:* $75. Electronic applications accepted. *Application Contact:* Chelsea Blanchet, Executive Assistant, 540-231-6779, Fax: 540-231-7157, E-mail: bchels1@vt.edu. *Interim Dean,* Rosemary Blieszner, 540-231-6779, Fax: 540-231-7157, E-mail: liberalartsdean@vt.edu.

College of Natural Resources and Environment Students: 174 full-time (85 women), 67 part-time (37 women); includes 22 minority (4 Black or African American, non-Hispanic/Latino; 4 Asian, non-Hispanic/Latino; 12 Hispanic/Latino; 2 Two or more races, non-Hispanic/Latino), 36 international. Average age 31. 103 applicants, 61% accepted, 57 enrolled. *Faculty:* 74 full-time (17 women). Expenses: Contact institution. *Financial support:* In 2016–17, 1 fellowship (averaging $24,256 per year), 23 research assistantships with full tuition reimbursements (averaging $26,209 per year), 26 teaching assistantships with full tuition reimbursements (averaging $22,466 per year) were awarded. Financial award application deadline: 3/1; financial award applicants required to submit FAFSA. In 2016, 102 master's, 20 doctorates awarded. Offers fisheries and wildlife (MS, PhD); forestry and forest products (MF, MS, PhD); geography (MS); geospatial and environmental analysis (PhD); natural resources (MNR). *Application deadline:* For fall admission, 8/1 for domestic students, 4/1 for international students; for spring admission, 1/1 for domestic students, 9/1 for international students. Applications are processed on a rolling basis. *Application fee:* $75. Electronic applications accepted. *Application Contact:* Arlice Banks, Executive Assistant, 540-231-7051, Fax: 540-231-7664, E-mail: arbanks@vt.edu. *Dean,* Dr. Paul M. Winistorfer, 540-231-5481, Fax: 540-231-7664, E-mail: pstorfer@vt.edu.

College of Science Students: 567 full-time (222 women), 47 part-time (19 women); includes 66 minority (14 Black or African American, non-Hispanic/Latino; 12 Asian, non-Hispanic/Latino; 29 Hispanic/Latino; 11 Two or more races, non-Hispanic/Latino), 247 international. Average age 27. 956 applicants, 17% accepted, 118 enrolled. *Faculty:* 299 full-time (92 women), 1 part-time/adjunct (0 women). Expenses: Contact institution. *Financial support:* In 2016–17, 156 research assistantships with full tuition reimbursements (averaging $21,863 per year), 379 teaching assistantships with full tuition reimbursements (averaging $18,980 per year) were awarded. Financial award application deadline: 3/1; financial award applicants required to submit FAFSA. In 2016, 75 master's, 71 doctorates awarded. Offers biological sciences (MS, PhD); biomedical technology development and management (MS); chemistry (MS, PhD); data analysis and applied statistics (MA); economics (MA, PhD); geosciences (MS, PhD); mathematics (MS, PhD); physics (MS, PhD); psychology (MS, PhD); statistics (MS, PhD). *Application deadline:* For fall admission, 8/1 for domestic students, 4/1 for international students; for spring admission, 1/1 for domestic students, 9/1 for international students. Applications are processed on a rolling basis. *Application fee:* $75. Electronic applications accepted. *Application Contact:* Teresa Price, Executive Assistant to the Dean and Grants Specialist, 540-231-6394, Fax: 540-231-3380, E-mail: tfprice@vt.edu. *Dean,* Dr. Sally C. Morton, 540-231-5422, Fax: 540-231-3380, E-mail: scmorton@vt.edu.

Intercollege Students: 175 full-time (82 women), 763 part-time (279 women); includes 217 minority (71 Black or African American, non-Hispanic/Latino; 1 American Indian or Alaska Native, non-Hispanic/Latino; 77 Asian, non-Hispanic/Latino; 43 Hispanic/Latino; 1 Native Hawaiian or other Pacific Islander, non-Hispanic/Latino; 24 Two or more races, non-Hispanic/Latino), 83 international. Average age 33. 626 applicants, 74% accepted, 373 enrolled. Expenses: Contact institution. *Financial support:* In 2016–17, 100 research assistantships with full tuition reimbursements (averaging $23,321 per year), 10 teaching assistantships with full tuition reimbursements (averaging $20,748 per year) were awarded. Financial award application deadline: 3/1; financial award applicants required to submit FAFSA. In 2016, 91 master's, 18 doctorates awarded. Offers genetics, bioinformatics and computational biology (PhD); information technology (MIT); macromolecular science and engineering (MS, PhD); translational biology, medicine, and health (PhD). *Application deadline:* For fall admission, 8/1 for domestic students, 4/1 for international students; for spring admission, 1/1 for domestic students, 9/1 for international students. Applications are processed on a rolling basis. *Application fee:* $75. Electronic applications accepted. *Vice President and Dean for Graduate Education,* Dr. Karen P. DePauw, 540-231-7581, Fax: 540-231-1670, E-mail: kpdepauw@vt.edu.

Pamplin College of Business Students: 255 full-time (101 women), 156 part-time (56 women); includes 95 minority (21 Black or African American, non-Hispanic/Latino; 49 Asian, non-Hispanic/Latino; 13 Hispanic/Latino; 12 Two or more races, non-Hispanic/Latino), 73 international. Average age 33. 310 applicants, 59% accepted, 150 enrolled. *Faculty:* 126 full-time (38 women), 3 part-time/adjunct (1 woman). Expenses: Contact institution. *Financial support:* In 2016–17, 2 fellowships with full tuition reimbursements (averaging $21,222 per year), 3 research assistantships with full tuition reimbursements (averaging $24,988 per year), 46 teaching assistantships with full tuition reimbursements (averaging $20,054 per year) were awarded. Financial award application deadline: 3/1; financial award applicants required to submit FAFSA. In 2016, 167 master's, 8 doctorates awarded. Offers accounting and information systems (MACIS); business (PhD); business administration (MBA, MS); hospitality and tourism management (MS, PhD). *Application deadline:* For fall admission, 8/1 for domestic students, 4/1 for international students; for spring admission, 1/1 for domestic students, 9/1 for international students. Applications are processed on a rolling basis. *Application fee:* $75. Electronic applications accepted. *Application Contact:* Kimberly Ridpath, Executive Assistant, 540-231-6601, Fax: 540-231-4487, E-mail: ridpathk@vt.edu. *Dean,* Dr. Robert T. Sumichrast, 540-231-6601, Fax: 540-231-4487, E-mail: busdean@vt.edu.

Virginia-Maryland Regional College of Veterinary Medicine Students: 589 full-time (415 women), 39 part-time (27 women); includes 103 minority (18 Black or African American, non-Hispanic/Latino; 1 American Indian or Alaska Native, non-Hispanic/Latino; 31 Asian, non-Hispanic/Latino; 26 Hispanic/Latino; 27 Two or more races, non-Hispanic/Latino), 31 international. Average age 26. 55 applicants, 69% accepted, 33 enrolled. *Faculty:* 99 full-time (47 women), 1 (woman) part-time/adjunct. Expenses: Contact institution. *Financial support:* In 2016–17, 3 fellowships (averaging $52,728 per year), 21 research assistantships with full tuition reimbursements (averaging $25,682 per year), 38 teaching assistantships with full tuition reimbursements (averaging $23,510 per year) were awarded. Financial award application deadline: 3/1; financial award applicants required to submit FAFSA. In 2016, 48 master's, 126 doctorates awarded. Offers biomedical and veterinary sciences (MS, PhD); public health (MPH); veterinary medicine (DVM). *Application deadline:* For fall admission, 8/1 for domestic students, 4/1 for international students; for spring admission, 1/1 for domestic students, 9/1 for international students. Applications are processed on a rolling basis. *Application fee:* $75. Electronic applications accepted. *Application Contact:* Shelia Steele, Executive Assistant, 540-231-7910, Fax: 540-231-3505, E-mail: ssteele@vt.edu. *Dean,* Dr. Cyril R. Clark, 540-231-7910, Fax: 540-231-3505, E-mail: cvmdean@vt.edu.

VT Online Offers advanced transportation systems (Certificate); aerospace engineering (MS); agricultural and life sciences (MSLFS); business information systems (Graduate Certificate); career and technical education (MS); civil engineering (MS); computer engineering (M Eng, MS); decision support systems (Graduate Certificate); eLearning leadership (MA); electrical engineering (M Eng, MS); engineering administration (MEA); environmental engineering (Certificate); environmental politics and policy (Graduate Certificate); environmental sciences and engineering (MS); foundations of political analysis (Graduate Certificate); health product risk management (Graduate Certificate); industrial and systems engineering (MS); information policy and society (Graduate Certificate); information security (Graduate Certificate); information technology (MIT); instructional technology (MA); integrative STEM education (MA Ed); liberal arts (Graduate Certificate); life sciences: health product risk management (MS); natural resources (MNR, Graduate Certificate); networking (Graduate Certificate); nonprofit and nongovernmental organization management (Graduate Certificate); ocean engineering (MS); political science (MA); security studies (Graduate Certificate); software development (Graduate Certificate).

VIRGINIA STATE UNIVERSITY, Petersburg, VA 23806-0001

General Information State-supported, coed, comprehensive institution. *Graduate housing:* Room and/or apartments available on a first-come, first-served basis to single students; on-campus housing not available to married students. Housing application deadline: 5/1. *Research affiliation:* Medical College of Virginia/Virginia Commonwealth University (biology), The College of William and Mary (biology), University of Massachusetts (biology), Rolls Royce USA (engineering), C-CAM Technologies (engineering).

GRADUATE UNITS

College of Graduate Studies *Program availability:* Part-time, evening/weekend. Offers interdisciplinary studies (MIS).

College of Education Offers administration and supervision (M Ed); education (M Ed, MS, Ed D); educational administration and supervision (Ed D); school and community counseling (M Ed, MS).

College of Engineering and Technology Offers computer science (MS); engineering and technology (M Ed, MS); mathematics (MS); mathematics education (MS).

College of Humanities and Social Sciences *Program availability:* Part-time, evening/weekend. Offers criminal justice (MS); economics (MA); humanities and social sciences (M Ed, MA, MS); media management (MA).

College of Natural and Health Sciences Offers behavioral and community health sciences (PhD); biology (MS); clinical health psychology (PhD); clinical psychology (MS); general psychology (MS); natural and health sciences (MS, PhD).

VIRGINIA THEOLOGICAL SEMINARY, Alexandria, VA 22304

General Information Independent-religious, coed, graduate-only institution. *Graduate faculty:* 26 full-time (11 women), 29 part-time/adjunct (11 women). *Tuition:* Full-time $13,800; part-time $636 per credit hour. *Required fees:* $140. *Graduate housing:* Rooms and/or apartments available on a first-come, first-served basis to single and married students. Typical cost: $4040 per year ($5650 including board) for single students; $14,400 per year ($16,310 including board) for married students. Room and board charges vary according to board plan, campus/location and housing facility selected. Housing application deadline: 5/1. *Student services:* Campus employment opportunities, child daycare facilities, exercise/wellness program, international student services, low-cost health insurance, multicultural affairs office, services for students with disabilities, writing training. *Library facilities:* Bishop Payne Library plus 1 other. *Collection:* Students can reserve study rooms.

Computer facilities: 20 computers available on campus for general student use. A campuswide network can be accessed from student residence rooms. Online class registration is available.
Website: http://www.vts.edu/

General Application Contact: Rachel Holm, Associate Director for Admissions, Financial Aid and Housing, 703-370-6600.

GRADUATE UNITS

Graduate and Professional Programs Students: 220. *Faculty:* 26 full-time (11 women), 29 part-time/adjunct (11 women). Expenses: Contact institution. *Financial support:* Career-related internships or fieldwork, Federal Work-Study, and institutionally sponsored loans available. *Program availability:* Part-time. Offers Christian spirituality (D Min); educational leadership (D Ed Min, D Min); ministry development (D Min); theology (M Div, MA). *Application deadline:* For fall admission, 5/1 for domestic students. *Application fee:* $0. *Application Contact:* Rachel Holm, Associate Director for Admissions, Financial Aid and Housing, 703-370-6600.

VIRGINIA UNION UNIVERSITY, Richmond, VA 23220-1170

General Information Independent-religious, coed, comprehensive institution. *Graduate housing:* Room and/or apartments available on a first-come, first-served basis to single students; on-campus housing not available to married students.

GRADUATE UNITS

Evelyn R. Syphax School of Education, Psychology and Interdisciplinary Studies Offers curriculum and instruction (MA).

Samuel DeWitt Proctor School of Theology *Program availability:* Part-time, evening/weekend. Offers theology (M Div, D Min).

VIRGINIA UNIVERSITY OF LYNCHBURG, Lynchburg, VA 24501-6417

General Information Independent-religious, coed, comprehensive institution. *Enrollment:* 64 full-time matriculated graduate/professional students (25 women), 4 part-time matriculated graduate/professional students (2 women). *Enrollment by degree level:* 10 master's. *Graduate faculty:* 6 full-time, 4 part-time/adjunct (all women). *Tuition:* Full-time $8200; part-time $4100 per credit hour. *Required fees:* $400. Tuition and fees vary according to campus/location and program. *Graduate housing:* Room and/or apartments available on a first-come, first-served basis to single students; on-campus housing not available to married students. Typical cost: $1860 per year ($4260 including board). Room and board charges vary according to board plan. Housing application deadline: 9/5. *Student services:* Campus safety program, career counseling, exercise/wellness program, services for students with disabilities. *Library facilities:* Mary Jane Cachelin Library.

Computer facilities: 10 computers available on campus for general student use. A campuswide network can be accessed from student residence rooms and from off campus.
Website: http://www.vul.edu/

General Application Contact: Houston Walthall, Admissions Director, 434-528-5276 Ext. 1130, Fax: 434-528-4257, E-mail: hwalthall@vul.edu.

GRADUATE UNITS

Graduate Programs Students: 64 full-time (25 women), 4 part-time (2 women). *Faculty:* 6 full-time (0 women), 4 part-time/adjunct (all women). Expenses: Contact institution. *Program availability:* Online learning. Offers Christian ministry (M Div); ministry (D Min). *Application Contact:* Houston Walthall, Admissions Director, 434-528-5276 Ext. 1130, Fax: 434-528-4257, E-mail: hwalthall@vul.edu.

VITERBO UNIVERSITY, La Crosse, WI 54601-4797

General Information Independent-religious, coed, comprehensive institution. *Graduate housing:* Room and/or apartments available on a first-come, first-served basis to single students; on-campus housing not available to married students. Housing application deadline: 4/2.

GRADUATE UNITS

Graduate Program in Nursing *Program availability:* Part-time. Offers nursing (DNP). Electronic applications accepted.

Graduate Programs in Education *Program availability:* Part-time, evening/weekend. Offers cross-categorical special education (Certificate); director of instruction (Certificate); director of special education and pupil services (Certificate); early childhood (Certificate); education (MAE); literacy coaching (Certificate); PreK-12 principal/supervisor of special education (Certificate); principal (Certificate); reading specialist endorsement (Certificate); reading teacher (Certificate); reading teacher 5-12 endorsement (Certificate); reading teacher K-8 endorsement (Certificate); superintendent (Certificate); talented and gifted endorsement (Certificate); Wisconsin

school business administrator (Certificate). Weekend courses available in summer. Electronic applications accepted.

Master of Arts in Servant Leadership Program *Program availability:* Part-time, evening/weekend. Offers ethical leadership in organizations (Certificate); servant leadership (MA). Electronic applications accepted.

Master of Business Administration Program *Program availability:* Part-time, evening/weekend. Offers general business administration (MBA); health care management (MBA); international business (MBA); leadership (MBA); project management (MBA). Electronic applications accepted.

Master of Science in Mental Health Counseling Program *Program availability:* Part-time, evening/weekend. Offers addiction counseling (MS); child and adolescent counseling (MS); complementary health and wellness counseling (MS). Electronic applications accepted.

WAGNER COLLEGE, Staten Island, NY 10301-4495

General Information Independent, coed, comprehensive institution. CGS member. *Enrollment:* 2,301 graduate, professional, and undergraduate students; 193 full-time matriculated graduate/professional students (105 women), 249 part-time matriculated graduate/professional students (191 women). *Enrollment by degree level:* 420 master's, 22 doctoral. *Graduate faculty:* 33 full-time (18 women), 31 part-time/adjunct (18 women). Tuition and fees vary according to degree level. *Graduate housing:* Room and/or apartments available on a first-come, first-served basis to single students; on-campus housing not available to married students. Typical cost: $13,000 (including board). Room and board charges vary according to board plan. Housing application deadline: 4/1. *Student services:* Campus employment opportunities, campus safety program, career counseling, child daycare facilities, exercise/wellness program, free psychological counseling, international student services, multicultural affairs office, services for students with disabilities, teacher training, writing training. *Library facilities:* August Horrmann Library. *Collection:* Books: 70,465 (physical), 180,000 (digital/electronic); Serial titles: 79,532 (physical); Databases: 61. Weekly public service hours: 120; students can reserve study rooms. *Research affiliation:* Staten Island University Hospital.

Computer facilities: 230 computers available on campus for general student use. A campuswide network can be accessed from student residence rooms and from off campus. Online class registration is available.
Website: http://www.wagner.edu/

General Application Contact: Robert Herr, Dean of Enrollment, 718-420-4242, Fax: 718-390-3105, E-mail: robert.herr@wagner.edu.

GRADUATE UNITS

Division of Graduate Studies Students: 202 full-time (107 women), 206 part-time (166 women); includes 83 minority (33 Black or African American, non-Hispanic/Latino; 1 American Indian or Alaska Native, non-Hispanic/Latino; 19 Asian, non-Hispanic/Latino; 25 Hispanic/Latino; 2 Native Hawaiian or other Pacific Islander, non-Hispanic/Latino; 3 Two or more races, non-Hispanic/Latino), 13 international. Average age 28. 267 applicants, 84% accepted, 182 enrolled. *Faculty:* 33 full-time (18 women), 31 part-time/adjunct (18 women). Expenses: Contact institution. *Financial support:* In 2016–17, 298 students received support. Career-related internships or fieldwork, unspecified assistantships, and alumni fellowship grants available. Financial award application deadline: 4/1; financial award applicants required to submit FAFSA. In 2016, 196 master's awarded. *Program availability:* Part-time, evening/weekend. Offers accounting (MS); business administration (MBA); childhood education/students with disabilities (MS Ed); early childhood education/students with disabilities (birth-grade 2) (MS Ed); educational leadership (MS Ed, Certificate); finance (MBA); health care administration (MBA); international business (MBA); literacy (B-6) (MS Ed); management (Exec MBA); marketing (MBA); microbiology (MS); school district leadership (MS Ed, Certificate); secondary education 7-12 (MS Ed); secondary education/students with disabilities (MS Ed). *Application deadline:* For fall admission, 5/1 priority date for domestic students, 3/1 priority date for international students; for spring admission, 11/1 priority date for domestic students, 10/1 priority date for international students. Applications are processed on a rolling basis. *Application fee:* $50. *Application Contact:* Patricia Clancy, Assistant Coordinator of Graduate Studies, 718-420-4464, Fax: 718-390-3105, E-mail: patricia.clancy@wagner.edu. *Coordinator,* Dr. Jeffrey Kraus, 718-390-3254, Fax: 718-390-3456, E-mail: jkraus@wagner.edu.

WAKE FOREST UNIVERSITY, Winston-Salem, NC 27106

General Information Independent, coed, university. CGS member. *Graduate housing:* On-campus housing not available.

GRADUATE UNITS

Graduate School of Arts and Sciences *Program availability:* Part-time. Offers accountancy (MSA); analytical chemistry (MS, PhD); arts and sciences (MA, MA Ed, MALS, MS, MSA, PhD); biology (MS, PhD); computer science (MS); counseling (MA); English (MA); health and exercise science (MS); inorganic chemistry (MS, PhD); liberal studies (MALS); mathematics (MA); organic chemistry (MS, PhD); physical chemistry (MS, PhD); physics (MS, PhD); psychology (MA); religion (MA); secondary education (MA Ed); speech communication (MA). Electronic applications accepted.

School of Business Students: 699 full-time (314 women); includes 142 minority (77 Black or African American, non-Hispanic/Latino; 4 American Indian or Alaska Native, non-Hispanic/Latino; 24 Asian, non-Hispanic/Latino; 27 Hispanic/Latino; 10 Two or more races, non-Hispanic/Latino), 73 international. Average age 28. 1,169 applicants, 63% accepted, 486 enrolled. *Faculty:* 57 full-time (13 women), 10 part-time/adjunct (3 women). Expenses: Contact institution. *Financial support:* Scholarships/grants available. Financial award applicants required to submit FAFSA. In 2016, 446 master's awarded. *Program availability:* Evening/weekend. Offers assurance services (MSA); business (MA, MBA, MS, MSA); business administration (MBA); business analytics (MS); management (MA); tax consulting (MSA); transaction services (MSA). *Application deadline:* Applications are processed on a rolling basis. *Application fee:* $100. Electronic applications accepted. *Application Contact:* Tamara Paquee, Administrative Assistant, 336-758-5422, Fax: 336-758-5830, E-mail: busadmissions@wfu.edu. *Dean,* Charles Iacovou, 336-758-5422, Fax: 336-758-5830, E-mail: busadmissions@wfu.edu.

School of Law Offers law (LL M, MSL, JD, SJD). LL M program is designed for foreign law graduates in American law. Electronic applications accepted.

School of Medicine Offers medicine (MS, MD, PhD). Electronic applications accepted.

Graduate Programs in Medicine Offers biochemistry (PhD); cancer biology (PhD); comparative medicine (MS); health sciences research (PhD); medicine (MS, PhD); microbiology and immunology (PhD); molecular and cellular pathobiology (MS, PhD); molecular genetics and genomics (PhD); molecular medicine (MS, PhD); neurobiology and anatomy (PhD); neuroscience (PhD); pharmacology (PhD); physiology (PhD). Electronic applications accepted.

Virginia Tech-Wake Forest University School of Biomedical Engineering and Sciences Offers biomedical engineering (MS, PhD). Electronic applications accepted.

WALDEN UNIVERSITY, Minneapolis, MN 55401
General Information Proprietary, coed, university. CGS member.

GRADUATE UNITS

Graduate Programs *Program availability:* Part-time, evening/weekend, online only, 100% online. Electronic applications accepted.

Richard W. Riley College of Education and Leadership *Program availability:* Part-time, evening/weekend, online only, 100% online. Offers adult education (Post-Master's Certificate); adult learning (Graduate Certificate); college teaching and learning (Graduate Certificate); community college leadership (Ed D); curriculum, instruction and assessment (Ed D, Ed S, Graduate Certificate); developmental education (Graduate Certificate); early childhood administration, management, and leadership (Graduate Certificate); early childhood education (Ed D, Ed S); early childhood public policy and advocacy (Graduate Certificate); early childhood studies (MS); education (MS, PhD); educational administration and leadership (Ed D); educational leadership and administration (principal preparation) (Ed S); educational technology (Ed D, Ed S, Post Master's Certificate); elementary reading and literacy (Graduate Certificate); engaging culturally diverse learners (Graduate Certificate); enrollment management and institutional marketing (Graduate Certificate); higher education (MS); higher education and adult learning (Ed D); higher education leadership and management (Ed D); higher education leadership for student success (Graduate Certificate); instructional design and technology (MS, Postbaccalaureate Certificate); integrating technology in the classroom (Graduate Certificate); mathematics 5-8 (Graduate Certificate); mathematics K-6 (Graduate Certificate); online teaching for adult educators (Graduate Certificate); reading, literacy, and assessment (Ed D, Ed S); science K-8 (Graduate Certificate); special education (Ed D, Ed S, Graduate Certificate); special education (K-age 21) (MAT); teacher leadership (Graduate Certificate); teaching adults English as a second language (Graduate Certificate); teaching adults in the early childhood field (Graduate Certificate); teaching and diversity in early childhood education (Graduate Certificate); teaching English language learners (grades K-12) (Graduate Certificate); teaching K-12 students online (Graduate Certificate). Electronic applications accepted.

School of Counseling *Program availability:* Part-time, evening/weekend, online only, 100% online. Offers addiction counseling (MS); clinical mental health counseling (MS); counselor education and supervision (PhD); marriage, couple, and family counseling (MS); school counseling (MS). Electronic applications accepted.

School of Health Sciences *Program availability:* Part-time, evening/weekend, online only, 100% online. Offers clinical research administration (MS, Graduate Certificate); health education and promotion (MS, PhD); health informatics (MS); health services (PhD); healthcare administration (MHA, DHA); leadership and organizational development (MHA); public health (MPH, Dr PH, PhD, Graduate Certificate); systems policy (MHA). Electronic applications accepted.

School of Information Systems and Technology *Program availability:* Part-time, evening/weekend, online only, 100% online. Offers information systems (Graduate Certificate); information systems management (MISM); information technology (MS, DIT). Electronic applications accepted.

School of Management *Program availability:* Part-time, evening/weekend, online only, 100% online. Offers accounting (MBA, MS, DBA); advanced project management (Graduate Certificate); applied project management (Graduate Certificate); auditing (Graduate Certificate); bridge to business administration (Post-Doctoral Certificate); bridge to management (Post-Doctoral Certificate); business management (Graduate Certificate); communication (MBA); corporate finance (MBA); digital marketing (Graduate Certificate); entrepreneurship (DBA); entrepreneurship and small business (MBA); finance (MS, DBA); global supply chain management (DBA); healthcare management (MBA, DBA); human resource management (MBA, MS, Graduate Certificate); human resources management (DBA); information systems management (DBA); international business (MBA, DBA); leadership (MBA, MS, DBA, Graduate Certificate); management (MS, PhD); managerial accounting (Graduate Certificate); marketing (MBA, MS, DBA); project management (MBA, MS, DBA); self-designed (MBA, DBA); social impact management (DBA); technology entrepreneurship (DBA). Electronic applications accepted.

School of Nursing *Program availability:* Part-time, evening/weekend, online only, 100% online. Offers adult-gerontology acute care nurse practitioner (MSN); adult-gerontology nurse practitioner (MSN); education (MSN); family nurse practitioner (MSN); informatics (MSN); leadership and management (MSN); nursing (PhD, Post-Master's Certificate); nursing practice (DNP); psychiatric mental health (MSN). Electronic applications accepted.

School of Psychology *Program availability:* Part-time, evening/weekend, online only, 100% online. Offers clinical psychology (MS); forensic psychology (MS); industrial organizational (MS, PhD); online teaching in psychology (Post-Master's Certificate); organizational psychology and development (Postbaccalaureate Certificate); psychology (MS, PhD); psychology respecialization (Post-Doctoral Certificate). Electronic applications accepted.

School of Public Policy and Administration *Program availability:* Part-time, evening/weekend, online only, 100% online. Offers criminal justice (MPA, MPP, MS, Graduate Certificate); criminal justice and executive management (MS); criminal justice leadership and executive management (MS); emergency management (MPA, MPP, MS); general program (MPA, MPP); global leadership (MPA, MPP); government management (Graduate Certificate); health policy (MPA, MPP); homeland security (MPA, MPP); homeland security and policy coordination (MPA, MPP); international nongovernmental organizations (MPA, MPP); law and public policy (MPA, MPP); local government management for sustainable communities (MPA, MPP); nonprofit management (Graduate Certificate); nonprofit management and leadership (MPA, MPP, MS); online teaching in higher education (Post-Master's Certificate); policy analysis (MPA); public management and leadership (MPA, MPP, Graduate Certificate); public policy (Graduate Certificate); public policy and administration (PhD); strategic planning and public policy (Graduate Certificate); terrorism, mediation, and peace (MPA, MPP). Electronic applications accepted.

School of Social Work and Human Services *Program availability:* Part-time, evening/weekend, online only, 100% online. Offers addictions and social work (DSW); advanced clinical practice (MSW); clinical expertise (DSW); criminal justice (DSW); disaster, crisis, and intervention (DSW); family studies and interventions (DSW); human and social services (PhD); medical social work (DSW); military social work (MSW); policy practice (DSW); social work (PhD); social work administration (DSW); social work in healthcare (MSW); social work with children and families (MSW). Electronic applications accepted.

WALDORF UNIVERSITY, Forest City, IA 50436
General Information Independent-religious, coed, comprehensive institution.

GRADUATE UNITS

Program in Organizational Leadership Offers criminal justice leadership (MA); emergency management leadership (MA); fire/rescue executive leadership (MA); human resource development (MA); public administration (MA); sport management (MA); teacher leader (MA).

WALLA WALLA UNIVERSITY, College Place, WA 99324
General Information Independent-religious, coed, comprehensive institution. *Enrollment:* 1,894 graduate, professional, and undergraduate students; 169 full-time matriculated graduate/professional students (129 women), 24 part-time matriculated graduate/professional students (16 women). *Enrollment by degree level:* 193 master's. *Tuition:* Part-time $592 per quarter hour. *Graduate housing:* Rooms and/or apartments available on a first-come, first-served basis to single and married students. *Student services:* Campus employment opportunities, career counseling, free psychological counseling, international student services, low-cost health insurance, multicultural affairs office, services for students with disabilities. *Library facilities:* Peterson Memorial Library plus 3 others.

Computer facilities: Computer purchase and lease plans are available. A campuswide network can be accessed from student residence rooms and from off campus. Online class registration, online forum, online classifieds, online student directory are available. Website: http://www.wallawalla.edu/

General Application Contact: Pamela Cress, Associate Vice President for Graduate Studies, 509-527-2421, Fax: 509-527-2237, E-mail: pam.cress@wallawalla.edu.

GRADUATE UNITS

Graduate Studies Students: 169 full-time (129 women), 24 part-time (16 women); includes 42 minority (4 Black or African American, non-Hispanic/Latino; 23 American Indian or Alaska Native, non-Hispanic/Latino; 7 Asian, non-Hispanic/Latino; 7 Hispanic/Latino; 1 Native Hawaiian or other Pacific Islander, non-Hispanic/Latino), 1 international. Expenses: Contact institution. *Financial support:* Research assistantships, teaching assistantships, career-related internships or fieldwork, Federal Work-Study, scholarships/grants, tuition waivers (partial), and unspecified assistantships available. Support available to part-time students. Financial award application deadline: 4/30; financial award applicants required to submit FAFSA. In 2016, 106 master's awarded. *Program availability:* Part-time, evening/weekend. Offers biology (MS). *Application deadline:* Applications are processed on a rolling basis. *Application fee:* $50. Electronic applications accepted. *Application Contact:* Sarah Thomas, Administrative Assistant, 509-527-2421, Fax: 509-527-2237, E-mail: sarah.thomas@wallawalla.edu. *Associate Vice President for Graduate Studies,* Pamela Cress, 509-527-2421, Fax: 509-527-2237, E-mail: pam.cress@wallawalla.edu.

School of Education and Psychology Expenses: Contact institution. *Financial support:* Research assistantships, teaching assistantships, Federal Work-Study, and tuition waivers (partial) available. Support available to part-time students. Financial award application deadline: 4/30; financial award applicants required to submit FAFSA. *Program availability:* Part-time. Offers curriculum and instruction (M Ed, MA, MAT); educational leadership (M Ed, MA, MAT); literacy instruction (M Ed, MA, MAT); students at risk (M Ed, MA, MAT); teaching (MAT). *Application deadline:* For fall admission, 4/1 priority date for domestic students. Applications are processed on a rolling basis. *Application fee:* $50. Electronic applications accepted. *Application Contact:* Dr. Joe G. Galusha, Dean of Graduate Studies, 509-527-2421, Fax: 509-527-2237, E-mail: joe.galusha@wallawalla.edu. *Dean,* Denise Dunzweiler, 509-527-2212, Fax: 509-527-2248, E-mail: denise.dunzweiler@wallawalla.edu.

Wilma Hepker School of Social Work and Sociology Expenses: Contact institution. *Financial support:* Career-related internships or fieldwork, Federal Work-Study, and scholarships/grants available. Support available to part-time students. Financial award application deadline: 4/30; financial award applicants required to submit FAFSA. *Program availability:* Part-time. Offers social work (MSW). *Application deadline:* For fall admission, 7/15 priority date for domestic students. Applications are processed on a rolling basis. *Application fee:* $50. Electronic applications accepted. *Application Contact:* Dr. Heather Vonderfecht, Program Director, 509-527-2584, Fax: 509-527-2237, E-mail: heather.vonderfecht@wallawalla.edu. *Dean,* Dr. Susan B. Smith, 509-527-2443, Fax: 509-527-2270, E-mail: susan.smith@wallawalla.edu.

WALSH COLLEGE OF ACCOUNTANCY AND BUSINESS ADMINISTRATION, Troy, MI 48083
General Information Independent, coed, upper-level institution. *Enrollment:* 2,423 graduate, professional, and undergraduate students; 38 full-time matriculated graduate/professional students (17 women), 1,544 part-time matriculated graduate/professional students (781 women). *Enrollment by degree level:* 1,582 master's. *Graduate faculty:* 24 full-time (12 women), 54 part-time/adjunct (18 women). *Tuition:* Full-time $20,355; part-time $13,695 per year. *Graduate housing:* On-campus housing not available. *Student services:* Campus employment opportunities, career counseling, international student services, services for students with disabilities, writing training. *Library facilities:* Vollbrecht Library plus 1 other. *Collection:* Books: 23,586 (physical), 2,695 (digital/electronic); Serial titles: 515 (physical), 23,818 (digital/electronic); Databases: 72. Weekly public service hours: 113.

Computer facilities: 400 computers available on campus for general student use. A campuswide network can be accessed from off campus. Online class registration is available. Website: http://www.walshcollege.edu/

General Application Contact: Heather Rigby, Director of Admissions and Academic Advising, 248-823-1610, Fax: 248-689-0938, E-mail: hrigby@walshcollege.edu.

GRADUATE UNITS

Graduate Programs Students: 1,134 (597 women); includes 254 minority (143 Black or African American, non-Hispanic/Latino; 6 American Indian or Alaska Native, non-Hispanic/Latino; 58 Asian, non-Hispanic/Latino; 33 Hispanic/Latino; 14 Two or more races, non-Hispanic/Latino), 81 international. Average age 33. 387 applicants, 82% accepted, 248 enrolled. *Faculty:* 24 full-time (12 women), 54 part-time/adjunct (18 women). Expenses: Contact institution. *Financial support:* In 2016–17, 55 students received support. Career-related internships or fieldwork and scholarships/grants available. Financial award application deadline: 6/30; financial award applicants required to submit FAFSA. In 2016, 352 master's awarded. *Program availability:* Part-time, evening/weekend, 100% online, blended/hybrid learning. Offers business administration (MBA); chief information officer (MS); chief security officer (MS); cybersecurity (MSIT); finance (MAC); financial management (MSF); financial services (MSF); human resources management (MS); international business (MS); marketing (MS); program management office (MS); strategic management (MS); taxation (MST). *Application* *deadline:* Applications are processed on a rolling basis. *Application fee:* $35. Electronic applications accepted. *Application Contact:* Heather Rigby, Director of Admissions and Academic Advising, 248-823-1600, Fax: 248-689-0938, E-mail: hrigby@walshcollege.edu. *Interim Chief Academic Officer/Executive Vice President,* Dr. Mike Rinkus, 248-823-1269, Fax: 248-689-0920, E-mail: mrinkus@walshcollege.edu.

WALSH UNIVERSITY, North Canton, OH 44720-3396

General Information Independent-religious, coed, comprehensive institution. CGS member. *Enrollment:* 2,819 graduate, professional, and undergraduate students; 239 full-time matriculated graduate/professional students (151 women), 322 part-time matriculated graduate/professional students (233 women). *Enrollment by degree level:* 555 master's, 103 doctoral, 3 other advanced degrees. *Graduate faculty:* 26 full-time (14 women), 46 part-time/adjunct (21 women). *Tuition:* Full-time $11,970. Full-time tuition and fees vary according to program. *Graduate housing:* Room and/or apartments available on a first-come, first-served basis to single students; on-campus housing not available to married students. Typical cost: $5430 per year ($10,240 including board). Room and board charges vary according to board plan and housing facility selected. Housing application deadline: 7/15. *Student services:* Campus employment opportunities, campus safety program, career counseling, exercise/wellness program, free psychological counseling, international student services, low-cost health insurance, multicultural affairs office, services for students with disabilities, teacher training, writing training. *Library facilities:* Brother Edmond Drouin Library. *Collection:* Books: 97,575 (physical), 254,114 (digital/electronic); Serial titles: 995 (physical), 82,413 (digital/electronic); Databases: 167. Weekly public service hours: 79. *Research affiliation:* North Canton Public Schools (straight A grants (student development)), Research Foundation of the Carolinas (surgery), Akron General Health System (patient satisfaction), Mercy Medical Center (orthopedics, nursing, physical therapy), Akron Children's Hospital (orthopedics).

Computer facilities: 336 computers available on campus for general student use. A campuswide network can be accessed from student residence rooms and from off campus. Online class registration is available. Website: http://www.walsh.edu/

General Application Contact: Audra Dice, Director of Graduate Admissions, 330-490-7181, Fax: 330-490-7165, E-mail: adice@walsh.edu.

GRADUATE UNITS

Graduate Programs Students: 239 full-time (151 women), 322 part-time (233 women); includes 48 minority (29 Black or African American, non-Hispanic/Latino; 3 American Indian or Alaska Native, non-Hispanic/Latino; 4 Asian, non-Hispanic/Latino; 9 Hispanic/Latino; 3 Two or more races, non-Hispanic/Latino), 11 international. Average age 34. 393 applicants, 48% accepted, 141 enrolled. *Faculty:* 39 full-time (21 women), 53 part-time/adjunct (30 women). Expenses: Contact institution. *Financial support:* Research assistantships available. Financial award application deadline: 12/31. *Program availability:* Part-time, evening/weekend, online learning. Offers clinical mental health counseling (MA); healthcare management (MBA); leadership with principal license (MA Ed); management (MBA); marketing (MBA); parish administration (MA); pastoral ministry (MA); physical therapy (DPT); reading literacy (MA Ed); religious education (MA); school counseling (MA); student affairs in higher education (MA). *Application deadline:* Applications are processed on a rolling basis. *Application fee:* $25. Electronic applications accepted. *Application Contact:* Audra Dice, Director of Graduate Admissions, 330-490-7181, Fax: 330-244-4680, E-mail: adice@walsh.edu. *Associate Vice President for Academic Affairs,* Dr. Linda Barclay, 330-490-7264, Fax: 330-490-7371, E-mail: lbarclay@walsh.edu.

Gary and Linda Byers School of Nursing Students: 43 full-time (34 women), 56 part-time (50 women); includes 7 minority (3 Black or African American, non-Hispanic/Latino; 1 American Indian or Alaska Native, non-Hispanic/Latino; 1 Asian, non-Hispanic/Latino; 2 Hispanic/Latino). Average age 36. 32 applicants, 88% accepted, 23 enrolled. *Faculty:* 6 full-time (all women), 10 part-time/adjunct (8 women). Expenses: Contact institution. *Financial support:* In 2016–17, 1 student received support, including 1 research assistantship (averaging $3,870 per year). Financial award application deadline: 12/31; financial award applicants required to submit FAFSA. In 2016, 10 master's, 6 doctorates awarded. *Program availability:* Part-time, evening/weekend, online only, 100% online. Offers academic nurse educator (MSN); adult acute care nurse practitioner (MSN); clinical nurse leader (MSN); nursing practice (DNP). *Application deadline:* Applications are processed on a rolling basis. *Application fee:* $25. Electronic applications accepted. *Application Contact:* Audra Dice, Graduate and Transfer Admissions Counselor, 330-490-7181, Fax: 330-244-4680, E-mail: adice@walsh.edu. *Director of Graduate Nursing Programs,* Dr. Maria Pappas-Rogich, 330-490-7283, Fax: 330-490-7371, E-mail: mpappas@walsh.edu.

WARNER PACIFIC COLLEGE, Portland, OR 97215-4099

General Information Independent-religious, coed, comprehensive institution. *Graduate housing:* On-campus housing not available.

GRADUATE UNITS

Graduate Programs *Program availability:* Part-time, evening/weekend. Offers human services (MA); not-for-profit leadership (MS); organizational leadership (MS); teaching (MAT).

WARNER UNIVERSITY, Lake Wales, FL 33859

General Information Independent-religious, coed, comprehensive institution. *Graduate housing:* Room and/or apartments available on a first-come, first-served basis to single students; on-campus housing not available to married students. *Student services:* Career counseling, services for students with disabilities. *Library facilities:* Pontious Learning Resource Center.

Computer facilities: 75 computers available on campus for general student use. A campuswide network can be accessed. Website: http://www.warner.edu/

General Application Contact: Bob Mobley, Dean of Admissions, 800-309-9563, Fax: 863-638-7290, E-mail: bob.mobley@warner.edu.

GRADUATE UNITS

School of Business Expenses: Contact institution. *Financial support:* Scholarships/grants available. Financial award applicants required to submit FAFSA. *Program availability:* Part-time, evening/weekend, online learning. Offers accounting (MBA); business administration (MBA); human resource management (MBA); international business (MBA); management (MSMC). *Application deadline:* Applications are processed on a rolling basis. *Application fee:* $50. Electronic applications accepted. *Application Contact:* Judianne Steibly, Graduate Academic Advisor, 863-638-3702, Fax: 863-638-4907, E-mail: admissions@warner.edu. *Program Director,* Cindy Polston, 863-638-7689.

School of Education Expenses: Contact institution. *Financial support:* Scholarships/grants available. Financial award applicants required to submit FAFSA. *Program availability:* Part-time, evening/weekend, online learning. Offers curriculum and instruction (MAEd); elementary education (MAEd); science, technology, engineering, and mathematics (STEM) (MAEd). *Application deadline:* Applications are processed on a rolling basis. *Application fee:* $50. Electronic applications accepted. *Application Contact:* Torshanda Howard, Admissions Advisor, 863-638-7501, Fax: 863-638-4907, E-mail: admissons@warner.edu. *Dean,* Dr. Bill Rigel, 863-638-7207, Fax: 863-638-4907, E-mail: bill.rigel@warner.edu.

WARREN WILSON COLLEGE, Asheville, NC 28815-9000

General Information Independent-religious, coed, comprehensive institution. *Graduate housing:* Room and/or apartments guaranteed to single students; on-campus housing not available to married students.

GRADUATE UNITS

MFA Program for Writers *Program availability:* Online learning. Offers creative writing (MFA). Electronic applications accepted.

WARTBURG THEOLOGICAL SEMINARY, Dubuque, IA 52004-5004

General Information Independent-religious, coed, graduate-only institution. *Graduate housing:* Rooms and/or apartments available on a first-come, first-served basis to single and married students. Housing application deadline: 4/30. *Research affiliation:* Menighetsfakultet, Augustana Theologische Hochschule.

GRADUATE UNITS

Graduate and Professional Programs *Program availability:* Online learning. Offers diaconal ministry (MA); ministry (M Div); theology (MA). Electronic applications accepted.

WASHBURN UNIVERSITY, Topeka, KS 66621

General Information City-supported, coed, comprehensive institution. *Graduate housing:* Room and/or apartments available on a first-come, first-served basis to single students; on-campus housing not available to married students.

GRADUATE UNITS

College of Arts and Sciences *Program availability:* Part-time, evening/weekend. Offers arts and sciences (M Ed, MA, MLS); clinical psychology (MA); curriculum and instruction (M Ed); educational leadership (M Ed); liberal studies (MLS); reading (M Ed); special education (M Ed). Electronic applications accepted.

School of Applied Studies *Program availability:* Part-time, evening/weekend, online learning. Offers addiction counseling (MA); applied studies (MA, MCJ, MHS, MSW); clinical social work (MSW); criminal justice and legal studies (MCJ); health care education (MHS).

School of Business *Program availability:* Part-time, evening/weekend. Offers accountancy (M Acc). Electronic applications accepted.

School of Law Offers global legal studies (LL M); law (MSL, JD). Electronic applications accepted.

School of Nursing *Program availability:* Part-time. Offers clinical nurse leader (MSN); nursing (DNP); psychiatric mental health nurse practitioner (Post-Graduate Certificate).

WASHINGTON ADVENTIST UNIVERSITY, Takoma Park, MD 20912

General Information Independent-religious, coed, comprehensive institution. *Graduate housing:* Rooms and/or apartments available to single and married students.

GRADUATE UNITS

MBA Program *Program availability:* Part-time, evening/weekend, online learning. Offers business administration (MBA).

Program in Counseling Psychology *Program availability:* Part-time. Offers counseling psychology (MA).

Program in Health Care Administration *Program availability:* Part-time. Offers health care administration (MA).

Program in Nursing - Business Leadership *Program availability:* Part-time. Offers nursing - business leadership (MSN).

Program in Nursing - Education *Program availability:* Part-time. Offers nursing - education (MS).

Program in Professional Counseling Psychology *Program availability:* Part-time. Offers professional counseling psychology (MA).

Program in Public Administration *Program availability:* Part-time. Offers public administration (MPA).

Program in Religion *Program availability:* Part-time. Offers religion (MAR).

WASHINGTON & JEFFERSON COLLEGE, Washington, PA 15301

General Information Independent, coed, comprehensive institution.

GRADUATE UNITS

Graduate and Continuing Studies

WASHINGTON AND LEE UNIVERSITY, Lexington, VA 24450-0303

General Information Independent, coed, comprehensive institution. *Enrollment:* 2,160 graduate, professional, and undergraduate students; 329 full-time matriculated graduate/professional students (148 women). *Enrollment by degree level:* 329 doctoral. *Graduate faculty:* 34 full-time (13 women), 33 part-time/adjunct (5 women). *Student services:* Campus employment opportunities, campus safety program, career counseling, exercise/wellness program, free psychological counseling, international student services, low-cost health insurance, multicultural affairs office services for students with disabilities, writing training. *Library facilities:* James G. Leyburn Library plus 2 others. *Collection:* Books: 1 million (physical), 321,493 (digital/electronic); Serial titles: 66,967 (digital/electronic); Databases: 441. Study areas open 24 hours, 5–7 days a week; students can reserve study rooms. *Research affiliation:* Future of Privacy Forum (data privacy, data security, and related fields).

Computer facilities: 176 computers available on campus for general student use. A campuswide network can be accessed from student residence rooms and from off campus. Online class registration is available. Website: http://www.wlu.edu/

General Application Contact: Lisa Rodocker, Director of Admissions, 540-458-8503, Fax: 540-458-8586, E-mail: rodockerl@wlu.edu.

GRADUATE UNITS

School of Law Students: 329 full-time (148 women); includes 65 minority (16 Black or African American, non-Hispanic/Latino; 2 American Indian or Alaska Native, non-Hispanic/Latino; 9 Asian, non-Hispanic/Latino; 27 Hispanic/Latino; 11 Two or more races, non-Hispanic/Latino), 9 international. Average age 23. 1,911 applicants, 47%

accepted, 117 enrolled. *Faculty:* 34 full-time (13 women), 33 part-time/adjunct (5 women). Expenses: Contact institution. *Financial support:* In 2016–17, 310 students received support. Fellowships, research assistantships, career-related internships or fieldwork, Federal Work-Study, institutionally sponsored loans, and scholarships/grants available. Financial award application deadline: 2/15; financial award applicants required to submit FAFSA. Offers law (JD). *Application deadline:* For fall admission, 3/1 priority date for domestic and international students. Applications are processed on a rolling basis. *Application fee:* $0. Electronic applications accepted. *Application Contact:* Lisa Rodocker, Director of Admissions, 540-458-8503, Fax: 540-458-8586, E-mail: rodockerl@wlu.edu. *Dean,* Brant Hellwig, 540-458-8502, Fax: 540-458-8488, E-mail: hellwigb@wlu.edu.

WASHINGTON STATE UNIVERSITY, Pullman, WA 99164

General Information State-supported, coed, university. CGS member. *Graduate housing:* Rooms and/or apartments available on a first-come, first-served basis to single and married students. Housing application deadline: 3/1. *Research affiliation:* Battelle–Pacific Northwest National Laboratory (biochemistry, engineering).

GRADUATE UNITS

Carson College of Business *Program availability:* Online learning. Offers accounting (M Acc); business (M Acc, MBA, PhD). Programs also offered at the Tri-Cities, Vancouver, and Global (online) campuses.

College of Agricultural, Human, and Natural Resource Sciences *Program availability:* Part-time, online learning. Offers agricultural, human, and natural resource sciences (MA, MS, PhD, Graduate Certificate); animal sciences (MS, PhD); apparel, merchandising, design, and textiles (MA); biological and agricultural engineering (MS, PhD); crop sciences (MS, PhD); entomology (MS, PhD); horticulture (MS, PhD); interior design and landscape architecture (MA, MS); plant pathology (MS, PhD); prevention science (PhD); soil sciences (MS, PhD). Programs also offered at the Global (online) campuses. Electronic applications accepted.

School of Economic Sciences Offers agricultural economics (PhD); economics (PhD). Programs offered at the Pullman campus. Electronic applications accepted.

School of Food Science *Program availability:* Part-time. Offers food science (MS, PhD). Programs offered at the Pullman campus. Electronic applications accepted.

School of the Environment Offers environmental and natural resource sciences (PhD); natural resource sciences (MS). Program applications must be made through the Pullman campus.

College of Arts and Sciences Offers American studies (MA, PhD); applied mathematics (MS, PhD); archaeology (MA, PhD); arts and sciences (MA, MFA, MPA, MS, PhD, Graduate Certificate); chemistry (MS, PhD); clinical psychology (PhD); criminal justice and criminology (MA, PhD); cultural anthropology (PhD); English (MA, PhD); evolutionary anthropology (MA, PhD); experimental psychology (PhD); fine arts (MFA); foreign languages and cultures (MA); history (MA, PhD); mathematics (MS, PhD); mathematics teaching (MS, PhD); physics and astronomy (MS, PhD); sociology (MA, PhD). Electronic applications accepted.

School of Biological Sciences Offers biological sciences (MS, PhD). Programs are offered at the Pullman campus.

School of Music *Program availability:* Part-time. Offers music (MA). Electronic applications accepted.

School of Politics, Philosophy and Public Affairs *Program availability:* Online learning. Offers bioethics (Graduate Certificate); political science (MA, PhD); public affairs (MPA). MPA, MA, and PhD programs also offered at the Vancouver campus; Graduate Certificate offered through Global (online) campus. Electronic applications accepted.

School of the Environment Offers environmental and natural resource sciences (PhD); environmental science (MS); geology (MS, PhD); natural resource science (MS).

College of Education Offers counseling psychology (PhD); cultural studies and social thought in education (PhD); curriculum and instruction (Ed M, MA); education (Ed M, MA, MIT, Ed D, PhD); educational leadership (Ed M, MA, Ed D, PhD); educational psychology (MA, PhD); English language learners (Ed M, MA); language, literacy and technology (PhD); literacy education (Ed M, MA); mathematics education (PhD); special education (Ed M, MA, PhD); sport management (MA); teacher leadership (Ed D); teaching (MIT). Electronic applications accepted.

College of Medicine Offers medicine (MS); speech and hearing sciences (MS).

College of Nursing Offers advanced population health (MN, DNP); family nurse practitioner (MN, DNP); nursing (PhD); psychiatric/mental health nurse practitioner (DNP); psychiatric/mental health practitioner (MN). Programs offered at the Spokane, Tri-Cities, and Vancouver campuses.

College of Pharmacy Offers health policy and administration (MHPA); nutrition and exercise physiology (MS); pharmacy (Pharm D). Programs offered at the Spokane campus.

College of Veterinary Medicine Students: 519 full-time (394 women); includes 76 minority (1 Black or African American, non-Hispanic/Latino; 2 American Indian or Alaska Native, non-Hispanic/Latino; 18 Asian, non-Hispanic/Latino; 26 Hispanic/Latino; 29 Two or more races, non-Hispanic/Latino). Average age 26. 1,288 applicants, 16% accepted, 132 enrolled. *Faculty:* 32 full-time (6 women), 45 part-time/adjunct (12 women). Expenses: Contact institution. *Financial support:* In 2016–17, 446 students received support, including 28 fellowships with full tuition reimbursements available, 87 research assistantships with full tuition reimbursements available (averaging $23,000 per year), 34 teaching assistantships with full tuition reimbursements available (averaging $22,000 per year); career-related internships or fieldwork, Federal Work-Study, institutionally sponsored loans, scholarships/grants, traineeships, health care benefits, and unspecified assistantships also available. Support available to part-time students. Financial award application deadline: 1/31; financial award applicants required to submit FAFSA. In 2016, 18 master's, 99 doctorates awarded. Offers immunology and infectious diseases (MS, PhD); molecular biosciences (MS, PhD); neuroscience (MS, PhD); veterinary medicine (MS, DVM, PhD); veterinary science (MS, PhD). *Application deadline:* For fall admission, 9/15 for domestic and international students; for spring admission, 8/1 for international students. *Application fee:* $60. Electronic applications accepted. *Application Contact:* Andrew Wade, Program Coordinator, 509-335-6133, E-mail: awade@vetmed.wsu.edu. *Dean,* Dr. Bryan Slinker, 509-335-9515, Fax: 509-335-0160, E-mail: vetmed-dean@vetmed.wsu.edu.

Paul G. Allen School for Global Animal Health Students: 20 full-time (9 women); includes 2 minority (1 Black or African American, non-Hispanic/Latino; 1 Native Hawaiian or other Pacific Islander, non-Hispanic/Latino). Average age 29. 2 applicants, 100% accepted, 2 enrolled. *Faculty:* 14 full-time (4 women), 13 part-time/adjunct (6 women). Expenses: Contact institution. *Financial support:* In 2016–17, 27 students received support, including 13 fellowships with full tuition reimbursements available, 23 research assistantships, 2 teaching assistantships; institutionally sponsored loans, scholarships/grants, traineeships, health care benefits, and unspecified assistantships also available. Financial award application deadline: 3/1. In 2016, 1 master's, 9 doctorates awarded. Offers immunology and infectious diseases (MS, PhD). *Application deadline:* For fall admission, 1/10 priority date for domestic and international students; for spring admission, 7/1 priority date for domestic and international students. *Application fee:* $75. Electronic applications accepted. *Application Contact:* Rebecca Manning, Administrative Manager, 509-335-5861, Fax: 509-335-6328, E-mail: manningr@wsu.edu. *Director, Paul G. Allen School for Global Animal Health,* Dr. Thomas Kawula, 509-335-5861, Fax: 509-335-6328, E-mail: tom.kawula@vetmed.wsu.edu.

The Edward R. Murrow College of Communication Offers communication (MA, PhD); strategic communication (MA). MA in strategic communication offered at the Global (online) campus. Electronic applications accepted.

Voiland College of Engineering and Architecture Offers architecture (M Arch); civil engineering (MS, PhD); engineering and architecture (M Arch, METM, MS, PhD, Certificate); engineering and computer science (MS); engineering and technology management (METM, Certificate); environmental engineering (MS).

The Gene and Linda Voiland School of Chemical Engineering and Bioengineering Offers chemical engineering and bioengineering (MS, PhD).

School of Electrical Engineering and Computer Science *Program availability:* Part-time. Offers computer engineering (MS); computer science (MS); electrical engineering (MS); electrical engineering and computer science (PhD); electrical power engineering (MS). MS programs in computer engineering, computer science and electrical engineering also offered at Tri-Cities campus; MS in electrical power engineering offered at the Global (online) campus.

School of Mechanical and Materials Engineering *Program availability:* Part-time. Offers materials science and engineering (MS, PhD); mechanical engineering (MS, PhD). MS programs also offered at Tri-Cities campus. Electronic applications accepted.

WASHINGTON UNIVERSITY IN ST. LOUIS, St. Louis, MO 63130-4899

General Information Independent, coed, university. CGS member. *Graduate housing:* Rooms and/or apartments available on a first-come, first-served basis to single and married students.

GRADUATE UNITS

Brown School Students: 281 full-time (235 women); includes 105 minority (37 Black or African American, non-Hispanic/Latino; 14 American Indian or Alaska Native, non-Hispanic/Latino; 20 Asian, non-Hispanic/Latino; 15 Hispanic/Latino; 1 Native Hawaiian or other Pacific Islander, non-Hispanic/Latino; 18 Two or more races, non-Hispanic/Latino), 47 international. Average age 25. 1,003 applicants, 281 enrolled. *Faculty:* 54 full-time (31 women), 87 part-time/adjunct (61 women). Expenses: Contact institution. *Financial support:* In 2016–17, 267 students received support, including 35 fellowships, 48 research assistantships; Federal Work-Study, scholarships/grants, and unspecified assistantships also available. Support available to part-time students. Financial award applicants required to submit FAFSA. In 2016, 239 master's, 5 doctorates awarded. Offers American Indian/Alaska native (MSW); children, youth and families (MSW); epidemiology/biostatistics (MPH); health (MSW); health policy analysis (MPH); individualized (MSW); mental health (MSW); older adults and aging societies (MSW); public health sciences (MSW); social and economic development (MSW); social work (PhD); violence and injury prevention (MSW). MSW/M Div and MSW/MAPS offered in partnership with Eden Theological Seminary. *Application deadline:* For fall admission, 12/15 priority date for domestic and international students; for winter admission, 3/1 priority date for domestic and international students. Applications are processed on a rolling basis. Electronic applications accepted. *Application Contact:* Office of Admissions and Recruitment, 314-935-6676, Fax: 314-935-4859, E-mail: brownadmissions@wustl.edu. *Director of Admissions and Recruitment,* Jamie L. Adkisson, 314-935-3524, Fax: 314-935-4859, E-mail: jadkisson@wustl.edu.

The Graduate School Students: 1,881 full-time (842 women), 732 international. 3,749 applicants, 21% accepted, 319 enrolled. Expenses: Contact institution. *Financial support:* Fellowships, research assistantships, teaching assistantships, career-related internships or fieldwork, scholarships/grants, traineeships, health care benefits, tuition waivers (full and partial), and unspecified assistantships available. In 2016, 283 master's, 172 doctorates awarded. Offers aging and development (PhD); anthropology (PhD); art history and archaeology (AM, PhD); chemistry (PhD); Chinese (MA); Chinese and comparative literature (PhD); Chinese language and literature (PhD); classics (MA, PhD); comparative literature (PhD); dance (MFA); earth and planetary sciences (PhD); East Asian studies (MA); economics (PhD); educational research (PhD); elementary education (MA Ed); English and American literature (PhD); French (PhD); French and comparative literature (PhD); French language and literature (PhD); Germanic languages and literatures (PhD); Hispanic languages and literatures (PhD); history (PhD); Islamic and Near Eastern studies (MA); Japanese (MA); Japanese and comparative literature (PhD); Japanese language and literature (PhD); Jewish studies (MA); mathematics (MA, PhD); music (MA, PhD); philosophy (PhD); philosophy-neuroscience-psychology (PhD); physics (PhD); political science (PhD); secondary education (MAT); Spanish (PhD); Spanish and comparative literature (PhD); statistics (MA, PhD); theater and performance studies (MA); writing (MFA). *Application deadline:* For fall admission, 1/15 for domestic students. Applications are processed on a rolling basis. *Application fee:* $45. Electronic applications accepted. *Application Contact:* Bridget Coleman, Director of Admissions, 314-935-8753, Fax: 314-935-4887. *Dean/Vice Chancellor for Graduate Education,* Dr. William Tate, 314-935-7355, Fax: 314-935-4887.

Division of Biology and Biomedical Sciences Offers biochemistry (PhD); computational and molecular biophysics (PhD); computational and systems biology (PhD); developmental, regenerative, and stem cell biology (PhD); ecology (PhD); evolution, ecology and population biology (PhD); human and statistical genetics (PhD); immunology (PhD); molecular cell biology (PhD); molecular genetics and genomics (PhD); molecular microbiology and microbial pathogenesis (PhD); neurosciences (PhD); plant and microbial biosciences (PhD). Electronic applications accepted.

Olin Business School Students: 638 full-time (248 women), 621 part-time (209 women); includes 270 minority (57 Black or African American, non-Hispanic/Latino; 2 American Indian or Alaska Native, non-Hispanic/Latino; 153 Asian, non-Hispanic/Latino; 20 Hispanic/Latino; 1 Native Hawaiian or other Pacific Islander, non-Hispanic/Latino; 37 Two or more races, non-Hispanic/Latino), 418 international. *Faculty:* 97 full-time (22 women), 44 part-time/adjunct (13 women). Expenses: Contact institution. Offers accounting (MS); business (EMBA, M Acc, MBA, MS, DBA, PhD); business administration (EMBA, MBA, PhD); corporate finance and investments (MS); customer analytics (MS); finance (MS, DBA); leadership (MS); quantitative finance (MS); supply chain management (MS). Electronic applications accepted. *Application Contact:*

Information Contact, 314-935-6880, Fax: 314-935-4887, E-mail: graduateschool@artsci.wustl.edu. *Dean*, Dr. Mahendra Gupta, 314-935-6344.

Sam Fox School of Design and Visual Arts Offers architecture (M Arch, MLA); design and visual arts (M Arch, MFA, MLA, MUD); urban design (MUD).

Graduate School of Art Students: 44 full-time (25 women); includes 6 minority (1 Black or African American, non-Hispanic/Latino; 1 American Indian or Alaska Native, non-Hispanic/Latino; 2 Asian, non-Hispanic/Latino; 1 Hispanic/Latino; 1 Two or more races, non-Hispanic/Latino), 9 international. Average age 28. 47 applicants, 91% accepted, 20 enrolled. *Faculty*: 16 full-time (7 women), 5 part-time/adjunct (3 women). Expenses: Contact institution. *Financial support*: In 2016–17, 44 students received support. Fellowships with partial tuition reimbursements available, Federal Work-Study, institutionally sponsored loans, scholarships/grants, and unspecified assistantships available. Financial award application deadline: 2/15; financial award applicants required to submit FAFSA. In 2016, 22 master's awarded. Offers visual art (MFA). *Application deadline*: For fall admission, 1/15 for domestic and international students. *Application fee*: $40. Electronic applications accepted. *Application Contact*: Prof. Patricia Olynyk, Director of the Graduate School of Art, 314-935-5884, Fax: 314-935-8413, E-mail: olynyk@wustl.edu. *Director of the College and Graduate School of Art*, Prof. Heather Corcoran, 314-935-6500, Fax: 314-935-4862, E-mail: hcorcoran@wustl.edu.

School of Engineering and Applied Science *Program availability*: Part-time, evening/weekend. Offers aerospace engineering (MS, PhD); biomedical engineering (MS, D Sc, PhD); chemical engineering (MS, D Sc); computer engineering (MS, PhD); computer science (MS, PhD); computer science and engineering (M Eng); engineering and applied science (M Eng, MCE, MCM, MEM, MIM, MPM, MS, MSEE, MSEE, MSI, D Sc, PhD); environmental engineering (MS, D Sc); materials science (MS); mechanical engineering (M Eng, MS, PhD). Electronic applications accepted.

School of Law Offers law (LL M, MJS, JD, JSD). Electronic applications accepted.

School of Medicine Offers applied health behavior research (MS); audiology (Au D); clinical epidemiology (MPHS); clinical investigation (MS); deaf education (MS); health behavior planning and evaluation (Graduate Certificate); health services (MPHS); medicine (MPHS, MS, MSOT, Au D, DPT, MD, OTD, PPDPT, PhD, Certificate, Graduate Certificate); movement science (PhD); occupational therapy (MSOT, OTD); physical therapy (DPT); psychiatric and behavioral health sciences (MPHS); quantitative methods (MPHS); rehabilitation and participation science (PhD); speech and hearing sciences (PhD).

Division of Biostatistics *Program availability*: Part-time. Offers biostatistics (MS); genetic epidemiology (Certificate). Electronic applications accepted.

See Close-Up on page 907.

WAYLAND BAPTIST UNIVERSITY, Plainview, TX 79072-6998

General Information Independent-religious, coed, comprehensive institution. *Graduate housing*: Rooms and/or apartments available on a first-come, first-served basis to single and married students.

GRADUATE UNITS

Graduate Programs *Program availability*: Part-time, evening/weekend, online learning. Offers accounting (MBA); Christian ministry (MCM); counseling (MA); criminal justice (MACJ); divinity (M Div); education administration (M Ed); education diagnostics (M Ed); education literacy (M Ed); elementary certification (M Ed); English (M Ed); English as a second language (M Ed); general business (MBA); government administration (MPA); health care administration (MAM, MBA); higher education administration (M Ed); history (MA); homeland security (MPA); human resource management (MAM, MBA); human resources (M Ed); humanities (MAH); instructional leadership (M Ed); instructional technology (M Ed); international management (MBA); justice administration (MPA); leadership training and development (M Ed); management (MBA, D Mgt); management information systems (MBA); multidisciplinary science (MS); organization management (MAM); project management (MBA); religion (MA); science education (M Ed); secondary certification (M Ed); social studies (M Ed); special education (M Ed); sports administration and management (M Ed). Electronic applications accepted.

WAYNESBURG UNIVERSITY, Waynesburg, PA 15370-1222

General Information Independent-religious, coed, comprehensive institution. *Graduate housing*: Room and/or apartments available on a first-come, first-served basis to single students; on-campus housing not available to married students. Housing application deadline: 8/1.

GRADUATE UNITS

Graduate and Professional Studies *Program availability*: Part-time, evening/weekend. Offers business (MBA); counseling (MA); counselor education and supervision (PhD); criminal investigation (MA); education (M Ed); nursing (MSN); nursing practice (DNP); special education (M Ed); technology (M Ed). Electronic applications accepted.

WAYNE STATE COLLEGE, Wayne, NE 68787

General Information State-supported, coed, comprehensive institution. CGS member. *Graduate housing*: Room and/or apartments available on a first-come, first-served basis to single students; on-campus housing not available to married students. *Research affiliation*: Nebraska Business Development Center, Social Sciences Research Center.

GRADUATE UNITS

Department of Health, Human Performance and Sport *Program availability*: Part-time, evening/weekend. Offers exercise science (MSE); organizational management (MS). Electronic applications accepted.

School of Business and Technology *Program availability*: Part-time, evening/weekend, online learning. Offers business and technology (MBA).

School of Education and Counseling *Program availability*: Part-time, evening/weekend. Offers alternative education (MSE); business and information technology education (MSE); communication arts education (MSE); counseling (MSE); counselor education (MSE); curriculum and instruction (MSE); early childhood education (MSE); education and counseling (MSE, Ed S); educational administration (MSE, Ed S); elementary administration (MSE); elementary and secondary administration (MSE); elementary education (MSE); English as a second language (MSE); English education (MSE); family and consumer sciences education (MSE); guidance and counseling (MSE); industrial technology and vocational education (MSE); learning communities (MSE); mathematics education (MSE); music education (MSE); school counseling (MSE); science education (MSE); secondary administration (MSE); social science education (MSE); special education (MSE).

WAYNE STATE UNIVERSITY, Detroit, MI 48202

General Information State-supported, coed, university. CGS member. *Enrollment*: 27,298 graduate, professional, and undergraduate students; 6,213 full-time matriculated graduate/professional students (3,154 women), 3,698 part-time matriculated graduate/professional students (2,160 women). *Enrollment by degree level*: 5,915 master's, 3,704 doctoral, 292 other advanced degrees. *Graduate faculty*: 873. Tuition, state resident: full-time $14,746; part-time $614.40 per credit hour. Tuition, nonresident: full-time $31,939; part-time $1330.81 per credit hour. *Required fees*: $1186; $49.40 per credit hour. $285.86 per semester. Tuition and fees vary according to course load and program. *Graduate housing*: Rooms and/or apartments available on a first-come, first-served basis to single and married students. Typical cost: $6077 per year ($9747 including board) for single students. Room and board charges vary according to board plan and housing facility selected. *Student services*: Campus employment opportunities, campus safety program, career counseling, child daycare facilities, exercise/wellness program, free psychological counseling, grant writing training, international student services, multicultural affairs office, services for students with disabilities, teacher training, writing training. *Library facilities*: David Adamany Undergraduate Library plus 5 others. *Collection*: Books: 2 million (physical), 1 million (digital/electronic); Serial titles: 63,572 (physical), 105,564 (digital/electronic); Databases: 750. Weekly public service hours: 138; study areas open 24 hours, 5–7 days a week. *Research affiliation*: Detroit Medical Center, Henry Ford Health System, John A. Dingell VA Medical Center, Karmanos Cancer Institute, Health Resources and Services Administration, Karmanos Cancer Institute.

Computer facilities: A campuswide network can be accessed from student residence rooms. Online class registration is available.
Website: http://www.wayne.edu/

General Application Contact: Deirdre S. Baker, Office of Graduate Admissions, 313-577-4723, Fax: 313-577-0131, E-mail: gradadmissions@wayne.edu.

GRADUATE UNITS

College of Education Students: 457 full-time (340 women), 942 part-time (688 women); includes 505 minority (384 Black or African American, non-Hispanic/Latino; 5 American Indian or Alaska Native, non-Hispanic/Latino; 25 Asian, non-Hispanic/Latino; 48 Hispanic/Latino; 1 Native Hawaiian or other Pacific Islander, non-Hispanic/Latino; 42 Two or more races, non-Hispanic/Latino), 60 international. Average age 35. 831 applicants, 42% accepted, 254 enrolled. *Faculty*: 62. Expenses: Contact institution. *Financial support*: In 2016–17, 342 students received support, including 4 fellowships with tuition reimbursements available (averaging $11,307 per year), 12 research assistantships with tuition reimbursements available (averaging $17,994 per year), 5 teaching assistantships with tuition reimbursements available (averaging $17,994 per year); Federal Work-Study, scholarships/grants, traineeships, health care benefits, and unspecified assistantships also available. Support available to part-time students. Financial award applicants required to submit FAFSA. In 2016, 384 master's, 40 doctorates, 65 other advanced degrees awarded. *Program availability*: Part-time, evening/weekend, 100% online, blended/hybrid learning. Offers education (M Ed, MA, MAT, Ed D, PhD, Certificate, Ed S); health education (M Ed); kinesiology (M Ed, PhD); sports administration (MA). *Application deadline*: For fall admission, 6/1 priority date for domestic students, 5/1 for international students; for winter admission, 10/1 priority date for domestic students, 9/1 priority date for international students; for spring admission, 2/1 priority date for domestic students, 1/1 priority date for international students. *Application fee*: $0. Electronic applications accepted. *Application Contact*: Janice Green, Assistant Dean, 313-577-1620, E-mail: jwgreen@wayne.edu. *Dean*, Dr. R. Douglas Whitman, 313-577-1620, E-mail: dwhitman@wayne.edu.

Division of Administrative and Organizational Studies Students: 83 full-time (58 women), 223 part-time (148 women); includes 151 minority (126 Black or African American, non-Hispanic/Latino; 3 American Indian or Alaska Native, non-Hispanic/Latino; 4 Asian, non-Hispanic/Latino; 8 Hispanic/Latino; 10 Two or more races, non-Hispanic/Latino), 14 international. Average age 39. 143 applicants, 43% accepted, 38 enrolled. *Faculty*: 11. Expenses: Contact institution. *Financial support*: In 2016–17, 96 students received support, including 1 fellowship with tuition reimbursement available (averaging $11,000 per year), 4 research assistantships with tuition reimbursements available (averaging $17,949 per year); scholarships/grants and unspecified assistantships also available. Support available to part-time students. Financial award applicants required to submit FAFSA. In 2016, 53 master's, 9 doctorates, 34 other advanced degrees awarded. *Program availability*: Part-time, 100% online, blended/hybrid learning. Offers college and university teaching (Certificate); educational administration and supervision (Ed S); educational leadership (M Ed); educational leadership and policy studies (Ed D, PhD); educational technology (Certificate); learning design and technology (M Ed, Ed D, PhD, Ed S); online teaching (Certificate). *Application deadline*: For fall admission, 6/1 priority date for domestic students, 5/1 priority date for international students; for winter admission, 10/1 priority date for domestic students, 9/1 priority date for international students; for spring admission, 2/1 priority date for domestic students, 1/1 priority date for international students. Applications are processed on a rolling basis. *Application fee*: $50. Electronic applications accepted. *Application Contact*: Janice Green, Assistant Dean, 313-577-1605, E-mail: jwgreen@wayne.edu. *Assistant Dean*, Dr. William Hill, 313-577-9316, E-mail: ad2107@wayne.edu.

Division of Teacher Education Students: 106 full-time (73 women), 351 part-time (276 women); includes 115 minority (76 Black or African American, non-Hispanic/Latino; 10 Asian, non-Hispanic/Latino; 20 Hispanic/Latino; 1 Native Hawaiian or other Pacific Islander, non-Hispanic/Latino; 8 Two or more races, non-Hispanic/Latino), 12 international. Average age 37. 242 applicants, 37% accepted, 74 enrolled. *Faculty*: 29. Expenses: Contact institution. *Financial support*: In 2016–17, 101 students received support, including 3 fellowships (averaging $11,409 per year); research assistantships with tuition reimbursements available, Federal Work-Study, scholarships/grants, and unspecified assistantships also available. Support available to part-time students. Financial award applicants required to submit FAFSA. In 2016, 178 master's, 19 doctorates, 17 other advanced degrees awarded. *Program availability*: Part-time, blended/hybrid learning. Offers art education (M Ed); bilingual/bicultural education (M Ed, Certificate); career and technical education (M Ed); curriculum and instruction (Ed D, PhD, Ed S); early childhood education (M Ed); elementary education (M Ed, MAT); English as a second language (Certificate); English education (M Ed); foreign language education (M Ed); mathematics education (M Ed); reading (M Ed, Ed S); reading, language and literature (Ed D); science education (M Ed); secondary education (MAT); social studies education (M Ed); special education (M Ed, MAT, Ed D, PhD, Ed S). *Application deadline*: For fall admission, 6/1 priority date for domestic students, 5/1 priority date for international students; for winter admission, 10/1 priority date for domestic students, 9/1 priority date for international students; for spring admission, 2/1 priority date for domestic students, 1/1 priority date for international students. Applications are processed on a rolling basis. *Application fee*: $50. Electronic applications accepted. *Application Contact*: Janice Green, Assistant Dean, 313-577-1605, E-mail: jwgreen@wayne.edu. *Assistant Dean*, Dr. Kathleen Crawford-McKinney, 313-577-0122.

Division of Theoretical and Behavioral Foundations Students: 211 full-time (179 women), 237 part-time (196 women); includes 167 minority (119 Black or African American, non-Hispanic/Latino; 1 American Indian or Alaska Native, non-Hispanic/Latino; 10 Asian, non-Hispanic/Latino; 17 Hispanic/Latino; 20 Two or more races, non-Hispanic/Latino), 24 international. Average age 32. 294 applicants, 34% accepted, 72 enrolled. *Faculty:* 12. Expenses: Contact institution. *Financial support:* In 2016–17, 92 students received support, including 2 research assistantships with tuition reimbursements available (averaging $17,994 per year); fellowships with tuition reimbursements available, teaching assistantships with tuition reimbursements available, Federal Work-Study, scholarships/grants, health care benefits, and unspecified assistantships also available. Support available to part-time students. Financial award applicants required to submit FAFSA. In 2016, 87 master's, 12 doctorates, 14 other advanced degrees awarded. *Program availability:* Evening/weekend. Offers applied behavior analysis (Certificate); counseling (M Ed, MA, Ed D, PhD, Ed S); counseling psychology (MA); education evaluation and research (M Ed, Ed D, PhD); educational psychology (M Ed, PhD); rehabilitation counseling and community inclusion (MA); school and community psychology (MA); school psychology (Certificate). *Application deadline:* For fall admission, 6/1 priority date for domestic students, 5/1 priority date for international students; for winter admission, 10/1 priority date for domestic students, 9/1 priority date for international students; for spring admission, 2/1 priority date for domestic students, 1/1 priority date for international students. Applications are processed on a rolling basis. *Application fee:* $50. Electronic applications accepted. *Application Contact:* Janice Green, Assistant Dean, 313-577-1605, E-mail: jwgreen@wayne.edu. *Assistant Dean,* Dr. Cheryl Somers, 313-577-1670, E-mail: c.somers@wayne.edu.

College of Engineering Students: 1,204 full-time (222 women), 382 part-time (78 women); includes 113 minority (35 Black or African American, non-Hispanic/Latino; 58 Asian, non-Hispanic/Latino; 9 Hispanic/Latino; 1 Native Hawaiian or other Pacific Islander, non-Hispanic/Latino; 10 Two or more races, non-Hispanic/Latino), 1,179 international. Average age 27. 4,150 applicants, 44% accepted, 466 enrolled. *Faculty:* 105. Expenses: Contact institution. *Financial support:* In 2016–17, 381 students received support, including 23 fellowships with tuition reimbursements available (averaging $15,878 per year), 69 research assistantships with tuition reimbursements available (averaging $19,550 per year), 114 teaching assistantships with tuition reimbursements available (averaging $19,176 per year); Federal Work-Study, scholarships/grants, tuition waivers (full and partial), and unspecified assistantships also available. Support available to part-time students. Financial award applicants required to submit FAFSA. In 2016, 448 master's, 42 doctorates, 1 other advanced degree awarded. *Program availability:* Part-time, evening/weekend. Offers alternative energy technology (MS, Graduate Certificate); biomedical engineering (MS, PhD); chemical engineering (MS, PhD); civil engineering (MS); computer engineering (MS, PhD); computer science (MS, PhD); data science and business analytics (MS); electric-drive vehicle engineering (MS, Graduate Certificate); electrical engineering (MS, PhD); engineering (MS, MSET, PhD, Certificate, Graduate Certificate, Postbaccalaureate Certificate); engineering management (MS); industrial engineering (MS, PhD); injury biomechanics (Graduate Certificate); manufacturing engineering (MS); materials science and engineering (MS, PhD, Graduate Certificate); mechanical engineering (MS, PhD); systems engineering (Certificate). *Application deadline:* For fall admission, 6/1 priority date for domestic students, 5/1 priority date for international students; for winter admission, 10/1 priority date for domestic students, 9/1 priority date for international students; for spring admission, 2/1 priority date for domestic students, 1/1 priority date for international students. Applications are processed on a rolling basis. *Application fee:* $50. Electronic applications accepted. *Application Contact:* Graduate Program Coordinator, E-mail: engineeringgradadmissions@eng.wayne.edu. *Dean,* Dr. Farshad Fotouhi, 313-577-3776, E-mail: fotouhi@wayne.edu.

Division of Engineering Technology Students: 5 full-time (0 women), 6 part-time (0 women); includes 2 minority (1 Asian, non-Hispanic/Latino; 1 Hispanic/Latino), 2 international. Average age 42. 22 applicants, 73% accepted, 1 enrolled. *Faculty:* 1. Expenses: Contact institution. *Financial support:* Career-related internships or fieldwork and scholarships/grants available. Financial award applicants required to submit FAFSA. In 2016, 8 master's awarded. Offers engineering technology (MSET). *Application deadline:* For fall admission, 6/1 priority date for domestic students, 5/1 priority date for international students; for winter admission, 10/1 priority date for domestic students, 9/1 priority date for international students; for spring admission, 2/1 priority date for domestic students, 1/1 priority date for international students. Applications are processed on a rolling basis. *Application fee:* $50. Electronic applications accepted. *Application Contact:* Ellen Cope, Graduate Program Coordinator, 313-577-0409, E-mail: escope@wayne.edu. *Division Chair,* Dr. Ece Yaprak, 313-577-0875, E-mail: yaprak@eng.wayne.edu.

College of Fine, Performing and Communication Arts Students: 120 full-time (65 women), 143 part-time (96 women); includes 95 minority (67 Black or African American, non-Hispanic/Latino; 3 Asian, non-Hispanic/Latino; 13 Hispanic/Latino; 12 Two or more races, non-Hispanic/Latino), 16 international. Average age 33. 292 applicants, 34% accepted, 72 enrolled. *Faculty:* 39. Expenses: Contact institution. *Financial support:* In 2016–17, 134 students received support, including 5 fellowships (averaging $16,000 per year), 34 research assistantships with tuition reimbursements available (averaging $18,087 per year), 27 teaching assistantships with tuition reimbursements available (averaging $17,994 per year); career-related internships or fieldwork, scholarships/grants, health care benefits, and unspecified assistantships also available. Financial award applicants required to submit FAFSA. In 2016, 52 master's, 10 doctorates, 4 other advanced degrees awarded. *Program availability:* Online learning. Offers art (MA, MFA); art history (MA); communication (PhD); communication and new media (Graduate Certificate); communication studies (MA); composition/theory (MM); conducting (MM); dispute resolution (MADR, Graduate Certificate); fine, performing and communication arts (MA, MADR, MFA, MM, PhD, Graduate Certificate); health communication (Graduate Certificate); jazz performance (MM); journalism (MA); media arts (MA); media studies (MA); music (MA); music education (MM); orchestral studies (Certificate); performance (MM); public relations and organizational communication (MA); theatre (MA); theatre and dance (MA). *Application deadline:* For fall admission, 6/1 priority date for domestic students, 5/1 priority date for international students; for winter admission, 10/1 priority date for domestic students, 9/1 priority date for international students; for spring admission, 2/1 priority date for domestic students, 1/1 priority date for international students. Applications are processed on a rolling basis. *Application fee:* $50. Electronic applications accepted. *Application Contact:* Deirdre S. Baker, Director, Office of Graduate Admissions, 313-577-8141, E-mail: gradadmissions@wayne.edu. *Dean,* Dr. Matthew Seeger, 313-577-5342, Fax: 313-577-5342, E-mail: matthew.seeger@wayne.edu.

College of Liberal Arts and Sciences Students: 903 full-time (507 women), 379 part-time (209 women); includes 232 minority (120 Black or African American, non-Hispanic/Latino; 1 American Indian or Alaska Native, non-Hispanic/Latino; 27 Asian,

non-Hispanic/Latino; 47 Hispanic/Latino; 37 Two or more races, non-Hispanic/Latino), 301 international. Average age 31. 2,305 applicants, 26% accepted, 321 enrolled. *Faculty:* 310. Expenses: Contact institution. *Financial support:* In 2016–17, 710 students received support, including 61 fellowships with tuition reimbursements available (averaging $17,221 per year), 83 research assistantships with tuition reimbursements available (averaging $20,468 per year), 332 teaching assistantships with tuition reimbursements available (averaging $19,137 per year); scholarships/grants, health care benefits, and unspecified assistantships also available. Support available to part-time students. Financial award applicants required to submit FAFSA. In 2016, 227 master's, 98 doctorates, 3 other advanced degrees awarded. *Program availability:* Part-time, evening/weekend, online learning. Offers advanced macroeconomics (PhD); Africa (PhD); America (PhD); analytical chemistry (PhD); anthropology (MA, PhD); applied mathematics (MA, PhD); applied sociological research methodology (MA); Asia (PhD); audiology (Au D); behavioral and cognitive neuroscience (PhD); biochemistry (PhD); biological sciences (MA, MS); cell development and neurobiology (PhD); chemistry (MA, MS); classics (MA); clinical psychology (PhD); cognitive, developmental and social psychology (PhD); communication disorders and science (PhD); criminal justice (MS); dietetics (Postbaccalaureate Certificate); econometrics (MA); economic development (Graduate Certificate); employment and labor relations (MA); English (MA); Europe (PhD); evolution and organismal biology (PhD); film and media studies (PhD); food science (PhD); gender (PhD); geology (MS); German (MA); health economics (MA, PhD); history (MA); industrial organization (MA, PhD); industrial/organizational psychology (MA, PhD); inorganic chemistry (PhD); international economics (MA, PhD); labor (PhD); labor and human resources (MA); labor economics (PhD); language learning (MALL); liberal arts and sciences (MA, MALL, MPA, MS, MUP, Au D, PhD, Graduate Certificate, Postbaccalaureate Certificate); linguistics (MA); literary and cultural studies (PhD); macroeconomics (MA); mathematical statistics (MA, PhD); mathematics (MA, MS); microeconomics (MA); modern languages (PhD); molecular biology and biotechnology (PhD); molecular biotechnology (MS); Near Eastern languages (MA); nutrition (PhD); nutrition and food science (MA, MS); organic chemistry (PhD); philosophy (MA, PhD); physical chemistry (PhD); physics (MA, MS, PhD); political science (MA, PhD); public administration (MPA); public history (MA); pure mathematics (PhD); rhetoric and composition studies (PhD); Romance languages (MA); science and technology (PhD); social work (PhD); sociology (MA, PhD); speech-language pathology (MA); urban studies and planning (MUP); world history (PhD, Graduate Certificate). *Application deadline:* For fall admission, 6/1 priority date for domestic students, 5/1 priority date for international students; for winter admission, 10/1 priority date for domestic students, 9/1 priority date for international students; for spring admission, 2/1 priority date for domestic students, 1/1 priority date for international students. Applications are processed on a rolling basis. *Application fee:* $50. Electronic applications accepted. *Application Contact:* Deirdre Baker, Director, Graduate Admissions, 313-577-8141, E-mail: gradadmissions@wayne.edu. *Dean,* Wayne Raskind, 313-577-2519, E-mail: raskind@wayne.edu.

Center for Peace and Conflict Studies *Faculty:* 13. Expenses: Contact institution. *Financial support:* Scholarships/grants available. Financial award applicants required to submit FAFSA. Offers peace and security studies (Graduate Certificate). *Application deadline:* For fall admission, 6/1 priority date for domestic students, 5/1 priority date for international students; for winter admission, 10/1 priority date for domestic students, 9/1 priority date for international students; for spring admission, 2/1 priority date for domestic students, 1/1 priority date for international students; for summer admission, 2/1 priority date for domestic students, 1/1 priority date for international students. Applications are processed on a rolling basis. *Application fee:* $50. Electronic applications accepted. *Professor and Program Director,* Dr. Fred Pearson, 313-577-3453, E-mail: ab3440@wayne.edu.

College of Nursing Students: 138 full-time (132 women), 152 part-time (130 women); includes 73 minority (45 Black or African American, non-Hispanic/Latino; 15 Asian, non-Hispanic/Latino; 6 Hispanic/Latino; 7 Two or more races, non-Hispanic/Latino), 20 international. Average age 35. 252 applicants, 41% accepted, 62 enrolled. *Faculty:* 33. Expenses: Contact institution. *Financial support:* In 2016–17, 93 students received support, including 39 fellowships with tuition reimbursements available (averaging $9,421 per year), 5 teaching assistantships with tuition reimbursements available (averaging $25,600 per year); scholarships/grants and unspecified assistantships also available. Support available to part-time students. Financial award applicants required to submit FAFSA. In 2016, 74 master's, 16 doctorates, 10 other advanced degrees awarded. *Program availability:* Part-time. Offers nursing (MSN, DNP, PhD, Graduate Certificate). Doctoral program admits for fall only. *Application fee:* $50. Electronic applications accepted. *Application Contact:* 313-577-4082, Fax: 313-577-6949, E-mail: nursinginfo@wayne.edu. *Dean, College of Nursing,* Dr. Laurie Lauzon Clabo, 313-577-4082, E-mail: laurie.lauzon.clabo@wayne.edu.

Eugene Applebaum College of Pharmacy and Health Sciences Students: 697 full-time (448 women), 45 part-time (23 women); includes 100 minority (17 Black or African American, non-Hispanic/Latino; 2 American Indian or Alaska Native, non-Hispanic/Latino; 62 Asian, non-Hispanic/Latino; 9 Hispanic/Latino; 1 Native Hawaiian or other Pacific Islander, non-Hispanic/Latino; 9 Two or more races, non-Hispanic/Latino), 61 international. Average age 25. 749 applicants, 34% accepted, 197 enrolled. *Faculty:* 28. Expenses: Contact institution. *Financial support:* In 2016–17, 164 students received support, including 3 fellowships with tuition reimbursements available (averaging $32,181 per year), 14 research assistantships with tuition reimbursements available (averaging $24,503 per year); scholarships/grants, health care benefits, and unspecified assistantships also available. Financial award application deadline: 3/31; financial award applicants required to submit FAFSA. In 2016, 97 master's, 135 doctorates, 1 other advanced degree awarded. *Program availability:* Part-time, evening/weekend. Offers anesthesia (MS); medicinal chemistry (MS, PhD); nurse anesthesia (MS, Certificate); occupational therapy (MOT); pediatric anesthesia (Certificate); pharmaceutics (MS, PhD); pharmacology and toxicology (MS, PhD); pharmacy (Pharm D); pharmacy and health sciences (MOT, MS, DPT, PhD, Pharm D, Certificate); physical therapy (DPT); physician assistant studies (MS). *Application fee:* $50. Electronic applications accepted. *Application Contact:* Dr. Mary K. Clark, Assistant Dean, Office of Student and Alumni Affairs, 313-577-1716, Fax: 313-577-5589, E-mail: cphsinfo@wayne.edu. *Dean,* Dr. Serrine S. Lau, 313-577-1716, E-mail: serrine.lau@wayne.edu.

Law School Students: 379 full-time (162 women), 58 part-time (26 women); includes 63 minority (35 Black or African American, non-Hispanic/Latino; 1 American Indian or Alaska Native, non-Hispanic/Latino; 9 Asian, non-Hispanic/Latino; 3 Hispanic/Latino; 15 Two or more races, non-Hispanic/Latino), 13 international. Average age 27. 684 applicants, 53% accepted, 138 enrolled. *Faculty:* 40 full-time (15 women), 27 part-time/adjunct (12 women). Expenses: Contact institution. *Financial support:* In 2016–17, 353 students received support. Fellowships, Federal Work-Study, and scholarships/grants available. Support available to part-time students. Financial award application deadline: 6/30; financial award applicants required to submit FAFSA. In 2016, 16 master's, 133 doctorates awarded. Offers corporate and finance law (LL M);

labor and employment law (LL M); law (JD); taxation (LL M); United States law (LL M). *Application deadline:* For fall admission, 7/1 for domestic students, 5/1 priority date for international students. Applications are processed on a rolling basis. *Application fee:* $0. Electronic applications accepted. *Application Contact:* Kathy Fox, Assistant Dean of Admissions, 313-577-3937, Fax: 313-993-8129, E-mail: lawinquire@wayne.edu. *Interim Dean*, Lance Gable, 313-577-3933, E-mail: jbenson@wayne.edu.

Mike Ilitch School of Business Students: 219 full-time (105 women), 941 part-time (406 women); includes 314 minority (186 Black or African American, non-Hispanic/Latino; 3 American Indian or Alaska Native, non-Hispanic/Latino; 68 Asian, non-Hispanic/Latino; 33 Hispanic/Latino; 24 Two or more races, non-Hispanic/Latino; 88 international. Average age 30. 1,119 applicants, 49% accepted, 329 enrolled. *Faculty:* 32. Expenses: Contact institution. *Financial support:* In 2016–17, 174 students received support, including 1 fellowship with tuition reimbursement available (averaging $18,000 per year), 2 research assistantships with tuition reimbursements available (averaging $18,000 per year), 5 teaching assistantships with tuition reimbursements available (averaging $18,000 per year); scholarships/grants, health care benefits, and unspecified assistantships also available. Support available to part-time students. Financial award applicants required to submit FAFSA. In 2016, 203 master's, 1 doctorate, 3 other advanced degrees awarded. *Program availability:* Part-time, evening/weekend. Offers accounting (MS, Postbaccalaureate Certificate); business (Graduate Certificate); business administration (MBA, PhD); data science (MS); entrepreneurship and innovation (Postbaccalaureate Certificate); finance (MS); information systems management (Postbaccalaureate Certificate); taxation (MST). Application deadline for PhD is February 15. *Application deadline:* For fall admission, 7/1 for domestic students, 5/1 priority date for international students; for winter admission, 11/1 for domestic students, 9/1 priority date for international students; for spring admission, 3/1 for domestic students, 1/1 priority date for international students. Applications are processed on a rolling basis. *Application fee:* $50. Electronic applications accepted. *Application Contact:* Kiantee N. Rupert-Jones, Director, 313-577-4511, Fax: 313-577-9442, E-mail: gradbusiness@wayne.edu. *Dean, School of Business Administration,* Dr. Robert Forsythe, 313-577-4501, E-mail: robert.forsythe@wayne.edu.

School of Library and Information Science Students: 90 full-time (69 women), 376 part-time (312 women); includes 74 minority (38 Black or African American, non-Hispanic/Latino; 2 American Indian or Alaska Native, non-Hispanic/Latino; 4 Asian, non-Hispanic/Latino; 17 Hispanic/Latino; 2 Native Hawaiian or other Pacific Islander, non-Hispanic/Latino; 11 Two or more races, non-Hispanic/Latino), 3 international. Average age 32. 265 applicants, 73% accepted, 120 enrolled. *Faculty:* 11 full-time (7 women), 30 part-time/adjunct (20 women). Expenses: Contact institution. *Financial support:* In 2016–17, 107 students received support. Fellowships with tuition reimbursements available, scholarships/grants, health care benefits, and unspecified assistantships available. Support available to part-time students. Financial award applicants required to submit FAFSA. In 2016, 145 master's, 34 other advanced degrees awarded. *Program availability:* Part-time, evening/weekend, 100% online, blended/hybrid learning. Offers archival administration (Graduate Certificate); information management (Graduate Certificate); library and information science (MLIS, Spec); public library services to children and young adults (Graduate Certificate). *Application deadline:* For fall admission, 7/1 for domestic students, 5/1 priority date for international students; for winter admission, 10/1 priority date for domestic students, 9/1 priority date for international students; for spring admission, 2/1 priority date for domestic students, 1/1 priority date for international students. Applications are processed on a rolling basis. *Application fee:* $50. Electronic applications accepted. *Application Contact:* Academic Services Officer II, 313-577-1825, E-mail: asklis@wayne.edu. *Dean*, Dr. Sandra Yee, 313-577-4059, E-mail: aj0533@wayne.edu.

School of Medicine Students: 1,472 full-time (649 women), 129 part-time (63 women); includes 480 minority (80 Black or African American, non-Hispanic/Latino; 6 American Indian or Alaska Native, non-Hispanic/Latino; 315 Asian, non-Hispanic/Latino; 46 Hispanic/Latino; 33 Two or more races, non-Hispanic/Latino), 144 international. Average age 26. *Faculty:* 229. Expenses: Contact institution. *Financial support:* In 2016–17, 1,155 students received support, including 67 fellowships with tuition reimbursements available (averaging $24,294 per year), 94 research assistantships with tuition reimbursements available (averaging $26,850 per year); Federal Work-Study, scholarships/grants, health care benefits, and unspecified assistantships also available. Support available to part-time students. Financial award applicants required to submit FAFSA. In 2016, 65 master's, 286 doctorates, 8 other advanced degrees awarded. Offers anatomy and cell biology (MS, PhD); basic medical sciences (MS); biochemistry and molecular biology (MS, PhD); cancer biology (MS, PhD); clinical and translational science (Graduate Certificate); family medicine and public health sciences (MPH, Graduate Certificate); genetic counseling (MS); immunology and microbiology (MS, PhD); medical physics (MS, PhD, Graduate Certificate); medical research (MS); medicine (MPH, MS, MD, PhD, Graduate Certificate); molecular medicine and genomics (MS, PhD); pathology (PhD); pharmacology (MS, PhD); physiology (MS, PhD); psychiatry and behavioral neurosciences (PhD). Electronic applications accepted. *Application Contact:* Dr. Kevin Sprague, Associate Dean of Admissions. *Dean*, Dr. Jack Sobel, 313-577-1335, Fax: 313-577-8777, E-mail: ad6283@wayne.edu.

School of Social Work Students: 515 full-time (442 women), 150 part-time (128 women); includes 251 minority (179 Black or African American, non-Hispanic/Latino; 4 American Indian or Alaska Native, non-Hispanic/Latino; 11 Asian, non-Hispanic/Latino; 29 Hispanic/Latino; 1 Native Hawaiian or other Pacific Islander, non-Hispanic/Latino; 27 Two or more races, non-Hispanic/Latino), 17 international. Average age 31. 809 applicants, 36% accepted, 200 enrolled. *Faculty:* 24. Expenses: Contact institution. *Financial support:* In 2016–17, 119 students received support, including 5 fellowships with tuition reimbursements available (averaging $18,800 per year), 2 research assistantships with tuition reimbursements available (averaging $21,593 per year), 2 teaching assistantships with tuition reimbursements available (averaging $17,994 per year); scholarships/grants and unspecified assistantships also available. Financial award applicants required to submit FAFSA. In 2016, 356 master's, 2 doctorates, 20 other advanced degrees awarded. *Program availability:* Part-time, evening/weekend. Offers alcohol and drug abuse studies (Certificate); clinical social work theory and practice (Certificate); disabilities (Certificate); gerontology (Certificate); social welfare research and evaluation (Certificate); social work (MSW, PhD); social work and anthropology (PhD); social work and gerontology (PhD); social work and infant mental health (MSW, PhD); social work practice with families and couples (Certificate). Application deadlines: April 1 for MSW, December 19 for PhD. *Application deadline:* Applications are processed on a rolling basis. *Application fee:* $50. Electronic applications accepted. *Application Contact:* Shantalea Johns, Interim Director of Admissions, 313-577-4409, E-mail: shantalea@wayne.edu. *Interim Dean*, Dr. Jerrold Brandell, 313-577-4409, E-mail: aa4537@wayne.edu.

WEBBER INTERNATIONAL UNIVERSITY, Babson Park, FL 33827-0096

General Information Independent, coed, comprehensive institution. *Enrollment:* 701 graduate, professional, and undergraduate students; 44 full-time matriculated graduate/professional students (21 women), 6 part-time matriculated graduate/professional students (2 women). *Enrollment by degree level:* 50 master's. *Graduate faculty:* 11 full-time (3 women), 1 part-time/adjunct (0 women). *Tuition:* Full-time $16,104; part-time $2013 per course. One-time fee: $310. *Graduate housing:* Room and/or apartments guaranteed to single students; on-campus housing not available to married students. Typical cost: $8696 per year ($13,432 including board). Room and board charges vary according to board plan and housing facility selected. *Student services:* Campus employment opportunities, campus safety program, career counseling, exercise/wellness program, international student services, services for students with disabilities. *Library facilities:* Grace and Roger Babson Library. *Collection:* Books: 1,041 (physical); Databases: 127. Weekly public service hours: 70; students can reserve study rooms.

Computer facilities: 92 computers available on campus for general student use. A campuswide network can be accessed from off campus. Online class registration is available.
Website: http://www.webber.edu/

General Application Contact: Rebecca Coleman, MBA Admissions Counselor, 863-638-2910, Fax: 863-638-1591, E-mail: admissions@webber.edu.

GRADUATE UNITS

Graduate School of Business Students: 44 full-time (21 women), 6 part-time (2 women); includes 11 minority (5 Black or African American, non-Hispanic/Latino; 5 Hispanic/Latino; 1 Two or more races, non-Hispanic/Latino), 11 international. Average age 27. 32 applicants, 69% accepted, 18 enrolled. *Faculty:* 11 full-time (3 women), 1 part-time/adjunct (0 women). Expenses: Contact institution. *Financial support:* In 2016–17, 11 students received support. Scholarships/grants and unspecified assistantships available. Financial award application deadline: 8/16; financial award applicants required to submit FAFSA. In 2016, 16 master's awarded. *Program availability:* Part-time, evening/weekend, 100% online. Offers accounting (MBA); business (MBA); criminal justice management (MBA); international business (MBA); sport business management (MBA). *Application deadline:* For fall admission, 7/1 for international students. Applications are processed on a rolling basis. *Application fee:* $50 ($75 for international students). Electronic applications accepted. *Application Contact:* Lacy Edwards, Admissions Counselor and MBA Coordinator, 863-638-2910, Fax: 863-638-1591, E-mail: admissions@webber.edu. *Dean*, Dr. Nikos Orphanoudakis, 863-638-2910, Fax: 863-638-1591, E-mail: orphanoudakisn@webber.edu.

WEBER STATE UNIVERSITY, Ogden, UT 84408-1001

General Information State-supported, coed, comprehensive institution. *Enrollment:* 26,809 graduate, professional, and undergraduate students; 328 full-time matriculated graduate/professional students (154 women), 369 part-time matriculated graduate/professional students (201 women). *Enrollment by degree level:* 697 master's. *Graduate faculty:* 92 full-time (44 women), 5 part-time/adjunct (1 woman). Tuition, state resident: full-time $4389; part-time $1548.87 per credit hour. Tuition, nonresident: full-time $13,169; part-time $9294.56 per credit hour. *Required fees:* $782; $575.46 per credit hour. $9.50 per term. Tuition and fees vary according to course level and program. *Graduate housing:* Room and/or apartments available on a first-come, first-served basis to single students; on-campus housing not available to married students. Typical cost: $3448 per year ($6079 including board). Room and board charges vary according to board plan, campus/location and housing facility selected. *Student services:* Campus employment opportunities, campus safety program, career counseling, child daycare facilities, exercise/wellness program, free psychological counseling, grant writing training, international student services, low-cost health insurance, multicultural affairs office, services for students with disabilities, teacher training, writing training. *Library facilities:* Stewart Library. *Collection:* Books: 411,661 (physical); Serial titles: 370 (physical). *Research affiliation:* Raytheon Training Corporation (education).

Computer facilities: Computer purchase and lease plans are available. 650 computers available on campus for general student use. A campuswide network can be accessed from student residence rooms and from off campus. Online class registration is available.
Website: http://www.weber.edu/

General Application Contact: Scott Teichert, Director of Admissions, 801-626-7670, Fax: 801-626-6045, E-mail: scottteichert@weber.edu.

GRADUATE UNITS

College of Engineering, Applied Science and Technology Expenses: Contact institution. Offers computer engineering (MS). *Application Contact:* Scott Teichert, Director of Admissions, 801-626-7670, Fax: 801-626-6045, E-mail: scottteichert@weber.edu. *Dean*, Dr. David L. Ferro, 801-626-6303, E-mail: dferro@weber.edu.

College of Health Professions Students: 134 full-time (71 women), 21 part-time (9 women); includes 6 minority (1 Black or African American, non-Hispanic/Latino; 5 Hispanic/Latino), 2 international. Average age 35. *Faculty:* 16 full-time (11 women), 1 (woman) part-time/adjunct. Expenses: Contact institution. *Financial support:* In 2016–17, 40 students received support. Scholarships/grants available. Financial award application deadline: 4/1; financial award applicants required to submit FAFSA. In 2016, 39 master's awarded. *Program availability:* Part-time, evening/weekend. Offers health administration (MHA); health professions (MHA, MSN, MSRS); radiologic sciences (MSRS). *Application deadline:* For fall admission, 3/15 for domestic students, 2/20 for international students. Applications are processed on a rolling basis. *Application fee:* $60 ($90 for international students). Electronic applications accepted. *Application Contact:* Ann Gessel, Office Manager, 801-626-7127, Fax: 801-626-7683, E-mail: anngessel@weber.edu. *Dean*, Dr. Yasmin Simonian, 801-626-7117, Fax: 801-626-7683, E-mail: ysimonian@weber.edu.

School of Nursing Students: 68 full-time (58 women), 3 part-time (all women); includes 2 minority (both Hispanic/Latino). Average age 36. *Faculty:* 7 full-time (all women), 1 (woman) part-time/adjunct. Expenses: Contact institution. *Financial support:* In 2016–17, 21 students received support. Scholarships/grants available. Financial award application deadline: 4/1; financial award applicants required to submit FAFSA. In 2016, 17 master's awarded. Offers nurse practitioner (MSN). *Application deadline:* For fall admission, 4/1 priority date for domestic students. *Application fee:* $60 ($90 for international students). Electronic applications accepted. *Application Contact:* Robert Holt, Director of Enrollment, 801-626-7774, Fax: 801-626-6397, E-mail: rholt@weber.edu. *MSN Program Director,* Dr. Melissa Neville, 801-626-6204, Fax: 801-626-6397, E-mail: mneville@weber.edu.

College of Social and Behavioral Sciences Students: 5 full-time (2 women), 23 part-time (9 women); includes 7 minority (3 Black or African American, non-Hispanic/Latino;

1 American Indian or Alaska Native, non-Hispanic/Latino; 2 Hispanic/Latino; 1 Two or more races, non-Hispanic/Latino). Average age 35. *Faculty:* 6 full-time (0 women), 1 part-time/adjunct (0 women). Expenses: Contact institution. *Financial support:* In 2016–17, 1 student received support. Scholarships/grants available. Financial award application deadline: 4/1; financial award applicants required to submit FAFSA. In 2016, 12 master's awarded. *Program availability:* Part-time, evening/weekend, online only, 100% online. Offers criminal justice (MCJ); social and behavioral sciences (MCJ). *Application deadline:* For fall admission, 7/29 for domestic students; for spring admission, 12/11 for domestic students; for summer admission, 4/1 for domestic students. Applications are processed on a rolling basis. *Application fee:* $60 ($90 for international students). *Application Contact:* Faye Medd, Enrollment Director, 801-626-6146, Fax: 801-626-6145, E-mail: fmedd@weber.edu. *Dean,* Dr. Francis Harrold, 801-626-6232, Fax: 801-626-7130, E-mail: francisharrold@weber.edu.

Jerry and Vickie Moyes College of Education Students: 48 full-time (24 women), 111 part-time (86 women); includes 10 minority (4 Asian, non-Hispanic/Latino; 4 Hispanic/Latino; 2 Two or more races, non-Hispanic/Latino), 5 international. Average age 35. *Faculty:* 18 full-time (12 women). Expenses: Contact institution. *Financial support:* In 2016–17, 38 students received support. Institutionally sponsored loans, scholarships/grants, tuition waivers (full and partial), and unspecified assistantships available. Support available to part-time students. Financial award application deadline: 4/1; financial award applicants required to submit FAFSA. In 2016, 45 master's awarded. *Program availability:* Part-time, evening/weekend. Offers athletic training (MSAT); curriculum and instruction (M Ed); education (M Ed, MSAT). *Application deadline:* For fall admission, 5/15 for domestic students; for spring admission, 9/15 for domestic students; for summer admission, 1/15 for domestic students. Applications are processed on a rolling basis. *Application fee:* $60 ($90 for international students). *Application Contact:* Nathan Alexander, College of Education Recruiter, 801-626-7427, E-mail: nathanalexander@weber.edu. *Dean,* Dr. Jack Rasmussen, 801-626-6273, Fax: 801-626-7427, E-mail: jrasmussen@weber.edu.

John B. Goddard School of Business and Economics Students: 97 full-time (27 women), 123 part-time (32 women); includes 9 minority (1 Black or African American, non-Hispanic/Latino; 1 American Indian or Alaska Native, non-Hispanic/Latino; 2 Asian, non-Hispanic/Latino; 4 Hispanic/Latino; 1 Two or more races, non-Hispanic/Latino), 11 international. Average age 34. *Faculty:* 20 full-time (5 women), 2 part-time/adjunct (0 women). Expenses: Contact institution. *Financial support:* In 2016–17, 32 students received support. Scholarships/grants available. Financial award application deadline: 4/1; financial award applicants required to submit FAFSA. In 2016, 108 master's awarded. *Program availability:* Part-time, evening/weekend. Offers business administration (MBA); business and economics (M Acc, M Tax, MBA). *Application deadline:* For fall admission, 5/1 for domestic students; for spring admission, 9/1 for domestic students. *Application fee:* $60 ($90 for international students). Electronic applications accepted. *Application Contact:* Mara Sikkink, Coordinator of Academic Advisement, 801-626-6534, Fax: 801-626-6747, E-mail: marasikkink@weber.edu. *Dean,* Dr. Jeffery W. Steagall, 801-626-7253, Fax: 801-626-6687, E-mail: jeffsteagall@weber.edu.

School of Accounting and Taxation Students: 25 full-time (12 women), 12 part-time (4 women); includes 3 minority (1 Asian, non-Hispanic/Latino; 2 Hispanic/Latino), 6 international. Average age 30. *Faculty:* 7 full-time (2 women). Expenses: Contact institution. *Financial support:* In 2016–17, 19 students received support. Scholarships/grants available. Financial award application deadline: 4/1; financial award applicants required to submit FAFSA. In 2016, 42 master's awarded. *Program availability:* Part-time, evening/weekend. Offers accounting (M Acc); taxation (M Tax). *Application deadline:* For fall admission, 8/1 for domestic students; for spring admission, 12/1 for domestic students; for summer admission, 4/1 for domestic students. *Application fee:* $60 ($90 for international students). Electronic applications accepted. *Application Contact:* Dr. Larry A. Deppe, Graduate Coordinator, 801-626-7838, Fax: 801-626-7423, E-mail: ldeppe1@weber.edu. *Program Director,* Dr. Ryan Pace, 801-626-7562, Fax: 801-626-7423, E-mail: rpace@weber.edu.

Telitha E. Lindquist College of Arts and Humanities Students: 13 full-time (10 women), 78 part-time (54 women); includes 11 minority (1 Black or African American, non-Hispanic/Latino; 3 Asian, non-Hispanic/Latino; 4 Hispanic/Latino; 3 Two or more races, non-Hispanic/Latino), 2 international. Average age 33. *Faculty:* 22 full-time (13 women), 1 part-time/adjunct (0 women). Expenses: Contact institution. *Financial support:* In 2016–17, 23 students received support. Scholarships/grants and tuition waivers (full and partial) available. Financial award application deadline: 4/1; financial award applicants required to submit FAFSA. In 2016, 37 master's awarded. *Program availability:* Part-time, evening/weekend. Offers arts and humanities (MA, MPC); communication (MPC); English (MA). *Application deadline:* For fall admission, 4/1 for domestic students. Applications are processed on a rolling basis. *Application fee:* $60 ($90 for international students). Electronic applications accepted. *Application Contact:* Scott Teichert, Director of Admissions, 801-626-7670, Fax: 801-626-6045, E-mail: scottteichert@weber.edu. *Dean,* College of Arts and Humanities, Dr. Scott Springer, 801-626-6424, Fax: 801-626-7422, E-mail: arts_humanities@weber.edu.

WEBSTER UNIVERSITY, St. Louis, MO 63119-3194

General Information Independent, coed, comprehensive institution. *Enrollment:* 2,573 full-time matriculated graduate/professional students (1,431 women), 8,798 part-time matriculated graduate/professional students (5,000 women). *Enrollment by degree level:* 11,096 master's, 39 doctoral, 236 other advanced degrees. *Graduate faculty:* 199 full-time (88 women), 875 part-time/adjunct (316 women). *Tuition:* Full-time $21,900; part-time $730 per credit hour. Tuition and fees vary according to campus/location and program. *Graduate housing:* Room and/or apartments available on a first-come, first-served basis to single students; on-campus housing not available to married students. Typical cost: $7680 per year. Room charges vary according to housing facility selected. Housing application deadline: 4/1. *Student services:* Campus employment opportunities, campus safety program, career counseling, exercise/wellness program, free psychological counseling, international student services, multicultural affairs office, services for students with disabilities, teacher training, writing training. *Library facilities:* Emerson Library. *Collection:* Books: 260,133 (physical), 70,612 (digital/electronic); Serial titles: 1,167 (physical), 180 (digital/electronic); Databases: 165. Weekly public service hours: 91; study areas open 24 hours, 5–7 days a week; students can reserve study rooms. *Research affiliation:* Literacy Investment for Tomorrow.

Computer facilities: Computer purchase and lease plans are available. 714 computers available on campus for general student use. A campuswide network can be accessed from student residence rooms and from off campus. Online class registration is available.
Website: http://www.webster.edu/

General Application Contact: John Massena, Director of Undergraduate and Graduate Admission, 314-968-7114, E-mail: johnmassena24@webster.edu.

GRADUATE UNITS

College of Arts and Sciences Expenses: Contact institution. *Financial support:* Career-related internships or fieldwork and Federal Work-Study available. Support available to part-time students. Financial award application deadline: 4/1; financial award applicants required to submit FAFSA. *Program availability:* Part-time, evening/weekend, online learning. Offers arts and sciences (GM Acc, MA, MS, MSN, DNAP, Graduate Certificate); biological sciences (MS); counseling (MA); counseling psychology (MS); environmental management (MS); gerontology (MS); human services (MA); international nongovernmental organizations (MA); international relations (GM Acc); legal studies (MA, Graduate Certificate); nurse anesthesia (DNAP); nurse educator (MSN). *Application deadline:* Applications are processed on a rolling basis. *Application fee:* $35 ($50 for international students). *Application Contact:* Sarah Nandor, Director, Graduate and Transfer Admissions, 314-968-7109, E-mail: gadmit@webster.edu. *Dean,* Dr. David Carl Wilson, 314-968-7160, Fax: 314-963-6043, E-mail: wilson@webster.edu.
Institute for Human Rights and Humanitarian Studies Expenses: Contact institution. Offers international human rights (MA). *Application Contact:* Sarah Nandor, Director, Graduate and Transfer Admissions, 314-968-7109, E-mail: gadmit@webster.edu. *Dean,* Dr. David Carl Wilson, 314-968-7160, Fax: 314-963-6043, E-mail: wilson@webster.edu.

George Herbert Walker School of Business and Technology Expenses: Contact institution. *Financial support:* Career-related internships or fieldwork and Federal Work-Study available. Support available to part-time students. Financial award application deadline: 4/1; financial award applicants required to submit FAFSA. *Program availability:* Part-time, evening/weekend, online learning. Offers business and organizational security management (MA, MBA); business and technology (MA, MBA, MHA, MHA, MPA, MS, D Mgt, DM, Graduate Certificate); cybersecurity (MS); decision support systems (MBA); digital marketing management (Graduate Certificate); environmental management (MBA); finance (MBA, MS); forensic accounting (MS); gerontology (MBA); government contracting (Graduate Certificate); health administration (MHA); health care management (MA); health services management (MA); human resources development (MA, MBA); human resources management (MA, MBA); information technology management (MA, MBA, MS); international business (MA, MBA); international relations (MBA); management (D Mgt); management and leadership (MA, MBA); marketing (MA, MBA); media communications (MBA); nonprofit leadership (MA); nonprofit revenue development (Graduate Certificate); organizational development (Graduate Certificate); procurement and acquisitions management (MA, MBA); public administration (MPA); space systems operations management (MS); Web services (MBA). *Application deadline:* Applications are processed on a rolling basis. *Application fee:* $35 ($50 for international students). *Application Contact:* Sarah Nandor, Director, Graduate and Transfer Admissions, 314-968-7109, E-mail: gadmit@webster.edu. *Interim Dean,* Dr. Thomas Johnson, 314-968-5951, Fax: 314-968-7077, E-mail: deansbt@webster.edu.

Leigh Gerdine College of Fine Arts Expenses: Contact institution. *Financial support:* Fellowships, teaching assistantships, career-related internships or fieldwork, and Federal Work-Study available. Support available to part-time students. Financial award application deadline: 4/1; financial award applicants required to submit FAFSA. *Program availability:* Part-time, evening/weekend. Offers art history and criticism (MA); church music (MM); composition (MM); fine arts (MA, MFA, MM); jazz studies (MM); music (MA); music education (MM); organ (MM); performance (MM); piano (MM); voice (MM). *Application deadline:* Applications are processed on a rolling basis. *Application fee:* $35 ($50 for international students). *Application Contact:* Sarah Nandor, Director, Graduate and Transfer Admissions, 314-968-7109, E-mail: gadmit@webster.edu.

School of Communications Expenses: Contact institution. *Financial support:* Career-related internships or fieldwork and Federal Work-Study available. Support available to part-time students. Financial award application deadline: 4/1; financial award applicants required to submit FAFSA. *Program availability:* Part-time, evening/weekend, online learning. Offers advertising and marketing communications (MA); communications (MA); communications management (MA); media communications (MA); media literacy (MA); new media production (MA); public relations (MA). *Application deadline:* Applications are processed on a rolling basis. *Application fee:* $35 ($50 for international students). *Dean,* Brenda Fyfe, 314-968-6913.

School of Education Expenses: Contact institution. *Financial support:* Career-related internships or fieldwork and Federal Work-Study available. Support available to part-time students. Financial award application deadline: 4/1; financial award applicants required to submit FAFSA. *Program availability:* Part-time, online learning. Offers applied educational psychology (MA, Ed S); communication arts (MA, MAT); early childhood education (MA, MAT); education (MA, MAT, MET, Ed S); education and innovation (MA); educational technology (MET); elementary education (MAT); mathematics for educators (MA); middle school education (MAT); multidisciplinary studies (MAT); multimodal literacy for global impact (MA); reading (MA); secondary school education (MAT); special education (MA, MAT); teaching English as a second language (MA); transformative learning in the global community (Ed S). *Application deadline:* Applications are processed on a rolling basis. *Application fee:* $35 ($50 for international students). *Application Contact:* Sarah Nandor, Director, Graduate and Transfer Admissions, 314-968-7109, E-mail: gadmit@webster.edu. *Dean,* Brenda Fyfe, 314-968-6913, Fax: 314-968-7118, E-mail: fyfebv@webster.edu.

WEILL CORNELL MEDICINE, New York, NY 10065

General Information Independent, coed, graduate-only institution. *Graduate housing:* Rooms and/or apartments guaranteed to single students and available on a first-come, first-served basis to married students. Housing application deadline: 4/30. *Research affiliation:* Memorial Sloan-Kettering Cancer Center (cancer), Houston Methodist Hospital (general medicine and surgery), The Rockefeller University (biomedical research), New York Methodist (general medicine and surgery), Hospital for Special Surgery (orthopedics), Burke Medical Research Institute (neurology).

GRADUATE UNITS

Weill Cornell Graduate School of Medical Sciences Offers biochemistry, cell and molecular biology (MS, PhD); chemical biology (PhD); clinical epidemiology and health services research (MS); computational biology and medicine (PhD); health informatics (MS); health sciences (MS); immunology (MS, PhD); medical sciences (MS, PhD); neuroscience (MS, PhD); pharmacology (MS, PhD); physiology, biophysics and systems biology (MS, PhD). Electronic applications accepted.

Weill Cornell/Rockefeller/Sloan-Kettering Tri-Institutional MD-PhD Program Offered jointly with The Rockefeller University and Sloan-Kettering Institute. Electronic applications accepted.

WENTWORTH INSTITUTE OF TECHNOLOGY, Boston, MA 02115-5998

General Information Independent, coed, comprehensive institution. *Enrollment:* 4,136 graduate, professional, and undergraduate students; 76 full-time matriculated graduate/professional students (35 women), 126 part-time matriculated graduate/professional students (30 women). *Enrollment by degree level:* 202 master's. *Graduate faculty:* 25 full-time (12 women), 29 part-time/adjunct (10 women). *Tuition:* Full-time $35,100; part-time $1100 per credit hour. *Required fees:* $1740. *Graduate housing:* Room and/or apartments available on a first-come, first-served basis to single students; on-campus housing not available to married students. Typical cost: $13,013 (including board). Housing application deadline: 5/1. *Student services:* Campus employment opportunities, campus safety program, career counseling, exercise/wellness program, international student services, low-cost health insurance, multicultural affairs office, services for students with disabilities. *Library facilities:* Wentworth Alumni Library plus 1 other. *Collection:* Books: 51,085 (physical), 229,005 (digital/electronic); Serial titles: 211 (physical), 27,903 (digital/electronic); Databases: 77. Weekly public service hours: 95.

Computer facilities: Computer purchase and lease plans are available. 320 computers available on campus for general student use. A campuswide network can be accessed from student residence rooms and from off campus. Online class registration is available.
Website: http://www.wit.edu/

General Application Contact: Martha Sheehan, Director of Admissions and Marketing, 617-989-4661, Fax: 617-989-4399, E-mail: sheehanm@wit.edu.

GRADUATE UNITS

Department of Architecture Students: 75 full-time (34 women), 3 part-time (2 women); includes 14 minority (5 Black or African American, non-Hispanic/Latino; 3 Asian, non-Hispanic/Latino; 2 Hispanic/Latino; 4 Two or more races, non-Hispanic/Latino), 7 international. Average age 24. 121 applicants, 83% accepted, 69 enrolled. *Faculty:* 14 full-time (7 women), 13 part-time/adjunct (5 women). *Expenses:* Contact institution. *Financial support:* In 2016–17, 88 students received support, including 87 fellowships (averaging $6,100 per year), 37 teaching assistantships (averaging $2,700 per year). Financial award application deadline: 5/1; financial award applicants required to submit FAFSA. In 2016, 78 master's awarded. Offers architecture (M Arch). *Application deadline:* For fall admission, 1/15 priority date for domestic and international students. Applications are processed on a rolling basis. *Application fee:* $50. Electronic applications accepted. *Application Contact:* Kelly Hutzell, Director of Graduate Programs, 617-989-4494, E-mail: hutzelk@wit.edu. *Architecture Department Chair,* Michael Macphail, 617-989-4455, E-mail: macphailm@wit.edu.

Master of Engineering in Civil Engineering Program Students: 17 part-time (4 women); includes 4 minority (2 Black or African American, non-Hispanic/Latino; 1 Hispanic/Latino; 1 Two or more races, non-Hispanic/Latino), 1 international. Average age 27. 10 applicants, 100% accepted, 10 enrolled. *Faculty:* 12 part-time/adjunct (4 women). *Expenses:* Contact institution. *Financial support:* Scholarships/grants available. Support available to part-time students. Financial award application deadline: 8/1; financial award applicants required to submit FAFSA. In 2016, 7 master's awarded. *Program availability:* Part-time-only, evening/weekend. Offers construction engineering (M Eng); infrastructure engineering (M Eng). *Application deadline:* For fall admission, 8/1 for domestic and international students. Applications are processed on a rolling basis. *Application fee:* $50. Electronic applications accepted. *Application Contact:* Martha Sheehan, Director of Admissions and Marketing, 617-989-4661, Fax: 617-989-4399, E-mail: sheehanm@wit.edu. *Director of Graduate Programs,* Philip Hammond, 617-989-4594, Fax: 617-989-4399, E-mail: hammondp1@wit.edu.

Master of Science in Construction Management Program Students: 1 (woman) full-time, 50 part-time (13 women); includes 11 minority (6 Black or African American, non-Hispanic/Latino; 1 American Indian or Alaska Native, non-Hispanic/Latino; 1 Hispanic/Latino; 3 Two or more races, non-Hispanic/Latino). Average age 30. 46 applicants, 83% accepted, 27 enrolled. *Faculty:* 38 part-time/adjunct (11 women). *Expenses:* Contact institution. *Financial support:* Scholarships/grants available. Support available to part-time students. Financial award application deadline: 8/1; financial award applicants required to submit FAFSA. In 2016, 23 master's awarded. *Program availability:* Part-time-only, evening/weekend, 100% online, blended/hybrid learning. Offers construction management (MS). *Application deadline:* For fall admission, 8/1 for domestic and international students; for spring admission, 12/20 for domestic and international students. Applications are processed on a rolling basis. *Application fee:* $50. Electronic applications accepted. *Application Contact:* Martha Sheehan, Director of Admissions and Marketing, 617-989-4661, Fax: 617-989-4399, E-mail: sheehanm@wit.edu. *Director of Graduate Programs,* Philip Hammond, 617-989-4594, Fax: 617-989-4399, E-mail: hammondp1@wit.edu.

Master of Science in Facility Management Program Students: 22 part-time (18 women); includes 4 minority (2 Black or African American, non-Hispanic/Latino; 2 Two or more races, non-Hispanic/Latino). Average age 38. 23 applicants, 83% accepted, 12 enrolled. *Faculty:* 26 part-time/adjunct (7 women). *Expenses:* Contact institution. *Financial support:* Scholarships/grants available. Support available to part-time students. Financial award application deadline: 8/1; financial award applicants required to submit FAFSA. In 2016, 9 master's awarded. *Program availability:* Part-time, evening/weekend, online only, 100% online, blended/hybrid learning. Offers facility management (MS). *Application deadline:* For fall admission, 8/1 for domestic and international students. Applications are processed on a rolling basis. *Application fee:* $50. Electronic applications accepted. *Application Contact:* Martha Sheehan, Director of Admissions and Marketing, 617-989-4661, Fax: 617-989-4399, E-mail: sheehanm@wit.edu. *Director of Graduate Programs,* Philip Hammond, 617-989-4594, Fax: 617-989-4399, E-mail: hammondp1@wit.edu.

Online Master of Science in Technology Management Program Students: 30 part-time (8 women); includes 11 minority (4 Black or African American, non-Hispanic/Latino; 5 Asian, non-Hispanic/Latino; 2 Hispanic/Latino). Average age 32. 19 applicants, 89% accepted, 14 enrolled. *Faculty:* 17 part-time/adjunct (6 women). *Expenses:* Contact institution. *Financial support:* Scholarships/grants available. Support available to part-time students. Financial award application deadline: 8/1; financial award applicants required to submit FAFSA. In 2016, 10 master's awarded. *Program availability:* Part-time-only, evening/weekend, online only, 100% online. Offers technology management (MS). *Application deadline:* For fall admission, 8/1 for domestic and international students; for spring admission, 12/20 for domestic and international students. Applications are processed on a rolling basis. *Application fee:* $50. Electronic applications accepted. *Application Contact:* Martha Sheehan, Director of Admissions and Marketing, 617-989-4661, Fax: 617-989-4399, E-mail: sheehanm@wit.edu. *Director of Graduate Programs,* Philip Hammond, 617-989-4594, Fax: 617-989-4399, E-mail: hammondp1@wit.edu.

WESLEYAN COLLEGE, Macon, GA 31210-4462

General Information Independent-religious, Undergraduate: women only; graduate: coed, comprehensive institution. *Graduate housing:* Room and/or apartments available on a first-come, first-served basis to single students; on-campus housing not available to married students. Housing application deadline: 5/1.

GRADUATE UNITS
Department of Business and Economics Offers business administration (EMBA); business and economics (EMBA).
Department of Education *Program availability:* Part-time. Offers early childhood education (MA).

WESLEYAN UNIVERSITY, Middletown, CT 06459

General Information Independent, coed, university. CGS member. *Enrollment:* 3,206 graduate, professional, and undergraduate students; 232 full-time matriculated graduate/professional students (106 women), 2 part-time matriculated graduate/professional students. *Graduate faculty:* 146 full-time (38 women), 8 part-time/adjunct (3 women). *Graduate housing:* Rooms and/or apartments available on a first-come, first-served basis to single and married students. Housing application deadline: 7/1. *Student services:* Campus employment opportunities, campus safety program, career counseling, exercise/wellness program, free psychological counseling, international student services, low-cost health insurance, services for students with disabilities, writing training. *Library facilities:* Olin Memorial Library plus 1 other. *Collection:* Books: 1.2 million (physical), 502,915 (digital/electronic); Serial titles: 999 (physical), 74,957 (digital/electronic); Databases: 213. Weekly public service hours: 113. *Research affiliation:* Woods Hole Oceanographic Institution, Cold Spring Harbor Laboratory.

Computer facilities: Computer purchase and lease plans are available. 1,600 computers available on campus for general student use. A campuswide network can be accessed from student residence rooms and from off campus. Online class registration, electronic portfolio, course drop/add, learning management system, software training are available.
Website: http://www.wesleyan.edu/

General Application Contact: Cheryl-Ann Hagner, Director, Graduate Student Services, 860-685-2223, Fax: 860-685-2439, E-mail: chagner@wesleyan.edu.

GRADUATE UNITS
Graduate Liberal Studies Program Expenses: Contact institution. *Financial support:* Scholarships/grants available. Support available to part-time students. *Program availability:* Part-time, evening/weekend. Offers liberal arts (M Phil); liberal studies (MALS); writing (Graduate Certificate). *Application deadline:* For fall admission, 7/10 for domestic students; for spring admission, 11/6 for domestic students; for summer admission, 4/16 for domestic students. Applications are processed on a rolling basis. *Application fee:* $100. *Application Contact:* Sarah-Jane Ripa, Associate Director, Student Services and Outreach, 860-685-3345, Fax: 860-685-2901, E-mail: sripa@wesleyan.edu. *Director,* Jennifer Curran, 860-685-3338, Fax: 860-685-2901, E-mail: jcurran@wesleyan.edu.

Graduate Studies Students: 124 full-time (65 women); includes 55 minority (9 Black or African American, non-Hispanic/Latino; 36 Asian, non-Hispanic/Latino; 10 Hispanic/Latino). Average age 26. 346 applicants, 15% accepted, 30 enrolled. *Faculty:* 77 full-time (20 women). *Expenses:* Contact institution. *Financial support:* In 2016–17, 93 students received support, including 93 teaching assistantships (averaging $30,570 per year); research assistantships, health care benefits, tuition waivers (full), and unspecified assistantships also available. Financial award application deadline: 4/15. In 2016, 29 master's, 15 doctorates awarded. Offers astronomy (MA); biochemistry (PhD); cell and developmental biology (PhD); chemical physics (PhD); composition (MA); computer science (MA); earth and environmental sciences (MA); ethnomusicology (MA, PhD); evolution and ecology (PhD); genetics and genomics (PhD); inorganic chemistry (PhD); mathematics (MA, PhD); molecular biology (PhD); molecular biophysics (PhD); molecular genetics (PhD); neurobiology and behavior (PhD); organic chemistry (PhD); physical chemistry (PhD); physics (PhD); theoretical chemistry (PhD). *Application fee:* $0. Electronic applications accepted. *Application Contact:* Cheryl-Ann Hagner, Director of Graduate Student Services, 860-685-2223, Fax: 860-685-2439, E-mail: chagner@wesleyan.edu. *Director of Graduate Studies,* Dr. Ann C. Burke, 860-685-3518, E-mail: acburke@wesleyan.edu.

WESLEY BIBLICAL SEMINARY, Jackson, MS 39206
General Information Independent-religious, coed, graduate-only institution.

GRADUATE UNITS
Graduate Programs *Program availability:* Part-time. Offers apologetics (MA); Biblical languages (M Div); Biblical literature (MA); Christian studies (MA); context and mission (M Div); honors research (M Div); interpretation (M Div); ministry (M Div); spiritual formation (M Div); teaching (M Div); theology (MA). Electronic applications accepted.

WESLEY COLLEGE, Dover, DE 19901-3875
General Information Independent-religious, coed, comprehensive institution. *Graduate housing:* On-campus housing not available.

GRADUATE UNITS
Business Program *Program availability:* Part-time, evening/weekend. Offers environmental management (MBA); executive leadership (MBA); management (MBA). Executive leadership concentration also offered at New Castle, DE location.
Education Program *Program availability:* Part-time, evening/weekend. Offers education (M Ed, MA Ed, MAT).
Environmental Studies Program *Program availability:* Part-time, evening/weekend. Offers environmental studies (MS).
Nursing Program *Program availability:* Part-time, evening/weekend. Offers nursing (MSN). Electronic applications accepted.

WESLEY THEOLOGICAL SEMINARY, Washington, DC 20016-5690
General Information Independent-religious, coed, graduate-only institution. *Graduate housing:* Rooms and/or apartments available to single and married students. Housing application deadline: 7/1.

GRADUATE UNITS
Graduate and Professional Programs *Program availability:* Part-time. Offers theology (M Div, MA, MTS, D Min).

WEST CHESTER UNIVERSITY OF PENNSYLVANIA, West Chester, PA 19383
General Information State-supported, coed, comprehensive institution. CGS member. *Enrollment by degree level:* 2,127 master's, 146 doctoral, 203 other advanced degrees. *Graduate faculty:* 269 full-time (149 women), 52 part-time/adjunct (40 women). Tuition, state resident: full-time $8694; part-time $483 per credit. Tuition, nonresident: full-time $13,050; part-time $725 per credit. *Required fees:* $2399; $119.05 per credit. Tuition and fees vary according to campus/location and program. *Graduate housing:* Room and/or apartments available on a first-come, first-served basis to single students; on-campus housing not available to married students. Typical cost: $6638 per year ($10,098

including board). Room and board charges vary according to board plan and housing facility selected. Housing application deadline: 5/1. *Student services:* Campus employment opportunities, campus safety program, career counseling, exercise/wellness program, free psychological counseling, international student services, multicultural affairs office, services for students with disabilities, teacher training, writing training. *Library facilities:* Francis Harvey Green Library plus 1 other. *Collection:* Books: 734,356 (physical), 1 million (digital/electronic); Serial titles: 2,066 (physical), 100,390 (digital/electronic); Databases: 314. Weekly public service hours: 107. *Research affiliation:* Pennsylvania Equine Toxicology and Research Laboratory (chemistry), Temple University Collaborative on Community Inclusion of Individuals with Psychiatric Disabilities (social work), University of Pennsylvania (social work), University of Connecticut Human Rights Institute Research Program on Economic and Social Rights (social work), The Soldier's Project (social work), Independent Blue Cross (IBC) (nursing).

Computer facilities: Computer purchase and lease plans are available. 2,500 computers available on campus for general student use. A campuswide network can be accessed from student residence rooms and from off campus. Online class registration, virtual software are available.
Website: http://www.wcupa.edu.

General Application Contact: Office of Graduate Studies, 610-436-2943, Fax: 610-436-2763, E-mail: gradstudy@wcupa.edu.

GRADUATE UNITS

College of Arts and Humanities Students: 78 full-time (48 women), 168 part-time (104 women); includes 25 minority (9 Black or African American, non-Hispanic/Latino; 1 Asian, non-Hispanic/Latino; 9 Hispanic/Latino; 1 Native Hawaiian or other Pacific Islander, non-Hispanic/Latino; 5 Two or more races, non-Hispanic/Latino), 7 international. Average age 31. 146 applicants, 90% accepted, 80 enrolled. *Faculty:* 76 full-time (31 women), 5 part-time/adjunct (3 women). Expenses: Contact institution. *Financial support:* Scholarships/grants and unspecified assistantships available. Financial award application deadline: 2/15; financial award applicants required to submit FAFSA. In 2016, 82 master's, 7 other advanced degrees awarded. *Program availability:* Part-time, evening/weekend. Offers arts and humanities (M Ed, MA, MM, MS, Certificate, Teaching Certificate); business ethics (Certificate); communication studies (MA); English (MA); French (Teaching Certificate); German (Teaching Certificate); health care ethics (Certificate); history (M Ed, MA); history and literature (MM); Holocaust and genocide studies (MA); Kodaly methodology (Certificate); languages and cultures (MA); music education (MM, Teaching Certificate); music technology (Certificate); music theory, history, and composition (MM); Orff-Schulwerk (Certificate); performance (MM); philosophy (MA); philosophy: applied ethics (MA); piano pedagogy (MM, Certificate); publishing (Certificate); secondary English (Teaching Certificate); Spanish (Teaching Certificate); teaching English as a second language (MA, Certificate). *Application deadline:* For fall admission, 5/15 for international students; for spring admission, 10/15 for international students. Applications are processed on a rolling basis. *Application fee:* $50. Electronic applications accepted. *Application Contact:* Office of Graduate Studies and Extended Education, 610-436-2943, Fax: 610-436-2763, E-mail: gradstudy@wcupa.edu. *Dean of the College of Arts and Humanities,* Dr. Timothy V. Blair, 610-436-2489, E-mail: tblair@wcupa.edu.

College of Business and Public Management Students: 133 full-time (72 women), 416 part-time (198 women); includes 140 minority (101 Black or African American, non-Hispanic/Latino; 1 American Indian or Alaska Native, non-Hispanic/Latino; 14 Asian, non-Hispanic/Latino; 19 Hispanic/Latino; 5 Two or more races, non-Hispanic/Latino), 9 international. Average age 32. 397 applicants, 86% accepted, 252 enrolled. *Faculty:* 30 full-time (14 women), 8 part-time/adjunct (6 women). Expenses: Contact institution. *Financial support:* Scholarships/grants and unspecified assistantships available. Financial award application deadline: 2/15; financial award applicants required to submit FAFSA. In 2016, 125 master's, 18 other advanced degrees awarded. *Program availability:* Part-time, evening/weekend, 100% online, blended/hybrid learning. Offers administration (Certificate); business and public management (MA, MBA, MPA, MS, MSA, MURP, Certificate, DPA); criminal justice (MS); geographic information systems (Certificate); geography (MS); geography and planning (MURP); human resource management (MPA, MS, Certificate); human resources management (DPA); non profit administration (Certificate); nonprofit administration (MPA); public administration (MPA); public policy and administration (MPA); urban and regional planning (MPA, Certificate). *Application deadline:* For fall admission, 5/15 for international students; for spring admission, 10/15 for international students. Applications are processed on a rolling basis. *Application fee:* $50. Electronic applications accepted. *Application Contact:* Office of Graduate Studies and Extended Education, 610-436-2943, Fax: 610-436-2763, E-mail: gradstudy@wcupa.edu. *Interim Dean,* Dr. Jeffery L. Osgood, Jr., 610-436-2930, Fax: 610-436-3170, E-mail: josgood@wcupa.edu.

School of Business Students: 44 full-time (23 women), 213 part-time (82 women); includes 37 minority (16 Black or African American, non-Hispanic/Latino; 11 Asian, non-Hispanic/Latino; 9 Hispanic/Latino; 1 Two or more races, non-Hispanic/Latino). Average age 32. 202 applicants, 83% accepted, 126 enrolled. *Faculty:* 13 full-time (6 women), 2 part-time/adjunct (1 woman). Expenses: Contact institution. *Financial support:* Scholarships/grants and unspecified assistantships available. Financial award application deadline: 2/15; financial award applicants required to submit FAFSA. In 2016, 41 master's, 16 other advanced degrees awarded. *Program availability:* Part-time, evening/weekend, 100% online. Offers business analytics (Certificate); business education (MBA); entrepreneurship (Certificate); project management (Certificate). *Application deadline:* For fall admission, 5/15 for international students; for spring admission, 10/15 for international students. Applications are processed on a rolling basis. *Application fee:* $50. Electronic applications accepted. *Application Contact:* Office of Graduate Studies and Extended Education, 610-436-2943, Fax: 610-436-2763, E-mail: gradstudy@wcupa.edu. *MBA Director/Graduate Coordinator,* Dr. Brian Halsey, 610-425-5000 Ext. 4444, E-mail: mba@wcupa.edu.

College of Education and Social Work Students: 355 full-time (293 women), 606 part-time (524 women); includes 219 minority (154 Black or African American, non-Hispanic/Latino; 7 Asian, non-Hispanic/Latino; 37 Hispanic/Latino; 21 Two or more races, non-Hispanic/Latino), 3 international. Average age 30. 674 applicants, 72% accepted, 316 enrolled. *Faculty:* 56 full-time (40 women), 21 part-time/adjunct (17 women). Expenses: Contact institution. *Financial support:* Scholarships/grants and unspecified assistantships available. Financial award application deadline: 2/15; financial award applicants required to submit FAFSA. In 2016, 255 master's, 53 other advanced degrees awarded. *Program availability:* Part-time, evening/weekend, 100% online, blended/hybrid learning. Offers applied studies in teaching and learning (M Ed); autism (Certificate); clinical mental health counseling (MS); counseling (Certificate); early childhood education (M Ed); education and social work (M Ed, MS, MSW, Ed D, Certificate, Post Master's Certificate, Teaching Certificate); education for sustainability (Certificate); educational technology (Certificate); entrepreneurial education

(Certificate); grades 4-8 (Teaching Certificate); grades preK-4 (Teaching Certificate); higher education counseling (Post Master's Certificate); higher education counseling/student affairs (MS, Certificate); literacy (Certificate); literacy coaching (Certificate); policy, planning, and administration (Ed D); reading (M Ed, Teaching Certificate); school counseling (M Ed); social work (MSW); special education (Teaching Certificate); special education (M Ed); transformative education and social change (MS); universal design for learning and assistive technology (Certificate). *Application deadline:* For fall admission, 5/15 for international students; for spring admission, 10/15 for international students. Applications are processed on a rolling basis. *Application fee:* $50. Electronic applications accepted. *Application Contact:* Office of Graduate Studies and Extended Education, 610-436-2943, Fax: 610-436-2763, E-mail: gradstudy@wcupa.edu. *Dean,* Dr. Kenneth D. Witmer, Jr., 610-436-2321, Fax: 610-436-3102, E-mail: kwitmer@wcupa.edu.

College of Health Sciences Students: 205 full-time (170 women), 239 part-time (182 women); includes 103 minority (84 Black or African American, non-Hispanic/Latino; 7 Asian, non-Hispanic/Latino; 10 Hispanic/Latino; 2 Two or more races, non-Hispanic/Latino), 18 international. Average age 32. 602 applicants, 54% accepted, 179 enrolled. *Faculty:* 51 full-time (39 women), 11 part-time/adjunct (9 women). Expenses: Contact institution. *Financial support:* Scholarships/grants and unspecified assistantships available. Financial award application deadline: 2/15; financial award applicants required to submit FAFSA. In 2016, 148 master's, 12 other advanced degrees awarded. *Program availability:* Part-time, evening/weekend. Offers adapted physical education (Certificate); adult-gerontology clinical nurse specialist (MSN); community nutrition (MS); emergency preparedness (Certificate); exercise and sport physiology (MS); general physical education (MS); gerontology (Certificate); health care management (Certificate); health sciences (M Ed, MA, MPA, MPH, MS, MSN, DNP, Certificate, Teaching Certificate); integrative health (Certificate); nursing (DNP); nursing education (MSN); public health (MPH); school health (M Ed); school nurse (Certificate); speech-language pathology (MA); sport management and athletics (MPA). *Application deadline:* For fall admission, 5/15 for international students; for spring admission, 10/15 for international students. Applications are processed on a rolling basis. *Application fee:* $50. Electronic applications accepted. *Application Contact:* Office of Graduate Studies, 610-436-2943, Fax: 610-436-2763, E-mail: gradstudy@wcupa.edu. *Dean,* Dr. Linda Adams, 610-436-2825, Fax: 610-436-2860, E-mail: ladams@wcupa.edu.

College of the Sciences and Mathematics Students: 116 full-time (70 women), 188 part-time (89 women); includes 64 minority (22 Black or African American, non-Hispanic/Latino; 28 Asian, non-Hispanic/Latino; 8 Hispanic/Latino; 6 Two or more races, non-Hispanic/Latino), 25 international. Average age 30. 114 applicants, 10 enrolled. *Faculty:* 56 full-time (25 women), 7 part-time/adjunct (5 women). Expenses: Contact institution. *Financial support:* Scholarships/grants and unspecified assistantships available. Financial award application deadline: 2/15; financial award applicants required to submit FAFSA. In 2016, 114 master's awarded. *Program availability:* Part-time, 100% online. Offers applied and computational mathematics (MS); applied statistics (MS, Certificate); biology (MS, Teaching Certificate); chemistry (Teaching Certificate); clinical psychology (Psy D); computer science (MS); computer security (information assurance) (Certificate); general science (Teaching Certificate); geoscience (MS); industrial/organizational psychology (Certificate); information systems (Certificate); mathematics (MA, Teaching Certificate); mathematics education (MA); physics (Teaching Certificate); psychology (MA); sciences and mathematics (MA, MS, Psy D, Certificate, Teaching Certificate); Web technology (Certificate). *Application deadline:* For fall admission, 5/15 for international students; for spring admission, 10/15 for international students. Applications are processed on a rolling basis. *Application fee:* $50. Electronic applications accepted. *Application Contact:* Office of Graduate Studies, 610-436-2943, Fax: 610-436-2763, E-mail: gradstudy@wcupa.edu. *Interim Dean,* Dr. Jack Waber, 610-436-3521.

WEST COAST UNIVERSITY, North Hollywood, CA 91606
General Information Proprietary, coed, comprehensive institution.
GRADUATE UNITS
Graduate Programs

WESTERN CAROLINA UNIVERSITY, Cullowhee, NC 28723
General Information State-supported, coed, university. CGS member. *Enrollment:* 10,805 graduate, professional, and undergraduate students; 692 full-time matriculated graduate/professional students (478 women), 872 part-time matriculated graduate/professional students (562 women). *Enrollment by degree level:* 1,359 master's, 127 doctoral, 74 other advanced degrees. *Graduate faculty:* 233 full-time (110 women), 36 part-time/adjunct (17 women). Tuition, state resident: full-time $2174. Tuition, nonresident: full-time $7377. *Required fees:* $1442. Part-time tuition and fees vary according to course load. *Graduate housing:* Room and/or apartments available on a first-come, first-served basis to single students; on-campus housing not available to married students. Typical cost: $10,100 (including board). Room and board charges vary according to board plan and housing facility selected. *Student services:* Campus employment opportunities, campus safety program, career counseling, child daycare facilities, exercise/wellness program, free psychological counseling, international student services, low-cost health insurance, multicultural affairs office, services for students with disabilities, teacher training, writing training. *Library facilities:* Hunter Library. *Collection:* Weekly public service hours: 96; study areas open 24 hours, 5–7 days a week; students can reserve study rooms. *Research affiliation:* North Carolina Center for the Advancement of Teaching.

Computer facilities: Computer purchase and lease plans are available. A campuswide network can be accessed from student residence rooms and from off campus. Online class registration is available.
Website: http://www.wcu.edu/

General Application Contact: Admissions Specialist, 828-227-7398, Fax: 828-227-7480, E-mail: gradsch@email.wcu.edu.

GRADUATE UNITS

Graduate School *Program availability:* Part-time, evening/weekend, online learning.

College of Arts and Sciences *Program availability:* Part-time, evening/weekend. Offers arts and sciences (MA, MPA, MS, Graduate Certificate); biology (MS); chemistry (MS); history (MA); political science and public affairs (MPA); teaching English as a second language or foreign language (MA).

College of Business *Program availability:* Part-time, evening/weekend, online learning. Offers accountancy (M Ac); business administration (MBA); entrepreneurship (ME); project management (MPM).

College of Education and Allied Professions *Program availability:* Part-time, evening/weekend, online learning. Offers education and allied professions (MA); general psychology (MA).

College of Fine and Performing Arts *Program availability:* Part-time. Offers art and design (MFA); fine and performing arts (MFA).

College of Health and Human Sciences *Program availability:* Part-time, evening/weekend. Offers communication sciences and disorders (MS); health and human sciences (MHS, MPT, MS, MSN, MSW, DPT, PMC); health sciences (MHS); nursing (MS, DNP, Post-Master's Certificate, Postbaccalaureate Certificate); physical therapy (DPT); social work (MSW).

Kimmel School of Construction Management and Technology *Program availability:* Part-time, evening/weekend, online learning. Offers construction management (MCM); construction management and technology (MCM).

WESTERN CONNECTICUT STATE UNIVERSITY, Danbury, CT 06810-6885

General Information State-supported, coed, comprehensive institution. *Graduate housing:* Rooms and/or apartments available on a first-come, first-served basis to single and married students. Housing application deadline: 4/1. *Research affiliation:* Smithsonian Institution Affiliations Program, The Jane Goodall Institute, Center for Financial Forensics and Informational Security, New England Educational Assessment Network, American Society for Microbiology.

GRADUATE UNITS

Division of Graduate Studies *Program availability:* Part-time.

Ancell School of Business *Program availability:* Part-time. Offers accounting (MBA); business (MBA, MHA, MS); business administration (MBA); health administration (MHA); justice administration (MS).

Maricostas School of Arts and Sciences *Program availability:* Part-time. Offers arts and sciences (MA, MAT, MFA); biological and environmental sciences (MAT); creative and professional writing (MFA); earth and planetary sciences (MA); history and non-Western cultures (MA); literature (MA); mathematics (MA).

School of Professional Studies *Program availability:* Part-time. Offers adult gerontology clinical nurse specialist (MSN); adult gerontology nurse practitioner (MSN); clinical mental health counseling (MS); curriculum (MS); instructional leadership (Ed D); instructional technology (MS); nursing education (Ed D); reading (MS); school counseling (MS); special education (MS).

School of Visual and Performing Arts *Program availability:* Part-time. Offers illustration (MFA); music education (MS); painting (MFA); visual and performing arts (MFA, MS).

WESTERN GOVERNORS UNIVERSITY, Salt Lake City, UT 84107

General Information Independent, coed, comprehensive institution.

GRADUATE UNITS

College of Business *Program availability:* Evening/weekend. Offers information technology management (MBA); integrated healthcare management (MS); management and strategy (MBA); strategic leadership (MBA). Electronic applications accepted.

College of Health Professions *Program availability:* Evening/weekend. Offers healthcare management (MBA); leadership and management (MSN); nursing education (MSN). Electronic applications accepted.

College of Information Technology *Program availability:* Online learning. Offers cybersecurity and information assurance (MS); data analytics (MS); information technology management (MS).

Teachers College *Program availability:* Evening/weekend, online learning. Offers curriculum and instruction (MS); educational leadership (MS); educational studies (MA); educational studies (5-12) (MA); elementary education (K-8) (MAT, Postbaccalaureate Certificate); elementary education (PreK-8) (MAT); English language learning (K-12) (MA); instructional design (MAT); learning and technology (M Ed, MA); management and innovation (M Ed); mathematics (5-12) (MAT, Postbaccalaureate Certificate); mathematics (5-9) (MAT, Postbaccalaureate Certificate); mathematics education (5-12) (MA); mathematics education (5-9) (MA); mathematics education (K-6) (MA); measurement and evaluation (M Ed); science (5-12) (Postbaccalaureate Certificate); science (5-9) (MAT, Postbaccalaureate Certificate); science education (5-12) (MA); science education (5-9) (MA); social science (5-12) (MAT, Postbaccalaureate Certificate); special education (MAT, MS). Electronic applications accepted.

WESTERN ILLINOIS UNIVERSITY, Macomb, IL 61455-1390

General Information State-supported, coed, comprehensive institution. CGS member. *Graduate housing:* Rooms and/or apartments available on a first-come, first-served basis to single and married students. *Student services:* Campus employment opportunities, campus safety program, career counseling, exercise/wellness program, free psychological counseling, international student services, low-cost health insurance, multicultural affairs office, services for students with disabilities, teacher training, writing training. *Library facilities:* Leslie Malpass Library plus 4 others. *Collection:* Books: 1 million (physical), 50,866 (digital/electronic); Databases: 126. *Research affiliation:* National Council of Teachers of English (English and journalism), Petroleum Research Fund (chemistry), Bayer Crop Services (agriculture), McDonald's Corporation (education), The Ceres Trust (agriculture), Quad Cities Manufacturing Lab (engineering).

Computer facilities: 632 computers available on campus for general student use. A campuswide network can be accessed from student residence rooms and from off campus. Online class registration is available.

Website: http://www.wiu.edu/

General Application Contact: Dr. Nancy Parsons, Associate Provost and Director of Graduate Studies, 309-298-1806, Fax: 309-298-2345, E-mail: grad-office@wiu.edu.

GRADUATE UNITS

School of Graduate Studies Expenses: Contact institution. *Financial support:* Research assistantships with full tuition reimbursements, teaching assistantships with full tuition reimbursements, and unspecified assistantships available. Financial award applicants required to submit FAFSA. *Program availability:* Part-time, online learning. Application fee: $30. Electronic applications accepted. *Associate Provost and Director of Graduate Studies,* Dr. Nancy Parsons, 309-298-1066, Fax: 309-298-2345, E-mail: grad-office@wiu.edu.

College of Arts and Sciences Expenses: Contact institution. *Financial support:* Research assistantships with full tuition reimbursements, teaching assistantships with full tuition reimbursements, and unspecified assistantships available. Financial award applicants required to submit FAFSA. *Program availability:* Part-time. Offers arts and sciences (MA, MLAS, MS, PhD, Certificate, SSP); biology (MS); chemistry (MS); clinical/community mental health (MS); community development and planning (Certificate); English (MA); environmental GIS (Certificate); environmental science: large river ecosystems (PhD); general experimental psychology (MS); geography (MA); GIS analysis: GIS applications (Certificate); history (MA); liberal arts and sciences (MLAS); literary studies (Certificate); mathematics (MS); physics (MS);

political science (MA); professional writing (Certificate); school psychology (SSP); sociology (MA); teaching writing (Certificate); zoo and aquarium studies (Certificate). *Application deadline:* Applications are processed on a rolling basis. *Application fee:* $30. Electronic applications accepted. *Application Contact:* Dr. Nancy Parsons, Associate Provost and Director of Graduate Studies, 309-298-1806, Fax: 309-298-2345, E-mail: grad-office@wiu.edu. *Dean,* Dr. Susan Martinelli-Fernandez, 309-298-1828.

College of Business and Technology Expenses: Contact institution. *Financial support:* Research assistantships, teaching assistantships with full tuition reimbursements, and unspecified assistantships available. Financial award applicants required to submit FAFSA. *Program availability:* Part-time. Offers accountancy (M Acct); applied statistics and decision analytics (MS); business administration (MBA, Certificate); business analytics (Certificate); business and technology (M Acct, MA, MBA, MS, Certificate); computer science (MS); economics (MA); educational technology specialist (Certificate); engineering technology leadership (MS); instructional design and technology (MS); instructional media development (Certificate); online and distance learning development (Certificate); supply chain management (Certificate); technology integration in education (Certificate); workplace learning and performance (Certificate). *Application deadline:* Applications are processed on a rolling basis. *Application fee:* $30. Electronic applications accepted. *Application Contact:* Dr. Nancy Parsons, Associate Provost and Director of Graduate Studies, 309-298-1806, Fax: 309-298-2345, E-mail: grad-office@wiu.edu. *Interim Dean,* Dr. William Bailey, 309-298-2442.

College of Education and Human Services Students: 281 full-time (155 women), 490 part-time (329 women); includes 108 minority (48 Black or African American, non-Hispanic/Latino; 1 American Indian or Alaska Native, non-Hispanic/Latino; 7 Asian, non-Hispanic/Latino; 39 Hispanic/Latino; 13 Two or more races, non-Hispanic/Latino), 26 international. Average age 30. 436 applicants, 84% accepted, 199 enrolled. Expenses: Contact institution. *Financial support:* Research assistantships with full tuition reimbursements, teaching assistantships with full tuition reimbursements, and unspecified assistantships available. Financial award applicants required to submit FAFSA. *Program availability:* Part-time, evening/weekend, online learning. Offers college student personnel (MS); counseling (MS Ed); curriculum and instruction (MS Ed); education and human services (MA, MS, MS Ed, Ed D, Certificate, Ed S); educational and interdisciplinary studies (MS Ed, Certificate); educational leadership (MS Ed, Ed D, Ed S); health sciences (MS); health services administration (Certificate); kinesiology (MS); law enforcement and justice administration (MA); police executive administration (Certificate); reading (MS Ed); recreation, park, and tourism administration (MS); special education (MS Ed); sport management (MS); teaching English to speakers of other languages (Certificate). *Application deadline:* Applications are processed on a rolling basis. *Application fee:* $30. Electronic applications accepted. *Application Contact:* Dr. Nancy Parsons, Associate Provost and Director of Graduate Studies, 309-298-1806, Fax: 309-298-2345, E-mail: grad-office@wiu.edu. *Dean,* Dr. Erskine Smith, 309-298-1690.

College of Fine Arts and Communication Students: 108 full-time (74 women), 23 part-time (13 women); includes 11 minority (10 Black or African American, non-Hispanic/Latino; 1 Hispanic/Latino), 12 international. Average age 27. 258 applicants, 49% accepted, 54 enrolled. Expenses: Contact institution. *Financial support:* Research assistantships with full tuition reimbursements, teaching assistantships with full tuition reimbursements, and unspecified assistantships available. Financial award applicants required to submit FAFSA. *Program availability:* Part-time. Offers communication (MA); communication sciences and disorders (MS); fine arts and communication (MA, MFA, MM, MS, Certificate); museum studies (MA, Certificate); music (MM); theatre (MFA). *Application deadline:* Applications are processed on a rolling basis. *Application fee:* $30. Electronic applications accepted. *Application Contact:* Dr. Nancy Parsons, Associate Provost and Director of Graduate Studies, 309-298-1806, Fax: 309-298-2345, E-mail: grad-office@wiu.edu. *Dean,* Billy Clow, 309-298-1618.

Illinois Institute for Rural Affairs Students: 6 full-time (4 women), 1 (woman) part-time; includes 2 minority (1 Hispanic/Latino; 1 Two or more races, non-Hispanic/Latino). Average age 35. 10 applicants, 100% accepted, 7 enrolled. Expenses: Contact institution. Offers community and economic development (MA). *Application deadline:* Applications are processed on a rolling basis. *Application fee:* $30. Electronic applications accepted. *Director,* Dr. Christopher Merrett, 309-298-2281, E-mail: cd-merrett@wiu.edu.

WESTERN KENTUCKY UNIVERSITY, Bowling Green, KY 42101

General Information State-supported, coed, comprehensive institution. CGS member. *Graduate housing:* Room and/or apartments guaranteed to single students; on-campus housing not available to married students. Housing application deadline: 4/1. *Research affiliation:* Bowling Green Field Station for Animal Studies (U.S. Fish and Wildlife Service), Roybal Center (gerontology).

GRADUATE UNITS

Graduate Studies *Program availability:* Part-time, evening/weekend, online learning.

College of Education and Behavioral Sciences *Program availability:* Part-time, evening/weekend, online learning. Offers adult education (MAE); clinical psychology (MA); counseling (MA Ed); education and behavioral sciences (MA, MAE, MS, Ed D, Ed S); educational leadership (Ed D); elementary education (MAE, Ed S); exceptional education: learning and behavioral disorders (MAE); exceptional education: moderate and severe disabilities (MAE); experimental psychology (MA); general psychology (MA); industrial/organizational psychology (MA); instructional design (MS); interdisciplinary early childhood education (MAE); library media education (MS); literacy education (MAE); middle grades education (MAE); school administration (Ed S); school counseling (P-12) (MA Ed); school principal (MAE); school psychology (Ed S); secondary education (MAE, Ed S); student affairs in higher education (MA Ed).

College of Health and Human Services *Program availability:* Part-time, evening/weekend. Offers athletic administration and coaching (MS); communication disorders (MS); health and human services (MHA, MPH, MS, MSN, MSW, DPT); healthcare administration (MHA); nursing (MSN); physical education (MS); physical therapy (DPT); public health (MPH); recreation and sport administration (MS); social work (MSW).

Gordon Ford College of Business *Program availability:* Part-time, evening/weekend. Offers applied economics (MA); business (MA, MBA); business administration (MBA).

Ogden College of Science and Engineering *Program availability:* Part-time, evening/weekend. Offers agriculture (MA Ed, MS); biology (MS); chemistry (MA Ed, MS); computational mathematics (MS); computer science (MS); geoscience (MS); homeland security sciences (MS); mathematics (MA, MS); physics (MA Ed); science and engineering (MA Ed, MS); technology management (MS).

Potter College of Arts and Letters Program availability: Part-time, evening/weekend, online learning. Offers art education (MA Ed); arts and letters (MA, MA Ed, MPA); communication (MA); criminology (MA); education (MA); English (MA Ed); folk studies (MA); French (MA Ed); German (MA Ed); history (MA, MA Ed); literature (MA); music (MA Ed); organizational communication (Graduate Certificate); political science (MPA); sociology (MA); Spanish (MA Ed); teaching English as a second language (MA); writing (MA).

WESTERN MICHIGAN UNIVERSITY, Kalamazoo, MI 49008

General Information State-supported, coed, university. CGS member. *Graduate housing:* Rooms and/or apartments available on a first-come, first-served basis to single and married students. Housing application deadline: 7/1. *Research affiliation:* Argonne National Laboratory (particle physics), Central States Universities, Inc., Ames Research Center (manufacturing education), Copper Development Association, Inc. (plastics extrusion), Pharmacia and Upjohn Company (electron microscopy), Flowserve Corporation (mechanical pumps and seals).

GRADUATE UNITS

Graduate College Program availability: Part-time, evening/weekend.

College of Arts and Sciences Program availability: Part-time. Offers anthropology (MA); applied and computational mathematics (MS); applied economics (MA, PhD); arts and sciences (MA, MFA, MIDA, MPA, MS, PhD, Graduate Certificate); behavior analysis (MA, PhD); biological sciences (MS, PhD); chemistry (MS, PhD); clinical psychology (PhD); communication (MA); comparative religion (MA, Graduate Certificate); creative writing (MFA, PhD); earth science (MA); English (MA, PhD); English teaching (MA); geographic information science (Graduate Certificate); geography (MA); geosciences (MS, PhD); health care administration (MPA, Graduate Certificate); history (MA, PhD); industrial/organizational behavior management (MA); international development administration (MIDA); mathematics education (MA, PhD); nonprofit leadership and administration (Graduate Certificate); philosophy (MA); physics (MA, PhD); political science (MA, PhD); public administration (PhD); science education (MA, PhD); sociology (MA, PhD); Spanish (MA, PhD); statistics (MS, PhD, Graduate Certificate).

College of Education and Human Development Program availability: Part-time. Offers athletic training (MS); career and technical education (MA); counseling psychology (MA, PhD); counselor education (MA, PhD); education and human development (MA, MS, Ed D, PhD, Ed D S, Graduate Certificate); educational leadership (MA, PhD, Ed S); educational technology (MA, Graduate Certificate); evaluation, measurement and research (MA, PhD); family and consumer sciences (MA); interdisciplinary education (PhD); literacy studies (MA); organizational learning and performance (MA); practice of teaching (MA); socio-cultural studies of education (MA); special education (MA, Ed D); sport management (MA); teaching children with visual impairments (MA).

College of Engineering and Applied Sciences Program availability: Part-time. Offers chemical and paper engineering (MS, MSE, PhD); civil and construction engineering (MSE); computer engineering (MSE); computer science (MS, PhD); electrical and computer engineering (PhD); electrical engineering (MSE); engineering and applied sciences (MS, MSE, PhD); engineering design, manufacturing, and management systems (MS); engineering management (MS); industrial engineering (MSE, PhD); mechanical engineering (MSE, PhD).

College of Fine Arts Program availability: Part-time. Offers art education (MA); fine arts (MA, MM, Graduate Certificate); music (MA); music composition (MM); music conducting (MM); music education (MM); music performance (MM); music therapy (MM).

College of Health and Human Services Program availability: Part-time. Offers audiology (Au D); health and human services (MA, MS, MSM, MSN, MSW, Au D, PhD, Graduate Certificate); interdisciplinary health services (PhD); nursing (MSN); occupational therapy (MS); orientation and mobility (MA); orientation and mobility of children (MA); physician assistant (MSM); social work (MSW); speech pathology and audiology (MA); vision rehabilitation therapy (MA).

Haworth College of Business Program availability: Part-time. Offers accountancy (MSA); business (MBA, MSA); business administration (MBA).

WESTERN NEW ENGLAND UNIVERSITY, Springfield, MA 01119

General Information Independent, coed, comprehensive institution. Enrollment: 3,833 graduate, professional, and undergraduate students; 468 full-time matriculated graduate/professional students (276 women), 618 part-time matriculated graduate/professional students (342 women). Enrollment by degree level: 426 master's, 658 doctoral, 2 other advanced degrees. Graduate faculty: 237 full-time (96 women), 33 part-time/adjunct (9 women). Tuition and fees vary according to program. *Graduate housing:* Rooms and/or apartments available to single and married students. Typical cost: $9230 per year for single students. Room charges vary according to board plan and housing facility selected. Housing application deadline: 3/9. *Student services:* Campus employment opportunities, campus safety program, career counseling, exercise/wellness program, free psychological counseling, international student services, services for students with disabilities, teacher training, writing training. *Library facilities:* D'Amour Library plus 1 other. *Collection:* Books: 107,000 (physical), 26,728 (digital/electronic); Serial titles: 46 (physical), 98,700 (digital/electronic); Databases: 122. Weekly public service hours: 97; study areas open 24 hours, 5–7 days a week. *Research affiliation:* New England Center for Children (applied behavior analysis).

Computer facilities: 530 computers available on campus for general student use. A campuswide network can be accessed from student residence rooms and from off campus. Online class registration is available.
Website: http://www.wne.edu/

General Application Contact: Matthew Fox, Director of Admissions for Graduate Students and Adult Learners, 413-782-1410, Fax: 413-782-1777, E-mail: study@wne.edu.

GRADUATE UNITS

College of Arts and Sciences Students: 226 part-time (183 women); includes 31 minority (9 Black or African American, non-Hispanic/Latino; 1 American Indian or Alaska Native, non-Hispanic/Latino; 11 Asian, non-Hispanic/Latino; 9 Hispanic/Latino; 1 Two or more races, non-Hispanic/Latino), 13 international. Average age 29. 144 applicants, 47% accepted, 59 enrolled. Faculty: 117 full-time (56 women). Expenses: Contact institution. Financial support: In 2016–17, 6 fellowships with tuition reimbursements were awarded. Support available to part-time students. Financial award application deadline: 4/15; financial award applicants required to submit FAFSA. In 2016, 66 master's, 4 doctorates awarded. Program availability: Part-time-only, evening/weekend, online learning. Offers applied behavior analysis (MS); arts and sciences (M Ed, MA, MAET, MAMT, MFA, MS, PhD); behavior analysis (MFA); creative writing (MFA); curriculum and instruction (M Ed); English for teachers (MAET); mathematics for teachers (MAMT); public relations (MA). Application fee: $30. Electronic applications accepted. Application

Contact: Matthew Fox, Director of Admissions for Graduate Students and Adult Learners, 413-782-1410, Fax: 413-782-1777, E-mail: study@wne.edu. Dean, Dr. Saeed Ghahramani, 413-782-1218, Fax: 413-796-2118, E-mail: sghahram@wne.edu.

College of Business Students: 136 part-time (60 women); includes 13 minority (6 Black or African American, non-Hispanic/Latino; 4 Asian, non-Hispanic/Latino; 3 Hispanic/Latino), 4 international. Average age 30. 102 applicants, 33% accepted, 30 enrolled. Faculty: 36 full-time (12 women). Expenses: Contact institution. Financial support: Application deadline: 4/15; applicants required to submit FAFSA. In 2016, 93 master's awarded. Program availability: Part-time, evening/weekend, online learning. Offers accounting (MSA); business (MBA, MS, MSA); general business (MBA); organizational leadership (MS); sport management (MBA). Application deadline: Applications are processed on a rolling basis. Application fee: $30. Electronic applications accepted. Application Contact: Matthew Fox, Director of Admissions for Graduate Students and Adult Learners, 413-782-1410, Fax: 413-782-1777, E-mail: study@wne.edu. Dean, Dr. Rob Kleine, 413-782-1395, E-mail: rob.kleine@wne.edu.

College of Engineering Students: 123 part-time (17 women); includes 10 minority (1 Black or African American, non-Hispanic/Latino; 2 Asian, non-Hispanic/Latino; 6 Hispanic/Latino; 1 Two or more races, non-Hispanic/Latino), 55 international. Average age 30. 476 applicants, 28% accepted, 33 enrolled. Faculty: 35 full-time (4 women). Expenses: Contact institution. Financial support: In 2016–17, 6 fellowships with tuition reimbursements were awarded. Financial award application deadline: 4/15; financial award applicants required to submit FAFSA. In 2016, 48 master's, 2 doctorates awarded. Program availability: Part-time, evening/weekend, online learning. Offers business and engineering information systems (MSEM); civil engineering (MS); electrical engineering (MSEE); engineering (MS, MSEE, MSEM, MSME, PhD); engineering management (MSEM, PhD); general engineering management (MSEM); industrial engineering (MS); mechanical engineering (MSME); mechatronics (MSEE, MSME); production and manufacturing systems (MSEM); quality engineering (MSEM). Application deadline: For fall admission, 1/15 priority date for domestic students. Applications are processed on a rolling basis. Application fee: $30. Electronic applications accepted. Application Contact: Matthew Fox, Director of Admissions for Graduate Students and Adult Learners, 413-782-1410, Fax: 413-782-1777, E-mail: study@wne.edu. Dean, Dr. S. Hossein Cheraghi, 413-782-1285, E-mail: cheraghi@wne.edu.

College of Pharmacy Students: 294 full-time (183 women); includes 43 minority (11 Black or African American, non-Hispanic/Latino; 1 American Indian or Alaska Native, non-Hispanic/Latino; 20 Asian, non-Hispanic/Latino; 11 Hispanic/Latino), 2 international. Average age 24. 341 applicants, 43% accepted, 75 enrolled. Faculty: 28 full-time (12 women), 3 part-time/adjunct (1 woman). Expenses: Contact institution. Financial support: Scholarships/grants available. Financial award application deadline: 4/15; financial award applicants required to submit FAFSA. In 2016, 66 doctorates awarded. Offers pharmacy (Pharm D). Application deadline: For fall admission, 3/1 for domestic students. Applications are processed on a rolling basis. Application fee: $150. Electronic applications accepted. Application Contact: Lori Berg, Assistant Director of Pharmacy Admissions, 413-796-2073, Fax: 413-796-2266, E-mail: rxadmissions@wne.edu. Dean, Dr. Evan T. Robinson, 413-796-2323, E-mail: erobinson@wne.edu.

Division of Occupational Therapy Faculty: 5 full-time (all women). Expenses: Contact institution. Financial support: Unspecified assistantships available. Financial award application deadline: 4/15; financial award applicants required to submit FAFSA. Offers occupational therapy (OTD). Application deadline: Applications are processed on a rolling basis. Electronic applications accepted. Application Contact: Matthew Fox, Director of Admissions for Graduate Students and Adult Learners, 413-782-1410, Fax: 413-782-1777, E-mail: study@wne.edu. Chair and Director of Occupational Therapy, Dr. Cathy Dow-Royer, 413-782-1423, E-mail: cathy.dow-royer@wne.edu.

School of Law Students: 174 full-time (93 women), 133 part-time (82 women); includes 80 minority (41 Black or African American, non-Hispanic/Latino; 4 American Indian or Alaska Native, non-Hispanic/Latino; 12 Asian, non-Hispanic/Latino; 23 Hispanic/Latino). Average age 32. 645 applicants, 55% accepted, 72 enrolled. Faculty: 21 full-time (12 women), 30 part-time/adjunct (8 women). Expenses: Contact institution. Financial support: Career-related internships or fieldwork, Federal Work-Study, and scholarships/grants available. Support available to part-time students. Financial award application deadline: 4/15; financial award applicants required to submit FAFSA. In 2016, 15 master's, 105 doctorates awarded. Program availability: Part-time, evening/weekend. Offers estate planning and elder law (LL M, MS); law (JD). Application deadline: For fall admission, 3/15 priority date for domestic students. Applications are processed on a rolling basis. Application fee: $0. Electronic applications accepted. Application Contact: Amy Mangione, Assistant Dean of Law/Director of Law Admissions, 413-782-1286, Fax: 413-796-2067, E-mail: admissions@law.wne.edu. Dean/Professor, Eric Gouvin, 413-796-2031, E-mail: eric.gouvin@law.wne.edu.

See Display on next page and Close-Up on page 909.

WESTERN NEW MEXICO UNIVERSITY, Silver City, NM 88062-0680

General Information State-supported, coed, comprehensive institution. *Graduate housing:* Rooms and/or apartments available on a first-come, first-served basis to single and married students. Housing application deadline: 6/30.

GRADUATE UNITS

Graduate Division Program availability: Part-time, evening/weekend, online learning. Offers interdisciplinary studies (MA); occupational therapy (MOT); social work (MSW). Electronic applications accepted.

School of Business Program availability: Part-time, online learning. Offers business administration (MBA). Electronic applications accepted.

School of Education Program availability: Part-time, online learning. Offers bilingual education (MAT); educational leadership (MA); elementary education (MAT); reading (MAT); secondary education (MAT); special education (MAT); TESOL (teaching English to speakers of other languages) (MAT). Electronic applications accepted.

WESTERN OREGON UNIVERSITY, Monmouth, OR 97361

General Information State-supported, coed, comprehensive institution. *Graduate housing:* Room and/or apartments available on a first-come, first-served basis to single students; on-campus housing not available to married students. *Research affiliation:* Teaching Research Institute (education).

GRADUATE UNITS

Graduate Programs Program availability: Part-time, evening/weekend, online learning.

College of Education Program availability: Part-time, evening/weekend, online learning. Offers bilingual education (MS Ed); deaf education (MS Ed); early childhood special education (MS Ed); education (MAT, MS, MS Ed); health (MS Ed); humanities (MAT, MS Ed); information technology (MS Ed); initial licensure (MAT); mathematics (MAT, MS Ed); rehabilitation counseling (MS); science (MAT, MS Ed); secondary education (MAT, MS Ed); social science (MAT, MS Ed); special education (MS, MS Ed).

College of Liberal Arts and Sciences Program availability: Part-time, evening/weekend. Offers contemporary music (MM); criminal justice (MA, MS); liberal arts and sciences (MA, MM, MS).

WESTERN SEMINARY, Portland, OR 97215-3367

General Information Independent-religious, coed, graduate-only institution. *Graduate housing:* On-campus housing not available.

GRADUATE UNITS

Graduate Programs *Program availability:* Part-time, evening/weekend, online learning. Offers biblical and theological studies (MA, G Dip); biblical studies (Certificate); chaplaincy (MA); coaching (MA); counseling (MA, Certificate); divinity (M Div); intercultural studies (MA, D Miss, Certificate, G Dip); Jewish ministry (MA); pastoral care to women (MA); pastoral counseling (M Div); theology (Th M); youth ministry (MA).

WESTERN SEMINARY–SACRAMENTO CAMPUS, Sacramento, CA 95821

General Information Independent-religious, coed, graduate-only institution.

GRADUATE UNITS

Graduate Certificate Programs *Program availability:* Online learning. Offers Bible (Graduate Certificate); coaching (Graduate Certificate); pastoral care to women (Graduate Certificate); theology (Graduate Certificate); youth and family (Graduate Certificate).

Graduate Diploma Programs Offers Bible and theology (Graduate Diploma); ministry (Graduate Diploma); pastoral care to women (Graduate Diploma).

Master of Divinity Program Offers divinity (M Div).

Program in Biblical and Theological Studies Offers biblical and theological studies (MA).

Program in Marital and Family Therapy Offers marital and family therapy (MA).

Program in Ministry and Leadership Offers ministry and leadership (MA).

WESTERN SEMINARY–SAN JOSE CAMPUS, Los Gatos, CA 95032-4520

General Information Independent-religious, coed, graduate-only institution. *Graduate housing:* On-campus housing not available.

GRADUATE UNITS

Graduate Programs *Program availability:* Part-time, evening/weekend, online learning. Offers Bible and theology (Graduate Diploma); Bible, camp and conference ministry (CGS); Biblical and theological studies (MA); coaching (CGS); expositional ministry (M Div); marital and family therapy (MA); ministry (Graduate Diploma); ministry and leadership (MA); pastoral care to women (CGS, Graduate Diploma); pastoral ministry (M Div); theology (CGS); youth and family (CGS). Electronic applications accepted.

WESTERN STATE COLLEGE OF LAW AT ARGOSY UNIVERSITY, Irvine, CA 92618-3601

General Information Proprietary, coed, graduate-only institution. *Graduate housing:* On-campus housing not available.

GRADUATE UNITS

Professional Program *Program availability:* Part-time, evening/weekend. Offers law (JD). Electronic applications accepted.

WESTERN STATE COLORADO UNIVERSITY, Gunnison, CO 81231

General Information State-supported, coed, comprehensive institution.

GRADUATE UNITS

Graduate Programs in Education *Program availability:* Online learning. Offers education administrator leadership (MA); reading leadership (MA); teacher leadership (MA).

Program in Creative Writing *Program availability:* Online learning. Offers mainstream genre fiction (MFA); poetry (MFA); screenwriting (MFA).

Program in Environmental Management *Program availability:* Online learning. Offers integrative land management (MEM); sustainable and resilient communities (MEM).

WESTERN THEOLOGICAL SEMINARY, Holland, MI 49423-3622

General Information Independent-religious, coed, graduate-only institution. *Graduate housing:* Rooms and/or apartments available on a first-come, first-served basis to single and married students. Housing application deadline: 5/1.

GRADUATE UNITS

Graduate and Professional Programs *Program availability:* Part-time, 100% online, blended/hybrid learning. Offers divinity (M Div); ministry (D Min); theology (M Th, MA); urban pastoral ministry (Graduate Certificate). Electronic applications accepted.

WESTERN UNIVERSITY OF HEALTH SCIENCES, Pomona, CA 91766-1854

General Information Independent, coed, graduate-only institution. *Enrollment by degree level:* 589 master's, 3,274 doctoral. *Graduate faculty:* 305 full-time (153 women), 67 part-time/adjunct (29 women). *Tuition:* Full-time $23,331. *Required fees:* $40. Tuition and fees vary according to course level, course load, degree level, program and student level. *Graduate housing:* Rooms and/or apartments available on a first-come, first-served basis to single and married students. Typical cost: $1389 per year for single students; $1389 per year for married students. Room charges vary according to campus/location and housing facility selected. *Student services:* Campus employment opportunities, campus safety program, career counseling, exercise/wellness program, free psychological counseling, grant writing training, international student services, low-cost health insurance, services for students with disabilities, teacher training. *Library facilities:* Pumerantz Library plus 1 other. *Collection:* Books: 19,940 (physical), 1,850 (digital/electronic); Serial titles: 762 (physical), 27,772 (digital/electronic); Databases: 75. Weekly public service hours: 91; students can reserve study rooms. *Research affiliation:* Fulgent (biomedical research), Neuralstem (biomedical research), Novartis Pharmaceuticals (biomedical research), Novo Nordisk (biomedical research), Merck & Company, Inc. (biomedical research), Aspire Biomet, Inc (cancer research).

Computer facilities: 56 computers available on campus for general student use. A campuswide network can be accessed. Online class registration is available. Website: http://www.westernu.edu/

General Application Contact: Admissions Office, 909-469-5335, Fax: 909-469-5570, E-mail: admissions@westernu.edu.

GRADUATE UNITS

College of Allied Health Professions Students: 374 full-time (249 women), 52 part-time (32 women); includes 231 minority (20 Black or African American, non-Hispanic/Latino; 101 Asian, non-Hispanic/Latino; 74 Hispanic/Latino; 2 Native Hawaiian or other Pacific Islander, non-Hispanic/Latino; 34 Two or more races, non-

Hispanic/Latino), 4 international. Average age 28. 3,113 applicants, 8% accepted, 171 enrolled. *Faculty:* 26 full-time (19 women), 2 part-time/adjunct (0 women). Expenses: Contact institution. *Financial support:* Scholarships/grants available. Financial award application deadline: 3/2; financial award applicants required to submit FAFSA. In 2016, 98 master's, 75 doctorates awarded. Offers allied health professions (MS, DPT); health sciences (MS); physical therapy (DPT); physician assistant studies (MS). *Application deadline:* For fall admission, 11/1 for domestic and international students. *Application fee:* $60. Electronic applications accepted. *Application Contact:* Karen Hutton-Lopez, Director of Admissions, 909-469-5650, Fax: 909-469-5570, E-mail: admissions@westernu.edu. *Dean,* Dr. Stephanie Bowlin, 909-469-5390, Fax: 909-469-5438, E-mail: sbowlin@westernu.edu.

College of Dental Medicine Students: 274 full-time (134 women); includes 168 minority (5 Black or African American, non-Hispanic/Latino; 3 American Indian or Alaska Native, non-Hispanic/Latino; 113 Asian, non-Hispanic/Latino; 31 Hispanic/Latino; 1 Native Hawaiian or other Pacific Islander, non-Hispanic/Latino; 15 Two or more races, non-Hispanic/Latino), 6 international. Average age 28. 2,843 applicants, 6% accepted, 69 enrolled. *Faculty:* 39 full-time (18 women), 18 part-time/adjunct (7 women). Expenses: Contact institution. *Financial support:* Scholarships/grants available. Financial award application deadline: 3/2; financial award applicants required to submit FAFSA. In 2016, 67 doctorates awarded. Offers dental medicine (DMD). *Application deadline:* For fall admission, 12/1 for domestic and international students. Applications are processed on a rolling basis. *Application fee:* $60. Electronic applications accepted. *Application Contact:* Marie Anderson, Director of Admissions, 909-469-5335, Fax: 909-469-5570, E-mail: admissions@westernu.edu. *Dean,* Dr. Steven Friedrichsen, 909-706-3911, E-mail: sfriedrichsen@westernu.edu.

College of Graduate Nursing Students: 303 full-time (253 women), 33 part-time (30 women); includes 218 minority (10 Black or African American, non-Hispanic/Latino; 1 American Indian or Alaska Native, non-Hispanic/Latino; 104 Asian, non-Hispanic/Latino; 73 Hispanic/Latino; 1 Native Hawaiian or other Pacific Islander, non-Hispanic/Latino; 29 Two or more races, non-Hispanic/Latino), 2 international. Average age 33. 536 applicants, 38% accepted, 127 enrolled. *Faculty:* 20 full-time (17 women), 16 part-time/adjunct (11 women). Expenses: Contact institution. *Financial support:* Fellowships, research assistantships, teaching assistantships, and scholarships/grants available. Support available to part-time students. Financial award application deadline: 3/2; financial award applicants required to submit FAFSA. In 2016, 91 master's, 17 doctorates awarded. *Program availability:* Part-time, evening/weekend, blended/hybrid learning. Offers administrative nurse leader (MSN); clinical nurse leader (MSN); nursing (MSN, DNP); nursing practice (DNP). *Application fee:* $60. Electronic applications accepted. *Application Contact:* Kathryn Ford, Director of Admissions/International Student Advisor, 909-469-5335, Fax: 909-469-5570, E-mail: admissions@westernu.edu. *Dean,* Dr. Mary Lopez, 909-706-3860, Fax: 909-469-5521, E-mail: mlopez@westernu.edu.

College of Optometry Students: 331 full-time (247 women); includes 212 minority (11 Black or African American, non-Hispanic/Latino; 124 Asian, non-Hispanic/Latino; 38 Hispanic/Latino; 39 Two or more races, non-Hispanic/Latino), 23 international. Average age 27. 756 applicants, 22% accepted, 74 enrolled. *Faculty:* 29 full-time (14 women), 6 part-time/adjunct (2 women). Expenses: Contact institution. *Financial support:* Career-related internships or fieldwork, scholarships/grants, and traineeships available. Financial award application deadline: 3/2; financial award applicants required to submit FAFSA. In 2016, 73 doctorates awarded. Offers optometry (OD). *Application deadline:* For fall admission, 5/1 for domestic and international students. Applications are processed on a rolling basis. *Application fee:* $65. Electronic applications accepted. *Application Contact:* Marie Anderson, Director of Admissions, 909-469-5335, Fax: 909-469-5570, E-mail: admissions@westernu.edu. *Dean,* Dr. Elizabeth Hoppe, 909-706-3497, E-mail: ehoppe@westernu.edu.

College of Osteopathic Medicine of the Pacific Students: 1,301 full-time (626 women); includes 575 minority (16 Black or African American, non-Hispanic/Latino; 1 American Indian or Alaska Native, non-Hispanic/Latino; 380 Asian, non-Hispanic/Latino; 81 Hispanic/Latino; 2 Native Hawaiian or other Pacific Islander, non-Hispanic/Latino; 95 Two or more races, non-Hispanic/Latino), 16 international. Average age 27. 11,178 applicants, 5% accepted, 298 enrolled. *Faculty:* 70 full-time (30 women), 22 part-time/adjunct (6 women). Expenses: Contact institution. *Financial support:* Scholarships/grants and unspecified assistantships available. Financial award application deadline: 3/2; financial award applicants required to submit FAFSA. In 2016, 314 doctorates awarded. Offers osteopathic medicine (DO). *Application deadline:* For fall admission, 2/1 for domestic and international students. Applications are processed on a rolling basis. *Application fee:* $65. Electronic applications accepted. *Application Contact:* Susan Hanson, Director of Admissions, 909-469-5335, Fax: 909-469-5570, E-mail: admissions@westernu.edu. *Dean,* Dr. Paula Crone, 541-259-0206, Fax: 541-259-0201, E-mail: pcrone@westernu.edu.

College of Pharmacy Students: 539 full-time (356 women), 9 part-time (5 women); includes 361 minority (18 Black or African American, non-Hispanic/Latino; 1 American Indian or Alaska Native, non-Hispanic/Latino; 284 Asian, non-Hispanic/Latino; 39 Hispanic/Latino; 19 Two or more races, non-Hispanic/Latino), 19 international. Average age 27. 1,167 applicants, 32% accepted, 149 enrolled. *Faculty:* 45 full-time (21 women), 2 part-time/adjunct (1 woman). Expenses: Contact institution. *Financial support:* Scholarships/grants available. Financial award application deadline: 3/2; financial award applicants required to submit FAFSA. In 2016, 12 master's, 132 doctorates awarded. Offers pharmaceutical sciences (MS); pharmacy (MS, Pharm D). *Application deadline:* For fall admission, 11/1 for domestic and international students. *Application fee:* $65. Electronic applications accepted. *Application Contact:* Kathryn Ford, Director of Admissions, 909-469-5335, Fax: 909-469-5570, E-mail: admissions@westernu.edu. *Dean,* Dr. Daniel Robinson, 909-469-5533, Fax: 909-469-5539, E-mail: drobinson@westernu.edu.

College of Podiatric Medicine Students: 150 full-time (49 women); includes 76 minority (5 Black or African American, non-Hispanic/Latino; 33 Asian, non-Hispanic/Latino; 16 Hispanic/Latino; 22 Two or more races, non-Hispanic/Latino), 1 international. Average age 27. 411 applicants, 24% accepted, 36 enrolled. *Faculty:* 10 full-time (5 women), 4 part-time/adjunct (1 woman). *Financial support:* Scholarships/grants available. Financial award application deadline: 3/2; financial award applicants required to submit FAFSA. In 2016, 25 doctorates awarded. Offers podiatric medicine (DPM). *Application deadline:* For fall admission, 6/30 for domestic and international students. Applications are processed on a rolling basis. *Application fee:* $0. Electronic applications accepted. *Application Contact:* Marie Anderson, Director of Admissions, 909-469-5335, Fax: 909-469-5570, E-mail: admissions@westernu.edu. *Dean,* Dr. Lawrence B. Harkless, 909-706-3933, E-mail: lharkless@westernu.edu.

College of Veterinary Medicine Students: 426 full-time (338 women); includes 185 minority (15 Black or African American, non-Hispanic/Latino; 1 American Indian or Alaska Native, non-Hispanic/Latino; 61 Asian, non-Hispanic/Latino; 80 Hispanic/Latino; 1 Native Hawaiian or other Pacific Islander, non-Hispanic/Latino; 27 Two or more races,

non-Hispanic/Latino), 7 international. Average age 27. 622 applicants, 43% accepted, 104 enrolled. *Faculty:* 51 full-time (25 women), 6 part-time/adjunct (2 women). Expenses: Contact institution. *Financial support:* Institutionally sponsored loans, scholarships/grants, and veterans' educational benefits available. Financial award application deadline: 3/2; financial award applicants required to submit FAFSA. In 2016, 105 doctorates awarded. Offers veterinary medicine (DVM). *Application deadline:* For fall admission, 9/15 for domestic and international students. *Application fee:* $50. Electronic applications accepted. *Application Contact:* Karen Hutton-Lopez, Director of Admissions, 909-469-5650, Fax: 909-469-5570, E-mail: admissions@westernu.edu. *Dean,* Dr. Phil Nelson, 909-469-5661, Fax: 909-469-5635, E-mail: pnelson@westernu.edu.

Graduate College of Biomedical Sciences Students: 47 full-time (22 women); includes 38 minority (6 Black or African American, non-Hispanic/Latino; 1 American Indian or Alaska Native, non-Hispanic/Latino; 16 Asian, non-Hispanic/Latino; 13 Hispanic/Latino; 2 Two or more races, non-Hispanic/Latino), 1 international. Average age 26. 319 applicants, 15% accepted, 39 enrolled. *Faculty:* 8 full-time (1 woman), 5 part-time/adjunct (2 women). Expenses: Contact institution. *Financial support:* Scholarships/grants available. Financial award application deadline: 3/2; financial award applicants required to submit FAFSA. In 2016, 40 master's awarded. Offers biomedical sciences (MS); medical sciences (MS). *Application deadline:* Applications are processed on a rolling basis. *Application fee:* $50. Electronic applications accepted. *Application Contact:* Kathryn Ford, Director of Admissions/International Student Advisor, 909-469-5335, Fax: 909-469-5570, E-mail: kford@westernu.edu. *Dean,* Dr. Michel Baudry, 909-469-8271, E-mail: mbaudry@westernu.edu.

WESTERN WASHINGTON UNIVERSITY, Bellingham, WA 98225-5996

General Information State-supported, coed, comprehensive institution. CGS member. *Graduate housing:* Rooms and/or apartments available on a first-come, first-served basis to single and married students. Housing application deadline: 5/1. *Research affiliation:* Golden Associates, American Metals Technology, Teck Cominco Ltd., Research Corporation, Dreyfus Foundation, NARSAD (mental health).

GRADUATE UNITS

Graduate School *Program availability:* Part-time. Electronic applications accepted.

College of Business and Economics *Program availability:* Part-time, evening/weekend. Offers business and economics (MBA, MP Acc). Electronic applications accepted.

College of Fine and Performing Arts *Program availability:* Part-time. Offers fine and performing arts (M Mus, MA); music (M Mus). Electronic applications accepted.

College of Humanities and Social Sciences *Program availability:* Part-time. Offers anthropology (MA); communication sciences and disorders (MA); English (MA); exercise science (MS); experimental psychology (MS); history (MA); humanities and social sciences (M Ed, MA, MS); mental health counseling (MS); political science (MA); school counseling (M Ed); sport psychology (MS). Electronic applications accepted.

College of Sciences and Technology Offers biology (MS); chemistry (MS); computer science (MS); geology (MS); mathematics (MS); natural science/science education (M Ed); sciences and technology (M Ed, MS). Electronic applications accepted.

Huxley College of the Environment *Program availability:* Part-time. Offers environment (M Ed, MS); environmental education (M Ed); environmental science (MS); geography (MS); marine and estuarine science (MS). Electronic applications accepted.

Woodring College of Education *Program availability:* Part-time, online learning. Offers continuing and college education (M Ed); education (M Ed, MA, MIT); educational administration (M Ed); elementary education (M Ed); rehabilitation counseling (MA); secondary education (MIT); special education (M Ed); student affairs administration (M Ed). Electronic applications accepted.

WESTFIELD STATE UNIVERSITY, Westfield, MA 01086

General Information State-supported, coed, comprehensive institution. *Enrollment:* 6,383 graduate, professional, and undergraduate students; 261 full-time matriculated graduate/professional students (193 women), 319 part-time matriculated graduate/professional students (211 women). *Enrollment by degree level:* 543 master's, 37 other advanced degrees. *Graduate faculty:* 48 full-time (21 women), 60 part-time/adjunct (39 women). Tuition, state resident: part-time $318 per semester hour. Tuition, nonresident: part-time $318 per semester hour. *Required fees:* $75 per semester. Tuition and fees vary according to course load and program. *Graduate housing:* On-campus housing not available. *Student services:* Career counseling, exercise/wellness program, free psychological counseling, low-cost health insurance, multicultural affairs office. *Library facilities:* Governor Joseph B. Ely Library. *Collection:* Books: 139,363 (physical), 156,760 (digital/electronic); Serial titles: 612 (physical), 26,637 (digital/electronic); Databases: 90. Weekly public service hours: 92; students can reserve study rooms.

Computer facilities: 727 computers available on campus for general student use. A campuswide network can be accessed from student residence rooms and from off campus. Online class registration, online transcripts, online billing information, Web portal are available.

Website: http://www.westfield.ma.edu/

General Application Contact: Shelly Henrichon, Coordinator of DGCE Admissions, 413-572-8022, Fax: 413-572-5227, E-mail: mhenrichon@westfield.ma.edu.

GRADUATE UNITS

College of Graduate and Continuing Education Students: 261 full-time (193 women), 319 part-time (211 women); includes 92 minority (22 Black or African American, non-Hispanic/Latino; 3 American Indian or Alaska Native, non-Hispanic/Latino; 5 Asian, non-Hispanic/Latino; 51 Hispanic/Latino; 11 Two or more races, non-Hispanic/Latino), 2 international. Average age 32. 260 applicants, 79% accepted, 142 enrolled. *Faculty:* 48 full-time (21 women), 60 part-time/adjunct (39 women). Expenses: Contact institution. *Financial support:* In 2016–17, 16 students received support. Unspecified assistantships and SOS scholarships for education majors only available. Financial award application deadline: 3/1; financial award applicants required to submit FAFSA. In 2016, 197 master's, 16 other advanced degrees awarded. *Program availability:* Part-time, evening/weekend. Offers accounting (MS); applied behavior analysis (MA); biology teacher education (M Ed); chemistry teacher education (M Ed); counseling (MA); criminal justice (MS); criminal justice administration (MPA); early childhood education (M Ed); elementary education (M Ed); English (MA); forensic mental health counseling (MA); general science teacher education (M Ed); history teacher education (M Ed); mathematics teacher education (M Ed); mental health counseling (MA); moderate disabilities, 5-12 (M Ed); moderate disabilities, preK-8 (M Ed); non-profit management (MPA); physical education teacher education (M Ed); public management (MPA); reading specialist (M Ed); school adjustment counseling (MA); school guidance counseling (MA); secondary education (M Ed); secondary education-biology (M Ed); secondary education-chemistry (M Ed); secondary education-general science (M Ed); secondary education-history (M Ed); secondary education-mathematics (M Ed); secondary education-physical education (M Ed); social work (MSW); special education (M Ed); vocational technical education (M Ed). *Application deadline:* For fall admission, 6/30 for domestic students; for spring admission, 10/31 for domestic students; for summer admission, 3/31 for domestic students. Applications are processed on a rolling basis. *Application fee:* $50. Electronic applications accepted. *Application Contact:* Shelly Henrichon, Coordinator of DGCE Admissions, 413-572-8022, Fax: 413-572-5227, E-mail: mhenrichon@westfield.ma.edu. *Interim Dean of Graduate and Continuing Education,* Dr. Shelley Tinkham, 413-572-8030, Fax: 413-572-5227, E-mail: shelleytinkham@westfield.ma.edu.

WEST LIBERTY UNIVERSITY, West Liberty, WV 26074
General Information State-supported, coed, comprehensive institution. *Enrollment:* 90 full-time matriculated graduate/professional students (60 women), 84 part-time matriculated graduate/professional students (60 women). *Enrollment by degree level:* 174 master's. *Graduate faculty:* 6 full-time (3 women). Tuition, state resident: full-time $7074; part-time $393 per credit. Tuition, nonresident: full-time $11,124; part-time $618 per credit. *Student services:* Campus employment opportunities, career counseling, exercise/wellness program, international student services, services for students with disabilities. *Library facilities:* Paul N. Elbin Library.
Computer facilities: Computer purchase and lease plans are available. A campuswide network can be accessed from student residence rooms and from off campus. Online class registration is available.
Website: http://www.westliberty.edu/

GRADUATE UNITS
College of Education Expenses: Contact institution. Offers education (MA Ed). Electronic applications accepted. *Dean,* Dr. Keely Camden, 304-336-8247, E-mail: kcamden@westliberty.edu.

School of Professional Studies Expenses: Contact institution. Offers justice leadership (MPS); organizational leadership (MPS). *Application deadline:* Applications are processed on a rolling basis. *Dean,* Dr. Thomas Michaud, 304-217-2800, E-mail: tmichaud@westliberty.edu.

WESTMINSTER COLLEGE, New Wilmington, PA 16172-0001
General Information Independent-religious, coed, comprehensive institution. *Enrollment:* 1,252 graduate, professional, and undergraduate students; 50 part-time matriculated graduate/professional students (37 women). *Enrollment by degree level:* 50 master's. *Graduate faculty:* 4 full-time (2 women), 21 part-time/adjunct (15 women). *Tuition:* Full-time $1362; part-time $454 per semester hour. One-time fee: $235.50 full-time. *Graduate housing:* On-campus housing not available. *Student services:* Career counseling, multicultural affairs office, services for students with disabilities. *Library facilities:* McGill Memorial Library plus 1 other. *Collection:* Books: 160,296 (physical), 771,138 (digital/electronic); Serial titles: 89 (physical), 30,100 (digital/electronic); Databases: 70. Weekly public service hours: 104; students can reserve study rooms.
Computer facilities: Computer purchase and lease plans are available. 144 computers available on campus for general student use. A campuswide network can be accessed from student residence rooms and from off campus. Online class registration is available.
Website: http://www.westminster.edu/
General Application Contact: Dr. Robert L. Zorn, Graduate Director, 724-946-7055, Fax: 724-946-6158, E-mail: rornrl@westminster.edu.

GRADUATE UNITS
Graduate School Expenses: Contact institution. *Financial support:* Career-related internships or fieldwork and scholarships/grants available. *Program availability:* Part-time, evening/weekend. Offers school counseling (M Ed, Certificate); school principal K-12 (M Ed); school superintendent (Certificate); special education and reading specialist (M Ed, Certificate). *Application deadline:* For fall admission, 8/15 priority date for domestic students; for spring admission, 1/8 priority date for domestic students. Applications are processed on a rolling basis. *Application fee:* $35. *Application Contact:* Dr. Darwin W. Huey, Graduate Education Director, 724-946-7186, Fax: 724-946-6158, E-mail: hueydw@westminster.edu. *Director,* Dr. Robert L. Zorn, 724-946-7031, Fax: 724-946-6158.

WESTMINSTER COLLEGE, Salt Lake City, UT 84105-3697
General Information Independent, coed, comprehensive institution. *Enrollment:* 2,692 graduate, professional, and undergraduate students; 352 full-time matriculated graduate/professional students (206 women), 213 part-time matriculated graduate/professional students (112 women). *Enrollment by degree level:* 565 master's, 2 other advanced degrees. *Graduate faculty:* 51 full-time (29 women), 49 part-time/adjunct (24 women). *Tuition:* Full-time $14,631; part-time $1045 per credit hour. *Required fees:* $182; $13 per credit hour. Tuition and fees vary according to course load and program. *Graduate housing:* Room and/or apartments available on a first-come, first-served basis to single students; on-campus housing not available to married students. Typical cost: $9908 (including board). *Student services:* Campus employment opportunities, campus safety program, career counseling, exercise/wellness program, free psychological counseling, grant writing training, international student services, low-cost health insurance, multicultural affairs office, services for students with disabilities, teacher training, writing training. *Library facilities:* Giovale Library plus 1 other. *Collection:* Books: 95,039 (physical), 364,687 (digital/electronic); Databases: 56. Students can reserve study rooms. *Research affiliation:* Key Bank (entrepreneurship), Zions Bank (entrepreneurship), International Psychotherapy (clinical training).
Computer facilities: 200 computers available on campus for general student use. A campuswide network can be accessed from student residence rooms and from off campus. Online class registration is available.
Website: http://www.westminstercollege.edu/
General Application Contact: Ron Headings, Associate Vice President for Enrollment Management and Student Success, 801-832-2200, Fax: 801-832-3101, E-mail: admission@westminstercollege.edu.

GRADUATE UNITS
The Bill and Vieve Gore School of Business Students: 120 full-time (43 women), 124 part-time (45 women); includes 47 minority (8 Black or African American, non-Hispanic/Latino; 1 American Indian or Alaska Native, non-Hispanic/Latino; 15 Asian, non-Hispanic/Latino; 18 Hispanic/Latino; 5 Two or more races, non-Hispanic/Latino; 12 international. Average age 34. 97 applicants, 79% accepted, 56 enrolled. *Faculty:* 19 full-time (5 women), 20 part-time/adjunct (7 women). Expenses: Contact institution. *Financial support:* In 2016–17, 87 students received support. Career-related internships or fieldwork, scholarships/grants, unspecified assistantships, and tuition reimbursements, tuition remission available. Financial award applicants required to submit FAFSA. In 2016, 119 master's, 10 other advanced degrees awarded. *Program availability:* Part-time, evening/weekend, 100% online. Offers accountancy (M Acc); business administration (MBA, Certificate); technology commercialization (MBA). *Application deadline:* For fall admission, 5/20 priority date for domestic and international students; for spring admission, 10/7 priority date for domestic and international students; for summer admission, 2/5 priority date for domestic and international students. Applications are processed on a rolling basis. *Application fee:* $50. Electronic applications accepted. *Application Contact:* Ashley Williams, Director of Graduate Admissions, 801-832-2213, Fax: 801-832-3101, E-mail: awilliams@westminstercollege.edu. *Interim Dean, Bill and Vieve Gore School of Business,* Melissa Koerner, 801-832-2600, Fax: 801-832-3106, E-mail: mkoerner@westminstercollege.edu.

Master of Science in Mental Health Counseling Program Students: 19 full-time (18 women), 11 part-time (8 women); includes 3 minority (1 Asian, non-Hispanic/Latino; 1 Hispanic/Latino; 1 Two or more races, non-Hispanic/Latino). Average age 31. 23 applicants, 70% accepted, 10 enrolled. *Faculty:* 4 full-time (all women), 1 (woman) part-time/adjunct. Expenses: Contact institution. *Financial support:* In 2016–17, 2 students received support. Career-related internships or fieldwork, scholarships/grants, unspecified assistantships, and tuition reimbursements, tuition remission available. Support available to part-time students. Financial award applicants required to submit FAFSA. In 2016, 17 master's awarded. *Program availability:* Part-time, evening/weekend. Offers mental health counseling (MSMHC). *Application deadline:* For fall admission, 2/1 priority date for domestic and international students. Applications are processed on a rolling basis. *Application fee:* $50. Electronic applications accepted. *Application Contact:* Ashley Williams, Director of Graduate Admissions, 801-832-2213, Fax: 801-832-3101, E-mail: awilliams@westminstercollege.edu. *Director,* Colleen Sandor, 801-832-2422, E-mail: csandor@westminstercollege.edu.

Program in Professional Communication Students: 24 full-time (14 women), 9 part-time (6 women); includes 5 minority (1 American Indian or Alaska Native, non-Hispanic/Latino; 1 Asian, non-Hispanic/Latino; 2 Hispanic/Latino; 1 Native Hawaiian or other Pacific Islander, non-Hispanic/Latino), 2 international. Average age 35. 4 applicants, 50% accepted, 1 enrolled. *Faculty:* 4 full-time (2 women), 3 part-time/adjunct (1 woman). Expenses: Contact institution. *Financial support:* Career-related internships or fieldwork, scholarships/grants, unspecified assistantships, and tuition reimbursements, tuition remission available. Support available to part-time students. Financial award applicants required to submit FAFSA. In 2016, 24 master's awarded. *Program availability:* Part-time, evening/weekend. Offers professional communication (MPC, MSC). *Application deadline:* For fall admission, 4/1 priority date for domestic and international students; for spring admission, 10/16 priority date for domestic and international students. Applications are processed on a rolling basis. *Application fee:* $50. Electronic applications accepted. *Application Contact:* Ashley Williams, Director of Graduate Admissions, 801-832-2213, Fax: 801-832-3101, E-mail: awilliams@westminstercollege.edu. *Director,* Dr. Helen Hodgson, 801-832-2821, Fax: 801-832-3102, E-mail: hhodgson@westminstercollege.edu.

School of Education Students: 56 full-time (46 women), 66 part-time (54 women); includes 26 minority (5 Black or African American, non-Hispanic/Latino; 5 Asian, non-Hispanic/Latino, 13 Hispanic/Latino; 2 Native Hawaiian or other Pacific Islander, non-Hispanic/Latino; 1 Two or more races, non-Hispanic/Latino), 5 international. Average age 34. 46 applicants, 89% accepted, 26 enrolled. *Faculty:* 13 full-time (10 women), 16 part-time/adjunct (10 women). Expenses: Contact institution. *Financial support:* In 2016–17, 39 students received support. Career-related internships or fieldwork, scholarships/grants, unspecified assistantships, and tuition reimbursements, tuition remission available. Support available to part-time students. Financial award applicants required to submit FAFSA. In 2016, 71 master's awarded. *Program availability:* Part-time, evening/weekend. Offers community leadership (MACL); education (M Ed); teaching (MAT). *Application deadline:* For fall admission, 6/3 priority date for domestic and international students; for spring admission, 10/16 priority date for domestic and international students; for summer admission, 1/22 priority date for domestic and international students. Applications are processed on a rolling basis. *Application fee:* $50. Electronic applications accepted. *Application Contact:* Ashley Williams, Director of Graduate Admissions, 801-832-2213, Fax: 801-832-3101, E-mail: awilliams@westminstercollege.edu. *Dean, School of Education,* Melanie Agnew, 801-832-2470, Fax: 801-832-3105.

School of Nursing and Health Sciences Students: 119 full-time (76 women), 2 part-time (1 woman); includes 15 minority (2 Black or African American, non-Hispanic/Latino; 1 Asian, non-Hispanic/Latino; 8 Hispanic/Latino; 1 Native Hawaiian or other Pacific Islander, non-Hispanic/Latino; 3 Two or more races, non-Hispanic/Latino), 2 international. Average age 32. 126 applicants, 54% accepted, 51 enrolled. *Faculty:* 10 full-time (7 women), 9 part-time/adjunct (5 women). Expenses: Contact institution. *Financial support:* In 2016–17, 7 students received support. Fellowships, career-related internships or fieldwork, unspecified assistantships, and tuition reimbursements, tuition remission available. Support available to part-time students. Financial award applicants required to submit FAFSA. In 2016, 54 master's awarded. Offers family nurse practitioner (MSN); nurse anesthesia (MSNA); public health (MPH). *Application fee:* $50. Electronic applications accepted. *Application Contact:* Ashley Williams, Director of Graduate Admissions, 801-832-2213, Fax: 801-832-3101, E-mail: awilliams@westminstercollege.edu. *Dean,* Dr. Sheryl Steadman, 801-832-2164, Fax: 801-832-3110, E-mail: ssteadman@westminstercollege.edu.

WESTMINSTER SEMINARY CALIFORNIA, Escondido, CA 92027-4128
General Information Independent-religious, coed, primarily men, graduate-only institution. *Graduate housing:* On-campus housing not available.

GRADUATE UNITS
Programs in Theology *Program availability:* Part-time, evening/weekend. Offers Biblical studies (MA); historical theology (MA); theological studies (M Div, MA).

WESTMINSTER THEOLOGICAL SEMINARY, Philadelphia, PA 19118
General Information Independent-religious, coed, primarily men, graduate-only institution. *Graduate housing:* Room and/or apartments available on a first-come, first-served basis to single students; on-campus housing not available to married students.

GRADUATE UNITS
Graduate and Professional Programs *Program availability:* Part-time. Offers apologetics (Th M); Biblical and urban studies (Certificate); Biblical counseling (MA); biblical studies (MAR); Christian studies (Certificate); church history (Th M); counseling (M Div); general studies (M Div, MAR); hermeneutics and Bible interpretations (PhD); historical and theological studies (PhD); historical theology (Th M); New Testament (Th M); Old Testament (Th M); pastoral counseling (D Min); pastoral ministry (M Div,

D Min); systematic theology (Th M); theological studies (MAR); urban missions (M Div, MA, MAR, D Min).

WEST TEXAS A&M UNIVERSITY, Canyon, TX 79016-0001

General Information State-supported, coed, comprehensive institution. CGS member. *Enrollment:* 9,901 graduate, professional, and undergraduate students; 2,454 matriculated graduate/professional students. *Enrollment by degree level:* 2,441 master's, 13 doctoral. *Graduate housing:* Room and/or apartments available on a first-come, first-served basis to single students; on-campus housing not available to married students. *Student services:* Campus employment opportunities, career counseling, child daycare facilities, exercise/wellness program, free psychological counseling, international student services, low-cost health insurance, multicultural affairs office, services for students with disabilities, writing training. *Library facilities:* Cornette Library plus 3 others. *Collection:* Books: 305,487 (physical), 516,531 (digital/electronic); Serial titles: 12,207 (physical), 12,592 (digital/electronic); Databases: 181. Weekly public service hours: 91; students can reserve study rooms. *Research affiliation:* Owens Corning (sports exercise), Pantex (chemistry), Agriculture Experiment Station (agriculture), Engineering Experiment Station (math, science).

Computer facilities: Computer purchase and lease plans are available. 1,200 computers available on campus for general student use. A campuswide network can be accessed from student residence rooms and from off campus. Online class registration is available.
Website: http://www.wtamu.edu/

GRADUATE UNITS

College of Agriculture and Natural Sciences Expenses: Contact institution. *Financial support:* Teaching assistantships available. Financial award applicants required to submit FAFSA. *Program availability:* Part-time. Offers agricultural business and economics (MS); agriculture (MS, PhD); agriculture and natural sciences (MS, PhD); animal science (MS); biology (MS); chemistry (MS); environmental science (MS); plant, soil and environmental science (MS). *Application deadline:* For fall admission, 8/1 for domestic students; for spring admission, 12/1 for domestic students; for summer admission, 5/1 for domestic students. Applications are processed on a rolling basis. *Application fee:* $40 ($75 for international students). Electronic applications accepted. *Application Contact:* Dr. Dean Hawkins, Dean, E-mail: dhawkins@wtamu.edu. *Dean,* Dr. Dean Hawkins, E-mail: dhawkins@wtamu.edu.

College of Business Expenses: Contact institution. *Financial support:* Application deadline: 2/1; applicants required to submit FAFSA. *Program availability:* Part-time, evening/weekend, 100% online, blended/hybrid learning. Offers accounting/business administration (MPA); business (MBA, MPA, MS); business administration (MBA); finance and economics (MS). *Application deadline:* For fall admission, 8/1 for domestic students, 6/1 for international students; for spring admission, 12/1 for domestic students, 11/1 for international students; for summer admission, 5/1 for domestic students. Applications are processed on a rolling basis. *Application fee:* $40 ($75 for international students). Electronic applications accepted. *Application Contact:* Dr. LaVelle Mills, Associate Dean, 806-651-3866.

College of Education and Social Sciences Students: 705. Expenses: Contact institution. *Program availability:* Part-time, evening/weekend, online learning. Offers counseling (MA); criminal justice (MA); curriculum and instruction (M Ed); education and social sciences (M Ed, MA, MAT, MS); educational diagnostician (M Ed); educational leadership (M Ed); instructional design and technology (M Ed); psychology (MA); reading education (M Ed); school counseling (M Ed); social work (MS); teaching (MAT). *Application deadline:* For fall admission, 8/1 for domestic students; for spring admission, 12/1 for domestic students; for summer admission, 5/1 for domestic students. Applications are processed on a rolling basis. *Application fee:* $40 ($75 for international students). Electronic applications accepted. *Application Contact:* Dr. Eddie Henderson, JD, Dean, 806-651-3622, E-mail: ehenderson@wtamu.edu. *Dean,* Dr. Eddie Henderson, JD, 806-651-3622, E-mail: ehenderson@wtamu.edu.

College of Fine Arts and Humanities Expenses: Contact institution. *Financial support:* Application deadline: 2/1; applicants required to submit FAFSA. *Program availability:* Part-time, evening/weekend. Offers communication (MA); English (MA); fine arts and humanities (MA, MFA, MM); history (MA); studio art (MFA). *Application deadline:* For fall admission, 8/1 for domestic students, 6/1 for international students; for spring admission, 12/1 for domestic students, 11/1 for international students; for summer admission, 5/1 for domestic students. Applications are processed on a rolling basis. *Application fee:* $40 ($75 for international students). Electronic applications accepted. *Application Contact:* Dr. Jessica Mallard, Dean, 806-651-2780.

School of Music Expenses: Contact institution. *Financial support:* Fellowships, research assistantships, teaching assistantships with partial tuition reimbursements, career-related internships or fieldwork, Federal Work-Study, institutionally sponsored loans, and tuition waivers (partial) available. Support available to part-time students. Financial award applicants required to submit CSS PROFILE or FAFSA. *Program availability:* Part-time. Offers music (MA); performance (MM). *Application deadline:* For fall admission, 8/1 for domestic students, 5/1 for international students; for spring admission, 12/1 for domestic students, 10/30 for international students; for summer admission, 5/1 for domestic students. Applications are processed on a rolling basis. *Application fee:* $40 ($75 for international students). Electronic applications accepted. *Director,* Dr. Robert Hansen, 806-651-2862, E-mail: rhansen@wtamu.edu.

College of Nursing and Health Sciences Students: 235. Expenses: Contact institution. *Program availability:* Part-time, evening/weekend. Offers communication disorders (MS); family nurse practitioner (MSN); nursing (MSN); nursing and health sciences (MS, MSN); sport management (MS); sports and exercise sciences (MS). *Application deadline:* For fall admission, 8/1 for domestic students; for spring admission, 12/1 for domestic students; for summer admission, 5/1 for domestic students. *Application fee:* $40 ($75 for international students). Electronic applications accepted. *Application Contact:* Collette Loftin, Assistant Professor, 806-651-2653. *Dean,* Dr. J. Dirk Nelson, E-mail: jdnelson@wtamu.edu.

Program in Interdisciplinary Studies Expenses: Contact institution. *Financial support:* Application deadline: 2/1; applicants required to submit FAFSA. *Program availability:* Part-time, evening/weekend. Offers interdisciplinary studies (MA, MS). *Application deadline:* For fall admission, 8/1 for domestic students, 6/1 for international students; for spring admission, 12/1 for domestic students, 11/1 for international students; for summer admission, 5/1 for domestic students. Applications are processed on a rolling basis. *Application fee:* $40 ($75 for international students). Electronic applications accepted. *Application Contact:* Dr. Rex Pjesky, Associate Dean of Graduate School and Research, 806-651-2737.

School of Engineering, Computer Science and Mathematics Expenses: Contact institution. *Financial support:* Research assistantships, teaching assistantships, Federal Work-Study, institutionally sponsored loans, and tuition waivers (partial) available. Support available to part-time students. Financial award applicants required to submit FAFSA. *Program availability:* Part-time. Offers engineering technology (MS); mathematics (MS). *Application deadline:* For fall admission, 8/1 for domestic students, 5/1 for international students; for spring admission, 12/1 for domestic students, 10/30 for international students; for summer admission, 5/1 for domestic students. Applications are processed on a rolling basis. *Application fee:* $40 ($75 for international students). Electronic applications accepted. *Dean,* Dr. Emily Hunt, 806-651-5257, E-mail: ecs@wtamu.edu.

WEST VIRGINIA SCHOOL OF OSTEOPATHIC MEDICINE, Lewisburg, WV 24901-1196

General Information State-supported, coed, graduate-only institution. *Enrollment by degree level:* 847 doctoral. *Graduate faculty:* 63 full-time (32 women). Tuition, state resident: full-time $19,450. Tuition, nonresident: full-time $49,200. Full-time tuition and fees vary according to student level. *Graduate housing:* On-campus housing not available. *Student services:* Campus employment opportunities, campus safety program, career counseling, exercise/wellness program, multicultural affairs office, services for students with disabilities. *Library facilities:* James R. Stookey Library. *Collection:* Books: 3,119 (physical), 1,188 (digital/electronic); Serial titles: 12 (physical), 6 (digital/electronic); Databases: 40. Weekly public service hours: 93; study areas open 24 hours, 5–7 days a week; students can reserve study rooms.

Computer facilities: 19 computers available on campus for general student use. A campuswide network can be accessed from off campus.
Website: http://www.wvsom.edu/

General Application Contact: Patricia A. Perkins, Interim Director of Admissions, 304-647-6336, Fax: 304-647-6384, E-mail: pperkins@osteo.wvsom.edu.

GRADUATE UNITS

Professional Program Students: 847 full-time (418 women); includes 217 minority (30 Black or African American, non-Hispanic/Latino; 1 American Indian or Alaska Native, non-Hispanic/Latino; 139 Asian, non-Hispanic/Latino; 32 Hispanic/Latino; 15 Native Hawaiian or other Pacific Islander, non-Hispanic/Latino). Average age 27. 4,855 applicants, 9% accepted, 212 enrolled. *Faculty:* 63 full-time (32 women), 1 part-time/adjunct (0 women). Expenses: Contact institution. *Financial support:* In 2016–17, 17 students received support, including 15 teaching assistantships with full tuition reimbursements available (averaging $45,250 per year); Federal Work-Study, scholarships/grants, tuition waivers (full), and unspecified assistantships also available. Financial award application deadline: 4/1; financial award applicants required to submit FAFSA. In 2016, 184 doctorates awarded. Offers osteopathic medicine (DO). *Application deadline:* For fall admission, 2/15 for domestic students. Applications are processed on a rolling basis. *Application fee:* $80. Electronic applications accepted. *Application Contact:* Gwen Byrd, Director of Admissions, 304-647-6336, Fax: 304-647-6384, E-mail: gbyrd@osteo.wvsom.edu. *President,* Dr. Michael D. Adelman, 304-645-4859, E-mail: madelman@osteo.wvsom.edu.

WEST VIRGINIA STATE UNIVERSITY, Institute, WV 25112-1000

General Information State-supported, coed, comprehensive institution. *Graduate housing:* Rooms and/or apartments available on a first-come, first-served basis to single and married students. Housing application deadline: 9/1.

GRADUATE UNITS

Biotechnology Graduate Program Offers biotechnology (MA, MS). Electronic applications accepted.

Master of Science Program in Law Enforcement and Administration Offers law enforcement and administration (MS). Electronic applications accepted.

Media Studies Graduate Program Offers media studies (MA). Electronic applications accepted.

WEST VIRGINIA UNIVERSITY, Morgantown, WV 26506

General Information State-supported, coed, university. CGS member. *Enrollment:* 28,488 graduate, professional, and undergraduate students; 4,634 full-time matriculated graduate/professional students (2,426 women), 1,644 part-time matriculated graduate/professional students (1,078 women). *Enrollment by degree level:* 3,324 master's, 2,954 doctoral. *Graduate faculty:* 872 full-time (355 women), 119 part-time/adjunct (53 women). Tuition, state resident: full-time $8568. Tuition, nonresident: full-time $22,140. Tuition and fees vary according to program. *Graduate housing:* Rooms and/or apartments available on a first-come, first-served basis to single and married students. Housing application deadline: 1/22. *Student services:* Campus employment opportunities, campus safety program, career counseling, child daycare facilities, exercise/wellness program, free psychological counseling, grant writing training, international student services, low-cost health insurance, multicultural affairs office, services for students with disabilities, teacher training, writing training. *Library facilities:* Downtown Library Complex plus 5 others. *Collection:* Books: 2.4 million (physical); Serial titles: 89,824 (physical); Databases: 390,341. Study areas open 24 hours, 5–7 days a week; students can reserve study rooms. *Research affiliation:* Federal Bureau of Investigation (FBI) (biometrics research), NASA IV and V Center (software verification/validation), Research Partnership for an Energy Secure America (energy research), Florida Agricultural and Mechanical University (plasma physics), University of Pittsburgh/Carnegie Mellon University (energy research), National Energy Technology Laboratory (fossil energy and environmental research).

Computer facilities: Computer purchase and lease plans are available. 1,800 computers available on campus for general student use. A campuswide network can be accessed from student residence rooms and from off campus. Online class registration is available.
Website: http://www.wvu.edu/

General Application Contact: Dr. Tracey L. Sheetz, Director, Graduate Admissions, 304-293-7173, Fax: 304-293-8657, E-mail: graded@mail.wvu.edu.

GRADUATE UNITS

College of Business and Economics Expenses: Contact institution. *Financial support:* Fellowships, research assistantships, teaching assistantships, career-related internships or fieldwork, Federal Work-Study, institutionally sponsored loans, scholarships/grants, health care benefits, tuition waivers (full and partial), unspecified assistantships, and administrative assistantships available. Financial award application deadline: 2/1; financial award applicants required to submit FAFSA. *Program availability:* Part-time, online learning. Offers business administration (MBA); business and economics (MA, MBA, MPA, MS, MSIR, PhD, Certificate); industrial relations (MSIR). *Application deadline:* For fall admission, 10/15 priority date for domestic and international students; for spring admission, 3/1 priority date for domestic and international students. Applications are processed on a rolling basis. *Application fee:* $60. Electronic applications accepted. *Application Contact:* Dr. Gerald Blakely, Professor/Director for Graduate Programs, 304-293-5505, Fax: 304-293-7188, E-mail: gerald.blakely@

mail.wvu.edu. *Interim Dean*, Dr. Nancy H. McIntyre, 304-293-7800, Fax: 304-293-4056, E-mail: nancy.mcintyre@mail.wvu.edu.

Division of Accounting Expenses: Contact institution. *Financial support:* Research assistantships, teaching assistantships, Federal Work-Study, institutionally sponsored loans, and unspecified assistantships available. Financial award application deadline: 2/1; financial award applicants required to submit FAFSA. *Program availability:* Part-time, evening/weekend. Offers accounting (MPA, PhD). *Application deadline:* For fall admission, 6/30 priority date for domestic students; for spring admission, 11/15 for domestic students. Applications are processed on a rolling basis. *Application fee:* $50. Electronic applications accepted. *Application Contact:* Dr. Robert Maust, Professor of Public Accounting, 304-293-7842, Fax: 304-293-5652, E-mail: robert.maust@mail.wvu.edu. *Director*, Prof. Timothy Pearson, 304-293-7847, Fax: 304-293-0635, E-mail: timothy.pearson@mail.wvu.edu.

Division of Economics and Finance Expenses: Contact institution. *Financial support:* Fellowships with full tuition reimbursements, research assistantships with full tuition reimbursements, teaching assistantships with full tuition reimbursements, Federal Work-Study, institutionally sponsored loans, and tuition waivers (full and partial) available. Financial award application deadline: 3/1; financial award applicants required to submit FAFSA. Offers business analysis (MA); developmental financial economics (PhD); environmental and resource economics (PhD); international economics (PhD); mathematical economics (MA); monetary economics (PhD); public finance (PhD); public policy (MA); regional and urban economics (PhD); statistics and economics (MA). *Application deadline:* For fall admission, 3/1 priority date for domestic and international students. Applications are processed on a rolling basis. *Application fee:* $50. Electronic applications accepted. *Application Contact:* Nicki Metts, Program Assistant II, 304-293-7859, Fax: 304-293-5652, E-mail: nicki.metts@mail.wvu.edu. *Director*, Dr. William N. Trumbull, 304-293-7860, Fax: 304-293-2233, E-mail: william.trumbull@mail.wvu.edu.

College of Creative Arts Expenses: Contact institution. *Financial support:* Research assistantships, teaching assistantships, career-related internships or fieldwork, Federal Work-Study, institutionally sponsored loans, scholarships/grants, health care benefits, tuition waivers (partial), and administrative assistantships available. Financial award applicants required to submit FAFSA. *Program availability:* Part-time. Offers creative arts (MA, MFA, MM, DMA, PhD). *Application deadline:* For fall admission, 3/1 priority date for domestic students, 2/15 for international students; for spring admission, 11/1 for domestic students, 9/15 for international students. Applications are processed on a rolling basis. *Application fee:* $60. Electronic applications accepted. *Application Contact:* Records Officer, 304-293-4841, Fax: 304-293-2533, E-mail: rachel.hanks@mail.wvu.edu. *Dean*, Dr. Paul Kreider, 304-293-4841 Ext. 3109, Fax: 304-293-6896, E-mail: paul.kreider@mail.wvu.edu.

School of Art and Design Expenses: Contact institution. *Financial support:* Research assistantships with full tuition reimbursements, teaching assistantships with full tuition reimbursements, Federal Work-Study, institutionally sponsored loans, tuition waivers (full and partial), and graduate administrative assistantships available. Financial award application deadline: 3/15; financial award applicants required to submit FAFSA. Offers art education (MA); art history (MA); ceramics (MFA); graphic design (MFA); painting (MFA); printmaking (MFA); sculpture (MFA); studio art (MA). *Application deadline:* For fall admission, 3/1 for domestic students, 2/15 for international students; for spring admission, 10/15 for domestic and international students. *Application fee:* $45. *Application Contact:* Records Officer, 304-293-4841, Fax: 304-293-2533, E-mail: rachel.hanks@mail.wvu.edu. *Interim Chair*, Alison Helm, 304-293-4841 Ext. 3140, Fax: 304-293-3136, E-mail: alison.helm@mail.wvu.edu.

School of Music Expenses: Contact institution. *Financial support:* Research assistantships with full and partial tuition reimbursements, teaching assistantships with full and partial tuition reimbursements, Federal Work-Study, institutionally sponsored loans, and tuition waivers (partial) available. Financial award application deadline: 2/1; financial award applicants required to submit FAFSA. Offers music composition (MM, DMA); music education (MM, PhD); music history (MM); music industry (MA); music performance (MM, DMA); music theory (MM). *Application deadline:* For fall admission, 3/15 priority date for domestic students, 2/15 priority date for international students; for spring admission, 10/15 for domestic students, 9/15 for international students. Applications are processed on a rolling basis. *Application fee:* $45. *Application Contact:* Molly Weaver, Coordinator, 304-293-4807, E-mail: molly.weaver@mail.wvu.edu.

College of Education and Human Services Expenses: Contact institution. *Financial support:* Fellowships, research assistantships, teaching assistantships, career-related internships or fieldwork, Federal Work-Study, institutionally sponsored loans, health care benefits, tuition waivers (full and partial), and administrative assistantships available. Financial award applicants required to submit FAFSA. *Program availability:* Part-time, evening/weekend, online learning. Offers autism spectrum disorder (5-adult) (MA); autism spectrum disorder (K-6) (MA); communication sciences and disorders (PhD); counseling (MA); counseling psychology (PhD); curriculum and instruction (Ed D); early intervention/early childhood special education (MA); education and human services (MA, Ed D, PhD); educational leadership studies (PhD); educational psychology (MA); elementary education (MA); gifted education (1-12) (MA); higher education curriculum and teaching (MA); instructional design and technology (MA, Ed D); low vision (PreK-adult) (MA); multicategorical special education (5-adult) (MA); multicategorical special education (K-6) (MA); secondary education (MA); severe/multiple disabilities (K-adult) (MA); special education (MA, Ed D); vision impairments (PreK-adult) (MA). *Application deadline:* For fall admission, 8/1 for domestic students; for spring admission, 1/1 for domestic students; for summer admission, 5/1 for domestic students. *Application fee:* $60. Electronic applications accepted. *Application Contact:* Dr. M. Cecil Smith, Associate Dean for Research and Graduate Education, 304-293-2174, Fax: 304-293-3802, E-mail: mcecil.smith@mail.wvu.edu. *Dean*, Dr. Gypsy Denzine, 304-293-5703, Fax: 304-293-7565, E-mail: gypsy.denzine@mail.wvu.edu.

College of Law Expenses: Contact institution. *Financial support:* Fellowships, research assistantships, teaching assistantships, career-related internships or fieldwork, Federal Work-Study, institutionally sponsored loans, scholarships/grants, health care benefits, tuition waivers (full), unspecified assistantships, and administrative assistantships, resident assistantships available. Support available to part-time students. Financial award application deadline: 3/1; financial award applicants required to submit FAFSA. *Program availability:* Part-time. Offers law (JD). *Application deadline:* For fall admission, 2/1 for domestic and international students. Applications are processed on a rolling basis. *Application fee:* $60. Electronic applications accepted. *Application Contact:* Beth Pierpont, Assistant Dean for Admissions and Student Financial Support, 304-293-7320, E-mail: beth.pierpont@mail.wvu.edu. *Assistant Dean for Admissions and Student Financial Support*, Beth Pierpont, 304-293-7320, E-mail: beth.pierpont@mail.wvu.edu.

College of Physical Activity and Sport Sciences Expenses: Contact institution. *Financial support:* Research assistantships, teaching assistantships, career-related internships or fieldwork, Federal Work-Study, institutionally sponsored loans, health care benefits, tuition waivers (full and partial), and administrative assistantships available. Support available to part-time students. Financial award application deadline: 2/1; financial award applicants required to submit FAFSA. Offers athletic training (MS); coaching and sport education (MS); coaching and teaching studies (Ed D); physical education/teacher education (MS, PhD); sport and exercise psychology (MS, PhD); sport coaching (MS); sport management (MS). *Application deadline:* For fall admission, 12/15 for domestic students, 10/1 for international students. *Application fee:* $60. Electronic applications accepted. *Application Contact:* Sean Bulger, Online Program Coordinator, 304-293-0845, Fax: 304-293-4641, E-mail: sean.bulger@mail.wvu.edu. *Online Program Coordinator*, Sean Bulger, 304-293-0845, Fax: 304-293-4641, E-mail: sean.bulger@mail.wvu.edu.

Davis College of Agriculture, Forestry and Consumer Sciences Expenses: Contact institution. *Financial support:* Fellowships, research assistantships, teaching assistantships, career-related internships or fieldwork, Federal Work-Study, institutionally sponsored loans, tuition waivers (full and partial), and unspecified assistantships available. Financial award application deadline: 2/1; financial award applicants required to submit FAFSA. *Program availability:* Part-time. Offers agriculture, forestry and consumer sciences (MLA, MS, MSF, PhD); animal breeding (MS, PhD); biochemical and molecular genetics (MS, PhD); cytogenetics (MS, PhD); descriptive embryology (MS, PhD); developmental genetics (MS); experimental morphogenesis/teratology (MS); human genetics (MS, PhD); immunogenetics (MS, PhD); life cycles of animals and plants (MS, PhD); molecular aspects of development (MS, PhD); mutagenesis (MS, PhD); oncology (MS, PhD); plant genetics (MS, PhD); population and quantitative genetics (MS, PhD); regeneration (MS, PhD); reproductive physiology (MS, PhD); teratology (PhD); toxicology (MS, PhD). *Application deadline:* For fall admission, 6/1 priority date for domestic students, 6/1 for international students; for spring admission, 1/5 for domestic and international students. Applications are processed on a rolling basis. *Application fee:* $60. Electronic applications accepted. *Application Contact:* Dr. Dennis K. Smith, Associate Dean, 304-293-2275, Fax: 304-293-3740, E-mail: denny.smith@mail.wvu.edu. *Dean*, Dr. Dan J. Robison, 304-293-2395, Fax: 304-293-3740, E-mail: dan.robison@mail.wvu.edu.

Division of Forestry Expenses: Contact institution. *Financial support:* Research assistantships, teaching assistantships, career-related internships or fieldwork, Federal Work-Study, institutionally sponsored loans, and tuition waivers (full and partial) available. Financial award application deadline: 2/1; financial award applicants required to submit FAFSA. *Program availability:* Part-time. Offers forest resource science (PhD); forestry (MSF); recreation, parks and tourism resources (MS); wildlife and fisheries resources (MS). *Application deadline:* Applications are processed on a rolling basis. *Application fee:* $50. *Application Contact:* Dr. Dennis K. Smith, Associate Dean, 304-293-2275, Fax: 304-293-3740, E-mail: denny.smith@mail.wvu.edu. *Division Director*, Dr. Joseph F. McNeel, 304-293-2941 Ext. 2471, Fax: 304-293-2441, E-mail: joseph.mcneel@mail.wvu.edu.

Division of Plant and Soil Sciences Expenses: Contact institution. *Financial support:* Research assistantships with full tuition reimbursements, teaching assistantships with full tuition reimbursements, Federal Work-Study, institutionally sponsored loans, and tuition waivers (full and partial) available. Financial award application deadline: 2/1; financial award applicants required to submit FAFSA. Offers agronomy (MS); entomology (MS); environmental microbiology (MS); horticulture (MS); plant pathology (MS). *Application deadline:* Applications are processed on a rolling basis. *Application fee:* $50. *Application Contact:* Dan Panaccione, Chair of the PSS Graduate Committee, 304-293-8819, Fax: 304-293-2960, E-mail: danpan@wvu.edu. *Chair of the PSS Graduate Committee*, Dan Panaccione, 304-293-8819, Fax: 304-293-2960, E-mail: danpan@wvu.edu.

Division of Resource Management and Sustainable Development Expenses: Contact institution. *Financial support:* Research assistantships, teaching assistantships, Federal Work-Study, institutionally sponsored loans, and tuition waivers (full and partial) available. Financial award applicants required to submit FAFSA. *Program availability:* Part-time. Offers agricultural and extension education (MS, PhD); agricultural and resource economics (MS); human and community development (PhD); natural resource economics (PhD); resource management (PhD); resource management and sustainable development (PhD); teaching vocational-agriculture (MS). *Application deadline:* Applications are processed on a rolling basis. *Application fee:* $50. *Application Contact:* Dr. Dennis K. Smith, Associate Dean, 304-293-3740, E-mail: denny.smith@mail.wvu.edu. *Director*, Dr. Timothy T. Phipps, 304-293-6253 Ext. 2474, Fax: 304-293-3752, E-mail: tphipps@mail.wvu.edu.

Eberly College of Arts and Sciences Expenses: Contact institution. *Financial support:* Fellowships with full tuition reimbursements, research assistantships with full tuition reimbursements, teaching assistantships with full tuition reimbursements, career-related internships or fieldwork, Federal Work-Study, institutionally sponsored loans, scholarships/grants, health care benefits, tuition waivers (full and partial), unspecified assistantships, and graduate administrative assistantships available. Financial award application deadline: 2/1; financial award applicants required to submit FAFSA. *Program availability:* Part-time, evening/weekend, online learning. Offers African history (MA, PhD); African-American history (MA, PhD); American history (MA, PhD); American public policy and politics (MA); analytical chemistry (MS, PhD); Appalachian/regional history (MA, PhD); applied mathematics (MS, PhD); applied physics (MS, PhD); arts and sciences (MA, MFA, MPA, MS, MSW, PhD); astrophysics (MS, PhD); behavior analysis (PhD); cell and molecular biology (MS, PhD); chemical physics (MS, PhD); clinical psychology (MA); communication in instruction (MA); communication studies (PhD); communication theory and research (MA); condensed matter physics (MS, PhD); corporate and organizational communication (MA); creative writing (MFA); discrete mathematics (PhD); East Asian history (MA, PhD); elementary particle physics (MS, PhD); energy and environmental resources (MA); English (MA, PhD); environmental and evolutionary biology (MS, PhD); European history (MA, PhD); forensic biology (MS, PhD); French (MA); genomic biology (MS, PhD); geographic information systems (PhD); geography (MA, PhD); geography-regional development (PhD); geology (MS, PhD); geomorphology (MS, PhD); geophysics (MS, PhD); GIS/cartographic analysis (MA); history of science and technology (MA, PhD); hydrogeology (MS, PhD); inorganic chemistry (MS, PhD); interdisciplinary mathematics (MS); international and comparative public policy and politics (MA); Latin American history (MA); linguistics (MA); literary/cultural studies (MA, PhD); materials physics (MS, PhD); mathematics for secondary education (MS); neurobiology (MS, PhD); organic chemistry (MS, PhD); paleontology (MS, PhD); petroleum geology (PhD); petrology (MS, PhD); physical chemistry (MS, PhD); plasma physics (MS, PhD); political science (PhD); public administration (MPA); public policy analysis (PhD); pure mathematics (MS); regional development (MS, PhD); sociology (MA, PhD); solid state physics (MS, PhD); Spanish (MA); statistical physics (MS); statistics (MS); stratigraphy (MS, PhD); structure (MS, PhD); teaching English to speakers of other languages (MA); theoretical chemistry (MS, PhD); theoretical physics (MS, PhD); writing (MA). *Application deadline:* For spring

admission, 2/15 priority date for domestic and international students. Applications are processed on a rolling basis. *Application fee:* $45. Electronic applications accepted. *Application Contact:* Dr. Fred L. King, Associate Dean for Graduate Studies, 304-293-4611 Ext. 5205, Fax: 304-293-6858, E-mail: fred.king@mail.wvu.edu. *Dean,* Dr. Mary Ellen Mazey, 304-293-4611, Fax: 304-293-6858, E-mail: mary.mazey@mail.wvu.edu.

School of Social Work Expenses: Contact institution. *Financial support:* Research assistantships with full tuition reimbursements, teaching assistantships with full tuition reimbursements, career-related internships or fieldwork, Federal Work-Study, institutionally sponsored loans, scholarships/grants, tuition waivers (full and partial), and stipends available. Financial award application deadline: 3/1; financial award applicants required to submit FAFSA. *Program availability:* Part-time. Offers aging and health care (MSW); children and families (MSW); community mental health (MSW); community organization and social administration (MSW); direct (clinical) social work practice (MSW). *Application deadline:* For fall admission, 3/1 for domestic students. *Application fee:* $45. *Application Contact:* Patricia Chase, 304-293-5132, Fax: 304-293-5936, E-mail: rachel.stein@mail.wvu.edu.

Reed College of Media Expenses: Contact institution. *Financial support:* Research assistantships, teaching assistantships, career-related internships or fieldwork, Federal Work-Study, institutionally sponsored loans, health care benefits, tuition waivers (full and partial), and administrative assistantships available. Financial award application deadline: 2/1; financial award applicants required to submit FAFSA. *Program availability:* Part-time, online learning. Offers digital marketing communications (Graduate Certificate); integrated marketing communications (MS, Graduate Certificate); journalism (MSJ). *Application deadline:* For fall admission, 3/1 priority date for domestic students, 3/1 for international students. *Application fee:* $60. Electronic applications accepted. *Application Contact:* Dr. Steve Urbanski, Director of Graduate Studies/Associate Professor, 304-293-6797, Fax: 304-293-3072, E-mail: steve.urbanski@mail.wvu.edu. *Dean,* Dr. Maryann Reed, 304-293-3505 Ext. 5409, Fax: 304-293-3072, E-mail: maryann.reed@mail.wvu.edu.

School of Dentistry Expenses: Contact institution. *Financial support:* Research assistantships, teaching assistantships, Federal Work-Study, institutionally sponsored loans, scholarships/grants, health care benefits, and tuition waivers (partial) available. Financial award application deadline: 3/1; financial award applicants required to submit FAFSA. Offers dentistry (DDS). *Application deadline:* For fall admission, 11/1 for domestic and international students. Applications are processed on a rolling basis. *Application fee:* $60. Electronic applications accepted. *Application Contact:* Dr. Sheila Price, Associate Dean for Admissions, Recruitment, and Access, 304-293-1980, E-mail: sprice@hsc.wvu.edu. *Dean,* Dr. Tom Borgia, 304-293-2521, E-mail: aborgia@hsc.wvu.edu.

School of Medicine Expenses: Contact institution. *Financial support:* Fellowships, research assistantships, teaching assistantships, career-related internships or fieldwork, Federal Work-Study, institutionally sponsored loans, health care benefits, tuition waivers (full and partial), and administrative assistantships available. Financial award applicants required to submit FAFSA. *Program availability:* Part-time, evening/weekend. Offers medicine (MHS, MOT, MS, DPT, MD, PhD, Graduate Certificate); occupational therapy (MOT); physical therapy (DPT). *Application deadline:* Applications are processed on a rolling basis. *Application fee:* $60. Electronic applications accepted. *Application Contact:* Lisa M. Salati, Assistant Vice President, Graduate Education, 304-293-7759, Fax: 304-293-3080, E-mail: lsalati@hsc.wvu.edu. *Executive Dean,* Dr. Clay Marsh, 304-293-6607, Fax: 304-293-6627, E-mail: clay.marsh@hsc.wvu.edu.

Graduate Programs at the Health Sciences Center Expenses: Contact institution. *Financial support:* Fellowships, research assistantships, teaching assistantships, career-related internships or fieldwork, Federal Work-Study, institutionally sponsored loans, tuition waivers (full and partial), and graduate administrative assistantships available. Financial award applicants required to submit FAFSA. *Program availability:* Part-time, evening/weekend, online learning. Offers biochemistry and molecular biology (PhD); cancer cell biology (PhD); cellular and integrative physiology (PhD); exercise physiology (MS, PhD); health sciences (MS, PhD); immunology and microbial pathogenesis (PhD); neuroscience (PhD); pharmaceutical and pharmacological sciences (PhD). *Application deadline:* For spring admission, 3/15 for domestic students. *Application fee:* $50. *Application Contact:* Claire Noel, Assistant Director for Health Sciences Graduate Program, 304-293-7116, Fax: 304-293-9257, E-mail: cnoel@hsc.wvu.edu. *Associate Vice President, Health Sciences Center Research and Graduate Education,* Dr. Thomas Saba, 304-293-7206, Fax: 304-293-7038, E-mail: tsaba@hsc.wvu.edu.

School of Nursing Expenses: Contact institution. *Financial support:* Teaching assistantships, Federal Work-Study, institutionally sponsored loans, health care benefits, tuition waivers (partial), and administrative assistantships available. Financial award application deadline: 2/1; financial award applicants required to submit FAFSA. *Program availability:* Part-time, online learning. Offers nurse practitioner (Certificate); nursing (MSN, DNP, PhD). *Application deadline:* For fall admission, 6/1 for domestic students. *Application fee:* $60. Electronic applications accepted. *Application Contact:* Brandy Sue Toothman, Program Assistant III, 304-293-4298, Fax: 304-293-2546, E-mail: btoothman@hsc.wvu.edu. *Dean,* Dr. Tara Hulsey, 304-293-6521, Fax: 304-293-6826, E-mail: tmhulsey@hsc.wvu.edu.

School of Pharmacy Expenses: Contact institution. *Financial support:* Research assistantships, teaching assistantships, career-related internships or fieldwork, Federal Work-Study, institutionally sponsored loans, health care benefits, tuition waivers (full and partial), and unspecified assistantships available. Financial award application deadline: 3/1; financial award applicants required to submit FAFSA. Offers administrative pharmacy (PhD); behavioral pharmacy (MS, PhD); biopharmaceutics/pharmacokinetics (MS, PhD); clinical pharmacy (Pharm D); industrial pharmacy (MS); medicinal chemistry (MS, PhD); pharmaceutical chemistry (MS, PhD); pharmaceutics (MS, PhD); pharmacology and toxicology (MS); pharmacy (MS); pharmacy administration (MS). *Application deadline:* For fall admission, 3/1 priority date for domestic and international students. *Application fee:* $60. Electronic applications accepted. *Application Contact:* Dr. Mary L. Euler, Associate Dean for Student Services, 304-293-7806, Fax: 304-293-5483, E-mail: mleuler@hsc.wvu.edu. *Interim Dean,* Dr. Mary K. Stamatakis, 304-293-5101, Fax: 304-293-5483, E-mail: mkstamatakis@hsc.wvu.edu.

School of Public Health Expenses: Contact institution. *Financial support:* Research assistantships, teaching assistantships, scholarships/grants, and health care benefits available. Financial award application deadline: 2/1; financial award applicants required to submit FAFSA. *Program availability:* Part-time, online learning. Offers biostatistics (MS); community health/preventative medicine (MPH); public health sciences (PhD); school health education (MS). *Application deadline:* For fall admission, 4/15 priority date for domestic students; for spring admission, 12/1 for domestic students. Applications are processed on a rolling basis. *Application fee:* $60. *Application Contact:* Leah Adkins, Senior Program Coordinator, 304-293-1097, E-mail: leadkins@hsc.wvu.edu. *Senior Program Coordinator,* Leah Adkins, 304-293-1097, E-mail: leadkins@hsc.wvu.edu.

Statler College of Engineering and Mineral Resources Expenses: Contact institution. *Financial support:* Fellowships, research assistantships, teaching assistantships, career-related internships or fieldwork, Federal Work-Study, institutionally sponsored loans, health care benefits, tuition waivers (full and partial), unspecified assistantships, and administrative assistantships available. Financial award application deadline: 2/1; financial award applicants required to submit FAFSA. *Program availability:* Part-time. Offers aerospace engineering (MSAE, PhD); chemical engineering (MS Ch E, PhD); civil engineering (MSCE, MSE, PhD); computer engineering (PhD); computer science (MS, PhD); electrical engineering (MSEE, PhD); industrial engineering (MS, PhD); industrial hygiene (MS); material science and engineering (MSMSE); mechanical engineering (MSME, PhD); mining engineering (MS Min E, PhD); occupational safety and health (PhD); petroleum and natural gas engineering (MSPNGE, PhD); safety management (MS); software engineering (MSSE). *Application deadline:* For fall admission, 4/1 for international students; for winter admission, 4/1 for international students; for spring admission, 10/1 for international students. Applications are processed on a rolling basis. *Application fee:* $60. Electronic applications accepted. *Application Contact:* Dr. David A. Wyrick, Associate Dean, Academic Affairs, 304-293-4334, Fax: 304-293-5024, E-mail: david.wyrick@mail.wvu.edu. *Dean,* Dr. Eugene V. Cilento, 304-293-4821 Ext. 2237, Fax: 304-293-2037, E-mail: gene.cilento@mail.wvu.edu.

WEST VIRGINIA WESLEYAN COLLEGE, Buckhannon, WV 26201

General Information Independent-religious, coed, comprehensive institution. *Graduate housing:* Room and/or apartments available to single students; on-campus housing not available to married students.

GRADUATE UNITS

Department of Education Offers education (M Ed).

Department of Exercise Science Offers athletic training (MS).

Department of Nursing Offers family nurse practitioner (MS, Post Master's Certificate); nurse administrator (MS); nurse educator (MS); nurse-midwifery (MS); nursing administration (Post Master's Certificate); nursing education (Post Master's Certificate); psychiatric mental health nurse practitioner (MS).

MBA Program *Program availability:* Part-time, evening/weekend. Offers business administration (MBA).

Program in Creative Writing Offers creative writing (MFA).

WHEATON COLLEGE, Wheaton, IL 60187-5593

General Information Independent-religious, coed, comprehensive institution. CGS member. *Enrollment:* 2,901 graduate, professional, and undergraduate students; 249 full-time matriculated graduate/professional students (158 women), 108 part-time matriculated graduate/professional students (54 women). *Enrollment by degree level:* 278 master's, 79 doctoral. *Graduate faculty:* 30 full-time (10 women), 12 part-time/adjunct (7 women). *Tuition:* Full-time $19,080; part-time $795 per credit hour. Tuition and fees vary according to degree level and program. *Graduate housing:* Rooms and/or apartments available on a first-come, first-served basis to single and married students. Typical cost: $6010 per year ($9920 including board) for single students; $10,670 per year ($14,580 including board) for married students. Room and board charges vary according to board plan and housing facility selected. Housing application deadline: 4/1. *Student services:* Campus employment opportunities, campus safety program, career counseling, exercise/wellness program, free psychological counseling, grant writing training, international student services, multicultural affairs office, services for students with disabilities, writing training. *Library facilities:* Buswell Memorial Library. *Collection:* Books: 518,164 (physical), 226,974 (digital/electronic); Serial titles: 389 (physical), 6,182 (digital/electronic); Databases: 249. Weekly public service hours: 94; students can reserve study rooms.

Computer facilities: 325 computers available on campus for general student use. A campuswide network can be accessed from student residence rooms and from off campus. Online class registration, financial information, degree requirements evaluation are available.
Website: http://www.wheaton.edu/

General Application Contact: Dusty Di Santo, Director of Graduate Admissions, 630-752-5195, Fax: 630-752-7047, E-mail: graduate.admissions@wheaton.edu.

GRADUATE UNITS

Graduate School Students: 249 full-time (158 women), 108 part-time (54 women); includes 71 minority (19 Black or African American, non-Hispanic/Latino; 1 American Indian or Alaska Native, non-Hispanic/Latino; 23 Asian, non-Hispanic/Latino; 16 Hispanic/Latino; 12 Two or more races, non-Hispanic/Latino), 47 international. Average age 30. 408 applicants, 83% accepted, 222 enrolled. *Faculty:* 30 full-time (10 women), 12 part-time/adjunct (7 women). Expenses: Contact institution. *Financial support:* Career-related internships or fieldwork, Federal Work-Study, scholarships/grants, and unspecified assistantships available. Financial award application deadline: 3/1; financial award applicants required to submit FAFSA. In 2016, 167 master's, 11 doctorates awarded. *Program availability:* Part-time. Offers Biblical and theological studies (PhD); Biblical archaeology (MA); Biblical exegesis (MA); Biblical studies (MA); Christian formation and ministry (MA); clinical mental health counseling (MA); clinical psychology (Psy D); counseling ministries (MA); elementary education (MAT); evangelism and leadership (MA); general theological studies (MA); historical and systematic theology (MA); history of Christianity (MA); intercultural studies (MA); intercultural studies/teaching English as a second language (MA); marriage and family therapy (MA); missional church movements (MA); missions (MA); secondary education (MAT); teaching English as a second language (Certificate). *Application deadline:* For fall admission, 1/1 priority date for domestic students, 1/1 for international students; for spring admission, 11/1 for domestic students. Applications are processed on a rolling basis. *Application fee:* $30. Electronic applications accepted. *Application Contact:* Dusty Di Santo, Director of Graduate Admissions, 630-752-5195, Fax: 630-752-7047, E-mail: graduate.admissions@wheaton.edu. *Dean,* Dr. Nicholas Perrin, 630-752-5933, E-mail: graduate.dean@wheaton.edu.

WHEELING JESUIT UNIVERSITY, Wheeling, WV 26003-6295

General Information Independent-religious, coed, comprehensive institution. *Graduate housing:* Rooms and/or apartments available on a first-come, first-served basis to single and married students.

GRADUATE UNITS

Department of Business *Program availability:* Part-time, evening/weekend. Offers accounting (MSA); business administration (MBA). Electronic applications accepted.

Department of Education *Program availability:* Part-time, evening/weekend, online learning. Offers education (MEL). Electronic applications accepted.

Department of Nursing *Program availability:* Part-time, evening/weekend, online learning. Offers nursing (MSN). Electronic applications accepted.

Department of Physical Therapy Offers physical therapy (DPT). Electronic applications accepted.

Department of Social Sciences *Program availability:* Part-time, evening/weekend. Offers social sciences (MSOL). Electronic applications accepted.

WHEELOCK COLLEGE, Boston, MA 02215

General Information Independent, coed, primarily women, comprehensive institution. *Graduate housing:* Room and/or apartments available on a first-come, first-served basis to single students; on-campus housing not available to married students. Housing application deadline: 5/1.

GRADUATE UNITS

Graduate Programs *Program availability:* Part-time, evening/weekend, online learning. Offers education (MS, MSW).

Division of Arts and Sciences Offers human development (MS). Electronic applications accepted.

Division of Child and Family Studies *Program availability:* Part-time, online learning. Offers family studies (MS); family support and parent education (MS); family, culture, and society (MS). Electronic applications accepted.

Division of Education *Program availability:* Online learning. Offers early childhood education (MS); education leadership (MS); elementary education (MS); language, literacy, and reading (MS); teaching students with moderate disabilities (MS). Electronic applications accepted.

Division of Social Work Offers social work (MSW). Electronic applications accepted.

WHITTIER COLLEGE, Whittier, CA 90608-0634

General Information Independent, coed, comprehensive institution. *Graduate housing:* On-campus housing not available.

GRADUATE UNITS

Graduate Programs *Program availability:* Part-time, evening/weekend. Offers educational administration (MA Ed); elementary education (MA Ed); secondary education (MA Ed).

WHITWORTH UNIVERSITY, Spokane, WA 99251-0001

General Information Independent-religious, coed, comprehensive institution. *Graduate housing:* Room and/or apartments available on a first-come, first-served basis to single students; on-campus housing not available to married students. Housing application deadline: 5/1.

GRADUATE UNITS

Master of Arts in Theology Program *Program availability:* Part-time, evening/weekend. Offers theology (MA).

School of Business *Program availability:* Part-time, evening/weekend. Offers business (MBA). Electronic applications accepted.

School of Education *Program availability:* Part-time, evening/weekend, online learning. Offers administration (M Ed); counseling (M Ed); education (M Ed, MAT, MIT); elementary education (M Ed); gifted and talented (MAT); school counselors (M Ed); secondary education (M Ed); social agency/church setting (M Ed); special education (MAT); teaching (MIT).

WICHITA STATE UNIVERSITY, Wichita, KS 67260

General Information State-supported, coed, university. CGS member. *Enrollment:* 14,474 graduate, professional, and undergraduate students; 1,321 full-time matriculated graduate/professional students (719 women), 1,330 part-time matriculated graduate/professional students (683 women). *Enrollment by degree level:* 1,959 master's, 503 doctoral, 189 other advanced degrees. *Graduate faculty:* 403 full-time (159 women), 21 part-time/adjunct (12 women). *Graduate housing:* Rooms and/or apartments available on a first-come, first-served basis to single and married students. *Student services:* Campus employment opportunities, campus safety program, career counseling, child daycare facilities, exercise/wellness program, free psychological counseling, grant writing training, international student services, low-cost health insurance, multicultural affairs office, services for students with disabilities, teacher training, writing training. *Library facilities:* Ablah Library plus 2 others. *Collection:* Books: 1.9 million (physical), 428,856 (digital/electronic); Serial titles: 281 (physical), 76,462 (digital/electronic); Databases: 250. Weekly public service hours: 92; study areas open 24 hours, 5–7 days a week; students can reserve study rooms. *Research affiliation:* Spirit Aerosystems (aerospace engineering), General Atomics (aerospace engineering), Wesley Medical Center (industrial and manufacturing engineering), NASA (aerospace engineering), Airbus (aerospace engineering), NetApp (computer engineering).

Computer facilities: 1,500 computers available on campus for general student use. A campuswide network can be accessed from student residence rooms and from off campus. Online class registration, learning management system are available. Website: http://www.wichita.edu/

General Application Contact: Jordan Oleson, Admissions Coordinator, 316-978-3095, Fax: 316-978-3253, E-mail: jordan.oleson@wichita.edu.

GRADUATE UNITS

Graduate School Students: 1,321 full-time (719 women), 1,330 part-time (683 women); includes 454 minority (115 Black or African American, non-Hispanic/Latino; 12 American Indian or Alaska Native, non-Hispanic/Latino; 111 Asian, non-Hispanic/Latino; 159 Hispanic/Latino; 2 Native Hawaiian or other Pacific Islander, non-Hispanic/Latino; 55 Two or more races, non-Hispanic/Latino), 574 international. Average age 31. 2,344 applicants, 56% accepted, 601 enrolled. *Faculty:* 403 full-time (159 women), 21 part-time/adjunct (12 women). Expenses: Contact institution. *Financial support:* In 2016–17, 445 research assistantships with partial tuition reimbursements (averaging $11,200 per year), 401 teaching assistantships with partial tuition reimbursements (averaging $10,264 per year) were awarded; fellowships, career-related internships or fieldwork, Federal Work-Study, institutionally sponsored loans, scholarships/grants, traineeships, health care benefits, and unspecified assistantships also available. Support available to part-time students. Financial award application deadline: 4/1; financial award applicants required to submit FAFSA. In 2016, 805 master's, 92 doctorates, 3 other advanced degrees awarded. *Program availability:* Part-time, evening/weekend, 100% online, blended/hybrid learning. *Application deadline:* For fall admission, 7/15 priority date for domestic students, 4/1 for international students; for spring admission, 12/1 priority date for domestic students, 8/1 for international students. Applications are processed on a rolling basis. *Application fee:* $50 ($65 for international students). *Application Contact:* Jordan Oleson, Admissions Coordinator, 316-978-3095, Fax: 316-978-3253, E-mail: jordan.oleson@wichita.edu. *Dean of the Graduate School/Associate Vice President of Research and Technology Transfer,* Dr. Dennis R. Livesay, 316-978-3095, Fax: 316-978-3253, E-mail: dennis.livesay@wichita.edu.

College of Education Expenses: Contact institution. *Program availability:* Part-time, evening/weekend, 100% online, blended/hybrid learning. Offers counseling (M Ed); education (M Ed, MAT, Ed D, Ed S); educational leadership (M Ed, Ed D); educational psychology (M Ed); exercise science (M Ed); learning and instructional design (M Ed); school psychology (Ed S); special education (M Ed); sport management (M Ed); teaching (MAT). *Application Contact:* Jordan Oleson, Admissions Coordinator, 316-978-3253, Fax: 316-978-3253, E-mail: jordan.oleson@wichita.edu. *Dean,* Dr. Shirley Lefever, 316-978-3301, Fax: 316-978-3302, E-mail: shirley.lefever@wichita.edu.

College of Engineering Expenses: Contact institution. *Program availability:* Part-time, evening/weekend. Offers aerospace engineering (MS, PhD); biomedical engineering (MS); computer networking (MS); computer science (MS); electrical engineering (MS); electrical engineering and computer science (PhD); engineering (MEM, MS, PhD); engineering management (MEM); industrial engineering (MS, PhD); mechanical engineering (MS, PhD). *Application Contact:* Jordan Oleson, Admissions Coordinator, 316-978-3095, Fax: 316-978-3253, E-mail: jordan.oleson@wichita.edu. *Dean,* Dr. Royce O. Bowden, 316-978-3400, Fax: 316-978-3853, E-mail: royce.bowden@wichita.edu.

College of Fine Arts Expenses: Contact institution. *Program availability:* Part-time. Offers fine arts (MFA, MM, MME); music (MM); music education (MME); studio arts (MFA). *Application Contact:* Jordan Oleson, Admissions Coordinator, 316-978-3095, Fax: 316-978-3253, E-mail: jordan.oleson@wichita.edu. *Dean,* Dr. Rodney E. Miller, 316-978-3389, Fax: 316-978-3951, E-mail: rodney.miller@wichita.edu.

College of Health Professions Expenses: Contact institution. *Program availability:* Part-time. Offers aging studies (MA); communication sciences and disorders (MA, Au D, PhD); health professions (MA, MPA, MSN, Au D, DNP, DPT, PhD); nursing (MSN); nursing practice (DNP); physical therapy (DPT); physician assistant (MPA). *Application Contact:* Jordan Oleson, Admissions Coordinator, 316-978-3095, Fax: 316-978-3253, E-mail: jordan.oleson@wichita.edu. *Dean,* Dr. Sandra C. Bibb, 316-978-3600, Fax: 316-978-3025, E-mail: sandra.bibb@wichita.edu.

Fairmount College of Liberal Arts and Sciences Expenses: Contact institution. *Program availability:* Part-time, evening/weekend, 100% online, blended/hybrid learning. Offers anthropology (MA); applied mathematics (PhD); biological sciences (MS); chemistry (MS, PhD); clinical (PhD); communication (MA); community (PhD); creative writing (MFA); criminal justice (MA); earth, environmental, and physical sciences (MS); English (MA); history (MA); human factors (PhD); liberal arts and sciences (MA, MFA, MPA, MS, MSW, PhD); liberal studies (MA); mathematics (MS); physics (MS); public administration (MPA); social work (MSW); sociology (MA); Spanish (MA). *Application Contact:* Jordan Oleson, Admissions Coordinator, 316-978-3095, Fax: 316-978-3253, E-mail: jordan.oleson@wichita.edu. *Dean,* Dr. Ronald Matson, 316-978-3100, Fax: 316-978-3234, E-mail: ron.matson@wichita.edu.

Institute for Interdisciplinary Creativity Expenses: Contact institution. Offers innovation design (MID). *Application Contact:* Jordan Oleson, Admissions Coordinator, 316-978-3095, Fax: 316-978-3253, E-mail: jordan.oleson@wichita.edu. *Graduate Coordinator,* Dr. Jeremy Patterson, 316-978-3010, E-mail: jeremy.patterson@wichita.edu.

W. Frank Barton School of Business Expenses: Contact institution. *Program availability:* Part-time, evening/weekend. Offers accounting information systems (M Acc); business (EMBA, M Acc, MA, MBA); economic analysis (MA); financial economics (MA); international economics (MA); taxation (M Acc). *Application Contact:* Jordan Oleson, Admissions Coordinator, 316-978-3095, Fax: 316-978-3253, E-mail: jordan.oleson@wichita.edu. *Dean,* Dr. Anand Desai, 316-978-3200, Fax: 316-978-3845, E-mail: anand.desai@wichita.edu.

WIDENER UNIVERSITY, Chester, PA 19013-5792

General Information Independent, coed, comprehensive institution. *Enrollment:* 6,402 graduate, professional, and undergraduate students; 1,409 full-time matriculated graduate/professional students (877 women), 1,402 part-time matriculated graduate/professional students (1,120 women). *Enrollment by degree level:* 1,417 master's, 1,312 doctoral, 82 other advanced degrees. *Graduate faculty:* 167 full-time (97 women), 177 part-time/adjunct (92 women). Tuition and fees vary according to degree level and program. *Graduate housing:* Rooms and/or apartments available on a first-come, first-served basis to single students and available to married students. Housing application deadline: 5/30. *Student services:* Campus employment opportunities, career counseling, child daycare facilities, exercise/wellness program, free psychological counseling, international student services, multicultural affairs office, services for students with disabilities, teacher training, writing training. *Library facilities:* Wolfgram Memorial Library. *Research affiliation:* Small Business Administration, Riverfront Development Corporation (engineering, management), Advanced Technology Center (engineering).

Computer facilities: 710 computers available on campus for general student use. A campuswide network can be accessed from student residence rooms and from off campus. Online class registration is available. Website: http://www.widener.edu/

General Application Contact: Dr. Roberta Nolan, Assistant to Associate Provost for Graduate Studies, 610-499-4125, Fax: 610-499-4676, E-mail: gradmc@mail.widener.edu.

GRADUATE UNITS

College of Arts and Sciences Students: 25 part-time (14 women); includes 12 minority (9 Black or African American, non-Hispanic/Latino; 1 Asian, non-Hispanic/Latino; 1 Hispanic/Latino; 1 Two or more races, non-Hispanic/Latino). Average age 31. 30 applicants, 50% accepted, 6 enrolled. *Faculty:* 9 full-time (2 women), 8 part-time/adjunct (1 woman). Expenses: Contact institution. *Financial support:* Career-related internships or fieldwork and institutionally sponsored loans available. Support available to part-time students. Financial award application deadline: 4/1. In 2016, 13 master's awarded. *Program availability:* Part-time, evening/weekend. Offers arts and sciences (MA, MPA); criminal justice (MA); liberal studies (MA); public administration (MPA). *Application deadline:* Applications are processed on a rolling basis. *Application fee:* $25 ($300 for international students). *Application Contact:* Dr. Roberta Nolan, Assistant to Associate Provost for Graduate Studies, 610-499-4125, Fax: 610-499-4676, E-mail: gradmc@mail.widener.edu. *Dean,* Dr. Sharon Meaghar, 610-499-4007, E-mail: smmeagher@widener.edu.

Commonwealth Law School Students: 236 full-time (112 women), 50 part-time (44 women); includes 51 minority (22 Black or African American, non-Hispanic/Latino; 3 American Indian or Alaska Native, non-Hispanic/Latino; 13 Asian, non-Hispanic/Latino; 13 Hispanic/Latino). Average age 25. 506 applicants, 67% accepted, 66 enrolled. *Faculty:* 17 full-time (8 women), 18 part-time/adjunct (6 women). Expenses: Contact institution. *Financial support:* Fellowships, research assistantships, career-related internships or fieldwork, Federal Work-Study, institutionally sponsored loans, and scholarships/grants available. Support available to part-time students. Financial award application deadline: 2/15; financial award applicants required to submit FAFSA. *Program availability:* Part-time. Offers law (JD). *Application deadline:* For fall admission, 5/15 for domestic students. Applications are processed on a rolling basis. *Application fee:* $60. Electronic applications accepted. *Application Contact:* John Benfield, Associate Dean for Admissions and Administration, 302-477-2210, Fax: 302-477-2224, E-mail: jsbenfield@widener.edu. *Dean,* Christian Johnson, 302-477-2100, Fax: 302-477-2282, E-mail: cajohnson2@widener.edu.

Delaware Law School Students: 479 full-time (252 women), 38 part-time (29 women); includes 128 minority (70 Black or African American, non-Hispanic/Latino; 12 American Indian or Alaska Native, non-Hispanic/Latino; 14 Asian, non-Hispanic/Latino; 26 Hispanic/Latino; 6 Two or more races, non-Hispanic/Latino; 39 international. Average age 26. 735 applicants, 80% accepted, 126 enrolled. *Faculty:* 24 full-time (13 women), 42 part-time/adjunct (15 women). Expenses: Contact institution. *Financial support:* Career-related internships or fieldwork, Federal Work-Study, institutionally sponsored loans, and scholarships/grants available. Support available to part-time students. Financial award application deadline: 2/15; financial award applicants required to submit FAFSA. *Program availability:* Part-time, 100% online. Offers corporate and business law (MJ); corporate law and finance (LL M); health law (LL M, MJ, D Law); higher education compliance (MJ); juridical science (SJD); law (JD). *Application deadline:* For fall admission, 5/15 for domestic students; for spring admission, 12/1 for domestic students. Applications are processed on a rolling basis. *Application fee:* $60. *Application Contact:* Barbara L. Ayars, Assistant Dean of Admissions, 302-477-2210, Fax: 302-477-2224, E-mail: barbara.l.ayars@law.widener.edu. *Dean,* Rod Smolla, 302-477-2100, Fax: 302-477-2282, E-mail: rasmolla@widener.edu.

Graduate Programs in Engineering Students: 9 full-time (3 women), 16 part-time (2 women); includes 2 minority (1 Asian, non-Hispanic/Latino; 1 Hispanic/Latino), 8 international. Average age 29. 75 applicants, 19% accepted, 8 enrolled. *Faculty:* 18 full-time (2 women), 7 part-time/adjunct (0 women). Expenses: Contact institution. *Financial support:* In 2016–17, 5 teaching assistantships with partial tuition reimbursements (averaging $8,000 per year) were awarded; research assistantships and unspecified assistantships also available. Financial award application deadline: 3/15. In 2016, 12 master's awarded. *Program availability:* Part-time, evening/weekend. Offers biomedical engineering (M Eng); chemical engineering (M Eng); civil engineering (M Eng); electrical engineering (M Eng); engineering (M Eng); engineering management (M Eng); mechanical engineering (M Eng). *Application deadline:* For fall admission, 8/1 priority date for domestic students, 4/1 priority date for international students; for winter admission, 2/1 priority date for international students; for spring admission, 12/1 priority date for domestic students, 9/1 priority date for international students. Applications are processed on a rolling basis. *Application fee:* $0. Electronic applications accepted. *Assistant Dean/Director of Graduate Programs,* Rudolph Treichel, 610-499-1294, Fax: 610-499-4059, E-mail: rjtreichel@widener.edu.

School of Business Administration Students: 50 full-time (26 women), 129 part-time (53 women); includes 48 minority (35 Black or African American, non-Hispanic/Latino; 6 Asian, non-Hispanic/Latino; 5 Hispanic/Latino; 1 Native Hawaiian or other Pacific Islander, non-Hispanic/Latino; 1 Two or more races, non-Hispanic/Latino), 27 international. Average age 34. 154 applicants, 49% accepted, 43 enrolled. *Faculty:* 14 full-time (6 women), 6 part-time/adjunct (2 women). Expenses: Contact institution. *Financial support:* In 2016–17, 11 research assistantships with full tuition reimbursements were awarded; career-related internships or fieldwork, Federal Work-Study, and traineeships also available. Support available to part-time students. Financial award application deadline: 5/1. In 2016, 45 master's awarded. *Program availability:* Part-time, evening/weekend, 100% online, blended/hybrid learning. Offers business administration (MBA, MHA, MS); health and medical services administration (MBA, MHA); taxation (MS). *Application deadline:* For fall admission, 8/1 priority date for domestic students; for spring admission, 12/1 for domestic students. Applications are processed on a rolling basis. *Application fee:* $25 ($300 for international students). Electronic applications accepted. *Application Contact:* Ann Seltzer, Graduate Enrollment Administrator, 610-499-4305, E-mail: apseltzer@widener.edu. *Interim Dean,* Dr. Catherine Morgan, 610-499-4300, Fax: 610-499-4615.

School of Education, Hospitality, and Continuing Studies Students: 97 full-time (64 women), 201 part-time (143 women); includes 56 minority (44 Black or African American, non-Hispanic/Latino; 1 American Indian or Alaska Native, non-Hispanic/Latino; 2 Asian, non-Hispanic/Latino; 8 Hispanic/Latino; 1 Two or more races, non-Hispanic/Latino), 32 international. Average age 39. 139 applicants, 88% accepted. *Faculty:* 34 full-time (22 women), 37 part-time/adjunct (14 women). Expenses: Contact institution. *Financial support:* Career-related internships or fieldwork, tuition waivers (full and partial), and unspecified assistantships available. Support available to part-time students. Financial award application deadline: 5/1. In 2016, 45 master's, 21 doctorates awarded. *Program availability:* Part-time, evening/weekend. Offers adult education (M Ed); counseling in higher education (M Ed); counselor education (M Ed); early childhood education (M Ed); educational foundations (M Ed); educational leadership (M Ed); educational psychology (M Ed); elementary education (M Ed); English and language arts (M Ed); health education (M Ed); higher education leadership (Ed D); home and school visitor (M Ed); human sexuality (M Ed, PhD); mathematics education (M Ed); middle school education (M Ed); principalship (M Ed); reading and language arts (Ed D); reading education (M Ed); school administration (Ed D); science education (M Ed); social studies education (M Ed); special education (M Ed); technology education (M Ed). *Application deadline:* Applications are processed on a rolling basis. *Application fee:* $25 ($300 for international students). Electronic applications accepted. *Application Contact:* Dr. Roberta Nolan, Director of Graduate Admissions, 610-499-4125, E-mail: rdnolan@widener.edu. *Dean,* Dr. Shawn Fitzgerald, 610-499-4294, Fax: 610-499-4623, E-mail: smfitzgerald@widener.edu.

School of Human Service Professions Students: 512 full-time (395 women), 807 part-time (712 women); includes 515 minority (360 Black or African American, non-Hispanic/Latino; 4 American Indian or Alaska Native, non-Hispanic/Latino; 28 Asian, non-Hispanic/Latino; 89 Hispanic/Latino; 1 Native Hawaiian or other Pacific Islander, non-Hispanic/Latino; 33 Two or more races, non-Hispanic/Latino), 11 international. Average age 34. 1,251 applicants, 34% accepted, 271 enrolled. *Faculty:* 64 full-time (39 women), 70 part-time/adjunct (34 women). Expenses: Contact institution. *Financial support:* Fellowships, research assistantships, teaching assistantships, career-related internships or fieldwork, Federal Work-Study, institutionally sponsored loans, tuition waivers (partial), unspecified assistantships, and stipends available. Support available to part-time students. Financial award applicants required to submit FAFSA. In 2016, 232 master's, 96 doctorates awarded. *Program availability:* Part-time, evening/weekend, 100% online, blended/hybrid learning. Offers human service professions (M Ed, MS, MSW, DPT, Ed D, PhD, Psy D). *Application Contact:* 610-499-4372, E-mail: gradmc@mail.widener.edu. *Dean,* Dr. Paula T. Silver, 610-499-4351, Fax: 610-499-4277, E-mail: ptsilver@widener.edu.

Center for Social Work Education Students: 74 full-time (63 women), 676 part-time (606 women); includes 375 minority (287 Black or African American, non-Hispanic/Latino; 2 American Indian or Alaska Native, non-Hispanic/Latino; 12 Asian, non-Hispanic/Latino; 56 Hispanic/Latino; 1 Native Hawaiian or other Pacific Islander, non-Hispanic/Latino; 17 Two or more races, non-Hispanic/Latino). Average age 33. 307 applicants, 60% accepted, 156 enrolled. *Faculty:* 15 full-time (9 women), 16 part-time/adjunct (9 women). Expenses: Contact institution. *Financial support:* In 2016–17, 11 students received support, including 6 fellowships; career-related internships or fieldwork, Federal Work-Study, institutionally sponsored loans, and unspecified assistantships also available. Support available to part-time students. Financial award applicants required to submit FAFSA. In 2016, 138 master's, 7 doctorates awarded. *Program availability:* Part-time, 100% online, blended/hybrid learning. Offers social work education (MSW, PhD). *Application deadline:* For fall admission, 3/1 for domestic students. Applications are processed on a rolling basis. *Application fee:* $25 ($300 for international students). Electronic applications accepted. *Application Contact:* Jill L. Brinker, Secretary, 610-499-1513, Fax: 610-499-4617, E-mail: socialwork@widener.edu. *Associate Dean and Director,* Dr. Paula T. Silver, 610-499-1150, Fax: 610-499-4617, E-mail: socialwork@widener.edu.

Institute for Graduate Clinical Psychology Students: 163 full-time (124 women), 16 part-time (11 women); includes 42 minority (10 Black or African American, non-Hispanic/Latino; 15 Asian, non-Hispanic/Latino; 13 Hispanic/Latino; 4 Two or more races, non-Hispanic/Latino), 3 international. Average age 25. 208 applicants, 31% accepted. *Faculty:* 15 full-time (6 women), 18 part-time/adjunct (10 women). Expenses: Contact institution. *Financial support:* Research assistantships, teaching assistantships, career-related internships or fieldwork, Federal Work-Study, institutionally sponsored loans, scholarships/grants, and stipends available. In 2016, 26 doctorates awarded. Offers clinical psychology (Psy D). *Application deadline:* For fall admission, 12/31 for domestic students. *Application fee:* $75. Electronic applications accepted. *Application Contact:* Ellen Madison, Admissions Coordinator, 611-499-1206, Fax: 610-499-4625, E-mail: ellen.t.madison@widener.edu. *Associate Dean/Director,* Dr. Virginia Brabender, 610-499-1208, Fax: 610-499-4625, E-mail: graduate.psychology@widener.edu.

Institute for Physical Therapy Education Students: 114 full-time (59 women), 4 part-time (2 women); includes 15 minority (4 Black or African American, non-Hispanic/Latino; 1 American Indian or Alaska Native, non-Hispanic/Latino; 5 Asian, non-Hispanic/Latino; 3 Hispanic/Latino; 2 Two or more races, non-Hispanic/Latino). Average age 24. 82 applicants, 93% accepted. *Faculty:* 8 full-time (5 women), 1 (woman) part-time/adjunct. Expenses: Contact institution. *Financial support:* Teaching assistantships, Federal Work-Study, institutionally sponsored loans, and scholarships/grants available. Financial award application deadline: 5/1; financial award applicants required to submit FAFSA. In 2016, 53 doctorates awarded. Offers physical therapy education (MS, DPT). *Application deadline:* For fall admission, 1/30 for domestic students. Applications are processed on a rolling basis. *Application fee:* $40. *Application Contact:* 610-499-4372, E-mail: gradmc@mail.widener.edu. *Associate Dean and Director,* Dr. Robin L. Dole, 610-499-1159, Fax: 610-499-1231, E-mail: robin.l.dole@widener.edu.

School of Nursing Students: 32 full-time (30 women), 182 part-time (165 women); includes 80 minority (55 Black or African American, non-Hispanic/Latino; 20 Asian, non-Hispanic/Latino; 3 Hispanic/Latino; 2 Two or more races, non-Hispanic/Latino), 5 international. Average age 33. 64 applicants, 47% accepted, 25 enrolled. *Faculty:* 12 full-time (all women), 4 part-time/adjunct (3 women). Expenses: Contact institution. *Financial support:* Career-related internships or fieldwork, Federal Work-Study, and traineeships available. Support available to part-time students. Financial award application deadline: 4/1. In 2016, 64 master's, 12 doctorates awarded. *Program availability:* Part-time, evening/weekend. Offers nursing (MSN, DN Sc, PhD, PMC). *Application deadline:* For fall admission, 7/1 for domestic students; for winter admission, 3/1 for domestic students; for spring admission, 11/1 for domestic students. Applications are processed on a rolling basis. *Application fee:* $25 ($300 for international students). Electronic applications accepted. *Dean,* Dr. Laura Dzurec, 610-499-4214, E-mail: lcdzurec@widener.edu.

WILBERFORCE UNIVERSITY, Wilberforce, OH 45384
General Information Independent-religious, coed, comprehensive institution.
GRADUATE UNITS
Program in Rehabilitation Counseling Offers rehabilitation counseling (MS).

WILFRID LAURIER UNIVERSITY, Waterloo, ON N2L 3C5, Canada
General Information Province-supported, coed, comprehensive institution.
GRADUATE UNITS

Faculty of Graduate and Postdoctoral Studies *Program availability:* Part-time, evening/weekend. Electronic applications accepted.

Faculty of Arts *Program availability:* Part-time. Offers agency (MA); arts (M Sc, MA, MES, MIPP, PhD); body politics (MA); Canadian political studies (MA); community (MA); comparative politics/international relations (MA); cultural representation and social theory (MA); English (MA); English and film (PhD); environmental and resource management (MA, MES, PhD); environmental science (M Sc, MES, PhD); gender, sexuality and embodiment (MA); geomatics (M Sc, MES, PhD); globalization, identity and social movements (MA); health, family and well-being (MA); history (MA, PhD); human geography (MES, PhD); internationalization, migration and human rights (MA); media, technology and culture (MA); religion and culture (MA); religious diversity of North America (PhD); self (MA); visual communication and culture (MA). Electronic applications accepted.

Faculty of Music Offers music (MMT). Electronic applications accepted.

Faculty of Science Offers behavioral neuroscience (M Sc, PhD); chemistry (M Sc); cognitive neuroscience (M Sc, PhD); community psychology (MA, PhD); integrative biology (M Sc); mathematics for science and finance (M Sc); physical activity and health (M Sc); science (M Sc, MA, PhD); social and developmental psychology (MA, PhD). Electronic applications accepted.

Lyle S. Hallman Faculty of Social Work *Program availability:* Part-time. Offers Aboriginal studies (MSW); community, policy, planning and organizations (MSW); critical social policy and organizational studies (PhD); individuals, families and groups (MSW); social work practice (individuals, families, groups and communities) (PhD); social work practice: individuals, families, groups and communities (PhD). Electronic applications accepted.

School of Business and Economics *Program availability:* Part-time, evening/weekend. Offers accounting (PhD); business and economics (EMTM, M Fin, M Sc, MA, MBA, PhD); co-op (MBA); economics (MA); finance (M Fin); financial economics (PhD); full-time (MBA); marketing (PhD); operations and supply chain management (PhD); organizational behavior and human resource management (M Sc); organizational behaviour and human resource management (PhD); part-time (MBA); supply chain management (M Sc); technology management (EMTM). Electronic applications accepted.

School of International Policy and Governance Offers conflict and security (PhD); global environment (PhD); global governance (MIPP); global justice and human rights (PhD); global political economy (PhD); global social governance (PhD); human security (MIPP); international economic relations (MIPP); international environmental policy (MIPP); international policy and governance (MIPP, PhD); multilateral institutions and diplomacy (PhD).

Laurier Brantford Offers criminology (MA). Electronic applications accepted.

Waterloo Lutheran Seminary *Program availability:* Part-time. Offers divinity (M Div); multifaith spiritual care and counseling (Diploma); pastoral leadership (D Min); spiritual care and counseling (D Min); theology (M Th, MTS). Electronic applications accepted.

WILKES UNIVERSITY, Wilkes-Barre, PA 18766-0002

General Information Independent, coed, comprehensive institution. *Enrollment:* 5,552 graduate, professional, and undergraduate students; 544 full-time matriculated graduate/professional students (360 women), 2,447 part-time matriculated graduate/professional students (1,886 women). *Enrollment by degree level:* 2,438 master's, 553 doctoral. Tuition and fees vary according to degree level and program. *Graduate housing:* On-campus housing not available. *Student services:* Campus employment opportunities, career counseling, free psychological counseling, international student services, low-cost health insurance, multicultural affairs office, services for students with disabilities. *Library facilities:* Eugene S. Farley Library. *Collection:* Books: 168,516 (physical), 7,880 (digital/electronic); Serial titles: 55,000 (digital/electronic); Databases: 55. Students can reserve study rooms.

Computer facilities: Computer purchase and lease plans are available. 817 computers available on campus for general student use. A campuswide network can be accessed from student residence rooms and from off campus. Online class registration is available.

Website: http://www.wilkes.edu/

General Application Contact: Director of Graduate Education, 570-408-4234, Fax: 570-408-7846.

GRADUATE UNITS

College of Graduate and Professional Studies Students: 544 full-time (360 women), 2,447 part-time (1,886 women); includes 371 minority (178 Black or African American, non-Hispanic/Latino; 5 American Indian or Alaska Native, non-Hispanic/Latino; 51 Asian, non-Hispanic/Latino; 81 Hispanic/Latino; 7 Native Hawaiian or other Pacific Islander, non-Hispanic/Latino; 49 Two or more races, non-Hispanic/Latino), 43 international. Average age 35. Expenses: Contact institution. *Financial support:* Unspecified assistantships available. Financial award application deadline: 3/1; financial award applicants required to submit FAFSA. In 2016, 660 master's, 113 doctorates awarded. *Program availability:* Part-time, evening/weekend, 100% online, blended/hybrid learning. Offers creative writing (MA, MFA). *Application deadline:* Applications are processed on a rolling basis. *Application fee:* $45 ($65 for international students). Electronic applications accepted. *Application Contact:* Director of Graduate Enrollment, 570-408-4234, Fax: 570-408-7846.

College of Science and Engineering Students: 31 full-time (7 women), 27 part-time (5 women); includes 6 minority (1 Black or African American, non-Hispanic/Latino; 1 Asian, non-Hispanic/Latino; 2 Hispanic/Latino; 2 Two or more races, non-Hispanic/Latino), 24 international. Average age 27. Expenses: Contact institution. *Financial support:* Unspecified assistantships available. Financial award application deadline: 3/1; financial award applicants required to submit FAFSA. In 2016, 23 master's awarded. *Program availability:* Part-time. Offers bioengineering (MS); electrical engineering (MSEE); engineering management (MS); mathematics (MS); mechanical engineering (MS); science and engineering (MS, MSEE). *Application deadline:* Applications are processed on a rolling basis. *Application fee:* $45 ($65 for international students). Electronic applications accepted. *Application Contact:* Director of Graduate Enrollment, 570-408-4234, Fax: 570-408-7846. *Dean,* Dr. William Hudson, 570-408-4600, Fax: 570-408-7860, E-mail: william.hudson@wilkes.edu.

Jay S. Sidhu School of Business and Leadership Students: 35 full-time (17 women), 112 part-time (55 women); includes 17 minority (6 Black or African American, non-Hispanic/Latino; 4 Asian, non-Hispanic/Latino; 5 Hispanic/Latino; 2 Two or more races, non-Hispanic/Latino), 16 international. Average age 31. Expenses: Contact institution. *Financial support:* Unspecified assistantships available. Financial award application deadline: 3/1; financial award applicants required to submit FAFSA. In 2016, 59 master's awarded. *Program availability:* Part-time, evening/weekend. Offers accounting (MBA); entrepreneurship (MBA); finance (MBA); health care administration (MBA); human resource management (MBA); international business (MBA); operations management (MBA); organizational leadership and development (MBA). *Application deadline:* Applications are processed on a rolling basis. *Application fee:* $45 ($65 for international students). Electronic applications accepted. *Application Contact:* Director of Graduate Enrollment, 570-408-4234, Fax: 570-408-7846. *Dean,* Dr. Abel Adekola, 570-408-4701, Fax: 570-408-7846, E-mail: abel.adekola@wilkes.edu.

Nesbitt School of Pharmacy Students: 284 full-time (189 women); includes 32 minority (3 Black or African American, non-Hispanic/Latino; 1 American Indian or Alaska Native, non-Hispanic/Latino; 8 Asian, non-Hispanic/Latino; 5 Hispanic/Latino; 15 Two or more races, non-Hispanic/Latino), 2 international. Average age 22. Expenses: Contact institution. *Financial support:* Federal Work-Study and unspecified assistantships available. Financial award application deadline: 3/1; financial award applicants required to submit FAFSA. In 2016, 73 doctorates awarded. Offers pharmacy (Pharm D). *Application deadline:* Applications are processed on a rolling basis. *Application Contact:* Director of Graduate Enrollment, 570-408-4234, Fax: 570-408-7846. *Dean,* Dr. Bernard Graham, 570-408-4280, Fax: 570-408-7828, E-mail: bernard.graham@wilkes.edu.

Passan School of Nursing Students: 41 full-time (36 women), 733 part-time (663 women); includes 227 minority (151 Black or African American, non-Hispanic/Latino; 2 American Indian or Alaska Native, non-Hispanic/Latino; 25 Asian, non-Hispanic/Latino; 39 Hispanic/Latino; 4 Native Hawaiian or other Pacific Islander, non-Hispanic/Latino; 6 Two or more races, non-Hispanic/Latino). Average age 44. Expenses: Contact institution. *Financial support:* Unspecified assistantships available. Financial award application deadline: 3/1; financial award applicants required to submit FAFSA. In 2016, 15 master's, 19 doctorates awarded. *Program availability:* Part-time, online only, 100% online. Offers nursing (MSN, DNP). *Application deadline:* Applications are processed on a rolling basis. *Application fee:* $45. Electronic applications accepted. *Application Contact:* Director of Graduate Enrollment, 570-408-4234, Fax: 570-408-7846. *Dean,* Dr. Deborah Zbegner, 570-408-4086, Fax: 570-408-7807, E-mail: deborah.zbegner@wilkes.edu.

School of Education Students: 87 full-time (70 women), 1,496 part-time (1,111 women); includes 77 minority (11 Black or African American, non-Hispanic/Latino; 2 American Indian or Alaska Native, non-Hispanic/Latino; 12 Asian, non-Hispanic/Latino; 28 Hispanic/Latino; 3 Native Hawaiian or other Pacific Islander, non-Hispanic/Latino; 21 Two or more races, non-Hispanic/Latino). Average age 33. Expenses: Contact institution. *Financial support:* Unspecified assistantships available. Financial award application deadline: 3/1; financial award applicants required to submit FAFSA. In 2016, 524 master's, 21 doctorates awarded. *Program availability:* Part-time, evening/weekend, 100% online, blended/hybrid learning. Offers 21st century teaching and learning (MS Ed); art and science of teaching (MS Ed); classroom technology (MS Ed); early childhood literacy (MS Ed); educational development and strategies (MS Ed); educational leadership (MS Ed, Ed D); effective teaching (MS Ed); instructional media (MS Ed); instructional technology (MS Ed); international school leadership (MS Ed); international teaching and learning (MS Ed); middle level education (MS Ed); online teaching (MS Ed); reading (MS Ed); school business leadership (MS Ed); special education (MS Ed); teaching English to speakers of other languages (MS Ed). *Application deadline:* Applications are processed on a rolling basis. *Application fee:* $45. Electronic applications accepted. *Application Contact:* Director of Graduate Education, 570-408-4234, Fax: 570-408-7846. *Dean,* Dr. Rhonda Rabbitt, 570-408-4680, Fax: 570-408-7872, E-mail: rhonda.rabbitt@wilkes.edu.

WILLAMETTE UNIVERSITY, Salem, OR 97301-3931

General Information Independent-religious, coed, comprehensive institution. *Enrollment:* 2,665 graduate, professional, and undergraduate students; 527 full-time matriculated graduate/professional students (229 women), 96 part-time matriculated graduate/professional students (41 women). *Enrollment by degree level:* 345 master's, 278 doctoral. *Graduate faculty:* 47 full-time (16 women), 17 part-time/adjunct (4 women). *Graduate housing:* Room and/or apartments available on a first-come, first-served basis to single students; on-campus housing not available to married students. Housing application deadline: 6/1. *Student services:* Campus employment opportunities, campus safety program, career counseling, free psychological counseling, international student services, low-cost health insurance, multicultural affairs office, services for students with disabilities, teacher training. *Library facilities:* Mark O. Hatfield Library plus 1 other. *Collection:* Study areas open 24 hours, 5–7 days a week; students can reserve study rooms.

Computer facilities: A campuswide network can be accessed from student residence rooms and from off campus. Online class registration is available.
Website: http://www.willamette.edu/

General Application Contact: Office of Graduate Admissions, 503-370-6300.

GRADUATE UNITS

Atkinson Graduate School of Management Students: 155 full-time (69 women), 120 part-time (67 women); includes 39 minority (6 Black or African American, non-Hispanic/Latino; 2 American Indian or Alaska Native, non-Hispanic/Latino; 18 Asian, non-Hispanic/Latino; 8 Hispanic/Latino; 3 Native Hawaiian or other Pacific Islander, non-Hispanic/Latino; 2 Two or more races, non-Hispanic/Latino), 66 international. Average age 29. 208 applicants, 96% accepted, 104 enrolled. *Faculty:* 17 full-time (3 women), 18 part-time/adjunct (7 women). Expenses: Contact institution. *Financial support:* In 2016–17, 220 students received support. Federal Work-Study, scholarships/grants, and unspecified assistantships available. Financial award application deadline: 5/1; financial award applicants required to submit FAFSA. In 2016, 138 master's awarded. *Program availability:* Part-time, evening/weekend. Offers management (MBA). JD/MBA offered jointly with College of Law. *Application deadline:* 5/1 priority date for domestic and international students. Applications are processed on a rolling basis. *Application fee:* $100. Electronic applications accepted. *Application Contact:* Aimee Akimoff, Director of Recruitment, 503-370-6167, Fax: 503-370-3011, E-mail: aakimoff@willamette.edu. *Dean and Professor of Free Enterprise,* Dr. Debra J. Ringold, 503-370-6790, Fax: 503-370-3011, E-mail: dringold@willamette.edu.

College of Law *Program availability:* Part-time. Offers dispute resolution (LL M); law (MLS, JD); transnational law (LL M). Electronic applications accepted.

WILLIAM CAREY UNIVERSITY, Hattiesburg, MS 39401-5499

General Information Independent-religious, coed, comprehensive institution. *Graduate housing:* Room and/or apartments available on a first-come, first-served basis to single students; on-campus housing not available to married students. Housing application deadline: 8/15.

GRADUATE UNITS

College of Osteopathic Medicine Offers osteopathic medicine (DO).

Department of Psychology and Graduate Counseling *Program availability:* Part-time. Offers counseling psychology (MS).

School of Business *Program availability:* Part-time. Offers business (MBA).

School of Education *Program availability:* Part-time. Offers art education (M Ed); art of teaching (M Ed); elementary education (M Ed, Ed S); English education (M Ed); gifted education (M Ed); history and social science (M Ed); mild/moderate disabilities (M Ed); secondary education (M Ed).

School of Nursing *Program availability:* Part-time. Offers nursing (MSN).

WILLIAM JAMES COLLEGE, Newton, MA 02459

General Information Independent, coed, primarily women, graduate-only institution. *Graduate housing:* On-campus housing not available.

GRADUATE UNITS

Graduate Programs Offers applied psychology in higher education student personnel administration (MA); clinical psychology (Psy D); counseling psychology (MA); counseling psychology and community mental health (MA); counseling psychology and global mental health (MA); executive coaching (Graduate Certificate); forensic and counseling psychology (MA); leadership psychology (Psy D); organizational psychology (MA); primary care psychology (MA); respecialization in clinical psychology (Certificate); school psychology (Psy D). Electronic applications accepted.

WILLIAM JESSUP UNIVERSITY, Rocklin, CA 95765

General Information Independent-religious, coed, comprehensive institution.

GRADUATE UNITS

Program in Teaching *Program availability:* Evening/weekend. Offers single subject English (MAT); single subject math (MAT).

WILLIAM JEWELL COLLEGE, Liberty, MO 64068-1843

General Information Independent, coed, comprehensive institution.

GRADUATE UNITS

Department of Education Offers differentiated instruction (MS Ed).

WILLIAM PATERSON UNIVERSITY OF NEW JERSEY, Wayne, NJ 07470-8420

General Information State-supported, coed, comprehensive institution. CGS member. *Enrollment:* 10,583 graduate, professional, and undergraduate students; 313 full-time matriculated graduate/professional students (200 women), 1,048 part-time matriculated graduate/professional students (818 women). *Enrollment by degree level:* 1,163 master's, 35 doctoral, 163 other advanced degrees. *Graduate faculty:* 143 full-time (78 women), 93 part-time/adjunct (64 women). Tuition, state resident: full-time $12,480; part-time $611 per credit. Tuition, nonresident: full-time $20,263; part-time $992 per credit. *Required fees:* $1573; $77 per credit. Tuition and fees vary according to course load, degree level and program. *Graduate housing:* Room and/or apartments available on a first-come, first-served basis to single students; on-campus housing not available to married students. Typical cost: $9020 per year. Room charges vary according to board plan, campus/location and housing facility selected. Housing application deadline: 5/1. *Student services:* Campus employment opportunities, campus safety program, career counseling, exercise/wellness program, free psychological counseling, international student services, multicultural affairs office, services for students with disabilities, teacher training, writing training. *Library facilities:* David and Lorraine Cheng Library. *Collection:* Books: 369,216 (physical), 116,597 (digital/electronic); Serial titles: 3,772 (physical), 164,249 (digital/electronic); Databases: 126. Weekly public service hours: 102; students can reserve study rooms. *Research affiliation:* Sun Chemical (chemistry), Arysta Life Sciences (biology).

Computer facilities: Computer purchase and lease plans are available. 1,271 computers available on campus for general student use. A campuswide network can be accessed from student residence rooms and from off campus. Online class registration is available.
Website: http://www.wpunj.edu/

General Application Contact: Augustus Kubeyinje, Director of Graduate Admissions and Enrollment Services, 973-720-3641, Fax: 973-720-2035, E-mail: kubeyinjea@wpunj.edu.

GRADUATE UNITS

College of Education Students: 74 full-time (51 women), 607 part-time (515 women); includes 194 minority (42 Black or African American, non-Hispanic/Latino; 21 Asian, non-Hispanic/Latino; 116 Hispanic/Latino; 15 Two or more races, non-Hispanic/Latino), 1 international. Average age 35. 390 applicants, 83% accepted, 263 enrolled. *Faculty:* 36 full-time (25 women), 32 part-time/adjunct (27 women). Expenses: Contact institution. *Financial support:* Career-related internships or fieldwork, Federal Work-Study, scholarships/grants, and unspecified assistantships available. Support available to part-time students. Financial award application deadline: 4/1; financial award applicants required to submit FAFSA. In 2016, 170 master's awarded. *Program availability:* Part-time, evening/weekend. Offers curriculum and learning (M Ed); educational leadership (M Ed); elementary education (MAT); literacy (M Ed); professional counseling (M Ed); secondary education (MAT); special education (M Ed). *Application deadline:* For fall admission, 8/1 for domestic students, 4/1 for international students; for spring admission, 12/1 for domestic students, 11/1 for international students; for summer admission, 5/1 for domestic students, 2/1 for international students. Applications are processed on a rolling basis. *Application fee:* $50. Electronic applications accepted. *Application Contact:* Liana Fornarotto, Director of Education Enrollment and Certification, 973-720-2206, Fax: 973-720-2989, E-mail: fornarottol@wpunj.edu. *Dean,* Dr. Candace Burns, 973-720-2137, Fax: 973-720-3467, E-mail: burnsc@wpunj.edu.

College of Humanities and Social Sciences Students: 58 full-time (38 women), 62 part-time (46 women); includes 40 minority (9 Black or African American, non-Hispanic/Latino; 6 Asian, non-Hispanic/Latino; 21 Hispanic/Latino; 4 Two or more races, non-Hispanic/Latino), 4 international. Average age 32. 160 applicants, 55% accepted, 50 enrolled. *Faculty:* 35 full-time (19 women), 8 part-time/adjunct (5 women). Expenses: Contact institution. *Financial support:* Career-related internships or fieldwork, Federal Work-Study, scholarships/grants, and unspecified assistantships available. Support available to part-time students. Financial award applicants required to submit FAFSA. In 2016, 56 master's awarded. *Program availability:* Part-time, evening/weekend. Offers applied sociology (MA); clinical and counseling psychology (MA); clinical psychology (Psy D); creative and professional writing (MFA); English (MA); history (MA); political science and public policy (MA); public policy and international affairs (MA). *Application deadline:* For fall admission, 8/1 for domestic students, 4/1 for international students; for spring admission, 12/1 for domestic students, 11/1 for international students; for summer admission, 5/1 for domestic students, 2/1 for international students. Applications are processed on a rolling basis. *Application fee:* $50. Electronic applications accepted. *Application Contact:* Tinu Adeniran, Associate Director, Graduate Admissions, 973-720-2764, Fax: 973-720-2035, E-mail: adenirant@wpunj.edu. *Dean,* Dr. Kara Rabbitt, 973-720-2180, Fax: 973-720-2955, E-mail: rabbittk@wpunj.edu.

College of Science and Health Students: 63 full-time (53 women), 199 part-time (171 women); includes 110 minority (14 Black or African American, non-Hispanic/Latino; 45 Asian, non-Hispanic/Latino; 44 Hispanic/Latino; 7 Two or more races, non-Hispanic/Latino), 2 international. Average age 33. 118 applicants, 98% accepted, 83 enrolled. *Faculty:* 30 full-time (19 women), 24 part-time/adjunct (24 women). Expenses: Contact institution. *Financial support:* Career-related internships or fieldwork, Federal Work-Study, scholarships/grants, and unspecified assistantships available. Support available to part-time students. Financial award applicants required to submit FAFSA. In 2016, 51 master's, 2 doctorates awarded. *Program availability:* Part-time, evening/weekend. Offers biology (MS); biotechnology (MS); communication disorders (MS); exercise and sport studies (MS); nursing (MSN); nursing practice (DNP). *Application deadline:* For fall admission, 8/1 for domestic students, 4/1 for international students; for spring admission, 12/1 for domestic students, 11/1 for international students; for summer admission, 5/1 for domestic students, 2/1 for international students. Applications are processed on a rolling basis. *Application fee:* $50. Electronic applications accepted. *Application Contact:* Christina Aiello, Assistant Director, Graduate Admissions, 973-720-2506, Fax: 973-720-2035, E-mail: aielloc@wpunj.edu. *Dean,* Dr. Kenneth Wolf, 973-720-2194, Fax: 973-720-3414, E-mail: wolfk@wpunj.edu.

College of the Arts and Communication Students: 44 full-time (21 women), 19 part-time (9 women); includes 17 minority (7 Black or African American, non-Hispanic/Latino; 1 Asian, non-Hispanic/Latino; 8 Hispanic/Latino; 1 Two or more races, non-Hispanic/Latino), 12 international. Average age 30. 81 applicants, 75% accepted, 33 enrolled. *Faculty:* 23 full-time (10 women), 26 part-time/adjunct (7 women). Expenses: Contact institution. *Financial support:* Career-related internships or fieldwork, Federal Work-Study, scholarships/grants, and unspecified assistantships available. Support available to part-time students. Financial award applicants required to submit FAFSA. In 2016, 22 master's awarded. *Program availability:* Part-time, evening/weekend. Offers art (MFA); music (MM); professional communication (MA). *Application deadline:* For fall admission, 8/1 for domestic students, 4/1 for international students; for spring admission, 12/1 for domestic students, 11/1 for international students; for summer admission, 5/1 for domestic students, 2/1 for international students. Applications are processed on a rolling basis. *Application fee:* $50. Electronic applications accepted. *Application Contact:* Christina Aiello, Assistant Director, Graduate Admissions, 973-720-2506, Fax: 973-720-2035, E-mail: aielloc@wpunj.edu. *Dean,* Daryl Moore, 973-720-2232, E-mail: moored@wpunj.edu.

Cotsakos College of Business Students: 74 full-time (37 women), 161 part-time (77 women); includes 86 minority (25 Black or African American, non-Hispanic/Latino; 13 Asian, non-Hispanic/Latino; 39 Hispanic/Latino; 9 Two or more races, non-Hispanic/Latino), 30 international. Average age 31. 176 applicants, 69% accepted, 89 enrolled. *Faculty:* 19 full-time (5 women), 1 (woman) part-time/adjunct. Expenses: Contact institution. *Financial support:* Career-related internships or fieldwork, Federal Work-Study, scholarships/grants, and unspecified assistantships available. Support available to part-time students. Financial award applicants required to submit FAFSA. In 2016, 41 master's awarded. *Program availability:* Part-time, evening/weekend. Offers business administration (MBA). *Application deadline:* For fall admission, 8/1 for domestic students, 4/1 for international students; for spring admission, 12/1 for domestic students, 11/1 for international students; for summer admission, 5/1 for domestic students, 2/1 for international students. Applications are processed on a rolling basis. *Application fee:* $50. Electronic applications accepted. *Application Contact:* Tinu Adeniran, Assistant Director, Graduate Admissions, 973-720-2764, Fax: 973-720-2035, E-mail: adenirant@wpunj.edu. *Dean,* Dr. Siamack Shojai, 973-720-2964, Fax: 973-720-2809, E-mail: shojais@wpunj.edu.

WILLIAM PENN UNIVERSITY, Oskaloosa, IA 52577-1799

General Information Independent-religious, coed, comprehensive institution.

GRADUATE UNITS

College for Working Adults *Program availability:* Online learning.

WILLIAMS COLLEGE, Williamstown, MA 01267

General Information Independent, coed, comprehensive institution. *Graduate housing:* Room and/or apartments available on a first-come, first-served basis to single students; on-campus housing not available to married students. *Research affiliation:* Clark Art Institute.

GRADUATE UNITS

Graduate Program in the History of Art Offers development economics (MA); history of art (MA). MA in history of art offered jointly with Sterling and Francine Clark Art Institute. Electronic applications accepted.

WILLIAMSON COLLEGE, Franklin, TN 37067

General Information Independent-religious, coed, comprehensive institution.

GRADUATE UNITS

Program in Organizational Leadership *Program availability:* Evening/weekend. Offers organizational leadership (MA).

WILLIAM WOODS UNIVERSITY, Fulton, MO 65251-1098

General Information Independent-religious, coed, comprehensive institution. *Graduate housing:* On-campus housing not available.

GRADUATE UNITS

Graduate and Adult Studies *Program availability:* Part-time, evening/weekend. Offers administration (M Ed, Ed S); athletic/activities administration (M Ed); curriculum and instruction (M Ed, Ed S); educational leadership (Ed D); equestrian education (M Ed); health management (MBA); human resources (MBA); leadership (MBA); marketing, advertising, and public relations (MBA); teaching and technology (M Ed). Electronic applications accepted.

WILMINGTON COLLEGE, Wilmington, OH 45177

General Information Independent-religious, coed, comprehensive institution. *Graduate housing:* On-campus housing not available.

GRADUATE UNITS

Department of Education *Program availability:* Part-time. Offers reading (M Ed); special education (M Ed).

WILMINGTON UNIVERSITY, New Castle, DE 19720-6491

General Information Independent, coed, university. *Enrollment:* 15,240 graduate, professional, and undergraduate students; 2,829 full-time matriculated graduate/professional students (1,306 women), 3,505 part-time matriculated graduate/professional students (2,426 women). *Enrollment by degree level:* 5,784 master's, 550 doctoral. *Graduate faculty:* 69 full-time (37 women), 500 part-time/adjunct (267 women). *Tuition:* Full-time $8388; part-time $466 per credit. *Required fees:* $25 per semester. Tuition and fees vary according to degree level. *Graduate housing:* On-campus housing not available. *Student services:* Career counseling, free psychological counseling, international student services, services for students with disabilities, teacher training, writing training. *Library facilities:* Robert C. and Dorothy M. Peoples Library plus 1 other.

Computer facilities: 600 computers available on campus for general student use. A campuswide network can be accessed. Online class registration is available.
Website: http://www.wilmu.edu/

General Application Contact: Laura Morris, Director of Admissions, 302-295-1179, Fax: 302-328-5164, E-mail: infocenter@wilmu.edu.

GRADUATE UNITS

College of Business Students: 436 full-time (237 women), 1,202 part-time (739 women); includes 594 minority (474 Black or African American, non-Hispanic/Latino; 19 American Indian or Alaska Native, non-Hispanic/Latino; 64 Asian, non-Hispanic/Latino; 30 Hispanic/Latino; 3 Native Hawaiian or other Pacific Islander, non-Hispanic/Latino; 4 Two or more races, non-Hispanic/Latino), 153 international. Average age 35. 814 applicants, 98% accepted, 426 enrolled. *Faculty:* 17 full-time (7 women), 106 part-time/adjunct (46 women). Expenses: Contact institution. *Financial support:* Applicants required to submit FAFSA. In 2016, 594 master's, 23 doctorates awarded. *Program availability:* Part-time, evening/weekend. Offers accounting (MBA, MS); business administration (MBA, DBA); environmental stewardship (MBA); finance (MBA); health care administration (MBA, MSM); homeland security (MBA, MSM); human resource management (MSM); management information systems (MBA, MSN); marketing (MSM); marketing management (MBA); military leadership (MSM); organizational leadership (MBA, MSM); public administration (MSM). *Application deadline:* Applications are processed on a rolling basis. *Application fee:* $35. Electronic applications accepted. *Application Contact:* Laura Morris, Director of Admissions, 877-967-5456, E-mail: infocenter@wilmu.edu. *Dean,* Dr. Robert W. Rescigno.

College of Education Students: 248 full-time (176 women), 999 part-time (738 women); includes 244 minority (193 Black or African American, non-Hispanic/Latino; 17 American Indian or Alaska Native, non-Hispanic/Latino; 9 Asian, non-Hispanic/Latino; 19 Hispanic/Latino; 2 Native Hawaiian or other Pacific Islander, non-Hispanic/Latino; 4 Two or more races, non-Hispanic/Latino), 7 international. Average age 34. 672 applicants, 96% accepted, 348 enrolled. *Faculty:* 19 full-time (11 women), 178 part-time/adjunct (99 women). Expenses: Contact institution. *Financial support:* Applicants required to submit FAFSA. In 2016, 529 master's, 87 doctorates awarded. *Program availability:* Part-time, evening/weekend. Offers applied technology in education (M Ed); career and technical education (M Ed); educational leadership (Ed D); elementary and secondary school counseling (M Ed); elementary studies (M Ed); ESOL literacy (M Ed); higher education leadership (Ed D); instruction: gifted and talented (M Ed); instruction: teacher of reading (M Ed); instruction: teaching and learning (M Ed); organizational leadership (Ed D); school leadership (M Ed); secondary education (MAT); special education (M Ed). *Application deadline:* For fall admission, 4/30 for domestic students. Applications are processed on a rolling basis. *Application fee:* $35. Electronic applications accepted. *Application Contact:* Laura Morris, Director of Admissions, 877-967-5464, E-mail: infocenter@wilmu.edu. *Dean,* Dr. John C. Gray.

College of Health Professions Students: 157 full-time (146 women), 587 part-time (538 women); includes 181 minority (142 Black or African American, non-Hispanic/Latino; 7 American Indian or Alaska Native, non-Hispanic/Latino; 21 Asian, non-Hispanic/Latino; 9 Hispanic/Latino; 2 Native Hawaiian or other Pacific Islander, non-Hispanic/Latino), 10 international. Average age 39. 464 applicants, 99% accepted, 235 enrolled. *Faculty:* 9 full-time (8 women), 52 part-time/adjunct (50 women). Expenses: Contact institution. *Financial support:* Fellowships with tuition reimbursements and traineeships available. Financial award applicants required to submit FAFSA. In 2016, 240 master's, 19 doctorates awarded. *Program availability:* Part-time. Offers adult nurse practitioner (MSN); family nurse practitioner (MSN); gerontology nurse practitioner (MSN); nursing (MSN); nursing leadership (MSN); nursing practice (DNP). *Application deadline:* For fall admission, 4/1 for domestic students; for spring admission, 9/1 for domestic students. Applications are processed on a rolling basis. *Application fee:* $35. Electronic applications accepted. *Application Contact:* Laura Morris, Director of Admissions, 877-967-5464, E-mail: infocenter@wilmu.edu. *Dean,* Denise Z. Westbrook.

College of Social and Behavioral Sciences Students: 210 full-time (162 women), 444 part-time (325 women); includes 320 minority (285 Black or African American, non-Hispanic/Latino; 12 American Indian or Alaska Native, non-Hispanic/Latino; 9 Asian, non-Hispanic/Latino; 12 Hispanic/Latino; 1 Native Hawaiian or other Pacific Islander, non-Hispanic/Latino; 1 Two or more races, non-Hispanic/Latino), 4 international. Average age 35. 255 applicants, 100% accepted, 25 enrolled. *Faculty:* 8 full-time (5 women), 79 part-time/adjunct (35 women). Expenses: Contact institution. *Financial support:* Applicants required to submit FAFSA. In 2016, 248 master's awarded. *Program availability:* Part-time, evening/weekend. Offers administration of human services (MS); administration of justice (MS); clinical mental health counseling (MS); homeland security (MS). *Application deadline:* Applications are processed on a rolling basis. *Application fee:* $35. Electronic applications accepted. *Application Contact:* Laura Morris, Director of Admissions, 877-967-5464, E-mail: inquire@wilmcoll.edu. *Dean,* Dr. Edward L. Guthrie.

College of Technology Students: 1,316 full-time (321 women), 263 part-time (79 women); includes 71 minority (53 Black or African American, non-Hispanic/Latino; 5 American Indian or Alaska Native, non-Hispanic/Latino; 8 Asian, non-Hispanic/Latino; 4 Hispanic/Latino; 1 Two or more races, non-Hispanic/Latino), 1,437 international. Average age 26. 856 applicants, 100% accepted, 332 enrolled. *Faculty:* 5 full-time (1 woman), 114 part-time/adjunct (31 women). Expenses: Contact institution. In 2016, 756 master's awarded. *Program availability:* Part-time, evening/weekend. Offers geographic information systems (MS); information assurance (MS); information systems technologies (MS); Internet/Web design (MS); management and management information systems (MS). *Application deadline:* Applications are processed on a rolling basis. *Application fee:* $35. Electronic applications accepted. *Application Contact:* Laura Morris, Director of Admissions, 877-967-5464, E-mail: infocenter@wilmu.edu. *Dean,* Dr. Mary Ann K. Westerfield.

WILSON COLLEGE, Chambersburg, PA 17201-1285

General Information Independent-religious, coed, primarily women, comprehensive institution.

GRADUATE UNITS

Graduate Programs *Program availability:* Evening/weekend. Offers accounting (M Acc); choreography and visual art (MFA); education (M Ed); healthcare management for sustainability (MHM); humanities (MA); management (MSM); nursing (MSN). Electronic applications accepted.

WINEBRENNER THEOLOGICAL SEMINARY, Findlay, OH 45840

General Information Independent-religious, coed, graduate-only institution. *Enrollment by degree level:* 61 master's, 5 doctoral. *Graduate faculty:* 7 full-time (2 women), 22 part-time/adjunct (8 women). *Tuition:* Full-time $14,175; part-time $525 per credit hour. *Required fees:* $450; $150 per trimester. Tuition and fees vary according to degree level. *Graduate housing:* On-campus housing not available. *Student services:* Campus safety program, career counseling, free psychological counseling, international student services, multicultural affairs office, services for students with disabilities, writing training. *Library facilities:* Shafer Library plus 1 other. *Collection:* Books: 42,350 (physical), 43 (digital/electronic); Serial titles: 2 (physical), 4 (digital/electronic). Weekly public service hours: 95; study areas open 24 hours, 5–7 days a week.

Computer facilities: 224 computers available on campus for general student use. Online class registration, X are available.
Website: http://www.winebrenner.edu/

General Application Contact: Jim Smarkel, Director of Enrollment Management, 419-434-4220, Fax: 419-434-4267, E-mail: admissions@winebrenner.edu.

GRADUATE UNITS

Graduate Programs Students: 16 full-time (10 women), 50 part-time (23 women); includes 12 minority (8 Black or African American, non-Hispanic/Latino; 2 Asian, non-Hispanic/Latino; 2 Two or more races, non-Hispanic/Latino), 2 international. Average age 41. 25 applicants, 76% accepted, 12 enrolled. *Faculty:* 7 full-time (2 women), 22 part-time/adjunct (8 women). Expenses: Contact institution. *Financial support:* In 2016–17, 32 students received support, including 3 teaching assistantships with partial tuition reimbursements available (averaging $1,575 per year); research assistantships, institutionally sponsored loans, scholarships/grants, unspecified assistantships, and denominational discounts, spousal discounts also available. Financial award application deadline: 7/1; financial award applicants required to submit FAFSA. In 2016, 8 master's, 2 doctorates awarded. *Program availability:* Part-time, 100% online, blended/hybrid learning. Offers clinical counseling (MA); family ministry (MA); practical theology (MA); theological and ministerial studies (M Div, D Min); theological studies (MA). *Application deadline:* For fall admission, 8/15 priority date for domestic students, 7/15 priority date

for international students; for winter admission, 12/15 priority date for domestic students, 11/15 priority date for international students; for spring admission, 4/15 priority date for domestic students, 3/15 priority date for international students. Applications are processed on a rolling basis. *Application fee:* $30. Electronic applications accepted. *Application Contact:* Jim Smarkel, Director of Enrollment Management, 419-434-4220, Fax: 419-434-4267, E-mail: admissions@winebrenner.edu. *Academic Dean,* Dr. Joel W. Cocklin, 419-434-4250, Fax: 419-434-4267, E-mail: jcocklin@winebrenner.edu.

WINGATE UNIVERSITY, Wingate, NC 28174

General Information Independent-religious, coed, comprehensive institution. *Enrollment:* 3,193 graduate, professional, and undergraduate students. *Graduate housing:* Rooms and/or apartments available on a first-come, first-served basis to single and married students. Housing application deadline: 8/15. *Student services:* Campus employment opportunities, career counseling, free psychological counseling, services for students with disabilities, teacher training. *Library facilities:* Ethel K. Smith Library. *Collection:* Books: 96,673 (physical); Databases: 110. Students can reserve study rooms.

Computer facilities: 80 computers available on campus for general student use. A campuswide network can be accessed from student residence rooms and from off campus. Online class registration is available.
Website: http://www.wingate.edu/

GRADUATE UNITS

Department of Physical Therapy Expenses: Contact institution. Offers physical therapy (DPT). *Application Contact:* Dr. Kevin E. Brueilly, Program Director, 704-233-8344, E-mail: k.brueilly@wingate.edu. *Program Director,* Dr. Kevin E. Brueilly, 704-233-8344, E-mail: k.brueilly@wingate.edu.

Harris Department of Physician Assistant Studies Expenses: Contact institution. Offers physician assistant studies (MPAS). *Application Contact:* Carolyn R. Little, Secretary/Admissions Assistant, 704-233-8993, E-mail: clittle@wingate.edu.

Porter B. Byrum School of Business Expenses: Contact institution. *Financial support:* Federal Work-Study and scholarships/grants available. Support available to part-time students. Financial award application deadline: 8/1; financial award applicants required to submit FAFSA. *Program availability:* Part-time, evening/weekend. Offers accounting (MAC); corporate innovation (MBA); finance (MBA); general management (MBA); healthcare management (MBA); marketing (MBA); project management (MBA). *Application deadline:* For fall admission, 8/15 priority date for domestic students; for spring admission, 12/15 priority date for domestic students. Applications are processed on a rolling basis. *Application fee:* $50. Electronic applications accepted. *Application Contact:* Mary Maye, Administrative Assistant to the Dean, 704-233-8148, Fax: 704-233-8146. *Dean,* Dr. Peter Frank, 704-233-8148, Fax: 704-233-8146, E-mail: pfrank@wingate.edu.

School of Pharmacy Expenses: Contact institution. *Financial support:* Fellowships, research assistantships, teaching assistantships, career-related internships or fieldwork, and scholarships/grants available. Financial award application deadline: 5/30. Offers pharmacy (Pharm D). *Application deadline:* For fall admission, 2/1 for domestic and international students. Applications are processed on a rolling basis. *Application fee:* $0. Electronic applications accepted. *Application Contact:* Jean Tarlton, Coordinator of Pharmacy Admissions, 704-233-8324, Fax: 704-233-8332, E-mail: jtarlton@wingate.edu. *Vice Provost, Levine College of Health Sciences/Dean,* Dr. Robert Supernaw, 704-233-8015, Fax: 704-233-8332, E-mail: supernaw@wingate.edu.

School of Sport Sciences Expenses: Contact institution. Offers sport management (MA). *Application deadline:* For fall admission, 7/1 for domestic students; for spring admission, 12/1 for domestic students. Electronic applications accepted. *Application Contact:* Dr. Dawn Norwood, Program Director, 980-359-1036, E-mail: masm@wingate.edu. *Dean,* Dr. Travis L. Teague, 704-233-8297, E-mail: t.teague@wingate.edu.

Thayer School of Education Expenses: Contact institution. *Financial support:* Scholarships/grants available. Support available to part-time students. Financial award applicants required to submit FAFSA. *Program availability:* Part-time, evening/weekend. Offers community college executive leadership (Ed D); educational leadership (MA Ed, Ed S); elementary education (MA Ed, MAT). *Application deadline:* For fall admission, 8/15 priority date for domestic students; for spring admission, 12/15 for domestic students. Applications are processed on a rolling basis. *Application fee:* $0. *Application Contact:* Theresa Gibson, Director of the Graduate Education Program, 980-359-1023, E-mail: t.gibson@wingate.edu. *Interim Dean,* Dr. Annette D. Digby, 704-233-8473, E-mail: a.digby@wingate.edu.

WINONA STATE UNIVERSITY, Winona, MN 55987

General Information State-supported, coed, comprehensive institution. Tuition, state resident: part-time $388.17 per credit. Tuition, nonresident: part-time $585.65 per credit. *Required fees:* $38.99 per credit. Part-time tuition and fees vary according to degree level, program and reciprocity agreements. *Graduate housing:* Room and/or apartments available to single students; on-campus housing not available to married students. Housing application deadline: 3/2. *Student services:* Campus employment opportunities, campus safety program, career counseling, child daycare facilities, exercise/wellness program, free psychological counseling, international student services, low-cost health insurance, services for students with disabilities. *Library facilities:* Darrel W. Krueger Library. *Collection:* Books: 344,659 (physical), 50,000 (digital/electronic); Serial titles: 2,097 (physical), 34,000 (digital/electronic); Databases: 100. Weekly public service hours: 99; students can reserve study rooms.

Computer facilities: Computer purchase and lease plans are available. 50 computers available on campus for general student use. A campuswide network can be accessed from student residence rooms and from off campus. Online class registration is available.
Website: http://www.winona.edu/

General Application Contact: Patricia Cichosz, Office Manager, School of Graduate Studies, 507-457-5038, E-mail: gradoffice@winona.edu.

GRADUATE UNITS

College of Education Expenses: Contact institution. *Financial support:* Fellowships, career-related internships or fieldwork, Federal Work-Study, and unspecified assistantships available. Support available to part-time students. *Program availability:* Part-time, evening/weekend. Offers addiction counseling (Certificate); clinical mental health counseling (MS); education (MS, Certificate, Ed S); education leadership (MS, Ed S); human services (MS); multicultural education (Certificate); organizational leadership (MS); professional leadership (MS); school counseling (MS); special education (MS); sport management (MS). *Application deadline:* For fall admission, 8/8 priority date for domestic students; for spring admission, 2/15 for domestic students. Applications are processed on a rolling basis. *Application fee:* $20. *Application Contact:* Patricia Cichosz, Office Manager, Graduate Studies, 507-457-5038, E-mail: pcichosz@winona.edu. *Dean,* Dr. Tarrell Portman, 507-457-5570, E-mail: tportman@winona.edu.

College of Liberal Arts Expenses: Contact institution. *Financial support:* Career-related internships or fieldwork, Federal Work-Study, and unspecified assistantships available. Support available to part-time students. Financial award applicants required to submit FAFSA. *Program availability:* Part-time. Offers English (MS); liberal arts (MA, MS); literature and language (MA); TESOL (MA). *Application deadline:* For fall admission, 7/26 priority date for domestic students; for spring admission, 12/8 for domestic students. Applications are processed on a rolling basis. *Application fee:* $20. *Application Contact:* Patricia Cichosz, Office Manager, Graduate Studies, 507-457-5038, E-mail: pcichosz@winona.edu. *Dean,* Dr. Peter Miene, 507-457-5017, E-mail: pmiene@winona.edu.

College of Nursing and Health Sciences Expenses: Contact institution. *Financial support:* Research assistantships with partial tuition reimbursements, Federal Work-Study, traineeships, and unspecified assistantships available. Support available to part-time students. Financial award application deadline: 8/15; financial award applicants required to submit FAFSA. *Program availability:* Part-time, online learning. Offers adult-gerontology acute care nurse practitioner (MS, DNP, Post Master's Certificate); adult-gerontology clinical nurse specialist (MS, DNP, Post Master's Certificate); adult-gerontology primary care nurse practitioner (MS, DNP, Post Master's Certificate); family nurse practitioner (MS, DNP, Post Master's Certificate); nurse educator (MS); nursing and organizational leadership (MS, DNP, Post Master's Certificate); practice and leadership innovations (DNP, Post Master's Certificate). *Application deadline:* For fall admission, 12/1 for domestic and international students. *Application fee:* $20. *Application Contact:* Patricia Cichosz, Office Manager, Graduate Studies, 507-457-5038, E-mail: pcichosz@winona.edu. *Dean,* Dr. William J. McBreen, 507-457-5122, E-mail: wmcbreen@winona.edu.

WINSTON-SALEM STATE UNIVERSITY, Winston-Salem, NC 27110-0003

General Information State-supported, coed, comprehensive institution. *Graduate housing:* On-campus housing not available.

GRADUATE UNITS

Department of Occupational Therapy Offers occupational therapy (MS). Electronic applications accepted.

Department of Physical Therapy Offers physical therapy (DPT). Electronic applications accepted.

MAT Program *Program availability:* Part-time, evening/weekend, online learning. Offers middle grades education (MAT); special education (MAT). Electronic applications accepted.

Program in Business Administration *Program availability:* Part-time, evening/weekend, online learning. Offers business administration (MBA). Electronic applications accepted.

Program in Computer Science and Information Technology *Program availability:* Part-time. Offers computer science and information technology (MS). Electronic applications accepted.

Program in Health Administration Offers health administration (MHA).

Program in Nursing *Program availability:* Part-time, evening/weekend, online learning. Offers advanced nurse educator (MSN); family nurse practitioner (MSN); nursing (DNP). Electronic applications accepted.

Program in Rehabilitation Counseling *Program availability:* Part-time, online learning. Offers rehabilitation counseling (MRC). Electronic applications accepted.

WINTHROP UNIVERSITY, Rock Hill, SC 29733

General Information State-supported, coed, comprehensive institution. CGS member. *Enrollment:* 6,109 graduate, professional, and undergraduate students; 460 full-time matriculated graduate/professional students (345 women), 321 part-time matriculated graduate/professional students (240 women). *Enrollment by degree level:* 781 master's, 35 other advanced degrees. Tuition, state resident: full-time $14,312; part-time $599 per credit hour. Tuition, nonresident: full-time $27,570; part-time $1153 per credit hour. *Graduate housing:* Rooms and/or apartments available on a first-come, first-served basis to single and married students. Typical cost: $5170 per year ($8500 including board) for single students; $5170 per year ($8500 including board) for married students. Room and board charges vary according to board plan and housing facility selected. Housing application deadline: 3/1. *Student services:* Campus employment opportunities, campus safety program, career counseling, exercise/wellness program, free psychological counseling, international student services, low-cost health insurance, multicultural affairs office, services for students with disabilities. *Library facilities:* Dacus Library plus 1 other. *Collection:* Books: 438,816 (physical), 15,746 (digital/electronic); Serial titles: 12,205 (physical), 15,873 (digital/electronic); Databases: 127. Weekly public service hours: 49; study areas open 24 hours, 5–7 days a week; students can reserve study rooms.

Computer facilities: Computer purchase and lease plans are available. 620 computers available on campus for general student use. A campuswide network can be accessed from student residence rooms and from off campus. Online class registration, university services are available.
Website: http://www.winthrop.edu/

General Application Contact: The Graduate School, 800-411-7041, Fax: 803-323-2204, E-mail: gradschool@winthrop.edu.

GRADUATE UNITS

College of Arts and Sciences *Program availability:* Part-time. Offers arts and sciences (MA, MLA, MS, MSW, Certificate, SSP); biology (MS); dietics (Certificate); English (MA); history (MA); human nutrition (MS); liberal arts (MLA); psychology (MS, SSP); social work (MSW). Electronic applications accepted.

College of Business Administration *Program availability:* Part-time, evening/weekend, online learning. Offers business administration (MBA). Electronic applications accepted.

College of Education *Program availability:* Part-time. Offers agency counseling (M Ed); education (M Ed, MAT); educational leadership (M Ed); physical education (MAT); school counseling (M Ed); secondary education (M Ed); special education (M Ed). Electronic applications accepted.

College of Visual and Performing Arts *Program availability:* Part-time. Offers art (MFA); art administration (MA); art education (MA); conducting (MM); music education (MME); performance (MM); visual and performing arts (MA, MFA, MM, MME). Electronic applications accepted.

WISCONSIN LUTHERAN COLLEGE, Milwaukee, WI 53226-9942

General Information Independent-religious, coed, comprehensive institution.

GRADUATE UNITS
College of Adult and Graduate Studies

WISCONSIN SCHOOL OF PROFESSIONAL PSYCHOLOGY, Milwaukee, WI 53225-4960

General Information Independent, coed, graduate-only institution. *Graduate housing:* On-campus housing not available.

GRADUATE UNITS
Program in Clinical Psychology *Program availability:* Part-time, evening/weekend. Offers clinical psychology (MA, Psy D).

WITTENBERG UNIVERSITY, Springfield, OH 45501-0720

General Information Independent-religious, coed, comprehensive institution.
GRADUATE UNITS
Graduate Program

WOLFORD COLLEGE, Naples, FL 34108

General Information Proprietary, coed, graduate-only institution.
GRADUATE UNITS
Graduate Programs Offers nurse anesthesia (MSNA, DNAP).

WON INSTITUTE OF GRADUATE STUDIES, Glenside, PA 19038

General Information Proprietary, coed, graduate-only institution. *Enrollment by degree level:* 71 master's, 10 other advanced degrees. *Graduate faculty:* 9 full-time (5 women), 21 part-time/adjunct (16 women). *Student services:* Career counseling, writing training. *Library facilities:* Won Institute Library plus 1 other. *Collection:* Books: 4,987 (physical), 5 (digital/electronic); Databases: 3. Study areas open 24 hours, 5–7 days a week; students can reserve study rooms.

Computer facilities: 4 computers available on campus for general student use. Online class registration is available.
Website: http://www.woninstitute.edu/

General Application Contact: Jennifer Cake, Enrollment Management Counselor, 215-884-8942 Ext. 219, Fax: 215-884-9002, E-mail: jennifer.cake@woninstitute.edu.

GRADUATE UNITS

Acupuncture Studies Program Students: 54 full-time (42 women); includes 8 minority (1 Black or African American, non-Hispanic/Latino; 6 Asian, non-Hispanic/Latino; 1 Hispanic/Latino), 1 international. Average age 33. Expenses: Contact institution. Offers acupuncture studies (M Ac). *Application deadline:* For fall admission, 6/15 for domestic students. Applications are processed on a rolling basis. *Application fee:* $75. Electronic applications accepted. *Application Contact:* Jennifer Cake, Lead Enrollment Management Counselor, 215-884-8942 Ext. 212, E-mail: jennifer.cake@woninstitute.edu. *Chair,* Ben Griffith, 215-884-8942, Fax: 215-884-8942, E-mail: ben.griffith@woninstitute.edu.

Program in Chinese Herbal Medicine Expenses: Contact institution. *Financial support:* Scholarships/grants available. Offers Chinese herbal medicine (Certificate). *Application deadline:* For fall admission, 8/1 for domestic students. Applications are processed on a rolling basis. *Application fee:* $75. Electronic applications accepted. *Application Contact:* Jennifer Cake, Enrollment Management Counselor, 215-884-8942 Ext. 219, Fax: 215-884-9002, E-mail: jennifer.cake@woninstitute.edu. *Acupuncture and Chinese Herbal Medicine Chair,* Dr. Janet Leidy, 215-884-8942, Fax: 215-884-9002, E-mail: chp.director@woninstitute.edu.

Won Buddhist Studies Program Expenses: Contact institution. *Financial support:* Application deadline: 8/1. *Program availability:* Part-time. Offers Won Buddhist studies (MWBS). *Application deadline:* For fall admission, 8/1 for domestic students; for spring admission, 12/1 for domestic students. Applications are processed on a rolling basis. *Application fee:* $75. *Application Contact:* Jennifer Cake, Enrollment Management Counselor, 215-884-8942 Ext. 219, E-mail: jennifer.cake@woninstitute.edu. *Chair,* Rev. Dr. Sanghyeon Cheon, 215-884-8942, E-mail: wbschair@woninstitute.edu.

WOODBURY UNIVERSITY, Burbank, CA 91504-1099

General Information Independent, coed, comprehensive institution. *Graduate housing:* Room and/or apartments available on a first-come, first-served basis to single students; on-campus housing not available to married students.

GRADUATE UNITS

School of Architecture Offers architecture (M Arch, MIA, MS Arch).

School of Business *Program availability:* Part-time, evening/weekend. Offers business administration (MBA); organizational leadership (MA).

WOODS HOLE OCEANOGRAPHIC INSTITUTION, Woods Hole, MA 02543-1541

General Information Independent, coed, graduate-only institution. CGS member. *Graduate housing:* Rooms and/or apartments guaranteed to single students and available on a first-come, first-served basis to married students.

GRADUATE UNITS

MIT/WHOI Joint Program in Oceanography/Applied Ocean Science and Engineering Offers applied ocean science and engineering (PhD); biological oceanography (PhD); chemical oceanography (PhD); marine geology and geophysics (PhD); physical oceanography (PhD). Program offered jointly with Massachusetts Institute of Technology. Electronic applications accepted.

WORCESTER POLYTECHNIC INSTITUTE, Worcester, MA 01609-2280

General Information Independent, coed, university. CGS member. *Enrollment:* 6,642 graduate, professional, and undergraduate students; 1,231 full-time matriculated graduate/professional students (437 women), 832 part-time matriculated graduate/professional students (195 women). *Enrollment by degree level:* 1,631 master's, 365 doctoral, 67 other advanced degrees. *Graduate faculty:* 165 full-time (40 women), 84 part-time/adjunct (13 women). *Graduate housing:* Rooms and/or apartments available on a first-come, first-served basis to single and married students. *Student services:* Campus employment opportunities, campus safety program, career counseling, exercise/wellness program, free psychological counseling, grant writing training, international student services, low-cost health insurance, multicultural affairs office, services for students with disabilities, teacher training, writing training. *Library facilities:* George C. Gordon Library. *Collection:* Books: 249,084 (physical), 1.1 million (digital/electronic); Serial titles: 5,533 (physical), 76,238 (digital/electronic); Databases: 380. Weekly public service hours: 107; students can reserve study rooms. *Research affiliation:* U.S. Army Research Laboratory (materials science and engineering), United States Advanced Battery Consortium LLC (advanced battery recycling), SRI International (educational software), Toyota Motor Company (automotive safety technology), MathWorks Inc. (Internet of Things (IoT)), University of Massachusetts Medical School at Worcester (basic transitional and clinical medical research).

Computer facilities: Computer purchase and lease plans are available. 860 computers available on campus for general student use. A campuswide network can be accessed from student residence rooms and from off campus. Online class registration, online course content are available.
Website: http://www.wpi.edu/

General Application Contact: Lynne Dougherty, Administrative Assistant, 508-831-5301, Fax: 508-831-5717, E-mail: grad@wpi.edu.

GRADUATE UNITS

Graduate Studies and Research Students: 1,231 full-time (437 women), 832 part-time (195 women); includes 245 minority (44 Black or African American, non-Hispanic/Latino; 3 American Indian or Alaska Native, non-Hispanic/Latino; 100 Asian, non-Hispanic/Latino; 74 Hispanic/Latino; 1 Native Hawaiian or other Pacific Islander, non-Hispanic/Latino; 23 Two or more races, non-Hispanic/Latino), 900 international. Average age 28. 3,704 applicants, 56% accepted, 772 enrolled. *Faculty:* 171 full-time (37 women), 92 part-time/adjunct (16 women). Expenses: Contact institution. *Financial support:* Research assistantships, teaching assistantships, career-related internships or fieldwork, institutionally sponsored loans, scholarships/grants, health care benefits, tuition waivers, and unspecified assistantships available. Financial award application deadline: 1/1; financial award applicants required to submit FAFSA. In 2016, 681 master's, 42 doctorates awarded. *Program availability:* Part-time, evening/weekend, 100% online, blended/hybrid learning. Offers aerospace engineering (MS, PhD); applied mathematics (MS); applied statistics (MS); biochemistry (MS, PhD); bioinformatics and computational biology (MS, PhD); biology and biotechnology (MS); biomedical engineering (M Eng, MS, PhD, Graduate Certificate); bioscience administration (MS); biotechnology (PhD); chemical engineering (MS, PhD); chemistry (MS, PhD); civil and environmental engineering (Advanced Certificate, Graduate Certificate); civil engineering (ME, MS, PhD); computer and communications networks (MS); computer science (MS, PhD, Advanced Certificate, Graduate Certificate); construction project management (MS); data science (MS, PhD, Graduate Certificate); electrical and computer engineering (Advanced Certificate, Graduate Certificate); electrical engineering (M Eng, MS, PhD); environmental engineering (M Eng, MS); financial mathematics (MS); fire protection engineering (MS, PhD, Advanced Certificate, Graduate Certificate); impact engineering (MS); industrial mathematics (MS); interactive media and game development (MS); interdisciplinary social science (PhD); learning sciences and technologies (MS, PhD); manufacturing engineering (MS, PhD); manufacturing engineering management (MS); master builder (M Eng); materials process engineering (MS); materials science and engineering (MS, PhD); mathematical sciences (PhD, Graduate Certificate); mathematics (MME); mechanical engineering (MS, PhD, Graduate Certificate); physics (MS, PhD); physics for educators (MS); power systems management (MS); robotics engineering (MS, PhD); social science (PhD); system dynamics (MS, Graduate Certificate); systems engineering (MS, Graduate Certificate); systems modeling (MS). *Application deadline:* For fall admission, 1/1 priority date for domestic and international students; for spring admission, 10/1 priority date for domestic and international students. Applications are processed on a rolling basis. *Application fee:* $70. Electronic applications accepted. *Application Contact:* Lynne Dougherty, Administrative Assistant, 508-831-5301, Fax: 508-831-5717, E-mail: grad@wpi.edu. *Dean,* Dr. Terri Camesano, 508-831-5380, E-mail: grad@wpi.edu.

Foisie Business School Students: 237 full-time (139 women), 186 part-time (67 women); includes 35 minority (4 Black or African American, non-Hispanic/Latino; 17 Asian, non-Hispanic/Latino; 12 Hispanic/Latino; 2 Two or more races, non-Hispanic/Latino), 221 international. 645 applicants, 62% accepted, 144 enrolled. *Faculty:* 20 full-time (12 women), 16 part-time/adjunct (1 woman). Expenses: Contact institution. *Financial support:* Career-related internships or fieldwork, institutionally sponsored loans, scholarships/grants, and unspecified assistantships available. Financial award application deadline: 6/1; financial award applicants required to submit FAFSA. In 2016, 150 master's awarded. *Program availability:* Part-time, evening/weekend, 100% online, blended/hybrid learning. Offers information technology (MS); management (Graduate Certificate); marketing and technological innovation (MS); operations design and leadership (MS); technology (MBA, MS). *Application deadline:* For fall admission, 6/1 priority date for domestic and international students; for spring admission, 11/1 priority date for domestic students, 10/1 priority date for international students. Applications are processed on a rolling basis. *Application fee:* $70. Electronic applications accepted. *Application Contact:* Eileen Dagostino, Recruiting Operations Coordinator, 508-831-4665, Fax: 508-831-5720, E-mail: edag@wpi.edu. *Executive Director,* Melissa Terrio, 508-831-4665, Fax: 508-831-4665, E-mail: biz@wpi.edu.

WORCESTER STATE UNIVERSITY, Worcester, MA 01602-2597

General Information State-supported, coed, comprehensive institution. *Enrollment:* 6,471 graduate, professional, and undergraduate students; 170 full-time matriculated graduate/professional students (146 women), 511 part-time matriculated graduate/professional students (392 women). *Enrollment by degree level:* 580 master's, 101 other advanced degrees. *Graduate faculty:* 52 full-time (39 women), 28 part-time/adjunct (12 women). Tuition, state resident: part-time $150 per credit. Tuition, nonresident: part-time $150 per credit. *Graduate housing:* On-campus housing not available. *Student services:* Campus employment opportunities, campus safety program, career counseling, exercise/wellness program, free psychological counseling, international student services, low-cost health insurance, multicultural affairs office, services for students with disabilities, teacher training, writing training. *Library facilities:* Worcester State University Library. *Collection:* Books: 144,910 (physical), 140,521 (digital/electronic); Serial titles: 129 (physical), 56,397 (digital/electronic); Databases: 133. Weekly public service hours: 100.

Computer facilities: Computer purchase and lease plans are available. 500 computers available on campus for general student use. A campuswide network can be accessed from student residence rooms and from off campus. Online class registration is available.
Website: http://www.worcester.edu/

General Application Contact: Sara Grady, Associate Dean, Graduate Studies and Professional Development, 508-929-8130, Fax: 508-929-8100, E-mail: sara.grady@worcester.edu.

GRADUATE UNITS

Graduate Studies Students: 170 full-time (146 women), 511 part-time (392 women); includes 80 minority (25 Black or African American, non-Hispanic/Latino; 5 American Indian or Alaska Native, non-Hispanic/Latino; 6 Asian, non-Hispanic/Latino; 32 Hispanic/Latino; 12 Two or more races, non-Hispanic/Latino), 13 international. Average age 33. 853 applicants, 58% accepted, 271 enrolled. *Faculty:* 52 full-time (39 women), 28 part-time/adjunct (12 women). Expenses: Contact institution. *Financial support:* Career-related internships or fieldwork, scholarships/grants, and unspecified assistantships available. Financial award application deadline: 3/1; financial award

applicants required to submit FAFSA. In 2016, 205 master's, 128 other advanced degrees awarded. *Program availability:* Part-time, evening/weekend. Offers accounting (MS); biotechnology (MS); community and public health nursing (MSN); early childhood education (M Ed); education (M Ed, CAGS, Ed S, Postbaccalaureate Certificate); elementary education (M Ed); English (MA); English as a second language (M Ed, Postbaccalaureate Certificate); health care administration (MS); health education (M Ed); history (MA); leadership and administration (M Ed, CAGS, Ed S); managerial leadership (MS); middle school education (M Ed, Postbaccalaureate Certificate); moderate disabilities (M Ed, Postbaccalaureate Certificate); non-profit management (MS); nurse educator (MSN); occupational therapy (MOT); reading (M Ed, CAGS, Ed S, Postbaccalaureate Certificate); school psychology (CAGS, Ed S); secondary education (M Ed, CAGS, Ed S); Spanish (MA); speech-language pathology (MS). *Application deadline:* For fall admission, 6/15 for domestic and international students; for spring admission, 11/1 for domestic and international students; for summer admission, 4/1 for domestic and international students. Applications are processed on a rolling basis. *Application fee:* $50. Electronic applications accepted. *Application Contact:* Sara Grady, Associate Dean, Graduate Studies and Professional Development, 508-929-8787, Fax: 508-929-8100, E-mail: sara.grady@worcester.edu. *Associate Vice President for Continuing Education/Dean of the Graduate Studies,* Dr. Roberta Kyle, 508-929-8111, Fax: 508-929-8100, E-mail: rkyle@worcester.edu.

WORLD MEDICINE INSTITUTE, Honolulu, HI 96821

General Information Independent, coed, graduate-only institution. *Graduate housing:* On-campus housing not available.

GRADUATE UNITS

Program in Acupuncture and Oriental Medicine *Program availability:* Part-time, evening/weekend. Offers acupuncture and Oriental medicine (M Ac OM).

WRIGHT INSTITUTE, Berkeley, CA 94704-1796

General Information Independent, coed, graduate-only institution. *Graduate housing:* On-campus housing not available. *Student services:* Campus employment opportunities, career counseling, services for students with disabilities. *Library facilities:* The Wright Institute Library plus 2 others.

Computer facilities: A campuswide network can be accessed. Online class registration is available.
Website: http://www.wi.edu/

General Application Contact: John Pitts, Director of Admissions, 510-841-9230 Ext. 170, Fax: 510-841-0167, E-mail: jpitts@wi.edu.

GRADUATE UNITS

Doctoral Program in Clinical Psychology Expenses: Contact institution. *Financial support:* Research assistantships, teaching assistantships, career-related internships or fieldwork, Federal Work-Study, and scholarships/grants available. Financial award applicants required to submit FAFSA. Offers clinical psychology (Psy D). *Application deadline:* For fall admission, 1/5 priority date for domestic and international students. *Application fee:* $50. Electronic applications accepted. *Application Contact:* John Pitts, Director of Admissions, 510-841-9230 Ext. 171, E-mail: jpitts@wi.edu. *Dean,* Dr. Gilbert Newman, 510-841-9230 Ext. 110, E-mail: gnewman@wi.edu.

Master of Arts in Counseling Psychology Program Expenses: Contact institution. *Financial support:* Career-related internships or fieldwork, Federal Work-Study, and scholarships/grants available. Financial award applicants required to submit FAFSA. *Program availability:* Part-time, evening/weekend. Offers counseling psychology (MA). *Application deadline:* Applications are processed on a rolling basis. *Application fee:* $50. Electronic applications accepted. *Application Contact:* John Pitts, Director of Admissions, 510-841-9230 Ext. 171, E-mail: jpitts@wi.edu. *Program Director,* Dr. Milena Esherick, 510-841-9230 Ext. 144.

WRIGHT STATE UNIVERSITY, Dayton, OH 45435

General Information State-supported, coed, university. CGS member. *Enrollment:* 16,655 graduate, professional, and undergraduate students; 2,710 full-time matriculated graduate/professional students (1,391 women), 862 part-time matriculated graduate/professional students (490 women). *Enrollment by degree level:* 2,957 master's, 873 doctoral, 186 other advanced degrees. *Graduate faculty:* 749 full-time (232 women), 354 part-time/adjunct (195 women). Tuition, state resident: full-time $9952; part-time $622 per credit hour. Tuition, nonresident: full-time $16,960; part-time $1060 per credit hour. *Graduate housing:* Rooms and/or apartments available on a first-come, first-served basis to single and married students. *Student services:* Campus employment opportunities, campus safety program, career counseling, child daycare facilities, exercise/wellness program, free psychological counseling, grant writing training, international student services, low-cost health insurance, multicultural affairs office, services for students with disabilities, teacher training, writing training. *Library facilities:* Paul Laurence Dunbar Library plus 1 other. *Collection:* Books: 870,406 (physical), 446,609 (digital/electronic); Serial titles: 520 (physical), 48,115 (digital/electronic); Databases: 130. Weekly public service hours: 105; students can reserve study rooms. *Research affiliation:* Wright-Patterson Air Force Base (research and development, systems and logistics), Veterans Administration Medical Center, Scott-Kettering Magnetic Resonance Research Laboratory (medical science), Edison Biotechnology Center, Edison Materials Technology Center (processing).

Computer facilities: Computer purchase and lease plans are available. 2,500 computers available on campus for general student use. A campuswide network can be accessed from student residence rooms and from off campus. Online class registration, student webpages, Lap tops 2 Go, office software programs are available.
Website: http://www.wright.edu/

General Application Contact: Lisa Lewandowski, Associate Director of Graduate Admissions, 937-775-3747, Fax: 937-775-2453, E-mail: lisa.lewandowski@wright.edu.

GRADUATE UNITS

Graduate School Students: 2,710 full-time (1,391 women), 862 part-time (490 women); includes 528 minority (254 Black or African American, non-Hispanic/Latino; 6 American Indian or Alaska Native, non-Hispanic/Latino; 117 Asian, non-Hispanic/Latino; 78 Hispanic/Latino; 2 Native Hawaiian or other Pacific Islander, non-Hispanic/Latino; 71 Two or more races, non-Hispanic/Latino), 977 international. Average age 30. 4,534 applicants, 51% accepted, 1101 enrolled. Expenses: Contact institution. *Financial support:* In 2016–17, 36 fellowships with full tuition reimbursements, 212 research assistantships with full tuition reimbursements, 141 teaching assistantships with full tuition reimbursements were awarded; career-related internships or fieldwork, Federal Work-Study, institutionally sponsored loans, tuition waivers (full and partial), and unspecified assistantships also available. Support available to part-time students. Financial award applicants required to submit FAFSA. In 2016, 1,370 master's, 168 doctorates, 190 other advanced degrees awarded. *Program availability:* Part-time, evening/weekend, 100% online, blended/hybrid learning. *Application deadline:* For fall admission, 5/15 for international students; for spring admission, 9/30 for international students; for summer admission, 2/15 for international students. Applications are processed on a rolling basis. *Application fee:* $40. Electronic applications accepted. *Application Contact:* Lisa Lewandowski, Associate Director of Graduate Admissions, 937-775-3747, Fax: 937-775-2453, E-mail: lisa.lewandowski@wright.edu. *Vice President for Research and Graduate Studies,* Dr. Robert Fyffe, 937-775-3336, Fax: 937-775-2357, E-mail: robert.fyffe@wright.edu.

College of Education and Human Services Expenses: Contact institution. *Financial support:* Fellowships with full tuition reimbursements, research assistantships, teaching assistantships, career-related internships or fieldwork, Federal Work-Study, institutionally sponsored loans, tuition waivers (full and partial), and unspecified assistantships available. Support available to part-time students. Financial award applicants required to submit FAFSA. *Program availability:* Part-time, evening/weekend. Offers adolescent to young adult education (M Ed); advanced curriculum and instruction (Ed S); advanced educational leadership (Ed S); chemical dependency (MRC); classroom teacher education (M Ed, MA); counseling (M Ed, MA, MS); education and human services (M Ed, MA, MRC, MS, Ed S); intervention specialist (M Ed); pupil personnel services (M Ed); rehabilitation counseling (MRC). *Application fee:* $25. *Application Contact:* John Kimble, Associate Director of Graduate Admissions and Records, 937-775-2957, Fax: 937-775-2453, E-mail: john.kimble@wright.edu. *Dean,* Dr. Gregory R. Bernhardt, 937-775-2822, Fax: 937-775-4855, E-mail: gregory.bernhardt@wright.edu.

College of Engineering and Computer Science Expenses: Contact institution. *Financial support:* Fellowships with full tuition reimbursements, research assistantships with full tuition reimbursements, teaching assistantships with full tuition reimbursements, Federal Work-Study, institutionally sponsored loans, tuition waivers (full and partial), and unspecified assistantships available. Support available to part-time students. Financial award applicants required to submit FAFSA. *Program availability:* Part-time, evening/weekend. Offers aerospace systems engineering (MSE); biomedical engineering (MS); computer engineering (MSCE); computer science (MS); computer science and engineering (MS, MSCE, PhD); electrical engineering (MSEE); engineering (PhD); engineering and computer science (MS, MSCE, MSE, MSEE, PhD); industrial and human factors engineering (MS); materials science and engineering (MSE); mechanical engineering (MSE); renewable ande clean energy (MSE). *Application fee:* $25. *Application Contact:* John Kimble, Associate Director of Graduate Admissions and Records, 937-775-2957, Fax: 937-775-2453, E-mail: john.kimble@wright.edu. *Dean,* Dr. Bor Z. Jang, 937-775-5001, Fax: 937-775-5009, E-mail: bor.jang@wright.edu.

College of Liberal Arts Expenses: Contact institution. *Financial support:* Fellowships with full tuition reimbursements, research assistantships with full tuition reimbursements, teaching assistantships with full tuition reimbursements, Federal Work-Study, institutionally sponsored loans, and unspecified assistantships available. Support available to part-time students. Financial award applicants required to submit FAFSA. *Program availability:* Part-time. Offers criminal justice and social problems (MA); English (MA); history (MA); humanities (M Hum); liberal arts (M Hum, MA, MM, MPA); music (MM); public administration (MPA). *Application fee:* $25. *Application Contact:* John Kimble, Associate Director of Graduate Admissions and Records, 937-775-2957, Fax: 937-775-2453, E-mail: john.kimble@wright.edu. *Dean,* Dr. Charles S. Taylor, 937-775-2225, Fax: 937-775-2707, E-mail: charles.taylor@wright.edu.

College of Nursing and Health Expenses: Contact institution. *Financial support:* Fellowships, research assistantships, teaching assistantships, Federal Work-Study, institutionally sponsored loans, and unspecified assistantships available. Support available to part-time students. Financial award application deadline: 6/1; financial award applicants required to submit FAFSA. *Program availability:* Part-time, evening/weekend. Offers administration of nursing and health care systems (MS); adult gerontology clinical nurse specialist (MS); adult-gerontology acute care nurse practitioner (MS); family nurse practitioner (MS); neonatal nurse practitioner (MS); nursing and health (MS); pediatric nurse practitioner-acute care (MS); pediatric nurse practitioner-primary care (MS); psychiatric mental health nurse practitioner (MS); school nurse (MS). *Application deadline:* For fall admission, 4/15 priority date for domestic students. *Application fee:* $25. *Application Contact:* Theresa A. Haghnazarian, Director of Student and Alumni Affairs, 937-775-2342, Fax: 937-775-4571, E-mail: theresa.haghnazarian@wright.edu. *Dean,* Dr. Patricia A. Martin, 937-775-3131, Fax: 937-775-4571, E-mail: patricia.martin@wright.edu.

College of Science and Mathematics Expenses: Contact institution. *Financial support:* Fellowships, research assistantships, teaching assistantships, career-related internships or fieldwork, Federal Work-Study, institutionally sponsored loans, tuition waivers (full and partial), and unspecified assistantships available. Support available to part-time students. Financial award applicants required to submit FAFSA. *Program availability:* Part-time, evening/weekend. Offers anatomy (MS); applied mathematics (MS); applied statistics (MS); biochemistry and molecular biology (MS); biological sciences (MS); biomedical sciences (PhD); chemistry (MS); earth science education (MST); environmental sciences (PhD); geological sciences (Graduate Certificate); geophysics (MS); human factors and industrial/organizational psychology (MS, PhD); mathematics (MS); microbiology and immunology (MS); physics (MS, MST); physiology and neuroscience (MS); science and mathematics (MS, MST, PhD, Graduate Certificate). *Application fee:* $25. *Application Contact:* John Kimble, Associate Director of Graduate Admissions and Records, 937-775-2957, Fax: 937-775-2453, E-mail: john.kimble@wright.edu. *Dean,* Dr. Michele Wheatly, 937-775-2611, Fax: 937-775-3068, E-mail: michele.wheatly@wright.edu.

Raj Soin College of Business Expenses: Contact institution. *Financial support:* Fellowships, research assistantships, teaching assistantships, career-related internships or fieldwork, Federal Work-Study, institutionally sponsored loans, and unspecified assistantships available. Support available to part-time students. Financial award applicants required to submit FAFSA. *Program availability:* Part-time, evening/weekend. Offers accountancy (M Acc); business (M Acc, MBA, MIS, MS); business administration (MBA); information systems (MIS); logistics and supply chain management (MS); management information technology (MBA); social and applied economics (MS). *Application fee:* $25. *Application Contact:* Michael Evans, Director of MBA Programs, 937-775-2437, Fax: 937-775-3545, E-mail: michael.evans@wright.edu. *Dean,* Dr. Berkwood Farmer, 937-775-3242, Fax: 937-775-3545, E-mail: berkwood.farmer@wright.edu.

School of Medicine Expenses: Contact institution. *Financial support:* Fellowships, research assistantships, teaching assistantships, and unspecified assistantships available. Financial award applicants required to submit FAFSA. Offers aerospace medicine (MS); health promotion and education (MPH); medicine (MPH, MS, MD, PhD); pharmacology and toxicology (MS). *Application Contact:* Dr. Paul G. Carlson, Associate Dean for Student Affairs and Admissions, 937-775-2934, Fax: 937-775-3672, E-mail: paul.carlson@wright.edu. *Dean,* Dr. Howard Part, 937-775-3010, Fax: 937-775-3672, E-mail: howard.part@wright.edu.

School of Professional Psychology Expenses: Contact institution. *Financial support:* Fellowships, teaching assistantships, career-related internships or fieldwork, Federal Work-Study, institutionally sponsored loans, and unspecified assistantships available. Financial award application deadline: 4/15; financial award applicants required to submit FAFSA. Offers clinical psychology (Psy D). *Application deadline:* For fall admission, 12/15 for domestic students. *Application fee:* $30. *Application Contact:* Leona L. Gray, Director, Student Services and Admissions, 937-775-3492, Fax: 937-775-3493, E-mail: leona.gray@wright.edu. *Dean,* Dr. John R. Rudisill, 937-775-3490, Fax: 937-775-3434, E-mail: john.rudisill@wright.edu.

WYCLIFFE COLLEGE, Toronto, ON M5S 1H7, Canada

General Information Independent-religious, coed, graduate-only institution. *Graduate housing:* Rooms and/or apartments guaranteed to single students and available on a first-come, first-served basis to married students. Housing application deadline: 5/1.

GRADUATE UNITS

Division of Advanced Degree Studies *Program availability:* Part-time. Offers theology (MA, Th M, D Min, PhD, Th D). PhD, D Min, MA offered jointly with Toronto School of Theology; Th D, Th M with University of Toronto.

Division of Basic Degree Studies *Program availability:* Part-time. Offers Christian Studies (Diploma); theology (M Div, M Rel, MTS). M Div, M Rel, MTS offered jointly with University of Toronto.

XAVIER UNIVERSITY, Cincinnati, OH 45207

General Information Independent-religious, coed, university. *Graduate housing:* On-campus housing not available.

GRADUATE UNITS

College of Arts and Sciences *Program availability:* Part-time. Offers arts and sciences (MA); English (MA); health care mission integration (MA); theology (MA); urban sustainability and resilience (MA). Electronic applications accepted.

College of Social Sciences, Health and Education Offers clinical psychology (Psy D); coaching education and athlete development (M Ed); criminal justice (MS); health services administration (MHSA); industrial-organizational psychology (MA); occupational therapy (MOT); social sciences, health and education (M Ed, MA, MHSA, MOT, MS, MSN, DNP, Ed D, Psy D, PMC); sport administration (M Ed).

School of Education Offers children's multicultural literature (M Ed); clinical mental health counseling (MA); education (M Ed, MA, MS, Ed D); educational administration (M Ed); elementary education (M Ed); human resource development (MS); Montessori education (M Ed); reading (M Ed); school counseling (MA); secondary education (M Ed); special education (M Ed). Electronic applications accepted.

School of Nursing *Program availability:* Part-time, evening/weekend. Offers nursing (MSN, DNP, PMC). Electronic applications accepted.

Williams College of Business *Program availability:* Part-time, evening/weekend. Offers accountancy (MS); business (Exec MBA, MBA, MS); business administration (Exec MBA, MBA); business intelligence (MBA); finance (MBA); health industry (MBA); international business (MBA); marketing (MBA); values-based leadership (MBA). Electronic applications accepted.

XAVIER UNIVERSITY OF LOUISIANA, New Orleans, LA 70125

General Information Independent-religious, coed, comprehensive institution. *Graduate housing:* On-campus housing not available.

GRADUATE UNITS

College of Pharmacy Offers pharmacy (Pharm D). Electronic applications accepted.

Graduate School *Program availability:* Part-time, evening/weekend. Offers counseling (MA); curriculum and instruction (MA); educational leadership (MA).

Institute for Black Catholic Studies *Program availability:* Part-time. Offers pastoral theology (Th M).

YALE UNIVERSITY, New Haven, CT 06520

General Information Independent, coed, university. CGS member. *Graduate housing:* Rooms and/or apartments available on a first-come, first-served basis to single and married students. Housing application deadline: 6/1. *Research affiliation:* Howard Hughes Medical Institute, J.B. Pierce Foundation (environmental physiology), Haskins Laboratories (speech, hearing, reading).

GRADUATE UNITS

Graduate School of Arts and Sciences *Program availability:* Part-time. Offers African studies (MA); African-American studies (PhD); American studies (PhD); anthropology (M Phil, MA, PhD); applied mathematics (M Phil, MS, PhD); Arabic and Islamic studies (MA, PhD); archaeological studies (MA); archaeology of the ancient Near East (MA, PhD); arts and sciences (M Phil, MA, MS, PhD); Assyriology (MA, PhD); astronomy (PhD); behavioral neuroscience (PhD); biochemistry, molecular biology and chemical biology (PhD); biogeochemistry (PhD); biophysical chemistry (PhD); cell biology (PhD); cellular and developmental biology (PhD); cellular and molecular physiology (PhD); classics (M Phil, MA, PhD); climate dynamics (PhD); clinical psychology (PhD); cognitive psychology (PhD); comparative and historical sociology (PhD); comparative literature (PhD); computer science (MS, PhD); cultural sociology and social theory (PhD); developmental psychology (PhD); East Asian languages and literatures (PhD); East Asian languages and literatures and film studies (PhD); East Asian studies (MA); ecology and evolutionary biology (PhD); economics (PhD); Egyptology (MA, PhD); English language and literature (MA, PhD); environmental sciences (PhD); experimental pathology (MS, PhD); film studies (PhD); forestry (PhD); French (M Phil, MA, PhD); genetics (PhD); geochemistry (PhD); geophysics (PhD); German (PhD); global affairs (MA); Graeco-Arabic studies (MA, PhD); history (M Phil, MA, PhD); history of art (PhD); history of science and medicine (MS, PhD); immunobiology (PhD); inorganic chemistry (PhD); international and development economics (MA); Italian language and literature (PhD); Latin American literature (PhD); linguistics (PhD); Luso-Brazilian and Spanish/Spanish American literatures (PhD); mathematics (M Phil, MS, PhD); medieval Slavic literature and philology (PhD); medieval studies (M Phil, PhD); meteorology (PhD); molecular biophysics and biochemistry (PhD); music history (MA); music theory (MA); neurobiology (PhD); neuroscience (PhD); Northwest Semitic, Bible, comparative Semitics (MA, PhD); oceanography (PhD); organic chemistry (PhD); paleontology (PhD); paleooceanography (PhD); petrology (PhD); philosophy (PhD); physical and theoretical chemistry (PhD); physics (PhD); plant sciences (PhD); Polish literature (PhD); political science (PhD); religious studies (PhD); Renaissance studies (PhD); Russian and East European studies (MA); Russian literature (PhD); Slavic languages and literatures and film studies (PhD); social stratification and the life course (PhD); social/personality psychology (PhD); solar and terrestrial physics (PhD); Spanish peninsular literature (PhD); statistics (MA, PhD); tectonics (PhD).

School of Engineering and Applied Science *Program availability:* Part-time. Offers applied physics (MS, PhD); biomedical engineering (MS, PhD); chemical engineering

(MS, PhD); electrical engineering (MS, PhD); engineering and applied science (MS, PhD); environmental engineering (MS, PhD); mechanical engineering (MS, PhD).

School of Architecture Offers architecture (M Arch, M Env Des, MEM, PhD). Electronic applications accepted.

School of Art Students: 127 full-time (65 women); includes 17 minority (8 Black or African American, non-Hispanic/Latino; 5 Asian, non-Hispanic/Latino; 4 Hispanic/Latino), 35 international. Average age 28. 1,003 applicants, 6% accepted, 61 enrolled. *Faculty:* 10 full-time (5 women), 35 part-time/adjunct (12 women). Expenses: Contact institution. *Financial support:* In 2016–17, 110 students received support, including 61 teaching assistantships (averaging $2,000 per year); Federal Work-Study, scholarships/grants, and unspecified assistantships also available. Financial award application deadline: 3/1; financial award applicants required to submit FAFSA. In 2016, 61 master's awarded. Offers graphic design (MFA); painting/printmaking (MFA); photography (MFA); sculpture (MFA). *Application deadline:* For fall admission, 1/4 for domestic and international students. *Application fee:* $100. Electronic applications accepted. *Application Contact:* Patricia Ann DeChiara, Director of Academic Affairs, 203-432-2600, E-mail: artschool.info@yale.edu. *Dean,* Marta Kuzma, 203-432-2606.

School of Drama Offers acting (MFA, Certificate); design (MFA, Certificate); directing (MFA, Certificate); dramaturgy and dramatic criticism (MFA, DFA); playwriting (MFA, Certificate); sound design (MFA, Certificate); stage management (MFA, Certificate); technical design and production (MFA, Certificate); theater management (MFA). Electronic applications accepted.

School of Forestry and Environmental Studies Students: 320 full-time. Average age 27. 600 applicants, 150 enrolled. *Faculty:* 32 full-time, 50 part-time/adjunct. Expenses: Contact institution. *Financial support:* In 2016–17, 240 students received support. Fellowships, research assistantships, teaching assistantships, career-related internships or fieldwork, Federal Work-Study, institutionally sponsored loans, scholarships/grants, and health care benefits available. Support available to part-time students. Financial award application deadline: 2/15; financial award applicants required to submit FAFSA. In 2016, 152 master's, 15 doctorates awarded. *Program availability:* Part-time. Offers environmental management (MEM); environmental science (MES); forest science (MFS); forestry (MF); forestry and environmental studies (PhD). *Application deadline:* For fall admission, 12/15 priority date for domestic and international students. *Application fee:* $80. Electronic applications accepted. *Application Contact:* Rebecca DeSalvo, Director of Enrollment Management and Diversity Initiatives, 800-825-0330, Fax: 203-432-5528, E-mail: fesinfo@yale.edu. *Dean, School of Forestry and Environmental Studies,* Dr. Ingrid Burke, 203-432-5109, Fax: 203-432-3051.

School of Music Students: 211 full-time (87 women); includes 43 minority (2 Black or African American, non-Hispanic/Latino; 23 Asian, non-Hispanic/Latino; 8 Hispanic/Latino; 10 Two or more races, non-Hispanic/Latino), 76 international. Average age 23. 1,512 applicants, 10% accepted, 108 enrolled. *Faculty:* 28 full-time (9 women), 33 part-time/adjunct (7 women). Expenses: Contact institution. *Financial support:* In 2016–17, 211 students received support, including 211 fellowships (averaging $34,000 per year); Federal Work-Study and scholarships/grants also available. Financial award application deadline: 5/30; financial award applicants required to submit FAFSA. In 2016, 72 master's, 3 doctorates, 23 ADs awarded. Offers music (MM, MMA, DMA, AD, Certificate). *Application deadline:* For fall admission, 12/1 for domestic and international students. *Application fee:* $150. Electronic applications accepted. *Application Contact:* Suzanne M. Stringer, Director of Student Services, 203-432-1962, Fax: 203-432-7448, E-mail: suzanne.stringer@yale.edu. *Dean,* Robert Blocker, 203-432-4160, Fax: 203-432-7542.

School of Nursing *Program availability:* Part-time, online learning. Offers nursing (MSN, DNP, PhD, Post Master's Certificate). Electronic applications accepted.

Yale Divinity School *Program availability:* Part-time. Offers divinity (M Div, MAR, STM). Electronic applications accepted.

Yale Law School Students: 632 full-time (301 women). Average age 26. 2,735 applicants, 9% accepted, 210 enrolled. *Faculty:* 66 full-time, 103 part-time/adjunct. Expenses: Contact institution. *Financial support:* Application deadline: 3/15; applicants required to submit FAFSA. Offers law (LL M, MSL, JD, JSD, PhD). *Application deadline:* For fall admission, 2/28 for domestic students. Applications are processed on a rolling basis. *Application fee:* $60. Electronic applications accepted. *Application Contact:* Asha Rangappa, Associate Dean, 203-432-4995, E-mail: admissions.law@yale.edu. *Dean,* Robert Post, 203-432-1660.

Yale School of Management Offers accounting (PhD); business administration (MBA); financial economics (PhD); management (MBA, PhD); marketing (PhD); organizations and management (PhD).

Yale School of Medicine *Program availability:* Part-time. Offers biological and biomedical sciences (PhD); computational biology and bioinformatics (PhD); immunology (PhD); medicine (APMPH, MM Sc, MPH, MS, MD, PhD); microbiology (PhD); molecular biophysics and biochemistry (PhD); molecular cell biology, genetics, and development (PhD); neurobiology (PhD); neuroscience (PhD); pharmacological sciences and molecular medicine (PhD); pharmacology (PhD); physician associate (MM Sc); physiology and integrative medical biology (PhD). Electronic applications accepted.

Yale School of Public Health *Program availability:* Part-time. Offers applied biostatistics and epidemiology (APMPH); biostatistics (MPH, MS, PhD); chronic disease epidemiology (MPH, PhD); environmental health sciences (MPH, PhD); epidemiology of microbial diseases (MPH, PhD); global health (APMPH); health management (MPH); health policy (MPH); health policy and administration (APMPH, PhD); occupational and environmental medicine (APMPH); preventive medicine (APMPH); social and behavioral sciences (APMPH, MPH). MS and PhD offered through the Graduate School. Electronic applications accepted.

YESHIVA BETH MOSHE, Scranton, PA 18505-2124
General Information Independent-religious, men only, comprehensive institution.
GRADUATE UNITS
Graduate Programs

YESHIVA DERECH CHAIM, Brooklyn, NY 11218
General Information Independent-religious, men only, comprehensive institution.
GRADUATE UNITS
Graduate Program Offers Talmudic studies (PhD).

YESHIVA KARLIN STOLIN RABBINICAL INSTITUTE, Brooklyn, NY 11204
General Information Independent-religious, men only, comprehensive institution. *Graduate housing:* On-campus housing not available.

GRADUATE UNITS
Graduate Programs

YESHIVA OF NITRA RABBINICAL COLLEGE, Mount Kisco, NY 10549
General Information Independent-religious, men only, comprehensive institution.
GRADUATE UNITS
Graduate Programs

YESHIVA SHAAR HATORAH TALMUDIC RESEARCH INSTITUTE, Kew Gardens, NY 11418-1469
General Information Independent-religious, men only, comprehensive institution.
GRADUATE UNITS
Graduate Programs

YESHIVATH VIZNITZ, Monsey, NY 10952
General Information Independent-religious, men only, comprehensive institution.
GRADUATE UNITS
Graduate Programs

YESHIVATH ZICHRON MOSHE, South Fallsburg, NY 12779
General Information Independent-religious, men only, comprehensive institution.
GRADUATE UNITS
Graduate Programs *Program availability:* Part-time.

YESHIVA UNIVERSITY, New York, NY 10033-3201
General Information Independent, coed, university. *Graduate housing:* On-campus housing not available.
GRADUATE UNITS

Azrieli Graduate School of Jewish Education and Administration *Program availability:* Part-time, evening/weekend. Offers Jewish education and administration (MS, Ed D, Specialist).

Benjamin N. Cardozo School of Law Students: 992 full-time (506 women), 85 part-time (48 women); includes 277 minority (65 Black or African American, non-Hispanic/Latino; 88 Asian, non-Hispanic/Latino; 112 Hispanic/Latino; 1 Native Hawaiian or other Pacific Islander, non-Hispanic/Latino; 11 Two or more races, non-Hispanic/Latino), 69 international. Average age 25. 2,475 applicants, 56% accepted, 272 enrolled. *Faculty:* 61 full-time (24 women), 92 part-time/adjunct (38 women). Expenses: Contact institution. *Financial support:* In 2016–17, 745 students received support, including 87 research assistantships (averaging $1,599 per year); career-related internships or fieldwork, Federal Work-Study, institutionally sponsored loans, scholarships/grants, health care benefits, and tuition waivers (full and partial) also available. Support available to part-time students. Financial award application deadline: 3/1; financial award applicants required to submit FAFSA. In 2016, 70 master's, 391 doctorates awarded. *Program availability:* Part-time. Offers comparative legal thought (LL M); dispute resolution and advocacy (LL M); general studies (LL M); intellectual property law (LL M); law (JD). *Application deadline:* For fall admission, 4/1 priority date for domestic students; for spring admission, 12/1 for domestic students. Applications are processed on a rolling basis. *Application fee:* $50. Electronic applications accepted. *Application Contact:* David G. Martinidez, Dean of Admissions, 212-790-0357, Fax: 212-790-0482, E-mail: lawinfo@yu.edu. *Dean of Admissions,* David G. Martinidez, 212-790-0357, Fax: 212-790-0482, E-mail: lawinfo@yu.edu.

Bernard Revel Graduate School of Jewish Studies *Program availability:* Part-time. Offers Jewish studies (MA, PhD).

Ferkauf Graduate School of Psychology *Program availability:* Part-time. Offers clinical health psychology (PhD); clinical psychology (Psy D); mental health counseling psychology (MA); psychology (MA, PhD, Psy D); school/clinical-child psychology (Psy D).

Graduate Programs in Arts and Sciences Offers mathematical sciences (PhD); mathematics (MA); quantitative economics (MS); speech-language pathology (MS).

Sy Syms School of Business *Program availability:* Part-time. Offers accounting (MS); business (EMBA); marketing (MS).

Wurzweiler School of Social Work *Program availability:* Part-time, evening/weekend. Offers social work (MSW, PhD).

YORK COLLEGE OF PENNSYLVANIA, York, PA 17403-3651
General Information Independent, coed, comprehensive institution. *Enrollment:* 4,739 graduate, professional, and undergraduate students; 45 full-time matriculated graduate/professional students (31 women), 170 part-time matriculated graduate/professional students (116 women). *Enrollment by degree level:* 205 master's, 10 doctoral. *Graduate faculty:* 21 full-time (12 women), 14 part-time/adjunct (4 women). Tuition and fees vary according to program. *Graduate housing:* On-campus housing not available. *Student services:* Campus employment opportunities, campus safety program, career counseling, exercise/wellness program, free psychological counseling, international student services, services for students with disabilities, writing training. *Library facilities:* Schmidt Library.

Computer facilities: A campuswide network can be accessed from student residence rooms and from off campus. Online class registration is available. Website: http://www.ycp.edu/

General Application Contact: Katie Schwienteck, Director of Transfer Admissions, 717-815-2257, Fax: 717-849-1607, E-mail: admissions@ycp.edu.

GRADUATE UNITS

Graham School of Business Students: 2 full-time (1 woman), 68 part-time (31 women); includes 7 minority (2 Black or African American, non-Hispanic/Latino; 1 Asian, non-Hispanic/Latino; 1 Hispanic/Latino; 3 Two or more races, non-Hispanic/Latino). Average age 32. 39 applicants, 79% accepted, 20 enrolled. *Faculty:* 11 full-time (3 women), 4 part-time/adjunct (1 woman). Expenses: Contact institution. *Financial support:* In 2016–17, 3 students received support. Scholarships/grants available. Financial award applicants required to submit FAFSA. In 2016, 22 master's awarded. *Program availability:* Part-time, evening/weekend. Offers continuous improvement (MBA); financial management (MBA); health care management (MBA); management (MBA); marketing (MBA); self-designed (MBA). *Application deadline:* For fall admission, 7/15 priority date for domestic students, 5/1 for international students; for spring admission, 11/15 priority date for domestic students, 9/1 for international students; for summer admission, 4/15 priority date for domestic students. Applications are processed on a rolling basis. *Application fee:* $0. Electronic applications accepted. *Application*

Contact: MBA Office, 717-815-1491, Fax: 717-600-3999, E-mail: mba@ycp.edu. *MBA Director,* Nicole Cornell Sadowski, 717-815-1491, Fax: 717-600-3999, E-mail: ncornell@ycp.edu.

Master of Education Program Students: 54 part-time (39 women), 1 international. Average age 33. 51 applicants, 67% accepted, 30 enrolled. *Faculty:* 3 full-time (2 women), 5 part-time/adjunct (2 women). Expenses: Contact institution. *Financial support:* Scholarships/grants available. Financial award applicants required to submit FAFSA. In 2016, 4 master's awarded. *Program availability:* Part-time, evening/weekend. Offers educational leadership (M Ed); educational technology (M Ed); reading specialist (M Ed). *Application deadline:* For fall admission, 7/15 priority date for domestic students; for spring admission, 11/15 priority date for domestic students; for summer admission, 4/15 priority date for domestic students. Applications are processed on a rolling basis. *Application fee:* $0. Electronic applications accepted. *Director, Master of Education Program,* Dr. Joshua D. DeSantis, 717-815-1936, E-mail: jdesant1@ycp.edu.

Stabler Department of Nursing Students: 43 full-time (30 women), 48 part-time (46 women); includes 12 minority (5 Black or African American, non-Hispanic/Latino; 3 Asian, non-Hispanic/Latino; 1 Hispanic/Latino; 3 Two or more races, non-Hispanic/Latino). Average age 34. 85 applicants, 26% accepted, 21 enrolled. *Faculty:* 7 full-time (all women), 5 part-time/adjunct (1 woman). Expenses: Contact institution. *Financial support:* In 2016–17, 1 student received support. Scholarships/grants available. Financial award applicants required to submit FAFSA. In 2016, 22 master's, 4 doctorates awarded. Offers adult gerontology clinical nurse specialist (MS); adult gerontology nurse practitioner (MS, Post-Master's Certificate); nurse anesthetist (DNP); nurse educator (MS); nursing practice (DNP). *Application fee:* $0. Electronic applications accepted. *Application Contact:* Allison Malachosky, Administrative Assistant, 717-815-1243, E-mail: amalacho@ycp.edu. *Graduate Program Director,* Dr. Kimberly Fenstermacher, 717-815-1383, Fax: 717-849-1651, E-mail: kfenster@ycp.edu.

YORK UNIVERSITY, Toronto, ON M3J 1P3, Canada

General Information Province-supported, coed, university. CGS member. *Graduate housing:* Rooms and/or apartments available on a first-come, first-served basis to single and married students. *Research affiliation:* Imperial Oil Limited, National Palace Museum, Unicorn Children's Foundation (developmental and learning disorders), Smithsonian Institution (astronomy, physics, space), Beijing Municipality (management training), German Academic Exchange (German studies).

GRADUATE UNITS

Faculty of Graduate Studies *Program availability:* Part-time, evening/weekend. Offers communication and culture (MA, PhD); environmental studies (MES, PhD); interdisciplinary studies (MA); social and political thought (MA, PhD). Electronic applications accepted.

Faculty of Education *Program availability:* Part-time. Offers education (M Ed, PhD). Electronic applications accepted.

Faculty of Fine Arts *Program availability:* Part-time. Offers art history (MA, PhD); composition (MA); dance (MA, MFA, PhD); design (M Des); film (MA, MFA, PhD); fine arts (M Des, MA, MFA, PhD); music (PhD); musicology and ethnomusicology (MA); theatre (MFA); theatre and performance studies (MA, PhD); visual arts (MFA, PhD). Electronic applications accepted.

Faculty of Health Offers critical disability studies (MA, PhD); health (M Sc, M Sc N, MA, PhD); kinesiology and health science (M Sc, MA, PhD); nursing (M Sc N); psychology (MA, PhD).

Faculty of Liberal Arts and Professional Studies Offers disaster and emergency management (MA); economics (MA, PhD); English (MA, PhD); gender, feminist and women's studies (MA, PhD); geography (M Sc, MA, PhD); history (MA, PhD); human resources management (MHRM, PhD); humanities (MA, PhD); liberal arts and professional studies (M Sc, MA, MHRM, MPPAL, MSW, PhD); linguistics and applied linguistics (MA, PhD); philosophy (MA, PhD); political science (MA, PhD); public policy, administration and law (MPPAL); social anthropology (MA, PhD); social work (MSW, PhD); sociology (MA, PhD).

Faculty of Science *Program availability:* Part-time, evening/weekend. Offers biology (M Sc, PhD); chemistry (M Sc, PhD); industrial and applied mathematics (M Sc); mathematics and statistics (MA, PhD); physics and astronomy (M Sc, PhD); science (M Sc, MA, PhD).

Glendon Campus Offers French studies (MA, PhD); public and international affairs (MA); translation (MA).

Lassonde School of Engineering Offers computer science (M Sc, PhD); earth and space science (M Sc, PhD); engineering (M Sc, PhD).

Osgoode Hall Law School *Program availability:* Part-time, evening/weekend. Offers law (LL M, JD, PhD). Electronic applications accepted.

Schulich School of Business *Program availability:* Part-time, evening/weekend. Offers accounting (M Acc); administration (PhD); business (MBA); business analytics (MBA); finance (MF); international business (IMBA). Electronic applications accepted.

YO SAN UNIVERSITY OF TRADITIONAL CHINESE MEDICINE, Los Angeles, CA 90066

General Information Private, coed, graduate-only institution. *Graduate housing:* On-campus housing not available.

GRADUATE UNITS

Program in Acupuncture and Traditional Chinese Medicine *Program availability:* Part-time, online learning. Offers acupuncture and traditional Chinese medicine (MATCM).

YOUNGSTOWN STATE UNIVERSITY, Youngstown, OH 44555-0001

General Information State-supported, coed, comprehensive institution. CGS member. *Graduate housing:* Room and/or apartments available on a first-come, first-served basis to single students; on-campus housing not available to married students. *Research affiliation:* Ohio Supercomputer Center (computational chemistry and physics), Northeast Ohio Medical University (medicine), Parker-Hannifin Corporation (engineering technology), Ohio Mass Spectrometry Consortium (chemistry and biology), BioRemedial Technologies Inc. (environmental bioremediation).

GRADUATE UNITS

Graduate School *Program availability:* Part-time, evening/weekend.

Beeghly College of Education *Program availability:* Part-time, evening/weekend. Offers adolescent/young adult education (MS Ed); community counseling (MS Ed); content area concentration (MS Ed); early childhood education (MS Ed); education (MS Ed, Ed D); educational administration (MS Ed); educational leadership (Ed D); educational technology (MS Ed); gifted and talented education (MS Ed); literacy (MS Ed); middle childhood education (MS Ed); school counseling (MS Ed); special education (MS Ed).

Bitonte College of Health and Human Services *Program availability:* Part-time, evening/weekend. Offers criminal justice (MS); health and human services (MHHS, MPH, MS, MSN, DPT); nursing (MSN); physical therapy (DPT); public health (MPH).

College of Fine and Performing Arts *Program availability:* Part-time, evening/weekend. Offers fine and performing arts (MM); jazz studies (MM); music education (MM); music history and literature (MM); music theory and composition (MM); performance (MM).

College of Liberal Arts and Social Sciences *Program availability:* Part-time. Offers applied behavior analysis (MS); economics (MA); English (MA); environmental studies (MS); financial economics (MA); gerontology (MA); history (MA); industrial/institutional management (Certificate); liberal arts and social sciences (MA, MS, Certificate); risk management (Certificate).

College of Science, Technology, Engineering and Mathematics *Program availability:* Part-time, evening/weekend. Offers analytical chemistry (MS); applied mathematics (MS); biochemistry (MS); chemistry education (MS); civil and environmental engineering (MSE); computer engineering (MSE); computer science (MS); computing and information systems (MCIS); electrical engineering (MSE); environmental biology (MS); industrial and systems engineering (MSE); inorganic chemistry (MS); mechanical engineering (MSE); molecular biology, microbiology, and genetic (MS); organic chemistry (MS); physical chemistry (MS); physiology and anatomy (MS); science, technology, engineering and mathematics (MCIS, MSE); secondary mathematics (MS); statistics (MS).

Williamson College of Business Administration *Program availability:* Part-time, evening/weekend. Offers accounting (MBA); business administration (MBA, Certificate); enterprise resource planning (Certificate); marketing (MBA).

CLOSE-UPS OF INSTITUTIONS OFFERING GRADUATE AND PROFESSIONAL WORK

ACADEMY OF ART UNIVERSITY
Graduate Programs

Programs of Study

Academy of Art University offers Master of Arts (M.A.), Master of Fine Arts (M.F.A.), Master of Architecture (M.Arch.), and Master of Arts in Teaching (M.A.T.) degrees as well as an Art Teaching Credential. Courses are available online and in San Francisco in the following areas of study: Acting (speech, improv, physical acting), Advertising (creative strategy, art direction, copywriting), Animation & Visual Effects (background painting/layout design, character development, storyboard art, 3-D modeling, VFX/compositing), Architecture (structures, materials and methods of construction, design process, structural and environmental systems), Art Education (learning to teach in museums, developmental psychology, teaching art in the community and in the California K–12 classroom), Art History (Renaissance art, American art history, ancient art history, looking at art, philosophy), Art Teaching Credential (learning to teach both children and adults), Fashion (design, knitwear, merchandising, textiles, product design, costume design), Fashion Costume Design (2-D concept design, 3-D production for film, research for costume needs, story and character costume design), Fashion Journalism (fashion writing, editorials for magazines, newspaper writing, fashion news), Fine Art (painting, printmaking, sculpture), Game Development (game engines, prototyping, level design, game art, 3-D modeling), Graphic Design (corporate and brand identity, package design, print and collateral), illustration (traditional and comic book), Industrial Design (furniture design, product design, toy design), Interior Architecture & Design (commercial and residential design), Jewelry & Metal Arts (fashion jewelry design, enameling, stone setting, casting, welded and fabricated sculpture), Landscape Architecture (plant design, elements in landscape, grading and drainage, urban open spaces), Motion Pictures & Television (cinematography, directing, editing, producing, production design, screenwriting), Multimedia Communications (journalism, editing, short-form documentary), Music Production & Sound Design for Visual Media (harmony, arranging, orchestration, music production techniques, scoring for film, sound design), Photography (architecture, advertising, digital documentary, editorial, fashion, fine art, landscape, photojournalism, portraiture), Visual Development (concept art for animation, film and games, digital painting, character design, cinematic storytelling, maquettes, environment creation), Web Design & New Media (user experience design, interactive design, new media, web design), and Writing for Film, Television & Digital Media (writing, pitching, and the business side of being a professional writer).

Academy of Art University graduate candidates engage in a unique interdisciplinary approach to master's degree preparation. Comprised of studio work and academic investigation, the programs prepare students for the rigors of the industry. Attainment of the various master's degrees requires the graduate candidate to successfully complete studio courses, directed study, academic study, and electives. Total units required to graduate varies depending on the degree.

Academy of Art University also offers revolutionary online graduate degree programs that provide the same exceptional education offered on campus, but with greater flexibility. Studying online allows students to balance course work with career, family, and other responsibilities. The Academy's accreditation assures the highest standard of education, instruction, and effectiveness. Online classes teach students the skills and techniques used by professional artists and designers, skills which can help students make the most of their creative abilities.

Facilities

Academy of Art University's state-of-the-art facilities offer students the tools they need to prepare for professional careers in art and design. The Academy invests in top-notch equipment to ensure it remains on the cutting edge of technology. Learning on industry-standard equipment, students gain hands-on experience.

Academy of Art University students have access to an array of digital tools. The School of Game Development and the School of Animation & Visual Effects provide the latest equipment, as well as a video and Cintiq lab, green screen studio, and sound booth. The School of Web Design & New Media houses a usability lab with the most current software, while the School of Music Production & Sound Design for Visual Media offers the latest sound design and video editing tools.

The School of Advertising is designed to look, feel, and function like an ad agency. Located in the heart of San Francisco's Financial District, the School of Graphic Design has the latest industry tools that enable students to have a seamless transition into post-graduation work. The School of Illustration is housed in a unique historic building in San Francisco's Union Square

District. The original libraries, meeting rooms, theater, and a ballroom have been transformed into drawing/painting studios and classrooms.

Both undergraduate and graduate students in Architecture and Interior Architecture & Design share an 800 square-foot materials library and plotting room, as well as a model shop. The School of Industrial Design offers multiple shop facilities and a 3-D computer lab. The School of Landscape Architecture benefits from being located in San Francisco, the hub of urban landscape design.

Fashion students have access to studio facilities for women's, men's, and children's wear, as well as textile design, knitwear design, fashion merchandising, and marketing. In 2005, the Academy's School of Fashion was the first school to premiere collections of recent graduates at Mercedes-Benz Fashion Week at Bryant Park and continues with this tradition today. Surrounded by world-renowned museums and galleries, the School of Fine Art and the School of Art History facilities include thousands of square feet of studio space with everything students need to bring their individual visions to life.

The School of Motion Pictures & Television and the School of Acting facilities include a postproduction facility, green screen studio, screenwriting lab, custom-built voiceover room, and several soundstage studios. Students of the School of Multimedia Communications have access to a cutting-edge radio studio and television studio, complete with robotic cameras, anchor desks and interview sets, teleprompters, and green screens. The School of Photography facilities are equipped with both traditional and digital photographic technology.

The library provides state-of-the-art digital tools, making it possible for students to access extensive art and design image resources and information on demand. The Academy Resource Center offers all students free learning support services that include study hall tutoring, academic coaching, English as a second language support programs, a writing lab, and a multimedia language lab.

Financial Aid

Academy of Art University offers financial aid packages consisting of loans, interest-free payment plans, and work-study to eligible students. As financial aid programs, procedures, and eligibility requirements change frequently, applicants should contact the Financial Aid office at 79 New Montgomery Street, 4th Floor, San Francisco, California 94105, or by telephone at 800-544-2787 (U.S. only) or 415-274-2222 to check current requirements.

Cost of Study

For 2016–17, tuition was $982 per credit unit for graduate study. There is a $50 application fee and a $95 enrollment fee. Course fees average $400 per semester, depending on the class and area of study. Tuition and fees are subject to change at any time. Through the Academy, students already have access to most of the expensive technical equipment necessary for their area of study. Estimated graduate expenses for a full-time student are $26,452 per academic year.

Student Group

The master's programs accommodate more than 4,000 students. Of those, 63 percent are women and 54 percent are international. Approximately 33 percent of the students receive financial aid.

Student Outcomes

Academy of Art University guides students to professional creative futures. Firms hiring Academy of Art University graduates include Pixar, NBC, Apple, Nike, Publicis/Hal Riney, Louis Vuitton, Williams-Sonoma Inc., Mazda, Electronic Arts, Architecture Planning Interiors, Carnal Comics, Hang Art Gallery, Architecture International, Blizzard, BMW, Tesla Motors, DreamWorks, and many others.

Location

Strategically located in the heart of San Francisco, Academy of Art University's campus is ideal for emerging artists and designers. Academy students benefit from the location which is centered within the creative industry, near Silicon Valley, Pixar Animation Studios, LucasArts, and more. Beautiful San Francisco is more than an inspiring backdrop for creative students. From its museums and theaters to its diverse population, the city is renowned as a center for technology, design, arts, and culture.

Academy of Art University has created a vibrant community of artists and designers, providing students with the opportunity to collaborate among disciplines to bring their dreams to life. This community enables students to grow as artists and designers, and develop a solid network of colleagues within their field.

The University

In 1929, Academy of Art University founder Richard S. Stephens—the advertising Creative Director of *Sunset* magazine—acted on his belief that "aspiring artists and designers, given proper instruction, hard work, and dedication, can learn the skills needed to become successful professionals." His new school of advertising art consisted of 46 students meeting in one room on San Francisco's Kearny Street.

The instructors, who were professional artists, brought real-world problems, situations, solutions, and practical experience to the students. Based on this idea, the school's philosophy was formulated: hire established professionals to teach the art and design professionals of tomorrow. At that time, advertising consisted primarily of illustrations, photos, and copy. Consequently, it became necessary to teach beginning students the fundamentals of drawing, painting, color, light, and photography, as well as layout and typography.

When Richard A. Stephens succeeded his father as President in 1951, the Foundations Department was added, ensuring all students mastered the principles of traditional art and design. Illustration soon expanded to include fine arts (drawing, painting, sculpture, and printmaking), and advertising design led to the School of Graphic Design. Fashion (design, textiles, and merchandising) and an Interior Design School were also added. In 1966, the Academy officially became a college, and a decade later began to offer the Master of Fine Arts degree. By 1992, there were more than 2,500 students.

The leadership of the Academy was then turned over to the third generation. Dr. Elisa Stephens, granddaughter of the founder, quickly determined that the small School of Web Design & New Media had enormous potential to prepare students for multimedia careers with companies such as Pixar, Adobe, and Disney.

Today, Academy of Art University is the largest accredited private art and design university in the nation with an enrollment of nearly 13,000. Approximately 37 percent of the student body is made up of international students. The Academy has over 40 facilities that house classrooms, studios, galleries, and residence halls. The students, who are admitted through an open-enrollment policy, aspire to earn A.A., B.A., B.S., B.F.A., B.Arch., M.A., M.F.A., M.A.T., or M.Arch. degrees or an Art Teaching Credential. Students can study in San Francisco or through the Academy's flexible online programs.

The Academy maintains a system of courtesy shuttles to connect the different points of the campus, all of which are located within the city limits of San Francisco. The instructors, who are working art and design professionals, are drawn from all around the world to the Academy and the creative and intellectual center that is the Bay Area. Extensive senior-year internship programs allow students to gain valuable experience and develop strong portfolios in their chosen field before graduation.

Academy of Art University is an accredited member of the Western Association of Schools and Colleges (WSCUC), National Association of Schools of Art and Design (NASAD), Council for Interior Design Accreditation (CIDA) for BFA-IAD and MFA-IAD, National Architectural Accrediting Board (NAAB) for B.Arch. and M.Arch., and California Commission on Teacher Credentialing (CTC).

What Sets the Academy Apart

The Academy is one of the few art and design schools that believes in nurturing the whole artist; this includes developing athletic ability along with artistic talent. Students can participate in intercollegiate, intramural, and club sports, and with Pacific West honors and national championships, the University offers basketball, baseball, softball, cross country, track and field, soccer, golf, volleyball, and tennis for its students to partake. Furthermore, the Academy is proud to be the only higher arts education institution in the U.S. to have an NCAA athletics program.

Faculty

Academy of Art University has assembled a faculty of top creative professionals. These award-winning industry leaders have a passion for inspiring the next generation of artists and designers. With a focus on hands-on experience, instructors guide students to achieve their full creative potential. Specific information about faculty members can be found on the University's website at www.academyart.edu.

Applying

Admission to the master's programs requires official transcripts indicating at least the completion of a bachelor's degree, submission of a portfolio of work (portfolio requirements vary by discipline), a statement of intent outlining graduate study goals, and a resume. Admission to the program is permitted at the beginning of each semester. Additional materials may be required. Students should contact the Graduate Admissions Office for further details.

Correspondence and Information

Academy of Art University Graduate Admissions
P.O. Box 193844
San Francisco, California 94119
United States
Phone: 415-274-2222
800-544-2787 (toll-free in the U.S. only)
Fax: 415-618-6287
E-mail: info@academyart.edu
Website: http://www.academyart.edu

Academy of Art University, Downtown San Francisco Campus.

THE COLLEGE OF NEW JERSEY

Graduate Programs

 For more information, visit http://petersons.to/collegeofnewjerseygrad

Programs of Study

The College of New Jersey (TCNJ) offers the following advanced degrees: Master of Arts (M.A.) in counselor education (areas include school counseling; clinical mental health counseling; and marriage, couple, and family counseling and therapy) or English (literature); Master of Arts in Teaching (M.A.T.) in early childhood education, elementary education, secondary education (iSTEM math, iSTEM science, and iSTEM technology education), special education/elementary; five-year programs (for TCNJ undergraduate students only) in education of the deaf and hard of hearing/elementary education, special education, urban education, and English; Master of Education (M.Ed.) in educational leadership–principal certification, educational leadership: instruction (a collaborative program in conjunction with the Regional Training Center), elementary and secondary education (off-site Global Program only), reading K–12, special education, special education/teacher of the blind or visually impaired, Integrative Science, Technology, Engineering, and Math (iSTEM), or teaching English as a second language; Master of Science in Nursing (M.S.N.) in adult/gerontological primary care nurse practitioner studies, clinical nurse leader studies, family nurse practitioner studies, neonatal nurse practitioner studies, or school nurse certification (instructional and non-instructional options); and Educational Specialist (Ed.S.) in marriage, couple, and family therapy.

Graduate certificate programs and/or post-master's programs are offered in adult/gerontological primary care nurse practitioner studies, family nurse practitioner studies, school nurse certification (instructional and non-instructional options), bilingual education (main campus and off-site Global Program), educational leadership–principal certification, instructional licensure–teacher of preschool–grade 3, learning disabilities teacher/consultant studies, teacher of students with blindness and visual impairments studies, reading specialist studies, student assistance coordinator studies, teacher certification for international schools (off-site Global Program only), teacher of students with disabilities, teaching English as a second language, or gender studies.

Global opportunities in education are also available for graduate students. Graduate global programs at TCNJ have been in existence for over thirty-five years and provide course work leading toward master's-level degrees in education and certification in teaching, administration, and substance abuse counseling. Courses are taught by TCNJ faculty members and other internationally recognized professors. Courses are offered June through July at TCNJ sites in Mallorca, Spain; Bangkok, Thailand; Lisbon, Portugal; and Johannesburg, South Africa. During the academic year, courses are available in Cairo, Egypt; Hsinchu, Taiwan; and Ho Chi Minh City, Vietnam.

For the convenience of the majority of graduate students who pursue degrees while employed full-time, graduate courses held on the Ewing campus are offered during the day and in the evening.

Research Facilities

TCNJ offers a state-of-the-art library that serves as an exciting intellectual, cultural, and social center for the College community. The five-story, 135,000-square-foot facility will provide cutting-edge services to the TCNJ community well into the twenty-first century. In addition to housing traditional library collections and services in an atmosphere that is both friendly and elegant, a key feature of the recently built library is its wide array of carefully considered and thoughtful amenities, which make using the facility both a pleasure and a convenience. The library provides twenty-four group-study rooms (one reserved for graduate students), ample and comfortable seating, tables and carrels, and both WiFi and LAN Internet access throughout, with power connections available at every carrel and study table. Special design features include a café, a secure, late night/24-hour study area, and a 105-seat multipurpose auditorium. The library also houses the Instructional Technology Services facility, creating ideal one-stop shopping for students working on projects.

Library collections include more than 560,000 volumes and 200,000 microforms as well as subscriptions to more than 1,400 periodicals. The library also subscribes to more than seventy-five electronic indexes covering more than 14,000 scholarly journals, including full-text resources. A media facility offers viewing and listening equipment as well as sound recordings, videos, and interactive computer software. PCs are available for public access to electronic resources. Collections are constantly augmented by new acquisitions, and interlibrary loan and document delivery services are available to students. The library is also an active participant in a number of library networks and maintains cooperative arrangements with many regional academic libraries, from which students may borrow directly. TCNJ librarians are an important resource in and of themselves. In addition to

advanced studies in library and information science, each subject librarian has additional graduate degrees in one of the major academic areas, and students are encouraged to consult them in person and online.

In addition to providing new library facilities for the College community, TCNJ has met the challenge of the computer field's phenomenal growth with installations of computer facilities in each of its seven schools.

Financial Aid

The College of New Jersey offers financial aid to qualified matriculated students through a combination of loans, assistantships, and/or student employment opportunities. To be considered for all financial aid programs, students must submit the Free Application for Federal Student Aid (FAFSA) to the College Financial Assistance Office. Graduate assistantships are available to qualified full-time students on a competitive basis. Prospective students must apply through the Office of Graduate Studies by April 15 to be considered for a graduate assistantship.

Cost of Study

Tuition for graduate courses for the 2017–18 academic year is $915.52 per semester hour of credit for New Jersey residents and $1,334.91 per semester hour of credit for out-of-state residents. Additional fees include ID, student center, computer access and service fees, and health insurance (for full-time students). Tuition and fees are subject to change by action of the New Jersey State Legislature.

Living and Housing Costs

As the majority of TCNJ's graduate students attend classes part-time in the evenings, the College does not offer on-campus housing for graduate students. Graduate students who seek housing in the area may obtain assistance from the Office of Residence Life.

Student Group

The College of New Jersey has an enrollment of approximately 6,500 undergraduate students and 1,000 graduate students.

Student Outcomes

The College of New Jersey's excellent reputation has afforded graduates outstanding opportunities when entering their professional fields. Many TCNJ graduates receive job placements through various on-campus recruitment programs sponsored by the Office of Career Services.

Location

The College of New Jersey is located on 289 tree-lined acres in suburban Ewing, New Jersey, 7 miles from the state capital in Trenton. Woodlands and two lakes surround the academic and residential buildings. More than thirty-five buildings make up the physical plant, most of which are built in the classic Georgian Colonial architecture. The campus is 30 miles from Philadelphia and 60 miles from New York's theaters, museums, and other attractions. The nearby towns of Princeton and New Hope offer additional cultural activities.

The College

Founded in 1855, the College has grown from its early years as a teachers' college to a multipurpose institution comprising seven schools: Arts and Communication; Business; Education; Engineering; Humanities and Social Sciences; Nursing, Health, and Exercise Science; and Science. Graduate study is available in the Schools of Education, Humanities and Social Sciences, and Nursing, Health, and Exercise Science.

TCNJ introduced its first advanced degree program, a Master of Science in elementary education, in 1947. Over the years, the number of graduate programs has steadily increased. At present, there are more than fifty specialized graduate degree and certificate programs.

TCNJ's academic programs are accredited by the Middle States Association of Colleges and Schools, the National Council for Accreditation of Teacher Education (NCATE)/Council for the Accreditation of Educator Preparation (CAEP), the Council for the Accreditation of Counseling and Related Educational Programs (CACREP), Commission on Collegiate Nursing Education (CCNE), and other appropriate professional associations.

Applying

Students of proven ability with undergraduate degrees in appropriate fields are eligible to apply for graduate study. Applications should be submitted online (http://graduate.tcnj.edu/apply) along with a $75 nonrefundable application fee. Transcripts of all previous college or university work and other supporting documentation, as noted on the website, should be

The College of New Jersey

forwarded to the Office of Graduate and Advancing Education. Acceptable scores on the appropriate national standardized tests are required for most degree and initial teacher certificate programs.

Application deadlines for matriculation and non-matriculation for the various graduate programs are located on the Graduate Studies website (http://graduate.tcnj.edu/apply).

Correspondence and Information

Office of Graduate and Advancing Education
Green Hall, Room 111
The College of New Jersey
P.O. Box 7718
2000 Pennington Road
Ewing, New Jersey 08628
United States
Phone: 609-771-2300
Fax: 609-637-5105
E-mail: graduate@tcnj.edu
Website: http://graduate.tcnj.edu

DEANS AND PROGRAM COORDINATORS

SCHOOL OF HUMANITIES AND SOCIAL SCIENCES
Jane Wong, Dean; Ph.D.

Graduate Program Coordinator
English: Jo Carney, Ph.D., Iowa.

SCHOOL OF EDUCATION
Suzanne McCotter, Dean; Ph.D., Georgia.

Graduate Program Coordinators
Counselor Education: Mark Woodford, Ph.D., Virginia. Marion Cavallaro, Ph.D., Ohio State. Atsuko Seto, Ph.D., Wyoming. Stuart Roe, Ph.D., Penn State.
Deaf and Hard of Hearing/Elementary Education Five-Year Program: Barbara Strassman, Ed.D., Columbia Teachers College.
Early Childhood Education: Jody Eberly, Ph.D., Rutgers.
Educational Leadership–Instruction: Alan Amtzis, Ph.D., Boston College.
Educational Leadership–Principal: Donald Leake, Ph.D., Ohio State.
Elementary and Early Childhood Education (M.A.T.): Arti Joshi, Ph.D., Syracuse.
Instructional Licensure–Teacher of Preschool–Grade 3: Jody Eberly, Ph.D., Rutgers.
Reading K–12: Matthew Hall, Ph.D., NYU.
Secondary Education: Donald Leake, Ph.D., Ohio State.
Special Education: Amy Dell, Ph.D., Rochester.
TESOL/Bilingual Education: Yiqiang Wu, Ph.D., Texas A&M.

SCHOOL OF NURSING, HEALTH, AND EXERCISE SCIENCE
Carole Kenner, Dean; Ph.D., Indiana.

Graduate Program Coordinators
Nursing: Connie Kartoz, Ph.D., Pennsylvania.

MAJOR RESEARCH PROJECTS, AWARDS, GRANTS, AND INITIATIVES

School of Education
Intoxicated Drivers' Resource Center (IDRC); Dr. Cassandra Gibson and the TCNJ Clinic, School of Education.
Community Reinforcement and Family Training (CRAFT); Dr. Cassandra Gibson and Dr. Mark Woodford, School of Education.
Collegiate Recovery Support and Environmental Change (CRC); Dr. Cassandra Gibson, School of Education.
Trenton Violence Reduction Strategy (TVRS); Dr. Cassandra Gibson, School of Education.
LifeChoices; Dr. Cassandra Gibson and Dr. Stuart Roe, School of Education.
Creating a team of highly qualified professionals for English language learners (CTHQP) grant; Dr. Yiqiang Wu, School of Education.
Adaptive Technology Center grant; Dr. Amy G. Dell, School of Education.
Preparing special and elementary educators to use inquiry and design-based learning; Dr. Amy Dell, School of Education.
Provisional Teacher Program; Dr. Anthony Evangelisto, School of Education.
TECH-NJ (Technology, Educators, and Children with Disabilities–New Jersey); Dr. Amy G. Dell, School of Education.
Deaf/Blind Family and Community Educational Support; Dr. Jerry Petroff, School of Education.
Conversation analysis of native/non-native speakers; Dr. Jean Wong, School of Education.
Facilitating transition from school to employment for individuals with challenging behavior; Dr. Shridevi Rao, School of Education.
Issues of literacy and teaching elementary students of color; Dr. Deborah Thompson, School of Education.
Fulbright Scholar Award to teach at the University of Bahrain, Bahrain Teachers College; Dr. Lynnette Mawhinney, School of Education

School of Nursing, Health and Exercise Science
Advanced education nursing traineeship program; Dr. Claire Lindberg, School of Nursing
HIV symptom distress project; Dr. Claire Lindberg, School of Nursing.

School of Humanities and Social Sciences
The reception of Dante and Chaucer within the work of their literary successors; Dr. Glenn Steinberg, School of Culture and Society.
Book-length research project in family memoir based on research and interviews: "The Seven: A Family Holocaust Story"; Ellen Friedman, School of Humanities and Social Sciences.
Research in Early Modern Grammars and Spelling Books; Felicia Steele, School of Humanities and Social Sciences.
"'Universal Mixing' and Interpenetrating Standing: Disability and Community in Melville's Moby-Dick"; Harriet Hustis, School of Humanities and Social Sciences.
Executive Director of the Thornton Wilder Society, which is headquartered at TCNJ, and co-founder and officer of the Edward Albee Society; Lincoln Konkle, School of Humanities and Social Sciences.
Thornton Wilder: New Perspectives; Lincoln Konkle, School of Humanities and Social Sciences.
Thornton Wilder and The Puritan Narrative Tradition; Lincoln Konkle, School of Humanities and Social Sciences.
National Endowment for the Humanities Fellowship; Michael Robertson, School of Humanities and Social Sciences.
Worshipping Walt: The Whitman Disciples; Michael Robertson, School of Humanities and Social Sciences.
Walt Whitman, Where the Future Becomes Present; David Blake and Michael Robertson, School of Humanities and Social Sciences.

The clock tower above Green Hall, the main administrative building on campus, is a well-known symbol of TCNJ tradition.

TCNJ offers a state-of-the-art library that serves as an exciting intellectual, cultural, and social center for the College community.

COLLEGE OF STATEN ISLAND
OF THE CITY UNIVERSITY OF NEW YORK
Graduate Degree Programs

Programs of Study

The College of Staten Island (CSI) offers master's degrees in Accounting (M.S.); Biology (M.S.); Business Management (M.S.); Cinema and Media Studies (M.A.); Clinical Mental Health Counseling (M.A.); Computer Science (M.S.); Education: Childhood (elementary) Education (M.S.Ed.), Adolescence (secondary) Education (M.S.Ed.), Special Education (grades 1–6) (M.S.Ed.), Special Education (grades 7–12) (M.S.Ed.), Teaching of English to Speakers of other Languages (M.S.Ed.); English (M.A.); Environmental Science (M.S.); History (M.A.); Liberal Studies (M.A.); Neuroscience and Developmental Disabilities (M.S.); Nursing: Adult-Gerontological Health Nursing (M.S.); Social Work (M.S.W.); and Electrical Engineering (M.E.).

Post-master's degrees are awarded in Education: School District Leader, School Building Leader and School District Leader (dual certificate) and in Nursing: Adult-Gerontological Health Nursing. Advanced certificates are offered in Autism Spectrum Disorders, Business Analytics of Large-Scale Data, Cultural Competence, Bilingual Education, Public History, and Teaching of English to Speakers of other Languages (online and in-classroom). The College of Staten Island offers an Adult-Gerontological Health Nursing (D.N.P.) program and a Clinical Doctorate in Physical Therapy (D.P.T.).

In addition, the College offers the following doctoral programs jointly with the Graduate Center of the City University of New York (CUNY): Biochemistry (Ph.D.), Biology (Ph.D.), Computer Science (Ph.D.), Nursing (Ph.D.), Physics (Ph.D.), and Polymer Chemistry (Ph.D.).

Research Facilities

The Center for Developmental Neuroscience and Developmental Disabilities is supported jointly with the New York State Institute for Basic Research (IBR). The center conducts, promotes, and sponsors research, education, and training in the developmental neurosciences, with special emphasis on research and educational programs in the specific field of developmental disabilities. The center provides for collaborative efforts between the College and IBR in offering the master's degree in Neuroscience and Developmental Disabilities, as well as with the University's doctoral programs in biology (subprogram in neuroscience), and in psychology (subprogram in learning processes). The center provides advanced research training for graduate students.

The Center for Environmental Science provides support for research and policy recommendations concerning environmental problems. One of the major purposes of the center is to define and solve environmental problems on Staten Island and its environs through research that includes studies of respiratory diseases, toxic and carcinogenic chemicals in the air, and the population at risk for lung cancer.

The Center for the Study of Staten Island: Staten Island Project (SIP) is designed to integrate the work of the College with the public affairs concerns of the people of Staten Island. To that end, it mediates and facilitates the collaboration of the College's faculty, students, and staff with government, civic organizations, and businesses in order to identify and assist in finding solutions to the borough's pressing public issues. The center serves as an information and consultation resource to prepare citizens and leaders to make better-informed decisions about public life; it fosters the development of faculty research and graduate education through engagement with the community; and it builds bridges to other public affairs institutes and local communities as a spur to innovations in public life on Staten Island.

The Center for Interdisciplinary Applied Mathematics and Computational Sciences brings together a diverse group of research faculty members and students with interests in interdisciplinary applications of mathematics and computational science. The center's activities include the use of the campus supercomputer, faculty collaboration, grant writing, student mentoring and research, and sponsored lectures.

The CUNY High-Performance Computing Center (HPCC) is located on the CSI campus. Goals of the HPCC are to: support the scientific computing needs of university faculty, student, staff, and their public and private sector partners; create opportunities for the CUNY research community to develop new partnerships with the government and private sectors; and leverage the center's capabilities to acquire additional research resources for its faculty and graduate students in existing and major new programs.

Financial Aid

The Office of Student Financial Aid administers federal and state grant, loan, and work-study programs to assist students with financial need to attend the College of Staten Island. Students should contact the Office of Student Financial Aid early in the admission process to discuss eligibility requirements and responsibilities. Graduate assistant positions are available for full-time graduate students in some departments. Information about these positions may be obtained from the individual program departments. The College of Staten Island also recognizes academic excellence through scholarship programs which offer assistance to students as well. For more information about the scholarship programs, prospective students can visit www.csi.cuny.edu/advancement/scholarships.html.

Cost of Study

For the 2017–18 academic year, tuition for master's programs for New York State residents is $440 per credit, or $5,225 per semester for 12 or more credits. Tuition for non-state residents is $805 per credit. Tuition for the Master in Social Work program is $580 per credit, or $6,895 per semester for New York State residents. Tuition for non-state residents is $940 per credit. Tuition for the Master of Engineering program is $520 per credit, or $6,115 per semester for New York State residents. Tuition for non-state residents is $895 per credit. Tuition for the Clinical Doctorate in Physical Therapy program for New York State residents is $645 per credit, or $5,635 per semester. Tuition for non-state residents is $1,015 per credit. Tuition for the Doctorate in Nursing Practice program for New York State residents is $580 per credit, or $6,895 per semester. Tuition for non-state residents is $940 per credit.

College of Staten Island of the City University of New York

Living and Housing Costs

For the 2017–18 academic year, students living with parents budget a minimum of $1,364 for books and supplies, $1,088 for local transportation, $3,020 for meals and personal expenses, and $4,290 for housing. Students living away from parents budget the same amounts for books, supplies, and transportation, plus $18,060 for food, housing, and personal expenses for a nine-month academic year. The College of Staten Island's first on-campus student housing is now open. Floor plans and rates are available online at www.csi.cuny.edu/housing.

Student Group

Nearly 1,000 graduate students enrolled at the College of Staten Island in the 2016 fall semester. The graduate population reflects a wide range of ethnicity, social and economic backgrounds, educational and professional experiences, and aspirations.

Location

The College of Staten Island is located in New York City in the Borough of Staten Island. Completed in 1994, the 204-acre campus of the College of Staten Island is the largest one for a college in New York City. Set in a park-like landscape, the campus is centrally located on Staten Island and is accessible by automobile and public transportation.

The College

The College of Staten Island is a college of the City University of New York that offers exceptional opportunities to all its students. Programs in the liberal arts and sciences and professional studies lead to bachelor's and associate degrees, in addition to the graduate programs previously listed.

Graduate Program Faculty Heads

A full listing of graduate program directors, contact information, and office hours is available at the College website. Please visit http://www.csi.cuny.edu/graduatestudies and click on "Graduate Programs and Requirements."

Applying

Requirements for admission and application deadlines vary by program and department. Students should contact the Graduate Admissions' Office for additional information or to arrange an admissions interview or campus tour.

Correspondence and Information

Sasha Spence, Associate Director for Graduate Admissions
Office of Recruitment and Admissions
North Administration Building (2A), Room 103
College of Staten Island
2800 Victory Boulevard
Staten Island, New York 10314
Phone: 718-982-2019
Fax: 718-982-2500
E-mail: masterit@csi.cuny.edu
Website: http://www.csi.cuny.edu/graduatestudies

Graduate students at the College of Staten Island are provided with the tools and opportunities they need to make positive contributions to society. CSI students perform research with faculty from every academic discipline on campus, using the College's state-of-the-art equipment and facilities.

Instructors at the College of Staten Island are committed to each graduate student's success. Whether offering guidance on a rigorous course of study, engaging students in stimulating research, or sharing their professional experiences, CSI faculty members help students shape and achieve their goals.

COLORADO SCHOOL OF MINES

Graduate School

 For more information, visit http://petersons.to/coloradoschoolofminesgrad

Programs of Studies

Specialized and focused, Colorado School of Mines (Mines) is a unique research university with an extensive array of resource-related programs. The need for Mines' rare mix of expertise has never been greater. The availability and sustainable use of natural resources is one of the world's greatest challenges, and Mines' graduates and faculty members are creating solutions.

Those interested in pursuing a graduate degree find significant academic and research opportunities in globally significant growth areas:

- Engineering—mechanical, electrical, civil and environmental, chemical and biological, nuclear
- Environment—environmental engineering science, chemistry, hydrology
- Geotechnics—geology, petroleum, mining, geophysics, underground construction and tunneling
- Business—mineral and energy economics, engineering and technology management

Graduate degree options range from Master of Engineering, Master of Science (thesis and non-thesis options), and Ph.D.'s.

Research

Mines is a global leader in research and the advancement of technology. Led by world-class faculty, the research conducted at Mines enhances the educational experience of its graduates. Students have the opportunity to actively participate in research at every level of their education.

With an annual research budget of more than $55 million and a faculty that has pioneered numerous advances in a wide range of technical fields, opportunities to conduct innovative research is virtually unlimited. Graduate students are able to work hand-in-hand with researchers at Mines and from around the world on both applied and academic research problems. Proximity to a number of governmental research facilities such as the U.S. Geological Survey, the National Renewable Energy Laboratory, the U.S. Bureau of Reclamation, and the National Institute of Standards and Technology provides unparalleled access to a wide variety of scholars, facilities, and research opportunities.

Research spans many highly relevant areas, with a specific focus on energy and environmental stewardship. Mines' first-rate facilities and partnerships with industry, national laboratories, other universities, funding agencies, and international institutions help maintain its cutting-edge research and have a significant impact on real-world problems. Research is a cooperative effort in the Mines community; more information can be found at http://www.minesnewsroom.com/.

Financial Aid

At Mines, the awarding policy gives priority to the neediest students, as determined by the FAFSA. In the last academic year, more than $27.9 million of financial assistance was awarded. Typically more than 85 percent of the student body receives some form of aid, which includes scholarships, grants, loans, or work-study employment.

Cost of Study

For the 2017–18 academic year, full-time (9–15 credits) tuition per semester is $8,085 for residents and $17,610 for nonresidents. Mandatory fees are $1,109. The estimated cost of books and supplies is $750 per semester. More information on tuition and fees is available online at www.mines.edu/Costs_GS.

Living and Housing Costs

The Apartments at Mines Park house undergraduate and graduate degree seeking students. Single student housing is available in 1, 2, and 3 bedroom apartments. Family housing is available in 1 and 2 bedroom apartments. Additional information on Mines Park is available from the Department of Residence Life or online at http://residencelife.mines.edu/Apartments-at-Mines-Park.

In addition, Golden and the surrounding communities—Lakewood, Arvada, Denver, Boulder, and Littleton—offer other affordable housing options (http://residencelife.mines.edu/Off-Campus-Housing-Resources).

Student Group and Outcomes

The Graduate School at Mines draws together nearly 1,300 graduate students from the United States and over sixty other countries, and encourages problem investigation from diverse, real-world perspectives. Together, faculty and staff members and undergraduate and graduate students build a strong community of shared interests. The Mines community understands the challenges that can arise in leaving a home community to attend graduate school and works collectively to help maintain those community ties while building and growing new ones.

A graduate student at Colorado School of Mines becomes an important member of a community that is dedicated to generating new knowledge and educating students and professionals in fields related to the:

- discovery and recovery of the Earth's resources, their conversion to materials and energy, and their utilization in advanced processes and products
- economic and social systems necessary to ensure the prudent and provident use of Earth's resources in a sustainable global society
- preservation and stewardship of the Earth's environment

Mines' renowned reputation, attained through the tremendous work of its students, faculty and staff; its high admission standards; and its alumni network combine to give students an edge in the job market. Mines' strong master's and professional degrees are extremely valuable and more than just precursors to a doctoral degree. More than 96 percent of the recipients of Mines' master's and professional degrees find employment by graduation. More than 70 percent of these graduates are employed in industry, with the remainder employed by governmental agencies or matriculating into doctoral degree programs.

Location

Mines is located in Golden, Colorado, in the foothills of the Rocky Mountains, 15 miles west of Denver's downtown business district. Golden, a thriving community of 17,000, offers outdoor adventure with small-town atmosphere and convenient access to big-city attractions. With more than 300 days of sunshine each year, Golden is a great place to visit or live in during any season. Founded during the Gold Rush of 1859, Golden is one of Colorado's oldest communities and served as the Capital of Colorado Territory from 1862 to 1867. Golden retains its small-town character and remains the seat of Jefferson County. Historic buildings and homes have been preserved and blend with new construction throughout the downtown area, which offers many shops and restaurants.

The school has some big-name neighbors in Golden, including the National Renewable Energy Laboratory, a frequent research partner, and Coors Brewing Company.

Colorado School of Mines

Outdoor enthusiasts will find the proximity of the Mines campus to Colorado's Rocky Mountains an exciting prospect. Colorado offers a legendary abundance of activity in its nearby mountains, open spaces, and parks including alpine skiing, snowboarding, cross-country skiing, snowshoeing, mountain climbing, river rafting, hiking, biking, camping, exploring and fishing—to name a few.

The Mines campus features beautifully renovated historical architecture, as well as award-winning, new, state-of-the-art buildings.

The School

Colorado School of Mines is a public research university devoted to engineering and applied science. Founded in 1874, Mines' role and mission has remained constant and is written in the Colorado statute as:

"The Colorado School of Mines shall be a specialized baccalaureate and graduate research institution with high admission standards. The Colorado School of Mines shall have a unique mission in energy, mineral, and materials science and engineering and associated engineering and science fields. The school shall be the primary institution of higher education offering energy, mineral and materials science and mineral engineering degrees at both the graduate and undergraduate levels." *(Colorado Revised Statutes, Section 23-41-105)*

Mines offers all the advantages of a world-class research institution with a size that allows for personal attention. Innovative ideas have the chance to flourish and with a strong work ethic, students have the opportunity to help drive positive change locally, nationally, and globally.

Applying

The Graduate School at Mines is open to graduates from four-year baccalaureate programs at recognized colleges and universities. Admission to all graduate programs is competitive, based on an evaluation of academic performance (undergraduate or graduate), test scores, and references. Each department evaluates applications separately and admissions decisions are based on distinct admission criteria.

All application materials are submitted to the Office of Graduate Studies. Once an application file is complete, it is forwarded to the academic department review committee. Prospective students should consult the Graduate Admissions website at www.mines.edu/graduate_admissions for more information.

Correspondence and Information

Office of Graduate Studies
Colorado School of Mines
Student Center E140
Golden, Colorado 80401
United States
Phone: 303-273-3247
800-446-9488 Ext. 3247
E-mail: grad-app@mines.edu
Website: http://www.mines.edu

Finding innovative solutions to global challenges.

Focused on responsible stewardship of the earth and its resources.

DARTMOUTH COLLEGE
School of Graduate and Advanced Studies

 For more information, visit http://petersons.to/dartmouthcollege-grad

Programs of Study

Since 1885, graduate and advanced studies at Dartmouth has combined world-class research facilities with an outstanding faculty. Dartmouth's graduate programs facilitate innovation, support collaboration, and deliver a unique blend of research opportunities and individualized education.

The School of Graduate and Advanced studies at Dartmouth offers master's and doctoral degrees across a broad range of programs, including several interdisciplinary programs and doctoral programs connected to the professional schools at Dartmouth. There are 16 programs leading to the Ph.D., 12 on the master's track, and 7 cross-disciplinary programs.

Master's degrees are offered in chemistry, comparative literature, computer science, digital music, engineering, earth sciences, liberal studies, health care delivery, health policy and clinical practice, physics and astronomy, and quantitative biomedical sciences.

Doctoral programs are offered in biochemistry, biology, chemistry, cognitive neuroscience, computer science, earth sciences, ecology evolution ecosystems and society, engineering, experimental and molecular medicine, genetics, health policy and clinical practice, mathematics, microbiology and immunology, physics and astronomy, psychological and brain sciences, and quantitative biomedical science.

Special interdisciplinary training programs include environmental sciences, Master of Engineering Management, medical physics, M.D./M.S. program in biomedical engineering, Ph.D. engineering innovation program, M.D./Ph.D. program, and Ph.D./MBA program.

The School supports over 1,000 students from 62 countries, including the United States. The graduate alumni network connects more than 4,000 graduates.

The School of Graduate and Advanced Studies has fused the liberal arts tradition with research and believes that intense collaboration among brilliant people and strong departments accelerates discovery. It seeks to develop scholars who can approach problems from multiple perspectives and who can work across fields of study.

Research Facilities

Graduate and postdoctoral education at Dartmouth is more intimate than at the big research universities it is often compared to. Faculty members lead small, intense, research teams and students enjoy unparalleled access to leaders in their fields.

Dartmouth boasts world-class research and teaching facilities designed to promote cross-disciplinary intellectual exchange. A physical sciences center and chemistry building house science programs, libraries, computer labs, and service shops, encouraging students and faculty from different fields to interact. The medical complex offers state-of-the-art research facilities created to provide training in life sciences programs.

Financial Aid

Dartmouth offers full financial support to all students in doctoral programs. Financial support includes a paid yearly stipend or fellowship. Financial aid at the master's level varies by program.

Living and Housing

There are several options off campus; information is available through the Dartmouth Real Estate Office (https://realestate.dartmouth.edu) and Craigslist. There will be housing information on the graduate studies' electronic bulletin board. The classified advertisement section of the Valley News (local newspaper) is another source.

Student Life

Roughly 1,050 graduate students attend Dartmouth, enjoying a coeducational college community built for them and the 4,276 undergraduates. Campus cultural life centers around the Hopkins Center for the Performing Arts, which sponsors an active film society, two full concert series, and a very active drama program. Facilities are available for students interested in joining a musical group or participating in arts workshops including sculpture, painting, and design. Graduate students also have access to the extensive Dartmouth College Athletic Facilities, and can participate in a variety of clubs, including the Dartmouth Graduate Outing Club.

Dartmouth's Entrepreneurial Network helps students learn valuable entrepreneurial skills, and offers strategic advice and mentoring to prepare students to leverage their knowledge and abilities.

The Dartmouth Career Network is a professional network of thousands of alumni who are willing to advise students and fellow alumni on their career path.

The Faculty

Dartmouth faculty members are experts in their fields, renowned for their scholarship in their respective disciplines and for their teaching ability. The faculty is accessible and available for consultation with students. The small program sizes ensure close collaborative relationships between faculty and students.

Students across the disciplines also interact with faculty at the professional schools including the Tuck School of Business, Thayer School of Engineering, and Geisel School of Medicine ensuring breadth of knowledge while pursuing their specific graduate program.

Location

Dartmouth is located in Hanover, New Hampshire on the western side of the state in the scenic Upper Connecticut River Valley. The river forms the border between Vermont and New Hampshire. Its location provides a gateway to nature in all seasons both on land and water, and is a 2–3 hour drive from Boston. The Dartmouth Coach travels daily to Boston and to New York City. Montreal, Canada is also just a few hours away.

Dartmouth College

The University

Founded in 1769, Dartmouth is a member of the Ivy League and consistently ranks among the world's greatest academic institutions. Dartmouth has forged a singular identity for combining its deep commitment to outstanding undergraduate liberal arts and graduate education with distinguished research and scholarship in the arts and sciences.

Professional and graduate programs across Dartmouth's schools—Geisel School of Medicine, the School of Graduate and Advanced Studies, Thayer School of Engineering, and the Tuck School of Business—have a distinguished history of training practitioners and scholars whose discoveries and expertise change the world.

Application and Admissions Information

The School of Graduate and Advanced Studies admits the most highly qualified applicants whose academic backgrounds and personal and professional experiences have prepared them for achievement and excellence in graduate studies.

Applications generally include a completed application form, undergraduate transcripts, three letters of recommendation, and scores from the General Test of the Graduate Record Examinations (GRE).

Application requirements vary by program; exact requirements can be obtained from each department. The complete list of programs online (http://dartmouth.edu/education/departments-programs-arts-sciences) includes links to department websites.

Dartmouth is committed to the principle of equal opportunity for all its students, faculty, employees, and applicants for admission and employment. Please see our non-discrimination policy and information for students with disabilities.

Correspondence and Information

Ruth Friend, Admissions Coordinator
School of Graduate and Advanced Studies
Suite 6062, Room 437
Dartmouth College
37 Dewey Field Road
Hanover, New Hampshire 03755-1419
Phone: 603-646-8193
E-mail: Ruth.E.Friend@Dartmouth.edu
Website: http://dartmouth.edu/education/graduate-schools

GODDARD COLLEGE
Graduate Programs

 For more information, visit http://petersons.to/goddardcollegegrad

Goddard College

Programs of Study

Individualized Master of Arts: Students seeking an Individualized M.A. at Goddard pursue a question, project, or career interest that is interdisciplinary, trans-disciplinary, and personally absorbing. The program requires students to complete 48 hours of credit over four semesters. The program is available at the Plainfield, Vermont campus.

Master of Arts in Education: The M.A. in Education program offers professional concentrations and licensure curriculum. Students can choose an individualized non-licensure focus in community education or dual-language studies, or complete a traditional M.A. in Education or School Counseling degree program ending in professional licensure.

All tracks are offered at the Plainfield location, while the non-licensure individual focus track is also available at the college's Seattle, Washington campus.

Master of Arts in Health Arts and Sciences: The M.A. in Health Arts degree program teaches students how to foster health and healing practices. Students can focus on body and movement therapies, botanical medicine and ethnobotany, community and environmental health, men's health, nutritional health, expressive arts, integrative health systems, integrative nursing, mind-body studies, ecopsychology, women's health and midwifery, and cross-cultural healing. The M.A. in Health Arts degree program is offered at the Plainfield campus.

Master of Arts in Psychology and Counseling: Goddard awards M.A. degrees in both psychology and clinical mental health counseling according to Council of Applied Master's Programs in Psychology specifications. Coursework is completed over four or five semesters of low-residency learning at the Plainfield campus.

Goddard also offers a sexual orientation concentration to both psychology and counseling students, as well as to non-licensure track students and as a continuing education option for professionals.

Master of Fine Arts (M.F.A.) in Creative Writing: Students in Goddard's M.F.A. program each graduate with a completed novel, a collection of stories or poems, a screenplay, a collection of plays, a memoir, or a graphic novel script. Each student's study plan is individually tailored to meet their ambitions and interests. Paired with a faculty member, the student receives a series of packets containing criticism, highlights of particularly excellent work, and reading assignments.

A unique feature of the M.F.A. program is the requirement for a teaching practicum, which can occur at grade schools, community centers, colleges, or any level in between, whether the student aspires to teach after finishing the degree or not.

Master of Fine Arts (M.F.A.) in Interdisciplinary Arts: One of the only graduate programs in the world committed to art as a transformational practice, Goddard's M.F.A. in Interdisciplinary Arts program is designed to support artists with diverse life experiences and goals ranging from the social or political, to the aesthetic, spiritual, or autobiographical. Goddard's learning community supports the development of a robust, lifelong art practice. The program envisions making art as a form of critical thinking that integrates research and interdisciplinary problem-solving and engages ethically in public contexts.

Students can enroll in the M.F.A. in Interdisciplinary Arts at two locations: Plainfield, Vermont—Goddard's historic main campus—or Port Townsend, Washington—a vibrant arts community on the Pacific Coast.

Financial Aid

While Goddard's admissions process is need-blind (meaning income has no bearing on whether a student is admitted), the College commits to offer as much aid as possible to every eligible admitted student. Approximately 90 percent of the students who apply to Goddard's graduate and undergraduate programs are independent, working adults.

The College participates in the Federal Student Aid program. Students receive aid in the form of subsidized and unsubsidized federal loans, and the College awards more than $450,000 in institutional scholarships and grants. Applicants are encouraged to complete the Free Application for Federal Student Aid as soon as they start the application process.

Cost of Study

Tuition in Goddard's graduate programs varies by degree. Specific details on tuition and fees can be found online at www.goddard.edu/tuition.

Living and Housing Costs

Room and board costs are assessed for the period of the 8-day residency that starts the semester. Current room and board costs are available online at goddard.edu/tuition.

Student Group

Students have the opportunity to experience the pleasures and challenges of editing with the student-run literary journal, *Pitkin Review*. Publishing workshops are offered at every residency of the M.F.A. in Creative Writing program, and faculty members are available to address questions about publishing.

Location

The Plainfield, Vermont campus, located just outside Montpelier, is a sprawling former farm with a manor garden, woods, and Victorian-period architecture. The buildings were added to the National Register of Historic Places in 1996. The Port Townsend, Washington campus is located at Fort Worden, a former Victorian-era Army base with beaches, trails, and a seaside town within walking distance.

The M.A. in Education degree program is available at Goddard's new Columbia City campus, in one of Seattle's most ethnically and racially diverse neighborhoods.

The Faculty

Faculty members at Goddard give students personalized feedback every three weeks during the semester, helping students organize their work, understand their subject matter, and find their way in the world. One such faculty member is Professor Kyle Bass. A member of the Drama Guild of America, Professor Bass has been a finalist for both the Princess Grace Award and the Pushcart Prize. His works have appeared onstage in New York City, Syracuse, and foreign venues. In addition to his teaching duties, Professor Bass serves as drama editor of the acclaimed journal *Stone Canoe* where he has edited works by such noted authors as Kenneth Lin, Rogelio Martinez, and Chiori Miyagawa.

Professor Deborah Brevoort is a two-time winner of the Frederick Loewe Award for American Musical Theater. Her play, *Signs of Life*, won the Jane Chambers Award and was a Pinter Review Prize for Drama Gold Medalist. Her interests as a writer have always had an international focus, and her works have often featured theatrical conventions and forms from around the world to explore contemporary American subjects, such as her use of Japanese Noh drama to highlight the utter American-ness of Elvis in her *Blue Moon over Hawaii*.

Professor Sharon Cronin is coauthor of *Soy Bilingüe: Language, Culture, and Young Latino Children*. Dr. Cronin has over 25 years of experience in bilingual education and is a lead researcher in the Teaching Umoja Participatory Action Research 15-Year Commitment, which examines the ethnic identity, bicultural, cross-cultural, and tri-literacy development of children of color in Port Royal and Moore Town, Jamaica.

Goddard College

The College

The mission of Goddard College is to advance cultures of rigorous inquiry, collaboration, and lifelong learning, where individuals take imaginative and responsible action in the world.

Students at Goddard work with faculty to direct their studies according to their personal and professional interests, goals, gifts, and desires. Students develop the capacity to understand their lives in an ever-changing social context, and thereby to take meaningful action in the world. They are encouraged to question received knowledge and the status quo and to create new understandings of the world and of human experience. As a collaborative interdependent learning community, Goddard respects, includes, and appreciates differing perspectives. The College community challenges themselves and each other to embrace uncertainty, experiment, and imagine unexpected outcomes. Goddard's faculty and students recognize their interconnectedness with others and with the earth, and hold their scholarship and actions to the highest standards of integrity, authenticity, and compassion.

Goddard recognizes that teaching and learning are fully realized when they include a wide range of people, cultures, experiences, abilities, and fields of knowledge. Understanding that access to resources and social and political power are not equally distributed, the College offers the means to explore and articulate a wide range of personal and cultural understandings of well-being and justice, and to take action to create a more-just world. In addition to keeping education affordable, Goddard seeks to create academic and campus environments that all learning community members can use. The College also recognizes the increasing impact of human activity on the planet's limited resources. In educational and institutional practices, Goddard is committed to thoughtful and sustainable action that increases individual and social capacity for environmental stewardship and an improved future.

Goddard College has embodied this educational philosophy and these values for nearly 150 years. Initially chartered as a Universalist seminary in 1863, Green Mountain Central Institute, later renamed Goddard Seminary, exemplified the inclusive, socially engaged values of its community. Goddard College's founder, Royce "Tim" Pitkin, was a graduate of Goddard Seminary and a student of John Dewey. Alarmed by the rise of fascism in Europe, Pitkin founded Goddard College in 1938 to unite the liberal values of the seminary with Dewey's belief that interactive, self-directed education could help build civil, democratic societies. An experimenting college, Goddard has continually offered new educational models in response to societal needs. It was one of the first colleges to include adult learning in its charter, the first to develop a low-residency model for higher education, and the first to offer residential programs for single parents receiving public assistance. The College continues to grow and change along with its students, who come to Goddard to transform themselves, their communities, and their world.

Applying

Prospective students need to apply online. There is a $65 application fee. The GRE is not required. Applicants must submit an application essay, three letters of recommendation, and official transcripts. Applicants should visit http://www.goddard.edu/admissions and click through to "Graduate Admissions" in the right-hand menu for specific instructions on applying.

Correspondence and Information

Goddard College
123 Pitkin Road
Plainfield, Vermont 05667
United States
Phone: 800-906-8312 (toll-free)
Fax: 802-454-1029
E-mail: admissions@goddard.edu
Website: http://www.goddard.edu/admissions

INDIANA STATE UNIVERSITY

College of Graduate and Professional Studies

 For more information, visit http://petersons.to/indianastategrad

Programs of Study

Indiana State University (ISU) offers more than 75 graduate programs ranging from a graduate certificate or a master's, education specialist, or doctoral degree in the Colleges of Arts and Sciences; Business; Education; Nursing, Health, and Human Services; and Technology.

Programs available are as follows:

The College of Arts and Sciences

Art (M.A.)

Biology (M.S.)

Biology and Spatial and Earth Sciences (Ph.D.).

Clinical Mental Health Counseling (M.S.)

Clinical Psychology (Psy.D.)

Computer Science (M.S.)

Communication (M.A.)

Communication Disorders (M.A. and M.S.)

Criminology and Criminal Justice (M.A. and M.S.)

Earth and Quaternary Sciences (M.S.)

Educational Technology (M.S.)

Electronics and Computer Technology (M.S.)

English (M.A.)

Geography (M.A.)

History (M.A. and M.S.)

Human Resource Development for Higher Education (M.S.)

Industrial Technology (M.S.)

Linguistics/TESL/cross linguistics (M.A.)

Master of Fine Arts (M.F.A.)

Master of Music (M.S.)

Master of Public Administration (M.P.A.)

Master of Social Work (M.S.W.)

Mathematics (M.A. and M.S.)

Occupational Therapy (M.S.)

Political Science (M.A. and M.S.)

Psychology (M.A. and M.S.)

Science Education (M.S.)

The College of Arts and Sciences (continued)

Special Education (M.A. and M.S.)

Student Affairs and Higher Education Career (M.S.)

Technical Education

The College of Business

Master of Business Administration (M.B.A.)

The College of Education

Curriculum and Instruction (M.Ed. and Ph.D.)

Educational Administration (Ph.D.)

Elementary Education (M.Ed.)

Guidance and Psychological Services (Ph.D.)

School Administration (Ed.S.)

School Administration and Supervision (M.Ed.)

School Counseling (M.Ed.)

School Psychology (M.Ed. and Ed.S.)

The College of Nursing, Health, and Human Services

Athletic Training (M.S.)

Health and Safety (M.A. and M.S.)

Nursing (M.S.)

Physician Assistant Studies (M.S.)

Physical Education (M.A. and M.S.)

Sport Management (M.S.)

The College of Nursing, Health, and Human Services

Doctor of Athletic Training (D.A.T.)

Doctor of Nursing Practice (D.N.P)

Doctor of Physical Therapy (D.P.T.)

The College of Technology

Technology Management (Ph.D.)

Research Facilities

Indiana State University's Cunningham Memorial Library houses more than 2.5 million items, subscribes to more than 5,000 periodicals, and provides access to more than 20,000 full-text electronic periodicals. These can be accessed through an online system that also connects with other college libraries in Terre Haute and Indiana. The ISU library provides collaborative workstations to facilitate group and collaborative research. All students enrolled at ISU have access to a wireless network that allows them to access the Internet from most locations on the campus. Several departments offer specialized research facilities. The Instructional and Research Technology Services offers services (at no cost to students) that include statistical design

consultation, research design consultation, design and analysis of sample research surveys, and presentation of statistical graphs and tables.

Financial Aid

Eligible graduate students may apply for institutional graduate assistantships through the respective academic departments. ISU graduate assistantships include a stipend and a tuition fee waiver. The tuition fee waivers are exclusive of building and student services fees, for up to 18 hours per academic year. For policies regarding graduate assistantships and fee waivers, students should visit the College of Graduate and Professional Studies website.

The Office of Student Financial Aid assists ISU graduate students in obtaining further educational funding. The office can be contacted at 812-237-2215 or at ISU-finaid@mail.indstate.edu.

Cost of Study

Tuition and fees for the 2017–18 academic year are $404 per semester hour for in-state students, $513 per semester hour for out-of-state students, and $793 per semester hour for international students.

Living and Housing Costs

Indiana State University offers furnished and unfurnished apartment-style housing for graduate students at its University Apartments. Each apartment is self-contained with its own bedroom(s), bathroom, living/dining area, and kitchen with an electric range, refrigerator, and garbage disposal. Utilities, wifi, and free local telephone service are also included. Additional information about ISU's Residential Life living options is available at indstate.edu/reslife.

Student Group

Since 1927, ISU's graduate programs have prepared students for careers in a wide range of teaching, research, and service professions. The campus has the highest diversity of students among four-year institutions in Indiana. Approximately 10 percent of the graduate students are international and 33 percent are out-of-state students.

Location

The campus is located adjacent to the central business district of Terre Haute, Indiana, which is an industrial and commercial city of approximately 61,000 located in west-central Indiana. Cultural activities include amateur and professional theatrical productions, symphonies, and art exhibits. Excellent county and state parks are within easy driving distance. The city is convenient to the four major metropolitan areas of Indianapolis, St. Louis, Chicago, and Cincinnati.

The University and the School

Indiana State University has been listed as one of the nation's best-value colleges by the Princeton Review for 13 years running. Indiana State University has grown during its 140-year history from Indiana State Normal School to Indiana State Teachers College and Indiana State College to full university status. With a graduate student population of approximately 2,000, students can be assured of a close mentoring experience and significant research opportunities within their academic program.

Applying

Applications to the College of Graduate and Professional Studies can be submitted online, by mail, or in person.

Prospective applicants should visit the College of Graduate and Professional Studies website at http://indstate.edu/graduate and check with their respective departments for specific deadlines and additional required admissions materials. Students generally receive a response acknowledging receipt of the application and other communication within one to two weeks. Once admitted, students receive instructions regarding academic advisement and registration.

International students must submit a TOEFL score of 550 or better and an Affidavit of Financial Support. For additional requirements and documentation, prospective students should visit the Graduate School website or the International Programs and Services at indstate.edu/international.

Indiana State University

Correspondence and Information

Dr. Lynn M. Maurer, Dean and Chief Research Officer

College of Graduate and Professional Studies
Indiana State University
Terre Haute, Indiana 47809-1904
United States
Phone: 812-237-3005
    800-444-GRAD (4723) (toll-free)
Fax: 812-237-8060
E-mail: ISU-GradStudy@mail.indstate.edu
Website: http://indstate.edu/graduate

For U.S. applicants, mail to:
Graduate Admissions
Indiana State University
Welcome Center 318 North Sixth Street
Terre Haute, Indiana 47809-1904
Phone: 812-237-3005
    800-444-GRAD (4723) (toll-free)
Fax: 812-237-8060
E-mail: ISU-GradInfo@mail.indstate.edu

For international applicants, mail to:
Graduate Admissions
Indiana State University
Welcome Center 318 North Sixth Street
Terre Haute, Indiana 47809-1904
United States
Phone: 812-237-3005
    800-444-GRAD (4723) toll-free)
Fax: 812-237-8060
E-mail: ISU-GradInfo@mail.indstate.edu
Website: http://indstate.edu/graduate

THE FACULTY

Deans
Lynn M. Maurer, Ph.D.; Dean and Chief Research Officer, College of Graduate and Professional Studies.
Christopher Olsen, Ph.D.; Dean, College of Arts and Sciences.
Brien N. Smith, Ph.D.; Dean, Scott College of Business.
Janet Buckenmeyer, Ph.D.; Dean, Bayh College of Education.
Caroline Mallory, Ph.D.; Dean, College of Nursing, Health, and Human Services.
Kara Harris, Ph.D.; Dean, College of Technology.

Directors of Graduate Degree Programs
Art: Nancy Nichols-Pethick, M.F.A., Assistant Professor.
Athletic Training: Lindsey Eberman, Ph.D., Assistant Professor.
Biology: Rusty Gonser, Ph.D., Professor.
Business Administration: Jeff Harper, Ph.D., Professor.
Center for Science Education: Carolyn S. Wallace, Ph.D., Associate Professor and Director.
Clinical Psychology: Liz O'Laughlin, Ph.D., Professor.
Communication: Mary Kahl, Ph.D., Professor and Chairperson.
Communication Disorders and School Counseling, School, and Educational Psychology: Vicki Hammen, Ph.D., Associate Professor.
Counseling Psychology: Tonya Balch, Ph.D., Assistant Professor.
Criminology and Criminal Justice: DeVere Woods, Ph.D., Associate Professor and Chairperson.
Curriculum, Instruction, and Media Technology: Susan Kiger, Ph.D., Associate Professor and Chairperson.
Educational and School Psychology: Carrie Ball, Ph.D., Assistant Professor.
Educational Leadership, Administration, and Foundations: Steve Gruenert, Ph.D., Professor and Chairperson.
Electronics, Computer, and Mechanical Engineering Technology: Joe Ashby, Ph.D., Assistant Professor.
Elementary, Early, and Special Education: Karen Liu, Ph.D., Professor.
English: Kit Kincade, Ph.D., Associate Professor.
Earth and Environmental Systems: C. Russell Stafford, Ph.D., Professor and Chairperson.
Health, Safety, and Environmental Health Sciences: Eliezer Bermudez, Ph.D., Associate Professor and Chairperson.
History: Richard Schneirov, Ph.D., Professor.
Human Resource Development: Tad Foster, Ph.D., Professor.

Industrial Technology: Michael Hayden, Ph.D., Professor.
Languages, Literatures, and Linguistics: Leslie Barratt, Ph.D., Professor and Chairperson.
Mathematics and Computer Science: Ralph Oberste-Vorth, Ph.D., Professor and Chairperson.
Mental Health Counseling: Catherine Tucker, Ph.D., Assistant Professor.
Music: Paul Bro, Ph.D., Professor and Chairperson.
Nursing: Susan Eley, Ph.D., Associate Professor and Chairperson.
Physical Education: Jolynn Kuhlman, Ph.D., Associate Professor.
Political Science: Michael Chambers, Ph.D., Professor and Chairperson.
Psychology: Veanne Anderson, Ph.D., Associate Professor.
Public Administration: Stan Buchanan, Ph.D., Associate Professor.
Recreation and Sport Management: Athanassios Strigas, Associate Professor.
School Administration and Supervision: Steve Gruenert, Ph.D., Professor and Chairperson.
School Counseling, M.Ed., and Licensure Programs: Tonya Balch, Ph.D., Assistant Professor.
School Psychology: Carrie Ball, Ph.D., Assistant Professor.
Student Affairs and Higher Education: William, Barratt, Ph.D., Associate Professor.
Technology Education: Kara Harris, Ed.D., Assistant Professor.
Technology Management: Ali Mehran Shahhosseini, D.Eng., Associate Professor.

Dede Plaza is home to Indiana State University's iconic fountain. The fountain is surrounded by seating for students to congregate with friends or study in the warmth of the sun.

Indiana State University sits in the heart of downtown Terre Haute. The aerial view highlights the Vigo County Courthouse, Sycamore Towers, and in the distance, a view of the Wabash River.

KANSAS STATE UNIVERSITY
Graduate School

Programs of Study

The Graduate School at Kansas State University offers preparation for a variety of scholarly and research careers and a wide range of professional positions through advanced study in more than 39 doctoral, 74 master's, 4 educational doctoral programs, and 44 certificate programs. Opportunities for research and scholarly activities exist in the areas of agriculture, architecture and design, business administration, education, engineering, food science, genetics, human ecology, humanities and fine arts, natural sciences, security studies, social sciences, veterinary medicine, and many others. Most programs are offered at the main Manhattan campus. A limited number of programs are offered at the K-State Polytechnic and K-State Olathe campuses and via distance education through the K-State Global Campus.

A minimum of 30 semester hours of graduate credit is required for a master's degree, with some academic programs requiring more. The Graduate School recognizes the following plans for a master's degree as part of the degree program: thesis option (students complete a thesis for 6–8 hours credit); report option (students complete a written report on research or a problem in the major field for 2 hours credit); and course work option (the degree program consists of course work only, but includes evidence of advanced work such as term papers, objects of art, music, or designs). Not all programs offer all three options.

Doctoral programs require 90 semester hours and educational doctoral programs require 94 semester hours beyond the bachelor's degree. Both degrees require original research and a dissertation. Students with a master's degree may transfer up to 30 hours of that degree toward a doctoral degree upon approval from the supervisory committee.

Research Facilities

K-State respects and admires the enthusiastic scholarship graduate students bring to the university. A vast library network houses more than 2 million books and provides online access to thousands of journals, databases, and books. Students receive dynamic training as they perform research alongside faculty in leading facilities. The Sensory and Consumer Research Center provides students with the opportunity to perform qualitative and quantitative consumer research. Atomic, molecular, and optical physics students work with ultrafast intense lasers in the James R. Macdonald Lab. K-State was selected as the location of the National Bio and Agro-Defense Facility in 2008. More than 85 additional specialized research centers unite researchers across disciplines and drive innovative research and discoveries at K-State. A complete list of research facilities and centers is available online at http://www.k-state.edu/directories/research-facilities.html.

Financial Aid

Many forms of financial assistance are available to graduate students, including graduate teaching or research assistantships, fellowships, scholarships, and loans. The Office of Student Financial Assistance administers federal assistance programs and a work-study program. Teaching and research assistantships are awarded on a competitive basis by individual departments. Research assistants qualify to pay tuition at resident rates if appointed to at least a 0.4 assistantship. Up to 10 hours of tuition is paid for fall and spring semesters for students who have a 0.5 teaching assistantship.

Cost of Study

Tuition in 2017–18 is $414.60 per credit hour for Kansas residents and $935.90 per credit hour for nonresidents. Some colleges have additional tuition surcharges and equipment fees. Graduate students are considered full-time if enrolled in at least 6 credit hours and employed on an assistantship. In addition to tuition, campus privilege fees range from $43.10 to $431 per semester.

Living and Housing Costs

The Jardine Apartment Complex features more than 700 on-campus apartments for students and families. One- to four-bedroom units are available and prices start at $495 per month. Residence hall meal plans are also available to Jardine residents. Numerous other off-campus apartments and housing options are also available. Monthly rates for off-campus apartments in Manhattan start around $550 for a one-bedroom and $800 for a two-bedroom.

Student Group

Approximately 4,000 graduate students from more than 92 countries around the world attend K-State. More than half of all graduate students at K-State are full-time students. Approximately 56 percent of all graduate students are female.

Student Outcomes

Students with advanced degrees from K-State are highly sought by employers. Students often receive multiple job offers and many find employment well before graduation. K-State graduates are leaders within all levels of public, private, and business sectors and government agencies.

Frequent employers of K-State graduates include: the National Institutes of Health, Argonne and Sandia National Labs, Nintendo, Merck, Pfizer, Cargill, Kellogg's, Hershey Foods, Anheuser-Busch, Motorola, Texas Instruments, Rockwell International, and Sprint.

Location

K-State's main campus is located on 668 acres in Manhattan, Kansas, approximately 125 miles west of Kansas City. With a population of more than 56,000, Manhattan has many urban amenities but still retains the best qualities of a small town. Manhattan features a regional airport, public and private schools, and a variety of shopping, entertainment, arts, and recreational activities.

Two additional campus locations in Kansas—Salina and Olathe—complement the main campus in Manhattan.

The University

Founded in 1863 as America's first land-grant university, K-State is an internationally recognized comprehensive research institution with academic programs offered in a lively intellectual and cultural atmosphere. In 1996, the university was one of only ten universities selected to receive the National Science Foundation's Recognition Award for the Integration of Research and Education. The university has since launched an ambitious planning initiative with a goal of being recognized as a top 50 public research university by 2025. One of the plan's main goals is to improve the scholarly experience for graduate students and advance a culture of excellence that attracts highly talented, diverse graduate students and produces graduates who are recognized as outstanding in their respective professions.

Applying

Applicants should complete the online application via the Graduate School website at www.k-state.edu/grad.

Applications for U.S. citizens and permanent residents are accepted year round. International residents must apply by January 8 for fall enrollment, August 1 for spring enrollment, and December 1 for summer enrollment. Application materials and deadlines for individual degree programs may vary. Contact each department for specific requirements and information.

Correspondence and Information

Graduate School
Kansas State University
119 Eisenhower Hall
Manhattan, Kansas 66506-1103
Phone: 785-532-6191
        800-651-1816 (toll-free in the U.S.)
Fax: 785-532-2983
E-mail: grad@k-state.edu
Website: http://www.k-state.edu/grad

GRADUATE PROGRAMS

For more information about the degrees offered within each department and contact information, prospective students should visit http://catalog.k-state.edu/content.php?catoid=2&navoid=634.

COLLEGE OF AGRICULTURE

Agribusiness
Agricultural Economics
Agricultural Education and Communication
Agronomy
Animal Sciences and Industry
Entomology
Grain Science
Horticulture
Plant Pathology

Kansas State University

COLLEGE OF ARCHITECTURE, PLANNING, AND DESIGN
Architecture
Community Development
Environmental Design and Planning
Interior Architecture and Product Design
Landscape Architecture
Regional & Community Planning

COLLEGE OF ARTS AND SCIENCES
Art
Biology
Chemistry
Communication Studies
Economics
English
Geography
Geology
History
Mass Communications
Mathematics
Microbiology
Modern Languages
Music
Physics
Political Science
Psychology
Public Administration
Security Studies
Sociology
Statistics
Theatre

COLLEGE OF BUSINESS ADMINISTRATION
Accountancy
Business Administration

COLLEGE OF EDUCATION
Academic Advising
Adult Learning and Leadership
Counseling and Student Development
Curriculum and Instruction
Educational Leadership
Master of Arts in Teaching
Special Education

COLLEGE OF ENGINEERING
Architectural Engineering
Biological and Agricultural Engineering
Chemical Engineering
Civil Engineering
Computer Science
Electrical Engineering
Engineering Management
Industrial Engineering
Mechanical Engineering
Nuclear Engineering
Operations Research
Software Engineering

COLLEGE OF HUMAN ECOLOGY
Apparel and Textiles
Dietetics
Family and Community Services
Family Studies and Human Services
Gerontology
Hospitality Administration
Human Ecology
Human Nutrition
Kinesiology
Nutrition, Dietetics, and Sensory Sciences
Personal Financial Planning

COLLEGE OF VETERINARY MEDICINE
Biomedical Science
Pathobiology
Physiology

INTERDISCIPLINARY PROGRAMS
Biochemistry
Food Science
Genetics
Leadership Communication
Public Health

KANSAS STATE POLYTECHNIC
Technology

KANSAS STATE OLATHE
Applied Science and Technology

A graduate student explains her research during one of the many research forums held on campus each year. Graduate Student Council also provides travel funding for graduate students to present their research at national and international conferences.

Part of the Manhattan campus. Eisenhower Hall, home of the Graduate School, is one of the oldest remaining buildings on campus.

MASSACHUSETTS COLLEGE OF ART AND DESIGN

Graduate Programs

 For more information, visit http://petersons.to/mcad-grad

Programs of Study

Founded in 1873, Massachusetts College of Art and Design (MassArt) is the nation's first and only freestanding, publicly supported college of art and design, and the first to grant a degree. The college offers a variety of disciplines including architecture, industrial design, fine arts, and art education, with graduate and undergraduate programs that prepare students to participate in the creative economy as designers, fine artists, and art educators.

The opportunity to work and create in a diverse community of innovative, hard-working artists, designers, and educators fosters a learning environment that encourages multidisciplinary practice and dialogue, a central value of the graduate programs.

MassArt awards the Master of Fine Arts (M.F.A.) degree in five separate fine arts disciplines: 2D Fine Arts, 3D Fine Arts, Design, Media Arts: Film/Video, and Media Arts: Photography. Admission to the M.F.A. program is highly competitive and attracts a global pool of applicants with professional portfolios who are interested in pursuing intensive study in the fine arts.

The full-residency M.F.A. program requires a full-time commitment over two years. The Low-Residency Fine Arts Program spans three years, and is highlighted by annual, six-week intensive summer residencies in Boston that allow artists who work across disciplines to develop a self-directed course of study.

MassArt also awards the following additional graduate degree programs: Master of Architecture (M.Arch.), Master of Arts: Teaching/Art Education (M.A.T.), and Master of Design Innovation (M.Des.).

M.F.A. in 2D Fine Arts: This program combines painting, drawing, and printmaking practices and techniques, with the emphasis on each student's evolution as an artist. Students have individual studios distributed throughout the FA2D undergraduate department, allowing for interaction between students that becomes dynamic when graduates participate in lectures, open houses, exhibitions, field trips, social media, and teaching assistantships.

The primary form of graduate studio instruction is critique. Three critiques are scheduled throughout the semester. During the third, called Review Board, students present their semester's work for critical review by their peers, resident faculty, an outside critic, and other invited guests. The capstone is the M.F.A. Thesis Exhibit, where students select and install their work in MassArt's Bakalar & Paine Galleries.

M.F.A. in 3D Fine Arts: This program focuses on creating the artistic object in one of five media: ceramics, fibers, glass, metals (jewelry and metalsmithing), and sculpture. Students study structure, form-making, idea development, tool handling, and studio safety, then advance to classes that develop and refine their aesthetic vision and build their technical, conceptual, and critical skills in their chosen medium.

M.F.A. in Film/Video: This program provides a personalized, intense environment where students acquire advanced skills in production and develop an informed perspective on film/video that is individual, political, conceptual, abstract, visceral, and visionary. The curriculum is enriched by the weekly screenings of The MassArt Film Society, drawing on a wide range of films and videos and often including a live discussion with the artist. Students have access to state-of-the-art facilities and resources, including advanced high-definition digital film and video production equipment, and more.

M.F.A. in Media Arts: Photography: This program teaches photography as fine art with an emphasis on personal vision, experimentation, and an understanding of the history of photography and the body of criticism that impacts it. The curriculum covers both analog and digital production, and offers a variety of elective courses providing a strong foundation for critical thinking, collaboration, and a career in photographic arts. The 11,000-square-foot photography facility offers three-studio digital capability with large-format printers, Flextight scanners, and 40 workstations. Analog black and white developing and printing areas are central to the curriculum, with two large-gang darkrooms, individual darkrooms, and a non-silver darkroom.

M.F.A.: Fine Arts (Low-Residency in Boston): This program is ideal for artists who work across disciplines in that it allows self-directed students to develop a course of study that might involve a combination of media, technologies, and techniques. The six-week summer residencies in Boston foster an intense studio environment and establish creative collaborations.

Students live on campus in the Artists' Residence or in off-campus housing of their choosing. Between residencies, students work under the guidance of artist/mentors through monthly studio visits and critiques, returning to campus in January for midterm reviews.

M.F.A. in Design: The Dynamic Media Institute (DMI) at MassArt offers an M.F.A. program for anyone passionate about the future of dynamic media in communication design. Students are fine artists, designers, architects, engineers, programmers, educators, and others who pursue a unique thesis vision through a rigorous practice of research, prototyping, and writing. Students emerge with a rich body of original work, empowered to become leading educators, practitioners, and entrepreneurs.

Master of Design Innovation (M.Des.): This program integrates deep expertise in design practice with business discipline in a broad-based curriculum that uses market challenges and social initiatives as the context for learning. The full-time, two-year interdisciplinary curriculum is intended for students who want to lead the design and planning of new products, services, environments, systems, and organizations.

Master of Architecture (M.Arch.): This full-residency program offers two tracks. Track I is designed for students who hold a bachelor's degree in fields other than architecture. Track II is intended for students with a bachelor's degree in architecture and professional portfolios. Accredited by the National Architecture Accrediting Board, the M.Arch. program combines professional requirements with hands-on design, and builds experience focused on community-based teaching and working spaces. Visiting architects, engineers, and related professionals enrich discussions in design critique.

Master of Arts: Teaching/Art Education (M.A.T.): This program provides artists with substantive, graduate-level education in teaching. The curriculum was developed for students with strong backgrounds in studio work who want to teach in schools, museums, social service agencies, or community agencies. The program leads to the Initial

Teacher License in Massachusetts while also providing the course work requirements for a Professional Teacher License.

Art Galleries

There are galleries located all across MassArt's campus, from the Arnheim and Brant galleries in South Hall, to the Student Life Gallery in the Kennedy Building, and the Godine Family Gallery in North Hall. Curated and managed by students and faculty, these galleries enrich the campus and curriculum through the presentation of departmental exhibitions (http://www.massart.edu/Galleries/Campus_Galleries.html).

As the largest free, contemporary art venue in New England, MassArt's Bakalar & Paine Galleries showcase some of the most exciting and influential artists from the world. Curated exhibitions feature both rising talents and well-known artists in exhibitions that are a public resource for the college, Boston, and beyond. (http://www.massart.edu/Galleries/Bakalar_and_Paine_Galleries.html).

The President's Gallery features exhibitions celebrating innovation in all artistic disciplines, the work of artists being honored and celebrated by the college, and the outstanding achievements of MassArt's alumni, staff, and students.

Faculty and Visiting Artists

The core faculty at MassArt comprises a diverse group of accomplished artists, artisans, designers, architects, programmers, engineers, filmmakers, photographers, and educators. Many have received prestigious fellowships, and exhibit and publish worldwide. Students are also exposed to working designers and artists through the Visiting Artist Program, which features lectures, seminars, workshops, and classroom interaction.

Financial Assistance

More than 80 percent of MassArt graduate students receive financial assistance in some form, including federal loans, scholarships, and assistantships.

Cost of Study

Graduate tuition for summer 2017 to spring 2018 is $780 per credit. Graduate students pay on a per-credit basis. The tuition fee per credit varies with the program, but does not vary based on the residency status of the student.

Living and Housing Costs

MassArt's Artists' Residence offers a few co-ed apartments to graduate students. For a double room, the total cost is $5,940 per semester. For a single room, the total cost is $6,495 per semester. The estimated cost for off-campus living expenses is about $18,722 for nine months and $24,959 for twelve months.

Student Group

MassArt's graduate students come from 18 countries. A full 20 percent of MassArt's students are international, including Fulbright Scholars.

Location

The MassArt campus in downtown Boston encompasses more than a million square feet of studios, workshops, and galleries within walking distance of three world-class museums.

Applying

Applicants to Massachusetts College of Art and Design are evaluated according to standards that gauge abilities and talent in the arts along with potential, motivation, and desire. There is no one formula that determines an applicant's potential for success. In evaluating an applicant, the admissions committee tries to be flexible, sensitive, and personal.

Admission to degree programs at Massachusetts College of Art and Design is extremely competitive. Each year the number of applicants for admission far exceeds the number of spaces available. This is true at all levels of admission, although the competition for admission to specific programs may vary from year to year.

Required items include the online application, a $90 application fee (paid online), statement of purpose, resume, official post-secondary/college transcripts, two letters of reference, and a portfolio. Students applying to the M.Arch. program must submit additional items with their application; specific details are available at https://massart.edu/node/721.

International applicants must meet the graduate application requirements as well as the additional requirements specific to international applicants, including official transcript translation and evaluation and scores on the TOEFL/IELTS (for non-native English speakers). Additional information can be found at https://massart.edu/international-students-0.

For a tour of MassArt's facilities, prospective graduate students should contact gradadmissions@massart.edu or 617-879-7203.

Correspondence and Information

Graduate Admissions
Massachusetts College of Art and Design
621 Huntington Avenue
Boston, Massachusetts 02115
United States
Phone: 617-879-7222
E-mail: gradadmissions@massart.edu
Website: https://massart.edu/graduate-admissions

The Tower Building on the MassArt campus.

MISSOURI STATE UNIVERSITY
Graduate College

 For more information, visit http://petersons.to/missouristateu-grad

Programs of Study

The Graduate College at Missouri State University (www.graduate.missouristate.edu) offers outstanding academic programs that prepare students for lifelong success. The college has over 100 graduate programs including master's degrees, specialist degrees, clinical doctoral degrees, cooperative degree programs, and certificate programs. In addition, it offers full- and part-time options, evening programs, online courses and programs, and blended formats, all of which enable students to earn their degrees while managing their personal and professional lives.

Missouri State University offers 52 **graduate certificate programs** (generally 12 credits) in special areas. Many of these can be expanded into a master's degree, or earned in conjunction with a master's degree in a related area.

Missouri State University has **Master of Arts (M.A.)** degree programs in several disciplines including Communication, English, History, Religious Studies, Teaching, and Writing. In addition there is a Teaching and Learning (M.A.T.L.) program available to cohorts in the Southwest Missouri area K–12 school districts. These programs give students opportunities to build upon previous study and professional experience to acquire the knowledge and skills needed to advance their careers or pursue doctoral study.

Students who are interested in earning **Master of Science (M.S.)** degrees can choose from more than 20 programs at Missouri State University including Agriculture, Applied Anthropology, Applied Behavior Analysis, Athletic Training, Biology, Cell and Molecular Biology, Chemistry, Child Life Studies, Communication Sciences and Disorders, Computer Information Systems, Computer Science, Counseling, Criminology and Criminal Justice, Cybersecurity, Defense and Strategic Studies, Early Childhood and Family Development, Geospatial Sciences in Geography, Geology and Planning, Health Promotion and Wellness Management, Interdisciplinary Studies, Materials Science, Mathematics, Physician Assistant Studies, Plant Science, Project Management, Psychology, and Student Affairs in Higher Education.

Individuals who are interested in earning advanced degrees in education, training, or instruction can choose from several **Master of Science in Education (M.S.Ed.)** programs including Early Childhood Special Education, Educational Administration, Educational Technology, Elementary Education, Literacy, Secondary Education, and Special Education.

Missouri State also offers several **other master's degree programs**, such as: Accountancy (MAcc.), Applied Second Language Acquisition (M.A.S.L.A.), Business Administration (MBA), Global Studies (M.G.S.), Health Administration (M.H.A.), Health Administration and Public Health dual-degree program, Music (M.M.), Natural and Applied Science (M.N.A.S.), Nursing–Nurse Educator (M.S.N.), Occupational Therapy (M.O.T.), Professional Studies (MPS), Public Administration (M.P.A.), Public Health (M.P.H.), Social Work (M.S.W.), and Visual Studies (M.F.A.).

MSU offers two **Specialist (Ed.S.)** programs: Educational Administration, and Counseling and Assessment. There is also a Specialist in Education, Teacher Leadership (SETL) program available to cohorts in the Southwest Missouri area K–12 school districts.

Individuals who are interested in **professional doctoral programs** will find Missouri State to be a great fit. Offerings include: Audiology (Au.D.); Educational Leadership (Ed.D.)—a cooperative program with the University of Missouri; Nurse Anesthesia (D.N.A.P.); Nursing (D.N.P.); Pharmacy (Pharm.D.)—a cooperative program with the University of Missouri Kansas City; and Physical Therapy (D.P.T.).

All students are assigned an academic adviser in their graduate program, and work closely with that adviser throughout the pursuit of their degree/certificate. Most of the Missouri State University master's programs provide for either a thesis, seminar/degree paper option, or internship option as the research component to be completed in partial fulfillment of the degree

Financial Aid

Missouri State proudly offers approximately 500 graduate assistantships each year to qualified grad students. These assistantships are offered in teaching, research, and/or administrative areas. In exchange for working the required 20 hours per week on campus, students receive a tuition fee waiver which covers up to 15 credit hours in the fall or spring semesters, and a stipend. The 2017–18 stipend amount is $8,772 (for the 9-month academic year). More information about graduate assistantships is available online at http://graduate.missouristate.edu/currentstudents/FeeWaiver.htm.

There are also a limited number of scholarships available to qualified graduate students. The most popular scholarships are the MOGO, Need-Based, and Midwest Student Exchange Program. A complete list of scholarships and qualifying requirements can be found at http://www.missouristate.edu/FinancialAid/scholarships/Graduate.htm.

Cost of Study

Base tuition for graduate students for 2017–18 is $268 per credit hour for Missouri residents and $539 per credit hour for nonresidents. Base tuition for online courses is $285 per credit hour for Missouri and Non-Missouri residents. (Note: Some graduate programs charge more than the base tuition.)

Student services fees are assessed in addition to tuition and are based on the total credit hours for which a student enrolls. (Note: Intersession courses, iCourses, Internet/online courses, courses taught in a location other than the Springfield campus, and courses scheduled to meet on the Springfield campus fewer than four times are excluded from student services fees.) Additional details regarding tuition and fees are available at http://www.missouristate.edu/registrar/costs.htm.

Location

Missouri State University's main campus is located in Springfield, Missouri, in the Midwestern region of the United States. The city of Springfield, Missouri, and the surrounding Ozarks provide numerous services and activities to meet the needs of its citizens. Missouri's third largest city is within a 500-mile radius of nearly 50 percent of the U.S. population. Springfield has the feel of a big city with the convenience of a small town, including friendly people, an affordable cost of living, and healthcare options that are among the best in the country. The city offers an array of options in terms of entertainment, the arts, sports, recreation, and entertainment. Downtown Springfield is less than a mile from the MSU campus.

The University

Founded in 1905, and now with a strong public affairs mission, Missouri State University serves more than 24,000 traditional and non-traditional students from over 80 countries, every state, and every county in Missouri, offering nearly 200 undergraduate degrees and graduate programs. The University is committed to providing graduate programs that meet the needs of a changing workforce and positively impact the region, state, nation, and world.

MSU seeks to be the university of choice to develop successful students who excel academically and in ethical leadership, cultural competence and community engagement.

Applying

Prospective students should review the Graduate Catalog to review the admission requirements for the Graduate College and their program of interest. Some programs require additional materials such as letters of recommendation, a resume, and a departmental or program application. Applicants should check with the program and the test requirements section of the Graduate Catalog for any standardized tests requirements. MSU's GRE school code is 6665. Students are required to submit official transcripts showing their bachelor's degree course work and any graduate-level work. Electronic transcripts should be sent to GraduateAdmissions@missouristate.edu through a clearinghouse or university's Registrar.

Interested students are encouraged to apply online. The online system allows applicants to apply and pay the fee, return to complete a saved application, check the status of an application, and change or add a graduate program.

After the Graduate College receives the application materials, they will be evaluated against the admission requirements. Applications will then be forwarded to their program for a program admission decision. Competitive programs cannot accept all students who meet the minimum requirements. The program's decision will be submitted to the Graduate College admission's office, which will notify the student via e-mail and/or mail.

International students need to complete an International Student Application, fulfill the academic requirements for admission, provide documentation of financial support, and submit an official TOEFL score if English is not the student's primary language. The minimum TOEFL score requirement is 79 or more for graduate applicants. Complete admission requirements for international students are available on the University's website at http://international.missouristate.edu/services/70306.htm.

Correspondence and Information

Dr. Julie Masterson, Graduate College Dean
Misty Stewart, Recruitment Coordinator
Graduate College
Missouri State University
901 South National Avenue
Springfield, Missouri 65897
United States
Phone: 417-836-5335 (Main Office)
417-836-5331 (Admissions)
E-mail: GraduateAdmissions@missouristate.edu
Website: www.graduate.missouristate.edu

Missouri State University campus and downtown Springfield, Missouri.

Missouri State University's main entrance, Bear Boulevard and National Avenue.

MISSOURI WESTERN STATE UNIVERSITY

Graduate Programs

 For more information, visit http://petersons.to/mwsu-grad

Programs of Study

Missouri Western State University (MWSU) offers a variety of graduate degree and certificate programs to help students at every life stage increase their potential and advance their careers through the Craig School of Business, Graduate School, School of Fine Arts, College of Liberal Arts and Sciences, and College of Professional Studies.

For example, the Master of Applied Science programs integrate advanced training in science and technology blended with business and professional skills. Similarly, the Master of Applied Arts programs focus on the skills in writing and the arts that are in high demand by employers. Most graduate programs are designed to be completed in two years, and graduate certificates can usually be completed within one year. Classes are offered primarily in the late afternoon and evenings to help accommodate working professionals.

Master of Business Administration (MBA): This degree program provides students from all types of educational backgrounds a broad business foundation in areas such as finance, accounting, marketing, and management with a focus on analytical decision-making and decision-making processes. This AACSB-accredited degree has four tracks available: general business, life and animal sciences, enterprise resource planning, and forensic accounting.

Master of Science (M.S.) in Information Technology Assurance Administration: This 36-credit program provides practical understanding about computer forensics, data protection, and network security. It also introduces students to policy, legal, and ethical issues regarding information security.

Master of Information Management (M.I.M.): This program, with a concentration in enterprise resource planning (ERP), trains students to apply ERP methods in a variety of business settings. Its 30-credit curriculum focuses on SAP software and provides in-depth understanding of business processes.

Missouri Western State University offers five **Master of Applied Science (M.A.S.)** programs, including Chemistry, Industrial Life Science, Engineering Technology Management, and Sport and Fitness Management.

M.A.S. in Chemistry: This 35-credit program provides advanced training in industry-focused chemistry with cross-training in business and communications.

M.A.S. in Industrial Life Science: This 35-credit program integrates biology and chemistry with skills-based course work in business fundamentals, intellectual property, project management, and laboratory management.

M.A.S. in Engineering and Technology Management: This 33-credit program focuses on applied research and hands-on experience to prepare students for a variety of positions including assembly line supervisor, plant manager, and secondary or post-secondary teacher.

M.A.S. in Sport and Fitness Management: This 33- to 36-credit program prepares graduates to manage and lead in areas such as intercollegiate and professional sports, and sport, fitness, and recreation facilities.

The **Master of Applied Science in Assessment** includes three options: K–12 Cross Categorical Special Education, Teaching English to Speakers of Other Languages (TESOL), and Writing. These programs are offered completely online.

K–12 Cross Categorical Special Education: This 33-credit option provides teachers with strategies for teaching learners with mild to moderate disabilities in inclusive kindergarten through 12th grade classrooms.

Teaching English to Speakers of Other Languages (TESOL): This 33-credit option provides students with the specific skill set and knowledge to teach English language learners and advocate for TESOL educational programs.

Writing: This 33-credit option helps teachers improve their abilities to teach writing. Focus areas include applying innovative methods to writing, evaluating writing, developing writing assignments, and integrating writing into curricula.

Master of Applied Arts in Digital Media: This program trains students for the digital arts workplace. Students strengthen their creative thinking skills and obtain hands-on and team-based experience. The 38-credit program allows students to successfully address the challenges that businesses, digital artists, and media professionals face in the 21st-century business environment.

The interdisciplinary, 33-credit **Master of Applied Arts in Written Communication** has two options: Technical Communication and Writing Studies.

Technical Communication: This option is ideal for individuals who want to advance their careers in business, government, and industry. It helps them improve their writing, supervisory, training, and technical communication skills.

Writing Studies: The Writing Studies option is designed for educators who want to strengthen their writing as a content area and for individuals interested in teaching at the post-secondary level. Students will improve their knowledge base in pedagogy and theory and their ability to use technology as a teaching tool.

Master of Science in Nursing (M.S.N.): The M.S.N. program prepares students for leadership roles in nursing practice. Its 32-credit curriculum has two tracks: Health Care Leadership and Nurse Educator. Both programs help graduates emerge as advocates for excellence and leaders in nursing, and nurse education and training.

Master of Applied Science (M.A.S.) in Forensic Investigations: This 36-credit program provides broad-based knowledge of the field and strengthens students' professional expertise in law enforcement investigation. The curriculum is taught by forensic investigation specialists and law enforcement professionals.

Graduate Certificates: Missouri Western State University offers seven graduate certificate programs, most associated with full master's-level programs: Digital Media, Forensic Investigation, Nurse Educator, Professional Skills, Teaching of Writing, Teaching English to Speakers of Other Languages (TESOL), and Technical Communication.

Research Facilities

The MWSU Library maintains over 228,000 volumes and holds more than 1,150 journal titles. It is also a State Government Documents Depository. Microfilm, company annual reports, CD-ROM products, pamphlet files, newspapers, and Internet resources provide additional unique information for users. Through its computer-based catalog and circulation system, students can gain quick access to the Library's collection. The TOWERS online catalog and 75 plus online databases are also available via the Web. Professionally trained librarians provide individual assistance to students and other users. Reference Chat, Book-a-Librarian, and My Librarian are specialized services to help student or faculty researchers. The Library has access to a national database of over 120 million items, assuring that clients can usually obtain the specific item needed. Group information instruction is enhanced by the availability of a specially equipped computer classroom within the library.

Financial Aid

Degree-seeking graduate students are generally eligible for scholarships and loans. A limited number of graduate assistantships may be offered by individual graduate programs when available. Assistantships may include a stipend and in-state tuition for up to 18 credits per academic year (not including summers). More information on assistantships and scholarships is available on the Graduate School website. International students who are fully admitted may be eligible for International Excellence Scholarships.

Cost of Study

Tuition for the 2017–18 academic year is $336 per credit hour for in-state students and $604 per credit hour for out-of-state and international students. Beginning in the fall semester of 2017, students accepted to the Graduate School who are U.S. citizens from Arkansas, Illinois, Iowa, Kansas, Kentucky, Nebraska, Oklahoma, and Tennessee will be eligible for in-state tuition under the **Griffon Rate**.

Housing

On-campus housing is available for graduate students primarily in Griffon Hall's apartments. Each apartment consists of four single bedrooms, two bathrooms, a shared living space, and a full kitchen. Each bedroom has built-in closets and a desk. For added convenience only two people share a bathroom. Other housing options are available. More information can be found on the Residential Life website (www.missouriwestern.edu/reslife).

Missouri Western State University

Location

The University's main campus is located on more than 700 wooded acres in historic St. Joseph, Missouri. This bustling city of approximately 76,000 residents offers many amenities including arts and culture, entertainment and nightlife, restaurants and shopping, and sports and recreation. St. Joseph is 35 minutes north of the Kansas City International Airport, providing convenient access to the university and an easy commute from the Kansas City metro area.

The University

Missouri Western State University offers high-quality, student-centered education that emphasizes applied learning and community service. It provides 83 degree programs, 119 majors, and 61 minors.

The university also has many co-curricular and recreational options including nearly 80 clubs and organizations, cultural events, and NCAA Division II athletics. In addition, it provides extensive support services including the Center for Academic Support, Counseling Center, Disability Services, Center for Multicultural Education, Student Health Center, Career Development Center, and International Student Services.

Applying

Applications can be submitted electronically through the Graduate School website (http://www.missouriwestern.edu/graduate). A bachelor's or master's degree from an accredited college or university with a minimum GPA of 2.75 (on a 4.0 scale) is required for graduate admission. Some programs require a 3.0 GPA and/or additional admission materials (such as GMAT, examples of representative work, letters of recommendation, personal statement). International students must have a TOEFL score of 79 or better (use code 6625 for automatic score submission) or an IELTS score of 6.0 or better for full admission. All international transcripts must be evaluated for U.S. equivalencies.

The application deadline for fall admission is July 15; for spring admission, November 1; and for summer admission, April 29. Certain programs may have earlier deadlines; applicants should consult the department offering their desired degree program for more information. It is recommended that international students apply by May 15 for fall admission and October 15 for spring admission.

Applications are submitted online, and required documents may be uploaded directly. Applicants should check individual graduate program requirements for any additional documents or materials that may be required for admission. Once all application materials have been submitted, applications are forwarded to the specified graduate program for evaluation and final admission decision. Competitive programs may not be able to accept all applicants who meet the minimum requirements. Final program admission decisions are communicated to the Graduate School which will then notify students by mail or e-mail.

Correspondence and Information

Dr. Ben D. Caldwell, Dean of Graduate Studies
Tina Washburn, Admissions Coordinator
Missouri Western State University Graduate School
4525 Downs Drive
St. Joseph, Missouri 64507
United States
Phone: 816-271-4394
E-mail: graduate@missouriwestern.edu
Website: http://www.missouriwestern.edu/graduate

The Glenn Marion Memorial Clock Tower has been an icon at the center of the Missouri Western State University campus since 1997. The beautiful clock tower fills the campus with music throughout the day.

The Griffon Plaza greets visitors on the east side of the Missouri Western State University campus. The mythical Griffon has been the mascot and symbol of the University since 1918 and was chosen because it is a guardian of education. Its wings are spread in the shape of the state of Missouri to signify the bond between the university and the state.

Programs of Study

Quinnipiac University is a dynamic, challenging, and supportive academic community, offering more than 30 outstanding graduate programs that give students a strong foundation for their careers with both rigorous academic preparation and in-depth practical experience.

The School of Health Sciences and School of Nursing offer a range of programs for students interested in the health professions, including the Master of Health Science (M.H.S.) with specializations in advanced medical imaging and leadership, cardiovascular perfusion, medical laboratory sciences, pathologists' assistant, physician assistant, and radiologist assistant; the Master of Social Work (M.S.W.); the Doctor of Nursing Practice (D.N.P.), with tracks including adult-gerontology nurse practitioner, family nurse practitioner, nurse anesthesia, care of populations, and nursing leadership; and the Master of Science in Nursing Operational Leadership. Also offered are the Doctor of Physical Therapy (D.P.T.) (freshman entry only), the Doctor of Occupational Therapy (D.O.T.), and the Master of Science (M.S.) in Molecular and Cell Biology (College of Arts & Sciences). The Frank H. Netter M.D. School of Medicine offers the Doctor of Medicine (M.D.) and the Anesthesiologist Assistant programs.

The School of Business offers the Master of Business Administration (M.B.A.). Students can choose the general M.B.A. or from among the following tracks: finance, health care management, and supply chain management. Other degree programs include the Master of Science (M.S.) in Business Analytics and the M.S. in Organizational Leadership. Graduate certificates are available in Long Term Care Administration and Health Care Compliance.

The School of Communications offers the M.S. programs in Journalism and Sports Journalism; the M.S. in Public Relations; the M.S. in Interactive Media; and graduate certificates in social media and user experience design.

The School of Education offers the Master of Arts in Teaching (M.A.T.), elementary and secondary; the Sixth-Year Diploma in Educational Leadership; the M.S. in Instructional Design; the M.S. in Teacher Leadership; the M.S. in Special Education; and the Certificate of Completion in Special Education.

The School of Law offers the Juris Doctor (J.D.), J.D./M.B.A., J.D./Master of Environmental Law and Policy (with Vermont Law School), J.D./M.S.W., and the Master of Laws (L.L.M.) in Health Law.

Most graduate programs range in length from one to three years. Both full- and part-time study are available in most programs, and a number of programs and tracks are offered online. All graduate programs at Quinnipiac University share three key foundations: instruction is provided by faculty members with the highest available academic credentials and practicing professionals; every graduate student has the opportunity to earn practical experience through residencies, internships, thesis research, special projects, clinical rotations, consulting practicums, or small laboratory classes; and study builds upon both undergraduate education and professional experience.

Research Facilities

The university features facilities on both academic campuses with state-of-the-art equipment for research and professional preparation across disciplines. The Mount Carmel Campus features biology laboratories for candidates in the master's programs in Molecular and Cell Biology and Medical Laboratory Sciences. M.B.A. and other business students practice analytical finance methods, conduct trading simulations, develop financial models, analyze economic databases, and study stocks, bonds, currency, and interest rates at the Terry W. Goodwin '67 Financial Technology Center, with real-time financial data from markets all over the world. For students in the School of Communications, the Ed McMahon Mass Communications Center offers a fully digital high-definition television studio, multimedia lab, audio production studio, master edit room, video editing lab, a media innovation classroom and lab modeled after a working newsroom, and an equipment loan room with a full complement of remote audio and video production gear.

The North Haven Campus is home to the cutting-edge Center for Medicine, Nursing and Health Sciences, with learning labs including a professional SimMan suite of life-size patient simulators, a pediatric and neonatal lab, magnetic resonance simulators and 3-D workstations, an orthopedics lab, a rehabilitative sciences lab, a clinical skills lab, an intensive care unit, a health assessment lab, a physical diagnostics lab, a motion analysis lab, an operating room suite with two additional high fidelity simulation rooms, and 48 prosection stations.

At the School of Law, the Center for Health Law and Policy and the Center on Dispute Resolution offer legal research opportunities. Other university institutes and centers include the Alternative Investments Institute, the National Institute for Community Health Education, the Center for Women and Business, the Center for Interprofessional Healthcare Education, the Bristol-Myers Squibb Center for Science Teaching and Learning, the Bioanthropology Research Institute, and the Albert Schweitzer Institute. Most recently, the university's Frank H. Netter M.D. School of Medicine has established the Institute for Primary Care, the Institute for Rehabilitation Medicine, and the Institute for Global Public Health.

Financial Aid

Graduate students are eligible to apply for several options to fund their education. Both full- and part-time students can apply for federal fixed-rate student loans.

The university offers institutional funds through a select number of merit-based scholarships to qualified full-time incoming (non-online) graduate students within certain disciplines: M.B.A., cardiovascular perfusion, journalism, medical laboratory sciences, molecular and cell biology, nursing, pathologists' assistant, physician assistant, public relations, radiologist assistant, and social work.

All full-time, on-ground domestic graduate students are also eligible to apply for an institutional need-based grant.

The university offers graduate assistantships on a limited basis to both full- and part-time students.

Students in the Master of Arts in Teaching (M.A.T.) program also receive reduced tuition rates while they are participating in the internship semesters of the program.

Students applying to programs in law, medicine, or through QU Online, should consult the website for financial aid information.

Cost of Study

Tuition in 2017–18 is $1,010 per credit hour for most on-campus graduate programs. Student fees are $40 per credit (not to exceed $360 per semester), and there is a $25 summer registration fee.

Living and Housing Costs

Hamden, North Haven, and surrounding communities in Greater New Haven offer a wide array of housing options for graduate students in a range of prices, including apartment complexes, rentals within multi-unit homes, and single family houses for rent. There is also a limited amount of on-campus housing available for graduate students. The university's Office of Residential Life maintains a listing of off-campus housing and can provide information about on-campus housing. In addition, the Quinnipiac Offices of Graduate Admissions and Graduate Student Affairs can provide information about the locales and communities within commuting distance of the campuses.

Student Group

Quinnipiac University enrolls approximately 7,000 undergraduates and 3,000 graduate students. Of the university's graduate student population, approximately 52 percent are enrolled in full-time programs, and 48 percent are enrolled in part-time programs. Many graduate students come from the Northeast region and northern mid-Atlantic region. Certain programs also attract graduate students from across the United States and internationally.

Location

The university's graduate programs are located on two beautiful, state-of-the-art campuses in Hamden and North Haven, Connecticut, located just outside of New Haven, approximately 90 minutes from New York City and two hours from Boston. The Mount Carmel Campus in Hamden is home to graduate programs in business, communications, and molecular and cell biology. The North Haven Campus is home to graduate programs in health sciences, nursing, education, law, and medicine. A third campus, York Hill, features the TD Bank Sports Center, home to Quinnipiac's Division I hockey and basketball teams, and the Rocky Top Student Center, featuring stunning views of Long Island Sound and a fitness facility, open to graduate students.

The University

Quinnipiac University is nationally recognized as a dynamic center for higher learning in the Northeast and is consistently ranked among the best master's-level universities in the North in *U.S. News & World Report*'s Guide to America's Best Colleges and its Best Online Graduate Business Programs. The Princeton Review has included Quinnipiac among its Best Business Schools and Best Law Schools.

Applying

Applicants should check the requirements on the university website for the specific program to which they plan to apply. Applications should be submitted online and by sending required materials to the Office of Graduate Admissions. International students should visit the website for application information; students from non–English-speaking countries must supply a notarized translation of their transcripts as well as Test of English as a Foreign Language (TOEFL) or International English Language Testing System (IELTS) scores.

Correspondence and Information:

Office of Graduate Admissions
Quinnipiac University
275 Mount Carmel Avenue
Hamden, Connecticut 06518-1940
United States
Phone: 203-582-8672
800-462-1944 (toll-free)
E-mail: graduate@qu.edu
Website: www.QU.edu

THE FACULTY

Quinnipiac faculty members demonstrate a high level of commitment to their fields, and notable faculty members work in each of the graduate areas of study. The following are key members of the Quinnipiac University faculty.

Matthew L. O'Connor, Ph.D., Dean of the School of Business and Professor of Finance, has published extensively in peer-reviewed journals and is an active participant at professional conferences. Recipient of the 2005 Excellence in Teaching Award by the university's Center for Excellence in Teaching and Service to Students, Dean O'Connor currently teaches courses in applied portfolio management.

Mark Contreras, M.B.A., recently joined the university as Dean of the School of Communications. Prior to joining Quinnipiac, he served as chief executive officer of Calkins Media, Inc. He is former chairman of the Newspaper Association of America (now known as the News Media Association) and the American Press Institute, one of the media industry's leading training, development, and research institutions.

Anne Dichele, Ph.D., Dean of the School of Education, is a former classroom teacher and director of Quinnipiac's master's in teaching program. She is the founder of Side By Side Charter School, one of Connecticut's first state-funded charter schools, where she serves as chairperson of the board of directors. Her scholarship has appeared in numerous journals and publications and her first book of original poetry was recently published.

Jennifer Gerarda Brown, J.D., is the Dean of the School of Law. Her research looks at LGBT rights, dispute resolution, and the professional responsibilities of lawyers, and she has contributed to numerous publications on the topics of marriage equality and the theory and practice of negotiation. Dean Brown was founding director of Quinnipiac Law's Center on Dispute Resolution.

Bruce M. Koeppen, M.D., Dean of the School of Medicine and Vice President of Health Affairs, has directed and published research on kidney function, has earned numerous awards for teaching, and has more than three decades of experience as a medical school professor and administrator.

William C. Kohlhepp, D.H.S., is Dean of the School of Health Sciences and teaches medical microbiology and infectious diseases. His professional experience includes clinical practice as a physician assistant, administrative directorship of an area occupational health center, and service as an officer or board member of several national physician assistant organizations.

Jean W. Lange, Ph.D., Dean of the School of Nursing, teaches clinical scholarship in addition to her administrative role. Her clinical experience encompasses cardiology, critical care, and neurology, and her academic work focuses on senior and Hispanic health issues. Dr. Lange is a Fellow of the American Academy of Nursing.

Allan Smits, Ph.D., is the Associate Dean of Sciences and Graduate Programs in the College of Arts and Sciences, which includes the M.S. in Molecular and Cell Biology program. He has been named an outstanding professor by the university's Center for Excellence in Teaching and Service to Students.

Students at Quinnipiac join a welcoming community that is supportive and collaborative.

Quinnipiac's campuses provide state-of-the-art resources in a dynamic and architecturally distinctive setting.

SALISBURY UNIVERSITY
Graduate Studies and Research

Programs of Study

Graduate study at Salisbury University (SU) provides baccalaureate degree holders from the United States and abroad with opportunities for professional advancement and personal enrichment. The graduate curriculum is designed to assist students in attaining greater mastery of their fields of specialization, improving skills in pursuing independent study, and increasing professional knowledge and ability through the study of new findings in areas of special interest.

Master's degree programs available at SU include the following: applied biology (M.S.), applied health physiology (M.S.), athletic training (M.S.A.T.), business administration (M.B.A.), conflict analysis and dispute resolution (M.A.), education (M.Ed.: curriculum and instruction; educational leadership; post-secondary education track; reading specialist), English (M.A.), geographic information systems management (M.S.), history (M.A.), mathematics education (M.S.M.E.), nursing (M.S.), social work (M.S.W.), and teaching (M.A.T.).

Doctoral programs are available in education (Ed.D.: contemporary curriculum theory and instruction in literacy) and nursing (D.N.P.: post-B.S.; post-masters).

A graduate certificate program is offered in Teaching English to Speakers of Other Languages (TESOL); also available are a post-master's Literacy Educator certificate program and a post-baccalaureate certificate in Higher Education.

Research Facilities

Salisbury University is home to Henson Science Hall, a $42 million science education and research building, and the new $117 million Patricia R. Guerrieri Academic Commons, the largest academic building in University history. An epicenter for learning, research, and creativity, it houses SU Libraries, the Nabb Research Center for Delmarva History and Culture, a Graduate Student Commons, and numerous academic centers and services.

Financial Aid

A limited amount of financial aid in the form of graduate assistantships from the University and scholarships from the Maryland State Scholarship Administration (Maryland residents only) are available each year to selected graduate students. Students applying for aid must complete the Free Application for Federal Student Aid (FAFSA) and indicate Salisbury University (title IV code of 002091). Students may also apply online at www.fafsa.ed.gov. For more information about financial assistance, prospective students should contact the Financial Aid Office at 410-543-6165 or finaid@salisbury.edu, or visit www.salisbury.edu/admissions/finaid/graduate.html.

Graduate assistants are eligible to receive a stipend and tuition waiver of up to 18 credits per fiscal year. To be eligible for the waiver, students must enroll for a minimum of 6 credits in both the fall and spring terms. Tuition is waived only for graduate courses applicable toward master's degree requirements. The tuition waiver does not include waiver of fees. A full-time assistantship requires a time commitment of approximately 20 hours per week, and a half-time assistantship requires 10 hours per week. For details, prospective students should visit www.salisbury.edu/gsr/gradstudies/grad_assistantships.html or consult the Graduate Assistantship section of the Graduate Student Handbook.

Enrolled graduate students are eligible for competitive research and funding opportunities within their academic schools and for Research and Presentation Grants providing up to $500 to support scholarly projects and presentations.

Cost of Study

All graduate tuition rates are charged on a per credit-hour basis; there is no full-time tuition rate. Prospective students should visit www.salisbury.edu/cashiers for information and an updated listing of tuition, fees, special course fees, and other related expenses. Tuition and fees for each semester may be changed and new ones established at any time by action of the Board of Regents of the University System of Maryland.

Living and Housing Costs

Salisbury University does not offer on-campus housing for graduate students; however, there are numerous off-campus housing options nearby. Prospective students should visit SU's Commuter and Connections' website at www.salisbury.edu/commuters.

Student Group

The Graduate Student Council (GSC) at SU provides opportunities for intellectual, professional, personal, and social development through grants, advocacy, public presentation of research, graduate community events, and campus service. The GSC is part of the campus' Governance Consortium.

Student Outcomes

SU offers a network of over 47,000 alumni nationwide.

Location

With a regional population of roughly 99,000, Salisbury is the cultural and economic hub of Delmarva (containing portions of Delaware, Maryland, and Virginia), a historically and ecologically rich peninsula located between the Atlantic Ocean and Chesapeake Bay. The city is 30 minutes west of the beaches of Assateague and Ocean City, Maryland; about 2 hours from Baltimore, Maryland; Wilmington, Delaware; Norfolk, Virginia; and Washington, D.C.; and 4½ hours from New York City.

The University

A member of the University System of Maryland, SU is a regionally accredited four-year comprehensive institution offering 59 distinct graduate and undergraduate programs.

Applying

To be considered for admission, the Salisbury University application, all transcripts and supporting documents, and $65 nonrefundable application fee must be submitted. For questions regarding the application process, prospective students should call the Office of Graduate Studies at 410-548-3546. For more information about specific program admission requirements, including priority application deadlines, applicants should contact the appropriate graduate program director. Additional information can be found online at www.salisbury.edu/gsr/gradstudies/admissions.html.

Correspondence and Information

Office of Graduate Studies
Holloway Hall 262
Salisbury University
1101 Camden Avenue
Salisbury, Maryland 21801
Phone: 410-548-3546
Fax: 410-677-0052
E-mail: graduateadmissions@salisbury.edu
Website: http://www.salisbury.edu/gsr/gradstudies/

Salisbury University

GRADUATE PROGRAMS AND THEIR DIRECTORS

Applied Biology (M.S.)
Dana Price, Ph.D., Graduate Program Director:
410-543-6498, dlprice@salisbury.edu.
http://www.salisbury.edu/gsr/gradstudies/MSBIOpage.html

Applied Health Physiology (M.S.)
Carlton Insley, Ph.D., RRT-NPS, RPFT, ACSM-CES; Graduate Program Director:
410-677-0145, rcinsley@salisbury.edu.
http://www.salisbury.edu/gsr/gradstudies/MSAHPHpage.html

Athletic Training (M.S.A.T.)
Kelly Fiala, Ph.D., Graduate Program Director:
410-543-6335, kafiala@salisbury.edu.
http://www.salisbury.edu/hss/atgrad/default.html

Business Administration (M.B.A.)
Yvonne Downie, Graduate Program Director:
410-548-3983, yxdownie@salisbury.edu.
http://www.salisbury.edu/gsr/gradstudies/MBApage.html

Conflict Analysis and Dispute Resolution (M.A.)
Vitus Ozoke, Ph.D., Graduate Program Director:
410-677-0276, vaozoke@salisbury.edu.
http://www.salisbury.edu/gsr/gradstudies/CADRpage.html

Education (Ed.D., M.Ed)
Ed.D.: Judith Franzak, Ph.D., Graduate Program Director:
410-677-0238, jkfranzak@salisbury.edu.
http://www.salisbury.edu/gsr/gradstudies/EDDpage.html
M.Ed. Curriculum and Instruction: Diana Wagner, Ph.D., Graduate Program Director:
410-677-5490, dmwagner@salisbury.edu.
http://www.salisbury.edu/gsr/gradstudies/MEDpage.html.
M.Ed. Education Leadership: Doug DeWitt, Ph.D., Graduate Program Director:
410-543-6286, dmdewitt@salisbury.edu.
http://www.salisbury.edu/gsr/gradstudies/MEDpage.html.
M.Ed. Reading Specialist: Joyce Wiencek, Ph.D., Graduate Program Director:
410-543-6288, bjwiencek@salisbury.edu.
http://www.salisbury.edu/gsr/gradstudies/MEDpage.html

English (M.A.)
Christopher Vilmar, Ph.D., Graduate Program Director:
410-677-6511, csvilmar@salisbury.edu.
http://www.salisbury.edu/gsr/gradstudies/ENGpage.html

Geographic Information Systems Management (M.S.)
Stuart Hamilton, Ph.D., Graduate Program Director:
410-548-3518, sehamilton@salisbury.edu.
http://www.salisbury.edu/gsr/gradstudies/GISpage.html

History (M.A.)
Celine Carayon, Ph.D., Graduate Program Director:
410-677-3251, cxcarayon@salisbury.edu.
http://www.salisbury.edu/gsr/gradstudies/HISTpage.html

Mathematics Education (M.S.M.E.)
Jennifer Bergner, Ph.D., Graduate Program Director:
410-677-5429, jabergner@salisbury.edu.
http://www.salisbury.edu/gsr/gradstudies/MSMEpage.html

Nursing
D.N.P.: Lisa Seldomridge, Ph.D., RN, Graduate Program Director:
410-543-6413, laseldomridge@salisbury.edu.
http://www.salisbury.edu/gsr/gradstudies/DNPpage.html
M.S.: Lisa Seldomridge, Ph.D., RN, Graduate Program Director:
410-543-6413, laseldomridge@salisbury.edu.
http://www.salisbury.edu/gsr/gradstudies/MSNpage.html

Social Work (M.S.W.)
Vicki Root, Ph.D., Graduate Program Director:
410-677-3948, vbroot@salisbury.edu.
http://www.salisbury.edu/gsr/gradstudies/MSWpage.html

Teaching (M.A.T.)
Regina Royer, Ed.D., Graduate Program Director:
410-548-3949, rdroyer@salisbury.edu.
http://www.salisbury.edu/gsr/gradstudies/MATpage.html

Teaching English to Speakers of Other Languages (TESOL)
http://www.salisbury.edu/english/grad/tesolID.html#tesol

SU's Patricia R. Guerrieri Academic Commons, opened fall 2016, houses SU Libraries, the Nabb Research Center, and a Graduate Student Commons.

Conway Hall has been cited as one of the nation's best designed higher education buildings.

SCHOOL FOR INTERNATIONAL TRAINING

Graduate Institute

 For more information, visit http://petersons.to/sitgradinst

Programs of Study

School for International Training (SIT) Graduate Institute prepares students from across the globe to be intercultural, effective leaders, professionals, and citizens and fosters a worldwide network of individuals and organizations committed to responsible global citizenship. SIT's graduate and professional development programs are rooted in the experiential education model, where learning occurs at the nexus of theory and practice. Since 1964, SIT Graduate Institute has trained students to become highly skilled practitioners who have a commanding knowledge of the theoretical basis of their profession, experience in the field, and an awareness of their own capabilities, values, and ethics.

SIT offers programs in multiple fields. In order to accommodate diverse professional and personal objectives, programs of varying duration and format are offered on SIT's historic 200-acre campus in Vermont; at the SIT Graduate Institute Washington, DC Center; online; and at overseas field sites.

SIT graduates start nonprofit organizations, work in the field of international education, teach English as a second language, become government and civic leaders, and achieve success in the private sector in highly diverse entities across the globe. Students gain the leadership capabilities and cross-cultural competencies to advance international understanding, work effectively in multicultural environments, and foster a more socially just and economically sustainable world.

Some of the SIT Graduate Institute degree options include:

- M.A. in Climate Change and Global Sustainability (Iceland and Tanzania)
- M.A. in Global Leadership and Social Innovation (Washington, DC; online; and India)
- M.Ed. in Global Youth Development and Leadership (Brattleboro, Vermont)
- M.A. in International Education (Brattleboro, Vermont, or online with short residencies in Vermont)
- M.A. in Intercultural Service, Leadership, and Management (self-designed program)
- M.A. in Peace and Justice Leadership (Brattleboro, Vermont)
- M.A. in Sustainable Development (full-time in Brattleboro, Vermont or Washington, DC, or part-time in Washington, DC)
- M.A. in Teaching English to Speakers of Other Languages (Brattleboro, Vermont, or online with short residencies in Vermont)

Degree Components

Coursework: Students attend classes in Vermont or Washington, DC; in global centers around the world; or online. Coursework includes core classes, degree-specific courses, and electives.

Professional Practice: Students spend several months working with an organization of their choosing that is relevant to their professional goals. This practicum may be an unpaid internship or a full-time, paid position and may take place in the United States or an international site. The practicum gives students an opportunity to practice what they've learned in class and develop a deeper understanding of their chosen field.

Capstone Paper or Teaching Portfolio: The final project investigates a question related to professional practice, integrates theory and practice, contributes to the student's chosen field, assesses what the student has learned, and demonstrates professional competencies.

Financial Aid

SIT is committed to ensuring students can successfully access funding for their graduate education. SIT's Financial Aid Office provides guidance on all aspects of graduate financial aid throughout the application process and beyond.

SIT students finance their degrees through a variety of resources, such as SIT scholarships, scholarships from external foundations, SIT partnership and affiliate program awards, on-campus employment, student loans, and personal and family funds. Approximately 95 percent of SIT Graduate Students receive scholarship and grant funding from SIT.

U.S. students and permanent residents are encouraged to learn about the Public Service Loan Forgiveness Program and income-based repayment plans offered through the Federal Student Loan program.

Cost of Study

Cost of attendance varies by graduate program. Tuition and costs associated with each degree can be found on each program's web page.

Student Group

SIT students represent a wide variety of socioeconomic backgrounds and come from across the globe. They have worked for educational institutions, for NGOs, and in the public and private sectors. They may be teachers, international education professionals, social justice and human rights activists, or returned Peace Corps volunteers. Students include experienced professionals who want to sharpen their skills, mid-career professionals seeking to change careers or boost their credentials, and recent college graduates.

The latest group of students in Vermont is made up of about 30 percent international students. Students have an average of four years of intercultural experience as well as four years of professional experience. Thirty-two percent of students have studied abroad before applying to SIT, 12 percent served in the Peace Corps, and 10 percent in AmeriCorps. Of the 65 percent of students who chose to share their racial identity, 10 percent identify as black or African American, 5 percent identify as Hispanic American, and 5 percent identify as Asian American.

At SIT's Center in Washington, DC, about 40 percent are international students. Students have an average of two years of intercultural experience as well as five years of professional experience. Fifty percent of students have studied abroad before applying to SIT, 20 percent served in the Peace Corps, and 6 percent served in AmeriCorps. Of the 50 percent of students who chose to share their racial identity, 13 percent identify as black or African American, 10 percent identify as Hispanic American, and 5 percent identify as Asian American.

Location

SIT's master's degree programs span the globe in scope and substance. Through a vast network of faculty, experts, universities, NGOs, and organizations, and established SIT program facilities in more than 30 countries, SIT Graduate Institute is able to offer elective field courses and access to practicum sites in locations around the world in addition to innovative master's degree programs that take students across the globe, with terms in Europe, Asia, and Africa.

SIT's 200-acre campus in Brattleboro, Vermont, is home to SIT Graduate Institute programs and SIT Study Abroad administrative offices. Each year, about half the student body lives in residences on campus. Campus resources include residence halls, an internationally focused library, technology and media services, a café, and a shuttle bus to downtown Brattleboro.

Conveniently located in the center of the U.S. capital, SIT Graduate Institute's center in Washington, DC, is also home to World Learning's International Development and Exchange Programs. Students have access to World Learning's professional development staff and to experts from other organizations and agencies based in Washington, DC, including speakers, guest lecturers, mentors, and project supervisors, as well as other learning resources.

The Institute

School for International Training (SIT) Graduate Institute equips students with theoretical knowledge, field experience, and professional skills. Programs are based on an experiential learning model and a commitment to social justice and intercultural communication. SIT offers on-campus and low-residency options in Vermont and Washington, DC, as well as innovative master's degree programs that take students across the globe.

SIT's graduate and professional development programs are rooted in the experiential education model, where learning occurs at the nexus of theory and practice. Students become highly skilled practitioners who have experience in the field; a commanding knowledge of the theoretical basis of their professions; and awareness of their own capabilities, values, and ethics.

School for International Training is accredited by the New England Association of Schools and Colleges.

The Faculty

SIT Graduate Institute faculty members practice what they teach.

With expertise in conflict transformation, international development, English and foreign language learning, international education, social justice, management, and human rights, faculty at SIT Graduate Institute come together at an institution that bridges practice and theory.

SIT faculty have worked across the world as consultants, trainers, and developers in the business, nonprofit, education, and public sectors. They are the founders and directors of NGOs and have consulted on projects for the U.S. State Department, NGOs, and other public- and private-sector organizations and agencies. Many SIT faculty are returned Peace Corps volunteers. They have published research on diverse topics ranging from sustainable industrial development to human trafficking to brain-friendly learning and the role of technology in language teaching.

SIT faculty, affiliated faculty, and practitioners-in-residence from across its globe-spanning network provide valuable resources and professional connections for SIT students in the areas of language teaching, international education, international exchange, and development.

Applying

SIT Graduate Admissions strives to create a diverse and experienced student body to enhance the learning experience both inside and outside the classroom. The SIT admissions staff works one-on-one with every applicant to facilitate a well-informed and multidimensional admissions experience.

Program start dates vary. Some programs have flexible start dates. Applicants should check the website or speak with an admissions counselor to find out when the program they're interested in begins.

Admission to a master's or certificate program, requires the following: a U.S. bachelor's degree or equivalent, demonstrated English language ability, intercultural and professional experience, and demonstrated ability to use experience as a source of learning. The GRE exam is not required.

Applicants whose first language is not English and who did not graduate from an English-speaking institution in a country whose official language is English must submit test scores for the TOEFL (Test of English as a Foreign Language), the IELTS (International English Language Testing System), or the PTE (Pearson Test of English).

Applicants to SIT's low-residency programs must be currently working in their field of study and must have experience and familiarity with instructional technology, distance learning, and/or independent learning.

More specific admissions requirements for each degree can be found on each program's web page.

Application deadlines and financial aid deadlines vary by program. Specific information is available at graduate.sit.edu/admissions. Admissions decisions are made on a rolling basis. Admissions decisions will be sent initially via e-mail; an official paper copy will also be sent by mail.

Correspondence and Information

Vermont Campus:
SIT Graduate Institute
1 Kipling Road
Brattleboro, Vermont 05302
Telephone: 800-336-1616
Outside the U.S.: +1-802-258-3510
E-mail: admissions@sit.edu
Website: graduate.sit.edu
DC Center:
SIT Graduate Institute
1015 15th Street, NW
Washington, DC 20005

Programs of Study

Education at Springfield College is all about taking action. Graduate students at Springfield College put their classroom education to practice through fieldwork and service learning. It's a learning advantage based on the College's historic mission, the Humanics philosophy, which calls for educating students in spirit, mind, and body for leadership in service to others. Humanics is at the base of everything the College does—in academics, athletics, and student life.

With an international reputation for educating tomorrow's leaders in some of the most vital career fields, Springfield College provides students with a competitive edge—top-quality academic preparation, research opportunities in state-of-the-art facilities, and real-world experience before graduating.

Springfield's graduate programs provide students with the employable skills and knowledge needed to advance their education and increase their job prospects and are taught by faculty members who are passionate about their disciplines. The programs integrate experiential learning opportunities, including fieldwork, internships, practicum, and research. Graduate courses at Springfield College challenge students to gain knowledge from the classroom, experience in the field, and think outside the box. Students leave Springfield College with a degree and real, applicable expertise in their fields.

Springfield offers a variety of master's degree programs including: art therapy/counseling, business administration, education (concentrations: in special education initial [preK–8, 5–12], elementary initial, secondary initial), exercise science and sport studies (concentrations: athletic training, clinical exercise physiology, exercise physiology, sport and exercise psychology, strength and conditioning), human services, occupational therapy, physical education (concentrations: adapted physical education, advanced-level coaching, athletic administration, health promotion and disease prevention, physical education teacher licensure, physical education teacher–professional licensure), physician assistant, psychology and counseling (concentrations: athletic counseling, clinical mental health counseling, industrial/organizational psychology, school counseling, student personnel administration in higher education), rehabilitation counseling and services (concentrations: general counseling, counseling and casework, pediatric and developmental disability counseling, psychiatric rehabilitation, and substance abuse counseling), social work (concentrations: M.S.W. weekday program, M.S.W. weekend program in Worcester and Springfield, advanced standing program, post-master's certificate program in trauma-informed practice), and sport management and recreation (concentrations: sport management, recreation management, therapeutic recreation management). Doctoral degree programs are also available: Ph.D. in Physical Education with specializations in sport and exercise psychology, exercise physiology, and teaching and administration; Doctor of Physical Therapy (D.P.T.); and Doctor of Psychology (Psy.D.) in counseling psychology.

Research Facilities

The campus is home to numerous research facilities, including a medical simulation lab, featuring high-fidelity 3G adult and baby patient simulator mannequins that respond to treatment as human patients would. The exercise physiology/biomechanics lab is where many graduate students conduct their own research, as well as working closely with faculty advisors on exciting new endeavors.

Financial Aid

Springfield College offers fellowships and associateships that assist in paying for tuition. During the 2016–17 academic year, Springfield College administered a total of $3.3 million in fellowship funding to graduate students. For some graduate students, AmeriCorps positions provide additional funding and professional opportunity that supplement their education. Federal financial aid, in the form of loans, is also available to those who qualify.

Cost of Study

The price per credit hour for graduate courses at Springfield College is $1,017. There is a graduate student fee of $215, which only applies to students taking nine or more credits.

Living and Housing Costs

Springfield College offers on-campus and off-campus housing options for graduate students. Housing costs range from $6,800 to $13,640 per academic year. Meal plans vary and there are many options from which to choose.

Student Group

Springfield College has 2,200 undergraduate students and 1,094 graduate students on the main campus and 1,600 nontraditional adult students at eight regional campuses across the country. Students come from 32 states, mostly from the northeastern corridor of the United States, and seven countries outside of the United States. The majority of undergraduate and graduate students reside on campus.

Student Outcomes

Springfield's graduate students are motivated, innovative, and focused on success, all while working to improve the world around them. According to a recent post-graduation survey, 97 percent of 2015–16 master's and doctoral graduates are employed or seeking advanced education.

Springfield College

Location

Located on the shores of Lake Massasoit, Springfield College is home to beautiful landscaping and top-notch facilities that combine function with artistry, while maintaining the historic beauty of the campus. Students have the best of both worlds—a campus located within a city with a classic New England charm.

The College

Springfield College provides a caring and inclusive environment, geared toward sharing ideas and research while collaborating with faculty members and other students. Founded in 1885, the college has maintained the same mission since day one—educating students in spirit, mind, and body for leadership in service to others. Being civically minded is celebrated at Springfield College and giving back to the community is a frequent occurrence at the college, whether it's through a group-organized service project or the annual Humanics in Action Day, where the college closes down for a day and students, faculty, and staff head out into the community to participate in service projects.

Faculty

The College's classrooms provide an environment where discussions are welcomed and faculty members will always know students by name. Class sizes are small, with an approximate 13:1 student-to-faculty ratio. Approximately 84 percent of full-time faculty members have earned the highest degrees attainable in their areas of expertise, and 70 percent hold doctorates.

Applying

Each graduate program has its own admissions requirements. Specific details about the requirements, as well as the graduate admissions process, are available online at springfield.edu/gradadmissions.

Correspondence and Information

Office of Graduate Admissions
Springfield College
263 Alden Street
Springfield, Massachusetts 01109
United States
Phone: 413-748-3225
TTY: 413-748-3383
E-mail: graduate@springfieldcollege.edu
Website: springfield.edu/gradadmissions

TEMPLE UNIVERSITY
Graduate School

Graduate School

⭐ For more information, visit http://petersons.to/templeugrad

Programs of Study

Doctor of Philosophy programs are offered in Africology and African American studies, anthropology, art history, bioengineering, biology, biomedical sciences (cancer biology and genetics, infectious disease and immunity, molecular and cellular biosciences, neuroscience, organ systems and translational medicine), business administration (accounting, finance, human resource management and organizational behavior, interdisciplinary study, international business administration, management information systems, marketing, risk management and insurance, strategic management, tourism and sport), chemistry, civil engineering, communication sciences and disorders, computer and information science, criminal justice, dance, decision neuroscience, documentary arts and visual research, economics, education (applied linguistics, educational psychology, literacy and learners, math and science education, special education, urban education), electrical engineering, engineering, English, environmental engineering, epidemiology, geography and urban studies, geoscience, health policy, history, kinesiology (athletic training, integrative exercise physiology, psychology of movement), mathematics, mechanical engineering, media and communication, music (composition, music studies, music theory, musicology), music education, music therapy, neuromotor science, pharmaceutical sciences (medicinal chemistry, pharmaceutics, pharmacodynamics), philosophy, physics, political science, psychology (brain and cognitive sciences, clinical psychology, developmental psychology, social psychology), religion, school psychology, social and behavioral health sciences, sociology, Spanish, and statistics.

The Doctor of Musical Arts is offered in music performance (bassoon, cello, clarinet, double bass, euphonium, flute, French horn, harp, historical keyboard, oboe, percussion, piano, trombone, trumpet, tuba, viola, violin, voice). The Doctor of Education degree is offered in educational leadership and higher education. Other specialized doctoral degrees include the Doctor of Athletic Training, Doctor of Nursing Practice (adult-gerontology primary care, family-individual across the lifespan primary care), Clinical Doctorate in Occupational Therapy, Doctor of Physical Therapy, and executive Doctor of Business Administration.

Master's degree programs are available in accomplished teaching; accountancy; actuarial science; adult and organizational development; Africology and African American studies; applied behavior analysis; architecture; art education; art history; athletic training; bioengineering; biology; biomedical sciences (cancer biology and genetics, general biomedical sciences, infectious disease and immunity, molecular and cellular biosciences, neuroscience, organ systems and translational medicine); business administration (business analytics, business management, enterprise risk management, entrepreneurship, financial management, health sector management, human resource management, innovation management, marketing management, strategic management); business analytics; career and technical education (business, computer and information technology; industrial education; marketing education); chemistry; choral conducting; city and regional planning; civil engineering; clinical research and translational medicine; collaborative piano and chamber music; collaborative piano and opera coaching; communication management (conflict management and dispute resolution, strategic communication and cross-cultural leadership); computational data science; computer science; counseling psychology; criminal justice; dance; digital innovation in marketing; early childhood education; early childhood education and special education; economics; educational psychology; electrical engineering; engineering management; English; environmental engineering; epidemiology; financial analysis and risk management; financial engineering; geography and urban studies; geology; global clinical and pharmacovigilance regulations; globalization and development communication; health administration; health informatics (cybersecurity for healthcare professionals, healthcare data analytics, population health management); higher education (access and success, institutional

effectiveness, student affairs leadership); history; human resource management; information science and technology; information technology auditing and cybersecurity (cybersecurity, information technology auditing); innovation management and entrepreneurship (entrepreneurship, innovative strategy, technology and innovation management); instrumental conducting: wind-band emphasis; investment management; jazz studies; journalism; kinesiology (athletic training, integrative exercise physiology, psychology of movement); landscape architecture; liberal arts; marketing (enterprise marketing management, marketing research and insight, strategic advertising and marketing); mathematics; mechanical engineering; media studies and production; mediaXarts: cinema for new technologies and environments; middle grades education (language arts, mathematics, mathematics and language arts, mathematics and science, science, science and language arts, social studies); middle grades and special education (language arts, mathematics, mathematics and language arts, mathematics and science, science, science and language arts, social studies); music; music composition; music education; music history; music performance (bassoon, cello, clarinet, classical guitar, double bass, euphonium, flute, French horn, harp, harpsichord, oboe, percussion, piano, saxophone, trombone, trumpet, tuba, viola, violin, voice); music technology; music theory; music therapy; musical theater studies; neuromotor science; neuroscience: systems, behavior and plasticity; occupational therapy; opera; oral biology; pharmaceutical sciences (medicinal chemistry, pharmaceutics, pharmacodynamics); philosophy; physician assistant; physics; piano pedagogy; political science; psychological research; public policy; recreation therapy; regulatory affairs and quality assurance; religion; school leadership (curriculum supervision, principal leadership, reform and change leadership); secondary education (English, mathematics, science, social studies, world/foreign languages); secondary education and special education (English, mathematics, science, social studies, world/foreign languages); social work; sociology; Spanish; special education (autism spectrum disorders, mild disabilities, severe disabilities); speech, language and hearing science; sport business (athletics administration, recreation and event management, sport analytics, sport marketing and promotions); sport business executive program; statistics; string pedagogy; taxation; teacher leadership; teaching English to speakers of other languages; tourism and hospitality management (hospitality operations management, tourism and hospitality marketing); travel and tourism; urban bioethics; urban education; urban school leadership; and vocal arts. Also offered are an executive M.B.A. and an Ed.S. in school psychology.

Master of Fine Arts degree programs are available in ceramics/glass, creative writing, dance, fibers and materials studies, film and media arts, graphic and interactive design, metals/jewelry/CAD-CAM, musical theater collaboration, painting, photography, printmaking, sculpture, and theater (acting, design, directing, playwriting). Master of Public Health degrees are offered in applied biostatistics, environmental health, epidemiology, health policy and management, and social and behavioral sciences. The Professional Science Master's (P.S.M.) degree is offered in applied sociology, bioinformatics, bioinnovation, biotechnology, computer and systems security, cyber defense and information assurance, forensic chemistry, geographic information systems, high-performance computing for scientific applications, and scientific writing (marketing/regulatory writing, popular scientific writing).

Rounding out the offerings are 100 graduate, post-master's, and specialty certificates in a range of disciplines.

Research Facilities

The world-class Science Education and Research Center (SERC) opened in fall 2014 with leading-edge laboratories to fully support moving scientific breakthroughs from the lab to the real world. To promote scientific collaboration, SERC offers breakout rooms and offices, storage and support areas, and seminar and conference rooms in addition to classroom space. The Materials Research Facility houses three X-ray diffractometers; a transmission electron microscope; and an accurate-mass quadrupole time-of-flight mass spectrometer, which offers superior sensitivity and data quality for profiling, identifying, characterizing, and quantifying compounds. The Research and Instructional Support Facility is home to glass-blowing design services and a computer numerical-control milling machine that enables the design and manufacture of an array of tools, prototypes, and products essential for advanced research. Less than 2 miles north of the main academic campus, on the Health Sciences Center campus at Broad and Ontario Streets, excellent and varied facilities for research are accessible. Finally, the University libraries contain more than 4 million bound volumes and are custodians of thousands of special collections of rare books and primary archival sources.

Financial Aid

Graduate students are eligible for financial assistance from private, University, state, and federal sources. The Office of Student Financial Services (http://sfs.temple.edu/) administers loans, grants, work-study, and other forms of financial aid. Students can contact the SFS office directly at 215-204-2244 for additional information.

Cost of Study

Resident tuition for the 2017–18 academic year ranges from $701 per credit for the Physician Assistant M.M.S. in the Lewis Katz School of Medicine to $2,300 per credit for the Fox School of Business and Management's executive D.B.A. Nonresident tuition ranges from $736 per credit for the Physician Assistant M.M.S. to $2,300 per credit for Fox School's executive D.B.A. A breakdown of tuition by school/college or program, in some cases, is available at http://bulletin.temple.edu/graduate/tuition-fees/.

Living and Housing Costs

On-campus housing is limited. For information on availability, students can contact the Office of University Housing and Residential Life at 215-204-7184 or visit http://housing.temple.edu/graduate.

Student Group

With a student body of more than 38,000 students, Temple University is one of the largest universities in the country. Since becoming a part of the Commonwealth System of Higher Education, it has increasingly emphasized upper-division and graduate work. Although the institution historically served the greater metropolitan area of southeastern Pennsylvania, Temple University now consistently attracts a significant and growing portion of the student body worldwide.

Location

With a population of more than 1.5 million, Philadelphia is the fifth-largest city in the country. It offers a variety of cultural attractions, including a world-renowned symphony orchestra, professional repertory theater, historic shrines, parks, and sports facilities. The climate is temperate, with an average temperature in winter of 38 degrees and 74 degrees in summer.

The University

With a rich heritage of populist tradition, Temple University provides students with an opportunity for education of high quality without regard to race, creed, or station in life. Affiliation with the Commonwealth System of Higher Education undergirds Temple's character as a public institution. Temple's academic programs are conducted on five campuses in Philadelphia and its nearby suburbs.

Applying

Departmental deadlines for admissions and financial aid vary. Applicants should consult a particular program's page in the Graduate Bulletin (http://bulletin.temple.edu/graduate/) and the program's website, which is identified on the program's Contacts tab in the Graduate Bulletin. Notification regarding admission and financial aid is made following the screening of the application.

Correspondence and Information

Zebulon V. Kendrick, Ph.D.
Vice Provost for Graduate Education
Temple University
501 Carnell Hall
1803 North Broad Street
Philadelphia, Pennsylvania 19122-6104
United States
Phone: 215-204-1380
Fax: 215-204-8781
E-mail: grad@temple.edu
Website: http://www.temple.edu/grad

FACULTY HEADS

Graduate School: Zebulon V. Kendrick, Ph.D., Vice Provost.
Beasley School of Law: Gregory N. Mandel, J.D., Dean.
Center for the Performing and Cinematic Arts, including Boyer College of Music and Dance and the School of Theater, Film and Media Arts: Robert T. Stroker, Ph.D., Dean.
College of Education: Gregory M. Anderson, Ph.D., Dean.
College of Engineering: Keyanoush Sadeghipour, Ph.D., Dean.
College of Liberal Arts: Richard Deeg, Ph.D., Dean.
College of Public Health: Laura A. Siminoff, Ph.D., Dean.
College of Science and Technology: Michael L. Klein, Ph.D., Dean.
Fox School of Business and Management: M. Moshe Porat, Ph.D., Dean.
Kornberg School of Dentistry: Amid I. Ismail, Dr.P.H., Dean.
Lew Klein College of Media and Communication: David Boardman, M.A., Dean.
Lewis Katz School of Medicine: Larry R. Kaiser, M.D., Dean.
School of Pharmacy: Peter H. Doukas, Ph.D., Dean.
School of Podiatric Medicine: John A. Mattiacci, D.P.M., Dean.
School of Sport, Tourism and Hospitality Management: M. Moshe Porat, Ph.D., Dean.
Tyler School of Art: Susan E. Cahan, Ph.D., Dean.

Two-story lobby of the Science Education and Research Center (SERC) on Temple University's main campus. This LEED Gold Registered structure has 247,000 square feet of space across 7 floors.

TUFTS UNIVERSITY
Graduate School of Arts and Sciences

 For more information, visit http://petersons.to/tuftsuniv-arts-sciences

Programs of Study

The Graduate School of Arts and Sciences at Tufts University offers master's, certificate, and doctoral programs in the natural sciences, social sciences, and the arts and humanities.

The Doctor of Philosophy (Ph.D.) degree is offered in biology, chemistry, chemistry/biotechnology, child study and human development, cognitive science, economics and public policy, education, English, history, human developmental economics, mathematics, physics, psychology, and theatre and performance studies. A highly selective interdisciplinary doctorate is available in other areas. Tufts also offers a Doctor of Occupational Therapy.

The Master of Arts degree may be earned in art history, art history and museum studies, child study and human development, classics, digital tools for premodern studies, diversity and inclusion leadership, education, English, French, German, history, history and museum studies, museum education, music, philosophy, school psychology, and urban and environmental policy and planning. The Master of Science is offered in biology, chemistry, chemistry/biotechnology, economics, education, environmental economics and urban planning, environmental policy and planning, mathematics, occupational therapy, and physics. The Master of Arts in Teaching is available in education with concentrations in art, early childhood education, secondary education, and child study and human development. The Master of Fine Arts degree is awarded through the School of the Museum of Fine Arts (SMFA) at Tufts. Tufts also offers the Master of Public Policy degree. Certificate programs are available in community environmental studies, early childhood technology, environmental management, interdisciplinary studio art, management of community organizations, museum studies, occupational therapy, program evaluation, school-based practice for occupational therapy, science education, and urban justice and sustainability.

Full-time students can take one course per semester, for both a grade and credit, through cross-registration agreements with Boston College, Boston University, and Brandeis University.

Research Facilities

The Tufts University library system includes the Tisch Library, the Lilly Music Library, the Edward Ginn Library of The Fletcher School, and the W. Van Alan Clark, Jr. Library at the SMFA. Through Tufts' membership in the Boston Library Consortium, graduate students also have library privileges at the Massachusetts State Library, the Woods Hole Oceanographic Institute, the Boston Public Library, and the libraries of Amherst College, Boston College, Boston University, Brandeis University, the Massachusetts Institute of Technology, Northeastern University, the University of Connecticut, the University of Massachusetts, the University of New Hampshire, Wellesley College, and Williams College. Theatre performance study students have access to the Harvard Theatre Collection.

Special research facilities for science and engineering students include the campus-based Science and Technology Center, housing selected areas of research in physics and electrical and chemical engineering as well as laboratory facilities in biology, chemistry, psychology, and electrical and civil engineering, and the Collaborative Learning and Innovation Complex (CLIC), housing the departments of physics and astronomy, occupational therapy, community health, child study and human development and faculty working in human-centered engineering. Students are encouraged to pursue collaborative research at off-site facilities, which have included Fermilab, the Woods Hole Oceanographic Institute, and Brookhaven Laboratories. Many student and faculty researchers carry out collaborative research with colleagues at nearby Boston universities.

Financial Aid

In 2017–18, the Graduate School of Arts and Sciences awarded more than $13 million in tuition scholarships. Teaching and research assistantships are available, as are some fellowships. Tufts also awards need-based financial aid through the Federal Perkins Loan, Federal Work-Study, and Federal Direct Student Loan programs.

Cost of Study

Tuition for most master's programs for 2017–18 is $49,892, and is only charged in the student's first year. The 2017–18 tuition for the occupational therapy Master of Science program is $49,892 charged for two years; the school psychology Master of Arts and educational specialist program is $43,680 charged for two years; the urban and environmental policy and planning Master of Arts program is $35,980 charged for two years; and the Master of Fine Arts program is $45,008 charged for one year. Part-time tuition in 2017–18 is $4,990 per course. The 2017–18 tuition for doctoral programs is $29,936, and is charged for five years. The 2017–18 tuition for Doctor of Occupational Therapy students is $49,892, and is charged for one year. Other charges include student health insurance, a health service fee, and a student activity fee.

Living and Housing Costs

Living expenses are estimated at about $1,200 a month, including food, housing, utilities, transportation, and textbook costs. There is limited on-campus housing for graduate students. Rents for one-bedroom apartments in Medford and Somerville begin at approximately $1,200 per month. The cost of sharing an apartment averages about $750 per person, and over 90 percent of students share apartments with at least one other individual. A public transportation system serves the greater Boston area and provides easy access to and from the campus, while a free, local shuttle runs throughout the academic year, providing easy access between campus, the subway, and Boston.

Student Group

In 2016–17, 971 students were enrolled in the Graduate School of Arts and Sciences. Of these, 68 percent were women and 22 percent were international students.

Location

The main campus, which spans the Medford-Somerville city line, is 7 miles from downtown Boston, a city where the arts (music, drama, and dance), museums, and sporting events abound. Cape Cod beaches and the mountains and forests of Maine, New Hampshire, and Vermont can be easily reached.

The University

Chartered as a liberal arts college in 1852, today Tufts is a small, selective, private university offering opportunities for undergraduate, graduate, and professional education to more than 7,500 students. The Graduate School of Arts and Sciences, the School of Engineering, The

Fletcher School of Law and Diplomacy, The Friedman School of Nutrition Science and Policy, The Sackler School of Graduate Biomedical Sciences, The Cummings School of Veterinary Medicine, The School of Dental Medicine, and The School of Medicine offer graduate and/or professional education. The university is accredited by the New England Association of Schools and Colleges.

Applying

Deadlines for applications vary by program. Applicants applying to a degree program are required to submit three letters of recommendation, a resume, official transcripts from all colleges and universities attended, and a personal statement. Most departments also require the results of the Graduate Record Examinations (GRE). Students whose native language is not English must submit official results of the Test of English as a Foreign Language (TOEFL).

Correspondence and Information

Office of Graduate Admissions
Tufts University
Bendetson Hall
Medford, Massachusetts 02155
United States
Phone: 617-627-3395
E-mail: gradadmissions@tufts.edu
Website: http://asegrad.tufts.edu

FIELDS OF STUDY AND FACULTY ADVISERS

Art: Lisa Bynoe
Art and Art History: Karen Overbey
Biology: Catherine Freudenreich
Chemistry: Samuel Thomas
Child Study and Human Development: Martha Pott (M.A. program); Tama Leventhal (Ph.D. program)
Classics: Marie-Claire Beaulieu
Digital Humanities: Marie-Claire Beaulieu
Diversity and Inclusion Leadership: Ellen Pinderhughes and Sabina Vaught
Economics: Jeffrey Zabel
Economics and Public Policy: Margaret McMillan
Education: Susan Barahal (Art Education); Sabina Vaught (Educational Studies); Brian Gravel (Elemetary Education); Cynthia Robinson (Museum Education); Steven Luz-Alterman and Laura Rogers (School Psychology); David Hammer (STEM Education); Linda Beardsley (Teacher Education)
English: Elizabeth Ammons
French: Gerard Gasarian
German: Markus Wilczek
History: Steven Marrone

Interdisciplinary Doctorate: Robert Cook
Mathematics: Kim Ruane
Music: Stephan Pennington
Museum Studies: Cynthia Robinson
Occupational Therapy: Gary Bedell and Janet Curran Brooks
Philosophy: Patrick Forber
Physics: Danilo Marchesini
Psychology: Ayanna Thomas
Theatre Performance Study: Noe Montez
Urban and Environmental Policy and Planning: Barbara Parmenter

THE UNIVERSITY OF TAMPA
Graduate Programs

THE UNIVERSITY OF TAMPA

 For more information, visit http://petersons.to/utampagrad

Programs of Study

The University of Tampa (UT) is a private nonprofit institution located on the west coast of Florida that offers graduate programs in business, nursing, education, creative writing, and exercise and nutrition science. *U.S. News & World Report* ranks UT among the Best Business Schools (with a Best Part-Time M.B.A. program) and Best Nursing Schools, as well as among the Top 25 Regional Universities in the South. UT has also been included in the *Forbes* annual ranking of America's Best Colleges every year since 2010. Likewise, The Princeton Review includes UT in its lists of Best Southeastern Colleges and Best 382 Colleges.

Graduate Business Programs for Full-Time and Working Students: The University of Tampa offers eight graduate degree programs in business including an M.B.A., Professional M.B.A., and Executive M.B.A. and five specialized master's programs. The Master of Business Administration gives students nine concentration options:

- Business analytics
- Cybersecurity
- Entrepreneurship
- Finance
- Information systems management
- Innovation management
- International business
- Marketing
- Nonprofit management

M.B.A. students may choose to enroll in the full-time/day program or part-time/evening program. Full-time business students typically complete the program in as few as twelve months. This schedule also applies to UT's M.S. in Accounting, M.S. in Cybersecurity, M.S. in Entrepreneurship, M.S. in Finance, and M.S. in Marketing programs.

Working professionals who want to earn their M.B.A. may choose to apply for UT's part-time Professional M.B.A. (P.M.B.A.) or the unique Executive M.B.A. (E.M.B.A.), which is designed for professionals with seven or more years of work experience. E.M.B.A. classes are held on alternate Saturdays and focus on the most current problem-solving and decision-making practices. The program takes two years to complete and includes a ten-day study abroad trip during the second year.

The Sykes College of Business is AACSB (Association to Advance Collegiate Schools of Business) accredited.

Graduate Programs in Education and Instructional Design: UT's Master of Education (M.Ed.) in Curriculum and Instruction program enjoys a solid, long-established relationship with Tampa Bay area school districts and administrators. The program helps develop and extend the teaching and leadership skills of certified teachers. The M.Ed. in Educational Leadership prepares educators for administrative roles and covers topics such as instructional leadership, school budgeting and finance, and community relations. Education classes are offered in the evenings, on weekends, and during summers, allowing students to complete either M.Ed. program in as little as a year.

The M.S. in Instructional Design and Technology program addresses a growing field in learning and human performance, providing an interdisciplinary approach to its study. It emphasizes theories of learning and cognition, multimedia development, systematic instructional design, technology, and open learning environments. The hybrid classroom-online curriculum allows students to complete the program within two years.

Criminology and Criminal Justice Graduate Degree Programs: UT's M.S. in Criminology and Criminal Justice prepares students for both practitioner and management careers in criminal justice and public safety. It is ideal for those embarking on a new career or seeking advancement in law enforcement, corrections, victim advocacy, or criminal justice management. It also provides preparation for doctoral studies. Students may choose between thesis and non-thesis tracks, with degree completion in two years.

Master of Science in Exercise and Nutrition Science: This internationally recognized program focuses on the relationship between exercise physiology and nutrition, with the goal of optimizing athletic performance. During a one-year course of study, students undertake numerous hands-on experiences in UT's Human Performance Research Lab, combined with rigorous classroom learning. Students may begin the program in the summer, fall, or spring semester.

Master of Science in Nursing: The M.S.N. program at UT offers graduate-level study with adult/gerontology and family nurse practitioner concentrations, all in a part-time format. Students benefit from UT's numerous clinical affiliations, and are well equipped to serve as primary care providers in a variety of settings. Admission to the program is competitive.

Master of Fine Arts in Creative Writing: UT's Master of Fine Arts in Creative Writing is a low-residency program intended to develop the skills of poets, fiction, and creative nonfiction writers through supportive critique and mentoring. Students attend four ten-day working residencies on campus, followed by semester-long faculty mentorships designed to support an individualized plan of study. The program takes approximately two years to complete.

Research Opportunities for Graduate Students

UT faculty members conduct and coordinate research in numerous fields across the disciplines. The Naimoli Institute for Business Strategy connects groups of students with more than 600 Tampa Bay area enterprises to conduct strategic evaluations and make performance improvement recommendations.

Research done by students in UT's renowned Human Performance Research Lab has been presented at the National Strength and Conditioning Conference.

Financial Aid and Scholarship Opportunities

The University of Tampa prides itself on its competitive graduate tuition rates. UT offers a limited number of merit-based scholarships for graduate students. Each program also offers graduate assistantship positions, which provide a tuition waiver for up to 12 credit hours per semester, plus a stipend. Reimbursement and stipend amounts vary by program. Graduate assistants are expected to work 20 hours per week for an academic or administrative office and to carry a full course load. Part-time employment is also available on campus.

Cost of Study

For the 2017–18 academic year, tuition for most graduate programs is $603 per credit hour. The cost for the Executive M.B.A. program is $47,460 for the entire two-year program. The M.F.A. in Creative Writing program is $8,815 per semester.

The University of Tampa

Living and Housing Costs

Most UT graduate students choose to live off campus. However, on-campus housing is also available, primarily in Urso or Straz halls. Costs for on-campus housing range from $3,742 to $4,985 per semester, depending on the room chosen. Students living on campus are also required to purchase a meal plan, with costs ranging from $1,376 to $2,552 per semester.

Student Life

UT's graduate student body reflects the global nature of the city and the school. For example, about 40 percent of the University's graduate business students come from outside the United States. UT enrolls students from more than 140 countries and all 50 states, providing opportunities for diverse cultural and educational exchange.

Location

The University's 110-acre campus is located in downtown Tampa, just north of Hillsborough Bay and a short drive from Gulf Coast beaches. The city is a cultural crossroads where national and global corporations offer opportunities for internships, networking, and job recruitment.

The University

Known for academic excellence, personal attention, and real-world experience in its undergraduate and graduate programs, UT offers more than 200 programs of study, including 15 master's degree programs and numerous study-abroad opportunities. Boasting a $265 million annual budget and a $1 billion estimated annual economic impact, UT serves approximately 9,000 undergraduate and graduate students.

Applying

The University of Tampa has rolling admissions. Applicants are advised to submit applications and supporting documents by June 1 for the fall semester, which begins in August. The deadline for the spring semester is November 1.

In general, applicants should submit a complete online application, the application fee, completed bachelor's degree official transcripts, two recommendation letters, and a personal statement and resume. For most graduate business programs, a GMAT or GRE score is required; TOEFL or IELTS scores are required for international applicants.

Correspondence Information

Joshua Stagner, Ed.D.
Director of Graduate and Continuing Studies
The University of Tampa
401 West Kennedy Boulevard
Tampa, Florida 33606-1490
United States
Phone: 813-257-3016
E-mail: jstagner@ut.edu
Website: www.ut.edu/graduate

WASHINGTON UNIVERSITY IN ST. LOUIS

Graduate School

 For more information, visit http://petersons.to/washingtonustlouisgrad

Programs of Study

The Graduate School offers more than thirty programs leading to the doctorate (Ph.D.) and to the Master of Arts (A.M.). In addition, programs are offered leading to the Master of Arts in Education (M.A.Ed.), Master of Arts in Teaching (M.A.T.), and Master of Fine Arts in Writing (M.F.A.W.).

Opportunities for combining a degree available through the Graduate School with a degree from one of the University's professional schools (business, law, medicine) are also available.

Research Facilities

The Washington University community is served by a network of libraries designed to meet the instructional and research needs of faculty members, students, and staff members. Washington University libraries contain the largest collection of any private academic library system between the Mississippi River and California. John M. Olin Library, the central University library, and twelve school and departmental libraries house many important and unique collections and provide state-of-the-art computerized information retrieval. The combined holdings include more than 3 million books and bound periodicals, 18,000 current serial subscriptions, and access to thousands of electronic journals and databases. For more information, students can visit http://library.wustl.edu.

More than thirty centers and institutes provide a spectrum of research opportunities. They include the Center for Air Pollution Impact and Trend Analysis; Center for the Study of American Business; Center for American Indian Studies; Business, Law, and Economics Center; Arts and Sciences Computing Center; Institutes for Biomedical Computing; McDonnell Center for Cellular and Molecular Neurobiology; Construction Management Center; Carolyne Roehm Electronic Media Center; Center for Engineering Computing; Center for Genetics in Medicine; McDonnell Center for Studies of Higher Brain Function; Center for the History of Freedom; Office of International Studies; International Writers Center; Center for the Study of Islamic Societies and Civilizations; Management Center; Fred Gasche Laboratory for Microstructured Materials Technologies; Markey Center for Research in Molecular Biology of Human Disease; Center for Optimization and Semantic Control; Center for Plant Science and Biotechnology; Center for the Study of Public Affairs; Center for Robotics and Automation; Social Work Research Development Center; McDonnell Center for Space Sciences; Center for the Application of Information Technology; and Urban Research and Design Center.

Financial Aid

The majority of full-time students receive financial support. Financial assistance in the form of scholarships, fellowships, and traineeships is offered annually on a competitive basis through the Graduate School from government, private, or endowed sources. Also available are scholarships and, in applied social sciences, clinical internships; grants and fellowships in national competition; and loans. Specific information may be obtained from the departmental or administrative unit to which the student intends to apply.

Cost of Study

Tuition for the 2017–18 academic year for the Graduate School is $50,650. The cost per credit unit is $2,110.

Living and Housing Costs

Many graduate students live in University-owned apartments, some with data connections and shuttle bus service. Listing information for these units as well as non-University housing is available through the University's Apartment Referral Service (http://offcampushousing.wustl.edu/). Average rent ranges from $500 to $1,000 per month.

Student Group

Of the more than 14,000 people attending Washington University, more than 5,000 are graduate students; approximately 2,000 of them are enrolled in the Graduate School. Students come to Washington University from all fifty states and more than eighty international locations.

Location

Washington University has two campuses that lie at opposite ends of Forest Park (one of the largest municipal parks in the nation). The campuses are approximately 5 miles west of downtown St. Louis. The Danforth campus is the location of the Graduate School of Arts and Sciences and all other schools of the University except Medicine. The latter is located on the east, or medical campus. The Division of Biology and Biomedical Sciences is also located on the medical campus. Free shuttle buses run between the campuses on a regular schedule.

The St. Louis area has nearly 2.4 million residents. The cost of living is affordable. The University's central location provides easy access to the zoo, museums, Science Center, Missouri Botanical Gardens, St. Louis Symphony, Opera Theatre, St. Louis Repertory Theatre, Black Repertory Theatre, Blues hockey, Rams football, and Cardinals baseball. Outdoor adventure beyond the city can be found in the Ozark Mountains and on the rivers of Missouri. Camping, hiking, floating, rock climbing, and spelunking are among the many possibilities within a few hours' drive of St. Louis.

The Graduate School

The Graduate School is a charter member of both the Association of Graduate Schools and the Council of Graduate Schools. The School provides a physical and academic environment in which inquiry, intellectual growth, and discovery can thrive and flourish.

Applying

Prospective students may apply online. Applicants should check with the department or program to which they are applying, as application deadlines vary. Most programs require GRE scores. For international students whose native language is not English, most programs require an official copy of a TOEFL score.

Correspondence and Information

Graduate School
Campus Box 1187
Washington University in St. Louis
One Brookings Drive
St. Louis, Missouri 63130-4899
United States
Phone: 314-935-6880
Fax: 314-935-4887
E-mail: GraduateSchool@wustl.edu
Website: http://graduateschool.wustl.edu

FACULTY HEADS, DEGREES OFFERED, AND DEPARTMENTAL INTERESTS

Anthropology (Ph.D.): T. R. Kidder (trkidder@wustl.edu). Sociocultural anthropology (including medical anthropology), archaeology, physical anthropology (including primate studies, paleontology and human biology).

Art History and Archaeology (A.M., Ph.D.): Liz Childs (ecchilds@wustl.edu). Ancient, medieval, Renaissance, early modern, European, modern and contemporary European and American, Asian art history; classical archaeology.

Division of Biology and Biomedical Sciences (Ph.D.): John Russell (800-852-9074, toll-free); e-mail: DBBSPhDAdmissions@wustl.edu).

    Biochemistry: Peter Burgers (DBBSPhDAdmissions@wustl.edu). Metabolic regulation, signal transduction, receptors, membrane channels and transporters, membrane structure and dynamics, membrane trafficking, cholesterol and lipid metabolism, nucleic acid-protein structure interactions and function, DNA replication and repair, recombination, transcription, translation, enzyme kinetics, cancer biology, cell cycle regulation, apoptosis, cell motility, cytoskeleton, cell division, extracellular matrix, vascular biology, aging, senescence, telomere biology, heat-shock proteins, prion proteins, gene expression, RNA editing and binding proteins, microbial pathogenesis, parasitology, virology, drug design and metabolism, plant natural products, photosynthesis and plant energy production, molecular imaging in cells and tissues, carbohydrate metabolism, proteases.

    Computational and Molecular Biophysics: Daved Fremont (DBBSPhDAdmissions@wustl.edu). Structural biology, protein and nucleic acid kinetics and thermodynamics, single-molecule enzymology, protein design, nanoscience, ion channels and lipid membranes, computational biophysics.

    Computational and Systems Biology: Barak Cohen (DBBSPhDAdmissions@wustl.edu). Systems biology, genomics, sequence analysis, regulatory networks, synthetic biology, metagenomics, metabolomics, proteomics, single cell dynamics, high-throughput technology development, applied math and mathematical models of biological processes, computational biology, comparative genomics, personalized medicine, next generation sequencing and its applications, bioinformatics.

Developmental, Regenerative, and Stem Cell Biology: Kerry Kornfeld and James Skeath (DBBSPhDAdmissions@wustl.edu). Development, stem cell biology, regenerative biology, cell biology, genetics, cell signaling, the biology of cancer, epigenetics, circadian rhythms, systems biology.

Evolution, Ecology, and Population Biology: David Queller (DBBSPhDAdmissions@wustl.edu). Population ecology, community ecology, plant and animal evolution, microbial evolution, evolution of behavior, phylogenetics, systematics, theoretical and experimental population genetics.

Human and Statistical Genetics: Patrick Jay and John Rice (DBBSPhDAdmissions@wustl.edu). Human genetics, statistical genetics, functional genomics, molecular genetics, Mendelian disease, complex disease, Mammalian genetics, systems biology.

Immunology: Eugene Otiz (DBBSPhDAdmissions@wustl.edu). Cellular immunology; molecular immunology; lineage development; autoimmunity; cancer immunotherapy; transcription factors; epigenomics; mucosal immunity; innate immunity; bacterial, viral, and parasite immunity; immune evasion; antigen processing and presentation; dendritic cells; T cell signaling; antigen receptor diversification.

Molecular Cell Biology: Heather True-Krob and Jason Weber (DBBSPhDAdmissions@wustl.edu). Cell adhesion, protein trafficking and organelle biogenesis, cell cycle, receptors, signal transduction, gene expression, metabolism, cytoskeleton and motility, membrane excitability, molecular basis of diseases.

Molecular Genetics and Genomics: Tim Schedl and James Skeath (DBBSPhDAdmissions@wustl.edu). Genetics, genetic basis of disease, genomics, epigenetics, genetic engineering, genome editing, model organism genetics, development, cell biology, molecular biology, complex traits, bioinformatics, systems biology.

Molecular Microbiology and Microbial Pathogenesis: David Sibley (DBBSPhDAdmissions@wustl.edu). Host-pathogen interactions, cellular microbiology, comparative genomics, molecular microbiology, microbial pathogenesis, pathogen discovery, emerging infectious diseases, microbial physiology, microbial ecology and energetics, virology, bacteriology, mycology, parasitology.

Neurosciences: Lawrence Snyder and Erik Herzog (DBBSPhDAdmissions@wustl.edu). Neurobiology, neurology, functional imaging, behavior, cognition, computational neuroscience, electrophysiology, sensory systems, motor systems, neuroglia, neuronal development, learning, memory, language, synaptic plasticity, mind, consciousness, neurodegeneration, diseases of the nervous system, neuronal injury, clinical neuroscience, motor control, biological rhythms, connectivity mapping.

Plant and Microbial Bioscience: Joseph Jez and Petra Levin (DBBSPhDAdmissions@wustl.edu). Cell biology, development, physiology, signaling, development, metabolic regulation, photosynthesis, bioenergy, protein structure-function, synthetic biology, biogeochemistry, environmental microbiology, ecology, population genetics, molecular evolution.

Business (Ph.D.): Anjan Thakor (phdinfo@olin.wustl.edu). Accounting, business economics, finance, marketing, organizational behavior, strategy, operations and manufacturing management.

Chemistry (Ph.D.): Bill Buhro (chemistry-admissions@wustl.edu). Bioinorganic, biological, bioorganic, biophysical, materials, nuclear, organic, organometallic, physical, polymer, radiochemistry, spectroscopy, theoretical.

Classics (A.M., Ph.D.): Timothy Moore (classics@wustl.edu). Greek and Latin language and literature, ancient performance, philosophy, history, and material culture.

Comparative Literature (Ph.D.): Lynne Tatlock (ltatlock@wustl.edu). World literature; literary theory; translation studies; global and multicultural theory; comparative drama; comparative arts; studies in literature, politics, and society; narrative theory; media ecologies, histories, and poetics.

Earth and Planetary Sciences (Ph.D.): Viatcheslav Solomatov (mwysession@wustl.edu). Planetary sciences, geology, geobiology, geochemistry, geodynamics.

East Asian Languages and Cultures (A.M., J.D./A.M., Ph.D.): Rebecca Copeland (ealc@wustl.edu). Chinese; Japanese; Chinese fiction, theater, poetry, modern literature; Japanese modern and classical fiction; translation theory; East Asian studies.

Economics (Ph.D.): John Nachbar (nachbar@wustl.edu). Economic theory, industrial organization, political economy, public economics, macroeconomics, public finance, development economics.

Education (M.A.Ed., M.A.T., Ph.D.): Kit Wellmon (kwellman@wustl.edu). Teacher education, educational studies, urban education, policy studies, science and math education, second language research.

English and American Literature (Ph.D.): Wolfram Schmidgen (wschmidg@wustl.edu). Medieval, early modern, early American, eighteenth-century British, nineteenth-century British, nineteenth-century American, twentieth-century British, twentieth-century American, African-American literature and culture, Irish literature, Anglophone postcolonial literature, gender and sexuality studies, modernism, poetry and poetics, theory.

Film and Media Studies (A.M.): Gaylyn Studlar (gstudlar@wustl.edu). Criticism, history, and theories of film and electronic media; all moving image forms of visual culture.

Germanic Languages and Literatures (Ph.D.): Matt Erlin (merlin@wustl.edu). German literature and culture from the Middle Ages through the twenty-first century, intellectual history, film and media studies, gender studies, Holocaust studies, history of the book, digital humanities.

History (Ph.D.): Peter Kastor (pjkastor@wustl.edu). Seventeenth- through nineteenth-century America, twentieth-century America, African history, central Europe, early modern Europe, East Asian history, history of American political culture, international urban history, Middle East, religion in the medieval Mediterranean world.

Institute of Materials Science and Engineering (Ph.D.): Kathy Flores (floresk@wustl.edu). Materials structure, properties, processing, and performance, particularly as related to materials for energy harvesting and storage; materials for environmental remediation and sustainability; materials for regenerative medicine; metallic glasses and other structurally complex materials; plasmonics, photonics, and materials for sensors and imaging; and computational materials science.

Jewish, Islamic, and Near Eastern Languages and Cultures (A.M.): Nancy Berg (nberg@wustl.edu). Islamic and Near Eastern studies (Islamic history, Arabic language and literature, modern Middle East history), Jewish studies (Hebrew Bible, Rabbinic literature, Jewish history, modern Hebrew literature).

Mathematics (A.M., Ph.D.): John McCarthy (mccarthy@wustl.edu). Algebra, algebraic geometry, real and complex analysis, differential geometry, topology, mathematical statistics, survival analysis, modeling, statistical computing for massive data, Bayesian regularization, bioinformatics, longitudinal and functional data analysis, statistical computation, application of statistics to medicine.

Movement Science (Ph.D.): Gammon Earhart (earhartg@wustl.edu). Philosophy of human movement function and dysfunction, with special emphasis on bioenergetics, biomechanics, and biocontrol.

Music (A.M., Ph.D.): Todd Decker (tdecker@wustl.edu). Musicology, ethnomusicology, theory, piano performance and pedagogy.

Performing Arts (A.M.): Mark Rollins (mark@wustl.edu). Theater studies, performance studies, dance.

Philosophy (Ph.D.): Ron Mallon (rmallon@wustl.edu). Ethics, social and political philosophy, history of philosophy, philosophy of law, philosophy of science, philosophy of mind, philosophy of language, theory of knowledge, aesthetics.

Philosophy/Neuroscience/Psychology (Ph.D.): Ron Mallon (pnp@wustl.edu). Philosophy of mind and language, with a special emphasis on the philosophical dimensions of psychology, neuroscience, and linguistics.

Physics (Ph.D.): Mark Alford (alford@wustl.edu). Experimental: astrophysics and space sciences, condensed matter and material physics, applications in biology and medicine, nuclear physics. Theoretical: astrophysics, biophysics, condensed matter and materials physics, elementary particles, many-body theory.

Political Science (Ph.D.): Jim Spriggs (jspriggs@wustl.edu). American politics, comparative politics, formal theory, international politics, law and courts, normative theory, political methodology.

Psychological & Brain Sciences (Ph.D.): Deanna Barch (dbarch@wustl.edu). Behavior/brain/cognition, clinical, development and aging, social/personality.

Rehabilitation and Participation Science (Ph.D.): Carolyn Baum (baumc@wustl.edu). Science of rehabilitation and participation with special emphasis placed on neurorehabilitation, performance, and community participation.

Romance Languages and Literatures (Ph.D.): Michael Sherberg (sherberg@wustl.edu). French language and literature, Latin American and Iberian literature and languages, Spanish and comparative literature.

Social Work (Ph.D.): Renee Cunningham Williams (williamsr@wustl.edu). Mental health, disparities, social and economic development, addictions, aging, child welfare, civic service, disabilities, health, poverty and social policy. Social determinants of health, health disparities, health promotion and disease prevention, health policy, dissemination and implementation, epidemiology, global health.

Speech and Hearing Sciences (Ph.D.): William Clark (elliottb@wustl.edu). Speech and hearing sciences, clinical audiology, deaf education, speech and language, sensory neuroscience.

The Writing Program (M.F.A.W.): David Schuman (dschuman@wustl.edu). Fiction, creative nonfiction, poetry-writing workshops and academic courses.

Programs of Study

A better job, financial security, and personal satisfaction are just some of the end goals for students seeking to earn an advanced degree through graduate study at Western New England University. From business to communication, creative writing to behavior analysis, and programs for teachers and engineers, students gain essential skills and expertise for success in their careers.

Programs in Communication, Accounting, and Curriculum and Instruction are offered entirely online and were developed specifically for that delivery model. Most of the Business and Engineering master's programs follow a blended model, allowing students to study completely online or attend select live sessions on campus. This flexibility enables working professionals to learn at their own pace. Education programs are offered in late afternoon and early evening to accommodate the schedules of working teachers. The low-residency M.F.A. in Creative Writing program includes four short-term residencies with author mentors, and the M.S. in Sport Leadership and Coaching includes two short-term residencies.

The University is regionally accredited by the New England Association of Schools and Colleges.

The **College of Arts and Sciences** offers the following graduate programs:

- Master of Arts in Communication with a public relations concentration
- Master of Arts in English for Teachers
- Master of Arts in Mathematics for Teachers
- Master of Education in Curriculum and Instruction
- Master of Fine Arts in Creative Writing
- Master of Science in Applied Behavior Analysis
- Ph.D. in Behavior Analysis

The **College of Business** offers the following graduate programs:

- Master of Business Administration (M.B.A.)
- Master of Science in Accounting (M.S.A.)
- M.S.A. with Forensic Accounting and Fraud Investigation concentration
- Master of Science in Organizational Leadership (M.S.O.L.)
- Master of Science in Sport Leadership and Coaching (M.S.L.C)
- J.D./M.B.A. combined degree program
- J.D./M.S.A. combined degree program
- J.D./M.S.O.L. combined degree program
- Pharm.D./M.B.A. combined degree program
- Pharm.D./M.S.O.L. combined degree program

The **College of Engineering** offers these graduate programs:

- Master of Science in Civil Engineering (M.S.C.E.)
- Master of Science in Electrical Engineering (M.S.E.E.)
- M.S.E.E. with Mechatronics concentration
- Master of Science in Engineering Management (M.S.E.M.)
- Master of Science in Industrial Engineering (M.S.I.E.)
- Master of Science in Mechanical Engineering (M.S.M.E.)
- M.S.M.E. with Mechatronics concentration
- M.S.E.M./M.B.A. combined degree program

- Ph.D. in Engineering Management
- J.D./M.S.E.M. combined degree program

The University also offers programs though the College of Pharmacy and Health Sciences and the Law School. These include the Juris Doctor, the Doctor of Pharmacy, and the Doctor of Occupational Therapy.

Financial Aid

To be considered for financial aid, a student must have final approval into a degree program and be enrolled in a minimum of 3 credits per term. Financial need-based resources, including grants and low-interest federal loans, may be available for eligible students.

Cost of Study

Western New England University is committed to keeping a high-quality private education affordable for its students. Western New England's graduate tuition rates are some of the most affordable in the region. Tuition for graduate programs is as follows:

College of Arts and Sciences:

- Online M.Ed.: $662 per credit
- M.A.E.T., and M.A.M.T.: $359 per credit
- M.A. in Communication: $769 per credit
- M.F.A. in Creative Writing: $615 per credit
- M.S. in Applied Behavior Analysis: $1,051 per credit
- Ph.D. in Behavior Analysis: $1,312 per credit

College of Business:

- M.B.A., M.S.A., M.S.O.L., and M.S.L.C.: $824 per credit

College of Engineering:

- M.S.C.E., M.S.E.E., M.S.E.M., M.S.I.E., and M.S.M.E.: $1,101 per credit
- Ph.D. in Engineering Management: $1,312 per credit

Living and Housing Costs

Graduate students have the option of living on campus. Housing costs range between $9,600 and $12,432, depending upon the apartment type and duration (10 to 12 months).

Career Development

The Career Development Center assists students and alumni with career planning, occupational exploration, and job search strategies. The center's staff members implement the University's strong commitment to the development of a student's career decision-making by providing individual career advising and assistance in identifying career options.

The Career Development Center staff brings students in contact with employers through dynamic on-campus recruiting, employer information sessions, and career fairs. In addition, students are assisted with resources for part-time and summer employment. A weekly newsletter is published online at www.wne.edu/careercenter and serves as one tool for alerting students to employment opportunities, internships, recruiting schedules, and career-related workshops and activities.

Location

Western New England University's beautiful 215-acre suburban campus is located in Springfield, Massachusetts, the cultural urban center of the western part of the state. Perhaps best known as the birthplace of basketball and home of the Naismith Memorial Basketball Hall of Fame, Springfield is midway between New York and Boston and on the road between New York and Canada. Springfield is ideally located for travel in all directions, and there is convenient access from the University to both the Mass Pike and Interstate 91.

Faculty

With an average class size of 20, students work closely with the University's full-time faculty members who bring outstanding professional and academic credentials to the classroom. On average, 85 percent of graduate courses are taught by full-time faculty members. Ninety percent of the faculty hold terminal degrees in their field.

Additional details about the faculty for specific departments/programs can be found at wne.edu.

The University

Originally established in 1919 to serve working adults, Western New England University is renowned for its innovative programs, culture of collaboration, and faculty members who are focused on student success. Today that commitment continues through the University's graduate programs on campus and online.

Accredited by AACSB International, the College of Business is widely respected throughout the region for the caliber of its flagship M.B.A. program, sought-after M.S.A. degree, and dynamic new offering in organizational leadership. The College of Arts and Sciences offers high-quality master's programs for teachers at an affordable tuition rate and an immersive M.F.A. in Creative Writing program. The College's master's and doctoral programs in Behavior Analysis have positioned the University as a global leader in research and education in that discipline. Accredited by the Association of Behavior Analysis International (ABAI), the Ph.D. in Behavior Analysis program has been cited by the ABAI as ranking third in total scholarly publications out of 74 programs. The thriving College of Engineering is recognized as an educational leader by major corporations in the northeast who seek out graduates of the University's master's and combined engineering/business and law degree programs.

Applying

Western New England University has a rolling admissions policy for most programs, not a set admission deadline. Admission decisions are typically released within two to three weeks of an application being complete. The University urges prospective students to apply as early as possible in relation to the anticipated start date. Most of the graduate programs offer multiple entry points annually. Graduate students can apply online at www.wne.edu/gradapp.

Correspondence and Information

Office of Graduate Admissions
Western New England University
1215 Wilbraham Road
Springfield, Massachusetts 01119
United States
Phone: 413-782-1517
      800-325-1122, Ext. 1517 (toll-free)
E-mail: study@wne.edu
Website: wne.edu/grad

APPENDIXES

Institutional Changes
Since the 2017 Edition

Following is an alphabetical listing of institutions that have recently closed, merged with other institutions, or changed their names or status. In the case of a name change, the former name appears first, followed by the new name.

Alliant International University–México City (Mexico City, Mexico): *closed.*

The American College (Bryn Mawr, PA): *name changed to The American College of Financial Services.*

Andover Newton Theological School (Newton Centre, MA): *now affiliated with Yale Divinity School.*

Argosy University, Washington DC (Arlington, VA): *name changed to Argosy University, Northern Virginia.*

The Art Institute of Dallas, a campus of South University (Dallas, TX): *name changed to The Art Institute of Dallas, a branch of Miami International University of Art & Design.*

Bard Graduate Center: Decorative Arts, Design History, Material Culture (New York, NY): *name changed to Bard Graduate Center.*

Bexley Hall Episcopal Seminary (Columbus, OH): *merged into a single entry for Bexley Seabury Seminary (Chicago, IL).*

Blessing-Rieman College of Nursing (Quincy, IL): *name changed to Blessing-Rieman College of Nursing & Health Sciences.*

California Maritime Academy (Vallejo, CA): *name changed to California State University Maritime Academy.*

California National University for Advanced Studies (Northridge, CA): *closed.*

California School of Podiatric Medicine at Samuel Merritt University (Oakland, CA): *merged as a unit into Samuel Merritt University (Oakland, CA).*

Calvary Bible College and Theological Seminary (Kansas City, MO): *name changed to Calvary University.*

Carolina Graduate School of Divinity (Greensboro, NC): *closed.*

Centenary College (Hackettstown, NJ): *name changed to Centenary University.*

Charlotte School of Law (Charlotte, NC): *will not be enrolling new students for the fall 2017 term.*

Colorado Heights University (Denver, CO): *closed.*

Colorado Technical University Denver South (Aurora, CO): *name changed to Colorado Technical University Aurora.*

The Commonwealth Medical College (Scranton, PA): *name changed to Geisinger Commonwealth School of Medicine.*

Connecticut College (New London, CT): *will not be accepting graduate program applications for the 2017-18 academic year.*

Daniel Webster College (Nashua, NH): *merged into Southern New Hampshire University (Manchester, NH).*

DeVry College of New York (New York, NY): *name changed to DeVry College of New York–Midtown Manhattan Campus.*

DeVry University (Glendale, AZ): *now a DeVry University center and no longer profiled separately.*

DeVry University (Mesa, AZ): *now a DeVry University center and no longer profiled separately.*

DeVry University (Phoenix, AZ): *name changed to DeVry University–Phoenix Campus.*

DeVry University (Alhambra, CA): *closed.*

DeVry University (Anaheim, CA): *now a DeVry University center and no longer profiled separately.*

DeVry University (Fremont, CA): *name changed to DeVry University–Fremont Campus.*

DeVry University (Long Beach, CA): *name changed to DeVry University–Long Beach Campus.*

DeVry University (Oakland, CA): *now a DeVry University center and no longer profiled separately.*

DeVry University (Oxnard, CA): *closed.*

DeVry University (Palmdale, CA): *now a DeVry University center and no longer profiled separately.*

DeVry University (Pomona, CA): *name changed to DeVry University–Pomona Campus.*

DeVry University (San Diego, CA): *name changed to DeVry University–San Diego Campus.*

DeVry University (Colorado Springs, CO): *now a DeVry University center and no longer profiled separately.*

DeVry University (Jacksonville, FL): *name changed to DeVry University–Jacksonville Campus.*

DeVry University (Miramar, FL): *name changed to DeVry University–Miramar Campus.*

DeVry University (Orlando, FL): *name changed to DeVry University–Orlando Campus.*

DeVry University (Alpharetta, GA): *name changed to DeVry University–Alpharetta Campus.*

DeVry University (Decatur, GA): *name changed to DeVry University–Decatur Campus.*

DeVry University (Duluth, GA): *now a DeVry University center and no longer profiled separately.*

DeVry University (Chicago, IL): *name changed to DeVry University–Chicago Campus.*

DeVry University (Downers Grove, IL): *now a DeVry University center and no longer profiled separately.*

DeVry University (Elgin, IL): *now a DeVry University center and no longer profiled separately.*

DeVry University (Gurnee, IL): *now a DeVry University center and no longer profiled separately.*

DeVry University (Naperville, IL): *now a DeVry University center and no longer profiled separately.*

DeVry University (Tinley Park, IL): *name changed to DeVry University–Tinley Park Campus.*

DeVry University (Merrillville, IN): *now a DeVry University center and no longer profiled separately.*

DeVry University (Henderson, NV): *name changed to DeVry University–Henderson Campus.*

DeVry University (North Brunswick, NJ): *name changed to DeVry University–North Brunswick Campus.*

DeVry University (Paramus, NJ): *now a DeVry University center and no longer profiled separately.*

DeVry University (Charlotte, NC): *name changed to DeVry University–Charlotte Campus.*

DeVry University (Columbus, OH): *name changed to DeVry University–Columbus Campus.*

DeVry University (Seven Hills, OH): *name changed to DeVry University–Seven Hills Campus.*

DeVry University (Fort Washington, PA): *name changed to DeVry University–Ft. Washington Campus.*

DeVry University (King of Prussia, PA): *closed.*

DeVry University (Nashville, TN): *name changed to DeVry University–Nashville Campus.*

DeVry University (Irving, TX): *name changed to DeVry University–Irving Campus.*

DeVry University (Arlington, VA): *name changed to DeVry University–Arlington Campus.*

DeVry University (Chesapeake, VA): *name changed to DeVry University–Chesapeake Campus.*

DeVry University (Manassas, VA): *closed.*

Ellis University (Oakbrook Terrace, IL): *closed.*

Everest University (Largo, FL): *closed.*

Everest University (Largo, FL): *closed.*

Everest University (Orlando, FL): *closed.*

Frank Lloyd Wright School of Architecture (Scottsdale, AZ): *name changed to School of Architecture at Taliesin.*

Hillsdale Free Will Baptist College (Moore, OK): *name changed to Randall University.*

Houston College of Law (Houston, TX): *name changed to South Texas College of Law Houston.*

Humphreys College (Stockton, CA): *name changed to Humphreys University.*

ITT Technical Institute (Indianapolis, IN): *closed.*

John Marshall Law School (Chicago, IL): *name changed to The John Marshall Law School.*

Lakehead University–Orillia (Orillia, ON, Canada): *name changed to Lakehead University.*

Long Island University–Hudson at Rockland (Orangeburg, NY): *merged into a single entry for Long Island University–Hudson (Purchase, NY) by request from the institution.*

Mary Baldwin College (Staunton, VA): *name changed to Mary Baldwin University.*

The Master's College and Seminary (Santa Clarita, CA): *name changed to The Master's University.*

Mayo Graduate School (Rochester, MN): *name changed to Mayo Clinic Graduate School of Biomedical Sciences.*

Mayo Medical School (Rochester, MN): *name changed to Mayo Clinic School of Medicine.*

Mayo School of Health Sciences (Rochester, MN): *name changed to Mayo Clinic School of Health Sciences.*

National College of Natural Medicine (Portland, OR): *name changed to National University of Natural Medicine.*

Oregon College of Art & Craft (Portland, OR): *name changed to Oregon College of Art and Craft.*

Our Lady of the Lake University of San Antonio (San Antonio, TX): *name changed to Our Lady of the Lake University.*

Phillips Graduate Institute (Encino, CA): *name changed to Phillips Graduate University.*

Pinchot University (Seattle, WA): *acquired by Presidio Graduate School (San Francisco, CA).*

Purdue University Northwest (Westville, IN): *merged into a single entry for Purdue University Northwest (Hammond, IN).*

Rabbi Isaac Elchanan Theological Seminary (New York, NY): *merged into Yeshiva University (New York, NY).*

Saint Joseph's College (Rensselaer, IN): *closed.*

School of the Museum of Fine Arts, Boston (Boston, MA): *merged as a unit into Tufts University (Medford, MA).*

Seabury-Western Theological Seminary (Evanston, IL): *name changed to Bexley Seabury Seminary.*

Seminary of the Immaculate Conception (Huntington, NY): *no longer degree granting.*

Summit University (Clarks Summit, PA): *name changed to Clarks Summit University.*

Tennessee Wesleyan College (Athens, TN): *name changed to Tennessee Wesleyan University.*

Texas A&M University at Galveston (Galveston, TX): *merged as a unit into Texas A&M University (College Station, TX).*

Waldorf College (Forest City, IA): *name changed to Waldorf University*

Abbreviations Used in the Guides

The following list includes abbreviations of degree names used in the profiles in the 2017 edition of the guide. Because some degrees (e.g., Doctor of Education) can be abbreviated in more than one way (e.g., D.Ed. or Ed.D.), and because the abbreviations used in the guides reflect the preferences of the individual colleges and universities, the list may include two or more abbreviations for a single degree.

DEGREES

A Mus D	Doctor of Musical Arts
AC	Advanced Certificate
AD	Artist's Diploma
	Doctor of Arts
ADP	Artist's Diploma
Adv C	Advanced Certificate
AGC	Advanced Graduate Certificate
AGSC	Advanced Graduate Specialist Certificate
ALM	Master of Liberal Arts
AM	Master of Arts
AMBA	Accelerated Master of Business Administration
APC	Advanced Professional Certificate
APMPH	Advanced Professional Master of Public Health
App Sc	Applied Scientist
App Sc D	Doctor of Applied Science
AstE	Astronautical Engineer
ATC	Advanced Training Certificate
Au D	Doctor of Audiology
B Th	Bachelor of Theology
BN	Bachelor of Naturopathy
CAES	Certificate of Advanced Educational Specialization
CAGS	Certificate of Advanced Graduate Studies
CAL	Certificate in Applied Linguistics
CAPS	Certificate of Advanced Professional Studies
CAS	Certificate of Advanced Studies
CASR	Certificate in Advanced Social Research
CATS	Certificate of Achievement in Theological Studies
CBHS	Certificate in Basic Health Sciences
CCJA	Certificate in Criminal Justice Administration
CE	Civil Engineer
CEM	Certificate of Environmental Management
CET	Certificate in Educational Technologies
CGS	Certificate of Graduate Studies
Ch E	Chemical Engineer
Clin Sc D	Doctor of Clinical Science
CM	Certificate in Management
CMH	Certificate in Medical Humanities
CMM	Master of Church Ministries
CMS	Certificate in Ministerial Studies
CNM	Certificate in Nonprofit Management
CPC	Certificate in Professional Counseling
	Certificate in Publication and Communication
CPH	Certificate in Public Health
CPM	Certificate in Public Management
CPS	Certificate of Professional Studies

CScD	Doctor of Clinical Science
CSD	Certificate in Spiritual Direction
CSS	Certificate of Special Studies
CTS	Certificate of Theological Studies
CURP	Certificate in Urban and Regional Planning
D Admin	Doctor of Administration
D Arch	Doctor of Architecture
D Be	Doctor in Bioethics
D Com	Doctor of Commerce
D Couns	Doctor of Counseling
D Des	Doctorate of Design
D Div	Doctor of Divinity
D Ed	Doctor of Education
D Ed Min	Doctor of Educational Ministry
D Eng	Doctor of Engineering
D Engr	Doctor of Engineering
D Ent	Doctor of Enterprise
D Env	Doctor of Environment
D Law	Doctor of Law
D Litt	Doctor of Letters
D Med Sc	Doctor of Medical Science
D Mgt	Doctor of Management
D Min	Doctor of Ministry
D Miss	Doctor of Missiology
D Mus	Doctor of Music
D Mus A	Doctor of Musical Arts
D Phil	Doctor of Philosophy
D Prof	Doctor of Professional Studies
D Ps	Doctor of Psychology
D Sc	Doctor of Science
D Sc D	Doctor of Science in Dentistry
D Sc IS	Doctor of Science in Information Systems
D Sc PA	Doctor of Science in Physician Assistant Studies
D Th	Doctor of Theology
D Th P	Doctor of Practical Theology
DA	Doctor of Accounting
	Doctor of Arts
DACM	Doctor of Acupuncture and Chinese Medicine
DAH	Doctor of Arts in Humanities
DAIS	Doctor of Applied Intercultural Studies
DAOM	Doctorate in Acupuncture and Oriental Medicine
DAT	Doctorate of Athletic Training
	Professional Doctor of Art Therapy
DBA	Doctor of Business Administration
DBH	Doctor of Behavioral Health
DBL	Doctor of Business Leadership
DC	Doctor of Chiropractic
DCC	Doctor of Computer Science
DCD	Doctor of Communications Design
DCE	Doctor of Computer Engineering
DCFT	Doctor of Couple and Family Therapy
DCL	Doctor of Civil Law
	Doctor of Comparative Law

DCM	Doctor of Church Music
DCN	Doctor of Clinical Nutrition
DCS	Doctor of Computer Science
DDN	Diplôme du Droit Notarial
DDS	Doctor of Dental Surgery
DE	Doctor of Education
	Doctor of Engineering
DED	Doctor of Economic Development
DEIT	Doctor of Educational Innovation and Technology
DEL	Doctor of Executive Leadership
DEM	Doctor of Educational Ministry
DEPD	Diplôme Études Spécialisées
DES	Doctor of Engineering Science
DESS	Diplôme Études Supérieures Spécialisées
DET	Doctor of Educational Technology
DFA	Doctor of Fine Arts
DGP	Diploma in Graduate and Professional Studies
DH Sc	Doctor of Health Sciences
DHA	Doctor of Health Administration
DHCE	Doctor of Health Care Ethics
DHL	Doctor of Hebrew Letters
DHPE	Doctorate of Health Professionals Education
DHS	Doctor of Health Science
DHSc	Doctor of Health Science
DIT	Doctor of Industrial Technology
	Doctor of Information Technology
DJS	Doctor of Jewish Studies
DLS	Doctor of Liberal Studies
DM	Doctor of Management
	Doctor of Music
DMA	Doctor of Musical Arts
DMD	Doctor of Dental Medicine
DME	Doctor of Manufacturing Management
	Doctor of Music Education
DMEd	Doctor of Music Education
DMFT	Doctor of Marital and Family Therapy
DMH	Doctor of Medical Humanities
DML	Doctor of Modern Languages
DMP	Doctorate in Medical Physics
DMPNA	Doctor of Management Practice in Nurse Anesthesia
DN Sc	Doctor of Nursing Science
DNAP	Doctor of Nurse Anesthesia Practice
DNP	Doctor of Nursing Practice
DNP-A	Doctor of Nursing Practice - Anesthesia
DNS	Doctor of Nursing Science
DO	Doctor of Osteopathy
DOT	Doctor of Occupational Therapy
DPA	Diploma in Public Administration
	Doctor of Public Administration
DPDS	Doctor of Planning and Development Studies
DPH	Doctor of Public Health
DPM	Doctor of Plant Medicine
	Doctor of Podiatric Medicine
DPPD	Doctor of Policy, Planning, and Development
DPS	Doctor of Professional Studies
DPT	Doctor of Physical Therapy
DPTSc	Doctor of Physical Therapy Science
Dr DES	Doctor of Design

Dr NP	Doctor of Nursing Practice
Dr OT	Doctor of Occupational Therapy
Dr PH	Doctor of Public Health
Dr Sc PT	Doctor of Science in Physical Therapy
DrAP	Doctor of Anesthesia Practice
DRSc	Doctor of Regulatory Science
DS	Doctor of Science
DScPT	Doctor of Science in Physical Therapy
DSJS	Doctor of Science in Jewish Studies
DSL	Doctor of Strategic Leadership
DSS	Doctor of Strategic Security
DSW	Doctor of Social Work
DTL	Doctor of Talmudic Law
	Doctor of Transformational Leadership
DV Sc	Doctor of Veterinary Science
DVM	Doctor of Veterinary Medicine
DWS	Doctor of Worship Studies
EAA	Engineer in Aeronautics and Astronautics
EASPh D	Engineering and Applied Science Doctor of Philosophy
ECS	Engineer in Computer Science
Ed D	Doctor of Education
Ed DCT	Doctor of Education in College Teaching
Ed L D	Doctor of Education Leadership
Ed M	Master of Education
Ed S	Specialist in Education
Ed Sp	Specialist in Education
EDB	Executive Doctorate in Business
EDBA	Executive Doctor of Business Administration
EDM	Executive Doctorate in Management
EE	Electrical Engineer
EJD	Executive Juris Doctor
EMBA	Executive Master of Business Administration
EMFA	Executive Master of Forensic Accounting
EMHA	Executive Master of Health Administration
EMHCL	Executive Master in Healthcare Leadership
EMIB	Executive Master of International Business
EMIR	Executive Master in International Relations
EML	Executive Master of Leadership
EMPA	Executive Master of Public Administration
EMPL	Executive Master in Public Leadership
EMS	Executive Master of Science
EMTM	Executive Master of Technology Management
Eng	Engineer
Eng Sc D	Doctor of Engineering Science
Engr	Engineer
Exec MHA	Executive Master of Health Administration
Exec Ed D	Executive Doctor of Education
Exec MBA	Executive Master of Business Administration
Exec MPA	Executive Master of Public Administration
Exec MPH	Executive Master of Public Health
Exec MS	Executive Master of Science
G Dip	Graduate Diploma
GBC	Graduate Business Certificate
GDM	Graduate Diploma in Management
GDPA	Graduate Diploma in Public Administration
GEMBA	Global Executive Master of Business Administration
GM Acc	Graduate Master of Accountancy
GMBA	Global Master of Business Administration

GP LL M	Global Professional Master of Laws
GPD	Graduate Performance Diploma
GSS	Graduate Special Certificate for Students in Special Situations
IEMBA	International Executive Master of Business Administration
IMA	Interdisciplinary Master of Arts
IMBA	International Master of Business Administration
IMES	International Master's in Environmental Studies
Ingeniero	Engineer
JCD	Doctor of Canon Law
JCL	Licentiate in Canon Law
JD	Juris Doctor
JM	Juris Master
JSD	Doctor of Juridical Science
	Doctor of Jurisprudence
	Doctor of the Science of Law
JSM	Master of the Science of Law
L Th	Licenciate in Theology
LL B	Bachelor of Laws
LL CM	Master of Comparative Law
LL D	Doctor of Laws
LL M	Master of Laws
LL M in Tax	Master of Laws in Taxation
LL M CL	Master of Laws in Common Law
M Ac	Master of Accountancy
	Master of Accounting
	Master of Acupuncture
M Ac OM	Master of Acupuncture and Oriental Medicine
M Acc	Master of Accountancy
	Master of Accounting
M Acct	Master of Accountancy
	Master of Accounting
M Accy	Master of Accountancy
M Actg	Master of Accounting
M Acy	Master of Accountancy
M Ad	Master of Administration
M Ad Ed	Master of Adult Education
M Adm	Master of Administration
M Adm Mgt	Master of Administrative Management
M Admin	Master of Administration
M ADU	Master of Architectural Design and Urbanism
M Adv	Master of Advertising
M AEST	Master of Applied Environmental Science and Technology
M Ag	Master of Agriculture
M Ag Ed	Master of Agricultural Education
M Agr	Master of Agriculture
M App Comp Sc	Master of Applied Computer Science
M App St	Master of Applied Statistics
M Appl Stat	Master of Applied Statistics
M Aq	Master of Aquaculture
M Ar	Master of Architecture
M Arc	Master of Architecture
M Arch	Master of Architecture
M Arch I	Master of Architecture I
M Arch II	Master of Architecture II
M Arch E	Master of Architectural Engineering
M Arch H	Master of Architectural History

M Bioethics	Master in Bioethics
M Biomath	Master of Biomathematics
M Cat	Master of Catechesis
M Ch E	Master of Chemical Engineering
M Cl D	Master of Clinical Dentistry
M Cl Sc	Master of Clinical Science
M Comm	Master of Communication
M Comp	Master of Computing
M Comp Sc	Master of Computer Science
M Coun	Master of Counseling
M Dent	Master of Dentistry
M Dent Sc	Master of Dental Sciences
M Des	Master of Design
M Des S	Master of Design Studies
M Div	Master of Divinity
M E Sci	Master of Earth Science
M Ec	Master of Economics
M Econ	Master of Economics
M Ed	Master of Education
M Ed T	Master of Education in Teaching
M En	Master of Engineering
M En S	Master of Environmental Sciences
M Eng	Master of Engineering
M Eng Mgt	Master of Engineering Management
M Engr	Master of Engineering
M Ent	Master of Enterprise
M Env	Master of Environment
M Env Des	Master of Environmental Design
M Env E	Master of Environmental Engineering
M Env Sc	Master of Environmental Science
M Fin	Master of Finance
M Geo E	Master of Geological Engineering
M Geoenv E	Master of Geoenvironmental Engineering
M Geog	Master of Geography
M Hum	Master of Humanities
M IDST	Master's in Interdisciplinary Studies
M Jur	Master of Jurisprudence
M Kin	Master of Kinesiology
M Land Arch	Master of Landscape Architecture
M Litt	Master of Letters
M Mark	Master of Marketing
M Mat SE	Master of Material Science and Engineering
M Math	Master of Mathematics
M Mech E	Master of Mechanical Engineering
M Med Sc	Master of Medical Science
M Mgmt	Master of Management
M Mgt	Master of Management
M Min	Master of Ministries
M Mtl E	Master of Materials Engineering
M Mu	Master of Music
M Mus	Master of Music
M Mus Ed	Master of Music Education
M Music	Master of Music
M Pet E	Master of Petroleum Engineering
M Pharm	Master of Pharmacy
M Phil	Master of Philosophy
M Phil F	Master of Philosophical Foundations
M Pl	Master of Planning
M Plan	Master of Planning

M Pol	Master of Political Science	MAA	Master of Applied Anthropology
M Pr Met	Master of Professional Meteorology		Master of Applied Arts
M Prob S	Master of Probability and Statistics		Master of Arts in Administration
M Psych	Master of Psychology	MAAA	Master of Arts in Arts Administration
M Pub	Master of Publishing	MAAAP	Master of Arts Administration and Policy
M Rel	Master of Religion	MAAD	Master of Advanced Architectural Design
M Sc	Master of Science	MAAE	Master of Arts in Art Education
M Sc A	Master of Science (Applied)	MAAS	Master of Arts in Aging and Spirituality
M Sc AC	Master of Science in Applied Computing	MAASJ	Master of Arts in Applied Social Justice
M Sc AHN	Master of Science in Applied Human Nutrition	MAAT	Master of Arts in Applied Theology
M Sc BMC	Master of Science in Biomedical Communications		Master of Arts in Art Therapy
M Sc CS	Master of Science in Computer Science	MAB	Master of Agribusiness
M Sc E	Master of Science in Engineering		Master of Applied Bioengineering
M Sc Eng	Master of Science in Engineering	MABA	Master's in Applied Behavior Analysis
M Sc Engr	Master of Science in Engineering	MABC	Master of Arts in Biblical Counseling
M Sc F	Master of Science in Forestry	MABE	Master of Arts in Bible Exposition
M Sc FE	Master of Science in Forest Engineering	MABL	Master of Arts in Biblical Languages
M Sc Geogr	Master of Science in Geography	MABM	Master of Agribusiness Management
M Sc N	Master of Science in Nursing	MABS	Master of Arts in Biblical Studies
M Sc OT	Master of Science in Occupational Therapy	MABT	Master of Arts in Bible Teaching
M Sc P	Master of Science in Planning	MAC	Master of Accountancy
M Sc Pl	Master of Science in Planning		Master of Accounting
M Sc PT	Master of Science in Physical Therapy		Master of Arts in Communication
M Sc T	Master of Science in Teaching		Master of Arts in Counseling
M SEM	Master of Sustainable Environmental Management	MACC	Master of Arts in Christian Counseling
			Master of Arts in Clinical Counseling
M Serv Soc	Master of Social Service	MACCT	Master of Accounting
M Soc	Master of Sociology	MACD	Master of Arts in Christian Doctrine
M Sp Ed	Master of Special Education	MACE	Master of Arts in Christian Education
M St	Master of Studies	MACH	Master of Arts in Church History
M Stat	Master of Statistics	MACI	Master of Arts in Curriculum and Instruction
M Sys E	Master of Systems Engineering	MACIS	Master of Accounting and Information Systems
M Sys Sc	Master of Systems Science	MACJ	Master of Arts in Criminal Justice
M Tax	Master of Taxation	MACL	Master of Arts in Christian Leadership
M Tech	Master of Technology		Master of Arts in Community Leadership
M Th	Master of Theology	MACM	Master of Arts in Christian Ministries
M Tox	Master of Toxicology		Master of Arts in Christian Ministry
M Trans E	Master of Transportation Engineering		Master of Arts in Church Music
M U Ed	Master of Urban Education		Master of Arts in Counseling Ministries
M Urb	Master of Urban Planning	MACML	Master of Arts in Christian Ministry and Leadership
M Vet Sc	Master of Veterinary Science	MACN	Master of Arts in Counseling
MA	Master of Accounting	MACO	Master of Arts in Counseling
	Master of Administration	MAcOM	Master of Acupuncture and Oriental Medicine
	Master of Arts	MACP	Master of Arts in Christian Practice
MA Comm	Master of Arts in Communication		Master of Arts in Church Planting
MA Ed	Master of Arts in Education		Master of Arts in Counseling Psychology
MA Ed/HD	Master of Arts in Education and Human Development	MACS	Master of Applied Computer Science
			Master of Arts in Catholic Studies
MA Ext	Master of Agricultural Extension		Master of Arts in Christian Studies
MA Islamic	Master of Arts in Islamic Studies	MACSE	Master of Arts in Christian School Education
MA Min	Master of Arts in Ministry	MACT	Master of Arts in Communications and Technology
MA Miss	Master of Arts in Missiology	MAD	Master in Educational Institution Administration
MA Past St	Master of Arts in Pastoral Studies		
MA Ph	Master of Arts in Philosophy		Master of Art and Design
MA Psych	Master of Arts in Psychology		
MA Sc	Master of Applied Science	MADR	Master of Arts in Dispute Resolution
MA Sp	Master of Arts (Spirituality)	MADS	Master of Animal and Dairy Science
MA Th	Master of Arts in Theology		Master of Applied Disability Studies
MA-R	Master of Arts (Research)	MAE	Master of Aerospace Engineering

	Master of Agricultural Economics	MAM	Master of Acquisition Management
	Master of Agricultural Education		Master of Agriculture and Management
	Master of Applied Economics		Master of Applied Mathematics
	Master of Architectural Engineering		Master of Arts in Management
	Master of Art Education		Master of Arts in Ministry
	Master of Arts in Education		Master of Arts Management
	Master of Arts in English		Master of Avian Medicine
MAEd	Master of Arts Education		Master of Aviation Management
MAEE	Master of Agricultural and Extension Education	MAMC	Master of Arts in Mass Communication
MAEL	Master of Arts in Educational Leadership		Master of Arts in Ministry and Culture
MAEM	Master of Arts in Educational Ministries		Master of Arts in Ministry for a Multicultural Church
MAEP	Master of Arts in Economic Policy		
	Master of Arts in Educational Psychology	MAME	Master of Arts in Missions/Evangelism
MAES	Master of Arts in Environmental Sciences	MAMFC	Master of Arts in Marriage and Family Counseling
MAET	Master of Arts in English Teaching	MAMFT	Master of Arts in Marriage and Family Therapy
MAF	Master of Arts in Finance	MAMHC	Master of Arts in Mental Health Counseling
MAFE	Master of Arts in Financial Economics	MAMS	Master of Applied Mathematical Sciences
MAFLL	Master of Arts in Foreign Language and Literature		Master of Arts in Ministerial Studies
MAFM	Master of Accounting and Financial Management		Master of Arts in Ministry and Spirituality
MAFS	Master of Arts in Family Studies	MAMT	Master of Arts in Mathematics Teaching
MAG	Master of Applied Geography	MAN	Master of Applied Nutrition
MAGU	Master of Urban Analysis and Management	MANT	Master of Arts in New Testament
MAH	Master of Arts in Humanities	MAOL	Master of Arts in Organizational Leadership
MAHA	Master of Arts in Humanitarian Assistance	MAOM	Master of Acupuncture and Oriental Medicine
MAHCM	Master of Arts in Health Care Mission	MAOT	Master of Arts in Old Testament
MAHG	Master of American History and Government	MAP	Master of Applied Politics
MAHL	Master of Arts in Hebrew Letters		Master of Applied Psychology
MAHN	Master of Applied Human Nutrition		Master of Arts in Planning
MAHR	Master of Applied Historical Research		Master of Psychology
MAHS	Master of Arts in Human Services		Master of Public Administration
MAHSR	Master in Applied Health Services Research	MAP Min	Master of Arts in Pastoral Ministry
MAIA	Master of Arts in International Administration	MAPA	Master of Arts in Public Administration
	Master of Arts in International Affairs	MAPC	Master of Arts in Pastoral Counseling
MAICS	Master of Arts in Intercultural Studies	MAPE	Master of Arts in Physics Education
MAIDM	Master of Arts in Interior Design and Merchandising	MAPM	Master of Arts in Pastoral Ministry
			Master of Arts in Pastoral Music
MAIH	Master of Arts in Interdisciplinary Humanities		Master of Arts in Practical Ministry
MAIOP	Master of Applied Industrial/Organizational Psychology	MAPP	Master of Arts in Public Policy
		MAPS	Master of Applied Psychological Sciences
MAIS	Master of Arts in Intercultural Studies		Master of Arts in Pastoral Studies
	Master of Arts in Interdisciplinary Studies		Master of Arts in Public Service
	Master of Arts in International Studies	MAPT	Master of Practical Theology
MAIT	Master of Administration in Information Technology	MAPW	Master of Arts in Professional Writing
		MAQRM	Master's of Actuarial Science and Quantitative Risk Management
MAJ	Master of Arts in Journalism	MAR	Master of Arts in Reading
MAJCS	Master of Arts in Jewish Communal Service		Master of Arts in Religion
MAJPS	Master of Arts in Jewish Professional Studies	Mar Eng	Marine Engineer
MAJS	Master of Arts in Jewish Studies	MARC	Master of Arts in Rehabilitation Counseling
MAL	Master in Agricultural Leadership	MARE	Master of Arts in Religious Education
	Master of Athletic Leadership	MARL	Master of Arts in Religious Leadership
MALA	Master of Arts in Liberal Arts	MARS	Master of Arts in Religious Studies
MALCM	Master in Arts Leadership and Cultural Management	MAS	Master of Accounting Science
			Master of Actuarial Science
MALD	Master of Arts in Law and Diplomacy		Master of Administrative Science
MALER	Master of Arts in Labor and Employment Relations		Master of Advanced Study
			Master of American Studies
MALL	Master of Arts in Language Learning		Master of Animal Science
MALP	Master of Arts in Language Pedagogy		Master of Applied Science
MALS	Master of Arts in Liberal Studies		

	Master of Applied Statistics
	Master of Archival Studies
MASA	Master of Advanced Studies in Architecture
MASC	Master of Arts in School Counseling
MASD	Master of Arts in Spiritual Direction
MASE	Master of Arts in Special Education
MASF	Master of Arts in Spiritual Formation
MASJ	Master of Arts in Systems of Justice
MASLA	Master of Advanced Studies in Landscape Architecture
MASM	Master of Aging Services Management
	Master of Arts in Specialized Ministries
MASP	Master of Arts in School Psychology
MASS	Master of Applied Social Science
	Master of Arts in Social Science
MAST	Master of Arts in Science Teaching
MASW	Master of Aboriginal Social Work
MAT	Master of Arts in Teaching
	Master of Arts in Theology
	Master of Athletic Training
	Master's in Administration of Telecommunications
Mat E	Materials Engineer
MATCM	Master of Acupuncture and Traditional Chinese Medicine
MATDE	Master of Arts in Theology, Development, and Evangelism
MATDR	Master of Territorial Management and Regional Development
MATE	Master of Arts for the Teaching of English
MATESL	Master of Arts in Teaching English as a Second Language
MATESOL	Master of Arts in Teaching English to Speakers of Other Languages
MATF	Master of Arts in Teaching English as a Foreign Language/Intercultural Studies
MATFL	Master of Arts in Teaching Foreign Language
MATH	Master of Arts in Therapy
MATI	Master of Administration of Information Technology
MATL	Master of Arts in Teaching of Languages
	Master of Arts in Transformational Leadership
MATM	Master of Arts in Teaching of Mathematics
MATRN	Master of Athletic Training
MATS	Master of Arts in Theological Studies
	Master of Arts in Transforming Spirituality
MAUA	Master of Arts in Urban Affairs
MAUD	Master of Arts in Urban Design
MAURP	Master of Arts in Urban and Regional Planning
MAW	Master of Arts in Worship
MAWSHP	Master of Arts in Worship
MAYM	Master of Arts in Youth Ministry
MB	Master of Bioinformatics
MBA	Master of Business Administration
MBA-AM	Master of Business Administration in Aviation Management
MBA-EP	Master of Business Administration–Experienced Professionals
MBAA	Master of Business Administration in Aviation
MBAE	Master of Biological and Agricultural Engineering
	Master of Biosystems and Agricultural Engineering
MBAH	Master of Business Administration in Health
MBAi	Master of Business Administration–International
MBAICT	Master of Business Administration in Information and Communication Technology
MBC	Master of Building Construction
MBE	Master of Bilingual Education
	Master of Bioengineering
	Master of Bioethics
	Master of Biomedical Engineering
	Master of Business Economics
	Master of Business Education
MBEE	Master in Biotechnology Enterprise and Entrepreneurship
MBET	Master of Business, Entrepreneurship and Technology
MBI	Master in Business Informatics
MBIOT	Master of Biotechnology
MBiotech	Master of Biotechnology
MBL	Master of Business Leadership
MBLE	Master in Business Logistics Engineering
MBME	Master's in Biomedical Engineering
MBMSE	Master of Business Management and Software Engineering
MBOE	Master of Business Operational Excellence
MBS	Master of Biblical Studies
	Master of Biological Science
	Master of Biomedical Sciences
	Master of Bioscience
	Master of Building Science
	Master of Business and Science
	Master of Business Statistics
MBST	Master of Biostatistics
MBT	Master of Biomedical Technology
	Master of Biotechnology
	Master of Business Taxation
MBV	Master of Business for Veterans
MC	Master of Classics
	Master of Communication
	Master of Counseling
	Master of Cybersecurity
MC Ed	Master of Continuing Education
MC Sc	Master of Computer Science
MCA	Master of Commercial Aviation
	Master of Communication Arts
	Master of Criminology (Applied)
MCAM	Master of Computational and Applied Mathematics
MCC	Master of Computer Science
MCD	Master of Communications Disorders
	Master of Community Development
MCE	Master in Electronic Commerce
	Master of Chemistry Education
	Master of Christian Education
	Master of Civil Engineering
	Master of Control Engineering
MCEM	Master of Construction Engineering Management
MCEPA	Master of Chinese Economic and Political Affairs
MCHE	Master of Chemical Engineering

MCIS	Master of Communication and Information Studies
	Master of Computer and Information Science
	Master of Computer Information Systems
MCIT	Master of Computer and Information Technology
MCJ	Master of Criminal Justice
MCL	Master in Communication Leadership
	Master of Canon Law
	Master of Christian Leadership
	Master of Comparative Law
MCM	Master of Christian Ministry
	Master of Church Ministry
	Master of Church Music
	Master of City Management
	Master of Communication Management
	Master of Community Medicine
	Master of Construction Management
	Master of Contract Management
MCMin	Master of Christian Ministry
MCMM	Master in Communications and Media Management
MCMP	Master of City and Metropolitan Planning
MCMS	Master of Clinical Medical Science
MCN	Master of Clinical Nutrition
MCOL	Master of Arts in Community and Organizational Leadership
MCP	Master of City Planning
	Master of Community Planning
	Master of Counseling Psychology
	Master of Cytopathology Practice
	Master of Science in Quality Systems and Productivity
MCPC	Master of Arts in Chaplaincy and Pastoral Care
MCPD	Master of Community Planning and Development
MCR	Master in Clinical Research
MCRP	Master of City and Regional Planning
	Master of Community and Regional Planning
MCRS	Master of City and Regional Studies
MCS	Master of Chemical Sciences
	Master of Christian Studies
	Master of Clinical Science
	Master of Combined Sciences
	Master of Communication Studies
	Master of Computer Science
	Master of Consumer Science
MCSE	Master of Computer Science and Engineering
MCSL	Master of Catholic School Leadership
MCSM	Master of Construction Science and Management
MCT	Master of Commerce and Technology
MCTM	Master of Clinical Translation Management
MCTP	Master of Communication Technology and Policy
MCTS	Master of Clinical and Translational Science
MCVS	Master of Cardiovascular Science
MD	Doctor of Medicine
MDA	Master of Dietetic Administration
MDB	Master of Design-Build
MDE	Master in Design Engineering

	Master of Developmental Economics
	Master of Distance Education
	Master of the Education of the Deaf
MDH	Master of Dental Hygiene
MDI	Masters of Disruptive Innovation
MDM	Master of Design Methods
	Master of Digital Media
MDP	Master in Sustainable Development Practice
	Master of Development Practice
MDR	Master of Dispute Resolution
MDS	Master in Data Science
	Master of Dental Surgery
	Master of Design Studies
	Master of Digital Sciences
ME	Master of Education
	Master of Engineering
	Master of Entrepreneurship
ME Sc	Master of Engineering Science
ME-PD	Master of Education–Professional Development
MEA	Master of Educational Administration
	Master of Engineering Administration
MEAE	Master of Entertainment Arts and Engineering
MEAP	Master of Environmental Administration and Planning
MEB	Master of Energy Business
MEBD	Master in Environmental Building Design
MEBT	Master in Electronic Business Technologies
MEC	Master of Electronic Commerce
Mech E	Mechanical Engineer
MED	Master of Education of the Deaf
MEDS	Master of Environmental Design Studies
MEE	Master in Education
	Master of Electrical Engineering
	Master of Energy Engineering
	Master of Environmental Engineering
MEECON	Master of Energy Economics
MEEM	Master of Environmental Engineering and Management
MEENE	Master of Engineering in Environmental Engineering
MEEP	Master of Environmental and Energy Policy
MEERM	Master of Earth and Environmental Resource Management
MEH	Master in Humanistic Studies
	Master of Environmental Health
	Master of Environmental Horticulture
MEHS	Master of Environmental Health and Safety
MEIM	Master of Entertainment Industry Management
	Master of Equine Industry Management
MEL	Master of Educational Leadership
	Master of English Literature
MELP	Master of Environmental Law and Policy
MEM	Master of Engineering Management
	Master of Environmental Management
	Master of Marketing
MEME	Master of Engineering in Manufacturing Engineering
	Master of Engineering in Mechanical Engineering
MENR	Master of Environment and Natural Resources
MENVEGR	Master of Environmental Engineering

MEP	Master of Engineering Physics	MGBA	Master of Global Business Administration
MEPC	Master of Environmental Pollution Control	MGC	Master of Genetic Counseling
MEPD	Master of Environmental Planning and Design	MGCS	Master of Genetic Counselor Studies
MER	Master of Employment Relations	MGD	Master of Graphic Design
MERE	Master of Entrepreneurial Real Estate	MGE	Master of Geotechnical Engineering
MERL	Master of Energy Regulation and Law	MGEM	Master of Global Entrepreneurship and Management
MES	Master of Education and Science		
	Master of Engineering Science	MGIS	Master of Geographic Information Science
	Master of Environment and Sustainability		Master of Geographic Information Systems
	Master of Environmental Science	MGM	Master of Global Management
	Master of Environmental Studies	MGMA	Master of Greenhouse Gas Management and Accounting
	Master of Environmental Systems		
MESM	Master of Environmental Science and Management	MGP	Master of Gestion de Projet
		MGPS	Master of Global Policy Studies
MET	Master of Educational Technology	MGREM	Master of Global Real Estate Management
	Master of Engineering Technology	MGS	Master of Gender Studies
	Master of Entertainment Technology		Master of Gerontological Studies
	Master of Environmental Toxicology		Master of Global Studies
METM	Master of Engineering and Technology Management	MGsc	Master of Geoscience
		MH	Master of Humanities
MEVE	Master of Environmental Engineering	MH Sc	Master of Health Sciences
MF	Master of Finance	MHA	Master of Health Administration
	Master of Forestry		Master of Healthcare Administration
MFA	Master of Financial Administration		Master of Hospital Administration
	Master of Fine Arts		Master of Hospitality Administration
MFALP	Master of Food and Agriculture Law and Policy	MHB	Master of Human Behavior
MFAM	Master's of Food Animal Medicine	MHC	Master of Mental Health Counseling
MFAS	Master of Fisheries and Aquatic Science	MHCA	Master of Health Care Administration
MFC	Master of Forest Conservation	MHCD	Master of Health Care Design
MFCS	Master of Family and Consumer Sciences	MHCI	Master of Human-Computer Interaction
MFE	Master of Financial Economics	MHCL	Master of Health Care Leadership
	Master of Financial Engineering	MHE	Master of Health Education
	Master of Forest Engineering		Master of Human Ecology
MFES	Master of Fire and Emergency Services	MHE Ed	Master of Home Economics Education
MFG	Master of Functional Genomics	MHEA	Master of Higher Education Administration
MFHD	Master of Family and Human Development	MHHS	Master of Health and Human Services
MFIN	Master of Finance	MHI	Master of Health Informatics
MFM	Master of Financial Management		Master of Healthcare Innovation
	Master of Financial Mathematics	MHID	Master of Healthcare Interior Design
MFPE	Master of Food Process Engineering	MHIHIM	Master of Health Informatics and Health Information Management
MFR	Master of Forest Resources		
MFRC	Master of Forest Resources and Conservation	MHIIM	Master of Health Informatics and Information Management
MFRE	Master of Food and Resource Economics		
MFS	Master of Food Science	MHK	Master of Human Kinetics
	Master of Forensic Sciences	MHM	Master of Healthcare Management
	Master of Forest Science	MHMS	Master of Health Management Systems
	Master of Forest Studies	MHP	Master of Health Physics
	Master of French Studies		Master of Heritage Preservation
MFST	Master of Food Safety and Technology		Master of Historic Preservation
MFT	Master of Family Therapy	MHPA	Master of Heath Policy and Administration
	Master of Food Technology	MHPCTL	Master of High Performance Coaching and Technical Leadership
MFWCB	Master of Fish, Wildlife and Conservation Biology		
		MHPE	Master of Health Professions Education
MFWS	Master of Fisheries and Wildlife Sciences	MHR	Master of Human Resources
MFYCS	Master of Family, Youth and Community Sciences	MHRD	Master in Human Resource Development
		MHRIR	Master of Human Resources and Industrial Relations
MG	Master of Genetics		
MGA	Master of Global Affairs	MHRLR	Master of Human Resources and Labor Relations
	Master of Government Administration		
	Master of Governmental Administration	MHRM	Master of Human Resources Management
		MHS	Master of Health Science

	Master of Health Sciences
	Master of Health Studies
	Master of Hispanic Studies
	Master of Humanistic Studies
MHSA	Master of Health Services Administration
MHSM	Master of Health Systems Management
MI	Master of Information
	Master of Instruction
MI Arch	Master of Interior Architecture
MIA	Master of Interior Architecture
	Master of International Affairs
MIAA	Master of International Affairs and Administration
MIAM	Master of International Agribusiness Management
MIAPD	Master of Interior Architecture and Product Design
MIB	Master of International Business
MICLJ	Master of International Criminal Law and Justice
MICM	Master of International Construction Management
MID	Master of Industrial Design
	Master of Industrial Distribution
	Master of Innovation Design
	Master of Interior Design
	Master of International Development
MIDA	Master of International Development Administration
MIDC	Master of Integrated Design and Construction
MIDP	Master of International Development Policy
MIDS	Master of Information and Data Science
MIE	Master of Industrial Engineering
MIHTM	Master of International Hospitality and Tourism Management
MIJ	Master of International Journalism
MILR	Master of Industrial and Labor Relations
MIM	Master in Ministry
	Master of Information Management
	Master of International Management
	Masters of International Marketing
MIMLAE	Master of International Management for Latin American Executives
MIMS	Master of Information Management and Systems
	Master of Integrated Manufacturing Systems
MIP	Master of Infrastructure Planning
	Master of Intellectual Property
	Master of International Policy
MIPA	Master of International Public Affairs
MIPD	Master of Integrated Product Design
MIPER	Master of International Political Economy of Resources
MIPM	Master of International Policy Management
MIPP	Master of International Policy and Practice
	Master of International Public Policy
MIPS	Master of International Planning Studies
MIR	Master of Industrial Relations
	Master of International Relations
MIRD	Master of International Relations and Diplomacy

MIRHR	Master of Industrial Relations and Human Resources
MIS	Master of Imaging Science
	Master of Industrial Statistics
	Master of Information Science
	Master of Information Systems
	Master of Integrated Science
	Master of Interdisciplinary Studies
	Master of International Service
	Master of International Studies
MISE	Master of Industrial and Systems Engineering
MISKM	Master of Information Sciences and Knowledge Management
MISM	Master of Information Systems Management
MISW	Master of Indigenous Social Work
MIT	Master in Teaching
	Master of Industrial Technology
	Master of Information Technology
	Master of Initial Teaching
	Master of International Trade
	Master of Internet Technology
MITA	Master of Information Technology Administration
MITM	Master of Information Technology and Management
MJ	Master of Journalism
	Master of Jurisprudence
MJ Ed	Master of Jewish Education
MJA	Master of Justice Administration
MJM	Master of Justice Management
MJS	Master of Judicial Studies
	Master of Juridical Studies
MK	Master of Kinesiology
MKM	Master of Knowledge Management
ML	Master of Latin
	Master's in Law
ML Arch	Master of Landscape Architecture
MLA	Master of Landscape Architecture
	Master of Liberal Arts
MLAS	Master of Laboratory Animal Science
	Master of Liberal Arts and Sciences
MLAUD	Master of Landscape Architecture in Urban Development
MLD	Master of Leadership Development
	Master of Leadership Studies
MLE	Master of Applied Linguistics and Exegesis
MLER	Master of Labor and Employment Relations
MLI Sc	Master of Library and Information Science
MLIS	Master of Library and Information Science
	Master of Library and Information Studies
MLM	Master of Leadership in Ministry
MLPD	Master of Land and Property Development
MLRHR	Master of Labor Relations and Human Resources
MLS	Master of Leadership Studies
	Master of Legal Studies
	Master of Liberal Studies
	Master of Library Science
	Master of Life Sciences
	Master of Medical Laboratory Sciences

MLSCM	Master of Logistics and Supply Chain Management	
MLT	Master of Language Technologies	
MLTCA	Master of Long Term Care Administration	
MLW	Master of Studies in Law	
MLWS	Master of Land and Water Systems	
MM	Master of Management	
	Master of Mediation	
	Master of Ministry	
	Master of Missiology	
	Master of Music	
MM Ed	Master of Music Education	
MM Sc	Master of Medical Science	
MM St	Master of Museum Studies	
MMA	Master of Marine Affairs	
	Master of Media Arts	
	Master of Ministry Administration	
	Master of Musical Arts	
MMAL	Master of Maritime Administration and Logistics	
MMAS	Master of Military Art and Science	
MMB	Master of Microbial Biotechnology	
MMC	Master of Manufacturing Competitiveness	
	Master of Mass Communications	
	Master of Music Conducting	
MMCM	Master of Music in Church Music	
MMCSS	Master of Mathematical Computational and Statistical Sciences	
MME	Master of Management in Energy	
	Master of Manufacturing Engineering	
	Master of Mathematics Education	
	Master of Mathematics for Educators	
	Master of Mechanical Engineering	
	Master of Mining Engineering	
	Master of Music Education	
MMEL	Master's in Medical Education Leadership	
MMF	Master of Mathematical Finance	
MMFC/T	Master of Marriage and Family Counseling/ Therapy	
MMFT	Master of Marriage and Family Therapy	
MMG	Master of Management	
MMH	Master of Management in Hospitality	
	Master of Medical Humanities	
MMI	Master of Management of Innovation	
MMIS	Master of Management Information Systems	
MML	Master of Managerial Logistics	
MMM	Master of Manufacturing Management	
	Master of Marine Management	
	Master of Medical Management	
MMP	Master of Marine Policy	
	Master of Medical Physics	
	Master of Music Performance	
MMPA	Master of Management and Professional Accounting	
MMQM	Master of Manufacturing Quality Management	
MMR	Master of Marketing Research	
MMRM	Master of Marine Resources Management	
MMS	Master in Migration Studies	
	Master of Management Science	
	Master of Management Studies	
	Master of Manufacturing Systems	

	Master of Marine Studies	
	Master of Materials Science	
	Master of Mathematical Sciences	
	Master of Medical Science	
	Master of Medieval Studies	
MMSE	Master of Manufacturing Systems Engineering	
MMSM	Master of Music in Sacred Music	
MMT	Master in Marketing	
	Master of Math for Teaching	
	Master of Music Therapy	
	Master's in Marketing Technology	
MMus	Master of Music	
MN	Master of Nursing	
	Master of Nutrition	
MN NP	Master of Nursing in Nurse Practitioner	
MNA	Master of Nonprofit Administration	
	Master of Nurse Anesthesia	
MNAL	Master of Nonprofit Administration and Leadership	
MNAS	Master of Natural and Applied Science	
MNCL	Master of Nonprofit and Civic Leadership	
MNCM	Master of Network and Communications Management	
MNE	Master of Nuclear Engineering	
MNL	Master in International Business for Latin America	
MNM	Master of Nonprofit Management	
MNO	Master of Nonprofit Organization	
MNPL	Master of Not-for-Profit Leadership	
MNpS	Master of Nonprofit Studies	
MNR	Master of Natural Resources	
MNRD	Master of Natural Resources Development	
MNRES	Master of Natural Resources and Environmental Studies	
MNRM	Master of Natural Resource Management	
MNRMG	Master of Natural Resource Management and Geography	
MNRS	Master of Natural Resource Stewardship	
MNS	Master of Natural Science	
MO	Master of Oceanography	
MOD	Master of Organizational Development	
MOGS	Master of Oil and Gas Studies	
MOL	Master of Organizational Leadership	
MOM	Master of Organizational Management	
	Master of Oriental Medicine	
MOR	Master of Operations Research	
MOT	Master of Occupational Therapy	
MP	Master of Physiology	
	Master of Planning	
MP Ac	Master of Professional Accountancy	
MP Acc	Master of Professional Accountancy	
	Master of Professional Accounting	
	Master of Public Accounting	
MP Aff	Master of Public Affairs	
MP Th	Master of Pastoral Theology	
MPA	Master of Performing Arts	
	Master of Physician Assistant	
	Master of Professional Accountancy	
	Master of Professional Accounting	
	Master of Public Administration	
	Master of Public Affairs	

MPAC	Master of Professional Accounting		Master of Physical Therapy
MPAID	Master of Public Administration and International Development		Master of Practical Theology
		MPVM	Master of Preventive Veterinary Medicine
MPAP	Master of Physician Assistant Practice	MPW	Master of Professional Writing
	Master of Public Administration and Policy		Master of Public Works
	Master of Public Affairs and Politics	MQF	Master of Quantitative Finance
MPAS	Master of Physician Assistant Science	MQM	Master of Quality Management
	Master of Physician Assistant Studies		Master of Quantitative Management
MPC	Master of Professional Communication	MQS	Master of Quality Systems
	Master of Professional Counseling	MR	Master of Recreation
MPD	Master of Product Development		Master of Retailing
	Master of Public Diplomacy	MRA	Master in Research Administration
MPDS	Master of Planning and Development Studies		Master of Regulatory Affairs
MPE	Master of Physical Education	MRC	Master of Rehabilitation Counseling
MPEM	Master of Project Engineering and Management	MRCP	Master of Regional and City Planning
			Master of Regional and Community Planning
MPFM	Master of Public Financial Management	MRD	Master of Rural Development
MPH	Master of Public Health	MRE	Master of Real Estate
MPHE	Master of Public Health Education		Master of Religious Education
MPHM	Master in Plant Health Management	MRED	Master of Real Estate Development
MPHS	Master of Population Health Sciences	MREM	Master of Resource and Environmental Management
MPHTM	Master of Public Health and Tropical Medicine		
MPI	Master of Product Innovation	MRLS	Master of Resources Law Studies
MPIA	Master of Public and International Affairs	MRM	Master of Resources Management
MPL	Master of Pastoral Leadership	MRP	Master of Regional Planning
MPM	Master of Pastoral Ministry	MRRD	Master in Recreation Resource Development
	Master of Pest Management	MRS	Master of Religious Studies
	Master of Policy Management	MRSc	Master of Rehabilitation Science
	Master of Practical Ministries	MS	Master of Science
	Master of Professional Management	MS Cmp E	Master of Science in Computer Engineering
	Master of Project Management	MS Kin	Master of Science in Kinesiology
	Master of Public Management	MS Acct	Master of Science in Accounting
MPNA	Master of Public and Nonprofit Administration	MS Accy	Master of Science in Accountancy
MPNL	Master of Philanthropy and Nonprofit Leadership	MS Aero E	Master of Science in Aerospace Engineering
		MS Ag	Master of Science in Agriculture
MPO	Master of Prosthetics and Orthotics	MS Arch	Master of Science in Architecture
MPOD	Master of Positive Organizational Development	MS Arch St	Master of Science in Architectural Studies
MPP	Master of Public Policy	MS Bio E	Master of Science in Bioengineering
MPPA	Master of Public Policy Administration	MS Bm E	Master of Science in Biomedical Engineering
	Master of Public Policy and Administration	MS Ch E	Master of Science in Chemical Engineering
MPPAL	Master of Public Policy, Administration and Law	MS Cp E	Master of Science in Computer Engineering
MPPGA	Master of Public Policy and Global Affairs	MS Eco	Master of Science in Economics
MPPM	Master of Public Policy and Management	MS Econ	Master of Science in Economics
MPPPM	Master of Plant Protection and Pest Management	MS Ed	Master of Science in Education
		MS El	Master of Science in Educational Leadership and Administration
MPRTM	Master of Parks, Recreation, and Tourism Management		
		MS En E	Master of Science in Environmental Engineering
MPS	Master of Pastoral Studies		
	Master of Perfusion Science	MS Eng	Master of Science in Engineering
	Master of Planning Studies	MS Engr	Master of Science in Engineering
	Master of Political Science	MS Env E	Master of Science in Environmental Engineering
	Master of Preservation Studies		
	Master of Prevention Science	MS Exp Surg	Master of Science in Experimental Surgery
	Master of Professional Studies	MS Mat E	Master of Science in Materials Engineering
	Master of Public Service	MS Mat SE	Master of Science in Material Science and Engineering
MPSA	Master of Public Service Administration		
MPSG	Master of Population and Social Gerontology	MS Met E	Master of Science in Metallurgical Engineering
MPSIA	Master of Political Science and International Affairs	MS Mgt	Master of Science in Management
		MS Min	Master of Science in Mining
MPSL	Master of Public Safety Leadership	MS Min E	Master of Science in Mining Engineering
MPT	Master of Pastoral Theology	MS Mt E	Master of Science in Materials Engineering

MS Otol	Master of Science in Otolaryngology
MS Pet E	Master of Science in Petroleum Engineering
MS Sc	Master of Social Science
MS Sp Ed	Master of Science in Special Education
MS Stat	Master of Science in Statistics
MS Surg	Master of Science in Surgery
MS Tax	Master of Science in Taxation
MS Tc E	Master of Science in Telecommunications Engineering
MS-R	Master of Science (Research)
MSA	Master of School Administration
	Master of Science in Accountancy
	Master of Science in Accounting
	Master of Science in Administration
	Master of Science in Aeronautics
	Master of Science in Agriculture
	Master of Science in Analytics
	Master of Science in Anesthesia
	Master of Science in Architecture
	Master of Science in Aviation
	Master of Sports Administration
	Master of Surgical Assisting
MSAA	Master of Science in Astronautics and Aeronautics
MSABE	Master of Science in Agricultural and Biological Engineering
MSAC	Master of Science in Acupuncture
MSACC	Master of Science in Accounting
MSACS	Master of Science in Applied Computer Science
MSAE	Master of Science in Aeronautical Engineering
	Master of Science in Aerospace Engineering
	Master of Science in Applied Economics
	Master of Science in Applied Engineering
	Master of Science in Architectural Engineering
MSAEM	Master of Science in Aerospace Engineering and Mechanics
MSAF	Master of Science in Aviation Finance
MSAG	Master of Science in Applied Geosciences
MSAH	Master of Science in Allied Health
MSAL	Master of Sport Administration and Leadership
MSAM	Master of Science in Applied Mathematics
MSANR	Master of Science in Agriculture and Natural Resources
MSAPM	Master of Security Analysis and Portfolio Management
MSAS	Master of Science in Administrative Studies
	Master of Science in Applied Statistics
	Master of Science in Architectural Studies
MSAT	Master of Science in Accounting and Taxation
	Master of Science in Advanced Technology
	Master of Science in Athletic Training
MSB	Master of Science in Biotechnology
	Master of Science in Business
	Master of Sustainable Business
MSBA	Master of Science in Business Administration
	Master of Science in Business Analysis
MSBAE	Master of Science in Biological and Agricultural Engineering
	Master of Science in Biosystems and Agricultural Engineering
MSBCB	Master's in Bioinformatics and Computational Biology

MSBE	Master of Science in Biological Engineering
	Master of Science in Biomedical Engineering
MSBENG	Master of Science in Bioengineering
MSBH	Master of Science in Behavioral Health
MSBM	Master of Sport Business Management
MSBME	Master of Science in Biomedical Engineering
MSBMS	Master of Science in Basic Medical Science
MSBS	Master of Science in Biomedical Sciences
MSBTM	Master of Science in Biotechnology and Management
MSC	Master of Science in Commerce
	Master of Science in Communication
	Master of Science in Computers
	Master of Science in Counseling
	Master of Science in Criminology
	Master of Strategic Communication
MSCC	Master of Science in Community Counseling
MSCD	Master of Science in Communication Disorders
	Master of Science in Community Development
MSCE	Master of Science in Chemistry Education
	Master of Science in Civil Engineering
	Master of Science in Clinical Epidemiology
	Master of Science in Computer Engineering
	Master of Science in Continuing Education
MSCEE	Master of Science in Civil and Environmental Engineering
MSCF	Master of Science in Computational Finance
MSCH	Master of Science in Chemical Engineering
MSChE	Master of Science in Chemical Engineering
MSCI	Master of Science in Clinical Investigation
MSCID	Master of Science in Community and International Development
MSCIS	Master of Science in Computer and Information Science
	Master of Science in Computer and Information Systems
	Master of Science in Computer Information Science
	Master of Science in Computer Information Systems
MSCIT	Master of Science in Computer Information Technology
MSCJ	Master of Science in Criminal Justice
MSCJA	Master of Science in Criminal Justice Administration
MSCJS	Master of Science in Crime and Justice Studies
MSCLS	Master of Science in Clinical Laboratory Studies
MSCM	Master of Science in Church Management
	Master of Science in Conflict Management
	Master of Science in Construction Management
	Master of Supply Chain Management
MSCMP	Master of Science in Cybersecurity Management and Policy
MSCNU	Master of Science in Clinical Nutrition
MSCP	Master of Science in Clinical Psychology
	Master of Science in Community Psychology
	Master of Science in Computer Engineering
	Master of Science in Counseling Psychology
MSCPE	Master of Science in Computer Engineering
MSCPharm	Master of Science in Pharmacy
MSCR	Master of Science in Clinical Research

MSCRP	Master of Science in City and Regional Planning
	Master of Science in Community and Regional Planning
MSCS	Master of Science in Clinical Science
	Master of Science in Computer Science
	Master of Science in Cyber Security
MSCSD	Master of Science in Communication Sciences and Disorders
MSCSE	Master of Science in Computer Science and Engineering
MSCTE	Master of Science in Career and Technical Education
MSD	Master of Science in Dentistry
	Master of Science in Design
	Master of Science in Dietetics
MSDM	Master of Security and Disaster Management
MSE	Master of Science Education
	Master of Science in Education
	Master of Science in Engineering
	Master of Science in Engineering Management
	Master of Software Engineering
	Master of Special Education
	Master of Structural Engineering
MSECE	Master of Science in Electrical and Computer Engineering
MSED	Master of Sustainable Economic Development
MSEE	Master of Science in Electrical Engineering
	Master of Science in Environmental Engineering
MSEH	Master of Science in Environmental Health
MSEL	Master of Science in Educational Leadership
MSEM	Master of Science in Engineering and Management
	Master of Science in Engineering Management
	Master of Science in Engineering Mechanics
	Master of Science in Environmental Management
MSENE	Master of Science in Environmental Engineering
MSEO	Master of Science in Electro-Optics
MSES	Master of Science in Embedded Software Engineering
	Master of Science in Engineering Science
	Master of Science in Environmental Science
	Master of Science in Environmental Studies
	Master of Science in Exercise Science
MSESE	Master of Science in Energy Systems Engineering
MSET	Master of Science in Educational Technology
	Master of Science in Engineering Technology
MSEV	Master of Science in Environmental Engineering
MSF	Master of Science in Finance
	Master of Science in Forestry
	Master of Spiritual Formation
MSFA	Master of Science in Financial Analysis
MSFCS	Master of Science in Family and Consumer Science
MSFE	Master of Science in Financial Engineering
MSFM	Master of Sustainable Forest Management
MSFOR	Master of Science in Forestry
MSFP	Master of Science in Financial Planning

MSFS	Master of Science in Financial Sciences
	Master of Science in Forensic Science
MSFSB	Master of Science in Financial Services and Banking
MSFT	Master of Science in Family Therapy
MSGC	Master of Science in Genetic Counseling
MSH	Master of Science in Health
	Master of Science in Hospice
MSHA	Master of Science in Health Administration
MSHCA	Master of Science in Health Care Administration
MSHCPM	Master of Science in Health Care Policy and Management
MSHE	Master of Science in Health Education
MSHES	Master of Science in Human Environmental Sciences
MSHFID	Master of Science in Human Factors in Information Design
MSHFS	Master of Science in Human Factors and Systems
MSHI	Master of Science in Health Informatics
MSHP	Master of Science in Health Professions
	Master of Science in Health Promotion
MSHR	Master of Science in Human Resources
MSHRL	Master of Science in Human Resource Leadership
MSHRM	Master of Science in Human Resource Management
MSHROD	Master of Science in Human Resources and Organizational Development
MSHS	Master of Science in Health Science
	Master of Science in Health Services
	Master of Science in Homeland Security
MSHSR	Master of Science in Human Security and Resilience
MSI	Master of Science in Information
	Master of Science in Instruction
	Master of System Integration
MSIA	Master of Science in Industrial Administration
	Master of Science in Information Assurance
MSIB	Master of Science in International Business
MSIDM	Master of Science in Interior Design and Merchandising
MSIE	Master of Science in Industrial Engineering
MSIEM	Master of Science in Information Engineering and Management
MSIM	Master of Science in Industrial Management
	Master of Science in Information Management
	Master of Science in International Management
MSIMC	Master of Science in Integrated Marketing Communications
MSIMS	Master of Science in Identity Management and Security
MSIR	Master of Science in Industrial Relations
MSIS	Master of Science in Information Science
	Master of Science in Information Studies
	Master of Science in Information Systems
	Master of Science in Interdisciplinary Studies
MSISE	Master of Science in Infrastructure Systems Engineering
MSISM	Master of Science in Information Systems Management
MSISPM	Master of Science in Information Security Policy and Management

MSIST	Master of Science in Information Systems Technology
MSIT	Master of Science in Industrial Technology
	Master of Science in Information Technology
	Master of Science in Instructional Technology
MSITM	Master of Science in Information Technology Management
MSJ	Master of Science in Journalism
	Master of Science in Jurisprudence
MSJC	Master of Social Justice and Criminology
MSJFP	Master of Science in Juvenile Forensic Psychology
MSJJ	Master of Science in Juvenile Justice
MSJPS	Master of Science in Justice and Public Safety
MSL	Master of School Leadership
	Master of Science in Leadership
	Master of Science in Limnology
	Master of Sports Leadership
	Master of Strategic Leadership
	Master of Studies in Law
MSLA	Master of Science in Legal Administration
MSLB	Master of Sports Law and Business
MSLFS	Master of Science in Life Sciences
MSLP	Master of Speech-Language Pathology
MSLS	Master of Science in Library Science
MSLSCM	Master of Science in Logistics and Supply Chain Management
MSLT	Master of Second Language Teaching
MSM	Master of Sacred Ministry
	Master of Sacred Music
	Master of School Mathematics
	Master of Science in Management
	Master of Science in Medicine
	Master of Science in Organization Management
	Master of Security Management
	Master of Supply Management
MSMA	Master of Science in Marketing Analysis
MSMAE	Master of Science in Materials Engineering
MSMC	Master of Science in Mass Communications
MSME	Master of Science in Mathematics Education
	Master of Science in Mechanical Engineering
	Master of Science in Medical Ethics
MSMFT	Master of Science in Marriage and Family Therapy
MSMHC	Master of Science in Mental Health Counseling
MSMIT	Master of Science in Management and Information Technology
MSMLS	Master of Science in Medical Laboratory Science
MSMOT	Master of Science in Management of Technology
MSMP	Master of Science in Medical Physics
	Master of Science in Molecular Pathology
MSMS	Master of Science in Management Science
	Master of Science in Marine Science
	Master of Science in Medical Sciences
MSMSE	Master of Science in Manufacturing Systems Engineering
	Master of Science in Material Science and Engineering
	Master of Science in Mathematics and Science Education

MSMus	Master of Sacred Music
MSN	Master of Science in Nursing
MSNA	Master of Science in Nurse Anesthesia
MSNE	Master of Science in Nuclear Engineering
MSNS	Master of Science in Natural Science
	Master of Science in Nutritional Science
MSOD	Master of Science in Organization Development
	Master of Science in Organizational Development
MSOEE	Master of Science in Outdoor and Environmental Education
MSOES	Master of Science in Occupational Ergonomics and Safety
MSOH	Master of Science in Occupational Health
MSOL	Master of Science in Organizational Leadership
MSOM	Master of Science in Oriental Medicine
MSOR	Master of Science in Operations Research
MSOT	Master of Science in Occupational Technology
	Master of Science in Occupational Therapy
MSP	Master of Science in Pharmacy
	Master of Science in Planning
	Master of Speech Pathology
	Master of Sustainable Peacebuilding
MSPA	Master of Science in Physician Assistant
MSPAS	Master of Science in Physician Assistant Studies
MSPC	Master of Science in Professional Communications
MSPE	Master of Science in Petroleum Engineering
MSPH	Master of Science in Public Health
MSPHR	Master of Science in Pharmacy
MSPM	Master of Science in Professional Management
	Master of Science in Project Management
MSPNGE	Master of Science in Petroleum and Natural Gas Engineering
MSPPM	Master of Science in Public Policy and Management
MSPS	Master of Science in Pharmaceutical Science
	Master of Science in Political Science
	Master of Science in Psychological Services
MSPT	Master of Science in Physical Therapy
MSpVM	Master of Specialized Veterinary Medicine
MSRA	Master of Science in Recreation Administration
MSRE	Master of Science in Real Estate
	Master of Science in Religious Education
MSRED	Master of Science in Real Estate Development
	Master of Sustainable Real Estate Development
MSRLS	Master of Science in Recreation and Leisure Studies
MSRM	Master of Science in Risk Management
MSRMP	Master of Science in Radiological Medical Physics
MSRS	Master of Science in Radiological Sciences
	Master of Science in Rehabilitation Science
MSS	Master of Security Studies
	Master of Social Science
	Master of Social Services
	Master of Software Systems
	Master of Sports Science
	Master of Strategic Studies
	Master's in Statistical Science
MSSA	Master of Science in Social Administration

MSSCM	Master of Science in Supply Chain Management	MTE	Master in Educational Technology
MSSD	Master of Arts in Software Driven Systems Design		Master of Technological Entrepreneurship
	Master of Science in Sustainable Design	MTESOL	Master in Teaching English to Speakers of Other Languages
MSSE	Master of Science in Software Engineering	MTHM	Master of Tourism and Hospitality Management
	Master of Science in Special Education	MTI	Master of Information Technology
MSSEM	Master of Science in Systems and Engineering Management	MTID	Master of Tangible Interaction Design
MSSI	Master of Science in Security Informatics	MTL	Master of Talmudic Law
	Master of Science in Strategic Intelligence	MTM	Master of Technology Management
MSSIS	Master of Science in Security and Intelligence Studies		Master of Telecommunications Management
MSSL	Master of Science in School Leadership		Master of the Teaching of Mathematics
MSSLP	Master of Science in Speech-Language Pathology		Master of Translational Medicine
MSSM	Master of Science in Sports Medicine	MTMH	Master of Tropical Medicine and Hygiene
	Master of Science in Systems Management	MTMS	Master in Teaching Mathematics and Science
MSSP	Master of Science in Social Policy	MTOM	Master of Traditional Oriental Medicine
MSSPA	Master of Science in Student Personnel Administration	MTPC	Master of Technical and Professional Communication
MSSS	Master of Science in Safety Science	MTR	Master of Translational Research
	Master of Science in Systems Science	MTS	Master of Theatre Studies
MSST	Master of Science in Security Technologies		Master of Theological Studies
MSSW	Master of Science in Social Work	MTWM	Master of Trust and Wealth Management
MSSWE	Master of Science in Software Engineering	MTX	Master of Taxation
MST	Master of Science and Technology	MUA	Master of Urban Affairs
	Master of Science in Taxation	MUCD	Master of Urban and Community Design
	Master of Science in Teaching	MUD	Master of Urban Design
	Master of Science in Technology	MUDS	Master of Urban Design Studies
	Master of Science in Telecommunications	MUEP	Master of Urban and Environmental Planning
	Master of Science Teaching	MUP	Master of Urban Planning
MSTC	Master of Science in Technical Communication	MUPDD	Master of Urban Planning, Design, and Development
	Master of Science in Telecommunications	MUPP	Master of Urban Planning and Policy
MSTCM	Master of Science in Traditional Chinese Medicine	MUPRED	Master of Urban Planning and Real Estate Development
MSTE	Master of Science in Telecommunications Engineering	MURP	Master of Urban and Regional Planning
	Master of Science in Transportation Engineering		Master of Urban and Rural Planning
MSTL	Master of Science in Teacher Leadership	MUS	Master of Urban Studies
MSTM	Master of Science in Technology Management	MUSA	Master of Urban Spatial Analytics
	Master of Science in Transfusion Medicine	MVP	Master of Voice Pedagogy
MSTOM	Master of Science in Traditional Oriental Medicine	MVPH	Master of Veterinary Public Health
MSUASE	Master of Science in Unmanned and Autonomous Systems Engineering	MVS	Master of Visual Studies
		MWBS	Master of Won Buddhist Studies
MSUD	Master of Science in Urban Design	MWC	Master of Wildlife Conservation
MSUS	Master of Science in Urban Studies	MWPS	Master of Wood and Paper Science
MSW	Master of Social Work	MWR	Master of Water Resources
MSWE	Master of Software Engineering	MWS	Master of Women's Studies
MSWREE	Master of Science in Water Resources and Environmental Engineering		Master of Worship Studies
MT	Master of Taxation	MWSc	Master of Wildlife Science
	Master of Teaching	MZS	Master of Zoological Science
	Master of Technology	Nav Arch	Naval Architecture
	Master of Textiles	Naval E	Naval Engineer
MTA	Master of Tax Accounting	ND	Doctor of Naturopathic Medicine
	Master of Teaching Arts		Doctor of Nursing
	Master of Tourism Administration	NE	Nuclear Engineer
MTC	Master of Technical Communications	Nuc E	Nuclear Engineer
MTCM	Master of Traditional Chinese Medicine	OD	Doctor of Optometry
MTD	Master of Training and Development	OTD	Doctor of Occupational Therapy
		PBME	Professional Master of Biomedical Engineering
		PC	Performer's Certificate
		PD	Professional Diploma
		PGC	Post-Graduate Certificate

PGD	Postgraduate Diploma
Ph L	Licentiate of Philosophy
Pharm D	Doctor of Pharmacy
PhD	Doctor of Philosophy
PhD Otol	Doctor of Philosophy in Otolaryngology
PhD Surg	Doctor of Philosophy in Surgery
PhDEE	Doctor of Philosophy in Electrical Engineering
PMASE	Professional Master's in Applied Systems Engineering
PMBA	Professional Master of Business Administration
PMC	Post Master Certificate
PMD	Post-Master's Diploma
PMS	Professional Master of Science
	Professional Master's
Post-Doctoral MS	Post-Doctoral Master of Science
Post-MSN Certificate	Post-Master of Science in Nursing Certificate
PPDPT	Postprofessional Doctor of Physical Therapy
Pro-MS	Professional Science Master's
Professional MA	Professional Master of Arts
Professional MBA	Professional Master of Business Administration
Professional MS	Professional Master of Science
PSM	Professional Master of Science
	Professional Science Master's
Psy D	Doctor of Psychology
Psy M	Master of Psychology
Psy S	Specialist in Psychology
Psya D	Doctor of Psychoanalysis
S Psy S	Specialist in Psychological Services
Sc D	Doctor of Science
Sc M	Master of Science
SCCT	Specialist in Community College Teaching
ScDPT	Doctor of Physical Therapy Science

SD	Doctor of Science
	Specialist Degree
SJD	Doctor of Juridical Sciences
SLPD	Doctor of Speech-Language Pathology
SM	Master of Science
SM Arch S	Master of Science in Architectural Studies
SMACT	Master of Science in Art, Culture and Technology
SMBT	Master of Science in Building Technology
SP	Specialist Degree
Sp Ed	Specialist in Education
Sp LIS	Specialist in Library and Information Science
SPA	Specialist in Arts
Spec	Specialist's Certificate
Spec M	Specialist in Music
Spt	Specialist Degree
SSP	Specialist in School Psychology
STB	Bachelor of Sacred Theology
STD	Doctor of Sacred Theology
STL	Licentiate of Sacred Theology
STM	Master of Sacred Theology
tDACM	Transitional Doctor of Acupuncture and Chinese Medicine
TDPT	Transitional Doctor of Physical Therapy
Th D	Doctor of Theology
Th M	Master of Theology
TOTD	Transitional Doctor of Occupational Therapy
VMD	Doctor of Veterinary Medicine
WEMBA	Weekend Executive Master of Business Administration
XMA	Executive Master of Arts

INDEXES

Profiles, Displays, and Close-Ups

Peterson's Graduate & Professional Programs: An Overview 2018

Directories and Subject Areas

Following is an alphabetical listing of directories and subject areas. Also listed are cross-references for subject area names not used in the directory structure of the guides, for example, "City and Regional Planning (*see* Urban and Regional Planning)."

Graduate Programs in the Humanities, Arts & Social Sciences

Addictions/Substance Abuse Counseling
Administration (*see* Arts Administration; Public Administration)
African-American Studies
African Languages and Literatures (*see* African Studies)
African Studies
Agribusiness (*see* Agricultural Economics and Agribusiness)
Agricultural Economics and Agribusiness
Alcohol Abuse Counseling (*see* Addictions/Substance Abuse Counseling)
American Indian/Native American Studies
American Studies
Anthropology
Applied Arts and Design—General
Applied Behavior Analysis
Applied Economics
Applied History (*see* Public History)
Applied Psychology
Applied Social Research
Arabic (*see* Near and Middle Eastern Languages)
Arab Studies (*see* Near and Middle Eastern Studies)
Archaeology
Architectural History
Architecture
Archives Administration (*see* Public History)
Area and Cultural Studies (*see* African-American Studies; African Studies; American Indian/Native American Studies; American Studies; Asian-American Studies; Asian Studies; Canadian Studies; Cultural Studies; East European and Russian Studies; Ethnic Studies; Folklore; Gender Studies; Hispanic Studies; Holocaust Studies; Jewish Studies; Latin American Studies; Near and Middle Eastern Studies; Northern Studies; Pacific Area/Pacific Rim Studies; Western European Studies; Women's Studies)
Art/Fine Arts
Art History
Arts Administration
Arts Journalism
Art Therapy
Asian-American Studies
Asian Languages
Asian Studies
Behavioral Sciences (*see* Psychology)
Bible Studies (*see* Religion; Theology)
Biological Anthropology
Black Studies (*see* African-American Studies)
Broadcasting (*see* Communication; Film, Television, and Video Production)
Broadcast Journalism
Building Science
Canadian Studies
Celtic Languages
Ceramics (*see* Art/Fine Arts)
Child and Family Studies
Child Development
Chinese
Chinese Studies (*see* Asian Languages; Asian Studies)

Christian Studies (*see* Missions and Missiology; Religion; Theology)
Cinema (*see* Film, Television, and Video Production)
City and Regional Planning (*see* Urban and Regional Planning)
Classical Languages and Literatures (*see* Classics)
Classics
Clinical Psychology
Clothing and Textiles
Cognitive Psychology (*see* Psychology—General; Cognitive Sciences)
Cognitive Sciences
Communication—General
Community Affairs (*see* Urban and Regional Planning; Urban Studies)
Community Planning (*see* Architecture; Environmental Design; Urban and Regional Planning; Urban Design; Urban Studies)
Community Psychology (*see* Social Psychology)
Comparative and Interdisciplinary Arts
Comparative Literature
Composition (*see* Music)
Computer Art and Design
Conflict Resolution and Mediation/Peace Studies
Consumer Economics
Corporate and Organizational Communication
Corrections (*see* Criminal Justice and Criminology)
Counseling (*see* Counseling Psychology; Pastoral Ministry and Counseling)
Counseling Psychology
Crafts (*see* Art/Fine Arts)
Creative Arts Therapies (*see* Art Therapy; Therapies—Dance, Drama, and Music)
Criminal Justice and Criminology
Cultural Anthropology
Cultural Studies
Dance
Decorative Arts
Demography and Population Studies
Design (*see* Applied Arts and Design; Architecture; Art/Fine Arts; Environmental Design; Graphic Design; Industrial Design; Interior Design; Textile Design; Urban Design)
Developmental Psychology
Diplomacy (*see* International Affairs)
Disability Studies
Drama Therapy (*see* Therapies—Dance, Drama, and Music)
Dramatic Arts (*see* Theater)
Drawing (*see* Art/Fine Arts)
Drug Abuse Counseling (*see* Addictions/Substance Abuse Counseling)
Drug and Alcohol Abuse Counseling (*see* Addictions/Substance Abuse Counseling)
East Asian Studies (*see* Asian Studies)
East European and Russian Studies
Economic Development
Economics
Educational Theater (*see* Theater; Therapies—Dance, Drama, and Music)
Emergency Management
English
Environmental Design
Ethics
Ethnic Studies
Ethnomusicology (*see* Music)
Experimental Psychology
Family and Consumer Sciences—General
Family Studies (*see* Child and Family Studies)
Family Therapy (*see* Child and Family Studies; Clinical Psychology; Counseling Psychology; Marriage and Family Therapy)
Filmmaking (*see* Film, Television, and Video Production)
Film Studies (*see* Film, Television, and Video Production)
Film, Television, and Video Production
Film, Television, and Video Theory and Criticism
Fine Arts (*see* Art/Fine Arts)

Folklore
Foreign Languages (*see* specific language)
Foreign Service (*see* International Affairs; International Development)
Forensic Psychology
Forensic Sciences
Forensics (*see* Speech and Interpersonal Communication)
French
Gender Studies
General Studies (*see* Liberal Studies)
Genetic Counseling
Geographic Information Systems
Geography
German
Gerontology
Graphic Design
Greek (*see* Classics)
Health Communication
Health Psychology
Hebrew (*see* Near and Middle Eastern Languages)
Hebrew Studies (*see* Jewish Studies)
Hispanic and Latin American Languages
Hispanic Studies
Historic Preservation
History
History of Art (*see* Art History)
History of Medicine
History of Science and Technology
Holocaust and Genocide Studies
Home Economics (*see* Family and Consumer Sciences—General)
Homeland Security
Household Economics, Sciences, and Management (*see* Family and Consumer Sciences—General)
Human Development
Humanities
Illustration
Industrial and Labor Relations
Industrial and Organizational Psychology
Industrial Design
Interdisciplinary Studies
Interior Design
International Affairs
International Development
International Economics
International Service (*see* International Affairs; International Development)
International Trade Policy
Internet and Interactive Multimedia
Interpersonal Communication (*see* Speech and Interpersonal Communication)
Interpretation (*see* Translation and Interpretation)
Islamic Studies (*see* Near and Middle Eastern Studies; Religion)
Italian
Japanese
Japanese Studies (*see* Asian Languages; Asian Studies; Japanese)
Jewelry (*see* Art/Fine Arts)
Jewish Studies
Journalism
Judaic Studies (*see* Jewish Studies; Religion)
Labor Relations (*see* Industrial and Labor Relations)
Landscape Architecture
Latin American Studies
Latin (*see* Classics)
Law Enforcement (*see* Criminal Justice and Criminology)
Liberal Studies
Lighting Design
Linguistics
Literature (*see* Classics; Comparative Literature; specific language)
Marriage and Family Therapy
Mass Communication
Media Studies
Medical Illustration
Medieval and Renaissance Studies
Metalsmithing (*see* Art/Fine Arts)

Middle Eastern Studies (*see* Near and Middle Eastern Studies)
Military and Defense Studies
Mineral Economics
Ministry (*see* Pastoral Ministry and Counseling; Theology)
Missions and Missiology
Motion Pictures (*see* Film, Television, and Video Production)
Museum Studies
Music
Musicology (*see* Music)
Music Therapy (*see* Therapies—Dance, Drama, and Music)
National Security
Native American Studies (*see* American Indian/Native American Studies)
Near and Middle Eastern Languages
Near and Middle Eastern Studies
Near Environment (*see* Family and Consumer Sciences)
Northern Studies
Organizational Psychology (*see* Industrial and Organizational Psychology)
Oriental Languages (*see* Asian Languages)
Oriental Studies (*see* Asian Studies)
Pacific Area/Pacific Rim Studies
Painting (*see* Art/Fine Arts)
Pastoral Ministry and Counseling
Philanthropic Studies
Philosophy
Photography
Playwriting (*see* Theater; Writing)
Policy Studies (*see* Public Policy)
Political Science
Population Studies (*see* Demography and Population Studies)
Portuguese
Printmaking (*see* Art/Fine Arts)
Product Design (*see* Industrial Design)
Psychoanalysis and Psychotherapy
Psychology—General
Public Administration
Public Affairs
Public History
Public Policy
Public Speaking (*see* Mass Communication; Rhetoric; Speech and Interpersonal Communication)
Publishing
Regional Planning (*see* Architecture; Urban and Regional Planning; Urban Design; Urban Studies)
Rehabilitation Counseling
Religion
Renaissance Studies (*see* Medieval and Renaissance Studies)
Rhetoric
Romance Languages
Romance Literatures (*see* Romance Languages)
Rural Planning and Studies
Rural Sociology
Russian
Scandinavian Languages
School Psychology
Sculpture (*see* Art/Fine Arts)
Security Administration (*see* Criminal Justice and Criminology)
Slavic Languages
Slavic Studies (*see* East European and Russian Studies; Slavic Languages)
Social Psychology
Social Sciences
Sociology
Southeast Asian Studies (*see* Asian Studies)
Soviet Studies (*see* East European and Russian Studies; Russian)
Spanish
Speech and Interpersonal Communication
Sport Psychology
Studio Art (*see* Art/Fine Arts)
Substance Abuse Counseling (*see* Addictions/Substance Abuse Counseling)
Survey Methodology

Sustainable Development
Technical Communication
Technical Writing
Telecommunications (*see* Film, Television, and Video Production)
Television (*see* Film, Television, and Video Production)
Textile Design
Textiles (*see* Clothing and Textiles; Textile Design)
Thanatology
Theater
Theater Arts (*see* Theater)
Theology
Therapies—Dance, Drama, and Music
Translation and Interpretation
Transpersonal and Humanistic Psychology
Urban and Regional Planning
Urban Design
Urban Planning (*see* Architecture; Urban and Regional Planning; Urban Design; Urban Studies)
Urban Studies
Video (*see* Film, Television, and Video Production)
Visual Arts (*see* Applied Arts and Design; Art/Fine Arts; Film, Television, and Video Production; Graphic Design; Illustration; Photography)
Western European Studies
Women's Studies
World Wide Web (*see* Internet and Interactive Multimedia)
Writing

Graduate Programs in the Biological/Biomedical Sciences & Health-Related Medical Professions

Acupuncture and Oriental Medicine
Acute Care/Critical Care Nursing Administration (*see* Health Services Management and Hospital Administration; Nursing and Healthcare Administration; Pharmaceutical Administration)
Adult Nursing
Advanced Practice Nursing (*see* Family Nurse Practitioner Studies)
Allied Health—General
Allied Health Professions (*see* Clinical Laboratory Sciences/Medical Technology; Clinical Research; Communication Disorders; Dental Hygiene; Emergency Medical Services; Occupational Therapy; Physical Therapy; Physician Assistant Studies; Rehabilitation Sciences)
Allopathic Medicine
Anatomy
Anesthesiologist Assistant Studies
Animal Behavior
Bacteriology
Behavioral Sciences (*see* Biopsychology; Neuroscience; Zoology)
Biochemistry
Bioethics
Biological and Biomedical Sciences—General Biological Chemistry (*see* Biochemistry)
Biological Oceanography (*see* Marine Biology)
Biophysics
Biopsychology
Botany
Breeding (*see* Botany; Plant Biology; Genetics)
Cancer Biology/Oncology
Cardiovascular Sciences
Cell Biology
Cellular Physiology (*see* Cell Biology; Physiology)
Child-Care Nursing (*see* Maternal and Child/Neonatal Nursing)
Chiropractic
Clinical Laboratory Sciences/Medical Technology
Clinical Research
Community Health
Community Health Nursing
Computational Biology

Conservation (*see* Conservation Biology; Environmental Biology)
Conservation Biology
Crop Sciences (*see* Botany; Plant Biology)
Cytology (*see* Cell Biology)
Dental and Oral Surgery (*see* Oral and Dental Sciences)
Dental Assistant Studies (*see* Dental Hygiene)
Dental Hygiene
Dental Services (*see* Dental Hygiene)
Dentistry
Developmental Biology Dietetics (*see* Nutrition)
Ecology
Embryology (*see* Developmental Biology)
Emergency Medical Services
Endocrinology (*see* Physiology)
Entomology
Environmental Biology
Environmental and Occupational Health
Epidemiology
Evolutionary Biology
Family Nurse Practitioner Studies
Foods (*see* Nutrition)
Forensic Nursing
Genetics
Genomic Sciences
Gerontological Nursing
Health Physics/Radiological Health
Health Promotion
Health-Related Professions (*see* individual allied health professions)
Health Services Management and Hospital Administration
Health Services Research
Histology (*see* Anatomy; Cell Biology)
HIV/AIDS Nursing
Hospice Nursing
Hospital Administration (*see* Health Services Management and Hospital Administration)
Human Genetics
Immunology
Industrial Hygiene
Infectious Diseases
International Health
Laboratory Medicine (*see* Clinical Laboratory Sciences/Medical Technology; Immunology; Microbiology; Pathology)
Life Sciences (*see* Biological and Biomedical Sciences)
Marine Biology
Maternal and Child Health
Maternal and Child/Neonatal Nursing
Medical Imaging
Medical Microbiology
Medical Nursing (*see* Medical/Surgical Nursing)
Medical Physics
Medical/Surgical Nursing
Medical Technology (*see* Clinical Laboratory Sciences/Medical Technology)
Medical Sciences (*see* Biological and Biomedical Sciences)
Medical Science Training Programs (*see* Biological and Biomedical Sciences)
Medicinal and Pharmaceutical Chemistry
Medicinal Chemistry (*see* Medicinal and Pharmaceutical Chemistry)
Medicine (*see* Allopathic Medicine; Naturopathic Medicine; Osteopathic Medicine; Podiatric Medicine)
Microbiology
Midwifery (*see* Nurse Midwifery)
Molecular Biology
Molecular Biophysics
Molecular Genetics
Molecular Medicine
Molecular Pathogenesis
Molecular Pathology
Molecular Pharmacology
Molecular Physiology
Molecular Toxicology
Naturopathic Medicine
Neural Sciences (*see* Biopsychology; Neurobiology; Neuroscience)

Neurobiology

Neuroendocrinology (see Biopsychology; Neurobiology; Neuroscience; Physiology)

Neuropharmacology (see Biopsychology; Neurobiology; Neuroscience; Pharmacology)

Neurophysiology (see Biopsychology; Neurobiology; Neuroscience; Physiology)

Neuroscience

Nuclear Medical Technology (see Clinical Laboratory Sciences/ Medical Technology)

Nurse Anesthesia

Nurse Midwifery

Nurse Practitioner Studies (see Family Nurse Practitioner Studies)

Nursing Administration (see Nursing and Healthcare Administration)

Nursing and Healthcare Administration

Nursing Education

Nursing—General

Nursing Informatics

Nutrition

Occupational Health (see Environmental and Occupational Health; Occupational Health Nursing)

Occupational Health Nursing

Occupational Therapy

Oncology (see Cancer Biology/Oncology)

Oncology Nursing

Optometry

Oral and Dental Sciences

Oral Biology (see Oral and Dental Sciences)

Oral Pathology (see Oral and Dental Sciences)

Organismal Biology (see Biological and Biomedical Sciences; Zoology)

Oriental Medicine and Acupuncture (see Acupuncture and Oriental Medicine)

Orthodontics (see Oral and Dental Sciences)

Osteopathic Medicine

Parasitology

Pathobiology

Pathology

Pediatric Nursing

Pedontics (see Oral and Dental Sciences)

Perfusion

Pharmaceutical Administration

Pharmaceutical Chemistry (see Medicinal and Pharmaceutical Chemistry)

Pharmaceutical Sciences

Pharmacology

Pharmacy

Photobiology of Cells and Organelles (see Botany; Cell Biology; Plant Biology)

Physical Therapy

Physician Assistant Studies

Physiological Optics (see Vision Sciences)

Podiatric Medicine

Preventive Medicine (see Community Health and Public Health)

Physiological Optics (see Physiology)

Physiology

Plant Biology

Plant Molecular Biology

Plant Pathology

Plant Physiology

Pomology (see Botany; Plant Biology)

Psychiatric Nursing

Public Health—General

Public Health Nursing (see Community Health Nursing)

Psychiatric Nursing

Psychobiology (see Biopsychology)

Psychopharmacology (see Biopsychology; Neuroscience; Pharmacology)

Radiation Biology

Radiological Health (see Health Physics/Radiological Health)

Rehabilitation Nursing

Rehabilitation Sciences

Rehabilitation Therapy (see Physical Therapy)

Reproductive Biology

School Nursing

Sociobiology (see Evolutionary Biology)

Structural Biology

Surgical Nursing (see Medical/Surgical Nursing)

Systems Biology

Teratology

Therapeutics

Theoretical Biology (see Biological and Biomedical Sciences)

Therapeutics (see Pharmaceutical Sciences; Pharmacology; Pharmacy)

Toxicology

Transcultural Nursing

Translational Biology

Tropical Medicine (see Parasitology)

Veterinary Medicine

Veterinary Sciences

Virology

Vision Sciences

Wildlife Biology (see Zoology)

Women's Health Nursing

Zoology

Graduate Programs in the Physical Sciences, Mathematics, Agricultural Sciences, the Environment & Natural Resources

Acoustics

Agricultural Sciences

Agronomy and Soil Sciences

Analytical Chemistry

Animal Sciences

Applied Mathematics

Applied Physics

Applied Statistics

Aquaculture

Astronomy

Astrophysical Sciences (see Astrophysics; Atmospheric Sciences; Meteorology; Planetary and Space Sciences)

Astrophysics

Atmospheric Sciences

Biological Oceanography (see Marine Affairs; Marine Sciences; Oceanography)

Biomathematics

Biometry

Biostatistics

Chemical Physics

Chemistry

Computational Sciences

Condensed Matter Physics

Dairy Science (see Animal Sciences)

Earth Sciences (see Geosciences)

Environmental Management and Policy

Environmental Sciences

Environmental Studies (see Environmental Management and Policy)

Experimental Statistics (see Statistics)

Fish, Game, and Wildlife Management

Food Science and Technology

Forestry

General Science (see specific topics)

Geochemistry

Geodetic Sciences

Geological Engineering (see Geology)

Geological Sciences (see Geology)

Geology

Geophysical Fluid Dynamics (see Geophysics)

Geophysics

Geosciences

Horticulture

Hydrogeology
Hydrology
Inorganic Chemistry
Limnology
Marine Affairs
Marine Geology
Marine Sciences
Marine Studies (*see* Marine Affairs; Marine Geology; Marine Sciences; Oceanography)
Mathematical and Computational Finance
Mathematical Physics
Mathematical Statistics (*see* Applied Statistics; Statistics)
Mathematics
Meteorology
Mineralogy
Natural Resource Management (*see* Environmental Management and Policy; Natural Resources)
Natural Resources
Nuclear Physics (*see* Physics)
Ocean Engineering (*see* Marine Affairs; Marine Geology; Marine Sciences; Oceanography)
Oceanography
Optical Sciences
Optical Technologies (*see* Optical Sciences)
Optics (*see* Applied Physics; Optical Sciences; Physics)
Organic Chemistry
Paleontology
Paper Chemistry (*see* Chemistry)
Photonics
Physical Chemistry
Physics
Planetary and Space Sciences
Plant Sciences
Plasma Physics
Poultry Science (*see* Animal Sciences)
Radiological Physics (*see* Physics)
Range Management (*see* Range Science)
Range Science
Resource Management (*see* Environmental Management and Policy; Natural Resources)
Solid-Earth Sciences (*see* Geosciences)
Space Sciences (*see* Planetary and Space Sciences)
Statistics
Theoretical Chemistry
Theoretical Physics
Viticulture and Enology
Water Resources

Graduate Programs in Engineering & Applied Sciences

Aeronautical Engineering (*see* Aerospace/Aeronautical Engineering)
Aerospace/Aeronautical Engineering
Aerospace Studies (*see* Aerospace/Aeronautical Engineering)
Agricultural Engineering
Applied Mechanics (*see* Mechanics)
Applied Science and Technology
Architectural Engineering
Artificial Intelligence/Robotics
Astronautical Engineering (*see* Aerospace/Aeronautical Engineering)
Automotive Engineering
Aviation
Biochemical Engineering
Bioengineering
Bioinformatics
Biological Engineering (*see* Bioengineering)
Biomedical Engineering
Biosystems Engineering
Biotechnology
Ceramic Engineering (*see* Ceramic Sciences and Engineering)
Ceramic Sciences and Engineering
Ceramics (*see* Ceramic Sciences and Engineering)

Chemical Engineering
Civil Engineering
Computer and Information Systems Security
Computer Engineering
Computer Science
Computing Technology (*see* Computer Science)
Construction Engineering
Construction Management
Database Systems
Electrical Engineering
Electronic Materials
Electronics Engineering (*see* Electrical Engineering)
Energy and Power Engineering
Energy Management and Policy
Engineering and Applied Sciences
Engineering and Public Affairs (*see* Technology and Public Policy)
Engineering and Public Policy (*see* Energy Management and Policy; Technology and Public Policy)
Engineering Design
Engineering Management
Engineering Mechanics (*see* Mechanics)
Engineering Metallurgy (*see* Metallurgical Engineering and Metallurgy)
Engineering Physics
Environmental Design (*see* Environmental Engineering)
Environmental Engineering
Ergonomics and Human Factors
Financial Engineering
Fire Protection Engineering
Food Engineering (*see* Agricultural Engineering)
Game Design and Development
Gas Engineering (*see* Petroleum Engineering)
Geological Engineering
Geophysics Engineering (*see* Geological Engineering)
Geotechnical Engineering
Hazardous Materials Management
Health Informatics
Health Systems (*see* Safety Engineering; Systems Engineering)
Highway Engineering (*see* Transportation and Highway Engineering)
Human-Computer Interaction
Human Factors (*see* Ergonomics and Human Factors)
Hydraulics
Hydrology (*see* Water Resources Engineering)
Industrial Engineering (*see* Industrial/Management Engineering)
Industrial/Management Engineering
Information Science
Internet Engineering
Macromolecular Science (*see* Polymer Science and Engineering)
Management Engineering (*see* Engineering Management; Industrial/Management Engineering)
Management of Technology
Manufacturing Engineering
Marine Engineering (*see* Civil Engineering)
Materials Engineering
Materials Sciences
Mechanical Engineering
Mechanics
Medical Informatics
Metallurgical Engineering and Metallurgy
Metallurgy (*see* Metallurgical Engineering and Metallurgy)
Mineral/Mining Engineering
Modeling and Simulation
Nanotechnology
Nuclear Engineering
Ocean Engineering
Operations Research
Paper and Pulp Engineering
Petroleum Engineering
Pharmaceutical Engineering
Plastics Engineering (*see* Polymer Science and Engineering)
Polymer Science and Engineering
Public Policy (*see* Energy Management and Policy; Technology and Public Policy)

Reliability Engineering
Robotics (*see* Artificial Intelligence/Robotics)
Safety Engineering
Software Engineering
Solid-State Sciences (*see* Materials Sciences)
Structural Engineering
Surveying Science and Engineering
Systems Analysis (*see* Systems Engineering)
Systems Engineering
Systems Science
Technology and Public Policy
Telecommunications
Telecommunications Management
Textile Sciences and Engineering
Textiles (*see* Textile Sciences and Engineering)
Transportation and Highway Engineering
Urban Systems Engineering (*see* Systems Engineering)
Waste Management (*see* Hazardous Materials Management)
Water Resources Engineering

Graduate Programs in Business, Education, Information Studies, Law & Social Work

Accounting
Actuarial Science
Adult Education
Advertising and Public Relations
Agricultural Education
Alcohol Abuse Counseling (*see* Counselor Education)
Archival Management and Studies
Art Education
Athletics Administration (*see* Kinesiology and Movement Studies)
Athletic Training and Sports Medicine
Audiology (*see* Communication Disorders)
Aviation Management
Banking (*see* Finance and Banking)
Business Administration and Management—General
Business Education
Communication Disorders
Community College Education
Computer Education
Continuing Education (*see* Adult Education)
Counseling (*see* Counselor Education)
Counselor Education
Curriculum and Instruction
Developmental Education
Distance Education Development
Drug Abuse Counseling (*see* Counselor Education)
Early Childhood Education
Educational Leadership and Administration
Educational Measurement and Evaluation
Educational Media/Instructional Technology
Educational Policy
Educational Psychology
Education—General
Education of the Blind (*see* Special Education)
Education of the Deaf (*see* Special Education)
Education of the Gifted
Education of the Hearing Impaired (*see* Special Education)
Education of the Learning Disabled (*see* Special Education)
Education of the Mentally Retarded (*see* Special Education)
Education of the Physically Handicapped (*see* Special Education)
Education of Students with Severe/Multiple Disabilities
Education of the Visually Handicapped (*see* Special Education)
Electronic Commerce
Elementary Education
English as a Second Language
English Education
Entertainment Management

Entrepreneurship
Environmental Education
Environmental Law
Exercise and Sports Science
Exercise Physiology (*see* Kinesiology and Movement Studies)
Facilities and Entertainment Management
Finance and Banking
Food Services Management (*see* Hospitality Management)
Foreign Languages Education
Foundations and Philosophy of Education
Guidance and Counseling (*see* Counselor Education)
Health Education
Health Law
Hearing Sciences (*see* Communication Disorders)
Higher Education
Home Economics Education
Hospitality Management
Hotel Management (*see* Travel and Tourism)
Human Resources Development
Human Resources Management
Human Services
Industrial Administration (*see* Industrial and Manufacturing Management)
Industrial and Manufacturing Management
Industrial Education (*see* Vocational and Technical Education)
Information Studies
Instructional Technology (*see* Educational Media/Instructional Technology)
Insurance
Intellectual Property Law
International and Comparative Education
International Business
International Commerce (*see* International Business)
International Economics (*see* International Business)
International Trade (*see* International Business)
Investment and Securities (*see* Business Administration and Management; Finance and Banking; Investment Management)
Investment Management
Junior College Education (*see* Community College Education)
Kinesiology and Movement Studies
Law
Legal and Justice Studies
Leisure Services (*see* Recreation and Park Management)
Leisure Studies
Library Science
Logistics
Management (*see* Business Administration and Management)
Management Information Systems
Management Strategy and Policy
Marketing
Marketing Research
Mathematics Education
Middle School Education
Movement Studies (*see* Kinesiology and Movement Studies)
Multilingual and Multicultural Education
Museum Education
Music Education
Nonprofit Management
Nursery School Education (*see* Early Childhood Education)
Occupational Education (*see* Vocational and Technical Education)
Organizational Behavior
Organizational Management
Parks Administration (*see* Recreation and Park Management)
Personnel (*see* Human Resources Development; Human Resources Management; Organizational Behavior; Organizational Management; Student Affairs)
Philosophy of Education (*see* Foundations and Philosophy of Education)
Physical Education
Project Management
Public Relations (*see* Advertising and Public Relations)
Quality Management
Quantitative Analysis

Reading Education
Real Estate
Recreation and Park Management
Recreation Therapy (*see* Recreation and Park Management)
Religious Education
Remedial Education (*see* Special Education)
Restaurant Administration (*see* Hospitality Management)
Science Education
Secondary Education
Social Sciences Education
Social Studies Education (*see* Social Sciences Education)
Social Work
Special Education
Speech-Language Pathology and Audiology (*see* Communication Disorders)
Sports Management
Sports Medicine (*see* Athletic Training and Sports Medicine)

Sports Psychology and Sociology (*see* Kinesiology and Movement Studies)
Student Affairs
Substance Abuse Counseling (*see* Counselor Education)
Supply Chain Management
Sustainability Management
Systems Management (*see* Management Information Systems)
Taxation
Teacher Education (*see* specific subject areas)
Teaching English as a Second Language (*see* English as a Second Language)
Technical Education (*see* Vocational and Technical Education)
Transportation Management
Travel and Tourism
Urban Education
Vocational and Technical Education
Vocational Counseling (*see* Counselor Education)